Who'sWho in Medicine and Healthcare™

Published by Marquis Who's Who®

Titles in Print

Who's Who in America®
Who's Who in America Junior & Senior High School Version
Who Was Who in America®
  Historical Volume (1607–1896)
  Volume I (1897–1942)
  Volume II (1943–1950)
  Volume III (1951–1960)
  Volume IV (1961–1968)
  Volume V (1969–1973)
  Volume VI (1974–1976)
  Volume VII (1977–1981)
  Volume VIII (1982–1985)
  Volume IX (1985–1989)
  Volume X (1989–1993)
  Volume XI (1993–1996)
  Index Volume (1607–1996)
Who's Who in the World®
Who's Who in the East®
Who's Who in the Midwest®
Who's Who in the South and Southwest®
Who's Who in the West®
Who's Who in American Education®
Who's Who in American Law®
Who's Who in American Nursing®
Who's Who of American Women®
Who's Who of Emerging Leaders®
Who's Who in Entertainment®
Who's Who in Finance and Industry®
Who's Who in Medicine and Healthcare™
Who's Who in Religion®
Who's Who in Science and Engineering®
Index to Marquis Who's Who® Publications
The *Official* ABMS Directory of Board Certified Medical Specialists®

Available on CD-ROM

The Complete Marquis Who's Who® on CD-ROM
ABMS Medical Specialists *PLUS*™

Who'sWho in Medicine and Healthcare™

1997~1998

First Edition

MARQUIS
Who'sWho®
121 Chanlon Road
New Providence, NJ 07974 U.S.A.

Who'sWho in Medicine and Healthcare™

Published by Marquis Who's Who, a division of Reed Elsevier Inc.

International Standard Book Number 0-8379-0000-X (Classic Edition)
0-8379-0001-8 (Deluxe Edition)
International Standard Serial Number 0000-1708

Manufactured in the United States of America

Table of Contents

Preface

With the publication of the First Edition of *Who's Who in Medicine and Healthcare*, Marquis Who's Who recognizes today's leaders in the teaching, practice, planning, financing, and delivery of healthcare.

Medical professionals worldwide are facing new demands for accessible, high-quality care at a reasonable cost. *Who's Who in Medicine and Healthcare* identifies those whose achievements place them at the forefront of the evolving healthcare system. It is a reference tool specifically designed to facilitate communication between healthcare professionals of all specializations. Its paramount purpose is to provide healthcare professionals and other interested readers with a vehicle for identifying achievers throughout the diverse medical community; for gaining insight into the purpose and progress of their peers' work and accomplishments; and for networking with those of similar or related interests.

This volume contains the biographies of approximately 27,800 medical administrators, educators, researchers, clinicians, and other healthcare leaders. While the majority of them come from the United States, many come from over 85 other nations. Their careers span more than 100 distinct specialties, including dentistry, medical education, geriatrics, gynecology, hospital administration, internal medicine, mental health, nuclear medicine, nursing, optometry, pediatrics, pharmaceuticals, public health, research, social work, speech pathology, substance abuse, surgery, and many more. Also included are those professions which provide support to the healthcare industry, such as communications; association, governmental, and industrial administration; corporate management; and legal practice.

Inclusion in *Who's Who in Medicine and Healthcare* is determined solely by reference value. Positions of responsibility, contributions to the field, and noteworthy individual accomplishment are vital factors in the final selection of listings for the book. Neither wealth nor social position is a criterion.

As in all Marquis Who's Who publications, the Biographee's own recommendations and ultimate approval ensure the accuracy of the sketches. In those instances where individuals of distinct reference value failed to supply biographical information, Marquis staff members carefully researched the necessary data. Asterisks denote such sketches.

Marquis Who's Who editors and researchers diligently prepare each biographical listing. However, errors may occur. We regret all such errors and invite Biographees and readers to report them to the publisher so that corrections can be made in subsequent editions.

Board of Advisors

Marquis Who's Who gratefully acknowledges the following distinguished individuals who have made themselves available for review, evaluation, and general comment with regard to the publication of the First Edition of *Who's Who in Medicine and Healthcare.* The advisors have enhanced the reference value of this edition by the nomination of outstanding individuals for inclusion. However, the Board of Advisors, either collectively or individually, is in no way responsible for the final selection of names appearing in this volume, nor does the Board of Advisors bear responsibility for the accuracy or comprehensiveness of the biographical information or other material contained herein.

Dr. Gerard P. Boe
Executive Director
American Medical Technologists

Dr. Thomas C. Dolan
President
American College of Healthcare Executives

Dr. Charles H. Hartman
Executive Director
American College Health Associations

Sonya A. Healy
Former Director of Patient Care Services
University of California, San Diego, Medical Center

Dr. Carla A.B. Lee
Associate Professor, School of Nursing
Clark College

Abbey S. Meyers
President and CEO
National Organization of Rare Disorders

Dr. Frederick W. Oehme
Fellow
American Academy of Clinical Toxicology, Kansas State University

Dr. Cory SerVaas
President and CEO
Benjamin Franklin Literary and Medical Society

Dr. Mervyn F. Silverman
President
American Foundation for AIDS Research

Standards of Admission

The foremost consideration in selecting Biographees for *Who's Who in Medicine and Healthcare* is the extent of an individual's reference interest. Such reference interest is judged on either of two factors: (1) the position of responsibility held, or (2) the level of achievement attained by the individual.

Admissions based on the factor of position include:

Elected members of the Institute of Medicine

Deans of medical, dental, and nursing schools

Directors and officers of the American Board of Medical Specialties and American Medical Association

Administrators and department heads within the U.S. Department of Health and Human Services, National Institutes of Health, Centers for Disease Control, and National Cancer Institute

State health department and licensing board heads

Executive officers of major health maintenance organizations, pharmaceutical companies, insurance companies, and other medical equipment and service companies

Recent winners of major awards from the top U.S. medical and health-related associations

All living American winners of the Nobel Prize of Physiology and Medicine

Admission for individual achievement is based on qualitative criteria. To be selected, a person must have attained conspicuous achievement.

Key to Information

[1] COOKE, NANCY ELIZABETH, [2] health care company executive; **[3]** b. Troy, N.Y., February 18, 1955; **[4]** d. Joseph and Carolyn (James) C.; **[5]** m. Joel Kevin Sullivan, Aug. 27, 1988; **[6]** children: Calvin Thomas, Katelyn Alyssa. **[7]** BS cum laude, SUNY Albany, 1977. **[8]** Cert. CPA. **[9]** Corp. accts. mgr., Tri-State Med. Ptnrs., N.Y.C., 1977-83; exec. dir., 1983-88; v.p. 1988-92; exec. v.p. HealthSystems Corp., Syracuse, N.Y., 1992—. **[10]** Vis. lectr., Onondaga C. C., 1992-93; cons. on healthcare and bus. edn., 1992—. **[11]** Contbr. articles to trade mags. **[12]** Chmn. planning com., Greater Onondaga Task Force on AIDS, 1992-93; bd. of trustees, Lake Dist. Shelter for Women, 1993— , United Way 1994— . **[13]** With USNG, 1977-82. **[14]** Recipient Comty. Svc. award, Syracuse, 1993. **[15]** Mem. Assn. of Healthcare Profls., Health Care Execs. Forum, Soroptimist Internat. **[16]** Democrat. **[17]** Episcopalian. **[18]** Home: 44 Pleasant St Syracuse NY 13244 **[19]** Office: HealthSystems Corp 100 Corporate Circle Syracuse NY 13240

KEY

[1]	Name
[2]	Occupation
[3]	Vital statistics
[4]	Parents
[5]	Marriage
[6]	Children
[7]	Education
[8]	Professional certifications
[9]	Career
[10]	Career-related activities
[11]	Writings and creative works
[12]	Civic and political activities
[13]	Military
[14]	Awards and fellowships
[15]	Professional and association memberships, clubs, and lodges
[16]	Political affiliation
[17]	Religion
[18]	Home address
[19]	Office address

Table of Abbreviations

The following abbreviations and symbols are frequently used in this book.

*An asterisk following a sketch indicates that it was researched by the Marquis Who's Who editorial staff and has not been verified by the Biographee.
A Associate (used with academic degrees only)
AA, A.A. Associate in Arts, Associate of Arts
AAAL American Academy of Arts and Letters
AAAS American Association for the Advancement of Science
AACD American Association for Counseling and Development
AACN American Association of Critical Care Nurses
AAHA American Academy of Health Administrators
AAHP American Association of Hospital Planners
AAHPERD American Alliance for Health, Physical Education, Recreation, and Dance
AAS Associate of Applied Science
AASL American Association of School Librarians
AASPA American Association of School Personnel Administrators
AAU Amateur Athletic Union
AAUP American Association of University Professors
AAUW American Association of University Women
AB, A.B. Arts, Bachelor of
AB Alberta
ABA American Bar Association
ABC American Broadcasting Company
AC Air Corps
acad. academy, academic
acct. accountant
acctg. accounting
ACDA Arms Control and Disarmament Agency
ACHA American College of Hospital Administrators
ACLS Advanced Cardiac Life Support
ACLU American Civil Liberties Union
ACOG American College of Ob-Gyn
ACP American College of Physicians
ACS American College of Surgeons
ADA American Dental Association
a.d.c. aide-de-camp
adj. adjunct, adjutant
adj. gen. adjutant general
adm. admiral
adminstr. administrator
adminstrn. administration
adminstrv. administrative
ADN Associate's Degree in Nursing
ADP Automatic Data Processing
adv. advocate, advisory
advt. advertising
AE, A.E. Agricultural Engineer
A.E. and P. Ambassador Extraordinary and Plenipotentiary
AEC Atomic Energy Commission
aero. aeronautical, aeronautic
aerodyn. aerodynamic
AFB Air Force Base
AFL-CIO American Federation of Labor and Congress of Industrial Organizations
AFTRA American Federation of TV and Radio Artists
AFSCME American Federation of State, County and Municipal Employees
agr. agriculture
agrl. agricultural
agt. agent
AGVA American Guild of Variety Artists
agy. agency
A&I Agricultural and Industrial
AIA American Institute of Architects
AIAA American Institute of Aeronautics and Astronautics
AIChE American Institute of Chemical Engineers
AICPA American Institute of Certified Public Accountants
AID Agency for International Development
AIDS Acquired Immune Deficiency Syndrome
AIEE American Institute of Electrical Engineers
AIM American Institute of Management
AIME American Institute of Mining, Metallurgy, and Petroleum Engineers
AK Alaska
AL Alabama
ALA American Library Association
Ala. Alabama
alt. alternate
Alta. Alberta
A&M Agricultural and Mechanical
AM, A.M. Arts, Master of
Am. American, America
AMA American Medical Association
amb. ambassador
A.M.E. African Methodist Episcopal
Amtrak National Railroad Passenger Corporation
AMVETS American Veterans of World War II, Korea, Vietnam
ANA American Nurses Association
anat. anatomical
ANCC American Nurses Credentialing Center
ann. annual
ANTA American National Theatre and Academy
anthrop. anthropological
AP Associated Press
APA American Psychological Association
APGA American Personnel Guidance Association
APHA American Public Health Association
APO Army Post Office
apptd. appointed
Apr. April
apt. apartment
AR Arkansas
ARC American Red Cross
arch. architect
archeol. archeological
archtl. architectural
Ariz. Arizona
Ark. Arkansas
ArtsD, ArtsD. Arts, Doctor of
arty. artillery
AS American Samoa
AS Associate in Science
ASCAP American Society of Composers, Authors and Publishers
ASCD Association for Supervision and Curriculum Development
ASCE American Society of Civil Engineers
ASHRAE American Society of Heating, Refrigeration, and Air Conditioning Engineers
ASME American Society of Mechanical Engineers
ASNSA American Society for Nursing Service Administrators
ASPA American Society for Public Administration
ASPCA American Society for the Prevention of Cruelty to Animals
assn. association
assoc. associate
asst. assistant
ASTD American Society for Training and Development
ASTM American Society for Testing and Materials
astron. astronomical
astrophys. astrophysical
ATLA Association of Trial Lawyers of America
ATSC Air Technical Service Command
AT&T American Telephone & Telegraph Company
atty. attorney
Aug. August
AUS Army of the United States
aux. auxiliary
Ave. Avenue
AVMA American Veterinary Medical Association
AZ Arizona
AWHONN Association of Women's Health Obstetric and Neonatal Nurses

B. Bachelor
b. born
BA, B.A. Bachelor of Arts
BAgr, B.Agr. Bachelor of Agriculture
Balt. Baltimore
Bapt. Baptist
BArch, B.Arch. Bachelor of Architecture
BAS, B.A.S. Bachelor of Agricultural Science
BBA, B.B.A. Bachelor of Business Administration
BBB Better Business Bureau
BBC British Broadcasting Corporation

BC, B.C. British Columbia
BCE, B.C.E. Bachelor of Civil Engineering
BChir, B.Chir. Bachelor of Surgery
BCL, B.C.L. Bachelor of Civil Law
BCLS Basic Cardiac Life Support
BCS, B.C.S. Bachelor of Commercial Science
BD, B.D. Bachelor of Divinity
bd. board
BE, B.E. Bachelor of Education
BEE, B.E.E. Bachelor of Electrical Engineering
BFA, B.F.A. Bachelor of Fine Arts
bibl. biblical
bibliog. bibliographical
biog. biographical
biol. biological
BJ, B.J. Bachelor of Journalism
Bklyn. Brooklyn
BL, B.L. Bachelor of Letters
bldg. building
BLS, B.L.S. Bachelor of Library Science
BLS Basic Life Support
Blvd. Boulevard
BMI Broadcast Music, Inc.
BMW Bavarian Motor Works (Bayerische Motoren Werke)
bn. battalion
B.&O.R.R. Baltimore & Ohio Railroad
bot. botanical
BPE, B.P.E. Bachelor of Physical Education
BPhil, B.Phil. Bachelor of Philosophy
br. branch
BRE, B.R.E. Bachelor of Religious Education
brig. gen. brigadier general
Brit. British, Brittanica
Bros. Brothers
BS, B.S. Bachelor of Science
BSA, B.S.A. Bachelor of Agricultural Science
BSBA Bachelor of Science in Business Administration
BSChemE Bachelor of Science in Chemical Engineering
BSD, B.S.D. Bachelor of Didactic Science
BSEE Bachelor of Science in Electrical Engineering
BSN Bachelor of Science in Nursing
BST, B.S.T. Bachelor of Sacred Theology
BTh, B.Th. Bachelor of Theology
bull. bulletin
bur. bureau
bus. business
B.W.I. British West Indies

CA California
CAA Civil Aeronautics Administration
CAB Civil Aeronautics Board
CAD-CAM Computer Aided Design–Computer Aided Model
Calif. California
C.Am. Central America
Can. Canada, Canadian
CAP Civil Air Patrol
capt. captain
cardiol. cardiological
cardiovasc. cardiovascular
CARE Cooperative American Relief Everywhere
Cath. Catholic
cav. cavalry
CBC Canadian Broadcasting Company
CBI China, Burma, India Theatre of Operations
CBS Columbia Broadcasting Company
C.C. Community College
CCC Commodity Credit Corporation
CCNY City College of New York
CCRN Critical Care Registered Nurse
CCU Cardiac Care Unit
CD Civil Defense
CE, C.E. Corps of Engineers, Civil Engineer
CEN Certified Emergency Nurse
CENTO Central Treaty Organization
CEO chief executive officer
CERN European Organization of Nuclear Research
cert. certificate, certification, certified
CETA Comprehensive Employment Training Act
CFA Chartered Financial Analyst
CFL Canadian Football League
CFO chief financial officer
CFP Certified Financial Planner
ch. church
ChD, Ch.D. Doctor of Chemistry
chem. chemical
ChemE, Chem.E. Chemical Engineer
ChFC Chartered Financial Consultant
Chgo. Chicago
chirurg. chirurgical
chmn. chairman
chpt. chapter
CIA Central Intelligence Agency
Cin. Cincinnati
cir. circle, circuit
CLE Continuing Legal Education
Cleve. Cleveland
climatol. climatological
clin. clinical
clk. clerk
C.L.U. Chartered Life Underwriter
CM, C.M. Master in Surgery
CM Northern Mariana Islands
CMA Certified Medical Assistant
cmty. community
CNA Certified Nurse's Aide
CNOR Certified Nurse (Operating Room)
C.&N.W.Ry. Chicago & North Western Railway
CO Colorado
Co. Company
COF Catholic Order of Foresters
C. of C. Chamber of Commerce
col. colonel
coll. college
Colo. Colorado
com. committee
comd. commanded
comdg. commanding
comdr. commander
comdt. commandant
comm. communications
commd. commissioned
comml. commercial
commn. commission
commr. commissioner
compt. comptroller
condr. conductor
Conf. Conference
Congl. Congregational, Congressional
Conglist. Congregationalist
Conn. Connecticut
cons. consultant, consulting
consol. consolidated
constl. constitutional
constn. constitution
constrn. construction
contbd. contributed
contbg. contributing
contbn. contribution
contbr. contributor
contr. controller
Conv. Convention
COO chief operating officer
coop. cooperative
coord. coordinator
CORDS Civil Operations and Revolutionary Development Support
CORE Congress of Racial Equality
corp. corporation, corporate
corr. correspondent, corresponding, correspondence
C.&O.Ry. Chesapeake & Ohio Railway
coun. council
CPA Certified Public Accountant
CPCU Chartered Property and Casualty Underwriter
CPH, C.P.H. Certificate of Public Health
cpl. corporal
CPR Cardio-Pulmonary Resuscitation
C.P.Ry. Canadian Pacific Railway
CRT Cathode Ray Terminal
C.S. Christian Science
CSB, C.S.B. Bachelor of Christian Science
C.S.C. Civil Service Commission
CT Connecticut
ct. court
ctr. center
ctrl. central
CWS Chemical Warfare Service
C.Z. Canal Zone

D. Doctor
d. daughter
DAgr, D.Agr. Doctor of Agriculture
DAR Daughters of the American Revolution
dau. daughter
DAV Disabled American Veterans
DC, D.C. District of Columbia
DCL, D.C.L. Doctor of Civil Law
DCS, D.C.S. Doctor of Commercial Science
DD, D.D. Doctor of Divinity
DDS, D.D.S. Doctor of Dental Surgery
DE Delaware
Dec. December
dec. deceased
def. defense
Del. Delaware
del. delegate, delegation
Dem. Democrat, Democratic
DEng, D.Eng. Doctor of Engineering
denom. denomination, denominational
dep. deputy
dept. department
dermatol. dermatological
desc. descendant
devel. development, developmental
DFA, D.F.A. Doctor of Fine Arts
D.F.C. Distinguished Flying Cross
DHL, D.H.L. Doctor of Hebrew Literature
dir. director
dist. district
distbg. distributing
distbn. distribution
distbr. distributor
disting. distinguished
div. division, divinity, divorce
divsn. division
DLitt, D.Litt. Doctor of Literature
DMD, D.M.D. Doctor of Dental Medicine
DMS, D.M.S. Doctor of Medical Science
DO, D.O. Doctor of Osteopathy
docs. documents
DON Director of Nursing
DPH, D.P.H. Diploma in Public Health
DPhil, D.Phil. Doctor of Philosophy
D.R. Daughters of the Revolution
Dr. Drive, Doctor
DRE, D.R.E. Doctor of Religious Education
DrPH, Dr.P.H. Doctor of Public Health, Doctor of Public Hygiene
D.S.C. Distinguished Service Cross

DSc, D.Sc. Doctor of Science
DSChemE Doctor of Science in Chemical Engineering
D.S.M. Distinguished Service Medal
DST, D.S.T. Doctor of Sacred Theology
DTM, D.T.M. Doctor of Tropical Medicine
DVM, D.V.M. Doctor of Veterinary Medicine
DVS, D.V.S. Doctor of Veterinary Surgery

E, E. East
ea. eastern
E. and P. Extraordinary and Plenipotentiary
Eccles. Ecclesiastical
ecol. ecological
econ. economic
ECOSOC Economic and Social Council (of the UN)
ED, E.D. Doctor of Engineering
ed. educated
EdB, Ed.B. Bachelor of Education
EdD, Ed.D. Doctor of Education
edit. edition
editl. editorial
EdM, Ed.M. Master of Education
edn. education
ednl. educational
EDP Electronic Data Processing
EdS, Ed.S. Specialist in Education
EE, E.E. Electrical Engineer
E.E. and M.P. Envoy Extraordinary and Minister Plenipotentiary
EEC European Economic Community
EEG Electroencephalogram
EEO Equal Employment Opportunity
EEOC Equal Employment Opportunity Commission
E.Ger. German Democratic Republic
EKG Electrocardiogram
elec. electrical
electrochem. electrochemical
electrophys. electrophysical
elem. elementary
EM, E.M. Engineer of Mines
EMT Emergency Medical Technician
ency. encyclopedia
Eng. England
engr. engineer
engring. engineering
entomol. entomological
environ. environmental
EPA Environmental Protection Agency
epidemiol. epidemiological
Episc. Episcopalian
ERA Equal Rights Amendment
ERDA Energy Research and Development Administration
ESEA Elementary and Secondary Education Act
ESL English as Second Language
ESPN Entertainment and Sports Programming Network
ESSA Environmental Science Services Administration
ethnol. ethnological
ETO European Theatre of Operations
Evang. Evangelical
exam. examination, examining
Exch. Exchange
exec. executive
exhbn. exhibition
expdn. expedition
expn. exposition
expt. experiment
exptl. experimental
Expy. Expressway
Ext. Extension

F.A. Field Artillery
FAA Federal Aviation Administration
FAO Food and Agriculture Organization (of the UN)
FBA Federal Bar Association
FBI Federal Bureau of Investigation
FCA Farm Credit Administration
FCC Federal Communications Commission
FCDA Federal Civil Defense Administration
FDA Food and Drug Administration
FDIA Federal Deposit Insurance Administration
FDIC Federal Deposit Insurance Corporation
FE, F.E. Forest Engineer
FEA Federal Energy Administration
Feb. February
fed. federal
fedn. federation
FERC Federal Energy Regulatory Commission
fgn. foreign
FHA Federal Housing Administration
fin. financial, finance
FL Florida
Fl. Floor
Fla. Florida
FMC Federal Maritime Commission
FNP Family Nurse Practitioner
FOA Foreign Operations Administration
found. foundation
FPC Federal Power Commission
FPO Fleet Post Office
frat. fraternity
FRS Federal Reserve System
FSA Federal Security Agency
Ft. Fort
FTC Federal Trade Commission
Fwy. Freeway

G-1 (or other number) Division of General Staff
GA, Ga. Georgia
GAO General Accounting Office
gastroent. gastroenterological
GATE Gifted and Talented Educators
GATT General Agreement on Tariffs and Trade
GE General Electric Company
gen. general
geneal. genealogical
geod. geodetic
geog. geographic, geographical
geol. geological
geophys. geophysical
geriat. geriatrics
gerontol. gerontological
G.H.Q. General Headquarters
GM General Motors Corporation
GMAC General Motors Acceptance Corporation
G.N.Ry. Great Northern Railway
gov. governor
govt. government
govtl. governmental
GPO Government Printing Office
grad. graduate, graduated
GSA General Services Administration
Gt. Great
GTE General Telephone and ElectricCompany
GU Guam
gynecol. gynecological

HBO Home Box Office
hdqs. headquarters
HEW Department of Health, Education and Welfare
HHD, H.H.D. Doctor of Humanities
HHFA Housing and Home Finance Agency
HHS Department of Health and Human Services
HI Hawaii
hist. historical, historic
HM, H.M. Master of Humanities
HMO Health Maintenance Organization
homeo. homeopathic
hon. honorary, honorable
Ho. of Dels. House of Delegates
Ho. of Reps. House of Representatives
hort. horticultural
hosp. hospital
H.S. High School
HUD Department of Housing and Urban Development
Hwy. Highway
hydrog. hydrographic

IA Iowa
IAEA International Atomic Energy Agency
IATSE International Alliance of Theatrical and Stage Employees and Moving Picture Operators of the United States and Canada
IBM International Business Machines Corporation
IBRD International Bank for Reconstruction and Development
ICA International Cooperation Administration
ICC Interstate Commerce Commission
ICCE International Council for Computers in Education
ICU Intensive Care Unit
ID Idaho
IEEE Institute of Electrical and Electronics Engineers
IFC International Finance Corporation
IGY International Geophysical Year
IL Illinois
Ill. Illinois
illus. illustrated
ILO International Labor Organization
IMF International Monetary Fund
IN Indiana
Inc. Incorporated
Ind. Indiana
ind. independent
Indpls. Indianapolis
indsl. industrial
inf. infantry
info. information
ins. insurance
insp. inspector
insp. gen. inspector general
inst. institute
instl. institutional
instn. institution
instr. instructor
instrn. instruction
instrnl. instructional
internat. international
intro. introduction
IRE Institute of Radio Engineers
IRS Internal Revenue Service
ITT International Telephone & Telegraph Corporation

JAG Judge Advocate General
JAGC Judge Advocate General Corps
Jan. January
Jaycees Junior Chamber of Commerce
JB, J.B. Jurum Baccalaureus

JCB, J.C.B. Juris Canoni Baccalaureus
JCD, J.C.D. Juris Canonici Doctor, Juris Civilis Doctor
JCL, J.C.L. Juris Canonici Licentiatus
JD, J.D. Juris Doctor
jg. junior grade
jour. journal
jr. junior
JSD, J.S.D. Juris Scientiae Doctor
JUD, J.U.D. Juris Utriusque Doctor
jud. judicial

Kans. Kansas
K.C. Knights of Columbus
K.P. Knights of Pythias
KS Kansas
K.T. Knight Templar
KY, Ky. Kentucky

LA, La. Louisiana
L.A. Los Angeles
lab. laboratory
L.Am. Latin America
lang. language
laryngol. laryngological
LB Labrador
LDS Latter Day Saints
LDS Church Church of Jesus Christ of Latter Day Saints
lectr. lecturer
legis. legislation, legislative
LHD, L.H.D. Doctor of Humane Letters
L.I. Long Island
libr. librarian, library
lic. licensed, license
L.I.R.R. Long Island Railroad
lit. literature
litig. litigation
LittB, Litt.B. Bachelor of Letters
LittD, Litt.D. Doctor of Letters
LLB, LL.B. Bachelor of Laws
LLD, L.L.D. Doctor of Laws
LLM, L.L.M. Master of Laws
Ln. Lane
L.&N.R.R. Louisville & Nashville Railroad
LPGA Ladies Professional Golf Association
LPN Licensed Practical Nurse
LS, L.S. Library Science (in degree)
lt. lieutenant
Ltd. Limited
Luth. Lutheran
LWV League of Women Voters

M. Master
m. married
MA, M.A. Master of Arts
MA Massachusetts
MADD Mothers Against Drunk Driving
mag. magazine
MAgr, M.Agr. Master of Agriculture
maj. major
Man. Manitoba
Mar. March
MArch, M.Arch. Master in Architecture
Mass. Massachusetts
math. mathematics, mathematical
MATS Military Air Transport Service
MB, M.B. Bachelor of Medicine
MB Manitoba
MBA, M.B.A. Master of Business Administration
MBS Mutual Broadcasting System
M.C. Medical Corps
MCE, M.C.E. Master of Civil Engineering
mcht. merchant
mcpl. municipal
MCS, M.C.S. Master of Commercial Science
MD, M.D. Doctor of Medicine
MD, Md. Maryland
MDiv Master of Divinity
MDip, M.Dip. Master in Diplomacy
mdse. merchandise
MDV, M.D.V. Doctor of Veterinary Medicine
ME, M.E. Mechanical Engineer
ME Maine
M.E.Ch. Methodist Episcopal Church
mech. mechanical
MEd., M.Ed. Master of Education
med. medical
MEE, M.E.E. Master of Electrical Engineering
mem. member
meml. memorial
merc. mercantile
met. metropolitan
metall. metallurgical
MetE, Met.E. Metallurgical Engineer
meteorol. meteorological
Meth. Methodist
Mex. Mexico
MF, M.F. Master of Forestry
MFA, M.F.A. Master of Fine Arts
mfg. manufacturing
mfr. manufacturer
mgmt. management
mgr. manager
MHA, M.H.A. Master of Hospital Administration
M.I. Military Intelligence
MI Michigan
Mich. Michigan
micros. microscopic, microscopical
mid. middle
mil. military
Milw. Milwaukee
Min. Minister
mineral. mineralogical
Minn. Minnesota
MIS Management Information Systems
Miss. Mississippi
MIT Massachusetts Institute of Technology
mktg. marketing
ML, M.L. Master of Laws
MLA Modern Language Association
M.L.D. Magister Legnum Diplomatic
MLitt, M.Litt. Master of Literature, Master of Letters
MLS, M.L.S. Master of Library Science
MME, M.M.E. Master of Mechanical Engineering
MN Minnesota
mng. managing
MO, Mo. Missouri
moblzn. mobilization
Mont. Montana
MP Northern Mariana Islands
M.P. Member of Parliament
MPA Master of Public Administration
MPE, M.P.E. Master of Physical Education
MPH, M.P.H. Master of Public Health
MPhil, M.Phil. Master of Philosophy
MPL, M.P.L. Master of Patent Law
Mpls. Minneapolis
MRE, M.R.E. Master of Religious Education
MRI Magnetic Resonance Imaging
MS, M.S. Master of Science
MS, Ms. Mississippi
MSc, M.Sc. Master of Science
MSChemE Master of Science in Chemical Engineering
MSEE Master of Science in Electrical Engineering
MSF, M.S.F. Master of Science of Forestry
MSN Master of Science in Nursing
MST, M.S.T. Master of Sacred Theology
MSW, M.S.W. Master of Social Work
MT Montana
Mt. Mount
MTO Mediterranean Theatre of Operation
MTV Music Television
mus. museum, musical
MusB, Mus.B. Bachelor of Music
MusD, Mus.D. Doctor of Music
MusM, Mus.M. Master of Music
mut. mutual
MVP Most Valuable Player
mycol. mycological

N. North
NAACOG Nurses Association of the American College of Obstetricians and Gynecologists
NAACP National Association for the Advancement of Colored People
NACA National Advisory Committee for Aeronautics
NACDL National Association of Criminal Defense Lawyers
NACU National Association of Colleges and Universities
NAD National Academy of Design
NAE National Academy of Engineering, National Association of Educators
NAESP National Association of Elementary School Principals
NAFE National Association of Female Executives
N.Am. North America
NAM National Association of Manufacturers
NAMH National Association for Mental Health
NAPA National Association of Performing Artists
NARAS National Academy of Recording Arts and Sciences
NAREB National Association of Real Estate Boards
NARS National Archives and Record Service
NAS National Academy of Sciences
NASA National Aeronautics and Space Administration
NASP National Association of School Psychologists
NASW National Association of Social Workers
nat. national
NATAS National Academy of Television Arts and Sciences
NATO North Atlantic Treaty Organization
NATOUSA North African Theatre of Operations, United States Army
nav. navigation
NB, N.B. New Brunswick
NBA National Basketball Association
NBC National Broadcasting Company
NC, N.C. North Carolina
NCAA National College Athletic Association
NCCJ National Conference of Christians and Jews
ND, N.D. North Dakota
NDEA National Defense Education Act
NE Nebraska
NE, N.E. Northeast
NEA National Education Association
Nebr. Nebraska
NEH National Endowment for Humanities
neurol. neurological
Nev. Nevada
NF Newfoundland

NFL National Football League
Nfld. Newfoundland
NG National Guard
NH, N.H. New Hampshire
NHL National Hockey League
NIH National Institutes of Health
NIMH National Institute of Mental Health
NJ, N.J. New Jersey
NLRB National Labor Relations Board
NM New Mexico
N.Mex. New Mexico
No. Northern
NOAA National Oceanographic and Atmospheric Administration
NORAD North America Air Defense
Nov. November
NOW National Organization for Women
N.P.Ry. Northern Pacific Railway
nr. near
NRA National Rifle Association
NRC National Research Council
NS, N.S. Nova Scotia
NSC National Security Council
NSF National Science Foundation
NSTA National Science Teachers Association
NSW New South Wales
N.T. New Testament
NT Northwest Territories
nuc. nuclear
numis. numismatic
NV Nevada
NW, N.W. Northwest
N.W.T. Northwest Territories
NY, N.Y. New York
N.Y.C. New York City
NYU New York University
N.Z. New Zealand

OAS Organization of American States
ob-gyn obstetrics-gynecology
obs. observatory
obstet. obstetrical
occupl. occupational
oceanog. oceanographic
Oct. October
OD, O.D. Doctor of Optometry
OECD Organization for Economic Cooperation and Development
OEEC Organization of European Economic Cooperation
OEO Office of Economic Opportunity
ofcl. official
OH Ohio
OK Oklahoma
Okla. Oklahoma
ON Ontario
Ont. Ontario
oper. operating
ophthal. ophthalmological
ops. operations
OR Oregon
orch. orchestra
Oreg. Oregon
orgn. organization
orgnl. organizational
ornithol. ornithological
orthop. orthopedic
OSHA Occupational Safety and Health Administration
OSRD Office of Scientific Research and Development
OSS Office of Strategic Services
osteo. osteopathic
otol. otological
otolaryn. otolaryngological

PA, Pa. Pennsylvania
P.A. Professional Association
paleontol. paleontological
path. pathological
PBS Public Broadcasting System
P.C. Professional Corporation
PE Prince Edward Island
pediat. pediatrics
P.E.I. Prince Edward Island
PEN Poets, Playwrights, Editors, Essayists and Novelists (international association)
penol. penological
P.E.O. women's organization (full name not disclosed)
pers. personnel
pfc. private first class
PGA Professional Golfers' Association of America
PHA Public Housing Administration
pharm. pharmaceutical
PharmD, Pharm.D. Doctor of Pharmacy
PharmM, Pharm.M. Master of Pharmacy
PhB, Ph.B. Bachelor of Philosophy
PhD, Ph.D. Doctor of Philosophy
PhDChemE Doctor of Science in Chemical Engineering
PhM, Ph.M. Master of Philosophy
Phila. Philadelphia
philharm. philharmonic
philol. philological
philos. philosophical
photog. photographic
phys. physical
physiol. physiological
Pitts. Pittsburgh
Pk. Park
Pky. Parkway
Pl. Place
P.&L.E.R.R. Pittsburgh & Lake Erie Railroad
Plz. Plaza
PNP Pediatric Nurse Practitioner
P.O. Post Office
PO Box Post Office Box
polit. political
poly. polytechnic, polytechnical
PQ Province of Quebec
PR, P.R. Puerto Rico
prep. preparatory
pres. president
Presbyn. Presbyterian
presdl. presidential
prin. principal
procs. proceedings
prod. produced (play production)
prodn. production
prodr. producer
prof. professor
profl. professional
prog. progressive
propr. proprietor
pros. atty. prosecuting attorney
pro tem. pro tempore
PSRO Professional Services Review Organization
psychiat. psychiatric
psychol. psychological
PTA Parent-Teachers Association
ptnr. partner
PTO Pacific Theatre of Operations, Parent Teacher Organization
pub. publisher, publishing, published
pub. public
publ. publication
pvt. private

quar. quarterly
qm. quartermaster
Q.M.C. Quartermaster Corps
Que. Quebec

radiol. radiological
RAF Royal Air Force
RCA Radio Corporation of America
RCAF Royal Canadian Air Force
RD Rural Delivery
Rd. Road
R&D Research & Development
REA Rural Electrification Administration
rec. recording
ref. reformed
regt. regiment
regtl. regimental
rehab. rehabilitation
rels. relations
Rep. Republican
rep. representative
Res. Reserve
ret. retired
Rev. Reverend
rev. review, revised
RFC Reconstruction Finance Corporation
RFD Rural Free Delivery
rhinol. rhinological
RI, R.I. Rhode Island
RISD Rhode Island School of Design
Rlwy. Railway
Rm. Room
RN, R.N. Registered Nurse
roentgenol. roentgenological
ROTC Reserve Officers Training Corps
RR Rural Route
R.R. Railroad
rsch. research
rschr. researcher
Rt. Route

S. South
s. son
SAC Strategic Air Command
SAG Screen Actors Guild
SALT Strategic Arms Limitation Talks
S.Am. South America
san. sanitary
SAR Sons of the American Revolution
Sask. Saskatchewan
savs. savings
SB, S.B. Bachelor of Science
SBA Small Business Administration
SC, S.C. South Carolina
SCAP Supreme Command Allies Pacific
ScB, Sc.B. Bachelor of Science
SCD, S.C.D. Doctor of Commercial Science
ScD, Sc.D. Doctor of Science
sch. school
sci. science, scientific
SCLC Southern Christian Leadership Conference
SCV Sons of Confederate Veterans
SD, S.D. South Dakota
SE, S.E. Southeast
SEATO Southeast Asia Treaty Organization
SEC Securities and Exchange Commission
sec. secretary
sect. section
seismol. seismological
sem. seminary
Sept. September
s.g. senior grade
sgt. sergeant
SHAEF Supreme Headquarters Allied Expeditionary Forces
SHAPE Supreme Headquarters Allied Powers in Europe
S.I. Staten Island

S.J. Society of Jesus (Jesuit)
SJD Scientiae Juridicae Doctor
SK Saskatchewan
SM, S.M. Master of Science
SNP Society of Nursing Professionals
So. Southern
soc. society
sociol. sociological
S.P.Co. Southern Pacific Company
spkr. speaker
spl. special
splty. specialty
Sq. Square
S.R. Sons of the Revolution
sr. senior
SS Steamship
SSS Selective Service System
St. Saint, Street
sta. station
stats. statistics
statis. statistical
STB, S.T.B. Bachelor of Sacred Theology
stblzn. stabilization
STD, S.T.D. Doctor of Sacred Theology
std. standard
Ste. Suite
subs. subsidiary
SUNY State University of New York
supr. supervisor
supt. superintendent
surg. surgical
svc. service
SW, S.W. Southwest
sys. system

TAPPI Technical Association of the Pulp and Paper Industry
tb. tuberculosis
tchg. teaching
tchr. teacher
tech. technical, technology
technol. technological
tel. telephone
Tel. & Tel. Telephone & Telegraph
telecom. telecommunications
temp. temporary
Tenn. Tennessee
Ter. Territory
Ter. Terrace
TESOL Teachers of English to Speakers of Other Languages
Tex. Texas
ThD, Th.D. Doctor of Theology
theol. theological
ThM, Th.M. Master of Theology
TN Tennessee
tng. training
topog. topographical
trans. transaction, transferred
transl. translation, translated
transp. transportation
treas. treasurer
TT Trust Territory
TV television
TVA Tennessee Valley Authority
TWA Trans World Airlines
twp. township
TX Texas
typog. typographical

U. University
UAW United Auto Workers
UCLA University of California at Los Angeles
UDC United Daughters of the Confederacy
U.K. United Kingdom
UN United Nations
UNESCO United Nations Educational, Scientific and Cultural Organization
UNICEF United Nations International Children's Emergency Fund
univ. university
UNRRA United Nations Relief and Rehabilitation Administration
UPI United Press International
U.P.R.R. United Pacific Railroad
urol. urological
U.S. United States
U.S.A. United States of America
USAAF United States Army Air Force
USAF United States Air Force
USAFR United States Air Force Reserve
USAR United States Army Reserve
USCG United States Coast Guard
USCGR United States Coast Guard Reserve
USES United States Employment Service
USIA United States Information Agency
USMC United States Marine Corps
USMCR United States Marine Corps Reserve
USN United States Navy
USNG United States National Guard
USNR United States Naval Reserve
USO United Service Organizations
USPHS United States Public Health Service
USS United States Ship
USSR Union of the Soviet Socialist Republics
USTA United States Tennis Association
USV United States Volunteers
UT Utah

VA Veterans Administration
VA, Va. Virginia
vet. veteran, veterinary
VFW Veterans of Foreign Wars
VI, V.I. Virgin Islands
vice pres. vice president
vis. visiting
VISTA Volunteers in Service to America
VITA Volunteers in Technical Assistance
vocat. vocational
vol. volunteer, volume
v.p. vice president
vs. versus
VT, Vt. Vermont

W, W. West
WA Washington (state)
WAC Women's Army Corps
Wash. Washington (state)
WATS Wide Area Telecommunications Service
WAVES Women's Reserve, US Naval Reserve
WCTU Women's Christian Temperance Union
we. western
W. Ger. Germany, Federal Republic of
WHO World Health Organization
WI Wisconsin
W.I. West Indies
Wis. Wisconsin
WSB Wage Stabilization Board
WV West Virginia
W.Va. West Virginia
WWI World War I
WWII World War II
WY Wyoming
Wyo. Wyoming

YK Yukon Territory
YMCA Young Men's Christian Association
YMHA Young Men's Hebrew Association
YM & YWHA Young Men's and Young Women's Hebrew Association
yr. year
YT, Y.T. Yukon Territory
YWCA Young Women's Christian Association

zool. zoological

Alphabetical Practices

Names are arranged alphabetically according to the surnames, and under identical surnames according to the first given name. If both surname and first given name are identical, names are arranged alphabetically according to the second given name.

Surnames beginning with De, Des, Du, however capitalized or spaced, are recorded with the prefix preceding the surname and arranged alphabetically under the letter D.

Surnames beginning with Mac and Mc are arranged alphabetically under M.

Surnames beginning with Saint or St. appear after names that begin Sains, and are arranged according to the second part of the name, e.g. St. Clair before Saint Dennis.

Surnames beginning with Van, Von, or von are arranged alphabetically under the letter V.

Compound surnames are arranged according to the first member of the compound.

Many hyphenated Arabic names begin Al-, El-, or al-. These names are alphabetized according to each Biographee's designation of last name. Thus Al-Bahar, Neta may be listed either under Al- or under Bahar, depending on the preference of the listee.

Also, Arabic names have a variety of possible spellings when transposed to English. Spelling of these names is always based on the practice of the Biographee. Some Biographees use a Western form of word order, while others prefer the Arabic word sequence.

Similarly, Asian names may have no comma between family and given names, but some Biographees have chosen to add the comma. In each case, punctuation follows the preference of the Biographee.

Parentheses used in connection with a name indicate which part of the full name is usually deleted in common usage. Hence Chambers, E(lizabeth) Anne indicates that the usual form of the given name is E. Anne. In such a case, the parentheses are ignored in alphabetizing and the name would be arranged as Chambers, Elizabeth Anne. However, if the name is recorded Chambers, (Elizabeth) Anne, signifying that the entire name Elizabeth is not commonly used, the alphabetizing would be arranged as though the name were Chambers, Anne. If an entire middle or last name is enclosed in parentheses, that portion of the name is used in the alphabetical arrangement. Hence Chambers, Elizabeth (Anne) would be arranged as Chambers, Elizabeth Anne.

Where more than one spelling, word order, or name of an individual is frequently encountered, the sketch has been entered under the form preferred by the Biographee, with cross-references under alternate forms.

Who'sWho in Medicine and Healthcare™

Biographies

AABERG, THOMAS M., SR., academic administrator, ophthalmology educator; b. St. Paul, Sept. 5, 1936; m. Judith S. Young, June 17, 1961; children: Thomas M. Jr., Leigh, Sarah. BA, Dartmouth Coll., 1958, MS, 1959; MD, Harvard U., 1961; MS in Preventative Medicine, U. Okla., 1968. Diplomate Am. Bd. Ophthalmology. Asst. prof. ophthalmology Med. Coll. Wis., Milw., 1969-71, assoc. prof. ophthalmology, 1971-76, prof. ophthalmology, 1976-88; chmn. dept. ophthalmology Sch Medicine Emory U., Atlanta, 1988—. Surgeon USPHS, 1966-68. Office: Emory Eye Ctr 1365-B Clifton Rd NE Atlanta GA 30322

AAGAARD, GEORGE NELSON, medical educator; b Mpls., Aug. 16, 1913; s. George N. and Lucy T. (Nelson) A.; m. Lorna D. Docken, Aug. 26, 1939; children: Diane Louise, George Nelson, Richard Nelson, David Nelson, Steven Nelson. B.S., U. Minn., 1934, M.B., 1936, M.D., 1937. Intern Mpls. Gen. Hosp., 1936-37; successively fellow, instr., asst. prof. internal medicine U. Minn. Med. Sch., 1941-47, assoc. prof., dir. continuing med. edn., 1948-51; prof. medicine, dean Southwestern Med. Sch., U. Tex., 1952-54; dean U. Washington Sch. Medicine, 1954-64, prof. medicine, 1954-78, disting. prof. medicine and pharmacology, 1978—, head div. clin. pharmacology, 1964-79; mem. Nat. Adv. Council for Health Research Facilities USPHS, 1954-58; mem. nat. adv. heart council NIH, 1961-65; mem. spl. med. adv. group VA, 1970-74; chmn. bd. trustees Network for Continuing Med. Edn., 1966-78. Bd. dirs., editorial bd.: Western Jour. Medicine. Mem. Am. Heart Assn. (trustee), Assn. Am. Med. Colls. (pres. 1960-61), AMA (dir., chmn. com. continuing profl. edn. programs 1972), Pharm. Mfrs. Assn. Found. (mem. sci. adv. com. 1967-74), Am. Soc. Clin. Pharmacology and Therapeutics (pres. 1977, Elliott award 1983), N.Y. Acad. Scis., A.A.A.S., Washington, King County med. socs., Alpha Omega Alpha. Home: 8001 Sand Point Way NE Apt 66C Seattle WA 98115-6356

AANESTAD, SAMUEL MARK, surgeon; b. Bismarck, N.D., July 16, 1946; s. Wilhelm C.D. and Harriet E. (Witta) A.; m. Susan Lee Thompson, Aug. 30, 1969; children: Kaesa, Erik, Kirstin. AB in Zoology, UCLA, 1969, DDS, 1973; MPA, Golden Gate U., 1991. Pvt. practice Grass Valley, Calif., 1980—; chmn. coun. on legislation, mem. dental PAC bd., Calif. Dental Assn., Sacramento, 1993—. Trustee Grass Valley Sch. Dist., 1983-94, chmn. 1986, 91. Paul Harris fellow Rotary. Mem. Pierre Fauchard Acad., Sadi Fontaine Acad. Republican. Office: 1364 Whispering Pines Ln #3 Grass Valley CA 95945

AANSTOOS, CHRISTOPHER MICHAEL, psychology educator; b. Saipan Island, U.S. Trust Ter., Apr. 4, 1952; s. Anthony Matthew and Frances Henrietta (Jambrick) A.; children: Megan Elizabeth, Lucas Mathew. BA, Mich. State U., 1974; MA, Duquesne U., 1976, PhD., 1982. Instr. Pa. State U., McKeesport, 1979-82; asst. prof. psychology State U. West Ga., Carrollton, 1982-87; assoc. prof., 1987-92, prof., 1992—, chmn., 1995-96; contracted rschr. Pitts. Sch. Dist., 1979; manuscript reviewer Harcourt, Brace, Jovanovich, N.Y., 1983, New Ideas in Psychology, 1984-85, Saybrook Inst., 1986, Metaphor and Symbolic Activity, 1985-88, Sage, 1989, Guilford, 1990. Editor Exploring the Lived World, 1984, The World of the Infant, 1987, Human Growth and Development, 1990; Studies in Humanistic Psychology, 1991; Jour. The Humanistic Psychologist, 1984—; assoc. editor Jour. Theoretical and Philosophical Psychology, 1986-89; cons. editor Jour. Phenomenological Psychology, 1982—; contbr. over 60 articles to profl. jours., books. Coord. Fund Drive Am. Heart Assn., State U. West Ga., 1985; vol. West Ga. Coll. Speakers Bur., 1983—. Faculty Rsch. grantee State U. West Ga., 1983-85, 89-90, 92-93. Mem. APA (exec. bd. divs. 24, 32, program chmn. div. 24 1991), AAUP, Human Sci. Research Assn. (program chmn. 1984), Southeastern Psychol. Assn., Assn. Qualitative Research Psychology (chmn. program com. 1987), Chess Fedn. (West Ga.), Phi Beta Kappa. Home: 2175 Hog Liver Rd Carrollton GA 30117-9308 Office: State U West Ga Psychology Dept Carrollton GA 30118

AARON, BERNARD MARK, gastroenterologist; b. N.Y.C., Dec. 6, 1945; s. Max and Esther (Lieberman) A.; m. Susan J. Aaron, June 23, 1974; children: David, Robert; stepchildren: Ellen Grenger, Cassandra Magzamen. Student, Hobart Coll., Geneva, N.Y., 1962-65; MD, SUNY, Bklyn., 1969. Diplomate Am. Bd. Internal Medicine and Gastroenterology. Straight med. intern St. Vincent's Hosp., N.Y.C., 1969-70, resident in medicine, 1970-71; resident in medicine Greenwich (Conn.) Hosp., 1971-72; fellow in gastroenterology Manhattan VA Hosp., 1972-74; acting chief gastroenterology Stonybrook Med. Sch., Northport, N.Y., 1976-77; staff physician Med. Ctr. Ocean County, Point Pleasant and Brick, N.J., 1977—, Jersey Shore Med. Ctr., Neptune, N.J., 1977—; clin. instr. medicine Robert Wood Johnson Med. Sch., New Brunswick, N.J., 1979—. Fellow Am. Coll. Gastroenterology; mem. ACP, Am. Soc. Gastrointestinal Endoscopy, N.Y. Soc. Gastrointestinal Endoscopy. Office: 459 Jack Martin Blvd Brick NJ 08724

AARON, CHARLES ROUNTREE, physician assistant; b. Anderson, S.C., Mar. 22, 1953; s. Ira Edward and Lottie Vickery (Rountree) A.; m. Rebecca Jan Moore, June 4, 1983; children: Rachel Vickery, Matthew Charles. BS in Biology, Ga. So. U., 1976; BS in Med. Sci., physician assoc. degree, Emory U., 1978. Cert. physician asst., N.C.; cert. Nat. Cert. Coun. Physician Assts. Physician asst. Hawkins County Hosp., Rogersville, Tenn., 1979-85, Beaver Family Care Assocs., Beckley, W.Va., 1985-95, Healthways Family Med. Ctr., Charlotte, N.C., 1995—. Mem. Am. Assn. Physician Assts., N.C. Assn. Physician Assts., W.Va. Assn. Med. Assts., Mechlenburg Med. Soc. Home: 1124 Sunny View Cir Matthews NC 28105

AARONSON, HERBERT G., psychiatrist; b. Phila., Feb. 8, 1927; s. Harry A. and S.B. (Belavsky) A.; m. Harriet B. Shulman, June 3, 1934; children: Gary, Arthur, Debra, Nina. BA, Temple U., 1950; MA, Columbia U., 1951; MD, Jefferson Med. Coll., 1957. Diplomate Am. Bd. Psychiatry and Neurology. Intern so. div. Albert Einstein Med. Ctr., Phila., 1957-58; resident Norristown State Hosp., Norristown, Pa., 1958-61; Arthur P. Noyes fellow in psychiatry Norristown State Hosp., 1961-62; pvt. practice Wyncote, Pa., 1962-91; dir. med. svcs. Prudential Ins. Co., Horsham, Pa., 1991—. Sgt. AUS, 1945-46. Office: Prudential Ins Co 250 Gibraltar Rd Horsham PA 19044-0911

ABAYAZED, OMER EL FAROUK HASSAN, surgeon; b. Cairo, Egypt, Mar. 22, 1944; came to U.S., 1995; s. Khairi Hassan Abayazed and Swar Fatima Mohamed. MBBCH, Med. Acad. Dresden, 1973; FACH in Surgery, Hannover U., 1983; MD, U. Dusseldorf, 1984. Registrar Dept. Orthop./Traumatology, Kharoum, Sudan, 1974-76; registrar surgery Marien Hosp., Osnabruca, Germany, 1976-78, St. Raphael Hosp., Ostercappela, Germany, 1978-81; specialist surgeon Stadt Klinker, Osnabruca, 1981-85, Rashid Hosp., Dubai, UAE, 1985—; lectr. surgery Dubai Med. Coll., 1987—. Mem. German Med. Assn. Home: PO Box 9023, Dubai United Arab Emirates Office: Rashid Hosp, Dubai United Arab Emirates

ABBAS, HISHAM IBRAHIM, physician; b. Mansoura, Egypt, Mar. 20, 1955; arrived in Saudi Arabia, 1988; s. Ibrahim Abbas Abdou and Iglal Ibrahim Amjn; m. Gihan Moustafa Ahmed, Aug. 16, 1987; children: Amjra Hisham, Aya Hisham. MBBCh, Mansoura U., 1980. Diplomate. Gen. practitioner Gen. Hosp., Mansoura, 1980-83; orthopaedic intern Gen. Hosp., Port Said, Egypt, 1983-85, dermatology intern, 1985-87; dir. PHC, Dawadmy, Saudi Arabia, 1990-91, Al Garrara, Saudi Arabia, 1991—. Office: Al Garara Dispensary, Al Bejadya, Riyadh 11931, Saudi Arabia

ABBASI, TARIQ AFZAL, psychiatrist, educator; b. Hyderabad, India, Aug. 13, 1946; came to U.S., 1976, naturalized, 1983; s. Shujaat Ali and Salma Khatoon (Siddiqui) A.; m. Kashifa Khatoon, Nov. 10, 1972; children—Sameena, Omar, Osman. B.S., Madrasa-I-Aliya, Hyderabad, 1964; M.B.B.S., Osmania Med. Coll., Hyderabad, 1970; Diploma in Psychol. Medicine, St. John's Hosp., U. Sheffield (Eng.), 1976. Diplomate Am. Bd. Psychiatry and Neurology; diplomate in psychiatry Royal Coll. Physicians of Eng. Sr. house officer St. John's Hosp., Lincoln, Eng., 1972-73, registrar, 1973-76; resident in psychiatry Rutgers Med. Sch., Piscataway, N.J., 1976-79, chief resident, 1979, dir. adult in-patient services Community Mental Health Ctr., Rutgers Med. Sch., also asst. prof. psychiatry, 1979-82; staff psychiatrist Northville Regional Psychiat. Hosp. (Mich.), 1982-83, div. dir., 1983—; cons. psychiatrist Rahway State Prison (N.J.), 1979-82; clin. instr. psychiatry Wayne State U. Med. Sch., Detroit. Mem. Am. Psychiat. Assn., Mich. Psychiat. Soc. Office: Northville Regl Psychiat Hosp 41001 7 Mile Rd Northville MI 48167-2655 also: 33200 Dequindre Rd Ste 200 Sterling Heights MI 48310-5916 also: 999 Haynes St Ste 245 Birmingham MI 48009-6775

ABBETT, WILLIAM S., dean. Dean Mich. State U. Coll. Human Medicine, East Lansing. Office: Mich State U A110 E Fee Hall East Lansing MI 48824*

ABBOTT, ANN AUGUSTINE, social worker, educator; b. Green Bay, Wis., July 6, 1943; d. Walter A. and Ethel D. Augustine. BS in Psychology, St. Norbert Coll., W. DePere, Wis., 1965; MSS in Social Work (U.S. Children's Bur. fellow), Bryn Mawr Coll., 1969, PhD (NIMH fellow), 1977; postgrad. in Higher Edn. Adminstrn., Higher Edn. Resource Sevcs. Summer Inst. for Women, Bryn Mawr (Pa.) Coll., 1978. Acad. tutor, counselor Devereux Schs., Devon, Pa., 1965-67; psychol. clinic coord. Pa. State U., University Park, 1969-71; social worker Tidewater Mental Health Clinic, Williamsburg, Va., 1971-72; adj. prof. Pa. State U., King of Prussia, 1973-75; vis. lectr. Community Coll. of Phila., 1975-76; asst. prof. dir. social work, community psychology Widener U., Chester, Pa., 1976-81, project dir. Univ. Yr. for Action, 1976-81, project cons. Adult Competency Tng. Grant, 1976-81; with sch. social work Rutgers U., Camden, N.J., 1981—, assoc. prof., 1987—, assoc. dean, 1993—; faculty fellow NIAAA/NIDA/OSAP, 1990-93. Tennis coach Nat. Jr. Tennis League, Phila., 1974-76; budget rev. bd. United Way, vice-chair allocations com., 1979-86. Vocation Rehab. Tng. grantee, 1964. Fellow Am. Orthopsychiat. Assn., Coll. Physicians of Phila.; mem. Nat. Assn. Social Workers (nat. bd. mem. region IV 1988-91, del. assembly rep. 1978-89, pres. Pa. state chpt. 1987-89, nat. pres.-elect. 1992-93, nat. pres. 1993-95), Coun. on Social Work Edn., Am. Group Psychotherapy Assn., Internat. Fed. of Social Workers (v.p. for N. Am. 1994-96). Home: PO Box 637 Villanova PA 19085-0637 Office: Rutgers U Social Work Dept 327 Cooper St Camden NJ 08102-1519

ABBOTT, CYNTHIA ALLEN, nurse administrator; b. Ponca City, Okla., Dec. 15, 1954; d. Thomas J. and Peggy Joan (Fugate) Allen; children: Michael Charles, Caroline Alyssa Allen. BSN, Okla. U., 1978; MSN, U. Tex., Austin, 1987, PhD, 1993. RN, Okla.; cert. perioperative nursing. Commd. 2d lt. U.S. Army, 1978, advanced through grades to lt. col., 1993; charge nurse Eisenhower Army Med. Ctr., Ft. Gordon, Ga., 1978-79, head nurse neurol. surg. svcs., 1979-80; oper. room staff devel. coord. 98th Gen. Hosp., Nuremberg, Germany, 1980-81; head nurse ctrl. material supply 98th Gen. Hosp., Nuremberg, 1981-83; head nurse oper. rm. gen. surgery svcs. Darnall Army Community Hosp., Ft. Hood, Tex., 1983-84; mem. assoc. faculty U. Tex. Sch. Nursing, San Antonio, 1988-90; sr. instr. operating rm. br., nursing sci. divsn. Acad. Health Scis., U.S. Army, Ft. Sam Houston, Tex., 1987-90; dir. perioperative nursing svcs. Ireland Army Cmty. Hosp., Ft. Knox, Ky., 1993-94, dir. patient care svcs. of surg. svcs. team, 1994; sr. nurse rschr. Ctr. for Health and Edn. Studies, Acad. Health Scis., Ft. Sam Houston, Tex., 1995—; chmn. patient/home health nursing Healthcare 2020 Futures Trisvc. Initiative, 1995—; presenter in field. Mem. editorial bd.: Seminars in Perioperative Nursing, 1992-93, Pathways, 1992-93; contbr. articles to profl. jours. Lt. col. U.S. Army, 1978—. Named ROTC Disting. Mil. Grad., U. Okla., 1978; decorated Expert Field Med. badge, Army Commendation medal with 4 oakleaf clusters, Meritorious Svc. medal with oakleaf cluster, 1995, Dr. Anita Newcomb McGee award Daughters of the Am. Revolution, 1995; named Army Surg. Gen. Nurse of Yr., 1995. Mem. ANA, Assn. Operating Rm. Nurses, Inc. (nat. com. on edn., rep. region VI, del. 36th Congress, Anaheim, Calif., 1989, chmn. nat. com. on edn., del. 37th Congress, Houston, 1990, chmn. nat. com. on edn., del. 38th Congress, Atlanta, 1991, nursing rsch. com., del. 39th Congress, Dallas, 1992, nursing rsch. com., chair-elect, del. 40th Congress, Anaheim, 1993, chmn. program com. San Antonio AORN chpt. 1987, mem. task force on data elements and unlicensed assistive personnel 1993-94, co-chair rsch. and legis coms., 28th annual symposium planning com. 1988, chmn. rsch. com., newsletter com. 1989-90, moderator/chmn. 29th annual symposium, sec. 1988-90, pres.-elect., chmn. bylaws com. 1990-91, pres. 1991-92, bd. dirs. nominating com. 1992-93), Tex. Nurses Assn., Sigma Theta Tau (Delta Alpha chpt. policy and bylaws com. 1988-90), Phi Kappa Phi. Methodist. Home: 6903 S Jamestown Tulsa OK 74136 Office: Ctr for Health Edn Studies CHES MCCS-HR AMEDD Ctr/Sch Acad Health Scis Fort Sam Houston TX 78234

ABBOTT, DAVID T., physician assistant; b. San Francisco, June 2, 1948; s. Vera Gordon Worth; m. Theresa Susan Petronico (div. 1979); 1 child, Jason; m. Mary Beth Roberts; children: Tammy, Beth, Amy. AS, Am. River Coll., Sacramento, 1974; BS, U. Okla., Norman, 1979. Respiratory therapist Mercy San Juan Hosp., Sacramento, 1973-77; physician asst. Dept. Justice, Fed. Prison Svc., El Reno, Okla., 1980-95, Federal Transfer Ctr., Oklahoma City, 1995—; lectr. in field. With U.S. Army, 1967-70. Mem. Am. Correctional Assn. (charter mem. planning com. 1984). Republican. Episcopalian. Home: 353 Chickasaw Ln Yukon OK 73099-5707 Office: Federal Transfer Ctr 7400 S McArthur Blvd Oklahoma City OK 73036-1000

ABBOTT, MARLENE LOUISE, nursing agency administrator; b. Hornell, N.Y., Aug. 11, 1935; d. George Wilfred and Eloise Lois (Simpson) Little; m. Robert Leroy, Mar. 16, 1953; children: Valarie, Kimberley, Steven, Tracey. AAS in Nursing, Corning Community Coll., 1968; BSN, Ariz. State U., 1984. Registered psychiatric community mental health nurse. R.N. ICU-CCU Arnot-Ogden Hosp., Elmira, N.Y., 1968-70, Good Samaritan Hosp., Phoenix, 1972-73; R.N. Scottsdale (Ariz.) Meml. Hosp., 1973-74; inservice dir. Mohave Gen. Hosp., Kingman, Ariz., 1974-75; school nurse Manzanita Elem. Sch., Kingman, 1975-77; R.N. staff surgical VA Med. Ctr., Phoenix, 1979-83; R.N. med., surgical Humana Hosp., Phoenix, 1983-84; R.N. psychiatric staff Camelback Hosp., Phoenix, 1984-86; owner, adminstr. Tri-Nursing, Inc., Phoenix, 1986—; bd. dirs. Career One/Ariz. Coll., Phoenix, 1987-89. Precinct committeewoman Dem. Party, Phoenix, 1987-92, state committeewoman, 1990—; candidate Ariz. State Senate, 1990; mem. Phoenix Community Coun. Mem. ANA, Ariz. Assn. Health Care Agencies (pres. 1988-89), Phoenix C. of C. Office: Tri Nursing Inc 18223 N 45th Ave Glendale AZ 85308-1615

ABBOTT, REGINA A., neurodiagnostic technologist, consultant, business owner; b. Haverhill, Mass., Mar. 5, 1950; d. Frank A. and Ann (Drelick) A. Student, Pierce Bus. Sch., Boston, 1967-70, Seizure Unit Children's Hosp. Med. Ctr. Sch. EEG Tech., Boston, 1970-71. Registered technologist. Tech. dir. electrodiagnostic labs. Salem Hosp., 1972-76; lab. dir. clin. neurophysiology Tufts U. New Eng. Med. Ctr., Boston, 1976-78; clin. instr. EEG program Laboure Coll., Boston, 1977-81; adminstrv. dir. dept. Neurology Mt. Auburn Hosp., Cambridge, Mass., 1978-81; tech. dir. clin. neurophysiology Drs. Diagnostic Service, Virginia Beach, Va.; tech. dir. neurodiagnostic ctr. Portsmouth Psychiatric Ctr., 1981-87; founder, pres., owner Commonwealth Neurodiagnostic Services, Inc., 1986—; co-dir. continuing edn. program EEG Tech., Boston, 1977-78; mem. adv. com. sch. neurodiagnostic tech. Laboure Coll., 1977-81, Sch. EEG Tech. Children's Hosp. Med. Ctr., Boston, 1980-81; assoc. examiner Am. Bd. Registration of Electroencephalographic Technologists, 1977-83; mem. guest faculty Oxford Medilog Co., 1986; cons. Nihon Kohden Am., 1981-83; cons., educator Teca Corp., Pleasantville, N.Y., 1981-87; allied health profl. staff mem. Virginia Beach Gen. Hosp., Humana Hosp. Bayside, Virginia Beach; clin. evaluator Calif. Coll. for Health Scis., 1995—. Contbr. articles to profl. jours. EIL scholar, Poland/USSR, 1970; recipient Internat. Woman of Yr. award in bus. and sci. Internat. Biographical Ctr., London, 1993-94, Woman of Yr. award Am. Biographical Inst., 1993. Mem. NAFE, Am. Soc. Electroneurodiagnostic Technologists, New Eng. Soc. EEG Technologists (bd. dirs., sec., tng. and edn. com., faculty tng. and edn.), Am. Assn. Electrodiagnostic Technologists, Epilepsy Soc. Mass. Office: Commonwealth Neurodiagnostic Svcs Inc 400 Biltmore Ct Virginia Beach VA 23454-3459

ABBOUD, FRANCOIS MITRY, physician, educator; b. Cairo, Egypt, Jan. 5, 1931; came to U.S., 1955, naturalized, 1963; s. Mitry Y. and Asma (Habac) A.; m. Doris Evelyn Khal, June 5, 1955; children: Mary Agnese, Susan Marie, Nancy Louise, Anthony Lawrence. Student, U. Cairo, 1948-52; M.B., B.Ch., Ein Chams U., 1955; D (hon.), U. Lyon, France, 1991; DSc (hon.), Med. Coll. Wis., 1994. Diplomate Am. Bd. Internal Medicine, Am. Bd. Cardiovascular Disease (bd. govs. 1987-93). Intern Demerdash Govt. Hosp., Cairo, 1955; resident Milw. County Hosp., 1955-58; Am. Heart Assn. research fellow cardiovascular labs. Marquette U., 1958-60; Am. Heart Assn. advanced research fellow U. Iowa, 1960-62, asst. prof., 1961-65, assoc. prof. medicine, 1965-68, prof. medicine, 1968—, prof. physiology and biophysics, 1975—, Edith King Pearson prof. cardiovascular rsch., 1988—; dir. cardiovascular div., 1970-76, chmn. dept. internal medicine, 1976—, dir. cardiovascular center, 1974—; attending physician U. Iowa Hosps., 1961—, VA Hosp., Iowa City, 1963—; chmn. rsch. rev. com. Nat. Heart, Lung and Blood Inst., 1978-80, adv. coun., 1995—. Editor Circulation Rsch., 1981-86, Procs. of the Assn. Am. Physicians, 1995—; assoc. editor Advances in Internal Medicine, 1991-96; editl. bd. Medicine, 1992—. Recipient European Traveling fellowship French Govt., 1948, NIH Career Devel. award, 1962-71. Master ACP; mem. Inst. Medicine NAS, AMA, Am. Soc. Clin. Investigation, Ctrl. Soc. for Clin. Rsch. (pres. elect 1984-85, pres. 1985-86), Soc. Exptl. Biology and Medicine, Am. Heart Assn. (bd. dirs. 1977-80, past chmn. rsch. coms., award of Merit 1982, Disting. Achievement award 1988, CIBA award for hypertension rsch. 1990, pres. elect 1989-90, pres. 1990-91, Gold Heart award 1995), Am. Fedn. Clin. Rsch. (pres. 1971-72), Assn. Univ. Cardiologists, Assn. Profs. Medicine (Robert H. Williams Disting. Chmn. of Medicine award 1993, bd. dirs. 1993—), Assn. Am. Physicians (treas. 1979-84, councillor 1984-89, 89—, pres.-elect 1989-90, pres. 1990-91), Am. Physiol. Soc. (chmn. circulation group 1979-80, chmn. clin. physiology sect. 1979-83, publ. com. 1987-90, Wiggers award 1988), Am. Clin. and Climatological Assn. (councillor 1992), Am. Soc. Pharmacology and Exptl. Therapeutics (award exptl. therapeutics 1972), Internat. Soc. Hypertension (Merck Sharp & Dohme Internat. award for rsch. in hypertension 1994), Sigma Xi, Alpha Omega Alpha (bd. dirs. 1989—). Home: 24 Kennedy Pky Iowa City IA 52246-2780 Office: U Iowa Coll Medicine Dept Internal Medicine Iowa City IA 52242*

ABBRECHT, PETER HERMAN, medical educator; b. Toledo, Nov. 27, 1930; s. Hermann Richard and Paula Katherine (Schwenk) A.; m. Anne Patterson Lampman, Feb. 16, 1957; children—Elaine, Brian. B.S., Purdue U., 1952; M.S., U. Mich., 1953, Ph.D. in Chem. Engring, 1957, M.D., 1962. Diplomate: Am. Bd. Internal Medicine, Am. Bd. Pulmonary Disease. Sr. chem. engr. Minn. Mining & Mfg. Co., Detroit, 1956-58; intern U. Calif. Hosp., L.A., 1962-63; mem. faculty U. Mich. Med. Sch., Ann Arbor, 1963-80; prof. physiology U. Mich. Med. Sch., 1972-80; resident in internal medicine U. Mich. Hosp., 1971-72, fellow in pulmonary disease, 1974-75; chmn. bioengring. program U. Mich. Med. Sch., 1972-77, prof. medicine, 1976-80; prof. medicine and physiology Uniformed Svcs. U. of Health Scis., Bethesda, Md., 1980—, chmn. dept. physiology, 1987—; cons. physician Walter Reed Army Med. Ctr., 1980—; guest scientist Naval Med. Rsch. Inst., 1980-82; vis. prof. bioengring. U. Calif., San Diego, 1973; dir. physiology and biomed. engring. program NIGMS, NIH, 1977-78; cons. VA, NASA, Air Force Office Sci. Rsch.; cons. NSF, mem. nat. rsch. resources adv. coun., 1975-78; cons., mem. biomed. rsch. tech. com. NIH, 1986-90, chmn., 1989-90; mem. U.S. Nat. Com. on Biomechanics, 1994-96. Editor in chief Internat. Jour. Biomed. Engring, 1972-74, Annals Biomed. Engring., 1978-84; mem. editorial bd. Jour. Biomechanics; contbr. articles to profl. jours. Recipient outstanding research award Mich. Heart Assn., 1960; research career devel. award NIH, 1969-73. Fellow ACP, Am. Coll. Chest Physicians; mem. AAAS, Biomed. Engring. Soc. (dir. 1970-72), Am. Physiol. Soc., Am. Thoracic Soc. Home: 2806 Spencer Rd Bethesda MD 20815-3877

ABBRUZZESE, CARLO ENRICO, physician, writer, educator; b. Rome, Italy, May 28, 1923; came to U.S., 1951, naturalized, 1959; s. Aurelio and Maria (Sbriccoli) A.; m. Silvia Ramirez-Lemus; children: Marco A., Carlo M., Eric L., Christopher E., Romana S. Liceo-Ginnasio, Dante Alighieri, Roma, 1935-43; Facoltà di Medicina e Chirurgia, Università di Roma, 1943-49; DSc, London Inst. Applied Rsch., 1973. Lic. med. dr. Italy, European Community, Calif. Resident in tropical subtropical diseases U. Rome, 1950-51; intern Woman's and Highland Park Gen. hosps., Detroit, 1951-53; resident in family practice Saratoga Gen. Hosp., Detroit, Columbus Hosp., Newark, 1953-57; gen. practice occupational and sport medicine Rome, 1949-51, Oakland, Calif., 1958-75, Santa Ana, Calif., 1975-84; dir. emergency and outpatient depts. Drs. Hosp. Santa Ana, Calif., 1975-77; dir. North Bristol Family Med. Clinic, Rsch. and Diagnostic Lab. Author: Storia della Psicologia, 1949, Roma, L'ascoltazione Stetoscopica del cuore, RCA italiana, 1953, L'ascoltazione stetoscopica, 1955, 56, 83, 86, Roma, 1986, Esercitazioni di diagnostica ascoltatoria, 1983, 86; founder, pub., editor-in-chief ESDNA, Rome, 1983, ESDI, Rome, 1986; pub. Med. Newsletter, 1987; contbr. articles to profl. jours. Founder, leader polit. youth movements, Rome, 1943-47; co-founder, nat. chmn. U.S. divorce reforms orgns., 1975; UN rep. on violation of due process and domestic human rights, 1977; exec. officer Men Internat., Calif.; active Nat. Italian Am. Found. Decorated Commendatore di Merito, 1950, Gran Croce Merito del Lavoro, Internat. Bus. Corp., 1981; Fulbright fellow, 1951-53. Fellow Am. Acad. Family Physicians; mem. AMA, Calif. Med. Assn., Orange County Med. Assn., Ordine dei Medici di Roma, Societá Italiana di Chirurgia, Union Am. Physicians, Am. Acad. Family Practice (co-founder). Office: 316 N Bristol St Santa Ana CA 92703-3811

ABBRUZZESE, JOHN ANTHONY, JR., psychologist, retired administrator, educator; b. Pitts., Dec. 19, 1928; s. John A. and Frances (Curcio) A.; m. Jean Dezzutti, Sept. 27, 1952; children: John A. III, Mark R., Eugenia F. BS, U. Pitts., 1949, MEd, 1954; PhD, Western U., San Diego, 1957. Cert. tchr., sch. adminstr., psychologist, Pa. Chemistry and physics tchr. various locations, Pa., 1950-51, 53-55; tchr. spl. edn., psychyol. examiner Allegheny County schs., 1955-56; psychologist Monroe County schs., Pa., 1956-66; asst. supt. Monroe County schs., 1966-69, supt., 1969-71; pvt. practice psychology, 1962—; mem. staff Pocono Med. Ctr., Pa., 1968—; asst. exec. dir. Colonial Northampton Intermediate Unit, Pa., 1971-73, dir. spl.

edn., 1973-82, exec. dir., 1982-93, exec. dir. emeritus, 1993—. Contbr. articles to profl. jours. Bd. dirs. Easter Seal Soc., Monroe County, Pa., 1957-85. Sgt. U.S. Army, 1951-53. Recipient numerous awards for profl. and civic contbns., including Brace for an Ace award Easter Seals Soc., 1970, Silver Beaver award Boy Scouts Am. Minsi Trails Coun., 1992. Mem. Am. Assn. Sch. Adminstrs., Am. Vocat. Assn., Nat. Assn. Sch. Psychologists, Nat. Rehab. Assn., Coun. Exceptional Children. Coun. Adminstrs. and Suprs. Spl. Edn., Pa. Assn. Chief Sch. Adminstrs., Lehigh Valley Psychol. Assn., Pa. Psychol. Assn., Mideast Pa. Sch. Psychologists Assn., Pa. Vocat. Assn., Pa. Assn. Sch. Adminstrs., Rotary, Pa. Schoolmen, Phi Delta Kappa. Democrat. Roman Catholic. Home: Locust Ln RR 1 Box 1026 Stroudsburg PA 18360 Office: 1320 N 5th St Stroudsburg PA 18360

ABCARIAN, HERAND, surgeon, educator; b. Ahvaz, Iran, Jan. 23, 1941; came to U.S., 1966; s. Joseph and Stella (Banki) A.; m. Karen Jane Berger, May 10, 1969; children: Gregory, Ariane, Margot. MD, Teheran U., 1965. Diplomate Am. Bd. Colon and rectal Surgery (exec. dir., sec.-treas.). Rotating intern Cook County Hosp., Chgo., 1966-67, resident gen. surgery, 1967-71, resident colon and rectal surgery, 1971-72, chmn. colon and rectal surgery, 1972-93; head dept. surgery U. Ill. Coll. Med., Chgo., 1989—; mem. Am. Bd. Colon and Rectal Surgery, exec. dir., 1987—; mem. Am. Bd. Med. Spltys., mem. exec. com., 1993—. Assoc. editor Diseases of Colon and Rectum, 1981-95. Fellow ACS (various coms. and offices), Am. Soc. Colon and Rectal Surgeons (sec. 1985-87, pres. 1988-89); mem. Soc. Am. Gastroendoscopic Surgeons (founder), Sydney Soc. Colon and Rectal Surgeons (hon.). Republican. Roman Catholic. Office: U Ill 820 S Wood St # 515 Chicago IL 60612-7310

ABDEL-DAYEM, HUSSEIN MAHMOUD, physician, educator; b. Cairo, Egypt, Apr. 5, 1934; s. Mahmoud Abdel-Dayem and Shafika El-Syed; m. Ayda M. El-Shirbiny, Sept. 19, 1968; children: Amani, Essmaeel. MBBCh, Cairo U., 1959, MD in Radiotherapy, 1967. Diplomate Am. Bd. Nuclear Medicine, Am. Bd. Radiotherapy. Lectr. radiotherapy Faculty of Medicine Cairo U., 1960-70; sr. registrar Kuwait Cancer Control Ctr., 1970-71; clin. assoc. prof. SUNY, Buffalo, 1970-72; dir. radiotherapy & nuclear medicine Erie County Med. Ctr., Buffalo, 1972-81; prof., chmn. dept. nuclear medicine Kuwait U., 1981-90; adj. mem. Meml. Sloan-Kettering Cancer Ctr., N.Y.C., 1990-91; chief nuclear medicine svc. St. Vincent's Hosp. & Med. Ctr., N.Y.C., 1992—; prof. radiology N.Y. Med. Coll., Valhalla; pres. Asia & Oceania Fedn. Nuclear Medicine & Biology, 1988-92. Mem. editorial bd. European Jour. Nuclear Medicine, 1992—, Jour. Nuclear Medicine, 1995—. Home: 71 Hoover Dr Cresskill NJ 07626-1705 Office: St Vincent's Hosp 153 W 11th St New York NY 10011-8305

ABD EL FATTAH, SAID MOHAMMED, surgeon; b. Cairo, Mar. 15, 1948; s. Mohammed Abd El Fattah and Sania Afifi (Nasser) Kheith; m. Salwa El Sayed Heba, Mar. 1, 1981. MBBCh, U. Cairo, 1971; MD, Al Azhar U. Med. officer Ministry of Health, Cairo, 1972-73; registrar Ministry of Health, Muscat, Oman, 1980-85, sr. registrar, 1985-88, sr. specialist, 1988-95; sr. house officer Health Ins., Cairo, 1973-75, registrar, 1975-80; trauma surgeon Ministry of Health, 1988-90, laproscopic surgeon, 1992-94, rschr. thyroid surgery, 1995-96. Author: Varicocele & Maile Infertility, 1981; contbr. articles to profl. jours. Office: Ministry of Health, PO Box 1331-111, Muscat Sultanate of Oman, Muscat Oman

ABDELLAH, FAYE GLENN, retired public health service executive; b. N.Y.C., Mar. 13; d. H.B. and Margaret (Glenn) A. BS in Teaching, Columbia U., 1945, MA in Teaching, 1947, EdD, 1955; LLD (hon.), Case Western Res. U., 1967, Rutgers U., 1973; DSc (hon.), U. Akron, 1978, Cath. U. Am., 1981, Monmouth Coll., 1982, Ea. Mich U., 1987, U. Bridgeport, 1987, Georgetown U., 1989; D Pub. Svc. (hon.), Am. U., 1987; LHD (hon.), Georgetown U., 1989, U. S.C., 1991; D Pub. Svc., U. S.C., 1991. RN. Commd. officer USPHS, Rockville, Md., 1949, advanced through grades to rear adm., 1970, asst. surgeon gen., chief nurse officer, 1970-87, dep. surgeon gen., 1981-89, chief nursing edn. br., div. nursing, 1949-59; surgeon gen. USPHS, 1989; chief rsch. grants br. Bur. Health Manpower Edn., NIH, HEW, Rockville, 1959-69; dir. Office Rsch. Tng. Nat. Ctr. for Health Svcs. R & D, Health Svcs. Mental Health Adminstrn., Rockville, 1969; acting dep. dir. Nat. Ctr. for Health Svcs. R & D, Rockville, 1971, Bur. Health Svcs. Rsch. and Evaluation, Health Resources Adminstrn., Rockville, 1973; dir. Office Long-Term Care, Office Asst. Sec. for Health, HEW, Rockville, 1973-80; exec. dir. grad. sch. nursing uniformed svcs., dean, prof. U. Health Scis., Bethesda, Md., 1993—; exec. dir., acting dean; prof. nursing, Emily Smith chair U. S.C., Columbia, 1990-91; dean, prof. Grad. Sch. Nursing, Uniformed Srvs. U. Health Scis., 1993—. Author: Effect of Nurse Staffing on Satisfactions with Nursing Care, 1959, Patient Centered Approaches to Nursing, 1960, Better Patient Care Through Nursing Research, 1965, 2d edit., 1979, 3d edit., 1986, Intensive Care, Concepts and Practices for Clinical Nurse Specialists, 1969, New Directions in Patient Centered Nursing, 1972, Preparing Nursing Research for the 21st Century, 1994; contbr. articles to profl. jours. Recipient Mary Adelaide Nutting award, 1983, hon. recognition ANA, 1986, Oustanding Leadership award U. Pa., 1987, 99, Disting. Svc. award, 1973-89, Surgeon Gen.'s medal and medallion, 1989, Allied-Signal Achievement award in aging, 1989, Gustav O. Lienhard award Inst. Medicine, NAS, 1992. Fellow Am. Acad. Nursing (charter, past v.p., pres.); mem. Am. Psychol. Assn., AAAS, Assn. Mil. Surgeons U.S., Sigma Theta Tau (Disting. Rsch. Fellow award 1989), Phi Lambda Theta. Home: 3713 Chanel Rd Annandale VA 22003-2024

ABDELNOOR, ALEXANDER MICHAEL, immunologist, educator; b. N.Y.C., Jan. 18, 1941; s. Michael Dib and Evelyn Isber (Massabni) A.; m. May Khalil Achkar, Aug. 25, 1970; children: Natalie, Michael, Cheryl. BS in Pharmacy, Am. U., Beirut, Lebanon, 1964; PhD, U. Mich., 1969. Postdoctoral fellow U. Mich., Ann Arbor, 1969-70; NIH postdoctoral fellow Temple U., Phila., 1970-72; lab. dir. Fanar (Lebanon) Rsch. Inst., 1973-76; from asst. prof. to assoc. prof. Am. U., Beirut, 1977-84, prof., 1984—, chmn. dept. microbiology and immunology faculty medicine, 1992—. Author: (with others) Cellular Antigens, 1972, Benefical Effects of Endotoxins, 1983; contbr. articles to Infection and Immunity, Annals of Saudi Medicine, Jour. Immunology and Immunopharmacology. F.G. Novy fellow U. Mich., Ann Arbor, 1969. Mem. Am. Assn. Immunologists, Am. Soc. Microbiology, N.Y. Acad. Scis., Internat. Endotoxin Soc., Am. Assn. Blood Banks, Am. Soc. Histocompatability and Immunogenetics. Office: Am U Beirut 850 3rd Ave New York NY 10022-6222

ABDEL SALAM, ISAM MOHAMED, surgeon; b. Omdurman, Sudan, Feb. 20, 1948; s. Mohammed Abdel Salam Egail and Acia Khider Mohammed; m. Gamar El Tayeb Ibrahim, Aug. 28, 1980; children: Mohamed, Yousra, Aala, Ola. MBBS, Khartoum Med. Sch., 1972. Registrar surgery M.O.H. & U of K, Khartoum, Sudan, 1976-77; dept. head M.O.H., Khartoum, Sennar, Sudan, 1979-81; sr. registrar St. Vincents, Dublin, 1981-83; cons. surgeon M.O.H. & U of K., 1983-88; sr. cons. surgeon M.O.H., Al Ain, United Arab Emirates, 1988—. Contbr. articles to profl. jours. Fellow Royal Coll. Surgeons Ireland; mem. Irish Soc. Gastroenterology, Emirate Med. Assn. (organizer), Assn. Laparoscopists. Moslem. Office: Al Ain Hosp, Al Jimi St PO box 1006, Al Ain United Arab Emirates

ABDULLA, MOHAMED, physician, educator; b. Alwaye, Kerala, India, Dec. 8, 1937; s. Mohamed Moulavi and Nacheema Mohamed; m. Nasemma Abdulla, Jan. 16, 1976; children; Nadia, Sabina. BSc, U. Punjab, Labore, Pakistan, 1958; MB, U. Lund, Sweden, 1974, MD, 1978, PhD, 1985. Cert. specialist in clin. chemistry. Sales officer Packages Ltd., Lahore, 1960-62; lab. technician Tottenham County Sch., London, 1962-64; engr. PLM, Malmö, Sweden, 1964-67; researcher McMaster U., Hamilton, Ont., Can., 1967-69; rsch. assoc. Swedish Med. Bd., Dalby, 1970-76; physician, researcher U. Hosp., Lund, 1976-88; prof., chmn. Baqai Med. Coll., Karachi, Pakistan, 1988-90; prof. Hamdard U., New Delhi, 1990—; dir. Primary Care Med. Ctr., Punjab Med. Ctr., Lahore, Pakistan; organizer internat. sci. meetings, Sweden, Denmark, Norway, U.S.A., Japan, Portugal, Turkey, India and Pakistan; sci. advisor to several pharm. cos. worldwide; cons. WHO, UNESCO, IAEA; mem. UN team to Chernobyl, 1990. Editor: Nutrition and Old Age, 1979, other books, 1975-90; contbr. over 200 articles to profl. jours. Founder, v.p. UNESCO Inst., Lyon, France. Fellow Swedish Med. Soc.; mem. Internat. Soc. Trace Element Rsch. in Humans (sec. 1985-88), Internat. Coll. Nutrition, Internat. Union Elementologists (v.p. 1984—), Pronutria Internat. (dir. 1993—). Home: Harjagersvägen 9, S 232 54 Åkarp Sweden Office: Hamdard U, PO Box 5133, S 220 05 Lund Sweden

ABDULLAH, SYED MOHAMMAD, surgeon; b. Peshawar, Pakistan; came to U.S., 1966; m. Ghazala M. Abdullah; 5 children. FSc, U. Peshawar, 1960; MB, BS, King Edward Med. Coll., Lahore, Pakistan, 1965. Diplomate Am. Bd. Surgery, Am. bd. Family Practice, Am. Bd. Abdominal Surgery. Rotating intern Pottsville (Pa.) Hosp., 1967; resident in surgery Atlantic City Hosp., 1968-69, Sacred Heart Hosp., Allentown, Pa., 1969-71; resident in surg. pathology Luth. Med. Ctr., Cleve., 1971-72; fellow in surgery St. Joseph Hosp., Mason City, Iowa, 1972-73; chief surgery Gardner (Kans.) Med. Ctr., 1973-77, Osborne (Kans.) Meml. Hosp., 1977-81; pvt. practice Okeechobee, Fla., 1981—; mem. med. staff HCA Raulerson Meml. Hosp., Okeechobee, 1981—. Fellow ACS, Internat. Coll. Surgeons; mem. Am. Soc. Colon and Rectal Surgeons, Am. Assn. Gastrointestinal Endoscopic Surgeons, Am. Coll. Gastroenterologists, Fla. Med. Assn., Okeechobee Med. Soc. Office: 202 NE 19th Dr Okeechobee FL 34972

ABE, KAZUHIKO, psychiatry educator; b. Kurume, Fukuoka-ken, Japan, Mar. 16, 1933; s. Ietsugu and Fusako (Ushijima) Abe; m. Hiroko Kumamaru, Jan. 26, 1969; 1 child, Shuei. MD, Kyushu U., Fukuoka, Japan, 1958; D in Med. Sci., Osaka City U., Japan, 1965. Resident Dept. Psychiatry, Osaka, 1959-63; asst. Osaka City U. Med. Sch., 1963-66, assoc. prof. psychiatry, 1969-78; vis. researcher Inst. Psychiatry Maudsley Hosp., London, 1966-68; prof., chmn. dept. psychiatry Univ. of Occupational and Environ. Health, Kitakyushu, Japan, 1978—. Mem. editorial bd. Internat. Jour. Mental Health, N.Y., 1970-88, Stress Medicine, Chichester, Eng., 1986—, Schizophrenia Rsch., Amsterdam, 1989—, Psychiat. Genetics, London, 1990—, Neuropsychiat. Genetics, N.Y., 1993—; contbr. articles to profl. jours. Recipient Rsch. grant Ministry Health and Welfare, Tokyo, 1976-78, '90-92. Mem. World Fedn. Socs. Biol. Pshychiatry (liaison com. psychiat. genetics 1989-91), Internat. Soc. Psychiat. Genetics (bd. dirs. 1994—), Japanese Soc. Biol. Psychiatry (trustee 1991-94). Office: U Occupational & Enviro Health, Yahata-Nishiku, Kitakyu 807, Japan

ABEL, ELIZABETH A., dermatologist; b. Hartford, Conn., Mar. 16, 1940; d. Frederick A. and Rose (Borovicka) A.; m. Barton Lane; children: Barton, Geoffrey, Suzanne. Student, Colby-Sawyer Coll., 1957-60; BS, Wash. Hosp. Ctr. Sch. Med. Tech., 1961, U. Md., 1965; MD cum laude, U. Md., 1967. Diplomate Am. Bd. Dermatology. Intern San Francisco Gen. Hosp., 1967-68; resident in medicine, fellow in oncology U. Calif. Med. Ctr., San Francisco, 1968-69; resident in dermatology NYU Med. Ctr., 1969-72, chief resident, 1971-72, USPHS research trainee in dermatology, 1972-73; dep. chief dept. dermatology USPHS Hosp., S.I., N.Y., 1973-74; instr. clin. dermatology Columbia U. Coll. Physicians and Surgeons, N.Y.C., 1974-75; instr. clin. dermatology Stanford (Calif.) U. Sch. Medicine, 1975-77, clin. asst. prof. dermatology, 1977-82, asst. prof. dermatology, 1982-90, clin. assoc. prof., 1990—; asst. editor Jour. Am. Acad. Dermatology; mem. med. adv. bd. The Nat. Psoriasis Found. Contbr. articles to sci. jours. Mellon Found. fellow, 1983, 87. Fellow Am. Acad. Dermatology; mem. N.Am. Clin. Dermatologic Soc., Soc. Investigative Dermatology, San Francisco Dermatologic Soc., Internat. Soc. Dermatology Surgery, Dermatology Found., Pacific Dermatologic Assn., Women's Dermatologic Soc., Noah Worcester Dermatologic Soc., Alpha Omega Alpha. Episcopalian. Office: 525 South Dr Ste 115 Mountain View CA 94040-4211

ABEL, FLORENCE CATHERINE HARRIS, social worker; b. Phila., Dec. 28, 1941; d. Wilber Fiske and Melda Elizabeth (Beitzel) Harris; m. David Lynn Abel, Jan. 22, 1983. B.S., High Point (N.C.) U., 1963; M.S.W., U. Md., 1972. Bd. cert. social worker; Diplomate in Clin. Social Work. Social work asst. Calvert County (Md.) Dept. Social Svcs., Prince Frederick, 1964-69; social work asst. Prince George's County (Md.) Dept. Social Svc., Hyattsville, 1969-71; social worker Md. Children's Aid and Family Svc., Towson, Md., 1972-80, Crownsville (Md.) Hosp. Ctr., 1980-86; field instr. U. Md. Sch. Social Work, 1985-86; chairperson Social Work Peer Rev. Com., 1982-83; cons. Contact Balt., 1974-79; counselor Family Life Ctr., Columbia, Md., 1974-80; mem. citizens adv. coun. N.W. Mental Health Balt. County, 1977-78. sec. bd. dirs. Christian Counseling Assocs., Columbia, 1978-90, family therapist, 1978—, social work supr., 1990—; dir. Dayspring Counseling Svc., Bowie, Md. 1994—. mem. Faith at Work Team, Columbia, 1973-75, Calvert County Commn. on Aging, 1967-68, Evang. Women's Caucus, Washington, 1976-85, N.W. Coalition Social Agys., Balt. County, 1978. Author: The Beitzel Family a History of the Descendants of John George Beitzel, 1986, The Shadow of His Hand: The Biography of Melda B. Harris, 1995. Vice pres., treas. bd. dirs. Wheaton Animal Hosp., Inc., Kensington, Md.; sec. local bd. adminstrn. Dayspring Wesleyan Ch., Bowie, Md., 1996. Lic. cert. social worker, Md. Mem. NASW, Register Register Clin. Social Workers, Assn. Certified Social Workers, Md. Conf. Social Concern, Christian Assocs. for Psychol. Studies. Democrat. Presbyterian. Home: 120 Hedgewood Dr Greenbelt MD 20770-1611 Office: 9630 Santiago Rd Ste 101 Columbia MD 21045-3907

ABEL, FRANCIS LEE, physiology educator; b. Iowa City, Apr. 12, 1931; s. Earl Lester A.; m. Evelyn Joyce Reischauer, Sept. 11, 1954 (div. Mar. 1974); children: Wanda, Donna, Carolyn; m. Anne Elizabeth Sutherland, June 9, 1974; 1 child, Jonathan. AA, Creston Jr. Coll., 1950; BA in Physics, U. Kans., 1952; MD, Harvard U., 1957; PhD in Physiology, U. Wis., 1960. Postdoctoral fellow, postdoctoral trainee Wis. Heart Assn. USPHS, Madison, 1958-60; intern in pediatrics Children's Hosp., L.A., 1960-61; from asst. prof. to prof. dept. physiology Sch. Medicine Ind. U., Indpls., 1962-75; prof., chmn. dept. physiology Sch. Medicine U. S.C., Columbia, 1975—; interim dean Sch Medicine U. S.C., Columbia, 1976, assoc. dean basic sci. affairs, 1976-78; vis. prof. dept. biomed. engring. U. So. Calif., L.A., 1970; vis. prof. dept. kinesiology Simon Fraser U., Burnaby, B.C., Can., 1982; vis. prof. dept. physiology U. Limburg, Maastricht, The Netherlands, 1989-90; cons. Eli Lilly & Co., Indpls., 1965-68, VA Hosp., Columbia, 1976-80. Coauthor: Basic Physiology for the Health Sciences, 1975, Cardiovascular Function, Principles and Applications, 1979, Functional Aspects of the Normal Hypertrophied and Failing Heart, 1984. Recipient Career Devel. award NIH, 1968-73, Nat. Rsch. Svc. award NIH, 1989-90. Fellow Cardiovascular sect. Am. Physiol. Soc.; mem. Am. Physiol. Soc., Am. Heart Assn., Biomed. Engring. Soc. (sr.), Shock Soc. (councillor 1980-82). Office: USC Dept Physiology Columbia SC 29208

ABEL, MARK, dermatologist; b. Bklyn., Jan. 25, 1948; s. David and Ada (Schumer) A.; 1 child, Lisa. BS in Biology, Rensselaer Polytech Inst., 1966; MD, Albany Med. Coll., 1970. Intern Albany Med. Ctr., 1970-71; commd. 2d lt. U.S. Army, 1970, advanced through grades to lt. col. Fellow Am. Acad. Dermatology; mem. AMA, N.J. Med. Soc., Ocean County Med. Soc. Office: 1541 Hwy 88 Brick NJ 08723

ABELLI, LUIGI, biologist; b. Rome, Feb. 12, 1957; s. Gian Luca and Maria (Monaco) A.; m. Angela Vittoria Goletti, Sept. 24, 1988. Degree in biol. scis., U. La Sapienza, Rome, 1981. Researcher Menarini Ricerche Sud, Pomezia/Rome, 1982-90, supr. respiratory disease unit, 1989-90; rsch. fellow scis. faculty U. Tuscia, Viterbo, Italy, 1991—, asst. prof. devel. biology, 1995—; vis. scientist dept. histochemistry Hammersmith Hosp., London, 1993-94. Contbr. articles to sci. publs. Mem. sat. Geog. Soc.,sEuropean Neuropeptide Club, N.Y. Acad. Scis., European Soc. Comparative Endocrinology, Italian Embryology Group, Italian Cytoskeleton Group. Home: Via Monfalcone 2/B, 01100 Viterbo Italy Office: Tuscia U Faculty Scis, VS Camillo de Lellis, 01100 Viterbo Italy

ABELMANN, WALTER H., internist; b. Frankfurt, Germany, May 16, 1921; s. Arthur and Else (Weill) A.; m. Rena J. White, June 8, 1958; children: Karen, Nancy, Ruth, Arthur, Charles. AB magna cum laude, Harvard Coll., 1943; MD, U. Rochester, 1946. Diplomate Am. Bd. Internal Medicine. Prof. medicine Harvard Med. Sch., Boston, 1972-91, prof. medicine emeritus, 1991—; prof. medicine Harvard-MIT Div. Health Sci. & Tech., Cambridge, 1974—; chief cardiology Beth Israel Hosp., Boston, 1974-78, physician, 1974-88, dir. cardiovascular rsch., 1978-88, sr. physician, 1989—; interim co-dir. Harvard-MIT Div. Health Sci. & Tech., Cambridge, 1990-92; cons. in cardiology Mt. Auburn Hosp., Cambridge, 1957—; lectr. medicine Tufts U., Boston, 1968-91; cons. in cardiology Children's Hosp., Boston, 1970-91. Contbr. over 250 articles to profl. jours. Recipient Paul Dudley White award, Am. Heart Assn., 1979. Fellow ACP, AAAS, Am. Coll. Cardiology; mem. New Eng. Cardiovascular Soc. (pres. 1965-66), Assn. Am. Physicians, Am. Soc. Clin. Investigation, Am. Univ. Cardiologists. Home: 975 Memorial Dr Apt 406 Cambridge MA 02138-5755 Office: Beth Israel Hosp 330 Brookline Ave Boston MA 02215-5400

ABELOFF, ABRAM JOSEPH, retired surgeon; b. N.Y.C., Mar. 19, 1900; s. Samuel and Rebecca Esther (Rogow) A.; m. Gertrude Theresa Kopsch, May 15, 1953; 1 son, Tobias Samuel. A.B., Columbia U., 1922, M.D., 1926. Diplomate: Am. Bd. Surgery. Sub-surg. intern Presbyn. Hosp., N.Y.C., 1926-27; surg. intern Lenox Hill Hosp., 1927-29; research asst. Inst. Pathology U. Freiburg, Germany, 1929; surg. service Frankfurt U., Germany, U. Vienna, Austria, 1930; adj. surgeon Beth Israel Hosp., 1930-37; assoc. surgeon Neurol. Hosp., N.Y.C., 1930-33; asst. adj. surgeon Lenox Hill Hosp., 1930-36, attending surgeon clinic, 1930-36, chief surgeon, 1936-42, adj. attending, 1936-46, assoc. surgeon, 1946-54, attending surgeon, 1954-65, hon. cons. surgeon, 1965—, charge service, 1971; surgeon Lexington Sch. for Deaf, 1947-68; asso. clin. prof. surgery NYU, 1947—. Hon. mem. exec. com., emeritus chmn. med. adv. bd. Am. Jewish Joint Distbn. Com.; adv. bd. Paul Baerwald Sch. Social Work, Parks; past pres., treas., now trustee Physicians Home; bd. visitors Watson Libr. Met. Mus. Art, 1976-94; trustee Columbia U., 1959-65. Col. M.C. AUS, 1942-46; hosp. comdr. 256th Sta. Hosp., 19th Field Hosp., 21st Sta. Hosp., 113th Gen. Hosp., Lawson Gen. Hosp. surg. cons. Persian Gulf Command. Decorated Legion of Merit; Distinctive Service Cross of State of N.Y.; recipient Disting. Service medal Columbia U. Alumni Fedn., 1963; Distinctive Achievement award Stuyvesant High Sch., 1965; Alumni Silver medal Coll. Phys. & Surg., 1969; Meritorious Service Unit citation Lawson Gen. Hosp. Fellow ACS, Brazilian Coll. Surgeons; mem. N.Y. Acad. Medicine, N.Y. Surg. Soc. (past council mem.), AMA, N.Y. State and County med. socs., Assn. Alumni Coll. Phys. and Surg. Columbia U. (pres. 1956-57), N.Y. Hist. Soc. (life). Club: Grolier (N.Y.C.). Home: 150 E 77th St New York NY 10021-1922

ABELOFF, MARTIN DAVID, medical administrator, educator, researcher; b. Shenandoah, Pa., Apr. 4, 1942; s. Aaron Harry and Cele (Freid) A.; m. Diane Kaufman, Jan. 7, 1967; children: Elisa, Jennifer. Student, Franklin and Marshall Coll., 1959-61; AB, Johns Hopkins U., 1963, MD, 1966. Diplomate Am. Bd. Internal Medicine, subspecialty in med. oncology. Intern U. Chgo. Hosps. and Clinics, 1966-67; clin. assoc. Balt. Cancer Rsch. Ctr., 1967-69; sr. asst. resident in medicine Beth Israel Hosp., Boston, 1969-70; fellow in clin. hematology New Eng. Med. Ctr., Boston, 1970-71; fellow in clin. oncology Sch. Medicine Johns Hopkins U., Balt., 1971-72, instr. in medicine, 1972-75, asst. prof. oncology, 1974-79, asst. prof. medicine, 1975-80, prof. medicine, 1980—; Eli Kennerly Mashall Jr. prof. oncology Johns Hopkins U.; prof. & dir. Johns Hopkins Oncology Ctr., 1992; numerous vis. professorships and lectrs. including INstitut Jules Bordet, Brussels, Milton S. Hershey Med. Ctr., Nat. Cancer Inst., U. Ariz., SUNY, Stony Brook, U. So. Calif., U. Chgo., U. Md., Boston U., Mayo Clinic, others; advisor St. George's Soc., Am. Cancer Soc., 1974-84; chmn. psychosocial com. Ea. Coop. Oncology Group, 1979-83; cons. reviewer for clin. oncology rev. com. divsn. cancer treatment Nat. Cancer Inst., Bethesda, Md., 1980—. Editorial bd. Lung Cancer, 1985—, PDQ, NCI, 1986-88, Cancer Rsch., 1993; assoc. editor Jour. Clin. Oncology, 1987—, Oncology, 1987—; assoc. editor, editorial bd. Cancer Treatment Reports, 1980-83; editor Clin. Oncology, 1992—, Oncology News Internat.; sect. editor Annals of Surg. Oncology, 1993—; adv. bd. The Med. Letter, 1991—; mem. editorial adv. bd. Health After 50, 1989—; contbr. numerous articles to profl. jours., chpts. to books. Bd. dirs. Md. divsn. Am. Cancer Soc., 1985-86. Mem. Am. Soc. Clin. Oncology (mem. ednl. com. 1978-80, mem. program com. 1981-83, chmn. program 1983-84, bd. dirs. 1984-87, chmn. com. on patterns of care 1986-87, chmn. ad-hoc com. for FDA liaison 1988-89, pres. 1991-92), Am. Assn. Cancer Rsch., Internat. Assn. for Study of Lung Cancer, Am. Assn. Cancer Edn., Phi Beta Kappa. Office: Johns Hopkins Oncology Ctr 600 N Wolfe St Rm B157 Baltimore MD 21287-8943

ABELS, B. CLIFFORD, JR., general and vascular surgeon; b. Greensboro, N.C., Nov. 27, 1958; s. Byron Clifford and Elizabeth (Pollok) A. BA, U. N.C., 1981; MD, Emory U., 1985. Diplomate Am. Bd. Surgery. Resident in gen. surgery Vanderbilt U., Nashville, 1986-91; fellow in vascular surgery Baylor U. Med. Ctr., Dallas, 1991-92; pvt. practice surgery Gainesville, Ga., 1992-95, Charlotte, N.C., 1995—. Fellow ACS (assoc.); mem. H. William Scott Soc., Jesse Thompson Soc. Office: Charlotte Surg Group PA 3535 Randolph Rd Ste 201-W Charlotte NC 28211

ABELSON, HERBERT TRAUB, pediatrician, educator; b. St. Louis, Feb. 19, 1941; s. Benjamin J. and Ann (Traub) A.; m. Constance Faye Caldwell, May 17, 1968; children: Matthew, Rebecca, Jonathan and Daniel (twins). AB with high honors, U. Ill., 1962; MD, Washington U., St. Louis, 1966. Diplomate Am. Bd. Pediatrics (examiner 1988—, bd. dirs. 1992—, sec.-treas. 1995, chmn.-elect 1995-96), Am. Bd. Pediatric Hematology-Oncology. Intern pediatrics U Colo. Med. Ctr., Denver, 1966-67; resident Boston Children's Hosp., 1969-71; staff assoc. Nat. Cancer Inst. NIH, Bethesda, Md., 1967-69; Jane Childs Meml. Fund for Med. Rsch. fellow NIH, 1971, spl. postdoctoral fellow, 1972; teaching fellow Med. Sch. Harvard Coll., Boston, 1970-71, instr. pediatrics, 1973-74, asst. prof., 1974-79; tutor in med. scis., 1977-79; assoc. prof. Harvard Coll., Boston, 1979-83; vis. prof., Ctr. for Cancer Rsch. MIT, Cambridge, 1982-83; prof., chmn. dept. pediatrics Med. Sch. U. Wash., Seattle, 1983-95; prof., chmn., physician-in-chief dept. pediatrics U. Chgo., 1995—; rsch. fellow in hematology Children's Hosp. Med. Ctr., Boston, 1971-73; rsch. assoc. in biology MIT, 1971-73; mem. pediatric residency rev. com. Accreditation Coun. for Grad. Med. Edn.; mem. exec. com. Am. Med. Sch. Pediatric Dept. Chmn. Assoc. editor Pediatric Annals; contbr. articles to profl. jours. Lt. comdr. USPHS, 1967-69. Recipient Rsch. Career Devel. award NIH, 1975-80. Fellow Am. Acad. Pediatrics; mem. Am. Soc. Hematology (mem. sci. subcom. on pediatric hematology 1987-91), Am. Assn. Cancer Rsch., Am. Soc. Clin. Oncology, Soc. Pediatric Rsch., Am. Pediatric Soc. Office: Univ Chgo Dept Pediatrics 5841 S Maryland MC 1051 Chicago IL 60637

ABERCROMBIE, STONEY ALTON, family physician; b. Six Mile, S.C., Dec. 9, 1949; s. William Morris and Mildred Marette (Ellenburg) A.; m. Donna Gay Underwood, June 17, 1973; children: Jonathan Edward, Kristina Katherine. BS, Clemson U., 1972; MD, Med. U. S.C., 1976. Diplomate Am. Bd. Family Practice; lic. physician, S.C. Family practice intern Greenville (S.C.) Hosp. System, 1976, family practice resident, 1979-80; pvt. practice Seneca (S.C.) Med. Assocs., 1981-88; asst. residency dir. Self Meml. Hosp., Greenwood, 1989-90; residency dir. and dir. med. edn. Med. U. S.C., Charleston, 1990—; prof. family medicine MUSC, 1995—; staff physician Oconee Meml. Hosp., Seneca, 1981-88, chief of staff, 1988, bd. trustees, 1987-88; mem. utilization rev. com. Oconee Geriatric Ctr., 1981-87; asst. med. dir. Greenwood Health Care Ctr., 1990—, chmn. utilization rev. com., 1990—; med. dir. Greenbrook Manor Nursing Home, 1989-93; lectr. in field. Contbr. articles to profl. jours. Founder Oconee County Prenatal Clinic for Indigent OB Patients, 1983; mem. Upstate S.C. Emergency Svcs. Coun., 1981-84, Upstate S.C. Perinatal Adv. Com., 1981-84, Teen Pregnancy Prevention Coun., Oconee, 1988; mem. Gov.'s Task Force on Primary Health Care in Oconee County, 1984, Med.-Industry Com. for Health Care in Oconee County, 1984-85; bd. visitors Lander U., Greenwood, 1991-93; bd. advisors Vocat. Rehab. Ctr., Greenwood, 1991-94; bd. trustees Greenwood Literacy Coun., 1994-97, chmn. 1996, mem. century club Clemson U., 1981—, mem. IPTAY, 1981—, alumni loyalty fund vol., 1984; active Gideon's Internat., 1984—. Recipient disting. svc. to mankind award Rotary, 1995, Halford award excellence in human medicine S.C. AHEC, 1996. Fellow Am. Bd. Family Practice; mem. AMA, Am. Acad. Family Physicians (reviewer Huffington Libr. 1991—, pub. com. 1994-96), S.C. Acad. Family Physicians (bd. trustees 1987—, editor S.C. Family Physician, v.p. 1995, pres. 1996, 97), Soc. of Tchrs. Family Practice, S.C. Med. Assn. (liability case reviewer 1990—, assoc. chmn. CME com. 1995—), Greenwood Med. Soc. (pres. 1992-93), Clemson Alumni Physicians Soc. (charter), Med. U.S.C. Alumni Assn. (Alumni Assn. centennial Recognition List 1992), Assn. of Family Practice Residency Dirs. (charter, S.C. chpt. chmn. 1994—), Emerald City Rotary Club (bd. dirs. 1989-96, pres. 1992-93). Republican. Ch. of God. Office: Self Meml Hosp Family Practice Residency 160 Academy Ave Greenwood SC 29646-3808

ABERGER, FRANK JOSEPH, gastroenterologist; b. N.Y.C., Sept. 7, 1952; s. Edward W. and Victoria J. (DiPaola) A.; m. Jenny Ann Wren, Nov. 23,

1980; children: Michael, Caitlin, Christopher. AB in Biology, Ind. U., Bloomington, 1974; MD, Ind. U., Indpls., 1977. Internal medicine resident St. Vincent Hosp., Indpls., 1977-80, gastroenterology fellow, 1980-82; gastroenterologist Joplin, Mo., 1982-84; staff gastroenterologist Gundersen Clinic, LaCrosse, Wis., 1984—, chief gastroenterologist, 1992—, vice chmn. internal medicine, 1993—. Fellow Am. Coll. Gastroenterology; mem. Am. Gastroent. Assn., Am. Soc. Gastrointestinal Endoscopy, Wis. State Med. Soc., LaCrosse County Med. Soc. Roman Catholic. Office: Gundersen Clinic 1836 S Ave LaCrosse WI 54601

ABERMAN, ARNOLD, dean. Dean faculty medicine U. Toronto, 1995—. Office: Univ Toronto, 215 Huron St, Toronto, ON Canada M5S 1A1 Office: Univ Toronto, Med Scis Bldg, 1 Kings College Cir Rm 2109, Toronto, Canada*

ABERMAN, HAROLD MARK, veterinarian; b. Chgo., Aug. 5, 1956; s. Howard Oscar and Goldie Esther (Imyak) A. BS, Purdue U., 1979, MSE, 1987, BSE, 1986, DVM, 1983. NIH postdoctoral fellow Purdue U., W. Lafayette, 1983-87; sr. rsch. scientist Howmedica Inc. subsidiary of Pfizer, Rutherford, N.J., 1987-88; prin. rsch. scientist Howmedica div. Pfizer, Rutherford, N.J., 1988-90, asst. dir., 1990-96, dir., 1996—; adj. prof. N.C. State U., Raleigh, 1988—, Miss. State U., Starkville, Miss., 1990—, Purdue U., 1991—. Contbr. articles to profl. jours. Mem. ASME, Am. Vet. Med. Assn., Am. Animal Hosp. Assn., Ortho. Rsch. Soc., Soc. Biomechanics, Acad. Surg. Rsch. Jewish. Home: 28 Glen Rd Ringwood NJ 07456-2331 Office: Howmedica 359 Veterans Blvd Rutherford NJ 07070-2564

ABERNATHY, CHARLES OWEN, toxicologist; b. Brunswick, Ga., Nov. 18, 1941; s. William Owen and Marcelle Louise (Francony) A.; m. Mary Mella Dees, Nov. 18, 1973. AB, Asbury Coll., Wilmore, Ky., 1964; MS, U. Ky., 1966; PhD, N.C. State U., 1970. Postdoctoral fellow U. Calif., Berkeley, 1970-73; pharmacologist VA Med. Ctr., Washington, 1973-84; pharmacologist office of toxic substances EPA, Washington, 1984-86; toxicologist Office Water, EPA, Washington, 1986—; rsch. toxicologist VA Med. Ctr., Washington, 1984-89. Contbr. over 60 articles to sci. jours., chpts. to books. Vol. tutor Bapt. Boys Home, Raleigh, N.C., 1967-69; vol. blood drive ARC, Washington, 1978. Recipient Employee Recognition award EPA, 1988, bronze medal, 1993, 96. Mem. Soc. Toxicology (chmn. awards com. risk assessment sect. 1989-90), Soc. for Exptl. Biology and Medicine, N.Y. Acad. Scis., Soc. Environ. Geochemistry and Health, Internat. Soc. Study of Xenobiotics. Home: 4718 River Rd Bethesda MD 20816-3035 Office: EPA 401 M St SW Washington DC 20460-0001

ABERNATHY, VICKI MARIE, nurse; b. L.A., Feb. 14, 1949; d. James David and Margaret Helen (Quider) Abernathy; m. Dirk Klaus Ernst Wiese, Aug. 15, 1968 (div. 1973); 1 child, Zoe Erde. Student, U. Calif., Riverside, 1966-67, L.A. City Coll., 1968-69; AA in Nursing, Riverside City Coll., 1971-74. RN, Calif.; cert. med.-surg. nurse; cert. ACLS. Staff nurse Riverside (Calif.) County Hosp., 1974, Oceanside (Calif.) Community Hosp., 1974-76; with Scripps Hosp., Encinitas, Calif., 1976—, ambulatory surgery unit and endoscopy coord., 1981-94, staff nurse short stay unit, 1994—. Mem. ACLU, Calif. Nurses Assn., San Diego Zool. Soc., San Elijo Lagoon Conservancy. Democrat.

ABIDI, S. MANZOOR, neurologist; b. Lucknow, India, Jan. 9, 1940; came to the U.S., 1965; s. S. Maqbool and Afsar Begum (Zaki) Abidi; children: Nicholas, Zeena. MD, King George's Med. Coll., 1962. Rotating intern King George's Med. Coll., Lucknow, 1962-63, med. resident, 1963-65; internal medicine resident Huron Road Hosp., Cleve., 1965-66; psychiatry resident Phila. Gen. Hosp., 1966-68; neurology resident Temple U. Hosp., Phila., 1968-71; pvt. practice Regional Neurol. Group, N.J., 1973-78, Neurol. Regional Assocs., Maple Shade, N.J., 1978—; asst. neurologist Cooper Med. Ctr., Camden, N.J., 1972-73, assoc. neurologist, 1974, attending neurologist, 1975-72; asst. neurologist Pa. Hosp., Phila., 1972-74; neurologist Garden State Cmty. Hosp., 1973-77, chief neurology, 1977-88, attending neurologist, 1989-92, mem. exec. com. bd. trustees; neurologist JFK Meml. Hosp./Univ. Med. Ctr., 1980-85, attending neurologist, 1985—; chief attending neurologist Undwrood Meml. Hosp., Woodbury, N.J., 1975-79, attending neurologist, 1979-82; assoc. neurologist Burlington County Meml. Hosp., Mount Holly, N.J., 1975-84, chief divsn. neurology, 1984-94; consulting neurologist So. Ocean County Hosp., Manahawkin, N.J., 1975—; attending neurologist Zurbrugg Meml. Hosp., Riverside, N.J., 1984-85; cons. neurologist Hampton Hosp., Rancocas, N.J., 1986-94. Mem. AMA, Am. Acad. Neurology, Am. Electroencephalography Soc., N.J. State Med. Soc., Burlington County Med. Soc., Acad. Medicine N.J., Phila. Neurol. Soc. Home: 4 Silverwood Rd Moorestown NJ 08057 Office: Neurol Regional Assocs 504 Rt 38 E Maple Shade NJ 08052

ABIRI, MOHAMMED, surgeon; b. Teheran, Iran, Mar. 16, 1933; came to U.S., 1959; s. Majid and Esmath (Farhoumand) A.; m. Terry Campbell, Sept. 1963 (div. 1975); children: Mark, Paul, Leila, David; m. Katherine Bradford, Dec. 1980; 1 child, Matthew. MD, Teheran U., Teheran, 1958. Diplomate Am. Bd. Surgery. Intern Beth David Hosp., N.Y.C., 1959-60; resident Seydenham Hosp., N.Y.C., 1960-61, Bklyn. Hosp., 1961-64; fellow Sloan-Kettering Meml. Hosp., N.Y.C., 1964-65; mem. surg. staff St. Joseph's Hosp., Providence, 1969—, Fatima Hosp., Providence, 1969—, Miriam Hosp., Providence, 1969—, Roger Williams Hosp., Providence, 1969—, Cranston (R.I.) Gen. Hosp., 1991—. Mem. ACS, Providence Surg. Soc. Office: 725 Reservoir Ave Cranston RI 02910-4448

ABLE, KENNETH PAUL, biology educator; b. Louisville, Feb. 5, 1944; s. William Morris and Viola (Bridwell) A.; m. Mary Allen, Jan. 27, 1967; 1 child, Joshua. BS, U. Louisville, 1966, MS, 1968; PhD, U. Ga., 1971. Asst. prof. SUNY, Albany, 1971-77, assoc. prof., 1977-84, prof., 1984—. NSF grantee, 1974—. Fellow Animal Behavior Soc., Am. Ornithologists' Union (treas. 1981-85); mem. Internat. Soc. Behavioral Ecology, Am. Soc. Naturalists, Am. Birding Assn. (dir. 1986-95). Office: SUNY Dept Biology 1400 Washington Ave Albany NY 12222-0100

ABLE, LUKE WILLIAM, retired pediatric surgeon, consultant; b. Pt. Arthur, Tex.; s. James Levert and Minnie Maude (Branson) A.; m. Mary Beth Able, June 7, 1937 (div. Dec. 1984); children: Luke William, Stephen Smith; m. Margaret Galloway, Dec. 29, 1984 (dec. Dec. 1993); m. Hester Finke, July 14, 1995. BA, U. Tex., 1933, MD, 1940. Diplomate Am. Bd. Surgery and Pediat. Surgery. Extern So. Pacific Hosp., 1939; intern, surg. resident Hermann Hosp., Houston, 1940-43; resident in gen. and cardiovasc. surgery Boston Children's Hosp., 1946-48; pvt. practice Tex., 1948; clin. prof. surgery Baylor Med. Coll., Houston, 1950—; surgeon-in-chief, head dept. surgery Tex. Children's Hosp., Houston, 1954-87, surgeon-in-chief, head dept. surgery emeritus, 1987—; active staff/cons. St. Luke's Episcopal Hosp., Meml. Sys., Meth. Hosp., Hermann Hosp., Tex. Children's Hosp.; teaching assoc. U. Tex., Houston. Author: Siamese Twins, 1968; contbr. numerous articles to surg. and med. jours., chpts. to med. and surg. books. Lt. USNR, 1943-46, PTO. Decorated Purple Heart, Silver Star. Mem. ACS (Outstanding Presentation award), AMA, Am. Med. Soc., Am. Acad. Pediats. (surg. sect. 1949—, Outstanding Presentation award), Am. Pediats. Surg. Assn. (charter), Am. Trauma Assn., Tex. Med. Soc., Tex. Pediat. Soc., Tex. Surg. Soc. (v.p. 1953—, pres. 1987, Comty. Svc. award), Tex. Assn. Pediat. Surgeons (past pres.), Houston Pediat. Soc., Houston Surg. Soc. (pres. 1969-70, Outstanding Surgeon of Yr. 1991, Comty. Svc. award). Harris County Med. Soc. (sec. 1958). Republican. Baptist. Home: 18734 Murrell Rd Hockley TX 77447-9781 Office: Pediat Surgery Cons 6624 Fannin Ste 1590 Houston TX 77002-7616

ABLIN, RICHARD JOEL, immunologist, educator; b. Chgo., May 15, 1940; s. Robert Benjamin and Minnie Edith (Gordon) A.; m. Linda Lee Lutwack; 1 son, Michael David. A.B., Lake Forest Coll., 1962; Ph.D. in Microbiology, SUNY-Buffalo, 1967. Diplomate Am. Bd. Clin. Immunology and Allergy. Grad. asst. dept. biology SUNY-Buffalo, 1963-65, research asst., summer 1963, research fellow, 1965-66; USPHS postdoctoral fellow dept. microbiology Sch. Medicine, lectr., lab instr., 1966-68; instr., research asst. Rosary Hill Coll., 1965-66; research cons. program med. edn. AID, Paraguay, 1968; dir. div. immunology Millard Fillmore Hosp. Rsch. Inst., Buffalo, 1968-70; head sect. immunology, renal unit Meml. Hosp. of Springfield, 1970-73; dir. sect. immunobiology div. urology dept. surgery Cook County Hosp. and Hektoen Inst. for Med. Research, Chgo., 1973-75, sr. sci. officer div. immunology, 1976-83; sr. mem. sci. staff, clin. immunologist Cook County Hosp., 1973-75; asst. prof. medicine So. Ill. U., 1971-73; assoc. prof. microbiology Univ. Health Sci. (Chgo. Med. Sch.), 1973-74; research assoc. prof. urology, dir. immunology unit dept. urology SUNY, Stony Brook, 1983-89; pres., dir. Robert Benjamin Ablin Found. for Cancer Rsch., Skokie, Ill., 1979—; dir. sci. investigation Innapharma, Inc., Suffern, N.Y., 1991—; mem. Univ. Senate, 1986-89, 89-92, Univ. Governing Coms., 1984-92; acad. del. United Univ. Professions, 1986-88, 88-90. Editor: Allergologia et Immunopathologia, 1980-84; contbg. editor: Current Perspectives in Allergology and Immunopathology, 1974-84; assoc. editor Jour. Investigational Allergology and Clin. Immunology (formerly Allergologia et Immunopatholgia), 1985-95, Seminars in Immunopathology and Oncology, Ill. Med. Jour., 1975-88; adv. editor: Jour. Cancer, 1976—; assoc. editor: Low Temperature Medicine, 1975—; mem. internat. editl. staff: Medikon, 1974—; mem. editl. bd. Immunology and Allergy Practice, 1979—, Am. Jour. Reproductive Immunology and Microbiology, 1980-91, Cellular and Molecular Biology, 1985-87, Early Pregnancy: Biology and Medicine, 1995—; mem. sci. bd.: Chemistry Today, 1991—, TumorDiagnostik and Therapie, 1980—; mem. editl. acad. Internat. Jour. of Oncology, 1996—; mem. editl. adv. bd. Med. Sci. Rsch., 1984—; contbr. numerous articles to profl. jours. and texts. Chief Sangamo Nation Y-Indian Guides, Springfield, 1972-73; mgr. Skokie Indians' Boys' Baseball, Ill., 1973-74, 77, 80, 81, bd. dirs., 1979-83, exec. v.p., 1981-82; mgr. Little League Three Villages, Setauket, N.Y., 1986; cubmaster N.W. Suburban coun. Boy Scouts Am., 1974-78, asst. scoutmaster, 1975-77; mem. exploring divsn. Suffolk County coun. Boy Scouts Am., 1985-88; pres., dir. Spirit of Chgo. Hockey Club Found., Skokie, Ill., 1982—. Recipient Nat. Pres. Leader's Dist. Boy Scouts Am., 1975; named Cubmaster of Yr. Boy Scouts Am., 1977. Fellow Am. Coll. Allergy and Immunology, Am. Coll. Cryosurgery (v.p. 1977-79, parliamentarian 1977-79, adv. bd. 1977-78, 80-81, 84-95), Indian Cryogenics Coun. (hon.); mem. AAAS, Am. Assn. Cancer Rsch., Am. Assn. Immunologists, Brit. Assn. Surg. Oncology, Buffalo Collegium Immunology, Internat. Soc. Andrology, Internat. Soc. Chronobiology, Internat. Soc. Cryosurgery (pres. 1977-80, hon. life pres.), Internat. Soc. Immunology Reprodn., Japan Soc. Low Temperature Medicine, N.Y. Acad. Scis., Soc. Leukocyte Biology, Soc. Cryobiology, Soc. Protozoologists, Soc. Study Reprodn., Soc. Exptl. Biology and Medicine, Transplantation Soc., Nat. Registry Microbiologist (cert. specialist in pub. health and med. lab. microbiology), Cryoimmunotherapeutic Study Group (chmn.), Sigma Xi.

ABLOW, KEITH RUSSELL, psychiatrist, journalist, author; b. Boston, Nov. 23, 1961; s. Allan Murray and Jeanette Norma (Mezansky) A. ScB, Brown U., 1983; MD, Johns Hopkins U., 1987. Reporter Newsweek, N.Y.C., 1984; columnist Balt. Evening Sun, Boston Herald, 1985-89, Washington Post, 1990—; intern in psychiatry Tufts U.-New Eng. Med. Ctr. Hosps., Boston, 1987-88, resident, 1988-91; chief resident 1991—, 1991-92; columnist Washington Post, 1990—; cons. psychiatrist WCVB TV, Boston, 1992—; med. dir. Tri-City Mental Health Ctr., 1992-94; assoc. med. dir. Heritage Health Systems, 1993-94; corr. Med. News Network, 1993—; med. dir. FHC New Eng., 1994-96; outpatient psychiatrist Boston Regional Med. Ctr., 1996—; med. editor Lifetime Med. TV, L.A. and Astoria, N.Y., 1986-89. Author: Medical School: Getting In, Staying In, Staying Human, 1987, How to Cope With Depression, 1989, To Wrestle With Demons, 1992, Anatomy of a Psychiatric Illness, 1993, The Strange Case of Dr. Kappler, 1994. Trustee White Pines Coll., Chester, N.H., 1989-91. Recipient Optimate award Am. Soc. Profl. Italians, 1990. Mem. AAAS, AMA (sr. editor, creative cons. Pulse 1986-87, Jerry L. Pettis award 1987), Am. Psychiat. Assn., Am. Med. Writers Assn. (Will Solimene award 1991, 92, Best Trade Book, 1993). Democrat. Home: 4 Breakwater Dr Chelsea MA 02150-4038

ABLOW, RONALD CHARLES, radiology director, pediatric radiologist; b. Salem, Mass., June 1, 1932; s. Benjamin and Eva (Smith) A.; m. Judith Ablow. AB in Physics cum laude, Harvard U., 1954, MBA, 1956; MD, U. Rochester, 1962; MA (hon.), Yale U., 1974. Diplomate Am. Bd. Radiology. Instr. radiology, assoc. attending radiologist Yale U., New Haven, 1966-67, asst. prof. radiology, attending radiologist, 1967-69, prof. radiology and pediatrics, 1973-84, clin. prof. radiology and pediatrics, 1984—; dir. radiology New Haven unit Yale New-Haven Hosp., 1973-75; chief pediatric radiology Yale-New Haven Hosp., 1974-84; asst. clin. prof. radiology U. Calif., San Francisco, 1971-73, Stanford (Calif.) U., 1971-73; assoc. CEO of radiology Mt. Zion Hosp./Med. Ctr., San Francisco, 1969-73; dir. radiology St. Luke's-Roosevelt Hosp. Ctr., N.Y.C., 1984—, pres., CEO, 1996—; prof. radiology Coll. Physicians and Surgeons Columbia U., N.Y.C., 1984—; cons. dir. radiology Beth Israel Med. Ctr., N.Y.C., 1991-94, chmn. radiology, 1994-96; mem. com. on practice of commn. on physics and radiation proction Am. Bd. Radiology, 1985-87, examiner, Louisville, 1987-88; specialist site visitor Accreditation Coun. for Grad. Med. Edn., 1988—. Contbr. articles to profl. jours. Timothy Dwight Coll. fellow Yale U., 1977-84. Fellow Am. Coll. Radiology, N.Y. Acad. Medicine; mem. Am. Roentgen Ray Soc., Radiol. Soc. N.Am., N.Y. Acad. Scis., N.Y. Roentgen Ray Soc. (pres. 1993-94), Conn. Radiology Soc., Assn. Univ. Radiologists, Silverman Soc., Soc. for Magnetic Resonance Imaging, Soc. Pediatric Radiology, Soc. Thoracic Radiology. Office: St Lukes's-Roosevelt Hosp Ctr 114th St Amsterdam Ave New York NY 10025

ABOULAFIA, SHARON J., health facility administrator, educator; b. N.Y.C., Sept. 29, 1958; d. Albert and Rita (Litshutz) A.; m. Steven Oken, Nov. 22, 1987; children: Melisa Hana Oken, Adam Chad Oken. BSN, Buffalo U., 1980; MSN, Hunter City U., 1984. RN, N.Y.; cert. critical care nurse, nursing adminstr., BCLS and ACLS instr. Clin. nurse ICU Univ. Hosps. Cleve., 1980-82; charge nurse, insvc. coord. N.Y. Hosp.-Cornell Med. Ctr., N.Y.C., 1982-84; clin. coord. ICU St. Lukes/Roosevelt Hosp. Ctr., N.Y.C., 1984-87; assoc. DON surgery/ICU div. SUNY-Health Sci. Ctr., Bklyn., 1987-90; asst. dir. nursing QI/RM Bronx-Lebanon (N.Y.) Hosp. Ctr., 1990—; cons. adjunct prof. clin. specialist grad. program SUNY Health Sci. Ctr., Bklyn., 1989-90; supr. part time Florence Nightingale Nursing Home, N.Y.C., 1984-85; clin. mgr. part time Home Health Care Am., N.Y.C., 1985-87; adj. faculty mem. masters clin. nurse spcialist track Columbia U. Grad. Sch. Nursing, 1985-89; presenter in field. Mem. AACCN, Am. Orgn. Nurse Execs., Sigma Theta Tau. Home: 9 Glen Ave Roslyn NY 11576

ABRAHAM, RAYMOND A., physician, surgeon; b. Evansville, Ind., Aug. 21, 1920; s. Harry and Mamie (Gordon) A.; m. Susan Gelfand; children: Michael, Rachel. AB, Ind. U., 1942, MD, 1944. Diplomate Am. Bd. Ophthalmology. Physician, surgeon Long Beach, Calif.; chief dept. ophthalmology Long Beach Meml. Med. Ctr., 1972-75; assoc. clin. prof. U. Calif., Irvine. Office: Calif Inst Eye Surgery & Vision Care 3840 Woodruff Ave # 102 Long Beach CA 90808

ABRAHAMS, JOSEPH ISAAC, psychiatrist; b. Dallas, Sept. 27, 1916; s. Harry George and Sarah (Galperin) A.; m. Apr. 20, 1948 (div. Nov. 1976); 1 child, Lisa Ann. MD, Emory U., 1939. Diplomate Am. Bd. Psychiatry and Neurology. Intern City Hosp., N.Y.C., 1939-41; resident in psychiatry St. Elizabeths Hosp., Washington, 1946-47, dir. group psychotherapy, 1947-50, cons., 1952-70; pvt. practice Washington, 1950-70, San Diego, 1970—; staff psychiatrist Atascadero (Calif.) State Hosp., 1990—; cons. fed. Prison Svc. NIMH, Washington, 1952-70, Bethesda (Md.) Naval Med. Svc., 1952-70, Mesa Vista Hosp., 1970-74. Organizer Workshop on County Polit. Orgn., San Diego, 1985; bd. dirs. San Diego County Dem. Cen. Com., 1988-90. Capt. M.C., AUS, 1941-46. Recipient Plaque, St. Elizabeths Hosp., 1970. Fellow Am. Psychoanalytic Assn. (life), Am. Psychiat. Assn. (life); mem. San Diego Psychoanalytic Soc. (sec. 1974-75), San Diego Psychoanalytic Inst. (sr. faculty), Wash. Pschoanalytic Soc. Jewish.

ABRAHAMS, MICHAEL LEWIS, social worker, consultant; b. N.Y.C., May 7, 1950. BA, Vassar Coll., 1972; MSW, U. Tenn., 1978. Counselor Spl. Approaches in Juvenile Assistance, Washington, 1974-76; cons. Methadone Treatment Program, Alexandria, Va., 1976; dep. coord. Alexandria Schs. Drug Edn. Office, 1976-77; social worker Prince William Dept. Social Svc., Manassas, Va., 1978-81; dir. Affiliated Cmty. Counselors Inc., Rockville, Md., 1983-86, 1985-89; pvt. practice Germantown, Md., 1988—; program advisor Beacon Coll., Washington, 1978-81; therapist Mental Health Assocs., Adelphi, Md., 1983-86; pvt. practice, Washington, 1984-94. Vol. quarry task force Boyds (Md.) Civic Assn., 1984-90. Mem. NASW, Greater Wash. Soc. for Clin. Social Work. Office: 18 Executive Park Ct Germantown MD 20874-2645

ABRAHAMSON, DALE RAYMOND, cell biology educator, researcher; b. Washington, June 18, 1949; s. Sherman R. and Katherine (Seglem) A.; m. Susan K. Spell, Aug. 14, 1971; 1 child, Katherine L. BA, U. Va., 1971, George Mason U., 1976; PhD, U. Va., 1981. Postdoctoral fellow Harvard Med. Sch., Boston, 1980-83; asst. prof. U. Ala., Birmingham, 1983-87, assoc. prof., 1987-92, prof., 1992—. Contbr. articles to profl. Rsch. grantee NIH, 1985—. Mem. Am. Assn. Anatomists, Am. soc. for Cell Biology, Am. Soc. Nephrology, Am. Heart Assn. (rsch. grantee 1986—). Office: U Ala Uab # 302 Birmingham AL 35294-0019

ABRAIRA, CARLOS, endocrinologist, physician; b. Buenos Aires, Argentina, Mar. 25, 1936; came to U.S., 1963, naturalized, 1976; s. Jose B. and Maria (Cela) A.; m. Rosa Saffier, July 11, 1963; children—Daniel, Irene. Bacchalaureate, U. Buenos Aires, 1953, M.D., 1962. Diplomate Am. Bd. Internal Medicine. Intern, Mercy Hosp., Chgo., 1963-64; resident Mt. Sinai Hosp., Chgo., 1964-66; fellow in medicine Northwestern U. Hosp., Evanston, Ill., 1966-67; fellow in endocrinology Michael Reese Hosp., Chgo., 1967-69, attending physician-medicine, 1969-70; asst. prof. medicine U. Ill. Abraham Lincoln Sch., Chgo., 1970-78, assoc. prof. medicine, 1978-83; assoc. prof. medicine Loyola U., Chgo., 1984—, prof. medicine, 1986—; chief endocrinology Hines VA Hosp. (Ill.), 1972—; lectr. Am. Diabetes Assn., 1984, 89-90, 94, 95; coord. diabetes program Chgo. Med. Soc. Midwest Clin. Conf., 1980-83. Editor: How to Be Your Own Diabetes Manager, 1983. Contbr. articles to profl. jours. Chmn. Nat. VA Coop Study in Diabetes, 1989—. Grantee Allstate Found., 1966, VA, 1981, 88—, Sugar Assn., 1983. Fellow ACP, Am. Coll. Nutrition; mem. Am. Diabetes Assn. (pres. Ill. affiliate, 1989-91), Am. Soc. Clin. Nutrition, Am. Inst. Nutrition, Am. Fedn. Clin. Research (sr.), Endocrine Soc. Office: Hines VA Hosp 111A 5th And Roosevelt Rd Hines IL 60141

ABRAMOWICZ, JACQUES SYLVAIN, obstetrician, perinatologist; b. Paris, Dec. 5, 1948; s. Theodore Dov and Sara Ethel (Cukiernik) A.; m. Annie Sternelicht, Aug. 1, 1972; children: Shelly, Ory. MD, Sackler Sch. Medicine, Tel-Aviv, 1975. Diplomate Israel Bd Obstetrics and Gynecology. Rotating intern Tel-Aviv Mcpl. Med. Ctr., 1973-74; resident dept. ob-gyn. Sapir Med. Ctr., Kfar-Saba, Israel, 1978-85; rsch. registrar ultrasound dept. ob-gyn. King's Coll. Hosp., London, 1981; resident dept. gen. surgery Sapir Med. Ctr., 1982-83, resident dept. urology, 1983; cons. Timsit Inst. Reproductive Medicine, Tel-Aviv, 1986-87; dir. clin. rsch. Div. Maternal-Fetal Medicine, Ea. Va. Med. Sch., Norfolk, 1987-89; assoc. researcher Jones Inst. Reproductive Medicine, Norfolk, 1989; dir. perinatal ultrasound, asst. prof. dept. ob-gyn. U. Rochester Med. Ctr., 1990-93, assoc. prof., 1993—, assoc. prof. radiology, 1995—. Contbr. articles to profl. jours. including Am. Jour. Ob-Gyn., Obstet. Gynecology, Jour. Ultrasound Medicine, Prenatal Diagnosis, Am. Jour. Perinatology, Fetal Therapy, Jour. Perinatal Medicine, also chpts. to books; referee various jours. Maj. Israel Def. Forces, 1974-78. Mem. Am. Inst. Ultrasound in Medicine (sr., internat. rels. com. 1988-91, standards com. 1991-93, mfrs. commendation panel 1991-93, chair mfrs. commendation panel 1993-94, bioeffects com. 1994—), N.Y. Acad. Sci., Soc. Perinatal Obstetricians, Internat. Perinatal Doppler Soc., Internat. Fetal Med. and Surg. Soc. Jewish. Office: U Rochester Dept Ob/Gyn Box 8668 601 Elmwood Ave Rochester NY 14642-0001

ABRAMOWITZ, JOEL, endocrinology educator; b. Bklyn., July 1, 1947; s. Sam and Freda (Goldberg) A.; m. Adele Florence Rosenzweig, Oct. 10, 1993. BS, Bklyn. Coll., 1969; MS, L.I. U., 1971; PhD, Wayne State U., 1977. Postdoctoral fellow Baylor Coll. Medicine, Houston, 1977-80, instr., 1980-81; asst. prof. Iowa State U., Ames, 1981-85, assoc. prof., 1985-88; assoc. prof. Baylor Coll. Medicine, Houston, 1988—. Editl. bd. Endocrinology, 1991-94, Am. Jour. Physiology: Endocrinology and Metabolism, 1995—. Fellow AAAS; mem. Endocrine Soc., Am. Heart Assn., Am. Soc. Nephrology, Soc. for the Study of Reproduction, N.Y. Acad. Sci. Office: Baylor Coll Medicine Dept Medicine 6565 Fannin St # F505 Houston TX 77030-2704

ABRAMS, ARTHUR JAY, physician; b. Camden, N.J., Apr. 9, 1938; s. Morris and Sophia Sarah (Kates) A.; m. Marianne Ritto Abrams, June 8, 1963; children: Suzanne Beth, Cheryl Lyn, Robert Dwight. BA, Rutgers U., Camden, N.J., 1959; MD, Hahneman U., Phila., 1963. Diplomate Am. Acad. Dermatology. Intern Madigan Army Med. Ctr., Tacoma, Wash., 1963-64; resident, chief resident Letterman Army Med. Ctr., San Francisco, 1964-67; dermatologist, Far East cons. 249th Gen. Hosp. U.S. Army, Tokyo, 1967-69; asst. chief dermatologist Tripler Army Med. Ctr., Honolulu, 1969-70; staff dermatologist El Camino Hosp., Mountain View, Calif., 1970—; clin. assoc. prof. dermatology Stanford U. Med. Ctr., 1979—; dermatology cons. San Jose (Calif.) State U., 1994—; maj. U.S. Army, 1963-70. Mem. AMA, Calif. Med. Assn., Pacific Dermatological Assn., San Francisco Dermatological Soc. Office: 763 Altos Oaks Dr Ste 4 Los Altos CA 94024

ABRAMS, CHARLES S., oncologist, hematologist, educator. MD, Yale U., 1984. Resident in internal medicine Temple U. Hosp., Phila., 1984-85; resident in internal medicine U. Pa. Hosp., Phila., 1985-87, fellow in hematology and oncology, 1987—, attending physician, asst. prof. hematology and oncology, 1992—. Grantee Am. Heart Assn., 1995-96. *

ABRAMS, GARY MITCHELL, neurologist, educator; b. N.Y.C., June 9, 1949; s. Abraham and Harriet (Vogel) A.; m. Joan Roth, July 4, 1971; children: Bryan Curtis, Lindsey June, Elizabeth Sara. BA, SUNY, Buffalo, 1970; MD, U. Pitts., 1974. Diplomate in neurology Am. Bd. Psychiatry and Neurology. Med. intern Presbyn.-U. Hosp., Pitts., 1974-75; neurology resident Columbia-Presbyn., N.Y.C., 1975-77, chief resident in neurology, 1977-78; fellow in neuroendocrinology Columbia U., N.Y.C., 1978-79, asst. prof. neurology, 1980-87, assoc. prof., 1987-95; asst. attending neurologist Presbyn. Hosp., N.Y.C., 1980-87; attending neurologist Helen Hayes Hosp., West Haverstraw, N.Y., 1982-95, chief of neurology, 1985-93, med. dir., 1986-93; dir. rehab. U. Calif. San Francisco/Mt. Zion Med. Ctr., 1995—; assoc. prof. neurology U. Calif., San Francisco, 1995—. Pres. Leonia (N.J.) Bd. Health, 1989-95. Recipient Tchr.-Investigator Devel. award NIH, 1980-85; Nat. Inst. for Med. Rsch. fellow in peptide chemistry, London, 1979-80. Fellow Am. Acad. Neurology; mem. Am. Soc. Neurorehab. (cert.), Am. Congerss Rehab. Medicine. Office: U Calif San Francisco Mt Zion Med Ctr 1600 Divisadero St San Francisco CA 94115

ABRAMS, HERBERT LEROY, radiologist, educator; b. N.Y.C., Aug. 16, 1920; s. Morris and Freda (Sugarman) A.; m. Marilyn Spitz, Mar. 23, 1943; children: Nancy, John. BA, Cornell U., 1941; MD, Downstate Med. Ctr., N.Y., 1946. Diplomate: Am. Bd. Radiology. Intern L.I. Coll. Hosp., 1946-47; resident in internal medicine Montefiore Hosp., Bronx, N.Y., 1947-48; resident in radiology Stanford U. Hosp., 1948-51; practice medicine specializing in radiology Stanford, Calif., 1951-67; faculty Sch. Medicine Stanford, 1951-67, dir. div. diagnostic roentgenology, 1961-67, prof. radiology, 1962-67; Philip H. Cook prof. radiology Harvard U., 1967-85, now prof. emeritus, chmn. dept. radiology, 1967-80; prof. radiology Stanford U. Sch. Medicine, 1985-90, prof. emeritus, 1990—; clin. prof. U. Calif. Sch. Medicine, San Francisco, 1986—; radiologist-in-chief Peter Bent Brigham Hosp., Boston, 1967-80; chmn. dept. radiology Brigham and Women's Hosp., Boston, 1981-85; radiologist-in-chief Sidney Farber Cancer Inst., Boston, 1974-85; R.H. Nimmo vis. prof. U. Adelaide, Australia; mem.-in-residence Ctr. for Internat. Security and Arms Control Stanford U., 1985—; mem. radiation study sect. NIH, 1962-66; cons. to hosps., profl. socs.; mem. com. disability U.S. Presidents, 1995—. Author: (with others) Angiocardiography in Congenital Heart Disease, 1956, Congenital Heart Disease, 1965, Coronary Arteriography: A Practical Approach, 1983, Brigham Guide to Diagnostic Imaging, 1986, Assessment of Diagnostic Technology in Health Care; editor: Abrams' Angiography, 3d edit., 1983; author: The President Has Been Shot: Confusion, Disability and the 25th Amendment, 1992, 94; mem. editorial bd. Investigative Radiology; editor-in-chief, founder Cardiovascular and Interventional Radiology, 1978-88, Postgraduate Radiology, 1983—. Nat. Cancer Inst. fellow, 1950; Spl. Research fellow Nat. Heart Inst., 1960, 73-74; David M. Gould Meml. lectr. Johns Hopkins, 1964; William R. Whitman Meml. lectr., 1968; Leo G. Rigler lectr. Tel-Aviv U., 1969; Holmes lectr. New Eng. Roentgen Ray Soc., Boston, 1970; Ross Golden lectr. N.Y. Roentgen Ray Soc., N.Y.C., 1971; Stauffer Meml. lectr. Phila. Roentgen Ray

Soc., 1971; J.M.T. Finney Fund lectr. Md. Radiol. Soc., Ocean City, 1972; Aubrey Hampton lectr. Mass. Gen. Hosp., Boston, 1974; Kirklin-Weber lectr. Mayo Clinic, 1974; Crookshank lectr. Royal Coll. Radiology, 1980; Alpha Omega Alpha lectr., vis. prof. U. Calif. Med. Sch., San Francisco, 1961-65; W.H. Herbert lectr. U. Calif.; Caldwell lectr. Am. Roentgen Ray Soc., 1982; Percy lectr. McMaster Med. Sch., 1983; Charles Dotter lectr. Soc. Cardiovascular and Interventional Radiology, 1988; Philip Hodes lectr. Jefferson Med. Coll., 1988; David Gould Meml. lectr. Johns Hopkins U., 1991; Henry J. Kaiser sr. fellow Center for Advanced Study in Behavioral Sci., 1980-81; Hymer Friedell lectr. Western Reserve Sch. Medicine, 1993. Hon. fellow Royal Coll. Radiology (Gt. Britain), Royal Coll. Surgery (Ireland), Am. Coll. Radiology, Am. Coll. Cardiology; mem. Assn. Univ. Radiologists (Gold medal 1984), Inst. Medicine, Am. Heart Assn., Am. Soc. Nephrology, Radiol. Soc. N.Am. (Gold medal 1995), N.Am. Soc. Cardiac Radiology (pres. 1979-80), Internat. Physicians for Prevention of Nuclear War (founding v.p., participant Nobel Peace prize 1985), Soc. Cardiovasc. Radiology, Soc. Chmn. Acad. Radiology Depts. (pres. 1970-71), Nat. Coun. Health Tech. Assessment, Inst. of Medicine, NAS, NIH (chmn. consensus panel on MRI, internat. blue ribbon panel radiation effects rsch. found. Hiroshima 1996), Phi Beta Kappa, Alpha Omega Alpha. Home: 714 Alvarado Stanford CA 94305 Office: Stanford U Sch Medicine Stanford CA 94305

ABRAMS, JAMES HOWARD, ophthalmologist; b. Kansas City, Kans., May 26, 1948; s. William H. and Evelyn (Rashbaum) A.; m. Nadine Phyllis Levin, Apr. 9, 1988; children: Loren William, Briana Michelle. AB, U. Pa., 1970; MD, U. Kans., 1974. Intern UCLA Harbor Gen. Hosp., 1974-75, resident, 1975-76; resident Mayo Clinic, Rochester, Minn., 1976-79; pvt. practice Daly City, Millbrae, Calif., 1980—; bd. dirs. Physicians Surgery Ctr., Daly City, Pacific Eye Physicians, Burlingame, Calif. Fellow Am. Acad. Ophthalmology; mem. Calif. Med. Assn., Am. Soc. Cataract and Refractive Surgery. Office: 901 Campus Dr Ste 205 Daly City CA 94015

ABRAMS, JULES CLINTON, psychologist; b. Phila.; s. Abraham and Sara (Rubinoff) A.; m. Ellen Shuman, Aug. 7, 1955; children—Richard, Robbi, Larry, Nancy. Student, La Salle Coll., 1944-45; A.B., Temple U., 1948, M.A., 1949, Ph.D., 1955; student, U. Toronto, 1949-50. Psychologist Sklar Sch., Phila., 1956-60; dir. Reading Improvement Inst., Pa., 1955-64; prof. psychiatry, head sect. psychology, dir. Inst. for Learning; dir. div. of psychology Hahnemann Med. Coll., Phila., 1968-89. assoc. dean, dir. Inst. for Grad. Clin. Psychology Widener U., Chester, Pa., 1989—; prof. Johns Hopkins, 1975-83. Author: Diagnosis, Correction, and Prevention of Reading Disabilities; Contbr. numerous articles to profl. jours. Pres. Parkway Day Sch., Phila., 1966-76; pres. Nat. Coun. Schs. Profl. Psychology. Fellow Am. Psychol. Assn.; mem. Assn. for Child Psychoanalysis, AAAS, Internat. Reading Assn., N.Y. Acad. Sci., Nat. Acad. Neuropsychologists, Multi-disciplinary Acad. Clin. Edn., Nat. Coun. Schs. and Programs Profl. Psychology (pres.), Council for Exceptional Children, Sigma Xi. Home: 1505 Paper Mill Rd Glenside PA 19038-7029 Office: 255 S 17th St Philadelphia PA 19103-6231

ABRAMS, JULIE MARIE, counseling psychologist; b. Bryn Mawr, Pa., Aug. 26, 1962; d. Robert Marlow and Patricia Ann (Theobald) A. BA in Psychology cum laude, Davidson Coll., 1984; MS, U. Fla., 1988, PhD, 1992. Intern in psychology Counseling Ctr. So. Ill. U., Carbondale, 1989-90; student counseling specialist sexual assault recovery svc. U. Fla., Gainesville, 1991-92, psychologist, 1992-94, interim coord., 1994-95; psychologist U. Fla., 1995—; rsch. team, cons. Fla. Vocat. Rehab. Program Dist. III, Gainesville, 1986-89; asst. to editorial rev. bd. Jour. Counseling and Devel., 1986-87. Contbr. articles to profl. jours. Crisis phone counselor Alachua County Crisis Ctr., Gainesville, 1985-86; mem. sexual battery com. City of Gainesville, 1988—. Fellow U. Fla. Grad. Coun., 1984-85, O. Ruth McQuown, 1989-90. Mem. APA, NOW. Office: U Fla CARE Student Health Care Ctr PO Box 117500 Gainesville FL 32611

ABRAMS, REID ALLEN, surgeon, educator; b. San Antonio, July 26, 1955. BA in Biology, Lawrence U., 1977; MD, U. Colo., 1982. Diplomate Am. Bd. Orthopaedic Surgery, with cert. of added qualifications in hand surgery; lic. physician, Calif., Colo., Washington. Intern then resident in orthopedic surgery U. Colo. Health Scis. Ctr., Denver, 1982-87; fellow pediatric orthopedics Children's Hosp. and Health ctr., San Diego, 1987-88; fellow hand and microvascular surgery Brigham and Women's Hosp., Boston, 1988-89; gen. orthopedist Group Health Coop. Puget Sound, 1989-90; asst. prof. in residence, chief hand & microvascular surgery U. Calif. Med. Ctr., San Diego, 1990—. Contbr. numerous articles to profl. jours. Mem. Acad. Orthopaedic Soc., Am. Acad. Orthopaedic Surgeons, Am. Soc. Surgery of the Hand, Kiros Soc., Phi Sigma. Office: U Calif Med Ctr Orthopedic Surgery 200 W Arbor Dr San Diego CA 92103-1911

ABRAMS, RICHARD STEPHEN, physician; b. St. Louis, Mo., June 15, 1946; s. Edwin P. and Marjorie (Rothman) A.; m. Carol Grossman, June 26, 1973; children: Brian, Katie. BA, Northwestern U., 1968; MD, U. Mo., 1972. Diplomate ACP, 1975. Chmn. Premier Healthcare Ptrns., 1995—; med. dir. clinical info. sys., Rose Med. Ctr., Denver, Co., 1990-95. Author: Medical Complications During Pregnancy, 1983, Gestatorial Diabetes, 1990, Handbook Of Medical Problems In Pregnancy, 1990, Will It Hurt The Baby?, 1993. Trustee, Garland Sch., Denver, 1990-95. Office: 4545 E. 9th Ave. #670 Denver CO 80220

ABRAMS, WILLIAM BERNARD, pharmaceutical company executive, physician; b. Atlantic City, July 15, 1922; s. Joseph and Zelda (Coleman) Salzberg; m. Berenda Weinberg Abrams, Mar. 4, 1945. children: James C., Andrew P., Joseph T., Julie A. BS in Biology, Rutgers U., 1944; MD, Jefferson Med. Coll. Phila., 1947. Diplomate Am. Bd. Internal Medicine. Intern Atlantic City Hosp., 1947-48; fellow pediatric rsch. Children's Hosp. Phila., 1949-50; fellow cardiology Phila. Gen. Hosp., 1950-51; resident in medicine St. Louis U. Hosp., 1953-54; pvt. practice internal medicine, 1955-59; asst. med. dir. Hoffman-La Roche, Inc., Nutley, N.J., 1959-62, dir. dept. clin. pharmacology, 1962-71; dir. clin. rsch. Ayerst Labs., N.Y.C., 1971-72, v.p., 1972-75; exec. dir. clin. pharmacology Merck Sharp & Dohme Rsch. Labs. divsn. Merck & Co., Inc., West Point, Pa., 1975-81, exec. dir. sci. devel., 1981-93; cons., 1993-95; spl. govt. employee, dir. Office Profl. Devel. FDA, 1988-91; instr. bacteriology Jefferson Med. Coll., 1948-49, instr. then assoc. in medicine, 1959-64; attending physician Newark City Hosp., 1959-71; part-time physician chest svc. VA Hosp. East Orange, N.J., 1956-58, ward physician, 1954-55; cons. clin. pharmacology Newark Presbyn. Hosp., 1955-71, dept. clin. pharmacology Newark Beth Israel Med. Ctr., 1962-71; rsch. assoc. prof. medicine Hahnemann Med. Coll. Phila., 1964-67, vis. prof. medicine Likoff Cardiovascular Inst., 1977-87; attending physician Martland Hosp. unit, clin. assoc. prof. medicine N.J. Coll. Medicine and Dentistry, 1967-75; adj. prof. medicine Jefferson Med. Coll. and Hosp., 1977—; geriatric adv. panel U.S. Pharmacopeia Convention, 1990-95; speaker numerous profl. nat. and internat. mtgs., symposia, others. Co-editor Merck Manual of Geriatrics, 1986—; contbr. numerous articles, abstracts to profl. jours., chpts. to textbooks. With U.S. Army, 1951-53. Fellow NIH, 1949-51. Fellow ACP, Am. Coll. Cardiology (gov. N.J. 1970-73, Cummings Humanitarian award 1969, 74); mem. Am. Soc. for Pharmacology and Exptl. Therapeutics, Am. Fedn. Clin. Rsch., Am. Heart Assn. (adv. bd. coun. high blood pressure rsch., bd. govs. Southeastern Pa. affiliate), Essex County N.J. Heart Assn. (past pres., trustee), N.J. Heart Assn. (trustee), Drug Info Assn. (Disting. Career award 1988), Am. Soc. Clin. Pharmacology and Therapeutics (pres. 1975-76, Henry W. Elliott Disting. Svc. award 1986), Internat. Soc. Hypertension, Pharm. Mfrs. Assn. Found. (clin. pharmacology adv. com. 1974-94), N.J. Acad. Medicine, N.Y. Acad. Scis., Am. Fedn. Aging Rsch. (bd. dirs.), Coun. Geriatric Cardiology, Alliance for Aging Rsch. (bd. dirs.), Internat. Leadership (adv. bd), Geriatric Clinical Pharmacology (honoree annual William B. Abrams award 1996—), Alpha Omega Alpha. Office: Merck Manuals Sci Devel West Point PA 19486

ABRAMSON, CLARENCE ALLEN, pharmaceutical company executive, lawyer; b. Ft. Worth, Oct. 15, 1932; s. Samuel and Katherine (Berg) A.; m. Maureen L. Foley, May 15, 1962; children: Steven T., Eric M., Katherine M. BBA, U. Tex., 1952, JD, 1954. Bar: Tex. 1954, N.Y. 1963, N.J. 1972, Pa. 1974. Ptnr. Wynne & Wynne, Dallas, 1954-61; atty. SEC, Washington, 1961-62; of counsel Mobil Oil Corp., N.Y., The Hague and London, 1962-69; internat. gen. counsel Merck & Co., Inc., Rahway, N.J., 1970-86, assoc. gen. counsel, 1986-89, sec., chief counsel, 1989-90, v.p., sec., 1991-93; pres. Health Care Ventures Internat., Inc., Scotch Plains, N.J., 1994—; dir., founder Poly Pharm Inc., N.Y.C., 1993—; co-founder, mng. dir. Gulf Stream Pharms., LLC, Boca Raton, Fla., 1995; bd. dirs. Handy & Harman, Inc., Polypharm, Inc., Acorda Therapeutics, Inc.; bd. dirs., chmn. bd. Gulfstream harma LLC, Scotch Plains; mem. adv. bd. Inst. Circadian Physiology, Cambridge, Mass.; adj. prof. legal studies Montclair State U. Trustee Cmty. Health Law Project. Mem. ABA, Tex. Bar Assn., N.J. Bar Assn., Pa. Bar Assn., N.Y. State Bar Assn. Office: 27 Blackbirch Rd Scotch Plains NJ 07076-2941

ABRAMSON, EDWARD GERALD, urologist; b. Washington, Oct. 23, 1940; s. Alfred and Beatrice Sylvia (Oxenburg) A.; m. Lynn Elise Nyberg, Jan. 19, 1985; 1 child, Lauren Allison. BA in Am. Civilization, U. Pa., 1962; Md, U. Va., 1967. Diplomate Am. Bd. Urology. Intern George Washington U. Hosp., Washington, 1967-68, jr. resident, 1968-69, resident in urology, 1969-71, chief resident urology, 1971-72; pvt. practice Alexandria Urol. Assoc., P.C., 1972—; chief of urology Alexandria Hosp., 1980—; asst. clin. prof. George Washington U. Sch. of Medicine, 1976—. Fellow ACS; mem. AMA, Am. Urologic Assn., Med. Soc. of Va. Office: Alexandria Urol Assocs PC 1707 Osage St #301 Alexandria VA 22302

ABRAMSON, HANLEY NORMAN, pharmacy educator; b. Detroit, June 10, 1940; s. Frederick Jacob and Lillian (Kampner) A.; m. Young Hee Kim, Aug. 1, 1967; children: Nathaniel, Deborah, Stephen. BS in Pharmacy, Wayne State U., 1962; MS in Pharm. Chemistry, U. Mich., 1963, PhD in Pharm. Chemistry, 1966. Registered pharmacist. Rsch. assoc. The Hebrew U., Jerusalem, Israel, 1966-67; asst. prof. Wayne State U., Detroit, 1967-73, assoc. prof., 1973-78, prof., 1978—, chmn. dept. pharm. sci., 1986-95, interim dean Coll. of Pharmacy and Allied Health Professions, 1987-88, assoc. dean, assoc. provost, 1991-95. Author numerous published articles in field of medicinal chemistry. Bd. trustees 1st Bapt. Ch. of Oak Park, Mich., 1974-78; deacon Bloomfield Hills (Mich.) Bapt. Ch., 1986-89. Recipient rsch. grants Mich. Heart Assn., Detroit, 1967-76, Nat. Cancer Inst., Bethesda, Md., 1982-91. Mem. Am. Chem. Soc., Am. Pharm. Assn., Am. Assn. Colls. Pharmacy, AAAS, Am. Assn. Pharm. Scientists. Baptist. Home: 5530 Hammersmith Dr West Bloomfield MI 48322-1452 Office: Wayne State U 101 Shapero Hall Detroit MI 48202

ABRAMSON, LEONARD, healthcare organization executive; b. 1938. BS, Pa. State U., 1954. V.p. Spectro Industries, Jenkintown, Pa., 1969-72, R H Med. Svcs., Inc., Phila., 1972-76; with Health Maintenance Orgn. of Pa., Phila., 1976-81; exec. v.p., dir. U.S. Health Care System of Pa., Inc., Blue Bell, 1981—; chmn. & CEO U.S. Healthcare System of P.A., 1996—. Office: US Healthcare Inc PO Box 1109 980 Jolly Rd Blue Bell PA 19422-1962*

ABRAMSON, SARA JANE, radiologist, educator; b. New Orleans, La., May 12, 1945; m. Walter Squire; children: Harrison, Russell, Zachary, Andrew. BA, Sarah Lawrence Coll., 1967; postgrad., Tulane U., 1967-69; MD, Mt. Sinai Sch. Medicine, 1971. Diplomate Am. Bd. Radiology, cert. added qualifications pediat. radiology. Intern in pediatrics Mt. Sinai Hosp., N.Y.C., 1971-72, resident in pediatrics, 1972-73; resident in radiology St. Luke's Children's Mercy Hosp., Kansas City, Mo., 1973-76; asst. prof. radiology U. Mo., 1976-79, Harvard U. Med. Sch., Cambridge, Mass., 1979-81; fellow in pediatric radiology Children's Hosp., Boston, 1979-81; asst. prof. radiology Columbia Coll. Physicians & Surgeons, N.Y.C., 1981-88, assoc. prof. radiology, 1988-93; assoc. attending radiologist Babies Hosp. Columbia Presbyn. Med. Ctr., N.Y.C., 1981-93, dep. dir. Div. Pediatric Radiology, 1992-93; assoc. prof. radiology Med. Coll. Cornell U., Ithaca, N.Y., 1993—; assoc. attending radiologist, assoc. mem. Mem. Sloan-Kettering Cancer Ctr. Mem. Hosp., N.Y.C., 1993—; apptd. to radiology elective program Columbia U. Med. Sch., N.Y.C., 1981-93, radiology residency program reevaluation, 1984-93, affirmative action com., 1987-90, program coord. affiliated hosps. teaching program, 1991-93, med. student advisor, 1991-93; mem. faculty coun. Columbia U., 1987-93; mem. resident selection com. Columbia-Presbyn. Med. Ctr., N.Y.C., 1985-93, quality assurance com., 1987-91, practice rev. com., 1991-93; cons. in pediatric radiology Blythedale Children's Hosp., 1982—, Bet Israel Hosp., N.Y.C., 1983—, Harlem Hosp., N.Y.C., 1983—, N.Y. Foundling Hosp., 1988—, Lenox Hill Hosp., 1990—, Morristown Meml. Hosp., 1990—; lectr., presenter in field. Contbr. over 40 articles to profl. jours., chpts. to books. Named Radiology Tchr. of Yr., Columbia Coll. Physicians and Surgeons, 1992. Fellow Am. Coll. Radiology (del. N.Y. chpt. 1991—, alt. del. 1984-91); mem. AMA, Soc. for Pediat. Radiology, Radiology Soc. N.Am., European Soc. for Pediat. Radiology, Soc. Thoracic Radiology, Am. Assn. Ultrasound in Medicine, Am. Assn. Women in Radiology, N.Y. Roentgen Soc. (sec.-treas. 1991-94, v.p. 1996—, moderator, pediat. program chair spring conf. 1991, guest lectr. spring conf. 1990), Nat. Children's Cancer Study Group, Caffey Soc., Neuhauser Soc., Kirkpatrick Soc. Office: Sloan-Kettering Cancer Ctr 1175 York Ave New York NY 10021-7169

ABRAMS-SMITH, PAULA SARA, psychologist; b. N.Y.C., Nov. 22, 1951; d. Arnold and Naomi Frances (Gettenberg) Abrams; children: J.N. Smith, Z.H. Smith; cert. Institute Montesano, Switzerland, 1969; B.A., U. Wash., Seattle, 1972; M.S., Nat. Coll. Edn., 1974; Ph.D., Northwestern U., 1977; exec. tng. program Harvard Bus. Sch., Buffalo, 1980-81; m. James Theodore Smith, Nov. 23, 1979. Program coordinator spl. edn. programs Abraham Lincoln Center, Chgo., 1973-74; tchr., psychologist, program supr. Developmental Inst. (formerly Dysfunctioning Child Center), Michael Reese Hosp. and Med. Center, Chgo., 1974-78; mgr. and child psychologist of child rsch. dept. rsch. and devel. Fisher-Price Toys, East Aurora, N.Y., 1978-83, corp. cons., 1983-85; asst. adj. prof. devel. psychology SUNY, Buffalo, 1980-84; clin. dir. Infant Initiative Programs; chair human svcs. dept., child and youth svcs. dept. Medaille Coll., Buffalo, 1993—; cons. HMS Assocs., N.Y. State Dept. Pub. Health, Rural Health Networks, 1993-95. Mem. Amherst Players, 1978-79; dir. western N.Y. region U.S. Olympic Com.; dir. Children's Centre, Inc., 1984—; mem. exec. bd. Buffalo Dive Club; coach lightweight men's crew West Side Rowing Club; translator World University Games, Buffalo, 1993. Mem. AAAS, N.Y. Acad. Scis., Am. Psychol. Assn., N.Y. Met. Assn. Applied Psychology, Nat. Assn. Underwater Instrs. (instr.), New Programs Developmental Inst. (asst. dir. Michael Reese Hosp. and Med. Ctr. 1985-89), Phi Delta Kappa. Editor Sch. Psychology Internat. Jour., 1980-90.

ABROMAITIS, STANLEY CLINTON, health care corporation executive; b. Detroit, Nov. 19, 1946; s. Stanley Louis and Marguerite Irene (Fotherby) A.; m. Kay Marie Van Den Beldt, Nov. 13, 1971; children: Sonia, Stephanie. BBA, Western Mich. U., Kalamazoo, 1971; MBA, U. Louisville, 1990. Engr. Ford Motor Co., Louisville, 1972-76; v.p. Action Advt. Corp., Ft. Lauderdale, Fla., 1976-80; regional mgr. Am. Sign & Indicator, Spokane, Wash., 1980-82; nat. account mgr. Fed. Sign Corp., Chgo., 1982-87; v.p. Quality Rehab. Svcs., Louisville, 1988-94; pres. Healthcare Cons., Louisville, 1990-94; v.p. Caretenders HealthCorp., Louisville, 1994—; mem. adv. bd. U. Ky. Sanders-Brown Ctr., Lexington, 1992-96, devel. bd. U. Ky. Coll. Allied Health Profls., 1996—, Ombudsman Program, Louisville, 1990-94. Host, prodr. weekly TV show Alzheimer's Life Line, 1992-96. Health advisor U.S. Senator McConnell, Washington, 1992; del. Gov.'s Health Care Reform, Frankfort, Ky., 1992; chmn. Gov.'s Task Force on Alzheimers, Frankfort, 1994-95; del. White House Conf. on Aging, Washington, 1995; chpt. pres. Alzheimer's Assn., Louisville, 1992-95, nat. bd. dirs., Chgo., 1996. Named Tchr. of Yr. Lees Coll., 1992; recipient Leadership award Alzheimer's Assn., Louisville, 1993. Mem. Am. Coll. Health Care Adminstrn. (faculty mem.), Ky. Assn. Gerontology, Nat. Coalition on Aging, Am. Soc. on Aging, MBA Assn. (pres. 1988). Republican. Roman Catholic. Office: Caretenders HealthCorp Ste 400 100 Mallard Creek Rd Louisville KY 40207

ABRUTYN, ELIAS, medical educator; b. Jersey City, N.J., Apr. 15, 1940; s. Samuel Bruce and Eva A.; m. Leslye Silver, Dec. 23, 1978; 1 child, Alex, Adam. BA, U. Pa., 1960; MD, U. Pitts., 1966. Intern Hosp. of U. Pa., Phila., 1966-67, resident, 1967-68; resident, instr. internal medicine U. Pa., VA Hosp., Phila., 1970-71; asst. prof. medicine U. Pa., Phila., 1972-78; asst. prof. medicine Med. Coll. Pa., Phila., 1978-79, assoc. prof. medicine, 1979-82, prof. medicine, 1982—; assoc. dean vets. affairs Med. Coll. Pa., Hahnemann U., Phila., 1991-95, vice chmn. medicine; adj. assoc. prof. medicine, U. Pa., 1979-84, 84-95. Assoc. editor Annals of Internal Medicine, 1978—; mem. editl. bd. Infectious Disease Practice, 1991—, Clinical Performance and Quality Health Care, 1995—. With USPHS, 1968-70. Sr. scholar clin. epidemiology unit U. Pa. Sch. Medicine, 1989-93, 93-95; recipient Heard award in Surgery, 1965. Fellow Am. Coll. Physicians, Infectious disease Soc.; mem. AMA (alt. del. 1991-94), Am. Fedn. Clin. Rsch., Am. Pub. Health Assn., Am. Soc. Microbiology, Soc. Healthcare Epiedmiology Am. (treas. 1991-95, v.p. 1996), Nat. Found. Infectious Diseases (sec. Pa. chpt. 1985-91), Pa. Med. Soc., Pa. Soc. Infectious Disease, Phila. County Med. Soc., Hosp. Infection Soc. (England), Epidemic Intelligence Svc. Alumni Assn., Alpha Omega Alpha. Office: VA Med Ctr 38th & Woodland Aves Philadelphia PA 19104-4594

ABTS, GWYNETH HARTMANN, dietitian; b. Union, Ill., Oct. 31, 1923; d. William John and Olga Anna (Krause) Hartmann; m. Rufus Heath Jr., Apr. 6, 1942 (div. Dec. 1945); m. Harold Henry Abts, Feb. 14, 1948; children: Leigh, Michael, Patricia. BS, U. Ill., 1945; postgrad., U. Oreg., 1945-46, U. Ill., Elgin, 1957, No. Ill. U., 1966, 74, 82, 87. Registered dietitian, Ill. Clin. dietitian St. Joseph Hosp., Elgin, 1947; asst. dietitian French Hosp., San Francisco, 1948-50, Elgin State Hosp., 1950-58; dietary cons. Ill. Youth Commn., Springfield, 1958-70; food adminstr. Ill. Dept. of Corrections, Springfield, 1970-85; mem. Food and Nutrition Cou. on Govt. Commodities, Springfield, 1980-85; bd. dirs. Ill. Nutrition Assn., Urbana, 1983. Pres. PTO, Geneva, 1972. McHenry County Home Econ. scholar U. Ill., 1941-45. Mem. Am. Dietetic Assn. (citizens ambassador program to Australia and New Zealand), Fox Valley Home Economists, West Suburban Dietetic Assn., AAUW. Lutheran. Home: 1505 Dunstan Rd Geneva IL 60134-3327

ABUL-HAJ, SULEIMAN KAHIL, pathologist; b. Palestine, Apr. 20, 1925; s. Sheik Khalil and S. Buteina (Oda) Abul-H.; BS, U. Calif. at Berkeley, 1949; M.S., U. Calif. at San Francisco, 1951, MD, 1955; m. Elizabeth Abood, Feb. 11, 1948; children: Charles, Alan, Cary; came to U.S., 1946, naturalized, 1955. Intern, Cook County Hosp., Chgo., 1955-56; resident U. Calif. Hosp., San Francisco, 1949, Brooke Gen. Hosp., 1957-59; chief clin. and anatomic pathology Walter Reed Army Hosp., Washington, 1959-62; assoc. prof. U. So. Calif. Sch. Medicine, Los Angeles, 1963—; sr. surg. pathologist L.A. County Gen. Hosp., 1963; dir. dept. pathology Cmty. Meml. Hosp., Ventura, Calif., 1964-80, Gen. Hosp. Ventura County, 1966-74; dir. Pathology Service Med. Group, 1970—; cons. Calif. Tumor Tissue Registry, 1962—, Camarillo State Hosp., 1964-70, Tripler Gen. Hosp., Hawaii, 1963-67, Armed Forces Inst. Pathology, 1960—. Bd. dirs. Tri-Counties Blood Bank, Am. Cancer Soc. Served to maj., M.C., U.S. Army, 1956-62. Recipient Borden award Calif. Honor Soc., 1949; Achievement cert. Surgeon Gen. Army, 1962. Fellow Am. Soc. Clin. Pathologists, Coll. Am. Pathologists; mem. Internat. Coll. Surgeons, World Affairs Council, Jonathan Club. Contbr. articles to profl. jours. Research in cardiovascular disease, endocrine, renal, skin diseases, also cancer. Home and Office: 105 Encinal Way Ventura CA 93001-3317

ABU-ZIDAN, FIKRI MAHMOUD, surgeon; b. Derna, Libya, May 19, 1957; arrived in New Zealand, 1995; s. Mahmoud Abdallah and Faheema Mousa (Salman) A.; m. Iman Ahmad Raad, Mar. 27, 1989; children: Mohammad, Yousef. MD, Aleppo (Syria) U., 1981; FRCS, Glasgow, U.K.; PhD, Linköping (Sweden) U., 1995. Internship Allepo U. Hosp., 1980-81; anatomy demonstrator Faculty of Medicine, Kuwait, 1981-83; surgeon Univ. Hosp., Kuwait, 1983-93; residency in surgery Mubarak Alkabeer Teaching Hosp., Kuwait, 1985-90; rsch. fellow Linköping U., 1993-95; rsch. fellow in surg. sci. Auckland (N.Z.) Univ. Hosp., 1996—. Contbr. numerous articles and abstracts to profl. jours. Lions Rsch. Found. grantee, 1994. Fellow Royal Coll. Physicians and Surgeons U.K. Office: Auckland Hospital Univ, Park Rd Bag 92024 dept Surg, Auckland New Zealand

ACASTER, LINDA DIANE, chiropractor; b. Somerville, N.J., Jan. 9, 1952; d. Horace Leroy and Dorothy Tekla (Stoeckel) A.; 1 child Brandon. Student, Syracuse U., 1971-73; BA magna cum laude, No. Ill. U., 1975; AS, San Diego Community Coll., 1982; D Chiropractic, Palmer Coll. Chiropractic, 1985. Tech. illustrator DMJM, San Diego, 1979; illustration supr. Rosenblatt & Son, Inc., San Diego, 1979-82; chiropractic assoc. Chapman Chiropractic, Chula Vista, Calif., 1987; pvt. practice chiropractic, radiology, phys. therapy, sports injuries, thermography Poway, Calif., 1988—; mem. Practice Mgmt. Assocs., 1988—. Mem. Calif. Chiropractic Assn., Internat. Acad. Clin. Thermographers, Christian Chiropractic Assn., Applied Spinal Biomech. Engring. Assn., Poway C. of C., Soroptimists, Sigma Phi Chi. Office: 13323 Poway Rd Poway CA 92064-4625

ACCARDI, LISA ANN, long term care coordinator, nurse consultant; b. Haverhill, Mass., July 24, 1962; d. Anthony George Accardi and Shirley Ann (Welch) McClean. LPN, Whittier Regional Vocat.-Tech., 1985. LPN Hannah Duston Long Term Care, Haverhill, Mass., 1985-90; LPN program coord. J.T. Berry Rehab. Ctr., North Reading, Mass., 1985-90; charge LPN Acad. Manor Nursing Home, Andover, Mass., 1990-91; nurse cons., program coord. Residential Resources, Salem, N.H., 1991-92; LPN Acad. Manor Nursing Home, Andover, 1992—. Roman Catholic. Home: 196C N Main St # 6 Salem NH 03079-1822 Office: Acad Manor Nursing Home 89 Morton St Andover MA 01810-2036

ACEE, MARY LYNN, counselor, social worker; b. Utica, N.Y., June 12, 1955; d. John J. and Pierina (Mattacola) A. BA in Sociology, SUNY, Geneseo, 1977; MSW, SUNY, Buffalo, 1988. Cert. social worker Acad. Cert. Social Workers. Case mgr. of community support system Neighborhood Ctr., Utica, N.Y., 1980-84, 85-86; dir. community residence Cath. Charities, Rome, N.Y., 1984-85; rsch. asst. SUNY, Buffalo, 1986; tng. specialist Crisis Svcs., Buffalo, 1986-89; counselor, med. social worker Buffalo Gen. Hosp., 1989—. Fellowship Am. Cancer Soc., 1987. Mem. NASW, SUNY at Buffalo Sch. of Social Work Grad. Student Assn. (v.p.). Office: Buffalo Gen Hosp Social Work Dept 100 High St Buffalo NY 14203-1126

ACHAUER, BRUCE MICHAEL, plastic surgeon. MD, Baylor U., 1967. Intern San Francisco Gen. Hosp., 1967-68; resident in gen. surgery U. Calif., Irvine, 1970-74, rsch. in plastic surgery, 1974-76, adj. prof. surgery, 1994—; fellow in plastic surgery Queen Victoria Hosp., East Grinstead, U.K., 1976; mem. staff U. Calif. Irvine Med. Ctr., Orange, 1977—, St. Joseph Hosp., 1977—; mem. active staff Children's Hosp. of Orange County, 1977—; pvt. practice plastic surgery; mem. courtesy staff Med. Ctr. of GGG, 1985—, Western Med. Ctr., 1977—; dir. Am. Bd. Plastic Surgery, 1995—. Fellow Am. Acad. Pediatrics; mem. ABA, AAPS, ACPA, ASPRS, ASSH. Office: 1140 W La Veta Ave # 810 Orange CA 92668-4223

ACHOR, LOUIS JOSEPH MERLIN, psychology and neuroscience educator; b. Clarendon, Tex., Jan. 2, 1948; s. Merlin Farr and Aileen (Arneson) A.; m. Sharon Lyn Slack, Nov. 7, 1970; children: Shawn Joseph, Amy Christina. BA in Psychology, UCLA, 1971, MA in Zoology, 1972; PhD in Psychobiology, U. Calif., Irvine, 1977. NIMH predoctoral fellow U. Calif., Irvine, 1974-76, trainee, 1972-74, 76-77; asst. prof. in psychology Baylor U., Waco, Tex., 1978-85, assoc. prof. psychology, 1986-91, assoc. prof. neurosci. and psychology, 1991—; dir. undergrad. programs in neurosci. and psychology Baylor U., 1992-94; jour. and conf. reviewer; judge Ctrl. Tex. Regional Sci. Fair, 1979—, mem. sci. rev. com., 1991-92; instr. Baylor U. for Young People, 1991-93; mem. pre-med./pre-dental adv. com. Baylor U., 1994—. Contbr. articles to profl. jours. Chmn. Nat. and Internat. Scholarships Com. Baylor U., 1986-90; asst. scoutmaster Boy Scouts Am., 1989-93. Recipient Young Investigator award Baylor U., 1982. Mem. AAAS, AAUP (Baylor chpt.), Am. Psychol. Soc. (charter), Soc. for Neurosci., Faculty for Undergrad. Neurosci. (charter, funding sources com. 1992—, councilor exec. com. 1993—, sec. 1994—, chmn. com. to establish a nat. honor soc. in neurosci. 1994—), Assn. Neurosci. Depts. and Programs, Internat. Brain Rsch. Orgn., Tex. Assn. Advisors for Health Professions, Sigma Xi (Baylor U. chpt. sec.-treas. 1988-89, v.p. 1989-90, pres. 1990-92), Psi Chi (advisor 1985—, scholarship established in his honor Baylor U. 1986. Home: 10005 Treeline Dr Waco TX 76712-8529 Office: Dept Psychology and Neurosci Baylor U Waco TX 76798

ACHORD, JAMES LEE, gastroenterologist, educator; b. Dayton, Ohio, Sept. 24, 1931; s. Lonnie M. and Ethel E. (Collins) A.; m. Patsy Jane Moore, Dec. 18, 1954; children: J. Michael, Ann Elizabeth, Andrew P. Student, Emory U., 1949-52, MD, 1956. Intern Emory Hosp., 1956-57; resident Emory U., Atlanta, 1959-62, instr., assoc. prof., 1962-71; med. dir. Med. Ctr.

Cen. Ga., Macon, 1971-75; assoc. dean, prof. East Tenn. State Sch. Medicine, Johnson City, 1975-76; prof., dir. div. digestive diseases U. Miss. Med. Ctr., Jackson, 1976—. Editor(book revs.) Am. Jour. Gastroenterology, 1985-91, Dig. Dis. Sci., 1994—; contbr. numerous articles and editorials to profl. jours. and chpts. to books. Capt. U.S. Army, 1957-59. Fellow ACP (gov. Miss. chpt. 1993—); mem. ACP, Am. Coll. Gastroenterology (pres. 1983-84), Am. Assn. Study Liver Disease, Am. Gastroent. Assn., Am. Soc. Gastroenterologic Endoscopy. Office: U Miss Med Ctr 2500 N State St Jackson MS 39216-4500

ACHRAFI, HADI, cardiologist, consultant; b. Nichabocre, Iran, May 24, 1941; s. Massih and Hachmat (Arbabe) A.; m. Michele LeRwyet, Nov. 28, 1978; children: Farchad, Soraya. MD, U. Paris, 1973. Intern, then resident dept. cardiology Ctrl. Gen. Hosp., Troyes, France, 1969-72; assoc. prof. Nat. U. Teheran, Iran, 1978, 79, 80; cardiac ressucitation cardiologist Nat. U. Teheran, Paris, 1981; pvt. practice Chartres, France, 1982—. Contbr. articles to med. jours. Recipient physician's award Mass. Postgrad. Med. Inst., 1988. Mem. AAAS (invited), Am. Heart Assn. (sci. coun.), French Soc. Cardiology, European Soc. Cardiology, French Coll. Vascular Pathology, French Coll. Cardiac Stimulation, N.Y. Acad. Scis. Office: Residence Topaze, 8 Rue GD Faubourg, 28000 Chartres France

ACHTEL, ROBERT ANDREW, pediatric cardiologist; b. Bklyn., May 5, 1941; s. Murray and Amelia (Ellian) A.; m. Erica Noel Woods, Mar. 10, 1963; children: Bergen Alison, Roland Hugh. BA, Adelphi U., 1963; MD, U. Cin., 1967. Diplomate Am. Bd. Pediatric Cardiology. Intern, Cin. Children's Hosp., 1967-68; resident in pediatrics Yale U., 1968-69, fellow in pediatric cardiology, 1969-71; clin. instr. pediatrics U. Calif.-Davis, 1972-73, clin. asst. prof., 1977-83; asst. prof. pediatrics, U. Ky., 1973-76; dir. pediatric ICU, Sutter Meml. Hosp., Sacramento, 1977-85, dir. pediatric Cardiology, 1982—, chmn. instl. rev. com., 1981-85; chmn. dept. pediatrics Mercy Hosp., Sacramento, 1981-83, vice chmn. pediatrics, 1983-85, 95—; dir. pediatric ICU, 1982-83; dir. Laurel Hills Devel. Ctr., 1985-89.; chmn. rsch com. Sutter Inst. for Med. Rsch., 1989—; trustee, mem. exec. com. Sutter Hosps. Found., vice chmn., 1992-93, CEO Access Care, 1994-95, med. dir. FastServe Med. Group, 1995; mem. tech. adv. com. pediat. cardiology State of Calif.; CEO AccessCare; chmn. regional instnl. rev. bd. Sutter/CHS Ctrl., 1996. Contbr. articles in cardiovascular rsch. Bd. dirs. Sutter Meml. Hosp. Found., 1986—; bd. dirs. Sutter Found., 1989, trustee, 1989—. Maj. M.C., USAF, 1971-73. Recipient grants from Heart Assn., U. Ky. Tobacco and Health Rsch. Found. Mem. Am. Heart Assn. (dir. Sacramento chpt., mem. councils congenital heart disease and atherosclerosis and cardiovascular surgery), Am. Coll. Chest Physicians, Am. Acad Pediatrics, S.W. Pediatric Cardiology Soc., So. Soc. Pediatric Rsch. Office: Pediatric Cardiology Assocs 5609 J St Ste A Sacramento CA 95819-3948

ACKER, VIRGINIA MARGARET, nursing educator; b. Madison, Wis., Aug. 11, 1946; d. Paul Peter and Lucille (Klein) A. Diploma in Nursing, St. Mary's Med. Ctr., Madison, 1972; BS in Nursing, Incarnate Work Coll., San Antonio, 1976; MS in Health Professions, S.W. Tex. State U., 1980; postgrad., U. Tex., 1992-93. RN, Wis., Tex. Staff nurse St. Mary's Hosp., Milw., 1972-73, Kenosha Meml. Hosp., Wis., 1973-74, S.W. Tex. Meth. Hosp., San Antonio, 1974-75, Met. Gen. Hosp., San Antonio, 1975-76; instr. Bapt. Meml. Hosp. System Sch. Nursing, San Antonio, 1976-83; dir. nursing Meml. Hosp., Gonzales, Tex., 1983-84; instr., dir. nursing Victoria Coll., Cuero, Tex., 1984-86; dir. nursing Rocky Knoll Health Care Facility, Plymouth, Wis., 1986-87, Unicare Health Facilities, Milw., 1987-88; coord. nursing edn. St. Nicholas Hosp., Sheboygan, Wis., 1989-90; instr. U. Wis. Oshkosh, 1990-92, St. David's Hosp., Austin, Tex., 1992-95, Bailey Sq. Surg Ctr., 1995—. Roman Catholic. Avocations: cross-stiching, reading, camping, fishing. Home: 2103 Four Oaks Ln Austin TX 78704-4624

ACKERMAN, GARY EDWIN, obstetrician, gynecologist; b. Phoenix, Aug. 27, 1945; s. Sol S. and Sylvia G. (Hordes) Saul; m. Ellen Ana Saitz, Dec. 27, 1970; children: Beth, Joshua, Jennifer, Benjamin. BS, Columbia U., 1968; MD, SUNY, N.Y.C., 1972. Diplomate Am. Bd. Obstetrics and Gynecology, Nat. Bd. Med. Examiners; lic. physician, Tex. Intern, resident in ob-gyn. Maimonides Med. Ctr., Bklyn., 1972-76; fellow in reproductive endocrinology U. Tex./Southwestern Med. Sch., Dallas, 1978-80; pvt. practice Dallas, 1980—; instr. dept. ob-gyn. U. Tex. southwestern Med. Sch., 1980-81, asst. prof., 1981-89, assoc. prof., 1989—; attending staff ob-gyn. Parkland Meml. Hosp., Dallas, 1980—, dir. ob-gyn. emergency room, 1989—, dir. faculty sexual assault exam and testimony program, 1993—, med. dir. cryopreservation program for human spermatozoa, 1984—, Zale-Lipshy Univ. Hosp., Dallas, 1989—; cons. St. Paul Med. Ctr., Dallas, 1980—; cynecol. cons. VA Med. Ctr., Dallas, 1982—. Contbr. numerous articles and abstracts to profl. jours. Maj. M.C. U.S. Army, 1976-78; lt. col. USAR Grantee Wyeth-Ayerst, 1988-91, 94—, 95—, Serono Labs., 1988-92, 89-92, Parke-Davis, 1990-93, Genzyme Corp., 1991-95, Syntex Labs., Inc., 1991-93, TAP Pharms., Inc., 1992-93, Zeneca Pharms., 1992-94, R.W. Johnson Pharm. Rsch. Inst., 1994-96, 94—, Rhône-Poulenc Rorer, 1995—. Fellow ACOG; mem. N.Y. Acad. Scis., Am. Soc. Reproductive Medicine, Tex. Med. Assn., Dallas County Med. Assn., Sigma Xi. Office: Univ of Texas Southwestern Med Sch 5323 Harry Hines Blvd Dallas TX 75235-7200

ACKERMAN, GLEN NEIL, neurologist; b. Stamford, Conn., Jan. 31, 1955; s. Louis Arnold and Edith (Rozinski) A.; children: Bradley, Corey, Alyssa. MD, Northwestern U., 1980. Intern Rush Presbyn. St. Luke's, Chgo., 1980-81; neurology resident Northwestern Meml. Hosp., Chgo., 19801-84; asst. clin. prof. Mich. State U., East Lansing, 1984—; pvt. practice East Lansing, 1984—; dir. Parkinson's Disease Clinic Mich. State U., 1995—. Fellow Am. Acad. Neurology; mem. Alpha Omega Alpha, Phi Beta Kappa. Office: Neurology Cons 1729 E Saginaw Ste 220 Lansing MI 48912

ACKERMAN, JEROME LEONARD, radiology educator; b. Bklyn., Jan. 4, 1950. BS in Chemistry, SUNY, Stony Brook, 1971; PhD in Physical Chemistry, MIT, Cambridge, 1976. Postdoctoral fellow U. Calif., Berkeley, 1976-77; asst. prof. chemistry U. Cin., 1977-82, assoc. prof. chemistry, 1982-85; asst. prof. radiology Harvard Med. Sch., Boston, 1985-95, assoc. prof. radiology, 1995—; dir. NMR spectroscopy Mass. Gen. Hosp., Charlestown, 1985—; cons. in field. Editor: (book) Advanced Tomographic Imaging Methods for the Analysis of Materials, 1991; contbr. numerous articles to profl. jours. Mem. Internat. Soc. for Magnetic Resonance in Medicine, Experimental Nuclear Magnetic Resonance Conf. (mem. exec. com. 1991—). Office: Biomaterials Lab NMR Ctr Mass Gen Hosp Rm 2301 149 13th St Boston MA 02129

ACKERMAN, PAUL ADAM, pharmacist; b. Cleve., Oct. 6, 1945; s. Kenneth Edwin and Jane (Hand) A.; m. Charity Reba Schierhorst, June 5, 1971; 1 child, Adam. BS, U. Fla., 1969. Lic. pharmacist, Fla., Ga. Pharmacist Robalo Pharmacy, Lake Park, Fla., 1969-73, Tru Valu Drugs, Lake Worth, 1973-77, Village Pharmacy, Tequesta, Fla., 1977-79, Shoppers Drug Mart, Palm Beach Garden, Fla., 1979-86; pharmacy mgr. Walgreen's, Palm Beach Garden, 1986—. Member Airports and Aviation Adv. Com., Palm Beach County, Fla., 1985—; mem. adv. bd. Coll. of Pharmacy, U. Fla., 1986—; bd. dirs. Am. Cancer Soc., Palm Beach County, 1983-89. Recipient Pharmacy Disting. Svc. Alumnus award U. Fla., 1991. Mem. Am. Pharmacy Assn., Fla. Pharmacy Assn. (exec. com. Tallahassee chpt. 1984-85, 88, chmn. Acad. Pharmacy Practice 1987-88, bd. dirs. ho. of dels. 1988-90, vice-speaker 1991, speaker 1992, pres.-elect 1996-97, Practitioner Merit award 1990), Palm Beach County Pharmacy Assn. (pres. West Palm Beach, Fla. chpt. 1983-85, Joe Price Pharmacist of Yr. 1985), Fla. Aero Club, Jupiter Elks, Palm Beach Gardens Moose, Masons, Shriners, Phi Lambda Sigma. Republican. Home: 12931 Inshore Dr West Palm Beach FL 33410-2005 Office: Walgreens 7170 Fairway Dr West Palm Beach FL 33418-3763

ACKERMAN, SIGURD HOWARD, psychiatrist; b. Millville, N.J., Feb. 25, 1940; s. William H. and Ethel (Kessler) A.; m. Cecelia M. McCarton, Apr. 25, 1983; children: Elizabeth, Rebecca, McCarton. BA, Harvard U., 1962; MD, Tufts U., 1966. Intern Kings County Hosp., Bklyn., 1966-67, resident in medicine, 1967-68; resident in psychiatry Montefiore Med. Ctr., Bronx, 1970-73; dir. psychiatry St. Lukes/Roosevelt Hosp. Ctr., N.Y.C., 1989—; med. dir., exec. v.p. St. Luke's Roosevelt Hosp. Ctr., N.Y.C., 1991-93; prof. clin. psychiatry Columbia U. Coll. Physicians and Surgeons, N.Y.C., 1989—, assoc. dean, 1991-93. Rsch. Scientist Devel. award level I and II, NIMH, 1976-84. Home: Pinebrook Rd # 2 Bedford NY 10506-1615 Office: St Lukes Roosevelt Hosp Ctr Amsterdam Ave New York NY 10023-7409

ACKERMAN, SYLVIA C., psychotherpaist; d. Joseph and Rose (Cohen) Bernhardt. BA, Hunter Coll., 1958; MA, New Sch. Social Rsch., 1960; postgrad., Yeshiva U., 1960-62. Cert. tchr.; cert. hypnotherapist. Group therapist Leroy Hosp. and TOPS, N.Y.C.; dir. psychodrama, mem. faculty Moreno Inst., Moreno ACad.; psychotherapist Cen. Queens (N.Y.) Psychotherapy Ctr. Author: International Handbook of Group Psychotherapy. Mem. Am. Psychol. Assn., Am. Soc. Group Psychotherapy and Psychodrama, Nat. Acad. Counselors and Family Therapists, Am. Assn. Counseling and Devel., Am. Psychol. Assn. (hypnosis div.), Am. Coun. Hypnosis, Phi Beta Kappa, Psi Chi, Mensa. Home: 89-15 Parsons Blvd Apt 1-l Jamaica NY 11432-6005

ACKERMAN, VALENTINE PETER, microbiologist; b. Sydney, NSW, Australia, Apr. 29, 1926; s. Valentine Peter and May Claribel (Hanson) A.; m. Maureen Lyle Stewart, Jan. 4, 1958; children: John, Mark, Elizabeth. BA, Sydney U., 1948, MB, BS, 1957; PhD, Australian Nat. U., 1965. Intern Royal North Shore Hosp., Sydney, 1957-58; intern Royal Alexandra Hosp. Children, Sydney, 1958-59, resident pathologist, 1959-61; scholar Australian Nat. U., Canberra, 1961-64; head bacterial products sect. Nat. Biol. Standards Lab., Canberra, 1964-71; head dept. microbiology Royal North Shore Hosp., Sydney, 1971-91; cons. Medisan Pathology, Sydney, 1992—; chmn. Microbiology Quality Assurance Programme, Sydney, 1981-92. Co-author: Microbiology: An Introduction, 1991; contbr. over 40 articles to profl. jours. Fellow Royal Coll. Pathologists Australasia; mem. Nat. Assn. Testing Authorities (chmn. microbiology ltech. group 1986-92). Home: 2 Manns Ave, Greenwich, Sydney NSW 2065, Australia Office: Medisan Pathology, 200 The Boulevarde, Fairfield Heights 2165, Australia

ACKERMANN, JOAN O'GORMAN, healthcare administrator, educator; b. Bronx, N.Y., June 21, 1941; d. John J. and Bridget (Coffey) O'Gorman; children: Barbara, Karen. AAS/RN, Pace Coll., Pleasantville, N.Y., 1972; BS in Nursing, Pace U., 1978; MS, L.I. U., 1984. Coord. alzheimer unit St. Joseph's Med. Ctr., Yonkers, N.Y., dir. day care program; adminstr. Thirty Thirty Park Healthcare Ctr., Bridgeport, Conn.; exec. dir. The Smith House Health Care Ctr., Stamford, Conn.; adj. prof. Iona Coll., New Rochelle, N.Y. Contbr. articles to profl. jours. Mem. Am. Coll. Healthcare Adminstrs., Nat. Coun. on Aging, Sigma Theta Tau. Home: 128 1st Ave Pelham NY 10803-1405

ACKERS, GARY KEITH, biophysical chemistry educator, researcher; b. Dodge City, Kans., Oct. 25, 1939; s. Leo Finley and Mabel Ida (Hostetler) A.; m. Clarissa Melba Cheney, May 12, 1984; children: Lisa, Sandra, Keith. BS in Chemistry and Math., Harding Coll., Searcy, Ark., 1961; PhD in Physiol. Chemistry, Johns Hopkins U., 1964. Instr. physiol. chemistry Johns Hopkins U. Sch. Medicine, Balt., 1965-66, prof. biology and biophysics, 1977-89, dir. Inst. Biophys. Rsch., 1987-89; asst. prof. biochemistry U. Va. Sch. Medicine, Charlottesville, 1966-67, assoc. prof., 1967-72, prof. biochemistry and biophysics, 1972-77; prof. biochemistry and molecular biophysics, head dept. Washington U., St. Louis, 1989—; instr. physiology Marine Biol. Labs., Woods Hole, Mass., 1974-76; chmn. Gordon Conf. on Proteins, 1985. Mem. editorial bd. Analytical Biochemistry, 1970-79, Biophys. Chemistry, 1973-78, Proteins, Structures, Functional Genetics, 1991—; contbr. over 100 articles to sci. jours. Guggenheim fellow, 1972-73; recipient NIH Merit award, 1987. Mem. Biophys. Soc. (coun. 1972-74, 80-83, pres. 1984-85, Cole rsch. award 1994), Am. Chem. Soc. (program chair biol. chem. divsn. 1994), Am. Soc. Biochem. Molecular Biology. Office: Washington U Med Sch Dept Biochem and Molecular Biophysics 660 S Euclid Ave Saint Louis MO 63110-1010*

ACKLAND, MICHAEL KINGSLEY, orthopaedic surgeon; b. Ottawa, Ont., Can., Sept. 23, 1955; came to U.S., 1992; s. Kingsley and Helen Iris (Truesdell) A.; m. Erin Therese O'Sullivan, June 18, 1983; children: Leone, Joseph, Michael Jesse. MD, Ottawa U., 1980. Intern U. Toronto (Ont., Can.), 1981; resident Ottawa (Ont., Can.) U., 1985; cons. orthopaedic surgeon St. Vincent de Paul Hosp, Brockville, Ont., Can., 1985-92, Brockville Gen. Hosp., 1985-92, A. Barton Hepburn Hosp., Ogdensburg, N.Y., 1991-92; owner, dir. Ling Clinic Phusiotherapy Ctr., Brockville, 1990-92; cons. orthopaedic surgeon Cape Cod Hosp., Hyannis, Mass., 1992—; med. dir. Cape Cod Hosp., 1995—; chmn. dept. rehab. medicine Brockville Gen. Hosp., 1987-92. Recipient W. Keon award Ottawa U., 1983. Mem. Mass. Med. Soc. (ho. del. 1994—, legis. com. 1995—), Fla. West Arthroscopy Assn., Can. Med. Assn., Ont. Med. Assn. Anglican. Office: Ackland Sports Medicine Inc 130 North St Hyannis MA 02601

ACKLIN, JIMMY DAVID, family medicine physician, educator; b. Conway, Ark., Apr. 23, 1957; s. Travis Henderson and Alta Ruth (Davis) A. BS in Zoology, U. Ark., Fayetteville, 1979; MD, U. Ark. for Med. Scis., Little Rock, 1983. Diplomate Am. Bd. Family Practice. Intern, resident U. Ark., Fort Smith, 1983-86, asst. prof. family medicine, 1986-93; assoc. prof. family medicine U. Ark. for Med. Scis., Ft. Smith, 1993—; med. dir. paramedic courses West Ark. C.C., Ft. Smith, 1990—; med. dir. Care Network Hospice, Ft. Smith, 1994—. Pres., founder Ft. Smith Fights AIDS, Inc., 1988—; bd. dirs. Dist. II AIDS Consortium, N.W. Ark., 1992—, Western Ark. Rsch. Found., Inc., Ft. Smith, 1995—. Fellow Am. Acad. Family Physicians; mem. AMA, Ark. Med. Soc., Ark. Acad. Family Physicians, Soc. Tchrs. of Family Medicine. Home: 1535 Pleasant Mountain Dr Van Buren AR 72956 Office: U Ark Med Sch Health Edn Ctr 612 S 12th St Fort Smith AR 72901

ACOSTA, FRANK XAVIER, psychologist, educator; b. L.A., Apr. 2, 1945; s. Gilbert Lascurain and Virginia (Posada) A.; m. MaryAnn Gonzales, June 30, 1979; children: Robert Xavier, Jeanette Marie. BS in Psychology magna cum laude, Loyola U., L.A., 1968; MA, UCLA, 1970, PhD in Clin. Psychology, 1974. Lic. psychologist, Calif. Rsch. asst. Neuropsychiat. Inst., UCLA, 1968-71, vis. assoc. prof., 1984-85; clin. psychology intern VA Outpatient Clinic, L.A., 1971-72, L.A. Psychiat. Svc., 1972-73, Long Beach VA Hosp., Calif., 1973-74; clin. psychologist L.A. County/U. So. Calif. Med. Ctr., L.A., 1974—; dir. Spanish-Speaking Clinic, Adult Psychiat. Clinic, 1975—; from assoc. dir. to dir. clin. psychol. internship trg. prog, 1986—; asst. prof. psychiatry Sch. Medicine, U. So. Calif., L.A., 1974-80, assoc. prof. clin. psychiatry, 1980-84, assoc. prof. psychiatry and behaviorl scis., 1984—; mem. allied health profl. staff U. So. Calif. Univ. Hosp., 1991—; cons. Spanish Speaking Mental Health Rsch. Ctr., L.A., 1974-88; cons., reviewer NIMH, 1977—. Author: (with J. Yamamoto and L. Evans) Effective Psychotherapy for Low-Income and Minority Patients, 1982 (Behavioral Sci. Book Club selection 1983); mem. editorial bd. Hispanic Jour. Behavioral Scis., 1981-85; contbr. chpts. to books, articles to profl. jours. Mem. psychol. rev. panel med. svcs. and occupational health and safety divs. of personnel dept. City of L.A., 1986-93; cons. Nat. Coalition Hispanic Mental Health and Human Svcs. Orgns., Washington, 1976-88; chair Nat. Rsch. Council, Evaluation Panel Psychology, Ford Found. Doctoral Fellowships Minorities Program, Washington, 1986-89. Rsch. grantee Social Sci. Rsch. Council, L.A., 1976, NIMH, 1977-84; Ford Found. postdoctoral minorities fellow NRC, 1984; recipient faculty rsch. prize, dept. psychiatry U. So. Calif. Sch. Medicine, 1977. Fellow APA (accreditation com. 1977-80); mem. Western Psychol. Assn., Interam. Soc. Psychology, Calif. State Psychol. Assn., Los Angelees County Psychol. Assn. Democrat. Roman Catholic. Office: U So Calif Sch Medicine Dept Psychiatry & Behavioral Sci 1937 Hospital Pl Los Angeles CA 90033-1073

ACQUAVIVA, SANDRA BIHARY, critical care nurse; b. Pitts., Sept. 23, 1957; d. John and Patricia (Neuhof) Bihary; m. Robert C. Acquaviva, Sept. 2, 1980. BSN, Carlow Coll., 1980; MS in Nursing, Widener U., 1988. RN, Pa., Del. Staff nurse coronary ICU, Montefiore Hosp., Pitts., 1980-81; staff nurse med.-surg. unit Med. Ctr. Del., Wilmington, 1981-83; staff nurse coronary ICU Med. Ctr. Del, Wilmington, 1983-85, asst. head nurse, 1985-88; clin. rsch. assoc. ICI Ams Inc, Wilmington, 1988-90, specialist in drug registration, 1990-92; sr. specialist drug registration ICI Ams Inc., Wilmington, 1992—; asst. mgr. Drug Registration Marketed Products Group Zeneca, Inc., Wilmington, 1992-95, mgr. Drug Regulatory Affairs, 1995—. Mem. AACN, Drug Info. Assn., Regulatory Affairs Profl. Soc. Home: 131 Bunting Dr Wilmington DE 19808-1969

ACQUAVIVA, TERESA, family nurse practitioner; b. Washington, Feb. 21, 1956. BSN, U. Md., Balt., 1978; MSN, Cath. U., 1985. CFNP. Clin. nurse Johns Hopkins Hosp., Balt.; case mgmt. cons. Hospice Care of Washington; staff nurse George Washington U. Hosp., Washington; family nurse practitioner Community Med. Care, Washington. Mem. Nurse Practitioner Assn. D.C., Sigma Theta Tau.

ACTOR, PAUL, microbiologist, consultant; b. N.Y.C., Mar. 17, 1933; m. Ruthe Hoenig, June 9, 1955; children: Carol F., Jeffrey K., Neil A. BA, CUNY, 1955; PhD, Rutgers U., 1959. Sr. rsch. scientist Squibb Inst. for Med. Rsch., New Brunswick, N.J., 1959-63; from dir. microbiology to dir. tech. licensing Smith Kline-French Labs., Phila., 1963-90; pres. Paul Actor Assocs., Phoenixville, Pa., 1990—; sci. adv. bd. Panax Pharm. Corp., N.Y.C., 1990—, CytRx Corp., Norcross, Ga., 1991—. Contbr. over 100 articles to profl. jours. Bd. dirs. Help Counseling Svcs., West Chester, Pa., 1975—. Fellow Am. Acad. Microbiology, Infectious Disease Soc. Am. Office: 632 Pickering Ln Phoenixville PA 19460-2550

ADAIR, IRMALEE TRAYLOR, social worker; b. Portsmouth, Ohio, Jan. 5, 1920; d. Finley Arving and Lora Alice (Nickell) Traylor; m. James Russell Adair; children: Jacqueline, Robert, Celeste, Marquita. AA in Social Work, Chipola Jr. Coll., 1980; BA in Social Work, U. West Fla., 1983; MSW, Fla. State U., 1985. Cert. gerontologist, community info. counselor. Sr. aide Guardian Office ESSH, Trevose, Pa.; interviewer, subcontractor Nat. Analysts, Phila.; social worker Hill House Manor, Bensalem, Pa.; ret. Mem. NASW, Fla. State U. Alumni Assn., U. West. Fla. Alumni Assn., Am. Assn. Retired Persons. Home: 8415 C Silver Way Tampa FL 33615-6003

ADAM, ELAINE T., medical and surgical nurse; b. Pulteney, N.Y., Apr. 20, 1943; d. Bernard Lewis and Josephine (Kennedy) Thompson; m. Gerald Adam, July 14, 1962; children: Sandra, Michael, Karen. Grad., St. James Mercy Sch. Nursing, Hornell, N.Y., 1975; Lic. Practical Nurse, Geneva Sch. Practical Nursing, 1961. Admissions coord.-supr., emergency rm. nurse, surg. nurse St. James Mercy Hosp., Hornell, N.Y., emergency outpatient surgery clinic nurse, day chg. nurse RHCF; developer organ procurement program. Home: 45 Maple St Canisteo NY 14823-1356

ADAM, EVELYN THERESA, educator, consultant; b. Lanark, Ont., Can., Apr. 9, 1929; d. Ewart Francis and Anna Irene (Dowdall) A. RN, Hotel Dieu Hosp., Kingston, Ont., 1950; B in Nursing, U. Montreal, 1966; M in Nursing, UCLA, 1971; hon. doctorate Laval U., Quebec City, 1992. Gen. duty nurse Deep River Hosp., Ont., 1951-52, Sunnybrook Hosp., Toronto, Ont., 1952-54; gen. duty and head nurse Montreal Neurol. Inst., 1954-61; gen. duty nurse Hopital Cantonal, Lausanne, Switzerland, 1961, Hopital Ste-Justine, Montreal, 1962-63; clin. instr. Montreal Rehab. Inst., 1963-64; lectr. U. Montreal Faculty of Nursing, 1966-69, asst. prof., 1971-77, assoc. prof., 1977-83, prof., 1983-89, prof. emeritus, 1989—, faculty sec. 1982-89; lectr., cons. in field., 1989—. Author: Etre Infirmiere, 1979, To be a Nurse, 1980, translations in Dutch, Spanish, Italian, Portuguese, and Japanese; author, editor (with Lauzon and Adam) La Personne Agee et des Besoins, 1996. Contbr. articles to profl. jours. Mem. Order of Nurses of Que. (Merit badge 1995). Avocations: swimming, cooking, theatre. Office: Faculty of Nursing U Montreal, PO Box 6128 Sta A, Montreal, PQ Canada H3C 3J7

ADAMAVAGE, ANN WILDES, speech pathologist; b. Raleigh, N.C., July 29, 1962; d. James Elbert and Linda Gail (Ellis) Wildes; m. Roger Scott Adamavage, June 13, 1981; children: Lindy Ann, Lori Beth. BEd, Valdosta State Coll., 1985, MS in Pathology, 1987. Speech pathologist Funston Elem., Reedy Creek Elem. Colquitt County Schs., Moultrie, Ga., 1985-86, speech pathologist Stringfellow Elem., Vereen Multi Handicap, 1986-89; speech pathologist Valdosta (Ga.) City Schs., 1990-95, Cobb County Schs., Marietta, Ga., 1995—. Mem. Ga. State Task Force to Review Regulations and Procedures for SLPs, 1993; dir., leader Girls in Action, Valdosta Area Chs., 1982-91; asst. team leader Vacation Bible Sch., Valdosta Bapt. Assn., 1989-90, assn. GA dir., 1992—. Mem. Ga. Assn. Speech and Hearing. Home: 4373 Inlet Rd Marietta GA 30066

ADAMIS, MARY K., medical educator. Instr. Beth Israel Hosp., Boston. Office: Beth Israel Hosp 330 Brookline Ave Boston MA 02215*

ADAMKIEWICZ, VINCENT WITOLD, microbiology and immunology educator, researcher; b. Poland, Nov. 27, 1924; came to Can., 1951; s. George and Zofia (Lewicka-Rogala) A.; m. Lidia Maria Gowor, July 11, 1953; children—Pavel, Marek, Tomek, Misio, Macio. B.Sc. in Biology, U. Bristol, 1948, B.Sc. in Chemistry with honors, 1949, M.S. in Pharmacology, 1950; Ph.D. in Exptl. Medicine, U. Montreal, 1954. Asst. prof. biology U. St. Francis Xavier, Antigonish, N.S., Can., 1951-52; chemist F.W. Horner Ltd., Montreal, Que., Can., 1954-56; asst. prof. physiology U. Montreal, 1956-60, assoc. prof., 1960-67, prof. microbiology and immunology, 1967—. Contbr. numerous articles to profl. jours. Pres. Can. Polish Congress, Que., 1969-71, Can. Polish Welfare Inst., Montreal, 1980-82. With Polish Underground Army, 1942-44; Polish Army under Brit. command, 1945-46. Mem. Am. Physiol. Soc. (emeritus); founding mem. Can. Soc. for Immunology, Can. Pharmacological Soc., Can. Biochem. Soc. Home: 5507 Cote St Antoine, Montreal, PQ Canada H4A 1R3 Office: U Montreal, Faculty of Medicine, Montreal, PQ Canada H3C 3J7

ADAMO, JOSEPH ALBERT, biologist, educator, researcher; b. Hoboken, New Jersey, October 22, 1938; s. Anthony and Helen Annamarie (Hornfeck) A.; BA, Jersey City State Coll., 1964; MS (Univ. fellow), Fairleigh Dickinson U., 1967; postgrad. (Fulbright-Hayes fellow) U. Philippines, Los Banos, 1973-74; PhD, Rutgers U., 1975; children: Thomas Anthony, Jo Anne, Samantha, Connie. Instr. botany Fairleigh Dickinson U., 1965-66; asst. prof. biology Jersey City State Coll., 1966-67; prof. Ocean County Coll., 1967—, chmn. sci. dept., 1981-91, co-dir. auto-tutorial units in biology, 1968—, dir. Environ. Ctr., 1978—; prof. Georgian Court Coll., 1991—. Fulbright-Hays fellow Internat. Rice Rsch. Inst., Los Baňs, 1973-74. Served with USAF, 1955-59. Recipient Hammond Sci. award Jersey City State Coll., 1964. Mem. Am. Soc. Microbiology, Soc. Nematologists, Am. Phytopathol. Soc., Iota Mu Pi, Phi Theta Kappa, Phi Sigma. Achievements include research in genetically engineered microorganisms and DNA transfer in the environment. Home: 185 Maple Ave Toms River NJ 08753-7023 Office: Ocean County Coll Dept Biology Toms River NJ 08753

ADAMS, BRENDA THERESA, nurse, educator; b. Bklyn., Oct. 14, 1945; d. Clarence and Rebecca (Gholson) Guess; m. Kenneth O. Adams, June 4, 1966; children: Kenneth O, Jr., Anthony, Reneé, Darryl, Joy. BA, New Sch. for Social Rsch., 1991, MS, 1992. RN, N.Y. Adminstrv. supr. Hempstead (N.Y.) Gen. Hosp. Med. Ctr., 1978-93; coord. patient edn. Syosset (N.Y.) Hosp., 1993-96; adminstrv. supr. North Shore Health Sys., Manhasset, N.Y., 1993—; mem. adj. faculty St. Joseph's Coll., Patchogue, N.Y., 1994—. Med. exec. scholar Hempstead Gen. Hosp., 1985.

ADAMS, CATHERINE, nursing educator; b. Trenton, N.J., Mar. 13, 1936; d. Richard H. and Ruth L. (Bullock) A.; children: Phoebe, Heather. BS, U. Conn., 1957; MS, Boston U., 1960; EdD, U. Mass., 1980. RN, N.Y. Instr. NYU, N.Y.C.; asst. prof. U. Conn., Storrs, U. Mass., Amherst; prof. Russell Sage Coll., Troy, N.Y. Author: MICA: Problems and Solutions in Treating the Mentally Ill/Chemically Addicted (videotape), 1990; (with Macione) Handbook in Psychiatric Mental Health Nursing, 1983; contbr. articles to profl. jours. Mem. ANA, Nat. League Nursing, Soc. Edn. and Rsch. Psychiat. Nursing, Nat. Women's Studies Assn., Nat. Assn. History Nursing, Sigma Theta Tau. Home: 183 2d St Troy NY 12180

ADAMS, CHRISTINE BEATE LIEBER, psychiatrist, educator; b. Greensboro, N.C., June 20, 1949; d. Paul Lieber Adams and Marjorie Pinckney (Quackenbos) Ould; 1 child, Justin McKendree Adams-Tucker. Student, Agnes Scott Coll., 1967-69; BA in English Lit. with honors, U. Fla., 1971, MD, 1976. Diplomate Am. Bd. Psychiatry and Neurology (examiner 1985), Am. Bd. Child Psychiatry (examiner 1984, 91), Nat. Bd. Med. Examiners. Resident in gen. psychiatry U. Louisville Sch. Medicine, 1976-78, fellow in child psychiatry, 1978-80, asst. clin. prof. dept. psychiatry and behavioral scis., 1981—, attending psychiatrist consultation-liaison svc., 1992, 93; pvt. practice, Louisville, 1980—; med. advisor Social Security Adminstrn., HHS, Louisville, 1986—; child psychiatry cons. Seven Counties Svcs., Ky. Dept.

Human Resources, 1989,, 93; physician advisor Healthcare Rev. Corp., Louisville, 1993—; reviewer Am. Jour. Psychiatry, 1983—; cons. So. Ind. Mental Health and Guidance Ctr., Jeffersonville, 1981-83, U. Fla., 1982; presenter in field. Contbr. articles to med. jours., chpts. to books. Bd. dirs. Gainesville (Fla.) Women's Health Ctr., 1973-75; mem. Jefferson County (Ky.) Juvenile Justice Commn., 1982-86. Recipient award Nat. Psychiat. Endowment Fund, 1980. Fellow Am. Acad. Child and Adolescent Psychiatry (com. on rights and legal matters 1984-92); mem. Am. Psychiat. Assn. (mem. com. family violence and child sexual abuse 1987-94), Am. Orthopsychiat. Assn., Am. Acad. Psychiatry and Law, Nat. Com. for Prevention Child Abuse, Ky. Psychiat. Assn., Ky. Acad. Child Psychiatry (sec.-treas. 1980-81, pres.-elect 1981-82, pres. 1982-83). Office: Med Arts Bldg Ste 3364 1169 Eastern Pky Louisville KY 40217-1417

ADAMS, CHRISTOPHER BERTLIN, neurosurgeon; b. Birkenhead, Lancashire, England, Apr. 7, 1939; s. Geoffrey Turner and Dora Eileen (Bertlin) A.; m. Sarah Isobel Holland, Jan. 12, 1957; children: Nicholas, Justin, Sam, Poppy, Henry, Belinda, George, Alex, Tom, Arabella. Student, Cambridge (Eng.) U., 1957-61, Guys Hosp., London, 1961-66. Resident Nat. Hosp., Queens Square, London, 1967, Dept. of Neurosurgery, Oxford, Eng., 1968; sr. resident neurosurgical dept. Guys-Maudsuey Hosp., London, 1969-71; cons. neurosurgeon Radcliffe Infirmary, Oxford, 1972—. Found. scholar Pembroke Coll., Cambridge, 1957. Fellow Royal Coll. Surgeons; corr. mem. Am. Assn. Neurol. Surgeons, Soc. British Neurosurgeons. Home: 29 Charlbury Rd, Oxford OX2 GUU, England Office: Felstead House, 23 Banbury Rd, Oxford OX2 6NX, England

ADAMS, DAVID BENNION, psychologist; b. Salt Lake City, May 21, 1945; s. Ferrell Harrison and Maurine (Bennion) A. B.A., U. Utah, 1968, M.S. (Kappa Sigma fellow), 1972, Ph.D. in Psychology cum laude, 1976. Staff psychologist Granite Mental Health Ctr., 1972-74; dir. Juvenile Alcohol Program, 1974-75; clin. supr. Adolescent Residential Treatment Ctr., 1974-79; pvt. practice clin. psychology, Salt Lake City, 1976—, also clin. dir. Am. Community Youth Services, 1979-82, Intermountain Youth Care, 1982-90, Interstate Youth Svcs., 1992-93, Youth Svcs. Internat. Utah, 1993-94; instr. U. Utah, Brigham Young U.; program coord. Children's div. Charter Summit Hosp. Local dist. Dem. del., 1972. Served with USAR, 1963-71. Lic. and cert. psychologist, Utah; cert. marriage and family counselor, Utah. Mem. Am. Psychol. Assn., Utah Psychol. Assn., Utah Psychologists in Pvt. Practice, Zero Population Growth, Nat. Register for Health Service Providers in Psychology, Sierra Club, Utah Assn. Juvenile and Adult Corrections, Kappa Sigma. Contbr. articles to profl. jours. Home: 1036 Countrylane Rd Salt Lake City UT 84117-4158 Office: 7138 Highland Dr Ste 105 Salt Lake City UT 84121-3755

ADAMS, DAVID DORIUS, physician assistant; b. Bingham Canyon, Utah, Oct. 25, 1943; s. Dorius Olney and Van Dyne (Hutchings) Madsen; m. Annette Halterman, Apr. 24, 1970; children: John David, Julia, Jeana Kristine, Eliza Joy, Jacob Lyle, Jennifer. BS, So. Utah U., 1972. Registered physician asst. Physican asst. Family Med. Ctr.-Dr. Lester J. Petersen, M.D., Rexburg, Idaho, 1972—; mem. selection com. U. Utah Medex Demonstration Project, Salt Lake City, 1973-81. Pres. Rexburg Kiwanis, 1979-80. With U.S. Army Med. Corps, 1968-70, Vietnam. Decorated Bronze star, D.S.M. with oak leaf cluster; named one of Outstanding Young Men of Am., 1976, Outstanding Young Men in Cmty., Rexburg, 1979. Republican. Mem. LDS Ch. Home: 1569 W 930 S Rexburg ID 83440 Office: Family Med Ctr # 1 Professional Plz Rexburg ID 83440

ADAMS, DIANE LORETTA, physician; b. St. Louis, Nov. 3, 1948; m. William McKinley Adams; children: Kareem McKinley, Dawn Caron, Akeem Michael. BS, Howard U., 1969; MD, N.J. Med. Sch., 1976; MPH, resident in gen. preventive medicine, Johns Hopkins U., 1980. Resident in family practice Howard U. Hosp., Washington, 1976-79; chief med. officer USCG Shipyard, Curtis Bay, Md., 1980-83, Bur. Engraving and Printing, Washington, 1983-85; med. officer St. Elizabeth Hosp., Washington, 1985-86; rsch. analyst Office Asst. Sec. Health, Rockville, Md., 1987-90; chief minority health svcs. rsch. program Agy. Health Care Policy and Rsch., Rockville, 1990-93; congl. fellow office of Congressman Louis Stokes U.S. Ho. of Reps., Washington, 1990; med. officer Agy. Health Care Policy and Rsch., Rockville, 1993—; cons. rep. AIDS Task Force, 1987-93; pres. Scholarship Search, Inc., 1991-93; lectr. intensive bioethics Georgetown U. Kennedy Inst. Ethics, 1991. Editor: Health Issues for Women of Color: A Cultural Diversity Perspective, 1995. Recipient Adminstrs. Outstanding Cmty. Svc. award Agy. Health Care Policy & Rsch., 1996. Mem. Am. Coll. Preventive Medicine, Alpha Kappa Alpha (Outstanding Comt. Svc. award 1981-85). Home: 17032 Barn Ridge Dr Silver Spring MD 20906-1106

ADAMS, DOUGLASS FRANKLIN, radiologist, educator, medical ethicist; b. Lewiston, Maine, Aug. 5, 1935; s. Shirah Devoy and Olive (Colburn) A.; m. Eleanor Pohleven, Aug. 15, 1954; children: Stanford, Jennifer, Jason. BA, Stetson U., 1957; BS, Wake Forest Coll., Winston-Salem, N.C., 1957; MD, Bowman Gray Sch. Medicine, Winston-Salem, 1960; SM, MIT, 1974; AM, Harvard U., 1990. Intern Phila. Gen. Hosp., 1960, resident in radiology, 1961; resident in radiology, then fellow Am. Cancer Soc., Stanford U. Hosp., 1963-66; radiologist Peter Bent Brigham Hosp., Boston, 1967-79, Brigham and Women's Hosp., Boston, 1981—; instr. Stanford U. Med. Sch., 1966-67; mem. faculty Harvard U. Med. Sch., 1967-79, 81—, assoc. prof. radiology, 1976-82, prof. radiology, 1982—; prof. radiology, chmn. dept. U. Mich. Med. Sch., 1979-81. Mem. editl. bd. profl. jours. Capt. M.C., USAF, 1961-63. Sloan fellow MIT, 1974; James Picker Found. scholar, 1967-70. Mem. Am. Coll. Radiology, Assn. Univ. Radiologists, Radiol. Soc. N.Am., Alpha Omega Alpha. Home: 9 Riverview Ter Dover MA 02030-2249 Office: 75 Francis St Boston MA 02115-6110

ADAMS, DUNCAN DARTREY, medical researcher, physician; b. Hamilton, Waikato, New Zealand, Apr. 18, 1925; s. H. Dartrey C. and Eliza Veitch (Duncan) A.; m. Yvonne Joan Macfarlane, Apr. 2, 1958 (dec. 1988); children: Christopher, Julia. MB ChB, Otago U., Dunedin, New Zealand, 1949, MD, 1962, DSc, 1962. Lectr. J.B. Collip's Lab., London, Ont., 1954; rsch. fellow Med. Rsch. Coun., New Zealand, 1951-53, rsch. officer, 1955-70, dir. autoimmunity rsch. unit, 1971-85; rsch. officer dean's dept. Otago Med. Sch., Dunedin, 1986—; vis. prof. Univ. Sheffield, Eng., 1964; vis. scientist Clin. Rsch. Centre, Med. Rsch. Coun., London, 1974-75. Contbr. 122 med. rsch. papers to profl. jours. With Merchant Navy, 1944. Recipient Van Meter prize Am. Goiter Assn., 1958, Organon Rsch. award Endocrine Soc., 1976, Mallinkrodt prize 8th Internat. Thyroid Congress, 1980, Medal for Contbns. to Biomed. Sci., Univ. Pisa, 1986; Am. Acad. Microbiology fellow, 1985. Fellow Royal Australasian Coll. Physicians (travelling scientist 1989). Home: 123 Cliffs Rd, St Clair, Dunedin New Zealand Office: Otago U Faculty of Medicine, Box 913, Dunedin New Zealand

ADAMS, GORDON DEWEY, physician; b. Red Cloud, Nebr., Mar. 26, 1932; s. James Dewey and Vivi Hildegarde (Swanson) A.; m. Gloria June Bauermeister, Aug. 29, 1954; children: Jane Marie, Jeffrey Dwight, Jennifer Louise. BS in Medicine, U. Nebr., 1956, MD, 1956. Diplomate Am. Bd. Surgery. Intern then resident Wayne County Gen. Hosp., Eloise, Mich., 1956-63; pvt. practice Norfolk (Nebr.) Med. Group, 1963—, med. dir., pres., 1978-95; bd. dirs. Luth. Cmty. Hosp., Norfolk, Firstier Bank, Norfolk; mem. staff Our Lady of Lourdes Hosp., Norfolk, Luth. Cmty. Hosp. Contbr. articles to profl. jours. Bd. dirs. Norfolk City Housing Authority, 1970—, chmn. bd., 1981—; bd. dirs. Boulevard Village Low Rent Housing, 1970—, chmn. bd., 1981—; area med. advisor Nebr. Dept. Edn., 1965-94; mem. State of Nebr. Bur. of Examining Bds., 1994—. Capt. USAR, 1957-59. Fellow ACS, Southwestern Surg. Congress; mem. AMA, Nebr. Med. Assn. (del. Madison county 1983—, bd. counselors 1990-96), N.E. Nebr. Med. Soc. (pres. 1982-84), Lions. Republican. Lutheran. Office: Norfolk Med Group 900 Norfolk Ave Norfolk NE 68701

ADAMS, H. RICHARD, physiatrist; b. Springfield, Mo., Oct. 5, 1945; s. Roy J. and Carmen A. (Coteron) A.; m. Cheryl A. Bachman, June 6, 1970; 1 child, Eric R. MD, U. Calif., Irvine, 1980. Diplomate Am. Bd. Phys. Medicine and Rehab. Assoc. med. dir. Meml. Med. Ctr., Long Beach, Calif., 1985—. Mem. AMA, Nat. Brain Injury Found., Rotary. Office: Rehab Assocs Med Group 701 28th St Ste 416 Long Beach CA 90806

ADAMS, HEIDI R., health facility administrator; b. Balt., Aug. 12, 1969; d. Ronald A. and Gwen (Giles) Rooks; m. Raylon K. Adams, May 29, 1995. BS in Psychology, Hampton U., 1991; MS in Legal and Ethical Studies, U. Balt., 1993; MS in Health Svcs. Adminstrn., George Washington U. Case mgr. Alliance, Inc./Sheppard Pratt Hosp., Balt., 1991-93; staff specialist, recruiter Inroads, Inc., Balt., 1992-94; adminstrn. resident Kennedy Krieger Inst., Balt., 1994-96. Mem. Am. Pub. Health Assn., Am. Coll. Health Care Execs., Nat. Assn. Health Svc. Execs. Mem. Ch. of Christ. Home: 505 Stamford Rd Baltimore MD 21229

ADAMS, JEANNE MASTERS, community health nurse, consultant; b. N.Y.C., Oct. 1, 1934; d. Thomas J. Coleman and Ann Mahon; children: Timothy, Christopher, Annmarie, Jeanne, Martin. AAS, Bergen Community Coll., 1974; BSN, Dominican Coll., 1976; MS in Nursing, Hunter Grad. Sch. of Nursing, 1976; PhD, CUNY, 1995. Occupational health nurse med. dept. N.Y. Daily News, N.Y.C.; asst. prof. sch. of nursing Hunter Coll., N.Y.C.; lectr., clin. instr. Bergen Community Coll., Paramus, N.J.; surg. nurse Columbia Presbyn. Hosp., N.Y.C.; educator, coord. health promotion Fashion Inst. Tech., N.Y.C., 1989—. Mem. N.Y. Acad. Sci., Sociologist Practice Assn., ANA. Home: PO Box 407 Park Ridge NJ 07656-0407

ADAMS, JIMMY GLENN, neonatologist, pediatrician; b. Longview, Tex., Mar. 22, 1948; s. Ewing and Virginia (Tremont) A.; m. Cristie Lee Owen, Aug. 31, 1971 (div. 1990); children: Amy, Erin; m. Rosey Daschelle Klinger, Sept. 21, 1993. BS, Tex. Christian U., 1971; DO, Des Moines Osteo. Coll., 1973. Diplomate Am. Bd. Pediat., Am. Bd. Neonatology and Perinatology. Resident in pediat. La. State U., 1973-75; fellow in neonatology Georgetown U., 1975-77; pvt. practice Lafayette, La., 1977—. Office: 107 Montrose Ave Ste D Lafayette LA 70503

ADAMS, JIMMY WAYNE, osteopath; b. Rockymount, Va., July 21, 1953; s. Mose Chitwood and Nellie June (Hall) A.; m. Mary Virginia Hunter, May 19, 1996. BA in Psychology, Roanoke Coll., Salem, Va., 1982; DO, Kirksville Coll. Osteo. Med., 1991. Diplomate Am. Bd. Osteo. Med. Examiners. Family med. intern Doctors Hosp., Columbus, Ohio, 1991-92, resident in diagnostic radiology and nuclear medicine, 1992-94; resident in phys. medicine and rehab. Med. Coll. Va., Richmond, 1994-96, attending physician episodic care unit, emergency dept., 1994-95; med. dir. Commonwealth Diagnostics and Rehab., Richmond, 1995—; mental helth therapist Roanoke Valley Psychiat. Ctr., Salem, 1992-95; pres. 7 med. corps. in Ohio and Va.; clin. instr. Ohio U. Coll. Osteo. Medicine, Columbus, 1993-94. Squadron comdr. North Ctrl. Mo. Composite Squadron, CAP USAF Aux., Kirksville, Mo., 1988-90. Mem. AMA, Am. Osteo. Assn., Christian Med. and Dental Soc., Am. Osteo. Acad. Sports Medicine, Am. Acad. Phys. Medicine and Rehab., Va. Osteo. Acad. Medicine, Psy Chi, Pi Gamma Mu, Iota Tau Sigma. Roman Catholic. Home: 708 Holbein Pl Richmond VA 23225 Office: 428 French St Pearisburg VA 24134

ADAMS, JOANNA BLOOD FAUCHER, health education specialist; b. Moscow, Idaho, Jan. 21, 1944; d. Harold Clifton and Marjorie Alene (Jones) Blood; m. Dwayne John Adams, Aug. 12, 1989; children: Michelle, Greg, Marjorie-Ann, Peter; stepsons: Chris, Matt, Jon. BS, U. Idaho, 1966, postgrad., 1966-68; postgrad., Boise State U., 1976-82. Newsletter editor, membership dir. C. of C., Coeur d'Alene, Idaho, 1983-85; Women, Infants and Children educator Panhandle Health Dist., Coeur d'Alene, 1985-90; AIDS educator Panhandle Health Dist., Coer d'Alene, 1985-87, cholesterol risk reduction program coord., 1986—, smoking cessation coord., 1987-94, health educator, 1987—; dist. coord. Idaho's Ptnrs. in Health Program, 1992—, dist. health promotion coord., 1994—; presenter CDC Chronic Disease Nutrition Conf., Kansas City, Mo., 1993; site facilitator CDC Nat. Videoconf., 1995; mem. city walk com. Mayor's Health Com., Coeur d'Alene, 1988-90. Bd. dirs. U. Idaho Family and Consumer Scis. Alumni Bd., 1993-96, sec., 1994-96; asst. coach Baseball, Soccer, Basketball, Coeur d'Alene; scout leader, 1988-92; bd. dirs. The Women's Forum, 1987-88; bd. dirs. Am. Cancer Soc., Kootenai County, 1993—. Named Outstanding Program Tobacco Educator Am. Heart Assn., 1990. Mem. AAUW (groumet pres. 1990-92), Soroptimist Internat. (awards chair 1989-91, legis. chair 1990-93), Am. Heart Assn. (bd. mem., devel. chair 1985-88, program chair 1988-91, adv. bd. 1994-95), Parent Tchr. Assn., Idaho Ptnrs. in Health (state steering com., Svc. award 1991), Toastmasters Internat. (cert., v.p. 1986-87, Western States region chair 1985-86), Coeur d'Alene Sunrise Rotary. Methodist. Home: 1928 Canyon Dr Coeur D Alene ID 83814-9007 Office: Panhandle Health Dist #1 2195 Ironwood Ct Coeur D Alene ID 83814-2628

ADAMS, JOHN PLETCH, orthopaedic surgeon; b. Ashburn, Md., Feb. 22, 1922; s. John William and Norm Emma (Fletch) A.; m. Nancy Ellen Murphy; 1 child, John P., Jr. BS, U. Md., 1943; MD, Washington U., St. Louis, 1945; MPH, Harvard U., 1978. Diplomate Am. Bd. Orthopaedic Surgery. Intern Wilmington (Del.) Gen. Hosp., 1945-46; resident Duke U., Durham, N.C., 1949-52; prof. and dept. chmn. George Washington U. Sch. of Medicine, Washington, 1953-87, prof. emeritus, 1987—. Councilman Lewes, Del., 1990-92, Mayor, 1992-94. Capt. U.S. Army Med. Corps, 1946-49. Named Am.-Brit. Exchange fellow, 1959. Fellow Am. Acad. Orthopaedic Surgery, Am. Coll. Surgeons, So. Surgical Assn.; mem. Am. Orthopaedic Assn., Am. Soc. for Surgery of the Hand (pres. 1971), Alpha Omega Alpha. Republican. Episcopalian. Home and Office: 804 Bay Ave Lewes DE 19958

ADAMS, JULIE KAREN, clinical psychologist; b. Portland, Oreg., Dec. 12, 1955; d. Allen Hays and Susanna Angelina (Meyers) A. B degree, Willamette U., 1977; M degree, Ctrl. Wash. U., 1982; cert. in bus. adminstrn., U. Wash., 1986; D degree, Pacific U., 1992. Lic. clin. psychologist; cert. counselor, sch. psychologist, Wash. Sch. psychologist Highline Sch. Dist., Seattle, 1987-90; psychology intern Elmcrest Psychiat. Hosp., Portland, Conn., 1990, clinician, 1991; rsch. asst. Yale U., New Haven, Conn., 1991; clinician Advanced Clin. Svcs., Seattle, 1991-93; postdoctoral fellow U. Wash., Seattle, 1991-93; acad. counselor Johns Hopkins U., Balt., 1993; behavior intervention specialist Edmonds (Wash.) Sch. Dist., 1993-94, Marysville Sch. Dist., Marysville, Wash., 1994—; instr. Seattle U., 1995—; guest spkr. in field to profl. assns., also Pacific U., U. Oreg., 1989—. Contbr. articles to profl. jours. Mem. tng. com., kids week com., nursing home com., pub. policy com. Jr. League of Seattle, 1988—; health care researcher Wash. State Legis., Olympia, 1993; campaigner Bush for Pres., Seattle, 1988, 92; rsch. asst. to state senator Oreg. State Legis., Salem, 1985; press page nat. conv. Rep. Nat. Com., Detroit, 1980; student grad. v.p., faculty rep. com. Pacific U. Sch. of Profl. Psychology, 1989-90. Mem. APA (health psychology com. student rep. 1992-93), Wash. Psychol. Assn., Willamette U. Alumni Assn. (bd. dirs. 1983-88), Vols. for Outdoor Wash. (bd. dirs. 1986-87), City Club of Seattle (membership com. 1986-88), Jr. League Seattle, Psi Chi, Beta Alpha Gamma. Home: 1038 NE 125th St Seattle WA 98125-4000

ADAMS, KELLY LYNN, emergency physician; b. High Point, N.C., Oct. 17, 1959; d. Roger Lee and Kathryn Maxine (Floyd) A. AA in Gen. Studies, U. Md., 1979; BA in Biology, Va. Intermont Coll., 1980; DO, Southeastern Coll. Osteo. Med., 1988. Cert. Am. Coll. Osteopathic Family Physicians. Emergency physician Humana South Broward, Hollywood, Fla., 1989-91; family practice physician Adams and Herzog, DO, PA, Plantation, Fla., 1990-91; emergency physician Homestead (Fla.) AFB, 1991-92, Mariners Hosp., Tavernier, Fla., 1991-93, Meml. Hosp., Pembroke Pines, Fla., 1992-96, Comp Health, Salt Lake City, 1996—. Recipient Cert. of Merit, State of Fla. and Fla. N.G., 1992. Mem. AMA, Am. Osteo. Assn., Fla. Osteo. Med. Assn., Broward County Osteo. Med. Assn., Assn. Emergency Physicians, Mensa. Republican. Office: 5722 S Flamingo Rd # 273 Fort Lauderdale FL 33330

ADAMS, LAMAR TAFT, physician; b. Hiawassee, Ga., Apr. 9, 1938; s. Cecil Taft and Julia Nadine (Wilson) A.; B.S., Wake Forest U., 1959; M.D., Bowman Gray Sch. Medicine, 1965. Intern, N.C. Bapt. Hosp., 1965-66, resident in internal medicine, 1966-69; staff physician VA Hosp., Mountain Home, Tenn., 1971-72; chief med.-surg. services Ga. Regional Hosp., Augusta, 1973-74; asst. prof., med. dir. physician's asst. tng. program Med. Coll. Ga., Augusta, 1974-75; practice medicine specializing in internal medicine, Monroe, Ga., 1975—. Served with USAF, 1969-71. Mem. Phi Rho Sigma. Baptist. Contbr. articles to med. jours. Home: PO Box 669 Monroe GA 30655-0669 Office: 305 S Broad St Monroe GA 30655-2119

ADAMS, LARRY EDWARD, speech pathologist, educator; b. Bell, Calif., Sept. 2, 1945; s. James Edward Adams and Jamie Lee (Mathis) Pruitt; m. Carroll Rebecca Miller, Apr. 16, 1977. BS, Henderson State U., Arkadelphia, Ark., 1972; PhD, Northwestern U., 1976. Asst. prof, then assoc. prof. U. So. Miss., Hattiesburg, 1976-80, dir. speech-hearing clinic, 1977-79, rsch. coord., 1979-80; vis. rsch. prof. U. Ala., Birmingham, 1979, assoc. prof., dir. speech clinic, 1980-84, vice chmn., dir. speech and hearing clinic, 1990—; prof., chmn. U. Ala., 1990—. Contbr. articles to profl. publs., chpt. to book; patentee electronic device. Fellow Am. Speech-Lang.-Hearing Assn.; mem. Am. Cleft Palate Assn., Ala. Speech and Hearing Assn., Pine Harbor Yacht Club (commodore 1985-86). Home: 329 Turnberry Rd Birmingham AL 35244-3291 Office: U Ala #503 Speech & Hearing Clinic Birmingham AL 35294-0001

ADAMS, LINAS JONAS, gastroenterologist; b. Akron, Ohio, May 2, 1955; s. Vladas and Veronika (Somkaite) A.; m. Elaine Kay Bulchik, Aug. 30, 1980; children: Jillian, Jonas, Nikolas, Madeline. MD, U. Autonoma of Guadalajara, Mex., 1978. Diplomate Am. Bd. Internal Medicine with subspecialty in gastroenterology; lic. physician, Tenn., Ky. Rotating intern St. Thomas Hosp. Med. Ctr., Akron, 1978-79; intern in internal medicine Tijuana BC Mex./Mexican Social Svc., 1979-80; resident Akron City Hosp., 1980-83; fellow in gastroenterology U. Ky. Med. Ctr., Lexington, 1983-86, clin. scholar, 1985-86; staff physician VA Hosp., Lexington, 1985-88; asst. prof. medicine U. Ky. Med. Ctr., Lexington, 1986-88; clin. asst. prof. medicine U. Tenn. Med. Ctr., Knoxville, 1988-89, asst. prof. medicine, 1989-94, assoc. prof. medicine, 1994—; physician dir. nutritional support team VA Med. Ctr., Lexington, 1984-86, fellowship dir. divsn. digestive diseases and nutrition, 1985-86, dir. therapeutic endoscopy, 1985-88, med. supr. D.R.G. allocations, 1985-88; co-dir. drug studies divsn. digestive diseases and nutrition U. Ky., 1985-88; dir. gastroenterology clinic U. Tenn. Med. Ctr., Knoxville, 1988—, dir. gastro-intestinal endoscopic, diagnostic and therapeutic lab., 1989—, chief divsn. gastroenterology and nutrition, 1989—; med. cons. Contbr. numerous articles to profl. jours., chpts. to books. Grantee U. Tenn. Physicians Med. Edn. and Rsch. Found., 1993—, Karl Storz Endoscopy-Am., Inc., 1990-91, VA, 1987-88, Smith, Kline and French, 1986-88, VA Coop. Studies Program, 1986-90, Upjohn Co., 1986-87, Eli Lilly and Co., 1985-87. Fellow Am. Coll. Gastroenterology; mem. ACP, Nat. Assn. Residents and Interns, Am. Gastroenterology Assn., Am. Soc. Parenteral and Enteral Nutrition, Am. Soc. Gastrointestinal Endoscopy, Ky. Soc. Gastrointestinal Endoscopy, Knoxville Acad. Medicine, Tenn. Med. Assn., tenn. Soc. Gastrointestinal Endoscopy, Crohn's Colitis Found. Am., Am. Soc. Internal Medicine, So. Med. Assn., Internat. Assn. Pancreatology, Am. Lithotripsy Soc., Am. Endosonography Club. Office: University Gastroenterology Physicians Office Bldg 1924 Alcoa Hwy # 100 Knoxville TN 37920-1511

ADAMS, MARILYN LEE, nurse; b. Mechanicsburg, Pa., Sept. 14, 1940; d. Earl Wingert and Mary Jayne (Burgner) Pyke; m. James Wesley Adams, Sept. 4, 1964; children: Timothy Allen, Pamela Sue. BS in Nursing, Messiah Coll., 1963; MA in Health Svc. Mgmt. and Human Resource Devel., Webster U., 1988. Cert. rehab. RN. Staff nurse Harrisburg Hosp. (Pa.), 1963-64; nursing instr. Ark. Bapt. Hosp., Little Rock, 1964-67, neurosurg. nurse, 1969-74; rehab. staff nurse Cen. Bapt. Hosp., Little Rock, 1974-77; unit nursing supr. Ark. Rehab. Inst., Little Rock, 1977-85, rehab. nurse educator, 1986-90, dir. of nursing Ctrl. Ark. Rehab. Hosp., 1990—; speaker, cons. in field. Author patient handbook, 1975. Leader Little Rock council Girl Scouts U.S., 1976-82; Ark. Regional Med. Program grantee, 1974. Mem. Ark. Organization for Nurse Excutives, Assn. Practitioners in Infection Control (sec. 1980-83), Assn. Rehab. Nurses (charter, state pres. 1986-88, dir.-at-large 1995—, sec. 1989-90, pres. 1990-94), Harrisburg Hosp. Nursing Alumni, Ark. Quilters Guild., Toastmasters (charter mem., sgt. at arms 1987-88). Republican. Baptist. Home: 2120 Deerwood Dr Hensley AR 72065-9608 Office: Ctrl Ark Rehab Hosp 2201 Wildwood Ave North Little Rock AR 72116-5074

ADAMS, RICHARD GEORGE, physician, educator; b. Natchez, Miss., Feb. 12, 1948; s. Richard George and Lillian (Johnson) A.; m. Regina Drake, Nov. 1988; children: Akinwale, Adekoya, Olaniyan, Abiola; m. Dina Hitalia, Apr. 4, 1989. BS in Biology, Tougaloo Coll., 1970; MD, Med. Coll. Wis., 1974. Diplomate Am. Bd. Internal Medicine, Nat. Bd. Med. Examiners. Dir. med. ICU Howard U. Hosp., Washington, 1982—, chief critical care tchg. program, 1983—, assoc. prof. dept. medicine, 1987—; chmn. Dr. Dan com. Howard U. Hosp., 1983—, chmn. pharm. and therapeutics com., 1992—, chmn. spl. care com., 1984—. Chmn. ACLS task force Washington Metro. Heart Assn., 1992-93, affiliate faculty ACLS, 1992—, v.p., 1993-94, pres.-elect, 1994—. Fellow Am. Coll. Chest Physicians (assoc.); mem. Med. Soc. D.C., Nat. Med. Soc. Office: Howard Univ Hosp 2041 Georgia Ave NW Washington DC 20060

ADAMS, ROBERT BARRY, pathologist; b. Birmingham, Ala., July 24, 1928; children: Jeanmarie, Robert Barry Jr. BS in Chemistry & Biology, Birmingham So., 1950; MD, Med. Coll. Ala., 1956. Rotating intern Lloyd Noland Hosp., Fairfield, Ala., 1956-57; pathology resident Bapt. Meml. Hosp., Memphis, 1957-59; mem. med. corps U.S. Army, San Antonio, 1959-61; instr., prof. Med. Coll. Ala., Birmingham, 1961-64; dir. pathology lab. Bapt. Med. Ctr., Montgomery, Ala., 1964-79, St. Margaret's Hosp., Montgomery, Ala., 1972—; med. dir. Ala. Reference Lab., Montgomery, 1972—, Ala. Reference Lab./LabSouth, Montgomery, 1995—; pres. Ala. Assn. Pathologists, Birmingham, 1969-71, Med. Coll. Ala. Alumni Assn., 1993-95; edn. leader Sch. Med. Tech. Bapt. Hosp., St. Margaret's Hosp., Auburn U. Montgomery, Ala. Reference Lab., 1968—. Pres., bd. trustees Judson Coll., Marion, Ala., 1985-88; pres. Nat. Coll. Ala. Alumni, Birmingham, 1993-95; sec.-treas. Montgomery County Med. Soc., 1990-92. Recipient Algernon Sidney Sullivan award Judson Coll., 1985. Mem. AMA, Am. Soc. Clin. Pathology, Am. Assn. Blood Banks (inspector 1963-86), Am. Soc. Nuc. Medicine, Coll. Am. Pathologists, Med. Soc. Montgomery County, Cornerstone Soc., Alpha Omega Alpha. Baptist. Office: Ala Reference Labs Inc 543 S Hull St Montgomery AL 36103

ADAMS, ROBERT HENRY, psychiatrist; b. Ft. Wayne, Ind., Feb. 27, 1937; s. Max Remond and Winifred (Wilson) A.; m. Carmona Marie McClanahan, June 10, 1958; children: Tamra, Bradley, Terri, Andrea. BA, Ind. U., 1959, MD, 1963. Diplomate Am. Bd. Med. Psychotherapists. Psychiatrist Prairie View Mental Health Ctr., Newton, Kans., 1971-74; psychiatrist, med. dir. Coles County Mental Health Ctr., Mattoon, Ill., 1974, Grant-Blackford Mental Health Ctr., Marion, Ind., 1974-75; psychiatrist Howard Community Hosp., Kokomo, Ind., 1975-78, med. dir., 1978-90; clin. dir. psychiat. medicine Mercy Hosp., Cadillac, Mich., 1990-94; staff psychiatrist No. Mich. Cmty. Mental Health Ctr., Petoskey, 1995—; cons. USAF, Grissom AFB, Ind., 1980-90. Bishop Ch. of Jesus Christ of Latter-day Saints, Kokomo, 1978-83, stake presidency, 2d counselor Lafayette (Ind.) stake, 1987-90, pres. Cadillac br., 1992-94. Mem. Am. Psychiat. Assn., Assn. Mormon Counselors and Psychotherapists. Republican. Office: No Mich Cmty Mental Health One McDonald Dr Petoskey MI 49770

ADAMS, ROBERT MONROE, retired dermatologist, educator; b. Pasadena, Calif., May 4, 1926; s. Oscar D. and Mamie (Butler) A.; m. Lorene Tassi, Mar. 21, 1948; children: Cynthia, Gregory. AB with distinction, Stanford U., 1946, MD, 1950. Diplomate Am. Bd. Dermatology. Rotating intern San Francisco City and County Hosp., 1949-50; resident in internal medicine Tripler Army Hosp., Honolulu, 1950-52; pvt. practice in family medicine Stockton, Calif., 1952-64; dermatologist Palo Alto (Calif.) Med. Clinic, 1967-75; resident in dermatology Stanford (Calif.) U. Med. Ctr., 1964-67, fellow in dermatology, 1966-67, dir. Contact Dermatitis and Occupational Skin Disease Clinic, 1967-96; from instr. to clin. prof. dermatology Stanford U., 1966-82, clin. prof. dermatology, 1982-96; mem. staff Stanford U. Hosp., 1967-96; pvt. practice in dermatology Menlo Park, Calif., 1975—; ret., 1996; dir. or co-dir. various profl. courses and symposia; guest lectr. many sci. confs. and ednl. instns., most recently Skin and Cancer Found. Seminar, Sidney, Australia, 1992, Cypress Found., Carmel, Calif., 1994, U. Calif., San Francisco, L.A. and Davis, numerous occasions. Author: (textbooks) Occupational Contact Dermatitis, 1969, Occupational Skin Disease, 1983, 2nd edit., 1990; co-author: Color Text of Contact

Dermatitis, 1992; editor: Occupational Medicine, State of the Art Reviews, 1986; contbr. 13 chpts. to books; founding editor Am. Jour. Contact Dermatitis, editor-in-chief, 1989-92, mem. editl. bd., 1992—; mem. editl. bd. Jour. Am. Acad. Dermatology, 1986—, Health Hazards of the Workplace Report, 1989; contbr. numerous articles and revs. to sci. jours. Recipient Jean Spencer Felton award for Excellence in Sci. Writing, 1983. Mem. AMA (mem. adv. panel on med. standards 1979-83), Am. Acad. Dermatology (mem. task force on contact dermatitis 1976-91, Gold award for Teaching 1981, bd. dirs. 1989-93), Calif. Med. Assn. (mem. adv. panel on occupational medicine 1975-83), We. Occupational Med. Assn. (pres. 1983-84), Am. Soc. for Contact Dermatitis (pres., founder 1989-91), Am. Conf. Govtl. Indsl. Hygienists, San Francisco Dermatology Soc. (pres. 1985-86), Soc. for Investigative Dermatology, Pacific Dermatol. Assn., Internat. Soc. for Tropical Dermatology, Santa Clara Med. Soc., Brit. Assn. Dermatologist (hon.), Mex. Acad. Dermatology (hon.), Chilean Soc. Dermatology (hon.), Venezuelan Soc. Dermatology (hon.), Chinese Contace Dermatitis Rsch. Group (hon.). Home: 555 Laurel Ave Apt 108 San Mateo CA 94401-4157 Office: 1300 University Dr Ste 8 Menlo Park CA 94025

ADAMS, SARAH VIRGINIA, family counselor; b. San Francisco, Oct. 23, 1955; d. Marco Tulio and Helen (Jorge) Zea; m. Glenn Richard Adams, Mar 22, 1980; children: Mark Vincent, Elena Giselle, Johnathan Richard. BA, Calif. State U., Long Beach, 1978, MS, 1980; postgrad., Fuller Theological Sem., Pasadena, 1990—. Lic. marriage, family, child counseling. Tutor math. and sci. Montebello, Calif., 1979-82; behavioral specialist Cross Cultural Psychol. Corp., L.A., 1979-80; psychol. asst. Legal Psychology, L.A., 1980-82, Eisner Psychol. Assocs., L.A., 1982-83; assoc. dir. Legal Psychodiagnosis and Forensic Psychology, L.A., 1982-83; adminstrv. dir. Diagnostic Clinic, Calif., 1983-85; dir. Diagnostic Clinic of West Covina, Calif., 1985-87; owner Adams Family Counseling Inc., Calif., 1987—; tchr. piano, Montebello, 1973-84; ins. agent Am. Mut. Life Ins., Des Moines, 1982-84. Fellow Am. Assn. Marriage and Family Therapists, Am. Psychol. Assn.; mem. NAFE, Calif. Assn. Marriage and Family Therapists, Calif. State Psychol. Assn., Calif. Soc. Indsl. Medicine and Surgery, Western Psychol. Assn., Psi Chi, Pi Delta Phi. Republican. Roman Catholic. Office: Adams Family Counseling Inc 260 S Glendora Ave # 101 West Covina CA 91790-3041

ADAMS, TIM GARDINER, JR., emergency physician; b. Dearborn, Mich., June 15, 1959; s. Tim Gardiner and Leah (Dutenhaver) A.; m. Ennette Emily Henry, Aug. 15, 1987; children: Charles Douglas, Emily Patrice, Olivia Layne. BA in Chemistry, BA in Math., Denison U., Granville, Ohio, 1981; MD, U. Mich., 1985. Diplomate Am. Bd. Family Practice, Am. Assn. Physician Specialist, Am. Bd. Emergency Medicine. Resident gen. surgery Wayne State U., Detroit, 1985-87; resident family practice St. John Hosp. & Med. Ctr., Detroit, 1988-91, chief resident, 1990-91; staff emergency physician Oakwood Hosp.-Annapolis Ctr., Wayne, Mich., 1987—; assoc. med. dir. emergency svcs. Saratago Hosp., Detroit, 1996—; assoc. med. dir. emergency svcs. Seaway Ctr. Oakwood Hosp., Trenton, Mich., 1995—; med. dir. emergency svcs. Heritage Ctr. Oakwood Hosp., Taylor, Mich., 1990—; chief emergency dept. Oakwood Hosp., Heritage Ctr., Taylor, 1990—, chmn. ethics com., 1995—, chmn. code blue com., 1990—; mem. med. control adv. bd. and quality rev. com. HEMS, Inc., Westland, Mich., 1991—. Fellow Am. Acad. Family Physicians; mem. Am. Coll. Emergency Physicians, Assn. Emergency Physicians, Am. Assn. Physician Specialists. Home and Office: Gard Adams 1824 N Evangeline Dearborn Heights MI 48127

ADAMS, WAYNE VERDUN, pediatric psychologist, educator; b. Rhinebeck, N.Y., Feb. 24, 1945; s. John Joseph and Lorena Pearl (Munroe) A.; m. Nora Lee Swindler, June 12, 1971; children: Jennifer, Elizabeth. BA, Houghton Coll., 1966; MA, Syracuse U., 1969, PhD, 1970; postgrad., U. N.C., Chapel Hill, 1975. Asst. prof. Colgate U., Hamilton, N.Y., 1970-75; chief psychologist Alfred I. DuPont Inst., Wilmington, Del., 1976-86; dir. div. psychology, dept. pediatrics Alfred I. DuPont Inst., Wilmington, 1987—; mem. Del. Bd. Licensure in Psychology, 1983-86, bd. pres., 1986; assoc. prof. pediat. Thomas Jefferson Coll. Medicine, Phila., 1995—. Cons. editor Jour. Pediatric Psychology, 1980-83, guest reviewer, 1984—; co-author 3 nationally used psychol. tests in field; contbr. articles to profl. jours. Fellow Am. Psychol. Assn.; mem. Soc. Pediatric Psychology, Del. Psychol. Assn. (exec. com. 1979-82, pres. 1981-82). Office: Alfred I DuPont Inst Div Psych PO Box 269 Wilmington DE 19899-0269

ADAMSHICK, PAMELA ZENZ, nursing educator; b. Monroe, Mich., Apr. 21, 1952; d. John Thomas and Helen (Strimbel) Zenz; m. George Adamshick, Aug. 30, 1975; children: Justin, Jacqueline. BSN cum laude, Mercy Coll. Detroit, 1974; MSN, U. Ill. Med. Ctr., Chgo., 1977. RN, Pa. Staff nurse U. Chgo., Billings Hosp., 1974-76; instr. nursing Lewis U., Romeoville, Ill., 1978-79; clin. nurse specialist St.Jospeh Hosp., Joliet, Ill., 1979-80; asst. prof. nursing Northampton Community Coll., Bethlehem, Pa., 1988-91; instr. Sch. Nursing St. Luke's Hosp., Bethlehem, Pa., 1991—; part-time staff nurse Lehigh Valley Hosp., Allentown, Pa., 1986—. Mem. Psychiat. Edn. Planning Com. Lehigh Valley Hosp. Recipient M. H. Nursing Grad. fellow. Home: 972 Bridle Path Rd Allentown PA 18103-4680

ADAMSON, GEOFFREY DAVID, reproductive endocrinologist, surgeon; b. Ottawa, Ont., Can., Sept. 16, 1946; came to U.S., 1978, naturalized, 1985; s. Geoffrey Peter Adamson and Anne Marian Allan; m. Rosemary C. Oddie, Apr. 28, 1973; children: Stephanie, Rebecca, Eric. BSc with honors, Trinity Coll., Toronto, Can., 1969; MD, U. Toronto, 1973. Diplomate Am. Bd. Ob-Gyn., Am. Bd. Laser Surgery; cert. Bd. Reproductive Endocrinology. Resident in ob-gyn. Toronto Gen. Hosp., 1973-77, fellow in ob-gyn., 1977-78; fellow reproductive endocrinology Stanford (Calif.) U. Med. Ctr., 1978-80; practice medicine specializing in infertility Los Gatos, Calif., 1980-84; instr. Stanford U. Sch. Medicine, 1980-84; clin. asst. prof. Stanford U. Sch. Medicine, Calif., 1984-92; clin. assoc. prof. Stanford U. Sch. Medicine, 1992-95; clin. prof. Stanford U. Sch. Medicine, Calif., 1995—; assoc. clin. prof. Sch. Medicine U. Calif., San Francisco, 1992—. Mem. editl. adv. bd. Can. Doctor mag., 1977-83, numerous others; contbr. numerous articles to sci. jours., mags.; editor: (textbook) Endoscopic Management of Gynecologic Disease. Ontario Ministry of Health fellow, 1977-78. Fellow ACS, Royal Coll. Surgeons Can., Am. Coll. Ob-Gyns.; mem. AAAS, AMA, Am. Assn. Gynecol. Laparoscopists (adv. bd.), Am. Soc. Reproductive Medicine (numerous coms.), Soc. Reproductive Endocrinologists (charter), Soc. Reproductive Surgeons (charter, bd. dirs., sec., treas.), Soc. Assisted Reproductive Tech. (treas., dir.), Pacific Coast Fertility Soc. (dir., sec.), Pacific Coast Ob-Gyn. Soc., Soc. Gynecologic Surgeons, San Francisco Ob-Gyn. Soc., Bay Area Reproductive Endocrinologists Soc. (founding pres.), Gynecol. Laser Soc., N.Y. Acad. Scis., Shufelt Gynecol. Soc., Peninsula Gynecol. Soc. (past pres.), Calif. Med. Assn., San Mateo County Med. Assn., Santa Clara County Med. Assn., Am. Fedn. Clin. Rsch., Nat. Resolve (sec., dir.), Can. Assn. Interns and Residents (hon. life, pres. 1977-79, bd. dirs. 1974-79, rep. AMA resident physician sect. 1978-79, rep. Can. Med. Protective Assn. 1975-78, rep. Can. Med. Assn. 1975-78, Disting. Svc. award 1980), Profl. Assn. Interns and Residents Ont. (bd. dirs. 1973-76, v.p. 1974-75, pres. 1975-76), Royal Coll. Physicians and Surgeons Can. (com. exams. 1977-80), Ont. Med. Assn. (sec. interns and residents sect. 1973-74). Home: 16520 S Kennedy Rd Los Gatos CA 95032-6406 Office: 540 University Ave # 200 Palo Alto CA 94301-1912

ADAMSON, THOMAS C., rheumatologist; b. Pasadena, Calif., Mar. 7, 1951; s. Thomas C. and Susan E. (Huncilman) A.; m. Ellen R. Rund; children: Emily, Gregory. BS, U. Mich., 1972, MD, 1977. Diplomate Am. Bd. Internal Medicine, Am. Bd. Rheumatology. Resident in internal medicine Henry Ford Hosp., Detroit, 1977-80; fellow in rheumatology Scripps Clinic, La Jolla, Calif., 1980-82; chief div. rheumatology, dir. managed care Sharp Rees-Stealy, San Diego, 1982—. Fellow Am. Coll. Physicians. Office: Sharp Rees-Stealy 2001 4th Ave San Diego CA 92101

ADASHI, ELI Y., obstetrician, gynecologist. MD, U. Tel Aviv, Israel, 1972. Diplomate Am. Bd. Obstetrics-Gynecology, Am. Bd. Reprodn. Endocrinology. Intern Met. Gen. Hospital, Tel Aviv, Israel, 1972-73; resident ob.-gyn. Tufts U. Sch. Medicine, Boston, 1974-77; fellow reprodn. endocrinology Johns Hopkins U., Balt., 1977-78; fellow reprodn.-endocrinology U. Calif. San Diego, La Jolla, 1978-81; mem. med. staff U. Md. Hosp., Balt., 1981—; prof. ob.-gyn., physiology U. Md., Balt., 1981—; private practice in ob.-gyn. Balt., 1981—. ACOG, Am. Fedn. Surgeons, Endocrine Surgeons, Soc. Gastro Enterology. Office: U Md Sch Medicine 405 W Redwood St 3d Fl Baltimore MD 21201*

ADATTO, IRVING JACK, physician; b. Chgo., Oct. 23, 1930; s. Leon and Sophie (Hasdai) A.; m. Tobey helene Heackley, June 29, 1952; children: Jeffrey, Steven, Nancy. BS, U. Ill., Chgo., 1952; MD, U. Ill., 1954. Diplomate Am. Bd. Internal Medicine, Am. Bd. Cardiovascular Diseases. Intern Cook County Hosp., Chgo., 1954-55; resident in gen. internal medicine U. Ill. Hosps., Chgo., 1955-57, fellow in clin. cardiology, 1957-59; chmn. cardiac bd. Luth. Gen. Hosp., Park Ridge, Ill., 1963-66, chmn. dept. medicine, 1968-69, chief CCU, 1965-72; pres. Maine Ridge Med. Assocs., Des Plaines, Ill., 1972—. Author: (booklets) Living with Heart Disease, 1973, Hypertension, 1975. Fellow Am. Coll. Chest Physicians (emeritus), Am. Coll. Cardiology. Office: Maine Ridge Med Assocs ltd 9301 Golf Rd Des Plaines IL 60016

ADCOCK, IAN MICHAEL, medical educator, research scientist; b. London, Sept. 23, 1960; s. Arthur Edward and Gwendolin Nora (Brampton) A.; m. Carolanne Ruth Brown, Apr. 17, 1993. BS, U. London, 1983 PhD, 1987. Rsch. fellow MRC Brain Metabolism Unit, Edinburgh, Scotland, 1986-87, St. Georges Hosp., London, 1987-90; rsch. fellow Nat. Heart and Lung Inst., London, 1990-93, lectr., 1993—. Patentee in field; contbr. articles to profl. jours. Travel grantee Royal Soc. (U.K.), 1990, rsch. grantee Glaxo, 1993; Med. Rsch. Coun. fellow, 1987. Mem. Endocrine Soc., Biochem. Soc., Am. Thoracic Soc. Office: Nat Heart & Lung Inst, Imperial Coll Dovehouse St, London SW3 GLY, England

ADDISON, ALEXANDER, retired general practitioner; b. Atchencoil T.E., Kerala, India, Aug. 23, 1930; arrived in Scotland, 1936; s. Alexander John and Lilian (Mair) A.; m. Joan Wood, Aug. 24, 1955; children: John, Lindsay, Gordon. MB, ChB, Aberdeen U., Scotland, 1954; D in Obstetrics, Royal Coll. Obstetricians, 1960; postgrad., Royal Coll. Gen. Practitioners, 1981. House surgeon, physician Woodend Gen. Hosp., Aberdeen, 1954-55; jr. med. specialist Royal Army Med. Corps, Glasgow, 1955-58; sr. house officer Bellshill Maternity Hosp., Lanarkshire, 1958-59; gen. practitioner Lanarks, Scotland, 1959-95; physician Lady Home Hosp., Douglas, Lanarkshire, 1959-95; hon. surgeon St. Andrews Ambulance Assn., 1959-89; chmn. Scottish Assn. Gen. Practitioner Hosps., 1985-87, Lanarkshire Area Med. Com., 1982-86, Lanarkshire Local Med. Com., 1988-95; mem. Scottish Coun., 1984—, Scottish Com. Med. Commn. Accident Prevention, 1976—. Past chmn. Douglas sect. Royal British Legion; founding mem. Lanark Round Table. Mem. British Med. Assn. (chmn. Lanark div. 1979-82, fellowship 1993), Douglas Curling Club (sec. 1981-91, chmn. 1991). Home: 7 Addison Dr, Douglas ML11 0PZ, Scotland

ADDUCCI, JOSEPH EDWARD, obstetrician, gynecologist; b. Chgo., Dec. 1, 1934; s. Dominee Edward and Harriet Evelyn (Kneppreth) A.; m. Mary Ann Tiertje, 1958; children—Christopher, Gregory, Steven, Jessica, Tobias. B.S., U. Ill., 1955; M.D., Loyola U., Chgo., 1959. Diplomate Am. Bd. Ob-Gyn., Nat. Bd. Med. Examiners. Intern Cook County Hosp., Chgo., 1959-60; resident in ob-gyn Mt. Carmel Hosp., Detroit, 1960-64; practice medicine specializing in obstetrics and gynecology Williston, N.D., 1966—; chief staff, chmn. obstetrics dept. Mercy Hosp., Williston, mem. governing bd., 1996; clin. prof. U. N.D. Med. Sch., 1973—; mem. gov. bd. Mercy Hosp. Cath. Health Corp. Mem. N.D. Bd. Med. Examiners, 1974—, past chmn.; project dir. Tri County Family Planning Svc.; past pres. Tri County Health Planning Coun.; mem. governing bd. Mercy Hosp., Williston, N.D. With Med. Corps, AUS, 1964-66. Fellow Am. Soc. Abdominal Surgeons, ACS (regent N.D. 1990—), Am. Coll. Obstetrics and Gynecologists (sect. chmn. N.D.), Internat. Coll. Surgeons (regent 1972-74, 88-89), Am. Fertility Soc., Am. Assn. Internat. Lazar Soc., Gynecol. Lataropists, N.D. Obstetricians and Gynecologists Soc. (pres. 1966, 76); mem. Am. Soc. for Colposcopy and Colpomicroscopy, Am. Soc. Cryosurgery, Am. Soc. Contemporary Medicine and Surgery, Am. Assn. Profl. Ob-Gyn., Pan Am. Med. Assn., Am. Coll. Surgeons (regent 1989— N.D.). Lodge: Elks. Home: 1717 Main St Williston ND 58801-4244 Office: Medical Ctr OB GYN Williston ND 58801

ADDY, JAN ARLENE, clinical nurse, educator; b. Balt., Apr. 16, 1951; d. James Anderson and June Annette (Windsor) Briggle; m. Rick Edward Addy, Feb. 26, 1988; children: Brittany Anissa, Richard Michael. AA in Nursing, Essex Community Coll., Balt., 1972; BSN, U. San Francisco, 1976; MS, U. Md., Balt., 1979; postgrad., Nova Southeastern U. Cert. sch. health nurse, pub. health nurse. Sr. staff nurse Francis Scott Key Med. Ctr., Balt., 1980-87; clin. instr. Harford Community Coll., Bel Air, Md., 1987-88; primary nurse and nurse educator U. Md., Balt., 1987—; asst. prof. Baltimore City C.C., 1994—; mem. rev. faculty for Nat. State Bd. Exam. for Nursing; mem. adj. faculty Catonsville C.C., 1994; instr. jr. students St. Joseph's Hosp. Sch. Nursing, Towson, Md., 1979-80; clin. instr., skills instr. Essex C.C., 1978-79; mem. U. Md. Med. Sys. Partnership Program, Frederick Douglas H.S. Contbr. articles to profl. jours. Mem. ASCD, Nat. Soc. Trauma Nurses, Nat. Nursing Staff Devel. Orgn., Emergency Nurses Assn., C.A.R.E., Sigma Theta Tau (program com. Pi chpt.).

ADEBIMPE, VICTOR ROTIMI, psychiatrist; b. Iji, Kwara, Nigeria, Nov. 6, 1945; came to U.S., 1972; s. Solomon Olawepo and Bolaji Adebimpe; m. Folasade Oluremi Ogunlana, Apr. 29, 1972; children: Oluseyi, Babatunde, Olajumoke. BS, U. Ibadan, Nigeria, 1968; MD, U. Ibadan, 1971. Intern Bapt. Hosp., Ogbomosho, Nigeria, 1971-72; resident Mo. Inst. Psychiatry, St. Louis, 1972-75; attending psychiatrist U. Pitts., 1975-79; med. dir. No. Commn. Mental Health Ctr., Pitts., 1979-82; sr. lectr. U. Ilorin, Ilorin, Nigeria, 1982-84; dir. psychiatry St. Johns Health & Hosp. Ctr., Pitts., 1984-90; med. dir. Charles R. Drew Community Mental Health Ctr., Phila., 1987-92; dir. adult psychiatry Mercy Psychiat. Inst., Pitts., 1990-95, pres. med. staff, 1992-95; adj. asst. prof. psycniatry Allegheny U. Health Scis., 1996; attending psychiatrist Mercy Providence Hosp., Pitts., 1996. Contbr. articles to profl. jours. Med. dir. Luth. Youth & Family Svcs., Zelienople, Pa., 1996. Mem. AAAS, Am. Psychiat. Assn., Nat. Med. Assn. Baptist. Office: Allies Behavioral Ctr 275 Gateway Twrs Pittsburgh PA 15222-1616

ADEBONOJO, FESTUS O., medical educator; b. Lagos, Nigeria, May 6, 1931; came to U.S., 1952; naturalized, 1989; s. Samuel A. and Regina O. Adebonojo; m. Leslie J. Goodale, Nov. 26, 1987; children: William, David, Andrew, Geoffrey. B.S., Yale U., 1956, M.D., 1960. Diplomate Am. Bd. Pediatrics. Intern in pediatrics Yale New Haven (Conn.) Hosp., 1960-61, resident in pediatrics, 1961-63; pediatrician Permanente Med. Group, San Rafael, Calif., 1964-71; asst. prof. pediatrics U. Pa., Phila., 1971-76; assoc. prof. U. Pa, Phila., 1976-77; prof. pediatrics, chmn. U. Ife, Ile-Ife, Nigeria, 1977-78, dean Sch. Medicine, 1978-80; sr. research fellow J. Stokes Research Inst., Children's Hosp., Phila., 1980-82; prof. pediatrics Cornell U., N.Y.C., 1982-84; prof., chmn. pediatrics Meharry Med. Coll, Nashville, 1984-88, James H. Quillen Coll. Medicine, East Tenn. State U., Johnson City, 1988—. Author: How Baby Grows, 1985. Bd. dirs. Family Service Agy., Marin County, Calif., 1965-71; bd. dirs. Econ. Opportunity Council, Marin County, 1966-71, chmn., 1970-71; mem. Gov.'s Task Force on Healthy Children, Tenn., 1984-87. Mem. Am. Pediatric Soc. Office: East Tenn State U James H Quillen Coll Medicine PO Box 70578 Johnson City TN 37614-0578

ADEKSON, MARY OLUFUNMILAYO, therapist; b. Ogbomoso, Nigeria; came to U.S., 1988; d. Gabriel and Deborah Williams; children: Adedayo, Babatunde. BA in English and Am. Lit., Brandeis U., 1975; MEd in Guidance and Counseling, Obafemi Awolowo U., Ile-Ife, Nigeria, 1987; PhD, Ohio U., 1996. English tchr. Cen. Sch. Bd., Ibadan, Nigeria, 1976-88; acting prin. Abe Tech. Coll., Ibadan, 1978; coord. guidance svcs. Min. Edn., Ile-Ife, 1984-88; part-time lectr. Obafemi Awolowo U., Ile-Ife, 1986-88; vice prin. Olubuse Meml. High Sch., Ile-Ife, 1987-88; grad. asst. Ohio U., Athens, 1988-91; vol. contract worker, trainer Careline, Tri-County Mental Health Ctr., Athens, 1988-92; vol. My Sister's Place, Athens, 1989, Good Works Athens, 1989, Montgomery County Hotline, 1994; contract worker Tri County Activity Ctr., Athens, 1989-92, therapist II Woodland Ctr., Gallipolis, Ohio, 1991-92; part-time lectr. U. Md., 1993, coord. tutorial svcs.; dir. Christian Book Ctr., Ile-Ife; vol., part-time counselor DWI program Prince George's County Health Dept., Hyattsville, Md.; counselor Potomac Healthcare Found. Mountain Manor Treatment Program. Vol. Montgomery County Police Dept.; mem. Alcohol and Other Drug Abuse Adv. Coun., Montgomery County, Md.; mem. adv. com. Germantown (Md.) Libr.; mem. Gaithersburg (Md.) City Adv. Com.; chmn. bd. dirs. Faith Enterprises, Germantown. Recipient Gold medal West African Athletic Assn., 1965; Internat. Peace scholar P.E.O., 1990-91, Wien Internat. scholar Brandeis U., 1973-75. Mem. ACA, Am. Mental Health Counselors Assn. Network on Children and Teens (membership chair 1991-92, chair 1993—), Am. Assn. Counseling and Devel. (award for internat. grad. students 1990), Counseling Assn. Nigeria (planning com. 1986), Am. Rehab. Counselors Assn., Am. Mental Health Counseling Assn., Assn. Multicultural Counseling and Devel., Oyo State Assn. Guidance Counselors (chmn. Oranmiyan local govt. area 1986-88), Chi Sigma Iota (program coord. ou chpt. 1990).

ADELMAN, HAROLD MICHAEL, rheumatologist, educator; b. Far Rockaway, N.Y., May 8, 1942; s. Sam and Evelyn (Miller) A.; m. Maralyn Helaine Gartner, Aug. 22, 1965; children: Sharon, Matthew. BA in Psychology, Hunter Coll. CUNY, 1964; MD, Bologna U., 1969. Diplomate in internal medicine and rheumatology Am. Bd. Internal Medicine. Intern Brookdale Hosp. Med. Ctr., Bklyn., 1970-71, resident internal medicine, 1971-73; fellow in rheumatology Albert Einstein Coll. Medicine, Bronx, 1973-75; pvt. practice Tampa, Fla., 1975-85; staff physician James A. Haley VA Hosp., Tampa, 1985-88, asst. chief med. svc., 1988—; prof. medicine U. South Fla., Tampa, 1995—. Contbr. articles to profl. jours. Capt. USAR, 1970-75. Fellow ACP, Am. Coll. Rheumatology. Jewish. Office: James A Haley VA Hosp 13000 Bruce B Downs Blvd Tampa FL 33612

ADELMAN, MILTON HARRIS, anesthesiologist; b. N.Y.C., Dec. 19, 1910; s. Samuel D. Adelman and Sadye (S.) A.; married, Jan. 15, 1950 (dec. 1990); 1 child, Samuel R. BS cum laude, NYU, 1931; MD, U. Md., Balt., 1935. Diplomate Am. Bd. Anesthesiology. Intern Hosp. for Joint Diseases, N.Y.C., 1936-38, assoc. attending anesthesiologist, 1941-46; resident in medicine Mt. Sinai Hosp., N.Y.C., 1938-39; resident anesthesiology Michael Reese Hosp., Chgo., 1939-41; anesthesiologist Mt. Sinai Hosp., N.Y.C., 1942-79, cons., clin. prof. emeritus, 1979—; clin. prof. anesthesiology NYU, N.Y.C., 1991—. Contbr. publs. to profl. jours. Maj. M.C., 1942-46, ETO. Fellow Am. Coll. Anesthesiology, N.Y. Acad. Medicine; mem. Am. Soc. Anesthesiology, N.Y. Soc. Anesthesiology (life). Republican. Jewish. Home: 29 Shawnee Rd Scarsdale NY 10583-2210 Office: NYU Sch Medicine 560 1st Ave New York NY 10016-6402

ADELSBERG, HARVEY, hospital administrator; b. Bronx, N.Y., Aug. 5, 1931; s. Joseph and Becky (Rindner) A.; BA, NYU, 1953, MPA, 1960, postgrad., 1960-65; m. Miriam Levine, June 20, 1964; children: Jonathan, Risa, Seth. Adminstrv. resident Beth David Hosp., N.Y.C., 1953-54; adminstrv. asst. Met. Jewish Geriatric Center, Bklyn., 1954-58; asst. dir. Kingsbrook Jewish Med. Center, Bklyn., 1958-61; asst. dir. Hosp. for Joint Diseases, N.Y.C., 1961-64; exec. dir. Theresa Grotta Center for Restorative Services, Caldwell, N.J., 1964-70; asst. dir. Mt. Sinai Hosp., N.Y.C., 1970-72; cons. med. care and svcs. to aged Fedn. Jewish Philanthropies, N.Y.C., 1972-74; exec. dir. Daus. of Miriam Center for Aged, Clifton, N.J., 1974-76, exec. v.p., 1977—; adj. asst. prof. health care adminstrn., Bernard M. Baruch Coll., Mt. Sinai Sch. Medicine, CUNY, 1973—, U. Medicine and Dentistry, N.J., 1995; mem. adv. com. Rutgers U., 1969—; mem. adj. prof. N.J. Grad. Sch. Pub. Health, 1995; cons. Consulting Svcs. Inst., 1995, mem. N.J. Licensing Bd. for Nursing Home Adminstrs., 1969—, vice chmn., 1969-77; mem. Adv. Council on Aging, Livington, N.J., 1977—. Trustee Hosp. and Council Met. N.J., 1967-70, Health and Hosp. Council So. N.Y., 1972-74, N.J. Assn. Non-Profit Homes for Aging, 1976—, Jewish Community Housing Corp., Paterson, N.J., 1975—; trustee tng. Dist, 1199J, 1990; agt. Daus. of Miriam Found., 1984; v.p. Solomon Schechter Day Sch. of Essex and Union, 1980—; trustee Synagogue of Suburban Torah Center, Livingston, 1978—; bd. govs. Greater N.Y. Hosp. Assn., 1972-74; v.p. Temple Beth Shalom, Livingston, 1970-71, 73, trustee, 1968-70, 75—; mem. governing com. Camp Ramah, Wingdale, N.Y., 1979—; exec. bd. Jewish Communal Svc. Assn. 1993—. Fellow Am. Coll. Hosp. Adminstrs., Am. Coll. Nursing Home Adminstrs., Am. Geriatric Soc., Am. Pub. Health Assn.; mem. Am., N.J. hosp. assns., Hosp. Exec. Club. Mem. B'nai B'rith (v.p. 1960-64). Home: 27 Tuxedo Dr Livingston NJ 07039-2452 Office: 155 Hazel St Clifton NJ 07011-3423

ADELSON, BERNARD HENRY, physician; b. Tampa, Fla., Mar. 16, 1920; s. Edward H. and Esther (Hadesman) A.; m. Martha Stein, June 13, 1950; children: Duffie Ann, Edward H., David E. BS, Northwestern U., Evanston, Ill., 1942, PhD, 1946, MD, 1951. Diplomate Am. Bd. Internal Medicine. Intern Jackson Meml. Hosp., Miami, Fla., 1950-51; resident Evanston Hosp., 1951-53, Cook County Hosp., Chgo., 1953-54; prof. clin. medicine Northwestern U., Chgo., 1980—; assoc. chmn. dept. medicine Evanston Hosp., 1979—, dir. program on med. ethics, 1985—, chair instl. ethics com., 1989—. Capt. U.S. Army, 1955-57. Fellow AAAS, Am. Coll. Physicians (Clinician Laureate 1989, 90), Royal Soc. Medicine. Office: Evanston Hosp 2650 Ridge Ave Evanston IL 60201-1718

ADELSON, ELLEN, social worker; b. Tulsa, June 18, 1936; d. Herbert and Roseline (Nadel) Gussman; m. Stephen Jay Adelson, June 23, 1957; children: David, Bob, Jim, Tom. BA in Sociology and Anthropology, Cornell U., 1958; MSW in Clin. Social Work, U. Okla., 1976. Cert. social worker, Okla. Clin. social worker Clin. Social Work Svcs., Tulsa, 1976-78; pvt. practice Tulsa, 1978—; bd. mem. Family & Children's Svcs., Tulsa, 1973-78; mem. adv. bd. Child Devel. Program, Norman, Okla., 1975-76; bd. mem. At Risk Bd., Tulsa, 1979-80, A New Leaf, Tulsa, 1979-80; bd. trustees, vice chair adminstrn. bd. coun., chair steering com. devel., chmn. adv. coun. dean arts & scis., chmn. regional campaign com., com.mem. acad. affairs & campus life, com. mem. alumni affairs & devel., Herbert Johnson Mus. Art adv. bd., Pres. Coun. Cornell Women, pres. emeritus Cornell Club Okla. Cornell U.; bd. trustees, chmn. vis. com. rare books & manuscripts dept. McFalin Libr., mem. TURC adv. bd., adv. bd. dept. engring. U. Tulsa. Home: 2811 E 28th St Tulsa OK 74114 Office: Ste 300 1980 Utica Sq Med Ctr Tulsa OK 74114

ADELSON, MARK DAVID, gynecologic oncologist; b. Cleve., Aug. 14, 1955; s. Robert Mortimer and June Elaine (Gold) A.; m. Katherine Lee Rosewinkel, Sept. 24, 1988; children: Leah May, Cara Grace. Student, Mich. State U., 1973-76; MD, Med. Coll. Ohio, 1979. Diplomate Am. Bd. Med. Examiners, Am. Bd. Ob-Gyn; cert. gynecologic oncologist. Resident in ob-gyn Emory U. Sch. Medicine, Atlanta, 1979-83; fellow in gynecologic oncology M.D. Anderson Hosp., U. Tex., Houston, 1983-85; asst. prof., dir. gynecologic oncology Dept. Ob-Gyn., SUNY Health Sci. Ctr., Syracuse, 1985-89, assoc. prof. dir. gynecologic oncology, 1989-93; pres. Comprehensive Gynecology, Syracuse, N.Y., 1993—; adv. bd. Hospice of Cen. N.Y., Syracuse, 1988—. Editorial bd. Clin. Practice of Gynecology, 1989—, Jour. of Gynecologic Surgery, 1990—; editor: Clinical Practice of Gynecology, 1991; author: (with others) Textbook of Gynecology, 1990, Clinical Obstetrics and Gynecology, 1990; contbr. articles to profl. jours. Rsch. grant Am. Cancer Soc., 1976; scholarship in clin. nutrition Joseph Goldberger AMA, 1976. Fellow ACS, Am. Coll. Ob-Gyn.; mem. Beta Beta Beta, Alpha Omega Alpha. Office: Comprehensive Gynecology 730 S Crouse Ave Ste 203 Syracuse NY 13210-1746

ADELSTEIN, S(TANLEY) JAMES, physician, educator; b. N.Y.C., Jan. 24, 1928; s. George and Belle (Schild) A.; m. Mary Charlesworth Taylor, Sept. 20, 1957; children—Joseph Burrows, Elizabeth Dunster. B.S., M.I.T., 1949, M.S., 1949, Ph.D. in Biophysics (Nat. Found. fellow), 1957; M.D., Harvard U., 1953. Med. house officer Peter Bent Brigham Hosp., Boston, 1953-54; sr. asst. resident physician Peter Bent Brigham Hosp., 1957-58, chief resident, 1959-60; fellow Howard Hughes Med. Inst., 1957-58, Henry A. and Camilus Christian fellow, 1959-60; Moseley Traveling fellow Harvard U., 1958-59; instr. anatomy Harvard Med. Sch., 1961-65, asst. prof., 1965-68, assoc. prof. radiology, 1968-72, prof., 1972-89, Paul C. Cabot prof. med. biophysics, 1989—, dean for acad. programs, 1978—; mem. Nat. Coun. for Radiation Protection Measurements, 1978—, dir., 1980—, v.p. 1982—; cons. Med. Found. fellow, 1960-63; Walter Daudy lectr. John Hopkins U., 1996. Mem. editorial bd. Investigative Radiology, 1972-80, Postgrad. Radiology, Radiation Rsch., 1990-94; assoc. editor Jour. Nuclear Medicine, 1975-81; contbr. articles to profl. jours. Trustee Am. Bd. Nuclear Medicine, 1972-78; mem. fellowship adv. com. Whitaker Found., 1991—. NIH Career Devel. awardee, 1965-68; Fogarty Sr. Internat. fellow, 1976; recipient Walter Dandy Izetorer award, 1996. Fellow AAAS, Am. Coll. Nuclear Physicians; mem. Am. Chem. Soc., Biophys. Soc., Assn. for Radiation Rsch., Radiation Rsch. Soc. (councillor 1975-78), Soc. Nuclear Medicine (trustee 1970-74, Blumgart award 1983, Aebersold award 1986), Boylston Med. Soc., Inst. Medicine, Sigma Xi, Tau Beta Pi, Alpha Omega Alpha. Office: Harvard Med Sch 25 Shattuck St Boston MA 02115-6027

ADENWALLA, SHABBIR TAHER, orthodontist, import/export and financial consultant; b. Cambay, Gujarat, India, Jan. 11, 1954; came to U.S., 1979; s. Taher Mohammedali and Banu T. (Poonawalla) A.; m. Durriya R. Parekh, Oct. 5, 1978; children: Muneera, Maria, Zahabiyah. B in Dental Surgery, Mysore U., Manipal, India, 1978; MS, Tufts U., 1983; DMD, Boston U., 1983. Lic. dentist Ohio, Mass., Northeastern U.S., Hong Kong, India. Research fellow Tufts U., Boston, 1981-83; orthodontist Orthodontic Assocs., Inc., Lowell, Mass., 1983-84; orthodontic dir. Horizon Dental Group Internat., Inc., Lorain, Ohio, 1984—. Contbr. articles to profl. jours. Recipient Cert. Indian Soc. Periodontology, 1978-79, Cert. Supreme Governing Body of Acad. Gen. Edn., 1978-79; fellow Supreme Governing Body of Acad. Gen. Edn., 1978; C.V. Mosby scholar Boston U., 1983. Mem. Jaycees. Moslem. Home: 1951 Coes Post Run Cleveland OH 44145-2022 Office: Horizon Dental Group 17535 Rosbrough Dr Ste 211 Middlesburg Heights OH 44130

ADER, ROBERT, psychology educator; b. N.Y.C., Feb. 20, 1932; s. Nathan and Mae (Levine) A.; m. Gayle Simon, June 2, 1957; children: Deborah, Janet, Norine, Leslie. BS, Tulane U., 1953; PhD honorus causa, Cornell U., 1957; MD with honors, U. Trondheim, Norway, 1992. Rsch. instr. dept. of psychiatry Sch. of Medicine and Dentistry, U. Rochester, N.Y., 1957-61, asst. prof., 1961-64, assoc. prof., 1964-68, prof., 1968-83, dir. divsn. behavioral and psychosocial medicine, 1982—, George L. Engel prof. dept. psychiatry, 1983—; vis. prof. Rudolf Magnus Inst. for Pharmacology, Utrecht, The Netherlands, 1970-71; Salmon lectr. N.Y. Acad. Medicine, N.Y.C., 1989; fellow Ctr. for Advanced Study in Behavioral Studies, Stanford, Calif. Editor: Psychoneuroimmunology, 1981, 2d edit., 1991, Experimental Foundations of Behavioral Medicine: Conditioning Approaches, 1988; editor-in-chief Brain, Behavior and Immunity, 1986—; contbr. numerous articles to profl. jours. Fellow Acad. Behavioral Medicine Rsch. (pres. 1984-85), Soc. for Behavioral Medicine; mem. Am. Psychosomatic Soc. (pres. 1979-80), Internat. Soc. Devel. Psychobiology (pres. 1981-82), Acad. Behavioral Medicine Rsch. (pres. 1984-85), Psychoneuroimmunology Rsch. Soc. (founding pres. 1993-94). Home: 9 Park Acre Rd Pittsford NY 14534-2735 Office: 300 Crittenden Blvd Rochester NY 14642

ADEY, DEBORAH BACHTOLD, nephrologist; b. Glendale, Calif., July 28, 1955; d. Donald Robert Bachtold and Kay Faith (Chubb) Green; m. Paul Vittori, Aug. 12, 1976 (div.); m. Geoffrey Robert Adey, Sept. 24, 1988; children: Amy Nicole Ward, Allison Sydney. BA, Calif. State U., 1979; MD, U. Colo. Health Scis. Ctr., 1989. Diplomate Am. Bd. Internal Medicine. Med. tech. St. Lukes Presbyn. Hosp., Denver, 1980-86; resident, fellow in nephrology Med. Ctr. Hosp. Vt., Burlington, 1989-94; fellow nephrology Mayo Clinic, Rochester, Minn., 1994—. Mem. Am. Soc. Nephrology. Lutheran. Home: 845 2d St NW Rochester MN 55901-2776

ADISMAN, I. KENNETH, prosthodontist; b. N.Y.C., Aug. 3, 1919; s. Joseph and Frances (Gertz) A.; m. Joan Sugarman, Aug. 27, 1957; children: Leslie, Kathryn. Student, Mich. State Coll., 1935-37; D.D.S., U. Buffalo, 1940; M.S., NYU, 1960. Diplomate: Am. Bd. Prosthodontics (examiner; pres. 1980). Attending dentist NYU Med. Center, U. Hosp., N.Y.C., 1960-78; prof. dept. prosthodontics and occlusion, dir. maxillofacial prosthetics Dental Center, 1978-86, chmn. dept. prosthodontics, 1978-86, dir. advanced edn. program in prosthodontics, dir. implant dentistry; clin. prof. sch. dentistry U. N.C., Chapel Hill, 1992—; attending dentist Meml. Hosp., N.Y.C., 1976-78; pres. Greater N.Y. Acad. Prosthodontics Rsch. Found., 1980; pres., dir. Internat. Cir. Courses, Inc. of Am. Prosthodontic Soc.; prof. emeritus Coll. Dentistry, NYU. Chmn. editorial coun. Jour. Prosthetic Dentistry, 1985—. Served to maj. Dental Corps, U.S. Army, 1942-46. Recipient Alumni Achievement award Coll. of Dentistry, NYU, 1988, Sch. Dental Medicine, U. Buffalo, 1990, Carl O. Boucher Disting. Svc. award Fedn. Prosthodontic Orgns., 1992. Fellow Acad. of Prosthodontics (pres. 1988-89), Acad. Maxillofacial Prosthetics; mem. Am. Coll. Prosthodontists (past pres. N.Y. sect.), Am. Coll. Dentists, Internat. Coll. Dentists, Greater N.Y. Acad. Prosthodontics, Nat. Acad. Practice, N.Y. Acad. Dentistry, N.Y. Acad. Sci. Club: The Carolina.

ADJAMAH, KOKOUVI MICHEL, physician; b. Lome, Togo, West Africa, Jan. 21, 1942; s. Carl Yao and Antoinette Afi (Tourné) A.; m. Francoise Legendre, July 30, 1975; children: Isabelle, Celine. MS, U. Paris, 1970, MD, 1973, MPH, 1974, M of Human Ecology, 1975, M of Clin. Toxicology-Pharmacology, 1976. Pub. health physician Dreux, France, 1973-74; gen. practice medicine, homeopathy, acupuncture, holistic medicine Vernouillet, France, 1976; expert in human ecology Paris, 1976, cons. clin. pharmacology, 1977—. Author: Onchocerchosis in West Africa, 1973; contbr. aritcles to profl. jours. Fellow Rabelais Med. Brotherhood; mem. French Com. for Med. Lexicon, Soc. Functional Medicine, French Soc. Pharmacology-Toxicology (assoc.), Social Medicine Club, Human Rights Assn., XVIII Century Studies Assn., History of Justice Assn. Quaker. Home: 25 rue Chailloy Garnay, Vernouillet 28500 Eure et Loir France Office: 5 Ter rue Louis Jouvet, Vernouillet 28500 Eure et Loir France

ADJEI, ALEX ASIEDU, internist, oncologist, pharmacologist; b. Kumasi, Ghana, Apr. 21, 1955; came to U.S., 1989; s. James Kwaku and Juliana (Owusua) A. MBChB, U. Ghana, 1982; PhD, U. Alta., Can., 1989. Diplomate Am. Bd. Internal Medicine. Med. officer Ghana Med. Sch., Accra, 1983-84; clin. rsch. fellow U. Alberta, Edmonton, Can., 1987-89; med. resident Howard U. Hosp., Washington, 1989-91, chief med. resident, 1991-92; sr. clin. fellow Oncology Clin. Ctr. Johns Hopkins Hosp., Balt., 1992-95; asst. prof. Mayo Med. Sch., Rochester, Minn., 1995—; mem. Grad. Student's Coun., Edmonton, 1984-86. Contbg. author book in field, 1988. Named Best Student, Ghana Med. Sch., 1979, Resident of Yr., D.C. Gen. Hosp., 1991; recipient Travel award Nat. Cancer Inst., Can., 1988, rsch. scholarship Alberta Heritage Found., Edmonton, 1985-89. Mem. AAAS, ACP, Am. Assn. Cancer Rsch., Am. Soc. Internal Medicine, Am. Soc. Hematology, N.Y. Acad. Scis. Home: 12443 White Bridge Ln NE Rochester MN 55906 Office: Mayo Clinic Div Med Oncology 200 First St SW Rochester MN 55905

ADKERSON, DONYA LYNN, clinical counselor; b. Mattoon, Ill., Oct. 5, 1959; d. Edwin Dwayne and Sonya Jeanne (Abernathie) Adkerson; m. George Anthony Ferguson, May 20, 1990; 1 child, Tiana Jo Berry. MA, So. Ill. U., Edwardsville, 1983. Outpatient dir. Children's Ctr. for Behavioral Devel., Centerville, Ill., 1983-90; pvt. practice psychotherapy Evaluation & Therapy Svc., Edwardsville, 1991-92; dir. Alternatives Counseling, Inc., 1993—; cons. St. Louis City Juvenile Ct., 1991-94, Covenant Children's Home, 1991-93. Co-author: Adult Sexual Offender Assessment Packet, 1994. Pres. Ill. Network for Mgmt. Abusive Sexuality, 1991; clin. mem. Assn. for Treatment of Sex Abusers, exec. bd., 1994—, mem. ethics and stds. com.; mem. Cmty. Coordinating Coun. Domestic Violence, 1996—; mem. Adolescent Perpetrator Network, 1987-95; exec. bd. Arts League Players Theatre, Edwardsville, 1986—; former chmn. Metro-East Task Force on Sexual Offenders. Mem. ACA, Ill. Counseling Assn., Ill. Mental Health Counselors Assn. Office: Alternatives Counseling 1 Mark Twain Plz Edwardsville IL 62025

ADKINS, ROYCE T., obstetrician, gynecologist; b. Springfield, Tenn., Oct. 1, 1958; s. Royce H. and Anne Dale (Terrell) A.; m. Cheri M. Adkins, June 20, 1981; children: Joshua, Zachary, Adam. adminstrv. chief resident ob-gyn. dept., Vanderbilt U., 1988-89, resident selection com., 1988, co-chmn. ob/gyn. dept. symposium on malpractice, 1988; numerous other hosp. activities; presenter in field. Fellow Am. Coll. Ob-Gyn, Am. Coll. Surgeons; mem. AMA, Tenn. Med. Assn., Am. Fertility Soc., Am. Uro-Gynecol. Soc., Am. Soc. for Colposcopy and Cervical Pathology, Nashville and Mid. Tenn. Ob-Gyn Soc., Nashville Acad. Medicine, Soc. Laparoensocopic Surgeons, Phi Eta Sigma, Phi Beta Kappa, Alpha Omega Alpha. Office: Growdon Van Hooydonk Bressman Adkins 2201 Murphy Ave Nashville TN 37203

ADKINS, WARREN YOUNG, otolaryngologist. MD, Med. Coll. S.C., 1965. Diplomate Am. Bd. Otolaryngology. Intern Shands Tchg. Hosp., Gainesville, 1965-66, resident in gen. surgery, 1966-67, resident in otolaryngology, 1967-70; fellow in head and neck surgery UCLA Med. Ctr., 1972-73; mem. staff Med. U. Hosp., Charleston, S.C., 1974—; prof., chmn. otolaryngology dept. Med. U. S.C., 1974—. Mem. Am. Assn. Otolaryngologists and Head and Neck Surgeons, Am. Laryngology Assn., Am. Otolaryngology Soc., Am. Soc. of Head and Neck Surgeons, ABEA. Office: Med Univ SC Faculty Otolaryngology 171 Ashley Ave Charleston SC 29425-0001*

ADKINSON, N. FRANKLIN, JR., clinical immunologist; b. Forest City, N.C., May 18, 1943; s. N. Frank and Estelle (Stembridge) A.; m. Judy F. Hyder, Aug. 20, 1966; children: Anna Estelle, Carter F. BA with highest honors, U. N.C., Chapel Hill, 1965; MD, Johns Hopkins U., 1969. Intern, resident in internal medicine Johns Hopkins U., Balt., 1969-71, asst. prof. medicine, 1973-81, assoc. prof., 1981-87, prof. medicine, 1987—; co-dir. div. allergy and clin. immunology Johns Hopkins Sch. of Medicine, Balt., 1991—; mem. immunolog. scis. study sect. NIH, Bethesda, Md., 1982-86, allergy immunology rev. com., 1987-91; clin. assoc. Lab. of Immunology, NIH, 1971-73. Editor: Allergy: Principles and Practice, 4th edit., 1993; mng. editor: Updates in Allergy and Immunology, 1989—; contbr. over 200 articles to profl. jours. Lt. comdr. USPHS, 1971-73. Recipient Allergic Disease Acad. award Nat. Inst. Allergy and Infectious Disease, 1975. Fellow Am. Acad. Allergy and Immunology; mem. Am. Soc. Clin. Investigation, Collegium Allergologica Internat., Am. Climatological Assn. Episcopalian. Office: Johns Hopkins Allergy & Asthma Ctr 5501 Hopkins Bayview Cir Baltimore MD 21224-6821

ADKISON, MARLA GALEEN, nursing consultant; b. Wellington, Kans., Apr. 8, 1948; d. Gale M. and Hazel C. (Wright) Aldrich; m. Herbert J. Adkison, Apr. 11, 1969; children: Joseph, Denise, Jason. ADN, San Jacinto Coll., 1968; BSN, U. Tex., Galveston, 1988. Nursing supr. Women's Hosp., Houston, 1975-77, Charter Med. Hosp., Pasadena, Tex., 1978-83; nursing instr. San Jacinto Coll., Houston, 1983-89; nurse cons. Fisher, Gallagher, Lewis, Houston, 1989—. Mem. NAACOG, Am. Assn. Legal Nurse Cons., Tex. Assn. Vocat. Nurse Educators. Home: 6906 Redwood Falls Dr Pasadena TX 77505-4414 Office: 1000 Louisiana 70th Fl Houston TX 77002

ADLAND, MARVIN LEON, psychiatrist, educator; b. Chgo., Dec. 24, 1919; s. Isadore Jack and Anna Rella (Falk) A.; m. Marilyn Friend, Oct. 22, 1947; children: Peter F., Susan F., Jonathan F., Elizabeth F. BS, U. Chgo., 1940, MD, 1943. Diplomate Am. Bd. Psychiatry and Neurology; cert. Am. Psychoanalytic Assn. Intern Milw. (Wis.) County Hosp., 1944; resident psychiatry Sheppard-Pratt Hosp., Towson, Md., 1944-46; resident to assoc. med. dir. Chestnut Lodge Hosp., Rockville, Md., 1948-63; pvt. practice Chevy Chase, Md., 1963—; supervising and tng. psychoanalyst Washington (D.C.) Psychoanalytic Inst., 1957—; clin. prof. psychiatry Georgetown Univ., Washington, 1971—. Contbr. articles to profl. jours. Capt. U.S. Army, 1946-48. Fellow Am. Psychiat. Assn. (life); mem. Washington Psychoanalytic Soc. (pres. 1991-93). Home and Office: 5521 Uppingham St Bethesda MD 20815-5507

ADLER, BARBARA ANN, social worker, consultant; b. Chgo., July 6, 1938; d. Joe and Sarah (Kesselman) Moret; widowed; 1 child, Karyn A. AA with honors, Lake Mich. Coll., 1976; BA cum laude, Western Mich. U., 1978, MSW, 1981. Cert. social worker, Mich.; lic. marriage and family therapist. Dir. Coll. Vocat. Edn. Rasmussen Bus. Coll., St. Paul; pres. The Fashion Mart, Inc., South Haven, Mich.; dir. Coll. Vocat. Edn. Mich. Dunes Correctional Facility, 1985-87; pvt. practice South Haven; adj. faculty Southwestern Mich. Coll., Dowagiac, Mich., Lake Mich. Coll., Benton Harbor, Mich. Active Citizen Amb. Program-Law Enforcement Adminstrn. Delegation, Shanghai and Manila, 1987, China, 1987, 88; citizen amb. to Russia, 1990; mem. City Coun., South Haven, 1993—. Recipient award of Appreciation, Commendation Dept. Social Svc. State of Mich., 1979, hon. fellowship Office Substance Abuse Western Mich. U. Mem. NASW, Internat. Soc. Prevention Child Abuse, Am. Assn. Marriage and Family Therapists, Am. Soc. Criminology, Mich. League for Human Svcs. (chair S.W. Mich. Total Living Ctrs.). Home: 38 Lake Shore Dr South Haven MI 49090-1131

ADLER, CHARLES IRWIN, oral surgeon; b. N.Y.C., Oct. 2, 1942; s. Joe and Anna (Pessy) A.; m. Iris Diane Levy, June 13, 1965; children: Richelle Teri, Melissa Ellen. BS, Bklyn. Coll., 1964; DDS, NYU, 1968. Diplomate Am. Bd. Oral and Maxillofacial Surgery. Oral surgeon Jackson Heights, N.Y., 1968—. Trustee Temple Israel of Great Neck, N.Y., 1985-93. Capt. USAF, 1971-73. Fellow Am. Assn. Oral and Maxillofacial Surgeons, Am. Dental Soc. of Anesthesiology; mem. ADA. Office: 33-53 82d St A01 Jackson Heights NY 11372

ADLER, CHARLES SPENCER, psychiatrist; b. N.Y.C., Nov. 27, 1941; s. Benjamin H. and Anne (Greenfield) A.; m. Sheila Noel Morrissey, Oct. 8, 1966 (dec.); m. Peggy Dolan Bean, Feb. 23, 1991. BA, Cornell U., 1962; MD, Duke U., 1966. Diplomate Nat. Bd. Med. Examiners, Am. Bd. Psychiatry and Neurology. Intern Tucson Hosps. Med. Edn. Program, 1966-67; psychiat. resident U. Colo. Med. Sch., Denver, 1967-70; pvt. practice medicine specializing in psychiatry and psychosomatic medicine Denver, 1970—; chief divsn. psychiatry Rose Med. Ctr, 1982-87; co-founder Applied Biofeedback Inst., Denver, 1972-75; prof. pro tempore Cleve. Clinic, 1977; asst. clin. prof. psychiatry U. Colo. Med. Ctr., 1986—, chief psychiatry and psychophysiology Colo. Neurology and Headache Ctr., 1988-95; med. dir. Colo. Ctr. for Biobehavioral Health, Boulder, 1994—; bd. dirs. Acad. Cert. Neurotherapists. Author: (with Gene Stanford and Sheila M. Adler) We Are But a Moment's Sunlight, 1976, (with Sheila M. Adler and Russell Packard) Psychiatric Aspects of Headache, 1987; contbr. (with S. Adler) sect. biofeedback med. and health ann. Ency. Britannica, 1986; chpts. to books, articles to profl. jours.; mem. editorial bd. Cephalalgia: an Internat. Jour. of Headache, Headache Quar. Emeritus mem. Citizen's Adv Bd. Duke U. Ctr. Aging and Human Devel. Recipient Award of Recognition, Nat. Migraine Found., 1981; N.Y. State regents scholar, 1958-62. Fellow Am. Psychiat. Assn.; mem. AAAS (rep. of AAPB to med. sect. com.), Am. Assn. Study Headache, Internat. Headache Soc. (chmn. subcom. on classifying psychiat. headaches), Am. Acad. Psychoanalysis (sci. assoc.), Colo. Psychiat. Soc., Biofeedback Soc. Colo. (pres. 1977-78), Assn. for Applied Psychophysiology and Biofeedback (rep. to AAAS, chmn. ethics com. 1983-87, bd. dirs. 1990-93, Sheila M. Adler cert. honor 1988). Jewish. Office: 955 Eudora St Apt 1605 Denver CO 80220-4341

ADLER, DAVID AVRAM, psychiatrist; b. N.Y.C., Aug. 25, 1947; s. Jack and Myril (Stangen) A.; m. Jill Sonneborn, Oct. 5, 1975; children: Jonathan Michael, Eliza Kate. BA, U. Rochester, 1969; MD, Yale U., 1973. Diplomate Am. Bd. Psychiatry and Neurology. Internship, residency Mass. Mental Health Ctr., 1973-76; dir. South Boston Ct. Clinic, Bay Cove Mental Heatlh Ctr., Boston, 1976-79; dir. partial hospitalization programs New Eng. Med. Ctr., Boston, 1979-82; dir. aftercare svcs. Bay Cove Mental Health Ctr., Boston, 1979-86; asst. chief div. adult psychiatry New Eng. Med. Ctr. Hosps., Boston, 1982-83; assoc. chief div. adult psychiatry New Eng. Med. Ctr. Hosps., 1983-84, dir. ambulatory adult psychiatry svcs., 1983-86, chief divsn. adult psychiatry, 1984-93, sr. psychiatrist, 1993—; adj. scientist The Health Inst., NEMC, 1993—; assoc. prof. psychiatry Tufts U. Sch. Medicine, Boston, 1984-90, prof. psychiatry, 1990—, vice chair faculty senate, 1995—; adj. assoc. prof. Simmons Coll. Sch. Social Work, Boston, 1986-91, adj. prof., 1991—; assoc. The Levinson Inst., Belmont, Mass., 1987-93; sr. cons. The Levinson Inst., Waltham, Mass., 1993—. Author 2 books; contbr. articles to profl. jours. Mem. cen. physicians planning com. Tufts Associated Health Plan, Waltham, Mass., 1983-88. Recipient Ten Yr. Disting. Svc. award Bay Cove Human Svcs., Boston, 1988, Henry Solomon Rsch. award Mass. Mental Health Ctr., Boston, 1975. Fellow Am. Psychiat. Assn.; mem. Group for Advancement Psychiatry (chair com. on psychopathology 1981-92, publ. bd. 1994—, chmn. publs. bd. 1996), Mass. Psychiat. Soc., Mass. Med. Soc. Office: New Eng Med Ctr Hosps PO Box 1007 750 Washington St Boston MA 02111

ADLER, HILTON C., plastic surgeon; b. N.Y.C., Apr. 19, 1952; s. Leonard Adler and Helen Sherman; m. Jaimie Fisher, May 1984; children: Shelley and Nomi. BS in Biology cum laude, U. Pitts., 1974; MD, U. Monterrey, Mex., 1978; 5th Path, Downstate Med. Sch., 1979. Diplomate Am. Bd. Plastic Surgeons. Resident in gen. surgery U. Miami-Jackson Meml. Hosp., Fla., 1979-80, Beth Israel Med. Ctr., N.Y.C., 1980-82; resident, then chief resident in plastic surgery Albany (N.Y.) Med. Ctr., 1983-854; fellow in head and neck surgery Beth Israel Med. Ctr., N.Y.C., 1981; fellow in burn surgery Albany Med. Ctr. Hosp., 1983; fellow in plastic surgery Westchester County Med. Ctr., Valhalla, N.Y., 1985-86; fellow in plastic/aesthetic surgeons Metropolitan Plastic Surgeons, N.Y.C., 1986; attending Brookhaven Meml. Hosp., Patchogue, N.Y., 1987—, Mather Meml. Hosp., Port Jefferson, N.Y., 1987—, St. Charles Hosp. and Rehab. Ctr., Port Jefferson, N.Y., 1987—, SUNY Hosp., Stony Brook, 1987—, N. Shore Surgi-Ctr., Smithtown, N.Y., 1991—; clin. instr. SUNY, Stony Brook. Mem. ACS, Am. Soc. Plastic Reconstructive Surgeons, Internat. Coll. Surgeons, Northeastern Soc. Plastic Surgeons, N.Y. Regl. Soc. Plastic Surgeons, Med. Soc. State N.Y., Suffolk Acad. Medicine. Office: Suffolk Plastic Surgeons 181 Belle Meade Rd East Setauket NY 11733

ADLER, JONATHAN ADAM, ophthalmologist; b. Queens, N.Y., Oct. 11, 1960; s. Albert and Joan Toby (Feldman) A.; m. Andrea Beth Futerman, June 24, 1984; children: Andrew, Clark, Ellis. BS, Muhlenberg Coll., Allentown, Pa., 1982; MS, Georgetown U., 1983, MD, 1987. Diplomate Am. Acad. Ophthalmology. Intern Med. Coll. Ga., Atlanta, 1987-88; resident Georgetown U. Ctr. for Sight, Washington, 1988-91; ptnr. Manatee Eyel Clinic, Bradenton, Fla., 1991—. Contbr. articles to profl. jours. Treas. Manatee Coun. on Aging, Bradenton, 1994—; team physician Manatee Sharks, 1996. Mem. Lions. Jewish. Home: 4468 Baycedar Ln Sarasota FL 34241 Office: Manatee Eye Clinic 217 Manatee Ave E Bradenton FL 34208

ADLER, LEE PAUL, nuclear radiologist; b. New Brunswick, N.J., Aug. 1, 1956; s. Orville and Rosita (Solomon) Adler; m. Karel Debra Kovnat, Dec. 9, 1984; 1 child, Sarah Alexis Kovnat Adler. BSE magne cum laude, Princeton U., 1977; MD, U. N.C., 1981. Diplomate Am. Bd. Radiology, Am. Bd. Nuclear Medicine. Radiology resident Hahnemann U. Hosp., Phila., 1981-85; fellow nuclear medicine Temple U. Hosp., Phila., 1985-87; asst. prof. radiology Case Western Res. U., Cleve., 1987-95, assoc. prof. radiology, 1995—, asst. prof. medicine (oncology), 1989-95, assoc. prof. medicine, 1995—; refresher course faculty Radiol. Soc. N.Am.; invited lectr. Am. Acad. Orthopedics, Am. Pharm. Assn., Am. Coll. Radiology, Soc. of Nuclear Medicine; chair multicenter nat. study of cost effectiveness of PET scanning of breast cancer; bd. dirs. Inst. for Clin.; adj. mem. diagnostic radiology study sect. NIH, 1996. Author numerous sci. papers, abstracts, book chpts.; editor-in-chief Cirtual Nuclear Medicine Textbook, 1996; editor Newer Radionuclide Imaging Techniques in Oncology; PET and SPECT, 1989; reviewer Radiology, Jour. of Nuclear Medicine, Jour. of Clin. Oncology, European Heart Jour., Nat. Cancer Inst. (Can.), Am. Heart Assn. (Cleve. chpt.). V.p. bd. dirs. U. Radiologists Cleve., 1995—. Recipient Best Abstract award Phila. Nulcear Med. Conf., 1987, Editor's Recognition award with distinction Radiology; State of Ohio grantee, 1988, NIH grantee, 1993—. Mem. Radiol. Soc. N.Am., Soc. Nuclear Medicine, Am. Coll. Radiology, Phi Beta Kappa, Tau Beta Pi, Sigma Xi. Office: Univ Hosps Radiology Dept 2074 Abington Rd Cleveland OH 44106-2602

ADLER, LINDA, mental health nurse, educator, quality assessment coordinator; b. Neptune, N.J., Nov. 28, 1946; d. David and Gertrude (Kaufman) Silverstein; m. Michael Adler, Apr. 7, 1968; children: Sandy, Carrie, Charles. Diploma, Newark Beth Israel Hosp., 1967; BSN, Elmhurst (Ill.) Coll., 1980; AS in Acctg., Brookdale Sch., Lincroft, N.J., 1982; MS in Psychiat. Nursing, U. Pa., 1989. Cert. gerontol. nurse. Infection control nurse, dir. staff devel. Amboy Care Ctr., Perth Amboy, N.J., 1981-87; instr., asst. DON, Marlboro (N.J.) Psychiat. Hosp., 1987—; adj. nursing instr. Brookdale C.C., Lincroft, N.J. Mem. ANA (cert. clin. nurse specialist psychiat. nursing, cert. profl. healthcare quality), Phi Kappa Phi. Home: 7 Gettysburg Dr Englishtown NJ 07726-1701

ADLER, MARTIN WILLIAM, neuropharmacologist; b. Phila., Oct. 30, 1929; s. Jack and Sonia (Coopersmith) A.; m. Toby Wisotsky, June 28, 1953; children: Charles Howard, Eve Robin. BA, NYU, 1949; BS, Bklyn. Coll. Pharmacy, 1953; MS, Columbia U., 1957; PhD, Albert Einstein Coll. Medicine, 1960. Instr. Temple U. Sch. Medicine, Phila., 1960-63, asst. prof., 1963-66, assoc. prof., 1966-73, prof., 1973—; chmn. biomed. rsch. rev. com. Nat. Inst. on Drug Abuse, Rockville, Md., 1980-82, 89-93; exec. officer Coll. on Problems of Drug Dependence, Washington, 1986—. Author: 5 book chpts., 6 major revs.; editor: (book) Factors Affecting Action of Narcotic Drugs, 1976, Testing of Drugs of Abuse, 1990; contbr. over 100 articles to profl. publs. Sgt. U.S. Army, 1953-55, Korea. Grantee Nat. Inst. on Drug Abuse, 1973—, dir. tng. grant, 1989—. Fellow AAAS, Coll. on Problems of Drug Dependence, Am. Coll. Neuropsychopharmacology; mem. Am. Soc. Pharmacology and Exptl. Therapeutics. Jewish. Office: Temple U Sch Medicine 3420 N Broad St Philadelphia PA 19140-5104

ADLER, MILTON LEON, psychologist; b. Bronx, N.Y., June 11, 1926; s. Siegmund and Josephine (Eppsteiner) A.; m. Margrit Klein, Mar. 5, 1948; children: Sandra Ellen, Mark Lawrence. BS, Rutgers U., 1951; MS, CUNY, 1952; postgrad., NYU, 1952-53; PhD, U. Ill., 1963. Lic. psychologist, Ill. Psychiat. case worker N.J. Neuropsychiat. Inst., Blauenberg, 1953; clin. psychology intern, staff psychologist Manteno (Ill.) State Hosp., 1953-57; regional psychologist Ill. Inst. Juvenile Research, Champaign, 1957-66; sr. psychologist, clin. supr., subregion dir. Herman M. Adler Children's Center, Champaign, 1966-74; cons. psychologist Frederic Chusid and Co., Chgo., 1963-64; lectr. psychology Ill. State U., Normal, 1974-75; instr. psychology Parkland Coll., Champaign, 1979-80; pvt. practice clin. counseling, cons. psychology Urbana, Ill., 1965-90; mem. staff Cole Hosp., 1985-88; med. cons. Ill. Dept. Rehab. Svcs. and Disability Determination Svcs., 1986-90; presenter growth in groups seminars and workshops on personal growth and interpersonal relationships Stress Mgmt. Svcs. Contbr. workshops/seminars for community and profl. groups on anxiety, risk-taking/and interpersonal relationships, and personal growth, workshops on group psychotherapy to profl. insts. With USAAF, 1944-47. Fellow Am. Group Psychotherapy Assn. (mem. fellowship com. 1982—, dir. 1974-76, instr. tng. inst., mem. inst. com.); mem. Internat. Group Psychotherapy Assn., Ill. Assn. Maternal and Child Health (dir. bd. dirs. 1975-83, v.p. 1980-81, pres-elect 1981-82 pres. 1982-83, workshop, seminar presenter), Champaign-Urbana State Employees Assn. (past v.p., pres.), Ill. Group Psychotherapy Soc. (workshop presenter, council rep., awards of distinction 1977, 83, v.p., pres.-elect 1980-81, pres. 1982), Am. Psychol. Assn. (divs. psychotherapy, ind. practice, cons., community, humanistic group psychotherapy and family psychology), Nat. Assn. Sch. Psychologists, Am. Assn. for Counseling and Devel., Am. Assn. Mental Health Counselors, Ill. Psychol. Assn. (clin. sect.), Ill. Acad. Criminology, Ill. Assn. for Counseling and Devel., Ill. Assn. Mental Health Counselors, Nat. Assn. Disability Examiners, Am. Acad. Psychotherapists, Am. Legion, N. Am. Hunting Club, Phi Delta Kappa. Democrat. Unitarian-Universalist. Home: 1507 W University Ave Champaign IL 61821-3132

ADLER, VIVIAN A., nurse; b. N.Y.C., May 4, 1956; d. Erich R. and Amely (Zippert) A. BSN, Columbia U., 1979, MSN, 1986. Staff nurse, inpatient psychiatry Montefiore Med. Ctr., Bronx, N.Y.; nursing practitioner, psychiat. emergency rm. St. Luke's-Roosevelt Hosp., N.Y.C.; clin. nurse specialist Vets. Outreach Ctr., Bklyn., Queens Hosp. Ctr., Jamaica, N.Y., Bklyn. VA Med. Ctr., 1993—; HIV counselor, nusring educator, pvt. practitioner psychotherapy; asst. prof. Iona Coll. Sch. Nursing. Mem. Network of N.Y. Clin. Specialists Psychiat. Mental Health Nursing. Mem. ANA (cert. clin. specialist psychiat.-mental health adult nursing), N.Y. State Nurse's Assn.

ADLERSBERG, JAY BEN, internist, rheumatologist; b. Pitts., Nov. 25, 1944; s. Herman and Mathilda (Marshall) A.; 1 child, Zoe. BS magna cum laude, U. Pitts., 1965; MD, U. Pa., 1969. Diplomate Am. Bd. Internal Medicine, Nat. Bd. Med. Examiners. Intern in internal medicine NYU Med. Ctr., N.Y.C., 1969-70; jr. asst. resident, asst. resident medicine Bellevue Hosp., NYU Med. Ctr., N.Y.C., 1970-72; NIH fellow in rheumatology/immunology NYU Med. Ctr., N.Y.C., 1972-74; asst. prof. medicine divsn. rheumatic diseases/immunology Albert Einstein Coll. Medicine, Bronx, 1974-80; assoc. attending physician Bronx (N.Y.) Mcpl. Hosp. Ctr., 1976-80; attending physician Beth Israel Med. Ctr., N.Y.C., 1980—, Lenox Hill Hosp., N.Y.C., 1986—; asst. prof. medicine Mt. Sinai Sch. Medicine, N.Y.C., 1980—; assoc. attending physician Hosp. for Joint Diseases/Orthopaedic Inst., N.Y.C., 1980—; attending physician Hosp. Albert Einstein Coll. Medicine, 1974-80, Montefiore Hosp. Med. Ctr., Bronx, 1974-76; teaching asst. in medicine NYU Med. Ctr., 1972-74; teaching fellow in rheumatology Bellevue Hosp., 1972-74; keynote speaker Jonas Salk Scholarship Awards

CUNY, 1993. Contbg. corr. ABC News Now, 1992—; weekly med. corr. The Health Show, ABC, 1987-90; med. reporter Eyewitness News, WABC-TV, N.Y., 1984—; co-host Arthritis Telethon, WOR-TV, N.Y.C., 1982-86; guest host Healthline, WNYU-AM Radio, N.Y.C., 1980; contbr. weekly health column Bridgehampton (N.Y.) Sun, 1980-81. Master of ceremonies gala Cystic Fibrosis Found., 1990, S.I. Hospice Assn., 1990; mem. med. and sci. com. N.Y. chpt. Arthritis Found., 1985-88. Am. Cancer Soc. grantee, 1977-79. Fellow Am. Coll. Rheumatology; mem. AMA, N.Y. Acad. Scis., Am. Rheumatism Assn., N.Y. Rheumatism Assn., Med. Soc. County of N.Y., Med. Soc. State of N.Y., Phi Beta Kappa. Office: 220 E 69th St New York NY 10021-5737

ADMAN, RAYMOND LANCE, pathologist; b. Columbus, Ohio, Apr. 24, 1940. BS, Ohio U., 1961; PhD, Brandeis U., 1966; MD, Miami (Fla.) U., 1973. Diplomate Am. Bd. Pathology. Intern in medicine U. Wash., Seattle, 1973-74, resident in pathology and lab. medicine, 1974-78; pathologist Northgate Hosp., Seattle, 1982-83, Flagler Hosp., St. Augustine, Fla., 1984—. Comdr. USNR, 1979-81. Office: Flagler Hospital 400 Health Park Blvd Saint Augustine FL 32086

ADNOT, JOHN, micrographic surgeon, dermatologist; b. N.Y.C., Nov. 15, 1950. BS, Mercer U., 1973; MD, U. South Fla., 1976. Diplomate Am. Bd. Dermatology. Commd. officer U.S. Army, 1976, advanced through grades to lt. col., 1986; resident in family practice Madigan Army Med. Ctr., Tacoma, 1976-79; brigade surgeon 82nd Airborn Divsn., Ft. Bragg, N.C., 1979-82; resident in dermatology Brooke Army Med. Ctr., Ft. Sam Houston, Tex., 1982-85, fellow in Mohs micrographic surgery, 1986-87; chief medicine and dermatology U.S. Army Hosp., Ft. Leonard Wood, Mo., 1985-86; chief surg. unit dermatology svc. Fitzsimons Army Med. Ctr., Aurora, Colo., 1987-89; resigned U.S. Army, 1989; pvt. practice, Ft. Worth, 1989—. Contbr. articles to med. jours. Fellow Am. Acad. Dermatology, Am. Soc. for Dermatologic Surgery, Am. Coll. Mohs Micrographic Surgery and Cutaneous Oncology; mem. AMA, Tex. Med. Assn., Tarrant County Med. Assn., North Tex. Dermatol. Surg. Soc. (pres. 1995-96). Office: 4200 S Hulen St Ste 400 Fort Worth TX 76109-4911

ADOLPHSON, PER YNGVE, orthopaedic surgeon; b. Stockholm, May 2, 1951; s. Yngue Karl and Lilian Ester (Jonsson) A.; divorced; children, Dan, Ulf. Med. Cert., Karolinska Inst., Stockholm, 1978, DMS, 1992, PhD. Cert. orthopaedic surgeon. Specialist in orthopaedic surgery Karolinska Inst., Stockholm, 1983. Contbr. articles to med. jours. Mem. Swedish Orthopaedic Assn. Office: Danderyd Hosp, S-18288 Stockholm Danderyd, Sweden

ADOM, EDWIN NII AMALAI, psychiatrist; b. Accra, Ghana, West Africa, Jan. 12, 1941; came to U.S., 1960; s. Isaac Quaye and Julianna Adorkor (Brown) Adom; m. Margaret Odarkor Lamptey; children: Edwin Nii Nortey Jr., Isaac Michael Nii Nortei. BA, U. Pa., 1963; MD, Meharry Med. Coll., 1968; FRSH (Eng.), Royal Soc. Health, 1974. Diplomate Am. Bd. Psychiatry and Neurology. Intern Pa. Hosp., Phila., 1968-69; resident in psychiatry Thomas Jefferson U. Med. Ctr., Phila., 1969-72; clin. asst. prof. psychiatry U. Pa. Sch. Medicine, Phila., 1972—; cons. psychiatrist St. Joseph Hosp., Phila., 1976-80, Stephen Smith Home for the Aged, Phila., 1976-85, Mercy Douglas Human Svcs. Ctr., Phila., 1977-79, St. Ignatius Home for the Aged, Phila., 1978-85; attending psychiatrist Belmont Ctr. for Comprehensive Health Care, 1987—; cons. psychiatrist psycho-social dept. Horizon House Rehab. Ctr., Phila., 1987-89; cons. psychiatrist U.S. Dept. Labor, Workmen's Compensation Div., Phila., 1987—, House Staff of the U. Pa. Hosp., Phila., 1989—; cons. The Grad. Hosp., Phila., 1976—; with State of Pa. Bur. Disability Determination, 1975—; attending psychiatrist West Phila. Mental Health Consortium, 1972—, med. dirs., 1991—. Ghana Govt. scholar U. Pa., 1960-68; recipient Citizen Citation Chapel of the Four Chaplains, 1974; named to African Am. Wall of Fame, Phila. Fellow Royal Soc. Health (Eng.), Thomas Bond Soc.; mem. Am. Psychiat. Assn., Am. Acad. Psychiatry and the Law, Nat. Med. Assn. (Black Pioneers in Medicine), Black Psychiatrists Am. (exec. 1975-77), Am. Soc. Clin. Psychopharmacology, Pa. Psychiat. Soc., Med. Soc. Ea. Pa., Phila. Psychiat. Soc., N.Y. Acad. Sci., World Fedn. Mental Health, Phila. Acad. Family Psychiatrists, Nat. Geog. Soc. Presbyterian. Office: Med Towers 255 S 17th St Ste # 2704 Philadelphia PA 19103-6227

ADREON, BEATRICE MARIE RICE, pharmacist; b. Huntington, W.Va., July 23, 1929; d. Lloyd Emerson and Beatrice (Odell) Rice; student Mary Washington Coll., 1947-49; B.S. in Pharmacy, Med. Coll. Va., 1952; M.A. in Spl. Studies and Women's Studies, George Washington U., 1976; m. Harry Barnes Adreon, Jr., Dec. 27, 1952. Summer vol. worker pharmacies De Paul Hosp., Norfolk, Va., 1949, U.S. Marine Hosp., Norfolk, 1950; pharmacist Washington Clinic, 1954-71; counselor George Washington U., 1976-77, cons. gerontology health scis. dept., 1977—; cons. medicine control traffic patterns nursing homes Cross & Adreon, Washington, 1962-87; founder, pres. Pharmacy Counseling Services, Inc., 1978—. Instr. advanced first aid ARC, 1952—, civil def. instr., 1952—; vol. Spanish Edn. Devel. Center, Washington, 1972; mem. Arlington (Va.) Community Services Bd., 1980-83; chmn. com. substance abuse. Recipient Arnold and Marie Schwartz award in pharmacy, 1980. Mem. Acad. Pharmacy Practice and Mgmt., Am. Pharm. Assn., Va. Pharm. Assn., Potomac Pharmacists Assn., Am. Inst. History of Pharmacy, Nat. Council Patient Info. and Edn. (task force pub. info.), Panhellenic Assn., Kappa Epsilon. Episcopalian (mem. bishop's com. neighborhood services 1967-69, chmn. services for aged div. 1967-69). Contbr. articles in field to profl. jours. Home: 4524 19th Rd N Arlington VA 22207-2352 Office: Pharmacy Counseling Svcs Inc 950 N Glebe Rd # 140 Arlington VA 22203-1824

ADRIAN, ERLE KEYS, JR., anatomist, educator; b. Temple, Tex., Apr. 18, 1936; s. Erle Keys and Gladys Lillian (Posey) A.; m. Gwendolyn Margaret Scharlach, July 27, 1962; children: Sabrina Lynn, Erle Paul, Don Arthur. BA, Rice U., 1958; MA, U. Tex., Galveston, 1961, PhD, 1967; MD, Harvard U., 1963. Lic. Bd. Med. Examiners, Tex. Instr. in anatomy med. br. U. Tex., Galveston, 1963-65, from asst. to assoc. prof. med. br., 1965-69; assoc. prof. Health Sci. Ctr. S.A. U. Tex., San Antonio, 1969-74, prof. Health Sci. Ctr. S.A., 1974—, acting chmn. dept. anatomy Health Sci. Ctr. S.A., 1980-81, dep. chmn. dept. cellular and structural biology Health Sci. Ctr. S.A., 1981—. Author several book chpts., teaching films; contbr. articles to profl. jours. Trustee Boerne (Tex.) Ind. Sch. Bd., 1974-77, 79-82. USPHS grantee, 1969-79. Mem. Am. Assn. Anatomists. Democrat. Methodist.

ADROUNIE, V. HARRY, public health administrator, scientist, educator, environmentalist; b. Battle Creek, Mich., Apr. 29, 1915; s. Haroutune Asadour and Dorthy (Kalaidjian) A.; m. Emalea Riley, June, 1943 (div. Jan. 1980); children: Harry Michael, Vee Patrick; m. Agnes M. Slone, June 26, 1981. BS, St. Ambrose U., 1940, BA, 1959; MS in Environ. Health, Western States U. Profl. Studies, 1984, PhD in Environ. Health, 1984, PhD in Pub. Health, 1984. Diplomate Am. Bd. Indsl. Hygiene, Am. Acad. Sanitarians; registered sanitarian, Calif., Mich., Pa., N.C. Enlisted U.S. Army, 1941, commd. 2nd. lt., 1943; advanced through grades to lt. col. USAF, ret., 1968; tech. dir. ARA Environ. Svcs., 1968-70; dir. environ. health div. Chester County (Pa.) Health Dept., 1970-75, Berrien County (Mich.) Health Dept., 1975-78; prof. environ. health Sch. Pub. Health U. Hawaii, Manoa, 1978-80; dean, prof. Sch. Pub. Health, Western States U. Profl. Studies, Mo., 1980-83; ret., 1983; vis. prof. environ. and pub. health Am. U., Armenia, 1995; USAF rep. U.S. Interdepartmental Com. on Nutrition for Nat. Def., 1959-61; cons. Health Mobilization Program USPHS Surgeon Gen., 1961-62; mem. USAF Surgeon Gen.'s med. goodwill tour all S.Am. countries, 1960; chmn., vis. assoc. prof. dept. environ. health Am. U. Beirut, 1963-66, chmn. dept. environ. health, 1964-66; charter mem. RSH-UN Welfare Relief Agy. Pub. Health Examining Bd. for Mid. East, 1963-66, UNWRA cons., 1964-66; founder, coord. 1st and 2d Environ. Health Symposium of Mid. East, 1965-66; mem. Mich. Hazardous Waste Policy Com., 1990-91, Mich. Mustfa Fin. Policy Bd., 1994—; adj. instr., mem. adv. com. environ. health Ferris State Coll., Big Rapids, Mich., 1974-75, 77-78. Contbr. numerous articles to profl. jours.; author many manuals and tng. booklets for USAF and several books. Mem. environ. issues com. Bush for Pres. Campaign, Washington, 1988; co-chmn. Barry County (Mich.) Bush for Pres. Campaign, Barry County Abraham for U.S. Senate Campaign, 1994; chmn. Barry County Solid Waste Planning and Oversight com., 1981—; vice chmn. Hastings City Planning Commn., 1984—; mem., co-founder sci. adv. and policy bd. Mich. Ground Water Survey, Inc., 1983—, chmn., 1988-91; chmn. adv. coun. South Ctrl. Mich. Commn. on Aging, 1981-91; mem. UL Underwriters adv. coun. environ. and pub. health, 1996—; past adult leader Boy Scouts Am. Decorated Legion of Merit, USAF; named Alumnus of Yr., Hastings H.S., 1961; recipient Walter S. Mangold award Nat. Environ. Health Assn., 1963, spl. recognition Mich. Environ. Health Assn., 1980, Concerned Citizen award World Safety Orgn., 1992, Safety Person of World Safety Orgn., 1992, Safety Person of Yr. award World Safety Orgn., 1993. Mem. VFW (life), APHA (emeritus v.p., emeritus conf. 1993, pres.-elect 1994-95, pres. 1995-97), Mich. Assn. Local Environ. Health Adminstrs. (pres., founder 1976), Nat. Environ. Health Assn. (life, pres. 1961-62), Assn. Mil. Surgeons U.S. (life), Internat. Pub. Health Soc. (charter-emeritus), Nat. Coun. Internat. Health, NRA (life, cert. rifle marksmanship instr.), World Safety Orgn. (bd. dirs. 1986-95, cert. bd. 1987—, editl. bd. 1988—), Mich. Environ. Health Assn. (pres. 1991-92), Air Force Assn., Am. Legion (comdr. 1989-90), Indonesian Environ. Health Assn. (co-founder), Lions, Elks (life), Moose, Kiwanis (pres. 1985-86). Home: 1905 N Broadway Hastings MI 49058-1056

ADWERS, JAMES ROBERT, medical director, physician, surgeon; b. Omaha, May 8, 1943; s. Robert E. and Mary (Heagy) A.; m. Mary Shaffer, Nov. 28, 1964; children: John Bradley, Ryan James. BS in Medicine, U. Nebr., 1965, MD, 1969. Diplomate Am. Bd. Surgery. Intern U. Nebr. Med. Ctr., Omaha, 1969-70, chief resident surgery, 1973-74; pvt. practice surgery Omaha, 1976-90; med. dir. Technomed Internat., Danvers, Mass., 1990-92, Becton Dickinson Acute Care, Franklin Lakes, N.J., 1992-95; regional v.p. corp. med. affairs dept. surg. group C.R. Bard, Inc., Murray Hill, N.J., 1995—. Maj. U.S. Army Med. Corps, 1974-76. Fellow ACS, ACP (execs.), Am. Coll. Gastroenterology; mem. AMA, Am. Soc. for Minimally Invasive Surgery. Republican. Episcopalian. Office: CR Bard Inc 730 Central Ave Murray Hill NJ 07974

AFFELDT, JOHN ELLSWORTH, physician; b. Lansing, Mich., May 26, 1918; s. John Ferdin and Pearl Heald (Gardner) A.; m. Nancy Faye Spomer, Sept. 2, 1942; children—John C., Elizabeth Affeldt Westberg, Cindy L. B.S., Andrews U., Berrien Springs, Mich., 1939; M.D., Loma Linda (Calif.) U., 1944. Intern Detroit Gen. Hosp., 1943-44; resident in internal medicine White Meml. Hosp., Los Angeles, 1946-49; fellow in pulmonary physiology Harvard Sch. Pub. Health, 1949-51; med. dir. Rancho Los Amigos Hosp., Downey, Calif., 1956-64, Los Angeles County Dept. Hosps., 1964-72, Los Angeles County Dept. Health Services, 1972-77; pres. Joint Commn. Accreditation Hosps., Chgo., 1977-86; med. advisor Beverly Enterprises, Pasadena, Calif., 1986—. Served with AUS, 1944-47. Mem. AMA, ACP, Am. Congress Rehab. Medicine, Inst. Medicine Western Soc. Clin. Rsch., L.A. County Med. Assn., Calif. Assn. Med. Dirs. (pres. 1993-94). Home: 5140 Bareback Sq PO Box 8432 Rancho Santa Fe CA 92067-8432

AFFONSO, DYANNE D., dean, nursing educator. BSN, U. Hawaii, 1966; MN in Nursing, U. Wash., 1967; MA in Clin. Psychology, U. Ariz., 1980, PhD in Clin. Psychology, 1982. Asst. prof. sch. nursing U. Miss., 1967-68; OB staff nurse, night charge nurse Kinchloe AFB Hosp., Mich., 1968-70; instr. sch. nursing U. Hawaii, 1970-73; asst. prof. coll. nursing U. Ariz., 1974-77, assoc. prof. coll. nursing, 1978, coord. psychiatric mental health nursing coll. nursing, 1982-84, joint appointment in psychology dept. psychology, 1983; assoc. prof. sch. nursing U. Calif., San Francisco, 1984-87, prof. sch. nursing, 1988; prof., dean sch. nursing Emory U., Atlanta, 1993—, assoc. prof. women's & children's divsn. sch. pub. health, 1993—. Contbr. articles to profl. jours.; presenter in field. Mem. NAS (mem. inst. medicine 1994), NIH (mem. adv. coun. nat. inst. child health & human devel. 1979-83, mem. agenda com. nat. inst. child health & human devel. 1982, mem. scientific rev. com. nat. ctr. nursing rsch. 1986, mem. adv. coun. nat. ctr. nursing rsch. 1986-88, mem. steering com. rsch. patient outcomes nat. ctr. nursing rsch. 1991, sec.'s conf. 1993, charter mem. adcv. coun. office rsch. on women's health 1995). Office: Emory U Sch Nursing Atlanta GA 30322-1100*

AFFRONTI, LEWIS FRANCIS, SR., microbiologist, educator; b. Rochester, N.Y., Aug. 12, 1928; s. John and Mary (Least) A.; m. Aileen Ledford, June 2, 1956; children—John, Lewis, Mary Louise, Eileen. BA, U. Buffalo, 1950, MA, 1951; PhD, Duke U., 1958. Rsch. assoc. Buffalo VA Hosp., 1951-52, Roswell Meml. Cancer Inst., 1954, TB Henry Phipps Inst. U. Pa., 1957-58; asst. prof. Sch. Medicine, George Washington U., Washington, 1962-65, assoc. prof., 1965-72, prof. microbiology, 1972-93; prof. emeritus, 1994—; chmn. dept. microbiology Sch. Medicine, George Washington U., Washington, 1973-93; cons. AVCO Rsch. Corp., VA Hosp., Martinsburg, W.Va., VA Hosp. Ctr., Wilmington, Del.; U.S. rep. WHO Conf. on Skin Test Antigens and Vaccines, Geneva, 1966; mem. med. adv. bd. VA, Wilmington. Mem. editorial bd. Infection and Immunity, 1972-78. Commd. officer USPHS, 1958-62; served with USAF, 1952-54. NIH Spl. fellow, 1969; Nat. Tb fellow for Internat. Conf. on Tb Moscow, 1971; Nat. Tb fellow for Internat. Conf. on Tb Tokyo, 1973; Washington Acad. Sci. fellow; Recipient WHO Exchange Rsch. Workers award, 1970, Scientist Emeritus award Soc. Expl. Biology & Medicine, Washington, 1994; interacad. exchange program award Nat. Acad. Sci., 1980. Fellow Am. Acad. Microbiology, Assn. Med. Sch. Microbiology Chmn. (sec.-treas. 1976-86, bd. dirs. 1976-86), Washington Acad. Sci.; mem. Am. Soc. Microbiology, Am. Assn. Immunologists, Reticuloendothelial Soc., Am. Thoracic Soc., Assembly on Microbiologists and Immunologists (sec. 1971-72), The Protein Soc., Toastmasters Internat. (Atlanta), KC, Sigma Xi (local pres. 1986-87). Office: George Washington U Med Ctr Dept Microbiology 2300 I St NW Washington DC 20037-2337

AFIELD, WALTER EDWARD, psychiatrist, service executive; b. N.Y.C., Dec. 28, 1935; s. Walter Edward and Mollie Evelyn (MCGovern) A.; m. Nancy Browning, Dec. 27, 1973; children: Walter Edward, Neva Browning. AB, U. Pa., 1956; MD, Johns Hopkins U., 1960. Intern Grady Meml. Hosp., Atlanta, 1960-61; fellow in psychiatry Harvard U., Cambridge, Mass., 1961-64, 66-67; asst. prof. psychiatry Johns Hopkins U., Balt., 1967-70, dir. dept. child psychiatry, 1967-70; prof. U. South Fla. Coll. Medicine, 1970-74, chmn. dept. psychiatry, 1970-74; exec. dir. Tampa Bay Neuropsychiat. Inst., Tampa, Fla., 1970—; chmn., chief exec. officer The Mental Health Programs Corp., Tampa, 1985-92. Author: The Children of Resurrection City, 1970; contbr. articles to profl. jours. Pres. Fla. Lyric Opera, 1976—. Capt. USAF, 1964-66. Fellow Am. Coll. Psychiatrists; mem. AMA, Am. Acad. Neurology, University Club, Tampa Yacht Club. Republican. Roman Catholic. Home: 4619 W Bay To Bay Blvd Tampa FL 33629-7610 Office: 5820 W Cypress Ste B Tampa FL 33607-2369

AFKARI, ELIZABETH ANN, geriatrics nurse, administrator; b. Lawrence, Mass., July 3, 1932; d. Raymond F. and Pearl (Frye) Taylor; m. Iraj Afkari, Aug. 3, 1963 (div.); 1 child, Semene Anne. Diploma, Presbyn. Hosp., N.Y.C., 1956; BSN, Columbia U., 1957, EdM, 1967. Cert. gerontol. nurse. Dir. nursing and allied health Passaic County Community Coll., Paterson, N.J.; asst. dir. nursing for staff devel. Sinai Hosp. of Balt.; instr. U. Md., Balt.; diabetes edn. coord. VA Med. Ctr., Ft. Howard, Md. Mem. ANA, Md. Nurses Assn. (fin. com. Dist. 2 1989), Huntington's Soc. Am. (treas., v.p., pres.-elect Md. chpt.), Pi Lambda Theta, Kappa Delta Pi. Home: 382 Ellsworth Pl Joppa MD 21085-3808

AFLAGUE, JOHN M., mental health nurse, educator, administrator; s. N.G. and Helen (Morris) A. Diploma in Nursing, Mt. Auburn Hosp. Sch. Nursing, Cambridge, Mass., 1977; BSN magna cum laude, Northeastern U., Boston, 1980; MS in Psychiat. and Mental Health Nursing, Boston U., 1987; postgrad., 1992—. RN, Mass. Staff nurse Mt. Auburn Hosp., Cambridge, 1977-80, Tobey Hosp., Wareham, Mass., 1980-81, Northeastern U., Boston, 1981-95, Mass. Gen. Hosp., Boston, 1984-95; dir., asst. prof., coord. psychiat. mental health nursing Lasell Coll., Newton, Mass., 1995—; instr., clin. supr. Medford (Mass.) Pub. Schs., 1979; lectr., clin. instr. Shepard-Gill Sch. Practical Nursing, Mass. Gen. Hosp., 1982-84, Laboure Coll., 1987, 92-94, Quincy (Mass.) Coll., 1991-94, Mass. Bay C.C., Wellesley Hills, 1991-94; clin. instr. acad. advisor Boston U. Sch. Nursing, 1987-88; lectr., lab. instr. Roxbury C.C., Boston, 1991-94; baccalaureate curriculum com. Northeastern U., Boston, 1979-80, psychiat. clin. nurse specialist, 1994-95, coord. psychiat. /mental health svcs., 1994-95; patient tchg. com. Mass. Gen. Hosp., 1984-85; instr. Simmons Coll., Boston, 1992-94; psychosocial cons. Curry Coll., Milton, Mass., 1993-94; cons. and lectr. in field. Vol. local chpt. Am. Cancer Soc., action com. AIDS, Boston. Thorne Found. scholar, 1976. Mem. ANA (cert. clin. specialist adult psychiat./mental health nursing 1988), Am. Coll. Health Assn., Nat. League for Nursing, Mass. Nurses Assn., Mass. Coalition Nurse Practitioners, Upper Cape Cod RN's Assn. (scholar 1977), Mt. Auburn Hosp. Nurses Alumnae Assn. (v.p. 1977-78, scholar for clin. and acad. excellence 1977), Nat. League for Nursing, Sigma Theta Tau. Home: 148 Lagrange St Boston MA 02132-3023 Office: Lasell Coll Newton MA 02166

AFRA, FUESUN, dentist, orthodontist; b. Istanbul, Turkey, Oct. 1, 1965; arrived in Germany, 1970; d. Ahmet Nihat and Gueler (Ozcelikel) Evic; m. Sina M. Afra, Jan. 18, 1996. Abitur, Recklinghausen, Germany, 1986; dentist degree, Goetting U., Germany, 1992; orthodontist degree, Cologne (Germany) U., 1996. Dentist Lange & Ptnrs., Germany, 1992-94; orthodontic asst. Cologne U., 1994—. Bd. dirs. German-Turkish Chamber Medicine, 1993-96. Office: U Cologne, Kerpernestr 32, 50932 Cologne Germany

AFZELIUS, BJÖRN ARVID, cell biology educator; b. Stockholm, Sweden, June 30, 1925; s. Nils Arvid and Margarethe (Thirring) A.; m. Ulla Elisabeth Fogelberg, May 24, 1957; children: Görel T.E., Boel A.M. PhD, Stockholm U., Sweden, 1957; MD (hon.), Karolinska Inst., Stockholm, 1981; PhD (hon.), U. Siena, Italy, 1986. Rsch. fellow Johns Hopkins U., Balt., 1957-58; lectr. Stockholm U., 1958-68, prof., 1968—. Author: Anatomy of the Cell, 1966. Home: Docentbacken 15, S-10405 Stockholm Sweden

AGALLIANOS, DENNIS DIONYSIOS, psychiatrist; b. Galati, Romania, Jan. 1, 1923; came to U.S., 1957; s. Dionysios Nicholas and Eleni (Craciun) A.; m. Georgia-Lee Virginia Foden, June 20, 1964; 1 child, Helen Penelope. BA, Classical Gymnasium, Galati, Romania, 1941; MD, Victor Babes Med. Sch., Cluj, Romania, 1948. Diplomate Am. Bd. Psychiatry and Neurology. Gen. practice Rumania, 1948-49; staff physician Polikliniki Athinon, Athens, Greece, 1954-56; intern, resident French Hosp., N.Y.C., 1957-58; resident in psychiatry Brattleboro Retreat, 1958-60; resident and staff psychiatrist Spring Grove State Hosp., Balt., 1960-64, chief of div., 1965-68; staff psychiatrist Brattleboro (Vt.) Retreat, 1969-71, chief of admission svc., 1971-75, chief of profl. svc., 1976-80, dir. older adult program, 1980-92; asst. prof. clin. psychiatry Dartmouth Med. Sch., Hanover, N.H., 1978-95,, 1995—; Brattleboro (Vt.) Retreat, 1980-92, Mental Health Svcs. of Southeastern Vt., 1992-95, Brattleboro, 1992—. Contbr. various articles to profl. jours. Pres. Parish Council St. George Greek Orthodox Ch., Keene, N.H., 1985-86; sustaining mem. Greek Orthodox Archdiocese of North and South Am., 1966—; founding father United Greek Orthodox Charities, 1967. Recipient Grant NIMH; Exemplary Psychiatrist award Nat. Alliance Mentally Ill, 1994. Fellow Am. Psychiat. Assn. (life), AMA, Vt. Psychiat. Assn., Vt. State Med. Soc. Greek Orthodox. Home: PO Box 759 Brattleboro VT 05302-0759 Office: Brattleboro Retreat 75 Linden St Brattleboro VT 05301-0803

AGARD, EMMA ESTORNEL, psychotherapist; b. Bronx, N.Y.. BA, Queens Coll.; MSW, Fordham U., 1962; cert. in Psychoanalytic Psychotherapy, Tng. Inst. for Mental Health, 1979; cert. in Child and Adolescent Psychotherapy, Postgrad. Ctr. for Mental Health, 1982. Supr. social work Foster Care Div., N.Y.C., 1968-72; asst. dir. Henry St. Settlement Urban Family Ctr., N.Y.C., 1972-74; tng. analyst, sr. supr. Tng. Inst. for Mental Health, N.Y.C., 1974—; pvt. practice psychotherapist N.Y.C., 1974—; lectr. social work Columbia U., N.Y.C., 1977-90; adj. asst. prof. NYU, 1978-80; field instr. N.Y.C. Housing Authority, 1974-80; dist. dir., cons. Am. Consultation Ctrs., Bklyn. and N.Y.C., 1985—, dir. Park Slope br. Mem. Albemarle-Kenmore Neighborhood Assn., Bklyn., 1974—, dir. Park Slope br. Fellow N.Y. State Soc. Clin. Social Work Psychotherapists (pres. Bklyn. chpt. 1988-91); mem. Profl. Soc. Tng. Inst. for Mental Health (sec.), Nat. Assn. Social Workers (diplomate), Acad. Cert. Social Workers, Nat. Coalition 100 Black Women, Delta Sigma Theta. Address: 221 E 21st St Brooklyn NY 11226-3903

AGEE, JAMES EVERETT, urologist; b. Detroit, Nov. 11, 1954; s. James Lawrence and Joan Carol (Klink) A.; m. Kristy Rene Richardson, Oct. 19, 1991; 1 child, Henry. BS, U. Pa., 1976; MD, U. Mich., 1980. Diplomate Am. Bd. Urology. Intern U. Calif., Davis, 1980-81, resident, 1981-82; resident U. Cin., 1982-85; urologist Beaver Med. Clinic, Redlands, Calif., 1985—. Office: Beaver Medical Clinic PO Box 3001 Redlands CA 92373-0307

AGHAJANIAN, GEORGE KEVORK, medical educator; b. Beirut, Apr. 14, 1932; father Am. citizen; s. Ghevont M. and Araxi (Movsessian) A.; m. Anne E. Hammond, Jan. 10, 1959; children: Michael, Andrew, Carol, Laura. AB, Cornell U., 1954; MD, Yale U., 1958. Asst. prof. psychiatry Sch. of Medicine Yale U., New Haven, 1965-68, assoc. prof. psychiatry Sch. of Medicine, 1968-70, assoc. prof. psychiatry and pharmacology Sch. of Medicine, 1970-74, prof. psychiatry and pharmacology Sch. of Medicine, 1974—, founds. fund prof. Sch. of Medicine, 1985. Contbr. more than 275 articles to profl. jours. Capt. U.S. Army, 1963-65. Recipient Founds. Fund Rsch. prize Am. Psychiat. Assn., 1981, Scheele medal Swedish Acad. Pharmacy, 1981, Merit award NIH, 1990-2000. Fellow Am. Coll. Neuropsychopharmacology (Efron award 1975); mem. Soc. for Pharmacology and Exptl. Therapeutics, Soc. for Neurosci., Internat. Brain Rsch. Orgn. Office: 34 Park St New Haven CT 06519-1109

AGID, YVES ALEXANDRE, medical educator; b. Nile, France, Nov. 13, 1940; s. René and Sylvia (Gadd) A.; m. France Basdevant, June 18, 1976; children: Isabelle, David. MD, U. Paris, 1973, cert. neuropsychiatry, 1973, DSc, 1976. Intern Paris, 1967, chief de clinique, 1973, assoc. prof. exptl. medicine, 1979-85, prof. cell biology, 1985; dir. INSERM, Paris, 1985; chef de svc. C.H.U. Pitie-Salpetrière, Paris, 1994—; prof. medicine Classe Exceptionelle, Paris, 1992. Lt. French Med. Svc., 1967-68. Recipient Prix de l'Academie des Scis., 1983, Prix de l'Academie de Medecine, 1994, Prix Athena, 1994. Home: 25 bis rue de Ecoles, 75005 Paris France Office: Fedn Neurologie Groupe Hosp, Pitie-Salpetriere, 75651 Paris France

AGLIETTA, MASSIMO, medical educator; b. Biella, Italy, Dec. 30, 1951; s. Attilio Aglietta and Iride Baietto; m. Franca Fagioli, 1993; 1 child, Anna. MD, Turin (Italy) Med. Sch., 1976, specialist in internal medicine, 1981; specialist in oncology, Parma (Italy) Med. Sch., 1986. Rsch. fellow Radiobiol. Inst., Rijswijk, The Netherlands, 1976-78, Favretto Found., Turin, 1978-80; from asst. prof. to assoc. prof. U. Turin Med. Sch., 1980-90, prof., 1990—; head internal medicine dept. Turin U. II Med. Sch., Novara, Italy, 1990. Author: Myeloproliferative Diseases, 1987; contbr. over 150 sci. articles to profl. jours. Recipient Banno prize, 1989. Mem. Italian Soc. Cancer (councilor 1991—), Italian Soc. Ematologia Sp. (councilor 1991—), Internat. Soc. Hematology, Internat. Soc. Exptl. Hematology, Rotary Club Novara. Home: Via Dolores Bello 2, 28100 Novara Italy Office: Clinica Medica Univ, Via Mazzini 18, 28100 Novara Italy

AGORASTOS, THEODOROS, obstetrics and gynecology educator; b. Drama, Macedonia, Greece, Dec. 31, 1951; s. Agorastos and Paraskevi (Kassimidou) A.; m. Ioanna Ikonomou, July 27, 1977; 1 child, Agorastos. Diploma in medicine, Aristotelian U. Thessaloniki, Greece, 1975; MD U. Aachen, Germany, 1979. Jr. registrar dept. ob-gyn U. Aachen, 1975-81; lectr. Aristotelian U. Thessaloniki, 1982-87, asst. prof., 1987—; sec. gen. 4th Greek Congress Ob-Gyn, 1988. Author, editor: Fetale Epidermis und Vernix c., 1989, Handbook of Cardiotocography, 1991. With Greek Navy, 1981-82. Scholar Aristotelian U. Thessaloniki, 1970-71, German Acad. Exch. Svc., 1984, 86; fellow Alexander von Humboldt Found., Graz, Austria, Aachen, Stockholm, 1989-90; grantee Volkswagen Found., 1991. Mem. European Soc. Human Reprodn. and Embryology, European Assn. Gynecologists and Obstetricians, German Soc. Ob-Gyn, Greek Soc. Ob-Gyn (assoc. editor Hellenic Ob-Gyn 1985-94), Greek Soc. Gynecologic Oncology. Home: 87 Mitropoleos St, 546 22 Thessaloniki Greece Office: Hipprokrateion Hosp O-G Cl, 50 Papanastassiou St, 546 39 Thessaloniki Greece

AGRANOFF, BERNARD WILLIAM, biochemist, educator; b. Detroit, June 26, 1926; s. William and Phyllis (Pelavin) A.; m. Raquel Betty Schwartz, Sept. 1, 1957; children: William, Adam. MD, Wayne State U.,

1950; BS, U. Mich., 1954. Intern Robert Packer Hosp., Sayre, Pa., 1950-51; commd. surgeon USPHS, 1954-60; biochemist Nat. Inst. Neurol. Diseases and Blindness, NIH, Bethesda, Md., 1954-60; mem. faculty U. Mich., Ann Arbor, 1960—, prof. biochemistry, 1965—; R.W. Gerard prof. of neurosci. in psychiatry, 1991; rsch. biochemist Mental Health Rsch. Inst., 1960—, assoc. dir., 1977-83, dir. 1983-95, dir. neurosci. lab., 1983—; vis. scientist Max Planck Inst. Zellchemie, Munich, 1957-58, Nat. Inst. Med. Rsch., Mine Hill, Eng., 1974-75; Henry Russel lectr. U. Mich., 1987; cons. pharm. industry, govt. Contbr. articles to profl. jours. Fogarty scholar-in-residence NIH, Bethesda, Md., 1989-95; named Mich. Scientist of Yr. Mus. of Sci., Lansing, 1992. Fellow Am. Coll. Neuropsychopharmacology; mem. Am. Soc. Biochemistry and Molecular Biology, Am. Chem. Soc., Inst. Medicine, Internat. Soc. Neurochemistry (treas. 1985-89, chmn. 1989-91), Am. Soc. Neurochemistry (pres. 1973-75). Home: 1942 Boulder Dr Ann Arbor MI 48104-4164 Office: U Mich Neurosci Lab 1103 E Huron St Ann Arbor MI 48104-1630

AGRAWAL, KRISHNA CHANDRA, pharmacology educator; b. Calcutta, India, Mar. 15, 1937; naturalized; s. Prasadi Lal and Asarfi Devi (Agrawal) A.; m. Mani Agrawal, Dec. 2, 1960; children—Sunil, Lina, Nira. B.S. in Pharmacy, Andhra U., Waltair, India, 1959, M.S., 1960; Ph.D., U. Fla., 1965. Cert. in pharm. chemistry. Research assoc. dept. pharmacology Yale U. Sch. Medicine, New Haven, 1966-69, instr., 1969-70, asst. prof., 1970-76, assoc. prof., 1976; assoc. prof. dept. pharmacology Tulane U. Sch. Medicine, New Orleans, 1976-81, prof., 1981—; cons. mem. Southeastern Cancer Study Group, 1980-85; mem. adv. com. on instnl. grants Am. Cancer Soc., 1980-85; mem. AIDS and Related Rsch. Rev. Group NIH, 1989-94. Conbr. articles to profl. jours.; patentee radiosensitizers for hypoxic tumor cells and compositions; novel AZT analogs. Grantee Nat. Cancer Inst., 1976-89, WHO, 1979-82, La. Bd. Regents, 1981-82, Nat. Inst. Allergy and Infectious Diseases, 1987—, Dept. Def., 1994—. Fellow Am. Inst. Chemists; mem. Am. Chem. Soc., Am. Assn. Cancer Rsch., Internat. Soc. Antiviral Rsch., Radiation Rsch. Soc., Am. Soc. Pharmacology and Exptl. Therapeutics, Am. Soc. Hematology, Sigma Xi. Home: 26 Olympic Ct New Orleans LA 70131-8614 Office: Tulane U Sch Medicine Dept Pharmacology New Orleans LA 70112

AGRESTI, MIRIAM MONELL, psychologist; b. N.Y.C., Mar. 23, 1926; d. James McCloud and Marion Henrietta (Zippel) Monell; children: Robert, Carol. BS, Queens Coll., 1947; MA in Sci. Edn., Columbia U., 1949; PhD in Clin. Psychology, Yeshiva U., 1976; postgrad., Ackerman Inst. Family Therapy, 1977-81, L.I. Jewish Hosp. Human Sexuality Ctr. Psychology intern Creedmoor Psychiat. Center, Queens, N.Y., 1963-64, family therapist, 1964-69; psychologist Northeast Nassau Psychiat. Ctr., Kings Park, N.Y., 1969-72; adminstrv. dir. Friendship House Day Hosp., Glen Cove, N.Y., 1972-74; psychologist and team leader Ctrl. Islip (N.Y.) Psychiat. Ctr., 1974-75; tchr., coord. family therapy program Pilgrim Psychiat. Ctr., West Brentwood, N.Y., 1976-80; pvt. practice psychotherapy, 1977—; pres. Nassau County Med. Ctr., 1990-95; co-dir. L.I. Family Inst., 1976-79; cons. family therapy Cath. Charities, 1979, St. Vincent's Hall, 1979, Nassau County Mental Health Assn., 1980; adj. faculty Sch. Edn., C.W. Post Coll., L.I. U., 1972, CUNY, 1978-80, St. John's U., 1983, Hofstra U., 1985-88. Exec. dir. movie/videotape Beware the Gaps in Medical Care for Older People (1st prize Am. Film Festival). Lic. psychologist, N.Y. Diplomate Am. Bd. Family Psychology (fellow, pres. 1984-85). Fellow Am. Orthopsychiat. Assn., Internat. Council Sex Edn. and Parenthood of Am. U.; mem. APA, N.Y. State Psychol. Assn., Nassau County Psychol. Assn., Suffolk County Psychol. Assn., Am. Assn. for Marriage and Family Therapy (pres. L.I. chpt. 1981-83, sec. N.Y. state divsn. 1996—), Am. Orthopsychiat. Assn., Pi Lambda Theta. Unitarian. Address: 11 Wren Dr Woodbury NY 11797-3212

AGRUSS, NEIL STUART, cardiologist; b. Chgo., June 2, 1939; s. Meyer and Frances (Spector) A.; B.S., U. Ill., 1960, M.D., 1963; m. Teresa Marie Stafford; children—David, Lauren, Michael, Joshua, Susan. Intern, U. Ill. Hosp., Chgo., 1963-64, resident in internal medicine, 1964-65, 67-68; fellow in cardiology, Cin. Gen. Hosp., 1968-70, dir. coronary care unit, 1971-74, dir. echocardiography lab., 1972-74; dir. cardiac diagnostic labs., Central DuPage Hosp., Winfield, Ill., 1974—; asst. prof. medicine, U. Cin., 1970-74, Rush Med. Coll., 1976—. Chmn. coronary care com. Heart Assn. DuPage County, 1974-76; active Congregation Beth Shalom, Naperville, Ill. Served to capt. M.C. U.S. Army, 1965-67. Diplomate Am. Bd. Internal Medicine. Fellow ACP, Am. Coll. Cardiology, Am. Coll. Chest Physicians, Council Clin. Cardiology, Am. Heart Assn.; mem. AMA, DuPage County, Ill. State Med. Socs., Am. Fedn. Clin. Research, Chgo. Heart Assn. Author and co-author publs. in field. Office: 454 Pennsylvania Ave Glen Ellyn IL 60137-4402

AGUAYO, ALBERT JUAN, neuroscientist. MD, U. Cordoba, Argentina, 1959; Dr. Honoris Causa, U. Lund, Sweden. Cert. specialist in neurology, Que., cert. EEG specialist, Que. Intern Port Arthut Gen. Hosp., 1960-61; resident in neurology Toronto Gen. Hosp., 1961-62, resident in medicine, 1962-63; resident in neurology Montreal Gen. Hosp., 1964-65; prof. neurology and physiology McGill U.; dir. Ctr. for Rsch. in Neurosci. McGill U. and Montreal Gen. Hosp. Rsch. Inst.; dir. Can. Network of Ctrs. of Excellence for the study of Neural Regeneration; mem. sci. adv. bds. and coms. including Med. Rsch. Can., Howard Hughes Med. Inst., Am. Paraplegic Assn., Ipsen Found., Max Planck Inst., Munich, Germany, Friedrich Miescher-Inst., Basle, Switzerland. Co-editor Current Opinion in Neurobiology; mem. editorial bd. European Jour. Neurosci., Experimental Brain Rsch., Brain Rsch., Synapse, Jour. of Neural Transplantation, Jour. of Chemical Transplantation, Jour. Neurobiology; mem. adv. bd. Neuroscis. Rsch.; mem. internat. adv. bd. NeuroReport. Decorated Order of Can.; recipient Gairdner Found. Internat. award, Ipsen award on Neural Plasticity, WH Helmerich III award for Outstanding Achievement in retina rsch., Leo Parizeau Prize in Biology Assn. Canadienne-Française pour l'Avancement des Sciences, 1993; rsch. fellow Banting Inst., U. Toronto, 1963-64, Montreal Gen. Hosp., 1965-66, traveling fellow McLaughlin Found., 1966-67. Fellow Royal Soc. Can.; mem. Inst. Medicine of the NAS (U.S), N-Am. Soc. for Neurosci. (pres.), Can. Neurol. Soc. (pres.), Can. Assn. of Neuroscientists (pres.), Third World Congress of the Internat. Brain Rsch. Orgn. (pres.). Office: Montreal Gen Hosp Neurosci Unit, 1650 Cedar Ave, Montreal, PQ Canada H3G 1A4

AGUAYO, MAGDALENA, physician assistant; b. Fort Collins, Colo., Dec. 28, 1942; d. Filigonio and Magdalena (Trujillo) Arellano; m. José Aguayo; children: Marisa, Lucia. BS, U. Colo., Denver, 1979; MS, U. Health Sci. Ctr., 1981. Cert. child health assoc. Child health assoc./physician asst. Denver (Colo.) Health & Hosps., 1981—. Home: 2122 W 28th Ave Denver CO 80211

AGUILAR, JUAN P., ophthalmologist; b. Santiago, Cuba, Sept. 21, 1950; s. Juan J. and Gladys E. (Guerra) A.; m. Ann E. Ballemd, Sept. 5, 1982; children: Jonathan, Rebecca. MD, U. Salamanca, 1978. Diplomate Am. Bd. Ophthalmology. Intern in internal medicine, gen. surgery Jackson Meml. Hosp., Miami, 1978-80; resident in ophthalmology SUNY, Buffalo, 1980-83; fellow in ophthalmic pathology The Wilmer Eye Inst., Balt., 1983-84; fellow in corneal disease, ophthalmic plastic surgery Kresge Eye Inst., Detroit, 1985-86; pvt. practice Biscayne Bay Eye Assocs., Miami, 1986-95, Greater Miami Med. Group, 1996—; founder, bd. dirs. Greater Miami Med. Group, 1996—. Mem. AMA, Am. Acad. Ophthalmology, Am. Assn. Ophthalmic Pathologists, Pan Am. Assn. Ophthalmology, Am. Israeli Ophthalmol. Soc., Fla. Med. Assn., Fla. Soc. Ophthalmology, Castroviego Soc., Wilmer Residents Assn., Dade County Med. Assn., Miami Ophthalmol. Soc.. Office: 2281 SW 27th Ave Miami FL 33145-3433

AGUILAR, SILVESTRE FRANCISCO, pediatrician; b. Santiago de Cuba, Cuba, Sept. 17, 1940; s. Silvestre Antonio and Gloria E. (Cabanas) A.; m. Maria L. Capin, Sept. 29, 1969; children: Montserrat, Pedro Jose. MD, U. Barcelona, 1969. Diplomate Am. Bd. Pediatrics. Intern Mercy Hosp., Rockville Ctr., N.Y., 1971-72; resident pediatrics Driscoll Hosp., Corpus Christi, Tex., 1972-73; resident psychiatry Southwestern Med. Sch., Dallas, 1973-74; resident pediatrics U. Tenn., Chattanooga, 1974-75; staff pediatrician Dallas North Med. Ctr., 1975—; clin. instr. pediatrics Southwestern Med. Sch., Dallas, 1975—; attending pediatrician Children's Med. Ctr., Dallas, 1975—, St. Paul Med. Ctr., Dallas, 1975—, Med. City of Dallas, 1975—, Presbyn. & RHD Meml. Hosp., 1975—; guest physician Spanish Radio Program, 1986—. Recipient Physician Recognition award AMA, 1975-83. Fellow Am. Acad. Pediatrics, Interamerican Coll. Physicians and Surgeons; mem. Dallas County Med. Soc., Tex. Med. Assn., World Med. Assn., Brookhaven Country Club. Republican. Roman Catholic. Office: Dallas North Med Ctr 2710 Valley View Ln Dallas TX 75234-4925

AGUILAR-BRYAN, LYDIA, medical educator, medical researcher; b. Mexico City, Feb. 25, 1951; m. Joseph Bryan; 1 child. MD, U. Nacional Autonoma de Mex., 1975; PhD in Population Studies, U. Tex., 1985. Rsch. assoc. Inst. Biomed. Rsch., U. Nacional Autonoma de Mex., Mexico City, 1985-86; rsch. assoc. Baylor Coll. of Medicine, Dept. of Medicine, Divsn. of Endocrinology, Houston, 1987-88, postdoctoral fellow, 1988-90, instr., 1990-91, asst. prof., 1991—. Contbr. articles to profl. jours. Postdoctoral fellow Juvenile Diabetes Found., 1988-90. Mem. AAAS, Am. Diabetes Assn. (Rsch. grantee 1995—), Biophys. Soc., Endocrine Soc. Office: Baylor Coll of Medicine Divsn Endocrinology 1 Baylor Plz Rm 537E Houston TX 77030*

AGUIRRE BIANCHI, RENATO, surgeon; b. Santiago, Chile, Nov. 10, 1943; s. Renato and Lina (Bianchi) Aguirre; m. Sara Aguirre, Nov. 30, 1968; children: Renato, Paula; m. Alejandra Gonzales, Mar., 1981; 1 child, Valeria. Bachiller, Internado Nacional Barros Arana, 1960; MD, U. Chile, 1969. Surg. resident Hosp. Salvador, Santiago, 1970-72; chief surgery Hosp. Juan Noe, Arica, Chile, 1973-83, Clinica Mutual, Arica, 1983-86; dir. Clinica Lautaro, Arica, 1982—. Contbr. articles to profl. jours. Recipient David Benavente award Sociedad de Cirujanos de Chile, 1976, Juan Gandulfo award, 1978. Fellow A.C.S., Internat. Cardiovascular Soc., Sociedad de Cirujanos de Chile; mem. Sociedad Medica del Norte (Chile) (founder), N.Y. Acad. Sci., Sociedad Chilena de Cirugia Toraxica y Vascular (founder), Colegio Brasileiro de Cirurgioes (corr.). Club: Arica's Yacht. Home: Lautaro 471, Arica Chile Office: Clinica Lautaro, Lautaro 487, Arica Chile

AGUS, ZALMAN S., physician, educator; b. Chgo., Apr. 3, 1941; s. Jacob B. and Miriam (Shore) A.; m. Sondra L. Lebow, June 26, 1963; children: David, Joel, Michael. BA, Johns Hopkins U., 1961; MD, U. Md., 1965; MA (hon., U. Pa., 1979. Diplomate Am. Bd. Internal Medicine, Am. Bd. Nephrology. Resident med. sch. U. Md., Balt., 1965-68; fellow nephrology U. Pa. Hosp., Phila., 1968-71, asst. prof., 1973-79, assoc. prof., 1979-86, chief renal sect., 1979-88, prof., 1986—. Contbr. over 100 articles to profl. jours. Chmn. bd. dirs. Harry B. Kellman Acad., Cherry Hil, N.J., 1981-83; bd. dirs. Congragation Beth El, Cherry Hill, 1978—; chmn. bd. Solomon Schecter Day Sch., San Antonio, 1972-73. Served to maj. USAF, 1971-73. Recipient Clin. Investigator award VA, 1973-76, Research Career Devel. award NIH, 1977-82. Fellow ACP; mem. Am. Heart Assn. (exec. com. coun. on the kidney 1984—, chmn. 1990-92), Am. Soc. for Clin. Investigation, Nat. Kidney Found. (regional v.p. 1987-89, Disting. Svc. award 1985). Democrat. Jewish. Office: Va Med Ctr Med Svc University and Woodland Ave Philadelphia PA 19104

AHERN, GEOFFREY LAWRENCE, behavioral neurologist; b. N.Y.C., Feb. 20, 1954. BA, SUNY, Purchase, 1976; MS, Yale U., 1978, PhD in Psychology, 1981, MD, 1984. Med. intern Waterbury (Conn.) Hosp., 1984-85; resident in neurology Boston U., 1985-88; fellow in behavioral neurology Beth Israel Hosp., Boston, 1988-90; instr. neurology Harvard Med. Sch., Boston, 1988-90; asst. prof. neurology and psychology U. Ariz., Tucson, 1990-96, assoc. prof., 1996—. Contbr. articles to profl. jours., chpts. to books. Mem. Am. Acad. Neurology. Office: Univ Med Ctr Dept Neurology 1501 N Campbell Ave Tucson AZ 85724

AHIMA, REXFORD SEFAH, neuroendocrinologist, internist; b. Accra, Ghana, Nov. 4, 1960; came to U.S., 1988; s. Lawrence and Grace (Kontoh) A.; m. Suzette Yaa Osei, June 9, 1990; 1 child, Afua Dedaa. BSc with honors, U. London, 1981; MD, U. Ghana, 1986; PhD, Tulane U., 1992. Diplomate Am. Bd. Internal Medicine. House physician, surgeon Korle Bu Teaching Hosp.-U. Ghana Med. Sch., Accra, 1986-87; rsch. assoc., instr./tutor in anatomy, physiology, neurosci. Tulane U. Sch. Medicine, New Orleans, 1988-92; house physician dept. medicine Albert Einstein Coll. Medicine, Yeshiva U., Bronx, N.Y., 1992-95; fellow joint program in endocrinology Harvard Med. Sch., Boston, 1995—. Contbr. articles to med. jours. Recipient Leo M. Davidoff award Albert Einstein Coll. Medicine, 1994, Owl Club award Tulane U. Med. Sch., 1989, Gold medal Anat. Soc. West Africa, 1991. Mem. ACP, Am. Assn. Anatomists. Office: Beth Israel Hosp Dept Med/ Harvard Med Sch Divsn Endo 330 Brookline Ave Boston MA 02215

AHLQUIST, DAVID ALAN, gastroenterologist, educator; b. Thief River Falls, Minn., July 28, 1951; s. Albert Charles and Virginia Julianne (Carlson) A.; m. Susan Lee Hirsekorn, Aug. 17, 1972; children: Aaron, Daniel, Brooke. BA, U. Minn., 1973; MD, Mayo Med. Sch., Rochester, Minn., 1977. Resident in internal medicine Mayo Grad. Sch., 1977-81, fellow in gastroenterology, 1981-83; pvt. practice Mayo Clinic, Rochester, 1983—, dir. endoscopy, 1989-92; asst. prof. medicine Mayo Med. Sch., 1983-87, assoc. prof. medicine, 1987-92, prof. medicine, 1992—; dir. colorectal tumor group Mayo Cancer Ctr., Rochester, 1995—. Contbr. chpt. to Textbook of Gastroenterology, 1991, 95; contbr. articles to New England Jour. Medicine, Annals Internal Medicine, Gastroenterology, Cancer, Jour. AMA. Mem. Am. Gastroenterol. Assn., Am. Soc. Gastrointestinal Endoscopy (rsch. com. 1990—), AAAS, Am. Assn. Cancer Rsch., Nature Conservancy, Nat. Audubon Soc., Sigma Xi. Office: Mayo Clinic 200 1st St SW Rochester MN 55905-0001

AHLSTROM, NANCY GAIL, nephrologist; b. Wichita, Kans., Oct. 26, 1959; d. Albert Neil and Mary Margaret (Bledsoe) A.; m. Gerald Bernard Stephanz, Dec. 30, 1989; 1 child, Megan Elizabeth; stepchildren: Emily Adele, Samuel Joseph. BS in Engring. summa cum laude, Wichita (Kans.) State U., 1981; MD, Kans. U., 1985. Diplomate Am. Bd. Internal Medicine and Nephrology. Intern in internal medicine U. Kans. Sch. Medicine, Wichita, 1981-82, resident in internal medicine, 1982-84; fellow in nephrology U. Fla., Gainesville, 1990; pvt. practice nephrology Kans. Nephrology Assocs., Wichita, 1990-94, Utah Valley Regional Med. Ctr., Provo, Utah, 1994—. Mem. AMA, Alpha Omega Alpha. Methodist.

AHMAD, ANWAR, radiologist; b. Peshawar, Pakistan, Apr. 15, 1945; s. Shams and Amtulaziz (Lateef) A.; m. Amtur R. Hameed, May 20, 1970; children: Attiya, Ghazala, Iftekhar. FSc, Islamia Coll., Peshawar, 1962; MBBS, Khyber Med. Sch., Peshawar, 1968. Cert. Am. Bd. Radiology. Gen. practice medicine Govt. Pakistan, Peshawar, 1968-71; med. missionary Ahmadiyya Mission, Banjul, The Gambia, 1971-75; attending physician VA Hosp., Hines, Ill., 1975-85, Mercy Hosp., Benton Harbor, Mich., 1985—; clin. instr. Chgo. Med. Sch., North Chicago, Ill., 1978—; program dir. residency tng., VA Hosp., Hines, 1982-85. Pres. suburban chpt. Ahmadiyya Muslim Mission, Glen Ellyn, Ill., 1982-85. Mem. AMA, Am. Soc. Therapeutic Radiology and Oncology, Am. Soc. Clin. Oncology, Am. Coll. Radiology, Radiol. Soc. N.Am., Am. Endocurie Therapy Soc., European Soc. Therapeutic Radiology and Oncology, Am. Endocurietherapy Soc., Internat. Assn. Study of Lung Cancer. Home: 1515 Cardinal Dr Saint Joseph MI 49085-9748 Office: PO Box 273 Saint Joseph MI 49085-0273

AHMAD, LAURA ANN, physician; b. San Francisco, Jan. 4, 1961; d. Nazir and Barbara Jean (Medina) A.; m. Anthony John Ujhazy, May 2, 1992; 1 child, Nicholas John. BS, U. So. Calif., 1983; MD, U. Calif., San Francisco, 1987. Diplomate Am. Bd. Internal Medicine. Intern and resident in internal medicine U. Colo. Health Sci. Ctr., Denver, 1984-90, fellow in geriat. medicine, 1990-92, instr. medicine, 1992-93; lectr. geriat. medicine U. Sydney, Australia, 1994—. Vol. St. John Ambulance Australia, Sydney, 1996. Recipient scholarship Rotary Internat. (Korea), 1991. Fellow Royal Australasian Coll. Physicians; mem. ACP, Am. Geriat. Soc., Am. Soc. Geriat. Medicine. Office: Ctr Edn & Rsch on Ageing, Hospital Rd, Concord NSW 2139, Australia

AHMANN, JOHN STANLEY, psychology educator; b. Struble, Iowa, Oct. 17, 1921; s. Henry Frank and Philomena (Wictor) A.; children—Sandi Ann, Sheri Kay, Gregory Steven, Shelly Joan. B.A., Trinity Coll., 1943; B.S., Iowa State U., 1947, M.S., 1949, Ph.D., 1951. Instr. profl. studies Iowa State U., 1949-51; asst. prof. div. ednl. psychology and psychol. measurement Cornell U., 1951-54, asso. prof., 1954-58, prof., 1958-60; prof. psychology Colo. State U., 1960-75; also asso. dir. Human Factors Research Lab., 1969-71, asst. to pres., 1961-64, head dept. psychology, 1962-64, acad. v.p., 1964-69; prof. edn. and psychology Iowa State U., Ames, 1975—; disting. prof. edn. Iowa State U., 1981—, chmn. dept. profl. studies, 1975-84; adj. prof. psychology and edn. U. Denver, 1971-76; vis. prof. Colo. State U., 1951, Wash. State U., 1960, Western Wash. U., 1970; Cons. research programs U.S. Dept. of Edn.; cons. for evalu. of ednl. programs in Colo., N.Y., La., Tex., Ark., Hawaii, Ga., Ariz., Ohio, Minn., Iowa; project dir. Nat. Assessment of Ednl. Progress, 1971-75; dir. various fed. and state sponsored research projects; honor lectr. Mid-Am. State U. Assn., 1976-77. Author: Statistical Methods in Educational and Psychological Research, 1954, Evaluating Student Progress, 6th edit, 1981, Evaluating Elementary School Pupils, 1960, Testing Student Achievements and Aptitudes, 1962, Measuring and Evaluating Educational Achievement, 2d edit, 1975, How Much Are Our Young People Learning?, 1976, Needs Assessment for Program Planning in Vocational Education, 1979, Academic Achievements of Young Americans, 1983; assoc. editor: Ednl. Studies, 1975-79. Served with USNR, 1943-46, PTO. Recipient Laureate award Iowa State U., 1975. Fellow AAAS, Am. Psychol. Assn.; mem. Am. Ednl. Research Assn., Nat. Council on Measurement in Edn., Sigma Xi, Phi Kappa Phi, Phi Delta Kappa, Phi Lambda Upsilon, Alpha Chi Sigma, Psi Chi. Home: 3105 Regatta Ln Apt 2 Fort Collins CO 80525-4727 Office: Iowa State Univ N 243 Quadrangle Ames IA 50011

AHMED, IQBAL, psychiatrist, consultant; b. Tumkur, Karnataka, India, Aug. 23, 1951; came to U.S., 1976; s. Rahimuddin Ahmed and Arifa (Banu) Rahimuddin; m. Lisa Suzanne Rose, Oct. 9, 1983; children: Yasmin, Jihan. BS, MB, St. John's Med. Coll., Bangalore, India, 1975. Diplomate in gen. psychiatry and geriatric psychiatry Am. Bd. Psychiatry and Neurology. Intern St. Martha's Hosp., Bangalore, India, 1974-75; resident in psychiatry U. Nebr. Med. Ctr., Omaha, 1976-79; fellowship in consultation Boston U. Sch. Medicine, 1979-81; staff psychiatrist in consultation liaison psychiatry Boston City Hosp., 1981-87, staff psychiatrist, geriatric psychiatry, 1983-85, dir. geriatric neuropsychiatry unit, 1985-87, dir. geriatric psychiatry, 1988-92; assoc. dir. consultation liaison psychiatry New England Med. Ctr., Boston, 1989-92; asst. prof. psychiatry Boston U. Sch. Medicine, 1981-87, Tufts U. Sch. Medicine, Boston, 1987-92; dir. med. student edn. in psychiatry Boston City Hosp., 1981-87; chief spl. svcs. Hawaii State Hosp., 1991-94, pres. med. staff, 1994-95, chief geriatric psychiatry, 1994—; assoc. prof. U. Hawaii John A. Burns Sch. Medicine, 1992—, co-dir. geriatric tng. program, 1995—, dir. psychiatry residency program, 1996—, mem. faculty senate, 1994—, v.p. senate, 1995—. Contbr. articles to profl. jours. Mem. Mass. State Dem. Party Minority Caucus, Boston, 1983. Mem. Am. Psychiat. Assn., Am. Neuropsychiat. Assn., Royal Coll. Psychiatrists, Acad. Psychosomatic Medicine, Am. Acad. Geriatric Psychiatry. Democrat. Office: Hawaii State Hosp 45-710 Keaahala Rd Kaneohe HI 96744-3528

AHMED, M. BASHEER, psychiatrist, educator; b. Hyderbad, India, June 7, 1935; came to U.S., 1968; s. M. Quameruddin and Aziz Fatima Ahmed; m. Shakila Khatoon, Dec. 7, 1967; children: Sameer, Araj. Osmania U., Hyderabad, 1954; MD, Dow Med. Coll., 1960. Diplomate Am. Bd. Psychiatry and Neurology, Am. Bd. Geriatric Psychiatry. Dir. psychiat. dept. St. Louis County Gen. Hosp., Clayton, Mo., 1969-71; dir. sound view Throngs Neck Community Mental Health Ctr., Bronx, N.Y., 1971-76; chief psychiatry VA Hosp., Dayton, Ohio, 1976-78; dir. psychiat. dept. John Peter Smith Hosp., Ft. Worth, 1978-82; pvt. practice, Ft. Worth, 1984—; dir. dept. psychiatry St. Joseph Hosp., Ft. Worth, 1985-89; chief staff Care Unit Hosp., Ft. Worth, 1989-94; dir. psych. geriatric unit Med. Plaza Hosp., Ft. Worth, 1992—; asst. prof. Albert Einstein Coll. Medicine, N.Y.C., 1971-76; prof. Wright State U. Med. Sch., Dayton, 1976-78, U. Tex. Southwestern Med. Sch., Dallas, 1978-88, U. Tex. Health Sci. Ctr., Ft. Worth, 1982—; chmn. dept. psychiatry Plaza Med. Ctr. East, 1995—. Contbg. author: Group Counseling and Psychotherapy, 1976, Administration of Mental Health, 1980. Life mem. Rep. Presdl. Task Force, Washington, 1986—. Hogg Found. grantee, 1980-81, U. Tex. Health Sci. Ctr. grantee, 1981. Fellow Am. Psychiat. Assn.; mem. AMA (Physician's Recognition award 1971—), Tex. Med. Assn., Tex., Soc. Psychiat. Physicians (pres. Tarrant County chpt. 1989-90), Tarrant County Med. Soc. (task force for homeless 1989-90), Islamic Med. Assn. (pres. 1978-79), Internat. Inst. Islamic Medicine. Home: 10 Home Place Ct Arlington TX 76016-3913 Office: 1015 S Henderson St Fort Worth TX 76104-2924

AHN, SAMUEL SEUNGHAE, vascular surgeon, researcher, consultant; b. Pusan, Korea, Feb. 9, 1954; came to U.S., 1959; s. Chai Ho and Sun Duk A.; m. Mi Ryu, Aug. 20, 1983; children: Justin, Alexander. BA in Biology, U. Tex., 1972-74; MD, U. Tex. Southwestern, 1974-78. Dimplomate Am. Bd. Surgery, Am. Bd. Med. Examiners; lic. Tex., Calif. Gen. surgery intern UCLA Med. Ctr., 1978-79, jr. resident gen. surgery, 1979-80, NIH rsch. fellow in surg. oncology, 1980-82, sr. resident gen. surgery, 1982-83, chief resident gen. surgery, 1983-84, clin. fellwo vascular surgery, 1984-85, rsch. fellow vascular surgery, 1985-86, attending surgeon, 1984—; asst. prof. surgery UCLA Med. Sch., 1986-93, assoc. clin. prof., 1994—; attending surgeon Sepulveda (Calif.) VA Med. Ctr., 1985-94; cons. surgeon UCLA Student Health Svcs., 1986—; surg. cons. Endovascular Equipment Cos., 1986-94; organizer facilities and programs in field; task force mem.; numerous com. appointments UCLA, 1985; guest lectr. and rsch. in field. Editor: (with W.S. Moore) Endovascular Surgery, 1989, 2d edit., 1992, (with J. Seeger) Endovascular Surgery for Peripheral Vascular Disease: Surgical Clinics of North America, 1992, (with D. Eton, K. Hodgson) Current Concepts in Endovascular Surgery, 1994; mem. editorial bd. Vascular Forum, 1993-94, Jour. Endovascular Surgery, 1994, Vascular Surgery, 1994; guest reviewer Jour. of Vascular Surgery, 1991-94, Postgraduate Vascular Surgery Jour., 1992-93, Surgery, 1992, Atherosclerosis and Thrombosis, 1992, Jour. of Am. Geriatrics Soc., 1992-93; abstractor Jour. of Vascular Surgery, 1994; contbr. chpts. books, articles to profl. jours. Mem. stroke coun. Am. Heart Assn., 1991—; vol. Korean Med. Missionary, 1969-88, Pub. Edn. of Cancer, 1980-83. East Tex. Chest Found. fellow East Tex. Chest Hosp., Tyler, 1976, Sigvaris award 1986; preceptee Am. Soc. Anesthesiologists, 1976; grantee E.R. Squibb and Sons. 1985-87, 85-86, Olympus Corp., 1985-86, UCLA Med. Aux., 1986, BioQuantum Tech., 1986-87, W.L. Gore and Assocs., 1986-87, 94, UCLA Sch. Medicine, 1986-87, NIH, 1987, 88, 93, Boston Scientific/Diasonics, 1989, Quadralogic Tech., Inc., 1990, Endo Vascular Instruments, Inc., 1993-94, Echocath and Acuson, 1993-94. Fellow Am. Coll. Surgeons; mem. AMA, Assn. Academic Surgery , Interant. Soc. Cardiovascular Surgery (N.Am. Chapter, rsch. fellow 1992, 93), So. Calif. Vascular Surg. Soc., Western Vascular Soc., Pacific Coast Surg. Assn., L.A. Surg. Soc., Acad. Surg. Rsch., Peripheral Vascular Surgery soc., Soc. Clin. Vascular Surgery, The Soc. for Vascular Surgery, Longmire Surg. Soc. Office: UCLA Med Ctr Ste #510 100 UCLA Medical Plz Los Angeles CA 90024-6970

AHR, PAUL ROBERT, clinical psychologist, management consultant; b. Irvington, N.J., Jan. 4, 1945; s. Wilbur Frederick and Marcella Elizabeth (Brady) A.; children: Thomas Brady, Andrew Travers. A.B. cum. laude, U. Notre Dame, 1966; Ph.D., Cath. U. Am., 1971; M.P.A., U. So. Calif., 1977. Postdoctoral fellow Harvard Med. Sch., Boston, 1972-73; dir. children's program Va. Dept. Mental Health and Mental Retardation, Richmond, 1973-74, dir. program analysis planning, 1974-75, asst. commr., 1975-79; dir. Mo. Dept. Mental Health, Jefferson City, 1979-86; pres. The Altenahr Group, Ltd., 1986—; pres. The Corp. Psychology Ctr., Inc., 1987—; lectr. U. Mo. Sch. Health Related Professions, Columbia, 1980, clin. assoc. prof. U. Mo. Sch. Medicine, 1980—; clin. assoc. prof. dept. psychiatry U. Mo., Kansas City, 1980—; assoc. clin. prof. St. Louis U. Sch. Medicine, 1982—. Served with USN, 1969-72. NIMH fellow, 1972-73, Vocat. Rehab. Adminstrn. fellow, 1966-69. Fellow Am. Coll. Mental Health Adminstrs.; mem. Am. Psychol. Assn. Roman Catholic. Office: The Altenahr Group Ltd 225 S Meramec Ave Ste 1032 Saint Louis MO 63105-3511

AHRENS, EDWARD HAMBLIN, JR., physician; b. Chgo., May 21, 1915; s. Edward Hamblin and Pauline (Forsyth) A.; m. Gertrude A. Fobes, Sept. 12, 1940; children: Sandra H., Peter Forsyth, Burgess. Grad., Hotchkiss Sch., 1933; BS magna cum laude, Harvard U., 1937, MD cum laude, 1941; MD (hon.), U. Lund, Sweden, 1976, U. Edinburgh, Scotland, 1988. Diplomate Am. Bd. Pediat. Intern Babies Hosp. of N.Y., 1942-43, chief resident, 1951-52; rsch. asst. Rockefeller U., 1946-49, assoc., 1952-58, assoc. prof., 1958-60, prof., 1960-85; prof. emeritus, 1985—. Pres. Mountain Top Arboretum, 1977—; mem. bd. mgrs. N.Y. Bot. Garden, 1981-93. Mem. NAS, Am. Soc. Biol. Chemists, Assn. Am. Physicians, Am. Soc. Clin. Investigation, Century Club, Phi Beta Kappa. Office: Rockefeller U 66th St and York Ave New York NY 10021

AHRENS, RICHARD AUGUST, nutrition educator; b. Manitowoc, Wis., Sept. 18, 1936; s. Richard William and Gladys LaVerne (Bierman) A.; m. Joan Ellen Morley, Aug. 19, 1961; children: Deborah Joan, Jill LaVerne, David Richard. BS, U. Wis., 1958; PhD, U. Calif., Davis, 1963. Rsch. physiologist USDA, Beltsville, Md., 1963-66; assoc. prof. U. Md., College Park, 1966-75, prof. nutrition, 1975—, coord. grad. program in nutrional scis., 1989-92; mgr. Open Workstation Lab., 1993—. vis. prof. Egerton U., Njoro, Kenya, 1987-88; vis. lectr. U. London, 1973; chmn. Md. Bd. Dietetic Practice, 1990-94. Author: Nutrition for Health, 1970; (with others) Food and the Consumer, 1973, Creative Wok Cooking, 1976, Creative Crepe Cooking, 1976; contbr. over 37 articles to profl. jours. Election judge Prince Georges County, Md., 1970-86. Treas. Boys and Girls Club, Berwyn Heights, Md., 1978-79. Grantee NIH, 1979-82, Nutrition Found., 1968-70. Recipient Excellence in Instrn. award coll. agriculture chpt. U. Md. at Coll. Park Alumni Assn., 1993. Fellow Am. Coll. Nutrition; mem. Md. Home Econ. Assn. (pres. 1982-83), Am. Inst. Nutrition, Am. Dietetic Assn., Sigma Xi. Republican. Lutheran. Avocation: beer and wine making. Home: 6216 Seminole Pl College Park MD 20740-2349 Office: Univ Md Nutrition and Food Sci College Park MD 20742

AI, EVERETT, ophthalmologist; b. N.Y.C., July 15, 1950. Student, SUNY, Stonybrook, 1967-69; BA, U. Iowa, 1971; MD, SUNY, Syracuse, 1975. Diplomate Am. Bd. Ophthalmology. Intern Northwestern U., Chgo., 1975-76, resident ophthalmology, 1976-79; fellowship disease of retina and vitreous Pacific Med. Ctr., 1979-80; fellow vitreoretinal surgery St. Lukes Hosp., Western Res. U., Cleve., 1981; asst. prof. dept. ophthalmology Northwestern U., Chgo., 1980-81, dir. ophthalmology residency program, 1980-81, dir. divsn. clin. echography, 1980-81; asst. clin. prof. U. Calif., Berkeley, 1983—; dir. retina unit CPMC, San Francisco, 1983—; ophthalmic examiner early treatment diabetic retinopathy study Pacific Presbyn. Med. Ctr., San Francisco, 1979-80, prin. investigator, 1983-89; retinal cons. Lakeside VA Hosp., Chgo., 1980-81, The Permanente Med. Group, Oakland, Calif., 1982-83, Fort Ord (Calif.) Army Med. Ctr., 1983—; assoc. examiner Am. Bd. Ophthalmology, San Francisco, 1985—; pres. Western Assn. for Vitreoretinal Edn., 1990-91; bd. dirs. Am. Diabetes Assn., San Francisco, pres., 1991-92; sci. reviewer Ophthalmology, 1990—; med. adv. bd. MID Labs., 1993—, Diabetes Interview, 1993—; active Diabetes 2000 Nat. Ops. Com., 1993—; presenter and lectr. in field. Contbr. articles to profl. jours. N.Y. State Regents Coll. scholar, 1967; Heed Ophthalmic fellow, 1979. Mem. Am. Acad. Ophthalmology (continuing ophthalmic video edn. com 1993—, nat. coord. for edn. courses 1993—), Am. Assn. Ophthalmology, Internat. Soc. for Ophthalmic Ultrasound, Assn. for Rsch. in Vision and Ophthalmology, Vitreous Soc., Calif. Assn. Ophthalmology (bd. dirs. 1991—), Calif. Med. Assn. (sect. asst. sec. sci. adv. panel on ophthalmology 1988-89, sci. program planner for ophthalmology 1988-89, ophthalmology sect. sec. sci. adv. panel on ophthalmology 1989-90, sect. chmn. 1990-91), Pacific Coast Oto-Ophthalmologic Soc. (sci. program com. 1991—, councillor 1991—), San Francisco Med. Soc., Soc. Heed Fellows, Ophthalmic Photographers' Soc. (med. adv. com. 1989—), Phi Beta Kappa. Office: Schatz McDonald Johnson Ai 1 Daniel Burnham Ct San Francisco CA 94109

AICKIN, DONALD RUSSELL, obstetrician/gynecologist, educator; b. Lower Hutt, New Zealand, Oct. 31, 1934; s. Ronald Patton and Ethel Marion (Moffat) A.; m. Jeanette Groom; children: Jill, Richard, Michael, Trudi. MB, Otago Med. Sch., Dunedin, New Zealand, 1958; MD, U. Melbourne, Australia, 1974. Resident Otago Hosp. Bd., Dunedin, 1959-62; traveling scholar Royal Women's Hosp., Melbourne, 1963-65; commonwealth scholar Queen Mother Hosp., Glasgow, Scotland, 1967-68; asst. dept. obstetrics U. Melbourne, 1968-72; prof., head ob-gyn. dept. Christchurch (New Zealand) Sch. Medicine, 1972—. Contbr. articles to profl. jours. Fellow Royal Coll. Ob-Gyn. London, Royal Coll. Surgeons Edinburgh, Royal Australian Coll. Surgeons, Royal New Zealand Coll. Ob-Gyn.; mem. Med. Rsch. Coun., Found. for Newborn (chmn. rsch. com. 1977—), Reproductive Medicine Found. (chmn. 1989—), Maternal Deaths Assessment Com. (chmn. 1989—). Office: Christchurch Sch Medicine, Dept Ob-Gyn Pvt Bag, Christchurch New Zealand

AIGES, HARVEY WAYNE, pediatrician, medical educator; b. N.Y.C., Jan. 13, 1947; s. Louis and Estelle (Rubin) A.; m. Judith Ann Moel, Mar. 20, 1982; 1 child, Laura. BA, Bklyn. Coll., 1967; MD, NYU, 1971. Diplomate Am. Bd. Pediats., Am. Bd. Pediat. Gastroenterology. Resident Bronx Mepl. Hosp. Ctr., 1971-74; chief resident in pediatrics Albert Einstein Coll. of Medicine, Bronx, 1974-75; pediatric fellow in gastroenterologist Med. Coll. Cornell U., Manhasset, N.Y., 1977-79; pediatric gastroenterologist North Shore Univ. Hosp., Manhasset, 1979—, chief clin. svcs., 1984—, vice chmn., 1989—. Author: Cystic Fibrosis, 1990, Pediatric Gastroenterologist, 1990; contbr. articles to profl. jours. Maj. U.S. Army, 1975-77. Fellow Am. Gastroenterologic Assn., Am. Assn. for Study of Liver Disease, Alpha Omega Alpha. Jewish. Office: North Shore Univ Hosp 300 Community Dr Manhasset NY 11030-3801

AIKAWA, JERRY KAZUO, physician, educator; b. Stockton, Calif., Aug. 24, 1921; s. Genmatsu and Shizuko (Yamamoto) A.; m. Chitose Aihara, Sept. 20, 1944; 1 son, Ronald K. A.B., U. Calif., 1942; M.D., Wake Forest Coll., 1945. Intern, asst. resident N.C. Baptist Hosp., 1945-47; NRC fellow in med. scis. U. Calif. Med. Sch., 1947-48; NRC, AEC postdoctoral fellow in med. scis. Bowman Gray Sch. Medicine, 1948-50, instr. internal medicine, 1950-53, asst. prof., 1953; established investigator Am. Heart Assn., 1952-58; exec. officer lab. service Univ. Hosps., 1958-61, dir. lab. services, 1961-83, dir. allied health program, 1969—, assoc. dean allied health program, 1983—, pres. med. bd.; assoc. dean clin. affairs asst. prof. U. Colo. Sch. Medicine, 1953- 60, asso. prof. medicine, 1960-67, prof., 1967—, prof. biometrics, 1974—, assoc. dean clin. affairs, 1974—; Pres. Med. bd. Univ. Hosps. Fellow ACP, Am. Coll. Nutrition; mem. Western Soc. Clin. Research, So. Soc. Clin. Research, Soc. Exptl. Biology and Medicine, Am. Fedn. Clin. Research, AAAS, Central Soc. Clin. Research, AMA, Assn. Am. Med. Colls., Phi Beta Kappa, Sigma Xi, Alpha Omega Alpha. Home: 3233 Lake Albano Cir San Jose CA 95135-1467 Office: U Colo Sch Medicine 4200 E 9th Ave Denver CO 80220-3706

AIKEN, LEWIS ROSCOE, JR., psychologist, educator; b. Bradenton Fla., Apr. 14, 1931; s. Lewis Roscoe and Vera Irene (Hess) A.; m. Dorothy Ree Grady, Dec. 16, 1956; children: Christopher, Timothy. BS, Fla. State U., Tallahassee, 1955, MA, 1956; PhD, U. N.C., 1960. Assoc. prof. psychology U. N.C., Greensboro, 1960-65; prof. Guilford Coll., Greensboro, 1966-74, Sacred Heart Coll., Belmont, N.C., 1974-76, U. Pacific, Stockton, Calif., 1977-79, Pepperdine U., Malibu, Calif., 1979-93. Author: General Psychology, 1969, Psychological and Educational Testing, 1971, Readings in Psychological and Educational Testing, 1973, Psychological Testing and Assessment, 1976, 8th edit., 1994, Later Life, 1978, 3d edit., 1989, Dying, Death and Bereavement, 1985, 3d edit., 1994, Assessment of Intellectual Functioning, 1987, 96, Assessment of Personality, 1989, 95, Personality: Theories, Research and Applications, 1993, Aging: An Introduction to Gerontology, 1994, Rating Scales and Checklists, 1996; also articles. Served to sgt. USMC, 1951-54. Fla. Lewis scholar, 1949-51, Gen. scholar, 1954-56; Emory U. fellow, 1957-58, U.S. Office Edn. postdoctoral fellow, 1968-69; NAS-NRC postdoctoral resident rsch. assoc., 1963-64. Fellow Am. Psychol. Assn., Am. Psychol. Soc.; mem. Am. Ednl. Rsch. Assn., Sigma Xi. Office: Pepperdine U Social Sci Divsn Malibu CA 90263

AIKEN, LINDA HARMAN, nurse, sociologist, educator; b. Roanoke, Va., July 29, 1943; d. William Jordan and Betty Philips (Warner) Harman; children: June Elizabeth, Alan James. BSN, U. Fla., 1964, M in Nursing, 1966; PhD in Sociology, U. Tex., 1973. Nurse Med. Ctr. U. Fla., Gainesville, 1964-65, instr. coll. nursing, 1966-67; instr. sch. of nursing U. Mo., Columbia, 1967-70, clin. nurse specialist sch. of nursing, 1967-70; program officer Robert Wood Johnson Found., Princeton, N.J., 1974-76, dir. rsch., 1976-79, asst. v.p., 1979-81, v.p., 1981-87; trustee prof. nursing and sociology U. Pa., Phila., 1988—; dir. Ctr. for Health Svcs. and Policy Rsch. U. Pa.; rsch. assoc. population studies ctr. U. Pa.; mem. Sec. Health and Human Svcs. Commn. on Nursing, 1988, Pres. Clinton's Nat. Health Care Reform Task Force, 1993; commr. Physician Payment Rev. Commn. nat. adv. coun. U.S. Agy. for Health Care Care Policy and Rsch. Author: Health Policy and Nursing Practice, 1981, Nursing in the 1980s, 1982, Applications of Social Science to Clinical Medicine and Health Policy, 1986, Evaluation Studies Rev. Ann., 1985, Charting Nursing's Future, 1991; assoc. editor Jour. Health and Social Behavior, 1979-81, Transaction Soc., 1985—; mem. editorial bd. Evaluation Quar., 1979-80, Med. Care, 1983—; contbr. articles to profl. jours. Mem. Adv. Council Social Security, 1982-83. Recipient Joint Secretarial commendation U.S. Dept. Health and Human Services and HUD, 1987; NIH Nurse Scientist fellow, 1970-73. Mem. ANA (Jessie M. Scott award 1984), Inst. Medicine, Nat. Acad. Scis., Nat. Acad. Social Ins., Am. Acad. Nursing (pres. 1979-80), Am. Sociol. Assn. (chair med. sociology sect. 1983-84), Sociol. Rsch. Assn., Coun. Nurse Rschrs. (Nurse Scientist of Yr. 1991), Sigma Theta Tau, Phi Kappa Phi. Home: 2209 Lombard St Philadelphia PA 19146-1107 Office: U Pa 420 Service Dr Philadelphia PA 19104-6020

AIKEN, LISA ANNE, psychologist, author, lecturer; b. Balt., July 8, 1956; d. Sidney Herbert and Janet Betty (Segall) A.; m. Ira Michaels, Aug., 1992. BA in Psychology summa cum laude, Towson State Coll., 1975; MA in Clin. Psychology, Loyola U., Chgo., 1977, PhD in Clin. Psychology, 1979. Lic. psychologist. Psychologist, cons. liaison psychiatry North Cen. Bronx (N.Y.) Hosp., 1980-82; chief psychologist Lenox Hill Hosp., N.Y.C., 1982-89; pvt. practice N.Y.C., 1982—; pub. nat. speaker 1988—; cons. Forest Hills Ind. Practice Assn., Queens, N.Y., 1989-92. Author: Why Me, God, 1996, Beyond Bashert: A Guide to Dating and a Better Marriage Enrichment, 1996, To Be a Jewish Woman, 1992; co-author: The Art of Jewish Prayer, 1991. Office: 145 W 96th St # 3F New York NY 10025-6449

AIKEN, ROBERT DENNIS, physician; b. Detroit, Sept. 4, 1950; s. Max Gordon and Hope (Collins) A.; m. Ellen Jayne Warren, Nov. 25, 1980; children: David, Caroline. BS, U. Mich., 1972; MD, Wayne State U., 1976. Med. resident Baylor Coll. Med., Houston, 1976-78; resident in Neurology Columbia Presbyn. Med. Ctr., N.Y.C., 1978-81; fellow in neurooncology Meml. Sloan Kettering Cancer Ctr., N.Y.C., 1981-83; assoc. prof. neurology Jefferson Med. Coll., Phila., 1983—; mem. Jefferson Cancer Inst. Fellow Coll. Physicians Phila.; mem. Am. Acad. Neurology, Assn. Rsch. Nervous and Mental Diseases, ASCO. Office: Thomas Jefferson U Hosp Ste 617 1015 Chestnut St Fl 617 Philadelphia PA 19107-4306

AILLON, ALEJANDRO JOSE, thoracic and cardiovascular surgeon; b. Cartagena, Colombia, Jan. 30, 1939; came to U.S., 1964; s. Ulpiano and Matilde (Perez) A.; children: Julie, Alexander, Natalie, Daniel. MD, U. Cartagena, 1963. Diplomate Am. Bd. Surgery, Am. Bd. Thoracic Surgery. Intern Charity Hosp New Orleans, 1964-65; resident in gen. surgery Church Home and Hosp., Balt., 1965-66, VA Hosp.-affiliated hosps. U. Tex. Southwestern Med. Sch., Dallas, 1968-72; resident in thoracic and cardiovasc. surgery U. Tex. Southwestern Med. Sch., 1972-74; thoracic and cardiovasc. surgeon Hertzler Clinic, Halstead, Kans., 1974—. Lt. comdr. M.C., USN, 1966-68. Fellow ACS, Am. Coll. Chest Physicians, Am. Coll. Cardiology, Soc. Thoracic Surgeons; mem. Kans. Med. Soc., Harvey County Med. Society, Southwestern Surg. Congress, Am. Soc. Cardiovasc. Interventionists, Internat. Soc. for Endovascular Surgery, Am. Heart Assn. Office: Hertzler Clinic 4th and Chestnut Sts Halstead KS 67056

AILLON, GONZALO ALBERTO, psychiatrist; b. Cartagena, Colombia, Aug. 28, 1940; came to U.S. 1967; s. Ulpiano and Matilde (Perez) A.; m. Cecilia Lecompte, June 6, 1967; children: Gonzalo A., Carlos G., Alfonso H. MD, U. Cartagena, 1964. Diplomate Am. Bd. Psychiatry and Neurology. Intern Univ. Hosp., Cartagena, 1964-65; intern in psychiatry/neurology Ellis Hosp., Schenectady, N.Y., 1967-68; resident in psychiatry Columbia Sch. Medicine U. Mo., St. Louis, 1968-73; chmn. dept. psychiatry Meth. Med. Ctr., Dallas, 1981-88; med. dir. psychiat. unit Meth. Med. Ctr., 1986-88; med. dir. The Haven Psychiat. Hosp., Desoto, Tex., 1988-90; founder, med. dir. Family Ctr. of the Southwest, Dallas, 1985-93, Day Treatment Ctr. of Dallas, 1989-95; clin. asst. prof. dept. psychiatry Southwestern Med. Sch., Dallas, 1983-89. Fellow Am. Psychiatric Assn.; mem. AMA, Hispanic Psychiatric Assn. Roman Catholic. Office: 1326 Stemmons Ave Dallas TX 75208-2342

AINSWORTH, ELAINE MARIE, occupational therapist; b. Jamestown, N.Y., July 24, 1948; d. Ralph Marion and Martha Elaine (Dunn) Sorenson; m. Stephen Marshall Ainsworth, Jan. 17, 1970 (div. Aug. 1973). BS in Edn., Edinboro State Coll., 1971; MS in Occupational Therapy, Columbia U., 1975. Mem. occupational therapy staff Warren (Pa.) State Hosp., 1975-77, chief occupational therapy staff, 1977; mem. occupational therapy staff Sheppard & Enoch Pratt Hosp., Towson, Md., 1978; pvt. practice Allentown, Pa., 1981-82; chief occupational therapy dept. Community Hosp. of Lancaster, Pa., 1982-86; asst. prof. Elizabethtown (Pa.) Coll., 1986-88, Alvernia Coll., Reading, Pa., 1996; chief occupational therapy dept. Lebanon (Pa.) VA Med. Ctr., 1989-90; owner Elaine Ainsworth & Assocs., Lancaster, 1991—; adv. bd. occupl. therapy dept. Alvernia Coll., Reading, Pa., 1995, Home Health Agy., Brethren Village, Lancaster, Pa., 1995, Northwestern Home Health Care/Svcs. Agy., 1994-95; cons. Mental Health Mgmt., Alexandria, Va., 1985, Stairways Agy., Erie, Pa., 1976, Hamot Med. Ctr., Erie, 1976, W.C.A. Hosp., Jamestown, N.Y., 1976; allied health Liaison Parkinson Support Group, Lancaster, 1983-86. Author: (with others) Core Curriculum for Home Health Care Nursing, 1993, 2d edit., 1995. Treas., bd. dirs. Orgn. for Responsible Care of Animals, Lancaster, 1988. Recipient scholarship Commonwealth of Pa., 1973-75. Mem. Am. Occupational Therapy Assn., Pa. Occupational Therapy Assn. (chair nominating com. 1980-81, chair program com. state conf. 1982). Office: 245 Butler Ave Ste 304 Lancaster PA 17601-6311

AINSWORTH, KRISTINE M., critical care nurse; b. Manchester, N.H., Jan. 10, 1959; d. Harry P. and Adoree Thomasina (Cote) A. BSN, St. Anselm Coll., 1981; MS in Family/Cmty. Health Nurse Practition, U. Mass., Lowell, 1996. Cert. CCRN. Staff nurse Elliot Hosp., Manchester, 1984—; ARNP Dr. Verani's Office, Londonderry, N.H., 1996. Mem. AACN (past pres. So. N.H. chpt.), N.H. Nurse Practitioner Assn., Sigma Theta Tau.

AIRD, ROBERT BURNS, neurologist, educator; b. Provo, Utah, Nov. 5, 1903; s. John William and Emily Dawn (McAuslan) A.; m. Ellinor Hill Collins, Oct. 5, 1935 (dec. 1988); children: Katharine (dec. 1992), Mary, John, Robert. BA, Cornell U., 1926. MD, Harvard Med. Sch., 1930. Diplomate Nat. Bd. Med. Examiners, Am. Bd. Psychiatry and Neurology. Intern Strong Meml. Hosp-U. Rochester (N.Y.) Sch. Medicine, 1930-31, resident, 1931-32; rsch. assoc. U. Calif., San Francisco, 1932-35, instr., 1935-39, from asst. to assoc. prof., 1939-49, prof. neurology, 1949-71, founder dept. neurology, 1947, chmn. dept. neurology, 1947-66, established Electroencephalographic Lab., 1940, dir. Electroencephalographic Lab., 1940-71; neurology cons. 9 hosps., Calif.; trustee Deep Springs Coll., Inyo County, Calif., 1959-71, dir. coll., 1960-66, hon. trustee, 1971—; founder No. Calif. chpt. Multiple Sclerosis Soc.; mem. five coms. NIH, Washington, 1953-63; rep. of AMA on Residency Rev. Bd., 1967-73; lectr. in field, U.S. and 10 fgn. countries. Author: Foundations of Modern Neurology: A Century of Progress, 1993, Conversations with Dr. Robert B. Aird: The Origins of Neuroscience at University California, San Francisco, 1995; sr. author: Management of Epilepsy, 1974, The Epilepsies-A Critical Review, 1984; coauthor: Clinical Neurology, 1955, Textbooks of Medicine, 1959, 62; editl. bd. Internat. Jour. Electroencephalography and Clin. Neurophysiology, 1945-65, Jour. Nervous and Mental Disorders, 1952-67; contbr. numerous articles to profl. jours. Founding chmn. William G. Lennox Trust Fund, 1961-69. Fulbright scholar, 1957-58; recipient Royer Significant Contbns. to Advancement of Neurology award, 1969, Hope Chest award Nat. Multiple Sclerosis Soc., 1962, 72, 82; founder vis. professorship in neurology U. Calif., San Francisco, 1949, endowed and named in his honor, 1973, professorship established, 1991, bldg. named in his honor Deep Springs Coll. (Medal of Honor, 1995), 1971, professorship, 1993. Mem. AAAS, Am. Epilepsy Soc. (hon. pres. 1959-60, Lennox award 1970), Am. Electroencephalographic Soc. (charter mem., pres. 1953-54), Am. Neurol. Assn. (v.p. 1955, 69, 72, sr. mem.), Pan-Am. Med. Soc. (N.Am. v.p. 1966), Calif. Acad. Sci. (life), Calif. Acad. Medicine, San Francisco Neurol. Soc. (co-founder, pres. 1951-52), Am. Bd. Qualification in Electroencephalography (founding chair), Western Soc. Electroencephalography (founder pres. 1946), Swedish Soc. of Med. Scis. (hon.), Argentina Assn. Neurol. and Psychology (hon.), Gold Headed Care Soc. (hon.), San Francisco Med. Soc. (hon.), Calif. Med. Assn. (hon.), others. Office: U Calif Dept Neurology M-794 PO Box 0114 San Francisco CA 94143-0518

AISENBERG, ALAN C., physician, educator, researcher; b. N.Y.C., Dec. 7, 1926; s. Jacob and Celia (Able) A.; m. Nadya Margulies, Oct. 2, 1952; children: James, Margaret. SB, Harvard U., 1945, MD, 1950; PhD, U. Wis., 1956. Diplomat Am. Bd. Internal Med. Internship & res. Presbyn. Hosp., N.Y.C., 1950-53; instr. in med. Harvard Med. Sch., Boston, 1956-62, asst. prof., 1962-69, assoc. prof., 1969-84, prof., 1984—; asst. physician Mass. Gen. Hosp., Boston, 1959-69, assoc. physician, 1969-84, physician, 1984—; mem. Clin. Trials Com. Nat. Cancer Inst., Bethesda, Md., 1977-82. Author over 140 articles on medicine to profl. jours. Recipient Guggenheim Fellowship, Guggenheim Found. Nat. Inst. for Med. Research, London, 1964-65. Mem. Am. Coll. of Physicians, Am. Soc. of Clin. Oncology, Am. Assn. Immunologists, Am. Fedn. for Clin. Research. Home: 124 Chestnut St Boston MA 02108-3318 Office: Mass Gen Hosp Fruit St Boston MA 02114-2620

AISNER, JOSEPH, oncologist, physician; b. Munich, Jan. 5, 1944; came to U.S., 1948; s. Philip and Faye Aisner; m. Seena Feldman, Aug. 31, 1969; children: Dara Lianna, Leon Andrew. BS in Chemistry, Wayne State U., 1965, MD, 1970. Intern Sinai Hosp. Detroit, 1970-71; resident Georgetown U. Hosp., Washington, 1971-72; commd. med. officer USPHS, 1972, advanced through grades to rank 05; clin. assoc. Nat. Cancer Inst., Balt., 1972-75, sr. investigator, 1975-78, chief med. oncology, 1978-81; resigned USPHS, 1981; chief med. oncology U. Md. Cancer Ctr., Balt., 1981-92, dep. dir. clin. affairs, 1982-88, ctr. dir., 1988-93; prof. medicine U. Medicine and Dentistry of N.J., New Brunswick, 1995—, prof. environ. and cmty. medicine, 1995—; prof. medicine U. Md., 1982-95, prof. oncology, 1982-95, prof. pharmacology, 1985-95, prof. clin. pharmacy, 1987-95, prof. epidemiology preventive medicine, 1993-95. Editor books; contbr. numerous chpts. to books and articles and abstracts to profl. jours. Bd. dirs. Md. Chpt. Am. Cancer Soc., 1988-94, Am. Assn. Cancer Edn., 1990; exec. com. Md. Cancer Consortium, chmn. breast cancer sect., 1992-93, chmn., 1993-95,; mem. Gov.'s Coun. Cancer Prevention, 1991, exec. com., 1991-95; bd. dirs. Md. Children's Cancer Found., 1991-95. nat. Cancer Inst. grantee, 1982-95. Fellow ACP; mem. Am. Fedn. Clin. Rsch., Am. Soc. Clin. Oncology (dir. edn. program 1985-86, bd. dirs. 1991-94), Am. Assn. Cancer Rsch., Cancer Leukemia Group B (bd. dirs. 1982-95, vice chair breast sect. 1980-86), Am. Radium Soc. (sci. program com. 1993-94). Home: 6 Cotswold Ln Warren NJ 07059 Office: Cancer Institute of NJ 303 George St # 501 New Brunswick NJ 08901

AISNER, MARK, internist; b. Boston, Feb. 27, 1910; s. Jacob and Sarah (Solomon) A.; m. Helen Cashman, June 27, 1948; children: Jonathan Alan, Susan Jane. AB, Harvard Coll., 1931; MD, Tufts U., 1935. Diplomate Am. Bd. Internal Medicine. Rsch. fellow physiology Tufts U. Sch. Medicine, Boston, 1935; residency Boston City Hosp., 1936-38; asst. prof. medicine Tufts U. Sch. Medicine, Boston, 1942-55, assoc. clin. prof. medicine, 1955-77, head course in phys. diagnosis, 1946-75; head course in physiology Tufts Dental Sch., Boston, 1938-43; chief cardiology Hahnemann Hosp., Boston, 1975-90; cons. staff Newton-Wellesley Hosp., Newton, Mass., 1991—, Faulkner Hosp., Boston, 1991—, Beth Israel Hosp., Boston, 1991—; vis. physician Holy Ghost Hosp. (now Youville Hosp.), Cambridge, Mass., 1943-53; attending physician Boston VA Hosp., 1947-75; chief cardiology Winthrop Comty. Hosp., 1950-75; active staff to cons. staff Faulkner Hosp., 1963—, Newton-Wellesley Hosp., 1938—; assoc. staff to cons. staff Beth Israel Hosp., 1938—; bio-med. cons. Naval Blood Rsch. Lab. Boston U. Sch. Medicine, 1993-94. Mem. editorial bd. New Eng. Jour. of Medicine, 1954-73; editor Disease-A-Month, 1954-59, editor emeritus, 1959—; contbr. articles to profl. jours. Trustee Countway Med. Libr., Boston, 1991—; mem. publs. com. Boston Med. Libr., 1992—; mem. Bd. of Registration in Medicine, Boston, 1981-84. Maj. M.C., U.S. Army, 1943-46. Recipient Bronze star U.S. Army, 1945, Army Commendation medal U.S. Army, 1946. Fellow Mass. Med. Soc., Am. Coll. Physicians; mem. Am. Coll. Physicians (Mass. Internist of Yr. 1991), Coun. Clin. Cardiology, Am. Heart Assn., AOA Honor Med. Soc. Home: 35 Evelyn Rd Waban MA 02168-1212

AIZAWA, KEIO, biology educator; b. Okaya, Japan, Feb. 13, 1927; s. Yukio and Chikae (Hanaoka) A.; m. Atsumi Aruga, Jan. 8, 1955; 1 child, Jun Aizawa. B, U. Tokyo, 1950, PhD, 1959. Insect pathologist, chief virus lab. Sericultural Expt. Sta., Ministry Agr. and Forestry, Tokyo, 1950-64; prof. biology Kyushu U., Fukuoka, Japan, 1964-90, prof. emeritus, 1990—; prof. biology Teikyo U., Utsunomiya, Japan, 1990—; subcom. mem. Internat. Com. on Taxonomy of Viruses, 1957-78, Internat. Com. on Systematic Bacteriology, 1973-78; mem. WHO Steering Com. on Biol. Control of Vectors, 1984-87. Author, contbr. 26 books on silkworm diseases, insect pathology, microbial control and microbial insecticides. Recipient prize Japanese Sci., Soc. Agrl. Scis., Tokyo, 1968, Louis Pasteur prize Commn. Séricicole Internat., La Mulatière, France, 1990, Sericultural Sci. prize Japanese Assn. Sericulture, 1991. Mem. Soc. Invertebrate Pathology (trustee 1968-72, hon.). Home: Aoba 3-23-5 Higashi-ku, Fukuoka 813, Japan

AIZAWA, MASUO, bioengineering educator; b. Yokohama, Aug. 31, 1942; s. Kaiji and Shin Aizawa; m. Hideko Aizawa, Oct. 1, 1971; 1 child, Gaku. BS in Engring., Yokohama Nat. U., 1966; D of Engring., Tokyo Inst. Tech., 1971. Rsch. assoc. Tokyo Inst. Tech., 1971-80; rsch. fellow Lehigh U., Bethlehem, Pa., 1974-75; assoc. prof. U. Tsukuba, Japan, 1980-86; assoc. prof. Tokyo Inst. Tech., 1985-86, prof., 1986—, dean faculty biosci. biotechnol., 1994—; coord. chmn. MITI Future Generation Project Bioelectronic Devices, Tokyo, 1991—. Author: Electrochemical Measurements, 1985, Electroenzymology, 1988, Biosensors, 1993; author, editor: Biocomputer, 1991. Mem. Soc. Elect. Chemistry (v.p. 1994—), Internat. Soc. Mol. Elect. Biocomputer (pres. 1994—). Home: 2-19-14 Amanuma, Suginami-ku, Tokyo 167, Japan Office: Tokyo Inst Tech, Dept Bioengrng Nagatsuta, Midori-ku Yokohama 226, Japan

AKELMAN, EDWARD, orthopedist; b. Sharon, Conn., Dec. 3, 1951; s. Herbert and Elizabeth (Clark) A.; m. Vickie Reynolds,Aug. 2, 1980; children: Christopher R., Matthew R. AB, Princeton U., 1975; MD, Dartmouth U., 1978. Diplomate Am. Bd. Orthop. Surgery. V.p. Univ. Orthopedics, Providence, 1989—; vice-chmn. dept. orthop. Brown U., Providence. Mem. New Eng. Hand Soc. (v.p.), R.I. Orthop. Soc. (v.p.).

AKERKAR, ANAND, biotechnologist; b. Bombay, India, Feb. 25, 1940; came to the U.S., 1969; s. Sakharam Bhaskar and Durgabai S. (Kashibai) A.; m. Shobha Anand, Nov. 8, 1965; children: Geetanjali, Sanket. PhD, Bombay U., 1968; MBA, NYU, 1972. Pres. Creative Scientific Tech., Great Neck, N.Y., 1986—; scientific advisor U.S. Congressman Benjamin Gilman, N.Y., 1976—. Contbr. 80 articles to profl. jours. Mem. N.Y. Acad. Scis., Am. Assn. for Clin. Chemistry. Republican. Home: 1 Ravenna Dr Pomona NY 10970-3607 Office: Creative Scientific Tech 55 Northern Blvd Great Neck NY 11021-4058

AKERS, DONALD LEA, JR., vascular surgeon; b. Knoxville, Tenn., May 7, 1955; m. Tammy Leigh Akers; 1 child, Laurea Ashley. BA, U. Tenn., 1977, postgrad., 1978-80; MD, U. Tenn. Ctr. for Health Scis., Memphis, 1984. Surg. technician City of Memphis Emergency Rm., 1981-83; rsch. asst. Dept. of Neuroanatomy U. Tenn., Memphis, 1982; intern in surgery Tulane U. Sch. of Medicine, New Orleans, 1984-85, resident in surgery, 1985-88, chief resident, 1988-89; clin. fellowship Divsn. of Vascular Surgery U. Cin. Med. Ctr., 1989-90, rsch. fellowship Divsn. of Vascular Surgery, 1990-91; asst. prof. Tulane Sch. of Medicine, New Orleans, 1991—; dir. vascular lab. Tulane Med. Ctr., New Orleans, 1991—; dir. McLano Vascular Lab. Med. Ctr. of La. at New Orleans, 1993—; dir., chief resident surg. rotation on vascular svc., 1992—, Tulane vascular fellowship, 1991-92, inpatient vascular surgery resident svcs. at MCLNO, 1991—, weekly teaching rounds on the Vascular Svc. Tulane Med. Ctr., 1994—. Recipient McDonald's Undergrad. scholarship U. Tenn., 1973-74, C.M. Gooch scholarship U. Tenn. Ctr. for Health Scis., 1981-84; named XXIII Maxwell Lapham lectr. Tulane Med. Alumni Assn., 1992. Office: Tulane U Med Ctr 1430 Tulane Ave New Orleans LA 70112-2699

AKERS, JAMES ERIC, medical practice marketing executive; b. Jonesboro, Ark., Oct. 14, 1945; s. Ward Eldridge and Dorothy Catherine (Erb) A.; m. Belinda Kay Pendleton, Sept. 3, 1973 (div.); 1 child, William Eric. BA in

Social Sci., Vanderbilt U., 1968; MDiv in Strategic Planning, Louisville Presbyn. Theol. Sem, 1971. Gen. mgr. TGI Fridays, Nashville, 1972-73, Annie Tigues Restaurant & Bar, Jacksonville, Fla., 1973-77; sales rep. Northwestern Mut. Life Ins. Co., Jacksonville, 1977-79, Peter Gregg Mercedes-Benz, Jacksonville, 1979-80; dir. life flight Bapt. Med. Ctr., Jacksonville, 1980-83, dir. spl. projects, 1983-84; dir. mktg. Jacksonville Faculty Practice Assn., 1984-88, v.p. planning, devel. and mktg., 1988—; v.p. mktg. Profl. Biling Systems Inc. subs. JFPA, 1986—, Fin.-Med. Mgmt. Svcs., 1989—, Physician Bus. Svcs. Inc., 1990; pres. Healthcare Mktg. Cons., Jacksonville, 1990—. Master of ceremonies Children's Miracle Network Telethon, Jacksonville, 1983, 84, 89, Am. Heart Assn., Jacksonville, 1988-90; chief auctioneer Sta. WJCT-TV, PBS, Jacksonville, 1983-88; campaign mgr. Senator Bill Bankhead, Jacksonville, 1984; pres. bd. dirs. Suicide Prevention Svcs., Jacksonville, 1983-89. Col. USAR, 1966—. Col. U.S. Army N.G., 1966—. Mem. Med. Group Mgmt. Assn., Acad. Practice Assembly, Am. Soc. Hosp. Based Emergency Air Med. Svcs. (bd. dirs.), Am. Coll. Healthcare Mktg., Acad. Health Svcs. Mktg., N.G. Officers Assn., Ye Mystic Revellers (team leader), Rotary (sec. Mandarin, Fla. 1983-84, Paul Harris fellow 1990). Republican. Presbyterian. Home: 8629 Royalwood Dr Jacksonville FL 32256 Office: Jacksonville Faculty Practice Assn PO Box 44008 Jacksonville FL 32231-4008

AKIL, HUDA, neuroscientist, educator, researcher; b. Damascus, Syria, May 19, 1945; came to U.S., 1968; d. Fakher and Widad (Al-Imam) A.; m. Stanley Jack Watson Jr., Dec. 21, 1972; children: Brendon Omar, Kathleen Tamara. BA, Am. U., Beirut, Lebanon, 1966, MA, 1968; PhD, UCLA, 1972. Postdoctoral fellow Stanford U., Palo Alto, Calif., 1974-78; from asst. prof. to prof. psychiatry and neuroscience U. Mich., Ann Arbor, 1979—; mem. adv. bd. Neurex Corp., Menlo Park, Calif., 1986—, Neurobiol. Techs., Inc., 1994—; sec. Internat. Narcotics Rsch. Conf., 1990-94. Editor: Pain and Headache: Neurochemistry of Pain, 1990; co-editor: Handbook of Experimental Pharmacology, 1990-91; contbr. over 250 articles to profl. jours. including 10 to Science and Nature, 1971-91. Rockefeller scholar, Beirut, 1963-66, Alfred P. Sloan fellow, Stanford, Calif., 1974-78; grantee Nat. Inst. Drug Abuse, Washington, 1978-95, NIMH, Washington, 1980-96, Markey Found., U. Mich., 1988—. Fellow Am. Coll. Neuropsychopharmacology, U. Mich. Soc. Fellows; mem. Inst. Medicine/NAS (mental health bd. 1991-95), Sci. Club. Office: Mental Health Rsch Inst 205 Zina Pitcher Ann Arbor MI 48109-2214

AKINS, ROBERT WILLIAM, surgeon; b. Cadillac, Mich., Apr. 22, 1915; s. Robert and Nellie Marie (Simons) A.; m. Donna Ruth Blynn, Aug. 12, 1966; children: Karen, Susan, Jeffrey. AB, Caloin Coll., 1943; DO, Kirksville Coll. Osteo. Med., 1946. Gen. practice osteopathy Antlers, Okla., 1946—. Mem. Sch. Bd., 17 yrs.; scoutmaster Boy Scouts m., 1960—. Mem. Lions. Home: Rt 1 Box 7145 Antlers OK 74523

AKIYAMA, HIDEKI, physician; b. Tokyo, Mar. 4, 1952; s. Masahide and Saeko (Iso) A.; m. Katsuko Noda, Apr. 23, 1983; children: Tetsuya, Takuya, Yuya. MD, Tokyo Med./Dental U., 1977, PhD, 1990. Diplomate Am. Bd. Internal Medicine, Am. Bd. Med. Hematology, Am. Bd. Med. Oncology. Intern, resident Tokyo Med./Dental U., 1977-79; rsch. fellow Tokyo Met. Inst. for Med. Sci., 1979-81; intern, resident Wayne State U., Detroit, 1981-84; fellow in hematology/oncology Temple U., Phila., 1984-86, Johns Hopkins U., Balt., 1986-89; staff Tokyo Met. Komagome Hosp., 1989—. Contbr. articles to profl. jours. Mem. ACP, Japan Soc. Clin. Hematology, Japan Hematol. Soc., Japanese Soc. Internal Medicine, Am. Soc. Hematology, Am. Soc. Clin. Oncology. Office: Tokyo Met Komagome Hosp, 3-8-22 Honkomagome Bunkyo, Tokyo 113, Japan

AKSIONOFF, ELIZABETH B., optometry educator; b. Queens, N.Y., Apr. 19, 1960; d. Nicholas and Elfriede Aksionoff; m. Michael Salshutz, June 2, 1991; children: Emily Sarah, Karen Michelle. BS, Cornell U., 1982; OD, SUNY, 1989. Resident VA Med. Ctr., Northport, N.Y., 1989-90; pvt. practice, N.Y.C., 1990-95; asst. clin. prof. SUNY Coll. Optometry, N.Y.C., 1990—. Contbr. chpts. to books and articles to profl. jours. Fellow Am. Acad. Optometry; mem. Am. Optometric Assn., N.Y. State Optometric Assn., Optometric Soc. City N.Y. Office: SUNY Coll of Optometry 100 E 24th St New York NY 10010

ALAIMO, MICHAEL JAMES, osteopath; b. N.Y.C., Feb. 16, 1964; s. Louis and Rosa Esther (Semidey) A.; m. Judith Chen, June 24, 1995. BS in Pharmacy, St. John's U., 1988; DO, N.Y. Coll. Osteo. Medicine, 1994. Diplomate Am. Bd. Osteo. Medicine, Nat. Bd. Med. Examiners; registered pharmacist, N.Y., Fla. Pharmacist Pathmark Drug Store, Rego Park, N.Y., 1988-89, Astoria, N.Y., 1989-90; intern, resident Peninsula Hosp. Ctr., Far Rockaway, N.Y., 1994-95; chief resident family practice Peninsula Hosp. Ctr., Far Rockaway, 1996—. Mem. Am. Osteo. Assn., Am. Acad. Osteopathy, Nat. Osteo. Found. Office: Peninsula Hosp Ctr 51-15 Beach Channel Dr Far Rockaway NY 11691

ALAMEDA, RUSSELL RAYMOND, JR., radiologic technologist; b. San Jose, Calif., Oct. 13, 1945; s. Russell Raymond and Rose Margaret (Manzone) A.; m. Gayle Evileen Allison, Feb. 16, 1969 (div. 1975); children: Lynda Rae, Anthony David. Student San Jose City Coll., 1963-65. Served with U.S. Navy, 1966-75; x-ray technician VA Hosp., Palo Alto, Calif., 1975-78; office mgr., radiologic technologist, responsible safety officer, orthopedic surgery Mountain View (Calif.), 1978—; owner, operator Ren-Tech, San Jose, 1982-87; radiologic technologist San Jose (Calif.) Med. Clinic, 1982-93. Mem. DeFrank Community Ctr. Recipient Mallinckrodt Outstanding Achievement award Mallinckrodt Corp., 1971. Mem. DAV (life), ACLU, NOW, Am. Registry of Radiologic Technologists, United We Stand Am., BAYMEC, Lamda Legal Def., Calif. Soc. Radiologic Technologists, Am. Soc. Radiologic Technologist. Democrat. Lutheran. Home: 165 Blossom Hill Rd # sp76 San Jose CA 95123 Office: Orthopedic Surgery 2500 Hospital Dr Bldg 7 Mountain View CA 94040-4115

ALAMSHAW, FREDDY RUSI, osteopath; b. Baroda, Gujrat, India, Apr. 13, 1969; s. Rusi and Chandrabala (Patel) A.; m. Anita Prasad, Dec. 1, 1991. BS, U. Calif., Riverside, 1991; MPH, UCLA, 1992; DO, Coll. Osteopathic Med. Pacific, Pomona, Calif., 1996. Respiratory therapy aide Hoag Mem. Hosp., Newport Beach, Calif., 1987; student asst. Fairview Devel. Ctr., Costa Mesa, Calif., 1988; rsch asst. U. Calif., Riverside, 1991; quality mgmt., cons. Hosp. of the Good Samaritan, L.A., 1991-92; quality assurance, cons. West L.A. VA, L.A., 1992—. Phi Delta Theta scholar, Edn. Found., 1990-91, Asian-Am. scholar COMP-Asian Am. Found., 1995. Mem. Am. Med. Student Assn., Am. Coll. Osteopathic Family Practitioneers, Asian-Am. Med. Student Assn., Am. Acad. Family Physicians, Student Osteopathic Med. Assn. Democrat. Zoroastrian.

ALARCON, JUAN ANTONIO, urologist; b. Guadalajara, Mex., Aug. 9, 1951; came to U.S., 1979; s. Jesus Pastor and Consuelo (Vargas) A.; m. Yvonne Morales, Dec. 1, 1991; 1 child, Juan Antonio. BS, Ignacio Zaragoza Coll., Mex., 1969; MD, Autonomous U. Guadalajara, 1977. Diplomate Am. Bd. Urology; lic. physician, Calif. Resident in gen. surgery Mt. Sinai Hosp. Med. Ctr., Chgo., 1981-82; resident in neurology Mt. Sinai Hosp./Louis Weiss Meml. Hosp./Children's Meml., Chgo., 1982-86; fellow UCLA, 1986-87; urologist Alarcon Urology Ctr., Monterey Park, Calif., 1987—, Santa Ana, Calif., 1988—; chief of surgery Monterey Park Hosp., 1993-95, chief of staff, 1996—. Office: Alarcon Urology 880 S Atlantic Blvd # 204 Monterey Park CA 91754

ALARCON, ROGELIO ALFONSO, physician, researcher; b. Yungay, Nuble, Chile, Feb. 14, 1926; came to U.S., 1954; s. Alfredo and Carmen Rosa (Carrasco) A. BS, U. Chile, Concepcion, 1943; MD, U. Chile, Santiago, 1950. Staff physician internal medicine U. Chile Hosp. Salvador, Santiago, 1951-52, Hosp. Gonzalez Cortez, Santiago, 1952-54; resident medicine Meml. Ctr. for Cancer and Allied Diseases, N.Y.C., 1955-56; fellow internal medicine George Washington U. Hops., George Washington Sch. Medicine, Washington, 1956-57; resident internal medicine Lemuel Shattuck Hosp., Boston, 1957-58; rsch. fellow pathology Children's Cancer Rsch. Found., Children's Hosp. Med. Ctr., Boston, 1958-60; rsch. assoc. Children's Cancer Rsch. Found., Boston, 1960-74, Harvard Med. Sch., Boston, 1962-76, Cancer Rsch. Inst., New Eng. Deaconess Hosp., Boston, 1974-76; staff physician Boston Children's Hosp. Med. Ctr., Wrentham, Mass., 1977-79; staff physician VA Med. Ctr., Phila., 1979-80, Bedford, Mass., 1980—. Contbr. articles to profl. jours. Mem. Am. Assn. for Cancer Rsch., N.Y. Acad. Scis., Nat. Assn. VA Physicians. Roman Catholic. Home: 33 Pond Ave Apt B-915 Brookline MA 02146-7128 Office: Bedford VA Med Ctr 200 Springs Rd Bedford MA 01730-1114

AL-ASKARI, SALAH, urologist; b. Baghdad, Iraq, Nov. 16, 1927; came to U.S., 1953; s. Abdul-Razzak and Wafia (Fakhri) A.; m. Catherine Elizabeth McCourt, Aug. 2, 1956; children: Yasamin, Laila, Mariam. MB, ChB, Royal Coll. Medicine, 1951; MS in Urology, NYU, 1959. Resident Bellevue Hosp., Cornell Surg. Div., N.Y.C., 1953-54; resident in urology Bellevue Med. Ctr., N.Y.C., 1955-57; fellow in urology NYU, 1958, instr., asst. prof., prof. urology, 1958—; dir. urology Bellevue Hosp., 1970—; urologist U. Hosp., N.Y.C., 1972—; cons. Manhattan VA Hosp., N.Y., 1966—. Mem. Am. Coll. Surgeons, Am. Bd. Urology (diplomate). Office: Bellevue Hosp Med Ctr 27th St & 1st Ave New York NY 10016

ALBANESE, ANTHONY JOHN, health facility administrator; b. Yonkers, N.Y., Nov. 12, 1948; s. Fredrick J. and Ann (Lambeiti) A.; m. Elisanne Albanese; children: Lauren, Jennifer, Leigh Ann. BS, St. Peters Coll., 1982; MS, Iona Coll., 1984. Pres. Pulmonary Outpatient Rehab. Svcs., Englewood, N.J., 1985-93; pres., CEO Best Healthcare Svc. Inc., Westwood, N.J., 1993—. Contbr. chpt. in books and articles to profl. jours. Bd. dirs. Am. Thoracic Soc.; pres. Am. Lung Assn. N.J., 1994-96; patron John Harms Theater. Mem. Apple Ridge Country Club. Office: Best Healthcare Svc Inc 354 Old Hook Rd Westwood NJ 07675-3246

ALBANI, ROBERTO, pediatrician, consultant; b. Asmara, Ethiopia, Aug. 21, 1943; s. Ernesto and Assunta (Riccio) A.; m. Maria Nella Mason, Jan. 13, 1968 (div. 1985); children: Odette, Marta. MD, Rome U. "La Sapienza", 1969. Intern in pediatrics Montefiore Hosp., N.Y.C., 1970-71; resident in pediatrics Flower & Fifth Ave. Hosp., N.Y.C., 1971-73; fellow in pediatric gastroenterology Albert Einstein Coll. Medicine, N.Y.C., 1973-76; cons. pediatric gastroenterology Rome Med. Sch., 1976—; sci. advisor Eurotrend Pub., Milan, 1985—. Author: Understanding Your Child, 1985, Treating Your Child, 1989, Feeding Your Child, 1996; contbr. numerous articles to profl. .jours.; author: (video) Parents Today, 1995. Pres. Sch. for Parents, Rome, 1990—. Fellow Am. Acad. Pediatrics (bd. cert.). Office: Via Livenza 6, 00198 Rome Italy

ALBAUM, JEAN STIRLING, psychologist, educator; b. Beijing, China, Jan. 11, 1932; came to U.S., 1936; d. Richard Henry and Emma Bowyer (Lueders) Ritter; m. B. Taylor Stirling, Aug. 15, 1953 (div. 1965); 1 child, Christopher Taylor Stirling; m. Joseph H. Albaum; stepchildren: Thomas Gary, Lauren Jean. BA, Beloit (Wis.) Coll., 1953; MS, Danbury (Conn.) State U., 1964, U. La Verne, Calif., 1983; PhD, Claremont (Calif.) Grad. Sch., 1985. Lic. ednl. psychologist, Calif. Spl. edn. tchr. Charter Oak (Calif.) Sch. Dist., 1966-80; psychologist, coord. elem. counseling Claremont Sch. Dist., 1980—; pvt. practice ednl. psychologist Encino, Calif., 1987—; clin. supr. Marriage, Family and Child Counselor Interns, Claremont, 1987—; sr. adj. prof. U. La Verne, 1988—; oral commr. Bd. Behavioral Sci. Examiners, Sacramento, 1989—. Contbr. articles to profl. jours. Hostess L.A. World Affairs Coun., 1980—; pres. Woodley Homeowner's Assn., Encino, 1986-89. Grantee Durfee Found., 1986, 92. Mem. Am. Psychol. Assn., Calif. Assn. Marriage, Family and Child Therapists, Calif. Assn. Lic. Ednl. Psychologists. Office: Edn Ctr 2080 N Mountain Ave Claremont CA 91711-2643

ALBECK, JOSEPH HENRY, psychiatrist; b. Scwandorf, West Germany, Feb. 6, 1946; came to U.S., 1949; s. Milton and Lonia (Goldfeld) A.; m. Isabelle Marie Bernadette Biseau, June 19, 1970; children: Simone, David, Margot. BA, Columbia U., 1966; MD, Harvard U., 1970. Diplomate Am. Bd. Psychiatry and Neurology. Intern NYU-Bellevue, N.Y.C., 1970-71; resident in psychiatry McLean Hosp., Belmont, Mass., 1973-76, asst. psychiatrist, 1981—; instr. psychiatry Harvard Med. Sch., McLean, Belmont, 1976—; dir. occupational psychiatry Community Care Systems, Inc., Boston, 1980-81; med. dir. Mystic Valley Unit Met. State Hosp., Waltham, Mass., 1981-84; psychiatrist-in-charge Alcohol and Drug Abuse Treatment Ctr., McLean Hosp., Belmont, 1987-92; psychiatrist Malden Hosp., 1993—; bd. dirs. One Generation After, Boston, Reconciliation Trust Inc., New England Holocaust Meml. Com. Contbr. articles to profl. jours.; author (poetry) Songs For the Last Survivor, 1989. Capt. U.S. Army, 1971-73. Mem. Am. Psychiat. Soc., Internat. Soc. for Traumatic Stress Studies (chmn. transgenerational interest area). Office: McLean Hosp 115 Mill St Belmont MA 02178-1041

ALBERS, JAMES WILSON, neurologist; b. Detroit, Oct. 28, 1943; s. James Milton and Willa Jean (Wilson) A.; m. Janet Mary Rakocy, May 10, 1968; children—Jeffrey, Matthew, Katherine, Elizabeth. B.S. in E.E., U. Mich., 1965, M.S., 1966; M.S., U. Mich., 1968, Ph.D., 1970, M.D., 1972. Diplomate Am. Bd. Neurology. Instr. neurology Mayo Clinic, Rochester, Minn., 1976; asst. prof. neurology Med. Coll. Wis., Milw., 1976-79; assoc. prof. neurology U. Mich., Ann Arbor, 1979-83, prof., 1983—, dir. neuromuscular program, 1979—. Contbr. articles to profl. jours. Recipient Henry W. Woltman award Neurology Dept. Mayo Clinic, 1978. Fellow Am. Acad. Neurology; mem. Am. Assn. Electromyography and Electrodiagnosis (bd. dirs. 1984—), Mich. Neurologic Assn. (sec. treas. 1985—), Sigma Xi, Eta Kappa Nu, Tau Beta Pi. Home: 3889 Waldenwood Dr Ann Arbor MI 48105-3006 Office: Univ Mich Med Ctr Dept Neurology B4952 CFOB Ann Arbor MI 48109

ALBERT, DANIEL MYRON, ophthalmologist, educator; b. Newark, Dec. 19, 1936; s. Maurice I. and Flora Albert; m. Eleanor Kagle, June 26, 1960; children: B. Steven, Michael. B.S., Franklin and Marshall Coll., 1958; M.D., U. Pa., 1962; M.A. (hon.), Harvard U., 1976; D honoris causa, Louis Pasteur U., Strasbourg, 1992. Diplomate: Am. Bd. Ophthalmology. Intern Hosp. U. Pa., 1962-63, resident, 1963-66; surgeon USPHS, 1966-68; NIH spl. fellow in ophthalmic pathology Armed Forces Inst. Pathology, 1968-69; practice medicine specializing in ophthalmology; assoc. surgeon Mass. Eye and Ear Infirmary, 1976-86, surgeon, 1986-92, dir. David G. Cogan eye pathology lab., 1979-92, surgeon, 1986-92; asst. prof. ophthalmology Yale U. Sch. Medicine, 1969-70, assoc. prof., 1970-75, prof., 1975-76; prof. ophthalmic pathology Harvard U. Med. Sch., 1976-84, David G. Cogan prof. ophthalmology, 1984-92; Frederick Allison Davis prof., chmn. dept. ophthalmology U. Wis., Madison, 1992—. Author: (with Scheie) A History of Ophthalmology at the University of Pennsylvania, 1965, Textbook of Ophthalmology, 8th edit. 1969, 9th edit. 1977; author: Jaegar's Atlas of Ophthalmology, 1972, (with Puliafito) Foundations of Ophthalmology, 1979; (with Jakosiec) Men of Vision, 1993, Atlas of Clinical Ophthalmology, 1996; (with Edwards) History of Ophthalmology, 1996; co-editor Principles and Practice of Ophthalmology, 1994; editor Archives of Ophthalmology, 1994—; contbr. articles to profl. jours. Recipient Friedenwald award, 1981, Von Sallmann award in vision and ophthalmology Internat. Conf. for Eye Rsch., 1988, award Humboldt Found., 1991, Mackenzie medal Scottish Ophthal. Soc., 1992, Jackson Meml. medal Am. Acad. Ophthalmology, 1996; William and Mary Greve scholar, 1978-79, scholar Alcon Rsch. Inst., 1984-85. Fellow ACS; mem. Am. Assn. Ophthalmic Pathology (Zimmerman medal 1993), Am. Acad. Ophthalmology (Jackson medal 1996). Jewish. Home: 1106 Wellesley Rd Madison WI 53705-2230 Office: U Wis Hosp and Clinics Dept Ophthalmology F4/334 600 Highland Ave Madison WI 53792-0001

ALBERT, DAVID EARL, biochemist; b. True, W.Va., Jan. 12, 1950; s. James Earl and Anna Pearl (Edwards) A.; m. Carol Ammons, Dec. 30, 1972 (div. 1981); 1 child, Christina Ann; m. Luann Perales, Oct. 3, 1981; children: Jennifer Lynn, Christina Ann, Jessica Marie, Amanda Sue, David James. BS in Pharmacy, Toledo U., 1973; D., Ohio Coll. Podiatric Medicine, 1977; MS in Biochemistry, Bowling Green State U., 1990. Assoc. chemist Owens-Ill., Toledo, 1980-85; rsch. assoc. Anatrace, Inc., Maumee, Ohio, 1985-89, sr. scientist, 1989-95; staff clin. chemist North Am. Sci. Assocs., Inc., Northwood, Ohio, 1995—; instr. chemistry Lourdes Coll., Sylvania, Ohio, 1989—. Mem. Am. Chem. Soc., Ohio Acad. Sci., Am. Assn. Clin. Chemists. Home: 3427 Grayling Pl Toledo OH 43623-1913

ALBERT, ENOCH HENRY, medical and surgical nurse; b. Springfield, Ill., Jan. 6, 1943; s. Enoch H. Sr. and Gena (Gresta) A.; m. Sharon J. Knopp; children: Heather M. Albert-Knopp, Eben M. Albert-Knopp, Colin D. Albert-Knopp. BA, So. Ill. U., 1965, MA, 1967; ASN, U. Maine, 1986; BSN, Graceland Coll., 1993. Cert. med./surg. nurse, ANCC, chemotherapy nurse. Staff nurse Togus VA Med. Ctr., Augusta, Maine, 1986-89, 94—, head nurse, 1989-94, patient care coord., 1995—; facilitator trainer, Maine Parent/Profl. Group, Augusta, 1987—. Contbr. articles to profl. jours. Bd. dirs. Mid-State Cerebral Palsy Ctr., Augusta, 1988-91. Capt. USAR, 1989—. Mem. Nat. Gerontol. Nursing Assn. (editl. bd.). Home: RR 1 Box 1095 Readfield ME 04355-9745

ALBERT, GERALD, clinical psychologist; b. N.Y.C., Nov. 13, 1917; s. Andrew I. and Eleanor (Walder) A.; divorced; m. Norma Holm Haskell, 1983; children: Jay Harvey, Laurie Ellen Albert Moxham. BA, CCNY, 1938; MA, New Sch. for Social Research, 1958; EdD, Columbia U., 1964; Cert. psychoanalytic tng. program, L.I. Inst. Mental Health, Queens, N.Y., 1964. Editor Vulcan and Creston Pubs., N.Y.C., 1939-45; nat. dir. advt., pub. relations Universal Pictures, div. ednl. films, N.Y.C., 1945-50; exec. dir. Advt. Enterprises and Continental Research Inst., Queens, N.Y., 1951-64; asst. to full prof. LIU, 1964-85, prof. Emeritus, 1985—; dir. L.I.U. C.W. Post Counseling Ctr., 1964-70; psychologist, supervising psychologist, clin. dir. L.I. Consultation Ctr., 1966-86, clin. cons., 1986-95; pvt. practice marriage and individual therapy, 1958—. Author: (cassette) How to Choose and Keep a Marriage Partner, 1980, The Wonderful Magic of No-Fault Living, 1990, Japanese edit., 1996; editor-in-chief Jour. Contemporary Psychotherapy, 1985-87; contbr. articles to profl. jours., author booklets. Recipient 1st prize Most Effective Communications/Newsletters Community Agys. Pub. Rels. Assn., 1983. Fellow Am. Assn. for Marriage & Family Therapy (L.I. Family Therapist of Yr. 1993, founder L.I. recorded telephone series 1995); mem. APA, Am. Soc. for Psychical Rsch., Soc. Clin. and Exptl. Hypnosis, Soc. Sci. Exploration, Internat. Soc. for Study of Subtle Energy and Energy Medicine. Office: 271 Merrick Ave East Meadow NY 11554-1549

ALBERT, N. ERICK, urologist; b. West Frankfort, Ill., July 27, 1945; s. Norman and Dorothy Dean (Trout) A.; m. Julie L. Wuorisalo, June 18, 1977; children: Alexander, Jillian. BS with honors, Tulane U., 1967; MD, U. Ill., 1971. Resident in surgery UCLA, 1971-73; resident in urology Yale U., New Haven, Conn., 1973-77; ptnr. Lodi (Calif.) Urol. Med. Group, Inc., 1980—; dir. Found. Med. Care, Stockton, Calif., 1985-88; chief dept. surgery Lodi Meml. Hosp., 1989-90; CEO ARTEL Med. Devel. Inc., Lodi, 1990-95; dir. Lodi Ind. Practice Orgn., 1994—; bd. dirs. ARTEL Med. Devel. Inc., Lodi, 1985—. Contbr. articles to profl. jours. Maj. U.S. Army, 1977-79. Yale U. fellow, 1975-76. Fellow ALS, Am. Urol. Assn.; mem. Calif. Med. Soc. Office: Lodi Urol Med Group Inc 830 S Ham Ln # 26 Lodi CA 95242

ALBERTAZZI, ALBERTO, nephrology educator; b. Bologna, Italy, Oct. 31, 1940; s. Giuseppe Albertazzi and Bruna Maldini; m. Pia Udina, Apr. 19, 1970; children: Valentina, Roberta, Vittorio, Giulia. Degree, U. Degli Studi, Bologna, 1966. Med. diplomate. Intern Inst. Med. Pathology U. Degli Studi, Bologna, 1962-66, fellow Inst. Nephrology, 1967-69, asst. prof. medicine, 1969-73, assoc. prof., 1973-77; prof. medicine and nephrology U. Degli Studi, Chieti, Italy, 1977—. Editor: Nefrologia-Dialisi-Trapianto, 1983. Capt. Italian Sanitary Corp, 1966-67. Mem. Internat. Soc. Nephrology, European Dialysis and Transplant Assn., Am. Soc. Artificial Internal Organs, Internat. Soc. Aftificial Organs. Home: Via Delle Fornaci 106, 66100 Chieti Abruzzo, Italy Office: Inst Nephrology S Camillo, Hosp, Via C Forlanini, 66100 Chieti Abruzzo, Italy

ALBERTI, OSWALDO, JR., pathology laboratory director; b. São Paulo, Brazil, Feb. 11, 1951; s. Oswaldo and Maria de Lourdes A.; m. Vania Nose, Apr. 2, 1976; children: Gustave, Erick, Philip. MD, State U. Campinas, 1975. Diplomate Am. Bd. Pathology. Resident Mercy Hosp., Des Moines, 1976-77, N.E. Deaconess Hosp., Boston, 1977-81, Brigham & Women's Hosp., Boston, 1981-83; lab. dir. pathology Imunotec, São Paulo, Brazil, 1983—. Mem. Coll. Am. Pathologists. Office: Imunotec, R Luis Gois 1945, 04043040 São Paulo Brazil

ALBERTINE, KURT H., anatomist, physiologist, educator; b. Newark, Nov. 29, 1952. BA, Lawrence U., 1975; PhD, Loyola U., Chgo., 1979. Asst. prof. anatomy U. South Fla., Tampa, 1984-86; rsch. asst. prof. pathology U. Pa., Phila., 1986-87, dir. pulmonary morphology lab. Inst. Environ. Medicine, 1986-88; asst. prof. medicine and physiology Jefferson Med. Coll., Phila., 1987-90, assoc. prof., 1990-93, dir. microscopy lab., 1987-93; assoc. prof. pediatrics, medicine and anatomy U. Utah, Salt Lake City, 1993—, dir. rsch. microscope facility, 1993—. NIH fellow, 1980-82; recipient New Investigator Rsch. award NIH, 1984-86. Mem. Am. Assn. Anatomists, Am. Thoracic Soc., Am. Physiol. Soc., N.Y. Acad. Scis., Microscopy Soc. Am., Sigma Xi. Office: U Utah Dept Pediatrics 50 N Medical Dr Salt Lake City UT 84132-0001

ALBERTO, PAMELA LOUISE, oral and maxillofacial surgeon, educator; b. Somerville, Mass., Apr. 13, 1954; d. Louis Leon and Pamela Marie (Spera) A.; m. Gregory John Wroclawski, Aug. 4, 1979; children: Daniel Alberto, Catherine Marie. BS, Rensselaer Poly. Inst., 1976; DMD, U. Pa., 1980. Cert. oral and maxillofacial surgeon. Clin. asst. prof. dept. oral/maxillofacial surgery N.J. Dental Sch., Newark, 1983-89, clin. assoc. prof. dept. oral/maxillofacial surgery, 1989—, dir. predoctoral edn. dept. oral/maxillofacial surgery, 1989—; pvt. practice Sparta, N.J., 1984—; dir. CPR N.J. Dental Sch., Newark, 1985—; dir. Dental Implant Ctr. Wallkill Valley Hosp., Sussex, N.J., 1988—. Recipient Outstanding Clin. Dentistry award Acad. Gen. Dentistry, 1980. Fellow Am. Assn. Oral and Maxillofacial Surgery, Am. Coll. Oral/Maxillofacial Surgery; mem. ADA, AAUP, Am. Assn. Dental Anesthesiology, Internat. Congress Oral Implantology, Psi Omega. Home: 549 Cherry Tree Ln Kinnelon NJ 07405-2229 Office: 17D Woodport Rd Sparta NJ 07871-2406

ALBERTS, RENÉE MILLER, substance abuse and mental health professional; b. N.Y.C., Oct. 17, 1930; d. Julius and Bertha (Brookner) Miller; m. Henry Celler Alberts, Jan 13, 1950; children: Jo Alberts Lord, Nina Alberts Charnley, Hope Alberts Megonical, Jody Alberts Naleppa. BA, Queens Coll., 1950; MA, U. Va., 1979; postgrad., Va. Poly. U.; cert. in community alcohol edn., Howard U. Med. Sch., 1973. Cert. substance abuse counselor, Va.; lic. profl. counselor, Va. Substance abuse counselor, asst. dir., then acting dir. Fairfax (Va.) Alcohol Safety Action Program, 1972-89; substance abuse coord. Mt. Vernon Ctr. Community Mental Health, Alexandria, Va., 1989—; v.p. Va. Coalition on Women, Alcohol and Drugs, Fairfax, 1985-86; mem. dual diagnosis subcom. Met. Washington Coun. Govts., 1990—; bd. apptd. Woman's Collaborative on HIV/AIDS, 1995—. Mem. No. Va. Clin. Counselors Assn. Office: Springfield Outpatient Unit Mt Vernon Ctr Cmty MH 8348 Traford Ln Springfield VA 22152-1650

ALBERTS, W. WATSON, health science administrator; b. Los Angeles, Dec. 31, 1929; s. Hugo William Alberts and Ruth Lucia Watson Marness; m. Marilyn Janice West; Mar. 22, 1959; children: Allison Christine, Allan Watson. AB in Physics with highest honors, U. Calif., Berkeley, 1951, PhD in Biophysics, 1956. Research physiologist Med. Ctr. U. Calif., San Francisco, 1955-56; biophysicist Mt. Zion Hosp. and Med. Ctr., San Francisco, 1956-72; grants assoc. NIH, Bethesda, Md., 1972-73; head rsch. contracts sect. Nat. Inst. Neurol. Disorders and Stroke, Bethesda, Md., 1974-75, asst. dir. contract research programs, 1975-77, dep. dir. div. fundamental neurosciences, 1978-94, acting Inst. dep. dir., 1989-90; administrv. dir. Smith Kettlewell Inst. and Dept. Visual Scis. U. Pacific, San Fransisco, 1977-78; mem. attending staff Mt. Zion Hosp. and Med. Ctr., San Francisco, 1956-72; cons. Donner Lab. Lawrence Berkeley Lab., Berkeley, 1959-64; lectr. U. Calif. Med. Ctr., San Francisco, 1969. Contbr. articles to profl. jours.; adv. editor: Jour. Biomedical Systems, 1969-72. Recipient NIH Rsch. Career Devel. award, 1963-68, NIH Award of Merit, 1983, NIH Dirs. Award, 1989, 91. Fellow AAAS; mem. Soc. for Neuroscience, Am. Physiol. Soc., Biophys. Soc., Planetary Soc., Fedn. Am. Scientists, Sierra Club, Phi Beta Kappa, Sigma Xi. Democrat.

ALBERTY, ROBERT ARNOLD, chemistry educator; b. Winfield, Kans., June 21, 1921; s. Luman Harvey and Mattie (Arnold) A.; m. Lillian Jane Wind, May 22, 1944; children—Nancy Lou, Steven Charles, Catherine Ann. B.S., U. Nebr., 1943, M.S., 1944, D.Sc., 1967; Ph.D., U. Wis., 1947; D.Sc., Lawrence U., 1967. Engaged in research blood plasma fractionation for U.S. Govt., 1944-46; mem. faculty U. Wis., 1947-67, prof. chemistry,

1955-67, assoc. dean letters and sci., 1961-63; dean U. Wis. (Grad. Sch.), 1963-67; prof. chemistry MIT, 1967-91, prof. emeritus, 1991—, dean Sch. Sci., 1967-82; cons. NSF, 1958-83, NIH, 1962-72; chmn. commn. on human resources NRC, 1974-77; dir. Colt Industries, 1978-88, Inst. for Def. Analysis, 1980-86; pres. phys. chemistry div. Internat. Union Pure and Applied Chemistry, 1991-93. Co-author: Physical Chemistry, 1996, Experimental Physical Chemistry, 3d edit., 1970. Guggenheim fellow Calif. Inst. Tech., 1950-51; recipient Eli Lilly award biol. chemistry, 1955. Fellow AAAS; mem. NAS, Inst. Medicine, Am. Chem. Soc. (chmn. com. on chemistry and pub. affairs 1978-80), Am. Acad. Arts and Scis. (coun. 1991-94), Phi Beta Kappa, Sigma Xi. Home: 7 Old Dee Rd Cambridge MA 02138-4633

ALBOM, MICHAEL JONATHAN, surgeon, educator; b. Hartford, Conn., Oct. 2, 1944; s. Milton Jeramiah and Clare (Marcus) A.; m. Lia Shuster, Jan. 22, 1983; children: Blair Ruth, Mark Jeffrey. BA, U. Conn., 1966; MD, Boston U., 1970. Diplomate Am. Bd. Med. Examiners, Am. Bd. Dermatology. Med. intern Hartford Hosp., 1970-71; resident in dermatology Boston U., 1971-74; skin cancer surgery fellow NYU, 1974-75; asst. prof. dermatology dept. dermatology NYU Med. Ctr., 1976-83, head surgery sect., skin and cancer unit, 1979-85, clin. assoc. prof., 1983-93, clin. prof., 1993—; attending surgeon dept. plastic surgery Manhattan Eye Ear & Throat Hosp., N.Y. Eye and Ear Infirmary; co-dir. Interspecialty Facial Surgery Congress, N.Y.C., 1983, 85. Contbr. articles to profl. jours., chpts. to med. books. Fellow Am. Soc. Dermatologic Surgery (bd. dirs. 1980-83, 1988-91), Am. Coll. Mohs Micrographic Surgery and Cutaneous Oncology (bd. dirs. 1987-90, sec.-treas. 1990-92, v.p. 1992-94, pres. 1994-96), Am. Acad. Dermatology (mem. task force dermatol. surgery 1979—, advanced surgery course dir. 1979-86, dir. surg. forum 1986-91); mem. AMA, Internat. Soc. Dermatologic Surgery (charter). Office: 33 E 70th St New York NY 10021-4946

ALBRECHT, CHARLES C., health facility administrator; b. Portsmouth, Ohio, Jan. 31, 1958; s. Roger August and Joan Carroll (Wallace) A. BS, Miami U., 1987, MS, 1989. Med. lab. tech. Mercy Hosp., Hamilton, Ohio, 1984-89; from case mgr. to exec. dir. AIDS Vols. Cin., 1989—; treas. Greater Cin. AIDS Consortium, 1992-95; v.p. HEAL Ohio, 1993-95. Mem. Greater Cin. AIDS Consortium, AIDS Action Coun., Nat. Soc. Fund Raising Execs. Office: AIDS Vols Cin 2183 Ctrl Pkwy Cincinnati OH 45214

ALBRECHT, GERALD THOMAS, JR., pediatric cardiologist; b. Balt., Jan. 19, 1953; s. Gerald Thomas Sr. and Dorothy Frances (Sullivan) A.; m. Pamela Sue Roberts, Apr. 16, 1983; children: Patrick S., Kevin H., Christine B. BA, U. Va., 1975, MD, 1983. Bd. cert. pediat. and pediat. cardiology. Pediat. cardiologist Pediat. Cardiology of Va., Richmond, 1988—. Fellow Am. Coll. Cardiology, Am. Heart Assn. (bd. mem. 1993—), Am. Acad. Pediats. Home: 1706 Tunbridge Dr Richmond VA 23233 Office: Pediat Cardiology Va Ste 401 7603 Forest Ave Richmond VA 23229

ALBRECHT, HELMUT HEINRICH, medical administrator; b. Trier, Fed. Republic Germany, Mar. 2, 1955; came to U.S., 1988; s. Heinrich Friedrich Paul and Ingeborg (Bräcker) A.; m. Gay Anne Wood, Oct. 12, 1984; children: Ingo, Ashley. MD, U. Hamburg and Heidelberg, Fed. Republic Germany, 1983; MS in Mgmt. and Policy, SUNY, Stony Brook, 1991, advanced cert. in health care mgmt., 1992. Intern in medicine and surgery Gen. Hosp. Hamburg-Altona, Dermatology U. Hosp., Eppendorf, 1982-83; rsch. asst. in pathology U. Heidelberg, 1983-84; asst. in gynecology and obstetrics City Hosp. Wiesbaden, Fed. Republic Germany, 1984-85; regional med. dir. BYK Gulden Pharms., Konstanz, Fed. Republic Germany, 1985-88; med. dir. Byk Gulden Pharma Group, Altana Inc., Melville, N.Y., 1988-92; med. dir. G.I. category Procter & Gamble Health Care, Cin., 1992-94; med. dir. G.I. products Procter & Gamble Pharms., 1994—; med. dir. Consumer Healthcare SmithKline Beecham, Parsippany, N.J.; Co-author, editor: Shopping Guide for Heidelberg, 1980. Co-author, editor: Shopping Guide for Heidelberg, 1980. Cons. Jr. Achievement. With Med. Svc., Fed. Republic Germany Air Force, 1974-76. Mem. AMA, Internat. Soc. Chronobiology, N.Y. Acad. Scis., Am. Acad. Pharm. Physicians, German Assn. Physicians in Pharm. Industry, Toastmasters Internat. (competent toastmaster). Home: 26 Clairview Denville NJ 07054 Office: SmithKline Beecham Consumer Healthcare 1500 Littleton Rd Parsippany NJ 07054-3884

ALBRECHT, RONALD FRANK, anesthesiologist; b. Chgo., Apr. 17, 1937; s. Frank William and Mabel Dorothy (Cassens) A.; m. Joyce Yvonne Burchfield, June 27, 1962; children: Ronald Frank II, Mark Burchfield, Meredith Ann. A.B., U. Ill., 1958, B.S., 1959, M.D., 1961. Diplomate Am. Bd. Anesthesiology. Intern U. Cin. Hosp., 1961-62; resident in anesthesiology U. Ill. Research and Ednl. Hosp., Chgo., 1962-64, attending physician, 1966-73, 89—; clin. assoc. NIH, Bethesda, Md., 1964-66; practice medicine specializing in anesthesiology Chgo., 1966—; asst. prof. anesthesiology U. Ill., Chgo., 1966-70, clin. assoc. prof., 1970-73, prof. anesthesiology, head dept. Coll. Medicine, 1989—; chief dept. anesthesiology U. Ill. Hosp., Chgo., 1989—; chmn. dept. anesthesiology Michael Reese Med. Ctr., Chgo., 1971—; prof. anesthesiology U. Chgo., 1973-89. Contbr. articles to profl. jours. Served to lt. comdr. USPHS, 1964-66. Fellow Am. Coll. Anesthesiologists; mem. AMA, Internat. Anesthesia Rsch. Soc., Am. Soc. Anesthesiologists, Assn. Anesthesists Gt. Britain and Ireland, Am. Physiol. Soc., Soc. Acad. Anesthesiology Chairs, Assn. Anesthesiology Program Dirs. (pres.-elect 1990-91, pres. 1991-93), Ill. Soc. Anesthesiologists (pres. 1980-81), Ill. State Med. Soc., Chgo. Med. Soc., Chgo. Soc. Anesthesiologists (pres. 1986-90), Assn. Univ. Anesthesiologists. Presbyterian. Home: 1020 Chestnut Ave Wilmette IL 60091-1732 Office: U Ill Chgo Coll Medicine MC/515 Dept Anesthesiology 1740 W Taylor St Ste 3200 Chicago IL 60612-7239

ALBRECHT, SUSAN ANN, nursing educator; b. Pitts., July 8, 1953; d. James Philip and Elizabeth K. (Dunn) Kenney; m. John A. Albrecht, May 24, 1975; children: Jill M., John A. Jr. BSN, U. Pitts., 1975, MNursing, 1978, PhD, 1981; M in Pub. Mgmt., Carnegie Mellon U., 1991. RN, Pa., Fla. Staff nurse South Hills Health System, Pitts., 1975-77, part-time, 1983—; asst. prof. undergrad. nursing program U. Pitts., 1979-87, asst. prof. grad. program in nursing, 1987-93, coord. doctoral program in nursing edn., 1992—, asst. dean, 1993—; nurse cons., Pitts., 1984—; Sigma Theta Internat. disting. lectr., 1995-97. Contbr. articles to profl. jours., chpts. to books. Am. Nurse's Found. scholar, 1994. Mem. ANA, Nat. League Nursing (item writer 1981-90, site visitor 1987—, nursing cons.). Roman Catholic. Home: 330 Wray Large Rd Clairton PA 15025-3836 Office: Office of Dean Victoria Univ Pittsburgh Pittsburgh PA 15261

ALBRECHTA, CAROL JEAN, critical care nurse; b. Hazleton, Pa., Nov. 12, 1958; d. John P. and Helen V. (Antanovich) Kravitz; m. Thomas S. Albrechta, May 2, 1987; 1 child, Thomas S. II. Diploma, Hazleton State Gen. Hosp., 1979. Cert. critical care nurse, ACLS, BLS instr. Med.-surg. staff nurse Hazleton (Pa.) St. Joseph's Med. Ctr., 1979-82, ICU staff nurse, 1982—.

ALBRIGHT, LAURIE JO, school psychologist; b. Toledo, Jan. 14, 1952; d. Lawrence Ray and Josephine Amelia (Knott) A.; m. Brian Lee Larson, Sept. 24, 1983; children: Timothy Martin, Bradley Ray. BA in Psychology magna cum laude, Cleve. State U., 1973, MA in Psychology, 1975. Lic. sch. psychologist, counselor with clin. endorsement, Ohio. Staff sch. psychologist Positive Edn. Program Early Intervention Ctr. East, Cleve., 1975-80, program coord., 1980—. Co-pres. Sch. Psychol. Ohio Polit. Action Com., 1987-89. Mem. Nat. Assn. Sch. Psychologists, Am. Psychol. Assn., Ohio Sch. Psychologist Assn. (pres. 1994-95), Cleve. Assn. Sch. Psychologists (pres. 1983-84), Ohio Assn. Masters in Psychology (founding bd. mem. 1994—). Office: Positive Edn Program 1827 E 101st St Cleveland OH 44106-4102

ALBUQUERQUE, EDSON XAVIER, pharmacology educator; b. Recife, Pernambuco, Brazil, Jan. 22, 1938. BS, Salesiano Coll., Recife, Brazil, 1953; MD, U. Recife, 1959; PhD, Fed. U. Pernambuco, U. Sao Paulo, U. Ill., 1962. Lectr. anatomy and physiology U. Recife, Pernambuco, Brazil, 1954-59; instr. pharmacology U. Ill., 1964-65; asst. prof. pharmacology U. Lund (Sweden), 1965-67; rsch. asst. prof. dept. pharmacology Schs. Medicine and Dentistry SUNY, Buffalo, 1968-69, assoc. prof. pharmacology, 1969-72, prof. pharmacology, 1972-73, prof., acting chmn., 1973-74; prof., chmn. dept. pharmacology and exptl. therapeutics U. Md., Balt., 1974—; titular prof. Fed. U. Rio de Janeiro; dir. molecular pharmacology tng. program Joint U. Md./Fed. U. Rio de Janeiro. Mem. editl. bd. and contbr. articles to profl. jours. C.A.P.E.S. fellow, 1959-62, Rockefeller Found. fellow, 1962-63, 63-64; Neuropharmacology grantee Nat. Inst. Neurological Diseases and Blindness, 1964-65; Neuropharmacology fellow Swedish Med. Rsch. Coun., IBRO/Unesco, 1965-67; Order of Grand Cross, Pres. of Brazil, 1995, Order of Rio Branco, 1996. Mem. AAAS, Am. Physiol. Soc., Am. Soc. Pharmacology and Exptl. Therapeutics (Otto Krayer award 1996), Am. Men and Women of Sci., Biophys. Soc. Am., Internat. Soc. Myochemistry, Internat. Brain Rsch. Orgn. (Latin Am. delegation), Latin Am. Soc. Physiol. Sci., Brazilian Pharmacology Soc., Soc. Toxicology, Soc. Neurosci., Third World Acad. Scis., Brazilian Acad. Sci. Office: U Md Dept Pharmacology & Exptl Therapeutics Sch of Medicine Baltimore MD 21201

ALBURTUS, MARY JO, social worker, consultant, trainer; b. Jersey City, Oct. 31, 1949; d. Wilson Vincent and Mary Therese (O'Neill) A. BA, Jersey City State U., 1973; MSW, Fordham U., 1982. Lic. social worker, N.J. Mgmt. analyst U.S. Dept. of Labor, N.Y.C., 1973-76; social worker/specialist Monmouth Family Ctr., Freehold, N.J., 1976-83; social work supr. Monmouth Family Ctr., Asbury Park, N.J., 1983-85; founder, group therapist Monmouth County Sexual Abuse Treatment Program, Red Bank, N.J., 1983-89; supr. community and program devel. Monmouth County Bd. Social Svcs., Neptune, N.J., 1985-90; pvt. practice clin. social worker, cons. Shrewsbury, N.J., 1988—; founder Monmouth County Sexual Abuse Coalition, 1981; social work specialist Family Svcs. Monmouth County Bd. Social Svcs., Neptune, 1990-91; adv. bd. Sexual Abuse Treatment Prog., Red Bank, 1983-89. Grantee Nat. Ctr. on Abuse and Neglect, 1980. Mem. NASW, Acad. Cert. Social Workers (diplomate social work), Mental Health Assn., Monmouth County Sexual Abuse Coalition, Task Force on Women and Alcohol. Office: 21 White St Shrewsbury NJ 07702-4440

ALBURY, CHARLES DONALD, JR., dentist; b. Miami, May 6, 1948; s. Charles Donald and Roberta Jean (Mowery) A.; m. Cynthia Therese Carter, Aug. 23, 1986; children: Vanessa Rihn, Julie Ann. AA, U. Fla., 1970; DMD, U. Louisville, 1974. Diplomate Am. Bd. Oral and Maxillofacial Surgery. Pvt. practice Nashville, 1977—. Mem. Am. Coll. Oral and Maxillofacial Surgeons, Internat. Congress of Oral Implantology. Office: 2400 Patterson St Ste 316 Nashville TN 37203-1562

AL-CHALABI, HATEM RASHEED, psychiatrist; b. Baghdad, Iraq, July 21, 1942; came to U.S., 1967; s. Rasheed K. and Sabiha (Bender) Al-C.; m. Nasreen M. Al-Roufie, Nov. 2, 1968; children: Luma, Ahmad, Edward, Joseph. MB, ChB, Baghdad U., 1965. Diplomate Am. Bd. Psychiatry and Neurology. Intern Kerbala Hosp., Iraq, 1965-66, Poly. Hosp., N.Y.C., 1967-68; pvt. practice Abu Saida, Iraq, 1966-67; resident in psychiatry N.Y. Med. Coll., N.Y.C., 1968-71; resident in neurology Downstate Med. Ctr., Bklyn., 1972-74; pvt. practice Dix Hills, N.Y., 1976—; asst. prof. psychiatry SUNY, Stony Brook, 1977-79; staff psychiatrist St. Vincent's Hosp., S.I., N.Y., 1971-72; attending psychiatrist Bklyn. Hosp., 1974-77, Gracie Square Hosp., N.Y.C., 1974-77; psychiatrist II. L.I. Devel. Ctr., Melville, N.Y., 1979-89; med. dir. Nassau Ctr., Woodbury, N.Y., 1983-85; cons. psychiatrist Cath. Charities, Bay Shore, N.Y., 1978-88, South Oaks Hosp., Amityville, N.Y., 1987—. Recipient recognition award Cath. Diocese Rockville Centre, 1989. Mem. Am. Psychiat. Assn., Suffolk County Psychiat. Soc. Home and Office: 24 Wedgewood Dr Huntington Station NY 11746-5825

AL-CHOKHACHY, MODHAFFER KHALAF, surgeon; b. Baghdad, Iraq, Apr. 10, 1930; came to U.S., 1948; m. Carolyn Ann Coombs, Apr. 10, 1964; children: Heather, David, Robert, Evan, Elissa. BS, Boston U., 1956, MD, 1956. Diplomate Am. Nat. Bd. Medicine, Am. Bd. Surgery. Intern, resident in surgery Boston City Hosp., 1956-61; resident in cancer surgery Western Mass. Hosp., Westfield, 1961; fellow in surgery Harvard Med. Sch., Boston, 1962-63; teaching fellow in surgery Newton (Mass.) Wellesley Hosp., 1963-64; pvt. practice, 1965—. Fellow ACS; mem. Mass. Med. Soc., Plymouth Dist. Med. Soc., Mass. Coll. Surgeons, New Eng. Endoscopy Soc., New Eng. Cancer Soc., Fly Caster's. Home: Ruffini Terr Box 3357 Plymouth MA 02361 Office: 143 Court St Plymouth MA 02360-3807

ALCON, SONJA LEE DE BEY GEBHARDT RYAN, retired medical social worker; b. Orange City, Iowa, Aug. 2, 1937; d. Albert Lee Gerard and Clarice Victoria (Brown) deBey; m. Richard J. Gebhardt, June 6, 1959; children: Russell, Cheryl, Kurt Gebhardt Ryan; m. George W. Ryan, Dec. 28, 1968; 1 dau., Alanna (dec.); m. David E. Alcon, July 20, 1985. C BA, Western Md. Coll., 1959; MSW, U. Md., 1973. Caseworker, Springfield State Hosp., Sykesville, Md., 1959-61; dir. social work dept. Hanover (Pa.) Gen. Hosp., 1966-96; field instr. We. Md. Coll., 1967-96; clin. assoc. prof. sch. social work and social planning U. Md., 1987-92; cons. Golden Age Nursing Home, Hanover, 1973-76, Carlisle (Pa.) Hosp., 1974-78, Hanover Vis. Nurse Assn., 1977-83, emergency svcs. Mental Health Clinic, 1972; chmn. profl. adv. com. Vis. Nurse Assn. of Hanover and Spring Grove, Inc., 1986-89; mem. social work adv. coun. Western Md. Coll., 1979, 80, 81, 94—. Bd. dirs. Hospice of York, 1980-82, Hanover chpt. ARC, 1976-79, Adams-Hanover Mental Health, 1973-76; pres. Human Svcs. Orgn., 1980, v.p., 1985-86; mem. adv. coun. Hanover Hospice, 1982-85; treas. Hanover Cmty. Progress Com., 1976-80; mem. Adams-Hanover Sheltered Workshop Com., 1968-70; bd. dirs. Hanover Cmty. Players, 1974-77, sec., 1982; organizer local chpt. Make Today Count and Preemie Parent Support Group, 1979; initiator, co-trustee Children's Cardiac Fund, 1979-92; mem. Hanover Oratorio Soc., 1964-85, adv. bd. United Cerebral Palsy South Cen. Pa., 1989-90; active YWCA, 1979-84; co-organizer Adams-Hanover chpt. Compassionate Friends, 1983; mem. vestry All Saints Episcopal Ch., 1973-74, 76-79, 83-86, vestry sec., 1975, diocesan del. Ctrl. Pa., 1978, 80-86, mem. altar guild, 1968-86, 92-95, treas. ch. women, 1979-83, ch. choir, soloist, 1975—, life mem.; life mem. Hanover Gen. Hosp. Aux.; mem. adv. group Inst. Pastoral Care, 1976-77; mem. adv. coun. Parents Anonymous, 1976-79, 85-92; adminstr. Hanover Gen. Hosp. Spl. Needs Fund, 1986—; cmty. adv. com. Healthsouth Rehab. York; co-facilitator I Can Cope classes Am. Cancer Soc., 1989-92; active Cmty. Needs Coalition, 1990—, South Ctrl. Pa. Orgn./Time Donation Coalition, 1994—; mem. Case Mgmt. Network South Ctrl. Pa., 1994—; vol. Hanover Hosp., Hanover Hosp. Aux., South Ctrl. Pa. Coalition Organ/Tissue Donation, Hanover Area Coun. Chs. Recipient York Daily Record Exceptional Citizen award, 1979, Spl. Recognition cert. Col. Richard McAllister chpt. DAR, 1980; finalist YWCA Salute to Women, 1986, 87. Mem. Nat. Assn. Social Workers, Acad. Cert. Social Workers (lic. social worker), Ea. Pa. Soc. Hosp. Social Workers, Am. Hosp. Assn. Soc. Hosp. Social Work Adminstrs., Hosp. Assn. Pa. Soc. for Social Work Adminstrs. in Health Care, Ctrl. Pa. Hosp. Social Workers (treas. 1981-85, v.p. 1987, pres. 1988), Md. Alumni Assn. (bd. dirs. 1983), Order Eastern Star (worthy matron 1985-86), Order of Amaranth (royal patron 1988-89, royal matron, 1995-96), Order of the White Shrine of Jerusalem (worthy high priestess 1994-95), Social Order of Beauceant (line officer 1996—), Commandery Ladies Aux. (pres. 1989-90), Elks Aux. (v.p. local club 1986-88). Home: RD # 3 Box 3305-M Spring Grove PA 17362

ALCORN, MERRITT OAKNEY, pathologist; b. Wynne, Ark., Nov. 5, 1920; s. Merritt Oakney and Martha Ellen (Keelty) A.; children: Merritt Keelty, George Lawrence, Mary Ellen Alcorn Cox, Charlotte Lee Alcorn Daughhetee. BS in Chemistry, U. Ark., 1941, MD, 1950. Diplomate Am. Bd. Pathology. Intern U. Ind., 1951; resident in pathology U. Louisville, 1962; engr. U.S. Army Ordinance, Hope, Ark.; pvt. practice Madison, Ind.; pathologist Madison and Lawrenceburg, Ind.; CEO Pathology Computer Systems, Madison. With USN. Home: 1955 Dugan Hollow Rd Madison IN 47250 Office: Pathology Computer Systems 601 Broadway Madison IN 47250-0009

ALDEN, INGEMAR BENGT, pharmaceutical executive; b. Stockholm, Feb. 23, 1943; s. Bengt Erik and Agnes (Eriksson) A.; m. Estelle Cuni Skrabanek, June 18, 1977; children: Lars, Sonja, Ingela. M.Social and Bus. Sci., Stockholm U., 1969. Field supr. Astra Lakemedel Sweden, Sodertalje, 1970-71, nat. sales mgr., 1971-72, mgr. mktg. and sales, 1973-74; internat. mktg. mgr. Astra Pharms., Sodertalje, 1975-76; dir. pharm. div. Astra Ltd., Watford, Eng., 1977-78; mng. dir. Merck Sharp & Dohme, Sweden, 1979-89; chief exec. officer Aldenco AB, 1989-91; dir. Pharma/Agro/Vet div. Svenska Hoechst AB, 1991-95; gen. mgr. Hoechst Marion Roussel AB, Stockholm, 1996—; bd. mem. Assn. Fgn. Pharm. Cos., Kronans Droghandel AB; chmn. Aldenco AB. Club: Rotary, RVC.

ALDERDICE, JOHN THOMAS, psychiatrist, politician; b. Lurgan, No. Ireland, Mar. 28, 1955; s. David and Annie Margaret Helena (Shields) A.; m. Joan Margaret Hill, July 30, 1977; children: Stephen, Peter, Anna. MB, BCh, BAO, Queens U., Belfast, No. Ireland, 1978. Jr. house officer Lagan Valley Hosp., Lisburn, No. Ireland, 1978-79; sr. house officer Belfast City Hosp., 1979-80, sr. registrar in psychotherapy, 1983-87; registrar Whiteabbey and Holywell Hosps., Antrim, No. Ireland, 1980-81, Shaftesbury Square Hosp., Belfast, 1981-82, Lissue Child Psychiatry Hosp., Lisburn, 1982-83; registrar Windsor House Belfast City Hosp., 1983; sr. tutor in psychiatry Queens U., Belfast, 1983-87; cons. psychotherapist Albertbridge Rd. Day Hosp., Belfast, 1988-91, cons. psychotherapist dept. psychotherapy, 1991—; dir. No. Ireland Inst. of Human Rels., 1990-95; exec. med. dir. South and East Belfast Health and Social Svcs. Trust, 1994—; hon. lectr. Queens U. of Belfast, 1990—. Contbr. articles on anorexia nervosa, psychotherapy, ethics and clin. psychiatry to med. jours. Vice chmn. Alliance Party No. Ireland, 1987, party leader, 1987—, leader Alliance del. to Brit.-Irish negotiations on future No. Ireland, 1991, 92—, leader Alliance del. at Forum for Peace and Reconciliation, Dublin Castle, 1994-96, leader Alliance delegation to All-Party Talks on future of No. Ireland, 1996; Westminster candidate for Parliament, 1987, 92; councillor City of Belfast, 1987—; mem. exec. com. European Liberal Dem. and Reform Party, Brussels, 1987-93, mem. ctrl. coun., 1993—, treas., 1995—; v.p. Liberal Internat., 1991—. Recipient Galloway medal Nat. Schizophrenia Fellowship No. Ireland, 1987. Fellow Ulster Med. Soc., Royal Acad. Medicine in Ireland; mem. Brit. Med. Assn., Royal Coll. Psychiatrists, Assn. for Psychoanalytic Psychotherapy (assoc.), Irish Forum for Psychoanalytic Psychotherapy, Nat. Liberal Club (London), Ulster Reform Club (Belfast). Presbyterian. Home: 55 Knock Rd, Belfast BT5 6LB, Northern Ireland Office: Alliance Party No Ireland, 88 University St, Belfast BT7 1HE, Northern Ireland also: City Hall, Belfast BT1 5GS, Northern Ireland

ALDERFER, CLAYTON PAUL, organizational psychologist, educator, author, consultant, administrator; b. Sellersville, Pa., Sept. 1, 1940; s. Joseph Paul and Ruth Althea (Buck) A.; m. Charleen Judith Frankenfield, July 14, 1962; children: Kate, Benjamin. BS with high honors, Yale U., 1962, PhD, 1966. Cert. Am. Bd. Profl. Psychology. Asst. prof. Cornell U., Ithaca, N.Y., 1966-68; asst. prof. Yale U., New Haven, 1968-70, assoc. prof., 1970-78; prof. Sch. Orgn. Mgmt., Yale U., New Haven, 1978-92, assoc. dean, 1982-84; prof. II Grad. Sch. Applied and Profl. Psychology Rutgers U., 1992—, dir. Orgnl. Psychology program, 1992—. Author: Existence, Relatedness and Growth, 1972, Learning from Changing, 1975; contbr. articles to profl. jours.; mem. editl. bd. Jour. Applied Behavioral Sci., 1978-89, editor, 1990—; mem. editl. bd. Family Bus. Rev., 1987—, Jour. Orgnl. Behavior, 1988-92; editor: Advances in Experiential Social Processes, vol. 1, 1979, vol. 2, 1980. Bd. dirs. NTL Inst., Arlington, Va., 1975-78, DATA, New Haven, 1989-92. Grantee Office Naval Research, 1970-74, 79-80, 82-86; recipient Cattell award, 1972, McGregor award, 1979. Fellow Am. Psychol. Assn., Soc. Applied Anthropology, Am. Psychol. Soc.; mem. Sigma Xi, Tau Beta Pi. Democrat. Lutheran. Office: Rutgers Grad Sch Applied Profl Psychology PO Box 819 Piscataway NJ 08855-0819

ALDERMAN, MICHAEL HARRIS, public health educator; b. New Haven, Mar. 26, 1936; s. Julius and Anna (Vener) A.; m. Betsy Feinstein, July 28, 1968; children—John F., Peter B. B.A. magna cum laude, Harvard U., 1958; M.D., Yale U., 1962. Intern Bronx Mcpl. Hosp. Ctr., N.Y., 1962-64; resident N.Y. Hosp.-Cornell Med. Ctr., N.Y.C., 1966-68; vis. prof. U. West Indies, Kingston, Jamaica, 1968-70; attending physician N.Y. Hosp., N.Y.C., 1982—; prof. pub. health Cornell U. Med. Coll., N.Y.C., 1980-84; prof. medicine Cornell U. Med. Coll., 1982-84; prof., chmn. dept. epidemiology and social medicine Albert Einstein Coll. Medicine, N.Y.C., 1984—; program dir. Robert Wood Johnson Found., Princeton, N.J., 1979-81; mem. cons. UN, N.Y.C., 1981; chmn. African Med. Rsch. Found., 1981-94; mem. N.Y. State Task Force on Clin. Guidelines & Med. Tech. Assessment, 1994; chmn. com. on pub. health and preventive medicine Nat. Bd. Med. Examiners, 1988; mem. 4th joint nat. com. on detection, evaluation and treatment high blood pressure Nat. Heart, Lung and Blood Inst., 1988, nat. high blood pressure edn. com. coordinating com. USPHS, 1989, 5th Joint Nat. Com. Detection, Evaluation and Treatment High Blood Pressure, 1991-92; vis. prof. cardiovascular medicine Oxford U., 1990-91. Mem. editl. bd. Jour. Urban Health; contbr. articles to med. jours. Mem. Council Fgn. Relations, N.Y.C., U.S. Civil Rights Commn., Albany, N.Y., 1972-76; U.S. Delegation to USSR, Moscow, 1979; trustee Sharon (Conn.) Hosp., Wallenberg Found., N.Y.; bd. dirs. N.Y. Planned Parenthood Assn., 1992—. Served to lt. cmdr. USPHS, 1964-66. Glorney Raisbeck fellow N.Y. Acad. medicine, 1967-68; WHO travelling fellow, 1973, 77. Fellow ACP, Am. Soc. Clin. Nutrition, Am. Fedn. Clin. Rsch., Royal Soc. Medicine, Am. Heart Assn. (coun. on epidemiology); mem. Nat. Coun. Internat. Health (bd. govs.), Am. Soc. Hypertension (pub. affairs com., exec. com., treas. 1991—, pres. elect 1994-96, pres. 1996—), N.Y. Acad. Medicine (vice chmn. pub. health com. 1988), Explorers Club, Century Assn., Harvard Club. Democrat. Jewish. Home: 1112 Park Ave New York NY 10128-1235 Office: Albert Einstein Coll Medicine 1300 Morris Park Ave Bronx NY 10461-1926

ALDERSON, GLORIA FRANCES DALE, rehabilitation specialist; b. Rainelle, W.Va., May 11, 1945; d. Orval Rupert and Juanita Rose (Nelson) Dale; m. Grayson Raines Alderson, June 3, 1964; children: John Grayson, James Leslie, Kathy LeDawn. ADN, U. Charleston; BS, W.Va. U. DON Charleston Area Med. Ctr., Charleston, 1977-84; head nurse Eye & Ear Clinic, Charleston, 1981-84; owner, operator ABZ Nursing, Kanawha County, W.Va., 1983-87; rehab. specialist W.Va., 1983—; bd. dirs. Profl. and Social Com. on Nursing. Bd. dirs. Urban Politics Symposium, Charleston, 1978; election campaign mgr. Rep. Party, Charleston. Scholarship Bd. Regents, 1974-77. Mem. AAUW, Am. Rehab. Profls., Internat. Platform Assn., Order Ea. Star. Home and Office: 1089 Highland Dr Saint Albans WV 25177-3675

ALDERSON, LOUIS EVERETT, biologist; b. Adrian, W.Va., Feb. 12, 1921; s. Frank Auburn and Charlotte Bierne (Walker) A.; m. Leta Gourley, Jan. 19, 1945; children: John Edward, David Walker. AB, U. W.Va., 1947; MS, U. Wyo., 1949; PhD, Pacific Western U., 1982. Grad. asst. Wyo. Game & Fish Dept., Laramie, 1948-49; dist. game mgr. W.Va. Conservation Commn., Hamlin, 1949-55; rsch. biologist U.S. Fish & Wildlife Svc., Ft. Worth, 1958-69; wildlife specialist Coastal Ecosystems Mgmt., Ft. Worth, 1972—, also bd. dirs. Author: B & O Monongah Memories, 1988. Occupational advisor Lincoln, Boone, and Logan Counties Draft Bds., Hamlin, 1949-55; precinct chmn. Tarrant County Rep. Com., Ft. Worth, 1970—; exec. coun. Internat. Student Assn., Ft. Worth, 1972-76; election judge Tarrant County Commrs. Ct., Ft. Worth, 1986—. Mem. Am. Soc. Mammalogists, Soc. Range Mgmt., Tex. Orgn. Endangered Species (bd. dirs. 1982-85), Wildlife Soc. (cert.) Sigma Xi. Republican. Home: 4541 Nolan St Fort Worth TX 76119-3415

ALDERSON, PHILIP OTIS, radiologist, educator; b. San Francisco, Aug. 11, 1944; s. Lloyd I. and Helen (Boekemeier) A.; m. Marjorie Jean Hawkins, June 13, 1970; children: Lisa Joanne, Kelly Suzanne. AB in Zoology, Washington U., St. Louis, 1966, MD, 1970. Diplomate Am. Bd. Nuclear Medicine, Am. Bd. Radiology (Diagnosis). Intern Jewish Hosp., Washington U. Med. Sch., St. Louis, 1970-71, resident in radiology and nuclear medicine, 1971-74; instr. in radiology Mallinckrodt Inst., Washington U. Med. Sch., St. Louis, 1974-75; from asst. to assoc. prof., dept. radiology Johns Hopkins Med. Inst., Balt., 1977-80; prof. radiology Columbia-Presbyn. Med. Ctr., N.Y.C., 1980—, James Picker prof., chmn. dept. radiology, 1990—; cons. Bur. Radiol. Health, FDA, Rockville, Md., 1980-82, mem. radiopharm. adv. com., 1980-82; bd. dirs. Am. Bd. Nuclear Medicine, 1990-95; invited spkr. numerous internat. confs.; holder 6 named lectureships. Author 4 books; contbr. numerous scientific articles to profl. jours. Maj. USAF, 1975-77. Recipient Alumni Achievement award Wash. U. Med. Sch., 1995; NIH grantee, 1974—. Fellow Am. Coll. Radiology (bd. chancellors 1993—), Am. Coll. Nuclear Physicians, N.Y. Acad. Medicine; mem. Fleischner Soc. (sec. 1989-92, treas. 1996—), N.Y. City Roentgen Soc. (v.p. 1989-90, pres. 1991-92), N.Y. State Radiol. Soc. (sec.-treas. 1991-93, pres. 1993-94), Soc. Nuclear Medicine (v.p. 1984-85, chmn. sci. program com. 1984-86), Assn. Univ. Radiologists (sec.-treas. 1994-95, pres. 1996—), Soc. Chmn. Acad. Radiology Depts. (rep. Coun. Acad. Socs. of Am. Assn. Med. Colls. 1990-95, pres. 1994-95), Omicron Delta Kappa. Office: Columbia-Presbyn Med Ctr Dept Radiology 630 W 168th St New York NY 10032-3702

ALDERTON, DARLENE DOROTHY, nurse, case manager; b. Detroit, Apr. 21, 1950; d. Edward Andrew and Alice Dorothy (Schultz) Grabowski; m. Jan Michael Uroda, Mar. 7, 1969 (div. Sept. 1978); 1 child, Pamela Ann; m. Daryl Kenneth Alderton, Aug. 18, 1979; 1 child, Bryan Edward. BSN, U. Mich., 1973; MSN, No. Mich. U., 1988. Cert. ins. rehab. specialist; cert. case mgr. Staff nurse respiratory ICU U. Mich. Hosp., Ann Arbor, 1973-76, staff nurse thoracic ICU, 1976-77, analgesic rsch. nurse, 1977-78, staff nurse hemodialysis, 1978-79; staff nurse ICU Marquette (Mich.) Gen. Hosp., 1978, staff nurse hemodialysis, 1979-81; patient edn. coord. F.A. Bell Meml. Hosp., Ishpeming, Mich., 1981-84; staff nurse float F.A. Bell Meml. Hosp., Ishpeming, 1984-85; asst. supr. nurses No. Mich. U. Health Ctr., Marquette, 1985-87, supr. nurses, 1987-91; asst. DON Marquette County Med. Care Facility, Ishpeming, 1991-92; med. svcs. specialist Hope Network-Pvt. Rehab., Marquette, 1992-94, Comprehensive Rehab. Assocs., Marquette, 1994-95, Ind. Rehab. Cons., Munising and Ishpeming, 1995—. Mem. planning com. Diabetes Update Workshop, Marquette, 1986-94; bd. mem. Marquette Area Diabetes Adv. Coun., 1986-93, ARC, Ishpeming, 1989-92; mem., co-founder Nat. Mine Sch. PTO, 1990—, pres., 1990-94; mem. planning com. Ishpeming (Mich.) Ind. Day Corp., 1990—; active Profl. Devel. Sch. Com., Marquette County, 1993-94, Citizens Task Force on Edn., Ishpeming, 1994-95. Scholar Marathon Oil/Edison/Crisco, 1968; grantee for diabetic rsch. No. Mich. U., Marquette, 1987-88. Mem. Phi Kappa Phi, Sigma Theta Tau. Home and Office: Rt 3 Box 1098 Ishpeming MI 49849

ALDIN, PETER, psychiatrist, educator; b. Schwerin, Germany, Oct. 29, 1932; came to U.S., 1952; m. Michèle Kenneth (div.). PhB, U. Paris, 1951; BA, CCNY, 1954, MA in Psychology, 1955; PhD Clin. Psychology, Clark U., 1957; MD, Boston U., 1964. Diplomate Am. Bd. Psychiatry and Neurology. Intern Maimonides Hosp., Bklyn., 1964-65; resident Hillside Hosp., Glen Oaks, N.Y., 1965-68, chief resident, 1966-67; attending staff St. Luke's-Roosevelt Hosp., N.Y.C.; teaching staff Columbia U. Sch. of Med., N.Y.C. Fellow Am. Psychiat. Assn. (past mem. exec. com., N.Y. County Dist. Br.), Am. Acad. Legal & Indsl. Medicine (sec. 1992—); mem. AMA. Office: 225 E 47th St Apt 1C New York NY 10017-2113

ALDOROTY, ROBERT ARTHUR, surgeon, educator; b. N.Y.C., July 24, 1954; s. David and Dorothy (Marino) A. BA in Chemistry and Biochemistry with honors, U. Pa., 1976; MA in Anatomy, Columbia U., 1978, MPhil in Anatomy, 1981, PhD in Anatomy and Cell Biology, 1984, MD, 1984. Lic. physician N.Y.; diplomate Am. Bd. Surgery added cert. in surg. critical care; diplomate Nat. Bd. Med. Examiners. Teaching asst. molecular and cell biology U. Pa., 1975-76; teaching asst. histology and gross anatomy Columbia U., N.Y.C., 1977-80; intern in surgery Mt. Sinai Med. Ctr., N.Y.C., 1984-85, resident in surgery, 1985-88, chief resident in surgery, 1988-89; assoc. instr. clin. surgery Mt. Sinai Sch. Medicine, CUNY, 1988-89, asst. prof. surgery, 1989—; asst. attending in surgery Mt. Sinai Svcs. Elmhurst (N.Y.) Hosp. Ctr., 1989—, dir. trauma svc., 1991—; asst. attending in surgery Mt. Sinai Hosp., N.Y.C., 1990—; speaker/presenter Am. Soc. Cell Biology, San Diego, 1974, SUNY, Stony Brook, 1981, U. Vt., 1984, Electrochem. Soc., 1985, Am. Phys. Soc., N.Y.C., 1987. Co-contbr. articles to profl. publs. including Jour. Cell Biology, Jour. Morphology, Jour. Gen. Physiology, Biophysics, Jour. Electrochem. Soc., others; co-contbr. chpt. to Electrical Double Layers in Biology, 1986. Recipient Upjohn award for excellence in rsch., 1984; grad. tng. grantee HEW, 1976-78. Fellow ACS; mem. AMA, Biophys. Soc. (presenter 1982, Samuel A. Talbot Meml. Fund Travel grantee 1982), Soc. Gen. Physiologists (presenter 1981), Med. Soc. of State of N.Y., N.Y. County Med. Soc., Sigma Xi. Office: Mt Sinai Med Ctr Elmhurst Hosp Dept Surgery 7901 Broadway Elmhurst NY 11373-3199

ALDOUS, RICHARD ALLEN, ophthalmologist; b. Salt Lake City, Jan. 8, 1930; s. Heber F. and June (Orrock) A.; m. LaRee Baird, Sept. 10, 1954; children: Kathleen, Julie, Michael, Annette, Sharon, John. BS, U. Utah, 1953, MD, 1956. Diplomate Am. Bd. Ophthalmology. Resident U. Calif., San Francisco, 1960; med. officer USAF, 1960-64; pvt. practice ophthalmologist Salt Lake City, 1964—. Capt. USAF, 1960-64. Fellow Am. Acad. Ophthalmology; mem. AMA, Utah Ophthalmol. Soc. (sec. 1969-72, pres. 1972-73). Mem. LDS Ch. Office: 857 E 2nd South Salt Lake City UT 84102

ALDRICH, CLARENCE KNIGHT, physician, educator; b. Chgo., Apr. 12, 1914; s. L. Sherman and Bessie A. (Knight) A.; m. Julie H. Murphy, Feb. 4, 1942; children—Carol K., Michael S., Thomas K., Robert F. B.A., Wesleyan U., 1935; M.D., Northwestern U., 1940. Faculty U. Minn. Med. Sch., 1947-55, asst. prof., 1947-52, assoc. prof., 1952-55; prof. psychiatry U. Chgo. Sch. Medicine, 1955-70, chmn. dept. psychiatry, 1955-64; prof., chmn. dept. N.J. Med. Sch., Newark, 1970-73; prof. psychiatry Sch. Medicine, U. Va., Charlottesville, 1973-77; prof. psychiatry and family medicine Sch. Medicine, U. Va., 1977-84, prof. emeritus, 1984—, mem. Ctr. Advanced Studies, 1981-84; vis. prof. psychiatry U. Edinburgh, 1963-64; dir. Blue Ridge Mental Health Ctr., 1973-75; Mayne guest prof. U. Queensland, Australia, 1986. Author: Psychiatry for the Family Physician, 1955, Introduction to Dynamic Psychiatry, 1966, (with C. Nighswonger) A Casebook for Pastoral Counseling, 1968, The Medical Interview: Gateway to the Doctor-Patient Relationship, 1993. Served from asst. surgeon to surgeon USPHS, 1940-46. Fellow Am. Coll. Psychiatrists, Am. Orthopsychiat. Assn., Am. Psychiat. Assn.; mem. Group for Advancement Psychiatry. Home and Office: 905 Cottage Ln Charlottesville VA 22903-1611

ALDRICH, DELL STANLEY, orthodontist; b. Southgate, Calif., July 31, 1938; s. Adelbert Carl and Marian Grace (Carlson) A.; m. Joanne Emily VanderByl, June 30, 1962 (div. 1976); children: Cheryl Marlene, Michelle Renee. AA, Glendale Coll., 1959; DDS, U. So. Calif., 1963, MS in Orthodontics, 1970. Intern U.S.C. Med. Ctr., L.A.; resident U. S.C. Sch. Dentistry, L.A.; clin. instr. fixed prosthetic dept. U. So. Calif., L.A., 1962-63, 66-68; pvt. practice instr. Swiss Dental Assn., Geneva and Zurich, Switzerland, 1970-71; instr. Internat. Post Doctorate Program, 1989-96; pvt. practice Descanso Med. Ctr., La Canada, Calif., 1972-93, Flintridge, Calif., 1993—. Author: Differential Response Incident to Tooth Movement, 1970; contbr. articles to profl. jours.; inventor, developer ultrasonic and fiber optic instruments; patentee in field. Mem. Rep. Presdl. Task Force, 1984. Capt. U.S. Army, 1963-66, Fed. Republic Germany. Mem. Am. Assn. Orthodontists, Pacific Coast Soc. Orthodontics, Am. Dental Assn., Calif. Dental Soc., Kiwanis, Tournament of Roses Assn., Omicron Kappa Epsilon Alumni Assn., Phi Kappa Phi. Address: 241 W Wilson St Apt 20 Costa Mesa CA 92627-5634

ALDRICH, NANCY ARMSTRONG, psychotherapist, clinical social worker; b. Taylorville, Ill., Oct. 4, 1925; d. Guy L. and Alice Irene (Hicks) Armstrong; m. Paul Harwood Aldrich, Sept. 30, 1949; children: Gregory Paul, Mark Douglas, Alice Ann Aldrich White, Ruth Lynne Aldrich Sammis. AB with highest honors, U. Ill., 1947, BS in Chemistry, 1948, MS in Chemistry, 1949; MSS, Bryn Mawr Coll., 1986. Lic. clin. social worker, Del., Pa. Parole bd. mem. State of Del., Dover, 1970-74; instr. continuing edn. U. Del., Newark, 1976-78, program specialist, 1978-83; founder Acad. Lifelong Learning; v.p. Aldrich Assocs. Inc., Landenberg, Pa., 1983—, psychotherapist, 1987—; psychotherapist Family Community Service Del. County, Media, Pa., 1986, Tressler Ctr. for Human Growth, Wilmington, Del., 1987-93; clin. affiliate Personal Performance Cons., 1990-94, Acorn, 1990—, CMG Health, 1991—, Inst. for Human Resources, 1993—, employee assistance program DuPont, 1992—, Champus, 1988—, HAI/Aetna, 1994—, Value Behavioral Health, 1993—, OPTUM, 1993—, Accord, 1996—; coord. human resources devel. program Tressler Ctr. for Human Growth, 1983-84. Pres. YWCA New Castle County, Wilmington, 1974-76; mem. Statewide Health Coordinating Coun., Del., 1978-79; bd. dirs., com. mem. United Way Del., Wilmington, 1975-84; trustee Unitarian Universalist House, Phila., 1992-94. Mem. AAUW (pres. Wilmington br. 1968-70, nat. resolutions com. 1971-72, fellowship gift named in her honor 1970), Del. Soc. Lic. Clin. Social Workers (pres. 1990-91), Del. Gerontol. Soc., Mental Health Assn. Del., Internat. Soc. Bioenergetic Analysis, Phi Beta Kappa, Phi Kappa Phi, Iota Sigma Pi. Office: 625 Chambers Rock Rd Landenberg PA 19350-1041 also: 1601 Milltown Rd Ste 8 Wilmington DE 19808-4047

ALDRIDGE, GWENDOLYN JOY, medical records administrator, clergy member; b. Lamesa, Tex., May 7, 1948. Accredited record tech., Am. Health Info. Mgmt; ordained minister, 1993. Adminstr. health info. med. Arts Hosp., 1974—; cons. Sage Health Care, Lamesa, 1990—, Lamesa Health Care Ctr. 1990—. Mem. Am. Heart Assn., Am. Cancer Soc. Home: 814 N 19th Lamesa TX 79331 Office: Med Arts Hosp Dept Adminstr Lamesa TX 79331

ALDY, MARY ELLEN, nurse aide; b. Denver, Feb. 15, 1961; d. Joseph and Neola (Brinley) A. BS in Human Svc., Met. State Coll., Denver, 1988; cert. in home health and nurse aide, E. Griffith Opportunity Sch., Denver, 1989. Lic. nurse aide, Colo.; cert. phys. therapy asst. Skills developer, outreach asst. Holistic Approaches to Ind. Living, Denver, 1986-87; residential living specialist Martin Luther Homes, Denver, 1987-88; presch. tchr. South Wadsworth Bapt. Ch., Denver, 1988-90; home health aide Swedish Home Health Care, Denver, 1990-91; nurse aide Brentwood Care Ctr., Denver, 1990-92, Julia Temple Ctr., 1992-94; nurse aide, cert. restorative nurse aide Univ. Hills Christian Living Campus, Denver, 1993-96; with Safeway, Denver, 1996—. Home: 2160 S Logan St Denver CO 80210-4428 Office: Safeway 2150 S Downing Denver CO 80210

ALEGRE, JOSE ALBERTO, family practice physician; b. Callao, Peru, Feb. 15, 1928; came to U.S., 1955; s. Max and Josefina (Benavides) A.; m. Joanne Martha Miller, Nov. 3, 1956; children: David, Barbara, Patricia, Dante, Joseph. BS, San Marcos U., Lima, Peru, 1950, MD, 1954. Diplomate Am. Bd. Family Practice. Physician VA, Leavenworth, Kans., 1959-61, Poplar Bluff, Mo., 1961-67, Prescott, Ariz., 1967-90. Fellow Am. Acad. Family Physicians; mem. AMA, Ariz. Med. Assn., Peruvian-Am. Med. Soc. Home: 3056 Chichicoi Ln Prescott AZ 86301-6911

ALEO, JOSEPH JOHN, pathology scientist, educator, academic research administrator; b. Wilkes-Barre, Pa., Oct. 8, 1925; s. Vincent and Martha (Lupino) A.; m. Fannie Ocuto, Aug. 28, 1949; children: Joseph John, James Robert. BS, Bucknell U., 1948; DDS, Temple U., 1953; PhD, U. Rochester, 1965. Commd. dental surgeon USPHS, 1953-54; pvt. practice dentistry Meshoppen, Pa., 1954-60; research fellow U. Rochester, N.Y., 1960-65; assoc. prof., chmn. dept. pathology Temple U., 1965-67, prof., chmn. dept., 1967-70, dean advanced edn. and research, 1970-87; cons., mem. standing coms. NIH, FDA, other gov. agencies, industries; vis. scholar U. Cambridge, 1971-72. Editorial bd., reviewer numerous sci. jours.; pub. over 100 papers, chpts., abstracts; rsch. connective tissue diseases; ascorbic acid transport in health and disease. Served with AUS, 1943-46. Decorated Bronze Star. Fellow AAAS, N.Y. Acad. Sci.; mem. numerous profl., sci., hon. socs. Home: 6610 Seawind Dr Fort Myers FL 33908-6160

ALEVY, DANIEL I., clinical psychologist; b. Long Beach, N.Y., May 29, 1929; s. Gabriel Moshe and Marie (Raphael) A.; children: Michael, Jonathan, Adam. BA, CCNY, 1954; PhD, Ind. U., 1960. Diplomate Am. Bd. Profl. Psychologists; lic. psychologist, Calif., Conn., N.Y. Field selection officer Peace Corps, Washington, 1964-70; psychology cons. New Haven (Conn.) Police Dept., 1969-78; chief psychologist Elmcrest Psychiat. Inst., Portland, Conn., 1979-81; asst. clin. prof. Yale U. Med. Sch., New Haven, 1969-91; dir. Psychology Intern Tng., Santa Barbara, Calif., 1991-94; care mgr. Green Spring Health Svcs., Chattanooga, 1995—; chmn. Human Resources Ctr. Conn., New Haven, 1968. Contbr. articles to profl. jours. Bd. dirs. New Haven Halfway House, 1973-76; unit commr. Quinnipiac coun. Boy Scouts Am., Hamden, Conn., 1985-86; bd. dirs. Big Bros./Big Sisters, South Cen. Conn., New Haven, 1985-86. With U.S. Army, 1950-52, Korea, Japan. USPHS fellow Ind. U., 1955-56. Mem. APA, Sigma Xi. Home: PO Box 3015 Stony Creek CT 06405-1615 Office: Green Spring Health Svcs 7P 801 Pine St # 7P Chattanooga TN 37402-2520

ALEXANDER, ARCHIE A., radiologist; b. Galveston, Tex., Jan. 23, 1953; s. Archie A. and Peggy Jean (Williamson) A.; m. Lory, May 24, 1981. BA, U. Tex., 1976; MD, U. Tex. Med. Br., 1981. Diplomate Am. Bd. Radiology. Asst. prof. radiology U. Fla. Health Sci. Ctr., Jacksonville, 1988-89; from asst. prof. to assoc. prof. radiology Thomas Jefferson Univ. Hosp., Phila., 1990—; Assoc. editor Radiology. Co-author: Urogenital Ultrasound, 1995. Fellow Coll. Physicians Phila.; mem. Am. Inst. Ultrasound in Medicine, Am. Coll. Radiology, Radiology Soc. N.Am., Cooley Soc., U. Tex. Med. Br. Alumni Assn. Office: Thomas Jefferson Univ Hosp Div Ultrasound 132 S 10th St 7 Main Philadelphia PA 19107

ALEXANDER, BARBARA LEAH SHAPIRO, clinical social worker; b. St. Louis, May 6, 1943; d. Harold Albert and Dorothy Miriam (Leifer) Shapiro; m. Richard E. Alexander. B in Music Edn., Washington U., St. Louis, 1964; postgrad., U. Ill., 1964-66; MSW, Smith Coll., 1970; postgrad., Inst. Psychoanalysis, Chgo., 1971-73, grad., child therapy program, 1976-80; cert. therapist Sex Dysfunction Clinic, Loyola U., Chgo., 1975. Diplomate in Clin. Social Work. Rsch. asst., NIMH grantee Smith Coll., 1968-70; probation officer Juvenile Ct. Cook County, Chgo., 1966-68, 70; therapist Madden Mental Health Ctr., Hines, Ill., 1970-72; supr., therapist, field instr. U. Chgo., U. Ill. Grad. Schs. Social Work; therapist Pritzker Children's Hosp., Chgo., 1972-82; therapist, cons., also pvt. practice, 1973—; pres. On Good Authority, 1992—; intern Divorce Conciliation Svc., Circuit Ct. Cook County, 1976-77. Contbr. articles to profl. jours. Bd. dirs., Grant Park Concerts Soc.; sec. Art Resources in Teaching. Recipient Sterling Achievement award Mu Phi Epsilon, 1964. Mem. Nat. Fed. Soc. for Clin. Social Work (chmn. 20th ann. conf., exec. bd.), Ill. Soc. Clin. Social Work (pres. 1986-90, bd. dirs., chmn. svcs. to mems. com., dir. pvt. practitioners' referral service), Assn. Child Psychotherapists, Amateur Chamber Music Players Assn., Jewish Geneal. Soc., Smith Coll. Alumni Assn. (bd. dirs., v.p. 1992-94). Home and Office: 6 Horizon Ln Galena IL 61036-9258

ALEXANDER, CHARLES, housing authority executive; b. Ft. Pierce, Fla., Dec. 10, 1942; s. George and Chris (Butler) A.; m. Ola M. Shelton, July 6, 1968; 1 child, Carlos David. BS, Troy State U., 1979, MS, 1987; MS, Troy State U., 1989. Enlisted U.S. Army, 1961, advanced through grades to master sgt., 1982; ret., 1984; from north area cluster mgr. to mgr. Columbus (Ga.) Housing Authority; exec. dir. Warner Robins (Ga.) Housing Authority, 1990; dir. youth counselors Elizabeth Canty, Warren Williams Apts., Columbus, 1988-90. Vol. worker Sta. FOXY-FM, Columbus, 1989-90; telephone operator United Negro Coll. Fund Campaign, Columbus, 1990; Omega chmn. membership A.J. McClung YMCA, Columbus, 1990. Mem. Nat. Assn. Housing R.O., Am. Assn. Ret. Persons, Omega Psi Phi (vice basileus 1987-89, basileus 1990). Methodist. Office: Warner Robins Housing Auth PO Box 2048 Warner Robins GA 31099-2048

ALEXANDER, DANIEL ROBERT, pathologist; b. Elizabeth, N.J., Oct. 22, 1962; s. Bernard David and Muriel Catherine (Sank) A.; m. Beth Kate Wenzel, May 26, 1991; children: Marin Rchel, Seth Morgan, Dylan Michael. BS, Rutgers U., 1984; MS, U. Medicine & Dentistry N.J., Newark, 1988; MD, U. Medicine & Dentistry N.J., New Brunswick, 1992. Diplomate Nat. Bd. Med. Examiners. Anatomic and clin. pathology resident SUNY Health Sci. Ctr., Syracuse, 1992—, intern in internal medicine, 1993-94. Contbg. author: Clinical Diagnosis and Management by Laboratory Methods, 19th edit., 1996; contbr. articles to med. jours. Mem. adminstrv. coun. on legislation N.J. Med. Soc., Lawrenceville, 1990-92. Mem. AMA, Coll. Am. Pathologists, Med. Soc. of State of N.Y., U.S. and Can. Acad. Pathology. Republican. Home: 27 Winthrop Rd Clark NJ 07066 Office: SUNY Health Sci Ctr 750 E Adams St Syracuse NY 13210

ALEXANDER, DAVID TODD, physician; b. N.Y.C., May 13, 1954; s. Albert Murry and Rhoda Naomi (Shapiro) A.; m. Patricia Agnes Darcy, May 23, 1982; 1 child, Colin, Locke. BS, Yale U., 1975; MD, Columbia U., 1979. Diplomate Am. Bd. Pediatrics. Resident in pediatrics Babies Hosp., N.Y.C., 1979-82; gen. pediat. fellow Children's Hosp., Phila., 1982-84; clin. asst. prof. pediatrics Thomas Jefferson U., Phila., 1984-87; asst. prof. pediatrics U. Pa., Phila., 1987-93; med. dir. Raymond Blank Children's Hosp., Des Moines, 1993—; clin. prof. of pediatrics U. Iowa Sch. of Medicine, 1995—. Office: Blank Childrens Hosp. 1200 Pleasant St Des Moines IA 50309

ALEXANDER, DUANE FREDERICK, pediatrician, research administrator; b. Balt., Aug. 11, 1940; s. Fred Lucas and Christiana H. (Showacre) A.; m. Marianne Ellis, June 23, 1963; children: Keith Duane, Kristin Marianne. B.S., Pa. State U., 1962; M.D., Johns Hopkins U., 1966. Diplomate Am. Bd. Pediatrics. Intern Johns Hopkins Hosp., Balt., 1966-67, resident, 1967-68, fellow, 1970-71; commd. officer USPHS, 1968—, now rear adm.; clin. assoc. Nat. Inst. Child Health and Human Devel., NIH, Bethesda, Md. 1968-70, asst. to sci. dir., 1971-74, asst. to dir., 1978-82, dep. dir., 1982-86 dir. Nat. Inst. Child Health and Human Devel., NIH, 1986—; staff pediatrician Nat. Commn. for Protection of Human Subjects of Research, 1974-78. Contbr. articles to profl. jours. Recipient Commendation medal USPHS, 1970, Meritorious Svc. medal USPHS, 1985, Spl. Recognition medal USPHS, 1985, Surgeon Gen.'s Exemplary Svc. medal, 1990, Irving B. Harris Lectureship award Soc. Behavioral Pediatrics, 1991, Pub. Svc. award Am. Coll. Ob-Gyn., 1992, Surgeon Gen.'s Medallion, 1993, Disting. Pub. Svc. award Am. Acad. Phys. Medicine and Rehab., 1993, Presdl. Citation, APA 1992; alumni fellow Pa. State U. Alumni Assn, 1993. Fellow Am. Acad. Pediatrics, Soc. Devel. Pediatrics, Am. Pediatric Soc., Assn. for Retarded Citizens. Methodist. Office: Nat Inst Child Health & Human Devel Bldg 31 Rm 2A03 31 Center Dr MSC 2425 Bethesda MD 20892-2425

ALEXANDER, EDWARD ALAN, medical educator; b. Paterson, N.J., Aug. 25, 1934; s. Paul Alton and Julia (Phillips) A.; m. Lois Diamond, June 15, 1958; children: Deborah, Peter. BA, Rutgers U., 1956; MD, Northwestern U., 1960. Intern King's County Hosp., Bklyn., 1960-61, jr. resident, 1961-62; jr. resident Boston City Hosp., 1964-65; nephrology fellow Boston U. Med. Ctr., 1965-67; physiology fellow Yale Med. Sch., 1967-69; asst. prof. Boston U. Med. Sch., 1969-73, assoc. prof., 1973-79, prof. medicine, 1979—; chief nephrology Boston City Hosp., 1972—. Office: Boston City Hosp 818 Harrison Ave Boston MA 02118

ALEXANDER, EDWARD GREENWOOD, JR., orthopaedic surgeon; b. Washington, May 19, 1940; s. Edward G. and Alice B. (Munsell) A.; m. Nancy Gervais Alexander, July 14, 1964 (div. June 1981); children Edward G. III, Jason D.; Jane Elizabeth Walker, Oct. 21, 1983;. Grad., G.W. U., 1966. Diplomate Am. Acad. Orthopaedic Surgeons. Intern Fairfax Hosp., 1966-67; resident Nat. Hosp. Med. Ctr., 1970-73; chief orthopaedic surgery Alexandria (Va.) Hosp., 1986-90, Nat. Hosp. Med. Ctr., Arlington, Va., 1993—. Capt. U.S. Army, 1967-70. Democrat. Office: No Va Orthopaedic Group # 106 2500 N Van Dorn St Alexandria VA 22302

ALEXANDER, GEORGE JAY, toxicologist; b. Paris, June 27, 1925; came to U.S., 1946; s. Max and Salomea (Rubin) A.; m. Rita Birnbaum, Apr. 29, 1958; 1 child, Mark. BS, Hobart Coll., 1949; PhD, Rutgers U., 1953. Rsch. fellow Rutgers Endowment Found., New Brunswick, N.Y., 1951-53; staff scientist Worcester Found., Shrewsbury, Mass., 1953-58; rsch. assoc. Columbia U., N.Y.C., 1958-60, from asst. prof. to assoc. prof. biochem. psychiatry, 1960-94; head behavioral toxicology N.Y. State Psychiat. Inst., N.Y.C., 1987-92; rsch. scientist N.Y. State Office of Mental Retardation and Devel. Disabilities, S.I., N.Y., 1992—; rsch. scientist V, N.Y. State Dept. Mental Hygiene, N.Y.C., 1977-92. Contbr. chpts. in books and articles to profl. jours. Exec. bd. dirs. Pub. Employees Fedn., N.Y.C., 1989-92; nat. exec. bd. dirs. Jewish Labor Com., N.Y.C., 1986—. Fellow Am. Philatelic Soc.; mem. Am. Soc. Chemistry and Molecular Biology, Soc. Exptl. Biology and Medicine, N.Y. Acad. Scis. Office: NY State Inst Basic Rsch Devel Disabilities 1050 Forest Hill Rd Staten Island NY 10314-6330

ALEXANDER, H. CLAY, surgeon, educator; b. N.Y.C., Feb. 3, 1935; s. Henry C. and Janet (Hutchinson) A.; m. Annalita Marsigli, 1963; 1 child, H. Clay; m. Paula T. Case, Jan. 12, 1977; 1 child, Grant; 1 stepchild, Reef. BA in English, Yale U., 1956; MD, Cornell U., 1961. Diplomate Nat. Bd. Med. Examiners. Intern surgery Columbia Presbyn. Med. Ctr., N.Y.C., 1961-62, resident, 1962-67; attending surgeon Roosevelt Hosp., N.Y.C., 1969-77, Doctors Hosp., Dallas, 1977—; asst. clin. prof. surgery Columbia Coll. Physicians and Surgeons, N.Y.C., 1969-77, U. Tex. Southwestern Med. Ctr., Dallas, 1979—; dir. surgery Gen. Hosp. Lakewood, Dallas, 1977-84. Bd. dirs. Physician's Direct Access; pres. Healthcare IPA, 1986—. Fellow ACS; mem. AMA, Am. Bd. Surgery, Soc. Laparoendoscopic Surgeons, Tex. Med. Assn. (alt. del. 1992—), Dallas County Med. Soc., Western Surg. Soc., Tex. Surg. Soc. Home: 8027 Abramshire Ave Dallas TX 75231-4714 Office: White Rock Surg Bldg 9335 Garland Rd Dallas TX 75218

ALEXANDER, JAMES WESLEY, surgeon, educator; b. El Dorado, Kans., May 23, 1934; s. Rossiter Wells and Merle Lydia Alexander; m. Maureen L. Strohofer; children: Joseph, Judith, Elizabeth, Randolph, John Charles, Lori, Molly. Student, Tex. Technol. Coll., 1951-53; MD, U. Tex., 1957; ScD, U. Cin., 1958-64; postgrad., U. Minn., 1966-67. Diplomate Am. Bd. Surgery, Am. Bd. Thoracic Surgery; lic. physician, Ohio. Intern Cin. Gen. Hosp., 1957-58; resident U. Cin.-Cin. Gen. Hosp., 1958-64; mem. faculty Coll. Medicine, U. Cin., 1962-64, 66—, prof. surgery, 1975—, dir. transplantation div., dept. surgery, 1967—, dir. surg. immunology lab., 1967—; dir. research Shriners Burns Inst., 1979-90; practice medicine and surgery Cin., 1966—; mem. staff U. Cin. Hosp., Bethesda Hosp., Cin. Children's Hosp., Christ Hosp., Good Samaritan Hosp., Jewish Hosp.; mem. study sect. NIH, 1983-87, 89-93, chmn., 1990-93. Author: (with R.A. Good) Fundamentals of Clinical Immunology, 1977; mem. editl. bd. Annals of Surgery, 1975—, Jour. Burn Care and Rehab., 1979—, Burns, Including Thermal Injury, 1985-92, Jour. Parenteral and Enteral Nutrition, 1991, Nutrition, 1991—, Transplantation Sci., 1991-94, Transplantatin, 1994—; contbr. over 600 articles to profl. jours. Served as capt. M.C., U.S. Army, 1964-66. Mem. AAAS, Am. Assn. for Surgery of Trauma, Am. Assn. Immunologists, Am. Burn Assn. (pres. 1984-85), ACS, Am. Soc. Transplant Surgeons (sec. 1985-87, pres. elect 1987-88, pres. 1988-89), Am. Soc. Parenteral and Enteral Nutrition, Am. Surg. Assn., Assn. for Acad. Surgery, Central Surg. Assn., Cin. Acad. Medicine, Cin. Curg. Soc., Halsted Soc., Immunocompromized Host Soc., Internat. Soc. for Burn Injuries, Internat. Soc. Surgery, Colombian Coll. Surgeons (hon.), Peruvian Acad. Surgery (hon.), St. Paul Surg. Soc. (hon.), Ohio Med. Assn., Soc. Univ. Surgeons, Surg. Biology Club, Surg. Infection Soc. (sec. 1981-84, pres.-elect 1985-86, pres. 1986-87), Tranplantation Soc., Shock Soc., Mont Reid Surg. Soc., Alpha Omega Alpha, Alpha Chi, Alpha Epsilon Delta, Phi Eta Sigma. Home: 2869 Grandin Rd Cincinnati OH 45208-3416 Office: U Cin Coll Medicine 231 Bethesda Ave Cincinnati OH 45267-0558

ALEXANDER, JOHN ROBERT, hospital administrator, internist; b. Tulsa, July 28, 1936; s. Hiram Marshall and Roberta Alice (Greene) A.; m. Marjorie Louise Okeson, Aug., 1958; children: Stephanie Maine, Paul Fulton, James Marshall, Cynthia Ann, Karen Louise, Robert Thomas. BS, U. Okla., 1958; MD, U. Okla., Oklahoma City, 1961. Intern St. John's Hosp., Tulsa, 1961-62, 1961-62; resident Meth. Hosp. of Dallas, Tex., 1962-65; resident in internal medicine Methodist Hosp. of Dallas, 1962-65; pres. Tulsa Internists, Ltd., 1974-89, Wheeling Med. Group, Inc., Tulsa, 1989-90; mem. staff St. John Med. Ctr., Tulsa, chief of staff, 1977-78, v.p. med. affairs, 1991—; vice chmn., bd. dirs. Physicians Liability Ins. Co., Oklahoma City; bd. dirs., mem. adv. coun. Okla. Bd. Nurse Registration and Nursing Edn., Oklahoma City; clin. prof. U. Okla. Coll. Medicine, 1974; mem. Okla. Bd. Med. Licensure and Supervision, Tulsa, 1993—, pres., 1995-96. Editor (report) Med. Edn. in Tulsa County, 1981. Pres. Tulsa County Heart Assn., 1970-71; elder Kirk of the Hills Presbyn. Ch., Tulsa, 1970—; med. dir. Wright City (Okla.) Free Health Clinic, 1975-80; chmn. bd. dirs. Tulsa County Health Dept., 1982; pres. bd. dirs. Tulsa Med. Edn., 1994—. Recipient Disting. Medical Svc. award U. Okla. Alumni Assn., 1995, Disting Svc. award Am. Heart Assn., 1971; named Friends of Nursing, Okla. Nurses Assn., 1990. Fellow ACP; mem. AMA (del. 1985—), Okla. State Med. Assn. (pres. 1989-90), Tulsa County Med. Soc. (pres. 1983), Tulsa Internists Soc.(pres. 1972), U. Okla. Alumni Assn. (pres. 1982-83), Rotary Club Will Rogers (pres. 1973-74), Alpha Omega Alpha. Republican. Home: 6733 S Gary Ave Tulsa OK 74136-4515 Office: St John Med Ctr 1923 S Utica Ave Tulsa OK 74104-6520

ALEXANDER, JONATHAN, cardiologist, consultant; b. N.Y.C., Nov. 29, 1947; s. Josef and Hannah (Margolis) A.; m. Karen Deborah Einhorn, Aug. 8, 1971; children: Jessica Beth, Daniel Lewis, Benjamin Joel. BA, Harvard U., 1968; MD, Albert Einstein Coll. Medicine, 1973. MD. Intern, resident Yale-New Haven Hosp., 1973-76; fellow dept. cardiology Sch. Medicine Yale U., New Haven, 1976-78, asst. clin. prof. medicine, 1978-83, assoc. clin. prof., 1983-95, clin. prof., 1995—; attending physician Danbury (Conn.) Hosp., 1978—, West Haven (Conn.) Vets. Hosp., 1978—, New Milford (Conn.) Hosp., 1980; dir. cardiac rehab. unit and nuclear cardiology Danbury (Conn.) Hosp., 1978—. Recipient Samuel Kushlan award Yale-New Haven Hosp., 1974, Revlon award 11th Internat. Congress Chemotherapy, 1983. Fellow ACP, Am. Coll. Cardiology (gov. Conn. 1993-

6), Conn. chpt. Am. Coll. Cardiology (pres. 1993-96), Conn. Hosp. Assn., Found. for Cmty. Health Care. Jewish.

ALEXANDER, KEITH N., hospital administrator; b. Youngstown, Ohio, Apr. 4, 1962; s. N. Ronald Alexander and Linda Sue (Cline) Blodgett; m. Megan Leishman, June 13, 1991; 1 child, Tyler Leishman. BS, Ohio State U., 1983, M. Health Adminstrn., 1988. House orderly Ohio State U. Hosp. and Clinics, Columbus, 1982-83; emergency rm. technician Mt. Carmel Med. Ctr., Columbus, 1983-88; adminstrv. resident Evanston (Ill.) Hosp. Corp., 1987; adminstrv. fellow St. Benedict's Hosp., Ogden, Utah, 1988-90; dir. ambulatory svcs. St. Francis Hosp. and Med. Ctr., Hartford, Conn., 1990-92; asst. CEO Mountainview Hosp., Payson, Utah, 1992-94; CEO Jordan Valley Hosp., West Jordan, Utah, 1994—. Bd. dirs. Hartford Primary Care Consortium, 1992-94. Named Asst. CEO of the Yr., HealthTrust, Inc., Western Region, 1993. Mem. Am. Coll. Healthcare Execs., West Jordan C. of C. (bd. dirs. 1994—). Office: Jordan Valley Hospital 3580 W 9000 S West Jordan UT 84088

ALEXANDER, KEVIN LEE, optometrist; b. Bowling Green, Ohio, July 9, 1951; s. Nelson Earl and Betty Louise (Bain) A.; m. Carol Louise Brown, May 28, 1988; children: Nicholas, Lindsay. BS, Ohio State U., 1974, OD, 1976, MS, 1977, PhD, 1979. Lic. optometrist, Ohio, Mich., Ind. Clin. asst. prof. Ohio State U., Columbus, 1979-86, 91-94, clin. assoc. prof., 1994—; pvt. practice optometry Columbus, 1981-87; ctr. dir. The Eye Ctr. of Toledo, 1987-94; optometrist Retina Vitreous Assocs., Toledo, 1994—. Editor: Lippincott's Manual of Primary Eyecare, 1995; author monograph; mem. editorial bd. Jour. Optometry and Visual Sci., 1994-96. Recipient Alumni award for disting. teaching Ohio State U., 1980. Fellow Am. Acad. Optometry; mem. Am. Optometric Assn., Ohio Optometric Assn. (past pres., Ohio Optometrist of Yr. 1989). Office: Retina Vitreous Assocs 2213 Cherry St Toledo OH 43608

ALEXANDER, ROBERT WAYNE, medical educator; b. Memphis, Mar. 19, 1941. AB, U. Miss., 1962; MS in Physiology, Emory U., 1967, PhD in Physiology, 1968; MD, Duke U., 1969. Diplomate Am. Bd. Internal Medicine, Am. Bd. Cardiovascular Disease. Intern in medicine Duke U., 1969-70, fellow in cardiology, 1974-76; resident in medicine U. Wash., 1970-71; asst. prof. medicine Harvard U., 1976-82, assoc. prof., 1982-88; assoc. phys. Brigham and Women's Hosp., Boston, 1982-88; asst. in medicine Beth Israel Hosp., Boston, 1982-88; chief of cardiology Emory U. Hosp., 1988—; dir. divsn. cardiology Emory U., 1988—, R. Bruce Logue prof. medicine, 1988—; staff assoc., sr. surgeon experimental therapeutics br. Nat. Heart and Lung Inst., Nat. Inst. Health, Bethsda, Md., 1971-74; vis. prof. Duke U. Med. Ctr., 1986, U. Tex. Southwestern Med. Ctr., Dallas, 1988, Mt. Sinai Med. Ctr., N.Y.C., 1990, Kobe U., Japan, 1992, Ohio State U., 1995; Pfizer vis. prof. U. Mich., 1993; Simon Dack vis. prof. Mt. Sinai Med. Ctr., 1995. Mem. editl. bd. Jour. Clin. Investigation, 1992—, Circulation Rsch., Advances in Pharmacology, Advances in Hypertension, all 1989-93; co-editor The Heart, 8th edit., 1993, sr. editor, 9th edit., 1995; circulation-cons. editor Jour. Am. Coll. Cardiology, 1993—. Recipient Rsch. Career Devel. award, 1977-82; Pfizer traveling fellow Clin. Rsch. Inst. Montreal, 1983. Fellow AAAS, Am. Coll. Cardiology, Am. Heart Assn. (v.p. rsch. 1995); mem. AMA, Assn. Am. Physicians, Am. Soc. Clin. Investigation, High Blood Pressure Rsch. Coun. Australia (hon. life), Am. Fedn. Clin. Rsch., Mass. Med. Soc., Henderson Med. Soc., Mass. Heart Assn., Am. Clin. and Climatological Soc. Home: 453 Argonne Dr NW Atlanta GA 30305

ALEXANDER, ROBERT WILLIAM, radiologist; b. Reading, Pa., May 30, 1924; s. Robert Mackey and Jessie Forbes (Smith) A.; m. Nancy Ann Wetty, June 19, 1964; children—William, Heather. Student Swarthmore Coll., 1942-44; M.D., Jefferson Med. Coll., 1948. Diplomate Am. Bd. Radiology. Intern, Phila. Gen. Hosp., 1948-49, resident in radiology, 1950-52; radiologist San Antonio Med. and Surg. Clinic, 1954, Hamburg, Pa. Hosp., 1965-94, Wernersville State Hosp., 1992—; practice medicine specializing in radiology, Reading, 1955—; cons. VA Hosp., Lebanon, Pa., Good Samaritan Hosp. Contbr. articles to profl. jours. Bd. dirs. Vis. Nurses Assn. Reading, 1959—, pres., 1984-93; bd. dirs. Reading chpt. Am. Lung Assn., 1960-92; chmn. profl. div. United Fund Reading, 1968; bd. dirs. Reading chpt. ARC, 1970-76, 78-84; pres. Berks County Tb Soc., 1970—, Levi Mengel Fund of Reading Mus. and Art Gallery; mem. Wyomissing Bd. of Health, 1984-90. With U.S. Army, 1952-54. Nat. Cancer Assn. fellow, 1952-53. Fellow Am. Coll. Radiology, Phila. Coll. Physicians; mem. AMA (del. 1974—, pres. 1985-86), Am. Med. Pol. Action Com. (bd. dirs. 1991—), Berks County Med. Soc. (pres. 1964), Pa. Med. Soc. (chmn. council govt. relations 1977-79, bd. dirs. ednl. and scientific trust. of PMS 1986—), Pa. Radiology Soc., N.Am. Radiology Soc., Phila., Radiology Soc., Blockly Radiology Soc., Reading-Berks C. of C. (dir. 1966-73). Republican. Lutheran. Clubs: Kiwanis (pres. Reading 1966), Berkshire Country (dir. 1964-69, life). Home: 1417 Old Mill Rd Reading PA 19610-2834 Office: 544 Elm St Reading PA 19601-3302

ALEXANDER, STEVEN, urologist, surgeon; b. Passaic, N.J., Aug. 23, 1934; s. Saul R. and Mildred (Hillman) A.; m. roselle Marcus, May 20, 1981; children: Heather, Craig. AB, Cornell U., 1956; MD, NYU, 1960. Diplomate Am. Bd. Urology. Attending urologist Beth Israel Hosp., Passaic, 1967—, v.p. med. affairs, 1992—; attending urologist Passaic Gen. Hosp., 1967—, St. Mary's Hosp., Passaic, 1967—; asst. clin. prof. urology Mt. Sinai Sch. Medicine, N.Y.C., 1976—; assoc. med. dir. U.S. Healthcare, Fairfield, N.J., 1994—; mem. adv. bd. Valley Nat. Bank, Wayne, N.J., 1986—; mem. med. mgmt. com. Premier Internal PPO, 1992—; presenter in field. Contbr. articles to profl. jours. Trustee Daus. of Miriam Ctr., Clifton, N.J., 1986—, Beth Israel Hosp., 1980-92. Recipient citation City of Passaic, 1978, Passaic Heart Assn., 1986, Profl. Svc. award Daus. of Miriam Ctr., 1992. Fellow ACS; mem. Am. Coll. Physician Execs., Am. Urol. Assn. (mem. exec. com. N.Y. sect. 1986-95), N.J. Urol. Soc. Office: 1011 Clifton Ave Clifton NJ 07013

ALFANO, MICHAEL CHARLES, pharmaceutical company executive; b. Newark, Aug. 8, 1947; s. Michael Ferdinand and Anne Marie (Barrington) A.; m. JoAnn Mary Coletta, Mar. 30, 1969; children: Michael Anthony, Kristin Lynn. Student, Rutgers U., 1965-67; DMD, U. Medicine and Dentistry of N.J., 1971; postgrad. in periodontics, Harvard U., 1971-74; PhD, MIT, 1975. Asst. prof. dentistry Fairleigh Dickinson U., Hackensack, N.J., 1974-77, assoc. prof., 1977-80, prof. with tenure, 1980-82, dir. Oral Health Research Ctr., 1977-82, asst. dean grad. affairs and research, 1981-82; v.p. dental research Block Drug Co., Inc., Jersey City, 1982-84, sr. v.p. R&D, 1987—, bd. dirs., 1988—, pres. dental products div., 1985-88, cons. office of chief exec., 1990—; cons. Nat. Inst. Dental Rsch., Bethesda, Md., 1976-82; apptd. nat. adv. dental rsch. coun. NIH, Bethesda, 1994—; apptd. vis. prof. Nat. Dairy Coun., Chgo., 1981; vis. sr. scientist Fairleigh Dickinson U., 1982-88; adj. prof. U. Medicine and Dentistry of N.J., Newark, 1985—; mem. sci. adv. coun. Office of Gov., State of N.J., 1981-84. Editor: Symposium on Nutrition, 1976; contbr. articles to profl. jours. and chpts. to books; patentee in field. Trustee Found. of U. Medicine and Dentistry of N.J., 1988—; adv. bd. Columbia U. Sch. Dental and Oral Surgery, 1990—; mem. program com. Am. Fund for Dental Health, 1991-93; bd. overseers Forsyth Dental Ctr., Boston, 1992—, U. Pa. Coll. Dental Medicine, 1992—. Recipient Leadership citation Newark YMCA, 1966, Disting. Alumnus award U. Medicine and Dentistry of N.J., 1986; NIH research grantee, 1974-82; NIH postdoctoral fellow, 1971-74. Fellow Am. Coll. Dentists, Am. Coll. of Prosthodontists (hon. fellow); mem. ADA (cons., Nat. Achievement award 1978), Internat. Assn. for Dental Rsch., Am. Assn. for Dental Rsch. (pres. N.J. chpt. 1985), Am. Inst. Nutrition. Independent. Roman Catholic. Home: 954 Arapaho Trl Franklin Lakes NJ 07417-2258 Office: Block Drug Co Inc 257 Cornelison Ave Jersey City NJ 07302-3113

ALFERT, HAROLD JOSEPH, urologist; b. N.Y.C., Mar. 7, 1939; s. Arthur S. and Rose (Bermak) A.; m. Franne Entalis, June 2, 1962 (div. Jan. 1980); children: Adam, Rebecca; m. Karen Vogel, Jan. 25, 1989. BS, Queens Coll., 1959; MD, Albert Einstein Coll. Medicine, 1963. Intern in surgery Yale-New Haven Hosp. Ctr., 1963-64, resident in surgery, 1964-65; resident in urology U. Va. Med. Ctr., 1968-71; asst. prof. urology Johns Hopkins Med. Sch., Balt., 1993—. Capt. USNR. Mem. Alpha Omega Alpha. Home: 1715 Westminster Way Annapolis MD 21401 Office: John Hopkins Bayview Dept Urology Med Ctr 4940 Eastern Ave Baltimore MD 21224

ALFIDI, RALPH JOSEPH, radiologist, educator; b. Rome, Apr. 20, 1932; s. Luca and Angeline (Panella) A.; m. Rose Esther Senesac, Sept. 3, 1956 (div. 1991); children: Suzanne, Lisa, Christine, Katherine, Mary, John; m. Mariella Boller, Aug. 29, 1992. A.B., Ripon (Wis.) Coll., 1955; M.D., Marquette U., Milw., 1959. Intern Oakwood Hosp., Dearborn, Mich., 1959-60; resident, chief resident, A.C.S. fellow U. Va., 1960-63; practice medicine, specializing in radiology Cleve., 1965—; staff mem. Cleve. Clinic, 1965-78, head dept. hosp. radiology, 1968-78; dir. dept. radiology Univ. Hosps., Cleve., 1978-92; cons. VA Hosp., Cleve.; chmn. dept. radiology Case Western Res. U. Sch. Medicine, 1978-92; chmn. staff Cleve. Clinic Found., 1975-76; bd. dirs. Cuyahoga Savs. and Loan, Cleve. Author: Complications and Legal Implications of Special Procedures, 1972, Computed Tomography of the Human Body: An Atlas of Normal Anatomy, 1977; editor: Whole Body Computed Tomography, 1977; contbr. articles to radiology jours. Served to capt., M.C. U.S. Army Res., 1963-65. Picker Found. grantee, 1969-70; NRC grantee, 1969-70. Fellow Am. Coll. Radiology; mem. AMA, Radiol. Soc. N. Am., Am. Roentgen Ray Soc., Am. Heart Assn., Soc. Cardiovascular Radiology, Soc. Gastrointestinal Radiology, Soc. Computed Body Tomography (pres. 1977-78), Eastern Radiol. Soc., Ohio Radiol. Soc., Cleve. Radiol. Soc. (pres. 1976-77). Roman Catholic. Club: Kirtland Country. Home: 2074 Abington Rd Cleveland OH 44106-2602 Office: U Hosps Cleve Radiology Dept 2074 Abington Rd Cleveland OH 44106-2602

ALFONSO, ANTONIO ESCOLAR, surgeon; b. Manila, Nov. 25, 1943; came to U.S., 1968, naturalized, 1978; s. Ricardo Lagdameo and Marita (Escolar) Alfonso; m. Teresita Nazareno, Apr. 25, 1970; children: Margaretta, Roberto. A.B. cum laude, Ateneo U., 1963; M.D. cum laude, U. Philippines, 1968. Diplomate: Am. Bd. Surgery. Intern U. Philippines-Philippine Gen. Hosp., 1968; instr. surgery Temple U., Phila., 1968-72; sr. fellow surg. oncology Meml. Sloan-Kettering Cancer Ctr., N.Y.C., 1972-74; dir. head and neck surgery service SUNY Downstate Med. Ctr., Bklyn., 1974—, assoc. dir. div. surg. oncology, 1974—, asst. prof. surgery, 1974-77, assoc. prof., 1977-82, prof., 1982—, vice-chmn. dept. surgery, 1988—; chmn. dept. surgery Bklyn. Hosp., 1982-88; chmn. Dept. Surgery L.I. Coll. Hosp., 1988—; cons. head and neck surgery Bklyn. VA Hosp., 1974—. Author: Principles of Surgery Oncology; contbr. articles in med. to profl. jours., chpts. to med. books. Recipient research essay prize N.Y. Colon and Rectal Surg. Soc., 1973; grantee Am. Cancer Soc., 1978. Mem. ACS (bd. govs. Bklyn.-L.I. chpt.), Assn. Acad. Surgeons, Am. Soc. Clin. Oncology, Am. Assn. Cancer Edn., Soc. Head and Neck Surgeons, N.Y. Surg. Soc. (treas. 1994), Bklyn. Surg. Soc. (pres. 1986-87), N.Y. Cancer Soc. (v.p. 1986-87, pres.-elect 1987-88, pres. 1988-89), Soc. Surg. Oncology, N.Y. Head and Neck Soc. (sec. 1993—), N.Y. Soc. Colon and Rectal Surgeons, Triboro Dirs. of Surgery Assn. (pres. 1989—), Phi Kappa Phi. Roman Catholic. Home: 50 Olive Pl Flushing NY 11375-5938 Office: LI Coll Hosp Dept Surgery 340 Henry St Brooklyn NY 11201-5525

ALFONSO, EDUARDO, ophthalmologist, educator; b. Cuba, Dec. 4, 1952; came to U.S., 1961; s. Candido and Margarite (Carcas) A.; m. Mary Romeu, Aug. 7, 1976; children: Angelica, Patricia, Eduardo. BA, Yale U., 1976, MD, 1980. Intern Mt. Sinai Hosp., U. Miami (Fla.), 1980; fellow Harvard U., Boston, 1984-86; resident in ophthalmology Bascom Palmer Eye Inst., U. Miami, Fla., 1980-84; prof. U. Miami, 1986—, dir. Microbiology Lab., Bascom Palmer Eye Inst., 1986—; dir. Microbiology Lab., Miami, 1986—; head Infection Control, Miami, 1986—. Contbr. articles to sci. publs. Fellow Am. Acad. Ophthalmology; mem. Phi Beta Kappa. Office: Bascom Palmer Eye Inst 900 NW 17th St Miami FL 33136-1119

ALFORD, BOBBY RAY, physician, educator, university official; b. Dallas, May 30, 1932; s. Bryant J. and Edith M. (Garrett) A.; m. Othelia Jerry Dorn, Aug. 28, 1953; children: Bradley Keith, Raye Lynn, Alan Scott. A.S., Tyler Jr. Coll., 1951; postgrad., U. Tex., 1951-52; M.D., Baylor U., 1956. Diplomate Am. Bd. Otolaryngology (dir. 1972-90, pres. 1985-86, exec. v.p. 1986-90). Intern Jefferson Davis Hosp., Houston, 1956-57; resident Baylor U. Coll. Medicine Affiliated Hosps. Program, 1957-60; mem. faculty Baylor U. Coll. Medicine, 1962—, prof. otolaryngology, 1966—, chmn. dept., 1967-95, v.p. and dean acad. and clin. affairs, 1984-88, exec. v.p., dean medicine, 1988—, disting. service prof., 1985—, interim chmn. dept. surgery, 1993-94; pres., CEO BaylorMedCare, Houston, 1994—; mem. rev. panel surgeon gen. on neurol. and sensory disease USPHS, 1965-67; cons. Nat. Inst. Neurol. Disease and Stroke, 1970-74; cons. to surgeon gen. U.S. Army, 1963-73; mem. nat. adv. coun. Neurol. and Communicative Disorders and Stroke, NIH, 1977-80, Deafness and Other Communicative Disorders, 1991-95; chmn. aerospace medicine adv. com. NASA, 1993-94, mem. nat. adv. coun., 1992-95, chmn. life microgravity scis. and applications adv. com., 1993-95. Author: Neurological Aspects of Auditory and Vestibular Disorders, 1964; Chief editor: A.M.A. Archives of Otolaryngology, 1970-79. Bd. dirs. Houston Acad. Medicine Tex. Med. Ctr. Libr., 1983-94. Recipient Herman Johnson award Baylor U. Coll. Medicine, 1956; spl. NIH fellow Johns Hopkins Hosp., 1961-62. Fellow ACS (bd. dirs. 1977-82); mem. NAS Inst. Medicine, Am. Laryngol. Assn., Soc. Univ. Otolaryngologists-Head and Neck Surgeons (sec. 1965-69), Am. Otol. Soc., Assn. Acad. Dept. Otolaryngology-Head and Neck Surgery, Am. Laryngol., Rhinol. and Otol. Soc., Am. Soc. Head and Neck Surgery (councillor 1978-80) Am. Acad. Otolaryngology-Head and Neck Surgery (pres. 1981), Am. Coun. Otolaryngology-Head and Neck Surgery (pres. 1980-81), Am. Bronchoesophagological Assn., Soc. Head and Neck Surgeons, Accustical Soc. Am., Collegium Oto-Rhino-Laryngologicum Amicitiae Sacrum, Johns Hopkins U. Soc. Scholars, Univ. Space Rsch. Assn. (bd. dirs. 1991-95), Tex. Corinthian Yacht Club (bd. dirs. 1978-80, 94-95), Doctor's Club (bd. govs. 1967-70, 91-93), Waterford Harbour Yacht Club, Lakewood Yacht Club, Alpha Omega Alpha. Office: Baylor Coll Medicine One Baylor Plz Houston TX 77030

ALFORD, BRAD ALAN, psychology educator; b. Tylertown, Miss., May 1, 1953; s. C.A. and Marilyn (Jackson) a.; m. Emily Cheryl Higgs, June 5, 1982; 1 child, Jason Alan Jackson. BA, Millsaps Coll., Jackson, Miss., 1976; MA, U. Miss., 1981, PhD, 1984. Diplomate in Clin. Psychology Am. Bd. Profl. Psychology; lic. psychologist, Pa. Program dir. Western Mental Health Inst., Bolivar, Tenn., 1984-85; clin. dir. N.W. Mental Health Ctr., Martin, Tenn., 1985-87; postdoctoral fellow U. Pa., Phila., 1987-88; asst. prof. psychology U. Ky., Lexington, 1988-89; asst. prof. psychology U. Scranton, Pa., 1989-92, assoc. prof., 1993—; prog. cons. Charter Psychiat. Hosp., Lexington, 1988-89. Contbr. chpts. to books and articles to profl. jours. Fellow Acad. Clin. Psychology; mem. APA, Assn. for Advancement of Behavior Therapy, Am. Psychol. Soc., Psi Chi. Home: 716 Timber Ridge Cir Greentown PA 18426-9173 Office: U Scranton Dept Psychology Scranton PA 18510-4596

ALFORD, NANCY BOYLAN, clinical psychologist; b. Portsmouth, Va., Oct. 12, 1941; d. Edwin Harry and Elizabeth Celia (Wood) B.; m. John Beckham Alford Jr., Aug. 6, 1960; children: Donna Lee, Roger W., Thomas Lee, Laura Jean, Joseph B. BS, Old Dominion U., Norfolk, Va., 1975, MS, 1977; D in Psychology, Fla. Inst. Tech., 1985; postgrad., Ea. Va. Family Therapy Sch., 1986. Dir. Aesop Schs., Inc., Portsmouth, Va., 1971-79; supervisor day treatment Halifax County Mental Health Ctr., Roanoke Rapids, N.C., 1979-82; coord. child and youth services Halifax County Mental Health Ctr., Roanoke Rapids, Va., 1985-88; psychology intern Ea. Va. Med. Sch., Norfolk, 1984-85; pvt. practice clin. psychology Roanoke Rapids, 1986—; cons. 6th Jud. Dist. Child Abuse Task Force, Roanoke Rapids, 1986—; evaluator Child Mental Health Evaluation Program, N.C., 1987—; guest lectr. in field. Temp. apptd. missionary So. Bapt. Fgn. Mission Bd., Belize, 1987—. mem. APA, N.C. Psychol. Assn., Southeastern Psychol. Assn., Am. Profl. Soc. On the Abuse of Children, Am. Assn. Marriage and Family Therapy (clin.), AAUW, FPPR (Can.), Psi Chi. Home: 13 Mulberry Ct Littleton NC 27850-9554 Office: 600 Jackson St # B Roanoke Rapids NC 27870-2604

ALGILANI, KAMRAN CAMERON, physician, surgeon, researcher; b. Uromia, Kurdistan, Iran, July 17, 1951; came to U.S., 1979; s. Fosch Pousho and Asma (Mohammadi-Nari) A.; m. Chilé Saleh Taha, Nov. 2, 1993; 1 child, Daniel Kamiar. BSc in Biology, Mashad (Iran) U., 1975; MSc in Microbiology, East Tenn. State U., 1982; DO, Okla. State U., 1990. Rschr. Tehran (Iran) Rehab. Ctr., 1977-79, Oral Roberts U., Tulsa, 1983-85, Okla. State U., Tulsa, 1985-86; intern Dallas Meml. Hosp., 1990-91; family practice resident N.E. Community Hosp., Bedford, Tex., 1991-93; pvt. practice Dallas, 1993—. Contbr. rsch. articles to profl. jours. Active with Kurdish-U.S. Orgn., Dallas, 1992—. 2d lt. Iranian Army, 1975-77. Mem. AMA, Am. Osteo. Assn., Terrant County Med. Assn., Okla. Osteo. Assn., Tex. Osteo. Med. Assn., Osteo. Physicians and Surgeons Calif. Office: PO Box 202438 Arlington TX 76006-8438

ALGRA, RONALD JAMES, dermatologist; b. Artesia, Calif., Feb. 23, 1949; s. Cornelius and Helena Joyce (De Boom) A.; m. Phyllis Ann Brandsma, July 31, 1970; children: Brian David, Stephanie Ann. BS in Chemistry, Calvin Coll., 1971; MD, Baylor Coll. Medicine, 1974; MBA, Pepperdine U., 1989. Diplomate Am. Bd. Dermatology. Intern Gen. Hosp. Ventura County, Ventura, Calif., 1974-75; resident in dermatology Baylor Coll. Medicine, Houston, 1975-78; pvt. practice Hawthorne, Calif., 1978-88; asst. med. dir. FHP, Inc., Fountain Valley, 1988-89, assoc. med. dir., 1990-91, med. dir., 1991-93, sr. med. dir., 1993, assoc. v.p. med. affairs, 1993-95; COO horses, zebras & unicorns, Irvine, Calif., 1995-96; exec., med. dir. SelectCare Health Plans, Longview, Wash., 1996—. Fellow Am. Acad. Dermatology; mem. AMA, Am. Coll. Physician Executives, Alpha Omega Alpha. Republican. Mem. Christian Reformed Ch. Office: SelectCare Health Plans Po Box 370 1338 Commerce #300 Longview WA 98632

AL-HASHIMI, IBTISAM, oral scientist, educator; b. Karbala, Iraq; d. Hadi A. and Rabab H. Al-H. B Dental Sci., Sch. Dentistry, Baghdad, 1973; MS, SUNY, Buffalo, 1985, PhD, 1989. Diplomate in Oral Surgery. Registrar Sch. Dentistry, Baghdad, 1975-81; postdoctoral assoc. SUNY, Buffalo, 1984-88, asst. prof., 1988-89; asst. prof. U. Pacific, San Francisco, 1989-90; dir. stomatology lab. Baylor Coll. Dentistry, Dallas, 1991—, dir. salivery dysfunction clinic, 1992—; clin. asst. prof. surgery U. Tex. Southwestern Med. Ctr., Dallas, 1996—; adv. com. mem. SS Found. (we. N.Y. chpt.) Buffalo, 1985-89, Dallas-Ft. Worth chpt., 1992—; mem. med. adv. bd., organizer Sjogren's Multispecialty Referral Ctr., 1996. Author: Proceeding of the Second Dows Symposium, 1987; contbr. articles to profl. jours. Mem. med. adv. bd. SS Found., 1995. Mem. AAAS, Am. Assn. Dental Schs., N.Y. Acad. Sci., Internat. Platform Assn., Internat. Assn. Dental Rsch., Libr. Congress Assn., Salivary Rsch. Group, Sigma Xi. Office: Baylor Coll Dentistry 3302 Gaston Ave Dallas TX 75246-2013

ALI, SHAIKH MOHAMAD, thoracic cardiovascular surgeon; b. Tehran, Iran, June 27, 1928; s. Ahmad and Massuma (Haydar) S.; m. Mahin Monique Mirzai, Oct. 20, 1968; children: Nader, Ladan. MD, U. Tehran, 1955. Diplomate Am. Bd. Surgery, Am. Bd. Thoracic Surgery; lic. physician Va., Calif., Md., D.C., Pa. Intern Nashville Gen. Hosp., 1956-57; resident in gen. surgery Balt. City Hosp., 1957, U. Louisville Med. Ctr., 1957-61; resident in thoracic and cardiovasc. surgery U. Alberta Hosp., Edmondton, Alta., Can., 1961-63; assoc. prof. U. Tehran Sch. Medicine, 1964-79; thoracic and cardio-vascular srugeon, prof. and chmn. Nat. U. Iran, Tehran, 1979-88; thoracic and vascular surgeon VA Med. Ctr., Wilkes-Barre, Pa., 1988—; assoc. prof. surgery Temple U., Phila., 1988—. Fellow ACS. Home: 34 S Main St #202 Wilkes Barre PA 18701 Office: VA Medical Ctr 1111 E End Blvd Wilkes Barre PA 18711

ALIBERTI, AMY MCCOY, health facility administrator; b. New Haven, Sept. 26, 1956; d. Donald S. and Anita Jeanne (Ayer) McCoy; m. Fred A. Aliberti. AB, Mt. Holyoke Coll., 1978; BS, Columbia U., 1980; MS, Russell Sage Coll., 1993. Staff nurse med.-surg. unit Albany (N.Y.) Med. Ctr., 1980-82, asst. head nurse med-surg. unit, 1982-84, nursing instr. med-surg. and pediatrics unit, 1984-88, staff nurse hemodialysis, 1988-89; nurse mgr. orthoneuro Albany Meml. Hosp., 1989-94, nurse mgr. hematology-oncology, 1994—. Mem. Nat. Assn. Orthopaedic Nurses (sec.). Home: 7247 Western Tpke Delanson NY 12053-3011 Office: Albany Meml Hosp 600 Northern Blvd Albany NY 12204-1004

ALIO, JORGE L., ophthalmologist, educator; b. Caracas, Apr. 4, 1953; arrived in Spain, 1960; s. Luciano and Lucia (Sanz) A.; m. Maria Lopez; children: Maica, Jorge. Grad. with honors, Inst. Cervantes, 1969; MD, U. Complutense, 1976, PhD, 1981. Resident in ophthalmology Clinica Concepción, Madrid, 1977-81; mem. staff Hosp. Miguel Servet, Zaragoza, Spain, 1981-83; head retinal svc. Hosp. Univ., Salamanca, Spain, 1984-86; prof. ophthalmology, chmn. U. Alicante, Spain, 1986—, head dept. surgery, 1991-93; fellow Wilmer Inst., Balt., 1985; dir. Ctr. to Prevent Blindness of Alicante, 1987—; founder, dir. Instituto Oftalmologico de Alicante, 1987—. Author 21 books; contbr. 237 articles to profl. jours. Founder, dir. Ctr. to Prevent Blindness of Alicante. Mem. Pres. Assn. Univ. Oftalmologica de Alicante. Office: Instituto Oftalmologico de Alicante, Avda de Denia 111, 03015 Alicante Spain

ALIOT, ETIENNE, cardiologist; b. Epinal, France, Dec. 14, 1946; s. Albert and Janine (Peiffer) A.; m. Christiane Marandel, Sept. 19, 1970; children: Delphine, Sophie, Romain. BA in Philosophy, St. Joseph U., Epinal, 1964; MD, U. Nancy, France, 1976. Intern U. Nancy, France, 1971-76, asst. prof. cardiology, 1976-83, assoc. prof., 1985, prof., chief dept. cardiology Hosp. Cen., 1989—; hon. prof. U. Okla., Oklahoma City, 1983-84; expert in cardiology Cour O'Appel, Nancy, 1988; cons. in field. Author, editor: Ventricular Tachycardia, 1987; editor (Books) Readaptation Cardiaque, 1987, Amiodarone Present or Future, 1991; contbr. articles and chpts. on cardiology to profl. jours. Capt. French Army, 1971-72. Fellow N.Am. Soc. Pacing, Am. Coll. Cardiology, European Soc. Cardiology (mem. working group on arrhythmias 1994), French Soc. Cardiology. Roman Catholic. Home: 21 Rue de Ludres, 54500 Vandoeuvre France Office: Hosp Cen, Dept Cardiology, 54037 Nancy France

ALIVIZATOS, PETER ALEXANDER, cardiothoracic surgeon; b. Athens, Greece, Nov. 28, 1937; came to U.S., 1970; s. Alexander and Anastasia (Zervou) A.; m. Margaret Sinclair, Feb. 28, 1976 (div. Oct. 1993). MD, Athens U. Med. Sch., 1962. Diplomate Am. Bd. Surgery, Am. Bd. Thoracic Surgery. Fellow in thoracic surgery Harvard Med. Sch., Cambridge, Mass., 1970-71; fellow in gen. surgery Lahey Clinic, Boston, 1971-72; fellow in thoracic surgery Baylor U. Med. Ctr., Dallas, 1972-73, dir. cardiothoracic transplantation, 1985—; resident in gen. surgery Boston U. Med. Ctr., 1973-78; resident in thoracic surgery Med. Coll. Va., Richmond, 1978-81; sr. registrar, thoracic surgeon Hosp. for Sick Children, London, 1981-82; clin. asst. heart transplantation Harefield Hosp., London, 1982-84. Contbr. over 30 articles to profl. jours. Lt. Greek Navy, 1962-65. Fellow ACS, Am. Coll. Chest Physicians, Am. Coll. Cardiology; mem. Soc. Thoracic Surgery, Internat. Soc. Heart and Lung Transplantation. Greek Orthodox. Office: 3600 Gaston Ave Ste 404 Dallas TX 75246-1804

ALKAWI, MUHAMMAD ZUHEIR, physician, neurologist; b. Damascus, Syria, Feb. 20, 1947; s. Jawdat and Siham Alkawi; m. Rima Alkawi, July 12, 1972; children: Ammar, Lina, Nour. MD, Damascus U., 1971. Diplomate Am. Bd. Psychiatry and Neurology. Intern in medicine Huron Rd. Hosp., Cleve., 1971-72; resident Ind. U., Indpls., 1972-75; clin. asst. prof. neurology Baylor U., Houston, 1976-93; clin. assoc. prof. neurology King Faisal U., Alkhober, Saudi Arabia, 1991—; head sect. of neurology King Faisal Specialist Hosp., Riyadh, Saudi Arabia, 1978-95; chmn. dept. medicine King Faisal Specialist Hosp., Riyadh, 1993—. Mem. editorial bd. Annals Saudi Medicine, 1988—, Neuroepidemiology, 1991—. Fellow ACP, Am. Acad. Neurology; mem. Riyadh Neurosci. Club (pres. 1984-85). Office: King Faisal Specialist Hosp, PO Box 3354, Riyadh 11211, Saudi Arabia

AL KHALIFA, MAAZ AL AMIN, medical researcher; b. Khartown, Sudan, Jan. 1, 1947; arrived in Sweden, 1991; s. Al Amin Alkhalifa and Fatima Mustafa (Omer) Mohamed; m. Hanan Awad Abubakr, Dec. 26, 1986; children: Rashid, Amin, Afnan. Diploma in Medicine, Faculty Medicine, Bratislava, Slovakia, 1977; specialist in urology, Lund (Sweden) U., 1989, M Med. Sci., 1990. Med. house officer Sudan, 1978-79, med. officer, 1979-81, med. inspector, 1981-82, registrar in surgery, 1982-84; rschr. Lund U., 1992—. Islam. Home: Kollegiv 45, 224 73 Lund Sweden Office: Lund U, Dept Urology, S-221 85 Lund Sweden

ALKON, ELLEN SKILLEN, physician; b. Los Angeles, Apr. 10, 1936; d. Emil Bogen and Jane (Skillen) Rost; m. Paul Kent Alkon, Aug. 30, 1957; children: Katherine Ellen, Cynthia Jane, Margaret Elaine. BA, Stanford U., 1955; MD, U. Chgo., 1961; MPH, U. Calif., Berkeley, 1968. Diplomate Nat. Bd. Med. Examiners, Am. Bd. Pediatrics, Am. Bd. Preventive Medicine in

Pub. Health. Chief sch. health Anne Arundel County Health Dept., Annapolis, Md., 1970-71; practice medicine specializing in pediatrics Mpls. Health Dept., 1971-73, dir. MCH, 1973-75, commr. health, 1975-80; chief preventive and pub. health Coastal Region of Los Angeles County Dept. Health Services, 1980-81; chief pub. health West Area Los Angeles County Dept. Health Services, 1981-85; acting med. dir. pub. health Los Angeles County Dept. Health, 1986-87, med. dir. pub. health, 1987-93; med. dir. Coastal Cluster Health Ctrs. L.A. County Dept. Pub. Health Svcs., 1993-96, CEO, med. dir., 1996—; adj. prof. UCLA Sch. Pub. Health, 1981—; adminstr. vis. nurses service, Mpls., 1975-80. Fellow Am. Coll. Preventive Medicine, Am. Acad. Pediatrics; mem. So. Calif. Pub. Health Assn. (pres. 1985-86), Minn. Pub. Health Assn. (pres. 1978-79), Am. Pub. Health Assn., Calif. Conf. Local Health Officers (pres. 1990-91), Delta Omega. Office: Comprehensive Health Ctr 1333 Chestnut Ave Long Beach CA 90813-2944

ALKSNE, JOHN F., dean. Dean U. Calif., La Jolla, 1995—. Office: U Calif San Diego Sch Medicine La Jolla CA 92093 Office: Univ Calif San Diego 9500 Gilman Dr La Jolla CA 92093*

ALLAN, MARGARET CATHERINE, psychologist; b. Edmonton, Can., Dec. 1, 1947; came to U.S., 1970; d. Edward Ainslie and Eileen Mary (Jones) A.; m. Allen Heimann, Oct. 21, 1970; 1 child, Matthew Wesley. BA, U. B.C., Vancouver, Can., 1970; MA, U. Iowa, 1975; MA in Sch. Psychology, U. Tex., 1992. Registered psychologist, B.C., cert. sch. psychologist. Ednl. rschr. Vancouver (Can.) Sch. Bd., 1976-77; program evaluator U. B.C., Vancouver, Can., 1977-79; evaluation coord. Coun. for Preschools, Vancouver, Can., 1980-81; curriculum developer Ministry Health, Vancouver, Can., 1981; rschr. Vancouver Health Dept., 1982; ednl. psychologist Children's Hosp., Vancouver, Can., 1982-83; test adminstr. Psychol. Corp., Austin, Tex., 1989; clinic supr., teaching asst. Learning Abilities Ctr., U. Tex., Austin, 1990-91; rsch. cons. Windsor (Can.)-Essex County Health Unit, 1990—. Author numerous rsch. publs. Founding dir. Assn. Parents of Hearing Impaired Children, B.C., 1981-85; regional coord. Terry Fox Youth Ctr., Vancouver, 1983-84; chmn. Christian Edn. Com., Shaughnessy Heights United Ch., 1979-87. U. Tex. at Austin grantee, 1989-91, A.G. Bell Assn. profl. devel. grantee, 1989, Internat. Sch. Psychology Assn., Cal Catterall grantee, 1991, U. Tex. Coll. Grad. Studies profl. devel. grantee, 1991, 93; recipient Christine Anderson Meml. scholarship, 1990, 91, U. Tex. at Austin, Coll. Edn. scholarship, 1990, 93. Mem. APA, ACA, Can. Psychol. Assn., Tex. Psychol. Assn., Am. Edn. Rsch. Assn., Nat. Coun. on Measurement in Edn., Jr. League Austin (sustaining mem.), Zarah Temple, Daus. of Nile, Alexander Graham Bell Assn. for Deaf. Office: U Texas 3616 Far West Blvd Ste 101-293 Austin TX 78731-3017

ALLARD, MARVEL JUNE, psychology educator, researcher; b. Detroit; d. Adrian Clarence and Marvel Claudia (Tremper) A.; m. James Donald Widmayer, Mar. 22, 1970 (div. Mar. 1982). AB, Mich. State U., MA, PhD. Rsch. assoc. Mich. State U., East Lansing, 1965-66; project dir., rsch. scientist Am. U., Washington, 1966-67; sr. staff Ops. Rsch., Inc., Silver Spring, Md., 1967-70; rsch. cons., 1970—; chair social and behavior sci., prof. psychology Worcester (Mass.) State Coll., 1973—; cons. Leasco Systems, Yankelovich Co., Middlesex County, others. Editor: Understanding Diversity: Rendings, Cases and Exercises, 1994; mem. editl. bd. Chronic Mental Illness and Aging newsletter; contbr. rsch. articles to profl. jours. Mem. Worcester County Hort. Soc.; bd. dirs. Girls, Inc., Worcester; pres., bd. trustees Worcester State Hosp. NSF fellow Mich. State U., 1959-64, Nat. fellow Assn. Am. Colls., 1985; scholar Mich. State U. and pvt. orgns., 1954-58, Phi Kappa Phi scholar Mich. State U.. Mem. APA (site visitor, mem. undergrad. cons. svc.). Home: 24 Curtis St Auburn MA 01501-3149 Office: Worcester State Coll 486 Chandler St Worcester MA 01602-2832

ALLBRIGHT, KARAN ELIZABETH, psychologist, consultant; b. Oklahoma City, Okla., Jan. 28, 1948; d. Jack Gahnal and Irma Lolene (Keesee) A. BA, Oklahoma City U., 1970, MAT, 1972; PhD, U. So. Miss., 1981. Cert. sch. psychologist, psychometrist; lic. psychologist, Okla., Ark. Psychol. technician Donald J. Bertoch, Ph.D., Oklahoma City, 1973-76; asst. adminstr. Parents' Assistance Ctr., Oklahoma City, 1976-77; psychology intern Burwell Psycho-ednl. Ctr., Carrollton, Ga., 1980-81; staff psychologist Griffin Area Psychoednl. Ctr., Ga., 1981-85; clinic dir. Sequoyah County Guidance Clinic, Sallisaw, Okla., 1985-88; psychologist Baker Psychiatric Clinic, Ft. Smith, Ark., 1988-90; cons. Harbor View Mercy Hosp., 1988-90, Bethany Hosp. Pavilion, 1992—; pvt. practice, Oklahoma City, 1990—; lectr. various orgns.; bd. dirs. workshops. Mem. Task Force to Prevent Child Abuse, Fayette County, Ga., 1984-85, Task Force on Family Violence, Spalding County, Ga., 1983-85; cons. Family Alliance (Parents Anonymous) Sequoyah County, Okla., 1985-88; assoc. bd. dirs. Lyric Theatre. Named Outstanding Young Women in Am., 1980. Mem. APA, Southeastern Psychol. Assn., Nat. Assn. Sch. Psychologists (cert. sch. psychologist), Okla. Psychol. Assn., Play Therapy Assn., Nat. Assn. Health Svc. Providers in Psychology, Psi Chi, Delta Zeta (chpt. dir. 1970-72). Democrat. Presbyterian. Home: 3941 NW 44th St Oklahoma City OK 73112-2517 Office: Northwest Mental Health Assocs 3832 N Meridian Ave Oklahoma City OK 73112-2820

ALLEGRA, MARISA IDA CALZOLARI, psychiatrist; b. Verbania, Torino, Italy; came to U.S., 1956, naturalized, 1962; d. Amilcare and Paola Bice (Alberizzi) Calzolari; MD summa cum laude, Bologna U., 1949; postgrad. Brown U., 1976. Diplomate Am. Bd. Psychiatry and Neurology; children: Ludwig Armand, David Paul, Christopher John. Pediatric and gen. practice medicine, Bologna, Italy, 1949-53; permanent staff physician Ospedale Maggiore, Bologna, 1953-56; resident in psychiatry Brown U., Providence, 1973-76, asst. clin. prof. dept. psychiatry and human behavior; pvt. practice medicine specializing in psychiatry, Providence, 1976—; cons. Family Svc., 1976-80. Pres. R.I. Civic Choral and Orch., 1974-76, bd. dirs., hon. pres., life mem.; bd. dirs. R.I. Philharm. Orch.; active R.I. Sch. Design. Fellow Bradley Hosp., Providence, 1976. Mem. AMA. Am. Psychiat. Assn., R.I. Med. Assn., Providence Med. Assn., N.Y. Acad. Scis., Butler Hosp. Staff Assn., Pan Am. Soc., Providence Preservation Soc., Newport Preservation Soc. Clubs: Conanicut Yacht (Jamestown, R.I.); Univ., Faculty, Brown (Providence), Arts. Home: 220 Blackstone Blvd Providence RI 02906-5801 also: 150 Bradley Pl Palm Beach FL 33480-3804

ALLEN, B. MARC, managed care executive; b. Balt.; s. Ralph A. and Frona B. A.; B.A., U. Balt., 1967, J.D., 1971; m. Judy E. Luray, Jan. 24, 1967; children—Lara Ann, Mason Luray. Mgr. med. affairs Md. Blue Cross, Balt., 1967-73; cons. Am. Health Systems, Boston, 1973-74; dir. field ops. Bay State PSRO, Boston, 1974-75; exec. dir. Essex Physicians' Rev. Orgn., South Orange, N.J., 1975; chmn., chief exec. officer Med. Rev. Corp., Randolph, N.J., MediChoice Provider Network, Randolph; cons. in field; guest lectr. health policy Rutgers U.; expert witness U.S. Senate Fin. Com., U.S. Select Com. on Aging. Active SSS, 1972-73, New Democratic Coalition, 1969-70; past-pres. Temple B'nai Or, Morristown, N.J. Mem. Nat. Health Lawyers Assn., Am. Med. Peer Rev., Inc. (chmn. task force on impact). Contbr. articles to profl. jours. Office: 1240 Sussex Tpke Randolph NJ 07869-2921

ALLEN, BERTHA LEE, social worker, family counselor; b. Bexley, Miss., Mar. 28, 1908; d. Charles H. and Winnie (McLeod) A. Student, Maryville Coll., 1928-29; BA, Miss. U. for Women, 1932; postgrad., U. Ala., 1936, La. State U., 1937, Miss. State U., 1939, U. Miss., 1940; MSW, Tulane U., 1949. Cert. tchr. life, Miss., social worker, La., Ala., Miss., first aid instr.; bd. cert. diplomate clin. social work. Tchr. high sch. English and Latin, Rocky Creek Sch., Lucedale, Miss., 1932-33, Agricola, Miss., 1933-36, Tchula, Miss., 1936-44; child welfare worker Miss. Dept. Pub. Welfare, Jackson, Columbus, Pascagoula, 1944-48; caseworker Columbia (Miss.) Tng. Sch., 1949-50; case work supr., chief social worker Osawatomie (Kans.) State Hosp., 1950-51; dir. casework Miss. Children's Home Soc., Jackson, 1952-54; casework supr. Child and Family Svc., Mobile, Ala., 1954-58; supr. casework practice Family Counseling Ctr., Mobile, 1958-65; caseworker ARC Disaster Svcs., Hurricane Betsy, New Orleans, 1965, Family Svc. Soc., New Orleans, 1965-66, Jewish Family and Children's Svc., New Orleans, 1966-71, Willow Wood, New Orleans Home for Jewish Aged, 1971-73; pvt. practice individual, marital and family counseling, New Orleans, Mobile, Lucedale, 1969—; cons. Wilmer Hall, Protestant Children's Home, YWCA, Mobile, 1954-65, Providence Nursing Home, New Orleans, 1972-77, Willow Wood, New Orleans Home for Jewish Aged, 1974-75. Bd. dirs. Mulherin Home for Spastic Children, Mobile, 1958-59; charter mem., sec. Miss. Mental Health Assn., 1953-54; mem. casework com. Mobile Coun. Social Agys., 1954-58, mem. interagy. planning com., 1958-62, mem. in-svc. tng. com., 1963-65; mem. program com. Southeastern Inst., Family Svc. Assn. Am., 1960; mem. planning com. Mobile County Mental Health Assn., 1964-65; sec. Assn. Maternity and Adoption Agys., New Orleans, 1969-70. Nat. Assn. Social Workers (diplomate), Acad. Cert. Social Workers, La. Soc. Clin. Social Work. Miss. Conf. Social Welfare, Ala. Conf. Social Work, Internat. Platform Assn., Oakliegh Garden Soc., Eta Sigma Phi. Presbyterian. Home and Office: 1050 Palmetto St Mobile AL 36604-3041 also: RR 9 Box 796 Lucedale MS 39452-8630

ALLEN, BRUCE ROYL, JR., social worker; b. Houston, Jan. 24, 1952; s. Bruce R. Allen Sr. and Violet R. (Bolton) Aaron; m. Linda Claire Jernigan, May 20, 1978; children: Gretchen, Kelsey. BS in Psychology, U. Houston, 1974, MSW, 1978. Lic. social worker, Ark. Sr. clinician Ozark Counseling Svc., Harrison, Ark., 1978-84; psychiat. social worker Charter Vista Hosp., Fayetteville, Ark., 1984-86; clin. social worker N.W. Ark. Counseling Assocs., Fayetteville, Ark., 1986—; faculty instr. Inst. for Reality Therapy, Canoga Park, Calif., 1988, U. Ark. at Little Rock Grad. Sch. Social Work. Mem. NASW (bd. dirs. 1986-88). Office: NW Ark Counseling Assocs 301 W Mountain Fayetteville AR 72701

ALLEN, CAROL MAUREEN EASLEY, public health nurse, educator; b. Huntington, W.Va., July 15, 1946; d. Paul Allen and Koneta Seona (Phillips) Easley; m. Gregory John Allen, June 1, 1980. BS, Columbia Union Coll., 1967; AM, NYU, 1970, PhD, 1983. RN, Mass.; cert. pub. health nurse, Calif. Pub. health nurse Yonkers (N.Y.) Health Dept., 1967-68, Neighborhood Maternity Ctr., Bronx, N.Y., 1969; instr., counselor Mt. Vernon (N.Y.) Sch. Practical Nursing, 1970-71; instr. divsn. nurse edn. NYU, N.Y.C., 1971-74; asst. prof. dept. nursing Andrews U., Berrien Springs, Mich., 1974-78, U. Mich., Ann Arbor, 1978-81; assoc. prof. Calif. State U., L.A., 1982-89; assoc. prof. grad. program nursing Northea. U., Boston, 1989-92; v.p. for acad. affairs Atlantic Union Coll., South Lancaster, Mass., 1992-95, acting pres., 1993; cmty. health nursing curriculum cons. So. Missionary Coll., Collegedale, Tenn., 1977, Andrews U., 1980, Rush U., Chgo., 1991; sec. Berrien County Child Abuse and Neglect Task Force, 1977-78; assoc. mem. Washtenaw County Comprehensive Health Planning Coun., Ann Arbor, 1980-81; exec. bd. U. Mich. Children's Ctr., Ann Arbor, 1980-81; chair exec. bd. Ark Child Devel. Ctr., Monrovia, Calif., 1986-88. Co-developer Easley-Storfjell Instruments for Caseload/Workload Analysis, 1977; contbr. articles, revs. to profl. jours., chpts. to books. Vol. IRS Vol. Income Tax Assistance Program, Monrovia, 1989. Mem. APHA (officer, chair pub. health nursing sect.), Mass. Pub. Health Assn., Sigma Theta Tau, Phi Delta Kappa, Phi Kappa Phi. Seventh-day Adventist. Home: 2900 Memory Ln Silver Spring MD 20904-9999

ALLEN, CHARLES UPTON, medical professional; b. Piqua, Ohio, Jan. 3, 1953; s. Charles Carlton and Mary Rebecca (Upton) A.; m. Nancy Lorena Sapp, July 14, 1974 (div. May 1979). BS, Duke U., 1975; postgrad., U N.C., 1976-90; MD, Wake Forest U., 1995. Rsch. technician psychology dept. Duke U., Durham, N.C., 1985-86, prosecutor, instr. anatomy dept., 1986-87; with anatomy dept. U. N.C., Chapel Hill, 1987-90; intern dept. surgery N.C. Bapt. Hosp., Winston-Salem, N.C., 1995—; swimming coach Chapel Hill Parks and Recreation dept., 1983-87. Author: Masters Swim Workouts, 1986. Mem. So. Poverty Law Ctr., Montgomery, Ala., 1987, Raleigh, 1987; bd. dirs. Hassle House Crisis Intervention Counseling Ctr., Durham, 1979, 80, 81. Mem. AMA, AAAS, N.C. Med. Soc., N.Y. Acad. Sci., N.C. Civil Liberties Union. Democrat. Presbyterian. Home: 2329 Rosewood Ave Winston Salem NC 27103-3638

ALLEN, CHARLOTTE HOBBS, medical technologist; b. Louisville, Nov. 21, 1951; d. Charles and Mabel Cleona (Jackson) Hobbs; m. Howard E. Allen, Jr., Sept. 29, 1986. BS, Tenn. State U., 1973; cert. in med. technology, Meharry Med. Coll., Nashville, 1973. Mem. staff Gen. Hosp., Louisville, So. Bapt. Hosp., New Orleans, Ben Taub Med. Ctr., Houston, Bd. of Health, Louisville, Clark Meml. Hosp., Jeffersonville, Ind. Mem. Am. Med. Technologists Assn., Assn. Clin. Lab. Scientists. Home: 3204 Wayside Dr Louisville KY 40216

ALLEN, CINDY, medical association administrator; b. Durand, Mich., Dec. 27, 1956; d. Lawrence Henry and Eunice Sophia (Lester) Sprague; m. Frank Michael Allen, Aug. 25, 1979; children: Shelly, Emily. RN, Lansing (Mich.) C.C., 1979; B in Health Sci., Western Mich. U., 1984, MPA, 1990. Cert. profl. in healthcare quality. RN Blodgett Meml. Med. Ctr., Grand Rapids, Mich., 1980-84, Butterworth Med. Ctrs., Grand Rapids, 1983-86, St. Mary's Hosp., Grand Rapids, 1984-87; quality assurance/risk mgr. Butterworth Ventures, Inc., Grand Rapids, 1986-92; dir. med. quality and credentialing Priority Health, Grand Rapids, 1992—; adj. prof. Davenport Coll.; presenter in field. Mem. Nat. Assn. for Health Care Quality, Am. Soc. for Quality Control, Mich. State Assn. Health Care Quality (regional rep. 1992-94, dir. 1994-96), Mich. Soc. Health Care Risk Mgmt., N.W. Mich. Assn. Health Care Quality (chairperson bylaws com. 1991-92, pres. 1992-94), Pi Alpha Alpha. Office: Priority Health 1231 E Beltline NE Grand Rapids MI 49505

ALLEN, CYNTHIA ANN, clinical psychologist; b. Columbus, Ohio, Sept. 24, 1959; d. William Thomas (dec.) and Mary Colletta (Paridon) A. BS, Ohio State U., 1981; MA, U. Dayton, 1984; PhD, Ohio State U., 1989. Lic. Ind. Health Professions Bur.; lic. psychology Ind. Psychology trainee Dayton (Ohio) Mental Health Ctr., 1982-84; assessment cons. Montgomery County Youth Employment Program, 1984; psychology trainee Timothy B. Moritz Forensic Unit, Columbus, 1984-85, Psychol. Svcs. Clin., Ohio State U., Columbus, 1985-86, Indsl. Commn. Ohio, J. Leonard Camera Ctr., Columbus, 1985-86; clin. psychology intern Ind. U. Med. Sch., Indpls., 1988-89; coord. evening therapy program St. Vincent Stress Ctr., Indpls., 1989-92; pvt. practice Ind. Psychiat. Consortium, Indpls., 1992-94; clin. psychologist corp. health svcs. Eli Lilly Co., Indpls., 1994—; grad. tchg. asst. dept. psychology Ohio State U., Columbus, 1985-87, grad. tchg. assoc., 1987-88; summer intern Columbus Devel. Ctr., 1987, 88; asst. clin. prof. Ind. U. Med. Ctr., Indpls., 1990—; adj. faculty mem., clin. asst. prof. psychology Dept. Psychiatry Ind. U. Med. Sch., 1991—. Vol. co-leader Alateen Group, Riverside Meth. Hosp., Columbus, 1982. Mem. APA, Ind. Psychol. Assn., Midwestern Psychol. Assn. (presenter). Roman Catholic.

ALLEN, DON LEE, dentistry educator; b. Burlington, N.C., Mar. 13, 1934; s. William Arthur and Gena (Davis) A.; m. Winifred Rouse, Aug. 2, 1958; children: Don Lee, Michael Denmark, Susan Winifred. Student, Elon Coll., 1952-55; DDS, U. N.C., 1959; MS in Periodontics, U. Mich., 1964. Instr. U. N.C. Sch. Dentistry, Chapel Hill, 1959-62; asst. prof. U. N.C. Sch. Dentistry, 1962-65, assoc. prof., 1965-69, prof., assoc. dean, 1969-70; prof., assoc. dean U. Fla. Coll. Dentistry, Gainesville, 1970-73; dean U. Fla. Coll. Dentistry, 1973-82; dean U. Tex. Dental Br. at Houston, 1982-92, William N. Finnegan prof. dental scis., 1985—, prof. Dept. Practice Mgmt., 1992—; univ. evaluation adminstr., 1993—; staff Shands Teaching Hosp., 1970-82; hon. prof. Tianjin Med. Coll., 1987; hon. lectr. Tokyo Dental Coll., 1986; nat. adv. coun. health profl. edn. HHS, 1978-82; commn. dental edn. and practice mem. Fedn. Dentaire Internat., 1981-87, vice-chmn., 1990, chmn. 1991-92; vice-chmn. Fedn. Dentaire Internat. Commn., 1991—, chmn. sect. dental deans and educators, 1994—; med. br. mem. Harris County (Tex.) Hosp. Dist., 1990-92; cons. USPHS, 1962-64, Coun. Dental Edn., 1970-78, 86-93, VA Hosp., Gainesville, 1970-82, commn. on dental accreditation appeal bd., 1995—; vis. prof. U. Stellenbosch, 1990, Kings Coll., London, 1993. Author: (with G. Hunter, W. McFall) Periodontics for the Dental Hygienist, 1968, 2d edit., 1974, 3d edit., 1980, 4th edit., 1987; contbg. editor: Gould Med. Dictionary. Active Y-Indian Guides, Chapel Hill, 1968-70, Gainesville, 1973-75; elder Presbyn. Ch., 1972-75, 78-82; mem. adminstrv. coun. Meth. Ch., 1990-94. Recipient teaching award U. N.C. Class of 1966; named Disting. Alumnus, Elon Coll., 1985. Fellow Am. Coll. Dentists (chmn. Fla. sect. 1980-81), Internat. Coll. Dentists (pres. 1981-82, master 1986); mem. ADA (coun. dental edn., commn. on dental accreditation 1978-86, chmn. 1984-86), Am. Acad. Peridontology, Am. Assn. Dental Schs. (pres. 1982-83), Internat. Assn. Dental Rsch., So. Conf. Dental Deans and Examiners (pres. 1983-84), Pierre Fauchard Acad., Houston Forum, Omicron Kappa Upsilon. Office: U of Tex Health Scis Ctr School Of Dentistry Houston TX 77225

ALLEN, DURWARD LEON, biologist, educator; b. Uniondale, Ind., Oct. 11, 1910; s. Harley J. and Jennie M. (LaTurner) A.; m. Dorothy Ellen Helling, Sept. 23, 1935 (dec.); children: Stephen R., Harley W., Susan E.; m. Suzanne E. Grieser, Oct. 21, 1985. A.B., U. Mich., 1932; Ph.D., Mich. State Coll., 1937; L.H.D. (hon.), No. Mich. U., 1971; D.A. (hon.), Purdue U., 1985. Game research biologist Mich. Dept. Conservation, 1935-46; wildlife research biologist U.S. Fish and Wildlife Service, Laurel, Md., 1946-50; asst. chief br. wildlife research U.S. Fish and Wildlife Service, Washington, 1951-54; prof. wildlife ecology Purdue U., West Lafayette, Ind., 1954-76, prof. emeritus, 1976—; mem. Adv. Bd. on Nat. Parks, Monuments and Historic Sites, U.S. Dept. Interior, 1966-72, chmn., 1971-72; chmn. Nat. Sci. Adv. Com. on Fish and Wildlife and Parks, U.S. Dept. Interior, 1975-76; adj. prof. Tex. Tech U., 1982. Author: Michigan Fox Squirrel Management, 1943, Pheasants Afield, 1953, Our Wildlife Legacy, 1954, 62, The Life of Prairies and Plains, 1967, Wolves of Minong, 1979, 93; editor: Pheasants in North America, 1956, Land Use and Wildlife Resources, 1970. Recipient medal of honor Anglers' Club of N.Y., 1956; inducted into Mich. Conservation Hall of Fame, Mich. United Conservation Clubs, 1985; named Sagamore of the Wabash, Ind. Gov., 1983. Fellow AAAS; mem. Wildlife Soc. (hon. life mem., pres. 1956-57, Annual Tech. Publ. award 1946, Annual Conservation Edn. award 1955, Leopold Meml. medal 1968), Am. Soc. Mammalogists, Ecol. Soc. Am., Washington Biologists' Field Club, Am. Inst. Biol. Scis., Am. Forestry Assn. (bd. dirs. 1983-88), George Wright Soc., Wilderness Soc., Outdoor Writers Assn. Am. (Jade of Chiefs award 1968, hon. life mem.), Nature Conservancy, Conservation Found., Nat. Parks and Conservation Assn., Nat. Wildlife Fedn. (ann. sci. award 1985), Ind. Acad. Sci. (named lectr. of yr. 1968), Nat. Audubon Soc. (bd. dirs. 1975-84, Audubon medal 1990), George Bird Grinnell Soc. (charter mem.), Boone and Crockett Club (emeritus), Cosmos Club, Explorers Club, Sigma Xi, Phi Sigma, Xi Sigma Pi, Seminarium Botanicum. Home: Westminster 2627 Calvin Ct West Lafayette IN 47906-1401

ALLEN, ELIZABETH HALLER, nurse; b. Cin., Sept. 26, 1963; d. Dale Stewart and Joyce Ann (Seifert) Haller; m. Kent Dorn Allen, Aug. 3, 1985. BSN cum laude, U. Cin., 1985. RN, Ohio, Ky. Staff nurse Children's Hosp. Med. Ctr., Cin., 1985-86; charge nurse, chmn. staff devel. St. Elizabeth Med. Ctr., Edgewood, Ky., 1986-87; nurse cons., rev. coordinator Health Svc. Rev., Franklin, Ohio, 1987-88; mgr. alternative care systems Health Svc. Rev., Franklin, 1988-91; mgr. quality assessment Integra Group, Cin., 1991—; profl. adv. bd. HMSS, Inc.; bd. dirs. Llanfair Retirement Cmty. Active Ch. of Savior, PTA. Mem. Nat. Assn. for Healthcare Quality, Ohio Assn. for Healthcare Quality, Ohio Continuum of Care Coun., The Ctr. for Healthcare Ethics. Republican. Home: 11093 Allenhurst Blvd W Cincinnati OH 45241-6610 Office: Integra Group 11499 Chester Rd Cincinnati OH 45246

ALLEN, GEORGE DESMOND, epidemiology nurse, surgical nurse; b. Trinidad and Tobago, July 24, 1952; s. George Nevielle and Ilene Gertrude Allen; m. Bernice Eileen Redman, Apr. 7, 1984; 1 child, Troy. BSN, CUNY, 1984; MS in Adminstrn., Cen. Mich. U., 1991. RN, N.Y.; CNOR; cert. in infection control. Staff nurse operating rm. Kings County Hosp., Bklyn., 1979-85; staff nurse operating rm. Interfaith Med. Ctr., Bklyn., 1986, nurse epidemiologist, infection control coord., 1986-91; sr. nurse epidemiologist, dir. infection control program Univ. Hosp. Bklyn., 1991—; staff nurse oper. rm. per diem St. Lukes ROosevelt Hosp., N.Y.C., 1986-95, Meth. Hosp., Bklyn., 1989—. Mem. APHA, Assn. Oper. Rm. Nurses (bd. dirs. 1990-91, v.p. Bklyn. chpt. 1992-93, pres. 1994-96), Assn. Practitioners in Infection Control, Nat. League Nursing, N.Y. State Nursing Assn. Democrat. Office: SUNY Univ Hosp Bklyn Box 37 450 Clarkson Ave Brooklyn NY 11203

ALLEN, GEORGE WHITAKER, physician, educator; b. Milledgeville, Ga., Feb. 8, 1928; s. Henry Dawson and Caroline (Reynolds) A.; m. Lis Margaret Jensen, Oct. 1, 1951 (div. 1973); 1 child, John Whitaker; m. Janice Alene Mandabach, Apr. 26, 1980. AB, Harvard U., 1948; MD, Columbia U., 1952. Diplomate Am. Bd. Otolaryngology. Intern, Presbyn. Hosp., N.Y.C., 1952-53; Jr. asst. resident in otolaryngology U. Chgo. Clinics, 1955-56, sr. asst. resident, 1956-57, resident, 1957-58, NIH spl. trainee, 1958-59; instr. dept. otolaryngology Northwestern U. Med. Sch., Chgo., 1959-60, asst. prof., 1961-64, assoc. prof., 1964—, dir. teaching and rsch., 1959-63, acting chmn. dept. otolaryngology, 1964-67; sole practice otolaryngology, Chgo., 1967—; attending physician Northwestern Meml. Hosp., Chgo., 1959—; vis. prof. U. Colo. Med. Sch., 1965; vis. prof. Emory U. Med. Sch., 1967; cons. Nat. Ctr. for Devices and Radiol. Health, FDA, 1983—. Served to 1st lt. M.C., U.S. Army, 1953-55. Recipient research award Am. Acad. Otolaryngology, 1960. Mem. AMA, Ill. Med. Soc., Chgo. Med. Soc., Chgo. Laryngological and Otological Soc., ACS, Triological Soc., Inst. Medicine Chgo., Am. Acad. Facial Plastic and Reconstructive Surgery, Am. Council of Otolaryngology, Sand Creek Country Club (Ind.), Nu Sigma Nu, Alpha Omega Alpha, Sigma Xi. Republican. Methodist. Club: Carlton (Chgo.). Contbr. articles to med. jours.; mem. editorial bd. Archives of Otolaryngology, 1960-69; co-author: (movie) Carcinoma of the Tonsil, 1960. Office: 150 E Huron St Ste 801 Chicago IL 60611-2912

ALLEN, HENRY L., pathologist; b. Phila., Apr. 26, 1945; s. Sydney and Edith A.; m. (div.); 1 child, Lisa E. BA, Pa. State U., 1967; MD in Vet. Medicine, U. Pa., 1971. From rsch. fellow to dir. toxicology and pathology Merck & Co., West Point, Pa., 1975-81, sr. investigator toxicology and pathology, 1981—.

ALLEN, HENRY WESLEY, biomedical researcher; b. Louisville, Oct. 16, 1927; s. John Turk and Irene Victoria (Slater) A.; m. Evelyn Chen, Dec. 29, 1968 (div. Dec. 1988); children: Lillian Chen, Rosaniline Chen, Dianne Chen. Student, U. Louisville, 1945-46, U. Chgo., 1946-47, U. So. Calif., 1960-61. Rschr. Loma Linda (Calif.) U., 1962-77, Am. Biologics, Chula Vista, Calif., 1977—. Author: International Protocols in Cancer Management, 1983, The Study of Reactive Oxygen Toxic Species and Their Metabolism, 1985, The Biochemistry of Live Cell Therapy, 1986; contbr. articles to Jour. of Theoretical Biology, Analytical Biochemistry, Nature, others. Office: Am Biologics 1180 Walnut Ave Chula Vista CA 91911-2622

ALLEN, JAMES DOUGLAS, dentist; b. Athens, Tenn., Apr. 4, 1958; s. John Douglas and Elizabeth Ann (Hale) A.; m. Jo Ena Oaks, June 18, 1977; children: Kristy Jo, Jamie Lin, Kathryn Noel. BA, U. Tenn., 1980; DDS, U. Tenn., Memphis, 1984. Cert. in prosthodontics Med. Coll. Ga., 1986, Am. Bd. Prosthodontists, 1989. Asst. prof. prosthodontics Med. Coll. Ga. Sch. Dentistry, Augusta, 1986-93, dir. craniomandibular pain clinic, 1986-92, dir. prosthodontic residency, 1990-93; pvt. practice, Nashville, 1993—; cons. VA Hosp., Augusta, 1989-93, Dublin, Fa., 1990-93; assoc. clin. prof. dentistry Vanderbilt U., 1994—. Instr. CPR Am. Heart Assn., Dallas, 1987-95. Recipient Southeastern Acad. Prosthodontics award (fixed), 1984. Fellow Am. Coll. Prosthodontists; mem. ADA, Tenn. Dental Assn., Nashville Dental Soc., Richard Doggett Dean & Margaret Taylor Dean Hon. Odontol. Soc., Omicron Kappa Upsilon. Republican. Baptist. Home: 514 Round Table Ct Murfreesboro TN 37129-1240 Office: 2285 Murfreesboro Pike Nashville TN 37217-3348

ALLEN, JANE ANN SMITH, toxicologist, geneticist; b. Longview, Tex., Jan. 13, 1951; d. Malcolm R. and Alta Bess Betty (Porter) Smith; m. Robert G. Allen; children: Kevin Timothy, Kathleen Claire. BA, U. Tex., 1971, PhD, 1974. Diplomate Am. Bd. Toxicology. Postdoctoral fellow Med. Sch. Yale U., New Haven, 1974-77; dir. toxicology agr. rsch. div. Am. Cyanamid, Princeton, N.J., 1977-86; prin. toxicologist Glaxo, Inc., Research Triangle Park, N.C., 1986—. Contbr. articles to profl. jours. NSF fellow, NIH fellow. Mem. ASTM, Soc. Toxicology, Genetic Toxicology Assn., Environ. Mutagen Soc., Phi Beta Kappa. Presbyterian. Office: Glaxo Wellcome Rm 9-2007 5 Moore Dr Durham NC 27709

ALLEN, JANICE FAYE CLEMENT, nursing administrator; b. Norfolk, Nebr., Aug. 19, 1946; d. Allen Edward and Hilda Bernice (Stange) Reeves; m. Roger Allen Clement, Oct. 6, 1968 (dec. July 1974).; m. August H. Allen, Sept. 17, 1988. RN, Meth. Sch. Nursing, Omaha, 1967; BS in Nursing, magna cum laude, Creighton U., 1978; MS in Nursing, U. Nebr., 1981; cert. in nursing adminstrn. With Meth. Hosp., 1967-68, 72-83, asst. head nurse, 1974-77, staff devel. nurse, 1977-81, dir. staff adminstrv. services, 1981-83; pub. health nurse Wichita-Sedgwick County Health Dept., Wichita, Kans., 1970-72; dir. nursing Meth. Med. Ctr., St. Joseph, Mo., 1983-84, Broadlawns Med. Ctr., Des Moines, 1984-93; dir. staff mgmt./infection control Ea.

N.Mex. Med. Ctr., Roswell, 1993—; adj. clin. faculty nursing Drake U. Nursing, Des Moines, 1986-93, mem. adv. bd., 1984-93, Cen. Campus Practical Nursing, 1984-93; mem. adv. bd. Des Moines Area Community Coll. Dist., 1987—, Des Moines Area C.C. Nursing Bd., 1987-93, Grandview Coll., 1988-93; bd. dirs. Vis. Nurse Svcs., 1988-93; assoc. Am. Coll. Healthcare Execs. Mem. Am. Nurses Assn., Am. Orgn. Nurse Execs., N.Mex. Nurses Assn. (bd. dirs. 1995), Cen. Iowa Nursing Leadership Conf. (pres. 1985), Colloquium Nursing Leaders Cen. Iowa, Iowa League for Nursing (treas. 1987-89, pres. 1989), Iowa Orgn. Nurse Execs. (treas. 1987, sec. 1989, pres.-elect 1993), Assn. Infection Control and Epidemiology, Sigma Theta Tau (pres. Zeta Chi chpt. 1990-92). Democrat. Presbyterian. Avocations: flying, sewing, golf, walking, reading. Home: 3201 Allison Dr Roswell NM 88201-1011 Office: Ea NMex Med Ctr 405 W Country Club Rd Roswell NM 88201-5209

ALLEN, JOHN R., orthopaedic surgeon; b. Somerset, Ky., July 25, 1946; s. Woodrow and Verna (Hail) A.; m. Robin Van Zytveld, Oct. 8, 1992 (div. Apr. 1987); children: Scott Spicer, Hilary Hail; m. Janet Lee Toth, June 27, 1991. BS, Davidson (N.C.) Coll., 1968; MD, U. Ky., 1972. Diplomate Nat. Bd. Med. Examiners, Am. Bd. Orthop. Surgery. Vis. fellow Oxford (Eng.) Med. Sch., 1972; intern in surgery NYU-Bellevue Hosp. Ctr., N.Y.C., 1972-73, surg. resident, 1973-74; orthop. surg. resident U. Va. Med. Ctr., Charlottesville, 1974-78; clin. fellow hip and implant surgery/teaching fellow Mass. Gen. Hosp./Harvard Med. Sch., Boston, 1978-79; asst. prof. orthop. surgery U. Ky., Lexington, 1979-82, asst. clin. prof. orthop. surgery, 1982—; pvt. practice Lexington, 1982—; staff orthop. surgeon Good Samaritan Hosp., Lexington, 1982—, chmn. dept. orthop., 1988-90. Adv. bd. Henry clay Meml. Found., Lexington, 1994—; bd. dirs. God's Pantry Food Crisis Ctr., Lexington, 1989-91; chmn. bd. deacons 2d Presbyn. Ch., Lexington, 1984; bd. dirs. Ky. Ednl. Med. Polit. Action Com., 1985-88; Ky. rep. Orthop. Rsch. and Edn. Found., 1984-86. Fellow Am. Acad. Orthop. Surgeons; mem. AMA, Ky. Orthop. Soc. (pres. 1987-88), Bluegrass Orthop. Soc. (pres. 1984-86), Fayette County Med. Soc. (v.p. 1989-90), Am. Orthop. Soc. for Sports Medicine, Am. Coll. Sports Medicine, So. Orthop. Soc., Clin. Orthop. Soc., The Melrose Club, Lexington Rotary, Harbour Run Yacht Club, Alpha Omega Alpha, Alpha Epsilon Delta, Omicron Delta Kappa. Democrat. Home: 1648 Richmond Rd Lexington KY 40502 Office: 135 E Maxwell St Ste 104 Lexington KY 40508

ALLEN, JULIA ELZADA, medical and surgical nurse; b. Las Vegas, Nov. 22, 1965; d. Leslie Otis and Pearl Marie (Palmeteer) Brown; children: Jennifer Dawn, Jacob Leslie, Jessica Kaye. ADN, Western Okla. State Coll., 1993. RN. Nurse Jackson County Meml. Hosp., Altus, Okla., 1993-94. Grad. mem. Western Okla. State Coll. Nursing Sch. Adv. Bd., 1993-94. Home: Rt 1 Box 150 Headrick OK 73549

ALLEN, MARC KEVIN, emergency physician; b. Bedford, Ind., Sept. 2, 1956; s. Robert Edward and Edna Ruth (Little) A.; m. Marita Ann Volk, May 13, 1995. AB, Washington U., St. Louis, 1978; MD, Wright State U., 1982. Diplomate Am. Bd. Emergency Medicine. Intern Mt. Sinai Med. Ctr., Cleve., 1982-83, resident in emergency medicine, 1984-85, rsch. dir. emergency med. residency, 1986—; attending physician Worcester (Mass.) City Hosp., 1985-86; flight physician Metro Lifeflight, Cleve., 1984—. Co-author: A Practical Approach Emergency Medicine, 1987. Co-chmn. YWCA, YMCA, 1977-78. Fellow Am. Coll. Emergency Medicine (councillor 1996—); mem. Assn. Air Med. Svcs., N.E. Soc. Emergency Med. (bd. dirs. 1992—), Phi Rho Sigma. Home: 485 Club Dr Aurora OH 44202 Office: Mt Sinai Med Ctr Emergency Dept One Mt Sinai Dr Cleveland OH 44106

ALLEN, NANCY JEAN, nursing educator; b. Indiana, Pa., Mar. 23, 1941; d. Frank and Ethel Viola (Glenn) Plusquellic; m. Ronald Dean Allen, June 6, 1969; children: Jennifer Allen Miller, Aaron Dean, Ian Woodruff. BSN, Alderson-Broaddus Coll., 1963; MS in Nursing Edn., Syracuse U., 1969. RN; cert. specialist in med.-surg. nursing. Instr. psychiat. nursing Harrisburg (Pa.) State Hosp., 1963-65; clin. instr. Brigham Young U., Provo, Utah, 1965-67; staff nurse med.-surg. unit Utah Valley LDS Hosp., Provo, 1966-67; part-time instr. Alderson-Broaddus Coll., Philippi, W.Va., summer 1968; instr., supr. psychiat. nursing SUNY Upstate Med. Ctr., Syracuse, 1969-71; instr. Syracuse (N.Y.) U., 1971-73; staff nurse U. Md. Med. Ctr., Balt., 1981-85; part time clin. instr. Howard County C.C., Columbia, Md., 1985—; part time shift dir. Howard County Gen. Hosp., Columbia, 1989—; part-time adminstr. Greater Laurel (Md.)-Beltsville Hosp., 1991-93; asst. RN coord. Ctrl. N.Y. Regional Med. Program, Syracuse, 1970-71. County rep. Citizens Adv. Com. to County Sch. Bd., Annapolis, Md., 1981-88; unit commr. Four Rivers Dist., Balt. Area coun. Boy Scouts Am., 1983—. Mem. ANA, Md. Nurses Assn. (treas. dist. 3 1992—, Md. del. to ANA ho. of dels. 1993—). Republican. Mem. LDS Ch. Office: Howard Community Coll Little Patuxent Pky Columbia MD 21044

ALLEN, ROBERT CARROLL, ophthalmologist; b. Balt., Nov. 18, 1950; s. Orville Albert and Lucy Patricia (Walker) A.; m. Janice Rosser, Sept. 10, 1977; children: Grant Rosser, Matthew Barratt, Robert Connor. BS, Duke U., 1972; MD, U. Va., 1975. Resident in ophthalmology U. Fla., Gainesville, 1977-80; fellow in ophthalmology Harvard U., 1980-82; assoc. prof. Emory U., Atlanta, 1982-84, U. Va., Charlottesville, 1984-94; chmn. dept. ophthalmology Med. Coll. Va., Richmond, 1994—. Author: Medial Therapy of Glaucoma, 1986. Bd. dirs. Covenant Sch., 1989—. Mem. Assn. for Rsch. in Vision and Ophthalmology, AMA, So. Med. Assn., Wilmer Residents Assn., Am. Acad. of Ophthalmology (Honor award 1989), Am. Soc. for Lase r Medicine and Surgery, Soc. of Heed Fellows, Mass. Eye and Ear Alumni Assn., Albemarle Med. Soc., Med. Soc. of Va., Va. Soc. of Ophthalmology (bd. dirs. 1986-87, chmn., ethics com. 1987—, v.p. 1988—), Am. Glaucoma Soc. Republican. Presbyterian. Home: 9009 Norwick Rd Richmond VA 23229 Office: Med Coll Va Dept Ophthlmlgy University Ave 1101 E Marshall St Rm 8022 Richmond VA 23298

ALLEN, ROBERT EDWARD, JR., physician assistant; b. Omaha, Mar. 27, 1950; s. Robert Edward and Virginia (Connor) A.; m. Christine Ann Rahm, July 16, 1985; children: Sean Edward, Erin Christine. Student, Brooke Army Hosp., San Antonio, 1968-69, St. Anthony Ctrl. Hosp., Denver, 1984-86. Cert. Nat. Bd. Orthopaedic Physician Assts.; cert. EMT, vocat. tchr., Colo.; lic. physician asst., Colo.; cert. BLS. Mem., patroller, instr. Nat. Ski Patrol, 1974-90; orthopaedic physician asst., orthopaedic technician Luth. Med. Ctr., Wheatridge, Colo., 1980-85, instr. EMT program, 1983-89; physician asst., mem. staff St. Joseph Hosp., Denver, 1985-87; physician asst. Denver Orthopedic Clinic and Inst. for Limb Preservation, 1987—; part-time EMT, Golden, Colo., 1980-84; lectr. continuing med. edn. Colo. Emergency Med. Svcs. Sys., also nursing staffs; manuscript reviewer William and Wilkins, Balt., 1993—; splty. lectr. oncology Clinicians Rev., Clifton, N.J., 1993—; insvc. lectr. in field. Exec. prodr. instrnl. videos; contbr. articles to profl. publs.; designer saw blade for arthroscopic anterior crucial ligament reconstrn.; co-designer antibiotic bead maker. Vol. Toys for Tots, Denver, 1992—. With Spl. Forces, U.S. Army, 1968-71, Vietnam. Fellow Am. Acad. Physician Assts., Am. Soc. Orthopedic Physician Assts.; mem. NRA. Lutheran. Home: 6777 W Mexico Pl Lakewood CO 80000 Office: Advanced Orthopedics Assocs 360 S Garfield ste 6300 Denver CO 80209

ALLEN, ROBERT ERWIN, physiologist; b. Lufkin, Tex., Oct. 9, 1941; s. John Franklin and Bonnie Mae (Smith) A.; BA, Stephen F. Austin State Coll., 1963; PhD, Vanderbilt Med. Sch., 1969; m. Roma Leah Trobaugh, Oct. 18, 1970; children: Jennifer Kay, David Whitfield. With NASA Marshall Space Flight Center, Huntsville, Ala., 1969-76, chief biometrics, 1972-74, chief biotech. br., 1975-76; spl. asst. to v.p. U. Ala. Med. Sch. Sys., 1975; exec. sec. NIH, Bethesda, 1976-78; spl. asst. to dir. med. rsch. svc. VA, Washington, 1978-87; dep. dir. AIDS Program Office VA Cen. Office, Washington, 1987-91; spl. asst. chief pub. health and environ. hazards officer Environ. Medicine and Pub. Health Dept. Vet. Affairs, Washington, 1991-95; spl. asst. to chief pub. health and environ. hazards officer, 1995. Home: 8 Jeb Stuart Ct Rockville MD 20854-6216 Office: Central Office VA Code 13 Washington DC 20420

ALLEN, SHEILA HILL, nursing executive, counselor, consultant; b. Imperial, Nebr., Sept. 28, 1935; d. Roger William and Lois Marion (Clayton) Hill; children: Steven Morgan, Lee-Ann Hill, Todd Everett, Andrew James. R.N., St. Lukes Sch. Nursing, 1958; BS, U. Denver, 1959. Cert. alcohol drug counselor, Calif. Asst. head nurse St. Lukes Hosp., Denver, 1959-62; dir. nursing Ridge Vista Mental Health, San Jose, Calif., 1973-75; dir. nursing svcs. Westwood Mental Health Facility, Fremont, Calif., 1975-89, dir. nursing svcs. Chem. Dependency Inst. No. Calif., Campbell, 1989-90; program dir. O'Connor Hosp. Recovery Ctr., San Jose, 1991-94; health facilities evaluator nurse State of Calif. Dept. Health Svcs. Licensing and Certification, 1995—. Bd. dirs., sec., Health Acctg. Svcs., Calif., 1984-89; co-founder, partner Health Acctg. Svcs., Fremont, 1984-89; co-owner Westwood Mental Health, 1984-89. Contbr. articles to profl jours. Mem. Calif. Assn. Alcoholism and Drug Abuse Counselors, Nat. Consortium Chem. Dependency Nurses, Brookridge Inst. Serving Addiction and Consciousness Profls., San Francisco Acad. Hypnosis, Nat. Coun. Alcoholism and Drug Dependence, Delta Gamma.

ALLEN, STEPHEN CHARLES, physician; b. Bristol, Avon, Eng., July 2, 1952; s. Thomas Ivan Charles and Iris Stella (Jarrett) A.; m. Julia Caroline Parr, Aug. 18, 1973; children: Katharine, Martin, Richard, Elizabeth. BSc with honors, Manchester (Eng.) U., 1973, MB ChB with honors, 1976, MD, 1981. Cert. qualified physician. House physician Withington Hosp., Manchester, 1976-77, Stepping Hill Hosp., Stockport, 1977; sr. house physician St. Mary's Hosp., Manchester, 1977-78, Withington Hosp., Manchester, 1978-79; registrar Manchester Royal Infirmary, 1979-81; sr. registrar Univ. Teaching Hosp., Lusaka, Zambia, 1981-83; rsch. fellow Manchester Royal Infirmary, 1983-84; lectr. Manchester U., 1984-86; cons. physician East Dorset Health Authority, Bournemouth, Eng., 1986—; clin. dir. Bournemouth Acute Unit, 1989—, Christchurch Hosp., 1991—; hon. lectr. Southampton (Eng.) U., 1990—; med. adviser Nursing Devel. Unit, Bournemouth, 1990—, Resource Mgmt. Unit, Christchurch, Eng., 1983—. Author: Geriatric Medicine for Students, 1988; author, editor: Case Studies in Medicine, 1988; author: (with others) Respiratory System in Old Age, 1991; contbr. articles to profl. jours. Com. mem. Age Concern, Bournemouth, 1990. Travelling scholar Dickenson Trust (UK), 1980. Fellow Royal Coll. Physicians Edinburgh, Royal Coll. Physicians London; mem. Brit. Geriatrics Soc., Wessex Physicians Club. Anglican. Office: Christchurch Hosp, Fairmile Rd, Christchurch BH23 2JX, England

ALLEN, STEPHEN D(EAN), pathologist, microbiologist; b. Linton, Ind., Sept. 8, 1943; s. Wilburn and Betty (Moffett) A.; m. Vally C. Autrey, June 17, 1964; children: Christopher D., Amy C. BA, Ind. U., 1965, MA, 1967; MD, Ind. U., Indpls., 1970. Diplomate Am. Bd. Pathology; cert. in anatomic and clin. pathology and med. microbiology. Intern in pathology Vanderbilt U. Hosp., Nashville, 1970-71; resident in pathology Vanderbilt U. Hosp., 1971-74; clin. asst. prof. pathology Emory U., Atlanta, 1974-77, asst. prof. clin. pathology Ind. U., Indpls., 1977-79; asst. prof. pathology Ind. U., 1979-81, assoc. prof. pathology, 1981-86, prof. pathology, 1986-92; prof. pathology and lab. medicine, 1992—; assoc. dir. div. clin. microbiology, dept. pathology Ind. U., 1977—, dir. grad. progam pathology, 1986—, sr. assoc. chmn. dept. pathology, 1990-91, dir. divsn. clin. microbiology dept. pathology/lab. medicine, 1992—; dir. disease control lab. divsn. Ind. State Dept. Health, 1994—. Co-author: Color Atlas of Diagnostic Microbiology, 4th edit. 1992, Introduction to Diagnostic Microbiology, 1994; contbr. articles to profl. jours. With USPHS, 1974-77. Fellow Coll. Am. Pathologists, Am. Acad. Microbiology, Am. Soc. Clin. Pathologists (coun. mem. microbiology 1983-89), Infectious Diseases Soc. Am., Soc. Sigma Xi; mem. Am. Bd. Pathology (trustee 1995—, chair microbiology test com., vice chair clin. pathology test com.), Masons (32d degreee), Shriners. Office: Ind U Hosp Rm 4430 550 N University Blvd Indianapolis IN 46202-5283

ALLEN, STEVEN LEE, hematologist, oncologist; b. Bklyn., Dec. 6, 1952; s. Morris and Ann A.; m. Barbara Helen Wolf, May 30, 1983; children: Jeremy Spencer, Peter Russell, Rebecca Rae. BS, CCNY, 1973; MD, Johns Hopkins U., 1977. Intern N.Y. Hosp. Cornell U., N.Y.C., 1977-78; resident N.Y. Hosp. Cornell U., 1978-80, fellow, 1980-83; instr. Cornell U. Med. Coll., N.Y.C., 1982-84; asst. prof. Cornell U. Med. Coll., 1984-90, assoc. prof. clin. medicine, 1990—; asst. attending physician North Shore U. Hosp., Manhasset, N.Y., 1983-90, assoc. attending physician, 1990-95, attending physician, 1995—; adj. assoc. prof. clin. medicine NYU Sch. Medicine, 1994—, N.Y. Coll. Osteo. Medicine, 1994—; prin. investigator Cancer and Leukemia Group B, 1989—. Contbr. articles to profl. jours. Jonas Salk scholar, 1973; W. Barry Wood Rsch. fellow, 1976, Jr. Faculty Clin. fellow, Am. Cancer Soc., 1984-86. Fellow Am. Coll. Physicians; mem. Am. Soc. Hematology, Am. Soc. Clin. Oncology, Am. Fedn. Clin. Rsch., Phi Beta Kappa (Sci. medal 1973). Office: North Shore U Hosp 300 Community Dr Manhasset NY 11030-3801

ALLEN, STEVEN PAUL, microbiologist; b. Oak Park, Ill., Nov. 6, 1958; s. Paul Samuel and Rosemary (Bieber) A.; m. Wendy Dianne Gunia, Sept. 11, 1982; children: Samantha Rose, Matthew David, Timothy Bryan. BS, U. Ill., 1980, PhD, 1990; MS, Iowa State U., 1982. Rsch. asst. Iowa State U., Ames, 1980-82; rsch. specialist U. Ill., Chgo., 1982-85; rsch. asst. U. Ill., Urbana, 1985-90; postdoctoral assoc. Monsanto Corp. Rsch., St. Louis, 1990-93; tech. specialist metabolic bus. team Abbott Lab., Abbott Park, Ill., 1993-95; mgr. STD/hepatitis rare reagent validations for infectious disease and assay devel. Abbott Lab., Abbott Park, 1995—. Contbr. numerous articles to profl. jours. Mem. Am. Soc. for Microbiology, Inst. of Food Technologists (fellowship 1989-90, merit fellowship 1987), Phi Kappa Phi, Gamma Sigma Delta, Sigma Xi. Office: Abbott Labs Dept 9K5 Bldg AP8B 100 Abbott Park Rd Abbott Park IL 60064

ALLEN, THERESA OHOTNICKY, neurobiologist, consultant; b. Torrington, Conn., Apr. 27, 1948; d. Frank Richard and Helen Theresa (Drozdenko) Ohotnicky; m. Thomas Atherton Allen, Aug. 12, 1972; children: Melanie Atherton, Abigail Baldwin. BA, U. Conn., 1970; MS, Villanova U., 1975; PhD, Duke U., 1978; cert. in bus. adminstrn., U. Pa., 1983. Realtor. Rsch. assoc. U. Pa., Phila., 1981-83; sci. dir. Drexel U., Phila., 1983-84; cons. on neurobiology to sci.-oriented cos., 1984—. Contbr. articles to profl. jours., also chpts. to books. Bd. dirs. Gladwyne (Pa.) Libr. League, 1986—, Athena Inst. for Women's Wellness, Haverford, Pa., 1989-93; trustee Gladwyne Libr., 1988—, pres., 1991-93; com. chmn. Jr. League Phila., 1989-90. Fellow Inst. Neurol. Scis., U. Pa., 1978-80, NIH, 1980-81. Mem. Phila. Skating Club, Humane Soc., Phi Beta Kappa. Episcopalian. Home: 1433 Waverly Rd Gladwyne PA 19035-1224 Office: 336 Conshohocken State Rd Gladwyne PA 19035-1336

ALLEN, THOMAS E., obstetrician, gynecologist; b. Bairdford, Pa., July 2, 1919; s. Emerson Ray and Lillie Mabel (McIntyre) A.; m. Judi Cannava, 1995; children: Catherine, Christine, Cynthia, Carolyn, Thomas J., Candace. BS, U. Pitts., 1940, MD, 1943. Diplomate Am. Bd. Ob-Gyn. Rotating intern U. Pitts., 1944, assoc. clin. prof. ob-gyn. Sch. Medicine; resident in gynegology Magee Hosp., Pitts., 1944-45, resident in ob-gyn., 1948-51; gen. practice medicine Oakmont, Pa., 1947-48; practice medicine specializing in ob-gyn. Pitts., 1951—; med. dir., co-founder Women's Health Service, Inc., Pitts., 1973-94; cons. ob-gyn Russelton Med. Group, New Kensington, Pa., 1953-73. Pres. Oakmont Sch. Bd., 1962-71; pres. bd. dirs. Am. Waterways Wind Orch., Pitts., 1970-93, chmn. bd. dirs., 1993—; bd. dirs. ACLU, Pitts., 1972-90. Served to capt. U.S. Army, 1945-47. Am. Legion and Buhl scholar, 1937. Fellow ACS, Am. Coll. Obstetricians and Gynecologists, Pan Pacific Surg. Assn., Pitts. Ob-gyn. Soc.; mem. AMA, county and state med. assns. Democrat. Club: Oakmont Country. Home: 301 Halket St Pittsburgh PA 15213-3104 Office: Womens Health Svcs Inc 221-225 Fifth Ave Pittsburgh PA 15222

ALLEN, THOMAS ERNEST, psychiatrist; b. Milw., Feb. 16, 1936; s. Thomas E. and Alice (Pfeifer) A.; m. Carol Israel, Oct. 19, 1963; children: Audrey, Ruth, Anna. AB, Princeton U., 1958; MD, Columbia U., 1962. Diplomate Am. Bd. Psychiatry and Neurology, Am. Bd. Child Psychiatry, Bd. Profl. Standards A Psa A. Intern San Francisco Gen. Hosp., 1962-63; resident in gen. psychiatry Columbia-Presbyn. Med. Ctr.-N.Y. State Psychiat. Inst., N.Y.C., 1963-66, resident in child psychiatry, 1965-66, chief resident, 1968-69; tng. in psychoanalysis Balt.-Wash. Psychoanalytic Inst., 1971-79; pvt. practice Towson, Md., 1974—; mem. med. staff Greater Balt. Med. Ctr., 1970—, Harbel Community Mental Health Ctr., 1980—. Contbr. articles to med. jours. With USPHS, 1966-68. Fellow Am. Psychiat. Assn., Am. Coll. Psychoanalysis; mem. Md. Psychiat. Soc. (pres. 1989-90), Md. Assn. for Pvt. Practice Psychiatrists (pres. 1985-86), Am. Assn. Pvt. Practice Psychiatrists (bd. dirs.), Balt. County Med. Assn. (pres. 1986), Md. Found. for Psychiatry (pres. 1991-92), Med Chi (v.p. 1993-94, treas. 1995-96, pres.-elect 1996-97), Balt.-Washington Soc. for Soc. for Psychoanalysis (pres. 1993-94). Democrat. Office: 7600 Osler Dr Ste 201 Baltimore MD 21204-7701

ALLEN, THOMAS WESLEY, medical educator, dean; b. Chgo., Sept. 13, 1938; s. Thomas and Helen Irene (Spitler) A.; m. Keith Mayo Capen, Oct. 6, 1988; children: Hilary, Roderick, Andrea. BA, Ottawa (Kans.) U., 1960; DO, Midwestern U., Chgo., 1964; DHL (hon.), U. New Eng., Biddeford, Maine, 1989. Diploamte Am. Bd. Internal medicine with subspecialty in pulmonary medicine, Am. Osteo. Bd. Internal Medicine. Intern Met. Hosp., Grand Rapids, Mich., 1964-65; resident in internal medicine Hosps. Chgo. Coll. Osteo Medicine, 1965-68; fellow in pulmonary medicine Northwestern U., 1969-70; from asst. to prof. medicine Chgo. Coll. Osteo. Medicine, 1968-87; pvt. practice Chgo., 1970-78; dean and v.p. acad. affairs and prof. medicine Midwestern U. Coll. Osteo. Medicine, Chgo., 1978-87; assoc. dean for acad. and clin. affars, prof. medicine U. Medicine and Dentistry of N.J. Coll. of Osteo. Medicine, 1987-91; provost, dean, prof. medicine Okla. State U. Coll. Osteo. Medicine, Tulsa, 1991—; mem. Nat. Adv. Coun. on Nat. Health Service Corps, Washington, 1994—, Nat. Adv. Coun. on Health Professions Edn., Washington, 1986-90. Editor-in-chief Jour. Am. Osteo. Assn., 1987—. Civic unit chair Tulsa Area United Way, 1995; trustee Village of Western Springs, Ill., 1981-85. Recipient Outstanding Achievement award Chgo. Coll. Osteo. Medicine Alumni Assn., 1993. Fellow Am. Coll. Osteo. Internists, Am. Coll. Chest Physicians; mem. Am. Osteo. Assn., Am. Assn. Colls. Osteo. Medicine, Am. Osteo. Acad. Sports Medicine, Am. Coll. Sports Medicine. Episcopalian. Home: 8911 S Florence Pl Tulsa OK 74137 Office: Okla State Univ College Osteopathic Med 1111 W 17th St Tulsa OK 74107

ALLEN, VICKI THOMAS, nutritionist, consultant; b. New Bern, N.C., Aug. 18, 1955; d. William Marshall and Vivian (Conway) Brantley; m. Rodney Dale Allen; 1 child, Brooke Ashley. AS, Pitt Community Coll., Greenville, N.C., 1976; BS magna cum laude, East Carolina U., 1982. Registered dietitian, N.C. Clin. dietitian Cape Fear Meml. Hosp., Wilmington, N.C., 1982-85, health promotion specialist, 1985-86, program coord., 1986-87, asst. dir. mktg., 1987-89, dir. outpatient nutrition svcs., 1989-90; dir. health svcs. New Hanover Med. Group, P.A., 1990—; cons. Duplin Gen. Hosp.; guest speaker on health topics Sta. WWAY-TV, Wilmington, 1987-89. Chmn. for ednl. and community programs, sec. New Hanover County Heart Assn., Wilmington, 1988-89, v.p., 1989—, pres. county affiliate Am. Heart Assn., New Hanover, 1991-92. Mem. Am. Dietetic Assn., N.C. Dietetic Assn., Coastal Carolinas Dietetics Assn. (treas. 1991-92), Phi Kappa Phi, Phi Upsilon Omicron. Republican. Office: New Hanover Med Group PA 1960 S 16th St Wilmington NC 28401-6647

ALLEN, WILLIAM CECIL, physician, educator; b. LaBelle, Mo., Sept. 8, 1919; s. William H. and Viola O. (Holt) A.; m. Madge Marie Gehardt, Dec. 25, 1943; children: William Walter, Linda Diane Allen Deardeuff, Robert Lee, Leah Denise Rogers. A.B., U. Nebr., 1947, M.D., 1951; M.P.H., Johns Hopkins U., 1960. Diplomate Am. Bd. Preventive Medicine. Intern Bishop Clarkson Meml. Hosp., Omaha, 1952; practice medicine specializing in family practice Glasgow, Mo., 1952-59; specializing in preventive medicine Columbia, Mo., 1960—; dir. sect. chronic diseases Mo. Div. Health, Jefferson City, 1960-65; asst. med. dir. U. Mo. Med. Ctr., 1965-75; assoc. coordinator Mo. Regional Med. Program, 1968-73, coordinator health programs, 1969—, clin. asst. prof. community health and med. practice, 1962-65, asst. prof. community health and med. practice, 1965-69, assoc. prof., 1969-75, prof., 1975-76, prof. dept. family and community medicine, 1976-87, prof. emeritus, 1987—; cons. Mo. Regional Med. Program, 1966-67, Norfolk Area Med. Sch. Authority, Va., 1965-66; governing body Area II Health Systems Agy., 1977-79, mem. coordinating com., 1977-79; founding dir. Mid-Mo. PSRO Corp., 1974-79, dir., 1976-84. Contbr. articles to profl. jours. Mem. Gov.'s Adv Council for Comprehensive Health Planning, 1970-73; trustee U. Mo. Med. Sch. Found., 1976—. Served with USMC, 1943-46. Fellow Am. Coll. Preventive Medicine, Am. Acad. Family Physicians (sci. program com. 1972-75, commn. on edn. 1975-80), Royal Soc. Health; mem. Mo. Acad. Family Physicians (dir. 1956-59, 76-82, alt. del. 1982-87, pres. 1985-86, chmn. bd. 1986-87), Mo. Med. Assn., Howard County Med. Soc. (pres. 1958-59), Boone County Med. Soc. (pres. 1974-75), Am. Diabetes Assn. (pres. 1978, dir. 1974-77), Mo. Diabetes Assn. (pres. 1972-73), Soc. Tchrs. Family Medicine, AMA, Mo. Public Health Assn., Am. Heart Assn. (program com. 1979-82), Am. Heart Assn. of Mo. (sec. 1980-81), Mo. Heart Assn. (sec. 1979-82, pres.-elect 1982-84, pres. 1984-86). Methodist. Office: U Mo M218 Medical Ctr Columbia MO 65203

ALLEN-CLAIBORNE, JOYCE G., clinical and educational psychologist; b. Columbus, Ga., Feb. 23 1948; d. Homer W. Jr. and Berneda C. Allen; m. Andrew J. Claiborne, Nov. 20, 1976 (dec.); 1 child, Jomo Abd-Allah Kenyatta Claiborne. BA cum laude, Spelman Coll., 1970; MA, U. Pitts., 1972, PhD (NIMH pub. health fellow, 1972-74), 1975. Lic. clin. psychologist; cert. sch. psychologist. Tchg. fellow U. Pitts., 1972, rsch. assoc., 1975-77; clin. psychologist Hillcrest Children's Ctr., Washington, 1977-78; pvt. practice clin. psychology, Washington, 1980-90, Albany, Ga., 1995—; psychologist, Region D, D.C. Pub. Schs., Washington, 1979-90; adj. prof. Union Grad. Sch., Clin., 1980-83; mem. rev. bd. Nat. Register Health Svc. Providers in Psychology, 1987-90; psychologist Dougherty County Sch. Sys., 1990—; part-time instr. dept. psychology, sociology, social work Albany (Ga.) State Coll., 1995-96. Adv. bd. St. Anselm's Abbey Day Camp, Washington. Mem. APA, Assn. Black Psychologists, Spelman Coll. Alumnae Club (pres. Albany chpt. 1996—), Delta Sigma Theta. Baptist. Home: 601 Freemont St Albany GA 31707-4507 Office: PO Box 1470 Albany GA 31702-1470

ALLENDER, JULIE ANN, psychologist; b. Elmhurst, Ill., Feb. 27, 1950; d. Frank and Edith (Gluklick) A.; m. Louis Zivic, May 18, 1980; 1 child, Jonathan Ephriam Allender-Zivic. BS in Psychology, U. Ill., 1973; MEd in Psychoednl. Processes, Temple U., 1974, EdD in Psychoednl. Processes, 1978. Lic. psychologist, Pa., Mass.; cert. sch. psychologist, Pa. Asst. prin. Beth Or Congregation Religious Sch., Spring House, Pa., 1977-78; dir. Homebased Businesswomen's Network, Lebanon, Pa., 1983-88; pvt. practice psychologist Lebanon, 1980—; staff cons. Good Samaritan Hosp., 1989—; former adj. faculty Community Coll. Phila., Temple U., Phila., Phila. Coll. Textile & Scis., Thomas Jefferson U. Med. Sch., Phila., Wheelock Coll., Boston, Pa. State U., Hershey, Reading; cons. med. staff Good Samaritan Hosp.; pvt. practice therapy, consultation and testing Pa. Coll. Optometry, Phila., Headstart, Chgo., Peabody (Mass.) Pub. Schs., Lynn (Mass.) Hist. Soc., Mich. Edn. Assn., Lansing, Dept. Agr. Extension Program, Lebanon, Pa., Lebanon Valley Coll., Annville, Pa., other orgns. Author: (book) End of My Rope: Gender Cooperation Model, 1996; contbr. articles to profl. jours. and newspapers, chpts. to books; participant media programs Sta. WRKO, Boston, 1983, Sta. WVLV, Lebanon, 1983-84, Sta. WAHT, Lebanon, 1988-90. Active Potential Reentry Opportunities in Bus. and Edn., 1986—, Homebased Businesswomen's Network of the Lebanon Valley, 1983-88; mem. women in bus. com. Lebanon C. of C., 1985-87; bd. dirs. Assn. for Humanistic Edn., 1983-87; mem. women's pavilion adv. bd. Lebanon Valley Gen. Hosp., 1986-90; bd. dirs. Interagency Mental Health Coun., Inc., 1995—. Mem. APA, ASTD, Pa. Psychol. Assn., Lancaster-Lebanon Psychol. Assn. (treas. 1990—), Orthopsychiat. Assn., Assn. for Humanistic Psychology. Jewish.

ALLEN PORTER, ESTHER, medical/surgical nurse; b. Jamaica, July 12, 1962; d. Delzago and Aneta (Dennis) A.; 1 chil, Courtney K.Y. Porter. AS, Nassau C.C., Garden City, N.Y., 1988. Asst. head nurse, surg. fl. North Shore Univ. Hosp., Manhasset, N.Y., 1992—.

ALLERTON, SAMUEL ELLSWORTH, biochemist; b. Three Rivers, Mich., Aug. 21, 1933; s. Sanford Ellsworth and Virginia Mary (Dickenson) A.; m. Theresa Mary Pawlak, Aug. 20, 1966; children: Adam Sanford, Eve Samantha. BA summa cum laude, Kalamazoo (Mich.) Coll., 1955; PhD, Harvard U., 1962. Teaching fellow Harvard U. Med. Sch., Boston, 1957-61; rsch. assoc. Rockefeller U., N.Y.C., 1961-65; asst. prof. U. So. Calif., L.A., 1965-69, assoc. prof., 1969—; cons. Woodroof Labs., Santa Ana, Calif., 1978-89. Contbr. articles to profl. jours. Bd. dirs. Huntington Beach (Calif.) Community Clinic, 1990-92. Named Outstanding Young Man of Am., Jaycee's, 1966. Mem. N.Y. Acad. Scis., Am. Coll. of Nutrition, Elks, Sigma Xi, Omicron Kappa Upsilon. Anglican. Office: Dentistry U So Calif University Park Mc # 0641 Los Angeles CA 90007

ALLESSIE, MAURITS ANTONIUS, physiologist; b. Gemert, The Netherlands, Aug. 14, 1945; s. Maurits Antonius and Petronella (Van Wel) A.; m. Paulina Jacoba Keepers, Mar. 4, 1968 (div. Aug. 1993); children: Martijn, Michiel, Chamila; m. Theodora Paulina Van de Waarsenburg, May 13, 1995; children: Sabine, Bram. MD, U. Amsterdam, 1968; PhD, U. Limburg, 1977. Asst. prof. U. Amsterdam, 1970-75; assoc. prof. U. Limburg, Maastricht, The Netherlands, 1975-84, prof., 1984—, chmn., 1990—. Editor: Atrial Fibrillation, 1994, Atrial and Ventricular Fibrillation, Mechanisms and Device Therapy, 1996; contbr. books on cardiac aarhythmias; contbr. articles to profl. jours. Recipient Fritz-Acker award German Soc. of Cardiology, 1994. Home: Arembergstraat 20, 5583 CD Waalre The Netherlands Office: Univ Limburg, Universiteitssingel 50, 6229 ER Maastricht The Netherlands

ALLEY, THOMAS ROBERTSON, psychology educator; b. Bryn Mawr, Pa., Oct. 20, 1953; s. Thomas R. and Ann (Higbee) A.; m. Pamela R. Pollack, July 31, 1977; children: Rebecca, Jennifer. BA, BS, Pa. State U., 1975; MA, U. Conn., 1979, PhD, 1981. Lectr. U. Conn., Storrs and Hartford, 1980-83; postdoctoral fellow U. Conn. Health Ctr., Farmington, 1981-84; asst. prof. psychology Clemson (S.C.) U., 1984-89, assoc. prof., 1989-92, prof. psychology, 1992—; vis. scholar Emory U., 1991-92. Editor: Social and Applied Aspects of Perceiving Faces, 1988; contbr. articles to profl. jours., chpts. to books. Mem. APS, Ea. Psychol. Assn., Psychonomic Soc., Internat. Soc. for Ecol. Psychology. Office: Clemson U Dept Psychology Clemson SC 29634-1511

ALLING, CHARLES CALVIN, III, oral-maxillofacial surgeon, educator, writer; b. Guthrie, Okla., Dec. 27, 1923; s. Charles Calvin Jr. and Bessie Palmer (Keller) A.; m. Laura Esther Freeland, May 10, 1947; children: Elaine Sue (Mrs. Andrew W. Lilliston Jr.), Rocklin David, Robert Freeland. AB, Ind. U., 1943, DDS, 1946; MS, U. Mich., 1954; DSc (hon.), Georgetown U., 1987. Diplomate Am. Bd. Oral and Maxillofacial Surgery (pres. 1983-84). Prof., chmn. dept. oral surgery U. Ala., Birmingham, 1969-81; oral-maxillofacial surgeon Drs. Alling & Alling, 1981—; adj. prof. Coll. Dentistry, U. Iowa; cons. ADA, U.S. Army Med. R & D Command, Surgeon Gen., VA; vis. prof. and lectr. Howard U., Georgetown U., Seoul U. Editor, author: Maxillofacial Trauma, 1988, Facial Pain, 3d edit., 1991, Oral Maxillofacial Surgery Clinics North America, 1973, 93, Impacted Teeth, 1993; mem. editorial bd. Oral Surgery, Oral Medicine, Oral Pathology; contbr. chpts. to books, articles to profl. jours. Bd. dirs. Kwang Myung Orphanage and Sch. for Blind, Inchon, Republic of Korea. With U.S. Army, 1943-69. Decorated Legion of Merit; Medaslha Le Rene Forte (Brazil); recipient U.S. Army Outstanding Civilian Svc. award, W.F. Harrigan award Bellevue Hosp., Sadi Fountaine award Alameda Med. Instns., Fauchard Disting. Svc. award, W.J. Gies Disting. Svc. award. Fellow Am. Coll. Dentists; mem. ADA, Am. Soc. Oral Surgeons (bd. dirs.), Am., Southeastern, Ala. Internat. Assn. Oral-Maxillofacial Surgeons, Chalmer Lyons Acad. Oral Surgery, 38th Parallel Dental Soc. (charter pres.), Greater Washington Soc. Oral Surgeons (charter pres.), Internat. Assn. Dental Rsch., Pan Pacific Implant Assn., Masons, Shriners, Phi Kappa Phi. Home: 1509 Panorama Dr Birmingham AL 35216-3316 Office: Drs Alling & Alling 1957 Hoover Ct Ste 206 Birmingham AL 35226-3622

ALLINSON, RICHARD WARD, physician; b. N.Y., Nov. 15, 1953; s. Francis Ward and Edith (Schmidt) A.; m. Wanda Carol Allinson, June 30, 1984; children: Elizabeth Carol, Francis Ward. BS, Univ. Ariz., 1975; MD, Univ. Tex. Health Sci., 1980. Diplomate Am. Bd. Ophthalmology. Internship Good Samaritan Hosp., Phoeniz, 1980-81; residency dept. ophthalmology Pa. State Univ. Coll. Medicine, Hershey, Pa., 1981-84; fellowship dept. ophthalmology Touro Infirmary, New Orleans, La., 1985-86; medical dir. Univ. Medical Ctr. Eye Clinic Univ. Ariz., 1989-91; dir. vitreoretinal svc. dept. ophthalmology Univ. Ariz., 1986-92; acting chief sect. of ophthalmology VA Medical Ctr., Phoenix, 1993; chief sect. ophthalmology VA Medical Ctr., Tuscon, Ariz., 1986-92; dir. retina svs. VA Adminstrn. Medical Ctr., Phoenix, 1992; clinical asst. prof. ophthalmology Univ. Ariz., 1986; credentialing com. St Joseph's Hosp., Phoenix, 1994, quality assurance com. VA Adminstrn. Medical Ctr., 1991-92, chmn. academic peer review com. Univ. Ariz., 1991-92, continuing medical edn. com., 1990-92; medical staff appeals com. Univ. Medical Ctr., 1987-88, 99-90, 89-90, 90-91, 91-92, ambulatory care com., 1989-91; staff Phoenix Bapt. Hosp., 1992, St. Jospeh's Hosp., 1993, VA Medical Ctr., 1993, St Luke's Medical Ctr., 1987. Author numerous books; contbr. articles to profl. jours. Vol. ophthalmological care to residents of Puerto Penasco, Mex., 1990. Recipient Physician award Univ. Medical Ctr., 1987, 88, 89, 90, 91; numerous rsch. grants. Mem. AMA, Am. Acad. Ophthalmology, Western Retina Study Club, Phoenix Ophthalmological Soc., Maricopa County Medical Soc., Ariz. Ophthalmological Soc., Ariz. Medical Assn., The Vitreous Soc., Tucson Ophthalmological Soc., Lions Club. Office: Richard W Allinson 3507 W Bethany Home Rd Phoenix AZ 85019

ALLISON, FRED, JR., physician, educator; b. Abingdon, Va., Sept. 8, 1922; s. Fred and Elizabeth Harriet (Kelly) A.; m. Clara Knox, Oct. 14, 1949; children: Rebecca Allison Parsley, Martha Allison Brown, Fred III, Robert Gardiner. B.S., Ala. Poly. Inst., 1944; M.D., Vanderbilt U., 1946. Diplomate: Am. Bd. Internal Medicine. Intern Vanderbilt Hosp., Nashville, 1946-47; resident Peter Bent Brigham Hosp., Boston, 1949-50; practice medicine specializing in internal medicine, 1946—; asst. prof. medicine Washington U., St. Louis, 1955; prof. medicine, head infectious disease dept. U. Miss., Jackson, 1955-68; vis scientist Rockefeller U., N.Y.C., 1966-67; prof. medicine, head dept. medicine La. State U., New Orleans, 1968-87; head La. State U. div. Charity Hosp., 1968-87; prof. medicine Vanderbilt U., Nashville, 1987—; clin. prof. medicine Meharry Med. Coll., Nashville, 1987; physician-in-chief Met. Nashville Gen. Hosp., 1987—. Served with U.S. Army, 1943-46, 47-49.

ALLISON, JANE SHAWVER, medical school administrator, management consultant; b. San Angelo, Tex., Dec. 29, 1938; d. Floyd McKinzie and Bertha J. (Hicks) Shawver; m. Cecil Wayne Allison, June 22, 1957; children: Jana Lea Jones, David Wayne, Don McKinzie. Student U. Denver, 1954, Northwestern U., 1955, Tex. Tech U., 1956-57, Midwestern U., Wichita Falls, Tex., 1958. Continuity writer, Sta. KFDX-TV, Wichita Falls, Tex., 1957-58; sec. Wichita Falls Symphony, Tex., 1968-70; adminstrv. asst. Coll. of Bus. Tex. Tech U., Lubbock, 1971-74, coord. programs dept. family medicine Tex. Tech. U. Health Sci. Ctr., 1974-77, adminstr. dept. family medicine, 1978-87, clin. adminstrv. dir. dept. family medicine, 1987—, vol. faculty grad. program in health orgn. mgmt. Coll. Bus. Adminstrn., 1993—, chmn. clin. adminstrs., 1994-95; cons. Family Practice Residency, Amarillo, Tex., 1984, Temple, Tex., 1984-85. Bd. dirs. Lubbock Symphony Orch., Inc., 1976-94, mem. nominating com., 1986, exec. com., 1987-88, v.p. 1988-89; bd. dirs. Helen A. Hodges Charitable Trust, Lubbock, 1983-95; mem. Tex. Tech U. Coll. Bus. Adminstrn. Lubbock Council, 1988—. Recipient Superior Achievement award Tex. Tech U. Health Scis. Ctr., 1987, HSC award of Excellence Tex. Tech U. Health Scis. Ctr., 1987; honoree 75th Birthday Celebration, Caprock Council Girl Scouts USA Mem. Med. Group Mgmt. Assn., Acad. Practice Assembly, Assn. Family Practice Adminstrs. (bd. dirs. 1993, 85, 87, 88, 94, 95, charter pres. 1984, chmn. steering com. 1983, chmn. 10th ann. celebration 1994, program co-chmn. and co-v.p. 1995-96, Jane S. Allison Ednl. Series Adminstrv. Issues established in her honor). Mem. Disciples of Christ. Club: Soroptimist Internat. (pres. 1986-87, regional parlimentarian, 1986-88, regional laws and resolutions chmn. 1988-90.). Office: Tex Tech U Health Sci Ctr Dept Family Medicine Lubbock TX 79430

ALLMAN, JAMES KIRK, physician's assistant; b. Arlington, Tex., Mar. 9, 1961; s. James Nathan Allman and Gloria (Kirk) Glass; m. Susan Lynn Garrity, Sept. 27, 1986; children: James Eric, Matthew Tyler. BS as Physician Asst., U. Okla., 1985. Bd. cert. physician asst. in primary care and surgery; lic. physician asst., Okla., N.Mex. Physician asst. Dennis E. Ester MD, Orthopedic Surgeon, Oklahoma City, 1985-95, Richard E. White, MD, N.Mex. Orthopedic Assoc., Albuquerque, 1995—; instr., assoc. prof. dept. family medicine U. Okla., Health Sci. Ctr., Coll. Medicine. Fellow Orthopedic Surgery-Am. Bd. Physician Asst. Practice; mem. Am. Acad. Physician Assts., Okla. Acad. Physician Assts., N.Mex. Acad. Physician Assts. Home: 5806 Broken Arrow Ln NW Albuquerque NM 87120-3046

ALLMAN, RICHARD MARK, physician, gerontologist; b. Columbus, Ohio, Feb. 23, 1955; m. Connie Lou Allman; children: Justin Mark, Philip Randolph. BA in Biology magna cum laude, W.Va. U., 1977, MD, 1980. Diplomate Am. Bd. Internal Medicine, sub.-bd. Geriatric Medicine; diplomate Nat. Bd. Med. Examiners. Internal medicine intern W.Va. U. Sch. Medicine, 1980-81, resident in internal medicine, 1981-83; fellow in internal medicine Johns Hopkins U., Balt., 1983-85; asst. in medicine, staff physician Johns Hopkins U./Hosp., Balt., 1985-86; staff physician U. Ala. Hosp., VA Med. Ctr., Birmingham, 1986—; asst. prof. medicine U. Ala., Birmingham, 1986-90, assoc. prof. medicine, dir. div. gerontology/geriatric med., 1990—, dir. Ctr. for Aging, 1992—, dir. Geriatric Edn. Ctr., 1993—; prin. clin. coord. Ala. Quality Assurance Found., Birmingham, 1995—; chief geriatrics sect. Birmingham VA Med. Ctr., 1990—. Assoc. editor Am. Jour. Medicine, 1988-92; mem. editorial bd. Advances in Wound Healing, 1989—, Jour. Am. Geriatrics Soc., 1994—; ad hoc reviewer for jours.; contbr. numerous articles to profl. jours. Recipient Lange Book award, 1977, Mosby Book award, 1978, John A. Hartford Found. award, 1991, others. Mem. ACP, Am. Fedn. for Aging Rsch., Assn. Dirs. Geriatric Acad. Programs (nat. coun. 1993—), Wound Healing Soc., Ala. Gerontol. Soc., So. Soc. for Clin. Investigation, Gerontol. Soc. Am., Am. Heart Assn. (coun. on epidemiology), Am. Geriatrics Soc., Am. Fedn. for Clin. Rsch. (Henry Christian Meml. award 1993), Soc. Gen. Internal Medicine, Phi Beta Kappa, Alpha Omega Alpha. Office: U Ala Ctr for Aging 933 19th St S Ste 201 Birmingham AL 35294-2041

ALLMEN, ROBERT JOSEPH, psychotherapist, priest; b. Rockville Centre, N.Y., Oct. 17, 1953; s. Henry and Patricia (Walsh) A. MDiv, CU, 1979, MS, 1980, DD, 1996. Pastor Good Shepherd Am. Cath. Ch., Hampton Bays, N.Y., 1989—; psychotherapist, exec. dir. Family Counseling Ctr. of L.I., Central Islip, 1989—. Ordained Am. Cath. Ch., 1980. Mem. Am. Orthopsychiat. Assn., Am. Soc. Pastoral and Wellness Counselors (cert.), Pax Christi USA, Civil Liberties, N.Y. State Coun. on Divorce Mediation, Guild of Holistic Practitioners. Democrat. American Catholic. Home and Office: 10 Faith Dr # 725 Hampton Bays NY 11946-2629

ALLOCCA, JOHN ANTHONY, medical research scientist; b. Bklyn., Aug. 27, 1948; s. Frank and Dorothy (Aulicino) A.; children: Jennifer, Jerry. AAS, SUNY-Farmingdale, 1972; BA, SUNY-Old Westbury, 1975; MS, Poly. Inst. N.Y., 1979; DSc, Pacific Western U., 1981. Adminstr. Hofstra U., 1967-71; psychotherapist Creedmore State Hosp., 1975-76; biomed. engr. Doll Rsch. Inc., 1971-77; rsch. scientist Albert Einstein Coll. Medicine, 1977-78; rsch. cons. L.I. Coll. Hosp., 1979-80; rsch. scientist, tech. dir. pulmonary labs. Mt. Sinai Med. Ctr., 1980-82; rsch. scientist Langer Biomech. Group, Inc., 1983-85; pres., rsch. scientist Andromeda Rsch., Inc., 1985-88, The Zibav Corp., 1988-89; pres. Allocca Tech. Inc., Smithtown, N.Y., 1989—. Author: Electrical/Electronic Safety, 1982, Electronic Instrumentation, 1983, Transducer Theory and Applications, 1983, Medical Instrumentation for the Health Care Professional, 1990, Physiology and Nutrition, 1986. Mem. IEEE, Assn. Advancement Med. Instrumentation, AAAS, Am. Assn. Physicists in Medicine, N.Y. Acad. Scis. Alumni Assn. Mt. Sinai Med. Ctr. Home and Office: 15 Tebelt Lane West Hurley NY 12491-5206

ALLRED, OLEN RUDOLPH, dentist; b. Brookhaven, Miss., Sept. 1, 1932; s. Elzie Middleton and Nellie Marie (Cowart) A.; m. Martha Ann Cupit, July 28, 1956; children: Gerald Wayne, James Olen, Terri Lynn, Cheryl Ann. BS, Stephen F. Austin U., 1954; DDS, U. Tex. Dental Br., Houston, 1957. Dentist pvt. practice Beaumont, Tex., 1957—. Pres. Lions Club North Beaumont, 1971; dep. dist. gov. Dist. 251 Lyons Internat., Beaumont, 1973-76; chmn. dentist United Appeals, Beaumont, 1977. Recipient fellowship Am. Coll. Dentist, 1992. Fellow Acad. Gen. Dentistry; mem. Sabine Dist. Dental Soc. (pres. 1989, Dentist of Yr. 1986), Tex. Dental Assn., Am. Dental Assn., No. Tex. Dental Br. Alumni (trustee 1989-91), Coun. Pub. Health Tex. Dental Assn. Republican. Baptist. Home: 1450 Continental St Beaumont TX 77706-3408 Office: 3635 Eastex Fwy Beaumont TX 77706-7529

ALLSHOUSE, MICHAEL JAMES, pediatric surgeon; b. U.S. Canal Zone, Panama, Feb. 24, 1954; s. Thomas James and Elsie Dale (Hamilton) A.; m. Denise Lynn Glass, Aug. 18, 1979; children: Anthony James, Victoria Lynn, Charles Michael. BS, Allegheny Coll., 1976; DO, Phila. Coll. Osteopathy, 1982. Diplomate Am. Bd. Surgery. Staff gen. surgeon Naval Hosp., Guam, 1988-90, Oakland, Calif., 1990-91; fellow in pediatric trauma Children's Nat. Med. Ctr., Washington, 1991-92; chief resident pediatric surgery The Children's Hosp., Denver, 1992-94; head div. pediatric surgery Naval Med. Ctr., San Diego, 1994—. Cmdr. USN, 1982-94. Recipient order of ancient chamorri Govt. Guam, 1990. Fellow Am. Coll. Surgeons. Home: 7685 Bromeliad Ct San Diego CA 92119-1535 Office: Naval Med Ctr 34800 Bob Wilson Dr San Diego CA 92135-5000

ALLUKIAN, MYRON, JR., government administrator, public health educator, dental educator; b. Cambridge, Mass., Jan. 6, 1939; s. Myron and Mary (Nahabedian) A.; m. Ruth Felice Losco, Oct. 11, 1975; children: Myron III, Kristin, Alison, Jason, Alexandra, Nathan. BS in Psychology, Tufts U., 1960; DDS, U. Pa., 1964; MPH, Harvard U., Boston, 1967. Chief dental health Bunker Hill Health Ctr., Mass. Gen. Hosp., Boston, 1969-77; dir. community dental programs Boston Dept. Health and Hosps., 1970-96, dir. personal health svcs., 1991-93; dir. cmty. dental programs Boston Pub. Health Dept., Pub. Health Commn., 1996—; assoc. vis. dentist Boston City Hosp., 1970-96, Boston Med. Ctr., 1996—; lectr. Georgetown U. Sch. Dentistry, 1979-89, Tufts Sch. Dental Medicine, 1994—, U. Mass. Sch. Pub. Health, 1984-93, U. Minn. Sch. Pub. Health, 1981-92, Forsyth Sch. for Dental Hygienists, Boston, 1970—, Boston U. Dental Sch., 1977—, Mich. Sch. Pub. Health, Ann Arbor, 1980—; assoc. clin. prof. Sch. Dental Medicine, Harvard U., 1977—, lectr. Sch. Pub. Health, 1991—; regional cons. Job Corps, U.S. Dept. Labor, New Eng., 1973—; corp. mem. Mass. Dental Svc. Corp., 1971-79; vis. prof. Columbia U. Sch. Dentistry, N.Y.C., 1991, mem., 1978-88; chmn., sec. Mass. Bd. Registration in Dentistry, 1980-86; mem. Am. Bd. Dental Pub. Health, treas., 1991-92, v.p., 1992-93, pres., 1993-94, diplomate, 1973—. Mem. editl. adv. com. Nation's Health, 1991-92; mem. editorial bd. Am. Jour. Pub. Health, 1979-82, Jour. Pub. Health Dentistry, 1985-89; editorial cons. Jour. Pub. Health Policy, 1985—; contbr. over 90 articles and abstracts to profl. jours., chpts. to books. Chmn. U.S. Surgeon Gen.'s Work Group on Fluoridation and Dental Health, 1990, Prevention Objectives for The Nation, 1978-80; mem. nat. dental tobacco-free steering com. Nat. Cancer Inst., 1989—; corp. mem. Boston Young Men's Christian Union, 1974—; clin. dental dir. New England AIDS Edn. and Tng. Ctr., 1991—, Northeast Regional Bd. Dental Examiners, mem., 1978—, steering com., 1980-86; adv. com. Boston Health Care for The Homeless, 1992-96, Nat. Bd. Examiners in Optometry, examination com., 1992—, chair pub. health/clin.- legal issues com., 1994—, Harvard Sch. Pub. Health Alumni Assn. Coun., 1992—, pres.- elect 1993-95, pres., 1995—, Mass. "Assist", 1991-93, chmn. Statewide Tobacco Control Planning Com., 1992, Pub. Health Mus. Mass., bd. dirs., 1992—, pres., 1993-94, cons. commn. dental accreditation Am. Dental Assn., 1996—; accreditation reviewer Coun. Edn. for Pub. Health, 1996—; bd. dirs. Urban Health Project, Harvard Med. Sch., 1996. Lt. Dental Corps, USN, 1964-66, Vietnam. Recipient cert. of appreciation U.S. Dept. Labor, 1981, Community Svc. award Health Planning Coun. Greater Boston, 1986, Disting. Faculty award Harvard Sch. Dental Medicine, 1986, Disting. Alumni award, 1996, Alumni Merit award U. Pa. Dental Sch., 1987, Exemplary Svc. award USPHS, 1990, Vision Svc. award Mass. Soc. Optometrists, 1992, Outstanding Achievement award Armenian-Am. Behavioral Sci. Assn., 1995; postdoctoral fellow Harvard Sch. Dental Medicine, 1969. Fellow Royal Soc. Health (hon.), Internat. Coll. Dentists; mem. APHA (pres. 1989-90), Inst. Medicine of NAS (com. educating dentists for the future 1992-93), Am. Assn. Pub. Health Dentistry (pres. 1984-85, spl. merit award 1987), Mass. Pub. Health Assn. (pres. 1977-78, Disting. Svc. citation 1988), Mass. Health Coun. (pres. 1977-78, ann. award 1989), Armenian-Am. Dental Soc. (pres. 1982-84, trustee 1985—, founding mem. 1978). Office: Cmty Dental Programs 1010 Massachusetts Ave Boston MA 02118-2600

ALLUMS, JAMES A., cardiovascular surgeon; b. Kountz, Tex., Sept. 28, 1937; m. Elizabeth Dee Walton, June 24, 1961; children: Ann Elizabeth, Sarah Dee, Benjamin Walton. BA, U. Tex., 1959; MD, U. Tex. Med. Br., 1962. Diplomate Am. Bd. Med. Examiners, Am. Bd. Surgery, Am. Bd. Thoracic Surgery, Am. Bd. Gen. Vascular Surgery. Rotating intern Phila. Gen. Hosp., 1962-63; resident gen. surgery Med. Br. U. Tex., Galveston, 1963-66, 68-69; ptnr. Thoracic and Cardiovascular Surg. Assocs., Beaumont, Tex., 1971—; clin. asst. prof. Dept. Thoracic and Cardiovascular Surgery, U. Tex. Med. Br., Galveston; active physician St. Elizabeth Hosp., chief of staff 1976-77, 87-88; active Beaumont, Bapt. Hosp. of S.E. Tex., Beaumont, Beaumont Regional Med. Ctr., Beaumont Regional Med. Ctr., Park Place Hosp.; courtesy staff St. Mary Hosp., Port Arthur, Mid Jefferson Hosp., Nederland, Tex.; cons. staff U. Tex. Med. Br. Hosp., Galveston; mem. cardiovascular com. Bapt. Hosp., 1991-93, 1996, physician, nurse ad hoc com., 1992; clin. asst. prof. Dept. of Surgery U. Tex. Med. Br. Hosp., 1993-94; OR com. St. Elizabeth Hosp., Beaumont, 1990-91, 93-94, cardiovascular quality assurance subcom., 1991-92, cardiovascular/coronary care com., 1990-91, 92-93, CCU quality assurance subcom. Contbr. articles to profl. jours. Capt. U.S. Army, 1966-68. Recipient J.C. Crager award Am. Heart Assn., 1992, Mr. East Tex. award Tyler County Dogwood Festival, 1993. Fellow ACS (gov. 1989-94, pres. South Tex. chpt. 1987), Am. Coll. of Angiology, Am. Coll. of Cardiology, Am. Coll. of Chest Physicians, Beaumont Acad. of Medicine; mem. AMA, Assn. of Am. Physicians and Surgeons, Bapt. Hosp. P.H.O., Beaumont Regional P.H.O., Jefferson County Med. Soc., Singleton Surg. Soc., Soc. of Thoracic Surgeons, So. Assn. for Vascular Surgery, So. Med. Assn., So. Thoracic Surg. Assn., St. Elizabeth Hosp. P.H.O., Tex. Med. Assn. (coun. on med. edn. 1985-92), Tex. Surg. Soc., Alumni Assn. of the U. of Tex. Med. Br. (pres. 1984-85)Phi Eta Sigma, Alpha Epsilon Delta. Office: T&C Surg Assocs 2955 Harrison #204 Beaumont TX 77702

ALMAGRO, URIAS ALCANTARA, pathologist; b. Dalaguete, Cebu, Philippines, Dec. 15, 1943; came to U.S., 1972; s. David M. and Juanita (Alcantara) A.; m. Amelia Louise Zwolinski, May 16, 1975; children: Alden, Brandon, Allison, Darren. BA, Southwestern U., Cebu City, 1964, MD, 1968. Instr. dept. microbiology and parasitology Southwestern U., Cebu City, 1968-69, instr. dept. pathology, 1969-72; rotating intern St. Joseph Hosp., Lorain, Ohio, 1972-73; pathology resident DePaul Hosp., Norfolk, Va., 1973-76; pathology resident Med. Coll. wis., Milw., 1976-78, asst. prof., 1978-85, assoc. prof., 1985—; pathologist Zablocki Vets. Affairs Med. Ctr., Milw., 1978—. Contbr. articles to profl. jours. Fellow Am. Coll. Pathologists, Am. Soc. Clin. Pathologists; mem. Wis. Soc. Pathologists. Roman Catholic. Home: 4035 S Wilshire Dr New Berlin WI 53151 Office: Zablocki VA Med Ctr 5000 W National Ave Milwaukee WI 53295

AL MAHASSENI, MOHAMMAD MARWAN, surgeon, educator; b. Damascus, Syria, Oct. 7, 1927; s. Fuad and Yusra (Seifi) al M.; m. Farida Nabulsi, Mar. 8, 1961; children: Fuad, Amr. MD, Damascus U., 1951; MS in Medicine, Paris U., 1962. Intern Damascus U. Hosp., 1950-51; resident Laënnec Hosp., Paris, 1952-55, Frenchay Hosp., Bristol, U.K., 1954, Shotley Bridge Hosp., Newcastle-upon-Tyne, U.K., 1958-59; fellow Broussais Hosp., Paris, 1961, St. Thomas Hosp., London, 1964; lectr. surgery Damascus U., Syria, 1955-60, assoc. prof. surgery, 1960-67, prof. surgery, 1967-79; prof. surgery King Abdulaziz U., Jeddah, Saudi Arabia, 1981-91, prof. and chmn. dept. surgery, 1983-86; dir. med. edn. King Abdulaziz Hosp. Ministry of Health, 1991. Co-author: Medical Dictionary Unified English/Arabic, 1973, Medical Dictionary Unified English/French/Arabic, 1983; author: Italian Words in Current Arabic, 1971; contbr. articles to profl. jours. Vice pres. Anti-Cancer Soc., Damascus, 1972-79; pres. League for Human Rights, Damascus, 1974—, Arab Com. for French Studies, Paris, 1974, French Inter-Univs. Com. French Studies, 1982. Lt. Syrian Army, 1951-52. Decorated Legion of Honor (Knight), Pres. French Republic, 1979. Mem. Societe Francaise de Pathologie Respiratoire, Soc. Thoracic Surgeons of G.B. and Ireland, Arab Acad. Moslem. Home: PO Box 9405, Jeddah 21413, Saudi Arabia Office: King Abdulaziz Univ, Jeddah Saudi Arabia

ALMANSA PASTOR, ANGEL F., chest physician; b. Malaga, Idem, Spain, Sept. 12, 1934; s. Salvador Almansa de Cara and Paula Pastor Roda; m. Isabel Mendez Peña, May 16, 1970; children: Maria Isabel, Angel, Paloma. Student Agustinos Coll., Malaga, 1943-47, Salesianos Coll., 1948-51; U. Grad., F. Medicine, Granada, 1957, Specialist Thoracic Surgeon, 1965, Specialist Pneumologie, 1980, Specialist Cardiologie, 1980. Diplomate Spain Bd. Med. Examiners. Asst. Hosp. Princesa, Madrid, 1958-59, Speziallungenklinik Hemer, Westfalhem, Fed. Republic Germany, 1969-76, U. Chirurg Klinik, Dusserdorf, 1961-65; chief pneumology Hosp. Civil Privincial, Malaga, 1966-75; med. dir. Hosp. Torax, Malaga, 1975—; prof. pneumologie Diputacion Provincial, Malaga, 1966, Valencia, 1965. Patentee blood circulation activator. Contbr. articles to profl. jours. Served with Spain Mil. Service, 1956-57. Pre-Univ. Grad. with honors, U. Granada, 1952; Med. Grad. with honors, F. Medicine, 1957. Fellow Am. Coll. Chest Physicians; mem. Coll. Internat. Angyologiae, Soc. Spain Patology A. Respiratorio, Soc. Spain Cardiologia, Soc. Andaluza Cardiologia, Soc. Spain Geriatria, Assn. Med. Naturistas. Roman Catholic. Club: Mediterraneo. Avocations: tennis; golfing. Office: San Lorenzo 2, Malaga 29001, Spain

ALMANSI, RENATO JOSEPH, psychoanalyst; b. Parma, Italy, Sept. 2, 1909; came to U.S., 1939; s. Dante G. and Ada B. (Torre) A.; widowed 1987; children: Stephen P., Susan B. MD, U. Rome, 1933; grad. student, N.Y. Psychoanalytic Inst., 1952-57. Diplomate Am. Bd. Psychiatry and Neurology. Clin. prof. psychiatry NYU, N.Y.C., 1979—. Contbr. articles to profl. jours. Fellow Am. Psychiat. Assn. (life); mem. N.Y. Psychoanalytic Soc., Psychoanalytic Assn. N.Y. Home and office: 200 E 89th St Apt 41B New York NY 10128-4308

ALMOND, CARL HERMAN, surgeon, physician, educator; b. Latour, Mo., Apr. 1, 1926; s. Hugh Herman and Sylvia (Morrison) A.; m. Nancy Ginn, June 18, 1964 (div. 1990); children: Carrie, Callie, Carl, Christopher. BS, Washington U., St. Louis, 1949, MD, 1953. Diplomate: Am. Bd. Surgery, Am. Bd. Thoracic Surgery. Rotating intern Los Angeles County Gen. Hosp., 1953-54; resident surgery U. Mich., Ann Arbor, 1954-56, jr. clin. instr. surgery, 1956-57, sr. clin. instr., 1957-58; fellow surg. pathology Barnes Hosp.-Washington U., St. Louis, 1956; sr. surg. resident in urology Baylor U. Affiliated Hosps., 1958-59; resident thoracic surgery U. So. Calif., Los Angeles, 1959, fellow thoracic surgery, 1962-63; staff surgeon Univ. Hosp., Columbia, Mo., 1959-78, dir. thoracic and cardiovascular surgery, 1968-77; dir. thoracic and cardiovascular surgery VA Hosp., Columbia; fellow Brompton Hosp., London, Eng., 1961; asst. prof. surgery U. Mo. Sch. Medicine, Columbia, 1959-64, asso. prof., 1964-69, prof., chief thoracic and cardiovascular surgery, from 1969; prof. and chmn. dept. surgery Sch. Medicine, U. S.C., Columbia, 1978-85, dir. gen. surgery residency program, 1979-85, assoc. dean clin. research and devel., 1986-90; vis. prof. U. Geneva, Switzerland, 1972-73; Mem. med. adv. panel FAA, 1970-75; mem. U.S. Commn. on UNESCO, 1983. Contbr. articles to profl. jours. Served with USNR, 1944-52. Fellow A.C.S.; mem. AMA, Boone County Med. Soc., Columbia Med. Soc., S.C. Med. Assn., S.C. Thoracic Soc., Am. Assn. Med. Colls., Frederick H. Coller Surg. Soc., St. Louis Surg. Soc., Am. Coll. Cardiology, Am., S.C. heart assns., Am. Soc. Artificial Internal Organs, Soc. Med. Cons. to Armed Forces, Am. Coll. Chest Physicians, So. Thoracic Surg. Assn., Central Surg. Soc., Am. Assn. Thoracic Surgery, So. Surg. Assn., S.C. Surg. Soc., Chest Club, Soc. Surg. Chairmen, Marion S. DeWeese Surg. Soc., Southeastern Surg. Soc., So. Surg. Soc., Internat. Cardiovascular Soc., Soc. Thoracic Surgeons, Sigma Xi, Nu Sigma Nu, Sigma Chi. Home: 2831 Gervais St Columbia SC 29204 Office: U SC Sch Medicine Dept Surgery Two Medical Park/Ste 300 Columbia SC 29203

ALMY, THOMAS PATTISON, physician, educator; b. N.Y.C., Jan. 10, 1915; s. Don Robinson and Marie (Pattison) A.; m. Katharine Whitin Swift, Nov. 12, 1943; children: Susan, Anne, Christine. A.B., Cornell U., 1935, M.D., 1939; M.A. (hon.), Dartmouth Coll., 1970. Intern N.Y. Hosp., 1939-40; resident medicine, 1940-43; from asst. prof. to prof. medicine Cornell U. Med. Coll., 1946-68; Nathan Smith prof. medicine, chmn. dept. Dartmouth Med. Sch., 1968-73, Third Century prof., 1973-85, prof. medicine and community medicine emeritus, 1985—; disting. physician VA, 1982-85; cons NIH, NRC, Am. Cancer Soc. Author articles in clin. physiology gastrointestinal disease and in med. edn. Recipient award of distinction Cornell U. Med. Coll. Alumni Assn., 1967. Master A.C.P. (bd. regents 1968-73); mem. Assn. Am. Physicians, Am. Gastroenterol. Assn. (pres. 1964, Julius Friedenwald medal 1976), Inst. Medicine NAS (sr. mem.). Home: 80 Lyme Rd Apt 222 Hanover NH 03755-1231

ALOIA, ROLAND CRAIG, scientist, administrator, educator; b. Newark, Dec. 21, 1943; s. Roland S. and Edna M. (Mahan) A. BS, St. Mary's Coll., 1965; PhD, U. Calif., Riverside, 1970. Postdoctoral fellow City of Hope,

Duarte, Calif., 1971-75; research biologist U. Calif., Riverside, 1975-76; asst. prof. Sch. of Medicine Loma Linda (Calif.) U., 1976-79; assoc. prof. Loma Linda (Calif.) U., 1979-89, prof. anesthesiology and biochemistry, 1989—; chemist VA, Loma Linda, 1979-94, chief rsch. ops., 1994—; pres., chmn. Loma Linda VA for Rsch. and Edn., 1988-94, pres., CEO, 1994—. Editor: Membrane Fluidity in Biology, Vols. 1-4, 1983, 85; sr. editor: (series) Advanced in Membrane Fluidity vols. 1-3, 1988, vol. 4, 1989, vol. 5, 1991, vol. 6, 1992. Pres. Riverside chpt. Calif. Heart Assn., 1979-80, 1984-86, bd. dirs., exec. com. mem., 1973-86. Calif. Heart Assn. fellow, 1971-73. Mem. Am. Chem. Soc., N.Y. Acad. Scis., Soc. Cell Biology, Sigma Xi (pres. Loma Linda chpt. 1991-92, pres.-elect 1990-91). Office: VA Med Ctr Rsch Svc 151 JL Pettis Loma Linda CA 92357

ALONSO, ANSELMO, surgeon; b. Aug. 5, 1958; s. Domingo and Lupe (Garcia) A.; m. Annabel Galva; children: Anselmo, Javier, Alejandro, Augusto, Andrea, Arianna. BS, Recinto U. Mayaguez, P.R., 1980; MD, U. P.R., San Juan, 1984. Diplomate Am. Bd. Surgery with subspecialty in surg. critical care, Am. Bd. Thoracic Surgery. Resident in gen. surgery Univ. Dist. Hosp., San Juan, 1984-89; resident in cardiothoracic surgery Ohio State U. Hosp., Columbus, 1990-92; heart transplant surgeon Omaha, Nebr., 1992—; asst. prof. surgery U. Nebr. Med. Ctr., Omaha, 1992—. Contbr. articles to profl. jours. Fellow ACS, Am. Coll. Cardiology, Am. Coll. Chest Physicians; mem. Assn. for Acad. Surgery, Internat. Soc. for Heart and Lung Transplantation, Soc. Thoracic Surgeons. Office: Univ of Nebr Med Ctr 600 S 42d St Omaha NE 68198-2315

ALONSO, VICTOR, physician; b. N.Y.C., Nov. 24, 1941; s. Victor and Mildred (Nieves) A.; m. Judith Leslie Wood, Jan. 15, 1965 (div. July 1968); 1 child, Pablo; m. Harriet Beatrice Hyman, Sept. 10, 1968; 1 child, Miguel. BFA, NYU, 1969; MA, San Francisco State U., 1970; MD, SUNY, Stony Brook, 1976. Diplomate Am. Bd. Internal Medicine, Am. Bd. Pulmonary Diseases. Resident Lincoln Hosp., Bronx, N.Y., 1976-79; pulmonary fellow Kings County Hosp., Bklyn., 1979-81; attending physician Bellevue Hosp., N.Y.C., 1981-85, Kings County Hosp., Bklyn., 1981—; pvt. practice Bklyn., 1985—. Office: 227 Smith St Brooklyn NY 11231

ALPER, RICHARD HENRY, pharmacology educator; b. Suffern, N.Y., Sept. 27, 1953. BS in Biology, SUNY, Stonybrook, 1975; PhD in Pharmacology, Mich. State U., 1981. Asst. prof. U. Kans., Kansas City, 1986-92, assoc. prof., 1992—. Mem. Am. Physiol. Soc., Soc. for Neurosci., Am. Soc. for Pharmacology and Exptl. Therapeutics. Office: U Kans Med Ctr 3901 Rainbow Blvd Kansas City KS 66160-7417

ALPERIN, RICHARD JUNIUS, biology educator; b. Phila., Dec. 16, 1941; s. Norman and Dorothy Edythe (Gross) A. AB, U. Pa., 1963, MS, 1965, PhD, 1969, postdoctoral, 1969-74. Registered embryologist, Utrecht, The Netherlands; diplomate scanning electron microscopy, McCrone Rsch. Inst., Chgo. From asst. prof. to prof. biology Community Coll. Phila., 1969—; cons. FDA, NASA; tech. expert ASTM, 1973-82; microbiology reviewer, W.C. Brown and Co., 1985-89; gen. biology reviewer, W.B. Saunders, 1989. Author: Studies on Hypoblast Function in Chick Blastoderm, 1969, Rimmonim Bells, 1980; mem. editorial bd. Biocompatibility of Plastics and Metals, 1973-82; editor: Submicroscopic Cytochemistry, 1974; contbr. articles to pofl. jours. Archival Trustee, Congregation Mickve Israel, Phila. 1982—. Recipient L.H. Bailey medals, Wissahickon Farm sch., 1955, Silver medal Naples Italy Acad. Sci., 1991; Medalha Pro Mundi Beneficio grantee, U. Pa. Biology Dept./Academia Brasileira de Ciencias Humans, 1975; Commonwealth Fund grantee, N.Y., 1969-74, grantee Junius, Inc., 1980—. Fellow Internat. Inst. Community Svc., Am. Soc. Zoologists, Am. Microscopical Soc.; mem. Internat. Biographical Soc. (dep. dir. gen. 1989—), AFL-CIO (pres. Local 2026 1972, chief delegate 1973—), N.Y. Acad. Scis., Pattern Recognition Soc., Pa. Geneal. Soc. Republican. Jewish. Home: 842 Lombard St Philadelphia PA 19147-1317 Office: Community Coll Phila Biology Dept 1700 Spring Garden St Philadelphia PA 19130-3936

ALPERIN, RICHARD MARTIN, clinical social worker, psychoanalyst; b. Mt. Vernon, N.Y., Oct. 16, 1946; s. Israel and Sara A.; children: Heather Nicole, Alexander Scott. BBA, Western Mich. U., 1968; MSW, Fordham U., 1974; DSW, Columbia U., 1982; postdoctoral diploma in psychotherapy and psychoanalysis, Adelphi U., 1988. Cert. social worker, N.Y.; lic. clin. social worker, N.J.; diplomate Am. Bd. Examiners in Clin. Social Work. Cons. Mt. Vernon Youth Bd., 1972-76; adj. faculty Marymount Manhattan Coll., N.Y.C., 1974-76; psychotherapist Riverdale Mental Health Clinic, N.Y.C., 1974-77; psychol. counselor, psychotherapist Ctr. Counseling and Psychol. Svcs. Ramapo (N.J.) Coll., 1976-81, adj. faculty, 1977-86, moderator evening forums, 1978, 80; counselor, psychotherapist Ctr. Counseling and Psychol. Svcs. SUNY, Purchase, 1981-82, 84-85, acting dir., 1982-84; clin. cons. Westside Ctr. for Family Svcs., N.Y.C., 1985-87; guest lectr. Cabrini Med. Ctr., 1979; pvt. practice psychotherapy and psychoanalysis Riverdale, N.Y., 1977—, Teaneck, N.J., 1980—, N.Y.C., 1984—; field instr. Sch. Social Work Columbia U., 1983-85; adj. assoc. prof. Sch. Social Svc Fordham U., 1985—; adj. asst. prof. Grad. Sch. Social Work NYU, 1989-91, mem. faculty, dean curriculum Rockland Inst. for Psychoanalysis and Psychotherapy, 1990—; mem. faculty Advanced Inst. Analytic Psychotherapy, 1992-95, Object Rel. Inst. Psychoanalysis and Psychotherapy, 1992—, Psychoanalytic Psychotherapy Study Ctr., 1994—, N.J. Inst. for Tng. in Psychoanalysis, 1994—. Co-editor: The Impact of Managed Care on the Practice of Psychotherapy: Innovation, Implementation, and Controversy, 1996; contbr. articles to profl. jours.; rsch. on psychotherapy, suicide and provision of preventative svcs. Nat. Jewish Welfare Bd. fellow Fordham U., 1972-74. Trainee NIMH Columbia U., 1978. Mem. NASW, N.Y. State Soc. Clin. Social Work (chair com. on psychoanalysis 1991-96), Adelphi Soc. Psychoanalysis and Psychotherapy, Am. Group Psychotherapy Assn., Inc., Ea. Group Psychotherapy Soc., Acad. Cert. Social Workers (cert.), Nat. Fedn. Soc. Clin. Social Work, Nat. Membership Com. Psychoanalysis Clin. Social Work (chair N.Y.-N.J. area 1992-94, treas. 1991-93), Alliance for Universal Access to Psychotherapy (founder, membership chair, mem. steering com. 1994-96), Nat. Study Group on Social Work and Psychoanalysis. Office: 121 Cedar Ln Teaneck NJ 07666-4457

ALPERN, JEFFREY B., cardiothoracic surgeon, heart transplant surgeon; b. Long Beach L.I., N.Y., Aug. 24, 1952; s. William and Grace A.; m. Randi Alpern, Mar. 1, 1986; 1 child, Madison. BS, Pa. State U., 1974; DO, Tex. Coll. Osteo. Medicine, 1979. Cert. Am. Osteo. Bd. Surgery. Cardiothoracic surgeon, pvt. practice Bethehem, Pa., 1984—; dir. cardiopulmonary transplantation Temple U. Hosp., Phila., 1986-92; cardiac transplant surgeon St. Christopher Hosp. for Children, Phila., 1988—; dir. cardiopulmonary transplantation Hahnemann U. Hosp., Phila., 1992-94; cardiac surgeon Phila. Coll. Osteo. Medicine (surg. quality assessment com.), 19868-95, rep. United Network of Organ Sharing, Phila., 1992-94; mem. cardiovasc. disease com. Pa. Osteo. Med. Assn., 1993-94. Contbr. articles to profl. jours.; prin. investigator Novacor artificial heart, 1992-94; critical care com. Tex. Heart Jour., 1986-94. Named Outstanding Alumnus Phila. Coll. Osteo. Medicine, 1986-95. Fellow Coll. of Physicians of Phila., Internat. Soc. Surgeons; mem. Internat. Soc. Heart and Lung Transplantation, Internat. Soc. Artificial Organs, Am. Soc. Artificial Organs, Soc. Critical Care Medicine, Assn. Acad. Surgery.

ALPERS, DAVID HERSHEL, physician, educator; b. Phila., May 9, 1935; s. Bernard Jacob and Lillian (Sher) A.; m. Melanie Goldman, Aug. 12, 1977; children: Ann, Ruth, Barbara. BA, Harvard U., 1956, MD, 1960. Intern Mass. Gen. Hosp., Boston, 1960-61, resident in internal medicine, 1961-62; instr. medicine Harvard U., 1965-67, assoc. in medicine, 1967-68, asst. prof., 1968-69; asst. prof. medicine Washington U., St. Louis, 1969-72, assoc. prof., 1972-73, prof., 1973—, dir. gastrointestinal divsn., 1969—. Author: (with others) Manual of Nutritional Therapeutics, 3rd edit., 1995; assoc. editor: Textbook of Gastroenterology, 2nd edit., 1995, Physiology of the Gastrointestinal Tract, 3rd edit., 1994; assoc. editor Jour. Clin. Investigation, 1977-82; editor Am. Jour. Physiology, Gastrointestinal and Liver Physiology, 1991—; contbr. articles and revs. to profl. jours., chpts. to books. With USPHS, 1962-64. Mem. Am. Soc. Clin. Investigation, Assn. Am. Physicians, Am. Gastroent. Assn. (pres. 1990-91), Am. Soc. Cell Biology, Am. Soc. Biol. Chemists, Am. Fedn. Clin. Rsch., Am. Soc. Clin. Nutrition. Office: Washington U Med Sch Dept Internal Medicine PO Box 8124 Saint Louis MO 63156-8124

ALPERT, HERMAN SAUL, psychiatrist; b. Potsdam, N.Y., Jan. 17, 1913; s. Israel Noah and Sarah (Lehrman) A.; m. Eileen Rita Picker, Mar. 31, 1946 (dec. 1970); children: Cheryl Lynne Alpert Sofer, Jeffery Neal; m. Harriet Menkes, Nov. 7, 1971; stepchildren: Margery Paula Karp, Peter Alan Lesnik. AB, U. Rochester, 1934; MD, Eclectic Med. Coll., Cin., 1938. Diplomate Am. bd. Psychiatry and Neurology. Intern Rockaway Beach (N.Y.) Hosp., 1938-39; resident in psychiatry Letchworth Village, N.Y. State Dept. Mental Hygiene, Thiels, 1939-42; supervising psychiatrist Marcy (N.Y.) State Hosp., 1946-47; sr. asst. psychiatrist out-patient dept. Mt. Sinai Hosp., N.Y.C., 1947-56; pvt. practice psychoanalysis, 1948-53; with N.Y. Psychoanalytic Inst., 1948-53; sr. clin. asst. psychiatrist group psychotherapy div. Mt. Sinai Hosp., N.Y.C., 1956-62, asst. attending then assoc. attending psychiatrist, 1962-84, attending psychiatrist group psychotherapy div., 1984—, supr. psychiat. residents group psychotherapy div., 1962—; pvt. practice N.Y.C., 1947—; Presenter, panelist at profl. confs.; interviewee local radio and TV programs. Contbr. articles to profl. publs. Violinist Mt. Sinai Symphony Orch., co-chair exec. com., 1969-88. Maj. U.S. Army, 1942-46, ETO. Fellow AMA (life), Am. Psychiat. Assn. (life), Am. Assn. Mental Deficiency (life), Am. Group Psychotherapy Assn., N.Y. Acad. Medicine, Am. Soc. Psychoanalytic Physicians, AAAS; mem. N.Y. Soc. Clin. Psychiatry, Pan-Am. Med. Assn., brit. Assn. Social Psychiatry, Phobia Soc. Am., N.Y. State Hosps. Med. Alumni Assn., Associated Alumni Mt. Sinai Med. Ctr., Ea. Group Psychotherapy Assn. (charter). Office: 133 E 73rd St # 2 New York NY 10021-3556

ALPERT, JOEL JACOBS, medical educator, pediatrician; b. New Haven, May 9, 1930; s. Herman Harold and Alice (Jacobs) A.; m. Barbara Ellen Wasserstrom, July 13, 1957; children: Norman, Mark, Deborah. AB, Yale U., 1952; MD, Harvard U., 1956. Diplomate Am. Bd. Pediatrics. Intern in medicine Children's Hosp. Med. Ctr., Boston, 1956-57, jr. asst. resident in medicine, 1957-58, chief resident for ambulatory svcs., fellow in medicine, 1961-62, from asst. to sr. assoc., 1962-72; exch. registrar St. Mary's Hosp. Med. Sch., London, 1958-59; from instr. to assoc. prof. Med. Sch., Harvard U., Boston, 1962-72, lectr., 1972; pediatrician in chief Boston City Hosp., 1972-92; prof. pediatrics and pub. health Boston (Mass.) U. Sch. Medicine, 1972—, chmn. dept. pediatrics, 1972-93, also prof. sociomed. scis. and pub. health law, 1980—; Dozer vis. prof. Ben. Gurion Sch. Medicine, Beersheva, Israel, 1979; Raine Found. vis. prof. U. Western Australia, Perth, 1983; James and Jean Davis Prestige visitor U. Otago, Dunedin, New Zealand, 1995; cons. USPHS, 1972—, Children's Hosp., Boston, 1972—; spl. cons. pres. N.Y.C. Health and Hosps. Corp., 1989; vis. prof. pediatrics Columbia Coll. Phys. and Surg., NYU Sch. Medicine; mem. med. adv. com. N.Y.C. Health and Hosps. Corp., 1989—. Author books, including: The Education of Physicians For Primary Care, 1974; also numerous papers. Mem. Town Meeting, Winchester, Mass., 1970-72; mem. exec. com. Mass. Com. for Children and Youth, Boston, 1975-82; chmn. adv. com. Mass. Poison Info. System, Boston, 1980-92; bd. dirs. Med. Found., Boston, 1992—. Capt. U.S. Army, 1959-61. Recipient numerous fed., non-fed. grants, 1965—, Lifetime Achievement award Mass. Poison Info. System, 1992; spl. fellow Nat. Ctr. Health Svcs. Rsch., London, 1971. Fellow Am. Acad. Pediatrics (Job Lewis Smith award 1992); mem. Inst. Medicine of NAS (mem. governing coun. 1993-95, mem. bd. families and children 1993-95, mem. task force on future of primary care 1994-96), Am. Pediatric Soc., Soc. Pediatric Rsch., Ambulatory Pediatric Assn. (pres. 1969, George Armstrong medal 1989, hon. mention for pub. health svc. Primary Care Achievement for Edn. award 1995), Mass. Assn. Pediat. Dept. Chmn. (chmn. 1976-78, 81-93), Yale Club, Harvard Club, Aescalapian Club, Lancet Club, St. Botolph Club, Alpha Omega Alpha. Jewish. Home: 224B Allandale Rd Chestnut Hill MA 02167-3200 Office: Boston U Sch of Medicine 818 Harrison Ave Boston MA 02118-2307

ALPERT, JOSEPH STEPHEN, physician, educator; b. New Haven, Feb. 1, 1942; s. Zelly Charles and Beatrice Ann (Kopsofsky) A.; m. Helle Mathiasen, Aug. 6, 1965; children: Eva Elisabeth, Niels David. BA magna cum laude, Yale U., 1963; MD cum laude, Harvard U., 1969. Diplomate: Am. Bd. Internal Medicine (cardiovascular disease). Successively intern, resident in internal medicine, fellow in cardiovascular disease Peter Bent Brigham Hosp.-Harvard U. Med. Sch., Boston, 1969-74; dir. Samuel A. Levine cardiac unit, asst. prof. medicine Peter Bent Brigham Hosp.-Harvard U. Med. Sch., 1976-78; prof., dir. div. cardiovascular medicine U. Mass. Med. Sch., Worcester, 1978-92, vice chm. Dept. Medicine, 1990—, Edward Budnitz prof. of cardiovascular medicine, 1988-92; Robert W. and Irene P. Flinn prof., chmn. dept. medicine U. Ariz., 1992—; cons. W. Roxbury VA Hosp., Boston, VA Med. Ctr., Tucson; sec., treas. med. staff U. Mass. Med. Ctr., 1979-81, pres. med. staff, 1981-82. Author: The Heart Attack Handbook, 1978, 2d edit., 1985, 3d edit., 1993, Cardiovascular Physiophathology, 1984; co-author: Manual of Coronary Care, 1977, 80, 84, 87, 93, Manual of Cardiovascular Diagnosis and Therapy, 1980, 84, 88, 96, Valvular Heart Disease, 1981, 87, Intensive Care Medicine, 1985, 2d edit., 1991, The Clinician's Companion, 1986, Modern Coronary Care, 1990, 2d edit., 1996, Diagnostic Atlas of the Heart, 1994, Cardiology for the Primary Care Physician, 1996; assoc. editor: Jour. History of Medicine and Allied Scis., 1977-80; editl. cons. Little, Brown & Co., Appleton-Century Crofts; mem. editl. bd. Am. Jour. Cardiology, 1985—, Archives Internal Medicine, 1987—, Heart and Lung, 1987-90, Cardiology, 1985—, assoc. editor, 1987—, editor-in-chief, 1991—; mem. editl. bd. Geriatric Cardiovascular Medicine, 1988-89, Am. Jour. Noninvasive Cardiology, 1987-95, Am. Heart Jour., 1992—, Internat. Jour. Cardiology, 1992—, European Heart Jour., 1995—; contbr. numerous articles to med. jours. Served to lt. comdr. USNR, 1974-76. Decorated Commendation medal, 1976; recipient Gold medal U. Copenhagen, 1968, Edward Rhodes Stitt award San Diego Naval Hosp., 1976, George W. Thorn award Peter Bent Bingham Hosp., 1977, Outstanding Tchr. award U. Mass. Med. Sch., 1981, 86, 87, 90, U. Ariz. Cardiology, 1995; Fulbright scholar Copenhagen, 1963-64; USPHS-Mass. Heart Assn. fellow, 1971-72; NIH spl. rsch. fellow, 1972-73. Fellow ACP, Am. Coll. Cardiology (jour. editl. bd. mem. 1983-86, chmn. tng. dirs. com. 1991—, bd. trustees 1996-2001), Am. Coll. Chest Physicians (gov. for Mass. 1983-85); mem. AAAS, Am. Heart Assn. (fellow coun. clin. cardiology, vice chmn. 1991-92, chmn. 1993-95, exec. com. 1986—), Am. Assn. History of Medicine, Am. Fedn. Clin. Rsch., Assn. Univ. Cardiologists, New Eng. Cardiovascular Club, Assn. Profs. of Medicine, Danish Cardiology Assn. (hon.), Argentine Heart Assn. (fgn. corr.), Aesculapian Club, Phi Beta Kappa, Sigma Xi, Alpha Omega Alpha. Office: 1501 N Campbell Ave Tucson AZ 85724-0001

ALPERT, LOUISE ANNETTE, cardiologist, internist; b. Chgo.; married Aug. 1977; 1 child. BA, U. Kans., 1970; MA, U. Chgo., 1974; MD, Ind. U., Indpls., 1983. Resident in internal medicine Ind. U.-Purdue U., Indpls., 1986-89; fellow in cardiology U. Chgo., 1989; pvt. practice Internal Medicine Assocs., Bloomington, Ind., 1989—. Office: Internal Medicine Assocs 719 S Rogers Bloomington IN 47403-2335

ALPERT, MARTIN JEFFREY, chiropractor; b. N.Y.C., Apr. 21, 1951; s. Sheldon Lee and Beatrice (Ostrager) A.; m. Elyse Shelly Sherman, Dec. 26, 1976; children: Chad, Mitchell. BA, Syracuse U., 1972; D Chiropractic, N.Y. Chiropractic Coll., 1976; MS, U. Bridgeport, 1979. Pvt. practice, Yonkers, N.Y., 1977-84, Hollywood, Fla., 1985, Coconut Creek, Fla., 1987-92, Miami, Fla., 1992-95, Ft. Lauderdale, Fla., 1985—, Orlando, Fla., 1994—. Maj. USAR, 1970-96. Mem. Am. Chiropractic Assn., Internat. Chiropractors Assn., Am. Acad. Pain Mgmt. (diplomate), Am. Coll. Sports Medicine, Fla. Chiropractic Assn., N.Y. Acad. Scis. Democrat. Home: 11095 NW 14th St Coral Springs FL 33071 Office: 3d Ave Chiropractic Ctr Inc 300 W Sunrise Blvd Ste 7 Fort Lauderdale FL 33311

ALPERT, SEYMOUR, anesthesiologist, educator; b. N.Y.C., Apr. 20, 1918; s. Louis and Ida (Freedman) A.; m. Cecile Bernadine Cohen, Sept. 7, 1941. AB, Columbia U., 1939; MD, SUNY Health Scis. Ctr., Bklyn., 1943; LLD (hon.), George Washington U., 1984. Diplomate Am. Bd. Anesthesiology. Intern Beth Israel Hosp., N.Y.C., 1943-44; resident in anesthesiology Gallinger Mcpl. Hosp., Washington, 1946-47; mem. faculty dept. anesthesiology George Washington U. Sch. Medicine and Hosp., Washington, 1948—, prof., 1961-83, prof. emeritus, 1983—; v.p. for devel. George Washington U., 1969-83, v.p. emeritus for devel., 1988—; cons. in anesthesiology Walter Reed Army Hosp., Washington, 1948-83, VA Hosp., Washington, 1948-70, D.C. Gen. Hosp., 1948-69, Mead Dental Hosp., 1949-69; dir. Jefferson Fed. Savs. and Loan Assn., 1979-82; adv. bd. Washington Fed. Savs. & Loan, 1982-89. Contbr. articles to med. jours. Bd. govs. Hebrew U., Jerusalem, 1968—; bd. govs. State of Israel Bonds, 1964—, nat. chmn. med. div., 1969-86; bd. dirs. Israel Investors Corp., 1965-82, exec. com., 1974-82; bd. dirs. Am. Friends of Hebrew U., 1966—, chmn. med. div., 1969-86, v.p., 1969-90, hon. v.p. 1990—; bd. dirs. Council Jewish Fedn. and Welfare Funds, 1966-73; examining physician Met. Police Boys Clubs, 1952-76; pres. United Jewish Appeal, 1966-67, exec. com., 1955—; bd. dirs. United Givers Fund, 1972-74; exec. com. Jewish Community Council, 1958-75; bd. mgrs. Adas Israel Congregation, 1963—; bd. dirs. Kaufmann Camp for Boys and Girls, 1964-78; bd. dirs. Jewish Community Found., 1966—, v.p., 1968-69; vice chmn. United Jewish Endowment Fund, 1984-86, pres. 1986-88. Served to capt. AUS, 1944-46. Recipient Man of Yr. award State of Israel Bonds, 1964; Freedom award, 1970; Disting. Svc. award Phi Delta Epsilon, 1971, 73; Torch of Learning award Am. Friends of Hebrew U., 1975; Med. award United Jewish Appeal, 1980; Achievement award Profl. Fraternity Assn., 1995. Fellow Am. Coll. Anesthesiology; mem. Am. Soc. Anesthesiologists (dir. 1963-66, trustee Wood Library Mus. Anesthesiology 1968-74, v.p. 1970-74), Md.-D.C. Soc. Anesthesiologists (pres. 1968-69), AMA, Med. Soc. D.C. (mem. numerous coms.), Jacobi Med. Soc., Pan Am. Med. Soc. (pres. 1967), Assn. Am. Med. Colls. (co-dir. nat. med. library study 1965-66), Assn. Univ. Anesthetists, Phi Delta Epsilon (nat. pres. 1961-62, exec. com. 1961—, exec. sec. 1963-72, v.p. bd. trustees 1972-73, pres. bd. trustees 1973-74), Cosmos Club (Washington), Woodmont Country Club (Rockville, Md.). Home: 2660 S Ocean Blvd Apt 502N Palm Beach FL 33480-5424 also: 2801 New Mexico Ave NW Apt 905 Washington DC 20007-3910

ALPHER, VICTOR SETH, clinical psychologist, consultant; b. Washington, Oct. 20, 1954; s. Ralph Asher and Louise Ellen (Simons) A. BA, U. Pa., 1976; PhD, Vanderbilt U., 1985. Lic. psychologist, Tex., Tenn.; diplomate in clin. psychology Am. Bd. Profl. Psychology. Grad. fellow Vanderbilt U., Nashville, 1981-85; asst. prof. U. Tex. Health Sci. Ctr., Houston, 1986-88, clin. asst. prof., 1989—; cons. Rsch. Inst. on Addictions, Buffalo, 1990—, Meml. Geriatric Evaluation and Resource Ctr., Houston, 1991—; bd. cons. Fla. Inst. Psychology, 1994—. Cons. reviewer Jour. Cons. and Clin. Psychology, 1995—; contbr. articles to profl. jours., including Jour. Cons. and Clin. Psychology, Jour. Personality Assessment, Jour. Psychopathology and Behavioral Assessment, Psychotherapy, and Jour. Applied Physiology. Fellow Acad. Clin. Psychology; mem. APA, Soc. Psychotherapy Rsch., Soc. Personality Assessment, Sigma Xi. Office: Weslayan Sta PO Box 270263 Houston TX 77277-0263

ALPHIN, REEVIS STANCIL, retired pharmacologist, consultant; b. Mt. Olive, N.C., Apr. 21, 1929; s. Fred and Clara (Dail) A.; m. Barbara Gilliam, Sept. 4, 1955; children: Robert S., Carla Gilliam. BA, U. N.C., 1951; MA, Duke U., 1956; PhD, Med. Coll. Va., Richmond, 1966. Pharmacologist Eli Lilly & Co., Indpls., 1956-60; group leader dept. pharmacology A. H. Robins & Co., Richmond, Va., 1960-66, head dept., 1966-72, assoc. dir. pharmacology, 1972-90, project mgr., 1986-90, ret.; cons. in field. Contbr. over 80 articles to profl. jours. Capt. USAF, 1951-53. Mem. Am. Physiology Soc., Am. Pharmacology Soc. Home and Office: 8525 Gilliam Rd Sanford NC 27330-9333

ALPREN, THOMAS V. P., ophthalmologist; b. East Orange, N.J., July 12, 1945; children: Jacob, Daniel, Emily. BA, Amherst Coll., 1967; MD, Tufts U., 1971. Diplomate Am. Bd. Ophthalmologist. Resident in ophthalmology Med. Coll. Wis., Milw., 1974-77, fellow in corneal disease, 1977-78; pvt. practice Milw., 1978—. Sr. asst. surgeon USPHS, 1972-74. Mem. Am. Acad. Ophthalmology, Am. Soc. Refractive Keratoplasty, Milw. Ophthal. Soc. Home: 3527 N Shepard Ave Shorewood WI 53211 Office: Ophthalmology Assocs SC 2500 W Layton Ave Milwaukee WI 53221

AL SAADI, ABDUL AMIR, clinical geneticist; b. Baquba, Iraq, Oct. 20, 1935; came to U.S., 1957; s. Majid Salih Al Saadi and Zahra (Jawad) Jabor; m. Karen Svendsen, Nov. 20, 1961 (div. Oct. 1986); children: Neda Marie, Yasmin Suzanne, Sami Amir, Laith Erik; mem. Cassandra Z. Eastman, Oct. 6, 1987. BA, U. Kans., 1958, MA, 1959; PhD, U. Mich., 1963. Diplomate Am. Bd. Med. Genetics. Rsch. assoc. Sch. Medicine U. Mich., Ann Arbor, 1963-66, assoc. prof., 1966-70; chief of genetics William Beaumont Hosp., Royal Oak, Mich., 1970—; dir. Sch. Histotech. William Beaumont Hosp., Royal Oak, 1976-89; clin. asst. prof. Sch. Medicine Wayne State U., Detroit, 1975—; clin. assoc. prof. health allied sci. Oakland U., Rochester, Mich., 1976—; clin. asst. prof. pediatrics Med. Coll. Ohio, Toledo, 1991—; mem. genetic disease adv. com. State of Mich., 1979—. Contbr. over 75 articles to profl. jours. Grantee Am. Cancer Soc., NIH. Fellow Am. Coll. Med. Genetics (founding mem.). Office: William Beaumont Hosp 3601 W 13 Mile Rd Royal Oak MI 48073-6712

AL-SAWWAF, MONQIDH MOHAMMED, surgeon; b. Baghdad, Iraq, 1950; s. Mohammed Mahmmod and Noria (Najmaldeen) Al-S. Student, Pahlavi U. Coll. of Medicine, Shiraz, Iran, 1967-70, MD, 1976. Diplomate Am. Bd. Surgery, Am. Bd. Surg. Critical Care. Resident Harlem Hosp., N.Y.C., 1976-81, fellow, 1981-83, asst. attending physician, 1983-86, assoc. attending physician, 1986-88, attending physician, 1988—, co-chief surgury ICU, 1987-89, chief surgery ICU, 1989—; instr. surgery Columbia U., N.Y.C., 1983—, asst. clin. prof., 1989—; researcher in clin. critical care Harlem Hosp., N.Y.C., Columbia U., N.Y.C., 1983—; lectr. in critical care. Contbr. articles to profl. jours. V.p. United Drs. Assn., 1990—. Mem. Am. Soc. Gastrointestinal Endoscopy, Internat. Coll. Surgeons, Soc. Critical Care Medicine. Office: Harlem Hosp Dept Surgery 506 Lenox Ave New York NY 10037

ALSBJOERN, BJARNE FINN, surgeon; b. Copenhagen, July 31, 1953. MD, U. Copenhagen, 1981, DMSc, 1991; specialist in plastic surgery and burns, 1993. Resident U. Copenhagen Hosps., 1981-94; chief surgeon burn unit U. Copenhagen-Huidovre Hosp., 1994—. Capt. Danish Mil., 1993. Office: Huidovre Hosp, Burn Unit, 2650 Copenhagen Denmark

ALSEVER, ROBERT NICHOLS, health facility administrator; b. Montclair, N.J., July 15, 1942; s. John Bellow and Janet Nichols (Gilbert) A.; m. Judith Rae Whitman, Apr. 29, 1944; children: Kristin, Jennifer. AB, U. Ariz., 1964; MD, U. Colo., 1969. Diplomate Am. Bd. Internal Medicine. Intern U. Calif., Irvine, 1969-70; resident U. Colo., Denver, 1970-72, fellow in endocrinology, 1972-74; pvt. practice So. Colo. Clinic, Pueblo, 1974-92; v.p. quality mgmt. Sisters of Charity Healthcare Sys., Cin., 1992—; med. dir. So. Colo. Health Plan, Puebo, 1989-90, St. Mary Corwin Regional Med. Ctr., Pubelo, 1990-92, trustee, 1989-90; med. adv. physician's coun. TDS Healthcare Corp., Atlanta, 1990-94; clin. prof. medicine U. Colo. Health Sci. Ctr., Denver, 1991—. Author: Handbook of Endocrine Tests in Adults, 1975, 2d edit. 78, Gynecologic Endocrinology, 1980, 2d edit., 1986; contbr. articles to profl. jours. Chairperosn Pueblo County Diabetes Task Force, 1983-85; elder 1st Presbyn. Ch., Pueblo, 1985-86, youth group educator, 1988—. Recipient Recognition award Colo. Diabetes Inst., 1990, Outstanding Speaker award Med. Info. Sys. Physicians, 1994, 95. Fellow ACP, Am. Coll. Clin. Endocrinology; mem. Am. Coll. Physician Execs., Am. Diabetes Assn., Colo. Soc. Endocrinology and Metabalism (v.p. 1981—), Eondocrine Soc. Home: 153 W Mangrum Ct Pueblo West CO 81007 Office: Sisters of Charity Healthcare Sys Inc 4815 List Dr Ste 111 Colorado Springs CO 80919

ALSIP, ANDEE, clinical neuroscience nurse; b. San Bernardino, Calif., Nov. 30, 1946; s. Edward and Lola Peggy (Hlavaty) A. AS, San Bernardino Valley Coll., 1980; BS in Nursing, Pacific Union Coll., 1986; MSN, Calif. State U., Dominguez Hills, 1991. Cert. neurosci. RN; cert. case mgr. Clin. nurse specialist in neurosci. Loma Linda (Calif.) U. Med. Ctr., 1991—, critical care educator, 1984-91, attending nurse, movement disorder team, Parkinson's surgery; part-time faculty U. Phoenix, 1993—; vol. asst. clin. prof. med.-surg. nursing Loma Linda U., 1994—; vol. assoc. prof. critical care nursing Calif. State U., Long Beach, 1993—. Contbr. articles to profl. jours. Mem. Am. Assn. Neurosci. Nurses, World Fedn. Neurosci. Nurses, Am. Assn. Critical Care Nurses, Sigma Theta Tau Internat. Home: 3777 N Arrowhead Ave San Bernardino CA 92405-2244 Office: LLUMC Dept Case Mgmt Rm 113 11234 Anderson St Loma Linda CA 92354

ALSON, ELI, psychologist; b. N.Y.C., Aug. 1, 1929; s. David and Katie (Beller) A.; m. Annette Shiffman, Oct. 28, 1956; children: Beth Fay, Amy Ruth. BA, Bklyn. Coll., 1952; PhD, U. Buffalo, 1959. Lic. psychologist, N.J.; cert. in biofeedback. Rsch. psychologist VA Med. Ctr., Lyons, N.J.,

1959-69, clin. psychologist, 1969-75, dir. psychology tng., 1975-84; dir. Biofeedback Clinic of Bernardsville (N.J.), 1980-87, Behavioral Medicine Clinic of VA Med. Ctr., Lyons, 1982-86; med. advisor Office of Hearings & Appeals, Social Security Adminstrn., Newark, 1986—; dir. Stress & Pain Mgmt. Ctr., St. Clares Riverside Med. Ctr., Boonton, N.J., 1987-91; cons. in behavioral medicine Life Performance Ctr., Denville, N.J., 1991—; adj. clin. prof. psychology L.I. U., Bklyn., 1976-84; adj. field supervisory faculty Rutgers U., Piscataway, N.J., 1976-84. Mem. profl. adv. com. Gov.'s Commn. for Study of Post-Traumatic Stress Disorders, 1990-91. Mem. Am. Psychol. Assn., N.J. Psychol. Assn., Biofeedback Soc. N.J. (pres. 1980, 91), Assn. for Applied Psychophysiology and Biofeedback (ethics com.). Home: 25 Kitchell Rd Denville NJ 07834-1321 Office: Life Performance Ctr 16 Pocono Rd # 302 Denville NJ 07834

ALSTER, MELISSA BETH, medical/surgical and oncological nurse; b. N.J., Apr. 4, 1966; d. Stanley Jay and Ann Lynn (Sutton) A. BSN, Towson State U., 1988. Cert. oncology nurse. Staff nurse Candler Gen. Hosp., Savannah, Ga., Humana Med. City of Dallas, Shady Grove Adventist Hosp., Rockville, Md.; sr. staff nurse Assocs. in Oncology and Hematology, Rockville. Mem. Oncology Nurses Soc., Rhone Poulenc-Rorer Taxotere Regional Nurse Spkrs. Bur., Sigma Theta Tau. Home: 307 Woodland Rd Gaithersburg MD 20877

ALTAY, GULTEKIN, physician, educator; b. Antalya, Turkey, Apr. 7, 1935; s. Omer and Gulsum (Ulus) A.; m. Cigdem Olcay, June 24, 1961; chidlren: Defne, Lale. MD, A.U. Med. Sch., Ankara, Turkey, 1960, specialist infectious disease, 1963. Resident Ankara Med. Sch., Turkey, 1960-63; MD Military Hosp., Enzurum, Turkey, 1963-65; fellow St. Louis U. Sch. Medicine, 1966-69; assoc. prof. Ankara Med. Sch., 1970-75, 76-80, prof., 1981—; rsch. fellow Ga. Med. Sch., 1975-76, assoc. prof., 1980-81. Lt. Marasal Cakmak Hosp., 1963-65. Mem. Turkish Microbiology Soc., Ankara Microbiology Soc. Home: Ceyhan Sok 25, 6530 Beysukent Ankara Turkey Office: Ibni Sina Hosp, Ankara Turkey

ALTCHEK, EDWARD M., neurosurgeon, educator; b. N.Y.C., Mar. 9, 1931; s. Isaac David and Fanny (Horowitz) A.; m. Florence Zeleznik, 1960 (div. 1968); children: Leslie Rachel, Glenn David, Michael Geoffrey; m. Roberta Louise Walsh, June 7, 1968; 1 child, Alexandra. BA in Psychology, NYU, 1951; BS in Biomed. Engring., N.Y. Inst. Tech., 1984; MD, Chgo. Med. Sch., 1955. Diplomate Am. Bd. Neurologic Soc. Intern L.I. Jewish Hosp., New Hyde Park, N.Y., 1955-56; resident neurosurgery Montefiore & Bronx Mcpl. Hosps., 1956-61; neurologic surgeon pvt. practice N.Y.C., L.I., 1961-76; prof. neuroanatomy St. George's Coll. of Medicine, Grenada, W.I., 1979-80; prof. engring. technology N.Y. Inst. Technology, Old Westbury, N.Y., 1984-91; asst. dir. rsch. inst. N.Y. Chiropractic Coll., Old Brookville, N.Y., 1987-90; assoc. prof. Touro Coll., Dix Hills, N.Y., 1992—. Patentee in field; contbr. articles to profl. jours. Mem. Soc. Automotive Engrs., Am. Assn. Med. Instrumentation. Republican. Jewish. Home: 181 Woodhull Ave Riverhead NY 11901-3513 Office: Touro Coll 135 Carman Rd Dix Hills NY 11746-5652

ALTCHULER, STEVEN IRA, psychiatry consultant, researcher; b. N.Y.C., Aug. 1, 1951; s. Murray and Lyn A. Altchuler; m. Debra A. Radack, Mar. 20, 1982; children: Joshua, Amy. BS, MIT, 1973, PhD, 1979; MD, Baylor Coll. Medicine, 1986. Nutritional physiologist NASA Johnson Space Ctr., Houston, 1978-82; cons. Tech., Inc., Houston, 1982-86; psychiatry cons. Mayo Clinic, Rochester, Minn., 1986—; med. dir. Mayo Psychiatry & Psychology Treatment Ctr., Rochester, 1993—; com. mem. Minn. Dept. Human Svcs., St. Paul, 1989-93; bd. dirs. Psychiatrists Mutual Ins. Co. Contbr. articles to profl. jours. Bd. dirs. Clear Lake Emergency Med. Corps., Houston, 1980-82; vol. Boy Scouts Am., Rochester, 1988—, exec. bd., v.p. Gamehaven coun., 1993—, nat. coun. mem., 1995—. Rock Sleyster fellow AMA, 1985, Laughlin fellow Am. Coll. Psychiatrists, 1990. Fellow Am. Sleep Disorders Assn.; mem. Am. Coll. Psychiatrists, Am. Psychiat. Assn. (Burroughs Wellcome fellow 1988, dir. purchasing group 1991—, assembly rep. 1989-90), Minn. Psychiat. Soc. (membership chmn. 1990-95, sec.-treas. 1993-95), Zumbro Valley Med. Soc. (ethics and religion com. 1988-95, exec. bd. 1994—). Office: Mayo Clinic 200 1st St SW Rochester MN 55905-0001

ALTEKRUSE, JOAN MORRISSEY, retired preventive medicine educator; b. Cohoes, N.Y., Nov. 15, 1928; d. William T. Dee and Agnes Kay (Fitzgerald) Morrissey; m. Ernest B. Altekruse, Dec. 17, 1950; children—Philip, Clifford, Lisa, Janice, Charles, Sean, Lowell, Patrick, E. Caitlin. AB, Vassar Coll., N.Y., 1949; MD, Stanford U., Calif., 1960; MPH, Harvard U., Cambridge, 1965; DPH, U. Calif., Berkeley, 1973. Cons., program dir. Calif. State Health Dept., 1966-69; mem. faculty U. Heidelberg, Germany, 1970-72; med. dir. regional office Fla. State Health Dept., 1972-75; prof., dir. health adminstrn. Sch. Pub. Health, U. S.C., Columbia, 1975-77; prof. preventive medicine Univ. S.C. Sch. of Medicine, Columbia, 1975-94, chmn. dept., 1979-89, disting. prof. emerita, 1994—; fellow, assoc. dir. Irish Peace Inst., U. LImerick, Ireland, 1990—; vis. scholar Ctr. for Rsch. in Disease Prevention, Stanford U., 1992; women in medicine liaison officer Assn. Am. Med. Colls., 1980-94; editl. bd. Aspen Publs. Mem. editorial bd. Family and Community Health Jour., Jour. Community Health; editorial adv. bd. VA Practitioner. Alumni councillor Harvard Sch. Pub. Health; docent, vol. bd. mem. Hunter Mus. Am. Art, Chattanooga. Lt. USMC, 1949-51; sr. surgeon USPHS, 1960-64. Recipient Adminstrn. award Women in Higher Edn., 1989, Achievement award S.C. Commn. on Women, 1990, Ann. award, 1991; WHO travel fellow, Eng., 1974; grantee NIH, NCI, Ctr. for Disease Control, pvt. founds. Fellow Assn. Tchrs. Preventive Medicine (Spl. Recognition award 1995); mem. Am. Bd. Preventive Medicine (trustee 1984-93), Am. Bd. Med. specialities (del. 1990-93), Am. Heart Assn. (S.C. affiliate pres. 1986, agenda planning com. 1987-89, women and minorities leadership com. 1989-92, Lifetime Achievement award 1992), Nat. Bd. Med. Examiners (comprehensive test com. 1986-92), Am. Womens Med. Assn. Democrat. Catholic.

ALTEMEIER, WILLIAM ARTHUR, pediatrician, administrator; b. Detroit, Oct. 3, 1936; s. William Arthur and Edna (Wyss) A.; m. Leslye Osbourne, June 17, 1961; children: Bill, Steven, Leah. BA in Chemistry, U. Cin., 1958; MD, Vanderbilt U., 1962. Resident in pediat. Vanderbilt U., Nashville, 1962-64, assoc. to prof., 1972-91, vice chairperson pediat., 1984-90, acting chairperson, 1984, 87-88; fellow in immunology U. Fla., Jacksonville, 1964-66, asst. prof., then assoc. prof., 1969-72; rsch. assoc. Walter Reed Rsch. Inst., Washington, 1966-69; chairperson dept. pediat. U. Mo., Columbia, 1990—; mem. Physicians Bus. Group U. Mo., 1990—. Editor: Pediatric Annuals, 1994. Capt. U.S. Army, 1964-69. Mem. Kiwanis (hon.). Office: Univ Hosp N708 Columbia MO 65212

ALTEMUS, ROXANNE, nurse; b. Johnstown, Pa., Nov. 15, 1959; d. Edward Valentine and Rose Marie (Lear) Bonk; m. Ron Lee Altemus, June 20, 1981; 1 child, Jennifer Rose. AD, Mt. Aloysius Coll., Cresson, Pa., 1991. Nurse Meml. Hosp., Johnstown, 1992—. Roman Catholic. Home: 130 Bayush St Johnstown PA 15902

ALTER, JOHN, otolaryngologist, facial cosmetic surgeon, educator; b. Hoffgastein, Austria, Feb. 6, 1946; came to U.S., 1948; s. Irving Israel and Clara Klara (Scotchinsky) A.; m. Denise Mary Webber, Apr. 17, 1982; children: Andrea Leah, Geoffrey Ian, Carolyn Clare, Leslie Nicole. BS, Wayne State U., 1967; DO, Des Moines Coll. Osteo. Medicine and Surgery, 1971. Diplomate Am. Bd. Otolaryngology, Am. Bd. Osteo. Otolaryngology & Facial Cosmetic Surgery. Intern, Botsford Hosp., Farmington, Mich., 1971-72; resident in surgery Providence Hosp., Southfield, Mich., 1972-73; resident in otolaryngology, facial cosmetic surgery Wayne State U., Detroit, 1973-76; practice medicine specializing in otolaryngology and facial cosmetic surgery, Pontiac, Mich., 1976—, Henry Ford Hosp., West Bloomfield, Mich., 1981—; clin. instr. Wayne State U. Med. Ctr., also local hosps.; past chmn. dept. otolaryngology and ophthalmology Pontiac (Mich.) Gen. Hosp., Huron Valley Hosp., Milford, St. Joseph Mercy Hosp. Mem. Simon Weisenthal Found., Zionist Orgn. Am., Sierra Club (West Bloomfield, Mich.). Fellow Am. Acad. Otolaryngology, Am. Facial Plastic and Reconstructive Soc., Osteo. Coll. Ophthalmology and Otohinolaryngology, Am. Acad. Cosmetic Surgery; mem. Am. Osteo. Assn., Oakland County Osteo. Assn., Mich. Osteo. Assn. Physicians and Surgeons, Mich. Otolaryn. Jewish. Office: 7001 Orchard Lake Rd Ste 230 West Bloomfield MI 48322-3604 also: 4000 Highland Rd Ste 100 Waterford MI 48328-2163

ALTER, MILTON, neurologist, educator; b. Buffalo, Nov. 11, 1929; s. Samuel and Rose (Schaffer) A.; m. Reina Rolnick, Aug. 31, 1952; children: David S., Daniel M., Michael A., Naomi T., Joel A. BA, U. Buffalo, 1951, MD, 1955; PhD, U. Minn., 1966. Diplomate Am. Bd. Psychiatry and Neurology. Intern U. Minn., Mpls., 1955-56; sr. surgeon USPHS, Bethesda, Md., 1956-62; fellow Med. Coll. S.C., Charleston, 1956-57, Dalhousie U., Halifax N.S., Can., 1957, Columbia U. Coll. Physicians and Surgeons, N.Y.C., 1957-58, Hebrew U., Jerusalem, Israel, 1960-62; mem. faculty, chief neurology svc. U. Minn., Mpls., 1962-76, Mpls. VA Hosp., 1967-76; chmn. dept. neurology Temple U., Phila., 1976-87; prof. neurology, dir. residency tng. Med. Coll. Pa., Phila., 1989-91, clin. prof. neurology, 1995; mem. sci. adv. bd. Nat. Multiple Sclerosis Soc., N.Y.C., Dystonia Med. Rsch. Found., Alzheimer Disease Assn.; peer reviewer Epidemiology and Disease Control 1 and 2, NIH, Bethesda, Md.; guest editor numerous profl. jours.; editor in chief Neuroepidemiology, 1989-96; contbr. numerous articles to med. jours., chpts. to books. Capt. USPHS; res., 1962. NIH grantee. Mem. AMA, Am. Acad. Neurology, Am. Neurol. Assn., Assn. Rsch. Nervous and Mental Diseases, Cen. Soc. Neurol. Rsch., Am. Epidemiology Soc.,World Fedn. of Neurol. Democrat. Jewish. Home: 236 Indian Creek Rd Wynnewood PA 19096-3404 Office: 2 Bala Plz IL1 Bala Cynwyd PA 19004

ALTINÖRS, NUR MEHMET, neurosurgery, educator; b. Izmir, Turkey, Jan. 5, 1950; s. Selahattin Armagan and Nimet Güzide (Ulueren) A.; m. Meltem Fatma Ogankulu, Aug. 3, 1976. MD, Med. Sch. of Ankara, 1974. Resident neurology dept. Hacettepe U., Ankara, 1974-75, resident neurosurgery, 1975-80; specialist neurosurgeon Mil. Hosp., Erzurum, Turkey, 1981-82; specialist neurosurgeon Social Security Hosp., Ankara, 1982-95, chief of the 2nd neurosurgery clinic, 1992-95; chmn. neurosurgery dept. Baskent U., Ankara, 1995—; mem. ethics com., coord. for residents of med. sch. Baskent U., 1995. Co-translator Translation of a Book from English to Turkish, 1979, Manual of Neurologic Therapeutics with Essentials of Diagnosis, 1982. Lt. Mil. 1981-82. Recipient Sports award Tarsus Am. Coll., 1968; Fulbright Partial grant Commn. for Ednl. Exch., 1966-67, 67-68. Mem. Turkish Neurosurg. Soc., European Assn. of Neurosurg. Socs., World Fedn. of Neurosurg. Socs. Home: Kizilirmak Cad 17/9, Ankara 06640, Turkey Office: Konur Sokak 31/2, Ankara 06640, Turkey

ALTMAN, ADELE ROSENHAIN, radiologist; b. Tel Aviv, Israel, June 4, 1924; came to U.S., 1933, naturalized, 1939; d. Bruno and Salla (Silberzweig) Rosenhain; m. Emmett Altman, Sept. 3, 1944; children: Brian R., Alan L., Karen D. Diplomate Am. Bd. Radiology. Intern Queens Gen. Hosp., N.Y.C., 1949-51; resident Hosp. for Joint Diseases, N.Y.C., 1951-52, Roosevelt Hosp., N.Y.C., 1955-57; clin. instr. radiology Downstate Med. Ctr., SUNY, Bklyn., 1957-61; asst. prof. radiology N.Y. Med. Coll., N.Y.C., 1961-65, assoc. prof., 1965-68; assoc. prof. radiology U. Okla. Health Sci. Ctr., Oklahoma City, 1968-78; assoc. prof. dept. radiology U. N.Mex. Sch. Medicine, Albuquerque, 1978-85. Author: Radiology of the Respiratory System: A Basic Review, 1978; contbr. articles to profl. jours. Fellow Am. Coll. Angiology, N.Y. Acad. Medicine; mem. Am. Coll. Radiologist, Am. Roentgen Ray Soc., Assn. Univ. Radiologists, Radiol. Soc. N.Am., B'nai B'rith Anti-Defamation League (bd. dirs. N.Mex. state bd.), Hadassah Club.

ALTMAN, KARL I., psychologist; b. Cleve., Nov. 22, 1942; s. Alfred A. and Etta (Fendrich) A.; m. Lois Ellen Goldstein, Aug. 22, 1965 (div. 1972) children: Ivy Shane Altman Briggs, Adam Michael; m. Sara Haavik, 1981; 1 child, Laurel Haavik. Student, John Carroll U., 1961-63; AB, Case Western Res. U., 1965; MA, N. Mex. State U., Univ. Park, 1967; PhD, U. Wis., Milw., 1971. Intern psychology Wood Vet. Hosp., Milw., 1970-71; postdoctoral fellow John F. Kennedy Inst. Johns Hopkins Hosp., Balt., 1971-72; from asst. to assoc. prof. Cmty. Health Kansas U. Child Rehab. Med. Ctr., Kansas City, Kansas, 1972-82; from adj. asst. to adj. assoc. prof. psychology U. Kansas, Lawrence, Kans., 1972-88, also courtesy assoc. prof. human devel., 1986-89; pvt. practice Lawrence, Kans., 1982—; dir. tng. Bureau Child Rsch Kansas U., Lawrence, 1982-88. Contbr. articles to profl. jours. Fellow NDEA, 1969; grantee Nat. Assn. Retarded Citizens, Kansas U. Med. Ctr., 1978, Dept. Health Edn. & Welfare, 1981; trainee NSF 1968; recipient Outstanding Achievement Psychology award Case Western Res. U., 1965. Mem. Assn. Advancement Behavior Therapy, Am. Psychol. Assn. Office: Lawrence Family Practice 500 Rockledge Rd Lawrence KS 66049

ALTMAN, KURT ISON, radiation biology educator; b. Breslau, Silesia, Germany, Oct. 13, 1919; came to U.S., 1935; s. Josef and Gretchen H. (Berju) A.; m. Babette S. Schaar, Sept. 3, 1945; children: Carl E., Theodore E., Peter. MD, U. Chgo., 1942; PhD, U. Rochester, 1963. Instr. George William Coll., Chgo., 1943-44; instr. dept. biochemistry U. Chgo., 1945-47, assoc. medicine dept. medicine, 1945-46; assoc. atomic energy project U. Rochester (N.Y.), 1947-63, assoc. dept. exptl. radiology, 1953-63, assoc. prof. dept. radiation biology, 1963—, asst. prof. dept. biochemistry, 1963-68, assoc. prof., 1968-83, prof. emeritus dept. biophysics, 1990—; isntr. physiol. chemistry U. Düsseldorf, Germany, 1973; instr. radiology Centre de l'Energie Nucléaire, Mol, Belgium, 1964-65, Forschungs Inst. Sandoz, Sandoz Pharm. Co., Vienna, 1978, Inst. for Medizin Forschungs Zentrum Jülich, 186-88, 91-94. Editor: Relative Radiation Sensitivity of Human Organ Systems, 1987, 89, 91, 94; contbr. articles to profl. jours.; assoc. editor Radiation Rsch., 1977-80. Eli Lilly fellow U. Chgo., 1939-40; grantee AEC, Dept. Energy, NIH, N.Y. State Health Dept., German Govt., 1950-75. Mem. Am. Assn. Biochemistry, Am. Soc. Radiation Rsch., N.Y. Acad. Scis. Home: 21 Waterford Cir Rochester NY 14618-5421 Office: U Rochester Dept Biophysics 601 Elmwood Ave Rochester NY 14642-0001

ALTMAN, LAWRENCE GENE, biologist; b. Flushing, N.Y., July 4, 1952; s. Mark Eugene and Roberta Mercedes (Baron) A. BA in Biology, Fordham U., 1972, MS, 1974, PhD, 1982. Mem. faculty Fordham U., N.Y.C., part-time 1979-81, Adelphi U., Garden City, N.Y., 1981-82; research biologist VA, West Haven, Conn., 1982-85; chmn. biology dept. Coll. of St. Elizabeth, Convent Station, N.J., 1985-86; asst. prof. div. sci. and math. Fordham U., N.Y.C., 1986-87; postdoctoral assoc. in pathology Yale U. Med. Sch., New Haven, 1982-85; cons. Coll. of New Rochelle, N.Y., 1980-81, Polyscis., Inc., Warrington, Pa., 1985-89, Columbia U. Coll. Physicians and Surgeons Dept. Microbiology, N.Y.C., 1986-88; curriculum cons. Sacred Heart U., Fairfield, Conn., 1990-91; part-time faculty Western Conn. State U., Danbury, 1990-91, asst. prof. biology anatomy and physiology, 1992-93, 94-95; pres. Cider Mill Pond Assn., Greenwich, Conn., 1994-96. Contbr. articles to profl. jours. Recipient Most Valuable Staff Mem. Faculty award Dowling Coll., 1975; Outstanding Performance award West Haven VA Med. Ctr., 1983; Fordham U. fellow, 1975-77. Mem. N.Y. Acad. Scis., Am. Soc. for Cell Biology, Electron Microscopy Soc. Am., AAAS, Conn. Electron Microscopy Soc., Sigma Xi. Avocations: Eagle scout; swimming; theater. Home: 304 Lansdowne Westport CT 06880-5649

ALTMAN, LAWRENCE KIMBALL, physician, journalist; b. Quincy, Mass., June 19, 1937; s. William S. and Esther (Kimball) A. A.B. cum laude, Harvard U., 1958; M.D., Tufts U., 1962. Diplomate: Am. Vet. Epidemiology Soc. Intern Mt. Zion Hosp., San Francisco, 1962-63; USPHS epidemic intelligence service officer Centers for Disease Control, Atlanta, 1963-66; med. resident, fellow U. Wash. Hosp., Seattle, 1966-69; med. corr., columnist The Doctors World N.Y. Times, 1969—; assoc. prof. medicine NYU, 1970—; vis. physician Serafimer Hosp., Karolinska Inst., Stockholm, Sweden, 1973; vis. scientist U. Wash., 1971; Chancellor's Disting. Lecture for Pub. Understanding of Sci., U. Calif., San Francisco, 1989. Author: Science of The Times, 1981, Who Goes First? The Story of Self-Experimentation in Medicine, 1987; contbr. chpts. to books, articles to profl. jours.; Ency. Brittanica, 1979, Grolier Ency., 1972-87. Recipient Howard W. Blakeslee award Am. Heart Assn., 1982, 83, 94, Claude Bernard award Nat. Soc. Med. Rsch., 1971, 74; Walter C. Alvarez award Am. Med. Writers Assn., 1980, Vincent Downing award 1988; journalism award Am. Acad. Pediat., 1982, pub. svc. award Nat. Kidney Found., George Polk award, 1986, journalism award Coll. Am. Pathologists, 1985, Med. Media Excellence award Friends Nat. Libr. Medicine, 1993. Fellow ACP, Am. Coll. Epidemiology, N.Y. Acad. Medicine; mem. Inst. Medicine/Nat. Acad. Scis., Am. Soc. Tropical Medicine and Hygiene, Soc. for Epidemiol., Am. Bd. Med. Spltys. (pub. 1986-88), Century Club (N.Y.C.), Harvard Club (N.Y.C. and Boston). Home: 140 W End Ave New York NY 10023-6131 Office: New York Times 229 W 43rd St New York NY 10036-3913

ALTMAN, LEONARD CHARLES, physician; b. Fresno, Calif., Sept. 1, 1944; s. Martin and Ida (Sharnoff) A.; m. Gaylene M. Bouska, Dec. 26, 1970; children: Jonathan David, Matthew Charles, Katherine Ann. BA, U. Pa., 1965; MD, Harvard U., 1969. Diplomate Am. Bd. Internal Medicine, Am. Bd. Allergy and Immunology, Nat. Bd. Med. Examiners. Intern, resident U. Wash. Affiliated Hosps., Seattle, 1969-71; sr. rsch. assoc. NIDR/NIH, Bethesda, Md., 1971-74; chief med. resident Harborview Med. Ctr., Seattle, 1974-75, chief allergy divsn., 1979—; asst. prof. medicine U. Wash., Seattle, 1975-79, assoc. prof. medicine, 1979-85, clin. assoc. prof. medicine, 1985-88, clin. prof. medicine, affiliate prof. environ. health, 1988—; ptnr. N.W. Asthma and Allergy Ctr., Seattle, 1985—; reviewer Alaska Soc. Tech. Found. Editor: Clinical Allergy and Immunology, 1984, Autoimmune Diseases, 1993; mem. editl. bd. Infection and Immunity; contbr. articles to profl. jours. Lt. col. USPHS. Mem. ACP, Am. Acad. Allergy and Clin. Immunology, Am. Assn. Immunologists, Am. Fedn. for Clin. Rsch., Am. Soc. for Microbiology, Clin. Immunology Soc., Infectious Disease Soc. Am., King County Med. Soc. (environ. health com. chmn. 1987—), Western Soc. for Clin. Rsch., Wash. State Med. Assn., Wash. State Soc. of Allergy and Immunology (sci. program com. chmn., v.p., pres.), Reticuloendothelial Soc., Puget Sound Allery Soc. (pres. 1977), N.W. Allergy Forum (sci. program com. chmn.), Physicians Bur. King County (adv. com., rep. on allergy), Seattle Acad. Internal Medicine, Alpha Epsilon Delta, Alpha Omega Alpha. Office: NW Asthma & Allergy Ctr Ste 200 4540 Sand Point Way NE Seattle WA 98105

ALTMAN, RICHARD STUART, periodontist; b. Phila., Apr. 12, 1933; s. Jules and Florence A.; m. Margaret Welham; children: David, Joanne Tate. BA, Penn State U., 1954; DDS, U. Pa., 1958; MS, George Washington U., 1972; postgrad., U.S. Naval Dental Sch., 1966-67, 71-73. Dentist Marine Corps Base, Camp Pendelton, Calif., 1958-59, 3rd marine Div., Okinawa, Japan, 1959-60, U.S. Naval Acad., Annapolis, Md., 1960-62, USS Essex, Quonset Point, R.I., 1962-64, Naval Air Sta., Quonset Point, R.I., 1964-66, Naval Support Activity, Naples, Italy, 1967-70, Naval Tng. Ctr., Orlando, Fla., 1970-71, Naval Hosp., Orlando, Fla., 1973-76, 76-78; ret., 1978; pvt. practice periodontology, Orlando, Fla., 1979—; cons. VA, Orlando, 1982—; trustee, past pres. Dental Found. of Cen. Fla., 1987—; adv. com. Coll. of Dentistry, U. Fla., 1989—; adj. faculty Valencia C.C., Orlando, 1979-84, adv. com., 1987-89; asst. examiner Bd. of Dentistry, Tallahassee, 1983-84. Recipient Beautification award Orlando C. of C., 1979, Golden Brick award, 1980. Fellow Am. Coll. Dentists; mem. ADA, Dental Soc. Greater Orlando (pres. 1988-89), Ctrl. Dist. Dental Soc. (sec. 1993-94, 2nd v.p. 1994-95, 1st v.p. 1995-96, pres. elect 1996—), Fla. Dental Assn., Fla. Soc. Periodontists (pres. 1991-92), Am. Acad. Periodontology, So. Acad. Periodontology (exec. coun. 1995—), Fla. Acad. Dental Practice Adminstrn., Pa. State Alumni Assn., U. Pa. Alumni Assn., U. Fla. Alumni Assn., Ret. Officers Assn., Am. Assn. Ret. Persons, Am. Heart Assn., U.S. Naval Dental Soc., Downtown Athletic Club Orlando. Home: 1110 Rollingwood Trl Maitland FL 32751-4849 Office: Richard S Altman DDS PA 338C N Magnolia Ave Orlando FL 32801-1609

ALTOMARI, MARK G., clinical psychologist; b. Ft. Monroe, Va., July 13, 1947; s. Guido and Mary Ann Altomari; m. Susan Alice Gross, Mar. 22, 1969; children: Alicia, Devin, Paul. BA, Villanova U., 1974; MA, West Chester State U., 1978; MS, Va. Poly. Inst. and State U., 1982, PhD, 1984. Lic. psychologist. Traffic hearing examiner Bur. Traffic Safety, Commonwealth of Pa., Harrisburg, 1973-78; behavioral specialist Community Svcs. Inc., Lancaster, Pa., 1977-78; counselor New River Valley Coun. on Alcoholism, Christiansburg, Va., 1981-82; psychology technician VA Med. Ctr., Salem, Va., 1981-82; case mgr. New River Valley Alcohol Safety Action Project, Christiansburg, 1982; clin. psychologist Va. Poly. Inst., Blacksburg, 1982-83; clin. psychology supr. Fulton (Mo.) State Hosp., 1984-86; pvt. practice clin. psychologist Columbia, Mo., 1986—; cons. Disability Determinations, Jefferson City, Mo., 1986—, Archdiocese of Jefferson City, 1987—, Fulton Police Dept., 1988—, Mo. State Hwy. Patrol, 1996—; cons. cert., forensic examiner Fulton State Hosp., 1986—; dir. of counseling William Woods Coll., Fulton, 1985—. Contbr. articles to profl. jours. Coach, mgr. Columbia Soccer Club, 1985; cons. Mo. Water Patrol, 1990—; fund raiser Clearview Neighborhood Assn., Columbia, 1990; assoc. chief justice Grad. Honor Ct.; pres. Strategy and Tactics Soc., Pottstown, Pa., 1975-80; dep. Pa. Athletic Commn., 1972. Senatorial scholar Commonwealth of Pa., 1971; rsch. co-grantee Gen. Motors, 1983. Mem. APA (divsn. clin. psychology, divsn. clin. hypnosis, psychology-law soc., neuropsychology divsn., divsn. psychologists in pub. svcs., divsn. pscyhologists in ind. practice), Mo. Psychol. Assn. Office: 916 N College Ave Columbia MO 65201-4784

ALTSCHUL, LARRY M., physician; b. N.Y.C., Jan. 17, 1952; s. Kurt Stephan and Paula (Sussman) A.; m. Mercedes Alfaro, Aug. 17, 1974; children: David, Jessica, Rebecca, Kurt, Erica. BA, CUNY, 1969-73; MD, SUNY, Buffalo, 1973-77. Diplomate Am. Bd. Internal Medicine. Resident in internal medicine Nassau County Med. Ctr., East Meadow, N.Y., 1977-80, fellowship in cardiology, 1980-82; co-dir. critical care unite Brunswick Hosp., Amityville, N.Y., 1986-90; co-chmn. spl. care com. Good Samaritan Hosp., West Islip, N.Y., 1995-96; adj. clin. prof. N.Y. Coll. Osteo. Medicine, Westbury, N.Y., 1996—. Fellow Am. Coll. Cardiology, Am. Coll. Chest Physicians, Am. Coll. Angiography, Am. Soc. Nuclear Cardiology. Home: 8 Talon Way Dix Hills NY 11795

ALTSCHULER, BRUCE ROBERT, research dentist; b. Bklyn., Feb. 17, 1947; s. Frank Philip and Sarah Gertrude (Cloder) A.; m. Ruth Phyllis Gass, Oct. 27, 1974; children: Joan Ellen, Wendy Karen, Cheryl Miriam. BA, Bklyn. Coll., 1967; DDS, Temple U., 1971. Lic. dentist, Md., Pa., Conn., Maine, N.Y. Commd. capt. USAF, 1971, advanced through grades to col., 1986; project scientist dental holography Dental Scis. Br., Brooks AFB, Tex., 1971-74, chief dental consultation, 1975-76; chief dental laser holography USAF Dental Investigation Svc., Brooks AFB, Tex., 1976-80; chief dental computer/laser tech. USAF Aerospace Medicine, Brooks AFB, Tex., 1980-82; chief avionics advanced systems rsch. group Info. Processing Br., Wright-Patterson AFB, Ohio, 1982-84; dep. optical processing Systems Avionics Div., Wright-Patterson AFB, 1985; dental resident Advanced Clin. Dentistry Residence Program, Eglin AFB, Fla., 1985-86; Air Force rsch. liaison, chief laser imaging U.S. Army Inst. Dental Rsch., Ft. Meade, Md., 1986-94; chief imaging robotics lab. Walter Reed Army Inst. Rsch. Dental Rsch. Detachment, Ft. Meade, Md., 1995—; clin. asst. prof. dept. diagnosis/roentgenology U. Tex. Health Sci. Ctr., San Antonio, 1976-80, dept. dental diagnostic svc., 1980-82; mem. dental x-ray subcom. 26 Am. Nat. Standards Inst., Washington, 1980-85; reviewer NIH Computer Aided Dentistry, Washington, 1987. Editor 3-D Machine Perception; patentee in field. Bd. dirs. Am. Cancer Soc., Bexar County, Tex., 1980-82, mem. pub. edn. com., 1980-82; campaign coord. Avionics Lab. Combined Fed. Campaign, Dayton, Ohio 1984; spl. award judge Alamo Regional Sci. Fair, San Antonio, 1980-82. Mem. ADA, Internat. Assn. Dental Rsch., Soc. Photo Optical Instrumentation Engrs., Air Force Assn., Armed Forces Communications, Electronics Assn., Tex. Dental Assn., Am. Mensa. Republican. Jewish. Home: PO Box 1151 Fort George G Meade MD 20755-3151 Office: US Army Inst Dental Rsch MCMR UDR USAF Fort George G Meade MD 20755

ALTSHULER, KENNETH Z., psychiatrist; b. Paterson, N.J., Apr. 11, 1929; s. Jacob and Altie (Freedman) A.; m. Gloria Seigel, June 14, 1952 (div. 1981); children: Steven, Lori, Dara; m. Ruth Collins Sharp, Dec. 5, 1987. B.A., Cornell U., 1948; M.D., U. Buffalo, 1952; D.Sc. (hon.), Gallaudet Coll., 1972. Intern Kings County Hosp., Bklyn., 1952-53; resident N.Y. State Psychiat. Inst., N.Y.C., 1955-58; asst. in psychiatry Columbia U., 1958-59, instr., 1959-63, research assoc., 1963-67, asst. clin. prof., 1967-71, assoc. clin. prof., 1971-75, prof., 1975-77; tng. analyst Columbia U. Psychoanalytic Clinic for Tng. and Research, 1969-77; project dir. Essential Aspects of Deafness, 1972-76, Trauma and Sleep Physiology, 1975-77; Stanton Sharp prof., chmn. psychiatry U. Tex.-Southwestern Med. Sch., Dallas, 1977—; tng. analyst New Orleans Psychoanalytic Inst., 1979-86, Dallas Psychoanalytic Inst., Tex., 1986—; chief of deafness unit Rockland State Hosp., Orangeburg, N.Y., 1966-77; cons. to NIH; dir. Am. Bd. Psychiatry and Neurology, 1990—, pres., 1996; mem. Nat. Bd. Med. Examiners, 1986-89, chmn. Part II psychiatry com., 1988-89. Co-author:

Managing Sleep Complaints, 1982; co-editor: Family and Mental Health Problems in a Deaf Population, 1963, Comprehensive Mental Health Services for the Deaf, 1966, Psychiatry and the Deaf, 1968, Expanded Mental Health Care for the Deaf, 1970, Depression: Mechanisms, Diagnosis and Treatment, 1986; others.; Contbr. articles to profl. jours. Mem. governing bd. Tex. Sch. for the Deaf, 1986-90. Served with USNR, 1953-55. Recipient Wilson award in genetics and preventive medicine, 1961, Disting. Community Service award Dallas County Mental Health Assn., 1986, Prism award, 1992, Disting. Alumnus award, SUNY, Buffalo, 1993, 1st Trailblazer award named in his honor, Dallas County Mental Health and Retardation Ctr., 1996; named Outstanding Psychiatrist, Tex. Soc. Psychiat. Physicians, 1996. Fellow Am. Psychiat. Assn. (cert. of achievement bd. hosp. psychiatry, cert. of significant achievement for deafness program, N.Y. State, 1976, for Mental Health Connections program, 1995), Am. Coll. Psychiatrists, Am. Coll. Psychoanalysts; mem. AAAS, AMA, Am. Psychoanalytic Assn., Assn. for Psychoanalytic Medicine (Merit award 1965), Tex. Med. Soc., Dallas County Med. Soc., Am. Psychopathol. Assn., Assn. Dirs. Med. Student Edn. in Psychiatry (founder, v.p. 1976-77), Am. Assn. Chmn. Depts. Psychiatry (pres. 1990-91), So. Assn. Rsch. Psychiatry (pres.-elect 1992-93, pres. 1993-94).

ALTUCCI, PAOLO, internal medicine educator; b. Naples, Italy, Feb. 17, 1934; s. Carlo and Lucia (Zitelli) A.; m. Giulia Guarino, Sept. 22, 1964; children: Carlo, Lucia. MD, Naples (Italy) U., 1957, postgrad., 1960; postgrad., Turin (Italy) U., 1964. Asst. prof. Naples (Italy) U., 1959-71, assoc. prof. clin. virology, 1971-73, assoc. prof. internal medicine, 1973-80, prof. internal medicine, 1980—; cons. prof. microbiology Naples U., 1963-80, cons. prof. infectious diseases, 1966-80, cons. prof. med. clinic, 1971-80; dir. dept. internal medicine "F. Magrassi" 2nd U. Naples, 1990—. Editor: Fisiopatologia Medica, 1971, Ricordo Di F. Magrassi, 1994; mem. editl. bd. Italian Jour. Internal Medicine, 1981. Travel fellow Naples U., 1958-59. Mem. Italian Soc. Therapy (sci. directory 1983—). Home: Via Timavo 39, 80126 Naples Italy Office: 2nd U Naples Dept Internal Medicine, Via Pansini 5, 80131 Naples Italy

ALTURA, BURTON MYRON, physiologist, educator; b. N.Y.C., Apr. 9, 1936; s. Barney and Frances (Dorfman) A.; m. Bella Tabak, Dec. 27, 1961; 1 child, Rachel Allison. BA, Hofstra U., 1957; MS, NYU, 1961, PhD (USPHS fellow), 1964. Diplomate Am. Coll. Forensic Examiners, 1996, Am. Bd. Forensic Medicine. Teaching fellow in biology NYU, N.Y.C., 1960-61, instr. exptl. anesthesiology Sch. Medicine, 1964-65, asst. prof. Sch. Medicine, 1965-66; asst. prof. physiology and anesthesiology Albert Einstein Coll. Medicine, N.Y.C., 1967-70, assoc. prof., 1970-74, vis. prof., 1974-78; prof. physiology SUNY Health Sci Ctr., Bklyn., 1974—, prof. medicine, 1992—; mem. Ctr. Cardiovascular and Muscle Rsch., 1995—; rsch. fellow Bronx Mcpl. Hosp. Center, 1967-76; mem. spl. study sect. on toxicology Nat. Inst. Environ. Health Scis., 1977-78; mem. Alcohol Biomed. Rsch. Rev. Com., Nat. Inst. Alcohol Abuse and Alcoholism, 1978-83, member, panel CNF bd. Inst. Med., NAS, 1996—. A Food bd. FTC; adj. prof. biology Queens Coll., CUNY, 1983-84; cons. NSF, VA Grants Rev. Commn., Nat. Heart, Lung and Blood Inst., CUNY, Miles Inst., Nat. Inst. Drug Abuse, FDA, USDA, Merck, Sharpe and Dohme, Millipore Corp., Internat. Ctr. Disabled, Upjohn Co., Bayer AG, Ciba-Geigy, Zyma SA, Genentech, Nova Biomed., Parke, Davis & Co., Chem. Def. Unit, Brit. Govt., Schering-Key Corp., Sterling Drug Co., Searle Pharm. Co., Niche Pharm. Inc., Chem. Def. Establishment, U.K., Am. Speech and Hearing Assn., Protina GmbH, Otsuka Pharm. Co., Japan; hon. pres. Internat. Symposium on Interactions of Magnesium and Potassium on Cardiac and Vascular Muscle, Montbazon, France, 1984; hon. pres., hon. lectr. Hungarian Soc. Electrochemistry, Budapest, 1995; organizer, condr. symposia; organizer workshop Nat. Inst. Alcohol Abuse and Alcoholism, 1992; condr., chmn. Gordon Rsch. Conf. on Magnesium in Biochem. Processes and Medicine, 1984; chmn., organizer First Internat. Workshop Unique Magnesium Sensitive Ion Selective Electrodes, Orlando, Fla., 1993; chmn. symposium Am. Soc. Nephrology, 1993; v.p. Fourth Internat. Symposium on Magnesium, Blacksburg, 1985; judge Am. Inst. Sci. and Tech., 1984, 85, 86, 88, 89, 90, 91, 93, Jr. Acad. N.Y. Acad. of Scis., 1987, 89, 90; mem. adv. council Nat. Found. for Addictive Drugs, 1986—; vis. prof. Yamaguchi U., Japan, 1988, 93, Beijing Coll. Traditional Chinese Medicine, People's Republic of China, 1988, Jiangsu Med. Coll., 1988, Beijing Med. U., 1988, Mass. Gen. Hosp., Harvard U. Med. Sch., 1989, U. Tokyo, 1993, Kokura Meml. Hosp. Kiyushi U. Japan, 1993, Yamaguchi U. Hosp., Japan, 1993, Tokyo U., 1993, Kyoto U. Sch. Medicine, 1993, Kumamoto U. Sch. Medicine, 1993, , U. Copenhagen-Herlev Hosp., 1994, U. Florence (Italy), 1994, U. Brussels-Erasmé Hosp., 1995, Humboldt U.-Charité Hosp., Berlin, 1995, U. Hamburg-Saarland, 1995, U. Birmingham, U.K., 1996; hon. prof. Yamaguchi U. Hosp., Japan, 1988; mentor Aaron Diamond fellowships, 1990—; vis. prof., hon. lectr. Inst. for Water, Soil, and Air Hygiene, Fed Health Inst., Berlin, 1991; vis. prof., hon. lectr. Max Planck Inst., Dortmund, Germany, 1992, 94, Yamonouchi Co. Ltd., Japan, 1993, Searle Co., Japan, 1993, Otsuka Pharm. Co., Japan, 1995; mem. working group convened by Congressman Durbin III, 1991; mem. Nat. Coun. on Magnesium and Cardiovasc. Disease, 1991—; keynote spkr. Internat. Symposium Blood, Gas and Electrolytes, Linköping (Sweden), 1994, 15th Ann. Magnesium Symposium, Kagoshima, Japan, 1995. Author: Microcirculation, 3 vols., 1977-80, Vascular Endothelium and Basement Membranes, 1980, Pathophysiology of the Reticuloendothelial System, 1981, Ionic Regulation of the Microcirculation, 1982; Handbook of Shock and Trauma, Vol. 1: Basic Science, 1983, Magnesium and the Cardiovascular System, 1985, Cardiovascular Actions of Anesthetic Agents and Drugs Used in Anesthesia, vol.,1986, vol. II, 1987, Magnesium, Stress and the Cardiovascular System, 1986, Magnesium in Biochemical Processes and Medicine, 1987, Magnesium in Clinical Medicine and Therapeutics, 1992, Unique Magnesium-Sensitive Ion Selective Electrodes, 1994; editor in chief: Physiology and Patho-physiology Series, 1976-81, Microcirculation, 1980-84, Magnesium: Exptl. and Clin. Research, 1981-89, Microcirculation, Endothelium and Lymphatics, 1984—, Magnesium and Trace Elements, 1990—; mem. editorial bd.: Jour. Circulatory Shock, 1973-85, Advances in Microcirculation, 1976-92, Jour. Cardiovascular Pharmacology, 1977-84, Prostaglandins, Leukotrienes and Fatty Acids, 1978—, Substance and Alcohol Actions/Misuse, 1979-84, Alcoholism: Clin. and Exptl. Research, 1982-87; assoc. editor: Jour. of Artery, 1974—; assoc. editor: Microvascular Research, 1978-85, Agents and Actions, 1981-88, Biogenic Amines, 1985-88, Jour. Am Coll. Nutrition, 1982-94; contbr. over 800 articles to profl. jours. Recipient Rsch. Career Devel. award USPHS, 1968-72, Silver medal for furthering French-U.S. sci. rels. Mayor of Paris, 1984, Medaille Vermeille, French Nat Acad. Medicine, 1984, Travel awards NIH, 1968, Am. Soc. Pharm. and Exptl. Therapeutics, 1969; grantee NIH, 1968—, NIMH, 1974-78, Nat. Heart Lung Blood Inst., 1974-86, Nat. Inst. Drug Abuse, 1979-83, Nat. Inst. Alcohol Abuse and Alcoholism, 1990—. Fellow Internat. Coll. Angiology, Am. Coll. Angiology, Am. Inst. Chemists, Am. Heart Assn. (mem. coun. on stroke 1973—, coun. basic sci. 1969—, coun. on thrombosis 1971—, coun. on circulation 1978—, coun. on high blood pressure 1978—, coun. on cardiopulmonary circulation, 1987—, cardiovasc. A study sect. 1978-81), Am. Coll. Nutrition, Am. Physiol. Soc. (mem. circulation group 1971—, pub. info. com. 1980-84, symposium organizer); mem. AAUP, AAAS, Biophysical Soc., Soc. for Magnetic Resonance, Am. Soc. Investigative Pathology, Am. Bd. Forensic Examiners, Am. Coll. Forensic Examiners (bd. cert. forensic examiners, 1996—), Microcirculatory Soc. (past mem. exec. coun., mem. nominating com. 1973-74), Soc. Exptl. Biology and Medicine (editl. bd. 1976-83), Am. Assn. for Clin. Chemistry (hon. lectr. 1989, 92, 94), Am. Pub. Health Assn., Am. Chem. Soc. (divsn. medicinal chemistry, divsn. analytical chemistry), Am. Soc. Pharm. and Exptl. Therapeutics (symposium organizer), Endocrine Soc., Harvey Soc., Am. Coll. Toxicology, Rsch. Soc. on Alcoholism (organizer several symposia), Soc. for Critical Care Medicine, Am. Thoracic Soc., Soc. for Neurosci., Shock Soc. (founder, hon. lectr.), Am. Fedn. Clin. Rsch., Microscopy Soc. Am., European Conf. Microcirculation (symposium organizer, hon. lectr.), Neurotrauma Soc., Internat. Anesthesia Rsch. Soc., Fedn. Am. Soc. Exptl. Biology (pub. info. com. 1981-86), Am. Inst. Nutrition (organizer mini-symposium), Am. Assn. Pathologists, Am. Soc. Investigative Pathology, Am. Soc. Microbiology, Internat. Soc. Thrombosis and Haemostasis, Internat. Soc. Biomed. Rsch. on Alcoholism (founding mem.), Biomed. Optics Soc., Internat. Soc. Biorheology, Soc. Leukocyte Biology, Soc. Environ. Geochemistry and Health, Soc. Neurosci., Soc. Cardiovasc. Pathology, Reticuloendothelial Soc. (hon. lectr.), Internat. Soc. Exposure Analysis, Soc. of Parenteral and Enteral Nutrition, Soc. Nutrition Edn., Soc. Scholarly Pub., Gerontol. Soc., Internat. Platform Assn., Am. Assn. Lab. Animal Sci., Am. Inst. Biol. Sci., Am. Microscopical Soc., Am. Soc. Zoologists, The Oxygen Soc., Am. Soc. Cell Biology, Am. Soc. Bone and Mineral Rsch., Am. Soc. Magnesium Rsch. (founder, pres., exec. dir. 1984—, symposium, workshop, organizer), N.Y. Acad. Scis., Am. Pub. Health Assn., N.Y. Heart Assn., N.Y. Soc. Electron Microscopy, Coun. Biology Editors, Internat. Anesthesia Soc., Internat. Soc. for Hypertension, Am. Soc. Hypertension (founding mem.), Am. Assn. Pharm. Scis., Nat. Coun. for Magnesium and Cardiovasc. Disease, Am. Med. Writers Assn., Am. Speech and Hearing Assn., Sigma Xi. Office: 450 Clarkson Ave Brooklyn NY 11203-2012

ALVAREZ, RAUL ALBERTO, physician; b. Holguin, Cuba, Aug. 7, 1956; came to U.S., 1967; s. Raul and Esperanza (Sedano) Alvarez; m. Maria Jose Sanjuan, Oct. 4, 1983; children: Raul Eduardo, Jessica Maria. MD, Cadiz Faculty Medicine, Spain, 1983. Diplomate Am. Bd. Internal Medicine. Resident in internal medicine St. Luke's Hosp., St. Louis, 1984-87; dir. emergency rm. svcs. Comprehensive Am. Care-HMO, Miami, Fla., 1987-88; primary care physician Greater Miami Med. Ctrs., North Miami Beach, Fla., 1991-94, Gratigny Cmty. Med. Ctr., North Miami Beach, 1995—; active med. staff Aventura Hosp. and Med. Ctr., 1991—, North Shore Hosp., Miami, 1994—, Parkway Regional Med. Ctr., Miami, 1991—. Fellow ACP (assoc.); mem. AMA (Physician Recognition award 1990, 93), Am. Soc. Internal Medicine. Republican. Roman Catholic. Home: 8861 NW 151st St Miami FL 33016 Office: Gratigny Cmty Med Ctr 845 NW 119th St North Miami Beach FL 33168

ALVAREZ-MARQUES, DESIDERIO MIGUEL, microbiologist; b. Aguilar, La Rioja, Spain, Oct. 4, 1951; s. Horacio and Esperanza (Marques) A.; m. Belen Lopez Hernandez, Aug. 1, 1980; children: Miguel, Alejandro. BSc, PhD, U. de Navara, Pamplona, 1975; Microbiology Bd., Clinica Univ., Pamplona, 1982. Asst. prof. microbiology U. Navarra, 1975-79; resident Clinica Universitaria, Pamplona, 1979-82; microbiologist City of Pamplona, 1983—. Contbr. articles to profl. jours. With Spanish Army, 1978-79. Recipient Beca Colaboracion award U. Navarra, 1974-75, Ayuda Investigacion award Gobierno de Navarra, 1985, 86, 94, 95. Home: Iturrama 28 1A, Pamplona Navarra, Spain 31007 Office: Microbiologia Ayuntamiento, San Saturnino 2, Pamplona Navarra, Spain 31001

ALVERIO, CARMEN ENID, occupational therapist; b. San Lorenzo, P.R., Sept. 13, 1960; d. Emilio and Carmen (Laureano) Alverio; m. Jose Manuel Girot, Oct. 17 (div.); 1 child, Jonathan Rene. BS in Occupational Therapy magna cum laude, U. P.R., 1982; MA in Edn. with high honors, U. Phoenix, P.R., 1992. Registered occupational therapist. Staff occupational therapist Nuestra Senora de Los Angeles Hosp., Rio Piedras, P.R., 1982, Brooke Army Med. Ctr., San Antonio, 1982-84; occupational therapist, asst. health care adminstr. U.S. Army Health Clinic, San Juan, P.R., 1984-85; occupational therapist, clin. supr. Letterman Army Med. Ctr., San Francisco, 1986; occupational therapist advisor USA Humanitarian Med. Team, El Salvador, Cen. Am., 1986-87; occupational therapist, asst. chief Martin Army Community Hosp., Columbus, Ga., 1987-88; program dir., instr., cons. Occupational Therapy Dept. Humacao U. Coll., 1990-92; English tchr. K-3d grade San Juan Apostle Catholic Sch., Caguar, P.R., 1993; mem. occupational therapy staff Font. Martelo Home Care Program, Humacao, P.R., 1994; prof. occupational therapy U. P.R., Humacao, 1994—. Contbr. articles to profl. jours. Vol. Am. Muscular Dystrophy Summer Camp, P.R., 1979, 2d Ann. Internat. Amputee Soccer Tournament, Seattle, 1987, Santa's Castle Non-Profit Toy Orgn., Ft. Benning, Ga.; mem. registration com. Army Med. Dept. Biathon Race, Ft. Benning, 1987; mem. asst. rescue team Earthquake Nat. Disaster, El Salvador, 1987; asst. mgr. Correo Centro Pvt. Postal Office, Humacao, 1992-94; chair cont. edn. com. P.R. Occupational Therapy Assn., 1993-94. Mem. Am. Occupational Therapists Assn., Tex. Occupational Therapists Assn., P.R. Occupational Therapists Assn., Officers Club. Home: PO Box 1265 San Lorenzo PR 00754-1265 Office: Occupational Therapy Dept U PR Humacao PR 00791

ALVERSON, JOY FERGUSON, nurse; b. Long Beach, Calif., Apr. 28, 1954; d. Ferdie Lawrence and Joyce (Berggren) Ferguson; m. Franklin Gray Alverson II, June 1, 1974; children: Nicholas, Clint. BS, Calif. State U., Long Beach, 1977. RN, Nev., Calif. Staff nurse Los Altos Hosp., Long Beach, 1977-78, Washoe Med. Ctr., Reno, 1979—; nurse Washoe County Sch. Dist., Sparks, Nev., 1988; staff nurse Sparks Family Hosp., 1990-95, Reno Med. Plaza, 1992-95; instr. prenatal Washoe Med. Ctr., 1985—. Instr. CPR ARC, Reno, 1982; helper jr. ski program Reno Recreation Dept., 1987-93. Mem. Beta Sigma Phi (sec. 1981—), Alpha Tau (various positions 1982-88), Alpha Chpt. Mem. Disciples of Christ.

ALVEY, DORIS MAY GIORDANO, hypnotherapist, nurse; b. N.Y.C., Nov. 1, 1945; d. Dominic Louis Giordono and Agnes (Victoria) Johnson; m. Lorenzo Marcello Margini, June 5, 1974 (div. 75); m. Clifford Charles Alvey, Apr. 11, 1981. RN, Queens Gen. Hosp. Sch. Nursing, 1966; BA in Psychology, Marymount Manhattan Coll., 1973; MS, CUNY, 1978; PhD in Hypnotherapy, Am. Inst. Hypnotherapy, Santa Ana, Calif., 1985. Cert. hypnotherapist, psychiat. and mental health nurse, biofeedback therapist. Nurse in charge Phoenix House Therapeutic Ctr., N.Y.C., 1968-70; research coordinator N.Y. Med. Coll., N.Y.C., 1971-74; pvt. practice psychotherapy N.Y.C., 1974-84; research coordinator UCLA Harbor Gen. Hosp., Torrance, Calif., 1985-86; dir., owner South Ctr. for Hypnosis and Health Edn., Costa Mesa, Calif., 1984—; psychiatric, alcohol cons. Comp Care, Tustin, Calif., 1984-85; home care cons. Med. Home Coll., L.A., 1986; psychiatric nursing supr. Coll., Cerritos, Calif., 1986—; instr. Golden West Coll., Calif., 1988; instr. Golden West Coll., 1988-89. Watercolor paintings exhibited in group shows including Madison Sq. Garden Art Show, 1981; contbr. poetry to mags. Cert. rev. hearing officer Orange County, Calif., 1989—. Therapist Who Cares Bayview Manor Home for Adults, Bklyn., 1980. Mem. Biofeedback Soc. Am., South Coast Metro Rotary, Calif. Dressage Soc., Am. Horse Show Assn. Episcopalian. Home: 357 Grenoble Ln Costa Mesa CA 92627-1412 Office: South Coast Ctr Hypnosis and Health Edn 3001 Red Hill Ave # 2 Costa Mesa CA 92626-4529

ALVINO, GLORIA, motivational speaker, writer, researcher; b. Revere, Mass., June 27, 1931; d. Alfonso and Mary (Scotti) A. Student, Boston U., 1949-51; BS in Pharmacy, Mass. Coll. Pharmacy and Allied Health Scis., 1955; MS in Health and Human Svcs., Columbia Pacific U., 1992. Registered pharmacist, Mass. Pharmacy mgr., 1955-59; owner Med. Ctr. Surg. Supply, Medi-Rents, Med. Ctr. Fitting Svc., Boston, 1959-94; founder, pres. Heart to Heart Assoc., Inc., Brookline, Mass., 1992—; lectr. on the human energy field in relation to sci. and healing, lectr. on combining traditional and complementary modalities of healthcare, lectr. on patient empowerment. Producer TV series: Heart to Heart on Health Issues. Mem. Toastmasters Internat. (officer), Yan Xin Qigong Internat.. Task Force on Energy Healing, Mind-Body Medicine Group. Home: 32 Clark Rd Brookline MA 02146-6030

ALVIR, JOSE MARIA JIMENEZ, biostatistician, epidemiologist, psychiatrist; b. Manila, The Philippines, Nov. 19, 1951; s. Jose Delgado and Gudelia (Jimnez) A.; m. Gloria Spielo, Jan. 12, 1980; 1 child, Marie-Therese. BA magna cum laude, U. of the Philippines, Quezon City, 1974; MPH, Columbia U., 1981, PhD, 1985. Rsch. scientist N.Y. State Rsch. Found. for Mental Hygiene, N.Y.C., 1982-84; sr. biostatistician Hillside Hosp., Glen Oaks, N.Y., 1985-94; assoc. dir. biostats. Hillside Hosp., Glen Oaks, 1994—; assoc. prof. Albert Einstein Coll. Medicine, Bronx, N.Y., 1995—; peer reviewer Archives of Gen. Psychiatry; grant reviewer NIH, CDC. Contbr. over 80 articles to profl. jours. including New Eng. Jour. Medicine., 1986—. Mem. Srathmore Vanderbilt Civic Assn., Manhasset, N.Y., 1988—, St. Mary's Ch. Choir, Manhasset, 1989—. Named Most Outstanding Grad. U. Philippines, 1974. Mem. Stats Assn.,. Roman Catholic. Office: Hillside Hosp Rsch 75-59 263d St Glen Oaks NY 11004

ALWARD, RUTH ROSENDALL, nursing consultant; d. Henry Rosendall and Freda Jonkman; m. Samuel Alward, Jan. 17, 1976. Diploma, Butterworth Hosp. Sch. Nursing, Grand Rapids, Mich.; RN, Hunter-Bellevue Sch. Nursing, N.Y.; BSN summa cum laude, Columbia U., MA, 1982, EdM, 1983; EdD, 1986. Sr. clin. nurse Wadsworth VA Hosp., L.A., 1966-68; exec. dir. nursing Care Corp, Grand Rapids, Mich., 1968-71; nursing cons. Humana Inc., Louisville, 1972-76; asst. prof., dir. nursing adminstrn. grad. prog. Hunter Coll., CUNY, N.Y.C., 1986-90; pres. Nurse Exec. Assocs., Inc., Washington, 1990—; series editor Delmar Pubs. Inc., Albany, 1993-96. Co-author: The Nurse's Shift Work Handbook, 1993, The Nurse's Guide to Marketing, 1991; contbr. articles to profl. jours.; mem. editorial adv. bd. Jour. of Nursing Adminstrn. Mem. Va Nurses Assn. (chair fin. com.), Nat. League Nursing (treas. D.C. chpt.), Coun. on Grad. Edn. for Adminstrn. in Nursing, Am. Orgn. Nurse Execs., Sigma Theta Tau. Home and Office: 2011 N St NW Washington DC 20036-2301

AMACHER, ARTHUR LOREN, neurosurgeon; b. Saskatoon, Sask., Can., Oct. 22, 1938; came to U.S., 1983; s. Arthur Melvin and Johanna Martha (Niebergall) A.; m. Jane Elizabeth Tomlinson, Sept. 20, 1961; children: Scott, Jon, Marc. MD, U. Western Ont., London, Can., 1962. Intern Victoria Hosp., London, Ont., 1962-63, resident (jr.) surgery, 1963-64, resident neurosurgery, 1965-67; chief resident neurosurgery Victoria Hosp., London, 1969-70; fellow anatomy and neuroanatomy U. Western Ont., 1964-65; resident (sr.) surgery Vets. Hosp., London, 1965; fellow neuropathology U. Toronto, 1967; resident neurosurgery Childrens Hosp. Med. Ctr. and Peter Bent Brigham Harvard U., 1968, chief resident, teaching fellow surgery, 1969; from lectr. to assoc. prof. clin. neuro-sci., surgery U. Western Ont., London, Can., 1970-83; prof. neurosurgery U. Conn., Farmington, 1983-87; neurosurgeon Geisinger Med. Ctr., Danville, Pa., 1987-95, chief, 1995—; cons. treatment alogitm USN, Washington, 1989, Via Cyemetrics, Bel Air, Md.; me.-legal cons. Jacobson, Maynard et al., Toledo, 1989-90. Author: Patient Care in Neurosurgery, 1990, Pediatric Head Injuries, 1988; contbr. articles to profl. jours., chpts. to books. Chorister Susquahanna Valley Chorale, Lewisburg, 1989—, Church Choir, Lewisburg, 1987—. Fellow ACS, Royal Coll. Surgeons of Can.; mem. N.Y. Acad. Sci., Pa. Neurosurg. Soc. (pres. 1997). Methodist. Office: Geisinger Med Ctr Danville PA 17822-1405

AMANN, KENNETH RAMSEY, substance abuse specialist, social worker; b. Bklyn., July 18, 1949; s. Howard and Helen (Ramsey) A.; m. Patricia Joan Roche, June 24, 1978; children: Katherine, Jan. BA in Psychology, Colgate U., 1971; MSW, Adelphi U., 1975, DSW, 1993. Bd. cert. diplomate social worker. Social worker L.I. Jewish Med. Ctr., New Hyde Park, N.Y., 1975-81, dir. adolescent treatment program Manhasset Day Ctr., 1981-84, dir. substance abuse svcs., assoc. dir. social work, 1984—; presenter to numerous nat. and internat. confs. Contbr. articles to profl. jours. Mem. Acad. Cert. Social Workers. Lutheran. Home: 616 De Mott Ave Baldwin NY 11510-1323 Office: LI Jewish Med Ctr PB # 4 New Hyde Park NY 11042

AMARAL, JOSEPH FERREIRA, surgeon; b. Pawtucket, R.I., Aug. 9, 1955; s. Joseph and Rosa (Ferreira) A.; m. Linda Watson, June 6, 1981; children: Courtney, Ashley, Gregory. BS in Biology summa cum laude, Providence Coll., 1977; MD, Brown U., 1981. Diplomate Am. Bd. Surgery, Am. Bd. Med. Examiners. Intern R.I. Hosp., Providence, 1981-82, resident, 1982-83; surg. rsch. fellow Brown U./R.I. Hosp., Providence, 1983-86; sr. surg. resident R.I. Hosp., Providence, 1986-88, adminstrv. chief surg. resident, 1988-89, ccord. surg. residency, asst. surgeon, asst. prof. Brown U., 1989-91, coord. surg. residency, dir. laparoscopic surgery, 1991-92, dir. laparoscopic surgery, asst. surgeon, assoc. prof., 1991-93, assoc. prof., surgeon, 1993—; treas. R.I. Hosp. Staff Assn., 1991-93; sec. R.I. Hosp. Surg. Found., 1992—; bd. dirs. R.I. Hosp. PHO; vis. surgeon hosps. in Australia, Argentina, Portugal, Austria, Rome, Singapore and Brazil. Contbr. articles to numerous profl. jours.; numerous internat., nat. and regional presentations; various scientific exhibits. Recipient Merck Clin. Achievement award, 1981, Haffenraffer Surg. Rsch. fellowship, 1983-85, 16th ACS scholarship, 1984-86, Young Investigators award Shock Soc., 1986, Residents Rsch. award Surg. Infection Soc., 1986. Fellow ACS, Internat. Coll. Surgeons; mem. AMA, AAAS, R.I. Med. Soc., Providence Surg. Soc., New Eng. Surg. Soc., Soc. Laproendoscopic Surgeons, Assn. Surg. Edn., Ctrl. N.Y. Surg. Soc. (hon.), Soc. Minimally Invasive Therapy, Am. Soc. Gastrointestinal Endoscopy, Am. Biatric Soc., Surg. Infection Soc., N.Y. Acad. Scis., Wound Healing Soc., Am. Soc. Eternal and Parenteral Nutrition, Shock Soc., Assn. Acad. Surgeons, Brown Med. Alumni Assn., Sigma Xi, Phi Sigma Tau, Sigma Pi Sigma. Office: R I Hosp Dept Surgery 2 Dudley St Ste 470 Providence RI 02903-4923

AMBACH, WALTER, physicist, educator; b. Innsbruck, Austria, Jan. 13, 1929; s. Alois and Leopoldine A.; m. Eva Prey, Aug. 13, 1955; 1 child, Edda. M rer. nat., U. Innsbruck, 1951, PhD in Physics, 1954, habilitation, 1962, prof. asst., 1974. Head dept. physics of snow and ice U. Innsbruck, 1974-76, prof., head Inst. Med. Physics, 1976—. Contbr. over 360 articles to internat. sci. jours. Recipient Felix-Kuschenitz award Austrian Acad. Scis., 1965. Mem. Austrian Soc. Med. Physics, German Soc. Med. Physics, Internat. Glaciological Soc., German Soc. Polar Rsch., other nat. socs. Office: U Innsbruck Inst Med Physics, Muellerstrasse 44, A 6020 Innsbruck Austria

AMBLER, ZDENĚK, neurologist, educator; b. Pilsen, Czechoslovakia, Dec. 2, 1940; s. Josef and Vlasta (Hodková) A.; m. Věra Novotná, Nov. 23, 1974; children: Tomás, Martina. MD, Charles U., Prague, 1963, PhD, 1980; DSc, Palacky U., Olomouc, Czech Republic, 1988. Diplomate Bd. Electromyography, Bd. Neurology. Physician Mil. Hosp., Pilsen, Czechoslovakia, 1963-71; asst. prof. Sch. Medicine, Charles U., Pilsen, 1971-84, assoc. prof., 1984-90, prof., chmn. dept. neurology, 1990—; vis. fellow Uppsala (Sweden) U., 1984; vis. prof. U. London, U. Nijmegen, The Netherlands, U. Edinburgh, Scotland, Oxford (Eng.) U., Duke U., Harvard U., 1991-95; rschr. on neuromuscular disorders, cerebrovascular disorders; nat. coord. Internat. Stroke Trial, 1991-96. Mem. editl. bd. Ces Slov Neurol Neurochir jour.; author: Ces a Slov Neruol. Neurochir, Electroenceph Clin. Neurophysiol; contbr. articles to profl. jours. Mem. Czech Soc. Neurology (mem. com. 1990—, chmn. sec. for neuromuscular disorders), Czech Soc. for Clin. Neurophysiology (mem. com. 1990—), European Fedn. Neurol. Socs. (mem. task force for continuous med. edn.). Office: Univ Hosp Dept Neurology, alej Svobody 80, 304 60 Pilsen Czech Republic

AMBORSKI, LEONARD EDWARD, chemist; b. Buffalo, Aug. 23, 1921; s. Nicholas Leon and Angeline (Laskowska) A.; m. Irene Kazmierclak, Oct. 3, 1944; children: Donna Marie, David Paul. BS, Canisius Coll., 1943; MA, SUNY, Buffalo, 1949, PhD, 1951. Cert. indsl. hygienist Am. Bd. Indsl. Hygiene; cert. EPA instr. in lead abatement and hazardous materials worker tng. Instr. physics Canisius Coll., 1943-44; physicist Carnegie Mellon Inst., Washington, 1944-45; with E.I. DuPont de Nemours & Co., Buffalo, 1945-90, staff scientist, 1973-90, environ. health cons., 1973-90; cons. in environ. health, 1990—; rsch. assoc. Toxicoloty Rsch. Ctr., SUNY, Buffalo. Patentee in field. Bd. dirs. Am. Lung Assn. of N.Y. State, Buffalo, 1985—; chmn. Tonawanda (N.Y.) Citizen Pre-Treatment Program, 1985-86, Tonawanda Hazardous Materials Adv. Com., Buffalo, 1985-88; chmn. local emergency planning commn. Buffalo and Erie County, N.Y., 1988—; mem. citizens adv. com. Remedial Action Plan for Niagara River. Recipient Indsl. and Hazardous Waste award N.Y. State Water Pollution Control Assn., 1989. Mem. Air Pollution Control Assn. (chmn. 1983-84, Svc. award 1984), Am. Chem. Soc., Am. Indsl. Hygiene Assn., Am. Bd. Indsl. Hygiene, Am. Pub. Health Assn., Am. Soc. Safety Engrs., Water Pollution Control Fedn. Republican. Roman Catholic. Home: 62 Wedgewood Dr Buffalo NY 14221-1469

AMBRE, JOHN JOSEPH, physician, toxicologist, clinical pharmacologist, researcher; b. Aurora, Ill., Sept. 14, 1937; s. Frederick Mathias and Cecelia Agnes (Petit) A.; m. Anita Marie Sievert, Nov. 3, 1962; children: Susan, Peter, Denise, Matthew. BS, Notre Dame U., 1959; MD, Loyola U., Chgo., 1963; PhD in Pharmacology, U. Iowa, 1972. Fellow Mayo Clinic, Rochester, Minn., 1966-68; asst. prof. medicine U. Iowa, Iowa City, 1972-75, assoc. prof., 1975-78; med. dir. CBT Labs., Highland Park, Ill., 1978-85; assoc. prof. medicine Northwestern U. Med. Sch., 1980-90; dir. dept. toxicology and drug abuse AMA, Chgo., 1990-95; dir. office med. info. scis. AMA, 1995—; cons. MetPath Labs., Teterboro, N.J., Abbott Labs., North Chicago, Time, Inc., Chgo., Motorola, Inc., Schaumburg, Ill., Fermi Lab, Batavia, Ill., Velsicol Chem. Corp., Chgo.; cons. Syntex Med. Diagnostics, lectr. symposium; expert witness; testifier various govt. congrl. hearings and subcoms. on drug testing; new drug application investigator appplication #32,040 FDA; mem. adv. panel on clin. toxicology and substance abuse USP-Drug Info, U.S. Pharmocopeial Conv., Inc., Washington; mem. consensus conf. on employee drug testing workgroup on analytical methods, spl. rev. com. office of extramural rsch. Nat. Inst. Drug Abuse; bd. dirs. Med. Rev. Officers Cert. Coun. Mem. subcom. on oversight and investigation U.S. Ho. of Reps. Com. on Energy and Commerce, 1988. Served as capt. U.S. Army, 1964-66. Recipient Nat. Rsch. award Nat. Inst. on Drug Abuse.

Mem. Am. Fedn. Clin. Research, Am. Soc. Pharmacology and Exptl. Therapeutics, Am. Soc. for Clin. Pharmacology and Therapeutics (chmn. clin. toxicology sect., mem. com. on substance abuse), Cen. Soc. for Clin. Rsch. (chmn. clin. pharmacology sect). Democrat. Author: Drug Assay, 1983; mem. editorial bd. Jour. Analytical Toxicology; contbr. articles to profl. jours., chpts. to books; TV appearance CBS Network News. Achievements include patent for 4-hydroxy glutethimide. Home: 1210 Walden Ln Deerfield IL 60015-3128 Office: AMA 515 N State St Chicago IL 60610-4320

AMBROSE, MARIANNE, psychologist; b. New Castle, Pa., Apr. 16, 1948; d. Peter and Rose (Galassi) A. BS in Secondary Edn., Kent (Ohio) State U., 1970, EdS in Sch. Psychology, 1972; postgrad., Ohio State U., 1973—. Intern sch. psychologist Ravenna (Ohio) City Schs., 1970-72; psychometric intern rschr. Akron (Ohio) U., 1972; sch. psychologist, intern supr. Hilliard (Ohio) City Schs., 1972—; pvt. practice psychology Columbus, Ohio, 1977—; psychologist, divorce mediator Tennenbaum & Assocs., Columbus, 1990—, Franklin County Domestic Rels. Ct., 1990—; bd. dirs., chmn. svc. com., exec. sec. N.W. Counseling Ctr., Columbus, 1982-88; condr. workshops in field; mental health cons. with parents and tchrs.; marriage and family counselor. Past pres., bd. dirs., treas. Upper Arlington (Ohio) Civitan Club, 1981—; dir. testing Hilliard City Schs., 1972-89, chmn. group testing com., 1977-89, mem. gifted com., 1976-79. Mem. NEA, Ohio Edn. Assn., Hilliard Edn. Assn. (treas. 1988-93), Ctrl. Ohio Psychol. Assn., Ohio Sch. Psychologist Assn., Nat. Assn. Sch. Psychologists, Acad. Family Mediators. Home: 6959 Literary Ln Dublin OH 43017 Office: Tennenbaum & Assocs 5151 Reed Rd Ste A-211 Columbus OH 43220-2553

AMBROSE, THOMAS ALBERT, II, orthopaedic surgeon; b. Las Vegas, Nev., Apr. 2, 1957; s. Thomas Anthony and Ida Ambrose; m. DeniseLynn Trimmer, Sept. 18, 1993; 1 child, Hunter Blair. BA, UCLA, 1979; MD, Ohio State U., 1983. Diplomate Nat. Bd. Med. Examiners, Am. Bd. Orthopaedic Surgery. House staff Riverside Meth. Hosp., Columbus, Ohio, 1983-88, Ohio State U. Hosp., Columbus, 1983-88, Columbus Children's Hosp., 1986-88; fellow The Children's Hosp., Denver, 1988-89; assoc. prof. Ind. U. Sch. Medicine, Indpls., 1989—; fellow AO/ASIF, Hannover, Germany, Basel, Switzerland, 1989. Fellow ACS, Am. Acad. Orthopaedic Surgeons; mem. AMA, Orthopaedic Trauma Assn., Mid Am. Orthopaedic Assn., Ind. Orthopaedic Soc. Office: Associated Orthopaedic Surgeons 541 Clinical Dr Ste 600 Indianapolis IN 46202-5233

AMBROSINI, PAUL JOHN, child psychiatry educator; b. N.Y.C., Apr. 27, 1950; s. S. Joseph and Lucia Virginia (Colaneri) A. Student, Fordham U., 1968-70; BA, Trinity Coll., Hartford, Conn., 1972; MD, Wake Forest U., 1976. Diplomate Am. Bd. Psychiatry and Neurology, Am. Bd. Child Psychiatry, Nat. Bd. Med. Examiners. Psychiat. intern Westchester div. N.Y. Hosp., White Plains, 1976-77, resident in psychiatry, 1977-79; fellow in child psychiatry N.Y. State Psychiat. Inst., Columbia U. Coll. Physicians and Surgeons, N.Y.C, 1979-81, rsch. fellow in child psychiatry, 1980-83, dep. med. dir. children's inpatient svc., 1982-83, instr., asst. prof. clin. psychiatry, 1981-85; acting med. dir. spl. treatment unit Manhattan Children's Psychiat. Ctr., N.Y.C, 1984-85; dep. dir. gen. clin. pediatric psychiatry Babies Hosp. Columbia-Presbyn. Med. Ctr., N.Y.C, 1985; asst. prof. psychiatry and pediatrics Case Western Res. U., Cleve., 1985-88; assoc. prof. psychiatry Ea. Pa. Psychiat. Inst., Med. Coll. Pa., Phila., 1988—, dir. child psychiatr. outpatient svcs., 1988—. Contbr. articles to med. jours. NIMH grantee, 1981-83, Case Western Res. U. grantee, 1986-87. Mem. Am. Acad. Child and Adolescent Psychiatry (rsch. com. 1988—, reviewer Jour. 1988—, editorial bd. jour. 1990—). Democrat. Roman Catholic. Home: 527 Penllyn Pike Penllyn PA 19422-1629 Office: Med Coll Pa 3200 Henry Ave Philadelphia PA 19129-1137

AMBROSIO, DEBORAH ANN, critical care nurse; b. N.Y., Aug. 21, 1959; d. Raphael J. and Lydia C. (Roman) A.; m. Bruce R. Mawhirter, Oct. 2, 1983. BSN, Adelphi U., 1981, MS, 1996. RN, N.Y. Primary nurse med./surg. unit St. Francis Hosp., Roslyn, N.Y., 1981-83, primary nurse RICU, 1983-86; asst. coord. nursing care L.I. Vascular Ctr., Roslyn, 1986-88, coord. nursing care, 1988-94, clin. nurse specialist, 1994—; adj. faculty mem. Sch. Nursing Adelphi U., 1994—. Contbr. to profl. jours. and newletters. Mem. AACCN, Am. Heart Assn. (cert. instr. CPR), N.Y. State Nurses Assn., Am. Coll. Nutrition, Soc. Peripheral Vascular Nursing, Soc. Non-Invasive Vascular Tech., Sigma Theta Tau (Alpha Omega chpt., exec. com., com. scholarship fund raising, corr. sec.).

AMBROSIO, THOMAS JAMES, pharmacist, researcher; b. Bklyn., Apr. 20, 1932; s. Pasquale and Fortunata Fetura (Annunziata) A.; m. Antonina Marie Bilello, June 26, 1954; children: Patrick James, Donna Marie. BS in Pharmacy, L.I. U., 1954; MS in Pharm. Sci., Rutgers U., 1966, PhD in Pharm. Sci., 1970. Pharmacist Katz Drug Store, Bklyn., 1954-57; research pharmacist Ortho Research Found., Raritan, N.J., 1957-70, Schering Pharm. Research Co., Kenilworth, N.J., 1970—; chmn. steering com. packaging sci. and engrng. program Rutgers U., New Brunswick, N.J., also moderator ann pharm. packaging conf.; co-adj. prof. Arnold and Marie Coll. Pharmacy, Bklyn., Rutgers U. Grad. Sch. Pharmacy; lectr. in field. Patentee in field. Mem. Somerset County (N.J.) Rep. Com. Served with U.S. Army, 1955-57. Schering research fellow, 1970-71. Mem. ASTM, Tech. Assn. Paper and Pulp, U.S. Pharmacopoeia. Roman Catholic. Club: Somerset Valley Players (Somerville, N.J.) (v.p. 1972-76). Office: Schering Pharm Research Co 2000 Galloping Hill Rd Kenilworth NJ 07033-0530

AMBRUS, JULIAN L., physician, medical educator; b. Budapest, Hungary, Nov. 29, 1924; came to U.S., 1949, naturalized, 1955; s. Alexander and Elizabeth Ambrus; m. Clara M. Bayer, Feb. 18, 1945; children: Madeline (Mrs. David Lillie), Peter, Julian, Linda (Mrs. Edward Broenniman), Steven, Katherine (Mrs. Thomas Cheney), Charles. Student, U. Budapest, 1942-47; M.D., U. Zurich, 1949; postgrad., Sorbonne, 1949-50; Ph.D. in Med. Sci, Jefferson Med. Coll., 1954; Sc.D. (hon.), Niagara U., 1984. Diplomate: Am. Bd. Clin. Chemistry, Am. Acad. Pain Mgmt. Research asst., instr. histology U. Budapest, 1943-45, demonstrator pharmacology, 1946-47; asst. pharmacology U. Zurich, 1947-49; asst. dept. therapeutic chemistry, virology and tropical medicine Inst. Pasteur, Paris, 1949; asst. prof., asso. prof., prof. Phila. Coll. Pharmacology and Sci., 1950-55; prin. cancer research scientist Roswell Park Meml. Inst. and Hosp., 1955-65, asst. to the dir., 1961-65; dir. Springville Labs., 1965-75, dir. cancer research, head dept. pathophysiology, 1975-89, mem. dept. medicine, 1989-92; asst. prof. pharmacology U. Buffalo Med. Sch., 1955-61, asso. prof. pharmacology, 1961-65, prof., 1965-72; chmn. Roswell Park div. exec. com. Grad. Sch., 1955-65; assoc. in internal medicine SUNY, Buffalo, 1961-64, asst. prof. internal medicine, 1964-66, prof. biochem. pharmacology, 1964-80, assoc. prof. internal medicine, 1966-71, prof., 1971—; prof., chmn. dept. exptl. pathology Grad. Sch., 1972-92; prof. emeritus, 1992—; attending physician Roswell Park Meml. Cancer Hosp., 1955-92, prof. emeritus Roswell Park Cancer Inst., 1992—; attending physician Buffalo Gen. Hosp., Erie County Med. Ctr., Children's Hosp. Buffalo, 1983—; cons. Millard Fillmore Hosp., Sisters of Charity Hosp., Buffalo, 1983—; dir. Instnl. Cancer Tng. Program, USPHS, 1956-65; mem. com. Thrombolytic agts. USPHS-NIH, 1960-66; cons. adv. com. on AMA Coun. Drugs; Blood Coagulation Components, Protein Found., Cambridge, Mass.; Bur. Drugs FDA, WHO, Geneva; commr. Lake Erie chpt. U.S. Pony Clubs, mem. intercollegiate polo com. Editor-in-chief: Revs. of Hematology Jour. Medicine; contbr. articles to profl. jours. Trustee Calasanctius Prep. Sch. for Acad. Gifted, 1964-92. Recipient first prize med. student paper Hungarian Med. Sch., 1947, 1st prize surgery U. Budapest, 1947, Nelson lectureship and medal U. Calif. Davis, 1972; named Disting. Alumnus Thomas Jefferson U., 1990, Knight Commander of the Equestrian Order of Holy Sepulcher of Jerusalem, 1991. Fellow ACP, AAAS, Am. Coll. Nuclear Physicians, Am. Coll. Angiology, Royal Soc. Medicine, Am. Coll. Pharmacology and Chemotherapy, Coun. on Clin. Cardiology, Am. Heart Assn., Internat. Coll. Angiology, Am. Geriat. Soc., N.Y. Acad. Sci., Internat. Soc. Hematology; mem. NAS (fgn. mem. Hungary), Am. Soc. Hematology, Am. Soc. Pathologists, Am. Soc. Nuclear Medicine, Am. Soc. Pharmacology and Exptl. Therapeutics, Am. Soc. Physiology, Am. Assn. Cancer Rsch., Am. Soc. Clin. Oncology, Fedn. Clin. Rsch., Soc. Exptl. Biology and Medicine, Assn. Am. Med. Colls., Cath. Physicians Guild (pres. 1985-86, 93-96), Sigma Xi, Rho Chi, Physiol. Soc. Phila., Radiation Rsch. Soc., Buffalo Zool. Soc. (chmn. Sci. Coun. 1965-66), Buffalo Acad. Medicine (pres. 1976-77). Home: 143 Windsor Ave Buffalo NY 14209-1020 also: West Hill Farm Emmerling Rd Boston NY 14025 Office: Buffalo Gen Hosp SUNY/B 100 High St Buffalo NY 14203-1126

AMBRUS, LORNA, medical, surgical and geriatrics nurse; b. Phila., June 17, 1956; d. Walter C. and Joan B. (Watts) Beilfuss; 1 child, Victoria Ambrus. LPN, Upper Bucks Vo-Tech., Perkasie, Pa., 1976; diploma, Gwynedd Mercy Coll., Gwynedd Valley, Pa., 1989. RN. Nurse Grandview Hosp., Sellersville, Pa., Quality Care, Allentown, Pa., Comprehensive Home Care, Doylestown, Pa., Doylestown Manor. Home: 118 Jefferson Ct Quakertown PA 18951-1417

AMEEN, LANE, psychiatrist; b. Hopewell, Va., Aug. 23, 1923; m. May Sams; children: Nancy, Robert. BA, U. Va., 1943, MD, 1946. Cert. psychiatrist. Intern Phila. Gen. Hosp., 1947, resident, 1948; resident Menninger Sch., Topeka, 1952; chief acute psychiatry VA Hosp., West Haven, Conn., 1953-79; assoc. clin. prof. Jonathan Edwards Coll., Yale U., New Haven, 1970—; sr. cons. Elmcrest Psychiat. Inst., Portland, Conn., 1971-81, med. dir., CEO, 1981—; vis. prof. U. Kuwait, 1980-81; psychiat. cons to Kuwait, 1991, 94. Capt. U.S. Army, 1948-50. Fellow Am. Psychiat. Assn.; mem. Jonathan Edwards Coll., Yale U. Alumni Assn. Office: Elmcrest Psychiat Inst 25 Marlborough St Portland CT 06480-1829

AMENT, RICHARD, anesthesiologist, educator; b. N.Y.C., Jan. 27, 1919; m. Esther Abrams, Apr. 18, 1943; children—Sara Lauren Baron, David S., Robert H., Victor C. M.D., U. Buffalo, 1942. Diplomate Nat. Bd. Med. Examiners, Am. Bd. Anesthesiology (sr. examiner, mem. nominating com. 1973-75, 78-83). Intern Buffalo Gen. Hosp., 1942-43, asst. in anesthesiology, 1949-54, asst. attending anesthesiologist, 1954-62, assoc. attending physician, 1962-63, attending physician, 1963-88; fellow in physiology U. Rochester, 1946-47; resident anesthesiology Bellevue Hosp., N.Y.C., 1947-49, Boston Childrens Hosp., 1949; clin. instr. anesthesiology U. Buffalo, 1949, asst. clin. prof., 1956; assoc. clin. prof. anesthesiology SUNY, Buffalo, 1960-71, clin. prof., 1971—, dir. anesthesia edn., 1978—, vice chmn. dept., 1987—, mem. faculty coun. Sch. Medicine, 1972-74, mem. admissions com., 1988-94; vis. prof. U. Md., 1975, U. Tex., Dallas, 1976, NYU, 1977, U. Colo., 1977, U. Wash., 1977, U. Tex., San Antonio, 1977; mem. panel on anesthesiology manpower Grad. Med. Edn. Nat. Adv. Com., 1979-81. Contbr. articles to med. jours. Trustee Temple Beth Zion, 1960-66, 68-75, pres., 1971-73; mem. nat. med. staff Nat. Jamboree; mem. nat. med. staff Boy Scouts Am., Colorado Springs, 1961, Valley Forge, 1964; mem. exec. bd. Greater Niagara Frontier coun., 1960-70, chmn. health and safety com. Buffalo Area coun., 1961-68, mem. exec. bd., 1959-70, rep. nat. coun., 1965-70; pres. Jewish Ctr. Greater Buffalo, Inc., 1970-72, 74-75, chmn. nominating com., 1977; bd. govs. Jewish Fedn. Greater Buffalo, Inc., 1964-69, 71-73, 77-79, 90-94, chmn. social planning com., 1968-69, v.p., 1977-79, 85-89, pres., 1990-92, chmn. planning and allocation com., 1985-89; vice chmn. Menorah Campus, 1993-96, chmn., 1996—. Capt., M.C. USAAF, 1943-46. Recipient Silver Beaver award, 1965, Alumni award NYU, 1985, Deans award SUNY-Buffalo, 1986. Fellow Am. Coll. Anesthesiologists (gov. 1973-75); mem. AMA (vice chmn. anesthesia sect. 1978-88, rep. to interspecialty adv. bd. 1978-80, rep. to coun. med. splty. socs. 1978-84, bd. dirs. 1980-84, treas. 1980-82, sec. 1983-84), Am. Soc. Anesthesiologists (pres. 1977, chmn. govt. affairs com. 1980-83, Disting. Svc. award 1985), N.Y. State Soc. Anesthesiologists (pres. 1967), World Fedn. Socs. of Anesthesiologists (sec. U.S. del. 1976-88, chmn. fin. com. 1980-84, treas. 1984-92, v.p. 1992-96), N.Y. State Med. Soc. (com. on forensic medicine 1965-67), Assn. U. Anesthesiologists, Erie County Med. Soc. (chmn. anesthesia study com. 1953-62), Coun. Jewish Fed. (bd. dirs. 1990-95).

AMENT, RICHARD RAND, psychologist; b. Merrill, Wis., Aug. 5, 1950; s. Jacob John and Edith Jean (Selner) A.; m. Mary Elizabeth Beau, Aug. 5, 1978; children: Adrianne Beth, Jacob John III, Breanne Beau. BS, U. Wis., Eau Claire, 1972; MSEd, U. Wis., Stout of Menominee, 1974. Sch. psychologist Wausau (Wis.) Sch. Dist., 1974—; mem. profl. adv. bd. Children with Attention Deficit Disorders North Cen. Wis., 1991-92. V.p. Montessori Presch., Inc., Wausau, 1986, pres., 1987, 93-95; bd. dirs., 1992-94; treas. Marathon County Reps., Wausau, 1977—; campaign mgr. Kasten for Assembly, Wausau, 1982; Marathon County chmn. Gov. Thompson for Wis. campaign, 1990, 94; county chmn. Bush for Pres. campaign, 1992; mem. St. Michael's Cath. Ch., 1991-92; county coord. Vannes for Congress, 1992; bd. dirs. Citizens for Neighborhood Schs., 1991-94; parent adv. bd. Horace Mann Mid. Sch., 1994-95; treas. Friends of Judge Howard campaign, 1996, Jacobson for Assembly campaign, 1996. Mem. Wis. Sch. Psychologists Assn. (mem. exec. bd. 1983-85), Sch. Psychologists of Wis.'s North (v.p. 1976-77, 81-82, pres. 1983-85). Home: 1800 Forest Valley Rd Wausau WI 54403-2038 Office: Wausau Pub Schs 415 Seymour St Wausau WI 54403-6267

AMENTA, PETER SEBASTIAN, anatomist, researcher, educator; b. Cromwell, Conn., Mar. 26, 1927; s. Peter and Mary (DeMauro) A.; m. Rose Phyllis Russo, June 20, 1953; children: Mary Vincenza, Rosemarie. Student, Conn. Wesleyan U., 1947-49; BS, Fairfield U., 1952; MS, Marquette U., 1954; PhD, U. Chgo., 1958. Undergrad. asst. Fairfield U., 1949-52; grad. asst. Marquette U., Milw., 1952-54, U. Chgo., 1955-58; instr., ind. investigator Marine Biol. Lab., Woods Hole, Mass., summer 1956; instr. anatomy Hahnemann Med. Coll., 1958-60, asst. prof. anatomy, 1960-63, assoc. prof., 1963-71, prof., 1972-94, prof. emeritus, 1994—, acting chmn. dept., 1973-75, chmn. dept., 1975-94; head microscopic anatomy Hahnemann Med. Coll., 1968-75, treas., exec. faculty mem., 1970-73, dir. divsn. electron microscopy, 1970-75; vis. prof. cytology Carmbirdge U., 1962, Rome U., 1966, 76, Estaco Agronomica Nat., Oeiras, Portugal, 1970, Edinburgh (Scotland) U., 1972, Cath. U., Rome, 1984, U. Ark., 1980, George Washington U., 1986, U. Padova, Italy, 1987, 91, Pa. Coll. Optometry, 1989-94, U. Man., Can., 1990; instr. Trenton Diocese H.S. Religion, 1967-72; lectr. in field. Author: Histology and Embryology Rev., 1977, 2d edit., 1983, Rev. of Med. Histology, 1977, Histology, 1973, 2d edit., 1978, 3d edit., 1983, 4th edit., 1990, Histology and Human Microanatomy, 5th edit., 1988, 6th edit., 1991, From Human Microanatomy to Pathology, 1996. Twp. chmn. Burlington County Juvenile Conf. Com., 1967-70; mem. Trenton Diocesan Pastoral Coun., 1968-73, vice chmn., 1970-72; dir St. Joan of Arc Choir, 1960-73. With AUS, 1946-47. Named Man of Year, Fairfield U., 1962; Distinguished Alumnus, Am. Jesuit U., 1967. Fellow AAAS; mem. AMA, Am. Assn. Anatomists, Assn. Anatomy Chmn. (emeritus mem., chmn. histology exam com. 1986-94), Albertus Magnus Guild of Cath. Scientists, N.Y. Acad. Scis., Am. Inst. Biol. Scis., Soc. for In Vitro Biology, Am. Soc. Photobiology, Internat. Congress Photobiology, Am. Soc. Zoologists, Hahnemann Alumni Assn. (hon.), Sigma Xi, Phi Sigma. Home: 110 24th St Avalon NJ 08202

AMER, MAGID HASHIM, physician; b. Cario, June 5, 1941; came to U.S. 1971; s. Hashim and Zeinab (Iskander) A.; m. Sabah El Sayed Shehata, Mar. 12, 1973; children: Sophi, Mona, Hoda. M.B.B.Ch., Cairo U. Med. Sch., 1963. Rotating intern Cairo U. Hosp., 1964-65; resident gen. surgery Northampton (UK) Gen. Hosp., 1968-69; resident internal medicine Worcester City Hosp., Mass., 1971-73, Lemuel Shattuck Hosp., Boston, 1973-74; fellow med. oncology Wayne State U., Detroit, 1974-76, asst. prof., 1977-78; cons. oncologist King Faisal Specialist Hosp., Riyadh, Saudi Arabia, 1978-84, head div. med. oncology, 1984-91, chmn. rsch. ethics com., 1986-91; pvt. practice oncology Maadi-Cairo, 1992—. Contbr. articles to profl. jours. Fellow Royal Coll. Physicians Can., ACP, Royal Coll. Surgeons Edinburgh; mem. Am. Soc. Clin. Oncology, Am. Assn. Cancer Research, Internat. Gynecol. Cancer Soc. Muslim. Home: 24 Rd 12, Maadi Cairo 11431, Egypt Office: Cairo Cancer Clinic, 33 Korniche El Nil St, Maadi Cairo 11431, Egypt

AMES, LOUISE BATES, child psychologist; b. Portland, Maine, Oct. 29, 1908; d. Samuel Lewis and Annie Earle (Leach) Bates; m. Smith Whittier Ames, May 22, 1930 (div. 1937); 1 child, Joan Ames Chase. AB, U. Maine, 1930, MA, 1933, ScD, 1957; PhD, Yale U., 1936; D.Sc., Wheaton Coll., 1967. Cert. psychologist, Conn. Research sec., personal asst. to Dr. Gesell Yale Clinc Child Devel., Yale Med. Sch., 1933-36, instr., 1940-44, asst. prof., 1944-50; curator Yale Films of Child Devel., 1944-50; co-founder Gesell Inst. Child Devel., dir. research, sec.-treas., 1950-65, asso. dir., chief psychologist, 1968, co-dir., 1971-77, acting dir., 1978, assoc. dir., 1978—; lectr. Child Study Ctr., Yale U., 1991—, emeritus asst. prof., 1993—. Syndicated newspaper columnist Parents Ask; host weekly TV broadcast on child behavior, WBZ, Boston, 1952-55; author 36 books including: (with others) The Gesell Institute's Child from One to Six; editorial bd. Jour. Learning Disabilities, Jour. Genetic Psychology. Mem. Conn. Psychol. Soc., Am. Psychol. Soc., Soc. Rsch. Child Devel., Internat. Coun. Psychologists (dir. 1945-47), Soc Projective Techniques (pres. 1970), Sigma Xi. Home: 283 Edwards St New Haven CT 06511-3719 Office: Gesell Inst Child Devel 310 Prospect St New Haven CT 06511-2187

AMES, RICHARD POLLARD, physician, educator, lecturer; b. Northampton, Mass., Aug. 4, 1932; s. Harold Leslie and Effie Melissa (Crowley) A.; m. Janet Ann Shaw, Oct. 7, 1961; children: Patricia Jean, Brian Shaw. BA cum laude, Williams Coll., 1954; MD, Columbia U., 1958. Diplomate Am. Bd. Internal Medicine, Am. Bd. Nephrology, Am. Bd. Med. Oncology, Am. Bd. Hematology. Fellow N.Y. Heart Assn. Presbyn. Hosp., N.Y.C., 1961-63; clin. assoc. Nat. Cancer Inst., Bethesda, Md., 1963-65; investigator Nat. Inst. Arthritis Metab., Paris, 1965-66, Whitehall Found., N.Y.C., 1967-70; nephrologist St. Luke's Roosevelt Hosp., N.Y.C., 1970—, chief hypertension clinic, 1973-94, dir. phys. diagnosis, 1981-94, assoc. dir. nephrology, 1990-93; dir. hypertension Am. Health Found., N.Y.C., 1972-82; clin. prof. Columbia U., N.Y.C., 1988—. Contributing author: Topics in Hypertension, 1980, Frontiers in Hypertension Res., 1981, Clinical Cardiovascular Therapeutics, 1989, Hypertension, 1995, Messerlis Cardiovascular Drug Therapy, 1996; co-editor: Medical Symposium Drugs, 1988. Asst. surgeon USPHS, 1963-65. Fellow ACP, AHA (mem. Coun. For High Blood Pressure Rsch.); mem. Phi Beta Kappa. Office: 16 E 90th St New York NY 10128-0676

AMES, STANLEY, obstetrician and gynecologist; b. Bklyn., Feb. 18, 1936; s. Jonas and Jean Ames; m. Arlene S. Litvinoff, 1958 (div. 1978); children: Leslie E., Alison M.; m. Georgia H. Dineen, July 17, 1988. BA, NYU, 1956; MD, Albert Einstein Coll. Medicine, 1960. Diplomate Am. Bd. Obstetrics and Gynecology. Intern Jewish Hosp., Bklyn., 1960-61; pvt. practice Las Vegas, Nev., 1967—; resident in ob-gyn. Albert Einstein Coll. Medicine, Bronx, 1961-65; chief ob-gyn. Sunrise Hosp., Las Vegas, 1973-74, 77-78, 81-82. Contbr. articles to profl. jours. Capt. USAF, 1965-67. Fellow ACS, Am. Coll. Obstetricians and Gynecologists (membership chmn. 1969-88). Office: 3196 Maryland Pkwy Las Vegas NV 89109

AMES, THOMAS-ROBERT HOWLAND, psychotherapist, educator; b. Daytona Beach, Fla., Feb. 22, 1930; s. Orris Kingsley and Helen-Margarett Geraldine (Reed) A. AA, U. Fla., Gainesville, 1951, BA, 1952; MA, NYU, 1960, EdD, 1981. Diplomate Am. Bd. Sexology. Purchasing asst. Beekman-Downtown Hosp., N.Y.C., 1954-56; claims adjuster Liberty Mutual Ins. Co., N.Y.C., 1956-58; dir .programs for developmentally disabled The Eastern Sch., N.Y.C., 1960-66; dir. of programs The Young Adult Inst., N.Y.C., 1966-67, exec. dir., 1967-71; dir. day camp for retarded children The Mental Retardation Inst. of N.Y. Med. Coll., N.Y.C., 1971; dir. community residence program Nassau County Assn. for Children with Learning Disabilities, Hempstead, N.Y., 1974-80; prof. human svcs. Borough of Manhattan Community Coll., CUNY, N.Y.C., 1970—; mem. N.Y.C. Mayor's Com. on Mental Retardation, 1966-68, adv. com. for training bds. dirs. of vol. agys. N.Y. State Office of Mental Retardation and Develop. Disabilities, 1985-87, adv. com. on develop. disabilities N.Y. State Office for the Aging, 1986-88, steering com. CUNY consortium for develop. disabilities studies, N.Y.C., 1991—; reviewer Nat. Info. Ctr. for Children and Youth with Handicaps, 1989-93; examiner Am. Bd. Sexology, 1990—; cons. Jamiaca (W.I.) Assn. for Mentally Handicapped Children, Ltd., 1965-67, NAMH, 1968-70, Joint Comn. on Mental Health of Children, Inc., 1968, N.J. Assn. for Children with Learning Disabilities, Inc., 1971-73, N.Y. Assn for Brain-Injured Children, Inc., 1971-74, The Adams Sch., Inc., 1974-78, The Burt Ctr., Inc., 1974-85, Springboard, Inc., 1977, The Hebrew Acad. for Spl. Children, Inc., 1982-85, Women in Need, Inc., 1989, Edwin Gould Svcs. for Children, Inc., 1995; task force on develop. disabilities Nat. Coun. of the Chs. of Christ in U.S., 1986-88; pres. Coalition on Sexuality and Disability, 1984-88; facilitator human sexuality dialogues sponsored by Cathedral St. John Divine, N.Y.C., 1993; cons. The Boy's Brotherhood Republic, Inc., 1994-95; serves on profl. adv. bds. of numerous social and rehab. agys. Author: (with others) Modification of Behavior of the Mentally Ill, 1974, Handbook on Learning Disabilities, 1974, Model Programs and New Technologies for People with Disabilities, 1986, Transitional Issues for Community Coalescence, 1990; mem. edtl. bd. Compendium of Sexology, 1991—; contbg. editor An Outline of Sexuality, 1993; contbr. numerous articles to profl. jours. Pres., chmn. bd. trustees The N.Y. League for Early Learning, Inc., N.Y.C., 1992—; pres. bd. dirs. Rockland County Assn. for Learning Disabilities, Inc., 1994—; v.p., vice chair, bd. trustees Young Adult Inst., N.Y.C., 1983—; v.p. sec. United World Partnerships on D.D., Inc., N.Y.C., 1988—; mem. cons. com. Nat. Soc. Children of Am. Revolution, 1992-94. Recipient Leadership and Svc. award Young Adult Inst., 1972, Disting. Svc. award, 1981, Spl. Svc. award, 1992, Citation for Outstanding Vol. Svcs., Gov. Cuomo, 1987, Leadership and Svc. award Nassau County ACLD, 1979, Meritorious Svcs. award Nat. Rehab. Assn., 1973, Cmty. Mental Health Soc. of B.M.C.C. award, 1981, Anne H. Berkman Meml. award Coalition on Sexuality and Disability, 1989, medal of Sexology For Life Time Achievement award The Am. Acad. of Sexology, 1995, Young Adult Inst., 1996; named in his honor The Thomas-Robert Howland Ames Residences, N.Y.C., 1993. Fellow Am. Assn. on Mental Retardation (life; region 10 exec. bd. 1973-74, Profl. award 1991), Am. Orthopsychiat. Assn., Am. Acad. Clin. Sexologists (founding), Royal Soc. Health, Nat. Rehab. Counseling Assn. (pres. met. N.Y.C. chpt. 1974, exec. bd. N.E. region 1974, leadership award 1974), Am. Soc. Group Psychotherapy and Psychodrama; mem. Nat. Soc. Ams. Royal Descent (life), Halifax Hist. Soc. (life), Order of Crown of Charlemagne in U.S.A. (life), Gen. Soc. Mayflower Descs. (life), Hereditary Order of Descs. of Colonial Govs. (life), Friends of St. George's Chapel, Windsor Castle (life, descendant mem.), Jamestowneife). Democrat. Episcopalian. Office: BMCC CUNY 199 Chambers St # N614 New York NY 10007-1079

AMIDON, ROGER LYMAN, health administration educator; b. Burlington, Vt., Apr. 8, 1938; s. Ellsworth L. and Mae (Liddle) A.; m. JoAnn Reiland, Aug. 1, 1968. B.A., U. Vt., 1960; M.A., U. Iowa, 1965, Ph.D. (USPHS trainee), 1968. Asst. prof. hosp. and health adminstrn. U. Iowa, 1968-73, asso. prof., 1973-77; prof., chmn. dept. health adminstrn. U. Okla., 1977-81; prof., chmn. dept. health adminstrn. U. S.C., 1981-88, on sabbatical, 1988-89, prof., grad. dir., 1989—; exec. sec. Nat. Center Health Services Research, 1975-76; dir. Am. Indian Grad. Program in Health Adminstrn., U. Okla., 1977-81; cons. Mackay Meml. Hosp., Taipei, Taiwan, 1993—. Contbr. articles to profl. jours. Served with M.S.C. U.S. Army, 1961-62. Mem. APHA, Am. Coll. Health Care Adminstrs., Am. Coll. Healthcare Execs., Am. Hosp. Assn. (life), Inst. Society, Ethics and Life Scis., Sigma Xi. Home: 234 Saluda Ave Columbia SC 29205 Office: U SC Sch Pub Health Dept Health Adminstrn Columbia SC 29208

AMIN, MOHAMMAD, urology educator; b. Sargodha, Pakistan, Jan. 1, 1942; came to U.S., 1964; s. Mohammad and Gulzar (Begum) Nawaz; m. Elizabeth Anne Howarth, May 25, 1973; children: Daniel, Omar. MB, BS, King Edward U., Lahore, Pakistan, 1963. Diplomate Am. Bd. of Urology. Intern Muhlenberg Hosp., Plainfield, N.J., 1964-65; resident in surgery Norton Hosp., Louisville, 1965-66; asst. prof. urology U. Louisville, 1971-74, assoc. prof., 1974-80, prof. urology, 1980—, resident in urology, 1966-69; med. officer Social Security, Pakistan, 1969-70; house officer urology Southmede Hosp., Bristol, Eng., 1970-71. Contbr. articles and book chpts. to profl. jours. Recipient Health Advancement award Nat. Kidney Found., 1981. Fellow ACS; mem. Am. Urol. Assn. Societe Internatioale D'Urologie, Univ. Club. Democrat. Islamic. Office: 210 E Gray St Ste 1000 Louisville KY 40202

AMINLARI, ALI, physician, ophthalmologist; b. Shiraz, Iran, Aug. 30, 1941; came to U.S., 1984; s. Mohammad H. and Halima (Aminlari) A.; m. Paymaneh Payman, Sept. 14, 1976; children: Amir, Eddie. MD, Pahlavi U., Shiraz, 1969; postgrad., U. Pa., 1975. Diplomate Am. Bd. Ophtahlmology. Fellow U. Pa., Phila., 1975-76; asst. prof. dept. ophthalmology Shiraz U., 1976-80, assoc. prof., 1980-84; rsch. fellow U. Pa., Phila., 1984-85; asst. prof. ophthalmology Pa. State U., Hershey, 1985-92, assoc. prof., 1992—. Contbr. articles to profl. jours. Fellow Am. Acad. Ophthalmology. Office: Hershey Med Ctr Hershey PA 17033

AMINO, NOBUYUKI, endocrinologist, educator; b. Kobe, Hyogo-ken, Japan, Dec. 4, 1940; s. Ichie and Ei (Yoshikawa) A.; m. Masae Tanaka, Oct.

17, 1969; children: Shingo, Ikuko. MD, Osaka U. Med. Sch., Japan, 1965. Clin. fellow Osaka U. Hosp., Japan, 1966-71; clin. asst. Osaka U. Hosp., 1974-78; rsch. fellow U. Chgo., 1971-73; asst. prof. Med. Sch. Osaka U., 1978-89, assoc. prof., 1989-92; prof. Med. Sch. Osaka U., 1992—. Recipient 1st Prize of Kozakai Nozomu, Clin. Pathology Rsch. Found., 1991, Annual award Japan Med. Assn., 1989, Prize, Asia and Oceania Thyroid Assn., 1989, 1st Annual award Japan Endocrine Soc., 1981, 6th Annual award Japan Thyroid Assn., 1977. Home: 5-60-38 Nanpeidai, Takatsuki Osaka 569, Japan Office: Osaka U Med Sch, 2-2 Yamadaoka, Suita Osaka 565, Japan

AMIRANA, M. T., surgeon; b. Bhanvad, India, Jan. 7, 1930; came to U.S., 1958; s. Tayob Amirana and Noorbai Abba; m. Annelene J. Vogt, July 30, 1959; children: Ebrahim, Omar, Jasmine. BS, Khalsa Coll., Bombay, 1953; MD, U. Heidelberg, Fed. Republic Germany, 1958. Instr. thoracic and cardiovascular surgery Albert Einstein Sch. Medicine, N.Y.C., 1966-67; pres. Rens County Med. Soc., Troy, N.Y., 1975-76; chmn. dept. surger Leonard Hosp., Troy, 1972-74, St. Mary's Hosp., Troy, 1981-83; pvt. practice, 1983—; adj. rsch. assoc. prof. Rensselaer Poly. Inst., Troy, 1968-74. Active Rens. County Med. Soc., Troy, 1967. Fellow Am. Coll. Surgeons, Am. Coll. Thoracic Surgeons; mem. N.Y. State Med. Soc. Home: 13 Brentwood Ave Troy NY 12180-1407 Office: 2416 21st St Troy NY 12180-1819

AMIRIKIA, HASSAN, obstetrician, gynecologist; b. Tehran, Iran, Dec. 10, 1937; came to U.S., 1966; d. Ahmad and Showkat (Asgari) Cheftsaz; m. Mino Vassigh Amirikia, Apr. 4, 1964; children: Arezo, Omid. MD, Tehran U., 1964. Cert. Am. Bd. Ob-Gyn. Intern Cook County Hosp., Chgo., 1966-67; resident Wayne State U., Detroit, 1967-71, fellow, 1971-72; practice medicine specializing in infertility Detroit, 1972—; asst. prof. Wayne State U., Detroit, 1972—; dir. ob-gyn. tng. dept. family medicine Wayne State U., Detroit, Mich., 1979—; dir. infertility and reproductive endocrinology St. Joseph's Hosp., Pontiac, Mich., 1990-93; chief staff Hutzel Hosp. Detroit Med. Ctr., 1993—; researcher effects of androgens on the ovary. Contbr. articles to profl. jours. Fellow ACS, Am. Coll. Ob-Gyn (Mich. sect.), Royal Coll. Physicians and Surgeons, Wayne County Med. Soc. (pres. 1995-96). Home: 1435 Lone Pine Rd Bloomfield Hills MI 48302-2632 Office: 4727 St Antoine St Detroit MI 48201-1461 also: 29877 Telegraph Rd Southfield MI 48034-1332

AMIRKHANIAN, JOHN DAVID, geneticist, researcher, educator; b. Iran, Nov. 10, 1927; came to U.S., 1979; s. Gregor D. and Astghik (Alexandrian) A.; m. Romelia Grigorian, Jan. 30, 1957; children: Varouj, Areg, Aspet. BSc in Biology, Tehran U., 1973; PhD in Genetics, King's Coll., U. London, 1977. Researcher on genetics of insect vectors of diseases Tehran U. Sch. Pub. Health, 1967-70; asst. prof. Sch. of Pub. Health Tehran U., 1977-79; rsch. scientist and assoc. Natural History Mus., L.A., 1980—; vis. prof. U. So. Calif., L.A., 1979-81; mem. faculty, sr. rsch. assoc. UCLA Sch. Medicine-King-Drew Med. Ctr., 1981-92; neonatal lung researcher, surfactant replacement models, mechanisms of lung surfactant damage by oxygen-derived species U. Calif., Davis, 1992—. Fellow Royal Micros. Soc. London, Linnean Soc. London; mem. AAAS, Inst. Biology, Genetics Soc. Eng., N.Y. Acad. Scis., Oxygen Soc. Office: U Calif Sch of Medicine Divsn Neonatology TB 193 Davis CA 95616

AMLAND, PETTER FRODE, plastic surgeon; b. Bergen, Norway, May 13, 1952; s. Sigurd Anfinn and Anne-Lotte (Geiger) A.; m. Karina Hyggen, Dec. 28, 1977. MD, U. Oslo, Norway, 1977; PhD (hon.), U. Tromsø, Norway, 1984. Surg. resident Tromsø, 1980-81, Kongsberg, Norway, 1981-83, Oslo, 1984-89; amanuensis rschr. Tromsø, 1983-84; plastic surg. resident Oslo, 1989-94, cons. plastic surgeon, 1994—; chief rsch. dept. plastic and reconstructive surgery Norwegian Nat. Hosp., Oslo, 1989-96. Contbr. articles to profl. publs. (Am. Coll. Medicine award 1995). Lt. Norwegian Army, 1979-80. Mem. Norwegian Med. Assn., Norwegian Assn. Plastic Surgery, Scandinavian Assn. Plastic Surgery. Evangelic-Lutheric. Home: Hoffsjef Lovenskioldsvei 6B, 0382 Oslo Norway Office: Norwegian Nat Hosp, Dept Plastic Surgery, Pilestredet 32, 0027 Oslo Norway

AMLICKE, ELIZABETH MARY, geriatrics nurse, nurse administrator; b. Abington, Pa., Apr. 28, 1941; d. Austin H. and Elizabeth M. (Hurd) Whitney; divorced; 1 child, Christopher John. Diploma in nursing, Mountainside Hosp., Glen Ridge, N.J., 1962. RN, N.J., Pa.; cert. in gerontology ANCC. Asst. dir. nursing, dir. nursing Pinewood Acres, Maple Shade, N.J., 1977-78, dir. nursing, 1978-79; staff nurse Delaware Valley Med. Ctr., Langhorne, Pa., 1979-81, head nurse, 1981-85; evening supr. Masonic Home N.J., Burlington Twp., 1983-85, nurse mgr., quality assessment and assurance nurse, 1983—, infection control nurse, 1993—, head nurse, 1985-88; instr. Burlington County Inst. Tech., Westampton, N.J., 1990—. Mem. ANA (cert. in gerontology). Home: 12 Windsor Rd Southampton NJ 08088

AMMANNATI, FRANCO, neurosurgeon; b. Florence, Tuscany, Italy, Sept. 16, 1951; s. Bruno and Franca (Ciappi) A.; m. Silvia Magni, June 3, 1979; children: Andrea, Damiano. MD, U. Florence, Italy, 1976. Cert. in neurology, neurosurgery, endocrinology, radiotherapy. Asst. neurosurg. dept. Ospedale Careggi, Florence, 1979-92, sr. asst. neurosurg. dept., 1992-96, eligibility for surgeon in chief neurosurg. dept., 1988—; contract-prof. neurophysiopathology U. Florence, 1993-96. Author 3 books in field; contbr. numerous articles to profl. jours. Mem. Italian Soc. Skull Base. Office: Ospedale Careggi Dept Neurosurgery, Viale Morgagni 85, 50134 Florence Italy

AMMERMAN, ROBERT THOMPSON, clinical psychologist; b. Madison, Wis., Mar. 4, 1959; s. Robert Ray and Joyce (Thompson) A.; m. Caroline Helm Bennett, June 1, 1985; children: Patrick Bennett, Evan Robert. AB, Vassar Coll., 1981; MS, U. Pitts., 1984, PhD, 1986. Supr. rsch. and clin. psychology Western Pa. Sch. for Blind Children, Pitts., 1986-95; asst. prof. psychiatry U. Pitts. Sch. Medicine, 1989-93; assoc. prof. psychiatry, 1993—; lectr. in psychology U. Pitts., 1986-92; pvt. practice Sewickley, Pa., 1988-92; assoc. prof. psychiatry and neurosurgery Med. Coll. of Pa. and Hahneman U., 1995—. Editor: (books) Children at Risk, 1990, Treatment of Family Violence, 1990, Case Studies in Family Violence, 1991, Assessment of Family Violence, 1992, Handbook of Behavior Therapy for Children and Adolescents, 1993, Handbook of Prescriptive Treatments for Children and Adolescents, 1993, Handbook of Aggressive and Destructive Behavior in Psychiatric Patients, 1994, Handbook of Prescriptive Treatments for Adults, 1994, Handbook of Child Behavior Therapy in the Psychiatric Setting, 1995, Advanced Abnormal Child Psychology, 1995. Grantee Nat. Inst. on Disabilities and Rehab. Rsch., U.S. Dept. Edn., 1987-90, 91-94, 94—, Vira I. Heinz Endowment, Pitts., 1988-91. Mem. Am. Psychol. Assn., Assn. for Advancement of Behavior Therapy, Internat. Soc. for the Prevention of Child Abuse and Neglect. Home: 1304 Beaver Rd Sewickley PA 15143-2008 Office: Allegheny Gen Hosp 320 E North Ave Pittsburgh PA 14212

AMMON, HERMANN PHILIPP THEODOR, pharmacologist, educator; b. Nuremberg, Bavaria, Germany, Jan. 24, 1933; s. Theodor and Käthe (Schatz) A.; m. Helga Ursula Grummt, Aug. 3, 1963; children: Susanne, Christiane. MD, U. Erlangen-Nuremberg, Fed. Republic of Germany, 1963, privat dozent, 1968. Rsch. fellow U. Erlangen-Nuremberg, Fed. Republic of Germany, 1965-70; asst. prof. Dept. Pharmacology, U. Erlangen, Nuremberg, Fed. Republic of Germany, 1971-74; instr. medicine Harvard Med. Sch., U. Harvard, Cambridge, Mass., 1970-71; assoc. prof. pharmacology Inst. Pharm. Scis., U. Tuebingen, Fed. Republic Germany, 1974-76; prof. U. Tübingen, Fed. Republic Germany, 1976—; dir. Inst. Pharm. Scis., U. Tuebingen, 1986-89, 95—. Author, editor: (handbook) Arzneimittelneben und Wechselwirkungen, 1981, 86, 91; editor, co-editor over 15 sci. jours. and books; contbr. 150 articles to profl. jours. Com. mem. Bundesgesundheitsamt, Berlin, 1978; bd. reviewers Deutsche Forschungsgemeinschaft, Bonn, Bad Godesburg, Fed. Republic of Germany, 1988. Mem. German Soc. for Pharmacology and Toxicology, German Diabetes Assn. (bd. dirs. 1989, pres. 1994-95), German Pharm. Soc. (bd. dirs. 1986, pres. 1996-99), Am. Diabetes Assn., Endocrine Soc. (U.S.), European Soc. for Study Diabetes, Lions (pres. Tuebingen 1983-84, gov. dist. IIISM 1992-93). Home: IM Kleeacker 30, D-72072 Tübingen Germany

AMMON, JOHN RICHARD, anesthesiologist; b. N.Y.C., 1948. MD, U. Pa., 1974. Cert. in anesthesiology. Intern Crozer Chester Med. Ctr., 1974-75; resident in anesthesiology Mass. Gen. Hosp., Boston, 1975-77; fellow in cardiac anesthesiology Stanford (Calif.) Med. Ctr., 1977-78. Mem. Am. Soc. Anesthesiology, Alpha Omega Alpha. Office: 300 W Berridge Ln Phoenix AZ 85013-1547*

AMON, ROBERT BICKFORD, physician, consultant; b. Grand Rapids, Mich., Sept. 24, 1940; s. Morris Frederick and Lorraine Florence (Hardesty) A.; m. Meredith Bess Raftshol, Aug. 19, 1961; 1 child, C. Malaika. MD, U. Mich., 1965; MPH, Harvard U., 1973. Diplomate Am. Bd. Dermatology, Am. Bd. Preventive Medicine. Intern U. Oreg. Hosps. and Clinics, Portland, Oreg., 1976—; resident Oreg. Health Scis. Univs.; pres. Dermatol. Consultants, PC, Portland, 1976—; clin. prof. dermatology Oreg. Health Sci U., Portland, 1980—. Home: 1700 SW Broadway Dr Portland OR 97201

AMOORE, JOHN ERNEST, biochemist; b. Matlock, England, Apr. 28, 1930; came to the U.S., 1962; s. Ronald Lewis and Kathleen (Winterton) A.; m. Annie Bodjayian, June 6, 1959; children: Ronald John, Marie Ani. BS in Biochemistry, Oxford U., 1952, PhD in Biochemistry, 1958. Registered environ. assessor, Calif. Rsch. chemist Western regional rsch. ctr. USDA, Albany, Calif., 1963-78; ptnr. Olfacto-Labs., El Cerrito, Calif., 1978—; mem. scientific adv. com. on acid deposition, Calif., 1983—. Author: Molecular Basis of Odor, 1970; contbr. 67 articles to profl. jours. 2d lt. British Army, 1954-56. Christopher Welch scholar, 1952. Mem. Assn. for Chemoreception Scis., Air and Waste Mgmt. Assn., Am. Water Works Assn., ASTM. Republican. Office: Olfacto-Labs 7701 Potrero Ave El Cerrito CA 94530-2023

AMORNMARN, RUMPA, physician; b. Rangoon, Burma, Oct. 2, 1946; came to U.S., 1972; s. Che Peng and Me Cho (Che) Moy; m. Surachai Sutha, July 19, 1980; one child, Ken. MD, Chulalongkorn U., Bangkok, 1967, Mahidol U., Bangkok, 1971. Diplomate Am. Bd. Radiology. Rotating internship Siriraj Hosp., Bangkok, 1971-72; internship VA Hosp., Washington, 1972-73; resident, fellow therapeutic radiology Johns Hopkins Cancer Ctr., Balt., 1973-77; staff mem. VA Med. Ctr., East Orange, N.J., 1977-81; asst. prof. radiation N.J. Med. Sch., Newark, 1978-81; asst. prof. dept. radiation oncology U. Md. Hosp., Balt., 1981-83; physician Univ. Hosp. of Jacksonville, Fla., 1983—; assoc. prof. radiology U. Fla., Jacksonville, 1983—; cons. Balt. City Hosp., 1976-77. Author numerous presentations; contbr. over 25 articles to profl. jours. Mem. Am. Soc. Therapeutic Radiologists, Am. Coll. Radiology, Duval County Med. Soc. Office: Radiation Oncology Ctr 655 W 8th St Jacksonville FL 32209-6511

AMOROSO, MARIE DOROTHY, retired medical technologist; b. Phila., Jan. 16, 1924; d. Salvatore and Clorinda (Gaudio) A. Med. Lab. Tech., Hahnemann Hosp., Phila., 1943; postgrad., Temple U., Phila., 1945-48, U. Pa., Phila., 1947-48, 1950. Registered EEG Technologist; cert. registered EEG Technologist. EEG technician Hahnemann Med. Coll., Phila., 1943-53, Phila. Gen. Hosp., 1953-62; histology technician Temple Med. Coll. Temple U., Phila., 1962-63; allergy technician Harry Rogers, M.D., Phila., 1963; EEG technologist Haverford (Pa.) State Hosp., 1963-85, Irvin M. Gerson, MD, Haverford, 1985-88; EEG technologist to pvt. physician Haverford State Hosp., 1985-88; ret., 1988; instr. EEG Osteopathic Med. Ctr. Sch. Allied Health, Phila., 1978-85. Editor: The Eastern Breeze, 1977-79; contbr. articles to profl. jours.; patentee in field. Mem. Am. Soc. Electroneurodiagnostic Technologists Inc., Western Soc. Electrodiagnostic Technologists, So. Soc. Electroneurodiagnostic Technologists Inc., Ea. Soc. EEG and Neurodiagnostic Technicians Assn. (sec. 1977-79), Phila. Regional EEG Technicians Assn. (exec. bd. dirs. 1967, sec. 1969), Ctrl. Soc. Electroneurodiagnostic Technologists, Ea. Assn. Electroencephalographers (subscriber). Home: 477 Brookfield Rd Drexel Hill PA 19026-1107 *Died, July 19, 1995.*

AMOROSO, SANTI, family physician; b. Santa Teresa di Riva, Messina, Italy, June 17, 1925; s. Gaetano Attilio and Francesca Erminia (Barbera) A.; m. Gabriella Lucia Malanga, June 12, 1952; children: Francesca Erminia, Gaetano Michael, Richard Paul, Marco Robert. MD, U. Rome, 1949. Lic. physician Md., Va.; diplomate Am. Bd. Family Practice. Rotating intern St. Mary's Meml. Hosp., Knoxville, 1953-54, resident in surgery and gen. practice, 1954-56, 57-59; mem. Overlea Med. Group, Balt., 1959-62, Perry Hall Med. Group, Balt., 1962-64; civil svc. physician Kirk Army Med. Ctr., Aberdeen Proving Grounds, 1977-78; pvt. practice Rome, 1964-77, 78—; cons. Clinica Villa Gina, Rome, 1982—. Translator: (from Italian to English) Giornale Italiano Di Ortopedia e Traumatologia, 1996. Capt. M.C. Italian Army, 1951, 82. Fulbright Travel grantee, 1953. Mem. AMA, Italian Med. Soc. Home and Office: Via di Villa Belardi 24, 00154 Rome Italy

AMOS, DENNIS B., immunologist; b. Bromley, Eng., Apr. 16, 1923; s. Benjamin and Vera (Oliver) A.; m. Solange M. Labesse, Aug. 25, 1949 (dec. 1980); children: Susan V., Martin D., Christopher I., Nigel P., Irene C.; m. Kay B. Veale, Mar. 9, 1984. MBBS, Guy's Hosp., London, 1951, MD, 1963. House officer Guy's Hosp., London, 1951-52, rsch. pathologist, 1952-55; prin. cancer rsch. scientist Roswell Park Inst., Buffalo, 1955-62; prof. immunology, exptl. surgery Duke U., Durham, N.C., 1962-93, prof. emeritus, 1993—; cons. NIH, Bethesda, Md., 1957—. Mem. Nat. Acad. Scis., Inst. of Medicine. Office: Duke Med Ctr PO Box 3010 Durham NC 27715-3010

AMOS, HAROLD, biomedical researcher, educator; b. Pennsauken, N.J., Sept. 7, 1919. BS, Springfield Coll., 1941, PhD in Bacteriology, 1952. Rsch. fellow Harvard Med. Sch., 1952-54; instr. bacteriology Springfield Coll., Boston, 1948-49; from assoc. to asst. prof. to assoc. prof. Harvard Med Sch., Boston, 1954-70, prof. microbiology and molecular genetics, 1970—; chmn. dept. microbiology Harvard Med. Sch., 1979—; Fulbright rsch. fellow Pasteur Inst., France, 1951-53; rsch. fellow Harvard Med. Sch., 1952-54; USPHS fellow, 1952-54, sr. rsch. fellow, 1958; mem. Nat. Cancer Adv. Bd., 1972—; trustee Josiah Macy Found., 1973—. Recipient Fulbright Rsch. fellow, 1951-52, Pub. Welfare medal NAS, 1995. Mem. Inst. Medicine-NAS, Am. Soc. Biol. Chemists, Tissue Culture Assn., Am. Soc. Microbiology. Office: Harvard Med Sch Dept Microbiol & Molec Gen 25 Shattuck St Boston MA 02115*

AMOS, LINDA K., nursing educator, college dean; b. Findlay, Ohio, Sept. 7, 1940; d. Blond G. and Dorotha (Brinkman) A. BS, Ohio State U., 1962, MS, 1964; EdD, Boston U., 1977. Asst. dean of baccalaureate affairs Boston U. Coll. Nursing, 1971-74, dean, prof., 1975-80; dean, prof. U. Utah Coll. Nursing, Salt Lake City, 1980—; chair Presdl. Commn. Status of Women U. Utah, 1995—; cons. Social Sci. Rsch. Inst., Boston. Contbr. articles to profl. jours. Chair Presdl. Commn. on Status of Women, U. Utah; bd. dirs. Utah Heart Assn. SErved with USPHS. Named for Outstanding Contbns. to the Nursing Profession, Utah Citizen's League for Nursing, 1989; recipient VA Chief Nurse award for promoting unity between edn. and practice, Mary Tolle Wright award for excellence in leadership Sigma Theta Tau, 1991. Fellow Am. Acad. Nursing (governing coun. 1986-90, selection com. 1995—); mem. ANA, Am. Assn. Colls. of Nursing (pres. 1984-86), Nat. Adv. Coun. on Nurse Tng., Sigma Theta Tau (internat. nominating com. 1995—).

AMOS, RICHARD E., director medical technology program; b. Akron, Ohio, Jan. 11, 1927; s. Richards E. and Hazel Marie (McCauley) A.; m. Mary Ellen Bridges, Nov. 11, 1950 (dec. Oct. 1969); children: Susan Ann, Richard E., Jane Kathryn, Charles B.; m. Marilyn G. Winter, Feb. 1, 1972. BS, U. Mich., 1949; MA, Ctrl. Mich. U., 1977; MS, U. Cin., 1982. Bacteriologist Ypsilanti (Mich.) State Hosp., 1950-51, St. Joseph Hosp., Joliet, Ill., 1951-52; bacteriologist, chief med. technologist Meml. Hosp., Elmhurst, Ill., 1952-55; pres., lab. dir. Arlington Labs., Inc., Columbus, Ohio, 1955-68; tech. dir. Consolidated Biomed. Labs., Columbus, Ohio, 1968-71; lab. dir. Diamond Shamrock Health Scis., Cleve., 1971-75; asst. dir. labs. Drs. Hosp., Massillon, Ohio, 1975-78, v.p. clin. svcs., 1978-85; dir. med. technology program U. Akron (Ohio), 1985—; mem. nursing program adv. com. Kent State U., New Philadelphia, Ohio, 1979-83; v.p., bd. trustees Vis. Nurse & Home Health Care, MAssillon, 1982-83; instr. health care mgmt. Stark Tech. Coll. Ganton, Ohio, 1983-85; ednl. cons. Med. Tech. Program, Children's Hosp. Akron, 1993—. With USN, 1945-46. Mem. Am. Acad. Med. Adminstrs., Am. Soc. Clin. Pathologists (assoc.). Home: 2055 Stabler Rd Akron OH 44313 Office: U Akron Akron OH 44325

AMSEL, BRAM JULES, cardiologist; b. Amsterdam, Netherlands, Mar. 3, 1949; s. Naftali Hersch and Ruth Henriette (Simons) A.; 1 child, Alon. SB in Applied Math. cum laude, Brown U., 1971; MD, U. Amsterdam, 1977, cert. in cardiology, 1983. Cardiologist-in-charge dept. cardiac surgery Univ. Hosp., Antwerp, Belgium, 1984—; lectr. U. Antwerp, Belgium, 1994—. With med. corps Army of Netherlands, 1977-78. Office: U Hosp of Antwerp, Wilrijkstraat 10, Edegem B-2650, Belgium

AMSTER, SUSAN M., physician assistant; b. Buffalo, Dec. 17, 1954; d. Saul and Marilyn (Michael) Gordon. BA, Hood Coll., 1976; physician asst. cert., St. Louis U., 1979; MBA, Sacred Heart U., 1994. Physician asst. resident Norwalk Hosp./Yale U., New Haven, 1982; sec. rsch. Nassau County Med. Ctr., Long Island, N.Y., 1976; vol. svcs. program Deaconess Hosp., St. Louis, 1976-77; emergency med. tech. Cmty. Hosp., St. Louis, 1977; physician asst. Hematology/Oncology Mobile Unit, Huntington, N.Y., 1979-80; pediat. physician asst. Norwalk Hosp., 1980-89; pediatric PA and practice mgr. Willows Pediatric Group, 1989—; pediatric physician asst. del. People to People Citizen Ambassador Program, China, 1992. Med. adv. vol. Asthma Camp for Kids, Camp Hazen, Conn., 1990—; pres. bd. dirs. Saugatuck Childcare Ctr., Westport, Conn., 1995—. Fellow Am. Acad. Physician Assts., Conn. Acad. Physician Assts. Office: Willows Pediat Group 129 Kings Hwy Westport CT 06880

AMSTERDAM, JAY D., psychiatrist, educator; b. Phila., Feb. 10, 1949. BA, Syracuse U., 1970; MD, Jefferson Med. Coll., 1974. Diplomate Am. Bd. Med. Examiners, Am. Bd. Psychiatry and Neurology; lic. physician, Pa., N.J. Intern in ob-gyn. Upstate Med. Ctr., Syracuse, N.Y., 1974; resident in psychiatry Thomas Jefferson U. Hosp., Phila., 1974-77, chief resident in psychiatry, 1976-77; sr. resident psychiat. rsch. svc. depression rsch. unit VA Med. Ctr., Phila., 1977-78; NIMH postdoctoral fellow in neuropsychopharmacology VA Med. Ctr./U. Pa. Hosp., Phila., 1978-79; asst. prof. psychiatry Thomas Jefferson U., Phila., 1978-83, adj. assoc. prof. psychiatry, 1983-88; dir. depression rsch. unit U. Pa. Hosp., Phila., 1979—; asst. prof. psychiatry U. Pa., Phila., 1979-86, assoc. prof. psychiatry, 1986-92, prof., 1992—; mem. instl. review bd. com. on studies involving human beings U. Pa., 1983—, faculty senate exec. com., 1987-88, univ. coun.,1987-88, undergrad. admissions and fin. aid, 1987-90, univ. facilities com., 1988-89, student affairs com., 1989-91, univ. disability bd., 1990-93; mem. student-faculty interaction com. U. Pa. Hosp. and Med. Sch., 1987-89, continuing med. edn. lecture series, 1986—, ad hoc com. on organ transplantation, 1988, pharmacy and therapeutics com., 1989-93, invetigational drug task force, 1991-92, mem. clin. svcs. steering com., 1985-86, residency tng. com., 1985-86, rsch. com., 1985-90, Sachar Rsch. Award com., 1985—; adj. assoc. prof. Wistar Inst. Antomy, Phila., 1988—; mem. program planning com. IV World Congress Biol. Psychiatry, Phila., 1984-85; sci. adv. com. 2nd Internat. Conf. on Viruses, Immunity and Mental Health, Montreal, Que., Can., 1988; program dir. organizating. com. 1st Internat. Conf. on Refractory Depression, Phila., 1988; mem. organizating com. 2nd Internat. Conf. on refractory Depression, Amsterdam, 1990-92; program organizer and dir. 3rd Internat. Conf. on Refractory Depression, 1992, Napa Valley, Calif., 1995; prin. or co-investigator 53 internat. drug trials. Editor: Pharmacology of Depression: Applications for the Outpatient Practitioner, 1990, Refractory Depression, 1991 (with J. Mendels) Psychobiology of Affective Disorders, 1980, (with W. Nolan, J. Zohar S. Roose) Refractory Depression, 1994; assoc. editor Jour. Affective Disorders, 1986—, referee; asst. editor Psychosomatics, 1987—; referee asst. editor Psychosomatics, 1987—; referee Archives Gen. Psychiatry, Am. Jour. Psychiatry, Biol. Psychiatry, Jour. Clin. Psychopharmacology, Jour. Neuropsychiatry and Clin. Neuroscience, Psychoneuroendocrinology, Psychiatry Rsch., Psychosomatics, Psychosomatic Medicien, Psychobiology; contbr. 125 articles to med. and sci. jours., 275 presentations, abstracts, and invited papers in field. Grantee NIMH, 1980-81, 1980-85, 89—, Jack Warsaw Fund, 1984—; Biomedical Rsch. Support grantee NIH, 1989-90. Fellow Am. Psychiat. Assn. (advisor mood disorders work group for DSM-IV 1989—, Marie H. Eldredge award 1986), Am. Bd. Med. Psychotherapists; mem. Am. Fedn. for Clin. Rsch., Am. Assn. History Medicine, Internat. Soc. Psychoneuroendocrinology, Internat. Soc. for Investigation of Stress, Soc. Biol. Psychiatry (membership com. 1988-91), Pa. Psychiat. Soc., Phila. Psychiat. Soc. (exec. coun. 1985—, chair clin. rsch. resource com. 1989—). Home: PO Box 1931 Cherry Hill NJ 08034-0128

AMTOFT-NIELSEN, JOAN THERESA, physician, educator, researcher; b. Reading, Pa., Jan. 31, 1940; children: Andre Christian, Nikolaj Johan, Anja. BS, Kutztown (Pa.) State U., 1960; MD, Ansalt U. Munchen, Fed. Republic Germany, 1965; DC, Nat. Coll., 1968; MD, U. Copenhagen, 1978; postgrad., Harvard U., 1989-90, 91. Regional dir. Pa. Acad. Sci., Reading, 1961; intern Cook County Hosp., Chgo., 1966-68; clin. instr. U. Copenhagen, 1975-80; proctor N.C. Coalition Health, Durham, 1985-87; founder, cons. Triangle PMS Ctr., Cary, N.C., 1987—, also bd. dirs. Contbr. articles to profl. jours. Bd. dirs. shelter St. Francis Ho., Chapel Hill, N.C., 1989—; bd. dirs., grant coordinator N.C. Coalition Chs., Raleigh; v.p. Danish Red Cross, 1975-80; cons. physician Handicapped Encounter in Christ, Raleigh, 1984-87. NSF grantee, 1961; recipient award Sardoni Found., 1964, Walter Morris Found., 1957, Community Svc. award K.C., 1989. Mem. Am. Acad. Holistic Physicians, European Acad. Preventative Medicine, AAUW (v.p. Raleigh chpt. 1987—), NAFE, Scandinavian Club. Republican. Roman Catholic. Home: 218 Rosebrooks Dr Cary NC 27513-3609

AN, HOWARD S., physician, educator; b. Buffalo, N.Y., Sept. 19, 1956; m. Sue Kao, 1984; children: Jennifer, Steven. Intern Med. Coll. Ohio, Toledo, 1982-83, resident in orthopaedics, 1983-88; spine fellowship Thomas Jefferson U. Hosp. and Pa. Hosp., Phila., 1988-89; asst. prof. Med. Coll. Wis., Milw., 1989-92, assoc. prof., 1992—, chief spine orthopaedics, 1989—; chief spine orthopaedics VA Hosp., Milw., 1992—, Lakeland Med. Ctr., Elkhorn, Wis., 1991, West Allis (Wis.) Meml. Hosp., 1993. Mem. Nat. Spine Network, Orthopaedic Rshc. Soc., Am. Acad. Orthopaedic Surgeons, Acad. Orthopaedic Soc. (N.Am. travel fellow 1990), Cervical Spine Rsch. Soc., Am. Spinal Injury Assn., N.Am. Spine Soc. (Rsch. award 1993), Scolios Rsch. Soc. (travel fellow 1995), Internat. Soc. for the Study of Lumbar Spine, Mid-Am. Orthopaedic Assn., Acad. Traveling Orthopaedic Soc., AMA, Milw. County Med. Soc., State Med. Soc. Wis., Blount-Schmidt Spine Soc. Wis., Wis. Orthopaedic Soc., Milw. Orthopaedic Soc., Jefferson Orthopaedic Soc. Home: 4645 Hastings Dr Brookfield WI 53045-8158 Office: Med Coll Wis Physicians & Clinics/Froedtert E 9200 W Wisconsin Ave Milwaukee WI 53226-0099

ANAEBONAM, ALOYSIUS ONYEABO, pharmacist; b. Udi, Nigeria, June 25, 1955; came to the U.S., 1980; s. George Nwoye and Maria Nneka (Ofoedu) A.; m. Nneka Chinyere Esimai, Feb. 21, 1992. BS in Pharmacy, U. Nigeria, 1978; PhD, Mass. Coll. Pharmacy, 1986. Registered pharmacist, Nigeria. Rsch. scientist Pfeiffer Pharm. Sci. Labs., Boston, 1981-86; product devel. scientist Fisons Corp., Bedford, Mass., 1986-89; mgr. analytical devel. Fisons Corp., Rochester, N.Y., 1989-91; dir. product devel. and quality control Ascent Pharms., Inc., Billerica, Mass., 1991-94, asst. v.p. product devel. and quality control, 1994—; cons. Al-Consult, Rochester, 1990—. Author: Chewable Tablets, 1990, 89; contbr. articles to profl. jours. Mem. Am. Assn. Pharm. Sci., Rho Chi, Beta Simga (gov. 1976-77). Roman Catholic. Home: 301 Arboretum Way Burlington MA 01803-3829

ANAGNOSTE, VIVIAN GABRIELA, pathologist; b. Risnov, Romania, Mar. 16, 1929; came to U.S., 1973; d. Carlo and Jenny (Zuckman) Androniu; 1 child, Nicole. Student, Medico-Pharmaceutic, Bucharest, Romania, 1947-53. Intern Inst. Dr. Cantacuzino, Bucharest, 1952-53; rsch. nutritionist Inst. Hygiene, Bucharest, 1953-57; attendant, clin. lab. Trauma Hosp., Bucharest, 1957-60, I.C. Frimu Hosp., Bucharest, 1960-63; lab dir. Pantelimon Hosp., Bucharest, 1963-71, G. Alexandrescu Hosp., Bucharest, 1971-73; resident in pathology Middlesex Gen. Hosp., New Brunswick, N.J., 1974-77; clin. instr. Raritot Valley Hosp., New Brunswick, 1977-78; lab. dir. Rolling Hills Hosp., Elkins Park, Pa., 1978-91, Franklin Square Hosp., Phila., 1991-92, Metpath, Horsham, Pa., 1992—. Mem. Coll. Am. Pathologists, Internat. Acad. Pathology, Am. Soc. Clin. Pathologists, Pa. Assn. Clin. Pathologists. Democrat. Christian Orthodox. Home: 1385 Mill Rd Jenkintown PA 19046-2530 Office: Corning Clin Labs 800 Business Ctr Dr Horsham PA 19044-3408

ANAND, SURESH CHANDRA, physician; b. Mathura, India, Sept. 13, 1931; came to U.S., 1957, naturalized, 1971; s. Satchit and Sumaran (Bai) A. m. Wiltrud, Jan. 29, 1966; children: Miriam, Michael. MB, BS, King George's Coll., U. Lucknow (India), 1954; MS in Medicine, U. Colo., 1962. Diplomate Am. Bd. Allergy and Immunology. Fellow pulmonary diseases Nat. Jewish Hosp., Denver, 1957-58, resident in chest medicine, 1958-59, chief resident allergy-asthma, 1960-62; intern Mt. Sinai Hosp., Toronto, Ont., Can., 1962-63, resident in medicine, 1963-64, chief resident, 1964-65, demonstrator clin. technique, 1963-64, U. Toronto fellow in medicine, 1964-65; rsch. assoc. asthma-allergy Nat. Jewish Hosp., Denver, 1967-69; clin. instr. medicine U. Colo., Denver, 1967-69; internist Ft. Logan Mental Health Ctr., Denver, 1968-69; pres. Allergy Assocs. & Lab., Ltd., Phoenix, 1974—; mem. staff Phoenix Bapt. Hosp., chmn. med. records com., 1987; mem. staff St. Joseph's Hosp., St. Luke's Hosp., Human Hosp., John C. Lincoln Hosp., Good Samaritan Hosp., Phoenix Children's Hosp., Tempe St. Luke Hosp., Desert Samaritan Hosp., Mesa Luth. Hosp., Scottsdale Meml. Hosp., Phoenix Meml. Hosp., Chandler (Ariz.) Regional Hosp., Valley Luth. Hosp., Mesa, Ariz.; pres. NJH Fed. Credit Union, 1967-68. Contbr. articles to profl. jours. Mem. Camelback Hosp. Mental Health Ctr. Citizens Adv. Bd., Scottsdale, Ariz., 1974-80; mem. Phoenix Symphony Coun., 1973-90; mem. Ariz. Opera Co., Boyce Thmpson Southwestern Arboretum; mem. Ariz. Hist. Soc., Phoenix Arts. Mus., Smithsonian Inst. Fellow ACP, Am. Coll. Chest Physicians (crit. care com.), Am. Acad. Allergy, Am. Assn. Cert. Allergists, Am. Coll. Allergy and Immunology (aerobiology com., internat. com., pub. edn. com. 1991-94); mem. AAAS, AMA, Internat. Assn. Allergy and Clin. Immunology, Ariz. Med. Assn., Ariz. Allergy Soc. (v.p. 1988-90, pres. 1990-91), Maricopa County Med. Soc. (del. ariz. Med. Assn., bd. dirs. 1996-98, exec. com. 1996-98), West Coast Soc. Allergy and Immunology, Greater Phoenix Allergy Soc. (v.p. 1984-86, pres. 1986-88, med. adv. team sports medicine Ariz. State U.), Phoenix Zoo, N.Y. Acad. Scis., World Med. Assn., Internat. Assn. Asthmology, Assn. Care of Asthma, Ariz. Thoracic Soc., Nat. Geog. Soc., Ariz. Wild Life Assn., Village Tennis Club. Office: 1006 E Guadalupe Rd Tempe AZ 85283-3044 also: Ste 206 6550 East Broadway Mesa AZ 85206-1752 also: 7331 E Osborn Dr Ste 340 Scottsdale AZ 85251-6422

ANANIA, WILLIAM CHRISTIAN, podiatrist; b. Long Branch, N.J., May 11, 1958; s. Joseph John and Marie (Forgione) A.; m. Pamela Capone, Dec. 18, 1982; 1 child, William Christian Jr. BS in Biology, Villanova U., 1980; D of Podiatric Medicine, Ohio Coll. Podiatric Medicine, 1984. Diplomate Am. Acad. Pain Mgmt., Nat. Bd. Podiatry Examiners; diplomate in podiatric surgery and medicine, Am. Podiatric Med. Specialties Bd. Resident James C. Giuffré Med. Ctr., Phila., 1984-86; pvt. practice Middletown, N.J., 1986—; cons. Fern Med., Boston, 1991. Chmn. editorial review bd. The Contemporary Podiatric Physician; assoc. editor: Jour. Current Podiatric Medicine, 1986-89; contbr. numerous articles to profl. jours. Treas. Middletown Township Housing Corp., 1994. Named Dr. of the Month Jour. Current Podiatric Medicine, 1986. Fellow Am. Soc. Podiatric Medicine, Am. Soc. Podiatric Dermatology, Nat. Soc. Conscious Sedation (med. advisor 1989—); mem. Am. Podiatric Med. Assn., Middletown Area C. of C. (bd. dirs. 19888-90, 2d v.p. 1990-91, pres. 1993). Home & Office: #673 112 Tindall Rd Middletown NJ 07748-2337

ANANTH, JAMBUR, psychiatrist, educator; b. Hassan, Mysore, India, Apr. 27, 1932; s. Venkata Subbaiah and Gundamma (Nanjundaiah) A.; m. Kamala Maroor, Apr. 23, 1971; 1 child, Kartik. MD, Kasturba Med. Sch., Manipal, India, 1960; Diploma in Psychol. Medicine, Nat. Inst. Mental Health, Bangalore, India, 1963. Diplomate Am. Bd. Psychiatry and Neurology. Asst. prof. McGill U., Montreal, Que., Can., 1969-74, assoc. prof., 1974-81; prof. UCLA, 1981—; chief clin. investigations dept. psychiatry McGill U., 1969-71, dir. edn. and research dept. psychiatry, 1971-72; dir. edn. and research St. Mary's Hosp., Montreal, 1972-76; dir. biol. psychiatry Allan Meml. Inst., Montreal, 1976-81. Contbr. articles to profl. jours.; adv. editor: Psychosomatics, 1978-87. Grantee Dept. Mental Health State of Calif., 1983. Fellow Collegeum Internat. Neuropharmocologicum, Royal Coll. Psychiatrists, Am. Psychiat. Assn. (pres. Que. dist. br. 1978-79). Home: 2709 Via Pacheco Palos Verdes Peninsula CA 90274-4351 Office: Harbor-UCLA Med Ctr Dept Psychiat PO Box 2910 Torrance CA 90509-2910

ANAPLE, ELSIE MAE, medical, surgical and geriatrics nurse; b. Urbana, Ohio, Apr. 22, 1932; d. Marion N. and Mae Irene (Newell) Bodey; div.; children: Glenn, Gretchen, Gloria, Giselle, Gregory, Gordon, Gary. BSN, Ohio State U., 1955. Cert. med.-surg. nurse. Night supr. Shriner's Burn Inst., Cin., 1971-73; clin. instr. med.-surg. Deaconess Hosp. Sch. Nursing, Cin., 1973-75; staff nurse Good Samaritan Hosp., Cin., 1960-92; clin. nurse, staff nurse Univ. Hosp.-U. Cin., 1984-95, asst. head nurse med. unit, 1992; ret., 1995; part-time nurse Mercy Hosp., Fairfield, Ohio, 1980—. Active Cin. chpt. ARC, Our Lady of Rosary Ch. Mem. ANA, Ohio Nurses Assn., S.W. Ohio Dist. Nurses Assn.

ANASTASI, GASPAR WALTER, plastic surgeon; b. N.Y.C., 1967. MD, U. Ottawa, 1959. Intern Stamford Hosp., 1959-60; resident in surgery St. Albans U.S. Naval Hosp., 1961-65; resident in plastic surgery NYU Sch. Medicine, 1965-67; attending plastic surgeon Boston U. Med. Ctr.; pvt. practice; part-time acad. faculty. Office: Boston U Med Ctr 88 E Newton St Boston MA 02118*

ANASTASIO, COLLEEN M., critical care nurse; b. Elizabeth, N.J., Aug. 23, 1964; d. Arthur and Josephine (Praschak) Dakin; m. Andrew Anastasio, Sept. 17, 1988; children: Andrew, Connor. BS, Rutgers U., 1987. Cert. CPR, critical care nurse. Staff nurse JFK Med. Ctr., Edison, N.J., 1987-88; staff relief nurse Kimberly Quality Care, Union, N.J., 1988-90; pacemaker nurse Deborah Heart and Lund Ctr., Browns Mills, NJ, 1990-92; staff relief nurse Shore Care, Neptune, N.J., 1990—; home care nurse Kimberly Quality Care, Eatontown, N.J., 1992-93.

ANASTASIOU, MARY M., pediatrician; b. Leicester, U.K., June 11, 1954; came to U.S., 1980; d. Thalis and Elli Michaelides; m. Stephen Anastasiou, Jan. 4, 1980; children: Alex, Christine. MD, U. Athens, Greece, 1979. Intern, resident Kaiser Hosp., Oakland, Calif., 1982-85; pvt. practice Pleasanton, Calif., 1985—. Mem. Am. Acad. Pediatrics (Chpt. 1), Calif. Med. Assn., Alameda Contra Costa Med. Assn. Home: 3501 Kamp Dr Pleasanton CA 94588 Office: #240 5565 W Las Positas Blvd Pleasanton CA 94588

ANBAR, MICHAEL, biophysics educator; b. Danzig, June 29, 1927; came to U.S., 1967, naturalized, 1973; s. Joshua and Chava A.; m. Ada Komet, Aug. 11, 1953; children: Ran D., Ariel D. MSc, Hebrew U., Jerusalem, 1950, PhD, 1953. Instr. chemistry U. Chgo., 1953-55; sr. scientist Weizmann Inst. Sci., 1955-67; prof. Frienberg Grad. Sch., Rehovoth, Israel, 1960-67; sr. rsch. assoc. NASA Ames Rsch. Ctr., 1967-68; dir. phys. sci. SRI Internat., Menlo Park, Calif., 1968-72; dir. mass spectrometry research ctr. SRI Internat., 1972-77; prof. biophysical sci., chmn. dept. Sch. Medicine, SUNY, Buffalo, 1977-90, Faculty prof., dir. Interdeptl. Clin. Biophysics Group, 1990—, exec. dir. Health Instrument and Device Inst., 1983-85; assoc. dean applied research Sch. Medicine, SUNY, 1983-85; v.p. R & D AMARA Inc, Amherst, N.Y., 1992—. Author: The Hydrated Electron, 1970, The Machine of the Bedside: Strategies for Using Technology in Parient Care, 1984, Clinical Biophysics, 1985, Computers in Medicine, 1986, Quantitative Dynamic Telethermometry in Medical Diabnosis and Management, 1994; editor-in-chief: Thermology, 1993; contbr. articles to profl. jours. With Israeli Air Force, 1947-49. Grantee in field. Mem. IEEE, AAAS, IEEE Computer Soc., IEEE Engring. in Biology and Medicine Soc., Assn. Am. Med. Colls., Am. Inst. Physics, Am. Chem. Soc., Am. Inst. Ultrasound in Mediicne, Am. Assn. Clin. Chemistry, Am. Assn. Dental Rsch., Am. Assn. Mass Spectrometry, Am. Acad. Thermology, Am. Assn. Med. Systems Informatics, N.Y. Acad. Scis., Internat. Assn. Dental Rsch., Radiation Rsch. Soc., Engring. in Medicine and Biology Soc., Internat. Med. Informatics Assn., Internat. Soc. Optical Engring. Office: SUNY 118 Cary Hall Buffalo NY 14214

ANCES, I. G(EORGE), obstetrician, gynecologist, educator; b. Balt., July 3, 1935; s. Harry and Fanny A.; m. Marlene Roth, Oct. 23, 1966; 1 son, Beau Mark. B.S., U. Md., 1956, M.D., 1959. Diplomate: Am. Bd. Obstetrics and Gynecology. Intern Ohio State U. Hosp., 1959-60; resident in obstetrics and gynecology Univ. Hosp., Balt., 1960-61, 63-65; mem. faculty U. Md. Med. Sch., Balt., 1966—; prof. obstetrics and gynecology U. Md. Med. Sch., 1975-83, dir. labs. obstetrics and gynecol. research and clin. labs., 1967-83, dir. div. adolescent obstetrics and gynecology and family planning, 1981-83;; prof. ob-gyn. Rutgers U. Sch. Medicine,, Camden,, N.J.,, 1983—; chmn. dept., 1983—. Contbr. chpts. to books, articles to profl. jours. Capt. sustaining fund drive Balt. Symphony Orch., Opera Co. Phila.; med. adv. com. Fire Dept. Balt. City. Served with USAF, 1961-63. Recipient awards Robert Wood Johnson Sch. Medicine, 1989, 92, 96. Fellow Am. Coll. Obstetrics and Gynecology; mem. Endocrine Soc., Soc. Gynecol. Investigation, Soc. Study Reprodn. (charter), Internat. Soc. Rsch. in Biology Reprodn. (charter), Md. Obstetrics and Gynecol. Soc. (sec. 1978-81, dir. 1979—), Med. and Chirurgical Soc. Md., Soc. Adolescent Medicine, Douglas Obstet. and Gynecol. Soc. (pres. 1984—), N.J. State Med. Soc. (chmn. neo-natal coop. So. Jersey 1986—), Phila. Ob-Gyn. Soc., English Speaking Union, Cooper Found., N.J. Conservation Coun., Harbour League Club, Sigma Xi. Clubs: Maryland, Towson Golf and Country. Home: 1 Lane Of Acres Haddonfield NJ 08033-3504 Office: Rutgers U Sch Medicine Dept Ob-Gyn 3 Cooper Plz Camden NJ 08103-1438

ANCRUM, CHERYL DENISE, dentist; b. Bklyn., Sept. 28, 1958; d. Ida Jackson. BA in Psychology, Harvard U., Cambridge, 1980; DDS, Columbia U., N.Y., 1986, MPH, 1989. Dentist. Credit analyst Hartford (Conn.) Nat. Bank, 1980-81; statistical coding instr./analyst Aetna Ins. Co., Hartford, Conn., 1981-82; dental asst. Gouverneur Hosp., N.Y.C., 1983; clk. typist Columbia Presbyn. Med. Ctr., N.Y.C., 1984-86; gen. practice resident Beth Israel Med. Ctr., N.Y.C., 1986-87; dental attending Montefiore Med. Ctr., Bronx, 1987-90; rsch. assoc./dentist North Central Bronx Hosp., 1989-90; dental dir. Manhattan Men's Ho. of Detention, N.Y.C., 1989—; dental extern N. Central Bronx. Hosp., 1985-86. Vol. St. John Episc. Hosp., Bklyn., 1974-75, Mt. Auburn Hosp., Cambridge, 1978, Harlem Hosp., N.Y.C., 1987-88; health adv. Harvard U., Cambridge, 1977-80; active Sutton for Mayor Campaign, Bklyn., 1977; mem. Girl Scouts U.S., Bklyn., 1969-75, Operation PUSH, Hartford, 1981-82, Hartford Black Women Network, 1980-82, Kuumba Singers, Harvard U., 1977-80, New Temple Singers, Cambridge, 1977-80; mem. tape commn. Bridge St. A.M.E. Ch., Bklyn., 1987-88; fin. sec. Flower Guild, Allen A.M.E. Church, Queens, 1994—; bd. dirs. F.I.S.H. of Uniondale, 1991-96. Recipient scholarship A Better Chance, 1973-76, Am. Fund for Dental Health, 1982-84, Clark Found., 1983-86, selected profl. fellowship AAUW, 1985-86, Letter of Commendation, Columbia U., 1983, Applewhite award, 1986, William Bailey Dunning award, 1986, Lester R. Cain Pathology prize, 1986; named to Outstanding Young Women of Am., 1983. Mem. ADA, N.Y. State Dental Soc., Acad. of Gen. Dentistry, Am. Assn. of Pub. Health Dentistry, Am. Profl. Practice Assn., Order of the Ea. Star (Elizabeth Moore chpt. sec. 1996—), Delta Sigma Theta (Nassau alumnae chpt. journalist, 1992-96, 2d v.p., 1995-96). Democrat. Mem. African Methodist Episcopal Ch. Home: 1043 Tulsa St Uniondale NY 11553-1615

ANDARY, MICHAEL THOMAS, physician; b. Columbia, S.C., Oct. 10, 1957; s. Lee Sha and Catherine (Hammond) A.; m. Ellen Monahan, May 6, 1983; children: Catherine, Caroline, William, Michelle. BS, Mich. State U., 1979; MD, Wayne State U., 1983; MS, U. Washington, 1989. Rsch. asst., tchg. asst. Mich. State U., East Lansing, 1978-79; rotating intern Wayne State U., 1983-84; asst. prof. Mich. State U., East Lansing, 1989-92, assoc. prof., 1993—; resident in phys. medicine and rehab. U. Wash., Seattle, 1984-87, instr., 1987-88; residency dir. dept. phys. medicine and rehab. Mich. State U., East Lansing, 1993-96. Editor: Physical Medicine and Rehabilitation Clinics of North America-Outpatient Management of Pain, 1993. U. Wash. fellow, 1987-88. Fellow Am. Acad. Phys. Medicine and Rehab., Am. Assn. Electrodiagnostic Medicine (chmn. rsch. com. 1995-96); mem. Internat. Assn. for the Study of Pain, Assn. Acad. Physiatrists. Roman Catholic. Office: Mich State Univ Coll Osteo Medicine B-401 W Fee East Lansing MI 48824

ANDERHUB, BETH MARIE, medical educator; b. St. Louis, Feb. 7, 1953; d. Anthony Pierre and Eleanor (Corich) A. A in Applied Sci., Forest Park C.C., St. Louis, 1974; BS in Radiologic Tech., U. Mo., 1975; MEd, St. Louis U., 1989, postgrad., 1989—. Cert. radiologic tech., nuclear medicine, abdominal sonography, ob-gyn sonography. Nuclear medicine and ultrasound technician VA Hosp., St. Louis, 1976-79; ultrasound technologist, sr. sonographer Deaconess Hosp., St. Louis, 1979-82, chief sonographer, 1982-83; assoc. prof., dir. ultrasound program St. Louis C.C., 1983—; chmn. accreditation com. Ultrasound Program, Englewood, Colo., 1990-95; v.p. Commn. on Accreditation for Allied Health Program, 1994-1996; lectr., presenter programs in field confs., symposia, colls., univs. Author: Manual on Abdominal Sonography, 1983, General Sonography, 1994; contbr. articles to profl. jours. Fellow Soc. Diagnostic Med. Sonographers (chmn. edn. com. 1984-86, contbg. editor Jour. Diagnostic Med. Sonography 1984-89, bd. dirs. 1986-89, v.p. 1989-91, pres.-elect 1991-93, pres. 1993-95, treas. ednl. found. 1988-91, other coms.), Am. Soc. Radiologic Technologists (bd. dirs. 1982-85, task force modality del. roles 1988-89, rep. sonography summit 1988, chmn. ultrasound com. 1980, 82-85, others), Am. Inst. Ultrasound in Medicine, Mo. Soc. Radiologic Technologists (pres. 1979-80, pres. 4th dist. 1978-79). Home: 12449 Dawn Hill Dr Maryland Hts MO 63043-3636 Office: St Louis C C 5600 Oakland Ave Saint Louis MO 63110-1316

ANDERLONIS-FULTON, MARY JO, critical care nurse, administrator; b. DuBois, Pa., Aug. 1, 1950; d. Joseph William and Jane Celine (Radzavich) Anderlonis; m. Robert Matthew Fulton, Aug. 21, 1987; 1 child, Robert Matthew Fulton Jr. Diploma in Nursing, Spencer Hosp. Sch. Nursing, Meadville, Pa., 1971; BA, Edinboro U., 1988; M.Healthcare Adminstrn., Gannon U., 1991. Staff nurse emergency dept. Hamot Med. Ctr., Erie, Pa., 1971-73, head nurse emergency rm., 1973-78, coord. emergency svc., 1978-79, dir. ambulatory svc., 1979-93; v.p. ops. Hamot Med. Ctr., 1993-95; chief nursing officer, 1995—. Nursing adv. com. Pa. Emergency Health Svc. Coun., Harrisburg, 1985-91, med. adv. com., 1988-90; founding mem. and bd. dirs. Erie SIDS, 1977; bd. dirs. St. Paul's Free Clinic, 1995—. Named Outstanding Young Woman of Am., Humanitarian of the Yr., Erie County EMS Coun.; recipient Dorothy Novello Award for Volunteerism Nursing Dept. of Hamot Med. Ctr., 1985. Mem. Emergency Nurses Assn., Am. Coll. Health Care Execs., Am. Orgn. Nurse Execs. Roman Catholic. Home: 2821 Lafayette Rd Erie PA 16506-2425 Office: Hamot Med Ctr 201 State St Erie PA 16550-0002

ANDERMAN, IRVING INGERSOLL, dentist; b. N.Y.C., June 10, 1918; s. Louis and Regina (Mandel) A.; m. Georgia Gordon, Feb. 14, 1943; children: Susan, Robert. BS, CCNY, 1938; DDS, NYU, 1942. Diplomate Am. Bd. Oral Electrosurgery. Pvt. practice Middletown, N.Y., 1946—; clin. instr. NYU, N.Y.C., 1947-48; vis. lectr. dental sch. NYU, N.Y.C., 1965-80, 9th Dist. Tchg. Ctr., Hawthorne, N.Y., 1965-94; adj. prof., chmn. dental hygiene adv. bd. Orange County C.C.,Middletown, 1965—; mem. Orange County Bd. Health, 1985-93. Co-author: Electrosurgery in Dental Practice, 1976, Dental Clinics of North America, 1982; contbr. articles to profl. jours. Chmn. Middletown Housing Authority, 1955—; disaster chmn. ARC, 1960-62; mem. exec. bd., dist. commr. Boy Scouts Am., Orange County, 1947—. Recipient gold medal 9th Dist. Dental Soc., 1984. Fellow Am. Coll. Dentists (Diamond Pin Svc. award), Am. Acad. Oral Medicine (acad.), Internat. Coll. Dentists, Soc. Physiology and Occlusion (pres.), Acad. Gen. Dentistry; mem. AAAS, Internat. Assn. Dental Rsch., n.Y. Acad. Scis., Kiwanis Internat. (pres., disting. svc. award 1979). Republican. Jewish. Office: 3 Linden Pl Middletown NY 10940-4803

ANDERSEN, ANITA MARIA, psychiatrist, osteopath; b. Calcutta, India, Nov. 6, 1954; came to U.S., 1963; d. Anthony Cajetan and Irene Eufemia (Azevedo) DiSouza; m. Gregory Alan Andersen, Sept. 6, 1982; 1 child, Lisa Marie. BS magna cum laude, N.E. Mo. State U., 1980; DO, Okla. State U., Tulsa, 1987. Rsch. asst. in biology NE. Mo. State U., Kirksville, 1978-80; resident in pathology U. Kans., Wichita, 1987-88, resident in psychiatry, 1988-92; resident and fellow in child psychiatry U. Kans., Kansas City, 1994-95. Regents scholar N.E. Mo. State U., 1976-80. Mem. AMA, Am. Med. Women's Assn. Roman Catholic.

ANDERSEN, BURTON ROBERT, physician, educator; b. Chgo., Aug. 27, 1932; s. Burton R. and Alice C. (Mara) A.; m. Susan Berg; children: Ellen C., Julia A., Brian E., Jennifer Berg. Student, Northwestern U., 1950-51; BS, U. Ill., Urbana, 1953; MS, U. Ill., Chgo., 1957; MD, U. Ill., 1957. Intern Mpls. Gen. Hosp., 1957-58; resident and fellow U. Ill. Hosp., 1958-61; clin. assoc. NIH, Bethesda, Md., 1961-64; asst. prof. U. Rochester, N.Y., 1964-67; assoc. prof. Northwestern U., 1967-70; prof. medicine and microbiology U. Ill., Chgo., 1970—, chief infectious diseases, 1986—; chief infectious diseases West Side VA Med. Ctr., 1970-90. Contbr. sci. research articles to profl. jours. Served as sr. surgeon USPHS, 1961-63. Fellow ACP; mem. Am. Assn. Immunologists, Am. Soc. for Clin. Research, Central Soc. for Clin. Research. Office: U Ill Sect Infectious Diseases 808 S Wood St Chicago IL 60612-7317

ANDERSEN, DANA KIMBALL, surgeon, educator; b. Utica, N.Y., Mar. 6, 1946; s. Cyril C. and Elizabeth (Kimball) A.; m. Ronnie Ann Rosenthal, Oct. 22, 1983. AB, Duke U., 1968, MD, 1972. Diplomate Am. Bd. Internal Medicine, Am. Bd. Surgery. Intern, resident internal medicine Duke U. Med. Ctr., Durham, N.C., 1972-73, resident gen. surgery, 1974, 76-79, instr. surgery, 1979-80; asst. prof. medicine and surgery SUNY-Downstate Med. Ctr., Bklyn., 1980-85, assoc. prof., 1985-89; prof. surgery and medicine, dir. surg. residency program U. Chgo., 1990—; clin. assoc. NIH, Balt., 1974-76; asst. in internal medicine Johns Hopkins U., Balt., 1974-76; cons. surgery VA Med. Ctr., Bklyn., 1982-89; dir. surg. research lab. SUNY Health Scis. Ctr., 1982-86, dir. surg. residency program, 1986-89. Contbr. articles to profl. jours., chpts. to books. Lt. comdr. USPHS, 1974-76. NIH grantee, 1983—; Am. Surg. Assn. Found. fellow, 1982-84. Fellow ACS; mem. Am. Surg. Assn., Assn. for Acad. Surgery (pres. 1989-90), Am. Gastroenterol. Assn., Soc. for Surgery of Alimentary Tract, Soc. Univ. Surgeons, Am. Assn. Endocrine Surgeons, Surg. Biology Club I, Sigma Xi, Alpha Omega Alpha. Episcopalian. Avocations: photography, sailing. Office: U Chgo Dept Surgery 5841 S Maryland Ave Chicago IL 60637-1463

ANDERSEN, LEIF PERCIVAL, physician; b. Copenhagen, Apr. 27, 1951; s. John Eivin Percival and Inger Viola Andrea (Wiberg) A.; m. Annemarie Skovshoved Petersen, July 23, 1977; children: Tine Skovshoved, Henrik Percival, Karsten Wiberg. MD, U. Copenhagen, 1982. Physician dept. organ surgery Cen. Hosp., Hillerød, Denmark, 1983; physician internal medicine Sundby Hosp., Copenhagen, 1984-86; med. doctor infectious diseases dept. medicine Rigshospitalet, Copenhagen, 1985-86; med. registrar clin. microbiolgoy Cen. Hosp., Hillerød, 1985; med. doctor dept. virology Statens Seruminstitut, Copenhagen, 1986-88; med. sr.registrar dept. clin. microbiology Rigshopitalet, Copenhagen, 1988-91; med. doctor dept. clin. microbiology Statens Seruminstitut, Copenhagen, 1992-93; med. sr. registrar dept. clin. microbiology Hillerød Hosp., 1994-95; sr. registrar dept. clin. microbiology Nat. U. Hosp., Copenhagen, 1995—; mem., coord. European study group on cellular immunology in helicobacter infections. Grantee Brochades pharma Denmark, 1988-92, Danish Med. Rsch. Coun., 1989—, Found. for Promotion of Med. Rsch., 1990-92; recipient Hoechst Denmark's Antibiotic award, 1992. Mem. Danish Med. Soc., Danish Helicobacter Pylori Study Group, Danish Soc. for Clin. Microbiology, Scandinavian Soc. for Antimicrobial Chemotherapy, European Soc. for Clin. Microbiology and Infectious Diseases, European Helicobacter Pylori Study Group (organizing com.), Am. Soc. Microbiology, Danish Soc. Gastroenterology. Office: Rigshospitalets Helicobacter Lab Dept Clin Microbiology, Juliane Mariesvej 22, DK 2100 Copenhagen 0, Denmark

ANDERSEN, LUBA, electrologist, electropigmentologist; b. Germany, Mar. 29, 1945; came to U.S., 1955; d. Osyp and Justyna (Drozd) Nahorniak; m. Roger A. Andersen, Dec. 9, 1989. A in Bus. and Acctg., DePaul U., 1977; BS in Commerce and Social Studies, LaSalle U., 1978; postgrad., U. Mich., 1984; cert., Ariz. Inst. Electrolysis, 1993. Cert. profl. electrologist, clin. electropigmentologist. From analyst to contr. Fed. Home Loan Bank, Chgo., 1965-83, v.p., contr., 1985-92; owner electrolysis and permanent cosmetic enhancement clinic The Electrolysis Connection, Tucson, 1993—. Mem. NAFE, Am. Soc. Women Accts. (chairperson bylaws com. 1981), Am. Electrology Assn., Electrologists Assn. Ill., Internat. Guild Profl. Electrologists, Inc., Fin. Mgrs. Soc., Soc. Cosmetic Profls., Assn. Clin. Electropigmentologists. Republican. Roman Catholic. Office: Electrolysis Connection Ste 110 3131 N Country Club Rd Tucson AZ 85716

ANDERSEN, MARIANNE SINGER, clinical psychologist; b. Baden nr. Vienna, Austria; came to U.S., 1940, naturalized, 1946; d. Richard L. and Jolanthe (Garda) Singer; 1 son, Richard Esten. BA, CUNY, 1950, MA, 1974; PhD, Fla. Inst. Tech., 1980. Rsch. assoc. Inst. for Rsch. in Hypnosis, N.Y.C., 1974-76, fellow in clin. hypnosis, 1976, dir. seminars, 1978-82, dir. edn., 1982—; psychotherapist specializing in hypnotherapy Morton Prince Ctr. for Hypnotherapy, dir. clin. services, 1981-82; dir. adminstrn. Internat. Grad. U., N.Y.C., 1974-77; pvt. practice psychotherapy, 1977—; adminstrv. coordinator Internat. Grad. Sch. Behavior Sci., Fla. Inst. Tech., 1978; co-dir. The Melbourne Group, 1983—; clin. instr. hypnotherapy Mt. Sinai Sch. Medicine, N.Y.C., 1996; lectr. hypnosis and hypnotherapy to mental and phys. health profls., 1977—. Author: (with Louis Savary) Passages: A Guide for Pilgrims of the Mind, 1972; rsch. on treatment obesity with hypnotherapy; book editor specializing in psychology and psychiatry including W.W. Norton Co., Sterling Pub. Co., E.P. Dutton Co., 1950-71. Fellow Soc. for Clin. and Exptl. Hypnosis; mem. Internat. Soc. for Clin. and Exptl. Hypnosis, Am. Psychol. Assn., N.Y. Acad. Scis. Home: 60 W 57th St New York NY 10019-3911

ANDERSEN, OLAF SPARRE, physiology educator, biophysicist; b. Hellerup, Denmark, Sept. 10, 1945; came to U.S., 1972; s. Erik Sparre and Kirsten (Kirketerp-Møller) A.; m. Johanne Juul Jørgensen, Dec. 22, 1973; children: Jesper S., Martin S. MD, U. Copenhagen, 1971. Postgrad. tng. Rockefeller U., N.Y.C., 1973; asst. prof. physiology Cornell U. Med. Coll., N.Y.C., 1973-77, assoc. prof., 1977-82; prof. Cornell U. Med. Ctr., N.Y.C., 1982—; mem. physiology study sect. NIH, Bethesda, Md., 1982-86. Assoc. editor Jour. Gen. Physiology, 1984-95, editor 1995—; contbr. articles to Biophys. Jour., Jour. Gen. Physiology, Biochemistry, Jour. Molecular Biology. Bd. dirs. N.Y. Heart Assn., 1985-95; pres. N.Y. affiliate Am. Heart Assn., 1992-93. Grantee A.W. Mellon Found., 1974-76, N.Y. Heart Assn., 1975-79, Irma T. Hirschl Fund, 1979-83. Mem. Biophys. Soc., Soc. Gen. Physiologists (pres.-elect 1995—), Am. Physiol. Soc., Soc. for Neurosci., Royal Danish Acad. Scis. and Letters (fgn. mem.). Office: Cornell U Med Coll 1300 York Ave New York NY 10021-4805

ANDERSEN, RONALD MAX, health services educator, researcher; b. Omaha, 1939; s. Max Adolph and Evangeline Dorothy (Wobbe) A.; m. Diane Borella, June 19, 1965; 1 dau., Rachel. B.S., U. Santa Clara, 1960; M.S., Purdue U., 1962, Ph.D., 1968. Research assoc. Purdue U., West Lafayette, Ind., 1962-63; assoc. study dir. Nat. Opinion Research Ctr., Chgo., 1963-66; research assoc. U. Chgo., 1963-77, assoc. prof., then prof. Grad. Sch. Bus., 1974-90, dir. Program in Health Adminstrn. and Ctr. for Health Adminstrn. Studies, 1980-90; Wasserman prof. dept. health svcs. and sociology UCLA, 1991—, chair dept. health svcs., 1993—; chmn. editl. bd. Health Adminstrn. Press, Chgo., 1980-83, 88—, Med. Care Rsch. & Rev., 1994—; mem. coms. Agy. for Health Care Policy and Rsch., Rockville, Md., 1970—. Author: A Decade of Health Services, 1967, Two Decades of Health Service, 1976, Total Survey Error, 1979, Health Services in the U.S., 1980, Ambulatory Care and Insurance Coverage in an Era of Constraint, 1987, Training Physicians, 1994. NIH fellow, 1960-62; grantee Robert Wood Johnson Found., 1983, Kaiser Family Found., 1983, Agy. for Health Care Policy and Rsch., 1982, WHO, 1990. Mem. Am. Sociol. Assn. (chmn. med. sociology sect. 1980-81, Disting. Med. Sociologist 1994), Nat. Acad. Scis., Nat. Inst. Medicine, Assn. for Health Services Research (dir. 1981-83), Am. Pub. Health Assn., Assoc. Univ. Program in Health Adminstrn. Roman Catholic. Home: 10724 Wilshire Blvd Apt 312 Los Angeles CA 90024-4453 Office: UCLA Sch Pub Health Los Angeles CA 90024

ANDERSEN, STEVE RICHARD, health care executive; b. Vermillion, S.D., Dec. 8, 1946; s. Elton Emil and Ruby Lee (Bagley) A.; m. Christie Joann Stater, June 14, 1969; children: Eric Steven, Amy Marie. AA in Natural Sci., Riverside City Coll., Calif., 1966; BS in Pharmacy, U. Pacific, 1970; MBA in Fin., Calif. State U., San Bernardino, 1982. Lic. pharmacist, Calif., Nev., Tex. Staff pharmacist Kaiser Found. Hosp., Sacramento, Calif., 1970-71, Riverside (Calif.) Gen. Hosp., 1971, St. Bernardine Med. Ctr., San Bernardino, Calif., 1971-74; dir. pharmacy svcs. St. Bernardine Med. Ctr., San Bernardino, 1974-82; dir. pharmacy svcs. Sisters of Charity Health Care System, Houston, 1982-85, dir. bus. devel., 1985-90, dir. planning and bus.

devel., 1990-93; v.p. planning and strategic devel. Sisters of Charity of Leavenworth(Kans.)/Health Svcs. Corp., 1994—; pres. Caritas, Inc., 1996—; bd. dirs. Primera Healthcare, L.L.C., St. James Cmty. Hosp.; pres. Caritas, Inc. Mgr. youth baseball, Spring, Tex., 1985; bd. dirs. Northland Cmty. Ch. Recipient Order of the Golden Sword, Am. Cancer Soc., San Bernardino, Calif., 1975. Mem. Am. Coll. Health Care Execs. (diplomate), Am. Soc. Hosp. Planners and Marketers. Office: Sisters Charity Leavenworth Health Svc Corp 4200 S 4th St Leavenworth KS 66048-5054

ANDERSEN, SUSAN MARIE, researcher, educator, clinician. BA in Psychology magna cum laude, U. Calif., Santa Cruz, 1977; PhD in Psychology, Stanford U., 1981. Asst. prof. psychology Univ. Calif., Santa Barbara, 1981-87; assoc. prof. NYU, N.Y.C., 1987-94, prof., 1994—; mem. grants panel, social and group processes rev. panel NIMH, 1992-94. Assoc. editor Jour. Social and Clin. Psychology, 1987-92, Social Cognition, 1993, Jour. Personality and Social Psychology, 1994-95; ad hoc reviewer Jour. Communication Rsch., Jour. Exptl. Psychology, Learning, Memory & Cognition, Jour. Exptl. Social Psychology, Jour. Personality, Jour. Rsch. in Personality, Jour. Social and Clin. Psychology, Motivation and Emotion; author numerous behavioral sci. articles and book chpts. NIMH grantee, 1985-86, 92—. Mem. APA, Am. Psychol. Soc., Soc. for Exptl. Social Psychology. Office: Dept Psychology NYU 6 Washington Pl Fl 4 New York NY 10003-6634

ANDERSON, ALLAMAY EUDORIS, health educator, home economist; b. N.Y.C., July 18, 1933; d. John Samuel and Charlotte Jane (Harrigan) Richardson; B.A., Queens Coll., CUNY, 1975; profl. mgmt. cert. Adelphi U., 1978; M.S. in Edn., Fordham U., 1984; m. Edgar Leopold Anderson, Jr., Apr. 14, 1957; 1 son, David Lancelot. Mem. staff sch. food service, dietitian Bd. Edn., N.Y.C., 1968-88; tchr. home and career skills Louis Armstrong Middle Sch., 1988; spl. edn. tchr. Manhattan High Sch., N.Y.C., 1989-95, coord AIDS resource, 1995, ret. 1995; profl. devel. cons., N.Y.C., 1978—; ptnr. Masiba Bldg. Corp., Corona, N.Y., 1975-82; adj. lectr. home econs. Queens Coll., 1987; owner AEA Devel. Svc., 1987—. Devel. coord. League for Better Community Life, Inc., 1977; treas. exec. bd., 1970-76; officer N.Y.C. Community Devel. Agy., 1980-83; mem. Kwanzaa Adv. Com. (P.R.) Urban Coalition, 1983, L.I. # 28 Episcopal Cursillo, 1991; vestry mem. youth ministries Grace Episcopal Ch., 1982-85, vestry mem., 1996—; mem. NAACP (local Women's History Month honoree). Recipient Elmcor Community Svc. award Elmcor Youth and Adult Activities, Inc., 1989. Mem. Nat. Soc. Fund Raising Execs., Langston Hughes Libr. Action Com. (bd. dirs. 1987—, treas. 1989), Queens Coll. Home Econs. Alumni Assn. (v.p., chmn. bylaws com. 1982), United Fedn. Tchrs./Retired Tchrs. Chpt., Libr. Action Com. (chair Kwanzaa 1994-96), Phi Delta Kappa. Office: 10013 34th Ave Flushing NY 11368-1052

ANDERSON, ARLO CONRAD, orthopedic surgeon; b. Jamestown, N.Y., Apr. 27, 1932; s. Conrad A. and Clara (Fluck) A.; m. Marjorie R. Anderson, June 4, 1964; children: John, Richard, Catherine. AB, Anderson (Ind.) U., 1955; MD, Jefferson U., 1961. Diplomate Am. Bd. Orthopedic Surgery, Am. Acad. Orthopedic Surgery, ACS. Intern Bryn Mawr (Pa.) Hosp., 1961-62; resident in gen. surgery Lankenau Hosp., Phila., 1962-63; resident in orthpedic surgery Geisinger Med. Ctr., Danville, Pa., 1963-66; pvt. practice Norristown (Pa.) Orthopedic Assocs., 1966—; chief orthopedic surgery dept. Sacred Heart Hosp., Norristown, Pa., 1990—; mem. attending staff orthopedic surgery dept. Sacred Heart Hosp., Norristown, 1966—, Montgomery Hosp., 1966—. Home: 1660 Williams Way Norristown PA 19403-3372 Office: Norristown Orthopedic Assocs 1308 Dekalb St Norristown PA 19401-3404

ANDERSON, ARTHUR OSMUND, pathologist, immunologist, army officer; b. N.Y.C., Mar. 12, 1945; s. Arthur Edmund and Florence Ranveig (Osmundsen) A.; m. Julane Kay Pynn, Oct. 4, 1969; 1 child, Phoebe MacDonald Anderson. BS, Wagner Coll., 1966; MD, U. Md., 1970. Diplomate Am. Bd. Pathology. Intern in pathology Johns Hopkins Hosp., Balt., 1970-71, fellow in exptl. pathology, 1970-74, resident in pathology, 1971-73; commd. 2d lt. U.S. Army, 1974, advanced through grades to col., 1988; asst. prof. biology and pathology U. Pa., Phila., 1980-83; prin. investigator pathology div. U.S. Army Med. Rsch. Inst. Infectious Diseases, Ft. Detrick, Md., 1974-80, chief respiratory immunity, 1983—, chmn. human investigational rev. bd., 1976-80, 84—. Contbr. numerous articles to profl. jours., chpts. to immunology text books. Decorated Meritorious Svc. medal; N.Y. State Regents scholar, 1962-66. Mem. Found. for Advanced Edn. in Scis., Am. Assn. Immunologists, Am. Assn. Pathologists, Kiwanis (pres. Frederick 1988-89), Beta Beta Beta, Omicron Delta Kappa. Republican. Office: US Army Med Rsch Inst Infectious Diseases Fort Detrick Frederick MD 21702

ANDERSON, BARRY STANLEY, health care educator; b. Atlanta, Sept. 6, 1942; s. Rex and Virginia A.; m. Katherine Krupp, Dec. 26, 1966 (div. 1973); 1 child, Jon Robert; m. Patricia Ann O'Neil, May 25, 1974; children: Russell Barry, Robert Bruce. AA, Foothill Coll., 1968; BA, San Francisco State U., 1976; MBA, U. N.D., 1984. V.p. Ventilation Assocs., Inc., Houston, 1971-74; program dir. Inst. Med. Studies, Berkeley, Calif., 1976-78; program dir. Sch. Respiratory Care, St. Alexius Med. Ctr., Bismarck, N.D., 1978-84, health care cons., dir. edn., 1984-87; mgr. respiratory care ops. Medisys Mgmt. System, 1988; program dir. Mt. Diablo Adult Edn. Ctr., Concord, Calif., 1988-91; ptnr. Profl. Data Resources, Vacaville, Calif., 1990-91, Virginia Beach, Va., 1991—; instr. Entrepreneurial Mgmt. Bus. Tng. Internat., Sacramento, 1988-90; adj. asst. prof. Chapman Coll., Vallejo, Calif., 1990-91; chmn. bd. dirs., pres. Creative Mktg., Inc., Bismarck (N.D.), Vacaville (Calif.), 1982—, Virginia Beach; v.p. Baby Products Ltd., 1987-88; asst. prof. U. of Mary, 1982-85; instr. bus. edn. div. Solano Community Coll., Suisun, Calif., 1988-91; asst. prof. Tidewater Community Coll., Virginia Beach, 1991—. Author: (with D. Quesinberry) Blood Gas Interpretations, 1974; mem. editorial adv. bd. Respiratory Mgmt.; contbr. articles to profl. jours. Mem. Am. Mktg. Assn., Am. Mgmt. Assn., Am. Hosp. Assn., Acad. for Health Svcs. Mktg., Assn. MBA Execs., Am. Coll. Healthcare Execs., Ctr. for Entrepreneurial Mgmt., U. N.D. Alumni Assn., Elks. Avocations: computer programming, writing, reading, lecturing, sailing. Office: Tidewater Community Coll 1700 College Cres Virginia Beach VA 23456-1918

ANDERSON, BRYAN K., ophthalmologist; b. Camden, S.C., Dec. 6, 1958; s. Arthur Bryan and Mary Ann (McAlister) A.; m. Tina Jean Patrick, June 60, 1981; children: Michael St. Bryan, Patrick Keith, Eric Nathaniel. BS, U. S.C., 1980, MD, 1984. Diplomate Am. Bd. Ophthalmology. Resident Roanoke (Va.) Meml. Hosp., 1984-85; resident in ophthalmology Vanderbilt U. Med. Ctr., Nashville, 1985-88; ophthalmologist Rock Hill (S.C.) Eye Ctr., 1988—. Bd. dirs. York County chpt. ARC, Rock Hill, 1989-95. Mem. S.C. Soc. Ophthalmology (bd. dirs. 1989—), Lions (bd. dirs. eye bank 1992—). Office: Rock Hill Eye Clinic 1565 Ebenezer Rd Rock Hill SC 29730

ANDERSON, CARLA LEE, psychologist; b. Edgeley, N.D., Nov. 26, 1930; d. Carl Erick and Ruth Johanna (Isaacson) Erickson; m. Wayne Perry Anderson, Dec. 22, 1952; children: Jerilyn, Debra, Rosalyn, Stephanie. BA, Jamestown Coll., 1952; MA, U. Del., 1964; MS, U. Mo., Columbia, 1977; PhD, U. Mo., 1978. Lic. psychologist, Mo. Tchr. Gilby (N.D.) High Sch., 1952-54, Moberly (Mo.) Jr. Coll., 1954-55, Hickman High Sch., Columbia, Mo., 1955-56; counseling intern U. Mo., Columbia, 1975-77; asst. prof. overseas counseling program Ball State U., Fed. Republic of Germany, 1979; psychologist Ctr. for Family & Individual Counseling, Columbia, 1979-96; pvt. practice Columbia, 1996—. Contbr. articles to profl. jours. Chair, bd. dirs. Unitarian-Universalist Ch., Columbia, 1985-86. Mem. Am. Psychol. Assn., Mo. Psychol. Assn., Mid-Mo. Network Women in Psychology (chair 1984-86). Home and Office: 1017 Prospect St Columbia MO 65203-2352

ANDERSON, CAROLE ANN, nursing educator; b. Chgo., Feb. 21, 1938; d. Robert and Marian (Harrity) Irving; m. Clark Anderson, Feb. 14, 1973; 1 child, Julie. Diploma, St. Francis Hosp., 1958; BS, U. Colo., 1962, MS, 1963, PhD, 1977. Group psychotherapist Dept. Vocat. Rehab., Denver, 1963-72; psychotherapist Prof. Psychiatry and Guidance Clinic, Denver, 1970-71; asst. prof., chmn. nursing sch. U. Colo., Denver, 1971-75; therapist, coordinator The Genessee Mental Health, Rochester, N.Y., 1977-78; assoc. dean U. Rochester, N.Y., 1978-86; dean, prof. Coll. Nursing Ohio State U., Columbus, 1986—; lectr. nursing sch. U. Colo., Denver, 1970-71; prin. investigator biomed. rsch. support grant, 1986-93, clin. rsch. facilitation grant, 1981-82; program dir. profl. nurse traineeship, 1978-86, advanced nurse tng. grant, 1982-85. Author: (with others) Women as Victims, 1986, Violence Toward Women, 1982, Substance Abuse of Women, 1982; editor Nursing Outlook, 1993—. Pres., bd. dirs. Health Assn., Rochester, 1984-86; mem. north sub area council Finger Lakes Health Systems Agy., 1983-86, longrange planning com., 1981-82; mem. Columbus Bd. Health; dir. Netcare Mental Health Ctr. Am. Acad. Nursing fellow. Mem. ANA, Am. Social. Assn., Ohio Nurses Assn., Am. Assn. Colls. Nursing (bd. dirs. 1992-94, pres.-elect 1994-96, pres. 1996—), Sigma Theta Tau. Home: 406 W 6th Ave Columbus OH 43201-3137 Office: The Ohio State Univ Coll Nursing 1585 Neil Ave Columbus OH 43210-1216

ANDERSON, CYNTHIA FINKBEINER SJOBERG, speech and language pathologist; b. Hastings, Mich., Dec. 7, 1949; d. Charles Lavern and Lois Mae (Kenyon) Finkbeiner; m. Peter Carl Sjoberg, Sept. 6, 1974 (div. Dec. 1981); 1 child, Hilary Kenyon; m. Donald Anderson, Sept. 16, 1985 BS, Western Mich. U., 1972, MA, 1974. Dir. speech Hackley Hosp., Muskegon, Mich., 1974-75; speech pathologist Grand Haven Pub. Schs., Mich., 1975—; dir. Ambucs Summer Lang. Clinic, Grand Haven, 1984—. Creator summer lang. program. Pres. Kiddie Carousel, Grand Haven, 1983-86; Stephen minister Christ Community Ch., Spring Lake, Mich., 1984—, elder, 1986—, mem. bd. trustees, 1991—; big sister Grand Haven, 1975-80; mem. allocations bd. Tri-Cities Area United Fund, 1995—; mem. bd. dirs. Camp Blue Bird, 1995—. Named Ambucs Nat. Therapist of Yr., 1985; recipient Excellence in Service award Grand Haven Pub. Schs., 1987. Mem. Am. Speech/Hearing/Lang. Assn. (cert.). Democrat. Home: 2102 Jane Ct Grand Haven MI 49417-2506 Office: Grand Haven Pub Schs 1415 S Beechtree St Grand Haven MI 49417-2843

ANDERSON, DENNIS LEE, pathologist; b. Des Moines, Aug. 2, 1943; s. Eldon LaRae and Virginia Faye (Mauck) A.; m. Linda Christine Anderson, Mar. 4, 1968; children: Eric Lee, Bryan Kristofer. MD, U. Health Scis., Des Moines, 1971. Diplomate Am. Bd. Pathology. Commd. 2d lt. USN, 1968, advanced through grades to comdr.; head hematology Madigan Army Hosp., Tacoma, 1975-76, head anatomic pathology, 1976-77; head pathology dept. UHS-COMS, Des Moines, 1977-78; head chemistry Oakland (Calif.) Naval Hosp., 1978-79; head anatomic pathology Great Lakes (Ill.) Naval Hosp., 1979-80; resident in anesthesia Portsmouth (Va.) Naval Hosp., 1980-81; head anatomic pathology Kansas City (Mo.) Med. Ctr., 1981-82; owner lab. Anpathic, Davenport, Iowa, 1982-88; head anatomic pathology USN, Jacksonville, N.C., 1988-89, Camp Pendelton, Calif., 1990-93; head dpe. pathology USN Hosp., Pensacola, Fla., 1993—. Author: (with ohters) Podiatric Medicine, 1988. Fellow Am. Bd. Pathology, Coll. Am. Pathologists; mem. NRA. Home: 3024 Knotty Pine Dr Pensacola FL 32505-1852

ANDERSON, DONALD LEE, psychologist b. Litchfield, Ill., May 31, 1929; s. Robert James and Nita Mae (MacDonald) A.; m. Jeanne Rodgers, Nov. 2, 1950; children: Cheryl, Kathy, Merri Lee. BA, W.J. Bryan Coll., Dayton, Tenn., 1951; PhD, U. Tex., 1971. Lic. psychologist, Tex.; ordained to ministry Bapt. Ch., 1950. Pastor 1st Bapt. Ch., Agua Dulce, Tex., 1951-53, Mathis, Tex., 1953-56, Kerrville, Tex., 1956-60, Kingsville, Tex., 1960-63; pastor Manor Bapt. Ch., San Antonio, 1963-72; exec. dir. Ecumenical Ctr. for Religion and Health, San Antonio, 1972—; clin. prof. U. Tex. Med. Sch., San Antonio; founding dir. Hospice San Antonio, 1983; mem. Christian edn. coordinating bd. Bapt. Conv. Tex., Dallas, 1985-93; mem. ethics com. Med. Ctr., S.W. Tex. Meth. Hosp., St. Luke's Hosp. Author: Better Than Blessed, 1982; contbr. articles to profl. jours. Recipient Liberty Bell award Young Lawyers Assn., 1977. Mem. Torch Club, Oak Hills Country. Baptist. Office: Ecumenical Ctr Religion & Health 8310 Ewing Halsell San Antonio TX 78229

ANDERSON, DOROTHY FISHER, social worker, psychotherapist; b. Funchal, Madeira, May 31, 1924; d. Lewis Mann Anker and Edna (Gilbert) Fisher (adoptive father David Henry Fisher); m. Theodore W. Anderson, July 8, 1950; children: Robert Lewis, Janet Anderson Yang, Jeanne Elizabeth. BA, Queens Coll., 1945; AM, U. Chgo., 1947. Diplomate Am. Bd. Examiners in Clin. Social Work; lic. clin. social worker, Calif.; registered cert. social worker, N.Y. Intern Cook County (Ill.) Bur. Pub. Welfare, Chgo., 1945-46, Ill. Neuropsychiat. Inst., Chgo., 1946; clin. caseworker, Neurol. Inst. Presbyn. Hosp., N.Y.C., 1947; therapist, Mental Hygiene Clinic VA, N.Y.C., 1947-50; therapist, Child Guidance Clinic Pub. Elem. Sch. 42, N.Y.C., 1950-53; social worker, counselor Cedarhurst (N.Y.) Family Service Agy., 1954-55; psychotherapist, counselor Family Service of the Midpeninsula, Palo Alto, Calif., 1971-73, 79-86, George Hexter, M.D., Inc., 1972-83; clin. social worker Tavistock Clinic, London, 1974-75, El Camino Hosp., Mountain View, Calif., 1979; pvt. practice clin. social work, 1978-92, ret., 1992; cons. Human Resource Services, Sunnyvale, Calif., 1981-86. Hannah G. Solomon scholar U. Chgo., 1945-46; Commonwealth fellow U. Chgo., 1946-47. Fellow Soc. Clin. Social Work (Continuing Edn. Recognition award 1980-83); mem. Nat. Assn. Social Workers (diplomate in clin. social work).

ANDERSON, DOUGLAS RICHARD, ophthalmologist, educator, scientist, researcher; b. Memphis, Apr. 7, 1938; s. William Arnold Douglas and Hariott Isabel (Gates) A.; m. Wirtley Anne Raine, Nov. 28, 1964; children: John Douglas, Wendy Anne, Michael Allen Scott. AB magna cum laude, U. Miami, Coral Gables, Fla., 1958; MD, Washington U., St. Louis, 1962. Diplomate Am. Bd. Ophthalmology (bd. dirs. 1988-95). Rotating intern U. Hosp. Cleve., 1962-63; staff assoc. Nat. Cancer Inst., Bethesda, Md., 1963-65; resident in ophthalmology U. Calif. Med. Ctr., San Francisco, 1965-68; rsch. fellow Howe lab. Mass. Eye and Ear Infirmary, Boston, 1968-69; asst. prof. U. Miami (Fla.) Sch. Medicine, 1969-75, assoc. prof., 1975-82, prof., 1982—; mem. nat. eye adv. coun. NIH, Bethesda, 1982-86, visual sci. study sect. A, 1972-76, chmn., 1975-76; bd. govs. Anne Bates Leach Eye Hosp., Miami, 1987-93, outpatient med. dir., 1993-95. Author: Testing the Field of Vision, 1982, Perimetry With and Without Automation, 1987, Automated Static Perimetry, 1992; contbr. over 200 sci. articles an book chpts.; coeditor: Discussions on Glaucoma, 1977, Automatic Perimetry in Glaucoma, 1985, Encounters in Glaucoma Research I: Receptors, 1994; assoc. editor Am. Jour. Opththalmology, Chgo., 1973-90. Mem., active med. staff Anne Bates Leach Eye Hosp., v.p., 1983-84, pres., 1984-86. Surgeon USPHS, 1963-65. Recipient William and Mary Greve Internat. Scholars award Rsch. to Prevent Blindness, Inc., 1978, Sr. Sci. Investigator award, 1986, 93, Recognition award Alcon Rsch. Inst., Ft. Worth, 1986; rsch. grantee Nat. Eye Inst., 1969-91, 93—, Am. Health Assistance Found., 1978-95, Glaucoma Rsch. Found., 1993-94. Fellow Am. Acad. Ophthalmology (councillor 1984-86, Gold medal 1972, Honor awards 1978, 83, Sr. Honor award 1992); mem. Am. Glaucoma Soc. (v.p. 1988-90, pres. 1990-92), Assn. for Rsch. in Vision and Ophthalmology (trustee 1983-88, pres. 1987), Am. Ophthal. Soc., Internat. Perimetric Soc. Home: 11880 SW 63rd Ave Miami FL 33156-4802 Office: Bascom Palmer Eye Inst PO Box 016880 900 NW 17th St Miami FL 33101-6880

ANDERSON, ELIZABETH HONORA, researcher, nurse practitioner; b. Yonkers, N.Y.; d. Harry C. and Ethel (Regan) Anderson. RN, St. Mary Hosp. Sch. Nursing, Waterbury, Conn.; BSN magna cum laude, U. Bridgeport (Conn.), 1971; MSN, Wayne State U., Detroit, 1977; PhD, U. Rochester (N.Y.), 1992. Adult nurse practitioner Charter Oak Terr./Rice Hts. Health Ctr., Hartford, Conn.; clin. instr./lectr. St. Joseph Coll., West Hartford, Conn.; rsch. asst. U. Rochester Sch. Nursing; advance practice nurse practitioner U. Rochester/AIDS Clinic; rsch. assoc., post doctoral fellow U. Rochester; asst. prof. U. Md., Balt.; nurse practitioner Balt. VA AIDS Clinic. Am. Nurses Found. scholar, 1990. Mem. ANA (coun. nurse rschrs.), Nurse Practitioner Assn. of Md., Ea. Nurses Rsch. Soc., Soc. for Behavioral Medicine. Home: 5413 Old Frederick Rd Baltimore MD 21229-2125 Office: U Md Sch Nursing Health Scis Facility Rm 138 685 W Baltimore St Baltimore MD 21201-1545

ANDERSON, FRANCES SWEM, nuclear medical technologist; b. Grand Rapids, Mich., Nov. 27, 1913; d. Frank Oscar and Carrie (Strang) Swem; m. Clarence A.F. Anderson, Apr. 9, 1934; children: Robert Curtis, Clarelyn Christine (Mrs. Roger L. Schmelling), Stanley Herbert. Student, Muskegon Sch. Bus., 1959-60; cert., Muskegon Community Coll., 1964; cert. adult edn. computer course, Fruitport Cmty. Schs., 1992. Registered nuclear med. technologist Am. Registry Radiol. Technologists. X-ray file clk., film librarian Hackley Hosp., Muskegon, Mich., 1957-59, radioisotope technologist and sec., 1959-65; nuclear med. technologist Butler Meml. Hosp., Muskegon Heights, Mich., 1966-70; nuclear med. technologist Mercy Hosp., Muskegon, 1970-79, ret., 1979. Mem. Muskegon Civic A Capella choir, 1932-39; mem. Mother-Tchr. Singers, PTA, Muskegon, 1941-48, treas. 1944-48; with Muskegon Civic Opera Assn., 1950-51; office vol. Alive '88 Crusade; mem. com. for 60th H.S. Class Reunion; mem. Sr. Harvest Day Com., Muskegon County, 1995; active Forest Park Covenant Ch., mem. choir, 1953-79, 83—, choir pres. 1992, 93, choir sec. 1963-69, Sunday Sch. tchr. 1954-75, supt. Sunday Sch., 1975-78, sec., treas. 1981-86, sec. 1991, 92, 93, mem. support team, sec. 1993, chmn. master planning coun., 1982; coord. centennial com. to 1981, ch. sec. 1982-84, 87, 91, 95-96, registrar vacation Bible sch. 1988, 89, 90. 91, treas., 1995, 96; co-chmn. Jackson Hill Old Timer's Reunion, 1982, 83, 85. Mem. Am. Registry Radiologic Technologists, Soc. Nuclear Medicine (cert. nuclear medicine technologist). Home: 5757 Sternberg Rd Fruitport MI 49415-9740

ANDERSON, GAIL V., obstetrician and gynecologist; b. Pensacola, Fla., Oct. 3, 1925; d. Parke Pleasant and Sarada M. (Thompson) A.; m. Alice Harriet Midghall, Nov. 6, 1923; children: Gail V. Jr., David C., Jerrold B., Walter P., Mark S. BA, BS, Columbia Union Coll., 1949; MD, Loma Linda U., 1953. Diplomate Am. Bd. Ob-Gyn. Resident in ob-gyn. D.C. Gen. Hosp., Washington, 1954-55, Georgetown U. Hosp., Washington, 1955-56; chief resident in ob-gyn. D.C. Gen. Hosp., Washington, 1956-57; dir. ob-gyn. L.A. County/U. So. Calif. Med. Ctr., 1958-70; prof. ob-gyn. U. So. Calif. Sch. Medicine, L.A., 1968—, prof., chmn. dept. emergency medicine, 1971—. Mem. South Pasadena Sch. Bd., 1971-77; cand. city coun. South Pasadena, 1980; dir. salerni Collegium, 1958-95, pres., 1992-93. With USN, 1943-46. Hartford Found. grantee, 1964. Fellow ACS, ACOG; mem. Am. Bd. Emergency Medicine (founder), Am. Coll. Emergency Physicians (charter). Republican. Home: 217 Oaklawn Ave South Pasadena CA 91030 Office: Univ of So Calif Dept of Emergency Medicine Sch of Medicine University Park Los Angeles CA 90007

ANDERSON, GARY RICHARD, social worker, educator; b. Lansing, Mich., Nov. 16, 1952; s. Richard J. and Carol Regina (Bentz) A.; m. Valerie Ann Glesnes, May 28, 1978; children: Lauren Marie, Elizabeth Joy. BRE, Baptist Coll., Grand Rapids, Mich., 1974; M in Social Work, U. Mich., 1976; PhD, U. Chgo., 1983. Child protective svcs. Mich. Dept. of Social Svcs., Ann Arbor, 1976-79; cons. Heartshare Human Svcs., Bklyn., 1983—; assoc. prof. CUNY, 1983-93, prof., 1993—; Cons. child welfare pvt. practice, N.Y. 1983—; dir. Nat. Resource Ctr. for Permanency Planning. Editor, Author Courage to Care, Responding to the Crisis of Children with AIDS, 1990, Health Care Ethics, 1987; Author monograph Children with AIDS, 1986. Mem. NASW, Council on Social Work Edn. Office: Hunter College School of Social Work 129 E 79th St New York NY 10021-0339

ANDERSON, GARY WILLIAM, physician; b. Summit, N.J., Nov. 10, 1951; s. Gotfried and Elise (Koch) A.; divorced; 1 child, Eric William George. BA, Seton Hall U., 1974; MA in Psychology, Fairleigh Dickinson U., 1977; MD, Autonomous U. Guadalajara, Mex., 1983. Intern Rutgers Med. Sch., New Brunswick, N.J., 1984; resident St. Joseph's Med. Ctr., Paterson, N.J., 1985; med. dir., dir. med. writing office of v.p. Sandoz Rsch. Inst., East Hanover, N.J., 1985—. Vol. med. dir., bd. trustees, exec. com. Sussex County (N.J.) Domestic Abuse Program, 1986—. Mem. AMA, Am. Med. Writers Assn., Am. Fedn. Clin. Rsch., Nat. Honor Soc. Psychology, Am. Acad. Family Physicians, N.J. Acad. Medicine. Republican. Office: Sandoz Rsch Inst RR 10 East Hanover NJ 07936

ANDERSON, GEORGE KENNETH, air force officer, physician; b. Providence, Feb. 17, 1946; s. George Raymond and Mildred (Caster) A.; m. Kimberly Kay Baker, May 18, 1968; children: George D., Ginger K. MD, U. Mich., 1971; MPH, Tulane U., 1973; postgrad., Nat. War Coll., Ft. McNair, Va., 1982-83. Diplomate Am. Bd. Preventive Medicine (chmn. 1991-95), Am. Bd. Med. Mgmt. (bd. dirs.). Intern Wilford Hall USAF Med Ctr., 1971-72; resident USAF Sch. Aerospace Medicine, 1973-75; commd. 2d lt. USAF, 1967, advanced through grades to maj. gen., 1993; comdr. USAF Hosp., Kunsan, Republic of Korea, 1975-76, 8th Tactical Hosp., Germany, 1976-79; mem. faculty USAF Sch. Aerospace Medicine, Brooks AFB, Tex., 1979-82; div. chief Office Surgeon Gen., Bolling AFB, Md., 1983-85, dep. dir., 1985-87; command surgeon Air Force Systems Command, Andrews AFB, Md., 1987-88; dir. med. inspection Air Force ISC, Norton AFB, Calif., 1988-90; comdr. Human Systems Ctr., Brooks AFB, 1990-94; deputy asst. sec. def. Health Svcs. Ops. and Readiness, Washington, D.C., 1994; chmn. Am. Bd. Preventive Medicine, 1991-95. Decorated Legion of Merit, Disting. Svc. medal. Fellow Am. Coll. Preventive Medicine, Am. Coll. Physician Execs., Aerospace Med. Assn. (Julian Ward award 1975); mem. AMA, Air Force Assn. (life). Office: The Pentagon Rm 3E336 Pentagon Rm 3E336 Washington DC 20301-1200

ANDERSON, GERALDINE LOUISE, laboratory scientist; b. Mpls., July 7, 1941; d. George M. and Viola Julia-Mary (Abel) Havrilla; m. Henry Clifford Anderson, May 21, 1966; children: Bruce Henry, Julie Lynne. BS, U. Minn., 1963. Med. technologist Swedish Hosp., Mpls., 1963-68; hematology supr. Glenwood Hills Hosp. lab., Golden Valley, Minn., 1968-70; assoc. scientist dept. pediatrics U. Minn. Hosps., Mpls., 1970-74; instr. health occupations Hennepin Tech. Coll., Brooklyn Park, Minn., 1974—, St. Paul Tech. Vocat. Inst., 1978-81; rsch. med. technologist Miller Hosp., St. Paul, 1975-78; rsch. assoc. Children's and United Hosps., St. Paul, 1979-88; sr. lab. analyst Cascade Med. Inc., Eden Prairie, Minn., 1989-90; lab. mgr. VA Med. Ctr., Mpls., 1990; technical support scientist INCSTAR Corp., 1990-94; reg. affairs product analysis coord. Medtronic Neurological, Mpls., 1995; quality assurance documentation coord. Lectec Corp., Stillwater, MN., Minnetonka, Minn.; clin. rsch. monitor, Eli Lilly Rsch. Labs., Indpls., 1995—; mem. health occupations adv. com. Hennepin Tech. Ctrs., 1975-90, chairperson, 1978-79; mem. hematology slide edn. rev. bd. Am. Soc. Hematology, 1976—; mem. flow cytometry and clin. chemistry quality control subcoms. Nat. Com. for Clin. Lab. Standards, 1988-92; cons. FCM Specialists, 1989—. Mem. rev. bd. Clin. Lab. Sci., 1990-91, The Learning Laboratorian Series 1991; contbr. and presenter In Svc. Rev. in Clin. Lab. Sci., audio taped study program for ASMT, 1992; contbr. articles to profl. jours. Mem. Med. Lab. Tech. Polit. Action Com., 1978—; charter orgns. rep. troop #534 Boy Scouts Am., Viking Coun., 1988-90; resource person lab. careers Robbinsdale Sch. Dist., Minn., 1970-79; del. Crest View Home Assn., 1981—; mem. sci. and math. subcom. Minn. High Tech. Council, 1983-88, mem. Women Scientists Speakers Bur., 1989-92; observer UN 4th World Conf. on Women, Beijing, 1995. Recipient svc. awards and honors Omicron Sigma. Mem. AAAS, AAUW, NAFE (Twin Cities network), Am. Med. Writers Assn., Women in Com. Inc., Assn. Clin. Pharmacology, Soc. Tech. Comm., Nat. Assn. Women Cons., Inc., Minn. Emerging Med. Orgns., Minn. Soc. Med. Tech. (sec. 1969-71), Am. Soc. Profl. and Exec. Women, Am. Soc. Clin. Lab. Sci. (del. to ann. meetings 1972—, chmn. hematology sci. assembly 1977-79, nomination com. 1979-81, bd. dirs. 1985-88), Twin City Hosp. Assn. (speakers bur. 1968-70), Assn. Women in Sci., World Future Soc., Minn. Med. Tech. Alumni, Am. Soc. Hematology, Internat. Soc. Analytical Cytology, Great Lakes Internat. Flow Cytometry Assn. (charter mem. 1992), Sigma Delta Epsilon (corr. sec. Xi chpt. 1980-82, pres. 1982-84, membership com. 1990-92, nat. nominations chair 1991-92, nat. v.p. 1992-93, nat. pres.-elect 1993-94, nat. pres. 1994-95), Alpha Mu Tau. Lutheran. Office: FCM Specialists 8400-33 Pl N Minneapolis MN 55427

ANDERSON, GREGORY LYMAN, psychology educator; b. Nebraska City, Nebr., Mar. 9, 1951; s. Lyman Eric and Jean Ann (Sand) A.; m. Linda Louise Wicker, Aug. 17, 1973 (div. Sept. 1985); m. Anne Louise Rollins, Nov. 19, 1988; 1 child, Lindsey Rollins. BS, U. Iowa, 1973; MS, Ea. Ky. U., 1976; PhD, U. Ky., 1986. Diplomte Am. Bd. Med. Psychotherapists. Ctr. dir. Mecklenburg Mental Health, Chase City, Va., 1975-82; teaching asst. U. Ky., Lexington, 1983-85; assoc. prof. psychology dept. family medicine Ea. Va. Med. Sch., Norfolk, 1986—; clin. psychologist Portsmouth (Va.) Family Medicine, 1986—; co-dir. behavioral medicine clinic Ghent Family Practice, Norfolk, Va., 1995—; cons. Dept. Corrections, Boydton, Va., 1976-82, Multidiscipline Child Abuse Team, Boydton, 1976-82, Psychiat. Inst. Hampton Roads, Norfolk, 1985-86, Tidewater AIDS Crisis Task Force, 1992-96; instr. Southside C.C., Alberta, Va., 1980-81. Contbr. articles to profl. jours. Mem. Port Norfolk Civic League, Portsmouth, 1990-95. Mem. APA, Am. Soc. Clin. Hypnosis, Va. Psychol. Assn., Internat. Soc.

for Study Dissociation, Internat. Soc. for Traumatic Stress Studies, Tidewater Acad. Clin. Psychologists, Am. Assn. Marriage and Family Therapists, Soc. Tchrs. Family Medicine, Internat. Soc. Hypnosis, Tidewater Songwriters Assn. (pres. 1990-96). Office: Portsmouth Family Medicine 2700 London Blvd Portsmouth VA 23707-3647

ANDERSON, HELEN ELIZABETH, occupational health nurse; b. Davenport, Iowa, Sept. 16, 1950; d. Donald Leroy and Virginia Katherine (Cherry) Wright; m. James Joseph Healy, Jan. 29, 1972 (div. Oct. 1981); children: Tiffany Virginia Healy, John T. Healy, David J. Healy; m. Loyal William Anderson, May 29, 1982; 1 child, Megan M. Anderson. Assoc., Black Hawk Coll., Moline, Ill., 1970. RN, Ill., Iowa, Ohio, Mich.; cert. occupl. health nurse, ABOHN. Head nurse, supr. East Moline State Hosp., 1970-74; private duty nurse Profl. Med. Coverage, Bettendorf, Iowa, 1978; office nurse Quad-Cities Pediat., East Moline, 1975-79; occupl. health nurse North Star Steel, Wilton, Iowa, 1979-95; contingent occupl. health nurse Rumpf/St. Vincent's, Toledo, 1995—. Mem. Am. Assn. Occupl. Health Nurses, Ctrl. Iowa Assn. Occupl. Health Nurses. Roman Catholic. Home: 8056 Littlefield Ct Sylvania OH 43560

ANDERSON, HOLLY GEIS, health facility administrator, commentator, educator; b. Waukesha, Wis., Oct. 23, 1946; d. Henry H. and Hulda (Sebroff) Geis; m. Richard Kent Anderson, June 6, 1969. BA, Azusa Pacific U., 1970. CEO Oak Tree Antiques, San Gabriel, Calif., 1975-82; pres., founder, CEO Premenstrual Syndrome Treatment Clinic, Arcadia, Calif., 1982—, Hormonal Treatment Ctrs., Inc., Arcadia, 1992-94; lectr. radio and TV shows, L.A.; on-air radio personality Women's Clinic with Holly Anderson, 1990—. Author: What Every Woman Needs to Know About PMS (audio cassette), 1987, The PMS Treatment Program (video cassette), 1989, PMS Talk (audio cassette), 1989. Mem. NAFE, The Dalton Soc. Republican. Office: PMS Treatment Clinic 150 N Santa Anita Ave Ste 755 Arcadia CA 91006-3113

ANDERSON, JAMES ALFRED, psychology educator; b. Detroit, July 31, 1940; s. Courtney Alfred and Catherine (Bullock) A.; m. Diana De Vincenzi, Nov. 1, 1969; 1 child, Eric David. BS, MIT, 1962, PhD, 1967. Postdoctoral fellow UCLA, 1967-71; research assoc. Rockefeller U., N.Y.C., 1971-73; asst. prof. cognitive and neural scis. Brown U., Providence, 1973-78, assoc. prof., 1978-85, prof., 1985—; chair dept. cognitive and linguistic scis., 1993—; chair Cognitive Functional Neurosci. Rev. Panel NIMH, 1992-94. Editor: (with G. Hinton) Parallel Models of Associative Memory, 1981, (with S. Lehmkuhle and W. Levy) Synaptic Modification, Neuron Selectivity and Nervous System Organization, 1985, (with E. Rosenfeld) Neurocomputing: Some Important Papers, 1988, (with E. Rosenfeld and A. Pellionisz) Neurocomputing 2, 1990, An Introduction to Neural Networks, 1995. Grantee NSF, 1979, 85, 91, Office Naval Rsch., 1986, 91. Mem. Cognitive Sci. Soc., Psychonomic Soc., Soc. for Neurosci., Soc. for Math. Psychology, Internat. Neural Network Soc. (mem. governing bd. 1987-95), Sigma Xi. Home: 1 Mathewson Rd Barrington RI 02806 Office: Brown U Dept Cognitive and Linguistic Scis 190 Thayer St Providence RI 02912-9067

ANDERSON, JAMES LINWOOD, pharmaceutical sales official; b. Bangor, Maine, June 8, 1949; s. Linwood Lamont and Helena May (Armitage) A.; m. Susan Grace Hughey, Aug. 23, 1974 (div. Aug. 1994). BS in Biology and Premedicine, U. Maine, 1971, MS in Physiology, 1972. Narcotics officer Maine State Police/Drug Enforcement Agy., 1973-74; sales rep. Wallace Labs., 1974-76, Hoechst-Roussell, Somerville, N.J., 1976-84; pharm. sales rep. I Miles (Bayer) Pharms., New Haven, 1984-90, ter. sales specialist, 1990-91, hosp. sales specialist, 1991-93, pharm. sales rep. II, 1994—. Coord. pastoral affairs Calvary Bapt. Ch., Manchester, N.H., 1976-80. Mem. USCG Aux. (flotilla comdr. New Bedford. Mass. 1992-94, divsn. capt. S.E. Mass. 1994-96, rear commodore Mass. and R.I. 1996—), Order of DeMolay (master councilor 1965-66, state master councilor 1966-67, chevalier 1967—). Home: 205 Stevenson St New Bedford MA 02745-3516

ANDERSON, JAMES WINGO, physician; b. Hinton, W.Va., Aug. 6, 1936; s. Fred Wingo and Georgia Lee (Whittaker) A.; m. Gay Veree Gilbert, June 21, 1957; children: Katherine, Steven. BS, W.Va. U., 1957; MD, Northwestern U., 1961; MS, Mayo Clinic, 1965. Intern Presbyn. Med. Ctr., Denver; resident, fellow Mayo Clinic, Rochester, Minn.; asst. prof. medicine U. Calif., San Francisco, 1968-73; prof. medicine, clin. nutrition U. Ky. Coll. Medicine, Lexington, 1973-96; pres., founder HCF Nutrition Found., Lexington, 1979—. Author: Diabetes-A Practical Guide to HEalty Living, 1981, Dr. Anderson's High Fiber Fitness Plan, 1994, Dr. Anderson;s Antioxident Antiaging, 1996. Trustee Georgetown (Ky.) Coll., 1988-96, chmn. bd. trustees, 1994-96. Capt. U.S. Army, 1965-68. Fellow Am. Coll. Physicians. Republican. Baptist. Home: 913 Tabor Lake Ct Lexington KY 40502 Office: VA Med Ctr 2250 Leestown Rd (IIIC) Lexington KY 40511

ANDERSON, JANICE RUTH, rehabilitation nurse, administrator; b. Effingham, Ill., Jan. 17, 1953; d. Harold J. and Avis Vivian (Rice) Schlicker; m. Arthur A. Anderson, Oct. 12, 1985. BSN, U. Mich., 1975; MSN, Columbia U., 1985. RN, N.C. Pub. health nurse Elem. Schs. of Durham, N.C., 1995—. Mem. Am. Assn. Cardiovascular Pulmonary Rehab., Am. Heart Assn., Sigma Theta Tau. Home: 916 Coker Dr Chapel Hill NC 27514-4406

ANDERSON, JEAN LORRAINE, nursing educator; b. Halifax, N.S., Apr. 22, 1945; d. Colin Francis and Elizabeth Florence (MacDonald) Livingstone; m. children: Colin Henry Michael, Sheena Margaret Isabel, Laura Mary Catherine, Sarah Christina Ann, Michelle Elizabeth Lynn. Diploma in Nursing, St. Martha's Hosp. Sch. Nursing, Antigonish, N.S., 1966; BS in Nursing, St. Francis Xavier U., Antigonish, N.S., 1970, MEd, 1988. Nurse, surgery St. Martha's Hosp., Antigonish, N.S., 1966-67; clin. instr. St. Martha's Hosp., Antigonish, 1981—; staff nurse ICU St. Joseph's Hosp., Victoria, B.C., 1967-68, nurse, 1967-68; nurse in charge Ranklin Inlet (N.W.T.) Nsg. Sta., 1970-76; staff nurse, maternity St. Martha's Hosp., Antigonish, 1979-81; nursing instr. St. Martha's Hosp. Sch. of Nursing, Antigonish, Can., 1981—. Roman Catholic. Home: RR 1 Merigomish, Pictou County, NS Canada B0K 1G0

ANDERSON, JOANN MORGAN, counselor; b. Detroit, Dec. 25, 1933; d. Verbon Anthony and Wanda Joan (Hutchison) Morgan; m. Robert Arthur Anderson; children: Carol Sue, Douglas Ross, Paul William. BA, U. Wash., 1957; MA, Fielding Inst., 1977. Self employed counselor Edmonds, Wash., 1976-78; dir. High Point Counseling Svc., Edmonds, 1978-80, Woodway Counseling Assn., Edmonds, 1980-86; mem. clin. staff N.W. Health Assocs., Edmonds, 1986-89, mem. sabbatical staff, 1989-90, mgr. property devel., 1989-91; pvt. counseling Edmonds, 1991—; workshop leader, Holland, England, New Zealand, 1993—; cons. Edmonds Sch. Dist. 15, 1979-82, Wash. Edn. Assn., 1980, Non-Profit Bds. Dirs., Seattle, 1985-87. Editor, columnist (quarterly newsletter), Living Well, 1987-90, (monthly newsletter) Creating Success, 1995—; author: Basics of Group Psychosynthesis, 1990. Vol. various agencies, 1957-76; pres. Stevens Meml. Hosp. Aux., Edmonds, 1964-65. Mem. AAUW, Am. Assn. Psychosynthesis (charter), Internat. Transactional Analysis Assn. (cert.), Am. Assn. Counseling and Devel., Assn. Transpersonal Psychology, Mortar Bd., PEO, Beta Gamma Sigma. Home and Office: 16010 73rd Pl W Edmonds WA 98026-4552

ANDERSON, JOHN ALBERT, physician; b. Ashtabula, Ohio, Jan. 25, 1935; s. Albert Gunnard Anderson and Martha Anetta (Bieshline) White; m. Nicole Jeanne Anderson, July 10, 1963; children: Carole Beno, John-Marc, Christopher B. BS, U. Ill., 1958, MD, 1960. Diplomate Am. Bd. Pediat., Am. Bd. Allergy and Immunology. Intern U. Ill., 1960-61; resident in pediat. U. Ill., Chgo., 1961-62, U.S. Naval Hosp., Bethesda, Md., 1964-65; fellow in allergy and immunology Children's Hosp., Washington, 1967-69; mem. sr. staff Henry Ford Hosp., Detroit, 1969—, dir. pediat. allergy fellowship program, 1969-77, dir. allergy and immunology program, 1977—, head divsn. allergy and immunology, dept. pediatrics, 1977—, chmn. dept. pediatrics, 1982-90; clin. prof. pediat., U. Mich., Ann Arbor, 1985-94; prof. pediat. Case Western Res. U., Cleve., 1994—; dir. Am. Bd. Allergy and Immunology, 1990—, sec., 1995—. Contbr. more than 50 articles to profl. jours. Lt. comdr. USN, 1962-66. Fellow Am. Acad. Allergy and Immunology (pres. 1990-91), Am. Acad. Pediat. (chmn. allergy sect. 1979-82), Mich. Allergy Soc. (pres. 1978-79); mem. Asthma and Allergy Found. Am. (dir. 1992—, v.p. med. affairs 1992-95, v.p. rsch. 1995—), Coun. Med. Speciality Soc. (bd. dirs. 1992-94), Am. Bd. Med. Specialists, Am. Bd. Allergy and Immunology, Sci. Advisors Internat. Life Scis. (allergy sect. 1990—). Home: 16543 Winchester Dr Northville MI 48167-2349 Office: Henry Ford Hosp # 1 Ford Pl Detroit MI 48202

ANDERSON, JOHN ARTHUR, dentist, prosthodontist; b. Orlando, Fla., Feb. 22, 1949; s. Arthur Carl and Carolyn Dorothy (Spizarny) A.; m. Joan Carol Scharfenberg, Dec. 28, 1971; children: Craig Andrew, Alan Edward. BA, Rollins Coll., 1971; DDS in Prosthodontics with distinction, Emory U., 1975; MS, U. Tex., 1980. Diplomate Am. Bd. Prosthodontics. Commd. USAF, 1971, advanced through grades to col., 1994; gen. dentist USAF, Wichita, Kans., 1975-77; resident in prosthodontics USAF, Houston, 1977-80; prosthodontist USAF, Homestead AFB, Fla., 1980-85; prosthodontist USAF, Bitburg AB, Germany, 1985-89, dental comdr., 1988-89; dep. dental comdr. USAF, MacDill AFB, Fla., 1989-93, prosthodontist, 1989-94; prosthodontist Fla. Dental Ctrs., Tampa, 1994-95, managing dentist, 1996—; mem. hosp. exec. com. USAF Hosp., Bitburg AB, 1988-89, MacDill AFB, 1989-93, disaster team chief, 1991-93; clin. asst. prof. U. Fla., Gainesville, 1996—. Columnist Sr. Connection/Fla. Sr., 1994—; contbr. articles to profl. jours. Adult leader Troop 22 Boy Scouts Am., Tampa, 1991—. Fellow Acad. Gen. Dentistry, Psi Omega (grad.); mem. Am. Dental Assn., Am. Coll. Prosthodontists, Am. Legion, Ret. Officers Assn., Fla. Dental Assn., Hillsborough County Dental Assn. Home: 4613 W Lamb Ave Tampa FL 33629 Office: 3308 S Dale Mabry Tampa FL 33629*

ANDERSON, JOHN BETHUNE, obstetrician, gynecologist; b. Phila., Sept. 26, 1943; s. Robert Neal and Agnes Lorena (McNaull) A.; m. Kathryn C. Gahagan, Aug. 28, 1965; 1 child, Jill Kathleen. BA, Brown U., 1965; MD, Jefferson Med. Coll., 1969. Diplomate Am. Bd. Obstetrics and Gynecology. Intern Reading (Pa.) Hosp. and Med. Ctr., 1969-70, resident, 1970-73, staff physician, 1973—; fellow in perinatal medicine Temple U. Health Scis. Ctr., Phila., 1973; chmn. sect. obstetrics Reading Hosp. and Med. Ctr., 1989—; clin. instr. U. Pa. Sch. Medicine, Phila., 1986-89, clin. asst. prof. ob.-gyn., 1989—. Fellow Am. Coll. Obstetricians and Gynecologists; mem. Am. Fertility Soc., AMA, Pa. Med. Soc. Office: 1340 Penn Ave Reading PA 19610-2132

ANDERSON, JOHN MICHAEL, physician; b. Phila., June 24, 1950; s. John Richard and Roberta Joan (Murtha) A.; m. Janet Delores Nye, Dec. 1973 (div. Feb. 1983); m. Linda Jean Cosner, Aug. 13, 1983; children: Melissa Jean, Rosanne Elizabeth, Stephen Jonathan, Daniel Clark. B, Mich. Tech. Univ., 1974; MD, Mich State. Univ., 1978; postgrad., Mayo Grad. Sch. Medicine, 1978-81. Asst. prof. Univ. Md. Sch. Medicine, Balt., 1982—; medical dir. Industrial Rehab. Ctr., Balt., 1988-90; outpatient medical dir. Sinai Hosp., Balt., 1990—; assoc. medical dir. Sinai Rehab. Ctr., Balt., 1991—; assoc. prof. Johns Hopkins Univ. Sch. Medicine, Balt., 1995—; medical dir. Return Program, Balt., 1985-89, Sinai Pain Rehab. Program, 1983-89, Cardiac Rehab. at Sinai, 1983-91. Contbr. articles to profl. jours. Active MADD,. Recipient CIBA Cmty. Svc. award CIBA Co., 1978, Teacher of Yr. award Sinai Hosp., 1986, Excellence in Teaching award, 1993. Mem. Am. Acad. Physical Medicine & Rehab., Md. Soc. Physical Medicine & Rehab., Internat. Assn. Study of Pain, West Mosby Vols., Gideons Internat., Am. Faculty Assn. Prison Fellowship. Republican. Home: 1134 Kingsbury Rd Owings Mells MD 21117 Office: Sinai Hosp Balt 2401 W Belvedere Ave Baltimore MD 21215

ANDERSON, JOHN RICHARD, entomologist, educator; b. Fargo, N.D., May 5, 1931; s. John Raymond and Mary Ann (Beaulieu) A.; m. Shereen V. Erickson, Mar. 26, 1955; children: Scott F., Lisa K., Steven F. BS, Utah State U., 1957; MS, U. Wis., 1958, PhD, 1960. Asst. prof. entomology U. Calif.-Berkeley, 1961-66, assoc. prof., 1967-70, prof., 1970-93, prof. emeritus, 1993—, assoc. dean research, 1979-85; trustee, past chmn. Alameda County (Calif.) Mosquito Abatement Dist., 1961-73, 79-93. Editoral bd.: Jour. Med. Entomology, 1968-72, Jour. Econ. Entomology, 1977-81, Thomas Say Found, 1968-72. Served with USN, 1950-54. Rsch. grantee; recipient Berkeley citation for Disting. Achievement, 1993. Fellow AAAS, Royal Entomol. Soc. (London); mem. Entomol. Soc. Am. (governing bd. 1987-90, C.W. Woodworth award Pacific br. 1988), Can. Entomol. Soc., Am. Mosquito Control Assn., Soc. Vector Ecologists, Nature Conservancy, Am. Mus. Natural History, Oreg. Nat. Resources Coun., Oreg. Nat. Desert Assn., High Desert Mus., Sierra Club, Xerces Soc. Home: 1283 NW Trenton Ave Bend OR 97701-1026 Office: U Calif Dept Dean Rsh Berkeley CA 94720

ANDERSON, KATHRYN DUNCAN, surgeon; b. Ashton-Under-Lyne, Lancashire, Eng., Mar. 14, 1939; came to U.S., 1961; m. French Anderson, June 24, 1961. BA, Cambridge (Eng.) U., 1961, MA, 1964; MD, Harvard U., 1964. Diplomate Am. Bd. Surgery. Intern in pediat. Children's Hosp., Boston, 1964-65; resident in surgery Georgetown U. Hosp., Washington, 1965-69, chief resident in surgery, 1969-70, attending surgeon, 1972-74, vice chmn. surgery, 1984-92; chief resident in pediat. surgery Children's Hosp., Washington, 1970-72, sr. attending surgeon, 1974-84; surgeon-in-chief Children's Hosp., L.A., 1992—; prof. surgery U. So. Calif. Fellow ACS (sec. 1992—), Am. Acad. Pediatrics (sec. surg. sect. 1982-85, chmn. 1985-86), Am. Pediatric Surg. Assn. (sec. 1988-91); Am. Surg. Assn., Soc. Univ. Surgeons. Office: Children's Hosp 4650 W Sunset Blvd Los Angeles CA 90027-6016

ANDERSON, KELLEY PIERCE, cardiologist; b. Chgo., Nov. 21, 1951; s. Herbert Lawrence and Jean Betty (Clough) A.; m. Susan E. Mann, Aug. 20, 1983. Intern, Michael Reese Hosp., Chgo., 1977-78, resident, 1978-80; BA in Psychology, U. Rochester, 1973, MD, 1977; intern, Michael Reese Hosp., Chgo., 1977-78, resident, 1978-80. Diplomate Am. Bd. Internal Medicine. Fellow in cardiology Stanford (Calif.) U., 1980-83; asst. prof. medicine U. Utah, Salt Lake City, 1983-94; assoc. prof. medicine U. Pitts. Med. Ctr., 1994—; dir. cardiac electrophysiology program U. Pitts., 1994—; dir. Electrophysiology Lab., U. Utah Med. Ctr., 1983-94. Editor-in-chief Cardiac Electrophysiology Rev.; mem. editorial bd. Annals Noninvasive Electrocardiology; contbr. articles to profl. jours. Advanced Research fellow Am. Heart Assn., 1982; recipient New Investigator Research award NIH, 1986. Fellow Am. Coll. Cardiology; mem. Am. Heart Assn.

ANDERSON, LEONARD LOUIS, laboratory administrator; b. Boston, Sept. 20, 1934; s. Everett Frank and Concetta (Vozzeilla) A.; m. M. Bernadette Judge, June 3, 1961; children: Christine, Eric, Lauren. BA, Harvard U., 1956; MA, Boston U., 1963; DSc, Sussex U., Brighton, Eng., 1974. Biochemist Gen. Foods Corp., Boston, 1956-57, Boston U. Med. Sch., 1959-60; rsch. biochemist Mass. Gen. Hosp., Boston, 1960-63, Tufts U., Boston, 1963-66; clin. researcher Lahey Clinic Found., Boston, 1966-79; biochemist Goddard Med. Assocs., Brockton, Mass., 1979-81; clin. rsearcher, supr. gen. lab. Biostat Lab., Brockton, 1981-84; lab. dir. New Eng. Sinai Hosp., Stoughton, Mass., 1984-88, St. John of God Hosp., Brookline, Mass., 1988—. Contbr. articles to sci. jours., chpt. to book. Soccer coach Bridgewater (Mass.) Youth Soccer Assn., 1980-86. With U.S. Army, 1957-59. Mem. Am. Fedn. Clin. Rsch., Am. Soc. Clin. Lab. Sci., N.Y. Acad. Scis., Mass. Archaeol. Soc. (field archaeologist 1979-86), Sigma Xi. Roman Catholic. Home: 353 Hayward St Bridgewater MA 02324-1912 Office: St John of God Hosp 296 Allston St Brookline MA 02146-1600

ANDERSON, LESLEY JEAN, surgeon; b. Darby, Pa., June 29, 1951; d. Kenneth and Frances A.; 1 child. BS, Pa. State U., 1972; MD, Hershey Med. Sch., 1976. Diplomate Am. Bd. Orthopedic Surgery. Orthopedic resident UCLA Med. Ctr., 1983; sports medicine fellow Blazina Clinic, Sherman Oaks, Calif., 1984; with Ortho Clinic Kaiser Permanente, San Francisco, 1977-79; cons. U.S. Dept. Labor, San Francisco, 1981—; pvt. practice Blazina Orthopedic Clinic, Sherman Oaks, 1984-85, Cal Pac Med Ctr., San Francisco, 1985-94; ptnr. Orthopedic Surgery Assocs., San Francisco, 1994—; orthopedic specialty rep. Cal Pacific Med. Svcs. Orgn., San Francisco, 1993-96, chair managed care com., 1994—. Editl. bd. Am. Acad. Ortho Surgeon, 1994—; contbg. author: The Knee, 1995 (Mosby award 1995), others. Asst. soccer coach, Vikings Soccer Club, San Francisco, 1993—. Lt. USPHS, 1976-77. Fellow AMA; mem. Calif. Med. Assn., San Francisco Med. Soc., Am. Assn. Phys. Human Rights (bd. dirs. 1988-89), Ruth Jackson Orthopedic Soc. Democrat. Episcopalian. Office: Orthopedic Surgery Assocs Ste 115 2100 Webster St San Francisco CA 94115

ANDERSON, LEWIS DANIEL, medical educator, orthopaedic surgeon; b. Greensboro, Ala., Oct. 13, 1930; s. Thomas Jefferson and Frances (Daniel) A.; m. Stella Stickney Cobbs, July 7, 1951; children: Evelyn Anderson McGehee, Lewis Daniel Jr., Tunstall Cobbs, Lida Anderson Cotton. Student, Emory U., 1947-49; MD, U. Pa., 1953; MS in Orthopedic Surgery, U. Tenn., 1960. Diplomate Am. Bd. Orthopaedic Surgery. Resident in surgery U. Pa., Phila., 1953-54, 56-57; resident in orthopedics Campbell Clinic U. Tenn., Memphis, 1957-60, mem. staff Campbell Clinic, 1966-77, asst. prof. orthopedic surgery, 1960-65, assoc. prof., 1965-71, prof., 1971-77, asst. dean for hosp. affairs, 1972-73, assoc. dean for hosp. affairs, 1973-75, asst. to chancellor clin. ops., 1975-77; prof., chmn. dept. orthopedic surgery U. South Ala., Mobile, 1977-92, clin. prof. dept. orthopedic surgery, 1992-93, prof. emeritus, 1993—, pres. Health Svcs. Found., 1979-82, 85-88, pres. med. staff, 1981-82, interim dean, 1886-87, v.p. for med. affairs, 1987-92; bd. examiner Am. Bd. Orthopedic Surgery, 1967-84; med. dir. City of Memphis Hosp., 1972-75. Editor: AAOS Instructional Course Lectures Vol. 35, 1986; contbr. to books. Lt. M.C., USNR, 1954-56. Fellow ACS, Am. Acad. Orthopedic Surgeons; mem. Internat. Soc. for Orthopedics and Trauma, Am. Orthopaedic Assn. (traveling fellow to U.K. 1967, Hon. Med. Soc. 1953), Am. Assn. Orthopedic Chmn., Ala. Orthopaedic Soc. (pres. 1986-87), Isle Dauphin Country Club. Office: U South Ala Med Ctr Dept of Orthopaedic Surgery 507 Mastin Mobile AL 36617

ANDERSON, LOIS ANN, medical technologist, consultant; b. York, Pa., Oct. 6, 1952; d. Charles Theodore and Charlotte Catherine (Lingg) Kochenour; m. George Stephen Anderson, Sept. 18, 1976; 1 child, James Thomas. BS, York Coll., Pa., 1974. Staff med. technologist Columbia (Pa.) Hosp., 1974-75, Meml. Hosp., York Pa., 1975-84; lab. technician, receptionist, asst. to adminstr. Hillcrest Women's Med. Ctr., York Pa., 1984-88; chemistry staff med. technologist Mercy Med. Ctr., Balt., 1988-91; chemistry staff med. technologists Cen. Labs., Timonium, Md., 1991-93; staff med. technologist Mercy Med. Ctr., Balt., 1993—; cons. Physician Office Lab. com., Balt., 1988-89; founder, facilitator Surviving Breast Cancer Support Group, York Cancer Ctr., 1993—; vol. Reach to Recovery, 1994—. Sec. PTA, York, 1985-86, mem. PTA, 1985-91; mem. Pa. Breast Cancer Coalition, 1993—. Mem. Am. Soc. Clin. Pathologists, Am. Soc. Med. Technology. Republican. Roman Catholic. Home: 485 Green Valley Rd York PA 17403-9577 Office: Merry Med Ctr 301 Saint Paul Pl Baltimore MD 21202-2102

ANDERSON, LOUISE MARIE, community health nurse; b. Darby, Pa., Dec. 16, 1950; d. Victor Joseph and Eleanor Suzanne (Snyder) Anderson; m. Justin Charles Sweeney, June 22, 1973 (div. Oct. 1986); m. Bradley Joseph Powers, Oct. 17, 1992. Diploma, Thomas Jefferson U., 1971; BSN, Villanova U., 1976. RN, Pa. Staff nurse Cmty. Nursing Svcs., Phila., 1973-76; dir. profl. svcs. Pa. Home Health Svcs., Bryn Mawr, 1978-84; mng. dir. St. Joseph's Health Svcs., Phila., 1984-87; exec. dir. Pa. Home Health Svcs., Phila., 1987-88; dir. profl. svcs. Homecall of Delaware Valley, West Chester, Pa., 1988-90; dir. profl. and clin. svcs. Kimberly Quality Care, Conshohocken, Pa., 1990-91; adminstr. Healthcare Svcs. Network, Kennett Square, Pa., 1991-95; dir. profl. svcs. MD Healthcare Svcs., Upper Darby, Pa., 1995—; cons. Home Care Mgmt. Assocs., Springfield, Pa., 1995—; counselor SID pilot program Cmty. Nursing Svcs., Phila., 1973-76; creator 1st cmty. based discharge planning program, 1978-80; developer home care svcs. for life care and SNF, 1991-95. Home: 187 New Garden Rd Avondale PA 19311

ANDERSON, MALCOLM FRANCIS, radiologist, educator; b. Leeds, Yorkshire, Eng., Mar. 7, 1935; came to U.S., 1973; s. Frank L. and Isobella C. (Simpson) A.; m. Valerie M. Meckiff, June 3, 1961; children: Victoria N. Anderson Benvegnu, Nicholas J.R. BSc in Physiology, U. London, 1957, MB, BS, 1960. Diplomate Am. Bd. Radiology. Intern St. George's Hosp., London; rotating intern Stanford U. Med. Sch., 1976; chief radiology svc. VA Med. Ctr., Fresno, Calif., 1964—, chief staff, 1989—; asst. prof. radiology Stanford (Calif.) U., 1964-73; assoc. clin. prof. U. Calif., San Francisco, 1964, prof. clin. radiology, 1988—, asst. dean, 1989—. Fellow Royal Coll. Radiologists, Coll. Physician Executives; mem. Soc. for Med. Decision Making, Soc. for Computer Applications in Radiology, Soc. Gastrointestinal Radiologists, Assn. Univ. Radiologists, Assn. Am. Gastroenterologists. Office: VA Med Ctr (11) 2615 E Clinton Ave Fresno CA 93703-2223

ANDERSON, MARK ALAN, physical therapist, educator; b. Garden City, Kans., July 10, 1953; s. Robert Deane and Glenda Lee (Benedict) A.; m. Vickie Jo Reifschneider, Sept. 4, 1976; 1 child, Benjamin Jacob. BS, U. Kans., 1975; MS, Fort Hays State U., 1979; PhD, U. Va., 1988. Chief phys. therapist Trego-Lemke Meml. Hosp., WaKeeney, Kans., 1975-77; cons. geriatric phys. therapist pvt. practice, N.W. Kans., 1976-79; pediatric phys. therapist Unified Sch. Dist. #489, Hays, Kans., 1977-78; asst. prof. phys. therapy U. Ctrl. Ark., Little Rock, 1979-80, U. Okla., Okla. City, 1980-85; adj. instr. HPER U. Va., Charlottesville, 1985-88, acad. sports medicine advisor, 1985-88; assoc. prof. phys. therapy U. Okla., Oklahoma City, 1988—, dir. grad. studies, 1990—; mem. sports medicine staff U.S. Paralympic Team, Barcelona, 1992, Atlanta, 1996, U.S. World U. Winter Games, U.S. Olympic Com., Jaca, Spain, 1995; med. dir. Jr. Nat. Wheelchair Chapionships, Edmond, Okla., 1994; sports medicine coord. Wheel Chair Sports USA, Internat. Games Planning Com., 1993—. Author: (with others) Techniques in Orthopedics, 1990, Athletic Injuries and Rehabilitation, 1996; reviewer Jour. Orthop. and Sports Phys. Therapy, 1991—, Jour. Phys. Therapy Edn., 1991—. Mem. Gov.'s Coun. on Phys. Fitness and Sports, 1989; vol. missionary trip, United Meth. Ch., Ulyanovsk, Russia, 1992, 94, Habitat for Humanity, Okla. City, 1995-96; vol. coach soccer, basketball Boys and Girls Club, Okla. City, 1995-96. Grantee: Found. for Phys. Therapy, 1988, U.S. Tennis Assn., 1989, Nat. Athletic Trainers Assn., 1991. Mem. Am. Phys. Therapy Assn. (registered phys. therapist), Nat. Athletic Trainers Assn. (cert., Eddie Wojecki Achievement award 1989), Am. Coll. Sports Medicine, Alpha Eta. Democrat. Methodist. Office: U Okla Health Scis Ctr CHB-237 PO Box 26901 Oklahoma City OK 73190

ANDERSON, MARK WENDELL, gastroenterologist; b. Berwyn, Ill., Feb. 20, 1964; s. Wendell Carl and Joyce Mae (Henn) A.; m. Michelle Gay Kreiner, May 9, 1992. BS in Biology, Hardin-Simmons U., Abilene, Tex., 1986; MD, Southwestern Med. Sch., Dallas, 1990. Cert. bd. internal medicine. Resident, intern in internal medicine U. Iowa, Iowa City, 1990-93; fellow in gasteroenterology U. Okla. Hosp., Oklahoma City, 1993—. Mem. Alpha Omega Alpha. Office: Carolina Gastroenterology 30 Memorial Medical Dr Greenville SC 29605

ANDERSON, MITCHELL, chiropractor; b. L.A., Aug. 9, 1963; s. Charles Terry and Anita Louise (Rose) A.; m. Patricia Elaine Evora, June 10, 1989. AA, Cerritos Coll., 1983; BS, Cleveland Chiropractic Coll., L.A., 1985; D of Chiropractic, Cleveland Chiropractic Coll., 1987; sports cert., L.A. Chiropractic Coll., 1988. Cert. chiropractor Nat. Bd. Chiropractic Examiners; bd. eligible/Diplomate Am. Bd. Chiropractic Sports Physicians; lic. chiropractor, Calif., Hawaii. Massage therapist/owner Body Work by Mitch, Downey, Calif., 1983-87; chiropractor Anderson Chiropractic Ctr., Los Alamitos, Calif., 1987—; referal doctor/owner Anderson Worker's Referal Svc., Orange, Calif., 1991—; physician Rossmor Athletic Club, Seal Beach, Calif., 1987—, Bretheren Christian High Sch., Cypress, Calif., 1988—; team chiropractor Anaheim Bullfrogs, 1993—; pres. Calif. Chiropractic Coun. on Sports Injuries and Phys. Fitness; physician 1992 Olympic Games, Barcelona, Spain, Profl. Rodeo, 1992—, 1996 Olympic Games, Atlanta. Mem. Am. Chiropractic Assn. (sports cert. 1989, coun. sports injuries 1988—), Fed. Internat. Chiropractic Sportive, Calif. Chiropractic Assn., Rotary, Masons (3 degree), Scottish Rite (32 degree). Republican. Baptist. Home: PO Box 5116 Los Alamitos CA 90720 Office: Anderson Chiropractic Ctr 10671 Los Alamitos Blvd Los Alamitos CA 90720-2148

ANDERSON, NANCY J., dermatologist; b. Battle Creek, Mich., July 19, 1950; d. Harold E. and Mary V. Anderson. BA cum laude, Andrews U., 1972; MD, Loma Linda U., 1976. Diplomate: Am. Bd. Dermatology, 1982. Intern, Loma Linda U. (Calif.), 1976-77, resident in internal medicine, 1977-78; family practice staff Kaiser Permanente, San Bernardino, Calif., 1978; resident in dermatology Henry Ford Hosp., Detroit, 1978-81, staff, 1981-82; assoc. prof. dermatology, pediatrics, pathology Loma Linda U., 1982—;

cons. Jerry L. Pettis VA Hosp., Loma Linda, San Bernardino County Hosp., 1982—. Mem. AMA, Calif., Med. Assn., San Bernardino Med. Soc. Republican. Contbr. articles to profl. jours. Office: Faculty Med Offices 11370 Anderson St Suite 2600 Loma Linda CA 92354

ANDERSON, PAUL NATHANIEL, oncologist, educator; b. Omaha, May 30, 1937; s. Nels Paul E. and Doris Marie (Chesnut) A.; BA, U. Colo., 1959, MD, 1963; m. Dee Ann Hipps, June 27, 1965; children: Mary Kathleen, Anne Christen; Diplomate Am. Bd. internal Medicine, Am. Bd. Med. Mgmt. Intern Johns Hopkins Hosp., 1963-64, resident in internal medicine, 1964-65; rsch. asso., staff assoc. NIH, Bethesda, Md., 1965-70; fellow in oncology Johns Hopkins Hosp., 1970-72, asst. prof. medicine, oncology Johns Hopkins U. Sch. Medicine, 1972-76; attending physician Balt. City Hosps., Johns Hopkins Hosp., 1972-76; dir. dept. med. oncology Penrose Cancer Hosp., Colorado Springs, Colo., 1976-86; clin. asst. prof. dept. medicine U. Colo. Sch. Medicine, 1976-90, clin. assoc. prof., 1990—; dir. Penrose Cancer Hosp., 1979-86, chief dept. medicine, 1985-86; founding dir. Cancer Ctr. of Colorado Springs, 1986-95; dir. Rocky Mountain Cancer Ctr., Colorado Springs, 1995—; med. dir. So. Colo. Cancer Program, 1979-86; pres., chmn. bd. dirs. Preferred Physicians, Inc., 1986-92; mem. Colo. Found. for Med. Care Health Standards Com., 1985, sec., exec. com., 1990, bd. dirs., pres. 1992-93; mem., chmn. treatment com. Colo. Cancer Control and Rsch. Panel, 1980-83; prin. investigator Cancer Info. Svc. of Colo., 1981-87. Editor Advances in Cancer Control; editorial bd. Journal of Cancer Progam Management, 1987-92, Health Care Management Review, 1988—. Mem. Colo. Gov.'s Rocky Flats Employee Health Assessment Group, 1983-84; mem. Gov.'s Breast Cancer Control Commn. Colo., 1984-89; pres., founder Oncology Mgmt. Network, Inc., 1985-95; founder, bd. dirs. Timberline Med. Assocs., 1986-87; founder, dir. So. Colo. AIDS project 1986-91; mem. adv. bd. Colo. State Bd. Health Tumor Registry, 1984-87; chmn., bd. dirs. Preferred Physicians, Inc., 1986-92; bd. dirs. Share Devel. Co. of Colo. Share Health Plan of Colo., 1986-90, vice chmn., 1989-91; bd. dirs., chmn. Preferred Health Care, Inc., 1991-92; mem. health care standards com., trustee Colo. Found. for Med. Care (PRO); mem. nat. bd. med. dirs. Fox Chase Cancer Ctr. Network, Phila., 1987-89; mem. tech. expert panel Harvard Resource-Based Relative Value Scale Study for Hematology/Oncology, 1991-92; founding dir. Colo. Healthcare Improvement Found., 1994-95. Served with USPHS, 1965-70. Diplomate Am. Bd. Internal Medicine, Am. Bd. Med. Oncology. Mem. Am. Soc. Clin. Oncology (chmn. subcom. on oncology clin. practice standards, mem. clin. practice com., rep. to AMA 1991—, mem. healthcare svcs. rsch. com., chmn. clin. guidelines subcom. 1993—), Am. Assn. Cancer Rsch., Am. Assn. Cancer Insts. (liaison mem. bd. trustees 1980-92), Am. Coll. Physician Execs., Am. Hospice Assn., Am. Soc. Internal Medicine, Nat. Cancer Inst. (com. for community hosp. oncology program evaluation 1982-83), Colo. Soc. Internal Medicine, Assn. Community Cancer Ctrs. (chmn. membership com. 1980, chmn. clin. rsch. com. 1983-85, sec. 1983-84, pres.-elect 1984-85, pres. 1986-87, trustee 1981-88), AAAS, N.Y. Acad. Scis., Johns Hopkins Med. Soc., AMA (mem. practice parameters forum 1989—, adv. com. to HCFA on uniform clin. data set), Colo. Med. Soc., Am. Mgmt. Assn., Am. Assn. Profl. Cons., Am. Soc. for Quality Control, Am. Acad. Med. Dirs., Am. Coll. Physician Execs., El Paso County Med. Soc., Rocky Mountain Oncology Soc. (chmn. clin. practice com. 1989-94, pres.-elect 1990, pres. 1993-95), Acad. Hospice Physicians, Coalition for Cancer, Colo. Springs Clin. Club, Alpha Omega Alpha. Contbr. articles to med. jours. Office: Rocky Mountain Cancer Ctr 110 East Monroe St Ste 200 PO Box 7148 Colorado Springs CO 80933-7148 also: 32 Sanford Rd Colorado Springs CO 80906-4233

ANDERSON, PETER JOSEPH, orthopedic surgeon; b. St. Paul, Aug. 10, 1959; s. Joseph N. and Ruth E. Anderson; m. Joella Voight, Aug. 29, 1987; children: Joseph R., Katelyn M. BA, Jamestown Coll., 1981; MD, Johns Hopkins U., 1985. Diplomate Am. Bd. Orthopaedic Surgery. Orthopedic resident Mayo Clinic, Rochester, Minn., 1990; orthopedic surgeon, pres. Ill. S.W. Orthopedics Ltd., Granite City, 1990—; chief of surgery St. Elizabeth Med. Ctr., Granite City, 1994—, chief of staff, 1996—; chief of surgery Anderson Hosp., Maryville, Ill., 1996—. Fellow AMA, Am. Acad. Orthopedic Surgery. Republican. Presbyterian. Office: Ill SW Orthopedics Ste 5 2044 Madison Granite City IL 62040

ANDERSON, RICHARD LELAND, health facility administrator; b. Appleton, Minn., July 27, 1944; s. Orrin Sidney and Eileen Irene (Brown) A.; m. Suzanne Lee Gustavson, Nov. 2, 1968; children: Carla Sue, Katherine, Gayle, Cynthia. BS in Pharmacy, U. Minn., 1968; MS in Pharmacy, N.D. State U., 1978; M in Health Adminstrn., Chapman U., 1995. Cert. pharmacist, Minn. Enlisted as pharmacist USN, 1974, advanced through grades to exec. officer, 1995; capt. US Naval Hosp., Okinawa, Japan, 1995—. Mem. Am. Coll. Healthcare Execs. (assoc.). Office: US Naval Hosp, Okinawa Japan

ANDERSON, RICHARD MCLEMORE, internist; b. Gainesville, Fla., Mar. 3, 1930; s. Montgomery Drummond and Myrtle (McLemore) A.; m. Leewood Shaw, Mar. 21, 1959; children: Richard McLemore Jr., Bruce Dexter. BS, U. Fla., 1951; MD, Emory U., 1958. Diplomate Am. Bd. Internal Medicine. Chief of staff Alachua Gen. Hosp., Gainesville, Fla. 1973-75; internist Gainesville, Fla., 1962—; Chmn. of bd. Santa Fe Health Care, Gainesville, 1984-91; bd. dirs. AV Med. Santa Fe. Pres. Rotary Club of Gainesville, 1980-81. Capt. USAF, 1951-54. Mem. AMA, Alachua County Med. Soc. (v.p. 1972), Fla. Med. Assn., Am. Soc. Internal Medicine. Presbyterian. Office: 106 SW 10th St Gainesville FL 32601-6201

ANDERSON, RICHARD POWELL, thoracic surgeon, educator; b. Seattle, June 1, 1934; s. Berton E. and Emmogene (Powell) A.; m. JoAnne Downing, June 21, 1958; children: Arlen, Alan. BS, U. Wash., Seattle, 1956, MD, 1959. Diplomate Am. Bd. Surgery, Am. Bd. Thoracic Surgery. Intern in surgery Johns Hopkins U., Balt., 1959-60, asst. resident, 1960-61, 63-66, resident surgeon, 1966-67; asst. prof. U. Calif., Davis, 1967-70; assoc. prof. U. Oreg. Med. Sch., Portland, 1970-74; chief cardiothoracic surgery Virginia Mason Clinic, Seattle, 1974—; clin. prof. U. Wash. Sch. Medicine, Seattle, 1965—. Contbr. numerous articles to profl. jours. Trustee Virginia Mason Med. Ctr., 1987—, Wash. affiliate Am. Heart Assn., 1987—. Sr. Surgeon USPHS, 1961-63. Fellow ACS, Am. Surg. Assn.; mem. AMA (com. on allied health 1988—), Soc. Thoracic Surgeons (sec. 1989—), Western Thoracic Surg. Assn. (pres. 1991), Am. Bd. Thoracic Surgery, Am. Assn. for Thoracic Surgery. Episcopalian. Office: Virginia Mason Med Ctr PO Box 900 Seattle WA 98111-0900

ANDERSON, ROBERT K., health care company executive; b. Brainerd, Minn., Oct. 20, 1935; s. Kenneth F. and Ida Anderson; m. Sydney M. Anderson, June 18, 1976; 1 child, Kimberly C.; children from previous marriage; Robert W., Richard K., Laura A. BEE, U. Minn., 1963. Co-founder, chief exec. officer, chmn. Valleylab, Inc., Boulder, Colo., 1969-85, chmn., 1986—; bd. dirs. Med. Devices, Inc., Pfizer Hosp. Products Group, Am. Med. Sys., Meritech, Inc., Camino Labs., Inc., Novacept, Inc., ReSound, Inc.; pres. Pfizer Health Care Ventures; chmn. bd. Contbr. articles to profl. jours.; patentee in field. Recipient Outstanding Achievement award U. Minn., 1992. Mem. IEEE, Health Industry Mfrs. Assn. (dir., mem. exec. com., treas. 1982-83), Assn. Advancement Med. Instrumentation (bd. dirs., corp. v.p. 1978-81), Young Pres.' Orgn. (edn. chmn. 1982, chpt. chmn. 1983, membership chmn. 1984), N.Y. Acad. Scis. Home: 7262 Old Post Rd Boulder CO 80301-3916 Office: Valleylab Inc 5920 Longbow Dr Boulder CO 80301-3202

ANDERSON, ROBERT LEROY, physician; b. Omaha, May 1, 1944; s. John Sheridan and Dorothy (Jones) A.; m. Amy Kathryn Svehla, June 29, 1975; children: Neil David, Alec Michael, Mark Alan. BA, U. Nebr., 1966; MD, U. Nebr. Med. Coll., Omaha, 1977. Diplomate Nat. Bd. Med. Examiners, Am. Bd. Surgery. Resident gen. surgery U. Nebr. Med. Ctr., Omaha, 1977-82; attending physician Mary Lanning Meml. Hosp., Hastings, Nebr., 1982—. Capt. USAF, 1967-73, Vietnam. Mem. Rotary. Office: 2115 N Kansas Hastings NE 68901

ANDERSON, ROBERT MAXWELL SCOTT, medical equipment manufacturers' representative; b. Bay City, Mich., Mar. 14, 1942; s. Raymond James and Elizabeth (Scott) A.; m. Barbara Ann Nase, June 4, 1966; children: Cheryl C., David S. BA and Scis., U.S. Mil. Acad., West Point, 1965; M Polit. Sci., U. Dayton, 1969; MBA in Health Care Adminstrn., George Washington U., 1973. Diplomate Am. Coll. Healthcare Execs.; cert. healthcare exec.; lic. nursing home adminstr. Nat. recruiter C. of C. of U.S., Washington, 1972; adminstrv. resident The Fairfax Hosp., Falls Church, Va., 1973; adminstrv. officer VA Med. Ctr., Washington, 1973-74; adminstrv. asst. to chief staff VA Med. Ctr., Chgo., 1975-76, asst. to chief staff, 1976-78; asst. med. dist. coord. Med. Dist. Office, Denver, 1978-79; asst. hosp. dir. trainee VA Med. Ctr., Omaha, 1979-80; asst. hosp. dir. VA Med. Ctr., Lincoln, Nebr., 1980-81; assoc. ctr. dir. VA Med. & Regional Office Ctr., Wilmington, Del., 1981-87; dir. VA Outpatient Clinic, Anchorage, 1987-91; asst. med. ctr. dir., assoc. med. ctr. dir. VA Med. Ctr., Memphis, 1991-95; dir. The Gateway Group, Germantown, Tenn., 1996—; cons. Memphis City Schs., 1995; mem. nat. planning com. VA Asst./Assoc. Dir. Forum, Wilmington, 1987; testified before Alaska Gov.'s Commn. on Healthcare, Antchorage, 1988; mem. regent's ad. com. Am. Coll. Healthcare Execs., Dover, Del., 1985-86; amateur radio operator FCC, 1988—. Editor: Cost Containment Sourcebook, 1984 (Cash award 1984). Chmn. ch. fin. com., Cordova, Tenn., 1994, 95, chmn. audit com., 1994, 95; vol. Alzheimer's Day Care, Inc., Bartlett, Tenn., 1994; vol. Tenn. Spl. Olympics, 1996, Arts Guild Telethon, 1996. Capt. U.S. Army, 1965-70, lt. col. U.S. Army Res., 1993. Recipient Leadership award Vietnam Vets. Am., Wilmington, Del., 1984, Letter of Appreciation Adminstr. Vets. Affairs, Washington, 1985, Meritorious Svc. medal U.S. Dept. Def., 1995, Cert. of Appreciation Adopt-A-Sch. Program, Memphis, 1995. Mem. Midsouth Health-care Execs., Memphis Fed. Exec. Assn., Am. Assn. Homes and Svcs., World Affairs Coun., Lions Club Internat. (v.p.). Home: 2264 Coathbridge Dr Germantown TN 38139-5422

ANDERSON, ROBIN ELLEN, federal public health service officer; b. Brockton, Mass., Nov. 17, 1953; d. Robert and Marilyn Eldredge (Hughes) Clark; m. Erik Dennis Anderson, Jan. 16, 1977; 1 child, Jill Meredith. Diploma, Holyoke Hosp. Sch. Nursing, Holyoke, Mass., 1974; BSN, SUNY, Albany, 1984; MBA, Marymount U., 1988. RN, Md. Evening charge nurse patient care unit Goddard Meml. Hosp., Stoughton, Mass., 1974-76, asst. head nurse patient care unit, 1976; staff nurse U.S.A.F., 1976-78; clin. nurse patient care unit nursing dept. Clin. Ctr., NIH, Bethesda, Md., 1978-79, acting head nurse endocrine patient care unit nursing dept., 1979-80; coord. ambulatory care nursing dept. Clin. Ctr., NIH, Bethesda, Md., 1980-86; assoc. investigator rsch. studies Nat Inst. Child Health and Human Devel., 1984-86; commd. officer USPHS, 1986; head nurse ambulatory care allergy, arthritis, child health Allergy, Arthritis, Child Health and Eye Nursing Svc. NIH, Bethesda, 1986-90; rsch. nurse specialist Nat. Inst. Nursing Rsch., NIH, Bethesda, 1990—; presenter in field. Contbr. articles to profl. jours. Recipient commendation medal USPHS, 1989, 95, Achievement medal, 1992. Mem. Am. Acad. Ambulatory Nursing Adminstrn. (nat. networking com., program planning com. Greater Washington area 1984-90), Commd. Officers Assn. USPHS, Assn. Nurses in AIDS Care, Res. Officers Assn. Methodist. Home: 30 Allenhurst Ct Gaithersburg MD 20878-1990 Office: Nat Inst Nursing Rsch NIH NIH Bldg 31 Rm 5B-03 Bethesda MD 20892

ANDERSON, RON JOE, hospital administrator, physician, educator; b. Chickasha, Okla., Sept. 6, 1946; s. Ted J. and Ruby (Harston) Anderson Benjamin; m. Sue Ann Blakely, Apr. 12, 1975; children: Sarah Elizabeth, Daniel Jerrod, John Charles. B.S. in Pharmacy, Southwest U. Okla., 1969; M.D., U. Okla., 1973. Diplomate Am. Bd. Internal Medicine, Am. Bd. Geriatrics. Intern U. Tex. Southwestern Med. Sch., Parkland Meml. Hosp., VA Hosp., Dallas, 1973-74, resident and chief resident in internal medicine, 1974-76; asst. prof. internal medicine U. Tex. Health Sci. Ctr., Dallas, 1976-81, asst. dean clin. affairs, 1979-82, prof. internal medicine, 1981—; med. dir. ambulatory-emergency services Dallas County Hosp. Dist., 1979-82, acting. med. dir., 1981-82, CEO, 1982—; chmn. Tex. Bd. Health, 1991-93; mem. task force on teaching hosps. Tex. Hosp. Assn., 1982—, task force on indigent health care, 1983-86; cons. on high blood pressure Am. Heart Assn., 1981-83; advisor Tex. Assn. Physician Assts.; chmn. Neighborhood Clinic Cooperating Com., Dallas, 1980-82; bd. dirs. Children's Oncology Services Tex., Dallas, 1982-86, Addison, Carrollton, Coppell, Farmers Branch chpt. Am. Heart Assn., 1978-80; mem. Tex. Gov.'s Task Force on Indigent Health Care, 1983-86, Tex. Health and Human Services Coordinating Council, 1983-86, Tex. Cancer Council, 1985-87, Spl. Task Force on Future of Long-Term Health Care for Tex., Mayor's Task Force on Internat. Devel., Dallas AIDS Planning Commn.; mem. Tex. Bd. Health, 1983—, chmn., 1983-87, 91—; mem. Dallas Council on Alcoholism and Drug Abuse, 1982, bd. dirs., 1982—, v.p., 1986, pres., 1987-88; mem. adv. com. program to improve maternal and infant care in South Robert Wood Johnson Found. Contbr. articles to profl. jours. Bd. dirs. Project Independence, Greater Dallas Ahead, 1985—, Kaiser Found. Health Plan Tex., 1991, Interfaith Housing Coalition; preceptor Dallas Ind. Sch. Dist. Talented and Gifted Program, 1977; mem. Dallas Commrs. Ct. Task Force on Mental Patients, 1979, Dallas Alliance, 1986—, Dallas Assembly, 1984—, Hogg Found. for Mental Health Commn. on Community Care of Mentally Ill, 1987—; adv. bd. Dallas Challenge, 19846; co-chmn. Tex. Response, 1985—; chmn. mission bd. 1st Bapt. Ch. of Oak Cliff, and others. Recipient Tex. Aging Leadership award, 1987, Community Service award Community and Migrant Health Ctrs. Tex., 1986, Tex. Leadership in Aging award Tex. 6th Annual Joint Conf. on Aging, 1987, Disting. Alumnus award S.W. U. Okla., 1987, James E. Peavy Meml. award Tex. Pub. Health Assn., 1988, Dallas Hist. Soc. award, Headliner award Dallas Press Club, Health Care Profl. of Yr. award Tex. Nurses Assn., 1990; named to Disting. Alumni Hall of Fame Southwestern Okla. State U., 1987. Fellow ACP; mem. AMA, Nat. Assn. Pub. Hosps. (bd. dirs., exec. com., chmn.-elect 1991, Safety Net awrd 1990), Nat. Pub. Health and Hosp. Inst. (bd. dirs., chmn. devel. com., chmn. 1991), Tex. Med. Assn., Dallas County Med. Soc., Am. Soc. Internat. Medicine, Soc. Gen. Internal Medicine, Dallas-Ft. Worth Hosp. Coun. (chmn.-elect 1991), Salesmanship Dallas Club. Democrat. Baptist. Home: 1022 Wind Ridge St Duncanville TX 75137 Office: Dallas County Hosp Dist Parkland Meml Hosp 5201 Harry Hines Blvd Dallas TX 75235-7708

ANDERSON, ROSS BARRETT, healthcare facility manager; b. Toronto, Ont., Can., Aug. 25, 1951; came to U.S., 1956; s. John Ross and Constance (Nielson) A.; m. Gladys Jeanette Vincent, Aug. 26, 1972; children: Christopher Matthew, John Ross II, Josiah Dan. Student, Boston U., 1970-73. Housekeeping supr. Parker Hill Med. Ctr., Roxbury, Mass., 1973-76; acct. mgr. Servicemaster Inc., 1973—; housekeeping mgr. Union Hosp., Lynn, Mass., 1976-77, Quincy (Mass.) City Hosp., 1977-78, St. Joseph's Hosp., Lowell, Mass., 1978-79; housekeeping mgr. Waltham Weston Hosp. and Med. Ctr., Waltham, Mass., 1979-86, support services mgr., 1986-90, dir. environ. svcs., 1991-93, chmn. customer svcs. bd., 1992; asst. dir. clin. engring. Good Samaritan Med. Ctr., Stoughton/Brockton, Mass., 1993-95; dir. environ. svcs. Harrington Meml. Hosp., Southbridge, Mass., 1995—. Mem. Boston Latin Sch. Assn., Scots Charitable Soc. Boston, Free Evang. Fellowship, Easton, Mass. Home: 389 Crescent St West Bridgewater MA 02379-1425 Office: Harrington Meml Hosp 100 South St Southbridge MA 01550

ANDERSON, SANDRA LEE, ambulatory surgery nurse; b. Eldorado, Ohio, July 30, 1940; d. Maurice Dale and Rachel Virginia (Baker) Harter; m. Richard W. Anderson, Oct. 2, 1971; children: William, Suzanne. Diploma, Miami Valley Hosp., Dayton, Ohio, 1962. Cert. ambulatory peri anesthesia nurse. Med. unit staff nurse Reid Meml. Hosp., Richmond, Ind., 1962-66; surg. unit head nurse Yale-New Haven Hosp., 1967-71, Danbury (Conn.) Hosp., 1972-74; ambulatory surgery nurse mgr. New Milford (Conn.) Hosp., 1987—; instr. breast self-exam. Am. Cancer Soc. Mem. Am. Soc. of Post Anesthesia Nurses, Conn. Soc. Post Anesthesia Nurse. Office: New Milford Hosp New Milford CT 06776

ANDERSON, STEPHEN ALAN, family psychology educator. BS, Babson Coll., 1970; MEd, Northeastern U., 1977; PhD, Kans. State U., 1982. Lic. marriage and family therapist, Conn.; cert. prevention profl., Conn. Mental health counselor McLean Hosp., Belmont, Mass., 1973-78; adminstrv. coord. Danvers State Psychiat. Hosp. Dept. Mental Health, Hawthorne, Mass., 1978; staff psychologist Mystic Valley Community Mental Ctr., Woburn, Mass., 1978-79; grad. teaching asst. Kans. State U., Manhattan, 1979-80, asst. instr., asst. dir. Family Ctr., 1980-82; asst. prof. Family Studies U. Conn., Storrs, 1982-87, assoc. prof. Family Studies, 1987-92; dir. marital & family therapy program, 1982-87; prof. family studies U. Conn., Storrs, 1992—, dean family studies, 1993-95. Co-author: Family Myths: Psychotherapy Implications, 1989, Personal, Marital and Family Myths: Theoretical Formulations and Clinical Strategies, 1989, Family Interaction: A Multigenerational Developmental Perspective, 1995; contbr. articles to profl. jours. Recipient Marriage and Family Therapy award for disting. svc. to profession Conn. Assn. for Marriage and Family, 1995. Mem. ACA, Am. Assn. for Marriage and Family Therapy, Internat. Network on Personal Relationships, Nat. Coun. of Family Rels. Home: 80 Maple Rd Storrs Mansfield CT 06268-2533 Office: Sch Family Studies U Conn Box U-58 348 Mansfield Rd Storrs CT 06269

ANDERSON, STEPHEN L., internist; b. Evanston, Ill., May 1, 1946; s. Harry C. and Marjorie J. (Brumleve) A.; m. Nancy R. Merriman, May 13, 1972; children: Michael, Matthew. BS, U. Notre Dame, 1968; MD, U. Cin., 1972. Diplomate Am. Bd. Internal Medicine. Pvt. practice internal medicine South Bend, Ind., 1975—; assoc. med. dir. Health Plus HMO, South Bend, 1985-88, bd. dirs., 1985-88; chmn. quality assurance com. Lincoln Nat. Health Plan, Ft. Wayne, Ind., 1989-92, Prin. Healthcare Ind., Ft. Wayne, 1993-94; med. dir. Select Health Network, South Bend, 1994—. Co-chmn. med. com. Spl. Olympics, 1987. Fellow Am. Coll. Physicians; mem. Am. Coll. Physician Execs., Ind. State Med. Assn. Democrat. Roman Catholic. Office: South Bend Internal Med 720 E Cedar South Bend IN 46617

ANDERSON, SUE ANN, nutritionist; b. Harrisburg, Ill., Jan. 8, 1947; d. Raymond E. and June J. (Tucker) Debes; m. Larry D. Anderson, 1978; children: Sara Elaine, Kevin Michael. BS, U. Ill., 1969; MS, Auburn U., 1972; PhD, Purdue U., 1974. Registered dietitian. Rsch. home econ. Armour Food Rsch., Oakbrook, Ill., 1969-70; asst. prof. Auburn (Ala.) U., 1975-78; staff scientist FASEB/Life Scis. Rsch. Office, Bethesda, Md., 1978-83, sr. staff scientist, 1984-93, assoc. dir., 1994; adj. prof. U. Va., Va. Tech. Grad. Sch., Falls Church, 1987. Mem. APHA, Am. Inst. Nutrition, Am. Dietetics Assn.

ANDERSON, SUSAN CARLYLE, family nurse practitioner; b. Chgo., Feb. 24, 1930; d. Carlyle Fairfax and Ellen Elizabeth (Davis) Anderson; m. John Schultz, Nov. 6, 1949 (div. June 1968); children: Joseph, Mary, William, Samuel, Benjamin; m. David T. Bottini, July 20, 1979 (div. Nov. 1987). BSN with high honors, San Diego State U., 1966; MS in Family Practice Nursing, U. Calif., Davis, 1974. Cert. nurse practitioner; RN, Calif. Staff nurse San Diego County Univ. Hosp., San Diego, 1966-67, pub. health nurse, 1967-72; nurse practitioner North County Health Svc., San Ramon, Calif., 1974-75; nurse practitioner/clinic coord. Davis Free Clinic, 1975-79; sch. nurse/educator Dept. of Def., Panama City, 1970-81; nurse practitioner, clin. instr. Santa Clara County Valley Med. Ctr., San Jose, 1981—; profl. performance com. San Diego County Health Dept., 1970-72; mem. coordinating com. Davis Free Clinic/Drug Abuse, 1974-79; program developer La Raza-Sacramento, 1976; bldg. and protocol cons. various instns., San Jose, 1981—. Mem. RN Profl. Assn. Home and Office: 4929 E Mountain View San Diego CA 92116

ANDERSON, THOR EDWIN, managed care executive; b. Ann Arbor, Mich., Feb. 10, 1949; s. Odin W. and Helen (Hay) A.; m. Jane L. Bowling, Apr. 5, 1975; children: Glenn Magni, Ashley Belle. BA, Antioch Coll., Yellow Springs, Ohio, 1972; MA in Bus., U. Wis., 1978. Asst. to project dir. Mountaineer Family Health Plan, Beckley, W.Va., 1973-75; planning analyst Divsn. Health Policy and Planning, SOWI, Madison, wis., 1975-76; Medicare program coord. Marshfield (Wis.) Clinic, 1979-80; mgr. corp. planning and rsch. WPS-Blue Shield, Madison, 1980-84; exec. dir. Physicians Health Plan of Fla., Tampa, 1984-87, Unity Health Plan, Springfield, Ill., 1988-89; contracts mgr. Sanus Health Plan, St. Louis, 1989-92; dir. produt and mkt. devel. Gencare/Physicians Health Plan, St. Louis, 1992-95, v.p. Medicare, 1995—; bd. dirs. Group Health Coop of SCWI, Madison, 1976-78. Home: 1531 Sugar Grove Ct Saint Louis MO 63146 Office: Gencare/PHP 77 Westport Pla Ste 500 Saint Louis MO 63146

ANDERSON, WILLIAM BANKS, JR., ophthalmology educator; b. Durham, N.C., June 14, 1931; s. William Banks and Mildred Ursula (Everett) A.; m. Nancy Eldridge Walker, Sept. 17, 1960; children: Mary Banks, Mark Eldridge, Elizabeth Perry. A.B., Princeton U., 1952; M.D., Harvard U., 1956. Diplomate: Am. Bd. Ophthalmology (dir. 1986-92). Intern Duke U. Med. Ctr., Durham, N.C., 1956-57, resident, 1959-62, asst. prof. ophthalmology, 1962-67, assoc. prof. ophthalmology, 1967-76, prof. ophthalmology, 1976—, acting chmn., 1991-92; mem. profl. adv. com. N.C. Div. Services to the Blind, Raleigh, 1972-84. Chmn. bd. trustees Durham Acad., 1975-77. Served to capt. M.C. U.S. Army, 1957-59. Fellow ACS; mem. Am. Ophthalmol. Soc. (sec.-treas. 1989—), Am. Acad. Ophthalmology (bd. dirs. 1986-89), Am. Bd. Ophthalmology (bd. dirs. 1986-93). Episcopalian. Home: 2401 Cranford Rd Durham NC 27706-2511 Office: Duke U Eye Ctr Erwin Rd Durham NC 27710

ANDERSON, WILLIAM HENRY, psychobiologist, educator; b. Phila., Nov. 10, 1940; s. William Henry Schoen and Elizabeth Winifred (Laverty) A.; m. Catherine Sacchetti, Oct. 7, 1967 (dec. Sept. 1991); 1 child, Jennifer Ann Gist. B.S., MIT, 1962; M.A., U. Pa., 1967; M.D., Thomas Jefferson U., 1967; M.P.H., Harvard U., 1977. Diplomate: Am. Bd. Psychiatry and Neurology. Intern. Pa. Hosp., Phila., 1967-68; resident in psychiatry Mass. Gen. Hosp., Boston, 1968-71, assoc. psychiatrist dept. psychiatry, 1976—, dir. postgrad. edn., 1976-81; instr. psychiatry Harvard U., Boston, 1973-75, asst. prof., 1975-81, asst. clin. prof., 1981-82, lectr., 1982—; chmn. psychiatry St. Elizabeths Hosp., Boston, 1981-92; dir. clinical svcs. Augusta Mental Health Inst.; asst. attending psychiatrist Mclean Hosp., Belmont, Mass.; Cons. Scientists' Inst. Pub. Info.; mem. Carnegie Coun. Ethics and Internat. Affairs. Contbg. editor: The New Physician, 1977-79; editorial bd. Topics in Geriatrics, 1981-87, Jour. Geriatric Psychiatry and Neurology. Served to lt. comdr., M.C. USNR, 1971-73. Fellow Am. Psychiat. Assn., Human Biology coun.; mem. AAAS, Am. Acad. Clin. Psychiatrists, Internat. Soc. Polit. Psychology, Coun. on Fgn. Rels. (lectr. to coms.), Med. Assn. P.R. (hon.), Mass. Med. Soc., Soc. Ethnobiology, U.S. Naval Inst., Boston Athenaeum (proprietor), Harvard Club of Boston, Union Club, Sigma Xi. Office: 34 Coolidge Hill Rd Cambridge MA 02138-5527

ANDERSON-CERMIN, CHERYL KAY, orthodontics educator; b. Osceola, Wis., Aug. 28, 1956; d. Darrell Duane and Barbara Carolyn (Paulson) Peterson; m. Paul Bradley Anderson, Aug. 12, 1978 (div. June 1986); m. Jonathan A. Cermin, Dec. 31, 1995; 1 child, Hayley Kristine. AA, Normandale C.C., Bloomington, Minn., 1977; BS, U. Minn., 1985, DDS, 1986; cert. in advanced grad. studies, Boston U., 1990. Intern Sch. Dental Medicine Harvard U., Boston, 1986-87; pvt. practice, Boston, 1988-90; rsch. fellow U. Tex. S.W. Med. Sch., Dallas, 1990-91, asst. prof. orthodontics, dir. orthodontics, 1991—. Bd. dirs. Life Enhancement for People, Dallas, 1993-94; sec. ch. coun. Shepherd of Life Luth. Ch., Arlington, Tex., 1993-94. Mem. ADA, Am. Assn. Orthodontists, Am. Cleft Palate Assn.

ANDERSON-IMBERT, ANA ISABEL, rheumatologist, health care facility administrator; b. Buenos Aires, Aug. 21, 1940; d. Enrique and Margot (Di Clerico) Anderson Imbert; m. Jack Joseph Himelbau, May 30, 1965 (div. 1988); children: Robert, Vanessa. BA, U. Mich., 1960, MS, 1963, MD, 1968. Diplomate Am. Bd. Internal Medicine. Resident Columbia Presbyn. Hosp., 1969-70; rheumatologist Permanente Med. Group Kaiser, Hayward, Calif., 1973—; asst. chief medicine Kaiser-Permanente Med. Ctr., Hayward, Calif., 1976-79; chief medicine Kaiser-Permanente Med. Ctr., Fremont, Calif., 1979-86, chief legal medicine, 1983-86, asst. physician in charge, 1986-87, physician in charge, 1987—; asst. physician-in-chief Kaiser Hayward Med. Ctr., 1988-96, physician-in-chief, 1996; apptd. to the Med. Bd. of Calif., 1993, pres. divsn. of faculty, 1996. Recipient fellow Cornell U., 1970-71, U. Calif. Med. Sch. fellow, 1971-72. Mem. ACP, Am. Rheumation Assn. Home: 909 Paramount Rd Oakland CA 94610-2438 Office: Kaiser-Permanente Med Ctr 27400 Hesperian Blvd Hayward CA 94545

ANDERSSON, BERNDT AKE SIGURD, surgeon, pediatrician; b. Norrköping, Sweden, Oct. 4, 1918; s. B. Gustav and Elin Susanna (Larsson) A.; m. Maud B. Lindberg, Feb. 18, 1952; children: Eva, Per, Lena. PhD, Karolinska Inst., Stockholm, 1948. Registrar Dept. Gen. Surgery and Pediatric Surgery, Karlshamn, Stockholm, Sweden, 1945-52; registrar, sr. surgeon Dept. Gen. Surgery, östersund, Sweden, 1952-59; sr. surgeon U. of Umeå, Sweden, 1959-72; head Dept. Gen. Surgery, Kristianstad, Sweden, 1972-83; head physician Social Ins. Svc., Kristianstad, Sweden, 1987-95. Contbr. articles to profl. jours.

ANDERSSON, LENNART N.E., chemist, researcher; b. Lönneberga, Sweden, Aug. 17, 1937; s. Karl E. and Olga W. (Karlsson) A.; m. Margareta K. Konradsson, June 8, 1974; children: Maria, Charlotta. MSc Pharm., Uppsala U., 1969. Mgr. Kabi AB, Stockholm, 1969-72, Kabivitrum AB, Stockholm, 1973-90, Kabi Pharmacia AB, Stockholm, 1991-92; chemist Kabi Pharmacia AB, Uppsala, 1992-95, Pharmacia & Upjohn, Uppsala, 1995—. Mem. Swedish Acad. Pharm. Scis. Home: Vallstanasvagen 81, S-19570 Rosersberg Sweden

ANDERSSON, TOMMY EVERT, cell biology educator; b. Karlskrona, Sweden, June 10, 1956; s. Evert Jonny and Inga Maria (Hakansson) A.; m. Anita Marianne Sjölander, Aug. 10, 1985; children: Jonatan, Kristina. PhD, U. Uppsala, Sweden, 1983. Rsch. assoc. dept. med. microbiology U. Linköping, 1984-88, assoc. prof. dept. cell biology, 1988-96; prof. exptl. pathology Lund U., Malmö, Sweden, 1996—. Contbr. articles to profl. jours. including Jour. Biol. Chem. and Proc. Nat. Acad. Fogarthy fellowship NIH, 1990; research Fernström Found., 1988, Odd Fellow Found., 1987. Mem. Am. Soc. for Cell Biology, Am. Soc. for Biochemistry and Molecular Biology, N.Y. Acad. Scis., Swedish Soc. Medicine. Home: Roddaregatan 30, S21611 Malmö Sweden Office: Lund Univ, Div Exptl Pathology, Divsn Exptl Pathology MAS, S20502 Malmö Sweden

ANDERT, JEFFREY NORMAN, clinical psychologist; b. Aberdeen, S.D., May 21, 1950; s. Norman Joseph and Irene Eleanor (Olson) A.; m. Diane Kay Dunham, May 29, 1971; Jason Ryan, Jonathan Erik, Justin Matthew. BA in Psychology, Augsburg Coll., 1971; MA in Psychology, Mankato (Minn.) State U., 1973; PhD in Psychology, U. So. Miss., 1976. Diplomate in Clin. Psychology Am. Bd. Profl. Psychology; lic. psychologist, Mich. Grad. asst. Mankato State U., Minn., 1972-73, U. So. Miss., Hattisburg, Miss., 1974-75; psychology intern Des Moines Child Guidance Ctr., Des Moines, 1975-76; clin. psychologist Battle Creek (Mich.) Child Guidance Clinic, 1976-80; pvt. practice Battle Creek, 1978—; pres., adminstrv. dir. Psychol. Cons. of Mich., P.C., Battle Creek, 1979—; administrv. dir. Chem. Dependency Resources, Battle Creek, 1982—; med. expert Office of Hearings and Appeals, Social Security Adminstrn., Lansing, Mich., 1986—. Contbr. articles to profl. jours. Pres., trustee Lakeview Pub. Sch. Dist., Battle Creek, 1991—; adult leader Boy Scouts Am., Battle Creek, 1988—. Disting. Svc. award, So. Cen. Mich. Substance Abuse Commn., Jackson, Mich., 1987. Fellow Acad. Clin. Psychology; mem. Assn. for the Advancement of Behavior Therapy, Am. Psychol. Assn., Mich. Psychol. Assn., Mich. Substance Abuse Program Dirs. Assn., South Cen. Mich. Substance Abuse Program Dirs. Assn. (pres. 1986-87). Lutheran. Home: 144 Waupakisco Bch Battle Creek MI 49015-3144 Office: Psychol Cons Mich PC 2518 Capital Ave SW Ste 2 Battle Creek MI 49015-4104

ANDO, SHIGERU, biology educator; b. Nagoya, Japan, Oct. 26, 1929; s. Kenji and Kikue (Ikai) A.; m. Youko Ishii, Apr. 8, 1958; children: Satoshi, Atsushi. BS, Nagoya U., 1954, MS, 1956, DSc, 1961. Instr. Nagoya U., 1959-68; assoc. prof. biology (biotelemetry) Aichi Kenritsu U., Nagoya, 1968-78, prof., 1978-95; cons. on harmful birds Chuubu Electric Power Co. Ltd., Nagoya, 1988-90; dir. investigation com. on natural nomument of cormorant, Nagoya, 1983. Co-author: Telemeter and Stimulator for Living, 1980, Sociology before Man, 1990; editor: Wild Herd, 1979. Mem. Com. Natural Properties, Aichi Prefecture, Nagoya, 1984—. Recipient award Found. for Sci. in Tokai, 1965, Ishida Found. for Sci., 1983; grantee Sakkoukai, 1964-66. Mem. Ecol. Soc. Japan. Home: 2-229 Shirotuchi Haruki, Tougou-cho Aichi-gun 470-01, Japan Office: Aichi Kenritsu U, 3-28 Takadacho, Nagoya 467, Japan

ANDOLF, ELLIKA MARGARETA, obstetrician, gynecologist; b. Uppsala, Sweden, Jan. 20, 1949; d. Nils Ake and Inger Anna (Svenson) Andolf; m. Per Vilhelm Aspenberg, Dec. 8, 1979; children: Ylva Aurora, Hedvig Elenora, Marta Lovisa. MD, U. Uppsala, 1976; PhD, U. Hosp. Lund, 1989. Intern Vasteras Hosp., 1976-82; obstetricians/gynecologist U. Hosp., Lund, 1983—, head ultrasound dept., 1995—, assoc. prof., 1996—. Mem. Swedish Soc. Gynecologists and Obstetrics, Swedish Soc. Obs-gyn. Ultrasound, Tennis Club of Lund. Lutheran. Home: Astrakanvagen 1, 223 56 Lund Sweden Office: Dept Ob/Gyn, Univ Hosp, 224 56 Lund Sweden

ANDONOPOULOS, ANDREW P., physician, researcher, educator; b. Patras, Achaia, Greece, Dec. 19, 1947; s. Panagiotis A. and Sophia (Kazanis) A.; m. Nicolitsa Georgiou, Aug. 18, 1973; children: Panagiotis, Constantinos, Joannis. MD, Sch. Medicine, Athens, 1971; PhD, Sch. Medicine, Patras, Greece, 1982. Cert. ECFMG, 1971, physician and surgeon Mich., 1977; diplomate AM. Bd. Internal Medicine, Am. Bd. Rheumatology, Bd. Internal Medicine, Greece, Bd. Rheumatology, Greece. Med. intern, resident Wayne State U., Detroit, 1974-77, rheumatology fellow, 1977-79; sr. registrar Patras U., Agios Andreas Hosp., Patras, Greece, 1980-86; dir. rheumatology divsn. Ioannina (Greece) Gen. Hosp., 1986-88; asst. prof. medicine, rheumatology U. Patras Med. Sch., 1989-93, assoc. prof. medicine, rheumatology, 1993—; chief divsn. rheumatology Patras U. Med. Sch., Greece, 1989—. Mem. editl. bd. Clinical and Experimental Rheumatology, 1988; contbr. chpts. to books, numerous articles to profl. jours. Doctor Greek War Navy, 1972-74. Fellow Am Coll. Physicians, Am. Coll. Rheumatology; mem. Greek Rheumatology Soc. Office: U Patras Sch Medicine, Box 1045, 261 10 Patras Greece

ANDONOV, NIKOLA BORIS, psychologist, consultant; b. Radovish, Macedonia, July 31, 1929; came to U.S., 1962; s. Boris Nikola and Zorka (Kaleova) A.; m. Mary Louise Andonov, July 4, 1974; 1 child, Nicole Marie. ThM, Sch. Tehology, Claremont, Calif., 1965; MA in Clin. Psychology, Fuller Grad. Sch. Psychology, Pasadena, Calif., 1969; PhD in Clin. Psychology, Calif. Sch. Profl. Psychology, L.A., 1973. Diplomate Am. Bd. Psychology. Intern Patton (Calif.) State Hosp., 1967-69; clin. psychologist, mgr., cons., surp. San Bernardino (Calif) County Dept. of Mental Health, 1969-82; pvt. practice San Bernardino, 1982—; mem. staff Cmty. Psychiatric Ctr., Fontane, Calif., 1991—, St. Bernardino (Calif.0 Med. Ctr., 1975—. Contbr. articles to profl. jours. With Macedonia Army, 1944-45. Mem. APA, Am. Soc. Psychology, Calif. Psychol. Assn. (exec. coun., chpt. rep.), Inland Psychol. Assn. (pres. 1983, Outstanding Svc./Leadership award 1983, 85, 89, 90, 94), So. Calif. Soc. Clin. Hypnosis, Rotary. Democrat. Methodist. Office: 2380 N Sierra Way San Bernardino CA 92405

ANDRAU, MAYA HEDDA, physical therapist; b. Digboi, Assam, India, Apr. 15, 1936; came to U.S., 1946; d. William Henry and Klara Irén Judit (Sima) Andrau; married, Sept. 1971 (div. July 1989); children: Francis Meher Traver, Darwin Meher Traver. BS in Phys. Therapy, Columbia U., 1958; MA in Social Anthropology, NYU, 1966. Lamaze cert. childbirth educator; lic. and registered phys. therapist. Phy. therapist Beekman-Downtown Hosp., N.Y.C., 1959-60; physiotherapist Stamford (Conn.) Hosp., 1963-64, Benedictine Hosp., Kingston, N.Y., 1966-69; pvt. practice in phys. therapy and lamaze Woodstock, N.Y., 1968-71; chief phy. therapist No. Duchess Hosp., Rhinebeck, N.Y., 1970-71; phy. therapist Waccamaw Pub. Health Dist., S.C. Dept. Health, Myrtle Beach, 1982-84; pain clinic specialist Pain Therapy Ctr. of Columbia (S.C.), Richland Meml. Hosp., 1986-87; phy. therapist Comprehensive Med. Rehab. Ctr., Conway, S.C., 1988-92; phys. therapist, instr. conditioning program Pawleys Island (S.C.) Wellness Inst., 1993; phys. therapist Total Care, Inc., 1993—; instr. phys. conditioning and therapeutic exercise courses, 1980—. Instr. Conditioning Program, Health Focus Brief for TV, 1990. Mem. Meher Spiritual Ctr., Inc., Alpha Kappa Delta. Follower of Avatar Meher Baba.

ANDRE, MICHAEL PAUL, physicist, educator; b. Des Moines, Apr. 25, 1951; s. Paul Leo and Pauline (Vermie) A.; m. Janice Joan Hanecak, Mar. 12, 1988. BA, Cen. U. Iowa, 1972; postgrad., U. Ariz., 1972-73; MS, UCLA, 1975, PhD, 1980. Assoc. engr. North Island Naval Air Sta., San Diego, 1970-71; rsch. assoc. Inst. Atmospheric Physics, Tucson, Ariz., 1972-73; mem. tech. staff Hughes Aircraft Co., L.A., 1973-74; postgrad. researcher UCLA, 1974-77; cons. L.A., 1975-84; med. radiologic physicist LACO/UCLA Olive View, L.A., 1977-81; sr. radiation physicist Cedars-Sinai Med. Ctr., L.A., 1979-84; chief med. physicist Dept. Vet. Affairs, San Diego, 1981—; prof. radiology, chief divsn.Physics and Engring, sch. medicine U. Calif., La Jolla, 1981—; qualified expert Calif. Radiol. Health Dept., Berkeley, 1979—; pub. spokesman Radiol. Soc., San Diego, 1987—; chmn. Nat. Physics Conf., San Diego, 1984-89. Editor: Physics and Biology of Radiology, 1988, Investigative Radiology, 1990—; contbr. articles to profl. jours. Mountain guide Sierra Club, L.A., 1977-80; dir. Ariz. PIRG, Tucson, 1973; jury foreman San Diego Dist. Ct., 1990; mountain guide Am. Alpine Inst., Peru, 1987. Rsch. grantee U. Calif.-San Diego Found., 1989—, NIH, Nat. Cancer Inst., 1986—, VA, 1989—, U.S. Army, 1994—. Mem. Am. Assn. Physicists in Medicine, Am. Inst. Ultrasound in Medicine, San Diego Radiol. Soc., Am. Inst. Physics, Soc. Photo-Optical Inst. Engrs. Office: U Calif Dept Radiology 9114 La Jolla CA 92093

ANDREASEN, NANCY COOVER, psychiatrist, educator; d. John A. Sr. and Pauline G. Coover; children: Robin, Susan. BA summa cum laude, U. Nebr., 1958, PhD, 1963; MA, Radcliffe Coll., 1959; MD, U. Iowa, 1970. Instr. English Nebr. Wesleyan Coll., 1960-61, U. Nebr., Lincoln, 1962-63; asst. prof. English U. Iowa, Iowa City, 1963-66; resident U. Iowa, 1970-73; asst. prof. psychiatry U. Iowa, Iowa City, 1973-77, assoc. prof., 1977-81, Andrew H. Woods prof. psychiatry, 1981—, dir. Mental Health Clin. Rsch. Ctr., 1987—; sr. cons. Northwick Pk. Hosp., London, 1983; acad. visitor Maudsley Hosp., London, 1986. Author: The Broken Brain, 1984, Introductory Psychiatry Textbook, 1991; editor: Can Schizophrenia be Localized to the Brain?, 1986, Brain Imaging: Applications in Psychiatry, 1988; book forum editor: Am. Jour. Psychiatry, 1988—, dep. editor, 1989-93, editor, 1993—. Woodrow Wilson fellow, 1958-59, Fulbright fellow Oxford U., London, 1959-60. Fellow Royal Coll. Physicians Surgeons Can. (hon.), Am. Psychiat. Assn., Am. Coll. Neuropharmacologists; mem. Am. Psychopathol. Assn. (pres. 1989-90), Inst. of Medicine of NAS. Office: U Iowa Hosps & Clinics 200 Hawkins Dr Iowa City IA 52242-1009

ANDREI, LINDA SUE, nursing consultant; b. Canton, Ohio, Nov. 17, 1948; d. Thurston Mack and Dorothy Mae (Beach) Phipps; m. Theodore Michael Andrei, June 6, 1975; children: Joshua Christian, Zachary Abraham. Diploma, Akron (Ohio) Gen. Med. Ctr., 1969; student, U. Akron, 1973-74. RN, Ohio, Maine. Office nurse Dr. Josephine Aronica, Norton, Ohio, 1969-72; head nurse Fallsview Mental Health Ctr., Cuyahoga Falls, Ohio, 1972-76; pvt. practice psychiat. observer Kennebec County Probate Ct., Augusta, Maine, 1985—; sch. nurse Sch. Adminstrn. Dist. 40, Waldoboro, Maine, 1993—; bd. dirs. Sheepscot Valley Regional Health Ctr. Home: 47 Bowman Mills Rd Washington ME 04574

ANDREOLI, KATHLEEN GAINOR, nurse, educator, administrator; b. Albany, N.Y., Sept. 22, 1935; d. John Edward and Edmunda Elizabeth (Ringlemann) Gainor; children: Paula Kathleen, Thomas Anthony, Karen Marie. B.S.N., Georgetown U., 1957; M.S.N., Vanderbilt U., 1959; D.S.N., U. Ala., Birmingham, 1979. Staff nurse Albany Hosp. Med. Ctr., 1957; instr. St. Thomas Hosp. Sch. Nursing, Nashville, 1958-59, Georgetown U. Sch., Nursing, 1959-60, Duke U. Sch. Nursing, 1960-61, Bon Secours Hosp. Sch. Nursing, Balt., 1962-64; ednl. coordinator, physician asst. program, instr. coronary care unit nursing inservice edn. Duke U. Med. Ctr., Durham, N.C., 1965-70; ednl. dir. physician asst. program dept. medicine U. Ala. Med. Ctr., Birmingham, 1970-75; clin. assoc. prof. cardiovascular nursing Sch. Nursing U. Ala. Med. Ctr., 1970-77, asst. prof. nursing dept. medicine, 1971, assoc. prof., 1972—, assoc. prof. nursing Sch. Pub. and Allied Health, 1973—; assoc. dir. Family Nurse Practitioner Program, 1976, assoc. prof. community health nursing Grad. Program, 1977-79, assoc. prof. dept. pub. health, 1978-79; prof. nursing, spl. asst. to pres. for ednl. affairs U. Tex. Health Sci. Ctr., Houston, 1979-82, acting dean Sch. Allied Health Scis., 1981; v.p. for ednl. services, interdisciplinary edn., internat. programs U. Tex. Health Sci. Ctr., 1983-87; v.p. nursing affairs Rush-Presbyn.-St. Lukes's Med. Ctr., Dean Rush U. Coll. Nursing, Chgo., 1987—; mem. nat. adv. nursing coun. VHA, 1992; cons. in field. Author, editor: (with others) Comprehensive Cardiac Care, 1983; editor: Heart and Lung, Jour. of Total Care, 1971; contbr. articles to profl. jours. Mem. adv. bd. Robert Wood Johnson Clin. Nurse Sch. Program; mem. vis. com. Vanderbilt U. Sch. Nursing; mem. Leadership Ill., 1991; mem. nat. nursing adv. com. Voluntary Hosp. Am., 1991; mem. governing coun. Inst. for Hosp. Clin. Nursing Edn. Am. Hosp. Assn., 1993. Recipient Founder's award N.C. Heart Assn., 1970, Disting. Alumni award Vanderbilt U. Sch. Nursing, 1985, Leadership Tex. award, 1985, Disting. Alumni award U. Ala. Sch. Nursing, 1991. Fellow Am. Acad. Nursing; mem. ANA, ACNA, Inst. Medicine, Nat. League Nursing, Ala. Heart Assn., Coun. Family Nurse Practitioners and Clinicians, Am. Heart Assn. Coun. Cardiovascular Nursing, Nat. Nursing Adv. Coun. Hosps. of Am., Sigma Theta Tau, Alpha Eta, Phi Kappa Phi. Roman Catholic. Home: 1212 S Lake Shore Dr Chicago IL 60610-2371 Office: Rush Presbyn-St Luke's Med Ctr 1653 W Congress Pky Chicago IL 60612-3833

ANDREOLI, THOMAS EUGENE, physician; b. Bronx, N.Y., Jan. 9, 1935. B.A. cum laude, St. Vincent Coll., 1956; M.D. magna cum laude, Georgetown U., 1960; ScD (hon.), St. Vincent Coll., Latrobe, Pa., 1987; PhD (hon.), Univ. Paris, 1993. Diplomate: Am. Bd. Internal Medicine and subspecialty in nephrology. Intern, resident in medicine Duke U., Durham, N.C., 1960-61, 64-65; assoc. prof. medicine and asst. prof. physiology Duke U., 1965-70; prof. medicine and physiology, dir. nephrology research and tng. center U. Ala. Sch. Medicine, Birmingham, 1970-78; prof., chmn. dept. internal medicine U. Tex. Med. Sch., Houston, 1979-87, Edward Randall III prof., chmn. dept. internal medicine, 1986-87; chief medicine Hermann Hosp., Houston, 1979-87; Nolan prof. and chmn. dept. internal medicine U. Ark. Coll. Medicine, Little Rock, 1988—. Author: Disturbances in Body Fluid Osmolality, 1977, Physiology of Membrane Disorders, 1978, 86, Cecil Essentials of Medicine, 1986, 90, 93, Molecular Biology of Membrane Transport Disorders, 1996; Editor Am. Jour. Physiology: Renal, Fluid and Electrolyte Physiology, 1976-83, Kidney Internat., 1985—; assoc. editor Annual Rev. Physiology, 1977-83, Am. Jour. Medicine, 1979-86; mem. editorial bd. Jour. Clin. Investigation, 1976-81, Mineral and Electrolyte Metabolism, 1977-80, Tex. Health Letter, 1980-88, Seminars in Nephrology, 1980—, Kidney Internat, 1981-85, Physiol. Revs., 1982-84. Recipient Louis Pasteur medal U. Louis Pasteur Strasbourg, France, 1995. Mem. ACP (master), Assn. Am. Physicians, Assn. Profs. Medicine, Am. Soc. Clin. Investigation, Am. Physiol. Soc., Am. Soc. Nephrology (coun. 1988-95, pres. 1993-94), Internat. Soc. Nephrology (exec. com. 1985—, v.p. 1995-97).

ANDRESEN, GRACIELA VAZQUEZ, clinical psychologist; b. Santiago, Cuba, Dec. 11, 1952; d. Abelardo and Graciela (Diaz) Vazquez-Perez; m. Stephen Richard Andresen, Aug. 9, 1975; children: Elizabeth Nicole, Jennifer Michelle. BS, Ohio State U., 1977; MA, U. Ill., 1981, PhD, 1989. Lic. clin. psychologist. Tchr. psychology dept. U. Ill., Urbana, 1978-79, therapist intern, 1979-81, instr. psychology dept., 1984-85; rsch. instr. U. Ill. Coll. Medicine, Urbana, 1989-93; postdoctoral assoc. U. Ill., Urbana, 1989-91, psychotherapist Psychol. Svcs. Ctr., 1990-91; rsch. assoc. Carle Found. Hosp., 1989-95; psychotherapist Assocs. in Clin. Psychology, Champaign, Ill., 1991-93, clin. psychologist, 1993—; grant reviewer Carle Found. Cancer Rsch. Com., Urbana, 1989-93. Contbr. articles to profl. jours. Bd. dirs. Jr. League of Champaign (Ill.)-Urbana, 1985-91, mem. Ill. State pub. affairs com. 85-87, pres. 1990-91; bd. dirs. Discovery Place Children's Mus., 1991-94, Am. Cancer Soc. 1992-96. Mem. APA, Ill. Psychol. Assn., Phi Kappa Phi. Office: Assocs in Clin Psychology 701 Devonshire Dr Champaign IL 61820-7337

ANDREW, CHRISTOPHER ROBERT, neurologist; b. Hull, Eng., Sept. 19, 1961; came to U.S., 1966; s. Norman and Sheila (Walker) A.; m. Tamara Leigh Miller; children: Joseph Arthur, Elizabeth Adrienne. BA, Northwestern U., 1983, MS, 1983; MD, U. Mo., 1988. Diplomate Am. Bd. Psychiatry and Neurology. Intern, resident Northwestern U., Chgo., 1988-92; staff physician Freeman Hosp., Joplin, Mo., 1992—; med. dir. Parkinson's and other Neurol. Disorder, Joplin, 1993—. Mem. Am. Acad. Neurology, Am. Bd. Electrodiagnostic Medicine, Joplin C. of C. Home: 1102 Rustic Ridge Joplin MO 64804

ANDREWS, BILLY FRANKLIN, pediatrician, educator; b. Graham, N.C., Sept. 22, 1932; s. Dean Franklin and Arlee (Byers) A.; m. Faye Rich, Dec. 25, 1953; children: Ann Elizabeth Feigenbaum, Billy Franklin Jr., David Ashley. Student, Brevard (N.C.) Coll., 1950, Elon Coll., 1951; BS cum laude, Wake Forest Coll., 1953; MD, Duke U., 1957. Diplomate Am bd. Pediatrics, 1963. Commd. 2nd lt. U.S. Army, 1956, advanced through grades to maj., 1962; intern Ft. Benning (Ga.) U.S. Army Hosp., 1957-58; resident in pediatrics Walter Reed Gen. Hosp., Washington, 1958-60; with mil. med. and allied scis. course Walter Reed Army Inst. Rsch., Washington, 1960-61; chief pediatric svc. Rodriguez U.S. Army Hosp., Ft. Brooke, P.R., 1961-63; chief pediatrics Tropical Med. Rsch. Lab., Ft. Brooke, P.R., 1963-64; res. U.S. Army, 1964; asst. prof. pediatrics U. Louisville, 1964-66, dir. newborn svcs., 1964-75, assoc. prof., 1966-68, prof., 1968—, dept. chmn. Sch. Medicine, 1969-93, chmn. emeritus, 1993—, dir. Comprehensive Health Care Ctr. for High Risk Infants and Children, 1968—; chief of staff Kosair Children's Hosp., Louisville, 1969-93; chief-of-staff emeritus Kosair Children's Hosp., 1993—; cons. div. maternal and child health Ky. Dept. Health, 1966—; lectr. Jour. Pediatrics Found., 1972; Staley Disting. Christian scholar Mary Baldwin Coll., Washington and Lee U., Sch. Medicine of U. Va., 1990; vis. scholar in med. history and ethics Green Coll., Oxford, Eng., 1993. Author: Children's Bill of Rights, 1968; editor: Small-for-Date Infants, 1970, The Newborn, Pediatric Clinics of North America, 1977, Aphorisms, Tributes and Tenets of Billy F. Andrews: In Walls, M.E., 1986, Ideals and Inspiration (F.R. Andrews), 1993, Words to Live By (F.R. Andrews), 1993; contbr. numerous articles to profl. publs.; inventor, poet. Pres. Kornhauser Libr., Health Scis. Ctr., 1981-82, 90-91. Recipient Helen B. Fraser award Norton-Children's Hosp., 1978, Award of Recognition, XVII Internat. Congress Pediat., Manila, 1983, Wisdom award of honor, eminent fellow The Wisdom Soc., 1991, The Billy F. Andrews, M.D. Endowed Chair in Pediat., U. Louisville, 1993, Winston Churchill medal of Wisdom Soc., Eminent Churchill Fellow of Wisdom Soc., 1993, Disting. Alumnus award Wake Forest U., 1983, The Billy F. Andrews, M.D. scholarship for pediat. U. Louisville Sch. Medicine, 1986, Festschrift to Billy F. Andrews, M.D., Jour. of Perinatology, 1995. Fellow ACP, Am. Acad. Pediatrics, Royal Soc. Medicine (London), N.Y. Acad. Scis., Internat. Biog. Assn.; mem. AAAS, AMA, Am. Pediatric Soc., Am. Osler Soc. (pres. 1996-97), Am. Soc. Law and Medicine, Soc. for Pediatric Rsch., So. Soc. Pediatric Rsch. (founding), Southeastern Perinatal Soc., Nat. Assn. Children's Hosps. and Related Instns., Ky. Med. Assn. (faculty Sci. Achievement award 1971, del. 1981-82), Jefferson County Med. Soc., Ky. Pediatric Soc., Louisville Pediatric Soc., U. Louisville Sch. Medicine Alumni Assn. (bd. govs. 1972-75), Univ. Pediatric Found. Inc. (pres. 1982-93), Internat. Assn. Bioethics, Order of Internat. Fellowship (Cambridge), Alpha Omega Alpha, others. Mem. United Church of Christ. Office: Kosair Charities Pediat Ctr 571 S Floyd St Ste 449 Louisville KY 40202

ANDREWS, CAROLYN ALICE, physicians assistant; b. El Paso, Tex., June 1, 1952; d. Charles Leonard and Barbara Alice (Davis) A.; m. Loomis Mayer, Sept. 3, 1983; children: Charles, John. BA in Biology, Randolph-Macon Women's Coll., 1974; BS, Baylor Coll. of Medicine, 1979; MS, L.I. U., 1994. Cert. physicians asst. Physicians asst. resident Montefiore Surg., Bronx, N.Y., 1979-80; physicians asst. Yonkers (N.Y.) Gen. Hosp., 1980-82; physicians asst. cardiology, cardiothoracic Montefiore Med. Ctr., Bronx, 1982—; sr. physicians asst. Montefiore Med. Ctr., Bronx, 1986—, physicians asst. com., 1988—; instr. Touro Coll. PA program. Contbr. articles to profl. jours. Clk. religious edn. Scarsdale Friends Meeting, 1991-95. Mem. Am. Acad. Physicians Assts., N.Y. State Soc. Physicians Assts. (election com. 1985), N.Am. soc. Pacing Electrophysiology (membership com. 1990-93), Com. Allied Profls. Democrat. Home: 20 Hunter Pl Croton NY 10520 Office: Montefiore Med Ctr 111 E 210th St Bronx NY 10467

ANDREWS, CLAUDE LEONARD, psychotherapist; b. Halifax County, N.C., Jan. 13, 1943; s. Leland Waverly and Annie Grey (Hyde) A.; m. Carol Gladys Cooper, June 10, 1967 (wid. Nov. 1986). BA, St. Andrews Coll., 1965; MDiv, Princeton (N.J.) Theol. Sch., 1969; MEd, U. Ga., 1972, ABD, 1974. Lic. psychol. assoc., N.C., marriage and family therapist, N.C., profl. counselor, N.C.; ordained to ministry Presbyn. Ch. Intern/chaplain U.N.C., Chapel Hill, 1967-68; intern/clin. chaplain Milledgeville (Ga.) State Hosp., 1970-71; minister Lavonia (Ga.) Presbyn. Ch., 1971-74; marital therapist U. Ga., Athens, 1971-73, teaching intern, 1972-74; psychologist Edgecombe-Nash Mental Health Ctr., Rocky Mount, N.C., 1974-76; dir., psychologist Tarboro (N.C.) Unit Mental Health Ctr., 1976-77; pvt. practice Creative Living Assocs., Tarboro, 1977—; cons. Albemarle Presbytery, Greenville, N.C., 1975-87, Presbytery of New Hope, Rocy Mount, 1987—, Tarboro Police Dept., 1987—, Edgecombe Sheriff's Dept., Tarboro, 1987—, Critical Incident Stress Debriefing Team, Coastal Plains Team, 1987—; cons. in mental health and psychology for N.E.E.D., Head Start. Mem. Rotary (past bd. dirs., sect.). Home: 309 St John St E Tarboro NC 27886-4413 Office: Creative Living Assocs 309 St John St E Tarboro NC 27886-4413

ANDREWS, DIANE RANDALL, nursing administrator, critical care nurse; b. Clinton, Iowa, Dec. 30, 1953; d. Eugene E. and Carol Lee (Walker) Randall; m. Thomas Wescott Andrews, Oct. 2, 1982; children: Christine, Charles. BSN, U. Iowa, 1976; MS, U. Ill., Chgo., 1981. RN, Fla., Ill. Unit leader/instr. Rush Presbyn. St. Lukes Med. Ctr., Chgo.; cons. Longwood, Fla.; trustee, mem. adv. com. Fla. Hosp. Coll. of Health Scis.; mem. adv. com. Fla. Hosp.; chair endowment oversight com. Fla. Hosp./Univ. of Ctrl. Fla. Author: After Anesthesia; former editor jour. Kaleidoscope; contbg. editor Jour. of the Fla. Med. Assn.; contbr. articles to profl. publs. Bd. dirs. Orange County Med. Soc. Alliance, Fla. Hosp. Golden Cir. of Friends, Fla. Hosp. Found., Fla. Med. Assn. Alliance, Jewish Family Svcs., Walt Disney Meml. Cancer Inst. State of Iowa scholar. Mem. Am. Soc. Post Anesthesia Nursing, Sigma Theta Tau. Home: 1821 Alaqua Dr Longwood FL 32779-3105

ANDREWS, EDSON JAMES, JR., radiologist; b. Tallahassee, Fla., Apr. 30, 1940; s. Edson James and Lola Irene (French) A.; m. Winifred Lynn Keller, Nov. 22, 1961; children: Michael Scott, James Brian. BA, U. Colo., 1962; MD, U. Fla., 1966. Diplomate Am. Bd. Radiology. Intern Charlotte (N.C.) Meml. Hosp., 1966-67; resident in radiology Barnes Hosp. of Washington U., Mallinckrodt Inst. Radiology, St. Louis, 1969-71; NIH postdoctoral fellow in cardiovascular radiology U. Fla., Gainesville, 1971-72; ptnr. Gadsden (Ala.) Radiology Assocs., 1972-77; staff radiologist West Fla. Hosp. Med. Ctr., Pensacola, 1977—, co-chair dept. nuclear cardiology, 1979—, chief nuclear medicine, 1982—, chmn. dept. radiology, 1993-95; bd. dirs. Med. Edn. and Rsch. Found. West Fla.; adj. assoc. prof. U. Fla. Coll. Med., 1985—; assoc. clin. prof. radiology U. South Ala., 1993—. Co-editor: (text) Color Atlas of First Pass Functional Imaging of the Heart, 1985; contbr. articles to profl. jours. Served with USPHS, 1967-69. Fellow Am. Coll. Radiology (councilor 1994—); mem. Am. Soc. Nuclear Cardiology (founding mem.), Soc. Nuclear Medicine, Radiol. Soc. N.Am., Am. Roentgen Ray Soc. Republican. Home: 2713 Del Mar Dr Gulf Breeze FL 32561-3015 Office: 8333 N Davis Hwy Pensacola FL 32514-6048

ANDREWS, JAMES CLAIRE, former dermatologist; b. Pleasant Plain, Iowa, Mar. 7, 1921; s. Claire Harrison and Lola Elizabeth (Crew) A.; m. Katherine Patricia McGinnis, June 21, 1947; 1 child, John Claire. BS, U. Notre Dame, 1945; MD, U. Mich., 1949. Diplomate Am. Bd. Dermatology. Intern St. Josephs Hosp., Lexington, Ky.; resident in dermatology U. Va. Hosp., Charlottesville, 1952-55; private practice in dermatology Charlottesville, Va., 1955-94; ret., 1994; cons. to various groups on skin disease and motor vehicle caused trauma. Contbr. articles to profl. pubs. Presenter children's auto restraints, motorcycle helmets, alcohol testing of drivers Gen. Assembly of Va., 1975—. Fellow Am. Acad. Dermatology; mem. Med. Soc. Va. (com. on hwy. safety 1978-81), Albemarle County Med. Soc., Washington Dermatol. Soc. (past pres.), Assn. for Advancement of Automotive Medicine (numerous offices including pres. 1979-80), Internat. Assn. for Automotive and Traffic Medicine (Achievement award 1981). Presbyterian. Home: 2529 Scottsville Rd Charlottesville VA 22902-7421

ANDREWS, JOHN THOMAS, nuclear medicine physician, consultant; b. Brighton, Sussex, England, Mar. 20, 1927; arrived in Australia, 1959; s. John James and Amelia (Marcantonio) A.; m. Iris Mary Groves, Aug. 20, 1957; children: Peter John, Michael, Steven Thomas, David. MBBS, London U., 1955; diploma of obstetrics, Royal Coll. Ob/Gyn., England, 1958; MD, U. Melbourne, 1979. Diplomate Am. Bd. Nuclear Medicine. House surgeon, asst. dept. anatomy London Hosp., 1955-57, jr. med. registrar, 1957-58; house physician Dover (Eng.) Hosp., 1955-57; med. registrar, clin. asst. in medicine Launceston (Tasmania, Australia) Hosp., 1959-61; trainee, then radiotherapist Cancer Inst. Melbourne, Australia, 1961-66; dir. nuclear medicine Royal Melbourne Hosp., 1966-92; part time dir. nuclear medicine Monash Med. Ctr., Melbourne, 1992—. Co-author: Nuclear Medicine: Clinical and Technological Bases, 1977; contbr. articles to profl. jours. Active Med. Assn. Prevention of War, 1981—. With Brit. Merchant Navy, 1943-48. Fellow Royal Australasian Coll. Physicians (Short Term Study grantee 1968), Royal Australasian Coll. Radiologists (Baker fellow 1969); mem. Australia and New Zealand Soc. Nuclear Medicine (chmn. accreditation bd., pres. 1979-80), Australia and New Zealand Assn. Physicians in Nuclear Medicine. Home: 400 New St, 3186 Brighton-Melbourne Victoria, Australia Office: Monash-Med Ctr Dept Nuclear Medicine, Clayton Rd, 3168 Clayton-Melbourne Victoria, Australia

ANDREWS, M. DEWAYNE, internist, educator; b. Enid, Okla., May 24, 1944; s. Mitchell S. and Truel Eva (Melton) A.; m. Rebecca Ellen Meltzer, Aug. 26, 1984. BS, Baylor U., 1966; MD, U. Okla., 1970. Diplomate Am. Bd. Internal Medicine. Resident internal medicine Johns Hopkins Hosp., Balt., 1970-71, U. Okla. Health Sci. Ctr., Oklahoma City, 1971-72, 74-76; asst. prof., assoc. prof., dir. residency program Dept. Medicine U. Okla., Oklahoma City, 1976-84; chief of medicine regional med. ctr., vice chmn. dept. medicine U. Tenn. Coll. Medicine, Memphis, 1984-86; vice chmn., chief gen. internal medicine, prof. Dept. Medicine U. Okla., Oklahoma City, 1986—; assoc. dean grad. med. edn. Coll. Okla. U. Okla., Oklahoma City, 1994—; chief of staff U. Hosp., Oklahoma City, 1992-94, med. dir., 1994—. Contbr. numerous articles in profl. jours. Bd. dirs. Chamber Orch. Oklahoma City, 1982-84; del. Okla. State Leadership Initiative to Soviet Union, 1988. Surgeon USPHS, 1972-74. Named Teaching & Research Scholar Am. Coll. Physicians, 1976-79; recipient Stollermen Award U. Tenn., 1986, Aesculapian award U. Okla. Coll. Medicine, 1989. Fellow Am. Coll. Physicians; mem. AMA, Am. Coll. Physician Execs., Soc. Gen. Internal Medicine, Alpha Omega Alpha. Episcopalian. Home: 3241 Lamp Post Ln Oklahoma City OK 73120-5620 Office: U Okla Health Sci Ctr PO Box 26901 Oklahoma City OK 73126

ANDREWS, PATRICIA AMANDA, pediatrician, educator; b. Easton, Pa., Sept. 23, 1939; d. Robert Tom and Gertrude Amanda (Cooper) A. BA, Russell Sage Coll., 1961; MS, Ind. U., 1965, MD, 1967; DSc (hon.), Russell Sage Coll., 1988. Intern M. Mary Hitchcock Meml. Hosp., Hanover, N.H., 1967-68; resident pediatrics Dartmouth-Hitchcock Med. Ctr., Hanover, 1968-69; resident pediatric neurology Med. Ctr. Ind. U., Indpls., 1969-70; resident pediatrics Dartmouth-Hitchcock Med. Ctr., Hanover, 1971; instr. medicine Med. Sch. Dartmouth Coll., Hanover, 1971-72; asst. prof. pediats. Med. Sch. Dartmouth Coll., 1972—, dir. child devel. program Med. Sch., 1971-82; med. dir. Laconia (N.H.) State Sch. and Tng. Ctr., 1982-84; cons. N.H. Divsn. Mental Health, 1971-76; cons. N.H. Spl. Edn. Bur., 1985-95. Mem. Canterbury (N.H.) Planning Bd., 1986-87; v.p. Canterbury Hist.Soc., 1986-88, pres., 1988-92. Mem. Am. Assn. Mental Retardation, Am. Acad. Cerebral Palsy and Devel. Medicine, N.H. Med. Soc., N.H. Pediatrics Soc. Home: PO Box 54 Canterbury NH 03224-0054 Office: Dartmouth Hitchcock Med Ctr Child Devel Ctr Lebanon NH 03756

ANDREWS, RICHARD VINCENT, physiologist, educator; b. Arapahoe, Nebr., Jan. 9, 1932; s. Wilber Vincent and Fern (Clawson) A.; m. Elizabeth Williams, June 1, 1954 (dec. Dec. 1994); children: Thomas, William, Robert, Catherine, James, John. BS, Creighton U., 1958, MS, 1959; PhD, U. Iowa, 1963. Instr. biology Creighton U., Omaha, 1958-60; instr. physiology U. Iowa, 1960-63; asst. prof. Creighton U., 1963-65, assoc. prof., 1965-68, prof. physiology, 1968—, asst. med. dean, 1972-75, dean grad. studies, 1975-85, dean emeritus, 1995—; vis. prof. Naval Arctic Rsch. Lab., 1963-72, U. B.C., 1985-86, U. Tasmania, 1993-94; cons. VA, NSF, NRC, ARS; plenary speaker USSR Symposium on Environment, 1970, Internat. Soc. Biomet., 1972. Contbr. articles to profl. jours. Served with M.C. U.S. Army, 1951-54. NSF fellow, 1962-63; NSF-NIH-ONR-AINA grantee, 1963—. Fellow Explorers Club, Arctic Inst. N.Am.; mem. Am. Physiol. Soc., Am. Mammal Soc., Endocrine Soc., Soc. Exptl. Biology and Medicine, Internat. Soc. for Biometeorology, Sigma Xi. Office: 2500 California St Omaha NE 68178

ANDREWS, ROBERT GEOFF, pediatrician, medical educator; b. Mpls., Jan. 28, 1949; s. James Edward and Marie Adelaide (Jones) A.; m. Carol Ann Chellino, July 1, 1979; 1 child, Joseph Einar. AB, Amherst Coll., 1972; MD, U. Minn., 1976. Diplomate Am. Bd. Pediats., Am. Bd. Pediat. Hematology and Oncology, Nat. Bd. Med. Examiners. Intern in pediats. New Eng. Med. Ctr., Boston, 1976-77, resident in pediats., 1977-79; fellow in pediat. hematology and oncology U. Wash. Sch. Medicine and Fred Hutchinson Cancer Rsch. Ctr., Seattle, 1979-83; pediats. instr. Sch. Medicine U. Wash., Seattle, 1983-84, asst. prof. Sch. Medicine, 1984-90, assoc. prof. Sch. Medicine, 1990—, rsch. affiliate Regional Primate Rsch. Ctr., 1987—; presenter more than 50 papers and abstracts at sci. and med. meetings. Contbr. more than 60 articles to profl. jours. Grantee Am. Cancer Soc., 1979-80, among others; fellow Am. Cancer Soc., 1983-86. Office: U Mpls F Hutchinson Cancer Rsch 1124 Columbia St Seattle WA 98104-2092

ANDREWS, SALLY MAY, healthcare administrator; b. Westfield, Mass., Feb. 29, 1956; d. Roger N. and Dorothy M. (Goodhind) A. Student, U. Conn., 1974-76; BA, Simmons Coll., Boston, 1978; MBA, Boston U., 1986. Payroll clk. Children's Hosp., Boston, 1978-79, asst. payroll supr., 1979-81, staff analyst dept. medicine, 1981-83, asst. adminstr. dept. medicine, 1983-86, adminstr. dept. medicine, 1986—. Bd. overseers Lasell Coll., Newton, Mass. Mem. Am. Mgmt. Assn., Adminstrs. of Internal Medicine, Assn. Adminstrs. in Acad. Pediatrics (pres. 1996—). Congregationalist. Office: Children's Hosp Dept Medicine 300 Longwood Ave Boston MA 02115-5724

ANDREWS, WILLIAM COOKE, physician; b. Norfolk, Va., June 7, 1924; s. Charles James and Jean Curry (Cooke) A.; m. Elizabeth Wight Kyle, Nov. 10, 1951; children—Elizabeth Randolph, William Cooke, Susan Carrington. A.A., Princeton U., 1946; M.D., Johns Hopkins U., 1947. Diplomate Am. Bd. Obstetrics and Gynecology. Intern N.Y. Hosp., 1947, resident in obstetrics and gynecology, 1948-50, 52-53; practice medicine specializing in obstetrics and gynecology Norfolk, Va., 1953-95; asst. in obstetrics and gynecology Cornell U. Med. Sch., 1948-50, 52-53; mem. attending staff Med. Ctr. Hosp.; prof. ob-gyn. Ea. Va. Med. Sch., Norfolk, 1975-95, prof. emeritus, 1995—, pres. faculty senate, 1976-77; mem. fertility and maternal health drug adv. com. FDA, 1979-83, chmn., 1982-83, cons., 1983-87; mem. sci. adv. bd. Alan Guttmacher Inst., 1992-94. Contbr. articles in field to profl. jours. Chmn. Norfolk Bicentennial Commn., 1969-71; mem. Community Facilities Commn., 1971-73, chmn., 1973-79; bd. dirs. Va. League for Planned Parenthood, 1966-68; pres. Norfolk chpt. Planned Parenthood, 1966-68. With M.C., USN, 1950-52. Named Hon. Officer of the Most Excellent Order of the Brit. Empire, Queen Elizabeth II, 1967; presented Order of Andres Bello, Pres. Carlos Andres Perez of Venezuela, 1992. Fellow Am. Coll. Obstetricians and Gynecologists (vice chmn. dist. IV 1985-88, chmn. 1988-91, v.p. 1992-93, pres.-elect 1993, pres. 1994-95, exec. bd. 1988-96), Am. Assn. Obstetricians and Gynecologists, Am. Gynecol. and Obstet. Soc., Royal Coll. Obstetricians and Gynecologists (hon.); mem. AMA, Am. Fertility Soc. (bd. dirs. 1970-73, pres. 1977, med. dir. 1986-88, exec. dir. 1988-92), Med. Soc. Va., Norfolk Acad. Medicine, Va. Tidewater Obstetricians and Gynecologists Soc., Continental Gynecol. Soc., South Atlantic Assn. Obs.-Gyns., Norfolk C. of C. (chmn. armed forces com. 1966-68, v.p. 1968-69, pres. 1970), Internat. Fedn. Fertility Socs. (asst. treas. 1974-80, pres. 1983-86, chmn. sci. program com. 1986-89, exec. com. 1989—), Navy League U.S. (pres. Hampton Roads coun. 1968-70, nat. dir. 1970-74), English Speaking Union U.S. (pres. Norfolk-Portsmouth br. 1964-66), Planned Parenthood Fedn. Am. (cons. nat. med. com. 1975-85, chmn. 1981-83), Norfolk Yacht and Country Club (commodore 1966). Presbyterian. Home and Office: 929 Graydon Ave Norfolk VA 23507-1207

ANDRICK, DAVID, health facility administrator; b. Indpls., Sept. 4, 1950; s. Gilbert Norman and Harriet J. (Narvell) A.; m. Nancy L. Kantor, Feb. 7, 1970 (div. Jan. 1976); 1 child, D. Maxwell; m. Janet Ann Hart, Nov. 4, 1977; children: Daniel, Rebecca. Student, Ball State U., 1969-70, Wright State U., 1990-91. Field engr. divsn. IBM, Cin., 1970-76; sales rep. R.T. French, Dayton, Ohio, 1976-78; regional sales mgr. 3M, Dayton, Ohio, 1978-80, Diacon Systems, Dayton, Ohio, 1980-82, Reynolds & Reynolds, Dayton, Ohio, 1982-87; asst. v.p. Cmty. Hosp., Springfield, Ohio, 1987-96; v.p. practice devel. Ohio Inst. Cardiac Care Inc., 1996—; faculty Nat. Inst. Physicians Recruitment, Atlanta, 1991-95, Ohio Hosp. Assn., Columbus, 1994-96; adv. bd. The Am. Coll. Med. Staff Devel., Atlanta, 1994-96. Contbr. articles to profl. jours. Bd. dirs. Northmont H.S. Soccer, Englewood, Ohio, 1986-88, Northmont Youth Football, Englewood, 1990-95, Ch. of Brethren, Dayton, 1990-93, Jr. Achievement, 1992-95. Mem. Am. Coll. Med. Staff Devel. (adv. coun. 1994-96, cert. med. staff recruiter 1994-97), Am. Hosp. Assn. (physician svcs. 1993-95), Ohio Hosp. Assn. (Soc. Healthcare Plan 1992-95), Alliance of Healthcare Mktg., Am. Mktg. Assn. Home: 1006 Meadowrun Englewood OH 45322

ANDRIOLE, GERALD LOUIS, urologist; b. Hazelton, Pa., Aug. 31, 1955; s. Gerald Louis and Irene Dorothy (Serratore) A.; m. Dorothy Potter, June 1, 1985; children: Gerald, Nicholas, Philip. BS summa cum laude, Pa. State U., 1976; MD, Jefferson Med. Coll., Phila., 1978. Diplomate Am. Bd. Urology, Nat. Bd. Med. Examiners; lic. physician, Md., Mo. Intern, resident in surgery Strong Meml. Hosp./U. Rochester, N.Y., 1978-80; resident in urology Brigham and Women's Hosp./Harvard Med. Sch., Boston, 1980-83; expert in urologic oncology Nat. Cancer Inst./NIH, Bethesda, Md., 1983-85; asst. prof. urologic surgery Washington U. Sch. Medicine, St. Louis, 1985-90, assoc. prof., 1990—; chief urology sect. St. Louis VA Med. Ctr., 1985-95; mem. staff Jewish Hosp., St. Louis, Children's Hosp., St. Louis, VA Hosp., St. Louis, St. Louis Regional Med. Ctr., Barnes Hosp., St. Louis. Author, editor, reviewer jours. Recipient 1st prize Radiol. Soc. N.Am., 1990, CIAO award for medicine, others; grantee Am. Cancer Soc., Nat. Cancer Inst., NIDDKD, NIH, Am. Found. for Urologic Disease/Nat. Kidney Found., others. Mem. ACS, Am. Assn. for Cancer Rsch., Am. Soc. Clin. Oncology, Am. Urol. Assn., Soc. Univ. Urologists, Soc. Urologic Oncology, Soc. for Basic Urologic Rsch., Nat. Urologic Forum. Office: Washington U Sch Medicine 4960 Children's Pl Saint Louis MO 63110

ANDRIS, JOSEPH JAMES, anesthesiologist. internist; b. Phila., May 24, 1950; s. Joseph James and Helen Irma (Thomas) A.; 1 child, Joseph James. BS in Biology, Villanova U., 1972; DO, Coll. Osteopathic Medicine, Phila., 1976. Diplomate Am. Bd. Anesthesiology. Rotating intern Riverside Hosp., Wilmington, Del., 1976-77; resident internal medicine Mercy Cath. Med. Ctr., Phila., 1977-80; resident in anesthesiology W.Va. U., 1991-94; pvt. practice internal medicine San Andreas, Calif., 1989-91, Phila., 1985-89; chief resident W. Va. U. Hosps., Morgantown, 1993-94, asst. prof., 1994—; scheduling operating rm. and medical bd. W.Va. Univ. Hosps., 1994—, mem. exec. com., 1994. Anesthesiologist Interplast, Palo Alto, Calif., 1993, Interplast, Morgantown, 1994—. Lt. commdr. U.S. Navy, 1980-83. Mem. Am. Soc. Anesthesiologists, W.Va. Med. Soc., Am. Bd. Anesthesiologists, Monowgalaia County Med. Soc. Home: 253 Riverview Ct Morgantown WV 26505 Office: W Va Univ Hosps Medical Center Dr Morgantown WV 26505

ANDRIST, CHRIS G., crime lab supervisor/forensic scientist; b. St. Francis, Kans., Oct. 20, 1955; s. Bill and Gerre (Ingamells) A.; m. Kimberly Anne Habegger, May 13, 1988. Grad., N.W. Inst. Med. Lab. Tech. 1976; BS, U. Kans., 1980; cert. in Scrology Tng., FBI Acad., 1992, cert. in Hair and Fiber Tng., 1996. cert. med. technologist. Lab. supr. N.W. Kans. Med. Ctr., Goodland, 1980-82; med. technologist Providence Hosp., Waco, Tex., 1982-84, Medicenter I and II, Waco, Tex., 1984-88; asst. mgr., tech. supr. Waco Clin. Pathology Lab., 1986-89; mgr. forensic toxicology Metwest Labs., Denver, 1989-91; criminalist, forensic serologist Jefferson County Sheriff's Dept., Golden, Colo., 1991—, Necrosearch Internat., Denver, 1993—; crime lab. supervisor/forensic scientist, 1996—; criminalistics adv. bd. Metro State Coll., Denver, 1994—. Mem. Am. Acad. Forensic Sci., Internat. Assn. Identification (bd. dirs. Rocky Mountain divsn., sec., 1996), Internat. Assn. Bloodstain Pattern Analysts, Rocky Mountain Assn. Bloodstain Pattern Analysts, Nat. Tech. Investigators Assn., Colo. Law Enforcement Officers Assn, Colo. Assn. Computer Crime Investigators, Jefferson County Critical Incident Response Team. Office: Jefferson County Sheriff's Dept 200 Jefferson County Pky Golden CO 80401

ANDRUZZI, ELLEN ADAMSON, nurse, marital and family therapist; b. Colon, Panama, Dec. 15, 1917; d. Charles and Annie Isabel (Grinder) Adamson; m. Francis Victor Andruzzi, May 28, 1941; children: Barbara F., Francis C., Judith E., Antonette T., John J. BS in Pub. Health Nursing, Cath. U. Am., 1947, MS in Nursing, 1951. Cert. clin. specialist, psychiat. nurse. Pub. health nurse Washington Health Dept., 1942-44; instr. psychiat. nursing St. Elizabeth's Hosp., Washington, 1948-57; dir. nursing Glenn Dale Hosp., Md., 1961-67; chief mental health nurse dept. human resources D.C. Govt., 1967-73; cons. NIMH, HHS, Rockville, Md., 1973-81; marital and family therapist TA Assocs., Camp Springs, Md., 1973-94; assoc. GWITA, Rockville, 1975-79; instr. Charles County C.C., LaPlata, Md., 1976-78, Prince George Community Coll., Largo, Md., 1973-81; assoc. Ctr. for Study of Human Systems, Chevy Chase, Md., 1976-94; nurse, psychotherapist pvt. practice. Author chpts. in books. Dist. co-capt. Prince Georgians for Glendening, Prince George County, Md., 1985-86; chmn. plan devel. com. So. Md. Health Systems Agy., Clinton, 1984-89, sec. governing body, 1978-80; chmn. Mental Health Adv. Com. Prince George County, Cheverly, Md., 1983-85; mem. Blue Ribbon Commn. on Health, Prince George's County, 1991-92; mem. Commn. Health, Prince George's County, 1992-94; mem. health com. and voter reporter League Women Voters. Recipient Disting. Nurse award St. Elizabeths Hosp., 1985, Paula Hamburger Vol award Mental Health Assn. Md., 1985, Recognition of Service award Md. Nurses Assn., 1983, Prince Georgian of the Yr. award, 1994, Vol. award Prince George's County, 1995. Fellow Am. Acad. Nursing, Am. Orthopsychiat. Assn.; mem. Internat. Transactional Analysis Assn. (clin.), Am. Nurses Assn., World Fedn. for Mental Health, Am. Assn. for Marriage and Family Therapy (clin.), Nat. Mental Health Assn. (v.p. 1984-87, bd. dirs. 1982-87), Mental Health Assn. Prince George County (pres. 1974-76, 87-88, Vol. of Yr. award 1993), Sigma Theta Tau (Kappa chpt., Excellence in Nursing award 1984). Democrat. Roman Catholic. Avocations: theatre, ballet, swimming, foreign travel.

ANDRZEJEWSKI, CHESTER, JR., immunologist, research scientist; b. Bridgeport, Conn., Mar. 20, 1953; s. Chester Sr. and Helen (Sholomicky) A.; m. Kathleen Marie O'Connor, Aug. 7, 1976; children: Nicholas Chester, Michael Yuri, Danielle Natalya. ScB, Brown U., 1975; PhD, Tufts U., 1981, MD, 1984. Diplomate Am. Bd. Pathology, Nat. Bd. Med. Examiners. Resident, fellow Hosp. U. Pa., Phila., 1984-88; staff pathologist Wilford Hall USAF Med. Ctr., Lackland AFB, Tex., 1988-92; med. dir., transfusion medicine and clin. immunology Wilford Hall USAF Med Ctr., Lackland AFB, 1989-92; med. dir. transfusion medicine, diagnostic immunology svcs. Baystate Med. Ctr., Springfield, Mass., 1992—; chief divsn. Baystate Reference Labs., 1994—; asst. prof. pathology Tufts U., 1993—. Contbr. articles to profl. jours. Sub-deacon Orthodox Ch. Am., 1977; mem. med. adv. com. N.E. region ARC Blood Svcs., 1993—, transfusion practices com., 1994—; adv. panelist on Mass. Peer Review Orgn., 1995—. Recipient Rsch. Fellowship award Mass. Lupus Found., 1979, Internat. Disting. Dissertation award Coun. Grad. Students in U.S. and Univ. Microfilms, 1981, Excellence Rsch. award Roche Labs., 1987, award Nat. Blind Found., 1987. Mem. Am. Assn. Clin. Pathologists, Mass. Soc. Pathologists (exec. com.), Clin. Immunology Soc., Coll. Am. Pathologists, Am. Soc. Apheresis, Assn. Med. Lab., Internat. Cord Blood Soc. (founding, charter). Mem. Orthodox Ch. Am. Home: PO Box 134 Somers CT 06071-1754 Office: Baystate Med Ctr Dept Pathology Springfield MA 01199

ANFINSEN, LIBBY ESTHER, social worker, clinical administrator; b. Jersey City, Dec. 20, 1931; d. Herman and Shirley Ann (Stiskin) Shulman; 2d m. Christian Boehmer Anfinsen, Mar., 1979; children: Mark H. Ely, Tobie R. Beckerman, Daniel J. Ely, David A. Ely. BA, Bklyn. Coll., 1954; MSW, NYU, 1956. Lic. cert. clin. social worker, Md.; diplomat in clin. social work. Clin. social worker NIH Clin. Ctr., Bethesda, Md., 1966-81; pvt. practice individual and group therapy Balt., Silver Spring, Md., 1980-95; dir. social svcs. Children's Hosp. and Ctr. for Reconstructive Surgery, Balt., 1983-85; social worker Balt. County Health Dept., Towson, Md., 1985-91; devel. disabilities adminstr. Balt. County Health Dept., Towson, Md., 1985-91; devel. disabilities adminstr. Balt. City Dept. Edn. Spl. Svcs. for Children with Learning Disorders, 1993-96; interviewer child Devel. Rsch. Jerome Riker Found. of Persecution of Holocaust Children, Balt. and N.Y C., 1983-95; mem. med. bd. NIH Clin. Ctr., Bethesda, Md. Contbr. articles to profl. publs. Comdr. USPHS, 1974-81. Mem. ACSW, NASW, Zionist Orgn. Am., Vols. for Israel, Israel Bond Prime Ministers Club, Israel Investment Club (Balt.). Jewish. Home: 4 Tanner Ct Baltimore MD 21208-1332

ANGEL, ARMANDO CARLOS, rheumatologist, internist; b. Las Vegas, N.Mex., Mar. 25, 1940; s. Edmundo Clemente and Pauline Teresa (Flores) Sanchez A.; m. Judith Lee Weedin, Aug. 5, 1961; children: Stephanie, Renee. BA, San Jose State U., 1963; MS, U. Ariz., 1970, PhD, 1971, M.D., 1977. Chemist Tracerlab, Inc., Richmond, Calif., 1963-67; prof. chemistry Pima Coll., Tucson, Ariz., 1971-74; intern U. N.Mex., Albuquerque, 1977-78, resident, 1978-80; resident VA Hosp., Lovelace Med. Ctr., Albuquerque, 1978-80; practice medicine specializing in internal medicine, Las Cruces, N.Mex., 1980-88; pvt. practice, El Paso, Tex., 1990—; dir. pain program Rio Vista Rehab. Hosp., 1992; med. dir. Ctr. for Rehab. and Evaluation, 1992; cons. minority biomed. sci. project NIH, Washington, 1970-74, Ednl. Assocs., Tucson, 1971-74. Author: Llevve Tlaloc No. 2, 1973. Treas. Nat. Chicano Health Orgn., Los Angeles, 1974-75; v.p. Mexican-Am. Educators, Tucson, 1973-74; pres. N.Mex. affiliate Am. Diabetes Assn., Albuquerque, 1983-85. Fellow U. Ariz., 1988-90. Fellow Am. Coll. Rheumatology; mem. AMA, Tex. Med. Soc., El Paso County Medical Soc., Am. Diabetes Assn., ACP, Dona Ana County Med. Soc. (pres. 1983), Am. Coll. Rheumatology, Am. Assn. Internal Medicine, Alpha Chi Sigma.

ANGELAKOS, EVANGELOS THEODOROU, physician, physiologist, pharmacologist, educator; b. Tripolis, Greece, July 15, 1929; came to U.S., 1948, naturalized, 1966; s. Theodore A. and Aglaia (Tsivericti) A.; m. Eleanor Pell, Aug. 28, 1954 (div. 1984); 1 son, Theodore; m. Elizabeth Hegnauer, Jan. 2, 1993. Student, Athens (Greece) U., 1947-48, Cornell U., 1950-51; MA, Boston U., 1953, PhD, 1956; MD, Harvard, 1959. Mem. faculty sch. medicine Boston U., 1955-68, prof. physiology, 1963-68; prof. dept. physiology and biophysics Hahnemann U., Phila., 1968—, chmn. dept., 1968-85, prof. dept. pharmacology and medicine, 1982—, interim dean sch. medicine, 1982-83, dean Grad. Sch., 1983-92, dep. dean sch. medicine, 1985-86, dir. Med. Sci. Track Program, 1982—; chmn. adv. com. biomed. research inst. Center for Research and Advanced Studies, U. Maine, Portland, 1971-80; research assoc. biomath. MIT, 1959-60; vis. scientist Karolinska Inst., Stockholm, 1962-63; cons. U.S. Army Labs. Environ. Medicine, Natick, Mass., 1964-72, NASA Electronics Research Center, Cambridge, Mass., 1966-68; Trustee, sec. bd. Hahnemann Med. Coll. and Hosp., Phila., 1977-81. Contbr. articles to sci. jours. and textbooks. Med. Found. Research fellow, 1959-60; USPHS Research and Career Devel. grantee, 1960-68. Home: 109 Wayside Dr Cherry Hill NJ 08034 Office: Hahnemann U Med Sci Track MS #344 Philadelphia PA 19102

ANGELIN, BO ANDERS, physician, clinical research educator, consultant; b. Stockholm, Aug. 16, 1949; s. Stig V. and Ingalill (Gewelius) A.; m. Kerstin Dahlin, June 23, 1973; children: Marcus, Julia. MD, U. Uppsala, Sweden, 1973; MD, PhD, Karolinska Inst., Stockholm, 1977. Asst. prof. dept. medicine Karolinska Inst., 1977-78, assoc. prof., 1978-80, assoc. prof. clin. rsch., 1980-91, prof., 1992—; sr. cons. Huddinge (Sweden) U. Hosp., 1980—. Office: Huddinge U Hosp, Dept Medicine, S-14186 Huddinge Sweden

ANGELINI, CORRADO ITALO, neurologist educator; b. Padova, Italy, Aug. 3, 1941; s. Giovanni and Marila (Gasparini) A.; m. Eicke Stehr, June 18, 1974; children: Margherita, Giovanni, Katia. MD, U. Padova, 1965. MD, Calif. From rsch. asst. to resident Mayo Clinic, Rochester, Minn., 1970-73; asst., assoc. prof. Padova (Italy) U., 1974-78, 80-93; prof. neurology Padua U., Padova, 1994—; vis. prof. UCLA, 1978-79, U. Colo., Denver, 1984; mem. med. commn. UIAA, 1986-96. Editor: MDR 80, 1981, MDR 90, 1991, Le Malattie Neuromuscolari, 1994. Capt. Italian Army, 1992. Jr. fellow Muscular Dystrophy Assn., 1984. Mem. Am. Acad. Neurology (assoc.), Am. Neurol. Assn. Office: U Padua, Dept Neurology, Padova Italy

ANGELO, E. JOANNE, child, adolescent and adult psychiatrist; b. Boston, Feb. 11, 1936; d. Gaspar and Eda (Polcari) A. AB, Mt. Holyoke Coll., 1957; MD, Tufts U., 1961. Diplomate Am. Bd. Psychiatry and Neurology. Pvt. practice Boston, 1969—; med. dir. Canarsie Mental Health Ctr., Bklyn., 1967-69; staff psychiatrist Community Mental Health Svc. Ctr., Boston, 1969-73; psychiat. dir. Laroure Ctr., South Boston, Mass., 1974-78; cons. Chandler Sch. for Women, Boston, 1971-72, Kennedy Meml. Hosp., Boston, 1971-74, St. Margaret's Hosp., Boston, 1976-83, North Suffolk Health Ctr., Boston, 1978-79; mem. staff St. Elizabeth's Hosp., Boston, Good Samaritan Hospice Boston. Office: 403 Commonwealth Ave Boston MA 02215-2326

ANGELOV, GEORGE ANGEL, pediatrician, anatomist, teratologist; b. Bulgaria, May 12, 1925; came to U.S., 1978; s. Angel Christov and Maria Angelov; m. Olga Valerie Minkova, Dec. 21, 1952; 1 child, Angel. MD, Sch. of Medicine, Sofia, Bulgaria, 1952. Pediatrician Distric Hosp., Bulgaria, 1952-53; asst. prof. Sch. of Medicine, Sofia, Bulgaria, 1953-64; prof. anatomy and anthropology Sch. of Biology, Sofia, Bulgaria, 1964-77; mgr. reproductive toxicology Lederle Labs., Pearl River, N.Y., 1979-89; cons. reproductive toxicology pvt. practice, Laguna Niguel, Calif., 1989—; assoc. dean Sch. of Biology, Sofia, 1970-72; vis. scientist Sch. of Medicine, Geneva, 1971, 74. Author: (textbook) Anatomy, 1970; mem. glossary com. Teratology Glossary, 1987-89; reviewer several sci. jours.; contbr. numerous sci. publs. on anatomy, teratology, and growth and devel. of adolescents to profl. jours. Mem. Teratology Soc. USA, European Teratology Soc., Human Biology Coun. USA, Free Union of Univ. Profs. of Anatomy. East Orthodox.

ANGERER, ROBERT CLIFFORD, biology educator, researcher; b. Columbus, Ohio, Nov. 4, 1944; s. Clifford Ackermann and Helena (Hurley) A.; m. Lynne Marie Musgrave, Dec. 27, 1966; children—Jennifer, Mark. B.S., Ohio State U., 1966; Ph.D., Johns Hopkins U., 1973; postgrad. Calif. Inst. Tech., 1973-78. Asst. prof. biology U. Rochester, N.Y., 1978-84, assoc. prof., 1984-89, prof., 1989—; mem. NIH DRG Molecular Biology Study Sect. Contbr. articles to profl. jours.; reviewer numerous jours. NIH fellow, 1970-72; Am. Cancer Soc./Am. Chem. Soc. fellow, 1973-77; USPHS grantee, 1978—, NSF, 1990—; recipient research career devel. award, 1984-89. Mem. Am. Soc. Cell Biology, Soc. Devel. Biology, Sigma Xi, Phi Beta Kappa. Home: 27 Chelmsford Rd Rochester NY 14618-1727 Office: Univ Rochester Hutchison Hall Rochester NY 14627

ANGLIM-GROTH, MARY ELIZABETH, pediatrics nurse; b. Utica, N.Y., Dec. 18, 1959; d. Thomas and Madeleine (Martyn) Anglim; m. Ken Groth, Jan. 5, 1985. Diploma, Peter Bent Brigham Hosp., Boston, 1983; BSN, Mercy Coll., Dobbs Ferry, N.Y., 1988; MSN, Mercy Coll., 1992; postgrad., Yale U., 1995—. RN, N.Y.; cert. pediatric nursing AANC. Staff nurse pediatrics Westchester County Med. Ctr., Valhalla, N.Y., 1983-85; asst. nursing care coord. Westchester County Med. Ctr., 1985-88; nurse clinician/clin. trial coord. N.Y. Med. Coll., Valhalla, 1988-90; clin. nurse specialist AIDS pediatric/maternal Westchester County Med. Ctr., Valhalla, 1990-93, staff nurse pediatric intensive care, 1993-96, acting clin. nurse specialist in pediat. critical care, 1994, nursing staff devel. specialist, 1994—; staff nurse pediat. ICU Yale New Haven Hosp., 1996—. Mem. ANA, N.Y. State Nurses Assn., Soc. Pediatric Nurses, Assn. Nurses in AIDS Care, Sigma Theta Tau.

ANGOLE, YUTUK ELEM, anaesthesiologist, consultant; b. Awelo-Lira, Uganda, May 22, 1933; Arrived in the Bahamas, 1978; s. Yusito and Eleseba (Agweng) Elem; m. Margaret Mary Alaba, Sept. 15, 1959; children: Joseph, Frederick, Juliette, Florence, Peter, June, Sanyu. GCE, Nyakasura, Fortportal, Uganda, 1953; A-Level, LMS, Makerere, Kampala, Uganda, 1960, MB ChB, 1964. Diplomate Royal Coll. of Anaesthetics. House officer Mulago Hosp., Kampala, 1961-63; med. officer Moroto (Uganda) Hosp., 1963-64; registrar Bishop-Stortforo Hosp., Britain, 1965-66; dep. chief med. officer Uganda Army, 1966-69; registrar anaesthesia Kings Coll. Hosp., England, 1969-73; cons. anaesthetist Bahamas Govt., 1978—; cons. anaesthetist Univ. Tchg. Hosp., 1973-78; dep. med. staff coord. Rand Meml. Hosp., Freeport, Bahamas, 1990—; lectr. in field. Mem. Red Cross, Freeport, 1990; mem. Knights of Columbus, Freeport, 1989. Maj. Uganda Army, 1966-69. Recipient O Level Hon. award Cambridge U., 1953. Fellow Royal Coll. Anaesthesiologists; mem. Assn. of Anaesthetists of England, Med. Assn. Bahamas. Roman Catholic. Home: 354 Coral Rd PO Box F40532, Freeport Grand Bahama Bahamas Office: Rand Meml Hosp-E Atlantic Mall E, PO Box F40071, Freeport Grand Bahama Bahamas

ANGRILLI, ALBERT, psychology educator; b. N.Y.C., Dec. 4, 1917; s. Peter and Antoinette (Levant) A.; m. Dorothy Sevush, Sept. 15, 1945 (dec. Aug. 1971); 1 child, Robert M.; m. Alma Shapiro, Aug., 1977. BS, NYU, 1949, MA, 1950, PhD, 1958. Lic. psychologist, N.Y.; diplomate Am. Bd. Profl. Psychology. Rsch. investigator Bellevue Hosp. Rapid Treatment Ctr., N.Y.C., 1945-49; clin. psychologist N.Y. State Traveling Child Guidance Clinics, Albany and Binghamton, N.Y., 1949-53; lectr. Queens Coll., CUNY, Flushing, 1953-58, asst. prof. edn., assoc. prof., prof., 1958-84, dir. Ednl. Clinic, 1946-76, prof. emeritus, 1984—, resident prof., adj. prof. grad. program in sch. psychology, 1984—; exam. asst. N.Y.C. Bd. Edn., 1962-80; cons., mem. faculty, vis. prof. Internat. Grad. Sch., Lugano, Switzerland, 1976-79, Bar Ilan U., Israel, 1972, P.R., 1979; cons. psychologist Sherut

La'am, Israel, 1972, sch. systems, N.Y. State, 1951; adj. prof. Fla. Inst. Tech. Sch. Profl. Psychology, Melbourne, 1979-90. Co-author: Child Psychology, 1981, Psychologia Infantil, 1984; also articles. Past pres. and bd. dirs. Queens County Mental Health Soc.; past liaison supr. Ferrini League; past bd. dirs. N.Y. State Mental Health Assn. Staff sgt. USAAF, 1942-45. Recipient cert. of merit N.Y.C. Dept. Health, 1957, cert. of honors contbn. Queens Coll. Sch. Edn., 1987. Fellow Am. Orthopsychiat. Assn. (life), Am. Acad. Sch. Psychologists; mem. APA, N.Y. State Psychol. Assn. Home: 105 Stone Oaks Dr Hartsdale NY 10530-1148 Office: Queens Coll Dept Edn and Community Programs Kissena Blvd Flushing NY 11367

ANGRIST, BURTON MORRIS, physician; b. N.Y.C., July 15, 1936; s. Alfred A. and Sylvia M. (Kasdan) A.; m. Anna Marie Katan, Apr. 2, 1976; 1 child, Laurel S. AB, Colby Coll., 1958; MD, Albert Einstein Coll. Medicine, 1962. Diplomate Am. Bd. Psychiatry and Neurology. Prof. Dept. Psychiatry NYU Sch. Medicine, 1980—; staff psychiatrist N.Y. VA Med. Ctr., 1980—. Editor: Schizophrenia & Pharmacologic Treatment; contbr. articles to profl. jours. and book chpts. Grantee NIMH, VA. Fellow Am. Coll. Neuropsychopharmacology, Collegium Internat. Neuropsychopharmacologium; mem. Psychiatry Rsch. Soc., Soc. Biol. Psychiatry. Office: Psychiatry 116A NY VA Med Ctr 423 E 23rd St New York NY 10010-5050

ANGUS, ROBERT CARLYLE, JR., health facility administrator; b. Grand Rapids, Mich., July 23, 1946; s. Robert Carlyle Sr. and Vicki I. (Weidman) Deiters; m. Elizabeth T. Angus, May 1990; children: Tamra, Robert M. BS, Donsbach U., Huntington Beach, Calif., 1985; PhD in Therapeutic Philosophy, World U., 1982. Registered cardiovascular technologist, pulmonary technologist, registered cardiology technologist, cert. respiratory therapy technician; lic. radiographer, respiratory care practitioner, hearing aid dispenser; cert. occupl. hearing conservationist. Dir. cardiopulmonary St. Mary's Hosp., Grand Rapids, Mich., 1970-74; Lectr. Muskegon (Mich.) Community Coll., 1974-76; dir. respiratory therapy Hackley Hosp., 1974-76; dir. cardiovascular, cardiopulmonary Am. Internat. Hosp., Zion, Ill., 1976-78; physician's asst. Dr. William J. Mauer; dir. med. svcs., clinic adminstr. Kingsley Med. Ctr., Arlington Heights, Ill., 1978-90; dir. med. diagnostics Celebration of Health Ctr., Inc., Bluffton, Ohio, 1990—; edn. cons. Brookhaven Med. Care Facility; lectr., advisor Muskegon Community Coll., 1974-76. Active Big Bros. Am., Muskegon, 1974-76. Mem. Nat. Bd. Cardiovascular Testing, Am. Cardiology Technologists Assn., Am. Assn. Respiratory Therapy, Nat. Soc. Cardiopulmonary Technologists, Coun. for Accreditation in Occupational Hearing Conservation, Clan MacInnes Soc.

ANILIONIS, ALGIS, molecular biologist; b. Halifax, Yorkshire, Eng., July 29, 1950; came to U.S., 1977; s. Jonas and Anna (Zizek) A.; m. Rita Heller, July 13, 1980; children: Deborah, Elizabeth. BA with honors, Oxford U., Eng., 1973; PhD, Edinburgh U., Scotland, 1977. Prin. investigator Repligen Corp., Cambridge, Mass., 1982-86; mgr. molecular biology Praxis Biologics, Rochester, N.Y., 1986-89, sr. prin. scientist, 1989-91; patent mgr. Oncogene Sci., Inc., Uniondale, N.Y., 1991-94; dir. intellectual property Cadus Pharm. Corp., Tarrytown, N.Y., 1994—; peer reviewer SBIR program NIH, Bethesda, Md., 1986-91; lectr. Ctr. for Profl. Advancement, East Brunswick, N.J., 1989-91. Author: (with others) Modern Approaches to Vaccines, 1989, Annual Reviews of Microbiology, 1978; contbr. articles to sci. jours. Phase I grantee, NIH, 1988, U.S. Patent Agt., 1993. Mem. AAAS, N.Y. Acad. Sci., Licensing Execs. Soc.

ANJARD, RONALD PAUL, SR., business and industry executive, consultant, educator, technologist, importer, author; b. Chgo., July 31, 1935; s. Auguste L. and Florence M. (Byrne) A.; m. Marie B. Sampler; children: Ronald Paul Jr., Michael P., Michele M., John R. BS in Metall. Engring., Carnegie Mellon U., 1957; MS/MBA in Indsl. Adminstrn., Purdue U., 1968; AS in Supervision, Ind. U., 1973; BS, U. State of N.Y., 1978; PDE, U. Wis., 1976; BA in Humanities, USNY, 1979; PhD in Edn., Columbia Pacific U., 1981, PhD in Metall. Engring., 1982; postgrad., Ind. U. Law Sch., 1975, La. State U., 1978, U. Calif., 1978; MS in Computer Resource Mgmt., Webster U., 1992; postgrad., U. Calif. Berkeley, 1978, La State U., 1979. Metallurgist U.S. Steel Corp., Braddock, Pa., 1956-57; metall. engr. Crucible Steel Co., Pitts., 1957-58; process engr. Raytheon Mfg. Co., Newton, Mass., 1958-59; program mgmt. engr. Delco Electronics div. GM, Kokomo, Ind., 1959-81; div. quality mgr. AVX Materials Div. Delco Electronics div. GM, Kokomo, 1981-82, div. quality mgr., JMI Electronic Materials div., 1982-83; v.p. engring. AG Tech, 1983—; pres. Anjard Internat. Cons., 1983, 86—, Anjard Solder Paste Tech., 1983—, Anjard Solder and Mfg. Tech., 1987—; corp. dir. quality Kaypro Corp., 1983-87; pres. Anjard Imports, 1965-80, 92—; sr. bank officer Mission Viejo (Calif.) Nat. Bank, 1986-87; v.p. mktg. Alpha Cast Products, 1987-93; v.p. adminstrn. Triage Network, 1988-93; sr. exec. broker Futures Investment Firm, 1983; quality cons. Gen. Dynamics, Convair, 1987, 92; SPC coord. Gen. Dynamics Electronics Div., 1989-94; distbr. Vertical Computer System, 1987; free-lance writer, photographer, 1966—; retail salesman Nurseryland, 1987-88; prof. Calif. Nat. U., 1993—, U. United States, 1995—; instr. Ball State U., 1970-71, 75-76, Kokomo Apprentice Program, 1971-81, Ind. Vocat. Tech. Coll., 1978-81, U. Phoenix, 1983, U. So. Calif., 1985-90, U. La Verne, 1985-92, Ala. A&M U., 1983, Chapman Coll., 1983-92, Nat. U., 1982-83, San Diego Community Coll., 1984—, U. Calif. San Diego, 1986-92, Golden State U., 1986-92, U. La Jolla, San Diego Job Corps, Union of Experimental Colls. and Univs., 1987—, Karanovich Counseling Ctr., Cen. Tex. Coll., 1987-92, numerous others; thesis mentor Columbia Pacific U., 1981—. Rev. editor Solid State Tech., rev. edit. Microelectronics and Reliability, 1982—, Ceram, 1985—, IEEE Circuits and Devices, 1985-93; contbr. to tech. and non-tech. publs. Pres. Greater Kokomo Assn. Chs., 1972-74; chmn. Diocesan Pastoral Council, Diocese Layfayette, Ind., 1977-78, diocesan ecumenical officer, 1972-78, diocesan impact coordinator, 1972-81; mem. Ascension Council, 1984—; active Ind. Council Chs., 1971-81; mem. San Diego Ecumenical Coun., 1995—; mem. Tierra Santa Town Council, 1988-90; councilman Howard County Council, Ind., 1981; trustee Clay Twp., 1970-75; dir. 5th dist. Ind. Twp. Trustees Assn.; vice chmn. Ind. State U. Young Republicans; del. Rep. State Conv., 1970, 74, 78, 80, dep. registration officer, 1970, 72, 74, 76, 80; mem. Rep. Nat. Com., 1970-75, mem. San Diego Rep. Cen. Com.; resolutions chmn. Young Reps. Conv., 1969; state minority chmn., dir. Howard County Young Reps.; regional dir. Leadership Tng. Sch.; chmn. 5th Dist. Young Reps.; mem. San Diego Rep. Cen. Com., 1985—; mem. Ind. State Com. for Med. Assistance, Ind. Citizens Adv. Council on Alcoholism, Ind. Citizens Council on Addictions, Mayor's Human Rights Com.; active Meshingomesia council Boy Scouts Am.; chmn. Clay Twp. Bicentennial Com., 1974-76; mem. exec. com. Kokomo Bicentennial Com., 1974-76; govt. agys. chmn. Howard County Bicentennial Com., 1974-76; capt. capital fund drive Sangralea Valley Boys Home Campaign, 1968; mem. San Diego Rep. Cen. Com., 1985—; regional bd. dirs. Drug Abuse Council, Howard County; bd. dirs., membership chmn. Mental Health Assn.; lector Ascension, San Diego, 1984—, mem. council, 1985-91, also numerous other civic activities. Served to capt., Ordnance Corps U.S. Army, 1957 Ind. Mental Health citations, 1969, 70, Howard County Mental Health citations, 1969, 70, Nat. Young Rep. Hard Charger award, 1970, Gen. Motors Community Service award, 1970, Jaycee Disting. Service award, 1970, Disting. Service award Ind. Young Reps., 1971, Layman of Year award K.C., 1971, Ind. Mental Health award, 1971-72, Heart Fund award, 1973, Ind. Gov.'s Vol. Action commendation, 1975, 78, award Greater Kokomo Council of Chs., 1975; named Outstanding Ind. Young Rep., 1970; fellow Harry S. Truman Library, 1974—. Fellow Internat. Soc. for Hybrid Microelectronics (Midwest regional dir., charter state pres., treas., v.p., publicity chmn., program chmn., others 1970), mem. Semicondr. Materials Soc., Am. Soc. Quality Control (editor non-periodic publs., electronics div.), Am. Soc. Metals, Am. Bar Assn., ASTM (chmn. subcoms. 1963-68), AIME , Kokomo Engring. Soc., Internat. Platform Assn., Internat. Brick Collector's Assn. (pres., gov. bd. 1983-93), Am. Indian Assn., Ind. Chess Assn., Nat. Hist. Soc., Ind. Hist. Soc., Howard County Hist. Soc. (bd. dirs.), Tippecanoe County Hist. Assn., Found. Ill. Archeology, Epigraphic Soc., Nat., Fla., Clearwater Audubon socs., N.Am. Acad. Ecumenists, Soc. Investigation of Unexplained, Ancient Astronaut Soc., Internat. Assn. for Investigation Ancient Civilizations (internat. dir. 1980—), Internat. UFO Registry, Kokomo Fine Arts Assn., Nat. Wilderness Soc., Whitewater Valley R.R. Assn., Kokomo Mgmt. Club (auditor 1970), Am. Hort. Soc., Nat. Greentown Glass Assn., San Diego Hist. Soc., San Diego Archeol. Soc., Calif. Archeol. Soc., San Diego Zool. Soc., Soc. for Hist. Archaeology, Soc. for Calif. Archaeology, San Diego Cymbidium Soc., San Diego Orch. and Soc., Nat. Acad. Ecumenists, Internat. Order St. Luke the Physician, Sigma Xi, numerous other organizations. Clubs: Kokomo Photo Guild, Ind. Chess, Donora Sportsman, Sycamore Racquet, Kokomo Rose Soc., Kokomo Astronomy, Kokomo Poetry, Kokomo Swim, East County Rep., Orion. Home: PO Box 420950 San Diego CA 92142-0950

ANJUR, SOWMYA SRIRAM, research scientist, educator; b. Ahmadi, Kuwait, Oct. 4, 1962; came to U.S. 1987; d. V.S. Krishna and Saraswathi (Venkitachalam) Moorthi; m. Sriram Padmanabhan Anjur, Aug. 22, 1991. BS in Biochemistry, Madras U., India, 1982; MS in Biochemistry, Bharathar U., India, 1984, MPhil in Biochemistry/Microbiology, 1986; PhD, Iowa State U., 1992. Biochemist ICCU, Modern Hosp., Salem, India, 1983-84; biochemist R&D Symbiotic Labs, Madras, India, 1984-85; chemistry lectr OCF High Sch., Madras, India, 1985-86; asst. prof. biochemistry Kongunadu Arts & Scis. Coll., Coimbatore, India, 1987; teaching asst. biology/zoology Iowa State U., Ames, 1987-92; lectr. U. Wis., Oshkosh, 1992; rsch. scientist Kimberly-Clark Corp., Neenah, Wis., 1993—; dietary cons. Hosp. Bd. Nutrition, Coimbatore, India, 1978-82; wastewater treatment cons. U. Madras, 1985-87, microbiology cons., 1984-86. Choreographer/performer solo Indian dance fundraisers: Bharathanatyam, 1979-82 (Best Dancer 1980, 81); dir. drama troupe: The Funsters, 1978-80. Group leader Nat. Adult Edn. Program, India, 1978-84; mgr. Nat. Svc. Scheme, India, 1978-84; team leader Community Social Svc. Projects, India, 1978-84; chief fundraiser Solo Bharathanatyam, 1979-82. Recipient Gold medal for proficiency Bharathiar U., India, 1984. Mem. IEEE, Soc. Engrs. in Medicine and Biology, Iowa Acad. Sci., Am. Soc. Animal Sci., Am. Dairy Sci. Assn., Soc. of Biol. Chemists (India), Am. Mensa, Gamma Sigma Delta. Home: 624 E Capitol Dr Appleton WI 54911-1209

ANKENBRUCK, MICHAEL JOSEPH, pharmacist; b. Ft. Wayne, Ind., Apr. 15, 1961; s. Donals Alfred and Rosemary Ann (Bonner) A.; m. Kimberly Ann Larrison, Sept. 8, 1984 (div. Dec. 1992); m. Kathy Jo Watters, Dec. 30, 1993; children: Nicholas Michael, Julia Christine. BS in Pharmacy, Purdue U., 1984. Pharmacist/mgr. Chronister Pharmacy, Ft. Wayne, 1984-89; outpatient pharmacy supr. Owen Healthcare, Bluffton, Ind., 1989-91, dir. pharmacy svcs., 1991—. Pres. bd. dirs. Park Free Clinic, Bluffton, 1994—. Recipient Recognition award Merck & Co., 1990. Fellow Am. Soc. Cons. Pharmacists; mem. Am. Soc. Health Systems Pharmacists, Ind. Soc. Hosp. Pharmacists (region II v.p. 1991—), Ind. Pharmacists Assn., N.E. Ind. Pharmacists Assn. (pres. 1989, continuing edn. chmn. 1990-93, Pharmacist of the Yr. 1990). Office: Caylor-Nickel Hosp 1 Caylor-Nickel Sq Bluffton IN 46714-2548

ANKERL, GUY CORNELIUS THOMAS, sociology educator, consultant, engineer, writer; b. Odenburg, Switzerland, May 30, 1933; s. Thomas and Cornelia (Faber) A.; m. Eva Polyanszky, Sept. 1, 1954 (dec. 1961); 1 child, Magnolia; m. Méry Jordan, June 27, 1978. BA, Oedenburg U., 1951; MArch in Engring., Tech. U., 1956; PhD in Social Sci., Freiburg U., 1965. Registered profl. engr., Switzerland. Prof. Mont. (Can.) U., 1966-72, MIT, Cambridge, Mass., 1972—, Inst. Inter-Univ. Geneva, 1980—; pvt. practice cons., Geneva, 1963—; advisor HIID, Harvard U., Cambridge, 1978—; expert Swiss NSF, Bern, Switzerland, 1976—; expert cons. Internat. Labour Office, Geneva, 1979—, UNESCO, 1994—. Author: Beyond Monopoly Capitalism and Monopoly, Socialism, 1978, Experimental Sociology of Architecture, 1983, Urbanization Overspeed in Tropical Africa, 1987. Contbr. articles to Internat. Herald Tribune Newspaper, Jour. of Geneva. Swiss NSF grantee, 1976. Mem. Rotary. Home: 3, rue St-Léger, Ch-1211 Geneva 11, Switzerland Office: MIT Cambridge MA 02139-7047

ANKNER, MARIE, nursing administrator; b. N.Y.C., May 10, 1951; d. Carmine P. and Betty (Stockl) Porcaro; m. Thomas J. Ankner, 1973; 2 children. Diploma in nursing, Westchester Sch. Nursing, 1972; BSN, Pace U., 1976, MSN with distinction, 1984. RN; cert. advanced nursing adminstrn. Staff nurse, MMTP, orthopedics-surg., ICU Jacobi Hosp., N.Y.C., 1975-93; supr. burn svc. Jacobi Hosp., Bronx, N.Y., 1978-84, ADN surg. svcs., 1984-86, assoc. dir. edn. and quality assurance, 1986-92, assoc. dir. regulatory affairs, 1993-95; ADN mgmt. svcs. Lawrence Hosp., Bronxville, N.Y., 1993-95; ADN II Jack D. Weiler Hosp. of Albert Einstein Coll. Medicine, 1995—; clin. instr. Coll. New Rochelle, 1996—. Recipient Regents scholarship, fed. traineeship. Mem. N.Y. Nurses Assn., N.Y. Quality Assurance Profls., Bronx Westchester Nurse Recruiters, Sigma Theta Tau.

ANLIKER, WAYNE L., optometrist; b. Emporia, Kans., Apr. 14, 1964; s. Glen Robert and Lorean Phyllis (Brown) A.; m. Dawn Marie Loechler, Aug. 9, 1986; children: Tyler Wayne, Danielle Marie. BS, Kans. State U., 1986; OD magna cum laude, U. Houston, 1990; postgrad. in Medicine, U. Kans., 1993—. Lic. optometrist, Kans. Optometrist G.L. Cockrell, OD, P.A., Emporia, Kans., 1990-92, Profl. Eyecare Corp., Overland Park, Kans., 1993—; rsch. asst. dept. ophthalmology U. Kans. Med. Ctr., Kansas City, 1994—. Mem. AMA, Kans. Med. Soc., Kiwanis (social svcs. chair 1991-92), Beta Sigma Kappa, Omega Chi Epsilon. Home: 919 N Sunset Dr Olathe KS 66061 Office: Profl Eyecare Corp 11205 W 95th St Overland Park KS 66214

ANLYAN, WILLIAM GEORGE, surgeon, university administrator; b. Alexandria, Egypt, Oct. 14, 1925; s. Armand and Emmeraude (Nazar) A.; children: William George, John Peter, Louise. BS magna cum laude, Yale U., 1945, MD, 1949; DSc (hon.), Rush Med. Coll., 1973. Diplomate Am. Bd. Surgery, Am. Bd. Thoracic Surgery. Intern, resident, instr., assoc. in surgery Duke Hosp., Durham, N.C., 1949-53; asst. prof. surgery Duke Hosp., Durham, 1953-58; prof. surgery Duke Hosp., Durham, N.C., 1961-89; assoc. dean Sch. Medicine Duke, 1963, dean, 1964-69, v.p. health affairs, 1969-83, chancellor health affairs, 1983-88, exec. v.p., 1987-88; chancellor Duke U., 1988-90, chancellor emeritus, 1990—; chmn. Durham VA Chancellor's Com., 1963-89, Pearl Health Svcs., Inc., 1983-85; surg. cons. Durham VA Hosp.; Markle scholar med. sci., 1953-58; chmn. regents Nat. Libr. Medicine, 1971-72; bd. trustees N.C. Sch. Sci. and Math., 1978-85, chmn. phys. facilities com., 1979, vice-chmn. of bd. trustees, 1981-84; mem. bd. visitors The U. Tex. Health Sci. Ctr. at Houston, 1980-88, Stanford U., 1985-87; chmn. Yale U. Coun. Com. on Med. Affairs, 1985-93. Mem. editorial bd. Pharos, 1968-93. Trustee The Duke Endowment, 1990—, Commn. on Future Structure of Vet. Health Care, 1990-92; chmn. Gov.'s Task Force on Better Health for N.C. in 2000, 1991—; mem. White House Sci. Coun., 1988-89. Recipient award for disting. achievement Modern Medicine, 1974; Gov.'s award for disting. meritorious service, 1978. Fellow ACS; mem. AMA (adv. com. med. sci. 1972—), Soc. Univ. Surgeons, Soc. Vascular Surgery, Internat. Cardiovascular Soc., Soc. Clin. Surgery, Am. Heart Assn., Soc. Med. Adminstrs. (pres. 1983-85), Inst. Medicine of Nat. Acad. Sci., Coun. Deans (chmn. 1968-69), AAMC Coun. Deans (chmn. 1968-69), So. Med. Assn., Coord. Coun. Med. Edn. (chmn. 1973-74), Surg. Biology Club II, Am. Surg. Assn., So. Surg. Assn., Halsted Soc., Allen O. Whipple Surg. Soc., Assn. Am. Med. Colls. (chmn. 1970-71, Abraham Flexner award 1980, WHO rep. 1981-84), Ind. Rsch. Roundtable NAS, Assn. Acad. Health Ctrs. (pres. 1975), Rsch. Am. (bd. dirs. 1989—, chmn. 1992-96), Rotary, Phi Beta Kappa, Sigma Xi, Alpha Omega Alpha. Home: 1516 Pinecrest Rd Durham NC 27705 Office: Duke Med Ctr Box 3626 Durham NC 27710

ANNAB, HASSAN ZUHEIR, pathologist; b. Aleppo, Syria, Oct. 24, 1950; s. Zuheir Hasan Annab and Widad Abdel-Hamid Mouhaffel; m. Madiha Hussein Mouhaffel, June 16, 1976; children: Muna, Yazan, Widad. MB BCh, U. Baghdad, Iraq, 1975. Diplomate Am. Bd. Pathology. Resident in pathology Bapt. Meml. Hosp., San Antonio, 1976-80; pvt. practice Annab Labs., Amman, Jordan, 1981—; examiner in pathology Jordan Med. Coun., 1987—; cons. Al-Bashir Hosp., Amman, 1986-88, Islamic Hosp., Amman, 1982—. Mem. Jordan Soc. Pathology (pres. 1994-96), Jordan Oncology Soc. (treas. 1993—). Office: Annab Labs, PO Box 1785, Amman 11118, Jordan

ANNIS, EDWARD R., surgeon; b. Detroit, Mar. 27, 1913; s. Edward Roland and Ethel Mary (Graham) A.; m. Betty McCue Starck, June 16, 1941; children: Joseph, Brian, Paul, Barbara, Marjorie, Kathleen, Timothy, Roberta. BS, U. Detroit, 1933; MD, Marquette Coll., 1938. Intern Milw. County Hosp., 1938; postgrad. surgery intern Cook County Hosp., Chgo., 1938-43; pvt. practice Miami, Fla., 1938-63, ind. cons., lectr., 1963—; cons. N.Am. Physicians Ins. Co., Am. coll. Legal Medicine, Drs. Legal Def. Inst. Co.; bd. dirs Cruise Am. Participant numerous radio and TVshows. Mem. adv. com. health care tech. assessment, Fla. State Ins. Commn., Cleve. Clinic Fla.; bd. dirs. Am. Inst. Med. Law; mem. Fla. State Pepper Commn. on Aging. Mem. AMA (speakers bur. 1961—, pres. 1963-64, trustee 1967-69), Am. Acad.Gen. Practice (hon.), Chamber of Commerce U.S. (bd. dirs., com. nation's health 1969-75), World Med. Assn. (pres. 1963-64, coun. emissary 1965-67), Internat. Coll. Surgeons (pres. U.S. sect. 1964-65), Soc. Air Force Clin. Surgeons (hon.), Fla. Med. Assn. (chmn. speakers bur. 1962—). Office: 9999 NE 2nd Ave Ste 303 Miami FL 33138-2346

ANNIS, LAWRENCE VINCENT, forensic clinical psychologist; b. Augusta, Ga., Dec. 28, 1946; s. Lawrence Vincent Sr. and Betty (Allen) An.; m. Kathy Ann Kirkwood, June 12, 1971 (div. 1973); m. Christy Adelle Baker, Aug. 23, 1982; children: Loren Adelle, Cathy Laurel. Lic. clin. psychologist, Fla. Behavior specialist Gracewood State Sch., Augusta, 1980-81; clin. dir. Youth Enrichment Services, Lumberton, N.C., 1982-83; clin. psychologist Fla. State Hosp., Chattahoochee, 1981-82, 83-84, internship dir., 1984-91; supervising psychologist Corrections Mental Health Inst., Chattahoochee, 1984-90; chief psychologist Fla. State Hosp., 1990-93, dir. psychol. svcs., 1993—; forensic cons. various corrections agys., 1985—. Contbr. chpts. to books, articles to profl. jours. Mem. Am. Psychol. Assn., S.E. Psychol. Assn., Am. Assn. for Correctional Psychology, Internat. Council Psychologists. Avocations: running; sailing. Office: Fla State Hosp Chattahoochee FL 32324

ANSARI, MOHAMMED RAFIULLAH, surgeon; b. Gokaram, Andhra Pradesh, India, Oct. 10, 1935; came to U.S., 1967, naturalized, 1977; s. Mohammed Mahboob Ali and Abbas (Bibi) A.; m. Raoof Yasmin, June 2, 1962; 1 child, Farrah Yasmin. B.S., Osmania U., India, 1957, M.B. B.S., 1962. Asst. surgeon Dist. Hosp., Karimnagar, India, 1963-67; intern St. Luke Hosp., St. Paul, 1967-68; resident Henry Ford Hosp., Detroit, 1968-73, staff surgeon, 1973—; clin. instr. surgery U. Mich., Detroit, 1976-80, clin. asst. prof., 1980—. Recipient Roy D. McClure Surg. award Henry Ford Hosp.-McClure Surg. Soc., 1971. Mem. AMA, Mich. State Med. Soc., ACS, Acad. Surgery of Detroit, Midwest Surg. Assn. Republican. Muslim. Home: 3016 Westman Ct Bloomfield Hills MI 48304-2062 Office: 2799 W Grand Blvd Detroit MI 48202

ANSELL, JULIAN S., physician, retired urology educator; b. Portland, Maine, June 30, 1922; s. Jacob M. and Anna Gertrude (Fieldman) A.; m. Eva Ruth Ballin, June 17, 1951; children: Steven, Jody, Carol, Ellen, Peter. BA, Bowdoin Coll., 1946; MD, Tufts U., 1951; PhD, U. Minn., 1959. Intern in surgery U. Minn. Hosps., Mpls., 1951-52, resident in urology, 1952-54; NIH fellow U. Minn., Mpls., 1954, instr., 1956-59; asst. prof., head urology U. Wash., Seattle, 1959-62, assoc. prof., head urology, 1962-64, prof., chair urology, 1965-87, prof. urology, 1987-92, prof. emeritus, 1992—. 2d lt. U.S. Army, 1943-46. Mem. Am. Alpine Club (N.Y.C.). Office: 3827 49th Ave NE Seattle WA 98105

ANSPAUGH, LYNN RICHARD, research biophysicist; b. Rawlins, Wyo., May 25, 1937; s. Solon Earl and Alice Henrietta (Day) A.; m. Barbara Anne Corrigan, Nov. 2, 1965 (div.); children: Gregory, Heidi; m. Larisa Fedorovna Kornushina, Sept. 27, 1993. BA, Nebr. Wesleyan U., 1959; M in Bioradiology, U. Calif., Berkeley, 1961, PhD, 1963. Biophysicist Lawrence Livermore (Calif.) Nat. Lab., 1963-74, group leader, 1974-75, sect. leader, 1976-82, div. leader, 1982-92, dir. Risk Scis. Ctr., 1992-95, dir. Dose Reconstruction program, 1995—; tchr. extension U. Calif., Berkeley, 1966-69; lectr. San Jose (Calif.) State U., 1975; guest lectr. UCLA, Stanford U., U. Calif., Davis, 1992—; faculty affiliate Colo. State U., Ft. Collins, 1979-83; cons. EPA, Washington, 1984-85, U. Utah, Salt Lake City, 1983-88; mem. U.S. del. UN Sci. Com. on Effects of Radiation, Vienna, 1987—; mem. Nat. Coun. on Radiation Protection and Measurements, 1989—. Contbr. articles to profl. jours. AEC fellow, 1959-61; fellow NSF, 1961-63. Fellow Health Physics Soc. (pres. environ. radiation sect. 1984-85, pres. No. Calif. chpt. 1986-87); mem. AAAS, Soc. for Risk Analysis, Internat. Union Radioecologists, Radioation Rsch. Soc., Sigma Xi. Mem. Evangelical Free Ch. Home: PO Box 2017 Danville CA 94526-7017 Office: Allegheny Gen Hosp 320 E North Ave Pittsburgh PA 15212

ANSTADT, GEORGE W., occupational medicine physician; b. Williamsport, Pa., Aug. 17, 1947; s. Vern Eugene and Jane Ann (Treon) A.; m. Nancy Jane Conrad, 1980; children: Jonathan, Jennifer. BS, Pa. State U., 1968; MD, Jefferson Med. Coll., 1970. Diplomate Am. Bd. Preventive Medicine (Occupational Medicine). Rotating intern Northwestern U., 1970-71; resident in occupational medicine U. Cin., 1974-76; sr. med. advisor Eastman Kodak Co., Rochester, N.Y., 1976—. Lt. comdr. M.C., USN, 1971-74. Mem. Am. Coll. Occupational and Environ. Medicine (nat. 1st v.p.). Home: 75 Panorama Trl Rochester NY 14625-1507 Office: Eastman Kodak Co 901 Elmgrove Rd Rochester NY 14653-5023

ANTELL, DARRICK EUGENE, plastic surgeon; b. Cleve., Feb. 22, 1951; s. E. James and Wanda H. (Kociecki) A.; m. Elizabeth Ann Sobottka, July 14, 1984; children: Gillian Elizabeth, Darrick Eugene, Leslie Jane. BS in Biology, Hobart Coll., 1973; DDS, Case Western Res. U. Dental, 1978; MD, Med. Coll. of Ohio, 1982. Cert. Am. Bd. Plastic Surgery. Surgery intern Stanford (Calif.) U. Med. Ctr., 1982-83, surgery resident, 1983-85; plastic surgery resident N.Y. Hosp. Cornell, N.Y.C., 1985-87; plastic and reconstructive surgeon St. Luke's/Roosevelt, N.Y.C., 1987—. Author: Plastic Surgery, 1991; contbr. articles to profl. jours. Bd. trustees East Side House Settlement, N.Y.C., 1991; bd. trustees adv. Girl Scouts of North Am., N.Y.C., 1991. Grantee Facial Proportions AM. Soc. for Aesthetic Plastic Surgery, 1987; recipient Pres. Citizenship award N.Y. State Med. Soc., 1992. Fellow Am. Coll. Surgeons; mem. AMA, Am. Soc. Plastic and Reconstructive Surgeons, Am. Soc. Aesthetic Plastic Surgery, Am. Soc. Maxillofacial Surgeons Parliamentarian, N.Y. Regional Soc. Plastic and Reconstructive Surgeons, Am. Acad. Cosmetic Dentistry, Interplast, Lipoplasty Soc., Herbert Conway Soc., Univ. Sch. Alumni Adv. Coun., Union Club. Office: 850 Park Ave New York NY 10021-1845

ANTESKI, MICHAEL, physician; b. Boston, July 22, 1937; s. Michael and Aldona Isabel (Sinkovich) A. AB, Boston U., 1959, MD, 1963. Intern Newton-Wellesley Hosp., Newton, Mass., 1963-64, resident in medicine, 1967; resident in medicine New Eng. Deaconess Hosp., Boston, 1964; staff physician Columbia Point Health Ctr., Boston, 1974-76; physician in western states Indian Health Svc., 1976-81; dir. Cmty. Health Ctr., Loving, N.Mex., 1981-82; physician Mil. Processing Sta., Boston, 1982-91; chief med. officer Med. Processing Sta., Boston, 1988-89; staff physician Addiction Ctr. Hosp., Bridgewater, Mass., 1989-91; pvt. practice, Attleboro, Mass., 1991—. Author: Twilight of the Gods, 1994. Capt. M.C., U.S. Army, 1965-67, Korea. Mem. AMA. Office: Gen Health Care Inc 66 S Washington St North Attleboro MA 02760

ANTHONISEN, NICHOLAS R., respiratory physiologist; b. Boston, Oct. 12, 1933. AB, Dartmouth Coll., 1955; MD, Harvard U., 1958; PhD in Exptl. Medicine, McGill U., 1969. Intern medicine N.C. Meml. Hosp., 1958-59, jr. asst. resident, 1959-60; sr. asst. resident respiratory dept. Royal Victoria Hosp., 1963-64; demonstrator medicine McGill U., 1964-66, from asst. to assoc. prof. exptl. medicine, 1969-73, prof., 1973-75; prof. medicine U. Man., Winnipeg, 1975—. Scholar Med. Rsch. Coun. Can., 1969-71. Mem. Can. Soc. Clin. Investigation, Can. Thoracic Soc., Am. Physiol. Soc., Am. Soc. Clin. Investigation, Am. Thoracic Soc. Office: U Man, 753 McDermot Ave, Winnipeg, MB Canada R3E 0W3*

ANTHONY, ADAM, physiology educator; b. Buffalo, Oct. 19, 1923; s. John and Rozalia (Piechowicz) Chmielowski; m. Barbara Oakes, June 20, 1949 (div. Oct. 1986); children: Heather Lee, Brian Adam. BA, SUNY, Buffalo, 1943; MS, Marquette U., 1948; PhD, U. Chgo., 1952. Asst. prof. Pa. State U., University Park, 1952-57, assoc. prof., 1957-61, prof., 1961—. Contbr. and co-contbr. numerous articles to profl. jours. With U.S. Army, 1943-46. John M. Prather scholar U. Chgo., 1950-52; recipient Darbaker award Pa. Acad. Scis., 1966, 68,69, C.I. Noll Outstanding Teaching award, 1990, Pa. State U., 1990. Mem. AAAS, Am. Physiol. Soc., Phi Lambda Upsilon, Phi Sigma, Sigma Xi. Office: Pa State U 418 Mueller University Park PA 16802

ANTHONY, VERNICE DAVIS, public health officer; b. Jan. 10, 1945; m. Eddie Anthony; 3 children. BSN, Wayne State U., 1970; MPH, U. Mich.,

1976. RN, Mich. Staff nurse Children's Hosp. Mich., Detroit; pub. health nurse, adminstr. community health field svcs. Detroit Health Dept.; health officer Wayne County, Detroit; div. chief Office Local Health Svcs. Mich. Dept. Pub. Health, Lansing, chief Office Police Devel. and Evaluation, dir. dept., 1991—; mem. nat. adv. coun. on maternal, infant and fetal nutrition USDA; former mem. state task forces on infant mortality, access to care and status minority health. Former mem. bd. dirs. United Community Svcs., St. John's Hosp.; former mem. health com. New Detroit Inc.; charter mem. Mich. Health Policy Forum; mem. exec. com. Greater Area Health Coun.; mem. alumni bd. U. Mich., Ann Arbor; bd. dirs. Mich. div. Am. Cancer Soc. Recipient achievement award Nat. Assn. Counties, 1985, 86. Mem. Mich. Health Officers Assn. (past pres., svc. award 1989), Mich. Assn. for Local Pub. Health (former mem. exec. coun., svc. award). Office: Public Health Dept 4323 N Logan St PO Box 30195 Lansing MI 48909

ANTHONY, VIRGINIA QUINN BAUSCH, medical association executive; b. Odessa, Tex., June 9, 1945; d. William Francis and Florence Elizabeth (Decker) Quinn; m. E. James Anthony; 1 child, Justin. B.A., Mt. Holyoke Coll., 1967. Exec. dir. Am. Acad. Child and Adolescent Psychiatry, Washington, 1973—. Mem. Am. Soc. Assn. Execs. Office: Am Acad Child and Adolescent Psychiatry 3615 Wisconsin Ave NW Washington DC 20016-3007

ANTHONY-PEREZ, BOBBIE COTTON MURPHY, psychology educator, researcher; b. Macon, Ga., Nov. 15, 1923; d. Solomon Richard and Maude Alice (Lockett) Cotton; m. William Anthony, Aug. 22, 1959 (dec.); 1 child, Freida; m. Andrew Silviano Perez, June 20, 1979. BS, DePaul U., 1953, MS, 1954; MS, U. Ill., 1959; PhD, U. Chgo., 1967; MA, DePaul, 1975. Tchr. Chgo. Pub. Schs., 1954-68; math. coord. U. Chgo., 1965; prof. Chgo. State U., 1968-95, coord. Black Studies Program, 1982-83; with psychol. svcs. Chgo. Pub. Schs., 1971-72; rsch. coord. Urban Affairs Inst., Howard U., Washington, 1978; coordinator Higher Edn. Careers Counseling Campus Ministry, Ingleside Whitfield Parish, 1978-84, comms. chmn., 1991-92, 95; coord. Black Studies Chgo. State U., 1990-94. V.p. Community Affairs Chatham Bus. Assn., 1981-85, asst. sec., 1985-86, sec., 1986-87, directory com., 1987, 88; bus. rels. chmn. Chatham Avalon Park Cmty. Coun., 1984—, newsletter editor, 1993—; bd. dirs. United Meth. Found. at U. Chgo., 1980-84, Community Mental Health Council, Inc., 1979-83; pub. edn. chairperson Chatham Avalon Unit Am. Cancer Soc., 1977-88, 90—, pub. info. chairperson, 1988-94; pres. Aux. Chgo. Chpt. Tuskegee Airmen, Inc., 1994, 95. NSF fellow, 1957, 58, 59; recipient numerous awards religious, civic and ednl. instns. and assns. Mem. Am. Psychol. Assn., Internat. Assn. Applied Psychology, Internat. Assn. Cross-Cultural Psychology, Internat. Assn. Ednl. and Vocat. Guidance, Assn. Black Psychologists (pres. Chgo. chpt.), Chgo. Psychol. Assn., Nat. Council Tchrs. Math., Am. Ednl. Research Assn., Midwest Ednl. Research Assn., Am. Soc. Clin. Hypnosis, Midwestern Psychol. Assn. Methodist. Contbr. numerous articles to profl. jours. Office: Chgo State U Dept Psychology 9501 S King Dr Chicago IL 60628-1502

ANTIA, KERSEY H., industrial and clinical psychologist, consultant; b Surat, Gujarat, India, Jan. 7, 1936; came to U.S. 1965; s. Hormasji and Dinsa R. (Mistry) A.; m. Dilshad K. Khambalta, Dec. 18, 1966; children: Anahita, Mazda, Jimmy. AB with honors, U. Bombay, 1958; MS, Tata Inst. Social Scis., Bombay, 1960, N.C. State U., 1969; PhD, Ind. No. U., 1976. Lic. psychologist, Ill.; cert. social worker, Ill. Personnel mgr., welfare officer Tata Steel and Tata Chem., 1960-65; research asst. psychology dept. N.C. State U., 1966-67, U. N.C., 1967-69; project dir. Behavior Systems, Inc., Raleigh, N.C., 1969-70; dir. Midwest Inst. Human Resources, Tinley Park, Ill., 1972—. Lang. scholar U. Bombay, 1954-56. Mem. Am. Psychol. Soc., Assn. for the Advancement of Psychology, Am. Acad. of Pain Mgmt., Am. Bd. of Profl. Disability Cons. Zoroastrian. Home: 8318 138th Pl Orland Park IL 60462-1746 Office: Tinley Ctr 17730B Oak Park Ave Tinley Park IL 60477-3936

ANTON, DAVID MICHAEL, hospital consultant; b. Bklyn., Jan. 27, 1911; s. Saul and Grace A.; m. Audrey Keller, Oct. 16, 1941 (dec. 1989); m. Marjorie Swigert, Aug. 18, 1992. Chief hosp. operations VA br. office, Columbus, Ohio, 1946-47; asst. dir. VA Med. Ctr., Dearborn, Mich., 1947-53, Bklyn., 1953-54; asst. dir. med. ctr. VA Med. Ctr., N.Y.C., 1954-57; med. ctr. dir. VA Med. Ctr., Castle Point, N.Y., 1957-58; area dir. adminstrv. services VA Area Med. Office, Boston, 1958-63; dir. bldg. mgmt. service VA Central Office, Washington, 1963-66; dir. VA Med. Ctr., West Haven, Conn., 1966-70; hosp. dir. VA Med. Ctr., St. Louis, from 1970; asso. chief med. dir. VA, Washington, ret., 1974; hosp. cons., 1974—; Bd. dirs. Lakeview Ctr., Pensacola, Fla. Served to maj. Med. Service Corps AUS; Served to maj. Med. Service Corps USAAF, 1942-46, ETO. Recipient citations Am. Legion, U.S. Customs Port N.Y., 1957, Am. Legion dept. N.Y., 1957, dept. Conn., 1970, AMVETS Spl. Meritorious Commendation Nat., 1967, United Spanish War Vets dept. Conn., 1968, Vets. World War I dept. Conn., 1968, 70, D.A.V. dept. Conn., 1970; Nat. D.A.V. citation for distinguished Service, 1972; others; Adminstrs. Exceptional Service award and Chief Med.; Dirs. certificate for outstanding performance VA, 1971; Distinguished Service award; Gold medal VA, 1974. Fellow Royal Soc. Health (Eng.); mem. Am. Coll. Hosp. Adminstrs. (life), Assn. Mil. Surgeons U.S. (life), Fed. Hosp. Inst. Alumni Assn., Am. Hosp. Assn. (life), Am. Legion., Masons, Rotary (Paul Harris award 1989). Lodges: Masons, Rotary. Home: 10100 Hillview Rd Apt 306 Pensacola FL 32514-5453

ANTON ALBISU, ANTONIO, physician, researcher; b. Alcoy, Alicante, Spain, Sept. 2, 1966; s. Antonio Anton Delso and Maria Albisu Andrade; m. Nuria Orriols Mestres. BS, Sitges Inst., Barcelona, Spain, 1983; med. lic., Barcelona U., 1991. Respiratory resident Hosp. Sant Pan, Pau, 1991-95; respiratory physician Hosp. Sant Pan, Barcelona, 1996—. Contbr. articles to profl. jours. Mem. Spanish Soc. Respiratory Pathology (investigation scholar 1995). Office: Hosp Sant Pau, Sant Antoni Ma Claret 167, 08025 Barcelona Spain

ANTONIOU, PANAYOTIS A., surgeon; b. Patras, Achaia, Greece, Feb. 17, 1962; s. Antonios Antoniou and Maria Flogera; m. Argiro Paloumpi, May 17, 1986. MD, Nat. U. Athens (Greece), 1986. Resident surgery Army Share Fund Hosp., Athens, 1986-89; resident surgery Air Force Gen. Hosp., 1990-91, resident urology, 1991; pvt. practice Athens, 1991-92; rural community work Korinthos Gen. Hosp., 1992-93; resident in surgery Air Force Gen. Hosp., 1993-94; pvt. practice Athens, 1995—; trainer, rechr. endoscopic surgery program. Contbr. to 1 book, 30 articles to med. jours., 58 presentations to med. congresses. Mem. European Assn. Endoscopic Surgery, Soc. for Minimally Invasive Therapy, Internat. Gastro-Surg. Club, European Gastrotestinal Mobility Soc., Hellenic Surgical Soc., Greek Assn. Endoscopic Surgery and other Interventional Techniques, Assn. Med. Grads. Athens U., Hellenic Action Against Cancer, European Assn. Surgical Scis., Greek Assn. of HPB Surgeons. Orthodox. Home: Adrianoupoleos 33, 15669 Papagos Athens Greece

ANTOSZYK, ANDREW NICHOLAS, ophthalmologist; b. Bklyn., Feb. 28, 1958; s. Nicholas and Corinne Theresa (Allegretti) A.; m. Karen Ann Esposito, May 28, 1983; children: Brian Andrew, Jennifer Christine. BA, U. Albany, 1979; MD, N.Y. Med. Coll., 1983. Diplomate Am. Bd. Ophthalmology. Intern, resident Duke U. Eye Ctr., Durham, N.C., 1983-87, fellow, 1987-89; asst. prof. surgery Uniformed Svcs. U. Health Scis., Bethesda, Md., 1989—; cons. ophthalmologist Nat. Naval Med. Ctr., Bethesda, 1989-93, Walter Reed Army Med. Ctr., Washington, 1989-93, Malcolm Grow Med. Ctr., Camp Springs, Md., 1990-93; staff ophthalmologist Charlotte Eye, Ear, Nose & Throat Assocs., Charlotte, 1993—; asst. cons. prof. Duke U. Eye Ctr., 1994—; treas. Ind. Eye Care Providers, Inc., Charlotte, 1995—; assoc. examiner Am. Bd. Ophthalmology, 1992—; adv. com. Presbyn. Specialty Hosp., Charlotte, 1995—. Maj. USAF, 1989-93. Fellow Am. Acad. Ophthalmology; mem. AMA, Assn. Rsch. in Vision and Ophthalmology, Soc. Heed/Knapp Fellows, N.C. Med. Soc., N.C. Soc. Ophthalmology, Mecklenburg County Med. Soc. (alt. del.), Alpha Omega Alpha. Roman Catholic. Office: Charlotte EENT Assocs 1600 E 3d St Charlotte NC 28204

ANWAR, MUJAHID, neonatologist, educator; b. Rawalpindi, Punjab, Pakistan, Mar. 23, 1949; came to U.S., 1972; s. Mohamed Anwar and Aqeela Khatoon; m. Nishat Zedie, June 12, 1972. MB,BS, Nishtar Med. Coll., Multan, Pakistan, 1970. Diplomate Am. Bd. Pediatrics, Am. Bd. Neonatal-Perinatal Medicine. Intern in pediatrics Lincoln Hosp., Bronx, N.Y., 1972-73; resident in pediatrics N.Y. Infirmary, N.Y.C., 1973-75; fellow in neonatology Newark Beth Israel Med. Ctr., 1975-77; attending neonatologist St. Peter's Med. Ctr., New Brunswick, N.J., 1977—; asst. prof. pediatrics Robert Wood Johnson Med. Sch. U. Medicine and Dentistry N.J., New Brunswick, 1979-86, assoc. prof. pediatrics Robert Wood Johnson Med. Sch., 1986—; cons. Robert Wood Johnson Med. Ctr., New Brunswick, 1978—. Contbr. articles to Circulation Rsch., Pediatric Rsch., Am. Jour Physiology. Mem. AAAS, Am. Physiol. Soc., Soc. Pediatric Rsch., Soc. Neurosciences. Office: St Peter's Med Ctr 254 Easton Ave New Brunswick NJ 08901-1766

ANYANWU, CHUKWUKRE, alcohol and drug abuse facility administrator; b. Ogbor-Ugiri, Nigeria, Apr. 14, 1943; came to U.S., 1963; s. Peter Ebo and Eunice Ikwuaha (Madu) A.; m. Ngozi G. Nwaike, Jan. 10, 1980; children: Okechukwu-Pat, Adaku Cathy, Ikechukwu-Uzo, Uremegbulem, Kingsley-Ugo, Ucheckukwu. BS in Biology and Chemistry, St. Joseph's Coll., 1971; MS in Biochemistry, Fairleigh Dickenson U., 1972; postgrad., Temple U., 1979; MD, Cetec U., Dominican Republic, 1981. Postdoctorate Temple Hosp.; diplomatic envoy Nigeria, 1973-75; extern various hosps., Phila. area, 1977-79; obstetrician-gynecologist, cons. Lagos U. Teaching Hosp., Nigeria, 1983-84; cons. psychiatry St. Mary's Hosp., Phila., 1981-82; rsch. nuclear medicine Temple U. Hosp., Phila., 1980-81; chmn. A-B Assocs. Inc., Phila., 1970—; chief exec. officer, owner, founder A-B Assocs., Inc., Phila., 1989—; virolog rsch. A-B Assocs. Inc., Phila., 1979-82, owner, chief exec. officer, dir.; mem. staff dept. of psychiatry JFK Mental Health/Retardation, Phila., 1985-88; mem. staff dept. of drug and alcohol addiction Giuffré Med. Ctr., 1988-89; counselor in psychiatry Misericordia Hosp., Phila., 1987-88; mem. staff addiction svcs. Giuffre Med. Ctr., Phila., 1988—; founder, chief exec. officer AB Assocs. Am. Beats Addiction, Inc., Phila., 1989—; paper rev. cons. NIH, Alcohol, Drug Abuse and Mental Health Adminstrn.; mem. com. peer rev. Dept. HHS, USPHS, NIH; mem. healthy start-reduction of infant mortality Pub. Policy Phila. Dept. Pub. Health; panelist Phila. Empowerment Zone for HealthCare Providers. Author numerous poems; contbr. articles profl. jours. Senate candidate Imo State Govt., Nigeria, 1983; mem. free standing steering com, pub. policy com. and providers com. Health Start Initiative-Phila. Dept. Pub. Health, vice chmn. programs, federally funded programs for maternal infant care; Olympian athlete competing in pole vault, 1500 meters and 400 meter hurdles, Mex., 1968; bd. dirs. March of Dimes Birth Defects Found.; mem. Mayor's Office of Cmty. Svcs., City of Phila., 1994—; rep. Area D., Phila. Mem. AAAS, Am. Coll. Healthcare Execs., Pa. Cert. Addiction Counselors. Orgn. Nigerian Profs. USA (chmn. jud. com.), Fedn. Police Law Enforcement, Phila. Fraternal Order of Police, Interagy. Coun. Homeless. Democrat. Roman Catholic. Office: America Beats Addiction Inc PO Box 38127 Philadelphia PA 19140-0127

APARICIO, ALEJANDRO, internist; b. Havana, Cuba, May 25, 1953; s. Aparicio M. and Delia (Baldo) A.; m. Susan L. Constable, Mar. 18, 1989; 1 child, Alexander Brian. BS, U. Fla., 1976; MD, Universidad Central del Este, San Pedro de Macoris, Dominican Republic, 1981. Diplomate Am. Bd. Internal Medicine; cert. geriatrics. Chief resident in internal medicine Ravenswood Hosp. Med. Ctr., Chgo., 1985-86, coord. ambulatory care internal medicine residency program, 1986-87, acad. coord. med. students in internal medicine, 1987—, asst. program dir. internal medicine residency program, 1987—, dir. med. edn., 1990—; med. dir. Ballard-A Health Care Residence, Des Plaines, Ill., 1994—; pvt. practice, Chgo.; clin. asst. prof. U. Ill. Sch. Medicine, Chgo. Recipeint cert. of merit State of Fla. Mem. AMA, ACP, Am. Geriatrics Soc., Chgo. Med. Soc., Ill. State Med. Soc., Am. Med. Dirs. Assn.

APATOCZKY, ADRIENNE ELIZABETH, physician; b. Allentown, Pa., Dec. 22, 1964; d. Zoltan Louis and Elizabeth (Ferenczi) A.; m. Dave Alan Baucom, Sept. 18, 1993. BS, Muhlenberg Coll., 1986; DO, Phila. Coll. Osteo. Medicine, 1990. Internist Alley Med. Ctr., Berwick, Pa., 1995—. Roman Catholic. Home: 601 Race St Apt 8 Nescopeck PA 18600 Office: Alley Med Ctr 301 W 3rd St Berwick PA 18000

APFELBAUM, H. BARTON, physician, urologist; b. N.Y.C., June 9, 1936; s. Sydney Newton and Hilda (Casileman) A.; m. Sharon Jackson, Oct. 9, 1965; children: Paige, Carter. Grad., Dartmouth Coll., 1958; MD, George Washington U., 1962. Diplomate Am. Bd. Urology. Pvt. practice urologist Palm Springs, Calif., 1969—; asst. clin. prof. surgery/urology U. Calif., San Diego, 1984—. Bd. dirs. Mt. San Jacinto Winter Park Authority, Palm Springs, 1993—. Capt. USAR, 1964-66. Mem. Palm Springs Club (bd. dirs. 1992—). Office: 555 Tachevah Dr Palm Springs CA 92262

APGAR, FRANK ALAN, internist, educator; b. Charleston, W.Va., Dec. 1, 1949; s. Robert Raymond and Helen Elizabeth (Schonwald) A.; m. Elise Cheryl Davis, Nov. 2, 1974; children: Kevin W., Erin C. BS in Zoology, San Diego State U., 1972; MD, UCLA, 1976. Diplomate Am. Coll. Physicians. Intern UCLA Med. Ctr., 1976-77, internal medicine resident, 1977-79, gen. internal medicine fellow, 1979-80, adj. asst. prof., 1980-87, assoc. clin. prof. medicine, 1987-90; med. dir. UCLA Primary Care Group, 1988—; vice chief of med. staff HealthNet, 1988-90; regional nat. dir. Blue Shield Calif., Folsom, 1995—. Mem. ACP, Am. Coll. Physician Execs. Office: Blue Shield Calif 181 Blue Ravine Rd Folsom CA 95630-4704

APKING, MAUREEN J., nurse; b. Indpls., Sept. 4, 1959; d. Chester M. and Ruth E. (Matza) T.; m. William D. Apking, Nov. 1983. BSN, Coll. Mt. St. Joseph, 1981. Cert. psychiat. mental health nurse. Nursing supr. Meml. Southwest Hosp., Houston, 1984-87; nursing care coord. Stafford Meadows Hosp., Tex., 1987-88; head nurse VA Med. Ctr., Houston, 1988-90, San Francisco, 1990-91, Martinez, Calif., 1991; staff nurse M.I.C.U. Muskogee (Okla.) VA Med. Ctr., Muskogee, Okla., 1991-95, cmty. health nurse coord., 1995—. Mem. HAPN, NOVA.

APLINGTON, JAMES PAGE, physician; b. Waterville, Maine, July 1, 1940; s. Henry Webster and Katherine (Kumpf) A.; m. Carol Davis, May 16, 1964; children: Robert, Kimberly, Christina. AB, Amherst Coll., 1962; MD, Johns Hopkins Sch. Medicine, 1966. Surgical intern Duke Med. Ctr., Durham, N.C., 1966-67, surgical resident, 1967-68; resident orthopedic surgery Duke Med. Ctr., Durham, 1970-74; ptnr. Greensboro (N.C.) Orthopedic Ctr., 1974—; trustee Humana Hosp., Greensboro, 1983-87; pres. med. staff Wesley Long Hosp., Greensboro, 1985-86, chief of surgery, 1990-96. Mem. Guilford Coll. civic orgn., Greensboro, 1987-90, pres. 1989-90. Maj. U.S. Army, 1968-70. Fellow AAOS, ACS; mem. Sigma Xi. Home: 105 Manchester Pl Greensboro NC 27410 Office: The Greensboro Orthopedic Ctr 1401 Benjamin Pkwy Greensboro NC 27408

APONTE, JOSEF H., physician; b. N.Y.C., May 24, 1953; divorced Nov. 1994; children: Josef, Raoul, Christine; m. Christine ELizabeth Seiber, Oct. 19, 1995; children: Stephen Matthew. BA, Fordham U., 1975; MD, NYU, 1981. Staff dept. emergency medicine Sierra Med. Ctr., El Paso, Tex., 1989-90, Vista Hills Med. Ctr., El Paso, Tex., 1990, Brodesville (Fla.) Regional Med. Ctr., 1990-91, Med. Ctr. Ctr. Ga., Macon, 1991-93; asst. med. dir. Elyria (Ohio) Meml. Hosp. & Med. Ctr., 1994-95; assoc. dir. clin. ops., dept. emergency medicine Cleve. Clinic Found., 1995—; med. dir. paramedic program Lerain County C.C., Elyria, 1993—. Maj. U.S. Army, 1976-89. Decorated Army Commendation medal (2), Meritorious Svc. medal. Office: Cleve Clinic Found 9500 Euclid Ave Cleveland OH 44195

APOSTLE, CHRISTOS NICHOLAS, social psychologist; b. N.Y.C., Nov. 14, 1935; s. Nicholas Christos and Maria (Katsaros) A. BS, U. Colo., 1958; postgrad., New Sch. Social Rsch., CCNY, 1959, 69; MS in Social Psychology, U. Md., 1963. Interviewer Columbia U. Sch. Pub. Health, N.Y.C., 1962; rsch. supr. Nat. Opinion Rsch. Ctr., U. Chgo., N.Y.C., 1963; instr. Wagner Coll., S.I., N.Y., 1964, Hunter Coll., Bronx, N.Y., 1964, Hofstra U., Hempstead, N.Y., 1965; asst. prof. SUNY, Albany, 1965-68; founder, dir. rsch. Inst. Temporal and Durational Studies, Albany, 1970—; prin. scientist Booz-Allen Applied Rsch., Ft. Monmouth, N.J., 1968-70; instr. Rutgers U., Newark, 1968; bd. dirs. Effective Advt., Albany; arbitrator Better Bus. Bur., 1981-92. Author: Getting Through College Using Sociological Principles, 1966; editor Indian Sociol. Bull., 1966-69; contbr. articles to profl. jours. Bd. dirs. Albany Colonie C. of C., 1975-85, YMCA, Albany, 1979-82; committeeman Town of Colonie (N.Y.) Dem. Com., 1987-91. NYU fellow, 1963-65. Fellow Am. Sociol. Assn.; mem. N.Y. Acad. Scis., World Assn. Pub. Opinion Rsch. Democrat. Greek Orthodox. Office: Inst Temporal Durational Studies PO Box 557 Newtonville NY 12128

APOSTOL, JAMES VICTOR, surgeon, educator; b. Chgo., June 21, 1929; s. Spero and Mary (Deam) A.; divorced; children: Marianne, Andrea. BS, Northwestern U., Evanston, Ill., 1950, MD, 1954. Diplomate Am. Bd. Surgery. Inter then resident Cook City Hosp., Chgo., 1954-55, 57-61; fellow Meml. Hosp. for Cancer, N.Y.C., 1961-64; instr. surgery Northwestern U., 1965-66, assoc. in surgery, 1966-71, asst. prof. surgery, 1971—; mem. staff VA Lakeside Hosp., Chgo., 1965—, Northwestern Meml. Hosp., Chgo., 1970—. Capt. U.S. Army, 1955-57, Korea. Mem. ACS, Chgo. Surg. Soc., Soc. Surg. Oncology (James Ewing Soc. award 1964), Soc. Head and Neck Surgeons, Soc. Surgery of Alimentary Tract. Greek Orthodox. Office: 251 E Chicago Ave Ste 927 Chicago IL 60611

APPEL, ANTOINETTE RUTH, neuropsychologist; b. N.Y.C., Mar. 31, 1943; d. Leon S. and Augusta (Marienberg) A. B.A., U. Vt., 1964; M.A., Mt. Holyoke Coll., 1965; postgrad., Yeshiva U., 1965-66, Hofstra U., 1966; Ph.D., CUNY, 1972. Diplomate Am. Bd. Profl. Neuropsychology, Am. Bd. Forensic Examiners. Instr. C.W. Post Coll., Greenvale, N.Y., 1968-69; lectr., instr. Queens Coll., Flushing, N.Y., 1970-71; fellow in neurology, instr. ophthalmology Mt. Sinai Sch. Medicine, N.Y.C., 1971-74; adj. asst. prof. St. Francis Coll., Bklyn., 1974; asst. prof. dept. psychology So. Ill. U. Sch. Medicine, Carbondale, 1974-76; USPHS intern Conn. Valley Hosp., Middletown, Conn., 1976-77; asst. prof., asst. project coordinator dept. psychiatry Nat. Alcohol Research Ctr., U. Conn. Health Ctr., Farmington, 1977-79; neuropsychologist, asst. prof. program in medicine Brown U., Providence, 1979-82; adj. asst. prof. psychology U. R.I., Kingston and Providence, 1979-83; pvt. practice psychology, 1981-83; dir. Neuropsychol. Assessment and Treatment Ctr., Ctr. for Neuropsychology Services, Ft. Lauderdale, 1983-90, So. Inst. Forensic Neuropsychology, 1990—; invited speaker NATO Neuropsychology Congress, 1980, Internat. Council Psychology, 1980, 22 Internat. Congress of Psychology, 1980; cons. Narco Bio-systems, 1974-75; cons. to commr. mental health State of Conn., 1978-79. Bd. dirs. Sojourner House, 1979-80, Combined Hosp. Alcoholism Program, 1978, Hartford Interval House, 1978. Served with WAC, 1963. CUNY fellow, 1972; recipient Hartford Salute award, 1979; USPHS tng. fellow, 1966-67, NIMH predoctoral fellow 1967-70. Fellow Am. Coll. Forensic Examiners; mem. APA (mem. exec. bd.), Assn. Women in Psychology (mem. steering com.), Eastern Psychol. Assn. (chmn. 1980 conv.), Conn. Psychol. Assn. (coun. 1978-79), R.I. Psychol. Assn., N.Y. Acad. Scis., Sigma Xi, Psi Chi. Home: 6622 Racquet Club Dr Fort Lauderdale FL 33319-5026 Office: 1392 N University Dr Fort Lauderdale FL 33322-4734

APPEL, STANLEY HERSH, neurologist; b. Boston, May 8, 1933; married; 4 children. AB, Harvard U., 1954; MD, Columbia U., 1960. Diplomate Am. Bd. Psyciatry & Neurology. Intern medicine Mass. Gen. Hosp., 1960-61; resident neurology Mt. Sinai Hosp., 1961-62; rsch. assoc. Lab. Moleculat Biology NIH, 1962-64; chief rsch. assoc. Sch. Medicine U. Pa., 1965-66, asst. prof., 1966-67; assoc. of neurology Med. Ctr. Duke U., 1964-65, from assoc. prof. to prof. neurology, 1967-77, assoc. prof. biochemistry, 1968-77, chief divsn. neurology, 1969-77; prof. neurology, dept. chmn. Baylor Coll. Medicine, 1977—, chmn. program neurosci., 1977-89, dir. Jerry Lewis Neuromuscular Disorder Rsch. Ctr., 1977—. Recipient Rsch. Career Devel. award USPHS, 1965-70. Mem. Am. Acad. Neurology, Am. Soc. Biol. Chemistry, Am. Soc. Clin. Investigation, Am. Neurol. Assn. Office: Baylor Dept Neurology 6501 Fannin St # B302 Houston TX 77030-2703

APPELBAUM, BRUCE DAVID, physician; b. Lincroft, N.J., Apr. 24, 1957; s. John S. and Shirley B. (Wolfson) A. BS in pharmacy, Rutgers Coll., 1980; MS in pharmacology, Emory U., 1983, PhD in pharmacology, 1985; MD, Medical Coll. Ga., 1989. Diplomate Nat. Bd. Med. Examiners, Am. Bd. Psychiatry and Neurology. Rsch. assoc. Emory U. Dept. Pharmacology, Atlanta, 1985; resident physician U. Calif. Dept. Psychiatry, Irvine, Calif., 1989-93; pvt. practice Pacifica Therapists, Huntington Beach, Calif., 1993—; cons. Avalon Med. Group, Garden Grove, Calif., 1990—. Contbr. articles to profl. jours. Recipient Nat. Rsch. Svc. award Nat. Inst. Health, 1982-83, Ea. Student Rsch. Forum U. Miami Medical Sch., 1984, Nat. Student Rsch. Forum, 1987. Mem. AMA, Am. Psychiat. Assn., Orange County Psychiat. Soc., N.Y. Acad. Scis., Sigma Xi. Home: 18602 Creek Ln Huntington Beach CA 92648-1629 Office: 18811 Huntington St Ste 200 Huntington Beach CA 92648-6003

APPELBAUM, PAUL STUART, psychiatrist, educator; b. Bklyn., Nov. 30, 1951; s. Isidore W. and Celia (Bressler) A.; m. Diana Muir Karter, Nov. 9, 1953; children: Binyamin, Yonaton, Avigail. AB, Columbia U., 1972; MD, Harvard U., 1976. Diplomate Am. Bd. Psychiatry and Neurology. Intern Soroka Med. Ctr., Beersheva, Israel, 1976-77; resident Mass. Mental Health Ctr., Boston, 1977-80; Clin. fellow psychiatry Harvard Med. Sch., Boston, 1977-80; from asst. prof. to assoc. prof. psychiatry and law U. Pitts., 1980-84; assoc. prof. psychiatry Harvard Med. Sch., Boston, 1984-85; Zeleznik prof. psychiatry, dir. law and psychiatry program U. Mass. Med. Sch., Worcester, 1985—; chmn. dept. U. Mass. Med. Sch., Worcester, Mass., 1992—; vis. interdisciplinary prof. Law Ctr. Georgetown U., Washington, 1988-89; mem. commn. on mentally disabled ABA, Washington, 1982-87; task force on involuntary civil commitment Nat. Ctr. for State Cts., Williamsburg, Va., 1984-89, Rsch. Network on Mental Health and Law, John D. and Catherine T. Macarthur Found., Chgo., 1988-96; fellow Ctr. for Advanced Study in the Behavioral Scis., Stanford, Calif., 1996—. Author: Clinical Handbook of Psychiatry and the Law, 1982 (M.F. Guttmacher award 1982), 2d edit., 1991, Informed Consent: Legal Theory and Clinical Practice, 1987, Paul Appelbaum on Law and Psychiatry, 1989, Almost A Revolution: Mental Health Law and Limits of Change, 1994 (M.F. Guttmacher award 1996); contbr. articles to profl. jours. Nat. coord. Med. Mobilization for Soviet Jewry, Waltham, Mass., 1974-80; bd. dirs. Action for Soviet Jewry, Waltham, 1984-85, Torah Ctr., Sharon, Mass., 1987-88, Community Health Link, Worcester, Mass., 1992—. Recipient rsch. scientist devel. award NIMH, 1983; rsch. grantee President's Commn. on Ethical Problems in Medicine, Washington, 1982, John D. and Catherine T. MacArthur Found., 1988; fellow Ctr. for Advanced Study in Behavioral Scis., Palo Alto, Calif., 1996-97. Mem. Internat. Acad. Law and Mental Health, Am. Psychiat. Assn. (chair commn. on jud. action 1984-90, joint reference com. 1984-94, chair coun. on psychiatry and law 1990-94, Isaac Ray award 1990), Am. Acad. Psychiatry and the Law (councillor 1987-90, pres.-elect 1994-95, pres. 1995-96), Am. Soc. Law and Medicine, Mass. Psychiat. Soc. (pres.-elect 1991-92, pres. 1992-93). Jewish. Office: U Mass Med Ctr Dept Psychiatry Worcester MA 01655

APPENZELLER, OTTO, neurologist, researcher; b. Czernowitz, Romania, Dec. 11, 1927; came to U.S., 1963; s. Emmanuel Adam and Josephine (Metsch) A.; m. Judith Bryce, Dec. 11, 1956; children: Timothy, Martin, Peter. MBBS, Sydney U., Australia, 1957, MD, 1966; PhD, U. London, Eng., 1963. Diplomate Am. Bd. Psychiatry and Neurology. Prof. U. N. Mex., Albuquerque, 1970-90; vis. prof. McGill U., Montreal, 1977; hon. rsch. fellow U. London, Eng., 1983; vis. scientist Oxygen Transport Program Lovelace Med. Found., Albuquerque, 1990-92; pres. N.Mex. Health Enhancement and Marathon Clinics Rsch. Found., Albuquerque, 1992—; prof. exptl. neurobiology Bogomoletz Inst. Ukrainian Acad. Sci., Kiev, 1995—; U.S.-India exch. scientist NSF, 1992; Fogarty internat. exch. scientist, Kiev, Ukraine, 1993; mem. rsch. com. UNESCO Internat. Coun. Sports and Phys. Edn., 1978—; ref. Med. Rsch. Coun. New Zealand, 1986—, reviewer, 1988—; mem. editorial bd. numerous peer reviewed med. jours. Author: The Autonomic Nervous System, 5th edit., 1996; co-author: Headache, 1984; editor: Pathogenesis and Management of Headache, 1976, Health Aspects of Endurance Training, 1978, Sports Medicine, 3d edit., 1988, Jour. Headache, 1975-77, Annals of Sports Medicine, 1984-88; translator: Neurologic Differential Diagnosis (M. Mumentaler), 2d edit., 1992. Grantee Diabetes Rsch. and Edn. Found., 1988, Instituto C. Mondino U. of Pavia, Italy, 1992, 95; individual health scientist exch. program Fogarty Internat. Ctr., NIH to A.A. Bogomoletz Inst. Physiology, Kiev, 1993. Fellow ACP, Am. Acad. Neurology.

APPERSON, JEAN, psychologist; b. Durham, N.C., June 8, 1934; d. James Harry and Dorothy Elizabeth (Johnson) Apperson; m. Calvin Adams Pope, Mar. 23, 1956 (div. 1967); 1 child, Richard Allan. BA, U. S. Fla., 1966;

MA, Mich. State U., 1970, PhD, 1973. Cert. in psychoanalysis Mich. Psychoanalytic Coun., 1990. Teaching asst. Mich. State U., E. Lansing, 1968-69; psychiatric technician St. Lawrence Community Mental Health Ctr., Lansing, Mich., 1968-69; psychology intern St. Lawrence Community Mental Health Ctr., 1969-71, Mich. State U. Counseling Ctr., 1971-73; clin. psychologist U. Mich. Counseling Ctr., Ann Arbor, 1973-81; pvt. practice psychology and psychoanalysis Ann Arbor, 1974—; mem., chmn. Mich. Bd. Psychology, Lansing, 1984-91. Contbr. articles to profl. jours.; cons. editor Am. Psychol. Assn. Catalog of Selected Documents, 1975-80. USPHS grantee, 1969-70; NIMH grantee, 1970-71. Fellow Mich. Psychol. Assn. (chmn. women's issues com. 1981-83); mem. APA (com. on sci. and profl. ethics and conduct 1977-80), Mich. Soc. Psychoanalytic Psychology (treas. 1982-86), Mich. Psychoanalytic Coun. (teaching and supervising analyst, mem. at large 1991-93, tng. com. 1992—, pres.-elect 1993-95, pres. 1995-97), Assn. for Advancement Psychology, Am. Women in Psychology, Mich. Women Psychologists. Democrat. Unitarian. Home: 7224 Chelsea Manchester Rd Manchester MI 48158-9407 Office: 555 E William St Apt 23E Ann Arbor MI 48104-2428

APPIAH, AARON, ophthalmologist, vitreo-retinal surgeon; b. Kumasi, Ghana, May 25, 1956; came to U.S., 1975; s. Koki and Marcy (Awuah) A.; m. Rosemary Appiah, Nov. 21, 1987; children: Anne-Marie, Amaris, Aaron. BA, Harvard U., 1978, MD, 1982. Diplomate Am. Bd. Ophthalmology. Intern Mass. Gen. Hosp., 1982-83; resident N.Y. Eye and Ear Infirmary Ophthalmology, Tallahassee, Fla., 1983-86; fellowship Retina Found. Mass. Eye and Ear Infirmary Vitreoretinal Surgery, 1986-88; asst. prof. ophthalmology UCLA Med. Ctr., 1980-90; pvt. practice retinal surgery Alpha Eye Clinic, Tallahassee, 1990—; ptnr. Diabetes Ctr., Tallahassee Meml. Hosp., 1993—. Contbr. articles to profl. jours. Recipient Teaching award King-Drew Med. Ctr., 1990. Fellow AMA, Am. Acad. Ophthalmology, Vitreous Soc. Office: Alpha Eye Clinic 2160 Capital Cir NE Tallahassee FL 32308

APPLE, DAVID JOSEPH, ophthalmology educator; b. Alton, Ill., Sept. 14, 1941; s. Joseph Bernard and Margaret Josephine (Bearden) A. BS, Northwestern U., 1962; MD, U. Ill., 1966. Intern and resident in pathology Charity Hosp. La., La. State U., New Orleans, 1966-71; ophthalmology resident U. Iowa, Iowa City, 1977-80; prof. ophthalmology and pathology O'Brien Lab. Ocular Pathology, Tulane U. Sch. Medicine, New Orleans, 1980-81, U. Utah Health Scis. Ctr., Salt Lake City, 1981-88; dir. Ctr. for Intraocular Lens Rsch. U. Utah Sch. Medicine, 1984-88; prof. ophthalmology dept. Storm Eye Inst., Med. U. S.C., Charleston, 1988—, chmn. dept., 1988—, dir. Ctr. Intraocular Lens Rsch., 1988—; Assoc. prof. ophthalmology and pathology U. Ill. Eye and Ear Infirmary, Chgo., 1974-76; vis. rsch. prof. eye clinics U. Tuebingen, Germany, 1975-77, U. Bonn., Germany, and U. Minuch, 1981; lectr. U.K. Intraocular Soc., Turnberry, Scotland, 1989; cons. McGraw Hill Pub. Co., N.Y.C.; cons. prevention of blindness program WHO; Walter Wright lectr., Toronto, 1993. Author: Pathology of the Eye, 1980 (German and Japanese edits.), Ocular Pathology, 4th edit., 1991, Intraocular Lenses, 1989, 7 other books, numerous book chpts. and articles. Recipient Témoignage d'Honneur Can. Implant Soc., Montreal, 1986, Ridley medal, lectr. 6th European Intraocular Coun., Copenhagen, 1988, Choyce medal. Mem. Am. Acad. Ophthalmology (Binkhorst lectr. and medal 1988), Internat. Acad. Pathology, Am. Assn. Ophthalmic Pathologists, Internat. Soc. Eye Rsch., Theobald Soc., Verhoeff Soc., Lions, Nu Sigma Nu, Phi Kappa Epsilon. Home: 93 E Bay St Charleston SC 29401-2544 Office: Med U SC Storm Eye Inst Dept Ophthalmology 171 Ashley Ave Charleston SC 29425-0001

APPLEBAUM, EDWARD LEON, otolaryngologist, educator; b. Detroit, Jan. 14, 1940; s. M. Lawrence and Frieda (Millman) A.; children: Daniel Ira, Rachel Anne. A.B., Wayne State U., 1961, M.D., 1964. Diplomate: Am. Bd. Otolaryngology. Intern Univ. Hosp., Ann Arbor, Mich., 1964-65; resident Mass. Eye and Ear Infirmary Harvard Med. Sch., Boston, 1966-69; practice medicine specializing in otolaryngology Chgo., 1972—; assoc. prof. Northwestern U. Med. Sch., 1972-79; prof., head dept. otolaryngology, head and neck surgery Coll. Medicine, U. Ill., 1979—; mem. staffs. U. Ill. Hosp., Westside VA Med. Ctr. Author: Tracheal Intubation, 1976; mem. editorial bd. Am. Jour. Otolaryngology, Laryngoscope. Served as maj. U.S. Army, 1969-71. Recipient Anna Albert Keller Rsch. award Wayne State U. Coll. Medicine, 1964, Disting. Alumni award, 1989, William Beaumont Soc. Original Rsch. award, 1964. Fellow ACS, Am. Soc. for Head and Neck Surgery, Am. Acad. Facial Plastic and Reconstructive Surgery, Am. Acad. Otolaryngology, Head and Neck Surgery, Am. Laryngol., Rhinol. and Otol. Soc., Am. Laryngol. Assn., Am. Otol. Soc., Soc. Univ. Otolaryngologists, Head and Neck Surgeons (pres. 1988), Assn. Acad. Depts. Otolaryngology-Head and Neck Surgery (pres.). Home: 400 E Ohio St Apt 3803 Chicago IL 60611-3327

APPLEBAUM, ROBERT E., surgeon; b. Balt., Sept. 23, 1953; s. Frank and Shirley (Himelfarb) A.; m. Stephanie Harris, June 23, 1985; children: Aaron, Daniel, Samuel. BS, U. Md., 1974, MD, 1978. Surg. resident U. Md., Balt., 1978-87; cardiovascular and thoracic surgeon St. Francis Hosp., Blue Island, Ill., 1987—. Fellow ACS, Am. Coll. Cardiology; mem. Soc. Thoracic Surgeons. Office: Cardiovascular Med Assn 1613 York St Blue Island IL 60406

APPLEBY, ALAN, radiation science educator; b. Newcastle upon Tyne, Eng., Apr. 25, 1937; came to U.S., 1963; s. Henry James and Gladys Evelyn (Simpson) A.; m. Kathleen Anne Shippen, July 25, 1960; children: Sarah Kathleen, Emily Jane. BSc, U. Durham, Newcastle, Eng., 1958, PhD, 1963. Rsch. assoc. Brookhaven Nat. Lab., Upton, N.Y., 1963-65; sr. sci. officer Radiochem. Ctr., Amersham, Eng., 1965-67; asst. prof. radiation sci. Rutgers U., New Brunswick, N.J., 1967-71, assoc. prof., 1971-77, prof., 1977—; dir. Ea. Regional Radon Tng. Ctr., New Brunswick, 1989—; adj. prof. radiology, U. Medicine and Dentistry, N.J., Piscataway. Contbr. over 50 articles to profl. jours. Grantee: EPA, 1973, 89, 95, NIH, 1976, Monsanto Rsch. Co., 1980, Gen. Pub. Utilities Nuclear, 1981, N.J. Commn. on Cancer Rsch., 1988, 95. Mem. Health Physics Soc., Sigma Xi. Episcopalian. Office: Rutgers U Cook Campus Environ Sci Dept New Brunswick NJ 08903

APPLEGATE, CLARENCE WILLIAM, nephrologist; b. Toledo, Ohio, Dec. 5, 1944; s. Clarence William and Alice Freda (Sieler) A.; m. Patricia Childs, Aug. 24, 1968; children: Clarence Bruce, Mark Richard. BA, Oberlin Coll., 1966; MD, Harvard U., 1970. Intern, resident Duke U. Med. Ctr., Durham, N.C., 1970-75; founder, physician N. Fla. Nephrology Assocs., Tallahassee, 1975—; chmn. med. staff Talla Meml. Regional Med. Ctr., Tallahassee, 1993-94; mem. regional quality coun. Vivra, Inc., Laguna Hills, Calif., 1995-96. Mem. AMA, Am. Soc. Nephrology, Fla. Med. Assn., Fla. Soc. Nephrology, Capital Med. Soc. (pres., editl. bd. newspaper), Sierra Club. Republican. Lutheran. Office: N Fla Nephrology Assocs 1609 Physicians Dr Tallahassee FL 32308

APPLETON, ABRAHAM THEODORE, othopedic surgeon; b. N.Y.C., July 11, 1955. BA, Yeshiva U., 1976; MD, Columbia U., 1981. Surg. resident Roosevelt U.; orthopedic resident Hosp. for Spl. Surgery, U. Calif., San Francisco, orthopedic trauma fellow; orthopedic surgeon Hosp. Spl. Surgery, Jamaica Hosp., N.Y.C., N.Y. Hosp. of Queens, N.Y.C., Parkway Hosp., N.Y.C.

APPLETON, DANIEL RANDOLPH, JR., optometrist; b. Boston, June 24, 1942; s. Daniel Randolph and Dorothy (Cheney) A.; m. Sandra Marshall Appleton; children: Carole Lee, Deborah Ann, Danielle Marie, Suzanne Estelle, Seth Marshall. BS, Tufts U., 1965; OD, Mass. Coll. Optometry, 1969. Pvt. practice optometry Newburyport, Mass., 1965—; dir. pediatric clinic Mass. Coll. Optometry, 1969-71, clin. cons., 1971-72; bd. dirs. 1st and Ocean Nat. Bank. Mem. bd. incorporators Anna Jacques Hosp., Newburyport, Sch. Com., 1975-79, Newburyport sewer commn., 1972-79; 2d v.p. ARC. Recipient Com. Svc. award United Fund, 1983, Disting. Svc. award Lions Club, 1989. Mem. Am. Optometric Found., Am. Optometric Assn., Mass. Soc. Optometrists (past dist. chmn., exec. bd. dirs.), Jaycees (past pres.). Lodges: Rotary (pres. 1988), Shriners. Home: 89 Scotland Rd Newburyport MA 01951-1002 Office: 39 Green St Newburyport MA 01950-2652

APPLEWHITE, PHILIP BOATMAN, biologist, researcher; b. Hollywood, Calif., Sept. 14, 1938; s. Douglas Maury and Treva (Watts) A.; m. Harriet Branson, Aug. 10, 1963; children: Eleanor, Kate, Douglas. BA, Pomona Coll., 1960; MA, Yale U., 1962; PhD, Stanford U., 1965. Cons. Rand Corp., Santa Monica, Calif., 1962-63; instr. Stanford (Calif.) U., 1963-64; postdoctoral fellow Yale U., New Haven, 1964-67, asst. prof., 1967-71, asst. dean, 1971-73, rsch. fellow, 1977—; assoc. prof. SUNY, Purchase, 1973-77. Author: Organizational Behavior, 1965, Molecular Gods, 1981, (with others) Studies in Organizational Behavior, 2d edit., 1971, Focus-Biology, 1975, Understanding Biology, 1978; contbr. over 65 articles to profl. jours. Office: Yale U Biology Dept New Haven CT 06520

APRIL, ERNEST WILFRED, anatomist, educator, researcher; b. Salem, Mass., Nov. 6, 1939; s. Ernest W. and Dorothea (Bousquet) A.; m. Nancy M. Paetzold, Feb. 26, 1977; children—Jeremy, Geoffrey. B.S., Tufts U., 1961; Ph.D., Columbia U., 1969. Asst. prof. anatomy Columbia U., N.Y.C., 1969-76, assoc. prof. anatomy and cell biology, 1976—; cons. Nat. Bd. Med. Examiners, Phila., 1982—. Author: Anatomy, 1996, Anatomy Interactive, 1996; editor: Anatomy Pretest, 1995, Anatomy, 1996, Anatomy Interactive, 1996; contbr. articles to profl. jours. Councilman Borough of Rockleigh, N.J., 1983—. Served to lt. USN, 1961-63. NIH grantee, 1972-83. Mem. Am. Assn. Anatomists, Am. Assn. Clin. Anatomists, Biophys. Soc., Soc. General Physiologists, Am. Soc. Cell Biology, Sigma Xi. Republican. Home: Rockleigh Rd Rockleigh NJ 07647 Office: Columbia U Coll Physicians and Surgeons 630 W 168th St New York NY 10032

AQUAVELLA, JAMES VINCENT, ophthalmologist; b. N.Y.C., May 2, 1932; s. Charles and Loretta Marie (Sorrentino) A.; m. Constance E., May 1, 1960; children: John, Constance, Mary, Thomas. BA, Johns Hopkins U., Balt., 1952; MD, U. Naples, Italy, 1958. Diplomate Am. Bd. Ophthalmology. Pvt. practice specializing in ophthalmology Rochester, N.Y., 1963—; dir. Dept. Ophthalmology Park Ridge Hosp., Rochester, N.Y., 1974-84, chief of staff, 1972-74; med. dir. ROA Ambulatory Ctr., Rochester, 1980-90, chief ophthalmology, 1980-89; clin. prof. ophthalmology U. Rochester Med. Ctr., 1982—, dir. cornea rsch. lab., 1982—; cons. N.Y. State Dept. Health, 1987—. Contbr. over 300 articles to profl. jours. Bd. dirs. Meml. Art Gallery, Rochester, 1972—, Rochester Eye & Human Parts Bank, 1968-80. Recipient Commendation award, Cen. N.Y. Eye Bank, 1989, Rochester Eye Bank, 1980. Fellow Internat. Coll. Surgeons, Am. Acad. Ophthalmology; mem. AMA, Am. Coll. Physician Execs., Assn. for Rsch. and Vision in Ophthalmology, Contact Lens Assn. of Ophthalmologists (dir. 1972-82, Eye Bank Assn. Am., Pan Am. Assn. Ophthalmology (Honor award 1980, Sr. Honor award 1991), Castroviejo Soc. (dir. 1980-88, Commendation award 1985). Office: 919 Westfall Rd Rochester NY 14618-2670

AQUINO, ERNESTO PONCE DE LEON, urologist; b. Morong, Rizal, The Philippines, July 18, 1933; arrived in U.S., 1958; s. Filemon L. and Juana Reynoso (Ponce de Leon) Q.; m. Lourdes G. Cortez, May 5, 1988; 1 child, Gerard V. AA, U. Santo Tomas, Manila, 1951, MD, 1957. Diplomate Am. Bd. Urology. Resident in surgery and urology St. Louis U., 1958-64; pvt. practice Tammuning, Guam; bd. dirs. Guam Meml. Hosp., 1976-77. Mem. Am. Urol. Assn., Guam Med. Soc., Guam Sr. Golf Club (v.p. 1993-95), Kiwanis, Rotary. Office: Good Samaritan Clinic 416 San Antonio Tamuning GU 96911

AQUINO, JOSEPH MARIO, clinical psychologist; b. N.Y.C., Nov. 21, 1947; s. Joseph and Rose (Nasi) A.; m. Kathleen Ann Ryan, Oct. 6, 1990; children: Joseph Patrick, Ryan Thomas. BA in English, So. Ill. U., 1969, MS in Secondary Edn., 1976; PhD in Clin. Psychology, St. John's U., Jamaica, N.Y., 1987. Lic. psychologist, N.Y. Tchr. English Wappingers Cen. Schs., Wappingers Falls, N.Y., 1969-79; intern psychology Maimonides Med. Ctr., Bklyn., 1983-84; specialist in applied behavior sci. Builders for Family and Youth, Bklyn., 1984-85; trainee psychology and psychologist St. Vincent's Svcs., Bklyn., 1984-89; psychologist St. Christopher-Ottilie Svcs., Sea Cliff, N.Y., 1989—; pvt. practice psychology N.Y.C. area, 1989-96; guest lectr. St. John's U., 1990. Co-author: Situational Leadership for Principles, 1983; mem. editl. bd. Jour. urban Psychiatry, 1982-84; guest The Women's Line, WVOX 1460 AM, 1994; cited in newspaper articles; contbr. articles to profl. jours. Recipient citation VFW, Wappingers Falls, N.Y., 1977; Bethany House Achievement award Bethany House II, 1991; psychology teaching fellow St. John's U., 1981; cited in article Emergency mag., 1991. Mem. APA, N.Y. State Psychol. Assn., Westchester County Psychol. Assn. Office: 10 Rye Ridge Plz Ste 213 Rye Brook NY 10573-2828

ARABIN, BIRGIT, gynecologist; b. Siegen, Westfalen, Germany, Nov. 30, 1952; d. Hans and Margarethe Meta Mathilde (Meyer) A. MD, Free U., Berlin, 1978, Priv.-Docent, 1988; Specialist in Gynecology, U. Heidelberg, Germany, 1984. Rsch. fellow Free U., Brussels, 1978; rsch. fellow Free U., Berlin, 1979, cons., 1985-88; asst. prof. Free U./K.L. Benjamin Franklin, Berlin, 1988-93; resident U. Heidelberg, 1979-85; perinatologist Sophia Ziekenhuis Zwolle, Netherlands, 1993—; lectr. Free U., Berlin, 1988—, Sch. of Pub. Health, U. Hannover, Germany, 1993—; founder Clara Angela Found., Zwolle, 1994. Author: Uteroplacental and Fetal Blood Flow Measurements, 1992 (St. Pfannenstiel Price award 1990); author scientific publs. in field. Project leader Inst. Pub. Health, Hannover, 1994—. Home: Wallotstr 16, 14193 Berlin Germany Office: Sophia Ziekenhuis, Dr van Heesweg 2, 8025 AB Zwolle The Netherlands

ARAIZA, JOSEPH PHILLIP, physician; b. San Antonio, Mar. 3, 1952; s. William Garcia and Josephine (Villarreal) A.; m. Beatrix Dagmar Quickert, Nov. 22, 1986. BA, St. Mary's U., 1974; MD, Hahnemann Med. Coll., 1980. Diplomate Am. Bd. Emergency Medicine. Intern Hahnemann Hosp., Phila., 1980-81; resident in emergency medicine Darnall Army Hosp., Killeen, Tex.; clin. asst. prof. emergency medicine Mt. Sinai Sch. Medicine, N.Y.C., 1993—. Maj. U.S. Army, 1981-90. Fellow Am. Coll. Emergency Physicians. Office: Mt Sinai Med Ctr Emergency Dept 1 Gustave L Levy Pl New York NY 10029-6574

ARAKAWA, KASUMI, physician, educator; b. Toyohashi, Japan, Feb. 19, 1926; came to U.S., 1954, naturalized, 1963; s. Masumi and Fayuko (Hattori) A.; m. Juen Hope Takahara, Aug. 27, 1956; children: Jane Riet, Kenneth Luke, Amy Kathryn. M.D., Tokyo Med. Coll., 1953; Ph.D., Showa U. Sch. Med., Tokyo, 1984. Diplomate: Am. Bd. Anesthesiology. Intern Iowa Meth. Hosp., Des Moines, 1954-56; resident U. Kans. Med. Ctr., Kansas City, 1956-58, instr. anesthesiology, 1961-64, asst. prof., 1964-71, assoc. prof., 1971-77, prof., 1977-94; prof. emeritus, 1994—; Arakawa Disting. prof. anesthesiology U. Kans. Med. Ctr., Kansas City, 1990, Kasumi Arakawa professorship, 1994, prof. emeritus, 1994—; clin. assoc. prof. U. Mo.-Kans. City Sch. Dentistry, 1973—; dir. Kansas City Health Care, Inc. Fulbright scholar, 1954; civilian cons. USAF. Recipient Outstanding Faculty award Student AMA, 1970. Fellow Am. Coll. Anesthesiology; mem. Assn. Univ. Anesthetists, Acad. Anesthesiology (pres. 1986-87), Japan-Am. Soc. Midwest (v.p. 1965, 71). Home: 6116 W 50th St Shawnee Mission KS 66202-1756 Office: Univ Med Ctr 3901 Rainbow Blvd Kansas City KS 66160-7197

ARAMINI, ALEXIS JEAN, nurse, air force officer; b. Washington, Pa., Dec. 17, 1951; d. Alexander Julian and Jennie Frances (Kalish) Czernecki; m. William Fetcko, May 5, 1973 (div. Sept. 1976); m. Anthony James Aramini, Sept. 15, 1977; 1 child, Marc Anthony. B.S. in Nursing, U. Pitts., 1973; M.S., U. Md., 1985. Registered nurse. Staff nurse Washington Hosp., Pa., 1973-75, Children's Hosp., Pitts., 1975-76; clin. instr. W.Va. No. C.C., Wheeling, 1976-77; commd. officer USAF, 1977; charge nurse Malcolm Grow Med. Ctr., Andrews Air Base, Md., 1977-80, preceptor nurse interns, 1978-79; staff nurse USAF Hosp. Torrejon, Torrejon Air Base, Spain, 1980-83, childbirth educator, 1981-83; charge nurse USAF Hosp. Loring, Loring AFB, Maine, 1985-86; pediatric nurse practitioner USAF Hosp. Cannon AFB, N.Mex., 1987-94; PNP 1 Med. Group, Langley AFB, Va., 1994—; cons. sibling project NIH, Bethesda, Md.; poison prevention officer USAF Hosp. Torrejon, 1981-83. Mem. Boy Scout Coun., Torrejon, 1982-83. Mem. ANA, Assn. Care of Children's Health, Nurses' Assn. Am. Coll. Obstetricians and Gynecologists, Uniformed Nurse Practitioners Assn., Nat. Assn. Pediatric Nurse Assocs. and Practitioners. Democrat. Mem. Polish Catholic Ch. Avocations: sewing; cooking; biking; swimming. Home: 103 Runaway Ln Yorktown VA 23692 Office: 1 Medical Group SGOBP Langley AFB VA 23665

ARANAS, MARIA ELENA LIZARES, physician; b. Talisay, Negros, The Philippines, Mar. 22, 1937; came to U.S., 1961; d. Felix A. and Josefina (Kilayko) Lizares; m. Romeo Saavedra Aranas, Aug. 28, 1965; children: Michelle J., Melinda L., Marsha L., Maria Theresa L. AA, U. St. Thomas, Manila, 1955, MD, 1960. Diplomate Am. Bd. Family Practice. Intern St. Francis Hosp., Poughkeepsie, N.Y., 1961-62, resident in pathology, 1962-63; resident in pathology Wyckoff Heights Hosp., Bklyn., 1963-67, asst. pathologist, 1967-69; pvt. practice The Philippines, 1969-73, Spring Valley, Ill., 1975-77; physician Lincoln Devel. Ctr., 1977; with Ill. Dept. MHDD-Zeller Mental Health Ctr., Peoria, 1978—, med. dir., 1986-87, assoc. med. dir., 1987-89, staff physician, 1989—. Mem. Tazewell Med. Soc., Am. Acad. Family Practice, Ill. Acad. Family Practice. Roman Catholic. Home: 607 W Thousand Oaks Dr Peoria IL 61615-1399 Office: Zeller Mental Health Ctr 5407 N University St Peoria IL 61614-4736

ARANDA, JUAN M., cardiologist; b. San Juan, P.R., Feb. 2, 1942; married; seven children. BS in Chemistry magna cum laude, U. P.R., 1963, MD, 1967. Intern U. Dist. Hosp., U. P.R. Sch. of Medicine, San Juan, 1967-68, resident in internal medicine, 1968-70, chief resident internal medicine, 1970-71, instr. in medicine U. Dist. Hosp., 1970-71, asst. prof. medicine, 1977-78, assoc. prof. medicine, 1978-85, prof. medicine, 1985-87, clin. prof. medicine, 1987—; asst. prof. medicine U. Miami Sch. of Medicine, 1974-77, clin. assoc. prof. medicine, 1978-85; chief dept. of medicine, staff physician Beach Army Hosp., Fort Wolter, Tex., 1971-73; attending physician Jackson Meml. Hosp., Miami, 1974-77, U. Miami Hosp. and Clinics, 1974-77, Am. Hosp., Miami, 1975-77, Cedars of Lebanon Med. Ctr., 1975-77, Hialeah Cmty. Hosp., Fla., 1975-77; asst. chief cardiovascular lab. VA Hosp., 1976-77; chief cardiology sect. VA Hosp., San Juan, 1977-86; faculty staff Hosp. Pavia, San Juan, 1977—; cons. in cardiology Hosp. de Damas Ponce, P.R., 1978—; dir. cardiac catherization lab. Pavia Cardiovascular Inst., 1986—, chief cardiology sect., 1990, co-dir., 1990, chmn. cardiac bd. 1990, co-dir. cardiac catherization lab. Pavia Hosp., 1990; chmn. problem oriented records com. VA Hosp., Miami, 1975-77; exercise com. Heart Assn. of Greater Miami, 1975-77; hosp. R&D com. VA Hosp., San Juan, 1979, mem. hosp. R&D com., 1984-86; staff cardiologist med. svc. VA Hosp., MiaNOT BOLDmi, Fla., 1974-77; nat. bd. advisors Am. Biographical Inst., 1982—. Editor, coord. Jornadas de Cardiología, 1978-80; editl. bd. Revista Latina de Cardiología Euroamericana, 1978—;. Active Cmty. Leaders of Am., 1978—. Maj. U.S. Army, 1971-73, U.S. Army Res., 1973-78. Fellow Am. Coll. Cardiology (nat. chpt. rels. com. 1991-94, v.p. P.R. chpt. 1990-93, pres., organizer P.R. chpt. 1987-90), Internat. Coll. Angiology, Am. Coll. Chest Physicians (assoc.); mem. P.R. Med. Assn., Am. Heart Assn., P.R. Soc. of Cardiology, Pan Am. Med. Assn., Am. Fedn. for Clin. Rsch., So. Soc. of Clin. Investigation. Home: Ave Hostos 411 San Juan PR 00918

ARANOW, NORMAN, podiatrist; b. N.Y.C., Feb. 1, 1923; s. William Benjamin and Fannie Aranow; B.A., N.Y. U., 1947; Pod.D., L.I. U., 1950; D.P.M., M. J. Lewi Coll. Podiatric Medicine, 1970; m. Muriel Jane Stoff, Dec. 25, 1956; 1 dau., Barbara Jean. Pvt. practice podiatric medicine, N.Y.C., 1951—; cons. AGVA; prof. exptl. orthopedic tech. Fitzsimmons Gen. Hosp., Denver, 1944-46. Served with AUS, 1942-46. Fellow Am. Assn. Foot Specialists; mem. Acad. Exptl. Arthritis and Musculoskeletal Disorders of Dancers, Podiatry Soc. State N.Y., Affiliated Podiatrists of N.Y. Office: 580 5th Ave New York NY 10036-4701

ARANT, BILLY SUNDAY, JR., pediatrics educator, medical director; b. Greer, S.C., Aug. 21, 1940; s. Billy S. Sr. and Helen L. (Hendrix) A.; m. Margaret F. Jackson, Aug. 28, 1976; children: Sarah Meghan, Peter Jackson. BS in Pre-Medicine, Clemson U., 1961; MD, Med. Coll. S.C., 1965. Diplomate Am. Bd. Pediat., sub-board pediat. nephrology. Resident in pediatrics Med. Coll. Va., Richmond, 1965-68; post-doctoral fellow Albert Einstein Coll. Medicine, Bronx, N.Y., 1970-73; asst. prof. pediat. U. Tenn., Memphis, 1973-75, assoc. prof. pediat., 1975-80; assoc. prof. pediat. U. Tex. Southwestern Med. Ctr., Dallas, 1980-83, prof. pediat., 1983-92; prof., chmn. pediat. U. Tenn. Coll. Medicine, Chattanooga, 1992—; med. dir. T.C. Thompson Children's Hosp., Chattanooga, 1992—; asst. sec. gen. Internat. Pediat. Nephrology Assn., 1985-92; pres. med. staff Children's Med. Ctr., Dallas, 1992. Mem. editl. bd. Am. Jour. Kidney Diseases, 1986-96; contbr. more than 100 chpts. to med. textbooks and articles to profl. jours. Bd. dirs. Ronald McDonald House, Chattanooga, 1993—, T.C. Thompson Hosp. Found., Chattanooga, 1993—. Maj. U.S. Army, 1968-70. Rsch. grantee NIH, Bethesda, Md., 1974-92. Fellow Am. Acad. Pediat. (mem. exec. com. Tenn. chpt. 1992—); mem. Am. Soc. Pediat. Nephrology (sec.-treas. 1985-91, pres. 1992-93), Internsoc. Coun. for Rsch. of the Kidney and Urinary Tract (sec.-treas. 1991-94), Am. Pediat. Soc., Am. Soc. Nephrology, Am. Soc. Hypertension, Soc. Pediat. Rsch. Baptist. Office: TC Thompson Childrens Hosp 910 Blackford St Chattanooga TN 37403

ARAOZ, DANIEL LEON, psychologist, educator; b. Buenos Aires, Argentina, Apr. 23, 1930; came to U.S., 1951, naturalized, 1967; s. Jose Daniel and Maria Lia (Suarez) A.; m. Marie Carrese, July 27, 1991; BA, Gonzaga U., 1953, M.A., 1954; M.S.T., U. Santa Clara, 1961; MA, Columbia U., 1964, EdD, 1969; m. Dorita Catherine Smyth, July 17, 1964 (div. 1984); children: Leon Daniel, Nadine Victoria. Asst. chaplain Coll. Mt. St. Vincent, Bronx, N.Y., 1962-64; psychotherapist Bklyn. Ctr. Psychotherapy, 1966-67; psychotherapist Cmty. Guidance Svc., N.Y.C., 1965-72, supr., 1972-82; faculty Am. Inst. Psychotherapy and Psychoanalysis, N.Y.C., 1972-82; asst. prof. psychology CUNY, 1970-73; assoc. prof. counseling L.I. U., 1973-82, prof., 1982—, chmn. dept. counsel & devel., 1995—; dir. L.I. Inst. Ericksonian Hypnosis, 1992—. Clin. psychologist, Ill., Pa. Diplomate in counseling psychology and family psychology Am. Bd. Profl. Psychology; diplomate in clin. hypnosis Am. Bd. Psychol. Hypnosis. Fellow APA, Am. Inst. Psychotherapy and Psychoanalysis, Am. Soc. Psychosomatic Dentistry and Medicine, Acad. Counseling Psychology, Acad. Family Psychology; mem. Am. Assn. Sex Educators, Counselors and Therapists, Am. Assn. Marriage and Family Therapy (supr. 1973—), Pa. Psychol. Assn., Am. Mgmt. Assn. (unit trainer 1987-94). Democrat. Editor-in-chief Am. Jour. Family Therapy, 1973-76, jour. adv., 1977—; author: Hypnosis and Sex Therapy, 1982; Hypnosex, 1982; Self-Transformation Through the New Hypnosis, 1984; The New Hypnosis, 1985, 95, The New Hypnosis in Family Therapy, 1987; Selbst Hypnose: Kreative Imagination in Beruf und Alltag, 1992, Reengineering Yourself, 1994, Solution-Oriented Brief Therapy for Adjustment Disorders, 1995; co-editor: Hypnosis Questions & Answers, 1986; contbr. articles to profl. jours. Home: 66 Gates Ave Malverne NY 11565-1912 Office: LI U CW Post Northern Blvd Brookville NY 11548-1207

ARBEIT, ROBERT DAVID, physician; b. Jersey City, Aug. 16, 1947; s. Sidney Robert and Marie (Gluck) A.; m. Susan Abelson, Dec. 20, 1970; children: Jeffrey, Miriam. BA, Williams Coll., 1968; MD, Yale U., 1972. Diplomate Am. Bd. Internat. Medicine, Am. Bd. Infectious Disease. Intern then resident Yale-New Haven Hosp., New Haven, 1972-74; clin. assoc. Nat. Cancer Inst., Bethesda, Md., 1974-76; fellow Sidney Farber Cancer Inst., Boston, 1976-79; staff physician VA Med. Ctr., Boston, 1979—, asst. chief med. svcs., 1989-91, dir. infectious diseases rsch., 1991—, assoc. chief of staff, rsch., 1991—; asst. prof. Sch. Med. Boston U., 1979-87, assoc. prof. Sch. Med., 1987-95, prof. Sch. Med., 1995—. Contbr. articles to profl. jours. and books. Fellow Infectious Diseases Soc. Am., Am. Coll. Physicians; mem. Am. Soc. for Microbiology, Soc. Rsch. Adminstrs., Phi Beta Kappa, Alpha Omega Alpha. Office: VA Med Ctr 150 S Huntington Ave Jamaica Plain MA 02130-4817

ARBER, WERNER, microbiologist; b. Gränichen, Switzerland, June 3, 1929; married; 2 children. Ed., Aargau (Switzerland) Gymnasium, Eidgenössische Technische Hochschule, Zurich. Asst. Lab. Biophysics, U. Geneva, 1953-58, docent, then extraordinary prof. molecular genetics, 1962-70; research assoc. dept. microbiology U. So. Calif., 1958-59; vis. investigator dept. molecular biology U. Calif., Berkeley, 1970-71; prof. microbiology U. Basel (Switzerland), 1971, rector, 1986-88. Co-recipient Nobel prize for physiology or medicine, 1978. Mem. Nat. Acad. Scis. (fgn. assoc.). Office: Biozentrum der Universität, 70 Klingelbergstrasse, CH-4056 Basel Switzerland

ARBITELL, MICHELLE RENEÉ, clinical psychologist; b. Trenton, N.J., Oct. 24, 1962; d. John A. and Adele M. Arbitell. BA, Lehigh U., 1984; MA, Indiana U. of Pa., 1986, D Psychology, 1988. Diplomate Am. Bd. Forensic Examiners; lic. psychologist, Pa.; cert. counselor; cert. eye movement desensitization reprocessing. Clin. psychology intern Geisinger Med. Ctr., Danville, Pa., 1987-88; dir. behavioral medicine and neuropsychology

HealthSouth Rehab. Hosp., 1988—; mem. adv. bd. Blair County Pain Support Groups, Altoona, 1988—; pvt. practice psychology, cons., Altoona and State College, Pa., 1991-94; mem. Am. Bd. Forensic Examiners; invited lectr. Pa. State U., University Park, 1991—; presenter in field. Author: (with others) On Spouse Abuse..., 1985; (with others) Bulimics' Perceptions..., 1991. Fellow Pa. Psychol. Assn.; mem. APA, NAFE, Nat. Acad. Neuropsychology, Soc. Behavioral Medicine, Am. Bd. Forensic Examiners, Phi Beta Kappa, Psi Chi (v.p., sec. 1980-84). Office: HealthSouth Rehab Hosp Altoona Valley View Blvd Altoona PA 16602

ARBOUR, RICHARD B., critical care nurse, educator; b. Chester, Pa., Jan. 21, 1960; s. John G. and Patricia (Donlin) A.; m. Kathy Arbour, Aug. 25, 1984; children: Stephen Scott, Amanda Lynn. AS, Luzerne County Community Coll., Nanticoke, Pa., 1983; BS, King's Coll., Wilkes-Barre, Pa., 1981. Cert. critical care nurse, trauma nurse, cert. neurosci. nurse; ACLS instr., provider. Staff nurse Temple U. Hosp., Phila., Med. Coll. Pa., Phila.; nurse mgr., hosp. orientation coord. Skilled Nursing Inc., Flourtown, Pa.; staff nurse in pvt. practice Phila.; prof., nurse adult critical care med. ICU, Albert Einstein Med. Ctr., Phila.; clin. preceptor in field. Clin. editor Nursing Mag., 1992; contbr. numerous articles to profl. jours. Mem. AACN (program com. S.E. Pa. chpt., mem. nomination s com.), Am. Assn. Neurosci. Nurses, Faculty for Trends in Critical Care Nursing, others. Home: 5928 N 11th St Philadelphia PA 19141-3211

ARBUCKLE, L. DAVIS, urologist; b. Balt., Jan. 2, 1933; s. Lockhart Davis and Gladys (Whitehead) A.; m. Julia Carol Arbuckle, June 16, 1956; children: Douglas Stuart, William Lockhart, Nancy Waite. AB, Williams Coll., 1955; MS in Surgery, U. Va., 1962; MD, Cornell U., 1959. Diplomate Am. Bd. Urology. Intern U. Va., Charlottesville, 1959-60, resident in surgery, 1960-61, resident in urology, 1962-65; pvt. practice Fairlawn, Ohio, 1965—; chmn. dept. urology Akron (Ohio) Gen. Med. Ctr., 1973—, urology residency dir., 1973-83, chief staff, 1992-93; prof. urology, urology residency dir., Northeastern Ohio U. Coll. Medicine, Rootstown, 1983—. contbr. articles to profl. jours. NIH fellow U. Va., 1961-62; named Tchr. of Yr., Akron Gen. Med. Ctr., 1978, 81, 87. Fellow ACS; mem. Am. Urological Soc., Am. Med. Soc., Ohio State Med. Soc., Cleve. Urological Soc. (pres. 1980-81), Summit County Med. Soc. Home: 4023 Shaw Rd Akron OH 44333 Office: The Akron Clinic 3600 W Market St Fairlawn OH 44333

ARCADI, JOHN ALBERT, urologist; b. Whittier, Calif., Oct. 23, 1924; s. Antonio and Josephine (Ramirez) A; m. Doris M. Bohanan, Apr. 11, 1951; children: Patrick, Michael, Judith, Timothy, Margaret, William, Catherine. BS cum laude, U. Notre Dame, 1947; MD, Johns Hopkins U., 1950. Diplomate Am. Bd. Urology. Intern Johns Hopkins Hosp., Balt., 1950-51, resident, 1951-52, 53-55; instr. urology Johns Hopkins U., Balt., 1953-55, U. So. Calif., L.A., 1955-60; research assoc. Whittier (Calif.) Coll., 1957-70, research prof., 1970—; coord. prostate cancer rsch. Huntington Med. Rsch. Inst., Pasadena, Calif., 1993—; staff mem. urology sect. Presbyn. Hosp., Whittier, 1960—. Fellow AAAS, ACS; mem. Endocrine Soc., Am. Urology Assn., Am. Micros. Soc., Internat. Urol. Soc., Am. Assn. Clin. Anatomy, Am. Assn. Anatomists, Soc. for Basic Urologic Rsch., Soc. for Invertebrate Pathology. Republican. Roman Catholic. Home: 6202 Washington Ave Whittier CA 90601-3640 Address: PO Box 9220 Whittier CA 90608-9220

ARCANGELO, VIRGINIA POOLE, nursing educator, nurse practitioner; b. Phila., May 2, 1947; d. William Harold and Roberta Harriet (Wilson) Poole; m. Anthony Joseph Arcangelo, July 12, 1974; children: David, Kristi. BSN, U. Del., 1969; MSN, U. Pa., 1974; PhD, Temple U., 1991; cert. adult nurse practitioner, U. Pa., 1994; cert. family nurse practitioner, Thomas Jefferson U., 1995. Staff nurse med. unit Thomas Jefferson U. Hosp., Phila., 1969-70, head nurse med. unit, 1970-72, nurse clinician med. care program, 1974-77, part-time staff nurse med. care program, 1977-80, instr. dept. nursing Coll. Allied Health Scis., 1988-91, asst. prof., 1991—; instr. Frankford Hosp. Sch. Nursing, Phila., 1972-74, Helene Fuld Sch. Nursing in Camden County, Camden, N.J., 1983-88; family nurse practitioner Jefferson Family Medicine Assocs., 1994—; presenter in field. Contbr. articles to profl. publs. Mem. Evesham Twp. Bd. Edn., Marlton, N.J., 1988-94, v.p. 1990, pres., 1991-92; mem. Evesham Twp. Clean Cmtys. Com., Marlton, 1988-94; mem. thorough and efficient edn. com. Evesham Twp. Schs., Marlton, 1989-90. Grantee Thomas Jefferson U., 1990, 91, NARD Found., 1990. Mem. ANA, N.J. State Nurses' Assn. (mem. med./surg. divsn. com. 1982-84, mem. dist. 5 legis. com. 1986), Am. Acad. of Nurse Practitioner Nat. Organ. of Nurse Practitioner Faculites, Sigma Theta Tau (chair eligibility com. 1990). Home: 7 Knightswood Dr Marlton NJ 08053-2521 Office: Thomas Jefferson U 130 S 9th St Philadelphia PA 19107-5233

ARCARESE, STASIA JOAN, medical and surgical nurse, educator; b. Sayville, N.Y., Mar. 19, 1940; d. Stanley and Sophia (Mazurcyk) Ostrowski; m. Lawrence C. Arcarese, Dec. 29, 1962; children: Josephine, Stacey, Tina. BS, Plattsburgh (N.Y.) State U., 1962; MSN, Russell Sage Coll., Troy, N.Y., 1980. Cert. educator breast self-exam. Sch. nurse, tchr. SUNY, Plattsburgh, N.Y., 1962-63; prof. Clinton C.C., Plattsburgh, 1980—; oper. rm. staff nurse CVPH Med. Ctr., Plattsburgh, 1963; part-time coll. lab. instr. Plattsburgh State U., 1973-80. Mem. LWV (past pres., newsletter editor Plattsburgh area), N.Y. State Nurses Assn. (dist. 8 bd. dirs., past pres., newsletter editor), Sigma Theta Tau. Home: 118 Prospect Ave Plattsburgh NY 12901-1355

ARCE, A. ANTHONY, psychiatrist; b. San Juan, P.R., June 13, 1923; s. Angel and Juana (Baez) A.; m. Malvene Balkind, Oct. 7, 1971; children—Alan I. Scheer, Judith Ann Scheer, Michael Anthony Arce. B.S., Washington and Jefferson Coll., 1942; M.D., Temple U., 1946. Diplomate: Am. Bd. Psychiatry and Neurology; certified in adminstrv. psychiatry. Intern Mercy Hosp., Bay City, Mich. and; Frankford Hosp., Phila., 1946-47; dir. Aguadilla (P.R.) Dist. Hosp., 1947-48; chief health officer Utuado, P.R., 1950-51; physician U.S. Mil. Acad., West Point, N.Y., 1951-52; med. officer Pa. R.R., 1952-53; practice medicine Yonkers, N.Y., 1953-59; resident psychiatrist Payne Whitney Clinic, N.Y.C., 1959-62; asso. dir. psychiatry Grasslands Hosp., Valhalla, N.Y., 1962-67; dir. psychiatry Lincoln Hall Sch., Lincolndale, N.Y., 1967-68; dir. Bur. Aftercare Services N.Y. State Dept. Mental Hygiene, 1968-71; dir. Manhattan Psychiat. Center, Ward's Island, N.Y., 1971-76, Hahnemann Community Mental Health and Mental Retardation Center, Phila., 1976-84; pvt. practice medicine specializing in psychiatry, 1962—; prof. psychiatry, dep. chmn. dept. mental health svcs. Hahnemann U., 1976-85, prof., chmn., 1985-87, prof., dir. amb. svcs., 1987-91; prof., dep. chmn. dept. psychiatry Med. Coll., U. Pa., Phila., 1991—. Mem. president's council N.Y. U. Sch. Social Work, 1963-66; bd. dirs. P.R. Family Inst., N.Y.C., 1970-72. Served with AUS, 1943-46, 48-50. Mem. Am. Coll. Mental Health Adminstrs., Am. Coll. Psychiatrists, Am. Psychiat. Assn. (chmn. task force continuing care), Phila. Psychiat. Soc., Am. Assn. Psychiat. Adminstrs. (treas., pres.). Home: 7805 Chandler Rd Glenside PA 19038-7267 Office: Girard Med Ctr 2ADC 8th St & Girard Ave Philadelphia PA 19122-9999

ARCHAMBAULT, DENISE, social worker; b. Woonsocket, R.I., Apr. 14, 1949; d. Alfred and Marie (Leclerc) A.; children: Shawna Romano, Nicole Romano. BA in Sociology, Salve Regina Coll., 1971; MA in Counseling, R.I. Coll., 1979, MSW, 1985. Cert. Acad. Cert. Social Workers, social worker, R.I. Family counselor Ocean Tides, Narragansett, R.I., 1979-81; handicapped coord. Head Start, 1981-83; rehab. social worker Pawtucket (R.I.) Meml. Hosp., 1985-87; pvt. practice counselor Lincoln, R.I., 1983—; clin. oncology social worker R.I. Hosp., Providence, 1987-89, Hospice Care of R.I., 1989—; lectr. workshops dealing with cancer patients and families, grief, loss and bereavement. Mem. NASW (chair R.I. social workers oncology group), Nat. Assn. Oncology Social Workers, Assn. for Death Edn. and Counseling, No. R.I. Adult Day Care (bd. dirs.). Home: 451 River Rd Lincoln RI 02865-1424

ARCHER, PATTI JUNE, social worker; b. Parkersburg, W.Va., June 9, 1956; d. Audra Nile and Helen Juanita (Knotts) A. BA, Geneva Coll., 1974; MSW, W.Va. U., 1983. Cert. social worker, W.Va. Social worker We. Dist. Guide Ctr., Parkersburg, W.Va., 1976-81; dir. Horizons Group Home, Parkersburg, 1983-85; social worker Camden Clark Meml. Hosp., Parkersburg, 1985-87, St. Joseph Hosp., Parkersburg, 1987—; bereavement coord. Hospice, Parkersburg; therapist Fred Knez & Assocs., Vienna, W.Va.; cons. ServeCare Home Health, Parkersburg, Housecalls Home Health, Parkersburg. Vol. Good Samaritan Clinic, Parkersburg, 1994; chair family nurturing com. Habitat for Humanity, 1996; Sun. sch. tchr. First Luth. Ch., Parkersburg, 1994—. Civitan Club (award). Democrat. Office: St Joseph Hosp PO Box 327 Parkersburg WV 26104

ARCHIBALD, PATRICIA ANN, biology educator, college director; b. Olney, Ill., July 18, 1931; d. Stanley Ray and Mable Ellen (Seed) A. BS, Ball State U., 1953, MA, 1961; PhD in Botany, U. Tex., 1969. Tchr. biology Elkhart (Ind.) Sr. High Sch., 1958-64; prof. biology Slippery Rock (Pa.) U., 1969-94, dir. Office Acad. Grants, 1987-94; sci. adminstr. EPA, Washington, 1980-82; leader seminar group China Sci. and Tech. Exch. Ctr., 1989. Contbr. chpts. to books, articles to profl. jours. Recipient Fullbright Teaching Exch. award, 1962-63, Rsch. Exch. award IREX, 1977, NAS, 1978, Collection Expdn. award N.Y. Bot. Garden, 1984. Mem. Psychol. Soc. Am. (sec. 1982-84), Sigma Xi. Home: PO Box 429 895 Liberty St Grove City PA 16127-9002

ARCHIE, CAROL LOUISE, obstetrician and gynecologist, educator; b. Detroit, May 18, 1957; d. Frank and Mildred (Barmore) A.; m. Edward Louis Keenan III, Mar. 7, 1993. BA in History, U. Mich., 1979, postgrad. in Pub. Health Adminstrn., 1979-83; MD, Wayne State U., 1983. Diplomate Am. Bd. Ob-Gyn., Am. Bd. Maternal-Fetal Medicine. Resident ob-gyn. Wayne State U., Detroit, 1983-87; fellow in maternal fetal medicine UCLA, 1987-89, asst. prof. ob-gyn., 1987—; cons. Office Substance Abuse Prevention, Washignton, 1989—, NIH, Bethesda, Md., 1990—, RAND, 1995—. Peer reviewer jours. Obstetrics and Gynecology, 1989—, Am. Jour. Pub. Health, 1994—, Am. Jour. Obstetrics and Gynecology, 1993—; contbr. chpts. to books. Mem. internal rev. bd. Friends Med. Rsch., 1991—; bd. dirs. Matrix Inst. on Addictions, L.A., 1993—; bd. dirs., vice chair Calif. Advocates for Pregnant Women, 1993—; bd. dirs., asst. v.p. med. svcs. Venice (Calif.) Free Clinic, 1994—. Clin. Tng. grantee UCLA, 1993—; recipient Faculty Devel. award Berlex Found., 1992. Fellow ACOG; mem. AMA, APHA, Soc. Perinatal Obstetricians, Royal Soc. of Medicine (Eng.), Assn. Profs. of Gynecology and Obstetrics. Office: Dept Ob-gyn UCLA Sch Medicine Rm 22-132 10833 Le Conte Ave Los Angeles CA 90024

ARCHIE, VICTORIA ESTHER, social worker; b. N.Y.C., June 4, 1960; d. James Lee and Marjorie Ann (Booth) Archie; m. Titus Stanfield Boyce, Mar. 21, 1993; 1 child, Julissa Elizabeth Jameta. Student, New York U., 1978-79, Andrews U., 1979-81; BA with honors, L.I. U., 1983. Case worker N.Y.C. Adminstrn. for Children's Svcs., 1986—, supr. I, 1989—; child care mgmt. worker Pam O'Neill, N.Y.C., 1983—; home health care mgmt. Richmond Home Need Services, S.I., 1985-86. Prin. works exhibited at L.I. U. Named Outstanding Young Woman in Am., 1986. Mem. NAFE. Democrat. Seventh Day Adventist. Home: 193-15A 73d Ave #1C Fresh Meadows NY 11365 Office: NYC Adminstrn for Children's Svcs 16515 Archer Ave Jamaica NY 11433-1109

ARCOS, GEORGE JOHN, anesthesiologist; b. Bklyn., Mar. 5, 1956; s. John George and Elsie (Coronges) A.; m. Barbara Fedak, Aug. 23, 1980; 1 child, Nicholas John. BSBA with honors, U. Fla., 1979; D of Osteo. Medicine, N.Y. Coll. Osteo. Medicine, 1983. Diplomate Am. Acad. Pain Mgmt., Am. Osteo. Coll. Anesthesiologist. Chief anesthesiology Homestead (Fla.) AFB, 1988-90; asst. prof. anesthesiology U. Miami/Jackson Meml. Hosp., 1990—, NOVA-Southeastern U., Davie, Fla., 1990—; vice-chief anesthesiology Fla. Med. Ctr. South, Plantation, 1990—; dir. acute paiin svc., med. dir. post-anesthesia care unit, post-doctoral tng. com., surg. care rev. com., Fla. Med. Ctr. South, Plantation, 1990—; cons. Vital Signs, Inc., 1988; lectr. in field. Vol. Christian Med. Soc., Tex., 1995—; booster U. Fla., Gainesville, 1994—. Maj. USAF, 1986-90. Fellow Am. Osteo. Coll. Anesthesiologists; mem. Am. Soc. Anesthesiologists, Am. Osteo. Assn., Am. Soc. Regional Anesthesia, Fla. Soc. Anesthesiologists. Republican. Home: 11750 NW 27th Ct Plantation FL 33323 Office: Fla Med Ctr South 6701 W Sunrise Blvd Plantation FL 33324

ARD, JAMES GEORGE, family physician; b. St. Anthony, Idaho, Mar. 22, 1951; s. George Francis and Belva Jeanne (Spillman) A.; m. Amanda Middleton, Apr. 6, 1985 (div. Oct. 1992); 1 child, Hayley Elizabeth. AA, Ricks Coll., 1971; BS, Brigham Young U., 1979; DO, Mich. State U., 1984. Diplomate Am. Bd. Family Practice. Family physician Kaiser Permanente, Lahaina, Hawaii, 1995—. Mem. AMA, Am. Acad. Family Practice, Am. Med. Informatics Assn. Office: Kaiser Permanente 910 Wainee St Lahania HI 96761

ARDARY, DARLENE ANN, pediatrics nurse; b. Clearfield, Pa., Feb. 3, 1964; d. Richard Melvin and Doris Marie (McFadden) Kolbe; m. Bryan C. Ardary, July 27, 1985; 1 child, Alyssa Janel. Diploma, Cen. Pa. Sch. Nursing, 1986; student, Pa. State U., State College, 1982-83, 95—. Cert. pediatrics nurse; cert. ACLS, pediat. advanced life support. Nurse DuBois (Pa.) Regional Med. Ctr., 1986-89, Clearfield (Pa.) Hosp. Home Health, 1989—. Mem. parish nurse svc. Curwensville United Meth. Ch., coord. parish nurse pediat./well-baby program; mem. Clearfield County Immunization Task Force. Mem. PNA, ANA.

ARDINGER, ROBERT HALL, JR., physician, educator; b. Corona, Calif., Dec. 4, 1956; s. Robert Hall Sr. and Alice Marie (Schaal) A.; m. Holly Hutchison, Nov. 6, 1982; children: Andrew, Patrick. BS, Calif. State Polytech. U., 1979; MD, U. Calif., San Diego, 1983. Diplomate Am. Bd. Pediats. Intern U. Iowa, Iowa City, 1983-84, resident, 1984-86, fellow, 1986-89; instr. U. Rochester, N.Y., 1989-90; asst. prof. U. Kans., Kansas City, 1990-96, assoc. prof., 1996—. Fellow Am. Acad. Pediats., Am. Coll. Cardiology. Office: Kans U Med Ctr Dept Pediats 3901 Rainbow Blvd Kansas City KS 66160

AREKAPUDI, KUMAR VIJAYA VASANTHA, sanitarian, real estate agent; b. Angaluru, India, July 21, 1957; came to U.S., 1985, naturalized 1990; s. Rahgavendra Rao and Chandramma (Lingam) A.; m. Aruna Vallabhaneni, Sept. 4, 1988; 1 child, Raghava Chandra. BA, Osmania U., Hyderabad, India, 1984; MBA, Calif. Coast U., 1994. Patient transporter Ill. Masonic Med. Ctr., Chgo., 1985, psychiatric technician, 1985-88; communicable disease control investigator Chgo. Dept. Health, 1987-88, sanitarian, 1988-94; psychiatric technician Lincoln West Hosp., Chgo., 1988-91; real estate assoc. All Star Realty, Chgo., 1990; assoc. mgr. residential and comml. div. Century 21 Ben Garth Realty, Chgo., 1990-91; founder, pres., CEO Blue Planet Realty Inc., 1991—; sanitarian/team leader Mayor's Health and Sanitation Task Force for City of Chgo., 1994—. Chmn. Community Svcs. Indo Am. Dem. Orgn., Chgo., 1985-86, chmn. pub. relations, 1987-88; mem. 48th Ward Progressive Network, Chgo., 1985—; voting mem. Multiple Listing Svc. No. Ill., 1992—; signatary fair housing and equal opportunity with U.S. Dept. Housing and Urban Devel, approved selling broker; active Ams. for Change, 1992—. Recipient Merit citation Indo-Am. Dem. Orgn., Chgo., 1985, Cert. of Recognition Mayor of City of Chgo. for Earth Day participation, Million Dollar Sales award Chgo. Assn. Realtors, 1991, Coop. Sales award N.W. Real Estate Bd., 1991, Man of Yr. medal honor ABI, 1994; named Man of Yr. 1986. Mem. Am. Fedn. State County Mcpl. Employees Union (pres. club), Congl. Network Team, Ill. Environ. Health Assn., Candlewick Lake Assn., Chgo. Assn. Realtors (voting mem. multiple listing svc. 1991—, leader comm. network team 1993, polit. affairs com., equal opportunity com. 1993), North Side Real Estate Bd. (Coop. Sales award 1991), N.W. Real Estate Bd. (Coop. Sales award 1991), N.W. Suburban Assn. Realtors (voting 1992-94), RNA, Euthanasia Club Ill., Real Estate Fin. Planners Inc. Hindu. Home and Office: 5770 N Ridge Ave Chicago IL 60660-3444

ARELLANO, EUGENE WALTER, family practitioner, thoroughbred horse breeder; b. L.A., Nov. 4, 1927; s. Federico and Petrita Beaubien (Abreu) A.; m. Patti Ruth Ann Stewart, July 15, 1948 (div. Sept. 1967); children: Debra, Kim; m. Judith Ellen Boam, Oct. 21, 1969; children: Edward, Eugene, Melinda. Student, Stanford U., 1945-46; AA, UCLA, 1949; DO, Coll. Osteo. Physicians and Surgeons, L.A., 1953; MD, U. Calif., Irvine, 1962. Diplomate Am. Bd. Family Physicians. Intern Glendale (Calif.) Community Hosp., 1953-55; pvt. practice, Glendale, Calif., 1955—; attending med. staff Glendale Adventist Med. Ctr., 1978—; chief staff Glendale Community Hosp., 1975, pres.-elect, 1981-83. With U.S. Army, 1946-47; lt. col. USAF, 1976-77. Fellow Am. Acad. Family Physicians; mem. AMA (physician's recognition award 1981, 84, 87, 95-98), Calif. Med. Assn., World Med. Assn., Calif. Acad. Family Physicians, L.A. County Med. Assn., Glendale Dist. Med. Assn., Assn. Mil. Surgeons U.S., UCLA Alumni Assn. Republican. Roman Catholic. Office: 605 Meadow Grove St La Canada Flintridge CA 91011-3532

ARENBERG, DAVID, research psychologist, consultant, writer; b. Balt., Nov. 14, 1927; s. Morris and Dorothy (Silver) A.; m. Jeanne Brown, 1957 (dec. Aug. 1977); children: Mark W., Josh L.; m. Muriel Groubert, May 7, 1989. AB, Johns Hopkins U., 1951; PhD, Duke U., 1960. Rsch. psychologist NIH, Balt., 1960-89; cons. Delray Beach, 1989—. Co-author: New Directions in Memory and Aging, 1980, Normal Human Aging, 1984; assoc. editor Jour. of Gerontology, 1970-72; contbr. articles to profl. jours. With AUS, 1946-47, Japan. Vis. scholar U. Md., 1978-79. Fellow APA (pres. divsn. on adult devel. and aging, chmn. various divsn. coms. 1971-90). Democrat. Home and Office: 13665A Via Aurora Delray Beach FL 33484-1617

AREND, WILLIAM PHELPS, medical researcher; b. Utica, N.Y., Aug. 24, 1937; s. Ralph Wilcox and Frances Elizabeth (Clapp) A.; m. Ann Elizabeth Manes, June 5, 1964; children: Thomas Clapp, Christopher Austin, Jeffrey Phelps. BA, Williams Coll., 1959; MD, Columbia U., 1964. Intern U. Wash., Seattle, 1964-65, residency, 1965-66, 68-69, fellow, 1969-71, asst. prof. medicine, 1971-75, assoc. prof. medicine, 1975-81; prof. medicine U. Tex. Health Scis. Ctr., Houston, 1981-82, dir. div. rheumatology, 1981-82; prof. medicine, microbiology and immunology U. Colo. Health Scis. Ctr., Denver, 1983—, head. div. of rheumatology, 1983—; Scoville endowed prof. rheumatology, 1993—; chief arthritis sect. VA Hosp., Seattle, 1971-80; vis. scholar Corpus Christi Coll., 1980-81, Cambridge U. Editor Arthritis Rheumatism, 1995—; assoc. editor Jour. Clin. Immunology, Jour. Immunology, Jour. Clin. Investigation, 1993-95; contbr. numerous articles to profl. jours. Mem. exec. coun. Hall of Life, Denver Mus. Natural History; mem. adv. coun. NIAMS, NIH, 1995—. Lt. comdr. USPHS, 1966-68. Guggenheim Found. fellow, 1980-81. Fellow AAAS, ACP; mem. Assn. Am. Physicians, Am. Soc. Clin. Investigation, Am. Assn. Immunologists, Am. Coll. Rheumatology (bd. dirs. 1991-94), Western Assn. Physicians, Western Soc. Clin. Investigation (councilor 1976-79), Phi Beta Kappa. Episcopalian. Office: U Colo Health Scis Ctr 4200 E 9th Ave Denver CO 80220-3706

ARENOWITZ, ALBERT HAROLD, psychiatrist; b. N.Y.C., Jan. 12, 1925; s. Louis Isaac and Lena Helen (Skovron) A.; m. Betty Jane Wiener, Oct. 11, 1953; children: Frederick Stuart, Diane Helen. BA with honors, U. Wis., 1948; MD, U. Va., 1951. Diplomate Am. Bd. Psychiatry, Am. Bd. Child Psychiatry. Intern Kings County Gen. Hosp., Bklyn., 1951-52; resident in psychiatry Bronx (N.Y.) VA Hosp., 1952-55; postdoctoral fellow Youth Guidance Ctr., Worcester, Mass., 1955-57; dir. Ctr. for Child Guidance, Phila., 1962-65, Hahnemann Med. Service Eastern State Sch. and Hosp., Trevose, Pa., 1965-68; dir., tng. dir. Child and Adolescent Psychiat. Clinic, Phila. Gen. Hosp., 1965-67; asst. clin. prof. psychiatry Jefferson Med. Coll., Phila., 1974-76; exec. dir. Child Guidance and Mental Health Clinics, Media, Pa., 1967-74; med. dir. Intercommunity Child Guidance Ctr., Whittier, Calif., 1976—; cons. Madison Pub. Schs., 1957-60, Dane County Child Guidance Ctr., Madison, 1957-62, Juvenile Ct., Madison, 1957-62; clin. asst. prof. child psychiatry Hahnemann Med. Coll., Phila., 1966-74; asst. clin. prof. psychiatry U. Wis., Madison, 1960-62, clin. asst. prof. psychiatry, behavioral scis. and family medicine U. So. Calif., L.A., 1976—; mem. med. staff Presbyn. Intercommunity Hosp., Whittier, 1976—. Pres. Whittier Area Coordinating Coun., 1978-80; chmn. ethics com. Presbyn. Intercommunity Hosp. Flight officer, navigator USAF, 1943-45. Decorated Air medal, POW medal. Fellow Am. Psychiat. Assn., Am. Acad. Child Psychiatry; mem. AAAS, Los Angeles County Med. Assn., So. Calif. Psychiat. Soc., So. Calif. Soc. Child Psychiatry, Phila. Soc. Adolescent Psychiatry (pres. 1967-68). Office: Intercommunity Child Guidance Ctr 8106 Broadway Ave Whittier CA 90606-3118

ARESKOG, DONALD CLINTON, retired chiropractor; b. Bklyn., Aug. 6, 1926; s. Andrew Albert and Jennie Margaret (Dickson) A.; m. Julia Catherine Koskela, May 15, 1954. D Chiropractic, Logan Coll., St. Louis, 1950; Philosopher of Chiropractic, Atlantic States Chiropractic Coll. Ret., 1989; pvt. practice Bklyn., 1952-56, Wappingers Falls, N.Y., 1956-61, Poughkeepsie, N.Y., 1961-89; retired, 1989; bd. govs. Atlantic States Chiropractic Coll., Bklyn., 1954; research in field. Developer technique for removal of mental aberrations. Mem. Am. Chiropractic Assn. (speakers bur. 1964), Ednl. Rsch. Soc., Internat. Basic Rsch. Inst., Internat. Platform Assn., Wappingers Falls C. of C. (treas. 1959), Toastmasters. Home: 330 SE 20th Ave Apt 514 Deerfield Beach FL 33441-5181

AREVALO, CARLOS OSCAR, endocrinologist; b. Lima, Peru, Sept. 3, 1948; came to U.S., 1975; s. Oscar and Victoria (Troncoso) A.; m. Maria Elizabeth Paredes, May 30, 1975; children: Janice, Richard. BS, San Marcos U., Lima, 1967; MD, San Fernando Med. Sch., Lima, 1974. Diplomate Am. Bd. Internal Medicine, Am. Bd. Endocrinology. Chief endocrinology divsn. Mary Immaculate Hosp., Jamaica, N.Y., 1987-96; clin. asst. prof. medicine Albert Einstein Coll. Medicine, Bronx, N.Y., 1996. Mem. Am. Diabetes Assn., Endocrine Soc., Spanish Am. Med. Soc., Peruvian Am. Med. Soc. Roman Catholic. Office: 40-45 78th St Elmhurst NY 11373

ARFFA, ROBERT CRAIG, ophthalmologist, educator; b. New Haven, Sept. 16, 1953; s. Stanley H. and Shirley Arffa; m. Sharon Mary Keunik, June 7, 1981; children: Rachel, Lauren, Matthew. BA, Cornell U., 1975; MD, U. Conn., 1979. Intern medicine St. Elizabeth's Hosp., Brighton, Mass., 1979-80; resident ophthalmology Ind. U., Indpls., 1981-84; fellow ophthalmology, cornea and external disease La. State U., New Orleans, 1984-86; asst. prof. ophthalmology U. Pitts., 1986-91; assoc. prof. Med. Coll. Pa., Pitts., 1991—. Author: Graysen's Diseases of the Cornea, 1991. Fellow Am. Acad. Ophthalmology. Office: 420 E North Ave Pittsburgh PA 15200

ARIAS, IRWIN MONROE, physician, educator; b. N.Y.C., Sept. 4, 1926; s. Henry Robert and Sylvia (Hirsh) A.; m. Lyuba Varticouski; children: Jonathan, Linda, Wendy, Nancy. BS, Harvard U., 1947; MS, Columbia U., 1948; MD cum laude, State U., N.Y. Med. Ctr., 1952; M.D. cum laude, N.Y. Med. Center, 1952. Diplomate: Am. Bd. Internal Medicine. Intern Fourth Med. Svc. (Harvard) Boston City Hosp., 1952-54, asst. resident, 1954-55; USPHS fellow gastroenterology/liver disease Second and Fourth Med. Svc., 1955-56; fellow hematology Boston VA Hosp., 1954-55; rsch. fellow N.Y. Heart Assn.; sr. rsch. fellow Albert Einstein Coll. Medicine, 1956-58, asst. prof., 1960-64, assoc. prof., 1964-69; asst. vis. physician Bronx Mcpl. Hosp. Center, 1956-64, assoc., 1964-67, attending physician, 1969-84; prin. investigator USPHS GI tng. program; dir. program and chief div. gastroenterology-liver disease Albert Einstein Coll. Medicine, Bronx, 1967-84; prof. medicine Albert Einstein Coll. Medicine, 1969-84, vice chmn. dept. medicine, 1973-84; dir. Liver Rsch. Ctr., 1973-84, asso. chmn. academic devel., dept. medicine, 1980-84; prof., chmn. dept. physiology-pathophysiology Tufts U. Sch. Medicine, 1984—, prof. medicine; cons. Rockefeller Found., 1958-60, Pan Am. Union, 1959-63. Founding editor: Hepatology; editor: (with others) Glutathione: Metabolism and Function, 1976; author: The Liver: Biology and Pathobiology, 1980; contbr. (with others) numerous articles to sci. publs. Mem. overseas med. adv. bd. Tel Aviv U. Sch. Medicine, 1963-69; mem. nat. adv. bd. La Leche League, 1970—; trustee Mount Desert Island Biol. Lab., 1969-71; mem. adv. bd. Children's Med. Rsch. Ctr., Cin., 1976-81; mem. nat. bd. Am. Liver Found.; mem. bd. The Med. Found. Recipient numerous awards including Disting. Achievement awards Am. Gastroenterologic Assn., 1970, Disting. Achievement awards Am. Coll. Gastroenterologists, 1971, Disting. Achievement award Can. Gastroenterologic Assn., 1972; B.B. Vincent Lyons award Am. Gastroenterologic Assn., 1965; San Diego-Spl. fellow. E.B. Scripps Inst. for Comparative Biology, 1967; Disting. Commendation medal medicine U. Recife, Brazil, 1972; NIH Fogarty Found. scholar, 1985. Mem. AAAS, Am. Soc. Clin. Investigation (v.p.), Am. Assn. Study Liver Disease (Disting. Achievement award 1993-94), Am. Fedn. Clin. Rsch., Am. Gastroenterol. Assn., The Harvey Soc., Am. Physiol. Soc., Internat. Assn. Clin. Investigation, Internat. Assn. Study Liver, Assn. Am. Physicians, Alpha Omega Alpha. Home: 55 Fay Ln Needham MA 02194-2105 Office: Tufts U Sch Medicine Dept Physiology 136 Harrison Ave Boston MA 02111-1800

ARIMURA, AKIRA, biomedical research laboratory administrator, educator; b. Kagoshima, Japan, Dec. 26, 1923; came to U.S., 1965; s. Jyojiro and Kiyoko (Kajiwara) A.; m. Katsuko Yamashita, July 31, 1957; children: Jerome J., Mark M., Margaret M. BS, 7th Nat. Coll., Kagoshima, 1943; MD, Nagoya (Japan) U., 1951, PhD, 1957. James Hudson Brown postdoctoral fellow Yale U., New Haven, Conn., 1956-58; instr., rsch. assoc. Hokkaido U., Sapporo, Japan, 1961-65; instr. Tulane U., New Orleans, 1958-61, asst. prof., 1965-68, assoc. prof., 1968-73; prof. medicine Tulane U., New Orleans, 1973—; dir. U.S.-Japan Biomedical Rsch. Lab. Tulane U., Belle Chasse, La., 1985—; rsch. physician VA Hosp., New Orleans, 1965-80; mem. Endocrine Study Sect., NIH, 1978-82; adj. prof. anatomy Tulane U., New Orleans, 1979—, Physiology, 1989—, founder, dir. clin. RIA Lab., Tulane U. Med. Ctr., 1980-87, molecular neuroendo and diabetes lab. Belle Chasse, 1980-85, dir., 1985; vis. prof. Keio U., Tokyo, 1990—; founder U.S.-Japan Biomed. Rsch. Labs., Belle Chasse, 1985—; reviewer Jour. Clin. Endocrinology and Metabolism, Am. Jour. Physiology, Jour. Clin. Investigation, Sci., Life Sci., Procs. Soc. Exptl. Biology and Medicine, others. Mem. editorial bd. Peptides, Turkish Jour. Med. and Endocrine Jour.; contbr. articles to scholarly and profl. jours. Planner, initiator student exchange program Tulane U. and Keio U., New Orleans and Tokyo, 1986. Decorated with Order of Rising Sun, Gold Rays with Neck Ribbon, Govt. of Japan, 1995; named Fulbright scholar 1956. Mem. AAAS, Internat. Soc. Neuroendocrine, Endocrine Soc. U.S., Japan Endocrine Soc. (hon.), Hungarian Soc. for Endocrinology and Metabolism (hon.), Am. Physiology Soc., Am. Soc. Neurosci., Soc. Exptl. Biology and Medicine, N.Y. Acad. Scis., Japan Physiol. Soc. (hon.). Office: Tulane U Herbert Rsch Ctr US-Japan Biomed Rsch Labs 3705 Main St Belle Chasse LA 70037-3001

ARITA, GEORGE SHIRO, biology educator; b. Honolulu, Oct. 9, 1940; s. Ichimatsu and Natsu (Kimoto) A.; m. Harriet Yooko Ide, Dec. 26, 1964; children: Laurie Reiko, Daren Shizuo. BA, U. Hawaii, 1962, MS, 1964; MS, U. B.C., Vancouver, 1967; postgrad., U. Calif., Santa Barbara, 1967-71. Cert. community coll. tchr., Calif. Prof. biology Ventura (Calif.) Coll., 1971—, curator fish collection, 1976—, head dept. biology, 1989—. Author: (with others, lab. manual) Basic Concepts in Biology, 1981, Study Guide to Accompany Biology: Today and Tomorrow, 2d edit., 1984; contbr. articles on ichthyology to profl. jours. Fushiminomiya Meml. scholar U. Hawaii, 1961-62, Fisheries Assn. B.C. scholar U. B.C., 1964-65; NSF grad. trainee U. Calif. Santa Barbara, 1969-71. Mem. AAAS, Am. Soc. Ichthyologists and Herpetologists, Western Soc. Naturalists, Sigma Xi. Home: 94 Howard Ave Oak View CA 93022-9524 Office: Ventura Coll Dept Biology Ventura CA 93003

ARIYOSHI, TOSHIHIKO, retired toxicologist, educator; b. Fukuoka, Japan, July 1, 1930; m. Nobu Yasutake, Oct. 30, 1958; children: Sakiko, Noritaka. B in Pharmacy, Kyushu U., Fukuoka, 1954, PharmM, 1956, PharmD, 1964. Pharmacist Tachiarai Hosp., Fukuoka, 1958-60; from rsch. assoc. to assoc. prof. Nagasaki (Japan) U., 1960-74, prof., 1975-96, dean of students, 1986-88, ret., 1996. Author: Drug Metabolism, 1986; contbr. over 140 articles to profl. jours. Humboldt fellow Tubingen U. 1966-68; recipient award Japanese Min. Environ. Agy. 1991. Mem. Coun. Environ. Pollution Control of Nagasaki Prefecture (chmn. 1990-96).

ARJE, FRANCES BURTON, nurse; b. Whitestone, N.Y., Feb. 14, 1917; d. Frederick Francis and Ethel Mary (Coulter) Burton; diploma Creedmoor State Hosp. Sch. Nursing, 1942; B.S., Columbia, 1957, M.A., 1958, Ed.D., 1973; m. Sidney Lewis Arje, Sept. 28, 1942 (div. Aug. 1953); children—Andrew Coulter, Abigail Arje Wilson. Coordinator profl. info. services Comeback, Inc., N.Y.C., 1961-67; asso. prof. nursing Coll. of V.I., St. Thomas, 1967-69; curriculum devel. cons., adj. prof. dept. leisure studies N.Y. U. Sch. Edn., Health, Nursing and Arts Professions, 1969-86; research asso., asst. dir. Nursing Home Trainer Program, United Hosp. Fund N.Y., 1970-72; asso. dir. edn. and tng. South Beach Psychiat. Center, N.Y.C., 1973-83, also cons. gerontology to staff; pvt. practice mental health, family and gay couple counseling, 1973-89; vol. AIDS, Manasota, 1990-93, Esprit d'Corps, Ballet Eddy Toussaint, 1994-95. Recipient Honor award Creedmoor State Hosp. Sch. Nursing, 1942, letter of citation Comdr. Pacific Fleet, 1948, Undergrad. Study award Minn. Dept. Welfare, 1956-57, Mary M. Roberts fellowship award in journalism Am. Jour. Nursing Co., 1958-59, Grad. Rehab. Lit. award Nat. Rehab. Assn., 1967, HEW research awards, 1969-71, Editor's Choice award Nat. Libr. of Poetry, 1993. Mem. ANA, AAUP, AAUW, Gerontol. Soc., Am. Assn. Sex Educators and Counsellors, Tchrs. Coll., Columbia, Creedmoor State Hosp. Sch. Nursing alumni assns., Kappa Delta Pi. Unitarian. Co-author, editor: Psychiatric-Mental Health Nursing, 4th edit.; Recreation for Your Disabled Child; Guidelines for Parents, 1975; Guidelines for Action: Comprehensive Recreation Services for Disabled Children, 1975; A Modular Training Program for Therapeutic Recreation Technicians, 1975, More Moon Songs, Winds in the Night Sky, National Library of Poetry, 1993; contbg. author: Aging and Isolation, 1980. Home: 38-46 Pin Oaks St Sarasota FL 34232-1242

ARKY, RONALD ALFRED, medical educator; b. New Brunswick, N.J., June 26, 1929; s. Eugene and Ida (Glick) A.; m. Marie Mahoney, Sept. 14, 1963. AB, Cornell U., Ithaca, N.Y., 1951; MD, Cornell U., N.Y.C., 1955. Intern Bellevue Hosp., N.Y.C., 1955-56; resident N.Y. VA Hosp., 1958-60; fellow Thorndike Meml. Lab., Boston City Hosp., 1961-63; dir. diabetes clinic Boston City Hosp., 1966-71; Charles S. Davidson prof. medicine Harvard U. Med. Sch., Cambridge, Mass., 1984—; chmn. dept. medicine Mt. Auburn Hosp., 1971-93; pres. Assocs. Program for Dirs. Internal Medicine, 1990-91. Fellow AAAS; Master ACP, Peabody Soc. Harvard Med. Sch.; mem. Am. Diabetes Assn. (pres. 1979-80). Office: Francis W Peabody Soc Harvard Med Sch 260 Longwood Ave Boston MA 02115-5701

ARLING, BRYAN JEREMY, internist; b. Mpls., Dec. 10, 1944; s. Leonard Swenson and Marion (Schroeder) A.; m. Donna Dickson; children: Elissa, Jeremy, Timothy. BA summa cum laude, U. Minn., 1965; MD, Harvard U., 1969. Diplomate, Am. Bd. Internal Medicine. Intern Stanford (Calif.) Affiliated Hosps., 1969-70, resident in medicine, 1970-71; spl. asst. to adminstr. Health Sci. Mental Health Adminstrn. USPHS, Rockville, Md., 1971-73; instr., chief resident medicine George Washington U. Hosp., Washington, 1973-74; asst. prof. medicine George Washington U. Hosp., 1974-77; pvt. practice gen. internal medicine Washington, 1977—; clin. prof. medicine George Washington U., 1988—. Mem. adminstrv. bd. Chevy Chase United Meth. Ch.; mem. devel. com. Maret Sch., 1985—, co-chair ann. giving campaign, 1986-87, 87-88, trustee, 1991—, v.p., 1994—; question relevance reviewer Am. Bd. Internal Medicine, 1991-92, mem. com. on certifying and recertifying exam., 1992-93. Named One of Best Doctors in Town, Washington Mag, 1986, 95, One of Best Pediatricians and Internists, 1987; named Top Internist by other doctors, 1993, Best Doctors in Am., S.E. region, 1996. Mem. ACP, AMA, Am. Soc. Internal Medicine, D.C. Med. Soc., Acad. Medicine, Smithsonian Assocs., Friends of Kennedy Ctr., Harvard Club Washington, Nat. Trust for Hist. Preservation, Friends of Nat. Zoo, Common Cause, ACLU, Physicians for Social Responsibility, Columbia Country Club, Bahamas Air-Sea Rescue Assn. Home: 3803 Taylor St Bethesda MD 20815-4117 Office: 2440 M St NW Ste 817 Washington DC 20037-1404

ARLING, DONNA DICKSON, social worker; b. Jersey Shore, Pa., July 8, 1945; d. Eugene Robert and Helen (Bardo) Dickson; m. Bryan Jeremy Arling, Aug. 28, 1969; children: Elissa, Jeremy, Timothy. BS, Pa. State U., 1967; MSW, Smith Coll., 1969. Cert. diplomate in social work, Md.; lic. clin. social worker. Clin. social worker N. County Mental Health Ctr., Palo Alto, Calif., 1969-71, VA Hosp., Washington, 1971-77; pvt. practice clin. social work Washington, 1978—. Mem. Nat. Assn. Social Workers, Greater Washington Soc. Clin. Social Work, Smith Coll. Sch. Social Work Alumni Assn. (exec. com. 1979-82). Home: 3803 Taylor St Chevy Chase MD 20815-4117 Office: 1015 33rd St NW Washington DC 20007-3523

ARLOW, JACOB A., psychiatrist, educator; b. N.Y.C., Sept. 3, 1912; s. Adolph A. and Ida (Feldman) A.; m. Alice Diamond, Oct. 31, 1936; children: Michael Saul, Allan Joseph, Seth Martin. B.S., N.Y. U., 1932, M.D., 1936; Grad., N.Y. Psychoanalytic Inst., 1947. Diplomate: Am. Bd. Neurology and Psychiatry. Rotating intern Harlem Hosp., N.Y.C., 1936-38; resident neuropsychiatrist USPHS Hosp., Ellis Island, N.Y., 1938-39; resident psychiatrist Kings County Hosp., Bklyn., 1939; asst. psychiatrist mental hygiene clinic Kings County Hosp., 1941; asst. resident neurologist Montefiore Hosp., Bronx, N.Y., 1940-41; asst. neurologist Montefiore Hosp., 1942-44; resident psychiatrist N.Y. State Psychiat. Inst. and Hosp., N.Y.C., 1940-41; cons. psychiatrist Pride of Judea Children's Home, Bklyn., 1940-45; pvt. practice N.Y.C., 1942-92; lectr. N.Y. Psychoanaltyic Inst., 1948-50; instr. neurology Columbia Coll. Phys. and Surg., 1942-44, instr. psychiatry psychosomatic service of psychoanalytic clinic for tng. and research, 1947-51, John B. Turner vis. prof. psychiatry, 1967-68; research asso, instr. psychiatry Presbyn. Hosp.-Columbia Med. Center, 1944-51; clin. asst. prof. psychoanalytic medicine State U. N.Y. Coll. Medicine at N.Y.C., 1952-55, clin. assoc. prof., 1955-62, clin. prof., 1962-79; clin. prof. NYU, N.Y.C., 1979—; mem. faculty Ctr. Psychoanlytic Tng., N.Y.C.; prof. emeritus Albert Einstein Coll. Medicine, N.Y.C.; pvt. practice part-time N.Y.C., 1984—, Great Neck, N.Y., 1984—; faculty N.Y. Psychoanalytic Inst., 1956—; vis. prof. psychiatry La. State U. Sch. Medicine, 1969-70, Mt. Sinai Sch. Medicine, N.Y.C., 1972-73; vis. scholar Freud chair Hebrew U., Jerusalem, April, 1985; cons. Hillside Hosp., Glen Oaks, N.Y., 1989—. Author: Legacy of Sigmund Freud, 1956, (with Charles Brenner) Psychoanalytic Concepts and the Structural Theory, 1964, Psychoanalysis: Clinical Theory and Practice, 1991; editor: Selected Writings of Bertram D. Lewin; editor-in-chief Psychoanalytic Quar., 1970-79; mem. editl. bd. Psyche. Vice pres. Great Neck (L.I.) Coop. Sch.; trustee, sec. N.Y. Psychoanalytic Inst., 1956-59. Recipient Heinz Hartmann award, 1980; Lenox Hill Disting. Clinicians award, 1980; Vexillarius Excellentae award Pride of Judea Mental Health Ctr. Mem. AMA, Am. Psychoanalytic Assn. (pres. 1960-61, chmn. COPE 1962-66, bd. editors jours. 1958-60, chmn. bd. profl. standards 1967-70, Jour. award 1988); mem. Internat. Soc. Study of Time (coun.), Am. Coll. Psychoanalysts (Mary S. Sigourney award 1990, Henry Loughlin award 1991), Am. Psychiat. Assn., Psychosomatic Soc., N.Y. Psychoanalytic Inst. (pres. 1966-68), Internat. Psycho-Analytic Assn. (treas., v.p. 1961-69). Address: 94 Wildwood Rd Great Neck NY 11024-1223

ARM, JONATHAN PETER, physician; b. M'Tafa, Malta, Aug. 28, 1953; arrived in Eng., 1955; s. Donald Albert and Jeannie Roberts (Johnson) A.; m. Joy Caroline Hopping, Nov. 16, 1977; children: Jennifer, Hannah, Thomas. BA, Cambridge (Eng.) U., 1974, MA, 1978; MB, BS, London U., 1977, MD, 1990. Squadron leader RAF, Eng., 1974-84; med. officer RAF, Wattisham, Eng., 1979-80; specialist in medicine RAF Nolton Hall, Lincoln, Eng., 1980-82; sr. specialist RAF Hosp. Halton, Aylesbury, Bucks, Eng., 1982-84; rsch. asst. Guy's Hosp., London, 1985-88; lectr. UMDS United Med. and Dental Schs. Guy's and St. Thomas Hosps., London, 1990-92; rsch. fellow Harvard Med. Sch., Boston, 1988-90, asst. prof. in medicine, 1993—. Contbr. papers to profl. publs. Traveling fellow Med. Rsch. Coun., Harvard Med. Sch., 1988. Mem. AAAS, Am. Acad. Allergy and Immunology, Brit. Soc. Allergy and Clin. Immunology, Brit. Soc. Immunology, Royal Coll. Physicians. Office: Divsn Rheumatology and Immunology Brigham and Womens Hosp Boston MA 02115

ARMALY, MANSOUR F(ARID), ophthalmologist, educator; b. Shefa Amer, Palestine, Feb. 25, 1927; came to U.S., 1955, naturalized, 1965; s. Fareed M. and Fadwa M. (Bahouth) A.; m. Aida Makdisi, July 2, 1950; children: Raya, Fareed. B.A., Am. U., Beirut, 1947, M.D., 1952; M.Sc., U. Iowa, 1957. Diplomate: Am. Bd. Ophthalmology. Intern Am. U. Hosps., Beirut, Resident, 1952-55; research fellow U. Iowa, 1955-57, instr., 1957-58, asst. prof. ophthalmology, 1958-60, asso. prof., 1960-66, prof., 1966-70; prof., chmn. dept. ophthalmology George Washington U. Med. Center, 1970—; cons. in field; Univ. prof. U. Paraguay. Contbr. articles to profl. publs.; mem. editorial bd.: Investigative Ophthalmology, 1969-73, Ophthalmology Digest, 1971—; asso. editor: Archives Ophthalmology, 1970. Decorated knight Order of Cedars, Lebanon; recipient Alumni Gold Medal Am. U. Beirut; NIH grantee, 1957-69, 58-75, 58-63, 63-73, 68-73; Nat. Eye Inst. grantee, 1972, 73-76, 74-76. Fellow ACS, Internat. Coll. Surgeons; mem. AMA (Knapp award 1968, Hektoen Silver medal 1969, Merit award 1976), Am. Acad. Ophthalmology, Assn. for Research in Vision and Ophthalmology (Fight for Sight award 1966), Am. Ophthalmol. Soc., Internat. Glaucoma Com., Internat. Glaucoma Congress (Ann. Achievement award 1979), Pan Am. Glaucoma Soc. (pres. 1983-87), French Ophthalmologic Soc., Introcular Lens Implant Soc., Internat. Eye Found. Office: 2150 Pennsylvania Ave NW Washington DC 20037-2396

ARMBRISTER, DOUGLAS KENLEY, surgeon; b. Emory, Va., Feb. 20, 1934; s. Victor Stradley and Naomi Lucile (Byrd) A.; m. Nancy Sheri Douglas, Apr. 30, 1960 (div. Sept. 1995); children: Valere Lynn, Victor Kenley, Christopher Douglas, Karen Leigh. BA in English/German, BS in Chemistry/Biology, Emory and Henry Coll., 1955; MD, U. Va., 1959, MS in Surg. Rsch., 1962. Diplomate Am. Bd. Surgery. Intern in surgery U. Va., 1959-60, resident in surgery, 1960-62, 64-67; pvt. practice Marion, Va., 1967—; regional adv. group Va. Regional Med. Progarm, 1971; subarea coun. chmn. Southwest Va. PSBO, 1978-83; bd. dirs. Va. Health Quality Ctr.; pres. Smyth County Cmty. Hosp. Med Staff, 1973, chair surg. svcs., 1978—. Bd. visitors Emory and Henry Coll., 1982—. Capt. USAF, 1962-64. Fellow Am. Col. Surgeons: mem. Va. Surg. Soc. (malpractice review panel mem. 1972—), Med. Soc. Va. (review bd. dir. 1985-95, Southwest Va. Med. Soc., Muller Surg. Soc., Nat. Eagle Scout Assn., Blue Key Nat. Honor Soc. (pres. 1953). Methodist. Office: 590 Radio Hill Rd Marion VA 24354

ARMBRUSTER, PAULA, social work educator, university director; b. N.Y.C., June 30, 1935; d. William and Anna Bertha Armbruster; children: K. Levni, Elif-Lale A., Murat A. BA, U. Conn., 1956, MSW, 1974; MA, Yale U., 1964. Intelligence analyst Nat. Security Agy., Washington, 1956-62; clin. instr. social work Yale Child Study Center, Sch. Medicine, Yale U., New Haven, Conn., 1974-80, clin. asst. prof., 1980—, dir. social work tng., 1984—, dir. outpatient svcs., 1985—; fellow Pierson Coll., Yale U., 1976—; assoc. project dir. HEW tng. grant, asst. prof. residence U. Conn. Sch. Social Work, West Hartford, 1979-80; mem. adv. coun. U. Conn. Sch. Social Work, So. Conn. State U. Sch. Social Work; Johnson Wax fellow, vis. prof. U. Surrey (Eng.), 1984. Author, editor works in field. Chmn. regional adv. coun. Conn. Dept. Children and Youth Svcs., chmn. regional adv. couns.; bd. dirs. Cmty. and Family Svcs., YWCA, New Haven, Sylvan House, VISTA, New Haven Dept. Edn. Sch. Based Clinics Bd.; founder and bd. dirs. Leadership, Ednl. Partnership for Youth of New Haven; rep. of the Nat. Assn. Social Worker to the Nat. Consortium on Children's Mental Health Svcs., Washington, sec. 1993, pres.-elect 1995; mem. Yale Sch. Medicine Adv. Com. on Sch. Based Clinics, children and soc., Yale Child Study Ctr.; mem. manage care/med. oversight coun. Conn. Legis., chair quality assurance, 1995; nat. task force managed care implementation Western Pa.; nat. task force Sch. Bd. Mental Health Svcs. Western Pa.; expert adv. panel Office Adolescent Medicine. Mem. AAUP, Nat. Acad. Cert. Social Workers, Conn. Soc. Clin. Social Work, Nat. Assn. Social Workers (sec. Conn. chpt.), So. Conn. State U. Sch. Social Work, Mory's Assn., Yale Club, New Haven Lawn Club. Office: Yale Child Study Ctr 230 S Frontage Rd New Haven CT 06519-1124

ARMENTROUT, STEVEN ALEXANDER, oncologist; b. Morgantown, W.Va., Aug. 22, 1933; s. Walter W. and Dorothy (Gasch) A.; m. Johanna Ruszkay; children—Marc, Susan, Sandra, Nancy. A.B., U. Chgo., 1953, M.D., 1959. Intern U. Hosp., Cleve., 1959-60; resident in medicine, fellow Am. Cancer Soc. Western Res. U. Hosp., 1960-63; project dir. USPHS, 1963-65; asst. prof. Case Western Res. U. Med. Sch., 1965-71; mem. faculty U. Calif. Med. Sch., Irvine, 1971—; prof. medicine, chief divsn. hematology-oncology U. Calif. Med. Sch., 1978—, also dir. program in oncology.; pres. med. staff U. Calif.-Irvine Med. Ctr., 1983-85; researcher in multiple sclerosis. Mem. Am. Assn. Cancer Research, AAUP, ACP, Am. Cancer Soc. (chmn. bd. 1973, pres. Orange County chpt. 1985-86), AMA, Am. Soc. Clin. Oncology, Am. Soc. Hematology, Orange County Med. Assn., Am. Soc. Internal Medicine, Calif. Med. Assn., Cen. Soc. Clin. Research, Leukemia Soc. Am., Orange County Chief of Staff Council. Office: 101 City Blvd W Orange CA 92668-2901

ARMISTEAD, HAL WAYNE, osteopathic physician; b. Steubenville, Ohio, Dec. 30, 1954; s. George Rivers and Linda Stephanie (Ciotczyk) A.; m. Amelia Kathryn Roush, Sept. 5, 1981; 1 child, Shannon Ashley. AB, W.Va. U., 1977, W.Va. U., 1977; DO, W.Va. U., 1981; MHSA, U. Mich., 1996. Physician Oxford (Mich.) Ambulatory Care Ctr., 1982-84; pvt. practice Temperance, Mich., 1985-91, Bowling Green, Ohio, 1991-93; physician, asst. med. dir. Maumee (Ohio) Urgent Med. Care Ctr., 1991-96. Bd. dirs. ARC, Monroe, Mich., 1985-90, regional blood svcs. com., Lansing, Mich., 1985-90; bd. dirs. Am. Heart Assn., Wood County, Ohio, 1992-96, pres., 1995-96. Mem. Am. Osteopathic Assn., Am. Coll. Osteopathic Family Physicians (del. Ohio 1994), Mich. Assn. Osteopathic Physicians and Surgeons, W.Va. Soc. Osteopathic Medicine, Ohio Osteopathic Assn. (state del. 1995), Toledo Acad. Osteopathic Physicians & Surgeons (sec./treas. 1994-95), Am. Coll. Physician Execs. Home: 26520 Carrington Blvd Perrysburg OH 43551 Office: Maumee Urgent Care Ctr 1015 Conant St Maumee OH 43537

ARMISTEAD, WILLIS WILLIAM, university administrator, veterinarian; b. Detroit, Oct. 28, 1916; s. Eber Merrill and Josephine Brunell (Kindred) A.; m. Martha Sidney Clark, Sept. 17, 1938 (dec. 1964); children: Willis William, Jack Murray, Sidney Merrill; m. Mary Wallace Nelson, 1967. D.V.M., Tex. A&M Coll., 1938; M.Sc., Ohio State U., 1950; Ph.D., U. Minn., 1955. Diplomate: hon. diplomate; Am. Coll. Veterinary Surgeons, Am. Coll. Veterinary Preventive Medicine. Pvt. practice veterinary medicine, 1938-40; instr. Sch. Veterinary Medicine Tex. A&M U., 1940-42, asst. prof. to prof. Sch. Veterinary Medicine, 1946-53, dean Sch. Veterinary Medicine, 1953-57; dean Coll. Veterinary Medicine Mich. State U., East Lansing, 1957-74; dean Coll. Veterinary Medicine, U. Tenn., Knoxville, 1974-79, chmn. strategic planning adv. com., 1988-89; v.p. agr. U. Tenn. System, 1979-87; collaborator animal diseases and parasite rsch. divsn. Dept. Agr., 1954-65; cons., adviser commn. vetinary edn. of South So. Regional Edn. Bd., 1953-56; mem. gov.'s sci. adv. bd., 1958-60; nat. cons. to Air Force Surgeon Gen., 1960-62; mem. adv. coun. Inst. Lab. Animal Resources, NRC, 1962-66; pres. Assn. Am. Veterinary Med. Colls., 1964-65, 73-74, Spl. award, 1983; veterinary med. resident investigators selection com. U.S. VA, 1967-70; veterinary medicine rev. com. Bur. Health Professions Edn. and Manpower Tng., HEW, 1967-71; mem. Nat. Bd. Veterinary Med. Examiners, 1970-74; mem. adv. panel for veterinary medicine Inst. Medicine, NAS, 1972-74; mem. bd. agr. and renewable resources NRC, 1976-77; 1st Allam lectr. Am. Coll. Veterinary Surgeons, 1972; Conti Meml. keynote lectr. Ariz.-Calif.-Nev. Veterinary Conf., 1994. Contbg. author: Canine Surgery, rev. edit, 1957, Canine Medicine, rev. edit, 1959; editor: The N.Am. Veterinarian, 1950-56, Jour. Veterinary Med. Edn, 1974-80; assoc. editor: Jour. Am. Animal Hosp. Assn., 1964-70; contbr. tech. articles to profl. jours. Bd. dirs. Tenn. Farm bur. Fedn., 1979-87, Tenn. Coun. Coops., 1982-87, Tenn. 4-H Club Found., 1979-87, Tenn. Agrl. Hall of Fame, 1979-87; mem. Tenn. State Soil Conservation Com., 1979-87; mem. Southwide adv. com. So. Agribus. Forum, 1989-96. Maj. Vet. Corps AUS, 1942-46. Recipient Meritorious Svc. award Selective Svc. System, 1972; hon. alumnus Mich. State U., 1972; recipient Disting. Alumnus award Coll. Vet. Medicine, Tex. A&M U., 1980, 75th Anniversary Achievement award Tex. A&M U. Coll. Vet. Medicine, 1991; named V.P Emeritus, U. Tenn., 1987—. Mem. AAAS, U.S. Animal Health Assn., Am. Vet. Med. Assn. (pres. 1957-58, award 1977), Tex. Vet. Med. Assn. (pres. 1947-48), Mich. Vet. Med. Assn. (trustee Edn. and Sci. Trust 1970-74), Fedn. Assns. Schs. of Health Professions (pres. 1975), Tenn. Vet. Med. Assn. (Lifetime Achievement award 1995), Inst. Medicine of NAS, N.Y. Acad. Scis., Rotary (pres. 1987-88), Sigma Xi, Phi Kappa Phi, Alpha Zeta, Phi Zeta, Omega Tau Sigma (nat. Gamma award Ohio State U. 1962), Phi Eta Sigma, Gamma Sigma Delta, Omicron Delta Kappa. Episcopalian. Lodge: Rotary. Home: 1101 Cherokee Blvd Knoxville TN 37919-7852

ARMITAGE, DAVID TEMPLETON, physician, lawyer, consultant; b. Troy, N.Y.. BA, Muskingum Coll., 1961; MD, SUNY, Syracuse, 1965; JD, Augusta Law Sch., 1977. Bar: Ga. 1978, U.S. Dist. Ct. (so. dist.) Ga., 1978, U.S. Ct. Appeals (11th cir.) 1978, U.S. Ct. Appeals for the Armed Forces 1986, U.S. Supreme Ct. 1982; diplomate Am. Bd. Psychiatry and Neurology, Am. Bd. Family Practice, Am. Bd. Forensic Psychiatry. Commd. capt. U.S. Army, 1965, advanced through grades to col., 1980; chief child psychiatry U.S. Army Hosp., Frankfurt, Fed. Republic of Germany, 1970-73; chief dept. psychiatry U.S. Army Hosp., Ft. Gordon, Ga., 1973-74, chief cmty. med. health clinic, 1974-76; dir. psychiatric residency tng. Dwight David Eisenhower Army Med. Ctr., Ft. Gordon, Ga., 1976-80, chief dept. of psychiatry and neurology, 1980-84; chief divsn. of medico-legal rsch., dept. of legal medicine Armed Forces Inst. of Pathology, Washington, 1984-86, asst. chmn. profl. affairs dept. of legal medicine, 1986-87, assoc. dir., 1987-89, assoc. chmn. for forensic svcs., sr. medico-legal cons. dept. legal medicine, 1989-95; co-dir. Forensic Psychiatry Fellowship Program Walter Reed Army Med. Ctr., Washington, 1995—; cons. to surgeon gen. of the army in forensic psychiatry U.S. Army, Washington, 1982-92; prof. psychiatry Uniformed Svcs. Univ. of Health Scis., Bethesda, Md., 1984—; med. adv. U.S. Army Physical Disability Agy., Forest Glen, Md., 1995—. Author (with others) Legal Issues in Treating the Military Family, 1984; editor (with others) Legal Medicine: Legal Dynamics of Medical Encounters, 1988, edit., 1991; contbr. articles to profl. jours. Liaison Layhill Civic Assn. and Layhill Alliance, Silver Spring, Md., 1988. Decorated various mil. awards including Legion of Merit, Order of the Mil. Medal Merit Health Svcs. Command. Fellow Am. Acad. Child Psychiatry, Am. Psychiat. Assn., Am. Acad. Family Physicians; mem. Am. Acad. of Psychiatry and the Law (com. on children and law 1986-93).

ARMSTRONG, DAVID MILLAR, physiology educator, academic administrator; b. Workington, Cumbria, Eng., May 25, 1941; s. James and Jeannie Alexandra (Millar) A.; m. Lucinda Russell Kennedy, Aug. 12, 1964; children: Katharine Anne, James Graham. BA, Oxford (Eng.) U., 1963, BSc, 1965; PhD, Australian Nat. U., 1967. Lectr. in physiology U. Bristol, Eng., 1968-78, reader, 1978-84, prof., 1984—, dept. chair, 1990-95; bd. dirs. neuroscis. U.K. Med. Rsch. Coun., 1987-91. Editor: LocoMotor Neural Mechanisms in Arthropods and Vertebrates, 1991; mem. editorial bd. Jour. of Physiology, 1979-86. Med. Rsch. Coun. grantee, Wellcome Trust grantee, Action Rsch. grantee, Royal Soc. grantee. Mem. Physiol. Soc., Marine Biol. Assn., European Neurosci. Assn., Brain Rsch. Assn. Mem. Labour Party. Office: U BristolDept Physiology, University Walk, Bristol BS 8 1TD, England

ARMSTRONG, DAVID WILLIAM, biotechnologist, microbiologist; b. Ottawa, Ont., Can., Jan. 29, 1954; s. Robert Crosby Armstrong and Margaret Theresa (Larose) Shepherd; m. J. Elaine Robertson, June 10, 1978; 1 child, Laura Lynne. BSc with honors, U. Ottawa, Ontario, Can., 1978, MSc, 1980; PhD, Carleton U., Ottawa, 1984. Rsch. scientist Nat. Rsch. Coun., Ottawa, 1979—, head Tissue Regeneration Lab., 1985—; advisor Biotech. and Biomedicine, Canadian Space Agy., Ottawa, 1985-88. Named Ontario scholar, 1973; recipient Ontario Grad. scholarship, 1978-80. Mem. Can. Coll. Microbiologist (registered specialist), Tissue Culture Assn. Mem. United Ch. Office: Nat Rsch Coun, 1200 Montreal Rd, Ottawa, ON Canada K1A 0R6

ARMSTRONG, EDWARD BRADFORD, JR., oral and maxillofacial surgeon, educator, naval officer; b. Teaneck, N.J., Sept. 24, 1928; s. Edward Bradford and Ruth Elizabeth (Fippinger) A.; AB, U. Pa., 1950; DDS, N.Y.U., 1954; m. Dusanka Vladimirovna Jakovljevic, Nov. 5, 1960; children: Edward Bradford, III, James B., Hugh B. Commd. lt. j.g. U.S. Navy, 1954, advanced through grades to capt. 1971; intern oral surgery Roosevelt Hosp., N.Y.C., 1958, assoc. attending oral surgery, 1959—, attending oral surgeon out-patient dept., 1959—, chmn., moderator Oral Surgery Staff Confs., 1963-70; resident Carle Hosp., Urbana, Ill., 1959; assoc. attending oral surgeon Flower and Fifth Ave. hosps., N.Y.C., 1960-78; asst. attending oral surgeon Hackensack (N.J.) Hosp., 1963-65; adminstrv. officer Naval Res. Dental Co. 3-2, 1965-68, exec. officer, 1968-71, comdg. officer, 1971-73; comdt.'s rep. 3d Naval Dist., Naval Acad., 1972-78, 3d Naval Dist for Dentistry, 1973-75, group staff officer for dentistry and medicine, 1973-75, Ready Res. Unit 502, 1975-77, VTU 0207, 1977-79, ret., 1979; assoc. clin. prof. oral surgery N.Y. Med. Coll., 1963-93; adj. assoc. clin. prof. oral surgery Columbia U. Sch. Dentistry, 1973-89; chmn. bd. E. & R. Armstrong, Inc., Albany, N.Y., 1966-77; pres. Edward B. Armstrong, P.C., N.Y.C., 1979-90; dir. Songtime, Inc., Boston; dir., mem. exec. com. PGP Internat. Corps, Inc. Bd. dirs., trustee Christian Mission Farms of Paraguay, Inc., 1974-84; pres., trustee Central Bible Chapel, Palisades Park, N.J.; area rep., ann. giving U. Pa., 1960-68; Blue and Gold officer Naval Acad. Admissions Com.; sec. bd. dirs., trustee Boys' Club of N.Y. Health Svcs., Inc. Diplomate Am. Bd. Oral Surgery. Fellow N.Y. Acad. Dentistry (sec., dir., pres. 1979-80), Am., Internat. Colls. Dentists (life), Am. Coll. Oral and Maxillofacial Surgeons (founding), Am. Dental Soc. Anesthesiology (hon. life); mem. ADA (life, 1st dist. life), Am. Assn. Oral and Maxillofacial Surgeons (life, N.J. rep. Ho. of Dels. 1963-65), N.Y. Soc. Oral Surgeons (life, chmn. audit and budget com. 1972-79), First Dist. Dental Soc. (life), N.Y. Dental Soc., Bklyn. Dental Soc., Yokosuka Dental Soc. (hon.), Assn. Mil. Surgeons U.S., Mil. Order World Wars, Naval Res. Assn. (life), Union League (chmn. art com. 1973-76, bd. govs. 1974-77, 82-84, v.p. 1977-80, 85-88), Met. Club (bd. gov. 1992), N.Y.C., U. Pa. Club, U. Pa. Club of Met. N.J. (dir. 1982—), Acacia, Xi Psi Phi, Psi Omega (hon.),

Delta Sigma Delta. Mem. Plymouth Brethren Ch. Home: 110 Broad Ave Leonia NJ 07605-2003

ARMSTRONG, FRANK THEODORE, nuclear medicine technologist; b. Lynn, Mass., Aug. 4, 1967; s. James Francis Sr. and Myra Ethel (Giakoumis) A.; m. Sheryl Lee Keating, July 31, 1993. BA in Biology cum laude, Curry Coll., 1989; cert. nuclear medicine technologist, Salem State Coll., 1991; postgrad., U. New Eng. Coll. Osteopathic Medicine, 1993—. Cert. nuc. medicine technologist. Nuclear medicine technologist Salem (Mass.) Hosp., 1989-93, pathology asst., 1990-93; nuclear medicine technologist York (Maine) Hosp., 1993—; nuclear medicine technologist Mediq Imaging Svcs., North Andover, Mass., 1993—, Holter monitor technologist, 1995—; tchg. asst. UNECOM, Biddeford, Maine, 1994. Walkathon team leader Am. Cancer Soc., Salem, 1992; coord. Physicians for Social Responsibility, Biddeford, 1994. Neuroanatomy fellow UNECOM, 1995. Mem. Am. Coll. Gen. Practitioners, Am. Med. Student Assn., Am. Registry Radiologic Technologists, Student Osteopathic Surg. Assn., Undergrad. Am. Acad. Osteopathy. Home: 204 Pool St Unit # 5 Biddeford ME 04005 Office: U New Eng Coll Osteo Medicine 11 Hills Beach Rd Biddeford ME 04005

ARMSTRONG, JOANNE MARIE, clinical and consulting psychologist, business advisor, mediator; b. Cooperstown, N.Y., Nov. 26, 1956; d. William John and Joan Alice (Larsen) A.; m. Brian Joseph Yore, July 31, 1983; children: Mackensie A., Campbell A. BA, Trinity U., San Antonio, 1978; MA, U. Louisville, 1982, PhD, 1987. Lic. psychologist Wis., S.C. Mgmt. positions in ops., adminstrn. and purchasing Gentec Hosp. Supply Co., San Antonio and Dallas, 1978-79; rsch. asst. U. Louisville, 1980-81; therapist Seven Counties Svcs., Louisville, 1981-82; mental health profl. Head Start, Louisville, 1982-83; psychology intern Dallas VA Med. Ctr./Dallas Ghild Guidance Clinic, 1983-84; dir. Kaufman County Outreach Clinic, Tex. Dept. Mental Health-Mental Retardation, Terrell, 1984-85; clin. psychologist Nicolet Clinic/La Salle Clinic, S.C., Menasha, Wis., 1987-89; pvt. practice, Neenah, Wis., 1989-93; pvt. practice Spartanburg and Greenville, S.C., 1993—; founder Advisors to Bus. and Profls., 1995—; cons. Wellness Counseling Ctr., Appleton, Wis., 1989-93, Fox Valley Hosp., Green Bay, Wis., 1990-91, Brownell Ctr., Greenville, S.C., 1993—, Greenville Hosp. Sys. Mem. bd. Birthing Network, Neenah, 1988-93; mem. Citizens for Better Environ., Neenah, 1989-93. Rsch. fellow U. Louisville, 1985-86. Mem. APA, Nat. Register Health Svc. Providers in Psychology, S.C. Psychol. Assn., S.C. Assn. Profl. Psychologists, Family Firm Inst., Acad. Family Mediators, S.C. Coun. Mediation and Alt. Dispute Resolution, Upstate Mediation Network. Episcopalian. Office: 390 E Henry St Ste 206 Spartanburg SC 29302-2659 also: 330 Pelham Rd Ste 103B Greenville SC 29615-3111

ARMSTRONG, JOY DOROTHY, psychotherapy educator; b. New Haven, Aug. 15, 1935; d. John and Charlotte (Brokks) A. BA, Hood Coll., 1957; MA, U. Chgo., 1959. Lic. clin. social worker, Calif. Field work asst. prof. Sch. Social Service Adminstrn. U. Chgo., 1963-74; ctr. dir., psychiat. social worker North County Treatment Ctr., Palo Alto, Calif., 1974-79; psychiat. social worker West Valley Treatment Ctr., Los Gatos, Calif., 1979—; instr. West Valley Coll., Los Gatos, 1980—, San Jose (Calif.) Community Coll., 1980—; pvt. practice psychotherapist, cons., Los Gatos, 1978—; cons. Robert T. Dorris and Assocs. Inc., Van Nuys, Calif., Chem. Dependency INst., Campbell, Calif., 1985-86; seminar leader Seminars for Adult Children of Alcoholics, Los Gatos, 1985—l guest lectr. Kids are Spl., Cupertino, Calif., 1986. Mem. Nat. Assn. Social Workers, Calif. Assn. Marriage and Family Therapists, Assn. Labor-Mgmt. Adminstrs. and Cons. on Alcoholism Inc., Nat. Council on Alcoholism, Nat. Assn. Adult Children of Alcoholics, Physicians for Social Responsibility, San Jose C. of C. Women in Bus.

ARMSTRONG, LILLIAN M., clinical counselor; b. Caguas, P.R., Mar. 27, 1946; d. Victor and Maria C. (Martinez) Soto; m. Daniel B. Armstrong, June 7, 1964; children: Daniel B. II, Ann Marie. AA, AS, Miami Dade Community Coll., Miami, Fla., 1981; BS, Fla. Internat. U., 1984; MS, Barry U., 1986. Cert. adult edn. tchr., Fla. Clin. counselor Metatherapy Inst., Homestead, Fla.; adult edn. tchr. Dade County Pub. Sch., Homestead, Fla.; chem. dependency therapist Archdioses of Miami, St. Luke's Ctr., Miami; pvt. practice clin. therapist Inst. of Psychology, Coral Gables, Fla.; counselor, interventionist with at risk students and family Circles of Care, Inc., Melbourne, Fla.; dir. social svcs. Hacienda Girls Ranch, Melbourne, Fla.; clin. case mgr. Children Psychiatric Hosp., Palm Bay, Fla.; adult edn. tchr. Brevard County Pub. Schs., Melbourne, Fla. Named NCO Wife of the Month. Mem. Fla. Internat. U. Alumni Assn., Barry U. Alumni Assn. Home: PO Box 34037 Indialantic FL 32903-0937

ARMSTRONG, PETER, radiologist; b. London, Aug. 31, 1940; s. Alexander and Ada (Lapidas) A.; m. Carole Jennifer Gray, July 22, 1967; children: Damon (dec. 1972), Natasha, Jethro. MB BS, London U., 1962. Registrar in radiology Middlesex Hosp., London, 1964-66, sr. registrar in radiology, 1966-68; sr. registrar in radiology Guy's Hosp., London, 1968-70; cons. radiologist King's Coll. Hosp., London, 1970-77; prof. radiology U. Va., 1977-89; prof. radiology St. Bartholomew's Hosp., London, 1989—, clin. dir., 1990—. Author: (textbooks) Imaging of Diseases of the Chest, 1989, 2d edit., 1995, Diagnostic Imaging, 1989, 3d edit., 1994; editor: Critical Problems in Diagnostic Radiology, 1982; editor-in-chief Clinical Radiology, 1990-94. Fellow Royal Coll. Radiologists (warden 1994—). Office: St Bartholomew's Hosp, Acad Dept Radiology, London EC1A 7BE, England

ARMSTRONG, ROBERT BEALL, physiologist; b. Hastings, Nebr., Nov. 13, 1940; s. Edwin Ollis and Elena (Beall) A.; m. Ingrid Elizabeth Vaiciulenas, Apr. 9, 1966; children: Edwin John, Andrew Niel, Sarah Elizabeth. BA, Hastings Coll., 1962; MS, Wash. State U., 1970, PhD, 1973. Asst. prof. biology Boston U., 1973-78; assoc. prof. physiology Oral Roberts U., Tulsa, Okla., 1978-81, prof. physiology, 1981-85; prof. U. Ga., Athens, 1985-90, rsch. prof., 1990-92; Omar Smith prof., head dept. health and kinesiology Tex. A&M U., College Station, 1992—, Omar Smith chair, 1995—; disting. prof., 1995—; assoc. zoology Harvard U., Cambridge, Mass., 1977-87; external examiner Nat. U. Singapore, 1984-85; rsch. com. Am. Heart Assn., Athens, 1987-89. Assoc. editor Med. Sci. Sports Exercise, Indpls., 1985-87; contbr. articles to Jour. Applied Physiology, Am. Jour. Physiology. NSF fellow, 1970-73; grantee NIH, 1975—, Am. Heart Assn., 1981-89. Fellow Am. Coll. Sports Medicine (trustee 1986-88); mem. Am. Physiol. Soc. Office: Tex A & M U Dept Health & Kinesiology College Station TX 77843

ARMSTRONG, ROBERT BICKEL, internist; b. Parkersburg, W.Va., Jan. 28, 1933; s. Thomas Dorsey and Isabel (Holliday) A.; m. Joedy Lee Moreland, Aug. 25, 1956; children: Robert B. Jr., David B., Jennifer Lee. AB, W.Va. U., 1955; MD, Jefferson Med. Coll., Phila., 1959. Intern/resident in internal medicine U.S. Naval Hosp., Phila., 1959-63; fellow in gastroenterology Cleve. Clinic, 1967-68; pvt. practice internal medicine and gastroenterology Ohio Valley Gen. Hosp., Wheeling, W.Va., 1968-72; chief gastroenterology St. Joseph's Hosp., Phoenix, 1982-92; pvt. practice Physician's Profl. Corp., Phoenix, 1972-94; internist Ariz. State Hosp., Phoenix, 1994, Ariz. Managed Health Care, Peoria, Ariz., 1994—. Lt. comdr. USN, 1959-68. W. Va. U. Bd. Govs. scholar, 1950-54. Mem. ACP, AMA, Maricopa County Med. Soc., Am. Soc. Gastrointestinal Endoscopy, Alpha Epsilon Delta, Phi Alpha Theta, Alpha Kappa Psi, Alpha Omega Alpha. Episcopalian. Office: Family & Senior Care 13660 N 94th Dr #C2 Peoria AZ 85381-4836

ARMSTRONG, ROSA MAE, biologist; b. New Orleans, Apr. 9, 1937; d. Wilford Lloyd and Amelia Ann (Grayson) Christy; m. Willard Samuel Armstrong Jr., Dec. 24, 1958; 1 child, Anna Marie. BS, So. Univ, 1956; MA, U. Calif., Berkeley, 1958; PhD, U. Calif., San Francisco, 1965. Postdoctoral fellow Stanford (Calif.) U., 1965-67; lectr. anatomy U. Calif., San Francisco, 1967-73, asst. prof. anatomy, 1973-81; rsch. biologist Collagen Corp., Palo Alto, Calif., 1981-86, sr. rsch. biologist, 1986-91; sr. scientist Genetics Inst., Cambridge, Mass., 1992-94; sr. cons. Genetics Inst., Andover, Mass., 1995; prin. Rosa M. Armstrong Consulting, Cambridge, 1995—. Contbr. articles to profl. jours. Bd. dirs. United Way, Palo Alto, 1978-81; mem. Human Rels. Commn., Palo Alto, Stanford, 1978-81.

ARN, KENNETH DALE, physician, city official; b. Dayton, Ohio, July 19, 1921; s. Elmer R. and Minna Marie (Wannagat) A.; m. Vivien Rose Fontini, Sept. 24, 1966; children—Christine H. Hulme, Laura P. Hafstad, Kevin D., Kimmel R. B.A., Miami U., Oxford, Ohio, 1943; M.D., U. Mich., 1946. Intern Miami Valley Hosp., Dayton, Ohio, 1947-48; resident in pathology U. Mich., 1948-49, fellow in renal research, 1949-50; fellow in internal medicine Cleve. Clinic, 1950-52; pvt. practice specializing in internal medicine, pub. health and vocat. rehab. Dayton, 1952—; commr. of health City of Oakwood, Ohio, 1953—; assoc. clin. prof. medicine Wright State U., 1975—; mem. staffs Kettering Med. Ctr., Dayton, Miami Valley Hosp.; adj. assoc. prof. edn. Wright State U.; field med. cons. Bur. Vocat. Rehab., 1958—, Bur. Svcs. to Blind, 1975—; med. dir. Ohio Rehab. Svcs. Commn., 1979-87; mem. Pres.'s Com. on Employment of Handicapped, 1971—; chmn. med. adv. com. Goodwill Industries, 1960-75, chmn. bd. trustees 1985-87, chmn. rehab. com. 1987—; mem., chmn. lay adv. com. vocat. edn. Dayton Pub. Schs., 1973-82; exec. com. Gov.'s Com. on Employment Handicapped; bd. dirs. Vis. Nurses Assn. Greater Dayton; chmn. profl. adv. com. Combined Gen. Health Dist. Montgomery County. Trustee Luth. Social Svc. of Miami Valley, 1982-88. Named City of Dayton's Outstanding Young Man, Jr. C. of C., 1957; 1 of 5 Outstanding Young Men of State, Ohio Jr. C. of C., 1958; Physician of Yr., Pres.'s Com. on Employment of Handicapped, 1971; Bishop's medal for meritorious service Miami U., 1972. Mem. AMA, Ohio Med. Assn., Montgomery County Med. Soc. (chmn. com. on diabetic detection 1955-65, chmn. polio com. 1954-58), Nat. Rehab. Assn., Am. Diabetes Assn., Am. Profl. Practice Assn., Am. Heart Assn., Am. Pub. Health Assn., Ohio Pub. Health Assn., Aerospace Med. Assn., Fraternal Order Police, Dayton Country Club, Kiwanis, Royal Order Jesters, Masons (past potentate), Shriners, K.T., Scottish Rite (33 deg.), Nu Sigma Nu, Sigma Chi. Lutheran. Home: 167 Lookout Dr Dayton OH 45409-2238 Office: 30 Park Ave Dayton OH 45419-3426

ARNAOUT, M. AMIN, internist, educator; b. Sidon, Lebanon, Aug. 8, 1949; came to U.S., 1976; s. Aladdin A. and Insaf B. (Kobtan) A.; m. Amal I. Kawa, Feb. 14, 1975; children: Ramy, Rima. BS in Biology, Am. U. Beirut, 1969, MD, 1974. Diplomate Am. Bd. Internal Medicine, Nephrology. Fellow in nephrology Johns Hopkins U., Balt., 1976; fellow immunology Children's Hosp./Harvard Med. Sch., Boston, 1976-78; fellow in nephrology Brigham & Women's Hosp./Harvard Med. Sch., Boston, 1979-80; instr., asst. prof., assoc. prof. medicine Harvard Med. Sch., Boston, 1980-96; prof. medicine Harvard Med. Sch./Mass. Gen. Hosp., Boston, 1996—; dir. inflammation program Mass. Gen. Hosp., Boston, 1993—; prin. investigator NIH, Bethesda, 1983—, program project dir., 1989—. Patentee in field; contbr. numerous articles to profl. jours. Mem. Assn. Am. Physicians, Am. Assn. Immunology, Am. Soc. Nephrology, Am. Soc. Clin. Investigation. Office: Mass Gen Hospital Bldg 149 & 13th St Charlestown MA 02129

ARNASON, BARRY GILBERT WYATT, neurologist, educator; b. Winnipeg, Man., Can., Aug. 30, 1933; s. Ingolfur Gilbert and Elsie (Wyatt) A.; m. Joan Frances Morton, Dec. 27, 1961; children—Stephen, Jon, Eva. M.D., U. Man., 1957. Intern Winnipeg Gen. Hosp., 1956-57, resident in medicine, 1957-58; resident in neurology Mass. Gen. Hosp., Boston, 1958-62; asst. prof. neurology Harvard Med. Sch., Boston, 1965-71, assoc. prof., 1971-76; prof., chmn. dept. neurology U. Chgo. Pritzker Sch. Medicine, 1976—, dir. Brain Research Inst., 1985-94; mem. med. adv. bd. Nat. Multiple Sclerosis Soc., 1977—, Amyotrophic Lateral Sclerosis Soc. Am., 1976-79, Hereditary Disease Found., 1977-85. Contbr. articles to med jours. Nat. Multiple Sclerosis Soc. rsch. fellow, 1959-61, 62-64; grantee NIH, other founds. Mem. Am. Soc. Clin. Investigation, Am. Assn. Immunology, Am. Neurol. Assn., Am. Acad. Neurology, Am. Assn. Neuropathology, Soc. Neurosci. Home: 4832 S Ellis Ave Chicago IL 60615-1810

ARNAUD, AXEL, surgeon; b. Marseille, France, Mar. 21, 1955; s. Jean and Marianne (Petitjean) A.; m. Nicole Lusinchi, Oct. 30, 1984; children: Fanny, Francois. MD, Faculty Medicine, Marseille, France, 1984. Asst., chief clinic chirurgicale CHU de Marseille, 1984-88, cons. surgeon, 1988—; dir. R & D Ethicon France, Paris, 1992—, also bd. dirs.; mem. coun. R & D dirs. Johnson and Johnson. Patentee in field. Home: 194 Blvd Bineau, 92200 Neuilly France Office: 192 Ave Charles de Gaulle, 92200 Neuilly France

ARNAUD, CLAUDE DONALD, JR., physician, educator; b. Hackensack, N.J., Dec. 4, 1929; s. Claude Donald and Alice Marie (Minnet) A.; m. Deborah Krupp; children: Claude Michael, Ellen Marie. B.A., Columbia Coll., 1951; M.D., N.Y. Med. Coll., 1955. Intern St. Luke's Hosp., N.Y.C.; also resident and endocrine fellow Milwaukee County Hosp.; fellow U. Wis.; instr. biochemistry U. Pa., 1959-66; cons. dept. endocrine research Mayo Clinic, Rochester, Minn., 1967-77; head mineral research unit Mayo Clinic, 1972-74, head endocrine research unit, mineral research lab., 1974-77, assoc. prof. medicine Grad. Sch. Medicine, 1970-74, prof., 1974-77; prof. medicine and physiology U. Calif., San Francisco, 1977—; chief endocrine unit San Francisco VA Med. Ctr., 1977-89, chief div. gerontology and geriatric medicine, 1989-91, dir. Ctr. for Biomed. Rsch. on Aging, 1989-91, dir. program osteoporosis and bone biology, 1991—. Contbr. numerous articles to profl. jours. Served with M.C. U.S. Navy, 1957-59. NIH grantee, 1968—. Fellow AAAS, Am. Coll. Endocrinologists, Am. Assn. Clin. Endocrinologists; mem. NAS (com. on diet, health and chronic disease 1985-88), NIH (musculoskeletal study sect. 1985-89), Am. Fedn. Clin. Rsch., Am. Soc. Biol. Chemists, Am. Soc. Clin. Investigation, Am. Physiol. Soc., Assn. Am. Physicians, Endocrine Soc., Western Assn. Physicians, Am. Soc. Bone Mineral Rsch. (past pres.), Nat. Rsch. Coun.

ARNELL, RICHARD ANTHONY, radiologist; b. Chgo., Aug. 21, 1938; s. Tony Frank and Mary Martha (Oberman) Yaki; BA (Younker Achievement scholar), Grinnell Coll., 1960; MD, U. Iowa, 1964; m. Paula Ann Youngberg, June 28, 1964; children: Carla Ann, Paula Marie, Paul Anthony. With Innc., 1968—, v.p., 1970-78, sec., 1978-90, pres., 1990—, trustee pension and profit plan, 1979—; pres. Moline Radiology Assocs., S.C., 1990-93, Advanced Radiology, S.C., 1993—; mem. staff Luth. Hosp., Moline, 1968-88, dir. continuing med. edn. program for physicians, 1979-83, bd. dirs., 1977-83; mem. staff Moline Pub. Hosp., 1968-88, Hammond-Henry Dist. Ill., Geneseo, Ill., United Med. Ctr., 1989-92, chmn. radiology dept. United Med. Ctr., 1989-92; mem. staff Trinity Med. Ctr., 1992, chmn. radiology dept., 1992-94, med. dir. radiology dept., 1992—; pres. Moline Radiology Assocs., Inc., 1990-93; pres. Advanced Radiology, S.C., 1993—; trustee Midstate Found. for Med. Care, 1975-79, exec. com., 1976-79; v.p. Quad City HMO Health Plan, 1979; clin. lectr. U. Iowa, 1980—; pres. med. staff, dir. Quad City MRI Inc., 1988-89; pres. Moline Mgmt. Assocs., Inc., 1990—; chmn. mng. com. Metro MRI Ctr., Ltd. Partnership. Supt. Sunday Ch. Sch. St. John's Luth. Ch., Rock Island, Ill., 1974-79, mem. ch. cabinet, 1975-76; del. Chs. United of Scott and Rock Island counties, Ill., 1977; mem. nat. exec. com. Augustana Coll., Rock Island, Ill., 1977-81; assoc. chmn. profl. div. United Way, 1985; bd. dirs. Luth. Hosp. Found., 1981-84, pres., 1982-84; bd. dirs. Quad Cities Health Care Resources, Inc., 1984-88; chmn. Luth. Health Care Found., 1984-88, chmn. United Health Care Found., 1984-88, 1989-91. Recipient David Theophillus trophy for outstanding athlete Grinnell Coll., 1960; diplomate Am. Bd. Radiology, Am. Bd. Nuclear Medicine. Mem. Am. Coll. Radiology, Ill. Radiol. Soc., Am. Coll. Nuclear Medicine, Soc. Nuclear Medicine, AMA, Ill. (ho. of dels. 1974-79), Rock Island County (exec. com. 1974-79, peer-rev. com. 1975-79), Iowa-Ill. Central (pres. 1978) med. socs., Central Ill. Med. Assn. (v.p. 1977, pres. 1978), Ind. Physicians Assn. Western Ill. (dir. 1984-86, v.p. 1985, pres. 1986), World Med. Assn., Am. Coll. Med. Imaging., Short Hills Country Club. Home: 3904 7th Ave Rock Island IL 61201-2246 Office: 1505 7th St Moline IL 61265-2918

ARNER, LINDA ANN, geriatrics nurse; b. Butler, Pa., Jan. 16, 1952; d. Wycliffe Emerald and Lida Blanche (Zeitler) King; m. James L. Arner, Jan. 7, 1984; children: Christopher, Melissa. ADN with high honors, Community Coll. Allegheny Co., Pitts., 1977; BSN, Slippery Rock (Pa.) U., 1986; postgrad., Pa. State U., 1992—. Cert. gerontol. nurse. Staff nurse Titusville (Pa.) Hosp., 1977-81, Biomed. Applications of Butler, 1981-86, Hillcrest Nursing Ctr., Grove City, Pa., 1986-88, Butler VA Med. Ctr., 1988—.

ARNETT, EUGENE WILLIAM, medical facility administrator; b. Marshfield, Wis., Dec. 9, 1932; married. BS, U. Wis., 1955; M Health Care Adminstrn., U. Iowa, 1961. Adminstrv. intern Milw. County Med. Complex, 1960-61; pres. Meml. Hosp. of Taylor County, Medford, Wis., 1961—. Active various cmty. orgns. Recipient various awards in field. Fellow Am. Coll. Health Care Execs.; mem. Am. Hosp. Assn. (del. 1972-79, mem. com. 1972-79, bd. dirs. 1983-86, chmn.-elect 1987, chmn. 1988), Wis. Hosp. Assn. (bd. dirs. 1966-71, del. 1979-82, pres. 1970), Joint Commn. on Health Care Orgns. (bd. dirs. 1984-87, bd. dirs. 1990-92), Tri-State Hosp. Assn. (pres. 1974, bd. dirs. 1969-76). Office: Meml Hosp of Taylor County 135 S Glasgow St Medford WI 54451*

ARNHEIM, DANIEL LESLIE, psychologist; b. Pitts., Mar. 6, 1948; s. Richard Herman and Edith Libby (Levenson) A.; BS, U. Pitts., 1970; MS, Fla. State U., 1972, PhD, 1974; m. Barbara Ann Nuttridge, Dec. 6, 1969; children: Steven Paul, Michelle Ann. Clin. psychologist Fla. State Hosp., Chattahoochee, 1971; with Vocat. Rehab., Tallahassee, 1971-73; staff Regional Rehab. Center, Fla. State U., 1972-73; staff psychologist Spring Grove Hosp. Center, Balt., 1973—; cons.; prof. Essex C.C., 1981—, C.C. Balt., 1976—, Anne Arundel C.C., 1975-79, Loyola Coll., 1974-75, Catonsville C.C., 1976—; asst. prof. U. Md.-Baltimore County, 1983—; pvt. practice psychodiagnostics and therapy, 1975—; presentor workshops. Fla. State U. scholar, 1970-73; lic. psychologist, Md. Mem. Profl. Psychology Assn. Spring Grove Hosp. (pres. 1978-80), APA, Eastern Psychol. Assn., Balt. Psychol. Assn. (sec. 1984-85), Phi Kappa Phi. Editor Polaris, 1969-70; contbr. articles to profl. jours. Home: 10305 John Eager Ct Ellicott City MD 21042-1600 Office: 8 Sudbrook Ln Baltimore MD 21208-4135 also: 1101 N Calvert St Ste 201 Baltimore MD 21202

ARNHEIM, FALK KANTOR, physician; b. Pitts., June 18, 1917; s. Raymond F. and Bessie (Kantor) A.; m. Marian Louise Lambie, Nov. 17, 1943; children: David, Daniel, Louise. BS, U. Pitts., 1939, MD, 1943. Diplomate Am. Bd. Urology. Intern St. Francis Hosp., Pitts., 1943-44; resident in surgery Montefiore Hosp., Pitts., 1944; resident in urology Michael Reese Hosp., Chgo., 1947-50; mem. staff Montefiore Hosp., Pitts., 1950—, Passavant Hosp., Pitts., 1955-60, St. Clair Meml. Hosp., Pitts., 1955—; cons. urology Nat. Splty. Rev. Svc., Pitts., 1986—; mem. staff West Pa. Hosp., Pitts., 1970-80. Capt. U.S. Army, 1944-46, CBI. Fellow ACS; mem. AMA, Am. Urol. Assn., Am. Assn. Clin. Urologists. Office: 1050 Bower Hill Rd Pittsburgh PA 15243-1800

ARNOLD, CHARLES BURLE, JR., psychiatrist, epidemiologist, writer; b. Seattle, Aug. 13, 1934; s. Charles Burle and Ruth Helene (Hadley) A.; m. Sarah J. Slagle, Dec. 16, 1972; children: Geoffrey, Christopher, Jonathan. B.S. cum laude, U. Puget Sound, 1956; M.D., C.M., McGill U., 1960; M.P.H., U. N.C., 1965. Diplomate: Am. Bd. Preventive Medicine. Intern U. Wash. Hosp., Seattle, 1960-61; resident U. Wash. Hosp., 1961; physician Peace Corps, Bolivia, Washington, 1961-64; asst. prof. health adminstrn., asso. Carolina Population Center, U. N.C., Chapel Hill, 1965-69; asst. prof. Albert Einstein Coll. Medicine, Bronx, N.Y., 1969-72; prof. public adminstrn. and clin. assoc. prof. preventive medicine NYU, N.Y.C., 1972-83; adj. prof. pub. adminstrn. NYU, 1983—; med. dir., med. rels. Met. Life Ins. Co., 1983-91, v.p. med. rels., 1991-93; psychiat. resident North Shore Univ. Hosp., Manhasset, N.Y., 1993-96, chief resident, 1995-96; lectr. community health Mt. Sinai Med. Sch., N.Y.C., 1986-92; dir. Mahoney Inst. Health Maintenance, Am. Health Found., 1975-83, v.p. rsch., 1978-83, cons., 1983-86; chair Hitchcock Weekday Sch. Bd., 1986-92; chmn. Worksite Smoking subcom. N.Y. State Commn. on Smoking or Health, 1991-93. Editor, mem. exec. coun.: Transactions of Am. Acad. Ins. Medicine, 1988-93; assoc. editor Preventive Medicine Jour., 1975-83, sr. assoc. editor, 1983-85; editor Advances in Disease Prevention, 1981-83; editor-in-chief Statis. Bull., 1983-93; contbr. articles to profl. jours. Milbank Faculty fellow, 1967-74; OEO grantee, 1968-74; Population Council grantee, 1971-75; Health Research Council N.Y.C. grantee, 1972-75; Nat. Cancer Inst. grantee, 1975-83; Nat. Heart, Lung and Blood Inst. grantee, 1977-83; HEW Office Health Promotion grantee, 1978-80. Fellow Am. Coll. Preventive Medicine (pres. 1977-78); mem. N.Y. Acad. Medicine (com. on pub. health 1988—, vice chmn. 1992, chmn. 1993), Pan Am. Community Health Assn. (sec. 1971-77), Internat. AIDS Assn., Health Ins. Assn. Am. (chair com. on prevention and pub. health policy 1989-92). Home: 25 Forest Ln Scarsdale NY 10583-6403 Office: North Shore Univ Hosp 400 Community Dr Manhasset NY 11030-3815

ARNOLD, DAVID ALAN, surgeon; b. Sioux City, Iowa, Apr. 10, 1946; s. Allen and Mary Jean (Harjehausen) A.; m. Lana Beth Carlson, Sept. 11, 1971; children: Chad, Carl, Wade, Craig. BS, Morningside Coll., 1968; DO, Kirksville Coll. Osteo. Med., 1972. Intern Osteo. Hosp. of Maine, Portland, 1972-73; emergency rm. physician Bridgton (Mass.) Community Hosp., 1973; sr. med. officer Naval Air Sta., S. Weymouth, Mass., 1974-76; sr. flight surgeon Naval Air Sta., S. Weymouth, 1974-76; resident Des Moines (Iowa) Gen. Hosp., 1976-78; pvt. practice gen. surgery Davenport, Iowa, 1980—; med. dir. Quad City Regional Wound Care Ctr., Davenport, Iowa, 1995—; chmn. dept. surgery Davenport Med. Ctr., 1996; AMCCOM flight surgeon Rock Island (Ill.) Arsenal, 1986; founder Midwest Hernia Inst., Davenport, 1980—. Capt. USNR, 1990-91, Desert Shield/Desert Storm. Decorated Commendation medal Iowa Nat. Guard, 1980, Meritorious Svc. medal U.S. Army, 1984; named Flight Surgon of Yr., U.S. Army, 1984. Mem. Am. Osteo. Assn., Am. Coll. Osteo. Surgeons, Am. Soc. Abdominal Surgeons, Iowa Med. Soc., Scott County Osteo. Soc., Scott County Med. Soc. Office: Ste 430 1351 W Central Park Davenport IA 52804 also: Quad City Regional Would Care Ctr 3801 N Marquette St Davenport IA 52806

ARNOLD, JANET NINA, health care consultant; b. Poughkeepsie, N.Y., Apr. 23, 1933; d. Paul Dudley and Pauline Katherine (Board) Bartram; AB, Vassar Coll., 1955; postgrad. Sch. Med. Tech., Albany Med. Center, 1955-56; MS, Vassar Coll., 1963; MHSM, Webster Coll., 1981; m. Robert William Arnold, Dec. 19, 1954; children: Paul Dudley, Janet Elizabeth. Rsch. asst., med. technologist H. Aird Boswell, M.D., Troy, N.Y., 1956-59; teaching supr., adminstrv. cons. Vassar Bros. Hosp., Poughkeepsie, N.Y., 1959-69; adv. to med. lab., lectr. med. mycology Vassar Coll., Poughkeepsie, 1961-66; asst. adminstr., lab. mgr. Boulder (Colo.) Meml. Hosp., 1975-80; cons. hosp. planning Mercy Med. Center, Denver, 1981-82; clin. lab. dir./adminstr. Humana, 1982-85, cons. health care mgmt., 1982-85; with MRI, 1985—, ptnr., 1988; pres. Arnold and Assocs., 1992—; ptnr. InterExec (divsn. MRI), 1994—; acad./adminstrv. cons. U. Guam, Vassar Coll., Boulder Cmty. Hosp., Humana Int., 1990—, others. Sec., bd. dirs. Sanitas Fed. Credit Union, 1977-78, pres., 1979-82; teaching fellow Vassar Coll., 1961-63, unrestricted fund chmn., 1989-96. Contbr. NMC, 1988-92. NSF rsch. fellow, 1960-62. Mem. Am. Acad. Microbiology, Soc. for Gen. Microbiology, Am. Soc. Med. Technologists, Colo. Public Health Assn., Med. Mycological Soc. of the Ams. Republican. Episcopalian. Asso. editor Am. Jour. Med. Tech., 1980-88; contbr. articles to profl. jours. Home: 4195 Chippewa Dr Boulder CO 80303-3610

ARNOLD, JOHN HOWARD, cardiothoracic surgeon; b. Urbana, Ohio, Nov. 2, 1957; s. Russell G. and Zelpha M. (Faulkner) A.; m. Teresa M. Coon, Jan. 30, 1988; 1 child, Cyrus Levi. BA in Psychology, Case Western Res. U., Cleve., 1980; MS in Physiol. Chemistry, Ohio State U., 1982, MD, 1986. Resident gen. surgery Vanderbilt U. Med. Ctr., Nashville, 1986-92; resident cardiothoracic surgery U. Utah, Salt Lake City, 1992-94; attending cardiothoracic surgeon U. Cin., 1994-96; clin. assoc. dept. cardiothoracic surgery Cleve. Clinic Found., 1996—. Mem. AMA, Ohio Med. Assn., Cin. Med. Assn. Office: U Cin Divsn Cardiothoracic Surg 210 Bethesda ML 558 Cincinnati OH 45267

ARNOLD, KEVIN DAVID, psychologist, educational researcher; b. Massilon, Ohio, Jan. 7, 1957; s. Jack Olen and Arlene Adele (Harrold) A.; m. Cindi Englefield. BS, Grace Coll., 1979; MA, Ohio State U., 1981; advanced cert., Ctr. for Cognitive Therapy, N.Y., 1994, Atlanta Ctr. Cognitive Therapy, 1994. Diplomate Am. Bd. Med. Psychotherapists; lic. psychologist, Ohio; accredited divorce mediator Franklin County (Ohio) Ct. Common Pleas. Grad. rsch. assoc. Ohio State U., Columbus, 1980-83, rsch. assoc., 1983-84, prin. investigator deaf and blind project, 1984-94, asst. dir. Ctr. Spl. Needs Populations, 1988-93, asst. prof., 1988-92; psychologist Columbus, 1991—; dir. Ctr. for Cognitive and Behavioral Therapy Greater Columbus, 1990-95; founder, CEO Ohio Proficiency Test Rev., Inc., 1995—; v.p. Englefield & Arnold Pub., 1995—. Co-author: Passing the Ohio Proficiency Test, 1993, (test) Social Behavior Assessment Inventory, 1992; contbr. articles to profl. jours. Mem. adv. com. Teaching Rsch. Assistance to Children

Experiencing Sensory Impairments; fundraiser, cons. Dem. gubernatorial campaign, 1989-90, 1989-90. Deaf and Blind Ctr. grantee U.S. Dept. Edn., 1984-94, Sch. Psychology grantee, 1987-93, Evaluation Intervention Teams Ohio Dept. Edn. grantee, 1988-93, Drop-out Cost Study Ctr. Labor Rsch. grantee, 1990-91, Parent Satisfaction Study Ohio Devel. Disabilities Planning Coun. grantee, 1989-90, Tchr. Compentency Survey Study grantee, 1992-93. Mem. APA, Assn. for Advancement of Behavior Therapy, Acad. Family Mediators, Ohio Psychol. Assn. (mem. continuing edn. com.), Nat. Orgn. Legal Problems in Edn., Am. Psychology-Law Soc., Soc. Rsch. in Child Devel., Nat. Coun. Family Rels. Roman Catholic. Office: CCBT Ste E 2121 Bethel Rd Columbus OH 43220

ARNOLD, MARTIN LEON, biologist; b. Sumter, S.C., Sept. 19, 1959; s. Leon and Dorothy Adelle (Bramlett) A.; m. Cathy Faye McLeod, Aug. 15, 1981; children: Stacy Kaye, Justin Martin. AS, U. S.C., Sumter, 1979; BS, U. S.C., 1980. Cert. sr. reactor operator. Med. technician Tuomey Hosp., Sumter, S.C., 1977-81; records technician Richland Meml. Hosp., Columbia, S.C., 1979; instr. Sumter Tech. Edn. Ctr., Sumter, 1980; health physics technician Carolina Power & Light Co., Hartsville, S.C., 1981-85; reactor operator Carolina Power & Light Co., Hartsville, 1985—; cons. instr. Carolina Power & Light Co., Hartsville. Counselor Student Counselor Corp., 1978-80. Recipient Am. Legion scholarship, 1977, 79. Mem. Health Physics Soc., Am. Nuclear Soc., Profl. Reactor Operator Soc., Bishopville Rescue Squad (paramedic 1985—). Home: RR 1 Box 177 Mayesville SC 29104-9600 Office: Carolina Power & Light Co PO Box 790 Hartsville SC 29551-0790

ARNOLD, ROBERT, internist; b. Vancouver, Wash., Nov. 12, 1957; s. Stanley Arnold and Joan (Gleitsman) Huber; m. Nancy Levine, Dec. 5, 1996; children: Hillel, Shula, Brandon, Kirsten. Cert. med. ethics practicum, U. Tenn., Memphis, 1980; student, U. Tenn., Knoxville, 1981; BA in Biology and Philosophy, U. Mo., Kansas City, 1983, MD, 1983. Lic. physician, Pa.; diplomate Am. Bd. Internal Medicine. Gen. internal medicine resident R.I. Hosp., Providence, 1983-86; Robert Wood Johnson Found. clin. scholar U. Pa., Phila., 1986-88; fellow in pub. and health policy Kellogg Found., 1987; dir. clin. ethics tng. program U. Pitts. Sch. Medicine, 1988—, dir. fellowship in med. ethics, 1988—, asst. prof. divsn. gen. internal medicine, 1988-93, clin. coord. primary care internal medicine residency, 1990-93, asst. prof. dept. psychiatry, 1990—, assoc. dir. edn. Ctr. for Med. Ethics, 1992—, dir. Primary Care Residency Tng. Program, 1993-96, assoc. prof. medicine divsn. gen. internal medicine, 1994—, dir. ambulatory edn. divsn. gen. medicine; staff physician Pitts. AIDS Ctr. for Treatment; co-instr. U. Mo., Kansas City Sch. Medicine, 1980-81; grad. asst. U. Tenn., Knoxville, 1981; instr. Brown U. Program in Medicine, 1985; founder, co-dir. curriculum in med. ethics gen. internal medicine residency program R.I. Hosp., 1984-86; co-organizer, instr. ethics component of introduction to clin. medicine Brown U. Program in Medicine, 1985-86; instr. seminar in med. ethics U. Pa. Sch. Medicine, 1986-88; mem. data safety and monitoring bd. peripheral arterial disease-pilot study Nat. Heart, Lung and Blood Inst., 1993; abstractor APDIM Ednl. Clearinghouse Tchg. Med. Ethics, 1989—, Miles Annotated Bibliography Doctor-Patient Comm.-Med. Ethics, 1992; lectr. various univs., orgns., hosps.; mem. cons. ethics and human rights com. Presbyn. U. Hosp., 1988—, ethics cons., 1991—; preceptor summer premed. acad. enrichment program, 1991—; mem. faculty Ctr. for Med. Ethics Continung Edn. Program, 1992—; staff physician Rainbow Free Care Clinic, Pitts., 1992—. Author: (with C.W. Lidz and L. Fischer) The Erosion of Autonomy in Long-Term Care, 1992; mem. editl. bd. Jour. Gen. Internal Medicine, 1990-94; reviewer Am. Jour. Hosp. Pharmacy, Am. Jour. Medicine, Annals Internal Medicine, Archives Internal Medicine, Chest, Clin. Rsch., Digestive Diseases and Scis., Hastings Center Report, Jour. AMA, Jour. Am. Geriatrics Soc., Jour. Clin. Ethics, Jour. Gen. Internal Medicine, Kennedy Inst. Jour. Ethics, Milbank Meml. Quart., Oxford U. Press, Social Sci. and Medicine; contbr. articles to profl. jours., chpts. to books. Recipient Vice Chancellor award for outstanding cmty. svc., 1983, Mosby Book award, 1983; grantee Brown U., Providence, R.I., 1984-85, Pub. Health Svcs., DHHS, Washington, 1984, AIDS Commn., Phila., 1988, Richard K. Mellon Found., 1990, McArthur Found., 1989-90, Agy. for Health Care Policy Rsch., 1990-93, Nat. Ctr. for Nursing Rsch., 1992-95, HRSA, 1992, Greenwall Foudn., 1992, Agy. for Health Care Policy Rsch., 1993-97. Mem. ACP, APHA, Am. Acad. on Doctor and Patient, Am. Geriatric Soc. (legis. affairs com. Pa. chpt. 1992), Am. Fedn. Clin. Rsch., Am. Med. Women's Assn., Assn. Practical and Profl. Ethics, Carol F. Reynolds Hist. Soc., Physicians for Human Rights, Physicians for a Nat. Health Program, Physicians for Social Responsibility (mem. nat. bd. dirs. 1986-90, nat. treas. exec. com. 1989-90, mem. Pitts. steering com. 1988-91, chair 1990-91), Soc. Bioethics Consultation, Soc. Gen. Internal Medicine (mem. ethics com., co-chair 1994-95), Soc. Health and Human Values (resident interest group 1985-88, 1991-94, reviewer nat. meeting 1988-89, nat. program coord. 1991-92, treas., sec. 1990-92, coun. mem. 1989-92, pres.-elect 1996), Phi Kappa Phi, Omega Delta Kappa. Home: 854 Heberton Ave Pittsburgh PA 15206 Office: U Pitts Div Gen Int Med Montefiore U Hosp 9Wedicine 3459 5th Ave Pittsburgh PA 15213 also: Ctr Med Ethics Med Arts Bldg Ste 300 3708 5th Ave Pittsburgh

ARNOLD, ROBERT DON, medical clinic administrator; b. Odessa, Tex., Oct. 30, 1939; s. Paul G. and Genevieve (Bryan) A.; m. Barbara Sue, May 25, 1958; children: Scott Allen, Dayna Leanne. BA, Kans. State U., 1963. Acctg. clk. Gulf Oil Co., Morgan City, La., 1963-64; acct. Woods & Durham, CPA, Salina, Kans., 1964-65, Woods & Dunham, CPA, Beloit, Kans., 1965-68; dept. audit mgr. Blue Cross-Blue Shield, Tulsa, 1969-73; adminstr. Cooper Clinic, P.A., Ft. Smith, Ark., 1973-86, Murfreesboro (Tenn.) Med. Clinic, P.A., 1986-94; asst. v.p. med. practices Phoebe Putney Meml. Hosp., Albany, 1994—. Coun. mem. Cmty. Coun., Murfreesboro. Mem. Med. Group Mgmt. Assn. (Ark. pres. 1982, Nashville chpt. treas. 1988-89), Rotary. Home: 2510 Perth Ct Albany GA 31707-2014

ARNOLD, WATSON CAUFIELD, JR., pediatric nephrology physician; b. Waco, Tex., Jan. 12, 1945; s. Watson Caufield and Mary Rebecca (Maxwell) A.; m. Tricia Barr, Oct. 18, 1975; children: Thomas, Philip. BA, Tulane U., 1966; MD, U. Tex., Dallas, 1967. Diplomate Am. Bd. Pediatrics, Am. Bd. Pediatric Nephrology. Intern Med. Coll. Va., Richmond, 1970-71, resident in pediatrics, 1973-75; fellow U. Calif., San Francisco, 1975-76; from asst. to assoc. prof. of pediatrics U. Ark. Med. Sch., Little Rock, 1977-90; dir. pediatric nephrology Ark. Children's Hosp., Little Rock, 1978-90, med. dir. pediatric dialysis Unit, 1979-88, dir. transplantation, 1986-90, dir. renal sect. dept. pediatrics U. Ark. for Med. Scis., 1986-90, dir. metabolic div. dept. pediatrics, 1987-90; dir. pediatric nephrology Cook-Ft. Worth Children's Med. Ctr., 1990—. Assoc. editor: Pediatric Nephrology, London, 1990—; contbr. more than 80 articles to profl. jours. Pres. Nat. Kidney Found., Ark., Little Rock, 1985; bd. dirs. Nat. Kidney Found. of Tex., 1991—; mem. nat. ethics com. United Network Organ Sharing, 1989-92; bd. dirs. Ronald McDonald House, Ark; exec. com. mem. Camp Aldersgate, 1985-90, Ark. Regional Organ Recovery Agy., 1987-90; vice-chmn. Network X Coordinating Coun., 1980-81; mem. med. adv. com. Ark. Kidney Commn. State Dept. Rehab., 1978-90; pres. Cen. Ark. Pediatric Soc., 1985-86. Lt. USNR, 1971-73. Fellow Am. Acad. Pediatrics (exec. com. nephrology sect. 1986—, chmn. 1989-92, program co-dir. 1985-87); mem. Am. Inst. Nutrition, Am. Fedn. for Exptl. Biology, Am. Soc. for Clin. Nutrition, Am. Soc. for Parenteral and Enteral Nutrition, Am. Soc. Nephrology, Am. Fedn. Clin. Rsch., Am. Soc. Pediatric Nephrology (audit com. 1983), Am. Soc. Transplant Physicians, Internat. Soc. Pediatric Nephrology, So. Soc. for Pediatric Rsch., S.W. Pediatric Nephrology Study Group, Internat. Soc. Nephrology, Tex. Med. Soc., Tex. Soc. Pediatrics, Ft. Worth Pediatric Soc., Sigma Xi. Presbyterian. Home: 2412 Colonial Pky Fort Worth TX 76109-1031 Office: Cook/Ft Worth Childrens Ctr 801 W 7th St Fort Worth TX 76102-3510

ARNONE, THOMAS JOSEPH, osteopath; b. Rochester, N.Y., Mar. 14, 1960; s. Joseph Louis and Florence (Zaffuto) A.; m. Christine Bozzelli; children: Dominic, Gina. BS, SUNY, Fredonia, 1982; DO, N.Y. Coll. Osteo. Medicine/N.Y. Inst. Tech., 1986. Cert. family practice Am. Osteopathic Bd. Family Practice. From intern to resident in family medicine Delaware Valley Med. Ctr., Langhorne, Pa., 1986-88; pvt. practice osteo. medicine Rochester, 1988—; asst. prof. family medicine N.Y. Coll. Osteo. Medicine, Old Westbury, 1989—; med. dir. Lakeside Nursing Home, Brockport, N.Y., 1991—; clin. instr. family practice U. Rochester Sch. Medicine, 1992—. Active Rep. Nat. Com., Washington, 1992—. Fellow Rochester Acad. Medicine; mem. Am. Osteo. Assn., Am. Acad. Family Medicine, Monroe County Med. Soc. Roman Catholic. Office: 432 Hamlin Clarkson Tl Rd Hamlin NY 14464-9332

ARNOTT, ELLEN MARIE, medical case management and occupational health executive; b. Berwyn, Ill., Apr. 28, 1945; d. Howard Thomas and Catherine Marie (Stauber) Simon; m. John Michael Arnott, Dec. 16, 1967; children: John Michael II, Michelle Marie. BSN, Seton Hall U., 1981; MA, Tex. Woman's U., 1991. Cert. occupational health nurse, case mgr. Staff nurse oncology, med.-surgery, ICU, CCU, recovery, 1981-83, community health nurse, 1982-83; disability health nurse AT&T, 1983-84; mgr. health svcs. Lone Star Gas Co., 1985-86, Abbott Labs., 1986-88; corp. nursing supr. J.C. Penney, 1988-89; pres. Arnott & Assocs., Grapevine, Tex., 1989—, New Vision Nursecare, 1996—; wellness cons.; cons. health fair; occupl. health mgmt. cons.; workers compensation case mgmt. cons.; spkr. in field. CPR instr. trainer Am. Heart Assn.; vol. and facilitator SBE and smoking cessation Am. Cancer Soc., edn. com., skin cancer com.; CPR instr. to cmty.; first aid vol.; local rescue squad vol.; bd. dirs. Ctr. for Computer Assistance to the Disabled. Recipient Tex. State Achievement award for excellence in occupational health, 1990; named one of the Great One-Hundred Nurses of 1991, Dallas/Ft. Worth. Mem. Am. Assn. Occupational Health Nurses, Nat. Assn. Women Bus. Owners, Case Mgmt. Soc. Am., Tex. Assn. Occupational Health Nurses (fin. com. 1989-90, v.p. 1989-91), Dallas Tex. Assn. Occupational Health Nurses (hospitality com. 1985, edn. com. 1986-87, dir.-newsletter editor 1987, v.p. 1988-90, pres. 1991-93), ANA, Tex. Nurses Assn., Ctr. Computer Assistance to the Disabled (bd. dirs.), Omicron Delta Epsilon. Roman Catholic. Office: New Vision NurseCare PO Box 923 Grapevine TX 76099

ARNOTT, ERIC JOHN, ophthalmologist; b. Sunningdale, Berkshire, Eng., June 12, 1929; s. Robert and Cynthia Emita Amelia (James) A.; m. Veronica Mary Langue, Nov. 19, 1960; children: Stephen John, Tatiana Amelia, Robert Lauriston John. BA, Trinity Coll., Dublin, 1953, M.B., B.Ch., BAO, 1954; DO, U. London, 1956, FRCS, 1963, FC Ophth., 1989; FC Oph. (hon.), 1989. Houseman Royal Victoria Eye & Ear Hosp. and Adelaide Hosp., Dublin, 1953-54; resident surg. officer Moorfields Eye Hosp., London, 1959-60; sr. registrar U. Coll. Hosp., London, 1961-63; cons. ophthalmologist surgeon Royal Eye Hosp., London, 1965-74, Charing Cross Hosp., London, 1971-94; faculty U. London, 1966—, Royal Coll. Opthalmologists, London, 1966—. Co-author: Emergency Surgery, 1983, Intraocular Lens Implantation, 1987; contbr. articles to profl. jours.; developer, inventor totally encircling loop intraocular lens for implantation into the capsular bag of the eye after surgery; pioneer in small incisional cataract surgery; patentee in field. Founder, chmn. The Arnott Trust, The Great London Treasure Hunt. Fellow Royal Coll. Surgeons, Royal Coll. Ophthalmologists, Am. Acad. Ophthalmologists; mem. Order of St. John, Outpatient Ophthalmic Surgery Soc., London Med. Soc., Royal Soc. Medicine, European Phaco & Laser Soc. (pres. 1986-92), Kildare St. Club (Dublin), RAC, The Garrick Club (London). Home: Trottsford Farm, Headley, Nr Bordon, Hampshire England GU358TF Office: Arnott Eye Ctr & Laser Vision Ctr, 22 Harley St, London WIN 2BP, England

ARNSBERGER, BRADLEY KIRK, family nurse practitioner, physician assistant; b. Santa Cruz, Calif., Dec. 11, 1954; s. Frederick Wayne and Lillian Miranda (Kornmann) A.; m. Lorice Jean Weidman, Nov. 5, 1983; children: Amy Michelle, Ryan Bradley. AS, ASN with high honors, Cabrillo Coll., 1982; degree in Family Nurse Practitioner, U. Calif., Davis, 1984. RN, Calif.ly nurse practitioner; cert. physician asst. Nurse practitioner, physician asst. family practice, Susanville, Calif., 1982-88, Robert T. Petty D.O., Selma, Calif., 1988—; ptnr. A.W. Assocs., Santa Cruz, 1983-86; guest lectr. local hosp. and civic groups, 1988—; guest lectr. gynecology issues U. Calif., Davis. Provider of sideline med. care for football team Orosi H.S., Calif.; mem. sch. bd. Cathedral Christian Sch., 1994-95. Fellow Am. Acad. Physician Asst., Calif. Acad. Physician Assts. Home: 2507 Magnolia Court Kingsburg CA 93631 Office: Robert T Petty OD 2210 Arrants Selma CA 93662

ARNSTEIN, PAUL MICHAEL, medical and surgical clinical nurse specialist; b. Boston, Aug. 29, 1956; s. Saul and JoAnne (Willens) A.; m. Honor Arnstein, Oct. 2, 1982; children: Eric Daniel, Cody Aaron. BSN, St. Louis U., 1979; MSN, U. Utah, 1984. Nurse practitioner Garfield Meml. Hosp., Panquitch, Utah, dir. nursing, 1982-86; clin. nurse specialist Concord (N.H.) Hosp., 1986-94; rsch. fellow Boston Coll., 1994—; chmn., pres. N.H. Cancer Pain Initiative; investigator for pain rsch.; nurse practitioner Deaconess Hosp. Pain Program, 1995—. Contbr. articles to profl. jours. Mem. ANA (cert., clin. nurse specialist, med.-surg. nurse, cert. AANP, cert. family nurse practitioner), Am. Soc. Pain Mgmt. Nurses, New Eng. Pain Assn. Home: 12 Oxalis Way Concord NH 03303-3428

ARON, ALAN MILFORD, pediatric neurology educator; b. White Plains, N.Y., Oct. 15, 1933; s. Henri Jordan and Rosalind (Weinstein) A.; m. Sarah Deborah Bornstein, Dec. 29, 1963; children: Alexandra, Abigail, Adam. BS, Tufts U., 1954; MD, Columbia U., 1958. Diplomate Am. Bd. Pediatrics, Am. Bd. Psychiatry and Neurology with spl. competence in child neurology. Intern Grace New Haven Hosp. and Yale Med. Ctr., 1958-59; resident in pediatrics Babies Hosp. Columbia Presbyn. Med. Ctr., N.Y.C., 1959-61; Fellow Columbia Presbyn. Med. Ctr. and Neurologic Inst., N.Y.C., 1961—; pediatric neurologist Mt. Sinai Hosp., N.Y.C., 1961-64; dir. child neurology Mt. Sinai Sch. Medicine, N.Y.C., 1975—, prof. pediatrics and neurology, 1982—; pres. N.Y. Pediatric Soc., N.Y.C., 1980-81. Contbr. articles to profl. jours. Recipient Lucy Moses award Clin. Research Neurologic Inst., N.Y.C., 1964. Mem. AMA, Am. Acad. Pediatrics, Am. Acad. Neurology, Child Neurology Soc., Tri-State Child Neurology Soc. (pres. 1990-91), Profs. Child Neurology, Phi Beta Kappa. Democrat. Jewish. Office: Mt Sinai Sch Medicine 5 E 98th St New York NY 10029-6501

ARON, DAVID C., physician, educator; b. N.Y.C., Sept. 10, 1949; s. Paul H. and Beatrice R. (Feinstein) A.; m. Victoria Ortiz, Jan. 27, 1971; 1 child, Joshua G. BA, Columbia Coll., 1971, MD, 1975; MS in Clin. Rsch. Design, U. Mich., 1995. Diplomate Am. Bd. Internal Medicine, subspecialty bd. endocrinology and metabolism. Intern and resident U. Calif., San Diego, 1975-78; endocrinology fellow U. Calif., San Francisco, 1978-80; assoc. investigator VA Med. Ctr., Cleve., 1980-82, staff physician, 1982—, rsch. assoc., 1983-85, acting chief med. svc., 1996—; asst. prof. medicine Case Western Res. U., 1980-87, assoc. prof. medicine, 1987-93, prof. medicine, 1993—; cons. endocrinologist Marshall Island Project, Brookhaven (N.Y.) Nat. Labs., 1989-90; fellowship program dir. endocrinology Case Western Res. U., Cleve., 1993-95; chair sci. adv. com. Clin. Rsch. Ctr., Case Western Res. U., Cleve., 1994—; mem. med. adv. bd. Cushing's Support and Rsch. Found., Balt., 1995—. Editor: Cushing's Syndrome/Endocrinology and Metabolism Clinics of NA, 1994. W.O. Thompson Meml. Traveling scholar ACP, Phila., 1983. Fellow ACP; mem. AAAS, Am. Assn. Clin. Endocrinologists, Am. Diabetes Assn., Endocrine Soc., Soc. for Med. Decision Making, Alpha Omega Alpha. Office: Med Svc III (W) VA Med Ctr 10701 East Blvd Cleveland OH 44106

ARONOFF, BILLE LOUIS, surgical oncologist; b. Dallas, May 28, 1914; s. Joseph and Julia (Rubenstein) A.; m. Valerie K. Rosenthal, Feb. 7, 1942; children: Gail Aronoff Granek, Stephen, Nancy, Ronald. Student, U. Chgo., 1931-33, So. Meth. U., 1933-34; MD, Baylor U., 1938. Diplomate Am. Bd. Surgery, Am. Bd. Laser Surgery (v.p. 1983-89, pres. 1989—). Resident in surgery Parkland Meml. Hosp., Dallas, 1939-41, attending surgeon, 1945—; asst. prof. surgery Baylor U. Med. Sch., Dallas, 1941-43; fellow in surgery Lahey Clinic, Boston, 1943-44, Oschner Clinic, New Orleans, 1944; resident in surgery Meml. Hosp. for Cancer, N.Y.C., 1944-45; attending surgeon Baylor U. Med. Ctr. Hosp., 1945—, dir. surg. oncology, 1970—, dir. laser surgery, 1974—. Author: (with others) Lasers in General Surgery, 1989; editor jour. Lasers in Surgery and Medicine, 1980-88; mem. editorial bd. jour. Internat. Advances in Surg. Oncology, 1978—. Fellow ACS (mem. commn. on cancer 1972-82, chmn. field liaison and exec. com. 1978-82); mem. Internat. Soc. Lasers in Medicine and Surgery (pres. 1980-82), Am. Soc. Lasers in Medicine and Surgery, Soc. Surg. Oncology (exec. com. 1978-82), Soc. Head and Neck Surgery (exec. com. 1975-78), Am. Cancer Soc. (nat. bd. dirs. 1964—, hon. life mem. bd. 1978—, Nat. Div. award, Vol. of Yr. award 1978), Columbian Club (exec. com. 1953-56), Chapparal Club. Republican. Jewish. Home: 5551 Drane Dr Dallas TX 75209-5505

ARONOFF, GEORGE RODGER, medicine and pharmacology educator; b. Peoria, Ill., Mar. 6, 1950. BA in Chemistry with distinction, Ind. U., 1972; MD with honors, Ind. U., Indpls., 1975, MS in Pharmacology, 1984. Diplomate Am. Bd. Internal Medicine; diplomate Am. Bd. Internal Medicine Nephrology. Intern in internal medicine Ind. U., Indpls., 1975-76, resident, 1976-77, clin. fellow div. nephrology, 1977-78, chief resident in internal medicine Wishard Meml. Hosp., 1978-79, rsch. fellow div. nephrology, 1979-80, instr. phys. diagnosis, 1977-78, instr. medicine, 1978-79, from asst. prof. to assoc. prof. medicine, 1980-87, assoc. prof. pharmacology, 1985-87; prof. medicine, prof. pharmacology U. Louisville, 1987—; mem. staff Ind. U. Hosp., Indpls., 1980-87, Wishard Meml. Hosp., Indpls., 1980-87; mem. staff VA Med. Ctr., Indpls., 1980-87, Louisville, 1987—; mem. staff Jewish Hosp., Louisville, 1987—, Univ. Louisville (Ky.) Hosp., 1987—; fellow in clin. pharmacology Eli Lilly & Co., Indpls., 1979-80; acting dir. med. ICU Wishard Meml. Hosp., 1978-79, mem. exec. coun., 1977-78; mem. exec. coun. Med. Ctr. Ind. U., 1977-78, mem. adv. com. clin. rsch. ctr., 1981-87, mem. pharmacy & therapeutics com., 1983-87, mem. biomed. rsch. com., 1983-87, others; mem. R&D com. VA Med. Ctr., Indpls., 1981-84, Louisville, 1987—; mem. faculty coun. Ind. U.-Purdue U., Indpls., 1982-84, mem. athletic affiars com., 1982-84; mem. core group study com. dept. medicine Sch. Medicine U. Louisville, 1987—, mem. residency evaluation com., 1988—; mem. pharmacy and therapeutics com. Humana Hosp. U. Louisville, 1989—, chmn., 1989; William N. Creasy vis. prof. clin. pharmacology U. Oreg., Portland, 1986; presenter numerous profl. meetings. Mem. editorial bd. Am. Jour. Kidney Disease, 1981—, Antimicrobial Agents and Chemotherapy, 1981—, Seminars in Dialysis, 1990—; reviewer Kidney Internat., 1983—; cons. The Med. Letter, Inc., 1981—; contbr. U.S. Pharmacopeia Dispensing Info., 1981—, numerous articles and abstracts to profl. jours. Mem. Nat. Kidney Found. Ind., 1979-87, bd. dirs., 1985-87, mem. exec. com., 1985-87, bd. dirs. cen. Ind. chpt., 1985-87, chmn. fundraising, 1985-87; bd. dirs. Nat. Kidney Found. Ky., 1987—, exec. com., 1988—, pres. med. and sci. adv. bd., 1989—. Fellow ACP; mem. AAAS, Am. Fedn. Clin. Rsch., Am. Soc. Clin. Pharmacology and Therapeutics (med. edn. rev. com. 1984-86), Am. Soc. Nephrology, Cen. Soc. Clin. Rsch., Ky. State Med. Assn., Inter-Am. Soc. Chemotherapy (chmn. div. medicinal chemistry and pharmacology 1982-87), Jefferson County Med. Soc. (editorial bd. Louisville Medicine 1989—, editor 1990), (bd. of dirs.) Renal Physicians Assn.,1995—, Phi Eta Sigma, Phi Lambda Upsilon, Phi Beta Kappa, Alpha Omega Alpha, Sigma Xi. Office: U Louisville Kidney Disease Program 615 S Preston St Louisville KY 40202-1715

ARONOFF, MICHAEL STEPHEN, psychiatrist; b. Phila., Aug. 5, 1940; s. William Richard and Reva (Miller) A.; m. Carol R. Aronoff, Nov. 27, 1966; m. Dara Welles Aronoff, June 17, 1984; children: Amanda Susan, Jessica Ann. BA, Haverford Coll., 1962; MD, U. Pa., 1966; radiation biophysics cert., NIH, 1967; psychoanalysis cert., Columbia U., 1976. Diplomate Am. Bd. Forensic Examiners; cert. Am. Bd. Psychiatry and Neurology, Am. Bd. Forensic Psychiatry. Intern medicine U. Chgo., 1966-67; staff assoc. NIMH, Bethesda, Md., 1967-69; resident psychiatry Columbia U., NYSPI, N.Y.C., 1969-72, chief resident, 1971-72; rsch. adminstr. unit for volitional disorders NYSPI, 1972-74; chief psychiat. outpatient svcs. Lenox Hill Hosp., N.Y.C., 1976-79, dir. rsch. dept. psychiatry, 1988, attending physician, sr. med. staff, 1976—; clin. prof. psychiatry NYU Med. Ctr., N.Y.C.; assoc. prof. psychiatry N.Y. Med. Coll., Valhalla; clin. prof. NYU Med. Ctr., 1995—; radio talkshow host WFAS, White Plains, N.Y. Author: Sleep and Its Secrets: The River of Crystal Light, 1991; host, assoc. editor The Elderly; contbr. 2 book chpts, 50 articles to profl. jours., 2 PBS TV series. Talk show host Sta. WFAS AM 1230, White Plains, N.Y.; pres. Black Lake Assn., White Lake, N.Y., 1989—. Lt. comdr., surgeon USN/USPHS, 1967-69. Fellow APA (Falk fellow 1970, chmn. pub. affairs NYCDB), Am. Coll. Psychoanalysts, Am. Acad. Psychoanalysts; mem. Am. Pain Soc. (charter), N.Y. Soc. for Ericksonian Psychotherapy and Hypnosis (past exec. v.p.). Jewish. Office: 60 Riverside Dr # 16-E New York NY 10024-6171

ARONOVITCH, SHARON ANN, medical/surgical nurse; b. Kingston, Pa., May 21, 1955; d. Edward J. and Ann T. (Kwiatkowski) Turon; m. Charles D. Aronovitch, Jan. 7, 1983. AAS, Middlesex County Coll., 1975; BS, SUNY, Albany, 1984; MS, Russell Sage Coll., 1987; PhD, Adelphi U., 1994. RN, N.Y. Staff nurse med./surg. nursing svc. Riverdell Hosp., Oradell, N.J., 1975; staff nurse surgery nursing svc. Coll. Medicine & Dentistry Raritan Valley Hosp., Greenbrook, N.J., 1976-77; enterostomal therapy nurse gen. surgery dept. VA Med. Ctr., East Orange, N.J., 1978-81; patient care coord. med./surg. unit United Hosps. Med. Ctr., Newark, 1981-82; sales rep. ConvaTec div. E. R. Squibb & Sons, Inc., Princeton, N.J., 1982-83; head nurse intermediate care gerontology/cardiology wards Albany, N.Y., 1984-86; staff nurse ambulatory care svcs. nursing dept. VA Med. Ctr., Albany, N.Y., 1986-87; clin. nurse specialist/enterostomal therapy Albany Med. Ctr., 1987—, dir. enterostomal therapy nursing edn. program, 1991—, chair rsch. coun., 1995—; mem. skin integrity and elimination protocol work group N.Y. State Dept. Health, Albany, 1987; mem. work group on rehab. for people with ostomies Am. Cancer Soc., N.Y., 1989-91; mem. investigational review bd. Albany Medial Ctr., 1995—, co.-chair specialty device mgmt. com., 1995—. Contbr. articles to profl. jours. Mem. Wound, Ostome, Continence Nurses Soc. (co-editor newsletter N.E. regional chpt. 1983-85), Internat. Urol. Scis. Inc., N.Y. State Nurses Assn. (chairperson edn. and practice com. dist. 9 1987-89, mem. membership com. 1986-87), United Ostomy Assn. (mem. adv. bd. New Brunswick, N.J. chpt. 1978-83), Sigma Theta Tau. Home: 21 Leaf Rd Delmar NY 12054-2607

ARONOWITZ, JEROME DAVID, ophthalmologist; b. Bklyn., May 22, 1946; s. Nat and Eve (Rabinowitz) A.; m. Susan Mary Grimsley, June 13, 1976; children: Jessica, Ashley. BA in English, U. Mich., 1966; MD, U. Md., 1970. Intern Lenox Hill Hosp., N.Y.C., 1970-71; fellow in ophthalmology Mayo Clinic, Rochester, Minn., 1974-76; fellow in cataract surgery Pacific Hosp., Long Beach, Calif., 1977; pvt. practice, Margate, Fla., 1978—; pres. Surg. Eye Expdns., Boca Raton, 1978-85, treas., 1985—. Lt. comdr. USPHS, 1971-73. Fellow Am. Acad. Ophthalmology; mem. Broward County Ophthalmology Soc. (pres. 1982-83). Office: 5800 Colonial Dr Margate FL 33063-5682

ARONS, ELISSA BERON, psychiatrist; b. Phila., Mar. 19, 1945; d. Edward and Edna (Sloan) Beron; m. Daniel Leon Arons, Aug. 18, 1968; children: Rebecca S., Dara B., Abigail J. AB, Brown U., 1966; postgrad., Yale U., 1966-68; MD, Harvard U., 1970. Intern in pediatrics Children's Hosp. Med. Ctr., Boston, 1970-71; resident in psychiatry Mass. Mental Health Ctr., Boston, 1971-75; clin. instr. in psychiatry Harvard Med. Sch., Boston, 1975—; asst. psychiatry Beth Israel Hosp., Boston, 1975—; candidate Psychoanalytic Inst. New Eng., East, 1983-92, mem. faculty, 1992—. Mem. Am. Psychiat. Assn., Mass. Psychiat. Soc., Am. Psychoanalytic Assn. Home and Office: 40 Hampshire St Newton MA 02165-2946

ARONSON, CARL EDWARD, pharmacology and toxicology educator; b. Providence, Mar. 14, 1936; s. Carl Ivar and Ruth (Workman) A.; m. Marjorie Peck Boutelle, Dec. 17, 1960; children—Linda J., Kristen L. A.B., Brown U., Providence, 1958; Ph.D., U. Vt., Burlington, 1966; M.A., U. Pa., Phila., 1973. Asst. prof. pharmacology U. Pa. Sch. Medicine, Phila., 1971-75, assoc. prof. pharmacology, 1975-92; asst. prof. pharmacology and toxicology dept. animal biology U. Pa. Sch. Vet. Medicine, Phila., 1971-73, head labs. of pharmacology and toxicology, 1972-86, assoc. prof. pharmacology and toxicology, 1973-96; retired to emeritus status, 1996. Editor Veterinary Pharmaceuticals and Biologicals, 1978-79, 80-81, 82-83, 85-86; contbr. chpts. to books, articles to profl. jours. Active local sch. dist. coms. and other civic assns. Served to 1st lt. USAFR, 1958-65. Recipient Norden award for disting. tchg. U. Pa. Sch. Vet. Medicine, 1982, Legion of Honor, Chapel of the Four Chaplains, 1984, A.A.V.P.T. Svc. award, 1994. Fellow Am. Acad. Vet. Pharmacology and Therapeutics (pres. 1983-85, Svc. award 1994), Am. Acad. Vet. and Comparative Toxicology; mem. Am. Soc. Pharmacology and Exptl. Therapeutics, Am. Vet. Med. Assn., AAUP, Sigma Xi. Lutheran. Club: Bohemia River Mariners Sailing Assn. (treas. 1981-83, vice comdr. 1986, commodore 1987). Lodge: Masons (Greenville, R.I.). Office: U Pa Sch Vet Medicine Labs of Pharmacology & Toxicology 3800 Spruce St Philadelphia PA 19104

ARONSON, FREDERICK RUPP, physician; b. N.Y.C., Nov. 5, 1953; s. Morton Jerome and Margaret (Rupp) A.; m. Jennifer Ann Goldfarb; children: Jonathan George, Max David. BA, Johns Hopkins U., 1975; MPH,

Yale U., 1980, MD, 1980. Resident R.I. Hosp., Providence, 1980-83; clin. fellow New England Med. Ctr., Boston, 1983-84, rsch. fellow, 1984-86; asst. prof. Sch. Medicine Tufts U., Boston, 1986-88; rsch. fellow The Med. Found., Inc., Boston, 1986-88; asst. clin. prof. U. Calif., San Francisco, 1988-93; assoc. clin. prof. Sch. Medicine U. Vt., 1993—; attending physician Maine Ctr. Cancer Medicine, Portland, 1993—; dir. biol. response modifiers program U. Calif., San Francisco, 1988-93; vis. prof. Dalian Med. Coll., Shenyang Tumor Hosp. and Inst., China, 1992.; cons. in field. Contbr. chapters to various books, articles to profl. jours. Co-chmn. edn. com. Regional Cancer Found., San Francisco, 1989-91. Recipient Nat. Rsch. Svc. award Nat. Cancer Inst.; NIH grantee. Fellow ACP, Am. Fedn. Clin. Rsch., Am. Soc. Clin. Oncology, Am. Assn. Cancer Rsch., Am. Soc. Hematology. Democrat. Jewish.

ARONSON, PETER SAMUEL, medical scientist, physiology educator; b. Bklyn., Feb. 3, 1947; s. Harry Aronson and Sydelle (Pincus) Holtz; m. Marie Louise Landry, Sept. 25, 1977; children: Paul L., William L. AB, U. Rochester, 1967; MD, NYU, 1970; MA (hon.), Yale U., 1987. Diplomate Nat. Bd. Med. Examiners, Am. Bd. Internal Medicine (subspeciality Nephrology). Intern and resident in internal medicine U. N.C. Sch. Medicine, Chapel Hill, 1970-72; clin. assoc. Gerontology Rsch. Ctr., NIH, Balt., 1972-74; fellow in nephrology Yale U. Sch. Medicine, New Haven, 1974-77, asst. prof. medicine and physiology, 1977-81, assoc. prof. medicine and physiology, 1981-87, prof. medicine and cellular and molecular physiology, 1987—, C.N.H. Long prof. internal medicine, 1995—; chief sect. nephrology Yale U. Sch. Medicine, New Haven; established investigator Am. Heart Assn., 1981-86. Mem. editorial bd. Am. Jour. Physiology, 1982-86, 87-90, 96—, Kidney Internat., 1990-94, Jour. Biol. Chemistry, 1995—; cons. editor Jour. Clin. Investigation, 1993—; contbr. rsch. articles to profl. jours. With USPHS, 1972-74. Recipient Solomon Berson Med. Alumni Achievement award NYU, 1996. Fellow AAAS (electorate nominating com. sect. med. scis. 1993-95); mem. Assn. Am. Physicians, Am. Fedn. for Clin. Rsch., Am. Physiol. Soc. (program adv. com. 1982-84), Am. Soc. for Clin. Investigation (councillor 1986-88, editorial com. 1993—), Am. Soc. Nephrology (Young Investigator award 1985, Homer Smith award 1994), Am. Heart Assn. (exec. com. coun. on the kidney 1986-90), Internat. Soc. Nephrology, Soc. Gen. Physiologists, Salt and Water Club (sec. 1985-87), Phi Beta Kappa. Office: Yale School of Medicine Dept of Medicine/Nephrology PO Box 208029 New Haven CT 06520-8029

ARORA, PRINCE KUMAR, immunologist; b. New Delhi, India, Nov. 15, 1947; came to U.S., 1972, naturalized, 1981; s. Manohar Lal Narayana and Khem (Kumari) A.; BS with honors, Panjab U., 1970, MS with honors, 1973; PhD in Microbiology, Mich. State U., 1978; m. Kit-ying Barbara Chin, 1982; children: Hans Chin A., Naveen Chin A., Jason Chin Arora. Grad. research asst. Mich. State U., 1976-78; John E. Fogarty internat. vis. fellow lab. immuno-diagnosis Nat. Cancer Inst., NIH, 1978-79, John E. Fogarty internat. vis. fellow immunology br., 1979-82, staff fellow Lab. Molecular Genetics, Nat. Inst. Child Health and Human Devel., 1982-83, staff fellow Lab. Devel. and Molecular Immunity, Nat. Inst. Child Health and Human Devel., 1983-87; sr. scientist lab. neurosci. NIH, Bethesda, Md., 1987—. Recipient Gold medal Panjab U., 1971, Internat. Travel awards, 1983, 88, 89; Merit scholar, 1967-72. Mem. Am. Soc. Microbiology, N.Y. Acad. Scis., Am. Assn. Immunologists, Sigma Xi. Editor Internat. Jour. Neuroscience; reviewing editor various profl. jours.; contbr. articles to profl. jours. Home: 10108 Ashburton Ln Bethesda MD 20817-1730 Office: NIH Lab Neuosci Bldg 8 Neuosci Rm 111 Nidd Bethesda MD 20892

ARRA, MICHAEL JOSEPH, chiropractor; b. Bronx, N.Y., May 15, 1958; s. Joseph Michael and Gloria June (Danella) A.; m. Ruth S. Berman, Sept. 4, 1988. AAS, Queensborough C.C., Bayside, N.Y., 1979; BS, SUNY, 1990; D in Chiropractic magna cum laude, Life Chiropractic Coll., 1987. Chiropractic certification in spinal trauma Internat. Chiropractors Assn. Staff chiropractor NMS Diagnostics, Decatur, Ga., 1988-90; owner, chiropractor Boynton Beach, Fla., 1990—. Bd. dirs. Child Abuse Prevention Ctr., Boynton Beach, 1992-94. Recipient Caregivers award Adult Care Residence of Boynton Beach, 1991, 92. Mem. Am. Chiropractic Assn., Fla. Chiropractic Assn., Fedn. for Chiropractic Edn. and Rsch., Parker Chiropractic Resource Found, Boynton Sunrise Rotary Club (pres. elect 1995, bd. dirs. 1994). Office: 346 N Congress Ave Boynton Beach FL 33426

ARRIGHI, HENRY MICHAEL, epidemiologist; b. San Francisco, July 29, 1955; s. Enrico and Louise (Parodi) A.; m. Diane Del Fiorentino, June 12, 1984. BA, Whitman Coll., 1977; MSPH, UCLA, 1980; PhD, U. N.C., 1992. Grad. rsch. asst. UCLA, 1979-80; rsch. asst. U. Ark., Little Rock, 1980-82; epidemiologist Arabian-Am. Oil Co., Dhahran, Saudi Arabia, 1982-88; rsch. asst. U. N.C., Chapel Hill, 1988-92; epidemiologist Glaxo Wellcome Inc., Research Triangle Park, N.C., 1992-96, Amgen Inc., Thousand Oaks, Calif., 1996—; advisor Ark. Family Planning Coun., Little Rock, 1982; cons. King Faisol U., Dhahran, 1985, Ark. Dept. Health, Little Rock, 1982. Contbr. articles to profl. jours. Mem. APHA, Soc. for Epidemiol. Rsch., Delta Omega. Office: Amgen Inc 1840 DeHavilland Dr Thousand Oaks CA 91320

ARSENAULT, DEBRA ANN, physician; b. Seattle, Mar. 25, 1965; d. J. Paul and Ann (Bergstrom) A.; m. Ted Phillip Briski, May 25, 1996. BS, Whitworth Coll., 1987; DO, Coll. Osteo. Medicine, 1991. Commd. lt. USN, 1991; intern USN Naval Med. Ctr., San Diego, 1991-92, resident in ob-gyn., 1995—; gen. med. officer 1st Marine Air Wing, Fleet Marine Force, Okinawa, Japan, 1992-93; gen. med. officer emergency dept. Naval Hosp. Guam, 1993-95; mem. Exec. Com. Med. Staff, Agana, Guam, 1993-95; physician advisor Civic Action Team, 1994-95. Recipient cert. of appreciation Guam Police Dept., 1995. Fellow ACOG (jr.); mem. Am. Osteo. Assn. Home: 7 Antigua Ct Coronado CA 92118

ARSENAULT, JEANNE GAWRON, medical and surgical nurse specialist, educator; b. New Haven, June 6, 1958; d. Paul Frank Sr. and Dorothy (Krenicki) Gawron; m. Ronald Joseph Arsenault, June 12, 1982; children: Benjamin, Corynne. BSN, So. Conn. State U., 1980; MSN, U. N.C., Greensboro, 1986. RN, Conn.; cert. med.-surg. clin. specialist, clin. nurse specialist, ACLS. Clin. instr. VA Med. Ctr., Salisbury, N.C., 1982-85; staff nurse Mass. Gen. Hosp., Boston, 1980-81, Yale New Haven Hosp., 1981-82; clin. instr. VA Med. Ctr., West Haven, Conn., 1989—; clin. nurse specialist surg. and peripheral vascular surgery West Haven VA Hosp., 1993—; adj. prof. Yale Sch. Nursing, 1989—. Mem. health adv. com. Fairfield U. Home: 15 Carriage Dr Woodbridge CT 06525-1212

ARSENE, DOMINIQUE, gastroenterologist; b. Castres, France, Apr. 5, 1952; s. Rene and Richarde A.; m. Claire Chaneac, July 2, 1979. MD, U. Caen, France, 1982. Sr. registrar U. Hosp., Caen, France, 1976-80, chef de clinique asst., 1982-84, hosp. physician, 1985—, gastroenterologist, cons., 1994; sr. registrar St. Luc Hosp., Montreal, Can., 1980-81; gastroenterologist, cons. Dharan, Saudi Arabia, 1991-92. Author: Colorectal Tumors, 1995, Medical Pathology: Gastroenterology, 1995. Office: U Hosp, Ave de La Cote de Nacre, 14033 Caen France

ARSENEAU, JAMES CHARLES, physician; b. Syracuse, N.Y., Aug. 29, 1942; s. James Howard and Glenna Carolyn (Worth) A.; m. Jane Macy, July 2, 1966; children: Marc, David. AB, Syracuse U., 1964; MD, Albany Med. Coll., 1968. Intern and resident in medicine Strong Meml. Hosp., Rochester, N.Y., 1968-70, fellow in med. oncology, 1973-74; clin. assoc. med. br. Nat. Cancer Inst., Bethesda, Md., 1970-73; asst. prof. medicine U. Rochester, 1974-80, assoc. prof. medicine, 1980-83; head med. oncology unit Rochester Gen. Hosp., 1974-83; clin. assoc. prof. medicine Albany Med. Coll., 1985—; ptnr. Albany Regional Cancer Ctr., 1983—; Pres. med. staff St. Peter's Hosp., Albany, N.Y., 1993—. Author numerous chpts. in textbooks; contbr. articles to profl. jours. Sr. Asst. Surgeon USPHS, 1970-73. Mem. Am. Soc. Clin. Oncology, Albany County Med. Soc. (exec. com. 1993—), Am Radium Soc., Upstate N.Y. Soc. Med. Oncology/Hematology (pres. 1994—), Gynecologic Oncology Group (chmn. devel. therapeutic com. 1980—), Wolfert's Roost Country Club, Zeta Psi, Alpha Omega Alpha (pres. 1966-67). Home: 205 Graffunder Dr Albany NY 12204-1301 Office: Albany Regional Cancer Ctr 317 S Manning Blvd Albany NY 12208-1738

ARSENOVIC, ALEXANDER, physician; b. Beograd, Yugoslavia, Dec. 19, 1928; s. Ilija and Anna (Muk) A.; v. Vukosava Dokovic, Oct. 4, 1954; children: Ilija, Nanka Arsenovic Schneider. MD, U. Beograd, 1953. Diplomate Am. Bd. Family Practice, Am. Bd. Quality Assurance; lic. physician, Pa. Internist/infectologist Univ. Clinics, Beograd, 1954-58; specialist-infectologist, chief of clin. lab. Health Ctr. Vracar, Beograd, 1958-68; resident in family practice Edgewater Hosp., Chgo., 1969-70; internist VA Hosps., various locations, 1970-86; pvt. practice family practitioner and geriatritian Community Med. Ctr. of Burgettstown, Kansas City, Mo., 1986—. Fellow Am. Geriatrics Soc.; mem. Am. Acad. Family Practice. Home: 8207 NW Westside Dr Weatherby Lake MO 64152

ARSHAM, GARY, medical educator; b. Cleve., 1941; s. Sanford Ronald and Florence A.; m. Diana Silver, 1971. AB cum laude, Harvard U., 1963; MD, Case-Western Res. U., 1967; PhD, U. Ill., 1971. Fellow in med. edn. U. Ill., Chgo., 1968-71; asst. then assoc. dean curriculum devel., asst. prof. medicine and health scis. communication SUNY, 1971-72; assoc. prof., prof. health professions edn. U. of Pacific, San Francisco, 1972-79; chmn. Council on Edn. Pacific Med. Ctr., San Francisco, 1976-81; v.p. Arsham Cons., Inc , San Francisco, 1981—; adminstr. Pacific Vision Found., 1977-84, dir. edn., 1983—; mem. nat. adv. bd. John Muir Hosp. Med. Film Festival, 1981—; mem. task force on interdisciplinary edn. Nat. Joint Practice Commn., 1973-74; bd. dirs. U.S.-China Ednl. Inst., 1980—, sec., 1986-88, treas., 1993—; chair, CEO Nat. Accreditation Commn. for Schs. and Colls. of Acupuncture and Oriental Medicine, 1993—. Co-author: Diabetes: A Guide To Living Well, 1989, 2d edit. 1992; chief editor Family Medicine Reports, San Francisco, 1983. Fellow ACP; mem. Am. Assn. Individual Investors (chpt. bd. dirs. 1984-88), Am. Ednl. Rsch. Assn., Assn. Am. Med. Colls., Assn. Study Med. Edn., Assn. Hosp. Med. Edn. (past exec. com., sec.-treas.), Am. Diabetes Assn. (chpt. bd. dirs. 1984—, pres. 1990-91, v.p. Calif. 1992-93, pres.-elect 1993-94, pres. 1994-95, nat. bd. dirs. 1995—), Am. Assn. Diabetes Educators (assoc. editor 1985-92, bd. dirs. 1994—), Calif. Med. Assn., San Francisco Med. Soc., Harvard Club San Francisco (bd. dirs., past pres.), Harvard Alumni Assn. (bd. dirs. 1993-96), Lane Med. Soc., Tech. Security Analysts Assn. Office: Arsham Cons Inc PO Box 15608 San Francisco CA 94115-0608

ARTHUR, JEWELL KATHLEEN, dental hygienist; b. Bloomington, Ind., Apr. 12, 1947; d. Gerald E. and Wilma Kathleen (McDonald) Beyers; m. Leland Stanley Arthur, Sept. 21, 1968; children: Sherri Kay, Brian Lee. AS in Dental Hygiene, Ind. U., 1968. Lic./registered dental hygienist. Infection control mgr., dental hygienist Office Dr. Thomas Watkins, DDS, Bloomington, Ind., 1990—; speaker and presenter in field. Vice-chmn. precinct Rep. Com., Batholomew, 1987—; chmn. Batholomew Consolidated Sch. Aids Com., Columbus, 1988—; vice chair City of Columbus Bd. Zoning Appeals, 1989-93, Bartholomew County Pers. Adminstrn. Com., 1993—; councilwoman Batholomew County Coun., Columbus, Ind., 1993—;. Mem. Am. Assn. Ret. Persons, Am. Dental Hygienists Assn. (liaison 1989—, Disting. Svc. award 1994), Ind. Dental Hygienists Assn. (pres. 1986-87, del. 1991—, Comty. Svc. award 1991, Outstanding Dental Hygienists of Yr. award 1991), Ind. Pub. Health Assn. (chair legislation 1986-89), Driftwood Valley Dental Hygienists Assn. (trustee 1989-91), Assn. Ind. Counties, DAR-Joseph Hart, Order Eastern Star. Republican. Methodist. Home: 1800 Clover Ct Columbus IN 47203-3615

ARTURSSON, PER ARTUR SVEN, pharmaceutical researcher; b. Karlskoga, Sweden, Jan. 18, 1956; s. Sven Rudolf and Sivan Karin (Landsberg) A.; m. Karin Ingegerd Höjer, June 3, 1989; children: Sara, Björn. M in Pharmaceutics, Uppsala (Sweden) U., 1981, PhD, 1985, Docent, 1990. Rsch. pharmacist Med. Products Agy., Uppsala, 1986-87; vis. scientist Ciba-Giegy Pharms., Horsham, Eng., 1987-88; asst. prof. Uppsala U., 1988-92, prof., 1992-96; acad. sabbatical Gene Medicine Inc., The Woodlands, Tex., 1996—; acad. sabbatical Genemedicine Inc., The Woodlands, Tex., 1996. Recipient Rsch. award The Swedish Found. for Rsch. Without Exptl. Animals, 1994. Mem. Am. Assn. Pharm. Scientists, Swedish Pharm. Soc., Controlled Relase Soc., European Fedn. Pharm. Scientists.

ARTUSO, DOMINICK PAUL, surgeon, educator; b. Bklyn., May 10, 1957; s. Xavier Francis and Irene (DeMartini) A.; m. Barbara Voges, Sept. 12, 1987; children: Andrew, Alexander, Blake, Christian. BS, U. Notre Dame, 1978; MD, U. CETEC, Santo Domingo, Dominican Republic, 1981. Diplomate Am. Bd. Surgery, Am. Bd. Surg. Critical Care. Trauma attending Cmty. Med. Ctr., Scranton, Pa., 1987-91; dir. trauma svc. Lee Meml. Hosp., Ft. Myers, Fla., 1991-93; assoc. dir. surgery Waterbury Hosp., Conn., 1993-94; asst. prof. surgery N.Y. Med. Coll., Valhalla, 1994—. Mem. Soc. Crit. Care Medicine. Roman Catholic. Office: NY Med Coll Dept Surgery Munger Pavilion Valhalla NY 10595

ARTZ, TYRONE DEAN, orthopedic surgeon; b. Kingsley, Iowa, Apr. 22, 1941; s. Ted D. Artz and Marsaline June (Wink) Rawson; m. Kaelene Rae Jurgensen, Apr. 10, 1992. BS, Iowa State U., 1964; MD, U. Iowa, 1967. Intern Santa Clara Valley Med. Ctr., San Jose, Calif., 1967-68; resident dept. orthopedic surgery U. Wis., Madison, 1968-72; fellow hand surgery The Grace Hosp., Detroit, 1972-73; fellow hip surgery The Hosp. for Spl. Surgery, N.Y.C., 1973-74; pvt. practice orthpedic surgeon Wichita, 1974—; pres. Kans. Orthopedic Ctr., P.A., Wichita, 1990—, Rehab. Assocs. of Kans., Wichita, 1990—, Surgery Ctr. of Kans., Wichita, 1991—; Diplomate Am. Bd. Orthopedic Surgery, added qualification in hand surgery cert. Fellow ACS, Am. Acad. Orthopedic Surgeons, Am. Assn. for Hand Surgery, Am. Soc. for Surgery of the Hand, Am. Orthopedic Foot and Ankle Soc., Am. Soc. Outpatient Surgeons, Internat. Coll. Surgeons. Office: Kans Orthopedic Ctr PA 1507 W 21st St Wichita KS 67203

ARVANITAKIS, CONSTANTINE S., gastroenterologist; b. Thessaloniki, Greece, Nov. 9, 1939; s. Spyros and Terpsithea A.; m. Sanda Nousia, June 3, 1967; 1 child, Marianna. Diploma, Anatolia Coll, 1958; MD U. Thessaloniki, 1965, postgrad., 1976. Diplomate Am. Bd. Internal Medicine, Am. Bd. Gastroenterology. House physician Nat. Health Service, Eng., 1967-70; resident, fellow U. Wis., Madison, 1970-73; asst. prof. medicine U. Kans., Kansas City, 1973-77, assoc. prof., 1977-79; clin. assoc. prof. U. Kans., 1979—; assoc. prof. medicine U. Thessaloniki, 1979—; prof. medicine, 1996; dir. gastrointestinal unit, first dept. medicine U. Thessaloniki, AHEPA Gen. Hosp., 1980—. Author: Drug Treatment of Gastrointestinal Disease, 1970; chmn. editl. bd. Hellenic Jour. Gastroenterology Internat., Hepatogastroenterology, Internat. Jour. Pancreatology, Arch. Hepatogastroenterology Gut; editor: Helleniki Iatriki 1985, Gastroenterology Intern. NIH grantee, Bethesda, Md., 1978-80. Fellow ACP; mem. Am. Gastroenterology Assn., Hellenic Soc. Gastroenterology (bd. dirs. 1987-88, pres. 1996), Cen. Soc. Clin. Rsch., Am. Physiol. Assn., Internat. Assn. Pacreat (chmn. organizing com.), Gastroent. Rsch. Group, Am. Pancreatic Assn., Assn. Nat. European Mediterr Gastroenterology (pres.), European Gastroenterology Fedn. Coun., ERASMUS (coord. European course transfer sys. program, pres. 1st unit Europe Gastroent. Week Athens 1992), Hellenic Soc. of Gastroenterology (pres. 1996). Christian Orthodox. Office: 30 Aghias Sofias Str, 54622 Thessaloniki Greece also: U Thessaloniki, AHEPA Gen Hosp, Thessaloniki Greece

ARVANITIS, CYRIL STEVEN, surgeon, educator; b. Long Branch N.J., Sept. 16, 1926; s. Samuel and Sassa Alexandra (Nelopoulos) A., m. Victoria Pappaylion, Dec. 26, 1950 (div. Jan. 1976); children:Samuel James, Hope Alexandra; m. Eva Blomberg, Aug. 8, 1976. BS, Ursinus Coll , 1949; MD, Hahnemann Med. Coll., 1953. Diplomate Am. Bd. Surgery. Intern, Hahnemann Hosp., 1953-54, resident, 1954-58; teaching fellow Hahnemann Med. Coll., Phila., 1957-58, prof. surgery, 1979-91, chmn. emeritus, 1991—; attending surgeon Monmouth Med. Ctr., Long Branch, N.J., 1968-80, attending surgeon, 1958—, chmn. dept. surgery 1978-91, also program dir. surgery, acting dir. med. edn., trustee, 1993; acting asst. dean Hahnemann U. Sch. Medicine; vis. specialist Care-Medico, Afghanistan, 1975, vis. surgeon St. Anne's Hosp., Brunapeg, Zimbabwe, 1994; coord. of surgical svcs. Jaqueline M. Wilentz Comprehensive Breast Ctr.; surg. specialist St. Anne's Mission Hosp., Brunapeg, Zimbabwe, 1993. Contbr. to profl. jours. Served with USN, 1944-46. Recipient Hathaway award Hahnemann Med. Coll., Phila., 1953, surg. award, 1953. Fellow ACS (councillor, pres. elect N.J. chpt., pres. 1989, com. oper. room environment), Hellenic Surg. Soc. (hon.), N.J. Soc. Surgeons, South Eastern Surg. Soc., Hahnemann Surg. Soc.; mem. Archeological Inst. of Am., Assn. Program Dirs. Surgery (nat. steering com.), Modern Greek Studies Assn., AGHIA Olga Soc., Deal Country Club (N.J.), Sea Bright Beach Club. Greek Orthodox. Home: 3 Laurel Ln Rumson NJ 07760-1004 Office: 279 3rd Ave Long Branch NJ 07740-6205

ARVIEW, KATHLEEN YVONNE, geriatrics nurse; b. Tucson, Dec. 31, 1957; d. Merwin Lawrence and Betty Alice (Damrau) Saxe; m. Arthur Ray Arview, Mar. 18, 1986 (dec. Feb. 1992); 1 child, Bettina Raye. Lic. vocat. nurse, Howard County Jr. Coll., 1989. Cert. BLS instr.; cert. nurse aide instr. Nurse Scenic Mountain Med. Ctr. Hosp., Big Spring, Tex., 1989-91, Mt. View Lodge, Big Spring, 1991-92; staff devel. coord. Manor Park, Midland, Tex., 1993; treatment nurse Stanton (Tex.) Care Ctr., 1993-94; coord. infection control, quality assurance com. Mt. View Lodge, Big Spring, 1991-92; instr. BSL. Comdr. DAV Aux., Big Spring, 1986-87; asst. leader Girl Scout U.S. Home: 3814 N Holiday Hill Rd Apt 212 Midland TX 79707-3019

ARVYSTAS, MICHAEL GECIAUSKAS, orthodontist, educator, sculptor; b. Vilnius, Lithuania, Dec. 18, 1942; came to U.S., 1949; naturalized, 1961; s. Mykolas and Antanina (Kleiza) A.; m. Jane Grannis, 1969 (div. 1978); m. Mary Ruth Buchness, Nov. 2, 1992. B.A., Colgate U., 1965, D.M.D., Tufts U., 1969; cert. Columbia U., 1973. Diplomate Am. Bd. Orthodontics. Chief orthodontic sect. Morrisania City Hosp., Bronx, N.Y., 1973-76; dir. orthodontics ctr. for cranio facial disorders and cleft palate ctr. Montefiore Hosp. and Med. Ctr., Bronx, 1973—; chief orthodontic sect. N. Central Bronx Hosp., 1976-83; clin. prof. N.J. Dental Sch., Newark, 1974—, dir., lectr. undergrad. and postgrad. dental students, 1974—; lectr. in field; vis. prof. Albert Einstein Coll. Medicine, Bronx. Contbr. numerous articles to profl. jours., also chpts. to books. Served to capt. Dental Corps, USAF, 1969-71. Mem. ADA, First Dist. Dental Soc. N.Y.C., Am. Assn. Orthodontists, Northeastern Soc. Orthodontists, N.Y. Acad. Dentistry, Am. Acad. Esthetic Dentistry, Tufts U. Dental Alumni Assn., Orthodontic Alumni Soc. Columbia U., Colgate U. Alumni Assn., Sigma Xi. Office: 24 Washington Sq N New York NY 10011-9168

ARWIDSSON, HANS GJELLAN, pharmaceutical company executive; b. Torsås, Småland, Sweden, May 22, 1958; s. Arthur R. and Karin M-B (Gustavsson) A.; m. Kirsti Gjellan, May 30, 1992; children: Ingrid Viktoria, Karin Linnea. MSc in Pharmacy, U. Uppsala, Sweden, 1984, PhD in Pharmacy, 1991. Cert. pharmacist. Rsch. pharmacist Astra Läkemedel AB, Södertälje, Sweden, 1984-86, assoc. dir., 1988-94, dir., 1994-95, sr. dir., 1995—; assoc. dir. Astra Alab AB, Södertälje, 1986-88; vis. lectr. Swedish Acad. Pharm. Scis., Stockholm, 1991-93; vis. lectr. U. Uppsala, 1990-94. Contbr. articles to profl. jours.; patentee in field. With Swedish Air Force, 1978-80. Office: Astra Läkemedel AB, R&D Labs, S-75185 Södertälje Sweden

ASAPH, JAMES WELLINGTON, cardiothoracic surgeon; b. Ketchikan, Alaska, Jan. 24, 1937; s. Wallace Dean and Lela May (McGrath) A.; m. Gail Linnea Larson, Sept. 7, 1957 (div. Dec. 1964); m. Mary Ann Olszaowski, Dec. 31, 1966; 1 child, Ashleigh Em. BS, U. Idaho, 1958; MD, U. Oreg., 1962. Intern in surgery N.Y. Hosp./Cornell U. Med. Coll., N.Y.C., 1962-63, resident in surgery, 1963-69; fellow in cardiothoracic surgery U. N.C. Med. Sch., Chapel Hill, 1973-74, instr. cardiothoracic surgery, 1974; cardiothoracic surgeon Thoracic Clinic, Portland, Oreg., 1974—; pres., CEO Physicians of Providence, Portland, 1985-94; chief of surgery Providence Med. Ctr., Portland, 1992-94. Lt. col. U.S. Army, 1969-73. Decorated Legion of Merit. Mem. Multnomah County Med. Soc. (trustee 1989-93). Office: The Oregon Clinic 507 NE 47th St Portland OR 97213

ASBED, MONA H., healthcare administrator, university coordinator; b. Huntington, W.Va., Oct. 5, 1935; d. John Alfred and Esta Elma Houston; children: Steven, Jeffrey, Julie. BA, U. Mo., St. Louis, 1977, MEd, 1982. Lic. profl. counselor, clin. social worker, Mo. Coord. program alcohol and drug awareness Southern Ill. U., Edwardsville; sr. specialist substance abuse Cigna Health Plan-MCC subs., St. Louis; mgr. program CD treatment for women Normandy Osteopathic Hosp. South, St. Louis; family therapist Deaconess Hosp., St. Louis; pvt. practice; clin. supr. Personal Performance Cons., St. Louis; appeals coord. Medco Behavioral Care Systems, 1993-95; clin. mgr. People Resources, St. Louis, 1995—. Profl. mem. Nat. Coun. on Alcoholism and Drug Abuse. Mem. Am. Assn. Counseling and Devel., Coalition on Alcoholism and Other Chem. Dependencies (past pres., v.p.), MAAC (bd. dirs.), Chi Sigma Iota. Office: People Resources 10900 Manchester Rd Ste 201 Saint Louis MO 63122

ASBURY, ARTHUR KNIGHT, neurologist, educator; b. Cin., Nov. 22, 1928; s. Eslie and Mary (Knight) A.; m. Carolyn Holstein, May 17, 1980; children by previous marriage: Dana, Patricia Knight, William Francis. Grad., Phillips Acad., Andover, Mass., 1946; student, Stanford, 1947-48; B.S., U. Ky., 1951; M.D., U. Cin., 1958; M.A. (hon.), U. Pa., 1974. Intern in medicine Mass. Gen. Hosp., Boston, 1958-59; resident Mass. Gen. Hosp., 1959-63, fellow, 1963-65, staff neurologist, 1965-69; chief neurology San Francisco VA Hosp., 1969-74; prof. dept. neurology U. Pa., Phila., 1974—, chmn. dept. neurology, 1974-82; Van Meter prof. neurology U. Pa., 1983—; acting dean, exec. v.p. U. Pa. Sch. Medicine, 1988-89, vice dean for rsch., 1990-93, vice dean for faculty affairs, 1993—; teaching fellow Harvard Med. Sch., 1958-65, instr., 1965-68, assoc., 1968-69; assoc. prof. neurology U. Calif. at San Francisco, 1969-73, vice-chmn., 1969-74, prof., 1973-74; mem. nat. adv. neurol. disease & stroke coun. NIH, 1990-93. Sr. editor Blue Books of Practical Neurology, 1980—; assoc. editor Archives of Neurology, 1975-76; assoc. editor Annals of Neurology, 1976-81, chief editor, 1985-93; mem. editorial bd. Muscle and Nerve, 1977-89, Neurology, 1981-85, Jour. Neuropathology and Exptl. Neurology, 1981-83, Jour. Neurol. Scis., 1989—; contbr. chpts. to med. textbooks, articles to med. jours. V.p., bd. dirs. Forest Retreat Farms Inc., Carlisle, Ky., 1970-92. With AUS, 1951-53. Recipient Daniel Drake medal U. Cin., 1988; grantee UPHS, 1967-93, Muscular Dystrophy Assn., 1974-82. Fellow Am. Acad. Neurology (v.p. 1977-79); mem. Inst. of Medicine, Am. Neurol. Assn. (councillor 1976-81, pres. 1982-83), Am. Assn. Neuropathologists (v.p. 1983-84), Soc. Neurosci., Assn. Univ. Prof. Neurology (pres. 1980-82), World Fedn. Neurology (v.p. 1989-93), European Neurol. Soc. (hon.). Home: 408 S Van Pelt St Philadelphia PA 19146-1233 Office: U Pa Hosp Dept Neurology 3400 Spruce St Philadelphia PA 19104

ASCH, SUSAN MCCLELLAN, pediatrician; b. Cleve., Dec. 31, 1945; d. William Alton and Alice Lonore (Heide) McClellan; m. Marc Asch, Sept. 10, 1966; children: Marc William, Sarah Susan, Rebecca Janney. AB, Oberlin (Ohio) Coll., 1967; MA, Mich. State U., 1968, PhD, 1975; MD, Case Western Res., 1977. Diplomate Nat. Bd. Med. Examiners, Am. Bd. Pediatrics (task force, sub-bd. emergency pediatrics 1987-93), Am. Bd. Emergency Pediatrics. Instr. sociology Mich. State U., East Lansing, 1971-73; resident in pediatrics Children's Nat. Med. Ctr., Washington, 1977-80; asst. to dir. Office for Med. Applications of Rsch. NIH, Bethesda, 1980-81; pvt. practice in pediatrics Millinocket (Maine) Regional Hosp., 1981-84; assoc. dir. emergency Akron (Ohio) Children's Hosp., 1984-87; asst. prof. pediatrics Northeastern Ohio U. Coll. Medicine, 1984-87; dir. emergency St. Paul Children's Hosp., 1987-91; asst. prof. pediatrics U. Minn., 1987-93, clin. assoc. prof., 1993-96; pvt. practice in pediatrics Stillwater (Minn.) Med. Group, 1992—; nat. faculty PALS Am. Heart Assn., Mpls., Dallas, 1987-94; mem. task force, sub-bd. emergency pediatrics Am. Bd. Pediatrics, 1987-93. Assoc. editor Pediatric Emergency Medicine, 1992, contbr., 1992, 96. State bd. dirs., affiliate faculty PALS Minn. affiliate Am. heart Assn., 1988-93, 96—; chairperson SIDS task force, Minn. Dept. Maternal and Child Health, St. Paul, 1990-92. Mem. Am. Acad. Pediatrics (nat. faculty advanced pediatric life support 1989—, exec. com. sect. on emergency pediatrics 1988-90, chair Minn. emergency pediatric com. 1989-91, Svc. commendation 1991), Minn. Med. Assn. (emergency svcs. com. 1990), Rotary Internat., Alpha Omega Alpha (Ohio chpt., Minn. chpt.). Democrat. Quaker. Home: 34 N Oaks Rd North Oaks MN 55127-6325 Office: Stillwater Med Group 921 Greeley St S Stillwater MN 55082-5935

ASCHEN, SHARON RUTH, genetic counselor, psychotherapist, nurse; b. Chgo., May 10, 1948. MA, Loyola U., 1979; MS, U. Ill., 1978, BS, 1972; postgrad., Ind. U. Med. Sch., Indpls., 1993—. RN, Ind. Mental health clinician Northwestern Inst. of Psychiatry, Chgo., 1974-79; lectr. Loyola U., Chgo., 1979-81; staff therapist Edgewater-Uptown Community Mental Health Clinic, Chgo., 1980-81, dir. emergency svcs., 1981-84; pvt. practice counselor and psychotherapist Chgo., 1984-87; psychiat. nurse Charter Hosp. of Indpls., Indpls., 1988-92; nurse LaRue Carter Meml. Hosp., Indpls., 1992-93, CPC Valle Vista Hosp., Greenwood, Ind., 1993-94, Koala Hosp., Indpls., 1995—; pvt. practice psychotherapy Indpls., 1995—; clin. therapist

Schizophrenic Treatment Ctr, Indpls., 1996—. Author (handbook) Mental Status Examination, 1981, rev. 1991. Grantee Gt. Lakes Regional Genetics Group Edn. Initiative in Psychiat. Genetics, 1995—, NIMH Svcs.-Rsch. Br. Psychiat. Genetic Svcs. and Related Rsch. Mem. APA (assoc.), Am. Soc. for Genetic Counselors, Internat. Soc. for Nurses in Genetics, Ill. Psychol. Assn. (sec. 1983-84).

ASCHER, JOHN ALBERT, physician, pharmaceutical researcher; b. N.Y.C., Mar. 23, 1949; s. Hans Albert and Germaine (Samuel) A.; m. Marilyn Ruth Loftis, Oct. 1, 1988. AB, U. N.C., 1975, MD, 1980. Diplomate Am. Bd. Psychiatry and Neurology. Sr. clin. rsch. physician, dept. clin. neuroscis. Glaxo Wellcome, Inc., Research Triangle Park, N.C., 1986—. Mem. AMA, N.C. Psychiat. Assn. (chair pub. affairs com. Raleigh chpt. 1989-92), N.C. Med. Soc. (chief psychiatry sect. Raleigh chpt. 1990-93), Am. Psychiat. Assn. Democrat. Episcopalian. Office: Glaxo Wellcome Inc 5 Moore Dr Durham NC 27709-2700

ASCHER, NANCY LOUISE, surgeon; b. Detroit, Mar. 15, 1949; d. Meyer S. and Beckie (Berger) A.; m. John. P. Roberts, Dec. 10, 1992; children: Becky, John. AB, U. Mich., 1970, MD, 1974; PhD, U. Minn., 1985. Instr. surgery U. Minn., Mpls., 1982-85, staff surgeon, dir. liver transplant, 1982-87, assoc. prof., 1987; prof. surgery U. Calif., San Francisco, 1988—, chief transplant svc., 1989—, prof., vice chmn., 1993—; presenter in field. Contbr. articles to profl. jours. Schering scholar, 1979; recipient Koret Israel prize, 1993. Fellow Am. Coll. Surgeons (surg. forum com.); mem. AMA, AAAS, Am. Assn. Immunologists, Am. Soc. Transplant Surgeons (publs. and programs com., edn. com., chair edn. com., councilor-at-large), Am. Surg. Assn., Calif. Med. Assn., Minn. Surg. Soc. (scholar 1982), Mpls. Surg. Soc., San Francisco Med. Soc., Internat. Transplantation Soc. (sec. local orgn. com.), Soc. U. Surgeons, Soc. Clin. Surgery, Surg. Biology Club, Acad. Medicine Task Force, Pacific Coast Surg. Soc., Live Transplant Soc., Phi Beta Kappa, Phi Kappa Phi, others. Office: U Calif Box 0780 505 Parnassus Ave San Francisco CA 94143

ASCIONE, FRANK JOSEPH, pharmacy educator; b. Detroit, Nov. 12, 1946; s. Salvatore Enrico and Anne Nelse (Wagman) A.; m. Patricia Coughlin, Mar. 21,1974; children: Wendy, Mark. BS in Pharmacy, U. Mich., 1969, PharmD, 1973, MPH, 1977, PhD, 1981. Lic. pharmacist, Mich. Staff pharmacist St. Joseph Mercy Hosp., Ann Arbor, Mich., 1969-73; prog. dir. Am. Pharm. Assn., Washington, 1973-76; asst. to assoc. prof. pharmacy U. Mich., Ann Arbor, 1976—, assoc. dean, 1996—. Editor: Evaluations of Drug Interactions, 1976, Principles of Drug Information and Scientific Literature Evaluation, 1994; contbr. articles to profl. jours. Mem. Am. Pharm. Assn. (chmn. econ. and adminstrv. sci. sect. 1990-91, Acad. fellow 1994), Mich. Pharmacy Assn. (task force on patient edn. 1983-86, exec. bd. medal 1986), Am. Phub. Health Assn., Drug Info. Assn., Rho Chi. Home: 2340 Mershon Dr Ann Arbor MI 48103-6049 Office: U Mich Coll Pharmacy 428 Church St Ann Arbor MI 48109-1065

ASCUNCE, GIL, physician; b. Santa Clara, Calif., Mar. 18, 1946; s. Gil and Hilda (Gonzalez) A.; m. Consuelo C. Ascunce, Sept. 30, 1972; children: Aranzazu, Gil I., Gabriel. BA, Cath. U., 1967; MD, U. Salamanca, 1973. Resident Georgetown-D.C. Gen. Svc., 1973-76; pvt. practice Arlington, Va., 1978—; clin. instr. medicine Georgetown U., Washington, 1979—; chief clin. nutrition Arlington Hosp., 1980—. Fellow Am. Coll. Gastroenterology. Office: 1715 N George Mason Dr 410 Arlington VA 22205

ASGHARIAN, BAHMAN, biomedical researcher; b. Tehran, Iran, Nov. 14, 1958; came to U.S., 1976; s. Ali Mohammad and Behjat (Mashhoon) A. BS in Mech. Engring., SUNY, Buffalo, 1980, MS in Mech. Engring., 1982, PhD in Mech. Engring., 1988. Vis. lectr. SUNY, Buffalo, 1988-89; postdoctoral fellow NYU Med. Ctr., Tuxedo, N.Y., 1989-90; scientist I Chem. Industry Inst. Toxicology, Raleigh, N.C., 1990—. Contbr. articles to profl. jours. Mem. Am. Assn. Aerosol Rsch., Internat. Soc. Aerosols in Medicine. Office: Chem Industry Inst Toxicol 6 Davis Dr PO Box 12137 Durham NC 27709

ASH, LAWRENCE ROBERT, public health educator, administrator; b. Holyoke, Mass., Mar. 5, 1933; s. Lawrence Clifton and Alice (Sartini) A.; m. Luana Lee Smith, Aug. 4 1960; 1 child, Leigh I. BS in Zoology, U. Mass., 1954, MA in Zoology, 1956; PhD in Parasitology, Tulane U., 1960. Asst. parasitologist U. Hawaii, Honolulu, 1960-61; instr. Tulane U., New Orleans, 1961-65; med. parasitologist South Pacific Commn., Noumea, New Caledonia, 1965-67; asst. prof. pub. health UCLA Sch. Pub. Health, 1967-71, assoc. prof., 1971-75, prof., 1975-94, chmn. dept., assoc. dean, 1979-84, prof. emeritus, 1994—; panelist U.S. Panel on Parasitic Diseases, U.S.-Japan Program, Washington, 1972-78, chmn., 1978-84; cons. Naval Med. Rsch. Unit # 2 Taipei, China, Manila, 1970-80. Sr. author: Atlas of Human Parasitology, 1980, 4th rev. edit., 1997, Parasites: A Guide to Laboratory Procedures and Identification, 1987; co-author: Parasites in Human Tissues, 1995. NIH grantee, 1970-84. Fellow Royal Soc. Tropical Medicine and Hygiene; mem. Am. Soc. Tropical Medicine and Hygiene (councilor 1974-77), Am. Soc. Parasitologists (councilor 1972-75, 88-92, v.p. 1982-83). Home: 10400 Northvale Rd Los Angeles CA 90064-4432 Office: UCLA Sch Pub Health Los Angeles CA 90095-1772

ASH, MAJOR MCKINLEY, JR., dentist, educator; b. Bellaire, Mich., Apr. 7, 1921; s. Major McKinley Sr. and Helen Marguerite (Early) A.; m. Fayola Foltz, Sept. 2, 1947; children: George McKinley, Carolyn Marguerite, Jeffrey LeRoy, Thomas Edward. BS, Mich. State U., 1947; DDS, Emory U., 1951; MS, U. Mich., 1954; Doctoris Medicine Honoris Causa, U. Bern, 1975. Instr. sch. dentistry Emory U., Atlanta, 1952-53; instr. U. Mich., Ann Arbor, 1953-56, asst. prof., 1956-59, assoc. prof., 1959-62, prof., 1962—, chmn. dept. occlusion, sch. dentistry, 1962-87, dir. stomatognathic physiology lab., sch. dentistry, 1969-87, dir. TMJ/oral facial pain clinic, sch. dentistry, 1983-87, Marcus L. Ward prof. dentistry, 1984-89, prof. emeritus, rsch. scientist emeritus, 1989—; cons. N.E. Regional Dental Bd., 1989—; vis. prof. U. Bern, 1989, U. Tex., San Antonio, 1990—; pres. Basic Sci. Bd., State of Mich., 1962-74; cons. over the counter drugs FDA, Washington, 1985-89. Author, co-author 54 textbooks, 1958—; editor 4 books; contbr. 171 articles to profl. jours. Served to tech. sgt. Signal Corps, U.S. Army, 1942-45, ETO. Nat. Inst. Dental Research grantee, 1962-85. Fellow Am. Coll. Dentists, Internat. Coll. Dentists, European Soc. Craniomandibular Disorders; mem. AAAS, Am. Dental Assn. (cons. coun. on dental therapeutics 1982—, cons. coun. sci. affairs 1995—), N.Y. Acad. Scis., Washtenaw Dist. Dental Soc. (pres. 1963-64), Phi Kappa Phi. Presbyterian. Office: U of Mich Sch of Dentistry Ann Arbor MI 48109

ASH, PETER, psychiatrist; b. Bellefonte, Pa., Dec. 4, 1947; s. Philip and Ruth (Clyde) A.; m. Margaret R. Jaffe, Sept. 13, 1986; children: David, Marcia. AB, Harvard U., 1969; MD, U. Pa., 1973. Diplomate Am. Bd. Psychiatry and Neurology, also sub-bd. child psychiatry, sub-bd. forensic psychiatry. Intern Presbyn. Hosp., San Francisco, 1973-74; resident in psychiatry U. Mich., Ann Arbor, 1974-77, resident in child psychiatry, 1977-78, instr., 1978-84, asst. prof., 1984-86, clin. asst. prof. psychiatry, 1986-93; asst. prof. psychiatry Emory U., Atlanta, 1993—. Contbr. articles to profl. jours. Office: Grady Meml Hosp Dept Psychiatry 80 Butler St SE Atlanta GA 30335-3801

ASH, PHILIP, psychologist; b. N.Y.C., Feb. 2, 1917; s. Samuel Kieval and Estella (Feldstein) A.; m. Ruth Clyde, Sept. 16, 1945 (div. Dec. 1972); children—Peter, Sharon; m. Judith Nelson Cates, June 6. 1973; 1 son, Nelson E. B.S. in Psychology, City U. N.Y., 1938; M.A. in Personnel Adminstrn, Am. U., 1949; Ph.D. in Psychology, Pa. State U., 1949. Diplomate: Indsl. Psychlogy Am. Bd. Profl. Psychology. Analyst to unit chief occupational research Dept. Labor, 1940-47; research fellow Pa. State U., 1947-49, asso. prof., 1949-52; asst. to v.p. indsl. relatons Inland Steel, 1952-68; prof. psychology U. Ill., Chgo., 1968-80; prof. emeritus U. Ill., 1980—; dir. rsch. John E. Reid Assocs., Chgo., 1969-87; v.p. rsch. Reid Psychol. Sys., 1985-87; cons. London House, Inc., Park Ridge, Ill., 1987-94; dir. Ash, Blackstone & Cates, Blacksburg, Va., 1975—. Author: Guide for Selection and Placement of Employees, 2d edit., 1977, Volunteers for Mental Health, 1973, The Legality of Preemployment Inquiries, 1989, The Construct of Employee Theft Proneness, 1991, Preparing for Retirement: Guidelines and Information Sources, 1993, also other books, monographs and articles; editor: Forensic Psychology and Disability Evaluation, 1972. Mem. public adv. com. Chgo. Commn. Human Relations, 1957-80; retirement com. Chgo. Commn. Sr. Citizens, 1960-80; chmn. Ill. Psychologist Examining Com., 1963-72. Fellow AAAS, Am. Psychol. Assn. (pres. div. indsl. psychology 1968-69); mem. Ill. Psychol. Assn. (pres. 1963-64), Chgo. Psychol. Assn., Va. Psychol. Assn., Va. Applied Psychology Acad. (pres. 1992-93), Midwest Psychol. Assn., Am. Pers. and Guidance Assn., Acad. for Criminal Justice Scis., Am. Criminology Assn., Internat. Assn. Applied Psychology, Sigma Xi, Phi Beta Kappa, Psi Chi. Home: 817 Hutcheson Dr Blacksburg VA 24060-3211

ASH, WILLIAM JAMES, geneticist, scientific consultant, educator; b. N.Y.C., Nov. 3, 1931; s. William and Anna Marie (Ruegg) A.; m. Gertrude Louise Kehm, June 15, 1953; children: Annalee M., Barbara A. (dec.), William J., Jr., James J., Lydia A. BS, Cornell U., 1953, MS, 1958, PhD, 1960. Grad. research asst. Cornell U., 1955-59; dir. research Crescent Corp., Aquebogue, N.Y., 1964-65; research geneticist Cornell U., Ithaca, N.Y., 1959-64; asst. prof. W.Va. U., Morgantown, 1965-66; prof. St. Lawrence U., Canton, N.Y., 1966-81, Kuwait U., Arabian Gulf, 1976-78; program officer NSF, Washington, 1979-81; mem. sr. staff U.S.-Saudi Joint Commn., Riyadh, Saudi Arabia, 1982-83; pres. Adv. Assocs. Internat., Westhampton, N.Y., 1981-94; prof. SUNY-Stony Brook, 1985-91 . Contbr. articles to profl. jours. Committeeman Canton Republican Party, 1972-73; exec. officer Peconic Bay Power Squadron, Riverhead, N.Y., 1985—, comdr., 1986-88; scoutmaster Boy Scouts Am., Canton, 1967-69; coach U.S. Amateur Ice Hockey Assn., Canton, 1970-75. Served to capt. U.S. Army, 1953-65. Recipient Travel award Cornell U., 1963, Travel award NSF, 1983; NSF grantee, 1970-72, 79-81. Fellow Am. Dermatoglyphics Assn.; mem. Southampton Town Wildfowl Assn., Sigma Xi, Beta Beta Beta. Roman Catholic. Republican. Clubs: Cape Lookout Power Squadron, Alpenverein. Avocations: sailing; gardening; photography; travel; amateur radio, genealogy, celestial navigation. Home: 3507 Canterbury Rd New Bern NC 28562-7703

ASHBAUGH, JAMES LEWIS, health services administrator; b. Gary, Ind., Sept. 26, 1953; s. Donald Lowry and Florence (Lewis) A.; m. Barbara Joan White, Sept. 11, 1982; children: Adam, Laura. BA, Wabash Coll., 1975; M in Mgmt., Northwestern U., 1977. Diplomate Am. Coll. Healthcare Execs. Asst. adminstr. Luth. Gen. Hosp., Park Ridge, Ill., 1976-81; asst. v.p. No. Ill. Med. Ctr., McHenry, Ill., 1981-84; assoc. exec. dir. Humana Hosp., Lexington, Ky., 1984-89; assoc. exec. dir. Hoffman Estates (Ill.) Med. Ctr., 1989-93, COO, 1993; adminstr., CEO Vencor Hosp. Ft. Worth S., Mansfield, Tex., 1994—, Vencor Hosp. Ft. Worth W., 1994—; preceptor summer program U. Ky. BHA Program, Lexington, 1984, 89. Mem. Hoffman Estates C. of C. bd. dirs. 1989-93, sec., 1991, v.p. 1992, pres. 1993. Home: 5709 Champion Ct Arlington TX 76017 Office: Vencor Hosps. Fort Worth 815 Eighth Ave Fort Worth TX 76104

ASHBY, MICHELLE CONCETTA, critical care nurse; b. Lancaster, Pa., Nov. 14, 1964; m. Thomas L. Ashby. Diploma, St. Joseph Hosp. Sch. Nursing, Lancaster, Pa., 1986; BSN, Millersville (Pa.) U., 1992; MSN, U. Pa., 1995. RN, Pa., N.J.; cert. RN practitioner, Pa., CCRN, acute care nurse practitioner, adult critical care nurse practitioner. Staff nurse progressive care St. Joseph Hosp., Lancaster, 1986-88, staff nurse ICU/CCU/OHS, 1988-95, OHS care mgr., 1993-94; cardiovasc. nurse practitioner The Heart Group, Lancaster, 1995—. Mem. AACN, ANA, PNA, SCCM, Sigma Theta Tau. Home: 3672 Horizon Dr Lancaster PA 17601-1116 Office: The Heart Group Lancaster PA 17601

ASHBY, STEVEN JAMES, mental health administrator; b. Niagara Falls, N.Y., Jan. 27, 1948; s. Robert Earl and Dolores Marian (Palm) A.; m. Carol Dominian. BA in Psychology, SUNY, Stony Brook, 1970; MA in Psychology, U. Conn., 1972, PhD in Psychology, 1976. Chief psychologist, asst. adminstr. Woods Lane Sch., Gilman, Conn., 1971-72; psychologist, adminstr. Kolburne Sch., Southfield, Mass., 1972-73, dir. psychol. svcs., 1974-75; dir. personal rehab. svcs. Western Res. Psychiat. Habilitation Ctr., Northfield, Ohio, 1975-78, dir. cultural day svcs., 1978-79; dir. community svcs. Wiltwyck, N.Y.C., 1979-81; dir. Chestnut Hill Hosp., Traveler's Rest, S.C., 1983; chief svc., community svcs. Middletown (N.Y.) Psychiat. Ctr., 1981-83, 84-89; cons. Durham County Dept. Mental Health, Devel. Disabilities, and Substance Abuse Svc., Durham, N.C., 1989; dir. Durham County Dept. Mental Health, Devel. Disabilites and Substance Abuse Svcs., Durham, N.C., 1989—; cons. Chestnut Hill Hosp., 1983, Durham County Dept. Mental Health, Devel. Disabilities and Substance Abuse, 1989. Trustee Fordham -Fremont CMHC Gov. Bd., Bronx, N.Y., 1980-81; mem. Putnam County (N.Y.) Youth Bd., 1981. Recipient Community Svc. commendation, Fordham-Fremont CHMC Gov. Bd., 1981, Commrs. Award for Excellence in Quality Assurance, N.Y. State Office Mental Health, 1988. Mem. Am. Psychol. Assn., Assn. Mental Health Adminstrs. (Achievement commendation 1986). Democrat. Methodist. Office: Durham County Mental Health 300 N Duke St Durham NC 27701

ASHDOWN, FRANKLIN DONALD, physician, composer; b. Logan, Utah, May 2, 1942; s. Donald and Theresa Marie (Hill) A. BA, Tex. Tech. U., 1963; MD, U. Tex., 1967. Chief of med. Holloman Air Force Base, New Mexico, 1971-73; chief of staff Gerald Champion Mem. Hosp., Alamogordo, N.M., 1976, 91, 92; pres. Otero County Concerts Assn., Alamogordo, 1985-94, Otero County Med. Soc., Alamogordo, 1986; cons. New Mexico Sch. for Visually Handicapped, Alamogordo, 1973-76. Composer of more than 30 published and recorded works. Bd. dirs. Otero County Mental Health Assn., Alamogordo, 1973-77, Flickinger Found. for Performing Arts, 1995; bd. trustees Gerald Champion Meml. Hosp., 1992. Mem. Gerald Champion Mem. Hosp., N.M. Med. Soc., Am. Soc. Internal Med., ASCAP. Republican. Home: 1435 Rockwood Alamogordo NM 88310-3920 Office: 1301 Cuba Ave Alamogordo NM 88310-5727

ASHER, BERNARD W(OLFF), surgeon; b. Hamburg, Germany, Apr. 27, 1936; came to U.S., 1937; s. Frederick and Herta (Bechof) A.; m. Lilian L. Orba, Aug. 28, 1967; children: Robert, Elizabeth, Katherine. AB, Brown U., Providence, R.I., 1958; MD, SUNY, 1963. Diplomat Am. Bd. Surgery, 1969; recertified 1980. Intern New England Ctr. Hosp., Boston, 1963-64; surgical resident Boston City Hosp., 1964-66; chief surgical resident Bronx Lebanon Hosp. Ctr., N.Y.C., 1966-69; gen. surgeon Cuba (N.Y.) Meml. Hosp., 1969-70; gen. surgeon, chief of surgery Jones Meml. Hosp., Willsville, N.Y., 1970-71; gen. surgeon St. James Hosp., Hornell, N.Y., 1971-72, Genesee Meml. Jerome Hosp., Batavia, N.Y., 1972—. Bd. mem. Batavia (N.Y.) YMCA, 1976-80, Genesee County Bd. Health, Batavia, N.Y., 1984—; city councilman, Batavia, N.Y., 1978-82. Fellow ACS, Am. Coll. Gastroenterology; mem. Am. Soc. Gastrointestional Endoscopy, Flying Physicians Assn., Aircraft Owners and Pilots Assn. Office: 190 Washington Ave Batavia NY 14020-2113

ASHKIN, KENNETH TODD, neurologist, epileptologist; b. Monroeville, Pa., May 22, 1963; s. Martin and Marilyn Elaine (Ginsberg) A.; m. Audrey Lynn Lyons, July 2, 1992. BA, Lehigh U., 1985; MD, Med. Coll. Pa., 1987. Diplomate Am. Bd. Psychiatry and Neurology; cert. in neurophysiology and sleep medicine. Fellow epilepsy, sleep disturbances. Cleve. Clinic, 1991-93; neurologist Va. Neurologic Ctr., Alexandria, 1993-94, Mecklenburg Neurologic Assn., Charlotte, N.C., 1994—. contbr. articles to Am. Jour. of Physiology, Archives of Neurology. Mem. Am. Acad. Neurology. Home: 6506 Prett Ct Charlotte NC 28270 Office: Mecklenburg Neurol Assocs 1900 Randolph Rd Ste 1010 Charlotte NC 28207

ASHKINAZY, LARRY ROBERT, dentist; b. N.Y.C., Feb. 12, 1952; s. Philip and Kate (Scherer) A. BS, Bklyn. Coll., 1973; DDS, NYU, 1976. Cert. Nat. Bd. Dental Examiners. Gen. dental practice residency Cabrini Health Care Ctr., 1977; pvt. practice dentistry N.Y.C., 1977—; assoc. attending dentist Cabrini Healthcare Ctr., 1984—, assoc. attending in implantology, 1983-86, postgrad. instr. Inst. for Grad. Dentists, 1981-82; guest lectr. various pub. and profl. edn. instns.; health and sci. corr. Sta. WWOR-TV. Author: Dentistry, 1982; contbr. articles to profl. jours.; mem. editorial bd. Internat. Congress Oral Implantologists newsletter, 1982; various radio and TV appearances; patentee in field; trademarks Bionic Tooth, Tooth Plant. Health care providor Drs. with a Heart, N.Y.C., 1987; health care spokesman Jr. League, N.Y.C., 1978, Community Fair, N.Y.C., 1983. Recipient Cert. of Appreciation Greater N.Y. Dental Meeting, 1981, 87, Cert. of Appreciation NYU Dental Ctr., 1981. Fellow Acad. Gen. Dentistry, Acad. Dentistry Internat., Acad. Implants and Transplants, Am. Endodontic Soc., Internat. Congress Oral Implantologists; mem. Am. Dental Assn. (cert. appreciation 1980), Am. Acad. Oral Medicine, Internat. Analgesia Soc. , 1st Dist. Dental Soc. (oral health clinician 1978, speakers bur. subcom.chmn. 1984pub. and profl. relations com. 1982), Am. Prosthodontic Soc., Sociedad Venezolana de Implantodontologos, Am. Acad. Implant Dentistry (chmn. sci. exhibit com., 1984, edn. com. 1984, library com. 1984, membership com. 1983, N.Y. chmn. 1983 ann. meeting and world assembly. Dentistry Alumni, Alpha Omega. Club: Greater N.Y. Implant Study (pres. 1981—). Home and Office: 200 Central Park S New York NY 10019-1415

ASHLEY, CYNTHIA ELIZABETH, psychotherapist, human service administrator; b. Springfield, Mass., July 16, 1945; d. Elbridge and Evelyn (Lewis) Farnsworth; m. Henry T. Szela, Mar. 13, 1965 (div. Jan. 1993); children: Scott Anthony, Wendy Marie. Grad. high sch., West Springfield, Mass. Lic. cert. social worker, Mass., psychotherapist. Meals on wheels coord. Town of Granville, Mass., 1976-77; program coord. Highland Valley Elder Svcs., Northampton, Mass., 1977-80; v.p., treas. Western Mass. Phobia Soc., Springfield, Mass., 1982-85; pvt. practice Springfield, Mass., 1985—; pres., therapist Exposure Therapy Assocs., Inc., Springfield, Mass., 1986-88; founder, dir., therapist, specialist in anxiety disorders and phobias Exposure Therapy and Counseling Svcs., Agawam, Mass., 1988—; pvt. practice Sedona (Ariz.) Health and Wellness Ctr., 1995—; workshop leader Exposure Therapy and Counseling Svcs., West Springfield, 1988-93; founder nationwide counseling line for anxiety disorders, 1993—; dir. nat. mktg. and ind. distbrn. Global Health & Wellness, Inc., 1995-96; lectr. in field. Youth adviser YMCA, West Springfield, 1967-70. Mem. Am. Counseling Assn., Anxiety Disorder Assn. Am., Nat. Orgn. for In Vivo Therapists, Am. Mental Health Counseling Assn. Office: Exposure Therapy and Counseling South End Bridge Cir Agawam MA 01001

ASHLEY, DARLENE JOY, psychologist; b. N.Y.C., Oct. 29, 1945; d. George Geiger and Ann Debra (Bernstein) Munzer; m. Joseph Michael O'Brien, Sept. 23, 1974 (div. June 1981); 1 child, Sundara Amber; m. Roy William Fagan, Aug. 16, 1991. BA with honors, Antioch Coll., 1966; MA, NYU, 1973; PhD, Calif. Grad. Sch. Family Psychology, San Rafael, 1987. Lic. clin. psychologist, Hawaii, Calif.; diplomate Am. Bd. Med. Psychotherapists; lic. marriage, family and child counselor, Calif.; cert. Calif. Community Coll. instr., biofeedback therapist, Biofeedback Cert. Inst. of Am. Psychology instr. Coll. of the Redwoods, 1977-82; instr. psychology North Am. Coll., San Rafael, 1980; cons., psychol. examiner Hawaii Bd. Edn., Hilo, 1982; lectr. U. Hawaii, Hilo and Manoa (Honolulu), 1982—; predoctoral clin. psychology intern Redwood Ctr., Berkeley, Calif., 1983-85; pvt. practice psychotherapy, San Rafael and Berkeley, 1985-87; pvt. practice psychology, Darlene Ashley, PhD and Assocs., Kailua Kona, Hawaii, 1988—; workshop presenter, 1977—; instr. psychology Coll. of Redwoods, Ft. Bragg, Calif., 1978-82; presenter AM-FM Sta. KMPO, Caspar, Calif., AMú-FM Sta. KKON, Kealakekua, Hawaii. Author: Voluntary Controls Training Handbook, 1982; author: (cassette) Deep Relaxation, 1983. Bd. dirs. Friends of Child Advocacy Ctr., 1995—; mem. Task Force on Worker's Compensation Reform for Hawaii, 1994-95; proponent Ho. bill pertaining to psychologists, 1988; mem. com. Rep. Virginia Isbell's Fundraiser, Kailua-Kona, 1988—. Recipient rsch. grant NSF, Mus. Natural History, N.Y.C., 1965, NIMH, NYU, 1968-70, fellowship NIMH, 1969, Outstanding Rsch. award Biofeedback Soc. Calif., 1987. Mem. APA, NAFE, Assn. Applied Psychophysiology and Biofeedback, Hawaii Psychol. Assn., Biofeedback/Behavioral Medicine Soc. Hawaii. Office: 75-5744 Alii Dr Ste 237 Kailua Kona HI 96740-1740

ASHLEY, JOHN DEWITT, JR., physician; b. Bentonville, Ark., June 12, 1915; s. John Dewitt and Mattie India (Toler) A.; m. Ann Price, Aug. 4, 1966. BS in Medicine, U. Mo., 1938; MD, Med. Coll. of Va., 1940. Diplomate Am. Bd. Internal Medicine. Intern Univ. Hosps., Oklahoma City, 1940-42, resident internal medicine, 1942-44; pvt. practice medicine Newport, Ark., 1949—; clin. preceptor U. Ark. Med. Ctr., 1953—, mem. admissions com., 1976-78. Pres. Am. Heart Assn., 1965-66; chmn. Newport Housing Authority. Lt. col. U.S. Army, 1944-49, ret. Res. Named Citizen of Yr., Jackson County, Ark., 1960. Mem. Am. Physicians Art Assn. Home: 2000 Mclain St Newport AR 72112-3661

ASHLEY, ROBERT ALAN, medical products executive; b. Northwich, United Kingdom, Oct. 14, 1957; came to the U.S., 1989; s. Alan and Ursula Loraine (Howden) A.; m. Jacqueline Tregortha; children: Oliver, Mary, Louise. MA in Biochemistry, Oxford U., 1979. Team leader Amersham (United Kingdom) Internat., 1979-80, product mgr., 1980-83, sr. product mgr., 1983-87, sales mgr., 1988-89; bus. devel. mgr. Squibb Diagnostics, Princeton, N.J., 1989-90, product mgr., 1990-92, product dir., 1992-93, dir. bus. devel., 1994; v.p. comml. devel. CollaGenex Pharmaceuticals, Inc., Newtown, Pa., 1995—. Office: Collagenex Inc 301 S State St Newtown PA 18940

ASHLEY, SHARON ANITA, pediatric anesthesiologist; b. Goulds, Fla., Dec. 28, 1948; d. John H. Ashley and Johnnie Mae (Everett) Ashley-Mitchell; m. Clifford K. Sessions, Sept. 1977 (div. 1985); children: Cecili, Nicole, Erika. BA, Lincoln U., 1970; postgrad., Pomona Coll., 1971; MD, Hahnemann Med. Sch., Phila., 1976. Diplomate Am. Bd. Pain Mgmt., Am. Bd. Anesthesiologists. Intern pediatrics Martin Luther King Hosp., L.A., 1976-77, resident pediatrics, 1977-78, resident anesthesiology, 1978-81, mem. staff, 1981—. Named Outstanding Tchr. of Yr., King Drew Med. Ctr., Dept. Anesthesia, 1989, Outstanding Faculty of Yr., 1991. Mem. Am. Soc. Anesthesiologists, Calif. Med. Assn., L.A. County Med. Soc., Soc. Regional Anesthesia, Soc. Pediatric Anesthesia. Democrat. Baptist. Office: Martin Luther King Hosp 12021 Wilmington Ave Los Angeles CA 90059-3019

ASHMAN, GEORGE SUPPES, ophthalmologist; b. Johnstown, Pa., Apr. 26, 1940; s. Wilbur McClintock and Sara Ann Dibert (Suppes) A.; m. Suzanne Marie Weigel, Apr. 11, 1965; children: Laura, David, Kathy. AB, Franklin and Marshall Coll., 1962; MD, U. Pitts., 1966. Diplomate Am. Bd. Ophthalmology. Intern Conemaugh Valley Meml. Hosp., Johnstown, 1966-67; resident U. Pitts. Med. Ctr., Eye and Ear Hosp., 1969-72; pvt. practice Ophthalmic Assocs., Johnstown, 1972—. Trustee Johnstown Bank & Trust Co., 1990-96, Conemaugh Valley Meml. Hosp., 1985-93; dir., past pres. Cambria County Assn. for Blind and Handicapped, Johnstown, 1975-93; trustee, deacon Westmont Presbyn. Ch., Johnstown, 1975-81, 87-93. Lt. comdr. USPHS, 1967-69. Fellow ACS, Am. Acad. Ophthalmology, Pa. Acad. Ophthalmology; mem. AMA (Physician's Recognition award), Pa. Med. Soc., Am. Soc. Cataract and Refractive Surgery, Black Pyramid, Pi Gamma Mu. Republican. Office: Ophthalmic Associates PO Box 580 120 Main St Johnstown PA 15907

ASHMEAD, ALLEZ MORRILL, speech, hearing, and language pathologist, orofacial myologist, consultant; b. Provo, Utah, Dec. 18, 1916; d. Laban Rupert and Zella May (Miller) M.; m. Harvey H. Ashmead, 1940; children: Harve DeWayne, Sheryl Mae Harames, Zeltha Janeel Henderson, Emma Allez Broadfoot. BS, Utah State U., 1938; MS summa cum laude, U. Utah, 1952, PhD summa cum laude, 1970; postgrad., Idaho State U., Oreg. State Coll., U. Denver, U. Utah, Brigham Young U., Utah State U., U. Washington, U. No. Colo. Cert. secondary edn., remedial reading, spl. edn., learning disabilities; cert. ASHA clin. competence speech pathology and audiology; profl. cert. in orofacial myology. Tchr. pub. schs. Utah, Idaho, 1938-43; speech and hearing pathologist Bushnell Hosp., Brigham City, Utah, 1943-45; sr. speech correctionist Utah State Dept. Health, Salt Lake City, 1945-52; dir. speech and hearing dept. Davis County Sch. Dist., Farmington, Utah, 1952-65; clin., field supr. U. Utah, Salt Lake City, 1965-70, 75-78; speech pathologist Box Elder Sch. Dist., Brigham City, 1970-75, 78-84; teaching specialist Brigham Young U., Provo, 1970-73; speech pathologist Primary Children's Med. Ctr., Salt Lake City, 1975-77; pvt. practice speech pathology and orofacial myology, 1970-88; del. USSR Profl. Speech Pathology seminar, 1984, 86; participant numerous internat. seminars. Author: Physical Facilities for Handicapped Children, 1957, A Guide for Training Public School Speech and Hearing Clinicians, 1965, A Guide for Public School Speech Hearing Programs, 1959, Impact of Orofacial Myofunctional Treatment on Orthodontic Correction, 1982, Meeting Needs of Handicapped Children, 1975, Relationship of Trace Minerals to Disease, 1972, Macro and Trace Minerals in Human Metabolism, 1971, Electromotive Potential Differences Between Stutterers and Non-stutterers, 1970, Learning

Disability, An Educational Adventure, 1969, New Horizons in Special Education, 1969, Developing Speech and Language in the Exceptional Child, 1961, Parent Teacher Guidance in Primary Stuttering, 1951, numerous others; contbr. research articles to profl. jours. Student Placement chair Am. Field Service, Kaysville, Utah, 1962-66; ednl. del. Women's State Legis. Council, Salt Lake City, 1958-70; chairwoman fund raising Utah Symphony Orch., Salt Lake City, 1970-71; sec., treas. Utah chpt. U.S. Council for Exceptional Children, 1958-62, membership com. chair, 1962-66, program com. chair, 1966-68. Recipient Scholarship award for Higher Edn. U. Utah, Salt Lake City, 1969; Delta Kappa Gamma scholar, 1968; rsch. grantee Utah Dept. Edn., 1962. Mem. NEA, Utah Ednl. Assn., Am. Speech, Lang. Hearing Assn. (life, continuing edn. com. 1985, Ace award for Continuing Edn. 1984), Western Speech Assn., Internat. Assn. Orofacial Myology (life, bd. examiners, Sci. Contribution award 1982), Utah Speech, Hearing and Lang. Assn. (life, sec., treas. 1956-60), AAUW (Utah state bd. chair status of women 1959-62, Kaysville br. 1957-60, bd. dirs. Kaysville-Davis br. 1987-92, chair internat. rels. 1987-91, chair cultural interests Kaysville-Davis br. 1991-92), Delta Kappa Gamma (state scholarship award 1968, del. Woman's State Legis. Coun. 1958-70, profl. affairs chair 1963-67, tchr. of yr. award 1978), AAUW (bd. dirs. internat. rels. Kaysvile-Davis br., 1988-91), Sigma Alpha Eta, Theta Alpha Phi, Psi Chi, Zeta Phi Eta, Phi Kappa Phi. Republican. Mem. LDS Ch. Lodges: Daus. Utah Pioneers (parliamentarian Kaysville 1980-92, historian 1974-80, lesson leader 1992-95, capt. 1996—), Soroptimists (charter, bd. dirs. 1954-56, pres. Davis County chpt. 1965-69, Rocky Mountain regional bd. dirs. 1965-70, cmty. svc. award 1968, pub. svc. award 1970). Home: 719 E Center St Kaysville UT 84037-2138

ASHRAF, ELIZABETH ANN, pharmaceutical company executive; b. Troy, N.Y., July 2, 1947; d. Samuel S. and Rose (Earley) Basen; m. Mirza Khalil Ashraf, Feb. 14, 1976; children: Danial, David. BA in Biology, Coll. St. Rose, 1969; MS in Pharmacology, St. John's U., Queens, N.Y., 1976, PhD in Pharmacology, 1981. Rsch. biologist Microscopy for Biol. Rsch., Albany, N.Y., 1969-71; rsch. scientist N.Y.U., N.Y.C., 1973-74; rsch. coord. Winthrop Labs., N.Y.C., 1974-76; supr. Sterling Drug Inc., N.Y.C., 1976-78; sr. dir. med. comm. Ives Labs., N.Y.C., 1978-86; sr. dir. med. comms. Whitehall Robins N.J., Madison, 1986—. Fellow Am. Med. Writers Assn. (sec. 1987-88, Past Pres.' award Met. chpt. 1981-82, 88-89); mem. Am. Soc. for Reproductive Medicine, Rho Chi. Roman Catholic.

ASHWAZ, STEPHEN, pediatrician, child neurologist, educator; b. Bklyn., Feb. 23, 1945. MD, NYU, 1970. Resident Bellevue Hosp., N.Y.C., 1970-73; prof. pediatrics & child neurology Loma Linda (Calif.) Sch Medicine, 1976—. Child Neurology fellow U. Minn., Mpls., 1973-76. Fellow Am. Acad. Pediatrics, Am. Acad. Neurology; mem. Child Neurology Soc. (sec.-treas. 1992—). Office: Loma Linda U Sch Medicine Dept Pediatrics Loma Linda CA 92503

ASHWOOD, EDWARD R., medical educator; b. Camp Pendleton, Calif., Dec. 14, 1953; s. Carl R. and H. Marian (Youmans) A.; m. Candice A. Johnson, June 2, 1979. BSChemE, U. Colo., 1975; MD, U. Colo., Denver, 1979. Diplomate Am. Bd. Pathology, Am. Bd. Clin. Pathology. Resident in pathology U. Wash., Seattle, 1979-82, instr. dept. lab. medicine, 1983-85; mem. faculty dept. pathology U. Utah, Salt Lake City, 1985—; tech. v.p. ARUP Labs., Salt Lake City, 1985—. Editor: Tietz Textbook of Clinical Chemistry, 2d edit., 1994, Tietz Fundamentals of Clinical Chemistry, 4th edit., 1996. Fellow Coll. Am. Pathologists; mem. Acad. Clin. Lab. Physicians and Scientists (pres. 1994-95), Am. Assn. Clin. Chemistry, Am. Soc. Clin. Pathology. Office: ARUP Labs 500 Chipeta Way Salt Lake City UT 84108

ASKANAS-ENGEL, VALERIE, neurologist, educator, researcher; b. Poland, May 28, 1937; came to U.S., 1969, naturalized, 1975; d. Marian and Leontyne Hornik; m. W. King Engel; 1 dau., Eve Monique Kerr. MD, Warsaw Med. Sch., Poland, 1960, PhD, 1967; Doctor honoris causa, U. d'Aix-Marseille, France, 1987. Rotating intern Univ. Hosp. Warsaw Med. Sch., 1960-61, resident in neurology, 1961-64, fellow in neuromuscular diseases, 1964-65; asst. prof. neurology Warsaw Med. Sch., 1965-69; assoc. mem. Inst. Muscle Diseases, N.Y.C., 1969-73; asst. prof. NYU Med. Sch., 1973-77; sr. investigator NIH, Bethesda, Md., 1977-81; prof. neurology and pathology U. So. Calif., L.A., 1981—; co-dir. Neuromuscular Ctr. at Hosp. Good Samaritan, 1981—, Muscular Dystrophy Assn. Clinic, 1981—, The Jerry Lewis ALS Clin. and Rsch. Ctr., 1988—; v.p. 6th Internat. Congress on Neuromuscular Diseases, 1986, 7th, 1990, 8th, 1994; vis. prof. internat. congresses, Europe, S.Am., Can., Far East. Contbr. numerous articles, chpts., abstracts to med. publs. Recipient Dean's prize for outstanding research, 1967; Premio Associazione Stampa Medica Italiana Di Giurnal Italianalsmo Medico, 1980; grantee NIH, 1974-77, 83—, Muscular Dystrophy Assn., 1969-77, 81—. Fellow Am. Acad. Neurology, L.A. Acad. Medicine; mem. Soc. for Neurosci., Am. Neurol. Assn., d'Honneur de la Soc. Francaise de Neurologie, Am. Soc. Cell Biology, Am. Assn. Neuropathology, Histochem. Soc., Uruguayan Neurological Assn. (hon. mem.), L.A. County Med. Assn. Home: 527 S Arden Blvd Los Angeles CA 90020-4737 Office: U So Calif Neuromuscular Ctr Good Samaritan Hosp 637 Lucas Ave Los Angeles CA 90017-1912

ASKEN, MICHAEL JOSEPH, clinical psychologist; b. N.Y.C., May 28, 1950; s. Robert Charles and Rose N. A.; m. Irene Cecelia McCall, Aug. 7, 1983; Kimberly I., Kaitlyn N., Tristen R., Breton M. BA, Johns Hopkins U., 1972; MA, W. Va. U., 1974, PhD, 1976. Diplomate Am. Bd. Med. Psychotherapists; lic. psychologist, Pa. Adj. asst. prof. Pa. State U. Sch. of Medicine, Hershey, 1976—; adj. assoc. prof. Lebanon Valley Coll., Annville, Pa., 1976—; instr. Pub. Safety Inst., Harrisburg (Pa.) Area C.C, 1976—; clin. health psychologist Holy Spirit Hosp., Camp Hill, Pa., 1976—, Polyclinic Med Ctr., Harrisburg, Pa., 1976—. Author, co-editor; (books) Neuropsychological Assessment, 1987, Sport Psychology, 1987; author: (books) Dying to Win: Preventing Drug Abuse in Sports, 1990, Psycho Response: Psychological Skills for Emergency Responders, 1993. Mem. profl. edn. com. Am. Cancer Soc., Dauphin County, Pa., 1992—; cons. Camp Hill (Pa.) Fire Dept., 1990—. Fellow Am. Psychol. Assn., Pa. Psychol. Assn., Am. Bd. Med. Psychotherapists; mem. Soc. Behavioral Medicine, Acad. of Psychosomatic Medicine. Office: Polyclinic Med Ctr 2601 N Third St Harrisburg PA 17110

ASKENASE, PHILIP WILLIAM, medicine and pathology educator; b. Bklyn., June 7, 1939; s. Irving and Hilda Askenase; m. Marjorie Dopkin, June 21, 1967; children: Hilary, Isabel. BA in Physics magna cum laude, Brown U., 1961; MD cum laude, Yale U., 1965. Diplomate Am. Bd. Internal Medicine, Am. Bd. Allergy and Immunology. Intern, asst. resident in medicine Boston City Hosp., 1965-67; clin. assoc. arthritis and rheumatism sect. Nat. Inst. Arthritis and Metabolic Disease, NIH, 1957-59; Brit. Am. Heart fellow of Am. Heart Assn., London Hosp. Med. Coll., 1969-70; postdoctoral trainee in inflammatory diseases Yale U. Sch. Medicine New Haven, 1970-71, asst. prof. medicine, 1971-75, assoc. prof., 1975-82, assoc. prof. pathology, 1981-82, prof. medicine and pathology, 1982—, chief sect. clin. immunology dept. medicine, 1985—; attending physician Yale-New Haven Hosp., 1971—, West Haven (Conn.) VA Hosp., 1971—; vis. scientist immunoparasitology div. Nat. Inst. Med. Rsch., London, 1977-78; lectr. biology Yale U., 1981—, vis. prof. molecular immunology unit, 1991; hon. rsch. fellow tumor immunology unit dept. zoology Univ. Coll., London, 1984-85; mem. Yale Comprehensive Cancer Ctr., 1987—; ad hoc reviewer numerous med. jours; vis. prof., Woods Hole, Mass., 1980-84; mem. U.S.-Israel Binat. Sci. Found., 1982—, Med. Rsch. Coun. Can., NSF, Netherlands Cancer Found., Wellcome Truste, London, Med. Rsch. Coun., London, Can. Med. Rsch. Coun.; mem. adv. bd. spl. program in tropical diseases WHO; mem. pathology-A/study sect. NIH, 1976, mem. immunol. scis. study sect., 1983-87, ad hoc mem. allergy and immunology study sect. NIH, 1987-89. Mem. editl. bd. Jour. Clin. Immunology, 1983-88, Jour. Allergy and Clin. Immunology, 1980-85, Clin. and Diagnostic Lab. Immunology, 1983—; assoc. editor Jour. Immunology, 1976082; mem. editl. adv. bd. Jour. Molecular and Cellular Immunology, 1983—; contbr. over 200 articles, abstracts and revs. to med. jours., chpts. to books. Laurens Hammond grantee for cancer rsch., 1975-77, grantee NIH, 1987—. Fellow Am. Acad. Allergy; mem. AAAS, Am. Assn. Immunologists (membership com. 1978-82), Am. Assn. Physicians, Am. Fedn. Clin. Rsch., Am. Rheumatism Assn., Am. Soc. Clin. Investigation, Am. Soc. Tropical Medicine and Hygiene, Am. Thoracic Soc., Brit. Soc. Immunology, Clin. Immunology Soc., Collegium Internat. Allergogium, Conn. Allergy Soc., Histamine Rsch. Soc. N.Am., Reticuloendothelial Soc., Serotonin Soc., Skin. Pharmacology Soc., Soc. Investigative Dermatology, Interurban Clin. Club, Polish Acad. Arts and Scis. (fgn. corr.), Phi Beta Kappa, Alpha Omega Alpha. Office: Yale U Sch of Medicine 333 Cedar St New Haven CT 06520-8013

ASKENASY, ALEXANDER ROBERT, social psychologist; b. Frankfurt am Main, Germany; s. Robert Leon Kurt and Dorothea (Wernecke) A.; came to U.S., 1947, naturalized, 1953; B.A., U. Wis., 1950; A.M., Princeton U., 1954; Ph.D., Columbia U., 1962. Research asso. Psychol. Research Assos., Arlington, Va., 1956-58; project co-dir. World Fedn. Mental Health, N.Y.C., 1959-62; asso. prof. in research Am. U., Washington, 1963-69; research scientist N.Y. State Psychiat. Inst., N.Y.C., 1969—; research asso. in psychiatry Columbia U., N.Y.C., 1977-78, asst. prof. psychiatry, 1978—; field research, Peru, Germany, Belgium, Eng., Hawaii. Served with AUS, 1954-56. Walker fellow, 1951-52. Mem. Internat. Assn. Cross-Cultural Psychology, Internat., Am. sociol. assns., Soc. for Psychol. Study of Social Issues, AAUP, Internat. Soc. Polit. Psychology, Ea. Psychol. assns., World Fedn. Mental Health. Author: Attitudes toward Mental Patients: A Study across Cultures, 1974; Sources of the Ability to Estimate Foreign Attitudes, 1976; (with B.S. Dohrenwend and B.P. Dohrenwend) Effects of Social Class and Ethnic Group on Judgments of Stressful Life Events, 1977, The Psychiatric Epidemiology Research Interview Life Events Scale, 1982; also monographs on cross-cultural subjects, articles in profl. jours.; presented papers at internat. sci. congresses. Home: 900 W 190th St New York NY 10040-3633 Office: 722 W 168th St New York NY 10032-2603

ASKIN, STEPHEN JOHN, surgeon; b. Pitts., Oct. 4, 1935; s. Ralph John and Evalyn I. (Waterman) A.; m. Sandra Hernandez. AB, U. Princeton, 1957, MD, 1961. Cert. Am. Bd. Surgery. Intern, then resident Calif.-Pacific Med. Ctr. (formerly Presbyn. Med. Ctr.), San Francisco, 1961-68; pvt. practice gen. surgery various hosps., San Francisco, 1969—; chief dept. surgery St. Lukes Hosp., San Francisco, 1986-91. Capt. USAF, 1962-64. Mem. Calif. Med. Assn., San Francisco Med. Soc. (ins. mediation com., editl. bd.). Republican. Office: 1580 Valencia #702 San Francisco CA 94110

ASKREN, CARL COLWELL, plastic surgeon; b. Atlanta, Nov. 10, 1956; s. Edward Leroy and Anne Colwell Askren; m. Karen Ashe, June 4, 1983; children: Annette Nicole, Charles Colin. BS, Ga. Tech., Atlanta, 1978, MS, 1980; MD, Emory U., 1984. Diplomate Am. Bd. Plastic Surgery. Asst. clin. prof. U. Calif./San Francisco and Fresno Affiliated Hosps., Fresno, 1995—; med. dir. Cranio Facial Anomalies Panel, Valley Children's Hosp., Fresno, 1994—. Contbg. author: (book) Reoperative Aesthetic and Reconstructive Plastic Surgery, 1995; illustrator: (book) Cardiovascular Pathophysiology, 1987. Fellow ACS; mem. Am. Soc. Plastic and Reconstructive Surgeons. Office: Sierra Plastic Surgery 6153 North Thesta Ave Fresno CA 93710

ASMA, LAWRENCE FRANCIS, priest; b. Waukegan, Ill., Oct. 21, 1947; s. Francis Victor and Isabelle Amelia (Recktenwald) A. BA in English, U. Wis., Whitewater, 1969; MA in English, Ill. State U., 1974; MA in Scripture magna cum laude, De Andreis Sem., 1982, MDiv, 1983. Ordained priest Roman Cath. Chr., 1983. Dir. spritual formation Cardinal Glennon Coll., St. Louis, 1983-85, instr. theology dept., 1983-85; chaplain St. Vincent's Div. DePaul Health Ctr., St. Louis, 1985—; Bd. dirs. Rosati Stabilization Ctr., St. Louis, 1988-94; vice chmn. Rosati Stabilization Ctr., 1990-94. Local religious superior Congregation of the Mission, 1994—. With USNR, 1970-72, Vietnam. Mem. Assn. Mental Health Clergy (bd. cert.), Cath. Biblical Assn., Congregation of Mission, Sigma Tau Delta. Office: DePaul Health Center 12303 De Paul Dr Bridgeton MO 63044-2512

ASNIS, MARTIN, psychiatrist; b. N.Y.C., July 1, 1928; s. Sidney and Mary Asnis; m. Muriel Asnis. BS in Pharmacy, Fordham U., 1949; MD, U. of Padua, Italy, 1963. Diplomate Am. Bd. of Psychiatry and Neurology. Resident in psychiatry Mt. Sinai Hosp., N.Y.C., 1964-65, Hillside L.I. Jewish Hosp., N.Y.C., 1965-67; univ. psychiatrist Columbia U. Psychiat. div. Student Health Svc., 1968-74; attending psychiatrist St. Luke's-Roosevelt Hosp. Ctr., N.Y.C., 1968—. Mem. Am. Psychiat. Assn., N.Y. County Med. Soc.

ASPDEN, RICHARD MALCOLM, biophysicist, researcher; b. Malta, Sept. 23, 1955; s. Ronald and Sheila Beulah (Ducker) A.; m. Anne Maclean Goudie, Apr. 11, 1981; children: Jonathan Maclean, Mark Barnabas, Reuben Stuart. BA with 1st class honors, U. York, Eng., 1977; PhD, U. Manchester, Eng., 1981. Rsch. assoc. U. Manchester, 1983-88; Wellcome rsch. fellow U. Lund, Sweden, 1988-90, U. Manchester, 1990; Wellcome rsch. fellow U. Aberdeen, Scotland, 1990-91, rsch. fellow, 1991-92, Med. Rsch. Coun. sr. rsch. fellow, 1992—. Editor Lumbar Spine Disorders, 1995; contbr. over 50 articles to profl. jours. Mem. Instn. Physics and Engring. in Medicine and Biology, Soc. for Back Pain Rsch. (hon. sec. 1993-95). Office: U Aberdeen Dept Orthopaedics, Polwarth Bldg Foresterhill, Aberdeen AB25 2ZD, Scotland

ASPER, SAMUEL PHILIPS, medical administrator; b. Oak Park, Ill., July 14, 1916; m.Ann Carver, 1942; children: Ann, Lucy. AB, Baylor U., 1936; MD, Johns Hopkins U., 1940. House officer in medicine Johns Hopkins Hosp., Balt., 1940-41; rsch. fellow Thorndike Meml. Lab., Harvard U., 1941-42, 46-47; from instr. to prof. Sch. Medicine Johns Hopkins U., 1947-85, assoc. dean, 1957-68; v.p. med. affairs Johns Hopkins Hosp., 1970-73; emeritus prof. medicine Johns Hopkins U., 1985—; prof. internal medicine, dean faculty med. sci. Am. U., Beirut, 1973-78; chief staff Univ. Hosp., 1973-78; dep. exec. v.p. ACP, 1979-81; pres. Edn. Com. Fgn. Med. Grads., 1982-85, emeritus pres., 1985—. Major U.S. Army Med. Corps, 1942-45. Master ACP (pres. 1969-70, emeritus pres. 1985—); mem. Inst. Medicine/Nat. Acad. Sci., Endocrine Soc. (v.p. 1966-67), Assn. Am. Physicians, Am. Soc. Clin. Investigation. Address: PO Box 153 Gibson Island MD 21056

ASSADI, FARAHNAK, nephrologist; b. Rasht, Iran, July 18, 1943; came to U.S., 1970; s. Kazem and Khadijeh (Hankani) A.; m. Nassrin Jadali, Oct. 22, 1970; children: Kathryn, Steven. MD, Tehran U., 1969. Diplomate Am. Bd. Pediatrics, sub-bd. pediatric nephrology. Resident in pediatrics Hahnemann & Thomas Jefferson Univs., Phila., 1973-75; fellow in pediatric nephrology U. Pa. Sch. Med. Children's Hosp. Phila., 1975-77; asst. prof. pediatrics U. Med. Scis., Tehran, 1977-80; asst. prof. pediatrics U. Ill., Chgo., 1980-86, assoc. prof., 1986-90; prof. Med. Coll. Ga., Augusta, 1990-91, U. Pa., Phila., 1991-92; adj. prof. sch. life and health scis. U. Del., Wilmington, 1992-95; prof. pediatrics Jefferson Med. Coll., Phila., 1995—; chief divsn. pediatric nephrology Med. Coll. Ga., 1990-91; med. dir. children's program Children's Hosp. Phila., 1991-92; chief divsn. nephrology Thomas Jefferson U. Hosp., 1992—. Contbr. articles to profl. jours. Grantee numerous univ.-based and pharm. agys., 1983—. Mem. Soc. for Pediatric Rsch., Am. Soc. Pediatric Nephrology, Am. Soc. Nephrology, Internat. Pediatric Nephrology Assn., Am. Fedn. Clin. Rsch., Eastern Soc. Pediatric Rsch. Office: AI duPont Childrens Hosp Wilmington DE 19899

ASSIF, DAVID, dentist; b. Tel Aviv, Sept. 19, 1937; s. Naftali and Chasia (Garbuz) Ziniuk; m. Edna Sum, Aug. 28, 1962; children: Yifat, Guy, Efrat, Tal. DMD, Faculty Dental Medicine. Jerusalem, 1965. Coord., dep. head prosthodontics Sch. Dental Medicine Tel Aviv U., 1979-83, clin. lectr. in prosthodontics, 1979-83, sr. clin. lectr. in prosthodontics, 1983-92, clin. assoc. prof. in prosthodontics, 1992—, mem. in-charge of implant prosthodontics, 1995—. Contbr. articles to profl. jours., chpts. to books. Capt. Israel Armed Forces, 1955-75. Home: 40 Yehuda Hanassi St, Tel Aviv 69393, Israel Office: Tel Aviv U, Sch Dental Medicine, Tel Aviv 69978, Israel

ASTLER, VERNON BENSON, surgeon; b. Wyoming, Ohio, Sept. 5, 1925; s. Vernon Wolfert and Blanche (Benson) A.; m. Louise Menge, Aug. 9, 1949 (div.); children: Kim Louise, Kristy Lee, Douglas Vernon; m. Diane Rosacker, Dec. 31, 1969 (div.); m. Frances Croft, Mar. 21, 1991. Student, Miami U., Oxford, Ohio, 1943-45; MD, Temple U., 1949; MS, U. Mich., 1953. Diplomate Am. Bd. Surgery. Intern Univ. Hosp., Ann Arbor, Mich., 1949-50, resident, 1950-57; practice medicine specializing in surgery, Boynton Beach, Fla., 1958-90; mem. hon. staff Bethesda Hosp., Boca Raton Hosp.; past mem. Fla. Bd. Med. Examiners, pres., 1971-73; past mem. Fla. Council of 100. Served with M.C., AUS, 1953-55. Fellow ACS (life mem.), Coll. Physicians of Phila., Southeastern Surg. Congress; mem. AMA, Am. Hosp. Assn. (com. on physicians 1974-76), Am. Soc. Bariatric Physicians, Fla. Med. Assn. (life, gov. 1971-84, pres. 1975-76), Frederick A. Coller Surg. Soc., Delray Beach C. of C., Am. Legion, Sigma Nu, Phi Chi. Clubs: Sapphire Valley Country (N.C.). Lodges: Masons, Shriners, Kiwanis. Home: 4 Gatehouse Ct Asheville NC 28803

ASTON, EDWARD ERNEST, IV, dermatologist; b. Jersey City, Jan. 14, 1944; m. Kirsten Anita. B.A., U. Md.-College Park, 1966; M.D., U. Md.-Balt., 1969. Diplomate Am. Bd. Dermatology. Intern, Orange County Med. Ctr., Orange, Calif., 1969-70; resident U. Calif.-Irvine-Orange County Med. Ctr., 1971-74; practice medicine specializing in dermatology Fullerton Med. Clinic of Dermatology, Calif., 1974—. Office: 301 W Bastanchury Rd Fullerton CA 92635

ASTON, SHERRELL JERONE, plastic surgeon, educator; b. Nansemono County, Va., July 14, 1942; s. Walter Mathew, Jr. and Mary Louise (Bracy) A.; B.A., U. Va., 1964, M.D., 1968; m. Michelle Sykes, Nov. 24, 1967 (dec. July 1995); children—Walter Mathew III, Sherrell Jerone, Bradford Sykes. Intern, UCLA, 1968-69, resident, chief resident in surgery, 1969-73; Halsted fellow Johns Hopkins Hosp., 1971; resident, chief resident in plastic surgery NYU, 1973-75; chief plastic surgery service Manhattan VA Hosp., 1975-79; assoc. prof. plastic surgery NYU Med. Center, 1977-93, prof. surgery, 1993—; attending surgeon Inst. Reconstructive Plastic Surgery, NYU Med. Center; chmn. dept. plastic surgery, chmn. plastic surgery dept. Manhattan Eye, Ear and Throat Hosp., Bellevue Hosp. Diplomate Am. Bd. Surgery, Am. Bd. Plastic Surgery. Fellow ACS, N.Y. Acad. Medicine, Am. Soc. Plastic and Reconstructive Surgery; mem. N.Y. State, N.Y. County med. socs., Soc. Academic Surgeons, Pan Am. Med. Assn., Brazilian Plastic Surgery Soc., Am. Soc. for Aesthetic Plastic Surgery (pres. 1993-94), Am. Assn. for Accreditation Ambulatory Plastic Surgery Facilities (founding mem., dir. 1980—), Am. Assn. Plastic Surgeons. Author numerous surg. publs. Home: 765 Park Ave New York NY 10021-4254 Office: 728 Park Ave New York NY 10021

ASTRACHAN, BORIS MORTON, psychiatry educator, consultant; b. N.Y.C., Dec. 1, 1931; s. Isaac and Ethel (Kahn) A.; m. Batja Sanders, June 17, 1956; children: David Isaac, Joseph Henry, Michael Sanders, Ellen Beth Astrachan-Fletcher. BA cum laude, Alfred (N.Y.) U., 1952; MD, Albany Med. Coll., 1956. Lic. Ill., Conn.; bd. cert. in psychiatry. Intern, resident USN Hosp., St. Albans and Phila., N.Y., 1956-57, 57-58; asst. depot psychiatrist recruitment tng. depot USMC, Parris Island, S.C., 1958-61; resident in psychiatry dept. psychiatry Yale U., New Haven, 1961-63, from asst. prof. to assoc. prof. dept. psychiatry, 1963-71; dir. Conn. Mental Health Ctr., New Haven, 1971-87; prof. dept. psychiatry Yale U., New Haven, 1971-90; prof., head dept. psychiatry U. Ill., Chgo., 1990—; mem. NIMH Initial Rev. Group, Rockville, Md., 1987-90, chmn., 1989-91; mem. IBM Mental Health Adv. Bd., White Plains, N.Y., 1990—; mem. adv. bd. ADAMAA, Washington, 1985-86; mem. rsch. task force Pres. Commn. on Mental Health and Illness, Washington, 1977-78; vis. prof. U. Rotterdam, Amsterdam, 1986, Boston U., 1996. Co-author: (with Tischler) Quality Assurance in Mental Health, 1983; contbr. articles to profl. jours. (Citation classic 1986). Mem. SHCCC, Hartford, Conn., 1980s; mem. clin. adv. com. DMHDD, Chgo., 1995—; chair mental health task force DCFS, Chgo., 1993—; chair Mental Health Svc. Sys. Adv. Coun., Springfield and Chgo., Ill., 1992-95. Lt. comdr. USN, 1955-61. Fellow Am. Coll. Psychiatrists, Am. Psychiat. Assn. (life, trustee-at-large, Adminstrv. Psychiatry award 1995), Am. Assn. Psychiat. Adminstrs. (Past. Pres. award 1992); mem. AMA. Jewish. Home: 2902B 333E Ontario St Chicago IL 60611 Office: Dept Psychiatry M/C 913 912 S Wood St Chicago IL 60612

ASTWOOD, WILLIAM PETER, psychotherapist; b. N.Y.C., May 18, 1940; s. Henry Kenneth and Rose Margit (Eastby) A.; m. Sharon Lisa Sprung, June 10, 1979; 1 child, Jesse Jack. BA, CUNY, 1962; MA, NYU, 1967, PhD, 1975. Case worker, supr. dept. social services City N.Y., 1964-67; community orgn. trainer Block Communities, Inc., N.Y.C., 1967-68; field rep. Office Econ. Opportunity, N.Y.C., 1968-70, U.S. Dept. Health, Edn., Welfare, N.Y.C., 1970-71; pvt. practice Bklyn., 1971—; dir. family therapy div. DiMele Ctr. for Psychotherapy, N.Y.C., 1990—; bd. dirs. South Beach Psychiat. Ctr., Bklyn., 1976-78, N.Y. Group for Comprehensive Family Therapy, Mineola, 1988—; exec. bd. Met. Ctr. for Psychotherapy, N.Y.C., 1969-72. Co-author: Practicing Psychotherapy, 1980. Exec. bd. Social Service Employees Union, N.Y.C., 1965-67. Staff sgt. USANG, 1963-69. Mem. N.Y. Acad. Scis., Assn. for Humanistic Psychology, Am. Assn. Marriage and Family Therapy (clin.). Home: 394 Atlantic Ave Brooklyn NY 11217-1703 Office: 163 Clinton St Brooklyn NY 11201-4601

ATALA, ANTHONY JOHN, surgeon; b. July 14, 1958; s. Michael and Isabel Atala; m. Katherine Aala, May 13, 1985. BA, U. Miami, 1981; MD, U. Louisville, 1985, postgrad. in urology, 1990; postgrad. in pediatric urology, Harvard Med. Sch., Boston, 1992. Intern in surgery U. Louisville Sch. of Medicine, 1985-86, resident in surgery, 1986-87, resident in urology, 1987-89, chief resident in urology, 1989-90; rsch. fellow dept. surgery Children's Hosp., Harvard Med. Sch., Boston, 1990-91, clin. fellow dept. surgery, 1991-92, instr., 1992-93, asst. prof., 1993—, dir. lab. for tissue engring., 1993—, mem. investigations rev. bd., 1994; mem. med. adv. bd. Reprogenesis, Dallas, 1993, Urosurge, Iowa City, 1993, Surgijet, Boston, 1995, Nat. Office ARC, Washington, 1995, Nat. Kidney Found., Boston, 1994; mem. study sect. Am. Found. for Urologic Disease, Balt., 1994. Editor Tissue Engring., 1995; cons. Jour. Urology, 1993, Lancet, 1994, (book) Current Concepts in Tissue Engineering, 1995; contbr. articles to profl. jours. Med. adv. bd. Nat. Kidney Found., Boston, 1994; mem. investigations rev. bd. Harvard Med. Sch., Boston, 1994. Rsch. award ACS, 1990, Am. Acad. Pediat., 1993, Am. Soc. Plastic Surgery, 1994. Mem. AMA, AAAS, Am. Urol. Assn. (program com. 1989), Soc. for Basic Urol. Rsch. (program com. 1990). Office: Childrens Hosp/Harvard Med 300 Longwood Ave Boston MA 02193

ATAMIAN, SUSAN, nurse; b. Cambridge, Mass., Sept. 14, 1950; d. Raymond H. and Alice (Chakerian) A. BA, Simmons Coll., 1972, MS, 1995. RN, Mass.; cert. infection control. Staff nurse Mass. Gen. Hosp., Boston, 1972-74, pvt. duty nurse, 1975-76, staff nurse, 1976-77; rsch. asst. III U. Cinn. Hosp., 1980-81; rsch. study nurse Mass. Gen. Hosp., Boston, 1977-80, instr. nursing, 1982-84, sr. rsch. study nurse, 1984-87, dir. clin. rsch. nurse group, 1985-90, infection control nurse, 1988-90; infection control nurse clinician Mass. Gen. Hosp., Boston, 1990-92; staff nurse Kimberly Nurses, Orange, Calif., 1982; coord., clin. rsch., vascular surg. div. Mass. Gen. Hosp., 1992—; cons. nutrition and liver diseases, McGaw Labs., Santa Ana, Calif., 1980-81; chmn. faculty devel. libr. com. Shepard Gill Sch., Boston, 1983-84; mem. rsch. nurses forum, Mass. Gen. Hosp., 1992—. Class agt. 1972 Simmons Coll., 1972, 86—, mem. com. alumnae fund, 1987-89, reunion com., 1990—, com. on classes, 1991-92, class of 1972 reunion fund chair, 1991-92. Mem. ANA, Am. Nurses Found. Century Club, Assn. Practitioners Infection Control, Soc. for Vascular Nursing, Mass. Nurses Assn., Rsch. Nurses Forum Mass. Gen. Hosp., Simmons Coll. Nursing Honor Soc., Simmons Club Boston (bd. dirs. 1988-90, v.p. 1990-92, co-chmn. boutique 1992-94, mem. nominating com. 1994-95), Coun. Armenian Am. Nurses (chair resource com.), Sigma Theta Tau. Mem. Armenian Apostolic Ch. Office: Mass Gen Hosp Wang Acc Ste 458 Boston MA 02114

ATCHISON, DAVID ANDREW, optometry educator; b. Melbourne, Victoria, Australia, Apr. 5, 1954; s. Douglas Stuart and Margaret Louise (Newnham) A.; m. Janette Margaret Johnson, March 18, 1978; children: Stuart, Callum. BS in Optometry, U. Melbourne, 1975, MS in Optometry, 1978, PhD, 1984. Cert. optometrist. Optometrist Melbourne, 1976-83; demonstrator dept. optometry U. Melbourne; rsch. officer Sola Internat. Holdings, Adelaide, Australia, 1983-84; lectr. dept. optometry Queensland Inst. Tech., Brisbane, Australia, 1985, sr. lectr. Sch. of Optometry, 1989; assoc. prof. Sch. of Optometry, 1991—; mem. 4 coms. Standards Assn. Australia, 1986—; mem. com. SC172 ophthalmic optics Internat. Standards Orgn., 1989—. Contbr. articles to profl. jours. Fellow Am. Acad. Optometry (Garland W. Clay award 1980), Victorian Coll. Optometry; mem. Applied Vision Assn. (UK), Australian Optometrical Assn., Soc. for Photo-Illumination Engrs., Australian Optical Soc., Optical Soc. Am., Queensland U. of Tech. Found. (life). Office: Queensland U Tech Sch Optometry, Locked Bag No 2, Red Hill QLD 4059, Australia

ATER, STEWART BRUCE, child neurologist; b. Dayton, Ohio, Oct. 16, 1949; s. Tom Farris Ater and Marjorie Lee (Ewer) Wallace; m. Joann Lynnette Miller, Mar. 4, 1972; children: Mindy Michelle, Sean David. Pre-med. student, U. Colo., 1969-72; MD, Washington U., St. Louis, 1976. Diplomate Am. Bd. Pediat., Am. Bd. Psychiatry and Neurology, with spl. qualification in child neurology. Resident in pediatrics Case Western Reserve U., Cleve., 1976-78; resident in pediatrics U. Utah, Salt Lake City, 1978-79, resident in child neurology, 1979-82, fellow in epilepsy and clin. pharmacology, 1982-84; asst. prof. pediatrics and neurology U. Colo., Denver, 1984-88; fellow in neurophysiology Baylor U., Houston, Tex., 1988-89; pres. and neurologist Pediatric Neurology P.A., Houston, 1989—; cons., nat. speakers bur. Abbot Labs., Chgo., 1986-90; cons. Brenham (Tex.) State Sch., 1990-93; med. dir. pediatric neuropsychiat. staff West Oaks Hosp., Houston, 1990-92; cons., speaker Sigma Tau, Rome, Italy, 1991-93; profl. adv. bd. mem. Attention Deficit Disorders Assn. Mem. AMA, Am. Acad. Neurology, Am. Epilepsy Soc., Child Neurolgy Soc., Phi Beta Kappa. Democrat. Office: Pediatric Neurology PA 7737 SE Freeway Ste 955 Houston TX 77074

ATHANASSIOU, EVANGELOS THEMISTOKLIS, general surgeon, educator; b. Larissa, Greece, Aug. 29, 1948; s. Themistoklis and Catherine. Diploma agrl. engr., U. Salonika, Greece, 1971; diploma of med., U. Athens, Greece, 1979. With Sugar Factory S.A., Larissa, Greece, 1971; medical resident Mitilini Gen. Hosp., Mitilini, Greece, 1980-81, St. Savas Anticancer Hosp., Athens, Greece, 1980-82, Municipal Gen. Hosp., Athens, Greece, 1982-83; sr. house officer Mansfield Gen. Hosp., Nottingham, England, 1983-84, Bassetlaw Gen. Hosp., Worksop, England, 1984-89; rsch. fellow Nottingham U. City Hosp., Nottingham, England, 1989; pvt. practice Sapkas Pvt. Hosp., Larissa, Greece, 1990-95; asst. prof. surgery U. Thessaly Med. Sch., 1996—. Author: Surgical Horm Manipulation in Advanced Breast Cancer, 1985. Grantee Lemos Soc., Athens, London, 1984, 89. Mem. Greek Surgeons Soc., Greek Oncolog. Soc., British Med. Coun., Senology Soc. Home: 60 Hatziyianni Str, Larissa 412-21, Greece Office: 23 Papanastasiou Str, Larissa 412-22, Greece

ATIEA, SALAH HAMAD, surgeon; b. Alexandria, Egypt, Oct. 1, 1954; s. Hamad Atiea Metwally; m. Iman Ibrahim Ghanem, Feb. 20, 1986. MBChB, U. Alexandria, 1979, DSc, 1986. House officer Alexandria U., 1980; gen. practitioner Ministry of Health, Alexandria, 1981-83; resident in urology Ministry of Health, Matrouh, Egypt, 1983-84, resident in surgery, 1984-85, specialist in surgery, 1985-86, chief surgeon, 1987—; dir. Siwa Hosp., Matrouh, 1984-85, 86-87, Saloom Hosp., Matrouh, 1987. Home: Masaken El Awam, Matrouh Egypt Office: Alexandria, Matrouh Egypt

ATKINS, CLAYTON H., family physician, epidemiologist, educator; b. Beech Grove, Ind., Nov. 12, 1944; s. Amos H. Atkins and Edythe E. (Dale) Heneghan; m. Carole A. Kirlin, Aug. 2, 1974; children: Brenda M. Spencer, Craig N., Angela C. AB in Chemistry, Ind. U., Bloomington, 1965, MAT in Chemistry, 1967; MD, Ind. U., Indpls., 1969; BS summa cum laude in Math., Butler U., 1980. Diplomate Am. Bd. Family Practice. Rotating intern Meth. Hosp. Ind. Inc., Indpls., 1969-70; pvt. practice, Greenwood, Ind., 1970-94; mem. active staff family practice dept., 1970—; hosp. epidemiologist, mem. med. bd. dirs. St. Francis Hosp. and Health Ctrs., Beech Grove, 1989—, mem. exec. mgmt. com., 1995—; pres. med. staff St. Francis Hosp. and Health Ctrs., Beech Grove, Ind., 1995; mem. courtesy med. staff family practice dept. Cmty. Hosp. South, Indpls., 1970—; instr. NSF math. for high sch. tchrs. Ind. U., Bloomington, 1966-67; instr. microgiology Ind. Ctrl. Coll. (now U. Indpls.), 1968; adj. asst. prof. Butler U. Coll. Pharmacy, Indpls., 1991-95. With USAFR, 1971-77, 91— maj. med. corps. Fellow Am. Acad. Family Physicians; mem. AMA, Ind. Med. Assn., Inpls. Med. Soc., Assn. for Practitioners in Infection Control, Epidemiology, Inc., Soc. for Hosp. Epidemiology in Am., Math. Assn. Am., Sigma Xi, Phi Kappa Phi, Phi Delta Kappa, Alpha Epsilon Delta, Phi Lambda Upsilon, Phi Eta Sigma, Mu Alpha Theta. Home: 6506 Boulder Ct S Indianapolis IN 46217 Office: 100 N Madison Ave Ste 200 Greenwood IN 46142-3578

ATKINS, DIXIE LEE, critical care nurse; b. Elkin, N.C., Oct. 8, 1953; d. Charles Lee and Betty Lou (Southard) Cook; m. Ronnie Steven Atkins, Aug. 30, 1984; children: Sarah Kathryn, Carl Steven, William Shane. AD in Applied Sci., Surry C.C., Dobson, 1973; student, St. Joseph's Coll., North Windham, Maine, 1990—. Cert. provider ACLS, NRP, Am. Heart Assn. Indsl. nurse Brown-Wooten Mills Inc., Mount Airy, N.C.; relief charge nurse pediatrics Forsyth Meml. Hosp., Winston-Salem, N.C., 1973-78; charge nurse emergency rm. No. Hosp. Surry County, Mount Airy, 1979—; nursing supr. No. Hosp. of Surry County, Mount Airy, 1995—; instr., CEN, basic trauma life support, CPR; mobile intensive care nurse; provider advanced cardiac life support, PALS; provider NRP; neonatal recussitation provider; part-time instr. Surry C.C. Mem. Surry County chpt. MADD; bd. dirs. Dobson Rescue Squad; chairperson Surry Nursing Domiciliary Home Cmty. Adv. Com.; vol. ARC. Mem. Emergency Nurses Assn. Home: PO Box 992 407 Marion St Dobson NC 27017-8430

ATKINSON, A. KELLEY, insurance company executive; b. Tulsa, Okla., July 7, 1947; s. Milton A. Atkinson and Helen G. Brower; m. Patricia L. Morton, June 28, 1969 (dec. 1991); children: Gregory, Brent; m. Pamela A. Bender, Feb. 14, 1993. BS, Tex. Christian U., 1969; MBA, Ariz. State U., 1972. Sales rep. Mallinckrodt, Inc., Saint Louis, 1972-73, assoc. product mgr., 1973-74, regional sales mgr., 1974-76, mgr. market rsch. & data systems, 1976-77; mgr. product mktg. Intermedics, Inc., Freeport, Tex., 1977-79, dir. mktg., 1979-82, v.p. mktg., 1982-83; pres., COO Neuro Systems, Inc., Garland, Tex., 1983; pres. BoMed Mfg., Irvine, Calif., 1984; pres., CEO Physicians Health Plan Utah, Salt Lake City, 1984-87, United Health Care Ga., Atlanta, 1987—; Pres. Ga. Assn. HMOs, Atlanta, 1989, 94-96; adj. prof. Mercer U., Atlanta, 1990-92. Treas. Windward Cmty. Svcs. Assn., Alpharetta, Ga., 1995-96. Office: United Healthcare Ga 2970 Clairmont Rd NE Ste 300 Atlanta GA 30329-4412

ATKINSON, ARTHUR JOHN, JR., clinical pharmacologist, educator; b. Chgo., Mar. 22, 1938; s. Arthur John and Inez (Hill) A.; A.B. in Chemistry, Harvard U., 1959; M.D., Cornell U., 1963. Intern and asst. resident in medicine Mass. Gen. Hosp., Boston, 1963-65, chief resident and Howard Carroll fellow in medicine Passavant Meml. Hosp., Chgo., instr. in medicine Northwestern U., Chgo., 1967-68; fellow in clin. pharmacology U. Cin., 1968-69, asst. prof. pharmacology, 1969; vis. scientist dept. toxicology Karolinska Inst., Stockholm, Sweden, 1970; asst. prof. medicine and pharmacology Northwestern U., Chgo., 1970-73, assoc. prof., 1973-76, prof., 1976-94; corp. v.p. clin. devel. & med. affairs Upjohn Co., 1994-95; v.p. clin. rsch. & devel. & worldwide clin. pharmacology Pharmaciz & Upjohn, Inc., 1995—. Served with NIH, USPHS, 1965-67. Recipient Faculty Devel. award in clin. pharmacology Pharm. Mfrs. Assn., 1970-72; Burroughs Wellcome scholar in clin. pharmacology, 1972-77. Fellow ACP; mem. Central Soc. Clin. Research, Am. Soc. for Clin. Investigation, Am. Soc. Pharmacology and Exptl. Therapeutics (Harry Gold award 1989), Am. Soc. Clin. Pharmacology and Therapeutics (pres. 1995-96, Rawls Palmer award 1983), Am. Bd. Clin. Pharmacology (pres. 1996—), Assn. Am. Physicians, Chgo. Soc. Internal Medicine (pres. 1984-85), Alpha Omega Alpha. Clubs: Chgo. Yacht, Gull Lake Yacht. Mem. editl. bd. jours. Rational Drug Therapy, 1972-83, Clin. Pharmacology and Therapeutics, 1973—, Pharm. Revs., 1977—, Therapeutic Drug Monitoring, 1979-94. Home: 6176 Hidden Lake Cir Richland MI 49083 Office: Pharmaciz & Upjon Inc Kalamazoo MI 49001

ATKINSON, DAWSON ROSS, periodontist; b. New Orleans, Mar. 6, 1953; s. James Dawson and Kathryne (Winham) A.; m. Carol Jo Clark, Aug. 15, 1976; children: Christopher Ross, Emily Kathleen, Daniel Dawson. Student, Hendrix Coll., Conway, Ark., 1971-73; BS, Henderson State U., 1975; DDS, La. State U., 1980; MS, U. Mo., 1982. Pvt. practice periodontics Hot Springs, Ark., 1982—. Dist. advancement chmn. Boy Scouts of Am., Hot Springs, 1985—, theme co-chmn. Expo Boy Scouts of Am., 1987. Served with USN, 1972-74. Named Eagle Scout Boy Scouts of Am., 1970; recipient award Pierre Fuschard Dental Honor Soc., 1995. Fellow Internat. Coll. Oral Implantologists; mem. ADA, Ark. Dental Assn., Am. Acad. Periodontology (bd. eligible 1994), Ark. Soc. Periodontists (pres. 1984-85), Ark. Dental Assn., Garland County Dental Soc. (1st v.p. 1985-86), S.W. Dist. Dental Soc., S.W. Soc. Periodontists, Am. Acad. Oral Medicine. Methodist. Home: 209 Bafanridge St Hot Springs National Park AR 71901-8157 Office: 2633 Malvern Ave Hot Springs National Park AR 71901-8176

ATKINSON, HOLLY GAIL, physician, journalist, author, lecturer, human rights activist; b. Detroit, Oct. 20, 1952. BA in Biology magna cum laude, Colgate U., 1974; MD, U. Rochester, 1978; MS in Journalism, Columbia U., 1981. Diplomate Nat. Med. Bds. Intern in internal medicine Strong Meml. Hosp., Rochester, N.Y., 1978-79; rschr. Walter Cronkite's Universe show CBS News, N.Y.C., 1981-82; med. reporter CBS Morning News, N.Y.C., 1982-83; on-air co-host Bodywatch health show PBS, 1983-88; contbg. editor and health columnist New Woman mag., 1983-88; on-air corr., med. editor Lifetime Med. TV, 1985-89, sr. v.p. programming and med. affairs, 1989-93; assoc. editor Journal Watch, 1986-90; med. corr. Today Show NBC News, N.Y.C., 1991-94; exec. v.p. Reuters Health, N.Y.C., 1994—; editor HealthNews, 1994—; mem. trustee's com. U. Rochester, 1983-90. Author: Women and Fatigue, 1986. Vol. nat. and local level Am. Heart Assn., 1984-91, bd. dirs., chmn. nat. comms. com. Am. Heart Assn., 1987-91; bd. dirs. Phys. Human Rights, 1994—, NOW LDEF, 1996—. Recipient Young Achievers award Nat. Coun. Women, 1986, Achievement award Soc. Advancement Women's Health Rsch., 1995. Mem. Phi Beta Kappa. Office: Reuters Health Info Svc 825 8th Ave New York NY 10019-7416

ATKINSON, JOHN PEPPER, physician; b. Macon, Ga., Aug. 22, 1942; s. Harold Cook and Lily Emma (Sprott) A.; m. Wanda Watkins, Sept. 22, 1973; children: Thomas Harold, Steven Pepper. AB, Emory U., 1964; MD, Duke U., 1968. Intern Med. Coll. Ga., Augusta, 1968-69, resident, 1971-73; staff physician Gracewood State Sch. and Hosp., Augusta, 1973-74; pvt. practice internal medicine Macon, 1975—. With USN, 1969-71. Office: 420 Charter Blvd Macon GA 31210-4854

ATKINSON, RICHARD CHATHAM, university president; b. Oak Park, Ill., Mar. 19, 1929; s. Herbert and Margaret (Feuerbach) A.; m. Rita Loyd, Aug. 20, 1952; 1 dau., Lynn Loyd. Ph.B., U. Chgo., 1948; Ph.D., Ind. U., 1955. Lectr. applied math. and stats. Stanford (Calif.) U., 1956-57, assoc. prof. psychology, 1961-64, prof. psychology, 1964-80; asst. prof. psychology UCLA, 1957-61; dep. dir. NSF, 1975-76, acting dir., 1976, dir., 1976-80; chancellor, prof. cognitive sci. U. Calif., San Diego, 1980-95; pres. U. Calif., Oakland, 1995—. Author: (with Atkinson, Smith and Bem) Introduction to Psychology, 12th edit., 1996, Computer Assisted Instruction, 1969, An Introduction to Mathematical Learning Theory, 1965, Studies in Mathematical Psychology, 1964, Contemporary Developments in Mathematical Psychology, 1974, Mind and Behavior, 1980, Stevens' Handbook of Experimental Psychology, 1988. Served with AUS, 1954-56. Guggenheim fellow, 1967; fellow Ctr. for Advanced Study in Behavioral Scis., 1963; recipient Distinguished Research award Social Sci. Research Council, 1962. Fellow APA (pres. exptl. div. 1974, Disting. Sci. Contbn. award 1977, Thorndike award 1980), AAAS (pres. 1989-90), Am. Psychol. Soc. (William James fellow 1985), Am. Acad. Arts and Scis.; mem. Soc. Exptl. Psychologists, Nat. Acad. Scis., Am. Philos. Soc., Nat. Acad. Edn., Inst. of Medicine, Psychonomic Soc., Cognitive Sci. Soc., Cosmos Club (Washington), Explorer's Club (N.Y.C.). Home: 70 Rincon Rd Kensington CA 94707 Office: U Calif Office of Pres 300 Lakeside Dr Oakland CA 94612-3550

ATKINSON, TAMMY RAY, clinical laboratory administrator; b. Asheville, N.C., Oct. 7, 1958; d. Ray and Evelyn (Crawford) Brendle; m. Rodney J. Craig, July 13, 1979 (div. Mar. 1984); 1 child, Wayne Michael Craig; m. Donnie Paul Atkinson, Feb. 14, 1986; 1 child, Aarron Atkinson. AD in Med. Lab. Tech., Asheville Buncombe Tech. Coll., 1979; BS, Mars Hill (N.C.) Coll., 1989. Lab. technician Transylvania Hosp., Brevard, N.C., 1979-80, 83-89, Mission Hosp., Asheville, 1980-83; lab. supr. Newland Svc. Orgn., Brevard, 1989-93, Lab Corp., Asheville, 1993—. Republican. Baptist. Office: Lab Corp 2 Hendersonville Rd Asheville NC 28804

ATKINSON, WILLIAM JAMES, JR., retired cardiologist; b. Mobile, Ala., July 4, 1917; s. William J. and Gertrude (Smith) A.; m. Glenda E. Street, Oct. 29, 1949; children: Glenda Street, Regina Creswell, William James III. BA, Amherst Coll., 1939; MD, U. Pa., 1943; MS in Internal Medicine, St. Louis U., 1949. Intern, Phila. Gen. Hosp., 1943-44; resident in medicine St. Louis City Hosp., 1946-48; resident in cardiology St. Louis U., 1948-49; practice medicine specializing in internal medicine and cardiology, Mobile, Ala., 1949—; chief cardiac clinic Mobile City Hosp., 1950-60; electrocardiographer Mobile Infirmary, 1949-92, Providence Hosp., 1949-75; cardiologist Diagnostic and Med. Clinic, 1949-92; mem. staff U. South Ala. Med. Ctr. Hosp., Mobile Infirmary, Providence Hosp.; chmn. bd. Diagnostic and Med. Clinic P.A., 1973-92; clin. assoc. prof. medicine U. Ala., 1964-89; clin. assoc. prof. medicine U. South Ala., 1973-92; ret. Served as capt. M.C., AUS, 1944-46. Decorated Bronze Star. Diplomate Am. Bd. Internat. Medicine, Am. Bd. Cardiovascular Disease. Fellow ACP, Am. Coll. Cardiology, Am. Coll. Chest Physicians; mem. Am. Heart Assn., Ala. Heart Assn. (chmn. bd. 1956), AMA, Am. Soc. Clin. Pharmacology and Therapeutics, Mobile C. of C. Republican. Episcopalian. Clubs: Rotary, Mobile Country, Mobile Yacht. Home: 3965 Byronell Ct Mobile AL 36693-5502

ATLAN, PAUL, gynecologist; b. Algiers, Algeria, France, June 13, 1942; s. Gabriel Nathan and Rosine (Chemaoun) A.; m. Liliane Haddad, Dec. 26, 1968; children: Sophie, Catherine. MD, U. Paris, 1969, degree gynecology, 1973. Resident Psychiatric Hosp., Epinay, 1971-74; planning ctr. dir. Fontenay Sous Bois (France), 1973—; gynecologist St. Anne Psychiatric Hosp., 1980—, Hosp. Antoine Beclere; cons. RTL radio station, Paris, 1979-86; attaché First Paris Hosp., 1980—; dir. Internat. Conf. on Jewish Ethics and New Med. Procreation, conf. on Laws and Ethics for New Med. Procreations in French Nat. Assembly, 1988. Mem. French Psychosomatic Gynecological Soc. Office: 105 Rue de la Convention, 75015 Paris France

ATTINGER, CHRISTOPHER ERNST, medical educator; b. Lausanne, Switzerland, July 20, 1947; came to the U.S., 1952; s. Ernst Otto and Françoise (Daubige) A.; m. Lydia Henri, June 20, 1975; 1 child, Thalia. BS, Washington & Lee U., 1977; MD, Yale U., 1981. Bd. cert. plastic surgery. Resident in gen. surgery Brigham & Women's Hosp., Boston, 1981-86, vascular fellow, 1986-87; plastic surgery resident NYU, N.Y.C., 1987-89, hand surgery fellow, 1989-90; asst. prof. plastic, orthopedic surgery, otolaryngology Georgetown U., Washington, 1990-94, assoc. prof. plastic, orthopedic surgery, otolaryngology, 1994—. Fellow ACS, Am. Foot and Ankle Surgery (hon.); mem. Am. Soc. Plastic and Reconstructive Surgery, Am. Soc. for Reconstructive Microsurgery. Home: 455 Walker Rd Great Falls VA 22066 Office: Georgetown Univ Hosp 3800 Reservoir Rd Washington DC 20007

ATTIX, EDWARD ALLEN, orthopaedic surgeon; b. Detroit, Jan. 6, 1924; s. Edward Allen and Signa (Gilling) A.; widowed; 1 child, Edward Allen III. BA, Dartmouth Coll., 1946; MD, Johns Hopkins U., 1948. Resident U. Oreg., Portland, 1953-56; staff physician Ochsner Clinic, New Orleans, 1956-57; orthopaedic surgeon pvt. practice, Hattiesburg, Miss., 1957—. Capt. U.S. Army Med. Corps, 1951-53. Mem. Forum of Cicero. Office: 2601 Mamie St Ste 201 Hattiesburg MS 30401

ATWELL, CONSTANCE WOODRUFF, health services executive, researcher; b. Jan. 27, 1942. AB with high honors in psychology, Mount Holyoke Coll., 1963; MA, UCLA, 1965, PhD, 1968. Asst. prof. psychology Pitzer Coll., Claremont (Calif.) Grad. Sch., 1967-72, assoc. prof. psychology, 1972-77, prof. psychology, 1977-78; grants assoc. div. of rsch. grants NIH, Bethesda, Md., 1978-79; chief, Office of Clin. Applications of Vision Rsch. Nat. Eye Inst., NIH, Bethesda, 1979-88, asst. chief, Strabismus, Amblyopia and Visual Processing Br., 1980-81, chief, Strabismus, Amblyopia and Visual Processing Br., 1981-92, dep. assoc. dir. Extramural and Collaborative Programs, 1988-92; assoc. dir. for extramural activities Nat. Inst. Neurol. Disorders and Stroke, Bethesda, 1992—; rsch. proposal reviewer for the Nat. Found. March of Dimes, Nat. Inst. of Disability and Rehab. Rsch., Nat. Soc. to Prevent Blindness, U.S. Dept. Edn., NIH office of Program Planning and Evaluation, co-chair women's health issues; various adv. bds., exec. coms. and rsch. projects, co-chair improving peer rev. reinvention com. Contbr. articles to profl. publs. Reader for Recording for the Blind, 1973-78; trustee Claremont Collegiate Sch., 1975-77; chmn. guidance adv. com. Cabin John Jr. High Sch., 1980-81, exec. com., 1980—, pres. parent tchrs. assn., 1981-82; mem. exec. com. Winston Churchill High Sch. PTA, 1982-85. Recipient Nat. Merit scholarship, 1959-63; named Sara Williston scholar, Mary Lyon scholar. Mem. AAAS, Soc. for Neurosci., Assn for Women in Sci., Phi Beta Kappa, Sigma Xi. Office: Ninds 7550 Wisconsin Ave Bethesda MD 20892-9190

ATWILL, WILLIAM HENRY, physician; b. Jackson, N.C., July 10, 1932; s. Charles Bailey and Mary Frances (Beaman) A.; m. Agnes Craighead Pierce, June 10, 1955; children: William H. Atwill Jr., E. Bennett Atwill, Charles B. Atwill II. BS, Va. Mil. Inst., 1953; MD, U. Va., 1960. Diplomate Am. Bd. Urology. Surg. intern, then asst. resident U. Fla. Med. Ctr., Gainesville, 1960-62; rsch. fellow in urology Duke U. Med. Ctr., Durham, N.C., 1964; asst. resident, chief resident, instr. urology Duke U. Med. Ctr., 1965-68; pvt. practice urology Richmond, Va., 1968—; pres. Urology Inc., Richmond, 1989-95, 1989-95; pres. Urology, Inc., Richmond, 1989—; clin. prof. surgery Med. Coll. Va. and Va. Commonwealth U., Richmond, 1986—. Contbr. articles to profl. jours. Capt. USAF, 1953-56. Fellow ACS, Country Club of Va. Republican. Episcopalian. Office: Urology Inc 5224 Monument Ave Richmond VA 23226-1405

AU, MELINDA L., osteopathic family practice physician; b. Westminster, Calif., Sept. 23, 1962; d. William C.F. and Lola C. Au; m. James O. Mann, Dec. 8, 1990; 1 child, Matai M. BS in Zoology, Calif. State Poly. U., Pomona, 1985; DO, Kirksville Coll. Osteo. Medicine. Diplomate Am. Bd. Family Practice. Pvt. practice, San Diego, 1992-93, Encinitas, Calif., 1993-95; physician U. Calif.-San Diego Healthcare, Encinitas, 1995—. Mem. Am. Acad. Family Practice, Am. Osteo. Assn. Office: UCSD Healthcare Ste A204 477 N El Camino Real Encinitas CA 92024

AUBREY, ROGER FREDERICK, psychology and education educator; b. Waterloo, Iowa, Nov. 1, 1929; s. Earl F. and Ruth M. (Schminke) A.; children: Joshua, David, Christopher. A.B., U. Miami, 1954; M.A., U. Chgo., 1964; Ed.D., Boston U., 1975. Tchr. United Twp. High Sch., East Moline, Ill., 1959-62; counselor Sch. Dist. 133, Chgo., 1964-69; psychologist-counselor, dir. guidance U. Chgo. Lab. Schs., 1964-69; dir. guidance and health Brookline (Mass.) Schs., 1969-77; prof. psychology and edn. Vanderbilt U., Nashville, 1977—; cons. in field. Author: The Counselor and Drug Abuse Programs, 1973, Experimenting with Living: Pros and Cons, 1973, Career Development Needs of Thirteen Year Olds, 1978; editor: Practices of Guidance, 1972, Guidance: Strategies and Techniques, 1975; contbr. articles to profl. jours. Served with U.S. Army, 1951. Named Writer of Yr. Am. Sch. Counselor Assn., 1973. Mem. Assn. Counselor Edn. and Supervision (pres. 1973-74), Am. Psychol. Assn., Am. Personnel and Guidance Assn., Am. Ednl. Research Assn., AAAS. Democrat. Unitarian. Home: 1930 20th Ave S Nashville TN 37212-3712 Office: PO Box 322 Nashville TN 37202-0322

AUCHINCLOSS, HUGH, JR., transplant surgeon; b. N.Y.C., Mar. 15, 1949; s. Hugh and Katharine Lawrence (Bundy) A.; m. Laurie Hollis Glimcher, Aug. 26, 1973; children: Kalah, Hugh, Jake. BA Polit. Sci. and Econs. cum laude, Yale Coll., 1972; MA Econs., Yale U., 1972; MD, Harvard Med. Sch., 1976. Diplomate Am. Bd. Gen. Surgery. Asst. resident in surgery Mass. Gen. Hosp., Boston, 1976-79, 82-84, chief resident in surgery, 1985; asst. in surgery Mass. Gen. Hosp., 1985-87, asst. surgeon, 1987-90, dir. pancreas transplantation, 1990—; clin. fellow in surgery Harvard Med. Sch., Boston, 1977-85, instr. surgery, 1986-87, asst. prof. surgery, 1987-90, assoc. prof. surgery, 1990—; assoc. vis. surgeon Mass. Gen. Hosp., 1991—; tchr. to dir. Ulysses S. Grant Found., New Haven, Conn., 1967-69; asst. to coord. spl. ednl. program, Yale U., New Haven, Conn., 1969-70; various positions in field to mem. pancreas com., New Eng. Organ Bank, 199—, pancreas subcom., The United Network for Organ Sharing, 1991—; scientific adv. bd. Bio-Transplants, Inc., Diacrin, Inc.; mem. NIAID Task Force on Organ Transplantation; ad hoc mem. immunobiology study sect., NIH, 1994; active numerous coms. in field; presenter in field; lectr. numerous ednl. orgns. and univs. Assoc. editor: Jour. of Immunology, 1991-94; editorial bd.: Transplantation, 1992—, Xenotransplantation, 1993—, Xeno, 1993—; editorial adv. bd. Sandoz Edn. Series: Immunology and Immunotherapeutics, 1994; contbr. articles to profl. jours. and publs. Recipient Charles H. Dickerman Meml. prize in Econs., Yale U., 1971. Fellow Am. Coll. Surgeons; mem. Am. Assn. Immunologists, The Transplantation Soc., Mass. Med. Soc., Clin. Immunology Soc., Am. Soc. Transplant Surgeons, Boston Surg. Soc., Soc. Univ. Surgeons, Soc. Clin. Surgery, Dorchester Med. Club, New Eng. Surg. Soc., Alpha Omega Alpha, Phi Beta Kappa, others. Office: Mass Gen Hosp White 510 B Boston MA 02114

AUCHINCLOSS, SARAH SEDGWICK, psychiatrist; b. N.Y.C., Sept. 19, 1949. BA magna cum laude, Harvard U., 1971; MD, Yale U., 1976. Intern in gen. surgery Roosevelt Hosp., N.Y.C., 1976-77, resident in surgery, 1977-78; resident in psychiatry N.Y. Hosp., 1979-82; fellow in psycho-oncology Meml. Hosp., N.Y.C., 1981-83, attending psychiatrist, 1983—; pvt. practice N.Y.C., 1983—. Contbg. author: Psycho-oncology: The Psychiatric Care of the Patient with Cancer, 1989. Mem. Am. Psychiat. Assn., Am. Soc. for Psychosomatic Ob/Gyn. Office: 6 W 77th St # 1A New York NY 10024-5125

AUCOIN, PAULA J., infectious disease consultant, internist; b. Providence, Sept. 27, 1951; d. Frederic Joseph and Pauline (Pasqualetti) A.; m. Noel Alan Blagg, July 10, 1982; children: Lindsay, Kristin, Jennifer. BA, Cath. U., 1973; MD, Georgetown U., 1977. Diplomate Am. Bd. Internal Medicine, cert. in infectious diseases. Intern in internal medicine St. Vincent Hosp., Worcester, Mass., 1977-78, resident in internal medicine, 1978-80; fellow in infectious diseases U. Mass. Med. Ctr., Worcester, Mass., 1980-82; attending staff Berkshire Med. Ctr., Pittsfield, Mass., 1982—; asst. prof. Mass. Med. Ctr. Med. U., Worcester, 1982—; student clerkship coord. internal medicine Berkshire Med. Ctr., 1989—; chmn. ethics com. Berkshire Med. Ctr., 1996—, chmn. infection control com., 1988—. Mem. spkrs. bur. ARC, Pittsfield, 1988—. Mem. Infectious Diseases Soc. Am., Am. Soc. for Microbiology, Mass. Med. Soc., Berkshire Dist. Med. Soc. Office: Berkshire Phys & Surgeons 777 North St Pittsfield MA 01201

AUER, THOMAS HARPER, physician, army officer; b. Abington, Pa., July 7, 1949; s. Edward Thomas and Mary (Hedesh) A.; m. Patricia Ann Steiner, Dec. 19, 1971; children: Jeffrey, Elizabeth. BS, Ursinus Coll., 1971; MD, St. Louis U., 1975; student, U.S. Army War Coll., 1992-93. Diplomate Am. Bd. Family Practice. Commd. 2d lt. U.S. Army, 1978, advanced through grades to col., 1990; family physician U.S. MEDDAC, Wuerzburg, Germany, 1978-79, chief family practice, 1979-84, chief ambulatory patient care, 1984-86, dep. commdr., 1989-90; divsn. surgeon 3d Infantry Divsn., Wuerzburg, 1986-89; chief med. corps br. U.S. Army PERSCOM, Alexandria, Va., 1993-96; commdr. Womack Army Med. Ctr., Fort Bragg, N.C., 1996—. Bd. dirs. Found. USAFP, 1994—. Fellow Am. Acad. Family Physicians; mem. Am. Assn. Therapeutic Humor, Am. Coll. Sports Medicine, Am. Assn. Mil. Surgeons. Home: 7 Dyer St Fort Bragg NC 28307 Office: Womack Army Med Ctr Fort Bragg NC 28307

AUERBACH, ANITA L., clinical psychologist; b. Flushing, N.Y., Dec. 23, 1946; d. Ben and Gussie (Zuckerman) Weiss; B.A. cum laude, SUNY, Buffalo, 1968, M.A., 1970; Ph.D. (N.Y. State Regents fellow 1970-72), George Washington U., 1977; m. Steven Miles Auerbach, May 25, 1969. Chief research youth crime control project D.C. Dept. Corrections, 1970-74; intern clin. psychology No. Va. Tng. Center, Fairfax, 1974-75, staff psychologist, then chief psychol. services, 1975-79; pvt. practice clin. psychology, dir. Commonwealth Psychol. Assocs., Mc Lean, Va., 1979—; lectr. Washington Tech. Inst., 1972-74, George Mason U., 1978—; cons. in field. Adv. bd. family edn. project Joseph P. Kennedy, Jr. Found., 1977-79; mem. regional appeals bd. No. Va. Public Sch. System, 1977-79. Recipient N.Y. State Scholar Incentive award, 1969; diplomate Am. Bd. Med. Psychotherapists, Internat. Acad. Behavioral Medicine. Mem. Am. Psychol. Assn., Am. Soc. Clin. Hypnosis (approved cons.), Va. Acad. Clin. Psychologists, Va. Psychol. Assn., No. Va. Soc. Clin. Psychologists, Washington Soc. Study Clin. Hypnosis, Psi Chi, Alpha Lambda Delta. Author articles in field. Office: 1479 Chain Bridge Rd Mc Lean VA 22101-5730

AUERBACH, MARCI FAY, social worker; b. Denver, Aug. 19, 1955; d. Ralph and Carolyn Louise (Lipp) A. BA in Theatre, U. Colo., 1977; MSW, NYU, 1983. Lic. clin. social worker, Colo. Social worker Social Svc. Agy., Lod, Israel, 1983-84, Mercy Med. Ctr., Denver, 1984-85; regional mktg. dir. Am. Med. Svcs., Lakewood, Colo., 1985-86; dir. social svcs. The Greenery

Rehab. Group, Pacifica, Calif., 1987-88; case mgr. NeuroCare, Inc., Concord, Calif., 1988-90, exec. dir., 1990-93; dir. case mgmt. and managed care Mediplex Rehab., Denver, 1994-95; sr. social worker Shalom Park, Denver, 1995—; pvt. practice case mgr., 1988-93. Founder The Source, Denver, 1985. Presidents scholar NYU, 1982-83. Mem. Case Mgmt. Soc. Am. (founder, nat. bd. dirs. 1991-94, nat. edn. chair 1990-92), No. Calif. Case Mgmt. Soc. Am. (founder, eligibility com. CCM commn. 1995-96).

AUERBACH, SIDNEY, pathologist; b. Phila., 1928. AB in Biology, Temple U., 1955, MD, 1959; MS in Pathology, Wayne State U., 1964. Cert. anat. and clin. pathologist. Intern Detroit Receiving Hosp., 1959-60; assoc. pathologist Cabell Huntington (W.Va.) Hosp., 1964-65; co-dir. labs. Ancker Hosp., St. Paul, 1965-66; assoc. pathologist Glenwood Hills Hosp., Mpls., 1966-67; dir. labs. Rahway (N.J.) Hosp., 1967-68; dir. labs., chief pathology Jersey Med. Ctr., Jersey City, 1968—; instr. pathology and lab. medicine, U. Minn., Mpls. Contbr. articles to profl. jours. 1st lt. USAF, 1951-55; lt. comdr. USPHS. Fellow Am. Soc. Clin. Pathologists; mem. Am. Assn. Blood Banks, Coll. Am. Pathologists. Address: 340 E 93rd St New York NY 10128-5547

AUERBACK, ALFRED, psychiatrist; b. Toronto, Can., Sept. 20, 1915; came to U.S., 1939, naturalized, 1944; s. Murray M. and Lena (Breslin) A.; m. Molly Loy Friedman, June 21, 1942; children—Norman L., Sandra J., Diana K. Auerback Gleave. M.D., U. Toronto, 1938. Intern Toronto Gen. Hosp., 1938-39; resident French Hosp., San Francisco, 1939-40; resident in neurology and psychiatry U. Calif. Hosp., San Francisco, 1940-42; practice medicine specializing in psychiatry San Francisco, 1943-90; staff psychiatrist Sheppard Pratt Hosp., Towson, Md., 1942-43; staff U Calif.-San Francisco, 1943—, asst. clin. prof., 1953, assoc. clin. prof., 1962, clin. prof., 1970-83, clin. prof. emeritus, 1983—; cons. San Francisco Gen. Hosp., 1953-70; mem. Mental Health Adv. Bd. of San Francisco, 1962-77, chmn., 1967-70; bd. dirs. San Francisco Mental Health Assn., 1981-87; cons. Nat. Adv. Council on Alcohol Abuse and Alcoholism, Washington, 1971-76, Calif. Alcoholic Rehab. Commn., 1955-57; mem. Citywide Alcoholism Adv. Bd., San Francisco, 1972-74; chmn., 1972-73, 1st Pacific Congress of Psychiatry, Melbourne, Australia, 1975; chmn. psychiat. congresses, Tokyo, Jerusalem, 1963, Mexico City, Lima, Rio de Janeiro, Sao Paulo, 1964; chmn. psychiat. congresses Edinburgh, 1965. Editor: Schizophrenia, An Integrated Approach, 1959. bd. dirs., sec. Fontana East Apt. Cooperative, 1985-87. Recipient Royer award U. Calif., 1966, Fromm Inst. award, 1993. Fellow Am. Psychiat. Assn. (life, v.p. 1966), San Francisco Med. Soc. (bd. dirs. 1955), Am., Royal, Royal Australian, New Zealand colls. psychiatrists; mem. No. Calif. Psychiat. Soc. (pres. 1956, award 1990), Am. Assn. Social Psychiatry (councillor 1980-86), Mental Health Assn. (award 1986), Commonwealth Club, Masons, Pi Lambda Phi, Phi Delta Epsilon. Home: 1000 N Point St San Francisco CA 94109-8301

AUERBACK, SANDRA JEAN, social worker; b. San Francisco, Feb. 21, 1946; d. Alfred and Molly Loy (Friedman) A. BA, U. Calif., Berkeley, 1967; MSW, Hunter Sch. Social Work, 1972. Diplomate clin. social work. Clin. social worker Jewish Family Services, Bklyn., 1972-73; clin. social worker Jewish Family Services, Hackensack, N.J., 1973-78; pvt. practice psychotherapy San Francisco, 1978—; dir. intake adult day care Jewish Home for the Aged, San Francisco, 1979-91. Mem. NASW (cert., bd. dirs. Bay Area Referral Svc. 1983-87, chmn. referral svc. 1984-87, state practice com. 1987-91, regional treas. 1989-91, rep. to Calif. Coun. Psychiatry, Psychology, Social Work and Nursing, 1987—, chmn. 1989, 93, v.p. cmty. svcs. 1991-93, chair Calif. polit. action com. 1993-95), Am. Group Psychotherapy Assn., Mental Health Assn. San Francisco (trustee 1987—). Home: 1100 Gough St Apt 8C San Francisco CA 94109-6638 Office: 450 Sutter St San Francisco CA 94108-4206

AUERHAHN, CAROLYN, nursing educator; b. Sept. 21, 1945. Diploma Bellevue Sch. Nursing, 1966; BS summa cum laude, Pace U., 1979; MS Columbia U., 1981, EdD, 1996. RN, N.Y.; cert. adult nurse practitioner AANP; cert. adult nurse practitioner, geriatric nurse practitioner, ANCC. Staff nurse med.-surg. South Nassau Communities Hosp., Oceanside, N.Y., 1966; staff nurse pediatrics Nassau County Med. Ctr., Meadowbrook Hosp., East Meadow, N.Y., 1966-67; staff nurse St. John's Riverside Hosp., Yonkers, N.Y., 1971-78; staff nurse outpatient dept. Westchester County Med. Ctr., Valhalla, N.Y., 1980; clin. nurse specialist/adult nurse practitioner Westchester County Med. Ctr., Valhalla, 1981-87; pvt. practice diabetes nurse practitioner N.Y. Med. Coll., Valhalla, 1985-87; asst. prof. clin. nursing, dir. adult nurse practitioner and geriatric nurse practitioner program Columbia U. Sch. Nursing, N.Y.C., 1987—. Contbr. articles to profl. jours. Active AACN/NHSC Faculty Advocate/Minority Mentor project. Grant N.Y. State Health Dept., 1985-86. Mem. ANA, Am. Diabetes Assn., Am. Assn. Diabetes Educators, Rachmiel Levine Diabetes Found. (bd. dirs. 1983-87), Westchester-Putnam Diabetes Assn. (profl. edn. com. 1983-85), Am. Acad. Nurse Practitioners, N.Y. State Nurses Assn. (dist. 16, bd. dirs. 1984-85, nominating chair 1982-83), Bellevue Alumnae Assn., Sigma Theta Tau, Kappa Delta Pi. Home: 137 Jennifer Ln Yonkers NY 10710-1723

AUFDERHEIDE, ARTHUR CARL, pathologist; b. New Ulm, Minn., Sept. 9, 1922; s. Herman John and Esther (Sannwald) A.; m. Mary Lillian Buryk, Jan. 26, 1946; children: Patricia Ann, Tom Paul, Walter Herman. MD, U. Minn., 1946; DSc (hon.), Coll. of St. Scholastica, 1983. Chief dept. pathology Mpls. VA Hosp., 1952-53, St. Mary's Hosp., Duluth, Minn., 1953-57; chief dept. pathology Sch. Medicine U. Minn., Duluth, 1970-87, dean Sch. Medicine, 1974-75, dir. paleobiology lab. Sch. Medicine, 1977—; rsch. cons. anthropology lab. U. Colombia, Bogota, 1989—, Pigorini Mus., Rome, 1988, Archeol. Mus. of Tenerife, Canary Islands, 1989-90; chmn. sci. com. Cronos Rsch Project, Santa Cruz, Tenerife, 1991—. Co-editor: Paleopathology, 1991; contbr. numerous articles to profl. publs. Chmn. civil com. to devel. a degree-granting med. sch., Duluth, 1988. Capt. U.S. Army, 1947-49. Mem. Paleopathology Assn., N.Y. Acad. Scis. Democrat. Lutheran. Home: 4711 Colorado St Duluth MN 55804-1512 Office: U Minn 10 University Dr Duluth MN 55812

AUFDERHEIDE, KARL JOHN, biologist; b. Mpls., Aug. 17, 1948; s. Carl John and Janet Ruth (Landrum) A.; m. Cheryl D. Wrolson, Sept. 6, 1969; 1 child, Karen Ruth. BS, U. Minn., 1970, MS, 1972, PhD, 1974. Postdoctoral fellow Ind. U., Bloomington, 1974-77; postdoctoral fellow/instr. U. Iowa, Iowa City, 1977-79; asst. prof. Tex. A&M U., College Station, 1979-86, assoc. prof., 1986—; vis. scholar Ind. U., Bloomington, 1986. Author: Cellular Aspects of Pattern Formation, 1991; contbr. articles to profl. jours. Rsch. grantee, NIH-NIGMS, 1985-89, NIH-Inst. on Aging, 1981-86; NSF predoctoral fellow, 1971-74; NIH Nat. Rsch. Svc. awardee, 1975-77; recipient Teaching Excellence award, Tex. A&M Former Students Assn., 1989. Mem. AAUP, Soc. Protozoologists (chmn. edn. com. 1985-92), S.W. Soc. of Developmental Biologists (conf. organizer 1991). Office: Texas A&M Univ Dept Biology College Station TX 77843

AUGUSTIN, ANTOINE, physician, surgeon; b. Port-au-Prince, Haiti, Aug. 9, 1947; s. Marc and Lilianne (Perrault) A.; m. Yvette Edouard, Mar. 21, 1987; children: Ann Savannah, Alain. BS, Loyola U., Chgo., 1968; MD, Med. Coll. Wis., 1972; MPH, Harvard U., 1977. Diplomate Am. Bd. Surgery. Mem. surg. staff St. Vincent's Hosp., N.Y.C., 1972-75, 77-79; mem. pediat. surg. staff Children's Hosp., Boston, 1975-77; rsch. fellow Children's Hosp. Harvard Med. Sch., Boston, 1976-77; instr. surgery NYU, N.Y.C., 1978-79; staff surgeon St. Vincent's Ctr., Port-au-Prince, 1979-82; dir. St. Catherine Hosp., Port-au-Prince, 1982-85; pres., gen. dir. Inst. Haitien de l'Enfance, Port-au-Prince, 1985-91; pres., CEO MARCH/Citymed, 1991—; pres. Ctr. d'Analyse des Politiques de Santé, Port-au-Prince, 1991—; pres., CEO City Med. Svcs., Miami, Fla., 1994—; cons. U.S. AID, FAO, UNICEF, CARE, Basics, Save the Children, Caribbean Resources Inc., Poptech; treas. Eye Care Haiti, Port-au-Prince, 1986-90; gen. sec. Profamil, Port-au-Prince, 1989-93, Alliance pour l'Enfance, Port-au-Prince, 1989-91. Prodr.: (TV video) Naitre pour Vivre, 1987; contbr. articles to profl. jours. Grantee Pricor, Chevy Chase, Md., 1984, AID Office Population, Washington, 1986, Nat. Acad. Sci., Washington, 1987, 89. Mem. AMA, AAAS, Nat. Coun. for Internat. Health, Assn. Medicale Haitienne, Harvard Club. Home: Rte de la Montagne Noire, Petion-Ville Haiti Office: Inst Haitien de l'Enfance, 41 Rue Borno, Petion-Ville Haiti

AUGUSTYNIAK, WAYNE GERARD, physician assistant; b. Chgo., Dec. 27, 1948; s. Alphonse R. and Marianne (Zawacki) A.; children: Wayne G., Judd C.; m. Lisa J. Giles, Dec. 29, 1994. Student, Western Mich. U., 1967-68; degree in practical nursing, Lake Mich. Coll., 1969, ADN, 1973; BMS, Western Mich. U., 1975; postgrad., Ind. Wesleyan U., 1992. Cert. physician's asst. Mich.; RN, LPH, Mich. Orderly South Haven (Mich.) Cmty. Hosp., 1966-69, staff nurse ICU, surg. unit, 1973-74; oper. rm. nurse St. Joseph (Mich.) Meml. Hosp., 1969-73; physician's asst. Cedarwood Med. Ctr. P.C., St. Joseph, 1975-90, C.R. Alderdice MD, P.C., St. Joseph, 1990-91, South Haven After Hours Clinic, 1991-93; adj. clin. prof. medicine Western Mich. U., Kalamazoo, 1976-95; courtesy prof., instr. Lake Mich. Coll., Benton Harbor, 1977-83; instr. Southwestern Mich. Coll., Dowagiac, 1979-80; lectr. Ostomy Assn. Tchr. BLS Mich. Heart Assn. Mem. Allied Am. Urol. Assn., Acad. Physician's Assts., Mich. Acad. Physician's Assts. (pres.-elect 1981-82). Home: 00589 CR 215 Grand Junction MI 49056

AULD, JAMES S., educational psychologist. Grad., U. Nebr. Cert. sch. counselor, profl. counselor. Dir. testing, asst. prof., K-12 dir. guidance, kindergarten-12 dir. psychol. svcs. Author: Real Personality. Mem. APA, AACD, ASCD, Can. Psychol. Assn., Nebr. Profl. Counselors, Gold Key, nat. Disting. Svc. Registry for Counselors, Phi Delta Kappa. Office: PO Box 6228 Lincoln NE 68506-6228

AUNGST, BRUCE JEFFREY, pharmaceutical company scientist; b. Pottsville, Pa., Nov. 22, 1952; s. Roy Stewart and Grace M. (Rupp) A.; m. Judith M. Smith, Aug. 23, 1980; children: Matthew, Colleen, Christopher, Keenan, Mariette. BS, Pa. State U., 1974, MS, 1977; PhD, SUNY, Buffalo, 1982. Rsch. pharmacist DuPont, Wilmington, Del., 1981-85, sr. rsch. pharmacist, 1985-91; prin. rsch. scientist DuPont Merck, Wilmington, 1991—. Contbr. articles to profl. jours.; patentee in field. Mem. Am. Assn. Pharm. Scientists, Controlled Release Soc. Office: DuPont Merck PO Box 80400 Wilmington DE 19880-0400

AURDAL, BASTIAN WEIBERG, neurophysiologist, neurologist; b. Volda, Sunnmøre, Norway, May 31, 1931; s. Gustav Adolf Weiberg and Solveig Lisa (Lehne) A.; m. Ada Mathilde Frivold, Sept. 19, 1976. Cand. med., U. Oslo, 1958. Staff physician Nat. Ctr. for Epilepsy, Sandvika, Norway, 1977-79; asst. chief physician Univ. Hosp., Tromsøe, Norway, 1980-82; chief physician Hvidovre Hosp., Copenhagen, 1982-33; staff physician Nat. Hosp., Oslo, 1984-87; chief physician Ullevaal Hosp., Oslo, 1987—. Capt. Norwegian Air Force, 1960-61. Fellow European Soc. for Sleep Rsch.; mem. Norwegian Epilepsy Soc., Den Norske Laegeforening. Office: Ullevaal U Hosp, Kirkeveien 166, N-0407 Oslo Norway

AUSTEN, K(ARL) FRANK, physician, educator; b. Akron, Ohio, Mar. 14, 1928; s. Karl and Bertle (Jehle) A.; m. Joycelyn Chapman, Apr. 11, 1959; children: Leslie Marie, Karla Ann, Timothy Frank, Jonathan Arthur. AB, Amherst Coll., 1950; MD, Harvard U., 1954. Intern in medicine Mass. Gen. Hosp., 1954-55, asst. resident, 1955-56, sr. resident, 1958-59, chief resident, 1961, asst. in medicine, 1962-63, asst. physician, 1963-66, chief pulmonary unit, 1964-66; also cons. in medicine; practice medicine, specializing in internal medicine, allergy and immunology Mass. Gen. Hosp., Boston, 1962-66; USPHS postdoctoral research fellow Nat. Inst. Med. Research, Mill Hill, London, 1959-61; asst. in medicine Harvard Med. Sch., 1961, instr., 1961-62, asso. in medicine, 1962-64, asst. prof., 1965-66, assoc. prof., 1966-63, prof., 1969-72, Theodore B. Bayles prof., 1972—; physician-in-chief Robert B. Brigham Hosp., 1966-80; chmn. dept. rheumatology and immunology Brigham and Women's Hosp., 1980-95; dir. lab. inflammation and allergic disease rsch. Brigham and Women's Hosp., Boston, 1995—; mem. fellowship subcom. Arthritis Found., 1968-71, chmn., 1971; mem. coun. Infectious Disease Soc. Am., 1969-71; mem. arthritis tng. grants com. Nat. Inst. Arthritis and Metabolic Diseases, NIH, 1970-73, NHLB adv. coun., 1994—; mem. directing group, task force on immunology and disease Nat. Inst. Allergy and Infectious Diseases, 1972-73; bd. dirs. Arthritis Found., 1972-75, chmn. manpower study com., 1972-73, chmn. rsch. com. Multipurpose Arth. Ctr., 1972-76; chmn. rsch. com. Med. Found., Inc., 1972-76; mem. Am. Bd. Allergy and Immunology, 1973-78, Nat. Commn. on Arthritis and Related Musculoskeletal Diseases, 1975-76, Allergy and Immunology Rsch. com., NIAID, 1975-79, chmn., 1976-79; chmn. nomenclature com. Internat. Union Immunological Socs., 1983—; mem. adv. com. to the dir. NIH, 1986-90, mem. nat heart, lung and blood adv. coun., 1966-80. Mem. editorial bd. Arthritis and Rheumatism, 1968-81, Proc. of Transplantation Soc., 1968-82, Jour. Infectious Diseases, 1966-79, Jour. Exptl. Medicine, 1971—, Immunol. Communications, 1972-85, Clin. Immunology and Immunopathology, 1972-89, Proc. of Nat. Acad. Scis., 1978-83, Clin. and Exptl. Immunology, 1978-88, Internat. Jour. Immunopharmacology, 1984, Advances in Immunology, 1985—, Advances in Pharmacology, 1989—; contbr. articles to profl. jours. Trustee Amherst Coll., 1981—. Served to capt., M.C. U.S. Army, 1956-58. Mem. NAS (chmn. sect. on med. microbiology and immunology 1983-86), Inst. Medicine, Am. Soc. Pharm. and Exptl. Therapeutics, Am. Soc. Exptl. Pathology, Am. Assn. Immunologists (pres. 1977-78), Brit. Soc. Immunology, Am. Soc. Clin. Investigation, Am. Rheumatism Assn., ACP, Transplantation Soc., Am. Acad. Arts and Scis., Assn. Am. Physicians (recorder 1978-84, pres. 1989-90), Am. Acad. Allergy and Immunology (exec. com. 1970-72, sec. 1977-80, pres. 1981), Interurban Clin. Club, Fedn. Am. Soc. Exptl. Biology, Internat. Assn. Allergology and Clin. Immunology, Internat. Soc. Immunopharmacology (pres. 1994). Office: Brigham & Women's Hospital PBB-B-2 75 Francis St Boston MA 02115-6195 also: 250 Longwood Ave Rm 604 Boston MA 02115-5701

AUSTEN, W(ILLIAM) GERALD, surgeon, educator; b. Akron, Ohio, Jan. 20, 1930; s. Karl A. and Bertl (Jehle) A.; m. Patricia Ramsdell, Jan. 28, 1961; children: Karl Ramsdell, William Gerald, Jr., Christopher Marshall, Elizabeth Patricia. B.S., MIT, 1951; M.D., Harvard U., 1955; H.H.D. (hon.), U. Akron, 1980; D.Sc. (hon.), U. Athens, Greece, 1981; DS (hon.), Northeastern Ohio U., 1996. Diplomate Am. Bd. Surgery (bd. dirs. 1969-74, sr. mem. 1974—), Am. Bd. Thoracic Surgery (bd. dirs. 1984-90). Intern, then resident surgery Mass. Gen. Hosp., Boston, 1955-61, chief of surg. svcs., 1969—, surgeon-in-chief, 1989—; pres. and CEO Mass. Gen. Physicians Orgn., 1994—; Edward D. Churchill prof. surgery Harvard Med. Sch., Boston, 1974—; Mem. corp. MIT, 1972—, life mem., 1982—; bd. trustees Knight Found., vice-chmn. bd., 1991-96, chmn., 1996—, mem. 1986—; bd. dirs. Whitehead Inst. Biomed. Rsch., 1982-88; trustee Mass. Eye and Ear Infirmary, 1991—; trustee Partners HealthCare System, Inc., 1994—. Contbr. articles to med. jours. Mem. corp. MIT, 1972—, life mem., 1982—; trustee Knight Found., 1986—, vice-chmn., 1991-96, chmn., 1996—; bd. dirs. Whitehead Inst. Biomed. Rsch., 1982-88. Markle scholar, 1963-68. Fellow Royal Coll. Surgeons England (hon.), Am. Acad. Arts and Scis.; mem. ACS (regent 1982-91, chmn. bd. 1989-91, pres. 1992-93), Accreditation Coun. Grad. Med. Edn. (residency rev. com. for surgery 1988-93), Inst. Medicine of NAS, Assn. Acad. Surgery (pres. 1970), Soc. Univ. Surgeons (sec. 1967-70, pres. 1972-73), Am. Surg. Assn. (sec. 1979-84, pres. 1985-86), Am. Heart Assn. (pres. 1977-78), Mass. Heart Assn. (pres. 1972-74), New Eng. Cardiovascular Soc. (pres. 1972-73), Am. Assn. Thoracic Surgery (v.p. 1987-88, pres. 1988-89). Home: 163 Wellesley St Weston MA 02193-1556 Office: Mass Gen Hospital Dept of Surgery White 506 Boston MA 02114

AUSTIN, DAVID MAYO, social work educator; b. New Haven, June 9, 1923; s. Ralph Vernon and Helen Howe (Mayo) A.; m. Zuria Farmer; Clayton Mayo, Judith Ann, Paul Farmer. BA, Lawrence Coll., 1943; MS Social Adminstrn., Western Res. U., 1948; PhD, Brandeis U., 1969. Cert. social worker, Tex. Group worker U. Settlement, Cleve., 1948-51; assoc. neighborhood svcs. United Community Svcs. Met. Boston, 1951-54; planner, exec. dir. Spl. Youth Program, Roxbury, Mass., 1953-56; exec. sec. group work coun. Welfare Fedn. Cleve., 1957-61; planning dir. Greater Cleve. Youth Svcs. Planning Commn., 1961-63; assoc. dir. planning and rsch. Community Action Youth Cleve., 1963-64; lectr. Sch. Applied Social Scis. Case Western Res. U., Cleve., 1964-65; lectr. Florence Heller Grad. Sch. for Advanced Studies in Social Welfare Brandeis U., Waltham, Mass., 1968-71, assoc. prof., 1971-73; prof. Sch. Social Work U. Tex., Austin, 1973—, Bert Kruger Smith Centennial prof., 1987—, acting dean, 1991-92; vis. prof. Coll. Social Work U. Tenn., Knoxville, 1985-86, cons., 1979; vis. scholar Nelson Rockefeller Coll. Pub. Affairs and Policy, SUNY, Albany, 1986; chmn. state adv. bd. Mass. Dept. Pub. Welfare, Boston, 1970-73; chmn. task force on social work rsch. NIMH, 1988-91; cons. Hogg Found. for Mental Health, Austin, 1989; external reviewer Sch. Social Work Rutgers U., New Brunswick, N.J., 1985; vis. com. Mandel Sch. Applied Social Scis., Case Western Res. U., Cleve., 1993—. Author: (with others) Organization and the Human Services: Cross-Disciplinary Reflections, 1981, (monograph) A History of Social Work Education, 1986, The Political Economy of Human Service Programs, 1988; mem. editorial bd. Social Work, 1983-89; interim co-editor Jour. Applied Behavioral Sci., 1988-89; contbr. articles to profl. jours., publs. including Ency. of Social Work. Bd. dirs. Unitarian Universalist Svc. Com., Boston, 1983-88. Sgt. U.S. Army, 1943-46. Named Alumnus of Yr. Sch. Applied Social Scis. Case Western U., 1980; fellow NIMH, 1965-68; named Outstanding Grad. Tchr. U. Tex. at Austin, 1989. Mem. Acad. Cert. Social Workers (cert.), Nat. Assn. Social Workers (bd. dirs. 1963-66, chmn. human rights commn. 1964-67, pres. award Excellence Social Work Rsch. 1992), Coun. on Social Work Edn. (ho. dels. 1975-78, 79-82, ednl. planning commn. 1979-82), Am. Pub. Welfare Assn. (bd. dirs. 1980-82), Am. Soc. Pub. Adminstrn., Nat. Conf. Social Welfare (bd. dirs. 1980-83), Phi Beta Kappa, Phi Kappa Phi. Office: U Texas Sch of Social Work Austin TX 78712

AUSTIN, JOHN RILEY, surgeon, educator; b. St. Louis, Feb. 19, 1960; s. Thomas L. and Barbara (Riley) A.; m. Sara Beth Goehringer, May 16, 1987; children: Claire Frances, Emily Grace. BS with highest honors, U. Wyo., 1982; MD, U. Utah, 1986. Diplomate Am. Bd. Facial Plastic and Reconstructive Surgery, Am. Bd. Otolaryngology. Surg. intern U. So. Calif., L.A. County Med. Ctr., L.A., 1986-87, resident in head and neck surgery dept. otolaryngology, 1987-91; fellow in head and neck surg. oncology M.D. Anderson Cancer Ctr. M.D. Anderson Cancer Ctr. U. Tex., Houston, 1991-92; asst. surgeon, clin. instr. U. Tex., Houston, 1992-93; asst. prof., asst. surgeon M.D. Anderson Cancer Ctr. U. Tex., Houston, 1993-95, clin. asst. prof., 1995—; adj. asst. prof. dept. otorhinolaryngology/comm. disorders Baylor Coll. Medicine, 1993-95; otolaryngologic cons. dept. infectious diseases U. So. Calif., 1988-91; mem. utilization com. M.D. Anderson Cancer Ctr., U.Tex., 1993-95, mem. laser com., 1993-95; presenter in field. Cons. editor Head and Neck, Laryngoscope, Otolaryngology-Head and Neck Surgery, Cancer, 1993—, Archives of Otolaryngology; contbr. articles to profl. jours. Mem. Graduate Edn. com. U. Tex., 1994. Fellow ACS, Am. Acad. Otolaryngology (human resource com.); mem. AMA, Am. Acad. Facial Plastic and Reconstructive Surgery (mem. publs. com.), Tex. Med. Assn. (mem. physician oncology edn. program 1993—, mem. com. cancer 1993—), M.D. Anderson Assocs., Soc. Univ. Otolaryngologists, Tex. Assn. Otolaryngology, Sir Charles Bell Soc. (founding), Travis County Med. Soc. (jour. com.), Salerni Colegium, Phi Kappa Phi, Phi Beta Kappa, Sigma Nu. Methodist. Home: 3507 Cactus Wren Way Austin TX 78746 Office: 3705 Medical Pkwy Ste 310 Austin TX 78705

AUSTIN, KRISTINA HEIDI, ophthalmologist; b. St. Paul, Sept. 21, 1958; d. George Herbert and Shirley Corrine Austin; m. Ethan Adolphus Nicholls, June 4, 1988; 1 child, Olivia Austin Nicholls. BS, U. Wis., Milw., 1979; MD, Med. Coll. Wis., Wauwatosa, 1983. Diplomate Am. Bd. Ophthalmology. Intern Virginia Mason Hosp., Seattle, 1983-84; resident Stanford (Calif.) U. Med. Ctr., 1984-87; ptnr. physician Kaiser Permanente, Hayward, Calif., 1987-89, 91—; acting chief ophthalmology Palo Alto (Calif.) VA Hosp., 1990; ophthalmologist Eye Assocs., Sebastopol, Calif., 1989-91. Fellow Am. Acad. Ophthalmology. Office: Kaiser Permanente 27400 Hesperian Hayward CA 94545

AUSTIN, SIGRID LINNEVOLD, counselor; b. Madison, Wis., Aug. 15, 1939; d. Bernhard Olaf Johann and Agnes Elizabeth (Spiva) Linnevold; m. William Jerome Austin, May 16, 1962; children: Christopher Peter, Douglas Patrick, Colin Michael. BA, Barnard Coll., 1961; MS, Va. Commonwealth U., 1986. Lic. profl. counselor. Sr. counselor Peninsula Hosp., Hampton, Va., 1986-88; counselor Williamsburg (Va.) Ctr. for Therapy, 1988—; counselor outreach program Williamsburg Hosp., 1988—; counselor eating disorder program Williamsburg Hosp. Outreach, 1993; crisis counselor William & Mary Police Dept., 1993—; adj. faculty Va. Commonwealth U., Richmond, 1988-90. Asst. editor: (newsletter) The Addiction Letter, 1986-89; contbr. articles to profl. jours. Bd. dirs. Surry County Soc. Prevention of Cruelty to Animals, Surry, Va., 1993; active Nat. Trust Hist. Preservation, Washington, 1992-93, Nat. Conservancy, 1992-93. Scholar Sch. Pub. Affairs, Va. Commonwealth U., 1986. Mem. Internat. Assn. Eating Disorders, Nat. Assn. Alcohol and Drug Abuse, Va. Assn. Alcohol and Drug Abuse, Va. Mental Health Assn., Va. Assn. Clin. Counselors, Obsessive Compulsive Found., Phi Kappa Phi. Democrat. Lutheran. Office: Williamsburg Ctr Therapy 217 Mclaws Cir Ste 2 Williamsburg VA 23185-5649

AUSTIN, TERRI LOUISE, psychologist; b. Winona, Miss., May 11, 1952; d. Thomas Ward and Hazel Inez (Devine) A.; m. Willard James McCullough Sr., Dec. 24, 1977; 1 child, Bethany Joanna Austin McCullough. BS, Delta State U., 1973, MEd, 1974; PhD, U. Miss., 1981. Cert. sch. psychologist, educator. Tchr. various schs., Miss., Ark., 1974-77; rsch. asst. U. Miss. Bur. Edn. Rsch., Oxford, Miss., 1977-79; spl. edn. suprv. Chicot County SPED Coop., Lake Village, Ark., 1980-81; asst. prof. U. Ark.-Monticello, 1981-82; sch. psychologist E. Carroll Parish Spl. Edn. Svc., Lake Providence, La., 1982—; asst. prof. psychology Ark. State U., State University, 1990—; cons. Miss. Migrant Edn. Program, Oxford, 1978-80, Ednl. Planners & Evaluators, Oxford, 1977-79; consortium pres. Ednl. Testing Cons., Eudora, Ark., 1980—. Author: Affective Influences During Student Teaching, 1981; contbr. articles to profl. jours. Adult leader 4-H Club, Eudora, 1988—; mem. adminstv. bd. Scott Meml. Meth. Ch., Eudora, 1985-88; sec. Eudora Christian Sch. Bd., 1983-85, Chicot County Devel. Disabilities Coop., Lake Village, 1980-81; tchr. Sunday Sch. Eudora Baptist Ch. Sumners scholar, 1978-80, Gooch scholar, 1972-73, Faculty scholar, 1971-73. Mem. DAR (sec.), Nat. Assn. Sch. Psychologists, Ark. and La. Assn. Sch. Psychologists, Am. Ednl. Rsch. Assn., Carroll Ladies Investment Club (sr. ptnr.), Women of the Moose (sr. regent 1987-88), Kappa Delta Pi (pres. 1972-74), Phi Kappa Phi, Phi Delta Kappa, Delta Kappa Gamma. Home: 1080 Grand Lake Loop Eudora AR 71640-9713 Office: Spl Edn Svcs 603 4th St Lake Providence LA 71254-2913

AUSTRIAN, ROBERT, physician, educator; b. Balt., Apr. 12, 1916; s. Charles Robert and Florence (Hochschild) A.; m. Babette Friedmann Bernstein, Dec. 29, 1963; stepchildren: Jill Bernstein, Toni Bernstein. AB, Johns Hopkins U., 1937, MD, 1941; DSc honoris causa, Hahnemann Med. Coll., 1980, Phila. Coll. Pharmacy and Sci., 1981, U. Pa., 1987, SUNY, 1996. Diplomate: Am. Bd. Internal Medicine. House officer Johns Hopkins Hosp., 1941-50, asst. dir. med. out-patient dept., 1951-52; assoc. prof. medicine, then prof. medicine SUNY Coll. Medicine, 1952-62; John Herr Musser prof., chmn. rsch. medicine U. Pa. Sch. Medicine, 1962-86, prof. emeritus, chmn. emeritus, 1986—; attending physician Hosp. U. Pa.; Tyndale vis. lectr. and prof. Coll. Medicine U. Utah, 1964; spl. research on infectious diseases, bacterial genetics; mem. Meningococcal Infections Com., 1964-72, Commn. on Acute Respiratory Disease, 1965-72, Commn. Streptococcal and Staphylococcal Diseases, 1970-72, Armed Forces Epidemiol. Bd.; cons. surg. gen. U.S. Army Research and Devel. Command, 1966-69; mem. subcom. streptococcus and pneumococcus Internat. Com. Bacteriol. Nomenclature; mem. allergy and immunology study sect. Nat. Inst. Allergy and Infectious Diseases, 1965-69, mem. bd. sci. counselors, 1967-70, chmn., 1969-70; mem. WHO Expert adv. panel Acute Bacterial diseases, 1979—. Mem. editorial bd.: Jour. Bacteriology 1964-69, Am. Rev. Respiratory Diseases, 1963-66, Bacteriol. Rev., 1967-71, Jour. Infectious Diseases, 1969-74, Antimicrobial Agents and Chemotherapy, 1972-86, Infection and Immunity, 1973-81, Revs. of Infectious Diseases, 1979-89, Vaccine, 1983—. Trustee Johns Hopkins U., 1963-69. Served to capt. M.C. AUS, 1943-45. Recipient U.S. Typhus Commn. medal, 1947; Albert Lasker Clin. Med. Research award, 1978; Phila. award, 1979; Willard O. Thompson award Am. Geriatric Soc., 1981, others. Fellow ACP (master, James D. Bruce Meml. award 1979), N.Y. Acad. Scis., Am. Acad. Microbiology, AAAS (chmn. sect. on med. scis. 1975); mem. Assn. Am. Physicians, Am. Soc. Clin. Investigation, Am. Clin. and Climatol. Assn. (pres. 1984), Am. Soc. Microbiology (v.p. N.Y. br. 1961-62), Am. Philos. Soc., Nat. Acad. Scis., Soc. Exptl. Biology and Medicine, Harvey Soc., Am. Fedn. Clin. Rsch., Inst. Medicine (sr.), Balt. Med. Soc., Am. Assn. Immunologists, N.Y. Acad. Medicine (sec. sect. microbiology 1961-62), Phila. County Med. Soc. (Strittmatter award 1979), Coll. Physicians Phila. (Meritorious Svc. award 1980, pres.-elect 1986, pres. 1988-89), Interurban Clin. Club (pres. 1970), Infectious Disease Soc. Am. (pres. 1971, Maxwell Finland lecture award 1974, Bristol award 1986), Johns Hopkins Soc. Scholars, Phi Beta Kappa, Sigma Xi, Alpha Omega Alpha, Omicron Delta Kappa. Club: 14 W. Hamilton Street (Balt.).

AUSTRIN, HARVEY ROBERT, psychologist, educator; b. N.Y.C., Nov. 8, 1924; s. Benjamin Ralph and Rose Ruth (Rosen) A.; m. Miriam Charlotte Gottschalk, Mar. 28, 1948; children: Diane, Debra, Michael. BS, CCNY, 1945; MA, U. Ill., 1946; PhD, Ohio State U., 1950. Prof., clin. dir. St. Louis U., 1963-72, prof., 1972-90, prof. emeritus, 1990—; cons. psychologist V.A. state and local mental health programs, St. Louis, 1963—. Co-author: Learning Medical Terminology, 1995; assoc. editor Jour. of Profl. Psychology, 1978-81; contbr. articles to profl. jours.. Field selection officer U.S. Peace Corps, Washington, 1965-68. Fellow APA. Home and Office: 221 S Warson Rd Saint Louis MO 63124-1207

AUSUBEL, HERBERT, internist, oncologist; b. Bklyn., Nov. 18, 1929; s. Adolph and Frances (Einwohner) A.; m. Stephanie Gusikoff, Jan. 31, 1960; children: Ian, Lara. AB, NYU, 1950; MD, Harvard U., 1954. Diplomate Am. Bd. Internal Medicine. Intern medicine Bellevue Hosp., N.Y.C., 1954-55; resident medicine Bellevue Hosp./Meml.-Sloan Kettering, N.Y.C., 1957-59, Mt. Sinai Hosp., N.Y.C., 1959-60; pvt. practice Valley Stream, N.Y., 1960—; fellow oncology Meml. Sloan-Kettering Hosp., N.Y.C., 1962; attending physician medicine oncology Franklin Hosp., Valley Stream, 1962—, Mercy Hosp., Rockville Centre, N.Y., 1960—; mem. staff medicine L.I. Jewish Hosp., New Hyde Park, N.Y., 1960—. Lt. USN, 1955-57. Fellow ACP, Am.Coll. Medicine, Royal Soc. Medicine London. Office: 509 W Merrick Rd Valley Stream NY 11580

AUTEN, CAROL ELAINE, health records administrator; b. Chickasha, Okla., July 6, 1945; d. Thomas Hubert and Leona Wallace Owen; m. Melvin Ray Auten, June 28, 1968; 1 child, Krista Renae Auten. BS, E. Ctrl. Okla. State U., 1987. Sec. to dean of student affairs E. Tex. State U., Commerce, 1976-79; med. ward asst. VA Hosp., Muskogee, Okla., 1979-80; med. lab. asst. Carl Albert Indian Hosp., Ada, Okla., 1980-85; health records adminstr. Valley View Hosp., Ada, 1988, US Pub. Health Svc., Shawnee, Okla., 1988—; coord. commd. corps liason, awards U.S. Pub. Health Svc., Shawnee, 1990—, recruiter, 1990—; health records adv. bd. Gordon Cooper Vo-Tech., Shawnee, 1991-94; cons. Okla. City Urban Clinic, 1995-96. Contbr. articles to mags. Supporter E. Ctrl. Univ. Health Records Program, Ada, 1988—, Pottawatamie Tribal Job-Tng. Program, Shawnee, 1990—; cons. Native Am. Ctr. for Recovery, Shawnee, 1994. Lt. U.S. Commd. Corps, 1988—. Mem. Am. Health Info. Mgmt. Assn. (registered records adminstr.), Okla. Health Info. Mgmt. Assn., Commd. Officers Assn. U.S. Pub. Health Svc., Assn. Mil. Surgeons of the U.S. Republican. Baptist. Home: RRR 6 Box 348 B Ada OK 74820 Office: US Pub Health Svc 2001 S Gordon Cooper Shawnee OK 74801

AUTREY, KATHALEEN MARIE, addictions nurse; b. L.A., Feb. 23, 1958; d. Robert M. and Joy G. (Sullivant) Autrey; m. Danny M. Cassell, June 15, 1986 (div. Sept. 1990); 1 child, Christopher Daniel Autrey. BSN in Nursing and Psychology, Murray (Ky.) State U., 1982; postgrad., Ind. U., Indpls., 1993—. RN, Ky., Ind.; cert. addictions nurse. Staff nurse Lourdes Hosp., Paducah, Ky., 1980-84, St. Joseph's Hosp., Lexington, Ky., 1984-86; clin. nurse Welborn Hosp/Mulberry Ctr., Evansville, Ind., 1991—. Mem. Ind. State Nurses Assn., Sigma Theta Tau. Home: 1611 W Louisiana St Evansville IN 47710 Office: Welborn Hosp Mulberry Ctr 401 SE 6th St Evansville IN 47713

AUWERX, JOHAN HENRI, molecular biologist, medical educator; b. Diepenbeek, Limburg, Belgium, Oct. 4, 1958; s. Rene Auwerx and Maria Gilissen. B of Medicine, Cath. U., Leuven, Belgium, 1978, MD, 1982, PhD, 1990, Specialist in Endocrinology, 1987. Specialist internal medicine. Intern Royal Victoria Hosp., Montreal, Can., 1981; resident in medicine Cath. U., Leuven, 1982-84, fellow in endocrinology, 1984-86; sr. rsch. fellow U. Wash., Seattle, 1986-88; rsch. dir. CNRS, Lille, 1991—; assoc. prof. Cath. U., Leuven, 1989—; cons. Janssen Pharm. Industry, Beerse, Belgium, Ligand Pharm., La Jolla, Calif. Co-author/editor seven scientific books; contbr. articles to profl. jours. Recipient Horlait-Dapsens prize Belgium, 1985, Fulbright award, 1986, J. Fogarty Rsch. award NIH, 1987, ILSI Rsch. award Internat. Life Sci. Inst., USA/Europe, 1989, Morgagni Young Investigator award European Metabolic soc., Italy, 1991, F. De Waele award, Belgium, 1989, Boehring award, Belgium, 1991, Danone award, France, 1993. Mem. AAAS, Am. Fedn. Clin. Rsch., Am. Heart Assn. (fellow coun. on atherosclerosis 1989), Am. Soc. Microbiology, European Atherosclerosis Soc., Institut Francais de Nutrition, Belgian Lipid Club. Office: Institut Pasteur, 1 Rue Calmette, 59019 Lille France

AUZÊPY, PHILIPPE, physician; b. Paris, Jan. 3, 1931; m. Dominique Laurence; 4 children. MD, U. Paris, 1960. Sr. prof. medicine U. Paris XI, 1970—; head med. ICU, Hosp. de Bicêtre, Kremlin Bicetre, France, 1973—. Editor, author: Les accidents des medicaments, 1990; assoc. editor Revue du Praticien, 1961—, Reanimation et Urgences, 1990-95. Home: 20 Rue La Trémoille, F-75008 Paris France Office: Hosp de Bicêtre, Rue du Géneral Leclerc, F-94275 Le Kremlin-Bicêtre France

AVAKIAN, LAURA ANN, hospital administrator; b. DeSoto, Mo., July 6, 1945; d. Edward Ernest and Elizabeth (Gamel) McClary; m. Stephen Avakian, Dec. 30, 1969. BA, U. Mo., 1967; MA, Northwestern U., 1968. Instr. Sacramento (Calif.) State Coll., 1968-69; English tchr. Hathaway Brown Sch., Cleve., 1969-73; pers. profl. Huron Rd. Hosp., Cleve., 1974-76, dir. human resources, 1978-80; dir. employment Cleve. Clinic Found., 1976-78; v.p. human resources Beth Israel Hosp., Boston, 1980—. Assoc. editor Yearbook of Healthcare Management, 1990, 91, 92, 93. Mem. Mayor's Commn. on Comparable Worth, Boston, 1989-90. Mem. Am. Soc. Healthcare Human Resources Adminstrn. (bd. dirs. 1989-93, Pres. Leadership award 1989, Lit. award 1992, pres. 1994-95), Soc. Human Resource Mgmt. (Profl. Excellence award 1996), Mass. Health Care Human Resources Assn. (pres. 1987-88). Office: Beth Israel Hosp 330 Brookline Ave Boston MA 02215-5400

AVAKOFF, JOSEPH CARNEGIE, medical and legal consultant; b. Fairbanks, Alaska, July 15, 1936; s. Harry B. and Margaret (Adams) A.; m. Teddy I. Law, May 7, 1966; children: Caroline, Joey, John. AA, U. Calif., Berkeley, 1956, AB, 1957; MD, U. Calif., San Francisco, 1961; JD, Santa Clara U., 1985. Bar: Calif. 1987; diplomate Am. Bd. Surgery, Am. Bd. Plastic Surgery. Physicist U.S. Naval Radiol. Def. Lab., San Francisco, 1957, 59; intern So. Pacific Gen. Hosp., San Francisco, 1961-62; resident in surgery Kaiser Found. Hosp., San Francisco, 1962-66; resident in plastic surgery U. Tex. Sch. Medicine, San Antonio, 1970-72; pvt. practice specializing in surgery Sacramento, 1966-70; pvt. practice specializing in plastic surgery Los Gatos and San Jose, Calif., 1972-94; cons. to med. and legal professions, 1994—; clin. instr. surgery U. Calif. Sch. Medicine, Davis, 1967-70; chief dept. surgery Mission Oaks Hosp., Los Gatos, 1988-90; chief div. plastic surgery Good Samaritan Hosp., San Jose, 1989-91; expert med. reviewer Med. Bd. Calif., 1995—; presenter numerous med. orgns. Contbr. numerous articles to med. jours. Mem. San Jose Adv. Commn. on Health, 1975-82; bd. govs. San Jose YMCA, 1977-80. Mem. AMA, Calif. Med. Assn., Santa Clara County Bar Assn., Santa Clara County Med. Assn., Union Am. Physicians and Dentists, Phi Beta Kappa, Phi Eta Sigma. Republican. Presbyterian. Home: 6832 Rockview Ct San Jose CA 95120-5607

AVANT, GAYLE, political science educator; b. Mercedes, Tex., Aug. 23, 1940; s. George Clarence and Winnie Lela (Bagley) A.; m. Patricia Kay Coalson, Sept. 1, 1970; children—Samantha, Celia. B.A., U. Tex., 1962; M.A., U. N.C., 1965, Ph.D., 1969. Devel. Officer AID/State Dept., Washington, 1966-68; asst. prof. Miami U., Oxford, Ohio, 1968-70; assoc. prof. polit. sci. Baylor U., Waco, Tex., 1970—; vis. prof. Inst. Brit. and Am. Studies, U. Oslo, Norway, 1993. Author: En Extremis, 1976; editor: Foundations of Citizenship, 1990. Dir. Baylor Washington Program, 1985-92. Mem. Centex Pub. Adminstrn. Assn. (program chmn. 1991-93), S.W. Social Sci. Assn., Nat. Coun. Social Studies, Tex. Coun. for Social Studies, Am. Polit. Sci. Assn. Baptist.

AVANT, ROBERT FRANK, physician, educator; b. Chisholm, Minn., 1937; m. Betty Jensen, Dec. 28, 1962; children: Paul, Gregory, Todd. MD, U. Minn., 1963. Diplomate Am. Bd. Family Practice. Intern San Bernardino, Calif. County Hosp., 1963-64; chief of family practice Glenwood Hills Hosp., 1970-71, chief of staff, 1972; dir. family practice residency North Meml. Hosp., Mpls., 1973-77; asst. prof. dept. family practice and cmty. health U. Minn., 1973-77; chmn. dept. family medicine Mayo Clinic, Rochester, Minn., 1977-91, assoc. prof. family medicine, 1977-84; prof. family medicine Mayo Clinic, Rochester, 1984-93, Sanders prof. primary care, 1986-93; chmn. div. family medicine Mayo Clinic Jacksonville, 1991-93; dep. exec. dir. Am. Bd. Family Practice, Lexington, Ky., 1991—. Capt. MC, USAF, 1964-66. Office: Am Bd Family Practice 2228 Young Dr Lexington KY 40505-4219

AVCI, ADNAN, health products executive; b. Diyarbakir, Turkey, Nov. 1, 1961; s. Bulent and Lamia (Hasirci) A.; m. Micheline Mariette Juliette Debraz, Oct. 4, 1986; children: Celine, Julide. MD, Istanbul U., 1986. Product specialist Organon Teknika, Turkey, 1993-95, mgr. product, 1995—. Home: TM Efendi Cad 74/7, 81060 Goztepe Istanbul Turkey Office: Organon Teknika AS, Kayisdagi Cad 288/2, Sahray-1 Cedit, 81080 Erenköy Istanbul Turkey

AVENDANO, MANUEL G., nephrologist, consultant; b. Mex., Dec. 2, 1943; s. Manuel and Guadalupe (Garcia) A.; m. Martha C. Armenta, Mar. 14, 1969; children: Hugo J., Aldo R., Manuel A. Prof. nephrology Escuela de Medicina, Mexicali, Mex., 1975-90; chief internal medicine and surgery Hosp. Gen., Mexicali, Mex., 1978-90, pres. med. rsch., 1979-90; chief nephrology Hosp. Almater, Mexicali, Mex., 1990—, coord. renal transplant program, 1993—; nephrologist Mexicali, Mex., 1975—. Mem. Mex. Soc. Nephrology, Internat. Soc. for Periotneal Dialysis, Assn. Egresados Unam. Roman Catholic. Home: Atenas # 169 Frace-Villafontana, 21180 Mexicali Mexico Office: Renal Med Unit, Av Zaragoza # 1362, 21100 Mexicali Mexico

AVENI, CARL ANTHONY, clinical social worker; b. Boston, Aug. 11, 1944; m. Lorraine Mary Shea, Apr. 29, 1967; children: Madonna, Carl Anthony II, David. AB, Boston Coll., Chesnut Hill, Mass., 1967, MSW, 1972; advanced diploma health care adminstrn., Acad. Health Scis., Ft. Sam Houston, Tex., 1981. Lic. ind. clin. social worker, Mass.; diplomate Am. Bd. Examiners in Clin. Social Work. Clin. social worker VA Med. Ctr., Brockton, Mass., 1968—, assoc. coord. behavior therapy unit, 1973-82, coord., 1982-84, program evaluation coord. chronic rehab. svcs., 1983-84, adminstrv. coord. mental health coun.-clinic case confs., 1985-90; instr. social work sequence Ea. Nazarene Coll., Quincy, Mass., 1972-80; instr., cons. New Eng. Ctr. for Behavior Modification, Boston, 1974-75; cons. Paul Dever State Sch., Taunton, Mass., 1975-77; program evaluator, cons. Brockton Multisvc. Ctr., 1978—; instr. Boston U. Sch. Social Work, 1980—, R.I. Coll. Sch. Social Work, Providence, 1990—; counselor Brockton Family and Cmty. Resources, 1989-91. Author, editor: Behavior Therapy Orientation Handbook, 1985; also articles. Pres. Brockton Jaycees, 1978-79; cubmaster pack 16 Boy Scouts Am., Brockton, 1980-82, asst. scoutmaster troop 16, 1982-90. Recipient Merit award Old Colony Coun. Boy Scouts Am., 1985. Mem. NASW (chmn. nominating com. Mass. chpt. 1980-82), Acad. Cert. Social Wrokers, New Eng. Soc. for Behavioral Assessment and Therapy (life, pres. 1975-77), Massasoit Amateur Radio Assn. (pres. 1992—, treas. 1990-91). Home: 89 Manners Ave Brockton MA 02401-1420 Office: VA Med Ctr 940 Belmont St Brockton MA 02401-5596

AVENIA, RONALD JOSEPH, ophthalmologist; b. Bklyn., July 30, 1950; s. Joseph Vincent and Jeanette Mary (Racinski). BA, NYU, 1971; MD, Georgetown U., 1975. Diplomat Am. Bd. Ophthalmology. Pvt. practice ophthalmology Bloomsburg (Pa.) Hosp., 1979—. Fellow Am. Acad. Ophthalmology (Physicians Recognition award 1982-98); mem. AMA, Pa. Med. Soc., Columbia County Med. Soc. Office: Ste 302 410 Glen Ave Bloomsburg PA 17815-1200

AVERBOOK, BERYL DAVID, surgeon, educator; b. Superior, Wis., Aug. 17, 1920; s. Abraham B. and Clara (Zeichig) A.; student Superior State Tchrs. Coll., 1938-39; B.S., U. Wis., 1942, M.D., 1945; postgrad. U. Colo., 1948-50; m. Gloria Sloane, Apr. 2, 1955; children—Bruce Jeffrey, Allan Wayne. Diplomate Am. Bd. Surgery; cert. as having spl. qualifications in gen. vascular surgery. Intern Akron (Ohio) City Hosp., 1945-46; resident VA Hosp., Denver, 1948-50, Rochester (N.Y.) Gen. Hosp., 1950-51, VA Hosp., Los Angeles, 1951-54; practice medicine specializing in gen. surgery, Torrance, Calif., 1948—; instr. surgery U. Calif. at Los Angeles-Harbor Gen. Hosp., 1954-58; practice tumor and vascular surgery, Torrance, 1961—; asst. prof. surgery U. Calif. Med. Center, Los Angeles, 1958-61, asst. clin. prof. surgery, 1961-64; chief surg. services Los Angeles County Harbor Gen. Hosp., Torrance, 1954-61. Served to capt. M.C., AUS; Res. Fellow A.C.S.; mem. Am. Los Angeles County med. assns., N.Y. Acad. Scis., Los Angeles Acad. Medicine, Am. Geriatric Soc., Am. Assn. Med. Colls., Soc. Head and Neck Surgeons, Soc. Clin. Vascular Surgeons, Long Beach Surg. Soc. Contbr. articles to profl. jours. Home: 6519 Springpark Ave Los Angeles CA 90056-2223

AVERILL, JAMES REED, psychology educator; b. San Francisco, Nov. 29, 1935; s. Dupree Reed and Rosalie (Diamond) Averill. B.A., San Jose U., 1959; Ph.D., UCLA, 1966. Psychologist U. Calif.-Berkeley, 1966-71; mem. faculty U. Mass., Amherst, 1971—, prof. psychology, 1976—. Served with U.S. Army, 1954-57. Fulbright fellow W. Germany, 1959-60. Mem. APA, Am. Psychol. Soc., Internat. Soc. for Rsch. on Emotion. Office: U Mass Dept Psychology Amherst MA 01003

AVERSA, JAMES JOHN, optometrist; b. Passaic, N.J., Sept. 20, 1957; s. Joseph Leonard and Marie (Russo) A.; m. Karen Ann Comiskey, Nov. 18, 1989; children: Stephen, Emily. BSc, Montclaire State Coll., 1980; OD, Pa. Coll. Optometry, 1985. Resident in geriatric optometry Wilkes Barre (Pa.) VA Med. Ctr., 1985-86; staff optometrist Dr. Commins & Shok, Passaic, 1986-88, Dr. Morhstien & Kaufmann, Passaic, 1988-90, Dr. Lenny Fress, Fairlawn, N.J., 1988-90, Dr. Ken Bair, West Milford, N.J., 1990-94; pvt. practice Has Heights, N.J., 1990—; cons. vision therapy Oi Press, Fontlawn, N.J., 1988-90. Am. Optometric Assn. Roman Catholic. Home: 59 Seminole Ave Oakland NJ 07436

AVERY, DONALD ROBERT, hospital administrator; b. Peoria, Ill., Dec. 21, 1956; s. Robert Frederick and Helen Chambers (Dodds) A.; m. Fara Ann Haney, June 30, 1984; children: Amelia Claire, Meredith Fara. BS, U.S. Air Force Acad., 1978; MBA, U. Fla., 1986, M of Health Sci., 1986. Adminstrv. resident Bapt. Med. Ctr., Jacksonville, Fla., 1986, adminstrv. coord., 1987-88; asst. adminstr. South Ga. Med. Ctr., Valdosta, 1988—; mem. adv. bd. Lownde County 911 Ctr., Valdosta, 1991—. Bd. dirs. Am. Cancer Soc., Valdosta, 1990—, pres., 1993; elder, tchr. Westminster Presbyn. Ch., 1988—. Capt. USAF, 1978-84. Fellow Am. Coll. Healthcare Execs. (regents coun. 1993—); mem. Ga. Assn. Healthcare Execs. (pres. 1994), Kiwanis (bd. dirs. 1994). Republican. Office: South Ga Med Ctr 2501 N Patterson St Valdosta GA 31602

AVERY, G(AYLORD) JAMES, II, cardiovascular surgeon; b. Omaha, Apr. 22, 1945; s. Gaylord James and Laura Katherine (York) A.; m. Judith Liggett, May 2, 1980 (div. Nov. 1990); children: Benjamin, Christopher; m. Ann L. Woodcock, June 29, 1995. BA, Yale U., 1967; MD, Columbia U., 1971. Diplomate Am. Bd. Surgery, Thoracic Surgery. Ptnr. Hill Avery Hershon, San Francisco. Office: 2100 Webster Ste 512 San Francisco CA 94115

AVERY, GORDON BENNETT, medical educator, neonatologist; b. Beirut, Lebanon, Dec. 10, 1931; s. Bennett Franklin and Margaret Anne (Scales) A.; m. Ruth Elizabeth Butler, June 12, 1954 (div.); children: Melody Anne, Wendy Jean, Heidi Elizabeth; m. Penny Glass, Nov. 4, 1989; children: Alexander, Andrew, Anthony. AB, Harvard U., 1953; MD, U. Pa., 1958, PhD, 1959. Dir. div. neonatology Children's Hosp. Nat. Med. Ctr., Washington, 1963-90, physician-in-chief, 1990—; prof. dept. child health and devel. George Washington U., Washington, 1971—, prof., chmn. dept. pediatrics, Sch. Med. and Health Scis., 1990—; chief oper. officer Children's Rsch. Inst., Washington, 1990—; adv. com. FDA, Washington, 1979-83, 88-91; cons. Nat. Inst. Child Health and Human Devel., 1978—, Bethesda Naval Hosp., 1980—, Walter Reed Army Hosp., 1981—; mem. Mayor's adv. bd. on maternal and infant health, 1986-90. Editor: Neonatology, Pathophysiology and Management of the Newborn, 1975, 3d edit., 1987, 4th edit., 1994; co-editor: Atlas of Neonatal Procedures, 1983; edtl. bd. Pediat. Jour., 1980-86. Bd. dirs. Pathfinder, Boston, 1975-86, Children's Rsch. Inst., Washington, Children's Hosp., Children's Nat. Med. Ctr. Lt. Med. Svc. Corps., USN, 1958-63. Mem. Soc. for Pediatric Research, Am. Pediatric Soc., Am. Acad. Pediatrics (chmn. fetus and newborn com. 1977-90), National Capital Med. Found. (chmn. perinatal mortality com. 1979-82), Peruvian Pediatric and Surg. Socs. (hon.), Nat. Perinatal Assn. (legis. com.). Home: 4655 36th St S # 2B Arlington VA 22206-1748 Office: Children's Nat Med Ctr 111 Michigan Ave NW Washington DC 20010-2970

AVERY, MARY ELLEN, pediatrician, educator; b. Camden, N.J., May 6, 1927; d. William Clarence and Mary (Miller) A. AB, Wheaton Coll., Norton, Mass., 1948, DSc (hon.), 1974; MD, Johns Hopkins U., 1952; DSc (hon.), Trinity Coll., 1976, U. Mich., 1975, Med. Coll. Pa., 1976, Albany Med. Coll., 1977, Med. Coll. Wis., 1978, Radcliffe Coll., 1978; MA (hon.), Harvard U., 1974; LHD (hon.), Emmanuel Coll., 1979, Northeastern U., 1981, Russell Sage Coll., 1983, Meml. U., Newfoundland, 1993. Intern Johns Hopkins Hosp., 1953-54, resident, 1954-57; research fellow in pediatrics Boston, 1957-59, Balt., 1959-69; assoc. prof. pediatrics Johns Hopkins U., 1964-69; prof., chmn. dept. pediatrics McGill U. Med. Sch., 1969-74; prof. pediatrics Harvard U., 1974—; physician-in-chief Montreal Children's Hosp., 1969-74, Children's Hosp. Med. Center, Boston, 1974-85; mem. Med. Rsch. Coun. Can.; mem. study sect. NIH, 1968-71, 84-88. Author: The Lung and Its Disorders in the Newborn Infant, 4th edit., 1981, (with A. Schaffer) Diseases of the Newborn, 1971, 6th edit. (with H.W. Taeusch and R. Ballard), 1991; (with G. Litwack) Born Early, 1984; author, editor: (with L. First) Pediatric Medicine, 1988, 2nd edit., 1994; also articles; mem. editorial bd. Pediatrics, 1965-71, Am. Rev. Respiratory Diseases, 1969-73, Am. Jour. Physiology, 1967-73, Jour. Pediatrics, 1974-84, Medicine, 1985, Johns Hopkins Med. Jour., 1978-82, Clin. and Investigative Critical Care Medicine, 1990, New Eng. Jour. Medicine, 1990. Trustee Wheaton Coll. (1965-85), Radcliffe Coll., Johns Hopkins U., 1982-88. Recipient Mead Johnson award in pediatric rsch., 1968, Trudeau medal Am. Thoracic Soc., 1984, Nat. Medal of Sci. NSF, 1991; Markle scholar in med. scis., 1961-66. Fellow AAAS (dir. 1989), NAS, Internat. Pediatric Assn. (standing com. 1986-89), Am. Acad. Pediatrics, Am. Acad. Arts and Scis., Royal Coll. Physicians and Surgeons Can.; mem. Can. Pediatric Soc., Am. Physiol. Soc., Soc. Pediatric Rsch. (pres. 1972-73), Brit. Pediatric Assn. (hon.), Inst. Medicine (coun. 1987), Am. Pediatric Soc. (pres. 1990), Phi Beta Kappa, Alpha Omega Alpha. Office: 221 Longwood Ave Boston MA 02115-5817

AVEY, HARRY THOMPSON, JR., internist; b. Allahabad, India, Dec. 31, 1916; came to U.S., 1920; s. Harry Thompson and Sarah Ellis (Swezey) A.; m. Winnie Mae Starkey, Oct. 26, 1941 (dec. July, 1991); 1 child, Carl Thompson. BS, U. Wis., 1937, MD, 1939. Diplomate Am. Bd. Internal Medicine. Dir. admission and outpatient depts. Univ. Hosps., Okla. City, 1942-46; pvt. practice internal medicine Okla. City, 1946—; assoc. clin. prof. medicine U. Okla. Med. Sch., Okla. City, 1959-71, clin. prof. medicine, 1971—; chmn. dept. medicine Bapt. Med. Ctr., Okla. City, 1965-87. Major U.S. Air Force, 1951-53. Recipient Govs. award, Gov. of Okla., 1989. Fellow Am. Coll. Physicians. Republican. Presbyterian. Office: H. Thompson Avey MD 3435 NW 56th St Oklahoma City OK 73112-4414

AVIADO, DOMINGO M., pharmacologist, toxicologist; b. Manila, Aug. 28, 1924; came to U.S., 1946, naturalized, 1990.; s. Domingo Gatus and Severina O. (Mariano) A.; m. Asuncion Palma Guevara, Aug. 15, 1953; children: Maria Cristina Aviado Gentile, Carlos G., Domingo G., Maria Asuncion. Student, U. Philippines, 1940-46; M.D., U. Pa., 1948. From asst. instr. pharmacology to assoc. prof. U. Pa. Med. Sch., 1948-65, prof., 1965-77, acting chmn. dept., 1969-70; sr. dir. biomed. research Allied Chem. Corp., Morristown, N.J., 1977-80; pres. Atmospheric Health Scis., Inc., 1980—; founder, pres. Orphan Pharms. Inc., 1984-87; adj. prof. pharmacology Coll. Medicine and Dentistry N.J., Newark, 1977-84; vis. lectr. anesthesiology Albert Einstein Med. Center, 1955-77; vis. prof. pharmacology U. of East Med. Center, Philippines, 1959-77; vis. lectr. physiology Women's Med. Coll., Phila., 1961-62, Rutgers U., 1966-67; cons. Council for Drug Research, 1972-73, Poison Control Program of Phila., 1964-70; mem. clean air sci. adv. com. EPA, 1978-80. Author textbook, 11 monographs, 2 med. dictionaries; mem. editorial bd. Cardiology, 1967-79, Drug Info. Jour., 1974-77, Jour. Cardiovascular Pharmacology, 1979-84, Biol. Abstracts, 1984-90; La Riforma Medica, 1987-90, adv. editorial bd. Archives Internationales de Pharmacodynamie et de Therapie, 1965-77; editor inhalation sect. Jour. Pathology and Environ. Toxicology, 1978-80; interim editor Jour. Clin. Pharmacology, 1984-85; contbr. articles to profl. jours., chpts. to books. Recipient Linnaeus medal Stockholm, 1961, Purkinje medal Prague, 1963; Presdl. trophy for most outstanding Filipino, 1975; named Physician of Yr., Philippine Med. Assn., 1969, numerous other awards; Guggenheim fellow, 1962-63. Fellow Acad. Medicine N.J.; mem. Physiol. Soc. Phila. (pres. 1959-60), Am. Soc.Pharmacology and Exptl. Therapeutics (fin. com. 1965-70), Am. Physiol. Soc., Internat. Union Pharmacology (treas. 1965-66), Am. Coll. Clin. Pharmacology (bd. regents 1978-83), Soc. Toxicology, Coll. Physicians Phila., U. Pa. Sch. Medicine Nat. Alumni Coun. Home and Office: 225 Hartshorn Dr Short Hills NJ 07078-3225

AVILES, ALICE ALERS, psychologist; b. N.Y.C; d. Jose Oscar and Pauline (Irizarry) Alers; m. Jose A. Aviles, Aug. 13, 1954 (div. Oct. 1981); children: Jeffrey (dec.), Brian, Gregory. BS magna cum laude, SUNY, Oswego, 1955; MA, Queens Coll., 1978; PhD, Yeshiva U., 1984; postdoctoral diploma in psychoanalysis, Adelphi U., 1991. Lic. psychologist, N.Y. Tchr. elem. schs. Spring Valley, N.Y., 1955, Erlangen (Fed. Republic Germany) Am. Sch., 1955-56; tchr. elem. schs. Uniondale, N.Y., 1956, Freeport, N.Y., 1957-58, Island Park, N.Y., 1973-75; psychology clk. Fifth Ave. Ctr. for Counseling and Psychotherapy, N.Y.C., 1978-80; psychology intern St. Vincent's Hosp. and Med. Ctr., N.Y.C., 1980-81; psychologist Kingsboro Psychiat. Ctr., Bklyn., 1981-84; psychologist to assoc. psychologist South Beach Psychiat. Ctr., Bklyn., 1984-86; pvt. practice Valley Stream, N.Y., 1985—; from staff psychologist to sr. psychologist Luth. Med. Ctr., Bklyn., 1986-95; cons. Beach Terrace Care Ctr., Long Beach, N.Y., 1995—; mem. adv. com. Hispanic Counseling Ctr. of Family Svc. Assn. of Nassau County, Hempstead, N.Y., 1978-80. Ford found. grad. fellow, 1978-81. Mem. APA, N.Y. State Psychol. Assn., Nassau County Psychol. Assn. (mem. pvt. practice com. 1992-93), Adelphi Soc. Psychoanalysis and Psychotherapy. Office: 10 Valley Ln E North Woodmere NY 11581

AVILÉS, IVÁN, health services administrator; b. Utuado, P.R., July 7, 1960; s. Pertanio and Irma Iris (Medina) A.; m. Evelyn Feliciano, Mar. 19, 1988. BBA, Puerto Rico U., 1982; M on Health Svcs. Adminstrn., Pub. Health Grad. Sch., Rio Piedras, P.R., 1986. Hosp. adminstr. Mental Health Secretariat, Aguadilla, P.R., 1987-93; aux. adminstr. Sub-Regional Hosp. Dept. Health-AFASS, Aguadilla, P.R., 1993—. Mem. Health Svcs. Adminstr. Coll. P.R. Presbyterian. Home: HC-03 Box 12625 Aguadilla PR 00603-9708 Office: Hosp Sub-Regional Box 3968 Aguadilla PR 00605

AVIS, KENNETH EDWARD, emeritus pharmaceutical educator, consultant; b. Elmer, N.J., June 3, 1918; s. Clinton Fisk and Clara B. (Urion) A.; m. Irma Jeanette Hildreth, Feb. 19, 1943; children: John Neal, Carolyn Ruth, Beverly Jean. BS in Pharmacy, Phila. Coll. Pharmacy and Sci., 1942, MS, 1947, DSc, 1956. Asst. Phila. Coll. Pharmacy and Sci., 1946-48, from instr. to assoc. prof., 1948-61; assoc. prof. U. Tenn. Coll. Pharmacy, Memphis, 1961-67, prof., vice chmn., 1967-83, prof., chmn., 1983-88, emeritus prof., 1988—; cons. to pharm. cos., 1966—, Pan Am. Health Orgn., 1979-83; cons., expert FDA, 1968—; chmn. parenteral home health care com. Tenn. Bd. Pharmacy, 1984-86; mem. home health care adv. panel U.S. Pharmacopeia, 1990—. Editor: Pharmaceutical Dosage Forms: Parenteral Medications, 1984, 86, 2d edit. Vol. 1, 1991, Vol. 2, 1993, Vol. 3, 1993, Drug Mfg. Tech. Series, 1995—, Sterile Pharmaceutical Products: Process Engineering Applications, 1995, Biotechnology and Biopharmaceutical Manufacturing, Processing and Preservation, 1996; contbr. articles to profl. jours., chpts. to books. Pres. bd. trustees Evang. Christian Sch., Memphis, 1964-74; trustee Covenant Coll., Lookout Mountain, Ga., 1988-96; mem. various bds. Riveroaks Reformed Presbyn. Ch., Memphis, 1975—. Recipient Alumni award Phila. Coll. Pharmacy and Sci., 1977. Fellow Am. Assn. Pharm. Scientists; mem. Parenteral Drug Assn. (bd. dirs. 1960-77, pres. 1968-69, Schaugus Tech. Achievement award 1976, Rsch. Achievement award 1979). Republican. Home: 2176 Gorham Pl Germantown TN 38139-4256 Office: U Tenn 874 Union Ave Memphis TN 38163-2105

AVNER, SANFORD ELDON, pediatrician; b. Gallipolis, Ohio, Apr. 20, 1940; s. Max and Ruth (Burech) A.; m. Susan E. Messinger; children: David Bryan, Marc Thomas. BA, Yale U., 1962; MD, SUNY, Bklyn, 1966. Diplomate Am. Bd. Pediats., Am. Bd. Immunology, Am. Bd. Internal Medicine and Pediats. Sr. staff Nat. Jewish Hosp., 1972—; clin. prof. pediatrics U. Colo. Med. Ctr., 1974—; pres. Colo. Allergy and Asthma Ctrs., Aurora. Author (with others) : Allergic Disease Information-Adult, 1988. Served to capt. USAF, 1968-70. Recipient Air Force Commendation medal, 1970. Mem. Am. Acad. Allergy, Asthma, and Immunology (bd. dirs.), AMA, Physicians for Social Responsibility, Colo. Med. Soc., Am. Thoracic Soc., Aurora-Adams County Med. Soc. Home: 13 Red Fox Ln Englewood CO 80111-1440 Office: Colorado Allergy and Asthma Clinic 1450 S Havana St Ste 500 Aurora CO 80012-4030

AWAD, ATIF BOSHRA, nutrition educator; b. Beni Suef, Arab Republic of Egypt, Sept. 14, 1939; came to U.S., 1969; s. Boshra and Ogeni Awad; m. Nagwa A. Jacob; children: George, Michael, David, Ann Mary. MS, Ain Shams U., Cairo, Arab Republic of Egypt, 1966; PhD, Rutgers U., 1974. Registered dietitian. Postdoctoral fellow U. Iowa, Iowa City, 1974-76; assoc. prof. Kirksville (Mo.) Coll. Osteopathic, 1976-85; assoc. prof., dir. nutrition program SUNY, Buffalo, 1985—. Contbr. articles to Jour. Nutrition, Lipids. Postdoctoral fellow NIH, 1975-76; rsch. grantee NIH, 1978-80, USDA, 1981-84, Am. Heart Assn., 1985-86; named Researcher of Yr., Sigma Sigma Phi, 1983. Mem. Am. Inst. Nutrition, Am. Soc. for Biochemistry & Molecular Biology, Am. Oil Chemists Soc., Am. Dietetic Assn. Office: SUNY Nutrition Program 301 Parker Hall S Campus Buffalo NY 14214

AWAD, WILLIAM MICHEL, JR., hematologist, biochemist, educator; b. Shanghai, China, Nov. 5, 1927; came to U.S., 1943; s. William Michel and Lilian Teresa (Affounso) A.; m. Marilyn Suzanne Wells, June 1, 1957 (dec. 1991); children: Lily Anne, William Michel III; m. Josephine Alexandra Johnson, July 11, 1993. BS, Manhattan Coll., 1950; MD, SUNY-Downstate Med. Ctr., N.Y.C., 1954; PhD, U. Wash., 1965. Diplomate Am. Bd. Internal Medicine. Intern Kings County Hosp., N.Y., 1954-55; resident in pathology St. Vincent's Hosp., N.Y.C., 1955-56; resident in medicine Albert Einstein Med. Ctr., N.Y.C., 1956-57; fellow in medicine U. Minn. Hosp., Mpls., 1957-58; fellow in cardiology N.Y. Hosp., N.Y.C., 1958-59; asst. prof. to prof. medicine, biochemistry U. Miami, Fla., 1965—, prof. biochemistry, molecular biology, 1987—; chmn. rsch. peer rev. com. Fla. affiliate Am. Heart Assn., St. Petersburg, 1988-90. With U.S. Army, 1946-47. Grantee NIH, 1973. Republican. Roman Catholic. Office: Univ Miami Dept Medicine PO Box 16960 Miami FL 33101-6960

AWAIS, GEORGE MUSA, obstetrician, gynecologist; b. Ajloun, Jordan, Dec. 15, 1929; came to U.S., 1951; s. Musa and Meha (Koury) A.; m. Nabila Rizk, June 24, 1970. AB, Hope Coll., 1955; MD, U. Toronto, 1960. Diplomate Am. Bd. Obstetrics and Gynecology. Intern U. Toronto Hosps., Ont., Can., 1960-61, resident in obstetrics and gynecology, 1961-64, chief resident, 1965; chief resident Harlem Hosp., Columbia U., N.Y.C., 1966; asst. obstetrician and gynecologist Cleve. Met. Gen. Hosp., 1967, assoc. obstetrician and gynecologist, 1969; instr. obstetrics and gynecology Case Western Res. U., Cleve., 1967-70, asst. obstetrician and gynecologist MacDonald House, 1970, asst. prof., 1970, asst. clin. prof. dept. reproductive biology, 1971, asst. obstetrician and gynecologist Univ. Hosps., 1971; mem. staff, dept. gynecology Cleve. Clinic Found., 1971-91; chmn. dept. ob-gyn King Faisal Specialist Hosp. and Rsch. Ctr., Riyadh, 1975-76; cons. panel mem. Internat. Corr. Soc. Obstetricians and Gynecologists, 1971; emeritus staff Cleve. Clinic Found., 1991. Contbr. articles to publs. in field, papers, reports to confs., TV appearances, Saudi Arabia. Named Grand Officer of Order of Independence His Majesty King Hussein of Jordan, 1992. Fellow ACS, Am. Coll. Obstetricians and Gynecologists, Royal Coll. Surgeons Can.; mem. AMA, AAAS, Am. Infertility Soc., Arab Am. Med. Assn. (pres. 1991—, chmn. humanities relief 1996), Acad. Medicine of Cleve. Office: Cleve Clinic Found Emeritus Office 9500 Euclid Ave Cleveland OH 44195-0001

AXELRAD, CHARLES STEVEN, dentist; b. N.Y.C., Oct. 7, 1949; s. Nathaniel Richard and Betty (Nathanson) A.; m. Lorraine R Goldstein, June 10, 1972; children: Marisa Lauren, Jordan Eric. BS, SUNY, Stony Brook, 1970; DDS, NYU, 1974. Resident in gen. practice dentistry Bronx (N.Y.)-Lebanon Hosp. Ctr., 1974-75; pvt. practice Farmingdale, N.Y., 1975—. Contbr. articles to profl. jours. Vol. dentist United Cerebral Palsy, Roosevelt, N.Y., 1980. Nat. Inst. Dental Rsch. grantee, 1974. Fellow Acad. Gen. Dentistry; mem. ADA, Am. Assn. Endodontists, N.Y. State Dental Soc., Nassau County Dental Soc., Mid Island Study Club. Office: Farmingdale Dental Group PC 260 Merritts Rd Farmingdale NY 11735-3200

AXELROD, JULIUS, pharmacologist, biochemist; b. N.Y.C., May 30, 1912; s. Isadore and Molly (Leichtling) A.; m. Sally Taub, Aug. 30, 1938; children: Paul Mark, Alfred Nathan. BS, CCNY, 1933; MA, NYU, 1941, DSc (hon.), 1971; PhD, George Washington U., 1955, LLD (hon.), 1971; DSc (hon.), U. Chgo., 1965, Med. Coll. Wis., 1971, Med. Coll. Pa., 1974, U. Pa., 1986, Hahnemann U., 1987; LLD (hon.), CCNY, 1972; D honoris causa, U. Panama, 1972, U. Paris (Sud), 1982, Ripon Coll, 1984, Tel Aviv U., 1984; DSC (hon., McGill U., Montreal, 1989. Chemist Lab. Indsl. Hygiene, 1935-46; research assoc. 3d N.Y. U. research divsn. Goldwater Meml. Hosp., 1946-49; assoc. chemist sect. chem. pharmacology Nat. Heart Inst., NIH, 1949-50, chemist, 1950-53, sr. chemist, 1953-55; acting chief sect. pharmacology Lab. Clin. Sci. NIMH, 1955, chief sect. pharmacology, 1955-84; guest worker Lab. Cell Biology NIMH, 1984—; Otto Loewi meml. lectr. N.Y. U., 1963; Karl E. Paschkis meml. lectr. Phila. Endocine Soc., 1966; NIH lectr., 1967; Nathanson meml. lectr. U. So. Calif., 1968; James Parkinson lectr. Columbia U., 1971; Wartenberg lectr. Am. Acad. Neurology, 1971; Arnold D. Welch lectr. Yale U., 1971; Harold Carpenter Hodge distinguished lectr. toxicology U. Rochester, 1971; Bennett lectr. Am. Neurol. Assn., 1971; Harvey lectr., 1971; Mayer lectr. Mass. Inst. Tech., 1971; distinguished prof. sci. George Washington U., 1972; Salmon lectr. N.Y. Acad. Medicine, 1972; Eli Lilly lectr., 1972; Mike Hogg lectr. U. Tex., 1972; Fred Schueler lectr. Tulane U., 1972; numerous other hon. lectures; vis. scholar Herbert Lehman Coll. City U. N.Y., 1973; professorial lectr. George Washington U., 1959—; panelist U.S. Bd. Civil Service Examiners, 1958-67; mem. research adv. com. United Cerebral Palsy Assn., 1966-69; mem. psychopharmacology study sect. NIMH, 1970-74; mem. Internat. Brain Research Orgn.; mem. research adv. com. Nat. Found.; vis. com. Brookhaven Nat. Lab., 1972-76; bd. overseers Jackson Lab., 1974-88. Mem. editorial bd. Jour. Pharmacology and Exptl. Therapeutics, 1956-72, Jour. Medicinal Chemistry, 1962-67, Circulation Research, 1963-71, Currents in Modern Biology, 1966-72; mem. editorial adv. bd. Communication in Behavioral Biology, 1967-73, Jour. Neurobiology, 1968-77, Jour. Neurochemistry, 1969-77, Jour. Neurovisceral Relation, 1969, Rassegna di Neurologia Vegetativa, 1969—, Internat. Jour. Psychobiology, 1970-75; hon. cons. editor Life Scis, 1961-69; co-author: The Pineal, 1968; contbr. papers in biochem. actions and metabolism of drugs, hormones, action of pineal gland, enzymes, neurochem. transmission to profl. jours. Recipient Meritorious Rsch. award Assn. Rsch. Nervous and Mental Diseases, 1965; Gairdner award disting. rsch., 1967; Nobel prize in med. physiology, 1970; Alumni Disting. Achievement award George Washington U., 1968; Superior Service award HEW, 1968; Disting. Svc. award, 1970; Claude Bernard professorship and medal U. Montreal, 1969; Disting. Svc. award Modern Medicine mag., 1970; Albert Einstein award Yeshiva U., 1971; medal Rudolf Virchow Med. Soc., 1971; Myrtle Wreath award Hadassah, 1972; Leibniz medal Acad. Sci. East Germany, 1984; Salmon medal N.Y. Acad. Medicine, Bristol-Myers award for disting. rsch. in neurosci., 1989, Thudicum medal Brit. Biochem. Soc. (lectr.), 1989, Gerard medal Soc. Neuroscience, 1991. Felow AAAS, Am. Acad. Arts and Scis., Am. Soc. Neuropsychopharmacology; mem. German Pharmacol. Soc. (corr.), Am. Chem. Soc., Am. Soc. Pharmacology and Exptl. Therapeutics (Torald Sollmann award 1973), Nat. Acad. Scis., Am. Neurol. Assn. (hon.), Royal Soc. London (fgn.), Inst. Medicine (sr.), Am. Philos. Soc., Deutsche Academie Naturfoucher (East Germany), Am. Psychopathol. Assn. (hon.), Sigma Xi. Home: 10401 Grosvenor Pl Rockville MD 20852-4646 Office: NIH Dept Health Edn & Welfare Bldg 36 Rm 3A-15 9000 Rockville Pike Bethesda MD 20014

AXELROD, STEPHEN LEE, physician; b. Detroit, June 23, 1951; s. Reuben and Selma Josia (Kazanoff) A.; m. Paula Evans, May 24, 1986; children: Sydeny Lauren, Marc Robert. BS, U. Mich., 1972; MD, Wayne State U., 1977. Diplomate Am. Bd. Emergency Medicine, Am. Bd. Med. Mgmt. Intern Presbyn.-Denver Med. Ctr., 1977-78; emergency physician Emergency Cons. Inc., Petoskey, Mich., 1978-80, Colo. Emergency Med. Assocs., Thornton, 1980-87; physician, med. dir. Med. Ctrs. Colo., Denver, 1980-89; med. dir. Coors Brewing Co., Denver, 1990-94; pres. The Axelrod Group-Healthcare Cons., Denver, 1994-96; pres., CEO MD Network, LP, Denver, 1996—; clin. instr. Okla. Coll. Medicine and Surgery, Tulsa, 1982-87; chmn. credential com. Humana Hosp., Thornton, 1984-88; mem. editorial adv. bd. Medictr. Mgmt. jour., 1985-87. Mgmt. jour., 1985-87; editorial adv. bd. Medicenter Mgmt. jour., 1986-89. Physician Family Builders by Adoption- Fun Run, Denver, 1985-86, Community Home Health Care-Greek Marathon, Seattle, 1984; physician advisor Broomfield (Colo.) Vol. Ambulance Svc., 1980-83; corp. sponsor fin. com. Allied Jewish Fedn., Denver, 1987. Fellow Am. Coll. Emergency Physicians; mem. Colo. Med. Soc., Nat. Assn. Ambulatory Care (bd. dirs. 1984-86, cert. of recognition 1985), Am. Coll. Physician Execs., Am. Coll. Occupational Medicine. Home: 45 S Dexter St Denver CO 80222-1050 Office: MD Network LP 1200 17th St Ste 1950 Denver CO 80202-5835

AYAD, JOSEPH MAGDY, psychologist; b. Cairo, Egypt, May 21, 1926; s. Fahim Gayed and Victoria Gabour (El-Masri) A.; came to U.S., 1949, naturalized, 1961; B.A. in Social Scis., Am. U., Cairo, 1946; M.A. in Clin. Psychology (Univ. scholar), Stanford U., 1952; Ph.D. in Clin. Psychology (Univ. scholar), U. Denver, 1956; m. Widad Fareed Bishai, May 29, 1954; children—Fareed Merritt, Victor Maher, Michael Joseph, Mona Elaine. Translator Hoover Inst. War and Peace, Stanford U., 1950-51; asst. to chief psychologist Colo. Psychopathic Hosp., 1952-54; cons. Child Guidance Clinic, State Dept. Pub. Welfare, Denver, 1953-56; cons. psychologist Dept. Pub. Welfare, State of Tex., 1957-72; cons. psychologist Dept. Insts., Social and Rehab. Svc., State of Okla., 1960-72, N.Mex. Dept. Pub. Welfare, 1960-72; lectr. Fitzsimmons Army Hosp., Denver, 1953-54; vis. psychologist State Dept. Pub. Welfare, Child Guidance Clinic, Pueblo, Colo., 1953-54; staff psychologist Cons. Psychol. Svc., Denver, 1956-57, High Plains Neurol. Ctr., Amarillo, Tex., 1957—; pres. JMA Cattle Co., Amarillo, 1973—; v.p., treas. Filigon Inc., Amarillo, 1962-75, pres., 1976—. Mem. profl. adv. bd. Amarillo Mental Health Assn., 1968-69. Mem. Amarillo Child Welfare Bd., 1961-63; area chmn. U. Denver Fund Raising Campaign, 1963; mem. profl. adv. bd. St. Paul's Meth. Ch. Sch. for Children with Learning Disabilities, Amarillo, 1969-70. Recipient Grad. Sr. award in Philosophy Am. U. at Cairo, 1946. Mem. Am. Psychol. Soc., Am. Psychol. Assn., Internat. Assn. Applied Psychology, Am. Assn. Marriage and Family Therapists, Potter-Randall County (Tex.) Psychol. Soc. (pres. 1974), Tex. Psychol. Assn., Calif. Psychol. Assn. Presbyn. Club: Amarillo Country. Contbr. articles to profl. jours. Home: 4239 Erik Ave Amarillo TX 79106-6008 Office: 2301 W 7th Ave Amarillo TX 79106-6601

AYASSO, M. SAMIR, internist, gastroenterologist; b. Damascus, Syria, Oct. 1, 1953; came to U.S., 1984; s. Abdul-Rajak and Suad (Halabi) A.; m. Subhair Baha Taha, Jan. 17, 1990; children: Sara Su'ad, Sammy Zyde, Ali Evan. MD, Damascus U., 1978. Intern in medicine Shadyside Hosp., Pitts., 1984-85, resident in medicine, 1985-87, fellow in gastroenterology, 1987-89, mem. tchg. faculty, 1989—; pvt. practice gastroenterology, Pitts., 1989—. Mem. AMA, Am. Gastroenterology Assn., Am. Coll. Gastroenterology. Republican. Home: 4018 Mayflower Dr Murrysville PA 15668 Office: 5200 Centre Ave Ste 312 Pittsburgh PA 15232

AYDELOTTE, MYRTLE KITCHELL, nursing administrator, educator, consultant; b. Van Meter, Iowa, May 31, 1917; d. John J. and Larava Josephine (Gutshall) Kitchell; m. William O. Aydelotte, June 22, 1956; children—Marie Elizabeth, Jeannette Farley. B.S., U. Minn., 1939, M.A., 1947, Ph.D., 1955; postgrad., Columbia U. Tchrs. Coll., summer 1948. Head nurse Charles T. Miller Hosp., St. Paul, 1939-41; surg. teaching St. Mary's Hosp. Sch. Nursing, Mpls., 1941-42; instr. U. Minn., 1945-49; dir., dean State U. Iowa Coll. Nursing, 1949-57, prof., 1957-62; assoc. chief nurse VA Hosp. Rsch. for Nursing, Iowa City, 1963-64, chief nursing rsch., 1964-65; prof. U. Iowa Coll. Nursing, 1964-76, 82-88; exec. dir. Am. Nurses Assn., 1977-81; dir. nursing U. Iowa Hosps. and Clinics, 1968-76; mem. sci. adv. bd. Ctr. for Health Rsch. Wayne State U., 1972-76, Inst. Medicine, 1973—; cons. U. Minn., 1970, 82, 90, U. Rochester, 1971, U. Mich., 1970, 73, U. Colo., 1970-71, U. Hawaii, 1972-73, Ariz. State U., 1972, U. Nebr., 1972-73. Contbr. articles to profl. jours.; editorial bd.: Nursing Forum, 1969-72, Jour. Nursing Adminstrn, 1971. Mem., v.p. Iowa City Library Bd., 1961-67; mem. Johnson County Bd. Health, 1967-70; mem. adv. com. on family living courses Iowa City Bd. Edn., 1970-72. Served with Army Nurse Corps, 1942-46. Mem. Am. Nurses Assn., Am. Hosp. Assn., Am. Acad. Nursing, Sigma Theta Tau (research com. 1968-72). Home: 201 N 1st Ave Apt 308 Iowa City IA 52245-3614

AYERS, CARLOS R., internist, medical educator; b. Oakvale, W.Va., 1932. MD, U. Va., 1958. Diplomate Am. Bd. Internal Medicine. Intern U. Va. Hosp., Charlottesville, 1958-59, fellow in cardiology, 1962-64, sr. resident in internal medicine, 1963-64, mem. staff, 1964—; asst. resident internal medicine U. Utah Affiliated Hosps., 1961-62; asst. prof. internal medicine U. Va., Charlottesville, 1965-89, assoc. prof., 1969-74, prof., 1974—. Office: U of Va Hosp Dept of Internal Medicine PO Box 146 Charlottesville VA 22908-0146

AYERS, ERIC WYNTON, physician; b. Detroit, Feb. 21, 1962; s. William Sonny and Antis (Bankhead) A.; m. Diane Roberts, June 17, 1989; children: Symone Nichole, Bradley Wynton. BS in Microbiology, Mich. State U., 1995; MD, Wayne State U., 1989. Chief resident med./pediat. Wayne State U., Detroit, 1989-93, 93-94; physician-in-charge Burton Detention Ctr., Detroit, 1993—; asst. prof. Wayne State U., 1994—. Bd. dirs. Detroit High Sch., 1995—. Mich. State U. fellow, 1996. Fellow Am. Acad. Pediatrics; mem. Am. Coll. Physicians, Detrout Med. Soc., Soc. Adolscent Medicine. Office: U Health Ctr Detroit Med Ctr 4201 St Anthony Detroit MI 48221

AYERS, ROBIN MCCLENNY, optometrist; b. Norton, Va., June 6, 1963; d. William M. and Hazel J. (Justice) McClenny; m. Thomas Lyle Ayers, Jr., June 25, 1988; 1 child, Alexandra Nicole. BS, Bridgewater Coll. 1985; OD, So. Coll. Optometry, 1991. Lic. optometrist Va. Optometrist Blum, Newman, Blackstock and Assocs., Optometrists, Lynchburg and Roanoke, Va., 1991-93, Wilson and Ayers Optometrists, Lynchburg and Roanoke, 993—. Office: Doctors of Optometry PO Box 11769 Lynchburg VA 24506

AYLSWORTH, JOSEPH LYNN, JR., former health care services executive, property owners association executive; b. Phila., June 30, 1916; s. Joseph Lynn and Margaret Eleanor (Wanner) A.; m. Marjorie Jane Biedert, June 20, 1942; children: Susan C. Aylsworth Bushnell, Joseph Lynn, John Stephen; m. Barbara A. Post, May 22, 1982. Student in acctg., Peirce Jr. Coll., 1938. Register rep. Butcher and Sherrerd, Phila., 1946; pres. Mortgage Assocs., Inc., 1946-68; exec. v.p., dir. Am. Med. Affiliates, Inc., Jenkintown, Pa., 1968-90; pres., dir. Island Dune Owners Assn., Jensen Beach, Fla., 1990—. Chmn. Montgomery County chpt. Am. Cancer Soc., 1971; bd. dirs. Millcreek Community Hosp., Erie, Pa., Met. Hosp., Phila., St. Petersburg (Fla.) Gen. Hosp.; trustee emeritus Kirksville Coll. Osteo. Medicine. 1st lt. USAF, 1942-45. Decorated Air medal. Mem. Am. Nursing Home Assn., Health Care Facilities Assn. Pa., Phila. Mortgage Bankers Assn. (pres. 1959), Union League Club, Doylestown Country Club, Island Dunes Country Club (pres. 1992—). Republican. Presbyterian. Home: 8750 S Ocean Dr Jensen Beach FL 34957

AYRES, JAYNE LYNN ANKRUM, community health nurse; b. Reed City, Mich., Oct. 12, 1944; d. Quinten Wayne and Marshia Agetha (Crum) Ankrum; m. Ronald Francis Ayres, Apr. 16, 1977; children: Linda, Michele, Julie. ADN, Manatee C.C., Bradenton, Fla., 1975. RN, Fla., Ga. Staff nurse med.-surg., cardiac, oncology and float team Sarasota (Fla.) Meml. Hosp., 1975-77; nursing supr. Upjohn Healthcare Svcs., Sarasota, 1981-85; staff nurse Devereux Found., Kennesaw, Ga., 1986-89; staff nurse, supr. Vis. Nurse Health Sys., Metro, Atlanta, 1989—. Vol. ARC, M.U.S.T. Ministries Health Clinic for Homeless, Summer Olympics Games, 1996 Mem. Am. Legion (hon.), Fla. Nurses Assn. (hon.), Beta Sigma Phi.

AYRES, JOHN JAMES BREVARD, psychologist; b. Ocean City, Md., Aug. 2, 1939; s. Denward Collins and Irma White (Pointer) A.; m. Sheila Anne Petera, Sept. 9, 1961; children: Julie, John. BA, Coll William and Mary, 1961; MA, U. Ky., 1963, PhD, 1965. Rsch. asst. Pub. Health Svc. Hosp., Addiction Rsch. Ctr., Lexington, Ky., 1963-64; instr. psychology Boston U., 1966-67; from asst. to assoc. prof. U. Mass., Amherst, 1967-78, prof., 1978—; vis. prof. Western Wash. State Coll., Bellingham, 1973, U. Hawaii, Honolulu, 1982; vis. scholar U. Wash., Seattle, 1974. Assoc. editor Animal Learning and Behavior, 1980-84; contbr. articles to profl. jours. Capt. U.S. Army, 1965-67. Grantee DHEH, 1970-71, 76-78, NSF, 1976-91, NIMH, 1993-95; NSF fellow, 1963. Mem. Am. Psychol. Soc., Psychonomic Soc., Ea. Psychol. Assn. Home: 8 Laurel Ln Amherst MA 01002-2811 Office: U Mass Dept Psychology Amherst MA 01003

AYRES, JONATHAN GEOFFREY, respiratory medicine educator, physician; b. Potters Bar, Hertfordshire, Eng., Feb. 14, 1950. BSc, London U., 1971; MBBS, Guys Hosp., 1974; MD, U. London, 1984. Tng. Guys Hosp., London U., Brompton Hosp., Birmingham Heartlands Hosp., Birmingham U.; prof. respiratory medicine U. Warwick, Birmingham Heartlands Hosp., West Midlands, West Midlands, Eng. Contbr. papers to profl. publs. Fellow Royal Coll. Physicians; mem. Brit. Thoracic Soc. (sec. epidemiology sect.), Internat. Epidemiological Assn., Am. Thoracic Soc. Office: Birmingham Heartlands Hosp, Dept Resp Med Bordesley Green E, Birmingham B9 5SS, England

AYRES, STEPHEN MCCLINTOCK, physician, educator; b. Elizabeth, N.J., Oct. 29, 1929; s. Malcolm B. and Florence M. A.; m. Dolores Kobrick, June 11, 1955; children—Stephen, Elizabeth, Margaret. B.A., Gettysburg Coll., 1951; M.D., Cornell U., 1955. Intern N.Y. Hosp., N.Y.C., 1955; resident N.Y. Hosp., 1958-61; dir. cardio-pulmonary lab. St. Michael's Hosp., Newark, 1961-63, St. Vincent's Hosp. and Med. Center, N.Y.C., 1963-73; physician-in-chief St. Vincent Hosp., Worcester, Mass., 1973-75; prof., chmn. dept. internal medicine St. Louis U. Med. Center, 1975-85; dean Med. Coll. Va., Richmond, 1985-93; dean emeritus, dir. office internat. health program Med. Coll. Va./Va. Commonwealth U., Richmond, 1993—. Author: Care of the Critically Ill, 3d edit., 1988; co-author: Textbook of Critical Care, 1988, Nutritional Support of the Critically Ill, 1988; editor: Major Issues in Critical Care Medicine, 1984; contbr. articles to profl. jours. Chmn. bd. Found. for Critical Care, 1985—. Served with M.C., U.S. Army, 1956-58. Fellow A.C.P., Am. Coll. Cardiology, Am. Coll. Chest Physicians; mem. Soc. Critical Care Medicine (pres. 1979-80), Am. Lung Assn., Assn. Am. Physicians, Am. Soc. Clin. Investigation. Home: 5103 Cary Street Rd Richmond VA 23226-1644 Office: Med Coll Va MCV Sta Box 565 Richmond VA 23298

AYRES-DE-CAMPOS, DIOGO, obstetrician and gynecologist; b. Oporto, Portugal, Nov. 2, 1962; s. Nuno and Maria da Paz (Matos Graça) A.; m. Maria João Cardoso, June 19, 1993. MD, Oporto Faculty of Medicine, 1988. Resident Hosp. São João, Oporto, Portugal, 1989-96; staff ob-gyn. Hosp. São João, Oporto, 1991—. Contbr. articles to profl. jours. Rsch. grantee Portuguese Ministry of Health, 1995, Junta Nacional Investigação Cientifica Tecnológica, 1996. Mem. European Soc. Reproductive Medicine, European Soc. Gynecology, Portuguese Soc. Reproductive Medicine. Office: Hosp São João, Dept Obstetrics Gynecology, 4200 Oporto Portugal

AYYAGARI, KAMALAKAR RAO, surgeon; b. Mogallu, India, Aug. 16, 1944; came to U.S., 1971; s. Satyanarayana Rao and Mahalakshmi (A-trayapurapu) A.; m. Kalavathi Isola, Feb. 4, 1973; children: Subhadra, Sunil. MB, BS, Gandhi Med. U., Hyderabad, India, 1967. Diplomate Am. Bd. Surgery. Intern Gandhi Hosp., Secunderabad, India, 1968-69; med. officer AP Govt., India, 1969-71; intern St. John's Riverside Hosp., Yonkers, N.Y., 1971-72; resident in gen. surgery Misericordia Hosp., Bronx, N.Y., 1973-77; chmn. dept. surgery Irvington (N.J.) Gen. Hosp., 1991—. Fellow ACS; mem. AMA, N.J. Med. Soc., Essex County Med. Soc. Office: K Ayyagari MD PA 2010 Springfield Ave Maplewood NJ 07040-3437

AYYAGARI, RAMCHANDRA RAO, gynecologist, obstetrician; b. Kakinada, Andhra Pradesh, India, Feb. 5, 1953; s. Sambasiva Rao and Annapurna (Kondepudi) A.; m. Ellen B. Murszewski, May 4, 1985. B in Medicine and Surgery, U. Bombay, 1978. Resident in obstetrics and gynecology SUNY, Buffalo, 1979-83; physician Buffalo Gen. Hosp., 1983-84, Erie Med. Ctr., Buffalo, 1983-84; fellowship in reproductive endocrinology U. Ill., Chgo., 1984-86; assoc. prof. Kern Med. Ctr., Bakersfield, Calif., 1986—. Grantee ACOG, 1985. Mem. Am. Fertility Soc., Fallopius Internat. Soc., Ill. Perinatal Assn., Chgo. Assn. Reproductive Endocrinology. Office: Kern Med Ctr Dept Obs-Gyn 1830 Flower St Bakersfield CA 93305-4144

AZADIAN, HARRY Y., physician; b. Somerville, Mass., Dec. 21, 1934; s. Vahan and Grace B. (Emanatian) A.; m. Carol Ann Fitzpatrick, June 24, 1956; children: Lynn, Jeffrey, Todd. BS, Tufts U., 1956; MD, Harvard Med. Sch., 1960. Intern U. Calif. Hosps., San Francisco, 1960-61; resident in surgery Boston City Hosp. Harvard Surg. Svc., 1964-68, Harvard Svc., Boston, 1964-68; pvt. practice Cambridge, Mass., 1969-89; occupational physician Raytheon Co., Lexington, Mass., 1989—, corp. med. dir. Fellow Am. Coll. Surgeons, Am. Coll. Occupational Medicine. Republican. Office: Raytheon Co Med Dept 141 Spring St Lexington MA 02173-7899

AZAR, HENRY AMIN, medical historian, educator; b. Egypt, Dec. 21, 1927; s. Amin Antonios and Agnes Garabed (Nazaretian) A.; m. Rose Theresa Connell, Apr. 19, 1960; children: Henry Amin Jr., Philip John. BA, Am. U., Beirut, 1948, MD, 1952; MA in History, U. N.C., 1994, postgrad. Diplomate Am. Bd. Pathology. Intern N.Y.C. Hosp., 1952-53; resident Columbia-Presbyn. Hosp. Med. Ctr., N.Y.C., 1955-56, N.Y.-Cornell, Med. Ctr., N.Y.C., 1956-57, Mass. Meml. Hosp., Boston, 1957-58; asst. prof. pathology Am. U., Beirut, 1958-60; asst. prof. and assoc. prof. pathology Coll. Physicians and Surgeons, Columbia U., 1960-70; dir. surg. pathology, prof. U. Kans., 1970-72; chief lab. service James A. Haley Vets. Hosp., Tampa, Fla., 1972-83, chief anatomic pathology, 1983-92; prof. U. South Fla., 1973-92, prof. emeritus, 1992; adj. prof. path. U. N.C. Author: Multiple Myeloma and Related Disorders, 1973, Diagnostic Electron Microscopy: The Hemopoietic System, 1979, Pathology of Human Neoplasms, 1988, Ibn Zuhr (Avenzoar): The Taysîr and Its Translations into Latin with an Analysis of Selected Texts, 1994; contbr. articles to profl. jours. Fellow Coll. Am. Pathologists; mem. Assn. Vet. Chiefs Lab. Svc. (pres. 1981-83), Arthur Purdy Stout Soc. (sec. 1983-87, pres. 1990-91), Pathology Alumni Found. (emeritus trustee) Harvey Soc., Internat. Acad. Pathology (emeritus), Hematopathology Soc., Am. Assn. for History of Medicine, Soc. Internat. History of Sci. and Philosopy Arab Islam, Am. U. Beirut Alumni Assn. (pres. Tampa Bay chpt. 1985-87), History of Pathology Soc. (pres. 1996—). Syrian Orthodox. Home: 1700 Old Oxford Rd Chapel Hill NC 27514-2132

AZAR, MARY ELLEN, dentist; b. Johnstown, Pa., Apr. 1, 1958; d. Mitchell and Lillian Loretta (Audi) A.; m. Kenneth Christopher Carsto, Aug. 19, 1984. BA, Bucknell U., 1980; DMD, U. Pa., 1984. Resident Med. Coll. Pa., Phila., 1984-85; pvt. practice Skippack, Pa., 1985—; cons. Meadowood Life Care Community, Worcester, Pa., 1988-91. Bd. dirs. Weller Ctr. Health Edn., Easton, Pa., 1991-92. Mem. ADA, Jr. League Lehigh Valley, Delta Gamma. Office: Skippack Dental 4121 Skippack Pike PO Box 819 Skippack PA 19474-0819

AZARIK, ROBERT A., orthodontist; b. Bronx, N.Y., Mar. 27, 1955; s. Arthur and Anne (Mateosian) A.; m. Barbara Jane Habeshian, June 29, 1980; children: Stephen Haig, Philip Arthur. BS cum laude, Tufts U., 1977; DMD, Tufts U. Sch. Dental Medicine, 1980; MDS, U. Pitts., 1983. Diplomate Am. Bd. Orthop. Pvt. practice orthodontics Perkasie, Pa., 1983—. Mem. Am. Dental Assn., Am. Assn. Orthodontists, Phila. Soc. Orthodontists, Pa. Dental Assn., Pa. Soc. Orthodontists. Republican. Office: 1300 N 5th St Perkasie PA 18944

AZARNOFF, DANIEL LESTER, pharmaceutical company consultant; b. Bklyn., Aug. 4, 1926; s. Samuel J. and Kate (Asarnow) A.; m. Joanne Stokes, Dec. 26, 1951; children: Rachel, Richard, Martin. BS, Rutgers U., 1947, MS, 1948; MD, U. Kans., 1955. Asst. instr. anatomy U. Kans. Med. Sch., 1949-50, research fellow, 1950-52, intern, 1955-56, resident, Nat. Heart Inst. research fellow, 1956-58, asst. prof. medicine, 1962-64, assoc. prof., 1964-68, dir. clin. pharmacology study unit, 1964-68, assoc. prof. pharmacology, 1965-68, prof. medicine and pharmacology, 1968, dir. Clin.

Pharmacology-Toxicology Ctr., 1967-78, Disting. prof., 1973-78, also prof. medicine, 1965-67, pres. Sigma Xi Club, 1968-69, clin. prof. medicine, 1982—; Nat. Inst. Neurol. Diseases and Blindness spl. trainee Washington U. Sch. Medicine, St. Louis, 1958-60; asst. prof. medicine St. Louis U. Sch. Medicine, 1960-62; vis. scientist, Fulbright scholar Karolinska Inst., Stockholm, Sweden, 1968; sr. v.p. worldwide research and devel. G.D. Searle & Co., Skokie, 1978; pres. Searle Research and Devel., Skokie, 1979-85, Azarnoff Assocs., Inc., Evanston, Ill., 1987—, D.L. Azarnoff Assocs., Burlingame, Calif., 1986—; prof. pathology, clin. prof. pharmacology Northwestern U. Med. Sch., 1978-85; commr. Nat. Commn. on Orphan Diseases, 1985-87; chmn. bd. dirs. Alpha RX Corp., South San Francisco, Calif., 1992-94; professorial lectr. U. Chgo., 1978-86; dir. Second Workshop on Prins. Drug Evaluation in Man, 1970; chmn. com. on problems of drug safety NRC-NAS, 1972-76; bd. dirs. Oread, Inc., Lawrence, Kans., De Novo, Inc., Memlo Park, Calif., Cibus Pharms., Redwood City, Calif.; cons. numerous govt. agys. Editor: Devel. of Drug Interactions, 1974-77, Yearbook of Drug Therapy, 1977-79; series editor: Monographs in Clin. Pharmacology, 1977-84; mem. editorial bd. Drug Investigation, 1989—, others. Served with U.S. Army, 1945-46. Recipient Ginsburg award in phys. diagnosis U. Kanas. Med. Ctr., 1953, Outstanding Intern award, 1956, Ciba award for gerontol. rsch., 1958, Rectors medal U. Helsinki, 1968; named Disting. Med. Alumnus, U. Kans. Coll. Health Sci., 1995; John and Mary R. Markle scholar, 1964, William N. Creasy vis. prof. clin. pharmacology Med. Coll. Va., 1975; Bruce Hall Meml. lectr. St. Vincents Hosp., Sydney, 1976, 7th Sir Henry Hallett Dale lectr. Johns Hopkins U. Med. Sch., 1978. Fellow ACP, N.Y. Acad. Scis., Am. Assn. Pharm. Scientists (Rsch. Achievement award in clin. scis. 1995); mem. Am. Soc. Clin. Nutrition, Am. Nutrition Instn., Am. Soc. Pharmacology and Exptl. Therapeutics (chmn. clin. pharmacology divsn. 1969-71, mem. exec. com. 1966-73, 78-81, del. 1975-78, bd. publ. trustees), Am. Soc. Clin. Pharmacology and Therapeutics (Oscar B. Hunter Meml. award 1995), Am. Fedn. Clin. Rsch., Brit. Pharmacol. Soc., AMA (vice chmn. coun. on drugs 1971-72, editl. bd. jour.), Ctrl. Soc. Clin. Rsch., Royal Soc. for Promotion Health, Inst. Medicine of Nat. Acad. Scis., Soc. Exptl. Biology and Medicine (councillor 1976-80), Internat. Union Pharmacologists (sec. clin. pharmacology sect. 1975-81, internat. adv. com. Paris Congress 1978), GPIA (blue ribbon com. on generic medicine 1990), Sigma Xi.

AZIZKHAN, RICHARD GEORGE, pediatric surgeon; b. London, Aug. 10, 1953; came to U.S., 1964; s. Reza George and Helga Marianne (Behnke) A.; m. Jane Elizabeth Clifford, May 8, 1976; children: Richard Anthony, Kathryn Marie, Christine Elizabeth Ann. BS with honors, Dickinson Coll., Carlisle, Pa., 1972; MD, Pa. State U., 1975. Diplomate in gen. surgery, pediatric surgery and surg. critical care Am. Bd. Surgery. Resident in surgery U. Va., Charlottesville, 1976-78, 80-83; rsch. fellow in pediatric surgery Harvard Med. Sch. Boston Children's Hosp., 1978-80; fellow in pediatric surgery Johns Hopkins Univ., Balt., 1983-85; chief pediatric surgery U. N.C., Chapel Hill, 1985-93; surgeon-in-chief Child Hosp., Buffalo, 1993—; prof. surgery and pediats. SUNY, Buffalo, 1993—; mem. surgical adv. bd. Smith, Kline, Beecham, Phila., 1990—. Author: (med. text) Congenital Malformations: Prenatal Diagnosis and Management, 1990; contbr. over 90 articles to profl. jours. Recipient Upjohn Achievement award U. Va. Sch. Medicine, 1981, Hugh J. Warren Tchg. award, 1983, Battle Disting. Excellence in Tchg. award U. N.C. Sch. Medicine, 1988, Disting. Alumnus award Pa. State U., 1995; Schering scholar ACS, 1982; SmithKline & French fellow ACS, 1986, Pa. State U. Alumnae fellow, 1995. Fellow ACS, Am. Acad. Pediatrics, Am. Pediatric Surgery Assn. (program com. 1990-93), Pa. State U. Alumnae Assn. (life); mem. Assn. of Acad. Surgery (exec. coun. 1986-89), Alpha Omega Alpha. Roman Catholic. Office: Childrens Hosp Buffalo Burnett-Womack 229 H 219 Bryant St Buffalo NY 14222-2006

AZMAN, THOMAS, optometrist; b. Bari, Italy, Apr. 29, 1949; came to U.S., 1950; s. Abraham and Elizabeth A.; m. Ruth Roseberg, June 3, 1973; children: Bari Michael, Stephen Andrew, David Joshua, Benjamin Edward. BS in Psychology, U. Md., 1970; BS in Physol. Optics, U. Ala., 1974, D in Optometry, 1975. Lic. optometrist Md. Pvt. practice optometry Lutherville, Md., 1975—; rschr. for Bausch & Lomb, Polymer Tech., Ciba Vision, Vision Pharms., Varilux; guest lectr. various nursing homes, PTA meetings, schs., sr. citizen ctrs., Balt. County Dept. of Aging; guest on informative TV shows on eye care, Balt. stationWJZ-TV; vision screener for industry, schs., sr. citizen ctrs. Past bd. dirs. Hebrew Acad. Washington, Shomrei Emmunah; bd. dirs. Yeshivat Rambam, Balt., vol. lunch program supr; past vol. lunch supr. Beth Tifloh; active in Nat. Coun. Synagogue Youth; past pres. Binai Brith Hillel House, U. Md. Recipient commendation Balt. City Coun., 1977, citation Balt. Mayor, 1983, cert. appreciation, Med. Shoppe. Balt., 1983, cert. appreciation rep. 3d congressional dist. Md., 1984, 86, Church Hosp., Balt. 1986, Bausch & Lomb Clin. Investigation award 1992, Spl. Recognition award Yesivat Rambam, 1992, Talmudical Acad., Balt., Ner Israel Rabbinical Coll. cert. Md. Ho. Dels., 1995; named one of 20/20's Best and Brightest, 1993, one of Mds. most exceptional businesses Warfield Bus. Record Corp. Profiles, 1995. Mem. BBB, Am. Optometric Assn. (contact lens sect., low vision sect., sports vision sect. Optometric Recognition Continuing Edn. award 1981-94), Md. Optometric Assn., Greater Balt. Optometric Assn. (past treas.), Doctors with a Heart Program, Nat. Eye Rsch. Found., Nat. Acad. Sports Vision Interlens, C. of C. Balt. County, C. of C. Dundalk, Nat. Alumni Soc. U. Ala. (charter mem.). Home: 3315 Labyrinth Rd Baltimore MD 21215 Office: Azman Eyecare Specialists 1407 York Rd Ste 213 Lutherville MD 21093

AZMITIA, EFRAIN CHARLES, neuroscience educator, researcher; b. Tampa, Fla., Sept. 18, 1946; s. Efrain Carlos and Angela (Gutierrez) A.; m. Patricia Mack Whitaker, Apr. 19, 1984; children: Grace Angela, Charles Cyril; children: Bianka Maria, Anthea Theresa. BA, Washington U., St. Louis, 1968; MA, Cambridge U., 1976; PhD, Rockefeller U., 1973. Postdoctoral fellow NIMH, Washington, 1973-75, Nat. Inst Med. Research, London, 1975-76; vis. demonstrator Cambridge U., Eng., 1976-78; asst., then assoc. prof. Mt. Sinai Sch. Medicine, N.Y.C., 1978-83; prof. biology NYU, N.Y.C., 1983—; dir. neurohistology Hosp. Salpetriere, Paris, 1981-82; vis. scientist Weitzmann Inst., Rehovet, Israel, 1984, 87, Cold Spring Harbor Lab., 1990-91, U. Tsukuuba, Japan, 1994; organizer Washington Square Ctr. Neurol. Sci., N.Y.C., 1984, fellow; dir. NIA program project S100B: A glial/neuronal link to Alzheimer's, NIDA. Editor: (book) Cell and Tissue Transplantation into the Adult Brain, 1987, Brain Corticosterone Receptors, 1994; mem. editorial bd. Neurosci. Net, Brain Rsch., Synapse, Neurochem. Rsch., Restorative Neurology and Neurosci., Devel. Neurosci., Jour. Chem. Neuroanat.; contbr. articles to profl. jours. Found. Funds for Research Psychiatry postdoctoral fellow, 1973; grantee NIH, 1979—, NSF, 1979—, U.S. Israel Binat. Sci. Found., 1985-88; Irma T. Hirschl career scientist award, 1979-83. Fellow Am. Coll. of Neuropsychopharmacology, N.Y. Acad. Scis. (chmn. Biomed. sect. 1986-91), N.Y. Acad. Medicine (assoc.), Harvey Soc.; mem. Neurosci. Soc., European Brain and Behavior Assn., Cambridge Philos. Soc. Presbyterian. Clubs: Cajal, Serotonin (councillor 1986-90). Avocations: antiquary books, modern art, chess, fishing, golf. Home: 345 Split Rock Rd Syosset NY 11791-1508 Office: New York University Dept Biology Washington Sq N New York NY 10003-6635

AZZARITI, VIRGINIA, pediatrics nurse; b. Hazleton, Pa., Apr. 17, 1943; d. John and Mabel (Bertolini) Pachence; m. Louis Azzariti, Apr. 20, 1968; children: Jennifer, Anthony. BSN, Columbia U., 1966; BA in Biology, Chestnut Hill Coll., Phila., 1964; postgrad., Columbia U. RN, N.J., N.Y.; cert. pediatric nurse. Staff nurse Holy Name Hosp., Teaneck, N.J., NYU Med. Ctr., N.Y.C.; office nurse, mgr. Pedimedica, Teaneck. Mem. Am. Assn. Office Nurses.

BAASKE, DAVID MICHAEL, chemist, researcher; b. Milw., Feb. 15, 1947; s. David Daniel and Joan Kathleen (Heath) B.; m. Jan Elizabeth Hayes, Sept. 30, 1969 (div. Nov. 1990); children: Ian William, Erik Michael; m. Nancy Joan Teaters, Nov. 13, 1993. BS, Carroll Coll., Waukesha, Wis., 1969; MA, DePauw U., 1971; PhD, Purdue U., 1976. Rsch. chemist Arnar Stone Labs., Waukegan, Ill., 1977-82; group leader Am. Critical Care, Waukegan, 1982-85; sect. head Du Pont Critical Care/Am. Critical Care, Waukegan, 1985-89; sr. rsch. supr. Du Pont Pharms., Wilmington, Del., 1989-90; assoc. dir. The Du Pont Merck Pharm. Co., Wilmington, 1991-93; sr. dir. A.L. Pharma, Inc. (now Alpharma, Inc.), Balt., 1993—; presenter in field to profl. meetings and workshops. Contbr. over 25 articles to Am. Jour. Hosp. Pharmacy, Antimicrobial Agts. and Chemothrapy, Jour. Chromatography, Jour. Med. Chemistry, Jour. Pharm. Sci., Chromatography Newsletter, Am. Pharmacology, Analytical Chemistry, Drug Intelligence and Clin. Pharmacology, Acta Pharmaceutica Suecica, chpts. to books. Mem. Am. Chem. Soc., Am. Assn. Pharm. Scis., N.Y. Acad. Scis., Sigma Xi. Office: Alpharma 333 Cassell Dr Ste 3500 Baltimore MD 21224

BABA, TAKESHI, cell biologist. PhD, MD, Shinshu U., Matsumoto, Japan, 1988. Instr. Shinshu U. Sch. Medicine, Matsumoto, 1988-95; asst. prof. Yamanashi Med. U., Shimokato, Tamaho. Office: Yamanashi Med Univ, Dept Anatomy, 1110 Shomokato, Tamaho 409-38, Japan

BABB, HAROLD, psychology educator; b. Mosheim, Tenn., Sept. 4, 1926; s. Ray Edward and Mary Louise (Brown) B.; m. Marjorie Craig Leask (Sept. 27, 1947); children: Patricia Craig, Barbara Lou, David Edward. BA, Wayne State U., 1950; MA, Ohio State U., 1951, PhD, 1953. Asst. prof., assoc. prof., chmn. dept. psychology Coe Coll., 1953-58; prof., chmn. dept. psychology Hobart and William Smith Colls., 1958-63; NIH, NIMH exec. sec., grants specialist, 1963-64; prof., chmn. dept. psychology U. Mont., Missoula, 1964-71; prof. psychology SUNY-Binghamton, 1971-95, prof. emeritus, 1995—, chmn. dept., 1971-74. Contbr. articles on psychology to profl. jours. Served with USNR, 1944-46. NIMH research grantee, 1960-62; NSF research grantee, 1968-69. Fellow Am. Psychol. Assn., Am. Psychol. Soc.; mem. AAAS, AAUP, Ea. Psychol. Assn., Midwestern Psychol. Assn., Psychonomic Soc., Sigma Xi. Home: RR 1 Box 1957 Stanley Lake Rd Friendsville PA 18818 Office: Binghamton U Dept Psychology PO Box 6000 Binghamton NY 13902-6000

BABB, JOSEPH DOLBY, physician; b. Columbus, Ohio, Apr. 16, 1939; s. Joe A. and Dorothe (Dolby) B.; m. Anne Tanner Hammerlund, Sept. 2, 1969 (div. Apr. 1985); children: Elizabeth Anne, Peter Dolby; m. Margo Tregenza, Oct. 6, 1990. BA magna cum laude, Kenyon Coll., Gambier, Ohio, 1961; MD, Johns Hopkins U., 1966. Diplomate in internal medicine and cardiovascular diseases Am. Bd. Internal Medicine; cert. physician, Pa., Conn., N.C. Intern Mass. Gen. Hosp., Boston, 1966-67, resident in internal medicine, 1967-68, clin. and rsch. fellow, 1970-72; teaching fellow Harvard Med. Sch., Boston, 1970-72; asst. prof. med. cardiology Pa. State U. Sch. Medicine, Hershey, 1972-76, assoc. prof., 1976-80; chief of cardiology Bridgeport (Conn.) Hosp., 1980-95; clin. assoc. prof. medicine (cardiology) Yale U., New Haven, 1980-95; prof. medicine (cardiology) East Carolina U. Sch. Medicine, Greenville, 1995—. Bd. dirs., pres. Alcohol and Drug Dependency Coun., Westport, Conn., 1987-95. Maj. U.S. Army, 1968-70, Vietnam. Fulbright fellow, Utrecht, Netherlands, 1961-62. Fellow Am. Coll. Cardiology (gov. 1987-90, Am. Heart Assn. (coun. clin. cardiology), Soc. Cardiac Angiography and Intervention (trustee 1993—). Home: 3804 Charleston Ct Greenville NC 27834 Office: East Carolina U Sch Med PCMH Teaching Annex Rm 352 Greenville NC 27858-4354

BABBIE, ANDREA LYNN, nursing educator; b. Munhall, Pa.. BSN, U. Pitts., 1972, MSN, 1989. Staff nurse West Penn Hosp., Pitts., 1972-78, staff educator, 1978—, nurse recruiter, 1989, staffing coord., 1990. Mem. Scoliosis Assn., Nat. Nursing Staff Devel. Orgn., Sigma Theta Tau.

BABBITT, DONALD PATRICK, radiologist; b. Oshkosh, Wis., Aug. 24, 1922; s. James Sylvester and Loretta Gertrude (Sensenbrenner) B.; m. Elizabeth May Gerhard, Apr. 28, 1945 (dec. Nov. 1971); children—Patrick, Ann, James; m. Jill Ann Sieg, Jan. 29, 1975 (div. Apr. 1984); m. Katherine J. Zehren, Dec. 12, 1987. Student, U. Wis., River Falls, 1939-42; M.D., Med. Coll. Wis., 1946. Diplomate Am. Bd. Radiology. Intern Meth. Hosp., Indpls., 1946-47; resident Milw. Hosp. and Milw. Ch. Hosp., 1949-52; practice medicine specializing in radiology Milw.; mem. staff Milw. Children's Hosp., 1952—, chief radiology, 1964-82; mem. staff Milw. County Gen. Hosp., 1964—; cons. St. Mary's Hosp., Milw., 1968-76, attending staff, 1982-95; instr. radiology Med. Coll., Wis., 1958; assoc. prof. radiology Med. Coll., 1964-70, clin. prof. pediatrics, 1979—; assoc. clin. prof. radiology U. Wis. Center Health Scis., Madison, 1968-70, clin. prof., 1970—. Active Boy Scouts Am. (century mem.). Served to capt. M.C., AUS, 1947-49. Named Tchr. of Yr. Milw. Children's Hosp. Dept. Pediatrics, 1980. Fellow Am. Coll. Radiology (medallion in nuclear medicine 1959), Am. Acad. Pediatrics; mem. Am. Roentgen Ray Soc., European Soc. Pediatric Radiology, Soc. Pediatric Radiology, Radiol. Soc. N.Am., Wis. Radiol. Soc. (pres. 1976), Wis. State Med. Soc., Milw. Surg. Soc. (pres. 1978), Milw. Roentgen Ray Soc. (pres. 1975-77), Milwaukee County Med. Soc. (pres. 1974), Milw. Acad. Medicine, Milw. Pediatric Soc., AMA Med. Coll. Wis. Alumni Assn., Alpha Omega Alpha, Phi Chi. Roman Catholic. Club: Flying Physicians. Lodge: Rotary (Milw.). Home: 5904 Eagle Point Rd Hartford WI 53027-9211

BABCOCK, BRYAN CORYDON, health facility administrator; b. Seattle, May 9, 1961; s. Richard D. and Juanita J. (Simonsen) B.; m. Betsy Bridges, Nov. 16, 1984; children: Corydon Douglas, Lindsey Rebecca. BS in Zoology, U. Tex., 1983; MS in Health Care Adminstrn., Trinity U., 1985. Lic. pvt. pilot. Asst. v.p. Parkview Episcopal Med. Ctr., Pueblo, Colo., 1985-87; regional dir. Rose Med. Ctr., Denver, 1987-89; asst. adminstr. Charter Hosp. Savannah, Ga., 1989-90; CEO Glen Oaks Hosp., Dallas, 1990-92; v.p. Richardson Med. Ctr., Dallas, 1992-93; CEO Charter Hosp. Wichita, Kans., 1993—; legis. com. mem. Fedn. Am. Health Care Sys., Washington, 1993-95, bd. govs., 1993-95; owner Wings Over Wichita. Leadership com. mem. Kans. Hosp. Assn., Topeka, 1993-95; site counsel chmn. Unified Sch. Dist. 259, Wichita, 1994-95. Mem. Nat. Assn. Pvt. Health Care Sys., Am. Coll. Health Care Execs., Am. Pilot and Owners Assn., Tex. EXS, Wichita C. of C. (legis. com. 1993-95). Republican. Home: 285 S Dellrose Wichita KS 67218 Office: Charter Hosp Wichita 8901 E Orme Wichita KS 67207

BABCOCK, DOROTHY ELLEN, nursing educator; b. Phila., July 10, 1931; d. Peter Joseph and Dorothy Ambrosia (Muldowney) Kreinbihl; m. Clarence Otis Babcock, June 28, 1958; children: Donna Miller, Phyllis Pennington, Karen Nern. Diploma, Misericordia Hosp. Sch. Nursing, 1952; BSNEd, U. Pa., 1956; MSN, Cath. U. of Am., 1958. RN, Colo. Clin. specialist Denver Health & Hosps.; educator Metro State Coll. of Denver, Denver. Author: Introduction to Growth Development and Family Life, 3d edit., 1972; co-author: Raising Kids OK, 1986, Client Education Theory and Practice, 1995, Critical Thinking Applied to Nursing, 1996. Mem. Am. Assn. Marriage and Family Therapists, Colo. Nurses Assn., Nat. League for Nursing, Sigma Theta Tau. Home: 5 S Flower St Lakewood CO 80226-1206 Office: Met State Coll Campus Box 33 PO Box 173362 Denver CO 80217-3362

BABCOCK, NANETTE LEE, obstetrics nurse; b. Denver, Sept. 16, 1962; d. Joel Eugene and Virginia Lee (Cooper) B. BS in Nursing, Aurora U., 1986. cert. inpatient obstetrics. Staff RN oncology Dartmouth Hitchcock Med. Ctr., Lebanon, N.H., 1986-87, staff RN obstetrics, 1988—; RN obstetrics Am. Mobile Nurses, Inc., San Diego, 1992-94. Mem. Assn. Women's Health, Obstetric and Neonatal Nurses. Home: PO Box 222 Hanover NH 03755 Office: Dartmouth Hitchcock Med Ctr 1 Med Ctr Dr Lebanon NH 03556

BABCOCK, THOMAS FRANCIS, family practice physician; b. Corning, N.Y., Dec. 10, 1947; s. Willoughby W. and Mary Charlotte (Miller) B.; m. Phyllis Jeanne Dorman, June 6, 1970; children: Leslie Michelle, Gregory William. BS, Elmira Coll., 1970; MA, Ea. N.Mex. U., 1976; PhD, Tulane U., 1980; DO, U. Osteo. Medicine & Health, 1988. Cert. Am. Bd. Family Practice. Cons. archaeologist, v.p. Grand River Cons., Grand Junction, Colo., 1980-84; resident physician Broadlawns Med. Ctr., Des Moines, 1988-91; physician Jefferson (Iowa) Clinic, 1991-94, McFarland Clinic-Jefferson, Ames, Iowa, 1994—; chief of staff Greene County Med. Ctr., Jefferson, 1996—. Bd. dirs. Am. Heart Assn.-Greene County, Jefferson, 1991—,Cmty. Adult Day Care, Jefferson, 1994—. Maj. U.S. Army, 1971-73, Res., 1984—. Mem. Am. Acad. Family Practice, Iowa Osteo. Assn., Iowa Acad. Family Practice, Phi Kappa Phi, Sigma Sigma Phi. Republican. Roman Catholic. Home: 507 Rushview Dr Jefferson IA 50129 Office: McFarland Clinic Jefferson 1002 W Lincolnway Jefferson IA 50129

BABEKIR, ABDEL RAHMAN EL TAYEB, surgeon, consultant; b. Zeidab, Nile Province, Sudan, Jan. 1, 1947; s. El Tayeb Babekir El Hag and Fatima Osman Kheir; m. Widad Akoud Osman, Mar. 13, 1956; children: Wala, Wael, Loai, Leina. MBBS, U. Khartoum, Sudan, 1971; FRCS, R.C.S. England, 1975; FRCSE, R.C.S. Edinbrough, 1976. Intern Khartoum (Sudan) Civil Hosp., 1971-72, registrar in surgery, 1972-74; SHO in Surgery West Middlesex Hosp., London, 1974-75; registrar in surgery Kingston Hosp., London, 1976-77; registrar in cardiothoracic surgery Brook Hosp., London, 1977-78; asst. prof. faculty of medicine, Khartoum, Sudan, 1978-83; cons. surgeon Soba Hosp., Khartoum, 1978-83, Jeddah Nat. Hosp., Sudi Arabia, 1983-85, Al Hayatt Hosp., Al Ain, United Arab Emirates, 1996; head dept. surgery Dibba Hosp., United Arab Emirates, 1986-95. Mem. Sudanese Med. Assn. (acad. sec. 1981-83), Sudanese Assn. of Gastroenterologist, Collegium Internationale Chirurgial Digestivae. Moslem. Office: Al Hayatt Hosp, Hkalifa St PO Box 15541, Al Ain United Arab Emirates

BABONIS, ELEANOR ROSE, physician assistant program director; b. Dupont, Pa., Dec. 2, 1935; d. Stephen Natale and Margaret Rose (Cicchillitti) Rinaldi; m. Bernard Joseph Babonis, Dec. 29, 1956; children: Theresa Ann, Brian Gerard. BS, St. Joseph's Coll., 1980; MPA, Marywood Coll., 1984; postgrad., LaSalle U. Physician asst. Hershey (Pa.) Med. Ctr.; RN Pittston (Pa.) Hosp. Sch. Nursing; physician asst. program dir. King's Coll., Wilkes-Barre, Pa., 1977—. Vol. ARC, Wilkes-Barre, instr., 1991—; leader Girl Scouts Am., Dupont; health officer Boro of Dupont, Pa., 1991—. Fellow Am. Acad. Physician Assts. (various coms. 1977—), Pa. Soc. Physician Assts. (region chair 1980-90, sec./treas 1990—); mem. Pittston Hosp. Nurses Alumni Assn., Alpha Epsilon Delta. Home: 111 Ziegler St Dupont PA 18641-1919

BACH, JOHN ROBERT, physician; b. Jersey City, Oct. 30, 1950; s. John Joseph and Anne Karen Filan B.: m. Muguette Ballanger, May 31, 1984; 1 child, Gaveric Alexandre. BS, Stevens Inst., 1972; MD, UMDNJ, 1976. Intern in pediat. NYU, resident in phys. medicine and rehab.; prof. phys. med. rehab. N.J. Med. Sch., Newark, 1992—; vice-chmn. dept. phys. med. and rehab. N.J. Med. Sch., 1988—. Editor: Pulmonary Rehab., 1996, Noninvasive Ventilation, 1996. Recipient Clin. Excellence award U. Medicine and Dentistry, 1995, Excellence in Rsch. Writing award Assn. Acad. Physiatrists, 1990, 94. Mem. Am. Coll. chest Physicians, Acad. Phys. Med. & Rehab. (Best Rsch. Paper 1994). Home: 17 Woodbine Terr Sparta NJ 07871 Office: Univ Hosp Dept Phys Med & Rehab 150 Bergen Newark NJ 07103

BACH, SHELDON, psychoanalyst; b. Bklyn., May 18, 1925; s. Frank and Ida (Ruben) B.; m. Phyllis Beren, Jan. 7, 1982; children: Rebecca, Matthew. Cert., Sorbonne, Paris, 1947; PhD, NYU, 1960. Intern Jacobi Hosp., N.Y.C., 1957-58, staff psychologist, 1960-62; sr. psychologist Montefiore Hosp., N.Y.C., 1962-70; vis. staff Jacobi Hosp., Montefiore Hosp., N.Y.C., 1970-75; tng. analyst N.Y. Freudian Soc., N.Y.C., 1968—; assoc. prof. psychiatry Albert Einstein Coll. Medicine, N.Y.C., 1968-91; prof. psychology postdoctoral program NYU, N.Y.C., 1980—; tng. analyst Inst. for Psychoanalytic Tng., N.Y.C., 1987—. Cons. editor Psychoanalytic Psychology, 1983-86; author: Narcissistic States & the Therapeutic Process, 1985, The Language of Perversion and the Language of Love, 1994; co-editor: Rapprochement: Subphase of Separation-Individuation, 1980, Self & Object Constancy, 1986. Sgt. U.S. Army, 1943-46, ETO. Rsch. fellow NIMH, 1958; named Disting. Lectr. Postgrad. Ctr., N.Y.C., 1988, Weil Meml. Lectr. Inst. Psychoanalytic Tng., N.Y.C., 1989, Mahler Commemorative Lectr. Albert Einstein Coll. Medicine, N.Y.C., 1987. Mem. N.Y. Acad. Sci., Am. Psychol. Assn. (founding mem. div. psychoanalysis 1980). Office: 365 W End Ave New York NY 10024-6511

BACHELIS, LEONARD, psychologist. Lic. psychologist, N.Y. Pvt. practice psychology N.Y.C. Office: Behavior Therapy Ctr NY PC 115 E 87th St New York NY 10128-1136

BACHICHA, JOSEPH ALFRED, obstetrician, gynecologist, educator; b. Rock Springs, Wyo.; s. Alfred and Helen B. BA, Stanford U., 1977; MD, Boston U., 1982. Diplomate Am. Board of Obstetrics and Gynecology. Intern St. Luke's-Roosevelt Hosp., N.Y.C., 1982-83; resident in ob-gyn Stanford U. Hosp., Palo Alto, Calif., 1983-86; pvt. practice ob-gyn. Chgo., 1986-95; asst. prof. U. Calif., San Francisco, 1996—; cons. WHO, UN Family Planning Assn.; asst. prof. Northwestern U., Chgo., 1986-95; asst. prof. dept. ob-gyn. San Francisco Gen. Hosp., 1996—, dir. student health edn. dept. ob-gyn., 1995—; dir. Group Health Care for Women and Children, San Francisco, 1995—; dir. low-risk obstetrics, coord. undergrad. med. edn. Prentice Women's Hosp., Chgo.; mem. Liaison Com. on Med. Edn. Contbr. articles to med. jours. Mem. Chgo. Coun. Fgn. Rels. Rotary Found. grad. fellow, 1980; mem. Harvard Macy Scholars Inst., 1995. Fellow Am. Coll. Ob-Gyn., Assn. Profs. Gynecology and Obstetrics, Internat. Coll. Surgeons, Royal Soc. Medicine; mem. AMA, APHA, Am. Assn. Maternal and Neonatal Health, Am. Fertility Soc., Chog. Gynecol. Soc., San Francisco Med. Soc., Stanford U. Alumni Assn., Boston U. Sch. Medicine Alumni Assn., Phi Delta Epsilon. Roman Catholic.

BACHMAN, DAVID JACOB, retired nursing educator; b. Lebanon, Pa., Sept. 4, 1932; s. Walter M. Bachman Sr. Diploma, Jersey City Hosp., 1954; BSN, NYU, 1964; MS in Adult Edn., Coppin State Coll., 1985. CNOR. Asst. supr., instr. oper. rm. Mount Sinai Hosp., N.Y.C., 1969-71; instr. oper. rm. Sinai Hosp., Balt., 1973-77, Johns Hopkins Hosp., Balt., 1977-88, Union Meml. Hosp., Balt., 1988-94; ret., 1995. Mem. AORN (nat. coms., speaker nat. congress). Home: 1409 Plaza Apts Lebanon PA 17042

BACHMAN, DAVID M., ophthalmologist; b. Scranton, Pa., Aug. 10, 1951; s. Seymour W. and Natalie (Goodman) B. BA, Johns Hopkins U., 1973, MD, 1976. Resident in ophthalmology Stanford (Calif.) U. Hosp., 1977-80; fellow Nat. Eye Inst.-NIH, Bethesda, Md., 1980-82; pvt. practice ophthalmology Washington, 1982—; sr. ophthalmic surgeon Washington Hosp. Ctr., Washington, 1982—; clin. instr. ophthalmology George Washington Hosp., Washington, 1990—. Contbr. articles to profl. jours. Bd. dirs. Myasthenia Gravis Found., Washington, 1986—, Young Concert Artists, Washington, 1983—. Recipient Physician's Recognition award AMA, 1980, 83, 86, 93. Fellow Am. Acad. Ophthalmology; mem. Washington Ophthalmol. Soc., Med. Soc. D.C. Jewish. Office: 1133 20th St NW Ste B-150 Washington DC 20036-3402

BACHMAN, JANE A., optometrist; b. Milw., Feb. 10, 1966; d. Howard and Irene Karin (Gobel) B. BS in visual sci., Ill. Coll. Optometry, 1989, OD, 1991. Resident Ill. Eye Inst., Chgo., 1991-92, clin. instr., 1992-93, asst. prof., 1993—; cons. Chgo. Eye Inst., 1992—. Contbr. articles to profl. jours. Fellow Am. Acad. Optometry; mem. Ill Acad. Optometry. Office: Ill Coll Optometry 3241 S Michigan Ave Chicago IL 60616

BACHMAN, LILLIAN HELEN, dentist; b. Jackson Heights, N.Y., July 12, 1938; d. Curt and Lillian (Koch) B.; m. Alberto Lacoius, July 1, 1976 (div. 1987). BS, Queens Coll., 1959; DDS, Columbia U., 1963, Cert. in Pedodontics, 1966, MA, 1967. Pvt. practice N.Y.C., 1967—; sr. attending St. Luke's Roosevelt Med. Ctr., N.Y.C., 1993—; dir., sec.-treas. N.E. Regional Bd. Dental Examiners, Washington, 1994—. Mem. surrogate panel N.Y. State Commn. on Quality of Care for Mentally Disabled, 1990-94, mem. Carnegie Hill Neighbors; bd. dirs. 1065 Park Ave Corp.; mem. adv. couns. for occupational edn./N.Y. Bd. Edn., 1988-94. Recipient fellowship N.Y. Acad. of Dentistry, 1974. Fellow Internat. Coll. Dentists, Am. Coll. Dentists, Am. Acad. Pediatric Dentists, Internat. Acad. of Dentistry, Pi Lambda Theta; mem. ADA (vice-chmn. joint commn. on nat. dental exams 1990—), Am. Assn. Dental Examiners (pres. 1995-96), N.Y. State Dental Assn., First Dist. Dental Soc. Home: 1065 Park Ave New York NY 10128-1001 Office: 30 E 60th St # 906 New York NY 10022-1008

BACHMANN, FEDOR WOLFGANG, hematology educator, scientist; b. Zurich, Switzerland, May 23, 1927; naturalized, 1968; s. Theodor E. and Maria (Isler) B.; m. Edith I. Derendinger, Oct. 17, 1957; 1 child, Christian M. MD, U. Zurich, 1954. Diplomate Swiss Bd. Internal Medicine and Hematology. Intern, resident Med. Sch. U. Zurich, 1955-61; trainee USPHS Med. Sch. Washington U., St. Louis, 1961-64, asst. prof. Med. Sch., 1964-68; assoc. prof. Med. Sch. Rush-Presbyn.-St. Luke's Hosp., Chgo., 1968-73; dir. med. rsch. Schering Corp., USA, Lucerne, Switzerland, 1973-76; prof. medicine Med. Sch. U. Lausanne, Switzerland, 1976-92, prof. emeritus, 1992—; dir. hematology labs. U. Lausanne Med. Ctr., 1976-92, acting chmn. Dept. Medicine, 1980-81, provost, 1987-91; sci. coord. Thrombosis Rsch.

Inst., London, 1995—; vis. scholar pathology dept. Stanford (Calif.) U., 1986; vis. prof. U. Paris VI, 1991—. Editor: Progress in Fibrinolysis, vol. 6, 1983, Fibrinolytics and Antifibrinolytics, 1996; assoc. editor Fibrinolysis; contbr. over 200 articles to profl. jours.; editl. bd. Clin. and Lab. Haematology, 1979—, Thrombosis and Haemostasis, 1986-88, Schweizerische Medizinische Wochenscrift, 1986-88, Internat. Jour. Haematology, 1990—. Chmn. med. adv. bd. Nat. Hemophilia Found., Greater St. Louis chpt., 1966-68; chmn. nursing svcs. com. Dept. Health and Hosps., City of St. Louis, 1967-68; mem. manpower com. Bi-State Regional Health Program, St. Louis, 1968-69; vice chmn. med. adv. bd. Nat. Hemophilipa Found., Midwest chpt., Chgo., 1971-73, med. adv. bd., Nat. Hemophilia Soc., Switzerland, 1977-85; mem. sci. coun. Swiss Nat. Blood Transfusion Svc., 1978-82; mem. sci. coun. Swiss Cancer Inst., 1980-88; pres. Rsch. Found. on Atherosclerosis and Thrombosis, Lausanne-Le Mont, 1983—; pres. Sci. Coun. "Aging and Cardiovascular Disease" of the French Ministry of Industry and Rsch., 1985-86; mem. sci. coun. European Sch. Haematology, 1986—; mem. sci. coun. on biomaterials German Ministry of Tech., 1986-92. Capt. Swiss Army Med. Corps, 1955-56. Recipient prize Internat. Com. of Fibrinolysis, Amsterdam, 1988; grantee. NIH/USPHS, 1961-73, Swiss Nat. Sci. Found., 1977-92, Emil Barrell Found., 1955-57, Sandoz Found., 1981-84, Roche Found., 1979-80, Swiss Cancer League, 1979-84, Thrombosis and Atherosclerosis Found., 1983-92, Swiss Cardiology Found., 1986-87. Fellow ACP; mem. Internat. Soc. Thrombosis and Haemostasis (exec. coun. 1988-94), Am. Heart Assn. (coun. on thrombosis), N.Y. Acad. Scis., Internat. Soc. Haematology, Internat. Soc. Fibrinolysis and Thrombolysis (exec. coun. 1992-93), Am. Fedn. Clin. Rsch., Am. Soc. Hematology, Am. Physiol. Soc., Ctrl. Soc. Clin. Rsch., Swiss Med. Soc., Swiss Hematol. Soc. (pres. 1986-88), Swiss Soc. Angiology, Soc. of Medicine Vaudois, Swiss Soc. Internal Medicine, Swiss Soc. Biochemistry, French Soc. Haematology, German-Austrian Soc. Thrombosis and Haemostasis (exec. coun. 1989—), Argentinian Med. Soc. (hon.), Med. Soc. Vienna (corr.), European Thrombosis Rsch. Assn., Internat. Soc. and Fedn. Cardiology (coun. on thrombosis, pres. 1994—), Sigma Xi. Home: Chemin Praz-Mandry 20, 1052 Le Mont Switzerland Office: Hôpital Nestlé 2077, Centre Hospitalier Univ Vau, 1011 Lausanne Switzerland

BACHMANN, WILLIAM THOMPSON, dermatologist; b. Orange, N.J., Mar. 21, 1940; s. George Kirsten and Agnes Mary (Cunningham) B.; m. Carolyn Emily Koeber, Dec. 28, 1961 (div. June 1971); children: John Kirsten, William Thompson; m. Judith Richmond, June 20, 1981; 1 stepchild, Julia Garriga. AB, Williams Coll., 1962; MD, Boston U., 1966. Diplomat Am. Bd. Internal Medicine, Am. Bd. Dermatology. Intern St. Francis Hosp., Hartford, Conn., 1966-67, resident, 1967-68; resident Yale New Haven (Conn.) Hosp., 1971-72, 72-74; dermatologist Westerly (R.I.) Hosp. Lt. comdr. USN, 1969-71. Fellow Am. Coll. Physicians, Am. Acad. Dermatology; mem. New England Dermatological Soc., R.I. Med. Soc., Yale Soc. Attendings in Dermatology (st. attending mem.), Alpha Omega Alpha. Office: 39 East Ave Westerly RI 02891

BACHOP, MARTIN WILLIAM, clinical psychologist; b. Seattle, Aug. 23, 1952; s. William George and Rita Agnes (Schug) B.; 1 child, Matthew Bradley; m. Sharon Kaye Knighton, Apr. 28, 1990 and Sept. 24, 1994. AB magna cum laude, Princeton U., 1973; PhD, CUNY, 1982. Lic. psychologist. Rsch. asst. Tex. Rsch. Inst. Mental Scis., Houston, 1978; assoc. psychologist R. Weinberger, PhD and M. Katz, PhD, Houston, 1978; psychologist Mapleridge RTC, Mental Health Mental Retardation Authority of Harris County, Houston, 1979-81, Weinberger & Katz, P.C., Houston, 1981-85; pvt. practice Houston, 1985—; dir. psychological svcs. Charter Hosp. of Sugar Land, 1994-95. Recipient NIMH traineeship, 1973-76. Mem. APA, Tex. Psychol. Assn., Houston Psychol. Assn. (chmn. hosp. rels. com. 1987-89), Mental Health Assn. Office: 9034 Westheimer Ste 340 Houston TX 77063

BACHRACH, LYNN S., pharmaceutical contract research organization executive; b. N.Y.C., Feb. 26, 1951; d. Jesse Silberstein and Nancy (Cohen) Sawyer. BA, Antioch Coll., 1973. Saleswoman Dunhill Greater Phila., 1974-76, Meloy Labs., Phila., 1976-78, Physio Control, Phila., 1978-80, Datamedix, Phila., 1980-82; sr. v.p. C.P. Rehab. Corp. Midlantic, Phila., 1982-87; sr. v.p. sales and mktg., pres. C.P. Rehab. Corp., N.Y.C., 1987-89; pres. The Cardiac Rehab. Co. and Clin. Rsch. Group, Phila., 1989—. Mem. Drug Info. Assn., Assn. Clin. Pharmacology, Tech. Coun. Greater Phila., Am. Assn. Cardiovascular and Pulmonary Rehab., Tri-State Soc. for Cardiovascular and Pulmonary Rehab. Jewish. Office: The Cardiac Rhab Co PO Box 127 Haverford PA 19041-0127

BACHYRYCZ, FRANK JOSEPH, pharmacist; b. Danbury, Conn., Oct. 22, 1948; s. Frank and Margaret (DeSantis) B.; m. Maryanne Cristaldi, Aug. 29, 1970; children: Frank Jr., Rachel, Amy, Brian. BS in Pharmacy, U. Conn., 1971; MS in Health Care Adminstrn., Western Conn. State U., 1988. RPh, Conn. Staff pharmacist Norwalk (Conn.) Hosp., 1974-76; staff pharmacist Danbury (Conn.) Hosp., 1976-86, pharmacy supr., 1986—; adj. prof. Western Conn. State U., 1996. Chmn. devel. fund St. Gregory the Great Sch., Danbury, 1994—; pres. lay adv. St. Gregory Ch., Danbury, 1990; mem. Dem. Town Com., Danbury, 1974-78; mem. health and support svcs. com. Am. Cancer Soc., Danbury, 1990-95. Mem. Danbury Pharm. Assn. (sec. 1985—). Roman Catholic. Office: Danbury Hosp Dept Pharmacy 24 Hospital Ave Danbury CT 06810

BACKENROTH-OHSAKO, GUNNEL ANNE MAJ, psychologist, educator, researcher; b. Grums, Värmland, Sweden, June 12, 1951; parents: K. Hugo and Maj E.I.S. (Joelsson) B. BA, Göteborgs U., Gothenberg, Sweden, 1974; MA, Umeå U., Sweden, 1976; PhD, Stockholm U., 1983. Lic. psychologist, Sweden. Child psychologist Barn-och ungdomspsykiatriska Kliniken, Lidköping, Sweden, 1973-76; researcher, program leader Stockholm U., 1976-79, 1981—; psychologist, program leader Parental Assn. for Cooperation, Stockholm, 1979-81; univ. lectr. Stockholm U., 1988, assoc. prof., 1989; lectr. various univs.; cons. Stockholms läns Landsting, 1985-91, Sveriges Dövas Riksförbund, 1991-92, Nämnden för vårdartjänst, 1992—. Contbr. numerous articles to profl., acad. jours. Lecture award Singapore Assn. for the Deaf, 1984. Mem. Swedish Assn. for Psychologists (sci. adv. council), Internat. Assn. Human Relations Lab. Tng. (hon., life), Univ. Assn. Stockholm, Assn. for Female Researchers, Scandinavian Assn. for Research of the Deafs Mental Health, Internat. Round. Table for the Advancement of Counseling, Swedish Rorschach Assn., Internat. Assn. of Applied Psychology. Home: Skidbacken 4, S-17245 Sundbyberg Sweden Office: Stockholm U, Dept Psychology, S-10691 Stockholm Sweden

BACKMAN, MARGARET ESTHER, psychologist; b. Johnstown, Pa.; d. Peter Louis and Helen (McNulty) B. AB, Barnard Coll., 1960; MA, Columbia U., 1961, PhD, 1970; postdoctoral cert. clin. psychology, NYU, 1980-83. Cert. clin. psychologist. Dir. research Internat. Ctr. for Disabled, N.Y.C., 1973-78; dir. program devel. services, exec. dir. personnel devel. Coll. Bd., N.Y.C., 1978-80; clin. asst. prof. NYU Med. Ctr., N.Y.C., 1985—; psychologist health services dept. Barnard Coll., N.Y.C., 1985-95; clin. health psychologist N.Y. VA Med. Ctr., N.Y.C., 1995—; with panel on testing handicapped people Nat. Acad. Scis., Washington, 1979-81, adv. council research and tng. ctr. U. Wis.-Stout, Menomenie, 1976-82. Author: The Psychology of the Physically Ill Patient, 1989, Choosing a Therapist, 1994. Postdoctoral fellow Cancer Rehab. Med. Ctr. NYU, 1984-85. Mem. Am. Psychological Assn., Nat. Rehab. Assn. Office: Suite 902 30 E 40th St New York NY 10016

BACON, BARBARA MCNUTT, social worker; b. London, Nov. 6, 1946; came to U.S., 1952; d. Peter Joseph and Margaret (Stronge) O'Reilly; m. Michael McNutt, Nov. 15, 1969 (div. 1977); m. John Lockhart Bacon, Apr. 29, 1978; children: Patricia, Ann Catherine. BA, Ursuline Coll. for Women, 1968; postgrad., Harvard U., 1968-69; MEd, U. Ill., 1971; MSW, U. Iowa, 1981. Psychometrist Child Devel. Lab., Mass. Gen. Hosp. and Harvard Med. Sch., Boston, 1968-69; research assoc. Inst. Child Behavior and Devel., U. Ill., Champaign, 1969-78; clin. social worker Family and Children's Services, Davenport, Iowa, 1979-83; psychologist Gt. River Mental Health Ctr., Muscatine, Iowa, 1978-79; behavioral sci. coord. family practice residency program Mercy-St Luke's Hosp., Davenport, Iowa, 1979-82; family therapist Family Counseling Service, Albuquerque, 1984-88; pvt. practice Profl. Counseling Assocs., 1984-86; clin. dir. adolescent psychiatric program Charter Hosp., Albuquerque, 1987-89; psychotherapist Family Health Plan of Utah, 1990-95; cons. CIBA-Geigy Corp., Summit, N.J., 1975-77, Council for Children at Risk, Rock Island, Ill., 1981-83. Mem. Nat. Assn. Social Workers, Phi Beta Kappa. Republican. Roman Catholic.

BACON, BRUCE RAYMOND, physician; b. Amherst, Ohio, Nov. 7, 1949; s. Raymond Clifford and Cathryn E. (Fowell) B.; m. Joan Laurie Benson, June 26, 1971; children: Jeffrey Dale, Laurie Katherine. BA in chem., Coll. Wooster, 1971; MD, Case Western Reserve U., 1975. Diplomate Am. Bd. Internal Medicine and Gastroenterology. Asst. prof. medicine Case Western Reserve U., Cleve., 1982-87, assoc. prof. medicine, 1987-88; assoc. prof. medicine, chief gastroenterology sect. La. State U., Shreveport, 1988-90; prof. internal medicine, dir. gastroenterology divsn. St. Louis U. Sch. Medicine, St.Louis, 1990—. Co-author: Essentials of Clinical Hepatology, 1993; contbr. numerous articles to profl. jours. Fellow Am. Coll. Physicians, Am. Coll. Gastroenterology, Am. Soc. Clin. Investigation. Presbyterian. Office: St Louis U Health Sci Ctr 3635 Vista Ave Saint Louis MO 63110-2539

BACON, JANICE LYNNE, obstetrician-gynecologist; b. Detroit, May 22, 1954; d. Ronald Dennis and Shirley Elaine (Davey) B. BA, Jacksonville (Fla.) U., 1976; MD, U. S. Fla., 1979. Resident Richland Meml. Hosp., Columbia, S.C., 1979-84; asst. prof. U. S.C., Columbia, 1984—; mem. med. adv. bd., trustee Planned Parenthood, Columbia, 1987—. Mem. AMA, N.Am. Soc. Pediatric and Adolescent Gynecology (bd. dirs.), Am. Coll. Ob.-Gyn., Delta Delta Delta Alumnae Assn. Home: 3401 Heatherwood Rd Columbia SC 29205-1952 Office: U SC Sch Medicine Dept Ob-Gyn Two Richland Med Pk Ste 208 Suite 302 Columbia SC 29203

BACQUÉ, ANGELA, pharmacist; b. Elizabeth, N.J., Aug. 20, 1957; d. Giuseppe and Lucia (Corsentino) M.; m. Stephen Emile Bacqué, June 2, 1990; 1 child, Lucia Eve. BS, Rutgers U., 1981; MPA, Kean Coll., 1987. RPh, N.J.; cert. clin. diabetes educator. Pharmacy technician Holmdel (N.J.) Village Pharmacy, 1977-78, Elmora Pharmacy, Elizabeth, 1978; pharmacy extern Clark (N.J.) Drugs, 1980, Schering Corp., Kenilworth, N.J., 1980, Alexian Bros. Hosp., Elizabeth, 1980; pharmacist Rahway (N.J.) Hosp., 1981—, speaker edn. dept., 1981—, mem. speakers bur. community relations dept., nutritional support com., 1985-87, asst. pharmacy adminstr., 1987—; relief pharmacist Horowitz Pharmacy, Elizabeth 1981. Performer and asst. dir. various local plays, 1982-86. Co-recipient first recognition award by N.J. Small Bus.Devel. Ctr., 1992. Mem. N.J. Assn. Hosp. Pharmacists, Am. Pharm. Assn. (polit. action com. 1981—), Pharmacists Against Drug Abuse (lectr. 1986—), Am. Assn. Diabetes Educators, Cranford Dramatic Club (chmn. set painting 1985-87, v.p. prodn. 1988-90), Pi Alpha Alpha. Democrat. Roman Catholic. Home: 315 S Stiles St Linden NJ 07036-4403 Office: Rahway Hosp 865 Stone St Rahway NJ 07065-2797

BADALAMENT, ROBERT ANTHONY, urologic oncologist; b. Detroit, Mar. 20, 1954; s. Louis F. and Grace D. (Costello) B.; m. Providenee F. Vitale, Nov. 9, 1980; children: Louis F., Peter P., Grace F. BS in Biology, So. Meth. U., 1976; MD, Emory U., 1980. Diplomate Am. Bd. Urology. Surg. intern Henry Ford Hosp., Detroit, 1980-81, surg. resident, 1981-82, urologic resident, 1982-85; fellow in urologic oncology Meml. Sloan Kettering Cancer Ctr., N.Y.C., 1985-87; asst. prof. Ohio State U., Columbus, 1987-92, assoc. prof., 1992-95, prof. Sch. Pub. Health, 1995—; mem. attending staff Arthur James Cancer Ctr., Columbus, 1990-95, Crittenton Hosp., Rochester Hills, Mich., 1995—. Contbr. chpt. to book, articles to profl. jours. Fellow ACS; mem. AMA, Am. Soc. Clin. Oncology, Soc. Univ. Urologists, Soc. Urologic Oncology, Soc. for Basic Urologic Rsch., Am. Cancer Soc. (bd. trustees Mich. divsn.). Office: Rochester Urology PC Ste 420 1135 W University Dr Rochester Hills MI 48307-1831

BADDOURA, RASHID JOSEPH, emergency medicine physician; b. Beirut, Aug. 4, 1947; came to U.S., 1974; s. Joseph and Renée Baddoura; m. Rola Baddoura; children: Joseph, Philip, Karea. BS, Am. U. Beirut, 1970, MD, 1974. Diplomate Am. Bd. Emergency Medicine (examiner 1984-89), Am. Bd. Internal Medicine, Am. Bd. Pulmonary Diseases. Dir. emergency dept. Meml. Hosp., Danville, Va., 1981-84; corp. med. officer, mem. med. adv. bd. Coastal Group, Durham, N.C., 1981-86; assoc. dir. emergency dept. Valley Hosp., Ridgewood, N.J., 1986-90, dir. emergency dept., 1990—; mem. bd. Coastal Found. for Med. Edn., Durham, 1984-89; clin. asst. prof. emergency medicine Georgetown U., Washington, 1986-89. Fellow Am. Coll. Emergency Medicine; mem. Am. Coll. Physician Execs. Office: Valley Hosp Dept Emergency Medicine Ridgewood NJ 07451

BADEN, THOMAS JAMES, dermatologist; b. Coral Gables, Fla., Dec. 29, 1951; s. Thomas Benjamin and Helen (Threadgill) B.; m. Sandra Louise Bradley, June 22, 1974; children: Craig, Scott, Michael. AB in Chemistry, Duke U., 1973; MD cum laude, Emory U., 1977. Diplomate Am. Bd. Internal Medicine, Am. Bd. Dermatology. Internal medicine resident N.C. Meml. Hosp., Chapel Hill, 1977-80; dermatology resident N.C. Meml. Hosp., 1983-86; internist Toe Valley Med. Assn., Spruce Pine, N.C., 1980-83; dermatologist West Piedmont Dermatology Assn., Morganton, N.C., 1986—; consulting dermatologist Western Carolina Ctr., Broughton Hosp., Morganton, 1986—; staff dermatologist Grace Hosp., Morganton, 1986—. Contbr. articles to profl. jours. Troop leader Boy Scouts Am.; deacon First Bapt. Ch., Morganton. Fellow ACP, Am. Acad. Dermatology, Am. Soc. Dermatology Surgeons; mem. AMA, Christian Med. Soc. Office: West Piedmont Dermatology 111 Foothills Dr Morganton NC 28655-5152

BADER, HERMANN JOSEPH, pharmacologist, educator; b. Furtwangen, Germany, Nov. 23, 1927; s. Joseph Bernhard and Martha (Müllegger) B.; m. Gertraude Haack, May 1, 1958; children: Sylvia, Andreas, Raoul, Maureen, Gregor, Oliver, Niklas, Matthias, Dominik. MD, U. Munich, 1955. Rsch. assoc. dept. physiology U. Munich, 1954-56, intern dept. medicine, 1956-57, German Sci. Found. scholar, 1957-58, instr. dept. physiology; instr. dept. physiology Vanderbilt U., Nashville, 1959-60, asst. prof., 1960, 63-66 instr. U. Munich, Germany, 1960-61; asst. prof. dept. physiology U. Wurzburg, Germany, 1961-63; assoc. prof. dept. pharmacology and toxicology U. Miss. Sch. Medicine, Jackson, 1966-70, prof., 1970-72; prof., head dept. pharmacology and toxicology U. Ulm, Germany, 1972-96, emeritus prof., 1996—; dean sch. of medicine, 1974-75, 79-83. With German Infantry 1944-45, prisoner of war, U.S.A., 1945-46. Mem. Am. Soc. Pharmacology and Exptl. Therapeutics, German Soc. Pharmacology and Toxicology, Biophys. Soc. U.S.A., German Biophys. Soc., German Biol. Chemistry soc., German Phys. Soc. Roman Catholic. Home: Neue Welt 6, 89269 Voehringen-Illerberg Germany

BADET, JOSETTE FRANÇOISE, research scientist; b. Paris, Aug. 17, 1947; d. Roger Eugene and Jeannine Henriette (Robin) Genissel; m. Bernard Badet, Apr. 7, 1973 (div. Jan. 1991); 1 child, Claire. BA in Biochemistry, Faculté des Scis. d'Orsay, Paris, 1970, MS in Biophysics, 1971, PhD in Biophysics, 1973, DSc in Biology, 1981. Rsch. scientist Nat. Inst. Health & Med. Rsch., Paris, 1976-81, sr. scientist, 1982, 85-90, rsch. dir., 1991—. Contbr. articles to profl. jours. Recipient awards Ligue contre le Cancer, 1971-73, Assn. for Cancer Rsch., 1990-91, 93-94, 95-96. Mem. European Tissue Culture Soc., French Soc. Biochemistry & Molecular Biology, N.Y. Acad. Scis. Office: INSERM U427 Pharmacie, Ave du General de Gaulle, Ave de l'Observatoire, 75006 Paris France

BADETTI, ROLANDO EMILIO, health science facility administrator; b. Istanbul, Turkey, Mar. 25, 1947; s. Umberto and Iole (Bianchi) B.; m. Emanuela Ponte, Oct. 29, 1973; children: Barbara, Fabiana. PhD in Pharmacy, U. Padua, Italy, 1971. Mfg. supr. Gruppo Lepetit, El Jadida, Morocco, 1971-76, plant mgr., 1977-79; quality assurance mgr. Gruppo Lepetit, Milan, 1980-81, material mgr., 1982-83; tech. dir. Lirca Synthelabo, Milan, 1983-91; gen. mgr. asst. Arval, Milan, 1991-92; tech. dir. Laboratori UCB, Turin, 1992—. Office: Laboratori UCB SpA, Via Praglia 15, 10044 Pianezza Italy

BADGER, THOMAS MARK, pediatrics educator, researcher; b. Modesto, Calif., Mar. 21, 1945; s. Robert Albert and Valeria (Eaves) B.; m. Cheryl Ann Jordan, Aug. 26, 1967; 1 child, Mark Jordan. BS in Biology and Chemistry, Calif. State U., Fresno, 1968; MS in Audiology, U. Mo., 1970, PhD in Nutritional Biochemistry, 1973. Rsch. assoc. in biochemistry U. Mo., Columbia, 1973-74; instr. psychiatry and neuropharmacology Washington U., St. Louis, 1974-77; asst. prof. reproductive neuroendocrinology Harvard Med. Sch., Boston, 1977-82, assoc. prof., 1982-86; prof. pediatrics U. Ark. Med. Scis., 1986—; asst. in biochemistry Mass. Gen. Hosp., Boston, 1977-82, assoc. in biochemistry, 1982-86, dir. basic rsch. Vincent reproductive endocrine unit, 1979-86, dir. pediatric rsch. U. Ark. for Med. Scis., 1986—; dir. rsch. Ark. Children's Hosp., 1986—; dir. Ark. Children's Hosp. Rsch. Inst., 1993—; assoc. dean Coll. Medicine U. Ark. for Med. Scis., 1993—; dir. Ark. USDA Human Nutrition Ctr., 1995—. spl. cons. Rsch. Ctr. Nat. Inst. for Drug Abuse, 1978—, Nat. Inst. Alcohol and Alcohol Abuse, 1990—. NIH fellow, 1975-77. Mem. Soc. for Exptl. Biology and Medicine, Endocrine Soc., Soc. Neurosci., Soc. Pediatric Rsch., Am. Inst. Nutrition, Soc. Pediatric Rsch. Soc. Neuroendocrinology, Soc. Reproductive Endocrinology, Rsch. Soc. of Alcoholism, Coll. Problems of Drug Dependence, Internat. Brain Rsch. Orgn., Internat. Soc. Neuroscience, Sigma Xi, Phi Lambda Upsilon, Gamma Sigma Delta. Contbr. articles on endocrinology and nutrition to sci. jours.; research on nutrition, growth, development and reproduction, mechanisms of hormone and drug actions, effects of alcohol and drugs of abuse on brain function and development, physiology of hypothalamus and pituitary gland. Home: 13500 Rivercrest Dr Little Rock AR 72212-1465

BADILLO, DIANA, psychologist; b. Aguadilla, P.R., May 14, 1946; d. Daniel and Carmen (Jimenez) B.; m. Jose Vivaldy Martinez, Sept. 28, 1968; children: Dana, Melissa, Jose II. MA, U. P.R., 1970; PhD, CUNY, N.Y.C., 1984. Diplomate Am. Acad. Pain Mgmt. Psychologist Pediatric Ctr. for Handicapped Children, Santurce, P.R., 1971-75, Bronx Psychiat. Ctr., 1978-86; pvt. practice psychology Danbury, Conn., 1986—; adj. prof. Western Conn. U., Danbury, 1986—; neuropsychologist DATAHR, Inc., Brookfield, Conn., 1985-90; cons. Hartford Mental Health Ctr., 1986-87; neuropsychologist Danbury Hosp., 1990-95; adj. prof. N.Y. Med. Coll., 1990-95. Reviewer Jour. Pediatric Psychology, 1989—. P.R. Dept Labor scholar, 1970. Mem. Am. Psychol. Assn., Soc. of Neurosci., Am. Pain Soc., Hispanic Psychol. Assn., N.Y. Acad. Scis., Spanish Am. Cultural Assn. (cultural com. 1986—). Baptist. Office: 60 Old New Milford Rd Ste 3D Brookfield CT 06804-2427

BADMAJEW, PETER, physician; b. Warsaw, Poland, Feb. 19, 1929; came to U.S., 1967, naturalized, 1973; s. Wlodzimierz and Tamara (Brzozowski) B.; M.D., Med. Acad. Lodz (Poland), 1952. Cert. ACLS, 1966. Asst. in surgery County Hosp., Garwolin, Poland, 1952-57; sr. asst. First Surg. Clinic, Postgrad. Sch. Medicine, Warsaw, 1957-62; surg. fellow Surg. Med. Inst., U. Alta. (Can.), Edmonton, 1962-63; rotating intern St. Mary's Hosp., Passaic, N.J., 1964; dep. chief dept. thoracic surgery Sanatorium Otwock (Poland), 1965; asst. cardiosurg. dept. Univ. Hosp., Zurich, Switzerland, 1966-67; resident in surgery Wilson Meml. Hosp., Johnson City, N.Y., 1967-68; sr. resident thoracic dept. New Eng. Deaconess Hosp., Boston, 1968-69; pvt. practice medicine specializing in family practice, Jamesport, N.Y., 1969—; mem. staff Central Suffolk Hosp., Riverhead, N.Y. With Polish Home Army, 1943-44, in German prison camp, 1944-45. Cert. specialist in gen. surgery, Poland, advanced cardiac life support system, 1989, advanced trauma life support system, 1989, 93; diplomate Am. Bd. Family Practice, Am. Bd. Geriatrics. Fellow Am. Acad. Family Physicians; mem. AMA (Physician's Recognition award 1982, 83, 90, 93). Roman Catholic. Home and Office: Main Rd Jamesport NY 11947

BAER, CHAROLD LEE, nephrology nurse, educator; b. Dover, Ohio, July 15, 1946; d. Harold and Zelda Mae (Frantz) Morris; m. Richard C. Baer, Sept. 7, 1968. BSN, Ohio State U., 1968, MSN, 1970, PhD, 1977. Cert. critical care nurse. Instr. Ohio State U., Columbus, 1970-77; prof. Oreg. Health Scis. U., Portland, 1978—; chmn. adult health and illness dept. Oreg. Health Scis. U., Portland, 1978-83, 92-94. Contbr. articles to profl. jours. Fellow Am. Coll. Critical Care Medicine; mem. AACN, Am. Nephrology Nurses Assn., Soc. Critical Care Medicine, Sigma Theta Tau. Home: 8039 SW 62nd Pl Portland OR 97219-3120 Office: Oreg Health Scis U Dept Adult Health & Illness 3181 SW Sam Jackson Park Rd Portland OR 97201-3011

BAER, RUDOLF LEWIS, dermatologist, educator; b. Strasbourg, France, July 22, 1910; came to U.S., 1934, naturalized, 1940; s. Ludwig and Clara (Mainzer) B.; m. Louise Jeanne Grumbach, Nov. 6, 1941; children: John Reckford, Andrew Rudolph. MD, U. Basel, Switzerland, 1934; postgrad. dermatology, N.Y. Postgrad. Med. Sch., 1937-39; MD (hon.), U. Munich, 1981. Diplomate Am. Bd. Dermatology (mem. 1964-72, pres. 1969-70). Intern Beth Israel Hosp., N.Y.C., 1934-35; resident dermatology Montefiore Hosp., N.Y.C., 1936-37; faculty Columbia U. Sch. Medicine, 1939-48; dir. dept. dermatology Univ. Hosp., 1961-81; faculty NYU Sch. Medicine, 1948—, prof. dermatology, 1961—, chmn. dept. dermatology, 1961-81, George Miller MacKee prof., 1961-81; dir. dept. dermatology Bellevue Hosp. Center, 1961-81; surgeon gen. U.S. Army, FDA; mem. Internat. Com. Dermatology, 1967-82, pres., 1972-77; mem. com. on revision U.S. Pharmacopeia, 197--75; mem. commn. cutaneous diseases Armed Forces Epidemiologic Bd., 1967-72. Editor: Office Immunology, 1947, Atopic Dermatitis, 1955, Year Book Dermatology, 1955-65; also past mem. numerous editorial bds.; Author over 300 articles. Chmn. bd. Dermatology Found., 1974-77; bd. dirs. Rudolf L. Baer Found. for Skin Diseases, 1975—. Decorated Order of the Rising Sun (Japan), 1991; Dohi lectr. and recipient Dohi medal Japanese Dermatol. Soc., 1965; Von Zumbusch lectr. Munich, 1967, Hellerstrom lectr. Stockholm, 1970, O'Leary lectr. Mayo Clinic, Rochester, Minn., 1971, Robinson lectr. U. Md., 1972, Barrett Kennedy lectr., 1973, Louis A. Duhring lectr., 1974, Samuel M. Bluefarb lectr., 1975, Frederick J. Novy Jr. vis. scholar, 1978, Morris Samitz lectr., 1979, Ruben Nomland-Robert Carney lectr., 1979, Barrett Kennedy meml. lectr., 1980, A. Harvey Neidorff lectr., 1985, Ferdinand von Hebra meml. lectr., 1988, Alexander A. Fisher lectr., 1989, Stuart B. Fisher lectr., 1991, Tamotsu Imaeda lectr., 1991, Hermann Pinkus lectr., 1992; Walter C. Lobitz Jr. lectr., 1994; recipient von Hebra medal U. Vienna, 1988, Discovery award Dermatology Found., 1993. Fellow N.Y. Acad. Medicine (chmn. sect. dermatology 1963-64), Am. Acad. Dermatology (pres. 1974-75, Dome lectr. 1976, gold medal 1978, hon. mem. 1980), Am. Acad. Allergy, Am. Coll. Allergists; mem. AMA (chmn. sect. dermatology 1965-66), Am. Dermatol. Assn. (pres. 1977, hon. mem. 1992), Soc. Investigative Dermatology (pres. 1963-64, Stephen Rothman medal 1973, hon. mem. 1980), Am. Contact Dermatitis Soc. (hon.), Bronx Dermatol. Soc. (pres. 1952), N.Y. Dermatol. Soc. (pres. 1982-83, hon. mem. 1991), N.Y. Allergy Soc., N.Y. Acad. Scis., N.Y. County and State Med. Soc., World Congress Dermatology (hon. pres. 1992), Internat. League Dermatol. Socs. (pres. 1972-77, Alfred Marchionini gold medal 1977), Argentinian Dermatol. Soc. (hon. mem.), Austrian Dermatol. Soc. (hon. mem.), Brit. Dermatol. Soc. (hon. mem.), Brazilian Dermatol. Soc. (hon. mem.), Danish Dermatol. Soc. (hon. mem.), Finnish Dermatol. Soc. (hon. mem.), German Dermatol. Soc. (hon. mem., Karl Herxheimer medal 1995), Iranian Dermatol. Soc. (hon. mem.), Israeli Dermatol. Soc. (hon. mem.), Italian Dermatol. Soc. (hon. mem.), Japanese Dermatol. Soc. (hon. mem.), Mex. Dermatol. Soc. (hon. mem.), Polish Dermatol. Soc. (hon. mem.), Swedish Dermatol. Soc. (hon. mem.), Yugoslav Dermatol. Soc. (hon. mem.), Venezuelan Dermatol. Soc. (hon. mem.), Brazilian Nat. Acad. Medicine, Pacific Dermatol. Soc. (corr. mem.), Cuban Dermatol. Soc. (corr. mem.), French Dermatol. Soc. (corr. mem.), French Allergy Soc. Home: 1185 Park Ave New York NY 10128-1311 Office: 566 1st Ave New York NY 10016-6402

BAERG, RICHARD HENRY, podiatrist, administrator, educator; b. L.A., Jan. 19, 1937; s. Henry Francis and Ruth Elizabeth (Loven) B.; children from previous marriage: Carol Elizabeth, William Richard, Michael David, Yvette Marie, Brie Ann. AA, Reedley Coll., 1956; BS, Calif. Coll. Podiatric Medicine, 1965, DPM, 1968, MSc in Foot Surgery, 1970; MPH in Med. Adminstrn., U. Calif., Berkeley, 1971; ScD (hon.), N.Y. Coll. Podiatric Medicine, 1980; LittD (hon.), Ohio Coll. Podiatric Medicine, 1984; postgrad. Sch. Edn. and Pub. Health, U. Mich., 1973-1974; postgrad. Sch. of Bus. and Sch. of Edn., Harvard U., 1975. Diplomate Am. Bd. Podiatric Surgery (foot and ankle surgery), Am. Bd. Podiatric Orthopedics and Primary Podiatric Medicine (exec. dir. 1980-90), Am. Bd. podiatric Pub. Health (bd. dirs. 1980-89). Intern Highland Gen. Hosp., Oakland, Calif., 1969; resident in surgery Calif. Podiatry Hosp. (Pacific Coast Hosp.), San Francisco, 1970; acad. dean N.Y. Coll. Podiatric Medicine, N.Y.C., 1971-74; v.p., dean Calif. Coll. Podiatric Medicine, San Francisco, 1974-76; chief podiatric medicine Los Angeles County-U. So. Calif. Med. Ctr., 1976-78; dir. So. Calif. Podiatric Med. Ctr., 1976-78; pvt. practice Beverly Hills, Calif., 1976-78; pres. Ill. Coll. Podiatric Medicine, Chgo., 1978-79; mem. spl. med. adv. group to sec. Dept. Vets. Affairs, Washington, 1976-79, dir. podiatric service, dept. medicine and surgery, 1979-84, acting dir., 1984-86; health resources adminstrn. cons.

Dept. Health and Human Svcs., Washington, 1974-88; chief podiatry VA Med. Ctr., Loma Linda, Calif., 1984-89; dir. residency tng. Loma Linda Foot Clinic, 1990; exec. v.p., med. dir. Dr. Footcare Corp., Montclair, Calif., 1988-90; faculty podiatry U. N.C. Hosps., Chapel Hill, 1992—; clin. prof. Sch. of Podiatric Medicine Barry U., Miami, Fla., 1993—; clin. prof. Med. Sch., U. N.C., 1992—; assoc. clin. prof. Stanford U. Med. Sch., 1974-76; clin. prof. Pa. Coll. Podiatric Medicine, 1979-86, U. Osteo. Medicine and Health Sci., 1984-92; pres. Baerg & Assocs.; mem. podiatry adv. panel NAS Inst. Medicine, 1974; mem. bd. podiatric medicine Calif. dept. Consumer Affairs, 1989-90, chmn. residency, edn. and hosp. inspection com. Contbg. author: (text) Podiatric Medicine and Public Health, 1987; mem. editl. bd. Jour. Podiatric Edn., Yearbook of Podiatric Medicine and Surgery, Mil. Medicine Jour.; contbr. over 30 articles to profl. jours., 3 chpts. to textbooks. With M.C. U.S. Army and USN, 1958-64. Mead-Johnson fellow, 1968-69. Fellow Am. Podiatric Med. Assn. (com. on pub. health 1971-84, coun. podiatric edn. 1975-84, chmn. profl. edn. com. 1977-78, com. on hosp. 1980-85, Kenison award 1984, cert. appreciation 1990, com. on pub. health and preventive medicine), Am. Coll. Foot and Ankle Surgeons, Am. Coll. Foot & Ankle Orthopedics and Medicine (exec. dir. 1980-90), Acad. Ambulatory Foot Surgery; mem. APHA (governing coun. 1977-80, chmn. podiatric health sect. 1991-94, chmn. nominating com. 1994-96), Am. Acad. Podiatric Adminstrns. (exec. dir. 1990-91), Nat. Bd. Podiatric Med. Examiners (bd. dirs.), Assn. Podiatrists in Fed. Svc., Am. Assn. Colls. Podiatric Medicine (exec. com. 1973, pres. 1980-81), Assn. Mil. Surgeons U.S., Nat. Acads. of Practice (podiatric medicine 1985), N.C. Podiatric Med. Soc. (bd. dirs. ins. com. 1994—, chmn. zone III 1994—, rep. N.C. Health Care Reform Com. 1994—), Coun. Med. Sch. Affiliated Podiatrists (bd. dirs., dir. region 10), Mason (Scottish Rite, 32 degree), Sigma Pi Epsilon, Pi Delta. Republican. Home: 5017 Pine Cone Dr Durham NC 27707 Office: Chapel Hill Podiatry Clinic 1777 N Fordham Blvd Ste 203 Chapel Hill NC 27514-5885

BAERT, LUC, urologist, educator; b. Roeselare, Belgium, Jan. 27, 1938; s. Beatrix Declercg, Aug. 8, 1964; 1 child, Joort Carl Benedikte. MD, U. Leuven, Belgium, 1964. Cert. urologist. Chmn. dept. urology Kortriyk, Belgium, 1964-85, Cath. U., Leuven, Belgium, 1985—; clin. prof. urology U. So. Calif., 1990. Editor Benigh Proltotic Stzferplatic Springer, 1994. Home: Berken Hoflaan 31, 3001 Heverlee Belgium

BAERT, ROGER J. M., nuclear medicine physicist; b. Koewacht, Zeeland, The Netherlands, Feb. 4, 1941; m. Marjo J. P. van der Heijden, Aug. 23, 1965; 3 children. Student, Tech. U., Delft, The Netherlands, 1965, Med. Free U., Amsterdam, The Netherlands, 1976-80. Cert. clin. physics. Nuclear medicine appl. Philips Med. Sys., Eindhoven, The Netherlands, 1965-76; head nuclear med. dept. Spaarne Hosp., Haarlem, The Netherlands, 1976—; Mem. Dutch Soc. Nuclear Medicine (bd. dirs.), Dutch Soc. Clin. Physics (bd. dirs.), World Fedn. Nuclear Medicine and Biology (bd. dirs.). Home: Rio Grandelaan 45, NL2051LK Overveen The Netherlands Office: Spaarne Hosp, POB 1644, NL2003BR Haarlem The Netherlands

BAETEN, CORNELIUS G.M.I., colorectal surgeon; b. Maastricht, Limburg, The Netherlands, Apr. 4, 1949; s. Alfons M.I.H. and Gerarda M.A. (Steemans) B.; m. Karin J.J. Verstralen, Oct. 13, 1973; children: Coen, Martijn, Titia. MD, K.U.N., Nimjegen, The Netherlands, 1976; postgrad. in surgery, R.L., Maastricht, The Netherlands, 1982, PhD, 1985. Surgeon Acad. Hosp., Maastricht; asst. prof. surgery R.L. Hosp., 1990; cons. Bakken Rsch. Ctr., Maastricht. Contbr. articles to profl. jours. Mem. ASCRS, Ned. Ver. Weelkunde, Ned. Ver. Gastro-Enterology. Roman Catholic. Office: AZM Dept Surgery, PO Box 5800, 6202 A2 Maastricht The Netherlands

BAEZ, WILFRED JOHN, substance abuse counselor, educator; b. S.I., N.Y., Mar. 1, 1956; s. Wilfred John and Maureen Bernadette (Byrne) B.; m. Marcia Ann Cotton, Aug. 9, 1986; children: Nicolas Dale Cotton-Baez, Rebecca Ann Cotton-Baez. BA in Psychology, SUNY, Oswego, 1979; MA in Counseling Psychology, Calif. Inst. Integral Studies, 1981; PhD in Counseling Psycyhology, Columbia Pacific U., 1989. Nationally cert. alcoholism and addictions counselor II; N.Y. state credentialed alcoholism counselor. Psychology intern St. George Homes Residential Treatment Svcs., Berkeley, 1982-83, Southwest Mental Health Svcs., San Francisco, 1983-84; mental health counselor Bayview Hunters Point Found., San Francisco, 1984-85; dir clin svcs., dir. outpatient clinic, alcoholism counselor Alcoholism Coun. Tompkins County, Ithaca, N.Y., 1985-95; substance abuse counselor, educator Nazareth Coll. Counseling Svcs., Rochester, N.Y., 1995—. Mem. Tompkins County Domestic Violence Coalition, Criminal Justice Adv. Bd. and Alternatives to Incarceration Bd. of Tompkins County Bd. of Reps., Tompkins County Child Protective Svcs. Planning Com., Tompkins County PINS Planning Com., 1989, Tompkins County Mental Health Svcs. Screening Com., Tompkins County Stop DWI Program Bd., 1985, Tompkins County Homeless Case Mgmt. Team, 1990. Mem. Am. Assn. Counseling and Devel., N.Y. State Fedn. Alcoholism Counselors. Home: 1100 S Goodman Rochester NY 14620 Office: Alcoholism Coun Tompkins 201 E Green St Ithaca NY 14850-5634

BAGCHI, DEBASIS, toxicologist; b. Santipur, W. Bengal, India, Feb. 28, 1954; came to U.S., 1985; s. Tarak Chandra and Pratima (Ghatak) B.; m. Manashi (Bardhan) B.; 1 child, Dipanjali. BS in Chem. with hons., Jadavpur U., Calcutta, 1973, MS in Chem., 1976; PhD in Medicinal Chemistry, Jadavpur U., 1982; Diploma in Chem. Engring., Indian Inst. Chem. Engrs., Calcutta, 1979. Rsch. and devel. officer Berger India, Ltd., Calcutta, 1982-85; postdoctoral fellow Bowling Green (Ohio) State U., 1985-87, U. Conn., Farmington, 1987-88, 90; devel. mgr. Berger India Ltd., Calcutta, 1988-90; rsch. assoc. prof. Creighton U., Omaha, 1991—. Contbg. author: Lipid Chromatographic Analysis, 1994; contbr. articles to profl. jours. Grantee Health Future Found., Omaha, 1993, 94, Biomed. Rsch. Support Grant, NIH, 1992, Procter & Gamble Co., 1994, Nebrs. State Smoking and Cancer Grant, 1994. Fellow Am. Coll. Nutrition; mem. Soc. Toxicology, N.Y. Acad. Scis. Hindu. Home: 12113 Burdette Cir Omaha NE 68164 Office: Creighton U 2500 California Pla Omaha NE 68178

BAGDASARIAN, ARA DER, surgeon; b. New Britain, Conn., June 27, 1935; s. Richard Der and Elizabeth Der (Garabedian) B.; m. Renate Ziegler, July 31, 1965; children: Rainer, Sabrina, Kristofer. BA, Yale U., 1957; MD, Stanford U., 1961. Diplomate Am. Bd. Surgery. Sr. surgeon Bristol (Conn.) Hosp., 1975—, chmn. dept. surgery, 1975-80, 90-92. Capt. U.S. Army, 1963-65, West Germany. Decorated Army Commendation Medal, 1965. Fellow Am. Coll. Surgeons; mem. New England Vascular Surg. Soc., Hartford County Med. Soc., Conn. State Med. Soc. Office: 25 Newell Rd Ste D-21 Bristol CT 06010

BAGDASARIAN, BORIS, osteopath, researcher; b. Montebello, Calif., Nov. 9, 1964; s. Sarkis and Asia (Janikian) B.; m. Karine Ayvazi, Aug. 5, 1995. BS, U. So. Calif., 1987; DO (magna cum laude), Coll. Osteopathic Medicine Pacific, 1993. Diplomate Nat. Bd. Osteopathic Med. Examiners. Intern internal medicine White Meml. Med. Ctr., L.A., 1993-94, resident, 1993-96, chief resident, 1995-96; fellow hematology-oncology City Hope/Harbor UCLA Med. Ctr., 1996—; adv. bd. White Meml. Med. Ctr., 1995-96. Mem. AMA, ACP (assoc.), Calif. Med. Assn., L.A. County Med. Assn., Sigma Sigma Phi. Republican.

BAGGENSTOS, PIUS A., neurosurgeon; b. Gersau, Switzerland, May 29, 1939; came to U.S., 1972; s. Martin and Cecilia (Camenzind) B.; m. Jennifer O. Folkes, June 4, 1976; children: Martin, Peter. MD, U. Zurich, 1968. Diplomate Am. Bd. Neurol. Surgeons, Am. Bd. Pain Medicine. Resident neurology U. Hamburg, Germany, 1969-71, resudent neurosurgery, 1971-72; rotating intern Summerset Hosp., N.J., 1972; resident gen. surgery St. Peter's hosp., New Brunswick, N.J., 1972-73; resident neurosurgery Downstate Med. Ctr./ Kings County Hosp., Bklyn., 1973-78; asst. clin. prof. U. N.D. Med. Sch., Grand Forks, 1978-81; attending neurosurgeon St. James Cmty. Hosp., Butte, Mont., 1981—; attending neurosurgeon United Hosp., Grand Forks, 1978-81. Mem. Lions (pres. 1994-95). Office: Neurol/Neurosurg Clinic 400 W Porphyry Butte MT 59701

BAGGETT, BILLY, biochemist; b. Oxford, Miss., Oct. 23, 1928; s. Lee and Estelle (Brown) B.; m. Elvira Castro, Aug. 18, 1990; children: Sallie, William, Mary, Teresa, Lane. BA, U. Miss., 1947; PhD in Biochemistry, St. Louis (Mo.) U., 1952. Instr. biol. chemistry Harvard Med. Sch., Boston, 1952-57; asst. in biochem. rsch. Mass. Gen. Hosp., Boston, 1952-57; from asst. prof. to prof. U. N.C., Chapel Hill, 1957-69; prof. Med. U. S.C., Charleston, 1969—. Mem. Am. Chem. Soc., Am. Soc. for Biochemistry and Molecular Biology, Endocrine Soc., Am. Assn. for Cancer Rsch., Soc. for the Study of Reprodn. Home: 102 Shady Ln Isle of Palms SC 29451 Office: Med Univ SC 171 Ashley Ave Charleston SC 29425

BAGGS, JUDITH GEDNEY, critical care nurse, researcher, educator; b. Omaha, Sept. 7, 1942; d. Robert H. and Ellen Edith (Lindquist) Gedney; m. Raymond B. Baggs, June 3, 1962; children: Aaron, Joshua, Kassandra. BA, Reed Coll., Portland, Oreg., 1964; AS in Nursing, North Essex Community Coll., Haverhill, Mass., 1975; BS, Alfred (N.Y.) U., 1981; MS, U. Rochester, 1984, PhD, 1990. RN, N.Y. Asst. prof. U. Rochester, N.Y. Contbr. articles to profl. jours. Recipient Nat. Rsch. Service award, 1988-89, Nat. Inst. Nursing award 1994-97; Isabel Hampton Robb scholar, 1989; Sproull fellow, 1986-88. Mem. ANA, AACN, N.Y. State Nurses Assn., Sigma Theta Tau.

BAGLEY, DEMETRIUS H., urologist, educator, researcher; b. Whitefield, N.H., Aug. 21, 1945; s. Demetrius H. and Myrtle (Nolan) B.; m. Jacqueline L. Hickey, May 30, 1970; 1 child, D. Jacques. B.A., Johns Hopkins U., 1966, M.D., 1970. Diplomate Am. Bd. Urology. Intern Yale-New Haven Hosp., 1970-71; resident, 1971-72, 75-79; instr. Sch. Medicine, Yale U., New Haven, 1978-79; asst. prof. U. Chgo., 1979-83, assoc. prof., 1983; assoc. prof. urology Thomas Jefferson U., Phila., 1983-88, prof. urology, 1988—, prof. radiology, 1989—. Author: Endoscopic Urology: A Manual and Atlas, 1985co-author: Ureteroscopy, 1988, Techniques in Flexible Ureteroscopy, 1991, Smith's Textbook of Endourology; editor jour. Endourology, Surgical Endoscopy, Ultrasound and Interventional Technology, Diagnostic and Therapeutic Endoscopy; assoc. editor Diagnostic and Therapeutic Endoscopy; also numerous articles, 1968—. Served to asst. surgeon USPHS, 1972-75. Fellow ACS, Coll. Physicians Phila.; mem. Am. Urol. Assn., Internat. Soc. Urologic Endoscopy, Endourology Soc., Soc. Univ. Urologists, Am. Lithotripsy Soc., Soc. Internat. d'Urol., Phila. Urological Soc. (pres. 1995-96), Phila. Med. Club. Avocations: photography, antiques, fishing. Home: 506 Spruce St Philadelphia PA 19106-4112 Office: Thomas Jefferson U Dept Urology 1025 Walnut St Philadelphia PA 19107

BAGLEY, JOHN NEFF, social worker, consultant; b. Murray, Utah, Apr. 21, 1944; s. Ben and Marie (Pearson) B.; m. Meggin Catmull, Nov. 18, 1981. BS, U. Utah, 1966, MSW, 1973. Lic. clin. social worker, marriage and family counselor, Utah. Sch. social worker Salt Lake City Bd. of Edn., 1973-74; psychiat. social worker Holy Cross Hosp., Salt Lake City, 1974-76; alcohol and drug counselor County of Salt Lake, 1976-78; dir. Salt Lake City Recovery Ctr., 1978-79; clin. social worker Ctrl. Utah Counseling and Consultation, 1982—; mem. grad. faculty social work U. Utah, 1975—, Human Affairs, Ltd., Richfield, 1987—, Gunnison (Utah) Hosp., 1988—, U.S. Behavior Health, 1995—, Sorenson's Ranch Sch., Koosharem, Utah, 1990-96; with Employee Assistance Program Utah Power and Light Co., Richfield, 1986—, Bur. Land Mgmt., Richfield, 1986—, Dept. of Corrections, Gunnison, Utah, 1984—, Heritage Youth Svcs., 1996—. Capt. USAF, 1967-71, Vietnam. Home: 1109 N 2450 W Monroe UT 84754-3447 Office: Ctrl Utah Counseling & Cons 108 N Main PO Box 421 Richfield UT 84701

BAGLI, VINCENT JOSEPH, plastic surgeon; b. Paterson, N.J., Aug. 6, 1925; s. Charles Vincent Badagliacca and Teresa Jane (Viviano) B.; m. Dorothy Jesse Lalli, Oct. 25, 1952; children: Charles, Thomas, Susan, Jeanne, Mary, Carolyn, James, Robert, Patricia, Nancy, Regina, Christopher. MD, Georgetown U., 1951. Diplomate Am. Bd. Plastic Surgery. Commd. 1st lt. USAF, 1951, advanced through grades to maj., 1959, resigned, 1962; intern Walter Reed Army Med. Ctr., Washington, 1951-52; resident in surgery Brooke Army Hosp., San Antonio, 1952-53, Univ. Hosps. of Cleve., 1953-54; resident in plastic surgery St. Barnabas Hosp., Newark, 1955-57; chief plastic surgery Wayne (N.J.) Gen. Hosp., 1963-75, Hackensack (N.J.) Med. Ctr., 1975-91; pres. Bergen Plastic Surg. Group, Paramus, N.J., 1979-92; bd. dirs. Jersey Bank for Savs., Montvale; sec. Bergen Med. Ctr., Paramus, 1985-92; cons. plastic surgeon N.E. area Office Surgeon Gen., Washington, 1960-63; asst. prof. plastic surgery N.J. Coll. Medicine, Newark, 1968-92. Bd. dirs. Salesian Sisters of St. John Bosco, 1990—. Fellow Am. Coll. Surgeons; mem. N.J. Soc. Plastic Surgeons (pres. 1978-79), Am. Soc. Plastic and Reconstructive Surgery, Am. Soc. Aesthetic Plastic Surgeons, N.Y. Regional Soc. Plastic Surgery, Plantation Country Club (Ponte Vedra Beach, Fla.). Republican. Roman Catholic. Home: 111 Mayfair Ln Ponte Vedra Beach FL 32082-3917 Office: Bergen Plastic Surg Group One W Ridgewood Ave Paramus NJ 07652

BAGSHAW, MALCOLM A., radiation oncologist, educator; b. Adrian, Mich., 1925. MD, Yale U., 1950. Diplomate Am. Bd. Radiology. Surg. intern Grace-New Haven Hosp., 1950-51, resident in surg. pathology, 1951-52; resident in radiology U. Mich., 1953-56, clin. instr. radiology, 1955-56; instr. Stanford U., Palo Alto, Calif., 1956-59, asst. prof., 1959-62, assoc. prof., 1962-69, prof., 1969-92, prof. emeritus, 1992—, dir. div. radiation therapy, 1960-92, chmn. radiology dept., 1972-86, chmn. radiation oncology dept., 1986-92; resident etranger Inst. Gustave-Roussy, France, 1962-63; cons. radiation therapy VA Hosp., Palo Alto, Calif., 1960-92. Mem. AMA. Office: Stanford U Med Ctr 300 Pasteur Dr Palo Alto CA 94304-2203

BAHADUE, GEORGE PAUL, general and family physician; b. Havana, Cuba, June 29, 1954; came to U.S., 1959; s. Teodosio and Carmen (Chabali) B.; m. Lori Dee Stampler, June 11, 1983; children: Felicia Lynn, Suria, George Paul Jr. BS cum laude, U. Miami, Coral Gables, Fla., 1978; DO, Coll. Osteo. Medicine, Kirksville, Mo., 1982. Diplomate Nat. Bd. Examiners, Nat. Bd. Examiners for Osteo. Physicians and Surgeons. Am. Osteo. Assn. rotating intern Southeastern Med. Ctr., North Miami Beach, Fla., 1982-83, resident in internal medicine, 1984; pvt. practice gen. and family medicine North Miami Beach, 1984-92; with pediatric emergency room Parkway Regional Med. Ctr., North Miami Beach, 1993-94; gen. medicine and pediatrics Town & Country Med. Ctr., Miami, 1993—; with Internat. Health Svcs., North Miami Beach, 1994—, Camillus Health Concern, Miami, 1996—; asst. clin. prof. Southeastern U. Coll. Osteo. Medicine, North Miami Beach, 1984—; active dept. family medicine Parkway Hosp., North Miami Beach, 1990—; preceptor Coll. Osteo. Medicine of te Pacific, 1986. Del. annual conv. Student Osteo. Med. Assn., 1980; mem. Republican Senatorial Inner Circle, Washington, 1990; charter mem. U.S. Com. for the Battle of Normandy Mus., Washington, 1990; mem. Republican Presdl. Task Force, Washington, 1990 (Recognition award 1990), Psi Chi; vol. svc. to homeless Family Migrant Pediatric Clinic/Camillus Health Concern, 1994, also to victims of hurricane Andrew, 1993. Honors scholar and Jane P. Simmons Sci. scholar U. Miami, 1976-78; recipient Honors award City of North Miami Beach, 1984-90. Mem. Soc. Critical Care Medicine, Dade County Med. Assn., Delta Theta Mu, Alpha Epsilon Delta (v.p. 1976-77, del. nat. conv. Ala. 1977). Republican. Roman Catholic. Home: 19665 E Saint Andrews Dr Hialeah FL 33015 Office: Camillus Health Concern 726 NE 1st Ave Miami FL 33101

BAHL, SAROJ MEHTA, nutritionist, educator; b. New Delhi, India, Apr. 4, 1946; came to U.S., 1972; d. L.D. and G.D. Mehta; m. Vishwa Mittar Bahl; children: Rahul, Ragini. BS in Home Sci., Delhi U., 1965, MS in Nutrition, 1967, PhD in Nutrition, 1973. Lectr. Lady Irwin Coll., New Delhi, 1970-71; instr. U. N.D., Grand Forks, 1972-74; rsch. assoc. U. Tex. Med. Sch., Houston, 1976-78; asst. prof. U. Tex. Sch. Allied Health, Houston, 1979-87, assoc. prof., 1987—; program dir. Peace Corps, Houston, 1984. Co-author: Sports Nutrition, Nutritional Management of the AIDS Patient; contbr. articles to profl. jours. Den leader Boy Scouts Am., Hosuton, 1983; mem. ednl. com. March of Dimes, Houston, 1986—. Recipient several awards for teaching excellence; nominated for U.S. Prof. of Yr., 1993, 94. Mem. Am. Inst. Life Threatening Illness (assoc.), Soc. Nutrition Edn. (editor newsletter). Office: U Tex Sch Allied Health 7000 Fannin St Ste 2440D Houston TX 77030-5502

BAHR, CARMAN BLOEDOW, internist; b. Middletown, Ohio, Mar. 24, 1931; d. Edwin Louis and Berneice Mae (Bacon) Bloedow; m. Walter Julien Bahr, Aug. 28, 1968 (dec. Sept. 1971). BA cum laude, Miami U., Oxford, Ohio, 1952; MD, Ohio State U., 1956. Cert. diabetes educator, 1992. Intern St. Luke's Hosp., Chgo., 1956-57; resident U. Okla. Health Sci. Ctr., 1971; assoc. prof. medicine Okla. City VA-U. Okla. Health Sci. Ctr., 1971-93, prof. emeritus, 1993—. Fellow ACP; mem. AMA (Physician's Recognition award 1976, 79, 82, 85, 88, 91, 93), Am. Diabetes Assn. (chpt. pres. 1989, Rober Endress award 1985), Am. Assn. Diabetes Educators, Western Okla. Di abetes Educators, Am. Med. Women's Assn. Home: 5609 N Everest Av Oklahoma City OK 73111-6729 Office: VA Med Ctr 921 NE 13th S Oklahoma City OK 73104-5007

BAHR, ROBERT LAWRENCE, ophthalmology educator; b. N.Y.C., Ma 12, 1945; s. Henry H. and Lore S. (Barth) B.; m. Susan J. Steinberg, June 28 1970; children: Talia M., Danielle N., Jonathan A. BA, Williams Coll. 1967; MD, Harvard Med. Sch., 1971. Diplomate Am. Bd. Ophthalmology Am. Bd. Med. Examiners. Intern Mt. Sinai Hosp., N.Y.C., 1971-72; residen in ophthalmology Yale U., New Haven, 1972-75, fellow in glaucoma rsch. 1972-74; asst. prof. Ophthalmology Yale U. Sch. Medicine, New Haven 1975-82; ophthalmologist The R.I. Eye Inst., Providence, 1976—; asst. clin prof. Ophthalmology Brown Med. Sch., Providence, 1976—; chief ophthalmology Miriam Hosp., Providence, 1991—. Contbr. articles to profl. jours. Capt. USAR, 1972-78. Fellow Am. Acad. Ophthalmology; mem. Am. Soc. Cataract and Refractive Surgery, New Eng. Ophthalmological Soc., R.I. Soc. Eye Physicians and Surgeons, Univ. Club, Aesculapian Club. Jewish. Home: 41 Cooke St Providence RI 02906-3101 Office: The RI Eye Inst 150 E Manning St Providence RI 02906-5109 also: Eye Surgery Group 386 High St Fall River MA 02720-3347

BAHRANI, MAHMOUD ABDUL HADI, pediatrician; b. Baghdad, Mar. 28, 1938; s. Abdul Hadi Abdul Kareem and Ghania (Hussain) B.; m. Sundus Mohammed Ali Imam, Nov. 17, 1967; children: Saba, Abdul Hadi, Ghena, Hassan. MBChB, U. Baghdad, 1961. Diplomate Am. Bd. Pediatric Medicine. Intern Duke U. Med. Ctr., 1963; resident in pediatrics Case Western U. Hosp., Cleve., 1963-66, rsch. fellow in metabolism, 1967; dir. pediatrics Yarmook Hosp. U. Mustanseria, Baghdad, 1967-70, Al-Karama Hosp. U. Baghdad, 1970-79; pvt. practice Imam Hosp., Baghdad, 1979—. Contbr. articles to profl. jours. Gulf area cons. UNICEF, Baghdad, 1986. Res. lt. Iraqi Army, 1961-62. Mem. Iraqi Med. Assn., Iraqi Pediatric Assn. Islam. Home: PO Box 725, Amman 11821, Iraq

BAHRKE, MICHAEL STEVEN, sport psychologist, educator, research analyst; b. Racine, Wis., Nov. 6, 1949; s. Milton Anthony and Betty Jean (Ferch) B.; m. Sally Warner, Aug. 22, 1971; children, Ryan, Erin. BS, U. Wis., LaCrosse, 1971; MS, U. Wis., Madison, 1973, PhD, 1977. Asst. prof. U. Kans., Lawrence, 1977-83; rsch. dir. U.S. Army Phys. Fitness Sch., Ft. Harrison, Ind., 1983-91; lectr. U. Wis., Madison, 1991-92; project dir. dept. epidemiology/biostatistics, sr. rsch. analyst U. Ill., Chgo., 1992-94; dir. devel. Human Kinetics, Champaign, Ill., 1994—. Contbr. articles to profl. jours. Fellow Am. Coll. Sports Medicine; mem. Nat. Strength and Conditioning Assn. Roman Catholic. Home: 402 Arbours Dr Savoy IL 61874-9669 Office: Human Kinetics Dept Epidemiology/Biostats 1607 N Market St Champaign IL 61825-5076

BAIER, EDWARD JOHN, former public health official, industrial hygiene engineer, consultant; b. Pitts., Apr. 1, 1925; s. Edward O. and Lucy M. Baier; m. Grace Cecelia McDonald, Jan. 15, 1947; children: Edward Michael, Grace Cecelia. B.S., U. Pitts., 1946, M.P.H. (fellow), 1955. Lic. indsl. hygienist, Ill.; cert. in comprehensive practice of indsl. hygiene, internat. hazard control mgmt., hazardous materials mgmt.; cert. safety profl. Chief indsl. hygiene sect. Dept. Health State of Pa., 1956-68, dir. div. occupational health, 1968-71; dir. div. occupational health Dept. Environ. Resources, 1971; dir. Bur. Mines and Occupational Health and Safety, 1971-72; dep. dir. Nat. Inst. for Occupational Safety and Health, HEW, Rockville, Md., 1972-78; corp. dir. indsl. hygiene and toxicology Diamond Shamrock Corp., Cleve., Dallas, 1978-82; dir. tech. support OSHA, Dept. Labor, 1982-89; cons. in occupational and environ. health and safety, 1989—; lectr. in field. Contbr. articles to profl. jours. Chmn. West Shore council Boy Scouts Am., 1970-71; sec. Upper Allen Twp. (Pa.) Sewer Authority, 1970-72. Mem. Am. Conf. Govt. Indsl. Hygienists (chmn. 1968-69), Am. Indsl. Hygiene Assn. (pres. 1975-76, Cummings Meml. award, Edward J. Baier Tech. Achievement award 1984), Am. Acad. Indsl. Hygiene (founder, pres. 1987-88), Indsl. Hygiene Roundtable (steward 1975-76), Inst. Hazardous Materials Mgmt. (cert. hazardous materials mgrs. bd. examiners 1991—, bd. dirs. 1992—, vice chmn. 1993—), Nat. Am. Indian Safety Coun., N.Y. Acad. Scis., Pa. Soc. Profl. Engrs., Am. Bd. Indsl. Hygiene (bd. dirs. 1970-76). Roman Catholic.

BAIERLEIN, JEAN L., mental health counselor; b. Phila., Jan. 19, 1940; d. Paul and Anne (Merkle) Lennox; m. Ralph Baierlein, June 12, 1965; children: Eric, Jeff. BA, Swarthmore Coll., 1961; PhD, Boston U., 1967; MA, St. Joseph Coll., 1988. Rsch. technician Harvard Med. Sch./McLean Hosp., Belmont, Mass., 1961-62; NIH fellow Wesleyan U., Middletown, Conn., 1967-69; pvt. practice counselor Middletown, 1987—; psychotherapist Community Health Ctr., 1988-89; clin. supr. Sexual Assault Crisis Svc., Meriden, Conn., 1990—; organizer counseling workshops for disabled, 1984-87. Vol. Battered Women's Shelter, Middletown, 1985-87; mem. Conn. Coalition for Citizens with Disabilities, 1985—. Mem. ACA, Am. Mental Health Counselors Assn. Home and Office: 613 Main St Portland CT 06480-1142

BAIGIS, JUDITH ANN, nursing educator, university official; b. Washington, Pa., July 26, 1941; d. Andrew J. and Mary Margaret (Mitchell) Baigis; m. Robert Wachbroit, June 26, 1989. Diploma, Geisinger Hosp. Sch. Nursing, Danville, Pa., 1962; BS, NYU, 1968, PhD, 1979. RN, Md., D.C. Instr. nursing NYU, N.Y.C., 1970-73, CUNY Lehman Coll., Bronx, N.Y., 1973-79; dir. community health nursing program U. Pa. Sch. Nursing, Phila., 1979-87; dir. long-term care Johns Hopkins U. Sch. Nursing, Balt., 1987-92; assoc. dean for rsch. Georgetown U. Sch. Nursing, Washington, 1992—. Contbr. articles to nursing jours. Nat. Inst. Nursing Rsch. grantee, 1988-96. Mem. ANA, APHA, Am. Acad. Nursing, Assn. Community Health Nursing Educators. Office: Georgetown U Sch Nursing Box 571107 3700 Reservoir Rd NW Washington DC 20057-1107

BAIGROS, JOSE ALBERTO, chiropractor, researcher; b. Zarate, Argentina, Nov. 22, 1950; s. Julio and Maria Luisa (Falicoff) B.; m. Patricia Monica Sontag, Jan. 24, 1976; children: Paula Carcina, Marcela Florencia. MD, U. Buenos Aires, Argentina, 1973. Dir. Argentine Med. Chiropractic Ctr., Buenos Aires, 1978—; prof. biomechs. Ministry of Edn., Argentina, 1988; pres. Argentine Med. Chiropractic Ctr., Buenos Aires, 1992—; cmty. svc. Radio FM 88, Fla., Buenos Aires, 1996. Mem. Am. Acad. Pain Mgmt., Punta Chica (Argentina) Rotary Club, Club Belgrano Social. Home: Arribenos 1697, 1426 Buenos Aires Argentina Office: Arenales 961 1 3, 1061 Buenos Aires Argentina

BAILAR, JOHN CHRISTIAN, III, public health educator, physician, statistician; b. Urbana, Ill., Oct. 9, 1932; married; 4 children. BA, U. Colo., 1953; MD, Yale U., 1955; PhD in Stats., Am. U., 1973. Intern U. Colo. Med. Ctr., Denver, 1955-56; field investigator, biometry br. Nat Cancer Inst., NIH, Bethesda, Md., 1956-62, head demography sect., 1962-70, dir. 3d nat. cancer survey, 1967-70, dep. assoc. dir. for cancer control, 1972-74; editor-in-chief JNCI, 1974-80; dir. research service VA, Washington, 1970-72; lectr. in biostats. Harvard U., Cambridge, Mass., 1980-87; prof. McGill U., Montreal, 1987-95; chair dept. epidemiology and biostats. McGill U., Can., 1993-95; sr. scientist Office Disease Prevention and Health Promotion, Dept. HHS, Washington, 1983-92; chmn. dept. health studies U. Chgo., 1995—; sr. scientist health and environ. rev. divsn. EPA, 1980-83; lectr. epidemiology and pub. health Yale U., New Haven, Conn., 1958-83; mem. faculty math. and stats. USDA Grad. Sch., Washington, 1966-76; vis. prof. stats. SUNY, Buffalo, 1974-80; professorial lectr. George Washington U., Washington, 1975-80; cons. in biostats. and epidemiology Dana-Farber Cancer Inst., Boston, 1977-83; vis. prof. Harvard U., 1977-79; spl. appointment grad. faculty U. Colo. Med. Ctr., Denver, 1979-81; scholar in residence NAS, 1992-96. Mem. editorial adv. bd. Cancer Rsch., 1968-72; statis. cons. New Eng. Jour. Medicine, 1980-91; mem. bd. editors New England Jour. Medicine, 1992—; contbr. numerous articles to profl. jours.; editor JNCI, 1974-80. John D. and Catherine T. MacArthur Found. fellow, 1990-95. Fellow AAAS, Am. Coll. Epidemiology, Am. Statis. Assn. (chair-elect and chair biometric sect. 1979-81, chair sect. stats. and environment 1990); mem. Inst. of Medicine, Internat. Statis. Inst., Coun. Biology Editors (chair publishing policy com. 1983-89, pres.-elect, pres., past pres. 1986-89), Soc. Risk Analysis (founding chair Boston chpt. 1985-86). Office: U Chgo Divsn Biol Scis MC-2007 5841 S Maryland Ave Chicago IL 60637-1470

BAILE, CLIFTON A., biologist, researcher; b. Warrensburg, Mo., Feb. 8, 1940; s. Harold F. and Salome (Mohler) B.; m. Beth Lucile Hoover, Aug. 21, 1960; children: Christopher A., Marisa B. BS in Agr., Bus., Cen. Mo. State U., 1962; PhD in Nutrition, U. Mo., 1965; MA (hon.), U. Pa., 1979. NIH rsch. fellow Sch. Pub. Health Harvard U., Boston, 1964-66, from. instr. to asst. prof. Sch. Pub. Health, 1966-71; mgr. neurobiol. rsch. SmithKline Animal Health, Phila., 1971-75; from assoc. prof. to prof. Sch. Vet. Medicine U. Pa., Phila., 1975-82; disting. fellow, dir. R & D Monsanto Agrl. Co., St. Louis, 1982-95; adj. prof. nutrition Sch. Medicine Washington U., St. Louis, 1982—; adj. prof. dept. animal sci. U. Mo., 1982—; disting. prof. animal sci. and food and nutrition, spl. asst. to v.p. rsch. and exec. v.p. U. Ga. Rsch. Found.; presentor numerous seminars and symposiums. Contbr. over 225 articles and 200 abstracts to sci. jours. Ralston Purina rsch. fellow, 1962-64, NIH spl. postdoctoral fellow, 1969. Mem. Am. Soc. Animal Sci. (bd. dirs. 1990-93, animal growth and devel. award 1989), Am. Physiol. Soc., Am. Inst. Nutrition, Am. Dairy Sci. Assn. (Am. Feed Mgmt. award 1979), Soc. Neurosci. Office: Univ Ga 708 Boyd 6SRC Athens GA 30602-7401

BAILEY, BARBARA JEAN, retired nurse; b. Spooner, Wis., Oct. 13, 1932; d. Edward Rydberg and Linda C. (Nystrom); m. Charles Swanson, July 3, 1953 (dec. May 1980); children: Jerri, Jan, Joan, Jill; m. James D. Bailey, Sept. 18, 1981; children: Dianne, Andrea. Diploma in nursing, Hamline U., St. Paul, Minn., 1953. RN, Ariz. Staff nurse Rush City (Minn.) Community Hosp., 1953-54; supr. Indianhead Med. Ctr., Shell Lake, Wis., 1962-86; staff nurse Terraceview Living Ctr., Shell Lake, 1986-87; charge nurse ARA Living Ctr., Sun City, Ariz., 1987-88, Sun Grove Care Ctr., Sun City, 1988-93, Wooddale Healthcare Ctr., Sun City, Ariz., 1993—. Sec. Washburn County Rep. Party, Wis., 1986-87; county chmn. Kasten for Senator Com., Shell Lake, 1986. Mem. Shell Lake Lioness Club (sec. 1986-87), Mid-Week Lioness of Sun City (pres. 1992-93, v.p. 1995-96), Mid-Week Lions Club. Methodist. Home: 10402 W Sombrero Cir Sun City AZ 85373-1338

BAILEY, DAVID HOWARD, health facility administrator; b. Indpls., May 9, 1960; s. Robert L. and Ruth H. (Taylor) B.; m. Stephanie Rene Mertens; 1 child, Morgan Rene. A in Bus. Adminstrn., Ind. U., 1981, BS in Med. Records Adminstrn., 1984. Registered records adminstr. Dir. med. records Jasper County Hosp., Rensselaer, Ind., 1985-88; cons. Humana, Inc., Louisville, Ky., 1988-89; dir. quality enhancement St. Joseph Hosp. and Health Ctr., Kokomo, Ind., 1989-91; dir. info. mgmt. HCA L.W. Blake Hosp., Bradenton, Fla., 1991-95; dir. quality mgmt. Kokomo Rehab. Hosp., 1995—; owner Record Rev., Inc. Cons. Svc., Bradenton, 1991-95. Coord. hosp. United Way, Kokomo, 1995. Mem. Am. Health Info. Mgmt. Assn., Am. Coll. Health Care Execs. (assoc.), Ind. Health Info. Mgmt. Assn. (chmn. programs 1988-89, chmn. legis. 1989-90). Office: Kokomo Rehab Hosp 829 N Dixon Rd Kokomo IN 46901

BAILEY, DAVID MICHAEL, physician; b. Aberdeen, S.D., Oct. 18, 1951; s. Timothy Clement and Mary Bernadine (Artz) B.; m. Janis Lynn Cazzell. BS, Cen. Mo., 1974; MD, U. Okla., 1981. Diplomate Am. Bd. Internal Medicine, added qualifications in geriatric medicine. Intern in internal medicine U. Okla. Teaching Hosps., Oklahoma City, 1981-82, resident in internal medicine, 1982-84; staff physician St. Anthony Hosp., Oklahoma City, 1984—, vice chmn. dept. of medicine, 1988-91; pvt. practice Assocs. in Internal Medicine, Oklahoma City, 1984-91; staff physician Health South Rehab. Hosp., 1988—, sec. med. staff, 1988—; staff physician Okla. Neurosurg. Inst. Spine Ctr., Oklahoma City, 1991-96, Columbia Sr. Health, Oklahoma City, Okla., 1996—, Columbia Presbyn. Hosp., Oklahoma City, 1996—. Mem. AMA, ACP, ASIM, Okla. State Med. Assn., Okla. County Med. Soc. Office: Columbia Sr Health Physicians and Surgeons Bldg 2700 Villa Prom Oklahoma City OK 73107

BAILEY, DAVID NELSON, pathologist, educator; b. Anderson, Ind., June 21, 1945; s. Omer Nelson and Louise Genevieve (Hurst) B. BS with high distinction, Ind. U., 1967; MD, Yale U., 1973. Diplomate Nat. Bd. Med. Examiners, Am. Bd. Pathology (Clin. and Chem. Pathology). Clin. fellow dept. lab. medicine Yale U., 1973-75; asst. resident specializing in clin. pathology Yale-New Haven (Conn.) Hosp., 1975-76, chief resident specializing in clin. pathology, 1976-77; asst. prof. pathology U. Calif. San Diego, 1977-81, assoc. prof. pathology, 1981-86, prof. pathology, 1986—, head div. lab. medicine, 1983-89, 94—; acting chmn., 1986-88; chmn. dept. pathology U. Calif. San Diego, 1988—; dir. toxicology lab. U. Calif. Med. Ctr., San Diego, 1977—, dir. clin. labs., 1982—. Mem. editorial bd. Jour. Analytical Toxicology, 1979—, Clin. Chemistry Jour., 1983-93, Am. Jour. Clin. Pathology, 1991—; contbr. articles to profl. jours. Recipient Gerald T. Evans award Acad. Clin. Lab. Physicians and Scientists, 1993; Merit scholar Ind. U., 1963-65, Arthur R. Metz scholar, 1965-67. Mem. Calif. Assn. Toxicologists (pres. 1981-82), Acad. Clin. Lab. Physicians and Scientists (pres. 1988-89), Am. Assn. Clin. Chemistry, Am. Chem. Soc., Assn. Pathology Chmn. (sec.-treas. 1996—), Phi Lambda Upsilon, Alpha Omega Alpha. Office: U Calif Med Ctr San Diego Dept Pathology 200 W Arbor Dr San Diego CA 92103-8320

BAILEY, DEENA TAMARA, health care administrator; b. Haifa, Israel, June 13, 1947; came to U.S., 1960; d. Fred Ephraim and Devora (Glaser) Mansbacher; m. Wayne W. Bailey, Apr. 4, 1970 (div. 1977); 1 child, Devora Elyse. BS in Health Sci., U. Redlands, 1989; MHA, U. So. Calif., 1995. Mgr. dept. surgery Cedars-Sinai Med. Ctr., L.A., 1980-87; mgr. cardiovascular intervention ctr. Cedars-Sinai Med. Ctr., 1988-93; dir. Cardiology Mgmt. Svcs., 1993-94; adminstrv. resident UniHealth, Burbank, Calif., 1994-95; adminstrv. dir. UniHealth-Arroyo Seco Med. Group/Mgmt. Svcs., 1995—. Mem. Health Care Execs. So. Calif., Women in Health Adminstrn. (pres. 1993), Am. Coll. Cardiovasc. Adminstrs. (regional dir. 1990-92), Am. Coll. Health Care Execs., (assoc.), U. So. Calif. Health Svcs. Adminstrs. Alumni Assn. (pres. 1996-97), Med. Group Mgmt. Assn., Calif. Med. Group Mgmt. Assn., L.A. Med. Group Mgmt. Assn. Democrat. Jewish.

BAILEY, F(RANCIS) WILLIAM, social worker; b. Kingston, N.Y., Mar. 11, 1927; s. Frank Patrick and Catherine Dolores (Dugan) B.; m. Rosalie Marie Vuocolo, Apr. 19, 1952; children: Mary, Irene, Kathleen, William, Teresa. BS, St. Peters U., 1948; MS, Fordham U., 1950; postgrad., Rutgers U. Diplomate Am. Bd. Social Work; cert. social worker; lic. marriage counselor. Clin. coord. Mt. Carmel Guild Multi-Svc. Ctr., Newark, 1959-72; clin. coord., project dir. Cen. Bergen Community Mental Health Ctr., Paramus, N.J., 1972-77; asst. adminstr. Greystone Park Hosp., Parsippany, N.J., 1978-80; pvt. practice Paramus, 1970—. Pres. Mental Health Advocacy Group, Ft. Lee, N.J., 1990; mem. N.J. Community Mental Health Bd., Trenton, N.J., 1990. Mem. NASW, Mental Health Assn. N.J. (pub. policy com. 1980—). Roman Catholic. Office: 107 Stella Ct Paramus NJ 07652-3816

BAILEY, HAROLD RANDOLPH, surgeon; b. Palestine, Tex., Jan. 20, 1943; m. Kelly Curry Bailey. BA in Biology summa cum laude, Rice U., 1964; MD, U. Tex., 1968. Diplomate Am. Bd. Surgery, Am. Bd. Colon and Rectal Surgery (assoc. examiner 1985-89, bd. dirs. 1989—, chmn. examination com. 1994—, active examination com. 1992—); mem. residency rev. com. colon and rectal surgery, 1993—. Intern straight surg. Parkland Hosp., Dallas, 1968-69; resident gen. surgery U. Tex. Med. Sch./Hermann Hosp., Houston, 1969-73; fellow colon and rectal surgery Ferguson-Droste-Ferguson Hosp., Grand Rapids, Mich., 1973-74; clin. faculty U. Tex. Med. Sch., Houston, 1974—, dir. residency tng. program colon and rectal surgery, 1984—, clin. prof. surgery, 1986—; clin. asst. prof. surgery Baylor Coll. Medicine, 1980—, clin. faculty, 1986—; assoc. examiner Am. Bd. Colon and Rectal Surgery, 1985-89, bd. mem., 1989—, chmn. exam. com., 1994—, exam. com., 1992—, residency rev. com. colon and rectal surgery 1993—); chief staff Park Plaza Hosp., Houston, 1988-90. Bd. dirs. Am. Cancer Soc., Greater Houston unit, 1989—, v.p., 1991-93, pres., 1993-95; mem. vestry Palmer Meml. Episcopal Ch., Houston, 1979-83, 84-86, chmn. fin. com., 1984-86; mem. fund coun. Rice U., Houston, 1993-94, class fund drive chmn. 1993-95). Recipient George Waldron award Hermann Hosp., 1970, Violet Keller award, 1973; named to Good Housekeeping mag. 400 Best Doctors in U.S., 1991, Good Housekeepingmag. Best Cancer Doctors in U.S., 1993. Fellow ACS, Internat. Soc. Univ. Colon and Rectal Surgeons (program com. 1986), Am. Soc. Colon and Rectal Surgeons (treas., exec. coun. 1993—), Tex. Surg. Soc.; mem. AMA, Tex. Soc. Colon and Rectal Surgeons (pres. 1981, exec. sec. 1982-88), Soc. Am. Gastrointestinal Endoscopic Surgeons, Tex. Med. Assn., Tex. Soc. Gastrointestinal Endoscopy, Harris County Med. Soc., Houston Surg. Soc., Phi Beta Kappa, Alpha Omega Alpha. Office: Colon & Rectal Clinic 6550 Fannin St Ste 2307 Houston TX 77030-2723*

BAILEY, JOSELYN ELIZABETH, physician; b. Pine Bluff, Ark.; d. Joseph Alexander and Angeline Elaine (Davis) B.; B.Mus., Manhattanville Coll., 1952; M.Music Edn., Manhattan Sch. Music, 1954; M.D., Howard U., 1971. Straight med. intern Huntington Meml. Hosp., Pasadena, Calif., 1971-72, resident, 1972-74; fell in nephrology Wadsworth VA Hosp., Los Angeles, 1975-77; practice medicine specializing in internal medicine and nephrology, Torrance, Calif.; assoc. staff Torrance Meml., South Bay; active Little Company of Mary hosps.; attending staff Harbor Gen. Hosp.; clin. faculty Dept. Medicine, UCLA; active staff Bay Harbor Hosp., trustee, 1982—.

BAILEY, LEONARD LEE, surgeon; b. Takoma Park, Md., Aug. 28, 1942; s. Nelson Hulburt and Catherine Effie (Long) B.; m. Nancy Ann Schroeder, Aug. 21, 1966; children: Jonathan Brooks, Charles Connor. BS, Columbia Union Coll., 1960-64; postgrad., NIH, 1965; MD, Loma Linda U., 1969. Diplomate Am. Bd. Surgery, Am. Bd. Thoracic Surgery. Intern Loma Linda U. Med. Ctr., 1969-70, resident in surgery, 1970-73, resident in thoracic and cardiovascular surgery, 1973-74; resident in pediatric cardiovascular surgery Hosp. for Sick Children, Toronto, Ont., Can., 1974-75; resident in thoracic and cardiovascular surgery Loma Linda U. Med. Sch., 1975-76, asst. prof. surgery, 1976-86, prof. surgery, 1986—, dir. pediatric cardiac surgery, 1976—, chief div. cardiothoracic surgery, 1988-92, chair dept. surgery, 1992—. Mem. ACS, AATS, Am. Surg. Assn., Am. Coll. Cardiology, Western Thoracic Surg. Assn., Soc. Thoracic Surgery, Western Soc. Pediatric Rsch., Internat. Soc. for Heart Transplantation, Am. Heart Assn., Internat. Assn. for Cardiac Biol. Implants, Am. Soc. for Artificial Internal Organs, Pacific Coast Surg. Assn., Western Assn. Transplant Surgeons, Internat. Soc. for Cardiovascular Surgery, United Network for Organ Sharing, The Transplant Soc. Democrat. Adventist. Office: Loma Linda U Med Ctr Rm 2584 Loma Linda CA 92354

BAILEY, MARY ETTA, food services director; b. Chattanooga, Tenn., June 23, 1947; d. Walter Raymond and Elizabeth Bell; m. Bob Lee Bailey, Aug. 20, 1961; children: Sallie Josephine, Mary Elizabeth. AS, Northeast Coll., Rainsville, Ala., 1968; BS in Edn., Jacksonville State Coll., 1971; intern, U. Ala., Birmingham, 1973. Registered dietitian. Dietitian Huntsville (Ala.) Hosp., 1971-72; food svcs. dir. Bapt. Med. Ctr. DeKalb, Fort Payne, Ala., 1974—; cons. DeKalb County Jail, Fort Payne, 1983—. Mem. DeKalb County Bd. of Edn., Fort Payne, Ala., 1982—; dir. DeKalb Bapt. Assn. Discipleship Tng., Rainsville, Ala., 1986-91, 94—, Sunday sch. dir., 1991-93; chmn. DeKalb County Library Bd., 1992-94., treas. 1994—. Named Outstnding Dietetic Intern U. Ala., Med. Ctr. Birmingham, 1973. Mem. Am. Dietetic Assn., Ala. Dietetic Assn. (newsletter editor, 1976-78, sec. 1978-79, pres. elect, 1979, pres. 1980), Ala. Diabetes Assn., (sec. 1982-83). Democrat. Home: PO Box 387 Rainsville AL 35986-0387 Office: Bapt Med Ctr DeKalb 200 Medical Center Dr Fort Payne AL 35967-9545

BAILEY, ROBIN KEITH, physician assistant, perfusionist; b. St. Petersburg, Fla., Jan. 8, 1951; s. Albert Hugh and Kathleen Elizabeth (Badgley) B. AA, St. Petersburg Jr. Coll., 1973; BS in Pub. Rels. in Criminal Justice, U. Fla., 1976, B Health Sci., 1984; cert., Newark Beth Israel Med. Ctr., 1990. Cert. physician Nat. Cert. Commn. of Physician Assts. Paramedic Alachua County Emergency Med. Svc., Gainesville, Fla., 1972-78; perfusionist U. Fla./VA Med. Ctr., Gainesville, 1980-96; physician asst. U. Fla., 1984-96; with VAMC/USF, Tampa, 1996—; cons. in field. Contbr. articles to profl. pubs. Officer U.S. Army, 1978-81; lt. col. USAFR, 1981—. Mem. Am. Acad. Physician Assts., Fla. Acad. Physician Assts., Assn. Mil. Surgeons, Am. Heart Assn. (exec. com., ACLS instr., BCLS instr./trainer). Home: 200 SW Lincoln Cir N Saint Petersburg FL 33703

BAILEY, ROLAND JAMES, pediatrician; b. Clarksburg, W.Va., Aug. 7, 1932; s. Roland Gilson and Eleanor Ruth B.; m. Elizabeth Jane Moore, June 1; children: Mark, Scott, Lisa, Kimberly. AB, W.Va. U., 1953, BS, 1954; MD, Med. Coll. Va., 1957. Pediatrician pvt. practice, Parkesburg, W.Va., 1963—. Capt. USAF, 1940-63. Fellow Am. Acad. Pediatrics; mem. W Va. State Med. Assn., Parkesburg Acad. Medicine (pres. 1970). Baptist. Home: 23 Ashwood Dr Vienna VA 26105 Office: 600 18th St Ste 301 Parkersburg WV 26101

BAILEY, ROSS R., nephrologist; b. Christchurch, New Zealand, Aug. 31, 1941; s. John Brimfield and Frances Agnes (Dunford) B.; m. Marion Lesley Butterfield, 1964; four children. MB, BChir, Otago U., 1964, MD, 1970. House officer Canty Hosp. Bd., 1965-67; sr. med. registrar renal medicine Christchurch Hosp., 1968-69; fellow in medicine Charing Cross Hosp., London, 1969-71; sr. rsch. fellow renal unit Victoria Hosp., London, Ont., Can., 1971-72; renal physician Canty Hosp. Bd., 1972-79; head dept. nephrology Canty Area Health Bd., 1979-91; clin. lectr. Christchurch Sch. Medicine. Author: Single Dose Therapy of Urinary Tract Infection, 1983; contbr. articles to profl. jours., chpts. to books. Fellow Royal Coll. Physicians (U.K.), Royal Australia and New Zealand Soc. Nephrology (past pres.), New Zealand Soc. Nephrology, Renal Assn. U.K., Internat. Soc. Nephrology (councillor), Internat. Soc. Hypertension, Internat. Soc. Pediat. Nephrology, Internat. Coun. Nephrology (mem. coun.), Asian-Pacific Soc. of Nephrology (coun.). Office: Christchurch Hosp Nephr, Pvt Bag 4710, Christchurch New Zealand

BAILEY, WILFORD SHERRILL, parisitology educator, science administrator, university president; b. nr. Hartselle, Ala., Mar. 2, 1921; s. Ollis Wilford and Bessie (Widener) B.; m. Cratus Hester, May 30, 1942; children: Wilford Edward, Joe Sherrill, Margaret Ann, Sarah Jane. D.V.M., Auburn U., 1942, M.S., 1946, H.H.D., 1984; Sc.D., Johns Hopkins U., 1950. Instr. to head prof. dept. pathology and parasitology Sch. Vet Medicine, Auburn U., 1942-62; asso. dean Grad. Sch. and coordinator research, 1962-66, v.p. for academic affairs, 1966-72; health scientist adminstr. Inst. Allergy and Infectious Diseases, NIH, 1972-74; prof. dept. pathology and parasitology Auburn (Ala.) U., 1974-92, assoc. dean vet. medicine, 1979-80, pres., 1983-84, Univ. prof., 1984-92; research leader Regional Parasite Research Lab., U.S. Dept. Agr., Auburn, 1980-82; custodian Am. Soc. Parasitologists, 1952-79. Mem. NRC Coun., 1962-68; mem. tng. grant com. Nat. Inst. Allergy and Infectious Diseases, 1964-69, Nat. Adv. Allergy and Infectious Disease Coun., 1971-72, 75-78; mem. com. on animal health NRC, Nat. Acad. Sci., 1980-84; trustee Internat. Christian U., Vienna, Austria, 1990-95. Research fellow Am. Vet. Med. Assn.; Johns Hopkins Univ. scholar; NSF Sci. Faculty fellow; Rockefeller Found. scholar. Mem. Am. Vet. Med. Assn., Am. Soc. Parasitologists (pres. 1971), Am. Soc. Tropical Medicine and Hygiene (pres. 1977), Mortar Bd., Nat. Collegiate Athletic Assn. (sec.-treas. 1985-86, pres. 1987-88), Sigma Xi, Phi Kappa Phi, Alpha Phi Omega, Phi Zeta, Omicron Delta Kappa, Phi Beta Delta. Mem. Ch. of Christ. Home: 778 Moores Mill Rd Auburn AL 36830-6032 Office: Auburn Univ Dept Parasitology Auburn AL 36849

BAILEY, WILLIAM A., orthopaedic surgeon; b. Kansas City, Kans., Aug. 29, 1940; s. William Thorne and Valarie (Lynoon) B.; m. Kristine Hall, July 25, 1987; children: Brock, Maxwell, Madelyn. AB, Kans. U., 1962, MD, 1966. Diplomate Am. Bd. Orthopaedic Surgery. Intern surgery Kans. U. Med. Ctr., Kansas City, 1966-67, resident surgery, 1967-68; resident orthopaedic surgery Duke U., Durham, N.C., 1970-74; staff orthopaedic surgeon Lawrence (Kans.) Meml. Hosp., 1974—, chief surgery, 1978-80. Lt. comdr. USN, 1968-70, Vietnam. Fellow Am. Acad. Orthopaedic Surgery; mem. Alpha Omega Alpha. Office: Box 1898 Lawrence KS 66044

BAILEY-JONES, CARLA LYNN, nursing administrator; b. Balt., June 4, 1957; d. Carlton L. and Helen P. (Wales) B.; m. Dean C. Jones, Mar. 1988. BS in Nursing, U. Md., Balt., 1979; MS in Health Scis., Towson (Md.) State U., 1987. Nurse clinician I, charge nurse, clin. nurse U. Md. Med. Systems, Balt., 1981-87; maternal transport coord. U. Md. Med. Systems Hosp., Balt., 1979—; rsch. nurse Tokos Med. Corp., Balt., 1988-91; perinatal care coord. U. Md. Med. Systems/Hosp., 1993—; assoc. faculty U. Md. Sch. Nursing; mem. fetal and infant mortality rev. bd. Healthy Start; mem. State Commn. on Infant Mortality Prevention. Mem. Assn. Women's Health, Obstetric and Neonatal Nurses, State Commn. Infant Mortality Prevention, Md. Nurse's Assn., Nat. Perinatal Assn., Md. Perinatal Assn.

BAILIT, HOWARD L., medical association administrator; b. Boston, Dec. 17, 1937. DMD, Tufts U., 1962; PhD, Harvard U., 1967. From asst. prof. to prof. dept. behavior sci. & cmty. health U. Conn. Health Ctr., 1967-82; prof., head dept. health adminstrn. Sch. Pub. Health & Medicine, Columbia U., 1982-86; sr. v.p. health svc. rsch. Aetna Life and Casualty, Hartford, 1986—; mem. study sect. Nat. Ctr. Health Svc. Rsch., 1978-82, 86—, nat. affairs com., Am. Assn. Dental Rsch., 1978-82, future dentist com. ADA, 1983, com. cost mgmt. sys. Inst. Medicine-NAS, 1987—; cons. Rand Health Ins. Exp., 1979-86, Office of Quality Assurance, ADA, 1983—. Contbr. articles to profl. jours. Mem. NAS, Inst. Medicine-NAS, Am. Coll. Dentists. Office: Aetna Life & Casualty Co 451 Farmington Ave Hartford CT 06105-4424*

BAILLIE, THOMAS WILSON, anesthesiologist; b. Kilmarnock, Scotland, July 7, 1929; arrived in The Netherlands, 1969; s. John Wilson and Elizabeth (Paisley) B.; m. Anja Maria Lie, July 10, 1947; children: Jennifer, Kathleen, Maureen Kim. MB ChB, U. Glasgow, Scotland, 1952, MD, 1963. Anesthesiologist Glasgow Tchg. Hosp., 1956-63; anesthetist-in-charge Dumfries Hosps., Scotland, 1963-69; dir. anesthesia Red Cross Hosp., The Hague, The Netherlands, 1969-72; pvt. practice anesthesiologist Zutphen, The Netherlands, 1972-94; ret., 1994. Author: From Boston to Dumfries, 1966, 2d edit., 1969, The Dumfries Ether Diary, 1996; co-editor: Disasters-Medical Organization 1980; editor or co-editor several books on disaster medicine in English, Dutch and Italian. Capt. Royal Army Med. Corps, 1954-56. Fellow Royal Coll. Surgeons, Royal Coll. Anaesthetists; mem. Soc. Anaesthetists of Great Britain and Ireland, Dutch Soc. for Anesthesiology. Home: De Heurne 17, 7255 CK Hengelo The Netherlands

BAIN, DIANE MARTHA D'ANDREA, clinical nurse specialist in critical care; b. Westfield, Mass., June 29, 1949; d. John Anthony and Eva Margaret (Gerulis) D'Andrea; m. John Kenneth, Sept. 24, 1972. AS with hons., Quinsigamond Community Coll., 1971; BS with high hons., Worcester State Coll., 1977; MS with highest honors, U. Mass., Worcester, 1987. Staff and asst. head nurse MICU and crit. care St. Vincent Hosp., Worcester, 1971-77; instr. St. Vincent Hosp. Sch. Nursing, 1977-79; nurse educator critical care U. Mass. Hosp., Worcester, 1979-87, clin. nurse specialist critical care, 1987-93; assoc. faculty U. Mass. Grad. Sch. Nursing, Worcester, 1987-93, Worcester State Coll., 1987-93; presenter, lectr., cons. for regional orgns., agencies, and hosps. Reviewer for Applied Rsch. nursing jour., 1988-89; contbr. articles to profl. jours. Mem. AACN, Sigma Theta Tau, Iota Phi.

BAIN, JAMES ARTHUR, pharmacologist, educator; b. Langdon, N.D., May 22, 1918; s. James Hamilton and Mabel (Aldritt) B.; m. Eleanor Theo Hohaus, Dec. 5, 1947; children: Andrew J., Peter T. A.A., Wayland Jr. Coll., 1938; B.S., U. Wis., 1940, Ph.D., 1944. Research asst. McArdle Meml. Lab., U. Wis., 1940-44, Rockefeller fellow, 1946-47; research asso. U. Ill., 1947-50, asst. prof., then asso. prof., 1952-54; mem. faculty dept. pharmacology Emory U., 1954—, prof., 1954-89, chmn. dept., 1957-62, dir. div. basic health scis., 1960-76; exec. asso. dean Emory U. (Sch. Medicine), 1976-88, prof. emeritus, 1988—, cons. to dean, v.p., 1989-93; cons. to govt., nat. agys., industry, 1954—. Contbr. articles profl. jours. Mem. Am. Chem. Soc., Am. Soc. Pharmacology and Exptl. Therapeutics, AAAS. Home: 2275 Tanglewood Rd Decatur GA 30033

BAINTON, DOROTHY FORD, pathology educator, researcher; b. Magnolia, Miss., June 18, 1933; d. Aubrey Ratcliff and Leta (Brumfield) Ford; m. Cedric R. Bainton, Nov. 28, 1959; children: Roland J., Bruce G., James H. BS, Millsaps Coll., 1955; MD, Tulane U. Sch. of Medicine, 1958; MS, U. Calif., San Francisco, 1966. Postdoctoral rsch. fellow U. Calif., San Francisco, 1963-66, postdoctoral rsch. pathologist, 1966-69, asst. prof. pathology, 1969-75, assoc. prof., 1975-81, prof. pathology, 1981—, chair pathology, 1987-94, vice chancellor acad. affairs, 1994—; mem. Inst. of Medicine, NAS, 1990—. NIH grantee, 1978—. Fellow AAAS, Am. Acad. Arts & Scis.; mem. FASEB (bd. dirs.), Am. Soc. for Cell Biology, Am. Soc. Hematology, Am. Soc. Histochemists and Cytochemists, Am. Assn. of Pathologists. Democrat. Mem. Soc. of Friends. Office: Office of Acad Affairs U Calif San Francisco Med Scis Bldg Rm 115 San Francisco CA 94143-0400

BAINUM, STEWART WILLIAM, JR., health care and lodging company executive; b. Takoma Park, Md., Mar. 25, 1946; s. Stewart William Sr. and Jane Loretta (Goyne) B.; m. Sandra Ann Yarish, Sept. 26, 1987. BA, Pacific Union Coll., 1968; MBA, UCLA, 1970; postgrad. theology, Andrews U., 1971-72. V.p. Manor Care Inc., Silver Spring, Md., 1973-79, vice chmn., 1982-87, chmn., chief exec. officer, 1987—, also bd. dirs.; mem. Md. Ho. of Dels., Annapolis, 1979-83, Md. State Senate, Annapolis, 1983-87. Bd. dirs. Invest in Am., Washington, 1987; co-chmn. Dem. Forum, Montgomery County, Md., 1987; alt. del. Dem. Nat. Conv., San Francisco, 1984. Named Outstanding State Ofcl. of Yr., Young Democrats of Md., 1981; recipient Cert. of Merit, Common Cause of Md., Annapolis, 1982, 85, Torch of Liberty award Anti-Defamation League, Washington region, 1984. Office: Manor Care Inc 10750 Columbia Pike Silver Spring MD 20901-4427 Also: 4 Seasons Nursing Ctrs 10750 Columbia Pike Silver Spring MD 20901-4427*

BAIRD, HAYNES WALLACE, pathologist; b. St. Louis, Jan. 28, 1943; s. Harry Haynes and Mary Cornelia (Wallace) B.; m. Phyllis Jean Tipton, June 26, 1965; children: Teresa Lee, Christopher Wallace, Kelly Wallace. BA, U. N.C., 1965, MD, 1969. Diplomate Am. Bd. Pathology. Radio announcer, disc jockey, 1961-63; intern N.C. Meml. Hosp., Chapel Hill, 1969-70, resident in pathology, 1970-72, chief resident in pathology, 1972-73; assoc. pathologist Moses H. Cone Meml. Hosp., Greensboro, N.C., 1973—; practice medicine, specializing in pathology Greensboro, 1973—; adj. asst. prof. U. N.C., Chapel Hill, 1978-96, adj. assoc. prof., 1996—; clin. lectr. chemistry U. N.C., Greensboro, 1973—. Mem. adminstrv. bd. West Market St. United Meth. Ch., 1985-88, usher, 1988—; bd. dirs. Greensboro unit Am. Cancer Soc., 1980-81; mem. com. protection of rights of human subjects (Instl. Rev. Bd.) Moses H. Cone Meml. Hosp., 1989—. Fellow Coll. Am. Pathologists (ho. of dels. 1983-85, insp. commn. on lab. accreditation); mem. AMA, So. Med. Assn., Am. Soc. for Clin. Chemistry, Am. Soc. Cytology, Papanicolaou Soc. of Cytopathology, Am. Soc. Clin. Pathologists, Internat. Acad. Pathology, N.C. Med. Soc., Greater Greensboro Soc. Medicine, N.C. Soc. Pathologists (sec.-treas. 1977-79). Methodist. Home: 2805 New Hanover Dr Greensboro NC 27408-6705 Office: 1200 N Elm St Greensboro NC 27401-1004

BAIRD, PATRICIA ANN, physician, educator; b. Rochdale, Eng.; came to Can., 1955; d. Harold and Winifred (Cainen) Holt; m. Robert Merrifield Baird, Feb. 22, 1964; children—Jennifer Ellen, Brian Merrifield, Bruce Andrew. B.Sc. with honors, McGill U., 1959, M.D., C.M., 1963; DSc honoris causa, McMaster U., 1991; DUniv honoris causa, U. Ottawa, 1991. Intern Royal Victoria Hosp., Montreal, Que., Can., 1963-64; resident, fellow in pediatrics Vancouver Gen. Hosp., B.C., Can., 1964-67; instr. pediatrics U. B.C., Vancouver, 1968-72, asst. prof., 1972-77, assoc. prof., 1977-79, dept. head, 1979-89, prof., 1982-94, Univ. prof., 1994—; head dept. med. genetics Grace Hosp., Vancouver, 1981-89, Children's Hosp., Vancouver, 1981-89, Health Scis. Centre Hosp., 1986-89; med. cons. B.C. Health Surveillance Registry, 1977-90; chmn. genetics grants com. Med. Rsch. Coun., Ottawa, Ont., Can., 1982-87, mem. coun., 1987-90; mem. Nat. Adv. Bd. on Sci. and Tech. to Fed. Govt., 1987-91; mem. genetic predisposition study steering com. Sci. Coun. Can., 1987-90; chair Royal Commn. on New Reproductive Technologies, 1989-93; co-chair Nat. Forum Sch. and Tech. Couns., 1991; v.p. Can. Inst. for Advanced Rsch., 1991—; bd. dirs. Biomed. Rsch. Centre, 1986-89. Contbr. over 350 articles and abstracts to med. jours. Bd. govs. U. B.C., 1984-90. Fellow RCP Can., Can. Coll. Med. Geneticists (v.p. 1984-86); mem. Am. Soc. Human Genetics (chair nominating com. 1987-89), B.C. Med. Assn., Can. Med. Assn., Genetics Soc. Can., Genetic Epidemiology (adv. bd. 1991-94), Order B.C. Office: U BC, Dept Med Genetics, Vancouver, BC Canada V6T 1Z3

BAIRD, ROGER NEALE, surgeon; b. Edinburgh, Scotland, Dec. 24, 1941; s. John Allan and Margaret Edith (Shand) B.; m. Affra Mary Varcoe-Cocks, Oct. 12, 1968; children: Susan Catherine, Richard Douglas. BSc with honors, Edinburgh U., 1963, B of Surgery, 1966, ChM, 1977. House surgeon Royal Infirmary, Edinburgh, 1966-67, research scholar dept. clin. surgery, 1967-69, registrar, 1969-72; lectr. surgery Bristol (Eng.) U., 1973-77, sr. lectr., 1977-81, Long Fox lectr., 1981; cons. surgeon Royal Infirmary,

Bristol, 1981—. Author books on vascular surgery; contbr. articles to med. jours. Fulbright scholar Harvard U. Med. Sch., Boston, 1975-76. Fellow Royal Coll. Surgeons (Eng.) (examiner 1981-86, Hunterian prof. 1980, Kinmonth lectr. 1984), Royal Coll. Surgeons (Edinburgh) (Learmonth lectr. 1980); mem. Vascular Surg. Soc. Gt. Britain and Ireland (mem. council 1991-94), Assn. Surgeons Gt. Britain and Ireland (hon. treas. 1985-90), European Soc. Vascular Surgery, Internat. Cardiovascular Soc. (Brit. nat. del. 1982-90), Soc. Vascular Surgery. Club: Army and Navy (London). Home: 23 Old Sneed Park, Bristol BS9 1RG, England Office: Royal Infirmary, Bristol BS2 8HW, England

BAISCH, STEVEN DALE, pediatric intensivist; b. Glendive, Mont., May 30, 1955; s. Maynard Jack and Edith Maxine (Milne) B.; children: Christopher, Rebecca. BA with honors, Jamestown Coll., 1977; Calculus fellow, Harvard U., 1975; MD, U. N.D., 1981. Pediatric resident U. N.D. Med. Ctr., 1981-84, asst. chief resident, 1983-84; ptnr., pres. Panhandle Pediatric Clinic, P.C., Scottsbluff, Nebr., 1984-88; pres. Region West Pediat. Svcs., P.C., Scottsbluff, 1988-91; fellow pediatric critical care medicine U. Minn., Mpls., 1991-94; attending staff in pediats. critical care Children's Hosp. of St. Paul, 1992—; attending staff in pediatric critical care Children's Health Care, Mpls. and St. Paul, 1994—; instr. pediats. U. Nebr. Med. Ctr., Omaha, 1984-91, med. dir. Camp Cosmos-Diabetic Camp, Scottsbluff, 1984-91; dir. Asthma Care Tng. Program, Scottsbluff, 1986-91. Outstanding fellow teaching award, 1993; U. Minn. fellow, 1991-94. Fellow Am. Acad. Pediatrics (PREP award 1990). Office: Children's Hosp St Paul Pediat Critical Care 345 Smith Ave N Saint Paul MN 55102-2369

BAJIT, FERNANDO GAMBOA, surgeon; b. Penaranda, The Philippines, Apr. 13, 1941; came to U.S., 1964; s. Monico R. and Mercedes (Gamboa) B.; m. Winifreda Garcia, Aug. 14, 1965; children: Ronald, John, Robert. AA, U. Santo Tomas, Manila, 1958, MD, 1963. Diplomate Am. Bd. Surgery. Intern U. Santo Tomas, 1962-63; fellow V. Luna Gen. Hosp., Quezon City, The Philippines, 1963-64; intern Paterson (N.J.) Gen. Hosp., 1964-65; surgical resident Wyckoff Heights Hosp., Bklyn., 1965-70, emergency room svc., 1970-71, pvt. practice, 1972—; pvt. practice Marcy Ave Hosp., Bklyn., 1972—. Roman Catholic. Office: 529 Marcy Ave Brooklyn NY 11206-5660

BAJPAI, ERNEST THEOPHILUS, physician; b. Ranchi, Bihar, India, Oct. 4, 1929; came to the U.S., 1968; s. Charles Theophilus and Angelina (Brown) B.; m. Nomita Biswas, June 1, 1959; children: Minakshi, Enakshi. Student, St. Xavier Coll., Ranchi, 1949, Patna Sci. Coll., India, 1950; MB BS, Prince of Wales U., 1955. Diplomate internal medicine and geriat. medicine Am. Bd. Internal Medicine. Rotating intern St. Charles Hosp., Toledo, Ohio, 1968; resident in internal medicine Misericordia Hosp., Phila., 1969-72; emergency rm. physician Mercy Cath. Med., Phila.; physician Sycamore (Ohio) Med. Assn., Wenonah (N.J.) Med. Assn., 1975—. Fellow ACP; mem. Am. Med. Dirs. Assn. (cert. med. dir.). Democrat. Episcopalian. Home: 208 E Buttonwood St Wenonah NJ 08090 Office: Wenonah Med Assocs PA 107 E Mantua Ave Wenonah NJ 08090

BAKAITIS, VINCENT WILLIAM, JR., psychology educator; b. Washington, Pa., Feb. 4, 1941; s. Vincent William and Mary Josephine (Cario) B.; m. Nancy Thomas, 1961 (div. 1966); m. Karen Crain (div. 1995); 1 child, Celia. BA, Pa. State U., 1963; MA, New Sch. for Social Rsch., 1966. Researcher U. Chgo., Law Sch. Libr., 1963-64; social caseworker N.Y.C. Dept. Social Svc., 1964-67, social sci. supr., 1967-69; prof. behavioral sci. Dutchess Community Coll., Poughkeepsie, N.Y., 1969—; cons. N.Y. State Poison Ctr., Nyack, 1986—; rsch. assoc. Hudsonia/Bard Coll., 1989—, N.Y. State Mus. and Biol. Survey, Albany, 1990. Contbr. articles to profl. jours. Ednl. advisor, founder Mid-Hudson Mycol. Assn., Highland, N.Y., 1986—. Mem. N. Am. Mycol. Assn. Home: RR 4 Box 285 Pleasant Valley NY 12569-9436 Office: Dutchess Community Coll Pendell Rd Poughkeepsie NY 12601

BAKAY, ROY ARPAD EARLE, neurosurgeon, educator; b. Chgo., Mar. 5, 1949; s. Archie Joseph and Marjorie (Jordal) B.; m. Joann P. Feiertag; children: Mark, Scott, Candace, Jacqueline. BS, Beloit Coll., 1971; MD, Northwestern U., 1975. Diplomate Am. Bd. Med. Examiners, Am. Bd. Neurol. Surgeons. Intern U. Mich., Ann Arbor, 1975-76; resident in neurosurgery U. Wash., Seattle, 1976-82; acting instr., asst. in neurosurgery U. Wash. Med. Sch., Seattle, 1980-82, NIH fellow, 1981-82; asst. prof. sect. neurol. surgery Emory U. Med. Sch., Atlanta, 1982-88, dir. neurol. surgery resident rsch., 1984—, assoc. prof., 1988-93, prof., 1993—; mem. R & D Com. VA Med. Ctr., Decatur, Ga., 1982-86, sect. chief neurol. surgery, 1982-95; affiliate scientist neurobiology Yerkes Regional Primate Rsch. Ctr., Atlanta, 1982-95; vice chmn. dept. neurol. surgery, 1995—. Author: (with others) Yearbook of Science and Technology, 1989; abstractor Jour. Surg. Gynecology and Obstetrics, 1978—; mem. editorial bd. Jour. Contemporary Neurosurgery, 1987-93; mem. editorial rev. bd. Neurosurgery, 1994—; contbr. articles to profl. jours., chpts. to books. Chmn. profl. adv. bd. Ga. chpt. Epilepsy Found. Am., 1987-88; mem. adv. panel U.S. Congl. Office Tech. Assessment, Washington, 1988-90; profl. rep. Am. Cancer Soc., Atlanta, 1987-90. Recipient Resident Rsch. award Western Neurosurgery Soc., 1979, No. Pacific Soc.Neurology and Psychiatry, 1979, Soc. Neurology Anesthesists and Neurology Supportive Care, 1981; named one of Outstanding Athletes of Am., 1971, Am. Best Doctor, 1995—. Mem. AAAS, Soc. Neurosci., Am. Stereotactic and Functional Neurosurgeons (v.p. 1988-91, pres. 1991-93), Am. Assn. Neurol. Surgeons (chmn. GRAFT Registry Com. 1987—), Congress Neurol. Surgeons (v.p. joint com. 1988-91, pres. 1991-93). Presbyterian. Office: The Emory Clinic 1327 Clifton Rd NE Atlanta GA 30307-1013

BAKER, ALYSE OTVOS, speech and language clinician; b. Hackensack, N.J., Feb. 2, 1950; d. Emery George Otvos and Maude Vance; m. Charles M. Baker III, May 19, 1979; children: Bevin, Julie. BA in Psychology, Yale U., 1972; MA in Edn., U. Mich., 1973, MS in Speech Pathology, 1974; postgrad., U. Pitts., 1992. Lic. speech, lang. pathologist, Pa.; level II/ permanent cert. tchr. speech and lang. impaired, Pa. Speech, lang. clinician Allegheny Gen. Hosp./Assn. for Children Learning Disabities, Pitts., 1974-75; clin. supr. U. Pitts., 1975-82; learning disorders and speech lang. clinician W. Pa. Hosp., Pitts., 1975-82; speech, lang. clinician Rehab. Specialists, Pitts., 1987, Cranberry Clinic, NovaCare, Pitts, 1988-93; speech/lang. clinician Project D.A.R.T. (early intervention) Allegheny Intermediate Unit, Pitts., 1993—. Vol. Campaign to Install Seat Belts on Sch. Buses, North Allegheny Sch. Dist., 1988—. Mem. Am. Speech-Lang.-Hearing Assn. (cert. clin. competence in speech pathology, 7 awards continuing edn.), S.W. Pa. Speech-Lang.-Hearing Assn. (sec. 1983-85), Coun. for Exceptional Children (divsn. for children with comm. disorders and divsn. for children with learning disabilities), Yale Club of Pitts. (alumni schs. com. 1975-84, sec. bd. govs. 1982-83). Democrat. Unitarian. Home: 10145 Grubbs Rd Wexford PA 15090-9649 Office: Allegheny Intermediate Unit Project DART 4 Station Sq Fl 2 Pittsburgh PA 15219

BAKER, ANDREW HARTILL, clinical laboratory executive; b. London, Dec. 7, 1948; came to U.S., 1976; s. Charles David and Isobel Joyce (Taylor) B.; m. Susan Nancy Spector, Oct. 24, 1986; children: Laura, Sally, Thomas; 1 stepchild, Jason Fredson. Student, Framlingham Coll., Suffolk, Eng., 1961-66; diploma accountancy, City of London Polytechnique, 1968. Auditor Touche Ross, London, 1968-73; contr. Corning Ltd., Essex, Eng., 1974-76; div. contr. Corning Med., N.Y., 1977-79; asst. contr. Corning Glass Works, N.Y., 1980-82; sr. v.p. Metpath, Teterboro, N.J., 1982-85, pres., 1985-92; chmn., CEO Unilabs Corp., Hackensack, N.J., 1989—; pres. Corning Lab Svcs. Inc., Teterboro, 1990-92; founder, dir. Med. Diagnostic Mgmt., Inc.; proprietor, chmn. Hartill Ltd. Investment Co. Treas. United Way of Steuben County, Corning, N.Y., 1978-82; trustee Wayne Gen. Hosp., N.J., 1982-87. Fellow Inst. Chartered Accts. in Eng. and Wales. Mem. Ch. of Eng. Club: Honourable Arty. Co. (London). Home: 636 Winding Hollow Dr Franklin Lakes NJ 07417-2829 Office: Unilabs Corp 401 Hackensack Ave Hackensack NJ 07601-6411

BAKER, ARTHUR BARRINGTON, anesthesiologist, educator; b. Brisbane, Queensland, Australia, June 24, 1939; s. Arthur and Edna Loyla (Crothers) B.; m. Jane Elizabeth Colliss, July 29, 1971; children: Merinda, Alexander, Matthew. MB, BS, Queensland U., Australia, 1963; postgrad., Faculty of Anaesthetists, Australia, 1968, Faculty of Anaesthetists, Eng., 1968; DPhil, Oxford U., Eng., 1971. Reader in anaesthesia Queensland U., Brisbane, 1972-75; prof. anaesthesia and intensive care Otago U., Dunedin, New Zealand, 1975-92; Nuffield prof. anesthetics Sydney (Australia) U. at Royal Prince Alfred Hosp., 1992—; dean Faculty of Anaesthetists Melbourne, Australia, 1987-90. Author: Physiology of Artificial Ventilation, 1971. Home: PO Box 345, Concord West Australia NSW 2138 Office: Univ Sydney, Sydney Australia 2006

BAKER, BRINDA ELIZABETH GARRISON, infectious disease nurse; b. Groveland, Ga., May 9, 1946; d. Archie and Nora Lee (Haynes) Garrison; m. Jerome Baker, Feb. 1970 (div. 1972); children: Katrina Lenyse Adams, Kelbert Lenard Adams. Student, Savannah (Ga.) State Coll., 1964-68; LPN, Savannah Tech. Sch., 1968; ADN, Armstrong State Coll., 1984, BSN, 1990. RN, Ga.; cert. provider BLS, Am. Heart Assn. LPN Candler Gen. Hosp., Savannah, 1968-72, staff nurse Cross Country Traveling Corps, 1990; LPN Ga. Regional Hosp., Savannah, 1972-74, sr. staff nurse, 1989-92; LPN St. Joseph Hosp., Savannah, 1974-84, staff nurse, 1984-90; sr. nurse, clinic supr. Chatham County Health Ctr., Savannah, 1992-95, clinic supr., 1995—; part-time clin. instr. Armstrong State Coll., Savannah, 1991—. Mem. ANA, Ga. Nurses Assn., Assn. Nurses in AIDS Care. Democrat. Roman Catholic. Home: 1307 E 71st St Savannah GA 31404-5735 Office: Chatham County Health Dept 2011 Eisenhower Dr Savannah GA 31406-3905

BAKER, BRUCE EDWARD, orthopedic surgeon, consultant; b. Oswego, N.Y., Mar. 22, 1937; s. Elbert J. and Reatha (Hartranft) B.; m. Patricia Therese Gormel, Aug. 19, 1961; children: Brett, Clayton, Sean, Reatha. BSME, Syracuse U., 1959; MD, SUNY-Syracuse, 1965. Intern State U. Iowa, Iowa City, 1965-66, asst. resident, 1966-67; resident orthopaedics SUNY-Upstate Med. Ctr., Syracuse, 1969-72, NIH orthopaedic rsch. fellow, 1972-73, asst. prof. orthopaedic surgery, 1973-79, assoc. prof., 1979-86, prof., 1986-89; dir. univ. sports medicine svc. divsn. dept. orthopaedic surgery 1980-89; team physician, dir. sports medicine athletic dept., Syracuse U., 1973-93, orthopaedic cons. Student Health Ctr., 1973-93, staff SUNY Hosp., Syracuse, 1973-89, Syracuse VA Hosp., 1973-89, A.C. Silverman Pub. Health Hosp., 1973-77, Crouse-Irving Meml. Hosp., 1973—; cons. in field. Contbr. numerous articles to profl. jours. Capt. USAF, 1967-69. Recipient AMA Physicians Recognition award, 1978, Bronze medal award Am. Roentgen Ray Soc., 1980, Gold medal award Sound Slide Prodn. Conditioning, 1977; Syracuse U. scholar, 1955; N.Y. State Regents scholar, 1955-59; USPHS grantee, 1973-74; Hendricks Research fund grantee, 1973-75; NIH grantee, 1974-76, 76-77. Fellow ACS, Am. Acad. Orthopaedic Surgeons; mem. AMA, Med. Soc. State N.Y., Onondaga County Med. Soc., Orthopaedic Rsch. Soc., Am. Coll. Sports Medicine, N.Y. Soc. Orthopaedic Surgeons, Royal Soc. Medicine, Internat. Arthroscopy Assn., Arthroscopy Assn. N. Am., Bioelectric Repair and Growth Soc. Office: Ste 108A 475 Irving Ave Syracuse NY 13210-1756

BAKER, BRUCE LEE, psychology educator, consultant; b. Cambridge, Mass., July 23, 1940; s. Karl Watson and Elizabeth Cole (Bland) B.; m. Patricia McNeal, Feb. 24, 1966 (div. Oct. 1978); children: Kristen, Jason; m. Jan Blacher, Jan. 27, 1985; children: Alexander, Spencer. A.B. in Psychology, Brown U., 1962; Ph.D. in clin. Psychology, Yale U., 1966. Lic. psychologist, Calif. Asst. prof. psychology and social relations Harvard U., Cambridge, 1966-69, assoc. prof. edn., lectr. social relations, 1969-75; assoc. prof. psychology UCLA, 1975-77, prof., 1977—, chmn. Clinical Psychology, dir. training program in clinical psychology, 1985-91, vis. prof. Harvard U. Med. Sch., Boston, 1982-83; pvt. practice psychology, Los Angeles, 1979—; founder, dir. Camp Freedom, Ossipee, N.H., 1969-75; mem. profl. adv. bd. May Inst., 1987—; bd. trustees Bancroft, N.J., 1988—. Co-author: Abnormal Psychology, 1980, 2d rev. edit., 1986; Readings in Abnormal Psychology, 1981; As Close As Possible, 1977; Steps to Independence, 1975-83, rev. 2nd edit., 1988, 3rd edit., 1996; mem. editorial bd. Jour. Behavior Therapy and Exptl. Psychology, 1975—, Am. Jour. Mental Retardation, 1981-83, 85-87, 93—, Family Process, 1979-85, Jour. Intellectual and Devel. Disability, 1989—. Grantee Dept. Edn., 1984-90, Nat. Inst. Child Health and Human Devel., 1971-75, 77-83, Social and Rehab. Services Adminstrn., 1970-75. Fellow Am. Assn. Mental Retardation (pres. psychology divsn. 1993-95, bd. dirs. 1994-95, Rsch. award Region II 1986); mem. APA (Young Psychologist award 1969), Western Psychol. Assn. Democrat. Home: 111 N Irving Blvd Los Angeles CA 90004-3804 Office: Dept Psychology UCLA Los Angeles CA 90024

BAKER, CARL EDWARD, III, psychologist; b. Phila., Sept. 17, 1958; s. Carl Edward and Helene (Johnson) B. BA, Brown U., 1981; MA, U. Nebr., 1985. Instr. asst. Bucks County Community Coll., Newtown, Pa., 1987-89; instr. Del. County Community Coll., Media, Pa., 1990; lang. lab. instr. Del. Valley Friends, Bryn Mawr, Pa., 1990-91; tutorial coord. Peirce Jr. Coll., 1991-93; learning disabilities specialist U. of Arts, Phila., 1993—. Mem. AAAS, ASCD, APA (assoc.), N.Y. Acad. Scis. Home: 3030 Bogle Rd Bensalem PA 19020-1722

BAKER, CARLETON HAROLD, physiology educator; b. Utica, N.Y., Aug. 2, 1930; s. Harold George and Loretta (Darling) B.; m. Sara Frances Johnson, July 20, 1963; children: Elizabeth Ann, Janet Lee. BA, Utica Coll. of Syracuse U., 1952; MA, Princeton U., 1954, PhD, 1955. Asst. instr. Princeton (N.J.) U., 1952-54, asst. in research, 1954-55; asst. prof. Med. Coll. Ga., Augusta, 1955-61, assoc prof., 1961-67, prof., 1967; prof. physiology and biophysics U. Louisville Health Scis. Ctr., 1967-71; prof., chmn. dept. physiology and biophysics U. South Fla. Coll. of Medicine, Tampa, 1971-92, dep. dean for research and grad. studies, 1980-82, prof surgery, physiology and biophysics, dir. surg. rsch., 1992-95; clin. rsch. prof. physiology U. S.C. Coll. Medicine, Columbia, 1994—; rsch. com. mem. Am. Heart Assn., Louisville, 1969-71; rsch. com., bd. dirs. Am. Heart Assn. of Fla., Tampa, 1971-85; NIH program project site visit team, 1982-84, mem. LCME Accreditation Survey Team, 1980-81; vis. prof. U. S.C., 1994-95; cons. U. Louisville Grad. Sch., East Carolina U. Grad. Program. Editor: Microcirculatory Technology, 1986; mem. numerous editorial bds.; contbr. numerous articles in field. Pres. Augusta Choral Soc., 1963; v.p. Blount Rd. Homeowners Assn., Lutz, Fla., 1986-93. Grantee NIH, 1960-92, Am. Heart Assn., 1972—; recipient Svc. awards Am. Heart Assn. Fla., 1974, 77, Disting. Scientist award U. South Fla. Coll. Medicine, 1981, Outstanding Artist/Scholar award Phi Kappa Phi, 1991, Dean's Citation U. So. Fla. Coll. Medicine, 1991, Founder award, 1992. Fellow: Am. Physiol. Soc. (fellow cardiovascular sect. mem. com. 1982-85); mem. Microcirculatory Soc., European Microcirculatory Soc., Shock Soc. (mem. program coms.). Republican. Home: 4039 Old Waynesboro Rd Augusta GA 30906-9254 Office: U SC Coll Medicine Dept Physiology VAH Bldg 1 Columbia SC 29208-9999

BAKER, DEBBIE KAYE, hospice, psychiatric, mental health nurse; b. Altoona, Pa., Sept. 26, 1956; d. Daniel P. and Betty Rae (Manley) B. ASN, Mt. Aloysius Jr. Coll., Cresson, Pa., 1982; BS in Health Planning and Administrn., Pa. State U., 1992. RN, Pa. Staff charge nurse We. Psychiat. Inst., Pitts., 1982-87; staff nurse Altoona Hosp. Mental Health Ctr., 1987-88; dir. staff devel. Hillview Care Ctr., Altoona, 1989-91; dir. Community Nurse Hospice, Hollidaysburg, Pa., 1991-94; mental health case mgr. First Am. Home Care, Altoona, 1994-95; mental health regional coord. First Am. Home Care, State College, Pa., 1995—. Mem. Nat. League Nursing, Hospice Nurses Assn., Home Health Care Nurses Assn., Pa. Hospice Network.

BAKER, DIANE R.H., dermatologist; b. Toledo, Nov. 17, 1945. BS, Ohio State U., 1967, MD cum laude, 1971. Diplomate Am. Bd. Dermatology. Intern U. Wis. Hosp., Madison, 1971-72, resident in dermatology, 1972-74; resident in dermatology Oreg. Health Sci. Ctr., Portland, 1974-76; pvt. practce, Portland, 1976—; clin. prof. dermatology Oreg. Health Sci. U., 1986—; mem. med. staff Meridian Park Hosp., Tualatin, Oreg., 1981—. Mem. Am. Acad. Dermatology, Am. Dermatol. Assn., Oreg. Med. Assn., Oreg. Derm. Soc., Alpha Omega Alpha. Office: Dermatol Assocs 9495 SW Locust St Portland OR 97223-6665

BAKER, DONN CALVIN, hospital administrator; b. Alliance, Ohio, Jan. 16, 1958; s. William Donald and Marylan (Belcher) B.; m. Karlette Baker, July 11, 1987; children: Shea, Skyler. Bachelor, Coll. of Wooster, 1980; Master, George Washington U., 1983. Resident Upstate Med. Ctr., Syracuse, N.Y., 1982-83; asst. adminstr. Dallas Mem. Hosp., 1983-84, Stevens Park Hosp., Dallas, 1984-85, K Med. Ctrs., Dallas, 1985, Southwest Dallas Hosp., 1985-88, Children's Med. Ctr. Dallas, 1988-92, Erlanger Med. Ctr., Chattanooga, 1992—. Bd. dirs. Children's Advocacy Ctr., Chatta nooga, 1992, Goodwill Industries, Chattanooga, 1992, Ronald McDonal House, Chattanooga, 1992. Recipient First Steps award Benwood Found. 1994, Westside Multiculture award Robert Wood Johnson, 1995. Mem ACHE (affiliate), Tenn. Craniofacial Soc. (bd. dirs.), Kiwanis, Chattanooga C. of C. Republican. Presbyterian. Home: 911 Dunsiane Rd Signal Mountain TN 37377 Office: Erlanger Med Ctr 975 E Third St Chattanooga TN 37408

BAKER, DOROTHY ELLEN ELLIS, women's health nurse; b. Salisbury, Md., Nov. 26, 1948; d. Joseph Daniel and Mary Elizabeth (Smith) Ellis; m. Wayne R. Baker, Dec. 30, 1967; 1 child, Benjamin J. Grad., Louise Obici Sch. Nursing, Suffolk, Va., 1969; BSN, Wesley Coll., Dover, Del., 1987; MS, U. Del., 1988. Cert. clin. specialist in community health nursing. Asst. clin. mgr. Peninsula Regional Med. Ctr., Salisbury, Md., 1977-87; clin. nurse specialist, case mgr. Community Health Ctr., Princess Anne, Md., 1989-92; clinician, educator HIV program Med. Ctr. Del., Wilmington, 1992-93; educator, clinician in cmty. health nurse Salisbury (Md.) State U., 1994-95; corp. nurse mgr. Perdue Farms, Inc., Salisbury, Md., 1995—; adj. faculty MSN/FNP program, Wilmington (Del.) Coll., 1994—. Mem. APHA, Assn. Women's Health, Obstetric, and Neonatal Nurses, Am. Assn. Occupational Health Nurses, Sigma Theta Tau. Home: PO Box 25 Delmar DE 19940-0025 Office: Perdue Farms Inc PO Box 1537 Salisbury MD 21802-1537

BAKER, EARL HOMER, psychologist, educator, academic administrator; b. Amarillo, Tex., Aug. 3, 1946; s. Benjamin Harold and Narcesia (Cranmer) B.; m. Ambia Jane Campbell, Feb. 17, 1972; children: Douglas, Caroline, James, Steven. BS, Boise (Idaho) State U., 1971; MS, U. R.I., 1979, PhD, 1984. Lic. psychologist. Sch. psychologist Coventry (R.I.) Pub. Schs., 1980-86; dir. sch. psychology N.E. La. U., Monroe, La., 1986-96. Contbr. articles to profl. jours. Sgt. U.S. Army, 1967-69, Vietnam. Mem. APA, Nat. Assn. Sch. Psychologists, La. Psychol. Assn., La. Sch. Psychol. Assn. (pres.-elect 1992, pres. 1993), South Western Psychol. Assn. Office: 312 Grammont Ste 403 Monroe LA 71201

BAKER, EDWARD L., JR., physician, science facility executive; b. Chattanooga, Nov. 18, 1946; s. Edward Lamar and Sue B. Baker; m. Pamela Taylor, June 21, 1969; children: Justin, Ryan, Lindsay. BA, Vanderbilt U., 1968; MD, Baylor U., 1972; MPH, Harvard U., 1979, MS, 1980. Diplomate Am. Bd. Internal Medicine, Am. Bd. Occupational Medicine. Commd. USPHS, 1974—, advanced through grades to rear adm., 1995; asst. prof. Harvard U. Sch. Pub. Health, Boston, 1980-82, assoc. prof., 1982-85; asst. dir. Nat. Inst Occupl. Safety and Health Ctr. Disease Control, Atlanta, 1985-88, dep. dir. Nat. Inst. Occupl. Safety and Health, 1988-90, asst. surgeon gen., dir. Pub. Health Practice Program Office, 1990—; bd. dirs. Internat. Commn. on Occupl. Health, 1986-92. Author, editor 100 sci. articles and book chpts. Fellow Am. Coll. Epidemiology; mem. APHA, Am. Coll. Occupl. and Environ. Medicine (authorship award 1988), Soc. Occupl. and Environ. Health, Royal Soc. Medicine (London, vis. fellow). Home: 755 Kirk Rd Decatur GA 30030-4529 Office: Ctr Disease Control Pub Health Program Office (E20) 1600 Clifton Rd NE Atlanta GA 30333

BAKER, ELIZABETH RENWICK, obstetrician, gynecologist, educator; b. Washington, Sept. 24, 1949; d. Ralph Parr and Frances Elizabeth (Renwick) B. AB, Duke U., 1971, MD, 1975. Diplomate div. reproductive endocrinology Am. Bd. Ob-Gyn. Resident in ob-gyn Duke Med. Ctr., Durham, N.C., 1975-79; fellow in reproductive endocrinology and infertility Med. U. S.C., Charleston, 1979-81, clin. instr., 1980-81; asst. prof. ob-gyn Milton S. Hershey Med. Ctr., Hershey, Pa., 1981-86; assoc. prof. ob-gyn U. S.C. Sch. Medicine, Columbia, 1986-96. Mem. Duke Med. Alumni Exec. Coun., 1978-84, pres., 1985-86. S.C. State grantee, 1980-81. Fellow Am. Coll. Ob-Gyn; mem. AMA, Newberry County Med. Soc., S.C. Med. Assn., Bayard Carter Soc., Am. Fertility Soc., Internat. Fedn. Fertility Socs., So. Med. Assn., Founder's Soc. Duke U., DAR, Children of Condederacy, Duke/Davison Club (sec.-treas. 1989-90, pres. 1991-92). Republican. Presbyterian. Contbr. articles to profl. jours. Home: 1905 Main St Newberry SC 29108-3519 Office: Univ SC Med Sch Ob-Gyn 717 Poinsettia Pl Columbia SC 29205

BAKER, FLOYD WILMER, surgeon, retired army officer; b. Leavenworth, Kans., May 25, 1927; s. Floyd Winfield and Lolita Clare (Somers) B.; m. Darlene Marie Fulk, Apr. 10, 1949; children: Linda Marie, Diane Louise, Barbara Jayne. B.A., U. Kans., 1950, M.D., 1953; grad., Army Command and Gen. Staff Coll., 1964, Indsl. Coll. Armed Forces, 1967. Diplomate: Am. Bd. Surgery. Commd. 1st lt. U.S. Army, 1953, advanced through grades to maj. gen., 1980; intern Madigan Gen. Hosp., Tacoma, 1953-54; resident in gen. surgery Fitzsimons Army Hosp., Denver, 1955-59; dir. personnel and tng. Office of Surgeon Gen., 1970-71; comdg. gen. Brooke Army Med. Center, Ft. Sam Houston, Tex., 1974-78; Letterman Army Med Center, Presidio of San Francisco, 1978-81; chief surgeon U.S. Army, Europe; comdg. gen. U.S. Army 7th Med. Command,, 1981-83, U.S. Army Health Services Command, Ft. Sam Houston, 1983-86; retired U.S. Army, 1986. Served with USNR, 1945-46. Decorated Legion of Merit (2), Meritorious Service medal, Army Commendation medal (3), Air medal (2), Disting. Service medal. Fellow Am. Coll. Physician Execs.; mem. AMA, Soc. U.S. Army Flight Surgeons, Wilderness Med. Soc. Republican. Baptist. Home and Office: 1413 Wiltshire Ave San Antonio TX 78209-6050

BAKER, GEORGE RICHARD, nuclear medicine physician, internist; b. Tacoma, June 16, 1923; s. George William Baker and Evla B. Hopkins; m. Betty P. Baker, June 27, 1947; children: Delwyn, Carl, Bruce, Nancy. BS, U. Wash., 1945; MD, U. Oreg., 1948. Diplomate Am. Bd. Nuclear Medicine. Thyroid disease cons., pvt. practice nuclear medicine Boise, Idaho, 1957-95; ret., 1996; physician St. Lukes Hosp., Boise, 1957-95. Contbr. articles to profl. jours. Capt. USAF, 1951-53. Fellow Soc. Nuclear Medicine; mem. ACP. Home: 916 W Braemere Rd Boise ID 83702

BAKER, HELEN MARIE, health services executive; b. Tulsa, Oct. 12, 1946; d. Joseph Donald and Caroline Emma (Nelson) Waldhelm; m. Lewis Edward Browder, 1964 (div. 1966); m. Lawrence Selden Baker, Nov. 23, 1978; children: Lawrence Nelson, Marjorie Lyn. Student, U. Tex., 1965-66. Staff asst. to pres. White House, Washington, 1970-73; v.p. Mgmt., Systems, Sales, Inc., Washington, 1973-74, Inter-Am. Svcs., Inc., Washington and Tex., 1974-83; v.p. Med. Diversified Svcs. Inc., San Antonio, 1983-90, exec. v.p., 1990-92, also bd. dirs., pres., CEO, 1992—. Editor newsletter Physician and Family, 1983-86. Elder St. Andrew Presbyn Ch., San Antonio, 1986-89; sponsor San Antonio Symphony. Mem. San Antonio Mus. Assn. (sponsor), Club of Sonterra. Republican. Office: Med Diversified Svcs 15600 San Pedro Ave Ste 107 San Antonio TX 78232-3738

BAKER, HERMAN, vitaminologist; b. N.Y.C., Jan. 22, 1926; s. Harry and Fannie Baker; m. Shirley Levitz, Nov. 15, 1952; children: Elliott Robert, Joel Martin. BS, CCNY, 1946; MS, Emory U., 1948; PhD, NYU, 1956. Cert. specialist human nutrition Am. Bd. Nutrition. Research asst. Columbia U., N.Y.C., 1949-50; research assoc. Mt. Sinai Hosp., N.Y.C., 1950-60; assoc. prof. medicine N.J. Med. Sch., Jersey City, 1960-70; prof. medicine and preventive medicine N.J. Med. Sch., Newark, 1970—. Contbr. over 270 articles on metabolic imbalances to profl. jours.; author: Clinical Vitaminology: Methods and Interpretation. Home: 27 Wilk Rd Edison NJ 08837-2726 Office: NJ Med Sch Martland GB 159 65 Bergen St Newark NJ 07107-3001

BAKER, HOWARD ALLEN, physician, retired naval officer; b. Carleton, Mich., Sept. 5, 1914; s. Gilbert and Olive (Sweet) B.; m. Dorothy M. Bennett, Sept. 5, 1942; children: Howard Allen III, Denise Lynne, Laurie Elise. BS, Wayne State U., 1939, MD, 1943; postgrad., U. Pa., 1955; fellow in cardio-thoracic surgery, Cleve. Clinic, 1960. Diplomate, Am. Bd. Surgery. Intern Grace Hosp., Detroit, 1943-44; resident in surgery Grace Hosp., 1944-45, 46-48; pvt. practice surgery Detroit, 1948-51; commd. ensign USN, 1941, advanced through grades to capt., 1964, physician, surgeon various naval hosps., 1951-59; dir. phys. standards, Bur. Medicine and Surgery Dept. Navy, Washington, 1962-64; chief surgery Guantanomo Bay, Cuba, 1965; coord. allied and civilian med. svcs. USN, Vietnam, 1966-67; commanding officer naval hosp. USN, Corpus Christi, Tex., 1969-71; ret. USN, 1971; clin. asst. prof. surgery, Boston U., 1967-71; surg. cons., disability determination sect. Fla. Dept. Health and Rehab. Svc., Tallahassee, 1971-85, cons., 1989—. Recipient 15 mil. decorations including Bronze Star medal. Fellow ACS;

mem. I Corp Med. Soc. Vietnam, Phi Rho Sigma. Baptist. Home: 1010 American Eagle Blvd Sun City Center FL 33573-5171

BAKER, IRENA MIHELCIC, orthodontist, educator; b. Rijeka, Croatia, Nov. 11, 1955; d. Bogomir and Ana (Coza) Mihelcic; m. Doug G. Baker, July 23, 1983; children: Lucie F., Gordon D. DDS, U. Zagreb, Croatia, 1980; orthodontic cert., U. Louisville, 1983. Lic. orthodontist, Ky., Wash. Student instr. U. Zagreb, 1975-77, resident, 1980-81; staff U. Louisville, 1981-83, asst. prof., 1984-92; pvt. practice, Seattle, 1992—; clin. prof. U. Wash., Seattle, 1994—; cons. Ky. Commn. for Handicapped Children, Louisville, 1990-95, Kosair Children Hosp., Louisville, 1990-95. Recipient N. Keasling award N.Am. Begg Soc., 1986. Mem. ADA, Am. Assn. Orthodontists, Am. Assn. Women Dentists, Pacific Soc. Orthodontists, Wash. Dental Assn., Wash. Orthodontic Assn., Wash. Assn. Women Dentists (v.p. 1995). Democrat. Roman Catholic. Office: 4704 Rainier Ave S Seattle WA 98118-1658

BAKER, JOHN CHARLES, laboratory manager; b. Aberdeen, Wash., Mar. 14, 1954; m. Julie Carlson. AS, Grays Harbor Coll., 1974; BS in Biology cum laude, Seattle U., 1976; MBA, City U., 1989. Cert. med. tech. Tech. supr. Ake Labs., Tacoma, 1979-87; tech. supr. toxicology Tacoma Gen. Hosp., 1987-90, mgr. toxicology lab., 1990-92, mgr. chemistry and immunology lab., 1992—. Mem. Phi Theta Kappa. Home: 1908 N Oakes St # 17 Tacoma WA 98406-7502 Office: Tacoma Gen Hosp 315 S K St Tacoma WA 98405-4234

BAKER, JOHN THEODORE, osteopath; b. Hamilton, Ont., Can., Mar. 2, 1920; came to U.S., 1946; s. Carey White and Marie Margaret (Zoellner) B.; m. Mary Eleanor Brown, Jan. 12, 1946; children: Robert John, Wendy Joy, Colleen Dawn. DO, Chgo. Coll. Osteopathy, 1943. Lic. osteopath Mich., Ariz., Ga., Okla. Intern Art Centre Hosp., Detroit, 1945; pvt. practice family physician West Dearborn, Mich., 1946-72; med. dir./dir. med. edn. Garden City Osteo. Hosp., 1962-72, Saginaw (Mich.) Osteo. Hosp., 1972-77; dir. med. edn. Phoenix Gen. Hosp., 1977-79, Doctors Hosp., Atlanta, 1979-84; assoc. prof. Okla. Coll. Osteo. Medicine and Surgery, Tulsa, 1984-86; pvt. practice Phoenix, 1989-93; ret.; inspecter internship , cons. Am. Osteo. Assn., mem. com. post-dr. edn., cons. on internships. Team physician Little League Football, West Dearborn; camping physician Boy Scouts Am., Wayne County, MIch.; chmn. com. Dearborn YMCA; physician Boys Club of Am., West Dearborn; bd. dirs. Garden City Hosp., Chgo. Coll. Osteo. Medicine, Shadow Rock Ch. With Royal Can. Navy, 1943-45. Fellow Acad. Osteo. Dirs. Med. Edn. (hon.); mem. Chgo. Coll. Osteo Medicine Alumni Assn. (Gold Medallaion Club, pres., bd. dirs. 1964-88, Outstanding Alumni award 1983, 93), Am. Osteo. Assn. (hon.). Republican. Home: 1744 W Acoma Dr Phoenix AZ 85023

BAKER, JOSEPH WILMER, cardiothoracic surgeon; b. Washington, Oct. 31, 1957; s. Joseph Fred and Maria Isabelle (Flores) B.; m. Tracy Lea Brown; children: Kathryn Marie, Emily Jo. BS, Duke U., 1979, MD, 1983. Diplomate Am. Bd. Surgery, Am. Bd. Thoracic Surgery. Resident in gen. surgery U. Va., Charlottesville, 1983-89, chief resident in gen. surgery, 1988-89, resident in thoracic surgery, 1989-90, chief resident in thoracic surgery, 1990-91; cardiothoracic surgeon Cardiovascular Surg. Assoc., Roanoke, Va., 1991—. Fellow ACS, Soc. Thoracic Surgeons; mem. So. Thoracic Surg. Soc., Va. Surg. Soc., Muller Surg. Soc. Home: 5421 Levi Rd SW Roanoke VA 24018 Office: Cardiovascular Surg Assocs 102 Highland Ave SE Ste 303 Roanoke VA 24013

BAKER, L. DWIGHT, plastic surgeon; b. LaFayette, Ala., Jan. 16, 1951; s. Luther Dwight and Catherine Mae (Harris) B.; m. Dorris Loretta Handley, June 21, 1975; children: Elizabeth Handley, Catherine Handley, Clayton Handley. BS in Chemistry, Auburn (Ala.) U., 1973; MD, U. South Ala., Mobile, 1977. Diplomate Am. Bd. Surgery. Intern Carraway Meth. Med. Ctr., Birmingham, Ala., 1977-78, resident in surgery, 1978-82; practice gen. surgery La Grange, Ga., 1982-86, Montgomery, Ala., 1986-91; resident in plastic and reconstructive surgery Mayo Clinic, Rochester, Minn., 1991-93; pvt. practice plastic and reconstructive surgery Feagin, Owen & Baker, Dothan, Ala., 1993—; med. dir. Rehab. Assocs., Dothan, 1994-95. Fellow ACS, Southeastern Surg. Congress; mem. AMA, Houston County Med. Soc., Med. Assn. State of Ala., So. Med. Assn. Office: Feagin Owens & Baker 4300 W Main St Ste 43 Dothan AL 36301-1054

BAKER, LORI ANN, physical therapist; b. Detroit, July 16, 1957; d. Richard Gary and Mary Barbara (Vail) Griffith; m. Joseph Kurtyka, Nov. 22, 1980 (div. Sept. 1984); m. William Randall Baker, June 24, 1989; 1 child, Katherine Elisabeth Baker. BS, U. Mich., 1979; MBA, Kennesaw Coll., 1990. Phys. therapist Lansing Sch. Dist., Mich., 1979-81, Mich. Sch. for Blind, 1980-81, Ingham Med. Ctr., 1980-81; pediatric phys. therapist Toledo Hosp., 1981-84, Childrens Ortho Hosp. and Med. Ctr., Seattle, 1984-85; pediatric clin. specialist Kennestone Hosp., Marietta Ga., 1985-89, supr. acute care therapy, 1989-90; phys. therapist Am. Home Health Care, 1987-91; contract phys. therapist, 1990-91; clin. mgr. Atlanta Rehab. Inst., 1991-95; phys. therapist Grandview Health Care Ctr., Atlanta, 1995—, Lumpkin County Schs., Atlanta, 1995—, Global Rehab., 1996—. Mem. Am. Phys. Therapy Assn., Neurodevelopmental Treatment Assn. Avocations: stained glass; furniture refinishing, running, biking. Home: 402 Wild Hill Rd Woodstock GA 30188-1972 Office: 340 W Peachtree St NW Ste 250 Atlanta GA 30308-3517

BAKER, LOWELL HOWARD, neurologist; b. Mpls., Oct. 26, 1938; s. Abe Burton and Rose (Witzman) B.; children: Gary Scott, Barry Stewart, Deborah Sue. BA cum laude, Macalester Coll., 1960; MD, State U. of Iowa, 1964. Diplomate Am. Bd. of Psychiatry and Neurology. Intern Hennepin County Hosp., Mpls., 1965-68; resident neurology U. Minn., Mpls., 1968; fellow NIH, Bethesda, Md., 1970; neurologist Mpls. Clinic, 1970-72, Noran Neurology Clinic, Mpls., 1972-79, A.B. Baker Neurology Clinic, Mpls., 1979—; clin. prof. U. Minn., Mpls., 1981—; chief neurology Mt. Sinai Hosp., Mpls., 1980—; chief neuro scis. Met. Mt. Sinai, Mpls., 1976. Comdr. NIH, 1968-70. Fellow Am. Acad. Neurology; mem. Minn. Med. Soc., Hennepin County Med. Soc. Office: AB Baker Neurol Clinic 910 E 26th St # 425 Minneapolis MN 55404

BAKER, MARK EARLY, radiology educator; b. Pasadena, Calif., Mar. 2, 1953; s. William Edward and Virginia Markley (Voigtlander) B.; m. Deborah Lyn Saylor, Dec. 30, 1978; children: Rebekah Lyn, Jonathan Early. AB cum laude, Occidental Coll., 1974; student, U. Calif., Santa Barbara, 1970-71; MD cum laude, Loyola U., Chgo., 1978. Cert. in diagnostic radiology Am. Bd. Radiology. Intern internal medicine Loyola U. Affiliated Hosps., Maywood, Ill., 1978-79, resident internal medicine, 1979-80, resident radiology, 1980-83; fellow radiology Duke U. Med. Ctr., Durham, N.C., 1983-84, asst. prof. radiology, 1984-89, assoc. prof. radiology, 1989-94, chief section of abdominal imaging, 1992-94; head sect. abdominal imaging dept. radiology Cleve. Clinic Found., 1994—. Reviewer Am. Jour. Roentgenology, 1977, mem. editorial bd., 1979—; reviewer Radiology, 1977—; contbr. sci. papers and revs. to profl. jours.; co-author books. Clin. fellow Am. Cancer Soc., 1983; recipient Editor's Recognition award Radiology Jour., 1986-95. Mem. Am. Roentgen Ray Soc., Radiol. Soc. N.Am., Soc. Gastrointestinal Radiologists, Assn. Univ. Radiologists, AMA, Alpha Sigma Nu, Alpha Omega Alpha. Office: Cleveland Clinic Foundation Dept Radiology Hb6 9500 Euclid Ave Cleveland OH 44195-0001

BAKER, MARSHALL MANFRED, health facility administrator; b. Wichita, Kans., Aug. 26, 1943; s. Robert Winfred Baker; m. Kathleen Mary Nagel, June 7, 1969; children: Wendy Colleen, Robert Marshall, Brandon Matthew. AA in Gen. Bus., Wenatchee Valley Coll., 1966; BS in Bus. Mgmt., U. Idaho, 1968, MS in Bus. Adminstrn., 1970. Adminstrv. asst. Gritman Meml. Hosp., Moscow, Idaho, 1966-68; adminstr. Fronk Clinic, Honolulu, 1968; adminstrv. dir. Walla Walla (Wash.) Clinic, 1969-77; exec. dir. Ctrl. Ohio Med. Group, Columbus, 1977-84; exec. v.p. Anesthesia Med. Cons., Albuquerque, 1984-92; sr. v.p. Tulsa Regional Med. Ctr., 1992-94; exec. dir. St. Luke's Regional Med. Ctr., Boise, Idaho, 1994—. Pres. Idaho Theater Youth, 1996—. Fellow Am. Coll. Med. Practice Execs. (pres. 1990); mem. Med. Group Mgmt. Assn. (pres. Ohio chpt. 1984, N.Mex. chpt. 1987), Soc. Ambulatory Care Profls., Rotary Internat., Southwest Boise chpt. Office: St Luke's Regional Med Ctr 190 E Bannock St Boise ID 83712

BAKER, PAUL THORNELL, anthropology educator; b. Burlington, Iowa, Feb. 28, 1927; s. Palmer Ward Baker and Viola Isabelle (Thornell) Loughlin; m. Thelma Marion Shoher, Feb. 21, 1949; children—Deborah C., Amy L., Joshua S., Felicia B. Student, U. Miami, 1947-49; B.A., U. N.Mex., 1951; Ph.D., Harvard U., 1956. Researcher U.S. Army Q.M., Natick, Mass., 1952-57; asst. prof. anthropology Pa. State U., University Park, 1957-61, assoc. prof., 1961-65, prof., 1965-81, Evan Pugh prof. anthropology, 1981-87, Evan Pugh prof. emeritus, 1987—, head dept., 1980-85; sci. advisor Wenner-Gren Found., N.Y.C., 1980-83; mem. U.S. Commn. for UNESCO 1982-84, exec. commn. 1983-84. Editor: Biology of Human Adaptability, 1966, Man in the Andes, 1976, Biology of High Altitude Peoples, 1978, The Changing Samoans, 1986; co-author: (with G.A. Harrison, J.M. Tanner, D.R. Pilbeam) Human Biology, 1988. Served with U.S. Army, 1945-47. Recipient Huxley medal Royal Anthrop. Inst. Gt. Brit., 1982; decorated Yugoslavian Order of the Golden Star with Necklace, 1988; Fulbright research scholar, 1962; Guggenheim Found. fellow, 1974-75. Fellow Am. Anthrop. Assn. (assoc. editor jour. 1973-76); mem. NAS, Am. Assn. Phys. Anthropologists (pres. 1969-71, Charles R. Darwin Lifetime Achievement award 1993), Human Biology Coun. (pres. 1974-77), Internat. Assn. Human Biologists (pres. 1980-89), Internat. Union Anthropol. and Ethnol. Scis. (v.p. 1988-93, sr. v.p. 1993-98). Address: 47-450 Lulani St Kaneohe HI 96744-4717

BAKER, RICHARD EARL, JR., podiatrist; b. Plymouth, Mass., June 12, 1960; s. Richard Earl and Therese Mary (Broullard) B. BA, Holy Cros Coll., 1982; postgrad., Bridgewater State Coll., 1982-85; D of Podiatric Medicine, Ohio Coll. Podiatric Medicine, 1989. Podiatric resident West Roxbury (Mass.) VA Med. Ctr., 1989-90, chief podiatric resident, 1990-91; chief podiatry Providence VA Med. Ctr., 1991—; clin. prof. surgery Brown U. Sch. Medicine, Providence, 1993—. Contbr. articles to profl. jours. Recipient KTE Pres.'s award, 1988. Mem. Am. Podiatric Med. Assn., Am. Coll. Podopediatrics, Am. Coll. Foot Orthopedics, Amn. Bd. Podiatric Orthopedics. Roman Catholic. Home: 736A Park Ave Cranston RI 02910-2115 Office: Providence VA Med Ctr 830 Chalkstone Ave Providence RI 02908-4734

BAKER, RICHARD KENNETH GEORGE, communications company executive; b. London, Dec. 31, 1941; m. Joan Elizabeth Summers, Oct. 6, 1968; children: Richard, Kenneth, George. Audit clk. Price Waterhouse, London, 1967-68; asst. chief acct. Maxwell Communication Corp., London, 1968-70, treas., 1970-82; dep. fin. dir. to fin. dir. Maxwell Communication Corp., Oxford, Eng., 1982; dep. mng. dir. Maxwell Communication Corp., Oxford, 1984—; dir. Macmillan, Inc., N.Y.C., 1988—. Fellow Inst. Chartered Accts., Assn. Corp. Treas. Office: Maxwell Communications Corp, Maxwell House New Fetter Ln, London EC1N 2NE, England

BAKER, ROBERT N., neurologist; b. Inglewood, Calif., Mar. 25, 1923; s. Glyn Maynard and Ruth Elizabeth (Norton) B.; m. Noreen Jacquelyne Isaak, June 19, 1971; children: Mark, Kent, Melanie. BA, Park Coll., 1944; MD, U. So. Calif., 1950. Diplomate Am. Bd. Psychiatry & Neurology. From instr. to assoc. prof. neurology UCLA Med. Sch., L.A., 1950-70; prof. U. Nebr. Med. Sch., Omaha, 1970—. Capt. USAF, 1994-96. Grantee NIH, 1956-76. Fellow Am. Acad. Neurology (sec./treas. 1962-64), Am. Neurol. Assn.; mem. AMA, Colo. Med. Soc. Democrat. Unitarian. Home: 690 Summerset Ct Estes Park CO 80517 Office: Estes Park Specialty Clinic 555 Prospect Ave Estes Park CO 80517

BAKER, ROLLIN HAROLD, biologist; b. Cordova, Ill., Nov. 11, 1916; s. Charles Laurence and Minnie Louise (Perkins) B.; m. Mary Elizabeth Waddell, Mar. 21, 1939; children: Elizabeth Alice, Bruce Rollin, Byron Laurence. B.A., U. Tex., 1937; M.S., Tex. A. and M. U., 1938; Ph.D., U. Kans., 1948. Wildlife tech. Nat. Park Service, Texas Big Bend, summer 1937; field biologist Tex. Coop. Wildlife Research Unit, College Station, 1933-39; biologist Tex. Game and Fish Commn., 1939-43; asst. curator mammals Mus. Natural History, U. Kans., 1948-55, asst. instr., 1946-48, instr., 1948-49, asst. prof., 1949-54, assoc. prof. zoology, 1954-55; acting dir. Mus. Natural History, 1950-51; dir. mus., prof. zoology and fisheries and wildlife Mich. State U., East Lansing, 1955-82, dir., prof. emeritus, 1983—; curator Prairie Edge Mus., Eagle Lake, Tex., 1983—; leader mus. expdns. western states and Mex., for collecting and observating animal life, 1949-83; also vis. investigator Rockefeller Inst. Medicine, 1944. Author: Michigan Mammals, 1983; contbr. more than 180 articles to profl. jours. Served from ensign to lt. USNR, 1943-46; capt. Res., ret. Fellow AAAS; mem. Am. Soc. Mammalogists (dir. 1956-78), Wildlife Soc., Am. Ornithol. Soc. Southwestern Naturalists, Soc. Study Evolution, Soc. Systematic Zoology (coun. 1958-61), Ecol. Soc. Am., Tex. Soc. Mammalogists (hon.; pres. 1983-84), Explorers Club, Mich. Polar-Equator Club (pres. 1976-78), Rotary, Sigma Xi, Alpha Epsilon Delta, Beta Beta Beta, Phi Sigma, Tau Kappa Epsilon, Phi Kappa Phi. Home: 302 N Strickland St Eagle Lake TX 77434-1841

BAKER, RUBY LINDA, medical and surgical, intravenous therapy nurse; b. Ft. Bragg, Calif., Feb. 11, 1965; d. Eugene F. and Felia Sol (Abad) B. BSN, Emory U., Atlanta, 1988; Nat. Intravenous Therapy Cert., 1992. RN, N.J., Pa.; Cert. RN infusion. Staff nurse Emory U. Hosp., Atlanta, 1988-89, Hosp. U. Pa., Phila., 1989-91; staff nurse intravenous therapy Hahnemann U. Hosp., Phila., 1991-93, nurse, clin. coord. IV team, 1993-94; DON IV therapy Healthcare Pharmacy Svcs., Erdenheim, Pa., 1994-95; vascular access specialist Becten-Dickinson Vascular Access, 1995—; mem. Nurse Practice Coun., 1993-94; mem. instnl. rev. bd. Hahnemann U. Hosp., 1994. Mem. Intravenous Nurses Soc. Home and Office: 705 Aberdeen Ln Blackwood NJ 08012-5523

BAKER, SAUL PHILLIP, geriatrician, cardiologist, internist; b. Cleve., Dec. 7, 1924; s. Barnet and Florence (Kleinman) B. B.S. in Physics, Case Inst. Tech., 1945; postgrad., Western Res. U., 1946-47; M.Sc. in Physiology, Ohio State U., 1949, M.D., 1953, Ph.D. in Physiology, 1957; J.D., Case Western Res. U., 1981. Intern Cleve. Met. Gen. Hosp., 1953-54; sr. asst. surgeon Gerontology Br. Nat. Heart Inst, NIH, now Gerontology Research Ctr., Nat. Inst. Aging, 1954-56; asst. vis. staff physician dept. medicine Balt. City Hosps. (now Francis Scott Key Hosp.) and Johns Hopkins Hosp., 1954-56; sr. asst. resident in internal medicine U. Chgo. Hosps., 1956-57; asst. prof. internal medicine Chgo. Med. Sch., 1957-62; assoc. prof. internal medicine Cook County Hosp. Grad. Sch. Medicine, Chgo., 1958-62; assoc. attending physician Cook County Hosp., 1957-62; practice medicine specializing in geriatrics, cardiology, internal medicine Cleve., 1962-70, 72-93, cons., 1993—; head dept. geriatrics St. Vincent Charity Hosp., Cleve., 1964-67; cons. internal medicine and cardiology Bur. Disability Determination, Old-Age and Survivors Ins., Social Security Adminstrn., 1963—; cons. internal medicine City of Cleve., 1964—; medicare med. cons. Gen. Am. Life Ins. Co., St. Louis, 1970-71; cons. internal medicine and cardiology Ohio Bur. Worker's Compensation, 1964—; cons. cardiovascular disease FAA, 1973—; cons. internal medicine and cardiology State of Ohio, 1974—. Contbr. articles to profl. and sci. jours. Mem. sci. coun. Northeastern Ohio affiliate Am. Heart Assn.; former mem. adv. com. Sr. Adult div. Jewish Community Ctr. Cleve.; mem. vis. com. colls. Case Western Res. U.; former mem. com. older people Fedn. Community Planning Cleve. Fellow AAAS, Am. Coll. Cardiology, Gerontol. Soc. Am. (former Ohio regent), Am. Geriatrics Soc., Cleve. Med. Library Assn. (life); mem. Am. Physiol. Soc., AMA, Ohio Med. Assn., N.Y. Acad. Scis., Chgo. Soc. Internal Medicine, Am. Fedn. Clin. Research, Soc. Exptl. Biology and Medicine, Am. Diabetes Assn., Diabetes Assn. Greater Cleve. (profl. sect.), Am. Heart Assn. (fellow council arteriosclerosis), Nat. Assn. Disability Examiners, Nat. Rehab. Assn., Am. Pub. Health Assn., Acad. Medicine Cleve., Internat. Soc. Cardiology (council epidemiology and prevention), Am. Soc. Law and Medicine, Sigma Xi, Phi Delta Epsilon, Sigma Alpha Mu (past pres. Cleve. alumni club). Club: Cleve. Clinical (past sec.). Lodges: Masons (32 degree), Shriners. Home: PO Box 24246 Cleveland OH 44124-0246

BAKER, SUSAN P., public health educator; b. Atlanta, May 31, 1930; d. Charles Laban and Susan (Lowell) Pardee; m. Timothy Danforth Baker, June 23, 1951; children—Timothy D., David C., Susan L. A.B., Cornell U., Ithaca, N.Y., 1951; M.P.H., Johns Hopkins U., Balt., 1968. Rsch. assoc. Office of Chief Med. Examiner, Balt., 1968-81; rsch. assoc. Johns Hopkins Sch. Hygiene and Pub. Health, Balt., 1968-71, asst. prof., 1971-74, assoc. prof., 1974-83, prof. health policy and mgmt., 1983—, joint appointment in environ. health scis., 1975—, joint appointment in pediatrics, 1983—, dir. Injury Prevention Ctr., 1987-88, co-dir., 1938—, acting head div. pub. health, 1988-90, joint appointment emergency medicine Sch. Hygiene & Pub., 1991—; vis. prof. U. Minn. Sch. Pub. Health, 1975-87; chmn. nat. rev. panel for nat. accident sampling sys. Dept. Transp., Washington, 1976-81; vice chmn. com. on trauma rsch. Nat. Rsch. Coun., Washington, 1984-85; mem. adv. com. on injury control CDC, 1989—; commr. West Latir Ditch Assn., N.Mex., 1990; vis. lectr. in injury prevention Harvard Sch. Pub. Health, 1984-87; John T. Law meml. lectr. U. Calgary, Alta., 1984; expert panel Age 60 rule FAA, 1991-93; cons. and lectr. in field. Author: (monograph) Fatally Injured Drivers, 1970 (Prince Bernhard medal 1974), The Injury Fact Book, 1984, 2d edit., 1992, Saving Children: A Guide to Injury Prevention, 1991; contbr. articles to books and articles to profl. jours. Recipient Charles A. Dana award for pioneering achievements in health, 1989, Johns Hopkins U. Disting. Alumnus award, 1996. Fellow Am. Assn. Automotive Medicine (bd. dirs. 1971-76, pres. 1974-75, award of merit 1985); mem. APHA (governing coun. 1975-77, jour. bd. 1983-87), Am. Trauma Soc. (bd. dirs., Disting. Achievement award 1981, Stone Lectureship award 1985, Fitz Oration award 1996), Aerospace Med. Assn. (editl. bd. 1994—), Wing (hon.), Assn. for Surgery of Trauma (hon.), Phi Beta Kappa, Delta Omega. Office: Johns Hopkins U Sch Hygiene & Pub Health 624 N Broadway Baltimore MD 21205-1901

BAKER, THERESA SUZANNE, military officer, health science facility administrator; b. Bremerton, Wash., Mar. 10, 1952; d. William Henry and Irene (Manley) B.; m. Patrick John Pound, Aug. 4, 1979. A of Bus. Adminstrn., Highline Community Coll., Midway, Wash., 1972; BBA, Park (Mo.) Coll., 1975; M of Hosp. and Health Adminstrn., Xavier U., Cin., 1980. Commd. 2d lt. USAF, 1976, advanced through grades to lt. col., 1992; comdr. Med. Squadron Sect., Vandenberg AFB, Calif., 1976-77; adminstr. resource mgmt. USAF Hosp., Vandenberg AFB, 1977-78; adminstr. nursing services USAF Regional Hosp., March AFB, Calif., 1980-81, dir. med. logistics, 1981-82; dir. planning, ops. and tng. uniformed services U. of Health Scis., Bethesda, Md., 1982-84, dir. mil. med. field studies uniformed services, 1982-86, chief basic scis. dept. mil. medicine, 1984-86; adminstr. USAF Clinic, Vance AFB, Okla., 1986-89; adminstr., dir. resource mgmt., dir. personnel & adminstrn. Commander Med. Squadron Sect. Wiesbaden Med. Ctr., Germany, 1989-93; adminstr., dir. base med. svcs. Izmir Clinic, Turkey, 1993-95; joint regional med. planner Fifth U.S. Army, Ft. Lewis, Wash., 1995—. Contbr. articles to profl. jours. Instr. basic life Bethesda chpt. ARC, 1984-86. Recipient Outstanding Med. Service award U.S. Air Force Assn., 1977. Fellow Am. Coll. Healthcare Execs.; mem. Assn. Mil. Surgeons U.S., Am. Bus. Women's Assn. (Woman of Yr. 1977). Club: Toastmasters (Disting. Toastmaster 1985). Office: Fifth US Army JRMPO Mail Stop 108 Fort Lewis WA 98433-9500

BAKER, THOMAS, pharmacologist, toxicologist; b. Mineola, N.Y., Sept. 19, 1933; s. Raymond Ira and Agatha (Carroll) B.; A.B., Hunter Coll., CUNY, 1968; M.S., Grad. Sch. Med. Scis., Cornell U., 1971; m. Marion Whitaker, Nov. 11, 1951; children: Patricia Anne, Susan, Thomas, Peter, David, Marian. Rsch. asst. Med. Coll., Cornell U., N.Y.C., 1962-68, rsch. assoc., 1968-76, asst. prof. pharmacology, 1976-81, assoc. prof., 1981-82; dir. rsch. St. Joseph's Hosp. and Med. Ctr., Paterson, N.J., 1983-90, Monmouth Med. Ctr., Long Branch, N.J., 1990—. Mem. AAAS, N.Y. Acad. Scis., Am. Soc. Pharmacology and Exptl. Therapeutics, Soc. Neurosci., Internat. Union Pharmacology (sect. on toxicology), Soc. Exptl. Biology and Medicine, Soc. Toxicology (neurotoxicology specialty sect.), Internat. Soc. for Study of Xenbiotics, Internat. Soc. for Myochemistry, Mid-Atlantic Pharmacology Soc., N.J. State Soc. Anesthesiology. Contbr. articles to profl. jours. Office: Monmouth Med Ctr Dept Pediats and Radiology 300 2nd Ave Long Branch NJ 07740-6300

BAKER, THOMAS SANDS, employee assistance professional, minister; b. Phila., Mar. 2, 1944; s. Arthur D. and Louise (Miller) B.; m. Carole Lynn Rogers, Aug. 26, 1978; children: Wendy, Lindsay, Cary, Glenn. BA, Denison U., 1966; MDiv, Princeton (N.J.) Theol. Sem., 1969; DMin, Princeton Theol. Sem., 1993. Sr. counselor Carrier Found., Belle Mead, N.J., 1978-84; employee assistance counselor Priority Systems, Summit, N.J., 1984-85; mgr. REACH, Summit, 1985-86; assistance adminstr. Johnson & Johnson Baby Products, Skillman, N.J., 1986-89; dir. employee assistance program Johnson & Johnson World Hdqrs., New Brunswick, N.J., 1989—. Contbr. articles to profl. jours. Mem. Presbytery of New Brunswick, 1977—, Lawrence Twp. Drug Adv. Bd., Lawrenceville, N.J., 1988—, N.J. Task Force on Compulsive Gambling, Trenton, N.J., 1989—; coach Nat. Youth Sports Coaches Assn., Lawrenceville, 1988—; trustee Lees Coll., Jackson, Ky.; bd. dirs. Crawford House, Skillman, N.J., Trinity Counseling Svc., Princeton, N.J., 1994—. Mem. APHA, Nat. Assn. Drug and Alcoholism Counselors, N.J. Coun. on Compulsive Gambling. Office: Johnson & Johnson World Hdqrs 501 George St New Brunswick NJ 08901-1161

BAKER, TIMOTHY DANFORTH, physician, educator; b. Balt., July 4, 1925; s. Frank and Alice Elizabeth (Chandler) B.; m. Susan Lowell Pardee, June 23, 1951; children: Timothy, David, Susan. BA, Johns Hopkins U., 1948, MPH, 1954; MD, U. Md., 1952. Intern U. Md. Hosp., Balt., 1952-53; resident pub. health N.Y. State Dept. Pub. Health, N.Y.C., 1953-56; health officer Syracuse, N.Y., 1958-59; asst. and acting chief health USAID, India, 1956-58; assoc. prof. Johns Hopkins U. Sch. Pub. Health, Balt., 1959-67, asst. dean, 1959-77, prof. internat. health, health svcs. adminstrn., and environ. health, 1967—, pres. faculty gen. assembly, 1987—; dir. Hubert H. Humphrey scholars program Johns Hopkins U. Sch. Pub. Health, 1987—; v.p., dir. Univ. Assocs., 1973-77; vis. prof. epidemiology U. Minn., 1976; dir. Intermed., 1982—; cons. health planning, med. edn., Brazil, Burma, India, Indonesia, Taiwan, Saudi Arabia, Kuwait, Ukraine, Viet Nam, Md., Calif., D.C.; external examiner U. Singapore. Author: Health Manpower in a Developing Economy, Assessment of Health Status and Needs, International Health Perspectives; contbr. articles to profl. publs. First vice chmn. central com. Republican party, Balt.; del., nominating com. Republican party; bd. dirs., treas. Pan Am. Health Edn. Found. Served with USAF, 1943-45; USPHS, 1956-58. Fellow AAAS (govs. commn. on minority health, task force on violence); mem. Am. Pub. Health Assn. (chmn. epidemiology sect., internat. health sect., Lifetime Achievement award 1994), Md. Med. Soc. (chmn. health manpower com.), Md. Pub. Health Assn. (pres.), Balt. Med. Soc. (chmn. med. care com.), Omicron Delta Kappa, Delta Omega. Republican. Home: 4705 Keswick Rd Baltimore MD 21210-2322 Office: Johns Hopkins U Sch Hygiene 615 N Wolfe St Baltimore MD 21205-2103

BAKER, WINDA LOUISE (WENDY BAKER), social worker; b. Suwannee County, Fla., July 16, 1952; d. Austin Sidney Baker and Jessie Mae (Williams) Baker Jones. BA in Theology, Berkshire Christian Coll., 1974. Clk.-typist State of Fla., Tallahassee, 1974-76; cashier Tallahassee-Eastern Theatres, 1975-76; field rep. Commn. Human Relations, 1976-77; asst. to dir. retirement living, sec., receptionist Advent Christian Village, Dowling Park, Fla., 1977-79, admissions counselor, social worker, after 1979, multi-purpose worker, 1980; geriatric care worker Advent Christian Village, Dowling Park, Fla., 1983-85, med. transcriptionist, 1985, advt. sales staff, 1986-87; processor H&R Block, 1987-1988; legal sec., McAlpin, Fla., 1987—; geriatric care person , Valdosta, Ga., 1989-94, Alpharetta, 1994—. Vol. ARC and Asso. Charities, 1977—; founder Suwannee County Overeaters Anonymous, Live Oak, Fla., 1982; live-in companion for the elderly Serve Care Nursing Svcs. of South Ga., 1988-89, for Ann Mason, 1989-92. Mem. Suwannee County Mental Assn., Assn. Informed Travelers, Christian Fin. Planning, Inc., Cheeks Sch. Gymnastics Alumni. Republican. Advent Christian. Home: 495 N Main St Alpharetta GA 30201

BAKER DAILEY, ALICE ANN, 0physiologist, exercise educator; b. Durant, Okla., Oct. 25, 1946; d. Finis Cortz and Alice Joyce (Hamilton) Baker; m. John Arthur Dailey, Nov. 23, 1985; 1 child, Megan Michelle. BA in Music, U. Okla., 1968; MS, North Tex. State U., 1985. Cert. fitness instr. Am. Coll. Sports Medicine. Piano tchr. Dallas Ind. Sch. Dist., 1969-71; music tchr. Houston Ind. Sch. Dist., 1971-75; mail order adminstr. Neiman-Marcus, Dallas, 1978-81; exercise physiologist Tex. Instruments, Dallas, 1984-86, HealthCheck, 1985, Internat. Athletic Club of Dallas, 1985-87, Verandah Club, 1986-89, Goodbody's, 1988-90; owner, pres. Alice Ann Baker Exercise: Therapeutic Conditioning, Dallas, 1980-90, Physicalmind Method (formerly Pilateds Method), 1988—, PhysioSynthesis, 1991—; owner, pres. Oasis Physical Conditioning Ctr., Inc., 1991—; cons. Region 10 Edn. Svc. Ctr., Dallas, 1985, RepublicBank, Dallas, 1985, Crescent Spag Landry Ctr.; exec. producer and creator exercise video on therapeutic conditioning Warner Amex Community Svcs. Channel, Dallas, 1984-85; presenter in field; research paper presented conf. AAHPERD, Cin., 1986; contbr. articles to profl. jours. Provider continuing edn. credits, 1989—; founding mem. Inst. for Pilateds Method; active mem. Dallas Zoo, Dallas Mus. Art, Sci. Place. Mem. Am. Coun. on Exercise, Am. Coll. Sports Medicine, Internat. Dance Educators Assn., Dallas Dance Coun. (mem. bd.), Kappa Alpha Theta, Phi Kappa Lambda. Home: 5839 Kenwood Ave Dallas TX 75206-5589

BAKHSH, AHMAD, physician, researcher; b. Anga, Punjab, Pakistan, Mar. 1, 1958; s. Muhammad and Qudrat (Begum) B.; m. Adeeba Malik, Sept. 21, 1989; children: Wafa Malik, Iqra Malik. MB, BS, U. Punjab, Pakistan, 1986. House surgeon Holy Family Hosp., Rawalpindi, Pakistan, 1985-86; med. officer Gen. Hosp., Rawalpindi, 1986-89; community med. officer Rural Health Svcs., Rawalpindi, 1989-90; founder Epilepsy Adv. Ctr., Rawalpindi, 1989—; rsch. fellow in paediatric neurosurgy Quaide-Azam Post-Grad. Med. Coll., Islamabad; coord. Nat. Epilepsy Adv. Coun. Pakistan, Rawalpindi. Mem. Internat. League against Epilepsy, Internat. Bur. for Epilepsy, Epilepsy Found. Am., Brit. Epilepsy Assn., Epilepsy Found. Australia, Swiss League aginst Epilepsy. Islam. Home: Z1119 Ratta Rd, Rawalpindi, Punjab Punjab, Pakistan Office: Epilepsy Adv Ctr, Z-1119 Ratta Rd, Rawalpindi Punjab, Pakistan

BAKKER, CORNELIS B., psychiatrist, educator; b. Rotterdam, Holland, Jan. 6, 1929; came to U.S., 1953, naturalized, 1963; s. Willem and Poulina J. (Reiff) B.; m. Marianne K. Rabdau, June 11, 1955; children: Paul, James, Gabrielle. M.D. with honors, U. Utrecht, Holland, 1952. Intern Clinics of Rotterdam, 1952-53, Sacred Heart Hosp., Spokane, 1953-54; resident in psychiatry Eastern State Hosp., Medical Lake, Wash., 1954-56, U. Utrecht, 1956-57, U. Mich. Med. Sch., 1957-59; instr., research asso. psychiatry U. Mich., Ann Arbor, 1959-60; instr. psychiatry U. Wash., Seattle, 1960-63; asst. prof. U. Wash., 1963-67, assoc. prof., 1967-72, prof. psychiatry, 1972-79, dir. Adult Psychiat. Inpatient Service, 1961-68; dir. Adult Devel. Program, 1968-79; prof., head dept. psychiatry U. Ill. Coll. Medicine, Peoria, 1979-84; med. dir. dept. psychiatry Sacred Heart Med. Ctr., Spokane, 1984—; clin. prof. dept. psychiatry and behavioral scis. U. Wash. Sch. Medicine, Seattle, 1985—; psychiat. cons. Soc. Sec. Hearings and Appeals, 1963-79, Ketchikan Community Mental Health Center, 1972-77. Contbr. articles to profl. jours.; author: (with M.K. Bakker Rabdau) No Trespassing! - Explorations in Human Territoriality, 1973. Dutch Govt. scholar, 1951-52, 52-53; Fulbright grantee, 1953; Fogarty Sr. fellow U. Leuven, Belgium, 1977-78; recipient Significant Achievement award Am. Psychiatric Assn., 1975. Fellow Am. Psychiatric Assn., Am. Coll. Psychiatrists. Office: Sacred Heart Med Ctr Dept Psychiatry 101 W 8th Ave PO Box 2555 Spokane WA 99220-2555

BALABAN-KRAUSS, JUDY CHARLOTTE, home health care nurse; b. N.Y.C., Nov. 28, 1951; d. Dave and Rose (Gross) Balaban; m. David Krauss, Aug. 17, 1975; children: Lisa, Eli. BA, CCNY, 1973, BSN, 1978. Staff nurse Mt. Sinai Hosp., N.Y.C., 1978-79; nursing supr. Upjohn Health Care, Gainesville, Fla., 1979-81, Nationwide Home Care, Goshen, N.Y., 1982; owner, DON Wellness Home Care, Goshen, 1983—; mem. Orange County sub. area coun. Hudson Valley Health Systems Agy., Tuxedo, N.Y., 1984-86, Sullivan County sub. area coun. 1993—. Mem. Jewish Family Svc. Com., Middletown, N.Y., 1985-87. Mem. N.Y. State Assn. Health Care Providers. Office: Wellness Home Care South ST and Rte 17M 252 Main St Goshen NY 10924

BALADERIAN, NORA JEAN, psychologist; b. L.A., July 30, 1945; d. O. Eugene and Esther Marie (Wilke) Wald; m. Demetrio Roberto Zuniga Bolanos, Sept. 6, 1967 (div. 1969); 1 child, Margret E. Erickson. BA, Calif. State U., Northridge, 1967, MA, 1979; PhD, Sierra U., 1985. Dir., therapist Beverly Hills (Calif.) Counseling Ctr., 1983-94, Counseling Ctr. West L.A., 1994—; dir., rschr. Disability Abuse and Personal Rights Project SPECTRUM Inst., L.A., 1980—. Author: Survivors Handbook for Sexual Assault Survivors with Disability, 1986, Interviewing Skills to Use with Persons with Disabilities, 1992, Parent's Guidebook on Sexual Assault, 1993; co-author: Answers to Questions Adolescents Have About Sex, 1986. Commr. Personal Privacy Commn. Calif., Sacramento, 1980-82; co-chair Task Force on Family Diversity, L.A., 1986-88; chair Nat. Task Force on Abuse of Adults and Children with Disabilities, 1991—. Mem. Nat. Task Force on Abuse and Disability (dir. 1989—), Nat. Coalition on Abuse and Disability (immediate past chair 1993-95), State Task Force on Abuse of Disabled Children (chair 1989—), Am. Psychol. Assn., L.A. County Psychol. Assn. Office: Counseling Ctr West LA 2100 Sawtelle Blvd # 303 West Los Angeles CA 90025-6237

BALAKRISHNAN, KRISHNA (BALKI BALAKRISHNAN), biotechnologist, corporate executive; b. Chelakkara, Kerala, India, June 30, 1955; came to U.S., 1977.; s. S. Krishna Iyer and C.K. Parvathy (Ammal); m. Sheela Kalyanakrishnan, Dec. 12, 1984; children: Karthik, Purnima. MS in Chem., Indian Inst. Tech., 1977; PhD in Biophysical Chem., Stanford U., 1982. Tchr., rsch. asst. dept. biophysical chem. Stanford U., Calif., 1977-82; staff sci. DNAX, Ltd., 1982-84; sr. sci. Biogenex, Inc., 1984-85; dir. hybridoma scis. Berkeley Antibody Co., Calif., 1985—, v.p. rsch. & devel., 1988—; guest lectr., sci. adv. biotech. program Contra Costa Coll., 1992—; indsl. ptrn. Stanford-NIH grad. tng. program biotech., 1992—. Contbr. articles to profl. jours.; speaker in field; patent applications. Mem. AAAS, Am. Chem. Soc. Office: Berkeley Antibody Co 1223 South 47th St Richmond CA 94804-4609

BALANDA, KEVIN PETER, statistician; b. Brisbane, Queensland, Australia, Oct. 17, 1955; s. John Patrick and Joan Delphia (Setterfield) B. BSc in Math. with honors, U. Queensland, Australia, 1977, PhD in Math., 1982, MSc in Statistics, 1986. Sr. tutor U. Queensland, Brisbane, Australia, 1983-86, lectr., 1987, statistician, 1991—; epidemiologist Queensland Health, Brisbane, 1988-90; assoc. dir. Wesley Rsch. Inst., Brisbane, 1995; head statistics sect. Ctr. Health Promotion & Cancer Prevention Rsch., Brisbane, 1995—; cons. Queensland Health, 1991-95. Contbr. articles to profl. jours. Mem. Statistical Soc. Australia, Pub. Health Assn. (exec. Brisbane chpt. 1995—). Home: 93 Jean St, Q-4051 Grange Queensland, Australia Office: U Queensland Med Sch, Herston Rd, Q 4006 Herston Queensland, Australia

BALA-SUBRAMANIAN, AMMUNNI SANKARAN, radiologist; b. Madras, India, Mar. 27, 1938; came to U.S., 1975, naturalized, 1982; s. Aerulil Sankaran and Ammanni Nambiar; M.D., Madras (India) Med. Coll., 1964; m. Kamala Govind, Apr. 29, 1965; children—Tulsi Nila Bala, Anand N. Bala. Asst. surgeon Madras Med. Service, 1964-73; sr. resident officer in emergency medicine and orthopedic surgery Worcester Royal Infirmary, Nottingham Gen. Hosp., Redhill Gen. Hosp. (all Eng.), 1973-75; emergency physician Rochester (N.Y.) Gen. Hosp., 1975-76, staff in diagnostic radiology, 1976-79 ; chief dept. diagnostic radiology and ultrasound Arnold Gregory Meml. Hosp., Albion, N.Y., 1980-89, also pres. med. staff; past courtesy staff Medina (N.Y.) Meml. Hosp.; former chief VA Hosp., Batavia, N.Y., 1989-93; radiologist Va Med. Ctr., Tuskegee, Ala., 1993—; former dir. Western Buffalo Blue Shield. Bd. dirs. Orleans County Health Dept., Albion. Mem. Am. Inst. Ultrasound Medicine, Radiol. Soc. N.Am., Rochester Rontgen Ray Soc., Am. Coll. Radiology, Orleans County Med. Soc. Home: 330 Riversong Way Alpharetta GA 30202-5327

BALCH, WILLIAM RUSSELL, psychologist, educator; b. N.Y.C., Apr. 3, 1946; s. George and Frances (High) B.; m. Martha Arlene Giles, Dec. 27, 1969 (div. 1984); 1 child, Laura Alexis; m. Brenda Kay Martin, Feb. 1, 1992. BA, Haverford (Pa.) Coll., 1968; PhD, U. Minn., 1976. Teaching and rsch. asst. U. Minn., Mpls., 1971-76; instr. Davidson (N.C.) Coll., 1976-77; postdoctoral fellow U. Conn., Storrs, 1977-8; faculty mem. Pa. State U., Altoona, 1978—; mem. promotion and tenure coms. Pa. State U., Altoona, 1987—; chmn. behavior mgmt. com. Altoona Ctr., 1983-86. Contbr. articles to profl. jours. Trustee Humane Soc., Blair County, Pa., 1979-83. With U.S. Army, 1968-71. NIMH fellow, 1976. Mem. Am. Psychol. Soc., Ea. Psychol. Assn., Internat. Coun. Psychologists. Office: Pa State U Altoona PA 16601

BALDASSIN-LIGHT, DONNA MARIE, health services administrator; b. Bklyn., Jan. 12, 1956; d. Louis and Connie (Apicella) B.; m. Robert Light. BSN cum laude, U. Bridgeport, 1978; MPA in Health Care Mgmt., NYU, 1988. RN, N.Y. Staff nurse ICU, N.Y. Hosp.-Cornell Med. Ctr., N.Y.C., 1978-80; pub. health staff nurse Vis. Nurse Svc. N.Y., N.Y.C., 1980-84; patient svc. mgr. Home Care Specialty, N.Y.C., 1984-89; home care cons., 1989-91; dir. of bus. devel. Premier Health Alliance of N.Y., 1991—; devel. programs and svcs. for 18 N.Y.C. Hosps.; negotiates vendor contracts, facilitates hosp. adminstr. peer group meetings for ops., human resources and biomed. tech. Mem. Am. Hosp. Assn. Soc. for Healthcare Mktg. and Planning, Healthcare Bus. Woman's Assn. Home: 4 Horizon Rd G-8 Fort Lee NJ 07024-6743

BALDERSTON, DAVID CHASE, psychotherapist; b. Little Falls, N.Y., Nov. 8, 1933; s. Roy Burdette and Maude Elizabeth (Chase) B.; m. Jean Audrey Merrill, June 1, 1957. BA, Union Coll., Schenectady, 1955; EdD, Columbia U., 1970. Asst. prof. Montclair State Coll., Upper Montclair, N.J., 1964-69; adj. asst. prof. Hunter Coll., CUNY, 1969-71; pvt. practice psychotherapy, N.Y.C., 1970—. Bd. dirs. Gould Farm, psychiat. halfway house, Monterey, Mass., 1974-77; photographer Carnegie Hill Neighbors, N.Y.C., 1985—; lectr. Inst. for Asian Studies, N.Y.C. Mem. APA, Am. Group Psychotherapy Assn., Am. Assn. for Marriage and Family Therapy. Office: 1225 Park Ave Apt 8C New York NY 10128-1758

BALDERSTON, JEAN MERRILL, psychotherapist, writer; b. Providence, Aug. 29, 1936; d. Frederick Augustus and Helen May (Cleveland) Merrill; m. David Chase Balderston, June 1, 1957. BA, U. Conn., 1957; MA, Columbia U., 1965, EdD, 1968. Pvt. practice psychotherapist N.Y.C., 1968—; adj. faculty Douglas Coll. for Women, New Brunswick, N.J., Rutgers U., New Brunswick, Montclair State Coll., Upper Montclair, N.J., CUNY (Hunter Coll. & Queens Coll.), Columbia U., N.Y., Mt. St. Vincent U., Can., 1965-70; editorial bd. N.Y. Quarterly, N.Y.C., 1971-76. Poems have appeared in various lit. mags., and anthologies. Mem. APA, Am. Assn. Marital and Family Therapy, Poetry Soc. Am., Emily Dickinson Internat. Soc., Am. Scandinavian Found. Home and Office: 1225 Park Ave New York NY 10128-1758

BALDI, CHRISTOPHER LAWRENCE, cardiologist; b. West Long Branch, N.J., Feb. 26, 1961; s. Aldo G. Baldi and Judith (Lawrence) Forsyth; m. Mena Scavina, June 11, 1994. BS, U. Scranton, Pa., 1984; DO, U. Medicine & Dentistry N.J., Stratford, 1990. Rotating intern Kennedy Meml. Hosp./U. Med. Ctr., Stratford, 1990-91; resident internal medicine Geisinger Med. Ctr., Danville, Pa., 1991-94; cardiology fellow Grad. Hosp., Phila., 1994-97. Mem. CAP. Mem. AMA, ACP, Am. Osteo. Assn., Am. Coll. Cardiology, Am. Coll. Chest Physician. Home: Apt 704A 5500 Wissahickon Ave Philadelphia PA 19144

BALDRICK, PAUL, toxicologist; b. Londonderry, Northern Ireland, Feb. 27, 1962; s. Matthew and June (Galbraith) B.; m. Lynda Margaret Crighton; 1 child, Camilia Elizabeth. BSc 1st Class in Zoology, Durham (Eng.) U., 1983, PhD, 1987. Cert. biologist; registered toxicologist. Rschr. Durham U., 1983-87; study dir. Huntingdon (Eng.) Life Scis., 1988-92; sr. toxicologist Fisons Pharms., Loughborough, Eng., 1993-96, UCB Pharma, Braine l'Alleud, Belgium, 1996—. Contbr. articles to profl. jours. Mem. Inst. Biology, Brit. Toxicology Soc., Round Table. Mem. Ch. of Eng. Office: UCB SA Pharma Sector, Toxicological Rsch, Chemin du Foriest, B-1420 Brain l'Alleud LE11 ODY, Belgium

BALDWIN, BRIAN EUGENE, medical devices manufacturing company executive; b. Schuyler, Nebr., Jan. 24, 1931; s. George Willard and Edna Marie (Carlson) B.; m. Elizabeth Ann Voris, Dec. 18, 1954 (div. Mar. 1979); children: Laura, Gregory, Jeffery; m. Elizabeth Ann Stone, Dec. 22, 1979. BSME, Northwestern U., 1954, MS in Indsl. Engring., 1955. Mfg. engr. Shure Bros., Evanston, Ill., 1955-56; product devel. engr. Am. Hosp. Supply, Evanston, 1956-58; founder, pres. MPL, Inc., Chgo., 1958-74, HypoMed Corp., Skokie, Ill., 1974-86; chmn. ASIK A/S, Rødby, Denmark, 1978-81; chmn., CEO, Pharm. Basics, Inc., Denver, 1981-86; founder, chmn., CEO, Baxa Corp., Englewood, Colo., 1983—. Patentee over 20 med. and related devices. Counsel to pres. Eleanor Roosevelt Inst., Denver, 1993-94. Mem. Med. Device Mfrs. Assn. (bd. dirs. 1994—), Colo. Med. Device Assn. (founder, pres. 1995), Econ. Club Colo., Valley Country Club, Sigma Xi. Office: Baxa Corp 13760 E Arapahoe Rd Englewood CO 80112

BALDWIN, DAVID SHEPARD, physician; b. Rochester, N.Y., Sept. 5, 1921; s. Jacob and Anna B.; m. Halee Morris, June 24, 1945; children—Neil, Andrew, Daniel, James. B.A., U. Rochester, 1943, M.D., 1945. Intern Barnes Hosp., St. Louis, 1945-46; resident in medicine Bellevue Hosp., N.Y.C., 1946-48; fellow in medicine and physiology N.Y. U. Sch. Medicine, 1948-50, mem. faculty, 1950—, prof. medicine, co-dir. nephrology div., 1972—; attending physician, physician-in-chief hypertension nephritis clinic Bellevue Hosp.; attending physician N.Y. U. Hosp.; cons. nephrology VA Hosp., N.Y.C.; mem. med. adv. bd. council high blood pressure research Am. Heart Assn.; hon. trustee Nat. Kidney Found. N.Y. Author papers in med. jours., chpts. in books. Served as officer M.C. AUS, 1953-55. Mem. Am. Fedn. Clin. Research, Harvey Soc., Am. Heart Assn., Am. Soc. Nephrology, Am. Soc. Clin. Investigation, Internat. Soc. Nephrology, N.Y. Soc. Nephrology (pres. 1974-75), N.Y. Heart Assn. Home: 333 E 69th St New York NY 10021-5549 Office: 550 1st Ave New York NY 10016-6481 also: 20 E 68th St New York NY 10021-5844

BALDWIN, DEWITT CLAIR, JR., physician, educator; b. Bangor, Maine, July 19, 1922; s. DeWitt Clair and Edna Frances (Aikin) B.; m. Michele Albre, Dec. 27, 1957; children: Lisa Anne, Mireille Diane. BA, Swarthmore Coll., 1943; postgrad. Div. Sch., Yale U., 1943-45, MD, 1949. Diplomate Am. Bd. Med. Examiners, Am. Bd. Pediatrics, Am. Bd. Family Practice. Intern, then resident in pediatrics U. Minn. Hosps., Mpls., 1949-51; rsch. fellow Yale Child Study Ctr., New Haven, Conn., 1951-52; instr., asst. prof. pediatrics U. Washington Sch. Medicine, Seattle, 1952-57; resident in psychiatry Met. State Hosp., Waltham, Mass., 1957-58; chief resident in psychiatry Mass. Meml. Hosps., Boston, 1958-59; fellow in child psychiatry Boston City Hosp., 1959-61; asst. prof. pediatrics Harvard Med. Sch., Boston, 1961-67; prof., chmn. behavioral scis. and community health U. Conn. Health Ctr., Farmington, 1967-71; prof. chmn. behavioral scis. U. Nev. Sch. Medicine, Reno, 1971-73, dir. health scis. program, 1971-81, prof. psychiatry and behavioral scis., 1971-83, asst. dean rural health, 1977-83, prof. emeritus psychiatry and behavioral scis., 1983—; pres. Earlham Coll., Richmond, Ind., 1983-84, Connor Prairie Pioneer Settlement Mus., Noblesville, Ind., 1983-84; dir. office edn. research, 1984-88; dir. divsn. med. edn., rsch., info. AMA, Chgo., 1985-88, scholar-in-residence, 1991—; adj. prof. psychiatry and behavioral scis. Northwestern U. Med. Sch., 1986—; adj. prof. med. edn. U. Ill. Coll. Medicine, Chgo., 1988-93; pres. Med. Edn. and Rsch. Assocs., Inc., 1992—; trustee Friends World Coll., Huntington, N.Y., 1980-83; bd. dirs. Nat. League Nursing, N.Y.C., 1981-83, Gt. Lakes Colls. Assn., 1983-84, Am. Rural Health Assn., 1985-87; mem. Nat. Bd. Med. Examiners, 1979-88, Nat. Adv. Coun. Nursing Tng., 1978-92; mem. coun. acad. socs. AAMC, Washington, 1987-94. Author: (with others) Behavioral Sciences and Medical Education, 1983, other books; author, editor: (with others) Interdisciplinary Health Care Teams in Teaching and Practice, 1981, Interdisciplinary Health Team Training, 1978; contbr. over 100 articles to scholarly publs. Recipient Rsch. Career Devel. award USPHS, 1961-67, Louis Gorin award inrural health, 1991; Commonwealth Fund fellow, 1951-52, Milbank Fund fellow, 1968, Rural Health fellow WHO, 1976. Mem. Assn. Behavioral Scis. and Med. Edn. (pres. 1978-79, 90-91), Nev. Bd. Oriental Medicine (pres. 1976-83). Democrat. Mem. Soc. of Friends.

BALDWIN, H. JOHN, dean; b. Ashern, Man., Can., Feb. 24, 1940; came to the U.S., 1964; s. George Herbert and Margaret Edith (Mackey) B.; m. Marilyn Jean Halloran, Nov. 17, 1973 (dec. Nov. 1991). BSc in Pharmacy, U. Man., 1962; MS, Purdue U., 1967, PhD, 1969. Pharmacist Gurvey's Pharmacies, Winnipeg, Man., 1962-64; tchg. asst., instr. Purdue U., West Lafayette, Ind., 1964-68; asst. prof. pharmacy U. Mo., Kansas City, 1968-72, Ohio State U., Columbus, 1973-74; from assoc. prof. to prof., dept. chair W.Va. U., Morgantown, 1974-85; dean Sch. Pharmacy U. Wyo., Laramie, 1985—; bd. dirs. Pharmat, Lawrence, Kans. Co-editor: Pharmacy Ethics, 1991; contbr. articles to profl. jours. Amb. Laramie C. of C. Recipient Appreciation award Wyo. State Bd. Pharmacists, Jackson, 1993. Mem. Am. Assn. Colls. Pharmacy (sect. chair, sec.-treas. 1975-77), Am. Inst. History Pharmacy, Am. Soc. Health-Sys. Pharmacy, Am. Pharm. Assn. (treas.), Wyo. Pharmacists Assn., Laramie Country Club (bd. dirs.). Office: Sch Pharmacy Univ Wyo Box 3375 Laramie WY 82071

BALDWIN, HAROLD SCOTT, pediatrician; b. Honolulu, Md., Dec. 22, 1954. MD, U. Va. Sch. Medicine, 1981. Diplomate Am. Bd. Pediatrics. Intern U. Rochester/Strong Meml. Hosp., N.Y., 1982-86, resident in pediatrics; asst. prof. Children's Hosp., Phila.; fellow in pediatric cardiology U. Iowa Coll. Med., Iowa City, 1986-90. Recipient Established Investigator award Am. Heart Assn., 1995. Mem. AMA. Office: Children's Hosp Phila 3421 S & Civic Ctr Blvd Philadelphia PA 19104

BALDWIN, HELAINE RAE, clinical psychologist; b. Fond du Lac, Wis., Oct. 16, 1940; d. Raymond Edward and Bertha Helen (Schorer) Schrank; m. Keith R. Baldwin, Sept. 21, 1963; children: Laura, Steven, Jennifer. BS, U. Wis., 1962; MA, Roosevelt U., 1987; D in Psychology, Forest Inst., 1991. Lic. Psychologist, Ill. Clin. psychologist PsyCare, Schaumburg, Ill., 1990-93, Complete Psychol. Care, Hoffman Estates, Ill., 1993—. Mem. APA, Ill. Psychol. Assn., Chgo. Psychol. Assn., Am. Assn. of Christian Counselors. Office: Complete Psychol Care Ste 140 2200 W Higgins Rd Hoffman Estates IL 60195

BALDWIN, JOHN CHARLES, surgeon, researcher; b. Ft. Worth, Sept. 23, 1948; s. Charles Leon and Anabel (West) B.; m. Christine Janet Stewart, Mar. 31, 1973; children: Alistair Edward Stewart, John Benjamin West, Andrew Christian William. BA summa cum laude, Harvard U., 1971; MD, Stanford U., 1975; MA Privatim (hon.), Yale U., 1989. Diplomate Am. Bd. Internal Medicine, Am. Bd. Surgery, Am. Bd. Thoracic Surgery. Fellow in medicine Harvard Med. Sch., Boston, 1975-77, fellow in surgery, resident in surgery, 1977-81; resident in surgery Mass. Gen. Hosp., 1977-81; resident in cardiothoracic surgery Stanford (Calif.) U., 1981-82, chief resident cardiothoracic surgery, 1983, asst. prof., 1984-87; dir. heart-lung transplantation, transplant rsch. lab. Stanford U., 1986-87; prof. surgery and chief cardiothoracic surgery Yale U., New Haven, 1988-94; cardiothoracic-surgeon-in chief Yale-New Haven Hosp.; DeBakey/Bard prof., chmn. Baylor Coll. Medicine, Houston, 1994—; sr. attending physician, chief surg. svcs. Meth. Hosp., Houston, 1994—; sr. attending physician, surgeon in chief Ben Taub Gen. Hosp., Houston, 1994; dir. multi-organ transplant ctr. Meth. Hosp./Baylor U., Houston; dir. thoracic surgery residency program Coll. Medicine Baylor U., Houston; dir. thoracic surgery residency program Yale-New Haven Hosp., 1988-94; vis. lectr. Yale U., bd. permanent officers, 1988-94; cons. gen. thoracic surgery Waterbury (Conn.) Hosp. health Ctr., 1988-94; bd. dirs. United Network Organ Sharing, 1984-87; mem. clin. rsch. com. ad hoc rsch. grant rev. Cystic Fibrosis Found.; trustee New Eng. Organ Bank, 1988; mem. solid organ transplant com. Blue Cross & Blue Shield of Conn., 1990—; mem. sci. adv. bd. Alexion Pharms., Inc., 1991-94; bd. dirs. Baylor Coll. medicine Healthcare, Inc.; mem. adv. bd. Donate Life Found.; mem. exec. faculty Baylor Coll. of Medicine, pres.'s coun.; bd. dirs. New England chpt. Transplant Recipients Internat. Orgn., 1992-94. Co-editor: Thoracic Surgery, Oxford Textbook of Surgery, 1989—; editor: Cardiac Surgery: Principles and Techniques, 1994; assoc. editor Jour. Applied Cardiology, 1985-92; editorial bd. Jour. Thoracic and Cardiovascular Surgery, 1990—, Transplantation, 1990—, Transplantation Sci., 1992—, Andromeda Interactive Ltd., The Cardiovasc. System Interactive Teaching Program, 1993—; contbr. numerous articles and book chpts. in field. Mem. Harvard Club Schs. Com., Harvard Coll. Fund, Harvard U. Undergrad. Admissions Interview Com.; fellow Timothy Dwight Coll. Yale U., Yale U. Art Gallery Assocs.; mem. appointments and promotions com. Sch. Medicine, Yale U., 1991—, clin. scis. bldg. planning com., 1990—; bd. dirs. Neighborhood Music Sch. New Haven., 1989-92; bd. overseers Harvard U., 1995—; bd. permanent officers Yale U., 1988-94. John Harvard scholar, 1969, 70, Wendell scholar Harvard U., 1969, Rhodes scholar Oxford U., Alumni scholar Stanford Sch. Medicine, 1974 ; medalist Gothenburg (Sweden) Thoracic Soc., 1985; recipient Medaille de la Ville de Bordeaux French Thoracic Soc., 1987, travelling lectureship, 1988, Master Tchr. award Cardiovascular Revs. & Reports, 1990; travelling fellow Australia and New Zealand chpt., ACS, 1989; traveling lectureship, 1989. Fellow ACP, ACS, Royal Coll. Surgeons (Eng., traveling lectr. 1989), Am. Coll. Angiology, Am. Coll. Cardiology (mem. transplantation com. 1991—, chmn. task force cardiac donor procurement Bethesda Conf. 1992), Am. Coll. Surgeons (bd. govs. 1993—), Am. Coll. Chest Physicians, Mass. Med. Soc.; mem. AMA, AAAS, Am. Assn. Thoracic Surgery (mem. com. grad. edn. thoracic surgery 1992—, Evarts A. Graham Meml. Traveling Fellowship com. 1993—), Am. Soc. Transplant Surgeons (com. on heart transplantation 1986—, adv. com. in issues 1989—, chmn. subcom. on heart transplantation, physician payment reform commn. 1989—), Nat. Heart, Lung and Blood Inst. (cons. divsn. extramural affairs rev. br. 1990—), Assn. Acad. Surgery, Am. Physiol. Soc., Am. Heart Assn. (mem. rsch. grant pe—, coun. circulation, cert. of appreciation for outstanding svc. 1986), Am. Surg. Assn., Am. Thoracic Soc., Am. Soc. Artificial Internal Organs, Am. Soc. Extracorporeal Tech., Am. Assn. Lab. Animal Sci., Am. Organ Transplant Assn., Am. Venous Forum, Internat. Soc. Heart and Lung Transplantation (chmn. program com. 1988), Internat. Assn. Cardiac Biol. Implants, Internat. Fedn. Surg. Colls., Internat. Soc. Cardiovasc. Surgery, Internat. Soc. Cardio-Thoracic Surgeons, Internat. Soc. for Heart Rsch. (mem. Am. sect.), Internat. Soc. for Artificial Organs, Mediterranean Assn. for Cardiology and Cardiac Surgery, New Century Soc., Thoracic Surgery Found. for Rsch. and Edn., Norman E. Shumway Surg. Soc., New Eng. Surg. Soc., Pan Am. Med. Assn. (coun. on organ transplantation), North Am. Soc. Pacing and Electrophysiology, Societe Internat. de Chirurgie, Royal Soc. Medicine, Soc. Univ. Surgeons, Thoracic Surgery Dirs. Assn. (chmn. curriculum com. transplantation 1993), Transplantation Soc., Assn. Alumni of Magdalen Coll. Oxford U., Assn. Rhodes Scholars, Acad. Surg. Rsch., Assn. Surg. Edn., Assn. Program Dirs. in Surgery, Conn. Thoracic Soc., Harris County Med. Soc., Calif. Med. Assn., Calif. Thoracic Soc., Calif. Thoracic Soc. Respiratory Care Assembly, No. Calif. Cystic Fibrosis Found., So. Calif. Transplant Soc., Conn. Med. Soc., Conn. Soc. Am. Bd. Surgeons, Mass. Med. Soc., N.Y. Soc. Thoracic Surgery, New Haven County Med. Soc., Harvard Med. Alumni Assn. (assoc.), Physicians' Assn. New Haven County, Soc. Crit. Care Medicine, Soc. Thoracic Surgeons, Southeastern Surg. Congress, Southern Surg. Assn., Southwestern Surg. Congress, Tex. Surg. Soc., Halsted Soc., Houston Surg. Soc. Soc. for Organ Sharing, United Network for Organ Sharing, San Francisco Surg. Soc., Santa Clara Med. Soc., Stanford Med. Alumni Assn., Stanford Club Conn., Harvard Clubs San Francisco, Peninsula, N.Y.C., So. Conn., Houston, Boston, Mory's Assn., New Haven Lawn Club, Inner Quad Stanford U., The Hasty Pudding Club - Inst. 1770, Quinnipiack Club, Yale Club New Haven, Forum World Affairs, Ambs. Roundtable, Oxford Soc., Phi Beta Kappa, others. Office: Dept Surgery One Baylor Plz Houston TX 77030

BALDWIN, ROBERT LESH, biochemist, educator; b. Madison, Wis., Sept. 30, 1927; s. Ira Lawrence and Mary (Lesh) B.; m. Anne Theodora Norris, Aug. 28, 1965; children—David Norris, Eric Lawrence. B.A., U. Wis., 1950; D.Phil. (Rhodes scholar), Oxford (Eng.) U., 1954. Asst. prof., then asso. prof. biochemistry U. Wis., 1955-59; mem. faculty Stanford, 1959—, prof. biochemistry, 1964—, chmn. dept., 1989-94; vis. prof. Collège de France, Paris, 1972; mem. adv. panel biochemistry and biophysics NSF, 1974-76, NIH study sect. molecular and cellular biophysics, 1984-88. Assoc. editor Jour. Molecular Biology, 1964-68, 75-79; mem. editorial bd. Trends Biochem. Sci., 1977-84, Biochemistry, 1984—, Protein Sci., 1992—. Mem. Searle Scholars award panel, 1993-96; mem. adv. panel in biophysics Burroughs-Wellcome, 1995—. Recipient Wheland award in chemistry U. Chgo., 1995; Guggenheim fellow, 1958-59. Mem. NAS, Am. Soc. Biol. Chemists, Am. Chem. Soc., Am. Biophysics Soc. (coun. 1977-81), Am. Acad. Arts and Scis., Protein Soc. (coun. 1993-95, Stein and Moore award 1992). Home: 1243 Los Trancos Rd Portola Vally CA 94028-8125 Office: Stanford Med Sch Dept Biochemistry 300 Pasteur Dr Palo Alto CA 94304-2203

BALDWIN, WILLIAM RUSSELL, optometrist, foundation executive; b. Danville, Ind., July 29, 1926; s. Edward Claire and Letha Verona (Russell) B.; m. Honey Esther Fisher, Aug. 16, 1947; children: Linda Marie Smith (dec.), Leslie Ann Baldwin Bloom. BS, Pacific U., 1949, OD, 1951, ScD (hon.), 1991; MS, Ind. U., 1956, PhD, 1964; LHD (hon.), New Eng. Coll., 1982. Practice optometry, Beech Grove, Ind., 1951-54; dir. optometry clinic Ind. U., Bloomington, 1959-63; dean Coll. Optometry, Pacific U., Forest Grove, Oreg., 1963-69; pres. New Eng. Coll. Optometry, Boston, 1969-79; dean Coll. Optometry, U. Houston, 1979-90; pres. River Blindness Found., 1990-96. Author: (with C.R. Schick) Corneal Contact Lenses, Fitting Procedures, 1962; (with others) The Refractive State of the Eye, 1969, (with others) Pediatric Optometry, 1988; editor Vision Science Symposium, Ind. U., 1988, (with others) Refractive Anomolies, 1991. Mem. exec. com. Rep.

Cen. Com., Washington County, Oreg., 1963-69; chmn. arts, scis. div. Ind. Reps., 1962-63; chmn. Vellore India Hosp. Fund Drive, 1959-61 chmn. bd. River Blindness Found., 1996—; mem. men's adv. coun. Bloomington Hosp., 1959-63. Recipient Disting. Alumni Svc. award Ind. U., 1977, Pacific U., 1995, Gold Medal award Beta Sigma Kappa, 1968, Pres.'s medal New Eng. Coll. Optometry, 1977; named Man of Vision Prevent Blindness Mass.,1994, Lifetime Achievement award Prevent Blindness Am., 1995; Disting. scholar Nat. Acad. Practice, 1994. Fellow AAAS; mem. working group Nat. Rsch. Coun. Com. Vision of NAS, Am. Optometric Assn. (chmn. com. on rsch., chmn. task force on manpower, Disting. Svc. award 1992), Assn. Schs. Colls. Optometry (pres. 1974-76, chmn. internat. optometric edn.), Am. Acad. Optometry (chmn. sect. on edn. 1984-87), Tex. Soc. to Prevent Blindness (v.p. 1985-90), Nat. Soc. to Prevent Blindness (bd. dirs. 1988-96, chmn. 1st World Conf. on Optometric Edn. 1990), Rotary, Sigma Xi, Sigma Nu, Kappa Kappa Sigma.

BALDWIN-BEVERIDGE, MARTHA, psychotherapist, writer; b. Anniston, Ala., June 3, 1941; d. Henry Marcellus and Lucille Quintard (Brownlow) Martin; m. Andrew J. Haswell, Jr., Aug. 29, 1962 (div. 1972); children: Lucie Haswell Voves, Leigh Reece; m. Norwood P. Beveridge, 1993. BA, Wellesley (Mass.) Coll., 1963; MSW, U. Louisville, 1975. Lic. clin. social worker, Okla. Program dir., probation counselor City of Oklahoma City Mcpl. Ct., 1970-76; psychotherapist Options Now, Inc., Oklahoma City, 1975—; radio therapist Stas. KLTE-FM, Oklahoma City, 1985-88, KTOK, Oklahoma City, 1989—, KTOK, Oklahoma City, 1989—, KNTL, Oklahoma City, 1993-94, WKY, Oklahoma City, 1995; newspaper columnist Okla. Gazette, Oklahoma City, 1986-89; publisher Change of Heart Jour. for Healthy Living. Author: Self-Sabotage (originally pub. as Nurture Yourself to Success), 1987, Beyond Victim, 1988; creator (audio tape) Change of Heart: Healing the Trauma of Sexual Abuse, 1989, (video tape) Dyscovery: Stop Sabotaging Success, 1993; creator, voice Live Tips. Founder, dir. Friends of Oklahoma City monthly workshop Presbyn. Hosp., 1985-93. Recipient Layman's award for Outstanding Contribution to Law and Justice Okla. County Bar Assn., 1972. Mem. Jr. League of Oklahoma City (chair community rsch. 1968-69, vol. chair juv. ct. 1969-70, vol. mcpl. ct. 1970-71, edn. com. 1971-72). Episcopalian. Office: Options Now Inc 901 NW 62nd St Oklahoma City OK 73118-5827

BALE, JAMES FRANKLIN, JR., pediatric neurologist; b. Kalamazoo, Mich., Jan. 11, 1949; s. James F. and Marilyn J. Bale; m. Martha Jens, Oct. 12, 1974; children: Zachary, Jeffrey, Margaret. BS in Zoology, U. Mich., 1971, MD, 1975. Diplomate Nat. Bd. Med. Examiners, Am. Bd. Pediatrics, Am. Bd. Psychiatry and Neurology. Intern then resident in pediatrics U. Utah, Salt Lake City, 1975-77, resident in neurology, 1977-80, fellow in infectious diseases, 1980-81; fellow in neurovirology VA Med. Ctr.-U. Calif., San Francisco, 1981-82; asst. prof. U. Iowa Coll. Medicine, Iowa City, 1982-85, assoc. prof., 1985-90, prof., 1990—; examiner Am. Bd. Psychiatry and Neurology, 1986—. Author: Infections in Children, 1986, 2d edit., 1994; contbr. chpts. to Cytomegalovirus Infections, 1991. Mem. Child Neurology Soc. (ethics com. 1990—), Soc. Pediatric Rsch., Am. Acad. Neurology, Am. Acad. Pediatrics, Am. Pediatric Soc. Office: U Iowa Dept Pediatrics 2504 Jcp Univ Hospital Iowa City IA 52242

BALES, ROBERT FREED, social psychologist, educator; b. Ellington, Mo., Mar. 9, 1916; s. Columbus Lee and Ada Lois (Sloan) B.; m. Dorothy Louise Johnson, Sept. 14, 1941. B.A., U. Oreg., 1938, M.S., 1941; M.A., Harvard U., 1943, Ph.D., 1945. Research assoc. sect. on alcohol studies Yale U., 1944-45; instr. sociology Harvard U., Cambridge, Mass., 1945-47, asst. prof. sociology, research assoc. Lab. Social Relations, 1947-51, lectr. sociology, research assoc., 1951-55, assoc. prof., 1955-57, prof. social relations, 1957-86, prof. emeritus, 1986—, dir. Lab. Social Rels., 1960-67, chmn. social psychology program, dept. psychology and social rels., 1970-82; cons. psychology Harvard U. Health Svcs., 1970-82; vis. lectr. sociology and social psychology U. Mich., summer 1949, Columbia U., summer 1950; lectr. Salzberg Austria Seminar of Am. Studies, summer 1952, 56; Mem. bd. sci. counsellors NIMH, 1957-60. Author: Interaction Process Analysis: A Method for the Study of Small Groups, 1950, The Fixation Factor in Alcohol Addiction, 1980, (with Talcott Parsons, Edward A. Shils) Working Papers in the Theory of Action, 1953, (with Talcott Parsons, et al) Family, Socialization, and Interaction Process, 1955, (with Stephen P. Cohen and Stephen A. Williamson) SYMLOG, A System for the Multiple Level Observation of Groups, 1979, SYMLOG Case Study Kit and Instructions for a Group Self Study, 1980; contbr. to Group Dynamics, Research and Theory, 1953, The SYMLOG Practitioner, 1988, several other compilations; editor: (with A. Paul Hare and Edgar F. Borgatta) Small Groups, Studies in Social Interaction, 1955; author various instruments and booklets, sr. rsch., cons. SYMLOG Cons. Group, 1983-96. Trustee Ella L. Cabot Trust. Mem. APA, Am. Sociol. Assn., Eastern Sociol. Soc. (pres. 1962-63), Am. Acad. Arts and Scis., Am. Psychol. Soc., Soc. Exptl. Social Psychology, Boston Psychoanalytic Soc. (affiliate). Home and Office: 61 Scotch Pine Rd Weston MA 02193-1439

BALES, VIRGINIA S., healthcare administratorn. BA in Chemistry, Emory U., Atlanta, MPH. Asst. to deputy dir. Ctr. Disease Control and Prevention, 1988; asst. dir. ctr for health promotion in edn.; acting dir., dir. office on smoking and health, 1994—. Office: Dept Health & Human Services Nat Center Chronic Disease Preven Koger-Rhodes-Davidson Bldg Atlanta GA 30341

BALESTRIERO, FERDINANDO (FRED BALESTRIERO), health facility administrator; b. West Islip, N.Y., Aug. 29, 1964; s. Luigi and Mary (Avitto) B. AA, Broward C.C., Coconut Creek, Fla., 1985; B in Health Svcs. Adminstrn., Fla. Atlantic U., 1988; MS in Health Svcs. Adminstrn., Nova-Southeastern U., 1992. Cert. nursing home adminstr., Fla. Adminstr.-in-tng. Whitehall Boca Raton, Fla., 1988, Beacon Pointe Nursing Ctr., Sunrise, Fla., 1992; dir. mktg. Ocean Park Manor, Pompano Beach, Fla., 1993; asst. adminstr. Elysium of Boca Raton, 1993-94; adminstr. Golf Crest Nursing Home, Hollywood, Fla., 1994-95; dark rm. technician Columbia U. Hosp. and Med. Ctr., Tamarac, Fla., 1980—. Mem. Am. Coll. Health Care Execs., Am. Coll. Health Care Adminstrs. Roman Catholic. Home: 8101 NW 27th St Apt 3 Coral Springs FL 33065

BALFOUR, ANA MARIA, office manager; b. Buenos Aires, Dec. 16, 1942; came to the U.S., 1962; d. Alfredo Hector and Luisa (Zagnoni) Malaccorto; m. Guillermo Aylmer Balfour, July 10, 1964; children: Michele, Valeria, Alexandra. Student, U. Buenos Aires, 1961-62; BA, Am. U., 1964. Tchr. Ft. Rucker (Ala.) Middle Sch., 1964-65; med. asst. F.R. Leyva & G.A. Balfour, M.D., P.C., Washington, 1968-73, office mgr., 1973-88, adminstr., 19886. Contbr. articles to profl. jours. Fundraiser Operation Smile, Stone Ridge Country Day Sch.-Sacred Heart; docent The Kreeger Mus., Washington, 1996—. Mem. Comision Esperanza Dames Argentinas, So Others May Eat, Ivy Found., Com. Hispanic Designers, Com. Am.'s Film Festival. Roman Catholic. Home: 9802 Hill St Kensington MD 20895-3135 Office: FR Leyva GA Balfour MD PC 3301 New Mexico Ave NW Washington DC 20016-3622

BALGEMAN, RICHARD VERNON, radiology administrator, alcoholism counselor; b. Berwyn, Ill., Dec. 25, 1929; s. Vernon Ernest and Regina Marie (Fitzgerald) B.; m. Wauneta Frances Laird, Nov. 15, 1952; children: Marcia, Kathleen, Barbara, Daniel. Radiology technician, Cook County Grad. Sch. of Med., 1951; BA in Health Svc., Governor State U., 1976, MA in Sci., 1978. Cert. technologist. Radiology adminstr. Manteno (Ill.) Mental Health Ctr., 1951-84; adminstrv. asst. bus. office Shapiro Devel. Ctr., Kankakee, Ill., 1984-88; with St. James Hosp., Chicago Heights, Ill., 1990—. Inventor DuPont Cronex Tech. Aid, 1965. Village trustee Village of Manteno, 1969-72, chmn. planning commn., 1985-93; pres. Village View TV, Channel 10. With USNG, 1948-56. Gov.'s award Ill. Dept. Mental Health, Manteno, 1971; named Citizen of Yr. Manteno Hist. Soc., 1996. Mem. Am. Legion, Moose, Rotary. Roman Catholic. Home: 555 Park St Manteno IL 60950-1045

BALINSKY, BENJAMIN, retired psychology educator; b. N.Y.C., Oct. 26, 1913; s. Jacob and Jenny (Broder) B.; m. Ruth Goldberg, Oct. 10, 1937; children: Judith Knee, Frances Berger. BA, CUNY, 1935; MA, Columbia U., 1937; PhD, NYU, 1940. Lic. psychologist, N.Y.; diplomate in clin. psychology Am. Bd. Profl. Providers in Psychology. Intern, rschr. Bellevue Hosp., N.Y.C., 1935-39; psychologist Nat. Youth Adminstrn., N.Y.C., 1939-42; cons. War Dept., N.Y.C., 1942-44; psychologist, counselor Vocat. Adv. Svc., N.Y.C., 1945-47; instr. to prof. psychology CCNY, 1947-69; prof., chmn. psychology Baruch Coll., CUNY, 1969-79, prof. emeritus psychology, 1979—; chief cons.BFS Inc., 1960-89. Co-author: Counseling and Psychology, 1951, The Executive Interview, 1959; author booklets: The Selection Interview, 1962, Improving Personnel Selection Through Effective Interviewing, 1978. Lectr. Mental Hygiene Clinic, N.Y.C., 1989. Fellow AAAS, APA (Disting. Psychologist award 1990). Jewish.

BALINT, JOHN ALEXANDER, physician; b. Budapest, Hungary, Feb. 11, 1925; came to U.S., 1958; s. Michael M. and Alice (Szekely-Kovacs) B.; m. Jean M. Gibson, Jan. 15, 1949; children: Peter John, Jane Penelope. BA, Cambridge U., Eng., 1945, MBBChir, 1948; MRcP, Royal Coll. Physicians, London, 1952. House physician various London Hosps., 1949-53; registrar Cen. Middlesex Hosp., London, 1953-58; fellow in gastroenterology U. Cin., 1958-59; trainee in biochem. Johns Hopkins U. Balt., 1959-60; asst. prof. medicine U. Ala., Birmingham, 1960-63; assoc. prof., head div. of gastroenterology Albany (N.Y.) Med. Coll., 1963-68, prof., head div. of gastroenterology, 1968-81, prof., chair medicine, 1981-88, Beebe prof. of medicine, 1988-93, Beebe prof and dir. Ctr. for Med. Ethics, 1993—. Co-author several textbooks chpts.; contbr. 75 sci. papers and 80 abstracts to profl. publs. Squadron leader, Royal Air Force, 1950-52. Mem. Am. Physiol. Soc., Am. Soc. Clin. Investigation, Am. Gastroent. Assn., Brit. Soc. Gastroent., Am. Assn. Study Liver Disease. Office: Albany Med Ctr Dept Medicine Albany NY 12208

BALIS, MOSES EARL, biochemist, educator; b. Phila., June 19, 1921; s. Harry and Frances (Spector) B.; m. Bernice M. Lamborg, Dec. 30, 1945; children—Frances Andrea, Ellen Joyce. B.A., Temple U., 1943; M.S., U. Pa., 1947, Ph.D., 1949. With Sloan-Kettering Inst., 1949-87, head nucleoprotein metabolism sect., 1957—, asso. mem., 1960-65, mem., 1965-87, chief div. cell metabolism, 1970-87; chair inst. senate, 1981-83; cons. Sloan-Kettering Inst., 1987-91; asso. prof. Med. Coll. Cornell U., 1954-66, prof. biochemistry, 1966-87, chmn. biochemistry unit, 1969-74; owner M.E. Balis, Inc., Fla.; vis. lectr. Adelphi U., 1963-64; cons. chemistry dept. Manhattan Coll., 1981-86; mem. study sects. Am. Cancer Soc., NIH.; mem. planning com. Nat. Cancer Plan; mem. rev. com. Nat. Large Bowel Cancer Program, 1977-81; pres. Med. Research Investment Fund, 1984-89. Mem. editorial bd. Cancer Rsch., 1969-73; assoc. editor, 1974-82. Served to lt. (j.g.) USNR, 1944-46. Recipient Research Career award USPHS, 1963. Mem. Am. Chem. Soc. (past sect. chmn.), AAAS, Am. Cancer Soc., Am. Soc. Biol Chemistry and Molecular Biology, Harvey Soc., Am. Assn. Cancer Rsch., Sigma Xi. Home and Office: 11587 Pathway Ln Boynton Beach FL 33437-4932

BALISTRERI, WILLIAM FRANCIS, physician, pediatric gastroenterologist; b. Geneva, N.Y., June 24, 1944; s. Francis William and Mary (Yannotti) B.; m. Rebecca Ann McLeod, May 31, 1969; children: Anthony, Jennifer, William Phillip. Student, St. Bonaventure U., 1962; BA, SUNY, Buffalo, 1966; MD, U. Buffalo, 1970. Diplomate Am. Bd. Pediat., Sub. Bd. of Gastroenterology. Intern Children's Hosp. Med. Ctr., Cin., 1970-71, resident, 1971-72, postdoctoral fellow, 1972-74; rsch. fellow Mayo Clinic, Rochester, Minn., 1974; pediat. instr. Sch. Medicine U. Cin., 1972-74; staff pediatrician U.S. Naval Hosp., Phila., 1974-76; asst. prof. pediat. Sch. Medicine U. Pa., 1976-78; assoc. prof. pediat. Sch. Medicine U. Cin., 1978-83, assoc. prof. medicine Sch. Medicine, 1982-91, prof. pediat. Sch. Medicine, 1983—, prof. medicine, 1991—; bd. dirs. Am. Bd. Pediat., 1991—, chmn. sub-bd. of pediatric gastroenterology, 1991-93; mem. ednl. coun. Nat. Hepatology Detection and Treatment Prevention Program, 1993—. Author, editor: Pediatric Hepatology, 1990, Pediatric Gastroenterology and Nutrition, 1990, Jour. Pediatrics, 1995. Lt. comdr. USN, 1974-76. Recipient Disting. Alumnus award U. Buffalo, 1993. Mem. Am. Assn. for Study of Liver Disease (chair clin. com. 1993-96, coun. 1996—), N.Am. Soc. for Pediat. Gastroenterology and Nutrition (editor-in-chief Western Hemisphere Jour. 1991-95, pres. 1985-86), Am. Gastroenterol. Assn. Roman Catholic. Office: Children's Hosp Med Ctr Ambulatory Svcs 3333 Burnet Ave Cincinnati OH 45229-3026

BALK, ROBERT A., medical educator. BA, U. Mo., Kansas City, 1976, MD, 1978. Resident internal medicine U. Mo., Kansas City, 1978-81; fellow pulmonary and critical care medicine U. Ark., Little Rock, 1981-83, instr. medicine, 1981-83, asst. prof. medicine, 1983-85; staff physician Little Rock VA Med. Ctr., 1983-85; asst. prof. medicine Rush-Presbyn.-St. Luke's Med. Ctr., Chgo., 1985-88, assoc. prof., 1988—, asst. dir. sect. pulmonary medicine, 1985-90, med. dir. respiratory care svcs., 1985-93, med. dir. noninvasive respiratory care unit, 1985-87, co-dir. med. intensive care unit, 1986-88, dir. med. intensive care unit, 1988-95, assoc. dir. sect. pulmonary & crit. care medicine, 1993—, assoc. dir. sect. critical care medicine, 1995—, dir. pulmonary & critical care medicine fellowship tng. program, 1994—. Contbr. articles to profl. jours. Recipient Dedicated Svc. & Superior Individual Effort in Patient Care Alice Sachs Meml. award, 1991, Alfred Soffer Rsch. award Am. Coll. Chest Physicians, 1995. Office: Rush-Presbyn St Luke's Med Ctr 1753 W Congress Pky Chicago IL 60612*

BALKAM, JANE JOHNSTON, pediatric nurse practitioner; b. Callicoon, N.Y., Mar. 5, 1950; d. Alfred G. and Esther (Robinson) Johnston; m. Clifford Robert Balkam, Oct. 20, 1979; children: Matthew, Andrew, James, John. BSN, Georgetown U., 1972; MSN, U. Rochester, 1977. RN, D.C., Md.; cert. pediatric nurse practitioner; cert. lactation cons. Internat. Bd. Lactation Cons. Examiners, Inc. Nurse epidemiologist Med. Coll. of Va. Hosp., Richmond, 1973-75; cert. pub. health nurse Sullivan County Pub. Health Nursing Svc., Liberty, N.Y., 1975-76; instr. in nursing Georgetown U. Sch. Nursing, 1977-78; pediatric nurse practitioner Georgetown U. Community Health Plan, 1978-79; asst. prof. nursing The Cath. U. of Am., Washington, 1978-83, Maymount Coll. of Va., Arlington, 1983-84; pediatric nurse practitioner Arlington County Health Dept., 1981-86; program mgr., child and adolescent health program Div. of Family Health Svcs., Montgomery County Health Dept., Rockville, Md., 1985-89; pediatric nurse pracitioner, after hours care unit Kaiser Permanente Health Plan, Landover, Md., 1989—; owner breast pump rental bus., Sanvita Programs Corp. Lactation Franchise; lactation cons., 1991—; PNP, Prince George's County Health Dept., 1987; staff nurse Vis. Nurse Assn. D.C., 1981-83; speaker in field. Contbr. articles to profl. jours. Mem. Commn. on Children and Youth Montgomery County, Md., 1988-89 mem. maternal child health adv. bd. Regional Ctr. for Infants and Young Children, Rockville, Md., 1987; mem. self-assessment examination com. Nat. Bd. of Pediatric Nurse Practitioners and Assocs., 1984-87; chief proctor Washington Ctr., Nat. Bd. of Pediatric Nurse Practitioners and Assocs. Certifying Examination. 1983, 84; vol. nurse Kensington Clinic of Mobile Med. Care, Inc., 1980-82; vol. staff CUA Health Clinic, 1978-81. Fellow Nat Assn. of Pediatric Nurse Assocs. and Practitioners (cert., sec. Md.-Chesapeake chpt. 1981-83); mem. ANA (cert.), Md. Nurses Assn. (dist. V mem. nominating com. 1981-83, Internat. Lactation Cons. Assn., Lactation Cons. Assn. of Greater Washington, Sigma Theta Tau (recording sec. Tau chpt. 1978-80). Republican. Roman Catholic. Home: 4515 Gladwyne Dr Bethesda MD 20814-4710

BALL, ANDREW JUSTIN, urologist; b. Bristol, Eng., July 22, 1949; s. Keith Seymour and Joan Sybil (Godfrey) B.; m. Georgina Caroline Watson, Jan. 27, 1973; 1 child, Alexander Justin Clifford. M.B., Ch.B., U. Bristol, Eng., 1972; F.R.C.S., Royal Coll. Surgeons Eng., London, 1977; MD, U. Bristol, 1984. House physician Royal United Hosp., Bath, Eng., 1972; house surgeon Bristol Royal Informary, 1973; demonstrator anatomy U. Bristol, 1973-74; sr. house officer surgery and urology Bristol Royal Infirmary, 1974-75; registrar surgery U. Hosp. Cardiff, Wales, 1976-78; sr. registrar Royal Gwent Hosp., Newport, Wales, 1979; sr. registrar rsch. urology Ham Green Hosp., Bristol, Eng., 1980-82; sr. registrar urology Bristol Royal Infirmary, 1982-84; cons. urologist N.E. Thames Reg. Health Authority, Southend Dist., Eng., 1984—. Contbr. articles to profl. jours. Recipient DISA prize for contbn. to understanding of urinary tract function, Brit. Assn. Urol. Surgeons, 1982. Fellow Royal Soc. Medicine Eng., Royal Coll. Surgeons Eng.; mem. Brit. Med. Assn., Brit. Assn. Urol. Surgeons, European Assn. of Urology. Office: Wellesley Hosp, Eastern Ave, Southend on Sea SS2 4XH, England

BALL, CARROLL RAYBOURNE, anatomist, medical educator, researcher; b. Leakesville, Miss., Oct. 11, 1925; s. Marvin Hugh and Elizabeth (Hillman) B.; m. Jannie Vee Brooks, Sept. 5, 1947 (dec. 1954); children: Hugh Brooks, Peter Stephen; m. Sally Ann Montgomery, Mar. 22, 1963 (div. 1976); 1 child, Lou Ellen. BA, U. Miss., 1947, MS, 1948, PhD, 1963. Grad. asst. in zoology U. Miss., Oxford, 1946-48; instr. Duke U., 1948-51; instr. anatomy Med. Sch. W.Va. U., 1951-57; asst. prof. biology U. So. Miss., 1957-60; asst. prof. U. Miss. Med. Ctr., Jackson, 1963-66, assoc. prof., 1966-71, prof., 1971—. Contbr. numerous articles to profl. jours. Pres. Jackson Civil War Round Table, 1983-84; chmn. Hist. Coker House Restoration Project, 1984—; v.p. Magnolia chpt. Nat. Assn. Watch and Clock Collectors, 1980-82; bd. dirs. Miss. Hist. Soc., 1976-79, 85-88, 93-96. Lt. comdr. USNR, 1944-71, PTO. NIH predoctoral trainee, 1960-63; Miss. Heart Assn. grantee, 1963-66. Mem. Am. Assn. Anatomists, Soc. Exptl. Biology and Medicine, Am. Assn. Pathology, So. Assn. Anatomy, Miss. Acad. Sci., Hattiesburg Jr. C. of C. (sec. 1959-60), Order of First Families of Miss., Sigma Xi, Alpha Epsilon Delta, Theta Nu Sigma, Beta Beta Beta (pres. 1947-48), Omicron Delta Kappa, Pi Kappa Alpha (sec. 1943-44). Methodist. Home: 905 Pinehurst Pl Jackson MS 39202-1742 Office: U Miss Med Ctr Dept Anatomy 2500 N State St Jackson MS 39216-4500

BALL, GENE VIRGIL, rheumatologist, clinical immunologist, educator; b. Fairmont, W.Va., June 28, 1931; s. John Franklin and Rebecca Elvira (Rush) B.; m. Sara Jane Clark, June 7, 1959; children: Rebecca Anne, Hilary Elizabeth. MD, Vanderbilt U., 1959. Diplomate Am. Bd. Internal Medicine, Am. Bd. Subspeciality Rheumatology. Prof. of medicine U. Ala., Birmingham, 1971-86, Jane Knight Lowe prof. of medicine, 1986—, interim dir. divsn. clin. immunology and rheumatology, 1995-96; mem. subspeciality sect. Am. Bd. Internal Medicine, 1982-88; mem. arthritis adv. coun. FDA, 1988—. Assoc. editor: Arthritis & Rheumatism Jour., 1985-90, editorial bd., 1990—; editor: Dial Access: Southern Medical Association, 1977—; co-editor: Clinical Rheumatology, 1986; contbr. chpts. to books and over 50 articles to profl. jours. Pres. Ala. Zool. Assn., Birmingham. Named Best Physician, Town and Country Mag., 1978, 84, 89, Good Housekeeping, 1991. Fellow ACP, Am. Coll. Rheumatology (pres. S.E. sect. 1978); mem. Rotary (Birmingham), Summit Club (Birmingham), Alpha Omega Alpha. Office: U Ala University Station Birmingham AL 35294

BALL, JOHN DAVID, clinical psychologist; b. Newport News, Va., Nov. 27, 1948; s. David Joseph and Elaine (Parks) B.; m. Bonney Lee Wiggins, July 1, 1972; children: Michael David, Taylor Edwin. BA, U. Va., 1971, MEd, 1975, PhD, 1978. Clin. psychology intern USAF/Wilford Hall Med. Ctr., San Antonio, 1977-78; clin. psychologist Malcolm Grow USAF Med. Ctr., Washington, 1978-81; prof., co-dir. neuropsychology ctr. dept. psychiatry Ea. Va. Med. Sch., Norfolk, 1981—. Editor: Psychotherapy Training: Contextual & Developmental Influences on Setting Stages and Mind Sets, 1991; contbr. articles to profl. jours. Trustee Chesapeake Bay Acad. Lt. (j.g.) USNR, 1971-74, maj. USAFR, 1977—. Fellow Va. Acad. Clin. Psychology (newsletter editor 1983-87, mem. at large 1986-88, chair membership and by-laws com. 1989—), Soc. Personality Assessment; mem. APA, Internat. Neuropsychol. Soc. Episcopalian. Home: 1137 Kings Way Dr Virginia Beach VA 23455-5535 Office: Ea Va Med Sch PO Box 1980 Norfolk VA 23501-1980

BALL, JOHN ROBERT, healthcare executive; b. Opelika, Ala., July 16, 1944; s. John Cooper Jr. and Ellen Beverly (Williams) B.; m. Cornelia Anne Phillips, Aug. 13, 1966 (div. 1983); children: Kristen Anne, John Robert; m. Pamela Preston Reynolds, Jan. 9, 1988. AB, Emory U., 1966; JD, Duke U., 1971, MD, 1972. Research assoc. Duke U. Sch. Medicine, Durham, N.C., 1971-72, resident in medicine, 1972-74; asst. to dir. office asst. sec. for health USPHS, Rockville, Md., 1974-76; chief med. audit br. bur. quality assurance HEW, Rockville, 1976-77; sr. policy analyst Office Sci. and Tech. Policy Exec. Office of Pres., Washington, 1978-81; assoc. exec. v.p. ACP, Phila., 1981-86, exec. v.p., 1986-94, also fellow; sr. scholar Assn. Acad. Health Ctrs., Washington, 1994-95; exec. v.p., acting pres., CEO Pa. Hosp., Phila., 1995-96, pres., CEO, 1996—; Robert Wood Johnson clin. scholar George Washington U., Washington, 1977-79; bd. dirs. Pa. Hosp.; bd. dirs. Milbank Meml. Fund. Assoc. editor Jour. Am. Geriatrics Soc., 1984-86; mem. editorial bd. Internat. Jour. Tech. Assessment in Health Care, 1986-89, European Jour. Internal Medicine, 1988-94, Duke U. Law Jour., 1969-71; contbr. articles to profl. jours. Sr. surgeon USPHS, 1974-77. John Gordon Stipe scholar, Nat. Merit scholar, Emory U., 1962. Mem. Inst. Medicine of NAS, N.Y. Acad. Medicine, N.C. Bar Assn., Internat. Soc. for Tech. Assessment in Health Care, Am. Clin. and Climatol. Assn., Soc. Med. Adminstrs. Democrat. Office: Pa Hosp 800 Spruce St Philadelphia PA 19107-6192

BALL, JOSEPHINE, psychiatric nurse consultant; b. Balt., Oct. 8, 1931; d. Joseph Henry Gordon and Alma Lorraine (Taylor) Bey; m. Austin Louis Ball (div. 1984); children: Danita Elena Waddy, Cheryl Evita, Josette Austina. AA in Nursing, Community Coll. Balt., 1977; BA in Human Svcs., Antioch U., 1981, MA in Planning Adminstrn., 1982; Doctorate degree, Am. Inst. Hypnotherapy, Calif., 1993. Cert. psychiat. nurse, Md., cert. hypnotherapist. From receptionist to nurse asst. Crownsville (Md.) State Hosp., 1958-65; charge nurse Rosewood State Hosp., Owings Mills, Md., 1965-75; nurse Patuxent Penal Instn., Jessup, Md., 1975-77; nurse supr., outpatient liaison Spring Grove Hosp., Catonsville, Md., 1977-81, clin. nurse specialist, 1987—; primary nurse, part-time nurse Md. Gen. Hosp., Balt., 1981—; cons. Jorieum Health Affiliates, Balt., 1987—. Mem. Polit. Congress of Black Women, Balt., 1986, Com. to Elect Salima Siler Marriott, Balt., 1989—; mem. adv. bd. Lady Md. Found., Balt., 1987; pres. emeritus Black Women's Cousciousness Raising Assn., Balt., 1958; co-chair AIDS Walk '89, Balt., 1989; former vice chmn., com. chair Balt. City Commn. for Women, 1983; health com. Balt. Empowerment Zone Task Force. Mem. Am. Nurses Assn., Am. Bd. Hypnotherapy, Profl. Nurses Assn. Spring Grove, Liberty Med. Ctr. Aux., 31st St. Bookstore, Balt. Women's Coalition (Contemporary Woman of Yr. 1987), Balt. Women's Mentoring Project. Democrat. Baptist. Home: 2619 Woodland Ave Baltimore MD 21215-6523 Office: Spring Grove Hosp Catonsville MD 21228

BALL, PATRICIA ANN, physician; b. Lockport, N.Y., Mar. 30, 1941; d. John Joseph and Katherine Elizabeth (Hoffmaster) B.; m. Robert E. Lee, May 18, 1973; children—Heather, Samantha. B.S., U. Mich., 1963; M.D., Wayne State U., 1969. Diplomate Am. Bd. Internal Medicine, Am. Bd. Hematology, Am. Bd. Med. Oncology. Intern, resident Detroit Gen. Hosp., 1969-71; resident Jackson Meml. Hosp., Miami, Fla., 1971-72; fellow Henry Ford Hosp., Detroit, 1972-74; staff physician VA Hosp., Allen Park, Mich., 1974-77; practice medicine specializing in hematology and oncology, Bloomfield Hills, Mich., 1977—; mem. faculty dept. medicine Wayne State U. Sch. Medicine, Detroit, 1974—. Mem. Founders Soc., Detroit Inst. Arts. Mem. ACP, AMA, Mich. State Med. Soc., Oakland County Med. Soc., Mich. Soc. Hematology and Oncology, Alpha Omega Alpha. Avocations: photography; skiing. Office: 1575 S Woodward Ave Ste 210 Bloomfield Hills MI 48302-0561

BALL, WILLIAM, microbiology educator, consultant; b. Phila., Mar. 3, 1921; s. Jacob Edward and Elsie (Greenberg) B.; m. Sylvia Braslow, Nov. 27, 1947; children: David Stuart, Lisa Robin. BSc in Biology, Phila. Coll. Pharmacy and Sci., 1943, MSc in Biology, 1948, ScD in Biology, 1950. Instr. biology Phila. Coll. Pharmacy and Sci., 1946-50, 65-66; microbiologist Med. Arts Lab., Jenkintown, Pa., 1950-51; parasitologist Albert Einstein Med. Ctrs., Phila., 1952-54; dir., owner Park Labs., Phila., 1954-70; tech. dir. Damon Med. Lab., Trevose, Pa., 1970-80; cons. William Ball, Sc.D., Inc., Erdenheim, Pa., 1980-82; adj. prof. biology Beaver Coll., Glenside, Pa., 1982-92, ret. chmn. biology dept.; cons. in microbiology and serology VA Hosp., Phila., 1966-80; cons. in infection control and parasitology. Co-editor: Infection Control in Health Care Facilities, 1977, Immunological and Serological Aspects of Clinical Parasitology, 1981, Free Living Amoebas in Human Infections, 1981. Coord. Erdenheim Town Watch, 1984—. Capt. U.S. Army, 1943-46, PTO. Recipient Legion of Honor, Chapel of Four Chaplains, 1973. Mem. Am. Soc. for Microbiology (co-chmn., mem. workshop com. and symposium com. Ea. Pa. br.), Am. Assn. Bioanalysts (cert. bioanalyst clin. lab. dir.), Am. Acad. Microbiology (registered). Jewish. Home: 411 Glenway Rd Erdenheim PA 19038-7019

BALL, WILLIAM ABNER, chiropractor; b. Tift County, Ga., Apr. 29, 1936; s. William Winston and Martha Emma (Donnahoo) B.; m. Sara Margaret Core, Sept. 16, 1956; children: William Steven, Marlesa Lynn Ball Greiner. D in Chiropractic, X Ray and Spinography, Palmer Chiropractic Coll., Davenport, Iowa, 1958; cert. Physiolog. Therapeutics, Logan Chiropractic Coll., St. Louis, 1982; cert. Acitivator Specialist, Life Coll., Atlanta, 1984. Intern in chiropractic Lawson Chiropractic Clinic, Albany, Ga., 1958-59; pvt. practice chiropractic Thomasville, Ga., 1959—. Church organist, Thomasville, 1960-80. Mem. Nat. Inst. Chiropractic Rsch. (charter), Am. Chiropractic Assn., Ga. Chiropractic Assn., Parker Chiropractic Resource Found., Palmer Chiropractic Coll. Alumni Assn., Thomasville C. of C., Kiwanis Club. Home: 1701 Millpond Rd Thomasville GA 31757

BALL, WILLIAM AUSTIN, health facility director, researcher; b. L.A., Feb. 16, 1948; s. Joe Martin and Norma Lou (Schouweiler) B.; m. Rachel Yvette Jeanne Tullier, July 21, 1972. BA summa cum laude, Harvard Coll., 1970; student, Ecole Normale Supérieure, Paris, 1970-71; PhD, U. Mich., 1976; MD, U. Pa., 1983. Diplomate Am. Bd. Psychiatry. Asst. prof. psychology Swarthmore (Pa.) Coll., 1976-80; assoc. prof. psychiatry U. Pa., Phila., 1988—; dir. emergency svcs., 1994—; med. dir. inpatient psychiatry svc. Hosp. U. Pa., Phila., 1989—. Assoc. editor Jour. Genetic Psychology; contbr. articles to profl. jours. Recipient Rsch. Svc. award NIH, 1987, Earl Bond Teaching award 1991. Mem. Soc. for Neuroscience, Phi Beta Kappa. Office: Hosp U Pa Dept Psychiatry 3400 Spruce St Philadelphia PA 19104

BALL, WILLIAM JAMES, pediatrician; b. Charleston, S.C., Apr. 16, 1910; s. Elias and Mary (Cain) B.; BS, U. of South, 1930; MD, Med. Coll. S.C., 1934; m. Doris Hallowell Mason, July 9, 1938. Intern, Roper Hosp., Charleston, 1934-35; resident dept. pediatrics U. Chgo. Clinics, 1935-37; instr. pediatrics Med. Coll. S.C., 1938-42; practice medicine specializing in pediatrics, Charleston, 1938-42, Northwest Clinic, Minot N.D., 1946-51, Aurora, Ill., 1951-70; physician student Health Svc. No. Ill. U., 1970-72; mem. staff Copley Meml., Mercy Ctr. Health Care Svcs.; assoc. prof. Sch. Nursing, No. Ill. U., 1971-72. Mem. Bd. Health, Aurora, Ill., 1958-62; pediatrician, divsn. svcs. for crippled children U. Ill., 1952-86; pediatric cons. sch. dists. 129 and 131, Aurora, 1972-85, DeKalb County Spl. Edn. Assn., 1972-81, Sch. Assn. Spl. Edn. Dupage County, 1930-83, Mooseheart, Ill., 1970-83, Northwestern Ill. Assn. Handicapped Children; chmn. adv. com. Kane County Health Dept., 1986-95; pres. Kane County sub-area coun. Health Sys. Agy., Kane, Lake, McHenry Counties, 1977-78, sec., 1978-79. Served as capt. M.C., AUS, 1942-46; maj., 1946 to col., 1963, ret. 1970. Diplomate Am. Bd. Pediatrics. Recipient Golden Apple award Ill. Sch. Dist. 129, 1983, Shimkus award Aurora Vis. Nurses Assn., 1993. Fellow Royal Soc. Health, Am. Acad. Pediatrics; mem. AMA, Kane County Med. Soc. (pres. 1962), Am. Heart Assn., Am. Sch. Health Assn., Am. Cancer Soc., Am. Pub. Health Assn., Juvenile Protective Assn. of Aurora, The Ret. Officers Assn. (west suburban Chgo. chpt.), Phi Beta Kappa, Phi Chi, Pi Kappa Phi. Rotarian. Address: 433 S Commonwealth Ave Aurora IL 60506-5439

BALLANTYNE, CHRISTIE MITCHELL, medical educator; b. Houston, Sept. 13, 1955; m. Yasmine Attie, June 21, 1980; children: Maria Leyla, Christina, Katina. BA magna cum laude, U. Tex., 1977; postgrad., NYU, Madrid, Spain, 1977; MD cum laude, Baylor Coll. Medicine, 1982. Diplomate Am. Bd. Internal Medicine, Am. Bd. Internal Medicine subspecialty Cardiovascular Disease; cert. ACLS instr. Resident in internal medicine U. Tex. Southwestern Med. Sch., Dallas, 1982-85; fellowship in cardiology Baylor Coll. Medicine, Houston, 1985-87, instr. sect. atherosclerosis and cardiology dept. medicine, 1988-89, asst. prof. atherosclerosis & cardiology dept. medicine, 1989-95, assoc. prof. dept. medicine, 1996—; attending Ben Taub Gen. Hosp. Cardiac Catherterization Lab., Houston, 1988—, Lipid Metabolism and Atherosclerosis Clinic, The Meth. Hosp., Houston, 1988—, Ben Taub Coronary Care Unit, Houston, 1989—; faculty mem. Am. Heart Assn./Squibb Tng. Ctr. for Clin. Mgmt. of Lipid Disorders, Baylor Coll. Medicine, 1990; co-investigator Lipoprotein and Coronary Atherosclerosis Study, 1990; sci. grant rev. com. Am. Heart Assn. Tex. Affiliate, 1991—; pharmacy and therapeutics com. The Meth. Hosp., 1992—. Contbr. chpts. to books and articles to profl. jours. Recipient Mosby scholarship award, Grant-in-Aid awards Am. Heart Assn. Tex. Affiliate, 1989, 91, Sanofi-Winthrop Grant-in-Aid award, 1994, Established Investigator award, 1996, Clin. Investigator award Nat. Heart Lung and Blood Inst., NIH, 1990, Caroline Wiess Law award in Molecular Medicine, 1992; named fellow Am. Heart Assn./Bugher Found. Ctr. for Molecular Biology in the Cardiovascular Sys., 1987-89. Fellow ACP, Am. Coll. Cardiology, Coun. on Clin. Cardiology Am. Heart Assn., Coun. on Arteriosclerosis; mem. Am. Fedn. Clin. Rsch. (sch. rep. for Baylor 1992), Tex. Med. Assn., Harris County Med. Soc., Houston Cardiology Soc. (pres. 1996), Phi Kappa Phi, Phi Beta Kappa, Alpha Omega Alpha. Office: Baylor Coll Medicine Sect Atherosclerosis 6565 Fannin Ms # A601 Houston TX 77030

BALLARD, HARRY HAMPTON, general surgeon; b. Washington, Jan. 14, 1945; s. Wade Hampton and Alice (Hamilton) B.; m. Margaret Hilliard Shackford, June 11, 1966 (div. 1977); children: Jody Laurie, David Wade; m. Dolly Ruth Grant, Mar. 3, 1979; children: Stephen Richmond, Alice Hamilton. AB, U. N.C., 1966; MD, W.Va. U., 1971. Diplomate Am. Bd. Surgery. Med. intern Albert Chandler Med. Ctr., Lexington, Ky., 1971-72; resident in gen. surgery N.C. Meml. Hosp., Chapel Hill, 1975-80; fellow in peripheral vascular surgery Good Samaritan Hosp., Phoenix, 1980-81; surgeon New Bern (N.C.) Surg. Assocs., 1981—; clin. dir. peripheral vascular lab. Craven Regional Med. Ctr., New Bern, 1982—; mem. adv. bd. Br. Banking & Trust Co., New Bern, 1994—. Lay Eucharistic min. Christ Episcopal Ch., New Bern. Lt. comdr. USNR, 1972-75, Spain. Fellow ACS; mem. Peripheral Vascular Surgery Soc. Republican. Home: 4506 Monck Ct New Bern NC 28542 Office: New Bern Surg Assocs 701 Newman Rd New Bern NC 28562

BALLARD, IAN MATHESON, physician; b. Norristown, Pa., Jan. 13, 1937; s. Herbert Theodore Jr. and Margaret (Matheson) B.; m. Paula Ballard, Aug. 31, 1957 (div. 1982); children: Jennifer Ballard Hyde, Jill Ballard Hamilton, Ian Matheson Jr.; m. Helen Lyons Clothier, Apr. 16, 1982. AB, Lafayette Coll., 1958; MD, Temple U., 1962. Diplomate Am. Bd. Family Practice, Nat. Bd. Med. Examiners. Intern St. Luke's Hosp., Bethlehem, Pa., 1962-63, resident in internal medicine, 1965-66; pvt. practice Bethlehem, Pa., 1965-71; assoc. dir. Merck Sharpe & Dohme, West Point, Pa., 1971-73, Wyeth Lab., Phila., 1973-77; med. dir. Valley Forge Mil. Acad. and Jr. Coll., Wayne, Pa., 1973—, Home Health Corp. Am., King of Prussia, Pa., 1976—; assoc. dir. Bryn Mawr Family Medicine, 1977-85; med. dir. Wayne Nursing & Rehab., 1983—; dir. Wyeth Ayerst Labs., Phila., 1985-89, sr. dir. clin. devel., 1989—; attending staff Bryn Mawr (Pa.) Hosp., 1972—; exec. dir. worldwide safety surveillance Wyeth-Ayerst Labs., Phila., 1995—; adj. faculty Bryn Mawr Family Practice, 1995—. Contbr. articles to profl. jours. Pres. Radnor Twp. Bd. Health, Wayne, 1988. Comdr. USNR, 1963—. Fellow Am. Acad. Family Physicians, Am. Coll. Rheumatology; mem. Am. Soc. Internal Medicine, Am. Soc. Clin. Pharmacology and Therapeutics, St. Andrews Soc., Soc. Tchrs. of Family Medicine, Faculty of Pharm. Medicine, Freemasonry. Episcopalian. Home: 529 County Line Rd Radnor PA 19087-3718 Office: Wyeth Ayerst Labs PO Box 8299 Philadelphia PA 19101-0082

BALLARD, KAREN A., professional association administrator; b. Bklyn., Aug. 11, 1944; d. Ernest J. and Mary M. (O'Brien) B. BS in Nursing, Niagara U., 1966; MA, NYU, 1968. Asst. prof. CUNY; clin. supr. Mt. Sinai Med. Ctr., N.Y.C.; clin. nurse specialist Cornell Med. Ctr., N.Y.C.; dir. nursing practice N.Y. State Nurses Assn., Guilderland. Author: (video) Preparing Children for the Hospital Experience, 1985; contbr.: The Person With AIDS: A Nursing Perspective, 1986, 2d edit., 1991, Policy and Politics for Nurses, 2d edit., 1993. Recipient Jane Delano award N.Y.C. Registered Nurses Assn. 1989. Mem. ANA (cabinet on nursing practice 1982-84), N.Y. State Nurses Assn. (dir. 1972-78, nursing practice award 1984), Assn. Care Children's Health, Assn. Child and Adolescent Psychiat. Nurses.

BALLARD, MELISSA GAYLE BISHOP, nurse, administrator; b. Orlando, Fla., Jan. 18, 1971; d. Thomas Jr. and Blanche Alice (Whitt) Ingle; m. Robert Kiah Ballard, Apr. 16, 1994. ADN, A-B Tech. C.C., Asheville, N.C., 1993. RN, N.C. Med. records clk. Meml. Mission Hosp., Asheville, 1989-90; data entry clk. Pathologists Med. Labs., Asheville, 1990-91; dialysis technician Asheville Kidney Ctr., 1991-93, staff and charge nurse, 1993-94; nurse mgr. Hendersonville (N.C.) Dialysis Ctr., 1994—. Baptist. Office: Hendersonville Dialysis Ctr 500 Beverly Hanks Centre Hendersonville NC 28792

BALLARD, WILEY PERRY III, hematologist, oncologist; b. Atlanta, Mar. 30, 1952; s. Wiley Perry Jr. and Anne Sykes (Equen) B.; m. Jane Elliot Roberts, Aug. 15, 1992; 1 child, Wiley Perry IV. AB with high honors, Dartmouth Coll., 1974; MD, Emory U., 1978. Diplomate Am. Bd. Internal Medicine, Am. Bd. Med. Oncology, Am. Bd. Hematology. Intern in medicine N.Y. Hosp.- Cornell Med. Ctr., N.Y.C., 1978-79, resident in medicine, 1979-81, asst. chief resident in medicine, 1981, fellow in hematology-oncology, 1983-84, chief clin. fellow in hematology-oncology, 1984-85, asst. attending physician, 1985-87; fellow in infectious disease Tufts-New England Med. Ctr., Boston, 1981-82; fellow in gen. internal medicine Cornell U. Sch. of Medicine, N.Y.C., 1982-83; instr. in medicine Cornell U. Med. Coll., N.Y.C., 1984-86, asst. prof. medicine, 1986-87; attending physician Piedmont Hosp., Atlanta, 1987—; pvt. practice Atlanta, 1987—; mem. adv. bd. Am. Cancer Soc., Atlanta, 1990-92, v.p. med. affairs, 1992—, bd. dirs., 1993—, exec. com., 1993—. Contbr. articles to profl. jours. Bd. dirs. CHRIS Homes, 1991—. Clin. fellow Am. Cancer Soc., 1983-85, Kate Rosenberg fellow N.Y. Hosp.- Cornell Med. Ctr. Mem. ACP, Am. Soc. Clin. Oncology, Am. Soc. Hematology, Piedmont Driving Club, Peachtree Golf Club, Phi Beta Kappa, Alpha Omega Alpha. Episcopalian. Home: 562 Arden Oaks Ct NW Atlanta GA 30305-1955 Office: Peachtree Hematology-Oncology Ste 5015 95 Collier Rd Atlanta GA 30309-1710

BALLIET, PAUL ANTHONY, optometrist; b. Linton, N.D., Feb. 6, 1961; s. Theophil and Bertha (Wickenheiser) B.; m. Paula Kay Kalberer, 1986; children: Scott, Julia. Student, U. of Mary, Bismarck, N.D., 1979, Moorhead (Minn.) State U., 1980-82; BS in Visual Sci., So. Calif. Coll. Optometry, 1982, OD, 1986. Pvt. practice, Bismarck, 1986—. Office: Dakota Eye Inst 200 S 5th St Bismarck ND 58504

BALLING, LOUISE MARY, social worker; b. North Tonawanda, N.Y.; d. Leo and Mary Anna (Achatz) B. BA, D'Youville Coll., 1960; MSW, SUNY, Buffalo, 1970. Cert. social worker, N.Y. Med. social worker Deaconess Hosp. of Buffalo, N.Y., 1972-80; social worker N.Y. State Office of Mental Health, Helmuth, 1981-94, Buffalo, 1994—; developer high risk pregnancy index and rsch. study. Bd. dirs. Hist. Soc. of Tonawandas, 1985-92; vol. Albright Knox Art Gallery, Buffalo, 1978-91; docent Long Homestead, Tonawanda, 1982—. Mem. English Speaking Union. Home: 57 Park St Springville NY 14141-1116

BALLITCH, HAROLD A., physician, ophthalmologist; b. Jackson, Mich., Oct. 1, 1962; s. Harold A. and Helen M. (Warren) B.; m. Margaret L., June 1, 1985; children: Andrew S., Brian A., Rachel E. BA, Spring Arbor Coll., 1983. Diplomate Am. Bd. Ophthalmology. Chief resident Med. Coll. of Va., Richmond, 1991; clin. asst., prof. of ophthalmology Albany (N.Y.) Med. Coll., 1991-92; ophthalmologist Sandusky Opthalmologists, Mansfield, Ohio, 1992-94; physician/opthalmologist Ohio Eye Assn., Mansfield, 1994—. Contbr. articles to profl. jours. Fellow Am. Coll. Surgeons, Am. Acad. Ophthalmology; mem. Ohio State Med. Assn., Richland County Med. Soc., Ohio Ophthal. Soc. Home: 1614 Pin Oak Trail Mansfield OH 44906 Office: Ohio Eye Assocs 466 S Trimble Rd Mansfield OH 44906

BALLOW, MARK, physician, educator; b. Harrisburg, Pa., Sept. 8, 1943; m. Molly Ballow, June 25, 1967; children: Sarah, Mara, Andrew. BA, Rutgers U., 1965; MD, U. Chgo., 1969. Diplomate Nat. Bd. Med. Examiners, Am. Bd. Pediatrics, Am. Bd. Allergy and Immunology, Diagnostic Lab. Immunology. Intern, resident Yale-New Haven Hosp., 1969-71; fellow U. Minn., 1971-73; chief clin./exptl. immunology U. Conn. Health Ctr., Farmington, 1975-79, assoc. prof. pediatrics, 1979-85, prof. pediatrics, 1985-88; prof., chief allergy and immunology divsn. Children's Hosp. Buffalo, SUNY at Buffalo, 1988—; dir. Am. Bd. Allergy and Immunology, 1993—. Mem. Am. Acad. Allergy and Immunology (Carl Arbesman Meml. lectr. 1994), Soc. Pediatric Rsch., Clin. Immunology Soc., Am. Pediatric Soc., Phi Beta Kappa. Office: SUNY-Buffalo/Childrens Hosp Dept Allergy & Immunology 219 Bryant St Buffalo NY 14222-2006*

BALLWEG, RUTH MILLIGAN, physician assistant, educator; b. Feb. 29, 1944. BS in Sociology, So. Oregon State Coll., 1969; grad. MEDEX N.W. physician asst. program, U. Wash., Seattle, 1978, postgrad. study, present. Cert. State Bd. Med. Examiners, Oregon, Wash.; cert. Nat. Commn. on Cert. of Physician Assts. Asst. to dirs. honors program So. Oregon State Coll., Ashland, Ore., 1968; social worker and clinical asst. M. Kirk Gooding MD and William Sammons MD, Ashland, Ore., 1971-78; physician asst. M. Kirk Gooding MD, Ashland and Medford, 1978-80; childbirth educator Childbirth Education Assn. So. Oregon, Ashland and Medford, Ore., 1971-79; physician asst. Bremerton Kitsap County Health Dept., Bremerton, Wash., 1980-81; asst. program dir. MEDEX Northwest, Wash., 1984-85; dir. physician asst. program MEDEX Northwest, U. Wash. Sch. Med., 1985—; cons. N. Mex. State Policy Commn. on Physician Assts. Program Devel, 1993, Oregon Office Rural Health on Physician Assts. Program Feasibilty, 1992, Seattle Planned Parenthood Physical Assesment Updates for Nurse Practitioners and Physician Assts. 1987, Benton-Franklin County Health Dept. Indigent Care Plan, Richland Wash., 1983, Physician Asst. Program Devel, Oregon Health Scis. U., Portland, Ore., 1993, 1994, Nat. Health Svc. Corps. James Bowman and Assocs., San Francisco, 1992, 93, Stanford U. Fed. Contract on Deployment of Physician Assts. Nurse Practicioners and CNM's to Underserved Populations, 1992-93; mem. Nat. Adv. Bd. Nat. Health Svc. Corps, 1994—, mem. Alaska Workgroup on Primary Care Planning, Dept. Health, Rural Alaska Health Edn. Ctr., 1994, exec. com. Northwest Geriat. Edn. Ctr. U. Wash., 1989-92, asst. coord. rural tng. activities 1990-92; coord. Emerging Options Symposium, Seattle Ctr., Sept. 1982; co-dir. Sugarloaf Leadership Inst., Sugarloaf, Maine, 1993; lectr. Seattle Midwifery Sch. 1984-88, cons. 1984—, MEDEX Northwest, 1981-84; spkr., presenter for over 19 confs., profl. assns. colls. and orgns. in field. Co-Editor: Physician Assistant: A Guide to Clinical Practice, 1994; mem. editl. bd. Clinician Reviews, 1990-94, Physician Assistant, 1989-90; contbr. articles to profl. jours. adv. com. Northwest AIDS Edn. Ctr, U. Wash., 1991-92; mem. People to People USSR Rural Health Project, Sch. Pub. Health, Sch. Medicine, U. Wash 1986-88. Primary Care Health Policy fellow, Bureau Health Professions, 1992; Recipient Disting. Svc. award Nat. Indian Health Bd. 1987. Grantee MEDEX Northwest Fed. Tng. , Wash., Alaska, Mont. Ore. Idaho, 1985-94, Health Careers Opportunity award, 1987, 90, Model Edn. Projects Health Professions, 1990. Mem. Assn. Physician Asst. Programs (chair pub. rels and mktg. com. 1984, ad hoc regionalization com. 1986-88, mem. futures com., consortia chair, 1986-89, pres. elect 1989-90, pres. 1990-91, 91-92, chair external rels. com. 1991-94, co-dir. new program devel. project, bd. mem.-at-large 1993-95, UPJOHN Presidential award 1991), Am. Acad. Physician Assts.(ho. dels. alt. 1984-87, cons. to edn. coun.1989-90, mem. health reform task force, 1994), Wash. Acad. Physician Assts. (bd.mem. 1984-86, v.p. 1986-88, chair health policy coun. 1993-94, pres.-elect. 1993-94, pres. 1994-95, spl. recognition award, 1988), Oregon Soc. Physician Assts.(MEDEX northwest liason bd. dirs. 1981-92), Nat. Rural Health Assn. (mem. task force Barriers to Practice Non Physician providers, 1991-92, frontier constituency), Wash. Rural Health Assn. Office: MEDEX Northwest UWMC Roosevelt 4245 Roosevelt Way NE Seattle WA 98105-6920

BALOG, THERESA GALLAGHER, nursing educator; b. Pitts., Dec. 18, 1937; d. Bernard and Dorothy (Sherred) Gallagher; children: Megan Anne, Paul David. Diploma in nursing, Allegheny Valley Hosp., 1960; BSN, Duquesne U., 1963; M in Nursing, U. Pitts., 1968, PhD, 1984. RN, Pa. Nursing staff adminstr., educator Children's Hosp., Pitts., 1963-68; instr., asst. prof. nursing children and maternal nursing U. Pitts., 1968-72; tenured assoc. prof. nursing, coord. family nursing Duquesne U., Pitts., 1972-77; asst. prof. nursing, dir. pediatric affiliate program U. Pitts., 1977-81; asst. dean instrn., nursing Community Coll. Allegheny County, Pitts., 1981-88; dir. Sch. Nursing Uniontown (Pa.) Hosp., 1988-94; asst. prof., campus coord. nursing Pa. State U. Fayette campus, Uniontown, Pa., 1994—; adj. asst. prof. grad. program in nursing adminstrn. U. Pitts., 1987-90, asst. prof. Helene Fuld grantee, Eberly Family Charitable Trustee grantee, Vocat. Edn. grantee. Mem. Nat. League Nursing, Pa. League Nursing (bd. dirs.), Nightingale Awards of Pa. (trustee), Carebreak, Sigma Theta Tau (Rsch. award 1983, Leadership in Nursing.Excellence in Edn. award 1992). Home: 1564 St Andrews Dr Oakmont PA 15139

BALOG (GILLETTE), DAWN LOIS, motivational therapist, nutritionist; b. Lansing, Mich., May 5, 1940; d. Harold James and Edna Alice (Richmond) Gilpin; m. John Francis Balog, June 22, 1963; children—Monica Marie, Teresa Alice. B.A., Immaculate Heart Coll., 1974; M.S., Donsbach U., 1981, Ph.D., 1983. Cert. biofeedback therapist. Program dir. Life Fitness Center, Pasadena, Calif., 1980-83; program dir., co-founder Lifestyle Dynamics, Pasadena, 1983-94; founder Awareness in Action, Kapalua, Hawaii. Bd. dirs. Immaculate Heart Coll., Los Angeles. Mem. Calif. Inst. Tech. Assocs. (Pasadena). Office: Awareness In Action 500 Bay Dr #35B2 Lahaina HI 96761-9034

BALON, RICHARD, psychiatrist, educator; b. Olomouc, Czechoslovakia, Oct. 11, 1951; s. Ota and Marie (Sindylek) B.; m. Helena Rachel Zador, July 24, 1976. MD, U. Karlova, Prague, Czechoslovakia, 1976. Diplomate Am. Bd. Psychiatry and Neurology; bd. cert. in psychiatry in Czechoslovakia. Resident in psychiatry and clin. rsch. Psychiat. Rsch. Inst., Prague, 1978-81; resident in psychiatry Lafayette Clinic, Detroit, 1983-87; asst. prof. Wayne State U., Detroit, 1987-90, assoc. prof., 1990-96, prof., 1996—; dir. jr. med. students program in psychiatry Wayne State U., Detroit, 1989-92, dir. med. student edn. psychiatry, 1993—; staff psychiatrist Lafayette Clinic, Detroit, 1987-92, pres. med. staff, 1990-92; co-chair Mich. Tech. Adv. Rsch. com., 1991—. Contbr. chpts to books and articles to profl. jours. Recipient Travel fellowship award Am. Coll. Neuropsychopharmacology, 1987. Fellow Am. Psychiat. Assn. (1st ann. Nancy C.A. Roeske award 1991); mem. AMA, Internat. Soc. Psychoneuroendocrinology, Am. Assn. Suicidology, Soc. Biol. Psychiatry, Collegium Internat. Neuro-Psychopharmacologicum, Assn. Dirs. of Med. Student Edn. in Psychiatry, Am. Coll. Psychiatrists. Office: Univ Psychiat Ctr 2751 E Jefferson Ave Ste 200 Detroit MI 48207-4100

BALON, THOMAS WILLIAM, exercise physiologist; b. Albany, N.Y., Mar. 3, 1952; s. Paul Joseph and Lieschen (Heider) B.; m. Judith Lee Treadway, Aug. 3, 1985 (div.); 1 child, Tanya Lee. BS, SUNY, Brockport, 1975; PhD, U. Toledo, 1983. Postdoctoral fellow Boston U. Sch. Medicine, 1983-86; asst. prof. U. Iowa, Iowa City, 1986-92; rsch. scientist City of Hope Nat. Med. Ctr., Duarte, Calif., 1992—; book reviewer MacMillan Pub. Co., N.Y.C., 1988, W. C. Brown Co., Madison, Wis., 1990; guest reviewer Jour. of Applied Physiology, Bethesda, Md., 1987-91; prin. investigator NIH, 1990—, Am. Diabetes Assn., 1987. Contbr. articles to Jour. of Applied Psychology, Biochem. Jour., Am. Jour. Physiology, Jour. of Biol. Chemistry, also chpt. to book. Fellow Am. Coll. Sports Medicine; mem. Am. Diabetes Assn. (grantee), Am. Physiol. Soc. (assoc.). Roman Catholic. Office: City of Hope Nat Med Ctr Dept Diabetes Endocrin/Met Shapiro S 104 Duarte CA 91010*

BALSAM, RICHARD FREDRIC, cardiologist; b. Port Chester, N.Y., Mar. 8, 1938; s. Paul and Bertha (Jacobs) B.; m. Mary Kennedy, Feb. 18, 1989; children: Loren, Daniel. BS, Union Coll., Schenectady, N.Y., 1959; MD, Albany Med. Coll., 1964. Internal medicine intern Albany (N.Y.) Med. Ctr. Hosp., 1964-65, internal medicine resident, 1965-67; cardiac fellow VA, Albany, 1967-69; internist/cardiologist Pankin & Balsam, M.D., P.C., Albany, 1969-95, Cmty. Care Physicians, Albany, 1995—; cons. Searle Pharms., Albany, 1992-95; mem. pharmacy adv. com. St. Peter's Hosp., Albany, 1969—; pres., founder Rennaissance Med. Arts, Inc., 1986—. Mem. bd. dirs. Albany Symphony Orch., 1977-83; pres. Empire State Youth Orch. Bd., Albany, 1983-87. Capt. USAR, 1965-72. Mem. Am. Coll. Cardiology, Am. Coll. Sports Medicine, Am. Heart Assn., Am. Soc. Internal Medicine, Cardiac Soc. of Upstate N.Y. (pres.). Jewish. Office: 23 Hackett Blvd Albany NY 12208-3436

BALSAM, THEODORE, physician; b. N.Y.C., Apr. 11, 1931; s. Abraham and Esther (Golden) B.; m. Barbara Korn, Dec. 25, 1952; children: Hugh, Adrienne, Lisbeth. BA, NYU, 1952; MD, Chgo. Med. Sch., 1957; MPH, Johns Hopkins U., 1959. Diplomate Am. Bd. Internal Medicine. Intern Charity Hosp., New Orleans, 1957-58; fellow Johns Hopkins U., Balt., 1958-59; resident in medicine Bklyn. Hosp., 1959-61, fellow in gastroenterology, 1961-62; physician USPHS, S.I., 1962-64; pvt. practice Chgo., 1964—; pres. med. staff Louis A. Weiss Meml. Hosp., Chgo., 1976-78, 93-95, dir. patient hosp. orgn., 1996—. Mem. Sch. Bd., Lincolnwood, Ill., 1970-72. Fellow Am. Coll. Gastroenterology; mem. AMA, Ill. State Med. Soc., Chgo. Med. Soc. Office: Weiss Meml Hosp 4640 N Marine Dr Chicago IL 60640

BALSTER, ROBERT LOUIS, pharmacologist; b. St. Cloud, Minn., Oct. 12, 1944; s. Louis and Marion Mae (Vandergon) B.; m. Sandra Kay Herwig, June 25, 1966; 1 child, Sarah Elizabeth Balster. BS, U. Minn., 1966; PhD, U. Houston, 1970. Postdoctoral fellow in Psychiatry and Pharmacology U. Chgo., 1970-72; rsch. assoc. in Psychiatry Duke U., Durham, N.C., 1972-73; asst. prof. Pharmacology Med. Coll. Va., Richmond, 1973-78; assoc. prof. Med. Coll. Va., 1978-84, prof. Pharmacology, 1984—; dir. Ctr. for Drug and Alcohol Studies, 1993—; chair Drug Abuse Adv. Com., FDA, Rockville, Md., 1983-84. Contbr. over 200 articles to profl. jours. Recipient NIH Merit award, 1993—. Fellow Coll. on Problems of Drug Dependence (charter fellow, pres. 1995-96), Am. Coll. Neuropsychopharmacology, Am. Psychol. Assn. (pres. psychopharmacology divsn. 1989-90); mem. European Behavioral Pharmacology Soc. (coun. mem. 1986-94). Office: Va Commonwealth U Box 980310 Richmond VA 23298-0310

BALTA, ANDREW STEPHEN, oral and facial surgeon; b. Duquesne, Pa., Jan. 19, 1938; s. Andrew Victor and Eva Margaret (Kupra) B.; m. JoAnn Diremigio, Dec. 30, 1961; children: Andrew Brian, Stephen Adam. BS, U. Pitts., 1963; DMD, Pitts. Sch. Dental Medicine, 1968. Diplomate Am. Bd. Oral and Maxillofacial Surgery. Asst. instr. histology U. Pitts. Sch. Dental Medicine, 1966-67, asst. instr. anesthesia, 1972-73; oral and maxillofacial surgeon Henry Ford Hosp., Detroit, 1971-72; dist. commr. Pa. Blue Shield, Camp Hill, 1973-91; founder, CEO Ctr. for Facial and Jaw Surgery, Washington, Pa., 1993—; active staff oral and facial surgeon Henry Ford Hosp., Detroit, 1971-72; chief dept. oral and facial surgery Canonsburg, Pa., 1975-94, Washington (Pa.) Hosp., 1992; CEO, chief of staff Ctr. for Facial and Jaw Surgery, Washington, 1992. Pres. Bd. of Health, City of Washington, 1981-84; chief dental forensic examiner Washington County Coroner, 1983-91; pres. CVO United Way of Washington County, 1985-87, United Way of s.W. Pa., 1987-90; exec. com. Washington County Rep. Party, 1987. Recipient Disting. Svc. award United Way of S.W. Pa., Pitts., 1977, Presdl. citations Pa. Dental Assn. and Dental Soc. Western Pa., 1983-94, Scholars award and Masters award Am. Coll. Maxillofacial Surgeons, 1993-94; named Man. of Yr., Jaycees, Washington, 1990; Owens fellow and NIH fellow, 1966-67. Fellow Am. Soc. Oral and Maxillofacial Surgeons, Am. Coll. Oral Surgeons, Am. Acad. Cosmetic Surgery; mem. ADA, PSOMS, WPSOMS, NRA, Pa. Dental Assn., Dental Soc. West Pa., Washington Unit Am. Cancer Soc. (pres. 1980-81). Roman Catholic. Home: 51 Fitzwilliams Rd Washington PA 15301

BALTARO, RICHARD J., pathologist; b. Caracas, Venezuela, June 15, 1950; came to the U.S., 1964; s. Dimitri and Maria Silvana (Vici) B.; m. Laura E. Neece, Sept. 9, 1972; children: Elizabeth B., John C. BA, Earlham Coll., 1972; PhD summa cum laude, U. Rome, Italy, 1977; MD magna cum laude, Cath. U., Rome, 1983. Bd. cert. anatomic and clin. pathology Am. Bd. Pathology, cert. immunopathology Am. Bd. Pathology. Pathology resident Brown U., Providence, 1983-87; clin. pathology fellow George Washington U. Hosp., Washington, 1987-88; asst. in pathology George Washington Med. Sch., Washington, 1987-88; sr. staff fellow NIH Clin. Ctr. Immunology, Bethesda, Md., 1988-90; jr. active staff NIH Clin. Ctr., Bethesda, 1988-90; asst. prof. Marshall U. Sch. Medicine, Huntington, W.Va., 1990-93; dir. pathology residency program Marshall U. Sch. Medicine, Huntington, 1991-93; staff pathologist lab. svc. VA Med. Ctr., Huntington, 1990-93; pathologist Med. Arts Lab., Oklahoma City, 1993—; stockholder Med. Arts Lab., 1994—; ptnr. Med. Arts Pathologists, 1995; adj. assoc. prof. U. Okla. Health Sci., Oklahoma City, 1993—; assoc. dir. Histocompatibility, 1995—; dir. Microbiology Lab., 1993—, Med. Arts Lab, Oklahoma City, 1995—; expert witness, cons. Nat. Med. Adv. Svc., Bethesda, 1990—; bd. trustees John Marshall Med. Svcs., Inc.; residency adv. com., search com., chmn. ob-gyn. Marshall U. Sch. Medicine; spkr. in field. Contbr. articles to profl. jours. Recipient NIH grant, 1991. Fellow Coll. Am. Pathologists (lab. insp. 1985—), Am. Soc. Clin. Pathologists, Internat. Acad. Pathology, Acad. Clin. Lab. Physicians and Scientists, Am. Coll. Internat. Physicians, Assn. Clin. Scientists; mem. AMA, AAAS, Am. Soc. Microbiology, Am. Assn. for Clin. chemistry, Assn. Med. Lab. Immunologists. Office: Med Arts Lab 1111 N Lee Ave Ste 100 Oklahoma City OK 73103-2620

BALTASAR, ANICETO, physician, surgeon; b. Guadalupe, Caceres, Spain, Feb. 10, 1944; s. Pedro and Fidela (Torrejon) B.; m. Luisa Pazos, June 14, 1969; children: Belen, Ana. MD, Madrid Med. Sch., 1967. Surg. resident L.I. (N.Y.) Coll. Hosp., 1969-74; chief of surgery Virgen de los Lirios Hosp., Alcoy, 1974—. Mem. editl. bd. Obesity Surgery; contbr. articles to med. jours. Fellow ACS, Am. Soc. Bariatric Surgery; mem. Spanish Assn. Surgery, Assn. Vascular Surgery. Home: Cid 6J, 03800 Alcoy Spain Office: Virgen de los Lirios Hosp, Alcoy, 10385 Alicante Spain

BALTAZAR, ROMULO FLORES, cardiologist; b. Naga, Camarines Sur, Philippines, Oct. 15, 1941; came to U.S., 1970; s.Melecio Perez and Socorro (Flores) B.; m. Ophelia Zarzuela, June 6, 1970; children: Maria Cristina, Romulo Jr. BA, U. Philippines, 1961, MD, 1966. Intern U. Philippines, Philippine Gen. Hosp., 1965-66; resident medicine Philippine Gen. Hosp., 1966-69, chief resident medicine, 1969-70; instr. medicine U. Philippines, 1969-70; resident medicine Sinai Hosp., Balt., 1970-71, resident cardiology, 1971-73, assoc. cardiology, 1975-87, dir. non-invasive cardiology, 1987—; resident pediatric cardiology Johns Hopkins Hosp., Balt., 1971-72; fellow cardiology Maimonides Med. Ctr., N.Y.C., 1973-75; instr. medicine Johns Hopkins U. Sch. Medicine, Balt., 1977-87, asst. prof. medicine, 1987—; referee Archives of Internal Medicine, 1991—, JAMA, 1988. Contbr. articles to med. jours. Fellow ACP, Am. Coll. Cardiology, Am. Coll. Chest Physicians. Roman Catholic. Office: Sinai Hosp Balt Div Cardiology Baltimore MD 21215

BALTIMORE, DAVID, microbiologist, educator; b. N.Y.C., N.Y., Mar. 7, 1938; s. Richard I. and Gertrude (Lipschitz) B.; m. Alice S. Huang, Oct. 5, 1968; 1 dau., Teak. BA with high honors in Chemistry, Swarthmore Coll., 1960; postgrad., MIT, 1960-61; PhD, Rockefeller U., 1964. Research assoc. Salk Inst. Biol. Studies, La Jolla, Calif., 1965-68; assoc. prof. microbiology MIT, Cambridge, 1968-72, prof. biology, 1972-95; Ivan R. Cottrell prof. molecular biology and immunology MIT, 1994—; inst. prof. MIT, Cambridge, 1995—, Am. Cancer Soc. prof. microbiology, 1973-83, 94—, dir. Whitehead Inst. Biomed. Rsch., 1982-90; pres. Rockefeller U., N.Y.C., 1990-91, prof., 1990-94. Mem. editorial bd. Jour. Molecular Biology, 1971-73, Jour. Virology, 1969-90, Sci., 1986—, New Eng. Jour. Medicine, 1989-94. Bd. govs. Weizmann Inst. Sci., Israel; bd. dirs. Life Sci. Rsch. Found.; co-chmn. Commn. on a Nat. Strategy of AIDS; ad hoc program adv. com. on complex genome, NIH; mem. office AIDS rsch. adv. coun. NIH. Recipient Gustav Stern award in virology, 1970; Warren Triennial prize Mass. Gen. Hosp., 1971; Eli Lilly and Co. award in microbiology and immunology, 1971; Nat. Acad. Scis. U.S. Steel award in molecular biology, 1974; Gairdner Found. ann. award, 1974; Nobel prize in physiology or medicine, 1975. Fellow AAAS, Am. Med. Writers Assn. (hon.), Am. Acad. Microbiology; mem. NAS, Am. Acad. Arts and Scis., Inst. Medicine, Pontifical Acad. Scis., Royal Soc. (Eng.) (fgn.). Office: MIT 77 Massachusetts Ave Rm 68-380 Cambridge MA 02139-4301

BALTIMORE, RUTH BETTY, social worker; b. Wilkes-Barre, Pa., Feb. 27, 1926; d. Samuel Jr. and Theresa (Bergsmann) Bloch; m. Martin Joseph Baltimore, Feb. 6, 1949; children: Francie, Sandy. BA in Psychology, Skidmore Coll., 1948; postgrad., U. Scranton, 1965, 70. Sch. social worker Wyoming Valley West Sch. Dist., Kingston, Pa., 1966-89; retired; cons. in field. Co-author: (booklet) Guide for Teachers on Reporting Child Abuse, 1970. Bd. dirs. Youth Svcs. Commn., Wilkes-Barre, 1986-87, Victims Resource Ctr., Wilkes-Barre, 1990—; bd. dirs. Luz County Adv. Bd. Children and Youth, Wilkes-Barre, 1988—, vice chairperson, 1991, chairperson, 1992-96. Recipient Connie Coun. Svc. award Nat. Coun. Jewish Women, Wilkes-Barre, 1959. Mem. Valley Tennis and Swim Club (pres.-elect 1994, pres. 1995-96). Home: 630 Newberry Estate Dallas PA 18612

BALTZ, RICHARD JAY, health care company executive; b. Kingston, N.Y., June 6, 1952; s. Harold H. and Virginia K. (Luedtke) B.; m. Mary Melissa White, May 26, 1974; 1 child, Christopher Jay. BS, St. Lawrence U., 1974; MA, George Washington U., 1978. Lic. nursing home adminstr. Adminstr. Hudson Valley Sr. Residence, Kingston, N.Y., 1974-76; adminstr. resident/asst. Buffalo VA Med. Ctr., 1977-80, asst. chief Med. Adminstrv. Svc., 1980-83; chief Med. Adminstrv. Svc. Syracuse (N.Y.) VA Med. Ctr., 1984-86; assoc. dir. trainee Albany (N.Y.) VA Med. Ctr., 1987; assoc. med. ctr. dir. Togus (Maine) VA Med. Ctr., 1988-90, VA Med. Ctr., Jackson, Miss., 1990—; adj. prof. dept. health care adminstrn. U. Ala., Birmingham, 1990—. Bd. dirs. Kennebec, Maine unit Am. Cancer Soc., 1988-90, pres., 1989, 90, Maine divsn., 1988-90. Fellow Am. Coll. Healthcare Execs. Home: 138 Northwind Dr Brandon MS 39042-8680 Office: VA Med Ctr 1500 E Woodrow Wilson Ave Jackson MS 39216-5116

BALTZAN, MARCEL ALTER, physician; b. Saskatoon, Sask., Can., Oct. 31, 1929; s. David Mortimer and Rose Cristall Baltzan; children: Marcel Alter, Frances B., Zeba, Elizabeth Virginia; m. Nahid Ahmad, Mar. 21, 1992. B.Sc., McGill U., 1953, M.D., C.M., 1953. Physician Baltzan Assoc. Med. Clinic, Saskatoon, 1959—; prof., chmn. dept. medicine U. Sask., 1974-79; gov. Am. Coll. Physicians, Man. and Sask., Can., 1988-92. Contbr. articles to med. jours. Named Officer Order of Can., 1995. Fellow Royal Coll. Physicians and Surgeons of Can., ACP; mem. Can. Med. Assn. (pres. 1982-83). Club: Saskatoon. Office: Baltzan Associate Medical Clinic, 366 3d Ave S, Suite 200, Saskatoon, SK Canada S7K 1M5

BALYEAT, HAL DAVISON, ophthalmologist; b. Oklahoma City, Mar. 28, 1940; s. Ray Morton and Gladys Faye (Smith) B.; m. Marilyn Black, June 17, 1962; children: Elaine, Megan, Melinda, Hal Jr. BA, U. Okla., 1962, MD, 1966. Intern Henry Ford Hosp., Detroit, 1966-67, resident in ophthalmology, 1969-73; pvt. practice ophthalmologist Oklahoma City, 1973-76; ophthalmologist Dean A. McGee Eye Inst., Oklahoma City, 1976—. Contbr. articles to profl. publs. Chmn. bd. trustees Columbia Presbyn. Hosp., Oklahoma City, 1996—, chmn. dept. opthalmology, 1992—; mem. corp. bd. Presbyn. Health Found., Oklahoma City, 1990-96. Capt. USAF, 1967-69. Fellow Am. Acad. Ophthalmology (chmn. POACE 1991-96, editl. bd. Focal Points 1994-96, Honor award 1989); mem. Okla. Med. Sch. Alumni Assn. (pres. 1995—). Home: 6803 Avondale Dr Oklahoma City OK 73116 Office: Dean A McGee Eye Inst 608 Stanton L Young Blvd Oklahoma City OK 73104

BALZ, JAMES B., surgeon; b. Fargo, N.D., Apr. 1, 1946; s. Fredric and Betty Ann (Beal) B.; m. Lynn Margaret Owen, Aug. 25, 1969 (dec. Sept. 1979); children: Ryan, Sara, Reika; m. Jeanine Marie Greb, July 11, 1981. BA in Biology, U. Puget Sound, 1968; MD, St. Louis U., 1972. Chief of staff Eugene (Oreg.) Hosp., 1982-84; dept. chief of surgery Sacred Heart Hosp., Eugene, 1990-92, divsn. chief of surgery, 1994—; pvt. practice Eugene. Contbr. articles to profl. publs. Fellow ACS, Am. Soc. Colon and Rectal Surgeons, N.W. Soc. Colon and Rectal Surgeons; mem. AMA, Oreg. Med. Assn. Home: 1948 Olive Eugene OR 97384 Office: 3203 Willamette Eugene OR 97405

BALZAC, AUDREY FLOBELLE ADRIAN, psychologist; b. N.Y.C., May 5, 1928; d. Allen Isaac and Mildred Florence (Brown) Adrian; m. Ralph P. Balzac, Jr., May 3, 1961; children: Stephen Rafael, Elena Adrian, Rebecca Lisa. BA in Psychology with honors, Hunter Coll., 1951; MS with honors, Purdue U., 1952; ABD, Columbia U., 1963. Intern in psychology Howard Rusk Inst., NYU and Bellevue Hosp., N.Y.C., 1956-57; clin. psychologist Westchester Community Mental Health Bd., and Children's Ct., White Plains, N.Y., 1957-63; psychol. cons. div. Vocat. Rehab., N.Y.C., 1957—; pvt. practice, 1963—; research psychologist Psychiat. Inst., Columbia Presbyn. Med. Ctr., N.Y.C., 1955-57; cons. Pound Ridge Elem. Sch., 1975-76. Contbr. articles to Concerned Parent. Chairwoman Community Relations bd. Pound Ridge Jewish Community Ctr., 1975-79, treas., 1978-79; mem. Westchester Women's Adv. Bd., 1986-87; candidate Bedford Cen. Sch. Bd., 1987, 88; panelist No. Westchester Geriatric Com., Inc., 1992; mem. U.S. Postal Adv. Commn., 1993—; mem. consumer panel adv. bd. N.Y. State Electric & Gas Co., Binghamton, 1994—; spl. advisor Town of Pound Ridge supr., liaison to N.Y. State Electric & Gas Co., 1996—. Fellow Rusk Inst., 1956-57; research grantee Columbia U., 1960—. Fellow AAUW; mem. Am. Psychol. Assn., Eastern Psychol. Assn., N.Y. Soc. Clin. Psychologists, Soc. Psychol. Study of Social Issues, Am. Sociol. Assn., Sigma Xi, Psi Chi (treas. 1951-52). Jewish. Home: RR 4 Box 267 Kitchawan Rd Pound Ridge NY 10576-9682

BAMBAKIDIS, PETER, neurologist, educator; b. Akron, Ohio, Nov. 2, 1948; s. Nicholas and Zopigi (Dragoumanou) B.; m. Anna Savaris, Aug. 18, 1974; children: Athe, John A., Theodore. Student, U. Akron, 1966-67; BMus, Cleve. Inst. Mus., 1971, MMus, 1973; postgrad., U. Pitts., 1974-75, Ohio State U., 1978-80; MD, Case Western Res. U., 1984. Diplomate Am. Bd. Psychiatry and Neurology, Am. Bd. Clin. Neurophysiology. Resident in neurology Mayo Grad. Sch. Medicine, Rochester, Minn., 1984-88; fellow EEG Mayo Grad. Sch. Medicine, Rochester, 1988-89; pvt. practice Cleve., 1989-92; asst. prof. neurology Case Western Res. U., Cleve., 1992—; neurologist Fairview Med. Group, 1994—; violinist Akron Symphony Orch., 1966-67, Richmond (Va.) Sinfonia, Richmond Symphony Orch., 1973-74, West Australian Symphony Orch., Perth, 1976-78, Columbus (Ohio) Symphony Orch., 1978-80; freelance musician, 1967-73; tchg. asst. Cleve. Inst. Music, 1971-73; tchg. fellow dept. music U. Pitts., 1974-75; follow-up asst. regional pediat. intensive care transport sys. Rainbow Babies and Children's Hosp., Cleve., 1981-82; hosp. affiliations Fairview Gen. Hosp., Cleve., U. Hosps. Cleve., Metrohealth Med. Ctr., Cleve., St. John & Westshore Hosp., Westlake, Ohio, Luth. Med. Ctr., Cleve. Tuesday Musical Club scholar, 1968, Ranney Found. scholar, 1968, Hellenic U. Club scholar, 1983. Mem. Am. Acad. Neurology, Am. Clin. Neurophysiology Soc., U.S. Weight-lifting Fedn., Phi Kappa Lambda. Office: 18099 Lorain Ave # 225 Cleveland OH 44111

BAMBERGER, JULIA KATHRYN, social worker; b. Phila., Dec. 23, 1960; d. William Thomas and Julia Kathryn (O'Brien) B. BA in Social Work, Holy Family Coll., Phila., 1983. Cert. social worker. Recreational therapy asst., physical therapy asst. Ashton Hall Nursing Home, Phila., 1979-83; hairdresser asst. St. John Neumann Nursing Home, Phila., 1982-83; recreational therapy asst. Evangelical Manor, Phila., 1983; social worker The Consortium/Southwest Sr. Citizens Ctr., Phila., 1983-90; resource specialist Phila. Corp. for Aging, 1990-92, case mgr. Family Caregiver Support program, 1992—. Mem., chair Alzheimer's Disease and Related Disorders Assn., Phila., 1983—; vol. Ashton Hall Nursing Home, Phila., 1983-89; V.I.P. blood donor ARC, 1978—; solicitor Cath. Charities Appeal, 1979—; mem. Pro Life Coalition of Southeastern Pa., 1986—; soprano singer guitar Mass group Maternity Blessed Virgin Mary Roman Cath. Ch., Phila., 1977—; vol. Perpetual Adoration Soc. Our Lady of Fatima Roman Cath. Ch., 1988—. Recipient Cert. of Appreciation Alzheimer's Disease and Related Disorders Assn., 1985, 91, 95; named one of Outstanding Young Women Am., 1985, 86, 88. Mem. Social Svc. Workers Assn. Nursing Homes, Archbishop Ryan H.S. for Girls ALumnae Assn. (corr. sec. 1985—), Holy Family Coll. Alumni Assn. (rec. sec. 1985-90, cert. of appreciation 1984, 90, bd. dirs., class rep. 1983—, Disting. Alumni Svc. award 1992), Assn. Ch. Musician in Phila., Classic Thunderbird Club (bd. dirs. 1994-95), Epsilon Nu Cath. Adult Club, Phi Chi. Democrat. Home: 2016 Tomlinson Rd Philadelphia PA 19116-3933 Office: Phila Corp for Aging 642 N Broad St Philadelphia PA 19130-3409

BAMFORD, JOSEPH CHARLES, JR., gynecologist, obstetrician, educator, medical missionary; b. Paterson, N.J., Oct. 23, 1930; s. Joseph Charles and Luise (Whitehead) B.; m. Susan Jane Hall, Apr. 13, 1951; children: Joseph Charles III, Elizabeth Ann. BS, Rutgers U., 1952; MD, N.Y. Med. Coll., 1956. Diplomate Am. Bd. Ob-Gyn. Intern, U. Vt., 1956-57; resident in ob-gyn N.Y. Med. Coll., N.Y.C., 1957-60, asst. clin. instr. dept. ob-gyn, 1960-64, clin. instr., 1964-65, asst. prof., 1965-70, asso. prof., 1970-72, asst. dean, 1966-68, asso. dean, 1968-72, acting v.p. hosp. affairs, 1971-72; sect. chief psychosomatic ob-gyn Met. Hosp. Center, N.Y.C., 1963-72, chief svc., 1971-72; practice medicine specializing in ob-gyn, Paterson, N.J., 1962-66, St. Johnsbury, Vt., 1972-76; asst. obstetrician and gynecologist Flower and Fifth Ave. hosps., N.Y.C., 1960-66, asst. attending 1966-70, attending, 1970-72; asst. vis. obstetrician and gynecologist Met. Hosp. Center, N.Y.C., 1960-66, asso., 1968-70, vis., 1970-72; clin. asst. ob-gyn Paterson Gen. Hosp., 1962-64, asso. attending, 1964-66, attending, 1966-67, cons., 1967—; attending obstetrician and gynecologist Northeastern Vt. Regional Hosp., St. Johnsburg, 1972-76, cons., 1976—; vis. obstetrician and gynecologist St. Jude Missions Hosp., St. Lucia, 1986; med. officer Tumutumu Mission Hosp., Kenya, 1987-88; cons. Beatrice D. Weeks Meml. Hosp., Lancaster, N.H., 1972-80; chmn. subcom. for fact finding Mayor's Com. for Hosp. Facilities Planning, Paterson, 1964-66; chmn. med. adv. com. Passaic County (N.J.) Com. for Planned Parenthood, 1965-67; mem. N.J. Com. on Med. Edn., 1965-66; trustee Greater Paterson Gen. Hosp., 1966—. Pres. Lyndon State Coll. Found., 1980-84. Lt. comdr. USNR, 1960-52. Fellow Am. Coll. Obstetricians and Gynecologists (mem. com. on course coordination 1977-79); mem. No. New Eng. Acad. Medicine, Obstet. and Gynecol. Soc. N.Y. Med. Coll. (mem. exec. com. 1963-66), Vt. (mem. judicial com. 1975-77), Caledonia County (v.p. 1974-75) med. socs. Contbr. articles to profl. jours. Home: Box 724 Myrickview Vlg Dorset VT 05251

BANAS, JOHN STANLEY, obstetrician, gynecologist; b. Chgo., May 27, 1955; s. Edward Thomas and Stephanie Victoria (Gatz) B.; m. Kerry Jeanine Keenan, June 7, 1981; children: Melissa, Kevin, Daniel, Amanda. BS in Biology cum laude, Loyola U., Chgo., 1977; MD, Loyola U., Maywood, Ill., 1981; bd. eligible obstetrics and gynecology, SUNY, Buffalo, 1985. Diplomate Am. Bd. Ob-Gyn. Obstetrician-gynecologist Associated Obstetrics and Gynecology Inc., Ft. Wayne, Ind., 1985, Affiliated Obstetrics and Gynecology, Inc., Ft. Wayne, 1986-88, Kurten Med. Group, Racine, Wis., 1988-90, United Trinity Med Ctr., Moline, Ill., 1990—. Fellow Am. Coll. Obstetricians and Gynecologists; mem. AMA, Ill. State Med. Soc., Rock Island County Med. Soc. Roman Catholic. Home: 2130 Nathan Ct Bettendorf IA 52722-2100 Office: Trinity Med Ctr 501 10th Ave Moline IL 61265-1217

BANATVALA, JANGU, virology educator, consultant, researcher; b. London, Jan. 7, 1934; s. Edal and Ratti (Shrof) B.; m. Roshan Mugaseth, Aug. 15, 1959; children: Nicholas, Jonathan, Christopher, Emma. BA, Cambridge (Eng.) U., 1955, MA, 1958; MB BChir, London Hosp. Medicine, 1959, MD, 1964, diploma in child health, 1961, diploma in pub. health, 1961. House officer London Hosp., 1958-59; sr. house officer, pediatrician Gen. Hosp., Kettering, Eng., 1959-60; rsch. fellow dept. pathology Cambridge (Eng.) U., 1961-64; postdoctoral fellow Yale U., New Haven, 1964-65; sr. lectr., reader, then prof. clin. virology United Med. and Dental Sch. St. Thomas Hosp., London, 1965—; mem. senate, various coms. U. London, 1988—; chair adv. group hepatitis Dept. Health, London, 1990—; asst. registrar, 1984-85, registrar, 1985-87, v.p., 1987-90, coun. mem. & exec., 1993—; examiner in pathology U. London, U. Cambridge, Eng., U. West Indies, U. Riyadh. Co-editor: Principal Practice of Clinical Virology, 1987, 3d edit., 1994; editor: Viral Infections of the Heart, 1993; contbr. articles to profl. jours. Freeman City of London. Fellow Royal Soc. Medicine, Royal Soc. Hygiene and Tropical Medicine, Royal Coll. Pathologists (registrar 1985-87, v.p. 1987-90, mem. coun. 1993—), Royal Coll. Physicians; mem. Worshipful Soc. Apothecaries London. Home: Church End, Henham, Bishops Stortford CM22 6AU, England Office: Guys & St Thomas Hosp Trust, St Thomas Hospital, Lambeth Palace Rd, London SE1 7EH, England

BAND, HENRETTA TRENT, evolutionary biologist, researcher; b. Danville, Va., June 28, 1932; d. Oscar and Lucile (Allen) Trent; m. Rudolph Neal Band, July 16, 1955; 1 child, Elizabeth Lee. BS, Coll. William and Mary, 1954; PhD, U. Calif., Berkeley, 1959; postdoctoral, U. Calif., Davis, 1972-73. Lectr. zoology U. B.C., Vancouver, Can., 1959-60, 61-62; rsch. assoc. zoology, 1960-61, 62-63; rsch. assoc. zoology Mich. State U., East Lansing, 1963-65, asst. prof. zoology, 1965, asst. prof. natural sci. dept., 1967-68; ind. investigator East Lansing, 1968—; researcher Mt. Lake Biol. Sta. U. Va., Pembroke, 1986-92; organizer Genetic Load Symposium, Internat. Soc. History, Philosophy, Social Studies and Biology, Northwestern U., 1991, T.H. Huxley session Brandeis U., 1993. Contbr. articles to Va. Jour. Sci., Genetics, Biochem. Genetics, Am. Naturalist, DAR mag., Evolution, others. Rec. sec. Rep. Women's Club of Mid-Mich., Lansing, 1987-89, pres., 1989-91. Recipient Rep. Presdl. Legion of Merit; NIH fellow U. Calif., Berkeley, 1957-58, Amherst Coll., 1958-59, Cambridge (Eng.) U., 1965-66, U. Va. fellow, 1986. Mem. Mich. Acad. Sci., Arts and Letters (vice chmn. history of sci. and tech. 1991-92, chmn. 1992-94), N.Y. Acad. Sci., Internat. Soc. History, Philosophy and Social Studies of Biology, Mich. Entomol. Soc., Soc. for Cryobiology, Soc. for Study of Evolution, Phi Beta Kappa, Sigma Xi. Home: 5854 Smithfield Ave East Lansing MI 48823-2368

BANDA, GERALDINE MARIE, chiropractic physician; b. Orange, N.J., Oct. 15, 1951; d. Albert Joseph and Maria Grace B.; 1 adopted child, Gabriele Grace. BA, Seton Hall U., 1974; D of Chiropractic, N.Y. Chiropractic Coll., 1984. Cert. scoliosis mgmt. specialist. Staff writer The Herald News, Passaic, N.J., 1974-77; tchr. St. Genevieve's Roman Cath. Sch., Elizabeth, N.J., 1977-80; chiropractic physician Banda Chiropractic Office, Cranford, N.J., 1984—. Contbr. articles to profl. jours. and newspapers. Activist community svc. projects and scoliosis screenings, Cranford, 1984—. Named Outstanding Young Woman of Am., 1981. Mem. Am. Chiropractic Assn. (mem. coun. on diagnostic imaging), N.J. Chiropractic Soc., Cranford C. of C., N.J. Women's Bus. Owners Assn. Office: Banda Chiropractic Office 347 Lincoln Ave E Cranford NJ 07016-3157

BANDEIAN, JOHN JACOB, physician, surgeon; b. Gurin, Armenia, Mar. 15, 1912; s. John and Flora (Gureghian) B.; m. Alice M. Kechijian, Apr. 4, 1942; children: Natalie, John Jacob, Stephen H. BS, Harvard U., 1935; MD, Tufts U., 1941. Intern Med. Center Jersey City, 1941-42, Mass. Meml. Hosp., 1942; resident in diseases of chest Trudeau San., Saranac Lake, N.Y., 1943, in oncol. surgery, Pondville State Hosp., Walpole, Mass., 1943-45; fellow gynecology Mass. Gen. Hosp., Boston, 1945-46; surg. resident Beverly (Mass.) Hosp., 1946-48; practice surgery, Holyoke, Mass., 1948—; pres. John J. Bandeian M.D. Assocs., Inc. Vestryman, St. Paul's Ch. Diplomate Am. Bd. Surgery. Fellow ACS; mem. AMA, Mass. Med. Soc. (del.), Hampden Dist. Med. Soc. (pres. 1971-72), New Eng. Cancer Soc., Holyoke C. of C. Republican. Survivor of the Armenian Genocide by the Ottomon Turks. Home: 1265 Northampton St Holyoke MA 01040-1909 Office: 210 Pine St Holyoke MA 01040-4017

BANDEIAN, JOHN JACOB, JR., plastic surgeon, lawyer; b. Beverly, Mass., Dec. 15, 1946; s. John Jacob and Alice (Kechijian) B.; children: John J., William Joel. AB, Harvard Coll., 1969, MD, 1973; BMS, Dartmouth Coll., 1971; JD, U. Tenn., 1994. Diplomate Am. Bd. Plastic Surgery. Pvt. practice plastic surgery Bristol, Tenn., 1981—; pvt. practice law Bristol, 1995—. Mem. Am. Soc. Plastic and Reconstructive Surgeons, Tenn. Bar Assn. Office: 3169 W State St Bristol TN 37620

BANDEMER, NORMAN JOHN, healthcare consulting executive; b. Detroit, Sept. 13, 1949; s. Marvin Gustave and Helen Theresa (Jashinski) B.; m. Elaine Ellen Massie, Sept. 4, 1971; children: Norman John II, Marisa Nikol. BBA, Eastern Mich. U., 1971; MBA, Mich. State U., 1977. Field auditor Blue Cross and Blue Shield of Mich., Detroit, 1971-72; supr. State of Mich. Medicaid Program, Lansing, 1972-77; asst. dir. Mich. Hosp. Assn. Svc. Corp., Lansing, 1977-83; v.p. of operation Bronson/Beaumont Mgmt. Svcs., Kalamazoo, Mich., 1983-86; exec. dir. The Travelers Health Network, Grand Rapids, 1986-88; regional dir. Coopers & Lybrand, Detroit, 1988-90; mng. ptnr. First Consulting Group-Healthcare Consulting, Grand Rapids, 1990—; guest speaker Health Care Benefits, Direct Contracting, 1992. Author: Health Care Costs in Michigan, 1991, Medicaid Program in Mich., 1992. Hon. coach Mich. State U. Athletic Booster Club, East Lansing, 1987. Mem. Lansing City Club, Healthcare Fin. Mgmt. Assn., Mich. Assn. CPAs Healthcare Com., Mich. State U. Alumni Club. Roman Catholic. Office: First Consulting Group 7705 Tobemory Ct SE Ste 100 Ada MI 49301-9362

BANDER, THOMAS SAMUEL, dentist; b. Grand Rapids, Mich., Mar. 3, 1924; s. Samuel and Jennie (David) B.; m. DoLores Abraham, Sept. 7, 1947; children: Samuel T., Jacquelyn Marie. AS, Grand Rapids Jr. Coll., 1944; DDS, U. Mich., 1948. Pvt. practice dentistry Grand Rapids, Mich., 1948—. Pres. St. Nicholas Orthodox Ch., Grand Rapids, 1965. Served with U.S. Army, 1941-44, to capt. USAF, 1955-57. Fellow Am. Coll. Dentists, Internat. Coll. of Dentists, ADA, Acad. Operative Dentistry; mem. West Mich. Dental Soc. (pres. 1978), Mich. Dental Assn. (chmn. sci. program 1977-78), Kent County Dental Soc. (pres. 1965), Cascade Hills Country Club. Republican. Eastern Orthodox. Home: 616 Manhattan Rd SE Grand Rapids MI 49506-2077 Office: 2426 Burton St SE Grand Rapids MI 49546-4806

BANDLER, MARTIN, physician; b. Vienna, Austria, Oct. 2, 1930; came to U.S., 1954; s. Sidney and Sara (Feinsinger) B.; m. Frances Feffer; children: Bruce, Gail, Ruth. MD, Dalhousie U., 1954. With USN, 1957-59. Office: 954 President St Brooklyn NY 11215

BANDMAN, ELSIE LUCIER, mental health nurse, ethicist; b. Putnam, Conn., Sept. 16, 1920; d. Alfred J. Sr. and Lea (LeClair) Lucier; m. Bertram Bandman, Aug. 1951; 1 child, Nancy. Diploma, Hartford Hosp. Sch. Nursing, 1942; BS, Simmons Coll., 1949; MA, NYU, 1952; EdD, Columbia U., 1968. Sr. nurse Vis. Nurse Assn. Boston, 1949-51; staff nurse EENT Hartford (Conn.) Hosp., 1942-43; prof. Hunter Coll., N.Y.C., 1968-91; adj. prof. Hunter Coll., N.Y.C., 1991-95. Author: Nursing Ethics Through the Life Span, 3d edit., 1995, Critical Thinking in Nursing, 2d edit., 1995, Bioethics and Human Rights; contbr. chpts. to books and articles to profl. jours. 1st lt. Nurse Corps, U.S. Army, 1943-46. Recipient award for geriatrics in nursing Pace Coll., Alumnae award for rsch. Columbia U., Pres.'s award Hunter Coll., 1983, award for edn. N.Y. State Nurse's Assn., 1991, Presdl. Citation, N.Y. Counties RN Assn., Dist. 13, 1992. Mem. ANA, Am. Acad. Nursing, Soc. for Rsch. and Edn. in Psychiat. Nursing. Home: 555 Kappock St Bronx NY 10463-6420

BANDO, EIICHI, dental educator; b. Naruto, Tokushima, Japan, Feb. 8, 1943; s. Akira and Ayako Bando; m. Ikuko Bando, May 6, 1979; children: Naoko, Mayuko, Yuuichi. DDS, Tokyo Med. and Dental U., 1967, DDSc, 1971. Instr. Tokyo Med. and Dental U., 1971-79; prof. U. Tokushima, 1979—; dir. Tokushima U. Dental Hosp., 1991-93. Home: 3-22 Yoshinohon-cho, Tokushima 770, Japan Office: U Tokushima Sch Dentistry, 3-18-15 Kuramoto-cho, Tokushima 770, Japan

BANDT, PAUL DOUGLAS, physician; b. Milbank, S.D., June 22, 1938; s. Lester Herman and Edna Louella (Sogn) B.; m. Mary King, Aug. 26, 1962 (div. Feb. 1974); children: Douglas, Peggy; m. Inara Irene Von Rostas, Apr. 1, 1974; 1 child, Jennifer. BS in Edn. with distinction, U. Minn., 1960, BS in Medicine, 1966, D in Medicine, 1966. Diplomate Am. Bd. Diagnostic Radiology, Am. Bd. Nuclear Medicine. Intern U.S. Pub. Health Svc., San Francisco, 1966-68; physician U.S. Pub. Health Svc., Las Vegas, 1968-69; resident Stanford U., Palo Alto, Calif., 1969-72; physician Desert Radiologists, Las Vegas, 1972—; vice chief med. staff Desert Springs Hosp., Las Vegas; immediate past chief of staff U. Med. Ctr. So. Nev., Las Vegas. Contbr. articles on diagnostic radiology to profl. jours. With USPHS, 1966-69. Mem. AMA, Am. Coll. Radiology, Am. Coll. Nuclear Medicine, Clark Med. Soc. Office: Desert Radiologists 2020 Palomino Ln Las Vegas NV 89106-4812

BANDURA, ALBERT, psychologist; b. Mundare, Alta., Can., Dec. 4, 1925; came to U.S., 1949, naturalized, 1956; m. Virginia Varns; 2 children. B.A., U. B.C., 1949, D.Sc. (hon.), 1979; M.A. in Psychology, U. Iowa, 1951, Ph.D. in Psychology, 1952. Prof. psychology Stanford U., 1953—, David Starr Jordan prof. social sci. in psychology, 1973—. Author: (with R.H. Walters) Adolescent Aggression, 1959, (with R.H. Walters) Social Learning and Personality Development, 1963, Principles of Behavior Modification, 1969, Aggression, 1973, Social Learning Theory, 1977, Social Foundations of Thought and Action: A Social Cognitive Theory, 1986; editor: Psychological Modeling: Conflicting Theories, 1971, Self-Efficacy in Changing Societies, 1995. Guggenheim fellow, 1972. Fellow Am. Acad. Arts and Scis., Ctr. Adv. Study in Behavioral Sci.; mem. Am. Psychol. Soc. (William James award 1989), Inst. Medicine NAS, Am. Psychol. Assn. (Disting. Scientist award divsn. 12, 1972, Disting. Sci. Contbn. award 1980, pres. 1974), Calif. Psychol. Assn. (Disting. Scientist award 1973), Western Psychol. Assn. (pres. 1980), Internat. Soc. Research on Aggression (Disting. Contbn. award 1980), Soc. Child Devel., Inst. of Medicine. Office: Stanford U Dept Psychology Stanford CA 94305-2130

BANE, MARY JO, federal agency administrator; b. Princeville, Ill., Feb. 24, 1942; d. Fred W. and Helen (Callery) B.; m. Kenneth Winston, May 31, 1975. BS in Internat. Rels., Georgetown U., 1963; MAT, Harvard U., 1966, DEd, 1972. Tchr. English U.S. Peace Corps, Liberia, 1963-65; tchr. social studies Arlington (Mass.) Pub. Schs., 1966-67; tchr. English and social studies Brookline (Mass.) Pub. Schs., 1968-71; rsch. assoc. Ctr. Ednl. Policy Rsch. and Huron Inst. Harvard U., Cambridge, Mass., 1971-72, project co-dir. Ctr. Study of Pub. Policy, 1972-75, assoc. prof. edn., lectr. in sociology, 1977-80, assoc. prof. pub. policy, 1981-86, dir. Malcolm Wiener Ctr. for Social Policy, 1987-92, prof. pub. policy, 1986-90, Malcolm Wiener Prof. of Social Policy, 1990-92; lectr. in Sociology U. Mass., Boston, 1972-75; assoc. dir. Ctr. Rsch. on Women, asst. prof. edn., lectr. in sociology Wellesley (Mass.) Coll., 1975-77; dep. asst. sec. for program planning and budget analyst Office Planning and Budget U.S. Dept. Edn., Washington, 1980-81; exec. dep. commr. N.Y. State Dept. Social Svcs., 1984-86, commr., 1992-93; asst. sec. Adminstrn. for Children and Families Dept. Health and Human Svcs., Washington, 1993—; Ida Bean vis. prof. U. Iowa, 1980; chair bd. overseers panel study income dynamics Inst. Rsch. U. Mich., 1982-86; regents lectr. U. Calif., Berkeley, 1987; mem. adv. com. urban poverty NAS, 1986-90, chair com. child devel. rsch. and pub. policy, 1987-90; mem. pres. adv. coun. Columbia U. Tchrs. Coll., N.Y.C., 1988-92; mem. grants adv. coun. Smith Richardson Found., 1989-92; bd. dirs. Manpower Demonstration Rsch. Coun., 1989-92; active William T. Grant Found. Commn. on Work, Family and Citizenship, 1987-88. Author: (with others) Inequality: A Reassessment of the Effects of Family and Schooling in America, 1972, Here to Stay: American Families in the Twentieth Century, 1974, Japanese translation, 1981, (with George Masnick) The Nation's Families 1960-90, 1980; editor: (with Donald Levine) The Inequality Controversy, 1975, (with Manuel Carballo) The State and the Poor in the 1980s, 1984, (with Kenneth I. Winston) Gender and Public Policy: Cases and Comments, 1993, (with David Ellwood) Welfare Realities: From Rhetoric to Reform, 1994; contbr. articles to profl. jours. Fellow Nat. Acad. Pub. Adminstrn.; mem. Am. Sociol. Assn., Population Assn. Am., Assn. Pub. Policy Analysis and Mgmt. Office: Dept Health and Human Svcs Adminstrn Children and Families 901 D St SW Washington DC 20447-0002*

BANERJEE, PUSHPAL ROCKY, osteopath; b. Calcutta, India, Jan. 6, 1967; came to U.S., 1983; s. Malay Kumar and Namita (Chatterjee) B. BS cum laude, U. Pitts., 1990; DO, Phila. Coll. Osteo. Medicine, 1995. Intern U. Ark. for Med. Sci., Pine Bluff, 1995-96; emergency and internal medicine physician Bi County Hosp.-Mich. State U., Warren, 1996—; physician, coach White Hall (Ark.) H.S., 1995. Thomas Rowland Meml. scholar Phila. Coll. Osteo. Medicine, 1995. Mem. AMA, Am. Acad. Family Physicians, Am. Osteo. Assn., Ark. Med. Soc., Ark. Osteo. Med. Assn., Phila. Coll. Osteo. Medicine Athletic Alumni Assn., alpha Epsilon Delta, Phi Eta Sigma. Home: 1901 W 40th St Apt 321 Pine Bluff AR 71603

BANERJEE, RANJIT, molecular biologist, geneticist, researcher; b. Calcutta, India, June 6, 1948; came to U.S., 1974; s. Ajit Kumar and Maya (Mukherjee) B.; m. Marilyn Anita DeSciscio, July 28, 1984; children: Christopher Paul, Victoria Grace. MS in Genetics, NYU, 1979, PhD in Genetics, 1981. Teaching fellow NYU, 1975-80; rsch. fellow dept. pathology Temple U., Phila., 1981-83; rsch. scientist inst. cancer rsch. Columbia U. Coll. Physicians and Surgeons, N.Y.C., 1983-86; asst. prof. dept. neoplastic diseases Mt. Sinai Med. Ctr., N.Y.C., 1986-94; asst. prof. dept. microbiology and immunology N.Y. Med. Coll., Valhalla, 1995—. Contbr. articles to profl. jours. Mem. AAAS, Am. Assn. for Cancer Rsch., Am. Soc. for Microbiology. Office: NY Med Coll Dept Microbiol & Immunology BSB Rm 340 Box 1131 Valhalla NY 10595

BANES, JOAN NEILD, medical journal editor and society administrator; b. Paterson, N.J., Jan. 15, 1930; d. Horace and Gertrude Dorothea (Fozard) Neild; m. Nicholas Gerten, Jr., June 27, 1953 (div. 1968); m. Kenneth Charles Banes, May 17, 1969; stepchildren: Evan Sinclair, Lisa. BSc, Rutgers U., 1951, MSc, 1953. Biochemist Columbia U. Coll. Physicians and Surgeons, N.Y.C., 1961-75; biochemist, grants mgr. Cornell U. Med. Coll., N.Y.C., 1975-85; exec. dir. Am. Soc. Hypertension, N.Y.C., 1985-94; mng. editor Am. Jour. Hypertension, N.Y.C., 1988—; exec. dir. Nat. Med. Soc., N.Y.C., 1985—; cons. Hypertension Ctr., N.Y.C., 1985—. Contbg. author: Hypertension Manual, 1974; contbr. articles to med. jours. Mem. Am. Soc. Assn. Execs. Office: Am Jour Hypertension 515 Madison Ave Rm 1212 New York NY 10022

BANEVER, THOMAS CLARK, surgeon, educator; b. Bridgeport, Conn., Dec. 21, 1945; s. Marshall and Elizabeth (Clark) B.; m. Jennifer Burke, June 29, 1969; children: Gregory, Andrew, Seth, Sarah Kate, Abigail, Matthew, Emily, Rebecca, Nadia Marie. BA in Chemistry, Yale U., 1968; MD, Tufts U., 1972. Diplomate Am. Bd. Surgery. Intern. New Haven (Conn.) Hosp, 1972-73; resident in surgery U. Conn., Farmington, 1974-75; resident in surgery Hartford (Conn.) Hosp., 1976-78, pvt. practice, 1978—; asst. clin. prof. U. Conn. Med. Sch., Farmington, 1990—. Bd. dirs. Community Health Svcs., Hartford, 1980—. Fellow ACS; mem. AMA, Conn. State Med. Soc., Hartford County Med. Assn. (Community Svc. award 1992), Soc. Critical Care Medicine, Ea. Assn. Surg. Trauma, Physicians for Social Responsibility. Home: 31 Main St Farmington CT 06032-2229 Office: Thomas Clark Banever MD 100 Retreat Ave Ste 808 Hartford CT 06106-2528

BANEY, RICHARD NEIL, physician, internist; b. Phila., Apr. 13, 1937; s. Robert Emmet and Mary Elizabeth (Hedges) B.; m. Carolyn Vern Kurey, Feb. 17, 1962; children: Richard N. Jr., Michael D., Marisa V., Brian E. BS, Georgetown U., 1958; MD, U. Pitts., 1963. Diplomate Am. Bd. Internal Medicine, Am. Bd. Rheumatology. Intern VA & Parkland Hosp., Dallas, 1963-64; resident U. Pitts., 1967-70; internist Jess Parrish Hosp., Titusville, Fla., 1971-76; chief med. staff Jess Parrish Hosp., Titusville, 1974-76; internist Melbourne (Fla.) Internal Med. Assocs., Holmes Regional Med Ctr., 1976-95; sr. v.p. med. affairs Holmes Regional Med. Ctr., Melbourne, Fla., 1995-96; CEO Health First Physicians; trustee Holmes Regional Med. Ctr., Melbourne, 1984-95; founding dir., chmn. bd. dirs. Reliance Bank Fla., Melbourne, 1985-95; founding dir., chmn. bd. Bank Brevard, 1996—; bd. dirs. DBA Sys., Inc. Trustee Fla. Inst. Tech., Melbourne, 1986—, mem. exec. com., 1987—, vice chmn. bd. trustees, 1991—; pres. Canaveral chpt. Am. Heart Assn., Rockledge, Fla., 1973-74; chmn. bd. trustees Sea Pines Rehab. Hosp., Melbourne, 1992-94. Med. officer, lt. comdr. USN, 1964-67. Fellow ACP; mem. Am. Coll. Rheumatology, Am. Soc. Nuc. Medicine, Am. Coll. Physicians Execs., Underwater and Hyperbaric Med. Soc., Brevard County Med. Soc. (pres. 1977-78), Navy League U.S., Eau Gallie Yacht Club (commodore 1985-86), Coast Club (bd. dirs. 1985-91, chmn. bd. 1989-91). Republican. Office: Heartfelt Physicians Inc 1499 Harbor City Blvd Ste 201 Melbourne FL 32901-3276

BANGHAM, ROBERT ARTHUR, orthotist; b. San Antonio, Sept. 12, 1942; s. Robert Dave and Marguerite C. (Wyckoff) B. Student, Northwestern U., 1965, 71, 76, NYU, 1969, Washtenaw C.C., Ann Arbor, Mich., 1971; misc. courses in field, various hosps., and med. orgns. Cert. orthotist; ordained to ministry Jehovah's Witness Ch., 1957. Orthotic resident J. R. Reets, Ann Arbor, Mich., 1960-65; orthotist Dreher-Jouett, Inc., Chgo., 1965-68; cert. orthotist U. Mich., 1968-75, Wright & Filipis, Inc., Alpena, Mich., 1975-78; mgr., orthotist Hittenbergers, Concord, Calif., 1978-81, 88-90; mgr., cert. orthotist x, Oakland, Calif., 1981-90, Hittenbergers, Concord, Oakland, 1988-90; mktg. mgr. western region Nat. Orthotic Labs., Winter Haven, Fla., 1990; CEO Mobile Orthotic & Prosthetic Assocs., Antioch, Calif., 1990-95, Oakland, Calif., 1990-95; practitioner Lakeshore Orthotics & Prosthetics, Muskegon, Mich., 1995—; orthotics cons. Benchmark Med. Group, 1992—; cons. Health Careers Profl. Assn., Calif. State Dept. Edn., 1992—; presenter papers in field to profl. assns., hosps., govtl. bodies. Contbr. articles to profl. jours. Fellow Am. Back Soc. (internat. profl. rels. com., co-chair orthotics divsn., vice chair orthotics com., AAOP liaison rep. to ABS), Am. Acad. Neurological and Orthopedic Surgeons (head dept. orthotics); mem. Am. Prosthetic Assn., Am. Acad. Orthotics and Prosthetists (nat. dir. 1988-91, pres. Calif. chpt. 1986-87, chpt. dir. 1989-91, sci. com. chmn., societies com., charter chmn. Spinal Orthotics Soc. 1991, 92, sec. lower extremity orthotics soc., bd. dirs. No. Calif. chpt., past pres. No. Calif. chpt., rep. Calif. coalition Allied Health Profls. No. Calif. chpt., co-chmn. sci. edn. com. No. Calif. chpt.), Am. Orthotics and Prosthetics Assn. (bd. dirs., chair NSF program), Internat. Soc. Orthotists and Prosthetists, Calif. Coalition Allied Health Professions (pres. 1989-90). Home and Office: Mobile O & P Assocs 3230 Roosevelt Rd Ste A A-7 Muskegon MI 49441

BANIC, ANDREJ BORIS, plastic surgeon; b. Ljubljana, Slovenia, Dec. 5, 1947; arrived in Switzerland, 1989; s. Stanko and Sonja (Soudat) B.; m. Martina Geltac, Oct. 7, 1984; children: Borut, Matjaz, Stasa. MD, U. Ljubljana, 1973; PhD, U. Linkoping, Sweden, 1973. Specialist in surgery Univ. Clin. Ctr., Ljubljana, 1980-83; cons., asst. prof. Univ. Hosp., Kuwait, 1983-89; oberaztrof. Inselspital, Berne, Switzerland, 1989-93, lietender arzt, 1994—; privat dozent U. Berne, 1993. Grantee Swiss Nat. Sci. Found., 1994. Mem. Internat. Soc. for Burn Injuries, European Assn. Plastic Surgeons, Deutschsprachige Arbeitsgemeinschaft für Mikrochururgie. Roman Catholic. Home: Kappelenring 24A, 3032 Hinterkappelen Switzerland Office: Univ Hosp Inselspital, Dept Plastic Surgery, 3010 Bern Switzerland

BANIK, SAMBHU NATH, psychologist; b. Joypara, India, Nov. 7, 1935; s. PadmaL. and Kadambini B.; BSc, Calcutta U., 1956, MSc, 1958; PhD, Bristol U., 1964; m. Promila Roy, Nov. 16, 1968; children: Sharmila, Kakali. Staff psychologist Des Moines Child Guidance Center, 1965; sr. psychologist, dir. internship tng. Univ. Hosp. Saskatoon, Sask., Can., 1965-69; dir. psychol. services, 1969-71; asst. chief mental health svcs. Glenn Dale Hosp. and D.C. Village, 1971-81; chief South Cmty. Mental Health Center, Washington, 1981-84, chief child and youth svcs., 1984-88, clin. adminstr. NE/SE Family Ctr., Washington, 1988—; pres. Family Diagnostic and Therapeutic Ctr., Washington, 1993—; exec. dir. Pres.'s Com. on Mental Retardation HHS, Washington, 1990-93, cons. psychologist, 1993—; pres. Banik and Assocs. Family Diagnostic and Therapeutic Ctr., 1993—; v.p. devel., chmn. Third World Found., 1993—; asst. prof. U. Sask., 1965-71; vis. prof. Bowie State Coll. (Md.), 1972-81, Thakur Hariprasad Inst., India, 1994. Mem. nat. adv. coun. drug abuse, 1987-90; mem. advisory bd. ARC, Washington, 1987-90; founder, pres. Prabashi, Inc., 1974-78, Assn. Indians in Am., 1980-84; pres. U.S.-Asia Found., 1995—; v.p. India Cultural Coordinating Com., 1979-80; sec. gen. Asian Pacific Am. Cultural Heritage Council, 1981-82; treas. Asian Pacific Am. Heritage Council, 1982-84; mem. spl. com. 3d Conv. Asian Indians in N.Am., 1984, chmn. Indian Am. Forum Polit. Edn., Md., 1986-88, 94—; chmn. Third World Found. 1993—; advisory bd. Ednl. India Found., Inc., 1993—, Commonwealth Assn. for the Mentally Handcapped and Developmental Dis., 1992—; chmn. Internat. Cooperation and Coordinating Com. 11th World Congress on Mental Retardation, 1993-94. Recipient Dept. Human Svcs. Humanitarian award D.C., 1986, Cmty. Svcs. award Assn. Indians in Am., 1987, Citizen award Mayor of Balt., Ramkamal Sinha Meml. Gold medal, 1994, Excellence in Human Svc. award Bangalore 1994, Cmty. Svc. award U.S. Asia Found., 1995. Mem. APA, Am. Group Psychotherapy Assn., D.C. Psychol. Assn., Internat. Acad. Forensic Psychology, Nat. Health Svcs. Providers in Psychology. Contbr. articles to profl. jours. Home: 8606 Bradmoor Dr Bethesda MD 20817-3633

BANK, HARVEY L., biologist; b. Bklyn., Feb. 13, 1943; s. Myron and Ruth (Lefkowitz) B.; m. Ellen S. Shield (div.); children: Daniel, Laura, Michael. BA, Hunter Coll., 1965; PhD, Oak Ridge Nat. Labs., 1971. Assoc. prof. Med. U. S.C., Charleston, 1973-90; exec. dir. Beacon Light Ctr., Sedona, Ariz., 1990-92; co-dir. Ctr. for Pranic Restoration, Springfield, Ohio, 1992—. Author several book chpts.; mem. editl. bd. Crybiology Soc., 1983—; contbr. 75 articles to profl. jours.; patentee in field. Smith Klein & French fellow, 1973-74. Mem. Sigma Xi (pres. 1979-80). Home: 1330 E High St Springfield OH 45505-1126

BANKART, CHARLES PETER, psychologist, educator; b. Cambridge, Mass., May 24, 1946; s. Charles Lawrence and Marguerite (Merrill) B.; m. Brenda Madeline Bryant, Apr. 27, 1968; 1 child, Charles Allen. BA, Dartmouth Coll., 1967, PhD, 1972. Lic. psychologist, Ind. Prof. dept. psychology Wabash Coll., Crawfordsville, Ind., 1971—, dir. student counseling svc., 1975—; staff psychologist Wabash Valley Mental Health Ctr., West Lafayette, Ind., 1978, 86; vis. lectr. Waseda U., Tokyo, 1981-82, assoc. dean internat. divsn., 1989-90; psychologist Tokyo Cmty. Counseling Svc., 1981-82. Co-author: Psychology 73/74, 1973, Encyclopedia of Psychology, 1974, 3d edit., 1984, also rsch. reports in field. Mem. Am. Psychol. Soc., Assn Advancement of Behavior Therapy. Office: Wabash Coll PO Box 352 Crawfordsvlle IN 47933-0352

BANKS, BETTIE SHEPPARD, psychologist; b. Birmingham, Ala., June 8, 1933; d. Francis Wilkerson and Bettie Pollard (Woodson) Sheppard; B.A., Ga. State U., 1966, M.A., 1968, Ph.D., 1970; m. Frazer Banks, Jr., Mar. 22, 1952; children: Bettie Banks Daley, Lee Frazer Banks III. Clin. assoc. Lab. for Psychol. Svcs., Ga. State U., 1968-70; intern Ga. State U. Counseling Ctr., 1969-70, Ga. Mental Health Inst., Atlanta, 1970-71, psychologist, 1971-72, chief psychologist, 1973; pvt. practice, Atlanta, 1972—; adj. assoc. prof. clin. psychology Ga. State U.; adj. asst. prof. Dept. Psychiatry, Emory U., 1974-83, 94—; mem. peer rev. panel Ga. Med. Care Found., 1980-86, chmn., 1986-88. Diplomate in clin. psychology Am. Bd. Profl. Psychology; Nat. Register Health Svc. Psychology Providers, 1977—, Nat. Register Cert. Group Psychotherapists, 1994—. Fellow Ga. Psychol. Assn. (chmn. div. E 1980, program chair ann. meeting 1991, treas. divsn. F 1993-95, chair publicity divsn. F 1995—); mem. APA, Am. Acad. Psychotherapists (exec. com. 1980-82, sec. 1982-86, 94—, ann. workshop chair 1979, com. ann. Inst. and Conf. 1975, 86, com. ann. workshop 1984), Am. Group Psychotherapy Assn. (clin. mem., co-chair local host com. 1995 Ann. Inst. and Conf.), Atlanta Group Psychotherapy Soc. (bd. exec. com. 1982-83, 91-92, treas. 1995—), Southeastern Psychol. Assn. Episcopalian. Club: Jr. League. Cons. editor Voices, The Art and Science of Psychotherapy, 1978-84. Office: 18 Lenox Pointe NE Atlanta GA 30324-3171

BANKS, HENRY H., academic dean, physician; b. Boston, Mar. 9, 1921; s. Isaac and Bessie B.; m. Judith Epstein, June 1945; children: Nancy (Mrs. Curt Civin), Betsy (Mrs. David Epstein), Steven. AB cum laude, Harvard U., 1942; MD, Tufts U., 1945. Diplomate Am. Bd. Orthopedic Surgery (pres. 1978-79, exec. dir. 1979-86). Surg. intern Beth Israel Hosp., Boston, 1945-46; asst. resident in surgery Beth Israel Hosp., 1947-49; asst. resident orthopedic lab. and pathology Children's Hosp., Boston, 1949-50; asst. resident orthopedic surgery Children's Hosp., 1950-51, Mass. Gen. Hosp., Boston, 1951-52; chief resident orthopedic surgery Peter Bent Brigham Hosp., Boston, 1952, Children's Hosp. Med. Center, Boston, 1952-53; practice medicine, specializing in orthopedic surgery Boston, 1953—; prof. Tufts U. Sch. Medicine, 1970-90, prof. emeritus, 1990—, chmn. dept. orthopedic surgery, 1970-84, assoc. dean, 1972-82, sr. assoc. dean med. affairs, 1982, acting med. dean, then med. dean, 1983-90, dean emeritus, 1990—; dir. orthopedic surgery Boston City Hosp., 1970-74; orthopedic surgeon-in-chief New Eng. Med. Center Hosps., 1970-84; orthopedic surgeon children's Hosp. Med. Ctr., 1953-70, Peter Bent Brigham Hosp., 1953-70, chief orthopedic surgery, 1968-70. Author: A Century of Excellence: The History of Tufts University School of Medicine, 1893-1993, 1993; editor: The Pediatric Clinics of North America-Musculoskeletal Disorder I, 1967; guest editor: Clinical Orthopedics and Related Research, 1968, Orthopedic Clinics of North America, 1976, 78; contbr. articles to profl. jours. With M.C. AUS, 1945-47. Mem. AMA, ACS, Am. Orthopedic Assn. (v.p. 1986-87), Am. Acad. Orthopedic Surgeons, Am. Acad. Cerebral Palsy (pres.), Eastern Orthopedic Assn., Mass. Med. Soc., Internat. Soc. Orthopedic Surgery and Traumatology, Boston Orthopedic Club (pres.), Pediatric Orthopedic Soc., Am. Bd. Orthopedic Surgery (sec., pres. 1973-79, exec. dir. 1979-86, Univ. Club (Boston). Home: 54 Commonwealth Ave Boston MA 02116-3043 Office: 136 Harrison Ave Boston MA 02111-1800

BANKS, J. FRED, research scientist; b. Akron, Ohio, Nov. 17, 1963; s. Jon F. sr. and Barbara (Downing) B. BS, U. Louisville, 1986; PhD, Ind. U., 1992. Rsch. assoc. Ind. U., Bloomington, 1986-91; rsch. scientist Analytica of Branford, Conn., 1995—; scientific adv. bd. Cesone, Waterbury, Conn., 1994—. Contbr. articles to profl. jours. Mem. Am. Soc. for Mass Spectrometry, Am. Chem. Soc., Capillary Electrophoresis Soc. of New Eng. (adv. bd. 1994—), Am. Inst. Chemists (Outstanding Rsch. award 1985), Phi Kappa Phi. Home: 90 High St Clinton CT 06413 Office: Analytica of Branford 29 Business Park Dr Branford CT 06405

BANNER, BURTON, pediatrician; b. N.Y.C., Aug. 29, 1948. BA cum laude, CUNY, 1970; MD, SUNY, Bklyn., 1974. Diplomate Nat. Bd. Med. Examiners, Am. Bd. Pediatrics. Intern Nassau County Med. Ctr., 1974-75; resident in pediatrics Montefiore Med. Ctr., Bronx, N.Y., 1975-77; fellow in pediatric endocrinology NYU Med. Ctr., 1977-78; pvt. practice in pediatrics Staten Island, N.Y., 1974—; clin. asst. prof. N.Y.U. Med. Sch., N.Y.C., 1986—. Hon. com. mem. Juvenile Diabetes Found., Staten Island Br. Mem. Med. Soc. of the State of N.Y., Richmond County Med. Soc. Office: 2281 Victory Blvd Staten Island NY 10314

BANNING, MICHAEL D., healthcare company executive, consultant; b. Manila, Aug. 5, 1954; s. Robert Darrel and Ruth Elaine B.; m. Laura Jolene Banning, Aug. 15, 1986. ADN, Okla. State U., Oklahoma City, 1984; BSN, Langston U., 1991. RN, Okla.; cert. BLS. Relief charge nurse orthopedics-neurology St. Anthony Hosp., Oklahoma City, 1987-88; charge nurse intensive care-coronary care unit Bethany (Okla.) Gen. Hosp., 1986-87; staff nurse high risk newborn unit Oklahoma Meml. Hosp., Oklahoma City, 1984; relief charge nurse surgical unit and burn unit Children's Hosp. Okla., 1988-93, Children's Hosp. Heart Ctr., 1988-93; asst. dir. nursing Western Oaks Health Care Ctr., Bethany, Okla., 1993, Putnam City Convalescent Home, Bethany, 1993-94; ind. long-term care cons., 1994-95; owner, CEO, pres. Heritage Healthcare Enterprise, 1995—; corp. cons. long term care and home health care, 1995—. Inventor low rider safety bed. With U.S. Army, 1975-79. Mem. ANA, Okal. Nurses Assn. Office: 7916 NW 23rd St Ste 150 Bethany OK 73008-4950

BANSAL, VINOD KUMAR, nephrologist; b. Sriganganagar, India, Apr. 5, 1938; came to U.S., 1966; s. Balbir Singh and Usha Devi (Mittal) B.; m. Promilla Aggarwal, June 12, 1966; 1 child, Seema. ISc, Dungar Coll., 1955; MBBS, U. Rajasthan, 1960, MD, 1964. Diplomate Am. Bd. Internal Medicine, Am. Bd. Nephrology. Intern, resident S.M.S. Med. Coll. Hosp., Jaipur, India, 1960-62, jr. demonstrator in biochem., 1962-63; intern St. Boniface Gen. Hosp., Winnipeg, Can., 1969-70; resident U. Ill. Hosp., Chgo., 1970-73; fellow in renal disease U. Colo. Med. Ctr., Denver, 1966-67; fellow in renal metabolic disease Cedars Sinai Med. Ctr., L.A., 1967-68; fellow in renal physiology NYU Med. Ctr., 1968-69; asst. prof. Postgrad. Inst. Medicine, Chandigarh, India, 1971-72; attending physician Hines VA Hosp./ Loyola U. Med. Ctr., Maywood, Ill., 1973-87; from asst. prof. to prof., dir. hypertension ctr. Loyola U. Med. Ctr., 1987—; med. advisor Jour. Renal Nutrition, 1989-95. Fulbright found. grantee, 1993. Fellow Am. Coll. Physicians, Royal Coll. Physicians (Can.); mem. AMA, Am. Soc. Nephrology, Am. Soc. Hypertension, Assn. Indians Living in Am. (nat. v.p. 1992-94), Internat. Soc. Nephrology, Am. Fedn. Clin. Rsch., Am. Soc. Transplant Physicians, Nat. Kidney Found., Midwest Salt and Water Club. Office: Loyola U Med Ctr 2160 S First Ave Maywood IL 60153

BANTA, JAMES ELMER, physician, epidemiologist, university dean; b. Tucumcari, N.Mex., July 1, 1927; s. James Elmer and Edna Mae (Murnahan) B. M.D., Marquette U., 1950; M.P.H., Johns Hopkins U., 1954; diploma, U.S. Naval Med. Sch., 1952. Med. officer USN, 1950-60; capt. med. officer USPHS, 1960-69; dir. med. program Peace Corps, 1963-65; dir. Office Internat. Health, HEW, 1967-68; med. officer WHO, 1968-70; prof. public health U. Hawaii, 1970-73; dep. dir. Office Health, AID, State Dept., Washington, 1973-75; dean, prof. Sch. Public Health and Tropical Medicine, Tulane U., New Orleans, 1975-87; prof. Sch. Pub. Health U. Hawaii, Honolulu, 1987-88; clin. prof. dept. community and family medicine Georgetown U., Washington, 1990—; adj. prof. dept. health care scis. George Washington U., Washington, 1992—. Co-author: How to Travel the World and Stay Healthy, 1969, Year-round Travelers' Health Guide, 1978; Contbr. articles on epidemiology, microbiology and health to profl. jours. Served with USN, 1944-46. Recipient Outstanding Service award Georgetown U., 1965. Fellow AAAS, Am. Coll. Preventive Medicine, Am. Public Health Assn., Am. Heart Assn., Am. Coll. Epidemiology, Coll. Phys. Phila.; mem. ACLU, Common Cause, Environ. Action, AAUP, Assn. Schs. Public Health (pres. 1979-81), Sigma Xi, Phi Sigma, Delta Omega. Office: George Washington U Med Ctr 2300 I St Sw Washington DC 20037

BANTA, WILLIAM CLAUDE, biology educator; b. Long Beach, Calif., Nov. 13, 1941; s. Claude S. and Nedra K. (Baker) B.; m. Dawn Davis, Dec. 18, 1968 (div. 1974); m. Rochelle Barrios, May 28, 1975; children: Claude, Joshua, Jessica. BS in Zoology, U. Calif., Berkeley, 1963; PhD in Biology, U. So. Calif., 1969. Rsch. fellow Smithsonian Instn., Washington, 1969-70; mem. faculty, now prof. biology Am. U., Washington, 1970—; rsch. fellow U. Sydney, Australia, 1977; tchg. fellow Bamfield (B.C., Can.) Lab., 1985; co-chair, panelist NAS, Washington, 1987—; cons. taxonomist Dames & Moore, Seattle, 1990—. Contbr. articles to profl. publs., chpts. to books. Grantee in field; recipient numerous awards. Democrat. Home: 3605 Stewart Dr Bethesda MD 20815-4732 Office: Am U Dept Biology Washington DC 20016

BANUELOS, BETTY LOU, rehabilitation nurse; b. Vandergrift, Pa., Nov. 28, 1930; d. Archibald and Bella Irene (George) McKinney; m. Raul, Nov. 1, 1986; children: Patrice, Michael. Diploma, U. Pitts., 1951; cert., Loma Linda U., 1960. RN, Calif.; cert. chem. dependency nurse. Cons. occupational health svcs. Bd. Registered Nurses, 1984—; lectr., cons. in field. Recipient Scholarship U. Pitts. Mem. Dirs. of Nursing, Calif. Assn. Nurses in Substance Abuse. Home and Office: 15 Oak Spring Ln Laguna Beach CA 92656-2980

BAO, JOSEPH YUE-SE, orthopedist, microsurgeon, educator; b. Shanghai, China, Feb. 20, 1937; s. George Zheng-En and Margaret Zhi-De (Wang) B.; m. Delia Way, Mar. 30, 1963; children: Alice, Angela. MD, Shanghai First Med. Coll., 1958. Intern affiliated hosps. Shanghai First. Med. Coll.; resident Shanghai Sixth People's Hosp., orthopaedist, 1958-78, orthopaedist-in-charge, 1978-79, vice chief orthopaedist, 1979-84; rsch. assoc. orthopaedic hosp. U. So. Calif., L.A., 1985-90, 94—, vis. clin. assoc. prof. dept. orthopaedics, 1986-89; coord. microvascular svcs. Orthopaedic Hosp., L.A., 1989-91; clin. assoc. prof. dept. orthopaedics U. So. Calif., L.A., 1989—; attending physician Los Angeles County and U. So. Calif. Med. Ctr., L.A., 1986, 90—; cons. Rancho Los Amigos Med. Ctr., Downey, Calif., 1986. Contbr. articles to profl. jours., chpts. to books. Mem. Internat. Microsurgical Soc., Am. Soc. for Reconstructive Microsurgery, Orthopaedic Rsch. Soc. Home: 17436 Terry Lyn Ln Cerritos CA 90703-8522 Office: LA County Med Ctr Dept Orthopaedics 1200 N State St GNH 3900 Los Angeles CA 90033-4526

BAPTIST, ERROL CHRISTOPHER, pediatrician, educator; b. Colombo, Sri Lanka, Feb. 24, 1945; came to U.S., 1974; s. Egerton Cuthbert and Hyacinth Margaret (Colomb) B.; MB, BS, Faculty of Medicine, U. Ceylon, 1969; m. Christine Rosemary Francke, Aug. 7, 1976; children: Lauren Marianne, Erik Christopher. Intern, Colombo Gen. Hosp. and Children's Hosp., Colombo, Sri Lanka, 1969-70; resident house officer Dist. Hosp., Gampola, Sri Lanka, 1970-71; resident house officer Base Hosp., Kegalle, Sri Lanka, 1971-74; family practitioner, Marawila, Sri Lanka, 1974; resident physician in pediatrics Coll. Medicine and Dentistry N.J., Newark, 1975-77; practice medicine specializing in pediatrics, Rockford, Ill., 1977—; asst. prof. pediatrics U. Ill. Coll. Medicine, Rockford, 1977—, assoc. prof., 1994—; chmn. dept. pediatrics St. Anthony Med. Ctr., Rockford, 1986—. Recipient 9 Raymond B. Allen Instructorship awards U. Ill. Diplomate Am. Bd. Pediatrics. Fellow Am. Acad. Pediatrics; mem. So. Med. Assn. Roman Catholic. Home: 5112 Parliament Pl Rockford IL 61107-5066 Office: Mulford Village Office Park 461 N Mulford Rd Rockford IL 61107-5165

BAPTIST, JEREMY EDUARD, allergist; b. Chgo., Mar. 22, 1940; s. Arthur Henry and Margaret Jane (Beck) B.; m. Sylvia Evelyn Bonin, July 21, 1962; children: Sarah, Margaret, Catherine. BS in Physics, U. Chgo., 1960, PhD in Biophysics (USPHS predoctoral fellow), 1966; MD, U. Mo., Kansas City, 1978. Asst. prof. radiation biophysics U. Kans., 1966-73; claims authorizer Social Security Adminstrn., 1974-75; intern in medicine Northwestern U., 1978-79; allergist Speer Allergy and Asthma Clinic, Shawnee Mission, Kans., 1979—, v.p., 1985-90, pres., 1991—; v.p. Multiple Data Svcs., Leawood, Kans., 1992-94; clin. asst. prof. Sch. Medicine U. Kans. Med. Ctr., Kansas City, 1994—. Co-author: Handbook of Clinical Allergy, 1982; contbr. to Britannica Yearbook of Science and the Future, 1973, 74; mem. editorial bd. Topics in Allergy and Clinical Immunology, 1982-83. Mem. Ethnic Enrichment Commn. of Kansas City, Mo., 1988—. Brown-Hazen grantee, 1970. Fellow Am. Coll. Allergy, Asthma, and Immunology (com. on adverse reactions to foods 1989-93); mem. AMA, AAAS, So. Med. Assn., Kans. Med. Soc., Johnson County Med. Soc., N.Y. Acad. Scis., Internat. Corr. Soc. Allergists and Clin. Immunologists (asst.

editor Allergy Letters 1984-85, assoc. editor 1985-89, editor, 1991—, exec. dir. 1991—), Internat. Assn. Aerobiology, Pan-Am. Aerobiology Assn., Armenian Soc. Greater Kansas City (v.p. 1989-93, pres. 1993-95, chmn. 1995—), Vasa (chmn. Kansas City club 1986-90, 92-93, 96—), Sigma Xi. Mem. Reorganized Ch. of Jesus Christ of Latter-day Saints. Office: 5811 Outlook Dr Shawnee Mission KS 66202

BAR, ROBERT S., endocrinologist, educator; b. Gainesville, Tex., Dec. 2, 1943; s. Samuel and Emma (Kaplan) B.; m. Laurel Ellen Burns, June 23, 1970; children: Katharine June, Matthew Thomas. BS, Tufts Univ., 1964; MS in Biochemistry, Ohio State U., 1970, MD, 1970. Medicine intern Pa. Hosp., Phila., 1970-71; medicine resident Ohio State Univ., Columbus, 1971-72; asst. prof., dept. medicine Univ. Iowa, Iowa City, 1977-82, assoc. prof., dept. medicine, 1982-86, prof., dept. medicine, 1986—; acting dir. divsn. of endocrinology and metabolism, U. Iowa, 1985-90; dir. diabetes-endocrinology rsch ctr., U. Iowa, 1986—, nat. rsch. svc. award in endocrinology, 1984—, endocrinology fellowship program, 1979—, divsn. of endocrinology and metabolism, 1990—; mem. ad hoc study sect. NIH, 1985; mem. editorial bd. Jour. of Clin. Endocrinology and Metabolism, 1984-87; mem study sect. Nat. Veterans Adminstrn., 1984-87; v.p. rsch. Nat. Am. Diabetes Assn., 1987-88; mem. orgn. com. Endothelium and Diabetes Symposium, Melbourne, 1988; mem. study sect. numerous assns. and coms.; guest reviewer numerous jours. Editor Endocrinology, 1987-89, Advances in Endocrinology and Metabolism, 1989—. Mem. Am. Diabetes Assn., Am. Soc. for Clin. Investigation, Assn. Am. Physicians, Endocrine Soc., Ctrl. Soc. for Clin. Rsch., Sigma Xi. Office: U Iowa Hwy 6 West 3E19 VA Iowa City IA 52246

BARACH, BRUCE KERRY, plastic surgeon; b. Albany, N.Y., Sept. 13, 1956; s. Jack A. and June (Tucker) B.; m. Irene Dana Bodnar, Aug. 18, 1984; children: Christopher M., Bryan E. AB, Dartmouth Coll., 1978; MD, SUNY, Syracuse, 1982. Diplomate Am. Bd. Plastic Surgery. Intern in surgery Hartford (Conn.) Hosp., 1982-83; resident in surgery Santa Barbara (Calif.) Cottage Hosp., 1983-85; resident in plastic surgery St. Francis Meml. Hosp., San Francisco, 1985-88; pvt. practice Schenectady, N.Y., 1988—. Mem. AMA, Am. Soc. of Plastic and Reconstructive Surgeons, N.Y. State Med. Soc., Schenectady County Med. Soc., Alpha Omega Alpha. Office: 1201 Nott St Ste 303 Schenectady NY 12308-2589

BARAK, ANDREW PAUL, otorhinolaryngologist; b. Detroit, Dec. 12, 1952; s. Morrey Aaron and Shirley Lillian (Spoon) B.; m. Bethany Ann Heitzner, June 1, 1980; children—Sean Adam, Lindsey Danielle, Jay Evan. B.S., Wayne State U., 1974; D.O., Kirksville Coll. Medicine, 1978. Intern Garden City Osteo. Hosp., 1978-79; resident Met. Hosp., 1979-82, resident trainer, 1985—, assoc. prof. surgery, U. Mich.; practice medicine specializing in otorhinolaryngology, 1984—. Contbr. articles to profl. jours. Mem. Am. Osteo. Assn., Am. Osteo. Bd. Ophtholmology and Otorhinolaryngology, Mich. Osteo. Physicians and Surgeons, Kent County Osteo. Physicians and Surgeons, Am. Acad. of Otolaryn., Mich. Otologic Soc.; Democrat. Jewish. Lodge: Centennial. Avocations: baseball, hockey, golf.

BARANOWSKI, TOM, public health educator, researcher; b. Bklyn., Dec. 3, 1946; s. Joseph A. Baranowski and Vera (Maschkoff) Willard; m. Jimmie Dolores Miller, June 21, 1968 (div.); children: Tanya Elise, Todd Michael; m. Janice Carlson Henske, June 2, 1990. AB, Princeton (N.J.) U., 1968; MA, U. Kans., 1970, PhD, 1974. Teaching asst. U. Kans., Lawrence, 1970-71, 73-74; rsch. assoc., evaluator, acting dir. planning Kans. Regional Med. Program, Kansas City, 1971-73; rsch. scientist Health Care Study Ctr. Battelle Human Affairs Rsch. Ctrs., Seattle, 1974-76; rsch. assoc. div. consumer and continuing edn. W.Va. U. Med. Ctr., Charleston, 1976-78, asst. prof. dept. community medicine, coord., 1978-80; asst. prof. depts. pediatrics and preventive medicine U. Tex. Med. Br., Galveston, 1980-84, assoc. prof. dept. preventive medicine and community health, 1984-90; prof. dept. pediatrics, dep. dir. Ga. Inst. Prevention Med. Coll. of Ga., Augusta, 1990-92; prof., chair divsn. behavioral scis. and health edn. Emory U., Atlanta, 1992-95, mem. faculty grad. program nutrition and health, 1993-95; prof. behavioral scis. M.D. Anderson Cancer Ctr. U. Tex., Houston, 1995—; adj. prof. behavioral scis. U. Tex. Sch. Pub. Health, Houston, 1996—. Contbr. numerous articles to profl. jours. Chairperson sch. site program com. Am. Heart Assn., 1990-92, bd. dirs. Augusta div. Ga. affiliate. N.Y. State Regent's scholar, 1964, Princeton U. scholar, 1964-68; USPHS fellow U. Kans., 1969-71; recipient citation Am. Diabetes Assn., Health award Anne Mooney Sch. Mem. Am. Heart Assn., Am. Psychol. Soc., Am. Pub. Health Assn., Am. Sch. Health Assn., Assn. on Hypertension in Black Populations, Soc. Behavioral Medicine, Soc. Nutrition Edn., Southwestern Soc. for Rsch. in Human Devel. Home: 2225 Sheridan Houston TX 77030

BÁRÁNY, PETER FRANZ, nephrologist; b. Stockholm, Oct. 26, 1955; s. Franz Rudolf and Margareta Ruth Ingrid (Nyland) B.; m. Åsa Gunilla Wallje, May 3, 1986; children: Elsa, Aina. Grad. Med. Faculty, Karolinska Inst., Stockholm, 1983, Dr. Med. Sci., 1993. Lic. physician, Sweden. Resident in nephrology dept. renal medicine Huddinge U. Hosp., Stockholm, 1987-94, specialist in nephrology, 1994—. Contbr. articles to profl. jours. Mem. Swedish Soc. Nephrology, European Dialysis and Transplantation Assn., Internat. Soc. Nephrology, Internat. Soc. for Peritoneal Dialysis, Am. Soc. Nephrology (corr.). Office: Huddinge Univ Hosp, Dept Renal Medicine, S-14186 Stockholm Sweden

BARASCH, PHILIP MARC, physician; b. Bklyn., Nov. 12, 1951; s. Stanley S. and Millicent R. (Goodheart) B.; m. Violette Kasica, Nov. 8, 1954; 1 child, James. BS, CUNY, 1972; MD, SUNY, Bklyn., 1976. Diplomate Am. Bd. Psychiatry and Neurology. Intern in medicine Brookdale Med. Ctr., Bklyn., 1976-77; resident in neurology Kings County Med. Ctr.-SUNY, Bklyn., 1977-80, fellow in neurophysiology, 1980-81; sr. neurologist Bridgeport (Conn.) Hosp., 1981—. Mem. Am. Acad. Neurology, Phi Beta Kappa, Alpha Omega Alpha. Office: Neurol Specialists 2590 Main St Stratford CT 06497

BARASH, DAVID PHILIP, psychology and zoology educator; b. N.Y.C., Jan. 9, 1946; s. Nathan and Anne (Shaposnick) B.; m. Beverly Ann Osband, Jan. 20, 1966 (div. 1975); 1 child, Eva; m. Judith Eve Lipton, Mar. 10, 1977; children: Ilona, Nanelle. BA, Harpur Coll., 1966; MA, U. Wis., 1968, PhD, 1970. Asst. prof. psychology, zoology SUNY Coll., Oneonta, 1970-73; assoc. prof. U. Wash., Seattle, 1973-80, prof., 1980—. Author: Sociobiology and Behavior, 1977, 82, The Whisperings Within, 1979, Stop Nuclear War, 1982, Aging: An Exploration, 1983, The Caveman and the Bomb, 1985, The Hare and the Tortoise, 1986, The Arms Race and Nuclear War, 1987, The Great Outdoors, 1989, Introduction to Peace Studies, 1991, The L Word, 1992, Beloved Enemies, 1994. Fellow NSF, Ctr. Advanced Study in the Behavioral Scis., 1977-78, Bellagio Study and Conf. Ctr., 1984. Fellow AAAS. Democrat. Home: 20006 NE 116th St Redmond WA 98053-9610 Office: U Wash Psychology Dept Seattle WA 98195

BARBA, ROBERTA ASHBURN, retired social worker; b. Morgantown, W.Va., June 23, 1931; d. Robert Russell and Mary Belle (Rogers) Ashburn; m. Harry C. Barba, Jan. 28, 1956 (div. June 1963); 1 child, Gregory Robert; m. Robert Franklin Church, May 10, 1972. BSSW, W.Va. U., 1953; post-grad., U. Conn., Hartford, 1953-54; MSSW, NYU, 1957. Diplomate in Am. Bd. Examiners; lic. N.Y., W.Va. Pvt. practice W.Va., 1968—; evaluator P.A.C.E., Star City, W.Va., 1973-74; social worker Family Svc. Assn., Morgantown, W.Va., 1974-75, 85-87; human resources asst., social worker Sundale Rest Home, Morgantown, 1977-79; cons., residential svcs. specialist Coordinating Coun. for Ind. Living, Morgantown, 1983-88; provider W.Va. Dept. Welfare, Human Svcs., Morgantown, 1980-87; social worker maternity svcs. Monongalia County Health Dept., Morgantown, 1985-87; social worker Hospice of Preston County, Kingwood, W.Va., 1988-89; shelter worker, field work instr. Bartlett House W.Va. Sch. Social Work, Morgantown, 1986-90; case mgr. Region VI Area Agy. on Aging, Fairmont, W.Va., 1990-92; case mgr. geriatric program W.Va. U., Morgantown, 1992-95; ret., 1995. Author (with others) Working with Terminally Ill, 1990, (short fiction) Kids Know, 1992; freedom writer Amnesty Internat., 1987—. George Davis Bivens Found. grantee, 1953-54. Mem. NASW (charter mem., cert. diplomate), ACLU, NOW, Acad. Cert. Social Workers, W.Va. Human Resources Assn., W.Va. Child Care Assn., Monongalia County Coun. Social Agys, Phi Beta Kappa. Home: 429 Fairmont Rd Morgantown WV 26505-4244

BARBARA, JOHN A.J., microbiologist; b. Cairo, Egypt, Apr. 2, 1946; parent British citizens; s. Francis and Theresa (Micallef) B.; m. Gillian Barnes, Aug. 2, 1968; children: Claire, David. BA, Cambridge U., 1968, MA, 1969; MSc, Birmingham U., 1969; PhD, Reading U., 1972. Demonstrator Reading U., U.K., 1969-72; lectr. Reading U., 1972-74; head microbiology No. London Blood Ctr., 1974—; cons. Nat. Blood Authority, England, 1993—;. Author: Microbiology in Blood Transfusion, 1983; contbr. articles to profl. jours. Fellow Inst. Biology; mem. Royal Coll. Pathologists, Br. Blood Transfusion Soc. (pres.-elect 1994, pres. 1995—), Internat. Soc. Blood Transfusion, Am. Assn. Blood Banks, Assn. Clin. Microbiologists. Office: No London Blood Transfusion, Colindale Ave, London NW9 5BG, England

BARBEE, CHARLES WALKER, vascular surgeon; b. Hugo, Okla., July 2, 1939; m. Pattye Perryman; children: Sam, Ann, Adam. BA, U. Okla., Norman, 1961; MD, U. Okla., Oklahoma City, 1965. Diplomate Am. Bd. Surgery with subspeciality in vascular surgery; cert. in endovascular surgery Dorros Feuer Found., Milw.; lic. physician Okla., Minn., Calif., Colo., Mo., Ga. Rotating intern Presbyn. Hosp., Oklahoma City, 1965-66; resident in gen. surgery Mayo Clinic, Rochester, Minn., 1966-70; pvt. practice Columbia, Mo., 1972—; staff in vascular and gen. surgery Boone Hosp. Ctr., Columbia, 1972—, med. dir. vascular lab., 1978-95, chmn. transfusion com., 1984, chief of staff, 1992-93, chmn. credentials com., 1994-95), Columbia Regional Hosp., 1975—; courtesy staff Moberly (Mo.) Regional Med. Ctr., 1985—; cons. staff Cooper County Hosp., Boonville, Mo., 1985—, Lake Ozark Gen. Hosp., Osage Beach, Mo., 1986—; assoc. in vascular and gen. surgery St. mary's Health Ctr., Jefferson City, Mo., 1987—; courtest meml. and still campuses Capital Region Med. Ctr., Jefferson City, 1993—; lectr. in field; rep. Boone County chpt. Blood Svcs. Com., Mo./Ill. Regional Blood Svcs., 1982-85; founding mem., bd. dirs. Mo. Heart Inst., 1982—; clin. cons. Atrium Co., IMPRA, 1987; cons., faculty/lectr. Biosound Duplex Scanning Physician Tng., 1987—. Contbr. articles to profl. jours.; editor Boone Clinic Bull., 1980-88. Maj. M.C. U.S. Army, 1970-72. Fellow ACS, Am. Coll. Chest Physicians (assoc.); mem. AMA (Physician's Recognition award 1981, 84, 87, 93), Mo. Cardiovascular and Thoracic Surgeons (pres. 1980—), Mo. Med. Assn. (councilor hosp./med. staff sect. 1987—), Ctrl. Mo. Physicians and Surgeons Assn. (founding mem., bd. dirs., sec. and chmn. credentials com.), Am. Heart Assn. (stroke coun. and cardiovascular surgery coun.), Am. Coll. Physician Execs., Am. Thoracic Soc., Doctors Mayo Soc., Internat. Coll. Surgeons, GAteway Vascular Soc., Mayo Alumni Assn., Midwestern Vascular Surg. Soc., Mo. Thoracic Soc., Mo. State Surg. Soc., Pan-Pacific Surg. Assn., St. Louis Vascular Soc., Priestley Soc. (exec. coun.), Soc. Non-Invasive Vascular Tech., So. Med. Assn., Southwestern Surg. Congress. Office: Mo Cardiovascular/Thoracic Stephens Park Med Bldg 1701 E Broadway Columbia MO 65201

BARBENEL, JOSEPH CYRIL, biomedical engineer; b. London, Jan. 2, 1937; s. Tobias and Sarah (Cattel) B.; m. Lesley Mary Hyde Jowett, Aug. 6, 1960; children: Rachel, David, Daniel. BS, U. London, 1960, U. St. Andrews, 1966; MS, U. Strathclyde, 1967, PhD, 1979. House surgeon London Hosp., 1960; pvt. practice Nat. Health Svc., London, 1962-63; lectr. dental sch. and hosp. U. Dundee, United Kingdom, 1967-70; sr. lectr. U. Strathclyde, Glasgow, United Kingdom, 1970-82, reader, 1982-85, personal prof., 1985-89, prof., 1989-92, dept. head, 1992—. Co-editor 5 books; contbr. chpts. to books and articles to profl. jours. Gov. Hutchesons' Grammar Sch., Glasgow, 1989—. Capt. Brit. Army, 1961-62. Recipient Pres.' medal Soc. Cosmetic Scientists, 1994; grantee numerous orgns. Fellow Inst. Physics, Inst. Biology, Royal Soc. Edinburgh, Inst. Phys. Scis. in Medicine, Biol. Engring. Soc. (pres. 1988-89). Office: U Strathclyde, 106 Rottenrow, Glasgow G4 0NW, Scotland

BARBER, ALLISON, public relations executive; b. Gary, Ind., Jan. 28, 1964; d. Gary D. and Barbara L. (Yonan) Canaday; m. D. Linden, Nov. 26, 1988. BS, Temple U., 1986; MS, Ind. U., 1990. Office: ARC 2025 East St NW Washington DC 20006

BARBER, ANN MARIE TERESA, nurse; b. Phila., Nov. 17, 1965; d. John Nicholas and Marie Teresa (Mazloom) B. BSN, Villanova U., 1987, MS in Health Care Adminstrn., 1991. Cert. pediatric advanced life support. instr. neonatal advanced life support, emergency helicopter transport. Exec. asst. Nat. Com. for Clin. Lab. Standards, Villanova, Pa., 1985-87; nurse pediatric unit Osteopathic Med. Ctr., Phila., 1987-88; nurse neonatal ICU Hahnemann U. Hosp., Phila., 1988-90, asst. head nurse neonatal ICU, 1990-95; clin. coord. maternal and child health div. Hanhemann U. Hosp., Phila., 1993—; clin. assoc. Neonatal ICU Hahnemann U. Hosp., Phila., 1994—. Mem. editorial com. The Phila. Nurse, 1987-88. Mem. AACN, Nat. Assn. Neonatal Nurses, Villanova U. Nursing Alumni Assn. Republican. Roman Catholic.

BARBER, ANN MCDONALD, internist; b. Washington, Jan. 14, 1951; d. Charles Finch and Lois Helen (LaCroix) B. MS in Math., BS in Math., Stanford U., 1974; MD, Northwestern U., Chgo., 1981. Mathematician NIH, Bethesda, Md., 1974-76; program analyst engr. II Mass. Gen. Hosp., Boston, 1976-77; resident in internal medicine Northwestern U. Med. Ctr., Chgo., 1981-84; med. staff fellow NIH, Bethesda, 1984-87; sr. staff fellow Nat. Cancer Inst., Bethesda, 1987-91; computer scientist DOE, 1991-92; attending physician Providence Hosp., Washington, 1992—; v.p. Reliance Ins. Co., N.Y.C., 1996—; peer reviewer Annuals Of Internal Medicne, ACP, Phila., 1986—; cons. Inst. for New Generation Computer Tech., Tokyo, 1991. Contbr. articles to profl. jours. Vol. Zacchaeus Free Med. Clinic, Washington, 1990-96. Recipient Physician's Recognition award AMA. Fellow Royal Soc. Medicine London; mem. ACP, Am. Coll. Physician Execs., Am. Med. Info. Assn. Office: Reliance Ins Co Park Ave Plz 55 E 52d St New York NY 10055

BARBER, CATHERINE, physician assistant; b. Phila., Apr. 22, 1961; d. Frank Floyd and Mary Jo (Limeberry) Martin; m. David C. Barber. B in Med. Sci., Emory U., 1986. Physician assoc. Downtown Med. and Diagnostic Ctr., St. Petersburg, Fla., 1986—; adminstr. Downtown Med. and Diagnostic Ctr., St. Petersburg, 1990—; cons. Fla. State DPR, 1995-96; pub. spkr. in field. Mem. AAPA, FAPA. Office: Downtown Med & Diag Ctr 400 6th St South Saint Petersburg FL 33701

BARBER, DONNA BRIGMAN, critical care nurse; b. Moultrie, Ga., Jan. 17, 1962; d. Samuel Lindsey and Bobbie Faye (Foreman) Brigman; m. Anthony C. Barber, July 5, 1981; children: Christi Michelle, Matthew Brian, Lindsey Nicole. ADN, Gordon Coll., 1993. RN, Ga.; cert. critical care nurse, cert. emergency nurse. ICU nurse Spalding Regional Hosp., Griffin, Ga., 1993-96; cardiac care unit nurse So. Regional Med. Ctr., 1996—. Mem. AACN. Baptist.

BARBER, DOUGLAS BYRON, physician; b. Tripoli, Lybia, Sept. 4, 1959; s. Douglas and Isabelle Lucille (Parker) B.; m. Anna Nellie Gonzalez, June 18, 1988; children: Samuel Raphael, Elise Isabella. BS in Physics and Mathematics, Baylor U., 1982; MD, U. Tex., 1987. Diplomate Am. Bd. Phys. Medicine and Rehab. Assoc. Rehab. Assocs. N. Mex., Albuquerque, 1991-92, The Rehab. Group, San Antonio, 1992-93; staff physician Spinal Cord Injury Ctr. Audie L. Murphy Meml. Vets. Hosp., San Antonio, 1993-95, chief Spinal Cord Injury Ctr., 1995—; asst. prof. dept. rehab. medicine Health Sci. Ctr. U. Tex., San Antonio, 1993—. Contbr. articles to profl. jours. Fellow Am. Acad. Phys. Medicine and Rehab., Am. Paraplegia Soc., Am. Spinal Injury Assn., Assn. Acad. Physiatrists. Office: Dept Rehab Medicine 7703 Floyd Curl Dr San Antonio TX 78284

BARBER, EDWARD BRUCE, medical products executive; b. Chgo., Mar. 11, 1937; s. Edward Vanrennsaler and Alice (Reinertsen) B.; m. Louise Joy Griebler, May 23, 1964. BS, Lake Forest (Ill.) Coll., 1957; MBA, U. Chgo., 1958. Market rsch. cons. Container Corp. of Am., Chgo., 1959-61; pres. Christiansen & Barber Assoc. Ltd., Chgo., 1961—; chmn., CEO Odyssey Travel Ltd., Chgo., 1974—; founder, chmn. M.E. Team, Inc., South Plainfield, N.J., 1980—, also bd. dirs.; pres. Colts Necks Farms, Inc. 1990—; cons. Lab. Supply Co., Louisville, 1990—, Graham-Field Surg., Inc., Hauppage, N.Y., 1990—; ptnr. Wynne Med./Statco Med., 1996—, Sci. Supply Co., Schiller Park, Ill., 1990—; bd. dirs. Golden Eagle Travel, Huntington Beach, Calif. Mem. Internat. Assn. of Travel Agys., Health Industries Distbr. Assn., Masons. Republican. Lutheran. Office: Christiansen Barber Assocs Ste 310 6800 W Raven St Chicago IL 60631-2586

BARBER, JANICE DIANNE, mental health nurse; b. Allentown, Pa., Feb. 9, 1945; d. Elam Daniel and Arlene Helen (Deysher) Smith; children: Jeffrey Nasser, Janene Diane Barber. Diploma, Allentown Hosp. Sch. Nursing, 1966; BS in Psychology, St. Joseph's Coll., North Windham, Maine, 1982, postgrad. in health care adminstrn., 1990—; postgrad. cert. in gerontology, Cedar Crest Coll., Allentown, 1992. Cert. CPR, cert. in gerontology. Med.-surg. charge nurse Allentown Osteo. Hosp., 1966-67; charge nurse Liberty Nursing Ctr., Allentown, 1968-71; labor and delivery staff nurse Allentown Hosp., 1971-80, psychiat. unit primary nurse, 1980—; researcher in field. Mem. Am. Psychiat. Nurses Assn., Allentown Hosp. Sch. Nursing Alumnae Assn. Office: LVH 17th and Chew St Allentown PA 18103

BARBER, JOHN STEVEN, hospital executive; b. Dalhart, Tex., May 3, 1955; s. Clyde Oliver Jr. and Nancy Jo (Cox) B.; m. Sherri Ann Scott, Jan. 1, 1975; children: Serena Annette, Jared Shane. AA in Liberal Arts, York Coll., 1975; BS in Acctg., Harding U., 1978; MBA in Acctg., Valdosta State Coll., 1988. Staff acct. Reames & Son Constrn. Co., Valdosta, Ga., 1978-81; controller Ga. Home Rehab Svcs. Inc., Valdosta, 1981-86, Berrien County Nursing Ctr., Nashville, Ga., 1983-86; chief fin. officer Comprehensive Health Mgmt., Valdosta, 1985-86; asst. controller Healthcare of Berrien County, Nashville, 1986-87; chief fin. officer Healthcare of Dooly County, Vienna, Ga., 1987, Dooly Med. Ctr., Vienna, 1987-89, Dorminy Med. Ctr., Fitzgerald, Ga., 1989-90; co-adminstr. Dorminy Med. Ctr., 1990-93, adminstr., 1993—; mem. adv. bd. Americare Home Health Agy., Brunswick, Ga., 1990—; coun. mem. Ga. Hosp. Assn. Coun. Fin. and Mgmt., Atlanta, 1991—. Asst. scout master Boy Scouts Am., Gruver, Tex., 1972-74; mem. exec. bd. Cities in Schs., 1993—, Ben Hill County Bd. Health, 1993—. Mem. Ga. Rural Health Assn. (Rural Hosp. of Yr. 1990), Southwest Dist. Ga. Hosp. Assn., Woodpecker Trail Hosp. Consortium, Fitzgerald-Ben Hill C. of C. (econ. devel. com. 1993—), Rotary. Republican. Office: Dorminy Med Ctr PO Box 1447 Fitzgerald GA 31750-1447

BARBER, NIGEL WILLIAM THOMAS, psychologist, educator; b. Tullamore, Ireland, Nov. 7, 1955; came to U.S., 1982; s. George and Rebecca (Hardy) B.; m. Trudy Callaghan, June 25, 1979; 1 child, David. BA in English with honors, Trinity Coll., Dublin, Ireland, 1977; PhD in Psychology, CUNY, 1989. Instr. in psychology Bemidji State U., Minn., 1989-90; asst. prof. psychology Birmingham (Ala.)-So. Coll., 1990—. Mem. APA., Human Behavior and Evolution Soc. Office: Birmingham So Coll PO Box 549037 Birmingham AL 35201-0037

BARBETTA, MARIA ANN, health records administrator, consultant; b. Bristol, Pa., Mar. 20, 1956; d. Eugene Charles and Anna Barbetta. AA, Bucks County Community Coll., 1976; BS, Coll. Allied Health Professions, Temple U., 1978. Dir. med. records Cumberland Regional Health Plan, Vineland, N.J., 1978; dir. med. record dept. St. Mary Hosp., Langhorne, Pa., 1978—; cons. med. records St. Joseph's Home for Aged, Holland, Pa., 1983-94; spkr. on med. record topics to various orgns., nationally, 1983—; cons. on health info. mgmt., optical imaging syss., 1990—. Mem. Am. Mgmt. Assn., Nat. Med. Records Imaging Users Group (sec. 1992-93, chairperson 1994-95, past chairperson 1995-96), Am. Health Info. Mgmt. Assn. (contbg. author jour. 1992, 93), Pa. Health Info. Mgmt. Assn. (edn. com. 1985-87, 91-92, project mgr. strategic plan 1987-89, sec. 1990-91, edn. com. 1991-92), RTAS Med. Record Users Group (co-chair 1993-94, 94-95), Southeastern Pa. Health Info. Mgmt. Assn. (chmn. membership com. 1987-88, membership com. 1988-89, chmn. program and edn. 1989-90, sec. 1992-93, pres.-elect 1996—). Avocations: cross-country skiing, volunteer work, reading, traveling. Home: 4707 Grandview Ave Bensalem PA 19020-1011 Office: St Mary Hosp Langhorne-Newtown Rd Langhorne PA 19047

BARBO, DOROTHY MARIE, obstetrician, gynecologist, educator; b. River Falls, Wis., May 28, 1932; d. George William and Marie Lillian (Stelsel) B. BA, Asbury Coll., 1954; MD, U. Wis., 1958; DSc (hon.), Asbury Coll., 1981. Diplomate Am. Bd. Ob-Gyn. Resident Luth. Hosp. Milw., 1958-62; instr. Sch. Medicine Marquette U., Milw., 1962-66, asst. prof., 1966-67; assoc. prof. Christian Med. Coll. Punjab U., Ludhiana, India, 1968-72; assoc. prof. Med. Coll. Pa., Phila., 1972-87, prof., 1988-91; prof. U. N.Mex., Albuquerque, 1991—; med. dir. Women's Health Ctr., 1991—; acting dept. chair Christian Med. Coll., Punjab U., 1970; dir. Ctr. for Mature Woman Med. Coll. Pa. 1983-91; examiner Am. Bd. Ob-Gyn, 1984—; bd. dirs. Ludhiana Christian Med. Coll., N.Y.C., Svc. Master Co. Ltd., Downers Grove, Ill., 1982-91. Co-author: Care of Post Menopausal Patient, 1985; editor: Medical Clinics of N.A., vol. 71, 1987; contbr. chpt. to book. Student chpt. sponsor Christian Med. and Dental Soc., Phila., 1973-93, trustee, 1991-95, pres.-elect Nat. Christian Med. and Dental Soc.; tchr., elder Leverington Presbyn. Ch., Phila., 1988-91; interviewer Reader's Digest Internat. fellowships, Brunswick, Ga., 1982—; bd. dirs. Phila. chpt. Am. Cancer Soc., 1980-86, vol., 1984. Named sr. clin. trainee USPHS, HEW, 1963-65, one of Best Woman Drs. in Am. Harper Bazaar, 1985. Fellow ACS (sec. Phila. chpt. 1990), ACOG, Am. Fertility Soc.; mem. Obstet. Soc. Phila. (pres. 1989-90), Phila. Colposcopy Soc. (pres. 1982-84), Philadelphia County Med. Soc. (com. chmn. 1989-90), Alpha Omega Alpha. Office: U N Mex Dept Ob-Gyn 2211 Lomas Blvd NE Albuquerque NM 87131-6285

BARBOUR, EDMUND MARTIN, physician, gastroenterology consultant; b. Detroit, Mar. 4, 1940; s. Edmund Nicholas and Elizabeth (Thomas) B.; m. Judith Marie Barbour, July 31, 1965; children: Nicole, Michael. BA, Marquette U., 1962; MD, Med. Coll. Wis., Milw., 1966. Diplomate Am. Bd. Internal Medicine. Intern USPHS, Boston, 1966; resident USPHS Indian Health Divsn., Phoenix, 1967-68; resident, then chief resident Harper Hosp., Detroit, 1969-70; fellow in gastroent. Haden Hosp., Detroit, 1972, Wayne State Univ., Detroit, 1971; chief of medicine Oakwood Hosp., Dearborn, Mich., 1988-94, vice chief of staff, 1992-95; assoc. prof. medicine Wayne State U., Detroit, 1987—. Clin. cons. on two books. Fellow ACP; mem. AMA, Am. Soc. Gastrointestinal Endoscopy, Am. Soc. Internal Medicine, Am. Soc. Gastroenterology, Mich. Soc. Gastrointestinal Endoscopy (pres. 1978-81), Detroit Med. Club (pres. 1980), Mich. State Med. Soc., Mich. Soc. Internal Medicine, Wayne County Med. Soc., Essex Golf and Country Club (v.p. 1995-96). Roman Catholic. Office: 125 N Military Dearborn MI 48124

BARBOUR, PETER J., neurologist; b. Phila., Mar. 24, 1948; s. Samuel Hershl and Etta Adelade (Ostroff) B.; m. Barbara Susan Falk, Aug. 16, 1970; children: Joshua Michael, Jonathan Ross, Samuel Natt. BA in Biology, U. Pa., 1970; MD, Temple U., 1974. Diplomate Am. Bd. Neurology and Psychiatry, Am. Bd. Electrodiagnostic Medicine. Intern Good Samaritan Hosp., Portland, Oreg., 1975; resident in neurology Stanford U. Sch. Medicine, Palo Alto, Calif., 1978; clin. dir. neurodiagnostic lab. Lehigh Valley Hosp., Allentown, Pa., 1980-90, asst. chief divsn. neurology, 1985-90, co-dir. neurosci. regional resource ctr., 1987-94, chmn. allied health profl. com., 1987-89, chief divsn. neurology, 1990—; assoc. clin. prof. medicine Hahnemann U. Med. Sch., 1986-95; clin. assoc. prof. medicine Pa. State U. Coll. Medicine, 1995—. Author: Loose Ends, 1988; contbr. articles, short stories to profl. publs. Football coach South Parkland Youth Assn., Allentown, Pa., 1984-93. Fellow Am. Acad. Neurology, Am. Assn. Electrodiagnostic Medicine; mem. Phila. Neurol. Soc., Alpha Omega Alpha. Office: Lehigh Neurology 1210 S Cedar Crest Blvd Allentown PA 18103

BARBUTO, JOSEPH, psychiatrist, educator; b. Bklyn., Mar. 22, 1947. BS, Bklyn. Coll., 1969; MD, Albert Einstein Coll. Medicine, 1978. Diplomate Am. Bd. Psychiatry and Neurology, Nat. Bd. Med. Examiners. Rsch. asst. in chemistry, lectr. Bklyn. Coll., 1966-68, 71-73; rsch. asst. in biochemistry NYU Sch. Medicine, N.Y.C., 1969-71, instr. chemistry, 1972, 74; fellow, supr. Gestalt Ctr. for Psychotherapy, N.Y.C., 1978-79; pvt. practice N.Y.C.; instr. clin. psychiatry Cornell U. Med. Coll., N.Y.C., 1981-86, asst. clin. prof., 1986—; clin. affiliate N.Y. Hosp., N.Y.C., 1982-87, asst. attending psychiatrist, 1987—; cons. Meml. Sloan-Kettering Cancer Ctr., N.Y.C., New Rochelle Hosp. Med. Ctr.; examiner Am. Bd. Psychiatry and Neurology, 1994—. Contbg. author: Psychiatric Complications of AIDS; contbr. articles to med. jours. Am. Cancer Soc. fellow, 1983. Mem. Am. Psychiat. Assn. (com. on AIDS N.Y. chpt. 1986-91). Office: 6 W 77th St New York NY 10024-5125

BARCENAS, CAMILO GUSTAVO, physician; b. Managua, Nicaragua, Sept. 18, 1944; came to U.S., 1969; s. Camilo and Margarita (Levy) B.; M.D., U. Nicaragua, 1968; m. Aurora Cardenas, Dec. 22, 1969; children—Margarita, Marcela, Camilo. Diplomate Am. Bd. Internal Medicine. Intern, Managua (Nicaragua) Gen. Hosp., 1967-68, Mt. Sinai Hosp., U. Conn., 1969; resident internal medicine Baylor Coll. Medicine, Houston, 1970-72; chief resident St. Luke's Episcopal Hosp., Houston, 1971; chief resident VA Hosp., Houston, 1972; fellow nephrology U. Tex. Health Sci. Ctr., Dallas, 1972-74; practice medicine specializing in nephrology, Dallas, 1974-76, Houston, 1976—; chief home dialysis unit VA Hosp., Dallas, 1974-75, chief hemodialysis unit, 1975; chief nephrology sect. St. Luke's Episcopal Hosp., Houston, 1976—; chief nephrology Tex. Heart Inst., dir. renal transplant svc.; asst. prof. medicine U. Tex. Health Sci. Ctr., Dallas, 1974-75; clin. asst. prof. medicine Baylor Coll. Medicine, Houston, 1976-79, clin. asso. prof., 1979-85, clin. prof., 1985—. Gen. sec. Juventud Social Christiana, 1968. Fellow A.C.P.; mem. Internat. Soc. Nephrology, Houston Soc. Internal Medicine, Am. Soc. Nephrology, Harris County Med. Soc., Tex. Med. Assn., Colegio Medico Nicaraguense. Roman Catholic. Contbr. articles on nephrology to med. jours. Office: 6624 Fannin # 2510 Houston TX 77030-2604 also: 9197 Winkler St Bldg D Houston TX 77017

BARCH, FRANK J., internist; b. Cin., Sept. 15, 1948; s. Frank Norris and Miriam Louise (Glaub) B.; m. Jean-Marie Prestwidge, June 6, 1970; children: Seth, Keith. BS, Swarthmore Coll., 1970; postgrad., Haverford Coll., 1971; MD, Med. Coll. Pa., 1978. Diplomate Am. Bd. Internal Medicine, Am. Bd. Internal Medicine in Pulmonary Disease, Am. Bd. Internal Medicine in Critical Care. Asst. clin. prof. Med. Coll. Pa., Phila., 1980-90; attending physician West Park Hosp., Phila., 1980-90, AFL-CIO Union Med. Clinic, Phila., 1980-94; med. dir. respiratory care Phoenixville (Pa.) Hosp., 1980-94; chief pulmonary svc. Brandywine Hosp., Coatesville, Pa., 1983—, med. dir. respiratory care, 1988—; med. supr. Chester County Chest Clinic, Phoenixville, 1984—; cons. staff Bryn Mawr (Pa.) Rehab. Hosp., 1993—. Mem. Am. Thoracic Soc., Pa. Thoracic Soc., AMA, Pa. Med. Soc., Chester County Med. Soc., Nat. Assn. Med. Dirs. Respiratory Care, Am. Assn. Respiratory Care, Alpha Omega Alpha. Mem. Soc. Friends. Office: Lung Cons Ltd 750 S Main St Ste 302 Phoenixville PA 19460

BARCHAS, JACK DAVID, psychiatrist, educator; b. Los Angeles, Nov. 2, 1935; s. Samuel Isaac and Cecile Margaret (Pasarow) B.; m. Patricia Ruth Corbitt, Feb. 9, 1957; 1 son, Isaac Doherty. B.A., Pomona Coll., 1956; M.D., Yale U., 1961. Intern Pritzker Sch. Medicine, U. Chgo., 1961-62; postdoctoral fellow in biochemistry and pharmacology NIH, 1962-64; resident in psychiatry Stanford Med. Sch., 1964-67, instr., 1966-67, asst. prof., 1967-71, assoc. prof., 1971-76, prof., 1976—, Nancy Friend Pritzker prof. psychiatry and behavioral scis., 1976—; dir. Nancy Pritzker Lab. of Behavioral Neurochemistry, 1976—. Editor; author: Serotonin and Behavior, 1973, Neuroregulators and Psychiatric Disorders, 1977, Psychopharmacology from Theory to Practice, 1977, Catecholamines - Basic and Clinical Frontiers, 1979, Isoquinolines and Beta-Carbolines, 1981, Research on Mental Illness and Addictive Disorders: Progress and Prospects, 1984, Neuropeptides in Neurology and Psychiatry, 1986, In Situ Hybridization in Neurobiology, 1987, Perspectives in Psychopharmacology, 1988, Biological Rhythms and Mental Illness, 1988; contbr. articles to profl. jours. Served with USPHS, 1962-64. Recipient Psychopharmacology award Am. Psychol. Assn., 1970, Research Scientist award NIMH, 1980—. Fellow Am. Psychiat. Assn., Am. Coll. Neuropsychopharmacology; mem. Soc. Neurosci., Am. Coll. Neuropsychopharmacology (Daniel Efron award 1978), Am. Soc. Pharmacology and Exptl. Therapeutics, Am. Physiol. Soc., Am. Soc. Neurochemistry, Am. Chem. Soc., Am. Psychosomatic Soc., Psychiat. Research Soc., Soc. Biol. Psychiatry (A.E. Bennett award 1968), Am. Psychopathol. Assn., Inst. Medicine Nat. Acad. Scis. (chmn. bd. Mental Health and Behavioral Medicine). *

BARCHI, ROBERT LAWRENCE, neuroscience educator, clinical neurologist, neuroscientist; b. Phila., Nov. 23, 1946; s. Henry John and Elizabeth (Pesci) B.; m. Joan E. Mollman, Sept. 20, 1976; children: Jonathan Robert, Jennifer Elizabeth. BS, Georgetown U., 1963, MS, 1969; PhD, U. Pa., 1972, MD, 1973. Diplomate Am. Bd. Neurology and Psychiatry, Am. Bd. Med. Examiners. Resident in neurology U. Pa. Hosp., 1973-75; asst. prof. biochemistry U. Pa. Med. Sch., Phila., 1974-75, asst. prof. neurology and biochemistry, 1975-78, assoc. prof., 1978-81, prof., 1981—, David Mahoney prof. neurosci., 1985—, chmn. neurosci. grad. program, 1983-89, dir. Mahoney Inst. Neurol. Scis., 1983-96; vice-dean rsch. sch. medicine U. Pa. Med. Sch., 1989-91, chmn. dept. neurosci., 1992-95, chmn. depts. neurology and neurosci., 1995—; mem. med. adv. bd. Muscular Dystrophy Assn., 1982-94; mem. adv. bd. Cephalon Inc., 1992—, Phila. Ventures Inc., 1992—. Author: (with Rosenberg, Prusiner, DiMauro) Molecular and Genetic Basis of Neurological Disease, 2 edits.; mem. editorial bd. Muscle and Nerve Jour., 1981-82, 95—, Jour. Neurochemistry, 1981-90, Jour. Neurosci., 1988-91, Ion Channels, 1988—, Current Opinion Neurology and Neurosurgery, 1992—, The Neuroscientist, 1993—, Neurobiology of Disease, 1994—; contbr. chpts. to textbooks, numerous articles to profl. jours. Recipient Lindback award U. Pa., 1979, Javits award NIH, 1985. Fellow AAAS, Am. Acad. Neurology, Am. Neurol. Assn. (bd. councillors 1992-94); mem. NAS, Inst. Medicine, Biophys. Soc., Soc. for Neurosci. (pub. lectr. 1985), Am. Soc. Clin. Investigation, Assn. Am. Physicians, Phi Beta Kappa, Alpha Omega Alpha. Office: U Pa Depts Neurology & Neurosci 215 Stemmler Hall Philadelphia PA 19104

BARCUS, ANNE SHARON, social services administrator; b. Kansas City, Kans., Nov. 5, 1947; d. Roy Victor and Ella Agnes (Nixon) Barcus; divorced; children: Brion Dickerson, Aaron Dickerson. BS magna cum laude, Park Coll., 1985; postgrad., Columbia Pacific U., 1987-94. Cert. relapse prevention specialist; lic. minister Ch. of the Nazarene. Counselor Univ. Hosp., Kansas City, Mo., 1984-85, St. John's Hosp., Leawood, Kans., 1986, Synergy House, Parkville, Mo., 1986-87; team leader St. Mary's Hosp., Kansas City, 1987-88; relapse specialist South Coast Med. Ctr., Laguna Beach, Calif., 1988-89; program dir. Cedarvale, Stroud, Okla., 1989-90; adminstr. Cornerstone, Tustin, Calif., 1990-94; homeless shelter ops. dir. Cath. Charities Cmty. Svcs., Honolulu, 1994—; lectr. in field, 1988—; pres. Network of Profls., Kansas City, 1987. Co-author: The Slippery Slope, 1992. Mem. Employee Assistance Programs. Nazarene. Home: 98-040 Puaalii Way Aiea HI 96701

BARCUS, GILBERT MARTIN, medical products executive, business educator; b. N.Y.C., Sept. 20, 1937; s. Leon A. and Dorothy (Brownstein) B.; m. Sondra Ettin, May 6, 1961; children: David A., Ruth A. Barcus Feinberg. BS, NYU, 1959; MBA, L.I. U., 1969. Stock broker Ernst & Co., N.Y.C., 1962-65, Johnson & Johnson, 1965-80; sales mgr. McNeil Labs., Ft. Washington, Pa., 1965-75; mktg. mgr. USA Devices Ltd., New Brunswick, N.J., 1976-77; dir. product mgmt. TENS div. Stimtech, Inc., Mpls., 1977-78; products dir. Critikon, Inc., Raritan, N.J., 1979-80; v.p. mktg. Electro Biology, Inc., Fairfield, N.J., 1980-82; dir. sales, mktg. Medtronic/Med. Data Systems, Ann Arbor, Mich., 1982-85; v.p. corp. devel. Am. Biomaterials Corp., Princeton, N.J., 1985-86, sr. v.p., 1986-88; pres. Sandar Assocs., North Brunswick, N.J., 1980—; gen. mgr. Creative Care Sys., Maplewood, N.J., 1986-88; adj. prof. Middlesex Coll., Edison, N.J., 1987—; sales and mktg. staff Life Scis., Inc., Lebanon, N.H., 1988-90, Healthwatch, Inc., Vista, Calif., 1990-95, Lunar Corp., Madison, Wis., 1992-95, Norland Med. Systems, Fort Atkinson, Wis., 1995—, Norland Med. Sys.; lectr. dept. bus. Brookdale C.C., Bus. Week Mktg. Seminars, 1988, UN Soviet Econs. Mission, 1992; prof. mktg. Coll. S.I., CUNY, 1990—, chmn. bus. dept. curriculum adv. bd., 1995—; vis. prof. mktg. Montclair (N.J.) State U., 1992-94; vis. prof. Kingsborough Coll., 1995—. Author books; contbr. articles to profl. jours. Chmn. Marlboro (N.J.) Fire Commn., 1970-76; dir. Small Bus. Devel. Ctr. Middlesex County, 1988-91. Students in Free Enterprise fellow Walmart Found., 1992-95. Fellow Assn. Advancement Med. Instrumentation, Internat. Assn. Study of Pain; mem. Ann Arbor C. of C. (legis. com. 1981-84), NYU Alumni Assn. (dir. 1987-92), Travis Pointe County Club (Mich.), Princeton Club of N.Y. (program com.), NYU Clubm Forsgate County Club (v.p. 1986-91, house com. 1993—), Pi Lambda Phi. Home: 15 Wood Lake Ct North Brunswick NJ 08902

BARD, ENZO, molecular biologist, researcher; b. Luis Palacios, Santa Fe, Argentina, Oct. 18, 1938; came to U.S., 1972; s. Pablo and Sofia (Llernovoy) B.; m. Maria J. dos Reis, Jan. 6, 1965; children: Fabio D., Dario P., Hugo F. Pharmacist, La Plata Nat. U., 1960, PhD in Biochemistry, 1972. Head instr., dept. biochemistry La Plata (Argentina) Nat. Univ., 1966-72; rsch. assoc. Inst. Cancer Rsch. Fox Chase, Phila., 1972-74; rsch. cons. NYU Sch. of Medicine, N.Y.C.; vis. prof., dept. biology Univ. Ottawa, Ont., 1975-77; rsch. asst. prof. NYU Sch. of Medicine, N.Y.C., 1977-81; asst. prof. SUNY, Health Sci. Ctr. Coll. of Medicine, Bklyn., 1981-94, assoc. prof., 1994—; asst. prof. SUNY Health Sci. Ctr. Sch. Grad. Studies, Bklyn., 1983-94, assoc. prof., 1994—, dir. Lab. of Molecular diagnostics, 1995—. Contbr. chpts. to books and articles to Cell., Jour. Biol. Chemistry, Nucleic Acids Rsch., Jour. Cell Biology, Biochemistry and Cell Biology, Annals N.Y. Acad. Scis., Cell Vision. Recipient fellowship Damon Runyon Cancer Fund, Inst. for Cancer Rsch., 1972-74; rsch. grants Am. Cancer Soc., NYU Sch. of Medicine, 1979, SUNY Univ. Awards Program, SUNY Health Sci. Ctr. Bklyn., 1982, UNDP/World Bank/WHO, SUNY Health Sci. Ctr. Bklyn., 1985, Rsch. Found., SUNY Health Sci. Ctr. Bklyn., 1986. Mem. Am. Soc. for Cell Biology, Am. Soc. for Microbiology, N.Y. Acad. Scis. (chair biol. sci. 1989-90), Sigma Xi. Office: SUNY Health Sci Ctr Bklyn 450 Clarkson Ave Brooklyn NY 11203-2012

BARDACH, JOAN LUCILE, clinical psychologist; b. Albany, N.Y., Oct. 3, 1919; d. Monroe Lederer and Lucile May (Lowenberg) B. AB, Cornell U., 1940; AM in Psychology, NYU, 1951; PhD in Clin. Psychology, 1957; cert. in psychoanalysis and psychotherapy, NYU, 1970. Supr. clin. psychologist NYU Rusk Inst. Rehab. Medicine, 1959-61; asst. chief and acting chief psychologist Rusk Inst. Rehab. Medicine, 1962-65, dir. psychol. services, 1965-82; research psychologist, mem. faculty N.Y. Med. Coll., 1961-62; clin. prof. rehab. medicine (psychology) NYU, 1976—, supr. postdoctoral program psychoanalysis and psychotherapy, 1978—; pvt. practice clin. psychology and psychoanalysis N.Y.C., 1957—; non-govtl. orgn. rep. to UN Internat. Ctr. Sociol., Penal and Penitentiary Rsch. and Studies, Messina, Italy, 1985—; prin. investigator NIMH, 1976-81; mem. adv. bd. Coalition Sexuality and Disability, Planned Parenthood, 1983-89; cons. in field. Contbr. articles to profl. jours., chpt. to books. Recipient 3 awards for ednl. film, Choices: In Sexuality With Physical Disability, Internat. Film Festivals, Pioneer award for Sexual Attitude Reassessment Workshops The Coalition on Sexuality and Disability, 1989; NIMH fellow Inst. Sex Rsch., U. Ind., 1976. Fellow Am. Orthopsychiat. Assn.; mem. Am. Psychol. Assn., Am. Congress Rehab. Medicine, Sex Info. and Edn. Council U.S., Nat. Register Health Service Providers in Psychology, Eastern Psychol. Assn., N.Y. State Psychol. Assn. Home & Office: 50 E 10th St New York NY 10003-6223

BARDEN, ROBERT CHRISTOPHER, psychologist, educator, lawyer, public policy consultant; b. Richmond, Va., June 7, 1954; s. Elliott Hatcher and Jane Elizabeth Cole (Ferris) B.; m. Robin Jones, Nov. 14, 1987. BA summa cum laude, U. Minn., 1976, PhD in Clin. Psychology, 1982; postgrad., U. Calif., Berkeley, 1977; JD cum laude, Harvard U., 1992. Lic. consulting psychologist, Minn., Tex. Project asst. NSF, 1978-79; intern in psychology VA Med. Ctr., Stanford Med. Ctr., Palo Alto, Calif., 1979-80; dir. psychology Internat. Craniofacial Surg. Inst., Dallas, 1980-87; corp., civil litigation, family and health law atty. Lindquist and Vennum, Mpls., 1992—; asst. prof. psychology So. Meth. U., Dallas, 1980-84; asst. prof., dir. child clin. psychology U. Utah, Salt Lake City, 1984-87, rsch. faculty dept. surgery, 1987-93; vis. faculty, asst. prof. psychology Gustavus Adolphus Coll., St. Peter, Minn., 1988; pres. Optimal Performance Sys., Inc., Cambridge, 1989—; mem. Minn. Bd. Psychology, 1993—; adj. prof. law U. Minn. Law Sch.; cons. in field. Consulting editor Devel. Psychology, 1989; editor Harvard Jour. Law and Pub. Policy, 1990-91; contbr. to profl. publs. Project dir. ch. cmty. svc. projects, Mpls. and Cambridge, 1988—; mem. Minn. Bd. Psychology, 1993—, Higher Edn. Coordinating Bd., 1993-94; rep. Minn. Sixth Congl. Dist. Fellow NSF 1978, NIMH 1976, 77; Recipient Young Scholar award Found. for Child Devel., faculty scholar award W.T. Grant Found. 1987-89. Mem. ABA, APA, Soc. for Rsch. in Child Devel., Internat. Soc. Clin. Hypnosis, Harvard Law Sch. Soc. Law and Medicine, Lowell House Commons Rm. Harvard U., Nat.Assn. for Consumer Protection in Mental Health Practices (pres. 1995—), Sigma Xi, Phi Beta Kappa. Office: RC Barden & Assocs 4025 Quaker Lane N Plymouth MN 55441-1637

BARDIN, CLYDE WAYNE, biomedical researcher, developer of contraceptives; b. McCamey, Tex., Sept. 18, 1934; s. James A. and Nora Irene (Barnett) B.; m. Dorothy Kreiger, Aug. 11, 1978 (dec. Apr. 1985); m. Beatrice MacDonald, June 12, 1987; children: Charlotte E., Stephanie F. BA in Biology, Rice U., 1957; MS with honor, Baylor U., 1962, MD with honor, 1962; Docteur honoris cause, Université de Caen, France, 1990. Cert., licensed MD, Tex., Pa., N.Y. Resident in medicine N.Y. Hosp., N.Y.C., 1962-64; clin. assoc. NIH, Bethesda, Md., 1964-67, sr. investigator, 1967-70; assoc. prof. Milton S. Hershey Med. Ctr., Pa. State U., Hershey, 1970-72, prof. medicine, 1972-78; v.p. The Population Coun., N.Y.C., 1978-95; pres. Bardin LLC, a consulting co. to pharm. industry, banks and govts., 1996—; adj. prof. Rockefeller U., N.Y.C., 1978—, Cornell Med. Ctr., N.Y.C., 1985—; cons. WHO, 1972-73; chmn. bd. sci. counselors Nat. Inst. Child Health and Human Devel., Bethesda, 1982-83; chmn. endocrine study sect. NIH, Bethesda, 1977-79; mem. nat. prostate cancer task force Nat. Cancer Inst., 1973-78; endocrinologist Nat. Inst. Child Health and Human Devel., NIH, 1996—. Editor 13 books on medicine and endocrinology; mem. editl. bd. 16 sci. jours.; contbr. over 500 articles to sci. jours. Advisor internat. divsn. Ford Found., N.Y.C., 1975-79; bd. dirs. Harris and Harris Group, Inc., 1994—. Decorated Order of Comdr. of Lion (Finland); recipient Transatlantic medal Brit. Endocrine Socs., 1988; named fellow Josiah Macy Jr. Found., 1976-77, Disting. Alumnus Rice U., 1994, Disting. Alumnus N.Y. Hosp.-Cornell Med. Ctr., 1992. Mem. Am. Assn. Physicians, Am. Soc. Clin. Investigation, Am. Soc. Andrology (coun., v.p., pres. 1984-89, Serono award 1984, Disting. Andrologist award 1992), Endocrine Soc. (coun. 1976-79, pres. 1993-94, Sidney H. Ingbar Disting. Svc. award), Internat. Soc. Andrology (exec. coun. 1981-85), Internat. Assn. Axel Munthe Awards (bd. dirs. 1982-92), Internat. Com. Contraception Rsch. (chmn. 1978-95), Inst. Medicine. Democrat.

BARDWIL, MICHAEL FERRIS, general and vascular surgeon; b. Galveston, Tex., Feb. 21, 1955; s. John Michael and Mary Eileen (Mulholland) B.; m. Patricia Mary Langley, Dec. 13, 1986; children: Stephanie Anne, Travis Langley. AB, St. Louis U., 1977; MD, U. Tex., 1982. Diplomate Am. Bd. Surgery. Intern U. Tex. Med. Br., Galveston, 1982-83, resident in gen. surgery, 1983-88; fellow in vascular surgery Baylor Coll. Medicine, 1992-93; surgeon Kelsey Seybold Clinic, Houston, 1993—. Fellow ACS; mem. Southwestern Surg. Congress, Harris County Med. Soc., Houston Surg. Soc. Home: 4542 Nassau Dr Sugar Land TX 77479-2115 Office: Kelsey Seybold Clinic 6624 Fannin Houston TX 77030

BARE, JOSEPH LEE, microbiologist; b. San Angelo, Tex., Sept. 12, 1941; s. Leslie Thompson and June Grace (Tremble) B.; m. Betty Ann Dusek, Sept. 10, 1963; children: Joseph Lee II, Michael Edward. BA in Math., U. Tex., 1969, postgrad., 1975-79. Cert. clin. microbiologist. Lab. technician Tex. Dept. Health, Austin, 1963-69, microbiologist, 1969-82, chief of environ. microbiology, 1982-95, supr. lab. cert. br., 1995—; state milk, water, shellfish certification officer Tex. Dept. Health, Austin, 1982—. Mem. Am. Soc. Clin. Pathologists, Tex. Assn. Milk, Food and Environ. Sanitarians, Am. Waterworks Assn. Office: Tex Dept Health 1100 W 49th St Austin TX 78756-3101

BAREFOOT, BRENDA L., health facility administrator; b. Windber, Pa., Mar. 19, 1957; d. Gerald R. and Dorothy J. (Zimmerman) Mock; m. Arthur J. Barefoot, Aug. 19, 1978; 1 child, Joseph E. BSN, U. Pitts., 1979. Asst. adminstr., dir. nursing Pennknoll Village, Everett, Pa., 1980-85, adminstr., 1985-90; adminstr. Beacon Manor, Inc., Indiana, Pa., 1991, dir. quality assurance, 1991; mgmt. cons., dir. quality assurance Patriot Manor, Inc., Somerset, Pa., 1986—; owner, operator Bear's Den Lodge, Alban, Ont., Can., Barefoot's & Assocs., Alban, 1996—. Home: RR 1 Box 361 Alum Bank PA 15521-9667

BAREIS, DONNA LYNN, biochemist, pharmacologist; b. Abington, Pa., May 1, 1954; d. Walter Charles and Doris (Cameron) B.; m. Paul Joseph Amico, Jan. 24, 1981. BS in Biochemistry, Pa. State U., 1975; PhD in Pharmacology, Duke U., 1979. Staff fellow NIH, Bethesda, Md., 1979-81; pharmacologist U.S. Army Med. Rsch. Inst. Chem. Def., Aberdeen Proving Ground, Md., 1981-82; program mgr. U.S. Army C.E., Washington, 1982-83; sr. scientist Sci. Applications Internat. Corp., Joppa, Md., 1983-87; div. mgr. Sci. Applications Internat. Corp., Joppa, 1987-89; asst. v.p. Sci. Applications Internat. Corp., Frederick, Md., 1989-94, v.p., 1994—. Contbr. articles to sci. jours. Lighting designer Rockville (Md.) Musical Theater, 1980—; pres. Swan Point Condominium Assn., Columbia, Md., 1982-84. Mem. AAAS, Soc. for Risk Analysis, Cattail Creek Country Club (bd. dirs. 1995—), Sigma Xi. Home: 8805 Blue Sea Columbia MD 21046-1412

BARES, LUDEK FRANCIS, neurologist, consultant; b. Mlada Boleslav, Czech Republic, July 5, 1929; s. Francis and Ludmila (Kulhava) B.; m. Edith Kurzova, Dec. 4, 1954; children: Jindrich, Vilem. BA, Pekar Gymn. Coll., 1948; MD, Charles U., Prague, 1953, PhD in Med. Scis., 1984. Diplomate in neurology. Demonstrator, scientist Charles U. Sch. Medicine, 1951-52; resident, attending, vice head Regional Hosp., Carlsbad, 1953-57; head dept. Dist. Hosp., Rumburk, 1958-64, Prague-East, 1965-89; rsch. group leader Czech Acad. Scis., Prague, 1989-91; cons. dept. surgery Med. Sch., Prague, 1965-68, Dist. Hosp., Brandys, 1992—; sworn expert High Ct. of Justice, Prague, 1967—. Author: Cranio-vertebral Junction's Syndromes, 1990; co-author film; patentee. Mem. Am. Acad. Neurology (hon.), N.Y. Acad. Scis., Czech Neuroradiol. Soc. Roman Catholic. Home: Stara Boleslav, Stara Boleslav Czech Republic

BARGER, BARBARA ELAINE, medical and surgical nurse, nursing educator; b. Franklin, Pa., Oct. 11, 1952; d. Clarence Burton and Shirley Louise (Ream) Haylett; m. James Clair Barger, Oct. 25, 1986; 1 child, Jenny Lynn. AD, Clarion U.-Venango Campus, Oil City, Pa.; BA, Eastern Nazarene Coll., Wollaston, Mass. Instr. Palm Beach County Schs., Belle Glade, Fla.; charge nurse Franklin Regional Med. Ctr.; instr., PN coord. CCAVTS, Shippenville, Pa. Mem. Nat. League Nursing, Pa. Nurses Assn.

BARGER, BENJAMIN, psychologist; b. Zaire, Oct. 26, 1920; came to U.S., 1931; s. Gervase James and Myrtle Grace (King) B.; m. Marilyn Eloise McDaniel, Nov. 28, 1946; children: Lynn Marie Barger D'Louhy, Janette Arlene Barger Bledsoe, Karen Sue Barger Hunter. BA, George Washington U., 1947; PhD, Duke U., 1952. Diplomate Am. Bd. Profl. Psychology. Chief psychologist Mental Hygiene Clinic Ohio State U., Columbus, 1952-55, instr. dept. psychiatry, 1953-55, asst. prof., 1955-59, lectr. dept. psychology, 1956-58, guest lectr. Sch. Social Adminstrn., 1957-59; dir. psychol. svc. Columbus Psychiat. Inst. and Hosp., 1955-59; co-dir. to dir. mental health project U. Fla., Gainesville, 1959-65, dir., 1965-71, co-dir. spl. tng. project, 1970-74, lectr. dept. psychology, 1960-65, prof. dept. psychology, 1965-85, prof. clin. psychology, 1974-85, prof. emeritus, 1985—; cons. Project on Student Devel. in Small Colls., Plainfield, Vt., 1964-69; reviewer Juvenile Problems Rsch. Rev. Com., NIMH, Bethesda, Md., 1968-71; mem. adv. bd. Strategies for Change, Empire State Coll., Saratoga Springs, N.Y., 1970-74; cons. Memphis State U. Ctr. Higher Edn., Memphis, 1979-83. Contbr. chpts. to books. Staff sgt. U.S. Army, 1943-46, ETO. Project grantee NIMH, U. Fla., 1961-65, 65-70, 70-74. Fellow APA (divs. community psychology and population and environ. psychology 1970—); mem. Assn. Psychol. Type (sec., treas. S.E. div. 1986-89), Southeastern Psychol. Assn., Fla. Psychol. Assn. Democrat. Methodist. Home: 3029 NW 2nd Ave Gainesville FL 32607-2505

BARGER, JAMES DANIEL, physician; b. Bismarck, N.C., May 17, 1917; s. Michael Thomas and Mayte (Donohue) B.; m. Susie Belle Helm, 1945 (dec. 1951); m. Josephine Steiner, 1952 (dec. 1971); m. Jane Ray Regan, Apr. 21, 1980 (dec. Feb. 1991); children: James Daniel, Mary Susan, Michael Thomas, Mary Elizabeth. Student, St. Mary's Coll., Winona, Minn., 1934-35; A.B., U. N.D., 1939, B.S., 1939; M.D., U. Pa., 1941; M.S. in Pathology, U. Minn., 1949. Diplomate Am. Bd. Pathology; registered quality engr., Calif. Intern. Milw. County Hosp., Wauwatosa, Wis., 1941-42; fellow in pathology Mayo Found., Rochester, Minn., 1941-49; pathologist Pima County Hosp., Tucson, 1949-50, Maricopa County Hosp., Phoenix, 1950-51; chmn. dept. pathology Good Samaritan Hosp., 1951-63; assoc. pathologist Sunrise Hosp., Las Vegas, Nev., 1964-69, chief pathology dept., 1969-81, sr. pathologist, 1981—; former med. dir. S.W. Blood Bank, Blood Services, Ariz., Blood Services Nev.; treas. Commn. for Lab. Assessment, 1988; emeritus clin. prof. pathology U. Nev. Sch. Medicine, 1988. Served to maj. AUS, 1942-46. Recipient Sioux award U. N.D. Alumni Assn., 1975; recipient disting. physician award NSMA, 1983; ASCP-CAP Disting. Service award, 1985. Mem. AAAS, AMA, Am. Assn. Pathologists, Am. Assn. Clin. Chemists, Am. Assn. History Medicine, Coll. Am. Pathologists (gov. 1966-72, sec.-treas. 1971-79, v.p. 1979-81, pres. 1980-81, historian 1988—, Pathologist of Yr. 1977), Nev. Soc. Pathologists (AMA del. 1990), Am. Assn. Blood Banks, Am. Soc. Quality Control (sr. mem.), Am. Mgmt. Assn., Soc. Advancement Mgmt., Am. Soc. Clin. Pathologists, Am. Cancer Soc. (nat. dir. 1974-80), Nat. Acad. Practice Medicine (dist. practitioner 1984—, del. AMA Ho. Dels. 1989—), others. Lodge: Knights of St. Lazarus (comdr. 1983). Home: 1307 Canosa Ave Las Vegas NV 89104-3132 Office: 3196 S Maryland Pky # 405 Las Vegas NV 89109-2306

BARIE, PHILIP STEVEN, surgeon, educator; b. Buffalo, Aug. 18, 1953; s. Kenneth George and Eleanor Lucille (Davis) B.; m. Elaine Catherine Dash, May 31, 1981; children: Catherine, Steven, Alexandra. AB cum laude, MD, Boston U., 1977. Diplomate and surgical critical care cert. Am. Bd. Surgery. Jr. resident in surgery N.Y. Hosp.-Cornell Med. Ctr., N.Y.C., 1977-79; fellow in surgery and physiology Albany (N.Y.) Med. Coll., 1979-81; sr. resident in surgery N.Y. Hosp.-Cornell Med. Ctr., 1981-83, adminstrv. chief resident surgery, 1983-84; asst. prof. surgery Cornell U. Med. Coll., N.Y.C., 1984-89, assoc. prof., 1989—; attending surgeon, dir. surg ICU, N.Y. Hosp., N.Y.C., 1984—; cons. in surgery Cath. Med. Ctr., N.Y.C., 1985—; chmn. inst. rev. bd. Med. Coll. Cornell U., N.Y.C., 1988-92; cons. specialist, mem. med. control bd. Health Ins. Plan Greater N.Y., 1990—; cons. in critical care therapeutics U.S. Pharmacopeial Conv., 1991—. Co-editor: Surgical Intensive Care, 1993 (Best New Book in Med Scis. Assn. Am. Pubs. 1994); contbr. articles to profl. jours. Fellow ACS, Am. Coll. Critical Care Medicine; mem. N.Y. Acad. Medicine (sec. surg. sect. 1991-92), N.Y. Surg. Soc. (coun. mem.-at-large 1995—), Soc. Critical Care Medicine (sec.-treas. surg. sect. 1995-96, chair-elect surg. sect. 1996—), Am. Thoracic Soc., Am. Assn. for Surgery of Trauma (Peter C. Canizaro award 1992), Internat. Surg. Soc., Am. Physiol. Soc., Soc. Univ. Surgeons, N.Y. State Soc. Surgeons (bd. dirs. 1992—, sec. 1995—), N.Y. Acad. Scis., Surg. Infection Soc. (mem. coun. 1994—), Assn. for Acad. Surgery, Shock Soc., Ea. Assn. for Surgery of Trauma (bd. dirs. 1996—), Am. Med. Writers Assn. Office: NY Hosp-Cornell Med Ctr Dept Surgery 525 E 68th St New York NY 10021-4873

BARIK, SUDHAKAR, microbiologist, research scientist; b. Sainkula, Orissa, India, Aug. 14, 1949; came to U.S., 1980; s. Ananda Chandra and Sakhamani (Behera) B.; m. Dharashri Behera, Mar. 4, 1979; children: Santwana, Sambit. BSc, Utkal U., Orissa, 1972, MSc, 1974, PhD, 1979. Postdoctoral fellow U. Okla., 1980-82; rsch. assoc. U. Ill., Urbana, 1982-84, U. Ark., Fayetteville, 1984-87; asst. prin. scientist Atlantic Rsch. Corp., Alexandria, Va., 1987-88; prin. scientist, group leader ARCTECH, Inc., Chantilly, Va., 1988-92; sr. devel. microbiologist Lederle Labs. Am. Cyanamid Co., Pearl River, N.Y., 1992-94; group leader process devel. Wyeth-Lederle Vaccines and Pediat. Home Products, Inc., Pearl River, 1994—. Contbr. articles to profl. jours., chpts. to books. Fund raiser PTA, Annandale, Va., 1987-92; sci. fair judge for high schs., Annandale and Alexandria, 1987-92. Mem. AAAS, Am. Soc. Microbiology, Soc. Indsl. Microbiology. Home: 8 Ambrey Ln Thiells NY 10984-1608 Office: Lederle Labs 401 N Middletown Rd Pearl River NY 10965

BARIL, NANCY ANN, gerontological nurse practitioner, consultant; b. Paterson, N.J., May 10, 1952; d. Kenneth Gerald and Jeanette Elenore (Girodet) Keiser; m. Joel Mark Baril, Apr. 15, 1984; children: Jason Kenneth, Jennifer Jean. AA, Gulf Coast C.C., 1976; BS in Nursing, Fla. State U., 1978; M in Nursing, UCLA, 1983. Registered pub. health nurse, Calif.; ANA cert. gerontol. nurse practitioner. Charge nurse, nurse preceptor Cedar Sinai Med. Ctr., L.A., 1979-83; RN Nursing Svcs. Incorp., Sherman Oaks, Calif., 1980-83; nurse practitioner Santa Monica Peer Counseling Ctr., Santa Monica, Calif., 1983; nurse cons., gerontol. nurse practioner Summit Health Ltd., Burbank, Calif., 1983-85; nurse cons. Geriatric Assocs., Granada Hills, Calif., 1983-85; nurse cons., gerontol. nurse practitioner Care Enterprises West, Burbank, 1985-86; patient svcs. coord., gerontol. nurse practitioner ARA Living Ctrs., Glendale, Calif., 1986-87; DON, gerontol. nurse practitioner Astoria Convalescent Hosp. Sign of the Dove, Sylmar, Calif., 1988-91;

gerontol. nurse practitioner Balboa Plz. Med. Group, 1991—. Mem. PTA, Granada Hills, 1985. Mem. ANA, Calif. Coalition of Nurse Practioners, Calif. Nursing Assn., Gerontol. Soc., Sigma Theta Tau (rec. sec. 1983-85). Democrat. Episcopalian. Avocations: reading, crossword puzzles, gardening, jet-skiing. Home: 17831 Tuscan Dr Granada Hills CA 91344-1094 Office: Balboa Med Group 10605 Balboa Blvd Ste 200 Granada Hills CA 91344

BARISH, CHARLES FRANKLIN, internist, gastroenterologist, educator; b. Franklin, N.J., Jan. 5, 1955; s. Philip and Laura (Freedman) B.; m. Debrah Lee Kaufman, Aug. 13, 1977; children: Philip, Stefanie, Jacob. BS in Chemistry with high honors, U. Fla., 1976, MD, 1980. Bd. cert. diplomate Am. Bd. Internal Medicine with added qualifications in gastroenterology. Resident, fellow Bowman Gray Sch. Medicine, Winston-Salem, N.C., 1980-85; physician Wake Internal Medicine Cons., Raleigh, N.C., 1985—; pres. Wake Rsch. Assocs., Raleigh, 1985—; clin. asst., prof. medicine U. N.C. Sch. Medicine, Chapel Hill, 1985—; chmn. nutritional care com. Rex Hosp., Raleigh, 1987—. Author: (book chpt.) Gastroesophageal Reflux Disease, 1985; contbr. articles to med. jours. Pres. Jewish Comty. Ctr., Raleigh, 1995—; v.p. Jewish Fedn. Greater Raleigh, 1993—. Fellow ACP, Am. Coll. Gastroenterology; mem. AMA, Am. Gastroenterol. Assn., Am. Coll. Physician Execs., Am. Soc. Gastrointestinal Endoscopy, N.C. Med. Socs., Wake County Med. Socs., Crohn's and Colitis Found. Am., Am. Liver Found., B'nai Brith, Alpha Omega Alpha, Phi Kappa Phi, Alpha Epsilon Delta. Office: Wake Internal Medicine Cons Ste 300 3100 Blue Ridge Rd Raleigh NC 27612

BARISH, JULIAN I., psychiatrist; b. Sault Ste Marie, Mich., Mar. 12, 1917; s. Max and Nancy Barish; m. Judith Sophian, June 7, 1941; children: Richard K., Patricia L. Speckert. AB, U. Mich., 1938, MD, 1941, MS, 1948; cert. in psychoanalysis, Columbia U., 1955. Diplomate Am. Bd. Psychiatry and Neurology. Intern Bridgeport Hosp., Bridgeport, Conn., 1941-42; resident psychiatry Neuropsychiat. Inst., U. Mich. Med. Ctr., Ann Arbor, 1946-48; fellow in psychiatry, instr. psychiatry N.Y. Hosp.-Cornell Med. Ctr., N.Y.C., 1948-56; pvt. practice psychiatry and psychoanalysis N.Y.C., Larchmont, N.Y., 1949—; candidate, preceptor, collaborating psychoanalyst Columbia U. Psychoanalytic Ctr., N.Y.C., 1949-57, 72-77; asst. prof. psychiatry Grad. Sch. Psychiatry, Downstate Med. Ctr., Bklyn., 1956-58; co-founder, co-dir. The Psychiat. Treatment Ctr., N.Y.C., 1961-68; chief adolescent svc. Four Winds Hosp., Katonah, N.Y., 1968-70; assoc. clin. prof. psychiatry Mt. Sinai Med. Ctr., N.Y.C., 1974—; mem. nat. bd. Soc. for Sci. Study of Sex, N.Y.C., 1978-80; councillor Westchester Psychiat. Soc., White Plains, N.Y., 1971-73; chmn. com. on adolescent care Nat. Assn. Pvt. Psychiat. Hosps., Washington, 1965-68. Contbr. articles to profl. jours. Panelist youth conf. Westchester Citizens Com., Nat. Coun. on Crime & Delinquency Jr. Leagues, Scarsdale, N.Y., 1967; del. White House Conf. on Youth, Estes Park, Colo., 1971; participant Spl. Action Office for Drug Abuse Prevention, Conf. on Youth Oriented Drug Programs, Washington, 1972; prin. speaker Riveredge Hosp. Conf. on Hosp. Treatment Adolescents, Forest Park, Ill., 1968. Major Med. Corps, U.S. Army, 1942-46, ETO. Recipient Richard L. Frank M.D. Meml. award for Disting. Leadership in Adolescent Psychiatry, 1996. Fellow Am. Soc. Adolescent Psychiatry (life, pres. 1975-76), Am. Psychiat. Assn. (life, vice chmn. coun. on nat. affairs and social issues 1972-74); mem. AMA (life), Am. Psychoanalytic Assn. (life, cert.), Am. Acad. Psychoanalysis (life). Home and Office: 17 E 93rd St Apt A New York NY 10128-0667

BARKER, BARBARA YVONNE, respiratory therapist; b. Whittier, Calif., Apr. 19, 1951; d. Donald Wayne and Ruth Berta (Hagen) Schutt; m. Jimmy D.W. McWilson, Feb. 23, 1974 (div. Sept. 1980); m. Richard Alexander Barker, Aug. 01, 1987; 1 child, Christina Nicole. AS in Respiratory Therapy, Mt. San Antonio Coll., Walnut, Calif., 1971; BS in Bus. Adminstrn., U. Redlands, 1989; MPA, Marist Coll., 1996. Lic. nursing home adminstr., Calif.; registered respiratory therapist; lic. respiratory care practitioner. Neonatal respiratory therapist U. Calif.-San Diego Med. Ctr., 1971-74; respiratory therapy supr. Hillside Hosp., 1974-75; asst. dir. ops. J.D.W. McWilson and Assocs., 1975-77; sales rep. Baxter-Travenol Home Respiratory Therapy, 1984-86; clin. application specialist Infrasonics, Inc., 1987-88; respiratory therapist/clin. coord., nursing home adminstr. Sharp Health Care, 1977-84, 88-90; nursing home adminstr. Care West Anza, 1990, Brighton Pl. Spring Valley, San Diego, 1990-91; dir. respiratory care No. Dutchess Hosp., Rhinebeck, N.Y., 1991—; cons. health care delivery systems various acute and long term care orgns., Dutchess County, N.Y., 1991—; developer quality assurance program long term care facility, San Diego, 1990; med. products researcher devel. neonatal ventilator device FDA, San Diego, 1988; coord. regional healthcare seminar, Dutchess County, Marist Coll. Author quality assurance protocol durable med. equipment cos., San Diego Am. Lung Assn., 1989; developer instrnl. manuals for patients with chronic lung disease and asthma, San Diego, 1990. Bd. mem. San Diego chpt. Calif. Assn. Health Facilities, 1990-91; participant Christmas in April civic rebldg. program, Poughkeepsie, N.Y., 1992-93. Mem. Am. Assn. Respiratory Therapy, Calif. Soc. Respiratory Therapy (treas., bd. mem., edn. developer 1986-90), Calif. Assn. Health Facilities, Mid Hudson Repiratory Care Dirs. Assn. Democrat. Lutheran. Home: 2 Birch Hill Dr Poughkeepsie NY 12603-6132 Office: No Dutchess Hosp 10 Springbrook Ave Rhinebeck NY 12572-1115

BARKER, BEN D., dentist, educator; b. Burlington, N.C., Dec. 19, 1931; married; 3 children. BS, Davidson Coll., 1954; DDS, U. N.C., 1958; MEd, Duke U. From instr. to assoc. prof. fixed prosthodontics U. N.C., Chapel Hill, 1958-65, assoc. prof. preventive dentistry and dental sci., 1965-69, asst. dean, 1968-69, prof., assoc. dean, 1969-75, prof., dean Sch. Dentistry, 1981-89, prof. dept. dental ecol. Sch. Dentistry, 1989—; program dir. W. K. Kellogg Found., 1975-81; mem. Coun. Internat. Rels., 1979-83, Bd. Health Care Svc., NAS, 1987—, Comty. Estate Rsch. Agenda Aging and Comty. Health Prom. & Disability Rev., 1988-90; vis. prof. New Cross Hosp., London, 1972-73. Fellow Am. Coll. Dentists, Internat. Coll. Dentists; mem. ADA (mem. coun. dental edn. 1971—), Inst. Medicine-NAS. Office: U NC Sch Dentistry 310 Braver Hall CB 7450 Chapel Hill NC 27599-7450*

BARKER, CLYDE FREDERICK, surgeon, educator; b. Salt Lake City, Aug. 16, 1932; s. Frederick George and Jennetta Elizabeth (Stephens) B.; m. Dorothy Joan Bieler, Aug. 11, 1956; children: Frederick George II, John Randolph, William Stephens, Elizabeth Dell. BA, Cornell U., 1954, MD, 1958. Diplomate Am. Bd. Surgery. Intern Hosp. U. Pa., Phila., 1958-59, resident in surgery, 1959-64, fellow in vascular surgery, 1964-65; fellow in med. genetics U. Pa. Sch. Medicine, Phila., 1965-66, assoc. in surgery, 1964-68, assoc. in med. genetics, 1966-72; attending surgeon Hosp. U. Pa., Phila., 1966—; chief div. transplantation U. Pa. Sch. Medicine, Phila., 1966—, asst. prof. surgery, 1968-69, assoc. prof. surgery, 1969-73, prof. surgery, 1973—, J. William White prof. surg. research, 1978-82, chief div. vascular surgery, 1982—, Guthrie prof. surgery, 1982—, John Rhea Barton prof. surgery, 1983—, chmn. dept. surgery, 1983—; chief surgery Hosp. U. Pa., Phila., 1983—; dir. Harrison Dept. Surgery research U. Pa., Phila., 1983—; mem. immunobiology study sect. NIH; chmn. clin. practices U. Pa., 1987-89. Mem. editl. bd. Jour. Transplantation, 1977—, Clin. Transplantation, 1988—, Jour. Surg. Rsch., 1979-85, Jour. Diabetes, 1981-86, Archives of Surgery, 1987—, Transplantation Procs., 1990—, Surgery, 1991-95, Cell Transplantation, 1991—, Postgrad. Gen. Surgery, 1991-95, Jour. ACS, 1994—, Annals of Surgery, 1995—; contbr. articles to profl. jours. and textbooks. Markle Found. Scholar, 1968-74; NIH grantee, 1974—; recipient Merit award NIH, 1987-95. Fellow AOA, NAS (Inst. Medicine), ACS (com. Forum on Fundamental Surg. Problems 1983-88, vice chmn. 1987-88, bd. govs. 1994—, pres. Phila. chpt. 1991-92), Coll. Physicians Phila.; mem. AMA, Assn. Acad. Surgery, Am. Diabetes Assn., Am. Soc. Artificial Internal Organs, Am. Fedn. Clin. Rsch., Juvenile Diabetes Found., Soc. Univ. Surgeons, Am. Surg. Assn. (recorder 1991-96, pres. 1996-97), Soc. Clin. Surgery (chmn. membership 1984-85), Halsted Soc. (chmn. membership 1984-85, v.p. 1985-86, pres. 1986-87), Surg. Biology Club II, Soc. Vascular Surgery, Internat. Cardiovascular Soc., Internat. Surg. Group (treas. 1988-94, pres. 1994-95), Internat. Soc. Surgery (v.p. U.S. chpt. 1995-97), Transplantation Soc. (councilman 1978-84, 94—), Am. Soc. Transplant Surgeons (chmn. membership 1980-81, treas. 1988-91, pres. 1992-93), Am. Acad. Arts and Scis., Assn. Am. Physicians, Phila. Acad. Surgery (program chmn. 1984-86, v.p. 1986-88, pres. 1988-89), Greater Del. Valley Soc. Transplant Surgeons (pres. 1978-80). Home: 3 Coopertown Rd Haverford PA 19041-1012 Office: Hosp Univ Pa Dept Surgery 3400 Spruce St Philadelphia PA 19104

BARKER, EDWARD ALLAN, pathologist; b. Indpls., June 24, 1938; s. Don Allan and Gladys Mercer (Hazel) B.; m. Nancy Laura Whittles, June 10, 1960 (dec. May 1979); children: Lauri Allyn Cikatz, Melanie K. Briggs, Donna Lynn Johnson; m. Cara Lee Stack, Aug. 15, 1980; 1 child, Brandy Noel. BA in Zoology, U. Wash., 1960, MD, 1964, PhD in Exptl. Pathology, 1970; postgrad. in biophysics, U. Rochester, N.Y., 1964-66. Diplomate Am. Bd. Pathology. Asst. prof. pathology U. Wash., Seattle, 1970-76, assoc. prof., 1976-83; staff pathologist Group Health Cooperative, Seattle, 1983-85, St. Joseph Hosp., Denver, 1985-88; med. dir. Molecular Oncology, Inc., Gaithersburg, Md., 1988-93; v.p. med. affairs Oncogenetics, Inc., Phoenix, 1993-95; sr. pathologist Dianon Systems, Inc., Stratford, Conn., 1995—; cons. cytology and dermatopathology Pathology Assocs., Spokane, Wash., 1981-83. Contbr. articles to profl. jours. Soccer field construction com. King County Govt., Bellevue, Wash., 1975. Surgeon USPHS, 1966-68. Nat. Cancer Inst. Cytology Edn. grantee, 1980, Cancer Rsch. fellow, 1968. Fellow Coll. Am. Pathologists; mem. Internat. Acad. Pathology. Home: 7720 44th Ave NE Seattle WA 98115 Office: Molecular Oncology INc 414 Pontius Ave N Ste E Seattle WA 98109

BARKER, HAROLD GRANT, surgeon; b. Salt Lake City, June 10, 1917; s. Frederick George and Jennetta (Stephens) B.; m. Kathleen Butler, July 29, 1949; children: Janet Stephens, Douglas Reid. A.B., U. Utah, 1939, postgrad., 1939-41; M.D., U. Pa., 1943. Diplomate Am. Bd. Surgery. Intern. Hosp. U. Pa., 1943-44, asst. resident in surgery, 1947-51, sr. resident in surgery, 1951-52, asst. attending surgeon, 1952-53; also asst. instr., research fellow U. Pa., 1946-51, instr., research fellow, 1951-52, assoc. in surgery, 1952-53; asst. prof. surgery Columbia U., 1953-57, assoc. prof., 1957-68, prof., 1968-82, prof. emeritus, 1982—; asst. attending surgeon Presbyn. Hosp., 1953-57, assoc. attending surgeon, 1957-69, attending surgeon, 1969-89, cons. surgeon, 1989—, dir. med. affairs, 1974-82; pvt. practice, Phila., 1952-53, N.Y.C., 1953-88. Contbr. articles med. jours. Served from 1st lt. to capt., M.C. AUS, 1944-46, ETO. Fellow ACS; mem. Soc. U. Surgeons, N.Y. Surg. Soc., Am. Physiol. Soc., Soc. Exptl. Biology and Medicine, AMA, Halsted Soc., N.Y. State (chmn. surg. sect. 1961-62), N.Y. County med. socs., Am. Surg. Assn., N.Y. Gastroent. Assn., Société Internationale de Chirurgie, Soc. Surgery Alimentary Tract, Allen O. Whipple Surg. Soc., Am. Assn. History Medicine, Collegium Internationale Chirurgiae Digestivae. Republican. Presbyn. Clubs: Century Assn; Manursing Island (Rye, N.Y.); Am. Yacht. Home: 1 Forest Ave Rye NY 10580-4209

BARKER, JANE ELLEN, research biologist; b. Bangor, Maine, June 2, 1935; d. David Emmons and Eleanor (Stockman (Herrick) B. BA, U. Maine, 1957; MA, Wellesley Coll., 1959; PhD, U. Wis., 1967. Rsch. asst. Wellesley (Mass.) Coll., 1959-61; staff scientist Inst. Cancer Rsch., Putnam Meml. Hosp., Bennington, Vt., 1969-72; sr. staff fellow Nat Heart, Lung and Blood Inst., Bethesda, Md., 1972-77, sr. investigator, 1977-80; postdoctoral fellow Jackson Lab., Bar Harbor, Maine, 1967-69, staff scientist, 1980-92; sr. staff scientist Jackson Lab., Bar Harbor, 1992—, assoc. dir. for rsch., 1991-93. Contbr. numerous articles to profl. jours., chpts. to books. Mem. Am. Soc. Hematology, Am. Soc. Cell Biology, Soc. for Devel. Biology, Sigma Xi. Office: Jackson Lab Bar Harbor ME 04609

BARKER, MARTHA SMITH, retired mental health nurse; b. Columbia, S.C., Mar. 30, 1935; d. Lonnie Edward and Virginia Fairey (Faulkner) Smith; 1 child, Michele de Calverhall. BS in Nursing with honors, Med. U. S.C., 1980; M in Nursing, U. S.C., 1988. Instr. Med. U. S.C. Sch. Nursing, Charleston, 1960-67; asst. prof./dir. practical nurse program & ADN program Med. U. S.C. Coll. Allied Health Scis., Charleston, 1967-85; dir. nursing edn., staff devel. S.C. Dept. Mental Health, Columbia, 1985-93; retired, 1993, con. in psychiat. nursing issues, 1993—. Home: 164 Court Inn Ln Camden SC 29020

BARKER, ROBERT LOUIS, physician; b. Okinawa, Japan, Dec. 28, 1952; came to the U.S., 1953; s. Robert and Konnie (Maemori) B.; m. Ann D. Hutchinson, Dec. 28, 1975; children: Tanya, Trisha, Justin. BA, Andrews U., 1975; MD, Loma Linda U., 1978. Bd. cert. in internal medicine and critical care medicine. Resident internal medicine Kettering (Ohio) Med. Ctr., 1979-81; fellow in critical care Meml. Sloan Kettering Cancer Ctr., N.Y.C., 1982; assoc. program dir. internal medicine Kettering (Ohio) Med. Ctr., 1983—; pvt. practice South Dayton (Ohio) Acute Care Cons., Inc., 1983—, pres., 1987—; v.p., med. staff Kettering (Ohio) Med. Ctr., 1996. Founding mem. Found. for Critical Care, Washington, 1988; mem. Rep. Senatorial Inner Circle, Washington, 1991-95; chmn. computer integration Spring Valley Acad., Centerville, Ohio, 1994-96; pres. club mem. The Heritage Found., Washington, 1994-96. Clara Wiffenbach fellow Kettering (Ohio) Med. Ctr., 1982. Fellow ACP, Am. Coll. Critical Care Medicine, Am. Coll. Chest Physicians; mem. AMA, Am. Soc. Parenteral and Enteral Nutrition. Seventh-day Adventist. Office: S Dayton Acute Care Cons 33 W Rahn Rd Dayton OH 45429

BARKER, THOMAS CARL, health care administration educator, executive; b. Cedar Rapids, Iowa, May 25, 1931; s. Carl Edward and Bertha Olive (Simons) B.; m. Mary Irene Beorkrem, Sept. 1, 1952 (dec. 1995); children: Cheryl Lynn, Thomas Carl Jr. (dec.), Laura Ann, David Edward Student, Loras Coll., 1949-50, Coe Coll., 1950-51; BS, U. Iowa, 1954, MA, 1960, PhD, 1963. Acct. Wilson & Co., Cedar Rapids, Iowa, 1951-54; contract adminstr. Collins Radio Co., Cedar Rapids, 1956-57; with customer rels. The Cryovac Co., Cedar Rapids, 1957-58; bus. officer Mercy Hosp., Iowa City, Iowa, 1958-59; rsch. asst. U. Iowa, 1959-60, tchg. asst., 1961-63, asst. prof., 1963-64; adminstrv. assoc. U. Iowa Hosp., 1960-62; rsch. assoc. UAW Internat. Union, Detroit, 1964-67; dir. Mich. Health and Social Security Rsch. Inst., Detroit, 1964-67; lectr. health econs. Wayne State U., Detroit, 1966-67; Arthur Graham Glasgow prof., dir. Sch. Hosp. Adminstrn. Med Coll. Va., Richmond, 1967-71; prof., dean and CEO Sch. Allied Health Professions, Va. Commonwealth U., Richmond, 1969—; mem. com. on allied health edn. and accreditation AMA, chmn. com., 1988-91; served as mem. or cons. to various pub. health svcs., including NIH, Health Resources Adminstrn., VA, HEW agys.; mem. dean's com. VA Med. Ctr., Richmond, 1974—; mem. Ctrl. Va. Health Sys. Agy., 1976-88, pres., 1979-80; mem. Va. Health Coord. Coun., 1986-88. Contbr. articles to profl. jours. With USN, 1954-56; capt. Res., ret. Named Hon. Alumni, Med. Coll. Va. Fellow APHA, Am. Soc. Allied Health Professions (pres. 1975-76); mem. Am. Health Planning Assn., Assn. Univ. Programs in Health Adminstrn., Soc. Sons. Revolution in State of Va., Va. Assn. Allied Health Professions, Va. Hosp. Assn., Rotary (pres. Richmond club 1991-92), Phi Kappa Phi. Roman Catholic. Home: 4516 Croatan Rd Richmond VA 23235-1122 Office: 1200 E Broad St Richmond VA 23298-0233

BARKER, WILLIAM DANIEL, hospital administrator; b. New Orleans, July 21, 1926; s. William Daniel and Ada (Will) B.; m. Nancy Pool, Sept. 23, 1949; children: Nancy Louise, Julia Ann, William Daniel III, Marion DeVilbiss. B in Bus. Adminstrn., Emory U., 1949; M in Hosp. Adminstrn., Ga. State U., 1966. Bus. office mgr. Emory U. Hosp., Atlanta, 1949-50; asst. adminstr. Griffin (Ga.) Spalding County Hosp., 1950-51; adminstr. Winder-Barrow (Ga.) Hosp., 1951-52; hosp. field rep. Ga. Dept. Pub. Health, Atlanta, 1952-54, hosp. cons., 1954-55; asst. adminstr. Tri-County Hosp., Ft. Oglethorpe, Ga., 1955-60; asst. dir. Crawford Long Hosp. Emory U., Atlanta, 1960-73, adminstr., 1973-84, dir. hosps., 1984-90, exec. dir. hosp., 1987-90; ret., 1991; prof. Emory U., Atlanta, 1988-93; bd. dirs. Ga. Fed. Bank, Atlanta, Blue Cross Blue Shield Ga., Inc.; provider affairs com. Blue Cross Blue Shield Assn., United Network for Organ Sharing, bd. dirs., 1991—; bd. govs. SunHealth, Charlotte, N.C., chmn., 1988-89; bd. commrs. Joint Commn. on Accreditation of Healthcare Orgns., 1981-86; v.p. Greater Atlanta Coalition on Health Care, 1983-84; mem. Gov.'s Coun. Malpractice Ins., 1975-83, Medicaid Adv. Com. Ga. Dept. Human Resources, 1973-77, Health Facilities Planning Com. Met. Atlanta Coun. for Health, 1971-74, Atlanta Regional Commn. Emergency Med. Task Force 1969-73, Gov.'s Commn. on Nursing, 1970-71, adv. commn. Internat. Implant Registry, 1989—, vice-chmn., 1991, chmn., 1992; pres. Health Careers of Ga., Inc., 1969-70, Ga. Coun. Paramed. Edn., 1968. Contbr. articles to profl. jours. With U.S. Army, 1944-46. Recipient R.C. Williams award Ga. State U., 1966, Disting. Alumni award, Ga. State U., 1979, Disting. Svc. award. Ga. Med. Assn. Atlanta, 1980; Disting. Guest Lectr. Ga. State U., 1978. Fellow Am. Coll. Healthcare Execs. (regent 1972-75); mem. Am. Hosp. Assn. (chmn. 1979, Speaker of Ho. 1980, Disting. Svc. award 1987), Ga. Hosp. Assn. (pres. 1966-79, Gold Honor award of Excellence 1980), Ansley Golf Club. Baptist. Home: 50 S Prado St NE Atlanta GA 30309-3309

BARKHAUS, PAUL EDWARD, neurologist, electromyographer; b. Detroit, May 8, 1949; s. Edward R. and Virginia A. (Kuhn) B. BS in Biology, Wayne State U., 1972, MD, 1975. Diplomate Am. Bd. Psychiatry and Neurology, Am. Bd. Electrodiagnostic Medicine. Resident in neurology Wayne State U., Detroit, 1975-78; electromyography fellow U. Minn., Mpls., 1978-79; neuromuscular fellow U. Ariz., Tucson, 1979-80; asst. prof. in neurology U. Cin., 1980-85; assoc. in medicine (neurology) Duke U., Durham, N.C., 1986-87; asst. prof. in neurology U. Minn., Mpls., 1987-93; assoc. prof. of neurology Med. Coll. Wis., Milw., 1993—; ad hoc reviewer Muscle & Nerve, 1989—. Contbr. articles to Archives of Neurology, Muscle & Nerve, New Eng. Jour. Medicine, Electoencephalography & Clin. Neurophysiology. Mem. med. adv. bd. Wis. chpt. Myasthenia Gravis Found. Recipient Disting. Svc. award Wayne State U. Sch. of Medicine, 1975, Trainee award, Fed. of Western Socs. of Neurol. Scis., 1980; named Alumni Hall of Fame, Allen Park High Sch., 1987. Fellow Am. Acad. Neurology; mem. Minn. Med. Assn., Minn. Soc. Neurol. Scis., Am. Assn. Electrodiagnostic Medicine. Office: Neurology 127 Milwaukee VAMC Milwaukee WI 53295

BARKHUUS, ARNE, physician; b. Copenhagen, Aug. 24, 1906; came to U.S., 1937, naturalized, 1972; s. Carl and Alma (Langkilde) B.; m. Anneli von dem Hagen, Jan. 1941 (dec. 1947); m. Adda von Bruemmer, Feb. 1951. B.A., U. Copenhagen, 1926, M.D., 1933; postgrad., London Sch. Hygiene and Tropical Medicine, 1934, 36-37; Dr.P.H., Johns Hopkins U., 1938. Intern, then resident Blegdamshosp., Copenhagen, 1934, 36; med. officer Brit. Red Cross in Ethiopia, 1935-36; adviser Ministry Health, Caracas, Venezuela, 1938-39; lectr. dept. hygiene U. Calif. at Berkeley, 1940-42; mem. Milbank Meml. Fund, 1942-44; pub. health expert U.S. Fgn. Econ. Adminstrn. Mission to Ethiopia, 1944-45; cons. Def. Dept., 1945-46; with UN Dept. Trusteeship, 1946-55; pub. health expert, chief med. officer for Arab refugees, 1948; dir. health services regional office WHO, S.E. Asia, 1955-59, chief pub. health tng. sect., Geneva, 1959-60; sr. pub. health adminstr. African regional office, 1960-62; chief nat. health planning WHO, Geneva, 1962-68; prof. pub. health practice Columbia U., N.Y.C., 1969-73, adj. prof. pub. health, 1973-83; cons. WHO, AID, in Cambodia, 1968, The Philippines, 1972, Haiti and West Africa, 1974, Chad, 1976. Author: (with Hilleboe and Thomas) Approaches to National Health Planning, 1972; contbr. articles to profl. jours. Mem. Danish Med. Assn., AAAS. Club: Explorers. Home: 24 Beall Cir Bronxville NY 10708-2109

BARKOVICH, ANTHONY JAMES, pediatric neuroradiologist, educator, researcher; b. Ft. Lee, Va., July 29, 1952; s. Anthony and Mildred Margaret (Donner) B.; m. Karen Kaye Jernstedt, May 24, 1986; children: Matthew, Krister, Emil. BS in Chemistry, U. Calif., Davis, 1974; MS in Chemistry, U. Calif., Berkeley, 1977; MD, George Washington U., 1980. Diplomate Am. Bd. Radiology. Intern, then resident in radiology Letterman Army Med. Ctr., 1980-84; fellow in neuroradiology Walter Reed Army Med. Ctr., 1984-86; maj. U.S. Army, 1980-89; neuroradiologist Letterman Army Med. Ctr., San Francisco, 1986-89; prof. radiology, pediatrics, neurology and neurosurgery U. Calif., San Francisco, 1989—. Author: Pediatric Neuroimaging, 1995; editor: Magnetic Resonance Neuroimaging, 1994. Grantee NIH, 1993. Mem. Am. Soc. Neuroradiology (sec. 1994-96), Am. Soc. Pediatric Neuroradiology (pres. 1992-94), Soc. Pediatric Radiology, Soc. Neuroscience, AAAS. Office: UCSF-Dept Neuroradiology 505 Parnassus Ave San Francisco CA 94143

BARKSDALE, CHARLES MADSEN, psychoneuroendocrinologist; b. San Diego, June 20, 1947; s. Madsen Lewis and Esther Elizabeth (La Force) B. BA in Chemistry and Math., U. Calif. San Diego, 1970; MS in Biochemistry, Columbia Pacific U., 1982, PhD in Chemistry, 1983. Rsch. assoc. U. Calif. San Diego, U. Hosp., 1970-76; rsch. scientist Diagnostics Products, Inc., La Jolla, Calif., 1976-77; sr. rsch. assoc. Hyland Diagnostics, Costa Mesa, Calif., 1977-81; NIH postdoctoral fellow U. Wis., Madison, 1981-84, rsch. assoc. dept. psychiatry, 1984-86, rsch. scientist, 1986-88; rsch. assoc. pharmacokinetics and drug metabolism Parke-Davis Pharm. Rsch., Ann Arbor, Mich., 1988—; Contbr. articles to numerous profl. jours. Recipient NIH Postdoctoral Rsch. fellowship U. Wis., 1983. Fellow Royal Entomol. Soc. of London; mem. Internat. Soc. for Psychoneuroendocrinology, The Endocrine Soc., Soc. Adolescent Medicine, The Soc. Neurosci., Calif. Acad. Scis. (hon. life). Office: Parke-Davis 2800 Plymouth Rd Ann Arbor MI 48105-2430

BARKSDALE, DARRYLL WAYNE, physician; b. Meridian, Miss., July 15, 1954; s. Aaron A. and Esther (Brown) B.; m. Marcia Cretin, Apr. 15, 1989; 1 child, Aaron Travis. BA, La. State U., 1976; MS, U. So. Miss., 1978; DO, W.Va. Sch. Osteo. Medicine, 1986. Diplomate Am. Bd. Emergency Medicine, Nat. Bd. Osteo. Med. Examiners, Am. Osteo. Bd. Family Physicians, Am. Bd. Forensic Medicine, Am. Coll. Forensic Examiners; cert. instr. ATLS/ ACLS. Intern, resident Cuyahoga Falls Gen. Hosp., 1986-88; sr. coord. Community Orgn. for Drug Abuse Control, Shreveport, La., 1972-76; sr. planner So. Miss. Planning and Devel. Dist., Gulfport, 1978-80; coord. govt. svcs. U. So. Miss. Div. Continuing Edn., Hattiesburg, 1980-81; resident dept. family medicine Cuyahoga Falls (Ohio) Gen. Hosp., 1986-88; attending physician dept. emergency medicine Ocean Springs (Miss.) Hosp., 1988—; staff physician Tallmadge (Ohio) Family Practice Ctr., 1987-88, Primary Care Assocs., Gulfport, Miss., 1988-90; adminstrv. cons. City of Hattiesburg, Miss., 1977-78, 80, Cmty. Assocs., Inc., 1994—; disaster mgmt. cons. Editor: How to Export, 1979, Coastal Civil Defense Medical Mass Casualty Manual, 1979. Exec. committeeman Rep. Party, 1972-76, party nominee for police jury, 1973, Bossier Parish, La.; mem. so. adv. coun. Miss. Health Systems Agy., 1979-82; active Casino Vessel Hurricane Preparedness Plan, Miss. Gulf Coast, 1994. Recipient Community Svc. award Gulf Coast Women's Ctr., 1989, Ship Bell award Jackson County Port Authority, 1980. Fellow Assn. Emergency Physicians; mem. Am. Osteo. Assn., Am. Coll. Osteo. Family Physicians, Am. Coll. Osteo. Emergency Physicians, Am. Osteo. Coll. Occupational & Preventive Medicine, Am. Assn. Physician Specialists, Am. Acad. Emergency Physicians, Am. Coll. Physician Execs., Miss. Osteo. Med. Assn., U. So. Miss. Alumni Assn. (life), La. State U.-Shreveport Alumni Assn., N.W. La. Umpire Assn. (pres. 1972-74). Methodist. Home: 9924 Banana Island Dr Ocean Springs MS 39564-9513

BARLAND, PETER, rheumatologist, medical educator; b. N.Y.C., June 5, 1936; s. Samuel and Marion (Angxist) B.; m. Tina Saleh, Apr. 15, 1951; children: Susan, Julie. BA, NYU, 1955; MD, Yeshiva U., 1959. Intern Strong Meml. Hosp., Rochester, N.Y.; resident BMHC, Bronx, N.Y.; prof. medicine Albert Einstein Coll. Medicine, Bronx, 1965—; attending physician Montefiore Med. Ctr., Bronx, 1969—, dir. rheumatology divsn., 1992—, dir. immunodiagnostic lab., 1970—. Fellow Am. Coll. Rheumatology; mem. N.Y. Rheumatism Assn. (pres., sec.-treas. 1975). Office: Montefiore Medical Center 111 E 210th St Bronx NY 10467

BARLASCINI, CORNELIUS OTTAVIO, JR., physician; b. Richmond, Va., Oct. 5, 1956; s. Cornelio O. Sr. and Gloria Stella (Massucco) B.; m. Laura Amelia Petrelli, June 22, 1991; 1 child, Louis Ernest. BA, U. Va., 1979, MD, 1983. Intern, resident and fellow Med. Coll. Va., Richmond, 1983-88; assoc. dir. Diabetes Treatment Ctr., Columbus, Ga., 1988-95; chief endocrinology sect. South Ga. Med. Ctr. Contbr.: (textbook) Drug Therapy in Emergency Medicine, 1990; contbr. articles to profl. jours.; inventor in field. Recipient Sandra Tate Russell award Va. chpt. Am. Diabetes Assn., 1988. Fellow ACP; mem. The Endocrine Soc., Phi Beta Kappa. Office: 201 Pendleton Dr Valdosta GA 31602

BARLETTA, GIUSEPPE ANTONIO, cardiologist; b. Novara, Italy, Mar. 28, 1954; s. Francesco and Eleonora (Benevento) B.; m. Laura Ferrini, Mar. 7, 1981; 1 child, Tommaso. BS, U. Florence, 1978. Rsch fellow in cardiology U. Florence, Italy, 1980-82; cons. cardiologist Florence Hosp., 1981—, asst. chief physician, 1988—, chief cardiovascular ultrasound sect., 1994—; prof. U. Florence, 1993—. Co-author book on semeiotics; contbr. articles to profl. jours. Nat. Com. Rsch. fellow. Fellow Italian Group Haemodynamic Studies, European Heart Assn.; mem. Italian Soc. Cardiology. Home: Via Medaglie D'Oro N 43, 59100 Prato Florence Italy Office: U Florence Dept IM & Cardio, Viale Morgagni, 50134 Florence Italy

BARLOW, CARL MORTON, physician; b. N.Y.C., Dec. 8, 1925; s. David M. and Beatrice (Sarlin) B.; m. Shirley Lantner, Sept. 28, 1923 (dec. Apr. 1959); children: Richard Mark, Steven Joseph; m. June Williams, Oct. 9, 1935; 1 child, Carol Elizabeth. BA, NYU, 1946; DDS, Columbia U., 1950, MD, 1953. Diplomate Am. Bd. Plastic Surgery. Staff plastic surgery L.I. Jewish Hosp., Queens, 1963-71; chief div. plastic surgery Queens Hosp. Ctr., 1963-71; attending surgeon (sr.) Lenox Hill Hosp., N.Y.C., 1961-85; assoc. prof. micro-biology grad. div. Univ. City of N.Y., 1962-66; chmn. scientific program AMFA-Soc. Max Surgeons, Phila., 1968; chmn. med. econs. com. N.Y. Regional Soc. Plastic Surgery, N.Y.C., 1968-76; hon. surgeon Lenox Hill Hosp., N.Y.C., 1985—; guest lectr. William Alanson White Inst. Psychiatry, Psychoanalysis & Psychology, 1976-78; workshop dirl, instr. Am. Soc. Plastic Reconstruction Surgery. Contbr. articles to profl. jours. Capt. U.S. Army, 1955-57. Fellow ACS, N.Y. Acad. Medicine; mem. Am. Soc. Plastic and Reconstructive Surgery, Am. Soc. Maxillofacial Surgeons, N.Y. State Med. Soc., New York County Med. Soc., Explorers Club, Alpha Omega Alpha, Omicron Kappa Upsilon. Office: 799 Park Ave New York NY 10021-3275

BARLOW, CHARLES FRANKLIN, physician, educator; b. Mason City, Iowa, Nov. 10, 1923; s. Frank Richard and Marie Gertrude (McCabe) B.; m. Patricia Keith, June 30, 1953; children: Ellen, Margaret Katherine. Student, Coe Coll., 1941-43; S.B., U. Chgo., 1945, M.D., 1947; A.M. (hon.), Harvard, 1963. Intern Johns Hopkins Hosp., 1947-48; jr. asst. resident Boston Children's Hosp., 1948-49; resident neurology, then instr. neurology U. Chgo. Sch. Medicine, 1951-55; asst. prof., then asso. prof. U. Chgo., 1960-63; prof. neurology Harvard Med. Sch., 1963-90; neurologist-in-chief Children's Hosp. Med. Center, Boston, 1963-91, emeritus, 1991—; cons. Peter Bent Brigham Hosp., Boston, 1963—, Beth Israel Hosp., Boston, 1966—. Recipient McClintock Teaching award U. Chgo., 1963. Mem. Am. Neurol. Assn., Child Neurol. Soc., Am. Acad. Neurology. Home: 482 Jerusalem Rd Cohasset MA 02025-1144 Office: 300 Longwood Ave Boston MA 02115-5724

BARLOW, JOHN SUTTON, neurophysiologist, electroencephalographer, lexicographer; b. Raleigh, N.C., June 10, 1925; s. David Henry and Anne Mary (Sutton) B.; m. Sibylle E. Jahrreiss, Aug. 5, 1950; children: Thomas Walter, Robert Sutton, Lisa Katharine. BS, U. N.C., 1944, MS, 1948; MD, Harvard U., 1953. Diplomate Am. Bd. Cert. EEG. Clin. and rsch. fellow, asst. resident in neurology Mass. Gen. Hosp., Boston, 1953-57; clin. and rsch. fellow Harvard Med. Sch., Boston, 1953-57; rsch. assoc. in elec. engring. MIT, Cambridge, 1954-64, rsch. affiliate Rsch. Lab. of Electronics, 1964—; asst. neurology Mass. Gen. Hosp., Boston, 1957-61, neurophysiologist neurology svc., 1961—; rsch. assoc. neurology Harvard Med. Sch., Boston, 1961-69, prin. rsch. assoc., 1969-78, sr. rsch. assoc. neurology, 1979—; mem. neurology study sect. NIH, Bethesda, Md., 1966-70; mem. rev. panel on neurol. devices FDA, Washington, 1974-76; cons. dept. neurology VA Med. Ctr., Boston, 1979-89, part-time staff, 1989—; cons. dept. neurology New Eng. Med. Ctr., Boston, 1979—. Author: The Electroencephalogram: Its Patterns and Origins, 1993, A Chinese-Russian-English Dictionary, 1995; cons. editor EEG Clin. Neurophysiology, 1970-86; translator/editor books from the Russian, Czech and Chinese; contbr. articles and revs. to profl. jours. Served from ensign to lt. (j.g.) USN, 1944-46. Recipient Rsch. Career Devel. award NIH, 1962-71, Sr. Scientist award Alexander Von Humboldt Found., Göttingen, Germany, 1979, Sr. Scientist Exch. award NAS, U.S.A./USSR Acad. Scis., Moscow, 1982, 83, 88; rsch. grantee NIH, 1962-88; Fogarty Internat. fellow, 1979. Mem. Internat. Brain Rsch. Orgn., Am. EEG Soc. (pres. 1975-76), Am. Neurol. Assn., Am. Acad. Neurology, Soc. Neurosci., Am. Geophys. Union, Ea. Assn. EEG (pres. 1971-72), Assn. Asian Studies, European Assn. Chinese Studies, Dictionary Soc. North Am.

BARMAN, SUSAN MARIE, physiologist; b. Joliet, Ill., Aug. 28, 1949; d. Vernon Rutherford and Shirley Marie (Shea) B. BS in Biology, Loyola U., Chgo., 1971; PhD in Physiology, Loyola U., 1976. From research assoc. to asst. prof. Mich. State U., East Lansing, 1975-84, assoc. prof., 1984-94, prof., 1994—; sci. cons. NIH, Bethesda, Md., 1981, 83—. Contbr. articles to profl. jours. Recipient Merit award NIH Heart, Lung, Blood Inst., 1995—. Mem. Soc. for Neuroscience, American Physiological Soc., AAAS. Democrat. Roman Catholic. Office: Mich State U Dept Pharmacology East Lansing MI 48824

BARNARD, CYNTHIA, hospital administrator; b. Chgo., Sept. 19, 1955. BA magna cum laude, Bryn Mawr Coll., 1976; MM, Northwestern U., 1982. Cert. profl. healthcare quality. Mgr. health care mgmt. cons. svcs. Price Waterhouse, Chgo., 1985-86; mgr. Info. Ctr. Rush-Presbyterian St. Luke's Med. Ctr., Chgo., 1979-82; cons. Planmetrics, Chgo., 1980-81; programmer analyst Shared Med. Systems, King of Prussia, Pa., 1976-78; rsch. specialist Eagleville (Pa.) Hosp. and Rehab. Ctr., 1976, Chgo., 1976; programmer analyst Shared Med. Systems, King of Prussia, Pa., 1976-78; cons. Planmetrics, Chgo., 1980-81; mgr. Info. Ctr. Rush-Presbyterian St. Luke's Med. Ctr., Chgo., 1979-82; various to dir. quality strategies Northwestern Meml. Hosp., Chgo., 1982—; mgr. health care mgmt. cons. svcs. Price Waterhouse, Chgo., 1985-86; Presenter in field. Contbr. articles to profl. jours. and publs. Chair health care sector Lincoln Found. for Bus. Excellence, 1995—, vol. Sarah's Inn, 1995; mem. coms. Oak Park Temple, 1994—, others. Mem. Ill. Hosp. and Health Systems Assn. (blue ribbon quality adv. bd., other coms. 1994—), Women Health Execs. Network (various offices), Nat. Assn. Healthcare Quality, Am. Soc. Quality Control, Northwestern U. Profl. Women's Assn., Chgo. Health Execs. Forum, Healthcare Fin. Mgmt. Assn., Chgo. Area Hosp. Planning and Mktg. Assn.

BARNARD, DENIS ALAN, medical technologist; b. Ogden, Utah, Aug. 23, 1953; s. Wayne Taylor and Elaine (Child) B.; m. Angelina Louise Abraham, July 21, 1972; children: Sean Michael, Marc Colin. Student, Westminster Coll., 1972; AD Med. Lab. Tech., C.C. the Air Force, 1996, AD Mil. Instr., 1996. Commd. 2d lt. USAF, 1972, advanced through grades to sr. master sgt., various lab positions, 1974-93; supt. office clin. lab. affairs Armed Forces Inst. Pathology, Washington, 1993—; top 3 enlisted coun., air force adv. coun. Armed Forces Inst. Pathology, Washington, 1995. Selected Tri-Svc. Enlisted Member of Yr., Soc. Armed Forces Med. Lab. Scientists, 1995. Home: 939 Hillside Lake Terr Gaithersburg MD 20878

BARNARD, KATHRYN ELAINE, nursing educator, researcher; b. Omaha, Apr. 16, 1938; d. Paul and Elsa Elizabeth (Anderson) B. BS in Nursing, U. Nebr., Omaha, 1960; MS in Nursing, Boston U., 1962; PhD, U. Wash., Seattle, 1972; DSc (hon.), U. Nebr., 1990. Acting instr. U. Nebr., Omaha, 1960-61; acting instr. U. Wash., Seattle, 1963-65, asst. prof., 1965-69, prof. nursing, 1972—, assoc. dean, 1987-92; bd. dirs. Nat. Ctr. for Clin. Infant Programs, Washington, 1980—. Chmn. rsch. com. Bur. of Community Health Svcs., MCH, 1987-89. Recipient Lucille Petry award Nat. League for Nursing, 1968, Martha Mae Eliot award Am. Assn. Pub. Health, 1983, Professorship award U. Wash., 1985. Fellow Am. Acad. Nursing (bd. dirs. 1980-82); mem. Inst. Medicine; mem. Am. Nurses Assn. (chmn. com. 1980-82, Jessie Scott award 1982, Nurse of Yr. award 1984), Soc. Research in Child Devel. (bd. dirs. 1981-87), Sigma Theta Tau (founders award in research 1987). Democrat. Presbyterian. Home: 11508 Durland Ave NE Seattle WA 98125-5904 Office: University of Washington Family & Child Nursing Box 357920 Seattle WA 98195-7920

BARNARD, WILLIAM MARION, psychiatrist; b. Mt. Pleasant, Tex., Dec. 17, 1949; s. Marion Jaggers and Med (Cody) B. BA, Yale U., 1972; MD, Baylor U., 1976. Diplomate Am. Bd. Psychiatry and Neurology. Resident NYU/Bellevue Med. Ctr., 1976-79; liaison, consultation fellow L.I. Jewish/Hillside Med. Ctr., 1979-80; chief, liaison, consultation psychiatrist Queens (N.Y.) Med. Ctr., 1980-83; liaison, consultation psychiatrist Mt. Sinai Med. Ctr., N.Y.C., 1983-84; clin. asst. prof. NYU Med. Sch., N.Y.C., 1984-87; emergency psychiatrist VA Med. Ctr., N.Y.C., 1984-87; pvt. practice Pasadena, Calif., 1987—; chief psychiat. svc. Las Encinas Hosp., Pasadena, 1989, chief staff, 1990, med. dir. gen. adult. psychiat. svc., 1990-92, asst. med. dir., 1992; med. dir. CPC Alhambra Hosp., Rosemead, Calif., 1992—. Chmn. mental health com. All Saints AIDS Svc. Ctr., Pasadena, 1990-94, bd. dirs. , 1991-94; bd. dirs. Pasadena Symphony, 1989—, Whiffenpoof Alumni, New Haven, 1991—. Wilson scholar Yale U., 1973. Mem. APA, NYU-Bellevue Psychiat. Assn., Am. Soc. Addiction Medicine, Calif. Med. Assn., So. Calif. Psychiat. Soc., Acad. Psychosomatic Medicine, L.A. County Med. Assn., Amateur Comedy Club, Met. Opera Club, Yale Club N.Y.C. Republican. Episcopalian. Office: 2810 E Del Mar Blvd Pasadena CA 91107-4321

BARNATHAN, JACK MARTIN, chiropractor; b. Queens, N.Y., Aug. 19, 1959; s. Jack and Christa Bianca (Manschwedat) B. BBA, Adelphi U., 1981; D Chiropractic, N.Y. Chiropractic Coll., 1984. Community crisis counselor Reach of LongBeach, N.Y., 1981-84; chiropractic doctor Bethpage, N.Y., 1984—; dir. Coun. Chiropractic Care for Disabled; cons. Internat. Fedn. Bodybuilders, 1987—; postgrad. faculty N.Y. Chiropractic Coll., 1992—, Life Coll., Ga., 1992—; mem. '96 Atlanta Olympic Chiropractic Adv. Com., 1993—; participant Great Am. Workoutw, Washington, 1992; pres. Nassau County Coun. Phys. Fitness and Sports, 1992. Author: Muscle, Mind and More, 1996. Recipient Presdl. Cert. of Merit, 1992, Cert. of Commendation Pres. Coun. Phys. Fitness and Sports, 1992; aptd. Col. (hon.) Gov. of Ky., 1994. Mem. Internat. Chiropractors Assn. (pres. coun. on fitness, Sports Chiropractor of Yr. award 1993-94), Internat. Platform Assn., N.Y. Chiropractic Coll. Alumni Assn. (dir. bd.). Office: 627 Hicksville Rd Bethpage NY 11714-3414

BARNER, ANNABEL MONROE, pastoral counselor; b. Pitts., Nov. 30, 1925; d. Samuel North and Annabel (McKibben) Monroe; m. Charles Ray Barner, Aug. 14, 1948; children: Bruce Monroe, Craig McLean, Leslie Ann. BA, Ohio Wesleyan U., 1947; postgrad., Case Western Res. U., 1974-78; MA, Ashland Theol. Sem., 1979; MDiv (hon.), Pitts. Theol. Sem., 1984; postgrad., Gestalt Inst., 1988, Process Comm. Inst., 1992. Producing dir. WPGH and KDKA radio and TV stas., Pitts., 1943-47; comml. writer, traffic contr. Sta. WRFD and WMRN, Worthington and Marion, Ohio, 1947-50; tutor emotionally disturbed youth Rocky River (Ohio) Bd. Edn., 1967-83; pastoral counselor Rocky River Presbyn. Ch., 1972-82, Samaritan Counseling Ctr., Elyria, Ohio, 1983-88; chaplain Fairview (Ohio) Gen. Hosp., 1980-81; counselor-at-large Greater Cleve. Counseling Svc., Inter Ch. Coun., 1981—; instr. Ohio Wesleyan U., Delaware, 1947-50, teaching fellow, 1948-50; mem. steering com. West Side Extended Care Ctr., Cleve., 1978; field placement counselor emergency svcs. West Side Community Health, Cleve., 1978; psychol. counselor Welsh Home, Westlake, Ohio, 1980-82; pastoral counselor John Knox Presbyn. Ch., North Olmsted, Ohio, 1988—; trainer Kahler Comm., Little Rock, 1991. Author, editor explanations of laws and statutes, State of Miss., 1953-55; author radio scripts and documentaries, 1950; contbr. articles to profl. publs. Media spokesperson Clergy for Choice, Lorain County, Ohio, 1990—, Friends of the Libr., Rocky River, 1972—; organizer Linden Sch., Lorain, 1988; mem. Open Door West, Cleve., 1990—. Gestalt Inst. scholar, 1985, 86. Mem. NOW, Nat. Trust for Historic Preservation, Am. Assn. Pastoral Counselors, Greenpeace, World Wildlife Fund, Habitat for Humanity, Sierra Club, Cleve. Art Mus., Spring Valley Country Club, Delta Gamma, Theta Alpha Phi. Home: 2694 Goldwood Dr Cleveland OH 44116-3013 Office: John Knox Presbyn Ch 25200 Lorain Rd North Olmsted OH 44070-2057

BARNES, DAVID BENTON, school psychologist; m. Cheryle Kirkland; children: David, Matthew, Bryan. BSc with honors, Springfield Coll., 1958; MEd, U. Maine, 1962; EdD, Rutgers U., 1970. Cert. tchr., Maine. Asst. football coach Boston U., 1964-66; dir. Counselling Ctr., asst. prof. edn. Acadia U., Wolfville, N.S., Can., 1966-71, acting dean Sch. Edn., 1969-70, assoc. prof., 1970; chief psychologist Fundy Med. Health Ctr., Wolfville, 1971-73; psychologist Atlantic Child Guidance Ctr., 1974-77; supr. spl. svcs. Cape Breton County Sch. Bd., 1977-82, Lunenburg County Dist. Bd., 1982-87; sch. psychologist, spl. edn. adminstr. Bennington-Rutland Supervisory Union, Vt., 1987-90; psychologist N.W. Psycho-Ednl. Program, Rome, Ga., 1990-92, Chattahoochee-Flint RESA, Ellaville, Ga., 1992—; mem. adminstrv. task force for spl. edn. N.S. Dept. Edn.; mem. N.S. Adv. Coun. on Tchr. Edn.; mem. Met. Mental Health Planning Bd.; mem. Aqua Percept Nat. Adv. Bd.; founder Camp Recskill; founder, bd. dirs. Cape Breton Child Guidance Ctr.; adj. faculty mem. U. Coll. of Cape Breton, Acadia U., Walden U. Co-author: Special Educator's Survival Guide: Practical Techniques and Materials for Supervision and Instruction. Grantee Can. Govt., 1978-87, Province of N.S., 1978-79, N.S. Tchrs. Union, 1980-81, Internat. Youth Yr., 1985, Donner Found., Laidlaw Found., Windsor Found. Mem. Can. Univ. Counselors Assn., Atlantic Inst. Edn. (steering com. for counselor edn.), Assn. Profl. Staffs of Community Mental Ctrs. (sec.-treas.), Can. Assn. for Children With Learning Disabilties (v.p.), Provincial Assn. for Children with Learning Disabilities (bd. dirs.), N.S. Mental Health Assn. (bd. dirs.), Dartmouth Mental Health Assn. (v.p.), Cape Breton Mental Health Assn. (bd. dirs.), Coun. Exceptional Children, Assn. Psychologists N.C., Nat. Assn. Sch. Psychologists. Home: 309 Rigas Rd Americus GA 31709-2717

BARNES, DONALD WESLEY, medical educator, software developer; b. Greenville, N.C., June 28, 1944; s. William W. and Vivian N. (Neal) B.; m. Margaret Epes Maddex, Mar. 29, 1969; children: Robert W., Sarah M. BS in Chemistry, U. Richmond, 1966; PhD in Pharmacology, Med. Coll. Va., Richmond, 1971. Asst. prof. pharmacology East Carolina U. Sch. Medicine, Greenville, N.C., 1971-82; assoc. prof. pharmacology East Carolina U. Sch. Medicine, 1982-95, prof. pharmacology, 1995—; cons. EPA, Cin., 1979. Author (computer software) MacDogLab, 1990. Pres. Greenville Host Lions Club, 1995—, Greenville Band Boosters, 1987-88; elder 1st Presbyn. Ch., Greenville, 1990-93. Mem. Am. Soc. Exptl. Pharmacology Therapeutics, Internat. Soc. Study of Xenobiotics, Sigma Xi. Office: Sch Medicine East Carolina U Greenville NC 27858

BARNES, FREDERICK WALTER, JR., physician, medical educator; b. Cleve., Mar. 3, 1909; s. Frederick Walter and Susan (Anderson) B.; m. Catherine Gardner Bowden, Apr. 6, 1940; children: William Anderson, Susan Hammond Barnes Waldrop. A.B., Yale U., 1930; M.D., Johns Hopkins Med. Sch., 1934; Ph.D., Columbia U., 1943; D.Med. Sci. (hon.), Brown U., 1984. Intern Johns Hopkins Hosp., 1934-36; resident Children's Hosp., Boston, 1936-38; asst. prof. medicine and biochemistry Cin. Med. Sch., 1942-46; assoc. prof. medicine and biochemistry Johns Hopkins Med. Sch., 1946-62; co-founder Brown Med. Sch., Providence, 1962; prof. med. sci. Brown U., Providence, 1962—, chmn. studies in world interdependence, 1979. Author: The Cellular Cloud, 1995. V.p. Urban League R.I., 1965; bd. dirs. R.I. TB Assn., 1966—; mem. Urban Coalition, 1969—; bd. dirs. Progress for Providence, 1970; co-chmn. R.I. Nuclear Arms Referendum Com., 1982; mem. State Commn. on Nuclear Arms, 1982. Recipient W.W. Keene award in medicine, 1979, Spl. Service award Brown U., 1983, Frederick W. Barnes prize, 1990. Mem. Am. Soc. Biol. Chemists, Pediatric Research Soc., ACP, N.Y. Acad. Sci., Am. Osler Soc., Assn. Am. Med. Colls. (chmn. group student affairs N.E. 1970-71). Home: 355 Blackstone Blvd Apt 343 Providence RI 02906-4946

BARNES, GEORGE EDGAR, research scientist; b. San Antonio, Jan. 27, 1943; s. Milton Arnold and Bess (Cook) B.; m. Janet Esther Miller, Jan. 15, 1961; children: Terri Denise, Gregory Scott. BS, S.W. Tex. State U., 1967, MA, 1969; PhD, U. Tex. Health Sci. Ctr., 1974. Asst. prof. Tex. A&M U. Coll. Medicine, College Station, 1976-85; sr. scientist ALCON Labs., Inc., Ft. Worth, 1985-91, prin. scientist, 1992—. Patentee in field. Mem. Am. Soc. Pharmacology and Exptl. Therapeutics, Soc. Exptl. Biology, Assn. Rsch. in Vision Ophthalmology, Microcirculatory Soc. Office: ALCON Labs Inc 6201 S Fwy Fort Worth TX 76134

BARNES, HERMAN VERDAIN, internist, educator; b. Borger, Tex., Nov. 20, 1935; s. Herman Christian and June Loraine (Mays) B.; m. Joyce Elaine Ground, June 15, 1957; children: Bradlee, Brendie, Brannon, Shari. BA, McMurry U., 1958; MDiv, Yale U., 1961; MD, Vanderbilt U., 1965. Asst. prof. medicine Johns Hopkins Hosp., Balt., 1972-75; assoc. prof. of medicine and pediatrics sch. of medicine U. Iowa, Iowa City, 1975-78; prof. of medicine & pediatrics coll. of medicine U. Tenn., Chattanooga, 1978-83; prof. medicine and pediatrics, chmn. med. Sch. Medicine, Wright State U., Dayton, Ohio, 1983-94; chmn. med. edn. Ea. Va. Med. Sch., Norfolk, 1994—, dir. Ctr. for Generalist medicine, 1994—, prof. medicine, pediatric and family practice, 1994—. Co-author: Manual of Clinical Problems in Internal Medicine, 1990; editor-in-chief Jour. Adolescent Health Care, 1979-90; editor: Clinical Medicine: Selected Problems with Pathophysiologic Correlations, 1988; assoc. editor Debates in Medicine, 1987-89. Recipient Adele Hofmann award Am. Acad. Pediatrics, 1990. Fellow ACP (regent 1987-88, chmn. coun. med. socs. 1987-88, gov.-elect for Ohio 1991, gov. 1992—). Office: Eastern Va Med Sch PO Box 1980 Norfolk VA 23501-1980

BARNES, KAREN LOUISE, neurophysiologist; b. Cleve., Feb. 24, 1942; d. Bentley Tiffany and Margaret Evelyn (Rowlands) B.; m. William Elliott Garapick, Sept. 1, 1973. AB, Mount Holyoke Coll., 1963; AM, U. Mich., 1965; PhD, Case Western Res. U., 1970. Rsch. assoc. Case Western Res. U., Cleve., 1969-75, asst. prof., 1973-83, assoc. prof., 1983-90; profl. staff Cleve. Clinic Rsch. Inst., 1976—, chair rsch. program coun., 1987—; sect. head rsch. dept. neurology Cleve. Clinic, 1979-90; prof. dept. physiology Ohio State U., 1994—; asst. prof. John Carroll U., Cleve., 1969-73; rsch. psychologist Cleve. VA Hosp., 1973-75; cons. NIH, Washington, 1980—, NSF, Washington, 1987—, VA, Washington, 1983-88. Contbr. articles to profl. jurs. Asst. regional dir. Nat. Ski Patrol System, Ohio, 1976-77, trustee, 1985—. Mem. Soc. for Neurosci., Am. Acad. Neurology, Am. Physiol. Soc., Coun. Assn., U.S. Sailing Assn. (cert. race officer), Edgewater Yacht Club (chair Cleve. Race Week race com. 1989, 91—, fleet capt. 1982-83), Phi Beta Kappa, Sigma Xi. Office: Cleve Clinic Found Rsch Inst NC11 9500 Euclid Ave Cleveland OH 44195-0001

BARNES, MAGGIE LUE SHIFFLETT (MRS. LAWRENCE BARNES), nurse; b. nr. Spur, Tex., Mar. 29, 1931; d. Howard Eldridge and Sadie Adilene (Dunlap) Shifflett; m. T.C. Fagan, Jan. 1950 (dec. Feb. 1952); 1 child, Lawayne; m. Lawrence Barnes, Sept. 2, 1960. Student, Cogdell Sch. Nursing, 1959-60, Western Tex. Coll., 1972-76; postgrad. Meth. Hosp. Sch. Nursing, Lubbock, Tex., 1975; BSN, W. Tex. State U., 1977. RN, Tex.; cert. gerontol. nurse, Am. Nurses Credentialing Ctr. Fl. nurse D.M. Cogdell Meml. Hosp., Snyder, Tex., 1960-64, medication nurse, 1964-76, asst. evening supr., 1976-78, charge nurse, after 1978, evening nursing supr., 1980; nursing supr. Scurry, Borden, Mitchel, Fisher, Howard Counties, West Cen. Home Health Agy., Snyder, 1980-83; emergency rm. evening supr. Root-Meml. Hosp., 1983-89; dir. of nurses Snyder Oak Core Ctr., 1989-91, Mountain View Lodge, Big Spring, Tex., 1991-92, Med. Arts. Hosp. Home Health, 1992-93, Metplex Home Health Svcs., Snyder, 1993-94, ret. 1994; part time nurse 1994—; regional coord. home health svcs. Beverly Enterprises, 1983. Den mother Cub Scouts, Boy Scouts Am., Holliday, Tex., 1960-61; mem. PTA, Snyder, Tex., 1960-69; adv. Sr. Citizens Assn.; mem. Tri-Region Health Systems Agy., 1979—; mem. adv. bd. Scurry County Diabetes Assn., 1982—. Mem. Vocat. Nurses Assn. Tex. (mem. bd. 1963-65, div. pres. 1967-69), Emergency Dept. Nursing Assn. Apostolic Faith Ch. (sec., treas. 1956-58). Home: 8239 CR 473 Hermleigh TX 79526-9704

BARNES, MICHELLE LEE, cardiovascular thoracic surgery nurse; b. Tulsa, Okla., May 19, 1969; d. Michael Loy and Judith Lee (Weedin) B.; 1 child, Austin Loy. BSN, S.W. Okla. State U., 1993. RN, Okla., Tex.; cert. BLS, ACLS. Staff nurse Woodland Heights Med. Ctr., Lufkin, Tex., 1993-94, Midway Pk. Med. Ctr., Lancaster, Tex., 1994, Presbyn. Hosp. Dallas, 1994—. Baptist. Home: 165 N Old Orchard Apt 323 Lewisville TX 75067

BARNES, PETER JOHN, thoracic medicine educator, consultant, physician; b. Birmingham, Eng., Oct. 29, 1946; s. John and Eileen Gertrude (Thurman) B.; m. Olivia Mary Harvard-Watts, Sept. 11, 1976; children: Adam John Harvard, Toby Samuel Harvard, Julian Peter Harvard. MA, Cambridge (Eng.) U., 1973; DM, Oxford (Eng.) U., 1982, DSc, 1987. Registrar Univ. Coll. Hosp., London, 1975-78; Med. Rsch. Coun. rsch. fellow Royal Postgrad. Med. Sch., London, 1978-79, sr. lectr., 1983-85; sr. registrar Hammersmith Hosp., London, 1979-83, cons. physician, 1983-85; prof. clin. pharmacology Cardiothoracic Inst., London, 1985-87; prof. thoracic medicine Nat. Heart and Lung Inst., U. London, 1987—; cons. physician Royal Brampton Hosp., London, 1985—. Editor: Asthma, 1989, also 15 books; contbr. more than 500 articles on lung pharmacology and asthma to med. jours. Fellow Royal Coll. Physicians; mem. Brit. Thoracic Soc. (coun. 1990), Am. Thoracic Soc., Physiol. Soc., Brit. Pharmacology Soc. Office: Nat Heart and Lung Inst, Dovehouse St, London SW3 6LY, England

BARNES, RAMON MURRAY, chemistry educator; b. Pitts., Apr. 24, 1940; s. Jack N. and Sally L. (Silver) B.; m. Dorothy M. Soja, May 17, 1969. BS, Oreg. State U., 1962; MA, Columbia U., 1963; PhD, U. Ill., Champaign-Urbana, 1966. Lectr. Baldwin Wallace Coll., Bera, Ohio, 1967-68; materials engr. NASA Lewis Research Ctr., Cleve., 1968-69; postdoctoral fellow Iowa State U., Ames, 1969; asst. to prof. chemistry U. Mass., Amherst, 1969—; chmn. Winter Conf. on Plasma Spectrochemistry, 1980—. Mem. editorial bd. Jour. Analytical Atomic Spectrometry, Canadian Jour. Spectroscopy, Spectroscopy (Eugene), Spectroscopy Europe, Analytical Abstracts, Guangpuxue Yu (Spectroscopy and Spectral Analysis), Spectrochimica Acta Revs., Spectrochimica Acta Electronica; editor, pub. (newsletter) ICP Info. Newsletter, 1975—; editor six books; inventor in field; contbr. articles to profl. jours. Capt. USAR, 1966-68. Fellow AAAS; mem. Am. Chem. Soc., Royal Soc. of Chemistry, Soc. for Applied Spectroscopy, Optical Soc. Am., Spectroscopy Soc. of Can., Sox. Toxicology, Sigma Xi. Office: U Mass Chem Dept Lederle GRC Tower PO Box 34510 Amherst MA 01003-4510

BARNES, RICHARD NEARN, biology educator emeritus; b. Washington, Dec. 10, 1928; s. Wilbur Brents and Helen Fronica (Hottenfeller) B.; m. Mary Elizabeth DeLauter, Jan. 19, 1957; children: Kathryn Ann, Marcia Louise. AB, U. Calif., Berkeley, 1952; MA, U. Calif., Davis, 1957, PhD, 1962. Instr. Calif. State U., Sacramento, 1957-62; from asst. prof. to prof. biology Berea (Ky.) Coll., 1962-72, full prof., 1972-94, prof. emeritus, 1994. Cpl. U.S. Army, 1952-54, Korea. Office: Berea Coll Dept Biology Berea KY 40404

BARNES, SHERRY GALE, health information management educator; b. Ada, Okla., Mar. 14, 1953; d. Clarence Raymond and Bernice (Fugate) Shiplet; m. Stanley Gene Barnes, Sept. 1, 1972; children: Michael Gene, Amy Elizabeth. BS, East Ctrl. U., Ada, Okla., 1976; MPH, Okla. U., 1982. Registered record adminstr. Asst. prof. East Ctrl. U., Ada, 1976—; cons. McCall's Chapel Sch., Ada, 1985—. Mem. Okla. Health Info. Mgmt. Assn. (del. dir. 1993-95, edn. chair 1992-93, v.p. 1991-92). Home: Rt 6 Box 930 Ada OK 74820 Office: East Ctrl U Dept Health Info Mgmt Ada OK 74820

BARNES, WADDELL, medical educator; b. Macon, Ga., June 19, 1925; s. Aiden Emmett and Sarah (Hogan) B.; m. Martha Davis; children: David, Sarah, Allen; m. Phyllis Noren. Student, Mercer U., 1942-44; MD, Harvard U., 1949. Diplomate Am. Bd. Internal Medicine, Am. Bd. Med. Oncology. Intern, then resident in internal medicine Grady Meml. Hosp., Atlanta, 1949-50, 52-53; A.B. Coxe Research fellow Yale-New Haven Hosp., 1953-54, assoc. resident internal medicine, 1954-55; practice medicine specializing in internal medicine Macon, 1955-73, practice medicine specializing in oncology, 1974-81; chmn. dept. medicine Mercer U., Macon, 1981-91. Served to lt. (j.g.) M.C., USN, 1951-52. Mem. ACP, Am. Soc. Internal Medicine, Assn. Profs. of Medicine, Assn. Program Dirs. in Internal Medicine. Office: Mercer Univ Sch Medicine 844 Spring St Macon GA 31201-2113

BARNES, WILLIAM BROOK, health facility administrator; b. Gastonia, N.C., Dec. 11, 1957; s. Lynn Walker and Cozette Miriam (Brookshire) B.; m. Eyleen Mariam Runge, May 15, 1987. BA in History, U. N.C., 1981. Installation rep. HBO & Co., Dallas, 1981-84; regional sales mgr. Infostat Inc., Dallas, 1984-86; regional mgr. Mgmt. Systems Assocs., Raleigh, N.C., 1986-90; regional sales dir. Ameritech Health Connections, 1993-95; with account devel. dept. HBO & Co., 1992—. Mem. N.C. Leadership Forum, Raleigh, 1987, 88. Mem. Healthcare Fin. Mgmt. Assn., Am. Mgmt. Assn. Home: 270 Abington Dr NE Atlanta GA 30328-1268 Office: Mgmt Systems Assocs 207 Abington Dr NE Atlanta GA 30328-1203

BARNES-DANEIL, SIDNEY J., chiropractor; b. Monticello, Ark., Apr. 22, 1956; d. Robert Lee and Marjorie Nowell (Wheeler) B.; m. Mark Lewis Daniel, Jul. 4, 1987; children: Morgan, Evan, Peggy. BS in psychology, Univ. Ga., 1977; D in chiropractic cum laude, Life Chiropractic Coll., 1983. Chiropractor Cotton Exchange Chiropractic, Atlanta, 1983—; official chiropractor The Atlanta Ballet, 1987—, Australian Body Works, 1994—. Treas. ChiroNet, Atlanta, 1986-88. Mem. Alliance Of Women Chiropractors (founding), Backhead Women's Leads Club (dir. 1994, Leadership award

1994). Office: Cotton Exchange Chiropracti 3155 Roswell Rd # 140 Atlanta GA 30305

BARNESS, LEWIS ABRAHAM, physician; b. Atlantic City, N.J., July 31, 1921; s. Joseph and Mary (Silverstein) B.; m. Elaine Berger, June 14, 1953 (dec. Jan. 1985); children: Carol, Laura, Joseph; m. Enid May Fischer Gilbert, July 5, 1987; stepchildren: Mary, Elizabeth, Jennifer, Rebecca. A.B., Harvard U., 1941, M.D., 1944; M.A. (hon.), U. Pa., 1971. Intern Phila. Gen. Hosp., 1944-45; resident Children's Med. Center, Boston, 1947-50; asst. chief, then chief dept. pediatrics Phila. Gen. Hosp., 1951-72; vis. physician U. Pa. Hosp., 1952-57, acting chief, then chief, 1957-72; mem. faculty U. Pa. Sch. Medicine, 1951-72, prof. pediatrics, 1964-72; chmn. dept. U. So. Fla. Med. Sch., Tampa, 1972-88, prof. pediatrics, 1988—; vis. prof. Univ. Wis., 1987-92, prof. emeritus, 1993—. Author: Pediatric Physical Diagnosis Yearbook, edits. 1-6, 1957—; editor: Advances in Pediatrics, 1976—, Pediatric Nutrition Handbook, 3d edit., 1991; asst. editor Pediatric Gastroenterology and Nutrition, 1981-91; editl. bd. Cons., 1960-84, Pediatrics, 1978-83, Core Jour. Pediatrics, 1980—, Contemporary Pediatrics, 1984—, Jour. Clin. Medicine and Nutrition, 1985-95, Nutrition Rev., 1985-87. Mem. dietary guidelines adv. com. USDA. Served to capt. AUS, 1945-46. Recipient Lindback Teaching award U. Pa., 1963; Borden award nutrition, 1972; Noer Disting. Prof. award, 1980, Joseph B. Goldberger award in clin. nutrition, 1984, Joseph St. Geme Leadership award 7 pediatric socs., 1991. Fellow Am. Inst. Nutrition; mem. AAAS, Am. Pediatric Soc. (recorder-editor 1964-75, pres. 1985-86, John Howland award 1993), Soc. Pediatric Rsch., Am. Acad. Pediatrics (chmn. com. on nutrition 1974-81, Abraham Jacobi award 1991, Med. Edn. Lifetime Achievment award 1995), Dietary Guidelines Adv. Commn., USDA, Sigma Xi, Alpha Omega Alpha. Home: 1115 W Virginia Ave Tampa FL 33603-4538 Office: U South Fla Dept Pediat 12901 Bruce B Downs Blvd Tampa FL 33612-4742

BARNET, ROBERT JOSEPH, cardiologist, ethicist; b. Port Huron, Mich., Apr. 27, 1929; s. John A. and Ruth Elizabeth (Wittliff) B.; m. Helen Kresoja, Dec. 8, 1969; children: Benedict, Maria, Antonia, Peter, Elizabeth, Rebecca, Christina, Jacqueline, Ann. Student, Port Huron Jr. Coll., summers 1947, 49; MD, Loyola U., Chgo., 1951; BS in Chemistry magna cum laude, U. Notre Dame, 1954; MA in History, U. of Nev., 1986; MA in Philosophy, U. Notre Dame, 1988. Diplomate Am. Bd. Internal Medicine, Nat. Bd. Med. Examiners. Med. intern Boston City Hosp., 1954-55; rotating intern Mercy Hosp., Chgo., 1955; asst. resident in medicine Boston City Hosp., 1958-59; clin. and research fellow in cardiology Children's Med. Center and House of the Good Samaritan, Boston, 1959-60; cons. fellow in rheumatic fever pediatric service Boston City Hosp., 1959-60; acamedician Cath. Acad. Sci., Washington, 1995—; research fellow in pediatrics Harvard U., Boston, 1959-60; clin. fellow in cardiology Mass. Meml. Hosps., Boston, 1960-61; physician-in-charge St. Francis Mission Hosp., Solwezi, No. Rhodesia, 1961-62; vis. physician Solwezi Boma Rural Hosp., No. Rhodesia, 1961-62; dir. clinics, assoc. in medicine Stritch Sch. Medicine, Loyola U., Chgo., 1962-65; physician-in-charge Cardiac Clinic, Loyola U., Chgo., Fantus Outpatient dept. Cook County Hosp., Chgo., 1962-65, Hypertension Clinic, Fantus Outpatient dept. Cook County Hosp., 1962-65; lectr. in electrocardiography and cardiology Loyola U., Chgo., 1962-65; assoc. attending physician dept. medicine Cook County Hosp., 1962-63, attending physician, 1963-65; practice medicine specializing in cardiology Reno, 1965-87; med. staff Washoe Med. Center, 1965—, St. Mary's Hosp., 1965—; assoc. clin. prof. cardiology U. Nev.; also assoc. dir. Lab. Environ. Patho-Physiology, Desert Research Inst., U. Nev., Reno, 1965-68; dir. Cardiac Care unit Washoe Med. Center, 1965-83, exec. com., 1967-71, 73-77, vice chief dept. medicine, 1969, chief, 1970-71, 78, chief dept. emergency services, 1973-77; cons. in cardiology disability determination unit State of Nev., 1966-87, Crippled Children's Svc., 1966-76, Reno VA Hosp., 1967-80; asst. clin. prof. med. edn. U. Utah, 1968-71; cons. Churchill Pub. Hosp., Fallon, Nev., 1969-87, Pershing Gen. Hosp., Lovelock, Nev., 1969-87; clin. assoc. U. Nev., Reno, 1971-72, assoc. clin. prof. medicine, 1973-77, prof., 1978—; vis. scholar U. Notre Dame, 1989-90, 96—; prof. med. ethics St. Louis U., 1993-95. Contbr. articles to med. jours. Served with U.S. Army, 1955-58. Recipient Clin. Faculty Honor award for outstanding tchr. Loyola U., 1963-64; Acemedician Catholic Acad. of Sci. Fellow A.C.P. (bd. govs. 1980-85), Am. Coll. Cardiology (bd. govs. 1974-77), Am. Coll. Chest Physicians; mem. Nev., Washoe County med. socs., Am. Fedn. Clin. Research, Nev. Heart Assn. (bd. dirs., exec. com., pres. 1974-75). Home: 166 Greenridge Dr Reno NV 89509-3927

BARNETT, BARON GALE, prosthodontist; b. St. Cloud, Minn., Dec. 17, 1946; s. Edgar Clinton Barnett and Delores (Robertson) Kelly; m. Jean Drabbe, June 9, 1968 (div. 1982); children: Dirk, Kiva, Alex; m. Barbara Jean Masters, May 9, 1984. BA, U. Calif., Riverside, 1969; DDS, UCLA, 1973. Diplomate Am. Bd. Prosthodontics (examiner 1982—). Rotating intern Long Beach (Calif.) VA Hosp., 1973-74; resident in fixed prosthodontics Wadsworth VA Health Ctr., L.A., 1974-76; pvt. practice, Tualatin, Oreg., 1976—; coord. for Multnomah County, Oreg. Peer Rev., 1984-92; vis. lectr. dept. fixed prosthodontics Oreg. Health Scis. U., Portland, 1976-80; lectr. in field to profl. meetings. Contbr. articles to dental jours. Recipient Alumnus award UCLA, 1973. Fellow Am. Coll. Prosthodontics, Internat. Coll. Prosthodontics; mem. ADA, Acad. Osseointegration, Am. Acad. Restorative Dentistry, Pacific Coast Soc. Prosthodontics, Oreg. Dental Assn., Osseointegration Study Club So. Calif., Clackamas County DentL Soc. (editor 1978, treas. 1979, v.p. 1980), Omicron Kappa Upsilon. Home: PO Box 595 Lake Oswego OR 97034 Office: 7965 SW Mohawk St Tualatin OR 97062

BARNETT, BENJAMIN LEWIS, JR., physician; b. Woodruff, S.C., July 22, 1926; s. Benjamin Lewis and Mattie Bernice (Skinner) B.; m. Annalyne Louise Hall, Oct. 25, 1958; children: Benjamin Lewis III, Jane Kristen. B.S., Furman U., 1946, LL.D., 1978; M.D., Med. U. S.C., 1949. Diplomate Am. Bd. Family Practice (mem. exam. bd. 1975-81, dir. 1976-81, exec. com. 1979-81, pres. 1980-81). Intern Protestant Episcopal Hosp., Phila., 1949-50; pvt. practice gen. medicine Woodruff, 1950-70; assoc. prof. family practice Med. U. S.C., Charleston, 1970-74; prof. family practice Med. U. S.C., 1974-77, asst. dir. family practice residency program, 1970-75, chief undergrad. curriculum, 1970-77, vice chmn. dept. family practice, 1973-77, asst. dean for student affairs, 1975-77; mem. clin. staff Med. U. Hosp., Charleston County Hosp., 1970-77; Walter M. Seward prof., chmn. dept. family medicine U. Va. Med. Sch., 1977—, baccalaureate, 1986, mem. faculty senate, 1988-92; family medicine physician-in-chief U. Va. Med. Center Hosp., 1977—; chief of staff Woodruff Hosp., 1966-69; vis. lectr., cons. numerous med. schs.; Stoneburner lectr. Med. Coll. Va., 1975; Daniel Drake lectr. U. Cin., 1976; Robert P. Walton lectr. Med. U. S.C., 1978; Goodlark prof. U. Tenn., 1979; Roy J. Gerard lectr. Mich. State U., 1992; vis. scholar U. Mich. Med. Sch., 1984; vis. prof. Med. Coll. of Ga., 1982, Case Western Res. Sch. Medicine, 1984, U. Vt., 1988, U. N.Mex., 1991; Mack Lipkins vis. prof. U. Oreg., 1987, U. Utah, 1989; Donald J. Welter Meml. lectr. Med. Coll. Wis., 1989; Frederick Lytel Meml. lectr., Abington, Pa., 1989; Bradford Strock lectr. Harrisburg (Pa.) Gen. Hosp., 1989; 7th Leland Blanchard Meml. lectr. Soc. Tchrs. Family Medicine ann. meeting, Nashville, 1985; health officer, Town of Woodruff, 1950-54; keynote speaker Assn. Depts. Family Medicine, Clearwater, Fla., 1991; commencement speaker U. Va. Med. Sch., 1992; Grand Prof. Rounds St. Margaret's Hosp., Pitts., 1993; Julian Keith lectr. Bowman Gray Sch. Medicine, 1993; keynote speaker leadership conf. Fla. Med. Assn., Ponta Vedra, 1994, AHEC conf. S.C. Family Practice, Myrtle Beach, 1994; B. Leslie Huffman lectr. Med. Coll. of Ohio, Toledo, 1994; grad. speaker McLennan County Med. Edn. and Rsch. Found., Waco, Tex., 1995. Author: Between the Lines, 1989; editor: S.C. Family Physician, 1973-74; contbr. articles to med. jours. and chpts. to textbooks. Mem. Spartanburg County Bd. Edn., 1968-70, sec. 1969-70; trustee Bethea Bapt. Home for Aged, Darlington, S.C., 1972-73; mem. bd. trustees Furman U., 1994—. Named Citizen of Year Woodmen of World, 1968; recipient Golden Apple award for clin. teaching Student AMA, 1973; Thomas W. Johnson award Am. Acad. Family Physicians, 1976, Disting. Alumnus award Med. U. S.C., 1993. Mem. AMA (mem. residency rev. com. for family practice 1974-79), Va., Albemarle County med. socs., Soc. Tchrs. Family Medicine (v.p. 1974, sec.-treas. 1975, dir. 1981-85, cert. of excellence 1983, F. Marian Bishop award 1996), Am. Acad. Family Physicians, S.C. Acad. Family Physicians (v.p. 1973, pres. 1975-76), Spartanburg County Med. Soc. (v.p. 1968), Am. Philatelic Soc., Coun. Acad. Socs., Furman U. Alumni Assn. (dir. 1972-77), U. Va. Raven Soc., Alpha Omega Alpha (faculty councilor), Alpha Kappa Kappa (pres. 1948), Kappa Alpha (v.p. 1944). Baptist (deacon, chmn. bd.). Home: 2406 Northfields Rd Charlottesville VA 22901-1728

BARNETT, CRAWFORD FANNIN, JR., internist, educator, cardiologist, travel medicine specialist; b. Atlanta, May 11, 1938; s. Crawford Fannin and Penelope Hollinshead (Brown) B.; m. Elizabeth McCarthy Hale, June 6, 1964; children: Crawford Fannin III, Robert Hale. Student Taft Sch., 1953-56, U. Minn., 1957; AB magna cum laude, Yale U., 1960; postgrad. (Davison scholar) Oxford (Eng.) U., 1963; MD (Trent scholar), Duke, 1964. Intern internal medicine Duke U. Med. Center, Durham, N.C., 1964-65, resident, 1965; resident internal medicine Wilmington (Del.) Med. Ctr., 1965-66. dir. Tenn. Heart Disease Control Program, Nashville, 1966-68; pvt. practice medicine specializing in internal medicine and travel medicine, Atlanta, 1968—; dir. Travel Immunization Ctr., Atlanta; mem. staff Crawford Long, Northside, Grady Meml., West Paces, North Fulton, hosps. (all Atlanta); mem. teaching staff Vanderbilt Med. Ctr., Nashville, 1966-68, Crawford Long Meml. Hosp., 1969—; clin. instr. internal medicine, dept. medicine Emory U. Med. Sch., Atlanta, 1969—. Bd. govs. Doctors Meml. Hosp., 1971-80; bd. dirs. Atlanta Speech Sch., 1976-80, 92—, Historic Oakland Cemetery, 1976-86, So. Turf Nurseries, 1977-92, Tech Industries, 1978-92; bd. dirs. Am. Chestnut Found., 1990. Served as surgeon USPHS, 1966-68. Fellow Am. Geog. Soc., Royal Soc. of Tropical Medicine and Hygiene, Royal Geog. Soc., Royal Soc. Medicine, Explorers Club (life, N.Y.C.); mem. Am. Soc. Tropical Medicine and Hygiene, Am. Fedn. Clin. Rsch., Coun. Clin. Cardiology, AMA, Ga. Med. Assn., Atlanta Med. Assn., Am. Heart Assn., Ga. Heart Assn., Am. Soc. Internal Medicine, Ga. Soc. Internal Medicine, Am. Assn. History Medicine, Ga. Hist. Soc., Atlanta Hist. Soc. (bd. govs. 1976-84), Ga. Trust for Hist. Preservation, Nat. Trust Hist. Preservation, Internat. Hippocratic Found. Soc. (Greece), Faculty of History of Medicine and Pharmacy Worshipful Soc. Apothecaries of London, Atlanta Com. on Fgn. Relations (chmn. exec. com. 1972-88), So. Council Internat. and Public Affairs, Newcomen Soc., Atlanta Clin. Soc., Wilderness Med. Soc., Internat. Soc. Travel Medicine (founding), Travelers Century Club, Circumnavigators Club, South Am. Explorers Club, Victorian Soc. Am. (bd. advisers Atlanta chpt. 1971-86), Mensa, Gridiron, Piedmont Driving Club, Yale Club (dir. 1970-74), Nine O'Clocks Club, Pan Am. Doctors Club, Phi Beta Kappa. Episcopalian. Contbr. articles to profl. publs. Home: 2739 Ramsgate Ct NW Atlanta GA 30305-2830 Office: 3250 Howell Mill Rd NW Ste 205 Atlanta GA 30327-4187

BARNETT, FRANKLIN DEWEES, gynecologist; b. Ft. Thomas, Ky., Aug. 1, 1935; s. Harry and Elizabeth (McKeny) B.; m. Louise Baillod, Oct. 23, 1976; children: Julie, Brian, Kelly, Colin, Robert, Shelley. BS, Asbury Coll., 1957; MD, U. Kans., 1961. Intern Wesley Med. Ctr., Wichita, Kans., 1961-62; resident U. Okla., Oklahoma City, 1964-67; pvt. practice ob.-gyn. Midwest City, Okla., 1967—; clin. assoc. prof. U. Okla. Med. Sch., Oklahoma City; bd. dirs. Okla. Blood Inst. Councilman Midwest City, Okla., 1988-92. Mem. AMA, Am. Assn. Gynecol. Laparoscopists, Am. Fertility Soc., Am. Coll. Ob-Gyn., Midwest City Rotary (pres. 1994-95), Midwest City C. of C. Methodist. Office: Women's Health Care of Midwest City 238 N Midwest Blvd Oklahoma City OK 73110-4229

BARNETT, GORDON JAMES, psychoanalyst; b. Upton, Maine, Mar. 13, 1921; s. James and Grace Darling (Bragg) B.; divorced; children: Gordon James Jr., James Bragdon, Jayson Wayne. BS, U. N.H., 1943; MA, Columbia U., 1945, PhD, 1950; diploma, William. A. White Inst., 1961. Staff psychologist Salvation Army Guidance Bur., N.Y.C., 1945-48; clin. psychologist VA Hosp., N.Y.C., 1948-49, staff clin. psychologist neuropsychiat. unit, 1949-55, asst. chief clin. psychology, 1955-57. supr. psychotherapy postdoctoral program Gordon Derner Inst., Adelphi U., Garden City, N.Y., 1960—; pvt. practice, N.Y.C., 1955—. Translator: Hashish and Mental Illness; contbr. articles to profl. jours. Fellow APA; mem. William A. White Psychoanalytic Soc., Adelphi U. Psychoanalytic Soc., SAR (assoc.), Order Founders and Patriots. Mem. Soc. of Friends. Home and Office: 69 Washington Ave Garden City NY 11530-6237 Office: 903 Park Ave New York NY 10021-0338

BARNETT, GUY OCTO, physician, educator; b. Chula Vista, Calif., Sept. 18, 1930; married, 1958; three children. BA, Vanderbilt U., 1952; MD, Harvard U., 1956. Resident Peter Bent Brigham Hosp., 1956-61; clin. assoc. Nat. Heart Inst., 1958-60; investigator Am. Heart Assn., 1961-67; physician Mass. Gen. Hosp., 1979—; prof. medicine Harvard U., 1980—; lectr. elec. engr. MIT, 1972—. Fellow Inst. Medicine-NAS; mem. IEEE, Assn. Computing Machinery, Biomed. Engring. Soc., ACP, Am. Med. Informatics Assn. (bd. dirs. 1984—). Office: Mass Gen Hosp Lab of Computer Science Lab Computer Sci Boston MA 02114*

BARNETT, HENRY LEWIS, pediatrician, medical educator; b. Detroit, June 25, 1914; s. Lewis and Florence (Marx) B.; m. Shirley Blanchard, Oct. 19, 1940; children—Judith Florence, Martin David. Student, Dartmouth Coll., 1931-32; B.S., Washington U., St. Louis, 1938, M.D., 1938; DSc (hon.), Yeshiva U., 1995. Instr. dept. pediatrics Washington U. Sch. Medicine, 1941-43; asst. prof. dept. pediatrics Cornell U. Med. Coll., 1946-50; asso. prof., 1950-55; prof., chmn. dept. pediatrics Albert Einstein Coll. Medicine, 1955-72, asso. dean clin. affairs, 1970-72, Univ. prof., 1972-81, prof. emeritus, 1981—; dir. pediatric service Bronx Municipal Hosp. Center, 1955-64; dir. Internat. Study Kidney Disease in Children, 1967-81; med. dir. Children's Aid Soc., 1981—; cons. Appleton-Century-Crofts, 1981-83; Mem. WHO Infant Metabolism Team to, Netherlands and Sweden, 1950, WHO Sci. Group Pediatric Rsch., 1967; adv. bd. Internat. Pediatric Assn., 1969-74; cons. Cento Meeting Pediatric Edn. and Family Planning, Ankara, Turkey, 1972, Nat.Inst. Child Health and Human Devel., 1974-85; mem. bd. on maternal, child, and family health rsch. NRC, 1974-82; mem. coun. Found. for Child Devel., 1966—; chmn. med. adv. bd. Am. Council for Emigrees in Professions, 1974-83; trustee, mem. med. adv. com. Children's Aid Soc., 1977-81, recipient trustee award 1992; Felton Bequests vis. prof. Royal Children's Hosp., Melbourne, Australia, 1978; cons. Asian Study Renal Disease in Children, 1978-81. Contbr. articles to profl. jours.; Editor: Pediatrics, 13th-17th edits. Served to capt. M.C. AUS, 1943-46. Fellow Am. Acad. Pediatrics (E. Mead Johnson award 1949, Kidney award 1992); mem. N.Y. Acad. Sci., Inst. Medicine NAS, AAAS, Soc. Pediatric Rsch. (pres. 1959-60), Soc. Exptl. Biology and Medicine, Harvey Soc., Am. Pediatric Soc. (pres. 1981-82, John Howland award and medal 1984), Am. Soc. Clin. Investigation, Assn. Am. Physicians, Am. Soc. Nephrology (John P. Peters award 1988), Brit. Pediatric Soc. (hon.), Am. Physiol. Soc., N.Y. Acad. Medicine, Nat. Turkish Pediatric Assn. (hon.), Societe Francaise de Pediatre (corr.), Sigma Xi, Alpha Omega Alpha. Home: 118 W 79th St New York NY 10024-6445 Office: Children's Aid Soc 150 E 45th St New York NY 10017-3115

BARNETT, JANICE ELAINE, critical care nurse; b. Flagstaff, Ariz., Jan. 3, 1951; d. Garland and Evelyn Rose (Benson) Downum; m. Joe Edwin Barnett, Aug. 9, 1972; children: Analie Rose, Daniel Joseph. BA, U. Okla., 1972; BSN summa cum laude, Tex. Woman's U., 1989. Staff nurse in ICU Decatur (Tex.) Community Hosp. Mem. Mortar Board, Phi Beta Kappa, Sigma Theta Tau, Alpha Chi. Home: RR 1 Box 137 Ponder TX 76259-9601

BARNETT, JEFFREY EDWARD, psychologist; b. Oceanside, N.Y., Apr. 21, 1957. BS, SUNY, Oneonta, 1979; MA, PSYD, Yeshiva U., 1984. Diplomate Am. Bd. Med. Psychotherapists; lic. psychologist, D.C., Md., Tenn. Pvt. practice Annapolis, Md., 1988—; staff psychologist Walter P. Carter Ctr., Balt., 1989—; clin. asst. prof. psychiatry and pediatrics U. Md., Balt., 1990—; adj. asst. prof. Dept. Psychology Loyola Coll., Balt., 1996—. Contbr. articles to profl. jours. Capt. U.S. Army, 1983-87. Fellow Md. Psychol. Assn. (pres. 1996); mem. APA, Nat. Psychology Honor Soc., Sigma Xi (assoc.). Office: 8 Willow St Annapolis MD 21401-3147

BARNETT, JOANNE, nurse, health care facility administrator; b. Mineola, N.Y., June 13, 1954; d. John Joseph and Eleanor Joan (Clemens) Samuels; m. Greg John Barnett, Feb. 4, 1979; children: Kelly Lynn, Kristin Leigh. AS in Nursing, Valencia Community Coll., Orlando, Fla., 1976, AA, 1984; BS in Nursing, U. Cen. Fla., 1987. RN, Fla. Lic. practical nurse Cen. Gen. Hosp., Plainview, N.Y., 1972-73, Fla. Hosp., Altamonte Springs, Fla., 1973-76; RN Orlando Regional Med. Ctr., 1976-77, Fish Meml. Hosp., Deland, Fla., 1977-89; adminstrv. coord. Cen. Fla. Regional Hosp., Sanford, 1990—; cons. Orange Belt Pharmacy, Deland, 1985. Mem. Am. Nurses' Assn., Fla. Nurses' Assn (local dist. sec. 1986-90), Gold Key Soc., Sigma Theta Tau. Republican. Roman Catholic. Home: 392 Hampton Hills Ct De Bary FL 32713 Office: Ctrl Fla Regional Hosp 1401 W Seminole Blvd Sanford FL 32771-6737

BARNETT, JOEY VICTOR, pharmacologist, educator, researcher; b. Evansville, Ind., June 18, 1958; s. Victor Alan and Judy Kay (Kohlmeyer) B. BS in Biology, U. So. Ind., 1980; PhD in Pharmacology, Vanderbilt U., 1986. Rsch. intern Argonne (Ill.) Nat. Lab., U.S. Dept. Energy, 1981; rsch. fellow Brigham & Women's Hosp., Harvard Med. Sch., Boston, 1986-89, instr. medicine, 1989-92; asst. prof. medicine and pharmacology Vanderbilt U., Nashville, 1992—; rsch. investigator Tenn. affiliate Am. Heart Assn., 1993-95, established investigator Am. Heart Assn., 1996—. Co-author: Heart Failure: Basic Science and Clinical Aspects, 1993; contbr. articles and abstracts to profl. jours. Founding bd. dirs. Dismas House in Cen. Mass., Worcester, 1987-90. Mass. affiliate Am. Heart Assn. fellow, 1986-88; recipient Nat. Rsch. Svc. award Nat. Heart Lung and Blood Inst./NIH, Boston, 1988-90, Disting. Alumni award U. So. Ind., 1991. Mem. AAAS, N.Y. Acad. Scis., Ind. Acad. Sci., Basic Rsch. Coun. Am. Heart Assn., Sigma Zeta. Roman Catholic. Office: Vanderbilt U Divsn Cardiology 315 MRB II Nashville TN 27232-6300

BARNETT, LESTER ALFRED, surgeon; b. N.Y.C., Mar. 11, 1915; s. Benjamin and Rae Viola (Marcus) B.; m. Jean Wolfe, Apr. 16, 1939; children: Barbara Jane Barnett Grossman, James A. Student, Ohio State U., 1932-35; B.A. with spl. honors, George Washington U., 1936, M.D., 1939. Diplomate: Am. Bd. Surgery. Intern Gallinger Mcpl. Hosp., Washington, 1939-40; resident St. Peter's Gen. Hosp., New Brunswick, N.J., 1940-41, Walter Reed Gen. Hosp., Washington, 1942-43, Grasslands Hosp., Valhalla, N.Y., 1944-46; practice medicine specializing in surgery Long Branch, N.J., 1945-92, specializing in diseases of the breast, 1985-95; mem. staff Monmouth Med. Center, 1946-95, surgeon emeritus, 1995, dir. dept. surgery, 1961-71, pres. med. staff, 1970-73, trustee, 1975—; bd. mgrs. Monmouth Meml. Sch. Nursing, 1953-65; clin. prof. surgery Hahnemann U., 1970—; assoc. in surgery U. Pa. Sch. Medicine; cons. surgery Jersey Shore Med. Ctr., Neptune; sr. attending in surgery Monmouth Med. Ctr., 1993; chmn. adv. bd. to cancer ctr. Monmouth Med. Ctr., 1993—. Author sci. articles. Trustee Monmouth Coll., 1971-78. Served to 1st lt. M.C. AUS, 1942-43. Recipient Pinnacle award Monmouth Med. Ctr., 1990. Fellow Am. Coll. Gastroenterology, A.C.S.; mem. N.J. Med. Soc. (Golden Merit award 1989), Monmouth County Med. Soc. (pres. 1959-60). Jewish. Clubs: Hollywood Golf (Deal, N.J.); Ocean Beach (Elberon, N.J.); Masons, B'nai B'rith (past lodge pres.). Home: 675 Ocean Ave Apt 9C Long Branch NJ 07740-5155

BARNETT, MARGARET EDWINA, nephrologist, researcher; b. Ft. Benning, Ga., July 28, 1949; d. Eddie Lee and Margaret Thomas (Herndon) B. BS magna cum laude with distinction in Zoology, Ohio State U., 1969; MD, Johns Hopkins U., 1973; PhD in Cellular and Molecular Biology, Case Western Res. U., 1984; postgrad. Purdue U., 1992. Med. technologist blood bank Johns Hopkins Hosp., Balt., 1971-73; intern Greater Balt. Med. Ctr., Towson, Md., 1973-74; med. resident Cleve. Clinic Ednl. Found., 1974-75, Univ. Hosps. Cleve., 1975-76; nephrology fellow, 1976-78, med. teaching fellow, 1978-84; nephrology rounding physician Cmty. Dialysis Ctr., Cleve. and Mentor, Ohio, 1978-83; rsch. assoc. Case Western Res. U., Cleve., 1978-79, 83-84; physician emergency medicine Huron Regional Urgent Care Ctrs., Inc., Cleve., 1983-84; preceptor renal correlation conf., Case Western Res. Sch. Medicine, 1980-81, lectr. anatomy and histology 1979-83; asst. prof. medicine/nephrology Milton S. Hershey Med. Ctr. Pa. State U., Hershey, 1984-87, acting chief renal and electrolyte divsn., 1985, dir. peritoneal, 1986-87, assoc. dir. hypertension, 1986-87; pvt. practice medicine specializing in nephrology and hypertension Arnett Clinic, Lafayette, Ind., 1987-93; dir. outpatient dialysis St. Elizabeth Hosp. Med. Ctr., Lafayette; clin. assoc. faculty of Lafayette Ctr. Sch. Medicine Ind. U., 1987-93; clin. asst. prof. of medicine, Ind. U. Sch. Medicine, 1989-94, pharmacology clin. preceptor Purdue U., 1988-93; spl. guest lectr. hypertension Drug Cos., Ill., Ind., S.D., Ky., Ohio, Pa., 1988-94, Calif., 1995; assoc. dean rsch. and grad. studies Sch. Allied Health Scis. Ind. U., 1993-94, vis. prof. medicine dept. health info. adminstrn. Allied Health Scis., Ind., U., 1994, medicine dept. phys. therapy Nat. Inst. Fitness & Sport, 1993-94; dir. dialysis svcs. King/Drew Med. Ctr., L.A., 1994—; asst. prof. medicine Charles R. Drew U., 1994—, asst. dir. nephrology fellowship program, 1995—; faculty mem. Nat. Bur. Info. on Coronary Heart Disease Risk, 1991-94, mem. cardiorenal subcom., 1995—; rep. rsch. and grad. studies alumni adv. coun. Ohio State U., 1990-93. Del. in nephrology and hypertension citizen amb. program People to People Internat. to Russia, Belarus and Lithuania, 1994, Chinese Med. Assn. 80th Anniversary, Beijing, 1995, active, 1994—. Scholar GM, Leo Yassinoff, Alpha Epsilon Delta, Beanie Drake, Am. Heart Assn., 1977; recipient NIH-Nat. Rsch. Svc. award, 1979-82; Ohio div. Am. Heart Assn. grantee, 1980-81; Ohio Kidney Found. grantee, 1977-78; Pres.'s Scholarship award, 1967-69; AMA Physician Recognition award, 1984-87, various medals for slalom racing. Fellow ACP; mem. John Hopkins Med. and Surg. Soc., AMA (physician rsch. evaluation panel 1981-83), Internat. Soc. of Nephrology, Assn. Black Cardiologists, Inc., Am. Soc. Hypertension, Nat. Kidney Found., Am. Acad. Med. Acupuncture (assoc.), World Tae Kwon Do Fedn., Seoul, Korea, Mensa, Am. Film Inst., Phi Beta Kappa, Alpha Epsilon Delta, Alpha Kappa Alpha. Democrat. Avocations: slalom racing, Tae Kwon Do (2d degree black belt). Office: King/Drew Med Ctr 12021 S Wilmington Ave Los Angeles CA 90059

BARNETT, PATRICIA ANN, health care policy and strategies professional; b. Libertyville, Ill., June 26, 1950; d. Francis Gerald and Johanna Louise (Church) McKinley; m. Junior Edwin Barnett, July 31, 1971; stepchildren: Christopher, Tamara. Diploma, Michael Reese Sch. Nursing, 1971; BA in Labor Rels., Roosevelt U., 1982; JD, Loyola U., Chgo., 1988. RN, Ill.; bar: Ill. Charge nurse Michael Reese Hosp., Chgo., 1971-73; nurse adminstr. Ill. State Psychiat. Inst., 1973-79; lobbyist, assn. adminstr. Ill. Nurses Assn., 1979-85, dir., 1985-87; govt. affairs mgr. Squibb Corp., 1987-89; dir. reimbursement Bristol-Myers Squibb Co., Princeton, N.J., 1989-93; sr. mgr. health econs. and policy Genentech, Inc., South San Francisco, 1993—. Bd. dirs. Loop YWCA, Chgo., 1983-84, Coastside Adult Daycare Ctr. Mem. ANA, ABA, Ill. Nurses Assn. (bd. dirs., conv. del. 1977-79), Alpha Sigma Nu. Office: Genentech Inc 460 Pint San Bruno Blvd South San Francisco CA 94080

BARNETT, PETER RALPH, health science facility administrator, dentist; b. Bklyn., Oct. 21, 1951; s. Seymour and Betty Natalie (Cobbs) B.; m. Susan Clay, Jan. 27, 1990; children: Regina, Alexis, Alana. AB, Colgate U., 1973; DMD, U. Pa., 1977, MBA, 1979. Lic. dentist, Pa., N.J., N.Y. Dir. mgmt. sys. U. Pa. Sch. Dental Med., Phila., 1979-81, asst. dir. clinic mgmt., 1981-84; dir. profl. affairs Pearle Dental, Inc., Dallas, 1984-86, v.p. and dir. dental ops., 1986-87; dir. vision benefits Pearle Health Svcs., Inc., Dallas, 1987-88, v.p. managed vision care, 1988-91, sr. v.p. franchising and sales, 1991-92, sr. v.p. quality and franchising, 1992-93; assoc. Healthcare Venture Assocs., Irving, Tex., 1993-94; exec. dir. Prudential DMO, Atlanta, 1994-95; sr. v.p. and C.O.O. United Dental Care, Dallas, 1995—. Author and co-author several profl. articles on health care mgmt., fin., and mktg. Bd. dirs. PTA Brinker Elementary Sch. Plano, Tex. 1988-89. Mem. ADA, Beta Beta Beta. Democrat. Jewish. Home: 1304 Chippewa Dr Plano TX 75093 Office: United Dental Care 14755 Preston Rd Ste 300 Dallas TX 75240-7862

BARNHART, CHARLES CLIFTON, JR., physician, psychiatrist; b. Ft. Worth, Dec. 29, 1945; s. Charles Clifton Sr. and Vera Louise Barnhart; m. Katharine Lynn Small; children: Melanie, Colin. BS, Tex. Christian U., 1968; MA, U. Tex., 1971; MD, U. Tex., Galveston, 1974. Diplomate Am. Bd. Psychiatry and Neurology. Pvt. practice San Antonio, 1977-92; assoc. clin. prof. U. Tex. Health Sci. Ctr., San Antonio, 1977—; med. dir. Alamo Mental Health Group, San Antonio, 1982-94, Villa Rosa Hosp., San Antonio, 1992—; pres. Travis Quality Mgmt., Austin, 1994—, So. Managed Care, San Antonio, 1994—; CEO South Tex. Behavioral Health, San Antonio, 1995—. Office: Villa Rosa Hosp 5115 Medical Dr San Antonio TX 78229

BARNHART, WILLIAM DANIEL, internist; b. Wheeling, W.Va., Nov. 8, 1944; s. Harold and Hazel (Ingram) B.; m. Norma Lee Kerns, Aug. 23, 1969; children: Catherine, Daniel. BA, W.Va. U., 1967; MD, Northwestern U., 1971, MBA, 1988. Diplomate Am. Bd. Internal Medicine, Am. Bd. Geriatrics. Intern in medicine Wesley Meml. Hosp., Chgo., Fla., 1971-72; resident in medicine Emory U., Atlanta, 1972-74; instr. in medicine Northwestern U., Chgo., 1976-78; dir. primary care St. Masonic Med. Ctr., Chgo., 1978-95; program dir. internal medicine Weiss Hosp., U. Chgo., 1995—. Maj. U.S. Army, 1974-76. Fellow ACP, Inst. Medicine Chgo.; mem. Ill. Soc. of Internal Medicine (sec., treas.), Am. Geriatrics Soc., Am. Coll. of Legal Medicine, Am. Soc. Low Medicine, Am. Soc. Internal Medicine. Home: 1712 N Larrabee St Chicago IL 60614-5622 Office: Weiss Hosp U of Chgo 4646 N Marine Dr Chicago IL 60640

BARNHILL, JOHN WARREN, psychiatrist, educator; b. Oklahoma City, Mar. 4, 1959; s. John Willis and Patricia Beth (Dale) B. AB magna cum laude, Duke U., 1981; MD, Baylor Coll. Medicine, 1985; grad. Ctr. Psychoanalytic Tng. and Rsch., Columbia U., 1996. Diplomate Am. Bd. Psychiatry and Neurology. Resident in pediatrics Baylor Coll. Medicine, Houston, 1985-86; resident in psychiatry The N.Y. Hosp.-Cornell Med. Ctr., N.Y.C., 1986-89, instr., 1989—; pvt. practice, staff psychiatrist Cornell Med. Ctr., 1989-96; student co-chmn. Baylor Med. Admissions Com., 1983-85; co-chmn. N.Y.C. Residents Com., 1987-89. Contbr. articles to med. jours. Interviewer Duke Undergrad. Admissions Com., Houston, 1981-86, N.Y.C., 1987—. Rock Sleyster scholar AMA, 1984-85. Mem. Am. Psychiat. Assn. (rep. exec. coun. 1987-89), Am. Psychoanalytic Assn. Office: 823 Park Ave New York NY 10021-2849

BARNHILL, WILLIAM KEITH, nurse anesthetist, hypnotherapist; b. Blythe, Calif., Aug. 6, 1959; s. William Edgar Barnhill and Eva (Soto) Montes; m. Teresa Lynn, Dec. 9, 1993. AS, Palo Verde Coll., 1982; ADN, Coll. of the Desert, 1983; BSN, Calif. State U., San Bernardino, 1987; MHS, Tex. Wesleyan U., 1990; postgrad., La Salle U., 1990—. RN, Calif.; cert. nurse anesthetist. Staff nurse San Bernardino Cmty. Hosp., 1983-85, emergency dept. supr., 1985-87; commd. 2d lt. U.S. Army, 1985, advanced through grades to maj., 1990; staff nurse Nurse Corps U.S. Army, Ft. Bragg, N.C., 1987-89; airborne nurse anesthetist U.S. Army, Frankfurt, Germany, 1989-93; staff nurse anesthetist Nurse Corps U.S. Army, Ft. Campbell, Ky., 1994-95; resigned U.S. Army, 1995; pres., nurse anesthetist Sleepers Anesthesia Svc., P.C., Taylorville, Ill., 1995—. Author: Hypnosis: A Clinical Course for Healthcare Professionals, 1995. Mem. Am. Assn. Nurse Anesthetists, Nat. Assn. Conceptual Hypnosis (v.p. med. activities, cons. 1994—), Profl. Hypnosis Assn. Home and Office: 3603 Lake Dr Taylorville IL 62568

BARNHOUSE, LILLIAN MAY PALMER, retired medical surgical nurse, researcher, civic worker; b. Canton, Ohio, Sept. 26, 1918; d. Frank Barnard and Jenny Mildred (Leggett) Shear; m. Arnold Barnhouse, June 26, 1940; 1 child, James Wilson. Diploma, Aultman Hosp. Sch. Nursing, Canton, 1939. RN, Ohio, obstetrics specialty. Supr., 1943-44; nurse physician's office Canton, Ohio, 1943-49; ind. critical care nursing local hosps., 1953-68. Instr., blood bank worker ARC, 1940-70; mem. Rep. Nat Com., 1980—; vol. genetic researcher, 1972—; vol. in community. Mem. Ohio Nurses Assn. (past v.p., past chmn. dist. legis. com.), First Families of Ohio, Ladies Oriental Shrine.

BARNUM, BARBARA STEVENS, nursing educator; b. Johnstown, Pa., Sept. 2, 1937; d. William C. and Freda Inzes (Claycomb) Burkett; m. H. James Barnum (dec.); children: Lauren, Elizabeth, Catherine, Anne, Shauna, Sallee, David. AA in Nursing, St. Petersburg Jr. Coll., 1958; BPh, Northwestern U., 1967; MA, DePaul U., 1971; PhD, U. Chgo., 1976. RN, Ill., N.Y. Dir. nursing svcs. Augustana Hosp. and Health Care Ctr., Chgo., 1970-71; dir. staff edn. U. Chgo. Hosps. and Clinics, 1971-73; prof. U. Ill., Chgo., 1973-79; dir. div. health svcs., sci. and edn. Columbia U. Tchrs. Coll., N.Y.C., 1979-87; editor Nursing & Health Care Nat. League for Nursing, N.Y.C., 1989-91; editor div. nursing Columbia-Presbyn. Med. Ctr., Columbia U., N.Y.C., 1991-95; prof. Sch. Nursing Columbia U., N.Y.C., 1995—; chmn. bd. Barnum & Souza, N.Y.C., 1989-92; civilian cons. to surgeon gen. USAF, 1980-87. Author: Nursing Theory, Analysis, Application and Evaluation, 4th edit., 1994, Writing for Publication: A Primer for Nurses, 1995, (with K. Kerfoot) The Nurse as Executive, 4th edit., 1995, Spirituality and Nursing: From Traditional to New Age, 1996; editor: Nursing Leadership Forum, 1994—. Mem. governing bd. Nurses House, 1979-86, Nat. Health Coun., 1981-90, others. Fellow Am. Acad. Nursing (governing bd. 1982-84); mem. Sigma Theta Tau (Founders' award 1979). Home: 80 Park Ave Apt 15G New York NY 10016-2537 Office: Columbia U Sch Nursing 630 W 168th St New York NY 10032

BAROFF, GEORGE STANLEY, psychologist, educator; b. Bronx, N.Y., Nov. 27, 1924; s. Irving and Ida (Herman) B.; m. Rose Kislin, June 15, 1952 (dec. May 1992); children: Marina Binet, Roy James. BS in Zoology, George Washington U., 1948, MA in Clin. Psychology, 1950; PhD in Clin. Psychology, NYU, 1955. Research psychologist dept. med. genetics N.Y. State Psychiat. Inst., 1952-60; chief clin. psychologist Vineland (N.J.) Tng. Sch., 1960-63; assoc. prof. psychology U. N.C., Chapel Hill, 1963-67; prof. U. N.C., 1967—, dir. devel. disabilties tng. inst., 1964—; forensic psychologist with criminal defendants who may be mentally retarded, 1987—. Author: Mental Retardation: Nature, Cause and Management, 1974, 86, Developmental Disabilities: Psychosocial Aspects, 1991; contbr. articles to profl. jours. Served with U.S. Army, 1943-45. Mem. Am. Psychol. Assn., Am. Assn. Mental Retardation, N.C. Psychol. Assn. Jewish. Home: 417 Granville Rd Chapel Hill NC 27514-2723 Office: Univ NC Psychology Dept Chapel Hill NC 27599-3370

BARON, BRUCE, neuroradiologist; b. N.Y.C., Jan. 4, 1962; s. John and Edythe (Levenson) B.; m. Jill Ann Shebeck, May 24, 1992; 1 child, Madison Paige. BS, Allegheny Coll., 1983, U. Osteo. Medicine Health Sci., 1987. Diplomate Am. Bd. Radiology. Resident in surgery Allegheny Gen. Hosp., Pitts., 1987-89, resident in radiology, 1989-93; neuroradiology fellow Cleve. Clin., 1993-95; neuroradiologist, radiologist Midwest Med. Imaging, Omaha, 1995—. Contbr. articles to profl. jours. Recipient Merit award Omaha Midwest Clin. Soc., 1995. Mem. AMA, Am. Soc. Neuroradiology, Radiologic Soc. N.Am., Am. Roentgen Ray Soc., Am. Coll. Radiology, Am. Osteopathic Assn. Office: Midwest Med Imaging Ctr Inc Profl Plz West Ste 104 6751 N 72d St Omaha NE 68122

BARON, DAVID ALAN, cell biologist; b. Chgo., Aug. 14, 1951; s. Marvin and Charlotte (Sebel) B.; m. Susan Daneman Kay, June 12, 1983; children: Jacob, Zachary. BA, U. Chgo., 1972, PhD, 1979. Rsch. scientist Drug Sci. Found., Charleston, S.C., 1982-84; asst. prof. Med. U. S.C., Charleston, 1984-89; rsch. scientist Searle R&D, Skokie, Ill., 1989-93, group leader, 1993-94, sci. fellow, head of investigative toxicology, 1994—. Contbr. articles to profl. jours. Interviewer U. Chgo., 1988, 89. Post-doctoral fellow, Med. U. S.C., 1979-82. Mem. AAAS, Am. Soc. Cell Biology, Electron Microscopy Soc. Am., Drug Information Assn. Office: Searle R&D 4901 Searle Pky Skokie IL 60077-2919

BARON, JEFFREY, pharmacologist, educator; b. Bklyn., July 10, 1942; s. Harry Leo and Terry (Goldstein) B.; m. Judith Carol Rothberg, June 27, 1965; children: Stephanie Ann, Leslie Beth, Melissa Leigh. B.S. in Pharmacy, U. Conn., 1965; Ph.D. in Pharmacology, U. Mich., 1969. Rsch. fellow in biochemistry U. Tex. Southwestern Med. Sch., Dallas, 1969-71, rsch. asst. prof. biochemistry and pharmacology, 1971-72; asst. prof. pharmacology U. Iowa, Iowa City, 1972-75, assoc. prof. pharmacology, 1975-80, prof. pharmacology, 1980—; mem. chem. pathology study sect. NIH, Bethesda, Md., 1983-87, tech. rev. com. Nebr. Cancer and Smoking Disease Rsch. Program, Lincoln, 1984, environ. health scis. rev. com. NIH, Nat. Inst. Environ. Health Scis., Research Triangle Park, N.C., 1990-94. Contbr. numerous articles to profl. jours., chpts. to books. Recipient Rsch. Career Devel. award NIH, 1975-80, numerous rsch. grants NIH. Mem. Am. Soc. for Pharmacology and Exptl. Therapeutics, Am. Soc. Biochem. and Molecular Biology, Am. Assn. for Cancer Rsch., Soc. Toxicology, Internat. Soc. for Study Xenobiotics. Office: U Iowa Dept Pharmacology 2-270 Bowen Sci Bldg Iowa City IA 52242

BARON, JOHN ANTHONY, epidemiologist; b. Cin., Aug. 10, 1945; s. Gilbert W. and Carolyn Marie (Cahan) B.; m. Karen Ann Nielsen; children: Carolynne, Catherine. BA, Yale U., 1967; MS, Stanford U., 1968; MD, U. Mich., 1976; MSc, U. London, 1981. Diplomate Am. Bd. Internal Medicine. Math. statistician Nat. Ctr. for Health Statistics, Washington, 1969-71; chief med. resident dept. medicine Dartmouth Med. Sch., Hanover, N.H., 1979-80; asst. prof. Dartmouth Med. Sch., 1980-86; Milbank scholar Oxford U., Eng., 1981-82; assoc. prof. dept. medicine Dartmouth Med. Sch., Hanover, N.H., 1986-93; prof. medicine, cmty. and family medicine Dartmouth Med. Sch., Hanover, 1993—, sect. chief biostatistics & epidemiology, 1994—; faculty New Eng. Epidemiology Inst., Boston, 1987-92; vis. prof. Uppsala U. Cancer Unit, 1992-93. Contbr. articles to profl. jours. With USPHS, 1969-71. Recipient de Forest prize Yale U., 1967, Girshick prize Stanford U., 1967. Mem. Phi Beta Kappa. Office: Dartmouth Med Sch Hanover NH 03755-3861

BARON, MARTIN RAYMOND, psychology educator; b. Stamford, Conn., Oct. 27, 1922; s. Harry Isaac and Gertrude (Sondak) B.; m. Shirley Elaine Thalberg, July 28, 1945 (dec. Feb. 26, 1989); children: Carol Ann Baron Quirke, Cynthia Ellen Baron Keohane, Marcia Wendy; m. Joy Gray Bennett, Sept. 29, 1992. B.A., Yale U., 1943; M.A., State U. Iowa, 1948, Ph.D., 1949. Asst. prof. psychology Kent (O.) State U., 1949-53, assoc. prof., 1953-58, prof., 1958-71; prof. psychology U. Louisville, 1971-86, prof. emeritus, 1986—, chmn. dept., 1971-72; acting dean U. Louisville (Coll. Arts and Scis.), 1972-73, asst. v.p. for acad. affairs, 1973-76, asst. exec. v.p. planning, 1976-81. Assoc. editor: Behavioral Sci, 1973-92; contbr. articles to psychol. publs. Bd. dirs. Coalition for Homeless of Louisville and Jefferson County, Ky., 1986-94, Seven Counties Svcs. Inc., Louisville, 1989-95, chmn., 1990-92. With AUS, 1943-46. Mem. Am. Psychol. Assn., Midwestern Psychol. Assn., Southeastern Psychol. Assn., So. Soc. Philosophy and Psychology, Sigma Xi. Home: 1611 Spring Dr Apt 5C Louisville KY 40205-1341

BARON, MELVIN FARRELL, pharmacy educator; b. L.A., July 29, 1932; s. Leo Ben and Sadie (Bauchman) B.; m. Lorraine Ross, Dec. 20, 1953; children: Lynn Baron Friedman, Ross David. PharmD, U. So. Calif., 1957, MPA, 1973. Lic. pharmacist, Calif. Pres. Shield Health Care Ctrs., Van Nuys, Calif., 1957-83; v.p. Shield Health Care Ctrs., Inc. (C.R. Bard, Inc. subsidiary), 1983-86; pres. Merit Coll., 1988-92, PharmCom., L.A., 1990—; asst. prof. clin. pharmacy U. So. Calif., L.A., 1991—, asst. dean pharm. care programs, 1995—; adj. asst. prof. U. Without Walls, Shaw U., Raleigh, N.C., 1973; project dir. Hayne Found. Drug Rsch. Ctr. U. So. Calif., L.A., 1973; assoc. dir. Calif. Alcoholism Found., 1973-75; adj. asst. prof. clin. pharmacy Sch. of Pharmacy U. So. Calif., L.A., 1981-91; cons. Topanga Terr. Convalescent Hosp., 1970-80, Calif. Labor Mgmt. Plan for alcoholism programs and coords., 1974, Office of Alcoholism, State of Calif., Nat. In-Home Health Svc., 1975, Continuity of Life Team, 1975, others; vis. prof. Tokyo Coll. Pharmacy, 1994; lectr. Meijo U., Nagoya U., Japan, 1994. Adv. bd. Pharmacist Newsletter, 1980—. Chmn. Friends of Operation Bootstrap, 1967-77; svc. chmn. tng. coord. Am. Cancer Soc., San Fernando Valley, Calif., 1980; mem. adv. bd. L.A. VNA, 1982; bd. dirs. pres. QSAD, 1987-88; pres. bd. Everywoman's Village, 1988-89; bd. dirs. Life Svcs., 1988—; pres. bd. counselors, U. So. Calif., 1988-92, mem. Calif. State Bd. Pharmacy Com. on Student/Preceptor Manual, 1991-93. Named Disting. Alumnus of Yr., U. So. Calif., Sch. of Pharmacy Alumni Assn., 1979, U. So. Calif. Torchbearer, 1990-91, hon. mem. Phi Lambda Sigma, L.A., 1994. Mem. Am. Pharm. Assn., Am. Soc. Health Sys. Pharmacists, Calif. Pharmacist Assn., Am. Soc. Pub. Adminstrn., Am. Assn. Colls. of Pharmacy, Phi Kappa Phi, Rho Chi. Home: 323 San Vicente Santa Monica CA 90402-1629 Office: U So Calif. 1985 Zonal Ave Los Angeles CA 90033-1058

BARON, ROBERT ALAN, psychology and business educator, author; b. N.Y.C., June 7, 1943; s. Bernard Paul and Ruth (Schlossberg) B.; m. Sandra Faye Lawton, June 21, 1974; 1 child, Jessica Lynn. BS, CUNY, 1964; MS, U. Iowa, 1967, PhD, 1968. Asst. prof. U. S.C., 1968-71; assoc. prof. psychology Purdue U., West Lafayette, Ind., 1971-75, prof., 1975-87; prof., prof. mgmt. and chair Rensselaer Poly. Inst., 1991-93; vis. assoc. prof. U. Minn., 1972, U. Tex., 1974-75; vis. prof. Princeton U., 1977-78; vis. prof. mgmt. U. Wash., 1985; program dir. NSF, 1979-81; vis. fellow U. Oxford, Eng., 1982. Author: (with D. Richardson) Human Aggression, 2d edit., 1994, (with D. Byrne) Social Psychology, 1974, 8th edit., 1996, (with J. Greenberg) Behavior in Organizations, 1983, 6th edit., 1996, Psychology, 3d edit., 1995; contbr. numerous articles to profl. jours.; patentee apparatus for enhancing the environ. quality of work spaces. NSF grantee. Fellow Am. Psychol. Assn.; mem. Acad. Mgmt., Eastern Psychol. Assn. Home: 27 Sunnyside Rd Scotia NY 12302-2408 Office: Rensselaer Poly Inst Dept Mgmt Troy NY 12180-3590

BARON, THOMAS EDWARD, urologist; b. Chgo., Dec. 5, 1946; s. Edward Valerian and Eve Christina (Grabowski) B.; m. Linda Sue Wheeler, Jan. 3, 1981; children: Joseph, Pamela, John. BS, U. of Ill., 1968, MD, 1972, MBA, 1989. Diplomate Am. Bd. Urology. Urologist U.S. Army, Ft. Campbell, Ky., 1977-79; pvt. practice Mt. Airy, N.C., 1979-81; urologist Springfield (Ill.) Clinic, 1981—; pres. Clay Scarritt Ptnrship., Springfield, 1989-91; pres. Springfield Clinic Bd., 1985-87. Major, AUS, 1977-79. Fellow ACS. Home: 1908 Oak Creek Rd Springfield IL 02703 Office: Springfield Clinic 1025 S 7th St Springfield IL 02703

BARONDES, SAMUEL HERBERT, psychiatrist, educator; b. Bklyn., Dec. 21, 1933; s. Solomon and Yetta (Kaplow) B.; m. Ellen Slater, Sept. 1, 1963 (dec. Nov. 22, 1971); children: Elizabeth Francesca, Jessica Gabrielle. AB, Columbia U., 1954, MD, 1958. Intern, then asst. resident in medicine Peter Bent Brigham Hosp., Boston, 1958-60; sr. asst. surgeon USPHS, NIH, Bethesda, Md., 1960-63; resident in psychiatry McLean and Mass. Gen. hosps., Boston, 1963-66; asst. prof., then assoc. prof. psychiatry and molecular biology Albert Einstein Coll. Medicine., Bronx, N.Y., 1966-69; prof. psychiatry U. Calif., San Diego, 1969-86; prof., chmn. dept. psychiatry, dir. Langley Porter Psychiat. Inst. U. Calif., San Francisco, 1986-94, dir. Ctr. Neurobiology and Psychiatry, 1994—, Jeanne and Sanford Robertson Prof. Neurobiol. and Psychiatry, 1996—; pres. McKnight Endowment Fund for Neurosci., 1989—; mem. sci. adv. com. Chalres E. Culpeper Found.; mem. bd. sci. advisors Buck Ctr. for Rsch. in Aging; mem. sci. adv. com. Rsch. Am.; mem. governing coun. Internat. Brain Rsch. Orgn., 1994—. Author: Molecules and Mental Illness, 1993; mem. editorial bds. profl. jours.; contbr. numerous articles to profl. publs. Recipient Rsch. Career Devel. award USPHS, 1967, Elliott Royer award, 1989, P.H. Stillmark medal Estonia, 1989; Fogarty Internat. scholar NIH, 1979. Fellow AAAS, Am. Psychiat. Assn., Am. Coll. Neuropsychopharmacology; mem. Inst. Medicine Nat. Acad. Sci. Office: U Calif-San Francisco Langly Porter Psychiat Inst 401 Parnassus Ave San Francisco CA 94143-0984

BARONDESS, JEREMIAH ABRAHAM, physician; b. N.Y.C., June 6, 1924; s. Benjamin and Dora (Greenberg) B.; m. Sue Kaufman, Nov. 22, 1953 (dec. 1977); 1 child, James Joseph; m. Linda Hiddemen, Dec. 10, 1982. MD, Johns Hopkins U., 1949; DSc (hon.), Albany Med. Coll., Union U., 1978; LittD (hon.), N.Y. Inst. Tech., 1992; DMedSci (hon.), Med. Coll. Pa., 1993. Diplomate Am. Bd. Internal Medicine (bd. govs., council gen. internal medicine 1975-81). Intern, then asst. resident in medicine Osler Med. Svc. Johns Hopkins Hosp., 1949-51; asst. medicine Johns Hopkins U. Med. Sch., 1950-51; mem. virology sect., research div. Children's Hosp., Phila., also; rsch. fellow virology U. Pa. Med. Sch., 1951-53; asst. resident, then chief resident in medicine N.Y. Hosp.-Cornell U. Med. Center, 1953-55; mem. faculty Cornell U. Med. Coll., 1953—, clin. prof. medicine, 1971-78, prof. clin. medicine, 1978-87, Irene F. and I. Roy Psaty Disting. Prof. Clin. Medicine, 1987-89, William T. Foley Disting. Prof. in Clin. Medicine, 1989-90, adj. prof. clin. medicine, 1990, prof. emeritus, 1993—; mem. staff N.Y. Hosp., 1953—, attending physician., 1971—; chief pvt. med. svc., 1971-92; hon. staff mem. N.Y. Hosp., 1992—; assoc. chmn. dept. medicine, 1983-90; asst. vis. physician Bellevue Hosp., 1960-67; cons. medicine Meml. Hosp. Cancer and Allied Diseases, 1972-90; Alpha Omega Alpha vis. prof. U. P.R. Med. Sch., 1972; Meyerowitz meml. lectr. U. Rochester Sch. Medicine, 1980; disting. lectr. U. N.C., 1982; vis. prof. medicine U. Ill. Med. Sch., 1974, U. Va. Med. Sch., 1976, Mayo Clinic and Med. Sch., 1978, U. Iowa Sch. Medicine, 1979, U. Tex. Med. Ctr., 1986, 90, U. Pa., 1986, U. Va., 1989, N.Y. Med. Coll., 1990, SUNY Health Sci. Ctr., Bklyn., 1992; mem. nat. resources com. Johns Hopkins U., 1965—, trustee, 1977-94, trustee emeritus, 1994—, chmn. vis. com. Sch. Medicine, 1978-92. Author: (with A.M. Harvey and J. Bordley) Differential Diagnosis, (with J. McGovern and C. Roland) The Persisting Osler, 1985, (with C. Roland) The Persisting Osler II, 1994, (with A.H. Samiy and R.G. Douglas) Textbook of Diagnostic Medicine, 1987; editor: Diagnostic Approaches to Presenting Syndromes, 1971; co-editor Differential Diagnosis, 1994; mem. editl. bd. Forum on Medicine, Pharos, Internat. Jour. Technol. Assessment in Health Care, Jour. Royal Soc. Med.; contbr. articles to profl. jours. Served with AUS, 1943-46; Served with USPHS, 1951-53. Recipient Wiggers award Albany Med. Coll. Union U., 1978, Alfred Stengel award ACP, 1983; named Hon. Alumnus Cornell U. Med. Coll., 1974. Fellow AAAS, Royal Coll. Physicians London, ACP (chmn. bd. govs. 1973-75, bd. regents 1975—, pres.-elect 1977-78, pres. 1978-79, pres. emeritus 1988), Federated Coun. Internal Medicine, Royal Soc. Medicine, Royal Soc. Health, Royal Coll. Physicians Ireland (hon.); mem. Am. Clin. and Climatol. Assn. (coun. 1975-78, pres. 1994), Am. Osler Soc. (pres. 1983-84), Am. Fedn. Clin. Rsch., APHA, Assn. Am. Physicians, Harvey Soc., N.Y. Heart Assn., Inst. Medicine NAS (coun. 1979-81, co-chair coun. on health care tech., chair com. on managed care and chronic disease 1996), N.Y. Acad. Scis., N.Y. Acad. Medicine (pres. 1990—), Internat. Soc. Internal Medicine, Phi Beta Kappa, Alpha Omega Alpha (dir. 1978-79, pres. 1987-89), Century Club (N.Y.C.), Cosmos Club (Washington). Jewish. Home: 544 E 86th St New York NY 10028-7536 Office: NY Acad Medicine 1216 5th Ave New York NY 10029

BARONE, ANTHONY, anesthesiologist; b. N.Y.C., Aug. 18, 1938; s. Frank and Eleanor Rita (Ferraioli) B.; m. Maryann Joan Mieczkowski, May 18, 1963; children: Karen Lisa, John Christopher, Stephen Collins. AB, Columbia U., 1960; MD, N.Y. Med. Coll., 1964. Diplomate Am. Bd. Anesthesiology, Am. Acad. Pain Mgmt., Am. Bd. Anesthesiologists. Intern U.S. Naval Hosp., St. Alban's, N.Y.C., 1964-65, resident in anesthesiology, 1965-68; resident in anesthesiology Columbia Presbyn. Hosp., Albert Einstein Med. Ctr., N.Y.C., 1965-68; U.S. Naval Hosp., St. Albans, N.Y.; anesthesiologist Sacred Heart Hosp., Allentown, Pa., 1971—, also chmn. dept. anesthesiology, 1975-83, 87-90. Lt. commdr. USN, 1964-71, Vietnam. Fellow Am. Coll. Anesthesiologists. Roman Catholic. Office: Valley Anesthisia Inc 451 W Chew St Ste 406 Allentown PA 18102-3424

BARONE, BARTOLO MARIANO, neurological surgeon; b. Poughkeepsie, N.Y., May 15, 1934; s. Bartolo and Gertrude (Granata) B.; m. Marianne Masterton, July 20, 1957 (div. 1974); children: Florence, Caroline, Elizabeth; m. Mary Pringle Herrin, Sept. 21, 1974. BS, Georgetown U., 1955, MD, 1959; MS, McGill U., 1962. Diplomate Am. Bd. Neurol. Surgery. Intern U. Chgo., 1959; resident Montreal Neurologic Inst.-McGill U., 1960-55; postdoctoral fellow NIH, Montreal, Que., Can., 1960, 64; asst. prof. neurosurgery Georgetown U., Washington, 1965-66; clin. assoc. prof. neurol. surgery Med. U. S.C., Charleston, 1966-88, clin. prof., 1988—; pvt. practice Charelston, 1968—; pres. staff Roper Hosp., Charleston, bd. dirs., 1978-88. Author: Roper Hospital Nursing Manual, 1970; contbr. articles to jours. Intracerebral Hemorrage, Brain Tumors, Jour. U. S.C. Adv. coun. Pollution Control Bd. Charleston County, 1970-72; bd. dirs. Greater Charleston Safety Coun., 1985, Charleston Symphony Orch., 1987—. Lt. commdr. USN, 1966-68. Named Boss of Yr. Am. Bus. Woman's Assn., 1972; ACS fellow, 1970. Mem. S.C. Assn. Neurol. Surgeons (pres.), S.C. Med. Assn. (treas., sec., pres.-elect 1991, pres. 1992), Am. Assn. Neurol. Surgeons, Joint Underwriting Assn. S.C. (bd. dirs. 1979—, vice chmn. 1989), Charleston County Med. Soc. (pres.), Carolina Art Assn., Navy League U.S. (life), Carolina Yacht Club, Roper Found. (chmn. bd. dirs. 1987—). Republican. Roman Catholic. Home: 125 Doughty St Ste 400 Charleston SC 29403-5741 Office: Neurology Clin PA 125 Doughty St Ste 400 Charleston SC 29403-5741

BARONE, DONALD ANTHONY, neurologist, educator; b. Bklyn., Dec. 18, 1948; s. John Dominick and Nancy Anne (Salzano) B.; m. Kathleen Ann Kelley, May 22, 1976; children—Steven, Matthew, Daniel. AB, Rutgers U., 1970; DO, Phila. Coll. Osteo. Medicine, 1974. Diplomate Am. Bd. Psychiatry and Neurology, Am. Bd. Electro Diagnostic Medicine. Intern Kennedy Meml. Hosp., Stratford, N.J., 1974-75; resident in neurology U. Vt. Med. Ctr., Burlington, 1975-78; fellow in neuromuscular diseases Columbia-Presbyn. Med. Ctr., N.Y.C., 1978-79; practice medicine specializing in neurology Voorhees and Stratford, N.J., 1979—; clin. asst. prof. U. Medicine and Dentistry of N.J. Sch. Osteo. Medicine, Camden, 1979-88, clin. assoc. prof., 1988—; sect. head neurology Kennedy Meml. Hosp., Stratford, 1979—, dir. Muscular Dystrophy Assn. Clinic, 1984—; cons. Nat. Bd. Examiners for Osteo. Physicians and Surgeons, 1980—; med. adv. bd. Garden State chpt. Myasthenia Gravis Found.; profl. adv. com. Greater Delaware Valley chpt. Multiple Sclerosis Soc.; adv. com., Del. Valley Transplant Assn., 1987—; examiner Am. Bd. Psychiatry and Neurology, 1981—. Editorial reviewer Jour. of the Am. Osteopathic Assn., 1988—; contbr. articles to med. jours. Bd. dirs. Kennedy Health Care Found., 1992—; trustee Kennedy Meml. Hosps., Univ. Med. Ctr., 1995—; chmn. bd. trustees Kennedy Surg. Ctr., 1995—. Recipient Golden Apple award for teaching N.J. Sch. Osteopathic Med., 1987, 88, 89, 90, Excellence in Teaching award U. Medicine and Dentistry of N.J. Found., 1980. . Mem. Am. Acad. Neurology, Am. Assn. Electrodiagnostic Medicine (membership com., mem. hist. com.), Am. Osteo. Assn., N.J. Assn. Osteo. Physicians and Surgeons, Camden County Assn. Osteo. Physicians and Surgeons, Sigma Sigma Phi, Sigma Alpha Omicron. Roman Catholic. Office: Voorhees Profl. Bldg PO Box 330 102 White Horse Rd Ste 101 Voorhees NJ 08043-2504

BARONE, ROBERT MICHAEL, physician; b. Buffalo, Apr. 2, 1941; s. Michael Horace and Antoinette (Buscaglia) B.; m. Mary Margaret Wallis, Mar. 11, 1967; children: Susanne, Julie, Robert. BS, Georgetown U., 1962; MD, SUNY, Buffalo, 1966; MS in Surgery, U. Ill., 1970. Resident in surgery U. Ill., Chgo., 1967-72, fellowship in surg. oncology, 1972-74, asst. prof. surgery, 1972-74; chief oncology NRMC, Oakland, Calif., 1974-76; asst. prof. surgery U. Calif., San Diego, 1976-80, assoc. clin. prof. surgery, 1980—; staff surgeon Oncology Assocs. of San Diego, 1980—; dir. surg. oncology Sharp Healthcare, 1995—; prin. investigator NIH Studies of Hepatic Arterial Therapy, 1983-85, prin. investigator sentinel node studies for melanoma, for intraperitoneal chemotherapy for treatment of colorectal, ovarian, gastric carcinomas and sarcomas. Served to commdr. USNR, 1974-76. Recipient Research award Chgo. Surg. Soc., 1971. Fellow ACS (state chmn. 1983-89, mem. commn. cancer, pres. San Diego chpt. 1986-87); mem. Soc. Surg. Oncology, Soc. Head and Neck Surgeons, Am. Soc. Clin. Oncology, Warren Cole Soc. Office: Oncology Assocs 8008 Frost St Ste 300 San Diego CA 92123

BARR, DAVID CHARLES, healthcare executive; b. Camden, N.J., Apr. 10, 1950; s. John James and Margaret Ruth (Smith) B.; m. Susan Kae Moore; 1 child, David William. BBA, U. Miami, Coral Gables, Fla., 1972. Ptnr. Glazebrook Acctg. Agy., Miami, 1972-73; v.p. Fidelity Bank, Phila., 1973-81; chief fin. officer Pubco Corp., Tysons Corner, Va., 1981-83; v.p. Perpetual Am. Bank, Alexandria, Va., 1983-85; exec. v.p. Equibank, Pitts., 1985-86, Allegheny Beverage Corp., Cheverly, Md., 1986-87; mng. ptnr. Kane Maiwurm Barr Inc., Reston, Va., 1988-89; pres. Genesis Health Svcs., Kennett Sq., Pa., 1989—; exec. v.p. Genesis Health Ventures, Kennett Sq., Pa. Home: 45 Blue Stone Dr Chadds Ford PA 19317-9311 Office: Genesis Health Ventures 148 W State St Kennett Square PA 19348-3050

BARR, KATHLEEN MARGARET, nursing administrator; b. Pottsville, Pa., Feb. 17, 1951; d. Donald Edward and Theresa (Tracy) Dry; mem. Ronald L. Barr, Oct. 15, 1977; 1 child, Rebecca Anne. Nursing diploma, Sacred Heart Hosp., Allentown, Pa., 1972; BSN, U. Tex., San Antonio, 1983; MS, Chapman Coll., Sacramento, Calif., 1985. Cert. ANA, Healthcare Quality Cert. Bd., InterQual, Inc.; RN, Pa. Staff nurse intensive care Palmdale (Calif.) Gen., 1974-75, Upstate Med. Ctr., Syracuse, N.Y., 1975-77; charge nurse cardiothoracic unit Wilford Hall Med. Ctr., San Antonio, 1977-81; charge nurse spl. care Mather Hosp., Sacramento, 1983-87, staff devel. officer, 1987-88; chief nursing svcs. Zweibrucken (Germany) Air Base, 1988-91, Ramstein (Germany) Air Base, 1991-94; chief TRICARE flight Eglin AFB, Ft. Walton Beach, Fla., 1994—; mem. adv. bd. Advanced Home Health Care, Ft. Walton Beach, 1995—; advisor EMT/Paramedic Bd., San Antonio, 1977-83, Sacramento, 1983-88. Author: (booklet) You and Your Heart, 1980, (booklets) Total Quality Management, 1990. Named Master Instr. Quality Inst., 1994. Mem. C. of C. Niceville/Valparaiso (health and wellness com. chair 1995—), Rotary Internat. (chair cmty. affairs 1995—). Home: 103 Oakwood Cir Niceville FL 32578 Office: 96th Med Group 307 Boatner Rd Ste 114 Eglin AFB FL 32542

BARR, PERRY I., family practice physician; b. Phila., Apr. 9, 1932; s. Morris and Dorothy (Shaffer) B.; m. Malva Solkin, June 26, 1955 (div. Dec. 1973); children: Lawrence F., Jamie B. Tyszka. AB, U. Pa., 1954; DO, Phila. Coll. Osteo. Medicine, 1958. Diplomate Am. Coll. Osteo. Family Physicians. Pvt. practice Haddon Heights, N.J., 1960—; lectr. in field.

Mem. Am. Acad. Family Physicians, Am. Osteo. Assn. Sports Medicine, Am. Osteo. Assn., N.J. Assn. Osteo. Physicians and Surgeons, Camden county Soc. Osteo. Physicians. Jewish. Office: 15 Black Horse Pike Haddon Heights NJ 08035-1007

BARR, RICHARD ARTHUR, biology educator, researcher; b. Southport, N.Y., Mar. 12, 1925; s. Harold Arthur and Emma Marie (Ferguson) B.; m. Violet Marie Keens, Oct. 8, 1961; children: Robert Adrian, Elisa Marie. BS in Agrl., U. Vt., 1950, MS, 1955; PhD, Cornell U., 1963. Rose grower Elmira (N.Y.) Floral Products, 1950-55; rsch. asst. U. Vt., Burlington, 1953-56; rsch. asst. Cornell U., Ithaca, N.Y., 1958-61, tchg. and rsch. asst., 1958-61, rsch. assoc., 1961-64, asst. prof., 1964-66; asst. prof. biology U. Mo., St. Louis, 1966-68; assoc. prof. Shippensburg (Pa.) State Coll., 1968-72; prof. Shippensburg U., 1972-91, prof. emeritus, 1992—. With USN, 1943-46. Republican. Presbyterian. Home: 55 Rich Dr Shippensburg PA 17257-8625 Office: Shippensburg U Biology Dept Shippensburg PA 17257

BARR, RONALD JEFFREY, dermatologist, pathologist; b. Mpls., Jan. 5, 1945; s. Maxwell Michael and Ethel Deana (Ring) B.; m. Ulla Elisabet Edstam; children: Anna, Jessica, Sara. BA, Johns Hopkins U., 1967, MD, 1970. Diplomate Am. Bd. Pathology, Am. Bd. Dermatology. Intern U. Calif., San Diego, 1970-71, resident in pathology, 1971-75; resident in dermatology U. Calif., Irvine, 1975-78, fellow in dermatopathology, 1975-78, asst. prof. dermatology, 1977-83, assoc. prof. dermatology and pathology, 1983-86, prof. dermatology and pathology, 1987—, dir. Dermatopathology Lab., 1979—; prof., chmn. dept. dermatology U. Calif., Davis, 1986-87; bd. dirs. Am. Bd. Dermatology, 1989—. Contbr. more than 10 chpts. to books. more than 100 articles to profl. jours. Lt. USN, 1971-73. Fellow Am. Soc. Dermatopathology (pres. 1988-89); mem. Internat. Soc. Dermatopathology (exec. com.), Internat. Com. for Dermatopathology (sec.-treas. 1987-91, pres. 1992-93). Office: U Calif Irvine Med Ctr Dermatopathology Lab 101 The City Dr S Orange CA 92668-3201

BARR, SANFORD LEE, dentist; b. Chgo., Jan. 18, 1952; s. Mike and Bernice (Kaplan) B.; m. Randy Joyce Briskman, Dec. 24, 1973; children: Shelby Paige, Blake Jared, Taylor Ashley. BS, U. Ill., 1972; DDS, Northwestern U., 1976. Resident gen. practice VA Hosp., Chgo., 1976-77; gen. practice dentistry Chgo., 1977—; attending dentist Rush Med. Coll., Chgo., 1977—; asst. prof. Presbyn.-St. Luke's Hosp., Chgo., 1977—, Northwestern U. Sch. Dentistry, Chgo., 1977-83; cons. VA Hosp., Chgo., 1978—. Mem. adv. bd. Homehealth of Ill. Chgo., 1984—. Fellow Acad. Gen. Dentistry, Acad. Facial Aesthetics; mem. ADA, Acad. Hosp. Dentistry, Chgo. Dental Soc., Alpha Omega (treas. 1984, pres. elect 1988), Tau Delta Phi. Jewish. Lodge: B'nai B'rith (v.p. Chgo. chpt. 1984—). Home: 632 Dauphine Ct Northbrook IL 60062-2256 Office: 25 E Washington St Chicago IL 60602

BARR, SOLOMON EFREM, allergist; b. Washington, Mar. 24, 1929; s. Barney and Jennie Florence (Brickman) B.; B.A. (Emma K. Carr scholar 1948-49; Maria M. Carter scholar), George Washington U., 1951, M.D., 1954; m. Rita Zeasla Cohan, June 20, 1954; children—Linda, Steven, Carol, Sharon. Intern, Phila. Gen. Hosp., 1954-55; resident D.C. Gen. Hosp., 1957-58, George Washington U., 1959-60; practice medicine specializing in allergies, Silver Spring, Md., 1960-78, Rockville, Md., 1978—; mem. staff Holy Cross Hosp., George Washington U.; asso. clin. prof. medicine George Washington U. Sch. Medicine. Served as capt. M.C., U.S. Army, 1955-57. Recipient Freshman award in chemistry Alpha Chi Sigma, 1948, award in Chemistry, Sigma Kappa, 1948, John Ordronaux award in medicine George Washington U., 1954; diplomate Am. Bd. Internal Medicine, Am. Bd. Allergy and Immunology. Fellow Am. Acad. Allergy, A.C.P., Am. Coll. Allergists, Am. Assn. Cert. Allergists; mem. Washington Allergy Soc., Montgomery County, Md. State med. socs., AMA (Physician's Recognition award 1974-77, 77-80), Smith-Reed-Russell, William Beaumont, Jacobi Med. Soc. Washington, Phi Beta Kappa, Alpha Omega Alpha. Club: Phi Delta Epsilon Grad. of Washington (pres. 1971-72). Contbr. articles to med. publs., most recent on insect sting allergy. Home: 5713 Magic Mountain Dr Rockville MD 20852-3233 Office: 121 Congressional Ln Rockville MD 20852-1542

BARRAGAN MUNOZ, FERNANDO, plastic surgeon; b. Madrid, Spain, Jan. 23, 1941; s. Fernando Barragan and Josefina Munoz; m. Mabel Fernandez; children: Gustavo, Maria Fernanda, Stella Maris. Bachiller, Jose Maria Moreno, Buenos Aires, Argentina, 1958; lab. auxiliary, Oncology Inst., Buenos Aires, 1961; MD, U. Buenos Aires, 1964. Resident Inst. Oncology Roffo, Buenos Aires, 1965-70, chief clinic, 1970-73; plastic surgeon Hosp. Gen., Mar del Plata, Argentina, 1970-76; chief plastic surgery Clinic del Nino, Mar del Plata, 1970-76; dir. Inst. Europe Plastic Surgery, Barcelona, Spain, 1977-80; dir., prof. dir. Clinic Barragan Plastic Surgery, Madrid, 1980—. Author: The Plastic Surgery Boom, 1980, The Beauty of the Face, 1985, The Terrorist Act That Does Not Change the World, 1986. Mem. Am. Soc. Facial Surgery, Am. Acad. Aestetic Surgery, Soc. Spanish Oncology, Soc. Catalana of Surgery, Am. Acad. Cosmetic Surgery, Spanish Acad. M.D. Writers, Catalan Acad. Surgery, Spanish Acad. Oncology, Internat. Soc. Aestetic Plastic and Reconstructive Surgery (bd. dir.), Lions Club (Madrid). Office: Clinica Barragan Cirugia, Pio XII #22, 28036 Madrid Spain

BARRATT, CYNTHIA LOUISE, pharmaceutical company executive; b. El Paso, Tex., Feb. 13, 1953; d. John Edward and Louise Joy (Lacy) B.; m. Nat G. Adkins, Jr., Oct. 5, 1980. BJ, U. Tex., 1975. Buyer Joske's of Tex., San Antonio, 1975-80, Craigs of Tex., Houston, 1981-83; v.p. sales ops. Akorn, Inc., Abita Springs, La., 1980-86; CEO, chmn. bd. dirs. NGLC Corp., Richmond, Tex., 1983—; pres., CEO, bd. dirs. CynaCon/Ocusoft, Richmond, 1986—. Mem. NAFE, Rosenberg/Richmond C. of C., DAR, Ft. Bend County Mus. Assn. Office: OcuSoft Inc PO Box 429 Richmond TX 77406-0429

BARRATT, RAYMOND WILLIAM, biologist, educator; b. Holyoke, Mass., May 4, 1920; s. George A. and Elizabeth (Bretschneider) B.; m. Helen Ruggles, July 1943 (div. 1968); children: Marguerite E., William R.; m. Barbara H. Kellerup, Oct. 16, 1971. B.Sc., Rutgers U., 1941; M.Sc., U. N.H., 1943; Ph.D., Yale, 1948; M.A. (hon.), Dartmouth, 1958. Asst. plant pathology and horticulture U. N.H., 1943-44; rsch. assoc., asst. plant pathologist Conn. Agrl. Expt. Sta., 1944-45; rsch. assoc. biology Stanford (Calif.) U., 1948-53, rsch. biologist, acting asst. prof., 1953-54; mem. faculty Dartmouth Coll., 1954-70, prof. botany, 1958-62, prof. biology, 1962-70, chmn. dept., 1965-69, lectr. microbiology Med. Sch., 1962-70; prof. biology Humboldt State U., 1970-92, dean sci., 1970-84; mem. vis. staff Vt. Environ. Center, Ripton, summers 1970, 71; dir. Fungal Genetics Stock Ctr., 1970-85. Mem. Hanover Sch. Bd., 1964-68; mem. Dresden (N.H.) Sch. Bd., 1964-68, chmn., 1968. Mem. Genetics Soc. Am. (chmn. com. maintenance genetic stocks 1964-68), Sigma Xi, Alpha Zeta, Phi Sigma, Kappa Sigma. Home: 6949 Fickle Hill Rd Arcata CA 95521-9040

BARRERA, CECILIO RICHARD, research microbiology educator; b. Rio Grande, Tex., Nov. 30, 1942; s. Manuel and Rafaela (Trevino) B.; m. Rosalinda Benavides; children: Marisa, Cristina. BA, U. Tex., 1965, MA, 1967, PhD, 1970. NIH predoctoral trainee U. Tex., Austin, 1966-69; fellow Clayton Found. Biochem. Inst., Austin, 1970-75; asst. prof. biology N.Mex. State U., Las Cruces, 1975-81, assoc. prof., 1981—; assoc. dean grad. sch. N. Mex. State U., Las Cruces, 1994—; vis. asst. prof. U. Tex., San Antonio, 1974; mem. rev. panel NRC, Washington, 1984-87; mem. site visit team NIH, Washington, 1980; mem. various NSF panels. Contbr. articles to profl. jours. Mem. AAAS, Am. Soc. Microbiology (pres. N.Mex. br. 1979-81), Sigma Xi (pres. N.Mex. State U. chpt. 1983-84). Office: N Mex State U Grad Sch PO Box 30001 Las Cruces NM 88003-8001

BARRETT, BEATRICE HELENE, psychologist; b. Cin., Dec. 8, 1928; d. Oscar Slack and Helen (Kaiper) B.; m. Harold Sheffield Van Buren, Oct. 6, 1966 (div. Oct. 1985). BA, U. Ariz., 1950, MA, U. Ky., 1952; PhD, Purdue U., 1957. Lic. psychologist, Mass. Grad. tchg. asst. in psychology U. Ky., Lexington, 1950-52; psychology asst. Longview State Hosp., Cin., 1951, staff psychologist, 1952; staff psychologist Children's Outpatient and Cons. Svcs. Ind. U. Med. Ctr., Indpls., 1954-57, chief psychologist, 1957-59; instr. psychology Ind. U. Med. Sch., Indpls., 1956-60; rsch. assoc. dept. psychiatry Ind. U. Med. Ctr., Indpls., 1959-60; pvt. practice clin. psychology Indpls., 1957-60; research fellow in psychology Sch. of Medicine Harvard U., Boston, 1960-62; lectr. in spl. edn. Grad. Sch. Edn., Boston U., 1962-63; dir. psychol. rsch. Walter E. Fernald State Sch., Belmont, Mass., 1962-69; dir. behavior prosthesis lab. Walter E. Fernald State Sch., Belmont, 1963-92; chief psychologist, 1969-92; assoc. psychologist Enuice Kennedy Shriver Ctr for Mental Retardation, Inc., Waltham, Mass., 1982—; instr. Mass. Psychol. Ctr., 1972; lectr. in spl. edn. Lesley Coll. Grad. Sch., 1974-76; adj. assoc. prof. Northeastern U., 1983-92; psychology cons. Carter Meml. Hosp., Indpls., 1959-60; mem. exec. com. Boston Behavior Therapy Interest Group, 1973-74. Cons. editor, mem. adv. bds. various profl. jours.; contbr. numerous articles to profl. jours. Mem. Ind. Gov.'s Youth Coun., 1959-61; mem. spl. adv. com. on mental retardation Ind. Dept. Pub. Instrn., 1959-61; mem. task force Mass. Mental Retardation Planning Project, 1965-66; mem. adv. bd. Cambridge Ctr. for Behavioral Studies, 1981-87, 93-94, trustee, 1987-93, 94—, chair devel. com., 1987-89, mem. subcom. on planned giving, 1992-95, chmn. nominating com., 1992-93, mem., 1993—, exec. com., 1993, 94—, mem. subcom. on acad. and sci. programs, 1992—; treas. B.F. Skinner Found., 1996—; mem. com. on dance edn. Spl. Commn. on Performing Arts, 1976-77; mem. art acquisition com. DeCordova Mus., 1978-80, mem. contemporary arts coun., 1985-87; trustee Boston Repertory Ballet, 1977-79, Boston Ballet Co., 1970-76, sec. bd., 1974-75, exec. com., 1974-76. Grantee Nat. Assn. for Retarded Citizens, 1963, NIHM, 1963-76. Fellow APA, Mass. Psychol. Assn. (Ezra Saul Psychol. Svc. award 1979), Behavior Therapy and Rsch. Soc. (charter clin.); mem. Assn. for Mentally Ill Children (human rights com. 1979-81), Am. Acad. on Mental Retardation (v.p. 1969-74, at-large exec. com. 1975-77), Ea. Psychol. Assn., Assn. for Advancement Behavior Therapy, Assn. Behavior Analysis (jour. adv. bd. 1983-87, chair task force on right to effective edn. 1986-91, presdl. adv. group on edn. and pub. policy 1994-95), Stage Harbor Yacht Club (Chatham, Mass., race com. 1984-86), Sigma Xi, Phi Kappa Phi. Home: RFD 5 Box 236A Winter St Lincoln MA 01773

BARRETT, BERNARD MORRIS, JR., plastic and reconstructive surgeon; b. Pensacola, Fla., May 3, 1944; s. Bernard Morris and Blanche (Lischkoff) B.; BS, Tulane U., 1965; MD, U. Miami, 1969; m. Julia Mae Prokop, Nov. 26, 1972; children: Beverly Frances, Julie Blaine, Audrey Blake, Bernard Joseph. Surg. intern Meth. Hosp. and Ben Taub Hosp., Houston, 1969-70; resident in gen. surgery Baylor Coll. Medicine, Houston, 1970-71, UCLA, 1971-73; resident in plastic surgery U. Miami Affiliated Hosps., Fla., 1973-75, chief resident in plastic surgery, 1975; fellow in plastic surgery Clinica Ivo Pitanguy, Rio de Janeiro, Brazil, 1973; instr. surgery Baylor Coll. Medicine, 1970-71, clin. instr. plastic surgery, 1977-80, clin. asst. prof., 1980-90, clin. assoc. prof., 1991—; instr. surg. emergencies L.A. County Paramedics, 1972-73; plastic surgery coordinator for jr. med. students Sch. Medicine U. Miami, 1975; practice medicine specializing in plastic and reconstructive surgery, Houston, 1976—; pres., chmn. bd. dirs. Plastic and Reconstructive Surgeons, P.A., Houston, 1978—; chmn. Tex. Inst. Plastic Surgery, Houston; assoc. chief plastic surgery St. Luke's Episcopal Hosp., Houston, 1991—; attending physician Jr. League Clinic, Tex. Children's Hosp., Houston, 1977—; active staff St. Luke's Hosp., Houston, Meth. Hosp., Houston; clin. assoc. in plastic surgery U. Tex. Med. Sch., Houston, 1976—; instr. surg. emergencies Harris County Community Coll.; dir. Am. Physicians Ins. Exchange, Austin, vice chmn. bd. dirs., 1995—; past chief of staff, chief plastic surgery Travis Centre Hosp., Houston, 1985—; cons. physician Houston Oilers, 1978—; attending physician Ontario Motor Speedway, Calif., 1972-73. Bd. dirs. Plastic Surgery Ednl. Found., Chgo; mem. Fed. Coun. on Aging, Washington, 1991-93. Served to lt. comdr., M.C., USNR, 1969-74. Surg. exchange scholar to Royal Coll. Surgeons, London, 1968; hon. dep. sheriff Harris County, Tex. (Houston); diplomate Am. Bd. Plastic Surgery. Fellow ACS; mem. Am. Soc. Plastic and Reconstructive Surgeons, Royal Soc. Medicine, Michael E. DeBakey Internat. Cardiovascular Surg. Soc., Am. Soc. for Aesthetic Plastic Surgery, Denton A. Cooley Cardiovascular Surg. Soc., Tex. Med. Assn., Tex. Soc. Plastic Surgery, Harris County Med. Assn., Lipoplasty Soc. N.Am., Houston Soc. Plastic Surgery, D. Ralph Millard Plastic Surg. Soc. (pres. 1993-94, v.p. 1977-79, sec., treas. 1975-77, historian 1980—), U. Miami Sch. Medicine Nat. Alumni Assn. (bd. dirs. 1975-77), Alpha Kappa Kappa (pres., 1968-69). Clubs: Houston City, Houstonian; Royal Biscayne Racquet; Commodore (Key Biscayne, Fla.), Coral Beach and Tennis Club (Bermuda). Author: Patient Care in Plastic Surgery, 1982; Manuel de Ciudados en Cirugia Plastica, 1985. Author: Patient Care in Plastic Surgery, 2d edit., 1996; contbr. articles to med. publs., presentations to profl. confs.; inventor Barrett sterling surgigrip. Office: 6624 Fannin St Ste 2200 Houston TX 77030-2334

BARRETT, CODY, hospital director; b. Leghorn, Italy, Jan. 1, 1947; s. Othell and Anna (Pezza) B.; m. Donella McRae, Feb. 14, 1986. BA, Kean Coll., Union, N.J., 1975. Cert. Alcoholism Counselor, Cert. Employee Assistance Profl., Cert. Compulsive Gambling Counselor. Dir. addiction svc. East Orange (N.J.) Gen. Hosp., 1975—. Founder, ABC Nat. Conf. Recipient Citizen award City of Newark, 1986. Mem. N.J. Assn. Addiction Counselors, Kendo Club. Home: 5 Tompkins St West Orange NJ 07052-5109

BARRETT, CURTIS LEO, psychologist; b. Evansville, Ind., Jan. 10, 1936; s. Curtis Leo and Ina Rose (Hendrix) B.; m. Jane Lee Kraemer Dec. 12, 1959; children: Gary Curtis, Karen Jane Barrett Sherman, Gregory Travis. BS, Purdue U., 1958; MA, U. Louisville, 1965, PhD, 1968. Diplomate Am. Bd. Profl. Psychology. Asst. prof. U. Louisville, 1961-63, instr. grad asst. Coll. Arts and Scis., 1965-67, prof. Sch. of Medicine, 1968—; dir. psychol. svcs. Norton Psychiat. Clinic, Louisville, 1975—; dir. addictive disorders program, Louisville, 1983—; dir. backside project Churchill Downs, Louisville, 1989—; dir. project follow-through Ryan Family Found., Louisville, 1991—; cons. in field. Contbr. chpts. to books, articles to profl. jours. Chair citizens adv. bd. Citizens for Better Judges, Louisville, 1990; chair troop com. Boy Scouts Am., active YMCA. Recipient Disting. Svc. award Soc. Psychologists in Addictive Behaviors, 1989, award Leadership Louisville, Inc., 1989, Dedicated Teaching award Sch. Justice Adminstrn. So. Police Inst., 1990. Fellow Am. Acad. Forensic Psychology (continuing edn. com. 1987-90); mem. Am. Bd. Forensic Psychology (bd. dirs. 1987-92), Soc. Psychologists in Addictive Disorders (pres. 1982—, Disting. Svc. award 1979), Ky. Psychol. Assn. (pres. 1968—, Outstanding Svc. award 1979), Ky. Bd. Examiners in Psychology (chair 1973), Ky. Coun. Compulsive Gambling (pres.), Nat. Coun. on Compulsive Gambling (advisor). Presbyterian. Home: 2407 Willowbrook Ct Prospect KY 40059-9088 Office: PO Box 35070-PSY 200 E Chestnut St Louisville KY 40202-1822

BARRETT, DAVID M., urologist; b. Detroit, Mar. 25, 1942. MD, Wayne State U., 1968. Diplmate Am. Bd. Urology. Intern Detroit Gen. Hosp., 1968-69; resident in gen. surgery Mayo Clinic, Rochester, Minn., 1969-70, resident in urology, 1972-75, staff, dept. urology, 1975—, chair, dept. urology, 1991—; faculty Mayo Med. Sch., Rochester, Minn., 1986—. Mem. ACS. Office: Mayo Clinic, Urology Dept 200 First St SW Rochester MN 55905-0001

BARRETT, ELIZABETH ANN MANHART, nursing educator, psychotherapist, consultant; b. Hume, Ill., July 11, 1934; d. Francis J. and Grace C. (Manhart) Fridy; children: Joseph B., Jeffrey F., Paula G. Brown, Pamela M. Shetler Carpino, Scott D. BS in Nursing summa cum laude, U. Evansville, 1970, MA, 1973, MS in Nursing, 1976; grad. Gestalt Assocs. for Psychotherapy, 1982; PhD in Nursing, NYU, 1983; grad. Am. Inst. for Mental Imagery, 1995. Instr. nursing U. Evansville, Ind., 1970-73, asst. prof., 1973-76; staff nurse Welborn Bapt. Hosp., Evansville, 1975-76; staff nurse Bellevue Psychiat. Hosp., N.Y.C., 1976-79; clin. tchr. CUNY, 1977-82; asst. prof. Adelphi U., 1979-80; group practice Nurse Healers, 1979-82; pvt. practice psychotherapy, 1980—; nurse researcher Mt. Sinai Med. Ctr., N.Y.C., 1982-86, asst. dir. nursing, 1983-86; assoc. prof. Hunter Coll., N.Y.C., 1986-89, prof., 1994—, dir. grad. studies, 1989-92, coord. Ctr. for Nursing Rsch., 1993—; cons. Internat. Soc. Univ. Nurses; co-chair adv. com. Martha E. Rogers Ctr. for Study of Nursing Svc., 1994-96. Mem. com. Regional Health Planning Council, Evansville, 1974-77. Mem. editl. bd. Alt. Therapies in Health and Medicine, 1995—. Recipient Disting. Nursing Alumnus award NYU, 1994, Disting Nurse Rschr. award Found. N.Y. State Nurses Assn., 1995. Fellow Am. Acad. Nursing; mem. Am. Nurses Assn. (cert. psychiat.-mental health, coun. nurse rschrs.), Nat. League Nursing, Ea. Nursing Rsch. Assn. (charter), Soc. Rogerian Scholars (co-founder, 1st pres. 1988-90), NOW, Phi Kappa Phi, Sigma Theta Tau (Upsilon chpt. pres. 1986-88), Alpha Tau Delta, Sigma Xi. Home: 415 E 85th St Apt 9E New York NY 10028-6358 Office: Hunter Coll 425 E 25th St New York NY 10010-2547

BARRETT, EUGENE JOSEPH, researcher, medical educator, physician; b. Jersey City, N.J., May 22, 1946; s. Joseph Francis and Margaret (Harney) B.; m. Paul Marie Quiricani, Jan. 31, 1976; children: Nora, Matthew. BS in Physics, St. Peters Coll., Jersey City, N.J., 1968; MD, U. Rochester, 1975, PhD in Biophysics, 1975. Intern in medicine Strong Meml. Hosp., Rochester, N.Y., 1975-76, asst. resident in medicine, 1976-77; fellow in endocrinology and metabolism Yale U. Sch. Medicine, New Haven, Conn., 1977-80, asst. prof. medicine, 1980-85, assoc. prof. medicine, 1985-91, chief diabetes unit, 1988-91; prof. internal medicine and pediats. U. Va. Sch. Medicine, Charlottesville, 1991—; dir. U. Va. Diabetes Ctr., 1991—; dir. diabetes unit Yale U. Sch. Medicine, 1987-91; dir. diabetes ctr. U. Va., 1991—. Contbr. over 70 articles to profl. jours. Recipient Rsch. Career award NIH, 1981-85. Mem. NIH (mem. metabolism study sect. 1993-96), Am. Diabetes Assn. (bd. dirs. Va. affiliate 1993-96, mem. nat. profl. practice com., rsch. award 1996), Am. Heart Assn. (Established Investigator 1987-92, mem. Conn. affiliate grant rev. panel 1985-90, mem. grant rev. panel New Eng. region 1986-91, chair 1991), Am. Fedn. Clin. Rsch., Am. Soc. Clin. Investigation. Roman Catholic. Office: U Va Sch Medicine Diabetes Rsch Ctr PO Box 5116 # 4 Charlottesville VA 22905-5116*

BARRETT, LAWRENCE ARTHUR, II, oral and maxillofacial surgeon, educator; b. Providence, R.I., June 4, 1953; s. Lawrence Arthur and Eleanor Anna (Lang) B; m. Linda Diane Ganaway, June 24, 1978; children: Heather Breanne, Jason Lawrence, Christopher James, Ashley Kristen. BS in Zoology, U. Md., 1977; DDS, Georgetown U., 1981; cert. in oral and maxillofacial surgery, Washington Hosp. Ctr., 1988. Diplomate Am. Bd. Oral and Maxillofacial Surgery. Comdr. USN, 1981—; asst. fleet liaison officer Naval Regional Dental Ctr., San Diego, 1981-83; dept. head USS Dubuque, San Diego, 1983-85; dept. chmn. Naval Hosp., Subic Bay Republic, The Philippines, 1988-91; staff oral and maxillofacial surgeon Naval Med. Ctr., San Diego, 1991-92, asst. residency dir., 1993-95; dept. head USS Ranger, San Diego, 1992-93; dept. chmn. dental sch. Nat. Naval Dental Ctr., Bethesda, Md., 1995—; ACLS instr. Mil. Tng. Network, San Diego, 1989-93, affiliate faculty, Bethesda, 1995—; regional cons. oral and maxillofacial surgery Nat. Naval Dental Ctr., Bethesda, 1995—. Contbr. articles to profl. jours. Leader Cub Scouts Am., San Diego, 1993-94. Decorated Navy Commendation medal, 1985, 91, 93, Meritorious Svc. medal, 1995; recipient Mortar Bd., U. Md., 1977. Fellow Am. Assn. Oral Maxillofacial Surgeons; mem. Mil. Order Carabao Companero, Nat. Eagle Scout Assn. (life), Delta Sigma Delta, Phi Sigma. Republican. Home: 12165 Hidden Brook Terrace North Potomac MD 20878-3321 Office: Naval Dental Sch Nat Naval Dental Ctr 8901 Wisconsin Ave Bethesda MD 20889-5602

BARRETT, MARIHELEN EGGERT, public health administrator, pediatrics nurse; b. Phila., Aug. 28, 1947; d. Herbert Raymond and Phyllis Esther (Twining) Eggert; m. Melvin D. Barrett, July 31, 1976 (div. July 1990); children: Jason Bradford, Jordan Elizabeth Marie. BSN, U. Del., 1969, MSN, 1973; postgrad., U. Md., 1981-85. RN, Del.; cert. pediatric nurse practitioner. Staff nurse Del. Div. Pub. Health, 1969-70; charge nurse, pediatric unit and ICU Wilmington (Del.) Med. ctr., 1970-73; pub. health nurse, coord., clin. specialist, 1973-75; project dir., program of projects Title V Project State of Del., 1975-80; maternal and child health nursing con. Bur. of Nursing, 1980-83; project coord. State of Del. Family Planning and Title X Project, 1984-85; dir. maternal and child health svcs. Del. Divsn. Pub. Health, Dover, 1985-91; policy coord. HIV/AIDS Del. Health and Social Svcs., Del., 1991-92; pub. health adminstr., cmty. health sect., dir. children's health svcs. Del. Divsn. Pub. Health, Dover, 1992—; instr. U. fel., 1973, 76, 80, Wilmington Coll., 1979; speaker Med. Ctr. of Del., U. Pa., 1985, 86, 87, U. Del., 1982, 83, 85, 86, Del. Nurses Assn. Conv., 1974, nat. MCH Leadership Conf., N.Y., 1990, Nat. Health Edn. Conf., Washington, 1993. Mem. maternal and child task force Del. Health Coun., grant rev. team Better Homes Found., grant for Homeless Women Projects, 1990; bd. dirs. Read Aloud Del., 1986-87; mem. adv. com. for Pub. Law 94-142, Edn. of the Handicapped, Seaford Sch. Dist.; mem. regional clin. adv. network U.S. Surgeon's Office, Region III; staff coord. Del. Task Force on Infant Mortality, 1985-91; mem. interant. consultation team on perinatal health to Latvia and Lithuania, 1992; Medicaid Managed Care Policy coord. Del. Pub. Health, 1995—; mgmt. oversight pub. health implementation IDEA Part H Birth to Three Svcs., Del., 1992-95; med. managed care contract negotiations with Managed Care Orgns., 1995; mgmt. oversight Title V MCH Block grant fed. application and state wide neeeds assessment, 1994, 95. Mem. Del. Nurses Assn. (chmn. maternal and child health 1975-76), Perinatal Assn. of Del., Am. Acad. Pediatrics (Del. chpt.), Del. Pub. Health Assn. (bd. dirs. 1986, Del. MCH Leadership award 1995), Women's Agenda of Del. (leadership coun. 1988—), Assn. of Maternal and Child Health Programs (region III councilor, exec. coun. 1989-92). Office: Del Divsn Pub Health Federal and Water Sts PO Box 637 Dover DE 19903-0637

BARRETT, MARILYN WOODY, nursing administrator, educator, business consultant; b. Portsmouth, Va.; married; children. BSN, U. Md., Balt., 1972; MA, Cen. Mich. U., 1982; MPA, U. So. Calif., L.A., 1985, D of Pub. Adminstrn., 1986. RN, Md., Va. Assoc. prof. pub. adminstrn. Cen. Mich. U., Mt. Pleasant, 1986—; cons.; bd. dirs. The Nursing Spectrum, 1991—. Lt. col. USAR, ret. Mem. ANA (cert. in nursing adminstrn.), Phi Kappa Phi, Sigma Theta Tau.

BARRETT, O'NEILL, JR., medical educator; b. Baton Rouge, Mar. 21, 1929; s. O'Neill and Hazel (Lohman) B.; m. Elois Stone; children: Deborah Ann, Michael, William. BS in Biology, La. State U., 1949; MSc in Medicine, Baylor U., 1958; MD, La. State U., New Orleans, 1953. Diplomate Am. Bd. Internal Medicine, Am. Bd. Med. Oncology, Am. Bd. Hematology. Commd. 2d lt. U.S. Army, 1953, advanced through grades to col., 1968; intern Brooke Army Med. Ctr., San Antonio, 1953-54, med. resident, 1955-58; chief gen. medicine Madigan Army Hosp., Tacoma, 1960-62; asst. chief medicine Letterman Army Hosp., San Francisco, 1963-68; chief dept. medicine Tripler Army Med. Ctr., Honolulu, 1968-71; chief dept. medicine Walter Reed Army Med. Ctr., Washington, 1971-73, ret., 1973; chmn. dept. comprehensive medicine U. So. Fla. Sch. Medicine, Tampa, 1973-76; dir. div. gen. medicine U. S.C. Sch. Medicine, Columbia, 1976-86, chmn. dept. medicine, 1987-92, dir. clin. curriculum, 1992-94, disting. prof. emeritus, 1994—; assoc. counselor So. Med. Assn. Editor: Internal Medicine in Vietnam, 1982; mem. editorial bd. Med. History Vietnam-U.S. Army, 1972—, Archives of Internal Medicine, 1980-91; asst. editor Southern Med. Assn. Jour.; contbr. articles to profl. jours. Recipient 5 Outstanding Tchr. of Yr. awards U. S.C. Sch. Medicine. Fellow ACP, Am. Coll. Clin. Pharmacology; mem. Am. Soc. Hematology, Am. Soc. Clin. Oncology. Home: 2810 Chatsworth Rd Columbia SC 29223-1804 Office: U SC Sch Medicine Med Libr Bldg Garver's Ferry Rd Ste 316 Columbia SC 29201

BARRETT, RONALD KEITH, psychology educator, consultant, researcher; b. Bklyn., Aug. 17, 1948; s. Cyril and Dorothy (Addison) B.; B.S., Morgan State U., 1970; M.A., U. Pitts., 1974; Ph.D., 1977. Cert. clin. hypnotist. Program evaluator Right Start, U. Pitts., 1976-77; asst. prof. psychology Calif. State U.-Dominguez Hills, 1977-78; cons. psychologist Inglewood Child Devel. Ctr., Calif., 1977-78; cons. Social Service Bur., Richmond Dept. Pub. Welfare, Va., 1978; asst. prof. psychology Loyola Marymount U., Los Angeles, 1978—; lectr., cons., supr. standardized tests, reviewer, researcher. Contbr. articles to newspapers. Mem. APA, Assn. Death Edn. and Counseling, Internat. Assn. Trauma Counselors, Psi Chi, Alpha Phi Omega. Democrat. Home: 240 W Queen St Unit 3 Inglewood CA 90301 Office: Dept Psychology Loyola Marymount Univ Los Angeles CA 90045

BARRETT, VIRGINIA WHIPPLE, gerontology nurse, researcher; b. N.Y.C., Dec. 5, 1941; d. H. Morgan and Muriel Scott (Whipple) Hicks; m. Robert E. Barrett, June 4, 1966; children: Elizabeth, Robert. BSN, Columbia U., 1964, MEd, 1980, DrPH, 1988. RN, N.Y. Cons. community health nursing Columbia U., N.Y.C., assoc. rsch. scientist Ctr. for Geriatrics, mem. faculty Sch. of Nursing. Mem. joint editorial bd. Found. of Thanalology. Mem. APHA.

BARRETT, WARRICK LEE, physician; b. Fort Dix, N.J., Oct. 17, 1949; s. Ross Paige and Allyson Lightfoot (Warrick) B.; m. Gail Denise Nash, June

24, 1978; children: Stephanie Latrelle, Galen Randolph, Gregory Paige. AB cum laude, St. Louis U., 1971; MD, Cornell U., 1975. Diplomate Am. Bd. Family Practice, Am. Bd. Preventive Medicine. Intern Montefiore U. Hosp., Pitts., 1975-76; resident in family practice USAF Med. Ctr., Wright-Patterson AFB, Ohio, 1977-79; med. officer USAF, 1976-81; med. dir. Essex Group, Inc., Fort Wayne, Ind., 1981-88; staff physician Meth. Health Care Ctrs., Indpls., 1988-89; pvt. practice physician Indpls., 1989-90; augmentee physician USAF, MacDill AFB, Fla., 1990-91; med. dir. Navistar-Indpls., 1991-93, Subaru-Isuzu Automotive, Inc., Lafayette, Ind., 1993—; med. cons. Occupl. Health and Hygiene Corp., Lebanon, Ind., 1989—; commdr. 434th Med. Squadron, Grissom ARB, Ind., 1994—. Author: Johnny Bright, Champion, 1996. Mem. adv. bd. Am. Cancer Soc., Ft.Wayne, 1982-88; mem. adv. bd., CPR instr. ARC, Ft. Wayne, 1982-88; vol. team physician Snider/Northrop H.S., Ft. Wayne, 1982-88; vol. physician, bd. dirs. Metro Midget Football League, Ft. Wayne, 1982-88. Col. USAFR, 1991—. Fellow Am. Acad. Family Physicians, Am. Coll. Occupl. and Environ. Medicine; mem. AMA, Ind. State Med. Assn., Assn. Mil. Surgeons of the U.S., Alpha Sigma Nu, Beta Beta Beta. Home: 9313 Castle Knoll Blvd Indianapolis IN 46250 Office: Subaru-Isuzu Automotive Inc 5500 State Rd 38 East Lafayette IN 47905

BARRETT-CONNOR, ELIZABETH LOUISE, epidemiologist, educator; b. Evanston, Ill., Apr. 8, 1935; m. James D. Connor. BA, Mt. Holyoke Coll., 1956, DSc (hon.), 1985; MD, Cornell U., 1960; MD (hon.), U. Utrecht, The Netherlands, 1996. Diplomate Am. Bd. Internal Medicine, Nat. Bd. Med. Examiners. Instr. medicine U. Miami, Fla., 1965-68, asst. prof. medicine, 1968-70; asst. prof. community and family medicine U. Calif., San Diego, 1970-74, assoc. prof. community and family medicine, 1974-81, prof. community and family medicine, 1981—, acting chair dept. community and family medicine, 1981-82, chmn. dept. family and preventative medicine, 1982—; vis. prof. Royal Soc. Medicine, London, 1989; mem. hosp. infection control com. VA Med. Ctr., San Diego, 1971—. Contbr. articles to profl. jours. NIH grantee, 1970-95, Am. Heart Assn. grantee, 1980-81. Mem. Am. Heart Assn. (chmn. budget com. coun. on epidemiology 1987-88, chmn. coun. on epidemiology 1988-89), Am. Pub. Health Assn. (chmn. epidemiology sect. 1989—), Assn. Tchrs. Preventive Medicine (bd. dirs. 1987—), Inst. Medicine. Office: U Calif #0628 La Jolla CA 92093

BARRICKMAN, LES L., psychiatrist; b. Centerville, Iowa, Nov. 2, 1953; s. Bob and Margie (Gorden) B. BA, William Penn Coll., 1976; DO, Kirksville Coll. Osteopathic, 1982. Diplomate Am. Bd. Psychiatry and Neurology, Am. Bd. Adult Psychiatry, Am. Bd. Adolescent Psychiatry. Intern Des Moines Gen. Hosp., 1982-83; resident adult psychiatry U. Iowa Coll. Medicine, Iowa City, 1983-86, resident child/adolescent psychiatry, 1986-88, fellow adult psychiatry and NIMH psychoatric-epidemiology, 1988-89, assoc. faculty, 1989-90, instr., 1990-91, asst. prof., 1991-93; clin. asst. prof. U. N.Mex., 1995; dir. child/adolescent edn. tng. program U. Iowa, 1991-93. Mem. AMA, Am. Psychiat. Assn., Am. Acad. Child/Adolescent Psychiatry.

BARRICKS, MICHAEL ELI, retinal surgeon; b. Chgo., Feb. 22, 1940; s. Arthur Goetz and Ruth (Zuckerman) B.; m. Zondra Dell Natman, Jan. 18, 1992; 1 child, Charleigh Ruth. BA, Harvard Coll., 1961; MD, U. Chgo., 1965; PhD, Stanford U., 1973. Diplomate Nat. Bd. Med. Examiners; lic. physician, Calif. Intern then resident in surgery Stanford (Calif.) U., 1965-67, postdoctoral fellow, 1967-72; resident, fellow in ophthalmology Bascom Palmer Eye Inst., Miami, Fla., 1972-76; fellow in retinal surgery U. Calif., San Francisco, 1976-77; asst. prof., dir. retina svc. U. Tex., San Antonio, 1977-78; retinal surgeon, dir. retina svc. Permanente Med. Group., Oakland, Calif., 1979—; asst. clin. prof. U. Calif., San Francisco, 1980-92, assoc. clin. prof., 1993—; bd. dirs. Barricks Mfg. Co., Gadsden, Ala. Contbr. articles to profl. jours. Recipient Gold award Am. Acad. Pediatrics, Outstanding Physician award Kaiser Hosp., 1982; Nat. scholar Fisher Body Craftsmans Guild; USPHS fellow Stanford U., 1967-70, Atholl McBean fellow Stanford Rsch. Inst., 1970-71. Fellow Am. Acad. Ophthalmology; mem. Permanente Ophthalmologic Soc. (pres. 1981), Vitreous Soc. Office: Permanente Med Group 280 W MacArthur Blvd Oakland CA 94611

BARRILLEAUX, CHRISTOPHER NISSEN, gastroenterologist; b. Franklin, La., Dec. 4, 1954; s. Darel Adam and Mildred (Hebert) B.; m. Rhonda Leona Stein, May 28, 1977; children: Ian Michael, Simone Marie, Nicole Terése. BS, Tulane U., 1976, MD, 1980. Diplomate Am. Bd. Internal Medicine, sub.-bd. in Gastroenterology. Commd. capt. U.S. Army, 1980, advanced through grades to maj., 1986; intern, then resident in internal medicine Brooke Army Medical Ctr., Ft. Sam Houston, Tex., 1980-83; staff internist USAMEDDAC, 2nd Field Hosp., Bremerhaven, Federal Republic of Germany, 1983-84, USAMEDDAC, 67th Evacuation Hosp., Wuerzburg, Federal Republic of Germany, 1984-86; fellow in gastroenterology Brooke Army Medical Ctr., Ft. Sam Houston, Tex., 1986-88, staff gastroenterology, 1988-90; staff gastroenterology Mahorner Clinic, Kenner, La., 1990-91; staff, gastroenterology Browne-McHardy Clinic, Metairie, 1992—; asst. clin. prof. internal medicine U. Tex. Health Sci. Ctr., San Antonio, 1989-90, La. State U. Sch. Medicine, 1992—, Tulane U., 1993—. Contbr. articles to profl jours. Tulane scholar, 1973-76. Fellow ACP, Am. Coll. Gastroenterology; mem. Am. Gastroent. Assn., Am. Soc. Gastrointestinal Endoscopy, Nature Conservancy. Republican. Roman Catholic. Office: Browne-McHardy Clinic 4315 Houma Blvd Metairie LA 70006-2981

BARRIOCANAL, JOSE L., urologist; b. Asuncion, Paraguay, Mar. 31, 1942; s. Santiago and Ascencion (Feltes) B.; m. Emiliana Felicita Pena, Apr. 19, 1969 n (dec. Apr. 1992); children: Jose A., Maria Veronica, Nelson R. MD, Nat. U. Sch. Medicine, 1966. Resident in surgery, urology Hahnemann U., Phila., 1974-75; pvt. practice urology Nauticoke Meml. Hosp., Seaford, Del., 1975—. Fellow Am. Coll. Surgeons; mem. AMA, Am. Urol. Assn. Republican. Roman Catholic. Home: 64 North Shore Dr Seaford DE 19973 Office: 220 Pennsylvania Ave Seaford DE 19973

BARRIOS, ALFRED ANGEL, psychologist; b. N.Y.C., Oct. 1, 1933; s. Arthur Domingo and Carmen Maria (Vidal) B. BS, Calif. Inst. Tech., 1955; PhD, UCLA, 1969. Chem. engr. Mobil Oil Co., Torrance, Calif., 1955-57; instr. psychology East L.A. Coll., 1969-72, UCLA, 1972-73, Southwest Coll., L.A., 1973-74, Santa Monica (Calif.) Coll., 1975; psychologist Self-Programmed Control Ctr., L.A., 1972—, pres., 1975—. Author: Towards Greater Freedom and Happiness, 1978, The Stress Test, 1984, The Habit Buster, 1987; inventor Stress Control Biofeedback Card. Recipient Cancer Fedn. award for pioneering work in psychoneuroimmunology and cancer, 1996. Office: SPC Ctr 11949 Jefferson Blvd Ste 104 Culver City CA 90230-6336

BARRIOS, GEORGE G., colon rectal surgeon; b. Zamboanga, The Philippines, Apr. 24, 1943; came to U.S., 1973; s. Donaciano and Nemesia (Gatchalian) B.; m. Olga Cruz, Dec. 11, 1969; children: Kurt, Karl, Erik, Katrina. BA, Ateneo de Manila, Quezon City, The Philippines, 1963; MD, U. The Philippines, Manila, 1968. Diplomate Am. Bd. Surgeons, Am. Bd. Colon and Rectal Surgeons. Resident in gen. surgery SUNY, Buffalo, 1975-78; resident in colon/rectal surgery, Buffalo Gen. Hosp., 1978-79; colon rectal surgeon Buffalo (N.Y.) Med. Group; clin. asst. prof. Dept. Surgery, SUNY, Buffalo. Fellow Am. Coll. Surgeons, Am. Soc. Colon and Rectal Surgeons. Office: Buffalo Med Group 85 High St Buffalo NY 14203-1149

BARRON, MICHAEL PETER, physician, medical educator; b. Boston, Oct. 19, 1939; s. Albert Lewis and Harriet Helen (Isenberg) B.; m. Shirley Ann Lewis, May 27, 1967; children: Sylvia Diane, Mark Lewis Michael. AB, Brown U., 1962; MD, U. Vt., 1967. Intern U. Ky. Med. Ctr., Lexington, 1967, med. resident, 1970-72; asst. prof. emeritus Richmond, 1991—; pvt. practice Richmond, Ky., 1972—; vis. clin. instr. U. Ky. Med. Ctr., 1972-91. Surgeon USPHS, 1968-70. Named to Order of Ky. Cols. Mem. Am. Soc. Internal Medicine, Ky. Med. Assn., So. Med. Assn. Office: 632 Eastern Byp Richmond KY 40475-2330

BARRON, SUSAN, clinical psychologist; b. Chgo., May 13, 1940; d. Earl and Trixie (Chernoff) B.; m. Eugene Pratt, Jan. 18, 1975 (div. 1983). BBA, CCNY, 1960, MA, 1963; PhD, CUNY, 1973. Lic. psychologist. Intern psychologist Bellevue Psychiat. Hosp., N.Y.C., 1964-65, psychologist, 1966-67; teaching fellow CUNY, 1965-66; staff psychologist Lighthouse, N.Y. Assn. for the Blind, N.Y.C., 1968-71, sr. clin. psychologist, 1971-74; dir. psychol. counseling svcs. Peninsula Ctr. for the Blind, Palo Alto, Calif., 1974-75; cons. psychologist N.Y. State Commn. for Blind and Visually Handicapped, N.Y.C., 1975-78, 86—; dir. psychol. svcs. Thoms Rehab. Hosp., Asheville, N.C., 1978-79; state coord. psychol. svcs. N.Y. State Office Vocat. Rehab., Albany, 1979-85; founder, dir. Family Support Program ICU N.Y. Infirmary-Beekman Downtown Hosp., N.Y.C., 1982-84; cons. clin. psychologist N.Y. Hosp. Cornell U. Med. Ctr., 1987—; pvt. practice, 1987—; behavioral scientist diabetes control/complications trial NIH Cornell U. Med. Ctr., N.Y.C., 1987—; cons. clin. psychologist Joslin Ctr. for Diabetes St. Luke's-Roosevelt Hosp. Ctr./Columbia U. Phys. and Surg., N.Y.C., 1994-95; consulting clin. psychologist Joslin Ctr. Diabetes, St. Lukes-Roosevelt Hosp. Ctr., U. Hosp. of Columbia U. Coll. of Physicians and Surgeons, N.Y.C., 1994-95; mem. Nat. Human Svcs. Adv. Bd.-Retinitis Pigmentosa Found., Balt., 1975-82; cons. Del. State Commn. for Blind, 1975-78, Am. Found. Blind, 1974-82, Calif. Dept. Rehab., 1974-82, Hawaii State Svcs. Blind, 1974-82, Ariz. State Svcs. Blind, 1974-82, Nev. State Svcs. Blind, 1974-82; speaker Nat. Multiple Disabilities Conf., 1982, NAS, 1981; mem. adv. bd. doctoral psychology internship program Rusk Inst. of Rehab. Medicine, NYU Med. Ctr., 1979-84; behavioral scientist Diabetes Control and Complications Trial NIH-Cornell U. Med. Ctr., 1987—. Contbr. articles to profl. jours. Recipient Leadership award Alumni Assn. CCNY, 1960, 62, Rsch. award Retinal Dystrophy Soc., Australia, 1975, Charles H. Best medal for disting. svc. Am. Diabetes Assn., 1994. Fellow Am. Orthopsychiat. Assn.; mem. APA, AAAS, Calif. State Psychol. Assn., N.Y. Acad. Sci. Office: 40 Park Ave New York NY 10016

BARROS D'SA, AIRES AGNELO BARNABÉ, vascular surgeon, educator; b. Nairobi, Kenya, June 9, 1939; s. Inaçio Francisco Purificação Saude and Maria Eslinda Inês (Barros) D'Sa; m. Elizabeth Anne Thompson, May 12, 1972; children: Vivienne, Lisa, Miranda, Angelina. MB, BChir, B in Obstetrics, Queen's U. Belfast, Northern Ireland, 1965, MD with honors, 1975. Cert. Ednl. Coun. for Fgn. Med. Grads. House officer Royal Victoria Hosp., Belfast, 1965-66; demonstrator dept. anatomy The Queen's U. Belfast, 1966-67; registrar, sr. registrar Gen. and Specialist Surg. Rotation Program, Northern Ireland, 1969-76; sr. tutor dept. surgery The Queen's U. Belfast, 1974; rsch. fellow Royal Victoria Hosp., Belfast, 1974-75; calvert lect. Roy Victoria Hosp., 1975; clin. vascular fellow Providence Med. Ctr., Reconstructive Cardiovascular Rsch. Ctr., Seattle, 1977-78; mem. No. Ireland Coun. for Postgrad. Med. and Dental Edn., 1989—; cons. Vascular Surgeon, Royal Victoria Hosp., 1978; hon. lectr. Queen's U., Belfast; with Joint Vascular Rsch. Group, U.K., 1983; Clin. Rsch. Avaros Aovsy Oee DHSS NI 1986—, Rovsing and Tcherning lectr., Denmark, 1987. Editor (textbooks) Vascular Surgery: Current Questions 1991, Emergency Vascular Practice, 1996; mem. editl. bd. European Jour. of Vascular and Endovascular Surgery, 1987—; contbr. over 150 chpts. to books and articles to profl. jours.; prodr. (tchg. film) Carotid Endarterectomy, 1981 (Merit award 1981). Active Friends of the Ulster Orchestra, 1981—, Friends of the Fedn. Brit. Artists, 1989—. Named 77th James IV Surg. Traveller to N.Am., Australia and South-East Asia, 1983, Gore Visitor, Royal Australasian Coll. Surgeons, (hon. mem. Vascular Sec.), 1994; recipient Joint Lectureship, Royal Coll. Surgeons of Edinburgh and Acad. Medicine, Singapore, 1989. Fellow Royal Soc. Medicine, Royal Coll. Surgeons Edinburgh (examiner and representives on N. Ire. Coun. for Postgraduate Med. Edn., 1984-94), Royal Coll. Surgeons England (Hunterian professorship 1979, adviser 1988-93); mem. Surgical Rsch. Soc.,European Soc. for Surg. Rsch., Vascular Surg. Soc. Great Britain and Ireland (past coun. mem.), European Soc. Vascular and Cardiovascular Surgery, Internat. Union Angiology, 1992, Internat. Coll. Surgeons, 1995, Brit. Vascular Found. (grant-giving com. 1994—), Environ. Investigation Agy., Greenpeace, Friends of the Earth. Office: Royal Victoria Hosp, Grosvenor Rd, Belfast BT12 6BA, Northern Ireland

BARROW, HUGH WILL, JR., obstetrician, gynecologist; b. Atlanta, July 25, 1949; s. Hugh Will and Bonnie Jean (Spruill) B.; m. Susan Carol Hudson, Apr. 7, 1973; children: Hugh Will III, Lori Hudson. BS, U. Ga., 1971; MD, U. Ala., 1974. Diplomate Am. Bd. Ob-gyn. Intern Rutgers U., New Brunswick, 1975; resident in ob-gyn. Med. U. S.C., Charleston, 1979, clin. assoc. prof., 1983—; chief ob-gyn. Spartanburg (S.C.) Regional Med. Ctr., 1979; pvt. practice Kiesan, Barrow & Davis, Spartanburg, 1979—; clin. instr. Mary Black Sch. Nursing, 1986—. Designer Computer Interfaces. Bd. dirs. Spartanburg Blood Bank, 1986—; chmn. pack com. Cub. Scouts Am., 1983—. Fellow Am. Coll. Ob-gyn.; mem. Am. Fertility Soc., Spartanburg Ob-gyn. soc. (pres. 1985-87), Endometriosis Assn. Presbyterian. Office: Kiesau Barrow & Davis 118 Dillon Dr Spartanburg SC 29307-1018

BARRY, ANNE M., public health officer. BA in Occupl. Therapy, Coll. St. Catherine; JD, William Mitchell Coll. Law; MPH, U. Minn. Dep. commr. health Minn. Dept. Health, Mpls., commr. health, 1995—. Office: Minn Dept Health PO Box 9441 717 Delaware St SE Minneapolis MN 55440-9441

BARRY, HERBERT, III, psychologist; b. N.Y.C., June 2, 1930; s. Herbert and Lucy Manning (Brown) B. B.A., Harvard U., 1952; M.S., Yale U., 1953, Ph.D., 1957. USPHS-NIMH postdoctoral research fellow Yale U., 1957-59, asst. prof. psychology, 1960-61; asst. prof. psychology U. Conn., Storrs, 1961-63; research assoc. prof. pharmacology, Sch. Pharmacy U. Pitts., 1963-70, prof., Sch. Pharmacy, 1970-87, prof. pharmacology and physiology Sch. Dental Medicine, 1987-94, prof. pharm. scis. Sch. Pharmacy, 1995—; mem. alcohol rsch. rev. com. Nat. Inst. Alcohol Abuse and Alcoholism, 1972-76; mem. sociobehavioral subcom. AIDS rsch. rev. com. Nat. Inst. Drug Abuse, 1988-89. Author: (with H. Wallgren) Actions of Alcohol, 1970, (with A. Schlegel) Adolescence; An Anthropological Inquiry, 1991; field editor Psychopharmacology, 1974-91; contbr. articles to profl. jours. Mem. Allegheny County Dem. Com., 1984—. Recipient NIMH Research Scientist Devel. award, 1967-77. Fellow Am. Psychol. Assn. (council reps. 1975-76, pres. div. psychopharmacology 1980-81), Acad. Pharm. Sci. (chmn. sect. pharmacodynamics and drug disposition 1984-85), Am. Assn. Pharm. Scientists, AAAS, Am. Anthrop. Assn.; mem. Am. Soc. Pharm. Exptl. Therapeutics, Psychonomic Soc., Am. Coll. Neuropsychopharmacology, Phi Beta Kappa, Sigma Xi. Episcopalian. Home: 552 N Neville St Apt 83 Pittsburgh PA 15213-2830 Office: U Pitts 512 Salk Hall Pittsburgh PA 15261-0001

BARRY, JOAN, clinical researcher; b. N.Y.C., Sept. 17, 1953. BA in Polit. Sci., UCLA, 1978. Rsch. assoc. cardiovasc. divsn. UCLA Med. Ctr., 1980-83; rsch. assoc. cardiovascular div. Brigham and Women's Hosp., Boston, 1983—, assoc. scientist Ischemia Lab., 1987—; co-dir. Brigham Ischemia Group, Boston, 1989—; rsch. assoc. Harvard Med. Sch., 1987-93, prin. assoc. in medicine, 1993—; cons. Boston U. Sch. Medicine, 1983. Contbr. articles to profl. jours. Mem. Am. Heart Assn. (mem. pub. edn. forum com. 1982-83, cons. com. to enhance cardiac patient family support groups). Home: 55 Hallwood Rd Chestnut Hill MA 02167-2720 Office: Brigham and Womens Hosp Cardiovasc Divsn 75 Francis St Rm L2—196 Boston MA 02115-6110

BARRY, PATRICIA DOWLING, psychotherapist, consultant; b. St. Albans, Vt., Oct. 3, 1941; d. James Edward and Anita Lina (Wiegand) Dowling; m. Richard J. Barry, May 4, 1963 (div. July 1982); children: Michelle, Catherine, Elizabeth. BS, Cen. Conn. State U., 1976; MSN, Yale U., 1979; PhD, Union Inst., 1991. Asst. prof. U. Hartford, Conn., 1979-80; psychiatric liaison nurse cons. St. Francis Hosp., Hartford, 1980-85; pvt. practice specializing in psychotherapy Hartford, 1985-93; assoc. prof. Yale U. Sch. Nursing, 1989—, U. Conn. Sch. Nursing, 1989—; assoc. staff dept. of psychiatry Mt. Sinai/St. Francis Hosp., Hartford, Conn., staff dept. of psychiatry Hartford Hosp. Author: Psychosocial Nursing Assessment and Intervention, 1984, 3d edit., 1996, Mental Health and Mental Illness, 1985, 5th edit., 1994. Bd. dirs. LWV, West Hartford, 1976-78; chmn. bd. dirs. Blue Hills Hosp., Hartford, 1982-86. Recipient Disting. Alumna award Yale U., 1989, rsch. award Nat. Psychiat. Consultation-Liaison Nursing Conf., 1993. Mem. Conn. Nurses Assn. (sec. 1987-88, bd. dirs. 1986-92, Vera Keane Dist. Svc. award 1992), Conn. United for Rsch. Excellence (bd. dirs. 1991-94), Hartford Golf Club, Sigma Theta Tau. Roman Catholic. Home and Office: 60 Linnard Rd West Hartford CT 06107-1234

BARRY, RONALD EVERETT, biology educator; b. Great Barrington, Mass., Jan. 4, 1947; s. Ronald E. Sr., Florence E. (Olds) B.; m. Elaine A. DeConti, May 30, 1969; children: Pamela J., Lisa M. BA in Zoology, U. Conn., 1968; MA in Life Scis., Ind. State U., 1974; PhD in Zoology, U. N.H., 1978. Instr. Bates Coll., Lewiston, Maine, 1977-78; lectr. W.Va. U., Morgantown, 1979-80; asst. prof. Unity (Maine) Coll., 1980-84; prof. Frostburg (Md.) State U., 1984—; peer reviewer NSF, Jour. of Mammalogy, Can. Jour. of Zoology, Jour. of Wildlife Mgmt., Am. Midland Naturalist, Wildlife Soc. Bulletin, The Southwestern Naturalist; co-chmn. local arrangements com. for 70th ann. mtg. of the Am. Soc. Mammalogists, Frostburg State U., 1990. Author: (lab. manual) General Zoology: Laboratory Exercises, 1983; contbg. author: Mammal Species of the World, 1982, Laboratory Manual to Accompany Starr and Taggart's Biology: The Unity and Diversity of Life, 1987, 89, 92. Fulbright Sr. Rsch. fellow, Zimbabwe, 1991; co-author NSF grantee, 1981-84, Nat. Geographic grantee, 1991. Mem. Am. Soc. Mammalogists, Assn. Southeastern Biologists, AAAS, Sigma Xi. Home: 15405 Winchester Rd SW Cumberland MD 21502 Office: Dept of Biology Frostburg State Univ 130 Tawes Hall Frostburg MD 21532

BARSAN, ROBERT BLAKE, dentist; b. Akron, Ohio, Apr. 7, 1948; s. Emil O. and Letitia (Dobrin) B.; m. Cheryl Lee Adams, Dec. 16, 1972; children: Erin Lee, Kathleen Letitia. BS, U. Cin., 1970; DDS, Ohio State U., 1974. Resident U. Chgo., 1976; gen. practice dentistry Cuyahoga Falls, Ohio, 1976—. Contbr. editor Modern Dental mag., 1984-89. Fellow Acad. Gen. Dentistry; mem. ADA (chmn. CPR 1984-90), Am. Endodontic Soc., Akron Gnathological Soc. (pres. 1986), Am. Acad. Cosmetic Dentistry, Fedn. Dentaire Internat., Canton Akron Cleve. Orthodontic Study Club (pres. 1994). Home: 3084 Silver Lake Blvd Silver Lake OH 44224-3033 Office: 330 Stow Ave Cuyahoga Falls OH 44221-2516

BARSCHALL, HENRY HERMAN, physics educator; b. Berlin, Germany, Apr. 29, 1915; m. Eleanor A. Folsom; two children. A.M., Princeton U., 1939; Ph.D., Princeton, 1940; Dr. rer. nat. h.c., U. Marburg, Germany, 1982. Instr. Princeton U., 1940-41, U. Kans., 1941-43; mem. staff Los Alamos Sci. Lab., 1943-46, asst. div. leader, 1951-52; mem. faculty U. Wis., 1946—, prof. physics, 1950—, chmn. dept., 1951, 54, 56-57, 63-64, Bascom prof., 1973—; prof. emeritus, 1988—; assoc. div. leader Lawrence Livermore Labs., 1971-73; Vis. prof. U. Calif., Davis, 1972-73. Assoc. editor: Revs. Modern Physics, 1951-53; Assoc. editor: Nuclear Physics, 1959-72; editor: Phys. Rev. C, 1972-87; mem. editorial bd.: Jour. Phys. and Chem. Reference Data, 1979-84. Fellow Am. Phys. Soc. (chmn. div. nuclear physics 1968-69, mem. coun. 1983-85, sec.-treas. Forum on Physics and Soc. 1988-93, Bonner prize 1965), Am. Acad. Arts and Scis. (Midwest coun. 1992—); mem. Nat. Acad. Sci. (chmn. physics sect. 1980-83), Am. Inst. Physics (chmn. publ. bd. 1980-82, governing bd. 1983-88), NRC (assembly math. and phys. scis. 1980-83). Home: 1110 Tumalo Trl Madison WI 53711-3027

BARSKY, ARTHUR JOSEPH, III, physician, researcher; b. N.Y.C., Feb. 19, 1943; s. Arthur Joseph and Hannah (Kahn) B.; m. Susan Margot Saaz; children: Timothy Andrew, Amy Abigail, Emily Elizabeth. BA, Williams Coll., 1964; MD, Columbia U., 1969; Harvard Med. Sch., Boston. Diplomate Am. Bd. Psychiatry and Neurology. Med. intern Beth Israel Med. Ctr., N.Y.C., 1969-70; resident in psychiatry Mass. Gen. Hosp., Boston, 1973-76; instr. psychiatry Harvard Med. Sch., Boston, 1976-79, asst. prof. psychiatry, 1980-87, assoc. prof. psychiatry, 1987-96, prof., 1996—; dir. acute psychiatry svc. Mass. Gen. Hosp., Boston, 1976-85, dir. primary care psychiatry unit, 1979-93; dir. psychosomatic rsch. Brigham and Women's Hosp., Boston, 1993—. Author: Worried Sick: Our Troubled Quest for Wellness, 1988; contbr. articles to profl. jours. Chairman parish com. 1st Parish Unitarian Ch., Wayland, Mass., 1989-90. Fellow Am. Coll. Psychiatrists, Am. Psychiat. Assn.; mem. Am. Psychosomatic Soc., Am. Psychopathol. Soc. Home: 268 Prince St Newton MA 02165-2920 Office: Brigham & Women's Hosp 75 Francis St Boston MA 02115

BARTEK, GORDON LUKE, radiologist; b. Valpraiso, Nebr., Dec. 27, 1925; s. Luke Victor and Sylvia (Buner) B.; m. Ruth Evelyn Rowley, Sept. 10, 1949; children: John, David, James. BSc, U. Nebr., 1948, MD, 1949. Diplomate Am. Bd. Radiology. Intern Bishop Clarksen Hosp., Omaha, 1949-50; resident in medicine Henry Ford Hosp., Detroit, 1952-53, resident in radiology, 1953-56; staff radiologist Ferguson Hosp., Grand Rapids, Mich., 1956-76, Holland City Hosp., Mich., 1956-76, Logan Hosp., Utah, 1976-78, St. Lawrence Hosp., Lansing, Mich., 1978—; asst. clin. prof. dept. radiology Mich. State Univ. Coll. Medicine, 1977-93, asst. prof. radiology, 1993—; dir. Accord Ins. Co., Cayman Islands, 1983-90; organizer Care Choices HMO, Lansing, 1983, bd. dirs., 1983-93. Served to lt. USN, 1949-52. Fellow Am. Coll. Radiology; mem. Mich. Radiology Practice Assn. (bd. dirs. 1984—, chmn. western Mich. sect. 1970-71), Am. Coll. Radiology (councilor 1972-76). Republican. Roman Catholic. Club: Kent Country Club. Avocations: flying, photography, skiing, snorkeling. Home: 1350 Briarcliff Dr SE Grand Rapids MI 49546-9679

BARTEL, LAVON LEE, university administrator, foods and nutrition scientist; b. Salem, Oreg., Nov. 12, 1951; d. Harvey C. Bartel and Jeanne Marie (Siddall) Bartel Shelton; m. David George Struck, Sept. 14, 1974. BS with honors, Oreg. State U., 1973, MS, 1975; PhD, U. Wis., 1979. Registered dietitian; cert. family and consumer scientist. Teaching asst. Oreg. State U., Corvallis, 1973-75; rsch. asst. U. Wis., Madison, 1975-79; asst. prof. Whittier (Calif.) Coll., 1979-82; asst. prof. U. Vt., Burlington, 1982-87, extension specialist extension svc., 1987-89, assoc. dean, 1989-96, assoc. dir. dir. agr./life scis., ext. and natural resources, 1989-96; dir. U. Maine Coop. Ext., Orono, 1996—; cons. Vt. food industry, 1982-89; bd. dirs. Earth's Best, Middlebury, Vt., 1984-88. Contbr. articles to profl. jours. Mem. APHA, Nat. Ext. Com. USDA (chair New Eng. ext. dir. 1992-93), Vt. Dietetic Assn. (pres. 1989-90, chair coun. of practice 1987-88, chair 1993-94, hunger and malnutrition practice group 1994—), Vt. Home Econs. Assn. (sec.-treas. 1987-89), Inst. Food Technologists, Assn. Women in Sci., Ext. Coun. on Policy (budget com. 1993-94, program leadership com. 1995, co-chair strategic planning coun. 1996—), Phi Kappa Phi. Office: U Maine Coop Ext Sys Ext System 101 Libby Hall Orono ME 04469

BARTEL, PETER ROBERT, clinical neurophysiologist, researcher; b. East London, South Africa, Oct. 27, 1946; s. Arthur Edward and Rhoda Ruth (Winzel) B.; m. Jeanette DeJager. BA, Rhodes U., South Africa, 1970, BA with honors, 1971, MA, 1972; PhD, U. Natal, 1977. Cert. med. scientist and psychologist South African Med. and Dental Coun. Rschr. South African Coun. for Sci. and Indsl. Rsch., Johannesburg, 1972-81; med. scientist HF Verwoerd Hosp. and U. of Pretoria, Pretoria, South Africa, 1981—; South African del. Internat. Fedn. Clin. Neurophysiology, Freiburg, Germany, 1995—. Contbr. sci. papers to profl. jours. Mem. South African Soc. Clin. Neurophysiology (pres. 1995—), Royal Soc. South Africa, Neurol. Assn. South Africa. Home: PO Box 70489 The Willows, 0041 Gauteng South Africa Office: Dept Neurology, Pvt Bag X 169, 0001 Gauteng South Africa

BARTELS, JEAN ELLEN, nursing educator; b. Two Rivers, Wis., July 15, 1949; m. Terry D. Bartels, Aug. 14, 1971; children: Justin Dean, Ashlee Jill. Diploma, Columbia Hosp. Sch. Nursing, 1970; BS in Nursing with honors, Alverno Coll., 1981; MS in Nursing, Marquette U., 1983; PhD in Nursing, U. Wis., 1990. Staff nurse ICU Columbia Hosp., Milw., 1970-83; dean, prof. of nursing Alverno Coll., Milw., 1990—. Contbr. articles to profl. jours. Mem. ANA, AACN (bd. dirs.), Internat. Soc. for Sci. Study Subjectivity, NLN, Midwest Nursing Rsch. Soc., Am. Assn. Collegiate Schs. Nursing, Sigma Theta Tau, Phi Kappa Phi. Home: N24w22623 Meadowood Ln Waukesha WI 53186-8822 Office: Alverno Coll PO Box 343922 Milwaukee WI 53234-3922

BARTELS, LOREN JAY, surgeon, otolaryngologist; b. David City, Nebr., June 2, 1949; s. Lambert Loren and Constance (Owen) B.; m. Linda Rousku, Aug. 26, 1972; children: Mathew Jonathan, Lisa Joy. BA, U. South Fla., 1971, MD, 1974. Intern Geisinger Med. Ctr., Danville, Pa., 1975-76, resident, 1976-79; fellow House Ear Inst., L.A., 1979-80; attending physician Univ. Community Hosp., Tampa, Fla., 1982-92, 95—; cons. physician St. Joseph's Hosp., Tampa, 1983-92, 95—; attending physician James A. Haley Vets. Hosp., Tampa, 1980—, Tampa Gen. Hosp., 1980—; assoc. prof. surgery, neurology and radiology U. South Fla. Coll. Medicine, 1987—, dir. temporal bone course, 1981-94; chief Tampa Gen. Dept. Otolaryngology, 1994-96. Contbr. articles to profl. jours. Mem. ACS, AMA, Am. Acad. Otolaryngology-Head and Neck Surgery, Fla. Med. Assn., Hillsborough County Med. Assn., Fla. Soc. Otolaryngology (pres. 1990-91), Am. Neurotology Soc., N.Am. Skull Base Surgery Soc., Am. Otol. Soc., Triologic Soc., The Otosclerosis Study Group, Alpha Omega Alpha, Omicron Delta

Kappa, Phi Kappa Phi (vice pres.1970-71), Pi Mu Epsilon. Office: The Tampa Bay Hearing & Balance Ctr 4 Columbia Dr Ste 610 Tampa FL 33606

BARTELSTONE, RONA SUE, gerontologist; b. Bklyn., Jan. 10, 1951; d. Herbert and Hazel (Mittman) Canarick; m. Alan Joel Markowitz. BS in Social Welfare, SUNY, Buffalo, 1972; MSW, Ind. U., 1974. Licensed Clin. Social Worker, Fla. Diplomate of Social Work. Social worker YM-YWHA of Greater N.Y., 1974-75; dist. supr. N.Y.C. Housing Authority, Bklyn., 1975-77; field instr. Barry U. Sch. Social Work, 1980-81; project dir. United Family & Children's Svcs., 1977-81; faculty Miami Dade Community Coll., 1981-82; adult educator Sch. Bd. Dade County, 1981-82; med. social worker Mederi Home Health Agy., 1979-82; mem. adj. faculty Nova U., 1986-88; pvt. practice Rona Bartelstone Assocs., Inc., Ft. Lauderdale, Fla., 1981—; adj. faculty Fla. Internat. U., S.E. Ctr. on Aging, 1996; cons. and trainer in field. Contbr. articles to various mags. d. dirs. Jewish Vocat. Svcs., Miami, 1985-92; mem. funding panel Area Agy. on Aging, Miami, 1985-89; active Friends of the Family Counseling Svcs., Miami, 1983-88; adv. bd., chair internship subcom. Lynn U., 1993—; exec. bd. Fla. Geriatric CAre Mgrs., 1993—; chair tng. com., exec. v.p. Alzheimer's Assn., Miami, 1994-96; co-chair Nat. Acad. Cert. Care Mgrs., 1994—. Recipient Dade County Citizen of the Yr. award, 1982, NASW Social Worker of the Yr. award, 1982-83, Trail Blazer award, 1984, Up & Comers award in health care Price Waterhouse and So. Fla. Bus. Jour., 1990. Mem. NASW (treas. 1987-89), Gerontology Soc. Am., Am. Soc. on Aging, Nat. Coun. on Aging, Assn. Profl. Geriatric Care Mgrs. (pres. 1988-94, chmn. credential com. 1993—), Nat. Acad. Cert. Care Mgrs. (co-chmn. 1994—), Fla. Geriatric Care Mgrs. Assn. (exec. bd. 1993—). Democrat. Jewish. Home: 2365 N 37th Ave Hollywood FL 33021-3645 Office: 2699 Stirling Rd Ste 304C Fort Lauderdale FL 33312-6517

BARTHA, RICHARD, microbiology educator; b. Budapest, Hungary, Nov. 14, 1934; came to U.S., 1962; s. Imre and Irene (Pfann) B.; m. Susi E. Fels, Dec. 29, 1966; children: Miriam, Doris. Student, Eötvös U., Budapest, 1953-56; PhD, U. Göttingen, Germany, 1961. Postdoctoral trainee U. Wash., Seattle, 1962-64; rsch. assoc. Rutgers U., New Brunswick, 1964-66, asst. prof., 1966-69, assoc. prof., 1969-73, prof., 1973-84, prof. II, 1984—. Author: Microbial Ecology, 1981, 3d rev. edit., 1992; mem. editorial bd. Applied and Environ. Microbiology, 1974-83, Soil Sci., 1978, Indsl. Microbiology; contbr. articles to profl. jours. Fellow AAAS, Am. Acad. Microbiology; mem. Am. Soc. for Microbiology (lectr. summer 1976), Am. Found. for Microbiology (lectr. 1977-78), Soil Microbiology (chmn. 1968-69), Applied Microbiology (chmn. 1979-81), Theobald Smith Soc. (pres. 1990-91). Office: Cook Coll Lipman Hall Rutgers U New Brunswick NJ 08903

BARTHEL, HERMAN JOSEPH, family practice physician; b. Chgo., Sept. 3, 1958; s. Herman Otto and Irmgard (Bayerstoffer) B.; m. Cheryl Sue Forgey, Aug. 31, 1988; children: Jennifer, Robbie, Matt. BS in Microbiology, U. Notre Dame, 1980; DO, U. Health Scis., 1984; grad. tropical medicine course, Walter Reed Army Inst. Rsch., 1986; grad., Command and Gen. Staff Coll., 1992. Diplomate Am. Bd. Family Practice; cert. ATLS instr., ACLS instr. Commd. 2d lt. U.S. Army, 1980, advanced through grades to lt. col., 1996; intern Martin Army Cmty. Hosp., Ft. Benning, Ga., 1984-85, resident dept. family practice, 1985-87; family physician U.S. Army, Ft. Leavenworth, Kans., 1987-92; chief blue primary care clinic U.S. Army, Ft. Campbell, Ky., 1992—, chief family practice svc., 1992—, chief dept primary care, 1994; family physician Schofield Barracks, Hawaii, 1989-92; emergency physician Lawrence (Kans.) Meml. Hosp., 1987-89, Hawaii Permanente Med. Group, Honolulu, 1989-92, Northcrest Med. Ctr., Springfield, Tenn., 1992—; chief emergency med. svcs. U.S. Army, Schofield Barracks, 1989-92, preceptor for med. students, physician assts. and emergency nurse practitioners, 1987—. Contbr. articles to profl. jours. Decorated Combat Med. Badge, Army Commendation medal, Meritorious Svc. medal. Fellow Am. Acad. Family Practice; mem. Uniformed Svcs. Acad. Family Practice. Office: Blanchfield Army Cmty Hosp Dept Primary Care Cmty Med Fort Campbell TN 42223

BARTHOLOMEW, JAMES WILLIAM, biology educator; b. Ashtabula, Ohio, May 10, 1916; s. Joseph Arthur and Myrtle Mae (Mahan) B.; m. Helen Shirley Buzard, Sept. 2, 1943. BS in Biology cum laude, Ohio U., 1939, MS in Bacteriology, 1941; PhD in Bacteriology, U. Wis., 1944. Asst. prof. biology U. So. Calif., L.A., 1944-46; assoc. prof. U. So. Calif., 1946-52, prof. biology, 1953-81, prof. emeritus biology, 1981—; cons. in field. Contbr. articles to profl. jours.; chpts. to books. Fulbright scholar, 1950-51, lectr., 1958, 59. Mem. Am. Soc. Microbiology, Biol. Stain Commn. Home: 4717 Barcelona Way Oceanside CA 92056-5110

BARTLETT, DIANE SUE, clinical mental health counselor; b. Laconia, N.H., Dec. 6, 1947; d. Fred Elmer and Dorothy Pearl (Wakefield) Davis; m. Josiah Henry Bartlett, Aug. 23, 1980; 1 child by previous marriage, Fred Louis Hacker; 1 step child, Juliet. AA, Plymouth State Coll., 1982; B in Gen. Studies summa cum laude, U. N.H. Sch. for Lifelong Learning, 1984; MEd., Plymouth State Coll., 1988. Cert. clin. mental health counselor. Police comms. specialist Divsn. Motore Vehicles, Concord, N.H., 1970-76, br. office mgr., 1976-83, coord. motor vehicles registrations, 1983-84; tax collector City of Dover, N.H., 1984; intern Lakes Region Mental Health Divsn., Laconia, N.H., 1985; counselor Latchkey Pastoral Counseling, Laconia, 1984-87; family therapist, Children's Best Interest, Laconia, 1988—; mental health counselor Carroll County Mental Health Svcs., Wolfeboro, N.H., 1988-95; mental health counselor, pvt. practice, Ossipee, N.H., 1995—. Mem. Town of Moultonboro Sch. Feasibility Study Commn., 1978; adminstrv. bd. mem., chmn. pastor-parish rels. com. United Meth. Ch., Moultonboro, N.H., 1983—, N.H. annual conf., 1986-88, participant N.H. Ann. Conf. on Status and Role of Women, Concord, 1985—; mem. Friends of Families in Carroll County, 1995—. N.H. Charitable Found. grantee, 1985. Mem. Internat. Soc. for Study of Dissociation, Am. Counseling Assn., Am. Mental Health Counselors Assn. Avocations: skiing, swimming, reading, writing. Home: PO Box 14 Moultonborough NH 03254-0014 Office: Mountainside Bus Ctr 127 Rte 28 Ossipee NH 03864

BARTLETT, JAMES WILLIAMS, psychiatrist, educator; b. Balt., Feb. 2, 1926; s. James Williams and Margaret Baylor (Alexander) B.; m. Nancy Bieszad, May 8, 1954; children: John Alexander, Anne Lee, Thomas Martin. B.A., Harvard U., 1948; M.D., Johns Hopkins U., 1952. Mem. faculty U. Rochester Med. Center, N.Y., 1957—, prof. psychiatry, 1968-96; prof. emeritus psychiatry U. Rochester Med. Ctr., N.Y., 1996—; prof. health services U. Rochester Med. Center, N.Y., 1968-85, assoc. dean Sch. Medicine and Dentistry, 1966-83; med. dir. Strong Meml. Hosp., 1967-83; prof. psychiatry, dean faculty health sci. Aga Khan U., Karachi, Pakistan, 1990-93; also acting rector Aga Khan U. Served with USNR, 1944-46. Fellow Am. Psychiat. Assn. (life); mem. Assn. Am. Med. Coll., Soc. Med. Adminstrs., Western N.Y. Psychoanalytic Soc., Rochester Acad. Medicine.

BARTLETT, ROBERT HAWES, surgeon; b. Ann Arbor, Mich., May 8, 1939. BA, Albion (Mich.) Coll., 1960; MD cum laude, U. Mich., 1963. Diplomate Nat. Bd. Med. Examiners, Am. Bd. Surgery (examination cons. 1989-90), Am. Bd. Thoracic Surgery. Intern in surgery Peter Bent Brigham Hosp., Boston, 1963-64, asst. resident/sr. asst. resident, 1964-67, chief resident in thoracic surgery, 1968, chief resident surgeon, 1969; rsch. fellow in surgery Harvard Med. Sch., Boston, 1968, Arthur Tracy Cabot Teaching fellow in surgery, 1969; Harvey Cushing fellow and rsch. fellow in surgery Peter Bent Brigham Hosp./Harvard Med. Sch., Boston, 1969-70; asst. prof. surgery U. Calif., Irvine, 1970-73, assoc. prof. surgery, 1973-77, prof. surgery, 1977-80; prof. surgery U. Mich., Ann Arbor, 1980—; asst. in surgery Peter Bent Brigham Hosp., 1969-70; attending staff U. Calif.-Irvine/Orange County Med. Ctr., 1970-80, asst. dir. surg. svcs., 1970-80, dir. burn ctr., 1971-80; attending staff St. Joseph Hosp., Orange, Calif., 1970-80, Children's Hosp. of Orange County, 1970-80, VA Hosp., Long Beach, 1970-80, Wayne County Gen. Hosp., 1980-84, Westland Med. Ctr., 1984-85; attending staff U. Mich. Med. Ctr., 1980—, dir. SICU, 1980—, gen. surgery sect. head, 1981-87, dir. grad. edn., 1980-91, trauma/critical care divsn. chief, 1980-91, critical care divsn. chief, 1991—, program dir. surg. critical care fellowship, 1991—, dir. extracorporeal life support program, 1980—; lectr. in field; cons. in field to NIH, Nat. Heart and Lun Inst., Calif. Heart Assn., March of Dimes Found., numerous others. Editl. bd. Perfusion, 1985—, Critical Care, 1985—, Trans ASAIQ, 1986—, Internat. Jour. Biomaterials, Artificial Cells and Artificial Organs, 1987, Jour. Thoracic and Cardiovascular Surgery, 1992-94, SESATS; reviewer Sci., 1974, Chest, 1974-79, 83—, Jour. Applied Physiology, 1977, Heart and Lung, 1978—, New Eng. Jour. Medicine, 1981, 87-88, Surgery, 1984—, Am. Rev. Respiratory Disease, 1985—, Jour. Thoracic and CArdiovascular Surgery, 1987—, Artificial Organs, 1987—, Pediatrics, 1987—, Intensive Care Medicine, 1987—, Jour. Parenteral and Enteral Nutrition, 1988—, Jour. Critical Care, 1989—, Jour. AMA, 1993—, Am. Jour. Respiratory and Critical Care Medicine, 1993—; patentee in field; contbr. over 243 articles to profl. jours., chpts. to books; author: Mechanical Devices for Cardiopulmonary Assistance, Advances in Cardiology, Vol. 6, 1971, Hematological Analysis of extracorporeal Membrane Oxygenation, 1974, Extracorporeal Circulation for Cardiopulmonary Failure, Current Problems in Surgery, Vol. 15, 1978, Extracorporeal Life Support for Cardiopulmonary Failure, Current Problems in Surgery, Vol. 27, 1990; co-editor: Biologic and Synthetic Vascular Protheses, 1982, Life Support Systems in Invensive Care, 1984, Medical Education: A Surgical Perspective, 1986; editor: Respiratory Care of the Surgical Patient, 1980. Rsch. grantee Orange County Heart Assn., 1971, Donald E. Baxter Found., 1970-71, Calif. TB and Respiratory Disease Assn., 1971-72, NIH, 1972-75, 74-77, 76-79, 78-80, 81-84, 84-85, 84-85, 85-90, 90-92, Hearst Found., 1976-78, 79-80, 89-93, Thoratec Inc., 1983, Mead-Johnson, 1983, GM Corp., 1984-85, others; recipient Gibbon award Am. Soc. Extra-Corporeal Tech., 1992, Dwight E. Harken award Temple U., 1992, Kaiser Permanente Excellence in Teaching award, 1993. Mem. ACS, Am. Surg. Assn., Am. Assn. Thoracic Surgery, Am. Assn. for Surgery of Trauma, Assn. for Acad. Surgery, Ctrl. Surg. Soc., Coller Surg. Soc., Soc. Univ. Surgeons, Surg. Biology Club II, Surg. Infection Soc., Western Thoracic Surg. Assn., Am. Burn Assn., Am. Assn. History of Medicine, Am. Physiol. Soc., Am. Coll. Chest Physicians, Am. Soc. for Artificial Internal Organs (bd. trustees 1986-87, regulatory affairs com. 1985—, pres. 1984, others), Am. Thoracic Soc., Am. Trauma Soc., Extracorporeal Life Support Orgn., Internat. Soc. Artificial Organs, Mich. Soc. Critical Care, Perinatal Assn. Mich., Soc. Critical Ca for Med. and Biol. Engring. (charter mem.), Beta Beta Beta, Alpha Omega Alpha, Galens Hon. Med. Soc. Office: University of Michigan Dept Surgery Ann Arbor MI 48109

BARTNIK, ANNA MARIA, physician; b. Bytom, Silesia, Poland, Oct. 11, 1964; d. Mieczyslaw Marian and Wieslawa Teresa (Koziol) Bartnik; m. Miroslaw Mikuta, July 30, 1994; 1 child, Marta. MD, Med. Acad., Poznan, Poland, 1989. Physician Out Patients Diabetes Clinic, Inst. of Paediatrics, Kraków, Poland, 1990—. Co-editor, co-author: My Book About Diabetes for Insulin-Dependent Diabetes, 1990; contbr. articles to profl. jours. Mem. Polish Dietetic Assn., Polish Diabetic Assn., European Assn. for Study on Diabetes, N.Y. Acad. Scis. Office: Inst Paediatrics Dept, Diabetology Wielicka 265, 30-663 Kraków Poland

BARTOLO, DONNA MARIE, hospital administrator, nurse; b. Springfield, Ill., Mar. 21, 1941; d. Elmer Ralph Bartolomucci and Zoe (Rose) Cavatorta. Diploma in nursing, St. John's Sch. Nursing, Springfield, Ill., 1962; BS, Milliken U., 1976; MA, Sangamon State U., 1978. Pediatric nurse Springfield Clin., 1962-64, physician's asst., 1972-74; gynecol. nurse Watson Clin., Lakeland, Fla., 1964-66; cons. state sch. nurses Office of Edn. State of Ill., Springfield, 1974-78; assoc. dir. operating rm. svcs. Cedars-Sinai Med. Ctr., L.A., 1978-82, co-dir. div. nursing, 1981-82; surg. nurse Emory U. Hosp., Atlanta, 1966-70, asst. dir. nursing, surg. svcs., 1982-94, dir. surg. svcs., dir. nursing, 1994—, dir. nursing for surg. scis., 1995—; adj. prof. Nell Hodgson Woodruff Sch. Nursing Emory U. Mem. editorial bd. Perioperative Nursing Quarterly; contbr. articles to nursing jours. Mem. Org. Nurse Execs., Ga. Assn. Nurse Exec. (pres. elect, pres. 1992), Assn. Operating Rm. Nurses, Sigma Theta Tau (sec. 1990—). Home: 1328 Mill Glen Dr Dunwoody GA 30338-2720

BARTON, BEVERLY ETHEL, immunologist; b. N.Y.C., May 6, 1954; d. Al J. and Sally (Kirschenbaum) Feigen; m. Arnold B. Barton, June 18, 1978; children: Rachel Tamara, Jerusha Elana. BA, Johns Hopkins U., 1976, ScM, 1979; PhD, Stanford U., 1984. Scientist Allergan, Inc., Irvine, Calif., 1984-87; prin. scientist Schering-Plough Rsch. Inst., Kenilworth, N.J., 1987—. Contbr. articles and abstracts to profl. jours.; patentee prevention of lens-related tissue growth in eye, use of IL-6 to treat toxic shock. Mem. Am. Assn. Immunologists, Soc. for Exptl. Biology and Medicine, N.Y. Acad. Scis., Soc. Leukocyte Biology, Inflammation Rsch. Assn. Democrat. Jewish. Office: Schering-Plough Rsch Inst 2015 Galloping Hill Rd Kenilworth NJ 07033-1310

BARTON, EDWARD ELIOT, urologist; b. Salt Lake City, Sept. 3, 1951; s. E. Dale and Mary M. (Moreton) B.; m. Cynthia Blake, Dec. 9, 1979; children: Elizabeth, Michael, Robert, David, Andrew. BA, U. Utah, 1976, MD, 1979. Diplomate Am. Bd. Urology. Intern Providence Hosp., Southfield, Mich., 1979-80, staff urologist, 1984—; resident Henry Ford Hosp., Detroit, 1980-84; assoc. staff urologist Beaumont Hosp., Royal Oak, Mich., 1986—; del. Oakland County Med. Soc., Birmingham, Mich., 1989-96. With USAR, 1969-76. Recipient Physicians Recognition aard AMA, 1993-96. Fellow ACS; mem. Am. Urol. Assn. Office: Providence Med Bldg 22250 Providence Dr Ste 205 Southfield MI 48075-6215

BARTON, FLORIN EDWARD, retired social services administrator; b. Springfield, Ill., Oct. 4, 1912; s. Roland I. and Rose Ella (Jouett) B.; m. Vivian Gertrude Vancil, Apr. 11, 1937; children: Judith Lee Williamson, JoAnn Steffens. Dist. dir. Muscular Dystrophy Assn., Springfield, 1968-71; regional coord. Muscular Dystrophy Assn., St. Louis, 1971-77; cons. Cardiac Pulmonary Recussitation Telethon WCIA-TV, Champaign, 1977-79; dir. info. svc. on aging Ill. Presbyn. Home, Springfield, 1979-93; ret., 1993; mem. Presbytery Great Rivers Task Force on Aging, Peoria, Ill., 1981-91; pres. Springfield Ministry Coun., 1986-89. Author: (booklet) Manual to Assist Congregations in their Ministry to the Elderly, 1981; editor The Informer quar. periodical, 1971-91. Sec. DeMolay Legion of Honor, Springfield, 1976-91; fin. officer Contact Ministries, Springfield, 1983-86; mem. Ill. State DeMolay Found., Collinsville, 1985-91. Mem. Masons. Presbyterian. Home: 2525 S 5th St Springfield IL 62703-3801

BARTON, MICHAEL W., health care executive; b. Preston, Eng., Feb. 8, 1944; s. Frederick Cardell and Margaret Edith (Smith) B.; m. Barbara Anne Barclay, Nov. 6, 1971; children: Warren, Cathy, Tiffany, Jason. BA, U. N.C., 1968; MBA, Ga. So. U., 1973. Chief fin. officer Candler Gen. Hosp., Savannah, Ga., 1970-73; asst. corp. contr. Hosp. Affiliates Internat., Nashville, 1973-76; exec. dir. Flower & Fifth Ave. Hosp., N.Y.C., 1976-78; sr. v.p. Hosp. Affiliates Mgmt. Corp., Nashville, 1978-81; prin., founder Hosp. Mgmt. Profls. Inc., Brentwood, Tenn., 1981-91; pres., CEO, founder Health Horizons, Inc., Brentwood, 1991—, PriCare, Inc., Brentwood, 1996—. Bd. dirs., chmn. strategic planning Martin Meth. Coll., Pulaski, Tenn., 1994—; bd. dirs., exec. com. Dede Wallace Healthcare System, Nashville, 1994—, Tenn. Repertory Theatre, Nashville, 1993—; mem. nat. adv. com. Rocky Mountain Coll., Billings, Mont., 1994—. Mem. Rotary (treas. 1985-86). Republican. Methodist. Home: 115 Suffolk Crescent Brentwood TN 37027

BARTON, WALTER EARL, psychiatrist; b. Oak Park, Ill., July 29, 1906; s. Alfred John and Bertha Marion (Kalish) B.; m. Elsa Viola Benson, July 2, 1932 (dec. June 1989); children: John A. (dec.), Gail M., Paul B. BS, U. Ill., 1928; MD, U. Ill., Chgo., 1931, DSc (hon.), 1975. Diplomate Am. Bd. Psychiatry and Neurology. Resident and all posts to acting supt. Worcester (Mass.) State Hosp., 1931-42; fellow in neurology Queen Sq., London, 1938; supt. Boston State Hosp., 1945-63; med. dir. Am. Psychiat. Assn., Washington, 1963-74; dir., pres. Am. Bd. of Psychiatry, Evanston, Ill., 1962-70; clin. prof. Boston U. Med. Sch., 1952—; prof. Dartmouth Med. Sch., Hanover, N.H., 1974—; cons. staff Mary Hitchcock Meml. Hosp., Hanover, 1974—; cons. Sibley, Washington, NIMH, Rockville, Md., 1963-64; bd. trustees Joint Commn. Mental Illness, Washington, 1956-61; editorial bd. Adminstrn. and Policy in Mental Health Social Psychiat. and Hosp. and Community Psychiatry, 1972—. Author: Administration in Psychiatry, 1962, History and Influence, 1987, (with Gail Barton) Mental Health Administration, 1983, Ethics and Law in Mental Health Administration, 1983; contbr. over 175 articles to profl. pubs. and 10 books publ. Bd. dirs. Worchester (Mass.) Child Guidance Clinic, 1940, YMCA, 1940, Inst. of Pastorial Ch., Washington, 1941; mem. Coun. of Religion and Hearlth, Boston, 1941. Lt. col. U.S. Army Med. Corps, 1942-46. Recipient Nolan D.C. Lewis award N.J. Psychiat. Inst., 1962, Salmon medal N.Y. Acad. of Medicine, 1974. Fellow (life) AMA, ACP, Am. Psychiat. Assn. (pres. 1961-62, med. dir. 1963-74, administrv. psychiatry com. 1983, disting. svc. award 1973), Am. Coll. of Psychiatrist,(E.B. Bowis award 1970), Am. Coll. Mental Health Administrn. (pres. 1980-81), Kiwanis, Cosmos. Republican. Congregationalist. Home: RR 1 Box 188 Hartland VT 05048-9728 Office: Dartmouth Med Sch Lebanon NH 03756

BARTON BURKE, MARGARET, oncology nurse, educator; b. Kearny, N.J., Nov. 14, 1950; d. Gerard A. and Antoinette (Casaletto) Barton; m. Thomas M. Burke, Sept. 21, 1974; children: Amelia, Whitney Antoinette. BSN, William Paterson Coll., 1972; MS, Boston U., 1980; postgrad., U. R.I. Staff nurse Monmouth Med. Ctr., Long Branch, N.J., 1972-73; instr. Clara Maass Hosp., Belleville, N.J., 1973-74, Mass. Gen. Hosp., Boston, 1974-79; staff nurse Pondville Hosp., Walpole, Mass., 1980; instr. U. R.I., Kingston, 1981-82; coord. Dana-Farber Cancer Inst., Boston, 1983-87; instr. nursing dept. Regis Coll., Weston, Mass., 1987-90; coord. Mass. Cancer Pain Initiative, Boston, 1990-91; cons. oncology nursing West Roxbury, Mass., 1987—; adj. faculty Northeastern U., Dedham, Mass., 1983-85. Author: Cancer Chemotherapy A Nursing Process Approach, 1991 (Book of Yr. 1991), 2nd edit. 1996, Cancer Chemotherapy Designs for Nursing Care, 1992, Oncology Nursing Homecare Handbook, 1992, Oncology Nursing Drug Reference, 1993; editl. bd. Cancer Practice, 1992—, A Cancer Source Book for Nurses, 7th edit. Mem. adv. group on cancer pain Am. Cancer Soc., 1991. Lt. col. U.S. Army Nurse Corps, 1992. Mem. Oncology Nursing Soc. (cert., chairperson nat. congress 1993). Home and Office: 7 Rendall Rd West Roxbury MA 02132-1023

BARTSCH, RICHARD ALAN, school psychologist; b. Mpls., Dec. 31, 1950; s. Carl H. and Carol J. (Brusletten) B.; m. Nancy Rae Anderson, Aug. 26, 1972; children: Marcy, Jonathan, Jeffrey. BA, U. Minn., Duluth, 1973; MS in Edn., U. Wis., Superior, 1975. Cert. sch. psychologist, Mont.; nat. cert. sch. psychologist. Sch. psychologist Billings (Mont.) Pub. Schs., 1975—, supr. psychol. svcs., 1979—. Mem. NASP (del. 1989-93), Mont. Assn. Sch. Psychologists (pres. 1994-95). Home: 1804 S Mariposa Ln Billings MT 59102-2351 Office: Billings Pub Schs 415 N 30th St Billings MT 59101-1252

BARTUCCI, MARILYN ROSSMAN, medical and surgical nurse, researcher; b. Cleve., Sept. 11, 1952; d. Raymond E. and Esther (Verbic) Rossman; m. Albert J. Bartucci, Apr. 26, 1975; children: Nicholas Raymond, Grant Douglas, Amelia Rose. BSN, Marquette U., 1974; MSN, Case Western Res. U., 1979. Cert. clin. nurse specialist in med.-surg. nursing, clin. transplant coord. Staff nurse med. nursing div. Univ. Hosps. of Cleve., asst. head nurse med. nursing div., clin. nurse specialist, transplant program, head nurse mgr. transplant ctr.; mem. clin. faculty Frances Payne Bolton Sch. Nursing, Case Western Res. U., Kent State U. Sch. of Nursing. Contbr. chpts. to nursing books and articles to profl. jours. Mem. Nat. Kidney Found., Am. Nephrology Nurses Assn., Ohio Nurses Assn., Transplantation Soc., Northeastern Ohio (past pres.), N.Am. Transplant Coords. Orgn. (past sec. and councillor at large), Ohio Coalition of Nurses (specialty cert.), Greater Cleve. Nurses Assn. (past v.p.), ALpha Sigma Nu, Sigma Theta Tau. Home: 91 E 196th St Cleveland OH 44119-1031

BARTUNEK, HENRIETTA ANN, patient care coordinator; b. N.Y.C., Oct. 28, 1944; d. Arthur William and Myra (Kacalek) B. Diploma in nursing, St. Vincent's Hosp., 1965; BA in Psychology, Marymount Manhattan Coll., 1973. RN, N.Y., Fla.; cert. psychiat. and mental health nurse, ANCC. Head nurse St. Vincent's Hosp., N.Y.C., 1965-83; staff nurse Long Beach (Calif.) VA Hosp., 1984-85; staff nurse Devereux Hosp. of Fla., Melbourne, 1990, unit dir., 1991-92; assoc. patient care coord. Wuesthoff Hosp., Rockledge, Fla., 1992—; practitioner Therapeutic Touch. Mem. AAUW, Alliance for Holistic Healing. Roman Catholic. Home: 155 Hwy A1A # 104 Satellite Beach FL 32937

BARTUNEK, JAMES SCOTT, psychiatrist; b. Flint, Mich., Oct. 20, 1962; s. Steven James and Frances Annabelle (Peters) B.; m. Carol Lynn Tobis, Feb. 26, 1994; 1 child, Rebecca. BS, U. Mich., Flint, 1985; MD, Wayne State U., 1989. Resident in psychiatry Sinai Hosp. Detroit, 1989-92; mem. staff Crittenton Hosp., Rochester, Mich., 1993—. Mem. Am. Psychiat. Assn., Founder's Soc. Detroit Inst. Arts, U. Mich. Club, Wayne State U. Med. Alumni Club. Home: 3541 Hidden Forest Ct Orion MI 48359 Office: 1460 Walton Blvd Ste 215 Rochester Hills MI 48309-1779

BARTUNEK, ROBERT RICHARD, retired physician; b. Cleve., Dec. 3, 1914; s. Emil Arthur and Mae (Friedl) B.; m. Clare Elizabeth Lonsway, Dec. 30, 1943 (dec. July 1975); children: Jean Marie, Robert R., Thomas J.; m. Mary Anne Piotrkowski, July 23, 1978. A.B., Case Western Res. U., 1936, M.D., 1940. Diplomate: Am. Bd. Internal Medicine. Intern St. Alexis Hosp., Cleve., 1940-41; resident St. Alexis Hosp., 1941-42; fellow in medicine Cleve. Clinic., 1946-48; pvt. practice medicine, specializing in gastroenterology Cleve., 1949-91; mem. staff St. Alexis Hosp., 1948-91, dir. gastroenterology, 1949-81, dir. medicine, 1952-61, dir. labs., 1950-62; mem. staff St. Vincent Charity Hosp., Cleve., 1950—; dir. gastroenterology St. Vincent Charity Hosp., 1960-83, dir. emeritus, 1983—, dir. medicine, 1966-72, 80-81; assoc. mem. staff emeritus Met. Gen. Hosp.; cons. Marymount Hosp., Garfield Heights, Ohio; faculty mem. Case Western Res. U. Med. Sch., from 1952, up through ranks to assoc. prof., 1980. Mem. med. morals adv. bd. Cleve. Catholic Diocese. Served to lt. col. AUS, 1942-46. Decorated Bronze Star. Fellow Am. Coll. Gastroenterology (pres. 1963-64, Samuel Weiss award 1974), ACP, AAAS (council 1963-76); mem. Am. Geriatric Soc., Am. Soc. Gastrointestinal Endoscopy, Assn. Mil. Surgeons, Internat. Congress of Internal Medicine, Am. Soc. Internal Medicine, Cleve. Diabetes Assn. (dir. 1967-70), AMA, Ohio Med. Assn., Cleve. Acad. Medicine, L'Organisation Mondiale de Gastro-Enterologie (U.S. del. 1963-65), Nu Sigma Nu. Home: Beechwood 23446 Letchworth Rd Cleveland OH 44122 Office: St Vincent Charity Hosp 2351 E 22nd St Cleveland OH 44115-3111

BARTUS, RAYMOND THOMAS, neuroscientist, pharmaceutical executive, writer; b. Chgo., May 19, 1947; s. Frank A. and Katherine (Bogus) B.; m. Cheryl Marie Gyure, Feb. 11, 1967; children: Raymond T., Kristin Marie. B.A., California State U. Pa., 1968; M.S., N.C. State U., 1970, Ph.D., 1972. NRC postdoctoral fellow, research assoc. Naval Med. Rsch. Lab., Groton, Conn., 1972; scientist Parke-Davis Rsch. Labs., Ann Arbor, Mich., 1973-75, sr. scientist, 1975-78; sr. scientist Lederle Labs., Am. Cyanamid Co., Pearl River, N.Y., 1978-79, group leader neuroscience, dir. geriatric discovery program, 1979-88; sr. v.p. R & D, chief sci. officer Cortex Pharms. Inc., Irvine, Calif., 1988-91, interim pres., 1990, exec. v.p., chief oper. officer, 1991-92; chief sci. officer Cortex Pharms. Inc., Irvine, 1988-92; also bd. dirs. Cortex Pharms. Inc., Irvine, Calif.; sr. v.p. neurobiology Alkermes Inc., Cambridge, Mass., 1992—; prof. NYU Med. Ctr., 1979-94; adj. prof. U. Calif., Irvine, 1988-92, Tulane U., 1978-87, Tufts U., 1992—; cons. in field. Editor-in-chief, founder, Neurobiology of Aging, 1980-89; contbr. articles on neurosci. to profl. jours. Mem. Sci. Med. Bd., Soc. Neurosci., Am. Coll. Neuropsychopharm., N.Y. Acad. Sci., Alzheimers Assn., Brain Tumor Soc. Office: Alkermes Inc 64 Sidney St Cambridge MA 02139-4170

BARTUSKA, DORIS GORKA, physician; b. Nanticoke, Pa., Apr. 18, 1929; d. Edward Edmund and Sophie Constance (Wombal) Gorka; m. Anthony John Bartuska, June 23, 1951; children: Ann, Kathleen, Lisa, Karen, Christina, Mia. BS in Biology, Bucknell U., 1949; MD, Woman's Med. Coll. of Pa., 1954. Diplomate Am. Bd. Internal Medicine, Am. Bd. Endocrinology and Metabolism. Rotating internship Hosp. of the Woman's Med. Coll., 1954-55, resident in medicine, 1956-57; fellow in medicine Women's Med. Coll. Pa., 1955-56; traineeship in endocrinology Jefferson Med. Coll., 1957-58; NIH spl. fellow in molecular medicine Hosp. of the U. of Pa., 1966-68; assoc. prof. clin. pathology Med. Coll. Pa., Phila., 1971—, dir., div. endocrinology and metabolism, 1973-95, prof. medicine, 1977-96, prof. emeritus medicine, endocrinology, diabetes & metabolism, 1996—; bd. dirs. Pa. Blue Shield, Camp Hill; active numerous coms.; lectr. in field. Contbg. author book chpts. in field; contbr. articles to profl. jours. Mem. East Falls Community Coun., Key Contact for Pa. Med. Soc. Polit. Action; mem. Wilkes U. Adv. Coun., 1990. Recipient scholarships Wilkes-Barre (Pa.) C. of C., 1949, Bucknell U., Lewisburg, Pa., 1950, Kosciuszko Found., 1951; fellowships from Kate Hurt Mead, 1955, NIH, 1957, 66-68. Fellow ACP; mem. Am. Assn. Clin. Endocrinologists (bd. dirs.), Phila. Endocrine Soc.,

Phila. County Med. Soc. (pres. Pfahler Found. 1990-93), Pa. Med. Soc. (vice-chmn. ednl. and sci. trust 1986—), Am. Med. Women's Assn. (Calcium Nutrition Edn. award 1990, past pres.), Disting. Dau. of Pa., Am. Fedn. Clin. Rsch., AAAS, Assn. Women in Sci., Am. Thyroid Assn., Pa. Soc. Internal Medicine, AMA (del.), Phi Sigma, Alpha Omega Alpha (past pres.), others. Office: Med College of Pennsylvania 3300 Henry Ave Philadelphia PA 19129-1121

BARUCH, MONICA LOBO-FILHO, psychological counselor; b. Rio de Janeiro, Jan. 11, 1954; d. Max and Margot Lobo-Filho; m. Robert Karl Baruch, Dec. 30, 1973 (div. May 1985). BA in Psychology, U. Rochester, 1975; MA in Counseling Edn., U. Mo., Kansas City, 1978. Cert. Nat. Bd. Cert. Counselors. Tchr. curriculum devel. St. Patrick's Sch., Rio de Janeiro, 1974-76; tchr., soccer coach Pembroke Country Day Sch., Kansas City, Mo., 1977-78; tchr., trainer Berlitz Sch. Langs., Kansas City and Washington, 1976-79; counselor, cons. Youth Understanding, Washington, 1979-81; pvt. practice, 1981—; academic faculty counselor Georgetown U., Washington, 1982-90; newsletter editor, mem. exec. bd. Greater Washington Coalition of Mental Health Profls. and Consumers, 1996—. Co-author: Weight Control: A Guide for Counselors and Therapists, 1987. Named one of Outstanding Young Women in Am., 1981. Mem. ACA, Am. Mental Health Counselors Assn., Multiple Personality Study Group, Md. Mental Health Counselors Assn. (program chmn. 1989, exec. bd. 1993), Md. Assn. Counseling and Devel. (ethics com. 1990, chairperson profl. practice devel. 1996-97).

BARWINSKI, RICHARD CONRAD, healthcare administrator; b. Detroit, Mar. 5, 1951; s. Adam Frank and Jane Charlotte (Mastalerz) B.; m. Jennifer Lynn Pearson, July 12, 1986. BA, Western Mich. U., 1973; MA, U. Mich., 1979. Employee counselor Kelsey-Hayes Corp., Romulus, Mich., 1980; therapist Cen. Substance Abuse Svcs., Warren, Mich., 1980-81; therapist, coord. program and contract devel. Eastwood Community Clinics, Detroit, 1981-89; program dir. psychiat. svcs. Psychiat. Inst. at Malden (Mass.) Hosp., 1989-90; regional dir. Nat. Med. Enterprises, Washington, 1990-91, regional v.p. Mgmt. Svcs. divsn., 1991-93, sr. v.p., 1993-95; dir. bus. devel. Providence Health Sys., Seattle, 1995—. Vol. U.S. Peace Corps, Chaiyaphum, Thailand, 1974-76. Mem. Thai-Am. Assn.

BASARA, LISA RUBY, pharmacist; b. Allentown, Pa., June 16, 1967; d. John Joseph and Bernice Mary (Mulik) R.; m. T. Scott Basara, Mar. 28, 1992. BS in Pharmacy, Phila. Coll. of Pharmacy Sci., 1990; MBA, Drexel U., 1991; PhD, U. Miss., 1955. Registered pharmacist. Asst. dir. mktg. accounts Phila. Coll. of Pharmacy and Sci., 1989-92; rsch. asst. U. Miss., University, 1992-95; sr. market rsch. analyst Rhone-Poulenc Rorer Pharms., 1995—. Mem. Am. Mktg. Assn., Am. Pharm. Assn., Am. Soc. Hosp. Pharmacy. Office: RPR Pharms Rsch Inst Pharmacy 500 Arcola Rd Collegeville PA 19426

BASCH, DARLENE CHAKIN, clinical social worker; b. Bklyn., Oct. 12, 1954; d. Samuel Benedict and Vivian (Sidranski) Chakin; m. Loren Bernhardt Basch, May 31, 1982; children: Michael Oswald, Ethan Raphael. BS, Cornell U., 1976; M in Social Welfare, U. Calif., Berkeley, 1979. Lic. clin. social worker, Calif. Cottage clin. supr. St. Vincent's Sch., San Rafael, Calif., 1979-83; program dir. Jewish Family and Children's Service, San Francisco, 1983-84, therapist, program dir. family life edn., 1985-87; pvt. practice therapist Los Angeles, Calif., 1982—; clin. soc. worker Jewish Family Svc. L.A., 1988-95; workshop leader Unilex, San Francisco, 1985; sch. cons. LEarning Assocs., San Francisco, 1985-87; lead trainer, regional rels. coord. Spielberg's Survivors of the Shoah Visual History Found., L.A., 1995—; founding mem. 2d Generation Dialogue, N.Y.C., 1995—. Chmn. Generation-to-Generation, San Francisco, 1979-87; sec. Holocaust Library and Research Ctr., San Francisco, 1980-87; exec. com. mem. World Gathering of Holocaust Survivors, N.Y.C., 1980-81. Mem. NASW, Am. Orthopsychiat. Assn., Internat. Assn. Interactive Body Psychotherapy (exec. dir. 1994—), Soc. Clin. Social Work. Office: Ste 350 6310 San Vicente Blvd Los Angeles CA 90048

BASCI, LISA LEE, health services director, educator; b. Everitt, Pa., Oct. 8, 1962; d. Anthony John and Shirley Jean (Lee) B. BA in Psychology, Bloomsburg U., 1984; MA in Psychology, Marywood Coll., 1991. Residential program supr. Cmty. Svcs. Group, Bloomsburg/Lancaster, Pa., 1984-87; on call mental health del. CMSU MH/MR Program, Danville, Pa., 1985-87; caseworker for pregnant/parenting teens Ctrl. Susquehanna Intermediate Unit, Lewisburg, Pa., 1987-89; program dir. Cmty. Svcs. Group, Bloomsburg/Lancaster, 1989-95, sr. program dir., 1995—; adj. faculty Luzerne County C.C., Nanticoke, Pa., 1993—. Bd. dirs. Bloomsburg (Pa.) YMCA, 1988-91. Mem. Pa. Psychol. Assn., Pa. Mental Health Counselors Assn., Mid Penn Partial Hospitalization Assn. (sec. 1992—). Home: 211 Fair St Bloomsburg PA 17815 Office: Options-Cmty Svcs Group 150 E 9th St Ste #4 Bloomsburg PA 17815

BASEHART, EVA PAULINE ANNE, health facility administrator, consultant; b. Boston, Nov. 7, 1967; d. Richard and Eileen (McIsaac) Kaloshis; m. Mark C. Basehart, May 23, 1992. BS, Daemen Coll., 1989; EdM, SUNY, Buffalo, 1992. Registered med. records adminstr. Supr. med. records Children's Hosp. of Buffalo, N.Y., 1989-91; owner Universal Consulting Svcs., Buffalo, N.Y., 1991—; med. svcs. dir. Seneca Nat. Health Dept., Gowanda, N.Y., 1992-94; dir. med. records Buffalo (N.Y.) Columbus Hosp., 1995—; bd. dirs. N.W. Buffalo Cmty. Health Ctr. Office: Buffalo Columbus Hospital 300 Niagara St Buffalo NY 14201

BASELT, RANDALL CLINT, toxicologist; b. Chgo., Feb. 12, 1944; s. Benjamin Oliver and Vivian Marie (Rende) B.; m. Lana Mak, June 11, 1966; 1 child, David. BS in Chemistry, U. Ill., 1965; PhD in Pharmacology, U. Hawaii, 1972. Cert. Am. Bd. Forensic Toxicology, Am. Bd. Clin. Chemistry, Am. Bd. Toxicology, forensic alcohol supr., clin. toxicologist technologist, clin. chemist, clin. lab. toxicologist. Forensic toxicologist Office of Coroner, County of Orange, Calif., 1965-69; rsch. fellow dept. pharmacology U. Hawaii Sch. Medicine, Honolulu, 1969-72; NIH postdoctoral rsch. fellow Medizinisch-Chemisches Inst., U. Bern (Switzerland) Sch. Medicine, 1972-73; rsch. toxicologist Office of Coroner, San Francisco, 1973-75; chief toxicologist Office of Med. Examiner, Farmington, Conn., 1975-78; dir. toxicology and drug analysis lab. U. Calif. Med. Ctr., Sacramento, 1978-84; dir. Chem. Toxicology Inst., Calif., 1984—; asst. prof. lab. medicine U. Conn. Health Ctr., Farmington, 1975-78; assoc. prof. pathology U. Calif. Sch. Medicine, Davis, 1978-84; cons. drug abuse USN, 1983—, USAF, 1984—; accredited lab. inspector Nat. Lab. Cert. Program, 1988—. Author: Disposition of Toxic Drugs and Chemicals in Man, 4th. edit., 1994, Biological Monitoring Methods for Industrial Chemicals, 2d edit., 1988, Analytical Procedures for Therapeutic Drug Monitoring and Emergency Toxicology , 2d edit., 1987, (with M. Houts and R.H. Cravey) Courtroom Toxicology, 1980; editor 7 other books; founder, editor Jour. Analytical Toxicology, 1977—; mem. editorial bd. Jour. Forensic Scis., 1983—; contbr. articles to profl. jours. Mem. Am. Acad. Clin. Toxicology, Am. Assn. for Clin. Chemistry, Am. Indsl. Hygiene Assn., Calif. Assn. Toxicologists (past pres.), Internat. Assn. Forensic Toxicologists, Jour. Am. Med. Assn. (peer rev. com. 1985—), Soc. Forensic Toxicologists (bd. dirs. 1978-80, lab. survey com. 1982-83), Soc. Toxicology, Southwestern Assn. Toxicologists. Office: Chem Toxicology Inst 1167 Chess Dr # E Foster City CA 94404-1112

BASERGA, RENATO LUIGI, pathology educator; b. Meda, Milan, Italy, Apr. 11, 1925; came to U.S., 1949; s. Alessandro and Giuseppina (Annoni) B.; m. Jane Conrad, Dec. 23, 1954 (div. Sept. 1974); children: Susan Jane, Janice Rene; m. Beverly Lange, Oct. 12, 1974. MD, U. Milan, 1949. Diplomate Am. Bd. Pathology. Resident U. Milan, 1949-51; intern Columbus Hosp., Chgo., 1952-53; assoc. in oncology Chgo. Med. Sch., 1953-54; resident pathology St. Luke's Hosp., Chgo., 1955-58; instr. pathology Northwestern U., Chgo., 1958-60, asst. prof., 1960-64, assoc. prof., 1964-65; prof. Temple U., Phila., 1965-91, chmn. dept. pathology, 1980-91; prof. microbiology Thomas Jefferson U., Phila, 1991—; dep. dir. Kimmel Cancer Ctr., 1991; cons. Argonne (Ill.) Nat. Lab., 1959-65; sr. investigator Fels Rsch. Inst., Temple U., 1965-91; Louis Gross Meml. lectr. NYU, 1974; Searle lectr. Brit. Soc. Cell Biology, 1976; Wellcome vis. prof., 1984. Author: Autoradiography Techniques and Applications, 1969, Multiplication and Division in Mammalian Cells, 1976, The Biology of Cell Reproduction, 1985; editor: The Cell Cycle and Cancer, 1971. Served with vol. forces, 1943-45, Italy. Recipient rsch. career devel. award USPHS, 1964-65, Samuel Noble Found. award, 1989, Rous-Whipple award, 1990, Fred Stewart award, 1990; Maria Antoinetta Della Casa scholar, Milan, 1951; sr. rsch. fellow USPHS, 1958-60, Schiffer Meml. Lectr. Internat. Cell Soc. award, 1992, Susan Swerling lectureship Dana-Farber Cancer Ctr., 1993. Fellow AAAS. Office: Kimmel Cancer Inst Bluemle Life Scis Bldg 233 S 10th St Fl 6 Philadelphia PA 19107-5566

BASHAM-TOOKER, JANET BROOKS, retired geropsychologist, educator; b. Hampton, Va., Sept. 27, 1919; d. Thomas Westmore and Cora Evelyn Brooks; m. Linwood Cecil Basham (div. 1968); m. Frederick Fitch Tooker. BA cum laude, U. N.C., Greensboro, 1948; ABD in Psychology, Calif. State U., L.A., 1981; MA in Human Devel., Pacific Oaks Coll., 1984. Tchr., Calif. Grad. asst. psychology Duke U., Durham, N.C., 1948-49; tchr. Albuquerque City Schs., 1950-51; tchr. L.A. City Schs., 1953-54, counselor, 1981; lectr. L.A., 1988—; now ret.; docent Las Angelitas del Pueblo, L.A., 1971-74; active project with autistic children, through Pepperdine Univ., UCLA Neuropsychiatric Inst., L.A., 1974. Author numerous poems. Mem. planning com., women's conf. Commn. on Status of Women, Pasadena, Calif., 1982-85, sr. com. Task Force on Aging, San Marino, Calif., 1986-89, bd. dirs. United Way, Arcadia, Calif., 1984-88, Symphony Guild, Fayetteville, 1990; adv. mem. San Gabriel Presbytery Commn. on Aging, 1984-88; mem. grad. studies subcom. Calif. State U., L.A., 1975-78; v.p. San Marino Aux. Meth. Hosp., Arcadia, Calif., 1985-86; docent Duarte Hist. Soc., Calif., 1986-89; moderator sr. adults 1st United Presbyn. Ch., Fayetteville, 1990; facilitator fin. info. program for women AARP, Fayetteville, 1990; vol. in gerontology Fayetteville (Ark.) City Hosp., 1991, Health Care Unit, Butterfield Trail Village, Fayetteville, 1993; adv. com. Single Parent Scholarship Fund, Fayetteville, 1992. Recipient Margaret Noffsinger award Va. Intermont Coll., 1937. Mem. AAUW, Am. Soc. Aging, Mental Health Assn., Older Women's League, LWV, Phi Beta Kappa, Phi Theta Kappa. Republican. Presbyterian.

BASHARUTHULLA, MAHAMOOD SYED, cardiologist; b. Bangalore, India, Dec. 1, 1942; s. Syed Mahamood and Fathima Bebe Basharuthulla; m. Naseem Akhthar, Nov. 18, 1973; children: Syed Ifthekharulla, Syed Mahamood. MBBS, Bangalore Med. Sch., 1965. House officer Victoria, Vanivillas and Minto Hosps., Bangalore, 1966-67; sr. house officer Victoria Hosp., Bangalore, 1967; asst. surgeon grade II, med. officer Leprosorium Inst., Bangalore, 1967; sr. house officer St. Johns Hosp., Halifax, United Kingdom, 1967-68; with Newcastle Area Health Authority North Ormesby Gen. Hosp., 1970-71, med. registrar, 1971-73; pvt. practice Bangalore, 1973-75; locum med. registrar Norfolk and Norwich Dist. Hosp., United Kingdom, 1975; med. registrar, staff physician Dorset Area Health Authority, Dorset County Hosp., Dorchester, United Kingdom, 1975-77; med. registar, sr. resident med. officer Bromsgrove and Reditch Health Dist., United Kingdom, 1977-79; sr. physician, sr. med. officer, head occupational health Wycombe Gen. Hosp., United Kingdom, 1979-80; cons. physician, head critical care unit, cons. cardiologist Al-Adan Hosp., Kuwait, 1980—. Contbr. articles to profl. jours. All India Merit scholar Royal Coll. Physicians Edinburgh. Fellow Coll. Chest Physicians India, Royal Soc. Medicine London; mem. Royal Coll. Physicians and Surgeons Glasgow, Royal Coll. Physicians of Ireland, ACP, Soc. Occupational Medicine, Royal Coll. Physicians London, Internat. Coll. Angiology, Am. Coll. Cardiology. Home: PO Box 47457, Fahaheel Kuwait

BASILIO, ANTHONY JOSEPH, social services labor union administrator; b. Bklyn., Apr. 25, 1938; s. Joseph and Ann (Olshefski) B.; m. Mary Louise DeLucca, Aug. 26, 1967; children: Dianna Marie, Maryann Judith. BBA, St. John's U., 1959; MSW, Fordham U., 1966. Cert. social worker, N.Y., sch. social worker, N.Y. Caseworker N.Y.C. Dept. Social Svcs., 1961-65, unit supr., 1965-67, field instr., 1968-69, asst. adminstr. Office Staff Devel. and Tng., 1969-79; sr. case supr. N.Y.C. Dept. Income Maintenance, 1979-82; sr. svc. supr. N.Y.C. Dept. Gen. Svcs., 1982-85; trustee Social Svc. Employees Union Local 371, N.Y.C., 1982-85, sec.-treas., 1985—; trustee legal svcs. fund com., legal assistance com. Social Svc. Employees Union Local 371, N.Y.C., 1985—. Mem. exec. bd. social svcs. br. NAACP, N.Y.C., 1968-72. With U.S. Army, 1959-60. Recipient Fordham U. Sch. Social Svcs. Scholarship award N.Y. State Dept. Social Svcs., 1964-66. Mem. NASW, AFSCME (del. local 371 to dist. coun. 37), Acad. Cert. Social Workers, Social Svcs. Employee Union Local 371 (exec. com. mem.). Roman Catholic. Home: 2459 Gerritsen Ave Brooklyn NY 11229-5903 Office: Social Svc Employees Union Local 371 817 Broadway New York NY 10003-4709

BASINGER, KAREN LYNN, renal dietitian; b. Mechanicsville, Md., July 4, 1955; d. Leonard Marcus and Mary Jane (Harding) Brookbank; m. Joseph Andrew Basinger, Nov. 17, 1984; 1 child, James Marcus. BS, U. Md., 1977; MS, Hood Coll., 1987. Lic. nutritionist. Libr. technician Bowie (Md.) State Coll., 1973-79; instr. St. Mary's County Adult Edn., Leonardtown, Md., 1979-80; home economist Zamoiski Co., Balt., 1977-83; nutritionist/WIC coord. South County Health Plan, Prince Frederick, Md., 1979-80; nutritionist Walter Reed Army Med. Ctr., Washington, 1980-82; renal dietitian Mid Atlantic/BMA, Camp Springs, Md., 1982-87, Kidney Care Ctr., Landover, Md., 1987—; instr. dietary intern program Andrews AFB, 1988-91; lectr. in field. Mem. profl. adv. bd. Nat. Kidney Found./NCA, 1989-94; chair coun. on renal nutrition Nat. Kidney Found., 1993-94, program chair, 1990-92. Recipient Spl. Recognition Nat. Kidney Found./NCA, 1990, 92, Recognized Renal Dietitian/NCA, 1991, 94. Mem. Am. Nutritionists Assn., Am. Home Econs. Assn., Md. Home Econs. Assn. (bylaws chair 1982-94), Am. Dietetic Assn., Washington Metro. Coun. on Renal Nutrition (chair 1986-91, nutrition symposium chair 1989), U. Md. Alumni Assn. Democrat. Lutheran. Office: Kidney Care Ctr 1300 Mercantile Ln Ste 194 Landover MD 20785-5339

BASINGER, MICHAEL ANDREW, nurse; b. Mt. Pleasant, Pa., Aug. 29, 1955; s. Lloyd James and Helen (Hresko) B. BSN with honors, Pa. State U., 1982; MBA, Tulane U., 1988. RN; cert. critical care nurse. Staff nurse, charge nurse Henry Clay Frick Hosp., Mt. Pleasant, 1976-84; clin. coordinator Pendleton Meml. Meth. Hosp., New Orleans, 1984; dir. critical care Doctor's Hosp. of Jefferson, Metairie, La., 1984-87; v.p. nursing ops. Emergency Physician's Network, New Orleans, 1987—; nursing cons. Nat. Emergency Services, New Orleans, 1984-86. Named one of Outstanding Young Men Am., 1985. Mem. Am. Assn. Critical Care Nurses, La. State Nurses Assn., Am. Nurses Assn. Home: 2103 Jena St New Orleans LA 70115-5901

BASISTA, MICHAEL PAUL, family physician; b. N.Y.C., July 27, 1952; s. Aron Bernard and Irene (Sonnenschein) B.; m. Babette Ilene Harrison, Apr. 18, 1986; children: Andrew Harrison, Margeaux Harrison. BS, Poly. Inst. Bklyn., 1973; MMS, Rutgers U., 1975, MD, 1977. Diplomate, Am. Bd. Family Practice, Am. Bd. Med. Examiners. Resident Overlook Hosp., Summit, N.J., 1977-79; chief resident Overlook Hosp., 1979-80; assoc. dir. CIBA-GEIGY Corp., Summit, 1980-84; gen ptnr. Immedicenter, Clifton, N.J., 1984—; vis. clin. fellow Columbia U. Coll. Physicians and Surgeons, N.Y.C., 1977-80; clin. instr. dept. family medicine U. Medicine and Dentistry N.J.-Robert Wood Johnson Med. Sch. Fellow Am. Acad. Family Physicians, Acad. Medicine N.J.; mem. AMA, Passaic County Med. Assn., Rutgers Med. Sch. Alumni Assn. Office: Immedicenter 1358 Broad St Clifton NJ 07013-4222

BASKAR, JOHN F(REDERICK), pathobiologist, biomedical researcher; b. Madras, India, July 17, 1936; came to U.S., 1964; s. David V. Dhyriam and Leelavathy Jane Savarus; m. Nirmala Adhilingham, May 3, 1969. BS, U. Madras, 1959; MS, Howard U., 1967; ScD, Johns Hopkins U., 1975. Asst. Madras Secretariat, 1960-64; grad. teaching asst. Howard U., Washington, 1964-67; sr. technician Microbiol. Assocs., Inc., Bethesda, Md., 1967-69; NIH postdoctoral rsch. fellow in reproductive physiology Harvard U. Med. Sch., Boston, 1975-77, rsch. assoc., 1977-78; rsch. assoc. Lineberger Cancer Rsch. Ctr., U. N.C., Chapel Hill, 1978-84, mem., 1984-92, rsch. asst. prof. dept. microbiology and immunology, 1984-92, dir. microinjection and transgenic facility, 1988-92; assoc. prof. dept. microbiology and immunology and animal care Oreg. Health Scis. U., 1992—, dir. transgenics lab., 1992—. Contbr. numerous articles to profl. publs. John Hopkins U. scholar, 1971-75; Nat. Inst. Child Health and Human Devel. grantee, 1980-91. Mem. AAAS, Am. Soc. for Microbiology, Oreg. Cancer Ctr., N.Y. Acad. Scis., Sigma Xi. Biomed. researcher on effect of cytomegalovirus on embryonic devel. Office: Oreg Health Scis U Dept Animal Care L110 Portland OR 97201-4338

BASKIN, DAVID STUART, neurosurgeon; b. N.Y.C., Feb. 11, 1952; s. Norman and Selma (Schorr) B. BA with high honors, Swarthmore Coll., 1974; MD, Mt. Sinai Sch. Medicine, CUNY, 1978. Diplomate Am. Bd. Neurol. Surgery. Intern in surgery U. Calif., San Francisco, 1978-79, resident in neurosurgery, 1979-84; asst. prof. Baylor Coll. Medicine, Houston, 1984-89, assoc. prof., 1989-94, assoc. prof. anesthesiology, 1993-94; chief neurosurgery VA Hosp., Houston, 1984-92, attending neurosurgeon, 1992—; prof. neurosurgery Baylor Coll. Medicine, Houston, 1994—, prof. anesthesiology, 1994—; attending physician Meth. Hosp., Ben Taub Hosp., Tex. Children's Hosp., St. Luke's Episc. Hosp., Inst. for Rehab. and Rsch., Houston, 1984—, Tex. Orthopedic Hosp., 1994—. Contbr. numerous articles to profl. jours. Mem. Alzheimer's Exec. Coun. Recipient Acad. award Am. Acad. Neurol. Surgeons, 1983, Wakeman award for rsch. in neurosci., 1990, Disting. Alumni awadr Mt. Sinai Sch. Medicine, 1990. Fellow ACS, Stroke Coun. of Am. Heart Assn.; mem. AMA, Congress Neurol. Surgeons, Joint Sect. on Spinal Disorders of Congress Neurol. Surgeons/Am. Assn. Neurol. Surgeons, Pituitary Found. Am., AAAS, Rocky Mountain Neurol. Soc., So. Med. Assn., Houston Neurol. Soc., Pituitary Soc. Houston, Tex. Med. Assn., Harris County Med. Soc., Phi Beta Kappa, Sigma Xi, Alpha Omega Alpha. Office: Baylor Coll Medicine 6560 Fannin St Ste 944 Houston TX 77030-2706

BASKIN, FRANK ELLIS, social worker, educator; b. Phila., June 3, 1943. BS in Social Welfare, Temple U., 1965; MSW, U. Mich., 1967. Cert. Acad. Cert. Social Worker; bd. cert. diplomate; lic. ind. clin. social worker. Social worker VA Hosp., Phila., 1967-74, Phila. Geriatric Ctr., 1974-77; dir. social svc. Lowell (Mass.) Gen. Hosp., 1979-80; counselor Lowell Indsl. Ctr., 1981-83; pvt. practice Phila. and Lowell, 1977—; instr. Salem (Mass.) State Coll. Grad. Sch. Social Work, 1990—; instr. gerontology Framingham (Mass.) State Coll., 1996—; instr. dramatics Ea. Coop. Recreation Sch., 1991—, staff coord., 1995—; coord. project to develop practice stads. for nursing home social workers in Mass., 1993. Author: (with others) Play & Playfulness, 1990; author (with others) law which amends Mass. Legislation on nursing home abuse. Recipient Greatest Contbn. to Social Work Practice award NASW Mass. chpt., 1989. Home and Office: 18 E Meadow Ln Lowell MA 01854-1557

BASLER, JOSEPH W, urologist, educator; b. St. Louis, Aug. 28, 1952; s. John Joseph and Lucille Marie Basler; m. LaWana J. Gammon, June 11, 1988; children: Jim, Willie, Rebecca. BA in Biology, U. Mo., 1974, MA in Biology, 1976, MD, 1984; MA in Molecular Biology, SUNY, Buffalo, 1979, PhD in Molecular Biology, 1983. Diplomate Am. Bd. Urology. Resident surgeon U. Mo. Hosps. and Clinics, Columbia, 1984-86; resident surgeon Washington U., St. Louis, 1986-90, asst. prof. surgery, 1990—; rsch. asst., grad. tchg. asst. divsn. biol. scis. U. Mo., Columbia, 1975-76; grad. tchg. asst. dept. cell and molecular biology, SUNY, Buffalo, 1977-78, rsch. asst., 1977-80; guest spkr. Washington U. Sch. Medicine, 1990; acting chief urology Jewish Hosp., St. Louis, 1992-93, chief urology sect., 1994, mem. operating room com., cancer com., surg. rev. com., 1991—; mem. hosp. emergency room adv. com. Barnes Hosp., 1990-91, operating room com., 1991; mem. laser com. VA Hosp., 1992—, ethics com., 1994—; lectr. in field. Contbr. 35 articles to profl. pubs. Recipient Am. Cancer Soc. Devel. award, 1991-94. Mem. Mo. State Med. Assn., St. Louis Med. Assn., Am. Cancer Soc., Am. Urol. Assn., South Ctrl. Section Am. Urol. Assn., St. Louis Urol. Soc. Office: Washington U Ste 3304 216 S Kings Hwy Saint Louis MO 63110

BASS, ANTHONY VINCENT, optometrist; b. Amarillo, Tex., Oct. 10, 1946; s. John Morton Bass and Meredith Jean (Patching) Bass Rich; m. Jane Redmond Bridges, Aug. 22, 1969; children: Jonna, Mary Elizabeth, Alison. OD, U. Houston, 1972. Diplomate Internat. Assn. Bds. Examiners in Optometry. Optometric vol. Amigos de Las Americas, Nicaragua, summer 1972; optometrist in pvt. practice Amarillo, 1973—; mem. adv. coun. for optometry U. Houston, 1983; mem. adv. com. on children's vision Tex. Dept. Health, Austin, 1981-82. Mem. Am. Optometric Assn. (Optometric Recognition award 1981), Tex. Assn. Optometrists (bd. dirs. 1978-82, state pres. 1982-83), Amarillo South Rotary (bd. dirs. 1995). Baptist. Office: Coulter Profl Ctr 1900 Coulter Dr Ste I Amarillo TX 79106-1784

BASS, JONATHAN, dermatologist; b. Cleve., July 2, 1953; m. Stephany Schatel. AB, Washington U., St. Louis, 1975; MD, U. Cin., 1979. Intern in internal medicine Mt. Sinai Med. Ctr., Cleve., 1979-80, resident in internal medicine, 1980-81; resident in dermatology MetroHealth Med. Ctr., Cleve., 1981-84, staff dermatologist, dermatopathologist, 1986—; fellow in dermatopathology Cleve. Clinic Found., 1985-86; asst. prof. dermatology, sr. instr. pathology Case Western Res. U. Sch. Medicine, Cleve., 1986—. Fellow Am. Soc. Dermatopathology, Am. Acad. Dermatology, Ohio Dermatological Assn., Cleve. Dermatological Soc.; mem. AMA. Office: MetroHealth Med Ctr Dept Dermatology 2500 MetroHealth Dr Cleveland OH 44109

BASS, KARIN TRENT, women's health nurse; b. Vienna, Austria, Dec. 3, 1946; d. William Franklin and Ernestine (Slama) Trent; 1 child, Justin LaVerne. Diploma, Luth. Hosp of Md. Sch. of Nursing, Balt., 1967; B in Gen. Studies, U. N.H., Durham, 1975. RN, Md. Staff nurse GS-7 Naval Hosp., Portsmouth, N.H.; staff nurse VA Hosp., Balt.; head nurse Suburban Hosp., Bethesda, Md.; staff nurse Frederick (Md.) Meml. Hosp. Lt. (j.g.) USN, 1968-70, lt. comdr. USNR, 197080. Mem. ANA, NAACOG.

BASS, MARY CATHERINE, clinical social worker, psychotherapist; b. Magnolia, N.C., Aug. 10, 1941; d. Paul and Louise Katherine (Peterson) B. BA, Wake Forest U., 1963; MDiv, Southeastern Bapt. Theol. Sem., 1967; MSW, U. N.C., 1972; postgrad., Georgetown U., 1978-82. Cert. clin. social worker; cert. marital and family therapist; cert. med. psychotherapist; diplomate Am. Bd. Med. Psychotherapy. Tchr. biology and earth sci. James Kenan High Sch., Warsaw, N.C., 1963-64; social worker Bapt. Children's Home of N.C., 1967-68, 1969-71; unit coord. Meth. Home for Children, Raleigh, N.C., 1972-73; family counselor III and clin. supr. Family Svcs. for Wake County, Inc., 1973-81; contract counselor Life Enrichment Ctr., Raleigh, 1983-84; pvt. practice individual, marital and family psychotherapy Raleigh, 1981—; clin. social worker, clin. supr. social work staff Dorothea Dix Hosp., 1981-86; clin. assoc. individual, marital and family psychotherapy Carolina Psychiatry, Raleigh, 1986-94; dir. Ea. N.C. Family Ctr., 1994—; cons. Med. Staff Health Care Affiliate, Charter Northridge Hosp., 1986—, Holly Hill Hosp., 1991—, Duplin County Coop. Ext. Svcs., Kenansville, N.C., 1994—; clergy cons., counselor Pullem Meml. Bapt. Ch., Raleigh, 1970s; cons., supr. Bowen Family Therapy, 1981—; cons., med. psychotherapist Goshen Med. Ctr., 1994—; field faculty Sch. Social Work ECU, 1995; lectr. in field; condr. workshops in field. Contbr. to book: The Aggressive Adolescent, 1984. Active Friends of the Arboretum, Raleigh, 1985—. Mem. NASW, AAUW, Acad. Cert. Social Workers, N.C. Bd. Marital and Family Therapists, Am. Family Therapy Acad. (clin. mem.), Am. Forestry Assocs., N.C. Forestry Assocs., Carolina Farm Stewardship Assn. Home: 1210 Harwich Ct Raleigh NC 27609-3958 also: PO Box 63 Magnolia NC 28453 Office: 219 E Carron St PO Box 63 Magnolia NC 28453 also: 8404-B Glenwood Ave Raleigh NC 27613

BASS, PAUL, pharmacology educator; b. Winnipeg, Man., Can., Aug. 12, 1928; came to U.S., 1958; s. Benjamin and Sarah B.; m. Ruth Zipursky, May 31, 1953; children: Stuart, Susan. B.S. in Pharmacy, U. B.C., 1953, M.A. in Pharmacology, 1955; Ph.D. in Pharmacology, McGill U., 1957, fellow in Biochemistry, 1957-58; fellow in Physiology, Mayo Found., 1958-60. Research asst. Ayerst, McKenna & Harrison, Can., 1956; assoc. lab. dir. Parke, Davis & Co., 1960-70; prof. pharmacology Sch. Pharmacy and Sch. Medicine, U. Wis., Madison, 1970—. Mem. editorial bd.: Am. Jour. Physiology, 1976-79, 81-92, Jour. Pharmacology and Exptl. Therapeutics, 1980—; contbr. chpts. to books, articles to profl. jours. Mem. Am. Soc. Pharmacology and Exptl. Therapeutics, Am. Gastroent. Assn. Home: 153 Nautilus Dr Madison WI 53705-4329 Office: 425 N Charter St Madison WI 53706-1508

BASSECHES, MICHAEL, psychologist, educator; b. N.Y.C., Apr. 1, 1950; s. Maurice and Beatrice (Goodman) B.; m. Ruth Rachel Aronson, June 30,

1985; children: Joshua, Benjamin. B.A., Swarthmore Coll., 1972; Ph.D., Harvard U., 1978. Instr. psychology Swarthmore Coll., Pa., 1976-77; asst. prof. Cornell U., Ithaca, N.Y., 1978-85; fellow Clin. Devel. Inst., Belmont, Mass., 1984—, co-dir. extern program, 1985—, psychotherapist and cons. on adolescent and adult devel., 1985—; adj. faculty Mass. Sch. Profl. Psychology, 1986, mem. faculty, 1987-88; psychologist Bur. Study Harvard U., 1988—; instr. psychology Harvard Med. Sch., 1991—; assoc. prof., co-dir. clin. tng. PhD program clin. devel. psychology Suffolk U., 1995—; lectr. in field. Author: Dialectical Thinking and Adult Development, 1984. Contbr. articles to profl. jours., chpts. to books. Harvard U. fellow, 1972-76. Co-founder New Jewish Agenda, Ithaca, N.Y., 1983. Fellow Soc. for Values in Higher Edn.; mem. Mass. Assn. Psychoanalytic Psychologists, Jean Piaget Soc., Am. Psychol. Assn., Mass. Psychol. Assn., Perry Devel. Scheme Network, Phi Beta Kappa. Home: 15 Baskin Rd Lexington MA 02173-6928 Office: Suffolk U 41 Temple St Boston MA 02114

BASSETT, ALTON HERMAN, health care company executive; b. Hartford, Conn., Nov. 27, 1930; s. Arthur and Martha B.; m. Joan Tolley, Jan. 7, 1956; children: Linda, Barbara. BA, Middlebury (Vt.) Coll., 1953. Plant chemist Am. Viscose Corp., Front Royal, Va., 1955-58; rsch. dir. Chicopee Inc., div. Johnson & Johnson, Milltown and Dayton, N.J., 1958-88, cons., 1988-94; ret., 1994. Patentee in field. Lt. USMC, 1953-55. Republican. Home: 73 Harriet Dr Princeton NJ 08540-3934 Office: Products & Materials Rsch Johnson & Johnson Worldwide Dayton NJ 08810-0940

BASSETT, GEORGE SHELDON, orthopedic surgeon; b. Rochester, N.Y., July 22, 1950; s. Charles Frederick and Carolyn (Chestnut) B.; m. Ruth Carlson, Dec. 18, 1971; children: Julie, Jeffrey, Linda. BS, Wheaton Coll., 1972; MD, SUNY, Syracuse, 1976. Diplomate Nat. Bd. Med. Examiners, Am. Bd. Orthopedic Surgery. Asst. clin. prof. Wright State U., Dayton, Ohio, 1982-84; clin. asst. prof. Thomas Jefferson Med. Coll., Phila., 1987-88; from asst. prof. to assoc. prof. orthopedics U. So. Calif. Sch. Medicine, L.A., 1988-96; assoc. prof. orthopedics Washington U. Sch. Medicine, St. Louis, 1996—; orthopedic surgeon in chief, St. Louis Children's Hosp., 1996; dir. quality assurance Alfred I. duPont Inst., Wilmington, Del., 1985-88; chmn. clin. car evaluation com. Children's Hosp. L.A., 1989-93, chmn. resident evaluation com., 1990-93, chmn. med. quality review com., 1993-96. Fellow Am. Acad. Orthopaedic Surgeons, Am. Orthopaedic Assn., Pediatric Orthopedic Soc. N.Am., Scoliosis Rsch. Soc. Office: St Louis Children's Hosp One Childrens Place Saint Louis MO 63110-1077

BASSETT, JAMES GUERNSEY, retired surgeon; b. East Cleveland, Ohio, Sept. 9, 1919; s. Buell Southmayd and Miriam Christine (Jones) B.; m. Eleanor Helma Feldrappe, Dec. 21, 1943; 1 child, Sarah. AB, U. Mich., 1942; MD, Duke U., 1946. Diplomate Am. Bd. Surgery. Intern/resident in surgery Univ. Hosp., Ann Arbor, Mich., 1946-53; asst. prof. surgery Univ. Hosp., Ann Arbor, 1953-55; asst. prof. to prof. surgery Med. Coll. of Pa., Phila., 1955-87, chmn. dept. surgery, 1983-87; pvt. practice; attending surgeon Phila. Gen. Hosp., 1955-62, U.S.A. Vet. Hosp., Phila., 1955-87, Grad. Hosp. of U. of Pa., Phila., 1955-60. Capt. M.C. USAF, 1948-50. Mem. Am. Cancer Soc. (pres. 1975-76). Home: 840 Montgomery Ave #802 Bryn Mawr PA 19010

BASSETT, MARK LLEWELLYN, gastroenterologist; b. Westport, New Zealand, Oct. 3, 1948; s. John Mace and Grace (Matthews) B.; m. Olive Moira Mathers, 1971 (div. 1991); children: Hamish, Camilla; m. Jane Esther Yeend, Apr. 29, 1992; children: Clare, Nicholas, Katharine, Peter. MB ChB, Otago (New Zealand) Med. Sch., 1972; MD, U. Queensland, Australia, 1983. Resident med. officer Canberra (Australia) Hosp., 1973-75; gastroenterology registrar Woder Valley Hosp., Australia, 1976-77; gastroenterologist Woden Valley Hosp., 1988—; sr. lectr. U. Queensland, 1981-85, assoc. prof., 1985-86; gastroenterologist Auckland (New Zealand) Hosp., 1987; vis. scientist NIH, Bethesda, Md., 1984-85. Contbr. over 50 articles to profl. jours. NH&MRC med. postgrad. scholar, 1978-80; Schering Corp. travelling fellow, 1984. Fellow Royal Australasian Coll. Physicians; mem. Am. Assn. for Study of Liver Diseases, Gastroenterol. Soc. Am. Home: 14 Melbourne Ave, Deakin 2600, Australia

BASSINGTHWAIGHTE, JAMES BUCKLIN, physiologist, educator, medical researcher; b. Toronto, Sept. 10, 1929; s. Ewart MacQuarrie and Velma Emeline B.; m. Joan Elizabeth Graham, June 18, 1955; children: Elizabeth Anne, Mary, Alan, Sarah, Rebecca. B.A., U. Toronto, 1951, M.D., 1955; postgrad., Med. Sch. London, 1957-58; Ph.D., Mayo Grad. Sch. Medicine U. Minn., 1964. Intern Toronto Gen. Hosp., 1955-56; physician Internat. Nickel Co., Sudbury and Matheson, Ont., 1956-57; house physician Hammersmith Hosp., London; postgrad. Med. Sch. London, 1957-58; teaching asst. physiology U. Minn., Mpls., 1961-62; fellow Mayo Grad. Sch. Medicine, Rochester, Minn., 1958-64, instr., 1964-67, asst. prof., 1967-69, assoc. prof., 1969-72; vis. prof. Pharmacology Inst., U. Bern, Switzerland, 1970-71; asso. prof. bioengring. U. Minn., 1972-75; prof. physiology Mayo Grad. Sch. Medicine, 1973-75, prof. medicine, 1975; prof. bioengring., radiology and biomath U. Wash., Seattle, 1975—; dir. Ctr. for Bioengring., 1975-80; vis. prof. medicine and physiology McGill U., 1979-81; affiliate prof. physiology Limburg U., Maastricht, The Netherlands, 1990—; mem. study sect. NIH, 1970-74, 80-83; chmn. Biotech. Resources Adv. Com., 1977-79, chmn. 1st Gordon Rsch. Conf. on Water and Solute Transport in Microvasculature, 1976; chmn. workshop on metabolic imaging Nat. Heart, Lung and Blood Inst., 1985; Lewellen-Thomas lectr., U. Toronto, 1991; Coulter lectr. U. N.C., 1995; Oxford lectr. Internat. Magnetic Resonance Medicine, 1996. Author: (with L.S. Liebovitch and B.J. West) Fractal Physiology, 1994; contbr. over 200 articles to profl. publs. Recipient NIH Rsch. Career Devel. award, 1964-74, Louis and Artur Lucian award McGill U., 1979, Faculty Achievement award for outstanding rsch. U. Wash. Coll. Engring, 1993. Mem. AAAS, Am. Heart Assn. (coun. on circulation 1976—), Biophys. Soc. (assoc. editor Biophys. Jour. 1980-83), Biomed. Engring. Soc. (dir. 1971-74, pres. 1977-78, Alza award 1986, editor-in-chief Annals of Biomedical Engring. 1993—), Microcirculatory Soc. (mem. coun. 1975-78, 80-83, pres. 1990-91, Landis award 1995), Am. Physiol. Soc. (mem. circulation group, editorial bd. 1972-76, 79-83, mem. edn. com.), Internat. Union Physiol. Scis. (U.S.A nat. com. 1978-86, U.S. del. to assembly 1980, 83, 86, chmn. 1983-86, chmn Commn. on Bioengring. and Clin. Physiology 1986-87, chmn. satellite to 30th Congress on Endothelial Transport 1986, co-chmn. satellite on microvascular networks 1989). Home: 3150 E Laurelhurst Dr NE Seattle WA 98105-5333 Office: U Wash Ctr for Bioengring Box 35-7962 Seattle WA 98195-7962

BASSIOUNY, HISHAN SALAH, surgeon, educator; b. Cairo, Mar. 30, 1954; m. Sandra Bassiouny; children: Deenah, Faith-Iman. Mb. Bch. Diploma with honors, Cairo U., 1977. Diplomate Am. Bd. Surgery; lic. surgeon, Ill., Mich., Md. Intern Cairo U. Hosps., 1977-78; surg. externship Linz (Austria) Gen. Hosp., 1980-81; intern Md. Gen. Hosp., Balt., 1981-82; resident Henry Ford Hosp., Detroit, 1982-86, clin. vascular fellow, 1986-87; postdoctoral rsch. fellow, instr. surgery U. Chgo., 1987-89, asst. prof. surgery, 1989—, assoc. prof. surgery, 1996—, dir. non-invasive vascular lab; mem. staff U. Chgo. Med. Ctr., Little Co. Mary Hosp., Weiss Meml. Hosp., dir. non-invasive vascular lab. Contbr. chpts. to books and numerous articles to profl. jours. Recipient Louis Block award, 1989; grantee W.L. Gore, 1987-89, NIH, 1988—, Mellon Found., 1990, U. Chgo., 1992-93, Washington Sqare Found., 1992, Am. Heart Assn., 1995—. Fellow ACS; mem. AAAS, AAS, Am. Heart Assn. (sci. coun. 1992—, coun. atherosclerosis, coun. cardio-thoracic and vascular surgery), Am. Venous Forum, Midwestern Vascular Soc., North Am. Vascular Biology Orgn., Internat. Soc. Cardiovascular Surgery, Chgo. Surg. Soc., Peripheral Vascular Surg. Soc., Soc. Vascular Surgery. Office: U Chgo 5841 S Maryland Ave MC 5028 Chicago IL 60637*

BASSOS, CHARLES ALEXANDER, psychologist; b. Hartford, Conn., Mar. 12, 1943; s. Alexander and Evelyn (Dukakis) B.; m. Jane Highsmith, June 1, 1968 (div. 1976); 1 child, Alexander Charles; m. Zoe Marie Stanley, May 25, 1980; children: Christi Anne, Stephanie. BA, Wesleyan U., Middletown, Conn., 1965; MA, U. Cin., 1967, PhD, 1969. Lic. psychologist, Mich. Asst. prof. Mich. State U., E. Lansing, 1969-74; assoc. prof. Mich. State U., 1974-78, prof., 1978-82, assoc. dir. counseling ctr., 1980-81; pvt. practice psychology Lansing, 1981-89; mng. ptnr. Psychol. Health Sys., P.C., Lansing, 1984-88; pres. Psychol. Health Sys., P.C., 1988—, The Synton Group, Inc., Lansing, 1986—; lectr. in field. Contbr. articles to profl. jours. Treas., Holy Trinity Greek Orthodox Ch., Lansing, 1982-84, pres. 1991; mem. Order of AHEPA, Lansing, 1982—. Mem. Am. Psychol. Assn., Nat. Register of Health Svc. Providers, Mich. Psychol. Assn. (legis. com. 1986-88), Lansing Rotary Club. Eastern Orthodox Ch. Office: The Synton Group Inc 617 Seymour Ave Lansing MI 48933-1119

BASS-RUBENSTEIN, DEBORAH SUE, social worker, educator, consultant; b. Springfield, Ill., Jan. 21, 1951; d. Ralph and Dorothy Bernice (Feuer) Bass; m. Jeffrey Rubenstein, Oct. 12, 1975; children: Jonathan, Benjamin. BA, MSW, U. Ill., 1973. Social worker Dept. Human Resources, Washington, 1974-75; analyst Asst. Sec. for Planning and Evaluation, Washington, 1975-76, Adminstrn. for Pub. Svcs., Washington, 1976-79, Health Care Financing Adminstrn., Washington, 1979; sr. analyst OHDS, Washington, 1979-83, 84-87, Adminstrn. on Aging, Washington, 1983-84; dir. Office Human Devel. Svcs., Exec. Secretariat, HHS, Washington, 1987-90; cons. and pres. Deborah Bass Assocs., Manassas, Va., 1990—; assoc. faculty Johns Hopkins Sch. Continuing Studies, 1993; sec. U.S. com. Internat. Coun. on Social Welfare, Washington, 1991-93, bd. dirs., 1987-90; convenor Fed. Social Workers Consortium, Washington, 1986-90; participant Dartmouth-Hitchcock Med. Ctr. Project on Family Support, 1993; co-facilitator Unity in the Community, 1995—; mem. multi-cultural com. Prince William County Sch. Divsn., 1993—; chair civic affairs com., Congregation Ner Shalom Sisterhood., 1996—. Author: Caring Families, 1990, Helping Vulnerable Youths, 1992; contbr. Ency. Social Work, 1995. Chmn. Congregation Nev Shalom Sisterhood civic affairs com., 1996—; co-pres. Coles Sch. PTO, Manassas, 1987-88; bd. dirs. Mid-County Coalition, Prince William County, Va., 1986; mem. multi-cultural com. Prince William County Sch. Divsn., 1993—; co-facilitator Citizens of Faith/Citizens Concerned About Discrimination in Prince William County, 1994—. James scholar U. Ill., 1969-73. Mem. NASW (poetry com. 1988-90). Home and Office: 7092 Kings Arms Dr Manassas VA 22111-3237

BASSUK, ELLEN LINDA, psychiatrist; b. N.Y.C., Feb. 8, 1945; d. Irving and Molly (Pakarow) B.; children: Daniel, Sarah. BA, Brandeis U., 1964; MD, Tufts U., 1968; Dr.P.S. (hon.), Northeastern U., 1993. Diplomate Am. Bd. Psychiatry. Intern Mt. Auburn Hosp., Cambridge, Mass., 1968-69; resident psychiatry Univ. Hosp., Boston, 1969-70, Boston State Hosp., Boston, 1970-71; resident psychiatry Beth Israel Hosp., Boston, 1971-73, dir. psychiat. emergency svcs., 1974-82; fellow Bunting Inst., Cambridge, Mass., 1982-84; assoc. prof. psychiatry Harvard Med. Sch., Boston, 1983—; founder, pres. The Better Homes Fund, Newton, Mass., 1988—; mem. Com. on Health Care of Homeless Persons Inst. of Medicine, Washington, 1986-88. Editor: The Practitioners Guide to Psychoactive Drugs, 1977, 83, 91; series editor Plenum Press; editor-in-chief Am. Jour. Orthopsychiatry, 1994—; contbr. numerous articles to profl. jours. Fellow Am. Psychiat. Assn.; mem. Mass. Psychiat. Soc. Home: 20 Randolph Rd Chestnut Hill MA 02167-2338 Office: The Better Homes Found 181 Wells Ave Newton MA 02159-3344

BASTIANELLI, MILO, otorhinolaryngologist, plastic surgeon resident; b. East Orange, N.J., Mar. 20, 1966; s. Tito and Maria (Quattrini) B. BS, Monmouth U., 1988; DO, U. Medicine & Dentistry N.J., 1992. Intern Union (N.J.) Hosp., 1992-93, surg. resident, 1993-94, otorhinolaryngologist, facial plastic surgeon, 1994—. Recipient Trustee scholarship Monmouth Trustees, 1984-88, Biology Acad. award Monmouth Coll., 1988, Van Hoten scholarship U. Medicine & Dentistry of N.J., Stratford, 1989, Charles B. Matthes scholarship, 1989, Rudy Wadle scholarship Union Hosp., 1993. Mem. AMA, Am. Osteo. Assn., N.J. Assn. Osteo. Physicians and Surgeons. Republican. Roman Catholic. Home: 3010 Plaza Dr Woodbridge NJ 07095

BATALDEN, PAUL BENNETT, pediatrician, health care educator; b. Mpls., Dec. 4, 1941; s. Abner Bennett and Martha (Bjornstad) B.; m. LaVonne Marie Olson; children: Maren, Sonja. BA, Augsburg Coll. 1963; MD, BS, U. Minn., 1967. Diplomate Am. Bd. Pediatrics. Clin. assoc. Nat. Cancer Inst., Bethesda, Md., 1969; med. dir. Job Corps, Washington 1970-72; dir. Community Health Svc., Rockville, Md., 1972-73; dir., Bur. Community Health Svc., Rockville, 1973-75; pediatrician Park Nicollet Med. Ctr., Mpls., 1975-86, quality assurance dir., 1976-84, chief oper. officer, 1984-86; v.p. med. care, head quality resource group Hosp. Corp. of Am., Nashville, 1986-94; Breech chmn. Dept. Health Care Quality Improvement Edn. and Rsch. Henry Ford Health Sci. Ctr., 1990—; prof., dir. Ctr. Health-care Improvement Leadership Devel. Dartmouth Med. Sch.; founding chmn. Inst. for Healthcare Improvement; bd. dirs. Allina Health Sys. Author: Quality Assurance in Ambulatory Care, 1980; contbr. articles on quality in healthcare and aspects of pediatric practice to profl. jours. Regent Augsburg Coll., Mpls., 1978-90. Recipient Guild of Honor, 1963, Pub. Svc. award Nat. Med. Assn., 1974, Disting. Alumnus award Augsburg Coll., 1984. Mem. Inst. of Medicine of NAS, Am. Acad. Pediatrics, Minn. Med. Assn., Tenn. Med. Assn., Alpha Omega Alpha.

BATCHELOR, RUBY STEPHENS, retired nurse; b. Rocky Mount, N.C., Sept. 27, 1931; d. Paul Madison and Ruby Leign (Coggins) Stephens; m. Sherwood H. Batchelor, Nov. 1, 1952; children: Paula S. Liggon, G. Brooks. Diploma, Wilson Sch. Nursing, 1953; student, Atlantic Christian Coll. Cert. med./surg. nurse. Assessment nurse Wilson (N.C.) Meml. Hosp., head nurse pediatrics, primary care nurse ob./gyn. unit, primary care nurse med./surg. unit, primary care nurse psychiat. unit, 1991-93, ret., 1993; organizer Al-A-Non, Wilson, N.C., 1973. Deacon Westview Christian Ch., 1995, 96, 97. cjmn. membership com., 1996. Mem. N.C. Nurse's Assn. (past dist. pres.), Am. Nurses' Assn. Home: 1300 Dogwood Ln NW Wilson NC 27896-1420

BATDORF, ANN, critical care nurse; b. Danville, Pa., Mar. 17, 1956; d. William A. and Pearl L. (Klouser) Bressler; m. Theodore Batdorf, June 4, 1983; children: Amanda, Lindsey. BSN, Pa. State U., 1981. Cert ACLS, CPR, med.-surgical nursing. Nurse oncology Lewistown Hosp., 1982; nurse pediatrics Centre Community Hosp., 1983-91; nurse Ashland (Pa.) Regional Med. Ctr., 1991-92; nurse med. intermediate unit Milton S. Hershey Med Ctr., 1992-95, Hendry Gen. Hosp., Clewiston, Fla., 1995—. Mem. Pa. Nurses Assn., Ashland Nurses Assn. Home: 330 W Opisbo Ave Clewiston PA 33440

BATE, BRIAN R., psychologist; b. Cleve., July 4, 1940; s. Paul A. and Claire N. B.; children: Jennifer A., Julia L. BA in English, Western Res. U., 1963, MS in Psychology, 1965; PhD in Psychology, Case Western Res. U., 1972. Lic. psychologist, Ohio. Instr. Cuyahoga Community Coll., Parma, Ohio, 1969, from asst. prof. to prof. of psychology, 1970—; pvt. practice Cleve., 1972—. Contbr. articles to profl. jours. Nat. Merit Scholar Princeton U., 1958-61, Western Res. U., 1962-63; USPHS fellow, 1963-67. Mem. APA, Am. Fedn. Musicians, Gestalt inst. of Cleve., Nat. Register Health Svc. Providers in Psychology (cert.), Edelweiss Ski Club, Cleve. Buddhist Temple. Home and Office: 6511 Mill Rd Cleveland OH 44141-1560

BATE, MARILYN ANNE, psychologist; b. Dillonvale, Ohio, May 23, 1939; d. Louis Edward and Veronica (Koval) Dezera; m. Brian Richard Bate, Sept. 7, 1968 (div. Apr. 1976); children: Jennifer, Julia. BSc, Ohio State U., 1961; MA, Case Western Res. U., Cleve., 1965, PhD, 1974. Lic. psychologist. Elem. tchr., sch. psychologist Cleve. City Schs., 1961-67; sch. psychologist, spl. edn. coord. Cleveland Heights (Ohio), U. Heights, Ohio City Schs., 1967-70; sch. psychologist Mayfield (Ohio) City Schs., 1970-71, Cleve. City Schs., 1971-79, North Olmsted (Ohio) Schs., 1979-82; instr. Cuyahoga Community Coll., Cleve., 1967-82; pvt. practice Cleve., 1967-82; psychologist Dept. Def. Dependent Schs., Aviano, Italy, 1982-86; pvt. practice Columbus, Ohio, 1986—; ct. psychologist Franklin County Ct. Common Pleas, Columbus, 1987—. Mem. adv. bd. Eastpark Elem. Sch., Middleburg Heights, Ohio, 1985; vol. Son of Heaven, Columbus, 1989. Mem. APA, Am. Correctional Assn., Nat. Sch. Psychology Assn., Ohio Psychol. Assn. (mem. ethics com. 1986-92, exec. bd. 1992—), Ctrl. Ohio Psychol. Assn. (exec. bd. 1986—, treas. 1990-92, pres. 1993), European Sch. Psychology Assn. (treas. 1985), Ohio Sch. Psychology Assn. (co-chmn. ethics com. 1976-86 exec. bd. 1992—), Cleve. Sch. Psychology Assn. (pres. 1969-71). Home: 3390 Stonehenge Ct Columbus OH 43221-1578 Office: Franklin County Ct 373 S High St Columbus OH 43215-4591 also: 5151A Reed Rd Columbus OH 43220

BATEMAN, MILDRED MITCHELL, psychiatrist; b. Cordele, Ga., Mar. 22, 1922; married; 2 children. BS, J.C. Smith U., 1941; MD, Woman's Med. Coll. Pa., 1946. Staff physician Larkin (W.Va.) State Hosp., 1947-48, clin. dir., 1951-52, 55-58, supt., 1958-60; supr. dir. profl. svcs. W.Va. Dept. Mental Health, 1960-62; dir. State Capital, 1962-77; prof., chmn. psychiat. Sch. Medicine Marshall U., Huntington, W.Va., 1977-82, prof. psychiatry, 1982—; staff psychiatrist Huntington VA Med. Ctr., 1986—; mem. com. mental illness and mental retardation Commn. Aging, W.Va. Commn. Mental Retardation, Govt. W.Va. Commn. Status of Women & Coop. Health Statis. Adv. Com., Nat. Ctr. Health Statis.; trustee Menninger Found. Mem. AMA, Inst. Medicine-NAS, Am. Psychiat. Assn. (v.p. 1973, Warren Williams Disting. award 1991). *

BATES, ERIC RANDOLPH, physician; b. Ann Arbor, Mich., Apr. 10, 1950; s. Richard Chester and Signe (Hegge) B.; m. Nancy Joanne Fortino, Sept. 25, 1976; children: Andrew, Alexis, Evan. AB, Princeton U., 1972; MD, U. Mich., 1976. Diplomate Am. Bd. Internal Medicine with added qualifications in cardiovascular diseases. Instr. in internal medicine U. Mich., Ann Arbor, 1981-84, asst. prof. internal medicine, 1984-89, assoc. prof. internal medicine, 1989-95, prof. internal medicine, 1995—, dir. cardiac catheterization lab., 1994—. Fellow Am. Coll. Physicians, Am. Coll. Cardiology, Am. Coll. Chest Physicians, Am. Heart Assn. Office: B1-F245 Univ Hosp 1500 Medical Ctr Dr Ann Arbor MI 48109

BATES, GEORGE WILLIAM, obstetrician, gynecologist, educator; b. Durham, N.C., Feb. 15, 1940; s. George W. and Lillian M. (Streete) B.; m. Susanne Rayburn, Oct. 18, 1969; children: Jonathan Rayburn, Jeffrey William, Robert Wiser. BS, U. N.C., 1962, MD, 1965; SM, MIT, 1984. Diplomate Am. Bd. Ob-Gyn. (examiner 1984-93). Intern U. Ala., Birmingham, 1965-66; resident ob-gyn U. N.C., Chapel Hill, 1966-70; prof., chmn. ob-gyn U. Tenn., Knoxville, 1972-76; fellow reproductive endocrinology U. Tex., Dallas, 1976-78; prof., dir. reproductive endocrinology U. Miss. Med. Ctr., Jackson, 1978-86; prof. ob.-gyn. Coll. Medicine Coll. Medicine, Med. U. S.C., Charleston, 1986-90, dean, 1986-89; v.p. med. edn. Greenville (S.C.) Hosp. System, 1990-96; exec. v.p., chief med. officer Prin.Care, Inc., Brentwood, Tenn., 1996—. Co-author: Obstetrics and Gynecology for Medical Students, 1992, 95; editor: Manual of Clinical Problems in Obstetrics and Gynecology, 1982, 86, 90; contbr. numerous articles to profl. publs. Commr. coun. Boy Scouts Am., 1989-90, v.p. adminstrn., 1992, pres., 1993-94; elder Mt. Pleasant Presbyn. Ch. Maj. USAF, 1970-72. Morehead scholar, 1958; NIH rsch. trainee, 1976-78; Sloan fellow, 1983; recipient Eagle Scout award, 1955, Henry Fordham award, 1966, Golden Apple award, 1987, Silver Beaver award, 1989, Hon. Alumnus award Med. U. S.C., 1990, Disting. Eagle Scout award, 1991; named Prof. of Yr., U. Miss., 1980. Mem. ACOG (chmn. fin. com. 1990-94, health care commn. 1994—, Jr. Fellow Profl. of Y. award dist. IV 1991), AMA, AAAS, Assn. Profs. Ob-Gyn. Found. (bd. dirs. 1993), Am. Gyn.-Ob. Soc., Nat. Bd. Med. Examiners, Gynecol. Investigation, Am. Fertility Soc. (bd. dirs., treas. 1994—), Soc. Gynecol. Surgeons, Accreditation Coun. Grad. Med. Edn., So. Atlantic Assn. Obstets. and Gynecologists, Ctrl. Assn. Obstets. and Gynecologists, Endocrine Soc., Rotary, Alpha Omega Alpha. Office: Prin-Care Inc 109 West Park Dr Ste 420 Brentwood TN 37027

BATES, HAMPTON ROBERT, JR., pathologist; b. Roanoke, Va., Feb. 1, 1933; s. Hampton Robert and Mary Mildred (Crowder) B.; B.S., Roanoke Coll., 1953; M.D., Med. Coll. Va., 1957; m. Carole Harrison Young, Apr. 12, 1958; children—Hampton Robert III, Catherine Louise. Intern, Med. Coll. Va. Hosp., Richmond, 1957-58, resident in pathology, 1958-63; practice medicine specializing in pathology and nuclear medicine, Richmond, 1963-95, ret., 1995; pathologist Johnston-Willis Hosp., Chippenham Med. Ctr.; v.p. Clin. Lab. Consultants, Inc., Richmond, 1972-95; forensic pathologist Richmond Met. Area, 1959-95. Diplomate Am. Bd. Pathology, Am. Bd. Nuclear Medicine, Nat. Bd. Med. Examiners. Fellow Coll. Am. Pathologists (life); mem. AMA, AAAS, Med. Soc. Va., Richmond Acad. Medicine, Swedish Pathol. Soc. (corr.), Rokitansky Soc. Episcopalian. Club: Diogenes. Contbr. articles on descriptive, exptl. and forensic pathology to med. Jours. Home: 641 Mobrey Dr Richmond VA 23236-4148

BATES, JOSEPH HENRY, physician, educator; b. Little Rock, Sept. 19, 1933; s. Henry Ermer and Susan Elizabeth (Wallis) B.; m. Patsy McGinnis, Aug. 6, 1955; children—Patricia, Susan Elizabeth, Joseph Henry, III, Elisabeth Lee. BS, U. Ark., 1957, MD, 1957, MS, 1963. Diplomate: Am. Bd. Internal Medicine (pulmonary disease; mem. exam. bd.). Med. intern U. Ark. Med. Center, 1957-58, resident in internal medicine, 1958-61, fellow in infections diseases, 1961-63; clin. investigator Little Rock VA Med. Center, 1963-66; mem. faculty U. Ark. Med. Center, Little Rock, 1967—; prof. medicine U. Ark. Med. Center, 1973—, vice chmn. dept., 1978—; chief med. service Little Rock VA Hosp., 1970—; dir. Twin City Bank of North Little Rock. Author research papers in field, chpts. in books. Chmn. Ark. chpt. NCCJ, 1980; chmn. biracial commn. Little Rock public schs., 1977-79; bd. dirs. Am. Lung Assn., 1972-90. Served as officer M.C. AUS, 1956-65. Grantee USPHS, 1961-63; Grantee NIH, VA, also pvt. founds. and corps., 1963—. Mem. ACP (gov.), Am. Coll. Chest Physicians (gov.), Am. Fedn. Clin. Rsch., Am. Thoracic Soc. (pres. 1988-89), Infectious Disease Soc., So. Soc. Clin. Rsch., Am. Lung Assn. (pres. 1994-95), Aassn. Am. Physicians, Assn. Profs. Medicine. Presbyterian. Home: 5 Glenridge Rd Little Rock AR 72227-2208 Office: 300 E Roosevelt Rd Little Rock AR 72206-2304

BATES, SUSAN VIOLA, healthcare administrator, nurse; b. Columbus, Wis., May 23, 1951; d. Lester Otto and Lois Viola (Rath) Henning; children: Rebecca Sue, Kenneth Ryan; m. Bill D. Bates. BS in Nursing, Olivet Nazarene Coll., Kankakee, Ill., 1973; MS, Govs. State U., Park Forest South, Ill., 1977. RN, CAlif. Nurse's aide Columbus Community Hosp., Wis., 1967-69; nurse aide Riverside Hosp., Kankakee, 1971-73, nurse, 1973; nurse Palos Community Hosp., Ill., 1973-74; instr. St. Joseph Hosp. Sch. of Nursing, Joliet, Ill., 1974-76; project coord. Our Lady of Mercy Hosp., Dyer, Ind., 1976-78, asst. dir. nursing, 1978-80, dir. of spl. svcs., 1980-81; dir. of nursing svcs. Culver Union Hosp., Crawfordsville, Ind., 1981-84, dir. of patient svcs., 1984, asst. adminstr., 1984-86; dir. nursing, asst. adminstr. Visalia (Calif.) Cmty. Hosp., 1986-90, dir. quality and risk mgmt., 1990-95; case mgr. Kaweah Delta Hosp., Visalia, 1996—. Mem. Sigma Theta Tau. Republican. Nazarene. Office: Kaweah Delta Hosp Visalia CA 93277

BATEY, SHARYN REBECCA, clinical research scientist; b. Nashville, Apr. 19, 1946; d. Robert Thomas and Sue (Alred) B. BS in Pharmacy, U. Tenn., 1969, D of Pharmacy, 1975; MS in Pub. Health, U. S.C., 1984. Registered pharmacist, Tenn. Hosp. pharmacist Vanderbilt Hosp., Nashville, 1969-71, VA Hosp., Beckley, W.Va., 1971-72, Gainesville, Fla., 1972-73, Battle Creek, Mich., 1973-74; hosp. pharmacy resident VA Hosp., Memphis, 1974-76; psychopharmacy resident Menninger Found., Topeka, 1976-77; clin. pharmacist William S. Hall Psychiat. Inst., Columbia, S.C., 1977-82; asst. prof. U. S.C. Coll. Pharmacy, Columbia, 1977-83, asst. prof. Sch. Medicine, 1981-83, assoc. prof. Coll. Pharmacy and Sch. Medicine, 1983-89; prof., 1989; chief clin. pharmacy services and ednl. programs William S. Hall Psychiat. Inst., Columbia, 1982-89; clin. rsch. scientist Burroughs Wellcome Co., Research Triangle Park, N.C., 1989-95; clin. program head, Glaxo Wellcome, Inc., Research Triangle Park, 1995—; clin. drug research/drug devel. fellow U. N.C. and Burroughs Wellcome, Research Triangle Park, 1983-84; pharmacist cons. NIMH, Bethesda, Md., 1983-84, Health Care Fin. Adminstrn., Balt., 1985-89. Author audio visual programs Psychotropic Medication Education Program for Adults, Adolescents and Children, 1978, 84, 88, 89; contbr. articles on psychopharmacology to profl. jours. Recipient Significant Achievement award Am. Psychiat. Assn., 1980, Sci. Exhibit award Am. Psychiat. Assn., 1981. Mem. Am. Coll. Clin. Pharmacy, Am. Soc. Hosp. Pharmacists (chmn. edn. and tng. working group of psychopharmacy spl. interest group 1983-85, chmn. elect 1985-86, chmn. 1986-87, past chmn. 1987-88, project leader psycopharmacy specialty recognition petition 1986-89, psychopharmacy fellow selection com. 1986-88, chmn. psychopharmacy spl. practice group 1989), S.C. Dementia Registry (pres. user policy coun. 1989). Avocations: travel, reading. Home: 4824 Highgate Dr Durham NC 27713-9417 Office: Glaxo Wellcome Inc Research Triangle Park NC 27709

BATICH, CHRISTOPHER DAVID, biomedical engineer, educator; b. Jersey City, Dec. 25, 1943; s. Stephen and Eleanor (Goldie) B.; m. Mary Elizabeth Byrne; children: Laura, Stephen, Elizabeth. BS, Pa. State U.,

1965; PhD, Rutgers U., 1971. Quality control chemist White Labs., Kenilworth, N.J., 1965-67; post doctoral fellow U. Basel, Switzerland, 1971-74; staff scientist DuPont Cen. Rsch., Wilmington, Del., 1974-81; assoc. prof. materials sci. dept. U. Fla., Gainesville, 1981-89, prof., 1989—; v.p. Materials Cons., Inc., Gainesville, Fla., 1983—; assoc. dir. Biomed. Engring Ctr., Gainesville, 1989—; vis. scientist, Akzo Co., Obernburg, Fed. Republic of Germany, 1990-91. Co-editor: (book) Adhesion, 1989. Co-chmn. Homeowners Assn., Gainesville, 1985; mem. Aschaffenberg Protestant Chapel Parish Coun. (Military) 1991. Grantee NIH, 1989, Fla. Dept. Environ. Regulation, 1990, Def. Advanced Rsch. Projects Agy., 1990. Mem. AAAS, Am. Chem. Soc., Am. Soc. Artificial Internal Organs. Home: 3733 NW 40th St Gainesville FL 32606-6199 Office: U Fla Materials Engring 317 Mae Gainesville FL 32611

BATISTA, DENISE APARECIDA SANTOS, cytogeneticist, researcher; b. Sao Vicente, Brazil, July 7, 1955; came to U.S., 1991; d. Jose Santos and Marly (Martins) B. Grad. in biology, U. Sao Paulo, Brazil, 1980, MS in Biology, 1983, PhD in Genetics, 1987. Diplomate Am. Bd. Internal Medicine, Am. Bd. Pediat., Am. Bd. Pediatric Critical Care Medicine. Cytotechnologist Servico de Tocoginecologia e Genetica, Sao Paulo, 1984-87; asst. prof. U. San Paulo, Sao Paulo, Brazil, 1988-91; dir. genetics svcs. U. San Paulo, Botucatu, Brazil, 1988-91; rsch. assoc. Johns Hopkins U., Balt., 1991—; dir. cytogenetics Union Meml. Hosp., Balt., 1994—; chmn. pharmacy and therapeutics St. Joseph's Hosp. and Med. Ctr., Phoenix, 1993—; v.p., bd. dirs. Ariz. Pediatric Sub-Specialists, IPA, Phoenix, 1995—; pres. Pediatric Critical Care of Ariz., Ltd., 1990—. Fellow Nat. Coun. for Sci. and Tech. Devel., 1980, Protection and Investigation Found. of the State of Sau Paulo, 1981-86, postdoc. fellow, 1991-92. Fellow Am. Assn. Immunology; mem. Soc. Critical Care Medicine, Am. Coll. Physicians Execs. Office: Union Meml Hosp Dept Ob-Gyn 201 E University Pkwy Baltimore MD 21218

BATLLE, DANIEL, nephrologist; b. Barcelona, Spain, Feb. 11, 1950; came to U.S., 1975; s. Narciso and Francisca (Campi) B.; m. Joan Batlle, Mar. 11, 1983; children: Jordi, Nicholas, Natalie. MD, U. Barcelona, 1973. Diplomate Am. Bd. Internal Medicine and Nephrology. Resident Wayne State U., Detroit, 1975-77; nephrology fellow U. Ill., Chgo., 1977-79, asst. prof. medicine, 1980-85; assoc. prof. medicine Northwestern U., Chgo., 1985-89, prof. medicine, 1989—; chief divsn. nephrology, hypertension Northwestern U., 2d Northwest Meml. Hosp., Chgo., 1992—. Editorial bd. Seminars in Nephrology, 1987—, Am. Jour. of Kidney Diseases, 1988—, Hypertension, 1992—, The Kidney, 1992—. Fellow ACP, Am. Heart Assn. (high blood pressure coun.); mem. Nat. Kidney Found. (sci. adv. bd. 1987—, chmn. nominating com. sci. adv. bd. 1989-91, chmn. program com. clin. meeting 1993—), Am. Soc. for Clin. Investigation, Cen. Soc. for Clin. Rsch., Soc. Gen. Physiologists, Am. Physiol. Soc., Am. Soc. Nephrology, Internat. Soc. Nephrology, Am. Heart Assn., N.Y. Acad. Scis. Office: Northwestern U Med Sch 303 E Chicago Ave Chicago IL 60611-3008

BATSAKIS, JOHN GEORGE, pathology educator; b. Petoskey, Mich., Aug. 14, 1929; s. George John and Stella (Vlahkis) B.; m. Mary Janet Savage, Dec. 28, 1957; children: Laura, Sharon, George. Student, Va. Mil. Inst., 1947, Albion Coll., Mich., 1948-50; M.D., U. Mich., 1954. Diplomate Am. Bd. Pathology. Intern George Washington Univ. Hosp., Washington, 1954-55; resident in pathology U. Mich. Hosp., Ann Arbor, 1955-59; prof. pathology U. Mich., Ann Arbor, 1969-79; chmn. dept. pathology M.D. Anderson Hosp. U. Tex., Houston, 1981—; Ruth Legett Jones prof. U. Tex., Austin, 1982; cons. Armed Forces Inst. Pathology, 1972—, VA Hosp., Ann Arbor, 1968-79; Hayes Martin lectr. Am. Soc. for Head and Neck Surgery, 1994; Gunnar Holmgren lectr. Swedish Nat. Ear, Nose, Throat Meeting, 1994; William Christopherson lectr. U. Louisville Dept. of Pathology, 1995; external examiner U. Hong Kong Dental Sch., 1995—. Author: Tumors of the Head and Neck, 2d edit., 1979; editor Clin. Lab. Ann., 1981-86; co-editor Advances in Anatomic Pathology, 1994—; mem. editorial bd. 13 jours., 1974—; contbr. numerous articles to profl. jours. Trustee George C. Marshall Found., Lexington, Va., 1995—. Capt. U.S. Army, 1959-61. Recipient William H. Rorer award Am. Coll. Gastroenterology, 1972, Disting. Alumnus award Albion Coll., 1987, Reviewer of the Decade award AMA Archives Orolaryngology Head Neck Surgery, 1990, Presdl. award Am. Soc. Head and Neck Surgery, 1991, Harlan Spjut award Houston Soc. Clin. Pathologists, 1992, Honor award Am. Laryngologic Assn., 1995; Spl. Honored Guest of Am. Soc. for Head and Neck Surgery, 1993. Fellow ACP, Am. Soc. Clin. Pathologists, Am. Acad. Otolaryngology (assoc., honor award 1994), Coll. Am. Pathologists (chmn. commn. anatomic pathology), Royal Soc. Medicine. Republican. Episcopalian. Home: 1701 Hermann Dr Apt 3304 Houston TX 77004-7331 Office: MD Anderson Hosp Dept Pathology 1515 Holcombe Blvd Houston TX 77030-4009

BATSHAW, MARK LEVITT, pediatrician; b. Montreal, Que., Can., Sept. 19, 1945; s. Manuel G. and Rachel (Levitt) B.; m. Karen N. Korman, June 29, 1969; children: Elissa, Michael, Andrew. BA, U. Pa., 1967; MD, U. Chgo., 1971. Diplomate Am. Bd. Pediatrics. Resident in pediatrics Hosp. for Sick Children, Toronto, 1971-73; fellow in developmental pediatrics Kennedy Krieger Inst., Johns Hopkins U. Sch. Medicine, 1973-75; instr. Johns Hopkins U. Sch. Medicine, Balt., 1975-76, asst. prof., 1976-80, assoc. prof. pediatrics, 1980-88; W.T. Grant prof. pediatrics and neurology U. Pa. Sch. Medicine, Phila., 1988—; chief div. child devel. and rehab. Children's Hosp. of Phila., 1988—; physician-in-chief Children's Seashore House, Phila., 1988—; mem. NIH study NICHD, 1991-95. Author: Children with Disabilities, 3d edit., 1992, Your Child Has a Disability, 1991. Johns Hopkins U. fellow, 1973-75; Kennedy scholar, Kennedy Inst., 1983-86. Fellow Royal Coll. Physicians; mem. Am. Pediatric Soc. Office: Children's Seashore House 3405 Civic Center Blvd Philadelphia PA 19104-4302

BATSON, BLAIR EVERETT, pediatrician, educator; b. Hattiesburg, Miss., Oct. 24, 1920; s. Claud L. and Mary Eaton (Bryan) B.; m. Blanche Russell Desmond, 1976. B.A., Vanderbilt U., 1941, M.D., 1944; M.P.H., Johns Hopkins U., 1954. Intern Vanderbilt U. Hosp., 1944-45, asst. resident in pediatrics, 1948-49, resident pediatrician, 1949-50, instr. pediatrics Sch. Medicine, 1949-52; asst. resident dept. pediatrics Johns Hopkins Hosp., 1945-46; instr. pediatrics Johns Hopkins Sch. Medicine, 1952-54, asst. prof., 1954-55; instr. public health adminstrn., div. maternal and child health Sch. Hygiene and Public Health, 1952-54, asst. prof. public health adminstrn., 1954-55; prof. pediatrics U. Miss. Sch. Medicine, Jackson, 1955-90, prof. emeritus, 1990—, chmn. dept. pediatrics, 1955-88; chmn. health com., adv. council Miss. Children's Code Commn., 1958-61; chmn. Miss. Conf. on Handicapped Children, 1960-61; nat. adviser on children, public children's bur. HEW; ofcl. examiner Am. Bd. Pediatrics, 1963-91; pediatric cons. USAF, 1971-76. Trustee Easter Seal Research Found., 1969-74. Served to capt. M.C. AUS, 1946-48. Mem. Am. Acad. Pediatrics (Mead Johnson awards com. 1958-61, exec. com. child devel. sect. 1964-67, charter mem. sect. on community pediatrics 1968, hosp. car com. 1970, nominating com. 1973-74, exec. bd. 1974-80, chmn. govt. affairs council 1983-86, Grulee award 1986), AMA, So. Soc. Pediatric Research, Am. Assn. Med. Colls., So. Med. Assn. (sec. pediatric sec. 1956-58, pres. 1959), Vanderbilt Alumni Club (pres. chpt. 1960-64), Am. Pediatric Soc., Sigma Chi, Phi Chi. Home: 1692 Laurel St Jackson MS 39202-1270 Office: Univ Miss Med Center 2500 N State St Jackson MS 39216-4500

BATT, RONALD ELMER, gynecologist; b. Buffalo, Sept. 24, 1933; s. Elmer Lawrence and Mary Catherine (Roll) B.; student Niagara U., 1951-54; M.D., U. Buffalo, 1958; m. Carol Mary Schaab, Dec. 28, 1957; children: Paula, Douglas, Thomas, Neil, Jennifer, John; m. 2d, Kathleen Over Cansdale, May 19, 1982; stepchildren: William, James, Suzanne, Timothy, John, Mark. Intern, Millard Fillmore Hosp., Buffalo, 1958-59; resident in ob-gyn SUNY, Buffalo, 1959-60, 62-66; rsch. fellow Harvard U. Med. Sch., 1963-64; asst. in surgery Peter Bent Brigham Hosp., Boston, 1963-64; fellow in gynecologic surgery Mayo Clinic, 1965; practice medicine specializing in endometriosis and reproductive surgery, Buffalo, 1966—; prof. clin. gynecology, SUNY Buffalo. Served with M.C., USN, 1960-62. Co-author: Another Era: A Pictorial History of the School of Medicine and Biomedical Sciences, State University of New York at Buffalo 1846-1996; contbr. chpts. to books, articles to profl. jours. Fellow Royal Coll. Surgeons Can., Am. Coll. Obstetricians and Gynecologists, ACS; mem. Am. Soc. Reproductive Medicine, Soc. Reproductive Surgeons, Am. Assn. History Medicine, Internat. Soc. History Medicine. Co-author: The Chapel, 1979, Conservative Surgery for Endometriosis in the Infertile Couple, 1982, Another Era: A Pictorial History of the School of Medicine and Biomedical Science, State University of New York at Buffalo 1846-1996. Office: Millard Fillmore Suburban Hosp Campus 1542 Maple Rd Buffalo NY 14221-3625

BATTAGLIA, FREDERICK CAMILLO, physician; b. Weehawken, N.J., Feb. 15, 1932; m. Jane B. Donohue; children—Susan Kate, Thomas Frederick. BA, Cornell U., 1953; MD, Yale U., 1957; DSc (hon.), U. Ind. Diplomate: Am. Bd. Pediatrics. Intern in pediatrics Johns Hopkins Hosp., 1957-58; USPHS postdoctoral fellow biochemistry Cambridge (Eng.) U., 1958-59; Josiah Macy Found. fellow in physiology Yale U. Med. Sch., 1959-60; asst. resident, fellow in pediatrics Johns Hopkins Hosp., 1960-61; resident, fellow, 1961-62; USPHS surgeon lab. perinatal physiology NIH, San Juan, P.R., 1962-64; asst. prof., then asso. prof. Johns Hopkins Med. Sch., 1963-65; mem. faculty U. Colo. Med. Sch., Denver, 1965—; prof. pediatrics, prof. Ob-Gyn U. Colo. Med. Sch., 1969—, dir. div. perinatal medicine, 1970-74, chmn. dept. pediatrics, 1974-89; prof. pediatrics, 1989—; attending pediatrician Children's, Denver Gen., Fitzsimons Gen. hosps.; co-dir. newborn center Univ. Hosp., 1967-74. Assoc. editor: Pediatrics, 15th edit; med. progress contbg. editor: Jour. Pediatrics, 1966-74; mem. editorial bd.: European Jour. Ob-Gyn, 1971—; assoc. editor Biol. Neonate, 1979—; contbr. numerous articles med. jours. Mem. Assn. Am. Physicians, Am. Acad. Pediatrics (E. Mead Johns award 1969), Am. Gynecologic and Obstet. Soc., Soc. Pediatric Rsch. (pres. 1976-77), Perinatal Rsch. Soc. (pres. 1974-75), Western Soc. Pediatric Rsch. (pres. 1987—), Soc. Gynecol. Investigation, Am. Pediatric Soc. (pres. 1996), Internat. Congress Perinatal Medicine (pres. 1996), Soc. Gynecol. Investigation (coun. 1969-72), Soc. Exptl. Biology and Medicine, Inst. of Medicine, Phi Beta Kappa, Sigma Xi. Home: 2975 E Cedar Ave Denver CO 80209-3211 Office: U Colo Dept Pediatrics Health Scis Ctr 4200 E 9th Ave Denver CO 80262

BATTAGLIA, MASSIMO, clinical virologist, researcher; b. Pisa, Italy, June 15, 1948; s. Emilio and Giovanna (Tellini) B.; m. Mariella Masselli, June 29, 1981; 1 child, Luca. MD magna cum laude, U. Rome, 1974. Med. diplomate. Researcher Consiglio Nat. Rsch., Rome, 1976-79, 81-83, 85—, Pavia, Italy, 1979-81, 85; Rusconi Found. fellow U. Zürich, Switzerland, 1984; mem. biosafety commn. Polo Biologico Integrato Consiglio Nazionale Ricerche, Rome, 1992—. Contbr. articles to profl. jours.; patentee in field. Mem. AAAS, Am. Soc. for Microbiology, N.Y. Acad. Scis., Gruppo Italiano Citometria, Lega Italiana per Lotta contro Malattie Virali, WHO Collabroating Ctr., Italian Inst. Prevention Liver Diseases, Soc. In Vitro Biology (formerly Tissue Culture Assn.), Soc. Italiana Geriatri Ospedalieri, Gerontol. Soc. Am., Internet Soc., Mensa. Home: Via Filippo Eredia 19, 00146 Rome Italy Office: Consiglio Nat Rsch IMS CNR, Viale Marx 15, 00137 Rome Italy

BATTARBEE, HAROLD D., physiology educator; b. Highlands, Tex., July 25, 1940; s. Richard B. Battarbee and Evelyn (Johnson) Magers; m. Jane Robberson, July 27, 1966 (dec. June 1982); children: Brad Lee (dec. Apr. 1993), Elizabeth Lynn; m. Jeanie Parks, Feb. 11, 1982; children: Albert E. Sampsell, Craig D. Sampsell. Student, Lee Coll.; BS, U. Houston, 1966; PhD, Baylor Coll. Medicine, 1971. From rsch assoc. to predoctoral trainee Baylor Coll. Medicine, Houston, 1966-71; from inst. to assoc. prof. physiology La. State U. Med. Ctr., Shreveport, 1971-86, prof., 1986—; vice chmn. physiology dept. La. State U. Med. Ctr., Shreveport, 1987—; cons. U.S. Army Aeromed. Rsch. Lab., Ft. Rucker, Ala., 1982-85; subcom. on combat stress mem. U.S. Army Med. R&D Adv. com., Ft. Detrick, Md., 1982-84. Author rsch. publs. and textbooks; contbr. articles to profl. jours. Mem. Union of Concerned Scientists, 1988—, Zero Population Growth. With U.S. Army, 1960-63, Korea. Trantee La. State U. Bd. Regents, 1988-92. Mem. AAAS, AAUP, Am. Physiol. Soc., Am. Heart Assn. (grantee 1972—), Am. Gastroenterol. Assn. Home: 522 S Dresden Ct Shreveport LA 71115-3504 Office: La State U Med Ctr Dept Physiology and Biophysics PO Box 33932 Shreveport LA 71130-3932

BATTEGAY, RAYMOND, psychiatrist; b. Berne, Switzerland, June 27, 1927; s. Karl and Marguerite (Goetschel) B.; m. Shulamit Violet Fitaya, Sept. 13, 1955; children: Edouard, Manuel, Oscar. MD. Head physician Psychiatric Inpatient Clinic, Basel, Switzerland, 1958-67; sr. lectr. U. Basel, 1962-69; chief physician Basel U. Psychiatric Outpatient Dept., 1968—; prof. psychiatry U. Basel, 1969—, chmn. dept. psychiatry, 1976—; mem. adv. panel Group Analysis, London, Rivista Italiana di Gruppoanalisi, Revista de Psicologia y Psicoterapia de Grupo, Argentina. Author: The Human Being in the Group, 1967, 5th edit., 1976, vol. II, 1967, vol. III, 1969, Anxiety and Existence, 1970, 3d edit., 1996, Psychoanalytic Theory of Neuroses, 1971, 2d edit., 1973, paper, 1986, 2d edit., 1994, Narcissism and Object Relations, 1977, 3d edit., 1991, El Hombre en el Grupo, 1978, Aggression—A Means of Communication?, 1979, Angoscia ed Essere, 1980, Grenzsituationen (Border Situations), 1981, apaper, 1992, La Agresion, 1981, Depression, 1985, 3d edit., 1991, Die Hungerkrankheiten, 1982, El Hambre como Fenomeno Patologico, 1986, Autodestruktion, 1988, Hunger Diseases, 1991, others; co-editor Crisis, Gruppenpsychotherapie und Gruppendynamik; cons. editor Internat. Jour. Group Psychotherapy, Revista de Psicologia Y Psicoterapia de grupo, Revista Italiana di Gruppoanalisi. Pres. sci. subcommn. Swiss Fed. Commn. Against Alcoholism, 1971-81; mem. Swiss Found. for Alcohol Research, 1980-89, Regency of U. Basel, 1981. Fellow Am. Acad. Psychoanalysis, Am. Group Psychotherapy Assn., Internat. Assn. Group Psychotherapy (chmn. by-laws com., pres. 1977-80); mem. Collegium Internat. Neuro-Psychopharmacologicum, Swiss Med. Assn. Psychotherapy (pres. 1973-76), Deutsche Psychotherapeutische und sozialmed. Gesellsch. (corres. mem.), Federacao Latino-Americana de Psicoterapia Analitica de Grupo (corres. mem.), Deutsche Psychoanalytische Gesellschaft (corres. mem.), Deutsche Gesellsch. fur Psychiatrie und Nervenheilkunde (corres. mem.). Home: Marschalkenstrasse 25, 4054 Basel Switzerland Office: Kantonsspital Petersgraben 4, Psychiatrische U-Poliklinik, 4031 Basel Switzerland

BATTEN, KIM ROBIN, intensive care and coronary care nurse; b. Rolling Hills, Pa., Aug. 25, 1956; d. Clarence Robert and Mildred Dorothy (Bird) Fisher; m. Wayne Carroll Batten, Oct. 9, 1982; children: Laura Gaye, Jill Kristine. BA in Bibl. Christian Edn. summa cum laude, Fla. Bible. Coll., Hollywood, Fla., 1978; student, Ga. State U., 1981, Anne Arundel Cmty. Coll., Arnold, Md., 1985-86; ADN summa cum laude, Bucks County Cmty. Coll., Newtown, Pa., 1993. RN, Pa. Staff nurse, med. surg. Del. Valley Med. Ctr., Langhorne, Pa., 1993-94; staff nurse, oncology St. Mary Med. Ctr., Langhorne, Pa., 1994-95, staff nurse intensive care/coronary care, 1995—. Area coord. Perot for Pres. campaign, Newtown, Pa., 1992. Mem. Oncology Nursing Soc. Christian. Home: 9 Chicory Place Newtown PA 18940 Office: St Mary Medical Center Langhorne-Newtown Rd Langhorne PA 19047

BATTIES, PAUL TERRY, physician; b. Indpls., July 22, 1941; s. paul A. and Louise Terry B. AB, Ind. U., 1962, MD, 1965. Bd. eligible Internal Medicine and Cardiovascular Diseases. Rotating intern Detroit Gen. Hosp., 1965-66; internal medicine resident Wayne State U., Detroit, 1966-69, chief med. resident, 1969; cardiology fellow U. Ky., Lexington, 1971-73; mem. dean's coun., Ind. U. Sch. Medicine, 1989—. Mem. C. of C. Maj. USAF, 1969-71. Named Ind. Disting. Citizen of Yr., Indpls. Black Centennial Com., 1976. Fellow Am. Coll. Cardiology; mem. Assn. Black Cardiologists, Ind. Soc. Internal Medicine (pres. 1990-91), Aesculapian Med. Soc. (pres. 1982-84), NAACP (life), Ind. U. Alumni Assn., Am. Heart Assn. (past chmn. hypertension com., Marion County chpt.), Ind. State Med. Assn., Marion County Med. Assn., Am. Soc. Internatl Medicine, others. Methodist. Home: 10316 Coral Reef Way Indianapolis IN 46256 Office: 1633 N Capitol Ave # 510 Indianapolis IN 46202

BATTLE, ALLEN OVERTON, JR., psychologist, educator; b. Memphis, Nov. 19, 1927; s. Allen Overton and Florence Louise (Castelvecchi) B.; m. Mary Madeline Vroman, June 14, 1952; 1 son, Allen Overton, III. B.S., Siena Coll., 1949; M.A., Cath. U. Am., 1953, Ph.D., 1961; certificate in clin. psychology, U. Tenn. Coll. Medicine, 1953. Diplomate: in clin. psychology Am. Bd. Profl. Psychology, 1971. Instr. dept. psychiatry U. Tenn. Coll. Medicine, 1956-61, asst. prof., 1961-67, asso. prof., 1966-72, prof., 1972—; chief clin. psychologist U. Tenn. Mental Health Center, 1971-78, chief div. clin. psychology, 1974—; vis. lectr. Southwestern U. at Memphis, 1962-84; vis. prof. Rhodes Coll., 1984—. Author: Clinical Psychology for Physical Therapists, 1975, Suicide and Crisis Intervention Training Manuals, 1978, The Psychology of Patient Care: A Humanistic Approach, 1979; contbr. articles to profl. jours. Cons. USPHS, Suicide and Crisis Intervention Svc.; mem. Mayor's Commn. on Alcohol and Drug Abuse, 1974-77; bd. dirs. Runaway House, St. Peter's Home for Children, De Neuville Heights Sch. Family Svc. Decorated knight Russian Imperial Order; knight Order St. John of Jerusalem; recipient Disting. Svc. award Tenn. Dept. Mental Health, 1971. Mem. Am., Tenn. psychol. assns., Am. Anthrop. Assn., N.Y. Acad. Sci., AAAS, Brit. Soc. Projective Techniques, Sigma Xi. Home: 2220 Washington Ave Memphis TN 38104-3025 Office: 66 N Pauline St Memphis TN 38105-5105

BATTLE, PAUL, physician assistant; b. Cleve., July 4, 1956; s. Joseph J. and Julia Ann (Dalton) B.; m. Michele Hogl, Feb. 10, 1990; children: Matthew Paul, Daniel Michael. BS in Physiology, U. Calif., Davis, 1978; BS in Med. Sci., Emory U., 1981. Cert. physian asst. Nat. Cert. Com. of Physician Assts. Nurse attendant Delta Meml. Hosp., Antioch, Calif., 1977-79; physician asst. family practice surgery Office of David Pierpont MD, Ironwood, Mich., 1981-86, Ironwood Family Practice, 1986; physician asst. Am. Lake VA Med. Ctr., Tacoma, Wash., 1986-89, Group Health Coop., Olympia, Wash., 1989-96, Denver Orthopedic Specialists, 1996—; chief affiliate staff south region Group Health Coop., Tacoma, 1994-95. Medic U. Calif.-Davis Camp for Welfare Children, 1977, 78; physician asst. Mex. Medi., Med. Mission, Mexicali, 1994; physician asst., EMT instr. Gogebic County EMS, Ironwood, 1983; physician asst., lectr. Gogebic County Head Start, Ironwood, 1984. Fellow Am. Assn. Physician Assts.; mem. Wash. Assn. Physician Assts., Wash. Med. Assn. Roman Catholic. Home: 1712 Daisy Ct Broomfield CO 80020 Office: Denver Orthopedic 1601 E 19th Ave Ste 5000 Denver CO 80218

BATTY, HUGH KENWORTHY, physician; b. Kansas City, Kans.; s. James Jacob and Genevieve Adeline (Johnston) B.; m. Mercedes Aguirre, Mar. 17, 1979; 1 child, Henry Briton. BS in Zoology, U. Wash., 1970; PhD in Anatomy, U. Utah, 1974; MD, Ciudad Juárez, Mex., 1977. Intern, asst. resident St. Vincent's Med. Ctr., Bridgeport, Conn., 1977-78, resident, 1978-79, chief resident, 1979-80; pvt. practice Sheridan, Wyo., 1980—; chmn. dept. medicine Meml. Hosp. Sheridan, 1989, 91, 95, chmn. ICU, 1995. Contbr. articles to profl. jours. Eleanor Roosevelt Cancer Rsch. Found. grantee, 1972. Mem. ACP, Wyo. Med. Soc., Sheridan County Med. Soc. Office: 1260-62 W 5th St Sheridan WY 82801-2702

BATZER, GABRIELLE BEMIS, physician, psychiatrist; b. Arlington, Va., July 24, 1953; d. Lawrence Ralph and Grace Southall (Cock) Bemis; m. Wayne Batzer, Nov. 29, 1980; children: Darien Bemis Batzer, Eliot Bemis Batzer. BA, Lewis and Clark Coll., 1974; MD, Georgetown U., 1981. Diplomate in psychiatry and addiction psychiatry Am. Bd. Psychiatry and Neurology; diplomate Nat. Bd. Med. Examiners; cert. in addiction medicine Am. Soc. Addiction Medicine. Intern, resident Georgetown U. Hosp., Washington, 1981-86, fellow alcohol and drug svc., 1986-87; clin. instr. dept. pschiatry Georgetown U., 1986-87; cons. assoc. dept. psychiatry Duke U., Durham, N.C., 1987-91; psychiatrist (USPHS) Lee-Harnett Mental Health Ctr., Buies Creek, N.C., 1987-91; asst. prof. U. Hawaii Sch. Medicine, Honolulu, 1991—; dir. addiction psychiatry Hawaii State Hosp., Kaneohe, 1991-94; dir. substance abuse program VA, Honolulu, 1994—; bd. dirs. Pacific Inst. Chem. Dependency, Honolulu, 1993—; mem. Hawaii Adv. Commn. Drug Abuse and Controlled Substances, Honolulu, 1993—; mem. Hawaii State Coun. on Mental Health, Honolulu, 1993—; examiner Am. Bd. Psychiatry and Neurology, 1993—. Contbr. chpts. to books. Mem. Am. Psychiat. Assn., Am. Acad. Addiction Psychiatry (charter mem.), Am. Soc. Addiction Medicine, Hawaii Psychiat. Med. Assn., Hawaii Med. Assn. Episcopalian. Office: VA 116E Substance Abuse Treatment 300 Ala Moana Blvd Honolulu HI 96813

BAUCCIO, LISA RUTH, obstetric nurse, high-risk perinatal nurse; b. Pitts., May 4, 1967; d. Raymond D. and Ruthann L. (Stevens) Valentine; m. Carmen J. Bauccio, May 12, 1990; 1 child, Anthony M. BSN, Carlow Coll., 1989; postgrad., U. Pitts. RN, Pitts. Asst. patient care Forbes Regional Health Ctr., Monroeville, Pa., 1987-89; clin. nurse II West Penn Hosp., Pitts., 1989—, instr. obstet. edn., 1991—, mem. core com. critical care obstet. unit, 1992—; speaker perinatal outreach program West Pa. Hosp., Pitts., 1993—. Fellow Nightingale Soc.; mem. AWHONN, Sigma Theta Tau, Delta Epsilon Sigma, Phi Eta Sigma, Alpha Lambda Delta. Home: 4037 Impala Dr Pittsburgh PA 15239-2705 Office: West Penn Hosp Unit E5DR Labor/Delivery 4800 Friendship Ave Pittsburgh PA 15224-1722

BAUE, ARTHUR EDWARD, surgeon, educator, administrator; b. St. Louis, Oct. 7, 1929; s. Arthur Christian and Viola (Wegener) B.; m. Rosemary Dysart, Nov. 24, 1956; children: Patricia Sage Baue Nizen, Arthur Christian II, William Dysart. AB summa cum laude, Westminster Coll., 1950; MD cum laude, Harvard, 1954. Diplomate Am. Bd. Surgery (dir.), Am. Bd. Thoracic Surgery (dir.). Successively intern, resident, chief resident surgery Mass. Gen. Hosp., Boston, 1954-61; asst. prof. surgery U. Mo. Sch. Medicine, 1962-64; asst. prof., then assoc. prof. surgery U. Pa. Sch. Medicine, Phila., 1964-67; Harry Edison prof. surgery Washington U. Sch. Medicine, St. Louis, 1967-75; surgeon-in-chief, dir. dept. surgery Jewish Hosp., St. Louis, 1967-75; chief of surgery Yale-New Haven Hosp., 1975-85; prof., chmn. dept. surgery Yale U., 1975-85, Donald Guthrie prof. surgery, 1977-85; assoc. dean for clin. affairs St. Louis U. Sch. Medicine, 1985-86; v.p. for the med. ctr. St. Louis U., 1986-90, prof. surgery, 1986—; dir. surg. edn. St. Mary's Health Ctr.; cons. surgery Nat. Bd. Med. Examiners; cons. to chief of staff VAMC, St. Louis; chmn. NIH surgery B study sect., 1978-82; bd. dirs., med. dir. Healthcare Mgmt., Inc. Chief editor Archives of Surgery, 1977-88, sr. cons. editor, 1989-93; mem. editl. bd. JAMA, 1977-88, Circulatory Shock, Am. Jour. Physiology, 1975-87, Postgrad. Gen. Surgery, Jour. Shock, 1994—; sr. editor: Glenn's Thoracic and Cardiovascular Surgery; contbr. over 550 articles to profl. jours. Life trustee Westminster Coll.; trustee Nat. Commn. for Quality Health Care, 1986-92, HEalth Care Leadership Coun.; bd. dirs. United Way. Capt. USAF, 1959. John and Mary R. Markle scholar acad. medicine, 1963; recipient Rsch. Career Devel. award USPHS, 1965-68, Scientist of Yr. award Sigma Xi, 1991. Mem. ACs, AMA (trustee jour., editl. bd. jour.), Assn. Am. Med. Colls. (coun. acad. socs.), Am. Assn. Thoracic Surgery, Am. Coll. Cardiology, Am. Coll. Chest Physicians, Assn. Acad. Surgery, New Eng. Surg. Soc., Internat. Cardiovasc. Soc., Soc. Thoracic Surgeons, Soc. Univ. Surgeons, Soc. Vascular Surgery, Shock Soc., Internat. Fedn. Shock Socs. (pres. 1992-95), Internat. Vascular Soc. Surgery, Am. Assn. for Surgery of Trauma, Am. Assn. Artificial Internal Organs, Organ Failur Acad. (Trieste, Italy, hon. pres. 1983—), Am. Physiol. Soc., Soc. Critical Care Medicine, Am. Surg. Assn., Ctrl. Surg. Assn., Soc. for Surgery Alimentary Tract, Alpha Omega Alpha. Office: St Louis U Hosp 3635 Vista Ave Saint Louis MO 63110-2539

BAUER, A(UGUST) ROBERT, JR., surgeon, educator; b. Phila., Dec. 23, 1928; s. A(ugust) Robert and Jessie Martha-Maynard (Monie) B.; BS, U. Mich., 1949, MS, 1950, MD, 1954; M Med. Sci.-Surgery, Ohio State U., 1960; m. Charmaine Louise Studer, June 28, 1957; children: Robert, John, William, Anne, Charles, James. Intern Walter Reed Army Med. Ctr., 1954-55; resident in surgery Univ. Hosp., Ohio State U., Columbus, also instr., 1957-61; pvt. practice medicine, specializing in surgery, Mt. Pleasant, Mich., 1962-74; chief surgery Ctrl. Mich. Community Hosp., Mt. Pleasant, 1964-65, vice chief of staff, 1967, chief of staff, 1968; clin. faculty Mich. State Med. Sch., East Lansing, 1974; mem. staff St. Mark's Hosp., Salt Lake City, 1974-91; pvt. practice surgery, Salt Lake City, 1974-91; clin. instr. surgery U. Utah, 1975-91. Trustee Rowland Hall, St. Mark's Sch., Salt Lake City, 1978-84; mem. Utah Health Planning Coun., 1979-81. Served with M.C., U.S. Army, 1954-57. Diplomate Am. Bd. Surgery. Fellow ACS, Southwestern Surg. Congress; mem. AMA, Salt Lake County Med. Soc., Utah Med. Assn. (various coms.), Utah Soc. Certified Surgeons, Salt Lake Surg. Soc., Pan Am. Med. Assn. (affiliate), AAAS (affiliate), Sigma Phi Epsilon, Phi Rho Sigma. Episcopalian. Club: Zollinger. Contbr. articles to profl. publs., researcher surg. immunology. Office: PO Box 17533 Salt Lake City UT 84117-0533

BAUER, EUGENE ANDREW, dermatologist, educator; b. Mattoon, Ill., June 17, 1942; s. Eugene C. and Madge L. (Armer) B.; m. Gloria Anne Hehman, Feb. 19, 1966; children: Marc A., Christine A., J. Michael, Amanda F. BS, Northwestern U., 1963, MD, 1967. Diplomate Am. Bd. Dermatology, Nat. Bd. Med. Examiners. Intern Barnes Hosp., St. Louis,

1967-68; resident, fellow div. dermatology Washington U. Med. Ctr., 1968-70; instr. Washington U., St. Louis, 1971-72, asst. prof. dermatology, 1974-78, assoc. prof., 1978-82, prof., 1982-88; prof. chmn. Stanford U. Sch. Medicine, 1988-95; program dir. Gen. Clin. Rsch. Ctr., 1990-93; dean Stanford U. Sch. Medicine, 1995—. Contbr. numerous articles to profl. jours. Served to lt. comdr. USNR, 1972-74. Fellow Am. Acad. Dermatology; mem. Am. Fedn. Clin. Research, Am. Soc. Clin. Investigation, Am. Dermatol. Assn., Soc. Investigative Dermatology (bd. dirs. 1981-86, assoc. editor Jour. Investigative Dermatology 1982-87, pres.-elect 1994-95, pres. 1995-96), Ctrl. Soc. Clin. Rsch., Assn. Am. Physicians. Office: Stanford U Sch Medicine Office of the Dean M121 Stanford CA 94305

BAUER, JAMES HARVEY, orthopaedic surgeon; b. Lincoln, Nebr., July 13, 1931; s. Wilbert Clayton and Dorothy Alice (Mahan) B.; m. Marion Jeanette Morse, Sept. 12, 1953; children: Kenneth, Ronald, Robert. BS, U. Oreg., 1954, MD, 1956. Diplomate Am. Bd. Orthopaedic Surgeons, Am. Bd. Orthopaedic Surgery. Intern U. Calif., San Francisco, 1956-57, resident in orthopaedic surgery, 1957-59, 61-63, asst. clin. prof. orthopaedic surgery, 1964-73; gen. orthopaedic surgery Santa Rosa, Calif., 1963—. With USAF, 1957-59. Fellow Am. Orthopaedic Foot Soc., Am. Coll. Surgeons; mem. AMA, Sonoma County Medical Assn., Calif. Medical Assn., Calif. Orthopaedic Assn., Western Orthopaedic Assn., Am. Acad. Orthopaedic Surgery. Office: 4700 Woodview Santa Rosa CA 95405

BAUER, JOHN ANTHONY, medical researcher; b. Sept. 29, 1964; married; 1 child. BSc in Pharmaceutics magna cum laude, SUNY, Buffalo, 1986, PhD in Pharmaceutics, 1991. Grad. rsch. fellow dept. pharmaceutics SUNY, Buffalo, 1987-91, postdoctoral fellow, rsch. assoc., 1991-93, instr., 1992-93, rsch. asst. prof. Sch. Pharmacy, 1994-96; sci. cons. Condon & Taheri P.C. Patentee in field; contbr. articles to profl. jours. Grantee Baker Norton Pharms., Inc. Mem. Am. Assn. Pharm. Scientists, Am. Diabetes Assn. (Rsch. award 1996), Sigma Xi. Office: SUNY Dept Pharmaceutics 514 Hochstetter Hall Buffalo NY 14260

BAUER, MARK DOUGLAS, emergency physician; b. Loma Linda, Calif., Mar. 12, 1958; s. Carl Leroy Bauer and Myrna J. (Clevenger) Goss; m. Tina Marie Baugher, Aug. 18, 1985; children: Brendon, Brooke. BSBA, Union Coll., 1981; MD, Loma Linda U., 1986. Diplomate Am. Bd. Emergency Medicine. Resident in internal medicine Loma Linda (Calif.) U. Med. Ctr., 1986-88, resident in emergency medicine, 1988-91; emergency physician Sacred Heart Med. Ctr., Spokane, Wash., 1991-96. Fellow Am. Coll. Emergency Physicians. Office: Sacred Heart Med Ctr 101 W 8th Ave Spokane WA 99220

BAUER, RICHARD MICHAEL, viral immunologist; b. Kent, Ohio, July 15, 1959; s. Richard George and Patrica Ann (Line) B.; m. Marche Anne Margene, July 16, 1983. BA, Hiram Coll., 1981; MS, U. Akron, 1983; PhD, Ohio State U., 1987. Rsch. fellow U. Akron, Ohio, 1982; postdoctoral fellow Ohio State U., Columbus, 1987-88; scientist Baxter Healthcare, Mundelein, Ill., 1988-90, project leader, 1990-91; sr. scientist Ortho Diagnostics Systems, Inc., Raritan, N.J., 1991-93; sr. rsch. scientist Bayer, Tarrytown, N.Y., 1993—; adj. faculty mem. Allentown Coll. St. Francis de Sales, Center Valley, Pa. Contbr. articles to profl. jours. Mem. AAAS, Am. Soc. Microbiology, Nat. Audubon Soc., N.Y. Acad. Scis. Home: 20 Tiffany Dr Danbury CT 06811-4250 Office: Ortho Diagnostics Systems Inc RR 2 Raritan NJ 08869

BAUER, SANDRA RAMSEY, maternity nursing educator; b. Phila., Apr. 29, 1948; d. Clyde Robert and Adella (Curry) Ramsey; m. William L. Bauer III, Aug. 26, 1972; children: Meridith Ann, Sherrie Lynn. Diploma in nursing, Thomas Jefferson U. Hosp., 1969; BSN, U. Pa., 1973, MS in Nursing, 1982. RN, Pa. Maternity float nurse Abington (Pa.) Meml. Hosp., 1969-70, permanent team leader postpartum unit, 1970-72, part-time staff maternity unit, 1972-73, 74-76, mem. postpartum staff, 1973-74, instr. expectant parents course, 1977-79; instr. prepared childbirth program Holy Redeemer Hosp., Meadowbrook, Pa., 1980-83; instr. maternity nursing Frankford Hosp. Sch. Nursing, Phila., 1983-90, Roxborough Meml. Hosp. Sch. Nursing, Phila., 1990-94, Frankford Hosp. Sch. of Nursing, Phila., 1994—; nursing mother counselor Childbirth Edn. Assn. Greater Phila., Warminster, Pa., 1975-81. Sunday Sch. vol. Glenside (Pa.) United Meth. Ch., 1974—; adult vol. Freedom Valley coun. Girl Scouts U.S.A., 1981-92; pres., vol. nurse William Tennent High Sch. Marching Band Assn., Warminster, 1990—. Mem. Assn. Women's Health, Obstet. and Neonatal Nursing, Nurses Assn. Tchr. Effectiveness (treas. 1991-94), Thomas Jefferson U. Hosp. Sch. Nursing Alumni Assn., Sigma Theta Tau. Home: 195 Belair Rd Warminster PA 18974-3933 Office: Frankford Hosp Sch of Nursing 4918 Penn St Philadelphia PA 19124

BAUER, THEODORE JAMES, physician; b. Iowa City, Nov. 18, 1909; s. Charles A. and Anna (Braun) B.; m. Helen Mattes, Sept. 1, 1938; children: Jane Helen Bauer Gray, Virginia Ann Bauer Biedron, Martha Jean Bauer. MD, U. Iowa, 1933, BS, 1934. Diplomate Am. Bd. Preventive Medicine and Pub. Health. Intern U.S. Marine Hosp., N.Y., 1933-34; resident in internal medicine U.S. Marine Hosp., Chgo., 1934-36; spl. tng. USPHS, 1936-37; regional cons. venereal disease control Dist. 5, San Francisco, 1938-41; veneral disease control officer Dist. 5, Kansas City, 1941-42; chief nat. div. venereal disease Washington, 1948-53; med. officer in charge Communicable Disease Ctr., Altanta, 1953-56; asst. surgeon gen., dep. chief Bur. State Svcs., Washington, 1956-60; chief Bur. State Services, 1960-62; veneral disease control officer Chgo. Health Dept.; also med. officer charge Chgo. Intensive Treatment Ctr., 1942-48; med. dir. Becton, Dickinson and Co., 1962-67, sr. v.p. rsch. and med. affairs, 1967-75, dir., 1965-85, cons., 1975—; dir. Med. Rsch. Mgmt. Group Inc., 1985-89; assoc. prof. bacteriology and immunology Emory U., 1954-58; mem. adv. com. Inst. Agrl. Medicine U. Iowa, 1954-72; spl. lectr. on venereal diseases Georgetown U. Sch. Medicine, Washington, Calif. U., Northwestern U.; mem. expert com. on venereal infections, trepinematoses WHO; bd. dirs. Nat. Council, 1972-76; mem. Surgeon Gen.'s Adv. Com. on Community Health Services, Adv. Council on the Chronic Sick of N.J., N.J. Health Care Adminstrn. Bd., 1975-86. Editor: Jour. Venereal Disease Info; mem. editorial bd.: Am. Jour. Syphilis, Gonorrhea and Other Venereal Diseases. Mem. gov's. adv. council Chronic Sick of N.J. Recipient Disting. Service award USPHS, 1962, Disting. Service medal Pub. Health Service, Dept. Health, Edn., Welfare, 1962. Fellow Am. Pub. Health Assn. (chmn. program area com. drugs), Am. Colls. Physicians; mem. AMA, Am. Veneral Disease Assn., Am. Soc. Hygiene Assn. (internat. adv. com.), Pharm. Mfrs. Assn. (med. sect.), Am. Venereal Disease Assn. (Disting. Achievement award 1934-35), Scientific Research Soc. Am. (pres. Communicable Disease Ctr. Br. 1954), Am. Social Health Assn. (bd. dirs.), Nat. Adv. Community Health Com., Bergen County Tuberculosis and Health Assn. (bd. dirs.), U.S.-Mex. Border Pub. Health Assn. (hon. life), Assn. Mil. Surgeons U.S., Bergen County Med. Soc., Med. Assn. N.J., Sigma Xi. Democrat. Roman Catholic. Home and Office: 451 Weymouth Dr Wyckoff NJ 07481-1216

BAUER, TIMOTHY DANIEL, physician assistant; b. St. Paul, Aug. 12, 1947; s. Daniel Adolph and Catherine Carola (Bauman) B.; m. Joyce Ann Schultz, Oct. 12, 1969; children: Tracy, Timothy Jr. Student, U. N.D., 1970-73; BA, Eckerd Coll., 1983; MPH/Allied Health Scis., Pacific Western U., 1987; postgrad., U.S. Mil. Health Scis. Sch., 1987-90. Lic. physician asst., Wis., nursing home adminstr., Wis. Physician asst. USPHS/Indian Health Svc., Sisseton, S.D., 1972-75, Aniak, Alaska, 1972-75; physician asst. Dept. Vets. Affairs Med. Ctr., Tomah, Wis., 1975-92; physician asst. geriatric rsch., ednl and clin. ctr. Dept. Vets. Affairs Med. Ctr., Mpls., 1992—; region # 4 rep., chmn. Vets. Affairs Ctrl. Office, chief med. dir. PA Adv. Group, 1991—; mem. med. examiners bd. com. on certification of postgrad. edn. State Med. Soc. Wis., 1979-90. Mem. Aniak Dist. Sch. Bd., 1974, mem. Aniak City Coun., 1974; mem. R&D com. Wis. chpt. Am. Coll. Nursing Home Adminstrs., 1981. With USN, 1966-70, lt. USNR, 1986-94. Mem. Nat. Commn. on Cert. of Physician Assts. (cert.), Am. Acad. Physician Assts. (mem. Vets. Caucus), Vets. Affairs Physician Assts. Assn. (regional 4 bd. dirs. 1980-90, chmn. constitution and bylaws com. 1988-94, chief del. to Am. Acad. Physician Assts. 1989-93, pres.-elect 1991-92, pres. 1993-94), Wis. Acad. Physician Assts. (pres. 1979-80), Assn. Naval Physician Assts. (res. liaison bd. dirs. 1991-92), U.S. Naval Inst., Assn. Mil. Surgeons U.S., Naval Res. Assn., VFW, DAV, KC (sec. 1981, comptr. 1982, dep. grand knight 1982, grand knight 1983, 4th degree), St. Croix Valley Rod and Gun Club, Game Unltd. Hunting Club. Home: 739 Aldro Rd Hudson WI 54016 Office: Dept Vets Affairs 1 Veterans Rd 11-G Minneapolis MN 55417

BAUGH, BRADFORD HAMILTON, occupational and environmental health advisor; b. Seattle, Jan. 18, 1943; s. Sheppard McReynolds and Naomi Emma (Hugel) B.; m. Karyl Eileen Onstad, June 8, 1974; children: Taggart, Darin, Robyn, Patrick, Tracy. BS in Zoology, BS in Psychology, Wash. State U., 1972; MS in Biology, Ea. Wash. State U., 1976, BSN, 1983, MS in devel. psychology, 1992; postgrad., Kennedy-Western U., 1986—. Cert. med. lab. tech., Community Health Nurse. Environ. chemist, research and devel. USCG, Groton, Conn., 1975-76; occupational health advisor USCG, Alameda, Calif., 1983—; adj. prof. Whitworth Coll., Spokane, Wash., 1973-82; counselor Morning Star Ranch, Spokane, 1982-83; instr. Chapman Coll., Alameda, 1983—; indsl. hygienist, fire chief VA, American Lake, Wash., 1986-87; child mental health specialist Tamarack Ctr., Spokane, Wash., 1987-92; occupational and environ. health cons., Nine Mile Falls, Wash., 1987—; indsl. hygienist Wash. State U., Pullman, 1990-93; environ. protection specialist no. cluster USDA Agr. Rsch. Svc., Pullman, 1993—. With USCGR, 1961-93. Mem. Am. Med. Techs., Am. Indsl. Hygiene Assn., Am. Pub. Health Assn., Nat. Environ. Health Assoc., Am. Conf. of Gov. Indsl. Hygienists World Safety Orgn. Mormon. Home: PO Box 209 Nine Mile Falls WA 99026-0209 Office: USDA Agr Rsch Svc Pullman WA 99164-6216

BAUM, CAROL GROSSMAN, physician; b. N.Y.C., June 14, 1958; d. Jacob Joseph and Anita Pearl (Serbrinsky) Grossman; m. Michael Seth Baum, June 16, 1985; 1 child, Daniel Joseph. BS, CCNY, 1979; MD, NYU, 1983. Diplomate Nat. Bd. Med. Examiners, Am. Bd. Internal Medicine, Am. Bd. Allergy & Immunology. Resident in internal medicine St. Luke's Hosp., N.Y.C., 1983-86; fellow in allergy & clin. immunology Cornell U. Med. Coll., N.Y.C., 1986-88; pvt. practice internal medicine, allergy-clin. immunology N.Y.C., 1988-90; asst. attending allergy clinic N.Y. Hosp., N.Y.C., 1988—; dir. allergy clinic St. Luke's Hosp., N.Y.C., 1989-90 William F. Ryan Community Health Ctr., 1990; dir. dept. allergy and clin. immunology N.E. Permanente Med. Group, White Plains, N.Y., Stamford, Conn., 1990—; clin. instr. medicine, Cornell U. Med. Coll., N.Y.C.; asst. attending N.Y. Hosp., White Plains Hosp. Ctr., St. Agnes Hosp.; lectr., presenter in field. Contbr. articles to profl. jours. Fellow ACP, Am. Acad. Allergy, Asthma and Immunology; mem. AMA, Am. Med. Women's Assn., Westchester Med. Soc., N.Y. Acad. Scis., Am. Coll. Physician Execs., Phi Beta Kappa, Sigma Xi. Office: N E Permanente Med Group 210 Westchester Ave White Plains NY 10604-2914 also: NE Permanente Med Group 1266 E Main St Stamford CT 06901

BAUM, HOWARD BARRY, physician; b. Passaic, N.J., Feb. 14, 1952; s. Samuel and Ethel (Stuhlbach) B.; m. Carolyn Frey, Sept. 7, 1986; children: Eric, Evan. AB summa cum laude, Dartmouth Coll., 1973; MD, Cornell U. Med. Coll., 1977. Diplomate Am. Bd. Internal Medicine and Gastroenterology. Resident internal medicine Dartmouth-Hitchcock Med. Ctr., Hanover, N.H., 1977-80; fellow in gastroenterology The N.Y. Hosp., Cornell Med. Ctr., N.Y.C., 1980-82; ptnr. Passaic (N.J.) Med. Assocs., PA, 1982—; trustee Passaic Valley Profl. Stds. Rev. Orgn., 1983-84; trustee Passaic Beth Israel Hosp., 1987—, vice chmn. bd. trustees; dept. chief gastroenterology Passaic Beth Israel Hosp., Gen. Hosp. Ctr. at Passaic, 1990-91; governing body Region One Health Planning Consortium, N.J., 1991—. Co-founder Doctors Against Misusing Passaic's Environ. Resources, 1985; trustee Jewish Fedn. Greater Clifton, Passaic, 1987—; mem. steering com. PASS Plan, Passaic County, 1988—; v.p. Assn. Jewish Fedns. N.J., 1990-93. Recipient Arthur Palmer prize Cornell Med. Coll., 1977; named Disting. Health Profl. United Passaic Orgn., 1987. Fellow ACP; mem. AMA, Passaic County Med. Soc. (pres. 1993-95, v.p. 1991-92), N.J. Med. Soc., N.J. Gastroenterology Soc., Phi Beta Kappa. Office: Passaic Med Assocs 540 Broadway Passaic NJ 07055-1956

BAUM, JOSEPH HERMAN, retired biomedical educator; b. Chgo., Sept. 9, 1927; s. Herman and Esther (Rosenzweig) B.; m. Mireille Josephe Jomain, Mar. 23, 1970 (dec. 1978); stepchildren: Eric Morin, Arthur Morin; m. Susan Harding, Apr. 10, 1994; stepchildren: L. Stephanie Promish, Gordon MacDonald Promish. BS, Roosevelt U., 1953; PhD, Northwestern U., 1962. Instr. pathology Northwestern U., Chgo., 1962-63, asst. prof. pathology, 1963-68; assoc. prof. pathology Temple U., Phila., 1968-80, asst. dean grad. sch., 1972-78, prof. pathology, 1981-90, prof. emeritus, 1990—, asst. dean Sch. Medicine, 1986-89, acting dean Sch. Medicine, 1989-90, exec. cabinet, 1989-90; cons. in field. Committeeman Boy Scouts Am., Hatboro, Pa., 1974-78; bd. govs. St. Christopher's Hosp. for Children, Phila., 1989-90, Temple U. Hosp., 1989-90; chmn. South Ga. cmty. svc. bd. Ga. State Mental Health, Retardation, Substance Abuse Delivery System, 1994-96. With U.S. Army, 1944, col. inf. AUS, ret. Decorated Meritorious Svc. medal U.S. Army; recipient Lindback award for disting. tchg. C. & M. Lindback Found., 1981, Golden Apple award Student AMA, 1987. Mem. AAAS, Am. Soc. Cell Biology, Am. Soc. Investigative Pathology, Multidiscipline Edn. in Health Scis. (founding mem.), Internat. Acad. Pathology. Home: PO Box 5202 Quitman GA 31643-5202

BAUM, JULES LEONARD, ophthalmologist, educator; b. N.Y.C., Mar. 13, 1931; children from previous marriage: Jeffrey Stuart, Alison Rachel; m. Laura Klabin, 1990. AB, Dartmouth Coll., 1952; MD, Tufts U., 1956. NIH fellow in research in ophthalmology N.Y. U., 1958-59, researcher in ophthalmology, 1961-62; asst. prof. N.Y. U. (Med. Sch.), 1965-68; resident in ophthalmology Bellevue Hosp., N.Y.C., 1962-64; mem. faculty Tufts U. Med. Sch., 1968—, prof. ophthalmology, 1974-91; sr. surgeon New Eng. Med. Center Hosp., Boston, 1973-91; res. prof. Tufts U. Med. Sch., 1991—. Assoc. editor Ophthalmic Lit., 1967-85; mem. editl. bd. Investigative Ophthalmology and Vision Sci., 1978-82, Survey of Ophthalmology, 1970-79, Am. Jour. Ophthalmology, 1985-91, Ophthalmic Surgery, 1985-95, Cornea Jour., 1989—; contbr. articles to profl. jours. Served to capt. M.C. AUS, 1959-61. Recipient William Warner Hoppin award N.Y. Acad. Medicine; Alcon Rsch. Inst. award, 1991; NIH fellow, 1958-59, 64-65; Nat. Eye Inst. grantee. Fellow Royal Coll. Ophthalmologists; mem. Am. Acad. Ophthalmology (honor award 1979, sr. honor award 1990), Assn. Rsch. in Vision and Ophthalmology (trustee 1981-86, v.p. 1986), Castroviejo Soc. (exec. sec., treas. 1979-87, v.p. 1987-89, pres. 1989-91), Mass. Ophthalmology Soc. (sec. 1974-76), Ocular Microbiology Immunology Group (pres. 1990-91), Conferie des Chevaliers du Tastevin, Chaine des Rotisseur, Internat. Wine and Food Soc., Phi Beta Kappa. Jewish. Office: 1244 Boylston St Chestnut Hill MA 02167-2115 also: 16 Webster St Brookline MA 02146-4938

BAUM, STANLEY, radiologist, educator; b. N.Y.C., Dec. 26, 1929; s. Herman and Fannie (Harris) B.; m. Jeanne Masch, June 29, 1958; children: Richard Arthur, Laura Dianne, Carol Lisa. B.A., N.Y. U., 1951; M.D., U. Utrecht, Holland, 1957. Intern Kings County Hosp., N.Y.C., 1957-58; resident in radiology Grad. Hosp., U. Pa., Phila., 1958-61; trainee Nat. Cancer Inst., Bethesda, Md., 1958-61; fellow cardiovascular radiology Stanford (Calif.) U., 1961-62; instr. radiology U. Pa., Phila., 1962-63; asst. prof. U. Pa., 1963-66, assoc. prof., 1966-70, prof., 1970—, Eugene P. Pendergrass prof. radiology, 1977—, chmn. dept. radiology, 1975—; chmn. med. bd. Hosp. of U. Pa., 1983-86; chief cardiovascular radiology Mass. Gen. Hosp., Boston, 1971-75; prof. radiology Harvard Med. Sch., Boston, 1971-75; cons. Radiation Effects Research Found., Hiroshima, Japan, 1975—; cardiovascular rev. bd. Am. Heart Assn., 1970—. Editorial bd.: Investigative Radiology, 1970-80, New Eng. Jour. Medicine, 1975-76, Radiology, 1975—, Gastrointestinal Radiology, 1975-79, Jour. Continuing Edn, 1978-80, Postgrad. Radiology, 1980—. Fellow Am. Coll. Radiology, Am. Coll. Cardiology; mem. Inst. Medicine Nat. Acad. Sci., Soc. Cardiovascular Radiology (pres. 1974-76), Soc. Chmn. Acad. Radiology Depts. (pres. elect 1985-86, pres. 1986). Home: 401 W Moreland Ave Philadelphia PA 19118-4207 Office: U Pa 3400 Spruce St Philadelphia PA 19104*

BAUMAN, JONATHAN HUGH, psychiatrist; b. Bklyn., June 28, 1948; s. Morris and Rachel (Fialkoff) B.; m. Carol Ann Weiss, Dec. 22, 1973; children: Emily, Jacob. BA, U. Rochester, 1970; MD, Georgetown U., 1974. Diplomate Am. Bd. Psychiatry and Neurology, Am. Bd. Adolescent Psychiatry, Am. Bd. Med. Examiners. Resident U. Va. Hosp., Charlottesville, 1974-75, Georgetown U. Hosp., Washington, 1975-77; acting clin. dir. Upper Montgomery Community Mental Health Ctr., Olney, Md., 1977-79, cons. psychiatrist, 1977-84; clin. asst. prof. Georgetown U. Sch. of Medicine, Washington, 1977-84; med. staff Montgomery Gen. Hosp., Olney, 1977-84; staff psychiatrist Four Winds Hosp., Katonah, N.Y., 1984-85, program dir., 1985-92; med. dir., 1992—; clin. assoc. prof. Albert Einstein Coll. Medicine, N.Y.C., 1994—. Mem. Am. Psychiat. Assn. Jewish. Office: Four Winds Hosp 800 Cross River Rd Katonah NY 10536-9694

BAUMAN, MARK LEE, podiatrist; b. Bronx, N.Y., Dec. 14, 1952; s. Jerrold Paul and Helen M. (Goldin) B.; m. Terri Ann Maurer, Aug. 31, 1974; children: Erica, Jaime. BS, CCNY, 1973; MS, C.W. Post Coll., 1974; D of Podiatric Medicine, Pa. Coll. Podiatric Medicine, 1978. Diplomate Am. Bd. Podiatric Surgery. Podiatry resident James C. Giuffre Med. Ctr., Phila., 1978-80; pres., podiatrist Wexford Leas Podiatry Assocs., Cherry Hill, N.J., 1980—; panel cons. Mediq Rev. Svcs., Inc., Mt. Laurel, N.J., 1991—; med. opinion cons. to ins. cos., 1989—. Contbr. articles to profl. jours.; patentee in field. Pres. Men's Club Congregation Beth Jacob-Beth Israel, Merchantville, N.H., 1980-81; chmn. ritual com. Congregation Beth Tikvah, Marlton, N.J., 1989-92, v.p. ritual and adult edn., 1992-96. Fellow Am. Coll. Foot Surgeons; mem. Am. Podiatric Med. Assn. Democrat. Jewish. Office: Wexfordleas Podiatry Assocs 1949 Marlton Pike E Ste 7 Cherry Hill NJ 08003-2145

BAUMAN, ROBERT WARREN, JR., biology educator; b. Austin, Tex., June 9, 1953; s. Robert Warren and Frances E. (Schneider) B.; m. Michelle Cecilia Nugent, Dec. 19, 1982. BA in Biology, U. Tex., 1975, MA in Botany, 1978; PhD in Biology, Stanford U., 1986. Cert. secondary sch. sci. tchr., Tex. Tchr. Austin Independent Sch. Dist., 1975-77, Amarillo (Tex.) Independent Sch. Dist., 1978-79; dir. edn., dir. planetarium Don Harrington Discovery Ctr., Amarillo, 1986-88; asst. prof. biology Amarillo Coll., 1988-91, assoc. prof. biology, 1991-94; prof. biology, 1994—. Pres. Sonship Ministries, Inc., Amarillo, 1983—; mem. Eldon Durrett Scholarship Com., Amarillo, 1986; asst. dir. High Plains Regional Sci. Fair, Amarillo, 1989, dir. 1990. Mem. Amarillo C. of C. (edn. com. 1986-88). Office: Amarillo Coll PO Box 447 Amarillo TX 79178-0001

BAUMAN, SANDRA SPIEGEL, nurse practitioner, mental health counselor; b. N.Y.C., June 30, 1949; d. Siegmund and Ruth (Josias) S.; student Boston U., 1967-70; B.S. in Nursing, Adelphi U., 1971, postgrad., 1973-74; M.S. in Community Counseling, Barry Coll., 1981; postgrad. Fla. Atlantic U./Fla. Internat. U., 1982—, Gestalt Inst. Miami, 1982—; clin. specialist psychiat./mental health; m. H. Lee Bauman, Nov. 3, 1978 (div.); 1 child, Brandon Spiegel; m. P.McGrath, 1991. Staff nurse educator obstetrics Albert Einstein Hosp., N.Y.C., 1971-72, head nurse newborn nurseries, 1973-74; asst. instr. maternity nursing St. Johns Riverside Hosp., 1972-73; head nurse obstetrics and nurseries, high risk nursery Mt. Sinai Hosp., Miami Beach, Fla., 1974-78; clin. nursing supr., div. pediatrics Jackson Meml. Hosp., Miami, 1978, coordinator div. clin. edn., 1978-81, quality assurance coordinator Maternal-Child Hosp. Center, 1979-81, perinatal coordinator, 1980-81, also core nursing mem. child protection team, 1979-81, asst. adminstr. ob-gyn, 1981-82; adminstr. Meadowbrook Med. Center, Inc., Dania, Fla., 1982—; pvt. practice Psychotherapy, 1983—; asst. adminstr. nursing Miami Gen. Hosp., 1985, assoc. adminstr. pvt. care services, 1985—; asst. prof. Sch. Nursing, Fla. Internat. U., North Miami, 1982-84, coordinator child bearing and child rearing courses, 1982-84; mem. Fla. Bd. Nursing, 1979-85, vice chmn., 1981-82, chmn., 1982-85; CPR instr., 1978; dir. nursing HCA Grant Ctr. Hosp., Miami, 1986-89, asst. adminstr. Dr's Hosp., 1990-91; pvt. practice, 1991—; cons. State Fla., 1992-95; interim dir. nursing Charter Hosp., Miami, 1995-96; surveyor Fla. Correctional Med. Authority, 1996. Mem. Am. Nurses Assn. (regional editor 1980—), Fla. Nurses Assn., Fla. Soc. Nurse Execs., Fla. Nursing Adminstrn. Assn., Fla. Hosp. Assn., Fla. Nursing Adminstrn. Soc., Sigma Theta Tau. Contbr. articles to RN mag., Fla. Nursing News, Fla. Nurses Assn. Newsletter and Nursing Mgmt. Office: 7600 SW 57th Ct # 309 South Miami FL 33143-5404

BAUMAN, WILLIAM ALLEN, pediatrician, educator; b. N.Y.C., Nov. 23, 1923; s. Louis and Stella (Kraus) B.; m. Joan Carlsen, June 28, 1952; children—William Carlsen, Phillip Allen, Pamela Joan. Student Harvard U., 1942-43, 46; M.D., Columbia U., 1947, postgrad. in biostats. Sch. Pub. Health, 1960-63. Intern L.I. div. Kings County Hosp., Bklyn., 1947-48; resident Babies Hosp., N.Y.C., 1948-50; dir. pediatric clinic Vanderbilt Clinic, N.Y.C., 1954-65; practice medicine specializing in pediatrics, N.Y.C., 1953-75; dir. med. data processing Presbyn. Hosp., N.Y.C., 1966-74, assoc. attending pediatrician, 1973-75, emeritus staff, 1994—; v.p. med. adminstrv. services Group Health Inc., N.Y.C., 1974-77; chmn. bd. govs. Hillcrest Gen. Hosp.-Group Health Inc., 1975-79, attending pediatrician, 1975-79; sr. v.p. Health Services Group Health Inc., 1977-79; v.p. med. affairs Danbury Hosp., Conn., 1979-90; assoc. clin. prof. pediatrics Columbia U., 1973—; mem. med. bd. Maternity Ctr. Assn., 1969-95; chmn. faculty-student adv. bd. P&S Club, Coll. Physicians and Surgeons, Columbia U., 1970-90; chmn. com. on data processing N.Y. County Health Rev. Orgn., 1976-79. Contbr. articles to profl. jours. Served with M.C., USAF 1951-52. Fellow Am. Coll. Med. Informatics, N.Y. Acad. Medicine; mem. Am. Acad. Pediatrics, New York County Med. Soc., AMA, Med. Soc. State N.Y., (chmn. com. info. tech. in medicine 1967-93), Assn. Ambulatory Pediatrics, Assn. Computing Machinery, Soc. Computer Medicine (bd. dirs.), Bioengring. Inst., Am. Soc. Info. Scis., N.Y. Acad. Scis., N.Y. State Assn. Professions, Am. Assn. Med. Systems and Informatics (pres. 1983). Home and Office: 667 Heritage Hills Somers NY 10589-1900

BAUMANN, CAROL KAY, clinical nurse specialist; b. Summersville, Mo., Dec. 12, 1946; d. Vern Underwood and Jean E. (Lay) Hines; children: Joell Christine, Richard Douglas. Diploma, Barnes Hosp., St. Louis, 1967; BS in Nursing, St. Louis U., 1981, MS in Nursing Rsch., 1989. Cert. operating rm. nurse, RN 1st asst. Staff nurse Barnes Hosp., St. Louis, 1967-68, head nurse neurosurgery, 1969-71; staff nurse St. John's Mercy Hosp., St. Louis, 1980-81, neurosurgery specialty nurse, 1981-85; surgery edn. coord. Mo. Bapt. Med. Ctr., St. Louis, 1985-90; asst. head nurse neuro/ophthalmology oper. rm. Barnes Hosp., St. Louis, 1990-92; clin. nurse specialist St. Louis U. Med. Ctr., 1992—; speaker in field. Contbr. articles to profl. jours. Mem. Assn. Oper. Rm. Nurses, Am. Assn. Neurosci. Nurses (Gateway City chpt. 1988—, charter sec.-treas. 1988-89, pres. 1989-91), Am. Assn. Neurol. Surgeons (assoc.), Sigma Theta Tau. Home: 14515 Coeur Dalene Ct Chesterfield MO 63017-2401

BAUMANN, GREGORY WILLIAM, physician, consultant; b. Detroit, June 20, 1947; s. Alfred Louis Baumann and Marian (Bartholomew) Martens. BS, U. Mich., 1968, MD cum laude, 1972, MA in Telecom. Arts, 1993. Diplomate Am. Bd. Emergency Medicine. Intern Albert Einstein Coll. Medicine, Bronx Mcpl. Dept. Surgery, 1972-73; resident in neurology U. Mich., 1973-74; staff physician Foote Hosp., Jackson, Mich., 1974—, chmn. emergency med. dept., 1979-89, med. dir. emergency med. svcs. project, 1981-86, dir. ambulatory care, 1982-90; pres. Abcedarian Prodns., Inc., Ann Arbor, Mich.; cons. emergency med. svcs., Jackson, 1982—; mem. adv. life support tech. com. Mich. Dept. Pub. Health, Lansing, 1985-87; med. dir. Mich. Internat. Speedway, Bklyn., 1986—; chief med. examiner Jackson County, 1986-88; med. dir. Cleve. Indy Car Grand Prix. Bd. dirs. Hospice of Jackson, 1984-88; med. dir. Nazareth (Pa.) Speedway, 1987—, Calif. Speedway, 1996—. Recipient Merit award March of Dimes, 1970; rsch. grantee U. Mich. Med. Sch., 1972. Mem. AMA, Mich. Med. Soc., Jackson County Med. Soc., Kappa Tau Alpha. Lutheran. Office: PO Box 1086 Ann Arbor MI 48106-1086

BAUMANN, HAROLD C., optometrist; b. Phila., May 8, 1921; s. Jacob and Elizabeth (Largemann) B.; m. Mildred E. Robin, May 27, 1944; children: Roger M., Barbara L., John R., Nancy R. OD, Pa. State Coll. Optometry, 1943. Optometrist Frank Tamarkin, O.D., York, Pa., 1945-46; pvt. practice optometrist Pottstown, Pa., 1946—. Bd. mem. Creative Health Svcs., Pottstown, 1965—, chmn. bd. dirs., 1990-91. Capt. U.S. Army Air Corps, 1942-45, Pa. Nat. Guard, 1949-55. Mem. Berks County Optometric Soc. (pres.), Rotary Club Pottstown (pres. dist. 7430 1968-69, gov. dist. 7430 1987-88). Home: 917 Brookside Rd Pottstown PA 19464 Office: 1630 E High St Pottstown PA 19464

BAUMANN, PIERRE KONRAD, biochemist, psychopharmacologist, educator; b. Lucerne, Switzerland, Mar. 16, 1944; s. Konrad O. and Kaethe (Schürhoff) B.; m. Marie-Hélène Verweyen-Thenagels, May 30, 1968; children: Kathrin, André. Dipl. in chemistry, U. Basle, Switzerland, 1968; dr rer nat., Max Planck Inst. Psychiatry, Munich, 1974; dipl. clin. pharmacology, Swiss Soc. Clin. Pharmacology, 1988. Postdoctoral fellow State Rsch. Hosp., Galesburg, Ill., 1972; head biochemistry and clin. psychopharmacology unit Univ. Adult Psychiatry Dept., Prilly-Lausanne, Switzerland, 1972—; lectr. U. Lausanne, 1980; sec. Swiss Soc. Biol. Psychiatry, 1981-87; v.p. Soc. Neuropsychopharm., Nurenberg, Germany, 1996—. Editor: Biologische Psychiatrie der Gegenwart, 1992, Alpha-Acid Glycoprotein: Genetics, Biochemistry, Physiological Functions and Pharmacology, 1989, Transport Mechanisms of Tryptophan in Blood Cells, Nerve Cells, and at the Blood-Brain Barrier, 1978; contbr. articles to profl. jours. Home: CH 1302 Vufflens-la-Ville Switzerland Office: Dept U Psychiatry Adulte, Route de Cery, Ch-1008 Lausanne Switzerland

BAUMANN, ROBERT JAY, child neurology educator; b. Chgo., Oct. 22, 1940; s. Stephen S. and Evelyn (Hellerstein) B.; m. Judith Kravitz, Oct. 1964; children: Barbara, Stephen, Lauren. BS magna cum laude, Tufts U., 1961; MD, Western Res. U., 1964. Diplomate Am. Bd. Psychiatry and Neurology (examiner 1976—). Intern, resident in pediatrics and neurology U. Chgo. Hosps., 1965-69, fellow in child neurology, 1971-72; asst. prof. neurology U. Ky., Lexington, 1972-78, assoc. prof., 1987-92, prof., 1992—, assoc. prof. rehab., 1987—, assoc. prof. pediatrics, 1989-92, prof., 1992—, dir. regional neurology program, 1972—, dir. child neurology program, 1979—; cons. U.S. Commn. for Control Epilepsy, Washington, 1976; reviewer, cons. Nat. Inst. Neurol. Disease and Stroke, Bethesda, Md., 1979—; neuroepidemiology cons. Ky.-Ecuador Ptnrs. of Ams., Quito, 1987-91, Am. Acad. Pediatrics, 1991—, Instituto de Investigaciones, Facultad de Ciencias Medicas, U. Ctrl. Del Ecuador, Quito. Chmn. United Jewish Appeal Campaign, Lexington, 1986-87; v.p. Cen. Ky. Jewish Fedn., Lexington, 1988-92. Capt. M.C., USAF, 1969-71. Mem. Child Neurology Soc., Am. Acad. Neurology, Am. Acad. Pediatrics (neuroepidemiologic cons. 1992—), Am. Coll. Epidemiology, Soc. for Epidemiologic Rsch., Profs. Child Neurology (bd. dirs. 1988-92). Office: U Ky Dept Neurology Ky Clinic 800 Rose St Lexington KY 40536-0284

BAUMGARTEN, STEPHEN ROBERT, physician, urologist; b. Bklyn., Jan. 18, 1945; s. Jack Milton and Diane (Perlman) B.; m. Anne Glanzman, Apr. 27, 1990; children: Kelly Elizabeth, Stephen Paul, Amy. BA, Queens Coll., 1966; MD, SUNY, Bklyn., 1970. Diplomate Am. Bd. Urology. Surg. intern Maimonides Med. Ctr., Bklyn., 1970-72, resident in urology, 1974-77; pvt. practice in urology Bklyn., 1977—; asst. teaching attending Maimonides Hosp. and Coney Island Hosp., Bklyn., 1977-87; clin. instr. urology N.Y. Hosp. Cornell Med. Sch., N.Y.C., 1988—. Lt. comdr. USN, 1972-74. Fellow ACS; mem. N.Y. State Med. Soc., Am. Fertility Soc., Bklyn. L.I. Urologic Assn. Office: 2301 Ocean Ave Brooklyn NY 11229

BAUMGARTNER, JOHANN FRANZ, radiochemistry scientist, educator; b. Munich, May 3, 1929. Diploma in chemistry, Tech. U., Munich, 1954, D in Natural Sci., 1956. Prof. U. Heidelberg, Fed. Republic of Germany, 1964-76, U. Mainz, Fed. Republic of Germany, 1976-79, Tech. U., Munich, 1980—; dir. Inst. Heisse Chemie Kernforschungszentrum, Karlsruhe, Fed. republic of Germany, 1964-79. Recipient Otto Hahn prize City of Frankfurt, Fed. Republic of Germany, 1989. Mem. Acad. Sci. Lit. (assoc.). Office: Tech U, Dept of Chemistry, 85748 Munich Germany

BAUMLER, JEAN ANN, nurse; b. West Union, Iowa, Apr. 22, 1951; d. Melvin John and Rita Theresa (Lansing) Baumler; B.S.N., Viterbo Coll., LaCrosse, Wis., 1973; M.S., San Jose (Calif.) State U., 1980. RN, Hawaii; cert. gerontol. nurse., ANCC, gerontol. nurse practitioner, San Jose State U., arthritis self-help instr. Arthritis Found., Health supr. Camp Ehawee Scout Camp, LaCrosse, 1973; staff nurse, then asst. head nurse Letterman Army Med. Ctr., San Francisco, 1972-75; charge nurse Palo Alto (Calif.) VA Hosp., 1975-83, mem. inservice com. Extended Care Service, 1981-83; adult day health program coordinator Kuakini Med. Ctr., Honolulu, 1983-87, mem. various coms. 1984-87; quality assurance nurse analyst, Straub Clinic & Hosp., Honolulu, 1987-88, dir. nursing svcs. Lanalou Good Samaritan Ctr., 1988-91, on-call case mgmt., nurse cons. Community Long Term Care Svcs., 1987-91, on-call nurse Hospice Hawaii, 1991—. Treas. Fair Oaks 90 Homeowners Assn., 1980-83. Served with Nurse Corps, U.S. Army, 1972-75. Recipient Incentive award VA, 1978, Components Achievement medal USAR, 1981, First Lady's Outstanding Vol. award Hawaii, 1987. Mem. Geront. Soc. Am. (student rep. to biol. sci. sect. 1980), Hawaii Pacific Gerontol. Soc., Alzheimer's Disease & Related Disorders Assn. (founding mem., cons. San Jose and Menlo Pk, Calif. chpts. 1982-83, bd. dirs. Honolulu chpt., 1984-91, also chair edn. and pub. com. 1984-91, long term care com. 1987-92). Contbr. articles to profl. jours.; author book revs. and brochure. Home: 730 Makaleka Ave Apt 206 Honolulu HI 96816-1160 Office: Hospice Hawaii 445 Seaside Ave Ste 604 Honolulu HI 96815-2676

BAUMRIND, LYDIA, psychologist; b. Bklyn., May 5, 1954; d. Seymour Harvey and Rosalyn Muriel (Greenwald) B.; m. Gerry Oster; children: Michael, Samara. BA, Brandeis U., 1975; EdD, Boston U., 1983. Counselor Durg Rehab. Clinic, Mass. Gen. Hosp., Boston, 1975-77; therapist Project Turnabout, Weymouth, Mass., 1976-77, Mass. Gen. Hosp.-Boston Clinic, 1977-78; trainee, intern Greater Lawrence (Mass.) Mental Health Ctr., 1977-78; prof. Mass. Bay Community Coll., Wellseley, 1978-79; psychotherapist Ctr. for Human Behavior, Taunton, Mass., 1978-91; psychologist Brookline (Mass.) Ctr. for Adolescent and Adult Counseling, 1985—, also bd. dirs. Active sch. groups, Brookline, 1989—. Boston U. scholar, 1978. Mem. APA, Mass. Psychol. Assn., Nat. Register Health Providers in Psychology. Office: Brookline Ctr for Adolescent and Adult Counseling 1415 Beacon St # 324 Brookline MA 02146-4811

BAUMRIND, ROSALYN MURIEL GREENWALD, psychologist; b. N.Y.C., Aug. 3; d. Samuel Howard and Rose (Halpern) Greenwald; m. Seymour Harvey Baumrind, Dec. 31, 1949 (div. 1969); children: Martin Mark, Lydia, Sandra. BA magna cum laude, Bklyn. Coll., 1950, MA, 1954; PhD, Adelphi U., 1967. Cert. clin. psychologist, N.Y. High sch. tchr. N.Y.C. Bd. Edn., 1950-62, Hebrew Inst. L.I., 1957-62; psychologist, phys. medicine and rehab. Elmhurst Gen. Hosp., Queens, N.Y., 1964; asst. psychologist VA Hosp. Ft. Hamilton, Bklyn., 1965-67; asst. prof. sch. edn. Bklyn. Coll., CUNY, 1967-85; pvt. practice, supervision of psychotherapists N.Y.C., 1967—; cons. in field. Contbr. articles to profl. publs.; author TV tapes. Recipient award NIMH, 1963-65. Mem. Am. Acad Psychotherapists (exec. coun. 1984-90), Am. Psychol. Assn., Am. Group Psychol. Assn., Phi Beta Kappa. Home and Office: 141 E 37th St New York NY 10016-3117

BAUMSLAG, NAOMI, pediatrician; b. Republic of South Africa, July 19, 1936; d. Kalman and Braine (Ginsburg) B.; children: Victor, Barry, Ruth. MD, U. Witwatersrand, 1958; MPH, Johns Hopkins U., 1976. Intern, resident Baragwanath Hosp., Johannesburg, South Africa, 1959-62; dir. office internat. health nutrition divsn. Dept. Health and Human Svcs., Rockville, Md., 1979-84; pres. Womens Internat. Pub. Health Network, Bethesda, Md., 1987—; clin. prof. pediatrics Georgetown U. Med. Sch., Washington, 1987—. Author: A Women's Guide to Vaginal Yeast Infection, 1992, Mother and Child Health, 1994, Milk Money and Madness: The Battle for the Breast, 1995. Mem. adv. bd. La Leche League, Dearborn, Mich., World Alliance Breastfeeding Assns., Penang, Malaysia, 1994. Recipient Alumna award for Outstanding Alumnae Johns Hopkins Sch. Hygiene and Pub. Health, 1976. Mem. Am. Pub. Health Assn. (mem. governing coun. 1993-96), Nat. Coun. Internatal Health (mem. governing bd. 1990), UNICEF Nutrition Working Group. Home: 7100 Oak Forest Ln Bethesda MD 20817-2144 Office: Womens Internat Pub Health 7100 Oak Forest Ln Bethesda MD 20817-2144

BAUR, LEONARD HUBERT BERNHARD, cardiologist; b. Heerlen, Limburg, the Netherlands, Mar. 20, 1957; s. Leonard Johan Jozef and Lotte (Schulze) B.; m. Anna-Christina Huisintveld, Aug. 15, 1985; children: Onno, Renske, Joukje. MD, U. Limburg, Maastricht, the Netherlands, 1981. Cert. Ednl. Commn. for Fgn. Med. Grads. Resident internal medicine Juliana Hosp., Apeldoorn, the Netherlands, 1983-85; resident cardiology Univ. Hosp., Maastricht, 1985-88; cardiologist Univ. Hosp., Leiden, the Netherlands, 1988-90; cons. thoracic surgery Leiden, 1990-96; mgr. Heart Care Lab. Univ. Hosp., Leiden, 1996—; cons. thoracic surgery, Leiden, 1990—. Contbr. articles to profl. jours. Capt. Dutch mil., 1981-82. Roman Catholic. Office: Dept Cardiology AZL Bldg, 1C5P Rynsburgerweg 10, 2333 AA Leiden The Netherlands

BAURER, FREDERIC MARTIN, psychiatrist; b. N.Y.C., Sept. 28, 1957; s. Theodore and Blanche (Strow) B.; m. Sharon Pollak, Aug. 1, 1982; children: Elana Stevie, Danielle Toby, Talia Brooke. BA, Wesleyan U., Middletown, Conn., 1979; MD, Temple U., 1984. Diplomate Am. Bd. Psychiatry and Neurology, Am. Bd. Addiction Psychiatry. Intern Pa. Hosp., Phila., 1984-85; cons. project for homeless Catch, Inc., Phila., 1985-88; resident in psychiatry Inst. of Pa. Hosp., Phila., 1985-88; pvt. practice psychiatry Inst. of Pa. Hosp., 1988—; dir. Strecker Intensive Out-patient Program for Addictions, 1989—, Out-patient Addictions Treatment Svc., Phila., 1992—; psychiat. and addictions cons. Moss Rehab. Hosp., Phila., 1989-90; faculty psychoanalytic tng. program Phila. Psychoanalytic Inst., 1987-95, Phila. Psychotherapy tng. program; clin. assoc. psychiatry dept. psychiatry U. Pa. Recipient Adolescent Psychiatry award, Inst. Pa. Hosp., 1988. Mem. AMA, Am. Psychiat. Assn., Am. Psychoanalytic Assn., Am. Acad. Addiction Psychiatry, Phila. Psychoanalytic Soc. Democrat. Jewish. Office: Inst of Pa Hosp 111 N 49th St Philadelphia PA 19139-2718

BAUTISTA, ABRAHAM PARANA, immunologist; b. Davao, Philippines, Mar. 15, 1952; s. Eufronio Bernardo and Loreto (Parana) B. BS in Biology, Far Eastern U., Manila, Philippines, 1972; Diploma in Microbiology, U. Tokyo, 1978; MS, Aberdeen (Scotland) U., 1981, PhD in Immunology, 1984. Sr. rschr. lectr. U. Santo Tomas, Manila, 1976-81; rsch. scholar U. Aberdeen, 1979-84; rsch. assoc. East Carolina U., Greenville, N.C., 1984-89; asst. prof. La. State U. Med. Ctr., New Orleans, 1989-93, assoc. prof., 1993—. Guest editor, reviewer Jour. Leukocyte Biology, 1988—, Circulatory Shock, 1991—, Am. Jour. Physiology, 1991—, Alcohol, 1992—, Alcoholism Clin. and Exptl. Rsch., 1992—, Hepatology, 1993—, Gastroenterology, 1994—, Biochem. Pharmacol, 1995—, Internat. Jour. Cancer, 1995—; contbr. articles to over 60 sci. articles to profl. jours. NIH-NIAAA grantee, 1995—; travel fellow Am. Assn. for Study Liver Disease, 1990; Internat. scholar Brit. Coun., 1979; recipient Rsch. award in Medicine, U. Aberdeen, 1981-84, F.I.R.S.T. award/Rsch. grantee NIH, 1991—; named Internat. UNESCO, 1978. Mem. AAAS, Am. Assn. Immunology, N.Y. Acad. Scis., Inst. of Biology, Soc. for Leukocyte Biology, Rsch. Soc. of Alcoholism, Sigma Xi. Home: 103 Hollow Rock Ct Slidell LA 70461-3422 Office: La State U Med Ctr 1901 Perdido St New Orleans LA 70112-1328

BAUTISTA, FLOROSA AGUINALDO, pediatrician; b. Binakayan, Philippines, July 10, 1928; parents Florentino Sarao Sr. and Rosalia Sañez (Aguinaldo) B. BS in Zoology, U. Philippines, Manila, 1948; MD, U. Santo Tomas, Philippines, 1954. Diplomate Philippine Bd. Pediatrics. Intern Lynn (Mass.) Hosp., 1955-56; resident in pediatrics Charles V. Chapin Hosp., R.I., 1956-58, Foxboro (Mass.) State Coll. Med. Ctr., 1958-59; from sr. resident to asst. chief of dept. pediatrics Vets. Meml. Med. Ctr., Quezon City, Philippines, 1960-73; cons. physician in pediatric and adolescent medicine Cavite (Philippines) Med. Ctr., 1973—, Our Savior Hosp., Rosario, Philippines, 1973—. Author: Applied Pediatrics, 1968. Pres. Pastoral Council Our Lady of Fatima Parish, 1975-86, Catholic Women's Club, 1975-78; core leader Aliw Ng Espiritu Santo Prayer Group, Binakayan, 1975—; pres. Yellow Brigade of Kawit, 1986-87; co-chmn. Mcpl. Food and Agrl. Council Kawit, 1987; mem. sem. bd. Diocese of Imus, 1987. Recipient Global Distinction award Internat. Biog. Rsch. Inst., 1995-96; named Outstanding Layman, Binakayan chpt. KC, 1975, Most Outstanding Woman of Cavite, Philippine Fedn. Women's Clubs, 1992. Fellow Philippine Pediatric Soc. (pres. So. Tagalog chpt. 1980-82, bd. dirs. 1983-94, adviser 1995—, recipient appreciation plaque 1978, appreciation awards 1979-82); mem. Cavite Med. Soc. (treas. 1982-83, appreciation cert. 1970), Maternal and Child Health Assn. Philippines, Philippine Med. Women's Assn. (v.p. 1976-78), U. Santo Tomas Alumni Assn. (trustee 1982—, Outstanding Thomasian award 1985), Binakayan Women's Club (pres. 1979—), Makabayang Kabitenyo, Yellow Brigade Inc., Barangayette. Roman Catholic. Home: Bautista Compound, Binkayan, Kawit Cavite 4104, The Philippines Office: Cavite Med Ctr, Cavite City The Philippines

BAUWIN, PHILIPPE, industrial pharmacist; b. Namur, Belgium, Apr. 23, 1949; s. Pierre and Annette (Germain) B.; m. Christine Heylen, Sept. 19, 1972 (div. 1986); children: Valerie, Laurent. Degree of pharmacy with honors, U. Louvain, Belgium, 1972. Cert. indsl. pharmacist Belgian Ministry Health. Sci. documentalist Schering, Brussels, 1972-74; lab. mgr. Bayer, Brussels, 1974-78; quality assurance mgr. Vygon, Frameries, Belgium, 1978-83; pharmacist in charge Lohmann, Liege, Belgium, 1983-85; cons. in good mfg. practices Brussels, 1985-86; lab. mgr. Sherwood, Verviers, Belgium, 1986-92, SciMed, Verviers, 1992-95, Boston Sci., Verviers, 1995—. Naturalist, mem. Cercle Marie Anne Libert, Malmedy, 1986—; treas. Pharmacy Students Cir., Louvain, 1971; humanitarian aid Rumanian Towns Orgn., Verviers, 1991. Lt. Belgian Army, 1973-74. Summer sch. scholar Danish Govt., 1970. Mem. Nat. Assn. Suppliers Med. Devices, Pharm. Sci. Soc. Home: Rue du Naimeux 26, B-4802 Verviers Belgium Office: Boston Sci Europe, Zone Ind Petit-Rechain, B-4800 Verviers Belgium

BAWDEN, DAVID GEORGE, psychiatrist; b. Madison, Wis., Sept. 18, 1949; s. George Thomas and Esther Katheryn (Price) B.; m. Jan Ellen Schiro, Oct. 2, 1976; children: Kathryn, Emily. BA, U. Wis., 1971, MD, 1976; MA, U. Chgo., 1976. Diplomate Am. Bd. Psychiatry Neurology; cert. adminstrv. psychiatry. Intern Jewish Gen. Hosp., Montreal, Can., 1976-77; resident Allan Meml. Inst., Montreal, 1977-78, Michael Reese Hosp., Chgo., 1978-79; pvt. practice Chgo., 1979-84; med. dir. Charter Barclay Hosp., Chgo., 1985-95; exec. med. dir. U. Health Systems, Chgo., 1995—. Recipient Michael Littner award Inst. for Psychoanalysis, Chgo., 1988. Mem. AMA, Am. Psychiatric Assn. Office: U Hosp 1116 N Kedzie Chicago IL 60651

BAWDEN, HERBERT PERRY, JR., psychologist; b. Passaic, N.J., Apr. 27, 1943; s. Herbert P. and Agnes R. (Weglowski) B.; m. Donna Jean Hunter, Aug. 28, 1965; children: Jeffrey Allen, Jennifer Lynn, Stephanie Ann. BA in Psychology, Tusculum Coll., 1965; MS in Organizational Psychology, U. Tenn., 1969. Lic. psychologist, Pa.; diplomate Am. Bd. Vocat. Experts. Dir. spl. svcs. Personnel Rsch. Ctr., Phila., 1969-70; dir. ops. Wittreich Assocs., Inc., Phila., 1971; dir. spl. svcs. Personnel Rsch. Ctr., Phila., 1971-73; dir., sr. rsch. assoc., rsch. assoc., cons. Job Trials Rsch. Ctr., Phila., 1974-79; sect. rsch. specialist Colonial Penn Group, Phila., 1979-80; rsch. assoc., cons. Pleasantville (N.Y.) Ednl. Supply Co., 1981-82; ptnr. Selection Systems Rsch., Southampton, Pa., 1979-83; mng. dir. Personnel Rsch. Ctr., Haverford, Pa., 1983-85; owner, pres. Personnel Rsch. Ctr., Horsham, Pa., 1985—; cons. Profl. Exam. Svc., N.Y.C., 1985-93. Mem. Am. Psychol. Assn., Soc. Indsl. and Orgn. Psychology, Internat. Career Assessment Network, Nat. Coun. Measurement in Edn., Eastern Psychol. Assn., Pa. Psychol. Assn., N.Am. Assn. Masters in Psychology, Pa. Assn. Masters in Psychology. Home: 555 Buckstone Dr Southampton PA 18966-3617 Office: Personnel Rsch Ctr 316 Easton Rd Ste C Horsham PA 19044-2562

BAWDEN, JAMES WYATT, dental educator, dental scientist; b. St. Louis, Apr. 23, 1930; s. Leland Miller and Rose Helen (Watt) B.; m. Merrie C. Teat, Oct. 11, 1988; children: Steven L., Michael J., Timothy C., David W. D.D.S., U. Iowa, 1954, M.S., 1960, Ph.D., 1961. Gen. practice dentistry Glenwood Springs, Colo., 1956-58; mem. faculty Sch. Dentistry, U. N.C., Chapel Hill, 1961—, prof., 1965-77, Alumni disting. prof., 1977—, dean, 1966-74; mem. faculty Sch. Dentistry, U. Lund, Malmo, Sweden, 1974-75; vis. prof. Karlinska Inst., Stockholom, 1992-93; mem. med.-dental staff N.C. Univ. Hosp., Chapel Hill, 1975—, cons. various coms. NIH, Bethesda, Md., 1979—; mem. oral medicine and biology study sect. Nat. Inst. Dental Health, Bethesda, 1982-83; mem., past pres. So. Conf. Dental Deans and Examiners, 1966-74. Contbr. articles to profl. jours., dental textbooks and studies. Chmn. bd. dirs. United Fund, Chapel Hill, 1972. Served to lt. Dental Corps, USN, 1954-56. Recipient Disting. Svc. award Dental Found. N.C., 1974; named Disting. Educator, U. Iowa, 1985; USPHS postdoctoral fellow U. Iowa, 1958-61, Fogarty sr. internat. fellow NIH, 1992-93; grantee W.K. Kellogg Found., 1976-79, Nat. Inst. Dental Rsch., 1963-66, 75—. Fellow AAAS, Am. Acad. Pediatric Dentistry; mem. ADA (coun. dental edn. 1971-74), Inst. Medicine of NAS, Am. Assn. for Dental Rsch. (pres. 1984-85), N.C. Dental Soc. (Disting. Svc. award), Am. Assn. Dental Schs. (chmn. coun. of deans 1972-73), Internat. Assn. for Dental Rsch., Omicron Kappa Upsilon, Delta Sigma Delta. Office: Univ NC Sch Dentistry Chapel Hill NC 27514*

BAXT, WILLIAM G., medical educator; b. Mar. 31, 1941. BA, Brown U., 1963; MD, Yale U., 1967. Diplomate Am. Bd. Internal Medicine, Am. Bd. Emergency Medicine. Intern Columbia-Presbyn. Hosp., N.Y.C., 1967-68, resident in internal medicine, 1970-71, fellow in hematology, 1971-73; from asst. prof. medicine to prof. clin. medicine & surgery U. Calif., San Diego, 1973-94; prof., chmn. dept. emergency medicine U. Pa. Med. Ctr., Phila., 1994—; rsch. biologist U. Calif., La Jolla, 1976-77; med. dir. life flight aeromed. program U. Calif. Med. Ctr., San Diego, 1980-89, assoc. dir. divsn. emergency med. svcs., 1978-80, dir. dept. emergency medicine, 1980-94; chief emergency medicine svcs. U. Pa. Med. Ctr., 1994—. Co-author: (with others) Cellular Modification and Genetic Transformation by Exogenous Nucleic Acids, 1973, The Leukemia Cell, 1979, Systems Approach to Emergency Medical Care, 1983, Trauma: The First Hour, 1985; mem. editl. bd. Emergency Care Quar., Annals of Emergency Medicine; contbr. articles to profl. jours. Surgeon USPHS, 1968-70. Leukemia Soc. Am. scholar, 1976; recipient Physicians Recognition award AMA, 1985, Best Oral Clin. Sci. Paper U. Assn. for Emergency Medicine, 1988, Best Oral Methodology Paper Soc. for Acad. Emergency Medicine, 1990. Mem. Nat. Acad. Scis., Soc. for Acad. Emergency Medicine, Phi Beta Kappa. Home: 245 Maple Hill Gladwyne PA 19035 Office: Univ Pa Med Ctr 7 Silverstein Pavilion 3400 Spruce St Philadelphia PA 19104-4283*

BAXTER, CAROL, infant and child mental health psychiatric nurse; b. Greenville, N.C., Dec. 12, 1955; d. Aaron and Mary Louise (Long) B. BSN, Tex. Woman's U., 1977; MSN, Columbia U., 1986. Cert. clin. specialist in child psychiat. nursing, 1990. Pediatrics staff nurse Childrens Med. Ctr., Dallas; staff nurse in psychiatry St. Vincent's Hosp. and Med. Ctr., N.Y.C.; head nurse Bronx (N.Y.) Children's Psychiat. Ctr.; clin. specialist Parent-Infant Therapeutic Program, N.Y.C., The Infant-Parent Inst., Champaign, Ill. Mem. Postpartum Support Internat., Ill. Assn. for Infant Mental Health, Am. Red Cross.

BAXTER, GRANT MACDONALD, radiologist; b. Dundee, Scotland, Feb. 2, 1960; s. Norman and Muriel (Geekie) B.; m. Nuala Margaret Moss, Dec. 7, 1990; 1 child, Matthew Robert. MBChB, U. Dundee, 1983. Med. house officer Ninewells Hosp., Dundee, 1983-84; surg. house officer Crosshouse Hosp., Kilmarnock, Scotland, 1984; sr. med. house officer Monklands Hosp., Airdrie, Scotland, 1984-85; registrar in radiology Royal Infirmary, Glasgow, Scotland, 1985-88; sr. registrar Western Infirmary, Glasgow, 1988-93, cons. radiologist, 1993—. Contbr. articles to profl. jours. and chpts. to books. Recipient Finzi Rsch. Radiology prize Brit. Inst. Radiology, 1991, Kodak prize Scottish Radiol. Soc., 1991. Fellow Royal Coll. Radiologists (Ellis Barnett prize 1993); mem. Brit. Med. Ultrasound Soc., Am. Inst. Ultrasound in Medicine. Office: Western Infirmary NHS Trust, Dept Radiology, Dumbarton Rd, Glasgow G11 6NT, Scotland

BAY, SUSAN LOUISE, critical care nurse; b. Ottumwa, Iowa, Sept. 18, 1946; d. Stanley Leo and Emily Ella (Newlin) B. Diploma, St. Joseph Sch. Nursing, Ottumwa, Iowa, 1967; BSN, N.E. Mo. State U., Kirksville, 1971. RN, Nebr.; CEN; cert. BLS, ACLS. Staff nurse St. Joseph Hosp., Ottumwa, Iowa, 1967-71, Omaha VA Hosp., 1971-74; dir. nursing emergency dept. Immanuel Med. Ctr., Omaha, 1974-79, staff nurse-emergency dept., 1979—. Vol. mission to India, 1983. Mem. Emergency Nurses Assn., Disciplined Order of Christ (Nashville chpt.). Republican. Presbyterian.

BAYER, MANFRED ERICH, molecular biologist, physician; b. Goerlitz, Silesia, Germany, Sept. 22, 1928; came to U.S., 1962; s. Erich Ludwig and Erika Helen (Pelikan) B.; m. Margaret Helene Janssen, Aug. 26, 1958; children: Ada-Helen, Thora-Ilin. MD, U. Hamburg Eppendorf, Germany, 1956; Diploma in Tropical Medicine, Inst. Tropical Diseases, Hamburg, 1961. Approbation as physician. Neurology fellow U. Hosp. Hamburg, 1956-58; from rsch. fellow virology to assoc. mem. Inst. Tropical Diseases, Hamburg, 1958-60; from asst. to assoc. mem. molecular biology Inst. Cancer Rsch., Phila., 1962-86, sr. mem. molecular biology, 1986—; vis. scientist Inst. Cancer Rsch., Villejuif, Paris, 1961, Inst. Virology, Kyoto, Japan, 1977, Max Planck Inst., Freiburg, Germany, 1986, 1988; hon. vis. prof. Dalhousie U. Med. Sch., Halifax, N.S., Can., 1984—; affiliated prof. graduate sch., U. Pa., Phila. 1976—. Mem. editoral bd. Jour. Bacteriology, 1979-91; contbr. articles to profl. jours. NSF grantee, 1968-91, 92—, NIH, 1967-92. Mem. Am. Soc. Microbiology (chmn. div. ultrastructure 1984-85), Am. Soc. Cell Biology, Am. Soc. Virology, Can. Soc. Microbiologists (chmn. morphology sect. 1991-92).

BAYES, BEVERLEY JOAN, pediatrician; b. Regina, Can., Nov. 1, 1937; came to U.S., 1988; d. Frederick Charles and Sylvia Mae (Hickling) B.; m. Edgar Gibson Merson, May 25, 1988; children: Jennifer Alice Merson Hersberg, Andrew Charles Merson, Keith Graham Merson. MD, U. Toronto, 1961. Diplomate Am. Bd. Pediat. Pediat. Fairfax County (Va.) Health Dept., 1972-82, North Va. Pediat. Assoc., Falls Church, 1982—. Family life edn. com. Fairfax County Coun. PTAs, 1982-84, Fairfax County Sch. Bd., 1992-94. Fellow ACP, Am. Acad. Pediat. (program chair Va. chpt. 1992-93). Presbyterian. Office: North Va Pediat Assoc 107 N Virginia Ave Falls Church VA 22046

BAYÉS, RAMON, psychologist, educator; b. Barcelona, Spain, Sept. 29, 1930; s. Ramon Bayés and Trinidad Sopena; m. Angels Salsas, May 2, 1960; children: Ricard (dec.), Mireia. Diploma in electro-tech., Indsl. Sch., Spain, 1961; MA in Psychology, U. Barcelona, Spain, 1974, PhD, 1976. Asst. prof. Autonomous U. Barcelona, 1974-76, assoc. prof., 1977-82, prof., 1983—. Author: Una Introducción al método científico en Psicologia, 1974, Iniciación a la farmacologia del comportamiento, 1977, Psicologia y Medicina, 1979, Psicologia oncológica, 1985, Sida y Psicologia, 1995. Fellow Soc. Catalano-Balear de Cures Pal.liatives, Soc. Española Interdisciplinaria del SIDA; mem. APA, Soc. Behavioral Medicine, Interamerican Soc. Psychology, Col.lègi Oficial de Psicòlegs de Catalunya. Home: Alfonso XII 32, 08006 Barcelona Spain Office: Autonomous U Barcelona, PO Box 29, 08193 Bellaterra Spain

BAYLOR, DENIS ARISTIDE, neurobiology educator; b. Oskaloosa, Iowa, Jan. 30, 1940; s. Hugh Murray and Elisabeth Anne (Barbou) B.; m. Eileen Margaret Steele, Aug. 12, 1983; children: Denis Murray, Michael Randel; 1 stepchild, Michele Gonelli. BA Chemistry magna cum laude, Knox Coll., 1961, DS (hon.), 1989; MD cum laude, Yale U., 1965. Post-doctoral fellow Yale Med. Sch., New Haven, Conn., 1965-68; staff assoc. Nat. Inst. Neurological Diseases and Stroke, Bethesda, 1968-70; spl. fellow USPSH Physiological Lab. Cambridge U., Eng., 1970-72; assoc. prof. physiology U. Colo. Med. Sch., Denver, 1972-74; assoc. prof. physiology Stanford U., Calif., 1974-75, assoc. prof. neurobiology, 1975-78, prof. neurobiology, 1978—, chmn. dept. neurobiology, 1992-95; First Annual W.S. Stiles lecturer U. Coll., London, England, 1989; Jonathan Magnes lecturer Hebrew U., Jerusalem, Israel, 1990; Woolsey lecturer U. Wis., 1992; E. Hille lectr. U. Washington, 1995; mem. NIH Visual Scis. Study Sect., 1984-88, chmn., 1986-88; vis. com. med. scis. Harvard U., 1987-93; chmn. Summer conf. on Vision FASEB, 1989; Wellcome vis. prof. U. Miami, 1995; mem. sci. adv. com. Alcon Rsch. Inst., 1994—; trustee The Grass Found., 1995—. Mem. editorial bd. Jour. Physiology, 1977-84, Neuron, 1988-93, Jour. Neurophysiology, 1989—, Visual Neurosci., 1990-93, Jour. Neurosci., 1991—; contbr. articles to profl. jours. Recipient Sinsheimer Found. award, 1975, Mathilde Solowey award, 1978, Kayser Internat. award Retina Rsch. Found., 1988, Golden Brain award Minerva Found., 1988, Merit award Nat. Eye Inst., 1990, Alcon Rsch. Inst. award, 1991; Rank Optoelectronics prize Rank Orgn., Eng., 1980; Proctor medal Assn. Rsch. Visin & Ophthalmology, 1986. Fellow Am. Acad. Arts and Scis.; mem. NAS, Phi Beta Kappa, Alpha Omega Alpha. Office: Stanford U Sch Med Fair Bldg Stanford CA 94305

BAZARBASHI, MAHER A.N., physician; b. Aleppo, Syria, Aug. 9, 1958; s. Najdat A. B. and Afaf Baki; m. Cherin Kayali; children: Farah, Ahmed, Zinah. BS, Aleppo (Syria) U., 1978; MBBS, Riyadh Med. Sch., 1982. Diplomate Am. Bd. Internal Medicine, Pulmonary Subspecialty, Critical Care Subspecialty. Rotating intern in surgery, pediats., OB King Khaled U. Hosp., Riyadh, 1982-83; resident dept. medicine King Faisal Specialist Hosp. and Rsch. Ctr., Riyadh, 1983-85, dir. respiratory care and pulmonary function lab., 1991-93, program dir. pulmonary fellowship, 1992-93, acting head sect. pulmonary medicine dept. medicine, 1992-93, head sect. pulmonary medicine dept. medicine, 1993—, 1995—; PGY 1 dept. internal medicine St. Joseph Mercy Hosp., Pontiac, Mich., 1985-86; PGY 2 St. Joseph Mercy

Hosp., Pontiac, 1986-87, chief med. resident dept. internal medicine, 1987-88; first yr. clin. fellow dept. pulmonary and critical medicine U. Pitts., 1988-89; second yr. fellow dept. pulmonary and critical care medicine Wayne State U., Detroit, 1989-90, third yr. fellow dept. pulmonary and critical care medicine, 1990-91, clin. asst. prof. critical care divsn. dept. medicine, 1991; cons. pulmonologist, intensivist dept. medicine King Faisal Specialist Hosp. and Rsch. Ctr., Riyadh, 1991—; external examiner K.S.U. Med. Sch.; presenter in field. Contbr. articles to profl. jours. Mem. A.S.I.M. (assoc.), AMA, A.C.C.P., Mich. Soc. Critical Care Medicine. Office: KFSH & RC Dept Medicine, (MBC46) PO Box 3354, 11211 Riyadh Saudi Arabia

BEACH, JOHNSTON, psychologist, military officer; b. Albany, N.Y., Apr. 21, 1945; s. Charles Addison Wilson and Eleanor (Johnston) B.; m. Maureen Ethel Brandow, June 17, 1967; children—Brandon Kirk, Amy Maureen, Emily Renee. B.A., U. Rochester, 1967; M.A., U. Maine, 1969, Ph.D., 1975. Enlisted in U.S. Army, 1969, advanced through grades to col., 1982; assoc. prof. dept. behavioral scis. and leadership U.S. Mil. Acad., West Point, N.Y., 1981—. Decorated Bronze Star, Meritorious Service medal with 2 oak leaf clusters, Army Commendation medal. Mem. Am. Psychol. Assn. Republican. Presbyterian. Home: 19 Wilson Rd # A West Point NY 10996-1706 Office: US Mil Acad Dept Behavioral Scisience and Leadership West Point NY 10996

BEACH, ROBERT LEIGH, neurologist, educator; b. Milford, Conn., July 4, 1948; s. Richard Booth and Georgia B.; children: Alexander, Nicholas. BA in Chemistry, U. Conn., 1971, MS in Organic Chemistry, 1973, PhD in Physiology, Neurobiology, 1977; MD, U. Kans., 1987. Diplomate Am. Bd. Psychiatry and Neurology, Am. Bd. Clin. Neurophysiology; lic. Calif., N.C. NIH postdoctoral fellow dept. psychobiology U. Calif., Irvine, 1977-80, rsch. psychobiologist dept. psychobiology, 1980-81; rsch. physiologist VA Med. Ctr., Kansas City, Mo., 1981-84; adj. asst. prof. dept. neurology U. Kans. Sch. Medicine, Kansas City, 1981-82, rsch. asst. prof. dept. neurology, 1982-84, clin. instr. in neurology, 1991-92; resident in medicine Waterbury (Conn.) Hosp. (Yale U. Affiliate), 1987-88; neurology resident and chief resident UCLA dept. neurology, L.A., 1988-91, clin. neurophysiology fellow, 1991-92; assoc. prof. dept. neurology, divsn. neurosurgery U. N.C. Sch. of Medicine, Chapel Hill, 1992—; neuroscis program com., human tissue adv. com. U. N.C. Hosps., med. dir. epilepsy surgery program, telemetry lab., co-dir. adult epilepsy clinic, dir. epilepsy surgery ctr., attending physician neurology, epilepsy, telemetry svc.; lectr. and spkr. in field. Contbr. articles to profl. jours., chpts. to books. Vol. Venice Free Clinic 1991-92, Camp Carefree (Epilepsy Summer Camp) 1993—. Recipient Cold Spring Harbor summer fellowship, 1976, Dean's Acad. scholarship Kans. Sch. Medicine, 1984-86, Merck award, 1987; grantee Parke Davis, 1995-96, Cyberonics, 1995-9, Marion Merrell Dow, 1995-96, U. N.C. Rsch. Coun. 1994-95. Mem. AMA, N.C. Med. Assn., Nat. Assn. Epilepsy Ctrs., Soc. for Neurosci., Am. Soc. Cell Biologists, Internat. Soc. for Neurochemistry, Am. Acad. Neurology, Am. Epilepsy Soc., Am. Clin. Neurophysiology Soc., Phi Kappa Phi, Sigma Xi, Alpha Omega Alpha. Office: U NC Sch Medicine Dept Neurology CB # 7025 Chapel Hill NC 27599

BEACHAM, WILLIAM FELDER, obstetrician and gynecologist; b. New Orleans, Feb. 27, 1952; s. Daniel Winston and Jena (Jackson) B.; m. Lucinda Lozier, Oct. 14, 1989; 1 child, Christopher Winston. BS in Chemistry, Washington and Lee U., 1974; MD, Tulane U., 1978. Diplomate Am. Bd. Obstetrics and Gynecology. Resident in ob-gyn. Emory U., Atlanta, 1978-82; ptnr. North Oaks Ob-Gyn., Hammond, La., 1982—; chief of staff North Oaks Med. Ctr., Hammond, 1995. Bd. dirs. Richard Murphy Hospice, Hammond, 1991-93. Fellow ACOG; mem. So. Med. Assn., La. State Med. Soc., Tangipahou Parish Med. Soc. Home: 39601 River Oaks Dr Ponchatoula LA 70454 Office: North Oaks Ob-Gyn 15748 Medical Arts Plaza Hammond LA 70403

BEACHLEY, MICHAEL CHARLES, radiologist; b. Harrisburg, Pa., Nov. 14, 1940; s. Kenneth Gumbert and Carolyn Elizabeth (Jones) B.; m. Deborah Rowe Samson, July 27, 1963; children: Kenneth, Barbara, William. A.B., Dartmouth Coll., 1962, B.M.S., 1963; M.D., Harvard U., 1965. Diplomate Am. Bd. Radiology. Intern in surgery Med. Coll. Va., Richmond, 1965-66 resident in radiology Med. Coll. Va., 1966-69, instr. radiology, 1970, faculty, 1972—, acting chmn. dept. radiology, 1976, prof., 1977-87, chmn. dept. radiology, 1977-82, prof. radiation scis., 1981-87, prof. biophysics, 1980-82, prof. physiology and biophysics, 1982-87, clin. prof., 1987—; clin. prof. radiology U. Pitts., 1988—; chmn. Dept. Radiology St. Margaret Meml. Hosp., Pitts., 1987—; pres. Three Rivers Imaging Cons., Ltd., 1993-94, Duquesne Imaging Ltd., 1994—; med. dir. Radiology Ptnrs.; cons. McGuire VA Hosp., 1977—; fellow in radiol. pathology Armed Forces Inst. Pathology, Washington, 1969. Contbr. chpt. to book, revs. and med. articles to profl. jours. Vice-pres. College Hills Civic Assn., 1975-77. Served as maj. M.C. U.S. Army, 1970-72. Fellow Am. Coll. Radiology (pres. Va. chpt. 1982-83), Am. Coll. Angiology: mem. AMA, Am. Heart Assn., Radiol. Soc. N.Am. (chmn. bylaws com.), Am. Roentgen Ray Soc., Pitts. Roentgen Soc., Pa. Radiol. Soc., Pa. Med. Soc., Allegheny Med. Soc., Pa. Radiol. MSO (chmn. by-laws com., exec. com.), Dartmouth Club Western Pa., Harvard Club Western Pa. (treas.), Pitts. Field Club. Home: PO Box 331 Bakerstown PA 15007-0331 Office: St Margaret Meml Hosp 815 Freeport Rd Pittsburgh PA 15215-3301

BEAHM, CAROL ANN, emergency physician; b. Allentown, Pa., June 24, 1961; d. Robert William and Loretta Ann (Farnschlader) B. BS and BA, Wilkes U., 1983; DO, Univ. Osteopathic Medicine and Health Scis., 1985. Bd. cert. emergency medicine. Intern Millcreek Cmty. Hosp., Erie, Pa., 1989-90; emergency dept. physician Millcreek Cmty. Hosp., Erie, 1991-93; emergency medicine resident Met. Hosp., Grand Rapids, Mich., 1990-93; emergency dept. physician Pennock Hosp., Hastings, Mich., 1992-93, St. Francis Hosp., Hartford, Conn., 1993—; instr. PALS/ACLS, Conn., 1993—. Mem. Am. Osteo. Assn., Am. Coll. Osteo. Emergency Physicians, Am. Coll. Emergency Physicians.

BEAHRS, OLIVER HOWARD, surgeon, educator; b. Eufaula, Ala., Sept. 19, 1914; s. Elmer Charles and Elsa Katherine (Smith) B.; 1 child, Gean Beahrs Landy; m. Helen Edith Taylor, July 27, 1947; children: John Randolf, David Howard, Nancy Ann Beahrs Oster. B.A., U. Calif., Berkeley, 1937; M.D., Northwestern U., 1942; M.S. in Surgery, Mayo Grad. Sch. Medicine, 1949. Diplomate Am. Bd. Surgery. Fellow surgery Mayo Grad. Sch. Medicine, Rochester, Minn., 1942, 46-49; prof. surgery, 1966-79, prof. emeritus, 1979—; asst. surgeon Mayo Clinic, 1949-50, head sect. gen. surgery, 1950-79, vice chmn. bd. govs., 1964-75; Bd. dirs. Rochester Meth. Hosp.; trustee Mayo Found.; mem. cancer control and rehab. adv. com. Nat. Cancer Inst., 1975-84; mem. Am. Joint Com. on Cancer, 1975-78, exec. dir., 1980-92. Editor: Surgical Consultations; editorial bd.: Surgery, Surg. Techniques Illustrated; contbr. over 400 articles to profl. jours. Hon. life, bd. dirs. Am. Cancer Soc., 1975—; trustee Rochester Meth. Hosp.; adv. bd. Uniform Svcs. Univ. Health Scis.; med. cons. Pres. and Mrs. Reagan. Capt. USNR, 1942-64. Recipient Leadership and Humanitarian awards Am. Cancer Soc. Fellow Royal Coll. Surgery in Ireland (hon.), Royal Australasian Coll. Surgery (hon.); mem. AMA, ACS (mem. exec. com., bd. govs., chmn. cen. jud. com., long-range planning com., chmn. bd. govs., chmn. bd. regents, pres. 1988-89), Am. Group Practice Assn. (sec.-treas. 1974-75), Minn. Surg. Soc. (pres. 1960-61), Am. Thyroid Assn., James IV Assn. Surgeons, Am. Surg. Assn. (pres. 1979-80, chmn. com. on issues 1980-83), So. Surg. Assn., Cen. Surg. Assn., Western Surg. Assn., Soc. Head and Neck Surgeons (pres. 1966-67), Am. Assn. Endocrine Surgeons (pres. 1986-87), Am. Assn. Clin. Anatomists (pres. 1986-87), Soc. Surgery Alimentary Tract, Soc. Pelvic Surgeons (pres. 1983-84), Soc. Surg. Oncology, Am. Assn. Clin. Anatomists (pres.), Philippine Coll. Surgeons (hon.), Hellenic Coll. Surgery (hon.), L'Association Française de Chirurgie Française, Northwestern U. Alumni Assn. (merit award), Sigma Xi, Phi Kappa Epsilon, Phi Beta Pi, Theta Delta Chi. Republican. Methodist. Home: 1010 60th Ave SW Rochester MN 55902-8700 Office: 200 1st St SW Rochester MN 55905-0001

BEAL, DONALD GORDON, clinical psychology educator; b. Phoenix, Nov. 4, 1943; s. Charles Gordon and Jane Ann (Cramer) B.; m. Rayma Carol Kirkpatrick, June 14, 1969; 1 child, Kristin Rayma. PhD, Tex. Tech U., 1978. Asst. prof. Miami U., Oxford, Ohio, 1978-82; clin. asst. prof. U. Cin. Coll. Medicine, 1982-87; assoc. prof. clin. psychology Ea. Ky. U., Richmond, 1987—. Contbr. articles to profl. jours. 1st lt. U.S. Army, 1968-70. Mem. APA, Assn. for Advancement Behavior Therapy. Home: 1977 Twain Ridge Dr Lexington KY 40514-1806 Office: Ea Ky U Dept Psychology Richmond KY 40475

BEAL, MYRON CLARENCE, osteopathic physician; b. N.Y.C., Dec. 4, 1920; s. Clarence Joseph and Birdice Elvira (Flint) B.; m. Esther Naomi DeLong, Sept 11, 1948; children: Rebecca Johnson, Myron Flint, Shelley Rees, Julie Wilson, Christina Beal Bailey. A.B., U. Rochester, 1942; D.O., Chgo. Coll. Osteo. Medicine, 1945; M.S. in Physiology, U. Chgo., 1949. Asst. dir. clinics Chgo. Coll. Osteo. Medicine, 1946-49; instr. London Coll. Osteopathy, 1949-51; pvt. practice osteo. medicine Rochester, N.Y., 1951-74; prof. biomechanics Coll. Osteo. Medicine, Mich. State U., East Lansing, 1974-81; prof. family medicine Coll. Osteo. Medicine, Mich. State U., 1981-89, prof. emeritus, 1989—, acting chmn. biomechanics, 1975-77; Mem. Nat. Bd. Examiners for Osteo. Physicians and Surgeons, 1960-84, cons., 1984-89; mem. N.Y. State Bd. Medicine, 1961-73. Trustee Chgo. Coll. Osteo. Medicine 1969-93, chmn. bd. dirs. 1985-91. Fellow Am. Acad. Osteopathy (editor 1987—); mem. Am. Osteop. Assn., N.Y. State Osteo. Soc., Mich. Assn. Osteo. Physicians and Surgeons, Chgo. Osteo. Health Systems (bd. dirs. 1986-90) . Congregationalist. Office: 5873 Seneca Point Rd Naples NY 14512-9763

BEALE, MIA, holistic nurse; b. Phila., Apr. 17, 1948; d. Edward F. and Margaret Y. Beale; 1 child, Laurel Carangelo. AD, U. Maine, Augusta, 1978; Ed.M. in Consulting and Counseling, Harvard U., 1983; student, Bennington Coll., 1967. Cert. clin. specialist in adult psychiat. and mental health nursing. Community mental health nurse Kennebec Valley Regional Health, Augusta, 1980-82; nurse educator, clin. specialist Augusta Mental Health Inst., 1983-85; nursing instr. U. Maine, Augusta, 1983-84, 89-91; pvt. practice as nurse-healer and educator Bath, Maine, 1985—. Mem. Am. Holistic Nurses Assn. (Maine area coord.), Nurse Healers Profl. Assocs., Inst. Noetic Scis., Transpersonal Psychology Assn.

BEALE, SUSAN YATES, social worker; b. Saginaw, Mich., Nov. 17, 1943; d. William Miller and Dorothy LaVerne (Langdon) Yates; m. Henry B.R. Beale, Aug. 27, 1966; children: Andrew, Nathaniel. AB cum laude, Oberlin Coll., 1966; MA, U. Chgo., 1969. Lic. ind. clin. social worker; lic. cert. social worker; bd. cert. in clin. social work, NASW. Social worker West Side VA Hosp., Chgo., 1969-70, D.C. Dept. Human Resources, Washington, 1970-72, D.C. Pub. Schs., Washington, 1972-73; pvt. practice Washington, 1973-74; dir. social svc. Capitol Hill Hosp., Washington, 1974-80; social worker No. Va. Dialysis Ctr., Alexandria, 1982-87, Vis. Nurse Assn., Rockville, Md., 1987-89; sr. social worker Hospice of Washington, 1989-95; sr. social svcs. analyst Microeconomic Applications, 1982—; pres. Coping Ptnrs., Washington, 1996—. Tchr. Royal Scottish Country Dance Soc. Mem. Nat. Assn. Social Workers, Greater Washington Soc. Clin. Social Workers. Office: Coping Ptnrs 4354 Warren St NW Washington DC 20016-2438

BEALL, JAMES ROBERT, toxicologist, consultant; b. Stillwater, Okla., June 29, 1940; s. James Arthur and Annabel (Hess) B.; m. Sandra L. Morseth, Aug. 31, 1985; children by previous marriage—Jimmie Karlene, Sidney Sharleen, Tracy Darlene. A.A.S., Amarillo Coll., 1960; B.S., Okla. State U., 1963; M.S., U. Okla., 1965, Ph.D., 1970. Sect. leader toxicology Schering Corp., Lafayette, N.J., 1969-77 cert. in Toxicology, 1980—; biol. sci. administr. EPA, Washington, 1977-79; spl. asst. OSHA, Washington, 1979-80; sr. policy advisor, toxicologist U.S. Dept. Energy, Washington, 1980—; dir. Cytomed. Lab., 1970-71, Am. Bd. Toxicology, Washington, 1981-85, Toxicology Lab. Accreditation Bd., Washington, 1983-87; cons. in field. Author: Uterine Lipid Biosynthesis during Reproductive Cycles, 1970. Contbr. articles to profl. jours. Mem. Ambulance Squad, N.J., 1974-76.Recipeint of the Maryland Gov. award, 1992 Recipient plaque of appreciation Am. Bd. Toxicology, 1985; award of appreciation Consumer Product Safety Commn., 1981; cert. of appreciation Dept. Energy, 1980, 96, health div. FDA, 1982. Mem. Soc. Toxicology, Teratology Soc., Assn. Govt. Toxicologists (pres. 1983-88, bd. dirs. 1983-88), N.Y. Acad. Scis., Sigma Xi. Avocations: backpacking; photography; writing. Home: 4804 Old Middletown Rd Jefferson MD 21755-8315 Office: ER-72 GTN Dept Energy Washington DC 20585

BEAMISH, MARY E., medical and surgical and pediatrics nurse; b. Seattle, June 24, 1940; d. Howard F. and Eleanor (Bentley) Porter; children: Todd, Shawn, Kevin, Rebecca, Vince, Mark. Diploma, Meth. Hosp. Sch. Nursing, Mitchell, S.D., 1961. Staff nurse Lookout Meml. Hosp., Spearfish, S.D., Martin Luther Hosp., Anaheim, Calif., Children's Hosp., Orange, Calif., VA Med. Ctr., Ft. Meade, S.D.; staff nurse med./surg. Geneva (N.Y.) Gen. Hosp., 1992; staff nurse med./surg., oncology Thompson Hosp., Canandaigua, N.Y., 1992-96, Clark Manor Proprietary Home, Canandaigua, N.Y., 1996—, House of John - Care of Terminally Ill, Clifton Springs, N.Y., 1996—.

BEAN, DAVID KEITH, osteopathic physician, surgeon; b. Moberly, Mo., Jan. 22, 1948; s. Pollard and Lavonne (Conway) B.; m. Judith Ann Orlet, Apr. 24, 1976 (dec. Apr. 1988); 1 child, Emily Louise BS, NE Mo. State U., 1970; DO, Kirksville Coll. Osteo. Medicine, 1974. Cert. Am. Osteo. Bd. Family Practice, 1982. Intern, then resident in internal medicine Normandy Osteo. Hosps., St. Louis, 1974-77; practice medicine Ellisville Family Medicine, Inc., Mo., 1977-88; asst. clin. prof. family practice New Eng. Univ. Coll. Osteopathic Medicine; clin. instr. Kirksville (Mo.) Coll. Osteopathic Medicine; chmn. dept. gen. practice, Normandy Osteo. Hosps., St. Louis, v.p., St. Louis Assn. Osteo. Physicians and Surgeons; staff physician DePaul Health Ctr., St. Louis. Bd. dirs. Normandy Osteo. Med. Ctr. St. Louis and Normandy Osteo. Hosps., 1984-88; pres. Mo. State Bd. Registration for the Healing Arts. Named Mo. Physician of Yr., 1996. Mem. Am. Osteo. Assn., Mo. Assn. Osteo. Physicians and Surgeons (chmn. pub. relations com. 1983-90, Presidents award 1983), St. Louis Assn. Osteo. Physicians and Surgeons (v.p. 1979-88). Republican. Baptist. Avocations: music, piano. Home: RR 10 Box 130 Poplar Bluff MO 63901-9253 Office: Poplar Bluff Family Medicine Inc 2530 Lucy Lee Pkwy Poplar Bluff MO 63901

BEAN, GARY, physician; b. Laurens, Iowa, Dec. 12, 1949; s. Ralph Orwig and Marygery (Lofquist) B.; m. Elizabeth McMillan, Mar. 15, 1975 (div. Jan. 1989); m. Sandra K. Thore, May 28, 1994; 1 child, David Kirkpatrick. BS, Creighton U., 1972; MD, Bowman Gray Sch. Medicine, Winston-Salem, N.C., 1976. Diplomate Am. Bd. Family Practice. Residency in family medicine Womack Army Hosp., Fort Bragg, N.C., 1979; fellowship in family medicine U.N.C., Chapel Hill, 1982; faculty, family medicine Womack Army Hosp., Fort Bragg, N.C., 1979-82; pvt. practice Raleigh (N.C.) Family Physicians, 1982—; edn. com. chmn. Womack Army Hosp., 1980-82; chmn. family practice dept. Wake County Med. Ctr., Raleigh, 1985-87, sec. med. staff Raleigh Cmty. Hosp., 1986, pres., 1987-88; chmn. bd. trustees, 1993-95; sec. med. staff Wake County Med. Ctr., 1990-91; asst. clin. program family practice U. N.C., Duke U. Med. Ctr. Vol. Open Door Clinic, Raleigh. Maj. U.S. Army, 1976-82. Named Outstanding Family Practice Resident, Assn. U.S. Army, 1979; recipient Family Practice Tchr. of Yr. award Womack Army Hosp., 1980, 81, Army Commendation medal, 1982. Mem. Am. Acad. Family Physicians, N.C. Acad. Family Physicians (edn. chmn. 1990-92, asst. dir. 1988-90, dir. dist. 6 1990-92, v.p. 1991-93, pres. elect 1993-94, pres. 1994-95, mem. exec. com., nominating com., chmn. 1996), N.C. Med. Soc. (2d v.p. 1994-95, 1st v.p. 1995-96), Wake County Med. Soc., Wake County Family Physicians. Republican. Methodist. Office: Raleigh Family Physicians 1109 Dresser Ct Raleigh NC 27609-7302

BEAN, JAMES RICHARD, physician; b. Coshocton, Ohio, Apr. 24, 1948; m. Deborah R. Bean; children: Jeffrey, Alison, Lucy. BA, U. Va., 1970; MD, Tulane U., 1973. Intern in surgery U. Ky., 1974-75, resident in neurosurgery, 1975-80; neurosurgeon Neursurg. Assocs., Lexington, Ky., 1982—; pres., mem. med. staff Samaritan Med. Ctr., Lexington, 1991; vice chmn. Joint Coun. of State Neurosurg. Societies, Chgo., 1994—. Contbr. articles to profl. jours. Mem. AMA, Congress Neurol. Surgeons, Am. Assn. Neurol. Surgeons (chmn. com. 1995-96), Ky. Med. Assn., Fayette County Med. Soc., The Physician's Network (pres. 1994-96). Mem. AMA, Ky. Med. Assn. (chmn. com.), Congress Neurol. Surgeons, Ky. Neurosurg. Soc. (pres. 1989-90), AANS (chmn. com. 1995-96), FCMS, The Physician's Network (pres. 1994—). Office: Neurosurg Assocs 1401 Harrodsburg Rd B 485 Lexington KY 40504

BEANE, JUDITH MAE, psychologist; b. Durham, N.C., Mar. 28, 1944; d. Joseph William Sr. and Antoinette Gwathmey (Dew) Sr. BA, Campbell U., 1967; MRE, Golden Gate Bapt. Theol. Sem., Mill Valley, Calif., 1972; PhD, Profl. Sch. of Psychology, San Francisco, 1988. Lic. psychologist, Calif.; mental health therapist II, Northern Neck-Middle Peninsula Cmty. Svcs. Bd.; cert. rehab. provider. Home missionary So. Bapt. Home Mission Bd., Atlanta, 1967-69; loan officer Coop Credit Union, Corte Madera, Calif., 1969-70; emergency svcs. specialist Community Action Marin, San Rafael, 1976-78; program coord. Marin Treatment Ctr., San Rafael, Calif., 1980-85; church sec. St. Paul's Episcopal Church, San Rafael, 1979-81; psychol. intern Raleigh Hills Hops., Redwood City, Calif., 1984; psychol. asst. Lic. Psychologisis, San Anselmo, Calif., 1985-96; bd. dirs. The Open Door Ministries, Inc., Sausalito, Calif., 1971—; psychologist Mill Valley, Calif., 1992-93; cons. Ross (Calif.) Hosp., 1991. Guest speaker for Turn on Marin, San Rafael, Calif., 1985. Recipient award Marin County People Speaking, 1985. Mem. Am. Psychol. Assn. (assoc.), Calif. State Psychol. Assn., Marin County Psychol. Assn., Am. Counseling Assn. Baptist. Home: PO Box 172 Lancaster VA 22503-0172

BEARB, MICHAEL EDWIN, anesthesiologist; b. Beaumont, Tex., June 30, 1956; s. Edwin and Ella Lou (Broussard) B.; m. Joanne Ruth Patterson, Nov. 18, 1989; 1 child, Emily. BS in Psychology with highest honors, Lamar U., 1978; MD, U. Tex., Dallas, 1984. Diplomate Am. Bd. Anesthesiology. Intern St. Paul Hosp., Dallas, 1984-85; resident in anesthesiology Parkland Meml. Hosp., Dallas, 1985-87; fellow in cardio-thoracic anesthesiology The Cleve. Clin. Found., Cleve., 1987-88; instr. in anesthesiology Georgetown U. Hosp., Washington, 1988-90, asst. prof. anesthesiology, 1990-93, chmn. resident selection com., 1990-93, coord. cardiovasc. lectr. series, 1990-91, attending intensivist cardiovasc. ICU, 1989-93; staff cardiac anesthesiologist Jackson (Tenn.)-Madison County Gen. Hosp., 1993—. Author: (with others) Trauma Patients with Hemoglobinopathies in Textbook of Trauma Anesthesia and Critical Care, 1993. Fellow Am. Coll. Angiology; mem. AMA, Internat. Anesthesia Rsch. Soc., Soc. Cardiovascular Anesthesiologists, Am. Soc. Anesthesiologists, Civil War Soc., Smithsonian Inst., Phi Kappa Phi. Home: 69 Elmhurst Dr Jackson TN 38305-8546 Office: Cardiac Anesthesia Group 364 N Parkway Jackson TN 38301

BEARD, DOUGLAS WARD, orthopedic surgeon; b. Denver, July 24, 1959; s. Donald Y. Beard. BS in Sci./Biology, Creighton U., 1982, MD, 1986. Resident in orthopedics U. Nebr., Omaha, 1991; fellow in spine surgery Tulane U., New Orleans, 1991; fellow in spine trauma surgery Northwestern U., Chgo., 1992; dir. Spine Ctr. of Rockies, Ft. Collins, Colo., 1992—. Fellow Am. Acad. Orthopedics; mem. N.Am. Spine Soc., Denver Med. Soc. Office: Orthopedic Ctr of Rockies 2500 E Prospect Fort Collins CO 80525

BEARD, JUDI LYNNE, pharmacist; b. Johnson City, Tenn., Aug. 26, 1965; d. Isaac Aven and Virginia Dare (Jobe) Broyles; m. James Samuel Beard, June 7, 1986. Student, East Tenn. State U., Johnson City, 1983-86; BS in Pharmacy, Samford U., 1989. Lic. pharmacist, Tenn. Pharmacist, pharmacy mgr. Eckerd Drugs, Johnson City, 1988-89, Hosp. Pharmacy, Johnson City, 1989-90; pharmacist Howard's Pharmacy/Susong Pharmacy, Greeneville, Tenn., 1990—. Mem. Am. Pharm. Assn., Tenn. Pharm. Assn., First Dist. Pharm. Assn. Republican. Mem. Grace Brethren Ch. Office: Howard's Pharmacy 1305 Tusculum Blvd Ste 2 Greeneville TN 37745

BEARD, PAMELA BROUGH, medical, surgical, emergency nurse; b. Washington, Feb. 9, 1963; d. Bruce Alvin and Jane Virginia (Koethen) Brough; m. Robert Gordon Beard, July 7, 1990; children: Buffy, Barbie, Lucy. BA in Art History, Wheaton Coll., 1984, BA in Ancient Near Eastern Archeology, 1984; AAS in Nursing, Blinn Coll., Bryan, Tex., 1993. RN, Tex.; ACLS, Am. Heart Assn., TNCCP, ENPC Emergency Nurses Assn. Telecom. specialist City of Bryan Police Dept.h Ctr., Bryan, 1985-90; comm. specialist Brazos County Emergency Comm. Dist., Bryan, 1990-95; staff nurse St. Joseph Hosp. and Health Ctr., Bryan, 1993—. Past bd. mem., vol. Brazos County Rape Crisis Ctr., Bryan, 1985—; res. dep. sheriff Brazos County Sheriff's Dept., Bryan, 1988—. Mem. Tex. Nurse's Assn., Tex. Res. Law Officer's Assn., NRA. Roman Catholic. Home: 419 Gilbert St Bryan TX 77801 Office: St Joseph Regional Health Ctr 2801 Franciscan Dr Bryan TX 77802

BEARD, RODNEY RAU, physician, educator; b. Guinda, Calif., Dec. 27, 1911; s. Aiton Holmes and Mathilda Anne (Rau) B.; m. Marion Lucile Harper, July 3, 1938; children—Julie-Anne, Philip, Marian, Edin. A.B., Stanford U., 1932, M.D., 1938; M.P.H., Harvard U., 1940. Diplomate: Am. Bd. Preventive Medicine (trustee 1961-70), Am. Bd. Indsl. Hygiene. Intern Gorgas Hosp., C.Z., 1937-38; asst. resident Stanford U. Hosps., 1938-39; Rockefeller fellow in med. sci., 1939-40; med. officer Pacific-Alaska div. Pan Am. Airways, 1940-49; instr. med. sch. Stanford U., 1940-42, asst. prof., 1942-45, asso. prof., 1945-49, prof., chmn. dept. preventive medicine, 1949-69, prof. family, community and preventive medicine, 1969-77, prof. emeritus dept. health rsch. and policy, 1977—; dir. rehab. svc. Stanford U., 1955-60; med. cons. W.P. Fuller & Co., 1952-60; clin. prof. occupl. health U. Calif., Berkeley, 1952-64, lectr., 1964-72; vis. prof. U. Occupl. and Environ. Health Sch. Medicine, Japan, 1980; cons. surgeon gen. U.S. Army, 1941-45, 54-75, USAF, 1966-69, Calif. Dept. Pub. Health, 1952-90, VA, 1954-67, Calif. EPA, 1991—; vis. prof. Clinica del Lavoro, U. Milan, 1960-61. Author: (with W.P. Shepard et al) Essentials of Public Health, 2d edit., 1952, (with Joseph T. Noe) Patty's Industrial Hygiene and Toxicology, 1981, 2d edit., 1982, (with M. Lipsett and D. Shusterman) 3d edit., 1994; contbr. papers; mem. editl. bd. Archives Environ. Health, 1973—. Chmn. health coun. San Francisco Community Chest, 1941-44; pub. health com. San Francisco C. of C., 1951-54, San Francisco Bd. Health, 1954-59; mem. commn. A. com. aviation medicine NRC, 1942-45; mem. commn. environ. hygiene Armed Forces Epidemiol. Bd., 1954-73, dir., 1955-66; mem. nat. adv. heart coun. NIH, HEW, 1957-61; mem. nat. adv. coun. Nat. Inst. Environ. Health Scis., 1971-74; mem. nat. adv. coun. pub. health tng. USPHS, 1965-69; mem. hearing bd. San Francisco Bay Area Air Quality Mgmt. Dist., 1973-89; mem. tech. adv. com. Calif. Air Resources Bd., 1969-72; mem. subcom. on atherosclerosis of peripheral vascular disease study group Inter-Soc. Commn. for Heart Disease Resources, 1969-76; mem. joint residency rev. com. for preventive medicine AMA-Am. Bd. Preventive Medicine, 1971-76, chmn., 1972-76; mem. biometry and epidemiology contract rev. com. Nat. Cancer Inst., NIH, HEW, 1982-85. Fellow Am. Coll. Preventive Medicine (v.p. 1967), Am. Pub. Health Assn., Am. Occupational Medicine Assn. (sec. Western sect. 1945-46, pres. 1949), Am. Acad. Occupational Medicine; mem. AMA (sec. sect. preventive medicine 1964-69, chmn. 1970-72, mem. com. occupational toxicology 1969-72), Internat Commn. on Occupational Health (hon.), Am. Indsl. Hygiene Assn. (dir. 1956-60), Assn. Tchrs. Preventive Medicine (pres. 1958-59), Am. Heart Assn., Soc. Occupational and Environ. Health, Calif. Acad. Medicine, ACLU, Airline Med. Dirs. Assn. (hon.), Calif. Acad. Preventive Medicine, Sigma Xi, Delta Omega. Unitarian. Home: 511 Gerona Rd Palo Alto CA 94305-8451 Office: Stanford U Sch Medicine Dept Health Rsch & Policy Stanford CA 94305-5092

BEARDEN, ELIZABETH FRANCES, respiratory care therapist; b. Galveston, Tex., Aug. 24, 1954; d. Walter Bentley and Elken Sarah (Gibson) B.; m. J. Carl Goodwin. AAS, Tarrant County Jr. Coll., 1979. Respiratory therapy tech. Hurst (Tex.) Gen. Hosp., 1978-79; staff therapist, supervisor Meth. Hosp., Dallas, 1979-81; clin. coord. Dallas Rehab. Inst., 1981-85; from respiratory care practitioner to clin. supr. St. Luke's Episcopal Hosp., Houston, 1985—. Mem. Am. Assn. Respiratory Care, Tex. Soc. Respiratory Care (adult practitioner of yr. 1992, region sec. 1992-93, dist. sec. 1991-92), Greater Houston Soc. Critical Care Medicine. Office: St Lukes Episcopal Hosp 6720 Bertner 4-247 Houston TX 77030

BEARDMORE, HARVEY ERNEST, retired physician, educator; b. Windsor, Ont., Can., Feb. 4, 1921; s. Harold and Marjorie (Harvey) B.; m. Frances Seymour Barnes, Sept. 1, 1945 (dec. Aug. 1995); children: Richard, Anne Beardmore Psaila, Patricia Beardmore Muldoon, Ian, Carol Beardmore Lamb, Diane Beardmore Lobb. BSc, McGill U., Montreal, Can., 1946, Dr. Medicine, M Surgery, 1948. Cert. in pediatric surgery Am. Bd. Surgery. Intern Montreal Gen. Hosp., 1948-49; resident Queen Mary Vets. Hosp., Montreal, 1949-51; teaching fellow Tufts U., Boston, 1951-52; chief resident

Montreal Children's Hosp., 1952-54, mem. staff, 1954-92; practice medicine specializing in pediatric surgery Montreal, 1954-92; assoc. prof. surgery McGill U., 1954-92. Served with Princess Patricias Canadian Light Inf., 1943-45, Italy, N.W. Europe. Fellow Am. Acad. Pediatrics (chmn. sect. surgery 1972), A.C.S., Royal Coll. Surgeons Can.; mem. Can. Assn. Paediatric Surgeons (founding pres. 1967-72), Am. Pediatric Surg. Assn. (pres 1974), World Fed. Assn. Pediatric Surgeons (first pres. 1974-77). Club: Chevalier de la Chaine des Rotisseurs. Home: 4501 Sherbrooke St W Apt 5B, Montreal, PQ Canada H3Z 1E7

BEARDMORE, JOHN ALEC, genetics educator, researcher; b. Burton on Trent, Staffordshire, Eng., May 1, 1930; s. George Edward and Anne Jean (Warrington) B.; m. Anne Patricia Wallace, Dec. 26, 1953; children: Anne Virginia, James Wallace, Hugo John, Charles Edward. BSc in Botany with 1st class hons., U. Sheffield, 1953; PhD in Genetics, 1956. Research demonstrator U. Sheffield, Eng., 1954-56, lectr., 1958-61; Harkness fellow Columbia U., N.Y.C., 1956-58; prof. genetics, dir. lab. U. Groningen, Netherlands, 1961-66; prof., head of genetics dept. U. Wales, Swansea, 1966-87, dir. Inst. Marine Studies, 1983-87; head Sch. Biol. Sci. U. Wales, 1988-95, chmn. validation bd., 1994—, mem. vice-chancellor's bd., 1993—; vis. asst. prof. Cornell U., 1958; rsch. assoc. Rochester U., 1961; NSF fellow PA State U., 1966; vis. prof. Ghent U., 1992—; ednl. advisor to Coun. for Professions Supplementary to Medicine, 1991—. Editor: (with B. Battaglia) Marine Organisms, 1977; contbr. numerous articles to profl. jours. Hon. treas. Abbeyfield Homes, Swansea, 1990-95. Recipient medal U. Helsinki, 1980. Fellow Inst. Biology (hon. sec. 1980-85), Linnaean Soc. (coun. mem. 1989-93); mem. Natural Environ. Rsch. Coun. (aquatic life scis. com. 1982-87, chmn. 1984-87). Home: 153 Derwen Fawr Rd, Swansea SA2 8ED, Wales Office: U Wales Swansea, Sch Biol Scis, Swansea SA2 8PP, Wales

BEARDSLEY, G(EORGE) PETER, pediatric oncologist, biochemical pharmacologist; b. N.Y.C., Dec. 29, 1940; s. G. Austin Beardsley and Sylvia Lucy (Davis) Eden; m. Diana S., June 10, 1971; Christopher Eden Marchant. BS, MIT, 1967; PhD in Bioorganic Chemistry, Princeton U., 1971; MD, Duke U., 1974. Resident in pediatrics Yale U., New Haven, 1974-76; fellow pediatric hematology/oncology Harvard Med. Sch., Boston, 1976-79, instr. pediatrics, 1979-81, asst. prof. pediatrics, 1981-85; assoc. prof. pediatrics Yale U. Sch. Medicine, New Haven, 1985-92, assoc. prof. pharmacology, 1989-92, prof. pharmacology, prof. pediatrics, 1992—, chief pediatric hematology/oncology, 1986—, dir. pediatric oncology program Yale Comprehensive Cancer Ctr., 1986. Contbr. articles, book chpts. related to biochem. pharmacology, chemistry or drug design and devel.; holder 4 patents. V.p. The Tommy Fund, Inc., New Haven, 1986—. Recipient Whitaker Found. Rsch. award, 1979, Jr. Faculty Rsch. award, 1981, Faculty Rsch. award Am. Cancer Soc., 1989. Mem. Am. Chem. Soc., Am. Assn. Cancer Rsch., Soc. for Pediatric Rsch. Office: Yale U Sch Medicine 333 Cedar St PO Box 3333 New Haven CT 06510

BEARDSLEY, ROBERT EUGENE, microbiologist, educator; b. Walton, N.Y., June 11, 1923; s. Harrison R. and Margaret (Sliter) B.; m. Philomena E. Pecora, Aug. 28, 1948; children: Luisa M., Margaret R., Robert E. B.S., Manhattan Coll., 1950; A.M., Columbia U., 1951, Ph.D., 1960. Instr. Manhattan Coll., 1951-54, asst. prof., 1954-58, assoc. prof., 1958-68, prof., 1968-77; dir. Manhattan Coll. (Lab. Plant Morphogenesis), 1962-69, head dept. biology, 1969-77; prof. Iona Coll., New Rochelle, N.Y., 1977-89, prof. emeritus, 1989—; dean Iona Coll. (Sch. Arts and Sci.), 1977-83; vis. investigator Inst. Pasteur, Paris, 1966-67; Co-chmn. Scientists Com. Radiation Info., 1960. Contbr. articles to profl. jours. Dist. comdr. U.S. Power Squadrons, 1993. Served with AUS, 1943-46. Guggenheim fellow, 1966. Mem. Am. Pub. Health Assn., Am. Soc. Microbiologists, AAAS, Sigma Xi, Epsilon Sigma Pi. Home: 242 Mountaindale Rd Yonkers NY 10710-3512 Office: Iona Coll New Rochelle NY 10801

BEARE-ROGERS, JOYCE LOUISE, former research executive; b. nr. Pickering, Ont., Can., Sept. 8, 1927; d. Frederick John and Sarah May (Michell) Beare; m. Charles Graham Rogers, Dec. 30, 1961; 1 child, Anne Catherine. BA, U. Toronto, Ont., 1951, MA, 1952; PhD, Carleton U., Ottawa, Ont., 1966; DSc (hon.), U. Man., Winnipeg, Can., 1985, U. Guelph, Ont., Can., 1993. Rsch. assoc. U. Toronto, 1952-54; instr. Vassar Coll., Poughkeepsie, N.Y., 1954-56; chemist Food, Drug Directorate (name now Health Protect Br.), Ottawa, 1956-65, rsch. scientist, 1965-75; rsch. mgr. Bur. Nutritional Scis., Ottawa, 1975-91; rsch. mgr. Bur. Nutritional Scis., Ottawa, 1975-91; adj. prof. U. Ottawa, 1980-92; cons. Food and Agrl. Orgn. UN, 1992-94; Hilditch lectr. U.K., 1994. Editor: Methods for Nutritional Assessment of Fats, 1985, Fat Requirement for Development and Health, 1988; contbr. articles on dietary fats to profl. jours. Decorated Order of Can.; recipient Queen's Jubilee medal Govt. of Can., 1977, Medaille Chevreul award Inst. Corps Gras, 1984, Crompton award McGill U., 1986, Normann medal German Assn. for Fat Rsch., 1987, Commemorative medal for 125th Anniversary of Fedn. of Can., 1992. Fellow Royal Soc. Can., Am. Inst. Nutrition; mem. Am. Oil Chemists Soc. (pres. 1985-86), Internat. Soc. Fat Rsch. (pres. 1991-92), Can. Soc. for Nutrition Scis. (pres. 1984-85, Bordon award 1971, McHenry award 1993), Can. Biochem. Soc. Home: 41 Okanagan Dr, Nepean, ON Canada K2H 7E9

BEARISON, DAVID J., psychologist, educator; b. N.J., Feb. 22, 1944; s. Clarence C. and Fay (Soskin) B.; B.A., Pa. State U., 1965; research fellow Merrill Palmer Inst., 1965-66; M.A., Clark U., 1968, Ph.D., 1973; Asst. prof. City U. N.Y., 1973-78, assoc. prof. psychology, 1978-86, prof. psychology Doctoral Faculty, 1986—, head PhD program in Devel. Psychology, 1992—; sr. research asso. Center for Advanced Study in Edn., 1973-86; clin. fellow in psychiatry Harvard Med. Sch. and Children's Hosp. Med. Center, 1981-82; pvt. clin. practice, N.Y.C., 1975—; adj. prof. pediatrics Mt. Sinai Med. Sch., N.Y.C., 1988—; Davis fellow and vis. prof. psychology Hebrew U., Jerusalem, 1986-88; vis. scholar Rockefeller Found., Bellagio, Italy, 1989. Fellow Am. Psychol. Assn.; mem. Soc. Research in Child Devel., Internat. Soc. Study Behavioral Devel., Jean Piaget Soc. (dir.). Author: They Never Want to Tell You: Children Talk About Cancer; editor: Thought and Emotion: Developmental Perspectives, 1991; editor: Pediatric Psychooncology: Psychological Perspectives on Children with Cancer, 1994; mem. editorial bd. Human Devel., 1978-87, Sex Roles: A Jour. of Research, 1975—, Genetic Epistemologist, 1980-86, Jour. Applied Devel. Psychology, 1983—, Cognitive Development, 1990—; contbr. articles to profl. jours. Office: CUNY Grad Ctr 33 W 42nd St New York NY 10036-8003

BEARN, ALEXANDER GORDON, physician scientist, former pharmaceutical company executive; b. Surrey, Eng., Mar. 29, 1923; came to U.S., 1951; s. Edward Gordon B.; m. Margaret Slocum, Dec. 20, 1952; children: Helen Elliot, Gordon Clarence Frederic. Ed., Epsom Coll.; MB, BS, Guy's Hosp., U. London, Eng., 1945, MD, 1951; MD (hon.), U. René Descartes, Paris, 1974, Cath. U. Korea, 1968. Postgrad. Med. Sch., London, 1948-51; mem. staff Rockefeller Inst., Rockefeller U., N.Y.C., 1951-64, 88—, asso. prof., 1957-64, prof., sr. physician, 1964-66, adj. prof., vis. physician, 1966—; prof. medicine Cornell U., 1966-89, prof. emeritus, 1989—, Stanton Griffis Distinguished med. prof., 1976-80, chmn. dept., 1966-77; physician-in-chief N.Y. Hosp., 1966-77; sr. v.p. for med. and sci. affairs Merck, Sharp & Dohme Internat., Rahway, N.J., 1979-88; mem. Commn. Human Resources, Nat. Acad. Scis., 1974-77; chmn. div. med. scis. Assembly Life Scis., 1978-79; bd. sci. counselors Nat. Inst. Arthritis, Metabolism and Digestive Diseases, 1976-80; mem. Space Sci. Bd., 1978-79; cons. genetics tng. com., div. gen. med. scis. USPHS, 1961-65, cons. genetics study sect., 1966-70, coun. Fogarty Ctr NIH, 1990—; pres. Royal Soc. Medicine Found., Inc., 1976-78; now dir.; mem. bd. sci. overseers Jackson Lab., Bar Harbor. Editor: Am. Jour. Medicine; co-editor: Progress in Medical Genetics, 1962-87; asso. editor: Cecil-Loeb Textbook of Medicine; Contbr. articles to profl. jours. Trustee Rockefeller U., Helen Hay Whitney Found., Macy Found., Howard Hughes Med. Inst. Served as med. officer RAF, 1947-49. Recipient Alfred Benzon prize, Denmark, 1979. Fellow AAAS, Royal Coll. Physicians (Edinburgh, Scotland), Royal Coll. Physicians (London, Eng.); mem. Inst. Medicine NAS, Am. Philos. Soc., Assn. Am. Physicians, Am. Soc. Clin. Investigation, Am. Soc. Human Genetics (pres. 1971), Genetics Soc. Am., Am. Soc. Biol. Chemists, Soc. Exptl. Biology and Medicine, Harvey Soc. (pres. 1972-73, Harvey lectr. 1975), Harveian Soc. London (Coun. 1959), Assn. Physicians Great Britain and Ireland, Med. Rsch. Soc. Great Britain, Med. Soc. London, Knickabocker, Sigma Xi (pres. Rockefeller chpt. 1962-63), fgn. assoc. Norwegian Acad. Sci. and Letters, Century Assn., Knickerbocker Club, Crail Golf Club (Scotland). Presbyterian. Home: 1225 Park Ave New York NY 10128-1758 Office: Rockefeller Univ 1230 York Ave New York NY 10021-6307

BEARN, DAVID RUSSELL, orthodontist; b. Sheffield, Yorkshire, Eng., Sept. 9, 1963; s. Andrew Russell and Margaret Edith (Morse) B.; m. Ruth Olga Hetherington, Apr. 14, 1984; children: Amelia, Russell. B Dental Surgery, U. Sheffield, Eng., 1985; M Dentistry, U. Newcastle, Eng., 1993. House surgeon U. Sheffield, 1986-87; sr. house physician Dumfries Infirmary, Scotland, 1987-88; registrar U. Glasgow (Scotland) Dental Sch., 1989-90; career registrar U. Newcastle Dental Sch., 1991-94; lectr. U. Manchester, Eng., 1994—; adj. assoc. prof. U. N.C., Chapel Hill, 1996; referee Brit. Jour. Orthodontics, 1996—; rsch. fellow U. Manchester/Royal Coll. Surgeons London, 1996—. Contbr. articles to profl. jours. Fellow Royal Coll. Physicians and Surgeons Glasgow; mem. Brit. Orthodontic Soc., Manchester Med. Soc., Royal Coll. Surgeons London. Mem. Ch. of England. Home: 69 Hathersage Dr, Glossop Derbyshire SK13 8RG, England Office: U Manchester Dental Sch, Higher Cambridge St, Manchester M15 6FR, England

BEART, ROBERT W., JR., surgeon, educator; b. Kansas City, Mo., Mar. 3, 1945; s. Robert Woodward and Helen Elizabeth (Wamsley) B.; m. Cynthia Anne, Jan. 23, 1971; children: Jennifer, Kristina, Amy. AB, Princeton U., 1967; MD, Harvard U., 1971. Diplomate Am. Bd. Surgery. Intern, resident U. Colo.; prof. surgery Mayo Clinic, Rochester, Minn., 1976-87, Scottsdale, Ariz., 1987-92; prof. surgery U. So. Calif., L.A., 1992—. Maj. USMC, 1972-83. Fellow Am. Soc. Colon and Rectal Surgery (pres. 1994); mem. Commn. on Cancer (chmn.). Office: U So Calif Dept Surgery 1510 San Pablo St Ste 514 Los Angeles CA 90033-4586

BEASLEY, CLARK WAYNE, biologist; b. Pittsburg, Kans., June 6, 1942; s. Keith Paul and Laura Mae (Johnson) B.; m. Barbara Sue Allman, May 25, 1965; children: Craig Clark, Stacy Leigh. BS, Kans. State Coll. of Pittsburg, 1964; PhD, U. Okla., 1968. Instr. Mo. So. Coll., Joplin, 1968-69, Kans. State Coll. of Pittsburg, 1969; asst. prof., prof. McMurry U., Abilene, Tex., 1969—; cons. Fairleigh Dickinson Labs., Abilene, 1988; field worker Peoples Republic of China, 1990. Contbr. articles on zoology to profl. jours. Mem. Am. Microscopical Soc., Southwestern Assn. Naturalists, Tex. Acad. Sci., Beta Beta Beta, Phi Sigma, Sigma Xi, Omicron Delta Kappa. Home: 1258 Vine St Abilene TX 79602-3518 Office: McMurry U Dept Biology Abilene TX 79697

BEASLEY, ERNEST WILLIAM, JR., endocrinologist; b. Atlanta, May 7, 1924; s. Ernest William and Arrinda Elizabeth (Eidson) B.; M.D., Georgetown U., 1949; m. Ann Lee Jeffreys, July 1, 1950; children—Janet Ann, Ernest William III, Mary Elizabeth, Barbara Elaine. Intern, Walter Reed Hosp., Washington, 1949-50; resident in internal medicine VA Hosp.-Grady Meml. Hosp.-Emory U. Hosp., Atlanta; practice medicine specializing in family practice, Atlanta, 1955-65, in internal medicine, Atlanta, 1966-75, in endocrinology, Atlanta, 1975—; chief endocrinology and metabolism Ga. Bapt. Med. Center; assoc. dept. internal medicine Emory U.; cons. Ga. Assn. Retarded Children, 1955-65; dir. Diabetes Assn. Atlanta, 1976. Served with AUS, 1943-45, M.C., U.S. Army, 50-52. Diplomate Am. Bd. Internal Medicine, Sub-Bd. Endocrinology, Am. Bd. Family Practice Geriatrics. Fellow Am. Coll. Endocrinology; mem. AMA, Am. Assn. Clin. Endocrinologists, Med. Assn. Atlanta, Med. Assn. Ga., Am. Soc. Internal Medicine, Am. Diabetes Assn. Methodist. Club: Cherokee Country. Address: 960 Johnson Ferry Rd NE Ste 340 Atlanta GA 30342-1601

BEASLEY, ROBERT PALMER, epidemiologist, dean, educator; b. Glendale, Calif., Apr. 29, 1936. AB in Philosophy, Darmouth Coll., 1958; MD, Harvard U., 1962; MSc in Preventive Medicine, U. Wash., 1969. Diplomate Am. Bd. Preventive Medicine, Am. Bd. Internal Medicine. Intern King County Hosp., Seattle, 1962-63; resident CDC, USPHS, 1963-65, U. Wash., Seattle, 1965-67; resident preventive medicine U. Washington Hosp., Seattle, 1967-69; assoc. prof. dept. medicine, dept. epidemiology U. Wash., Seattle, 1969-72, assoc. prof. to rsch. prof., 1972-86; with U. Calif., San Francisco, 1986-87; dir. Am. U. Med. Ctr., Taipei, Taiwan, 1979—; dean Sch. Pub. Health, U. Tex. Health Sci. Ctr. at Houston, 1987—. Recipient King Faisal Internat. prize in medicine, 1985; co-recipient Mott medal GM Cancer Rsch. Found., 1987. Mem. Am. Epidemiological Soc., Am. Fedn. for Clin. Rsch., Am. Pub. Health Assn., Am. Soc. of Internal Medicine, Soc. for Epidemiological Rsch. Office: U Texas Health Sci Ctr Sch Pub Health Houston TX 77225

BEASLEY, WILLAIM ROBERT, oral and maxillofacial surgeon; b. Richmond, Va., Aug. 22, 1927; s. Joseph Dewitt and Jenneill Langford (Allison) B.; m. Elizabeth Boling Hurt, Dec. 27, 1952 (div. Aug. 1979); chldren: Mark, Jenneill, John, James; m. Joe Ann Perry, Aug. 27, 1980; stepchildren: Jill, Mala, Pamela. BS in Chemistry, U. Richmond, 1953; DDS, Med. Coll. Va., 1957. Diplomate Am. Bd. Oral and Maxillofacial Surgery. Asst. prof. oral and maxillofacial surgery U. Iowa Hosps., Iowa City, 1960-63; gen. med. staff St. Luke's Hosp., Cedar Rapids, 1963-65, Mercy Hosp., Cedar Rapids, 1963-65, Rockingham Meml. Hosp., Harrisonburg, Va., 1965—. Contbr. articles to profl. jours. Commr. City Planning Commn., Harrisonburg, 1994—; pres. Shenandoah Valley Choral Soc., Harrisonburg, 1970-71; pres. Rockingham unit Am. Cancer Soc., Harrisonburg, 1972-73. With USN, 1945-48. Fellow Am. Assn. Oral and Maxillofacial Surgeons; mem. ADA, Va. Soc. Oral Surgeons (pres. 1971-72), Va. Dental Assn., Am. Coll. Oral and Maxillofacial Surgery, Southeastern Soc. Oral and Maxillofacial Surgeons, Rotary of Harrisonburg (pres. 1977-78). Republican. Presbyterian. Home: 895 Summit Ave Harrisonburg VA 22801 Office: 2262 Bluestone Hills Dr Harrisonburg VA 22801

BEATTIE, EDWARD JAMES, surgeon, educator; b. Phila., June 30, 1918; m. Nicole Mary; 1 son, Bruce Stewart. B.A., Princeton U., 1939; M.D., Harvard U., 1943. Diplomate Am. Bd. Surgery, Am. Bd. Thoracic Surgery (mem. bd. 1960-69, chmn. bd. 1967-69). Intern, surg. resident Peter Bent Brigham Hosp., Boston, 1942-46; Mosely traveling fellow (Harvard) to U. London, Eng., 1946-47; surg. fellow, Markle scholar George Washington U., 1947-52; chief thoracic surgery Presbyn. Hosp., 1952-54; chmn. dept. surgery Presbyn.-St. Luke's Hosp., 1954-65; cons. thoracic surgery Hines VA Hosp., Ill., 1953-65, Chgo. Tb San., 1954-65, Ill. Research and Edn. Hosp., 1956-65, Rockefeller U. Hosp., 1978-83; prof. surgery U. Ill., 1955-65; prof. surgery Cornell U., 1965-83, emeritus, 1983—; prof. surgery, prof. oncology U. Miami, Fla., 1983-85; prof. surgery Mt. Sinai Sch. Medicine, N.Y.C., 1988-94, Albert Einstein Coll. Medicine, 1994—; chief thoracic surgery Meml. Hosp., N.Y.C., 1965-75, chmn. dept. surgery, 1966-78, chief med. officer, 1966-83, gen. dir., chief oper. officer, 1975-83; chief thoracic surgery, dir. Kriser Lung Cancer Ctr., dir. clin. cancer programs Beth Israel Med. Ctr., N.Y.C., 1985-95, dir. emeritus Kriser Lung Cancer Ctr., 1995, med. dir. Cancer Ctr., 1994—. Mem. editl. bd. Jour. Thoracic and Cardiovascular Surgery, 1962-83, Pediat. Digest, 1962-85, Cancer Clin. Trials, 1977-85, Internat. Advances in Surg. Oncology, 1977. Fellow A.C.S.; mem. Am. Assn. Thoracic Surgery, Am. Surg. Assn., Soc. Vascular Surgery, AMA, Central, Western surg. assns., Internat. Soc. Surgery, Soc. Clin. Surgery, Am. Radium Soc., Soc. Thoracic Surgeons, Transplantation Soc., Am. Assn. Med. Colls., Pan Am. Med. Assn., Am. Cancer Soc., Am. Fedn. Clin. Research, Soc. Surg. Oncology. Office: Beth Israel Med Ctr Cancer Ctr/Phillips ACC 10 E Union Sq New York NY 10003

BEATTIE, GEORGE CHAPIN, orthopedic surgeon; b. Bowling Green, Ohio, Sept. 24, 1919; s. George Wilson and Mary Turner (Chapin) B.; m. Nancy U. Fant, Mar. 1, 1947; children: Michael, Suzanne, Eric. BA, Bowling Green U., 1939; MD, U. Chgo., 1943. Diplomate Am. Bd. Orthopaedic Surgery. Commd. lt. (j.g.) MC USN, 1943, advanced through grades to lt. comdr., 1951; med. officer, intern U.S. Naval Hosp., Great Lakes, Ill., 1943-44; resident, fellow in orthopaedic surgery Lahey Clinic, Boston, 1944; ward med. officer orthopaedic services Naval Hosp., Guam, 1944-46; sr. med. officer USN, Manus Island, Papua New Guinea, 1946; resident tng. in orthopaedic surgery U.S. Naval Hosp. St. Albans, N.Y.C., 1947-48; resident in orthopaedic surgery Children's Hosp., Boston, 1949; asst. chief orthopaedic surgery U.S. Naval Hosp. Oak Knoll, Oakland, Calif., 1950-52; comdg. officer med. co. 1st Marine Div. Med. Bn., Republic of Korea, 1952-53; chief orthopaedic service Dept. Phys. Medicine and Navy Amputee Ctr. U.S. Naval Hosp., Phila., 1954; resigned USN, 1954; practice medicine specializing in orthopaedic surgery San Francisco, 1954—; co-chmn. handicapping conditions com. Health Action Study San Mateo County, 1965; 1st chmn. orthopaedic sect. surg. dept. Peninsula Hosp. and Med. Ctr., Burlingame, Calif., 1967, chmn. rehab. service, 1967-71, chmn. phys. therapy and rehab. com., 1956—, vice chmn. orthopaedic dept., 1973-76, chmn., 1977-79; med. dir. research and rehab. ctr. San Mateo (Calif.) County Soc. Crippled Children and Adults, 1958-63; mem. exec. com. Harold D. Chope Community Hosp., San Mateo, 1971-76, chief, co-chmn. orthopaedic sect., 1971-76; chief orthopaedic surg. sect. Mills Meml. Hosp., San Mateo, 1976-78; others. Contbr. articles to profl. jours. Active Indian Guides, 1972-77; pres. Calif. Easter Seal Soc., 1969-71. Decorated Bronze Star. Fellow Am. Acad. Orthopaedic Surgeons (exhibit com. 1979-86); mem. AMA (Billings Bronze medal 1954), Western Orthopaedic Assn. (pres., bd. dirs. 1986), Leroy Abbott Orthopaedic Soc. U. Calif. San Francisco (assoc. clin. prof.), Alpha Omega Alpha. Office: 1828 El Camino Real Ste 606 Burlingame CA 94010-3120

BEATY, HARRY NELSON, internist, educator, university dean; b. Brookfield, Mo., June 25, 1932; s. William Harry and Agnes Marie (Walton) B.; m. Georgia Kay Luther, July 30, 1955; children: Christopher, Kara Lynn. Student, U. Wash., 1950-54, M.D., 1958. Intern in medicine U. Minn., Mpls., 1958-59; resident in medicine U. Wash., Seattle, 1962-63; NIH fellow in medicine and biochemistry, 1963-65; instr. medicine U. Wash., 1965-67, asst. prof., 1967-71, assoc. prof., 1971-75, prof., 1975-77; prof., chmn. dept. medicine U. Vt., Burlington, 1977-83; prof., dean Med. Sch. Northwestern U., Chgo., 1983—; head infectious diseases Harborview Med. Ctr., Seattle, 1968-73; med. dir. Providence Med. Ctr., Seattle, 1973-77; chief med. service Med. Ctr. Hosp. Vt. Burlington, 1977-83; investigator Howard Hughes Med. Inst., 1965-66; bd. dirs. Becton, Dickinson & Co. Contbr. articles on infectious disease to med. to profl. jours., chpts. to med. textbooks. Served to lt. USN, 1959-63. Fellow ACP (sec. treas. Wash. chpt. 1975-76); mem. Assn. Profs. Medicine (chmn. task force manpower needs 1980-83), Infectious Diseases Soc. Am. (councillor 1979-82), Am. Soc. Clin. Investigation, Assn. Am. Med. Colls. (coun. deans adminstrv. bd., exec. coun. 1989—), Alpha Omega Alpha. Office: Northwestern U Med Sch 303 E Chicago Ave Chicago IL 60611-3008 also: Northwestern U 633 Clark St Evanston IL 60208-0001

BEAUCHAMP, BRUCE WILLIAM, physician; b. Portland, Oreg., Feb. 26, 1956; s. Auburn William and Elizabeth Ann (Nierling) B. Student, Portland C.C., 1974-77; BS in Biology & Gen. Sci., Portland State U., 1984; DO in Medicine & Surgery, Coll. Osteo. Medicine Pacific, 1988. Diplomate Nat. Bd. Osteo. Med. Examiners. Vol. paramedic Tualatin Valley Ambulance, Portland, 1974-84; paramedic Metrowest Ambulance, Hillsboro, Oreg., 1979-90; intern St. Joseph N.E. Heights Hosp., Albuquerque, 1988-89; emergency dept. physician Sierra Vista Hosp., Truth or Consequences, N.Mex., 1989-90, Samaritan Hosp., Moses Lake, Wash., 1990-92; resident in anesthesiology Allegheny Gen. Hosp., Pitts., 1992-95; staff anesthesiologist Davis Meml. Hosp, Elkins, W.Va., 1995—; med. dir. emergency med. svcs. Randolph County, W.Va., 1995-96; asst. physician advisor Moses Lake Fire & Ambulance, 1990-92; vol. educator Sierra Vista Hosp./Community, Truth or Consequences, 1990. Vol. ARC, Portland, 1972-82, Am. Heart Assn., Portland, 1980-82; community svc. vol. Allegheny County Amateur Radio Svc., Pitts., 1992—. Named one of Outstanding Young Men Am., 1986; recipient Cmty. Svc. awards Coll. Osteo. Medicine, Pomona, Calif., 1986, 87. Mem. Am. Soc. Anesthesiologists, Christian Med. & Dental Soc., Med. Amateur Coun, W.Va. Med. Soc., Am. Soc. Critical Care Anesthesiologists, Internat. Trauma Anesthesia and Critical Care Soc. Roman Catholic. Home: # 8 Applecreek Elkins WV 26241 Office: Davis Meml Hosp 612 Gorman Ave Elkins WV 26241

BEAUCHAMP, GEORGE ROBERT, ophthalmologist, medical products executive; b. Pontiac, Mich., Nov. 27, 1942; s. George Albert and Kathryn Elizabeth (McCarbery) B.; m. Suzanne Phillips Chelborg, Dec. 23, 1967; children: Christine Marie, Cynthia Lais. AB, U. Calif., Berkeley, 1965; MD, Northwestern U., 1968. Diplomate Am. Bd. Ophthalmology, Nat. Bd. Med. Examiners. Intern Walter Reed Army Med. Ctr., Washington, 1968-69, ophthalmology resident, 1970-73; chief ophthalmology svc. William Beaumont Army Med. Ctr., El Paso, Tex., 1973-74; asst. chief ophthalmology svc. Walter Reed Army Med. Ctr., 1974-75; pvt. practice Washington, 1976-83; dir. office of regional health affairs Cleve. Clinic Found., 1983-90; v.p., sr. v.p. Integrated Med. Systems (now subsidiary Eli Lilly and Co.), Golden, Colo., 1991—; clin. prof. ophthalmology U. Tex. S.W. Med. Ctr., Dallas, 1992—, pvt. practice pediat. ophthalmology, Dallas, 1991—; dir. Am. Bd. Ophthalmology, 1991—; pres. Nat. Children's Eye Care Found, 1987—; chmn. dept. ophthalmology Dr.'s Hosp., Washington, 1978-79; program dir., residency in ophthalmology Washington Eye Ctr. and Dr.'s Hosp., Washington, 1976-79; med. dir. Nat. Eye Found., 1975-79; clin. asst. prof. ophthalmology Georgetown U. Med. Ctr., 1980-83; various Internat. Eye Found. sponsorships in Peru, Bangladesh, Honduras; mem. corneal transplant tchg. team, Bangladesh, 1974, Malta, 1975, Saudi Arabia, 1977; cons. surgeon Queen Elizabeth Hosp., Bridgetown, Barbados, 1977; vis. prof. King Khaled Eye Specialist Hosp., Riyadh, Saudi Arabia, 1984, Hosp. Santo Toribio, Lima, Peru, 1986. Contbr. articles to profl. jours.; editl. rev. bd. Ophthalmic Surgery, 1984-95, Jou. Learning Disabilities, 1987—. Pres. Nat. Children's Eye Care Found., Dallas, 1986—, internat. rels. com., 1978-80, med. adv. bd., 1983-86, bd. dirs., 1984-87, exec. com. bd. dirs., 1984-87, fund-raising com., 1986-87, chmn. planning com., 1986-87. Major USAR, 1967-75. Fellow ACS, Am. Acad. Ophthalmology (fed. legis. subcom. 1981-83, ethics com. 1981-83, vice chmn. 1984-87, chmn. 1988-91, long range strategic planning com. 1986, coord. goals of ethics and quality of care, long range strategic planning 1986-88, chmn. com. on vision and learning disabilities 1982-88, joint com. on resident edn. 1986, task force on targeted exams. 1989, com. on residency and fellowship edn. 1987-91, quality of care com. 1986-91, chmn. panel writing quality of care preferred practice patterns for pediat. ophthalmology 1990-92, cons. ethics com. 1991-92, Honor award 1984); mem. Am. Hosp. Assn., Am. Ophthalmol. Soc., Am. Coll. Physician Execs., Am. Assn. Pediat. Ophthalmology and Strabismus (membership and credentials com. 1983-85, eye care for the children of Am. subcom. 1987-89, liaison com. to Nat. Children's Eye Care Found. 1986-88, long range strategic planning com. 1986-88, Honor award 1990), Am. Coll. Med. Informatics Assn., Internat. Strabismological Assn., Costenbader Alumni Soc. (sec.-treas. 1983-86). Home: 5604 Brushy Creek Trail Dallas TX 75252 Office: IMS/Lilly & Co 15000 West 6th Ave Golden CO 80401

BEAUDOIN, CAROL ANN, psychologist; b. Lowell, Mass., Mar. 30, 1949; d. Adrien P. and Rita J. (LeBlanc) B.; B.A. with honors, U. Fla., 1971; M.Ed. in Counseling, Boston U., 1973, Ed.D. in Counseling Psychology, 1979. Psychiat. aide U. Fla.-Shands Teaching Hosp., Gainesville, 1970-71; trainee VA Hosp., Gainesville, 1971-72; attendant Boston State Hosp., 1972, intern, 1973; intern Univ. Hosp., also Counseling Center, Northeastern U., Boston, 1973-74, Dorchester Mental Health Center, also Carney Hosp., 1974-75; staff psychologist Human Resource Inst., Boston, 1974-80, treatment team leader, 1975-80; pvt. practice psychology, Brookline, Mass., 1980—. Mem. Am. Psychol. Assn. Office: 1101 Beacon St Brookline MA 02146-5502

BEAUDRY, DIANE FAY PUTA, medical staff services director; b. Manitowoc, Wis., Mar. 6, 1947; d. Ruben William and Gertrude Katherine (Novak) Puta. BSN, Alverno Coll., 1971; MS in Ednl. Adminstrn., U. Wis., Milw., 1979, PhD in Urban Edn., 1991. Staff nurse St. Mary's Hosp., Milw., 1971-72, St. Anthony's Hosp., Milw., 1972-74; nurse coord. Pvt. Initiative in PSRO, Wis., 1974-75; insvc. instr. Deaconess Hosp., Milw., 1975-77, insvc. coord., 1977-81; dir. nursing staff devel./quality assurance Good Samaritan Med. Ctr., Milw., 1981-84, dir. quality assurance, 1984-85, dir. utilization mgmt., 1985-88; mgr. quality mgmt. Sinai Samaritan Med. Ctr., Milw., 1988-89, dir. med. staff svcs. and quality mgmt., 1989—. Author: (with others) Interdisciplinary QA: Issues in Collaboration, 1991; author poem. mem. Nat. Assn. for Healthcare Quality, Alverno Coll. Alumnae Assn., U. Wis. Alumni Assn., Delta Epsilon Sigma, Kappa Gamma Pi. Home: 11047 N Riverland Ct 36W Mequon WI 53092-4900 Office: Sinai Samaritan Med Ctr PO Box 342 Milwaukee WI 53201-0342

BEAUGRAND, MICHEL, physician, educator; b. Paris, Oct. 30, 1945; s. Henri and Christiane (Bertrand) B. BS, 1963; MD, Faculte de Medicine, Paris, 1974. Intern Assistance Publique de Paris, 1969-74; prof. hepatogastroenterology Faculte de Medicine, Paris, 1981—; mem. staff Hosp. Jean Verdier, Bondy, France. Office: Hosp Jean Verdier, Ave 14 Juillet, 93143 Bondy France

BEAVEN, MICHAEL ANTHONY, biomedical researcher; b. London, Eng., Dec. 4, 1936; came to U.S., 1962; s. Edward Beaven and Phyllis Georgina (Barker) Collins; m. Vida Helms, Feb. 2, 1964. B in Pharmacy, U. London, Eng., 1959, PhD, 1962. spkr. in field; cons. to various pharm. cos. Contbr. articles to profl. jours. and chpts. to books; mem. editl. adv. bd. various sci. jours., 1959-92. Recipient Dir.'s award NIH, 1989, Travel fellowship Japan Soc. for the Promotion of Sci., 1989. Mem. Am. Soc. Pharmacology and Exptl. Therapeutics, Am. Assn. Immunologists. Office: NIH Nat Heart Lung and Blood Inst Bethesda MD 20892-1760

BEAVER, WAYNE L., cardiologist; b. Ind., Jan. 12, 1943. MD, Ind. U., 1968. Pvt. practice cardiology Columbus, Ohio. Home: 8965 Dublin Rd Powell OH 43065 Office: 777 W State St #302 Columbus OH 43222

BECAN-MCBRIDE, KATHLEEN ELIZABETH, medical and cytogenetic technology educator; b. Houston, Feb. 24, 1949; d. Frank Ernest and Dorothy C. (Sturm) Becan; m. Mark Anerson McBride, July 11, 1970; children: Patrick Becan, Jonathan Aaron. BS in Biology, U. Houston, 1971, MEd in Allied Health, 1973, EdD in Higher Edn. Adminstrn., 1977. Med. technologist St. Luke's Episcopal Hosp., Houston, 1971-73; instr. dept. med. tech. U. Tex., Galveston, 1973-75; instr. med. lab. technician program Houston Community Coll., 1975-77; prof. dept. pathology, dir. program in med. tech. and cytogenetics U. Tex., Houston, 1977-91, prof. Grad. Sch. Biomed. Scis., 1986-92, chair dept. clin. lab. scis., 1991-92, prof. dept. clin. lab. scis., 1991, prof. dept. pathology and lab, medicine, 1991—; coord. Tex.-Mex. border health svcs. project, 1990—; asst. dir. Greater Houston Area Health Edn. Ctr., 1995—; instrnl. cons. Pvt. Industry Council, Houston, 1982-85, Peace Corps, Houston, 1984, ITT, Houston, 1985; ednl. research cons. Am. Soc. for Med. Tech., Houston, 1977-79, 83-84; ednl. cons. La. State Bd. Regents, Baton Rouge, 1985, Profl. Seminar Cons., Inc. Author: Textbook of Clinical Lab Sciences, 1982, (with others) Phlebotomy Handbook, 1984, 3d edit. 1993, 4th edit. 1996, Essentials for the Small Laboratory and Physician's Office, 1988, Phlebotomy Exam Review, 1990, 2d edit. 1993, 3rd edit. 1996; contbr. articles and monographs to Med. Lab. Scis. jour., chpts. to books; editor med. jours. Mem. adv. bd. for health occupation, adv. bd. com. for edn. evaluation Houston Ind. Sch. Dist., 1985-87; pres. for sch. with allied health scis. Faculty Goverance Orgn., U. Tex. Health Scis. Ctr., 1989-90; chair U. Tex. Health Scis. Ctr. Valley/Border Health Svcs. Projects, 1989-90; coord. Tex.-Mex. border health projects U. Tex. Houston Health Sci. Ctr., 1990—. Grantee U. Tex., Peace Corps, Pvt. Industry Council, Tex. Edn. Agy., ITT. Named one of Outstanding Young Women Am., 1979-82, 84; Grantee March of Dimes Nat. Found., 1989, Rio Grande Valley Project, 1988-89, 89-90, 90-91, 91-92, 92-93. Mem. Am. Soc. Med. Tech. (coms. chmn.), Tex. Soc. for Med. Tech. (chmn. coms.), Houston Soc. Clin. Pathologists, Tex. Soc. Allied Health Professions (bd. dirs. 1981-82, pres. 1984, 85), Am. Soc. Clin. Pathologists (R&D com. 1983-86, cert., computer testing com. 1989-93, phlebotomy exam com. 1992—), Health Edn. Tng. Ctr. Alliance Tex. (chair U. Tex. system Tex.-Mex. border health adv. coun. and exec. com.), Clin. Lab. Mgmt. Assn., Zonta Internat. Exec. Bus. and Profl. Woman's Orgn., Alpha Mu Tau, Omicron Sigma. Democrat. Roman Catholic. Avocations: tennis, jogging, soccer coaching and playing, piano. Home: 3806 Marlowe St Houston TX 77005-2044 Office: U Tex Houston Health Sci Ctr Tex-Mex Border Health Proj Coord Houston TX 77030

BECHER, ROBERT MCADOO, physician, surgeon; b. Springfield, Mass., Feb. 11, 1935; s. George David and Idabel Lydia (McAdoo) B.; m. Virginia Cornelia deRonde, July 8, 1967; children: Katherine Tansey, Robert David. AB, Harvard Coll., 1956; MD, Johns Hopkins U., 1960. Diplomate Am. Bd. Surgery. Intern Peter Bent Brigham, Boston, 1960-68; resident Hosp. and Affil. Med. Ctrs., Boston, 1968—. Capt. USAF, 1962-63, Eng. Fellow Am. Coll. Surgeons; mem. New Eng. Surg. Soc., Harvard Club of Boston, Beverly Yacht Club. Office: Park Surg Assocs Inc 966A Park St Stoughton MA 02072

BECHT, ADELINE CHARLOTTE, retired counseling psychology educator, consultant; b. Muskegon, Mich., Mar. 11, 1937. BA in Psychology, Cascade Coll., 1964; MEd in Counseling and Guidance, Lewis and Clark Coll., 1976; MA in Clin. Psychology, U. Oreg., 1982, DPhil in Counseling and Clin. Psychology, 1982. Founder, dir. corp. blind, deaf, deaf-blind adults Living Rehab. Ctr. Inc., Portland, Oreg., 1971-81; intern in psychology Riverside Hosp. (now named Pacific Gateway Hosp.), Portland, 1980-81; pvt. practice Portland, 1980-89; instr. communications, Am. sign lang. for the deaf Notre Coeur Coll., Portland, 1984-86; adj. prof. counseling psychology Lewis and Clark Coll., Portland, 1987-92; ret., 1992; vis. lectr., workshop facilitator spl. edn. Lewis and Clark Coll., Portland, 1971-92; cons. on deafness for psychiat. patients Pacific Gateway Hosp., Portland, 1974-92; vis. instr. deaf specialist tng. Western Oreg. State Coll., Monmouth, 1974-80. Contbr. articles to profl. jours. Mem. adv. bd. HEW, 1973-75; bd. dirs. Oreg. Coun. Orgns. Serving the Deaf, 1974-75. Home: 2600 SE Freeman Way # 5 Milwaukie OR 97222-4651

BECHTEL, SHERRELL JEAN, psychotherapist; b. Birmingham, Ala., Sept. 23, 1961; d. Lewis Eugene and Sarah Rozelle (Sherrell) B. BS in Social Work, U. Ala., Birmingham, 1989; MSW, U. Ala., Tuscaloosa, 1990. Cert. addiction specialist; cert. group psychotherapist; lic. clin. social worker, Tenn., Ga. Vol. counselor Planned Parenthood, Birmingham, 1986-88; intern Bradford Adult Chem. Dependency, Birmingham, 1989; rsch. staff asst. U. Ala., Tuscaloosa, 1989-90; intern counselor Bradford Adolescent Chem. Dependency, Birmingham, 1990; primary counselor The Crossroads, Chattanooga, 1990-92; owner S. J. Bechtel LCSW, CAS, Chattanooga, 1991—; rschr. Ala. Commn. Youth, Montgomery, 1989-90; trainer Legal and Jud. Aspects Child Welfare, Decatur, Ala., 1989; presenter Ala. Victim Compensation, Mobile, 1990; speaker Limestone Correctional Facility, Huntsville, 1990; lectr. Grad. Sch. Social Wk., Tuscaloosa, 1990, U. Tenn., Chattanooga. Subcom. mem. Atty. Gen. Alliance Against Drug Abuse, Birmingham, 1989; speaker Victims of Crime and Leniency, Tuscaloosa, 1990; planning com. Holistic Health Retreat, Birmingham, 1988; mem. Tenn. Coun. on Children and Youth-Legis./Policy. Mem. NASW (pres. student orgn. 1986-89), Tenn. Alcohol Drug Assn., Jewish Community Ctr., Phi Kappa Phi. Office: 7405 Shallowford Rd Ste 280 Chattanooga TN 37421-2662

BECICH, RAYMOND BRICE, healthcare consultant, mediator, trainer, educator; b. Chgo., Jan. 9, 1945; s. Nicholas Gabriel and Rose Christina (Spillar) B. BA, Ind. U., 1966; MS, Columbia U., 1968. Adminstrv. officer, then hosp. dir. Indian Health Svc., Harlem, Mont., 1968-72; hosp. dir. Indian Health Svc., Rapid City, S.D., 1972-78; hosp. adminstr. St. Elizabeth's Hosp., Washington, 1979-82, exec. officer, 1983-86; exec. officer NIH Clin. Ctr., Bethesda, Md., 1986-94; healthcare cons., mediator, trainer, educator, 1994—; adj. faculty Univ. Coll., U. Md., College Park, U. N.Mex., Albuquerque and Los Alamos, Coll. Santa Fe, Ctrl. Mich. U., Mt. Pleasant, 1995—. Bd. dirs. Ronald McDonald House, Washington, 1986-89; vol. Whitman-Walker Clinic, 1987-95. Fellow Am. Coll. Healthcare Execs. (life). Democrat.

BECK, ADRIAN ROBERT, surgeon, educator; b. N.Y.C., June 8, 1932; s. Alexander George and Frances (Price) B.; m. Marcia Perlmutter, Aug. 18, 1963; children—Adrienne, David. B.S., Union Coll., 1954; M.D., Albany Med. Coll., 1958. Diplomate: Am. Bd. Surgery, Am. Bd. Pediatric Surgery. Intern Beth Israel Hosp., N.Y.C., 1958-59; asst. resident surgery Mt. Sinai Hosp., N.Y.C., 1959-63; Dazian fellow in surg. research Mt. Sinai Hosp., 1960-61, chief resident, 1963-64; chief resident pediatric surgery Buffalo Children's Hosp., 1964-66; practice medicine specializing in pediatric surgery N.Y.C., 1968—; clin. prof. surgery Mt. Sinai Sch. Medicine, N.Y.C., 1978—, clin. prof. pediatrics, 1984—; attending surgeon, assoc. dir. divsn. pediatric surgery Mt. Sinai Med. Ctr.; attending surgeon, dir. divsn. pediatric surgery Beth Israel Med. Ctr.; attending pediatric surgeon Lenox Hill Hosp. Contbr. articles to profl. jours., chpt. to book. Fellow ACS, Am. Acad. Pediatrics; mem. Am. Pediatric Surg. Assn., N.Y. Acad. Sci., N.Y. Pediatric Soc., Harvey Soc., N.Y. Soc. Pediatric Surgery, N.Y. Surg. Soc., Soc. Surgery Alimentary Tract, Undersea and Hyperbaric Med. Soc. Home: 4919 Goodridge Ave Bronx NY 10471-3317 Office: 112 E 83rd St New York NY 10028-0880

BECK, DEBRA LOU, medical technologist; b. Elk City, Okla., Aug. 23, 1957; d. Rosco Donovan Mullenix and Janyce Lou (McGowan) DeLaRosa; m. Dennis Wayne Beck, Nov. 1, 1974; children: Angela, Amber. AAS in Med. Tech., Radiographic Tech., Southwestern Okla. State U., 1989. Gen. technologist Clinton (Okla.) Regional Hosp., 1989; supr. blood bank, microbiology Great Plains Regional Med. Ctr., Elk City, Okla., 1989-94; med., radiographic technologist Okla. West Physicians Group P.C., Weatherford, 1995—. Mem. Am. Med. Technologists (cert., Outstanding Med. Lab. Technician of Yr. 1988), Am. Registry of Radiol. Technologists (cert.), Okla. State Soc. Med. Technologists, Alpha Sigma Omega. Home: 415 MacArthur Blvd Elk City OK 73644

BECK, DONALD FRANK, health care financial consultant; b. Toledo, Oct. 6, 1942; s. Frank L. and Virginia D. (Lesniewicz) B.; children: Leslie Ann, Marjorie Marie, Donald Raymond. BBA, U.Toledo, 1970, MBA, 1975. CPA, Ohio, Miss., Tenn., Ill., Ark., Tex. Internal auditor Med. Coll. Ohio, Toledo, 1971-76; asst. controller Toledo Hosp., 1976-78; cons. TriBrook Inc., Chgo., 1977-78; hosp. controller Hosp. Corp. of Am., Nashville, 1978-79; controller Meth. Hosps. at Memphis, 1979-81; pres. D.F. Beck & Assocs., Memphis, 1981—; vis. prof. health care Auburn (Ala.) U., 1987; lectr. in field; adj. prof. acctg. Owens Coll., Perrysburg, Ohio, 1975-77; lectr. in health care fin. U. Miss. grad. program in healthcare adminstrn., 1982—. Mem. Am. Coll. Healthcare Adminstrs., Healthcare Fin. Mgmt. Assn., Nat. Writers Assn., Internat. Platform Assn., Am. Inst. CPA's, Tenn. Soc. CPA's, Tenn. Hosp. Assn., Toastmasters Internat., Assn. MBA Execs., K.C., Beta Gamma Sigma. Republican. Author: Basic Hospital Financial Management, 1980, Principles of Reimbursement in Healthcare, 1983, Basic Hospital Management, 2nd edito., 1988; mem. editorial bds. Healthcare Supr., So. Hosps., Topics in Hosp. Pharm. Mgmt.; contbr. articles to hosp. jours. Home: 569 N Mendenhall Rd Memphis TN 38117-1961 Office: PO Box 242146 Memphis TN 38124-2146

BECK, EUGEN ALEXANDER, physician; b. Basel, Switzerland, Nov. 27, 1933; s. Conrad Arthur Beck and Emma Jacot-Descombes; m. Charlotte Karrer, Mar. 12, 1964 (div.); children: Thomas, Michael, Catherine; m. Elsbeth Baertschi, June 14, 1984; 1 child, Anna. MD, U. Zurich, Switzerland, 1959, PhD, 1965. Mem. splty. bds. in internal medicine and hematology. Intern U. Zurich Hosp., 1960-61, 62-63, Neumünster Hosp., Zurich, 1961-62; research fellow Johns Hopkins Hosp., Balt., 1963-65; resident U. Hosp., Basel, 1965-70; vice chmn. cen. hematology lab. U. Hosp., Bern, 1970-87; pvt. practice Lugano, Switzerland, 1987—; prof. medicine U. Bern, 1970, hon. prof., 1987; cons. Swiss Nat. Sci. Found., U. Bern, 1986. Editor: Acta haematologica, 1984-88; co-author: Simple Laboratory Tests in Hematology, 1978, Variants of Human Fibrinogen, 1984, Laboratory Investigations in Hematology, 1988. Chmn. German Task Force for blood coagulation rsch., 1984. Postdoc. fellow U.S. Nat. Health Svc., 1963-65; rsch. grantee Swiss Nat. Sci. Found., 1965, 87. Home: Via Crocetta 12, Ch-6962 Viganello Ticino Switzerland Office: Via Beltramina 7 A, CH-6900 Lugano Ticino, Switzerland

BECK, GEORGE PRESTON, anesthesiologist, educator; b. Wichita Falls, Tex., Oct. 21, 1930; s. George P. and Amanda (Wilbanks) B.; m. Constance Carolyn Krog, Dec. 22, 1953; children: Carla Elizabeth, George P., Howard W. BS, Midwestern U., 1951; MD, U. Tex., 1955. Diplomate Am. Bd. Anesthesiology. Intern John Sealy Hosp., 1955-56; resident anesthesiology Parkland Meml. Hosp., Dallas, 1959-62, vis. staff, 1964—; practice medicine specializing in anesthesiology, Lubbock, Tex., 1964—; chief staff Meth. Hosp., Lubbock, 1967-68; asst. prof. anesthesiology Southwestern Med. Sch., Dallas, 1962-64, asst. clin. prof., 1964-71, prof. 1996—, assoc. clin. prof. anesthesiology U. Tex. Med. Br. at Galveston, 1971—; pres. Gt. Plain Ballistics Corp., 1967—; clin. prof. Tex. Tech. U. Sch. Medicine, 1986—, pres. found. bd., 1972-73. Author: The Ideal Anesthesiologist, 1960, Mnemonics as an Aid to the Anesthesiologist, 1961, Anterior Approach to Sciatic Nerve Block, 1962; inventor Beck Airway Airflow Monitor. Pres. Luth. Ch. council, pres. congregation, 1965-66. With USAF, 1956-59. Fellow Am. Coll. Anesthesiologists; mem. Am. Soc. Anesthesiologists, Tex. Soc. Anesthesiologists (pres. 1974) Tex. Med. Soc., Lubbock County Med. Soc., Lubbock Surg. Soc. (pres. 1969). Home: 4601 18th St Lubbock TX 79416-5713 Office: PO Box 16385 Lubbock TX 79490-6385

BECK, IRENE CLARE, educational consultant, writer; b. N.Y.C., Dec. 18, 1944; d. James E. and Helen (Carroll) Clare; m. William J. Beck, Aug. 9, 1986; children: Daniel, James Chesire. BA, St. Mary's Coll., 1966; MA, Fairfield U., 1977; EdD, U. Rochester, 1982. Cert. tchr., N.Y. Tchr. Elem. Sch., N.Y.C., 1966-68, Montessori Acad. N.Y., Bklyn., 1968-73; faculty Housatonic Community Coll., Bridgeport, Conn., 1975-77, Nazareth Coll., Rochester, N.Y., 1977-83; faculty dir. Sheppard Pratt Nat. Ctr. Human Devel., Balt., 1983-91; exec. dir. William & Irene Beck Found., 1987—; cons. Headstart Programs, Rochester, 1980-83, Family Day Care Tng., Rochester, 1980-83; presenter workshops and seminars. Author: Expect Respect, Let Me Tell You (manuals), (No Hang Ups (telephone audiotape), 1987, In Tune With Teens (booklet), 1990; weekly news col. Parents and Teens, 1987-90; freelance writer, 1986—; contbr. articles to profl. jours. Mem. AAUW (chair equity task force Ill. chpt.), PTA, Assn. Childhood Edn. Internat Home: 424-F W Armitage Ave Chicago IL 60614

BECK, JEROME JOSEPH, health care administrator, biomedical technologist; b. Mesa, Ariz., Nov. 7, 1957; s. Robert Leon and Marie Margaret (Curry) B.; m. Catherine Elizabeth Williams, June 27, 1981; 1 child, John Robert. BSBA, U. Phoenix, 1989. Cert. hemodialysis technologist Bd. of Nephrology Examiners Nursing & Tech. Dialysis unit housekeeper Good Samaritan Hosp., Phoenix, 1976-78, dialysis equipment technician, 1978-81, dialysis sr. equipment technician, 1981-83, coord. tech. staff devel., 1983-88, mgr. dialysis tech. svcs., 1988-89; dir. tech. svcs. East Valley Dialysis Svcs., Mesa, 1989-91, program dir., 1991-93; ops. mgr. Renalwest L.C. (formerly East Valley Dialysis Svcs.), Mesa, 1993—; dir. ops.; bd. dirs. Bd. Nephrology Examiners, Madison, Wis., 1990-92; mem. renal disease and detoxification com. Assn. for the Advancement of Med. Instrumentation, 1989-93; mem. technicians com. ESRD Network VI, Albuquerque, 1984-85; nephrology conf. lectr. nationwide. Mem. editl. adv. bd. Nephrology News and Issues, 1996—; contbr. articles to profl. jours. Mem. Nat. Assn. Nephrology Technologists (bd. dirs., western v.p. 1989-91, Torchbearer award 1994). Republican. Office: RENALWEST lc 1750 S Mesa Dr Ste 110 Mesa AZ 85210-6226

BECK, JOHN CHRISTIAN, physician, educator; b. Audubon, Iowa, Jan. 4, 1924; s. Wilhelm and Marie (Brandt) B. MD, McGill U., 1947, MSc, 1951, DSc (honoris causa), 1994; PhD (hon.), Ben Gurion U. of the Negev. Diplomate Am. Bd. Internal Medicine (chmn., dir.). Intern Royal Victoria Hosp., Montreal, 1947-48; sr. asst. resident Royal Victoria Hosp., 1948-49; practice medicine, specializing in endocrinology Montreal, 1964-74; physician-in-chief Royal Victoria Hosp., 1964-74; chmn. dept. medicine, dir. Univ. Clinic McGill U., 1964-74; prof. medicine U. Calif., San Francisco, 1974-79; dir. Robert Wood Johnson Clin. Scholars Program, 1974-79; prof. geriatric medicine and gerontology UCLA, 1979—, dir. academic geriatric resource ctr., 1984-90; dir. long term car gerontology ctr. UCLA/U. So. Calif., 1980-85; dir. Calif. Geriatric Edn. Ctr., 1987—, emeritus dir., 1993—; dir. Multicampus Program in Geriatric Medicine & Gerontology UCLA, 1979-93; pres. Am. Bd. Med. Spltys.; vis. prof. numerous univs.; Simeone lectr. Brown U., 1977; John McCreary Meml. lectr. U. B.C., 1985; Bruce Hall Meml. lectr. Garvan Inst. Med. Rsch., U. N.S.W., Sydney, Australia, 1989—; Allen T. Bailey Meml. lectr. U. Sask., Can., 1989. Mem. editorial bd. Jour. Clin. Endocrinology and Metabolism, Current Topics in Exptl. Endocrinology, Psychiatry in Medicine, Health Policy and Edn.; cons. editor Roche Lab. Series on Geriatrics and Gerontology; mem. editorial adv. bd. Jour. Am. Bd. Family Practice. Recipient Lifetime award Ben Gurion U. of Negev, Israel, 1985. Fellow ACP (master), AAAS, Royal Coll. Physicians (Can., mem. coun., Duncan Graham award 1990), Royal Coll. Physicians (London), Royal Soc. Can., Inst. of Medicine, Internat. Soc. Endocrinology (sec.-gen.), Can. Soc. Clin. Investigation (pres.), Endocrine Soc. (v.p., chmn. postgrad. assembly), Am. Fedn. Clin. Rsch. (coun. East div.), Can. Med. Assn. (postgrad. edn. com.), Am. Diabetes Assn., Can. Diabetes Assn., McGill Osler Reporting Soc. (sec.), Montreal Physiol. Soc., Can. Physiol. Soc., Laurentian Hormone Conf. (bd. dirs.), Can. Assn. Profs. Medicine (Ronald V. Christie award 1987), Am. Clin. and Climatological Assn., Assn. Am. Med. Colls., Can. Med. Protective Assn., Internat. Soc. Neuroendocrinology, Soc. Exptl. Biology and Medicine (mem. editorial bd. jour.), Western Assn. Physicians, Am. Geriatrics Soc. (Milo F. Leavitt Meml. award 1988), Gerontol. Soc. Am. (mem. editorial bd. jour., Joseph T. Freeman award 1990), Am. Fedn. on Aging Rsch. (Irving S. Wright award 1991), Sigma Xi, Alpha Omega Alpha. Home: 1562 Casale Rd Pacific Palisades CA 90272-2714 Office: UCLA Box 951687 Los Angeles CA 90095-1687

BECK, JOHN ROBERT, pathologist, information scientist; b. Cleve., Sept. 8, 1953; s. John Edward and Maralyn Janet (Smith) B.; m. Sharon Louise Dombkowski, Aug. 30, 1975; children: John Benjamin, Stefan Andrew, Meredith Louise. AB, Dartmouth Coll., 1974; MD, Johns Hopkins U., 1978. Diplomate Am. Bd. Pathology. Intern, then resident in pathology Dartmouth-Hitchcock Med. Ctr., Hanover, N.H., 1978-80, dir. bloodbank, 1984-89, dir. clin. pathology, 1987-89; fellow, clin. decision making New Eng. Med. Ctr., Boston, 1981; from asst. to assoc. prof. pathology Dartmouth Med. Sch., Hanover, 1982-89; prof., dir. biomed. info. communication ctr. Oreg. Health Scis. U., Portland, 1989-92; prof., v.p. info. tech. Baylor Coll. Medicine, Houston, 1992—; chmn. Health Outcome Techs., Inc., Portland, 1991—; cons. Nat. Libr. Medicine, Bethesda, Md., 1988-92. Editor-in-chief Med. Decision Making, 1989-94. Recipient Rsch. Career Devel. award Nat. Libr. Medicine, 1986. Fellow Am. Coll. Med. Informatics, Am. Soc. Clin. Pathologists (coun. chmn. 1991-93); mem. Soc. for Med. Decision Making (sec.-treas. 1985-87, v.p. 1987-88, pres. 1995-96), Acad. Clin. Lab. Physicians and Scientists (exec. councilor 1989-91, Young Investigator award 1981), Integrated Advanced Info. Mgmt. Sys. (chmn. 1994-96). Republican. Office: Baylor Coll of Medicine Info Tech 1 Baylor Plz Houston TX 77030-3411

BECK, JOHN ROLAND, environmental consultant; b. Las Vegas, N.Mex., Feb. 26, 1929; s. Roland L. and Betty L. (Shrock) B.; m. Doris A. Olson, Feb. 9, 1951; children: Elizabeth J., Thomas R., Patricia L., John William. BS, Okla. A&M U., 1950; MS, Okla. State U., 1957; postgrad., U. Tex., 1954, George Washington U., 1965. Registered sanitarian, Ohio, Ariz.; cert. wildlife biologist. Wildlife researcher King Ranch, Kingsville, Tex., 1950-51; faculty Inst. Human Physiology U. Tenn., Martin, 1954-55; rsch. biologist FWS, USDI, Grangeville, Idaho, 1955-57; ctr. dir. Job Corps, OEO, Indiahoma, Okla., 1965-67; supr. animal control biology FWS, USDI, 1953-69; operating v.p. Bio-Svc. Corp., Troy, Mich., 1969-78; pres. BECS Ltd., Prescott, Ariz., 1981-85; spl. asst. USDA - APHIS, Washington, 1986-87; prin. cons. Biol. Environ. Cons. Svc. Inc., Phoenix, 1978-93; faculty assoc. Ariz. State U., Tempe, 1980-89; expert witness in bus. evaluations, 1979-94; expert witness in pesticide litigations, 1989-94; participant fin. seminars, 1980-85. Sr. author: Managing Service for Success, 1987, 2d edit., 1991; columnist mo. column on pest control in 2 mags., 1980-88; contbr. articles to profl. jours. Life mem. Rep. Nat. Com., 1993—; mem. Rep. Senatorial Inner Cir., 1994—, Rep. Presdl. Roundtable, 1995—. Capt. USAR, 1950-62. Fellow Royal Soc. Health, N.Y. Explorers Soc.; mem. ASTM (chmn. pesticide com. 1979-81, ad hoc chmn. vertebrate pesticides 1994-95), Wildlife Soc., Sigma Xi. Republican. Baptist.

BECK, LIVIA GRÜNWALD, physician, psychiatrist; b. Bratislava, Czechoslovakia, Jan. 5, 1947; came to U.S., 1974; d. Dezider and Gizela (Reisz) G.; 1 child, Michael. MBCHB, Victoria U., Manchester, England, 1969-74. Resident in psychiatry Long Island Jewish Hosp. and Med. Ctr., N.Y.C., 1974-78, fellow in psychotherapy, 1978-80, staff psychiatrist Aftercare div., 1978-83, unit chief Adult Day Hosp., 1983—, supr. of residents, 1978-83; pvt. practice N.Y.C., 1980—; staff psychiatrist L.I. Jewish Hosp. and Med. Ctr. Geriatric Day Hosp., N.Y.C., 1991—, Holliswood Hosp., Jamaica Estates, N.Y., 1994—. Mem. Am. Psychiatric Assn. Jewish. Home and Office: 1110 Cedar Dr W New Hyde Park NY 11040-1206

BECK, MICHAEL HAWLEY, dermatologist, consultant; b. Stoke-on-Trent, Stafford., Eng., Oct. 20, 1948; s. William Hawley and June Aldersey (Davenport) B.; m. Gerralynn Judith Harrop, Mar. 18, 1978; children—James John William, Robin Michael Davenport. M.B., Ch.B., Liverpool U. Med. Sch., 1972, M.R.C.P., 1977. House officer Clatterbridge Hosp., Merseyside, Eng., 1972-73, sr. house officer, 1973-74; sr. house officer in gen. medicine Salford Health Authority, Manchester, 1975-77; registrar of gen. medicine Trafford Health Authority, Manchester, 1977; registrar in dermatology Salford Health Authority, 1977-79, sr. registrar, 1979-81; cons. dermatologist Northwest Regional Health Authority, Manchester, 1981—, chmn., 1985—; cons. in charge of contact dermatitis investigation, Manchester, U.K., 1981—; hon. assoc. lectr. U. Manchester, 1985—. Contbr. articles to med. jours. Fellow Royal Soc. Medicine (dermatol. sect. 1981—); mem. North of Eng. Dermatol. Soc., Dowling Club, Brit. Assn. Dermatologists, Ileostomy Assn. (dermatol. adv. 1982—), Brit. Contact Dermatitis Research Group (com. mem. 1981—). Ch. of Eng. Office: 23 St John Street, Manchester M30 4DT, England

BECK, MORRIS, allergist; b. Miami, Fla., Oct. 12, 1927; s. Max and Anna (Luks) B.; m. Hollis Schwartz, Aug. 6, 1960; children: Gayle Beck Finan, Anne Lin. BA, UCLA, 1949; MD, U. Zurich, Switzerland, 1957. Diplomate Am. Bd. Allergy and Immunology, Am. Bd. Pediatrics. Intern Queens Hosp. Ctr., 1958, resident in pediatrics, 1959-60; preceptor in allergy U. Miami (Fla.) Med. Sch., 1961-77; pvt. practice pediatrician Miami, 1961-77, pvt. practice allergist, 1978—; chief dept. allergy Miami Children's Hosp., 1986—, Miami VA Hosp., 1994—. With U.S. Army, 1950-52. Fellow Am. Coll. Allergy & Immunology, Am. Acad. Pediatrics, Am. Assn. Cert. Allergists; mem. Am. Acad. Allergy & Immunology, Am. Coll. Chest Physicians. Republican. Jewish. Home: 12015 SW 68th Ave Miami FL 33156-5406 Office: Ste B 240 7800 SW 87th Ave Miami FL 33173-3570

BECK, SHARON ELLEN, nursing educator, nursing administrator; b. Phila., Nov. 2, 1943; d. Albert and Ruth (Reiff) Bralow; m. Morton S. Beck, July 11, 1965; children: Paul, Lisa. BS, Adelphi U., 1965; EdM, Temple U., 1976; DNSc, Villanova U., 1985; DS in Nursing, Widener U., 1992. RN Abington (Pa.) Meml. Hosp., 1970-73; nursing instr. Abington (Pa.) Meml. Hosp. Sch. Nursing, 1973-82; psychiat. liaison nurse Abington (Pa.) Mem. Hosp., 1981-82, nurse mgr. psychiat. unit, 1982-85; asst. DON Fairmount Inst., Phila., 1985-86; nursing instr. psychiat. nursing Frankford Hosp. Sch. Nursing, Phila., 1986-89; asst. prof. La Salle U., Phila., 1989-95; asst. hosp. dir. nursing edn.-quality improvement Temple U., Phila., 1995—; teaching asst. Pa. State U., Abington, 1977-83; adj. faculty La Salle U., Phila., 1988, Pa. State U. Sch. Nursing, Abington, 1989; cons. North Phila. (Pa.) Health System; lectr. in field. Bd. dirs. Benjamin Rush Mental Health Ctr., 1972-79, pres., 1977-79; bd. dirs. Bldg. Blocks, 1990-91. Named Outstanding Young Woman, 1975. Mem. ANA (cert. nursing adminstrn.), Pa. Nurses Assn., Montgomery County Nurses Assn. (v.p. 1991—, pres.), Nat. League for Nursing, Pa. League for Nursing (bd. dirs., co-membership chair, Hadassah Nurses Couns. pres.), Southeastern League Nursing, Sigma Theta Tau (jr. advisor 1991-93, sr. advisor 1993-94), Phi Kappa Phi. Home: 7819 Clyde Stone Dr Elkins Park PA 19027-1111 Office: Temple U Broad 2 Ontario Philadelphia PA 19140

BECK, WILLIAM SAMSON, physician, educator, biochemist; b. Reading, Pa., Nov. 7, 1923; s. Myron Paul and Gertrude (Harris) B.; m. Helene Samuels, Oct. 24, 1947; children—Thomas Russell, Peter Dean; m. Hanne Troedsson, July 20, 1964; children—John Christopher, Paul Brooks. B.S. in Chemistry, U. Mich., 1943, M.D., 1946; A.M. (hon.), Harvard U., 1971. Diplomate Am. Bd. Internal Medicine. Instr., asst. prof. medicine UCLA, 1950-57; fellow in biochemistry NYU Coll. Medicine, 1955-57; mem. faculty dept. medicine Harvard U., Boston, 1957—; prof. Harvard U., 1979—, tutor in biochem. scis., 1957—; prof. div. health sci. and tech. Harvard-MIT, 1971—, chmn. admissions com., 1977-88; dir. clin. labs. Mass. Gen. Hosp., Boston, 1957-75, chief hematology unit, 1957-72, dir. hematology rsch. lab., physician, 1957—; mem. adv. coun. Nat. Inst. Arthritis, Metabolism and Digestive Diseases, NIH, 1971-74; mem. hematology study sect. NIH, 1967-71. Author: Modern Science and the Nature of Life, 1957, Life: An Introduction to Biology, 3d edit., 1991, (with K.F. Liem, G.G. Simpson), Human Design, 1971, Hematology, 5th edit., 1991 (CD-ROM) Hemavid, 1995; contbr. articles to profl. jours. Served with AUS, 1943-46. Mem. Am. Soc. Biochemistry and Molecular Biology, Am. Soc. Hematology (exec. com. 1979-84), Assn. Am. Physicians, Am. Soc. Clin. Investigation, Am. Assn.

Cancer Rsch. Home: 85 Arlington St Winchester MA 01890-3734 Office: Mass Gen Hosp Boston MA 02114

BECK, WINFRIED, orthopedic surgeon; b. Germany, June 2, 1943; s. Walter and Irmgard (Sieber) B.; m. Renate Thies, Feb. 17, 1971; 1 child, Roman. MD, U. Frankfurt, 1968. Intern Orthopedic U. Clinic, Frankfurt, 1968-77; orthopedic surgeon in pvt. practice Frankfurt, 1977—; rep. Gen. Med. Coun., Hessen County, 1976—. Editor, author: Pax Medica, 1986, Arzte Opposition, 1987; editor circular: Democratic Doctors, 1987; author: Desire on Health, 1990. Mem. Com. on Environment and Health, Med. Coun. Hessen, 1985—; activist for environment, peace apartheit, others. Mem. Dem. Drs. Assn. (chmn. 1987—), World Med. Assn. (coord. opposition in med. coun. 199916), Assn. Victims of Nazi Regime (dep. chmn. 1976-91), Internat. Physicians for Preventive Nuclear War. Office: Verein Demokratischer Arzte, Kurfuerstenstrasse 18, D-60486 Frankfurt Germany

BECKER, BARBARA WIEGERS, hospital administrator; b. Charleston, W.Va., Oct. 27, 1956; d. Conrad Bernard and Eleanor Margaret (Haney) Wiegers; m. Thomas Spagnol, Apr. 3, 1984; children: Stephanie and Stephen (twins); m. Scott Becker, Sept. 18, 1993. BS in Health Info. Mgmt., U. Pitts., 1978, MS in Health Adminstrn., 1994. Cert. RRA, CPHQ. Quality analyst Youngstown (Ohio) Hosp. Assn., 1978-79; quality coord. Citizens Gen. Hosp., New Kensington, Pa., 1979-82; dir. med. records Shawano (Wis.) Cmty. Hosp., 1982-83; dir. med records Greene County (Pa.) Meml. Hosp., Waynesburg, 1983-84; asst. dir. med. records Magee-Womens Hosp., Pitts., 1984-85; DRG coord. Magee-Womens Hosp., 1985-86, dir. quality assessment/improvement/utilization mgmt., 1986—. Mem. Nat. Assn. Healthcare Quality (nominating com. 1990-92, chmn. 1993-94), Am. Health Info. Mgmt. Assn. (chmn. state and local DRG/legis. com. 1986, 87, chmn. quality/risk mgmt. com. 1988, 89), Western Pa. Assn. Healthcare Quality (bd. dirs., parliamentarian). Office: Magee-Womens Hosp Forbes & Halket Sts Pittsburgh PA 15213

BECKER, BRUCE CARL, II, physician, educator; b. Chgo., Sept. 8, 1948; s. Carl Max and Lillian (Podzamsky) B. BS in Aero. and Astron. Engring., U. Ill., 1970; MSME, Colo. State U., 1972; postgrad. Wright State U., 1973-74; MD, Chgo. Med. Sch., 1978; MS in Health Svcs. Adminstrn., Coll. St. Francis, Joliet, Ill., 1984; Diploma in Spanish, U. Chgo., 1988; Diploma in Polish, Coll. of Du Page, 1989. Diplomate Am. Bd. Med. Mgmt. Resident in surgery U. N.C.-Chapel Hill, 1978-79, in family practice St. Mary of Nazareth Hosp. Ctr., Chgo., 1979-81, chmn., program dir. dept. family practice, 1985-90; clin. instr. Chgo. Med. Sch., 1982, affiliate instr., 1982-83, asst. prof., 1983, vice chmn. dept. family medicine, 1983-91; asst. dir. med. edn. St. Mary of Nazareth Hosp. Ctr., Chgo., 1981-82, dir. family practice residency, 1983-90, chief Family Practice Ctr., 1983-85, chmn. dept. family practice, 1985-90, med. dir. Home Health Svc., 1985—, med. dir. HMO-Ill., 1985—, mem. fin. com. governing bd., 1987-91, planning and devel. com. governing bd., 1990—, v.p. med. affairs, 1989—; mem. adv. com. family practice residency Ill. Dept. Health, 1991—. Contbr. articles to profl. jours. Mem. editorial rev. bd. Postgrad. Medicine, 1987-89. Mem. Pub. Health Svc. Adv. Network Dept. Health & Human Svcs., 1990-91; bd. dirs. Inn Care of Am. Midwest Region, 1991—; mem. dinner com. Ill. chpt. Lupus Found. Am., 1991. Capt., USAF, 1970-75. Recipient Literary Key award St. Mary of Nazareth Hosp. Ctr., 1981, 85. Fellow Am. Acad. Family Physicians (rep. to accreditation rev. com. for physician assts. 1989-94, chmn. 1991-93), Am. Coll. Physician Execs., Am. Coll. Health Care Execs.; mem. AMA, Ill. Acad. Family Physicians (commn. on internal affairs 1986, commn. pub. and govt. policy 1987-89, chmn. 1989-90, bd. dirs. 1988-92, chmn. pub. rels. and info. com. 1988-92, state rep. family practice res. act com. 1990-92, vice speaker, 1991-92), Soc. Tchrs. of Family Medicine, Assn. Am. Med. Colls., Alliance Continuing Med. Edn., Am. Coll. Occupl. Medicine, Am. Acad. Med. Adminstrs., Chgo. Med. Soc. (councilor for Chgo. Med. Sch. 1986-91, alt. councilor for Chgo. Med. Sch. 1991-95, physicians stress ad hoc com. 1989-90, vice chmn. 1990-91, adv. com. on pub. health policy 1990—, presdl. adv. com. 1991—), Ill. State Med. Soc. (coun. on edn. and manpower 1986-96, chmn. com. on CME activities 1991-96, chmn. subcom. physican placement and practice issues 1986-90, third party payment and processes com. IAFP rep. 1990-92), Phi Delta Epsilon. Roman Catholic.

BECKER, DONALD PAUL, surgeon, neurosurgeon; b. Cleve., 1935. MD, Case Western Res. U., 1961. Diplomate Am. Bd. Neurol. Surgery. Intern U. (Cleve.) Hosps., 1961-62, resident in surgery, 1962-63, resident in neurol. surgery, 1963-67; fellow in neurosurgery NIH, Bethesda, Md., 1966; prof., chief neurosurgery U. Calif. (L.A.) Med. Ctr., 1967—. Mem. ACS, AMA. Office: UCLA Medical Center Div Neurosurgery Box 957039 Los Angeles CA 90095-7039

BECKER, HERMAN ELI, retired pharmacist; b. N.Y.C., Mar. 27, 1910; s. Abraham Jacob and Esther (Sabin) B.; m. Mina Leah Schuchat, Sept. 13, 1936; children: Jerome David, Stanley Harold. Degree in pharmacy, Med. Coll. Va., 1931. RPh, Va. Pharmacist, asst. mgr. Peoples Drug Stores, Richmond, Va., 1931-38; pharmacist Grant Drug Store, Richmond, 1938-40; co-owner, mgr. Blvd. Grant Drug Co., Richmond, 1940-48; pharmacist, asst. mgr. Meadowbridge Pharmacy, Richmond, 1948-67; pharmacist, asst. drug buyer Gem Drug Co., Richmond, 1967-69; pharmacist St. Mary's Hosp., Richmond, 1969-71; pharmacist, asst. mgr. various pharmacies, Richmond, 1971-89. Mem. Henrico County, Va. adv. com. to Va. Ho. of Reps.; adv. com. Congressman Thomas J. Bliley Jr., 3d Congl. Dist. Va.; v.p., chmn. bd. Temple Beth El, Richmond, 1963-64, lay reader evening svcs.; bd. dirs. Beth Sholom Home for Aged, Richmond, 1979-84; active Richmond Jewish Ctr., 1990. Recipient Disting. Worker award Temple Beth El, 1965, Samuel Gerson award, 1978, Methuselah award Beth Sholom Home for Aged, 1984. Mem. Richmond Pharm. Assn. (pres. 1957-58, dist. pres. svc. award 1957, human rels. award 1962), Va. Pharm. Assn., Am. Acad. Gen. Pharmacy Practice, B'nai Brith, Masons, Omega Chi. Republican. Home: 5108 Downy Ln # 101 Richmond VA 23228-3950

BECKER, JAMES WILLIAM, physician assistant; b. N.Y.C., Aug. 22, 1956; s. Christian Paul and Virginia Theresa (Smith) B.; m. Katherine Ann Sickles, Nov. 14, 1981; children: Michael James, Kevin Andrew, Kelly Jean. BS in Biology, SUNY, Albany, 1979; BS in Allied Health, SUNY, Stony Brook, 1981. Diplomate Nat. Commn. on Cert. of Physician Assts. Physician asst. St. Francis Hosp., Port Washington, N.Y., 1981-82, Ga. Surg. Assocs., Atlanta, 1982—; chmn. bd. dirs. 5-Quad Vol. Ambulance, Albany, 1978-79; chmn. Specified Profl. Pers. Adv. Com., Atlanta, 1993—; vis. lectr. Emory U., Atlanta, 1992—. Contbr. chpt. to book. Lt., Wading River (N.Y.) Vol. Fire Dept., 1980-82. Fellow Am. Acad. Physician Assts., Ga. Assn. Physician Assts. (chmn. pub. edn. com. 1990-93), bd. dirs. 1990-91, Cmty. Svc. award 1986). Office: Ga Surg Assocs Ste 170 5667 Peachtree Dunwood Rd Atlanta GA 30342

BECKER, JAN HENDRIK R., surgeon, educator; b. Pretoria, Republic of South Africa, Aug. 17, 1947; s. Theunis Christoffel and Regina Catharina (Neser) B.; m. Laurel Rose Manley, Dec. 13, 1973; children: Inge, Christo, Karen-Marie. MB ChB, U. Pretoria, Republic of South Africa, 1972, M Medicine in Surgery, 1979. Intern U. Pretoria, 1973, registrar in surgery, 1975-79, sr. lectr. in surgery, 1981-82, asst. prof. surgery, 1982-87, prof. surgery, 1987—, head surgery, 1993—; med. officer Pretoria Gen. Hosp., 1974; sr. lectr. in pediatric surgery Yorkhill Children's Hosp., Glasgow, Scotland, 1980. Author: Werkboek in Kinderchirurgie, 1992; contbr. over 50 articles to profl. jours. Lt. col. South African Med. Corps, 1967—. Recipient various rsch. awards. Fellow South African Coll. Medicine, Royal Coll. Medicine Scotland. Home: 181 Mackenziestr, Pretoria 0181, South Africa Office: Dept Surgery, Po Box 667, Pretoria 0001, South Africa

BECKER, JEANNE LYNN, immunologist, researcher, educator; b. Pensacola, Fla., Oct. 28, 1958; d. William Martin and Rhogene Becker. BS, U. Fla., 1980; PhD, U. South Fla., 1986. Postdoctoral fellow Moffitt Cancer Ctr. U. South Fla., Tampa, 1986-88, clin. rsch. assoc. dept. surgery, 1988-90, asst. prof. ob.-gyn. dept., 1990—. Contbr. articles to profl. jours. Grantee U. South Fla., 1983, 84, 85, 91, Am. Cancer Soc., 1990, NASA, 1992; recipient Sigma Xi award, 1985. Mem. AAAS, N.Y. Acad. Scis., Soc. for Gynecol. Investigation, Soc. for In Vitro Biology, Internat. Endometriosis Assn. (sci. advisor 1992—), U. South Fla. McClintock Soc. for Jr. Women Faculty (founding mem. 1993). Office: U South Fla Dept Ob/Gyn 4 Columbia Dr Tampa FL 33606-3589

BECKER, MICHAEL ALLEN, physician, educator; b. N.Y.C., Oct. 3, 1940; s. David S. and Sylvia M. (Salomon) B.; m. Mary E. Baim; children: David, Jonathan, Abigail, Arielle, Daniel. BA, U. Pa., Phila., 1961, MD, 1965. Diplomate Am. Bd. Internal Medicine, with subspecialty in rheumatology. Intern Barnes Hosp., Washington U., St. Louis, 1965-66, resident, 1969-70; asst. prof. U. Calif., San Diego, 1972-77, assoc. prof., 1977-80; prof. medicine Pritzker Sch. Medicine U. Chgo., 1980—; mem. biochemistry study sect. NIH, Bethesda, Md., 1991-95. Contbr. over 85 rsch. articles ot profl. publs. Sr. asst. surgeon USPHS, 1966-69. Mem. Am. Soc. Clin. Investigation, Assn. Am. Physicians, Am. Coll. Rheumatology. Office: U Chgo Med Ctr MC0930 Chicago IL 60637

BECKER, NANCY MAY, nursing educator; b. Reading, Pa., July 28, 1949; d. Theodore R. and Minerva M. (Deiseroth) B. Diploma, Reading Hosp. Sch. Nursing, Pa., 1970; BS, Albright Coll., 1979; MS, U. Del., 1981. RN, Pa., Del. Nurse mgr. Cmty. Gen. Hosp., Reading, 1974-76; nurse educator Albright Coll., Reading, 1980-87; clin. nurse specialist Polyclinic Med. Ctr., Harrisburg, Pa., 1987-89; asst. prof. Lehigh Carbon C.C., Schnecksville, Pa., 1989-95, dir. nursing programs, 1995—. Mem. ANA (cert. clin. nurse specialist), AACN (cert. critical care nurse), Nat. League Nursing, Sigma Theta Tau.

BECKER, RALPH LEONARD, psychologist; b. Cin., July 15, 1927; s. Morris and Sarah Ruth B.; m. Evelyn Zeifman, Aug. 15, 1976. BA in Sci., Ohio State U., 1958, BS in Edn., 1960, MA in Psychology, 1961, PhD in Psychology, 1979. Lic. psychologist, Ohio; cert. counselor, Ohio. Spl. tchr. Columbus (Ohio) City Schs., 1962-64; staff psychologist Ohio Dept. Mental Retardation/Devel. Disabilities, Columbus, 1964-68, research scientist, 1968-72, research assoc., 1972-82; research dir. Elbern Pubs., Columbus, 1982—. Author: Reading-Free Vocational Interest Inventory, 1981, rev. edit. 1988, Occupational Title List, 1984, rev. edit. 1992, Becker Work Adjustment Profile, 1989; contbr. articles to profl. jours. Grantee State of Ohio, 1966, 67, U.S. Office of Edn., 1968. Fellow Am. Assn. on Mental Retardation; mem. Coun. for Exceptional Children, Ohio Psychol. Assn., Ohio State Alumni Assn., Am. Psychol. Assn. Office: Elbern Publs PO Box 09497 Columbus OH 43209-0497

BECKER, ROBERT JEROME, allergist, health care consultant; b. Milw., May 29, 1922; s. Jacob and Sarah (Saxe) B.; m. June Granof, June 25, 1950; children: Scott M., Jill Becker Wilson, Jon G. BS, U. Wis., Milw., 1943; MD, Med. Coll. Wis., 1949. Intern Michael Reese Hosp., Chgo., 1949-50; resident in internal medicine VA Hosp., Wood, Wis., 1950-53; resident in allergy Roosevelt Hosp., N.Y.C., 1955-56; pvt. practice specializing in allergy Joliet, Ill., 1956-82; founder, chmn. HealthCare COMPARE, 1982-90, chmn. emeritus, bd. dirs., 1990—; cons. health care utilization co., 1982-90; founder, pres. Becker Cons. Corp., 1990—; founder, chmn. Healthcare Communications Mgmt. Corp., 1990-93; med. dir. Quad river Found. Med. Care, 1976-84; pres. Am. Assn. Profl. Stds. Rev. Orgns., 1980-82; exec. v.p. Joint Coll. Allergy and Immunology, 1978-86; mem. adv. coun. Nat. Inst. Environ. Health Scis., 1984-88; bd. dirs. GMIS, Allerx, Am. Psych Sys.; chmn. Utilization Rev. Accreditation Commn., 1991-94, bd. dirs., 1994-96. Author articles in field. Pres. bd. edn. Joliet Twp. High Sch. Dist. 204, 1969-70, 75-76; mem. bus. adv. com. U. Ill. Sch. Bus., Chgo., 1987—. Recipient Clemens von Pirquet award Georgetown U. Internat. Interdisciplinary Ctr. Immunology, 1978; named Entrepreneur of Yr. Arthur Young/Venture Mag., 1988. Fellow ACP, Am. Acad. Allergy, Am. Coll. Allergists (pres. 1987), Am. Coll. Chest Physicians; mem. Ill. Soc. Internal Medicine (pres. 1984-86), Asthma and Allergy Assn. Am. (bd. dirs. 1987—), Asthma and Allergy Found. Am. (bd. dirs. 1990-94), Am. Managed Care and Rev. Assn. (bd. dirs. 1989-95), Am. Assn. Preferred Providers Assn. (bd. dirs. 1989—), Utilization Rev. Accreditation Commn. (chair 1991-94, bd. dirs. 1991—), Am. Assn. Preferred Provider Orgns. (bd. dirs. 1988-93), Am. Psychiat. Systems (bd. dirs. 1994—), Alpha Omega Alpha, Alpha Sigma Nu. Home: 2036 Intracoastal Dr Fort Lauderdale FL 33305-3636 Office: 1 Tower Ln Ste 1140 Villa Park IL 60181-4625

BECKER, ROBERT OTTO, orthopedic surgery educator; b. River Edge, N.J., May 31, 1923; s. Otto and Elizabeth (Blank) B.; m. Lillian J. Moller, Sept. 6, 1946; children: Lisa, Michael, Adam. B.A., Gettysburg Coll., 1946; M.D., NYU, 1948. Am. Bd. Orthopedic Surgery Nat. Bd. Med. Examiners. Intern Bellevue Hosp., N.Y.C., 1948-49; resident Mary Hitchcock Meml. Hosp., Hanover, N.H., 1950-51, SUNY Downstate Med. Ctr., 1953-56; practice medicine specializing in orthopedic surgery, 1956—; prof. orthopedics SUNY Upstate Med. Ctr., Syracuse, 1966—; clin. prof. orthopedics La. State Coll. Medicine, Shreveport, 1980—; v.p. rsch. Becker Biomagnetics, 1992—. Author: Electromagnetism and Life, 1982, The Body Electric, 1985, Cross Currents, 1990; editor: Mechanisms of Growth Control, 1981; patentee electric stimulation of growth. Served to 1st lt. USMC, 1951-53. Faculty exchange scholar SUNY, 1979; recipient Middletown research award VA, 1960, disting. alumnus award NYU Coll. Medicine, 1966, Nicolas Andry award Assn. Bone and Joint Surgery, 1979. Mem. AAAS, N.Y. Acad. Scis., Bioelectronics Soc., Internat. Soc. for Bioelectricity. Republican. Home: Star Route Lowville NY 13367 Office: Becker Biomagnetics Star Route Lowville NY 13367

BECKER, ROSEMARY M., retired gerontology nurse; b. East Newark, N.J., Sept. 4, 1928; d. James A. and Elizabeth J. (Berkise) Degnan; m. David J. Becker, Sept. 5, 1959; children: James, Cecelia Dietrick, Stephen, Susan, Ann, Maureen. Grad., RN, Jersey City Med. Ctr., 1949; BSN, Cath. U. Am., 1966. Cert. in gerontology. Head nurse Georgetown U. Hosp., Washington; staff nurse Providence Hosp., Washington, asst. dir. nursings nights; charge nurse Little Sisters of the Poor, Washington. Home: 5203 Wiley St Riverdale MD 20737-3042

BECKER, VICTORIA LORETTA, geriatrics nurse; b. Nationa Heights, Pa., Dec. 22, 1947; d. Emil Michael and Beatrice Bernadette (Scharle) B. Diploma, Allegany Valley Hosp. Sch. Nursing, 1970; BS in Profl. Arts, St. Joseph's Coll., 1983. Geriatric charge nurse Fair Winds, Inc., Sarver, Pa. Recipient Staff Nurse Recognition award Pa. Nurses Assn., 1984, 86. Mem. Pa. Nurses Assn. (Staff Nurse Recognition award 1984, 86). Roman Catholic.

BECKER, WILLIAM KIRBY, surgeon; b. Mpls., July 10, 1952; s. William Kirby and Joan Catherine (Moery) B.; m. Patricia Ann Gerardy, June 12, 1977; children: Amy, Anna. BS in Microbiology, U. Minn., 1973, MD, 1976, PhD, 1993. Diplomate Am. Bd. Surgeons. Program dir. William Beaumont Army Med. Ctr., El Paso, Tex., 1987-88, Brooke Arm Med. Ctr., Ft. Sam Houston, Tex., 1988-92; program dir. of surgery U. N.D., Grand Forks, 1992—. Contbr. numerous articles to prof. jours. Lt. Col. U.S. Armed Forces, 1981-93. Decorated Bronze Star; recipient Cert. of Appreciation, Ministry of Def. and Aviation, Saudi Arabia, 1991; recipient grant from Office of Resh. and Program Devel., 1993. Fellow, ACS; Mem. Soc. for Cryobiology, Soc. Critical Care Med., Internat. Soc. of Burn Injury, Am. Soc. for Microbiology, Lillehei Surgical Soc., Am. Burn Assn., Surgical Infection Soc. Office: Univ of North Dakota Surgery PO Box 9037 Grand Forks ND 58202

BECKER, WOLFGANG STEFAN, nuclear medicine physician; b. Uffenheim, Bavaria, Germany, Sept. 7, 1952; s. Peter and Gerda (Neubert) B.; m. Hedwig Zeptner, Nov. 10, 1978; children: Sabine, Sebastian. MD, U. Würzburg, Germany, 1978. Asst. physician dept. pathology U. Würzburg, 1979, asst. physician dept. nuclear medicine, 1981-88; prof. nuclear medicine U. Erlangen, Nuremburg, Germany, 1988-95; prof. nuclear medicine U. Göttingen, Germany, 1995—, dean European Sch. Nuclear Medicine, 1995—; presenter in field. Contbr. over 100 articles to profl. publs., chpts. to books. Mem. German Soc. Nuclear Medicine (Mallinckrodt prize 1988), numerous other med. and sci. orgns. Office: U Göttingen, Rob Koch Str 40, D-37075 Göttingen Germany

BECKERMAN, ROBERT CY, pediatrician, educator; b. Bklyn., Oct. 29, 1946; s. Edward and Beatrice (Sherman) B.; children: Sarah, Ashley, Mollye. BS, Dickinson Coll., 1968; MD, Jefferson Med. Coll., 1972. Cert. Nat. Bd. Med. Examiners, Bd. Pulmonary Disease subspecialty Am. Bd. Pediatrics. Intern Riverside Hosp., Newport News, Va., 1972-73; resident in pediatrics Children's Hosp./U. of Cin., 1973-75, devel. disability fellow, 1975-76; pulmonary fellow U. Ariz., Tucson, 1976-78; asst. prof. pediatrics U. Miami (Fla.) Sch. Medicine, 1978-79; dir. pediatric pulmonary and sleep lab. Tulane U. Sch. Medicine, New Orleans, 1980-90, prof. pediatrics, physiology, chief pediatric pulmonology, 1978—; chief pediat. pulmonology Constance Kaufman Ctr., New Orleans, 1988—; dir. fellowship program pediatric pulmonary sect. Tulane U. Sch. Medicine, New Orleans, 1983—; dir., head CF Ctr. La., New Orleans, 1987-92; dir. Pediatric Pulmonary Ctr. So. La., New Orleans, 1988-92, Pediatric Pulmonary Outreach Program, Lafayette, La., 1988—; med. dir. SIDS program Office Pub. Health/State of La.; chief med. cons. Audubon Zoo, New Orleans; med. cons. Friends of SIDS, La. Chpt. Sudden Infant Death Syndrome Found., New Orleans, Spinal Muscular Atrophy Assn. Exec. Com., New Orleans. Author: (with others) Practical Manual of Pediatrics, 2d edit., 1981, Current Pediatric Therapy, 13th edit., 1990, Respiratory Control Disorders in Infants and Children, 1992; editorial bd.: So. Med. Jour., 1993-96. Fellow Am. Coll. Chest Physicians (pediat. assembly), Am. Acad. Pediatrics; mem. Am. Thoracic Soc., La. Lung Assn., So. Soc. for Pediat. Rsch. Office: Tulane U Sch Medicine 1430 Tulane Ave New Orleans LA 70112-2699

BECKHAM, ERNEST EDWARD, clinical psychologist; b. Dallas, Jan. 8, 1950; s. Ernest and Audean (Croan) B.; m. Cecilia Elaine Owens, May 29, 1976; children: Michael Christopher, Matthew Taylor. BA in Physics, North Tex. State U., 1970; MDiv, Tex. Christian U., 1973, MA in Clin. Psychology, 1976; PhD, Tex. Tech U., 1980. Lic. psychologist, Okla. Instr. dept. psychiatry U. Okla. Coll. Medicine, Oklahoma City, 1980-82, asst. prof., 1982-88, assoc. prof., 1988-91; clin. assoc. prof., 1991—; also dir. Mood Disorders Clinic U. Okla. Coll. Medicine, Oklahoma City, 1989-91; psychologist Psychiat. Assocs., Edmond, Okla., 1991—; cons. Oklahoma City Manic Depressive Assn., 1984—. Editor: Handbook of Depression, 1985, 2nd edit., 1995; contbr. articles to profl. jours. Mem. APA, Okla. Psychol. Assn., Sigma Xi.

BECKHAM, SUSAN GAY, exercise physiologist, educator; b. Wichita, Kans., Mar. 27, 1956; d. Rex Larkin and Mary JoAnn (Maddox) Beckham. BS in Geology cum laude, S.W. Mo. State U., 1980; MS in Health Sci. magna cum laude, Okla. State U., 1984, postgrad. Geologist NEMO Coal, Moberly, Mo., 1980-81, Assoc. Elec. Coop., Springfield, Mo., 1981-82, Jim Winnek, Inc., Tulsa, 1982-84; fitness instr. Tulsa Racquetball Aerobics Club, Tulsa, 1983-85; exercise technician/leader cardiac rehab. Okla. State U. Health Fitness Ctr., Stillwater, 1983-84; exercise technician St. Francis Phys. Performance Ctr., Tulsa, 1985; fitness dir. Okla. Ctr. for Athletes, Oklahoma City, 1985-88; exercise physiologist/cons. Okla. Ctr. for Athletes, 1989-92; ptnr. Fitness, Inc., Carrollton, Tex., 1992-94; instr. North Lake Coll., Irving, Tex., 1994—; wellness dir. Lifestyle to Wellness, 1992-94; owner Rock Fitness & Sport Sci., 1995—; adj. asst. prof. U. Tex., Arlington, 1995—; owner Rock Fitness and Sports Sci. Ctr. Contbr. articles to profl. jours.; author: (with others) ARC Injury Manual, 1987, Clinical Sports Medicine, 1990. Mem. spl. projects com. ARC, 1989-90; active Gov.'s Coun. on Phys. Fitness & Sports, Okla., 1988—. Fellow Am. Coll. Sports Medicine; mem. Okla. Aerobic Tchrs. Assn. (co-founder, bd. dirs. 1986—). Methodist. Home: 8827 D Gaston Pkwy Dallas TX 75218-3929 Office: Univ of Tex Box 19259 Arlington TX 76019

BECKLAKE, MARGARET RIGSBY, physician, educator; b. London, May 27, 1922; d. James Thomas and Dorothy Mabel (Mills) B.; m. Maurice McGregor, Mar. 20, 1949; children: James, Margaret. MBBCh, U. Witwatersrand, 1944, MD, 1951, MD (hon.), 1974. Lectr. U. Witwatersrand, 1950-57; asst. prof. exptl. medicine McGill U., 1961-65, prof., 1967-96, prof. epidemiology and medicine, 1973-96, prof. emeritus, 1996—; career investigator Med. Rsch. Coun. Can., 1968-93. Contbr. articles to med. jours. Named hon. prof., U. Witwatersrand, 1984-85. Fellow Royal Coll. Physicians, Royal Soc. (Can.); mem. Am. Thoracic Soc., Can. Thoracic Soc., Am. Physiol. Soc. Home: 532 Pine Ave W, Montreal, PQ Canada H2W 1S6 Office: McGill U, Dept of Epidemiology & Biostats, 1110 Pine Ave W, Montreal, PQ Canada H3A 1A3

BECKLEY, JEANINE SUSAN, nuclear medicine technologist; b. Rome, N.Y., Jan. 31, 1964; d. Jerry Slater and Glada Ruth (Kingsbury) B. AA, Prince George's C.C., Largo, Md., 1989. Cert. nuclear medicine technologist. Nuc. medicine technologist Nuc. Cardiology Lab., Silver Spring, Md., 1989-93; chief nuc. medicine technologist So. Md. Nuc. Cardiology, Clinton, 1993-95; asst. chief nuc. medicine tech. Cardio Diagnostic Ctr., Chevy Chase, Md., 1995—; mem. rsch. apprentice program Naval Rsch. Lab., Washington, 1982; student rep. med. isotope tech. program Prince George's C.C., 1987-89. Acad. scholar Findlay (Ohio) U., 1982, music scholar, 1982, senatorial scholar Prince George's C.C., 1987-89. Mem. Soc. Nuclear Medicine, Am. Soc. Nuclear Cardiology (assoc.), Am. Soc. Radiologic Technologists. Republican. Methodist. Office: Cardio Diagnostic Ctr 5530 Wisconsin Ave # 740 Chevy Chase MD 20815 also: Laurel Park Animal Hosp 7401 Van Dusen Rd Laurel MD 20707

BECKMAN, HOWARD BRUCE, internist; b. Boston, May 8, 1947; s. Louis and Bernice (Andelman) B.; m. Ellen M. Leopold, Sept. 11, 1985; children: Liza, Renee, Alice, Micah. BA, Brandeis U., 1969; MD, Wayne State U., 1974. Diplomate Am. Bd. Internal Medicine with subspecialty in geriatrics. Jr. resident internal medicine Detroit Gen. Hosp., 1974-75, chief resident, 1977-78; sr. resident internal medicine Wayne State U., Detroit, 1975-77, asst. prof. medicine, 1979-88, residency coord., 1980-90, assoc. prof. medicine, 1988-90; assoc. prof. medicine U. Rochester, N.Y., 1990-95, prof. medicine and family medicine, 1995—; chief dept. medicine Highland Hosp., Rochester, 1990—; pvt. practice Highland Hosp., 1990—; mem. adv. bd. physician asst. program Rochester Inst. Tech., 1993—. Contbr. articles to profl. jours. Fellow ACP (subcom. mem. 1992-96), Am. Acad. on Physicians and Patients; mem. Am. Coll. Physician Execs., Physicians for Nat. Health Plan, Soc. Gen. Internal Medicine. Office: Highland Hospital 1000 South Ave Rochester NY 14620

BECKMEYER, HENRY ERNEST, anesthesiologist, medical educator; b. Cape Girardeau, Mo., Apr. 13, 1939; s. Henry Ernest Jr. and Margaret Gertrude (Link) B.; m. Virginia Hobson; children: Henry, James, Martha, Leigh, Hillary, Nicole. BA, Mich. State U., 1961; DO, U. Health Scis., 1965. Diplomate Am. Bd. Med. Examiners, Am. Osteo. Bd. Anesthesiology, Am. Acad. Pain Mgmt. Chief physician migrant worker program and op. head start Sheridan (Mich.) Community Hosp., 1967-69; resident in anesthesia Bi-County Community Hosp./DOH Corp., Detroit, 1969-71, chief resident, 1968-69; staff anesthesiologist Detroit Osteo. Hosp./BCCH, 1971-75; founding chmn. dept. anesthesia Humana Hosp. of the Palm Beaches, West Palm Beach, Fla., 1975-79; assoc. prof. Mich. State U., East Lansing, 1979-88, prof. anesthesia, 1988—, chmn. dept. osteo. medicine, 1985—; chief staff Mich. State U. Health Facilities, 1988-90, chmn. med. staff exec. and steering coms., 1988-90; chmn. of anesthesia St. Lawrence Hosp., Lansing, Mich., 1984-90, adminstrv. dir. dept. anesthesia, 1994—; chief of staff Sheridan Community Hosp., 1968-69; mem. adminstrv. coun. Mich. State U., 1988—, mem. acad. coun., 1992—, mem. faculty coun., 1992—, mem. clin. practice bd., bd. dirs. sports medicine; mem. internal mgmt. com. Mich. Ctr. for Rural Health; cons. Ministry Health, Belize C.A., 1993—; amb. Midwestern Univ. Consortium Internat. Activities, 1993; program chmn. Am. Russian Med. Exch., 1993—; bd. dirs. Belize Med. Partnership. Speaker Sta. WKAR, Mich. State U.; bd. dirs. Boy Scouts Am., W. Bloomfield, Mich., 1973-74, Palm Beach Mental Health, 1977-79, Care Choices HMO, Lansing, 1987-88. Fellow Am. Coll. Osteo. Anesthesiologists; mem. Am. Osteo. Coll. Anesthesiology (chmn. commn. on colls. 1988-89, cert. anesthesiology 1976), Soc. Critical Care Medicine, Internat. Anesthesiology Rsch. Soc., Am. Coll. Physician Execs., Am. Osteo. Assn. (spkr.), Am. Acad. Pain Mgmt. (cert. 1991), Am. Arbitration Assn., Mich. Pain Soc., Mich. Peer Rev. Orgn., Am. Soc. Regional Anesthesia, Soc. Security Disability Evaluation, Univ. Club, Phi Beta Delta. Republican. Office: Mich State U West Fee Hall East Lansing MI 48824

BECKTELL, PHOEBE JEAN, nurse, educator; b. Belle Fourche, S.D., Dec. 11, 1929; d. Wilfred Sinclair and Thelma Violet (Strain) Stevenson; m. Marvin Jack Becktell, June 22, 1957; children: Kathleen Jo Chervnsik, Patricia Jane Olson, M. Joel. BSN, U. Minn., 1952; MA, U. N.Mex., 1975,

PhD, 1986. Prof. emerita U. N.Mex., Albuquerque; primary care clinician, dir. nursing svcs. for therapeutic pre-sch., cons. to St. Jude's Express to provide humanitarian and health care to Indians of Mex. Contbr. articles to profl. jours. Intramural grantee, 1989; recipient Biomed. Rsch. Support, 1988, Fulbright Lectr. award to India, 1991-92. Mem. Sigma Theta Tau.

BECKWITH, CHARLES ALLAN, healthcare administrator, consultant; b. L.A., Feb. 15, 1940; s. Harry Spencer and Mary Dorothy (Riley) B.; m. Roberta Louise Sommerdorf, Nov. 27, 1963 (dec. Jan. 1966); m. Susan Ann Robinson, Aug. 24, 1969; 1 child, Mary Aileen. BS in Psychology, Loyola-Marymount U., 1962; cert., George Washington U., 1989; M of Profl. Studies: Hosp. and Health Svcs. Adminstrn., Cornell U., 1976. Adminstr. Grover M. Hermann divsn. Comty. Gen. Hosp. Sullivan County, Callicoon, N.Y., 1976-77; assoc. dir. Comty. Gen. Hosp. Sullivan County, Harris, N.Y., 1977-78; adminstr. for ambulatory care USPHS Hosp., Balt., 1978-81; program cons. Office Ambulatory Care Bur. Med. Svcs., Hyattsville, Md., 1981; adminstr. area contract health svcs., program/internal auditor Albuquerque Area Indian Health Svc., 1981-84, internal auditor Office of Area Dir., 1984; sr. internal auditor Calif. Area Indian Health Svc., Sacramento, 1984-89, spl. adminstrv. asst., 1989—; mem. health svcs. adminstrn. adv. bd. Sch. Pub. Adminstrn., U. So. Calif., 1988-93; adminstrv. residency preceptor for M. of Healthcare Adminstrn. students Sacramento campus U. So. Calif., 1992-94; presenter profl. papers ann. meeting USPHS Profl. Assn., Scottsdale, Ariz., 1988, 93; mem. Sloan Program Hosp. and Health Svcs. Adminstrn., Grad. Sch. Bus. and Pub. Adminstrn., Cornell U., 1976; presenter in field. Contbr. articles to profl. publs. Alumni admissions interviewer Johnson Grad. Sch. Mgmt., Cornell U., 1985—; co-master of ceremony duties for commemorative awards Indian Health Svcs. Honor Awards Ceremony, Rockville, Md., 1989, 91. Capt. USPHS, 1978—. Decorated Bronze Star medal; recipient Calif. Area Dir.'s award for Managerial Excellence for leadership in advancement of healthcare adminstrn., 1994, award of appreciation Combined Fed. Campaign Coord., 1993, award for Area Office with Best Overall Performance, U.S. Savs. Bond Campaign Coord., 1994, PHS Outstanding Svc. medal, 2 PHS Commendation medals, PHS Citation and Unit Citation. Fellow Am. Coll. Healthcare Execs. (membership examiner); mem. Commd. Officers Assn. Roman Catholic. Office: Calif Area Indian Health Ser 1825 Bell St Ste 200 Sacramento CA 95825-1020

BECKWITH, JONATHAN ROGER, geneticist; b. Cambridge, Mass., Dec. 25, 1935; s. Manuel and Mildred B.; m. Barbara Shutt, Dec. 26, 1960; children—Benjamin Hunter, Anthony Rhys. B.A., Harvard U., 1957, Ph.D., 1961. Mem. faculty Harvard U. Med. Sch., 1965—, prof. genetics, 1969—, Am. Cancer Soc. prof., 1979—; mem. Sci. for The People, 1971—; mem. Nat. Acad. Scis., 1984—. Recipient Eli Lilly award, 1970, Genetics Soc. Am. medal, 1993. Fellow AAAS; mem. Am. Acad. Arts and Scis., European Molecular Biology Orgn. (assoc.), Am. Soc. Exptl. Biologists, Am. Soc. Microbiology, Genetics Soc. Am. Home: 8A Appleton Rd Cambridge MA 02138-2226 Office: Harvard Univ Medical Sch Boston MA 02115

BEDELL, ARCHIE WILLIAM, family physician, educator; b. Detroit, Sept. 22, 1938; s. Archie Arnold and Mary (Barson) B.; m. Linda Suzanne Boos, Apr. 15, 1952; children: Robert, Marty, Jim, Amy. BS, Detroit Inst. Tech., 1961; MS in Biology, U. Detroit, 1963; MS in Human Anatomy, Wayne State U., 1964, PhD, 1967, MD, 1970. Diplomate Am. Bd. Family Practice. Med. intern Bon Secours Hosp., Grosse Point, Mich., 1969-71, Holden fellow, 1969-71; dir. inpatient tng. Bon Secours Hosp., Grosse Pointe, Mich., 1971-73; founding dir. family practice residency Bon Secours Hosp., Grosse Pointe, 1974-88; founding chmn. dept. family practice Henry Ford Hosp., Detroit, 1988-91, founding dir. family practice residency program, 1988-91; pvt. family practice Grosse Pointe, Mich., 1991-95; chmn., family practice Macomb Hosp., Warren, Mich., 1994; dir. family practice residency Mercy Hosp., Toledo, 1995—, dir. med. edn., 1995; trustee Detroit Inst. Tech., 1974-78; merit project bd. mem. Family Health Found. Am. Acad. Family Practice, Kansas City, Mo., 1982; chmn. bd. Mich. Health Coun., Lansing, 1996—. Provider Homeless, Toledo, 1995. Recipient Holden award Sisters of Bon Secour, Grosse Pointe, 1969, 71, Semmes award, 1970. Mem. Mich. Acad. Family Physicians (chmn. risk mgmt. 1980-90, bd. mem., v.p., pres.-elect 1994-95, pres. 1996—), Wyndgate County Club (founder). Methodist. Office: Mercy Family Practice Ctr 2127 Jefferson Toledo OH 43624

BEDELL, BARBARA ANN, nurse; b. Yonkers, N.Y., Dec. 23, 1939; d. George and Viola (Murphy) Pasquel; divorced; children: James, Timothy, Raymond, Terri Ann. AAS, Queensboro Community Coll., 1970; BSN, Adelphi U., 1983, MSN, 1988. Team leader Flushing (N.Y.) Hosp.; nurse Vis. Nurse Svcs., Flushing. Mem. Nat. Honor Soc. Nursing, Sigma Theta Tau. Home: 32-31 202nd St Bayside NY 11361-1017

BEDENKO, DIMITRI MITCHELL, psychiatrist; b. Zagreb, Croatia, Feb. 23, 1936; came to U.S. 1966; s. Dr. Rudolf and Marta (Thaller) B.; m. Victoria Ruzica Cargonja, July 29, 1961; 1 child, Alan Joseph. Maturity Cert., Classical Gymnasium, Zagreb, Croatia, 1954; MD, Zagreb U., 1961. Diplomate Am. Bd. Psychiatry and Neurology. Psychiatrist pvt. practice, White Plains, N.Y., 1972—; staff psychiatrist FDR VA Hosp, Montrose, N.Y., 1986—; attending MD United Hosp Med. Ctr., Port Chester, N.Y., 1973-91, Rye Psychiatric Hosp. Ctr., Rye, N.Y., 1972—; clinical asst. prof., N.Y. Med. Coll., Valhalla, N.Y. Maj., Med. Corps, U.S. Army, 1969-71, Ft. Jackson. Mem. AMA, Am. Psychiat. Assn. Office: 510 N Broadway White Plains NY 10603-3217

BEDFORD, MARY RUTH, dietitian, educator, consultant; b. Roswell, N.Mex., May 31, 1923; d. Sidney McHenry and Jennie Pearl (Hutchison) B. BS in Dietetics, James Madison U., 1943; MS, Kans. State U., Manhattan, 1971, PhD, 1975. Registered dietitian. Intern U. Colo. Med. Ctr., Denver, 1944; dietitian Presbyn. Med. Ctr., Denver, 1944-47, U. Iowa Hosps., Iowa City, 1947-51, Neb. State Tchrs. Coll., Chadron, 1951-52, State Home and Tng. Sch., Wheatridge, Colo., 1952-55; asst. chief dietetic service VA Med. Ctr., Ft. Lyon, Colo., 1955-56; chief dietitian Presbyn. Med. Ctr., Denver, 1956-63; cons. dietitian State Bd. Health, N.C., 1963-68; instr. Ind. State U., Terre Haute, 1968-72, Kans. State U., Manhattan, 1972-75; assoc. prof., dir. coordinated undergrad. program in dietetics Va. Poly. Inst. and State U., Blacksburg, 1975-83; prof. grad. program in dietetics M.G.H., Boston, 1983-86; vis. prof. U. So. Miss, Hattiesburg, 1986; lectr. in field; cons. Mem. editorial bds., contbr. articles to profl. jours;. Named one of Notable Americans of Bicentennial Era, 1976; recipient of award as designer of one of twenty-five outstanding foodservice facilities in U.S Insts. Mag. for Presbyn. Hosp., 1962; grantee Dept. HEW, 1977-81, VA, 1977-84, Va. Poly. Inst., 1976. Mem. Am. Dietetic Assn. (coun. edn. 1978-81, review panel accreditation 1986-89, bd. editors, medallion 1992), Acad. Mgmt., Am. Assn. Adult and Continuing Edn., Am. Sch. Food Service Assn. (cert. and personal devel. com. 1981-83, cert. adv. bd. 1983-84, chmn. coll. personnel sect. 1984-85, task force to develop master plan for edn. 1984, exec. bd. 1984-85, ad hoc nat. breakfast month com. 1984, ad hoc com. to determine sch. food service research needs 1984-85, chmn. coll. personnel sect. 1984-85, nominating com. 1985-86), Am. Soc. Hosp. Food Service Adminstrs. (chmn. spl. com. pubs. rev. 1982-83, research and devel. com. 1984,), Am. Assn. Higher Edn., Am. Ednl. Research Assn., Am. Home Econs. Assn. (co-chmn. instn. mgmt. sect. 1977-79), Am. Mgmt. Assn., Am. Soc. Tng. and Devel., Am. Soc. Allied Health Professions, Food Service Systems Mgmt. Edn. Council (nominating com. 1979-81, com. to study fins. 1981-83, treas. 1981-85, chmn. spl. com. pubs. rev. 1982-83, chmn. com. to develop guidelines for small grants 1983-85, chmn. 1987-89), Inst. Food Tech., Soc. Advancement Food Service Research, Soc. Foodservice Systems, Soc. Nutrition Edn., West Cen. Ind. Dietetic Assn. (chmn. edn. and service com., pres.-elect 1971-72), Raleigh Dietetic Assn. (pres.-elect 1964-65, pres. 1965-66), Denver Dietetic Assn. (pres.-elect 1954, pres. 1955), Phi Delta Gamma, Phi Upsilon Omicron, Omicron Nu. Mem. Christian Ch. Home and Office: 110 S Festival Dr Apt 5A El Paso TX 79912-5821

BEDFORD, ROBERT FORREST, anesthesiologist; b. Boston, Oct. 6, 1942; s. Nathaniel Forrest and Roberta Lelia (Skinner) B.; m. Faith Goodwin Andrews, Dec. 28, 1963; children: William, Eleanor, Sarah. AB in Biology, Princeton U., 1964; MD, Cornell U., 1968. Diplomate Am. Bd. Anesthesiology. Intern Va. Mason Hosp., Seattle, 1968-69; resident/fellow anesthesiology U. Pa. Hosp., Phila., 1969-72; chief anesthesiology, operating svcs. U.S. Walson Army Hosp., Ft. Dix, N.J., 1972-74; asst. clin. prof. anesthesiology Columbia U. Coll. Physicians and Surgeons, N.Y.C., 1974-77; from asst. prof. to prof. anesthesiology U. Va. Sch. Med., Charlottesville, Va., 1977-86; clin. prof. anesthesiology U. Va. Sch. Med., Charlottesville, 1990-96; chmn. dept. anesthesiology Meml. Sloan Kettering Cancer Ctr., N.Y.C., 1986-90; prof. anesthesiology U. South Fla., Tampa, 1996—; chief anesthesia svc. James Haley VA Med. Ctr., Tampa, 1996—; special govt. employee anesthetic and life support drug adv. com. FDA, Rockville, Md., 1991-94, 96—, acting dir. pilot drug divsn. 1994-95, divsn. anesthetics, 1995-96; assoc. examiner Am. Bd. Anesthesiology, Hartford, Conn., 1987-90. Contbr. over 85 articles to profl. jours., 15 chpts. to books. Maj. USAR, 1972-74. Grantee Found. Anesthesia Edn./Rsch., 1981; recipient Univ. Bordeaux II medal, 1988, Continuing Edn. award AMA, 1991-97. Mem. Soc. Neurosurg. Anesthesia (sec., treas., v.p., pres.), Va. Soc. Anesthesiologists (sec., treas., v.p., pres.), Am. Soc. Anesthesiologists (chair neurosci. com. 1986-88, resident rsch. essay award, 1973) Presbyterian. Home: PO Box 340 Shelterwood Farm Ivy VA 22945 Office: James Haley VA Med Ctr Anesthesia Svc 1300 Bruce B Downes Blvd Tampa FL 33600

BEDI, HARVINDER SINGH, neonatologist; b. Patiala, Punjab, India, Dec. 9, 1960; came to U.S., 1984; s. Harcharn S. and Narinder K. (Khanna) B.; m. Rajinder K. Sahni, Dec. 31, 1983; children: Munpal, Priya. MB, BS, Christian Med. Coll., Punjab, India, 1983. Diplomate Am. Bd. Pediatrics, Am. Sub-Bd. of Neonatal-Perinatal Medicine. Rotating intern Christian Med. Coll. and Hosp., Punjab, 1982-83; resident in pediatrics Hahnemann U. Hosp., Phila., 1985-88; postdoctoral fellow in neonatology Baylor Coll. Medicine, Houston, 1988-91; med. dir. neonatal ICU Clear Lake Regional Med. Ctr., 1991—. Contbr. articles to Pediatric Rsch. Fellow Am. Acad. Pediatrics; mem. AMA, Tex. Med. Assn., Harris County Med. Soc., Houston Pediatric Soc. Home: 15711 Sylvan Lake Dr Houston TX 77062-4724 Office: 500 Medical Center Blvd Webster TX 77598-4220

BEDIGUIAN, MARIAMIG JINX, operating room nurse; b. Neptune, N.J., July 13, 1956; d. Haig Leon and Mary (Durna) B. BSN, George Mason U., 1979. RN, Va., N.J.; cert. nurse operating room. Operating room staff nurse Jersey Shore Med. Ctr., Neptune, 1979—, clinical nurse IV, svc. leader gynecology and laser, 1992-94, svc. leader gen., gynecology and gentourinary endoscopy, 1994—; operating rm. staff nurse Monmouth Med. Ctr., Long Branch, N.J., 1994—; focus panel mem., oper. rm. cons. Ansell Med. Corp., Eatontown, N.J., 1993; oper. rm. cons. Armenian Gen. Benevolent Union, Saddle Brook, N.J., Plastic and Reconstructive Surgery Ctr., Yerevan, Armenia, 1992. Recipient Chief Residents award Jersey Shore Med. Ctr. Obs.-Gyn. Residency Program, 1993. Mem. Assn. Oper. Rm. Nurses (product fair co-chair 1987-90, 93, chair seminar com. 1985, chair program com. 1985-88, v.p. 1983-85, bd. dirs. 1985-89, 95—, audit com. 1987-88, Congress del. 1984, alt. del. 1987), Nat. Assn. Orthopaedic Nurses (bd. dirs. 1994—), Assn. Womens Health Obstetric and Neonatal Nurses, Am. Assn. Gynecologic Laparoscopists, N.J. State Nurses Assn., George Mason U. Sch. Nursing Alumni Assn., George Mason U. Alumni Assn., Mary Washington Coll. Alumni Assn., Armenian Students Assn., Phi Mu (rec. sec. 1977-78), Sigma Theta Tau. Home: 12 Inlet Ter Belmar NJ 07719-2142 Office: Jersey Shore Med Ctr 1945 Corlies Ave Neptune NJ 07753-4859

BEDINE, MARSHALL STEPHEN, physician; b. Bklyn., June 29, 1941; s. Alexander Leo and Sylvia Marilyn (Block) B.; m. Joyce Ruth Cohen, Aug. 21, 1966; children: Geoffrey Scott, Matthew David, Jeremy Evan. AB, Brown U., 1963; MD, Boston U., 1967. Diplomate Am. Bd. Internal Medicine, Am. Bd. Gastroenterology. Asst. prof. medicine Sch. Medicine Johns Hopkins U., Balt., 1972—. Contbr. articles to profl. jours., chpts. to books. Capt. USAR. Recipient Harry Greenstein Leadership award Associated Jewish Charities, 1979. Fellow Am. Coll. Physicians, Am. Coll. Gastroenterology; mem. Md. Soc. Internal Medicine (pres. 1987-89, disting. internist of yr. award 1993), Md. Soc. Gastrointestinal Endoscopy (pres. 1988-90), Balt. Bd. Jewish Edn. (pres. 1987-89). Office: 10751 Falls Rd Lutherville MD 21093

BEDWELL, DAVID M., medical educator; b. Paducah, Ky., Feb. 20, 1956; married; two children. BS, Purdue U., 1979; PhD, U. Wis., 1985. Rsch. specialist dept. biol. scis. Purdue U., West Lafayette, Ind., 1979-80; postdoctoral rsch. fellow Divsn. Biology Calif. Inst. Technology, Pasadena, 1986-88; assoc. scientist Comprehensive Cancer Ctr. U. Ala., Birmingham, 1988—; asst. prof. dept. microbiology U. Ala., 1988—, asst. prof. dept. cell biology, 1993—; mem. numerous coms. in field; grant reviewer in field. Contbr. articles to profl. jours. Mem. AAAS, Am. Soc. Microbiology, Genetics Soc. Am., Am. Soc. Cell Biology. Office: Dept Microbiology Bevill Biomed Rsch Bldg Univ Ala Birmingham Birmingham AL 35294-2170

BEDWELL, THEODORE CLEVELAND, JR., physician, association executive; b. Caddo Mills, Tex., Mar. 31, 1909; s. Theodore Clevel and Mary Rebecca (Gary) B.; m. Blanche Elizabeth Harper, June 1, 1935 1 dau., Beverly Anne. B.S., So. Meth. U., 1931; M.D., Baylor U., 1933; certificate indsl. medicine, Harvard Sch. Pub. Health, 1941; M.P.H., Johns Hopkins U., 1951. Diplomate, Am. Bd. Preventive Medicine and Pub. Health (aviation medicine 1953, occupational medicine 1956). Intern Baylor Hosp., Dallas, 1933-34; gen. practice medicine and surgery Longview, Tex., 1934-35; commd. 1st lt. M.C. U.S. Army, 1935; advanced through grades to maj. gen. USAF, 1963; staff duties various army hosp., 1935-40; grad. (Army Med. Field Service Sch.), 1940; chief indsl. medicine (Army Surgeon Gen. Office), 1940-42; grad. (USAAF Sch. Aviation Medicine), 1942; base surgeon, comdg. officer (USAAF hosps.), 1942-46; dep. surgeon (Air Material Command), 1946-47, surgeon, 1947-48; staff surgeon (5th Air Force) Nagoya, Japan, 1948-50; grad. (Air War Coll.), 1951-52; assigned Office Asst. Sec. Def. Health and Medicine, 1952-53; chief preventive medicine USAF Surgeon Gen.'s Office, 1953-56; dep. surgeon SAC, 1956-59, surgeon, 1959-61; comdr. USAF Aero. Med. Center, 1961, USAF Aero. Med. Center (Aerospace med. div. Air Force Systems Command), Brooks AFB, 1961-66; dir. staff Office Dep. Asst. Sec. Def., Health and Medicine dep. asst. sec. of def., health and med. Office Dep. Asst. Sec. Def., Health and Medicine, Washington, 1966-68; ret., 1968; chief med. officer Bur. Health Ins., Social Security Adminstrn., Balt., 1968-75; asst. v.p. sci. and profl. relations, dir. med. relations Pharm. Mfrs. Assn., Washington, 1975-79. Decorated D.S.M., Air Force medal with oak leaf cluster; Republic Korea Presdl. citation; recipient Distinguished Alumnus award So. Meth. U., 1966, Spl. Aerospace Medicine Honor Citation AMA, 1964. Fellow Am. Coll. Preventive Medicine (v.p. aviation medicine 1960-61), Aerospace Med. Assn. (pres. 1964-65), Royal Soc. Health (Eng.); mem. Soc. USAF Flight Surgeons (pres. 1961-62), Am. Pub. Health Assn., Assn. Mil. Surgeons, Internat. Acad. Aviation and Space Medicine, Phi Chi, Alpha Omega Alpha. Home: 1 Towers Park Ln Apt 416 San Antonio TX 78209-6420

BEEBE, BRADFORD MICHAEL, clinical psychologist; b. Valparaiso, Ind., Nov. 15, 1960; s. Frederick Liston Beebe and Kathleen Anne (Stoppelmoore) Gocek; m. Leslie Karen Delgado, July 14, 1991. BS, Fla. State U., 1984; MA, U. Louisville, 1987, PhD, 1992. Licensed clin. psychologist, Ky. Instr. U. Louisville, 1990-92; psychotherapist Seven Counties Svcs., Louisville, 1987-89; clin. therapist United Behavioral Systems, Louisville, 1991-94; staff psychologist INPSYCH/KY, Louisville, 1994—; intern ISUSCC, Normal, Ill., 1989-90. Grad. fellow U. Louisville, 1984-85. Mem. APA (assoc.), Ky. Psychol. Assn., Golden Key. Office: INPSYCH/KY 3430 Newburg Rd Louisville KY 40128

BEEBE, GILBERT WHEELER, epidemiologist; b. Mahwah, N.J., Apr. 3, 1912; s. Edwin P. and Gertrude Mabel (Gilbert) B.; m. Ruth Lillian White, Dec. 29, 1933; children: Alfred, Beatrice, Brian, Christopher. AB, Dartmouth Coll., 1933; AM, Columbia U., 1938, PhD, 1942. Statistician Nat. Commn. Maternal Health, N.Y.C., 1934-41; rsch. assoc. Milbank Meml. Fund, N.Y.C., 1939-41, tech. staff, 1941-46; cons./hist. div. U.S. Army, Washington, 1946-50, cons./Hoover Commn., 1948; profl. assoc. NRC/NAS, Washington, 1946-58; dir. Med. Follow-up Agy., Washington, 1958-77; chief, dept. stats. Atomic Bomb Casualty Commn., Hiroshima, Japan, 1958-60, chief, dept. epidemiology and stats., 1966-68, 73-75; various to statistician Nat. Cancer Inst., Bethesda, Md., 1977—; chief scientist Radiation Effects Rsch. Found., Hiroshima, 1975. Author: Fertility and Contraception in Southern Appalachians, 1942, Battle Casualties, 1952, Follow-up Study of War Neurosis, 1956; editor: Peripheral Nerve Regeneration, 1957. Capt. U.S. Army, 1943-46. Recipient Lectureship/Cutter Lectr., Harvard Sch. of Pub. Health, Boston, 1979, Spl. Recognition award Pub. Health Svc., Washington, 1983, Dir.'s award NIH, Washington, 1985. Fellow AAAS, Am. Pub. Health Assn. (Frost Lectr., N.Y.C. 1980), Am. Statis. Assn.; mem. Soc. for Epidemiol. Rsch., Radiation Rsch. Soc., Health Physics Soc., Am. Epidemiol. Soc., Internat. Epidemiol. Assn., Japan Radiation Rsch. Soc., Soc. for Risk Analysis. Home: 7311 Stafford Rd Alexandria VA 22307-1808 Office: National Cancer Inst Epn # 400 Bethesda MD 20892

BEEBE, RICHARD TOWNSEND, physician; b. Great Barrington, Mass., Jan. 22, 1902; s. John and Louise (Taylor) B.; m. Jean Wickersham, Aug. 10, 1932; children—Nancy Taylor, John Wickersham, Louise Townsend. B.S., Princeton U., 1924; M.D., Johns Hopkins, 1928; D.Sc. (hon.), Albany Med. Coll. of Union U., 1982. Diplomate: Am. Bd. Internal Medicine. Intern Johns Hopkins Hosp., 1928-29, asst. resident physician, 1930-32; residency tng. Thorndike Meml. Lab., Harvard, 1929- 30; asso. medicine Albany Med. Coll., 1932-37, asso. prof. medicine, 1937-48, prof. medicine, dir. dept., 1948-67, Distinguished prof. medicine, 1968—; asst. physician Albany Hosp., 1932-34, clin. asst. medicine, 1934-37, attending physician, 1937-48, dispensary physician in charge, 1941-48, physician in chief, 1948-67, sr. physician, 1967—; cons. internal medicine Albany VA Hosp. Author: Albany Medical College and Albany Hospital, A History: 1839-1982. Fellow ACP (master 1983); mem. AMA N.Y. State, Albany County med. socs., Am. Soc. Clin. Investigation, Am. Clin. and Climatol. Assn., Alpha Omega Alpha. Home: Schuyler Rd Albany NY 12211-1420 Office: Albany Med Coll Albany NY 12208

BEECHER, BRUCE JAMES, aeromedical physician assistant; b. Bethpage, N.Y., Dec. 11, 1958; s. Richard Patrick and Geraldine (Ward) B.; m. Nancy Fay Lewis Beecher, Dec. 30, 1994; children: Kara Koger, Alisha Koger, Amanda Beecher, Bruce Beecher Jr., Scott Koger. AS, Enterprise State Jr. Coll., Ala., 1989; BS as Physician Assoc., U. Okla., 1994. Cert. hyperbaric technologist Nat. Bd. Diving and Hyperbaric Medicine Technologists; cert. aeromed. physician asst. Commd. U.S. Army, advanced through grades to 1st lt.; aerospace physiology technician USAAMA, Ft. Rucker, Ala., 1976-80; air ambulance NCO/1st sgt. 63rd Med. Det (HA), Landstuhl, Germany, 1980-85; masterinstr CHT U.S. Army Sch. Aviation Medicine, Ft. Rucker, 1985-92; aeromed. physician asst. HHT 5/17 Air Cavalry, Camp Pelham, South Korea, 1995-96, HHT 3/4 Cavalry, Ft. Carson, Colo., 1996—; CHT nat. exam. cons. Nat. Bd. Diving & Hyperbaric Medicine Technologists, New Orleans, 1990-91. Editor: Study Guide for CHT Exam, 1991. Dir. AWANA youth program Ewell (Ala.) Bapt. Ch., 1987-89. Mem. VFW, Am. Acad. Physician Assts., Am. Coll. Sports Medicine, 38th Prallel Med. Soc. Republican. Baptist.

BEECHER, CHRISTOPHER WILLIAM WARD, science educator, consultant; b. N.Y.C., Aug. 20, 1948; s. William Ward and Delores (Laredo) B.; m. Louise Patry, May 29, 1981; children: Francis, William. BA in Anthropology, NYU, 1974, MS in Botany, 1980; PhD in Natural Product Chemistry, U. Conn., 1986. Vis. prof. U. Ill., Chgo., 1985-89, asst. prof., 1989-93, assoc. prof., 1993—; assoc. dir. Napralert, Chgo. Contbr. numerous articles to profl. jours. Grantee USDA, NIH. Fellow Am. Soc. Plant Physiology, Am. Soc. Pharmacology, Econ. Botany. Office: U Ill/COP (M/C 781) 833 S Wood St Chicago IL 60612-7229

BEECHER, GEORGE, otolaryngologist; b. Barranquilla, Colombia, Sept. 26, 1940; came to U.S., 1946; s. Hugo and Margaret (Hahn) B.; m. Judith Ann Holt, Oct. 1, 1965; 1 child, James Hugo. Student, Tufts Coll., 1958-59; MD, Louvain (Belgium) U., 1965. Rotating intern Phila. Gen. Hosp., 1965-66; surg. resident St. Michael's Hosp., Newark, 1966-67, N.J. Coll. of Medicine, Newark, 1970-71; ENT resident NYU/Bellevue Hosp. Ctr., N.Y.C., 1971-74; physician ptnr. Summit (N.J.) Med. Group, 1974-93; pvt. practice Warren, N.J., 1993—; mem. Bd. of Health, New Providence, N.J., 1990—; clin. instr. NYU/Bellevue Med. Ctr., N.Y.C., 1975—; staff attending Overlook Hosp., Summit, 1974—. Mem. Crippled Children's Commn., N.J., 1974—. Capt. U.S. Army, 1968-70, Vietnam. Decorated Bronze Star. Mem. AMA, N.J. Med. Soc., Am. Bd. Otolaryngology, Lions. Republican. Jewish. Office: 8 Mountain Blvd Warren NJ 07059-5614

BEEGHLY, JAMES H., psychiatrist; b. Pitts., Feb. 5, 1950; m. Helen M. Farrell. MD, W.Va. U. Diplomate in gen.psychiatry and child psychiatry Am. Bd. Psychiatry and Neurology. Resident in psychiatry Cooperstown, N.Y.; resident in psychiatry U. Iowa, Iowa City, asst. prof. psychiatry, 1985-89; psychiat. coord. MidEastern Iowa Cmty. Mental Heakth Ctr., Iowa City, 1989-92; pvt. practie psychiatry Iowa City, 1989—. Mem. AMA, Am. Psychiat. Assn., Am. Acad. Child and Adolescent Psychiatry. Office: 312 E College St Ste 200 Iowa City IA 52240

BEEGLE, EARL DENNIS, family physician; b. Ashland, Ohio, July 24, 1944; s. Ray Benjamin and Alice Mae (Imhoff) B.; m. Isabel Sloan-Kerr Adamson, Sept. 3, 1964; children: Ryan Benjamin, Kevin Ian. BA, Manchester Coll., 1967; MS, Purdue U., 1970; MB BChir, MD, BAO, Queen's U., Belfast, No. Ireland, 1978. Diplomate Am. Bd. Family Practice. Life scis. tchr. Elkhart (Ind.) Schs., 1967-72; house officer Nat. Health Svc. of U.K., No. Ireland and U.K., 1978-79; resident in family practice Riverside Hosp. Med. Coll. Ohio, Toledo, 1979-81; chief resident Med. Coll. Ohio, Toledo, 1981-82; pvt. practice Everett, Wash., 1982-93; med. dir. Providence Primary Care Network, Everett, 1993—; elected to credentials com. Providence Gen. Med. Ctr., 1996—; med. dir. Planned Parenthood, Everett, 1983-86; chmn. utilization Providence Hosp., Everett, 1987-90, chmn. quality assurance, 1991-92; chmn. dept. family practice Providence-Gen. Med. Ctr., Everett, 1993-94; dir. Sisters of Providence Health Plans, Seattle, 1993—. Active Friends of the Somme, No. Ireland, 1991—. NSF fellow, 1967-70. Fellow Am. Acad. Family Practice; mem. Irish and Am. Pediatric Soc., Snohomish County Med. Soc., Associated Physicians of Snohomish County (bd. dirs.), Internat. Soc. Travel Medicine. Office: Providence Claremont Clinic 5007 Claremont Way Everett WA 98203-3321

BEEKLEY, WILLIAM HARVEY, surgeon; b. N.Y.C., Mar. 15, 1940; s. Eugene Augustus and Irene Emily (Englehardt) B.; m. Judith Ann Moyer, Dec. 15, 1986. BA, Bowdoin Coll., 1962; MD, Boston U., 1966. Diplomate Am. Bd. Surgery. Intern Albany (N.Y.) Med. Ctr. Hosp., 1966-67; resident Boston City Hosp., 1967-72; staff surgeon Naval Hosp. Phila., 1972-74, Paoli (Pa.) Meml. Hosp., 1974-90, Boaz (Ala.) Albertville Hosp., 1990—. Lt. comdr. USN, 1972-74. Office: Boaz Surg Assocs PO Box 854 Boaz AL 35957

BEELER, CARL EDWARD, JR., emergency nurse, paramedic; b. Knoxville, Tenn., Dec. 30, 1953; s. Carl Edward and Frankie Lou (Keelen) B.; children: Michael Edward, April Marie; m. Lynn Marie Isaksen, Oct. 12, 1985; children: Sean Justin, Sara Elaine. AS in Nursing, East Tenn. State U., 1989. RN, Tenn.; cert. EMT, ACLS instr., BLS. Staff RN critical care Ft. Sanders Regional Med. Ctr., Knoxville, 1989-93, shift supr. critical care, 1993-94; staff RN cath lab. Ft. Sanders Parkwest Med. Ctr., Knoxville, 1994-95, staff RN emergency rm., 1995—. Mem. AACN, Emergency Nurses Assn. Home: 8241 Elm Hill Cir Knoxville TN 37919 Office: Ft Sanders Parkwest Med Ctr Parkwest Blvd Knoxville TN 37922

BEENKEN, SAMUEL WARNER, surgery educator, researcher; b. Sioux Falls, S.D., Nov. 7, 1951; s. Gilbert Merle and Juanita Marie (Low) B.; m. Esther Ruth Warkentin, Sept. 30, 1978; children: Andrew Samuel, Timothy Gilbert. MD, U. Man., Winnipeg, Can., 1975; cert. in head and neck surgery, U. Tex., Houston, 1988, cert. in surg. oncology, 1990. Diplomate Am. Bd. Surgery. Rotating intern Manitoba Affiliated Teaching Hosp., 1975-76; emergency med. officer St. Boniface Gen. Hosp., Winnipeg, 1976-82; resident in gen. surgery U. Man., 1982-86; rsch. fellow Man. Inst. Cell Biology, Winnipeg, 1986-87; fellow in head and neck surgery M.D. Anderson Cancer Ctr., Houston, 1987-88, rsch. fellow, faculty assoc., 1988-89, fellow in surg. oncology, faculty assoc., 1989-90; asst. prof. surgery U. Ala., Birmingham, 1990-94; assoc. prof. surgery U. Ala. Birmingham, 1995—; med. dir. Jiwan Jyoti Hosp., Robertsganj, India, 1979-80; assoc. scientist Wallace Tumor Inst., Birmingham, 1990—; head sect. head and neck surgery VA Med. Ctr., Birmingham, 1991. Contbr. articles to med. jours. Recipient Cancer Found. award U. Tex., 1989, Young Investigator award Am. Soc. Clin. Oncology, 1991, award Wendy Will Case Cancer Fund, 1992, Clin. Oncology Cancer Devel. award Am. Cancer Soc., 1992—, award Cancer Rsch. Found. Am., 1992-94; Terry Fox rsch. fellow Nat. Cancer Inst. Can.,

1986-87, R.A. MacBeth fellow Man. Cancer Soc., 1987-88, faculty clin. fellow U. Man., 1988-90. Fellow Royal Coll. Physicians and Surgeons Can.; mem. ACS, Soc. Head and Neck Surgeons, Am. Assn. Cancer Rsch., Am. Soc. Clin. Oncology, Soc. Surg. Oncology, Assn. Acad. Surgery, M.D. Anderson Assocs. Republican. Presbyterian. Office: U Ala 1922 7th Ave S Rm 321 Birmingham AL 35233-2006

BEERY, WILLIAM STOCKTILL, psychologist, management consultant, clergyman; b. Bklyn., Nov. 27, 1947; s. Edwin Newman and Evelyn Vivian (Onken) B.; m. Margaret Augusta Broz, May 30, 1970; children: William, Gabriele; m. Ellen Agnes Sommers, Feb. 28, 1981; children: Matthew, Jonathan. AB, Colgate U., 1969; MDiv, Yale U., 1972; PhD, NYU, 1983. Ordained to ministry Episcopal Ch., 1972; lic. psychologist in Conn., N.Y. Assoc. dir. V.I.P., Inc., Yonkers, N.Y., 1975-81; staff psychologist Sound Ctr., Rye, N.Y., 1981-82; exec. dir. Counseling and Testing Svc., YMCA, N.Y.C., 1983-85; ptnr. Personnel Corp. Am., Norwalk, Conn., 1985-88; pres. Exec. Devel. Internat., Inc., 1988—; elected mem. Darien rep. town meeting; mem. Darien Bd. Ethics, chmn. pub. safety com.; adj. assoc. St. Luke's Parish, Darien, Conn., 1984—, mem. vestry; pres. Friends of Gorham's Pond Inc. Watson fellow Yale U., 1972-80. Fellow Am. Assn. Pastoral Counselors; mem. Am. Psychol. Assn., Am. Assn. Counseling and Devel., Met. N.Y. Assn. for Applied Psychology, Am. Soc. for Tng. and Devel., Norwalk Yacht Club (bd. govs.). Avocations: skiing, tennis, scuba, gardening, sailing. Home: 223 Old Kings Hwy S Darien CT 06820-5931

BEESMER, SHIRLEY JEAN, community health nurse; b. Cortland, N.Y., Dec. 17, 1958; d. John Ezra and Marilyn Pearl (Green) B. LPN, SUNY, Morrisville, 1979; postgrad., Practical Bible Tng. Sch., Bible Sch. Park, N.Y., 1982. LPN Chenango Meml. Hosp., Norwich, N.Y., Med. Personnel Pool, Syracuse, N.Y.; sec., nurse Cen. N.Y. Bapt. Youth Camp, Marathon, N.Y.; LPN Quality Care, Syracuse. Home: HC 65 Box 405 De Ruyter NY 13052-9301

BEESON, MONTEL EILEEN, human services administrator, gerontologist; b. El Dorado, Ark., Dec. 22, 1939; d. Waymon Willett and Myrtle May (Roach) B. BS in Recreation, Calif. State U., Hayward, 1963; MA in Edn. and Human Devel., Holy Names Coll., Oakland, Calif., 1979. Lic. nursing home adminstr.; cert. community coll. instr.; cert. gerontology. Dist. exec. Ariz. Cactus-Pine Girl Scouts Coun., Phoenix, 1963-66, dist. exec. San Francisco Bay coun., Oakland, Calif., 1966-68, bus. mgr., 1968-71, exec. dir. Shabonee coun., Moline, Ill., 1971-73, Tongass-Alaska coun., Ketchikan, 1973-74, Muir Trail coun., Modesto, Calif., 1974-78; asst. adminstr. Beulah Home, Inc., Oakland, 1980-86; elder care cons., 1986—; exec. dir. Community Adult Day Health Svcs., Oakland, 1987-88; adminstr. Greenhills Retirement Ctr. Millbrae, Calif., 1988—. Mem. Am. Coll. Health Care Adminstrs., Am. Soc. on Aging. Avocations: cross-country skiing, history, travel, reading, music. Home: 3393 Kiwanis St Oakland CA 94602-4005

BEESON, PAUL BRUCE, physician; b. Livingston, Mont., Oct. 18, 1908; s. John Bradley and Martha Gerard (Ash) B.; m. Barbara Neal, July 10, 1942; children: John, Peter, Judith. Student, U. Wash., 1925-28; M.D., C.M., McGill U., 1933, D.Sc., 1971; D.Sc., Emory U., 1968, Albany Med. Coll., 1975, Yale U., 1975, Med. Coll. Ohio, 1979. Asst. Rockefeller Inst., 1937-39, Harvard Med. Sch., 1939-40; asst. prof. medicine Emory U. Med. Sch., 1942-46, prof., chmn. dept., 1946-52; Ensign prof. medicine, chmn. dept. internal medicine Yale Med. Sch., 1952-65; physician-in-chief univ. service Grace-New Haven Community Hosp., 1952-65; Nuffield prof. clin. medicine Oxford (Eng.) U., 1965-74; prof. medicine U. Wash., Seattle, 1974-81. Named Alumnus summa laude dignatus U. Wash., 1968, hon. knight comdr. Brit. Empire, 1973; recipient 50th Anniversary Gold medal Peter Bent Brigham Hosp., 1962; Bristol award Infectious Diseases Soc. Am., 1972; Kober medal Assn. Am. Physicians, 1973; Abraham Flexner award Assn. Am. Med. Colls., 1977; Willard Thompson award Am. Geriatrics Soc., 1984; Founders award So. Soc. Clin. Research, 1982; fellow Berkeley Coll.; fellow Yale; fellow Magdalen Coll. (hon.); fellow Green Coll. (hon.); fellow Oxford U. Fellow Royal Coll. Physicians (London), Royal Soc. Medicine (hon.); mem. Nat Acad. Scis., Am. Acad. Arts and Scis., A.C.P. (master, John Phillips Meml. award 1976, Disting. Tchr. award 1990), Soc. Expel. Biology and Medicine, Am. Soc. Clin. Investigation, Assn. Am. Physicians (pres. 1967), Assn. Physicians Gt. Britain and Ireland. Episcopalian. Home: 21013 NE 122nd St Redmond WA 98053-5323

BEETEL, DOROTHEA J., pediatric and school nurse; b. Riverside, N.J., Mar. 5, 1942; d. Joseph A. and Jean (Conda) Matlack; m. Robert J. Beetel, July 17, 1965; children: Mary Jean, Kevin, Kerry, Robert J. III. Diploma, St. Francis Hosp. Sch. Nursing, 1963; postgrad., Trenton State Coll. RN, N.J. Pvt. duty nurse Burlington County Nurses Registry, Mt. Holly, N.J.; asst. supr. Masonic Home, Burlington, N.J., coord. Alzheimer, spl. care patients; sch. nurse Our Lady of Sorrows Sch., Mercerville, N.J.; pediatric specialist Bayada Nurses, Cherry Hill, N.J.; med./legal investigator Marshall & Manion Law Office, Mt. Holly; sch. nurse Independent Child Study Team, Jersey City, N.J. Mem. St. Francis Hosp. Sch. Nursing Alumni Assn., Mercer County Sch. Nurses Assn. (assoc.). Home: 104 Gilbert Rd Bordentown NJ 08505-4003

BEFELER, DAVID, surgeon, educator; b. Bklyn., May 3, 1935. BA, Columbia U., 1955, MD, 1959. Diplomate Am. Bd. Surgery, Nat. Bd. Med. Examiners. Intern St. Vincent's Hosp., N.Y.C., 1959-60, resident in gen. surgery, 1960-64; pvt. practice, Westfield, N.J.; attending surgeon Overlook Hosp., Summit, N.J.; sec. med. staff, 1978-79, v.p. 1980-81, pres., 1982-84, chief surgery, 1990; asst. prof. clin. surgery N.J. Coll. Medicine; assoc. prof. Columbia. U. Coll. Physicians and Surgeons; presenter, lectr. in field; editl. cons. Patient Care Publs., Inc.; cons. in surgery N.Y. State Bd. Med. Examiners. Contbr. articles to med. jours. Officer M.C., U.S. Army, 1964-66. Fellow ACS, Am. Geriatrics Soc., Am. Coll. Gastroenterology, Internat. Coll. Proctology; mem. AMA, AAAS, N.Y. State Med. Soc., New York County Med. Soc., N.Y. Cancer Soc., Am. Med. Writers Assn., N.J. Med. Soc., N.J. Soc. Gasterenterology, Acad. Med. N.J., N.Y. Acad. Socs., Am. Soc. Cosmetic Breast Surgery, N.J. Soc. Gastrointestinal Endoscopy, N.J. Gastroenterology Soc., Soc. Laparoendoscopic Surgery, So. Am. Gastrointestinal Endoscopic Surgery, Phi Chi. Office: 507 Westfield Ave Westfield NJ 07090

BEGGS, SYBLE MARIE, program coordinator; b. Oklahoma City, Aug. 24, 1953; d. Frank V. and Rosetta Pairlee (Floyd) Kirby; m. Ernie Dale Beggs, Oct. 1, 1985; children: Wanda, Dawn. Diploma, Kiamichi VoTech, McAlester, Okla., 1978; BSN, East Cen. U., Ada, Okla., 1989. Staff nurse in critical care McAlester Regional Hosp., nurse mgr. Rehab. unit, adminstr., dir. skilled nursing facility, program coord., concurrent case mgmt.-utilization rev. Home: 416 E Osage Ave McAlester OK 74501-6453

BEGLEY, CARL EDWARD, psychologist; b. Springfield, Ky., Nov. 4, 1928; s. William Woodson and Jenny May (Logsden) B.; m. Mary Anaise Lanter, Jan. 25, 1958; children—Catherine, Joseph, Ellen. B.S., U. Ky., 1951, M.A., 1956, Ph.D., 1961. Lic. psychologist, Fla.; diplomate Am. Bd. Profl. Psychology. Intern Dept. Psychology U. Louisville, 1956-57; psychol. asst. Child Guidance, Lexington, Ky., 1957-59; sr. psychologist Ky. State Hosp., Danville, 1959-61; chief psychologist Mental Health Clinic, Jacksonville, Fla., 1961-68; part time psychologist Child Guidance Clinic, Jacksonville, 1968-71; pvt. practice psychology, Jacksonville, 1971—. Contbr. articles to profl. jours. Sec. Fla. State Bd. Examiners in Psychology, 1979. Mem. Am. Psychol. Assn., Fla. Psychol. Assn. (pres. Northeast Fla. chpt. 1984), Sigma Xi. Roman Catholic. Home: 1962 Largo Pl Jacksonville FL 32207-3921

BEGLEY, NAN ELIZABETH, psychotherapist, psychology educator; b. Springfield, Mass., Oct. 20, 1951; d. Howard George and Marguerite Rosalie (Christodolou) Gauthier; children: James, Taryn. AA, Springfield Tech. Community Coll., 1981; BA, Westfield State Coll., 1983, MA, 1985. Lic. marriage and family therapist, Mass., mental health counselor, Mass. Dir. parent empowerment project United Cerebral Palsy Inc., Springfield, 1983-84, dir., 1984-85, staff psychotherapist, 1985-87; staff psychotherapist Osborn Clinic, Agawam, Mass., 1985-92; pvt. practice Springfield, 1985—; prof. psychology Springfield Tech. Community Coll., 1985—, Springfield Coll., 1987—; staff psychotherapist Child Guidance Clinic, Springfield, Mass., 1991—; cons. spl. edn. area schs., Springfield, Agawam, Chicopee, Hampden and Wilbraham, Mass., 1985—. Active in pub. rels. and fundraising Springfield Tech. Community Coll., 1981-88; producer DGR Prodns. Theatre Co., Springfield, 1981—. Mem. APA (assoc.), ACA, Am. Assn. for Marriage and Family Therapy, Am. Assn. Mental Health Counselors, Mass. Assn. Mental Health Counselors.

BEHAN, JAMES MICHAEL, SR., physician assistant; b. Bklyn., Feb. 28, 1957; s. John Michael and Mary (Hynes) B.; m. Maryanne Lois Spinelli, July 14, 1979; children: James Jr., John, Peter. BS in Biology, St. Joseph's Coll., Bklyn., 1979; BS in Physician Asst., Touro Coll., 1981. Registered physician asst., N.Y. Physician asst. Jamaica (N.Y.) Hosp., 1981-82, Prison Health Svcs., Bklyn., 1986-88, Office of William A. Lois, MD, P.C., Bklyn., 1988—; supervising physician asst. St. John's Episcopal Hosp., Far Rockaway, N.Y., 1982—. EMT Flatlands Vol. Ambulance Corps, Bklyn., 1977—. Fellow Am. Acad. Physician Assts., N.Y. State Soc. Physician Assts.; mem. Am. Assn. Surgeon Assts. Roman Catholic. Home: 1836 E 51st St Brooklyn NY 11234 Office: St John's Episcopal Hosp 327 Beach 19th St Far Rockaway NY 11591

BEHAN, PETER OLIVER, neurologist, educator; b. Athy, Ireland, July 8, 1935; s. Patrick and Mary (Ryan) B.; m. Wilhelmina Mary Harcourt Hughes, Aug. 1968; children: Charlotte, Miles, Edmund. MB ChB, Leeds U., 1964, MD, 1979; DSc, Nat. U. Ireland, 1995. NIH traveling fellow Oxford (Eng.) U., 1969-70; chief resident in neurology U. Hosp., Boston, 1970-71, staff neurologist, 1971-73; neurology lectr. Glasgow (Scotland) U., 1973-74, cons. neurologist Inst. Neurol. Scis., 1974-77, sr. lectr., hon. cons. Ins. So. Gen. Hosp., 1977-80, reader in neurology, 1980-89, prof. neurology, 1989—; vis. prof. neurology Mass. Gen. Hosp.-Harvard U., Boston, 1980; cons. neurologist Nat. Health Svc., Scotland, 1971—. Editor: Clinical Neuroimmunology, 1986, Postviral Fatigue Syndrom, 1991; contbr. articles to profl. jours. including Brit. Med. Jour., Jour. Neuroloyg, Neurology and Psychiatry, among others. Patron Motor Neurone Disease Assn., Scotland, 1980—. Recipient Pattison medal, 1985, Internat. Dutch Myalgic Encephalomyelitis award, 1995; grantee Scottish Motorneurone Disease, 1982, NIH, 1986, Barclay Rsch. Trust, 1989. Fellow ACP, Royal Coll. Physicians (Scotland, Eng., Ireland); mem. Savile Club, Flyfishers Club. Office: Glasgow U Dept Neurology, So Gen Hosp, Glasgow G51 4TF, Scotland

BEHEN, DOROTHY SHERIN, medical/surgical nurse; b. Jackson Heights, N.Y., Oct. 14, 1939; d. George William and Helen I. (Thompson) Sherin; m. David E. Behen, Nov. 25, 1967. RN, Sisters of Charity Hosp., Buffalo, 1960; BSN, SUNY, Buffalo, 1975, MS in Nursing Adminstrn., 1992. Surgery coord. Sisters of Charity Hosp., Buffalo, 1979-83; staff nurse operating rm. Sisters of Charity Hosp., 1960-79; charge nurse oper. rm. Dept. Vets. Affairs Med. Ctr., Buffalo, 1983—. Mem. Assn. Oper. Rm. Nurses, Assn. Oper. Rm. Nurses of Western N.Y. (past treas., bd. dirs.).

BEHLING, CHARLES FREDERICK, psychology educator; b. St. George, S.C., Sept. 8, 1940; s. John Henry and Floy (Owings) B.; m. Jennifer Crocker; children: John Charles, Andrew Crocker. BA, U. S.C., 1962, MA, 1964; MA, Vanderbilt U., 1966, PhD, 1969. Asst. dean of students U. S.C., Columbia, 1962-63; asst. state news editor The State Newspaper, Columbia, 1963-64; asst. prof. psychology Lake Forest (Ill.) Coll., 1968-74; assoc. prof. Lake Forest Coll., 1974-88, chmn. dept., 1977-84; pvt. practice psychotherapy Lake Bluff, Ill., 1970-88, Buffalo, 1988-95; clin. assoc. prof. SUNY, Buffalo, 1988-95; dir. of undergraduate studies, 1989-95; adj. prof. U. Mich., Ann Arbor, 1995—; dir. intergroup rels., conflict and cmty., 1995—. Contbr. articles to profl. jours. Bd. dirs. Nat. Abortion Rights Action League, Planned Parenthood; mem. long-range planning com. Lake Bluff Bd. Edn. Named Outstanding Prof., Underground Guide to Colls., 1971, Birnbaum Guide, 1992, Outstanding Tchr., Lake Forest Coll., 1981, SUNY, Buffalo, 1991; NASA fellow. Mem. Am. Psychol. Assn., Soc. Psychol. Study of Social Issues, Assn. Humanistic Psychology, AAUP, Univ. S.C. Alumni Assn., Psi Chi, Sigma Delta Chi. Democrat. Home: 1325 Wynnstone Dr Ann Arbor MI 48105 Office: U Mich Dept Psychology Ann Arbor MI 48109

BEHM, JOHN ROBERT, physician; b. Marietta, Ohio, Dec. 13, 1953; s. Russell C. and Jean M. (Styles) B.; m. Lori Grace Smith, June 21, 1975 (div. Aug. 1976); m. Leslie Merrill Hallstead, Aug. 21, 1977. BS in Biology, Heidelberg Coll., 1976; DO, Mich. State U., 1990, cert. in secondary edn., 1983. Diplomate Am. Bd. Osteo. Family Physicians, Am. Acad. Family Practice. Grad. asst. dept. biophysics Mich. State U., 1977-78, rschr. dept. entomology, 1979-83, med. technician animal health diagnostic lab., 1983-84, rsch. technician plant rsch. lab., 1984-85; intern in osteo. medicine Lansing (Mich.) Gen. Hosp., 1990-91; resident Sparrow Family Practice, Lansing, 1991-93, chief resident, 1992-93; shift physician Mason (Mich.) Urgent Care Ctr., Delta Med. ctrs., Lansing area, Mich., 1991-93. V.p. Lansing Area Commodore Club, 1984; mem. exec. bd. Clerical Tech. Union, Mich. State U., 1982-83. Mem. AMA, Am. Osteo. Assn., Am. Acad. Family Practice. Democrat. Mennonite. Home: PO Box 947 Okemos MI 48805-0947 Office: Perry Family Practice 3337 Britton Rd Perry MI 48872-9706

BEHNER, ELTON DALE, dentist; b. Oberlin, Ohio, Sept. 6, 1952; s. Wayne Edwin and Velma Jean (Sevison) B.; m. Brenda Kay Crabtree, Aug. 18, 1974 (div. July 1982); m. Annette Lynn Brunst, Oct. 27, 1984: children: Nicolas, Ryan, Tadd. Student, Andrews U., 1971-74; BS, Loma Linda U., 1976; DDS, Ind. U., 1984. Dipolmate Am. Bd. Dental Examiners. Staff technologist clin. lab. Loma Linda (Calif.) U. Hosp., 1976-77, rsch. technologist, 1977-79; sr. technologist Ind. U. Hosp., Indpls., 1982-84; asst. prof. sch. dentistry Ind. U., Indpls.; grad. residency Ind. U. Med. Ctr., Indpls., 1984; owner Lakewood Dental Group, 1985—; coord., cons. dental svc. Am. Surgery Ctr., Indpls., 1987—; active mem. staff dental svc. Wishard Meml. Hosp., Indpls. Fellow Acad. Gen. Dentistry; mem. ADA, Ind. Dental Assn., Indpls. Dist. Dental Soc. Office: Lakewood Dental Group 5987 E 71st St Ste 103 Indianapolis IN 46220-4049

BEHNKE, MARYLOU, neonatologist, educator; b. Orlando, Fla., Sept. 1, 1950; d. Ernest Edmund and Elizabeth (Kolb) B. BS in Chemistry, U. Fla., 1972, MD, 1976. Diplomate Am. Bd. Pediatrics, Am. Bd. Neonatology-Perinatology. Intern dept. pediatrics Coll. Medicine, U. Fla., Gainesville, 1976-77, resident, 1977-79, chief resident, 1979-80, fellow in neonatology, 1981-83, asst. prof., 1979-81, 83-89, assoc. prof., 1989—; adj. asst. prof. Coll. Nursing, Gainesville, 1988-89, adj. assoc. prof., 1989—, mem. senate-at-large, 1984-89, mem. grad. studies faculty, 1988—; med. dir. neonatology ICU Shands Hosp., Gainesville, 1983-89, neonatal developmental follow-up program, 1989—; presenter at nat. and internat. meetings, 1981—; ad hoc mem. spl. rev. com. on human devel. rsch. NIH, 1991—, chair, 1993, 94. Mem. editl. bd. Death Studies, 1983-94; contbr. articles to med. jours., chpts. to books. Grantee NIH, 1984-87, 91—, Nat. Inst. on Drug Abuse, 1991—, Ctr. for Substance abuse Treatment, 1993—. Fellow Am. Acad. Pediatrics; mem. Fla. Med. Assn., Alachua County Med. Soc., Nat. Perinatal Assn., So. Soc. for Pediatric Rsch., Fla. Interagy. Coord. Coun. for Infants and Toddlers, Fla. Soc. Neonatal Perinatologists. Republican. Mem. Ch. of Christ. Home: 426 SW 40th St Gainesville FL 32607-2749 Office: J Hillis Miller Health Ctr Dept Pediatrics Box 100296 Gainesville FL 32610

BEHNKE, ROY HERBERT, physician, educator; b. Chgo., Feb. 24, 1921; s. Harry and Florence Alice (MacArthur) B.; m. Ruth Gretchen Zinszer, June 3, 1944; children: Roy, Michael, Donald, Elise. A.B., Hanover Coll., 1943; Ph.D. (hon.), 1972; M.D., Ind. U., 1946. Diplomate: Am. Bd. Internal Medicine. Intern Ind. U. Med. Center, 1946-47, resident, 1949-51, chief resident medicine, 1951-52; instr. medicine Ind. U. Sch. Medicine, Indpls., 1952-55, asst. prof. medicine, 1955-58, assoc. prof., 1958-61, prof., 1961-72; chief medicine VA Hosp., Indpls., 1957-72; prof. medicine U. South Fla. Coll. Medicine, Tampa, 1972—, chmn. dept. medicine, 1972-95, chmn. dept. head emeritus, 1995—; AMA rep. to residency rev. com. in internal medicine, 1970-75; mem. exec. and adv. com. Inter-Soc. Commn. Heart Disease Resources, 1968-72, chmn. pulmonary study sect., 1969-72; chmn. career devel. com. VA, 1980-83. Mem. Met. Sch. Bd. Washington Twp., 1968-72, pres., 1971; bd. dirs. Southside Community Health Center, 1968; trustee Tampa Gen. Hosp. Found., 1979-85; mem. research coordinating com. Am. Lung Assn., 1983-85, chmn., 1985-87, bd. dirs., 1983-87. Served with AUS, 1943-45, 47-49. Recipient Std. Oil Found. award Ind. U., 1971, Alumni Achievement award Hanover Coll., 1971; named Hon. Alumnus, USF Coll. Medicine, 1995; John and Mary Markle scholar, 1952, 57. Fellow and master ACP (gov. Fla. chpt. 1980-84, Laureate award 1991); fellow Am. Coll. chest Physicians; mem. AMA, Am. Fedn. Clin. Rsch., Ctrl. Soc. Clin. Rsch., So. Soc. Clin. Rsch., Alpha Omega Alpha. Home: 5111 Rolling Hill Ct Tampa FL 33617-1024 Office: Dept Internal Medicine 12901 N 30th St # 19 Tampa FL 33612-4742

BEHR, RAYMOND ANTHONY, psychiatrist; b. Johannesburg, South Africia, May 26, 1948; came to U.S., 1976; s. David Chone and Joan Roxanna (Lazarus) B.; m. Avril Pera Galasko; children: Gerald, Nadia, Warren. MD, U. Pretoria, South Africa, 1973. Diplomate Am. Bd. Psychiatry and Neurology (gen. psychiatry and child psychiatry). Intern Pretoria Gen. Hosp., 1974-75; resident in psychiatry L.I. Jewish Med. Ctr., New Hyde Park, N.Y., 1976-78, fellow in child psychiatry, 1978-80; med. dir. project outreach L.I. Jewish Med. Ctr., New Hyde Park, 1980-81, psychiat. cons. child devel. clinic, 1985-87, dir. adolescent day hosp., 1987-88; coord. law and psychiatry program L.I. Jewish Med. Ctr., Schneider Children's Hosp., New Hyde Park, 1988-93; psychiat. cons. Peninsula Counselling Ctr., Woodmere, N.Y., 1981-85; pvt. practice Great Neck, N.Y., 1980—; asst. clin. prof. psychiatry Albert Einstein Sch. Medicine Yeshiva U. Mem. AMA, Am. Psychiat. Assn., Am. Acad. Child and Adolescent Psychiatry, Am. Soc. Clin. Psychopharmacology.

BEHREND, FRANK LUDWIG, obstetrician, gynecologist; b. Berlin, Germany, July 1, 1938; came to U.S., 1947; m. Carole Triska; children: Robbie, Nichole. BA, Augustana Coll., 1961; MD, U. Ill., 1965. Diplomate Am. Bd. Ob-Gyn. Intern Cook County Hosp., Chgo., 1965-67, resident, 1967-70; practice medicine specilizing in ob-gyn. Valparaiso, Ind., 1970—. Mem. ACS, AMA, Am. Fertility Soc., Am. Soc. for Colposcopy and Cervical Pathology, Am. Assn. Gynecologic Laparoscopists, Am. Coll. Ob-Gyn., Calif. Med. Assn., Ind. Med. Assn. Porter County Med. Soc. Home: 2208 Wynnewood Dr Valparaiso IN 46383-2829 Office: Obstetrical & Gynecological Assocs Inc 1101 Glendale Blvd Valparaiso IN 46383-3724

BEHRENS, BEREL LYN, physician, academic administrator; b. New South Wales, Australia, 1940. MB, BS, Sydney (Australia) U., 1964. Cert. pediatrics, allergy and immunology. Pediatric pulmonary intern Royal Prince Alfred Hosp., Australia, 1964; resident Loma Linda (Calif.) U. Med. Ctr., 1966-68; with Henrietta Egleston Hosp. for Children, Atlanta, 1968-69, T.C. Thompson Children's Hosp., Chattanooga, 1969-70; instr. pediatrics Loma Linda U., 1970-72, with dept. pediatrics, 1972—, dean Sch. Medicine, 1986-91, pres., 1990—. Office: Loma Linda U Office of the President Loma Linda CA 92350*

BEHRENS, JEFFREY MARC, physician; b. Bklyn., Oct. 15, 1951; s. George I. and Leona A. (Strauss) B.; m. Donna J. Nenstiel, July 24, 1987; children: Michael, Jennifer. BS with honors, SUNY, Stony Brook, 1973; MD, N.Y. Med. Coll., 1976. Diplomate Am. Bd. Internal Medicine, added qualification in geriatrics; cert. Am. Bd. Quality Assurance and Utilization Rev. Physicians. Intern Nassau County Med. Ctr., East Meadow, N.Y., resident in internal medicine; pvt. practice L.I., N.Y., 1982-85, South Charleston, W.Va., 1985-87; group physician Davidson Med. Group, Lake Worth, Fla., 1988—; chief divsn. internal medicine JFK Hosp., Atlantis, 1992—; internist-in-charge cardiology clinic Walson Army Cmty. Hosp., Ft. Dix, N.J., 1980-81; instr. in medicine SUNY Health Scis. Ctr., Stony Brook, 1982-85; med. dirs. Bishop Gray Inn for Older People, Lake Worth, 1988-91; med. dir. Maclens (N.J.) Rehab. Nursing Home, 1992-95, Finnish Am. Nursing Home, 1993—; med. dir. Avaneé, Lake worth, 1995—. Vol. physician Healthright Clinic, Charleston, 1986-87. Capt. U.S. Army, 1979-82. Mem. AMA, ACP, Am. Soc. Internal Medicine, Fla. Med. Assn., Palm Beach County Med. Assn., So. Med. Assn. Office: Davidson Med Group 1640 S Congress Ave # 200 Lake Worth FL 33461-2142

BEHRENTS, ROLF GORDON, dental educator, orthodontist; b. Galesburg, Ill., July 21, 1947; s. Ellis Gordon and Alice Margaret (Norby) B.; m. Eileen Starkman, June 17, 1978; children: Nathaniel Eliott, Jenna Lauren. BA, St. Olaf Coll., 1969; DDS, Meharry Med. Coll., 1973; MS, Case Western Res. U., 1975; PhD, U. Mich., 1984. Program dir. orthodontics Case Western Res. U., Cleve., 1978-84; chmn. dept. orthodontics U. Tenn., Memphis, 1984—; grant reviewer NIH, Washington, 1986—; chmn. rev. panel Am. Assn. Orthodontics Found., St. Louis, 1992—. Author: Growth of the Aging Craniofacial Skeleton, 1985. Mem. ADA, Am. Assn. Orthodontics (Milo Hellman award 1975, 84). Office: U Tenn 875 Union Ave Memphis TN 38163

BEHRJE, WILLIAM JOHN, surgeon; b. N.Y.C., Apr. 30, 1940; s. William F. and Johanna G. (Brandes) B.; m. Pamala Lynn Harrison; children: Rolfe Tonis, Garth Francis, Rhett Brandon. BS in Biology, Wagner Coll., N.Y.C., 1961; MD, N.Y. Med. Coll., N.Y.C., 1965. Diplomate Nat. Bd. Med. Examiners, Am. Bd. Surgery. Surg. intern USPHS Hosp., Staten Island, N.Y., 1965-66, resident in surgery, 1966-70; asst. chief surgery USPHS Hosp., S.I., N.Y., 1970-72, dep. chief surgery, 1972-74; pvt. practice S.W. Mich. Surgery P.C., Kalamazoo, 1974—; chief dept. surgery Borgess Med. Ctr., Kalamazoo, Mich., 1994-96; assoc. clin. prof. surgery Mich.State U., Coll. Human Medicine, 1978—. Mem. ACS, Transplantation Soc. Mich., Pan Pacific Surg. Soc., Mich. State Med. Soc., Kalamazoo Acad. Medicine, Alpha Omega Alpha. Office: Southwest Mich Surgery PC 1717 Shaffer Kalamazoo MI 49001

BEHRMAN, RICHARD ELLIOT, pediatrician, neonatologist, university dean; b. Phila., Dec. 13, 1931; s. Robert and Vivian (Keegan) B.; m. Ann Nelson, Aug. 14, 1954; children: Amy Jane, Michael Jameson, Carolyn Ann, Hillary. A.B., Amherst Coll., 1953; J.D., Harvard U., 1956; M.D. (Univ. scholar), U. Rochester, 1960. Diplomate Am. Bd. Pediatrics (examiner). Intern Johns Hopkins Hosp., Balt., 1960-61; resident in pediatrics Johns Hopkins Hosp., 1963-65; asst. prof. pediatrics U. Oreg. Sch. Medicine, Portland, 1965-67; asso. prof. U. Oreg. Sch. Medicine, 1967-68; prof. U. Ill. Coll. Medicine, Chgo., 1968-71; prof., chmn. dept. pediatrics Columbia U. Coll. Physicians and Surgeons, N.Y.C., 1971-76; prof., chmn. dept. Case Western Res. U. Sch. Medicine, Cleve., 1976-81, dean Sch. Medicine, 1980-89, v.p. med. affairs, 1987-89; dir. dept. pediatrics Rainbow Babies and Children's Hosp., Cleve., 1976-81; dir. Ctr. for Future Children, David & Lucile Packard FD, prof. Stanford U., U. Calif., San Francisco, 1989; chmn. bd. maternal, child and family research Nat. Acad. Sci., NRC, 1977-80; dir. Lucile S. Packard Children's Hosp., Stanford. Author: Neonatology: Diseases of the Fetus and Infant, 1973, Neonatal-Perinatal Medicine, 1977; editor: Nelson's Textbook of Pediatrics, 1978, 83, 87, 92, 95, Essentials of Pediatrics, 1989, 93, The Future of Children, 1990; mem. editl. bd., sect. editor fetal and neonatal medicine Jour. Pediats., 1970-85; assoc. editor, mem. editl. bd., sect. editor fetal and neonatal medicine Pediat. Rsch. Jour., 1971-80. With USPHS, 1961-63. Served with USPHS, 1961-63. Whipple scholar, 1960-61; Wyeth pediatric fellow, 1963-65. Fellow Am. Acad. Pediatrics; mem. Soc. Pediatric Rsch. (v.p. 1976-77), Inst. Medicine of Nat. Acad. Scis., Am. Pediatric Soc., Perinatal Rsch. Soc. (coun. 1970-73), Soc. Gynecol. Investigation, Sigma Xi. Presbyterian. Club: Century Assn. Home: 15 Crest Rd Belvedere Tiburon CA 94920

BEIDEMAN, RONALD PAUL, chiropractor, college dean; b. Norristown, Pa., Mar. 22, 1926; s. Jonas Paul and Bertha May (Cane) B.; student Temple U., 1948; D. Chiropractic, Nat. Coll. Chiropractic, Chgo., 1952; postgrad. Wheaton Coll.; B.A., Lewis U., 1976; m. Lorraine Marian Barrett, Aug. 19, 1950 (dec.); children—Ronald Paul, J. Kirk; m. 2d, Peggy Ann Bartlett, May 31, 1980. Dir. dept. diagnosis Nat. Coll. Chiropractic, Chgo., 1952-66, sr. tenured prof., 1963—, registrar, 1966-78, dean admissions and records, 1973-88, ofcl. coll. historian, 1987—; dean of records 1988-94, coll. archivist, 1994—; exam. physician Chgo. Gen. Health Service, 1954-65; lectr. in field; pvt. practice chiropractic Chgo., 1954—; mem. nat. profl. standards rev. council, Health Care Financing Adminstrn., HHS, 1982; prof. Nat.-Lincoln Sch. Postgrad. Edn., 1964—; accrediting evaluator Council on Chiropractic Edn., 1978—, mem. task force panels on admissions Commn. on Accreditation, 1980, 84—; accrediting evaluator Western Assn. Schs. and Colls., 1985. Served with USAAF, 1944-46. Fellow Internat. Coll. Chiropractors (faculty); mem. Nat. Coll. Chiropractic (corp. sec. 1972-94), Nat. Bd. Chiropractic Examiners (chmn. test com. 1967-69), Ill., Chgo. chiropractic socs., Am. Chiropractic Assn. (vet. affairs com. 1979-81), Am. Legion (post comdr. 1957-58), Am., Ill. assns. Collegiate Registrars and Admissions Officers, Ill. Assn. Student Financial Aid Adminstrs., Nat. Assn. Coll. Admissions Counselors, Sigma Phi Kappa (grand chancellor), Lambda Phi Delta.

Author: In The Making of a Profession: The National College of Chiropractic 1906-1981, 1995; contbr. articles to profl. publs. Office: 200 E Roosevelt Rd Lombard IL 60148-4539

BEIERWALTES, WILLIAM HENRY, physician, educator; b. Saginaw, Mich., Nov. 23, 1916; s. John Andrew and Fanny (Aris) B.; m. Mary Martha Nichols, Jan. 1, 1942; children: Andrew George, William Howard, Martha Louise. A.B., U. Mich., 1938, M.D., 1941. Diplomate: Am. Bd. Internal Medicine and Nuclear Medicine. Intern, then asst. resident medicine Cleve. City Hosp., 1941-43; mem. faculty U. Mich. Med. Center, 1944—, prof. medicine, 1959—; dir. nuclear medicine, also dir. Thyroid Research Lab., 1952-86, cons., 1987—; cons. nuclear medicine depts. St. John Hosp., Detroit, Wm. Beaumont Hosp., Royal Oak and Troy, Mich., The UpJohn Co. Rsch. div., 1952-65, The Abbott Labs. Rsch. div., 1960-67; sr. med. cons. MD (Med. Fedn.), Bagdad, Iraq, 1963; mem. exec. com. Inst. Sci. and Tech., 1963; lectr. Nat. Naval Med. Ctr., 1964-88, Ctr. for Environ. Health Mich. State Dept. Health, 1988-89; Peter Heimann lectr. 34th meeting Internat. Congress Surgery, Stockholm, Sweden, 1991; adv. panel on radionuclide labeled compounds for tumor diagnosis Internat. AEC, 1974-75; mem. Mich. State Radiation Bd., 1980-84; co-chmn. Nat. Coop., Thyroid Cancer Therapy Group, 1978-81. Author: Clinical Use of Radioisotopes, 1957, Manual of Nuclear Medicine Procedures, 1971, Love of Live Autobiog. Sketches, 1996; contbr. numerous articles to profl. jours.; assoc. editor Jour. Lab. and Clin. Medicine, 1954-60; editl. bd. Jour. Nuclear Medicine, 1969-64, assoc. editor, 1975-81; editl. bd. Jour. Clin. Endocrinology and Metabolism, 1963; adv. bd. Annals of Saudi Medicine, 1986-90; patentee for monoclonal antibodies to HCG, and radionuclide in vivo biochem. imaging of endocrine glands, 1951; first to treat a patient for cancer with radio labeled antibodies, 1951; co-inventor radiopharms, 1971; originator of radioimmunodetection of human cancer; first description of cytogenetic evolution of thyroid cancer; first description of fall of serum antithyroid antibodies during pregnancy with rise after delivery, other med. techniques. Guggenheim fellow, 1966-67; Commonwealth Fund fellow, 1967; recipient Hevesy Nuc. Medicine Pioneer award, 1982, Disting. Faculty award U. Mich., 1982, Johann-Georg-Zimmerman Trust for Cancer Rsch. Sci. prize for greatest contbn. to treatment of thyroid cancer, 1983, WWJ 950 Detroit Citizen of Week award, 1994; named Internat. Man of Yr. Internat. Biog. Ctr., Cambridge, Eng., 1992-93. Mem. AMA (Outstanding Scientific Achievement award 1994), ACP, Am. Fedn. Clin. Rsch. (pres. 1954-55), Soc. Nuclear Medicine (pres. 1965-66, Disting. Educator's award 1989, The Best Doctors in Am. award 1993-95), Ctrl. Clin. Rsch. Club (pres. 1958-59), Am. Thyroid Assn. (v.p. 1964-65, 66-67, Disting. Svc. award 1972), Ctrl. Soc. Clin. Rsch. (councillor 1964-67, 67-71), Galens Med. Soc., Assn. Am. Physicians, Mich. Med. Soc., Am. Endocrine Soc., Am. Soc. Clin. Oncology. Home: 917 Whittier Rd Grosse Pointe MI 48230-1873

BEIERWALTES, WILLIAM HOWARD, physiologist, educator; b. Ann Arbor, Mich., Oct. 6, 1947; s. William Henry and Mary-Martha (Nichols) B.; m. Patricia Sue Olson, July 11, 1982; children: William N., Peter L., Nora R. BA, Kalamazoo Coll., 1969; PhD, U. N.C., 1978. Instr. Mayo Med. Sch., Rochester, Minn., 1979-81; sr. staff scientist Henry Ford Hosp., Detroit, 1981—; assoc. prof. Case Western Res. Sch. Medicine, Detroit, 1994—. Contbr. articles to profl. jours. With U.S. Army, 1971-72. Mem. Am. Physiol. Soc., Am. Heart Assn. (fellow coun. on high blood pressure 1992, honor roll coun. on kidney 1988, chair rsch. fellowship com. Mich. chpt. 1987-90, 92-94, established investigator 1983-88), Am. Soc. Nephrology, Inter-Am. Soc. Hypertension, Mich. Soc. Med. Rsch. (bd. dirs. 1988-94, pres. 1992-94), Nat. Kidney Found. Mich. (rsch. rev. com. 1984-85, 88). Presbyterian. Home: 535 Barrington Rd Grosse Pointe MI 48230-1721 Office: Henry Ford Hosp 2799 W Grand Blvd Detroit MI 48202-2608*

BEIGL, WILLIAM, physician, naturopath, hypnotist, acupuncturist, consultant; b. Chgo., July 9, 1950; s. William C. Beigl and Mary Tomlinson; m. Mavis Johnson, Aug. 5, 1977. BA in Elem. Edn., U. South Fla., 1971; D of Natural Medicine, Acad. Sci. of Man, Sussex, Eng., 1979. Founder "You Too Can Choose Happiness" System, 1975; pvt. practice hypnotherapy Chgo., 1977—, pvt. practice naturopathic medicine, acupuncture and oriental natural medicine, 1979—; mem. rsch. team Donsbach U., 1980; chief rschr. disease prevention B.P.H. Corp.; bd. dirs. Mid-West Hypnosis Conv.; cons. in field; 1st syndicated hypnosis columnist, 1982; CEO Bill Beigl Enterprises, Inc., 1992, World Hypnosis Orgn., Inc., 1992; guest presenter Paramedics 25th Anniversary Celebration, Phila., 1993, (with Lee Ramsey) Blair Cheese Fest, 1994; devised lowered casino game tables; expert witness on hypnosis Cook County Ct. Sys. Editor, pub. Portage Park News, 1980; originator Paramedic System, 1968 (honored by Pres. Johnson 1968, Pres. Nixon 1969, Pres. Reagan 1985); responsible for Ramped Curbs, Braille Markings on Elevators and Monuments, Handicapped Parking Space, Licence Plates and Pub. Accessibility for Wheelchairs, Lowered Casino Gaming Tables; author: Adventures in Hypnosis, 1990, 2d edit., 1991; contbg. author: Think & Grow Breasts, 1994; contbr. articles on natural healing and hypnosis to newspapers and mags.; patentee in field. Assoc. bd. mgrs. Robert R. McCormick chpt. Chgo. Boy's Club, 1975; mem. trauma unit Operation Desert Storm, 1991; vol. with Hurricane Andrew victims, 1992, Mississippi River flood victims, 1993, summer Centennial Olympics physician, Atlanta, 1996; bd. dirs. Kids Internat., 1996. Recipient award Congressman Sidney Yates, 1971, Disease Prevention award Better Positive Health Found., 1979, Pen and Quill award Nat. Bd. for Hypnotherapy and Hypnotic Anesthesiology, 1991, Excellence award Honeywell, 1994; named Chicagoan of Yr., Mayor Richard J. Daley, 1968, Chgo. Cath. of Yr., Cardinal John Cody, 1968, Illinoisan of Yr., Gov. Richard B. Ogilvie, 1968, One of 10 Outstanding Young Citizens, Chgo. Jaycees, 1980, Inspirational Mind of Four Profl. Championship Sports Teams, 1983-84, Citizen of Week, Sta. WBBM, 1984; appeared in Ripley's Believe It Or Not, 1984; honored by Gov. James R. Thompson, 1985, U.S. Senator Charles H. Percy, 1986; featured on CBS-TV Portrait Series, 1985, Cablevision's Good Neighbors, 1987; inducted into Internat. Hypnosis Hall of Fame, 1989. Mem. Internat. Naturopathic Assn. (cert., Naturopathic Physician Yr. 1985), Nat. Assn. Naturopathic Physicians (cert.), Nat. Guild Hypnotists (cert.), Assn. Advance Ethical Hypnosis (cert., past v.p., past sec. Ill. chpt., bd. dirs. 1986, participant the biggest hypnosis conv. 1988, co-chmn. world's largest and friendliest 1987-88, 89), World Hypnosis Orgn. (cert.), Am. Naturopathic Assn., Am. Soc. Clin. Hypnosis, Minn. Assn. Naturopathic Physicians (cert.), Hemlock Soc., Chgo. Meml. Assn., Boys Clubs Am. (life, Boy of Yr. 1968), Hospice, Midwest Pain Soc., Pain Clinic Physicians. Lodge: Moose. Office: 2521 W Montrose Ave Chicago IL 60618-1505

BEINFELD, MARGERY COHEN, neurobiology educator; b. Washington, Oct. 21, 1945; d. Robert Abraham and Mabel (Blake) Cohen; m. Solon Beinfeld, June 1970; children—Benjamin Ezra, Molly Toba. B.A., Washington U., St. Louis, 1968, Ph.D., 1973. Postdoctoral fellow St. Louis U., 1973-75, Washington U., St. Louis, 1975-79; staff fellow NIAMDD, NIH, Bethesda, Md., 1979-81; asst. prof. St. Louis U. Med. Sch., 1981-85, assoc. prof., 1985-88, prof., 1988-95; prof. Tufts U. Sch. Medicine, 1995—. Contbr. chpts. to books, articles to profl. jours. NIH grantee, 1976-79, 81—. Mem. AAAS. Democrat. Jewish. Avocations: gardening; camping; hiking; biking. Office: 136 Harrison Ave Boston MA 02111

BEINFIELD, MALCOLM SYDNEY, surgeon, educator; b. N.Y.C., Mar. 24, 1921; married Marjorie Koster, 1945; children: Harriet, Lynn, Bruce, Elizabeth. BA, Yale U., 1942; MD, SUNY, Downstate, 1945. Diplomate Am. Bd. Surgery. Intern Kings County Hosp., 1945-46; resident in pathology and surgery Cleve. City Hosp., 1946-47; resident in surgery Harlem Hosp., 1947-51; attending surgeon Norwalk Hosp., 1951—, dir. med. edn., 1953-57, dir. dept. surgery, 1966-69, dir. gen. surgery, 1969-72, asst. chief of staff, 1975-79; dir. Physicians Asst. Surg. Residency Program Norwalk Hosp./Yale U., 1975; instr. dept. anatomy Yale U., 1951-53, asst. clin. prof. surgery, now assoc. clin. prof. surgery, 1980—; assoc. clin. prof. health care scis. George Washington U., 1980—; ret.; mem. exec. com. Norwalk Hosp., 1966-69, 75-79, joint conf. com., 1975-79, cost containment com., 1978-79, trustee, 1976-79; adj. prof. clin. medicine King's Coll., 1990; preceptor physician asst. program Dept. Family Medicine and Practice, U. Wis., 1990; surg. cons. Westport Athletic Program, 1951—; bd. dirs. Bank Darien, 1989—, PHS, Inc. of Conn., 1984—, vice-chmn., 1990—; founding mem. Westport Nat. Bank, 1964, past bd. dirs.; bd. dirs. FIPA, Bank of Darien, 1989—; mem. credentialling com. Prucare, 1985—; presenter, panelist numerous confs. Surg. editor HospiMedica, 1984-86; editorial bd. Physician Assistants, 1988—; contbr. over 13 articles to profl. jours. Chmn. Red Cross Med. Svc., 1951-59; dir. Civil Def. Med. Svc., 1951-59; mem. Dem. Town Com., 1952-54. Recipient commendation for disting. svc. Am. Assn. Physician's Assts., 1988. Fellow ACS; mem. New England Cancer Soc. (by invitation). Home: 17 Hockanum Rd Westport CT 06880-2166

BEISNER, DONALD HENRY, ophthalmologist; b. Cedar Falls, Iowa, Mar. 30, 1939; s. Henry Fred and Mathilde Sophia (Tadge) B.; m. Judith Ann Gardner, July 13, 1963; children: Katherine Amy, Sarah Elizabeth (dec.), David Gardner. Student, Iowa State U., 1957-60; MD, U. Iowa, 1964, MS, 1970. Diplomate Am. Bd. Ophthalmology. Intern L.A. County Hosp., 1964-65; resident U. Iowa Hosp., Iowa City, 1967-70; surgeon Eye Ear Nose & Throat Assocs., Springfield, Mo., 1970-73; surgeon, v.p. Eye Surg. Assocs., Springfield, 1974-86, surgeon, pres., 1986-92; surgeon Mo. Eye Inst., Springfield, 1992—; Staff physician Cox Med. Ctr., 1970-95, St. John's Hosp., 1970-95, chmn. dept. Ophthalmology, 1973-75, mem.-at-large exec. com., 1982-83. Contbr. articles to profl. jours. Sec. bd. dirs. Hawaiian Eye Found., 1987—. Lt. USN, 1965-67. Recipient Sci. Achievement award Bausch & Lomb, 1957, scholarship Phi Eta Sigma, 1958, Phi Kappa Phi, 1960, Alpha Omega Alpha, 1964. Fellow ACS (credentials com. 1979-84), Am. Acad. Ophthalmology (adv. bd. Argus 1976-82). Home: 4131 E Saint Andrews Dr Springfield MO 65809 Office: Missouri Eye Inst 2900 S Fremont Springfield MO 65804

BEITZ, RICHARD THEODORE, JR., family physician, acute care physician; b. Greeley, Colo., Aug. 30, 1953; s. Richard Theodore and Geraldine Ann (Weiss) B.; m. Valerie Robin Finch, Dec. 27, 1974; children: Ryan Richard, Kevin Matthew, Eric Jonathan, Evan Nicholas. AS, C.C. Denver, 1980; BS in Biology, BA in Chemistry, Metropolitan State Coll., Denver, 1981; DO, U. Health Scis. Coll Osteo., Kansas City, Mo., 1986. Diplomate Am. Bd. Family Practice. Intern in family practice Womack Army Cmty. Hosp., Ft. Bragg, N.C., 1986-87; brigade surgeon HHC 2d Brigade 4th ID, Ft. Carson, Colo., 1987-89; resident in family practice D.D. Eisenhower Med. Ctr., Ft. Gordon, Ga., 1989-90; chief resident D.D. Eisenhower Med. Ctr., 1990-91; resident in family practice Eisenhower Army Med. Ctr., Ft. Gordon, Ga., 1991-92; staff physician 547th med. clearing co. U.S. Army, Saudi Arabia, Iraq, 1990-91; comdr. 547th gen. dispensary U.S. Army, Grafenwoehr, Germany, 1992-93; chief AMIC/PAC Evans Army Cmty. Hosp., Ft. Carson, Colo., 1994—; chmn. family advocacy com., Grafenwoehr, 1992-93; flight surgeon 547th Gen. Dispensary, Grafenwoehr, 1992-93, med. rev. officer, 1992-93; mem. hosp. pharmacy & therapeutics com. Evans Army Cmty. Hosp., 1994—, competency chmn., 1995—. Instr. ACLS Am. Heart Assn., Ft. Carson, 1995. Maj. U.S. Army, 1986—. Decorated Meritorious Svc. medal U.S. Army, 1988, 93, Army Commendation medal, 1989, 91. Mem. AMA (Physician Recognition award 1995), Am. Osteo. Assn., Am. Acad. Family Physicians, Uniformed Svcs. Acad. Family Practice. Lutheran. Office: Evans Army Cmty Hosp Fort Carson CO 80913

BEKKEDAHL, BRAD DOUGLAS, dentist; b. Williston, N.D., Nov. 23, 1957; s. Oliver Lawrence Jr. and Gudrun Joan (Sundby) B. BA, Jamestown (N.D.) Coll., 1979; BS, U. Minn., 1982, DDS, 1984. Gen. practice dentistry Williston, 1984—; chmn. dental staff Mercy Med. Ctr., 1991-93. Scoutmaster Boy Scouts Am., Williston, 1984-86; mem. pastoral com. Gloria Dei Luth. Ch., Williston, 1986-88, mem. coun., 1993-96, congregation pres., 1995; pres. Am. Legion Drum and Bugle Corps, Williston, 1986; edn. officer Luth. Brotherhood br. 8334, 1989-93; mem. exec. com. Raymond Family Cmty. Ctr., 1988-96; bd. dirs. Williston Band, 1988-96, pres. 1988-92; commr. Williston, 1996—; mem. Williston Pk. Bd., 1988-96, pres., 1988-92. Mem. ADA, N.D. Dental Assn., N.W. Dist. Dental Assn., Williston Dental Soc. (sec.-treas.), N.D. Amateur Hockey Assn. (v.p. 1990-93, cmty. rep., pres. 1986-90, pres. 1993—). Republican. Home: 2501 13th Ave W Williston ND 58801-3225 Office: PO Box 2443 2204 2d Ave W Williston ND 58801

BEKOFF, OSCAR, psychotherapist; b. Bklyn., Aug. 27, 1917; s. Irving and Eva (Horowitz) B.; m. Beatrice Mendelow, June 9, 1940; children: Roberta, Marc, Marjorie. BA, City U. L.A., 1979, MS in Psychology, 1981, Litt.D (hon.), 1984, PhD in Psychology, 1986. Fellow and Diplomate Am. Bd. Med. Psychotherapists and Diagnosticians; diplomate Internat. Acad. Behavioral Medicine Counseling and Psychotherapy. Pvt. practice psychotherapy & behavioral medicine Tamarac, Fla., 1982—; exec. v.p. Clinton Oil Co., 1961-67; asst. to the chmn. of the bd. Real Petroleum Co., 1968-71; pres. Nantod Corp., Brookville, N.Y., 1963-77; bd. govs. Behavioral Sci. Ctr., Nova U., Ft. Lauderdale, 1985-88; instr. continuing edn. Broward Community Coll., Coconut Creek, Fla., 1985, L.I. U., Greenvale, N.Y., 1984-88; prof. psychology dept. L.I. U. Developed Intra-Persona Therapy. Author: It's Yours for the Asking, 1988. Dist. commr. Boy Scouts Am., 1938-42; commr. City of N.Y., 1948; adv. bd. Fla. State Crime Commn., 1985—; cons., advisor Fla. Pepper Commn. on Aging, Tallahassee, 1990—. Recipient Cert. of Merit Nat. Coun. ARC, 1985, 50-Yr. Svc. award, 1990, Letter of Honor for pro bono work with the elderly from Pres. Ronald Reagan, 1988. Mem. Am. Assn. Counseling and Devel., Am. Assn. Family Counseling and Mediators (supr. 1986), Nat. Ski Patrol (life), Amateur Ski Instrs. Assn. (life, cert. ski instr. 1946—). Oddfellows, Masons (32 deg.). Jewish. Home: 7661 Granville Dr Tamarac FL 33321

BELAFSKY, MARK LEWIS, otolaryngologist; b. Perth Amboy, N.J., June 8, 1939; s. Henry A. and Rose (Buckner) B.; m. Betty M. Forman, Dec. 25, 1962; children: Caryn, Peter. BA, U. Pa., 1960; MD, Chgo. Med. Sch., 1964. Diplomate Am. Bd. Otolaryngology. Intern Thomas Jefferson U., Phila., 1964-65, resident, 1967-71; pvt. practive Cherry Hill, N.J., 1971—; chmn. bd. dirs. Our Lady of Lourdes Hosp., Camden, N.J., Rancocas Valley Hosp., Willingboro, N.J. Chmn. bd. dirs. med. adv. coun. N.J. State Athletic Control Bd., 1987—. Capt. U.S. Army, 1965-67, Vietnam. Fellow ACS, Am. Acad. of Otolaryngology & Head & Neck Surgery, Am. Soc. Head & Neck Surgery, Am. Soc. of Facial, Plastic & Reconstructive Surgery, Phila. Coll. of Physicians. Office: 1910 Route 70 E Cherry Hill NJ 08003-2123

BELANGER, WILLIAM A., health facility administrator; b. Cohoes, N.Y., Mar. 20, 1956; s. William R. and Helen C. (Califano) B.; m. Carol R. Holland, Mar. 28, 1980; children: William Kyle, Thomas Payne. BSBA in Acctg., U. Fla., 1978, MBA, 1979. Fin. specialist Humana Hosp., Kissimmee, Fla., 1980-82; assoc. exec. dir fin. Humana Hosp., Kissimmee, 1983-87, assoc. exec. dir., 1987-88, exec. dir., 1988-91; asst. adminstr. fin. Humana Hosp., St. Petersburg, 1982-83; dir. market planning Humana Ctrl. Fla. Office, Orlando, 1991-93; assoc. adminstr. bus. devel. Cape Fear Valley Med. Ctr., Fayetteville, N.C., 1993—. Home: PO Box 64524 Fayetteville NC 28311 Office: Cape Fear Valley Med Ctr PO Box 2000 Fayetteville NC 28302

BELCASTRO, PATRICK FRANK, pharmaceutical scientist; b. Italy, June 3, 1920; came to U.S., 1927, naturalized, 1943; s. Samuel and Sarah (Mosca) B.; m. Hanna Vilhelmina Jensen, July 6, 1963; children—Helen Maria, Paul Anthony. B.S., Duquesne U., 1942; M.S. (Am. Found. Pharm. Edn. fellow), Purdue U., 1951, Ph.D. in Pharmacy and Pharm. Chemistry (Am. Found. for Pharm. Edn. fellow), 1953. Instr. pharmacy Duquesne U., 1946-49; asst. prof. pharmacy Ohio State U., 1953-54; prof. indsl. pharmacy Purdue U., 1954-90, prof. emeritus, 1990—. Author: Physical and Technical Pharmacy, 1963; contbg. editor: (with others) Internat. Phar. Abstracts, 1970—, Pharm. Tech, 1977—; contbr. to: (with others) Jour. Pharm. Scis. Served with U.S. Army, 1942-46. Mem. Am. Pharm. Assn., Am. Soc. Hosp. Pharmacists, Am. Assn. Colls. Pharmacy, AAUP, Parenteral Drug Assn., Rho Chi, Phi Lambda Upsilon. Roman Catholic. Home: 327 Meridian St West Lafayette IN 47906-2603 Office: Purdue U Sch Pharmacy and Pharm Scis West Lafayette IN 47907

BELCHER, JAMES MICHAEL, periodontist; b. Kansas City, Kans., July 23, 1947; s. Milton Parks and Nina Sylvia (Schwab) B.; m. Carolyn Sue Siegel, May 8, 1976 children—Christopher, Jennifer. B.A. in Biochemistry, U. Kans., 1969; D.D.S., U. Mo.-Kansas City, 1973, cert. in periodontology, 1976. Practice dentistry specializing in periodontology, Lakeland, Fla., 1976—. Author: Immunology and Periodontal Disease, 1975; Data Base Systems for Periodontics, 1985. past bd. dirs. Girls Club of Lakeland; past chmn. Thunderbird dist. coun. Boy Scouts Am. Mem. Am. Acad. Periodontology, ADA, Fla. Dental Assn., West Coast Dental Assn., Polk County Dental Assn. (past pres.), Polk County Dental Study Club Assn. (past pres.), Fla. Acad. Practice Mgmt., Phi Kappa Sigma, Phi Psi Republican. Roman Catholic. Lodge: Kiwanis (past pres., past bd. dirs.). Home: 4313 Forest Hills Dr Lakeland FL 33813-1764 Office: James Belcher 3003 S Florida Ave Ste 201 Lakeland FL 33803-4050

BELCHER-REDEBAUGH-LEVI, CAROLINE LOUISE, nursing home administrator, nurse; b. Dixon, Ill., May 23, 1910; d. Charles R. and May Caroline (Barnes) Kreger; m. Richard E. Belcher, Nov. 24, 1934 (dec. 1964); children: Richard Charles (dec.), Mary; m. Charles H. Redebaugh, Dec. 3, 1966 (dec. 1979); m. Paul Levi, July 20, 1985 (dec. Sept. 1993). R.N., Katherine Shaw Bethea Sch. Nursing, 1930. Nurse, various hosps., 1930-49; adminstr. Orchard Glen Nursing Home, Dixon, Ill., 1949-76; coordinator Sr. Action Ctr., Springfield, Ill., 1977-87; charter mem. Ill. Nursing Home Adminstrs. Licensure Bd., 1970-76; mem. Sauk Valley Community Coll. Found., Dixon, Ill., 1988, adv. com. for sr. programs, 1988, chmn. ball com., 1989-90, Co Coun. on Aging, 1988, various adv. coms. advocating for srs. Contbr. articles to profl. jours. Mem. nat. adv. com., del. White House Conf. on Aging, 1961-81; v.p. Ill. Joint Council to Improve Health Care for Aged, 1953, pres., 1954; chair Sec. State George Ryan Adv. Com. Health Maintenance, 1991; charter mem. bd. dirs. Lee County Vol. Care Ctr., 1994, Free Health Clinic. Mem. Capitol City Rep. Women (v.p. 1983-90), Lee County Rep. Women, State Council on Aging, Am. Coll. Nursing Home Adminstrs. (charter, edn. com., pres.), Am. Nursing Home Assn. (v.p. 1953), Ill. Nurses Assn. (bd. dirs.), Ill. Nursing Home Adminstrs (charter), Sr. Illinoisian's Hall of Fame (charter). Home: 1420 Eustace Dr Dixon IL 61021-1742

BELETZ, ELAINE ETHEL, nurse, educator; b. N.Y.C., Jan. 5, 1944; d. Harry and Rose (Friedman) B. RN, Mt. Sinai Hosp., N.Y.C., 1968; BS in Nursing, Fairleigh Dickinson U., 1970; MA, NYU, 1974; MEd, Columbia U., 1978, EdD, 1979. Staff nurse ICU Mt. Sinai Hosp., 1968-70, asst. head nurse, 1970; adminstrv. supervisory relief nurse, 1973-74, 77-78; clin. instr. Roosevelt Hosp. Sch. Nursing, N.Y.C., 1970-73; nurse gerontologist St. Luke's Hosp. Ctr., N.Y.C., 1974; asst. dir. nursing Bklyn. Hosp., N.Y.C., 1975-77; asst. prof. nursing Hunter Coll., CUNY, 1978-81; v.p. nursing Mt. Sinai Hosp., Med. Ctr., Chgo., 1982-83; assoc. prof. nursing Villanova (Pa.) U., 1983—; lectr.; cons. nursing adminstrn., labor relations in health care; mem. task force on block grants. Ill. Dept. Health. Contbr. articles to profl. jours.; internat. cons. and lectr. Bd. dirs. Hadassah Nurses Coun., Phila., 1993-94; pres.-elect, 1994-96, pres. 96—. Recipient Disting. Achievement award Columbia U. Nursing Edn. Alumni Assn., 1989. Fellow Am. Acad. Nursing; mem. Am. Nurses Assn. (bd. dirs. 1982-87, mem. polit. action com. 1982-86), N.Y. State Nurses Assn. (treas. 1977-78, pres.-elect 1978-79, pres. 1979-81, bd. trustees, cert. of appreciation 1981, hon. recognition award 1987), Pa. Nurses Assn. (nominating com. 1985-86, chair polit. action com. 1990-92), N.Y. Counties Registered Nurses Assn. (nominating com. 1973, dir. 1975-78, Amanda Silvers award 1981), Shershower Benevolent Assn., Nursing Edn. Alumni Assn. (Leadership award 1989), Sigma Theta Tau, Phi Kappa Phi. Jewish. Office: Villanova U Grad Program Nursing Health Care Adminstrn Coll Nursing Villanova PA 19085

BELFER, MARK HARRIS, physician; b. Grand Rapids, Mich., Oct. 7, 1952; s. Gerald Charles and Sylvia Mae (Shinwell) B.; m. Nancy Lynn Sharp, June 9, 1974; children: Rachel, Aaron, Bret. BS, Mich. State U., 1974; DO, Coll. Osteo. Med. and Surgery, Des Moines, 1977. Diplomate Nat. Bd. Osteo. Med. Examiners, Am. Bd. Family Practice. Commd. U.S. Army, 1978, advanced through grades to maj., resigned, 1986; brigade surgeon U.S. Army, Bamberg, Fed. Republic Germany, 1978-80; gen. med. officer U.S. Army Health Clinic, Bamberg, 1980-81; family practice resident U.S. Army, Ft. Benning, Ga., 1981-83; dir. family practice ctr. Tripler Army Med. Ctr., Honolulu, 1983-86; pvt. practice family medicine Warren, Ohio, 1986-94; assoc. dir. Family Practice Residency Good Samaritan Hosp., Dayton, Ohio, 1994-95; asst. prof. Wright State U. Sch. of Medicine, 1994-95; program dir. Family Practice Residency St. Elizabeth Health Ctr., Youngstown, Ohio, 1995—; assoc. prof. Clin. Family Medicine Northeastern Ohio U. Coll. of Medicine, Rootstown, Ohio, 1995—; asst. clin. prof. U. Hawaii, Honolulu, 1983-86; with staff Trumbull Meml. Hosp., Warren, 1986-96, St. Joseph/Riverside Hosp., 1986-94; preceptor Northeastern Ohio U. Coll. Medicine, 1987; med. dir. Trumbull County Bd. Health, 1988-94; pres. Trumbull Mahoning Counties Acad. Family Physicians, 1990-93; dist. dir. Ohio Acad. Family Physicians, 1990-92; bd. dirs. Quality Physicians Care Corp., 1996. Advisor Med. Explorers Boy Scouts Am., Warren, 1986-94; pres.-elect Trumbull County Med. Soc., 1994. Fellow Am. Acad. Family Physicians; mem. Ohio Acad. Family Physicians (v.p. 1993-95, pres.-elect 1995-96), Am. Cancer Soc. (exec bd. Mahoning County unit 1995-96). Jewish. Lodge: B'nai Brith. Home: 8574 Reserve Ct Poland OH 44514 Office: St Elizabeth Health Ctr Family Health Ctr 1053 Belmont Ave Youngstown OH 44501

BELGOROD, BARRY MILES, surgeon; b. N.Y.C., Mar. 27, 1953; s. Howard H. and Madeline (Bloom) B.; B.A. summa cum laude, Queens Coll., 1973; M.D., U. Pa., 1977. Intern in internal medicine Pa. Hosp., 1977-78; resident in ophthalmology Manhattan Eye, Ear and Throat Hosp., N.Y.C., 1978-81, asst. attending surgeon, 1981—; asst. attending ophthalmologist N.Y. Hosp., 1982—; clin. instr. dept. ophthalmology Cornell U. Med. Coll., N.Y.C. Pres. BMB Patent Holding Corp. Patentee electronic photochromic lens, laser corneal surgery. Recipient Ira M. Goldin award, 1973; Charles A. Oliver Meml. prize in ophthalmology, 1977; N.Y. State Regents scholar, 1969-73; NSF Research fellow, 1972; Jonas Salk scholar, 1973-77; diplomate Am. Bd. Ophthalmology, Nat. Bd. Med. Examiners. Fellow Am. Acad. Ophthalmology, ACS, N.Y. Acad. Medicine; mem. N.Y. Acad. Scis., N.Y. County Med. Soc., Med. Soc. State N.Y., U. Pa. Alumni Assn., Jonas Salk Scholars Endowment Fund, Phi Beta Kappa, Sigma Xi, Beta Delta Chi. Office: 115 E 61st St New York NY 10021

BELK, LISA TRAVIS, health facility administrator; b. Charlotte, N.C., Oct. 22, 1967; d. Dale Martin and Joyce Arlene (Setzer) Travis; m. Michael Kenneth Belk, May 20, 1995. AAS, Ctrl. Piedmont Coll., 1988. Med. records clk. III Piedmont Behavioral Health, Monroe, N.C., 1988-89; health data analyst Presbyn.-Orthopedic Hosp., Charlotte, 1989-90; med. records dept. dir. Charter Pines Hosp., Charlotte, 1990-95; med. record dept. coord. Piedmont Behavioral Health, 1995—. Mem. Am. Health Info. Mgmt. Assn., N.C. Health Info. Mgmt. Assn. (sec. region VI 1989—, health info. mgmt. recruiter 1992-93). Baptist. Office: Piedmont Behavioral Health 1623 E Sunset Dr Monroe NC 28112

BELKER, ARNOLD M., urologist; b. Louisville, Feb. 27, 1934; s. I. Joseph and Margery (Weinberg) B.; m. Terry Marks, Oct. 20, 1958; children: Paul S., Jill H. BS, U. Louisville, 1955, MD, 1958. Diplomate Am. Bd. Urology. Intern New Eng. Med. Ctr. Hosp., Boston, 1958-59; resident in gen. surgery Louisville Gen. Hosp., 1961-62; resident in urology State U. Iowa Hosps., Iowa City, 1962-65; urologist Louisville Urology Assocs., PSC, 1965—; clin. prof. divsn. urology U. Louisville, 1983—. Guest editor Urologic Clinics of North America, 1987; contbr. over 50 articles to profl. jours. Bd. dirs. Jewish Hosp. Health Care Sys., Louisville, 1988—; mem. County Commr.'s Com. on Quality and Charity Trust, Louisville, 1990-91; mem. Gov.'s Task Force on Healthcare Costs and Quality, Frankfort, 1990-91. With USPHS, 1959-61. Mem. Soc. Reproductive Surgeons (pres. 1992-93), Jefferson County Med. Soc. (pres. 1990-91), Soc. for Study of Male Reprodn. (pres. 1995-96), Am. Soc. Andrology (pres. 1996—), U. Louisville Sch. Medicine Alumni Assn. (pres. 1985-86). Office: Louisville Urology Assocs 250 E Liberty St Ste 602 Louisville KY 40202

BELKIN, MICHAEL, ophthalmic researcher; b. Tel Aviv, Nov. 14, 1941; s. Yerachmeal and Gita Belkin; m. Ruth Miriam Loeb, Nov. 8, 1967; children: Tamar, Dan, Daphna. MA, Cambridge U., 1965; MD, Hebrew U., 1969. Chief physician, eye dept. Haddasah Univ. Hosp., Jerusalem, 1975-76; chief rsch. and devel. Mil. Med. Corps., Israel, 1976-79; head, Laser Lab. Tel Aviv Univ. Eye Rsch. Inst., 1981—; dir. Eye Rsch. Inst. Tel Aviv Univ. Med. Sch., 1981-91, prof. ophthalmol., 1987—, chmn., dept. ophthalmology, 1988-92; chmn. Adv. Com. on Ophthalmology, Israel, 1985-93; mem. World Coun. Ergoophthalmology, Stockholm, 1988—; vis. prof. Letterman Army Inst. Rsch., San Francisco, 1979-81, 89, 90, 94, 95. Contbg. author books in field, publs.; contbr. articles to profl. jours. Chmn. Ophthalmic Planning Com. for Nat. Emergencies, Israel, 1982-95; mem. Human Use in Sci. Experiment Com., Tel Hashomer, Israel, 1984—; bd. dirs. Ramot Ltd., Tel Aviv, 1988-95. Lt. col. Israeli Med. Corps, 1976-84. Recipient Landau

Rsch. prize Israel Med. Assn., 1976, Stein Rsch. prize Tel Aviv U., 1985, 88, 95, Merit award and medal Internat. Ophthalmol. Congress, 1990, Beatrice lectr. U.S. Army, 1990. Mem. Internat. Soc. for Eye Rsch., Assn. for Rsch. in Vision and Ophthalmology, Am. Acad. Ophthalmology, Internat. Soc. Ocular Trauma (founding), Israel Eye Rsch. Assn. (founding chmn. 1983-86). Office: Sheba Med Ctr, Eye Inst, 52621 Tel Hashomer Israel

BELL, CHAROLETTE RENEE, psychologist; b. St. Louis, Jan. 23, 1949. BA, Dillard U., New Orleans, 1970; MA, U. No. Colo., Greeley, 1973; EdD, U. No. Colo., 1976. Sch. psychologist Aurora (Colo.) Pub. Schs., 1974-76, Cherry Creek Schs., Englewood, Colo., 1976-78; psychologist Orangeburg (S.C.) Area Mental Health Ctr., 1978-79; prin. investigator 1890 research S.C. State Coll., 1979-83; private practice Columbia, S.C., 1983-87; research and program evaluator S.C. Inst. Poverty & Deprivation, 1987-88; rsch. and program evaluator coll. edn. U. S.C., 1988-89; cons. Calif. State U., San Marcos, 1989-90, assoc. prof. edn. Coll. of Edn., 1990—; founder, chairperson Citizens Against Sexual Assault, O'burg, S.C., Columbia Coalition Black Concerns, Cola, S.C., 1987—; exec. dir Project Soaring, Cola, 1986-87. Co-author: Discipline and Classroom Management, 1980, Added Dimensions in Fitness, 1984. Sec. Dem. Precinct Ward, Columbia, 1988. Home: PO Box 2111 San Marcos CA 92079-2111

BELL, DAVID SAMUEL HENRY, medical educator; b. Armagh, Northern Ireland, Jan. 13, 1944; came to U.S., 1975; s. James Smyth and Violet (Burgess) B.; m. Jocelyn Anne Johnson, Nov. 20, 1971; children: James, Michael, Andrew. MB, BCh, BAO, Queens U., Belfast, 1970. Diplomate Am. Bd. Internal Medicine. Fellow in Endocrinology U. Saskatchewan, Saskatoon, 1974-75; fellow in Endocrinology Greater Balt. Med. Ctr., Balt., 1975-76; cons. Georgetown (Ont.) Hosp., 1976-78; dir. internal medicine Connemaugh Hosp., Johnstown, Pa., 1978-80; assoc. prof. U. Ala., Birmingham, 1980-87; prof. medicine U. Ala., 1987—, dir. diabetes program, 1985—. Contbr. numerous articles to profl. jours. Fellow ACP, Royal Coll. Physicians (Edinburgh), Royal Coll. Physicians (Can.), Am. Coll. Endocrinology. Office: U Ala Med Sch 2000 6th Ave S Birmingham AL 35233

BELL, DOROTHY ANN COMFORT, rehabilitation nurse; b. Harrisburg, Pa., Sept. 11, 1958; d. Nathaniel Lawrence and Edwina Marie (Cox) Comfort; m. Lance Meade Bell, Aug. 19, 1989. Diploma, Richmond Meml Hosp Sch Nursing, Richmond, Va., 1979. Staff nurse Richmond Meml. Hosp., 1979, Johnston-Willis Hosp., Richmond, 1979-81, Sheltering Arms Rehab. Hosp., Richmond, 1981-85; staff nurse Univ. Hosp. Rehab. Ctr., Elizabethtown, Pa., 1985-87, 3-11 relief supr., 1987-83, 3-11 supr, 1989-90; rehab. counselor, cons. LRC Rehab. Consultants, Inc., Paoli, Pa., 1990-93; pediatric rehab. nurse Milton S. Hershey Med. Ctr., Hershey, Pa., 1993—; rehab. cons. LRC Rehab. Cons., Inc., Paoli, 1990-93. Mem. Hershey Cmty. Chorus, 1990—, publicity chmn. 1992, bd. dirs., 1994—, membership chmn., 1996—; recorder membership com. 1st United Meth. Ch., Hershey, 1992—. Mem. Assn. Rehab. Nurses (cert. rehab. RN, bd. dirs. Ctrl. Pa. chpt. 1994-96, membership chair Pa. chpt. 1996—), ARC (cert. 1979). Home: 344 Maple Ave Hershey PA 17033-1738 Office: Milton S Hershey Med Ctr PO Box 850 Hershey PA 17033-0850

BELL, FRANCES LOUISE, medical technologist; b. Milton, Pa., Apr. 28, 1926; d. George Earl and Kathryn Robbins (Fairchild) Reichard; m. Edwin Lewis Bell II, Dec. 27, 1950; children: Ernest Michael, Stephen Thomas, Eric Leslie. BS in Biology cum laude, Bucknell U., 1948; MT, Geisinger Meml. Hosp., 1949. Registered med. technologist. Med. technologist Burlington County Hosp., Mt. Holly, N.J., 1949-50, Robert Packer Hosp., Sayre, Pa., 1950, Carle Hosp./Clinic, Urbana, Ill., 1951-52, St. Joseph Hosp., Reading, Pa., 1972-83. Vol. Crime Watch, City Hall, Reading, 1985-90, Am. Heart Assn., Reading, 1956—, March of Dimes, Reading, 1956-72, Am. Cancer Soc., Reading, 1956-71, Multiple Sclerosis, Reading, 1956-72, Reading Musical Found., 1985-90, Hist. Soc. Berks County; corr. sec. women's aux., 1986-90; fin. sec. aux. Albright Coll., 1988-95; hospitality co-chmn. women's com. Reading Symphony Orch., 1985-90, editor yearbook women's com., 1992-96; editor yearbook Reading Symphony Orch. League, 1996—; chmn. hospitality Reading-Berks Pub. Librs., 1988-91; mem. Friends Reading Mus., Berks County Conservancy. Mem. AAUW (assoc. editor bull. 1961-63, cultural interests rep. 1967-68), Woman's Club of Reading (treas. 1986-88, fin. sec. 1991—), United Meth. Women, World Affairs Coun. Berks County, Libr. Soc. Albright Coll., Phi Beta Kappa. Republican. Methodist. Home: 1454 Oak Ln Reading PA 19604-1865

BELL, GUS KAISER, clinical psychologist, consultant; b. Knoxville, Tenn., June 27, 1927; s. Fred E. and Jean (Kaiser) B.; m. Norma Jean Maddox, Aug. 24, 1952; children: Ellen (dec.), Jeffrey, Linda. BA in Psychology with honors, Rhodes Coll., 1951; PhD in Clin. Psychology, U. Tenn., 1956. Psychometrist Oak Ridge (Tenn.) Sch. Adminstrn., 1953; psychology trainee VA Mental Hygiene Clinic, Knoxville, 1953-54, Kennedy VA Med. Teaching Group, Memphis, 1954-55; asst. clin. psychologist Psychol. Svc. Ctr., U. Tenn., Knoxville, 1955-56; clin. psychologist Knoxville Mental Health Ctr., 1955-56, Nashville Mental Health Ctr., 1956-58; sr. clin. psychologist, dir. tng. Dede Wallace Mental Health Ctr., Nashville, 1958-64, chief clin. psychologist, 1965-67; pvt. practice clin. and cons. psychology, Nashville, 1967—; cons. children and youth divsn. Mid. Tenn. Mental Health Inst., Nashville, 1964-95, YWCA TryAngle House, Nashville, 1978-91, Respite Coordination Svcs., Nashville, 1989-91. Mem. APA, Tenn. Psychol. Assn. (sec.-treas. 1963-64, pres. 1969-70), Southeastern Psychol. Assn., Nashville Area Psychol. Assn., Am. Soc. Clin. Hypnosis, Soc. for Clin. and Exptl. Hypnosis. Home: 4026 Aberdeen Rd Nashville TN 37205-1806 Office: 110 30th Ave S Ste 200 Nashville TN 37212-2519

BELL, JACK, psychologist; b. Conway, Ark., Aug. 11, 1952; s. William G. and Florine (Graham) B.; m. Ginny Rohlman, May 14, 1977; children; Jeremy, Jessica, Lauren. BA in Psychology, Hendrix Coll., 1975; MS in Sch. Psychology, U. Ctrl. Ark., 1977. Cert. sch. psychologist; lic. sch. psychologist. Psychologist II Ark. Dept. Youth Svcs., Alexander, 1977; psychol. examiner Conway Pub. Schs., 1977—; pres. Ind. Living Svcs., Conway, 1987; bd. dirs. 1st Cmty. Bank. Alderman Conway City Coun., 1979—; bd. dirs. United Way Faulkner County, Conway, 1989-92; past pres. Boys and Girls Club Conway, 1990. Recipient Ethel K. Millar award Evan Hendrix Coll., 1994. Fellow Conway Leadership Inst. (pres. Alumni Assn.); mem. Ark. Sch. Psychology Assn. (pres. 1981), Kiwanis (pres. Conway chpt. 1982-83). Democrat. Methodist. Home: 1171 Western Ave Conway AR 72032-3735

BELL, JAMES MILTON, psychiatrist, educator; b. Portsmouth, Va., Nov. 5, 1921; s. Charles Edward and Lucy (Barnes) B. Student, Va. State Coll., 1939-40; BS, N.C. Cen. U. (formerly N.C. Coll.), 1943; MD, Meharry Med. Coll., 1947. Diplomate in psychiatry and child psychiatry Am. Bd. Psychiatry and Neurology (examiner 1980—), Pan. Am. Med. Assn. (coun. psychiatry sect.); cert. N.Y. State Dept. Mental Hygiene. With Harlem Hosp., N.Y.C., 1947-48; asst. physician to clin. dir. Lakin (W.Va.) State Hosp., N.Y.C., 1948-51; fellow gen. psychiatry Menninger Sch. Psychiatry-Menninger Found., Topeka, 1953-56, tng. child psychiatry, 1957-58; resident Winter VA Hosp., Topeka, 1953-56; asst. sect. chief children's unit Topeka State Hosp., 1956-58; clin. teaching staff Menninger Sch. Psychiatry, 1956-58; clin. dir., psychiatrist Berkshire Farm Ctr. and Svcs. for Youth, Canaan, N.Y., 1959-86, sr. child and adolescent psychiatrist, 1986—; mem. N.Y. State post-Vietnam planning comm., 1968, vice chmn. subcom. on returning veteran, 1968; clin. asst. to clin. prof. psychiatry Albany Med. Coll., Union U., 1959—, mem. admission com., 1972-79; psychiatrist-in-charge Albany Home for Children, N.Y., 1959-77; staff psychiatrist Parsons Child and Family Ctr., 1977—, staff mem. adoption svc. and foster care, 1995—; asst. dispensary to dispensary psychiatrist Albany Med. Ctr. Clinic, 1960; trainee cons. Albany Child Guidance Ctr. Psychiat. Svc., Inc., 1961. cons. Keller U.S. Army Hosp., U.S. Mil. Acad., West Point, N.Y.; del. White House Conf. on Children, mem. exec. com., gov.'s state wide com., 1970; lectr. in field; spkr. in field worldwide; participant in confs., hosps., state/govt. coms. Contbr. numerous articles to profl. jours. Cons. Astor Home for Children, Rhinebeck, N.Y., 1965; instrnl. staff Frederick Amman Meml. Inst. Delinquency and Crime, St. Lawrence U., 1965-70; cons. adolescence N.Y. State Div. Youth, 1966-76, mem. med. rev. bd., 1974-76; mem. Child Abuse Adv. Coun., Albany; bd. dirs., mem. com. on proposed policy N.Y. Spaulding for Children, v.p., 1988-89; bd. dirs., exec. com. Guold Farm, Barrington, Mass.; life mem. NAACP; hon. life bd. mem. Parsons Child and Family Ctr., Albany, N.Y., 1995—. Capt. M.C., AUS, 1951-53; col. USAR, 1955-85, ret., 1985. Decorated Army Commendation medal, Meritorious Svc. medal, others, Plaque of Appreciation Com. of Physicians of Vol. Child Care Agencies, 1993, N.Y. Capital Dist. Coun. of Child and Adolescent Psychiatry, 1993, hon. Life Bd. Mem. Parsons Child and Family Ctr., Albany, N.Y., 1995; named Disting. Alumnus, Meharry Med. Coll., 1980; Tng. Inst. named in his honor Berkshire Farm Ctr. & Svcs. for Youth, 1996. Fellow AAAS (life), Am. Psychiat. Assn. (life, panelist on child & adolescent psychiatry 1963, chmn. coun. nat. affairs 1973-75, past vice-chmn.), Am. Acad. of Child and Adolescent Psychiatry (life, chmn. com. psychiat. facilities for children and adolescence 1973-75), Am. Orthopsychiat. Assn. (life, past dir.), Am. Soc. Adolescent Psychiatry (life), N.Y. Acad. Scis., Am. Coll. Psychiatrists (past mem. Stanley Dean award com.), Am. Psychopathol. Assn.; mem. AMA, Am. Acad. Polit. and Social Sci., Am. Soc. Addiction Medicine, Black Psychiatrists Am., Group for Advancement of Psychiatry (com. on child psychiatry), Inst. Religion and Health (charter), Coun. for Exceptional Children, Nat. Assn. Tng. Schs. and Juvenile Agys., Assn. N.Y. Educators of Emotionally Disturbed, Med. Soc. State N.Y. (life), Columbia Country med. assns., Child Care Workers (bd. dirs. N.Y.), Assn. Psychiat. Treatment of Offenders, N.Y. State Soc. Med. Rsch., N.Y. Capitol Dist. Coun. Child Psychiatry (pres. 1974), Am. Legion (life), Rotary (ann. participant youth leadership conf., Youth Leadership award 1992), Alpha Omega Alpha. Home: Hudsonview 175 Old Post Rd N Croton On Hudson NY 10520-1931 Office: Berkshire Farm Ctr & Svcs for Youth Canaan NY 12029

BELL, LEO S., retired physician; b. Newark, Nov. 7, 1913; s. Alexander M. and Marie (Saxon) B.; AB, Syracuse U., 1934; MD, 1938; m. Edith Lewis, July 3, 1938; children: Jewyl Linn, David Alden. Intern, N.Y.C. Hosp., 1938, Bklyn. Hosp., 1939-40; resident in pediatrics Sea View Hosp., N.Y.C., 1940-41, N.Y.C. Hosp., 1941-42; practice medicine specializing in pediatrics, San Mateo, Calif., 1946-86; mem. staff Mills Meml. Hosp., San Mateo, Peninsula Hosp. & Med. Ctr., Burlingame, Children's Hosp., San Francisco; assoc. clin. prof. pediatrics U. Calif. Med Sch., San Francisco, prof. clin. emeritus Stanford Med. Sch., Palo Alto; mem. curriculum & ednl. affairs comm. U. San Francisco Med. Sch., adminstv. coun.; med. columnist San Mateo Times. Bd. dirs. Mills Hosp. Found., San Mateo, U. Calif. San Francisco Hosp., San Mateo County Heart Assn., Hillsborough Schs. Found. (Calif.), 1980-83. Capt. as flight surgeon USAAF, 1942-46. Recipient bronze and silver medals Am. Heart Assn. Diplomate Am. Bd. Pediatrics. Fellow Am. Acad. Pediatrics, Am. Pub. Health Assn.; mem. Clin. Faculty Assn. (pres.), Calif. Fedn. Pediatric Socs. (pres.), Am. Fedn. Pediatric Socs. (pres.), Calif. Med. Assn., Am. Pub. Health Assn., Air Force Assn., AMA (alt. del. to ho. of dels.), Calif. Med. Assn. (ho. of dels.), San Mateo County Med. Assn., Internat. Snuff Bottle Soc., Hong Kong Snuff Bottle Soc., San Francisco Gem and Mineral Soc., World Affairs Coun. San Francisco, U. San Francisco Med. Sch. Clin. Faculty Assn. (coun., pres.), Peninsula Golf and Country Club, Commonwealth Club. Contbr. articles to profl. jours. Home: 220 Roblar Ave Burlingame CA 94010-6846 Office: PO Box 1877 San Mateo CA 94401-0946

BELL, LORI JO, psychiatric nurse, mental health counselor, infectious disease education specialist; b. Pitts., Dec. 16, 1960; d. John Spencer and Nancy Carol (Schleicher) B. ADN, C.C. Allegheny Co., Pitts., 1987; BS in Devel. Psychology, U. Pitts., 1984; MSEd in Cmty. Counseling, Duquesne U., 1996. Nat. cert. counselor, cert. in adult psychiat./mental health nursing, cert. crisis intervention, cert. pre/post HIV counseling. Primary counselor Mon Yough Mental Health/Mental Retardation, McKeesport, Pa., 1984; residential advisor Chartiers Mental Health/Mental Retardation, Bridgeville, Pa., 1985-87; counselor, 1985-87; psychiat. nurse in acute/admissions bldg. Eastern State Hosp., Williamsburg, Va., 1987; psychiat. nurse St. Francis Med. Ctr., Pitts., 1996; cmty. HIV/AIDS educator; microbiology tutor Duquesne U., 1994. Contbr. articles to profl. jours. Mem. ACA, ANA, APA, Am. Mental Health Counselor's Assn., Pa. Counseling Assn., Pa. Mental Health Counselor's Assn., Heath Psychology Assn., Internat. Critical Incident Stress Found., Internat. Assn. Addiction and Offender Counselors, Chi Sigma Iota. Home: 337 Shadowlawn Ave Pittsburgh PA 15216-1239

BELL, MELISSA LEE, health care consultant; b. Portland, Maine, July 26, 1956; d. John Ellis and Evangeline Rose Lee; m. Walter Bell Jr., Jan. 21, 1978; children: William, Michael. Diploma, Mercy Hosp., Portland, 1977; BSN, Westbrook Coll., 1984. RNC. Staff nurse labor and delivery Parkview Meml. Hosp., Brunswick, Maine, 1977; staff nurse neurology Maine Med. Ctr., Portland, 1977-78, staff nurse labor and delivery, 1978-85, per diem nurse, 1989—; office nurse to ob.-gyn. practice Portland, 1985-88; asst. dept. dir. Osteo. Hosp., Portland, 1988-89; health care advisor Preti, Flaherty, Beliveau & Pachius, Portland, 1989—; instr. BLS Am. Heart Assn., Maine, 1987—. Mem. NAACOG (legis. chair dist. 1 1991—, edn. com. 1986-90). Democrat. Methodist. Home: 34 Wythburn Rd South Portland ME 04106-5317

BELL, MICHAEL ANDREW, health services administrator; b. Ann Arbor, Mich., Nov. 6, 1968; s. Michael Allen and Linda Ann Bell; m. Julie Marie Smith, May 22, 1993. BS in Sports Medicine, Ea. Mich. U., 1990; M Health Svcs. Adminstrn., U. Mich., 1994. Lic. nursing home adminstr., Mich. Asst. adminstr. Frenchtown Nursing Care Ctr., Monroe, Mich., 1994-95; adminstr. Luth. Home, Monroe, 1995—. Instr. in swimming, CPR and first aid ARC, Monroe, 1984-86; bd. dirs., mem. steering com. Interfaith Vol. Caregivers, Monroe, 1995—. Named All-Am., U.S. Masters Swimming, 1991-94. Mem. Am. Coll. Healthcare Adminstrs., Am. Assn. Homes and Svcs. for the Aging, Monroe C. of C., Toastmasters Internat. Lutheran. Home: 611 Dane Dr Monroe MI 48162 Office: Lutheran Home 1236 S Monroe Monroe MI 48161

BELL, MICHAEL JOHN, physician, radiologist; b. Mpls., July 29, 1938; s. Willard J. and Marcella E. (Kuhlman) B.; m. Sheridan R. Michael, Feb. 26, 1966; children: Richard H., Stephen W. Student, Princeton U., 1956-57; BA, U. Minn., 1960, MD, 1963. Diplomate Am. Bd. Radiology, Am. Bd. Nuclear Medicine. Intern Tripler Army Med. Ctr., Honolulu, 1964-65, resident in radiology, 1967-69; resident in radiology Walter Reed Army Med. Ctr., Washington, 1969-70; chief of radiology Womack Army Hosp., Ft. Bragg, N.c., 1970-72; staff radiologist Mercy Hosp., Charlotte, N.C., 1972-92; chief dept. radiology, 1992—. Bd. dirs. Opera Carolina, Charlotte, 1991-94, Mercy Hosp. Found., Charlotte, 1995. Maj. U.S. Army, 1964-72. Mem. AMA, Am. Coll. Radiology, Radiol. Soc. N.Am., N.C. Med. Soc. Office: Mercy Hosp Dept Radiology 2001 Vail Ave Charlotte NC 28207

BELL, NANCY DENESE, patient abuse investigator; b. Shaker Heights, Ohio, Sept. 17, 1951; d. Louis and Rita (Sheber) B.; m. Eli Taub, Jan. 15, 1983; 1 child, Jennifer Taub. BA, SUNY, Albany, 1973, MSW, 1980. Cert. CSW Acad. Cert. Social Workers. Caseworker child protective svcs. Albany County Dept. Social Svcs., Albany, 1976-80, case planner protective svcs., 1980-86, supr. child protective svcs., 1982-86; patient abuse investigator N.Y. State Commn. on Quality of Care for Mentally Disabled, Albany, 1986—. Bd. dirs., past pres. Albany County Abuse Neglect Coun. Inc.; bd. dirs. Schenectady Citizens' Task Force on Child Abuse and Neglect; former v.p. Schenectady Hadassah. Mem. NASW. Home: 105 N Ferry St Schenectady NY 12305-1610

BELL, RANDALL WILLIAM, ophthalmic surgeon; b. N.Y.C., Jan. 20, 1938; s. William Randall and Frances Veronica (Dwyer) B.; children: Randall, Deborah, Kevin, Thomas, James; m. Maryanne Gallagher. BS, U.S. Mil. Acad., 1959; MD, Cornell U., 1966; grad., U.S. Army War Coll., 1983. Diplomate: Am. Bd. Ophthalmology, Nat. Bd. Med. Examiners. Commd. 2d Lt. U.S. Army, 1959, advanced through grades to brig. gen. Res., 1975; intern Walter Reed Gen. Hosp. U.S. Army, Washington, 1966-67, resident Walter Reed Gen. Hosp., 1967-70; chief ophthalmology Valley Forge (Pa.) Gen. Hosp. U.S. Army, 1970-72; practice medicine specializing in ophthalmology USAR 338th Med. Group, Wayne, Pa., 1972-83; comdg. gen. 2290th U.S. Army Hosp., Washington, 1981-85; mem. Surgeon's Gen.'s Adv. Council; mem. staff Scheie Inst., Presbyn. U. Pa. Med. Ctr., assoc. attending surgeon Wills Eye Hosp., Phila., Jefferson Hosp., Phila., Bryn Mawr (Pa.) Hosp.; sr. attending opthalmologist, mem. exec. com. Sacred Heart Hosp., Norristown; asst. prof. Thomas Jefferson U., Phila., 1972-76, U. Pa., 1978. Contbr. articles on ophthalmology to profl. jours. Bd. dirs. West Point Fund and Soc. Fellow ACS, Pa. Acad. Opthalmology and Otolaryngology, Am. Acad. Opthalmology, Phila. Coll. Physicians; mem. AMA, Pa. Med. Soc., Del. County Med. Soc., Assn. Research in Vision and Ophthalmology, Soc. Contemporary Ophthalmology, Soc. Mil. Ophthalmologists, Ophthalmic Club Phila. (pres. 1981-83), West Point Soc. Phila. (bd. govs. 1975—, pres. 1981-82), Assn. U.S. Army (life), Soc. Med. Cons. Armed Forces. Clubs: Merion Cricket, Merion Golf, Union League of Phila, Cornell. Home: 124 Bloomingdale Ave Wayne PA 19087-3929

BELL, RICHARD TRENT, physician; b. Balt., Mar. 14, 1946; s. Vernon Adam Veith and Clara Beatrice (Scull) B.; m. Karen Louise Taylor, Aug. 23, 1969; children: Kristin, Allison, Lauren. BA with honors, Lehigh U., 1968; MD, Jefferson Med. Coll., 1972. Diplomate Am. Bd. Internal Medicine/Pulmonary Diseases. Resident internal medicine Lankenau Hosp., Phila., 1972-75; fellow pulmonary diseases Einstein Med. Ctr., Phila., 1977-79; ptnr. Pulmonary Med. Assocs., West Reading, Pa., 1979—. Contbr. articles to profl. jours. Chmn. chpt. ARC of Berks County, Reading, Pa., 1989-91; dir. Am. Lung Assn. Pa., Harrisburg. Maj. USAF, 1975-77. Fellow ACP, Am. Coll. Chest Physicians; mem. AMA (alternate Pa. del. 1991—), Pa. Soc. for Pulmonary Disease (pres. 1991—), Berks County Med. Soc. (pres. 1988, chmn. bd. 1989-92), Pa. Med. Soc., Am. Thoraic Soc. Office: Pulmonary Med Assocs 301 S Seventh Ave Reading PA 19611-1410

BELL, ROBERT MAURICE, biochemistry educator, consultant; b. Lincoln, Nebr., Mar. 24, 1944; s. Robert Loyal and Faye Rogene (Pickell) B.; m. Barbara Ruth Miller, Apr. 6, 1966; children: Rae Jean Elizabeth, Scott Robert. BS, U. Nebr., 1966; PhD, U. Calif., Berkeley, 1970; postdoctoral study, Washington U., St. Louis, 1970-72. Asst. prof. Duke U. Med. Ctr., Durham, N.C., 1972, assoc. prof., 1978-84, prof. biochemistry, 1984—, James B. Duke prof. biochemistry, 1987—, dep. dir. Duke Comprehensive Cancer Ctr., 1987—, chmn. dept. molecular cancer biology, 1993-95; adj. prof. molecular biology Duke Comprehensive Cancer Ctr., 1995—; v.p. rsch. Glaxo Wellcome, Research Triangle Park, N.C., 1995—; cons. pharm. industry; co-founder Sphinx Pharms, chmn. sci. adv. bd., dir. ; cons. pharm. cos. Contbr. numerous articles and revs. to profl. jours. Rsch. grantee NIH, Bethesda, Md., 1974-95. Mem. Am. Soc. Biol. Chemistry and Molecular Biologists (assoc. editor Jour. Biol. Chemistry 1986-92, program com. 1986—, nominating com. 1988), Univ. Club (Durham). Office: Glaxo Wellcome Five Moore Dr Research Triangle Park NC 27709

BELL, SUSAN JANE, nurse; b. Columbus, Ohio, July 24, 1946; d. Donald Richard Bell and Martha Jane (McDowell) Nichols; m. Robert Earlin Ward, Oct. 24, 1964 (div. 1984); children: Duane Allen Ward, Melissa Jane Ward, Bryan Thomas Ward. Degree in nursing, Columbus Sch. Practical Nursing, 1986; ADRN, Columbus State C.C., 1989; student, Franklin U., 1993—. RN, Ohio; cert. CPR; notary pub., Ohio. Nurse's asst. Riverside Meth. Hosp., Columbus, 1970-80, Norworth Convalescent Ctr., Columbus, 1980-86; lic. practical nurse, charge nurse Heartland Thurber Care Ctr., Columbus, 1986-89; staff nurse Am. Nursing Care, Columbus, 1989—; medicare home visitation, staffing and pvt. duty nurse Telemed, Columbus, 1989—; asst. head nurse Northland Terr., Columbus, 1989; supr. Elmington Manor, Columbus, 1989; staff nurse cardiac step down unit Grant Hosp., Columbus, 1989-92; nurse med. ICU, CCU and pediatric ICU, 1992-93; charge nurse critical/skilled unit First Cmty. Village Health Care Ctr., Columbus, 1992-95; pres. Bell Mktg. Distbrs., pvt. duty ALS ventilator patients Med. Pers. Poole; regional claims rep. Fed. Resources Group. Rev. Am. Fellowship Ch. Mem. NAFE, ASPCA, YMCA, Internat. Clergy Assn., World Wildlife Fund., Nature Conservancy, Ohio Hist. Found. (archives/libr. divsn.).

BELL, THOMAS EUGENE, psychologist, educational administrator; b. Okmulgee, Okla., Feb. 20, 1945; s. Wilmer Ordell and Betty Jean (Good) Bell; m. Ramona Kay Ashlock, Aug. 26, 1965; 1 child, Stacie Lane. BA, Cen. State U., Edmond, Okla., 1972, MEd, 1975; postgrad., Okla. State U., 1986-88. Lic. profl. counselor, Okla. Psychometrist Guthrie (Okla.) Pub. Schs., 1975-79, sch. psychologist, 1979-89, dir. counseling, 1989-94; pvt. practice Edmond, 1994—. Developer Teen Buddies, 1990. With USAF, 1965-67. Recipient Parent Edn. award Okla. Juvenile Justice, Oklahoma City, 1991. Mem. Mensa Internat. (proctor 1979-86), Okla. Psychol. Assn. (rep. 1986-87), Okla. Sch. Psychology Assn. (area rep. 1987-88), Nat. Assn. Sch. Psychologists, Youth Suicide Prevention Assn. (v.p. 1991—). Democrat. Mem. Ch. of Christ. Home: 1101 Apollo Cir Edmond OK 73003-6013 Office: Meridian Med Tower Bldg 400 Ste A Ste 304 Oklahoma City OK 73120

BELL, WILLIAM ROBERT, hematologist, internist, educator, scientist; b. Greece, N.Y., Oct. 14, 1943; s. William Robert and Dorothy (Efing) B.; m. May 14, 1966; children: William R. III, George H., Elizabeth E. BS, U. Notre Dame, 1957; MS, George Washington U., 1961, Georgetown U./Harvard Med. Sch., 1962; MD, Harvard U., 1964. Intern Johns Hopkins U. Sch. Medicine, Balt., 1964-65, resident, 1967-68, chief resident, 1969-70, asst. prof. medicine, 1970, prof. medicine, radiology, nuclear medicine, 1978—, Edythe Harris Lucas-Clara Lucas Lynn prof. hematology, clin. dir., 1991—; rsch. assoc. NIH, Bethesda, Md., 1965-67; fellow U. London-Hammersmith Hosp., 1967-68; resident in medicine Peter Bent Brigham Hosp., Boston, 1968-69; cons. NIH, 1978—, Walter Reed Army Hosp., USN, Washington, Bethesda, 1978—. Contbr. articles to profl. jours.; patentee in field. Fellow ACP; mem. Am. Soc. Hematology, Am. Soc. Clin. Investigation, Phi Beta Kappa, Alpha Omega Alpha. Jewish. Home: 601 N Broadway Blalock 100Z Baltimore MD 21287-4928 Office: Johns Hopkins U Dept Medicine Blalock 1002 600 N Wolfe St Baltimore MD 21287-4928

BELL (JARRATT), CORINNE, psychologist; b. Holly Springs, Miss., July 6, 1943; d. Robert Norris and Laura Kathleen (Robinson) Reed; m. John Baker Jarratt; children: Jeffrey Kenneth Bell, Jennifer Bell Monroe, Joshua Brown Jarratt. BA with highest honors, U. Tenn., 1976, MA, 1978, PhD, 1985. Lic. psychologist, Tenn. Rsch. asst. Lakeshore Mental Health Inst., Knoxville, 1976; instr. psychology dept. Roane State C.C., Harriman, Tenn., 1978; cons., sch. psychologist dept. spl. edn. U. Tenn., Knoxville, 1979-80; pvt. practice psychology Knoxville, 1979—; founder, psychologist, ptnr. Clin. & Sch. Assocs., Knoxville, 1985-96; v.p. mktg. Lark Industries, Inc., Knoxville, 1994-95; founder, adminstr., psychologist Behavioral Health Ctr. Child & Adult Svcs., Knoxville, 1996—, bd. dirs., 1994—; cons. social svcs. Dept. Human Svcs., Tenn., 1985—. Contbr. articles to profl. jours. Mem. adv. bd. John Tarleton Children's Home, Knoxville, 1987-93, Florence Crittendon Agy., 1994—; bd. dirs. Sexual Assault Crisis Ctr., Knoxvile, 1987-94, Children's Ctr. Knoxville, 1995—; mem., cons. Knox County Child Abuse Rev. Team, Knoxville, 1982—; vol. Knox County Mental Health Assn. and Interfaith Health Clinic. Acad. scholar U. Tenn., 1974; rsch. grantee Knox County Children's Found., 1979. Mem. APA, Tenn. Psychol. Assn. (pub. rels. chair 1992-94), Knoxville Area Psychol. Assn. (treas. 1986-88, pub. rels. chair 1989-90, pres. 1990-91), Unified Psychology Coalition (co-founder, legis. chair/spokesperson 1989-92), Tenn. Assn. Sch. Psychologists, Mortar Bd., Phi Kappa Phi, Phi Beta Kappa. Episcopalian. Office: Behavioral Health Ctr Child & Adult Svcs 3624 Vandeventer Ave Knoxville TN 37919

BELLACK, ALAN SCOTT, clinical psychologist; b. N.Y.C., Nov. 27, 1944; s. Jack and Yetta B.; m. Barbara Bartlett, Nov. 16, 1969; children: Jonathan, Adam. B.S., CCNY, 1965; M.S., St. John's U., 1967; Ph.D., Pa. State U., 1970. Diplomate Am. Bd. Profl. Psychology. Asst. prof. psychology Pa. State U., 1970; mem. faculty U. Pitts., 1971-82, prof. psychology and psychiatry, 1980-82; prof. psychiatry Med. Coll. Pa., Phila., 1982-95, U. Md., 1995—; vice chmn., dir. clin. psychology Med. Coll. Pa., Phila.; chmn., dir. clin. psychology; prof. psychiatry U. Md. Sch. Medicine; cons. in field. Author: Behavioral Assessment: A Practical Handbook, 1976, 2nd edit., 1981, 3rd edit., 1988, Behavior Modification: An Introduction, 1977, Introduction to Clinical Psychology, 1980, The Clinical Psychology, Handbook, 1983, 2nd edit., 1991, others; editor: Clin. Psychology Rev., 1981—, Behavior Modification, 1977—; contbr. articles to profl. jours. USPHS fellow, 1968-70. Mem. Am. Psychol. Assn., Assn. Advancement Behavior Therapy. Office: Univ of Maryland at Balt Dept Psychiatry 685 W Baltimore St Baltimore MD 21201-1549

BELLACOSA, RICHARD ANTHONY, podiatrist; b. Newark, May 9, 1955; s. Anthony Vito and Irene Catherine (Sweeney) B.; m. Jody-Ann Caroline Jones, June 7, 1980; children: Keri, Mallory, Michael. BS in Biology, Wilkes Coll., 1978; DPM, Pa. Coll. Podiatric Medicine, 1980. Diplomate Am. Bd. Podiatric Surgery. Resident podiatric surgery Northlake (Ill.) Comty. Hosp., 1980-81, chief resident, 1981-82; pvt. practice podiatry Springfield, N.J., 1982-83, San Antonio Podiatry Assocs., 1983—; clin. instr. podiatry U. Tex. Health Sci. Ctr., San Antonio, 1983-91, clin. asst. prof., 1991—; bd. dirs. Surgictr., San Antonio, 1989-90; mem. written exam com. Am. Bd. Podiatric Surgery, San Francisco, 1992-95, exam. devel. com. Tex. State Bd. Podiatry Examiners, Austin, 1994-96. Contbr. articles to podiatric med. jours. Mem. Soc. Luke, The Physician, St. Luke's Hosp. Found., San Antonio, 1992-94. Fellow Am. Coll. Foot and Ankle Surgeons; mem. Am. Podiatric Med. Assn. (spl. adv. group on health care reform 1993, alt. ho. of dels. 1993), Tex. Podiatric Med. Assn. (bd. dirs. 1988-93, pres. 1993-94, Young Practitioner award 1989), Bexar County Podiatric Med. Soc. Roman Catholic. Office: San Antonio Podiatry Assocs 14615 San Pedro Ste 235 San Antonio TX 78232

BELLAN, GÉRARD LÉON, marine biologist; b. Cherbourg, Manche, France, Jan. 28, 1934; s. Auguste Guillaume and Raymonde Paule (Beaumanoir) B.; m. Denise Rose Santini, Aug. 30, 1961; 1 child, Raymonde-Gaëlle. Lic. Scis., U. Caen, Calvados, France, 1957; D Oceanography, U. Marseilles, Bches Rhone, France, 1959, D Natural Scis., 1964. Instr. U. Marseilles, 1957-59; rsch. attaché Nat. Ctr. Sci. Rsch., Marseilles, 1959-64, rsch. chargé, 1964-72, master rsch., 1972-83, dir. rsch., 1984—; advisor, cons. FAO, Rome, 1977-80; com. mem. Internat. Com. Sci. Exploration Mediterranean, Monaco, 1960-90, advisor, 1991—. Author: The Pollution of Sea, 1974, 3d edit., 1994; co-author: Pollution of Marine Water, 1976, Great Atlas of the Sea, 1984, Meditteranean Marine Ecosystems, 1985. Pres. Assn. for Help to Young Disabled, Marseilles, 1977-79, adminstr., 1969—. Recipient de Morgan-Vachon medal Acad. Scis., Marseille, 1989, 9th Gold Neptun, Alghero, Italy, 1991, Dioscuri-Men of the Sea prize Italian Naval League, 1994. Mem. AAAS, Soc. Ecology (v.p. 1988-90), French Soc. Zoology, Am. Zoologists Soc., Acad. Subaquatic Sci. 'd Technics (Gold Trident award 1989), Acad. Sci. So. Calif., Italian Soc. Marine Biology. Home: Clio D Parc Berger, 13009 Marseilles France Office: COM UMR CNRS DIMAR, Rue Batterie des Lions, 13007 Marseilles France

BELLANGER, BARBARA DORIS HOYSAK, biomedical research technologist; b. Syracuse, N.Y., Oct. 24, 1936; d. Edward George and Bernardine Elizabeth (Blaney) Hoysak; m. Ronald Patrick Bellanger, July 1, 1961; children: Laura Jeanne, Andrea Lynne, Janis Anne. BS, Syracuse U., 1958. Cert. lab. animal technician. Tech. asst. Bur. of Labs., Syracuse, 1958; rsch. scientist Bristol Labs., Syracuse, 1958-63; rsch. assoc. Syracuse Cancer Rsch. Inst., 1973—. Pres. CNS Northstars Band Parents, Inc., Cicero-North Syracuse, N.Y., 1986-87. Mem. Am. Assn. Lab. Animal Sci. (cert. lab. animal technician, sec. Upstate N.Y. br. 1990—, Technician of Yr. award 1992), N.Y. Acad. Scis., Alpha Gamma Delta (pres. Alpha alumnae chpt. 1959-60, treas. 1989—). Home: 410 David Dr North Syracuse NY 13212-1929 Office: Syracuse Cancer Rsch Inst Presdl Plz 600 E Genesee St Syracuse NY 13202-3111

BELL-BERTI, FREDERICKA RUTH, speech science educator; b. N.Y.C., Sept. 21, 1945; d. Victor Alfred and Helvi Sanelma (Maki) Bell; m. Ronald Edmund Berti, June 28, 1970. BS, CCNY, 1967; PhD, CUNY, 1973. Prof. speech sci. Montclair State Coll., Upper Montclair, N.J., 1972-79; assoc. prof. St. John's U., Jamaica, N.Y., 1980-87, prof., 1987—; research assoc. Haskins Labs., New Haven, 1973—; chercheur étranger Physiologie et Pathologie Cérébrales Hosp. Salpetrière, 1987; lectr. in field. Contbr. articles to profl. jours. Nat. Inst. Neurol. and Communicative Disorders and Stroke grantee, 1977-80. Fellow Acoustical Soc. Am., Am. Speech-Lang.-Hearing Assn.; mem. AAAS, Linguistic Soc. Am., Am. Cleft Palate Assn., Sierra Club, Sigma Xi. Presbyterian. Office: St John's U Dept Speech Comm Scis and Theatre 8000 Utopia Pky Jamaica NY 11432-1335 also: Haskins Labs 270 Crown St New Haven CT 06511-6610

BELLE-ISLE, DAVID RICHARD, health care corporate executive, educator, consultant; b. Springfield, Mass., Mar. 26, 1950; s. Richard Alfred and Eda (Carra) Belle-Isle; m. Gwen Roton, Jan. 1, 1988; children: Justin, Melissa, Michelle, Megan; stepchildren: Mandy, Megan. AA, Kendall Coll., 1969; BS magna cum laude, Springfield Coll., 1971, MEd, 1972; PhD, U. North Colo., 1975; postgrad., MIT, 1979-80. Asst. dean Western New Eng. Coll., Springfield, 1972-73, U. No. Colo., Greeley, 1973-75, W.Va. Inst. Tech., Montgomery, 1975-76; sr. cons. Digital Equipment Corp., Maynard, Mass., 1976-80; dir. corp. planning Martin Marietta Corp., Bethesda, Md., 1980-84; exec. dir. Sara Lee Corp., Chgo., 1984-86; sr. v.p. Electrolux Corp., Stamford, Conn., 1986-87; pres. David Belle-Isle Corp., Fairfield, Conn., 1987-88; chief human resources officer Epic Health Care Group, Dallas, 1988-94; pres. Tex. chpt. Nat. Esop Assn., 1992-94, Belle-Isle Insight Consulting, Inc., 1994—; prof. Suffolk U., Boston, 1976-78, Clark U., Worcester, Mass., 1977-79, U. Mich., Ann Arbor, 1985-87; bd. dirs. Mgmt. Techs., Houston. Mem. Grace Commn., U.S. Presdl. Pvt. Sector Study on Cost Control, Washington, 1983-84. Mem. Psi Chi Nat. Honor Soc. Republican. Home and Office: Belle-Isle Insight Consulting 2104 Sutton Pl Plano TX 75093

BELLES, ANITA LOUISE, health care researcher, consultant; b. San Angelo, Tex., Aug. 30, 1948; d. Curtis Lee and Margaret Louise (Perry) B.; m. John Arvel Willey, Jul. 13, 1969 (div. Aug. 1978); children: Suzan Heather, Kenneth Alan; m. John W. Portfield, Dec. 22, 1992. BA, U. Tex., 1972; MS in Health Care Adminstrn., Trinity U., 1984. dir. family planning Bexar County Hosp. Dist., Tex., 1987; mgmt. engr. Inpatient Support Applications, 1987-88; instr. grad. sch. health care adminstrn. S.W. Tex. State U.; researcher on cardiovascular rsch. on artificial heart and heart transplantation, San Antonio Regional Heart Inst., 1993. Regional emergency med. service tng. coordinator Bur. Emergency Med. Service, Lake Charles, La., 1978-79; exec. dir. Southwest La. Emergency Med. Service Council, Lake Charles, 1979-83; project coordinator Tulane U. Med. Sch., New Orleans, 1982-83; dir. La. Bur. of Emergency Med. Service, Baton Rouge, 1983-86; pres. Computype, Inc., San Antonio, 1983-86, Emergency Med. and Safety Assocs., La. and Tex., 1982—; dir. family planning Bexar County Hosp. Dist., Tex., 1987; mgmt. engr. Inpatient Support Applications, 1987-88; instr. grad. sch. health care adminstrn. S.W. Tex. State U. Editor A.L.E.R.T., 1980-83, San Antonio Executive News, 1987—, Family Living, 1987-88; feature writer Bright Scrawl, 1985-86; contbr. numerous articles on emergency med. services to profl. jours. Bd. dirs. Thousand Oaks Homeowner's Assn., sec., treas., 1985; active Trinity U. Health Care Alumni Assn., Jr. League San Antonio, The Parenting Ctr., Baton Rouge, 1982-83, Jr. League Lake Charles, 1982, Campfire Council Pub. Relations Com., Lake Charles, 1982; newsletter editor Community Food Co-Op, Newsletter Editor, 1979; vol. Lake Charles Mental Health Ctr., 1974. Recipient Outstanding Service award La. Assn Registered Emergency Med. Technicians, 1983, Southwest La. Assn. Emergency Med. Technicians, 1983; named Community Leader KPLC TV, Lake Charles, 1981, regional winner Assn U. Programs in Health Adminstrn., HHS Sec's. Competitions for Innovations in Health, 1982. Mem. Nat. Assn. Emergency Med. Technicians., Tex. Assn. Emergency Med. Technicians, Am. Coll. Health Care Execs., Am. Assn. Automotive Medicine, Southwest La. Assn. Emergency Med. Technicians (founding mem., v.p. 1979-80, CPR com. chmn. 1980-81, pub. relations com. chmn. 1981-82, bd. dirs. 1980-82), Am. Mgmt. Assn., Nat. Soc. Emergency Med. Service Adminstrs., Nat. Coalition Emergency Med. Services, Am. Composition Assn. Methodist.

BELLHORN, KURT CHARLES, clinical neuropsychologist; b. Allentown, Pa., May 3, 1962; s. Charles Keith and Carole Ann (Frable) B. BS in Psychobiology, Albright Coll., 1984; MA in Clin. Psychology, Fairleigh Dickinson U., 1988, PhD in Clin. Psychology, 1990. Instr. Fairleigh Dickinson U., 1984-89, Ramapo (N.J.) Coll., 1987; psychology intern U. Medicine & Dentistry of N.J., Newark, 1989-90; postdoctoral fellow in clin. neuropsychology Inst. of Living, Hartford, Conn., 1990-92; instr. U. Conn., 1991—; Trinity Coll., Hartford, 1991—; pvt. practice Hartford, 1992—; psychology extern Reading (Pa.) Rehab. Ctr., 1984, Project Youth Haven, Paterson, N.J., 1984-85; rsch. assts. Carrier Found., Belle mead, N.J., 1985-86; acad. counselor athletic counseling program Fairleigh Dickinson U., 1985-86; psychology extern Hudson County Meadowview Hosp., Secaucus, N.J., 1985-86; neuropsychol. extern East Orange (N.J.) VA, 1987; outpatient therapist divsn. psychol. svcs. Fairleigh Dickinson U., 1986-88; residence counselor Pequannock Valley Mental Health Ctr., Boonton, N.J., 1984-90; staff clin. neuropsychologist DATAHR Rehab. Inst., Brookfield, Conn., 1992-93; dir. neuropsychol. and assessment svcs. Inst. of Living, Hartford, Conn., 1993—, dir. postdoctoral program in clin. neuropsychology, 1993—, clin. psychology intern supr., 1991—. Contbr. articles to profl. jours. Pres. Walnutport (Pa.) Tennis League, 1978; program dir. Sta. WXAC-FM, Reading, 1982-83. Recipient Bausch & Lomb award, 1980, Psychobiology award, 1984. Mem. APA, Eastern Psychol. Assn., Conn. Neuropsychol. Soc., Nat. Acad. Neuropsychology, Internat. Neuropsychol. Soc., Nat. Register of Health Svc. Providers in Psychology, Conn. Neuropsychol. Soc. (sec. 1995—).

BELLI, MARILYN ANN, nursing educator; b. Rochester, N.Y., Sept. 3, 1943; d. Anthony D. and Irene M. (Paglia) B. Diploma, St. Mary's Hosp. Sch. Nursing, Rochester, 1964; A in Liberal Arts, Monroe C.C., Rochester, 1974; BSN, U. Rochester, 1975, MS in Cardiopulmonary Nursing, 1983. RN, N.Y. Staff nurse gen. med. unit St. Mary's Hosp., Rochester, 1964-84, staff nurse coronary care unit, 1964-76, assoc. nursing care coord. med.-surg. unit, 1976-77, assoc. nursing care coord. ICU, 1977-79, instr. nursing edn., 1978-83, nursing care coord., 1983-84; clinician II Park Ridge Hosp., Rochester, 1984-86; asst. prof. nursing Roberts Wesleyan Coll., Rochester, 1986-87; asst. prof. nursing, mem. adv. bd. Utica (N.Y.) Coll. of Syracuse U., 1987—; adj. asst. prof. nursing Alfred U., Rochester, 1984-90; mem., cons. clin. practice and edn. com. Oneida County Critical Care, Utica, 1991-93. Vol. Literacy Vols. Am., Oneida County, 1992—. St. Mary's Hosp. Women's Bd. scholar, 1974. Fellow Am. Thoracic Soc., Am. Lung Assn.; mem. AAUP, AACN (cert., sec. Mohawk Valley chpt. 1989-90, program chairperson 1990-92, pres. 1993-94, bd. dirs. 1990—), Profl. Nurses Ctrl. N.Y., Nat. League for Nursing, St. Mary's Alumnae Assn. (bd. dirs., program chairperson 1985-87), Am. Heart Assn., Sigma Theta Tau (Iota chpt.). Democrat. Roman Catholic. Home: B2A7 1735 Burrstone Rd New Hartford NY 13413-1039 Office: Utica Coll of Syracuse U 1600 Burrstone Rd Utica NY 13502-4857

BELLIN, HOWARD THEODORE, plastic surgeon; b. N.Y.C., Apr. 8, 1936; s. Maurice and Etta (Rosenbloom) B.; m. Christina Paolozzi, Oct. 27, 1964 (dec. Apr. 27, 1988); children: Marco, Andy. BA, Amherst Coll., 1957; MD, N.Y. Med. Coll., 1962. Diplomate Am. Bd. Plastic Surgery. Intern U. Calif. Hosp., San Francisco, 1962-63; resident Met. Hosp., N.Y.C., 1963-66; resident in plastic surgery Columbia Presbyn. Med. Ctr., N.Y.C., 1968-70; instr. in surgery Columbia Coll. Physicians and Surgeons, N.Y.C., 1968-70; asst. clin. prof. surgery N.Y. Med. Coll., N.Y.C., 1970-84, asst. clin. prof. demratology, 1975-83; chief plastic surbery Cabrini Med. Ctr., N.Y.C., 1973-80; pres. Cosmedica Plastic Surgery Ctr., N.Y.C., 1980—; pres. Cortec, Inc., N.Y.C., 1983—, Life Signs, Inc., N.Y.C., 1989—, Motor Vehicle Protection Systems, Inc., N.Y.C., 1993—. Author: Dr. Bellin's Beautiful You Book, 1981; patentee on cardiac monitoring system, 1991, portable EKG monitoring device, 1985, system for subliminal signals, 1992, systems for cancellation...artifacts, 1992, auto theft prevention system, 1995, patient monitor sheets, 1995. Capt. USAF, 1966-68. Fellow N.Y. Acad. Medicine; mem. AAAS, Am. Soc. Plastic and Reconstrv. Surgeons, Explorers Club (nominating com. 1985). Office: Cosmedica 105 E 73rd St New York NY 10021-3502

BELLING, DOROTHY IRMA, retired geriatrics and critical care nurse; b. North Tonawanda, N.Y., Dec. 13, 1924; d. George Martin and Josephine (Knoell) B. Diploma in nursing, Millard Fillmore Hosp., Buffalo; BS in Mgmt. and Supervision with honors, U. Buffalo, 1949; MAA in Mgmt. and Supervision with honors, Columbia U., 1959. RN, Md., N.Y. Clin. specialist Heart, Lung and Blood Inst., NIH, Bethesda, Md., 1966-78; night supr. Buffalo VA Hosp., 1959-61; head nurse med.-surg. unit Millard Fillmore Hosp., 1949-52; staff gerontology nurse Carriage Hill Bethesda., 1986-90; past chmn. task force on nursing practice NIH. Contbr. articles to nursing jours. Recipient nursing rsch. award NIH, 1981. Mem. ANA.

BELLINGHAM, CHARLES EDWARD, urologist; b. Newark, May 12, 1940; s. Lowell C. and Adelaine A. (Wright) B.; m. Mary Ellen McNamee (div.); children: Walter, Lisa, Deborah. BS, Allegheny Coll., 1962. MD, U. Medicine & Dentistry N.J., 1966. Diplomate Am. Bd. Urology. Intern Allegheny Gen. Hosp., Pitts., 1966-67; resident in gen. surgery VA Hosp., East Orange, N.J., 1969-70; resident in urology N.J. Coll. Medicine and Dentistry, Newark, 1970-73, instr. in urology, 1972-73; pvt. practice urology Bricktown, N.J., 1973—; chief urology Point Pleasant (N.J.) Hosp., 1981-86, Jersey Shore Med. Ctr., Neptune, N.J., 1982-86; chief of staff Med. Ctr. of Ocean County, N.J., 1986-88; aviation med. examiner FAA, 1986-91; chmn. urology sect. N.J. Acad. Medicine, 1989-91. Contbr. articles to profl. publs. Lt. comdr. USN, 1967-69. Fellow ACS, Internat. Coll. Surgeons, Soc. Surgeons N.J.; mem. AMA, Acad. Medicine N.J., Am. Assn. Clin. Urologists, Am. Fertility Assn., Am. Geriatric Soc., Am. Lithotriptor Soc., Am. Ultrasound Soc., Am. Urol. Assn., Monmouth County Med. Soc., Monmouth-Ocean Urology Soc., N.J. Med. Soc., Urology Soc. N.J. (sec. 1986-89, pres. 1989-90). Office: 224 Jack Martin Blvd E4 Brick NJ 08724

BELLIS, CARROLL JOSEPH, surgeon; b. Shreveport, La.; s. Joseph and Rose (Bloome) B.; m. Mildred Darmody, Dec. 26, 1939; children: Joseph, David. BS, U. Minn., 1930, MS in Physiology, 1932, PhD in Physiology, 1934, MD, 1936, PhD in Surgery, 1941. Diplomate Am. Bd. Surgery. Resident surgery U. Minn. Hosps., 1937-41; pvt. practice surgery Long Beach, Calif., 1945—; mem. staff St. Mary's Med. Ctr., Long Beach; cons. surgery Long Beach Gen. Hosp.; prof., chmn. dept. surgery Calif. Coll. Medicine, 1962—; surgical cons. to Surgeon-Gen., U.S. Army; adj. prof. surgery U. Calif. Author: Fundamentals of Human Physiology, 1935, A Critique of Reason, 1938, Lectures in Medical Physiology; contbr. numerous articles in field of surgery, physiology to profl. jours. Served to col. M.C. AUS, 1941-46. Recipient Charles Lyman Green prize in physiology, 1934, prize Mpls. Surg. Soc., 1938, ann. award Mississippi Valley Med. Soc., 1955; Alice Shevlin fellow U. Minn., 1932. Fellow ACS, Royal Soc. Medicine, Internat. Coll. Surgeons, Am. Coll. Gastroenterology, Am. Med. Writers Assn., Internat. Coll. Angiology (sci. council), Gerontol. Soc., Am. Soc. Abdominal Surgeons, Nat. Cancer Inst., Phlebology Soc. Am., Internat. Acad. Proctology, Peripheral Vascular Soc. Am. (founding); mem. AAAS, Am. Assn. Study Neoplastic Diseases, Mississippi Valley Med. Soc., N.Y. Acad. Scis., Hollywood Acad. Medicine, Am. Geriatrics Soc., Irish Med. Assn., Am. Assn. History Medicine, Pan Pacific Surgical Assn., Indsl. Med. Assn., L.A. Musicians Union (hon.), Pan Am. Med. Assn. (diplomate), Internat. Bd. Surgery (cert.), Internat. Bd. Proctology (cert.), Wisdom Soc. (wisdom award of honor), Sigma Xi, Phi Beta Kappa, Alpha Omega Alpha. Home: 904 Silver Spur Rd Ste 804 Rolling Hills Estates CA 90274

BELLISTON, EDWARD GLEN, medical facility administrator, consultant; b. Upland, Calif., Oct. 20, 1958; s. G. Howard and MaryAnn (Fitzgerald) B.; m. Kristine Marie Holmes, Aug. 12, 1981. BS, Brigham Young U., 1984, MHA, 1987. Cert. EMT. Admitting clk. Utah Valley Regional Med. Ctr., Provo, 1985; adminstrv. resident St. Benedict's Hosp., Holy Cross Health System, Ogden, Utah, 1986; fin. counselor Utah Valley Regional Med. Ctr., Provo, 1986, adminstrv. dir., 1986; regional clin. adminstrv. coord. Intermountain Health Care-IHC Physicians Svcs., Salt Lake City, 1989; sr. phys. cons. Intermountain Health Care-IHC Physicians Svcs., Salt Lake, 1990-95, dir. group opers.physics divsn., 1995—. Instr. gospel doctrine LDS Ch., Springville, Utah, 1989-91, bishopric Brigham Young U. 81st ward, 1991-93; welfare coord. LDS Ch., American Fork, Utah, 1994-95, Sunday sch. instr., 1996—; leader Boy Scouts Am., Springville, 1988; coord. Neighborhood Watch, 1994—. Mem. Med. Group Mgmt. Assn., Am. Coll. Healthcare Execs. Republican. Home: 363 W 1400 N American Fork UT 84003-2794 Office: IHC Physician Group Utah County Ste 5A 2230 N University Pkwy Provo UT 84604-1585

BELLM, JOAN, civic worker; b. Alton, Ill., June 20, 1934; d. Harvey Jacob and Alma Lorene (Roberts) Goldsby; m. Earl David Bellm, Oct. 1, 1955; children: David, Lori, Michael. Editor Best of IDEA newsletter, 1991—. Organist, dir. jr. choir St. Mary's Cath. Ch., 1958-78; mem. adv. bd. Carlinville (Ill.) Area Hosp., 1981-86; trustee Blackburn Coll., Carlinville, 1983-86; bd. dirs. Cath. Children's Home, Diocese of Springfield, Ill., 1986—; founder, bd. dirs., state networker Ill. Drug Edn. Alliance, 1982-86, pres., 1987-89; bd. dirs., nat. networker Nat. Fedn. Parents for Drug-Free Youth, Washington, 1984-86; mem. Ill. Gov.'s Adv. Coun. on Alcoholism and Substance Abuse, 1989-93; founder Drug Watch Internat., 1991, Internat. Drug Strategy Inst., 1993, invited participant Internat. Private Sector Conf. on Drugs, Seville, 1993, advisor U.N. Internat. Drug Ctrl. Program, 1994 ; numerous others. Recipient letter of endorsement Pres. of U.S., 1981, citation of recognition Ill. Dept., Am. Legion, 1981, Meritorious Svc. award, 1982, award Ill. Drug Edn. Alliance award, 1984, Southwestern Ill. Law Enforcement Commn., 1984, Carlinville Sch. Bd., 1985, Outstanding Svc. award Nat. Fedn. Parents, 1986, award Ill. Alcohol and Drug Dependence Assn., 1986, Optimist Internat., 1987, Ill. Drug Edn. Alliance, 1988, Outstanding Citizen award Blackburn U., 1989, Citizen of Yr. award, Carlinville, 1990. Home: PO Box 227 Carlinville IL 62626-0227

BELLO, MARY, physician; b. Paterson, N.J., Dec. 27, 1954; d. John Vincent and Rose (Piccirilli) B.; married, June 3, 1984; children: Michael Mutter, Jonathan Mutter. BA, Rutgers Coll., 1977; BS, L.I. U., 1980; MD, Ross U., 1984. Family physician pvt. practice; clin. dir. N.J. Med. Sch., 1994—. Republican. Roman Catholic. Office: 400 Franklin Tpk Ste 106 Mahwah NJ

BELLONE, JACK D., physician; b. Chgo., Oct. 4, 1942; s. Arthur P. and Ruth (Grubb) B.; m. Jo Ann J. Bellone, June 17, 1972; children: Chuck, Dustin, Rebecca, Natalie. BS, Iowa State U., 1964; DO, Chgo. Coll. Osteo. Medicine, 1969; MD, Loyola U., Maywood, Ill., 1975. Diplomate in internal medicine, hematology and med. oncology Am. Bd. Internal Medicine. Intern Ill. Masonic Med. Ctr., Chgo., 1970-71; resident in internal medicine Med. Coll. Ohio, Toledo, 1971-72; resident in internal medicine Hines (Ill.) VA Hosp., 1972-73, sr. resident in hematology and oncology, 1973-75; assoc. Joliet (Ill.) Med. Group, Ltd., 1975-82; pvt. practice Radiation Therapy Oncology Ctr., New Port Richey, Fla., 1982-84, Gulf Point Oncology, Hudson, Fla., 1984—; asst. clin. prof. medicine Loyola U., Stritch Sch. Medicine, 1976-82; mem. staff HCA Bayonet Point/Hudson Med. Ctr., HCA New Port Richey Hosp. Contbr. articles to profl. jours. Fellow ACP; mem. AMA, Fla. Med. Assn., Pasco County Med. Soc., Am. Soc. Clin. Oncology, Fla. Soc. Clin. Oncology. Office: Gulf Pointe Cancer Ctr 7651 Medical Dr Hudson FL 34667

BELLONI, FRANCIS LOUIS, physiologist; b. N.Y.C., Jan. 23, 1949; s. Francis Peter and Frances Marie (Asaro) B.; m. Susan Marie Kelly, May 1, 1971; children: Benjamin Francis. BS in Biology cum laude, Providence Coll., 1970; PhD in Physiology, U. Mich., 1975. Grad. teaching asst. U. Mich., Ann Arbor, 1971-75, postdoctoral fellow, 1975-78; rsch. asst. prof. U. Va., Charlottesville, 1979-81; asst. prof. N.Y. Med. Coll., Valhalla, 1981-86, assoc. prof., 1986-94, prof., 1994—, acting dean Grad. Sch. Basic Med. Scis., 1993—, vice provost/sci. affairs, 1996—. Editorial cons., contbr. articles and rsch. reports to numerous profl. jours. Bd. dirs. Cortlandt Am. Little League, Cortlandt Manor, N.Y., 1985-95; mem. long-range planning com. Lakeland Ctrl. Sch. Dist., 1990-92; mem. adv. bd. Town of Cortlandt Pks. and Recreation, 1991—; trustee, treas. Lakeland Edn. Found., 1994—. Mem. Am. Physiol. soc. (edn. com. 1990-93, chair edn. com. 1995—), Fedn. Am. Socs. for Exptl. Biology, Am. Heart Assn. (couns. on circulation 1987—, basic sci. 1992—). Roman Catholic. Office: NY Med Coll Dept Physiology Basic Scis Bldg Valhalla NY 10595

BELLO-REUSS, ELSA NOEMI, physician, educator; b. Buenos Aires, Argentina, May 1, 1939; came to U.S., 1972; naturalized, 1989; d. Jose F. and Julia M. (Hiriart) Bello; B.S., U. Chile, 1957, M.D., 1964; m. Luis Reuss, Apr. 15, 1965; children: Luis F., Alejandro E. Intern J.J. Aguirre Hosp., Chile, 1963-64; intern, then resident in internal medicine U. Chile, Santiago, 1964-66; pvt. practice medicine specializing in nephrology Santiago, 1967-72; prof. pathophysiology Sch. Nutrition U. Chile, 1970-72; Internat. NIH fellow U. N.C., Chapel Hill, 1972-74; vis. asst. prof. physiology U. N.C., Chapel Hill, 1974-75; Louis Welt fellow U. N.C.-Duke U. Med. Ctr., 1975-76; mem. faculty Jewish Hosp. St. Louis, 1976-83, asst. prof. medicine, physiology and biophysics Washington U. Sch. Medicine, St. Louis, 1976-86, assoc. prof. physiology dept. cell biology and physiology, 1986; assoc. prof. medicine U. Tex. Med. Br., Galveston, 1986-94, prof. dept. internal medicine and dept. phys. and biophys. medicine, 1994—, dir. Renal Clin, 1995—; mem. reviewers res. study sect. NIH, 1991-95; chair Women's Coun. Internat. Medicine U. Tex. Med. Bd. chpt., 1993—, mem. rsch. coun. Author: (with others) The Kidney and Body Fluids in Health and Disease, 1983; contbr. articles on nephrology and epithelial electrophysiology to med. and physiology jours. Mem. Internat., Am. Socs. Nephrology, Royal Soc. Medicine, Nat. Kidney Found. of S.E. Tex. (med. adv. bd., chairperson med. adv. bd., bd. dirs. 1994-95), Coun. of Women in Nephrology, Tex. Med. Assn., Am. Fedn. Clin. Rsch., Am. Soc. Renal Biochemistry and Metabolism, Internat. Soc. Renal Nutrition and Metabolism, Am. Physiology Soc., Am. Heart Assn., Kidney Coun., Soc. Gen. Physiologists, Math. Assn. Am., Gt. Houston and Gulf Coast Nephrology Assn., NIH Gen. Medicine B Study Sect. (mem. 1987-91), Reserve reviewer 1991-95, VA grant reviewer, Sigma Xi. Office: U Tex Med Br Dept Medicine Nephrology OJS 4 200 Galveston TX 77555-0562

BELLOS, JACK FRANK, dentist; b. San Antonio, Aug. 20, 1939; s. Photios Peter and Afrodite (Varessis) B.; m. Mary Jane Beck, July 26, 1969; children: Gregory, Amanda, Matthew, Thomas. BS in Pharmacy, U. Tex., 1962; DDS, U. Tex., Houston, 1969. Pharmacist Sommer's Drug Stores, San Antonio, 1962-63, Univ. Drug Store, San Antonio, 1963-65; pvt. practice gen. dentistry San Antonio, 1969—. Football coach YMCA. Fellow Tex. Dental Assn.; mem. ADA, San Antonio Dist. Dental Soc. Greek Orthodox. Home: 415 Rockhill Dr San Antonio TX 78209-2316 Office: 7231 Broadway St San Antonio TX 78209-3741

BELLOWS, ROBERT ALVIN, research physiologist; b. Bozeman, Mont., Aug. 22, 1934; s. Alvin O. and Lucy E. (Norman) B.; m. Laura Mae Pasha, Dec. 27, 1957; children: Donna Kay, William, Norman, David. BS, Mont. State U., 1956, MS, 1958; PhD, U. Wis., 1962. Registered profl. animal scientist. Rsch. physiologist USDA-Agrl. Rsch. Svc., Miles City, Mont., 1962-67, rsch. physiologist, investigations leader, 1967-71, rsch. physiology supr., 1971-79, rsch. leader, 1979-84, rsch. physiologist, 1984—; reviewer, cons. State Expt. Stas., USDA-Agrl. Rsch. Svc., Can., Mex., Egypt, Soviet Union, Kazakhstan, Kyrgyzstan, Nat. Cattleman's Assn., Angus, Hereford, Charolais and Simmental Breed Assn., 1971—; adj. prof. Mont. State U. Mem. Am. Soc. Animal Sci. (western dir. 1967, sec., pres. elect, pres. western sect. 1989-91, disting. svc. award 1983, animal mgmt. award 1993, sr. scientist of yr. 1994), Soc. for Study of Reproduction, Coun. Agrl. Sci. and Tech., Alpha Zeta. Office: US Dept Agr Agrl Rsch Svc Livestock & Range Rsch Lab Rte 1 Box 2021 Miles City MT 59301

BELMAN, A. BARRY, pediatric urologist; b. Columbus, Ga., Oct. 16, 1938; s. David Joseph and Ruth (Radin) B.; m. Paula Yonover, June 14, 1964; children: Peter, Lisa, Trina, Jessica. BA with distinction, U. Ariz., 1960; MD, Northwestern U., 1964, MS, 1969. Diplomate Am. Bd. Urology (exam. com. 1980-84, guest oral examiner). Intern Passavant Meml. Hosp., Chgo., 1964-65; resident dept. urology Northwestern U. Med. Sch., 1965-70, from instr. to assoc. prof. urology, 1969-76; attending pediatric urologist Children's Meml. Hosp., Chgo., 1970-76; assoc. prof. urology and pediatrics George Washington U. Sch. Medicine, Washington, 1976-78, prof. urology and pediatrics, 1978—; chmn. dept. pediatric urology Children's Hosp., Washington, 1976-96; cons. Nat. Naval, Walter Reed Army Hosps., NIH. Co-author: Genitourinary Problems in Pediatrics, 1981; assoc. editor: Clinical Pediatric Urology, 1976, co-editor, 2d edit., 1985, 3rd edit., 1992; mem. editorial bd. Current Problems in Urology, 1989-93, Jour. Urology, 1991—. Mem. AMA (rep. urology residency rev. com. 1995—), ACS, Am. Urol. Assn. (ped. cons., mem. residency edn. and fellowship com. Mid-Atlantic sect.), Am. Acad. Pediat. (sec. urology sect. 1984-87, chmn.-elect 1987-88, chmn. 1988-89), Soc. Pediat. Urology (mem. exec. com. 1990-96, pres. 1995-96), Cosmos Club. Office: Childrens Hosp Med Ctr 111 Michigan Ave NW Washington DC 20010-2970

BELMONT, HOWARD MICHAEL, physician; b. New Hyde Park, N.Y., Sept. 21, 1954; s. Joseph Irwin and Paula (Baker) B.; m. Suzanne Snipes, Mar. 2, 1996; children: David, Benjamin, Daniel. BA, Harvard U., 1976; MD, U. Pitts., 1980. Lic. physician, N.Y. Dir. lupus clinic Bellevue Hosp., N.Y.C., 1986-90; co-dir. lupus clinic Hosp. for Joint Diseases, N.Y.C., 1990-95, med. dir., 1995—; asst. prof. NYU Med. Ctr., N.Y.C., 1995. Office: Hosp for Joint Diseases 301 E 17th M St New York NY 10003

BELMONT, LARRY MILLER, health association executive; b. Reno, Apr. 13, 1936; s. Miller Lawrence and Madeline (Echante) B.; m. Laureen Metzger, Aug. 14, 1966; children: Miller Lawrence, Rebecca Madeline, Amie Echante, Bradley August. BA in Psychology, U. Nev., 1962; MPH, U. Mich., 1968; cert. in environ. mgmt., U. So. Calif., 1978; M in Pub. Adminstrn., U. Idaho, 1979. Rep. on loan to city health depts. USPHS, Los Angeles and Long Beach, 1962-63; advisor pub. health on loan to Alaska dept. health and welfare USPHS, Anchorage, 1963-64, Juneau and Anchorage, 1964-67; dep. dir. Wash./Alaska Regional Med. Program, Spokane, Wash., 1968-71; dir., sec.-treas. bd. of health Panhandle Health Dist., Coeur d'Alene, Idaho, 1971—; mem. adj. faculty Whitworth Coll., Spokane; presenter papers internat., nat., region, state confs., 1981-82; testifier congl. coms., Washington, 1973, 76, state legis. com., Idaho, 1972-82. Chmn. nominating com. Kootenai Econ. Devel. Council, Idaho, 1985, bd. dirs. 1981-86; mem. adv. com. Kootenai County Council Alcoholism, 1979-80; regional coordinator Gov.'s Com. Vol. Services, Idaho, 1979-80; chmn. Montessori Adv. Bd., Idaho, 1975-79; chmn. personnel com. North Idaho Hospice, 1985-88, bd. dirs. 1985-88; bd. dirs. North Idaho Spl. Services Agy., 1972-76; bd. dirs., vice chmn. Pub. Employees Credit Union, 1990-95; bd. dirs. United Way of Kootemai County, Inc., 1990-91; mem. nat. steering com. APEX/PH, 1987-91; active numerous other organizations. USPHS trainee U. Mich., 1967-68, EPA trainee U. So. Calif., 1978. Mem. Am. Pub. Health Assn., Nat. Assn. Home Health Agys. (chmn. legis. com. 1979-82, bd. dirs. 1978-81), Nat. Assn. County Health Ofcls. (bd. dirs. 1986-88, registry com. 1990), Idaho Pub. Health Assn. (bd. dirs., treas. 1973-77), Idaho Conf. Dist. Health Dirs. (vice-chmn. and chmn. 1993-95), Idaho Forest Owners Assn., Kootenai County Environ. Alliance, Washington Pub. Health Assn., Idaho Conservation League, Kootenai County Quality of Life Coalition, Ducks Ultd. Democrat.

BELMONT, MATTHEW RAMSDEN, anesthesiologist; b. N.Y.C., Sept. 5, 1959; s. Ronald John and Beverly Lucille (Simpson) B. BS, Georgetown U., 1981; MD, SUNY, Bklyn., 1986. Intern Meml. Sloane Kettering Cancer Ctr., N.Y.C., 1986-87; resident N.Y. Hosp.-Cornell Med. Ctr., 1987-90, rsch. fellow, 1990-91, instr. in anesthesia, 1991-92, asst. prof., 1992—. Contbr. articles and revs. to profl. jours. Mem. Am. Soc. Anesthesiologists, Internat. Anesthesia Rsch. Soc. Office: NY Hosp-Cornell Med Ctr 525 E 68th St Starr 1000 New York NY 10021

BELONICK, CYNTHIA ANN, psychiatric-mental health nurse; b. New Britain, Conn., Mar. 21, 1957; d. Steven and Anne (Kochanowski) B. Diploma, St. Francis Hosp. Sch. Nursing, Hartford, Conn., 1982; BA cum laude, U. Conn., 1979; MSN, Yale U., 1992. Cert. clin. specialist in adult psychiat. and mental health, advanced practice RN. Nurse educator The Inst. of Living, Hartford, Conn., 1993—. Contbr. Psychiat. Nursing Diagnoses: A Comprehensive Manual of Manual Health Care. Mem. Conn. Nurses Assn., Orthodox Christian Assn. Medicine, Psychology and Religion, Sigma Theta Tau, Delta Mu.

BELOVANOFF, OLGA, retired health care facility administrator; b. Buchanan, Sask., Can., July 1, 1932; d. Frederick Alexander and Dora (Konkin) B. Grad. high sch., Kamsack, Sask., Can. From clk. to adminstrv. officer Sask. Health Dept. Cancer Clinic, Saskatoon, 1951-78; bus. mgr. Sask. Cancer Found. Saskatoon Clinic, 1979-90; ret., 1990. Dir. Sask. Br. Can. Tenpin Fedn., Inc. Home: 420 3d Ave N, Saskatoon, SK Canada S7K 2J3

BELSTERLING, JEAN INNES, retired medical librarian; b. Phila., Feb. 2, 1928; d. George McNeely Belsterling and Mary Thornton (Innes) Bowman. Grad., Bryn Mawr Hosp. Sch. Nursing, 1948; BA, U. Pa., 1974; MS, Drexel U., 1976. RN, Pa. Nurse Bryn Mawr (Pa.) Hosp., 1948-51; commd. ensign USN, 1951, advanced through grades to lt. comdr., 1961; ret., 1971; med. libr. West Jersey Health System, Voorhees, N.J., 1976-90, ret., 1990; coord. S.W. N.J. Libr. Consortium, 1985-90. Deacon Trinity Presbyn. Ch., Cherry Hill, N.J., 1976-79, trustee, elder, 1984-87. Mem. AAUW, DAR, USN League. Home: 214 Shady Ln Marlton NJ 08053-2716

BELT, AUDREY E(VON), social worker, consultant; b. New Orleans, June 23, 1948. BS in Social Work, Grambling State U., 1970; MSW in Social Work Adminstrn., U. Mich., 1972. Adult probation officer City/County San Francisco Hall of Justice, 1973-74; child welfare worker dept. social svcs. City/County San Francisco, 1974-79; rsch. and planning specialist City of Ann Arbor (Mich.) Model Cities Interdisciplinary Agy; cons. in field. Grambling State U. scholar, 1966-70, U. Mich. scholar, 1971-72. Mem. ABA, NASW (edn. task force), Am. Orthopsychiat. Assn., Am. Humane Soc. (exec. asst. dir., sec. exec. bd.), Child Welfare League Am., N.Y. Acad. Scis., Smithsonian Rsch. Instn., Alpha Kappa Delta. Democrat. Roman Catholic. Home and Office: PO Box 424288 610 Polk St Apt 217 San Francisco CA 94103

BELVILLE, WILLIAM DONALD, urologist; b. Burlington, Vt., Oct. 19, 1945; s. Roy Glendon and Irene Germaine (LaRiviere) B.; m. Virginia Lorraine Paradin, June 5, 1971; children: Roy, Ryan, William Jr. BA, U. Vt., 1967, MD, 1971. Commd. 2d lt. U.S. Army, 1967, advanced through grades to col., ret., 1990; resident in urology Walter Reed Army Med. Ctr., Washington, 1974-78, fellow in urology, 1978-79; assoc. sect. head urology U. Mich. Hosps., Ann Arbor, 1990-93, assoc. prof. surgery, 1990—; undergrad. edn. dir. urology sect. U. Mich., 1992—; chair credentials com. U. Mich. Hosps., 1993—. Contbr. chpts. to books; reviewer: Urology Jour., 1994—. Decorated Commendation medal, Order of Mil. Med. Merit, Legion of Merit. Fellow ACS; mem. AMA, Soc. Govt. Svc. Urologists (pres. 1985-86), Am. Urologic Assn., Am. Assn. Clin. Urologists, Soc. Univ. Urologists. Office: U Mich Hosps 1500 E Medical Ctr Dr Ann Arbor MI 48109-0330

BEMAK, FREDERIC PAUL, psychology educator; b. Boston, Oct. 23, 1948; s. Walter I. and Ruth B. (Ruskin) B.; m. Adi Bemak (div. 1988); children: Amber, Lani. BA, Boston U., 1970; MEd, U. Mass., 1971, EdD, 1975. With Upward Bound Program, Amherst, Mass., 1970-75, dir., 1974-75; dir. Mass. Region I Adolescent Treatment Program, Northampton, 1977-79; clin. dir. tng. consortium U. Mass. Med. Sch., Worcester, 1980-82; assoc. dir. psychology dept. New Eng. Grad. Sch. Antioch U., Keene, N.H., 1982-86; asst. prof. U. Wis., Oshkosh, 1986-88, assoc. prof., coord. community human svcs. grad. program, 1989; dir. Human Svcs. Consortium U. Wis. System, 1987-89; chmn. dept. counseling/human svcs. Johns Hopkins U., Balt., 1989—; internat. cons. in field, Boliva, Barbados, Colombia, Mex., China, Hong Kong; vis. psychologist APA, 1982; vis. scholar Antioch U., 1984. Contbr. articles to profl. publs. Kellogg Found. fellow, 1988-90, World Rehab. Fund fellow, 1982; grantee El Salvador Nat. Assn. Psychologists-US. Embassy, 1990, Ptnrs. of Ams., 1984—, U.S. Dept. HHS, 1989-90, NIMH, 1991, U.S. Dept. Edn., 1993-94; Fulbright scholar, Brazil, 1995. Mem. ACA, APA, Ptnrs. Ams. (chmn. health com. 1990-95, bd. dirs. 1982-95). Office: Johns Hopkins U Div Edn 105 Whitehead Hall Baltimore MD 21218

BEMELMAN, WILLEM A., surgeon; b. Amsterdam, The Netherlands, Dec. 17, 1958; s. Wilhelmus Adrianus and Gerda J. H. (Den-Hartog) B.; m. Philomeen Kuijer, June 25, 1994. MD cum laude, U. Amsterdam, 1986, PhD, 1989. Lic. surgeon. Surg. fellow Acad. Med. Ctr., 1994; cons. gastrointestinal surgery Leiden (The Netherlands) Univ. Hosp., 1995—. Fellow MGEM. Office: U Leiden Hosp, Dept Surgery PO Box 9600, Leiden 2300, The Netherlands

BENACERRAF, BARUJ, pathologist, educator; b. Caracas, Venezuela, Oct. 29, 1920; came to U.S., 1939, naturalized, 1943; s. Abraham and Henriette (Lasry) B.; m. Annette Dreyfus, Mar. 24, 1943; 1 child, Beryl. B es L, Lycee Janson, 1940; BS, Columbia U., 1942; MD, Med. Sch. Va., 1945; MA, Harvard U., 1970; MD (hon.), U. Geneva, 1980; DSc (hon.), NYU, 1981, Va. Commonwealth U., 1981, Yeshiva U., 1982, U. Aix-Marseille, 1982, Columbia U., 1985, Adelphi U., 1988, Weizmann Inst., 1989, Harvard U., 1992, U. Bordeaux, 1993, U. Vienna, 1995. Intern Queens Gen. Hosp., N.Y.C., 1945-46; rsch. fellow dept. microbiology Med. Sch. Columbia U., 1948-50; charge de recherches Centre Nat. de Recherche Scientique Hosp. Broussais, Paris, 1950-56; asst. prof. pathology Sch. Medicine NYU, 1956-58, assoc. prof. Sch. Medicine, 1958-60, prof. Sch. Medicine, 1960-68; chief immunology Nat. Inst. Allergy and Infectious Diseases NIH, Bethesda, Md., 1968-70; Fabyan prof. comparative pathology, chmn. dept. Med. Sch. Harvard U., 1970-91; ret. Med. Sch., Harvard U., Cambridge, Mass., 1991; pres., CEO Dana-Farber Cancer Inst., 1980-91, Dana-Farber Inc., 1990-95; mem. immunology study sect. NIH; pres. Fedn. Am. Socs. Exptl. Biology, 1974-75; chmn. sci. adv. com. Centre d'Immunologie de Marseille. Bd. govs. Weizmann Inst. Medicine; mem. sci. adv. com. Children's Hosp. Boston; mem. award com. GM Cancer Rsch. Found., also chmn. selection com. Sloan prize, 1980. Capt. M.C. AUS, 1946-48. Recipient T. Duckett Jones Meml. award Helen Hay Whitney Found., 1976, Rabbi Shai Shacknai lectr. and prize Hebrew U. Jerusalem, 1974, Waterford award, 1980, Nobel prize, 1980, Corr. Emerite de l'Institut de la Sante et de la Recherche Scientifique, Nat. Medal of Sci. NSF, 1990. Fellow Am. Acad. Arts and Scis.; mem. NAS, Nat. Inst. Medicine, Am. Assn. Immunologists (pres. 1973-74), Brit. Assn. Immunology, French Soc. Biol. Chemistry, Internat. Union Immunology Socs. (pres. 1980-83). Home: 111 Perkins St Jamaica Plain MA 02130-4313 Office: Dana-Farber Cancer Inst 375 Longwood Ave Boston MA 02215-5328

BENACH, SHARON ANN, physician assistant; b. New Orleans, Aug. 28, 1944; d. Wilbur G. and Freda Helen (Klaas) Cherry; m. Richard Benach, Dec. 6, 1969 (div. Oct. 1976); children: Craig, Rachel. Degree, St. Louis U., 1978. Physician asst. VA Hosp., St. Louis, 1982-84, Maricopa County Health Svcs., Phoenix, 1984—. Served with USPHS, 1978-82. Recipient Outstanding Performance award HHS. Mem. Maricopa Faculty Assn. (div. internal medicine), Mensa. Jewish. Home: 5726 N 10th St No 5 Phoenix AZ 85014-2273

BENAGIANO, GIUSEPPE PINO, medical program director, medical educator; b. Rome, Oct. 15, 1937; s. Andrea and Maria Luisa (Piergili) B.; m. Orietta Bianchini, Oct. 4, 1965 (div. 1984); children: Marisa, Andrea; m. Stephanie Canwell, June 29, 1985. MD, U. Rome, 1961, specialist in ob-gyn., 1965. Supranumerary asst. prof. U. Rome, 1962-63, asst. prof., 1968-70, assoc. prof., 1970-73; Ford Fdn. fellow Karolinska Inst., Stockholm, 1966-67; rsch. specialist Population Coun., N.Y.C., 1967; med. officer WHO, Geneva, 1973-80, dir. spl. program rsch. in human reproduction, 1993—; prof., dir. Inst. Ob-Gyn. U. La Sapienza, Rome, 1981-93; cons. U.S. AID, Washington, 1982, 90. Editor: Progestogens in Therapy, 1982, Endocrine Mechanisms in Fertility Regulation, 1986, Immaginario Erotico e "Realta" Pornografica, 1989, Trattato di Fisiopatologia della Riproduzione Umana, 1993. Mem. Soc. Italiana di Sessuologia Clinica (pres. 1986-89), Soc. Advancement of Contraception (pres. 1992-95), Italian Soc. Ob-gyn. (com. chmn. 1990—), Internat. Fedn. Gynecologists and Obstetricians (jour. assoc. editor. 1989—), Internat. Com. Rsch. in Reproduction (founding mem., bd. dirs. 1981—). Roman Catholic. Home: 28 Chemin des Massettes, 1218 Grand Saconnex Geneva, Switzerland Office: WHO, Avenue Appia, 1211 Geneva 27, Switzerland

BENARESH, EHSANOLLAH, anesthesiologist; b. Kashan, Iran, Apr. 22, 1934; came to U.S., 1958; s. Leon and Cecile (Shaker) B.; m. Marcelle A. Gold, July 9, 1964; children: Lamont, Jennifer. BS, Alborz Coll., Teheran, Iran, 1951; MD, Teheran U., 1957. Diplomate, Am. Bd. Anesthesiology. Intern Beth David Hosp., N.Y.C., 1958-59; resident in anesthesia Bellevue Hosp., N.Y.C., 1959-61; chief resident in anesthesia Jewish Hosp. Bklyn., 1961-62; fellow in anesthesia, rsch. assoc. Flower-Fifth Ave. and Met. Hosp. Ctr., N.Y.C., 1962-65; rsch. assoc. in anesthesiology Hosp. for Joint Diseases, Bronx, N.Y., 1965-66; anesthesiologist, med. dir. Hurley Ave. Surgicenter, Kingston, N.Y., 1966-88; anesthesiologist Columbia-Green Med. Ctr., Hudson, N.Y., 1990-91; asst. prof. anesthesiology, anesthesiologist N.Y. Downtown Cornell Med. Ctr., N.Y.C., 1991—. Fellow Am. Coll. Anesthesiology; mem. Am. Soc. Anesthesiologists, N.Y. State Soc. Anesthesiologists, Med. Soc. State N.Y., Ulster County Med. Soc., Internat. Anesthesia Rsch. Soc. Home and Office: 3 Arapaho Ct Suffern NY 10901-4139

BEN-ASHER, M. DAVID, physician; b. Newark, June 18, 1931; s. Samuel Irving and Dora Ruth (Kagan)B.; m. Bryna S. Zeller, Nov. 22, 1956. BA, Syracuse U., 1952; MD, U. Buffalo Sch. Med., 1956. Intern E.J. Meyer Mem. Hosp., Buffalo, N.Y., 1956-57; resident Jersey City Med. Ctr., 1957-58; asst. chief med. service U.S. Army Hosp., Ft. McPherson, Ga., 1958-60; resident Madigan Gen. Hosp., Tacoma, Wash., 1960-62; chief gen. med. service Walson Army Hosp., Ft. Dix, N.Y., 1962-64; attending staff St. Mary's Hosp., Tucson, Ariz., 1964—; pvt. practice Tucson, 1964—; mem. Ariz. State Bd. Med. Examiners, 1978-88. Bd. dirs. Tucson Symphony, 1971-73; mem. Ariz. State Bd. Med. Examiners, 1978-88 (joint bd. for regulation of physicians' assts. 1990—); bd. trustees United Synagogue Am., 1981-87, nat. adv. bd., 1987-91. Mem. Pima County Med. Soc. (bd. dirs. 1971-77, pres. 1976), Ariz. Med. Assn., AMA, ACP. Democrat. Home: 3401 N Tanuri Dr Tucson AZ 85715-6735 Office: So Ariz Med Specialists 4711 N 1st Ave Tucson AZ 85718-5610

BENATAR, SOLOMON ROBERT, internist; b. Selukwe, Zimbabwe, Feb. 6, 1942; s. Haim Solomon and Suzette Sultana (Albagli) B.; m. Evelyn Mary Goldberg, Oct. 26, 1943; children: David, Michael, Brian. B Medicine, B Surgery, U. Capetown, Republic of South Africa, 1965. Fellow faculty anaesthestists Coll. of Medicine of South Africa, 1971; intern Groote Schuur Hosp., Capetown, 1966; pvt. practice Port Elizabeth, Republic of South Africa, 1967-68; resident anesthesiology Groote Schuur Hosp., U. Capetown, 1969-70; resident internal medicine Grooote Schuur Hosp., U. Capetown, 1971; rsch. fellow Northwick Park and Brompton Hosps., London, 1972; rsch. fellow, hon. resident Brompton Hosp. and Cardiothoracic Inst., London, 1973; cons. physician Groote Schuur Hosp. and U. Capetown, 1974—, prof., chmn. dept. medicine, 1980—; physician-in-chief dept. medicine Groote Schuur Hosp., Capetown, 1980—; dir. Bioethics Ctr. U. Capetown, 1992—; hon. registrar Coll. Medicine South Africa, 1978-80, elected councillor, 1980—, chmn. faculty medicine, 1980-91, v.p. 1986-95; internat. vis. scholar Hastings Ctr., N.Y.C., 1986; internat. advisor Jour. Respiratory Medicine; fellow Program in Ethics and the Professions, Harvard U., 1994-95; vis. prof. Harvard U. Med. Sch., 1994-95. Mem. editorial bd. South African Med. Jour., 1983-92. Trustee South Africa Med. Students Trust, 1980-90; mem. coun. U. Capetown, 1990—; chmn. selection com. Imperial Chem. Industries Rsch. Scholarship, 1992—, Sandoz Rsch. Scholarship, Johannesburg, 1989—; commr. U. Witswatersrand Enquiry on Baragwanath Hosp., 1988. Recipient African Oxygen Gold medal Coll. Medicine South Africa, 1971, Hamilton Maynard Meml. medal South African Med. Jour., 1977; rsch. fellow Imperial Chem. Industries, 1971. Fellow ACP (hon.), Royal Coll. Physicians, Coll. Medicine South Africa; mem. NAS, AAAS (fgn. hon.), Acad. Sci. South Africa (founder), Inst. Medicine. Jewish. Home: 41 Willow Rd Newlands, Capetown 7700, South Africa Office: U Capetown, Groote Schuur Hosp Observatory, Capetown 7925, South Africa

BENBOW, GREGORY ALLEN, emergency medicine physician, consultant; s. Kyle Cannon Benbow and Mary Eva (Moore) Thomas; m. Lisa Michelle McCanless, Aug. 2, 1996; children: Michael, Gabriel, Matthew. BA, U. Pa., 1983; DO, U. Health Scis., Kansas City, 1987. Diplomate Am. Bd. Family Practice. Emergency medicine physician Southeastern Emergency Medicine Physicians, Richmond, Va., 1993—. Lt. comdr. USN, 1990-93. Mem. Am. Acad. Family Physicians, Am. Assn. Physician Specialists, Assn. Mil. Surgeons of the U.S. Home: 15200 Powell Grove Rd Midlothian VA 23112

BENBOW, RICHARD ADDISON, psychological counselor; b. Las Vegas, Dec. 27, 1949; s. Jules Coleman and Bonnie Ray B. BBA, U. Nev. 1972, MS in Counseling, 1974; AAS in Bus. Mgmt. and Real Estate, Clark County Community Coll., 1980; PhD in Clin. Psychology, U. Humanistic Studies, 1986. Cert. tchr., Nev.; cert. clin. mental health counselor, secondary sch. counselor, Nev., substance abuse counselor, Nev., substance abuse program adminstr., Nev.; nat. cert. counselor. Jud. svcs. officer Mcpl. Ct. City of Las Vegas, 1983-88, pretrial program coord., 1988—; inmate classification technician Detention and Correctional Svcs., 1982-83; stress mgmt. cons. Mem. Biofeedback Soc. Am., Assn. Humanistic Psychology, Nat. Assn. Psychotherapists, Am. Counseling Assn., Am. Mental Health Counselors Assn., Am. Acad. Crisis Interveners, Jr. C. of C., U.S. Jaycees (presdl. award of honor 1978-79), Delta Sigma Phi. Democrat. Christian Scientist. Office: Mcpl Ct Intake Svcs City of Las Vegas 400 Stewart Ave Las Vegas NV 89101-2942

BENDA, KAREL, radiodiagnostician; b. Brno, Moravia, Czech Republic, Jan. 23, 1936; s. Emil Bruno and Alžběta (Musilová) B.; m. Jana Martínková, May 29, 1959 (div. 1985); 1 child, David; m. Marcela Roztočilová, Mar. 27, 1985. MD, Masaryk U., Brno, 1960; ScD, Charles U., 1980. Radiologist/lectr. Univ. Hosp., Olomouc, Czech Republic, 1961-76; rschr. Inst. Clin. and Exptl. Medicine, Prague, 1976-77; assoc. prof. Palacky U., Olomouc, 1978-84; prof. Masaryk U., Brno, 1985-89; head Radiol. Inst. Masaryk Univ. Hosp., Brno, 1989—; cons. Univ. Hosp., La Valletta, Malta, 1978, 90. Author: (monograph) Lymphedema of the Extremities, 1981 (Best Pub. award Czech Soc. Radiology 1982). Recipient Acad. Sport medal for orgn. Ministry of Edn., Prague, 1995. Fellow Internat. Coll. Angiology (sc. coun. 1987-92); mem. Internat. Soc. Lymphology (exec. com. 1994—), Czech Soc. Lymphology (pres. 1994—), Czech Soc. Radiology (hon.). Office: U Hosp Inst Radiodiagnostics, Jihlavská 20, 639 00 Brno Czech Republic

BENDA, LENORA, nurse; b. Flint, Mich., Apr. 11, 1940; d. George and Edith (Hanel) B. Diploma, Borgess Sch. Nursing, 1963; BS in Biology, Nazareth Coll., 1964; BSN, Marillac Coll., 1969; MSN, St. Louis U., 1971. Cert. nurse practitioner U. Colo., 1979. Coll. health nurse Nazareth Coll., Kalamazoo, 1963-64; staff nurse Lee Meml. Hosp., Dowagiac, Mich., 1964-65, St. John Hosp., Detroit, 1966-68; cardiovascular clin. specialist Borgess Hosp., Kalamazoo, 1971-79; adult nurse practitioner Internat. Com of Red Cross, Cath. Relief Svc., Bangkok, Thailand, 1980-82, SOME Health Svc., Washington, 1983-85, Health Care for Homeless, Washington, 1985-86, Christ House Med. Facility, Washington, 1986—. Nominee Nurse of Yr., Washington. Mem. Nurse Practitioner Assn. Home: 3300 Chauncey Pl # 302 Mount Rainier MD 20712-1001

BENDER, ARTHUR STILLMAN, internist; b. Springfield, Mass., July 7, 1938; s. Theodore George and Faye (August) B.; m. Susan Kathleen Gabroy, Nov. 2, 1963; children: Penelope Ann, Arthur Kenneth. BA, Yale U., 1959; MD, U. Va., 1963. Diplomate Am. Bd. Internal Medicine. Intern U. Va. Hosp., 1963-64, asst. resident, 1964-65, 66-67, hematology fellow, 1965-66, chief med. resident, 1967-68; pvt. practice Charlottesville, Va., 1970-73; founding ptnr. Internal Medicine, Ltd., Charlottesville, 1973—; pres. med. staff Martha Jefferson Hosp., Charlottesville, 1981-82, trustee, 1984-91, chmn. bd., 1989-90; mem. Martha Jefferson Hosp. Health Svcs. Corp. Bd., 1992—. Maj. U.S. Army, 1968-70, Korea. Office: Internal Medicine Ltd 1011 E Jefferson St Charlottesville VA 22902-5327

BENDER, DORIS RAE, pediatric psychiatric nurse; b. Cedar Rapids, Iowa, Mar. 4, 1950; d. Raymond William and Jutta Waltraud (Otte) B.; m. Michael Owen Hodges, Mar. 30, 1974 (div. 1978); 1 child, Matthew Karl. BS in Nursing, U. Iowa, 1972; MA in Health Service Mgmt. and Computer Resource Mgmt., Webster U., Denver, 1987. Head nurse Prince George's Gen. Hosp., Cheverly, Md., 1978-79, McAuley Neuropsychiat. Inst., St. Mary's Hosp., San Francisco, 1979-81; clin. mgr. Rocky Mountain Hosp., Denver, 1981-85; head nurse Bethesda PsycHealth Hosp., Denver, 1985-89, Nat. Jewish Ctr., Denver, 1989—. Capt. Nurse Corps, U.S. Army, 1970-78; lt. col. USAR. 1978—. Presbyterian. Office: Nat Jewish Ctr 1400 Jackson St Denver CO 80206-2761

BENDER, HARVEY W., JR., cardiac and thoracic surgeon; b. Corpus Christi, Tex., 1933. MD, Baylor U., 1959. Diplomate Am. Bd. Surgery. Intern. Johns Hopkins Hosp., 1959-60, res., 1960-61, 1963-67; surgeon John Hopkins Hosp., 1967-71; asst. prof. surgery John Hopkins U., Sch. Medicine, 1967-70; assoc. prof. surgery John Hopkins U. Sch. Medicine, 1970-71; sr. asst. surgeon US PHS, 1961-63; prof. surgery, chmn. cardiac and thoracic surgery Vanderbilt U. (Sch. Medicine), 1971—; cons. Va. Hosp., Balt., Md., 1968-71; consulting surgeon Good Samaritan Hosp., Balt., Md., 1968-71; formerly chmn. Am. Bd. Thoracic Surgery. Mem. Am. Assn. for Thoracic Surg., Am. Coll. of Surgeons, Am. Surgical Assn. Office: Vanderbilt U Hosp 2986 Venderbilt Clinic 1301 22nd Ave S Nashville TN 37232-5734

BENDER, JAMES FREDERICK, psychologist, educator, university dean; b. Dayton, Ohio, Apr. 6, 1905; s. Fred Jacob and Bertha (Zimmerman) B.; m. Anne Parsons, June 25, 1925; m. Gertrude Moller, Jan. 21, 1966 (div. 1967); m. Vera E. Sattler, Feb. 21, 1968. B.S., Columbia U., 1928, Ph.D., 1939; D.H.L. (hon.), Adelphi U., 1980. Lic. psychologist, N.Y. Psychol. examiner Personnel Bur., CCNY, 1928-37; lectr., adj. prof. psychology Bklyn. Poly. Inst., 1928-40; chmn. dept. speech, dir. Speech and Hearing Center; chmn. div. lang., lit. and arts Queens Coll., 1937-44; dir. Nat. Inst. Human Relations, 1944-54; pres. James F. Bender Assos., 1954-74; prof. bus. adminstrn. Adelphi U., Garden City, 1960-66; dean Adelphi U. (Sch. Bus.), 1964-66, acting dean, 1973-74; dean Center Banking and Money Mgmt., 1974-77, dean spl. programs, 1977-85; prof. bus. adminstrn. Pace Coll., 1966-68; prof. bus. adminstrn., dir. Enterprise Edn. N.Y. Inst. Tech., 1985-87; prof. C.W. Post Coll. of L.I. U.; dir. Money Mgmt. Inst., 1969-73; lic. psychologist, 1958—; dir. sales tng. Lehigh Nav. Coal Sales Co., 1965—; also dir.; sr. cons. Kimberly-Clark Corp.; dean Kimberly Clark Mktg. Inst., 1958-59; lectr. Columbia U., 1950-57, mem. alumni council, 1950-59; Cons. Adelphi-Suffolk Coll.; dir. Follett Corp., Tech Products, Profit Motivation Service, Inc., First Multifund Inc., First Multifund for Income, Inc., Tapewatchers Fund, Inc.; pres., dir. Enterprise Fund of Adelphi U., Inc., Fidelity N.Y. Savs. & Loan Assn., First Coinvestors Inc., 1985-88; chmn. exec. com. Nat. Schs. Com. Econ. Edn., 1965-81; chmn. Career Planning Comm. Nassau County, N.Y., 1966-67. Author: (with Victor A. Fields) Voice and Diction, 1944, The Technique of Executive Leadership, 1950, (with Lee Graham) Your Way to Popularity and Personal Power, 1950, How to Sleep, Personality Structure of Stuttering, How to Talk Well, 1949, Salesman's Mispronunciations, Make Your Business Letters Make Friends, 1952, Victory Over Fear, 1952, Profits from Business Letters, 1952, How to Sell Well, 1961, 10 Biggest Mistakes Speakers Make, 1963, Our Mixed and Mixed Up Economy, 1972, (with Judy Thornton Stark) You, 1973; also articles. Trustee Queens Speech and Hearing Service Center, 1941-73, Friends Acad., 1957-62, Human Resources Found., 1965—; chmn. Div. II Tri-State United Way, 1977; hon. chmn. N.Y. March of Dimes Dinner, 1975. Recipient Owl award as outstanding alumnus Sch. Gen. Studies Columbia U., 1973; Disting. Teaching award Am. Econ. Found.; L.I. Bus. Rev. Disting. Leadership award, 1975; Honor award Nassau County council Boy Scouts Am., 1980; James F. Bender endowed professorship named in his honor C.W. Post Center L.I. U., 1975; James F. Bender Vis. Professorship in banking and money mgmt. Adelphi U., 1980; hon. past commdr. Coeur De Lion Commandery No. 23, Knights Templar, 1986. Fellow AAAS, Am. Speech and Hearing Assn.; mem. Am. Speech Correction Assn. (past councillor), N.Y. State Assn. Applied Psychology (exec. com. 1942-44), Am. Psychol. Assn., N.Y. Met. Assn. Psychologists, N.Y. Soc. Clin. Psychologists, Nat. Vocat. Guidance Assn., Nat. Council Family Relations, Emerson Lit. Soc., Acad. Mgmt., Fin. Execs. Inst., Internat. Assn. Fin. Planning, Adelphi U. Alumni Assn. (hon.), Sigma Chi. Mem. Religious Soc. of Friends. Republican. Clubs: Columbia Univ, Garden City Country, Manhasset Bath and Tennis. Lodge: Masons.

BENDER, JOEL REED, health science association administrator; b. N.D., Oct. 9, 1947; m. Lynn Zagora Bender; children: Justin, Laura. BS, N.D. State U., Fargo, 1969; MSPH, U. N.C., Chapel Hill, 1972; PhD in Environ. Scis., Drexel U., Phila., 1974; MD, U. Ala., Birmingham, 1978. Diplomate Am. Bd. Preventive Medicine. Instr. Dept. Cmty. Medicine U. Ala., Birmingham, 1976-78; med. cons. Haskell Lab., Wilmington, Del., 1979-80, mgr. field svcs. divsn., 1980-81; sr. occupational health physician E.I. duPont de Nemours, Aiken, S.C., 1981-82; med. supr. E.I. duPont de Nemours, Chattanooga, 1982-84; med. dir. Conoco, Houston, 1984-87; v.p. health, safety & environ. Owens Corning, Toledo, 1987-95, v.p. health scis., CMO, 1995—; dir. Am. Indsl. Health Coun., Washington D.C., 1996—; pres. N.W. Ohio Hospice Assn., Toledo, 1996—; past mem. bd. dirs. Am. Coll. Occup. & Environ. Medicine, Arlington Heights, Ill. Contbr. numerous articles in field to profl. jours. Office: Owens Corning Fiberglass Tower Toledo OH 43659

BENDER, MAURICE, health science administrator, consultant; b. N.Y.C., July 22, 1918; s. Max and Leah (Levitin) B.; m. Rosine Winokur, Dec. 23, 1941; children: Laurie Ann, David Max. BA, Johns Hopkins U., 1938; BS in Pharmacy, Temple U., 1944, MS in Pharmacy, 1945; PhD, Georgetown U., 1950. Registered pharmacist, Pa., Md., Alaska. Bioassayist, Munch Lab., Upper Darby, Pa., 1943-45; pharmacologist Fish Tech. Lab., College Park,

Md., 1945-48; toxicologist, Army Med. Ctr., 1951-52; chemist Eastern Regional Research Lab., U.S. Dept. Agr., Phila., 1948-51; asst. prof. biochemistry Rutgers U., Newark, 1952-55; biochemist div. Indsl. Research and Services, Bur. Comml. Fisheries, U.S. Dept. Interior, Washington, 1955-58; pub. health research program analyst div. gen. med. services NIH, Bethesda, 1958-59, exec. sec. cancer chemotherapy study sect., 1959-60; chief research and tng. grants br. div. air pollution USPHS, Bethesda, 1960-65, asst. to adminstr. Health Services and Mental Health Adminstrn., Rockville, Md., 1970-72; asst. dir. Statewide Air Pollution Research Ctr., U. Calif.-Riverside, 1965-67; spl. asst. to commr. Nat. Air Pollution Control Adminstrn., HEW, Washington, 1967-68, dir. extramural research and devel. Consumer Protection and Environ. Health Service, 1968-70, team chmn. Fed. Assistance Streamlining Task Force, Office of Sec., 1970, dir. Arctic Health Research Ctr., Fairbanks, Alaska, 1972-73; exec. dir. Comprehensive Health Planning Council Spokane County, Inc., Spokane, Wash., 1973-76; exec. dir. Rock Island Health Council, Inc. (Ill.), 1976-77; health programs mgmt. and planning cons., Bellevue, Wash., 1977—; mem. King County Health Planning Council, Seattle, 1978—. Contbr. articles to profl. publs. Bd. dirs. Residence East, Bellevue, 1984; mem. service com. RSVP, Seattle, 1984. Served to cpl. AUS, 1942-43. Recipient Cert. of Honor, Temple U., 1969; spl. award USPHS, 1971. Fellow Am. Pub. Health Assn., Am. Inst. Chemists, Royal Soc. Health; mem. AMA (affiliate), Inst. Food Technologists (profl. emeritus), Am. Pharm. Assn., Am. Soc. Pub. Adminstrn., Am. Chem. Soc. (emeritus), AAAS, Wash. Acad. Sci. (emeritus), Am. Inst. Nutrition (emeritus), Delta Sigma Theta, Rho Pi Phi. Unitarian. Home: 1684-152 2d Ave NE Apt 103 Bellevue WA 98007-4278

BENDER, MICHAEL A., geneticist; b. N.Y.C., July 25, 1929; s. Clifford Arthur and Margaret (Rigg) B.; m. Belinda Susan Gilmer, June 1979; children: Michèle, Leslie, Sabina, William. BS, U. Wash., 1952; PhD, Johns Hopkins U., 1956. Postdoctoral fellow Johns Hopkins U., Balt., 1956-58, vis. prof. radiology, 1973-75; group leader Oak Ridge (Tenn.) Nat. Lab., 1958-69; assoc. prof. Vanderbilt U., Nashville, 1969-73; sr. scientist Brookhaven Nat. Lab., Upton, N.Y., 1975—; mem. Nat. Commn. on Radiation Protection, Bethesda, Md., 1987—; mem. editorial bd. Mutation Rsch., Radiation Protection Dosimetry. Contbr. articles to profl. publs. Fellow AAAS; mem. Radiation Rsch. Soc., Am. Soc. for Cell Biology, Am. Soc. Photobiology. Office: Brookhaven Nat Lab Med Dept 30 Bell Ave Upton NY 11973-9999

BENDER, PAMELA ANN, nurse; b. Hiedelberg, Germany, Aug. 22, 1961; d. Joseph Francis and loretta Kathryn (Yoder) B. BSN, Ea. Memonite Coll., 1983. RN, Ariz. Staff nurse Sierra Vista (Ariz.) Community Hosp., 1983-84; staff nurse neonatal ICU Maricopa Med. Ctr., Phoenix, 1984-86, staff nurse, 1986-90; staff nurse ICU, 1986-89; asst. head nurse surg. ICU Maricopa Med. Ctr., Phoenix, 1988-90; staff nurse ICU Meml. Hosp. Med. Ctr., Cumberland, Md., 1990-91, head nurse High Level Care Unit, 1991-92; staff nurse ICU Nurse Works Inc. Naval Hosp., Bethesda, Md., 1992-93; govt. svc. staff nurse Adult Pediatrics ICU Bethesda (Md.) Naval Hosp., 1993—. Mem. Am. Assn. Critical Care Nurses, NAFE. Methodist. Home: 18915 Port Haven Pl Germantown MD 20874-5381

BENDER, RANDI LAINE, occupational therapist; b. Omaha, July 17, 1947; d. Kenneth Norman and Lois (Harmon) Anderson; m. Howard Jeffrey Bender, May 22, 1971; children: Rebecca Jennifer, Heidi Julia (dec. March 1990). BS, U. Ill., 1970; MS, Calif. Coll. for Health Scis., 1996. Registered occupational therapist. Occupational therapist Westchester County Med. Ctr., Valhalla, N.Y., 1970-76, UCP Therapeutic Nursery, Washington, 1987-89, Edward Mazique Parent Child Ctr., Washington, 1989, Great Oak Ctr., Silver Spring, Md., 1989-92, Montgomery Primary Achievement Ctr., Silver Spring, 1993—; co-monitor Riverdale Presbyn. Ch.; actress Riverdale Players. Mem. Coun. for Exceptional Children, Am. Occupational Therapy Assn., DAR, Riverdale Presbyn. Ch. Democrat. Home: 4200 Sheridan St Hyattsville MD 20782-2137

BENDINELLI, MAURO GIUSEPPE, microbiology educator; b. Massarosa, Lucca, Italy, Dec. 20, 1934; s. Cino and Elda (Ricci) B.; m. Gabriella Moriconi, Oct. 30, 1968; children: Cino, Silvia. MD, U. Pisa (Italy), 1959; PhD, U. Rome, 1967. Rsch. asst. U. Pisa, 1959-65, asst. prof., 1967-69, assoc. prof., 1970-74, prof. microbiology, 1975—, chmn. dept. biomedicine, 1987-94, dir. Retrovirus Ctr., 1994—; vis. prof. U. South Fla., Tampa, 1980, 83. Editor: Mycobacterium Tuberculosis, Interactions with Immune System, 1988, Coksackieviruse A General Update, 1988, Virus Induced Immuno Suppression, 1990, Neuropathogenic Viruses and Immunity, 1991, Pseudomonas Aeruginosa as an Opportunistic Pathogen, 1993, Fungal Infections and Immunity, 1993, Pulmonary Infections and Immunity, 1994, Enteric Infections and Immunity, 1996, DNA Tumor Viruse: Oncogenic Mechanisms, 1996, Microorganisms and Autoimmune Disease, 1996. Home: Via Sant Antonio 1, I-56125 Pisa Italy Office: Dept Biomedicine, Via San Zeno 35, I-56127 Pisa Italy

BENENSON, ABRAM SALMON, epidomiologist; b. Napanoch, N.Y., Jan. 22, 1914; s. Jacob and Sonia (Mekler) B.; m. Regina Van Aalten, May 20, 1939; children: Michael W., Thomas R., James S., Sonia A. BA, Cornell U., Ithaca, N.Y., 1933; MD, Cornell U., N.Y.C., 1937. Diplomate Am. Bd. Pathology, Preventive Medicine, Microbiology. Commanding officer Tropical Rsch. Med. Lab., San Juan, 1952-54; dir. exptl. medicine U.S. Army, Ft. Detrick, Md., 1954-55; dir. immunology div. Walter Reed Inst. Rsch., Washington, 1957-60, dir. communicable disease and immunology, 1960-62; dir. sci. adv. SEATO Cholera Rsch. Lab., Dacca, East Pakistan, 1962-66; prof. preventive medicine and microbiology Jefferson Med. Coll., Phila., 1966-69; prof., chmn. dept. of community medicine U. Ky. Coll. of Medicine, Lexington, 1969-77; dir. Gorgas Meml. Lab., Panama, 1977-81; prof. divsn. of epidemiology biostats. Grad. Sch. Pub. Health, San Diego State U., 1982-92, prof. emeritus, 1992—, head, 1982-90; prof. dept. family and preventive medicine U. Calif., San Diego, 1982—; dir. com. immunization, dir. subcom. disease control Armed Forces Epidemiol. Bd., Washington. Editor: Control of Communicable Diseases in Man, 1970, 75, 80, 85, 90, 95; contbr. articles to profl. jours. Bd. dirs. Project Concern Internat. Task Force on AIDS, San Diego County. Col. U.S. Army, 1940-62. Recipient award for excellence APHA, 1991, John Snow award, 1992. Jewish. Home: 6619 Claremore Ave San Diego CA 92120-3121

BENENSON, ESTHER SIEV (MRS. WILLIAM BENENSON), nursing home administrator, gerontologist; b. Jerusalem (parents Am. citizens); d. Joshua and Anna (Sanders) Siev; B.S., Hunter Coll., 1972, M.S., 1974; M.Ed., Tchrs. Coll., Columbia U., 1976, Ed.D. in Gerontology, 1981; m. William Benenson, Sept. 15, 1957; children: Michael J., Sharon G., Amy L., Blanche S. Exec. dir. Flushing (N.Y.) Manor Nursing Home, 1959—, Flushing Manor Care Center, 1974—. Registered nurse. Adj. assoc. prof. C.W. Post Coll., L.I. U., 1972-77, also mem. adv. bd., dept. health care and public adminstrn.; mem. Bd. Examiners Licensing Nursing Home Adminstrs. N.Y. State, 1970-74; adv. council N.Y. State Health Planning Commn., 1974; bd. dirs. Health Systems Agy. of N.Y.C., 1994-96, 1st v.p. Queensboro Council Social Welfare. Fellow Am. Coll. Health Care Adminstrs., Am. Acad. Med. Adminstrs., Royal Soc. Health; mem. APHA, Soc. Public Health Educators, Gerontol. Soc., Soc. N.Y. State Health Facilities Assn. Inc., Greater N.Y. Health Care Facilities Assn.

BENES, SUSAN CARLETON, neuro-ophthalmologist; b. Cleve., Jan. 2, 1948; d. Edward Fulton and Rita Elyse (True) Carleton; m. James David Benes, Dec. 27, 1969; children: Jennifer, David, Olivia. BS, U. Mich., 1970, cert. tchr., 1969; MD, Med. Coll. Pa., 1975. Diplomate Am. Bd. Ophthalmology. Resident in internal medicine Lankenau Hosp., Phila., 1975-76; resident in ophthalmology Wills Eye Hosp., Phila., 1976-79, fellow in neuro-ophthalmology, 1979-80, staff physician Wills Eye and Grad. Hosp., 1980-81; lectr. in neuro-ophthalmology Kenyatta U., Nairobi, Kenya, 1980; asst. prof. neuro-ophthalmology Ohio State U., Columbus, 1981-86, assoc. prof., 1987—; cons., Quito, Ecuador, 1985, Dept. Energy in Marshall Islands, South Pacific, 1987; cons. surgeon blindness and malnutrition survey, Honduras, 1992; humanitarian aid, tchr., surgeon, Republic of Georgia, 1995. Contbr. chpts. to books, articles to profl. jours. Bd. govs. First Cmty. Ch.; leader Camp Fire Girls, Columbus, 1983-88. Recipient Wakian Service award Camp Fire, Inc., 1986; grantee NIH, 1984-87, 87-94. Fellow Am. Acad. Ophthalmology; mem. AMA, Ohio State Med. Assn., Franklin County Med. Soc., Alpha Omega Alpha, Kappa Kappa Gamma.

BENET, LESLIE ZACHARY, pharmacokineticist; b. Cin., May 17, 1937; s. Jonas John and Esther Racie (Hirschfeld) B.; m. Carol Ann Levin, Sept. 8, 1960; children: Reed Michael, Gillian Vivia. AB in English, U. Mich., 1959, BS in Pharmacy, 1960, MS in Pharm. Chemistry, 1962; PhD in Pharm. Chemistry, U. Calif., San Francisco, 1965; PharmD (hon.), Uppsala U., Sweden, 1987; PhD (hon.), Leiden U., The Netherlands, 1995. Asst. prof. pharmacy Wash. State U., Pullman, 1965-69; asst. prof. pharmacy and pharm. chemistry U. Calif., San Francisco, 1969-71, assoc. prof., 1971-76, prof., 1976—, vice chmn. dept. pharmacy, 1973-78, chmn. dept. pharmacy, 1978-96, dir. drug studies unit, 1977—, dir. drug kinetics and dynamics ctr., 1979—; chmn. dept. biopharm. scis., 1996—; mem. pharmacology study sect. NIH, Washington, 1977-81, chmn., 1979-81, mem. pharmacol. scis. rev. com., 1984-88, chmn., 1986-88; mem. generic drugs adv. com. FDA, Washington, 1990-94, mem. Sci. Bd., 1992—; mem. sci. adv. bd. SmithKline Beecham Pharms., 1989-92, Pharmetrix, 1989-92, Alteon, Inc., 1993—, TheraTech, Inc., 1993—; chmn. bd. AvMax, Inc., 1994—; bd. dirs. Medication Mgmt. Techs., Inc. Editor Jour. Pharmacokinetics and Biopharmaceutics, 1976—; assoc. editor Pharmacology and Therapeutics, 1995—; editl. bd. Pharmacology, 1979—, Pharmacy Internat., 1979-82, Pharmaceutical Rsch., 1983-95, ISI Atlas of Sci.: Pharmacology, 1988-89, Pharmaceutical News, 1994—, The Effect of Disease States on Drug Pharmacokinetics, 1976, Pharmacokinetic Basis for Drug Treatment, 1984, Pharmacokinetics: A Modern View, 1984, ISI Atlas of Sci.: Pharmacology, 1988-89, Integration of Pharmacokinetics, Pharmacodynamics and Toxicokinetics in Rational Drug Development, 1992, Clinical Applications of Mifepristone (RU486) and Other Antiprogestins, 1993; contbr. numerous articles to profl. jours. Appt. to Forum on Drug Devel. and Regulation, 1988. Fellow Acad. Pharm. Scis. (pres. 1985-86, chmn. basic pharmaceutics sect. 1976-77, mem.-at-large exec. com. 1979-83, Rsch. Achievement award 1982), AAAS (mem.-at-large exec. com. pharm. scis. sect. 1978-81, 91-95, chair 1996—), Am. Assn. Pharm. Scientists (pres. 1986, treas. 1987, bd. dirs. 1988-93, Disting. Pharm. Scientist award 1989, Disting. Svc. award 1996); mem. Inst. Medicine NAS (forum on drug devel. and regulation 1988-94, chmn. com. on antiprogestins, 1993, membership com. 1994—, chmn. other health professions sect. 1995—), AAUP, Am. Found. for Pharm. Edn. (bd. dirs. 1987—, Disting. Svc. "Profile" award 1993), Am. Coll. Clin. Pharmacology (Disting. Svc. award 1988), ISSX (councillor 1992-96, treas.-elect 1996—), Am. Pharm. Assn., Am. Soc. Clin. Pharmacology and Therapeutics (Rawls-Palmer award and lectureship 1995), Am. Soc. for Pharmacology and Exptl. Therapeutics, Generic Pharm. Industry Assn. (mem. blue ribbon com. on generic medicines 1990), Internat. Pharm. Fedn. (bd. pharm. scis. 1988-, chair 1996—), Drug Info. Assn., Am. Coll. Clin. Pharmacy (therapeutic frontiers lectr. 1995), Am. Assn. Colls. Pharmacy (Volwiler Rsch. Achievement award 1991, pres. 1993-94, bd. dirs. 1992-95), Sigma Xi, Rho Chi (Ann. Lecture award 1990), Phi Lambda Sigma. Home: 53 Beach Rd Belvedere CA 94920-2364 Office: U Calif San Francisco Dept Biopharm Scis San Francisco CA 94143

BÉNÉZECH, MICHEL HENRI, criminologist, researcher; b. Agen, France, Oct. 1, 1942; s. René and Marguerite (Charles) B.; m. Claude Christine Mandraut, Dec. 22, 1994. MD, U. Bordeaux, France, 1969, Forensic Physician, 1970, Psychiatrist, 1973, LLD, 1973. Diplomate in medicine and criminology. Lectr. Nat. Sch. Magistrature, Bordeaux, 1970-85; assoc. prof. forensic medicine U. Bordeaux, 1989-92; head dept. psychiatry Penitentiary System, Bordeaux, 1979—; lectr. law U. Bordeaux, 1980—; cons. in legal psychiatry, 1979—; expert in law cts., Bordeaux, 1974—; rsch. on mentally disordered offenders. Author: L'information en médecine, 1993; contbr. articles to profl. jours. Mem. World Forensic Psychiatry and Psychology Assn., Internat. Acad. Legal Medicine, N.Y. Acad. Scis. Office: Centre Hosp Charles Perrens, 121 Rue de la Béchade, 33076 Bordeaux France

BENFIELD, JOHN RICHARD, surgeon; b. Vienna, Austria, June 24, 1931; came to U.S., 1938, naturalized, 1945; s. Richard and Charlotte Lola Benfield; m. Joyce A. Cohler, Dec. 22, 1963; children: Richard L., Robert E., Nancy J. A.B., Columbia U., 1952; M.D., U. Chgo., 1955. Diplomate Am. Bd. Surgery, Am. Bd. Thoracic Surgery (bd. dirs. 1982-88). Intern Columbia-Presbyterian Hosp., N.Y.C., 1955-56; E.H. Andrews fellow in thoracic surgery U. Chgo., 1956-57; chief resident and instr. in surgery U. Chgo. Clinics, 1962-64, resident in surgery, 1956-57, 59-63; asst. prof. surgery U. Wis., 1964-67; asst. prof. UCLA, 1967-69, assoc. prof., 1969-73, prof., 1973-77, clin. prof., 1978-88; prof. surgery, chief cardiothoracic surgery, vice chmn. surgery U. Calif. Davis Med. Ctr., Sacramento, 1988-95, prof. surgery, chief thoracic surgery, 1995—; attending surgeon V.A Martinez Med. Ctr., 1988—; courtesy staff Kaiser Permanente Med. Ctr., Sacramento, 1988—; James Utley prof. surgery, chmn. dept. surgery Boston U., 1977; chmn. surgery City of Hope Nat. Med. Ctr., Duarte, Calif., 1978-87; bd. dirs. Am. Bd. Thoracic Surgery, 1982-88; cons. U.S. Naval Med. Ctr., San Diego, 1968-88; mem. sr. staff VA Wadsworth Med. Ctr., L.A., 1978-88. Editor Current Problems in Cancer, 1975-86; mem. editorial bd. Annals of Thoracic Surgery, 1979—, Annals of Surg. Oncology, 1994—; assoc. editor Annals of Thoracic Surgery, 1987—; contbr. articles to prof. jours., chpts. to books. Sec., trustee Univ. Synagogue, Los Angeles. Served as capt. M.C. U.S. Army, 1957-59, Korea. Grantee Life Ins. Med. Rsch., 1962-66, Am. Heart Assn., 1968-71; USPHS, 1971-92. Mem. ACS (bd. govs. 1982-88, 92—), Am. Surg. Assn., Am. Assn. Thoracic Surgery, Am. Assn. Cancer Rsch., Am. Med. Writers Assn., Internat. Assn. Study Lung Cancer, Internat. Soc. Surgery, Calif. Med. Soc., Ctrl. Surg. Assn., L.A. Acad. Medicine, The Royal Soc. Medicine (Gt. Britain), The Transplantation Soc., Soc. Thoracic Surgeons (v.p. 1994-95, pres. 1995-96), Soc. Univ. Surgeons, Pacific Coast Surg. Assn. (v.p. 1995-96), Soc. Surg. Oncology, Am. Coll. Chest Physicians (pres. 1996—), Western Thoracic Surgeons Assn. (pres. 1989-90), Internat. Soc. Surgeons, Thoracic Surgery Dirs. Assn. (pres. 1995—). Office: U Calif Davis Med Ctr 4301 X St Sacramento CA 95817-2214

BENHAMOU, GUY, physician; b. Oujda, Morocco, June 13, 1933; s. Rene and Claire Benhamou; m. Rachel Bensimon, 1960; children: Judith, Myriam, Dinah. MD, Faculty Medicine Paris. Prof. Faculty Medicine Paris, 1970—. Contbr. articles to profl. jours. Mem. Assn. Surgery, Nat. Coll. Surgery, Internat. Soc. Surgery, Nat. Soc. Gastroenterology. Home: 82 Bd Bineau, 92200 Neuilly/Seine Seine, France Office: Hosp Bichat 46R, Henri Huchard, 75018 Paris France

BENIAN, GUY M., medical educator. Asst. prof. Emory U. Sch. Medicine, Atlanta. Office: Emory U Sch Medicine Atlanta GA 30322*

BENISON, BETTY SUE, therapist; b. Irving, Ky., Aug. 25, 1933; d. Jack Everett Bryant and Mable Clara (Daniel) Welsh; m. Raymond Daniel Benison, May 25, 1959 (div. May 1977); 1 child, Brian Douglas; m. George Everett Robertson, Nov. 10, 1979 (dec. July 1987). BS, La. State U., 1955; MA, U. Mich., 1959; PhD, U. N.Mex., 1968; MS, Tex. Women's U., 1990. Diplomate Am. Bd. Sexology; cert. clin. hypnotherapist. Instr. C.E. Byrd H.S., Shreveport, 1955-56, Miss. State Coll. Women, Columbus, 1956-57, U. Mich., Ann Arbor, 1957-59; asst. prof. Stephen F. Austin Univ., Nacogdoches, Tex., 1959-60, U. North Tex., Denton, 1960-65, U. N.Mex., Albuquerque, 1965-69; prof. Tex. Christian U., Ft. Worth, 1969—. Fellow Soc. Pub. Health Assn., Am. Acad. Clin. Sexologists; mem. Internat. Med. & Dental Hypnotherapy Assn., AAUP, Phi Delta Kappa. Home: 3501 Bellaire Dr N #11 Fort Worth TX 76109-2109 Office: Tex Christian U 209 Rickel Bldg 3005 Fort Worth TX 76129

BENITEZ, JOHN GRISWOLD, medical toxicologist, emergency physician; b. St. Louis, July 1, 1957; s. Vicente and Jane (Griswold) B.; m. Linda Gail Allison, May 2, 1982. BA, So. Ill. U., 1978, MD, 1981; MPH, U. Pitts., 1995. Diplomate Am. Bd. Med. Toxicology, Am. Bd. Emergency Medicine. Intern surgery Southwestern Mich. Area Health Edn. Ctr., Kalamazoo, 1981-82; emergency physician Hillsboro (Ill.) Hosp., Hillsboro, Ill., 1982-84, Sarah Bush Lincoln Hosp., Mattoon, Ill., 1983-84; staff physician Community Health Improvement Ctr., Decatur, Ill., 1983-84; emergency physician St John's Hosp., Springfield, Ill., 1984-88; fellow in hyperbaric medicine St. Luke's Hosp., Milw., 1988; emergency med. svcs. project med. dir. Bromenn Med. Ctr., Normal, Ill., 1988-89; instr., fellow in clin. toxicology Vanderbilt U. Med. Ctr., Nashville, 1989-91; clin. toxicology fellowship dir., asst. prof. U. Pitts., 1991—; chmn. adverse drug reaction com. U. Pitts. Med. Ctr., 1991-95; med. dir. Pitts. Poison Ctr., 1993—; Intox Project Internat. Programme on Chemical Safety World Health Orgn., 1995—; emergency medicine edn. chmn. St. John's Hosp., Springfield, Ill., 1984-88; clin. assoc. Dept. Surgery So. Ill. U. Sch. Medicine, 1986-89; affiliate faculty, mem. AHA Ill. affiliate, Normal, 1988-89; asst. state dir. basic trauma life support, Normal, Ill., 1988-89. Med. cons. disaster svcs. ARC, Springfield, Ill., 1987-88. Recipient Am. Acad. Clin. Toxicology Rsch. award, 1990. Fellow Am. Coll. Emergency Medicine; mem. Am. Coll. Sports Medicine, Soc. Acad. Emergency Medicine, Am. Coll. Emergency Physicians (chmn. emergency med. svc. Ill. chpt. 1988-89), Am. Acad. Clin. Toxicology, Wilderness Med. Soc. Office: Toxicology Treatment Prgrm 200 Lothrop St Pittsburgh PA 15213-2546

BENJAMIN, BRY, internist; b. N.Y.C., Oct. 20, 1924; m. Marianne Benjamin. BS, Yale U., 1945; MD, Harvard Med. Sch., 1947. Diplomate Am. Bd. Internal Medicine. Intern Lenox Hill Hosp., N.Y.C., 1947-48; resident Goldwater Meml. Hosp., N.Y.C., 1948-50; fellow in psychosomatic medicine Cin. Gen. Hosp., 1950-51; resident in internal medicine SUNY, Bklyn., 1953-54; resident in comprehensive care Cornell U. Med. Coll., N.Y.C., 1954-55; asst. clin. prof. medicine Cornell Univ. Med. Coll., N.Y.C., 1957—; asst. attending physician N.Y. Hosp., 1957—; assoc. attending physician Manhattan Eye, Ear and Throat Hosp., 1979—; attending physician Beth Israel Hosp., N.Y.C., 1995—; researcher human ecology study program Cornell U., 1955-63. Fellow Am. Coll. Physicians, N.Y. Acad. Medicine; mem. AAAS, AMA, Am. Soc. Internal Medicine, Am. Psychomatic Soc., Am. Geriatric Soc., Am. Pub. Health Assn., N.Y. Soc. Internal Medicine, N.Y. State Med. Soc., N.Y. Acad. Scis., Harvey Soc., Choice in Dying, N.Y. County Med. Soc. (managed care task force 1996—, pub. health com. 1975—), Alpha Omega Alpha. Office: 14 E 63d St New York NY 10021

BENJAMIN, GEORGES CURTIS, emergency physician, consultant; b. Chgo., Sept. 28, 1952; s. George and Tessie Cozie (Edwards) B.; m. Yvette Josphanie Janisse; children: Stephanie, Kali. BS, Ill. Inst. Tech., 1973; MD, U. Ill., 1978. Diplomate Am. Bd. Emergency Medicine, Internal Medicine, Medical Examiners. Intern and resident internal medicine Brooke Army Medical Ctr., San Antonio, Tex., 1978-81; dept. emergency medicine Madigan Army Medical Ctr., Tacoma, Wash., 1981-83; chief emergency medicine Walter Reed Army Med. Ctr., Washington, 1983-87; chair. dept. com. health & ambulatory care Dist. Columbia Gen. Hosp., Washington, 1987-90; commr. pub. health Dist. Columbia, 1990-91; health policy cons., 1992-95; emergency physician Holy Cross Com. Hosp., Silver Spring, Md., 1991-95; dep. sec. Pub. Health State of Md., Balt., 1995—; emergency physician Patuxent Naval Air Station, Patuxent River, Md., 1989, Nisqually Clinic, Yelm, Wash., 1981-82, Allenmore Com. Hosp., Tacoma, 1981-82; house internist Greater Southeast Com. Hosp., Washington, 1985-87; clinical instr. emergency medicine, Georgetown U., 1988—; adj. prof. Health Care Scis., 1993, asst. prof. medicine Uniformed Svcs. U. Health Scis., Bethesda, Md., 1984-87, 90—. Editorial bd. Jour. Nat. Medical Assn., 1986-93; reviewer Am. Coll. Physician Execs., 1989—, Am. Jour. Emergency Medicine, 1986—, Military Medicine, 1983-87; contbr. articles to profl. jours. Bd. dirs. Hosp. Sock Children, Boarder Baby Project, Inc. Whiteman Walker Clinic Inc.; adv. bd. D.C. Commn. Pub. Health Disability and Injury Prevention Program, 1993, Montgomery County HIV/AIDS Citizens, 1992-93; bd. trustees Am. Cancer Soc.; bd. govs. Medico Chirurgical Soc. D.C.; mem. D.C. Emergency Med. Svcs. Com., 1990-91, D.C. State Health Coord. Coun., 1990-91; gov. commn. Welfare Policy State of Md., 1993. With M.C. U.S. Army, 1978-87, USAR, 1974-78. Recipient Cert. Recognition, 1993, Coun. Govs. Svc. award, 1991, Disting. Pub. Svc. award, 1991, Cert. Appreciation Best Friends of D.C., 1991, Cert. Appreciation D.C. Pub. Schs., 1991, Svc. award Medico Chirurgical Soc., 1990, Recognition award D.C.G.H. Medical/Dental staff, 1990; decorated Army Commendation medal, 1983, Commanders award, 1981, Eisenhower Proclamation medal, 1970. Fellow ACP, Am. Coll. Emergency Physicians (Nat. Key Contact 1987-90, 92-95, gov. affairs com. 1993, D.C. chpt. v.p. 1988-90, D.C. chpt. pres. 1989-90, liaison rep. emergency nurses assn. 1992-95, nat. health policy com. Dallas 1992-93); mem. APHA, Nat. Med. Assn. (mil. and aerospace medicine sect. sec. 1983, nat. co-chmn. 1985, 86, nat. chmn. 1987, emergency medicine nat. chmn. 1990-93), Medico Chirurgical Soc. (violence task force chmn. 1992-94), Am. Coll. Physicians Execs. Home: 108 Pembrooke View Ln Gaithersburg MD 20877-3783

BENJAMIN, LUDY THOMPSON, JR., psychology educator; b. Corpus Christi, Tex., Dec. 26, 1945; s. Ludy Thompson Sr. and Mary Kate (Jones) B.; m. Priscilla Kay Finlay, Dec. 12, 1964; children: Melissa Lane, Melanie Lee. BA in Psychology, U. Tex., 1966; postgrad., Auburn U., 1966-67; PhD in Psychology, Tex. Christian U., 1971. From asst. to assoc. prof. Nebr. Wesleyan U., Lincoln, 1970-78; dir. ednl. affairs Am. Psychol. Assn., Washington, 1978-80; prof. Tex. A&M U., College Station, 1980—; bd. advisors Archives of History of Am. Psychology, Akron, Ohio, 1980—. Author: Psychology, 1994, A History of Psychology, 1988, rev. 2d edit., 1996, Harry Kirke Wolfe, 1990; assoc. editor Am. Psychologist, 1985-95. Recipient Disting. Teaching award Am. Psychol. Found., 1986. Fellow APA (pres. history of psychology divsn. 1983-84, tchg. of psychology divsn. 1986-87); mem. Ea. Psychol. Assn. (pres. 1996-97). Office: Tex A&M U Dept Psychology College Station TX 77843

BENJAMIN, WILLIAM PHILIP, psychiatrist; b. Chgo., Feb. 14, 1922; s. Louis and Marion (Roth) B.; m. Adele Leah Conroy, Mar. 15, 1953 (div. June 1978); children: Michael David, Melanie Ann, Cynthia Joan; m. Marilyn Palughi, Oct. 15, 1983. BA, Bklyn. Coll., 1943; MD, U. Md., 1949. Diplomate Am. Bd. Neurology and Psychiatry. Intern N.Y.C. Hosp., 1949-50; resident Rockland State Hosp., Orangeburg, N.Y., 1950-51; fellow Menninger Sch. Psychiatry, Topeka, 1951-52, 54; asst. chief psychiatry Wright Patterson Air Force Base Hosp., Dayton, Ohio, 1952-54; resident Winter VA Hosp., Topeka, 1951-52, 54; chief women's svc. Winter VA Hosp., 1955-58; sr. staff psychiatrist Hillside Hosp., Glen Oaks, N.Y., 1958-89; dir. day hosp. Hillside div. L.I. Jewish Med. Ctr., New Hyde Park, N.Y., 1964-89; assoc. prof. clin. psychiatry med. sch. SUNY, Stony Brook, 1973—. Contbr. article to JAPA, 1959. Active speakers bur. Nassau Neuropsychiat. Soc. Recipient Citation for Disting. Svc. Nassau County Mental Health Assn., 1969. Fellow Am. Psychiat. Assn. (life), Nassau Acad. Medicine; mem. AAAS, Nassau Psychiat. Soc. (treas. 1965-66, sec. 1966-67, pres.-elect, 1967-68, pres. 1968-69, bd. dirs. 1969-74, chmn. community aspects com. 1963-64, chmn. ethics com. 1982-84), Nassau County Med. Soc., N.Y. State Med. Soc., Am. Coll. Physicians (assoc.), World Mental Health Assn. Home and office: 271 Grand Central Pky # 28H Floral Park NY 11005

BENKOVIC, STEPHEN JAMES, chemist; b. Orange, N.J., Apr. 20, 1938; s. Stephen and Mary (Zamadics) B.; m. Patricia Doran, June 10, 1961. A.B. in English Lit., Lehigh U., 1960, B.S. in Chemistry, 1960; Ph.D. in Organic Chemistry (NIH fellow 1961-63. Teeple fellow 1960-61), Cornell U., 1963. Research asso. U. Calif., Santa Barbara, 1964-65; asst. prof. chemistry Pa. State U., University Park., 1965-67; assoc. prof. Pa. State U., 1967-70, prof., 1970—, Evan Pugh prof., 1977, univ. chair in biol. scis., 1984, Univ. prof., Eberly chair in chemistry, 1986. Contbr. articles to profl. jours. Alfred P. Sloan Found. fellow, 1968-70; Guggenheim fellow, 1975; recipient NIH career devel. award., 1969-74, Pfizer award in enzyme chemistry Pa. State U., 1977, Gowland Hopkins award, 1986, Arthur Cope Scholar award, 1988, NIH Merit award, 1988, Alfred R. Bader award Am. Chem. Soc., 1995. Mem. Fedn. Am. Biologists., Am. Acad. Arts and Scis., Nat. Acad. Scis., Chem. Soc., Am. Chem. Soc. (Alfred Bader award 1995), Sigma Xi., Phi Beta Kappa. Home: 771 Teaberry Ln State College PA 16803-3183 Office: Pa State U 411 Wartik Laboratory University Park PA 16802-6300*

BEN-MEIR, MARC, psychologist, substance abuse counselor; b. Bronx, N.Y., June 23, 1946; s. Murray Norman and Shirley Lenora (Fox) Friedman; m. Aliza Assulin, June 22, 1971 (div. Apr. 1983); m. Candace Jo Drinnon, June 5, 1983 (div. Apr. 1994); children: Neil, Ron, Jonathan. AA in Human Cultural Devel., Brookdale Coll., Lincroft, N.J., 1979; BA in Humanities, Thomas Edison State Coll., Trenton, N.J., 1984; MA in Orgnl. Behavior cum laude, Norwich U., 1990; PhD in Orgnl. Psychology, La Salle U., 1992. Lic. chem. dependency counselor; cert. clin. hypnotherapist; cert. addictions counselor; lic. social work assoc.; ordained rabbi, Nov. 6, 1995. Enlisted U.S. Army, 1976, advanced through grades to capt., 1985, counselor, 1976-85; counselor USAF, Carswell AFB, Tex., 1986-91; dir., tng. coord. Nat. Vets. Outreach, State of Tex., Ft. Worth, 1990-91; owner Springhaven Addictions Clinic, Ft. Worth, 1992—; adj. prof. La Salle U. Author: Concepts in Prisoner Rehabilitation, 1991 (hon. mention 1991), The Frozen Mountain-How to Counsel Native Americans, 1994. Diplomat Am. Jewish Congress. With Tex. N.G. Mem. Internat. Assn. Pers. in Employment Security, Nat. Clin. Hypnotherapy Assn., Tex. Assn. Drug and Alcohol Counselors, Masons (32nd degree). Democrat. Jewish. Office: Springhaven Clinic Magnolia St Fort Worth TX 76117

BEN-MENACHEM, YORAM, radiologist; b. Jerusalem, Sept. 1, 1934; came to U.S., 1969; s. Haim and Eva (Beisem) Ben-M.; m. Sylvia Tizes, Dec. 24, 1957; children: Tamir, Gadi, Drory. M.D., Hebrew U., Jerusalem, 1960. Diplomate: Am. Bd. Radiology. Physician Israel Def. Forces, 1960-63; med. supt. Lilongwe (Malawi) Gen. Hosp., 1963-66; fellow in vascular radiology Thomas Jefferson U., Phila., 1969-72; prof. radiology U. Tex. Med. Sch., Houston, 1977-84, dir. vascular radiology, 1972-83; prof. radiology Baylor Coll. Medicine, Houston, 1985-87; prof. radiology, adj. prof. surgery U. Washington, Seattle, 1987-92; dir. dept. radiology Harborview Med. Ctr., Seattle, 1988-92; prof., vice chmn. dept. radiology U. Med. and Dentistry N.J., N.J. Med. Sch., Newark, 1992—; chief traumatologic radiology UMDNJ Univ. Hosp., Newark, 1992—; rep. to Trauma Task Force of Joint Commn. on Accreditation Health Care Orgns., 1988—. Author: Angiography in Trauma: A Work Atlas, 1981; cons. editor Orthopedics. Mem. Am. Soc. Emergency Radiology, Radiol. Soc. N.J., Am. Coll. Radiology, Radiol. Soc. N.Am., Soc. Cardiovasc. Intervention Radiology, Cardiovasc. Intervention Soc. Europe, Am. Roentgen Ray Soc., Internat. Wound Ballistics Assn. Jewish. Office: Univ Hosp UMDNJ Dept Radiology C-320 150 Bergen St Newark NJ 07103-2406

BENNER, CHARLES M., internist; b. Gary, Ind., Sept. 22, 1947; s. Myron E. and Ruth A. (Edwards) B.; m. Anne Meade, Jan. 30, 1970 (div. June 1980); m. Patricia Ann Gurny, June 12, 1981; children: Daniel (dec.), Mary E. BS, American U., 1973; MD, George Washington U., 1977. Diplomate Am. Bd. Internal Medicine. Instr. medicine Washington VA Med. Ctr., 1980-84; pvt. practice Silver Springs, Md., 1984—; vis. lectr. Johns Hopkins U., Balt., 1995—; v.p., med. dir. Primary Care Mid-Atlantic, LLC, Rockville, Md., 1994—; chmn. profl. adv. com. Adventist Home Health Care, Silver Spring, 1995-96; chmn. pharmacy & therapeutics com. Washington Adventist Hosp., Takoma Park, Md., 1989—, med. exec. com., 1989—. Served to staff sgt. USAF, 1969-73. Episcopal. Office: 11251 Lockwood Dr Silver Spring MD 20901

BENNETT, AMY SPEAR, nursing educator; b. Albuquerque, June 15, 1949; d. Edward D. and Amy (Clark) Spear; m. Gary W. Bennett, June 1, 1970; children: Amy Lee, Margaret, Katherine. Student, Cornell U., 1969-70; BA, Northwestern State U. of La., 1971, BS in Nursing, 1973; MS in Nursing, U. Pa., 1981; postgrad., Widener U., 1988—. Cert. med.-surg. nursing Am. Nurses Assn. Staff nurse Rolling Hill Hosp., Elkins Pk., Pa., 1973-77; nursing instr. Albert Einstein Med. Ctr. Sch. Nursing, Phila., 1977-80, Episcopal Hosp. Sch. Nursing, Phila., 1982—. Troop leader Girl Scouts Am., Wyncote, Pa., 1987—. Mem. ANA, NLN, AAUW, Acad. Med.-Surg. Nurses, Sigma Theta Tau. Democrat. Unitarian-Universalist. Home: 7931 Green Ln Wyncote PA 19095-1615 Office: Episcopal Hosp Sch Nursing 100 E Lehigh Ave Philadelphia PA 19125-1012

BENNETT, ANN CRISTINE, critical care nurse; b. Boise, Idaho, Nov. 9, 1955; d. Leo Peter and Elizabeth (Niichel) Ruffing; m. Steven Michael Bennett, Mar. 31, 1979; children: Kelly, Amanda, Brittany. BSN, Idaho State U., Pocatello, 1977. Cert. instr. ACLS, cert. provider pediat. advanced life support, Am. Heart Assn. Staff nurse ICU/CCU St. Alphonsus Med. Ctr., Boise, 1978-79; charge nurse CCU/ICU St. Anthony Hosp., Pocatello, Idaho, 1979-80; emergency dept. nurse mgr. Pocatello Reg. Med. Ctr., 1980-83; charge staff nurse emergency dept. Goddard Meml. Hosp., Stoughton, Mass., 1986-90; staff nurse Bay State Med. Ctr., Springfield, Mass., 1990—. Mem. AACN, Zonta, Phi Kappa Phi.

BENNETT, DEAN R., orthopaedic surgeon; b. Pitts., Sept. 6, 1952. BA in Chemistry, U. Calif., Irvine, 1974, BS in Biology, 1974; MD, U. Pitts., 1978. Diplomate Am. Bd. Orthopedic Surgeons. Intern in categorical gen. surgery Mercy Hosp., Pitts., 1978-79; resident in orthopaedic surgery U. Pitts., 1979-82, U. Glasgow, Scotland, 1982-83; staff physician sports medicine clinic Snomass Resort, Aspen, Colo., 1983-84; pvt. practice Vienna, Va., 1984-89, Arlington, Va., 1989-92; pvt. practice, v.p. Commonwealth Orthopaedics and Rehab., P.C., Herndon, Va., 1989—; chmn. dept. orthopaedics Fair Oaks Hosp., Fairfax, 1996; mem. staff Fairfax Hosp., Falls Church, Va., Reston (Va.) Hosp.; mem. orthopaedic steering com. Inova Health Sys., 1994—. Fellow Am. Acad. Orthopaedic Surgeons; mem. AMA, Med. Soc. Va., Fairfax County Med. Soc., Va. Orthopaedic Soc., Washington Orthopaedic Soc.. Office: Commonwealth Orthopaedics 13350 Franklin Farm Rd #220 Herndon VA 22071

BENNETT, DOROTHY CATHERINE, cell biology educator, researcher; b. Leicester, Eng., Feb. 16, 1954; d. Herbert William and Eileen Mary (Talbot) B.; m. Robert Frederick Brooks, Apr. 4, 1981; children: Rachel, Helen. BA with honors, Cambridge (Eng.) U., 1975, MA, 1979; PhD, London U., 1979; rsch. student, Imperial Cancer Rsch. Fund, London, 1975-79. Postdoctoral fellow Salk Inst., Calif., 1979-80, Imperial Cancer Rsch. Fund, London, 1980-83; from asst. prof. to assoc. prof. St. George's Hosp. Med. Sch., London, 1987-91, prof., 1993—; mem. adv. panel Vitiligo Soc., 1995—. Contbr. articles to sci., biomed., and cancer jours., also rev. chpts. to books. Mem. Amnesty Internat., Friends of the Earth, Save Brit. Sci. Soc. Cancer Rsch. Campaign grantee St. George's Hosp. Med. Sch., 1983-87; Runyon-Winchell Cancer Fund fellow, 1979, Imperial Cancer Rsch. Fund fellow, 1980-83; Fulbright-Hays sr. trave scholar, 1979-80. Mem. European Soc. for Pigment Cell Rsch., Brit. Assn. for Cancer Rsch., Brit. Soc. for Devel. Biology, Brit. Soc. for Cell Biology. Office: St George's Hosp Med Sch, Cranmer Ter, London SW17 ORE, England

BENNETT, EDWARD VIRDELL, JR., surgeon; b. Nashville, July 17, 1947; s. Edward Virdell and Florence Elaine (Nelson) B. BA in Biology, Fisk U., 1969; MD cum laude, Ohio State U., 1973. Fellow in surgery Johns Hopkins U., Balt., 1973-75; intern, then resident Johns Hopkins Hosp., Balt., 1973-75; resident in surgery and cardiothoracic surgery Albany Med. Ctr. Hosp., N.Y., 1975-80, instr. in surgery, 1976-80; asst. prof. surgery Health Ctr., U. Tex.-San Antonio, 1980-83; practice medicine specializing in cardiothoracic surgery, Sayre, Pa., 1983-91; chief cardiac surgery Guthrie Clin. Ltd., Sayre, 1990-91; mem. staff Robert Packer Hosp., Sayre, 1983-91; mem. Guthrie Clinic, Ltd., Sayre, 1983-91; cardiac surgeon Albany Cardiothoracic Surgeons, P.C., 1991—; mem. staff Albany Med. Ctr. Hosp., 1991—, St. Peters Hosp., Albany, 1991—; clin. asst. prof. surgery Albany Med. Coll., 1991—. Contbr. articles to med. jours. Producer med. motion picture. Fellow Am. Coll. Chest Physicians, Am. Coll. Cardiology, ACS; mem. Soc. Thoracic Surgeons, Internat. Soc. for Heart Transplantation, Sigma Xi, Alpha Omega Alpha, Omega Psi Phi. Republican. Episcopalian. Avocations: sailing; scuba diving; skiing. Office: Albany Cardiothoracic Surgeons 319 S Manning Blvd Ste 301 Albany NY 12208-1743

BENNETT, GERTRUDE KRISTINE, plastic surgeon; b. Douglas, Ga., May 16, 1948; d. Herman L. and G. Elizabeth B.; m. George Cierny III: children: Bennett Alec, Sylvie, Tessa Cierny. BA, Emory U., 1969; MD, Med. Coll. Ga., 1972. Diplomate Am. Bd. Plastic and Reconstructive Surgery. Intern and resident gen. surgery Norfolk (Va.) Gen. Hosp., 1973, resident surgeon various depts., 1974-75; chief resident gen. surgery VA Hosp., Hampton Roads, Va., 1975; plastic surgeon U. Tex. Health Sci. Ctr., Parkland Hosp., Dallas, 1975-76, 77, VA Hosp., Dallas, 1976, Peter Smith Hosp., Fort Worth, Tex., 1976-77, Children's Med. Ctr., Dallas, 1977; asst. prof. surgery divsn. plastic surgery U. Tex. Health Sci. Ctr., Dallas, 1978-79, Baylor U. Hosp., Dallas, 1978-79, Children's Med. Ctr., Dallas, 1978-79; consulting staff surgeon Shirners Burns Inst., Galveston, Tex., 1980-83; plastic surgeon Atlanta Plastic Surgery, 1993—; attending surgeon, St. Joseph's Hosp., Atlanta, Scottish Rite Children's Med. Ctr., Atlanta, Northside Hosp., Atlanta. Contbr. articles to profl. jours.; presenter at profl. meetings. Grantee: U. Tex. Health Sci. Ctr., 1979. Fellow ACS; mem. AMA, Am. Soc. Aesthetic Plastic Surgery, Ga. Med. Assn., Med. Assn. Met. Atlanta, Am. Soc. Plastic and Reconstructive Surgeons, Ga. Soc. Plastic and Reconstructive Surgeons, Assn. Women Surgeons. Office: Atlanta Plastic Surgery 975 Johnson Ferry Rd # 500 Atlanta GA 30342

BENNETT, HARRIET COOK, social worker, educator; b. Telfair County, Ga., Aug. 3, 1945; d. Harry A. and Amy H. Cook; B.A., LaGrange (Ga.) Coll., 1967; M.S.W., U. Ga., Athens, 1969; postgrad. Tulane U., 1970; m. Fredrick E. Bennett, Jr., June 6, 1971; children—Amy, Andrew. Med. social reviewer state rev. team, Dept. Family and Children Services, Atlanta, 1969-71; social worker/instr. U. Mo. Med. Center, Columbia, 1971-73; social worker Easter Seal Rehab. Center, Tampa, Fla., 1978-79, Children's Home Society Fla., St. Petersburg, 1984-95; dir. LaPetite Acad., Tampa, 1980, tchr. kindergarten, 1981-84; social worker Hillsborough County Pub. Sch. Sys., 1995—. Vol. cons. Desenzano, Italy, 1976-78; vol. fundraiser Nat. Kidney Found., Arthritis Found. Lic. clin. social worker. Mem. Northdale Civic Assn., Nat. Assn. Social Workers, Acad. Cert. Social Workers, Hillsborough County PTA. Methodist. Home: 16006 Honeysuckle Pl Tampa FL 33624-1723

BENNETT, JACQUELINE BEEKMAN, school psychologist; b. Santa Paula, Calif., Sept. 4, 1946; d. Jack Edward and Margaret Blanche (MacPherson) Beekman.; m. Thomas LeRoy Bennett Jr., Aug. 5, 1972; children: Shannon, Brian, Laurie. BA, U. Calif., Davis, 1968; MS, Colo. State U., 1975, PhD, 1984. Histologist Sch. Veterinary Medicine, Davis, 1969-71; sch. psychologist Poudre Sch. Dist. R-1, Ft. Collins, Colo., 1993-95; psychologist Brain Imaging Recovery Program, 1995—. Mem. augment panel Colo. State Grievance Bd., 1988—; nominating chmn. United Presbyn. Women, Timnath, Colo., 1982, pres., 1986; mem. Women and the Ch. com. Boulder Presbytery, Colo., 1985-86; elder Timnath Presbyn. Ch., 1985—. Mem. Colo. Soc. Sch. Psychologists (cert.), Nat. Assn. Sch. Psychologists (cert.), NEA, Am. Psychol. Assn., Ft. Collins Parents of Twins (pres. 1977-78), Sigma Xi, Phi Kappa Phi. Democrat. Club: Squaredusters (Ft. Collins) (v.p. 1977-78). Home: 213 Camino Real Fort Collins CO 80524-8907 Office: Poudre Sch Dist R-1 2407 La Porte Ave Fort Collins CO 80521-2211

BENNETT, JAMES PATRICK, healthcare executive, accountant; b. Huntsville, Ala., Oct. 20, 1957; s. Raymond Arthur and Shirley Marie (Breach) B.; m. Marcella Joanne Lakebrink, Sept. 28, 1979; children: Stephanie Erin, James Patrick Jr. BS, U. North Ala., 1979. CPA, Ala. With Ernst & Whinney, Birmingham, Ala., 1979-87, supr., 1983-86, sr. mgr., 1986-87; v.p. fin. Russ Pharms., Inc., Birmingham, 1987-89, v.p. ops., bd. dirs., 1989-91; group v.p. inpatient rehab. ops. HealthSouth Rehab. Corp., Birmingham, 1991-92, pres. inpatient ops., bd. dirs., 1992-95; pres. HealthSouth Rehab. Hosp., 1992-95; pres., COO Healthsouth Corp., Birmingham, 1995—; bd. dirs. Arthritis Found. Ala. chpt. Treas. Shelby Com. of 100, Birmingham, 1987-89; chmn. U. North Ala. Ann. Fund Drive, 1995; chmn. rehab. com. Fedn. Am. Hosps., 1995-96; hon. chmn. Birmingham Multiple Sclerosis Soc., 1996; bd. dirs. Birmingham chpt. Am. Cancer Soc., 1996, Am. Sports Medicine Inst., 1995—. Nominee Leadership Birmingham, 1994, 95; recipient Cmty. Leadership award Multiple Sclerosis Soc., 1994. Mem. AICPA, Ala. Soc. CPAs, Am. Mgmt. Assn., Healthcare Fin. Mgmt. Assn. (regional v.p. 1987-88, Outstanding Mem. 1987), Nat. Assn. Accts., Secession Golf Club, Greystone Golf Club, Shoal Creek Golf Club, Elks. Roman Catholic. Home: 3732 Shady Cove Dr Birmingham AL 35243-2448 Office: Healthsouth Corp Two Perimeter Park S Birmingham AL 35243

BENNETT, JAMES TOLIVER, pediatric orthopedist; b. New Orleans, Nov. 29, 1953; s. Joseph Walter and Alberta (Toliver) B.; m. Susan Pardue, Oct. 20, 1972; children: James Jr., Robert Clifton. BS in Engring., Tulane U., 1974, MD, 1978. Diplomate Am. Bd. Orthopedic Surgery. Assoc. prof. Tulane U., New Orleans. Contbr. articles to profl. jours. Bd. dirs. United Cerebral Palsy, New Orleans. Mem. Am. Acad. Orthop. Surgery, Am. Acad. Pediat., Scoliosis Rsch. Soc., Pediatric Orthop. Soc. N.Am. Republican. Presbyterian. Office: Tulane U 1430 Tulane Ave New Orleans LA also: Tulane Med Ctr Hosp & Clinic 1415 Tulane Ave New Orleans LA 70112-2605

BENNETT, JAY BRETT, medical equipment company executive; b. Durham, N.C., Dec. 13, 1961; s. James Leonard Jr. and Yoalder Kathleen (Brunson) B.; m. Trisha Helen Folds, Feb. 3, 1990; children: Lydia Helen, William Chisholm. BA in Econs., Wake Forest U., 1984; M Health Adminstrn., Duke U., 1986. Sr. cons. Ernst and Whinney (now Ernst and Young), Charlotte, N.C., 1986-89; assoc. dir. strategic planning SSI Med. Svcs., Inc., Charleston, S.C., 1989-92, dir. strategic planning, 1992-94; dir. planning and bus. devel. Hill-Rom, Inc., 1994—; adj. prof. bus. and econs. Coll. Charleston, 1995—. Mem. alumni coun. grad. program in health svcs. Mgmt. Fuqua Sch. Bus., Duke U., Univ. Hosp. and Health Adminstrn. Mem. Am. Coll. Healthcare Execs., Nat. Trust for Historic Preservation, Am. Hosp. Assn., Soc. for Healthcare Planning and Mktg., Nat. Soc. SAR, Ducks Unltd., Quail Unltd., Trout Unltd. Office: 4349 Corporate Rd Charleston SC 29405

BENNETT, JOE CLAUDE, university president; b. Birmingham, Ala., Dec. 12, 1933; s. Claude and Clara Lucille (Clark) B.; m. Nancy Miller, June 17, 1958; children: Katherine Diane, Miller, Clark Barton. A.B., Samford U., 1954; M.D., Harvard U., 1958; DSc (hon.), U. Ala., 1992. Diplomate Am. Bd. Internal Medicine (governing bd. 1987—, cert. exam. com. for 1989, ind. com. R & D, 1988—), Am. Bd. Rheumatology, Nat. Bd. Med. Examiners. Intern Univ. Ala. Hosp., Birmingham, 1958-59, resident, 1959-60; rsch. assoc. molecuar biology NIH, Bethesda, Md., 1962-64; sr. rsch. fellow div. biology Calif. Inst. Tech., Pasadena, Calif., 1964-65; asst. prof. dept. medicine, assoc. prof. dept. microbiology, asst. dir. div. clin. immunology and rheumatology U. Ala. Med. Sch., Birmingham, 1965-70; dir. div. clin. immunology and rheumatology U. Ala. Med. Sch., 1970-83, prof., chmn. dept. microbiology, 1970-82, prof., chmn. dept. medicine, 1982—, Spencer Prof. Med. Sci., 1992—, dir. multipurpose arthritis center, 1977-84, disting. faculty lectr., 1979; pres. U. Ala., Birmingham, 1993—; physician in chief U. Ala. Hosp.; vis. prof. U. Mo.-Columbia Sch. Medicine, 1987, U. Leiden, The Netherlands, 1988, Baylor U. Coll. Medicine, Houston, 1989, others; invited lectr. various univs., confs. including IX Pan-Am. Congress Rheumatology, Buenos Aires, 1986, U. Mo.-Columbia Sch. Medicine, 1987, Cornell Med. Sch., 1986, U. Colo., 1986; mem. sci. adv. bd. Merck Sharp & Dohme Rsch. Labs., 1987-89, Gorgas Meml. Inst. Tropical and Preventive Medicine, 1985—, others; mem. bd. health sci. policies, NIH, NAS, 1988—. Editor: Vistas in Connective Tissue Diseases, 1968; co-editor: Rheumatology and Immunology, 2d edit., 1986, Cecil Textbook of Medicine, 1988—, Cecil Essentials of Medicine; editor-in-chief Am. Jour. Medicine, 1986—, Arthritis and Rheumatism, 1975-80; mem. editorial bd. Protein and Peptide Revs., 1980—, Current Opinion in Rheumatology, 1988—, Arthritis and Rheumatism, 1969-75; contbr. numerous articles, papers, book revs., abstracts to profl. publs. Recipient Ala. Acad. Honor award, 1987, Seale Harris award So. Med. Assn., 1987; John and Mary R. Markle Found. scholar in acad. medicine, 1965-70; recipient Rsch. Career Devel. award NIH, 1965-75; fellow Arthritis and Rheumatism Found., Harvard Med. Sch., Mass. Gen. Hosp., 1960-62. Fellow AAAS (sec. N. Med. scis. nominating com. 1989—); mem. Am. Bd. Internal Medicine (exec. com. 1992), Federated Coun. of Internatl Medicine, Assn. of Am. Med. Colls. (adv. panel on biomed. rsch. 1991-92), Inst. Medicine NAS, ACP (master 1990), Am. Assn. Immunologists, Am. Fedn. Clin. Rsch., Am. Coll. Rheumatology (pres. 1981-82, bd. dirs. planning group 1986-87), Am. Soc. Biol. Chemists, Am. Soc. Clin. Investigation, Am. Soc. Microbiology, more. Home: 4101 Altamont Rd Birmingham AL 35213-2813 Office: Univ of Alabama-Birmingham 701 20th St S Birmingham AL 35233-2035

BENNETT, JOHN MORRISON, medical oncologist; b. Boston, Apr. 24, 1933; s. Theodore and Gladys B.; m. Carol F. Rosenblum, Dec. 22, 1957; children: Robert, Elizabeth, Douglas. A.B. cum laude, Harvard U., 1955; M.D. cum laude, Boston U., 1959. Intern Mass. Meml. Hosp., Boston, 1959-60; resident Beth Israel Hosp., Boston, 1960-62; instr. medicine Harvard Med. Sch., 1965-66; head morphology and histochem. sect. clin. pathology dept. NIH, 1966-68; asst. prof. medicine Sch. Medicine Tufts U., 1968-69; dir. outpatient labs. Boston City Hosp., 1968-69; dir. hematology and med. oncology Highland Hosp., Rochester, N.Y., 1969-74; prof. oncology in medicine, pathology and lab. medicine U. Rochester Sch. Medicine, 1976—; asso. dir. clin. affairs U. Rochester Cancer Center, 1978-94; head med. oncology unit Strong Meml. Hosp., Rochester, 1974-95. Editor: Leukemia Research, 1993, others; contbr. some 350 articles to profl. jours. Served with USPHS, 1966-68. Mem. ACP, AMA, Am. Soc. Clin. Oncology, Am. Soc. Hematology. Home: 335 Avalon Dr Rochester NY 14618-2731 Office: 601 Elmwood Ave Rochester NY 14642-0001

BENNETT, MARGARET ETHEL BOOKER, psychotherapist; b. Spartanburg, S.C., June 15, 1923; d. Paschal and Ovie (Grey) Booker. BS, N.C. A&T State U., 1944; MSW, U. Mich., 1947; PhD, Wayne State U., 1980. Diplomate Cert. Bd. Social Workers; cert. marriage counselor, cert. social worker, Mich. Caseworker, field instr. Family Svcs. Soc. Met. Detroit, 1947-52; caseworker, field instr., casework supr. Wayne County Cons. Center, 1952-60, Psychiat. Social Svcs., Wayne County Gen. Hosp., 1960-62; psychotherapist, field instr., asst. dir. Wayne County Mental Health Clinic, 1962-76; asst. dir. psychiat. social svc. Wayne County Psychiat. Hosp., 1976-77; dir. med. social svc. Wayne County Gen. Hosp., 1977-78; treatment cons. Project Paradigm, 1978-83; pvt. practice psychotherapy, Detroit, 1965—; psychotherapist, pres. Booker Bennett & Assocs., 1980—; founder Consultation Center of Ecorse, Mich., 1961; instr. Immanuel Luth. Coll., 1944-45; lectr. U. Mich., 1969-76. Bd. dirs. Crossroads, 1980-86; exec. coun. Episcopal Diocese of Mich., 1974-77, 80-83, exec. com. 1982-85, lic. lay reader, 1983—, healing min.; governing bd. Cathedral Ch. of St. Paul, Detroit, 1971-74, 76-77, 79-82, v.p. governing bd., 1977, sub-deacon, 1985—; bd. dirs. Cathedral Terr., 1981-87, U. Mich. Women, 1982-88, v.p., 1988-90, pres., 1990—, Wayne State U. Sch. Social Work Alumni Assn., 1981-86. Lic. Lay reader Episcopal Diocese Mich., 1983—, sub deacon Cathedral Ch. St. Paul, Detroit, Mich., 1985—; trustee bishop Page Found., 1986—; head verger, Cathedral Ch. St. Paul, Detroit, 1988—, lay eucharistic min. Episc. Diocese Mich., 1989—, chalice bearer, 1989—, healing min., 1995—, Dean's cross for Disting. Svc., 1993; active Verger's Guild Episc. Ch. Fellow Am. Orthopsychiat. Assn.; mem. Mich. Assn. Marriage and Family Therapy, Nat. Assn. Equal Opportunity in Higher Edn. (Disting. Alumni award), Am. Assn. Marriage and Family Therapy, Acad. Cert. Social Workers (cert.), Mich. Assn. Clin. Social Worker's Nat. Assn. Social Workers, Nat. Coalition 100 Black Women, Assn. Advancement Psychoanalysis, Phi Delta Kappa, Alpha Kappa Alpha. Democrat. Episcopalian. Co-author: The Handbook of Psychodynamic Therapy; contbr. articles to profl. jours. Home: 1971 Glynn Ct Detroit MI 48206-1742 Office: 11000 W Mcnichols Rd Detroit MI 48221-2357

BENNETT, MARY ELLEN, health care facility surveyor; b. Bklyn., May 13, 1944; d. Leon Alfred Thompson and Ruth Earle Kamrara; m. Jonas Shepard (div.); children: Jonas A. Shepard, Stephen K. Shepard, Tslané M. Shepard; m. Julian L. Bennett (div.); 1 child, Julian L. Bennett III. ADN, Mass. Bay C.C., 1971; student, Northeastern U., Boston, 1974; MPH, Boston U., 1979; EdD, U. Mass., 1991. RN, Mass. Rsch. clin. charge nurse Harvard U. Rsch. Clin. Ctr., Boston, 1971-73; physician asst. Roxbury (Mass.) Comprehensive Cmty. Health Ctr., 1974-80; clin. coord. Northeastern U., Boston, 1978-80; adminstr., mgr. Univ. Home Health Svcs., Brookline, Mass., 1980-81; nurse cons. Elm Hill Nursing Home, Roxbury, 1982-83; field ops. supr. Mass. Dept. Pub. Health, Boston, 1988-89, health care facility surveyor, 1983-88, 89—; chair sch. bd. Berea Seventh Day Adventist Acad., Dorchester, Mass., 1992—; lectr. in field. Contbr. articles to profl. jours. Recipient citations and awards. Seventh-day Adventist. Home: 38 Murray St West Peabody MA 01960

BENNETT, MICHAEL, pathologist, educator; b. Goose Creek, Tex., Feb. 11, 1936; s. Alvin Lowell and Jessie Lorena (Wintz) B.; m. Mary Allen Propes, June 4, 1960; children: Byron Craig, Marc Alan, Daniel Clay, Heather Ann. Student, U. Tex., 1954-57; MD, Baylor Coll. Medicine, 1961. Intern Cleve. Met. Gen. Hosp., 1961-62; resident in pathology Phila. Gen. Hosp., 1962-63, Buffalo Gen. Hosp., 1969-71; biologist Oak Ridge (Tenn.) Nat. Lab., 1963-65; sr. and assoc. rsch. scientist Roswell Park Meml. Inst., Buffalo, 1965-72; from assoc. prof. to prof. pathology Boston U. Sch. Medicine, 1972-81; prof. pathology U. Tex. Southwestern Med. Ctr., Dallas, 1981—; cons. Immunology Study Section, Bethesda, Md., 1981-84; mem. editorial bd. Jour. Immunology, 1984-87, Explt. Hematology, 1972-75, Nat. Immunology, 1984—. Assoc. editor Cancer Rsch. jour., 1985-89; contbr. articles to profl. publs. Recipient Rsch. Career Devel. award Nat. Cancer Inst., 1974-79, Best Cancer Rsch. Project Frances Stones Burns, 1973. Democrat. Home: 7235 Holyoke Dr Dallas TX 75248 Office: U Tex Southwestern Med Ctr 5323 Harry Hines Blvd Dallas TX 75235-9072

BENNETT, MICHAEL VANDER LAAN, neuroscience educator; b. Madison, Wis., Jan. 7, 1931; s. Martin Toscan and Cornelia (Vanderlaan) B.; m. Ruth Berman, July 19, 1963 (div. 1993); children: Nicholas Toscan, Elena Paula. BS, Yale U., 1952; DPhil, Oxford U., Eng., 1957. Research worker Coll. of Physicians and Surgeons Columbia U., N.Y.C., 1957-58, rsch. assoc., 1958-59, asst. prof. neurology, 1959-61, assoc. prof. neurology, 1961-66; co-dir. neurobiology Marine Biol. Lab., Woods Hole, Mass., 1970-74; prof. anatomy Albert Einstein Coll. Medicine, Bronx, N.Y., 1967-74, prof. neurosci., 1974—, chmn. neurosci., 1982-96, Sylvia and Robert S. Olnick Prof. of Neurosci., 1986—; Editor rev. jours.; contbr. articles to profl. jours. Hon. Pepsi Cola scholar, 1948, Rhodes scholar, 1952; Grass Fellow, 1958. Fellow AAAS; mem. NAS, Am. Physiol. Soc., Am. Soc. Cell Biology, Biophys. Soc., Soc. Neurosci., N.Y. Road Runners Club, Phi Beta Kappa. Office: Albert Einstein Coll of Medicine Dept Of Neurosci Bronx NY 10461

BENNETT, PAUL ANDREW, health science administrator, educator; b. Newburg, W.Va., Sept. 27, 1940; s. James Andrew and Ethel Florence (Shipp) B.; m. Alma Jean Muncy, June 15, 1963; 1 child, Jason Andrew. BS, W.Va. U., 1967, MS, 1969, EdD, 1972. Biology tchr., coach St. Francis H.S., Morgantown, W.Va., 1967-68; grad. lectr. in health W.Va. U., Morgantown, 1970-72; instr. health Ea. Ky. U., Richmond, 1969-70; grad. faculty in health E. Ky. U., Richmond, 1972-73; coord. health edn. Fla. Internat. U., Miami, 1973-75; chmn. dept. health, phys. edn. and recreation Alderson-Broaddus Coll., Philippi, W.Va., 1975-76, chmn. divsn. edn., 1976-78, chmn. dept. med. sci., 1978—, chmn. divsn. health scis., 1978—; pres. trustees Broaddus Hosp., Philippi, 1986—; trustee, bd. dirs. Davis Meml. Hosp., Elkins, W.Va., 1992—. V.p. Barbour County Bd. Edn., Philippi, 1988-94; pres. Barbour County Heart and Cancer Soc., Philippi, 1984-87. Served with USAF, 1958-62, Germany. HHS grantee, 1986—; Benedum Found. grantee. Mem. Assn. Physician Asst. Programs, W.Va. Assn. Physician Assocs., W.Va. Hosp. Assn. (trustee, bd. dirs.), W.Va. Primary Care Assn. (bd. dirs.), Masons, Shriners, Phi Delta Kappa, Eta Sigma Gamma. Republican. Methodist. Home: Rte 3 Box 38-H Philippi WV 26416 Office: Alderson-Broaddus Coll College Hill Philippi WV 26416

BENNETT, PAUL BERT, JR., medical researcher, educator; b. Camden, Ark., Mar. 15, 1954; s. Paul Bert and Constance Marie (Sizeland) B.; m. Connie T. Frenz, Aug. 1, 1981; children: Patrick Ehren, Christopher Paul. BA, U. Ark., 1976, PhD, 1982; postgrad., U. Rochester, 1982-85, Vanderbilt U., 1985-86. Instr. Vanderbilt U. Sch. Medicine, Nashville, 1986-87, asst. prof., 1987-93, assoc. prof., 1993—. Contbr. articles to profl. jours. Mem. editl. bd. Circulation Rsch. Jour., 1992—. NIH grantee, 1989—. Mem. Am. Heart Assn. (established investigator), Biophys. Soc., Soc. Gen. Physiologists. Home: 6002 Tattersall Ct Brentwood TN 37027 Office: Vanderbilt U Sch Medicine Dept Pharmacology Nashville TN 37232-6602

BENNETT, R. DAWN, social worker; b. Roanoke, Va., Nov. 16, 1937; d. Robert Lee and Pearl Lucille (Webber) Moore; m. Charles Peter Bennett, June 16, 1961; children: Michael Charles, Laura Dawn. BA, Baylor U., 1960; MSW, Norfolk State U., 1979. Lic. clin. social worker, Va. Clinician Cath. Family and Children's Svc., Norfolk, Va., 1979-83; social worker Multimodal Therapy, Norfolk, 1983-86; pvt. practice social work Virginia Beach, Va., 1986—. Vol. Habitat for Humanity, Hampton, Va., 1989-90. Mem. Nat. Assn. Social Workers, Va. Soc. Clin. Social Workers.

BENNETT, RICHARD CARL, social worker; b. Eau Claire, Wis., July 25, 1933; s. Ira Anthony and Marion Rhoda (Johnson) B.; BA, Hamline U., St. Paul, 1955; MS, George Williams Coll., 1957; MS (Lou Hougttellian fellow, Am. Lutheran Ch. fellow), U. Chgo., 1962; postgrad. Loyola U., Chgo., Roosevelt U., Chgo., Forest Inst., Chgo., Coll. Fin. Planning, Denver, Columbia Pacific U., 1990—; grad. in computer sci. Nat. Radio Inst.,1985, grad. in computerized acctg., 1988; grad. Ind. Family Mediation Tng., 1992; PhD Clayton Sch, Birmingham, Ala.; Diplomate Am. Bd. of Examiners in Clin. Social Work. m. Patricia Ann Work, Oct. 27, 1972; children: Matthew, Elizabeth, Kimberly, Timothy. Caseworker, Rock County Welfare Dept., Janesville, Wis., 1957-61; area dir. Luth. Family Service Oreg., Eugene, 1962-67; exec. dir. Family Service Travelers Aid, Fort Worth, 1967-70; mgr. agy. ops. Tarrant County United Way, Fort Worth, 1970-73; mile coord. Hands Accross Am., 1986, coord. Porter County Share Food, 1986-87; exec. dir.

Luth. Family Service N.W. Ind., Merrillville, 1973-80; exec. v.p. Listening Inc., 1979—; exec. dir. Inst. for Family Life Porter County, 1982-93; CEO Environtech, 1988-94; cons. Ind. sentencing; lectr. Calumet Coll., Hammond, Ind., 1988-94, Purdue U., Westville, 1991-94, adult edu. instr, Indiana U., coord. of telecourses Calumet Coll., 1989-91; cons. Support Group Adult Attention Deficit Disorder, 1992. Apptd. by gov. Ind. Social Work and Marriage and Family Therapist Cert. Bd., 1991; host TV show Life's Dimensions, 1985-90; cons. internat. bd. Parents without Ptnrs.; cons. numerous social agys. With USAR, 1958-62. Mem. Nat. Assn. Social Workers (dir. Ind. chpt.), Acad. Cert. Social Workers (diplomate in clin. social work), Assn. Marriage and Family Therapists, Nat. Orgn. Forensic Social Workers, Ind. Pub. Defender Coun., Assn. Family and Conciliatory Cts. Author: Second Opinion: A Holistic Approach to Treating Adults with ADD, 1994, Reversing Attention Deficit Disorder, 1996; author divorce mgmt. materials and newspaper column, Author: QSort 10 an interactive diagnostic/treatment to add aduct depression, 1996, Reversing Attention Disorders in adult, 1996. profl. manuals; pub. Step Families and Beyond, 1979—; editor: The Business of Social Work, 1983-84, ADD-Up Bi-monthly Newslatter dor ADD-Adults. Home and Office: 8716 Pine Ave Gary IN 46403-1441

BENNETT, ROBERT MARTIN, immunology, rheumatology educator; b. Berkhamsted, Eng., Nov. 30, 1940; came to U.S., 1972; s. Leonard and Gladys May (Young) R.; m. Jennifer Delmira Montagu, June 26, 1964 (div. Aug. 1986); children: Emma, Jeremy, Katrina; m. Sharon Rae Clark, Aug. 29, 1989. MD, U. London, 1964. Tutor Royal Postgrad. Med. Sch., London, 1970-72; instr. in medicine U. Chgo., 1972-73, asst. prof. medicine, 1973-76; assoc. prof. medicine Oreg. Health Scis. U., Portland, 1976-80, prof. medicine, 1980—; chmn. div. rheumatology Oreg. Health Scis. U. Editor: The Fibromyalgia Syndrome, 1996; author (chpt.) Mixed Connective Tissue Disease, 1996; editl. bd. Geriatrics, Jour. Musculoskeletal Pain, Arthritis and Rheumatism. Lt. RAF, 1964-70. Fellow ACP, Royal Coll. Physicians, Am. Coll. Rheumatology; mem. Am. Lupus Soc. (med. adv. bd. L.A. chpt. 1989-95). Republican. Office: Oreg Health Scis U 3181 SW Sam Jackson Park Rd Portland OR 97201-3011

BENNETT, ROBIN RAY, nephrologist, internist; b. New Orleans, Aug. 22, 1953; s. Milfred Ray and Evelyn (Ridgedell) B.; m. Cynthia Leigh Crain, Aug. 5, 1978; children: Matthew Ryan, Elizabeth Grace. BS in Chemistry, Southeastern La. U., 1975; MD, La. State U., 1978. Diplomate Am. Bd. Internal Medicine, Am. Bd. Nephrology. Commd. capt. U.S. Army, 1979, advanced through grades to maj.; flexible intern Brooke Army Med. Ctr., San Antonio, 1979-80, resident in internal medicine, 1980-82; fellow in nephrology Walter Reed Army Med. Ctr., Washington, 1982-84; staff nephrologist Eisenhower Army Med. Ctr., Augusta, Ga., 1984-87; resigned, 1979; pvt. practice, Alexandria, La., 1987—. Mem., chmn. adminstrv. bd. 1st United Meth. Ch., Alexandria. Fellow ACP; mem. Am. Diabetes Assn., Internat. Soc. Nephrology, Am. Soc. Nephrology, La. Med. Soc. Office: Freedman Clinic 1337 Centre Ct Alexandria LA 71315-3030

BENNETT, THOMAS LEROY, JR., clinical neuropsychology educator; b. Norwalk, Conn., Sept. 25, 1942; s. Thomas LeRoy and Gertrude Upson (Richardson) B.; m. Jacqueline Beekman, Aug. 5, 1972; children: Dean, Shannon, Brian, Laurie. B.A., U. N. Mex., 1964, M.S., 1966, Ph.D., 1968. Diplomate Am. Bd. Profl. Neuropsychology (examiner, treas. 1993-96, pres.-elect 1996—), Am. Bd. Forensic Examiners, Am. Bd. Profl. Disability Cons. Asst. prof. Calif. State U., Sacramento, 1968-70; assoc. prof., then prof. psychology and physiology Colo. State U., Ft. Collins, 1970—, coord. exptl. psychology sect., 1978-81, 92-95; pvt. practice neuropsychology Ft. Collins, 1981—; mem. allied health staff Poudre Valley Hosp., Ft. Collins; clin. dir. Brain Injury Recovery Program, Ft. Collins. Author: Brain and Behavior, 1977, The Sensory World, 1978, The Psychology of Learning and Memory, 1979, Exploring the Sensory World, 1979, Introduction to Physiological Psychology, 1982, The Neuropsychology of Epilepsy, 1992; also articles and book chpts.; mem. editorial bd. Cognitive Rehab., Archives Clin. Neuropsychology, Jour. Head Injury, Bulletin of Nat. Acad. Neuropsychology. Elder Timnath Presbyterian Ch. Fellow APA, Nat. Acad. Neuropsychology (editl. bd. Bull., bd. dirs. 1993-95, conv. chmn. 1993, 94), Am. Psychol. Soc., Am. Coll. Profl. Neuropsychology (pres.-elect 1996—); mem. Am. Coll. Forensic Examiners, Psychonomic Soc., Rocky Mountain Psychol. Assn., Soc. for Cognitive Rehab., Nat. Head Injury Found. (provider's coun.), Colo. Head Injury Found. (provder's coun.), Colo. Head Injury Found., Internat. Neuropsychol. Soc., Colo. Neuropsychol. Soc., Sigma Xi (named Colo. State U. Honored Scientist 1996). Home: 213 Camino Real Fort Collins CO 80524-8907 Office: Colo State U Dept Psychology Fort Collins CO 80523

BENNETT, WESLEY STEWART, cardiologist; b. Natchez, Miss., July 8, 1958; s. John Jackson and Mary (Nichols) B.; m. Lallie Lawson Owens, Mar. 22, 1986; children: John Jennings, Wesley Stewart, Lallie Elise. BS with honors, Tulane U., 1980; MD, U. Miss., 1984. Diplomate Am. Bd. Internal Medicine, Am. Bd. Cardivascular Diseases. Staff cardiologist Internal Medicine Clinic, Meridian, Miss., 1990—; chmn. dept. medicine Riley Meml. Hosp., Meridian, 1994-95, 1st v.p. med. staff, 1995-96; chmn. dept. medicine Jeff Anderson Med. Ctr., Meridian, 1994-95. Bd. Trustees, Meridian Grand Opera House, 1994-97. Fellow Am. Coll. Cardiologists. Methodist. Office: Internal Medicine Clinic 2113 11th St Meridian MS 39301

BENNETT, WILLIAM MICHAEL, physician; b. Chgo., May 6, 1938; s. Harry H. and Helen A. (Kaplan) B.; m. Sandra S. Silen, June 12, 1977; four children. Student, U. Mich., 1956-59; B.S., Northwestern U., 1960, M.D., 1963. Diplomate Am. Bd. Internal Medicine, Am. Bd. Nephrology, Am. Bd. Clin. Pharmacology. Intern U. Oreg., 1963-64; resident Northwestern U., 1964-66; practice medicine specializing in internal medicine Portland, Oreg. and; Boston; mem. staff Mass. Gen. Hosp., 1969-70; asst. prof. medicine U. Oreg. Health Scis. Center, 1970-74, asso. prof., 1974-78, prof. medicine and pharmacology, 1978—. Author: Pharmacology and Management of Hypertension, 1994, Manual of Nephrology, 1990, Drug Therapy in Renal Failure, 1994; contbr. articles to med. jours. Served with USAF, 1967-69. Fellow ACP; mem. Am. Soc. Nephrology (mem. coun.), Transplantation Soc., Internat. Soc. Nephrology, Am. Soc. Pharmacology and Exptl. Therapeutics. Office: Oreg Health Sci U Portland OR 97201

BENNIE, PETER, JR., physician assistant; b. Lakewood, Ohio, Feb. 23, 1958; s. Peter and Audrey Lynette (Hutchinson) B.; m. Patricia Delcarmen Lebron, May 8, 1982; children: Peter III, Lindsay Nicole. BS, U. Okla., Oklahoma City, 1985; M in Med. Sci., St. Francis Coll., Loretto, Pa., 1995. Cert. physician asst.; cert. surg. asst. Commd. 2d lt. USAF, 1985, advanced through grades to capt., 1990; family practice physician asst. 91 Strategic Hosp., Minot AFB, N.D., 1985-90; resident 74th Med. Group, Wright Patterson AFB, Ohio, 1990-91, orthopedic physician asst., edn. coord., 1995—; orthopedic physician asst., clin. officer in charge 8th Med. Group, Sheppard AFB, Tex., 1991-95. Youth coord. YMCA, Fairborn, Ohio, 1995—. Decorated Air Force Achievement medal, Air Force Commendation. Fellow Am. Acad. Physician Assts., Soc. Air Force Physician Asst., Physician Asst. in Orthopedic Surgery. Home: 6423 Pheasant Finch Ave Dayton OH 45424 Office: 74th Med Group 4881 Sugar Maple Dr Wright Patterson AFB OH 45433

BENNINGFIELD, ANNA BETH, family therapist, psychologist; b. Vernon, Tex., Feb. 7, 1940; d. Maurice Leon and Mary Geneva (Gaines) Oliver; m. Milo F. Benningfield, June 11, 1960; children: Milo Mark, Dana Beth. BA, U. Md., 1963; MA, Tex. Women's U., 1977; PhD, U. North Tex., 1982. Lic. psychologist, Tex. Tchr. McMichael Elem. Sch., Phila., 1967-68, Strickland Jr. High Sch., Denton, Tex., 1968-75; clin. psychologist Dallas Child Guidance Clinic, 1981-84; prin. Benningfield, Benningfield & Assocs., Dallas, 1984—; cons. psychologist Dallas Child Guidance Clinic, 1984—. Editor (newsletter) Contact, 1978-80; contbr. articles to profl. jours. Fellow Am. Assn. for Marriage and Family Therapy (Disting. Svc. award 1986 Tex. chpt., nat. pres. 1993-95); mem. APA, Am. Soc. Clin. Hypnosis, Dallas Psychol. Assn. (pres. 1986-87). Methodist. Office: Benningfield Benningfield Assocs 5310 Harvest Hill Rd Ste 290 Dallas TX 75230-5800

BENNION, SCOTT DESMOND, physician; b. Casper, Wyo., July 26, 1948; s. Desmond and Wanda Bennion; m. Mary Marie Blanton; children: Scott, Beau, Brandon. BS summa cum laude, U. Wyo., 1970, MS, 1972; MD, U. Utah, 1975. Diplomate Nat. Bd. Med. Examiners, Am. Bd. Internal Medicine, Am. Bd. Dermatology, Am. Bd. Dermatologic Immunology/Diagnostic and Lab. Immunology. Intern U. Rutgers Med. Sch., 1975-76, resident in internal medicine, 1976-78, chief resident dept. medicine, 1978; commd. 2d lt. U.S. Army, 1976, advanced through grades to col., 1991; resident in dermatology Fitzsimons Army Med. Sch., Denver, 1981-84, chief dept. clin. investigations, 1994—, chmn. lab. animal use and care com., 1994—; asst. chief dermatology svc. 98th Gen. Hosp., Nuremburg, Germany, 1986, chief dept. health clinics, 1987-88; chief immunodermatology sect. dermatology svc. Fitzsimons Army MC, Aurora, Colo., 1989—; command surgeon ARTASK, Kuwait, 1992; command surgeon joint task force Kuwait and Army Ctrl. Command-Forward, 1992; dermatology cons. to the Army Surgeon Gen., 1996. Contbr. chpts. to book: Military Dermatology Secrets of Dermatology, 1996, also articles to profl. pubs. Pres. Nuremburg Elem. Sch. PTSA; asst. cubmaster, cubmaster, chmn. Volksmarch com. Boy Scouts Am., 1986; bd. dirs. Foxrdige Improvement Assn., 1992—, pres., 1994—. Named to Order of Mil. Med. Merit, 1987; named Cubmaster of Yr. Bavaria dist. Boy Scouts Am., 1987. Mem. ACP, Am. Acad. Dermatology (mem. govt. medicine task force 1996—), Assn. Mil. Surgeons, Assn. Mil. Dermatologists (Residents award 1984, sec.-treas. 1990—, guest editor jour. 1991), Soc. for Investigative Dermatology, Phi Kappa Phi. Home: 7944 S Olive Dr Englewood CO 80112 Office: Fitzsimons Army MC Dept Clin Investigation Aurora CO 80045

BENOIT, JEAN-PIERRE ROBERT, pneumologist, consultant; b. Cotonou, Dahomey, May 19, 1930; s. Samuel Pierre and Renée (Meffre) B.; m. Isabelle Rappard, Apr. 10, 1969; children: Laurence, Arnaud. MD in Pneumo-phtisiology, Paris U., 1964, PhD in Econs., 1968. Intern in medicine Paris Hosp.; resident in pneumology-indsl. medicine Corbeil (France) Hosp.; sr. cons., dept. head Pneumology Hosp. Fontenoy, Chartres, France, 1970—; v.p. Ligue contre le Cancer, Chartres, 1990—. Contbr. articles to profl. jours. Officer French Med. Svc., 1957-59. Mem. Mem Am. Thoracic Soc., Soc. Pneumology de Langue Francaise, N.Y. Acad. Scis., Nat. Geog. Soc., European Respiratory Soc., Imagery Thoracic Soc. Office: Hôpital Fontenoy Ctr, Hospitalier, Chartres 28018, France

BENOIT, MARCEL M., nephrologist, internist; b. Haiti, Dec. 26, 1956; came to U.S., 1972; s. Pierre and Lucida (LaGuerre) B.; m. Josie Benoit, July 27, 1987; children: Janeeka, Jomar. BS, CCNY, 1979; postgrad., U. Liège, Belgium, 1979-84; MD, U. del Noreste, Tampico, Tamaulipas, Mex., 1987. From intern to chief resident, then attending physician Brookdale Hosp., N.Y.C., 1988—; CEO, dir. High Blood Pressure Ctr., Ctr. for Kidney Diseases, Flatbush Med. Ctr., Brookdale, N.Y., 1995—. Mem. Am. Coll. Physicians, Am. Soc. Internal Medicine, Nat. Kidney Found. Office: Flatbush Med Heights 1794 Flatbush Ave Brooklyn NY 11210

BENSCH, KLAUS GEORGE, pathology educator; b. Miedar, Germany, Sept. 1, 1928; (married); 3 children. M.D., U. Erlangen, Germany, 1953. Diplomate: Am. Bd. Pathology. Intern U. Hosps. of Erlangen, 1953-54; resident in anat. pathology U. Tex. and; M.D. Anderson Hosp., Houston, 1954-56, Yale, 1956-57; instr. pathology Yale Med. Sch., 1958-61, asst. prof., 1961-64, assoc. prof., 1964-68; prof. pathology Stanford Med. Sch., 1968—, acting chmn. dept. pathology, 1984-85, chmn. dept. pathology, 1985—. Office: Stanford U Med Sch Dept Pathology 300 Pasteur Dr Stanford CA 94305

BENSHOFF, DIXIE L., psychologist; b. Ravenna, Ohio, Apr. 11, 1950; d. Roy O. and Pauline B.; m. Timothy David Ludick; 1 child, David Grant Benshoff Ludick. BA, Hiram Coll., 1972; MEd, Kent State U., 1973, PhD, 1977. Diplomate Internat. Acad. Behavioral Medicine Counseling and Psychotherapy. Adminstrv. dir., clin. dir. health psychology Pain Mgmt. Ctr. Cleve. Clin. Found., 1994-96; pvt. psychologist and health svcs. con., Aurora, Ohio, 1980—; presenter in field. Mem. Am. Assn. Marriage and Family Therapists, Am. Psychol. Assn., Am. Pain Soc. Home: 250 Birchbark Trail Aurora OH 44202 Office: Portage Bluff 210 W Protage Trail Ext Ste 101 Cuyahoga Falls OH 44223

BENSKI, RAYMOND, physician, educator; b. Bridgeport, Conn., Sept. 18, 1931; s. Casimir Francis and Margaret (Phelke) B.; m. Sandra Laputz, Sept. 5, 1964; children—Bradley Raymond, Pamela Ann. B.S. in Pharmacy, U. Houston, 1954; M.D., U. Tex., 1962. Diplomat Am. Bd. Family Practice. Intern Green Hosp., San Antonio, 1962-63; chief staff Mid Jeff Hosp., Nederland, 1969, 80; co-dir. U. Tex. FPC Residency Program, Port Arthur, Tex., 1981-82, clin. assoc. prof., Galveston, 1982—. Committeeman, Republican Party of Tex., Austin, 1980-90; del. Rep. Nat. Conv., Detroit and Dallas, 1980-84; regional dir. Phil Gramm for Senate, SE Tex., 1984. Served to capt. MSC, U.S. Army, 1954-69. Mem. Jefferson County Med. Soc., Tex. Med. Assn., AMA, Tex. Acad. Family Physicians, Am. Acad. Family Physicians, VFW, Am. Legion. Republican. Episcopalian. Lodges. Masons. Avocation: personal computers. Home: 927 N 30th St Nederland TX 77627-6701

BENSON, J. ROBERT, physician; b. Springfield, Ill., Oct. 6, 1934; s. Ed B. and Catherine Juanita (Gable) B.; m. Betty Jane Beasley, Dec. 18, 1955; children: Kimberly, Susan, Elizabeth. BS, Washington U., 1956, MD, 1959. Diplomate Am. Bd. Surgery. Surgeon Riverside Clinic, Jacksonville, Fla., 1969—; chief of surgery Riverside Hosp., Jacksonville, 1975-80, med. staff, chief of staff, 1981-82, bd. dirs., 1978-82. Lt. col. U.S. Army, 1958-69. Fellow ACS, So. Assn. of Vascular Surgery (bd. dirs. 1986); mem. AMA, Fla. Surg. Soc., Fla. Yacht Club (bd. dirs. 1980, 84, rear commodore, 1994, vice commodore 1995, commodore 1996). Office: Riverside Clinic 2005 Riverside Ave Jacksonville FL 32210

BENSON, JOHN ALEXANDER, JR., physician, educator; b. Manchester, Conn., July 23, 1921; s. John A. and Rachel (Patterson) B.; m. Irene Zucker, Sept. 29, 1947; children: Peter M., John Alexander III, Susan Leigh, Jeremy P. BA, Wesleyan U., 1943; MD, Harvard Med. Sch., 1946. Diplomate Am. Bd. Internal Medicine (mem. 1969-91, sec.-treas. 1972-75, pres. 1975-91, pres. emeritus 1991—), Subsplty. Bd. Gastroenterology (mem. 1961-66, chmn. 1965-66). Intern Univ. Hosps., Cleve., 1946-47; resident Peter Bent Brigham Hosp., Boston, 1949-51; fellow Mass. Gen. Hosp., Boston, 1951-53; rsch. asst. Mayo Clinic, Rochester, Minn., 1953-54; instr. medicine Harvard U., 1956-59; head divsn. gastroenterology U. Oreg. Med. Sch., Portland, 1959-75, prof. medicine, 1965-93; prof. emeritus Oreg. Health Sci. U., Portland, 1993—; interim dean Sch. Medicine Oreg. Health Sci. U., 1991-93, dean emeritus, 1993—; cons. VA Hosps., Madigan Gen. Army Hosp. Editorial bd.: Am. Jour. Digestive Diseases, 1966-73; Contbr. articles to profl. jours. Mem.Oreg. Med. Ednl. Found., 1957-73; dir. Oreg. Med. Ednl. Found., 1967-73, pres., 1969-72; bd. dirs. N.W. Ctr. for Physician-Patient Comm., 1994—, Am. Acad. on Physician and Patient, 1994—. With USNR, 1947-49. Mem. AAS, AMA, ACP (master), Am. Gastroenterol. Assn. (sec. 1970-73, v.p. 1975-76, pres.-elect. 1976-77, pres. 1977-78), Am. Clin. and Climatol. Assn., Am. Soc. Internal Medicine, Western Assn. Physicians, North Pacific Soc. Internal Medicine, Am. Fedn. Clin. Rsch., Federated Coun. for Internal Medicine, Am. Assn. Study Liver Disease, Western Soc. Clin. Investigation, Soc. Health and Human Values, Assn. Health Svcs. Rsch., Inst. Medicine NAS (sr.), Phi Beta Kappa, Sigma Xi, Alpha Omega Alpha. Office: Oreg Health Scis U Sch Medicine L102 Portland OR 97201

BENSON, KAREN G., physician assistant, actress; b. N.Y.C.. BA, Emerson Coll., Boston; BS, Touro Coll., N.Y.C. Registered physician asst., N.Y. Salesperson Synanon, various cities, 1979-83; mgr. sales network Eagle Seafood, N.Y.C., 1983-86; physician asst. N.Y.C., 1990-95. Actress, singer leading role in Hair, Boston, 1968-71. Active PETA, Washington. Mem. AAPA, JAAP, N.Y. State Soc. Physician Assts., Actors Equity. Home: 85 4th Ave New York NY 10003

BENSON, MITCHELL CLARK, urologist; b. N.Y.C., Feb. 21, 1951; s. Stanley R. and Gladys R. (Rappaport) B.; m. Ronda Bixon, Dec. 6, 1986; children: Nicole, Michael. BS magna cum laude, Union Coll., 1973; MD, Columbia U., 1977. Intern in surgery Mt. Sinai Hosp., N.Y.C., 1977-78, resident in surgery, 1978-79; resident in urology The Presbyn. Hosp., N.Y.C., 1979-81; chief resident urology The Presbyn. Hosp., 1981-82, asst. prof. urology, 1984-89, assoc. prof. urology, 1989-95, prof. urology, 1995—; fellow in oncology John Hopkins Hosp., Balt., 1982-84; dir. urologic oncology Columbia Presbyn. Med. Ctr., N.Y.C., 1984— vice chmn. dept. urology, 1993—; cons. Shering Oncology, Kenicourt, N.J., 1990—. Author: Camprell's Urology; contbr. articles to profl. jours. Office: Columbia Presbyn Med Ctr 161 Ft Washington Ave New York NY 10032

BENTLEY, BONNIE J., medical and oncological nurse; b. Akron, Ohio, Mar. 11, 1940; d. Francis P. and Anna (Lebkisher) Mugrage; children: Santa, David, Christopher. RN, Akron Gen. Hosp. Sch. Nursing, 1961. Cert. med./surg. nurse, gerontology. Charge nurse Akron Manor Care, Smithville-Western, Wooster, Ohio, Barberton (Ohio) Citizens Hosp.; office nurse, oncologist, hematologist Dr. S. Hazra, M.D.; supr. Barberton Manor Care; cons. Akron. Home: 727 Carnegie Ave Apt 2C Akron OH 44314-1165

BENTLEY, JAMES DANIEL, medical association executive; b. Jamestown, N.Y., Feb. 17, 1945; s. John Alexander and Pauline Ruby (Norberg) B.; m. Lorraine Kay Anderson, June 17, 1967; children: Kimberly, Andrew. BA, Mich. State U., 1967; PhD, U. Mich., 1971. Asst. dir. teaching hosps. Assn. Am. Med. Colls., Washington, 1976-80, assoc. dir.teaching hosps., 1980-86, v.p. for clin. svcs., 1987-91; sr. v.p. policy Am. Hosp. Assn., Washington, 1991—; tech. advisor Health Care Financing Adminstrn., Washington, 1984-87. Mem. editorial bd. Health Adminstrn. Press, Ann Arbor, Mich., 1988-91. Pres. Ch. Coun. St. Luke Luth., Silver Spring, Md., 1986-88. Lt. USN, 1971-76; Bd. Dirs. Holy Cross Hosp. Silver Spring, Md. 1990—. Recipient trainership USPHS, 1967-71. Office: Am Hosp Assn Liberty Pl 325 7th St NW Washington DC 20004-2802

BENTON, ALLEN HAYDON, biology educator; b. Ira, N.Y., Sept. 4, 1921; s. Haydon Willey and Pearl Amelia (Diddy) B.; m. Marjorie Lois Hall, Aug. 16, 1947; children: Thomas Hall, Christopher Allen, Holly Anne. B.S., Cornell U., 1948, M.S., 1949, Ph.D, 1952. Jr. wildlife biologist U.S. Fish and Wildlife Service, 1949; asst. prof. biology SUNY-Albany, 1949-57, assoc. prof., 1957-62; prof. biology SUNY-Fredonia, 1962-73, disting. teaching prof., 1973-84, faculty exchange scholar, 1975-84, prof. emeritus, 1984—; vis. prof. Stephen F. Austin Coll., 1957, Concord Coll., Athens, W.Va., 1969-70, U. Minn. Biol. Sta., 1970; cons. Nuclear Fuel Services Inc., Fla. Arthropod Collection, Roger Tory Peterson Inst. for the Study of Natural History. Author: (with W.E. Werner Jr.) Field Biology and Ecology, 3rd edit., 1974, Atlas of Fleas of the Eastern United States, 1980, Manual for Field Biology and Ecology, 6th edit., 1983, Wild Worlds, 1988, Light and Natural, 1992; columnist Dunkirk (N.Y.) Evening Observer, Albany (N.Y.) Knickerbocker News; freelance writer on nature and sci.; contbr. articles to profl. jours. Served with cav. U.S. Army, 1942-46. Decorated Bronze Star; grantee Research Found. SUNY, 1963, 83; NSF grantee, 1972; E.N. Huyck Found. grantee, 1976-78. Mem. Am. Ornithologists Union, Am. Soc. Mammalogists, Wilson Ornithol. Soc., Fedn. N.Y. State Bird Clubs (pres.), Outdoor Writers Assn. Am., PTA (life), Sigma Xi, Phi Kappa Phi. Home: 292 Water St Fredonia NY 14063-2025

BENTRUP, ANNA, nuclear medicine physician; b. Budapest, Hungary, Mar. 16, 1950; arrived in Germany, 1973.; d. Josef and Suzsanna (Schulhof) Szekeres; m. Hans-Jürgen Bentrup, Sept. 15, 1973. MA, U. Budapest, 1973; MD, U. Münster, Germany, 1984. Cert. specialist in nuclear medicine. Resident Clinic for Cardiology, Bad Salzuflen, Germany, 1984-88, Heart Centre, Bad Oeynhausen, Germany, 1988-94; head physician dept. nuclear medicine U. Magdeburg, Germany, 1994—. Home: Koeckerwald 77a, 33739 Bielefeld Germany Office: U Magdeburg, Med Fakultaet, Leipziger Str 44, 39120 Magdeburg Germany

BENTZ, MICHAEL LLOYD, plastic and reconstructive surgeon; b. Pitts., May 9, 1958; s. Joe Denton and Ida Mae (Troxell) B.; m. Kim Marie Livingstone, Nov. 19, 1988. BA, Ind. U., 1980; MD, Temple U., 1984. Diplomate Am. Bd. Surgery, Am. Bd. Plastic Surgery, Nat. Bd. Med. Examiners. Resident in gen. surgery Temple U. Hosp., Phila., 1984-89; rsch. fellow U. Pitts., 1989-90, resident in plastic and reconstructive surgery, 1990-92; asst. prof. surgery and pediatrics U. Pitts., Pa., 1992—; instr. advanced trauma life support U. Pitts., 1989—. Contbr. articles to profl. jours. Rsch. grantee Am. Soc. for Surgery of Hand, 1990-91, Plastic Surgery Ednl. Found., 1991-92, 92-93; recipient 1st prize rsch. Ohio Valley soc. Plastic and Reconstructive Surgeons, 1990, Ivy Soc., 1991, Clin. Tour award Coller Soc., 1989, Humaneness in Medicine award Philadelphia County Med. Soc., 1989. Fellow ACS, Am. Acad. Pediatrics; mem. Am. Cleft Palate-Craniofacial Assn., Am. Soc. Plastic and Reconstructive Surgeons, Plastic Surgery Rsch. Coun. Republican. Presbyterian. Home: 2440 Dogwood Dr Wexford PA 15090-7705 Office: Childrens Hosp of Pitts DeSoto 4A447 3705 5th Ave Pittsburgh PA 15213-2524

BENTZEN, NIELS, physician, radiologist; b. Slagelse, Denmark, Jan. 3, 1920; s. Bent Becker and maria (Kaalund) B.; m. Elva Bentzen, July 29, 1945 (div. 1981); children: Benedikte, Henrik, Lars. MD, U. Copenhagen, 1946, Dr. of Philosophy, 1960. Intern Roskilde County Hosp., 1946-47; resident Randers Hosp., 1947-49, Rigshospitalet, Copenhagen, 1949-50; resident Finsen Inst., Copenhagen, 1950-51, 53-56, cons., 1960-90; resident The County Hosp., Gentofte, 1951-53, Sundby Hosp., Copenhagen, 1956-59. With Danish Army, 1943-48. Mem. Danish Soc. X-ray Diagnosticians, Danish Med. Soc., Danish Soc. Head and Neck Onchology, Christiansborg Club of 1914. Home: Danmarksvej 46B, DK-2800 Lyngby Denmark

BENYO, JOANNE, critical care nurse; b. Coaldale, Pa., Aug. 28, 1957; d. John and Teresa (Firkal) B. Diploma, Reading (Pa.) Sch. Nursing, 1978; BSN, N.Y. State Regents Coll., 1992; postgrad., Northeastern U., 1995—. RN, Mass.; CCRN; cert. ACLS, CPR instr. Staff nurse ICU/CCU, coord. hemodialysis unit Reading Hosp., 1978-85, staff nurse, angioplasty nurse, cardiac catheterization lab., 1985-87; staff nurse cardiac cath lab. Lahey Clinic., Burlington, Mass., 1992; staff nurse per diem ICU/CCU Newton-Wellsley Hosp., 1991-92, Cambridge Hosp., 1991-92; staff nurse transplantation Mass. Gen. Hosp., Boston, 1988-91; clin. leader interventional imaging Newton-Wellesley Hosp., 1993-96; clin. sys. specialist Ptnrs. Healthcare Sys., Inc., 1996—. Mem. Am. Assn. Critical Care Nurses, Am. Radiology Nurses Assn., Am. Coll. Cardiology, New Eng. Critical Care Soc. (founding mem.), Soc. Critical Care Medicine. Home: 9 Holt St Belmont MA 02178-4436

BEN-YOSEPH, YOAV, geneticist; b. Petah-Tikra, Israel, Jan. 8, 1941; came to U.S., 1975; s. Hanania and Deborah (Shaferman) Ben-Y.; m. Tova Roth, Aug. 23, 1964 (div. 1974); children: Roey, Gilad; m. Miriam Mendel, Dec. 24, 1974. BSc, Hebrew U., Jerusalem, 1965, PhD, 1973. Cert. Am. Bd. Med. Genetics. WHO fellow Middlesex Hosp., London, 1971; investigator Weizmana Inst. Sci., Rehovot, Israel, 1973-75; asst. prof. Northwestern U., Chgo., 1975-79, assoc. prof., 1979-81; assoc. prof. Wayne State U., Detroit, 1981-88, prof. genetics, 1988—. Contbr. 7 chpts. to books, 57 articles to profl. jours., and 52 publs. to abstracts. Bd. dirs. Bur. of Protective Analysis, Gary, Ind., 1976-87; adv. bd. Mucolipidosis IV Found., N.Y.C., 1985—. Roch Studienstiftung fellow, Switzerland, 1974; March of Dimes grantee, 1984, 86, 89. Mem. Am. Coll. Med. Genetics, Am. Soc. Human Genetics, N.Y. Acad. Scis., Soc. Inherited Metabolic Disorders, Soc. Pediatric Rsch. Jewish. Home: 5200 Anthony Wayne Dr Apt 1007 Detroit MI 48202-3976 Office: Wayne State U 550 E Canfield Ave Detroit MI 48201-1969

BENZ, EDWARD J., JR., physician, educator; b. Pitts., May 22, 1946; s. Edward John and Verna Marie (Cuddyre) B.; m. Margaret A. Vettese; children: Timothy Edward, Jennifer Kirsten. AB in Biology cum laude, Princeton U., 1968; MD magna cum laude, Harvard U., 1973. Diplomate Am. Bd. Internal Medicine; cert. hematology; lic. physician, Md., Pa. Resident Peter Bent Brigham Hosp., Boston, 1973-75; fellow pediatric hematology Children's Hosp. Med. Ctr., Boston, 1974-75; fellow adult hematology Yale U. Sch. of Medicine, New Haven, Conn., 1978-79; asst. prof. internal medicine Yale U. Sch. of Medicine, New Haven, 1979-82, assoc. prof. internal medicine, human genetics, 1982-87, prof. internal medicine, human genetics, 1987-92, chief sect. hematology, 1987-92, chmn. dean's curriculum task force, 1987-88, assoc. chmn. dept. internal medicine, 1988-92; Jack D. Myers prof., chmn. dept. medicine U. Pitts. Sch. Medicine, 1993-95; Sir William Osler prof., dir. dept. medicine Johns Hopkins U. Sch. Medicine., Balt., 1995—; physician-in-chief Johns Hopkins Hosp., Balt., 1995—; prof. molecular biology and genetics Johns Hopkins U. Sch. of Medicine, 1995—; research assoc. molecular hematology Nat. Heart, Lung, Blood Inst., Bethesda, Md., 1975-78; chmn. curriculum com. Yale Sch. of

Medicine, New Haven, Conn., 1985-88; lectr. Am. Assn. Blood Banks, 1986, William B. Castle, 1995; surgeon USPHS, 1975-78, Bethesda; adj. prof. biol. scis. Carnegie Mellon U., 1993-95. Author: Molecular Genetics Methods, 1987; co-editor: Hematology, Principles and Practice, 1990, 2d edit. 94; assoc. editor Blood, 1988-94; contbr. more than 150 articles to profl. jours. Recipient Career Devel. award nat. Inst. Health, 1982, Edward Paradiso Research award Cooley's Am. Found., N.Y.C., 1985, Basil O'Connor award March of Dimes, 1980. Fellow ACP, Molecular Med. Soc.; mem. Am. Soc. Clin. Investigation (nat. coun. 1987-91, pres. 1991-92), Assn. Am. Physicians, NIH (study sect. 1984—, chmn. 1993-95), Am. Fedn. Clin. Rsch., Am. Soc. Hematology (exec. coun. 1994), Am. Clin. and Climatological Soc., Am. Bd. Internal Medicine (hematology com.), Am. Soc. Human Genetics, Assn. Profs. Medicine, Interurban Clin. Club, Princeton Elm Club, Johns Hopkins Club, Phi Beta Kappa, Sigma Xi, Alpha Omega Alpha. Home: 2028 Knox Ave Reisterstown MD 21136 Office: Johns Hopkins Sch Medicine Dept Medicine Rm 9026 1830 E Monument St Baltimore MD 21205

BENZ, EDWARD JOHN, clinical pathologist; b. Pitts., June 11, 1923; s. Henry John and Gertrude Nora (Heffernan) B.; m. Verna Marie Cuddyre, June 20, 1945; children: Edward John, Thomas James, Gregory Paul, Mary Louise. BS, U. Pitts., 1943, MD, 1946; MS, U. Minn., 1952. Intern, St. Joseph's Hosp., Pitts., 1946-47; resident, fellow Mayo Found., Mayo Clinic, 1949-53; pathologist, dir. labs. St. Luke's Hosp., Bethlehem, Pa., 1953-84, v.p. med. affairs, 1984-89; med. dir. utilization rev. Sacred Heart Hosp., Allentown, PA., 1990—; adj. prof. microbiology Lehigh U., Bethlehem, 1956-64; pres. Lab. Clin. Pathology, Bethlehem, 1956-88, ret., 1988; cons. Palmerton (Pa.) Hosp., Allentown (Pa.) State Hosp.; past dir. Miller Meml. Blood Bank, Bethlehem Mem. adv. com. Pa. Sec. Health on Clin. Labs., 1973-89; mem. health sci. adv. com. Lehigh U., 1973-89. Trustee St. Luke's Hosp., 1968-71; pres. Pa. Assn. Clin. Pathologists, 1966-67. Served as capt. M.C., AUS, 1947-49. Fellow Coll. Am. Pathologists (past chmn. anat. path. commn., past del. from Pa.), Am. Soc. Clin. Pathologists; mem. Internat. Acad. Pathology, Am. Assn. Pathologists and Bacteriologists, Am. Assn. Blood Banks, Am. Coll. Physician Execs., Sigma Xi, Alpha Omega Alpha. Club: Saucon Valley Country (Bethlehem). Contbr. articles to profl. publs. Home and Office: 1564 Saucon Valley Rd Bethlehem PA 18015-5260

BENZIES, BONNIE JEANNE, clinical and industrial psychologist; b. Chgo., May 3, 1943; d. Roy Benzies and Margaret Lucille (Hernly) Benzies-Sorensen. BS, MacMurray Coll., 1965; MS, Ill. Inst. Tech., 1971, PhD, 1980. Lic. clin. psychologist; cert. nat./internat. cert. alcohol and other drug abuse counselor; cert. alcohol, tobacco and other drug abuse preventionist; diplomate, bd. cert. forensic examiner. Statistician, psychologist State of Ill., Chgo., 1966-73; psychologist State of Ill., Manteno, 1976-82; pub. svc. adminstr. State of Ill., Elgin, 1988—; psychologist Ingalls Meml. Hosp., Harvey, Ill., 1982-84, Cook County Juvenile Ct., Chgo., 1987-88; pvt. practice Chgo., Hanover Park, Palatine, Ill., 1984—; cons., trainer PREVENTION PLUS of Palatine, 1994—; grad. tchg. asst. Ill. Inst. Tech., Chgo., 1973-74; mem. staff Hoffman Estates Med. Ctr., Woodland Hosp., Hoffman Estates. Co-author psychol. test: Time Questionnaire, 1979. Mem. Nat. Task Force on Depressive Disorders, 1991—; mem. Statewide Subcom. on Mentally Ill Substance Abuser, 1991-93. MacMurray scholar, 1961-65, Am. Legion scholar, 1963-64; recipient Achievement award in addictions counseling Loop Coll., 1986. Mem. APA, Am. Assn. Christian Counselors, Am. Bd. Forensic Examiners, Chgo. Assn. for Psychoanalytic Psychology, Employee Assistance Profls. Assn., Christian Assn. Psychol. Studies, Internat. Critical Incident Stress Found., Inc., Palatine C. of C. Home and Office: Prevention Plus of Palatine 1531 E Anderson Dr Palatine IL 60067-4101

BENZINGER, ROLF HANS, molecular biologist; b. Rostock, Fed. Republic Germany, Dec. 4, 1935; came to U.S., 1948; s. Theodor Hans and Ilse (Koss) B.; m. Elizabeth Karges Bailey, Nov. 22, 1962 (div. 1982); children: Elinor Mae, Philip. BA, Johns Hopkins U., 1956, PhD, 1961. Postdoctoral fellow Max-Planck-Inst. fuer Biochemie, Munich, 1961-65; rsch. assoc. Lab. Biochimie Genetique, Geneva, 1965-67; asst. prof. biology Dept. Biology, U. Va., Charlottesville, 1967-70, assoc. prof. biology, 1970—; program assoc. NSF, Washington, 1984-85; instr. FBI Acad., Quantico, Va., 1988, 91. Contbr. articles to profl. jours. Recipient Rsch. Career Devel. award NIH, 1971-76. Fellow AAAS; mem. Am. Soc. for Microbiology (pub. affairs com.), Phi Beta Kappa, Delta Phi Alpha. Office: Univ Va 247 Gilmer Hall Charlottesville VA 22901

BENZO-BONACCI, ROSEMARY ANNE, health facility administrator; b. Utica, N.Y., Apr. 28, 1955; d. Rocco Anthony and Grace Lillian (Maggi) B.; m. Michael V. AAS, Mohawk Valley C.C., 1988; BS, New Sch. for Social Rsch., 1992, postgrad., 1994—. With Mohawk Valley C.C., Utica, 1977-89, alumni asst., 1989-93; dir. vol. svcs., pub. rels. and devel. Charles T. Sitrin Health Care Ctr., New Hartford, N.Y., 1993—; program dir. Youth Mentorship Activities Program in Health Care Svcs. Dept. Health N.Y. Pres. Vol. Horizons, 1993—, Coalition for Tobacco Control, 1994; bd. dirs., mem. task force pub. edn. sector Utica Coalition for a Smoke-Free Cmty., 1989-93, chair ann. coalition meeting, 1990-91; chair search com. for tech. asst. Mohawk Valley C.C., 1990. Mem. Mohawk Valley C.C. Alumni Assn. (bd. dirs. 1991-93). Democrat. Roman Catholic. Home: 16 Symphony Pl Whitesboro NY 13492-2227 Office: Charles T Sitrin Health Care Ctr Box 2050 Tilden Ave New Hartford NY 13413

BENZONI, THOMAS E., emergency physician; b. Canandaigna, N.Y., Oct. 8, 1956; s. Richard John and Sue Carol (Smith) B.; m. Noreen E. O'Shea, Aug. 3, 1979; children: Sharon, Rachel, Nicole, Peter. BS in Med. Technology, Creighton U., 1978; DO, Caoll. Osteo. Medicine/Surgery, 1983. Diplomate Am. Bd. Family Practice, Am. Bd. Emergency Medicine, ABOEM (EMS). Resident Creighton/St. Joseph Hosp., Omaha, Nebr., 1985-87; dir. emergency svcs. KRMC, Jackson, Ky., 1988-91; staff emergency dept. F.F. Thompson Hosp., Canandaigua, N.Y., 1991-94, Marian Health Ctr., Sioux City, Iowa, 1994—; dir. Marian Air Care, Sioux City, 1994—. Office: 801 5th St Sioux City IA

BEN-ZVI, JEFFREY STUART, gastroenterologist, internist; b. Bklyn., Aug. 19, 1957; s. Seymour and Doris (Salzman) B.-Z.; m. Julie Genuth, May 11, 1982; children: Chana, Adina, Ilana, Aviva, Samuel. BSc, CUNY, Bklyn., 1979; MD, Columbia U., 1983. Diplomate Am. Bd. Internal Medicine, Am. Bd. Gastroenterology; bd. cert. in geriatrics. Intern St. Luke's-Roosevelt Hosp., N.Y.C., 1983-84, resident in internal medicine, 1984-86, fellow in gastroenterology, 1986-88; asst. prof. clin. med. Columbia U., N.Y.C., 1988—. Contbr. articles to profl. jours. Med. dir./advisor Hatzolah Vol. Ambulance Corp., N.Y.C., 1985—. Fellow ACP, Am. Coll. Gastroenterology; mem. AMA, Am. Gastroent. Assn., Am. Soc. Internal Medicine. Home: 2414 Avenue R Brooklyn NY 11229 Office: 911 Park Ave New York NY 10021 Office: 315 W 57th St New York NY 10019 Office: 2800 Kings Hwy Brooklyn NY 11229

BERARDI, RICHARD DOMINICK, JR., physician; b. Bronxville, N.Y., July 31, 1961; s. Richard Sr. and Josephine (Solensky) B.; m. Anne Fico; children: Michael, David. BS in Biology, Purdue U., 1984, BS in Biochemistry, 1984; DO, N.Y. Coll. Osteo. Medicine, 1990. Diplomate Am. Bd. Internal Medicine. Intern Peninsula Hosp., Far Rockaway, N.Y., 1990-91; resident Mountainside Hosp., Montclair, N.J., 1991-92, OVerook Hosp., Summit, N.J., 1992-94; physician Pratt Med. Ctr., Fredericksburg, Va., 1994-95; assoc. dir., physician Cmty. Med. Assocs., Howell, N.J., 1995—; regional dir. Cmty. Med. Assocs., 1995. Mem. AMA, Am. Coll. Physicians, Am. Osteo. Assn., Am. Coll. Osteo. Internists. Roman Catholic. Office: Cmty Med Assocs 4521 Hwy 9 Howell NJ 07731

BERARDI, RONALD STEPHEN, pathologist, educator; b. Rochester, Pa., Jan. 12, 1943; s. Desiderio John and Florence (Salvaggio) B.; m. Diane Lenore Wytaske, June 17, 1967; children: Lenore Christine, James Ronald, Anne-Marie. BS in Chemstry, U. Pitts., 1963; MD, Loyola U., Chgo., 1967. Diplomate Am. Bd. Pathology. Intern Presbyn.-St. Lukes Hosp., Chgo., 1967-68, resident in pathology, 1968-69; resident in pathology Malcolm Grow USAF Med. Ctr., Washington, 1969-71, New Eng. Deaconess Hosp., Boston, 1971-72, U. Pitts. Health Ctr. Hosp., 1972-73; Sarah Mellon Scaife fellow in immunopathology U. Pitts., 1973-74; assoc. pathologist Latrobe (Pa.) Area Hosp., 1974-80, chief pathologist, dir. labs., 1980—; co-dir. labs. Henry Clay Frick Community Hosp. Latrobe Area Hosp., Mt. Pleasant, Pa., 1974-80; assoc. instr. U. Ill., Chgo., 1967-69; teaching fellow U. Pitts., 1972-74, teaching faculty, 1974-76; instr. Thomas Jefferson Coll. Medicine, Phila., 1977—; med. dir. Sch. Med. Tech. Ind. U. Pa., 1980—; lab. insp. Coll. Am. Pathology, Chgo., 1980—; chmn. infection control com., tissue transfusion com., cancer registry, cost containment com. Latrobe Area Hosp., 1980—. Reviewer jour. Cancer, 1994; editl. bd. Physicians News Digest 1994—; contbr. articles to profl. jours. Mem. Nat. Adv. Bd. Am. Security Council, Boston, 1985; mem. Rep. Presdl. Task Force, Washington, 1985-88; mem. Rep. Nat. Com., Washington, 1985. Senatorial scholar, 1961-63; mem. Rep. Senatorial Inner Circle, U.S. Senatorial Bus. Adv. Bd., 1988, state advisor to U.S. Congl. Adv. Bd.; U.S. Congressional Adv. Bd. (state advisor). Fellow Am. Soc. Clin. Pathologists, Coll. Am. Pathologists, U.S.-Can. Acad. Pathology Inc., Internat. Biographical Assn.; mem. Am. Assn. Blood Banks, AMA (Physicians Recognition award 1985), Am. Chem. Soc., N.Y. Acad. Scis., Internat. Platform Assn., Am. Biographical Inst. (disting. leadership award), Am. Inst. Chemists, Am. Med. Writers Assn., Westmoreland County Med. Soc. (editor bulletin), Pitts. Cancer Inst. (affiliate), Latrobe Country Club, Univ. Club, U.S. Senatorial Club, Phi Eta Sigma, Alpha Epsilon Delta. Roman Catholic. Home: 811 Spring St Latrobe PA 15650-2025 Office: Latrobe Area Hosp 2D West Ave Latrobe PA 15650

BERBOS, JAMES NICKOLAS, ophthalmologist; b. Aberdeen, S.D., Sept. 29, 1922; s. Nickolas James and Beryl (Norman) B.; m. Sarah Anna Sloan, Feb. 5, 1947; children; Jo Ann, Sally Ann, James N., Jr., Nancy Ann, Elizabeth Ann. BS in Medicine, U. S.D., 1945; MD in Medicine, U. Louisville, 1946. Diplomat Am. Bd. Ophthalmology. Intern Broadlawn Polk County Hosp., Des Moines, 1947; pvt. practice Aberdeen, S.D., 1948-50, 53-64; resident in ophthalmology U. Minn., Mpls., 1964-67; ophthalmologist Fullerton (Calif.) Eye, 1967-93; pres. St. Luke's Hosp., 1961; exec. com. St. Jude's Hosp., Fullerton, chief of surgery, 1982; speaker in field. Contbr. articles to profl. jours. Mem. Sch. Bd., Aberdeen, 1953. Lt. USN, 1950-53, Korea. Republican. Episcopalian. Home: 1812 Ladera Fullerton CA 92631

BERCEL, NICHOLAS ANTHONY, neurologist, neurophysiologist; b. Budapest, Hungary, Aug. 20, 1911; came to U.S., 1940; s. Desiré and Julia (Kapos) B.; m. Eva Mindszenti, Mar. 25, 1982; children: Diana, Anthony, Christopher, Patrick, Yvette. MD, U. Rome, 1936., 1940; Resident U. Rome, 1936-38, U. Paris, 1938-40; intern Swedish Hosp., Mpls., 1958—; assoc. prof. in physiology U. So. Calif., L.A., 1948-67; mem. staff St. John Hosp., Santa Monica, 1954-84; mem. staff dept. neurodiagnosis Queen of Angels Hosp., L.A., 1960-80; neuro-psychiat. cons. Social Security Adminstrn., West Los Angeles, 1958—. Author: Textbook on Etiology of Schizophrenia, Psychopathology, 1959; contbr. numerous articles to profl. publs., including Diseases of the Nervous System, Jour. of Neuropsychiatry, Jour. AMA, Calif. Medicine, Am. Jour. Med. Scis., others. Republican.

BERCIK, MICHAEL JAMES, orthopaedic surgeon; b. Elizabeth, N.J., Dec. 19, 1950; s. Steven Joseph and Catherine (Clarke) B.; m. Anamaria Bretao, Nov. 15, 1975; children: Marie, Lisa, Michael. BS, Georgetown U., 1972, MD, 1976. Diplomate Am. Bd. Orthop. Surgery. Resident in gen. surgery North Shore U. Hosp., Manhasset, N.Y., 1976-77; resident in orthop. surgery St. Luke's Hosp., N.Y.C., 1977-80; pvt. practice orthop. surgeon Michael J. Bercik, MD, PA, Elizabeth, 1980—; clin. instr. dept. orthop. surgery U. Medicine and Dentistry of N.J., Newark, 1994—. Fellow Am. Acad. Orthop. Surgeons, Am. Coll. Surgeons; mem. N.J. Orthop. Soc., Ea. States Orthop. Assn. Roman Catholic. Office: Michael J Bercik MD PA 711 Westminster Ave Elizabeth NJ 07208

BERCOVICI, EDWIN BYRL, ophthalmologist; b. Omaha, Mar. 2, 1938; s. Jacob and Ethelyn (Kramer) B.; m. Judith Ann Egan, Dec. 6, 1971; children: Alicia, Jeffrey, Robyn. AB, U. Omaha, 1960; MD, U. Nebr., 1963. Diplomate Am. Bd. Ophthalmology. Intern Grad. Hosp. of U. Pa., Phila., 1963-64; resident Ill. Eye and Ear Infirmary/U. Ill.; pres. Med. Eye Care, S.C., Milw., 1972—. Capt. USAF, 1964-66. Mem. Milw. Grad. Club (pres. 1986-88), Phi Delta Epsilon. Office: Med Eye Care SC 5678 W Brown Deer Rd Milwaukee WI 53223

BERCU, DANIEL GREGORY, emergency physician; b. St. Louis, July 6, 1952; s. Bernard Aran and Elizabeth Lee (Johnson) B.; m. Deborah Ann Douglas, Nov. 23, 1974; 1 child, Aran Scott. BS, Eastern Mich. U., 1976; DO, Mich. State U., 1981. Diplomate Am. Bd. Emergency Medicine; cert. ACLS, ATLS. Intern Pontiac (Mich.) Osteo. Hosp., 1981-82; pvt. practice Mesa, Ariz., 1982-83; part-time emergency physician Mesa (Ariz.) Gen. Hosp., 1982-83; dir. Urgent Care Ctr. St. Joseph Hosp., Phoenix, 1984-87; dir. emergency svcs. Marion (Ill.) Meml. Hosp., 1988-93, St. Mary's Hosp., Centralia, Ill., 1993—. Mem., health com., Sunday sch. tchr. First Bapt. Ch., Marion, 1990—. Fellow Assn. Emergency Physicians; mem. Am. Assn. Physician Specialists, Christian Med. and Dental Soc. Republican. Office: St Marys Hosp 400 N Pleasant Centralia IL 62801

BERDANIER, CAROLYN DAWSON, nutrition educator, researcher; b. East Brunswick, N.J., Nov. 14, 1936; d. Frederick H.C. and Mabelle (Virginia McNiven) Dawson; m. Charles Reese Berdanier, Aug. 10, 1957; children: Lynnette, Charles, Robert. BS, Pa. State U., 1958; MS, Rutgers U., 1963, PhD, 1966. Therapeutic dietitian St. Peters Hosp., New Brunswick, N.J., 1960-61; research asst. Rutgers U., 1961-63, grad. research fellow, 1963-66; postdoctoral fellow Rutgers U., 1966-67; research nutritionist Nutrition Inst. U.S. Dept. Agr., Beltsville, Md., 1968-75; asst. prof. nutrition U. Md., College Park, 1970-75; assoc. prof. biochemistry and medicine U. Nebr., Omaha, 1975-77; prof. U. Ga., Athens, 1977—, head dept. foods and nutrition Coll. Home Econs., 1977-88; nutrition study sect., NIH, 1987, 95; mem. review panel in human nutrition U.S. Dept. Agr. Competitive Grants Program, 1978, 79, 81. NIH fellow, 1966-67; recipient Ga. Nutrition Council award for Outstanding Contbns. to Research in Human Nutrition, 1982; Lamar Dodd award for research, 1984, Borden award Am. Home Econs. Assn., 1992, Outstanding Alumna award Pa. State U., 1995. Mem. Am. Diabetes Assn., Soc. Exptl. Biology and Medicine, Am. Inst. Nutrition, Am. Soc. Clin. Nutrition, Sigma Xi, Gamma Sigma Delta, Phi Kappa Phi, Sigma Delta Epsilon. Mem. editorial bd. Jour. Nutrition, 1977-81, FASEB Jour, 1987-93, Biochem Arch, 1990—, Nutrition Rsch., 1990—; contbr. articles to profl. jours.

BERDEL, WOLFGANG E., hematologist; b. Hamburg, Germany, Jan. 31, 1952; s. Walter C. and Sigrid Berdel; m. Jeannette Malin; children: Henrik, Ania, Julia, Nils Andrew. MD, U. Freiburg, Germany, 1979; PhD, U. Munich, 1985. Diplomate German Bd. Internal Medicine, German Bd. Hematology, European Bd. Med. Oncology. Postdoctoral fellow Max-Planck-Inst., Freiburg, 1978-79; resident, fellow Tech. U., Munich, 1979-87, vice dir. divsn. hematology and oncology, 1988-90; prof. medicine U. Berlin, 1990—; vis. prof. Emory U., Atlanta, 1987-88. Contbr. over 140 articles to profl. jours.; mem. editl. acad. Internat. Jour. Oncology; developer anticancer drugs. Stabsarzt, Bundeswehr, 1982. Recipient Best Basic Rsch. Presentation award Hellenic Anticancer Soc., 1994; Heisenberg scholar Deutsche Forschungsgemeinschaft, 1987. Mem. ASCO, ASH, AACR, EORTC, ESMO, German Cancer Soc. (Carlo Erba prize 1985). Office: Freie U Berlin, Fachbereich Humanmedizin, 12200 Berlin Germany

BERDEN, ELEANOR ALICE, pathologist, family physician; b. Milford, Del., Nov. 20, 1923; d. George Kennard and Clara May (Vosburg) B.; m. Wells Elton Hunt, Aug. 17, 1978 (div. Feb. 1962); 1 child, Michael Patrick Munyon (dec.). BS in Med. Biology, Mich. State U., 1945; MD, Woman's Med. Coll. Pa., 1953. Diplomate Am. Bd. Pathology, Am. Bd. Pathologic Anatomy, Am. Bd. Clin. Pathology. Intern E.W. Sparrow Hosp., Lansing, Mich., 1953-54, resident in anatomical pathology, 1954-56; resident in clin. pathology Detroit Gen. Hosp., 1956-58; chief pathologist Ingham Med. Ctr. and Eaton Rapids (Mich.) Cmty. Hosp., 1958-75; clin. pathologist Clinton Meml. Hosp., St. Johns, Mich., 1970-75; owner, dir. lab. Pathology Assocs. of Ctrl. Mich., P.C., Lansing, 1975-80; pvt. practice family medicine Lansing, 1975-80; med. dir. Toxicology Lab. Ctr., Inc., Lansing, 1977—; locum tenens McPherson Cmty. Hosp., Howell, Mich., 1977-80, Lansing Gen. Hosp., 1977-80; staff rev. physician Disability Determination Svc., State of Mich., Lansing, 1980-84, chief med. cons., 1984—. Cellist Mason Orchestral Soc. Mem. AMA, Am. Soc. Clin. Pathology, Nat. Assn. Disability Examiners, Mich. State Med. Soc., Ingham County Med. Soc. Congregationalist. Home: 2630 W Libbie Dr Lansing MI 48917 Office: Disability Determination Svc Mich Social Svcs Dept PO Box 30011 Lansing MI 48909-7511

BEREITER-HAHN, JÜRGEN, cell biologist; b. Innsbruck, Tirol, Austria, Apr. 21, 1941; arrived in Fed. Republic Germany, 1945; s. Werner and Dorothea (Dittrich) B-H.; m. Heidi Eisenmenger; 1 child, Isabel. D in Cell Biology, U. Frankfurt, Fed. Republic Germany, 1967, postgrad., 1972. Asst. U. Frankfurt, 1968-72, prof., 1972—. Author, editor: Biology of the Integument, 1986, Cytomechanics, 1987, Cell and Tissue Culture Models in Dermatological Research, 1993; author, editor video discs on cell biology; contbr. articles to profl. jours. Recipient medal of med. faculty Charles U., 1995. Fellow Royal Micros. Soc.; mem. Inst. Scientific Film Assn., German Assn. Biol. Chemistry, German Assn. Cell Biology. Office: Goethe U, Biozentrum Marie Curie str 9, D60439 Frankfurt Germany

BERENDSEN, PETER BARNEY, anatomist, educator; b. L.A., Calif.; s. Raymond George and Maudie Belle (Lowrance) B.; m. Sallyann Margaret Lawrence, Oct. 26, 1962; children: Thomas, Margaret, Raymond. BS, St. Mary's Coll., Moraga, Calif., 1960; MS, PhD, George Washington U., 1972. Rsch. asst. Armed Forces Inst. Pathology, Washington, 1962-65; rsch. assoc. U. Mich., Ann Arbor, 1965-67; guest worker NIH, Bethesda, Md., 1970-72; instr. U. Medicine and Dentistry N.J., Newark, 1972-73, asst. prof., 1973-81, assoc. prof., 1981—, asst. dean, 1990—. With U.S. Army, 1960-62. Am. Lung Assn. grantee, NIH grantee. Mem. Microscopy Soc. Am., Am. Assn. Anatomists, Microcirculatory Soc., Sigma Xi (chpt. pres. 1990-91). Home: 152 Rockwood Rd Florham Park NJ 07932-2644 Office: U Medicine and Dentistry NJ Lab Edn 185 S Orange Ave Newark NJ 07103-2714

BERES, MILAN, surgeon; b. Trebisov, Slovak Republic, Jan. 13, 1936; came to U.S., 1968, naturalized, 1974; s. Juraj and Barbara (Hrinova) B.; grad. Slovak U., 1955; M.D., P.J. Safarik U. (Slovak Republic), 1959; m. Terezia Marcinova, Nov. 17, 1962; children: Stephen, Milan Jr. Otolaryngologist, Univ. Hosp., Kosice, Slovak Republic, 1962-68; fellow in otolaryngology Cleve. Clin. Edni. Found., 1970-71; resident physician in otolaryngology and facial plastic and reconstructive surgery U. Conn. Health Center, Farmington, 1971-74, sr. attending physician, 1974-87, chief otolaryngology sect., 1987—, Bridgeport (Ct.) Hosp.; elected pres. Slovak-Am. Cultural Ctr., N.Y.C., 1991-94. Served with Czechoslovakian Army, 1960-61. Fellow ACS; mem. AMA (physicians recognition awards), Conn. Med. Assn., Fairfield County Med. Assn., Greater Bridgeport Med. Assn., Am. Acad. Otolaryngology, ACS, Internat. Corr. Soc. Ophthalmologists and Otolaryngologists, Am. Acad. Facial Plastic and Reconstructive Surgery, New England Otolaryn. Soc., Pan Am. Assn. Oto-rhino-laryngology Head and Neck Surgery. Roman Catholic. Contbr. articles to med. jours. Home: 31 Isinglass Ter Trumbull CT 06611-4038 Office: 1681 Barnum Ave Stratford CT 06497-5302

BERESFORD, RICHARD, medical and legal educator; b. Boulder, Colo., Oct. 1, 1930; s. Howard Chester and Mollie Lee (Bowles) B.; m. Suzanne Pigott, Dec. 29, 1955; 1 child, John W. Beresford. BA, Yale U., 1952; JD, Harvard U., 1955; MD, U. Colo., Denver, 1963. Bar: Colo. 1955; diplomate Am. Bd. Psychiatry and Neurology. Assoc. Holland & Hart, Denver, 1955-59; intern, resident N.Y. Hosp., Cornell Med. Ctr., N.Y.C., 1963-65, resident neurology, 1966-68; resident neurology U. Colo., Denver, 1965-66, asst. prof. medicine, 1968-71; assoc. prof. neurology Cornell U. Med. Ctr., N.Y.C., 1971-81, prof. neurology, 1981-91; dir. dept. neurology North Shore U. Hosp., Manhasset, N.Y., 1971-90; vis. prof. Cornell Law Sch., Ithaca, N.Y., 1977—; vis. scientist Sloan Kettering Inst., N.Y.C., 1978-80, 90-92; prof. neurology U. Rochester Sch. Medicine, 1991—. Author: Legal Aspects of Neurological Practice, 1975; contbr. articles in field to profl. pubs. With USN, 1956-57. Fellow Am. Acad. Neurology; mem. ABA, AAAS. Democrat. Office: Sch Law Cornell U Ithaca NY 14853

BERESIN, EUGENE VICTOR, psychiatrist; b. Phila., Jan. 26, 1950; s. Victor Eugene and Marcella Grace (Suskind) B.; m. Mary Michaela Moran, Sept. 6, 1981; children: Jade Moran, Caitlin Rebecca, Glennon Alexa, Zachary Ivan. BA, Princeton U., 1971; MA, U. Pa., 1974, MD, 1977. Diplomate Am. Bd. Psychiatry and Neurology. Intern in pediatrics Yale New Haven Hosp., 1977-78; resident in psychiatry Mass. Gen. Hosp., Boston, 1978-80; resident in child psychiatry Children's Hosp. Med. Ctr., Boston, 1980-82; dir. gen. residency tng. dept. psychiatry Mass. Gen. Hosp., Boston, 1990-92; assoc. dir. continuing edn. Dept. Psychiatry Mass. Gen. Hosp., Boston, 1982-92, dir. child psychiatry residency tng., 1984—, dir. gen. residency tng., 1990-92, pvt. practice of psychiatry, 1982—; dir. child psychiatry residency tng. McLean Hosp., Belmont, Mass., 1992—; asst. prof. psychiatry Harvard Med. Sch., 1993—. Contbr. numerous articles to profl. jours. Recipient Kenneth Appel Award in Psychiatry U. Pa. Med. Sch., 1977, Lowenberg Award in Pediatrics U. Pa., 1977, Dunlop Award in Psychiat. Research Mass. Gen. Hosp., 1980, Tchr. of Yr. award Assn. Acad. Psychiatry, 1995. Mem. Am. Assn. Dirs. Psychiat. Residency Tng., Am. Acad. Child & Adolescent Psychiatry, Am. Psychiat. Assn. Home: 80 School St Acton MA 01720-3626 Office: Mass Gen Hosp Dept of Psychiatry Bulfinch 444 Boston MA 02114

BEREST, MYRA, nursing administrator; b. Phila., Dec. 8, 1942; d. Samuel and Dorothy (Hoffman) B. AA, Bucks County Community coll., 1976; BS in Supervision and Mgmt. cum laude, Gwynerd Mercy Coll., 1978, MS in Nursing, 1986, postgrad. RN; lic. nursing home adminstr., Pa. Dir. nursing Doylestown (Pa.) Manor, 1979-84, asst. adminstr., 1982-84; supr. Arrow Home Healthcare Agy., Phila., 1984-85; dir. nursing Heritage Towers, Doylestown, 1985—; pres. A&M Health Care Svcs., Inc., Gwynedd Valley, Pa., 1990-93; lectr. health and human devel, nursing mgmt. of human resources Pa. State U., 1992. Mem. Pa. Assn. Non-Profit Homes for Aging (del. 1985—), Cen. Bucks Nursing Assn., Long-Term Care Nursing Adminstrs. Orgn. (corr. sec. 1984-86), Cen. Bucks County C. of C., Sigma Theta Tau, Phi Theta Kappa, Beta Sigma Phi (corr. sec., pres. Iota Theta chpt. 1989-90). Home: 612 N Shady Retreat Rd Apt 58 Doylestown PA 18901-2527

BERESTON, EUGENE SYDNEY, retired dermatologist; b. Balt., Feb. 21, 1914; s. Arthur and Sarah Bertha (Hillman) B.; m. Marion Ableman, Jan. 15, 1942 (dec. May 1975); children: Linda Bereston Katz, David, Michael; m. Bertha G. Kaufman, June 7, 1980; stepchildren: Felix Kaufman, Bruce Kaufman. A.B., Johns Hopkins U., 1933; M.D., U. Md., 1937; M.Sc., U. Pa., 1945, D.Sc., 1955. Diplomate Am. Bd. Dermatology. Intern Meml. Hosp., Johnstown, Pa., 1937-38, Mercy Hosp., Balt., 1938-39; resident in dermatology U. Pa., Phila., 1939-40, Montefiore Hosp., N.Y.C., 1940-41; practice medicine specializing in dermatology Balt., 1946-95; faculty U. Md., 1946—, prof. medicine in dermatology, 1972—; instr. dermatology Johns Hopkins U., 1946-60; chief dermatology Mercy Hosp., 1968-95; part-time chief dermatology VA Hosp., Washington, 1977-83; cons. dermatology VA Hosp. Balt., 1951-76, Spring Grove State Hosp., 1952-82. Bd. dirs., chmn. Religious Sch., Temple Oheb Shalom, 1960-72, trustee, 1977-80. Served to maj. M.C. AUS, 1941-46, PTO. Recipient research grant U.S. Army, 1951-57, award Ner Israel Rabbinical Coll., 1970. Fellow ACP, Am. Acad. Dermatology, Royal Soc. Health (Eng.), Royal Soc. Medicine; mem. AMA, Am. Legion (comdr. 1971-73), Dermatology Found., Md. Dermatol. Soc., Md. Med. Soc., Balt. City Med. Soc., Civitan Club (bd. dirs. Balt. chpt. 1964-78, 89-95), Johns Hopkins Club, Suburban Club. Home: 7 Slade Ave Apt 221 Baltimore MD 21208-5227

BEREZIN, ALEXANDRE, surgeon; b. Paris, Oct. 1, 1927; s. Berezin Simon and Fanny (Portnoi) B.; m. Nicole Lugan, Dec. 7, 1976; m. Denise Duval, June 6, 1956; children—Serge, Catherine. M.D., U. Paris. Resident Hosp. of Paris, 1955-59, asst., 1960-73; clinic chief U. Paris, 1960-61; chief ear/nose and throat dept. Hosp. Nanterre, 1973—; prof. U. Paris VII, 1975—; contbr. to field. Author: Practical Book of Eye, Ear, Nose and Throat, 1985, Practical Handbook of Daily Medicine, 1996; editor: Ellipses; contbr. numerous articles, tech. revs. to profl. lit. Served with arty. French Army, 1947. Mem. Laryngology Soc. Paris, French Soc. Laryngology (presenter), French Soc. Plastic and Reconstructive Surgery. Avocations: sailing, photography, video, writing. Home: 6 Rue Mirabeau, F-75016 Paris France

BEREZIN, MARTIN ARTHUR, retired psychiatrist; b. Wrentham, Mass., Sept. 14, 1912; s. Samuel and Fannie (Fliegleman) B.; m. Evelyn Polan, Jan. 14, 1942; children: Jane, Robert, Charles. BS, Boston U., 1934, MD, 1937. Diplomate Am. Bd. Psychiatry and Neurology. Intern Mars Meml. Hosp., Boston, 1937-39; resident Medfield State Hosp., Harding, Mass., 1939-40; prof. med. sch. Harvard U., Boston, 1947-79, prof. emeritus, 1979—; staff physician Beth Israel Hosp., Boston, 1947-87, McLean Hosp., Belmont, Mass., 1951-87; ret., 1987; tng. analyst Boston Pscyhoanalytic Soc., 1965-80. Editor: Geriatric Psychiatry, 1965; contbr. articles to profl. jours. Col. U.S. Army, 1940-46. Fellow Am. Pscyhiat. Assn. (Weinberg award 1987); mem. Am. Psychoanalytic Assn., Phi Beta Kappa. Home: 241 Perkins St Apt 105C Jamaica Plain MA 02130-4002

BERG, ARTHUR ZELIG, psychiatrist, educator; b. Phila., 1931. Student, U. Pa.; MD, Boston U., 1961. Diplomate Am. Bd. Psychiatry and Neurology. Internship Phila. Gen. Hosp., 1961-62; psychiatric residency Harvard-Mass. Gen. Hosp., Boston U.-Boston VA Hosp., Tufts U. spl. study unit, 1962-65; chief of psychiatry Beverly (Mass.) Hosp., 1969-83; vis. psychiatrist Mass. Gen. Hosp., Boston, 1983—; asst. clin. prof. Harvard Med. Sch., Boston, 1983—. Fellow Am. Psychiat. Assn. (life). Office: Parkhurst Med Bldg Beverly MA 01915

BERG, CHRISTINE DOROTHY, radiation oncologist; b. Chgo., Nov. 18, 1954; d. Roy Albert and Dorothy (Dahlberg) B.; m. Cyril Draffin, 1990. BS, Northwestern U., 1975, MD, 1977. Diplomate Nat. Bd. Med. Examiners, Am. Bd. Radiology in Therapeutic Radiology, Am. Bd. Internal Medicine in Internal Medicine and Med. Oncology. Resident in internal medicine Northwestern Meml. Hosp., Chgo., 1977-80; chief med. resident Northwestern Med. Hosp., Chgo., 1980-81; med. staff fellow Med. Oncology br. Nat. Cancer Inst., Bethesda, Md., 1981-84; radiation therapy resident Georgetown U. Hosp., Washington, 1984-86, clin. dir. benign breast disease svcs., 1987-88; dir. breast radiation therapy, dir. residency tng. program, assoc. prof. Georgetown U. Hosp., 1992—; clin. dir. Georgetown Radiation Medicine Assocs., Rockville, Md., 1986-92. Mem. editorial bd. Physicians Data Query, 1986—; contbr. articles to profl. jours. Bd. alumni councillors Northwestern U. Med. Sch., Chgo., 1988-94; interviewer Northwestern U. Alumni Admissions Coun., 1984—; bd. dirs. Rockville Cmty. Clinic, 1986-90. Mem. Am. Soc. Therapeutic Radiology and Oncology, Am. Soc. Clin. Oncology, ACP, AMA, Assn. of Residents in Radiation Oncology (exec. com. 1984-86), Alpha Omega Alpha. Office: Radiation Oncology Georgetown U 3800 Reservoir Rd NW Washington DC 20007-2196

BERG, IRWIN AUGUST, psychology educator; b. Chgo., Oct. 9, 1913; s. Bertil Sigfried and Clara (Anderson) B.; m. Sylvia Maria Taipale, Mar. 4, 1939; 1 dau., Karen Astrid (Mrs. A. C. Kirby). A.B. cum laude, Knox Coll., 1936; A.M., U. Mich., 1940, Ph.D., 1942. Asst. prof. psychology U. Ill., 1942-47; assoc. prof. Pomona Coll., 1947-48, Northwestern U., 1948-55; chmn. dept., prof. psychology La. State U., 1955-65, dean coll. arts and scis. emeritus, prof. psychology, 1965-79; Spl. cons. U.S. Dept. Labor, U.S. VA, La. State Dept. Hosps.; Mem. La. State Commn. on Law Enforcement and Adminstrn. Criminal Justice, 1968-73; mem. La. Bd. Licensing for Sanitarians. Author: Workbook in Psychology, 1961, Response Set and Personality Assessment, 1967; Co-editor: Conformity and Deviation, 1961, An Introduction to Clinical Psychology, 3d edit, 1966. Bd. dirs. Nat. Council on Arts and Scis., 1970-73. Mem. Am. Psychol. Assn. (pres. div. counseling psychology 1964), Southeastern Psychol. Assn. (pres. 1963), Southwestern Psychol. Assn. (pres. 1963-64), AAAS, AAUP, Phi Beta Kappa, Sigma Xi, Phi Kappa Phi, Phi Beta. Home: St James Pl 333 Lee Dr Apt 17G Baton Rouge LA 70808-4980

BERG, JANET M., mental health nurse; b. Port Arthur, Tex., Nov. 14, 1951; d. Peter and Helen B. (Merwin) Berg; m. Everett Siegel, May 5, 1985; children: Leigh P., Daniel J. BSN, U. Tex., 1978; MSN, U. Md., Balt., 1982. Staff nurse, clin. instr., shift coord. Johns Hopkins Hosp., Balt.; instr. nursing Johns Hopkins U. Sch. of Nursing, Balt. Mem. Am. Nurses Assn., Md. Nurses Assn., Sigma Theta Tau.

BERG, JEREMY M., chemistry educator. Prof., dir. dept. biophysics Johns Hopkins U., Balt. Recipient Pure Chemistry award Am. Chem. Soc., 1993, Eli Lilly Biological Chemistry award Am. Chem. Soc. 1995. Office: Johns Hopkins Univ Sch Dept Biophysics 720 Rutland Ave Baltimore MD 21205-2109

BERG, PATRICIA ELENE, molecular biologist; b. Dubuque, Iowa, Sept. 17, 1943; s. Clifford Jay and Dorothy Ruth (McKibben) Emerson; 1 child, Bridget K. Berg. S.B. in Math., U. Chgo., 1965; Ph.D. in Microbiology, Ill. Inst. Tech., 1973. Postdoctoral fellow U. Chgo., 1973-78; dir. genetic engring. Bethesda Rsch. Labs., Rockville, Md., 1978-80; expert NIH, Bethesda, 1980-82, sr. staff fellow, 1982-85, sr. staff fellow Nat. Inst. Digestive Diseases and Kidney, 1985-91; assoc. prof. div. of pediatric hematology/oncology Sch. Medicine U. Md., Balt., 1991—. Contbr. articles to profl. jours. Scholar U. Chgo., 1961-65, Ill. State U., 1965. Mem. N.Y. Acad. Scis., AAAS, Am. Soc. Microbiology, Sigma Xi. Democrat. Methodist. Club: Chesapeake Masters Swim Team. Avocations: swimming; reading. Office: U Md Sch Medicine Divsn Pediatric Hematology/Oncology BRB 10-015, 655 W Baltimore St Baltimore MD 21201-1544

BERG, SAUL R., obstetrician, gynecologist, educator; b. Pitts., Apr. 11, 1940; s. Harry S. and Betty H. Berg; m. Rhonda S. Cohen, June 2, 1963; children: Rebecca I., David J., Suzy H. BA, Washington and Jefferson Coll., 1961; MD, W.Va. U., 1965. Diplomate Am. Bd. Ob-Gyn. Intern Allegheny Gen. Hosp., Pitts., 1965-66; resident U. Pitts., 1966-70; pvt. practice, Pitts., 1972—; clin. assoc. prof. ob-gyn. Magee Women's Hosp., U. Pitts., 1972—; prof. U. Pitts., 1972—. Maj. USMC, 1970-72. Mem. AMA, Pa. Med. Soc., Allegheny County Med. Soc., Pitts. Ob-Gyn Soc. Office: 532 S Aiken Ave Pittsburgh PA 15232-1521

BERG, STACEY LYNN, pediatric oncologist; b. Pitts., Apr. 17, 1960. AB, Harvard U., 1981; MD, U. Pitts., 1985. Diplomate Am. Bd. Pediatrics, Am. Bd. Pediatric Hematology-Oncology. Resident Children's Hosp. Pitts., 1985-88; fellow pediatric hematology-oncology pediatric br. Nat. Cancer Inst., Bethesda, Md., 1988-91; biotech. fellow Nat. Cancer Inst., Bethesda, 1991-94; asst. prof. pediatrics Uniformed Scis. U. Health Scis., Bethesda, 1993-94, Tex. Childrens Hosp., Baylor Coll. Medicine, Houston, 1994—. Recipient travel award Am. Soc. Clin. Oncology, Washington, 1990. Mem. Am. Assn. Cancer Rsch., Phi Beta Kappa. Office: Tex Childrens Cancer Ctr 6621 Fannin MC3-3320 Houston TX 77030

BERGA, SARAH LEE, women's health physician, educator; b. San Benito, Tex., May 22, 1954; d. John Orrin and Nancy Estelle (Michael) B.; m. Frederick S. Sherman, Sept. 26, 1981 (div. 1994); children: Alexis Estelle, Nathaniel Abbott; m. Lockwood Hoehl, Oct. 28, 1995. BA, U. Va., 1976, MD, 1980. Diplomate Am. Bd. Ob-Gyn., Am. Bd. Reproductive Endocrinology. From asst. to assoc. prof. U. Pitts., 1988—; dir. reproductive endocrinology fellowship U. Pitts. Sch. of Medicine, 1995—; med. dir. menopause ctr. Magee-Womens Hosp.; fellowship dir. Reproductive Endocrinology, U. Pitts. Home: 5432 Northumberland St Pittsburgh PA 15217-1129 Office: U Pitts Magee Womens Hosp 300 Halket St Pittsburgh PA 15213-3108

BERGDOLL, MERLIN SCOTT, retired food microbiology educator; b. Petersburg, W.Va., Sept. 23, 1916; s. James E. and Rhoda (Sites) B.; m. Mildred Paddack, June 4, 1942 (div. Aug. 1973); children: Janice, Alice, Carol. BS in Agr., W.Va. U., 1940; PhD in Agrl. Biochemistry, Purdue U., 1946; D. honoris causa, U. Madrid, 1989. Instr. U. Chgo., 1946-50, asst. prof., 1950-56, assoc. prof., 1956-66; prof. U. Wis., Madison, 1966-88, prof. emeritus, 1988—. Mem. editorial bd. ASM jours., Applied & Clin. Microbiology; co-author: Toxic Shock Syndrome, 1990; contbr. over 170 articles to referred jours. Pres. Community Improvement Assn., Chgo., 1948-50; moderator Community Ch. Congregation, Chgo., 1950-60s; clk. of session Dale Height's Presbyn. Ch., Madison, 1970s. Fulbright fellow Fulbright Com., Brazil, 1987; grantee NIH. Mem. ACS, Am. Soc. for Microbiology, Inst. Food Microbiology, Am. Soc. Biol. Chemists. Baptist.

BERGELSON, JEFFREY MICHAEL, pediatrician , educator; b. Phila., 1950. MD, U. Penn., 1981. Diplomate Am. Bd. Pediatrics. Resident in pediatrics U. Calif., San Francisco, 1981-84; fellow in infectious diseases Children's Hosp., Boston; pediatrician Dana-Farber Cancer Inst., Boston; instr. pediatrics Harvard Med. Sch. Recipient Established Investigator award Am. Heart Assn., 1995. Office: Lab on Infectious Diseases Dana-Farber Cancer Inst 44 Binney St Boston MA 02215-6084*

BERGEN, DONNA CATHERINE, neurologist; b. Crawfordshire, Ind., Mar. 17, 1945; d. Donald Walter and Phyllis (Noland) B.; m. Thomas Arthur Madden, May 28, 1978. BA, Vassar Coll., 1967; MD, U. Ill., Chgo., 1971. Diplomate Am. Bd. Neurology and Psychiatry. Intern in internal medicine Evanston (Ill.) Hosp., 1971-72; resident in neurology Rush-Presbyn.-St. Luke's Med. Ctr., Chgo., 1972-75, asst. attending neurologist, 1975-82, assoc. attending neurologist, 1983-89, sr. attending neurologist, 1989—, dir. Electroencephalography Lab., 1975-88; asst. prof. dept. neurol. scis. Rush Med. Coll., 1975-82, assoc. prof. neurol. scis., 1982—, asst. chmn. dept. neurol. scis.; cons. neurologist Cook County Hosp., 1992—; mem. staff Rush North Shore Hosp., Chgo., 1993—; hon. clin. asst. electroencephalography Nat. Hosp. for Nervous Diseases, London, 1974, hon. clin asst. Evoked Potential Lab., 1981; cons. for neurology St. Basil's Clinic, Chgo., 1989—; mem. profl. adv. bd. Epilepsy Svcs. Northwestern Ill., 1986—, Epilepsy Svcs. of Greater Chgo., 1993—; cons., lectr. in field; organizer, moderator, presenter seminars in field; examiner Am. Bd. Qualification in Electroencephalography, 1982, 88, 96. Reviewer Neurology, 1987-96, Archives of Neurology, 1988-91, Electroencephalography and Clin. Neurphysiology, 1987-96, Epilepsia, 1990-93, Jour. AMA, 1989-96; contbr. articles, abstracts, revs., chpts. to profl. pubs. Grantee Lorex Pharms., 1986-87, Burroughs Wellcome Co., 1988-90, McNeil Pharm. Co., 1988-90, 89-92, Epilepsy Found. Am., 1988-89, Parke Davis, 1989-93, Wallace, 1989-91, 90-92, Marion Merrell Dow, 1990-92, 91, Cyberonics, 1990-92, Abbott Labs., 1991—, Dainippon Pharm. Co., 1993—, Atlena Labs., 1994—. Fellow Am. Acad. Neurology, Am. EEG Soc., Royal Soc. Medicine; mem. Am. Epilepsy Soc., Am. Acad. Neurology, Chgo. Neurol. Soc. (pres. 1992-93), Chgo. Neurol. Soc. (sec.-treas. 1989-90, v.p. 1991-92), Soc. for Clin. Autonomic Disorders, World Fedn. Neurology (founding mem., rsch. group on orgn. and delivery of neurol. svcs. 1990—), Alpha Omega Alpha. Office: Rush Med Coll 1725 W Harrison St Chicago IL 60612-3828

BERGENTZ, GUNNAR SVEN, orthopaedic surgeon; b. Vänersborg, Sweden, Aug. 8, 1949; s. Sven Gunnar and Margit (Andersson) B.; m. Synnove Lena Lindquist, Aug. 18, 1952; children: Kajsa, Pontus, Josefine, Rasmus. Civil Engr., Chalmers TH, Göteborg, 1973, MD, 1981. Cert. specialist in orthopedic surgery and gen. surgery. Asst. cons. Lasarettet, Lindesberg, Sweden, 1986, cons., 1986—. Capt. Swedish mil. Home: Talludden, 713 94 Nora Sweden Office: Lasarettet, 711 85 Lindesberg Sweden

BERGER, ALLAN SIDNEY, psychiatrist, educator; b. N.Y.C., Nov. 26, 1931; s. Nathan and Ida (Masor) B.; m. Lois Harriet Blumfield, Dec. 27, 1953; children: Karen, Gary, Jonathan. AB magna cum laude, Syracuse U., 1951; MD, SUNY, Bklyn., 1955. Diplomate Am. Bd. Psychiatry and Neurology, 1962; additional qualification in geriatric psychiatry cert., 1991. Intern L.I. Coll. Hosp., N.Y.C., 1955-56; resident Yale U. Sch. Medicine, New Haven, 1956-58, fellow Yale Child Study Ctr., 1958-59; pvt. practice Silver Spring, Md., 1961—; asst. chief D.C. Gen. Hosp., Washington, 1961-62; clin. prof. Georgetown U. Sch. Medicine, Washington, 1986—; cons. NIH, 1987-88; command cons. Nat. Naval Med. Ctr. Bethesda, 1990—; mem. physician expert panel VA, 1993-96. Contbr. articles to profl. jours. Cons. Peace Corps, 1962, Hebrew Home for the Aged, Rockville, Md., 1962-72. Recipient Vicennial Medalist award Georgetown U. Sch. Medicine, 1981. Mem. AMA, Mid-Atlantic Group Psychotherapy Soc. (bd. dirs. 1977-78), Metro. Washington Soc. Adolescent Psychiatry (treas. 1979-80, pres. 1982-83), Med. and Chirurgical Faculty Md. B'nai B'rith. Republican. Home and Office: 1302 Midwood Pl Silver Spring MD 20910-1645

BERGER, ANITA HAZEL, psychotherapist. adult educator; b. N.Y.C., Mar. 27, 1930; d. Harry William and Sadye (Lauzar) Fink; m. Ramon Francis Berger, May 6, 1951, (dec.); children: Elizabeth Harrie, Gideon Samuel. BA cum laude, Bklyn. Coll., 1951; MSW, U. Pa., 1953; postgrad., Columbia U., NYU. Cert. social worker, N.Y. Psychotherapist Jewish Community Svcs. L.I., N.Y.C., 1953-57; psychotherapist, field work instr. Jewish Family Svc., N.Y.C., 1957-60; supr. lower Manhattan social svc. dept., dir. student unit N.Y.C. Housing Authority, 1972-74; asst. prof. SUNY Grad. Sch. Social Work, Buffalo, 1974-75; psychotherapist Ch. Mission of Hope Family Svc., Erie County Mental Health Svcs., Buffalo, 1975-77; pvt. practice Providence, 1978—; instr. Brown Learning Community Brown U., 1988-92; cons., educator orgnl. and corp. leadership devel. Quest for Excellence, Providence, 1992—, staff assoc., 1992—; orgnl. cons., 1995—; cons. in field. Coord. Community Ctr. Art Show, N.Y.C., 1964-71; rep. community planning bd. 2 Congressman Koch's, N.Y.C., 1968-71; mem. adv. com. to bd. dirs. Mental Health Clinic, Buffalo, 1976-77; bd. dirs., chmn. tng. and edn. com., trainer Vols. in Action, Providence, 1979-85; mem. R.I. adv. com. U.S. Commn. on Civil Rights, 1981-85; rep. R.I. Coalition Against Bigotry, 1982-85; mem. allocations and budget com. United Way Southeastern New Eng., Providence, 1981-84; mem. R.I. Gov.'s Adv. Commn. on Women, 1982-85. Recipient Woman of Yr. award Providence Bus. and Profl. Women's Orgn., 1984. Fellow N.Y. State Soc. Clin. Social Work Psychotherapists; mem. Nat. Assn. Social Workers, R.I. Group Psychotherapy Assn. (pres. 1988-89), Alpha Kappa Delta. Jewish.

BERGER, BARBARA PAULL, social worker, marriage and family therapist; b. St. Louis, June 18, 1955; d. Ted and Florence Ann (Vines) Paull; m. Allan Berger, Dec. 27, 1980; children: Melissa Dawn, Tammi Alyse, Jessica Lauren. BS, U. Tex., 1977; MSSW, U. Wis.. 1978. Diplomate Am. Bd. Clin. Social Work; lic. social worker, Tex., Miss., Ky.; cert. marriage and family therapist. Clin. social worker Child and Family Svcs., Buffalo, 1980-81, United Cerebral Palsy Assn., St. Louis, 1982-83; clin. social worker/coord. Jewish Family Life Edn. Jewish Family Svc., Dallas, 1984-85, 88-90; instr. Miss. Delta C. C., Greenville, 1991; child and adolescent therapist United Behavioral Systems, Louisville, 1993-94; therapist CMG Health-Inpsych, Louisville, 1994—. Mem. NASW, Acad. Cert. Social Workers, Am. Assn. Marriage and Family Therapy, Phi Kappa Phi, Pi Lambda Theta, Omicron Nu. Home: 2719 Avenue Of The Woods Louisville KY 40241-6281

BERGER, BRUCE WARREN, physician, urologist; b. Auburn, N.Y., Sept. 25, 1942; m. Toni M. LeRoy, Aug. 27, 1966; children: Jill, David. BA, Cornell U., 1964; MD, Upstate Med. Ctr., 1968. Diplomate Am. Bd. of Urology, Nat. Bd. of Med. Examiners. Surg. intern Hosp. U. of Pa., Phila., 1968-69; surgery resident NYU Hosp.-Bellevue (N.Y.) Med. Ctr., 1969-70; resident in urology Johns Hopkins Hosp., Balt., 1972-76; urologist Cohen, Berger & Jaskulsky, P.A., Balt., 1976—; assoc. prof. clin. surgery urology U. Md., Balt., 1976—; attending, pres. med. staff Sinai Hosp., 1989-90, 94, 95, bd. dirs., 1989—; attending Northwest Hosp., Greater Balt. Med. Ctr. Maj. USAR, 1970-72, Vietnam. Mem. AMA, Balt. Med. Soc., Am. Assn. Clin. Urologists, Md. Urologists Assn. (pres. 1995-95), Am. Urologists Assn., The Associate Jewish Cmty. Fedn. (chmn. physicians divsn. 1991), Alpha Omega Alpha. Office: Cohen Berger & Jaskulsky PA 2411 W Belvedere Ave Ste 305 Baltimore MD 21215-5217

BERGER, EDWARD BENJAMIN, biofeedback therapist; b. Washington, Sept. 13, 1956; s. Meyer and Dorothy (Platt) B. BS in Psychology, U. Md., 1978, MA in Biomed. Health, 1981. Cert. biofeedback therapist, profl. counselor, stress mgmt. educator, pain mgmt. specialist. Biofeedback therapist Inst. for Behavioral Rsch., Silver Spring, Md., 1978-80, Behavioral Medicine Ctr., No. Va. Psychiat. Group, Fairfax, 1981-90; dir. biofeedback svcs. Behavioral and Phys. Medicine Assocs., Rockville, Md., 1991-94; biofeedback program dir. Ctr. for Physical Medicine and Rehab., Rockville, Md., 1995—. Mem. AACD, Assn. Applied Psychophysiology and Biofeedback, Am. Acad. Pain Mgmt., Am. Pain Soc., Biofeedback Soc. Washington, Md. and Va.

BERGER, E(VAN) ROY, medical oncologist and hematologist; b. Bklyn., Aug. 2, 1944; s. Theodore Trietsch and Ida (Elion) B.; m. Joan Carol Askins, Mar. 21, 1971; children: Allison Lara, Jessica Karen. BS in Chemistry, Bucknell U., 1966; MD, SUNY, Bklyn., 1970. Diplomate Am. Bd. Internal Medicine, sub-bds. med. oncology and hematology. Intern, resident in medicine Roosevelt Hosp.-Columbia Coll. Phys. and Surg., N.Y.C., 1970-73, fellow in hematology, 1973-74; fellow in med. oncology Meml. Sloan-Kettering Cancer Ctr., N.Y.C., 1974-75; pvt. practice North Shore Hematology-Oncology Assocs. P.C., East Setauket/Smithtown, N.Y., 1975—; chmn. tumor bd. St. John's Episcopal Hosp., Smithtown, 1977—; mem. Prostate Cancer Edn. Coun., N.Y.C., 1989—; chmn. Prostate Cancer Oncology Group, Grand Rapids, Mich., 1990—. Contbr. articles to profl. jours. Mem. AMA, Am. Soc. Hematology, Am. Soc. Clin. Oncology, Suffolk County Med. Soc., Am. Urolog. Assn. (affiliate),. Office: North Shore Hematology-Oncology 235 N Belle Mead Rd East Setauket NY 11733

BERGER, FRANK MILAN, biomedical researcher, scientist, former pharmaceutical company executive; b. Pilsen, Czechoslovakia, June 25, 1913; came to U.S., 1947, naturalized, 1953; s. Otto and Martha (Weigner) B.; m. Bozena Jahodova, Mar. 15, 1939 (dec. Nov. 1972); children: Franklin Milan, Thomas Jan; m. A. Christine Spade, May 21, 1975. M.D., U. Prague, Czechoslovakia, 1937, SUNY, 1948; D.Sc. (hon.), Phila. Coll. Sci. and Pharmacy, 1966. Research fellow physiology U. Prague, 1934-36, research asst. bacteriology, 1936-38; bacteriologist Czechoslovak State Inst. Health, 1938-39; sr. resident Monsall Hosp. Infectious Diseases, Manchester, Eng., 1941-43; chief pharmacologist Brit. Drug Houses, London, 1945-47; asst. prof. pediatrics U. Rochester, 1947-49; dir. research Carter-Wallace Inc., 1949-55, v.p., 1955-58; pres. Wallace Labs. div. Carter-Wallace Inc., Cranbury, N.J., 1958-73; mem. adv. council dept. biology Princeton U., 1961-74, lectr., prof., 1969-74; mem. sci. adv. com. Waksman Inst. Microbiology, Rutgers U., 1960-67; cons. Surgeon Gen., Walter Reed Army Med. Center, Washington, 1974-80; pres. Mario Negri Inst. Found. for Biomed. Research, Inc., 1973—; prof. psychiatry U. Louisville Med. Sch., 1974-90; hon. prof. microbiology Waksman Inst. Microbiology, Rutgers U., 1982. Fellow N.Y. Acad. Scis., Am. Coll. Neuropsychopharmacology, AAAS; mem. AMA, AAUP, Am. Pharm. Soc., Brit. Pharm. Soc., Can. Pharm. Soc., Am. Bacteriol. Soc., Soc. Exptl. Biology and Medicine, Am. Chem. Soc., Biometric Soc., Cosmos Club (Washington), Princeton Club (N.Y.C.), N.Y. Athletic Club, Sigma Xi. Office: 200 E 72d St New York NY 10021

BERGER, HAROLD RICHARD, physician; b. Elizabeth, N.J., Oct. 31, 1914; s. Abraham and Frances (Herield) B.; m. Minna Constance Wolfson, Aug. 21, 1944; children: Brian, Andrew, Alan, James. AB, Cornell U., Ithaca, N.Y.; MD, NYU Sch. Medicine. Diplomate Am. Bd. Pediatrics. Intern Elizabeth (N.J.) Gen. Hosp., 1940-41; maj. U.S. Med. Corp., 1941-46; resident in pediatrics Jersey City (N.J.) Med. Ctr., 1951-53; pvt. practice, 1946—; mem. child health program Elizabeth Bd. of Health, Hillside Bd. of Health; sch. physician Elizabeth Bd. Edn. Recipient award Am. Bd. Pediatrics, 1954. Mem. AMA, N.J. Med. Soc., Union County Med. Soc. Home: 987 Harding Rd Elizabeth NJ 07208 Office: 250 Elizabeth Ave Elizabeth NJ 07206

BERGER, HARVEY ROBERT, psychologist; b. Quincy, Mass., Nov. 3, 1927; s. Joel Joseph and Helen Esther (Stone) B.; m. Thelma Lee Cohen, July 11, 1954. BA, Tufts U., 1949, MA, 1950; PhD, U. Mo., 1953. Diplomate Am. Bd. Examiners Profl. Psychology, Prescribing Psychologists Register, cert. fellow; cert. prescribing psychologist. Psychologist Marblehead (Mass.) Pub. Schs., 1953-79; dir. psychol. svcs. federally assisted programs Salem (Mass.) Pub. Schs., 1967-76; cons. Revere (Mass.) Pub. Schs., 1979-90; nat. svc. officer Jewish War Vets. U.S.A., 1984—; assoc. prof. Salem State Coll., 1963; clin. dir. North Shore Psychol. Counseling and Testing Ctr., 1963-75; pres. Paul Revere Savs. & Loan Assn., 1971-76, William Dawes Realty Corp.; with U.S. Dept. Commerce, 1983-84. Mem. Nat. Commn. on Safety Edn., 1952-54; capt., Mass. comdt. U.S. Naval Cadet Program, 1966-86; col. Gov.'s staff Ky. N.G.; pres. Area Bd. on Mental Health and Retardation, 1975-78; vice chmn. Greater Lynn (Mass.) Coun. for Children, Mass. Office for Children, 1977-78; mem. governance bd. Greater Lynn Cmty. Mental Health Ctr., 1977-90; auditor Rep. City Com., Lynn, 1970-75; pres. Mass. Am. Legion Coll., 1964-66; pres. NEA Mut. Fund; chmn. bd. NEA Income Fund; trustee Ida C. Romanow Fund, Jewish Cmty. Rels. Coun. of Greater Boston; pres. Congregation Chevra Tehillim; diplomat World Jewish Congress. With U.S. Army, 1945-47. Sch. Alcohol Studies fellow Yale U., 1957, John F. Kennedy Libr. fellow. Fellow APA; mem NASP (life), NEA (life, Disting. Svc. award), VFW (life), DAV (life, past comdr.), Am. Assn. Mental Retardation, Am. Orthopsychiat. Assn., Royal Soc. Health, Am. in Torah (life, patron, benefactor), Soc. for Personality and Social Psychology, Internat. Assn. for the Scientific Study of Intellectual Disabilities, Nat. Assn. Sch. Counselors, Mass. Schoolmasters Club (life). Am. Psychology-Law Soc., Soc. for Advancement Social Psychology, Soc. for Psychol. Study Social Issues, Am. Security Coun. Found. (congl. adv. bd.), USN Meml. Found. (mem. nat. adv. coun.), Soc. Behaviorists, Religious Zionists Am. (life), Mass. Bar Assn., Am. Legion (life, past comdr.), Def. of Washington Garrison, Army and Navy Union USA, Mil. Order Purple Heart (life, comdr. Dept. Mass.), Navy League (life), U.S. Naval Inst. (life, Silver Citation award), Orders and Medals Soc. Am., Nat. Soc. Profs. (life), Am. Assn. Higher Edn. (life), Jewish War Vets (life, nat. svc. officer 1984—, Disting. Svc. award), Tufts Jumbo Club, Nat. Eagle Scout Assn., Masons (32 degree), Shriners (fire brigade chaplain), Legion of Honor, Order Ea. Star (auditor), Order of Amaranth (auditor), Phi Beta Kappa, Phi Delta Kappa. Home: 31 Tudor St Lynn MA 01902-4617 Office: John F Kennedy Federal Bldg Boston MA 02203

BERGER, HENRY GRANT, psychiatrist; b. Pitts., Aug. 9, 1943; s. Emanuel and Yolane (Brody) B. BA, Brandeis U., Mass., 1965; MD, U. Pa., Phila., 1969. Diplomate Am. Bd. Psychiatry and Neurology in both general and child and adolescent psychiatry. Pvt. practice psychiatry Phila.; staff psychiatrist Pennsylvania Hosp., Phila., 1986—; asst. clin. prof. psychiatry U. Pa., Phila., 1976—; intern UCLA-Wadsworth Hosp., 1969-70; resident in psychiatry U. Pa., Phila., 1970-72; fellow in psychiatry Phila. Child Guidance Clinic, 1972-74. Contbr. articles to profl. jours., chpts. to books. Mem. Phila. Soc. Adolescent Psychiatry (pres. 1990-91), Am. Psychiat. Assn., Acad. Child Psychiatrists. Home: 18 Druim Moir Philadelphia PA 19118 Office: 2401 Pennsylvania Ave Philadelphia PA 19130-3001

BERGER, HOWARD STEPHEN, psychiatrist; b. N.Y.C., Apr. 18, 1941; s. Morris Marvin and Lillian (Richel) B.; m. Frances Erica Rosen; children: Daniel, Jeffrey. BA, Amherst Coll., 1962; MD, U. Rochester, 1966. Diplomate Am. Bd. Psychiatry and Neurology, Gen. and Geriatric Psychiatry. Med. intern U. Pitts., 1966-67; surgeon USPHS, 1967-69; resident in psychiatry Sch. Medicine Boston U., 1969-72; assoc. dir. psychiatry inpatient svc. Boston City Hosp., 1972-73; asst. attending psychiatrist McLean Hosp., Belmont, Mass., 1973-75; chief of psychiatry The Meml. Hosp., Worcester, Mass., 1975-82; assoc. prof. psychiatry Med. Sch. U. Mass., Worcester, 1979—; clin. instr. in psychiatry Med. Sch. Harvard U., Boston, 1973—; chairperson psychiat. div. The Med. Ctr. of Cen. Mass./Meml., Worcester, 1982-91; pvt. practice Worcester, 1991—; bd. dirs. Cen. Mass. Health Systems Agy., 1986-88; mem. bd. corporators Worcester Fights Back, 1990—. Mem. Temple Emanuel, Worcester. Fellow Am. Psychiat. Assn.; mem. Mass. Psychiat. Soc., Mass. Med. Soc., Am. Acad. Psychiatrists in Alcoholism and Addictions, Am. Assn. Geriatric Psychiatry. Home: 65 Kinnicutt Rd Worcester MA 01602-1548 Office: 295 Lincoln St Worcester MA 01605-3639

BERGER, LORINDA JEAN, psychiatrist; b. Passaic, N.J., June 16, 1957; d. I. Andrew and Lita Berger. BA in Econs. and English, U. Fla., 1980; postgrad studies, Marshall U. Grad. Sch., 1982; OD, WV Sch. Osteopath. Medicine, 1988. Diplomate Am. Bd. Psychiatry and Neurology. Staff psychiatrist N. Phila. Health Systems, 1990—; psychiatrist People Acting To Help, 1994. Mem. Am. Psychiat. Assn., Physicians for Social Responsibility. Home: 306 Highland Rd Cheltenham PA 19012

BERGER, MELVIN, allergist, immunologist; b. Phila., Mar. 7, 1950. MD, Case Western Res. U., 1976. Internship, resident pediatrics Children's Hosp. Med. Ctr., Boston, 1976-78; fellow allergy & immunology Nat. Inst. Allergy & Infectious Diseases, Bethesda, Md., 1978-81; pediatrician Rainbow Babies, Cleve., 1984—, Children's Hosp., Cleve., 1984—; prof. peds. Case Western Res. U. Mem. Am. Acad. Pediatrics. Office: Rainbow Babies Hosp Div Pediatrics/Immunology Cleveland OH 44106

BERGER, NATHAN ALLEN, dean; b. Phila., July 8, 1940; s. Meyer and Lillian (Salko) B.; m. Sosamma John, June 23, 1968; children: Joshua S., Ravi B., Sarina H. AB, Temple U., 1962; MD, Hahneman U., 1966. Intern Michael Reese Med. Ctr., Chgo., 1967-68; rsch. assoc. NIH, Balt., 1968-71; assoc. prof. Washington U. Sch. Medicine, St. Louis, 1971-82; prof. medicine, biochemistry Case Western Res. U., Cleve., 1983-95, dir. cancer ctr., 1985—, interim dean, v.p. med. affairs, 1995-96, dean, 1996—; bd. trustees Edison Biotech. Am. Cancer Soc. Contbr. articles to profl. jours.; mem. editl. b. Jour. Clin. Investigation, Jour. Biol. Chemistry; others. Lt. comdr. USPHS, 1968-71. Fellow Washington U. Sch. Medicine, 1971-82; Leukemia Soc. Am.

scholar. Mem. Am. Soc. Hematology, Am. Soc. Biol. Chemists, Am. Soc. Clin. Oncology, Am. Soc. Cancer Rsch., Am. Soc. Clin. Investigation, Am. Assn. Physicians. Office: Case Western Res U 10900 Euclid Ave Cleveland OH 44106-4915

BERGER, PAUL STUART, physician; b. Bronx, N.Y., Mar. 26, 1954; s. Marvin and Marilyn (Kleinman) B.; m. Marilyn Debra Loewenstein, Mar. 8, 1978; children: Stephanie, Scott. BA, SUNY, Buffalo, 1975; MD, SUNY, Bklyn., 1979. Diplomate Am. Bd. Internal Medicine. Intern and resident in internal medicine Brookdale Hosp. Med. Ctr., Bklyn., 1979-82; fellow nephrology Albert Einstein Coll. of Medicine, Bronx, 1982-84; attending physician Good Samaritan Hosp., West Islip, N.Y., 1984—; pvt. practice Dix Hills Med. Assocs., PC, Commack, N.Y., 1984—; adj. clin. asst. prof. in medicine N.Y. Coll. of Osteo. Medicine, 1995—. Contbr. articles to profl. jours. Mem. AMA, Am. Soc. Nephrology. Office: Dix Hills Med Assocs PC 646 Commack Rd Commack NY 11725

BERGER, PETER BRUCE, cardiologist; b. N.Y.C., Apr. 22, 1956; s. Alexander and Phyllis (Belous) B.; m. Nina E. Charnoff, Nov. 20, 1983; children: Laura, Lisa. Student, Herriot-Walt U., Stony Brook, 1976-77; BSstgrad., SUNY, Stony Brook, 1978; MD, NYU, 1983. Intern, resident Boston City Hosp., 1983-86; fellow divsn. of cardiology Boston U. Hosp., Boston City Hosp.; cons. cardiac catheterization lab., coronary care unit Mayo Clinic, Rochester, Minn., 1990—, assoc. prof. Office: Mayo Clinic 200 1st St SW Rochester MN 55905

BERGER, RICHARD STANTON, dermatologist; b. Flint, Mich., July 30, 1940; s. Frederick S. and Millicent (Petschau) B.; m. Brenda Gorne (div.); children: Adam, Lauren; m. Janice Marie Berger, Feb. 10, 1978. MD, U. Mich., 1965. Intern Walter Reed Gen. Hosp., Washington, 1965-66; resident U. Mich., Ann Arbor, 1968-71; asst. prof. medicine and dermatology U. Mo., Columbia, 1971-73; assoc. dir. clin. rsch. Johnson & Johnson, New Brunswick, N.J., 1973-78; clin. asst. prof. medicine and dermatology Rutgers Med. Sch., New Brunswick, N.J., 1973-77; assoc. prof. medicine and dermatology U. Medicine and Dentistry of N.J., New Brunswick, 1977-87, clin. prof., 1987—, chief dermatology, 1979-95; chief dermatology Robert Wood Johnson Univ. Hosp., New Brunswick, 1979-95; pvt. practice Kendall Park, N.J., 1983—; cons. for several cos. and hosps., including Rutgers Cmty. Health Plan, New Brunswick, 1976-89, Personal Products Rsch. Divsn., Milltown, N.J., 1978-95, Chicopee Mfg. Co., Rsch. Divsn., Milltown, 1978-94, VA Hosp., Lyons, N.J., 1978—, Greenbrook Regional Ctr., Green Brook, N.J., 1980—; med. dir. Hilltop Rsch., East Brunswick, N.J., 1979—. Contbr. more than 100 articles to profl. jours. Capt. Med. Corps, U.S. Army, 1966-68. Fellow Am. Acad. Dermatology (Silver award for Tchg. Value 1985); mem. Middlesex County Med. Soc., Internat. Soc. for Dermatologic Surgery, Soc. for Investigative Dermatology, Inc., Assn. of Profs. of Dermatology, Inc., N.J. Dermatol. Soc., Dermal Clin. Evaluation Soc., Skin Pharmacology Soc. Office: 3270 State Rt 27 Kendall Park NJ 08824-1458

BERGER, RONALD OWEN, ophthalmologist; b. N.Y.C., May 21, 1943; s. John J. and Mildred (Reich) B.; m. Linda J. Katz, Feb. 27, 1972; children: Jacqueline, Danielle, Alexandra. BA, U. Mass., 1965; MD, U. Louisville, 1969. Staff physician Winsted (Conn.) Mem. Hosp., 1976—, Charlotte Hungerford Hosp., Torrington, Conn., 1976—; courtesy staff U. Conn. Hosp., Farmington, Conn., 1976—. Lt. Cmdr. USPHS, 1970-72. Office: Litchfield Hills Eye Phys 333 Kennedy Dr Torrington CT 06790

BERGER, SEYMOUR MAURICE, social psychologist; b. Bklyn., Jan. 7, 1928; s. Leo and Bessie Ida (Okun) Berger; m. Sara Marilyn Nappen, Sept. 7, 1952; children: Evelyn Joyce, Nancy Faith. B.S., Okla. A&M Coll., 1949; M.A., Columbia U., 1950; Ph.D., Cornell U., 1959. Instr. Trinity Coll., Hartford, Conn., 1958-59; from instr. to assoc. prof. Ind. U., Bloomington, 1959-69; prof. social psychology U. Mass., Amherst, 1969-95, prof. emeritus, 1995—, acting dean social and behavioral scis., 1991-92, dean social behavioral scis., 1992-95. Contbr. articles on social psychology to profl. jours.; mem. editorial bd. Jour. Personality and Social Psychology. Served with USNR, 1945-46; served with USAF, 1951-55. Fulbright sr. research scholar, 1975-76,83; spl. fellow NIH, 1965-66. Democrat. Jewish. Home: 459 Flat Hills Rd Amherst MA 01002-1219

BERGER, ULRICH, retired microbiology educator; b. Breslau, Germany, Dec. 5, 1919. MD, U. Wurzburg, Wurzburg, Fed. Republic of Germany, 1945. Med. diplomate. Asst. Hafen-Krankenhaus, Hamburg, Fed. Republic Germany, 1945-46; asst. Inst. Tropical Diseases, Hamburg, 1946-47, Inst. Hygiene, Hamburg, 1947-48, Inst. Cantonal d'Hygiene et de Bacteriology, Fribourg, Switzerland, 1948-51; chief lab. U. Dental Clinic, Hamburg, 1951-63; prof. med. microbiology U. Hamburg, 1962; dir. bacteriology dept. U. Inst. Hygiene, Heidelberg, Fed. Republic Germany, 1963-85. Author: Microbiology of Oral Cavity, 1956, 63; contbr. articles to profl. jours. and handbooks. Mem. Paul-Ehrlich Assn. for Chemotherapy, German Assn. for Hygiene and Microbiology. Home: Georg F Händel Str 18, D 69214 Eppelheim Baden, Germany

BERGER-KRAEMER, NANCY, speech and language pathologist, artist; b. N.Y.C., Aug. 15, 1941; d. George G. and Ruth (Kirsch) Berger; m. Aaron Kraemer, July 10, 1966; children: Lea, Steven. BA, Adelphi U., 1963; MS in Edn., Queens Coll., 1968; cert. clin. competency in speech pathology. Lic. and cert. speech and lang. pathologist, N.Y., N.J.; permanent cert. speech and hearing for handicapped, N.Y. Speech therapist Dist. # 24 Sch. Sys., Valley Stream, L.I., 1962-64; dir. speech and lang., hearing/speech pathologist Port Chester Sch. Dist., Rye, N.Y., 1965-66; speech and lang. pathologist Roselle Park (N.J.) Sch. Sys., 1966-67, Willis Sch. for Educationally Handicapped, Plainfield, N.J., 1967-68, St. Barnabas Med. Ctr., West Orange, N.J., 1971-73; pvt. practice Maplewood, N.J., 1968—; lectr., spkr., spl. edn. cons. in field. Numerous one-woman shows in N.J., N.Y., N.Y.C.; group exhbns. include N.J. Ctr. Visual Arts, Summit, N.J., City Without Walls, Newark, Bergen Mus., Jersey City Mus., Trenton City Mus., N.J. State Mus., Montclair Art Mus., Noyes Mus., Phoenix Gallery, Veridian Gallery, Pendar Gallery, Gallerie Ambiente, Germany, William Carlos Williams Ctr. for Arts, San Diego Art Inst., Stedman Art Gallery, New Brunswick, N.J., Fordham U.-Lowenstein Libr., N.Y.C., SUNY Gallery, Stony Brook, N.Y., Johnson & Johnson, Cali Assocs., Bellemead Devel. Corp., AT&T, Nabisco Brands, Beneficial Ins. Co., Prudential Ins. Co., Pleiades Gallery, N.Y.C., Art Ctr. No. N.J., Art Assn. Harrisburg, Stamford Art Assn., Princeton (N.J.) Art Assn., Bucknell U. Ctr. Gallery, NYU/Washington Sq. East Galleries, Newark (N.J.) Mus., The Waterloo Found. for the Arts, Inc., Stamford, others. Mem. Am. Speech Lang. Hearing Assn., Auditory Verbal Internat. (charter, lectr. 1975—), Alexander Graham Bell Assn., N.J. Speech and Hearing Assn.

BERGERON, PAUL PHILLIP, internist; s. Roger Joseph and Jean Marie (Campiola) B.; m. Margaret Alice Pothier, June 4, 1994. BA, Coll. of the Holy Cross, 1987; MD, U. Vt., 1994. Cert. BLS, ACLS. Teenage counselor Worcester Youth Guidance Assn., 1985-86; developmentally-delayed children camp counselor Greater Lawrence Ednl. Collaborative, 1986; mental health technician Holy Family Hosp., 1985-87; pharm. co. rep. 3M Pharms./3M Health Care, 1988-90; resident in internal medicine Stanford (Calif.) Health Svcs., 1994—. Mem. ACP (assoc.), Psi Chi. Office: Stanford Health Svcs Dept of Medicine S102 325 Pasteur Stanford CA 94305

BERGEY, GREGORY KENT, neurology educator, neuroscientist; b. Bryn Mawr, Pa., Nov. 9, 1949; s. Robert Harr and Kathryn (Schmidt) B.; m. Stefanie Friday Antonakos, Aug. 27, 1972; children: Alyssa Noelle, Alexander Christian. AB, Princeton U., 1971; MD, U. Pa., 1975. Diplomate Am. Bd. Psychiatry and Neurology, diplomate internal medicine. Intern internal medicine Yale U., New Haven, 1975-76, resident internal medicine, 1975-77; fellow neurophysiology Lab. Devel. Neurobiology Nat. Inst. Child Health and Human Devel., NIH, Bethesda, Md., 1977-79, 82; resident neurology Johns Hopkins, Balt., 1979-83; assoc. prof. U. Md. Sch. Medicine, Balt., 1989-96, prof. neurology and physiology, 1996—; dir. Md. Epilepsy Ctr. Md. Epilepsy Ctr., Balt., 1988—. Contbr. articles to med. jours. Lt. cmdr. USPHS, 1977-79, 81-82. Mem. Soc. for Neurosci., Am. Acad. Neurology, Am. Epilepsy Soc., Epilepsy Assn. Md. (bd. dirs. 1984—, pres. 1993-95). Office: 5207 Springlake Way Baltimore MD 21212-3421 Office: U Md Sch Medicine Dept Neurology 22 S Greene St Baltimore MD 21201-1544

BERGGREN, RONALD BERNARD, surgeon, emeritus educator; b. S.I., N.Y., June 13, 1931; s. Bernard and Florence (Schmidt) B.; m. Mary Beth Griffith, Nov. 25, 1954; children: Karen Berggren Murray, Eric Griffith. BA, Johns Hopkins U., 1953; MD, U. Pa., 1957. Diplomate Am. Bd. Surgery, Nat. Bd. Med. Examiners, Am. Bd. Plastic Surgery (bd. dirs. 1982-88, chmn. 1987-88). Asst. instr. surgery U. Pa., 1958-62, instr., 1962-65; gen. surg. resident Hosp. U. Pa., 1958-62, resident plastic surgery, 1963-64, chief resident plastic surgery, 1964-65; sr. resident surgery Phila. Gen. Hosp., 1962-63; asst. prof. surgery Ohio State U. Sch. Medicine, 1965-68, dir. div. plastic surgery, 1965-85, assoc. prof. surgery, 1968-73, prof. surgery, 1973-86, emeritus prof. surgery, 1986—; attending staff Ohio State U. Hosps., chief of staff, 1983-85, hon. staff, 1986—; attending staff, dir. div. plastic surgery Children's Hosp., Columbus, Ohio, 1965-90; v.p. Plastic Surgery Ednl. Found., 1984-85, pres., 1986-87; sec. Plastic Surgery Tng. Program Dirs., 1981-83, chmn., 1983-85; mem. med. adv. bd. Ohio Bur. for Children with Med. Handicaps, 1974—. Trustee Mid Ohio Health Planning Fedn., 1979-82, 84, PSRO, 1980-84, Scioto Valley Health Systems Agy., 1985-87; del. Coun. Med. Splty. Socs., 1982-90, dir., 1988-90. Recipient Disting. Svc. award Plastic Surgery Edn. Foun., 1990. Fellow ACS (gov. 1996—), mem. AMA, Ctrl. Surg. Soc., Columbus Surg. Soc., Am. Soc. Plastic and Reconstructive Surgeons (spl. hon. citation 1995), Ohio Valley Plastic Surg. Soc., Am. Cleft Palate Assn., Am. Assn. Plastic Surgeons (treas. 1982-85, v.p. 1988-89, pres. elect 1989-90, pres. 1990-91), Franklin County Med. Soc. (pres.-elect 1982-83, pres. 1983-84), Plastic Surg. Rsch. Coun. (chair 1975-76), N.Y. Acad. Scis., Am. Assn. Surgery Trauma, Assn. Acad. Surgery, Am. Burn Assn., Am. Trauma Soc., Am. Soc. Aesthetic Plastic Surgery (parliamentarian 1992-93), Am. Soc. Maxillofacial Surgery, Accreditation Coun. for Grad. Med. Edn. (rev. com. for plastic surgery 1983-90, mem. exec. com. 1987-90, 94, designate chmn. 1988, chmn. 1989, 94, institutional rev. com. 1996—), Coun. Med. Specialty Socs. (dir. 1989-90, sec. 1991-92, pres.-elect 1993, pres. 1994), Coun. Plastic Surgical Orgn. (convenor 1996—), Sigma Xi, Phi Kappa Psi, Alpha Kappa Kappa. Home: 9787 Windale Farms Cir Galena OH 43021-9609 Office: 3732 Olentangy River Rd Ste E Columbus OH 43214-3449

BERGIN, COLLEEN JOAN, medical educator; b. Foxton, New Zealand, May 13, 1953; came to U.S., 1981; d. Joseph Bernard and Mary Catherine (Butel) B; m. Niall C.T. Wilton, May 22, 1992; children: Tessa, Sophie. BS, Auckland Med. Sch., 1979. Resident U. B.C., Vancouver, Can., 1981-87; faculty Stanford (Calif.) U., 1989-92; assoc. prof. U. Calif., San Diego, 1992—. Contbr. articles to profl. jours. NIH Rsch. grantee, 1992—; Thoracic Radiology fellow Duke U., 1988. Mem. Am. Roentgen Ray Soc., Radiologic Soc. N.Am., Soc. Thoracic Radiology (stds. com. 1990-96), Soc. Magnetic Resonance. Democrat. Roman Catholic.

BERGLAS, STEVEN, clinical psychologist; b. N.Y.C., Nov. 26, 1950; s. Jerome Kenneth and Lena (Schneider) Berglas. BA, Clark U., 1972; PhD, Duke U., 1976. Research fellow Harvard U. Med. Sch., Boston, 1977-79; instr. psychiatry Harvard U. Med. Sch., 1979—; attending psychologist McLean Hosp., Belmont, Mass., 1985—; dir. Exec. Stress Clinic, Chestnut Hill, Mass., 1985—. Author: The Success Syndrome, 1986; co-author: Self Handicapping, 1990, Your Own Worst Enemy, 1994. Recipient undergrad. rsch. award NSF, 1971, Nat. Rsch. Svc. award NIMH, 1977-79, Career Scientist Devel. award Alcohol, Drug Abuse, and Mental Health Adminstrn, 1980-85. Mem. Am. Psychol. Assn., Phi Beta Kappa. Jewish. Office: McLean Hosp Harvard Med Sch 115 Mill St Belmont MA 02178-1041

BERGMAN, DONALD ARTHUR, endocrinologist; b. Bklyn., Apr. 6, 1946; s. Joseph and Clara Bergman; m. Susan Menin, June 23, 1970; 1 child, Melissa. AB, Dartmouth Coll., 1967; MD, Jefferson Med. Coll., 1971. Diplomate: Am. Bd. Endocrinology, Am. Bd. Internal Medicine. Ob-gyn. resident Mount Sinai Hosp., N.Y.C., 1971-72, med. resident, 1973-75, endocrinology fellow, 1975-77; clin. asst. prof. medicine Mount Sinai Sch. Medicine, N.Y.C., 1984—; med. intern NYU Hosps., 1972-73; pvt. practice N.Y.C., 1977—. Contbg. author: Mount Sinai Book of Nutrition; contbr. articles to profl. jours.; assoc. editor (jour.) Endocrine Practice. Capt. U.S. Army, 1971-77. Fellow ACP, Am. Coll. of Endocrinology; mem. Am. Assn. of Clin. Endocrinologists (bd. dirs. 1993—, chair practice stds. com. 1995—). Office: 1199 Park Ave (1F) New York NY 10128

BERGMAN, ERNEST L., retired horticulture educator; b. Munich, July 12, 1922; s. Willy and Julia (Steiner) Bergmann; came to U.S., 1946; m. Alice H. Adler, Feb. 15, 1948. B.S., Oreg. State U., 1955; M.S., Mich. State U., 1956, Ph.D., 1958. Asst. prof. plant nutrition Pa. State U., University Park, 1958-63, assoc. prof., 1963-70, prof., 1970-87; prof. emeritus, 1987—; internat. assignments in Argentine, Uruguay, Peoples Republic of China, Senegal and Mali. Contbr. articles to profl. jours. Chmn., Ferguson Twp. Bd. Adjustment, 1961-64, Patton Ferguson Joint Authority, 1964-74, Ferguson Twp. Bd. Suprs., 1974-79, Ctr. Region Coun. Govt., 1976; mem. Patton Ferguson Joint Authority, 1982—, Univ. Area Joint Authority, Ctr. Region Govt. Study Com., 1991-93. Fellow AAAS, Am. Soc. Hort. Sci.(bd. dirs. 1981-83, 86-87, v.p. internat. affairs 1986-87, Kenneth Post award 1968); mem. Internat. Soc. Hort. Sci., Am. Soc. Plant Physiologists, Pa. Plant Food and Protectant Edn. Soc. (man of yr. award 1983), Sigma Xi, Alpha Zeta, Gamma Sigma Delta. Lodge: Kiwanis (pres. 1976, dist. lt. gov. 1988). Office: 1421 Harris St State College PA 16803-3024

BERGMAN, HARRY, urologist; b. N.Y.C., Oct. 25, 1912; s. Sam and Pauline (Freedman) B.; m. Tillie Simon, Feb. 16, 1936 (dec. Feb. 1957); m. Mollie Holtzman, Apr. 2, 1958. M.D., U. Buffalo, 1934. Diplomate Am. Bd. Urology. Intern Lebanon Hosp., N.Y.C., 1934-36; resident Morrisania City Hosp., N.Y.C., 1942-43; attending urologist Morrisania City Hosp., 1958—; hon. vis. urologist, pvt. practice medicine specializing in urology Bronx and N.Y.C., 1936-78; attending urologist Bronx Lebanon Hosp. Center, 1953-79, cons., 1979—; staff Jewish Meml. Hosp., 1960-79, attending urologist, 1970-79, cons., 1979—; Flower-Fifth Ave. Hosp., Met. Hosp., all N.Y.C.; past dir. urology Hebrew Home for Aged, Riverdale, N.Y., to 1978; cons. staff St. Clare-St. Elizabeth's Hosp. Assn.; clin. prof. urology N.Y. Med. Coll., 1966—, U. Miami Med. Sch., 1983—. Numerous publs. in urol. lit.; editor-in-chief: The Ureter, 1967, 2d edit., 1981; co-editor column Urologic-Radiologic Revs. in N.Y. State Jour. Medicine; guest editor Ill. Med. Jour., 1969; contbr. to book Current Operative Urology, 1973, 2d edit., 1984, Current Urologic Therapy, 2d edit.; urologic book reviewer N.Y. State Jour. Medicine, Jour. AMA; designer 1st serial sect. biopsy instrument, 1942 (Am. Cancer Soc. award); abstractor internat. sect. Urology-Surgery, Gynecology & Obs. Surg Jour., internal sect. SGO Surgical Jour.-urology sect. Recipient Honor award Bronx physicians div. State of Israel-Fedn. Jewish Philanthropies, 1969; citation Am. Cancer Soc.; Gold medal award for achievement in medicine particularly urology Phi Lambda Kappa, 1989. Fellow ACS (exec. com. 1962—, pres. Bronx chpt. 1965—, life), Soc. Urologists and Engrs. (sr.), Am. Urol. Soc., N.Y. Acad. Medicine, N.Y. Acad. Medicine (life); mem. Am. Trauma Soc. (founder), Bronx County Med. Soc., Am. Soc. Clin. Urologists, N.Y. State Soc. Surgeons (dir.), Am. Geriatric Soc., Pan. Am. Med. Assn. (hon. life mem. sect. urology), Met. Med. Alumni U. Buffalo (pres. gen. alumni 1958—), Magicians Guild Am., Physicians Sq. Club Am., Alpha Omega Alpha. Lodge: Masons. Home: 4200 Hillcrest Dr Apt 219 Hollywood FL 33021-7900

BERGMAN, RONALD H., ophthalmologist; b. Sept. 24, 1963; s. Gary D. and Judith Bergman; m. Miriam Bergman; children: Zachery, Rachael. BS in Biology, U. Mich., 1985, MD, 1990. Intern Sinai Hosp. of Detroit, 1989-90, resident in ophthalmology, 1990-93; pvt. practice Ophthalmology Assocs., Southfield, Mich., 1990—. Office: Ophthalmology Assocs PC 26615 Green Field Southfield MI 48076

BERGMANN, DEIDRA ANN, surgeon; b. Bay Village, Ohio, July 11, 1953; d. Donald Charles and Roberta Mildred (Foust) B. AA, Miami (Fla.)-Dade C.C., 1975; BS in Biology, N.E. Mo. State U., 1981; DO, Nova Southeastern U., 1985. Bd. cert. gen. surgery Am. Bd. Osteo. Surgery. Intern Southeastern Med. Ctr., North Miami Beach, Fla., 1985-86; resident in gen. surgery Southeastern Med. Ctr. Nova Southeastern, North Miami Beach, 1986-90; intern, resident in gen. surgery Nova Southeastern U., North Miami Beach, Fla., 1985-90; surgeon Gen. Surg. Group Practice, Hollywood, Fla., 1990-95, Coral Springs, Fla., 1995—; oper. rm. technician Southeastern Med. Ctr., North Miami Beach, Fla., 1975-80; chief resident Southeastern Med. Ctr., North Miami Beach, 1987-88, 88-89; emergency medicine physician Emergency Med. Svcs. Assn., Ft. Lauderdale, Fla., 1988-90; clin. instr. surgery Southeastern U. Health Scis., North Miami Beach, 1990—; surg. rev. mem. Pembroke Pines (Fla.) Hosp., 1991-95. Lectr. Am. Cancer Soc., Hollywood, Fla., 1993. Mem. Am. Osteo. Assoc., Am. Coll. Osteo. Surgery, Fla. Osteo. Med. Assn., Broward County Osteo. Med. Assn., Soc. Laproscopic Surgeons. Office: 983 University Dr Coral Springs FL 33071

BERGMANN, FREDERICK GEORGE, urologist; b. Elizabeth, N.J., July 29, 1941; s. Ewald Howard and Frances Georgia (Beardsley) B.; m. Linda Lou Walker, Sept. 19, 1970; children: Crista Elise, Karen Michelle. AB, Cornell U., 1963; MD, Temple U., 1967. Diplomate Am. Bd. Urology. Intern, resident surgery D.C. Gen. Hosp., Washington, 1967-69; resident urology U. Md. Hosp., Balt., 1973-76, asst. clin. prof., vol., 1995—; urologist Patuxent Med. Group, Inc., Columbia, Md., 1976—. Maj. U.S. Army, 1969-73. Fellow Am. Coll. Surgeons; mem. AMA, Am. Urological Assn., Southern Med. Assn. (assoc. councilor 1994—), Med. Chirurgical Faculty of Md. (del. Ho. of Dels. 1986), Howard County Med. Soc. (sec., pres. 1986, 93). Office: Patuxent Med Group Inc 2 Knoll North Dr Columbia MD 21045

BERGMANN, MARGARET ANN, nurse; b. Boston, Jan. 1, 1959; d. John Howard and Helen Gertrude (Flanagan) B. BSN, Boston Coll., 1981; MS, U. Lowell, 1989. Resident care coord. Hebrew Rehab. Ctr. for Aged, Roslindale, Mass.; rsch. nurse practitioner Hebrew Rehab. Ctr. for Aged, Roslindale, Mass; staff nurse, geriatric neuropsychol. unit Boston City Hosp.; gerintol. nurse practitioner Urban Med. Group, Jamaica Plain, Mass. Mem. ANA, Mass. Coalition of Nurse Practitioners, Nurse Practitioner Coun. Mass. Nurses Assn. Home: 31 Knowlton St Somerville MA 02145-4225

BERGOLD, ORM, medical educator; b. Nuremberg, Germany, Apr. 30, 1925; s. Friedrich and Wilhelmine (Schering) B.; MD, Chgo. Med. Coll., 1974; DChemistry, Benjamin Franklin Inst., N.Y.C., 1976; MAcupuncture, Old Chinese Acupuncture Acad., Hong Kong, 1978; DSc (hon.), St. Andrew's Coll., London, 1965; REIKI Master, 1994; m. Sylvia Patricia Sanchez, 1983; children: Heike, Timm. Pres., Orm Bergold Chemie, Langlau and Bochum, Germany, 1953-63; pres. Inst. Med. Biophysics and Biochemistry, Campione, Switzerland, 1963-82; pres. Inst. Med. Biophysics and Biochemistry, San Jose, Costa Rica, 1982—, Inst. Biocybernetic and Natural Therapy, San Jose, 1985—; pres. Stress and Aging Control Inc., Panama, Costa Rica, 1986—; pres. AIDS Control, Inc., Panama, 1989—; prof. cybernetic medicine Academia Gentium Pro Pace, Rome, 1977—, senator, 1979—; prof. extraordinary U. Francisco Marroquin, Guatemala City, 1979—, senator, 1980—. Named Hon. Pres. Acad. for Biocybernetic Holistic Medicine, Rheda, Germany, 1990—, Man of Yr. Am. Biographical Inst., 1994; decorated grand cross Ordre Equestre de la San Croix de Jérusalem; chevalier du Tastevin. Author: Kybernetische Medizin, 1977, Cancer prophylaxis: a problem of early recognition and treatment, 1980, Cancer Treatment with Human Fibroblast Interferon, 1982, Cancer Treatment by Natural Remedies, 1983, Stress, Cortisol and Stress Diseases, 1989, AIDS Treatment, 1989; also articles. Home: PO Box 359-1250, Escazu Costa Rica

BERGSMA, DERK J., geneticist; b. Sioux Falls, S.D., Jan. 25, 1955; s. Derke Peter and Doris Elaine (Bielema) B.; m. Cheryl Lynn Venema, June 28, 1980; children; Kelley Marie, Suzanne Ruth, Emilie Jean. BA, Trinity Christian Coll., Chgo., 1977; PhD, U. Ill., 1982. Postdoctoral rsch. assoc. Baylor Coll. of Medicine, Houston, 1982-86, rsch. instr., 1986-87; sr. scientist, assoc. Smith, Kline, Beecham Pharms., Phila., 1987-89, sr. scientist, 1989-91, asst. dir., 1991-93, assoc. dir., 1993—. Contbg. author books in field; contbr. articles to profl. jours. Home: 271 Irish Rd Berwyn PA 19312 Office: Smith Kline Beecham Pharms 709 Swedeland King Of Prussia PA 19406

BERGSTEIN, JERRY MICHAEL, pediatric nephrology; b. Cleve., June 26, 1939; s. Sol R. and Hilda (Nittscoff) B.; m. Renee M. Hillman, July 7, 1963; children: Stephanie, Michael, Jeffrey. BA, UCLA, 1961; MD, U. Minn., 1965. Diplomate Nat. Bd. Med. Examiners, Am. Bd. Pediat., Am. Bd. Pediat. Nephrology; lic. physician, Ind. Intern in pediat. U. Minn., Mpls., 1965-66, jr. pediat. resident, 1966-67, chief pediat. resident, 1969-70, postdoctoral fellow in pediat. nephrology, 1970-73; asst. prof., head pediat. nephrology UCLA, 1973-77; assoc. prof. Ind. U. Sch. Medicine, Indpls., 1977-82, head pediat. nephrology, 1977—, prof., 1982—; mem. adv. bd. Nat. Kidney Found. Ind., 1980—; mem. adv. coun. Am. Heart Assn., 1988—. Mem. editl. bd. Child Nephrology and Urology, 1980-90, Pediat. Nephrology, 1995—; contbr. chpts. to books. Lt. comdr. USN, 1967-69. Recipient Fellowship USPHS, Washington, 1970; grantee Thrasher Fund, 1980, Amgen, 1990. Mem. Am. Soc. Nephrology, Am. Soc. Pediat. Nephrology, Am. Soc. Investigative Pathology, Soc. Exptl. Biology and Medicine. Office: James Whitcomb Riley Hosp for Children 702 Barnhill Dr Indianapolis IN 46202

BERGSTRÖM, K. SUNE D., biochemist; b. Stockholm, Jan. 10, 1916; s. Sverker B. and Wera (Wistrand) B.; m. Maj Gernandt, July 30, 1943. Docent physiol. chemistry, MD, Karolinska Inst., Stockholm, 1944, D. Med. Sci. in Biochemistry, 1944; D h.c., U. Basel, Switzerland, 1960, U. Chgo., 1960, Harvard U., 1976, Mt. Sinai Med. Sch., 1976, Med. Acad. Wroclaw, Poland, 1976, McMaster U., Hamilton, Can., 1988. Rsch. fellow U. London, 1938, Columbia U., N.Y.C., 1940-41, Squibb Inst. Med. Rsch., New Brunswick, N.J., 1941-42; asst. biochem. dept. Med. Nobel Inst., Karolinska Inst., Stockholm, 1944-47; rsch. fellow U. Basel, 1946-47; prof. physiol. chemistry U. Lund, Sweden, 1947-58; prof. chemistry Karolinska Inst., 1958-80, dean med. faculty, 1963-66, rector, 1969-77; chmn. bd. dirs. Nobel Found., Stockholm, 1975-87; pres. Royal Swedish Acad. Scis., 1983-85; chmn. WHO Adv. Com. Med. Research, Geneva, 1977-82; La Madonnina lectr., Milan, Italy, 1972; Dunham Lectr. Harvard U., 1972; Dohme lectr. Johns Hopkins U., 1972-73; Merrimon lectr. U. N.C., Chapel Hill, 1973; V.D. Mattia lectr. Roche Inst., 1974; Harvey lectr. Harvey Soc., N.Y.C., 1974; Gen. Amir Chand orator All India Inst., New Delhi, 1978; Cairlton lectr. U. Tex. Health Sci. Ctr., Dallas, 1979; mem. Swedish Med. Rsch. Coun., 1952-58, 64-70, Swedish Natural Sci. Rsch. Coun., 1955-62. Contbr. articles to sci. jours. Decorated Grand Officier de l'Ordre du Mérite, Paris, 1984; recipient Anders Jahre Med. prize, Oslo, 1972, Gairdner award U. Toronto, 1972, Louisa Gross Horwitz prize Columbia U., 1975, Francis Amory prize Am. Acad. Arts and Scis., 1975, Albert Lasker Basic Med. Rsch. award, N.Y.C., 1977, Robert A. Welch award, Houston, 1980, Nobel prize, 1982. Mem. Royal Swedish Acad. Scis., Swedish Acad. Engrng. Scis., Am. Acad. Arts and Scis., Am. Philos Soc. (Benjamin Franklin medal 1988), Am. Soc. Biol. Chemists, Acad. Scis. USSR, Academia Leopoldina (German Democratic Republic), Royal Soc. Edinburgh, Med. Acad. USSR, Finska Vetenskaps-Societeten, Swedish Soc. Med. Scis., Inst. of Medicine (sr.), NAS, fgn. assoc. NAS, Pontifical Acad. Scis., Città del Vàticano. Office: Karolinska Inst, Nobel Forum, Box 270, 17177 Stockholm Sweden

BERGSTRÖM, STEN RUDOLF, psychology educator; b. Uppsala, Sweden, Dec. 10, 1934; s. Rudolf Vilhelm and Maud Margit (Kihlberg) B.; m. Karin Birgitta Ahlstrand, Dec. 29, 1962 (div. 1966); children: Erik, Eleonora; m. Inga Lena Ahlstrand, June 13, 1970. BA, U. Uppsala, 1961, MA, 1965, PhD, 1969. Amanuensis Inst. Psychology U. Uppsala, 1961-65, asst. prof. Inst. Psychology, 1965-90, dir. studies Inst. Psychology, 1965-69, head of dept. Inst. of Psychology, 1969-86, head of dept Inst. of Applied Psychology, 1972-85, docent Faculty of Social Scis., 1969—; advisor Swedish Nat. Bd. Health and Welfare, Stockholm, 1970-75. Contbr. articles to sci. publs.; patentee in med. equipment field. Churchwarden Ch. of Sweden, Häggeby, 1977—; mem. Coun. of Archbishops Diocese, Uppsala, 1989—, Bd. of Archbishops Diocese, 1989—. Mem. Swedish Soc. Medicine, Swedish Soc. for Traffic Medicine, Rotary (past pres.). Lutheran. Home: Häggeby prästgård, S-74694 Bålsta Sweden

BERING, EVA, nursing administrator; b. Lebanon, Pa.; d. Harry R. and Minnie (Capretti) Greenawalt; children: Christine, Corey. Diploma, St. Joseph Hosp. Sch. Nursing, Lancaster, Pa., 1967; BSN, Lebanon Valley Coll., 1982; MS in Administrn., Cen. Mich. U., 1987; MSN, Widener U.,

1992. RN, Pa., cert. nursing administr. Head nurse ICU/CCU St. Joseph Hosp., Lancaster, 1976-82; dir. nursing Good Samaritan Hosp., Lebanon, 1982-85, v.p., 1985-91; v.p. nursing Westmoreland Hosp., Greensburg, Pa., 1992-93; v.p. patient svcs. Susquehanna Health Svcs., 1993-96, v.p. ops., 1996—. Mem. Am. Coll. Healthcare Execs. (assoc.), Am. Orgn. Nurse Execs., Pa. Orgn. Nurse Execs. (pres. 1994), South Ctrl. Nurse Execs. (bd. dirs., pres. 1990), Pa. Nurses Assn. (chair practice com. 1993-95).

BERK, H. RONALD, physician; b. Youngstown, July 3, 1952; s. Eli and Shirley (Rales) B.; m. Nancy Jane Woodward, Oct. 24, 1987; children: Daniel Lee, Hunter David. BA, Ohio State U., 1974, MD, 1977. Diplomate Am. Bd. Internal Medicine, Am. Bd. Psychiatry and Neurology, Am. Bd. Electrodiagnostic Medicine, Am. Bd. Clin. Neurophysiology, Am. Bd. Clin. Electroencephalography. Intern U. Pitts. Health Ctr., 1977-78, resident in internal medicine, 1978-80; resident in neurology Yale New Haven Hosp., 1981-82, U. Pitts., 1982-84; fellowship in neurodiagnostic medicine Cleve. Clinic Found., 1985; chief, Divsn. of Neurology Western Pa. Hosp., Pitts., 1994—, dir. Neuroelectrodiagnostic Lab., 1994—; assoc. clin. prof. in neurology U. Pitts., 1994—. Mem. Am. Acad. Neurology, Am. Coll. Physicians, Am. Assn. Electrodiagnostic Medicine. Office: Neurologic Neurosurg Assocs 3471 Fifth Ave # 810 Pittsburgh PA 15213

BERK, PAUL DAVID, physician, scientist, educator; b. Bklyn., Apr. 3, 1938; s. Charles and Helen (Goell) B.; m. Aviva Ancona, July 4, 1965 (div. Aug. 1990); children: Claire, Philip, Edward; m. Nicole Polak, 1991. B.A., Swarthmore Coll., 1959; cert., U. St. Andrews, Scotland, 1960; M.D., Columbia U., 1964. Diplomate Am. Bd. Internal Medicine, Am. Bd. Hematology. Intern Columbia-Presbyn. Med. Ctr., N.Y.C., 1964-65, resident, 1965-66, fellow in hematology, 1969-70; clin. assoc. metabolism br. Nat. Cancer Inst., Bethesda, Md., 1966-69; sr. investigator Nat. Cancer Inst., Bethesda, 1970-73; clin. asst. prof. medicine Georgetown U., Washington, 1971-75, clin. assoc. prof., 1975-77; chief sect. on diseases of the liver Nat. Inst. Arthritis, Metabolism and Digestive Diseases, NIH, Washington, 1973-77; prof. medicine Mt. Sinai Sch. Medicine, N.Y.C., 1977—, Albert and Vera List prof. medicine, 1980-89, prof. biochemistry, 1987—, Henry and Lillian Stratton prof. molecular medicine, 1989—, chief div. hematology, 1977-89, acting chief, 1989-90, chief div. liver disease, 1989—; adj. prof. Rockefeller U., 1987-89; cons. in liver disease NIH, 1978—, mem. adv. coun. Nat. Inst. Diabetes and Digestive and Kidney Diseases, 1990-94. Editor: (with others) Chemistry and Physiology of the Bile Pigments, 1977, Frontiers in Liver Disease, 1981, Myelofibrosis and the Biology of Connective Tissue, 1984, Hans Popper: A Tribute, 1992, Hepatic Transport and Bile Secretion, 1993, Polythemia Vera, 1994; editor-in-chief Seminars in Liver Disease, 1981-90, 96—, Hepatology, 1991-96; mem. editorial bd. Artificial Organs, 1979-92, Liver, 1980-93; contbr. articles to profl. jours. Served as sr. surgeon USPHS, 1966-69, 75-77. Recipient Merck award Columbia U., 1964; Fulbright scholar, 1959. Fellow ACP; mem. Am. Soc. Clin. Investigation, Assn. Am. Physicians, Am. Assn. Study of Liver Disease (councillor 1985—, v.p. 1988, pres. 1989), Internat. Assn. Study of Liver (councillor 1988-91), Am. Soc. for Hematology, Am. Clin. and Climatological Assn., Nat. Polycthemia Vera Study Group (vice chmn. 1978—), Soc. Exptl. Biol. Medicine (councillor 1993-96), N.Y. Soc. Study of Blood (pres. 1982-83), Sigma Xi, Phi Beta Kappa, Alpha Omega Alpha. Office: Mt Sinai Sch Medicine Box 1039 1 Gustave L Levy Pl New York NY 10029-6504

BERKELHAMER, JAY ELLIS, pediatrician; b. Tuscaloosa, Ala., Apr. 8, 1942; s. Louis H. and Belle F. B.; m. Jacqueline Beth Colman, June 12, 1966; children: Beth Carolyn, Sara Kay, Adam Colman. BS, U. Mich., 1963, MD, 1967. Resident U. Chgo., 1967-70, asst. prof., 1972-78, assoc. prof., 1978-84, prof., 1984-93, assoc. chair, dir. residency program, 1986-93, assoc. dean ambulatory care, 1983-88; chair pediatrics Henry Ford Health Sys., Detroit, 1993—; prof. pediatrics Case Western Res. U., Cleve., 1994—; clin. prof. pediatrics and communicable diseases U. Mich., Ann Arbor, 1994—. Lt. comdr. USPHS, 1970-72. Robert Wood Johnson Health Policy fellow NAS, Washington, 1978-79. Mem. Am. Acad. Pediatrics (pres. Ill. chpt. 1992), Chgo. Pediatric Soc. (pres. 1987, Archibald L. Hoyce award 1993), Ambulatory Pediatric Assn. (pres. 1986). Office: Henry Ford Health Sys 2799 W Grand Blvd Detroit MI 48202

BERKENBILE, GLEN LEE, retired surgeon; b. Creek County, Okla., July 25, 1922; s. Lawrence Wilburn and Zelma (Lee) B.; m. Martha Annette Perot, Feb. 3, 1945; children: Carol Sue, Sally Kay, Janis Lee. BS, Okla. State U., 1944; MD, U. Okla., 1946. Diplomate, Am. Bd. Surgery. Pvt. practice gen. medicine Purcell, Okla., 1949-53; pvt. practice surgery Muskogee, Okla., 1956-79; staff physician Glass-Nelson Clinic, Tulsa, 1979-87; ret., 1987; mem. Okla. State Bd. Med. Examiners, 1963-66, Okla. State Bd. Health, 1968-78. Capt., U.S. Army, 1947-49. Fellow ACS; mem. AMA, Okla. Surg. Assn. (pres. 1978-79), Okla. State Med. Soc., Tulsa County Med. Soc., Rotary. Republican. Methodist. Home: 2408 E 72nd Pl Tulsa OK 74136-5535

BERKENES, JOYCE MARIE POORE, family counselor; b. Des Moines, Aug. 29, 1953; d. Donald Roy and Thelma Beatrice (Hart) Poore; m. Robert Elliott Berkenes, Jan. 3, 1976; children: Tiffany Noelle, Cory Matthew. BA in Social Work and Biology, Simpson Coll., Indianola, Iowa., 1975. Resident counselor and group home mgr. Chaddock Boys Home, Quincy, Ill., 1976-78; social service dir. North Adams Nursing Home, Mendon, Ill., 1978; home tchr. Head Start, Camp Point, Ill., 1978-79, home tchr. supr./edn. and parent involvement coordinator, 1979-82; family counselor Iowa Children's and Family Services, Des Moines, 1982-85; family counselor and vol. coordinator Luth. Social Services, Des Moines, 1985-89; educator/social worker Parent-Infant Nurturing Ctr., Meth. Med. Ctr., Des Moines, 1989-95; social worker The Homestead, 1995—; mem. Greater Des Moines Child Abuse and Neglect Coun. Bd., Friends of New Parents Bd.; mem. racial justice com. YWCA; cons. in field, 1975-76. Democrat. Methodist. Home: 2901 NE 80th St Altoona IA 50009-9505 Office: The Homestead 8270 NE 12th St Runnels IA 50009

BERKMAN, CLAIRE FLEET, psychologist; b. New Orleans, Dec. 5, 1942; d. Joel and Margaret Grace (Fishler) Fleet; m. Arnold Stephen Berkman, Apr. 27, 1975; children: Janna Samantha, Micah Seth Siegel. BA, Boston U., 1964; EdM, Harvard U., 1966; EdD, Boston U., 1970. Asst. prof. Counseling Ctr., Mich. State U., East Lansing, 1971-75, assoc. prof., 1975-78, assoc. prof. dept. psychiatry, 1975-82, clin. assoc. prof., 1986-87; pvt. clin. practice, 1975—; cons. Cath. Family Social Service, Lansing, 1979-83; mem. adv. bd. Cir. Ct. Family Counseling Program, 1982-88. V.p. Kehillat Israel Synagogue, 1975-76, pres. 1992-94; bd. dirs. Jewish Welfare Fedn., Lansing, 1974-75, 84-87; mem. children's task force State Bar Mich., 1993-95. NDEA fellow, 1968-70. Mem. Am. Psychol. Assn., Mich. Psychol. Assn., Mich. Soc. Forensic Psychologists. Office: 4084 Okemos Rd Okemos MI 48864-3258

BERKMAN, MILTON DAVID, orthodontist; b. Syracuse, N.Y., Nov. 8, 1940; s. Isaac and Sarah (Weinstein) B.; DMD, Tufts U., 1965, MS, 1968; cert. in orthodontics Columbia U., 1972; cert. advanced gnathol. occlusion prins. and technique Found. Advanced Continuing Edn., 1981; diplomate Am. Bd. Orthodontics; m. Arlene Saltzman, Dec. 27, 1969; 1 child, Seth. Instr., U. Pa. Sch. Dental Medicine, 1969-70; asst. prof. dentistry Albert Einstein Coll. Medicine, Bronx, N.Y., 1972-77, asst. clin. prof., 1977-92 ; practice dentistry specializing in orthodontics and temporomandibular joint disorders, Scarsdale, N.Y.; assoc. attending dentist Westchester Med. Center, Valhalla, N.Y., 1981-92 ; orthodontist Center for Craniofacial Disorders, Montefiore Hosp., N.Y.C.; guest lectr. N.Y.U. Sch. Dentistry, 1981—. Served with Dental Corps, U.S. Army, 1968-70. Fellow Northeastern Gnathological Soc.; mem. Am. Assn. Orthodontists, Am. Cleft Palate Assn., ADA, Northeastern Soc. Orthodontists, N.Y. State Dental Soc., Northeastern Gnathol. Soc., Sigma Xi, Omicron Kappa Upsilon. Contbr. articles to profl. jours, contbr. chpts. to textbooks.

BERKOFF, CHARLES EDWARD, pharmaceutical executive; b. London, Sept. 29, 1932; came to U.S., 1963; s. Maurice and Dora (Landy) B.; children: Timothy, David, Kevin. BS in Chemistry, U. London, 1956, DIC, 1958; PhD, Imperial Coll., U. London, 1959. Chartered chemist. Dir. SmithKline Beckman Group, Phila., 1964-83; exec. v.p. ImuTech, Inc., Huntingdon Valley, Pa., 1983-84; pres., CEO Antigenics, Inc., Horsham, Pa., 1984-89; pres., chief exec. officer Creative Licensing Internat., Inc., Sarasota, Fla., 1987—, CEBRAL, 1987—; research assoc. Johns Hopkins U., Balt., 1959-60; sr. research fellow Southampton U., Eng., 1960-61; mem. Adv. Council Smithsonian Sci. Info. Exchange, Washington, 1976-82. Contbr. articles to profl. jours.; patentee numerous U.S. and fgn. patents. Monsanto Research fellow Imperial Coll. Sci. and Tech., 1956-59; Fulbright scholar, 1959-60; recipient Statue of Victory World Culture prize Centro Studi e Ricerche Delle Nazioni, 1985. Fellow Am. Chem. Soc., Royal Soc. Chemistry; mem. Am. Arbitration Assn., Entomol. Soc., Am. Inst. Chem. Engrs., Licensing Execs. Soc. Republican. Unitarian. Club: Engrs. Club of Phila. Office: PO Box 3376 Sarasota FL 34230-3376

BERKOVIC, SAMUEL FRANK, neurologist; b. Melbourne, Australia, Oct. 13, 1953; s. Alexander and Eva Clara (Fraenkel) B.; m. Helena Frima Makowski, Dec. 10, 1977; children: Penina, Jonathan, Naomi. MB BS, U. Melbourne, 1977, MD, 1985. Fellow Hamilton Fairly Univ. Melbourne, Australia, 1987-88; sr. lectr. Univ. Melbourne, 1989-94; dir. comprehensive epilepsy program Austin and Repatriation Med. Ctr., Heidelberg, Australia, 1994—; neurologist Austin and Repatriation Med. Ctr., Melbourne, 1987—; adj. prof. dept. neurology McGill U., Montreal, Can., 1989—; assoc. prof. dept. medicine U. Melbourne, 1995—; chmn. Commn. on Neuroimaging of Internat. League Against Epilepsy, 1994—. Contbr. numerous articles to profl. jours. Fellow Royal Australasian Coll. Physicians (Eric Susman prize 1993); mem. Am. Epilepsy Soc. (Rsch. Recognition award 1995), Am. Acad. Neurology. Home: 21 Brendan Ave, Melbourne Victoria 3108, Australia Office: Dept Neurology, Austin & Repatriation Med, Melbourne Victoria 3084, Australia

BERKOWITZ, AMY SILVERMAN, gerontology nurse; b. N.Y.C., Mar. 19, 1953; d. Albert and Leah (Binder) Silverman; m. David Berkowitz, June 15, 1975; children: Aaron, Leah, Daniel. BS in Nursing, Russell Sage Coll., 1975. RN, Pa.; cert. gerontol. nurse. Dir. infection control Cen. Park Lodge Nursing Home, Broomall, Pa., 1991-92, relief supr. and staff nurse, 1979-92; head staff nurse Martins Run Life Care Community, Media, Pa., 1992-95; dir. staff devel., employee health & infection control Haverford Rehab., Havertown, Pa., 1995—. Mem. Sigma Theta Tau, Psi Chi. Home: 2752 S Kent Rd Broomall PA 19008-2019

BERKOWITZ, CONCEIÇÃO MARIA, nurse anesthetist; b. Lisbon, Portugal, July 5, 1963; d. Gumercindo and Maria Luisa (Ribeiro) Ricardo; m. Richard Carl Berkowitz, June 23, 1990. BSN, Southeastern Mass. U., 1986; cert. nurse anesthetist, St. Joseph's Sch. Anesthesia, 1991. Portuguese interpreter ILGWU, Fall River, Mass., 1979-85; nurse R.I. Hosp., Providence, 1985-90; rsch. cons. Beth Israel Hosp., Boston, 1990; intravenous clinician Clin. IV Network, Providence, 1990-92; nurse anesthetist East Side Anesthesia, Providence, 1991-94; with St. Vincent Anesthesia Assocs., Worcester, Mass., 1994-95, Anesthesia Assocs. Kent County, Warwick, Mass. Eagle's scholar, 1981, 82; named Vol. of Yr. Charlton Meml. Hosp., 1977. Mem. Am. Assn. Nurse Anesthesists (cert.), Portuguese Am. Health Providers Assn. Home: 90 Stone Ridge Dr East Greenwich RI 02818-1612 Office: Kent County Anesthesia Assocs 455 Toll Gate Rd Warwick RI 02886

BERKOWITZ, LEONARD BRUCE, infectious diseases physician; b. Bklyn., Feb. 5, 1952; s. Harold N. and Sylvia (Paris) B.; m. Joan R. Brandstein, July 4, 1974; children: Jodi, Naomi. BA, SUNY, Buffalo, 1973; MD, SUNY, Bklyn., 1977. Diplomate Am. Bd. Internal Medicine, Sub-Bd. Infectious Diseases. Intern, resident, fellow SUNY Downstate Med. Ctr.-Kings County Hosp., Bklyn.; chief divsn. infection diseases Long Island Coll. Hosp., Bklyn., 1985—. Mem. Am. Coll. Physicians, Am. Soc. Microbiology, Infectious Disease Soc. Am. Office: LI Coll Hosp 340 Henry St Brooklyn NY 11201

BERKOWITZ, MARVIN, transplant consultant; b. Bklyn., June 16, 1939; m. Renay Lerman, Apr. 2, 1961; children: Jeffrey, Jonathan, Lisa. BA, L.I. U., 1961, MS, 1967. Biology tchr. N.Y.C. Bd. Edn., Bklyn., 1961-64; with Upjohn Co., Kalamazoo, Mich., 1964-95, hosp. mgr., 1978-80, dir. med. scis. liaison/immunology, 1980-93, worldwide dir. transplant, 1993-95; pres. Immunoledge Internat. Inc., Portage, Mich., 1995—. Patentee pharmaceutical product. Mem. Am. Soc. Clin. Pharmacology and Therapeutics, Am. Coll. Rheumatology, The Transplantation Soc., Internat. Soc. Liver Transplantation, Internat. Soc. Heart and Lung Transplantation, N.Y. Acad. Medicine. Home: 6544 Cypress Portage MI 49024 Office: Immunoledge Internat Inc PO Box 0931 Portage MI 49081-0931

BERKSON, DAVID M., cardiologist; b. Chgo., Oct. 16, 1928; s. Morris J. and Jennie (Goldman) B.; m. Joan Grieggs, Jan. 1, 1973; children from previous marriage: Michael, Matthew, Catherine. BS, U. Ill., 1949; MD, Northwestern U., 1953. Diplomate Am. Bd. Internal Medicine. Heart disease control officer Chgo. Dept. Health, 1963-90; chief of cardiology St. Joseph Hosp., Chgo., 1963—; prof. preventive medicine Northwestern U. Med. Sch., Chgo., 1982—. Contbr. over 130 articles to profl. jours., chpts. to books. Capt. USAF, 1955-57. Fellow ACP, Am. Coll. Cardiology, N.Y. Acad. Scis., Am. Heart Assn. Coun. Epidemiology and Prevention, Am. Heart Assn. Coun. on Arteriosclerosis (Heart of Yr. award 1984); mem. Chgo. Heart Assn. (bd. govs. 1990—, pres. 1981-82), Inst. Medicine (bd. govs. 1988—), Phi Beta Kappa, Alpha Omega Alpha. Office: 2800 N Sheridan Rd Chicago IL 60657

BERLAND, KAREN INA, psychologist; b. N.Y.C., Nov. 14, 1947; d. Max and Lillian (Graf) B. BA in Psychology, SUNY, Buffalo, 1969; MEd in Ednl. Psychology, U. Ill., 1971; D. Psychology, U. Denver, 1984. Cert. sch. psychologist, clin. psychologist. Sch. psychologist City Sch. Dist. Rochester (N.Y.), 1971-73, Denver Pub. Sch., 1973—; psychology intern Vets. Hosp., West Haven, Conn., 1983-84; psychologist Aurora (Colo.) Community Mental Health Ctr., 1985-92; expert witness Denver County Ct. Mem. APA, Colo. Soc. Sch. Psychologists (pres. 1986-87, leadership award 1987), Colo. Psychol. Assn. (PAC chair, treas.), Colo. Women's Psychologists (western regional dir. and Colo. rep. 1976-83), Assn. Advancement of Behavior Therapy, Mensa. Democrat. Jewish. Home: 1171 Forest St Denver CO 80220-4450

BERLIN, BYRON SANFORD, microbiologist, researcher; b. Detroit, Mar. 19, 1921; s. Charles Murrow and Rita (Greenberg) B.; m. Lillian Zaretsky, Nov. 9, 1946; children: Paul, Gabriel, Micheal, Joshua, Miriam, Hillelseth. BA, Wayne State U., 1943, MD, 1945. Diplomate Am. Bd Med. Microbiology. Intern Wayne County Gen. Hosp., Eloise, Mich., 1945-46; physician health svcs. U. Chgo., 1949, fellow in medicine, 1950-52, resident in medicine, 1952-54; rsch. faculty, Pub. Health U. Mich., Ann Arbor, 1954-67; assoc. prof. med. sch. Northwestern U., Chgo., 1967-80; coord. physician bur. lab. Mich. Dept. Health, Lansing, 1980-92. Author, editor: Internship-Continuing Medical Education, 1962, Control of Infections in Hospitals, 1966; author: (book chpts.) Biological Basis of Infectious Disease, 1978; contbr. articles to profl. jours. Capt. Med. Corps, U.S. Army, 1946-48. Mem. AAAS, Am. Assn. Immunologists, Soc. Exptl. Biologists & Medicine, Am. Soc. Microbiologists. Home: 940 Longfellow Dr East Lansing MI 48823-2474 Office: Biomed Data 940 Longfellow Dr East Lansing MI 48823-2474

BERLIN, CHARLES SEDER, psychiatrist, educator; b. Pitts., June 5, 1947; s. M. Lester and Sara (Seder) B.; m. Pamela M. Omenke, Aug. 21, 1968; children: Robin E., Kate L. BA with high distinction, U. Mich., 1969; MD, U. Pitts., 1973. Diplomate Am. Bd. Psychiatry and Neurology. Rotating intern U. Health Ctr. Hosps., U. Pitts., 1973; resident Western Psychiat. Inst. and Clinic, U. Pitts., 1973-76; pvt. practice adult and gen. psychiatry Pitts., 1976—; cons. Pub. Inebriate program Salvation Army, Pitts., 1975-76, Pitts. Ctr. Psychotherapy, 1976-81; dir. hosp. svcs. Allegheny East Mental Health Ctr., Pitts., 1976-78, med. dir., 1973-91; supr. psychotherapy U. Pitts., 1978-86, clin. asst. prof. psychiatry, 1973-93, clin. assoc. prof., 1993—; teaching cons. dept. family practice Forbes Health System, Pitts., 1982-91; cons. VA Med. Ctr., Butler, Pa., 1991-93, Western State Penitentiary, 1993—; mem. med. staff Western Psychiat. Inst. and Clinic, St. Francis Med. Ctr., Forbes Health Ctr. James B. Angell scholar, 1965. Fellow Am. Psychiat. Assn.; mem. Pa. Psychiat. Soc., Pitts. Psychiat. Soc. (pres 1989-90), Allegheny County Med. Soc., Phi Beta Kappa. Office: 417 S Craig St Ste 303 Pittsburgh PA 15213-3727

BERLIN, CHESTON MILTON, JR., pediatrician, educator; b. Pitts., Mar. 28, 1936; s. Cheston Milton and Gladys Irene (Vance) B.; m. Anne Risher, July 9, 1960; children: Jean Vance, Douglas Cheston, Alexander Lindsay, Gordon Johnston. BA, Haverford (Pa.) Coll., 1958; MD, Harvard U., 1962. Intern Boston Children's Hosp., 1962-63, resident in pediatrics, 1965-67; asst. prof. pediatrics U. Ala. Sch. Medicine, Birmingham, 1967-68, George Washington U. Sch. Medicine, Washington, 1968-71; assoc. prof. pediatrics Pa. State U. Coll. Medicine, Hershey, 1971-75, prof. pediatrics and pharmacology, 1975-86, univ. prof. pediatrics, prof. pharmacology, 1986—; pediatric panel mem. U.S. Pharmacopeia, Rockville, Md., 1970-75, 80—. Contbr. articles to profl. jours. Sr. asst. surgeon USPHS, 1963-65. Markle Found. scholar, 1969, 74; recipient Cheston M. Berlin Alumni Svc. award Pa. State U. Coll. Medicine, 1987. Mem. Am. Acad. Pediatrics, Am. Soc. Experimental Pharmacology and Therapeutics, Am. Soc. Clin. Pharmacology and Therapeutics, Am. Pediatric Soc., Phi Beta Kappa, Alpha Omega Alpha, Alpha Epsilon Delta. Episcopalian. Office: MS Hershey Med Ctr Dept Pediatrics PO Box 850 Hershey PA 17033-0850

BERLIN, DORIS ADA, psychiatrist; b. Newark, May 23, 1919; d. Samuel and Fanny (Lippman) B.; m. Saul R. Kelson; children: Joel, Tamar. BS in Pharmacy, Columbia U., 1940; MD, Med. Coll. Va., 1948; MPH in Community Mental Health, U. Mich., 1966. Cert. Am. Bd. Psychiatry and Neurology; lic. psychiatrist N.Y., Va., Ohio, Mich., Tex., Calif. Intern Beth Israel Hosp., N.Y.C., 1948-49; resident in psychiatry Bellevue Hosp., N.Y.C., 1949-52; pvt. practice N.Y.C., 1952-57, Toledo, 1957-66, Fishkill and Poughkeepsie, N.Y., 1984—; clin. asst. in psychiatry NYU Coll. Medicine, 1952-57; asst. in psychiatry U. Hosp., N.Y., 1952-53; clin. asst. vis. neuropsychiatrist Bellevue Hosp., N.Y., 1954-57; lectr. mental health Sch. Pub. Health U. Mich., 1966-68; dir. profl. edn. Toledo State Hosp., 1969-70; clin. assoc. prof. N.Y. Sch. Psychiatry, 1970-81; dir. residency program Hudson River Psychiat. Ctr., Poughkeepsie, 1970-83, others. Mem. citizen's adv. bd. Lucas County (Ohio) Welfare Dept., 1963-67, chair, 1965-66; bd. dirs. Jewish Family Svc., Toledo, 1969-70; mem. policy coun., rehab. com. Toledo Area Program on Drug Abuse, 1970; bd. dirs. Dutchess County Assn. for Sr. Citizens, 1993-96. Grantee NEH, 1979. Fellow Am. Psychiat. Assn. (chair editl. bd. Hosp. and Cmty. Psychiatric Jour., 1979-80, task force on cmty. mental health ctrs., 1983-88, com. on advertisers and exhibitors 1989-92, vice-chair lifers caucus, 1990-91, chair lifers orgn. 1992), Am. Coll. Psychiatrists (Laughlin fellowship com. 1976-79); mem. Am. Acad. Psychoanalysis (com. on psychoanalysis and cmty. mental health 1967-68), Dutchess County Med. Soc. (psychiatrists' rep. to coun. 1985—, treas. 1987). Home and Office: 66 Mitchell Ave Poughkeepsie NY 12603-3423

BERLIN, FRED SAUL, psychiatrist, educator; b. Pitts., July 27, 1941; s. Sidney Danial and Pauline (Ritt) B.; m. Mary Ann Pazics, Oct. 3, 1969; children: Debra, Alison, Samantha, Ryan. BS, U. Pitts., 1964; MA, Fordham U., 1966; PhD, Dalhousie U., Halifax, N.S., Can., 1970, MD, 1974. Intern McGill U. Sch. Medicine, Jewish Gen. Hosp., Childrens Hosp., Montreal, Can., 1974-75; psychiat. resident Johns Hopkins Hosp., Balt., 1975-76; Johns Hopkins exch. resident Maudsley Hosp., London, 1977; chief resident dept. psychiatry and behavioral sci. Johns Hopkins Hosp., Balt., 1977-78; assoc. prof. dept. psychiatry and behavioral sci. Johns Hopkins U. Sch. Medicine; dir. Sexual Disorders Clinic Johns Hopkins Hosp.; attending physician Johns Hopkins Hosp., mem. house staff coun., 1976-77, mem. adv. com. house staff coun., 1977-78, mem. utilization rev. com., 1977-78, gender identity com., 1980-81; mem. Johns Hopkins U. Med. Sch. Coun., 1982-84; mem. bd. student advisors Johns Hopkins U. Sch. Medicine, 1980—; bd. dir. Nat. Inst. for Study Prevention and Treatment Sexual Trauma. Contbr. numerous articles to profl. publs. Recipient cert. appreciation Balt. County Police, 1989, 93. Fellow Am. Psychiat. Assn.; mem. AMA, Am. Acad. Psychiatry and Law (pres. Chesapeake Bay chpt.), Md. Psychiat. Assn. (legis. com. 1989—). Office: John Hopkins Hosp 600 N Wolfe St Baltimore MD 21205-2110

BERLIN, JACOB BORIS, psychotherapist; b. N.Y.C., Apr. 16, 1924; s. Alexander and Martha (Aranow) B.; m. Anne Wright Morris, Apr. 26, 1947; children—Alexander, Ralph, Christopher, Letitia, Deborah. A.B., Harvard U., 1950; M.S.P.H., U. N.C., Chapel Hill, 1951; M.Div., Va. Theol. Sem., 1960; M.A., U. S.C., 1975; DMin Colo. Theol. Sem., 1986. Lic. marriage and family counselor, Ga.; ordained to ministry, Episcopal Ch., 1960. Sanitarian, Near East Found., Iranian area, 1951-57; vicar St. Andrew's Episcopal Ch., Pasadena, Md., 1960-64, St. Anne's Episcopal Ch., Damascus, Md., 1964-69; assoc. dir. pastoral Counseling Ctrs. of Augusta (Ga.), 1969-73; asst. prof. Sch. Nursing, Med. Coll. Ga., 1973-75; dir. St. Paul's Counseling Service, Augusta, 1975—; assoc. rector St. Paul's Episcopal Ch., Augusta, 1975-94 . Pres., Augusta Area Mental Health Assn., 1976-77; bd. dirs. Sr. Citizens Council, Augusta, 1975-76, Augusta Players, 1969-72, Housing Authority Adjudication Ct., Richmond County, 1973-75. Served with U.S. Army, 1942-45. Named Hon. Citizen of Sarlat, the Dordogne, France in recognition of service as OSS agt. with French resistance in World War II, 1985. Mem. Am. Assn. Pastoral Counselors (diplomate), Am. Assn. Marriage and Family Therapy (approved supr.). Office: St Paul's Counseling Svc 605 Reynolds St Augusta GA 30901-1431

BERLIN, JERRY D., biology educator; b. Trenton, Mo., Aug. 28, 1934; s. Ben F. and Clara (Gabrielson) B.; m. Ellen J. Fairchild, Aug. 17, 1958; children: Brenda, Paula, Dana. BS, U. Mo., 1960, MA, 1961; PhD, Iowa State U., 1964. Sr. scientist Battelle N.W. Labs., Richland, Wash., 1964-68; prof. biology Tex. Tech U., Lubbock, 1968-85, chmn. dept. biology, 1985-87; dean sci. and math. S.W. Mo. State U., Springfield, 1987-94, prof. biology, 1994—; del. mem. Peoples Republic of China, Beijing, 1981-82; workshop dir. U. Idaho, Moscow, 1985. Contbr. over 60 articles to profl. jours.; author lab manual: A Laboratory Manual for Cell Biology, 1986; editor Cotton Physiology, 1977. Chmn. Solid Waste Mgmt. Task Force, Springfield, 1988-90. NSF grantee, 1976-77, Velsicol Chem. Co., 1984-86; recipient Excellence in Teaching award, Tex. Tech. U., 1983. Mem. AAAS, Am. Soc. Cell Biology, Mo. Acad. Sci., Tex. Soc. for Electron Microscopy (pres. 1977-78). Office: SW Mo State U Dept Biology Springfield MO 65804

BERLIN, KATHRYN E., retired public health nurse; b. Pemberville, Ohio, Nov. 5, 1937; d. Jurdin Deforest and Janet Mary (Hathaway) Smith; m. Albert James Rubel, (div. Sept. 1972); children: Douglas James, Jeffrey Dean, Cynthia Sue, Craig Alan; m. James Vernon Berlin, July 1984. Diploma, Flower Hosp. Sch. Nursing, 1959. RN, Ohio. Head nurse, emergency rm. Flower Hosp., Toledo, 1959-62; occupational health nurse Brush Wellman-Berrylium, Elmore, Ohio, 1962-65; nurse, emergency rm., ICU, recovery rom. Wood County Hosp., Bowling Green, Ohio, 1967-68; office nurse Drs. H.W. Mannhard and R.J. Wherry, Bowling Green, 1968-73; occupational health nurse H.J. Heinz Co., Bowling Green, 1972-73; pub. health nurse Wood County Health Dept., Bowling Green, 1973-79; occupational health nurse Chrysler Machining, Perrysburg, Ohio, 1977-80; occupational nurse Hunt Wesson Foods, Perrysburg, 1979; charge nurse St. Charles Hosp., Toledo, 1979-80; pub. health nurse, nurse surveyer Ohio Dept. Health, Toledo, 1980-91; cert. reviewer Health Facilities in NWDO, 1980-91. Sunday sch. tchr., organist, officer United Meth. Ch., 1950-70; sr. 1st class Girl Scouts U.S. Mem. AARP, ANA, Ohio Nurses Assn., Wood County Dist. Nurses Assn. (treas. 1960), Toledo Zool. Soc., Flower Hosp. Alumni Assn. Home: Kitty Hawk Estates 18954 62nd Pl Live Oak FL 32060

BERLIN, LAURA JANE, psychologist, author; b. Bklyn., Apr. 21, 1947; d. Howard Bernard and Rose (Mandel) Corwin; m. Alfred G. Gladstone, June 12, 1983; 1 child, Michael Hamilton. BA, Queens Coll. of CUNY, 1968; PhD, Yeshiva U., 1988. Lic. sch. psychologist, N.Y. Psychologist Albert Einstein Coll. Medicine, Bronx, N.Y., 1968-85; freelance writer, 1988—. Co-author: The Language of Learning: Preschool Years, 1976, The Parents' Guide to Educational Software, 1991; co-author PLAI: Preschool Language Assessment Instrument, 1976. Home and Office: 45 Old Oak Rd West Hartford CT 06117-1849

BERLINER, ALLEN IRWIN, dermatologist; b. N.Y.C., Apr. 18, 1947; s. Joseph Benjamin and Ruth (Kaplan) B.; m. Edwina. BA, Queens Coll., 1967; MD, SUNY, Buffalo, 1971. Diplomate: Am. Bd. Dermatology. Intern Nassau County Med. Ctr., East Meadow, N.Y., 1971-72; resident in dermatology Boston U. Med. Ctr., 1974-76, chief resident, 1976-77; practice medicine specializing in dermatology Norwood, Mass., 1977—; asst. clin. prof. Tufts U., 1980-90, assoc. clin. prof., 1990—; chief dermatology sect.

Norwood Hosp., 1986—; assoc. staff Boston U. Hosp., Tufts-New Eng. Med. Ctr.; bd. dirs. Mass. Acad. Dermatology. Served as surgeon USPHS, 1972-74. Mem. Am. Acad. Dermatology, New Eng. Dermatol. Soc., Mass. Acad. Dermatology (pres. 1994-95). Office: 95 Chapel St Norwood MA 02062-3155

BERLINER, ROBERT WILLIAM, physician, medical educator, b. N.Y.C., Mar. 10, 1915; s. William Marcus and Anna (Weiner) B.; m. Leah Silver, Dec. 21, 1941; children: Robert William, Alice Hadler, Henry J., Nancy. BS, Yale U., 1936; MD, Columbia U., 1939; DSc (hon.), Med. Coll. Wis., 1973, Yale U., 1973. Intern Presbyn. Hosp., N.Y.C., 1939-41; resident Goldwater Meml. Hosp., N.Y.C., 1942-43, rsch. fellow, 1943-44, research asst., 1944-47; asst. in medicine NYU Coll. Medicine, 1943-44, instr. medicine, 1944-47; asst. prof. medicine Columbia U., 1947-50; rsch. assoc. dept. hosps., City of N.Y., 1947-50; chief Lab. Kidney and Electrolyte Metabolism, Nat. Heart Inst., NIH, Bethesda, Md., 1950-62, dir. intramural rsch., 1954-68; dir. labs. and clinics NIH, Bethesda, 1968-69, dep. dir. for sci., 1969-73; dean, prof. physiology and medicine Yale U., New Haven, 1973-84, dean emeritus, 1985—, prof. emeritus physiology and medicine, 1985—; dir. Pew Scholars Program in Biomed. Scis., New Haven, 1984-91; lectr. George Washington U. Sch. Medicine, 1951-73, Georgetown U. Schs. Medicine and Dentistry, 1964-73; mem. exec. com. assembly of life scis. NRC, 1973-78, chmn. div. med. scis., 1976-78. Contbr. articles to tech. jours. Served with USPHS, 1952-54. Recipient Disting. Service award HEW, 1962; Homer W. Smith Award in Renal Physiology, 1965, Alumni Award for Disting. Achievement, Coll. Physicians and Surgeons, Columbia U., 1966, Bicentennial Medal, 1967; Disting. Achievement award Modern Medicine, 1969; Research Achievement award Am. Heart Assn., 1970; Service award Assn. Chmn. Depts. Physiology, 1981; David M. Hume Meml. award Nat. Kidney Found., 1983; Mem. AAAS (bd. dirs., v.p. 1972), Am. Physiology Soc. (pres. 1967, Ray G. Daggs award 1982, Am. Soc. Clin. Investigation (pres. 1959), Am. Soc. Nephrology (pres. 1968), Internat. Soc. Nephrology (A.N. Richards award 1987), Assn. Am. Physicians (George M. Kober medal 1984), Inst. Medicine, Nat. Acad. Scis., (com. sci. and pub. policy 1978-81, council of acad. 1978-81), Soc. Exptl. Biology and Medicine (pres. 1978-81). Avocations: birdwatching, music. Home: 36 Edgehill Ter Hamden CT 06517-4016 Office: Yale Univ Sch Medicine 333 Cedar St New Haven CT 06520

BERLINSKY, ELLEN BETH, psychologist; b. Providence, Sept. 3, 1953; d. Everett and Sandra Marilyn (Pliner) B.; B.A. magna cum laude, Syracuse U., 1975; M.A., Columbia U., 1976; Ph.D., U. R.I., 1981; m. Gary L. Schine, Mar. 19, 1978; children: Adam Ross Berlinsky-Schine, Laura Jane Berlinsky-Schine. Lic. psychologist, Mass. Clin. psychologist No. R.I. Community Mental Health, Woonsocket, 1979-81; psychologist Counseling and Family Services, Taunton, Mass., 1981; clin. psychologist, asst. prof. U. Mass. Med. Ctr., Worcester, 1981-90; clin. psychologist Human Resource Inst., Norton, Mass., 1981-89; clin. psychologist Bridgewater (Mass.) Psychol. Assocs., 1985-88; cons. Applied Media Group, Providence, 1981-87; pvt. practice, Middleboro, Ma., 1989-94, Taunton, Mass., 1995—. Writer, narrator: (videotape) Getting Ready to Learn. Mem. Am. Psychol. Assn., Mass. Psychol. Assn., Phi Beta Kappa, Phi Kappa Phi. Author: (with Henry Biller) Parental Death and Psychological Development, 1982, (with Gary Schine) If the President Had Cancer, 1993, reissued as Cancer Cure, 1996. Home: 39 Brenton Ave Providence RI 02906-2414

BERLUCCHI, GIOVANNI, physiologist, educator; b. Pavia, Lombardy, Italy, May 25, 1935; s. Carlo Filippo and Elsa (Baraldi) B.; m. Maria Luigia Botta, July 14, 1960; children: Filippo, Silvia. MD, U. Pavia, 1959. Rsch. fellow in neurophysiology U. Pisa, Italy, 1960-69; asst. prof. Med. Sch., U. Pisa, 1969-74, prof., 1976-83; postdoctoral rsch. fellow Calif. Tech. Inst., Pasadena, 1964-65; rsch. assoc. anatomy dept. U. Pa., Phila., 1968; prof. Med. Sch. U. Siena, Italy, 1974-76; prof. U. Pisa, Italy, 1976-83; prof. Med. Sch. U. Verona, Italy, 1983—; mem. panel on human factors NATO, Brussels, 1979-81, chmn., 1981. Editor: Structure and Function of Cerebral Commissures, 1979; editor European Jour. Neurosci. Neuropsychologia, Exptl. Brain Rsch., Cognitive Brain Rsch. Mem. Academia Europaea, Academia Rodinensis Remediatione Stockholm, Accademia Fisiocritici, Academia dei Lincei, Accademia Nazionale Virgiliana, Internat. Brain Rsch. Orgn., European Neurosci. Assn. (councilor 1976-80), European Brain and Behavior Soc. (councilor 1971-75, 86-89), Soc. for Neurosci., Società Italiana Fisiologia, Società Italiana Neuroscienze. Office: U Verona Dept Sci Neurologiche e della Visione, Strada Le Grazie, I-37134 Verona Italy

BERLYNE, GEOFFREY MERTON, nephrologist, researcher; b. Manchester, Eng., May 11, 1931; came to U.S., 1976, naturalized, 1981; s. Charles Solomon and Miriam Hannah (Rosenthal) B.; m. Ruth Selbourne, June 7, 1969; children: Jonathan, Benjamin, Suzannah. B of Medicine and Surgery with honors, Manchester U., 1954, MD, 1966. Lectr. in medicine U. Manchester, 1961-62, sr. lectr., 1964-68, reader, 1969-70; prof. medicine and life scis. Negev (Israel) U., 1970-79; prof. medicine SUNY, Bklyn., 1976—; chief nephrology sect. Brooklyn VA Med. Center, 1976—; adj. prof. medicine Ben Gurion U. of Negev Faculty of Health Scis., Beer Sheter, Israel, 1995—. Author courses sci. topics, including renal diseases, 1966, electrolytes and body fluids, 1981; editor: Nephron; contbr. articles to profl. jours. Pres. area synagogue, 1982-90. Fellow Am. Coll. Nutrition; mem. Japanese Nephrology Soc. (named Disting Nephrologist 1979), Assn. Physicians Gt. Britain, Am. Fedn. Clin. Rsch. Jewish (chmn. 1970-74, pres. synagogue 1982-90). Office: Bklyn VA Hosp 800 Poly Pl Renal Sect III 800 Poly Pl Brooklyn NY 11209-7104

BERMAN, ARTHUR JEROME, gastroenterologist; b. N.Y.C., May 3, 1928; s. Henry and Frances (Sapir-Cohen) B.; m. Carol Michaelson, Oct. 25, 1959; children: Douglas, Judith, Susanne. BS, NYU, 1948, MD, 1951. Diplomate Am. Bd. Internal Medicine, Am. Bd. Internal Medicine-Gastroenterology, Nat. Bd. Med. Examiners. Intern Kings County Hosp., Bklyn., 1951-52; asst. resident Montefiore Hosp., Bronx, N.Y., 1952-53; asst. resident in pathology Montefiore Hosp., Bronx, 1955-56; asst. resident medicine Montefiore Hosp., 1956, 57-58; gastroenterology resident U.S. VA Hosp., N.Y.C., 1958-59; Fulbright fellow infectious diseases U. Tokyo, 1957; assoc. attending div. gastroenterology Dept. Medicine Montefiore Hosp., 1959—; dir. dept. medicine, chief sect. gastroenterology Lawrence Hosp., Bronxville, N.Y., 1963—; asst. clin. prof. medicine Albert Einstein Coll., Columbia Presbyn. Med. Ctr. Contbr. articles to profl. jours., chpt. to book. Fulbright scholar, 1957. Fellow ACP, Am. Coll. Gastroenterology; mem. AMA, Med. Soc. State of N.Y., Westchester County Med. Soc., Am. Gastroenterol. Assn., N.Y. Acad. Gastroenterology, N.Y. Soc. Gastrointestinal Endoscopy, Am. Soc. Gastrointestinal Endoscopy. Home: 10 Deer Hill Ln Scarsdale NY 10583-1048 Office: 1 Pondfield Rd W Bronxville NY 10708-2635

BERMAN, BARNETT, internist, educator; b. Balt., Aug. 8, 1922; s. Benjamin and Lena (Hyatt) B.; m. Mildred Sauber, Jan. 14, 1945; 1 child, Amy Berman Jackson. B.S., Northwestern U., 1945, M.B., 1949, M.D., 1950. Diplomate Am. Bd. Internal Medicine. Intern, Sinai Hosp., Balt., 1949-50, mem. staff, 1950-91; fellow, researcher Johns Hopkins Hosp., Balt., 1950-51; resident in medicine VA Hosp., Balt., 1953, Balt. City Hosp., 1953-55; practice medicine specializing in internal medicine, Balt., 1955-91, retired. Mem. staff Johns Hopkins Hosp.; mem. faculty Johns Hopkins U., Balt., 1953—, assoc. prof. medicine, 1973—. Contbr. articles to med. jours. Mem. Gov.'s Com. on Rehab. of Injured Workers, 1965-70; chmn. bd. trustees Balt. Hebrew Coll., 1972-74. Served to 1st lt. U.S. Army, 1942-46, 51-53. Fellow ACP; mem. Am. Soc. Internal Medicine, Md. Soc. Internal Medicine (pres. 1970), AMA, Md. Med. and Chirurg. Faculty, Johns Hopkins Med. Soc., Alpha Omega Alpha, Phi Rho Sigma. Democrat. Jewish. Home: 3119 Northbrook Rd Baltimore MD 21208-4524

BERMAN, BERNARD I., physician, surgeon; b. Bklyn., Feb. 5, 1922; s. Nathan Berman and Anna Zunder; 2 children. DO, Phila. Coll. Osteopathic Medicine, 1945; MD, Calif. Coll. Medicine, 1962. Diplomate Am. Bd. Family. Intern L.A. County Hosp., resident; pvt. practice; physician Kings Highway Hosp., Bklyn.; mem. staff Beth Israel Hosp. N.Y.C. Fellow Am. Acad. Family Practice. Office: 2017 63rd St Brooklyn NY 11204

BERMAN, BRIAN WILLIAM, pediatrician; b. Phila., Jan. 19, 1950; s. Milton and Estelle (Resnick) B.; children: Elizabeth, Jared, Amanda. BS, Pa. State U., 1971; MD, Temple U., 1975. Diplomate Am. Bd. Pediatrics, added qualifications in pediatric hematology and oncology. Chief divsn. gen. acad. pediatrics Rainbow Babies and Children's Hosp., Cleve., 1993—; assoc. prof. pediatrics Case Western Reserve U. Sch. Medicine, Cleve., 1990—. Fellow Am. Acad. Pediatrics; mem. Am. Soc. Hematology, Am. Soc. Pediatric Hematology and Oncology, Ambulatory Pediatric Assn., No. Ohio Pediatric Soc.

BERMAN, DAVID ALBERT, pharmacologist, educator; b. Rochester, N.Y., Nov. 4, 1917; s. Sam Moses and Anna (Newman) B.; m. Miriam Goodman, Aug. 13, 1945; children: Shelly, Judith. BS, U. So. Calif., 1940, MS, 1948, PhD, 1951. Instr. U. So. Calif. Med. Sch., L.A., 1952-54, asst. prof., 1954-58, assoc. prof., 1958-63, prof., 1963—. Contbr. articles to profl. jours. Mem. Calif. Rsch. Adv. Panel, San Francisco, 1970-82. Recipient Elaine Stevely Hoffman Achievement award, 1971, Merit award Am. Heart Assn., 1979, Faculty Achievement award Burlington No. Found., 1988, Tchg. award Kaiser Permanente, 1993. Mem. Am. Soc. Pharmacology and Exptl. Therapeutics, Sigma XI, Phi Kappa Phi. Home: 3304 Scadlock Ln Sherman Oaks CA 91403-4912 Office: U So Calif Med Sch 2025 Zonal Ave Los Angeles CA 90033-4526

BERMAN, DEAN A., otolaryngologist; b. N.Y.C., Feb. 14, 1952; s. Robert and Beverly B.; m. Jerilyn. DO, N.Y. Coll. Osteopath. Medicine, 1981. Intern Osteo. Med. Coll. Phila., 1981-82, resident, 1982-87; pvt. practice Massapequa, N.Y., 1987—. Office: 680 Broadway Massapequa NY 11758

BERMAN, DIANA LEONORA, psychiatric social worker; b. N.Y.C., July 14, 1932; d. Benjamin and Betty (Schwartz) Styler; m. Irwin Berman, Nov. 17, 1956 (dec. Jan. 1987); children: Kenneth, Benjamin. BA, U. Mich., 1953, MSW, 1955; cert. social work, Columbia U., 1970. Diplomate Am. Bd. Examiners in Clin. Social Work; lic. clin. social worker, N.J., N.Y. Social worker Jewish Child Care Assn., N.Y.C., 1955-59, Montefiore Hosp., N.Y.C., 1964-71; pediatric social worker Mountainside Hosp., Montclair, N.J., 1971-81; sch. social worker West Essex Regional Schs., West Caldwell, N.J., 1982-84; psychiat. social worker Essex County Hosp. Ctr., Cedar Grove, N.J., 1984-93; child abuse coord. Mountainside Hosp., Montclair, N.J., 1971-81, mem. speakers bur., 1971-81; cons. Assn. for Children N.J., Bloomfield, 1971-81. Pres. Inter-Agy. Coun., Bloomfield, 1978-81; active Sr. Citizens Adv. Coun. Montclair, 1994—. Mem. LWV, NASW (diplomate), AARP (bd. dirs. chpt. 131 1995—). Home: 530 Valley Rd Montclair NJ 07043-2729

BERMAN, EARL JOSEPH, physician, consultant; b. Savannah, Ga., July 19, 1960; s. Bernard David and Frances (Effel) B.; m. Anchell Farkas, Aug. 11, 1985; children: Blake David, Kelsey Lynn. BS in Microbiology, U. Ga., Athens, 1982; MD, Med. Coll. Ga., 1988; internship and residency in internal medicine, Meml. Med. Ctr., Savannah, 1988-91. Diplomate Am. Bd. Internal Medicine, Am. Bd. Med. Examiners. Clin. instr. Med. Coll. Ga., Augusta, 1991—; prin., pvt. practice in internal medicine Oconnee Med. Cons., Milledgeville, Ga., 1995—; clin. asst. prof. Mercer U. Sch. of Medicine, 1995—; founder Augusta (Ga.) Ind. Physician Orgn., 1993-95; med. dir. Oconnee Regional Med. Ctr. Sports Medicine, Milledgeville, 1995—; advisor Ga. Mil. Coll. Found., Milledgeville, 1995—. Contbr. articles to Jour. AMA, Chest. Recipient Med. Leadership award Med. Leadership Honor Soc., 1988, Nat. Rsch. award ACP, 1989, Soc. Tchrs. Family Medicine, 1990. Jewish. Office: Oconnee Med Cons 641 W Thomas Dr Milledgeville GA 31061

BERMAN, JOEL ARTHUR, physician; b. Cambridge, Mass., Nov. 9, 1932; s. Conrad and Dorothy Berman; m. Carole, June 11, 1957; children: Steven, Lori, Eric. BS, Tufts U., 1953, MD, 1957. Diplomate Am. Bd. Ob-Gyn. Intern Mt. Sinai Hosp., Cleve., Mass.; resident Yale-New Haven Hosp., New Haven; Pres. Obs & Gyn, Inc., Lynn, Mass., 1969-89. Capt. USAF, 1958-61. Fellow Am. Coll. Ob-gyn., 1966-89. Office: Obs-Gyn Inc 225 Boston St Lynn MA 01904

BERMAN, LISA MAURIN, oncological nurse; b. New Orleans, Dec. 1, 1961; d. Joseph LeBrun and Marilyn Rose (Torres) Maurin; married. BSN, Southea. La. U., 1983. RN, La., Colo., N.Y. Staff nurse East Jefferson Gen. Hosp., Metairie, La., 1983-84, Westpark Cmty. Hosp., Hammond, La., 1984-85; staff nurse Doctors Hosp. Jefferson, Metairie, 1985-86, charge nurse, 1986-87, acting head nurse, 1987, head nurse, 1987-88; charge and staff nurse Penrose Hosp., Colorado Springs, Colo., 1988-94; radiation oncology nurse Holy Cross Cancer Ctr., Mission Hills, Calif., 1994-95; clin. nurse III ambulatory nursing thoracic svc. Meml. Sloane Kettering Cancer Ctr., N.Y.C., 1995—. Recipient ONS Pearl Moore Career Devel. award, 1992. Mem. Oncology Nursing Soc. (pres. Pikes Peake S.E. Colo. chpt. 1990-92). Home: 32 Essex Rd Chatham NJ 07928 Office: Meml Sloane Kettering Cancer Ctr 1275 York Ave New York NY 10021-9999

BERMAN, PETER HENRY, physician educator; b. Vienna, Austria, Dec. 29, 1931; came to U.S., 1940; s. Paul and Alice (Kalman) B.; m. Lynne Moskowitz, Dec. 17, 1961; children: John K., Elizabeth, Michael C. BA, NYU, 1952, MD, 1957; MA (hon.), U. Pa., Phila., 1970. Asst. prof. medicine NYU, N.Y.C., 1965-69; assoc. prof. neurology U. Pa., 1969-80, prof. neurology, 1980—; dir. divsn. neurology Children's Hosp. Phila., 1969-94. Mem. editl. bd. jours. Pediatrics, 1989-95, Pediatric Neurology, 1985-91, Neuropediatrics, 1985—; contbr. chpts. to books and articles to profl. jours. Mem. Child Neurology Soc. (pres. 1991-93), Profl. of Child Neurology (pres. 1987-89). Democrat. Office: Childrens Hosp Phils Div Neurology Philadelphia PA 19104

BERMAN, RICHARD ANGEL, health and educational administrator; b. Cin., Jan. 23, 1945; s. Isidore Alexander and Cecilia (Angel) B.; m. Jean Berman; 1 child, Joshua. BBA with distinction, U. Mich., 1966, MBA with distinction, MHA, 1968. Spl. asst., asst. sec. health, dir. health policy Econ. Stblzn. Program, HEW, Washington, 1972-74; sr. program cons. Robert Wood Johnson Found., Princeton, N.J., 1974-77; asst. dean, assoc. hosp. dir. N.Y. Hosp.-Cornell Med. Ctr., N.Y.C., 1974-77; dir. N.Y. State Office Health Systems Mgmt., Albany, 1977-80; commr. N.Y. State Div. Housing and Community Renewal, 1981-83; exec. v.p. NYU Med. Ctr., N.Y.C., 1983-86; prof. health care mgmt. NYU Sch. Medicine, 1983-86; candidate for U.S. Congress 1986; spl. cons. McKinsey and Co., N.Y.C., 1987-90; v.p. Korn/Ferry Internat., N.Y.C., 1990-91; pres. N.Am. Howe-Lewis Internat., N.Y.C., 1991-92, pres., CEO, 1992-94; pres. Manhattanville Coll., Purchase, N.Y., 1994—; cons. in field. Contbr. articles to profl. jours. Chmn. N.Y. State Bldg. Code Coun., 1981-83; mem. N.Y. State Housing Fin. Agy., 1981-83, N.Y. Statewide Health Coord. Coun.; mem. adv. bd. Ctr. Hosp. Fin. and Mgmt.; bd. dirs. N.Y.C. Pub. Devel. Corp., 1985-90; mem. Prospective Payment Assessment Commn., 1989-95; mem. exec. com. N.Y. March of Dimes Bd., 1980-95; mem. Mayor's Mgmt. Adv. Task Force, 1991-93; mem. nat. adv. coun. Nat. Inst. for Nursing Rsch., NIH, 1991-94; trustee SUNY, 1993-95. Fellow Am. Coll. Health Care Execs., N.Y. Acad. Medicine (assoc.); mem. Am. Hosp. Assn., Am. Pub. Health Assn., Pub. Health Assn. N.Y., Nat. Acad. Sci. Inst. Medicine. Home: 4 Langeloh Ct Rye NY 10580 Office: Manhattanville Coll 2900 Purchase St Purchase NY 10577-2103

BERMAN, SIDNEY, psychiatrist; b. New Haven, Feb. 8, 1919; s. Benjamin and Pauline Muriel (Siegel) B.; m. Jenette Kelly, June 3, 1978; children: Robert Kelly, Barbara Kelly Titus, Leslie Jane Berman Oelsner. BA, Yale Coll., 1939; MD, Long Island Med. Coll., 1943. Diplomate Am. Bd. Psychiatry and Neurology. Intern, asst. resident in medicine and neurology Mt. Sinai Hosp., N.Y.C., 1943-46, resident in neurology, 1943-46; resident staff in psychiatry Fairfield State Hosp., 1948, The Psychoanalytic Clinic for Tng. and Rsch., 1948-49; asst. chief neuropsychiatry VA Hosp., Newington, Conn., 1951-53; chief open psychiat. sect. neuropsychiat. svc. VA Hosp., West Haven, Conn., 1953-54; pvt. practice New Haven, Conn., 1949—; asst. clin. prof. psychiatry Yale Med. Sch., New Haven, 1952-71, assoc. clin. prof., 1971—; attending psychiatrist Yale-New Haven Med. Ctr., 1960-89, emeritus, 1989—, sr. staff, 1990—; staff psychiatrist Yale U. Health Svc., 1961-89; psychiat. cons. Conn. Alcohol and Drug Abuse Commn., 1984-91. Contbr. 12 articles to profl. jours. Asst. concert master New Haven Civic Symphony Orch., 1973-86; psychiatrist-in-charge Conn. Alcohol Commn. Bridgeport Alcohol Clinic, 1949-51 Capt. AUS, 1946-48. Sterling Meml. scholar Yale, 1935-39; Branford Coll. fellow, 1980—. Fellow Am. Psychiat. Assn. (life); mem. AMA, Conn. Med. Assn., Conn. Psychiat. Assn. (pres. 1957-58). Office: 123 York St New Haven CT 06511

BERN, HOWARD ALAN, science educator, research biologist; b. Montreal, Que., Can., Jan. 30, 1920; m. Estelle Bruck, 1946; children: Alan, Lauren. BA, UCLA, 1941, MA, 1942, PhD in Zoology, 1948; PhD (hon.), U. Rouen, France, 1992; LLD (hon.), U. Hokkaido, Japan, 1994. Nat. Rsch. Coun. predoctoral fellow in biology UCLA, 1946-68; instr. in zoology U. Calif., Berkeley, 1948-50, asst. prof., 1950-56, assoc. prof., 1956-60, prof., 1960-89, prof. integrative biology, 1989-90, prof. emeritus, 1990—; rsch. endocrinologist Cancer Rsch. Lab., U. Calif., Berkeley, 1960—; chair group in endocrinology U. Calif., Berkeley, 1962-90, faculty rsch. lectr., 1988; rsch. prof. Miller Inst. for Basic Rsch. in Sci., 1961; vis. prof. pharmacology U. Bristol, 1965-66, U. Kerala, India, 1967, Ocean Rsch. Inst., U. Tokyo, 1971, 86, U. P.R., 1973, 74, U. Tel Aviv, 1975, Nat. Mus. Natural History, Paris, 1981, Toho U., Funabashi, Japan, 1982-84, 86-89, U. Hawaii, 1986, 91-93, Hokkaido U., 1992, 94, U. Fla., 1991, 92; James vis. prof. St. Francis Xavier U., Antigonish, N.S., 1986; Walker-Ames prof. U. Wash., 1977; disting. visitor U. Alta., Edmonton, Can., 1981; John W. Cowper Disting. vis. lectr. SUNY-Buffalo, 1984; Watkins vis. prof. Wichita (Kans.) State U., 1984; vis. scholar Meiji U., Tokyo, 1986; internat. guest prof. Yokohama City U., Japan, 1988, 95; lectr., spkr. in field; mem. adv. com. on instl. rsch. grants Am. Cancer Soc., 1967-70; mem. adv. com. Nat. Cancer Inst., 1975-79; mem. NIH adv. com. in Endocrinology and Metabolism GM Cancer Rsch. Found., 1984-85, Japan Internat. Prize in Biology Selection Com., 1987, 92, 96. Mem. editl. bd. Endocrinology, 1962-74, Gen. and Comparative Endocrinology, Jour. Exptl. Zoology, 1965-69, 86-89, Internat. Rev. Cytology, Neuroendocrinology, 1974-80, Cancer Rsch., 1975-78, Jour. Comparative Physiology B, 1977-84, Am. Zoologist, 1978-83, Acta Zoologica, Zool. Sci., Tokyo, Animal Biol., Italy; contbr. articles to profl. publs. Assoc. Nat. Mus. Natural History, Paris, 1980; mem. adv. com. Contra Costa Cancer Rsch. Fund, 1984—, Stazione Zoologica Anton Dohrn de Napoli, 1987-92. Recipient Disting. Tchg. award U. Calif., Berkeley, 1979, The Berkeley Citation, 1990, Disting. Svc. award Soc. Adv. Chicanos and Native Americans in Sci., 1990; Guggenheim fellow, 1951-52, NSF fellow U. Hawaii, 1958-59, fellow Ctr. for Advanced Study in Behavioral Scis., Stanford U., 1960, NSF fellow Stazione Zoologica, Naples, 1965-55, Japan Soc. Promotion of Sci. Rsch. fellow U. Toyama, Japan, 1993. Fellow NAS, AAAS, Am. Acad. Arts and Scis., Indian Nat. Sci. Acad. (fgn.), Società Nazionale di Scienze Lettere e Arti Napoli (fgn.), Calif. Acad. Sci., Accademia Nazionale dei lincei (fgn.); mem. Am. Soc. Zoologists (hon., pres. 1967), Am. Assn. Cancer Rsch., Am. Physiol. Soc., Endocrine Soc., Internat. Soc. Neuroendocrinology (coun. 1977-80), Exptl. Biology and Medicine (coun. 1980-83), Am. Soc. Molec. Marine Biol. Biotech., Western Soc. Naturalists, Japan Soc. Zootech. Sci. (hon.), Japan Soc. Comparative Endocrinology (hon.), Cosmos Club. Home: 1010 Shattuck Ave Berkeley CA 94707-2626 Office: U Calif Dept Integrative Biology Berkeley CA 94720-3140

BERN, LYNDA KAPLAN, women's health and pediatric nurse; b. N.Y.C., Apr. 17, 1960; d. Melvin and Marilyn Kaplan; m. Jay Bern, June 1986. BSN, SUNY, Binghamton, 1981. RN, N.Y., Md., D.C., Va., N.J. Clin. nurse Gt. Neck (N.Y.) Pediatrics, 1981-82, North Shore Ob-Gyn, Bayside, N.Y., 1982-84; clin. ladder level three nurse North Shore U. Hosp., Manhasset, N.Y., 1981-88; breast feeding cons., instr. childbirth preparation Shady Grove Adventist Hosp., Rockville, Md., 1989-90, 91-92; relief nurse Md. Profl. Staffing Svc., Bethesda, Md., 1989-92; staff nurse St. Peter's Med. Ctr., New Brunswick, N.J., 1993—; instr. maternal-child series St. Peter's Med. Ctr., 1994—; mgr. nursing hon. com. SUNY, mem. hosp. stds. of care com., nursing preceptor Adelphi Sr. Nursing Students, Vol. March of Dimes/Health Screening Fair. Nursing scholar Good Citizenship League.

BERN, MURRAY MORRIS, hematologist, oncologist; b. Montgomery, Ala., Feb. 26, 1944; s. Hymie and Ruth Edith (Schaeffer) B.; m. Nancy Frazee, Nov. 23, 1967; 1 child, Alan. BA, Vanderbilt U., 1966; MD, Tulane U., 1970. Diplomate Am. Bd. Internal Medicine, Am. Bd. Hematology, Am. Bd. Oncology. Intern, then resident New Eng. Deaconess Hosp., Boston, 1970-72; resident in medicine Boston City Hosp., 1972-73; Am. Cancer Soc. fellow Ctr. for Blood Rsch., Boston, 1973-75; sect. chief hematology New Eng. Deaconess Hosp., Boston, 1975-86; co-founder Cancer Ctr. of Boston, 1986; lab. dir. bone marrow transplantation Cancer Ctr. Boston, Boston and Plymouth, Mass., 1986—; dir. Cancer Ctr. of Boston and its stem cell support care, 1990—; asst. prof. medicine Harvard U., 1987-94, asst. clin. prof. medicine, 1978-87. Author, editor: Urinary Track Bleeding, 1985, Hematologic Disorders in Maternal and Fetal Medicine, 1990. Mem. bd. med. advisors Am. Cancer Soc., Mass., 1976-80, fellow, 1973-75; bd. dirs. N.E. region ARC, 1994—. Recipient Tullis award for rsch. Fellow ACP; mem. Am. Soc. Hematology (clin. practice com. 1996—), Am. Soc. Clin. Oncology. Office: Cancer Ctr Boston 125 Parker Hill Ave Boston MA 02120-2847

BERNACKI, RALPH JAMES, pharmacologist, researcher; b. Buffalo, Oct. 9, 1946; s. Roman Stanislaus and Emily (Dommer) B.; m. Celeste Agnes Wojtkowski; Aug. 16, 1969; children: Rachelle Emily, Gwen Marie. BS in Biology, Rensselaer Poly. Inst., 1968; PhD in Pharmacology, U. Rochester, 1972. Cancer rsch. scientist I, dept. exptl. therapeutics Grace Cancer Drug Ctr., Roswell Pk. Cancer Inst., Buffalo, 1972-74, cancer rsch. scientist II, dept. exptl. therapeutics, 1974-76, cancer rsch. scientist III, dept. exptl. therapeutics, 1976-77, cancer rsch. scientist IV, dept. exptl. therapeutics, 1977-80, cancer rsch. scientist V, dept. exptl. therapeutics, 1980-93; cancer rsch. scientist VI dept. exptl. therapeutics Roswell Park Cancer Inst., Buffalo, 1993—; rsch. prof., dept. pharmacology SUNY, Buffalo, 1975—; cons. Nat. Cancer Inst., Bethesda, Md., 1985—, Am. Cancer Soc., Atlanta, 1990—, U.S. Army Med. Rsch. and Materiel Command, 1995, various pharm. cos. Author (with others) several books on sci. and cancer rsch.; contbr. over 160 articles to sci. jours. Nat. Cancer Inst. grantee, 1975—. Mem. AAAS, Am. Assn. Cancer Rsch., Am. Soc. Pharmacology and Exptl. Therapeutics, Fedn. Am. Soc. Exptl. Biology, Roswell Pk. Assn. Scientists (pres. 1990-92), Sigma Xi. Republican. Roman Catholic. Office: Roswell Pk Cancer Inst Elm And Carlton St Buffalo NY 14263-0001

BERNARD, GEORGE W., cell, oral biology, and neurobiology educator; b. N.Y.C., Aug. 22, 1925; s. Meyer Welitskin and Helen (Grenadier) Luskin; m. Maxine Shear, Nov. 5, 1947 (div. Feb. 1971); children: Claudia, Nancy; m. Ellie Bragg Schiff, Aug. 24, 1986. AA, U. Fla., 1944; DDS, Wash. U., St. Louis, 1947; BA with honors, UCLA, 1963, PhD, 1967. Gen. practice resident Kingsbrook Hosp., N.Y.C.; from assoc. prof. to prof. anatomy, cell and oral biology UCLA, 1967—; chair dept. oral biology, 1992—; prof. neurobiology UCLA Sch. Medicine, 1995—; vis. prof. dept. cellular pathology Marie and Pierre Curie U., Paris, 1980-81; vis. prof. II U. degli Studi di Roma, 1995—; mem. Dental Rsch. Inst. UCLA, 1974, Cancer Ctr., 1977, grad. advisor Sch. Dentistry, 1985—; mem. oral biology and med. study sect. NIH, Bethesda, Md., 1978-81; cons. VA Hosp., Long Beach, Calif., 1980—. Editl. bd. Internat. Jour. Oral Biology; contbr. articles to profl. jours., chpts. to books. Served to capt. U.S. Army, 1952-53. NIH fellow, 1964-67, post doctoral fellow Inst. de Recherches Scientifiques, Villejuif, France, 1970-71. Fellow AAAS; mem. Am. Assn. Anatomists, Electron Microscopy Soc. Am., Am. Assn. Dental Rsch., Internat. Assn. Dental Rsch., Am. Soc. Bone and Mineral Rsch. Office: UCLA Sch Medicine Dept Neurobiology Los Angeles CA 90024

BERNARD, JAMES DONALD, dermatologist; b. Neptune, N.J., Dec. 15, 1938; s. Donald Joseph and Myrtle Marite (Boyd) B.; m. Tommie Lou Lowrey, May 31, 1969; B.S., Ariz. State U., 1961; D.O., U. Health Scis. Coll. Osteo. Medicine, Kansas City, Mo., 1969. Diplomate Am. Osteopathic Bd. Dermatology; cert. graphoanalysis. Intern Phoenix Gen. Hosp., 1969-70; resident in dermatology Detroit Osteo. Hosp., 1970-73; practice osteo. medicine specializing in dermatology, Atlanta, 1973—; chief of staff Ga. Osteo. Hosp., Atlanta, 1979-80. Served to 1st lt. MC, USAR, 1964-71. Fellow Am. Osteo. Coll. Dermatology (pres. 1977-78, sec.-treas. 1979—); mem. Am. Osteo. Assn., Ga. Osteo. Med. Assn. (pres. 1982-83). Ex officio mem. Am. Osteo. Bd. Dermatology, 1979—. Republican. Roman Catholic. Lodges: Civitan, K.C. Avocations: swimming; tennis. Home: 4330 Idlewood Ln Tucker GA 30084-6400 Office: 4480 Covington Hwy Ste A Decatur GA 30035-1215

BERNARD, RICHARD MONTGOMERY, physician; b. Long Beach, Calif., Feb. 21, 1925; s. Francis M. and Irma V. (Phillips) B.; m. Virginia Marie Thompson Hummel, Sept. 19, 1946 (div. Mar. 1971); children: Richard Jr., David, Mary, Danielle; m. Nancy Johnston, Nov. 18, 1971; children: Vivienne Kouba, N. Catherine Thompson. BS in Chemistry, U. Calif. Berkeley, 1945; MD, U. Chgo., 1950. Diplomate Am. Bd. Family Practice. Assoc. physician Dr. G. Alan Fisher, Gresham, Oreg., 1953-54; pvt. practice Westslope, Portland, Oreg., 1954-60, Beaverton, Oreg., 1960-86; assoc. with Dr. D. Graham R.M. Bernard, MD P.C., Beaverton, 1986-90; family practitioner St. Vincent Tanesbourne Med. Plz., Beaverton, 1990-91; locum tenens Oreg., 1991-92; family practitioner Providence Health Sys., Wilsonville, Oreg., 1992—; clin. prof. Oreg. Health Sci. U., Portland, 1994—. Capt. USNR, WWII, 1942-46, Korea, 1950-53, ret., 1985. Recipient award of meritorious achievement OHSU, 1988. Mem. Wilsonville Rotary, Wilsonville C. of C. (long range planning commn.). Republican. Home: 31530 SW Village Green Ct Wilsonville OR 97070 Office: Providence Health Sys 29890 Town Ctr Loop Ste E Wilsonville OR 97070

BERNARDIS, LEE LIVIUS, medical researcher; b. Graz, Austria, Sept. 18, 1926; came to U.S., 1961; s. Johannes Matthias and Sylvia (von Eyberger) B.; m. Barbara Abbott, May 24, 1958; 1 child, Glenn Allan. PhD, U. Graz, 1949, U. Western Ont., London, Can., 1961. Rsch. technician Children's Hosp., Toronto, Can., 1953-55; rsch. mem. Can. Packers Ltd., Toronto, 1956-57; rsch. asst. U. Western Ont., 1957-61; rsch. assoc. La. State U., New Orleans, 1961; rsch. assoc. U. Buffalo, 1961-63, rsch. assoc. prof., 1961-73; rsch. prof. surgery SUNY, Buffalo, 19732-80, rsch. prof. medicine, 1980—; assoc. rsch. carr. scientist VA Med. Ctr., Buffalo, 1973-94, rsch. clin. prof. orthop., 1994—, adj. prof. nutrition, 1994—. Contbr. articles and abstracts to profl. jours. Democrat. Home: 112 Bondcroft Dr Buffalo NY 14226-3427 Office: VA Med Ctr 3495 Bailey Ave Buffalo NY 14215-1129

BERNARDO, LISA MARIE, pediatrics nurse; b. McKeesport, Pa., Sept. 26, 1956; d. Anthony Nickolas and Dorothy Marie (Pastor) Bernardo; m. C. Richard Packer, Aug. 30, 1986. BSN, Duquesne U., Pitts., 1978; MSN, Widener U., Chester, Pa., 1983; PhD, NYU, 1993. Instr. nursing St. Francis Coll., Loretto, Pa., 1983-85; trauma clin. nurse specialist Children's Hosp. of Pitts., 1985-90; instr. nursing parent/child grad. prog. U. Pitts., 1988-90; clin. nurse specialist Children's Hosp., Pitts., 1990-92; clin. nurse specialist emergency dept. Children's Hosp. Pitts., 1992-96; asst. prof. U. Pitts. Sch. Nursing, 1996—. Recipient Mary LeMoyne Page award Children's Hosp. of Pitts., 1988, Micromedex Best Rsch. Abstract award, 1995; grantee Nat. Ctr. for Nursing Rsch., 1989, Emergency Nursing Found., 1992; ANA scholar. Mem. Emergency Nurses Assn. (Edn. award 1995, co-chair LUNAR project, uniform data set com., standing com. rsch.), Sigma Theta Tau. Home: 5256 Turner Rd Gibsonia PA 15044-9531

BERNDT, WILLIAM O., academic administrator, pharmacology educator; b. St. Joseph, Mo., May 11, 1933; s. Oscar Emil and Gertrude Ann (Muthig) B.; m. Bonnie Lou Lampe, Aug. 28, 1954; childen: Barbara, Carol, David, Mary Joan, Paul. BS, Creighton U., 1954; PhD, SUNY, Buffalo, 1959. Diplomate Am. Bd. Toxicology. From instr. to prof. pharmacology Dartmouth Med. Sch., Hanover, N.H., 1959-74; prof., chmn. pharmacology and toxicology Med. Ctr. U. Miss., Jackson, 1974-82; prof. pharmacology Med. Ctr. U. Nebr., Omaha, 1982—, dean grad. studies and rsch., 1982—, vice-chancellor academic affairs, 1985—; chmn. Cosmetic Ingredient Rev. Expert Panel, Washington, 1987-90, Gordon Rsch. Conf.: Mechanisms of Toxicity, Meriden, N.H., 1991; v.p. Am. Bd. Toxicology, Washington, 1988-92, pres. 1992. Contbr. chpts. to books and articles to profl. jours. Mem. pharm. study sect. NIH, Bethesda, Md., 1980-84; chmn. Who Task Group Nephrotoxicity Document, Bilthoven, The Netherlands, 1989. Capt. M.C., 1962-63. Fellow Acad. Toxicological Scis.; mem. Am. Soc. Nephrology, Am. Soc. Pharm. and Experimental Therapeutics, Soc. Toxicology, Inst. Soc. Study Xenobiotics, Internat. Soc. Nephrology, Am. Heart Assn. (established investigator 1964-69). Office: U Nebr Med Ctr 600 S 42nd St # 3022 Omaha NE 68105-1002

BERNE, ROBERT MATTHEW, physiologist, educator; b. Yonkers, N.Y., Apr. 22, 1918; s. Nelson and Julia (Stahl) B.; m. Beth Goldberg, Aug. 18, 1944; children: Julie, Amy, Gordon, Michael. AB, U. N.C., 1939; MD, Harvard U., 1943; DSc, Med. Coll. Ohio, 1973. Intern Mt. Sinai Hosp., N.Y.C., 1943-44; resident Mt. Sinai Hosp., 1946-48; rsch. fellow Western Res. U. Sch. Medicine, Cleve., 1948-49; instr. physiology Western Res. U. Sch. Medicine, 1949-50, sr. instr., 1950-52, asst. prof., 1952-55, assoc. prof., 1955-61, prof., 1961-66; prof., chmn. dept. physiology U. Va. Sch. Medicine, Charlottesville, 1966-88, Alumni prof. physiology, 1988-95; mem. sci. adv. bd. Alfred I. duPont Inst., 1988-94; prof. emeritus U. Va. Sch. Medicine, Charlottesville, 1995—; mem. evaluation com. on post doctoral fellowships in life scis. Nat. Acad. Scis., 1963-65; mem. physiology tng. com. NIH, 1964-65, mem. heart and vascular disease panel, nat. research and devel. demonstration rev. com., 1973-74; mem. tng. com. Nat. Heart Inst., 1966-70; mem. cardio-pulmonary tng. program VA, 1968-71; mem. physiology test Com. Nat. Bd. Med. Examiners, 1969-70, mem. study com., 1983-84; mem. panel on heart and blood vessel diseases, task force Nat. Heart, Lung, and Blood Inst., 1972, mem. heart and lung program project com., 1975-79, mem. hypertension task force, 1976-79; adminstrv. bd., council acad. socs. Assn. Am. Med. Colls., 1975, chmn. council acad. socs., exec. com., 1977-78, disting. service mem., 1982—; Nathanson Meml. lectr. U. So. Calif., 1973; mem. selection com. award for hypertension CIBA Found, 1975-77; Coordinating com. N.Y. State Doctoral Programs rev., 1982-89, bd. sci. counsel Nat. Heart Lung and Blood Inst., 1986-89; mem. Council Internat. Union Physiol. Scis., 1986—. Author: (with M.N. Levy) Physiology, 3d edit., 1993, Principles of Physiology, 1990, 2d edit., 1996, Case Studies in Physiology, 1994; editor: Circulation Rsch., 1970-75; sect. editor Am. Jour. Physiology, Jour. Applied Physiology, 1964-65; editl. bd. Circulation Rsch., 1961-70, 75—, Jour. Molecular and Cellular Cardiology, 1969-71, Proc. Soc. Exptl. Biology and Medicine FASEB Jour., 1962-64, Ann. Rev. Physiology, 1976-81, assoc. editor, 1980-82, editor, 1982. Trustee Cleve. Area Heart Soc., 1962-65, pres. sci. council, 1964-65; steering com. Circulation Group Physiol. Soc., 1969-71. Served with M.C. AUS, 1944-46. Recipient Carl J. Wiggers award, 1975, Va. Lifetime Sci. Achievement award 1988, Daggs award, 1990, Inventor or Yr. award U. Va. Alumni Assn., 1992. Fellow Am. Coll. Cardiology (hon.); mem. AAAS, NAS, Am. Acad. Arts and Scis., Am. Physiol. Soc. (mem. coun. 1970-72, mem. fin. com. 1966-70, 75-78, pres. 1972-73, publs. com. 1976-80, Perkins Meml. Award com. 1977-80), Am. Soc. for Clin. Investigation (award com. Lita Annenberg Hazen awards 1984-86, mem. nat. adv. com. Pew Scholars program 1984-89), Am. Heart Assn. (com. on med. edn. 1963-66, vice chmn. on coun. basic sci., mem. med. adv. bd. coun. high blood pressure rsch. 1976-78, 79-80, 83, chmn. publs. com. 1981-85, award of merit 1978, rsch. achievement award 1979, Gold Heart award 1985, Jacobi Medallion award 1987), Am. Physiol. Soc. (hon. membership com. 1987-89), Raven Soc. of U. Va., Cardiac Muscle Club, Assn. Chmn. Depts. Physiology (pres. 1970-71, teaching award 176), Microcirculatory Soc. (mem. coun. 1971-72, liaison com. 1973-75, chmn. Landis award com. 1977-78), Inst. of Medicine (membership com. 1984-85), Inst. of Medicine (membership com. 1984-85, bd. health scis. policy 1984-85), Phi Beta Kappa, Sigma Xi (v.p. 1984-85, pres. 1985-86), Alpha Omega Alpha. Home: 1851 Wayside Pl Charlottesville VA 22903-1630 Office: U Va Sch Med Dept Physiology Box 1116 MR4 Bldg Charlottesville VA 22908-0001

BERNEIS, KENNETH STANLEY, physician, educator; b. Bloomington, Ind., Dec. 25, 1951; s. Hans Ludwig and Regina (Fischhoff) B.; m. Karen Lou Sachs, Nov. 23, 1975; children: Erica, Erin, Ellen, Elaina, Elyse. B.S., U. Mich., 1973, M.D., 1977. Diplomate Am. Bd. Family Practice; cert. geriatrics. Intern-resident Bronson Hosp., and Borgess Med. Ctr., 1977-80; practice family medicine, Ostego, Mich., 1980—; pres., owner Ostego Family Physicians, P.C., 1981—; clin. instr. Mich. State U., 1980—; preceptor Southwestern Mich. Area Health Edn. Ctr., 1980—; chief of staff Pipp Community Hosp., 1982-85, vice-chief of staff, 1985-86, chief of staff 1986—, chief ob-gyn, 1985—, chief pharmacy and therapeutics, 1984—; chief quality assurance Minret Research Network, 1981—, mem. steering com., 1982—; med. dir. Bronson Healthcare Group Nursing Homes. Mem. AMA, NRA, Am. Geriatrics Soc. (cert.), Am. Acad. Family Physicians. Home: 131 N Sunset St Plainwell MI 49080-1296 Office: 900 Dix St Otsego MI 49078-1563 also: 1576 Main St Martin MI 49070

BERNENE, JAMES LOUIS, physician; b. Mt. Kiso, N.Y., July 31, 1940; s. James C. and Elizabeth B.; m. Diane N. Nicandri, June 17, 1943; children: J. Christopher, Melissa. BS, Middlebury Coll., 1963; MD, Albany Med. Coll. Diplomate Am. Bd. Internal Medicine. Resident, dir. Greenwich (Conn.) Hosp., 1976-81, Samaritan Health Svc., Phoenix, 1981-88; chmn dept. medicine, assoc. chmn. New Britan Gen. Hosp. - U. Conn., 1988—; prof. medicine U. Conn., Farmington, 1988—. Contbr. articles to profl. jours. Fellow Am. Coll. Physicians (gov. elect 1995—); mem. Conn. Endocrine Soc. (sec.). Office: New Britain Gen Hosp Dept Medicine 100 Grand St New Britain CT 06032

BERNER, JUDITH, mental health nurse; b. Tamaqua, Pa., June 19, 1938; d. Ralph Edgar and Ethel Mary (Williams) B Diploma in nursing, Temple U. Hosp., 1959; AS, Coll. of Ganado, 1975, MS in Community Health, D of Med. Adminstrn. (hon.); BA, Stephens Coll., 1977; MEd, U. Ariz., 1980; LD (hon.), U. Iceland. RN, Ariz., N.Mex., Pa. Nursing adminstr. Project HOPE Internat. Office & Hosp. Ship, Washington, 1970-72; assoc. adminstr. Navajo Nation Health Found., Ganado, Ariz., 1972-79; clin. instr. psychiat. nursing Mo. So. State Coll., Joplin, 1986; nurse/therapist Presbyn. Kaseman Hosp., Albuquerque, 1986-93; emergency svcs. clinician for mental health svcs. Presbyn. Healthcare Systems, also Hts. Psychiat. Hosp., Albuquerque, 1994—; regional clin. coord. Mental Health Svcs., Inc., 1995—. Mem. ANA (cert. in psychiat. and mental health nursing), AACD, Internat. Acad. Behavioral Medicine, Counseling and Psychotherapy, Inc.

BERNFIELD, LYNNE, psychotherapist; b. N.Y.C., Mar. 16, 1943; d. Meyer and Lilian Claire (Pastel) B.; m. Arthur Dawson Richards, June 16, 1982. BA, Hofstra U., 1964; MA, Asuza Pacific U., 1981. Lic. marriage, family, and child therapist, Calif., Fla. Founder, dir. Writers & Artists Inst., L.A., 1984—. Author: When You Can You Will, 1993. Mem. ASCAP, Calif. Assn. Marriage and Family Therapists, Am. Assn. Marriage and Family Therapists.

BERNFIELD, MERTON RONALD, pediatrician, scientist, educator; b. Chgo., Apr. 9, 1938; s. Harry B. and Adeline A. (Fischer) B.; m. Audrey A. Rivkin, Aug. 30, 1959; children: Susan, James. Mark. BS, U. Ill., 1957, MS, 1961; MD, U. Ill., Chgo., 1961. Intern U. Ill. Research Hosps., Chgo., 1961-62; asst. resident in pediatrics N.Y. Hosp.-Cornell U. Med. Center, N.Y.C., 1962-63; research assoc. NIH, Bethesda, Md., 1963-65; research investigator Nat. Inst. Child Health and Human Devel., U. Calif., San Diego, 1965-66; chief resident in pediatrics Stanford U. Med. Center, 1967; asst. prof. pediatrics Stanford U., 1967-70, assoc. prof., 1970-75, prof., 1975-89, Josephine Knotts Knowles prof. human biology, 1977-89, dir. med. scientist MD-PhD tng. program, 1974-77, chmn. program in human biology, 1977-80, dir. fellowship program in membrane pathobiology, 1975-85, dir. fellowship program in developmental and neonatal biology, 1982-89; dir. cystic fibrosis rsch. devel. program Stanford (Calif.) U., 1987-89; Clement A. Smith prof. pediatrics, prof. cell biology Harvard U Med. Sch., 1989—; chief div. newborn medicine Children's Hosp., Boston; chmn. newborn medicine Brigham and Women's Hosp., Boston, Beth Israel Hosp., Boston; mem. rsch. com. Cystic Fibrosis Found., 1972-76; mem developmental biology panel NSF, 1976-77; mem. physiol. chemistry research com. Am. Heart Assn., 1979-83; mem. craniofacial anomalies evaluation panel Nat. Inst. Dental Research, 1980-81; mem. health adv. com. Calif. Medfly Eradication Project, 1981-82; mem. sci. adv. bd. Collagen Corp., 1981-90; chmn. Neonatal Biology Group, 1984-91; chmn. Ciba Symposium, Basement Membranes and Cell Movement, 1984; chmn. Gordon Rsch. Conf. on Basement Membranes, 1986; cons. in field. Contbr. articles to profl. jours.; mem. editorial bd. Archives Biochemistry and Biophysics, 1972-79, Cell Differentiation and Devel., 1980-90, Jour. Craniofacial Genetics and Devel. Biology, 1980-83, Jour. Biol. Chemistry, 1987-93, Am. Jour. Respiratory Cell and Molecular Biology, 1988—, Cell Regulation/Molecular Biology of the Cell, 1989—; assoc. editor Developmental Biology, 1981-95; exec. editor MATRIX, 1989—; sect. editor Current Opinion in Cell Biology, 1988-92. Mem. working group Organ Systems Program Nat. Cancer Inst., 1986-89, selection com. Pediatric Scientist Tng. Program, Assn. Med. Sch. Pediatric Dept. Chairmen, 1987-91, Mid. Grades Life Sci. Adv. Bd. Carnegie Corp., N.Y., 1988—, Maternal and Child Health Rsch. Com. Nat. Inst. Child Health and Human Devel., 1988-92; mem. working group on Early Life and Adolescent Health Policy, Harvard U., 1989—; mem. sci. adv. bd. Neose Techs., 1992—, Peregrine Pharmaceuticals, 1993—, Exilexsis Pharms., Genzyme Corp., 1994—. With USPHS, 1963-66. Guggenheim fellow, 1972-73; Josiah Macy scholar, 1980-81; recipient Merit award Nat. Inst. Child Health and Human Devel., 1988. Mem. Am. Pediatrics Soc. (Centennial Symposium lectr. 1988), Am. Acad. Pediatrics, Am. Soc. for Biochemistry and Molecular Biology, Am. Soc. Cell Biology (chmn. pub. policy com., treas.), Internat. Soc. for Devel. Biology, Perinatal Research Soc., Soc. Devel. Biology (pres. 1991), Soc. Pediatric Research, Teratology Soc., Western Soc. Pediatric Research (Ross award 1973). Home: 25 Brimmer St Boston MA 02108-1040 Office: Harvard Med Sch Joint Program In Neonatal Boston MA 02115

BERNHANG, ARTHUR M., orthopaedic surgeon, sculptor; b. N.Y.C., June 21, 1934; s. Clare (Kessler) B.; m. Judy Lynne Pertz, Dec. 3, 1961. AB, U. Rochester, 1955; MD, Chgo Med. Sch., 1959. Diplomate Am. Bd. Orthopaedic Surgery. Intern Hosp. for Joint Diseases, N.Y.C., 1959-60, resident, 1960-64; pvt. practice Huntington, N.Y.; attending orthopaedist Huntington Hosp., 1970—; vis. prof. U. Papua New Guinea, 1986, Orthopeadics Overseas, Indonesia, 1989, Vietnam, 1993. Works shown at one man shows and exhbns. Lt. comdr. USNR, 1966-68. Fellow Royal Soc. Arts, Internat. Arthroscopy Assn., Internat. Soc. Orthopaedics and Traumatology, Am. Orthopaedic Soc. for Sports Medicine; mem. Explorers Club. Office: 124 Main St Huntington NY 11743-6922

BERNHARD, JEFFREY DAVID, dermatologist, educator; b. Buffalo, Oct. 31, 1951. AB, Harvard Coll., 1973; MD, Harvard Med. Sch., 1978. Diplomate Am. Bd. Dermatology. Chief resident dermatology Harvard Med. Sch., Boston, 1982—; fellow photomedicine Mass. Gen. Hosp., 1983; faculty U. Mass. Med. Sch., Worcester, 1983-86, dir. dermatology, assoc. prof., 1986—, assoc. dean for admissions, 1989-95, prof., 1992—. Author: Itch: Mechanisms & Management of Pruritus, 1994; mem. editl. bd. Jour. Am. Acad. Dermatology, asst. editor, Yearbook of Dermatology, Internat. Jour. Dermatology. Mem. Soc. for Investigative Dermatology, Royal Soc. Medicine, Sir. James Saunders Soc., Aesculapian Club Boston, Assn. Profs. Dermatology, New Eng. Dermatol. Soc. (pres. 1990-91). Office: U Mass Med Ctr 55 Lake Ave N Worcester MA 01655-0307

BERNHARD, MICHAEL IAN, pharmaceutical company executive; b. N.Y.C., Apr. 29, 1944; s. Seymour Jean and Ella (Mackler) B.; m. Deborah Gutcheon; children: Jessica Lauren, Adam David. BS, Tufts U., 1966; MS, NYU, 1969; PhD, Cornell U., 1976. Post-doctoral fellow Sloan-Kettering Inst., N.Y.C., 1976-78; asst. prof. U. Va., Charlottesville, 1978-80; acting chief monoclonal program NIH, Frederick, Md., 1980-82; assoc. dir. Coulter Immunology, Hialeah, Fla., 1982-83, Key Pharms., Miami, Fla., 1983-86, Schering Rsch., Inc., Miami and N.J., 1986-90; v.p. pharm. product devel. Block Drug Co., N.J., 1990-95; dir. iontophoretic patch devel. Becton Dickinson Transdermal Sys., Fair Lawn, N.J., 1995—; cons. in field. Contbr. numerous articles to profl. jours.; speaker in field. Recipient Outstanding Inst. Research award Sloan-Kettering Inst. for Cancer Research, 1975, Young Investigator award N.Y. State Health Research Council, 1975, 1978, Scientist of Yr. award Richard Molin Meml. Found. for Cancer Research, 1976, 1977, Pratt Found. award U. Va., 1979. Home: 11 Harvey Dr Summit NJ 07901-1204

BERNHARDT, MARCIA BRENDA, mental health counselor; b. Jersey, N.J., Aug. 22, 1938; d. Jerome and Mitzie (Cohen) B. BA, Fairleigh Dickinson U., 1960; MA, Columbia U., 1960-63, postgrad., 1968-70; postgrad., Hunter Coll., 1973-74. Nat. cert. counselor. Rsch. asst. Tchrs. Coll., Columbia U., N.Y.C., 1963-64; counselor JOIN, N.Y.C., 1965-66; project assoc. Bd. Higher Edn. N.Y., N.Y.C., 1966-68, Tchrs. Coll, Columbia U., N.Y.C., 1968-70; counselor Nassau Community Coll., Garden City, N.Y., 1970-72; rsch. scientist Div. for Youth, N.Y.C., 1972-73; rsch. assoc. Family Svc. Assn., N.Y.C., 1974-76; counselor Div. Blind Svcs., West Palm Beach, Fla., 1984-96; sec., chairperson adv. bd. com. Lighthouse for the Blind, West Palm Beach, 1984—. Mem. AAUW, NASW, ACA, Fla. Assn. for Counseling and Devel., Mental Health Counselor Assn. Greater Palm Beach County, Internat. Platform Assn., Guild for Internat. Piano Competition, Edna Hibel Soc. Democrat. Jewish. Home: Chatham B # 40 Cv West Palm Beach FL 33417-1807

BERNHEIMER, ALAN WEYL, microbiologist; b. Phila., Dec. 9, 1913; s. Eugene Seligman and Helen (Weyl) B.; m. Harriet Poller, MAr. 29, 1942; 1 child, Alan Jr. BS, Temple U., 1935, MA, 1937; PhD, U. Pa., 1942. Biology asst. Temple U., Phila., 1935-37; instr. bacteriology Pa. State Coll. Optometry, Phila., 1937-39; instr. bacteriology N.Y. U. Coll. Medicine, N.Y.C., 1941-45, asst. prof., 1945-52; assoc. prof. N.Y. U. Sch. Medicine, N.Y.C., 1952-58, prof., 1958-84, chmn. basic sci., 1969-74, prof. emeritus, 1984—; cons. in field; trustee Cold Springs Harbor Lab., 1963-68; mem. micro tng. com. NIH, 1960-62. Author: Reflectographs, 1965, Perspectives in Toxinology, 1977; editor: Mechanisms in Bacterial Toxinology, 1976. Fellow AAAS, N.Y. Acad. Sci.; mem. Am. Soc. Microbiology, Am. Acad. Microbiology, Am. Microscopical Soc., Mineralogical Soc. Am., Am. Assn. Immunologists. Home: 51 5th Ave New York NY 10003-4320 Office: NYU Med Sch 550 1st Ave New York NY 10016-6481

BERNHOFT, FRANKLIN OTTO, psychotherapist, psychologist; b. Fargo, N.D., Aug. 12, 1944; s. Otto and Irene Bernhoft; m. Dorothy Ann Larsen, Aug. 11, 1973; children: Kimberly, Brady, Heather. BA in English, N.D. State U., 1966; MA in Counseling Psychology, U. N.D., 1970; MA in English, Calif. State U., 1978; PhD in Counseling Psychology, Brigham Young U., 1985. Cert. therapist, hypnotherapist, counselor, secondary tchr.; lic. marriage, family and child counselor, ednl. psychologist. Instr. Chapman Coll., Brigham Young U., U. N.D., U.S. I.U.; staff trainer Sacramento (Calif.) County Office Edn., 1977-82; therapist Lodi and Stockton, Calif., 1985—; therapist, family fitness trainer, master trainer systematic helping skills, devel. capable people trainer U. Pacific Behavioral Medicine Clinic; co-founder prevention/intervention project, Sacto County, 1977; presenter in field. Contbr. articles to profl. jours. Lt. U.S. Army, 1968-69. H.H. Kirk R. Askanase scholar; cert. achievement Ft. Carson; decorated Bronze star, combat med. badge Nat. Def. Svc. Vietnam. Mem. Am. Assn. Counseling and Devel., Children with Attention Deficit Disorders, Nat. Assn. Sch. Psychologists, Assn. Mormon Counselors and Psychotherapists, Calif. Assn. Marriage and Family Therapists,Sacramento Area Sch. Psychologists Assn., Calif. Continuation Edn. Assn. (past treas.), Calif. Assn. Lic. Edn. Psychologists, Mensa, Blue Key, Phi Eta Sigma. Office: Creative Therapy 310 W Lockeford St Lodi CA 95240-2033

BERNI, GEORGE ALBERT, surgeon; b. Portland, Oreg., Oct. 29, 1950; s. Albert Hawthorne and Rose Marian Berni; m. Gretchen Cornwall; children: Samuel, Alex, Loree Kathryn. BA in Zoology, U. Wash., 1972, MD, 1975. Diplomate Am. Bd. Surgery and Gen. Surgery, Am. Bd. Gen. Vascular Surgery. Resident gen. surgery U. Wash., 1980-82, vascular fellow, 1982; chief surgery Harrison Meml. Hosp., Bremerton, Wash., 1988-92, asst. chief staff, 1993—. Contbr. articles to profl. jours. Recipient Robert S. Evans award. Mem. ACS, Pacific N.W. Vascular Soc. (pres. 1992-93), Internat. Soc. Cardiovascular Surgery, North Pacific Surg. Assn., Phi Beta Kappa, Alpha Omega. Office: Thoracic & Vascular Group 1225 Campbell Way # 101 Bremerton WA 98310-3323

BERNICK, JOAN MERLE, nursing educator; b. L.A.. AA, El Camino Coll., Torrance, Calif., 1979; BA, U. So. Calif., L.A., 1966. RN, Calif.; cert. diabetes educator. Clin. instr. Little Company of Mary Hosp., Torrance, 1979-88; diabetes nurse clinician Diabetes Treatment Ctr. Am., Lakewood, Calif., 1988-92; diabetes nurse specialist Advanced Diabetes Mgmt., Bellflower, Calif., 1992—. Mem. CASCADE (past pres.), Am. Assn. Diabetes Educators, Diabetes Teaching Nurses So. Calif., Am. Diabetes Assn.

BERNIER, CYNTHIA CAROL, critical care nurse; b. Maine, Sept. 27, 1942; d. Millard E. and Grace E. (Studivant) Leighton; m. Joseph D. Bernier, Sept. 5, 1981; children: Andrew S., Debra J. Kennedy. AD, Atlantic Union Coll., 1976; BSN, Westbrook Coll., 1987; MS, U. So. Maine, 1992. RN, Maine. Staff nurse ICU New Eng. Meml. Hosp., Stoneham, Mass., 1976-77, Emerson Hosp., Concord, 1977; unit mgr. Parkview Meml. Hosp., Brunswick, Maine, 1977—. Mem. AACCN (pres. So. Maine chpt.), Maine Mid. Nurse Mgrs. (sec.). Home: 15 Oak St Topsham ME 04086-1924

BERNIER, GEORGE MATTHEW, JR., physician, medical educator, medical school dean; b. Portland, Maine, June 29, 1934; s. George Matthew and Lillian Theresa (Wallace) B.; m. Mary Jane Marron, June 29, 1963; children: George Matthew, III, Elizabeth Wallace. A.B., Boston Coll., 1956; M.D., Harvard U., 1960. Intern Univ. Hosps., Cleve., 1960-61; resident Univ. Hosps., 1961-62, 65-66, U. Fla. Hosps., Gainesville, 1964-65; fellow in biochemistry U. Fla., 1962-64; instr. Case Western Res. U., Cleve., 1966-67, asst. prof. medicine, 1967-72, assoc. prof., 1972-75, prof., 1975-78; dir. div. med. oncology Univ. Hosps., Cleve., 1974-78; prof., chmn. dept. medicine Dartmouth Med. Sch., Hanover, N.H., 1978-86, Joseph M. Huber prof. medicine, 1982-86; dean, prof. medicine U. Pitts. Sch. Medicine, U. Pitts., 1987-95; dean medicine, v.p. acad. affairs U. Tex. Med. Br., Galveston, 1995—. Contbr. articles to profl. jours. Trustee Jackson Labs., Bar Harbor, Maine, 1973—. Served to lt. col. M.C. U.S. Army, 1967-70. Leukemia Soc. Am. scholar, 1970-75. Fellow A.C.P.; mem. Am. Soc. Hematology, Am. Soc. Clin. Oncology, Am. Soc. Clin. Investigation, Am. Assn. Immunologists., Assn. Am. Physicians, Am. Clin. and Climatological Assn. Office: U Tex Med Br 301 University Blvd Galveston TX 77555-0133

BERNIER, PETER DAVID, family practice physician; b. Portland, Maine, Sept. 21, 1950; s. Fredrick Joseph and Erleen Vivian (Ingals) B.; m. Gerri Anne Hendry; children: Jacky Nicole, Michelle Joli, Ryan Benjamin. BS, U. Wash., 1973; OD, Coll. Osteo. Medicine Pacific, 1983. Pvt. practice Union, Oreg., 1984-87, Gresham, Oreg., 1987-95; pvt. practice Springwater Clinic Portland Adventist Med. Group, Gresham, 1995—. Trustee Pleasant Harbor Mariners, Brinan, Wash., 1995—. Mem. Am. Osteo. Assn. Home: 27711 SE Haley Boring OR 97009 Office: 100 W Powell Blvd Gresham OR 97030-7055

BERNOCO, DOMENICO, immunogeneticist, educator; b. Cherasco, Cuneo, Italy, Apr. 6, 1935; s. Giuseppe and Lucia (Merlo) D.; m. Marietta Magdelene von Diepow, July 20, 1972. DVM, U. Torino, Italy, 1959; lic. vet. medicine, Rome, 1961; Libera Docenza, Ministry Pub. Instrn., Rome, 1971. Asst. prof. med. genetics U. Torino, 1961-70; mem. staff Basel (Switzerland) Inst. Immunology, 1970-76; assoc. rsch. immunologist dept. surgery UCLA, 1977-81; assoc. prof. vet. medicine reproduction U. Calif., Davis, 1981-94, prof. emeritus, 1994—. Contbr. 105 articles to profl. jours. Fellow Italian Nat. Coun. Rsch., 1962-63, Italian Ministry for Pub. Instrn., 1963-64, fellow for fgn. countries NATO, 1967-68. Mem. Am. Assn. Immunologists, Internat. Soc. Animal Genetics, Am. Soc. Histocompatibility and Immunogenetics. Home: 1002 Deodara Ct Davis CA 95616-5037 Office: Dept Population Health & Reproduction U Calif Sch Vet Medicine Davis CA 95616-8743

BERNS, KENNETH IRA, physician; b. Cleve., June 14, 1938; s. Charles and Delnet (Cohn) B.; m. Laura Louise Lawless, June 26, 1964; children: Jonathan Charles, Deborah Louise. Student, Harvard U., 1956-59; A.B., Johns Hopkins U., 1960, Ph.D., 1964, M.D., 1966. Intern Johns Hopkins Hosp., 1966-67; asst. prof. microbiology Johns Hopkins U. Sch. Medicine, 1970-74, asst. prof. pediatrics, 1970-76, asso. prof. microbiology, 1974-76; dir. Johns Hopkins U. Sch. Medicine (Year I program), 1973-76; prof., chmn. dept. immunology and med. microbiology, prof. pediatrics U. Fla. Coll. Medicine, Gainesville, 1976-84; R.A. Rees Pritchett prof., chmn. dept. microbiology Cornell U. Med. Coll., 1984—; Howard Hughes med. investigator, 1970-75; mem. microbiology test com. Nat. Bd. Med. Examiners, 1979-82, chmn., 1983-86, mem. exec. bd., 1986-95; mem. Recombinant DNA adv. com. NIH, 1980-83, chmn., 1982-83; mem. genetic biology panel NSF, 1981-84; Fogarty sr. internat. fellow virology dept. Weizmann Inst. Sci., Rehovot, Israel, 1982-83; ad hoc mem. Bd. Sci. Counselors, Nat. Inst. Allergy and Infectious Diseases, 1981-82, perm. mem., 1992—; del. U.S.-Japan Coop. Program on Recombinant DNA, 1981; mem. Internat. Com. Taxonomy of Viruses, 1981—; mem. virology study sect. NIH, 1985-89; mem. virology and microbiology adv. com. Am. Cancer Soc., 1985-89, liaison com. on med. edn., 1989-92; mem. composite com. U.S. Med. Licensing Exam., 1995-98. Served with USPHS, 1967-70. Recipient faculty research award Am. Cancer Soc., 1975-76; grantee NIH, 1970-76, 80—; grantee NSF, 1973-75, 77-80; grantee Am. Cancer Soc., 1970-72; Shell Oil fellow, 1963-64.

Mem. AAAS, NAS, Am. Acad. Microbiology, Am. Soc. Biol. Chemists, Am. Soc. Microbiology (bd. pub. and sci. affairs, pres.-elect 1995-96), Assn. Med. Sch. Microbiology Chairmen (counselor 1980-83, chmn. com. pub. policy 1979, pres. 1985), Am. Soc. Virology (pres. 1988-89), Soc. Gen. Microbiology, Soc. Pediatric Rsch., Internat. Union Microbiol. Socs. (v.p. 1990—), Inst. Medicine, Phi Beta Kappa, Sigma Xi. Home: 50 Sutton Pl S Apt 6C New York NY 10022-4182 Office: Cornell U Med Coll Dept Microbiology 1300 York Ave New York NY 10021-4805

BERNSTEIN, ALAN BARRY, medical manager, pediatrician; b. Bklyn., Dec. 4, 1951; s. Donald and Phyllis Estelle Bernstein; m. Mindy Jan Bender; 1 child, Gabriel Benjamin. BA in Biology with high distinction, U. Rochester, N.Y., 1973; MD, New York U., 1977; MPH in Maternal and Child Health, U. Calif., Berkeley, 1981; postgrad. Ambulatory Care Mgmt. Inst., Columbia U. Sch. Public Health, 1987-88. Diplomate Am. Bd. Pediatrics, Nat. Bd. Med. Examiners; lic. Mass., Calif., N.Y.; cert. Pediat. Advanced Life Support, BCLS-ACLS. Pediat. intern Babies Hosp.-Columbia Presbyn. Med. Ctr., N.Y.C., 1977-78, pediat. resident, 1978-80; asst. med. dir. Montefiore Health Ctr., Bronx, N.Y., 1981-84; med. dir. Cumberland Health Ctr., Bklyn., 1984-88; chmn. dept. pediats. Bklyn. Hosp. Ctr., 1988-90; v.p., regional med. dir. U.S. Healthcare-N.Y., Uniondale, 1990-95; chair dept. pediats. Newton (Mass.) Wellesley Hosp., 1993-95; sr. v.p. med. affairs, chief med. officer N.Y.C. Care Health Pland of N.Y., 1995—; asst. clin. prof. pediats. Albert Einstein Coll. Med., Bronx, 1981-84; clin. asst. prof. pediats. SUNY Health Sci. Ctr., Bklyn., 1984-90; adj. lectr. maternal-child health Columbia U. Sch. of Public Health, 1987—; med. cons. Positive Promotions, Bklyn., 1988—. Contbr. articles to profl. pubs. including Archives Pediat. Adolescent Medicine, abstracts, others. Vice-chmn. Bklyn. Perinatal Network, 1988-90. Fellow Am. Acad. Pediats. (mem. dist. II com. on homeless, mem. provisional com. on adminstrn. and mgmt. 1995—), Am. Coll. Preventive Medicine, Soc. for Adolescent Medicine, N.Y. Acad. Medicine; mem. APHA (sect. coun. maternal-child health 1990-93), Ambulatory Pediat. Assn. (coord. managed care spl. interest group 1994—, co-chmn. Region 2 1990-92), Am. Coll. Physician Execs. Home: 52 Hill St Rye NY 10580

BERNSTEIN, ALVIN STANLEY, psychophysiology and behavior science educator; b. Bklyn., Nov. 2, 1929; s. Joseph and Clara (Schwartz) B.; m. Elly Rattner, Sept. 1, 1968; 1 child, Peter S. BA, NYU, 1950; postgrad., Columbia U., 1950-51, U. Mass., 1952; PhD, U. Buffalo, 1958. Ward psychologist, rsch. ward adminstr. VA Hosp., Montrose, N.Y., 1958-66; asst. prof. Med. Sch. Cornell U., N.Y.C., 1965-66; from asst. to assoc. prof. Coll. of Medicine SUNY, Bklyn., 1966—, from asst. prof. to assoc. prof. clin. behavior Grad. Sch., 1970—, assoc. prof. neurol. and behavior sci. Coll. of Medicine, 1975—; sr. rsch. scientist Kings County Med. Ctr., Bklyn., 1970—; vis. prof. dept. psychology U. York, Eng., 1976; mem. rsch. rev. com. Psychopathology and Clin. Biology NIMH, 1979-81, spl. rev. coms., 1985, 88, cons. panel on nat. plan for schizophrenia rsch., 1987, NSF, 1988; cons. Nat. Sci. and Enging. Rsch. Coun., Can., 1982. Assoc. editor Psychophysiology Jour., 1986-94; contbr. numerous articles to profl. jours. Fellow NIMH, 1966-68, grantee, 1969-72, 75, 76-89. Fellow Internat. Orgn. for Psychophysiology; mem. Soc. for Psychophysiology Rsch. (bd dirs. 1989-92, chmn. by-laws com. 1990-92).

BERNSTEIN, IRA HARVEY, psychology educator; b. N.Y.C., Aug. 10, 1938; s. Louis and Sally (Cantor) B.; m. Linda Jean Greif, June 4, 1961; children: Cari Gaye, Dina Louise. BA, U. Mich., 1959; MA, Vanderbilt U., 1961, PhD, 1963. Instr. U. Ill., Urbana, 1963-64; clin. prof. U. Tex. S.W. Med. Sch., Dallas, 1976-78, 80-89; asst. prof. to prof. U. Tex., Arlington, 1965—; vis. prof. North Tex. State U., Denton, 1972. Author: Applied Multivariate Analysis, 1988, (with J.C. Nunnally) Psychometric Theory, 3d edit., 1994; contbr. over 70 articles to profl. jours. Mem. Dallas Police Review Bd., 1983-87. Recipient award Am. Med. Assn., 1969, Am. Acad. Ophthalnology-Otolaryngology, 1969. Democrat. Jewish. Office: Univ Tex Dept Psychology PO Box 19528 Arlington TX 76019

BERNSTEIN, JAMES ERNST, health company executive; b. N.Y.C., Mar. 23, 1939; s. Martin L. and Juliet (Danzinger) B.; m. Jean F. Duff, May 16, 1986; children: Martin, Sarah, Susanna, Rachel. BS, Harvard U., 1960; MD, Cornell U., 1964. Research assoc., asst. to pres. Salk Inst., La Jolla, Calif., 1971-73; exec. asst. to chmn. bd. suprs. San Diego County, 1973-75; dep. dir. health policy ctr. Georgetown U., Washington, 1975-76; exec. asst. to Chmn. Bd. Suprs. San Diego County, Washington, 1973-75; chmn. bd. SEEDCO, Washington, 1989—; coo Age Wave Inc, Emeryville, Calif., 1986-89, dir. 1989—, bd. dirs.; chmn. bd. Pharmsvc., Inc., 1991-93; chmn.Age Wave Health Svcs., 1994—; dir. MedMax Inc., 1995—; spl. expert in disease prevention and control NIH-Nat. Heart Lung and Blood Inst., 1976; rsch. assoc. to pres. Salk. Chmn. Nat. Health Found. Russia, 1992-94. Capt. USAR, 1965-75. Mem. AMA, Am. Occupational Med. Assn. Home: 2700 36th St NW Washington DC 20007-1421 Office: SEEDCO 1101 30th St NW Washington DC 20007-3708

BERNSTEIN, JERALD JACK, neuroscience and physiology educator; b. Bklyn., Mar. 30, 1934; m. Frances Ann Pitlick, 1986. BS, Hunter Coll., Bronx, N.Y., 1955; MS, U. Mich., 1957, PhD, 1959. Prof. neurosci. U. Fla. Sch. Medicine, 1965-80, prof. ophthalmology, 1967-80; chief lab. ctrl. nervous system regeneration VA Med. Ctr., Washington, 1980—; prof. neurol. surgery and physiology George Washington U. Sch. Medicine, Washington, 1980—; dir. lab. ctrl. nervous system regen and neuro-oncology VA Med. Ctr., Washington, 1993—. Recipient Elaine Snider award for Cancer Rsch., 1992; grantee NIH, 1965—, VA, 1980—; USPHS fellow Lab. Neuroanatomy, 1959-65. Mem. Soc. for Neurosci., Am. Soc. Investigative Pathology, Am. Assn. Cancer Rsch., Am. Soc. Neurochemistry, Internat. Devel. Neurosci., Internat. Soc. Neurochemistry, Internat. Brain Rsch. Orgn. Office: VA Med Ctr 50 Irving St NW Washington DC 20422-0001

BERNSTEIN, LIONEL M., gastroenterologist, educator; b. Chgo., Sept. 10, 1923; married, 1952; 3 children. BS, U. Ill., 1944, MD, 1945, MS, 1951, PhD in Physiology, 1954. Diplomate Am. Bd. Internal Medicine. Rsch. assoc. med. and clin. sci. U. Ill., 1952-53, instr. med. and physiology, 1953-54; chief metabolism rsch. divsn. Med. Nutrition Lab. Fitzsimmons Army Hosp., Denver, 1954-55; physician sr. grade VA Hosp., Sepulveda, Calif., 1955-56; chief gastroent. sect. VA Hosp., Hines, Ill., 1956-57, assoc. chief of staff, 1957-62; chief med. svcs. VA West Side Hosp., Chgo., 1962-67; dir. rsch. svc. VA Ctr. Office, 1967-70; assoc. dir. extramural programs Nat. Inst. Arthritis and Metabolism Disorders, 1970-73; dir. office program ops. HEW, 1973-74; spl. asst. Office Asst. Sec. Health, 1975-77; asst. dep. dir. rsch. and edn. Lister Hill Nat. Ctr. Biomed. Nat. Libr. Medicine, 1977-78, dir., 1978-83; prof. health professions edn. Coll. Medicine, acting head U. Ill., 1985-88, 88-90, prof. med. edn. Coll. Medicine, 1988—; vet. adminstrn. mem. Gen. Med. Study Sect., NIH, 1962-67; clin. prof. medicine George Washington U., 1982—; pres. Knowledge Sys., Inc., 1983—. Fellow AAAS, ACP; mem. Inst. Med.-NAS, AMA, Am. Gastroent. Assn., Am. Fedn. Clin. Rsch. Office: U Illinois Ctr Ednl Devel 808 S Wood St Chicago IL 60612-7300*

BERNSTEIN, RICHARD K., physician, diabetologist; b. N.Y.C., June 17, 1934; m. Anne E. Hendon, Dec. 23, 1956; children: Julie, Laura, Jeffrey, Lil. BA in Liberal Arts and Math., Columbia U., 1954, BS in Indsl. and Mgmt. Engring., 1955, postgrad., 1959-60, 1978; MD, Albert Einstein Coll. Medicine, 1982. Diplomate Nat. Bd. Med. Examiners. Indsl. engr., data processing mgr., pers. mgr. Nat. Silver Co., N.Y.C., 1955-58; asst. to exec. v.p. Clay Adams, Inc., N.Y.C., 1958-64, dir. rsch., devel. and mktg., 1964-67; corp. sec., dir. corp. planning Nat. Silver Industries, Inc., N.Y.C., 1967-78, cons., bd. dirs., 1978-82; med. intern N.Y. Med. Coll., Valhalla, 1982-83; pvt. practice ltd. to diabetes mellitus and baryatrics Mamaroneck, N.Y., 1983—; mem. com. on women Westchester County Med. Soc., N.Y., 1984—; adj. instr. medicine N.Y. Med. Coll.; cons. rehab. medicine Albert Einstein Coll. Medicine; asst. attending physician Peripheral Vascular Disease Jacobi Med. Ctr. Author: Diabetes: The Glucograf Method for Normalizing Blood Sugar, 1981, Diabetes, Type II, 1990; contbr. numerous articles to profl. jours. Mem. AMA, AAAS,IEEE, ASME, Nat. Flute Assn., Westchester Acad. Medicine, Am. Assn. Clin. Endocrinologists, Inst. Gen. Semantics, Internat. Soc. Gen. Semantics, Am. Assn. Diabetes Educators, Am. Diabetes Assn. (couns. on complications and nutritional scis.), Am. Med. Writers Assn. (exec. com. 1991—, chmn. awards com. 1991—), Nat. Assn. Sci. Writers, Engring. in Medicine and Biology Soc., European Assn. for Study of Diabetes, Astron. Soc. of Pacific, Amateur Astronomers Assn., Fedn. Am. Scientists, Inst. Indsl. Engrs. (life), Mensa, Intertel, Alpha Pi Mu. Office: 1160 Greacen Point Rd Mamaroneck NY 10543-4611

BERNSTEIN, ROBERT, retired physician, state official, former army officer; b. N.Y.C., Feb. 20, 1920; s. Morris and Rose (Gordich) B. BA, Vanderbilt U., 1942; MD, U. Louisville, 1946. Diplomate Nat. Bd. Med. Examiners, Am. Bd. Internal Medicine. Commd. 2d lt. U.S. Army, 1942, advanced through grades to maj. gen., 1973; intern Grasslands Hosp., Valhalla, N.Y., 1946-47; resident Walter Reed Army Med. Ctr., Washington, 1952-55, dep. comdr., 1972-73, comdg. gen., 1973-78; surgeon U.S. Mil. Assistance Command, Vietnam, 1970-72; ret., 1978; commr. for spl. health services Tex. Dept. Health, Austin, 1978-80; commr. of health Tex. Dept. Health, 1980-91; adj. prof. U. Tex. Health Sci. Ctr., 1982—. Contbr. articles to mil. and med. jours. Decorated D.S.M. with oak leaf cluster, Legion of Merit with two oak leaf clusters, Bronze Star with oak leaf cluster, Purple Heart. Fellow ACP; mem. Soc. Med. Consultants to Armed Forces, Internat. Soc. Internal Medicine, Phi Delta Epsilon, Phi Kappa Phi, Alpha Epsilon Pi, Alpha Omega Alpha. Home: 3805 Greystone Dr Austin TX 78731-1505

BERNSTEIN, SOL, cardiologist, educator; b. West New York, N.J., Feb. 3, 1927; s. Morris Irving and Rose (Leibowitz) B.; m. Suzi Maris Sommer, Sept. 15, 1963; 1 son, Paul. AB in Bacteriology, U. Southern Calif., 1952, MD, 1956. Diplomate Am. Bd. Internal Medicine. Intern Los Angeles County Hosp., 1956-57, resident, 1957-60; practice medicine specializing in cardiology L.A., 1960—; staff physician dept. medicine Los Angeles County Hosp. U. So. Calif. Med. Center, L.A., 1960—, chief cardiology clinics, 1964, asst. dir. dept. medicine, 1965-72; chief profl. services Gen. Hosp., 1972-74; med. dir. Los Angeles County-U So. Calif. Med. Center, L.A., 1974-94; med. dir. central region Los Angeles County, 1974-78; dir. Dept. Health Services, Los Angeles County, 1978; assoc. dean Sch. Medicine, U. So. Calif., L.A., 1986-94, assoc. prof., 1968—; med. dir. Health Rsch. Assn., L.A., 1995—; cons. Crippled Childrens Svc. Calif., 1965—. Contbr. articles on cardiac surgery, cardiology, diabetes and health care planning to med. jours. Served with AUS, 1946-47, 52-53. Fellow A.C.P., Am. Coll. Cardiology; mem. Am. Acad. Phys. Execs., Am. Fedn. Clin. Research, N.Y. Acad. Sci., Los Angeles, Am. heart assns., Los Angeles Soc. Internal Medicine, Los Angeles Acad. Medicine, Sigma Xi, Phi Beta Phi, Phi Eta Sigma, Alpha Omega Alpha. Home: 4966 Ambrose Ave Los Angeles CA 90027-1756 Office: 1640 Marengo St Los Angeles CA 90033

BERNSTEN, STEPHEN A., plastic surgeon; b. Chgo., Sept. 8, 1944; s. Harold Bernard and Emily Marie (Hauseman) B.; m. Trudy Susan Taitz, Nov. 24, 1962; children: Kimberly, Stephen Jr., Benjamin. BA, Lawrence U., 1966; MD, U. Wis., 1970, gen. surgery, 1974, plastic surgery, 1976. Diplomate Am. Bd. Plastic and Reconstructive Surgery. Ptnr., surgeon Madison (Wis.) Plastic Surgery Assocs., 1978-92; plastic surgeon Dean Clinic, Madison, 1992—. Maj. USAF, 1976-78. Fellow ACS; mem. AMA, Am. Soc. Plastic and Reconstructive Surgeons, Am. Soc. Aesthetic Surgeons, Madison Soc. Surgeons (pres. 1992), Alpha Omega Alpha, Phi Beta Kappa. Office: Dean Med Ctr 1313 Fish Hatchery Madison WI 53715

BERNTHAL, HAROLD GEORGE, health care company executive; b. Frankenmuth, Mich., June 11, 1928; s. Wilfred Michael and Olga Bertha (Stern) B.; m. Margaret Hrebek, Jan. 25, 1958; children: Barbara Anne, Karen Elizabeth, James Willard. B.S. in Chemistry, Mich. State U., 1950. Pres. Am. Hosp. Supply Corp., Evanston, Ill., 1974-85; chmn. Cobern Inc., Lake Forest, Ill., 1986—; bd. dirs. Nat. Standard Corp., Nalco Chem. Co., Butler Mfg. Co. Trustee Northwestern Meml. Hosp., Chgo., Valparaiso (Ind.) U., Wheat Ridge Found; governing mem. Chgo. Symphony Orch. Served with AUS, 1950-52. Mem. Health Industries Assn. (past pres.), Health Industry Mfr.'s Assn. (past mem. exec. com.), Pharm. Mfrs. Assn. (past chmn. med. device com.). Clubs: Chgo. Comml.; Knollwood; Old Elm. Office: 225 E Deerpath Rd Lake Forest IL 60045-1952

BERREY, BEDFORD HUDSON, physician; b. Carrollton, Mo., Apr. 20, 1922; s. Robert Wilson and Elizabeth Mary (Hudson) B.; student Kansas City Jr. Coll., Mo., 1939-40, U. Kans., 1940-42; BS in Medicine, U. Mo., 1943; MD, U. Colo., 1945; MA in Internat. Rels., Am. U., 1969; m. Marcia Lois Bagley, May 22, 1943; children: Elizabeth, Barbara, B. Hudson, Christopher, Michael. Intern, Kansas City Gen. Hosp., Mo., 1945-46; resident in pediatrics Denver Children's Hosp., 1946-47; practice medicine specializing in pediatrics, Kansas City, Mo., 1947-48, Harlingen, Tex., 1950-51; fellow in pediatrics Ochsner Clinic, New Orleans, 1949; commd. capt. U.S. Army, 1951, advanced through grades to col., 1967, ret., 1976; dep. asst. chief med. dir. VA, Washington, 1976-77; asst. state health commr. Va. Health Dept., Richmond, 1977-84; med. dir. Nat. Alliance Sr. Citizen, 1986-91; Pres. South Tex. Amateur Athletic Union, 1962-63; pres. PTA, Berlin, 1954, Denver, 1952. Decorated Legion of Merit with 2 oak leaf clusters. Diplomate Am. Bd. Pediatrics. Fellow Am. Acad. Pediatrics, ACP, Am. Coll. Physician Execs.; mem. Med. Soc. Va., Hudson Family Assn. (pres. 1989-90), Masons (32 degrees). Republican. (Washington); Army and Navy Country (Arlington, Va.). Lodges: Masons (32 degrees), Shriners. Home: 16 Evergreen Dr Lexington VA 24450-9209

BERREY, BEDFORD HUDSON, JR., orthopedic surgeon; b. Harlingen, Tex., Nov. 12, 1950; m. Rosalind Therese Mack Berrey, Apr. 5, 1975; children: Alison Elizabeth, Jillian Elise. BS, U.S. Mil. Acad., 1972; MD, U. Tex., Galveston, 1977. Diplomate Nat. Bd. Med. Examiners, Am. Bd. Orthopedic Surgery. Orthopedic resident Tripler Army Med. Ctr., Honolulu, 1977-81; fellow orthopedic oncology Mass. Gen. Hosp./Harvard Med. Sch., Boston, 1984-85; chief orthopaedic oncology Walter Reed Army Med. Ctr., Washington, 1985-87, chief orthopaedic surgery, 1987-93; assoc. prof. orthopaedic surgery U. Tex. Southwestern Med. Ctr., Dallas, 1993-96; prof., chmn. orthopedic surgery U. Fla., Gainesville, 1996—; orthopedic cons. Office of Surgeon Gen., U.S. Army. Gen., U.S. Army, col. AUS, 1972-93, ret. Decorated Bronze Star medal, Army Commendation medal, Meritorious Svc. medal, Army Achievement medal. Fellow ACS, Acad. Orthopaedic Soc., Am. Acad. Orthopaedic Surgeons; mem. Musculoskeletal Tumor Soc., Orthopaedic Rsch. Soc., So. Med. Assn., So. Orthopaedic Assn., West Point Med. Assn. (v.p. 1988-89), Soc. Mil. Orthopaedic Surgeons (pres. 1987-88), Residents Coun. Tripler Army Med. Ctr. (pres. 1980-81), Med. Assn. Panama Canal Area (sec.-treas. 1984-85), Army Navy Club. Republican. Office: Dept of Orthopaedic Surgery Univ Fla Coll Medicine PO Box 100246-HSC Gainesville FL 32610-0246

BERRY, ALAN RAYMOND, surgeon; b. Huddersfield, Yorkshire, Eng., Mar. 12, 1949; s. Raymond and Margaret Parkin (Matthews) B.; m. Gay Berry Bennet-Pitkin, Feb. 28, 1976; children: Nicola Margaret, Michael Alan, Ian Raymond. BS, U. Edinburgh, Scotland, 1970, ChM, 1981, MB BChir, 1973. House surgeon Royal Infirmary, Edinburgh, 1973; house physician City Hosp., York, Eng., 1974; surg. sr. house officer West Fife Hosp., Dunfirmline, Scotland, 1975; surg. registrar Royal Infirmary, Edinburgh, 1976-79; rsch. fellow U. Edinburgh, 1980-81; surg. tutor, lectr. U. Oxford, Eng., 1981-89; cons. surgeon Gen. Hosp., Northampton, Eng., 1989—; med. officer Oxford United Football Club, 1983-89. Contbr. to sci. jours. and surg. textbooks. Fellow Royal Coll. Surgeons Edinburgh, Royal Coll. Surgeons Eng.; mem. Assn. Coloproctology of Gt. Britain and Ireland (regional rep. 1996-99). Home: Maryland Farm House, Grendon Northants NNT 1JW, England Office: Northampton Gen Hosp, Dept Surgery, Northampton NN1 5BD, England

BERRY, ARNOLD JOEL, anesthesiologist, educator; b. Nashville, Aug. 28, 1948; s. Lester and Mamie Rebecca (Lebed) B.; m. Loraine Mendel, June 28, 1970 (div.); children: Michael, Jeremy; m. Heleen Becker, Nov. 15, 1986; 1 child, Samuel. A.B., Emory U., 1970; M.D., U. Pa., 1974. Diplomate Am. Bd. Anesthesiology. Intern, Hosp. U. Pa. Phila., 1974-75, resident in anesthesiology, 1975-77, research fellow in anesthesiology, 1977-78; practice medicine specializing in anesthesiology; asst. prof. anesthesiology Emory U., Atlanta, 1978-84, assoc. prof., 1984-94, prof., 1994—; lectr. in field. Mem. Am. Soc. Anesthesiologists (chmn. infection control policy task force), Internat. Anesthesia Research Soc., Assn. Am. Med. Colls. (rep. to coun. acad. socs.), AMA, Ga. Soc. Anesthesiologists, Soc. Cardiovascular Anesthesiologists, Soc. Edn. in Anesthesia (bd. dirs.), Phi Beta Kappa, Alpha Omega Alpha. Contbr. articles in field to profl. jours. Office: Emory Univ Hosp Dept Anesthesia Atlanta GA 30322

BERRY, JOHN CHARLES, clinical psychologist, educational administrator; b. Modesto, Calif., Nov. 29, 1938; s. John Wesley and Dorothy Evelyn (Harris) B.; A.B., Stanford, 1960; postgrad. Trinity Coll., Dublin, Ireland, 1960-61; Ph.D., Columbia, 1967; m. Arlene Ellen Sossin, Oct. 7, 1978; children—Elise, John Jordan, Kaitlyn. Research assoc. Judge Baker Guidance Center, Boston, 1965-66; psychology asso. Napa State Hosp., Imola, Calif., 1966-67, staff psychologist, 1967-75, program asst., 1975-76; program dir. Met. State Hosp., Norwalk, Calif., 1976-77; asst. supt. Empire Union Sch. Dist., Modesto, Calif., 1977-93, dep. supt., 1993—. Mem. Am. Psychol. Assn., Assn. Calif. Sch. Adminstrs., Sigma Xi. Contbg. author: Life History Research in Psychopathology, 1970. Home: 920 Eastridge Dr Modesto CA 95355-4672 Office: Empire Union Sch Dist 116 N Mcclure Rd Modesto CA 95357-1329

BERRY, JONI INGRAM, hospice pharmacist, educator; b. Charlotte, N.C., June 6, 1953; d. James Clifford and Patricia Ann (Ebener) Ingram; m. William Rosser Berry, May 29, 1976; children: Erin Blair, Rachel Anne, James Rosser. BS in Pharmacy, U. N.C., 1976, MS in Pharmacy, 1979. Lic. pharmacist, N.C. Resident in pharmacy Sch. Pharmacy, U. N.C., Chapel Hill, 1977-79, adj. asst. prof., 1985—; pharmacist Durham County Gen. Hosp., Durham, N.C., 1977-79; coord. clin. pharm. Wake Med. Ctr., Raleigh, N.C., 1979-80; co-dir. pharmacy edn. Wake Area Health Edn. Ctr., Raleigh, 1980-85; pharmacist cons. Hospice of Wake County, Raleigh, 1980—; co-owner Integrated Pharm. Care Systems, Inc., 1995—. Mem. editorial adv. bd. Hospice Jour., 1985-91, 94—, Jour. Pharm. Care in Pain and Symptom Mgmt., 1992—; reviewer Am. Jour. Hospice Care, 1986—; editor pharmacy sect. notes NHO Coun. Hospice Profls.; contbr. articles to profl. jours. Troop leader Girl Scouts U.S.A., Raleigh, 1987—, trainer, 1989-91, mgr. svc. unit, 1990-94; Sunday sch. tchr. St. Phillips Luth. Ch., Raleigh, 1990-92, 94-95, asst. min., 1995—. Recipient Silver Pinecone award Girl Scouts U.S., 1991, Golden Rule award J.C. Penney Co., 1991. Mem. Am. Pharm. Assn. (hospice pharmacist steering com. 1990—), Acad. of Pharmacy Practice and Mgmt. (mem.-at-large 1996—), Am. Soc. Hosp. Pharmacists, Nat. Hospice Orgn., Am. Pain Soc., N.C. Pharm. Assn. (Don Blanton award 1985, mem. continuing edn. com. 1986-87, com. chair 1981-84), N.C. Soc. Hosp. Pharmacists (bd. dirs. 1984-86, program com. 1988-91), Wake County Pharm. Assn. (sec. 1982-85), Rho Chi. Democrat. Office: Hospice Wake County 4513 Creedmoor Rd Fl 4 Raleigh NC 27612-3815

BERRY, KEEHN W., JR., cardiologist, educator; b. Birmingham, Ala., June 26, 1922; s. Keehn W. and Mary Lois (Brown) B.; m. Murray Brown, Mar. 1, 1949; children, Murray Johnston, Keehn W. III, Melissa Strange. BS, Yale U., 1944; MD, Columbia U., 1946. Intern Phila. Gen. Hosp., 1946-47, 1946-47, resident, 1949-52; pvt. practice Birmingham, 1952-88; chief cardiology St. Vincents Hosp., Birmingham, 1960-93, dir. med. clinic, 1993—; clin. prof. medicine Med. Coll. Ala., Birmingham, 1970—; mem. staff Lakeview Internal Medicine Assocs., Birmingham, 1988-93. Lt. (j.g.) USN, 1950-52. Cardiology fellow Phila. Gen. Hosp., 1950-51. Fellow ACP, Am. Coll. Cardiology, Coun. Clin. Cardiology; mem. Photography Guild Birmingham Mus. Art (pres. 1987-95). Home: 3024 Woodleigh Rd Birmingham AL 35223-1325

BERRY, MICHAEL A., physician, consultant; b. San Francisco, June 2, 1946; s. Charles Alden and Addella (Nance) B.; m. Mary Frances Cauthen, Mar. 5, 1977; children: Jennifer Alice, Michael David, Matthew Alden. BS, Tex. Christian U., 1968; MD, U. Tex., Dallas, 1971; MS, Ohio State U., 1977. Diplomate Am. Bd. Preventive Medicine (bd. dirs., trustee 1990, vice chmn. aerospace medicine). Intern in gen. surgery Wilford Hall USAF Med. Ctr., San Antonio, 1971-72; flight surgeon USAF, Madrid, Spain, 1972-75, chief physician, 1974-75; comdr. 401st Air Transport Hosp., 1974; flight surgeon USAF, Lakenheath, Eng., 1975-76; resident in aerospace medicine Ohio State U., Columbus, 1976-78, Johnson Space Ctr., Houston, 1976-78; chief flight medicine clinic NASA Johnson Space Ctr., 1978-81; ptnr. Preventive & Aerospace Medicine Cons., P.A., Houston, 1982—; adj. asst. prof. aerospace medicine U. Tex. Sch. Pub. Health, Houston, 1979—; vis. lectr. space medicine USAF Sch. Aerospace Medicine, Brooks AFB, Tex., 1979—. Author book chpts.; contbr. articles to profl. jours. V.p. Am. Heart Assn., 1979-80, pres., 1981-82, Mission Glen Elem. PTA, 1986; mem. fin. com. Mission Bend United Meth. Ch., 1984-88, mem. adminstrv. bd., 1985-89, chmn., 1987, 88. Maj. USAF, 1970-76. Decorated D.S.M. Fellow Am. Coll. Preventive Medicine (chair sci. program 1981); mem. AMA (Physicians Recognition award 1982), Aerospace Med. Assn. (pres. 1991-92, first v.p./pres.-elect 1989-91, v.p. 1988-89, chair sci. program 1985, mem. edn. and tng. com., mem. awards com., mem. exec. coun. 1984—, mem. exec. com. 1984—, Julian E. Ward Meml. award 1979), Civil Aviation Med. Assn., Soc. USAF Flight Surgeons, Soc. NASA Flight Surgeons (v.p. 1988, pres. 1990), Wilderness Med. Soc. (founding mem.), Internat. Acad. Aviation and Space Medicine (mem. com. selectors), Tex. Med. Assn., Harris County Med. Soc. Office: Preventive & Aerospace Med Cons PA 10777 Westheimer Ste 935 Houston TX 77042-3460

BERRY, NORMA JEAN, social worker; b. Charleston, W.Va., Jan. 7, 1946; d. Carl E. and Dora Lee (Hamm) Inman; m. Julian, July 5, 1974, (div. 1980); m. Vincent L. Swadis, Sept. 12, 1985. BS, Morris Harvey Coll., 1967; MSW, W.Va. U., 1975. Social Worker. Social worker Fla. State Dept. of Welfare, Crestview, 1968-69; asst. adminstr. Hilltop Home for the Elderly, Charleston, 1970-71; social worker W.Va. Dept. of Welfare, Charleston, 1971-74; social worker VA Hosp., Huntington, W.Va., 1974-82, Temple, Tex., 1982-1990; psychotherapist Minirth-Meier, Tunnell & Wilson Psychiat. Clinic, Belton, Tex., 1990-91; social worker Vets. Affairs Med. Ctr., Temple, Tex., 1991—; real estate agt. Bruzzese Realty Co., Huntington, 1980-81; salesperson Mary Kay Cosmetics, Temple, 1983-84. Recipient Outstanding Svc. award DAV, 1981. Home: 8920 Trailridge Dr Temple TX 76502-5210 Office: Olin E Teague Veteran Ctr Temple TX 76504

BERRY, RICHARD GARTH, medical director; b. Kingston, Jamaica, July 30, 1956; came to the U.S., 1978; s. Earnest I. and Eleanor (Burke) B.; m. Charlene I. Berry, Dec. 18, 1983; children: Kayla Renee, Kiana Nicole. AA, West Indies Coll., 1977; BS, Loma Linda U., 1981; MD, U. Calif., Irvine, 1989. Biology tchr. West Indies Coll. H.S., Mandeville, Jamaica, 1977-78; biology/sci. tchr. Pomona (Calif.) Adventist Jr. Acad., 1981-84; intern, resident Kaiser/UCLA, 1989-92, 1989-92; pres. Southeastern Med. Mgmt., Chapel Hill, N.C., 1993—; med. dir., lab.dir. Southeastern Med. Assn., Whiteville, N.C., 1993—; pres. N.Y. Health Recovery Ctr., Inc., Whiteville, 1995—; vice chief of medicine, dir. med. records Columbus County Hosp., Whiteville, 1995—. Author, editor: Medical Officer on Duty, 1992; author: The Western Journal of Medicine, 1993, Hospis Report, 1995. Mem. AMA, Calif. Med. Assn., N.C. Med. Soc. Seventh-Day Adventist. Office: Southeastern Med Assocs 109 N Powell Blvd Whiteville NC 28472

BERRY, ROBERTA MILDRED, civic worker; b. Medinah, Ill., Feb. 27, 1926; d. Judson Stewart and Anna Doretha (Neddermeyer) Lawrence; m. Moses Berry, June 29, 1948; children: Scott, Mark. B.Mus., Cornell Coll., 1948. Choir dir. Presbyterian, Methodist Chs., Cedar Rapids, Iowa, 1949-71; tchr. assoc. Cedar Rapids Cmty. Schs., 1963-73; dir. Pioneer Village, Cedar Rapids, 1982-83; dir. Linn Cmty. Food Bank, Cedar Rapids, 1983—; pres. Chs. United, Cedar Rapids, 1984-85, v.p. Iowa state bd., 1994—; orginator Grade Sch. Picture Lady Program, Cedar Rapids, 1968-69; pres. Seminole Valley Farm, Cedar Rapids, 1980-81; pres. Ch. Women United, Cedar Rapids, 1985-86, also bd. dirs., editor newsletter for Iowa State. Bd. dirs. YWCA, Cedar Rapids, 1970-72, Cedar Rapids Symphony Guild, 1983-88, Iowa Rails to Trails, Cedar Rapids, 1983-88; pres. Methwick Manor Aux., Cedar Rapids, 1985; sec. Council on Aging, Cedar Rapids, 1984-85; rep. Civic Newcomers, 1986-93; pres. Cedar Rapids Area Peace Network Guide; Guide Brucemore Hist. Home, 1982—. Mem. UN Assn. (Iowa state bd. 1993—, Linn County pres. 1996—). Clubs: Beethoven (pres. 1964-65), College (pres. 1965-66), PEO (pres. 1982-83), Demolay Mothers Aux (pres. 1974-75), Postal Workers Aux (pres. 1974-75) (Cedar Rapids). Avocations: oil painting, needlework, tennis, biking. Home: 1118 Maplewood Dr NE Cedar Rapids IA 52402-4710

BERS, DONALD MARTIN, physiology educator; b. N.Y.C., Dec. 13, 1953; s. Harold Theodore and Penny (Wall) B.; m. Kathryn Eileen Hammond, July

17, 1976; children: Brian Alexander, Rebecca Ann. BA, U. Colo., 1974; PhD, UCLA, 1978. Postdoctoral research fellow UCLA, 1978-79, asst. research physiologist, 1980-82, adj. asst. prof., 1981-87; postdoctoral research fellow Edinburgh (Scotland) U., 1979-80; asst. prof. U. Calif., Riverside, 1982-86, assoc. prof., 1986-89, prof., 1989-92, divisional dean, dir. biomed. scis. program, 1991-92; prof., chmn. dept. physiology Loyola U., Chgo., 1992—. Author: Excitation-Contraction Coupling and Cardiac Contractile Force, 1991; mem. editorial bd. Am. Jour. Physiology, Circulation Rsch., Jour. Pharm. and Exptl. Therapeutics, Jour. Molecular Cell Cardiology; contbr. articles to profl. jours. Bd. dirs. Am. Heart Assn., Riverside, 1985-92, pres., 1989-91. Fellow Am. Heart Assn., L.A., 1978-80, Brit.-Am., Am. Heart Assn., 1980-81; recipient New Investigator Rsch. award NIH, 1982-85, Rsch. Career Devel. award NIH, 1985-90. Mem. AAAS, Am. Physiol. Soc., Biophys. Soc., Internat. Soc. Heart Rsch., Soc. Gen. Physiology.

BERSAK, CAROLYN BETH, psychotherapist, educator; b. N.Y.C., Feb. 15, 1949; d. Sidney I. and Shirley (Greenstein) Love; m. David Bersak, May 27, 1973; children: Jennifer, Michael. BA in Psychology, Carnegie-Mellon U., 1971; MS in Casework, Columbia U., 1973; DSW, Adelphi U., 1986. Cert. social worker, N.Y.; diplomate N.Y. Soc. Clin. Social Work Psychotherapists (chair membership Mid-Hudson chpt. 1989—). Social work supr. Outpatient Alcohol Clinic, Kings County Hosp., Bklyn., 1974-77; social worker, team leader Outpatient Alcohol Clinic, Beth Israel Hosp., N.Y.C., 1977-79; staff therapist Mid-Hudson Consultation Ctr., Wappingers Falls, N.Y., 1979-82; unit supr. Family Svcs. of Duchess County, Poughkeepsie, N.Y., 1979-80; pvt. practice psychotherapy Poughkeepsie, 1981—; asst. prof. dept. social work Marist Coll., Poughkeepsie, 1980-81; instr., faculty advisor Sch. Social Work, Adelphi U., 1979-85; coord. dual degree program, instr., advisor SUNY-New Paltz, 1985-92; instr. YMCA, Poughkeepsie, 1985-89; presenter workshops in field. Contbr. articles to profl. publs. Mem. NASW, Acad. Cert. Social Workers. Home: 24 Tamidan Rd Poughkeepsie NY 12601-5239

BERSCHEID, ELLEN S., psychology educator, author, researcher; b. Colfax, Wis., Oct. 11, 1936; d. Sylvan L. and Alvilde (Running) Saumer; m. Dewey Mathias Berscheid, Nov. 21, 1959. BA, U. Nev., 1959, MA, 1960; PhD, U. Minn., 1965. Market rsch. analyst Pillsbury Co., Mpls., 1960-62; asst. prof. psychology and mktg. U. Minn., Mpls., 1965-66, asst. prof. psychology, 1967-68, assoc. prof., 1969-71, prof., 1971-88, Regents' prof. psychology, 1988—; mem. NRC Assembly Behavioral and Social Scis., 1973-77. Co-author: Interpersonal Attraction, 1969, 78, Equity: Theory and Research, 1978, Close Relationships, 1983, also numerous articles; mem. numerous editorial bds., past editorships. Recipient Disting. Scientist award Soc. Exptl. Social Psychology, 1993. Fellow APA (Donald T. Campbell award 1984, editor Contemporary Psychology Jour. 1985-91), Soc. for Personality and Social Psychology (pres. 1985), Soc. for Psychol. Study Social Issues; mem. Internat. Soc. for the Study Personal Relationships (pres. 1990-92), Soc. Exptl. Social Psychology (exec. bd. 1971-74, 77-80, 85-89, Disting. Scientist award 1993), Cosmos Club (Washington), Gown-in-Town Club. Presbyterian. Home: 506 Grand Hl Saint Paul MN 55102-2613 Office: U Minn Dept Psychology N309 Elliott Hall Minneapolis MN 55455

BERSH, PHILIP JOSEPH, psychologist, educator; b. Phila., Sept. 9, 1921; s. Michael and Sophie (Faggen) B.; m. Jacqueline Edith Fratkin, June 8, 1952; children: Lauren Helene, Marilyn Ellen. A.B., Temple U., 1944; A.M., Columbia U., 1947, Ph.D., 1949. Lectr. Columbia U., 1948-54, research assoc., 1951-54; lectr. U. Wis., 1951; chief intelligence and electronic warfare br. Rome Air Devel. Ctr., N.Y., 1954-62; lectr. Utica Coll., Syracuse U., N.Y., 1958-60, Hamilton Coll., 1961-62; chief combat systems div. U.S. Army Behavioral Sci. Research Lab., Washington, 1962-67, assoc. dir. human performance experimentation, 1966-67; lectr. George Washington U., 1966-67; prof. psychology Temple U., Phila., 1967—; vis. prof. dept. psychology Inst. Psychiatry U. London, 1979; cons. U.S. Army Research Inst. for Behavioral and Social Scis. Cons. editor: JSAS; Catalog Selected Documents in Psychology, 1976-79; mem. editorial bd. Jour. Exptl. Analysis of Behavior, 1980-83, 85-87; contbr. articles on psychology to profl. jours. Served with AUS, 1942-46, ETO. NRC postdoctoral fellow, 1950. Fellow Am. Psychol. Assn., AAAS, Am. Psychol. Soc.; mem. Assn. Behavior Analysis, Psychonomic Soc., Ctr. for Behavioral Studies, Ea. Psychol. Assn., Sigma Xi. Home: Cedarbrook Hill Apts # C223 Wyncote PA 19095

BERSON, BURTON LEONARD, orthopaedic surgeon; b. Bklyn., May 8, 1934; s. Ralph Rubin and Evelyn (Duboff) B.; div.; children: Deborah, Brad. BA, Harvard U., 1955; MD, U. Rochester, N.Y., 1959. Diplomate Am. Bd. Orthop. Surgeons. Intern and asst. resident surgery The N.Y. Hosp., N.Y.C., 1959-61; resident orthop. surgery Mount Sinai Hosp., N.Y.C., 1963-66, from asst. to assoc. attending orthop. surgeon, 1966—; attending orthop. surgeon Beth Israel N. Hosp., N.Y.C., 1970—; cons. orthop. surgeon Elmhurst City Hosp., Queens, N.Y., 1966—; chief arthroscopic surgery Mount Sinai Hosp., N.Y.C., 1976—, chief sports medicine dept. Mt. Sinai Hosp., 1976—; assoc. clin. prof. orthop. surgery, Mount Sinai Sch. of Medicine, N.Y.C., 1985—. Contbr. 20 sci. articles to profl. jours.; chpts. to 2 med. texts; numerous articles in pub. press; numerous med. and civic lectrs. Med. advisor 92d St YMHA, N.Y.C., 1980—, Eastern Tennis Assn., N.Y.C., 1985—; med. staff U.S. Nat. Open Tennis Tournament, N.Y.C., 1987-92, U.S. Maccabi Team. Caracas, Venezuela, 1987. Capt. U.S. Army med. corps, 1961-63. Recipient Kaplan fellowship, Mount Sinai Hosp., N.Y.C., 1966. Fellow Am. Acad. Orthop. Surgeons, Am. Coll. Surgeons, Am. Orthop. Soc. for Sports Medicine, Arthroscopy Assn. N. Am., Internat. Arthroscopy Assn. Office: 1100 Park Ave New York NY 10128

BERSON, ELIOT LAWRENCE, ophthalmologist, medical educator; b. Boston, 1937. MD, Harvard U., 1962. Intern Calif. Hosp., San Francisco, 1962-63; resident in ophthalmology Barnes and McMillan Hosps., St. Louis, 1963-66; clin. assoc. ophthalmologist Nat. Inst. Neurol. Diseases and Blindness, Bethesda, Md., 1966-68; asst. Mass. Eye and Ear Infirmary, Boston, 1968-73, asst. surgeon, 1974-78, dir. Berman-Gund Lab. for Study of Retinal Degenerations, Harvard Med. Sch., 1974—, assoc. surgeon in ophthalmology, 1979-84, surgeon in ophthalmology, 1984—; instr. Harvard U. Sch. Medicine, Boston, 1968-70, asst. prof., 1971-76, assoc. prof. ophthalmology, 1976-82, Chatlos prof. ophthalmology, 1982—. Surgeon USPHS, 1966-68. Mem. AMA, Assn. for Rsch. in Vision and Ophthalmology, Am. Acad. Ophthalmology, Am. Ophthal. Soc. Office: Berman-Gund Lab Mass Eye and Ear Infirmary 243 Charles St Boston MA 02114-3002

BERSON, HAROLD EUGENE, psychiatrist, neurologist; b. Bklyn., June 23, 1924; s. Ralph and Evelyn (Duboff) B.; m. Florence Berson, June 23, 1957; children: Diane, Denise. BA, NYU, 1945; MD, Chgo. Med. Sch., 1949. Diplomate Am. Bd. Psychiatry and Neurology, Nat. Bd. Med. Examiners, Pan Am. Med. Soc.; lic. psychiatrist, neurologist, N.Y., Fla. Intern Coney Island Hosp., Bklyn., 1949-50; resident in psychiatry VA Hosp., Northport, N.Y., 1950-51; resident in psychiatry and neurology VA Hosp., Bklyn., 1951-53; resident in nurology Kingsbrook Jewish Med. Ctr., Bklyn., 1953-54, 56-57; pvt. practice psychiatry Bklyn., 1957—, Manhattan, 1989—; attending physician Interfaith Med. Ctr., Bklyn., Kingshighway Hosp., Bklyn., Gracie Sq. Hosp., N.Y.C.; instr. neurology Downstate Med. Sch., 1957—; cons. Maimonides Hosp. and Med. Ctr., St. Lucie Fla.-Savannas Hosp.; mem. vaculty nat. Jud. Coll., U. Reno, Nev., 1979; lectr. and cons. in field. Lt. USN, 1954-56. Recipient AMA Physician Recognition award, 1969—. Fellow Am. Geriatric Soc., Am. Psychiat. Assn. (life; mem. liability ins. com. 1974-84, cons. to com. on spl. benefit program 1989-90, nat. nominating com. 1988-89, 91-92, Warren Williams award for Disting. Svc. to Psychiatry 1992, impaired physician com. 1992, founder and past chmn. Lifers Orgn. 1989); mem. Am. Acad. Neurology, Med. Soc. Kings County (asst. treas. 1990-91), Bklyn. Psychiat. Soc. (pres. 1971), Bklyn. Neurol. Soc. (pres. 1975), Ea. Psychiat. Soc., Med. Soc. State N.Y. (mem. mental health com. 1986—, interspclty. com. 1979-86), Assn. Am. Med. Colls., Am. Acad. Psychiatry and Law, others. Home: 2900 SE Dune Dr Stuart FL 34996-4935 Office: 200 E 61st St New York NY 10021-8550 also: 448 74th St Brooklyn NY 11209-2602

BERSTEIN, IRVING AARON, biotechnology and medical technology executive; b. Providence, Oct. 11, 1926; s. Robert Louis and Laura (Sperber) B.; m. Suzanne D'Amico, Apr. 16, 1972; children: Jonathan, Robert Laurance. ScB, Brown U., 1947; PhD, Cornell U., 1951. Assoc. tech. dir., sr. scientist Tracer Lab Inc., 1951-57; pres., tech. dir. Controls for Radiation, Inc., Cambridge, Mass., 1957-69, Controls for Radiation Inc. (aquired by Teledyne Inc.), Cambridge, Mass., 1969; v.p. Isotopes Inc. (subs. Teledyne Inc.), Cambridge, Mass., 1969-70; dir. med. div., v.p. AGA Corp., Secaucus, N.J., 1970-71; asst. dir. rsch. program devel. div. health sci. and tech. Harvard U.-MIT, 1972-86; founder and chmn. bd. Hygeia Scis. Inc., 1980-87; pres. Hygeia Scis., Inc. (merged Hygeia Scis. Inc. into Tambrands, Inc.), 1985-87; sr. sci. advisor Hygeia Scis., Inc., 1988-90; chmn. bd. Endogen, Inc., Boston, 1990-95, Bio-Delivery Scis., Inc., 1995—; pres. Berstein Tech Corp., 1980—; cons. for Med. and Biotech., Corp. Devel. Francis Wayland scholar; Cornell U. fellow. Mem. World Pres.'s Orgn., Forty-Niners (pres. N.E. chpt.), Harvard Club Boston, Cornell Club Boston, Sigma Xi. Home and Office: 42 Buckman Dr Lexington MA 02173-6040

BERSU, EDWARD THORWALD, anatomist; b. Duluth, Minn., May 6, 1946; s. Thorwald and Ella Margaret (Hagen) B. BA, U. Minn., Duluth, 1968; PhD, U. Wis., 1976. Assoc. prof. anatomy U. Wis. Med. Sch., Madison, 1976-82, 1982—. Author rsch. papers relating to the study of the relationship of the altered phenotypes associated with chromosomal aneuploidy. Staff sgt. USAF, 1968-72. Mem. Am. Assn. Clin. Anatomists, Teratology Soc. Lutheran. Home: 3811 Euclid Ave Madison WI 53711-1745 Office: U Wis Dept of Anatomy 1300 University Ave Madison WI 53706-1510

BERTELLE, LORRAINE, nurse administrator; b. Bklyn., Nov. 9, 1953; d. Stephen and Margaret (DiSanto) Casale; m. Anthony Bertelle, Sept. 1, 1974; children: Lauren Ann, Jacquelyn Suzanne, Antonia Kristine. AAS, Coll. Staten Island, 1993. RN, N.Y. Nurse adminstr. physician's office, Bklyn. Home: 7515 13th Ave Brooklyn NY 11228

BERTHA, NICHOLAS A., general surgeon; b. Dover, N.J., Aug. 29, 1963; s. Nicholas John and Susan Marion (Gibbs) B.; m. Dawn Marie Nicholls, Sept. 25, 1993. BS, Bucknell U., 1985; DO, U. Med. & Dental N.J., 1990. Intern. UMDNJ, Stratford, 1990-91; resident Morristown (N.J.) Med. Ctr., 1991-96. Mem. AMA, Am. Osteopathic Assn., Med. Soc. N.J. Home: Carriage House Jenks Hill Estate Bailey Hollow Rd Morristown NJ 07950

BERTHELSDORF, SIEGFRIED, psychiatrist; b. Shannon County, Mo., June 16, 1911; s. Richard and Amalia (Morschenko) von Berthelsdorf; m. Mildred Friederich, May 13, 1945; children: Richard, Victor, Dianne. BA, U. Oreg., 1934, MA, MD, 1939. Lic. psychiatrist, psychoanalyst. Intern U.S. Marine Hosp., Staten Island, N.Y., 1939-40; psychiat. intern Bellevue Hosp., N.Y.C., 1940-41; psychiat. resident N.Y. State Psychiat. Hosp., N.Y.C., 1941-42; research assoc. Columbia U. Coll. Physicians and Surgeons, N.Y.C., 1942-43; asst. physician Presbyn. Hosp. and Vanderbilt Clinic, N.Y.C., 1942-51; supervising psychiatrist Manhattan (N.Y.) State Hosp., 1946-50; asst. adolescent psychiatrist Mt. Zion Hosp., N.Y.C., 1950-52; psychiat. cons. MacLaren Sch. for Boys, Woodburn, Oreg., 1952-84, Portland (Oreg.) Pub. Schs., 1952-67; clin. prof. U. Oreg. Health Scis. Ctr., 1956—; tng. and supervising analyst Seattle Psychoanalytic Inst., 1970—. Author: Treatment of Drug Addiction in Psychoanalytic Study of the Child, Vol. 31, 1976, Ambivalence Towards Women in Chinese Characters and Its Implication for Feminism, American Imago, 1988, (with others) Psychiatrists Look at Aging, 1992. Bd. dirs., v.p. Portland Opera Assn., 1960-64, Portland Musical Co., 1987-92; bd. dirs., pres. Portland Chamber Orch., 1964-70, 92-94. Maj. USAF, 1943-46. Recipient Henry Waldo Coe award U. Oreg. Med. Sch., Portland, 1939, citation Parry Ctr. for Children, Portland, 1970. Fellow Am. Psychiat. Assn. (life), Am. Geriatrics Soc. (founding fellow); mem. Am. Psychoanalytic Assn. (life), Portland Psychiatrists in Pvt. Practice (charter, pres. 1958), Mental Health Assn. (bd. dirs., chmn. med. adv. com. 1952-60), Multnomah County Med. Soc. (pres.'s citation 1979), Oreg. Psychoanalytic Found. (founding mem.), Am. Rhododendron Soc. (bd. dirs., v.p. Portland chpt. 1956-58, Bronze medal and citation 1974), Am. Rhododendron Species Found. (bd. dirs. 1960-75), Phi Beta Kappa, Sigma Xi, Phi Sigma. Home and Office: 1125 SW St Clair Ave Portland OR 97205-1127

BERTHOLD, FRANK, pediatrician and oncologist; b. Dresden, Germany, May 4, 1948; s. Harald and Ilse (Lembcke) B.; m. Rosemarie Schwarzer; children: Christiane, Susanne. MD, Med. Sch. Dresden, 1978; PhD, U. Giessen, Germany, 1985. Physician asst. Cmty. Children's Hosp., Dresden, 1972-78; rsch. assoc. Children's Hosp., U. Giessen, 1978-82, sr. physician, 1983-86; rsch. assoc. Children's Hosp., U. Fhila., 1982-83; prof. Children's Hosp., U. Cologne, Germany, 1986—. Author: Clinical and Laboratory Investigations in Neuroblastoma. Bd. dirs. Psychosocial Network of Luth. Ch., Cologne, 1994—. Mem. German Soc. Pediatric Oncology and Hematology (treas. 1986—), German Soc. Pediatrics, Internat. Soc. Pediatric Oncology. Office: U Cologne Children's Hosp, Joseph-Stelzmann-str 9, D-50924 Cologne Germany

BERTI, PHYLLIS MAE, health information management specialist; b. Blue Island, Ill., Jan. 27, 1941; d. Louis J. and Helen Beatrice (Smola) Hankus; m. Jerome Leon Berti, May 27, 1967; children: James Louis, Jeffrey Jerome, Joseph Gregory, Cynthia Ann. AS in Health Info. Mgmt., Stark Tech. Coll., Canton, Ohio, 1992. Claims processor Mass. Mut. Ins. Co., Hazel Crest, Ill., 1981-84; physician billing rep. Ingalls Meml. Hosp., Harvey, Ill., 1984-87; coder, abstractor Timken Mercy Med. Ctr., Canton, 1987-89, Wooster (Ohio) Cmty. Hosp., 1989-92; coord. clin. records Quest Recovery Svcs., Canton, 1992-93; health info. mgmt. specialist So. Health Care Ctr., Southaven, Miss., 1994—. Mem. Am. Health Info. Mgmt. Assn. (long term care sect., accredited records technician), Miss. Health Info. Mgmt. Assn., Memphis Health Info. Mgmt. Assn. Home: 4178 Starlanding Rd E Nesbit MS 38651

BERTINO, JOSEPH ROCCO, physician, educator; b. Port Chester, N.Y., Aug. 16, 1930; s. Joseph and Madaleine (Posillipo) B.; m. Mary Patricia Hagemeyer, Sept. 29, 1956; children—Frederick, Amy Marie, Thomas Allen, Paul Phillip. Student, Cornell U., 1947-50; M.D., Downstate Med. Center N.Y., 1954. USPHS Research fellow U. Wash. Sch. Medicine, Seattle, 1958-61; mem. faculty Yale U. Sch. Medicine, 1961-87, assoc. prof. pharmacology and medicine, 1964-67, prof., 1967-87, Am. Cancer Soc. prof., 1975—; head program molecular pharmacology and therapeutics Sloan Kettering Ctr., 1987—; prof. medicine and pharmacology Cornell U. Sch. Medicine, N.Y.C., 1987—; cons. USPHS, 1966—; N.Y. State scholar for medicine, 1950-54. Contbr. articles to profl. jours. Recipient Honor medal Am. Cancer Soc., 1992. Mem. Am. Soc. for Clin. Investigation, Am. Soc. Hematology, Biol. Chemists, Pharmacology and Therapeutics. Home: 117 Sunset Hill Rd Branford CT 06405-6419 Office: Meml Sloan Kettering Cancer Ctr 1275 York Ave New York NY 10021-6007

BERTRAND, SCOTT RICHARD, chiropractic physician; b. Dayton, Ohio, May 13, 1954; s. Richard Earl and Eleanor Catherine (Swanson) B.; m. Theresa Jean Bertrand, Feb. 9, 1974 (div. 1977); m. Vicki Lynn Buckner, July 11, 1980; children: Stephanie Marie, Lucas Scott. BS, Wright State U., Fairborn, Ohio, 1978; postgrad., Ohio State U., 1980; DC, Life Chiropractic Coll., Marietta, Ga., 1984. Mgr. Holiday Health Spa, Dayton, Ohio, 1975-77; dir., chief of staff Arrowhead Clinics of Am., Jonesboro, Ga., 1984-90; pres. Diversified Tech., Marietta, 1980—; pres. The Fitness Concept. Inventor in field. With U.S. Army, 1973-76. Mem. Am. Chiropractic Assn., Mensa. Republican. Roman Catholic. Home: 1460 Sweet Bottom Cir Marietta GA 30064-5223 Office: Bertrand Chiropractic Ctr 3433 Main St Atlanta GA 30337-1911

BERUBE, LINDA L., women's health nurse; b. N.Y.C., Mar. 18, 1944. Diploma, Bellevue Hosp. Sch. Nursing, 1965; cert. adult nurse practitioner, U. Mass., 1977. RN, Mass. Women's health nurse practitioner, facilitator, coord. Cmty. Health Plan, Greenfield, Mass., 1993—. Mem. ANA, AWHONN (cert.), Am. Holistic Nurses Assn. (cert. holistic nursing), Mass. Nurses Assn. (expert witness program).

BERVEN, NORMAN LEE, counselor, psychologist, educator; b. Des Moines, May 14, 1945; s. Arthur N. and Ruth N. (Sharp) B.; m. Estella Stone, Oct. 11, 1969; 1 child, Jennifer. BS, U. Iowa, 1967, MA, 1969; PhD, U. Wis., 1973. Lic. Psychologist; cert. rehab. counselor, profl. counselor. Rehab. counselor San Mateo County Mental Health Svc., San Mateo, Calif., 1969-71; rsch. assoc. Internat. Ctr. for Disabled, N.Y.C., 1973-75; asst. prof. counseling and spl. svcs. Seton Hall U., South Orange, N.J., 1975-76; asst. prof. to prof. rehab. psychology, program chair U. Wis., Madison, 1976—; cons. to univ., govt. and pvt. non-profit programs. Editor: Rehab. Counseling Bull., 1985-92, assoc. editor, 1982-85, editorial bd., 1980-82, 92—; editorial bd. Rehab. Psychology, 1981—, Vocat. Evaluation and Work Adjustment Bull., 1980—, Assessment in Rehab. and Exceptionality, 1992—; contbr. articles to profl. jours., chpts. to books. Grantee U.S. Dept. Edn., 1986-89, 89-92, 90-93, 92-95, 93—, 95—, Spencer Found., 1981-82, Wis. Alumni Rsch. Found., 1979-80. Fellow APA (rehab., counseling and evaluation, measurement and stats. divsn.); mem. ACA (rsch. award 1986), Am. Rehab. Counseling Assn. (bd. dirs. N.J. chpt. 1975-76, disting. profl. award 1990, rsch. award 1981, 84, 86, 92, 93, 95), Nat. Rehab. Counseling Assn. (bd. dirs. Wis. chpt. 1981-83, Meritorious Svc. award 1992, Calif. chpt. 1971), Nat. Rehab. Assn. (bd. dirs. S.W. Wis. chpt., 1980—, San Mateo chpt. 1969-71, grad. lit. award 1968), Assn. for Counselor Edn. and Supervision, Assn. for Assessment in Counseling, Assn. for Specialists in Group Work, Vocat. Evaluation and Work Adjustment Assn. Home: 10 Southwick Cir Madison WI 53717-1415 Office: U Wis Madison Rehab Psychology 432 N Murray St Madison WI 53706-1407

BERZON, FAYE CLARK, retired nursing educator; b. New Britain, Conn., Sept. 26, 1926; d. Bernard Francis and Elizabeth Tillie (Gross) Clark; m. Harry Berzon, June 18, 1961. Diploma Beth Israel Hosp., 1947; BSN, Boston U., 1957, MSN, 1959; cert. advanced grad. studies, U. Mass., 1987, cert. in gerontology, 1993, adv. cert. in gerontology, 1994. Staff, head nurse, instr. Beth Israel Hosp., Boston, 1948-58; instr. nursing Simmons Coll., Boston, 1958-62, Cath. Labore Sch. Nursing, Dorchester, Mass., 1962-67; asst. prof. nursing Boston U. Sch. Nursing, 1967-70; div. chmn. human svcs. Massasoit C.C., Brockton, Mass., 1973-79, prof. nursing, 1970-92, chair nursing dept. 1988-91; mem. acad. adv. com. to Mass. Bd. Higher Edn., 1975-76; ombudsman in nursing home South Shore Elder Svcs., 1993—. Author: (with Govoni, Berzon, Fall) Drugs and Nursing Implications, 1965, Nursing Outlook, 1970. Vol., Milton (Mass.) Meals on Wheels, 1978-90. Bd. advisors New Eng. Sinai Hosp., 1996. Mem. ANA, Nat. League Nursing (scholar 1963-79, accreditation visitor 1976-86), Nursing Archives, Nat. Assoc. ADN, Mass. Assn. Older Ams., Mass. Gerontology Assn., Beth Israel Hosp. Nurses Alumnae Assn. (co-pres.), Hadassah-Landy-Kaplan Nurses Coun. (life), Sigma Theta Tau. Jewish. Home: 37 Brandon Rd Milton MA 02186-1615

BESCH, EMERSON LOUIS, physiology educator, past academic administrator; b. Hammond, Ind., June 9, 1928; s. Ernest Henry and Carolyn (Dieckmann) B.; m. H. Jean Whitstine, May 28, 1955; children: Karen J., Kevin D., Kathleen L., Kristine A. BS in Biology/Chemistry, S.W. Tex. State U., 1952, MA in Biology/Chemistry, 1955; PhD in Physiology, U. Calif., Davis, 1964. Grad. instr. biology dept. S.W. Tex. State U., San Marcos, 1954-55; research asst., NIH trainee U. Calif., Davis, 1960-64, research physiologist, lectr., 1964-67; research assoc. Pacific Missile Range, USN, Point Mugu, Calif., 1960-64; from assoc. to full prof., head dept. physiology Kans. State U., Manhattan, 1967-74, from assoc. to full prof. mech. engring., 1967-74; prof. mech. engring. U. Fla., Gainesville, 1974-93; prof. physiology U. Fla. Coll. Vet. Medicine, Gainesville, 1974-93, assoc. dean, 1974-87, acting dean, 1980-81, exec. assoc. dean, 1987-88, prof. emeritus, 1993—. Served to capt. USNR. Fellow Aerospace Med. Assn. (exec. council 1985-88, profl. excellence award 1987); mem. Am. Physiology Soc., Soc. for Exptl. Biology & Medicine, Aerospace Physiologist Soc. (pres. 1984-86), Am. Soc. Heating, Refrigerating & Air Conditioning Engring. Home: 15207 Rompel Trail Dr San Antonio TX 78232-4255 Office: U Fla Coll Vet Medicine PO Box 100144 Gainesville FL 32610-0144

BESCH, HENRY ROLAND, JR., pharmacologist, educator; b. San Antonio, Sept. 12, 1942; s. Henry Roland and Monette Helen (Kasten) B.; m. Frankie R. Drejer; 1 child, Kurt Theodore. B.Sc. in Physiology, Ohio State U., 1964, Ph.D. in Pharmacology (USPHS predoctoral trainee 1964-67), 1967; USPHS postdoctoral trainee, Baylor U. Coll. Medicine, Houston, 1968-70. Instr. ob-gyn. Ohio State U. Med. Sch., Columbus, 1967-68; asst. prof. Ind. U. Sch. Medicine, Indpls., 1971-73, assoc. prof., 1973-77, prof., 1977, Showalter prof. and chmn. pharmacology and toxicology, 1977—; dir. Ind. State Dept. Toxicology, Indpls., 1991—; Can. Med. Rsch. Coun. vis. prof., 1979, Swiss Fed. Tech. Inst. vis. prof., 1995; investigator fed. grants, mem. nat. panels and coms.; cons. in field. Contbr. numerous articles pharm. and med. jours.; mem. editorial bds. profl. jours. Fellow Brit. Med. Research Council, 1970-71; Grantee Showalter Trust, 1975—. Fellow Sm. Coll. Cardiology; mem. AAAS, Am. Assn. Clin. Chemistry, Am. Coll. Forensic Examiners, Am. Physiol. Soc., Am. Soc. Biochem. Molecular Biology, Am. Soc. Pharmacology and Exptl. Therpeutics, Assn. Med. Sch. Pharmacologists (exec. com. 1985—, pres. 1994-96), Biochem. Soc., Cardiac Muscle Soc., Internat. Soc. Heart Rsch. (exec. com. Am. sect. 1986-92), Nat. Acad. Clin. Biochemistry, N.Y. Acad. Scis., Sigma Xi. Office: Ind U Sch Medicine 635 Barnhill Dr Indianapolis IN 46202-5126

BESEMAN, SCOTT GREGORY, critical care nurse; b. Little Falls, Minn., Jan. 17, 1955; s. Kenneth Walter and Arlene Elizabeth (Schmidt) B. BSN, Augustana Coll., Sioux Falls, S.D., 1977. Cert. ACLS instr., ICU-CCU neonatal edn. program module, neonatal edn. AHEC, emergency nurse pediatric course, instr., trauma nurse core course. Asst. head nurse cardiac telemetry, emergency rm. nurse St. Luke's Regional Med. Ctr., Boise, Idaho; interpreter for deaf. Founder, pres., artistic dir. Knock 'Em Dead Prodns., Inc. Named one of Outstanding Young Men in Am., U.S. Jaycees; Armond Hanson scholar. Home: 1305 E Boise Ave Boise ID 83706-5162

BESHARSE, JOSEPH CULP, cell biologist, researcher; b. Hickman, Ky., Jan. 21, 1944; s. Herschell and June Elizabeth (Bush) B.; m. Janie Iris Robinson, Aug. 21, 1966; children: Joseph Galen, Kari Elizabeth. BA, Hendrix Coll., 1966; MA, So. Ill. U., 1969, PhD, 1973. Asst. prof. Old Dominion U., Norfolk, Va., 1972-75; postdoctoral fellow Columbia U., N.Y.C., 1975-77; asst. prof. Emory U. Sch. Medicine, Atlanta, 1977-80, assoc. prof., 1980-84, prof., 1984-89; prof., chmn. dept. anatomy & cell biology U. Kans. Sch. Medicine, Kansas City, 1989—; mem. study sect. NIH, Bethesda, Md., 1981-86, 92-96. Mem. editl. bd. Exptl. Eye Rsch., 1985—, Investigative Ophthalmology, 1987-92, Visual Neurosci., 1990-92; contbr. more than 85 articles to sci. jours. Rsch. grantee NIH, 1976-96; recipient Rsch. Career Devel. award, 1979-84, Alcon Rsch. award, 1993. M. Democrat. Office: U Kans Med Ctr Dept Anatomy & Cell Biology Kansas City KS 66160

BESJAKOV, DAN VIKTOR, pharmaceutical executive; b. Copenhagen, Aug. 3, 1961; s. Abraham Jakob and Henny (Seiden) B. DDS, Royal Dental Coll., Copenhagen, 1985; MBA, Columbia U., 1989. Rsch. assoc. Royal Dental Coll., 1984-85; pvt. practice as dentist Copenhagen, 1985-86; sales rep. Pharmacia, Inc., Odense, Denmark, 1986-87; mktg. assoc. Eli Lilly and Co., Indpls., 1989-90, internat. recruiting coord., 1990; sales mgr. Eli Lilly Denmark Inc., Copenhagen, 1990-91, product mgr., 1991-92; mgmt. cons. Aarsoe Nielsen & Ptnrs. Inc., Copenhagen, 1993; internat. product mgr. H. Lundbeck A/S, Copenhagen, 1993—. Scholarship Denmark-Am. Found., 1987, numerous others. Mem. Danish-Am. C. of C., Danish-Am. Soc., Columbia U. Alumni Assn. (counseling bd. dirs. 1989—). Home: 2251 Rippling Way Ct Apt E Indianapolis IN 46260-6551 Office: Lille Strandvej 26 5 sal, Hellerup Denmark DK-2900

BESNER, LANCE ALAN, psychiatrist; b. N.Y.C., Sept. 30, 1961; s. Marvin Besner and Sheila (Friedman) Kleiner; m. Marixie O. Zelen, Nov. 17, 1995. BA, Johns Hopkins U., 1982; MD, SUNY, Buffalo, 1986. Intern SUNY, Buffalo, 1986-87, resident in psychiatry, 1987-90, chief resident in psychiatry, 1989-90; med. dir. emergency svcs. div. behavioral svcs. St. Vincent Health Ctr., Erie, Pa., 1990-93, dir. residency tng. in psychiatry, family practice program, 1990-93. Mem. Am. Psychiat. Assn., Alpha Omega Alpha.

BESPALEC, DALE ANTHONY, clinical psychologist; b. Waukegan, Ill., Sept. 21, 1951; s. Anthony Frank Bespalec and Mildred B. (Glogovsky) Etolen; m. Marylou B. Bartholomae, June 23, 1973; 1 child, Christine Marie. BS magna cum laude with honors, Loyola U., 1973, MA, 1975,

PhD, 1978. Lic. psychologist, Wis. Staff cons. psychologist Behavior and Mgmt. Cons., Inc., Milw., 1977-79; instr. U. Wis.-Parkside, Racine, 1979; staff psychologist St. Michael Hosp. Mental Health Ctr., Milw., 1979-86, mgr. outpatient, 1986-90; pvt. practice Milw., 1979-88; clinical prof. Wis. Sch. Profl. Psychology, Milw., 1985—, dir. clin. tng., 1990-92; mgr. mental health program Community Meml. Hosp., Menomonee Falls, Wis., 1992-96; sr. staff psychologist Taycheeda Correctional Inst., Fond du Lac, Wis., 1996—; clin. instr. Med. Coll. Wis., Milw., 1981—; coord. Wis. Psychol. Assn. Diaster Response Team. Contbr. articles to profl. jours. Past v.p. internal devel. Grafton Jaycees; past mem. bd. dirs United Way Ozaukee County; vol. ARC, chair mental health function; active Riveredge Nature Ctr. Fellow NIMH, USPH, 1973-74. Mem. APA, Wis. Psychol. Assn. (mem. adv. coun. 1994—), Milw. Area Psychologist Assn. (pres. 1994—). Roman Catholic. Office: Taycheeda Correctional Inst N 7139 Hwy K Fond Du Lac WI 54935-9099

BESS, MICHAEL DAVID, physician; b. Kingsport, Tenn., June 21, 1962; s. Bennie Elizabeth (Chesser) B. BS, Va. Tech. U., 1984; DO, W.Va. Sch. Osteo. Medicine, 1989. Diplomate Am. Osteopathic Bd. Family Practice, Nat. Bd. Osteopathic Med. Examiners. Fishery biologist U.S. Fish and Wildlife Svc., Bowden, W.Va., 1984-85; staff physician Andover (Ohio) Med. Ctr., 1991-92; emergency physician St. Anthony Hosp., Michigan City, Ind., 1993-94, Good Samaritan Hosp., Vincennes, Ind., 1994-95; advisor Knox County Emergency Med. Svc., Vincennes, 1995. Mem. Niles (Ohio) Fraternal Order of Police, 1991. Mem. Am. Coll. Family Practice, Am. Osteo. Coll. Emergency Medicine, Am. Osteo. Assn., Am. Coll. Emergency Physicians, Am. Osteo. Aux. Methodist. Home: 13 Moss Point Rd Hattiesburg MS 39402

BESSEY, PALMER QUINTARD, surgeon; b. Glen Ridge, N.J., Aug. 14, 1944. MD, U. Vt., 1975. Diplomate Am. Bd. Surgeons, Am. Bd. Critical Care Surgery. Intern U. Ala. Hosp., Birmingham, 1975-76, resident in surgery, 1976-81; fellow metabolism, nutrition metabolism Brigham and Women's Hosp., Boston, 1981-83, fellow metabolism, 1981-83; surgeon, attending surgeon U. Rochester (N.Y.) Sch. Medicine and Dentistry, 1993—; dir. trauma, burns, and surg. critical care Strong Meml. Hosp., Rochester, 1993—; prof. surgery U. Rochester Sch. Medicine and Dentistry, 1993—. Mem. ACS, Assn. Acad. Surgery, Soc Univ. Surgeons, Am. Assn. Surgery Trauma, ASPEN, Soc. Critical Care Medicine, Ctrl. Surg. Assn., Am. Surg. Assn., Am. Bd. Surgery (bd. dirs.), Am. Burn Assn. Office: U Rochester Med Ctr Dept Surgery 601 Elmwood Ave Rochester NY 14642-8410

BESSMAN, ALICE N., physician, educator; b. Washington, Nov. 7, 1922; d. Lester and Janet (Nusbaum) Neuman; m. Samuel P. Bessman, July 3, 1945; children: Joel David, Ellen. BA, Smith Coll., 1943; MD, George Washington U., 1949. Am. Bd. Internal Medicine. Intern, resident George Washington U. Hosp., 1949-51, fellow in medicine, 1951-52,53-54; fellow in pediatrics Harvard U. and Mass. Gen. Hosp., Boston, 1952-53; instr. medicine Johns Hopkins Balt. City Hosp., 1955-68; assoc. prof. medicine U. So. Calif., L.A., 1969-79, prof. medicine, 1979-94; prof. emeritus, 1993; chief Rancho Los Amigos Med. Ctr., 1968-93, diabetes endocrine svc. Contbr. articles to profl. jours. and chpts. to books. Mem. Am. Fedn. for Clin. Rsch., AMA, Am. Diabetes Assn. (diabetes clinician of yr. award 1993), L.A. County Med. Assn., L.A. Soc. Internal Medicine, So. Calif. Diabetes Assn. Jewish. Office: Rancho Los Amigos Med Ctr 7601 Imperial Hwy Rm 256 Downey CA 90242-3456

BESSMAN, SAMUEL PAUL, biochemist, pediatrician; b. Newark, Feb. 3, 1921; s. Edward S. and Sara R. (Greenberg) B.; m. Alice Neuman, July 3, 1945; children: Joel David, Ellen. Student, Coll. William and Mary, 1938-41; M.D., Washington U., St. Louis, 1944. Intern, asst. resident St. Louis Children's Hosp., 1944-45; asst. prof. pediatrics George Washington U., 1947-54; dir. research Children's Hosp., Washington, 1947-54; asso. prof. pediatrics U. Md., 1954-59, prof. pediatric research, 1959-68, prof. biochemistry, 1962-68; prof., chmn. dept. pharmacology and nutrition U. So. Calif., 1968-91, prof. pediatrics, 1969-91, prof. emeritus, 1991—; dir. research Rosewood State Hosp., Md., 1962-68, Jewish Home for Retarded Children, Washington, 1962-68. Founding editor Biochem. Medicine; mem. editorial bd. Analytical Biochemistry. Pres. First Dist. Cmty. Coun., Balt., 1965; trustee Robert Lindner Found.; pres. Molly Towell Found., Alsam Found. Served with USPHS, 1945-47. Recipient Crawford Long award U. Ga., 1963, Creative Scholar award U. So. Calif., 1978, Maimonides award Technion, 1979, Disting. Sci. Achievement award Am. Heart Assn., 1984, Inst. for Advanced Studies award Louis Pasteur Libr. and Sci. Found., 1986, Alumni Achievement award Washington U. Med. Sch., 1994. Fellow AAAS, Am. Acad. Pediat.; mem. Am. Soc. Biol. Chemists, Soc. Pediat. Rsch., Am. Inst. Nutrition, Am. Soc. Pharmacology and Exptl. Therapeutics, Sigma Xi, Alpha Omega Alpha. Home: 7404 Woodrow Wilson Dr Los Angeles CA 90046-1323

BEST, KATHLEEN CLAIRE, physician assistant; b. Liberty, N.Y., Apr. 15, 1953; d. Joseph and Muriel J. (Berberich) Kutger; m. Wayne A. Best, Nov. 18, 1979; children: John M., Jill L. BS in Biology, SUNY, Binghamton, 1975; Physician Asst. Cert., USPHS Hosp., S.I., 1978. Cert. physician asst. House staff surgery Montefiore Med. Ctr., Bronx, 1978-79; physician asst. Surg. dept. Shands Hosp., Gainesville, Fla., 1980; physician asst. student infirmary U. Fla., Gainesville, 1980-81, physician asst. dept. neurosurgery, 1981-88; physician asst. Ocala (Fla.) Neurosurg. Ctr., 1988—. Com. chmn. Boy Scouts Am., Micanopy, Fla., 1991—; troop leader Girl Scouts U.S., 1995—; sec. Micanopy Fall Harvest Festival, 1993—. Fellow Am. Assn. Physician Assts.; mem. Fla. Assn. Physician Assts. Roman Catholic. Office: Ocala Neurosurgical Ctr 1105 SW 1st Ave Ocala FL 34474

BEST, KIM DONALD, physician assistant, nurse, educator; b. Norfolk, Nebr., Aug. 7, 1956; s. Richard Lee and Freda D. (White) B.; divorced; children: Rashelle D., Alison M. LPN, U.S. Army Hosp., El Paso, Tex., 1980; A Mgmt., El Paso C.C., 1984; BS, U. Okla., 1991. Enlisted man U.S. Army, 1974, advanced through grades to CW-2, 1992; aid U.S. Army, Germersheim, Germany, 1975-77, Ft. Huachuca, Ariz., 1977-78; LPN U.S. Army, Honolulu, 1980-83; instr. nursing U.S. Army, Ft. Bliss, Tex., 1983-89; physician asst. U.S. Army, Ft. Riley, Kans., 1991—; instr. Barton C.C., Junction City, Kans., 1991—; med. advisor 3/37 Armor Div., Ft. Riley, 1991—. Instr. CPR Am. Heart Assn. Mem. Am. Assn. Physician Assts. Lutheran. Home: HC 1 Box 1934 Silsbee TX 77656 Office: Fred Rural Health Care Clin Fred TX 77616

BEST, ROBERT GLEN, geneticist; b. Springfield, Ohio, Jan. 27, 1958; s. Richard Alexander and Ella Marie (Buss) B.; m. Sara Felicia Newton, June 2, 1984; children: Cami DeNeil, Heidi Amber, Adrian Alexander, Joshua Ellis. BS in Biochemistry, Lehigh U., 1981; MS in Toxicology, N.C. State U., 1983, PhD in Genetics/Toxicology, 1987. Diplomate Am. Bd. Med. Genetics. Med. geneticist, clin. cytogeneticist Richland Mem. Hosp., Columbia, S.C., 1986-89; from acting dir. to assoc. dir. clin. genetics U. S.C., Columbia, 1989-91, dir. clin. genetics, 1991—; assoc. prof. ob-gyn., dir. divsn. clin. genetics; cons. Hybritech Inc., San Diego, 1989—. Grantee March of Dimes, 1990, Ctrs. for Disease Control, 1993-96. Mem. Am. Soc. Human Genetics, Am. Soc. Hematology, European Soc. Human Genetics, Genotoxicity and Environ. Mutagenesis Soc. Home: 101 White Falls Cir Columbia SC 29212-1241 Office: U SC Dept Ob-Gyn Two Med Park # 301 Columbia SC 29203

BESTETTI, REINALDO BULGARELLI, clinical researcher, cardiologist; b. Ribeirao Preto, Brazil, Nov. 12, 1955; s. Reynaldo Antonio and Palmira Vera (Bulgarelli) B.; children: Gabriel Henrique, Giuliana. MD, Ribeirao Preto, 1980, grad. in Cardiology, 1983, MS, 1985, PhD, 1988. Rschr. Ribeirao Preto, 1989-94; prof. Uberaba (Brazil) Med. Sch., 1994—; dir. transplantation svc. S:Casa Hosp., Ribeirao, 1990-93. Contbr. articles to profl. jours. Office: Uberaba Med Sch, PO Box 118 Av Getulio Guarita 130, 38001970 Uberaba Minas Gerais Brazil

BETANCOURT, ANTONIO MIGUEL, psychiatrist, consultant; b. Santurce, P.R., Oct. 15, 1949; s. Antonio and Maria Teresa Betancourt; m. Brunilda Milagros Falcon, July 7, 1973; children: Mariel Milagros, Javier Antonio. MD, U. P.R., 1975. Diplomate Am. Bd. Psychiatry and Neurology. Resident in psychiatry Menninger Sch. of Psychiatry, Topeka, 1978; med. dir., dir. psychiatry Youth Ctr. of Topeka, 1978-79; chief consultation, liaison psychiatry sect. VA Hosp., San Juan, P.R., 1980-82; staff psychiatrist U. Dist. Hosp., San Juan, 1982-83; dir. consultation U. P.R. Sch. Medicine/U. Dist. Hosp., San Juan, 1983-84; staff psychiatrist U. Dist. Hosp., San Juan, 1984-86; pvt. practice San Juan, 1982-86; staff psychiatrist South Cen. Community Mental Health Ctrs., Inc., Bloomington, Ind., 1986-88; psychiat. cons. Fla. Dept. Corrections, Tallahassee, 1988-92, Ga. Dept. Corrections, Valdosta and Pelham, 1991—; instr. in psychiatry Med. Coll. of Va., Richmond, 1979-80; asst. prof. psychiatry U. P.R. Sch. Medicine, 1981-87, San Juan Bautista Sch. Medicine, San Juan, 1982-87, Ind. U. Sch. Medicine, Indpls., 1987-89; adj. prof. Fla. A&M U., Tallahassee, 1990-93; assoc. in medicine Fla. State U., Tallahassee, 1996—. Fellow Am. Psychiat. Assn., Fla. Psychiat. Soc., Capital Psychiat. Soc.; mem. Am. Soc. Clin. Hypnosis. Office: 1342 Timberlane Rd Ste 101 B Tallahassee FL 32312-1775

BETCHER, ALBERT MAXWELL, anesthesiologist; b. Jersey City, June 22, 1911; s. Jacob and Esther (Popkin) B.; m. Gertrude Weinberger, Sept. 22, 1940; children: Diane Trister Dodge, Peter Andrew, Robert William. BS, NYU, 1931; MD, St. Louis U., 1935. Diplomate Am. Bd. Anesthesiology (pres. 1974-75, bd. dirs. 1967-75). Rotating intern Jersey City Med. Ctr., 1935-36, resident in anesthesiology, 1937-38, staff anesthetist, 1938-41; staff anesthetist Hosp. Joint Diseases, N.Y.C., 1946—, dir. dept., 1947-76, sec. med. adv. bd., assoc. editor hosp. jour., 1960-69, pres., 1970-76; dir. dept. anesthesiology Beth Israel Med. Ctr., 1978-81, Nyack (N.Y.) Hosp., 1981-84; assoc. dir. profl. and acad. affairs Orthopedic Inst., N.Y.C., 1981—; asst. clin. prof. Albert Einstein Coll. Medicine, 1955-61, assoc. clin. prof., 1961-67; prof. Mt. Sinai Sch. Medicine CUNY, 1967-83, prof. emeritus, 1983—; mem. organizing com. Caribbean Symposium in Anesthesiology and Related Fields, P.R. Soc. Anesthesiologists and Tchrs. Hosp. San Juan, P.R., 1975—. Contbr. articles to profl. jours. Pres., chmn. bd. trustees Wood Libr.-Mus. Anesthesiology, 1956-69; trustee Anesthesia Found. Lt. col. M.C., AUS, 1941-46. Decorated Purple Heart, Bronze Star. Fellow Am. Coll. Anesthesiologists, ACP; mem. Am. Soc. Anesthesiologists (treas. 1958-61, pres. 1962-63, Disting. Service award 1975), N.Y. Acad. Medicine (sec. 1961-63, chmn. sect. anesthesiology and resuscitation 1963-64, trustee 1979-85), N.Y. Soc. Anesthesiologists (pres. 1955, speaker ho. dels. 1956-59), N.Y. State Med. Soc. (chmn. anesthesiology 1959-60), AMA (residency rev. com. for anesthesiology 1969-72, chmn. 1973), N.Y. Acad. Scis., AAAS, Acad. Anesthesiology, World Fedn. Socs. Anesthesiologists (del., chmn. finance com., U.S.A. mem. exec. com. 1976-84, v.p. 1984-86). Home: 1435 Lexington Ave New York NY 10128-1625 Office: 301 E 17th St New York NY 10003-3804

BETHCHKAL, JANET ANN, ophthalmologist; b. Racine, Wis., Apr. 6, 1957; d. James and Ann (Vernon) B. BS, Vassar Coll., 1979; MD, Rush Med. Coll., 1983. Diplomate Am. Bd. Ophthalmology. Intern in internal medicine Rush-Presbyn.-St. Luke's Med. Ctr., Chgo., 1983-84; resident in ophthalmology Northwestern U., Chgo., 1984-87; fellow in glaucoma Wills Eye Hosp., Phila., 1987-88; assoc. chmn. dept. ophthalmology U. Fla. Health Sci. Ctr., Jacksonville, 1988—; lead physician Eye Care Assoc. of North Fla., 1992—; mem. exec. bd. N.E. Fla. Assn. to Prevent Blindness, 1992—. Mem. com. mem. Nielson Organ Transplant Found., Jacksonville, 1990-92; coord. Reef Rsch. Team, Jacksonville, 1992—. Fellow Am. Acad. Ophthalmology; mem. Fla. Soc. Ophthalmology (sec.-treas., v.p., membership chair). Democrat. Home: 6335 Christopher Creek Rd W Jacksonville FL 32217 Office: U Fla Health Sci Ctr 653 W 8th St Jacksonville FL 32209

BETHJE, ROBERT, general surgeon, retired; b. Braunschweig, Fed. Republic of Germany, Nov. 15, 1922; came to U.S., 1923; s. Robert Paul and Elisabeth Augusta (Lieder) B.; m. Maria Vatral, June 11, 1955; children: Susan Leslie, Robert Eric, Alan Randolph. BS cum laude, CCNY, 1945; MD, N.Y. Med. Coll., 1949. Diplomate Nat. Bd., 1950, Am. Bd. Surgery, 1958. Asst. treas. Broome County Med. Soc., Binghamton, N.Y., 1964, v.p., 1965, pres., 1966; pres. med. staff Ideal Hosp., Endicott, N.Y., 1973-76, chief of surgery, 1971-77; chief of surgery Wilson Meml. Hosp., Johnson City, N.Y., 1979-80. Bd. dirs. Broome-Tioga Assn. for Retarded Children, Binghamton, 1983—. Capt. U.S. Army Med. Corps, 1951-53. Fellow Am. Coll. Surgeons; mem. Rotary (Endicott v.p. 1980-81, dir. 1981-84, pres. 1985-86). Home: 4 Ivanhoe Rd Binghamton NY 13903-1424

BETRUS, PATRICIA ANN, nursing educator, researcher; b. Bozeman, Mont., July 2, 1950; d. Thomas and Gladys (Barnes) Betrus. BSN, Ariz. State U., Tempe, 1976; BS, Ariz. State U., 1972; M of Nursing, U. Wash., 1979, PhD, 1985. RN, Wash; cert. clin. specialist psychiat. mental health. Dir. Mgmt. of Stress Response Clinic, U. Wash., Seattle, 1979-82; asst. prof. nursing U. Wash., 1986-92; assoc. prof. nursing, 1992—. Contbr. articles to profl. jours. Recipient Acad. Investigators grant NCNR. Mem. Sigma Theta Tau.

BETSINGER, PEGGY ANN, oncological nurse; b. St. Charles, Mo., Dec. 11, 1939; d. Edward and Dorothy (Brockgrietens) Oelklaus; m. Richard Betsinger, Mar. 17, 1964 (div. Mar. 1986); children: Bryon, Alicia. Diploma, St. John's Hosp. Sch. Nursing, St. Louis U., St. Louis, 1960; student, U. Colo., Colorado Springs, 1973, St. Joseph Coll., 1985. RN, Ohio, Mo.; cert. oncology-chemotherapy nurse. Charge nurse oncology unit Grandview Hosp., Dayton, 1976-81; asst. dir. nurses Alta Nursing Home, Dayton, Ohio, 1982-86; nurse oncology unit De Paul Hosp., St. Louis, 1986—. Vol. nurse ARC, 1971-74. Capt. Nurse Corps, USAF, 1961-64. Mem. Oncology Nursing Soc.

BETTEN, MICHAEL G., physician; b. N.Y.C., Nov. 23, 1940; m. Florence Eldensohn, Aug. 2, 1964; children: Paige, Jordan. BS, Cornell U., 1962; MD, Albert Einstein Coll. Medicine, 1966. Intern Jackson Meml. Hosp., Miami, Fla., 1966-67; resident Barnes Hosp., St. Louis, 1969-72; trustee Conn. Hosp. Assn., Wallingsford, 1992-94; mem. Conn. Motor Vehicle Adv. Bd., Meridan, 1993—. Comdr. USPHS, 1967-69. Fellow Am. Coll. Surgeons; mem. AMA, Am. Acad. Ophthalmologic, New England Ophthalmologic Soc., Conn. State Med. Soc., New London County Med. Assn. (pres.). Republican. Jewish. Home: 68 Wawecus Hill Rd Bozrah CT 06334 Office: Norwich Ophthalmology Group 130 New London Turnpike Norwich CT 06360

BETTIGOLE, MICHELLE RAHOCZY, medical and surgical nurse, health facility administrator; b. Danbury, Conn., Aug. 11, 1964; d. Endre S. and Arlene (Gereg) Rahoczy; m. Edward N. Bettigole, Sept. 3, 1989. BSN, St. Joseph Coll., West Hartford, Conn., 1986; MS, Rensselaer Poly. Inst., 1989. Staff nurse in med. ICU Hartford Hosp., 1986-89; nurse clinician Caremark Homecare, N.Y.C., 1989-91; med.-surg. insvc. coord. Drs. Hosp. div. Beth Israel Med. Ctr., N.Y.C., 1989-91; head nurse Bridgeport (Conn.) Hosp., 1991-93; dir. med.-surg. nursing St. Luke's Hosp., Newburgh, N.Y., 1993-94; nurse mgr. The Stamford (Conn.) Hosp., 1994-95, dir. quality planning and profl. devel., 1995—. Mem. ANA, Am. Assn. of Nurse Execs., Conn. Nurses' Assn., Kappa Gamma Pi, Sigma Theta Tau. Home: 365 S Benson Rd Fairfield CT 06430-6942

BETTS, HENRY BROGNARD, physician, health facility administrator, educator; b. New Rochelle, N.Y., May 25, 1928; s. Henry Brognard and Marguerite Meredith (Denise) B.; m. Monika Christine Paul, Apr. 25, 1970. A.B., Princeton, 1950; M.D., U. Va., 1954; DSc (hon.), Hamilton Coll., 1992. Diplomate: Am. Bd. Phys. Medicine and Rehab. Intern Cin. Gen. Hosp., 1954-55; resident, teaching fellow NYU Med. Center Inst. Rehab. Medicine (Rusk Inst.), N.Y.C., 1958-63; practice medicine, specializing in phys. medicine and rehab. Chgo., 1963—; staff physiatrist Rehab. Inst. Chgo., 1963-64, assoc. med. dir., 1964-65, med. dir., 1965-94, CEO, 1986-94, pres., CEO, 1994—; chmn. dept. phys. medicine and rehab. Northwestern U. Med. Sch., 1967-94, prof., 1967-94, Manguson prof., 1994—, assoc. mem. Robert H. Lurie Cancer Ctr., 1993—; cons. Northwestern Meml. Hosp., Chgo.; mem. adv. bd. Commn. on Future Structure of Vets. Health Care, Dept. Vets. Affairs, 1990-92, Vets. Adv. Com. on Rehab., 1990—; med. adv. com. Spl. Olympics Internat., 1991—. Contbr. articles to profl. jours. Bd. dirs. Nat. Com. Arts for Handicapped (now called Very Spl. Arts), 1981—; mem. traffic safety adv. coun. Ill. Sec. of State Office, 1992—; mem. adv. coun. on spinal cord and head injuries State of Ill. Dept. Rehab. Svc., 1993—. Recipient Disting. Svc. award Ill. Congress Orgns. Physically Handicapped, 1982, Disting. Svc. award Marine Scholarship Found., Chgo., 1993, Individual Leadership award Infinitec-United Cerebral Palsy, 1994, Disting. Pub. Svc. award Am. Acad. Phys. Medicine and Rehab., 1994, James Brady award Ill. Head Injury Assn., 1989, Disting. Svc. award Nat. Orgn. on Disabilities, 1989, Milton Cohen Disting. Career award Nat. Assn. Rehab. Facilities, 1990, Henry H. Kessler Human Dignity award Kessler Inst. Rehab. Inc., 1992, The Scopus award Am. Friends of the Hebrew U., 1995, The August W. Christmann award for Tech. and Info., City of Chgo. Mayor's Office for People with Disabilities and t MOPD Adv. Council, 1995; names Physician of Yr., Ill. Gov.'s Com., 1964, Exec. of Yr., Ill. Assn. Rehab. Facilities, 1989—; commended by Ill. Gen. Assembly, 1967; cited for meritorious svc. Pres.'s Com. on Employment of Handicapped, 1965. Mem. Ill. Med. Soc., Assn. Acad. Physiatrists (pres. 1968-69, bd. dirs. 1990—), Am. Congress Rehab. Med. (med. adv. com., pres. 1976-77; Gold Key 1984), Mid-Am. Soc. Phys. Med. and Rehab. (pres. 1969), Brain Trauma Found. (bd. dirs. 1990-93), Untied Cerebral Palsy Assn. Greater Chgo. (bd. dirs. 1990—). Home: 1727 N Orleans St Chicago IL 60614-5719 Office: Rehabilitation Inst 345 E Superior St Chicago IL 60611-3015

BETTS, WILLIAM EDWIN, JR., radiologist; b. Montclair, N.J., Oct. 8, 1925; s. WIlliam Edwin and Laura Amelia (Sanford) B.; m. Barbara Dyche, June 18, 1949; children: Christine, Lori, William, Tracy. BA, U. Pa., 1952; DO, Phila. Coll. Osteopathy, 1956, MS in Radiology, 1960. Intern Phila. Coll. Osteopathy, 1956-57, resident, 1957-60; chief of radiology Cmty. Hosp., Lancaster, Pa., 1960-90; pvt. practice, 1990—. Fellow Am. Osteo. Coll. Surgeons, Am. Coll. Gasteroenterology, Am. Osteo. Coll. Radiology. Home and Office: 1539 Center Rd Lancaster PA 17603

BETZ, JOHN EDWARD, physician assistant; b. Oil City, Pa., Jan. 25, 1942; s. Paul John and Katherine Elizabeth (McAlevy) B.; m. Pamela Carol Ard, Oct. 8, 1992. HN, USN Hosp. Corps Sch., 1965; Cert. Physician Asst., U. Wash., 1970. Emergency room technician Suburban Hosp., Bethesda, Md., 1967-69; physician asst. Fourteenth Ave. Med. Ctr., Othello, Wash., 1970—; bd. dirs. Wash./Ala. RMP, Seattle, 1972-74. With USN, 1964-66. Fellow Am. Acad. Physician Assts., Wash. State Acad. Physician Assts.; mem. Wash. State Med. Assn. Home: 925 Hamlet Othello WA 99344 Office: Fourteenth Ave Med Ctr 475 N 14th Ave Othello WA 99344

BETZ, RONALD PHILIP, pharmacist; b. Chgo., Nov. 26, 1933; s. David Robert and Olga Marie (Martinson) B.; BS, U. Ill., 1955; MPA, Roosevelt U., 1987; m. Rose Marie Marella, May 18, 1963; children: David Christian, Christopher Peter. Asst. dir. of pharmacy U. Ill., Chgo., 1959-62; dir. pharmacy Mt. Sinai Hosp., Chgo., 1962—; pres. Pharmacy Systems, Inc., 1982-89; teaching assoc. Coll. of Pharmacy, U. Ill., Chgo., 1977-88; adj. clin. asst. prof. pharmacy, U. Ill., 1988—; pres. Pharmacy Svc. and Systems, 1972-81; dir. Ill. Coop. Health Data Systems, 1976-80. Bd. dirs. Howard/Paulina Redevel. Corp., 1983-92. With U.S. Army, 1956-58. Mem. Am. Soc. Health Sys. Pharmacists, Ill. Pharm. Assn. (pres. 1975), Ill. Acad. Preceptors in Pharmacy (pres. 1972), No. Ill. Soc. Hosp. Pharmacists (pres. 1966), Kappa Psi. Democrat. Lutheran. Contbr. articles in field to profl. jours. Home: 1021 Sussex Dr Northbrook IL 60062 Office: 2750 W 15th Pl Chicago IL 60608-1704

BETZOLD, JOAN LEA, healthcare administrator, consultant; b. Madison, Wis., Jan. 16, 1955; d. William Burton Rathbun and Eva Joyce (Adams) Colgate; m. Victor Arthur Betzold, May 22, 1976 (div. July 1995); children: Gillian Lea, Travis Collins; m. Robert Lawrence Brown, Aug. 30, 1995. BS cum laude, U. Minn., 1977; MEd, U. Md., 1984. Dir. Therapeutic Recreation Manor Care Rossville, Balt., 1977-82; quality assurance specialist Manor Care Inc., Silver Springs, Md., 1982-86; freelance cons. Bel Air, Md., 1986-87; CEO Primavera TX Ctr., Culpepper, Va., 1987; regional dir. CAPS, Inc., Vienna, Va., 1988, v.p. profl. svcs., 1987-88; pres. PSC, Inc., Bel Air, 1986—; mem. Nat. Assn. Alcoholism and Drug Abuse Counselors Found., Nat. Treatment & Consortium Bd. Contbr. numerous articles to profl. jours. Treas. Calvary United Meth. Ch., Churchville, Md.; leader 4-H, Hartford County. Named Practitioner of Yr. Md. Rec. & Parks Assn., 1984; recipient numerous Markie awards for journalism. Mem. Soroptomist, Inc. Republican.

BEUERLEIN, SISTER JULIANA, hospital administrator; b. Lawrenceburg, Tenn., June 19, 1921; d. John Adolph and Sophia (Held) B. R.N., St. Joseph's Sch. Nursing, Chgo., 1945; BS in Edn., DePaul U., 1947; MS in Nursing Edn., Marquette U., 1954; postgrad., St. Louis U., 1966-69. Operating room supr. St. Joseph's Hosp., Alton, Ill., 1945-48; dir. sch. of nursing and nursing svc. Providence Hosp., Waco, Tex., 1948-56, St. Joseph's Hosp., Chgo., 1956-62; asst. adminstr. St. Joseph's Hosp., 1962-63; adminstrv. asst. St. Mary's Hosp., Evansville, Ind., 1963-65; adminstr. St. Mary's Hosp., 1965-73, pres. governing bd., 1965-73; adminstr. St. Joseph Hosp., Chgo., 1973-81; pres. governing bd. St. Joseph Hosp., 1973-75; adminstr. St. Thomas Hosp., Nashville, 1981-89; dir. spl. devel. programs Providence Hosp., Southfield, Mich., 1989—; Mem. governing bd. St. Vincent's Hosp., Indpls., 1969-73; mem. governing bd. St. Mary's Hosp., Milw., 1974-75, chmn., 1978-79; mem. governing bd. Providence Hosp., Southfield, Mich., 1975-78, chmn. governing bd., 1977-78; mem. Chgo. Health Systems Agy., 1976-79; mem. gov. bd. St. Thomas Hosp., Nashville, Hubbard Hosp., Nashville; pres. gov. bd. St. Vincent Hosp., Birmingham, Ala.; mem. Am. Hosp. Assn. Commn. on Nursing, 1980-89. Mem. bd. dirs. St. Mary's Med. Ctr., Evansville, Ind., Middle Tenn. Med. Ctr., Murfreesboro. Fellow Am. Coll. Hosp. Adminstrs. (com. on elections); mem. Cath., Tenn. Hosp. Assns., Nasville C. of C. (bd. dirs.). Office: Providence Hosp Devel Dept 22255 Greenfield Rd Ste 228 Southfield MI 48075-4818

BEUKER, FRIEDHELM MARIA, sports medicine physician; b. Berlin, Germany, June 22, 1932; s. Heinrich and Priska Maria (Lehmann) B. MD, U. Berlin, 1967; Dr.rer.habil, U. Dusseldorf, 1984. Faculty medicine Inst. Occupational Health, Frankfurt, East Germany, 1958-62, Inst. Sports Medicine, Berlin, 1963-67; sen. physician Sports Med. Inst., Leipzig, 1967-72; head Fitness-Sports Inst. of Highschool for Sports, Leipzig, 1972-82; cons. Ministry of Health and Sports, East Berlin, 1960-75, 83; dir. Inst. Sports Sci., Heinrich-Heine U., Dusseldorf, 1984—; v.p. DBKV e.V., Munich, 1987—; sec. med. com. IFBB, Montreal, 1988; mem. titulaire Ordinex, Paris, 1988—; v.p. German Soc. Leisure-Time; cons. in field of textile physiology, nutrition and sports. Author: Tests in Physical Fitness, 1992 (Gutsmuths award 1976). Recipient Hufeland medal, Ministry of Health, Berlin, 1972, Nat. Assn. Sports Medicine award, 1988-89. Roman Catholic. Home: Moerikestr 7, 40688 Merbusch Germany Office: Heinrich Heine U, Universitatsstr 1, 40225 Dusseldorf Germany

BEUSCH, GLADYS JEANETTE, optician; b. Ashley, N.D., Sept. 11, 1937; d. Adam and Eva (Woehl) Rott; m. Leroy Beusch, Sept. 11, 1955; children: Burton, Bradley, Glenda Schaefer, Bonita. Student, Ea. Mont. Coll., 1984. Am. Bd. Cert. Optician. Sales clk. Thompson Drugstore, McLaughlin, S.D., 1953-55; bookkeeper Banek Implement, McLaughlin, 1955-56; checker Jack and Jill Grocery, McLaughlin, 1967-68; sales clk. Thompson Drugstore, McLaughlin, 1968-69; stock clk. Brown Wholesale Drug Co., Rapid City, S.D., 1969; billing clk. Benson Optical Co., Rapid City, 1969-77; lab. tech. Benson Optical Co., Aberdeen, S.D., Billings, Mont., 1977-86; dispensing optician Benson Optical Co., Albuquerque, 1986-89; optician, mgr. Albuquerque (N.Mex.) Assocs. of Optometry, 1989—; owner Beusch Optical, Albuquerque, 1990-94. Vol. Montibello Retirement Home, Albuquerque, 1991-95. Fellow Nat. Acad. Opticianary; mem. Opticians Assn. Am., Far Western Conf. Opticians. Baptist. Home: 2117 Altez St NE Albuquerque NM 87112-2803

BEUTLER, ERNEST, physician, research scientist; b. Berlin, Sept. 30, 1928; came to U.S., 1936, naturalized, 1943; s. Alfred David and Kaethe (Italiener) B.; m. Brondelle Fleisher, June 15, 1950; children: Steven Merrill, Earl Bryan, Bruce Alan, Deborah Ann. Ph.B., U. Chgo., 1946, B.S., 1948, M.D., 1950; PhD (hon.), Tel Aviv U., Israel, 1993. Intern U. Chgo. Clinics, 1950-51; resident in medicine 1951-53; asst. prof. U. Chgo., 1956-59; chmn. div. medicine City of Hope Med. Ctr., L.A., 1959-78; chmn. dept. clin. rsch. Scripps Clinic and Rsch. Found., La Jolla, Calif., 1978-82, chmn. dept. basic and clin. rsch., 1982-89, chmn. dept. molecular and exptl. medicine, 1989—; clin. prof. medicine U. So. Calif., 1964-79, U. Calif. San Diego, 1979—; mem. hematology study sect. NIH, 1970-74, 89-91; Spinoza Chair U. Amsterdam, 1991. Author 8 books, numerous articles in med. jours.; mem. editorial bds. profl. jours. Adv. com. Blood Products FDA, 1984-88; nat. heart, lung, and blood adv. coun. mem. NIH, 1994-97. Recipient Gairdner award, 1975, Blundell prize, 1985, Nat. Heart, Lung, and Blood Inst. Merit award NIH,

1987, 5th ann. Excellence award Gen. Clin. Rsch. Program, 1993, Nat. Acad. Clin. Biochemistry Lectureship award Kodak Instruments, 1990, Mayo Soley award Western Soc. Clin. Investigation, 1992, City of Medicine award, 1994. Mem. NAS, Am. Acad. Arts and Scis., Assn. Am. Physicians, Am. Soc. Clin. Investigation, Western Assn. Physicians (pres. 1989), Am. Soc. Hematology (mem. exec. com. 1968-72, v.p. 1977, pres. 1979), Am. Soc. Human Genetics (mem. exec. com. 1968-72). Jewish. Home: 2707 Costebelle Dr La Jolla CA 92037-3518 Office: The Scripps Rsch Inst 10550 N Torrey Pines Rd La Jolla CA 92037-1027

BEUTNER, ERNST HERMAN, microbiology educator; b. Berlin, Germany, Aug. 27, 1923; came to U.S., 1923; s. Reinhard and Hermine (Aye) B.; children: Eric, Karen, Jean. BA, Pa. State U., 1947; PhD, U. Pa., 1951. Cert. Am. Bd. Med. Microbiology, Am. Bd. Med. Lab. Immunology, Am. Bd. Bioanalysis. Rsch. supr. Sias Labs. at Brook Hosp., Brookline, Mass., 1951-55; rsch. assoc. Harvard Sch. of Dental Medicine, Boston, 1955-56; prof. microbiology and dermatology SUNY at Buffalo, 1956—. Mem. editorial bd. Internat. Jour. of Dermatology Autoimmunity. Fellow Phila. Coll. of Physicians; mem. AAAS, Am. Soc. Microbiologists, Soc. Investigative Dermatology, Am. Acad. Dermatology, Soc. for History of Dermatology, Am. Assn. Immunologists, N.Y. Acad. Scis., Acad. Microbiology of ASM, Am. Acad. Dermatology, Japanese Soc. for Investigative Dermatology. Office: Univ at Buffalo SUNY Dept Of Microbiology Buffalo NY 14214

BEVAN, WILLIAM, retired foundation executive; b. Plains, Pa., May 16, 1922; s. William and Elizabeth Merle (Jones) B.; m. Dorothy Louise Chorpening, Feb. 17, 1945; children: William III, Mark Filbert, Philip Ross. AB with honors, Franklin and Marshall Coll., 1942, ScD, 1979; MA, Duke U., 1943, PhD, 1948, LLD, 1972; ScD, Fla. Atlantic U., 1968, Emory U., 1974, U. Md., 1981, Kans. State U., 1987; DHL, So. Ill. U., 1989. Instr. psychology Duke U., 1947, William Preston Few prof. psychology, 1974-92, prof. emeritus, 1992—, provost, 1979-83; instr., then asst. prof. psychology Heidelberg Coll., Tiffin, Ohio, 1946-48; mem. faculty Emory U., 1948-59, prof. psychology, 1958-59; prof. psychology, chmn. dept. Kans. State U., 1959-62, dean arts and scis., 1962-63, v.p. acad. affairs, 1963-66; fellow Center for Advanced Study Behavioral Scis., Stanford, Calif., 1965-66; sr. postdoctoral fellow NSF, 1965-66; v.p., provost Johns Hopkins U., Balt., 1966-70; prof. psychology Johns Hopkins U., 1966-74; exec. officer AAAS, 1970-74, pub. Science, 1970-74; mem. adv. bd. Univ. Coll., U. Md., 1978-86; bd. govs. Research Triangle Inst., 1979-82; v.p. John D. and Catherine T. MacArthur Found., Chgo., 1983-91, ret., 1991; mem. adv. bd. Ctr. Advanced Study U. Va., 1976-89, adv. coun. Sch. Medicine U. Chgo., 1984-89. Editorial adv. bd.: Am. Men and Women of Sci., 12th edit, 1972, Social Sci. Citations Index, 1972-77; contbr. articles to profl. jours. Trustee Human Resources Research Orgn., 1968-88, Franklin and Marshall Coll., 1971-76, Coll. Retirement Equity Fund, 1972-90, Ctr. for Creative Leadership, 1972-79, Bioscis. Info. Svc., 1974-80, Am. Psychol. Found., 1970-77, 83-89, Assn. Advancement of Psychology, 1974-78, William T. Grant Found., 1977-90, HumRRO Internat. Inc., 1985-89, Jackson Meml. Lab., 1986-90. With USNR, 1944-70. Fulbright scholar U. Oslo (Norway), 1952-53. Fellow Am. Psychol. Assn. (pres. 1982), AAAS; mem. Inst. Medicine of Nat. Acad. Sci., Psychonomic Soc., So. Soc. Philosophy and Psychology, History of Sci. Soc., Soc. Exptl. Psychologists, Am. Psychol. Soc., Phi Beta Kappa, Sigma Xi. Clubs: Cosmos (Washington); Century (N.Y.C.). Home: 21 Stoneridge Cir Durham NC 27705-5510

BEVAN, WILLIAM ARNOLD, JR., emergency physician; b. Sault St. Marie, Mich., June 23, 1943; s. William Arnold and Syneva Lois (Martin) B.; m. Martha Lynn Peterson, Dec. 29, 1973; children: Terry Eugene, Brian William, PAtrick Jon. BS, U. Minn., 1966, MD, 1970. Frmily practitioner VMMPC, Vail, Colo., 1972-83; emergency physician Vail Valley Emergency Physicians, 1983—; dir. Vail Valley Emergency Dept., 1992—. Trustee Shattuck St. Mary's Sch., Paribault, Minn., 1977—; football coach Battle Mountain H.S., Vail, 1978—. Named Man of Yr. Boy Scouts Am., 1966, 77. Mem. AMA, Rocky Mountain Med. Soc., Colo. Med. Soc. Republican. Lutheran. Home: 0025 Cottonwood Rd Eagle CO 81631 Office: Vail Valley Emergency Dept 181 W Meadow Dr Vail CO 81657

BEVEN, TERENCE, nuclear medicine physician; b. Baton Rouge, Mar. 30, 1933; s. John Lansing and Evelyn (Campbell) B.; m. Elizabeth Chotard O'Shea, Sept. 9, 1960; children: John Lansing, William O'shea, Evelyn Chotard. BS, La. State U., Baton Rouge, 1953; MD, La. State U., New Orleans, 1957. Diplomate Am. Bd. Nuc. Medicine, Am. Bd. Pathology (spl. competence in dermatology); lic. physician, La., Miss. Intern Charity Hosp. of La., New Orleans, 1957-58, resident, 1958-62; pvt. practice Baton Rouge, 1958—; dir. nuclear medicine Our Lady of Lake Regional Med. Ctr., Baton Rouge, 1964—; clin. assoc. prof. pathology La. State U.; vis. chief pathology Earl K. Long Hosp.; staff Woman's Hosp., Field Meml. Hosp., St. Helena Parish Hosp., Earl K. Long Meml. Hosp., Lane Meml. Hosp., Mary Bird Perkins Cancer Ctr.; lectr. in field. Contbr. articles to profl. jours. Mem. health affairs com. La. Assn. Bus. and Industry, Baton Rouge Found., Anglo-Am. Art Mus., La. Hist. Soc., Friends of La. State U. Libr., Southside Civic Assn.; bd. dirs. Arts and Sci. Ctr., 1971-74. Rsch. grantee Immunomedics, Inc., 1994, Cytogen Corp., Hybritech Corp., Amersham Corp., La. State U. Sch. Vet. Medicine/Our Lady of Lake Regional Med. Ctr./ Baton Rouge. Fellow Am. Coll. Nuclear Physicians (charter mem., alt. del. La. 1976-83, del. 1983-85, bd. regents 1986-87, 96—, pres. 1991, exec. com. 1987-89, mem. membership com. 1987—, profl. and pub. info. program com. 1987—, chair nuclear medicine imaging com. 1996, numerous other coms.), Am. Soc. Clin. Pathologists; mem. AMA (vice chmn. La. delegation, del. 1992—, CPT adv. com. representing ACNP 1992—, ref. com. E interim meeting 1995), Soc. Nuclear Medicine (bd. dirs. S.W. chpt. 1989-92, reviewer Jour. Nuclear Medicine 1987—, spl. com. on coding/RVU 1990—, conjoint ACNP/SNM govtl. rels. com. 1995—, coding com. 1995—), La. Soc. Nuclear Medicine (pres. 1980-81), La. State Med. Soc. (chmn. com. on nuclear medicine 1980-85, v.p. 1985-86, chmn. environ. subcom. 1988-91, alt. bd. mem. med. polit. action com. 1988-90, treas. 1990—, ho. of dels. 1972—), Ctrl. States Low Level Waste Mgmt. Group, Am. Inst. Ultrasound in Medicine, Soc. Magnetic Resonance Imaging, Inst. for Clin. P.E.T., Coll. Am. Pathologists (ho. of dels., legis. keyman for La. 1970-84), La. Pathology Soc. (sec.-treas. 1972-74, v.p. 1974-76, pres. 1976-78), Baton Rouge Acad. Internal Medicine (sec.-treas. 1978, v.p. 1979, pres. 1980), East Baton Rouge Parish Med. soc. (exec. com. 1983-84), Am. Soc. Dermatopathology, Am. Assn. Blood Banks, So. Med. Assn., Internat. Acad. Pathology, La. Pub. Health Assn., La. Environ. Health Assn., Baton Rouge C. of C., Am. Legion. Republican. Episcopalian. Office: Our Lady Lake Reg Med Ctr 5000 Hennessy Blvd Baton Rouge LA 70808

BEVER, CHRISTOPHER THEODORE, psychiatrist; b. Munich, Mar. 12, 1919; came to U.S., 1936, naturalized, 1943; s. Rudolf Paul and Maria (Bever) Berliner; m. Josephine Jordan Morton, Mar. 12, 1944; children: Christopher Theodore, Caroline Stakpole, Edward Watts, Sarah Sayward. AB cum laude, Harvard U., 1940, MD, 1943; postgrad., Washington Psychoanalytic Inst., 1947-53; diploma, Washington Sch. Psychiatry, 1952; MA in History, U. Md., 1993. Diplomate Am. Bd. Psychiatry. Intern Hartford (Conn.) Hosp., 1944; resident in psychiatry St. Elizabeths Hosp., Washington, 1947-48, psychiatrist, 1948-50; psychiatrist Washington Inst. Mental Hygiene, 1950-51; dir. Montgomery County Mental Hygiene Clinic, 1951-54; assoc. prof. psychiatry U. N.C., 1954-56; pvt. practice medicine specializing in psychiatry and psychoanalysis Washington, 1956—; dir. Washington Psychoanalytic Clinic, 1983-87; mem. faculty Washington Psychoanalytic Inst., 1954—, Washington Sch. Psychiatry, 1956—; mem. faculty George Washington U., 1957—, clin. prof., 1974-96, emeritus clin. prof., 1996—; cons. Ctr. for Mental Health, Washington, 1990-95. Bd. dirs. Cmty. Psychiat. Clinic, Bethesda, Md., 1958—, pres., 1973-75; bd. dirs. D.C. Inst. Mental Hygiene, 1966-73, pres., 1966-68, trustee, 1973-90; bd. dirs. Washington Sch. Psychiatry, 1983—, Washington Psychoanalytic Found., 1993—; trustee William Alanson White Found., Washington, 1974-84. Recipient Mary W. Allen award Washington Psychoanalytic Soc., 1991. Fellow Am. Psychiat. Assn. (life), Am. Orthopsychiat. Assn. (life), Am. Acad. Psychoanalysis; mem. AMA, Am. Psychoanalytic Assn. (life, cert. in psychoanalysis), Columbia (Md.) Study Group, Assn. for Advancement of Philosophy and Psychiatry (pub. Philosophy, Psychiatry and Psychology jour. 1995—). Democrat. Home and Office: 10450 Lottsford Rd Apt 1003 Mitchellville MD 20721-2745

BEVERIDGE, DEBRA IRENE METTY, speech language pathologist; b. Cumberland, Md., July 30, 1956; d. Howard James and Helen Cleo (Summers) Metty; m. Russell David Beveridge, July 8, 1989. BA, W.Va. U., 1978; MA, U. Conn., 1980, degree in Ednl. Adminstrn., 1996. Speech pathologist Southeast Conn. Hearing and Speech Ctr., Norwich, 1980-81, South Windsor (Conn.) Pub. Schs., 1981—, Dept. Mental Retardation State Conn., Newington, 1985-91. Mem. NEA, Am. Speech and Hearing Assn., South Windsor Edn. Assn. (sec. 1989-93), Conn. Edn. Assn., The Nature Conservancy. Office: Pleasant Valley Sch 591 Ellington Rd South Windsor CT 06074-4118

BEVERLEY, CORDIA LUVONNE, gastroenterologist; b. Jamaica, W.I., Oct. 19, 1950; d. Hurdley Aston and Joyce Ruby (Baker) B.; B.A., Hunter Coll., 1971; M.D., N.Y. U., 1975. Diplomate Am. Bd. Gastroenterology, Am. Bd. Internal Medicine. Intern, Columbia U., Harlem Hosp. Center, N.Y.C., 1975-76, resident in medicine, 1976-78; clin. fellow div. gastroenterology N.Y. Hosp./Cornell U. Med. Coll., N.Y.C., 1979-82; asst. physician Rockefeller U. Hosp., N.Y.C., 1978-81. Nat. Inst. Alcohol Abuse and Alcoholism postdoctoral fellow, 1980-82. Mem. Women's Med. Assn. N.Y.C. Office: 1085 Park Ave New York NY 10128-1168

BEVERLY, ZYLPHIA MARIE, case worker; b. San Antonio, May 23, 1956; d. Robert James Sr. and Mae Ruth (Douglas) Davis; married, Mar. 5, 1994. BS, Tex. Women's U., 1978; MA, St. Mary's U., 1982. Lic. profl. counselor Nat. Bd. for Cert. Counselor, Tex., chem. dependency counselor. Residential asst. Tex. Women's U., Denton; telephone crisis interventionist Contact Crisis Hotline, San Antonio; child care worker II Children Svc. Bur., San Antonio; psychol. evaluation technician Colonial Hills Hosp., San Antonio, case mgr., mental health provider; caseworker III Ctr. for Health Care Svcs., San Antonio. Mem. AACD, AM. Assn. for Mental Health, Tex. Assn. for Alcohol and Drug Abuse Counselors. Home: 315 Astoria Dr San Antonio TX 78220-1601

BEVINS, OKEY DAVID, medical facility executive; b. Williamson, W.Va., Feb. 10, 1943; s. Okey and Mary Ethel (Runyon) B.; m. Bobbie Frances Webb, Aug. 24, 1968; children: Laura Kathryn, Melissa Lynn. BSBA, Berea Coll., 1966; postgrad., U. Ala., 1974-75. From adminstrv. asst. to adminstr. Appalachian Regional Healthcare, Ky., 1966-82; adminstr. Norton (Va.) Cmty. Hosp., 1982-89, Healthcare & Retirement Corp., South Point, Ohio, 1989-90; ceo Ky. River Med. Ctr., Jackson, 1990—; cons. Dickinson County Med. Ctr., Clintwood, Va., 1993-94. Bd. deacons, moderator New Hope Cmty. Baptist Ch., Jackson, 1991—. Mem. Am. Coll. Healthcare Execs., Ky. Hosp. Assn., Lonesome Pine Country Club (pres. 1985-88). Office: Ky River Med Ctr 540 Jett Dr Jackson KY 41339

BEYENBACH, KLAUS WERNER, physiologist; b. Mainz, Germany, Mar. 19, 1943; came to U.S. 1962; s. Otto Georg and Maria (Eschenauer) B.; m. Christa-Maria Kuhn, Apr. 13, 1979; 1 child, Thomas Wischert. BA in Biology, St. Mary's U., San Antonio, 1968; MA in Zoology, S.W. Tex. State U., 1970; PhD in Physiology, Wash. State U., 1974. Postdoctoral fellow Nat. Kidney Found., Tucson, 1974-76, NRC, Urbana, Ill., 1976-78; asst. prof. physiology Cornell U., Ithaca, N.Y., 1978-82, assoc. prof. physiology, 1982-88, prof. physiology, 1988—; panel mem. NSF, 1989-92; mem. spl. study sect. NIH, 1989; trustee Mt. Desert Island Biol. Lab., Salisbury Cove, Maine, 1983-86; resident Bellagio Study and Conf. Ctr., 1995. Co-editor: Comparative Physiology, 1989-93. NIH predoctoral tng. fellow, 1972-74, sr. internat. fellow Fogarty Ctr., NIH, 1985; rsch. grantee, NIH, 1978-90, NSF, 1984—; recipient Sr. U.S. Scientist Humboldt award, 1991. Mem. AAAS, Am. Soc. Nephrology, Am. Physiol. Soc., Soc. Exptl. Biology, Alexander von Humboldt Assn. of Am. (v.p. 1994—). Office: Cornell Univ Dept Physiol Vrt # 826 Ithaca NY 14853

BEYER, KAREN HAYNES, social worker; b. Cleve. BA, Ohio State U., 1965; MSW, Loyola U., Chgo., 1969; postgrad. Family Inst., Northwestern U., 1979; MPA, Roosevelt U., 1992; CBA U. Ill. Chgo., 1995. Lic. clin. social worker Ill. With Cuyahoga County Div. Child Welfare, Cleve., 1965, Dallas County Child Welfare Unit, Dallas, 1966; with Luth. Social Svcs. Ill., Chgo., 1967-73; pvt. practice psychotherapy, family mediation, Schaumburg, Ill., 1975-93; therapist Family Svcs. Assn. Greater Elgin (Ill.), 1973-77, dir. profl. svcs., 1977-83; dir. HHS Village of Hoffman Estates, Ill., 1983-93; exec. dir. Larkin Ctr., Elgin, Ill., 1993—. Mem. NASW, Rotary. Unitarian. Office: Larkin Ctr 1212 Larkin Ave Elgin IL 60123-6042

BEYER, KARL HENRY, JR., pharmacologist; b. Henderson, Ky., June 19, 1914; s. Karl H. and Lennie M. (Beadles) B.; m. Camille Slobodzian, Nov. 9, 1979; children by previous marriage: Annette Matilda Beyer Mears, Katherine Louise Beyer Cranson. B.S., Western Ky. State Coll., 1935; Ph.M., U. Wis., 1937, Ph.D., 1940, M.D., 1943, Sc.D. (hon.), 1972. Asst. dir. pharmacol. research Sharp & Dohme, 1943-44, dir. pharmacol. research, 1944-50, asst. dir. research, 1950-56; dir. Merck Inst. Therapeutic Research, West Point, Pa., 1956-58; pres. Merck Inst. Therapeutic Research, 1961-66; v.p. life scis. Merck Sharp & Dohme, Research Labs., West Point, 1958-66; sr. v.p. research Merck Sharp & Dohme, Research Labs., 1966-73; vis. prof., guest lectr. U. Wis., 1958, Swedish U. Med. Schs., 1962, Howard U., 1964, Free U. Berlin, 1966; vis. prof. Milton S. Hershey Med. Center, Pa. State U., 1973—, Vanderbilt U. Sch. Medicine, 1973-79, Harvard U. Sch. Medicine, 1985-89; chmn. Cosmetic Ingredient Rev., 1976-86; bd. sci. advisers Merck Inst., 1973-77, 78-82 ; chmn. bd. Phila. Assn. Clin. Trials, 1980. Author: Pharmacological Basis of Penicillin Therapy, 1950, Discovery, Development and Delivery of New Drugs, 1978; contbr. articles to profl. jours. Recipient Gairdner Found. award, 1964; Modern Pioneers in Creative Industry award NAM, 1965; Modern Medicine Disting. Achievement award, 1967; Am. Pharm. Assn. Found. Achievement award, 1967; Disting. Service award Wis. Alumni Assn., 1968; Lasker award, 1975; Torald Sollmann award, 1978; Catell award Am. Coll. Clin. Pharmacology, 1980, Wis. Med. Alumni Citation, 1987; Pharm. Mfrs. Assn. Discoverer's award, 1988. Fellow ACP, AAAS, N.Y. Acad. Scis.; mem. NAS (drug rsch. bd. 1964-70), Am. Chem. Soc., Am. Physiol. Soc., Phila. Med. Soc., Am. Soc. for Pharmacology and Exptl. Therapeutics (pres. 1964-65), Fedn. Am. Soc. Exptl. Biology (pres. 1965-66), Phila. Coll. Physicians, Am. Therapeutic Soc., Soc. Toxicology, Am. Soc. Nephrology, Am. Heart Assn. (hypertension research award 1979, coun. circulation and renal sect.), Heart Assn. Southeastern Pa., Biol. Abstracts (trustee, treas. 1965-69). Home: PO Box 142 Gwynedd Valley PA 19437-0142

BEYER, TODD L., surgeon; b. St. Louis, Mar. 19, 1954; s. Robert and Gabriel (Sala) B.; m. Lois Joan Beyer (div.); 1 child, Heather Michelle. BS in Biology, U. Mo., 1975. Diplomate Nat. Bd. Osteo. Examiners for Osteo. Physicians and Surgeons, Am. Bd. Ophthalmology. Intern Normandy Osteo. Hosps., St. Louis, 1980-81; resident St. Louis U. Med. Ctr./Bethesda Eye Inst., St. Louis, 1981-84; asst. prof. U. Health Scis., Des Moines, 1984-86; fellow eye plastic surgery U. Ariz., Tucson, 1986-87; physician/surgeon Tallmadge (Ohio) Eye Inst., 1988-93; med. dir. System Optics, Tallmadge, 1993—. Contbr. articles to profl. jours. Rsch. grantee AMA, Physicians Recognition award 1986. Fellow Am. Soc. Ophthalmic Plastic and Reconstructive Surgeons, Am. Acad. Ophthalmology; mem. Summit County Med. Soc., Ohio Ophthalmologic Soc., Internat. Soc. Refractive Surgery, Phi Sigma Alpha. Office: System Optics 518 West Ave Tallmadge OH 44278

BEYER-MEARS, ANNETTE, physiologist; b. Madison, Wis., May 26, 1941; d. Karl and Annette (Weiss) Beyer. B.A., Vassar Coll., 1963; M.S., Fairleigh Dickinson U., 1973; Ph.D., Coll. Medicine and Dentistry N.J., 1977. NIH fellow Cornell U. Med. Sch., 1963-65; instr. physiology Springside Sch., Phila., 1967-71; teaching asst. dept. physiology Coll. Medicine & Dentistry N.J., N.J. Med. Sch., 1974-77, NIH fellow dept. ophthalmology, 1978-80; asst. prof. dept. ophthalmology U. Medicine and Dentistry N.J., N.J. Med. Sch., Newark, 1979-85, asst. prof. dept. physiology, 1980-85, assoc. prof. dept. physiology, 1986—, assoc. prof. dept. ophthalmology, 1986—; cons. Alcon Labs.; vis. assoc. prof. dept. ophthalmology U. Wis. Med. Sch., Madison, 1995—. Contbr. articles in field of diabetic lens and kidney therapy to profl. jours. Chmn. admissions No. N.J., Vassar Coll., 1974-79; mem. minister search com. St. Bartholomew Episcopal Ch., N.J., 1977, fund-raising chmn., 1978, 79; del. Episc. Diocesian Conv., 1977, 78; long range planning com. Christ Ch., Ridgewood, N.J., 1985-87, vestry, 1994-95. Recipient NIH Nat. Rsch. Svc. award, 1978-80, Found. CMDNJ Rsch. award, 1980; grantee Juvenile Diabetes Found., 1985-87, NIH, NEI grantee, 1980-95, Pfizer, Inc. grantee, 1985-89, 93—. Mem. Am. Physiol. Soc., N.Y. Acad. Scis., Soc. for Neurosci., Am. Soc. Pharmacology and Exptl. Therapeutics, Assn. for Rsch. Vision & Ophthalmology, Internat. Soc. for Eye Research, AAAS, The Royal Soc. Medicine, Internat. Diabetes Found., Am. Diabetes Assn., European Assn. Study of Diabetes, Aircraft Owners and Pilots Assn., Sigma Xi.

BEYNON, KAREN HEPPLEWHITE, pediatrics, medical and surgical nurse, administrator; b. Scranton, Pa., Feb. 3, 1942; d. Robert W. and Mary Ann (Davies) Hepplewhite. Diploma, Hahnemann Hosp. Sch. Nursing, Scranton, 1962; BSN, Wilkes U., 1985. RN, Pa.; cert. profl. in healthcare quality. Head nurse Children's Hosp. of Phila.; med./surg. pediatrics head nurse Moses Taylor Hosp., Scranton, dir. quality assessment. Mem. Nat. Assn. for Healthcare Quality (program chmn. 1996), Pa. Assn. for Healthcare Quality (newsletter editor 1995), Northeastern Pa. Assn. for Healthcare Quality (sec. 1989-90, pres. 1990-92).

BEYTH, REBECCA JENNIFER, physician; b. Sharon, Pa., Feb. 5, 1960; d. Frank Joseph and Ceila (Strecansky) B.; m. John C. Charnas, Mar. 4, 1989; children: Alexis K., Nicole K., Savannah R. BA magna cum laude, Case Western Res. U., 1982; MD, Jefferson Med. Coll., Phila., 1987. Diplomate Nat. Bd. Med. Examiners, Am. Bd. Internal Medicine; lic. physician, Mich., Ohio. Med. resident Mich. State U. Associated Hosps., East Lansing, 1987-90; gen. medicine fellow Case Western Res. U. and U. Hosps. Cleve., 1990-92, geriatric fellow, 1992-94, sr. instr. medicine, 1994-95; asst. prof. medicine Case Western Res. U. and U. Hosp. Cleve.; attending physician U. Hosps. Cleve., 1994—, Cleve. VA Med. Ctr., 1994—. Contbr. articles to profl. jours., chpts. to books. Mem. ACP (1st pl. prize best sci. paper 1988, cert. of merit 1990), Mich. State Med. Soc. (1st pl. prize for poster presentation ann. meeting 1989, 2nd pl. prize 1989), Soc. Gen. Internal Medicine (Assocs. award 1991, jr. faculty award 1995), Ctrl. Soc. Clin. Rsch. (assoc.), Am. Geriatric Soc. Office: U Hosp Cleve Dept Medicine Divsn Gen Internal Medicine 11100 Euclid Ave Rm 409 Cleveland OH 44106

BEZAHLER, HARVEY BERNARD, psychiatrist; b. N.Y.C., Nov. 1, 1930; s. Joseph and Bertha (Ablon) B.; m. Deborah Minkoff, Apr. 4, 1953, Ilene, Alysse, Lori. BA, NYU, 1952, MD, 1956. Cert. in child, adolescent, and adult psychoanalysis; cert. in psychiatry. Intern E.J. Meyer Meml. Hosp., Buffalo, 1956-57; resident Winter VA Hosp., Topeka, 1957-60, Menninger Hosp., Menninger Found., Topeka, 1958-59; Pvt. practice psychoanalysis N.Y.C., 1964—; clin. assoc. prof. psychiatry NYU Med. Ctr., N.Y.C., 1979—. Capt. USAR, 1960-62. Mem. Psychoanalytic Assn. N.Y. (pres. 1995—). Office: 14 E 4th St Apt 601 New York NY 10012-1141

BEZWODA, WERNER ROBERT, medical educator; b. Vienna, Austria, June 2, 1944; arrived in South Africa, 1952; s. Emil and Hetta (Gzicki) B.; m. Margaret Ann Sumner, Nov. 19, 1980. MB, BCh, U. Witwatersrand, Johannesburg, S. Africa, 1966, PhD, 1983. Intern Johannesburg Hosp., 1966-68, registrar medicine, 1968-72; physician, lectr. dept. medicine U. Witwatersrand, Johannesburg, 1972-81, sr. physician, sr. lectr., 1981-83, assoc. prof. medicine, 1983-93, prof. medicine, hematology and oncology, 1993—. Mem. S. African Soc. Med. Oncology (com. mem. 1990-93, chmn. 1994, Gold medal 1993), S. African Soc. Hematology (com. mem. 1989-92). Office: Univ Witwatersrand Dept Med, York Rd Parktown, Johannesburg South Africa

BHALLA, DEEPAK KUMAR, cell biologist, toxicologist, educator; b. Kasauli, India, Aug. 31, 1946; s. Khazan Chand and Shyama Bhalla; 1 child, Neel. BS, Punjab U., India, 1968, MS, 1969; PhD, Howard U., Washington, 1976. Postdoctoral fellow Harvard U., Boston, 1976-79; asst. rsch. cell biologist U. Calif., San Francisco, 1979-82; asst. prof. U. Calif., Irvine, 1982-86, assoc. prof., 1986-95; assoc. prof. Wayne State U., Detroit, 1995—; speaker in field. Contbr. articles and revs. to profl. jours. NIH grantee, 1985-88, 88—, Calif. Air Resources Bd. grantee, 1990—. Mem. AAAS, Am. Thoracic Soc., Am. Soc. Cell Biology, Soc. Toxicology. Office: OEHS-Sch Pharmacy 628 Shapero Hall Wayne State Univ Detroit MI 48202

BHALODKAR, NARENDRA CHANDRAKANT, cardiologist; b. Baroda, Gujarat, India, July 23, 1948; came to U.S., 1973, naturalized, 1980; s. Chandrakant G. and Pramila (Deo) R.; M.B., B.S., Baroda Med. Coll., India, 1971; m. Dina Rasiklal Bhatt, June 1, 1972; children—Ami, Neil, Samir. Rotating intern Luth. Med. Center, Cleve., 1973-74; resident in internal medicine Bronx Lebanon Hosp., 1974-76, cardiology fellow, 1976-78, asst. adj. dept. medicine, asso. cardiologist, 1978-80, asso. dept. medicine, 1980—; asst. prof. medicine Albert Einstein Coll. Medicine of Yeshiva U.; adj. asst. prof. dept. medicine Baylor Coll. of Medicine, Houston, 1992; acting dir. CCU Bronx Lebanon Hosp., 1992, assoc. dir. cardiac cath lab., 1992, dir. preventative cardiology, 1993, dir. CCU, 1993, dir. clin. study unit, 1994. Diplomate Am. Bd. Internal Medicine, Am. Bd. Cardiovascular Diseases. Fellow Am. Coll. Cardiology, N.Y. Cardiology Soc., ACP, Am. Heart Assn., Coun. Geriatric Cardiology, Am. Coll. Chest Physicians; mem. N.Y. State Soc. Internal Medicine. Hindu, Am. Assn. Physicians from India, Am. Assn. Cardiologists of Indian Origin, L.I. Heart Coun., Assn. Profl. Businessmen of the Bronx, Bronx County Med. Soc. Home: 1 Monterey Dr New Hyde Park NY 11040-1029 Office: 1650 Selwyn Ave Apt 8C Bronx NY 10457-7627

BHARDWAJ, ANISH, neuroscientist, medical educator; b. June 3, 1960. Diplomate Am. Bd. Neurology and Psychiatry. Intern Univ. Coll. Hosp., Ibadan, Nigeria, 1984-85; med. officer Sokoto Clinic, Nigeria, 1985-86; rsch. fellow dept. neurology Mt. Sinai Sch. Medicine, N.Y.C., 1987-89, resident in neurology, 1990-92, chief resident in neurology, 1992-93; resident in internal medicine Elmhurst Hosp., Mt. Sinai Sch. Medicine, N.Y.C., 1989-90; neurosci. crit. care fellow Johns Hopkins U. Sch. Medicine, Balt., 1993-95, nat. stroke assn. fellow, 1994-96, instr. depts. neurology, neurol. surgery, anesthesiology and crit. care medicine, 1995-96, dir. neurosci. crit. care fellowship tng. program, asst. prof. depts. neurology, neurol. surgery, anesthesiology and crit. care medicine, 1996—; staff attending neurosci. crit. care unit Johns Hopkins Hosp., Balt., 1995—. Contbr. articles to profl. jours.; ad hoc reviewer Jour. Cerebral Blood Flow and Metabolism, Crit. Care Medicine; spkr. in field. Fellow Am. Heart Assn. (mem. stroke coun., honorable mention Robert G. Siekert young investigator award in stroke 1995, clinician-scientist award 1996); mem. AMA, Am. Acad. Neurology, Nat. Stroke Assn. (fellowship career devel. award 1994), Soc. for Neurosci., Nigeria Med. Coun. Office: Johns Hopkins U Sch Medicine Meyer Bldg 8-140 600 N Wolfe St Baltimore MD 21287-7839

BHARGAVA, HEMENDRA NATH, pharmacologist, educator; b. Delhi, India, Sept. 30, 1942; m. Shakti Bhargava. B in Pharmacy, Banaras Hindu U., India, 1963, PharmM, 1965; PhD, U. Calif., San Francisco, 1969. Postdoctoral fellow U. Calif. Med. Sch., San Francisco, 1969-72, rsch. pharmacologist, 1972-74, lectr., 1974-75; asst. prof. pharmacology U. Ill. Med. Ctr., Chgo., 1975-78, assoc. prof., 1978-81, prof. pharmacology, 1981—; reviewer grants from NSF, Nat. Inst. on Drug Abuse, Ont. Mental Health Found (Can.). Contbr. over 530 articles to profl. jours., chpts. to books; reviewer manuscripts from 18 nat. and internat. jours. of pharmacology and neurosci. Recipient Madan Mohan Malviya prize Banaras Hindu U., 1963, Gold medal, 1965, Sr. Neurosci Rsch. Achievement award, 1991 and Rsch. Scientist Devel. award NIH, 1992—, Golden Apple award, 1980, Pride of India Gold medal, 1991, Mother India Internat. award, 1994; named to Chgo. Tribune's Tempo All-Prof. Team Acad. Champions, 1993; rsch. grantee NIH, Am. Heart Assn., Ill. Dept. Mental Health. Fellow Internat. Peptide Soc.; mem. Am. Soc. for Pharmacology and Exptl. Therapeutics, Am. Heart Assn. Met. Chgo., Am. Assn. Coll. of Pharmacy, Indian Acad. Neurosci., Soc. for Neurosci., Internat. Narcotic Rsch. Club. Office: U Ill at Chgo M/C 865 833 S Wood St Chicago IL 60612-7229

BHARGAVA, PUSHPA MITTRA, molecular biologist; b. Ajmer, Rajasthan, India, Feb. 22, 1928; s. Ram Chandra and Gayatri Devi Bhargava; m. Edith Manorama Patrick, Aug. 11, 1958; children: Vaneeta, Mohit. BS in Physics, Chemistry, Math., Lucknow U., 1944, MS in Organic Chemistry, 1946, PhD in Synthetic Organic Chemistry, 1949; DSc (hon.), U. Burdwan, 1988. Lectr. chemistry Lucknow U.; lectr. chemistry Osmania U., Hyderabad, India; rsch. fellow Regional Rsch. Lab., Hyderabad; project assoc. McArdle Meml. Lab. for Cancer Rsch., U. Wis., Madison; spl.

Wellcome rsch. fellow Nat. Inst. Med. Rsch., London; with staff Regional Rsch. Lab., Hyderabad, 1958-77; Eleanor Roosevelt Internat. Cancer Rsch. fellow Institut du Radium, Paris, 1971-72; dir. Centre for Cellular & Molecular Biology, Coun. Sci. Indsl. Rsch., Hyderabad, 1977-90, disting. fellow, 1990-93; life fellow Clare Hall, Cambridge, Eng., 1986; vis. prof. Coll. de France, Paris, 1992. Co-author: (with S. Shivaji) Proteins of Seminal Plasma, 1989; editor: Nucleic Acids: Structure, Biosynthesis and Function, 1965; contbr. articles to profl. jours; patentee in field. Recipient Watamull Mem. prize, 1962, award Fedn. Indian C. of C. and Industry, 1979, Nat. Citizen's award, India, 1988, Ranbaxy award, 1988, SICO award, 1990, Goyal prize, 1993, R.D. Birla award, 1994. Fellow NAS, Indian Acad. Scis., Indian Nat. Sci. Acad. (B.N. Chopra award 1989), Nat. Acad. Med. Scis. (India), World Acad. Arts and Scis.; mem. Biochem. Soc. (U.K.), Soc. for Study Reprodn. (fgn.), Am. Assn. for Cancer Rsch., Am. Fertility Soc., N.Y. Acad. Scis., Soc. Biol. Chemists India (past pres.), Guha Rsch. Conf. (founder), Indian Immunology Soc., Indian Assn. for Cancer Rsch., Assn. Biomed. Scientists, Indian Soc. for Chronobiology, Indian Acad. Social Scis. (past pres), Assn. for Promotion DNA Fingerprinting and Other DNA Techs. (pres.). Home: 12-5-27 Vijayapuri Tarnaka, Hyderabad 500 017, India Office: Anveshna Consultancy, 12-13-414/4 Street No 1, Tarnaka Hyderabad 500 017, India also: Indian Inst Chem Tech, Uppal Rd, Hyderabad 500 007, India

BHARTHUAR, ARUN, surgeon; b. Patna, Bihar, India, Jan. 27, 1951; s. Rajeshwari and Sarju Bala (Choudhary) Prasad; m. Kalpna Nath, Apr. 25, 1974; children: Alpana, Anupam, Arvind. BS, Prince Wales Med. Coll., 1974; MS in Surgery, Patna U., 1978. Registrar Dudley Rd. Hosp., Birmingham, Eng., 1979-81; surgeon civil asst. Bihar Health Svc., Bettiah, India, 1981-85; registrar surg. Nalanda Med. Coll. Hosp., Patna, India, 1985-88; surgeon specialist Prince Salman Hosp., Riyadh, Saudi Arabia, 1989-92; surgeon cons. Gen. Hosp., Misurata, Libya, 1992-93, Afif, Saudi Arabia, 1994—. Contbr. articles to profl. jours. Recipient award Pfizer Co., 1974. Mem. Assn. Surgeons India (life), Urology Assn. India. Home: Hari Niketan Rd #39, Patna 2 Bihar 800002, India Office: Afif Gen Hosp, PO Box 98, Afif Riyadh 11921, India

BHATNAGAR, GOPAL MOHAN, health scientist; b. Lucknow, India, July 15, 1937; came to U.S., 1963; s. Jagmohan Lal and Gopi Devi Bhatnagar. BSc, Lucknow U., 1955, MSc, 1957, PhD, 1961. Sr. rsch. fellow Nat. Chem. Lab., Poona, India, 1961-63; rsch. scientist Commonwealth Sci. and Indsl. Rsch. Orgn., Melbourne, Victoria, Australia, 1965-69; staff scientist Boston Biomed. Rsch. Inst., 1969-73; prin. assoc. Med. Sch. Harvard U., Boston, 1974-77; assoc. prof. Sch. of Medicine Johns Hopkins U., Balt., 1977-88; chemist FDA, Rockville, Md., 1988-91; sci. rev. adminstr. NIH, Bethesda, Md., 1991—. NIH grantee, 1976-86. Mem. Am. Soc. Biochemistry and Molecular Biology. Office: NIH/Nat Inst Child Health & Human Devel Div Sci Rev 6100 Executive Blvd Rm 5E01 Bethesda MD 20892

BHATNAGAR, KUNWAR PRASAD, medical educator; b. Gwalior, India, Mar. 21, 1934; came to U.S., 1967; s. Narayan Swaroop and Bhagwati Devi B.; m. Indu, Apr. 28, 1961; children: Divya B. Rouben, Jyoti B. Burruss. BS, Agra U., 1956; MS, Vikram U., 1958; PhD, SUNY, Buffalo, 1972. Asst. prof., assoc. prof., prof. U. Louisville Sch. Medicine, Anatomical Scis. & Neurobiology, 1972—. Editor: Bat Rsch. News, 1982-86; guest editor: Microscopy Rsch. & Technique, 1992; contbr. articles to profl. jours. Fellow Max Planck Inst. Brain Rsch., 1978, 86. Hindu. Home: 2651 Kings Hwy Louisville KY 40205-2648 Office: U Louisville Sch Medicine Dept Anatomical Sci and Neurobiol Louisville KY 40292

BHATTACHARYA, ARJUN, surgeon; b. Nagpur, India, Nov. 28, 1939; came to the U.S., 1971; s. Bhabani Charan and Sawla (Mukherji) B.; married, Jan. 3, 1968; children: Joyesha, Indraneel. MD, Med. Coll. Nagpur, 1962; MS in Surgery, Bombay U., 1967. Pres. med. staff Deaconess Hosp., St. Louis, 1985; dir. surgery fleet 22 USN, 1995—. Mem. editl. bd. St. Louis Met. Med. Mag., 1993-95. Capt. USN, 1992—; comdr. USNR, 1984-92, lt. comdr., 1983-84. Fellow ACS, Am. Coll. Occupational Medicine; mem. St. Louis Met. Med. Soc. (councillor 1995), Mo. State Med. Assn. (del. 1995), Rotary. Hindu. Home: 31 Dunleith Dr Ladue Saint Louis MO 63131 Office: 7200 Manchester Blvd Saint Louis MO 63143

BHATTACHARYYA, ASHIM KUMAR, pathology and physiology educator, researcher; b. Kanpur, Uttar Pradesh, India, July 9, 1936; came to U.S., 1966; s. Vishwa Nath and Ashalata (Bhattacharya) B.; m. Bani Chatterjee, July 10, 1966; children: Rupa, Gopa. BSc with honors, Calcutta U., 1957, MSc, 1959, PhD, 1965, DSc, 1989. Postdoctoral fellow U. Minn., Mpls., 1966-68; postdoctoral fellow U. Iowa, Iowa City, 1969-70, assoc. rsch scientist, 1970-74, rsch. scientist, 1974-75; asst. prof. pathology and physiology La. State U. Med. Ctr., New Orleans, 1975-80; assoc. prof. pathology and physiology La. State U., New Orleans, 1980-89, prof. pathology and physiology, 1989—. Contbr. 70 articles to profl. jours. Trustee India Assn. New Orleans, 1982-85, pres. La. Bengali Cultural Assn., 1985. Recipient Emery Goff Rsch. award, Am. Heart Assn.-La., New Orleans, 1977-78; sr. rsch. grantee, Am. Heart Assn.-La., 1976-77,1980-81. Fellow Coun. on Arteriosclerosis, Am. Heart Assn.; mem. Am. Physiol. Soc., Am. Inst. Nutrition, Am. Soc. for Clin. Nutrition, Sigma Xi. Hindu. Home: 1156 Elmeer Ave Metairie LA 70005-1616 Office: La State U Med Ctr Dept Pathology 1901 Perdido St New Orleans LA 70112-1328

BHATTI, IFTIKHAR HAMID, chiropractic educator; b. Lahore, Pahjab, Pakistan, Sept. 15, 1929; came to U.S., 1954; s. Hamid Khan and Akhtar (Hussain) B.; m. Sabahat Rafi, Dec. 17, 1961 (dec. 1992); children: Tanees, Tahir. BSc, U. Panjab, 1949, MSc, 1951; PhD, U. S.D., 1971. Prof. zoology Forman Christian Coll., Lahore, 1951-54, 57-61; biology instr. Swarthmore (Pa.) Coll., 1954-55, Haverford (Pa.) Coll., 1955-57; teaching fellow Woman's Med. Coll., Phila., 1961-63; biology prof. Buena Vista Coll., Storm Lake, Iowa, 1963-76; anatomy prof. Palmer Coll. Chiropractic, Davenport, Iowa, 1976—, chmn. dept., 1977-83, v.p. acad. affairs, 1988-91, dean of rsch. and grad. studies, 1991-95, asst. v.p. acad. affairs, 1994—, dean grad. and undergrad. studies, 1995—. Author: Human Embryology, 1988; contbr. articles to profl. pubis. Fellow Duke U., 1969. Mem. AAAS, Soc. Rsch. Adminstrn., Am. Pub. Health Assn., Iowa Microbeam Soc. Home: 1419 Tanglefoot Ln Bettendorf IA 52722-2413 Office: Palmer Inst Grad Studies & Rsch 741 Brady St Davenport IA 52803-5238

BHAVSAR, ASHA BIPIN, chemist, researcher; b. Ahmedabad, Gjurat, India, Dec. 25, 1955; came to U.S., 1987; d. Chandubhai L. and Dhahiben C. (Bhavsar) B.; m. Bipin K. Bhavsar, Dec. 4, 1978; 1 child, Kanan. BSc in Chem. Physics, M.G. Sci. Inst., Ahmedabad, 1976; MSc in Organic Chemistry, Sch. Sci., Ahmedabad, 1978. Product chemist Sims Lab., Ahmedabad, 1979-84; lab. supr. Maize Products, Ahmedabad, 1984-88; chemist Mut. Pharm., Phila., 1988-90; sr. chemist Whitehall Robins, Hammonton, N.J., 1990-92; asst. rsch. scientist Pfizer Inc., Groton, Conn., 1992—. Mem. Am. Chem. Soc., Union Pure and Applied Chemistry. Home: 18 Jean Dr East Lyme CT 06333 Office: Prizer Inc Eastern Point Rd Groton CT 06340

BHOPAL, RAJ SINGH, epidemiology and public health educator, physician; b. Moga, India, Apr. 10, 1953; s. Jhanda Singh and Bhagwanti Kaur (Rakhra) B.; m. Roma Mazumdar, June 21, 1981; children: Sunil, Vijay, Anand, Rajan. BS with honors, Edinburgh (Scotland) U., 1975, MB, BChir, 1978, MD, 1991; MPH, Glasgow (Scotland) U., 1985. House officer in medicine City Hosp., Edinburgh, 1978-79; house officer in surgery St. Bernard's Hosp., Gibralter, 1978-79; trainee gen. practitioner Edinburgh, 1980-81; sr. house officer in medicine Neville Hall Hosp., Abergavenny, Wales, 1981-82, East Birmingham Hosp., 1982; registrar then sr. registrar cmty. medicine Greater Glasgow Health Bd., 1983-85; lectr., hon. sr. registrar in cmty. medicine Glasgow U., Glasgow, 1985-88; sr. lectr. and cons. cmty. medicine U. Newcastle Upon Tyne, 1988-91; head dept. epidemiology, prof. chair epidemiology & pub. health Newcastle Med. Sch., U.K., 1991—; non-exec. dir., vice-chmn. Newcastle and North Tyneside Health Authority, 1992-96; respiratory infection task force Schering Plough Internat., 1993-96; mem. Health Edn. Authority of Eng. and Wales, 1996—. Mem. editl. bd. Jour. Epidemiology-Community Health, 1993—; contbr. over 70 articles to profl. jours. Gov. Coquet Park First Sch., Whitley Bay, U.K., 1992—; mem. health panel Racial Equality Coun., Newcastle, 1990-93. Fellow Soc. of Pub. Health (Maddison prize 1993, Neech prize 1995), Royal Coll. Physicians; mem. Faculty of Pub. Health Medicine (Littlejohn Gardner prize 1987), Brit. Med. Assn., Soc. for Soc. Medicine, Internat. Epidemiology Assn. Office: Med Sch Dept Epidemiology, Framlington Pl, Newcastle NE2 4HH, England

BHORE, JAY NARAYAN, psychiatrist; b. Kavalapur, Bombay, India, Sept. 12, 1915; came to U.S. 1958; s. Narayan Suleman and Chandra (Nandrekar) B.; m. Mary Elizabeth Singleton, June 17, 1960. BS, Govt. Coll., India, 1939; M.B.B.S., BJJ Med. Coll., India, 1943; MD, Northwestern U., Chgo., 1967. Med. officer Student Health Ctr., Bishop Coll., Calcutta, India, 1947-51; resident physician Jubar Sanatorium, Simla Hills, India, 1951-53; resident diseases of chest Mcpl. T.B. Sanatorium, Chgo., 1958-60; fellow neurology/psychiatry Northwestern U. Med. Sch., Chgo., 1960-61; rotating intern Augustana Hosp., Chgo., 1962; resident in psychiatry St. Joseph Hosp., London, Ont., Can., 1964-65, Northwestern U., Chgo., 1965-67; staff psychiatrist Downey (Ill.) VA Hosp., 1968-71, West Side VA Hosp., Chgo., 1970-73, VA Hosp., Woods, Wis., 1973; pvt. practice psychiatry Milw., 1974—; founder, pres. Rev. N.S. Bhore Meml., Kavalapur, India, 1975; pres. Rev. N.S. Bhore Mem. Evang. Assocs., Milw., 1976. Founder Free Pub. Libr., Kavalapur, 1980, Med. Clinic Day Care Ctr., Kavalapur, 1981, Chandra Hosp., Kavalapur, 1990. Mem. APA, AMA, Wis. Psychiat. Assn., Christian Med. Dental Soc., Am. Assn. Physicians from India. Presbyterian. Home and Office: 1543 N Prospect Ave Milwaukee WI 53202-2367

BHUTTA, OMAR IQBAL, psychiatrist; b. Pakistan, Oct. 3, 1945; came to U.S. 1970; s. M. Jamal and Amna (Bhutta) B.; m. Rita E. Ernst, Oct. 18, 1975; children: Omar Jamal, Daniel. MD, Punjab Univ., Pakistan, 1968. Bd. cert. psychiatrist with added qualifications in addiction psychiatry and geriatric psychiatry. Recipient; Am. Psychiatric Assn. fellowship 1987. Mem. AMA, Pitts. Psychiatric Soc., Pa. Med. Soc., Allegheny County Med. Soc., Psychiatric Physicians of Pa. Home: 5550 Beverly Pl Pittsburgh PA 15206-1427 Office: Clin Psychiatry Assn P C 1501 Locust St Ste 306 Pittsburgh PA 15219-5128

BIANCHI, MARIA, critical care nurse, adult nurse practitioner. Diploma, Catherine Laboure Sch. Nursing, 1979; Grad., Fitchburg (Mass.) State Coll., 1985; postgrad., Russell Sage Coll., Troy, N.Y.; adult nurse practitioner, Mass. Gen. Hosp., Boston. Cert. post-anesthesia care nurse; critical care specialist 1993. Recovery as mgmt. educator, mktg. and recruitment cons., cons. in critical care nursing; nurse mgr. ICU and pediatric ICU Baystate Med. Ctr., Springfield, Mass., 1980-89; recruitment and staff St. Francis Med. Ctr., 1989-92; advanced practice nurse U. Mass. Med. Ctr., Worcester, 1995—; critical care nurse Mass. Gen. Hosp., 1992-93, adult nurse practitioner, 1995-96; rsch. in pain, burn trauma, stress reduction, holistic methods for high risk individuals in maximum penitentiary. Mem. AACN, Am. Soc. Post-Anesthesia Nursing (Boston chpt. editl. cons.), Sigma Theta Tau. Office: 33 Duclos Dr Feeding Hills MA 01030-1409

BIANCHI, MARIE ANNE, gastroenterology, critical care, medical and surgical nurse; b. Rochester, N.Y., Jan. 29, 1956; d. Angelo J. and Ida A. (Guanciale) B. BSN, Skidmore Coll., 1978; MSN, U. Pa., 1984; diploma, Eurocentres, Florence, Italy, 1986; MBA, Rochester Inst. Tech. Mktg., 1993. Cert. gastroenterology nursing. Staff nurse gen. surgery Highland Hosp., Rochester, N.Y., 1978-81, staff nurse med. ICU, 1982; staff nurse med. ICU Strong Meml. Hosp., Rochester, 1982-85, 87-89; clin. intern Temple U. Hosp., Phila., 1983-84; rsch. asst. Rochester Gen. Hosp., 1987-89, quality assurance analyst, 1988-89; nurse mgr., clin. nurse specialist St. Mary's Hosp., Rochester, 1989-90; nurse leader gastrointestinal unit Strong Meml. Hosp., Rochester, 1991—. Recipient Profl. Nurse traineeship NIH, 1983-84. Mem. AACN, Soc. Gastroenterology Nurses and Assocs., Genesee Valley Nurses Assn., Sigma Theta Tau. Home: 1935 Clinton Ave N Rochester NY 14621-1007

BIANCHI, NÉSTOR OSCAR, physician; b. La Plata, Argentina, Apr. 18, 1931; s. Carlos J. and Sara A. (Adrogue) B.; m. Martha Susana Albarellos, Apr. 18, 1956; children: Carlos Marcelo, César Esteban. MD, U. La Plata, 1955; D Nutrition, U. Buenos Aires, 1957. Intern Hosp. Policlínico de La Plata, 1953-55, resident, 1956-58; resident Presbyn. Hosp., N.Y., 1961; head Lab. Cytogenetics Com. Investigaciones Científicas Y Técnicas, Buenos Aires, 1961-69; vis. prof. dept. anatomy La. State U., New Orleans, 1970; acting head dept. cell biology Gulf South Rsch. Inst., New Orleans, 1970-72; assoc. investigator Inst. Genetics of Santa Catalina, Lavallol, Buenos Aires, 1972-74; dir. Inst. Multidisciplinario de Biología Celular, La Plata, 1974—; vis. prof. U. Helsinki (Finladn), 1988-91; cons. orgn. Am. States, Washington, 1976-83, Internat. Atomic Energy Agy., Vienna, Austria, 1978-83, Sec. Sci. Tech., Argentina, 1989-91, Nat. Coun. Rsch., Argentina, 1989-91; sci. cons. Nat. Deputies and Senators, Province of Buenos Aires Reps., 1989-91. Author 3 books in field of molecular genetics, 230 papers on cytogenetics and molecular genetics. With Argentine Army, 1953-54. Recipient Tetrann. Rubén Cherny, Lucio Cherny Found., Argentina, 1977. Mem. Med. Coll. Province Buenos Aires, Club de Regatas. Roman Catholic. Home: 54 #959 - 20, 1900 La Plata Argentina Office: Inst Multidisciplinario de Biologia Celular, 526 e/10 y 11 CC 403, 1900 La Plata Argentina

BIANCHI-BIGELOW, CHERYL ANN, mental health facility director; b. Rochester, N.Y., July 1, 1957; d. Samuel Gene and Marlene Ann (Conte) Bianchi; m. Howard Francis Bigelow, Oct. 30, 1984; 1 child, Alexa Anne. BA in Sociology, SUNY, Cortland, 1979; MSW, Syracuse U., 1984. Cert. social worker, mental health and gerontology profl. Psychiat. social worker, psychotherapist, intern Hillside Children's Ctr., Rochester, 1982-83; psychiat. social worker Veteran's Hosp., Canadagula, N.Y., 1983-84; from clin. coord. to assoc. dir. DePaul Mental Health Svcs., Rochester, 1984-88, dir., 1987-92; chief exec. officer, pres. The Bread Harbor, Inc., Chatham, Mass., 1991—. Recipient Best Bus. Display of Christmas Spirit award Chatham Yule Bowl, 1993, Award of Excellence, Best Chefs of Cape Cod, 1994. Mem. NAFE, NASW, NASE, Chatham Merchants Assn., Chatham C. of C., U. Club Rochester, Women's Network, Phi Beta Kappa. Home: 56 Augustine St Rochester NY 14613-1425 Office: The Bread Harbor Inc Chatham MA 02633

BIANCHI PORRO, GABRIELE, medical clinician; b. Forli, Italy, May 27, 1938; s. Guido and Elsa (Giammarchii) Bianchi P.; m. Maddalena Petrillo, Nov. 8, 1969; 1 child, Michela. DM, U. Milan, 1962, diploma in gastroenterology, 1970; diploma in cardiology, U. Torino, Italy, 1966. Jr. asst. U. Milan, 1962-64, sr. asst., 1964-72; dep. head Sacco U. Hosp., Milan, 1972-75; chmn. dept. gastroenterology Sacco U. Hosp., 1975—. Editor: (series) Perspectives in Gastroenterology, 1985—; editor Italian Jour. Gastroenterology, Hepatogastroenterology jour. Named Disting. Citizen, Pres. of Italy, 1990. Mem. European Gastroenterology Club, European Assn. Gastroenterology and Endoscopy (pres. 1986-88), Italian Soc. Gastroenterology (v.p. 1985-87), Rotary. Roman Catholis. Home: Piazzetta Bossi 1, 20121 Milan Italy Office: Via del Lauro 10, 20121 Milan Italy

BIANCONI, GREGORY FREDERICK, family practitioner; b. Meriden, Conn., July 24, 1952; s. Natale P. and Constance (Siino) B.; m. Deborah Sisson-Bianconi, June 9, 1979; children: Matthew, Anna, Joseph. ScB, Brown U., 1974, MD, 1977. Diplomate Am. Bd. Family Practice. Resident Meml. Hosp., Pawtucket, R.I., 1977-80; staff physician Nat. Health Svc. Corps, Parsons, Tenn., 1980-83; pvt. practice Lisbon, Maine, 1983—; adj. instr. Family Practice Residency, U. Tenn., Jackson, 1980-83, Family Practice Residency, Central Maine Med. Ctr., Lewiston, 1983—. Adv. bd. Town of Lisbon, Maine, 1987—; bd. dirs. First Universalist Ch., Auburn, Maine, 1989-92. Fellow Am. Acad. Family Physicians. Unitarian-Universalist. Home: RR 1 Box 372 Lisbon Falls ME 04252-9706 Office: Lisbon Family Practice Two Rivers Med Ctr Lisbon ME 04250

BIASINI, VIRGINIA, social worker; b. N.Y.C., July 5, 1939; d. Albert Eugene and Irene Veronica (Kuzmiak) B. BA, Coll. Mt. St. Vincent, Bronx, N.Y., 1977; MSW, Hunter Coll. CUNY, 1980. Cert. social worker, N.Y., sch. social worker, N.J., clin. hypnotherapist Wellness Inst., Seattle; diplomate Am. Bd. Examiners in Clin. Social Work; lic. clin. social worker, N.J. Office mgr. Wiltwyck Sch. for Boys, N.Y.C., 1963-66; adminstrv. asst. to law ptnr. Acme Quilting Co., Inc., N.Y.C., 1966-73; adminstrv. asst. to chmn. bd. Calvary Hosp., Bronx, 1973-77, oncology social worker, 1977-78, patient rep. program coord., 1978-81; med. social worker Westchester Sq. Med. Ctr., Bronx, 1981-84, sr. social worker, supr., 1984-86; asst. dir. social work dept. Cabrini Med. Ctr., N.Y.C., 1986; dir. social work discharge planning dept. Westchester Sq. Med. Ctr., Bronx, 1986-90; individual, family and group social worker, counselor Kimball-Manchester Ambulatory Care Ctr. div. Kimball Med. Ctr., Whiting, N.J., 1990—; instr. field work Union Theol. Sem., 1978-79, Lehman Coll., CUNY, Bronx, 1988-90; mem. adj. faculty Coll. Mt. St. Vincent, 1981-82. Mem. NASW, Acad. Cert. Social Workers, Soc. Social Work Dirs., Nat. Soc. Social Work Dirs., Am. Hosp. Assn. Office: Kimball-Manchester Ambulatory Care Ctr 1100 Route 70 Whiting NJ 08759

BIBBO, MARLUCE, physician, educator; b. Sao Paulo, Brazil, July 14, 1939; d. Domingos and Yolanda (Ranciaro) B. M.D, U. Sao Paulo, 1963, Sc.D., 1968. Intern Hosps. das Clinicas, U. Sao Paulo, 1963; resident in morphology, 1964-66; instr. dept. morphology and ob-gyn U. Sao Paulo, 1966-68, asst. prof., 1968-69; fellow in cytology U. Chgo., 1969-70, asst. prof. sect. cytology dept. ob-gyn, 1971-73, assoc. prof., 1973-77, assoc. prof. pathology, 1974-77, prof. ob-gyn and pathology, 1978-92; assoc. dir. Cytology Lab., Approved Sch. Cytotech and Cytocybernetics, AMA-Am. Soc. Clin. Pathologists, 1970-91; dir. Cytology Lab., Phila., 1992; prof. pathology Thomas Jefferson U., Phila., 1992—, Warren R. Lane prof. pathology & cell biology, 1993—; mem. rsch. com. Ill. divsn. Am. Cancer Soc., 1976-91. Contbr. numerous articles to profl. jours. Fellow Internat. Acad. Cytology (pres.-elect, v.p. 1987, pres. 1992, dep. editor Acta Cytologica, editor 1995), Am. Soc. Clin. Pathologists (coun. on cytopathology); mem. Am. Soc. Cytology (exec. com., pres. 1982-83), U.S. Acad. Pathology, Can. Acad. Pathology, Soc. Analytical Cytology, Coun. Cytopathology. Home: 250 S 9th St Philadelphia PA 19107-5734 Office: Cytology Lab 132 S 10th St Philadelphia PA 19107-5244

BICE, JAMES BRADLEY, physician; b. Des Moines, Sept. 16, 1963; s. Harry Elmer and Ruth Lorrene (Sandeen) B.; m. Tiffany Elizabeth Braun, Aug. 15, 1992. BS cum laude, Drake U., 1986; D of Osteopathy, U. Osteo. Medicine & Health, 1990. Diplomate Am. Bd. Family Practice. Intern Oakland Gen. Hosp., Madison Heights, Mich., 1990-91; resident family practice Iowa Luth. Hosp., Des Moines, 1991-93; physician La Salle Clinic, Neenah, Wis., 1993-95, Mercy Med. Clinic, Indianola, Iowa, 1995—. Mem. bd. Juvenile Diabetes Found., Appleton, Wis., 1994-95. Mem. AMA, Am. Acad. Family Physicians, Am. Osteo. Assn., Am. Coll. Osteo. Family Physicians (del. 1994), Am. Coll. Sports Medicine, Sigma Sigma Phi, Alpha Epsilon Delta, Beta Beta Beta. Office: Mercy-Indianola Med Clinic 108 N Jefferson Indianola IA 50125

BICHSEL, HANS, physicist, consultant, researcher; b. Basel, Switzerland, Sept. 2, 1924; came to U.S., 1951; s. Paul and Anna Maria Bichsel; m. Sue O. Greenwalt, Sept. 12, 1959; children: Elizabeth Christine, Joseph Oliver. MA, U. Basel, 1951, PhD, 1951. Rsch. asst. Princeton (N.J.) U., 1951-55; rsch. assoc. Rice U., Houston, 1955-57; asst. prof. physics U. Wash., Seattle, 1957-59; affiliate prof. physics U. Wash., Seattle, 1992—; assoc. prof., prof. radiology U. Wash., Seattle, 1969-80; asst. prof., assoc. prof. physics U. So. Calif., L.A., 1959-68; assoc. prof. U. Calif., Berkeley, 1968-69; cons. Capitol Hill Cons., Seattle, 1980—; cons. Internat. Commn. on Radiation Units, Bethesda, Md., 1970—, Los Alamos (N.Mex.) Nat. Lab., 1978-83, IAEA, Vienna, Austria, 1990—; vis. scientist Nat. Inst. Radiol., Scis., Chiba, Japan, 1991, U. Sherbrooke Med. Sch., Que., Can.; referee Phys. Rev., Nuclear Instruments and Methods, Physics in Medicine and Biology, also others. Contbr. articles to profl. jours. Fellow Am. Phys. Soc.; mem. Swiss Phys. Soc. Home and Office: 1211 22nd Ave E Seattle WA 98112-3534

BICKEL, EARL YOUNT, orthopedic surgeon; b. Cedar Rapids, Iowa, July 2, 1928; s. Earl Alban and DeFoy (Goudy) B.; m. Linda Sue Gehl; children: Christopher W., Jonathan E., Heidi Joy. BA, Carleton Coll., Northfield, Minn., 1950; MD, U. Iowa, 1954. Diplomate Am. Bd. Orthopaedic Surgery. Intern U. Minn., Mpls., 1955, fellow in surgery, 1956; resident in orthopedic surgery U. Iowa, Iowa City, 1961; pvt. practice orthopedic surgery Iowa Med. Clinic, Cedar Rapids, 1961—; med. staff Mercy Med. Ctr., Cedar Rapids, St. Luke's Hosp., Cedar Rapids. Capt. U.S. Army, 1956-58. Mem. ACS (pres. Iowa chpt. 1996), AMA, Am. Acad. Orthopaedic Surgeons, Mid-Ctrl. States Orthopaedic Soc., Iowa State Orthopaedic Soc. (pres. 1978), Iowa State Orthopaedic Alumni Assn., Iowa State Med. Assn., Linn County Med. Assn. Office: IMC 600 7th St Cedar Rapids IA 52401-2112

BICKERTON, JOHN THORBURN, retired pharmaceutical executive; b. Windsor, Ont., Can., Apr. 6, 1930; came to U.S., 1972; s. Edward Levi and Catherine (Thorburn) B.; m. Natalie Katherine Kasurak, Aug. 20, 1955; children: Katherine, John, Paul. B in Commerce, Queen's U., Kingston, Ont., 1953. Auditor Price Waterhouse & Co., Windsor, 1953-57; asst. controller Parke Davis subs. Warner Lambert Co., Detroit, 1957-72; controller Warner Lambert Internat., Morris Plains, N.J., 1972-80, v.p. fin., 1980-82; v.p. fin. Parke Davis subs. Warner Lambert Co., Morris Plains, N.J., 1982-91, ret., 1991. Episcopalian. Home: 16 Summit Rd Morristown NJ 07960-2827

BICKFORD, BETH E., nurse; b. Warren, Ohio, Mar. 29, 1958; d. Duane W. and Jean Marie (Peterson) B. Student, Champion high sch., Warren, Ohio, 1976; BSc., Case We. Res. U., Cleve., 1981; Msc., U. Rochester, N.Y., 1987. Staff nurse U. Hosp. Cleve., 1981-82, U. Rochester, N.Y., 1982-84, Rochester Gen. Hosp., N.Y., 1984-86; dir. critical care services Clifton Springs Hosp. Clinic, N.Y., 1986-87; surgical clinical nurse specialist We. Res. Care System, Youngstown, 1987-92; clin. nurse analyst, 1992-94; dir. program svcs. Ohio Nurses Assn., Columbus, 1994—. Choir mem. St. Paul Luth. Ch., Westerville, Ohio 1995—. Recipient Pre-profl. scholar award Case We. Res. U. Cleve. 1978, Nip Heim award Case We. Res. U. Cleve. 1981. Mem. ANA, Ohio Nurses Assn., Am. Assn. Critical Care Nurses (grantee 1989), Midwest Nursing Rsch. Soc. Lutheran. Home: 2804 Albemarle Dr Columbus OH 43068 Office: 4000 E Main St Columbus OH 43213

BICKHAM, CHARLES EDWARD, JR., radiologist, educator; b. Bude, Miss., Nov. 29, 1918; s. Charles Edward and Luda (Oglesby) B.; m. Melba Scrivner, Dec. 22, 1944; children—Charles Edward III, Martha, Melissa. B.A., U. Ala., 1943; M.D., Jefferson Med. Coll., 1946. Diplomate Am. Bd. Radiology. Intern U.S. Naval Hosp., Jacksonville, Fla., 1947; resident in radiology Doctors Hosp., Washington, 1949, Garfield Meml. Hosp. and Emergency Hosp., Washington, 1952; practice medicine specializing in radiology, Washington, 1952—; clin. assoc. prof. radiology Uniformed Svcs. Univ. Health Scis. Med. Sch., Bethesda, Md., 1982-91; cons. radiologist Armed Forces Inst. Pathology, Washington, 1960-68, U.S. Naval Hosp., Bethesda, 1958-82, Washington Hosp. Ctr., 1958—; attending radiologist, vice chmn. dept. Doctors Hosp., 1958-73, chmn. dept., 1973-75; chmn. dept. radiology Suburban Hosp., Bethesda, 1975-88, chmn. emeritus; assoc. radiologist Sibley Meml. Hosp., Washington, 1968—; trustee Med. Svc. of D.C., 1966-75; mem. N-44 com. Am. Nat. Standards Inst. Contbr. articles to med. jours. Served with USN, 1943-45, 46-49, 50-51; lt. Res. ret. Fellow Am. Coll. Radiology (com. on Blue Shield program); mem. AMA (sect. coun. radiology 1978-79, adv. com. health policy agenda for the Am. people, 1983-86; physician's recognition award 1969, 72, 75, 79, 82), Med. Soc. D.C. (occupational health com., vice chmn. relative value com., mem. clin. efficacy rev. com.), Am. Roentgen Ray Soc. (exec. council 1972-77, fin. com. 1974-76, chmn. exec. council 1976-77, 2d v.p. 1977-79), Radiol. Soc. N.Am., So. Med. Assn. (chmn. elec. sect. radiology 1974), Pan Am. Med. Soc. (pres. 1978-79), Hippocrates Galen Med. Soc., Med. Arts Soc., William Earl Clark Gastroent. Soc., Eastern Radiol. Soc., Montgomery County Med. Soc. (affiliate), Med. and Chirurg. Faculty Md. Home: 5920 Searl Ter Bethesda MD 20816-2023

BICKNELL, BRIAN KEITH, dentist; b. Orlando, Fla., Mar. 8, 1957; s. Keith Arthur and Mary Lou (Papish) B.; m. Gina Rose Smajo; children: Michael Brian, Daniel Keith. BS, U. Notre Dame, 1979, U. Ill., Chgo., 1981; DDS, U. Ill., Chgo., 1983. Practice gen. dentistry Batavia, Ill., 1984—. Fellow Acad. Gen. Dentistry; mem. ADA, Ill. State Dental Soc., Fox River Valley Dental Soc. Roman Catholic. Home: 594 N Van Nortwick St Batavia IL 60510-1119 Office: 109 E Wilson St Batavia IL 60510-2658

BICKNELL, ELIZABETH HOWARD, nursing educator, community health nurse; b. Bangor, Maine, July 17, 1950; d. James Russell and Carolyn Delle (Quimby) Howard; m. Albert Francis Bicknell, Sept. 10, 1977; children: Jonathan Albert, Jason James. BSN, U. So. Maine, 1972; MS, Boston U., 1982. RN, Maine; cert. nursing adminstr.-advanced. Coord. geriatric nursing svcs. Bangor Mental Health Inst., 1975-77, asst. dir. nursing, 1977-83; assoc. prof. U. Maine, Orono, 1983—. Contbr. chpt. to Rural Nursing, vol. 2; contbr. articles to profl. jours. Mem. ANA, Maine Nurse's Assn., Maine Pub. Health Assn., Assn. Cmty. Health Nurse Educators, Sigma Theta Tau. Home: RR 2 Box 343 Orrington ME 04474-9614 Office: 243 Dunn Hall Orono ME 04469

BICKS, RICHARD OSCAR, internist, gastroenterologist; b. Bklyn., May 26, 1927; s. Nathan Hale and Rose (Oseasohr) B.; m. Marcia Bryan, July 31, 1955; children: Nathan A., Steven B., Sharon G. BS, Coll. William and Mary, 1946; MD, SUNY, Bklyn., 1950. Diplomate Am. Bd. Internal Medicine with subspecialty in gastroenterology. Intern Mt. Sinai Hosp., Cleve., 1950-51, resident in medicine, 1951-52; resident in pathology Mallory Inst. Pathology, Boston City Hosp., 1952-53; resident in medicine Beth Israel Hosp., Boston, 1953-54; USPHS fellow in gastroenterology U. Chgo., 1956; teaching fellow in medicine Harvard Med. Sch., Boston, 1953-54; USPHS rsch. fellow U. Chgo., 1956-58; asst. prof. medicine U. Tenn., Memphis, 1958-66, clin. assoc. prof. medicine, 1966-69, clin. prof., 1969—. Contbr. articles to profl. jours., chpts. to books. Pres. Opera Memphis, 1974-77; dir. exch. program Xian Med. U., China, 1978. Lt. comdr. USNR, 1954-62. NIH grantee, 1963-67. Fellow ACP; mem. Am. Gastroenterol. Assn., Am. Soc. Gastrointestinal Endoscopy. Office: 920 Madison Ave Memphis TN 38103

BIDDICK-LIEPINS, DIANE KAY, healthcare administrator; b. Madison, Wis., Nov. 8, 1954; d. Scott Hathaway and Betty Darlene (Womack) Biddick; m. Edgars Liepins, May 29, 1989. BS in Nursing, Wash. State U., Pullman, 1976; M of Mgmt. Info. Systems, West Coast U., 1986. Cert. nursing adminstr. Charge nurse Del Amo Hosp., Torrance, Calif., 1976-78; supr. mental health Kaiser Found. Hosp., L.A., 1978-81; asst. dept adminstr. So. Calif. Permanente Med. Group, L.A., 1981-84, dept. adminstr., 1984-89, adminstrv. asst., 1989-95; project mgr. So. Calif. Permanente Med. Group, Pasadena, 1995—. Sec., bd. dirs. Fair Oaks Homeowners Assn., 1988-89, v.p., 1989-91. Mem. ANA, Toastmasters Internat., Inc., Phi Kappa Phi, Alpha Chi. Republican. Lutheran. Office: So Calif Permanente Med Group 393 E Walnut Pasadena CA 91188

BIDDINGTON, WILLIAM ROBERT, university administrator, dental educator; b. Piedmont, W.Va., Mar. 30, 1925; s. William M. and Sadie (Vogtman) B.; m. Dolores E. Berrett, June 14, 1947; 1 son, William Berrett. Student, Potomac State Coll., 1942-43, Hampden-Sydney Coll., 1943-44; D.D.S. cum laude, U. Md., 1948. Diplomate: Am. Bd. Endodontics. Gen. practice dentistry Balt., 1949-59; instr. Balt. Coll. Dental Surgery, Dental Sch. U. Md., 1949-52, asst. prof., 1952-56, assoc. prof., 1956-59; prof., chmn. dept. endodontics Sch. Dentistry, W.Va. U., Morgantown, 1959-68; asst. dean Sch. Dentistry, W.Va. U., 1966-68, dean, 1968-91, interim v.p. academic affairs, 1979-80, interim v.p. health scis., 1981-82; v.p. Robert C. Byrd Health Scis. Ctr., Morgantown, 1991-92, sr. assoc. v.p., 1992-93, assoc. v.p., 1993—; interim dir. Ctr. on Aging W.Va. U. Sch. Medicine, 1993-95; Mem. at large, sec., vice chmn., chmn. adminstrv. bd., v.p. council deans Am. Assn. Dental Schs., 1974-78, pres., 1983-84. Served with USNR, 1942-46, 48-49. Fellow Am. Coll. Dentists (regent 1983-87, v.p. 1988-89, pres.-elect 1989-90, pres. 1990-91, pres. ACD Found. 1991-92); mem. ADA (joint commn. on nat. dental exams. 1979-84, commn. on dental health of the coun. on sports medicine of the U.S. Olympic Com. 1980-88, chmn. commn. 1988—, mem. com. on accreditation, coun. on dental edn. 1986-90), W.Va. Dental Assn., Monongahela Valley Dental Soc., Monongahela County Dental Soc. (pres. 1966), Am. Assn. Dental Schs., Internat. Assn. Dental Rsch., Am. Assn. Endodontists, Gorgas Odontological Soc., Psi Omega, Omicron Kappa Upsilon (pres. Supreme chpt. 1965-67). Home: RR 7 Box 720 Morgantown WV 26505-9124 Office: 1157 HSCN PO Box 9001 Morgantown WV 26506-9001

BIDLACK, WAYNE ROSS, nutritional biochemist, toxicologist, food scienti; b. Waverly, N.Y., Aug. 12, 1944; s. Andrew L. Bidlack and Vivian Pearl Cowles Williams; m. Wei Wang, July 29, 1995. BS, Pa. State U., 1966; MS, Iowa State U., 1968; PhD, U. Calif., Davis, 1972. Postdoctoral fellow U. So. Calif., Dept. Pharmacology, L.A., 1972-74; asst prof. sch. medicine U. So. Calif., 1974-80, assoc. prof., 1980-92, prof., 1992—, asst. dean student affairs, 1988-91, chmn. dept. pharmacology and nutrition, 1991-92; chmn. Dept. Food Sci. and Human Nutrition Iowa State U., Ames, 1992-95; dean coll. agrl. Calif. State Poly. U., Pomona, 1995—. Assoc. editor Biochem. Medicine and Metabolic Biology, 1986-87; book reviewer, abstract editor Jour. Am. Coll. Nutrition, 1995; assoc. editor Environmental Nutritional Interactions, 1996—. Chmn. Greater L.A. Nutrition Coun., 1982-83, So. Calif. Inst. Food Technologists, 1988-89, Toxicology and Safety Evaluation divsn. Inst. Food Technologists, 1989-90, food sci. communicator, 1986—; chmn. Nat. Coun. Against Health Fraud, 1983-85; mem. expert panel on foods and nurtrition, 1989-93. Recipient Outstanding Tchr. Award, U. So. Calif., Sch. Medicine, 1987-88, Meritorious Svc. award, Calif. Dietetic Assn., 1990, Disting. Achievement award, So. Calif. Inst. Food Technologists, 1990. Mem. Soc. Toxicology (chair awards com. food safety sect. 1993-94, chair 1994-95), Nat. Golden Key Soc. (hon.). Republican. Office: Calif State Polytech U Coll of Agrl 3801 W Temple Ave Pomona CA 91768

BIDWELL, ROBERT JAMES, pediatrics educator; b. Columbus, Ohio, Feb. 1, 1948; s. Laurence Earl and Helen Elizabeth (Cunningham). BA summa cum laude, U. Minn., 1976, MD, 1981. Diplomate Am. Bd. Pediatrics. Assoc. prof. U. Hawaii, Honolulu, 1988—; dir. adolescent medicine U. of the Sch. of Medicine, Honolulu, 1988—. Mem. Hawaii chpt. Am. Acad. Pediatrics, Soc. for Adolescent Medicine. Home: 610 Kumukahi Pl Honolulu HI 96825 Office: Kapiolani Med Ctr 1319 Punahou St Honolulu HI 96826-1032

BIDWICK SANDFORD, MARY A., adult nurse practitioner; b. Olney, Md., Sept. 30, 1958; d. Albert J. Jr. and Mary A. Bidwick; m. Clinton Sandford, June 16, 1990. BSN, U. Md., Balt., 1981, MSN, 1987; postgrad., Gallaudet U., Washington. Cert. adult nurse practitioner. Staff nurse Holy Cross Hosp., Wheaton, Md.; clin. nurse NIH, Bethesda, Md.; staff nurse Washington Hosp. Ctr. Med. Clinic; adult nurse practitioner Gallaudet Student Health Svc., Washington, Shady Grove Adventist Hosp., 1991—. Mem. Nurse Practitioner Assn. of D.C., Sigma Theta Tau. Home: 3036 Piano Ln Silver Spring MD 20904-6810

BIEBEL, CURT FRED, JR., dentist; b. St. Louis, Dec. 7, 1947; s. Curt F. and Jewell (Frank) B.; children: Betheny Doreen, Brendon Matthew. AB in Psychology, U. Mo., Columbia, 1970; DDS, U. Mo., Kansas City, 1974. Assoc. dentist Louis R. Nolan, Inc., St. Louis, 1976-79; gen. practice dentistry Chesterfield, Mo., 1979—. Capt. USAF, 1974-76. Mem. ADA, Greater St. Louis Dental Soc., Chgo. Dental Soc., Country Club of St. Albans, Forest Park Handball Assn., St. Louis Hinder Club. Office: 14378 Wood Lake Dr Chesterfield MO 63017-5714

BIEBER, MARK ALLAN, nutrition scientist, researcher; b. Cleve., Sept. 16, 1946; s. Lester and Ethel R. (Rubin) B. BS in Chemistry, U. Pitts., 1968; PhD in Biochemistry, Mich. State U., 1973. Cert. Am. Chem. Soc. Predoctoral trainee NIH, 1968-73; postdoctoral trainee NIH, Bethesda, Md., 1975-77; fell in pediatrics and human nutrition Columbia U. Coll. Physicans and Surgeons, N.Y.C., 1973-77; sr. nutritionist Best Foods, Union, N.J., 1977-79, prin. nutritionist, 1979-83, nutrition rsch. assoc., 1983—; $D, $D; mem. steering com. N.J. Nutrition Coun., 1978-82, Internat. Life Sci. Inst., Washington, 1986—. Contbr. articles to sci. jours. Chmn bd. Congregation Beth Simchat Torah, 1987-88. Fellow Mataheson Found., 1973-74. Fellow Am. Heart Assn., Am. Coll. Nutrition, Am. Oil Chemists Soc. (pres. N.E. region 1987-88, merit award 1989, chair health and nutrition divsn. 1994-96, chair divsn. coun. 1995-96), Am. Inst. Nutrition, Inst. Food Technologists, Soc. for Nutrition Edn. Democrat. Office: Best Foods 150 Pierce St Somerset NJ 08873-4185

BIEBUYCK, JULIEN FRANCOIS, anesthesiologist, educator; b. South Africa, Feb. 2, 1935; came to U.S., 1971, naturalized, 1985; s. Lucien Jean and Drix J. B.; m. Jeanette A. Sumner, May 10, 1961; children: Gavin L., Richard M., Clare E. M.B., U. Capetown, 1959; D.Phil., Oxford U., Eng., 1971. Diplomat Am. Bd. Anesthesiology. Nuffield scholar Oxford U., Eng., 1969-71; asst. prof. anesthesiology Harvard Med. Sch., Mass. Gen. Hosp., Boston, 1971-76; Eric A. Walker prof., chmn dept. anesthesia Pa. State U. Coll. Medicine, Hershey, 1977—, assoc. dean for acad. affairs, 1991—; mem. anesthetic and life support drugs adv. com. FDA, 1995—; faculty fellow, liaison com. on med. edn. Pa. State U. Coll. Medicine, 1995—. Mem. editorial bd. Anesthesiology; co-editor Current Opinion in Anaesthesiology; contbr. chpts. to books, articles to med. jours. Med. Found. fellow, 1972-76. Fellow Royal Coll. Anaesthetists (hon.), Australian and New Zealand Coll. Anaesthetists (hon.); mem. AMA, Assn. Univ. Anesthesiologists, Am. Soc. Anesthesiologists (com. on rsch.), Am. Physiol. Soc., Soc. Acad. Anesthesia Chmn. (past pres.), Coun. Acad. Socs. of Assn., Am. Med. Colls., Biochem. Soc. (London), Soc. Parenteral Nutrition, Soc. Neurosci., Soc. Neurosurg. Anesthesia, Pa. Med. Soc., Trinity Coll. Club, Harvard Club, Alpha Omega Alpha. Home: 2261 Gates Rd Hershey PA 17033-9513 Office: Pa State Univ Coll Medicine Milton S Hershey Med Ctr Dept Anesthesia Hershey PA 17033

BIEGEL, DAVID ELI, social worker, educator; b. N.Y.C., July 3, 1946; s. Jack and Estelle (Lentin) B.; B.A., CCNY, 1967; M.S.W., U. Md., 1970, Ph.D., 1982; m. Margaret S. Smoot, Jan. 31, 1976; 1 child, Geoffrey S. Field coordinator United Farm Workers, AFL-CIO, Balt., 1971; exec. dir. Junction, Inc., Westminster, Md., 1971-72; dir. office planning and program devel. Catholic Charities, Balt., 1973-76; center asso., dir. neighborhood and family services project for U. So. Calif., Washington Public Affairs Center, 1976-80; asst. prof. social work U. Pitts., 1980-85, assoc. prof., 1985-86; Henry L. Zucker Prof. social work practice, prof. sociology Mandel Sch. Applied Social Scis., Case Western Reserve Univ., 1987—, co-dir. Ctr. for Practice Innovations, 1991—; co-dir. Cuyahoga County Community Mental Health Rsch. Inst., Mandel Sch. Applied Social Sci. Case Western Reserve Univ., 1994—. cons. Vol. VISTA, Raton, N.Mex. and Balt., 1967-70 active Big Bros. Am., Balt., 1974-77. N.Y. State Incentive scholar, 1963-64; VISTA Fellows Program fellow, 1968-70. Fellow Gerontol. Soc. Am.; mem. APHA, Acad. Cert. Social Workers, Am. Orthopsychiat. Assn., Council Social Work Edn., Nat. Assn. Social Workers. Democrat. Jewish. Co-editor: Innovations in Practice and Service Delivery with Vulnerable Populations Series, Family Caregiving Applications Series; contbr. articles to profl. jours., books; coauthor 10 books.

BIEGEL, EILEEN MAE, hospital executive; b. Eau Claire, Wis., Nov. 13, 1937; d. Ewald Frederic and Emma Antonia (Conrad) Weggen; student Dist. One Tech. Inst., 1974, also part time, corr. student U. Wis., Madison; grad. mgmt. seminars; student Upper Iowa U., 1984—; m. James O. Biegel, Oct. 6, 1956; children: Jeffrey Alan, John William. Exec. sec. to pres. Broadcaster Services, Inc., Eau Claire, Wis., 1969-74; exec. sec. to exec. v.p. Am. Nat. Bank, Eau Claire, 1975-77; exec. asst. to pres. Luther Hosp., Eau Claire, 1977—, asst. corporate sec., 1984—; mem. exec. staff, 1985—; asst. corp. sec. Luther Health Care Corp., 1984—; mem. secretarial adv. council Dist. One Tech. Sch. 1975—; corp. sec. Northwest Health Ventures, 1988-92, bd. dirs. State pres. Future Homemakers Am., 1955; mem. governance com. Wis. Hosp. Assn. Cert. profl. sec., 1980; sec. bd. dirs. Chestnut Properties. Mem. Eau Claire Womens Network (founder, mem. steering com.), Profl. Secs. Internat. (chmn. goals and priorities com., pres. Eau Claire chpt. 1982-83), Wis. Hosp. Assn. (gov. com.). Home: 4707 Tower Dr Eau Claire WI 54703-8717 Office: 310 Chestnut St Eau Claire WI 54703-5230

BIEKER-BRADY, KRISTINA, molecular biologist; b. Fresno, Calif., Mar. 14, 1964; d. Fred William and Gayle (Van Houten) Bieker; m. David Paul Brady, July 27, 1991. BA, Swarthmore Coll., 1986; student, Harvard U., 1985-86; MA, Princeton U., 1988, PhD in Molecular Biology, 1991; JD, Boston Coll., 1996. Rsch. assoc. Whitehead Inst. for Biomed. Rsch., Cambridge, Mass., 1984-86; vis. scientist MIT, Cambridge, 1991-92; patent lawyer Fish and Richardson, Boston, 1992—. Contbr. articles to profl. jours. NIH predoctoral fellow, 1986-90; jr. fellow Soc. of Fellows, Harvard U., 1991-95. Mem. Sigma Xi. Home: 18 Carleton St Newton MA 02158-1604 Office: Fish and Richardson 225 Franklin St Boston MA 02110-2804

BIEL, LEONARD, JR., urologist; b. N.Y.C., Jan. 17, 1922; s. Leonard and Eleanor Roberta (Abrahams) B.; m. Lynn Arnstein, June 27, 1958; children: Pamela, Alix. AB, Yale U., 1943; MD, N.Y. Med. Coll., 1946. Diplomate Am. Bd. Urology. Intern Paterson (N.J.) Gen. Hosp., 1946-47; resident in surgery Flower and Fifth Ave. Hosps., N.Y.C., 1950-51, Bellevue Hosp., N.Y.C., 1951-52; resident in urology Mt. Sinai Hosp., N.Y.C., 1952-54; pvt. practice N.Y.C., 1954—; asst. attending physician Mt. Sinai Hosp., attending physician Beth Israel North, North Gen. Hosp. Capt. U.S. Army, 1947-49, ETO. Fellow ACS; mem. AMA, N.Y. Acad. Medicine, N.Y. Med. Soc., N.Y. County Med. Soc., Am. Urol. Assn. Home and Office: 114 E 90th St New York NY 10128

BIELAWSKI, REGINA MARIA, internist; b. Worcester, Mass., Sept. 15, 1957; d. Stefan and Aniela B.; m. William Gerard Dietrich, June 8, 1985; children: Catherine Ann., Elisabeth Ann. BA in Chemistry, Mount Holyoke Coll., South Hadley, Mass., 1979; MD, U. Mass., Worcester, 1983. Diplomate Am. Bd. Internal Medicine, Am. Bd. Geriatrics. Intern Albany (N.Y.) Med. Ctr. and Affiliated Hosps., 1983-84, resident, 1984-85; resident St. Vincent Hosp., Worcester, Mass., 1985-86; internist Fallon Clinic, Worcester, Mass., 1986-88; with Orange Park Internal Medicine, Fla., 1988-89; pvt. practice Orange Park, Fla., 1989—; med. dir. Heartland Health Care Ctr., Orange Park, 1990-94. Moderator Orange Park Jour. AMA Jour. Club, 1991-93. Mem. AMA, Am. Soc. Internal Medicine, Clay County Med. Soc. Office: 1895 Kingsley Ave Ste 805 Orange Park FL 32073

BIELKE, PATRICIA ANNE, psychologist; b. Bay Shore, N.Y., May 11, 1949; d. Lawrence Curtis and Marcella Elizabeth (Maize) Widdoes; m. Stephen Roy Bielke, July 10, 1971; children: Eric, Christine. BA, Carleton Coll., 1971; PhD, U. Minn., 1979. Lic. psychologist, Wis. Rsch. asst. Nat. Inst. Mental Health, Washington, 1972-74; sch. psychologist Roseville Pub. Schs., St. Paul, 1978-79; psychologist Southeastern Wis. Med. and Social Svcs., Milw., 1979-93; staff psychologist Elmbrook Meml. Hosp., 1986—; pvt. practice Brookfield, Wis., 1991—; Lic. psychologist, Wis.; cert. marriage & family therapist. Bd. dirs. LWV, Brookfield, 1984-88, Elmbrook Sch. Bd., 1989—. Mem. APA, Am. Assn. Marriage and Family Therapists. Home: 17455 Bedford Dr Brookfield WI 53045-1301 Office: 17000 W North Ave Brookfield WI 53005-4423

BIELORY, LEONARD, allergist, immunologist, medical school administrator; b. Neptune, N.J., Nov. 17, 1954; s. Max and Bessie (Spielberg) B.; m. Marilyn Miriam Gilan, July 5, 1981; children: Brett Phillip, Barry Mark, Amy Beth. BS, Lehigh U., 1976, MS, 1976, MD, N.J. Med. Sch., 1980. Intern, resident U. Md. Hosp., Balt., 1980-82; clin. assoc. NIH, Bethesda, Md., 1982-85; dir. divsn. allergy and immunology N.J. Med. Sch., Newark, 1985—, co-dir. immuno-ophthalmology svcs., 1992—; pres. med. staff Univ. Medicine and Dentistry N.J.-Univ. Hosp., 1993-95; chmn. clin. trial study sect. NIH, 1993; pres. med. staff ex-oficio mem. NIH Safety and Data Mgmt. Bd., 1993; bd. dirs Univ. Health Care Corp., acting med. dir., 1995—. Contbr. rsch. papers to profl. jours., chpt. to books. Bd. dirs. Congregation Israel, Springfield, N.J., 1988. Recipient Young Investigator award Am. Acad. Allergy and Immunology, 1985; Schering Corp. Travel grantee, 1985. Fellow ACP, Am. Acad. Allergy and Immunology; mem. Med. Soc. N.J.; Nat. Inst. of Health Clin. Treatment Study Section (chmn. 1993). Jewish. Office: NJ Med Sch Divsn Allergy & Immunology 90 Bergen St Ste 4700 Newark NJ 07103-2441

BIENENSTOCK, JOHN, physician, educator; b. Budapest, Hungary, Oct. 6, 1936; s. Maurice and Anne (Horn) B.; m. Dody Sanders, Nov. 24, 1961; children: Jimson Andrew, Adam Sebastian, Robin Anne. MB, BS, Westminster Med. Sch., London, 1960; postgrad., Harvard Med. Sch., 1964-66, SUNY, Buffalo, 1966-68. Fellow Harvard U. Med. Sch., Boston, 1964-66; Buswell fellow SUNY, Buffalo, 1966-68, asst. rsch. prof. medicine, 1967-68; asst. prof. medicine McMaster U., Hamilton, Ont., Can., 1968-74, assoc. dean rsch., 1972-78, prof. medicine and pathology, 1974—, chmn. dept. pathology, 1978-89, v.p. health scis., 1989—, dean health scis., 1992—; founder AB Biol. Supply Inc., 1977, Agritech Rsch. Inc., 1980; D.W. Harrington lectr. SUNY, Buffalo, 1986, Rayne vis. prof. U. Western Australia, Perth, 1987; cons. WHO, Geneva, 1970—; also cons. various pharm. cos. Editor: Immunology of Lung, 1984, Mast Cell Differentiation, 1986, Recent Advances in Mucosal Immunology, 1987, Handbook of Mucosal Immunology, 1994; contbr. over 350 articles to sci. jours. Chmn. bd. Dundas Valley (Ont.) Sch. Art, 1984-86; chmn., bd. dirs. Can. Red Cross Soc.; chmn. adv. com. nat. blood svcs., 1985-90. Recipient Purkynje medal Assn. Czechoslovak Socs., Prague, 1989, Ross A. McIntyre gold medal U. Nebr., Omaha, 1989. Fellow RCP (Can.), RCP (London), Royal Soc. (Can.); mem. Swiss Soc. Allergy and Immunology (hon.), , Can. Soc. Immunology (pres. 1985-87), Assn. Am. Physicians, Am. Soc. Clin. Investigation, Am. Thoracic Soc., Internat. Union Immunological Socs. (mem. coun.), Soc. Mucosal Immunology (pres. 1990-92), Coll. Internat. Allergologicum (pres. elect 1994). Jewish. Home: 50 Albert St, Dundas, ON Canada L9H 2X1 Office: McMaster U Faculty Health Scis, 1200 W Main St, Hamilton, ON Canada L8N 3Z5*

BIERENBAUM, MARVIN LEONARD, cardiology educator, consultant; b. Phila., Aug. 30, 1926; s. Bernhard and Anna (Eckert) B.; m. Nettie Bella Eiser, July 1, 1951; children: Michele Bierenbaum Reichstein, Robert. BS in Biology, Rutgers U., 1947; MD, Hahnemann Med. Coll., 1953; postgrad. in Epidemiology, The London Hosp., 1965. Diplomate Am. Bd. Internal Medicine. Intern Beth Israel Hosp., Newark, 1953-54; resident VA Hosp., Bklyn., 1954-57; cons. Montclair, N.J., 1957—; coord. and sr. pub. health physician heart disease control program N.J. State Dept. Health, Montclair, 1957-81; dir. Kenneth L. Jordan Cardiac Rsch. Group, Montclair, 1959—; clin. assoc. prof. medicine U. Medicine and Dentistry N.J., 1965—; dir. dept. medicine St. Vincent's Hosp., Montclair, 1969-82; med. dir. Disability Determination Svc., 1985-88; prof. community medicine Seton Hall U., South Orange, N.J., 1988—; resident cons. Netherlands Heart Assn., 1976-77, cons. N.J. Commn. for the Blind, 1981-85; regional med. adv. Social Security Adminstrn., 1973-85; hon. prof. medicine Chongqing Med. Sch., People's Republic China, 1987. Contbr. over 150 articles to profl. jours. Fellow coun. epidemiology Am. Heart Assn., fellow coun. atherosclerosis. With U.S. Army, 1945-46. Milbank Fund fellow, 1965. Fellow ACP, Am. Coll. Cardiology, Am. Soc. Clin. Nutrition, Am. Coll. Nutrion; mem. Am. Fedn. Clin. Rsch., Am. Inst. Nutrition, Am. Pub. Health Assn., Essex County (N.J.) Med. Soc. Office: Kenneth L Jordan Heart Fund 48 Plymouth St Montclair NJ 07042-2625

BIERKER, SUSAN, psychotherapist; b. Ft. Wayne, Ind., Jan. 9, 1939; d. Garland E. and Margaret D. (Mooney) Brenneman; m. George Bierker, Apr. 9, 1960 (div. 1977); children: Michael, Eric, Stephen, Matthew. BSW, San Francisco State U., 1960; MSW, Temple U., 1980. Lic. social worker, Pa.; diplomate in clin. social work Nat. Registrar of Clin. Social Workers. Supr. Children of Youth Svcs., Media, Pa., 1974-87; pvt. practice Devon, Pa., 1987—. Author: About Sexual Abuse. Mem. NASW, Acad. Cert. Social Workers. Democrat. Home: 317 Devonshire Rd Devon PA 19333-1060

BIES, ROGER DAVID, cardiologist; b. Athens, Ohio, May 28, 1956; s. Ronald Kenneth and Genivieve H. (Parlow) B.; m. Rhonda Jean Pope; children: Lucas, Tyler, Wade. BA, U. Colo., 1979, MD, 1986. Intern, resident U. Pitts., 1986-89; fellow in cardiology Baylor Coll. Medicine, Houston, 1987-92; asst. prof. medicine U. Colo. Health Scis. Ctr., Denver, 1993—; vis. asst. prof. Inst. Molecular Genetics, Houston, 1993; assoc. dir. cardiology U. Colo. Health Sci. Ctr., 1995—; dir. heart failure/transplant clinic VA Med. Ctr., Denver, 1993—, dir. pacemaker clinic, 1993—. Author: A Primer of Molecular Biology, 1992; contbr. articles to profl. jours., chpts. to books. Fellow Am. Coll. Cardiology; mem. Am. Fedn. Clin. Rsch. (grantee), Am. Heart Assn. Office: VA Med Ctr 1055 Clermont St Denver CO 80220

BIESELE, JOHN JULIUS, biologist, educator; b. Waco, Tex., Mar. 24, 1918; s. Rudolph Leopold and Anna Emma (Jahn) B.; m. Marguerite Calfee McAfee, July 29, 1943 (dec. 1991); children: Marguerite Anne, Diana Terry, Elizabeth Jane; m. Esther Aline Eakin, Mar. 9, 1992. B.A. with highest honors, U. Tex., 1939, Ph.D., 1942. Fellow Internat. Cancer Research Found., U. Tex., 1942-43, Barnard Skin and Cancer Hosp., St. Louis, also; U. Pa., 1943-44, instr. zoology, 1943-44; temporary research assoc. dept. genetics Carnegie Instn. of Washington, Cold Spring Harbor, 1944-46; research assoc. biology dept. Mass. Inst. Tech., 1946-47; asst. Sloan-Kettering Inst. Cancer Research, 1946-47, research fellow, 1947, assoc., 1947-55, head cell growth sect., div. exptl. chemotherapy, 1947-58, mem., 1955-58, assoc. scientist div., 1959-78; asst. prof. anatomy Cornell U. Med. Sch., 1950-52; assoc. prof. biology Sloan-Kettering div. Cornell U. Grad. Sch. Med. Scis., 1952-55, prof. biology, 1955-58; prof. zoology, mem. grad. faculty U. Tex., Austin, 1958-78; also mem. faculty U. Tex. (Coll. Pharmacy), 1969-71, prof. edn., 1973-78; prof. emeritus zoology U. Tex., Austin, 1978—; cons. cell biology M.D. Anderson Hosp. and Tumor Inst., U. Tex. at Houston, 1958-72; dir. Genetics Found., 1959-78; mem. cell biology study sect. NIH, 1958-63; Sigma Xi lectr. NYU Grad. Sch. Arts and Scis., 1957; Mendel lectr. St. Peter's Coll., Jersey City, 1958; featured spkr. on first Earth Day, Old Westbury Campus of N.Y. Inst. Tech., 1970; Mendel Club lectr. Canisius Coll., Buffalo, 1971; mem. adv. com. rsch. etiology of cancer Am. Cancer Soc., 1961-64, pres. Travis County unit, 1966, mem. adv. com. on personnel for rsch., 1969-73; counsellor Cancer Internat. Rsch. Coop., Inc., 1962-90; mem. cancer rsch. tng. com. Nat. Cancer Inst., 1969-72; gen. chmn. Conf. Advancement Sci. and Math. Teaching, 1966. Author: Mitotic Poisons and the Cancer Problem, 1958; mem. editorial bd. Year Book Cancer, 1959-72; mem. editorial adv. bd. Cancer Rsch., 1960-64, assoc. editor, 1969-72; cons. editor: Am. Jour. Mental Deficiency, 1963-68; mem. editorial bd. The Jour. of Applied Nutrition, 1987-91; contbr. articles to profl. jours. Research Career award NIH, 1962, 67, 72, 77. Fellow N.Y., Tex. acads. scis., AAAS; mem. Am. Assn. Cancer Research (dir. 1960-63), Am. Soc. Cell Biology, Am. Inst. Biol. Scis., Phi Beta Kappa, Sigma Xi (pres. Tex. chpt. 1963-64), Phi Eta Sigma, Phi Kappa Phi. Home: 2500 Great Oaks Pky Austin TX 78756-2908

BIFANE, JAMES L., health information manager; b. Johnstown, Pa., June 2, 1952; s. James M. and Alice (Davidson) B.; m. Deborah E. Good, June 16, 1979 (div. Mar. 1996); children: Vincent J., Angela D. BA, U. Pitts., 1974; BS, York Coll. Pa., 1979; MBA, U. Toledo, 1985. Registered record adminstr. Asst. dir. med. records U. Utah Med. Ctr., Salt Lake City, 1979-80; dir. med. records St. Charles Hosp., Toledo, 1980-86; dir. clin. data svcs. Good Samaritan Hosp. and Health Ctr., Dayton, Ohio, 1986-89; dir. health info. svcs. Meridia Hillcrest Hosp., Mayfield, Ohio, 1989-93; mgr. health info. svcs. Pa. State U. Hosp., Hershey Med. Ctr., 1993—; pres. Northwest Ohio Med. Bd. Assn., Toledo, 1982-84; mem. adv. bd. Sinclair Tech. Coll., Dayton, 1987-89. Contbr., supporter Elisabethtown (Pa.) Area Recreation Coun., 1993—, Elizabethtown Boys Club, 1993—; mem. fin. rev. com. West Geauga Sch. Dist., Chesterland, Ohio, 1991-92. Mem. Ohio Hosp. Assn. (polit. action com. 1986-96), Northwest Ohio Health Info. Mgmt. Assn. (v.p. 1992-93), Greater Dayton Area Hosp. Assn. (chmn. med. records com. 1988-89), Acacia Nat. Fraternity (life, pres. cons.), Hershey Italian Lodge, SAR, Alpha Chi. Republican. Office: Pa State Hershey Med Ctr PO Box 850 Hershey PA 17033-0850

BIGBY, MICHAEL ELLIOTT, dermatologist; b. Glen Cove, N.Y., Feb. 13, 1949; s. Laura Odessa Bigby; m. Judyann Rollins, Sept. 4, 1971; children: Kenan Ali, Naima Alexis. BA, Princeton U., 1971; MD, Harvard U., 1975. Intern, resident in medicine Mass. Gen. Hosp., Boston, 1975-78; instr. medicine U. Wash., Seattle, 1978-81, asst. clin. prof., 1981; dermatology resident Harvard Med. Sch., Boston, 1982-85, rsch. assoc., 1985-88, asst. prof. dermatology, 1991—; assoc. dermatologist Beth Israel Hosp., Boston, 1985—; asst. immunology Mass. Gen. Hosp., Boston, 1988-96; mem. adv. bd. dermatology sect. U.S. Pharm., Washington, 1985-95. Editor: Manual of Clinical Problems in Dermatology, 1992; book rev. editor Archives of Dermatology, 1985-93, editl. bd., 1993—; editl. bd. Jour. Am. Acad. of Dermatology, 1995—. V.p. Lupus Found. Am., Newton, Mass., 1991, pres., 1992. Lt. USPHS, 1978-81. Mem. Soc. Investigative Dermatology, Am. Assn. Immunologists, Sigma Xi, Phi Beta Kappa. Office: Dept of Dermatology Beth Israel Hosp 330 Brookline Ave Boston MA 02215

BIGELOW, LLEWELLYN BARRY, physician, psychiatrist, researcher; b. Ann Arbor, Mich., June 4, 1936; s. Barry and Marjorie (Moore) B.; m. Deborah Ellis, Apr. 7, 1963; children: Isabel, Anna. BA, Harvard U., Cambridge, Mass., 1957; MD, Harvard U., Boston, 1961. Diplomate Am.

Bd. Psychiatry and Neurology. Internship U. Ill. Rsch. Hosp., Chgo., 1961-62, med. resident, 1962-63; resident in psychiatry N.Y. Hosp. Payne Whitney Clinic, N.Y.C., 1963-66; staff assoc. NIH, Washington, 1966-68; permanent mem. staff Intramural Rsch. Program NIMH, Washington, 1969—, assoc. clin. dir., 1984-87, sr. scientist, 1987—; pvt. practice (part-time) Alexandria, Va., 1982—; clin. prof. psychiatry, George Washington U. Med. Sch., Washington, 1983—; cons. U.S. Dept. Justice, Washington, 1985—. Contbr. over 70 articles to profl. publs. Recipient Meritorious Svc. award USPH, Washington, 1985. Fellow Am. Psychiatric Assn.; mem. Soc. Biol. Psychiatry, Boylston Soc. Harvard Med. Sch. Home: 423 S Lee St Alexandria VA 22314 Office: NIMH Neurosci Ctr Ste 1200 2700 Martin Luther King Jr Ave SE Washington DC 20032-2698

BIGGER, JOHN THOMAS, JR., physician, educator; b. Cambridge, Mass., Jan. 17, 1935; s. John Thomas and Wilma Rebecca (Rushing) B.; m. Susan T. Harrison, 1982; children: Deborah Lynn, Nicholas Alexander. A.B., Emory U., 1955; M.D., Med. Coll. Ga., 1960. Diplomate: Am. Bd. Internal Medicine. Intern Bellevue Hosp., N.Y.C., 1960-61; resident in internal medicine Columbia U., 1961-64, fellow in cardiology, 1964-67, asst. prof. medicine and pharmacology, 1967-72, assoc. prof., 1972-75, prof., 1975—; dir. cardiology Columbia-Presbyn. Med. Ctr., 1978-87; attending physician Presbyn. Hosp., N.Y.C., 1975—; mem. pharmacology study sect., NIH, 1972-75, mem. cardiovascular and renal study sect., 1986-88. Mem. editorial bd. Circulation, 1970-76, 82-91, 93—, Jour. Pharmacology and Therapeutics, 1974-92, Stroke, 1976-80, Am. Jour. Medicine, 1979-89, Pharmacology, 1978-92, Jour. Cardiovascular Pharmacology, 1979-90, Am. Heart Jour., 1989—, Am. Jour. Cardiology, 1990—; contbr. articles to profl. jours. Elder Madison Ave. Presbyn. Ch., N.Y.C. With USN, 1962-63. Fellow N.Y. Acad. Scis.; mem. Assn. Univ. Cardiologists, Am. Coll. Cardiology, ACP, Am. Soc. Pharmacology and Exptl. Therapeutics, Am. Physiol. Soc., Biophys. Soc., N.Y. Heart Assn., Am. Heart Assn., Assn. Am. Physicians, Am. Soc. Clin. Investigation, Am. Fedn. Clin. Research, Coalition Against Sudden Cardiac Death, Alpha Omega Alpha. Democrat. Office: 630 W 168th St New York NY 10032-3702

BIGGERSTAFF, RANDY LEE, medical products executive, sports medicine rehabilitation consultant; b. Buffalo, Feb. 13, 1951; s. Dever Poole and Mary Martha (Smith) B.; m. Sue Ann Knobeloch, Nov. 26, 1977; children: Nicholas Lee, Amy Elizabeth. BS, U. Mo., 1973; MS in Health Mgmt., Lindenwood Coll., 1995. Dist. athletic tng. tchr. Granite City (Ill.) Community Sch. Dist., 1973-77; athletic trainer St. Louis Hummers, Profl. Softball Team, Valley Park, Mo., 1978-79; founder-ptnr., clinic dir. St. Louis Sports Medicine Clinic, Chesterfield, Mo., 1977-82; founder, clin. dir. Iowa Orthopedic Sports Medicine Clinic, Urbandale, 1982-84; clinic dir. St. Louis Orthopedic Sports Medicine Clinic, Chesterfield, 1984-86; ptnr., v.p. St. Louis Rehab. Sports Clinic, Crystal City, Mo., 1986-88; adminstr., regional dir. St. Louis Orthopedic Sports Medicine Clinic, Chesterfield, 1989-90; coord., trainer, cons. St. Luke's Hosp., Chesterfield, 1990-92; v.p. D. P. Biggs Cons. Ltd., Inc., 1992-93; pres. Phoenix Sports Med. Systems, St. Louis, 1993—; cons. Brentwood & Creve Coeur Skating, St. Louis, 1986—, Gateway Athletics, St. Louis, 1984—; med. coord. Show-Me-Bowl, St. Louis, 1979-82, Summer Biathalon Series, Essex Junction, Vt., 1989—. Contbr. articles to profl. jours. Sec. bd. overseers Lindenwood Coll., St. Charles, Mo., 1992-93, vice chmn., 1993-95, chair, 1995—, bd. dirs., 1995—. Inducted to Mo. Sports Medicine Hall of Fame, 1995. Mem. Nat. Athletic Trainers Assn. (cert., clin. corp. com., treas. M.A.A.T.A. dist. V), Mo. Athletic Trainer Assn. (registered, chair Hall of Fame com. 1991-94), Mid-Am. Athletic Trainers Assn. (treas.). Methodist. Home: 82 Shirecreek Ct Saint Charles MO 63303-5432 Office: Phoenix Sports Med Systems 13357 Olive St Rd Chesterfield MO 63017

BIGLAN, ANTHONY, medical educator; b. Bklyn., June 6, 1944. BA in Psychology, U. Rochester, N.Y., 1966; MA in Social Psychology, U. Ill., 1968, PhD in Social Psycology, 1971. Rsch. assoc., instr. dept. psychology U. Wash., 1969-72; vis. asst. prof. psychology U. Oreg., 1973-74, asst. prof., 1974-78, rsch. asst., 1977-78; psychologist Behavior Change Ctr., Springfield, Oreg., 1977-82; rsch. scientist Oreg. Rsch. Inst., Eugene, Oreg., 1979—; bd. dirs. Pacific Rsch. Inst., 1992—, bd. chmn., 1994. Contbr. numerous articles to profl. jours. including Jour. Behavioral Medicine, Drugs and Society, The Analyst, others. Bd. dirs. ACLU of Oreg., pres., 1989-91. Nat. Inst. of Drug Abuse grantee, 1991—, Nat. Cancer Inst. grantee, 1995-2000. Home: 2324 West 28th St Eugene OR 97405 Office: Oreg Rsch Inst 1715 Franklin Blvd Eugene OR 97403*

BIGLER, ERIN DAVID, psychology educator; b. L.A., July 9, 1949; s. Erin Boley and Natalie (Webb) B.; m. Janet Beckstrom, June 22, 1990; children: Alicia Suzanne, Erin Daniel. BS, Brigham Young U., 1971, PhD, 1974. NIH postdoctoral fellow Barrow Neurol. Inst., St. Joseph's Hosp. and Med. Ctr., Phoenix, 1975-77; asst. to prof. of psychology U. Tex., Austin, 1977-90; prof. psychology Brigham Young U., Provo, Utah, 1990—, chair dept. psychology, 1996—. Author: Diagnostic Clinical Neuropsychology, 1984, 2d edit. 1988, Neuropsychological Function and Brain Imaging, 1989, Traumatic Brain Injury, 1990, Attention Deficit Disorder, 1990, Handbook of Human Brain Function, 1995; assoc. editor: Archives of Clinical Neuropsychology, 1987—, Jour. Internat. Neuropsychol. Soc., 1994—; cons. editor: Jour. of Learning Disabilities, 1987—, Neuropsychological Review, 1989—, Psychological Assessment, 1989—. Recipient Significant Contbrn. in Head Injury Rsch. and Treatment award Tex. Psychol. Assn. and Health Care Internat., Austin, 1990, grant NIH, Phoenix, 1975-77, grant Hogg Found. Univ. Tex., Austin, 1980-82. Fellow Nat. Acad. Neuropsychology (pres. 1989-90); mem. Am. Psychol. Assn., Soc. for Neuroscience, Internat. Neuropsychological Soc. Democrat. Mem. LDS Ch. Office: Dept Psychology 1086 SWKT Brigham Young U Provo UT 84602

BIGOGNO, JAMES C., health services administrator; b. St. Louis, June 8, 1954; s. John F. and Dorothy M. (Davis) B.; m. Candie S., Aug. 21, 1976; children: Andrew, Kristopher, Landon, Tessa. B in Psychology, Washington U., St. Louis, 1976, MHA, 1978. Asst. adminstr. Christian Hosp., St. Louis, 1978-82; from asst. to sr. v.p. John C. Lincoln Hosp. and Health Ctr., Phoenix, 1981-86; CEO St. Croix Valley Meml. Hosp., St. Croix Falls, Wis., 1986-90; exec. v.p., CEO Owensboro-Daviess County Hosp., Owensboro, Ky., 1990-93; pres., CEO Howard Community Hosp., Kokomo, Ind., 1993—; preceptor Washington U. Health Adminstrn. Program; preceptor, Ind. Univ.-Purdue U. Grad. Leadership Owensboro, 1993. Fellow Am. Coll. Healthcare Execs.; mem. Rotary, Lions.

BIGOS, STANLEY JAMES, orthopedic surgery spine specialist, educator; b. Grand Island, Nebr., Jan. 20, 1946; s. Stanley Joseph and Dorothy Marie (Krumel) B.; m. Karen Marie Hartnett Graybeal, Mar. 31, 1970 (div. Feb. 1988); children: Kristen Elizabeth (dec.), Jennifer Leah, John Bradley; m. Kathleen Marie Boyle, Aug. 19, 1993. AA, Fairbury (Nebr.) Coll., 1966; BS in Phys. Therapy, U. Mo., 1970, MD, 1975. Chief phys. therapist Johnson & Carroll County Hosp., Warrensburg and Carrollton, Mo., 1970-71; clin. instr. U. Mo. Phys. Therapy, Columbia, 1972-76; surg. intern U. Mo. Med. Ctr., Columbia, 1975-76; resident orthopaedics U. Utah, Salt Lake City, 1976-80; spine fellow Alf Nachemson, Gothenburg, Sweden, Seattle, 1980-81; from asst. prof. to assoc. prof. U. Wash., Seattle, 1982-91, prof. orthopaedics, 1991—; adj. prof. environ. health, 1991—; adj. prof. Environ. Health, 1991—; founder, dir. Spine Resource Clinic, Seattle, 1985—; chmn. panel guide Agy. for Health Care Policy Rsch., Rockville, Md., 1991—; cons. U.K. Low Back Guidelines Com., 1993; guest lectr. Clemenson Lectrs., Denmark, 1993—; internat. guest lectr. in field. Author: Musculoskeletal Guide, 1983; guest editor Seminars in Spine, 1992; contbr. chpt. to book and articles to profl. jours. Co-founder, mem. Patrons Cystic Fibrosis, Seattle, 1985; pres. 65 Roses Club, Seattle, 1986-88. Named Friend of Man Wash. Gens., 1988. Fellow Am. Acad. Orthopaedic Surgeons (occupational health/outcomes com. 1989—, Kappa Delta award 1991); mem. Am. Orthopaedic Assn., N.Am. Spine Soc., Western Orthopaedic Assn., Internat. Assn. Study of Pain, Internat. Soc. Study Lumber Spine (west coast rep. 1987-91), Patrons Cystic Fibrosis (v.p. 1985-86, award of merit 1987). Office: U Wash Dept Orthopaedics Box 356500 Seattle WA 98195

BIGOT, JEAN-MICHEL ROGER, radiologist, educator; b. Paris, July 26, 1935; s. Alfred Georges and Simone (Cornevin) B.; m. Anne Le Guennec, Mar. 5, 1965; children: Christophe, Eric, Justine Alexandra. Student, Le Havre, Janson de Sailly, France, 1950-52; MD, U. Paris, 1968. Externe Hosp. Paris., 1956-62, intern, 1964-68, chief clinic, 1968-74; radiologist Hosp. St. Antoine, Paris, 1974-76; chief radiology service Hosp. Tenon, Paris, 1976—; prof. U. Paris, 1974—. Contbr. over 210 artices to French and fgn. med. jours. Mem. various French and European med. socs., Radiol. Soc. N.Am., Am. Roentgen Ray Soc., European Congress Radiology (sci. sec. 1983), Internat. Congress Radiology (sec. gen. 1989). Home: 16 Rue Fosses Saint Jacques, 75005 Paris France Office: Hopital Tenon, 4 rue de la Chine, 75020 Paris France

BIHARI, BERNARD, physician, scientist; b. Bronx, Nov. 11, 1931; s. Henry Jacob and Martha (May) B.; m. Margery Surle, Feb. 4, 1961 (div. 1975); children: Tamar, Aaron. AB, Cornell U., 1953; MD, Harvard U., 1957. Intern Beth Israel Hosp., Boston, 1957-58, resident in medicine, 1958-59; resident in neurology Mass. Gen. Hosp., Boston, 1959-60; resident in psychiatry Columbia Presbyn. Med. Ctr., N.Y.C., 1962-65; dir. drug addiction svc. Beth Israel Hosp., N.Y.C., 1969-72, dir. alcohol treatment program, 1972-75; commr. N.Y.C. Addictions Svc. Agy., 1975-78; dep. commr. N.Y.C. Dept. Health, 1978-80; assoc. prof. psychiatry SUNY, Bklyn., 1980—; dir. Kings County Addictive Disease Hosp., Bklyn., 1980-89; exec. dir. Community Rsch. Initiative, N.Y.C., 1989-91; med. dir. Found. for Integrative Rsch., 1992—; bd. dirs. Progenics, Inc., N.Y.C.; chmn. bd. dirs. AIDS Rsch. Treatment Inst. Corp., N.Y.C. 1st Lt. USPHS, 1960-62. Office: 29 W 15th St New York NY 10011-6810

BIHARI, MICHAEL, physician researcher; b. N.Y.C., Apr. 1, 1941; s. Henry and Martha (May) B.; m. Marion Sieder, Sept. 7, 1969; 1 child, Jonathan David. BA, U. Pa., 1962; MD, U. Chgo., 1966. Resident in pediatrics U. Chgo., 1966-69, fellow in pediat. nephrology, 1971-72; pediatrician Martin Luther King, Jr. Health Ctr., Bronx, N.Y., 1972-74; dir. Valentine Lane Family Practice, Yonkers, N.Y., 1974-80; dir. health ctr. Bronx Lebanon Hosp., 1980-86; med. dir., v.p. managed care Empire Blue Cross Blue Shield, N.Y.C., 1986-92; chief med. officer MD Health Plan, North Haven, Conn., 1992-93; med. dir. Aetna Health Plan N.Y., Purchase, 1994-96; sr. med. dir. Schering Plough, Kenilworth, N.J., 1996—. Maj. U.S. Army, 1969-71. Fellow Am. Acad. Pediatrics; mem. Am. Coll. Physican Execs. Office: Schering Labs 2000 Galloping Hill Rd Kenilworth NY 07033

BIHLDORFF, JOHN PEARSON, hospital director; b. Boston, Aug. 3, 1945; s. Carl Birger and Martha Bowling (McCandless) B.; AB, Harvard U., 1969; MPH, Yale U., 1971; m. Jane Sargent Lyman, Mar. 30, 1968; children: Jennifer, Nathan, David. With McMaster U. Med. Center, Hamilton, Ont., Can., 1971-77, assoc. exec. dir., 1975-77; dir. program planning, asst. prof. div. med. adminstrn. Vanderbilt U. Med. Center and Sch. Medicine, 1977-78; assoc. hosp. dir., COO U. Conn. Health Center-John Dempsey Hosp., Farmington, Conn., 1978-81; asst. exec. dir. U. Conn. Health Center, Farmington, 1981-82, hosp. dir., 1982-86; pres., CEO St. Luke's Health Found. and Hosp., New Bedford Mass., 1986-91; pres., CEO Newton-Wellesley Hosp. and NeWell Health System, Newton, Mass., 1991—; chmn. bd. dirs. VHA of Mass., Inc.; chmn. bd. dirs. VHA Healthfront; bd. dirs. Tufts Assocs. Health Plan, 1994-96. Home: 107 Elm St Canton MA 02021-1255

BILAK, MYRON, psychologist, consultant; b. Lorain, Ohio, Sept. 23, 1951; s. Wolodymyr and Jaroslawa (Drohomyrecka) B.; m. Sheila Moffatt, Nov. 27, 1982; children: Andrew Joseph, Michael Alexander. BA, Case Western Res. U., 1973; PhD, U. Fla., 1981. Lic. psychologist. Psychologist Gainesville, Fla., 1981—. Mem. Am. Psychol. Assn., Fla. Psychol. Assn. (treas. 1987—), Fla. Soc. Clin. Hypnosis (assoc.), Coun. Nat. Register Health Svc. Providers in Psychology. Ukrainian Catholic. Office: Behavioral Health Assocs 2631 NW 41st St Ste D1 Gainesville FL 32606-6689

BILANIUK, LARISSA TETIANA, neuroradiologist, educator; b. Ukraine, July 15, 1941; came to U.S., 1951; d. Yaroslav and Myroslava (Hryculak) Zubal; m. Oleksa-Myron Bilaniuk, Nov. 14, 1964; children: Larissa Indira, Laada Myroslava. BA, Wayne State U., 1961, MD, 1965. Diplomate Am. Bd. Radiology (cert. neuroradiology 1996). Resident in radiology Hosp. of U. Pa., Phila., 1966-70; fellow Fondation Ophtalmologique, Paris, 1972; assoc. in radiology U. Pa. Sch. Medicine, Phila., 1973-74, asst. prof., 1974-79, assoc. prof., 1979-82, prof., 1982—; with Children's Hosp. of Phila., 1992—; reviewer grants rsch. NIH, Washington, 1983-86, St. Goran lectr. Karolinska Inst., Stockholm, 1984; vis. prof. Grosshadern Clinics, U. Munich, 1988, Inst. Med. Radiology, Kharkiv, Ukraine, 1996; invited lectr. USSR, 1976, 90, People's Republic China, 1977, France, 1980, 82, 89, 94, 96, Japan, 1984, 90, Swden, 1984, 92, Eng., 1985, The Netherlands, 1985, Italy, 1986, 87, 90, 92, Germany, 1987, 95, Chile, 1993, Australia, 1995. Co-editor 3 radiology books; contbr. over 200 articles on radiology to med. jours. and chpts. to books. Rsch. fellow Cancer Rsch. Ctr., Heidelberg, Fed. Republic Germany, 1967-68. Fellow Am. Coll. Radiology; mem. Radiol. Soc. N.Am., Am. Soc. Neuroradiology, European Soc. Neuroradiology, Soc. for Pediatric Radiology, Soc. Magnetic Resonance in Medicine, Ukrainian Med. Assn. N.Am., Sigma Xi. Office: Childrens Hosp of Phila 324 S 34th St Philadelphia PA 19104-4345

BILDER, ROBERT MARTIN, JR., neuropsychologist; b. Summit, N.J., Oct. 25, 1956; s. Robert M. Sr. and Sally Elizabeth (Link) B. AB, Columbia U., 1978; PhD, CUNY, 1984. Lic. psychologist, N.Y., 1986. Neuropsychologist, asst. rsch. dir. Creedmoor Psychiat. Ctr., N.Y.C., 1983-87; asst. profl. psychologist Columbia Presbyn. Med. Ctr., N.Y.C., 1987-88; chief clin. neuropsychology Hillside Hosp., Glen Oaks, N.Y., 1988—; cognitive assessment specialist N.Y. Inst. for Aging, 1982-83; rsch. scientist N.Y. State Psychiatric Inst. & Hosp., 1982-83, rsch. assoc., 1984-86, dept. chief, 1986-87; instr. dept. psychiatry Columbia U., 1984-87; adj. asst. prof. CUNY, 1987—; asst. prof. psychiatry Albert Einstein Coll. Medicine, Yeshiva U., 1989-95, assoc. prof., 1995—; mem. adv. com. NIMH. Author book chpts., abstracts and presentations in field; contbr. articles, revs. to profl. jours. Mem. AAAS, APA, Am. Psychopathol. Assn., Am. Coll. Neurol. Psychiatry, Internat. Neuropsychol. Soc., Soc. Rsch. Psychopathology, N.Y. Acad. Scis., N.Y. Neuropsychology Group, N.Y. State Psychol. Assn., Soc. Biol. Psychiatry. Office: Hillside Hosp Rsch PO Box 38 Floral Park NY 11004-0038

BILES, JOHN ALEXANDER, pharmacology educator, chemistry educator; b. Del Norte, Colo., May 4, 1923; s. John Alexander and Lillie (Willis) B.; m. Margaret Pauline Off, June 19, 1943; children: Paula M. (Mrs. Patrick Murphy), M. Suzanne. B.S., U. Colo., 1944, Ph.D. (AEC fellow), 1949. Prof. pharm. chem. Midwestern U., 1949-50; asst. prof. pharm. chem. Ohio State U., 1950-52, U. So. Calif., Los Angeles, 1952-53; assoc. prof. U. So. Calif., 1953-57, prof., 1957—, dean, prof. pharm. scis., 1968-94, John Stauffer dean's chair in pharmacy, 1988-94; John Biles professorship, 1994—; bd. dirs. Marion Merrell Dow; cons. Allergan Pharms., 1953-68, Region IX Bur. Health Manpower Edn., Health Resources Adminstrn., 1973, Region X, 1974, Region VI, 1975, VA Ctrl. Office Pharmacy Svcs.; mem. Nat. Adv. Coun., Edn. for Health Professions, 1970-71, nat. study commn. on pharmacy, 1972-75; mem. adv. panel on pharmacy for study costs of educating profls. Nat. Acad. Scis., Inst. Medicine, 1973; mem. interdisciplinary tng. in health scis. com. Bur. Health Manpower Edn., 1972, post contrn. evaluation com., 1972, health facilities survey com., 1971; mem. adv. coun. Howard U. Coll. Pharmacy, 1985-90; bd. grants Am. Found. for Pharm. Edn., 1996—. Reviewer: Jour. of AMA, 1982-90. Bd. grantes Am. Found. Pharm. Edn., 1996—. Recipient Lehn and Fink Scholarship award, 1945, S.C. Assos. award for excellence in teaching, 1962. Fellow Acad. Pharm. Scis., Am. Assn. Pharm. Scientists; mem. Am., Cal. pharm. assns., Am. Cancer Soc. (mem. sci. adv. com. Los Angeles County), Am. Assn. Colls. Pharmacy (study commn. on pharmacy 1973-75, pres. 1990-91), Nat. Adv. Health Svcs. Coun. (bur. health svcs. rsch. 1974), Phi Kappa Phi. Office: U So Calif Sch Pharmacy 1985 Zonal Ave Los Angeles CA 90033-1058

BILFINGER, THOMAS VICTOR, surgeon, educator; b. Ridgewood, N.J., May 4, 1952; s. Victor Wilhelm and Heidi Erika (Muser) B.; m. Celia Betty Dameron; children: Elizabeth, Christine. MD, U. Zurich, Switzerland, 1978, ScD, 1979. Intern U. Chgo., 1980-81, rsch. fellow, 1981-82; resident in surgery U. Tex. Med. Br., Galveston, 1982-86, resident in cardiovascular surgery, 1986-88, instr. in surgery, 1988-89; asst. prof. surgery SUNY, Stony Brook, 1989-92, assoc. prof. surgery, 1992—; bd. dirs. cardiovascular intensive care unit SUNY, Stony Brook. Co-author: Evaluation of the Cardiac Surgical Candidate, 1992; mem. editl. bd. Advances in Neuroimmunology; contbr. articles to profl. jours. Recipient Rsch. grant U. Chgo., 1981, Rsch. grant Eli Lilly, 1989, Rsch. grant NIH, 1991. Fellow ACS, Am. Coll. Cardiology, Am. Coll. Chest Physicians; mem. Assn. for Acad. Surgery, Soc. Critical Care Medicine, Swiss Soc. Thoracic and Cardiovasc. Surgery, Soc. Thoracic Surgery. Office: SUNY Stony Brook Health Sc Ctr T19 Rm 080 Stony Brook NY 11794

BILFIUGER, THOMAS VICTOR, surgeon, researcher; b. Ridgewood, N.J., May 4, 1952; s. Victor W. and Heidi E. (Muses) B.; m. Celia B. Dameson, Aug. 10, 1988; children: Christine, Elizabeth. MD, U. Zurich, 1978, ScD, 1979. Diplomate Am. Bd. Surgery, Am. Bd. Thoracic Surgery. Intern U. Chgo., 1980-81, rsch. fellow, 1981-82; resident in surgery U. Tex. Med. Br., Galveston, 1982-86, cardiothoracic resident, 1986-88, instr. cardiothoracic surgery, 1988-89; asst. prof. SUNY, Stony Brook, 1989-93, assoc. prof., 1993—; rsch. assoc. SUNY, Old Westbury, 1993—. Editl. bd. Advances in Neuroimmunology, 1994—; contbr. over 50 articles to profl. jours. Grantee NIH, 1992, SUNY, 1994. Fellow ACS, Am. Coll. Cardiology, Am. Coll. Chest Physicians; mem. Soc. Thoracic Surgeons, Soc. Critical Care Medicine, Med. Soc. Switzerland. Office: SUNY HSC T-19 Rm 80 Stony Brook NY 11794

BILLADELLO, JOSEPH JOHN, physician, educator; b. N.Y.C., Nov. 1, 1952; s. Joseph and Julia (Colangelo) B.; m. Guadalupe Sanchez, June 29, 1981; 1 child, Laura Nicole. BS, SUNY, Stony Brook, 1973; MD, Georgetown U., 1978. Intern, resident Duke Univ. Hosp., Durham, N.C., 1978-81; fellow in cardiology Washington Univ. Sch. Medicine, St. Louis, 1981-85, instr. in medicine, 1985-86, asst. prof. medicine, 1986-91, assoc. prof. medicine, 1991—. Contbr. over 30 articles to profl. jours. Recipient Syntex scholars award Syntex Corp., Palo Alto, Calif., 1987-90; established investigator Am. Heart Assn., 1990-95. Home: 3 Oak Park Ct Saint Louis MO 63141-8427 Office: Washington Univ 660 S Euclid Ave Saint Louis MO 63110-1010

BILLAK, JAMES ROBERT, physican; b. Sharon, Pa., Aug. 18, 1950; s. Andrew A. and Paula R. (Capson) B.; m. Katie Moore Smith, Dec. 23, 1983; children: Shannon, J. C., Caron, Lauren. BS, U. Pitts., 1972; DO, Phila. Coll. Osteo. Medicine, 1976. Diplomat Am. Bd. Emergency Medicine. Intern Riverside Hosp., Wilmington, Del., 1976-77; resident in internal medicine Atlantic City Med. Ctr., 1977-80, mem. staff emergency medicine, 1981-83; mem. staff internal medicine Shore Meml. Hosp., Somers Point, N.J., 1980-81; dir. emergency medicine Youngstown (Ohio) Osteo. Hosp., 1983—; clin. prof. emergency medicine Ohio U. Coll. Osteo. Medicine, 1985—; affiliate physician Cleve. Clinic Found., 1993—; adj. clin. prof. emergency medicine Lake Erie Osteo. Coll. Medicine, 1996. Fellow Am. Coll. Emergency Physicians, Am. Acad. Emergency Medicine; mem. Am. Coll. Emergency Physicians, Wilderness Med. Soc., Phi Sigma Gamma. Home: 43736 Cameron Rd Wellsville OH 43968-9734

BILLER, HENRY BURT, psychologist, educator; b. Providence, Oct. 30, 1940; s. David and Thelma (Rodin) B.; m. Margery Salter, Oct. 7, 1979 (div. July 1993); children: Jonathan, Kenneth, Cameron, Michael, Benjamin. A.B. magna cum laude, Brown U., 1962; Ph.D. (USPHS fellow), Duke U., 1967. Asst. prof. psychology U. Mass., Amherst, 1967-69, George Peabody Coll., 1969-70; prof. U. R.I., Kingston, 1970—; cons. Northampton (Mass.) Welfare Dept., 1968-69, Protestant Youth Center, Baldwinville, Mass., 1969, Cape Cod (Mass.) Mental Health Center, 1970, Newport County (R.I.) Mental Health Center, 1970-71, VA Hosp., Providence, 1972-76, Emma Pendleton Bradley Hosp., Riverside, R.I., 1970-80, No. R.I. Mental Health Center, Woonsocket, 1980-82, No. R.I. Assn. for Retarded Citizens, Woonsocket, 1980-83, John E. Fogarty Ctr., North Providence, 1982—, Elmwood Community Ctr., Providence, 1992-93, Newport County Regional Spl. Ednl. Program, 1993-94, St. Joseph's Ctr. for Family Clin. Svcs., Providence, 1993-94; pvt. practice Warwick, R.I., 1970—. Author: Father, Child and Sex Role, 1971, Paternal Deprivation, 1974, Father Power, 1974, The Other Helpers, 1977, Parental Death and Psychological Development, 1982, Child Maltreatment and Paternal Deprivation, 1986, Stature and Stigma, 1987, Fathers and Families, 1993, (with Robert J. Trotter) The Father Factor, 1994; mem. editorial bd. Archives of Sexual Behavior, 1975—; cons. Editor Sex Roles, 1979—; assoc. editor Family Rels., 1980-81; contbr. chpts. to books, articles to profl. jours. Fellow Am. Psychol. Assn., Am. Psychol. Soc., Am. Assn. Applied and Preventive Psychology; mem. Phi Beta Kappa, Sigma Xi. Home: 4080 Post Rd Warwick RI 02886-9214 Office: U RI Dept Psychology Kingston RI 02881

BILLER, HUGH FREDERICK, medical educator; b. Milw., Sept. 11, 1934; s. Saul E. and Mildred (Wilson) B.; m. Diane Schumacher, July 28, 1958; 1 dau., Heather. M.C., Marquette, 1960. Intern Balt. City Hosps.; resident otolaryngology Johns Hopkins Hosp., 1964-67; asst. prof. Wash. U. Sch. Medicine, 1967-70, asso. prof., 1970-71; prof., chmn. dept. otolaryngology Mt. Sinai Sch. Medicine, N.Y.C., 1972-95. Served with AUS, 1962-64. Recipient Harris P. Mosher award, 1972. Mem. Am. Laryngologic Soc., Soc. U. Otolaryngologists, AMA, ACS, Am. Laryngol., Rhinol. and Otol. Soc., Am. Soc. Head and Neck Surgery (pres. 1984-85), Soc. Academic Surgeons, Am. Council Otolaryngology (dir. 1972-74). Office: 100th St and Fifth Ave 5 E 98th St New York NY 10029-6501

BILLER, JOSE, neurologist; b. Montevideo, Uruguay, Jan. 16, 1948. MD, U. de la Republica, Montevideo, Uruguay, 1974. Diplomate Am. Bd. Psychiatry and Neurology. Intern Columbus Hosp., Chgo., 1976-77; resident neurology Henry Ford Hosp., Detroit, 1977-78; resident neurolgy Loyola U. Hosp., Maywood, Ill., 1978-80; fellow cerebral vascular diseases Bowman Gray Sch. Med., Winston Salem, N.C., 1980-81; neurologist Northwestern Meml. Hosp., Chgo., 1983—; prof. Northwestern Sch. Medicine, Chgo., 1983—; prof., chmn. dept neurology Indiana U. Sch. Med. Author, co-author of more than 300 articles, book chpts., abstracts, 5 edited books. Fellow ACP, Am. Acad. Neurology; mem. Am. Neurology Assn., Am. Heart Assn. Office: Ind U Sch of Medicine Dept Neurology Emerson Hall 545 Barnhill Dr Indianapolis IN 46202-5124

BILLETER, MARIANNE, pharmacy educator; b. Durham, N.C., Feb. 28, 1963; d. Ralph Leonard and Nancy Jane (Chambers) B. BS in Pharmacy, Purdue U., 1986, PharmD, 1987. Cert. pharmacotherapy specialist. Pharmacy Commd. Officer Student Tng. and Extern Program, USPHS-FDA, Rockville, Md., 1983; radiopharmacy USPHS-NIH, Bethesda, Md., 1984; pharmacy Indian Health Svc. Commd. Officer Student Tng. and Extern Program, USPHS, Tahlequah, Okla., 1985; pharmacist Beaumont Hosp., Royal Oak, Mich., 1986; pharmacy resident U. Ky., Lexington, 1987-89, fellow in infectious diseases, 1989-90; asst. prof. Xavier Univ. of L.A., New Orleans, 1990—; relief pharmacist Ochsner Med. Instns., New Orleans, 1991-96; cons. Abbott Labs., Abbott Park, Ill., 1991—. Contbr. chpts. to books and articles to profl. jours. Mem. Am. Assn. Colls. Pharmacy, Am. Coll. Clin. Pharmacy, Am. Soc. Health-Sys. Pharmacists, La. Soc. Pharmacists, Soc. Infectious Diseases Pharmacists (bd. dirs.), Am. Soc. Microbiology. Office: Xavier Coll Pharmacy 7325 Palmetto St New Orleans LA 70125-1056

BILLIG, ROBERT EMMANUEL, psychiatric social worker; b. N.Y.C.; s. Benjamin and Pearl (Kwiat) B. BA, McKendree Coll., 1966; MS, Fort Hays (Kans.) State Coll., 1969; MSW, Marywood Coll., 1974. Diplomate Clin. Social Work Am. Bd. Examiners in Clin. Social Work; cert. hypnotherapist Nat. Bd. Hypnotherapist Examiners. Psychiat. social worker S.I. Devel. Center, 1974-76, Queens and Bklyn. Devel. Ctrs., 1976-79, Bellevue Psychiat. Hosp., N.Y.C., 1979-88; pvt. practice, 1988—; adminstr. Bellevue Cmty. Support Sys., 1983-86. Mem. Acad. Cert. Social Workers, Nat. Assn. Social Workers, N.Y. State Soc. Clin. Social Work Psychotherapists, Am. Soc. Group Psychotherapy and Psychodrama, Am. Bd. Hypnotherapy, Am. Assn. Profl. Hypnotherapist, Am. Assn. Behavioral Therapists, Mensa. Jewish. Home: 10 Park Ter E New York NY 10034-1504

BILLINGS, PATRICIA ANN COLLINS, nurse practitioner; b. San Diego, Jan. 31, 1946; d. Normon Clyde and Mary Asunda (Fantoni) Collins; m. George M. Whitehead, June 12, 1966 (div. Mar. 1975); children: Garrett Grafton Rayne, Sharna Raynel, Adrianna Megan, Autumn Leigh; m. Russell F. Billings II, Aug. 19, 1989. BS in Nursing, Loma Linda (Calif.) U., 1967, MPH, 1971; cert. Pediatric Nurse Practitioner, U. Calif, San Diego, 1979. RN, Calif., Idaho; cert. nurse practitioner, Idaho, Calif. Pub. health nurse San Bernardino County, Calif., 1967-72, San Diego County, 1974; sch. nurse, pediatric nurse practitioner Vista (Calif.) Unified Sch. Dist., 1974-85; pediatric nurse practitioner Sharp Rees-Stealy Med. Group, San Diego, 1985-94; pediatric nurse practitioners Pediatric Ctr., Twin Falls, Idaho, 1994—. Contbg. editor Pediatric Nursing, 1994—. mem. Pres.'s Coun., San Diego, 1984-85; bd. dirs. Idahoans Concerned With Adolescent Pregnancy, 1995—. Recipient USPHS scholarship, 1971. Fellow Nat. Assn. Pediatric Nurse Practitioners (cert. chmn. 1987-93); mem. Am. Acad. Pediats. (mem. Idaho chpt.), San Diego Assn. Pediatric Nurse Practitioners (legis. chair 1993-94, editor pedits. nursing assessment 1995—, 1993 Pediatric Nurse Practitioner of Yr.). Republican. Office: Pediatric Ctr 388 Martin St Twin Falls ID 83301-4544

BILLINGSLEY, JUDITH ANN SEAVEY, oncology nurse; b. Manchester, Conn., Aug. 4, 1947; d. John Frank and Carol Jean (Wood) Seavey; m. Michael Billingsley, June 7, 1969; children: Tamara Lynn, Tara Lynn. Diploma, Hartford Hosp. Sch. Nursing, 1968; student, Coll. of Albemarle, 1985-86, No. Va. C.C., 1990; grad. with honors, George Mason U., 1992. Cert. oncology nurse ANCC, 1995. Staff nurse ICU Manchester Meml. Hosp., 1968-69; staff nurse recovery rm. Burlingame (Calif.) Hosp. and Med. Ctr., 1972-73; staff nurse St. Joseph's Hosp., Atlanta, 1987-89; clin. nurse Alexandria (Va.) Hosp., 1989-91; admissions nurse Hospice of No. Va., 1991-92; neuro-oncology clin. rsch. nurse Winship Cancer Ctr. Emory U. Sch. Medicine, Atlanta, 1992—. Mem. Golden Key, Sigma Theta Tau, Alpha Chi. Home: 1273 Gray Squirrel Xing Marietta GA 30062-6275

BILLINGSLEY, MELVIN LEE, neuropharmacologist; b. Pitts., Oct. 3, 1953; s. m. and Mary (Niznik) B.; m. Elizabeth Magill, Sept. 14, 1991; children: Tyler D., Chelsea D., Andrew M. BS in Biophysics-Microbiology and Biology, U. Pitts., 1974; PhD, George Washington U., 1981; postdoctoral, Yale U., 1981-82. Rsch. asst. dept. pharmacology U. Pitts., 1974-75; pharmacologist Stuart Pharms. div. Imperial Chem. Industries, Wilmington, Del., 1975-77; postdoctoral fellow dept. pharmacology Yale U., New Haven, 1981-82; staff fellow sect. on biochem. pharmacology Nat. Heart Lung and Blood Inst., Bethesda, Md., 1982-84; asst. prof. pharmacology Hershey Med. Ctr. Pa. State U., Hershey, 1984-87, assoc. prof. Hershey Med. Ctr., 1987-91; prof. Hershey Med. Ctr., 1991—; dir. Pa. State U., Hershey, 1988—, acting dir. cell and molecular biology grad. program, 1989-90; reviewer grants Am. heart Assn., Pa. chpt., 1988-89, Ben Franklin Partnership, 1990—, Pub. Health Sci. (NIH), NSF, VA. Contbr. articles to jours. including Life Sci., Brain Rsch. Bull., Immunopharmacology, Jour. Biol. Chemistry, Jour. Neurochemistry, Biotechniques, Jour. Cyclic Nucleotide Rsch., Nature, Molecular Brain Rsch., Jour. Cell Biology, Devel. Brain Rsch., Biochem. Jour. and Stroke. Chmn. bd. dirs. Cen. Pa. Tech. Coun., Harrisburg, Pa., 1990-92. Fellow Pharm. Mfr.'s Assn., 1980-81, NIMH Nat. Rsch. Svc. award, 1982-84, Internat. Life Scis. Inst., 1986-89, March of Dimes, 1987-89, 89, 90; grantee numerous orgns. including Am. Heart Assn., Am. Cancer Soc., U.S. EPA, NIH, and NSF. Mem. AAAS, Soc. for Neurosci. (past pres. Susquehanna chpt.), Am. Soc. for Biochemistry and Molecular Biology, ASPET, Sigma Xi. Home: 202 Java Ave Hershey PA 17033-1463 Office: Pa State Coll Medicine PO Box 850 Hershey PA 17033-0850

BILYEU, ALAN DALE, family physician; b. Decatur, Ill., Aug. 31, 1946; s. Charles Thomas and Erma Elizabeth (Jacobs) B.; m. June Maureen Rarlsback, Mar. 2, 1976; children: Alison Elizabeth, Scott Marshall. MD, U. Ill., Chgo., 1975. Diplomate Am. Bd. Family Practice. Resident Cedar Rapis (Iowa) Med. Edn. Program, 1975-78; chair dept. family practice St. Mary's Hosp., Decatur, Ill., 1981-85, sec.-treas. med. staff, 1985-89, pres.-elect, pres., past pres., 1990—; med. practice Moweaqua Family Practice Ctr., 1978—; bd. dirs. Ctrl. Ill. Health Assocs., Decatur. Fellow Am. Acad. Family Physicians; mem. Ill. State Med. Soc. (del. 1994-96). Home: RR # 1 Box 104W Moweaqua IL 62550 Office: Moweaqua Family Prac Ctr 620 N Putnam Moweaqua IL 62550

BINDER, GORDON M., health and medical products executive; b. St. Louis, 1935. Degree in elec. engring., Purdue U., 1957; MBA, Harvard U., 1962. Formerly with Litton Industries, 1962-64; various fin. mgmt. positions Ford Motor Co., 1964-69; CFO Sys. Devel. Corp., 1971-81; v.p., CFO Amgen, Thousand Oaks, Calif., 1982-88, CEO, 1988—, chmn. bd., 1990—. Baker scholar Harvard U. Office: Amgen 1840 De Havilland Dr Thousand Oaks CA 91320-1701*

BINDER, MADELINE DOTTI, counselor; b. Chgo., Oct. 7, 1942; d. Martin and Anne (Sweet) Binder; children: Mark Nathan, Marla Susan. BEd, Nat. Coll. Edn., 1964, MS, 1972, MS in Human Svcs.-Counseling, 1993. Tchr., Rochester Schs. (Minn.), 1963-64, Orange County Schs., Orlando, Fla., 1967-68; reading cons. Palatine Schs. (Ill.), 1972-73; instr. Parent Effective Tng., Wilmette, Ill., 1974-76, tchr. Effectiveness Tng., 1974-76; pres. Profls. Diversified, Wilmette, Ill., 1976-89; remedial and enrichment reading tchr. Waukegan (Ill.) Pub. Schs., 1986; pres. Lifeline, 1989-90; mgmt. cons. World Wide Diamonds Assn., Schaumburg, Ill., 1979-89, Artistic Color, Dallas, 1983-87; Pearl direct distbr. Amway Corp., Ada, Mich., 1976-94; exec. distbr. NU Skin, 1992; distbr. Emerald-Starlight Internat., 1994—; psychotherapist, 1993—. Author: Organic Gardening, 1975, The Go-Getters Planner, 1986, Singles Guide to Chicagoland, 1995. Leader, Camp Fire Girls, Evanston, Ill., 1963, 75. Recipient Ednl. Scholarship, Nat. Coll. Edn., 1971. Mem. Phi Delta Kappa, Alpha Delta Omega. Jewish.

BINDER, MICHAEL ALAN, urologist; b. Bklyn., Sept. 17, 1955; s. Lee Stevens and Sylvia (Klempner) B.; m. Amy Dee Feder, May 30, 1982; children: Mara, Aaron, Anna. BA, Clark U., 1977; MD, SUNY, 1982. Resident surgery SUNY-Downstate, Bklyn., 1982-84, resident urology, 1984-87; pvt. practice urology Oil City, Pa., 1988-92; chmn. div. urology N.W. Med. Ctr., Oil City, Pa., 1988-92; pvt. practice Tampa, Fla., 1992—; affiliate Cleve. Clin. Coop.; chmn. divsn. urology Centurion Hosp. of Carrollwood (Fla.), 1992-94. Mem. Am. Urol. Assn., Fla. Urol. Soc., Greater Tampa Bay Urol. Soc., Am. Assn. Clin. Urologists. Republican. Jewish. Office: 14499 N Dale Mabry Hwy Ste 180 Tampa FL 33618-2071

BINDER, RICHARD ALLEN, hematologist, oncologist; b. Boston, Aug. 26, 1937; s. Harry Aron and Beatrice (Seltzer) B.; m. Elaine F. Kotell; children: Mark Stephen, Jonathan Stuart. BSChemE, Northeastern U., Boston, 1960; MD, Tufts U., Boston, 1964. Diplomate Am. Bd. Internal Medicine, also sub-bds. in Hematology and Med. Oncology. Intern in medicine/resident in medicine New Eng. Med. Ctr., Boston, 1964-66; resident in medicine Columbia Presbyn. Hosp., N.Y.C., 1966-67; fellow in hematology Mt. Sinai Hosp., N.Y.C., 1967-68; instr. Tufts U. Sch. Medicine, 1970-71; asst. prof. Georgetown U., Washington, 1971-75, assoc. clin. prof. medicine, 1975-78, clin. prof. medicine, 1978—; v.p. Inova Health Sys., 1994-95; assoc. chmn. dept. medicine Fairfax Hosp., 1978—, v.p. med. staff, 1989-91, pres. med. staff, 1992-94; bd. dirs. Inova Hosp., Hospice No. Va., v.p., 1966—; active Inova Hosps. Bd., 1988-95, Inova Health Sys. Bd., 1992-95, Hospice of No. Va. Bd., 1993—, vice-chmn., 1995—. Editor Hematology Rev.-Family Practice, 1979; contbr. articles to profl. jours. Maj. U.S. Army, 1968-70. Recipient Golden Apple, Georgetown U., 1975, 76, Vicentennial medal Georgetown U., 1991, Excellence in Teaching award Fairfax Hosp., 1994—. Fellow ACP; mem. Am. Soc. Hematology, Am. Soc. Clin. Oncology, Physicians for Social Responsibility, Fairfax Hosp. Assn. (bd. dirs. 1988-95), Alumni Assn. Tufts U. (bd. dirs. 1990—). Home: 6704 Bradley Blvd Bethesda MD 20817-3045 Office: Fairfax Hematology 3301 Woodburn Rd Annandale VA 22003-1229

BINDER, ROBERT EDWARD, orthodontics educator; b. Boston, Aug. 26, 1937; s. Harry and Beatrice Gertrude (Seltzer) B.; m. Ruth Susan Shepard, May 29, 1960; children: Rebecca Ellen, Jeffrey Steven. BSChemE, Northeastern U., 1960; DMD, Harvard U., 1966, cert. in orthodontics, 1969. Diplomate Am. Bd. Orthodontics. Assoc. orthodontics Harvard Sch. Dental Mediine, Boston, 1966-69; asst. prof. orthodontics U. Md. Sch. Dentistry, Balt., 1969-70; assoc. prof. U. Medicine and Dentistry of N.J., Newark, 1970-73, prof., 1973—, chmn. dept., 1970-85, prof. biomed. sci., 1979—; dir. orthodontics Univ. Hosp., Newark, 1975-82; co-dir. orthodontics Overlook Hosp., Summit, N.J., 1981—. Author: Orthodontic Technique; contbr. articles to profl. jours., chpts. to books. Fellow Internat. Coll. Dentists, 1975, Am. Coll. Dentists, 1982; NIH postdoctoral fellow, 1966-69. Mem. ADA, Am. Assn. Orthodontists, Angle Soc. Orthodontists (sec.-treas. 1995—), Hudson County Dental Soc. (pres. 1977-78), N.J. Soc. Orthodontists (program chmn. 1981-82). Office: U Medicine and Dentistry of NJ 110 Bergen St Newark NJ 07103-2400

BINDER, SHELDON CARL, surgeon; b. Boston, Sept. 18, 1934; s. Abraham and Ida (Goldman) B.; m. Marrlyn R. Taylor, June 2, 1962; children: Dawn N., Michael L. AB summa cum laude, Harvard U., Cambridge, Mass., 1956; MD cum laude, Harvard U., Boston, 1960. Diplomate Am. Bd. Surgery. Intern and resident in surgery Mass. Gen. Hosp., Boston, 1960-67; fellow in surg. oncology Mem. Sloan-Kettering Cancer Ctr., N.Y.C., 1967-68; attending surgeon Tufts-New Eng. Med. Ctr., Boston, 1968-76, Mt. Auburn Hosp., Cambridge, 1979-93; asst. prof. Tufts U. Sch. Medicine, Boston, 1968-76; chief surgery Youngstown (Ohio) Hosp Assn., 1977-78, VA Med. Ctr., Ft. Meade, S.D., 1994; prof. Northeastern Ohio Univs. Coll. Medicine, Rootstown, 1977-78; instr. Harvard U. Med. Sch., 1979-93; assoc. prof. U. S.D. Sch. Medicine, Sioux Falls, 1994; part-time pvt. practice Belmont, Mass., 1994—. Contbr. articles and monographs to med. jours. Lt. comdr. USPHS, 1962-64. Fellow ACS; mem. Assn. for Acad. Surgery, Boston Surg. Soc., Soc. Head and Neck Surgeons, Soc. for Surgery Alimentary Tract, Soc. Surg. Oncology, Am. Gastroent. Assn., New Eng. Cancer Soc., Am. Soc. Gen. Surgeons. Republican. Jewish. Home and Office: 41 Bow Rd Belmont MA 02178

BINDLER, RUTH, nursing educator; b. Saranac Lake, N.Y., Feb. 7, 1949; d. John Duncan and Alice Constance (Sullivan) McGillis; m. Julian Bindler, Aug. 11, 1973; children: Dana K., Ross J. BSN, Cornell U., 1971; MS in Child Devel., U. Wis., 1974. Staff nurse Meml.-Sloan Kettering Cancer Ctr., N.Y.C., 1971; pub. health nurse Dane County Pub. Health Dept., Madison, Wis., 1971-74; assoc.prof. Intercollegiate Ctr. Nursing Edn., Spokane, Wash., 1974—. Author: (with L. Howry and Y. Tso) Pediatric Medications, 1981, The Parent's Guide to Pediatric Drugs, 1986, (with Howry) Pediatric Drugs and Nursing Implications, 1991, 2d edit. 1996, (with J. Ball) Pediatric Nursing: Caring for Children, 1995; contbr. articles to profl. jours. Mem. ANA, Assn. for Care Children's Health, Sigma Theta Tau. Home: 10207 Sherman Rd Spokane WA 99204-9771

BINENBAUM, STEVE Z., cardiologist; b. Jerusalem, Dec. 18, 1937; came to the U.S., 1963; s. Nehemiah and Esther (Sandberg) B.; m. Nurit Ofi, Aug. 18, 1964; children: Gil, Rona. BSEE, Poly. U., Bklyn., 1965, MS in Bioengring., 1968, PhD, 1972; MD, Albert Einstein Coll. Medicine, 1982. Elect. engr. Otis Elevator Co., N.Y.C., 1965-66; rsch. assoc. Roche Med. Electronics, Caranbury, N.J., 1969-74; sr. project engr. Emergency Care Rsch. Inst., Phila., 1974-75; cons. tech. transfer Berkey Tech. Co., Woodside, N.Y., 1975-76; dir. biomed. engring. Washington Hosp. Ctr., 1976-78; dir. cardiac care unit VA Med. Ctr., East Orange, N.J., 1989-92, dir. cardiac cath lab., 1992—. Fellow Am. Coll. Cardiology, ACP; mem. Am. Heart Assn., N.Am. Soc. Pacing and Electrophysiology. Home: 490 Fairfield Rd East Windsor NJ 08520 Office: VA Med Ctr 385 Tremont Ave East Orange NJ 07018

BING, LOIS BLACK, optometrist; b. Newark, W.Va., Sept. 16, 1909; d. Louis Eckert and Jennie Clare (Fought) Black; m. James Augustus Bing, Oct. 26, 1931; 1 child, James DeCamp. AB, Coll. Wooster, 1931; BS, Ohio State U., 1948; OD, Mass. Coll. Optometry, 1962; D Ocular Sci. (hon.), Mass. Coll., 1962. Lic. Ohio State Bd. Optometry. Healthcare rep Cleve. Optometric Assn., 1955-80; pvt. practice Shaker Heights, Ohio, 1950-87, Middleburg Heights, Ohio, 1967—; adv. bd. Miracles & Motion-Metro-Health, 1993—; early intervention collaborative group, Clev., 1993—; chmn. Sch. Vision Forum and Reading Conf., Cleve., 1951—. Co-author: Vision and School Success, 1990; contbr. articles to profl. jours., chpts. to books. Elder emeritus Fairmount Presbyn. Ch., Cleveland Heights, Ohio. Mem. Am. Optometric Assn. (Apollo award 1962, chair vision problems of children & youth com., 1951-62, rep. nat. conf. cooperation in health edn. 1955-62), Am. Acad. Optometry (hon. life), Nat. Acads. Practice (disting. practioner 1984), Ohio Optometric Assn. (Vicere award 1952), Ohio Sch. Psychol. Assn. (hon. life), Ohio Coun. of Internat. Reading Assn. (hon. life), Cleve. Optometric Assn. (rep. Whitehouse Conf. Children & Youth 1960), Coll. Optometrists in Vision Devel., Delta Kappa Gamma (hon.). Republican. Home: 6995 Paula Dr Middelburg Heights OH 44130 Office: 7054 W 130th St Middleburg Heights OH 44130

BING, OSCAR HAROLD LEE, medical research administrator; b. N.Y.C., July 13, 1935; s. Herbert Maurice and Karolina Grete (Tuchmann) B.; m. Barbara Kay Nelson, May 13, 1976; children: David Charles, Michael Herbert, Benjamin Lee, William Nelson. BS, Washington & Lee U., 1956; MD, U. Md., 1961. Diplomate Am. Bd. Internal Medicine and Cardiovascular Disease. Intern Boston City Hosp., 1961-62; capt. med. corp. U.S. Med. Corp, Edgewood, Md., 1962-64; resident in medicine Georgetown U. Hosp., Washington, 1964-66; cardiology fellow New Eng. Med. ctr. Hosps., Boston, 1966-69; cardiologist Boston City Hosp., 1969-74, Beth Israel Hosp., Boston, 1974-81; assoc. chief of staff R & D Boston VA Med. Ctr., 1981—; instr. medicine Tufts U. Sch. Medicine, Boston, 1969-72, prof., 1981—; from asst. to assoc. prof. medicine Harvard Med. Sch., Boston, 1974-81; rsch. prof. medicine Boston U. Sch. Medicine, 1995—. Contbr. over 100 book chpts. and articles to profl. jours. Recipient Rsch. Career Devel. award NIH, 1975-80. Mem. Am. Heart Assn., Internat. Soc. Heart Rsch., Am. Physiologic Soc. (assoc.). Office: Boston VA Med Ctr 150 S Huntington Ave Jamaica Plain MA 02130-4817

BINGDE, TAN, physician; b. Guangzhou, Guangdong, People's Republic of China, July 29, 1928; s. Tan Ting-Jin and Deng Qiong-Xian B.; m. Tong Pei-Lan, Feb. 8, 1957; children: Tan Min, Tan Jiang-Tang. Student, Sun Yet-Sen Med. U., Guangzhou, China, 1946-52; M of Medicine, Sun Yet-Sen Med. U., 1960; MD, Guangdong Rsch. Instn., 1984. Asst. researcher Chinese Acad. Med. Scis., Beijing, China, 1953-60; chief of medicine Guangdong Prevention and Treatment Ctr., Guangzhou, China, 1961-70; dir., assoc. prof. Guangdong P/T Ctr. Occupational Disease, 1971-83, dir., prof., 1984—; committeeman of deliberative assembly of degree Beijing Med. U., 1985, Hua-Xi Med. U., Ghengtu, 1984-87, Tong-Ji Med. U., Wuham 1984-91, Sun Yet-Sen Med. U., Guangzhou, 1980-91. Chief editor Jour. Occupational Medicine, 1978-91; editor Chinese Jour. Indsl. Medicine, 1988-91; author: Clinical Toxiology, 1965, Occupational Leukopenia, 1982. Mem. Internat. Com. Occupl. Health, Chinese Med. Assn. (committeeman 1985-91), Guangdong Learned Soc. Labour Health & Occupational Medicine (dir. 1980—), Guangdong Learned Soc. Radioactive Protection (dir. 1980—). Office: Guangdong P/T Ctr Occupl Dis, 86 Yile Rd, Guangzhou 510260, People's Republic of China

BINGHAM, BART MATTHEW, health services administrator; b. St. Louis, Aug. 11, 1955; s. Max and Ann (Moore) B.; m. Kathy Jo Habel, Jan. 11, 1990; children: Anthony Michael, Jason Matthew, Rachael Elizabeth Ousley. BS in Adminstr., Ind. U., Indpls., 1977 Adminstr. Alexandria (Ind.) Convalescent Ctr., 1980-84; asst. adminstr. Parkview Convalescent Ctr., Elwood, Ind., 1977-80, adminstr., 1984-90, adminstr., owner, 1994; adminstr. Heritage House of New Castle, Ind., 1984-90. Pres. YMCA, Elwood, 1985, PTA, Elwood, 1985. Mem. Am. Coll. Health Care Adminstrs., Elks Club. Republican. Home: 1200 Cedar Ct Elwood IN 46036 Office: Parkview Progressive Care 2300 Parkview Ln Elwood IN 46036

BINKERT, ALVIN JOHN, hospital administrator; b. Ft. Atkinson, Wis., Oct. 20, 1910; s. John and Clara (Burrow) B.; m. Lucile Latton, June 4, 1939; children: Barbara L., Cynthia R. Binkert Elias. BA, U. Wis., 1931. With Haskins & Sells (CPAs), N.Y.C., 1931-41; comptr. Presbyn. Hosp., N.Y.C., 1941-48, asst. v.p., 1948-54, v.p., gen. mgr., 1954-57, exec. v.p., 1957-70, pres., 1970—, vice chmn. bd., 1975—, also trustee; trustee Sr. Med. Cons.'s, N.Y.C.; lectr. pub. health, adminstrv. medicine Columbia U., 1954—. Trustee Presbyn. Hosp. Mem. Greater N.Y. Hosp. Assn. (past pres., bd. govs.), Hosp. Assn. N.Y. State (past pres., trustee, del.), Am. Coll. Hosp. Adminstrs., Univ. Club, Key Biscayne Yacht Club. Home: 681 Harbor Ln Key Biscayne FL 33149-1713 Office: 622 W 168th St New York NY 10032-3702

BINKLEY, JAMES EDGAR, dentist; b. Hennessey, Okla., July 27, 1931; s. Floyd Halie and Faye Sincle (Keller) B.; m. Shirley Kathleen Weeks, Jan. 24, 1953; children—Kathleen Ann, James Michael. Student U. Okla., 1949-53; D.D.S., Kansas City Western Dental Coll., U. Mo., 1957. Gen. practice dentistry, Hennessey, 1957-58, 60—. Officer Hennessey Sch. Bd., 1961-66; mem. Republican Nat. Com.; former deacon 1st Christian Ch. Served to capt. U.S. Army, 1953-60. Recipient Service award Seoul Orphanage, Korea, 1959. Mem. ADA, Okla. Dental Assn., Northwest Dist. Dental Assn., Okla. Wildlife Fedn., U. Okla. Alumni Assn. (life mem.), Hennessey C. of C. (founding mem., 1st sec.-treas.), U.S. Golf Assn., Nat. Rifle Assn. Clubs: Hennessey Golf and Country (charter mem.); Bella Vista Golf and Country (Ark.); Fishing of Am. Lodges; Mason (32 degree), Order Eastern Star, Lions. Avocations: golf; fishing; hunting; coin collecting. Home: 214 E 3rd St Hennessey OK 73742-1506 Office: Binkley Dental Clinic Box 265 120 E Oklahoma Ave Hennessey OK 73742-0265

BINKS, TERRANCE ALAN, family practice physician, flight surgeon; b. Oak Park, Ill., Apr. 19, 1943; s. George Alvin and Ruth Mae (Naus) B.; m. Jenella Edwina Borden, Dec. 25, 1969; children: Jason Alan, Teri Nichole, Colleen Daniel, Kacie Alexander. BS, George Williams Coll., 1971; DO, Chgo. Coll. Osteopathic Med., 1979. From battalion surgeon to dir. med. svcs. NMCL, Quantico, Va. Home: 4803 Belmont Rd Downers Grove IL 60515 Office: DMS CDR USN NMCL MCB 2200 Lester St Quantico VA 22130

BINNIE, NANCY CATHERINE, nurse, educator; b. Sioux Falls, S.D., Jan. 28, 1937; d. Edward Grant and Jessie May (Martini) Larkin; m. Charles H. Binnie. Diploma, St. Joseph's Hosp. Sch. Nursing, Phoenix, 1965; BS in Nursing, Ariz. State U., 1970, MA, 1974. Intensive care charge nurse Scottsdale (Ariz.) Meml. Hosp., 1968-70, coordinator critical care, 1970-71; coordinator critical care John C. Lincoln Hosp., Phoenix, 1971-73; prof. nursing GateWay Community Coll., Phoenix, 1974—; coord. part-time evening nursing programs Gateway Community Coll., 1984—, interim dir. nursing, 1989, 91. Mem. Orgn. Advancement of Assoc. Degree Nursing, Practical and Assoc. Coun. Nursing Educators, Ariz. Coun. Nurse Educators. Office: Gateway C C 104 N 40th St Phoenix AZ 85034-1704

BIONDO, RAYMOND VITUS, dermatologist; b. N.Y.C., June 13, 1936; s. Joseph Pernice and Bena (Schwartz) B.; m. Mary McKinnon, Dec. 24, 1976. BA in Biology, U. No. Colo., 1960; MS in Biochemistry, U. Ark., 1963, BS in Medicine, 1967, MD, 1967. Diplomate Am. Bd. Dermatology. Asst. mgmt. analyst 389th USAF Hosp., Francis E. Warren AFB, Wyo., 1954-58; rsch. trainee NIH at U. Ark., Little Rock, 1961-63; rsch. biochemist VA Hosp., Little Rock, 1963-65; intern U. Cin. Med. Ctr., 1967-68; resident in dermatology U. Ark., Little Rock, 1968-71, asst. clin. prof. dermatology, 1971-90; pres. North Little Rock (Ark.) Dermatology Clinic, 1971-90. Contbr. rsch. articles to profl. publs. Mem. nat. adv. com. on scouting for the handicapped Boy Scouts Am., 1976-81, nat. chmn. med. exploring com., 1981-84, nat. coun., 1977—, nat. exploring com., 1977-92, nat. urban emphasis com. 1990—, nat. Jewish com. on scouting, 1981-84; mem. Ark. Kidney Disease Commn., 1979-83; bd. dirs. Cen. Ark. Health Systems Agy., 1984, Congregation B'nai Israel, Little Rock, 1982-84, Jewish Fedn. Ark., 1989-92; founder, pres. Am. Red Magen David for Israel, Ark., 1987-92. Staff officer USCG Aux. Flotilla, 1995. Recipient Outstanding Alumnus award U. No. Colo., 1977, Shofar award, 1992, William H. Spurgeon and Whitney M. Young awards Boy Scouts Am., 1981, Silver Antelope award, 1983, Silver Beaver award, 1977, Nat. Torch of Gold award, 1993, cert. of achievement in cmty. health promotion Ark. Dept. Health, 1983, vol. action award The White House, 1982, Gov.'s Vol. Excellence award, 1983, Ark. cert. appreciation for pub. svc., 1992, Father Joseph H. Biltz award Ark. Coun. Nat. Conf. of Christians & Jews, 1990, Nat. Disting. Svc. award Jewish War Vets. of the U.S., 1995; Golden Rule award finalist JC Penney Co./United Way of Pulaski County, 1996, Olympic Torch Relay nominee, 1996. Fellow Am. Acad. Dermatology (adv. bd. nat. dermatology program 1973-75); mem. AMA (physicians recognition award 1971-90, cert of appreciation 1984), Ark. Med. Soc. (ho. of dels. 1971—), Ark Dermatol. Soc. (pres. 1977), Pulaski County Med. Soc., Jewish War Vets U.S. (founder, comdr. Ark. post 436, nat. surgeon 1993-96, nat. asst. Boy Scout officer 1993-96, nat. White House liaison officer 1993-95, chapel of four chaplains Legion of Honor 1994, cert. apreciation Tex. dept. 1991, cert. merit 1992, Judge Lawrence Gubow Meml. hon. mention 1989, Humanitarian award 1996) Sigma Xi, Alpha Omega Alpha. Jewish. Home: PO Box 6361 North Little Rock AR 72124-6361

BIRA, PATRICK GERARD, healthcare administrator; b. St. Louis, Apr. 11, 1959; m. M. Ann Conrad; children: Emily, Claire, Ben, Nicholas. B Mgmt., Rockhurst Coll., 1980; M Health Adminstrn., St. Louis U., 1984, JD, 1984. Bar: Mo. 1985, Ill. 1985. Adminstrv. intern St. Anthony's Med. Ctr., St. Louis, 1983; corp. counsel intern West Jersey Health Sys., Camden, N.J., 1984; asst. to pres. St. Mary of Nazareth Hosp. Ctr., Chgo., 1985-88; CEO Perry County Meml. Hosp., Perryville, Mo., 1988—; treas. Med.Am. HealthNet, Inc., 1994; mgmt. cons. Perry County Nursing Home, Perryville, 1989—. V.p. Perryville Bus. and Edn. Coun., 1994; bd. dirs. St. Vincent's Fin. Commn., 1989-93; bd. dirs. St. Vincent's Parish Coun., 1993. Fellow Am. Coll. Healthcare Execs; mem. Mo. Health Lawyers Assn., Mo. Lic. Nursing Home Adminstrs., Mo. Hosp. Assn. (bd. dirs., Mo. svc. corp. 1992, pres. S.E. dist. coun. 1992), Perryville C. of C. (bd. dirs. 1991-92), Alpha Sigma Nu. Roman Catholic. Office: Perry County Meml Hosp 434 NW St Perryville MO 63775

BIRBARI, ADIL ELIAS, physician, educator; b. Ziguinchor, Senegal, May 26, 1933; s. Elias George and Sophia George (Nasrallah) B.; m. Micheline Michel Ghosn, Feb. 4, 1978; children: Yolande, Sophia. Baccalaureat II, Internat. Coll., Beirut, 1952; BS, Am. U., Beirut, 1955, MD, 1959. Fellow in hypertension Peter Bent Brigham Hosp., Boston, 1963-65, assoc. dir. hypertension lab, 1965-66; asst. prof. medicine and physiology Am. U., Beirut, 1967-72, assoc. prof. medicine and physiology, 1972-77; prof., chmn. dept. medicine Lebanese U., Beirut, 1987-90. Author: Kidney and Genetic Diseases, 1986, Manual of Clinical Hypertension; editor-in-chief Lebanese Med. Jour.; contbr. numerous articles to profl. jours. Fellow high blood pressure coun. Am. Heart Assn.; v.p. Lebanese Health Soc., Beirut, 1986; mem. Camille Shamoun Found., Beirut, 1992. Grantee Nat. Coun. Sci. Rsch., 1973-91. Fellow ACP, Internat. Coll. Angiology; mem. Lebanese Assn. Advancement of Sci. (sec. gen. 1974-92), Lebanese Soc. Nephrology and Hypertension (pres. 1975-93, editor-in-chief Jour. 1990-93), Lebanese Hypertension League (pres., editor-in-chief Jour. 1994), Nat. Coun. for Sci. Rsch. (Lebanon), Internat. Soc. Nephrology, Internat./European Soc. Hypertension, Am. Soc. Hypertension, Pan Arab Hypertension Soc. (v.p.). Office: Am Univ Beirut 850 3rd Ave Fl 18 New York NY 10022-6222

BIRCAN, MEHMET KÂMURAN, urologist, educator; b. Sivas, Turkey, June 11, 1959; s. Rasim and Meliha (Karahan) B.; m. Zelal Ekinci, Sept. 7, 1983; 1 child, Baris. MD, Hacettepe U., Ankara, Turkey, 1983. Medical diplomate. Gen. practitioner Dept. of Health, Eskisehir, Turkey, 1983-85; resident in urology Hacettepe U. Sch. Medicine, Ankara, 1985-90; asst. prof. urology Dicle U. Sch. Medicine, Diyarbakir, Turkey, 1990-94, assoc. prof. urology, 1994—; head dept. urology Dicle U. Sch. Medicine, Diyarbakir, 1994—. Contbr. articles to profl. jours. Mem. Turkish MD Assn. Office: Dicle U, Tip Fakultesi Uroloji ABD, 21280 Diyarbakir Turkey

BIRCH, NICHOLAS JOHN, biomedical science educator; b. Birmingham, Eng., Feb. 4, 1944; s. George Alfred and Constance (Hill) B.; m. Jennifer Grylls, Aug. 3, 1968 (div. 1983); children: Susanna Clare, Catherine Emma; m. Vance Joy Lomax, Dec. 14, 1988. BSc with honors, U. London, 1967; PhD, U. Sheffield, England, 1971. Rsch. fellow psychiatry U. Sheffield, England, 1971; rsch. fellow biochemistry U. Leeds, England, 1971-80, sr. rsch. fellow biochemistry, 1980-81; reader biomed. scis. Wolverhampton (England) Poly., 1981-88; prof. biomed. scis. U. Wolverhampton, 1988—; vis. prof. Coll. of Allied Health U. Montpellier, France. Author: 5 books, 216 publs. in sci. and med. jours. Recipient Bronze medal Acad Medicine, Paris, 1980; named Ky. Col, Commonwealth of Ky., 1992, hon. prof. U. Ky., Lexington. Fellow Inst. Biology (mem. coun. 1992-95); mem. Biochem Soc., Brit Pharmacol. Soc., The Physiol. Soc. Office: U Wolverhampton Biomed Rsch, 62-68 Lichfield St, Wolverhampton WV1 1DJ, England

BIRCHEM, REGINA, cell biologist, environment consultant, educator, writer; b. Sisseton, S.D., Dec. 20, 1938; d. Victor John and Hazel Mary (O'Brien) Birchem; m. Dan I. Bolef, Aug. 29, 1981. BS in Edn., U. N.D., 1964; MEd, U. Ga., 1970, PhD, 1977. Rsch. assoc. U. Ga., Athens, 1977-79, U. Colo., Boulder, 1979-80, Washington U., St. Louis, 1980-81; asst. prof. Fontbonne Coll., St. Louis, 1981-84; vis. asst. prof. U. South, Sewanee, Tenn., 1984; asst. rsch. prof. St. Louis U. Sch. Medicine, 1985-88; assoc.

prof. Pa. State U., McKeesport, Pa., 1988-90; assoc. prof. Florence Scott chair in devel. biology Seton Hill Coll., Greensburg, Pa., 1990-94; coord. Pitts. Beijing '95 and Beyond Coalition, 1995—; biology cons. Pa. Environ. Network, Yukon; cons. in edn. Contbr. numerous articles to profl. jours. in biology and electron microscopy, environment and peace; editl. bd. Haversack: A Franciscan Rev., 1987-94. Internat. cons. Women's Internat. League for Peace and Freedom, Geneva, 1989—; credentialed NGO del. to UN Earth Summit, Rio de Janeiro, Brazil, 1992, UN Conf. in Copenhagen, 1995, UN Conf. on Women, Beijing, 1995, UN Conf. on Human Settlements, Istanbul, Turkey, June 1996. Grantee NSF, 1969-70, 82, 84, 91, NIH, 1979-80; fellow NDEA, 1971-74. Mem. Am. Soc. for Cell Biology, Fedn. Am. Socs. for Experimental Biology, Pa. Acad. Sci., Sigma Xi. Roman Catholic.

BIRCHER, ANDREA URSULA, psychiatric mental health nurse specialist; b. Bern, Switzerland, Mar. 6, 1928; came to U.S., 1947; d. Franklin E. Bircher and Hedy E. Bircher-Rey. Diploma, Knapp Coll. Nursing, Santa Barbara, Calif., 1957; BS, U. Calif., San Francisco, 1961, MS, 1962; PhD, U. Calif., Berkeley, 1966. RN, Calif., Ill., Okla. Staff nurse, head nurse Cottage Hosp., Santa Barbara, 1957-58; psychiatric nurse, jr., sr. Langley-Porter Neuropsychiatric Inst., San Francisco, 1958-66; asst. prof. U. Ill. Coll. Nursing, Chgo., 1966-72; prof. U. Okla. Coll. Nursing, Oklahoma City, 1972-93, prof. emeritus, 1993—. Contbr. articles and papers to profl. jours. Recipient award for Outstanding Contributions to Faculty Governance U. Okla. Faculty Senate 1985, 93, others. Mem. AAUP, ANA, AAUW, Soc. for Edn. and Rsch. in Psychiat. Nursing, Nat. League for Nursing, N.Am. Nursing Diagnosis Assn., Internat. Platform Assn., Am. Assn. Ret. Persons, Ventura County writers Club, Sigma Theta Tau, Phi Kappa Phi. Republican. Home: 1161 Cypress Point Ln Apt 201 Ventura CA 93003-6074

BIRD, DONNA CLARICE, health services researcher; b. Saginaw, Mich., Mar. 1, 1950; d. Charles Van and Verna Clarice (Schuh) B. AB, Brown U., 1972; MSIA, Union Coll., Schenectady, N.Y., 1977; MA, Goddard Coll., 1985, U. Conn., 1991; ABD, U. Conn., 1995. Coord. health svc. devel. Whitney Young Health Ctr., Albany, N.Y., 1977-79; sr. health planner Health Systems Agy., Albany, 1979-85, primary care planner, 1985-87; adj. instr. Russell Sage Coll., Albany, 1985-88; cons. Dancing the Vision, Troy, N.Y., 1986-88; planning dir. United Way of the Capital Area, Hartford, Conn., 1989-92; rsch. asst. Edmund S. Muskie Inst. Pub. Affairs, Portland, Maine, 1992-94; rsch. assoc. Edmond S. Muskie Inst. Pub. Affairs, Portland, Maine, 1994—; adj. instr. U. So. Maine, 1992—. Author: Visionary Planning, 1985. Bd. dirs. Capital Dist. Cmty. Gardens, Inc., Troy, N.Y., 1981-84, Honest Weight Food Co-op, Albany, 1988. Mem. Am. Sociol. Assn., Ea. Sociol. Soc., Rural Sociol. Soc., Soc. for Applied Sociology, Phi Beta Kappa. Home: 82 Rackleff St Portland ME 04103-4439 Office: E Muskie Inst Pub Affairs Univ So Maine PO Box 9300 Portland ME 04104-9300

BIRD, JAMES DANIEL, SR., emergency medicine physician assistant; b. Yokosuka, Japan, Aug. 16, 1953; came to U.S., 1958; s. Leslie Duane and Yoshi (Seki) B.; m. Shirley Kay Vetarbo; m. Helen Elizabeth Higney, Aug. 11, 1979; children: Yoshi Meke, Elina Marie, Mariko Lee, James Daniel Jr. Student, Iowa State U., 1971-72, Colo. U., 1977-78; BS in Physician Asst., Mercy Coll., Detroit, 1980; diploma in Emergency Medicine, U. So. Calif., 1982. Cert. physician asst. with cert. in surgery and extended primary care by exams; cert. ACLS, ATLS, PALS, BLS. Physician asst. Kaiser Permanente, Northglenn, Colo., 1980-81, L.A. County/U. So. Calif. Med. Ctr., 1981-82, No. Mich. Health Svcs., Houghton Lake, Mich., 1982-83, Kingsburg (Calif.) Gen. Hosp., 1983-84, McDonnell-Douglas Svcs. Inc., Taif, Saudi Arabia, 1984-85, Iliuliuk Clinic, Unalaska, Alaska, 1985-86, 89—, Tanana Chiefs Conf. Inc., Ft. Yukon, Alaska, 1986-89, ARCO Alaska Inc.-Kuparuk River, North Slope, Alaska, 1986-89; cons. Cmty. Disaster Planning, Unalaska, 1992—; instr. ACLS Am. Heart Assn., Alaska, Mich., Calif., 1982-92; aeromedevac instr. State of Alaska, 1986—. Active civilian activities program ARCO Alaska Inc., 1995—. With U.S. Army, 1972-77. Fellow Internat. Travel Medicine Soc., Soc. Emergency Medicine Physician Assts. (founding), Red Blanket Soc.-L.A. County U. So. Calif. Med. Ctr. (founding), Am. Assn. Physician Assts.; mem. Am. Soc. Tropical Medicine and Hygiene, Undersea and Hyperbaric Med. Soc. (assoc.), Wilderness Med. Soc. Home: PO Box 920166 Dutch Harbor AK 99692 Office: Iliuliuk Family & Health Svcs Inc PO Box 144 Unalaska AK 99685

BIRD, JOHN WILLIAM CLYDE, physiology educator, scientist; b. Erie, Pa., Nov. 10, 1932; s. John Francis and Mabel (Reynolds) B.; m. Evelyn Jean Stutzman, Oct. 5, 1954; children—John Wallace, Jason Allen. B.A., U. Colo., 1958, M.A., 1959; Ph.D., U. Iowa, 1961. Mem. faculty Rutgers U., Piscataway, N.J.; now Disting. prof. physiology Rutgers U., Piscataway; cons. Beecham Products, Inc., NASA, Muscular Dystrophy Assn., Merck Pharm., Inc.; Fulbright prof., 1994. Contbr. numerous articles to profl. jours. NSF fellow Princeton U., 1964; Fulbright prof., 1964-65; Fulbright Research scholar, 1969-70; recipient Research Career Devel. award U.S. Govt., 1969-74. Mem. Am. Physiol. Soc., N.Y. Acad. Scis., Am. Soc. Cell Biologists, Internat. Com. Proteolysis (exec. com.). Mem. Religious Soc. of Friends. Home: 38 Juniper Ln Piscataway NJ 08854-5632 Office: Rutgers U PO Box 1059 Piscataway NJ 08855-1059

BIRD, KIMON TED, plant biotechnologist; b. San Antonio, Oct. 30, 1951; s. Claud E. and Ada M. (Fine) B.; m. Susan J. Carroll, Sept. 2, 1989. BA, U. Tex., 1973; MS, U. So. Calif., L.A., 1975; PhD, U. South Fla., 1979. Project mgr. Gas Rsch. Inst., Chgo., 1981-84; divsn. dir. Harbor Br. Oceanographic Inst., Ft. Pierce, Fla., 1984-90; program coord. marine biotech. U. N.C., Wilmington, 1990—; cons. FMC-Marine Colloids, Rockland, Maine, 1988—, Nat. Cancer Inst., Bethesda, Md., 1987, 90, USDA, Washington, 1994, Cal Bio Marine Inc., 1994, NOAA Office Global Programs, Silver Spring, Md., 1993—, Smithsonian Instn., Washington, 1996. Editor: Seaweed Cultivation for Renewable Resources, 1987; editor Applied Phycology Forum, 1990-95; mem. editorial bd. Jour. Applied Phycology, 1993—, Jour. Phycology, 1994—; contbr. over 50 articles to profl. jours. Grantee NSF, 1977, 85, 94, Fla. Sea 1989, NOAA 1991, 94, 96, NRC, 1993, N.C. Biotech. Ctr. 1990, 91, 92, Agy. Internat. Devel., 1992. Mem. AAAS, Phycological Soc. Am., Sigma Xi. Office: Univ NC 7205 Wrightsville Ave Wilmington NC 28403-7224

BIRD, RICHARD EARL, neurologist; b. Arlington, Va., Sept. 20, 1947; s. Ernest T. and Annie Bell (Casson) B.; m. Nanette Carolyn Usher, July 12, 1975; children: Shawna Lynne, Kathryn Marie. BA, Hobart Coll., 1969; MD, SUNY, Syracuse, 1973. Diplomate Am. Bd. Psychiatry and Neurology, Am. Bd. EEG. Intern St. Josephs Hosp., Syracuse, 1973-74; resident in neurology SUNY Upstate Med. Ctr., Syracuse, 1974-77; neurophysiology fellow U. Rochester (N.Y.) Strong Meml. Hosp., 1977-78; pvt. practice Salisbury, Md., 1978—; past pres., bd. dirs. Epilepsy Assn. Eastern Shore, Salisbury, 1981—; cons. Salisbury Musculoskeletal Clinic, 1993—. Bd. dirs., sec. Holly Ctr. Found., Salisbury, 1991—. Mem. AMA, Am. Acad. Neurology, Am. Med. EEG, Wicomico Med. Soc., Am. Assn. Orthop. Medicine. Democrat. Presbyterian. Office: Drs Bird & Baumann & Assocs 560 Riverside Dr B 204 Salisbury MD 21801

BIRD, SHARLENE, clinical psychologist; b. N.Y.C., Sept. 3, 1957; d. Rubin and Dina Bird. BA in Psychology & Hispanic Studies, Vassar Coll., 1979; MA in Applied Psychology, Adelphi U., 1986; MA in Human Resources Mgmt., New Sch. for Social Rsch., N.Y.C., 1987; PsyD in Clin. Psychology, Yeshiva U., 1992. Lic. psychologist, N.Y. Clin. extern St. Mary's Children & Family Svcs., Syosset, N.Y., 1980-81; behavior modifier Flower Hosp./Terence Cardinal Cooke, N.Y.C., 1981-82; clin. psychology extern Met. Ctr. for Mental Health, N.Y.C., 1986-87; clin. psychology intern NYU Med. Ctr./Bellevue Hosp., N.Y.C., 1989-90; postdoctoral fellow in human sexuality N.Y. Hosp./Cornell Med. Ctr., 1990-93, 96—; family therapist Roberto Clemente Family Guidance Ctr., N.Y.C., 1991-93, 96—; healthcare planning analyst Inst. for Family & Community Care, N.Y.C., 1993-96; pvt. practice N.Y.C., 1994—; supr. NYU Med. Ctr./Bellevue Hosp., N.Y.C., 1992—; part-time clin. instr. dept. psychiatry NYU Med. Ctr., 1995—; tng. cons. Inst. for Family and Comty Care, N.Y.C., 1993; weekly permanent radio talk show co-host Siempre a Tu Lado, Sta. WADO 1280-AM, 1992-95. Chair bd. dirs. Mothers of Children with AIDS, N.Y.C., 1991-93. Mem. APA, N.Y. State Psychol. Assn., Am. Orthopsychiat. Assn., Assn. Hispanic Health Profls. (bd. dirs., mem. at large 1995—), Am. Assn. Sex Educators, Counselors and Therapists, Am. Group Psychotherapy Assn., Assn. for Advancement of Behavior Therapy, Sigma Delta Phi. Office: 112 W 56th St Ste 15-S Rm C New York NY 10019-3834

BIRD, THOMAS D., neurologist; b. Newark, N.Y., Aug. 3, 1942; s. Donald and Virginia (Johnson) B.; m. Rosaline Merrill, July 1, 1967; children: Jeffrey, Caroline. BA, Dartmouth Coll., 1964; MD, Cornell U., 1968. Diplomate Am. Bd. Psychiatry and Neurology. Intern U. Wash. Med. Sch., Seattle, 1968-69, resident in neurology, 1969-70, 72-74; chief neurology VA Med. Ctr., Seattle, 1985—; prof. neurology & medicine U. Wash. Med. Sch., Seattle, 1988—; Editl. bd. Acta Neurologica Scandinavica, Annals of Neurology, European Neurology; contbr. more than 100 articles to profl. jours. Lt. comdr. USN, 1970-72. Grantee NIH, VA, Am. Health Assn. Found.; recipient Met. Life award for Alzheimer's Rsch., 1995. Mem. AAAS, Am. Soc. Human Genetics, Am. Neurol. Assn., Am. Acad. Neurology (Wartenburg prize 1992), Soc. Neurosci. Office: VA Med Ctr Dept Neurology 1660 S Columbian Way Seattle WA 98108

BIRDSONG, RICHARD HAMPDEN, ophthalmology resident, army officer; b. Jackson, Miss., Aug. 23, 1960; s. Walter Ernest Sr. and Marcia Lee (Morton) B.; m. Paula Doulaveris, Oct. 18, 1987; children: Toni Marie, Lauren Corinne. BS, Millsaps Coll., Jackson, 1982; MD, U. Miss. Med. Ctr., Jackson, 1986. Diplomate Am. Bd. Family Practice. Comd. 2d lt. U.S. Army, 1986, advanced through grades to maj., 1993; resident U.S. Army Hosp., Ft. Ord, Calif., 1986-89; staff physician U.S. Army Health Clinic, Katterbch, Germany, 1989-90, comdr., 1990-92; staff physician U.S. Army Hosp., Nüernberg, Germany, 1992-93, chief emergency svcs., 1993-94; resident in ophthalmology U.S. Army Med. Ctr., Washington, 1994—. Decorated Meriotoris Svc. medals (3), Amry Commendation medals (2), Army Achievement medal. Mem. Am. Ophthalmology Assn., Internat. Plastic Modeler's Assn. Republican. Greek Orthodox. Home: 1221 Noyes Dr Silver Spring MD 20910 Office: US Army Med Ctr Ophthalmology Svc Washington DC 20307

BIRK, ROBERT EUGENE, retired physician, educator; b. Buffalo, Jan. 7, 1926; s. Reginald H. and Florence (Diebolt) B.; m. Janet L. Davidson, June 24, 1950; children—David Eugene, James Michael, Patricia Jean, Thomas Spencer, Susan Margaret. A.B., Colgate U., 1948; M.D., U. Rochester, 1952. Diplomate Am. Bd. Internal Medicine. Intern, resident Henry Ford Hosp., Detroit, 1952-57, chief 2d med. div., 1961-66, asst. to chmn. dept. medicine, 1965-66; practice medicine specializing in internal medicine Grosse Pointe, Mich., 1966-89; sr. active staff St. John Hosp., 1966-89, chief dept. medicine, 1967-70, dir. health edn., dir. grad. med. edn., 1975-86, exec. dir. continuing med. edn., 1975-86; dir. med. affairs St. Clair Ambulatory Care Corp., St. Clair Home Care Services, 1980-89; v.p. clin. affairs St. Clair Health Corp., 1985-89; assoc. prof. medicine Wayne State U., 1969-89. Contbr. articles to profl. jours. Mem. trustee's coun. U. Rochester, 1973-75, Med. Ctr. alumni coun., 1974-75; corp. mem. bd. Boys Clubs Met. Detroit, 1973-89; bd. trustees St. John Hosp., Macomb Ctr., 1986-89; corp. mem. bd. Boys Clubs Met. Detroit, 1973-89; trustee Mich. Cancer Found., 1980-89, bd. dirs., 1982-85. With U.S. Army, 1943-46. Fellow ACP, Detroit Acad. Medicine; mem. AMA, Assn. Hosp. Med. Edn. (trustee region IV 1986-87), Mich. Assn. Med. Edn. (trustee 1985-86), Am. Soc. Internal Medicine, Am. Acad. Med. Dirs., Oyster Reef Golf Club, Alpha Tau Omega. Republican. Episcopalian. Home: 8 Eagle Claw Dr Hilton Head Island SC 29926-1853

BIRKHAHN, RONALD HUGO, clinical nutrition educator; b. Marshalltown, Iowa, Dec. 4, 1939; s. Hugo Robert and Florence Grace (Lyon) B.; m. Gertrude Oi-Yee Chan, Nov 22, 1969; childrenonald Henry, Robert Hugo. B.A., Cornell Coll., Mt. Vernon, Iowa, 1962; Ph.D., Purdue U., 1967. Asst. prof. Hanover Coll., Ind., 1967-73; research assoc. SUNY-Buffalo, 1973-76; asst. prof. Med. Coll. Ohio, Toledo, 1976-81. assoc. prof., 1981-90; cons. Travenol Labs., Deerfield, Ill., 1982—. Contbr. articles to profl. jours. and chpts. to scholarly texts. Inventor of synthetic compounds. British Am. Coll. Nutrition; mem. Am. Inst. Nutrition, Am. Physiology Soc., Am. Soc. Clin. Nutrition, N.Y. Acad. Sci. Office: Med Coll of Ohio PO 10008 Toledo OH 43699-0008

BIRKHEAD, RICHARD GARTNER, cardiologist; b. Syracuse, N.Y., May 4, 1957; s. Guthrie Sweeney Jr. and Louise (Gartner) B.; m. Gail Joseph, July 22, 1984; children: Andrew Gartner, Emily, Daniel Alexander. AB, Oberlin (Ohio) Coll., 1979; MD, SUNY, Syracuse, 1983. Diplomate Am. Bd. Internal Medicine. Intern then resident Roger Williams Hosp., Providence, 1984-86; chief resident Meml. Hosp., Pawtucket, R.I., 1987-89; fellow in cardiology St. Elizabeth's Hosp., Boston, 1989; assoc. cardiologist Merrimack Valley Cardiology, Inc., Chelmsford, Mass., 1989—; dir. cardiac catheterization lab. Lowell (Mass.) Gen. Hosp., 1991—. Fellow Am. Coll. Cardiology. Office: Merrimack Valley Cardiology Inc 27 Village Square Chelmsford MA 01824

BIRMINGHAM, JACQUELINE JOSEPH, nursing administrator, consultant; b. Niagara Falls, N.Y., June 22, 1938; d. James and Helen (Hammam) Joseph; m. Ronald Birmingham; children: Ruth Wendy Allerton, Sarah Ellen. BSN, Niagara U. Coll. Nursing, 1960; MS in Adminstrn., U. Hartford, 1983. Staff devel. instr. Hartford (Conn.) Hosp., 1977-83, dir. discharge planning, 1983-93; dir. continuity of care Chartwell Home Therapies, 1993—; civilian nat. cons. on discharge planning Air Force Surgeon Gen. Author: Discharge Planning for Case Managers, 1994. Mem. Am. Assn. Continuity Care (past pres.), Case Mgmt. Soc. Am., Am. Assn. Healthcare Execs. (assoc.), Sigma Theta Tau.

BIRNS, MARK THEODORE, physician; b. Bklyn., Sept. 24, 1949; s. Leon and Naomi B.; m. Ann Krieger, Aug. 15, 1976; children: Samantha Lynn, Michael Eric, Kevin Douglas. B.A., Case Western Res. U., 1971; M.D., Albert Einstein Coll. Medicine, 1974. Diplomate: Am. Bd. Internal Medicine, Am. Bd. Gastroenterology. Intern Bronx Mcpl. Hosp. Ctr. Albert Einstein Hosps., 1974-75, resident in medicine, 1975-77; fellow in gastroenterology U. Oreg. Health Scis. Ctr., 1977-79; asst. chief gastroenterology Walter Reed Army Med. Ctr., 1979-83; asst. prof. medicine U. Health Scis., 1980-83; emergency physician Shady Grove Adventist Hosp., part time, 1980-83, Frederick Meml. Hosp., Washington, 1980-83; practice medicine specializing in gastroenterology and endoscopic biliary surgery Rockville, Md., 1983—; active staff Shady Grove Adventist Hosp., sec. med. staff, 1986-87, chief gastroenterology sect., vice chmn. dept. medicine, 1988, 89, mem. exec. com., 1990-92, mem. laser com., 1992, 93, 94, 95, mem. OR com., 1996; assoc. clin. prof. medicine dept. gastroenterology Georgetown U., Washington, 1988—; active staff Suburban Hosp.; courtesy staff Montgomery Gen. Hosp., Holy Cross Hosp. Major contbg. author: Radiology of the Liver, Biliary Tract, Pancreas and Spleen, 1987. Served to maj. USAR. Fellow ACP, Am. Coll. Gastroenterology; mem. AMA (Physician Recognition award 1978, 81, 84, 87, 90, 93), Am. Fedn. Clin. Rsch., Am. Gastroent. Assn., Am. Soc. Gastrointestinal Endoscopy (postgrad. edn. com. 1991-92), Md. Soc. Gastrointestinal Endoscopy, William Earl Clark Soc., Montgomery County Med. Soc. Home: 11413 Twining Ln Rockville MD 20854-1860 Office: 9711 Medical Center Dr Ste 308 Rockville MD 20850-3323

BIRNSTIEL, MAX LUCIANO, molecular biologist researcher; b. Bahia, South Am., Brazil, July 12, 1933; s. Max and Dalila (Varella) B.; m. Margaret Chipchase, Nov. 10, 1961; children: Marcus, Kirsty. D in Natural Scis., Swiss Fed. Sch., Zurich, Switzerland, 1959; D in Natural Scis. (hon.), U. Fribourg, Switzerland, 1977; PhD (hon.), U. Lund, Sweden, 1978; D in Natural Scis. (hon.), U. Guelph, Can., 1991. Postdoctoral Calif. Inst. Tech., Pasadena, 1960-63; lectr. U. Edinburgh, Scotland, 1963-66, sr. lectr., 1966-69, reader, 1969-71, prof., 1971-72; prof., head U. Zurich, Inst. Molecular Biology II, Zurich, Switzerland, 1972-86; mng. dir. Rsch. Inst. Molecular Pathology, Vienna, Austria, 1986-96; cons. Helmut Horten Found., Villalta, Switzerland, 1989—. Recipient Otto-Naegeli prize Swiss Nat. Fund. Com., 1979, Gold Medal for Outstanding Achievements, City of Vienna, 1989. Mem. NAS, German Acad. Nat. Scientists, Brazilian Acad. Scis. (founding), Acad. Europaea, Soc. German Scientists and Physicians, Soc. Physicians, Austrian Acad. Scis. Office: Rsch Inst Molecular Pathol, Dr Bohr-Gasse 7, 1030 Vienna Austria

BIRO, LASZLO, dermatologist; b. Czechoslovakia, May 31, 1929; came to U.S., 1956; s. Sandor and Margaret (Klein) B.; m. Dolores Macchiaroli, July 9, 1961; children: David, Lisa, Deborah, Michele. M.D., Univ. Med. Sch., Debrecen, Hungary, 1953. Diplomate Am. Bd. Dermatology. Intern Kings County Hosp., Bklyn., 1957-58; resident Bellevue Hosp., N.Y.C., 1958-60; pvt. practice medicine specializing in dermatology N.Y.C., 1960-61, Bklyn., 1960—; cons. dept. dermatology Bklyn. Hosp.; chief dept. dermatology Luth. Med. Ctr.; clin. prof. dermatology SUNY, Downstate Med. Ctr., 1971—. Contbr. articles on skin tumors to profl. jours. Fellow ACP, Am. Acad. Dermatology, N.Y. Acad. Medicine; mem. AMA, Kings County Med. Assn., Bay Ridge Med. Soc. (pres. 1987-88), N.Y. State Dermatol. Soc., Bklyn Dermatol. Soc., Internat. Soc. Tropical Dermatology, N.Y. Acad. Scis., Am. Coll. Cryosurgery (v.p. 1996), Semmelweis Sci. Soc. (pres. 1985). Office: 9921 4th Ave Brooklyn NY 11209-8347

BIRON, CHRISTINE ANNE, medical science educator, researcher; b. Woonsocket, R.I., Aug. 8, 1951; d. R. Bernard and Theresa Priscilla (Sauvageau) B. BS, U. Mass., 1973; PhD, U. N.C., 1980. Rsch. technician U. Mass., Amherst, 1973-75; grad. researcher U. N.C., Chapel Hill, 1975-80; postdoctoral fellow Scripps Clinic and Rsch., La Jolla, Calif., 1980; fellow U. Mass. Med. Sch., Worcester, 1981-82, instr., 1983, asst. prof., 1984-87; vis. scientist Karolinska Inst., Stockholm, 1984; asst. prof. Sch. Medicine Brown U., Providence, 1988-90, assoc. prof., 1990-96, prof., 1996—; mem. AIDS and related rsch. study sect. 3 NIH, 1991-93; mem. exptl. immunology study sect. NIH, 1993—. Assoc. editor Jour. Immunology, 1990-94; bd. editors Proceedings of Soc. for Exptl. Biology and Medicine, 1993—; contbr. articles, revs. to sci. jours.; sect. editor Jour. Immunology, 1995—; editor Jour. Nat. Immunity, 1994—. Leukemia Soc. Am. fellow, 1981, Spl. fellow, 1983, scholar, 1987; grantee NIH, 1985—; rsch. grantee MacArthur Found., 1991—. Mem. AAAS, Am. Assn. Immunologists (co-chmn. symposium 1990, 94, 95, 96), Am. Soc. Virology, Sigma Xi. Office: Brown U Biomed Ctr Box G-B618 Providence RI 02912

BIRSKIE, JOSEPH STANLEY, physician; b. Scranton, Pa., Jan. 7, 1963; s. Joseph Stanley and Dolores (Figured) B.; m. Kimberlee Ann Conte, June 1989; children: Matthew, Tyler. BS in biology, Wilkes Univ., 1987; D in osteopathy, Kirksville Coll., 1991. Diplomate Nat. Bd. Medical Examiners, Am. Bd. Osteopathic Internal Medicine. Osteopathic intern Atlantic City (N.J.) Med. Ctr., 1991-92, internal medicine resideny, 1992-94; cardiology fellow Deborah Heart & Lung Ctr., Browns Mills, N.J., 1994—; mem. Med. Edn. and Libr. Com. Deborah Heart & Lung Ctr., 1995—. Contbr. articles to profl. jours. Named Intern of Yr. Atlantic City Medical Ctr., 1992. Mem. Am. Osteopathic Assn., AMA, Am. Coll. Cardiology, Kirskville Alumni Assn. Republican. Roman Catholic. Home: 181 E Mourning Dove Way Absecon NJ 08201

BISBEE, GERALD ELFTMAN, JR., investment company executive; b. Waterloo, Iowa, July 12, 1942; s. Gerald Elftman Bisbee and Maxine Cole Prather; m. Linda Elaine Ude, Aug. 22, 1970; children: Gerald Elftman III, Katherine Elizabeth. BA, North Cen. Coll., Naperville, Ill., 1967; MBA, U. Pa., 1972; PhD, Yale U., 1975. Adminstr. Med. Ctr. Northwestern U., Chgo., 1968-70; asst. prof. Yale U., New Haven, 1974-78, assoc. dir. health svcs., 1975-78; pres. Hosp. Rsch. and Ednl. Trust, Chgo., 1978-84; v.p., shareholder Kidder, Peabody & Co., N.Y.C., 1984-88; chmn., chief exec. officer Hanger Orthopedic Group, New Canaan, Conn., 1988-89, Apache Med. Systems, Inc., Washington, 1989—; adj. prof. Northwestern U., Kellogg Sch. of Mgmt., Evanston, Ill., 1979-83; mem. visiting com. Harvard U. Health Svcs., Boston, 1986-92, exec. adv. com. Weatherhead Sch. of Mgmt. Health Systems Program, Case Western Res. U., Cleve., 1984-86; bd. dirs. Cerner Corp., Yamaichi Funds, Inc., Geriatrics and Med. Ctrs., Inc., Choate-Rosemary Hall. Author: (book) Multihospital Systems: Policy Issues for the Future, 1981, co-author: Managing the Finances of Health Institutions, 1980, Financing of Health Care, 1979, Musculo-skeletal Disorders: Their Frequency of Occurrence and Their Impact on the Population of the United States, 1978. Mem. adv. com. Waveney Care Ctr., New Canaan, 1987. Grantee USPHS, Washington, 1972-75. Mem. Yale Club (N.Y.). Home: 110 Wellesley Dr New Canaan CT 06840-3530 Office: Apache Med Systems 1650 Tysons Blvd Mc Lean VA 22102-3915

BISBEE, WILLIAM CARPENTER, physician assistant; b. Waterville, Maine, Feb. 14, 1950; s. Spaulding Jr. and Carol (Carpenter) B.; m. Elaine Louise Simard, May 28, 1978; children: Kristen Danielle, Bryanne, Erica, Dana Suzanne. BA, Dartmouth Coll., Hanover, N.H., 1972; cert. physician asst., Yale U., 1978. Cert. physician asst., Pa., Maine. Physician asst. Penquis Orthopaedics, P.A., Dover-Foxcroft, Maine, 1978—. Mem. sch. bd. MSAD #68, Dover-Foxcroft, 1980-85, 95—; joint bd. mem. Foxcroft Acad./MSAD #68, Dover-Foxcroft, 1980-85; mem. adv. bd. Foxcroft Acad. Health Ctr., Dover-Foxcroft, 1990-96; deacon Dover-Foxcroft Congl. Ch./United Ch. Christ, 1990-94, vice moderator, 1994-96, moderator, 1996—. Named Maine Rural Physician Asst. of Yr., Downeast Assn. Physician Assts., State of Maine, 1995. Home: 40 Spring St Dover Foxcroft ME 04426 Office: Penquis Orthopaedics PA 45 Dwelley Ave Dover Foxcroft ME 04426

BISBING, STEVEN B., mental health law consultant, psychologist; b. Carlisle, Pa., May 12, 1956; s. Raymond H. and Patricia A. (Bricker) B.; m. Janet A. Vecchia, Sept. 12, 1987; children: Daniel Vecchia, Zoe Vecchia. AB in Human Rels., High Point Coll., 1978; MS in Clin. Psychology, U. Cen. Fla., 1986; PsyD, Fla. Inst. Tech., 1986; JD, Antioch Sch. of Law, Washington, 1986. Lic. psychologist, Md. Psychotherapist pvt. practice Takoma Park, Md., 1986-89, 90—; sr. damages analyst Med-Psych Corp., Gaithersburg, Md., 1987-90; forensic cons., psychol. expert Mental Health Consultation Analysis, Inc., Takoma Park, Md., 1987—. Co-author: Sexual Exploitation by Health Providers, 1987, Forensic Psychiatry and Psychology, 1988, Sexual Abuse by Professionals: A Legal Guide, 1995. Mem. APA, Am. Acad. Forensic Sci., Am. Coll. Legal Medicine (Pres. award 1988-94), Md. Psychol. Assn.

BISCHOFF, MARILYN BRETT, clinical social worker; b. Mt. Vernon, N.Y., Apr. 16, 1930; d. Arthur Cushman and Mary Kathryn (Clark) Brett; m. Walter A. Bischoff, Mar. 25, 1961; children: Holly, Robert. BA magna cum laude, CCNY, 1959; MSW, Columbia U., 1961; D in Social Work, Boston Coll., 1985; cert. gerontology, U. Mass., Dartmouth, 1995. Diplomate Clin. Social Work. Clin. social worker Providence Child Guidance Clinic, 1961-65, 69-73; pvt. practice clin. social worker Providence, Attleboro, Mass., 1965—; instr. Providence Coll., 1988-89; speaker in field. Active Attleboro (Mass.) Area Mental Health Assn., 1975-94. Columbia Univ. fellow, N.Y.C., 1959-60; Nat. Inst. Mental Health fellow, 1960-61. Mem. NASW (sec.-treas. S.E. Mass. chpt. 1967-68, mem. speaker's bur. R.I. chpt. 1987), Acad. Cert. Social Workers, R.I. Group Psychotherapy Soc. (membership com. 1985—), Am. Group Psychotherapy Assn., Columbia U. Alumni Assn., Attleboro Ski Club, Phi Beta Kappa. Home and Office: 10 Norfolk Row Attleboro MA 02703-1629

BISGARD, JAY CRISPIN, physician, retired air force officer; b. Denver, Oct. 26, 1942; s. William Howard and Doris Irene (Carlson) B.; m. Nonja Sherriel Fulsher, June 11, 1964; children: Kirsten Laurel, Erika Lynn. BA, Northwestern U., 1964, MD, 1967; MPH, Harvard U., 1971. Diplomate Am. Bd. Preventive Medicine in Aerospace Medicine. Commd. 2d lt. U.S. Army, 1963; transferred to USAF, 1974, advanced through grades to col., 1980; cons. to surgeon gen. USAF, Washington, 1977—, chief med. readiness, 1978-79; spl. asst. to asst. sec. health affairs Dept. Def., Washington, 1979-81, dep. asst. sec., 1981-84; comdr. USAF Hosp., Robins AFB, Ga., 1984-85; command surgeon Alaskan Air Command, Elmendorf AFB, 1985-86; ret. USAF, 1986; corp. med. dir. Atlantic Richfield Co., Los Angeles, 1986-87; v.p., corp. med. dir. GTE, Stamford, Ct., 1987-88; corp. med. dir. Pacific Bell, San Francisco, 1988-94; dir. health svcs. Delta Airlines, Atlanta, 1994—. Decorated Bronze Star, Legion of Merit, Def. Superior Svc. medal. Fellow Aerospace Med. Assn., Am. Coll. Preventive Medicine, Am. Coll. Physician Execs.; mem. Internat. Aviation & Space Medicine, Am. Coll. Occupational Medicine.

BISH, JEANNETTE LOUISE, nurse, educator; b. Willmar, Minn., Jan. 14, 1932; d. Jay L. and Hannah (Ostlund) Larson; m. Daniel W. Bish, Sept. 1, 1954; children: Elizabeth Bish Alvarez, Katherine Bish. Diploma, Northwestern, Mpls., 1953; degree, Am. Med. Records Assn., 1975; BA in Health Care, Stephens Coll., 1978; MA in Health Care Mgmt., Redlands U., 1981. RN. Neuropsychiat. nurse supr. Brooke Army Gen. Hosp., San Antonio, 1970; dir. nurses Pomona (Calif.) Psychiat. Hosp., 1971-72; nursing edn. dir. State of Calif., Pomona, 1973—; retired, 1986—. Lt. Army Nurse Corps, 1953-55. Mem. ANA, ARC, Hospice.

BISHOP, BARBARA STRELETZKY, adult nurse practitioner; b. Bklyn., Oct. 1, 1962; d. Donald C. and Eleanor (Galassi) Streletzky; m. Jon C. Bishop, Oct. 3, 1987. BSN, Pa. State U., 1984; postgrad., U. Md., 1988-91. Cert. neurosci. nurse, adult nurse practitioner. Rehab. intern Good Shepherd Rehab. Ctr., 1983; clin. nurse dept. medicine Johns Hopkins Hosp., 1984-85, clin. nurse neurosci. critical care unit, 1985-90, coord. dept. neuroscis., 1990-91; adult nurse practitioner in pvt. neurology practice Easton, Md., 1991-94; pvt. practice adult nurse practitioner Southeastern Neurology Group, Portsmouth, Va., 1994—; lectr. Nat. Nurse Practitioner Symposium, 1993-95; NPACE, 1995-96. Author: (with others) Myasthenia Gravis - A Manual for the Nurse; author Pathelogic Eye Signs: A Self Study Module, Management of the Orgeon Donor: A First Step in Transplantation. Mem. ANA, Md. Nurses Assn., Am. Assn. Neurol. Nurses, Sigma Theta Tau.

BISHOP, BEVERLY PETTERSON, physiologist; b. Corning, N.Y., Oct. 19, 1922; d. Elof B. and Bonnie (Hunderford) Petterson; m. Charles William Bishop, May 2, 1944; 1 child, Geoffrey. BA, Syracuse U., 1944; MA, Rochester U., 1946; PhD, U. Buffalo, 1958. Asst. in physiology Glasgow (Scotland) U., 1956-57; instr. physiology U. Buffalo, 1958-62, asst. prof., 1962-67; assoc. prof. SUNY, Buffalo, 1967-75, prof. of physiology, 1976—, Disting. Teaching prof., 1992. Author: Basic Neurophysiology, 1992; co-editor: Neural Control Respiratory Muscles, 1996; contbr. more than 125 articles to profl. jours. Mem. Am. Physiol. Soc. (councillor, chair coms. 1989-92), Soc. Neurosci., Am. Thoracic Soc., Am. Congress Rehab., Am. Assn. of Electrodiagnostic Medicine. Home: 508 Getzville Rd Buffalo NY 14226-2546 Office: SUNY Dept Physiology S Camp Buffalo NY 14214

BISHOP, ELIZABETH SHREVE, psychologist; b. Ann Arbor, Mich., Nov. 18, 1951; d. William Warner Jr. and Mary Fairfax (Shreve) B. AB, U. Mich., 1972; MA, Ohio State U., 1973, PhD, 1976. Lic. psychologist, Mich. Psychologist Franklin County Program for the Mentally Retarded, Columbus, Ohio, 1974, WC Mental Health, Willmar, Minn., 1977-83; chief psychologist Battle Creek (Mich.) Child Guidance Ctr., 1981; dir. psychometrics Meridian Profl. Psychol. Cons., East Lansing, Mich., 1983-92; pres. Arbor Psychol. Cons., Ann Arbor, 1991—. Troop leader Girl Scouts U.S.A., Minn., Mich., Ohio, 1971-87, trainer, 1993—. Assoc. Univ. London Inst. Edn., 1976. Fellow Am. Orthopsychiat. Assn.; mem. APA, AAUW, Mich. Psychol. Assn., Mich. Women Psychologists, Coun. for Exceptional Children (local pres. 1977-78), Internat. Coun. Psychologists, Internat. Sch. Psychology Assn., LWV (Willmar v.p. 1989-91). Home: 1612 Morton Ave Ann Arbor MI 48104-4441 Office: Arbor Psychol Cons 1565 Eastover Pl Ann Arbor MI 48104-6316

BISHOP, EMMETT RUCKER, JR., psychiatrist; b. Spartenburg, S.C., June 17, 1946; m. Jill Hudson; children: Emmett R., Adam Frazier. BS, U. Ga., 1968; MD, Med. Coll. Ga., 1972. Jr. asst. resident Inst. of Psychiat. and Human Behavior, Balt., 1972-73; resident in psychiatry Med. Coll. Ga., Augusta, 1973-75, asst. prof. psychiat., 1977-81, dir. undergrad. curriculum in psychiat., 1977-81, instr. in gen. medicine, 1980-81; cons. Augusta Area Community Health/VA Hosp., 1977-81; pvt. practice The Harbin Clinic, Rome, Ga., 1981-82; cons. Tidelands, Savannah, Ga.; med. dir. Clark Ctr. Eating Disorder Program, Savannah. Lt. comdr. USN, 1975-77. Mem. AMA, Coastal Ga. Psychiat. Soc. (treas. 1990-91), Med. Assn. of Ga., Ga. Psychiat. Assn. (trustee, pres. coastal chpt. 1987). Office: 515 # 63d St Savannah GA 31405-4344

BISHOP, JOHN MICHAEL, biomedical research scientist, educator; b. York, Pa., Feb. 22, 1936; married 1959; 2 children. AB, Gettysburg Coll., 1957; MD, Harvard U., 1962; DSc (hon.), Gettysburg Coll., 1983. Intern in internal medicine Mass. Gen. Hosp., Boston, 1962-63, resident, 1963-64; rsch. assoc. virology NIH, Washington, 1964-66, sr. investigator, 1966-68; from asst. prof. to assoc. prof. U. Calif. Med. Ctr., San Francisco, 1968-72, prof. microbiology and immunology, 1972—, prof. biochemistry and biophysics, 1982—; prof., dir. G.W. Hooper Rsch. Found. G.W. Hooper Rsch. Found., 1981—; Univ. prof. U. Calif. Med. Ctr., San Francisco, 1994—. Recipient Nobel prize in physiology or medicine, 1989, Biomed. Rsch. award Am. Assn. Med. Colls., 1981, Albert Lasker Basic Med. Rsch. award, 1981, Armand Hammer Cancer award, 1984, GM Found. Cancer Rsch. award, 1984, Gairdner Found. Internat. award, Can., 1984, Medal of Honor, Am. Cancer Soc., 1984; NIH grantee, 1968—. Fellow Salk Inst. (trustee 1991—); mem. NAS, Inst. Medicine. Office: U Calif Medical Ctr Dept Microbiology Box 0552 San Francisco CA 94143-0552

BISHOP, KATHERINE ELIZABETH, clinical social worker, psychotherapist; b. Sanford, Fla., May 17, 1952; d. George Donald Jr. and Katherine Elizabeth (Gordon) B.; m. Joseph A. Weckerle III, Mar. 19, 1977 (div. Nov. 1989); 1 child, Katherine. B of Social Work summa cum laude, U. Fla., 1970; BS in Social Work summa cum laude, U. Cen. Fla., 1974; MSW, Fla. State U., Tallahassee, 1979. Lic. clin. social worker, Fla.; qualified clin. social worker, Acad. Cert. Social Workers; diplomate in clin. social work, NASW; cert. eating disorder specialist, Internat. Assn. Eating Disorder Profls. Clin. social worker Community Mental Health Ctr. Orange Meml. Hosp., Orlando, Fla., 1975-84; coord. outpatient svcs. Mental Health Ctr. Orlando Reg. Med. Ctr., 1984-87, adminstrv. dir. Ctr. for Life Mgmt., 1987-89; dir. eating disorder program, with social work svcs. Glenbeigh Hosp. of Orlando, 1989—, with outpatient svcs., 1991—; clin. social worker in pvt. practice Winter Park, Fla., 1980—; adj. prof. U. Ctrl. Fla. Sch. Social Work, Orlando, 1994—; student supr. Fla. State U., 1986—, U. So. Fla., Tampa, 1988-89; nursing and edn. supr. U. Fla., 1987-89. Facilitator, organizer Project Cope: Families of Mentally Ill, 1981-88. Recipient 1st prize Fla. Poetry Contest, U. Cen. Fla., 1974. Mem. Nat. Assn. Social Workers, Mental Health Assn. Cen. Fla. (bd. dirs. 1982-88, Golden Bell fellowship award 1982), Internat. Assn. Eating Disorder Profls., Delta Tau Kappa. Democrat. Episcopalian. Office: 1065 W Morse Blvd Ste 202 Winter Park FL 32789-3747

BISHOP, MICHAEL D., emergency physician; b. Anna, Ill., Feb. 10, 1945; m. Mary Susan Wilkens, Dec. 28, 1965; children: Amy Elizabeth, Amanda Marie. AB, GreenvilleColl., 1967; MD, U. Ill., 1971. Diplomate Am. Bd. Emergency Medicine (oral examiner 1980—, dir. 1988-96, mem. exec. com. 1990-95, mem. several bd. coms., sec.-treas. 1991-92, pres.-elect 1992-93, pres. 1993-94). Intern Meth. Hosp. Dallas, 1971-72; emergency physician Bloomington (Ind.) Hosp., 1972—, Morgan County Meml. Hosp., Martinsville, Ind., 1978—, Fayette Meml. Hosp., Connersville, Ind., 1989—, Jackson County Meml. Hosp., Seymour, Ind., 1989—; gen. dir. Immediate Care Ctrs. in Ind., various cities, 1981—; asst. clin. prof. med. scis. Ind. U., Bloomington, 1980—; pres., CEO Unity Physician Group P.C., Bloomington, Ind., 1971—. Bd. trustee, Sunday sch. tchr. Ellettsville (Ind.) Christian Ch.; bd. dirs. Peoples State Bank, Ellettsville; bd. dirs., sec. Ellettsville Bancshares, Ellettsville Elem. Sch. Bldg. Corp. Fellow AMA, Am. Coll. Emergency Physicians (charter, pres. Ind. chpt. 1979-80, nat. councillor 1976-81, 83, mem. nat. multi hosp./multi state blue ribbon task force 1981, mem. nat. ins. com. 1976-77, mem. coun. long range planning com. 1981-82, mem. coun. steering com. 1983-85, chmn. medicare task force 1984-86, chmn. task force on physician payment reform 1986-88, mem. govt. affairs com. 1983-88, 89-93, chmn. 1984-87, 89-93, mem. nat. emergency medicine polit. action com. bd. trustees 1984-88, 89-93, chmn. 1987, 89-93, mem. fin. com. 1987-93, James D. Mills Outstanding Contribution to Emergency medicine award 1990, mem. awards com. 1991-93, mem. reimbursement com. 1992—, dir. 1995—, lectr. in field), Am. Heart Assn. (mem. Ind. affiliate faculty, advanced cardiac life support), Am. Coll. Physician Execs. (dir. 1995—), Soc. Acad. Emergency Medicine, Christian Med. Dental Soc., Ind. State Med. Assn., Med. Group Mgmt. Assn., Owen Monroe County Med. Soc. Office: Unity Physician Group PC 1155 W Third St Bloomington IN 47404

BISHOP, RODNEY PHILIP, physician; b. London, Mar. 22, 1932; came to U.S., 1993; s. Reginald Henry and Eileen Gertrude (Hill) B.; m. Ann Frances Margaret Swindale, July 17, 1965; children: James, Sarah, Amy. BA in Natural Sci., Cambridge (Eng.) U., 1955, MA in Natural Sci., 1959; MD, London Royal Coll., Eng., 1960; D in Pub. Adminstrn. (med. advocacy), Pacific Western U., 1988. Diplomate English Med. Bd., Can. Med. Bd. Intern Salvation Army Hosp., Winnipeg, Can., 1960-61; surg. tng. Salvation Army Hosp., Nagercoil, South India, 1962-64; maternity tng. Maternity Hosp., Aberdeen, Scotland, 1964-65; pvt. practice Bedfordshire, Eng., 1966-73, New Westminster, B.C., Can., 1974—; med. dir. Queens Park Extended Care Hosp., New Westminster, 1977-86; pres., rsch. Rodney Bishop Mgmt. Co., Inc., 1980—. Readership and youth group leader Episcopalian Ch., London, 1956-73. Lt. British Army, 1950-55. Mem. AMA, Brit. Med. Assn., Can. Med. Assn., N.Y. Acad. Sci. Episcopalian. Home: 4177 Patos Dr Ferndale WA 98248 Office: 211-301 E Columbia St, New Westminster, BC Canada V3L 3W5

BISHOP, RUTH ANN, nurse, hospital administrator; b. Millville, N.J., July 4, 1953; d. Richard James and Florence Mae (France) Bishop; children: Jessica Ann, Melissa Sue. ADN, Cumberland County Coll., Vineland, N.J., 1982. Med. investigator Cumberland County Coroners Office, Millville; staff RN ICU, emergency rm., OP, insvc. dept. Millville; asst. dir. nursing long-term care Absecon (N.J.) Manor; dir. nursing long-term care Cumberland Convalescent Ctr., Vineland; coord. patient edn. and nursing quality assurance Elmer (N.J.) Hosp.; dir total quality mgmt. South Jersey Hosp. Systems, Bridgeton, N.J., 1991—; instr. Arthritis Support Group. Mem. Am. Diabetes Assn., Am. Soc. for Quality Control, Am. AACN, Millville Hosp. Nurses Assn. (past pres.), So. Jersey Consortium, South Jersey Insvc. Exch., Am. Heart Assn. (instr., critical care cert., IV cert., ACLS), VHA Quality Connections Coun. (chmn. 1996—). Home: 1301 S Lincoln Ave #115 Vineland NJ 08360-6685 Office: South Jersey Hosp System 333 Irving Ave Bridgeton NJ 08302-2123

BISOL, SUSAN ANN, nursing administrator; b. Shirley, Mass., Aug. 14, 1954; d. Paul Shannon and Joan Martha (Cosenza) McCumber; m. Thomas James Bisol, May 1, 1981. Diploma, Leominster (Mass.) Hosp., 1975. BSN, Fitchburg State, 1980; MSN, Anna Maria Coll., Mass., 1987. RN, Mass., N.H.; cer. operating room nurse. Staff nurse emergency rm. Leominster (Mass.) Hosp., 1975-79, staff nurse oper. rm., 1980-83; surgical supr. Heywood Hosp., Gardner, Mass., 1983-86; nurse mgr. oper. rm. Burbank Hosp., Fitchburg, Mass., 1986-87; dir. nursing Mystic Nursing and Rehab. Ctr., Fitchburg, Mass., 1990-91; nurse mgr. surg. svcs. Henry Heywood Hosp., 1991-92; dir. surg. svcs. So. N.H. Regional Med. Ctr., Nashua, 1993—; faculty Fisher Coll. Mem. N.H. Orgn. Nurse Execs., Assn. Oper. Rm. Nurses, Sigma Theta Tau. Office: So NH Regional Med Ctr PO Box 2014 8 Prospect St Nashua NH 03061

BISORDI, JOSEPH EDMUND, nephrologist, medical center administrator; b. Mt. Vernon, N.Y., Sept. 18, 1949; s. Edmund P. and Winifred (Martin) B.; m. Carol Ann Keimig, May 18, 1975; children: John Edmund, Kathryn Elizabeth. BA, Manhattan Coll., 1971; MD, Georgetown U., 1975. Diplomate Am. Bd. Internal Medicine with subspecialty in nephrology. Resident internal medicine Geisinger Med. Ctr., Danville, Pa., 1975-77, chief resident, 1977-78, assoc. nephrology, 1980-93, v.p. clin. rsch., 1987—, dir. dept. nephrology, 1993—; fellow nephrology Albert Einstein Coll. Medicine, Bronx, 1978-80; clin. assoc. prof. medicine Thomas Jefferson Med. Coll., Phila., 1989—; mem. med. rev. bd. End Stage Renal Disease Network #24, King of Prussia, Pa., 1986-88, med. rev. chair Network #4, Pitts., 1988—; mem. forum, 1995—. Contbr. articles to profl. jours. Pres. Timberwood Homeowner's Assn., Danville, 1988-92. Rsch. fellow Nat. Kidney Found., 1978-79. Fellow ACP; mem. Am. Soc. Hypertension, Am. Soc. Nephrology, Am. Soc. Transplant Physicians, Internat. Soc. Nephrology, Hosp. Info. and Mgmt. Sys. Soc., Applied Rsch. Ethics Nat. Assn. (pres. 1989). Office: Geisinger Medical Center Dept. Nephrology Academy Ave Danville PA 17822-1410

BISSADA, NABIL KADDIS, urologist, educator, researcher, author; b. Cairo, Egypt, Sept. 2, 1938; s. Kaddis B. and Negma Bissada; m. Samia Shafik Henain, July 23, 1967; children: Sally, Nancy, Mary, Amy, Andrew. M.D., Cairo U., 1963. Diplomate Am. Bd. Urology. Intern Cairo Univ. Hosp., 1964-65; resident in surgery Babelsharia Gen. Hosp., 1965-69; resident in urology U. N.C. Hosp., 1970-72, chief resident, 1972-73; asst. prof. urology U. Ark., 1973-77, assoc. prof., 1977-79; cons. urologist King Faisal Specialist Hosp. and Rsch. Ctr., Riyadh, Saudi Arabia, 1979-87; prof., chief urologic oncology Med. U. S.C., 1987—; chief urologic surgery Ralph H. Johnson Med. Ctr., 1987—; co-chmn. Div. U., U.S. Sect. Internat Coll. Surgeons, 1989-91, chmn., 1991-93; frequent speaker to regional, nat. and internat. med. groups. Author: Lower Urinary Tract Function and Dysfunction: Diagnosis and Management, 1978; Pharmacology of the Urinary Tract and the Male Reproductive System, 1982; contbr. to hundreds of articles and books; pioneer, developer of several significant surgical and med. urologic treatment methods. Fellow ACS, Internat. Coll. Surgeons; mem. AMA, Am. Urol. Assn., Soc. Internat. D'Urologie, Soc. Urologic Oncology, Urodynamic Soc., Soc. Urology and Engring., Egypt Am. Urol. Assn. (pres. 1990-92), Arab Am. Urol. Assn. (pres. 1993—), Sigma Xi. Office: Med U of SC Med Ctr 171 Ashley Ave Charleston SC 29425-0001

BISSELL, MICHAEL GILBERT, pathologist; b. Ridgecrest, Calif., Mar. 5, 1947; s. Henry Robert and Margaret Alberta (Ezell) Benefiel; m. Sherrie L. Lyons, Mar. 27, 1977 (div. June 1990); children: Cassandra, Grahame; m. Lita A. Hill, Nov. 29, 1991. BS in Chemistry, U. Ariz., 1969, BS in Math., 1969; MD, Stanford U., 1975, PhD in Neurobiol., 1977; MPH, U. Calif., Berkeley, 1978. Diplomate Am. Bd. Pathology. Resident Martinez VA Med. Ctr. U. Calif., Davis, 1978-81; rsch. fellow NIMH, Bethesda, Md., 1981-84; asst. prof. pathology U. Chgo. Med. Ctr., 1984-88; dir. clin. pathology City of Hope Nat. Med. Ctr., Duarte, Calif., 1988-91; v.p./med. dir. Nichols Inst. Reference Lab., San Juan Capistrano, Calif., 1991-93; dir. lab. medicine, assoc. prof. pathology U. Texas, 1993—; ptnr. Biomed.-Environ. Cons., Richland, Wash., 1989—; speaker in field. Contbr. articles to profl. jours. Activist/lectr. Calif. Physicians Alliance, San Francisco, 1988—. Fellow Am. Soc. Clin. Pathologists (course dir. annual meeting), Coll. Am. Pathologists, mem. Nat. Com. Clin. Lab. Standards, Am. Assn. Clin. Chemistry, Clin. Lab. Mgmt. Assn. (treas.), Physicians for Nat. Health Program (activist, lectr.), Sierra Club, Sigma Xi. Democrat. Office: U Tex Med Br 11th and Texas Ave Galveston TX 77555

BISSONNETTE, DEBORA LEE, obstetrics birth center nurse; b. Newark, N.Y., Aug. 8, 1965; d. Leo A. and Clara A. (Perrault) B. Diploma cum laude, St. Joseph's Sch. Nursing, Syracuse, N.Y., 1986; BSN cum laude, Nazareth Coll., 1988. Staff nurse Rochester (N.Y.) Gen. Hosp., 1986; primary nurse Birth Ctr. Strong Meml. Hosp., Rochester, 1988—; nurse Lourdes Camp, Skaneatles, N.Y., summer 1987. Mem. PNO, EXCEL (exec. com., restructuring com. 1992—), Sigma Theta Tau. Roman Catholic. Office: Strong Meml Hosp 601 Elmwood Ave Rochester NY 14642-0001

BISTRIAN, BRUCE RYAN, internist, educator; b. Southampton, N.Y., Oct. 22, 1939; s. Peter and Mary Laura (Ryan) B.; m. Eleanor Alice Dix, Sept. 3, 1964; children: Tennille Ryan, Jordan Brooke, Britton Perry. BA, NYU, 1961; MD, Cornell U., 1965; MPH, Johns Hopkins U., 1971; PhD, MIT, 1975; AM (hon.) Harvard, 1990. Diplomate: Am. Bd. Internal Medicine; bd. cert. Critical Care Medicine. Intern Cornell U., N.Y.C., 1965-66; metabolism fellow U. Vt., Burlington, 1968-69, resident in medicine, 1969-70; from asst. clin. prof. to assoc. prof. Harvard U. Med. Sch., Boston, 1975-90, prof. medicine, 1990—; clin. assoc. physician research resources div. NIH, 1975-78; lectr. MIT, 1981-84. Mem. editorial bd. Jour. Parenteral and Enteral Nutrition, Jour. Nutritional Biochemistry and Metabolism, Harvard Health Letter, Women's Health, Critical Care Medicine; contbr. over 300 sci. articles to profl. publs. Served to capt. U.S. Army, 1966-68. Grantee Nat. Inst. Gen. Med. Scis., 1977-80; Nat. Inst. Arthritis, Metabolism and Digestive Disease, 1979-83, Nat. Inst. Arthritis, Diabetes, Digestive and Kidney Diseases, 1985—, Nat. Cancer Inst., 1984-87. Fellow Am. Coll. Nutrition, ACP; mem. Fedn. Am. Soc. Exptl. Biologists, Am. Soc. Clin. Nutrition (sec. 1993—), Am. Fedn. Clin. Research, Am. Soc. Parenteral and Enteral Nutrition (pres. 1989-90), Soc. Critical Care Medicine, Mass. Med. Soc. Presbyterian. Achievements include over 20 patents in field. Subspecialties: Nutrition (medicine); Biochemistry (medicine). Current work: Protein calorie malnutrition; total parenteral nutrition; nutrition and infection. Home: Argilla Rd Ipswich MA 01938 Office: New Eng Deaconess Hosp 194 Pilgrim Rd Boston MA 02215-5310

BISTRONG, HERBERT WALTER, internist; b. N.Y.C., May 22, 1934. BS, Coll. William and Mary, 1956; MD, U. Va., 1960. Diplomate Am. Bd. Internal Medicine; lic. physician, Mass., Va. Intern Nat. Naval Med. Ctr., Bethesda, Md., 1960-61; resident Naval Hosp., San Diego, 1964-67; pvt. practice Beverly, Mass., 1970—; cons. Naval Hosp., Boston, 1974; clin. instr. Boston U., 1968-74; staff internist Beverly Hosp., 1970—, chief medicine, 1978-80, v.p. med. staff, 1982-84, corporator, 1983—, pres. med. staff, 1991-93. Trustee Boston Med. Libr., 1979-82, N.E. Health Sys., 1995—. Fellow ACP, Mass. Med. Soc. (councilor, pres. Essex South dist. 1980-82). Office: 77 Herrick St Beverly MA 01915-2734

BITAR, DAVID E., colon and rectal surgeon; b. Portland, Oreg., Nov. 9, 1944; s. Emmanuel and Margaret Bitar; children: Elizabeth, David. BS, Westmont Coll., Santa Barbara, Calif., 1967; MD CM, McGill U., Montreal, 1971. Resident in surgery Mt. Zion Hosp., San Franciso, 1971-75; fellow Presbyn. Hosp., Dallas, 1975-76; pvt. practice colon and rectal surgery Berkeley, Calif., 1976—. Author: Cohn's Current Therapy, 1977. Fellow ACS, Am. Soc. Colon and Rectal Surgeons; mem. Calif. Med. Assn. Office: 2900 Telegraph Berkeley CA 94705

BITONTE, DAVID ALAN, anesthesiologist; b. Youngstown, Ohio, Apr. 4, 1954; s. Dominic Anthony and Helen Marie (Furr) B.; m. Laura Beth Stiver, Sept. 7, 1985; children: Elizabeth, David, Caroline. BS, U. Dayton, 1976; DO, Phila. Coll. Osteo. Medicine, 1980. Diplomate Am. Osteo. Bd. Anesthesiology. Intern Doctors Hosp., Columbus, Ohio, 1981; resident Warren (Ohio) Gen. Hosp., 1984, staff anesthesiologist, 1985-87; fellow Pain Therapy Cleve. Clinic, 1987; chief of Anesthesia Alliance (Ohio) Community Hosp., 1988—; bd. dirs. Phila. Coll. Osteo. Medicine Alumni Assn. Mem. Christopher Columbus Mutual Benefit, Alliance, 1988—; trustee Alliance Community Found., 1990—; bd. dirs. Stark County Med. Soc., Canton, Ohio, 1989—; bd. dirs. Mahoning Nat. Bank of Youngstown, Ohio. Am. Coll. Gen. Practitioners scholar, 1978. Fellow Am. Osteo. Coll. Anesthesiologists; mem. Am. Acad. Pain Mgmt., Am. Soc. Anesthesiology, Internat. Anesthesia Rsch. Soc., Ohio State Med. Assn., Ohio Osteo. Assn. Home: 4602 Beecwood Ave NE Paris OH 44669 Office: Alliance Community Hosp 264 E Rice St Alliance OH 44601-4341

BITSCH-LARSEN, LARS KRISTIAN, anesthesia and intensive care specialist; b. Herning, Denmark, May 12, 1945; s. Immanuel and Valborg (Larsen) B.-L.; m. Kate Lund Jensen; children: Kristian, Simon. MD, Copenhagen U., Denmark, 1973; Degree, Tech. Inst., 1976; diploma in health econs., 1993. Diplomate European Acad. Anaesthesia. Residency Växsjö, Lasaret, Sweden, 1984; specialist tng. Växsjö Lassaret, Sweden, 1984; specialist tng. Haukeland U., Bergen, Norway, 1985, cons. anaesthesia, 1986-88; dir. anaesthesia Kalundborg Sygehus, Denmark, 1989—; vice-chmn. staff com. Kalundborg Sugehus, Denmark, 1990-93, chief adminstrv. dr., also dir. clin. chemistry dept., dir. blood bank, 1994—; sci. advisor for developing monitoring systems Nimorod, 1992, dir. clin. chemistry lab., 1995, dir. blood bank, 1995—; chmn. County Ednl. Bd. Specialist Tng. Anaesthesia and Intensive Care, 1994. Author: Phsyologi in Anaesthesi, 1986, 2d edit., 1987; editor: pratical Respirator Therapy, 1986, 2d edit., 1987; contbr. articles to profl. jours. Chmn. County Adv. Com., Vestsjaelland, 1989—, Computer Implimentation Com., Kalundborg, 1990—. Grantee Vestsjaellands County, 1990, Comers & Industry Bd., 1991, 92. Mem. Engrs. Assn. (div. for risk evaluation), European Acad. Anaesthesia, European Cardiothoracis Anesthetist Assn., European Soc. Computing and Tech. in Anaesthesia, Nordic Neuroanesthist Assn., Lions. Office: Kalundborg Sygehus, Noerrre Alle 27, DK 4400 Kalundborg Denmark

BITTAR, EDWARD S., orthopaedic surgeon; b. N.Y.C., June 16, 1942. AB, Rutgers U., 1963; MD, Temple U., 1978; PhD, NYU, 1978. Diplomate Am. Bd. Orthopaedic Surgeons; lic. physician, Va., Fla. Intern in gen. surgery U. Fla. Coll. Medicine, Gainesville, 1978-79, resident in orthopaedics, 1979-82; chief resident Gainesville VA Med. Ctr., 1982-83; fellow in arthroscopy, arthroscopic surgery, sports medicine Orthop. Rsch. of Va., Richmond, Va., 1983; asst. prof. orthop. surgery U. Fla., Gainesville, 1984-87, assoc. prof., 1987—, assoc. chmn. dept. orthops., 1986-87, dir. med. edn. dept. orthops., 1984-87, co-dir. Orthop. Clinic, Student Health Svc., 1984-87, assoc. clin. prof., 1989—, co-dir. orthop. outreach program, 1992—; pres. Univ. Orthop. Assocs., Gainesville, 1986—; pvt. practice Palm Bay, Fla., 1987—; team physician Fla. Marlins Baseball Club, 1992—, Fla. Manatees, 1993—, Fla. State League Baseball, 1994, U. Fla. Gators, 1984-87, Brevard C.C., 1989—, Fla. Inst. Tech., 1989—, N.Y. Knights, 1992, Melbourne (Fla.) H.S., 1987—; chief orthop. surgery Gainesville VA Med. Ctr., 1984-87; mem. sci. adv. bd. Spinal Cord Rsch. Found., 1986-89; arthroscopy cons. Cabot Med., 1984-87, Lasersonics Corp., Becton Dickinson; mem. arthroscopy bd. Orthop. and Sports Medicine News, 1989—. Contbr. articles to profl. jours. Grantee VA Hosp., 1989; Meml. Sloan-Kettering Cancer Ctr. scholar. Fellow Am. Acad. Orthop. Surgeons; mem. Arthroscopy Assn. N.Am. (bd. trustees 1995—, psychomotor skills com. 1990—), Am. Bd. Med. Specialties, Fla. Orthop. Soc., Fla. Med. Soc., Brevard County Med. Soc., European Soc. Knee Surgery and Arthroscopy, Am. Soc. Sports Medicine, Internat. Arthroscopy Assn., Mensa. Office: Univ Orthopaedic Assocs 5200 Babcock St NE #111 Palm Bay FL 32905

BITTENBENDER, LEE R., dermatologist; b. Palo Alto, Calif., Feb. 17, 1946; s. Clark R. and Dollie Kathleen (Jones) B.; m. Marily Sue Buller, May 30, 1970 (div. 1994); children: Laura, Kyra. BA, U. Kans., 1968, MD, 1972. Diplomate Am. Bd. Dermatology, Nat. Bd. Med. Examiners; lic. physician Kans. State Bd. Healing Arts, Iowa State Bd. Healing Arts. Pvt. practice dermatology Lawrence, Kans.; intern St. Francis Hosp., Wichita, 1972-73; resident in dermatology U. Iowa, Iowa City, 1973-76. Fellow Am. Acad. Dermatology, Am. Soc. for Dermatologic Surgery; mem. Kans. Dermatol. Soc. (pres.), Iowa Dermatologic Soc., Kansas City Dermatol. Soc. (pres.). Office: Dermatology Ctr Lawrence 930 Iowa St Lawrence KS 66044

BITTNER, MARVIN JOEL, physician, educator; b. Lincoln, Nebr., Apr. 3, 1950; s. Morris Baer and Clarissa Louise (Hollander) B. SB, U. Chgo., 1972; MD, Harvard U., 1976. House officer dept. internal medicine U. Mich., Ann Arbor, 1976-79; fellow in infectious diseases U. Minn. Med. Sch., Mpls., 1979-81; asst. prof. med. microbiology and medicine Creighton U. Sch. Medicine, Omaha, 1981-91, assoc. prof., 1991—; assoc. prof. U. Nebr. Med. Ctr., Omaha, 1992—; staff physician VA Med. Ctr., Omaha, 1981—; physician travel clinic Douglas County Health Dept., Omaha, 1985—. Contbr. articles to Am. Jour. Infection Control, Archives Internal Medicine, Am. Jour. Medicine, Infection Control, Hosp. Practice, Jour Antimicrobial Agts. Chemotherapy, Clin. Infectious Diseases. Tng. fellow Venereal Disease Rsch. Fund., Am. Social Health Assn., 1980-81. Fellow ACP; mem. Infectious Disease Soc. Am., Sigma Xi (assoc.). Office: VA Med Ctr 111 D 4101 Woolworth Ave Omaha NE 68105-1873

BITTNER, NORMAN DOUGLAS, prosthodontist; b. Glen Ridge, N.J., July 8, 1930; s. Norman Meuser and Marion Jean (Reilly) B.; m. Nov. 24, 1958 (div. Nov. 1985); children: Elisabeth, Douglas, Christine. BSBA, Upsala Coll., 1953; DDS, U. Pa., 1957; prosthodontic cert., NYU, 1969. Pvt. practice, Peapack, N.J., 1959—; pres. N.D. Bittner & Co., investments; cons. on product devel. Warner Lambert Corp., Parsippany, Troy Hills, N.J., 1970-80, lectr., demononstrator new products, 1976-80; cons. Johnson & Johnson, New Brunswick, N.J., 1985, Prudential DMO, Livingston, N.J., 1985-90; expert witness on dental litigation and malpractice numerous ins. cos., N.J., 1985—; asst. prof. prosthodontics, 1968-75; lectr. investments and health care Felician Coll., Lodi, N.J., 1965—; lectr. U. Tokyo Dental Sch., 1976. Trustee Upsala Coll., East Orange, N.J., 1980-94; trustee Felician Coll., 1990—, chmn. fin. com., 1995—, also portfolio mgr. endowment. Lt. USN, 1957-59. Recipient certs. of appreciation for lectures various dental socs., 1970-79. Mem. Am. Prosthodontics Soc. (life), Am. Hanoverian Soc. (treas. 1980-90). Home and Office: 181 Main St Peapack NJ 07977

BIXBY, DENNIS ARTHUR, engineering manager; b. Essex, Eng., July 3, 1955; s. Harold James and Jemima Dale (Barnard) B.; m. Jill Ann Gamblin, July 11, 1981. BSEE with honors, U. of South Bank, London, 1986. Chartered engr. Group project engr. Elec. Corp. U.K., London, 1983-88; sr. elec. engr. Glaxo, Stevenage, 1988-92, site-wide project engr. elec., 1992-95, area project mgr., 1995; area project mgr. Glaxo Wellcome, Greenford, 1995—. Mem. CIBSE, Inst. Elec. Engrs. (sr. vice chmn. Bedfordshire area 1986-95). Office: Glaxo Wellcome, Greenford Rd, Greenford England

BIXLER, SANDRA J., cardiovascular clinical nurse specialist; b. Reading, Pa., Mar. 10, 1942; m. James Philip Bixler III, July 28, 1963; children: Kimberly, Karen, J. Philip IV. Diploma, Hahnemann Hosp., Phila., 1963; BSN, Widener U., 1988; MSN, U. Pa., 1992. RN, Pa. Office nurse Reading, 1965-67; PRN staff nurse St. Joseph Hosp., Reading, 1971-73, staff nurse ICU-CCU, 1973-80, asst. head nurse, 1980-84, staff developer, asst. head nurse, 1984-87, staff nurse cardiac cath lab., 1987-89, staff developer specialty care, 1989-90, ICU-CCU staff nurse, 1990-92; clin. nurse specialist cardiology practice St. Joseph Hosp., 1993—; pvt. practice clin. nurse specialist cardiology; cons. Springhouse Corp. Mem. AACN (cert. CCRN, rep. edn. network 1990-91, Southeastern chpt., sec. Greater Reading chpt. 1992-93, 94-95, chairperson membership com. 1992), Sigma Theta Tau.

BIXON, CHRISTINE TACKETT, chiropractor; b. Akron, Ohio, June 23, 1944; d. Elbert E. and Mary I. (Stumpf) Gruber; m. Roger D. Tackett, Aug. 19, 1967 (dec. June 1979); 1 child, Catherine J.; m. Lewis A. Bixon, July 3, 1983; 1 child, Michael D. BS, Georgetown U., 1967; DC summa cum laude, Life Chiropractic Coll., Marietta, Ga., 1981. Pvt. practice Longwood, Fla., 1983—. Mem. Internat. Chiropractic Assn., Nat. Inst. Chiropractic Rsch., Fla. Chiropractic Assn., Parker Rsch. Found. Office: 242 Highway 434 W Longwood FL 32750-4918

BIZZI, EMILIO, neurophysiologist, educator; b. Rome, Feb. 22, 1933; came to U.S., 1963, naturalized, 1982; s. Vittorio and Anna (Galeazzi) B.; m. Jane Stockton Shaw, Aug. 9, 1941. M.D. summa cum laude with highest honors, U. Rome, 1958. Postdoctoral trainee Inst. Med. Pathology, U. Siena, Italy, 1958-60; postdoctoral trainee Inst. Physiology, U. Pisa, Italy, 1960-63; research assoc. neurophysiol. lab., dept. zoology Washington U., St. Louis, 1963-64; vis. assoc. sci. physiology, lab. clin. sci. NIMH, Bethesda, Md., 1964-66; research assoc. dept. psychology MIT, Cambridge, 1966-67; lectr. dept. psychology MIT, 1967-68, assoc. prof. neurophysiology, 1969-72, prof. neurophysiology, 1972-80, Eugene McDermott prof. brain scis. and human behavior, 1980—; dir. Whitaker Coll., MIT, 1983-88, chmn. dept. Brain and Cognitive Scis., 1986—; adv. bd. Biomed. Engring. Ctr. for Clin. Instrumentation. Contbr. numerous chpts., articles, abstracts to profl. pubs.; editorial bd. Brain Theory Newsletter, 1980—, Jour. Motor Behavior, 1981—, Jour. Neurobiology, 1981—. Recipient Alden Spencer award Columbia U. Coll. Physicians and Surgeons, 1978, Whitaker Health Scis. award MIT, 1978, Hermann von. Helmholtz award 1992; Found. for Research in Psychiatry fellow, 1978—. Mem. Nat. Acad. Scis., Internat. Brain Research Orgn., Am. Acad. Arts and Scis., Am. Acad. Clin. Neurophysiol., AAAS, Am. Physiol. Soc., Soc. Neurosci. Office: MIT Dept Brain & Cognitive Scis Cambridge MA 02139

BIZZOCO, DREW FRANK, chiropractor; b. Bklyn., Feb. 5, 1961; s. Rose Josephine (Giglio) B. Student, Kingsboro Coll., 1978-79, Bklyn. Coll., 1980-81; D Chiropractic, N.Y. Chiropractic Coll., 1985; grad., Logan Chiropractic Coll., 1993. Diplomate in chiropractic neurology. Pvt. practice chiropractic Bklyn., 1987-93; chiropractor, owner, mgr. Spinecare, Bklyn., 1993—; quality assurance mgr. CHIRO, N.J., 1995—. Instr. T. Kang Tae Kwon Do, 1986—. Mem. Am. Chiropractic Assn., N.Y. State Chiropractic Assn. Republican. Office: Spinecare 3500 Nostrand Ave Brooklyn NY 11229

BJARNASON, SIBILLA EIRIKSDOTTIR, dentist, educator, researcher; b. Rezekne, Latvia, Jan. 27, 1938; arrived in Sweden, 1980; d. Eriks Alksnis and Vanda (Senake) Elksne; m. Reynir Bjarnason, May 18, 1965; children: Reynisdottir, Signy. DDS, Rigas Med. Inst., Riga, Latvia, 1961; PhD, Göteborg (Sweden) U., 1987; diploma (hon.), Latvian Med. Acad., Riga, 1995. Gen. practice dentistry Dental Clinic, Moscow, 1961-64, Tallin, USSR, 1964-65; pvt. practice Reykjavik, Iceland, 1965-80; clin. instr. Göteborg U., 1980-85, assoc. prof. dentistry, 1985—; rsch. adviser Latvian Med. Acad., 1990—. Contbr. articles to profl. jours. Recipient numerous rsch. grants. Mem. Internat. Assn. Dental Rsch., European Orgn. for Caries Rsch. (sr.), European Assn. for Pediatric Dentistry, Latvian Assn. Dental Rsch. (hon.). Home: Berzeliigatan 25, 412 53 Goteborg Sweden Office: Göteborg U, Medicinaregatan 12, 413 90 Goteborg Sweden

BJÖRKHOLM, ELISABET ANNA, gynecological educator; b. Stockholm, Oct. 13, 1941; s. Georg and Anna-Greta (Wahlstedt) B. MD, Karolinska Inst., 1967, PhD, 1980. With clin. gyn-obs. Danderyds Hosp., Sweden, 1968-70; surgeon Nacka and St. Erik Hosp., Stockholm, 1971-72; mem. clin. gyneacological oncology staff Radiumhemmet Karolinska Hosp., Stockholm, 1973—; assoc. prof. Karolinska U., 1983—. Contbr. articles to profl. jours. Mem. Swedish Med. Assn., Swedish Soc. Medicine, Internat. Gyneacologic Cancer Soc., Swedish Soc. Obs-gyn. Office: Karolinska Hosp, Dept Gyn/Oncology, S-17176 Stockholm Sweden

BJORKLUND, JANET VINSEN, speech pathologist; b. Seattle, July 31, 1947; d. Vernon Edward and Virginia Lea (Rogers) B.; m. Dan Robert Young, Dec. 04, 1971; children: Emery Allen, Alanna Vinsen, Marisa Rogers. Student, U. Vienna, Austria, 1966-67; BA, Pacific U., 1969; student, U. Wash., 1970-71; MA, San Francisco State U., 1977. Cert. clin. speech pathologist, audiologist. Speech pathologist, audiological cons. USN Hosp., Rota, Spain, 1972-75; traineeship in audiology VA Hosp., San Francisco, 1976; speech pathologist San Lorenzo (Calif.) Unified Schs., 1975-77, 78-81; dir. speech pathology St. Lukes Speech and Hearing Clinic, San Francisco, 1977-78; audiologist X.O. Barrios, M.D., San Francisco, 1977-81; cons. Visually Impaired Infant Program, Seattle, 1981-82; speech pathologist Everett (Wash.) Schs., 1982-94; speech-lang. pathologist, supr. Sultan (Wash.) Schs., 1995—; supr. pediat. programs speech pathology Group Health Coop. Puget Sound, Seattle, 1994; cons. Providence Hosp. Childrens Ctr., Everett, 1985-93, Pacific Hearing and Speech, 1988-93. Author: (with others) Screening for Bilingual Preschoolers, 1977, (TV script), Clinical Services in San Francisco, 1978, Developing Better Communication Skills, 1982. Chair Washington Mid. Sch. Site Coun., 1995—. Mem. Am. Speech-Lang. and Hearing Assn., Wash. Speech and Hearing Assn. (regional rep. 1985-86, chair licensure task force 1986-88, rep. Birth to Six Project 1988-91, pres. 1993), Pub. Edn. Adv. Com. (rep. 1995—), Phi Lambda Omicron (pres. Pacific U. chpt. 1968). Congregationalist.

BJORNDAL, ARNE MAGNE, endodontist; b. Ulstein, Norway, Aug. 19, 1916; s. Martin I. and Anne B.; B.S., State Coll. Volda, 1939; D.D.S., U. Oslo, 1947; D.D.S., U. Iowa, 1954, M.S., 1956; m. Katharine G. Benson, Jan. 12, 1952; children—Katharine, Kari, Lee. Instr., Coll. Dentistry U. Oslo, 1948-50, 51-53; intern Forsyth Dental Infirmary, Boston, 1950-51; mem. faculty U. Iowa, Iowa City, 1954—, prof., 1964—, founder, head dept. endodontics, 1956-80. Served to maj. Army NG, 1963-70. Decorated King Hakon 7th medal (Norway); diplomate Am. Bd. Endodontics; Fulbright scholar, 1950-51. Fellow Am. Coll. Dentistry; mem. ADA (service fgn. countries award 1979), Iowa Dental Assn. (life), Am. Assn. Endodontics, N.Y. Acad. Sci., Omicron Kappa Upsilon. Republican. Lutheran. Clubs: Optimists, Elks. Author: Anatomy and Morphology of Human Teeth, 1983. Home: 2510 Bluffwood Cir Iowa City IA 52245-3543 Office: Coll Dentistry U Iowa Iowa City IA 52242

BJORNES, OLE PEDER, physician, consultant; b. Arendal, Norway, Mar. 30, 1957; s. Clifford Mangor and Marie (Våje) B.; m. Antje Cläre Louise Ziegler, Nov. 30, 1985 (dec. Mar. 1994); children: Mathias, Christine. Candidate med., Rheinische Friedriche-Wilhelm U., Bonn, Germany, 1983. Home: Singslivn 6, N-4800 Arendal Norway

BJØRNØ, LEIF, industrial acoustics educator; b. Svendborg, Denmark, Mar. 30, 1937; s. Svend Aage Valdemar and Elna Marie Jensen. Student, U. Roskilde (Denmark), 1956; MSc in Mech. Engring., Tech. U. Denmark, Lyngby, 1962, PhD, 1967; diploma, Imperial Coll., London, 1971. Asst. prof. Tech. U. Denmark, Lyngby, 1967-69, assoc. prof., 1970-78, prof. indsl. acoustics, 1978—; prof. honoris causa Harbin U. Engring., 1994; vis. prof. Imperial Coll., London, 1969-70; chmn. mech. engring., v.p. Acad. Tech. Scis., 1989-93; chmn. bd. dirs. Brunata A/S, Sensor Tech. System A/S, Syd-Tek, Food Tech A/S; bd. dirs. Reson A/S, Reson Inc. USA, pres. 2d European Congress Underwater Acoustics, 1994. Author: Fluid Mechanics, 1972; author or co-author 8 books, 1 translation; editor Ultrasonics, 1973-94; contbr. 300 articles to internat. jours., conf. proceedings and books. Mem. Coun. of the Ch., Taastrup, 1977-80. Named Knight of the Order of Dannebrog, Her Majesty the Queen, Denmark, 1991. Fellow Acoustical Soc. Am., Inst. Acoustics U.K., South African Acoustical Inst., IEEE; mem. Soc. Exploration Geophysicists, Acoustical Soc. Japan, Acad. Tech. Scis., U.S. Naval Inst., Instr. Noise Control Engring. (corr.), Spanish Acoustical Soc. (hon.), Sigma Xi. Office: Tech U Denmark, Dept Indsl Acoustics, 2800 Lyngby Denmark

BJORNSSON, SIGURDUR, physician; b. Princeton, N.J., June 5, 1942; s. Bjorn Sigurdsson and Una (Johannesdottir) S.; children: Kristin, Björn, Signy Sif. MD, U. Iceland, 1968. Diplomate Am. Diplomate Am. Bd. Internal Medicine. Intern U. Iceland Hosp., Reykjavik, 1969; resident New Britain Gen. Hosp., Conn., 1972; fellow Roswell Park Meml. Inst., Buffalo, 1974; sr. cancer research internist Roswell Park Meml. Inst., Buffalo, 1974-78; research asst. prof. medicine SUNY, Buffalo, 1977-78; cons. med. oncologist City Hosp., Reykjavik, Iceland, 1978—; attending physician internal medicine and oncology St. Joseph's Hosp., Reykjavik, 1978—, chief dept. internal medicine, 1989-96; chief dept. hematology and oncology Reykjavik Hosp., 1996—; cons. med. oncologist U. Hosp., Reykjavik, 1978—; lectr. medicine and oncology U. Iceland, Reykjavik, 1978—. Bd. dirs. Icelandic Cancer Soc., Reykjavik, 1980, Icelandic Physicians for the Prevention Nuclear War, Reykjavik, 1983. Mem. Am. Soc. Clin. Oncology, Am. Assn. Cancer Research, European Soc. for Med. Oncology, Icelandic Med. Assn., Icelandic Assn. Med. Specialists (chmn.), Icelandic Soc. Internal Medicine, World Med. Assn. Home: Bergstadastraeti 78, 101 Reykjavik Iceland

BJORNSTAD, BRAD, physician, management consultant; b. Huron, S.D., June 5, 1952; s. Bruce Bjornstad and Norine Alyce (Hodgins) Dougherty; m. Kathryn Cecilia Corrigan, Sept. 5, 1949; children: Kathryn Angela, Julie Michelle. BA in Chemistry, U. South Fla., 1974, MD, 1977; M in Health Svc. Adminstrn., Coll. of St. Francis, 1996. Diplomate Am. Bd. Internal Medicine, Am. Bd. Geriatric Medicine, Am. Bd. Quality Assurance and Utiliation Rev. Physicians. Intern dept. internal medicine U. South Fla. Coll. Medicine, Tampa, 1977-78, resident dept. internal medicine, 1978-80, asst. prof. dept. internal medicine, 1980-81, fellow dept. allergy and immunology, 1980-81; pvt. practice Tampa, 1981-93; med. dir., pres. Tampa Bay Health Care Group, 1994—; trustee Ami Town and Country Hosp., 1986-93, chief staff, 1986-88, chmn. dept. medicine, 1982-85, mem. med. staff exec. co., 1982-90; cons. Iameter, Inc., San Mateo, Calif., 1990-93. Author: (with others) Risk Management Trends and Applications, 1988, (with others) Economic Credentialing in the Era of Integrated Health Care, 1993. Mem. governing bd. Hillpac, Tampa, 1990-93. Fellow ACP; mem. AMA (del. hosp. med. staff sect. 1987-93, chmn. fla. del. 1991-93), Am. Soc. Internal Medicine, Fla. Med. Assn. (ho. of dels. 1987—, chmn. coun. hosp. med. staffs 1991), Fla. Soc. Internal Medicine, Hillsborough County Med. Assn. (chmn. hosp. med. staff com. 1987-93, del.-at-large to exec. coun. 1989-91, trustee 1991-94, chmn. bd. trustees 1994-95), Greater Town and Country C. of C. Office: 12210 Bruce B Downs Blvd Tampa FL 33612-9211 Office: 12210 Bruce B Downs Blvd Tampa FL 33612-9211

BLACHER, RICHARD STANLEY, psychiatrist; b. N.Y.C., May 24, 1924; s. Charles and Bernardine (Zolotorofe) B.; m. Sara-Lee Rudolph, July 4, 1960 (dec. 1970); 1 child, Lisa; m. Marjory May Popky, Oct. 27, 1985. BA, Brown U., 1945; MD, U. Rochester, 1948; cert. in psychoanalysis, N.Y. Psychoanalytic Inst., 1963. Diplomate Am. Bd. Psychiatry and Neurology. Clin. asst. attending psychiatrist Mt. Sinai Hosp., N.Y.C., 1955-66, assoc. attending psychiatrist, 1966-74; assoc. clin. prof. Mt. Sinai Sch. Medicine, N.Y.C., 1967-74; clin. prof. Tufts U. Sch. Medicine, Boston, 1974-85, prof. psychiatry, 1985—, lectr. in surgery, 1977—; psychiatry lectr. Boston U. Sch. Medicine, 1995—; bd. dirs. Internat. Consortium for Study of Neurol. and Psychol. Reactions to Cardiac Surgery, 1980—. Editor: The Psychological Experience of Surgery, 1987; editl. bd. Found. of Thanatology, N.Y.C., 1988—, Wiley Series in Psychiatry, N.Y.C., 1987—; contbr. over 50 articles to profl. jours. Pres. Tenafly (N.J.) Nature Ctr. Assn., 1972; mem. steering com. Greater Boston Physicians for Social Responsibility, Cambridge, Mass., 1983-92; trustee Boston Civic Symphony Orch., 1993—. Fellow Am. Psychiat. Assn. (life); mem. Am. Psychoanalytic Assn., Internat. Psychoanalytic Assn., Am. Psychosomatic Soc., N.Y. Psychoanalytic Soc., Boston Psychoanalytic Soc. Jewish. Home and Office: 50 Plainfield St Newton MA 02168-1618

BLACK, ASA CALVIN, JR., anatomist, educator; b. Clarksville, Tenn., Jan. 2, 1943; s. Asa C. and Josephine Elizabeth Black; m. Cynthia Woods, Apr. 3, 1971; B.A., Vanderbilt U., 1965, Ph.D. in Anatomy (NIH predoctoral fellow), 1974. Assoc. U. Iowa, Iowa City, 1973-74, NIH postdoctoral fellow Coll. Medicine, 1974-75, asst. prof. dept. anatomy Coll. Medicine, 1975-85; assoc. prof. Mercer U. Sch. Medicine, 1985-95, prof. 1995—; instr. anatomy Vanderbilt U., Nashville, 1972-73. Mem. AAAS, Am. Assn. Anatomists, Anat. Soc. of Great Britain and Ireland, Internat. Soc. Biomed. Rsch. on Alcoholism, N.Y. Acad. Scis., Rsch. Soc. on Alcoholism, Am. Soc. Neurochemistry, Brit. Brain Research Assn., European Brain Behavior Soc., Internat. Soc. Neurochemistry, Sigma Xi, Alpha Chi Sigma. Contbr. chpts. to books, articles to biol. jours. Home: 1701 River Forest Dr Macon GA 31211-9635 Office: Mercer U Sch Medicine 1400 Coleman Ave Macon GA 31207-1000

BLACK, BETTY LYNNE, biologist, educator; b. St. Louis, Mar. 28, 1946; d. Samuel Richard and Roma Maxine (Fox) B. BA, Lindenwood Coll., 1967; MS, Vanderbilt U., 1969; PhD, Washington U., 1977. Grad. teaching asst. Vanderbilt U., Nashville, 1967-69; instr. Harris Tchr.'s Coll., St. Louis, 1969-72; grad. rsch. asst. Washington U., St. Louis, 1972-76, postdoctoral fellow dept. pathology sch. medicine, 1977-79; asst. prof. dept. zoology N.C. State U., Raleigh, 1979-85, assoc. prof., 1985-96, prof., 1996—. Contbr. articles to profl. jours. NIH fellow, 1977-79, grantee, 1984-87; NIH Rsch. Career Devel. award, 1986-91. mem. Soc. Devel. Biology, Am. Soc. for Cell Biology. Home: 5104 Carter St Raleigh NC 27612-3466 Office: NC State U Dept Zoology Box 7617 Raleigh NC 27695-7617

BLACK, BEVERLY HOLSTUN, psychiatric social worker; b. Thomaston, Ga., Sept. 27, 1942; d. Gordon Robinson and Louise (Hooten) Holstun; m. Frank Anderson Black, Dec. 27, 1963 (div. 1988); children: Sereina Louise, Margot Elisabeth; m. Michael Summers Lynch, Dec. 31, 1992. BA in English, U. Denver, 1963; MSW, U. S.C., 1979. Diplomate in social work. Tchr. Sumter County, S.C., 1975-77; clin. social worker Santee-Wateree Mental Health Ctr., Sumter, S.C., 1979-81; psychiat. social worker Ctr. for Personal and Family Growth, Valdosta, Ga., 1981-83; dir. Anxiety Disorders Ctr., Round House Psychiat. Ctr., Alexandria, Va., 1983—; speaker, lectr. on anxiety disorders, 1985—. Editor, expert videos for United Way, 1986, 87; appearances on TV as expert on anxiety disorders. Mem. adv. bd. No. Va. Women's Ctr., Vienna, 1985—; advisor 1st Family Support Ctr. in Air Force, Moody AFB, Valdosta, 1982, YMCA Women's Shelter, Sumter, 1980; mem. adv. bd. CIA, Washington, 1995—. Mem. AAUW, Nat. Assn. Social Workers. Republican. Baptist. Home: 6313 Mori St Mc Lean VA 22101-3153 Office: Round House Sq Psychiat Ctr 1444 Duke St Alexandria VA 22314-3403

BLACK, DEVERA GIGES, psychotherapist; b. Newark, Nov. 21, 1926; d. Bernard Edward and Belle (Demner) McCoy; m. Gerald Giges, July 6, 1952 (div. July 1975); children: Robert Eli, Laura Ellen; m. Stuart C. Black, Aug. 31, 1975. BA, Douglas Coll., 1948; MSW, Columbia U., 1951. Cert. social worker N.Y.; bd. cert. diplomate in social work. Med. social worker Maimonides Hosp., Bklyn., 1951-54; social work cons. Coll. of Dentistry NYU, N.Y.C., 1963-68; clin. social worker Westchester Jewish Community Svcs., White Plains and Yonkers, N.Y., 1968-78; pvt. practice South Salem, N.Y., 1977—; mem. faculty Core Energetic Inst., N.Y.C., 1981-90, Phoenica Pathwork Ctr., 1982-93. Nem. NASW, Soc. Clin. Social Work Psychotherapists. Home and Office: 71 Twin Lakes Rd South Salem NY 10590-1012

BLACK, HENRY RICHARD, physician; b. N.Y.C., June 1, 1942; s. David Robert and Beatrice (Morris) B.; m. Hannah Leah Rosenberg, Aug. 15, 1965; children—Matthew, Dana. A.B., Columbia U., 1963; M.D., NYU, 1967. Diplomate Am. Bd. Internal Medicine. Intern, Johns Hopkins Hosp., Balt., 1967-68, resident in internal medicine, 1970-71; resident Yale-New Haven Hosp., 1971-72, chief resident in internal medicine, 1974-75; fellow Yale U., 1972-74; practice medicine specializing in internal medicine and hypertension, New Haven, 1975-92; asst. prof. Yale U. Med. Sch., New Haven, 1975-79, assoc. prof. 1979-88, prof., 1988-92, dir. hypertension svcs., 1975-92; Charles J. and Margaret Roberts prof. and chmn. dept. preventive medicine, prof. internal medicine Rush-Presbyn.-St. Luke's Med. Ctr., Chgo., 1992—. Bd. dirs. Am. Heart Assn. Conn., 1985—, fellow council on hypertension. Contbr. articles to profl. jours. Served with USPHS, 1968-70. Fellow ACP, Internat. Soc. Hypertension; mem. Am. Fedn. Clin. Research, Columbia Coll. Alumni Assn. (bd. dirs. 1983-87, v.p. acad. affairs 1986-87), Am. Soc. Hypertension (exec. coun.). Jewish. Home: 1209 N Astor St # 4N Chicago IL 60610-2314 Office: Rush Presbyn St Lukes Med Ctr 1725 W Harrison St Chicago IL 60612

BLACK, JACINTH BAUBLITZ, clinical social worker; b. Corpus Christi, Tex., Feb. 17, 1944; m. Donald James Baublitz, Oct. 26, 1968 (div. June 1979); children: Jessica Ruth, Stefanie Elizabeth; m. Robert Drummond Black, Mar. 14, 1987. BA, Sam Houston U., 1965; MSW, Boston Coll., 1972; postgrad., Am. Assn. Sex Educators, Counselors and Therapists, Washington, 1976-77; advanced studies with Maxie Maultsby Jr., U. Ky., 1980. Cert. Acad. Social Workers, 1976; lic. social worker and marriage and family therapist, Mich.; diplomate Acad. Social Workers, 1988; nat. bd. cert. clin. hypnotherapist, 1995. Tchr. English and Spanish Brazosport Schs., Freeport, Tex., 1965-67; caseworker Harris County Child Welfare Unit, Houston, 1967-69; vocat. counselor Mass. Employment Security, Lowell, 1969-70; family therapist Cath. Family Service, Saginaw, Mich., 1973-75; contractual clin. social worker Midland-Gladwin Community Mental Health Ctr., 1975-80; pvt. practice clin. social work Midland, Mich., 1975—; adj. prof. psychology Northwood Inst., 1982-85; cons., lectr., speaker various profl. and lay orgns. Author: Relationshift, 1983, A Singles Guide to Tight Spots and Tricky Situations, 1986; newspaper advice columnist Bay Area Rev., 1985-89. Bd. dirs. Big Sisters Am., Inc., Midland, 1978-80; mem. bd. mgrs. Midland County Hist. Soc., 1996—. Mem. NASW. Episcopalian. Home: 4553 S Saginaw Rd Midland MI 48640-8554 Office: PO Box 2227 Midland MI 48641-2227

BLACK, SIR JAMES (WHYTE), pharmacologist; b. June 14, 1924. MB, ChB, U. St. Andrews; MD (hon.), U. Edinburgh, 1989; DSc (hon.), U. Glasgow, 1989. Asst. lectr. physiology U. St. Andrews, 1946; lectr. physiology U. Malaya, 1947-50; sr. lectr. U. Glasgow Vet. Sch., 1950-58; with ICI Pharms. Ltd., 1958-64; head biol. rsch., dep. rsch. dir. Smith, Kline & French, Welwyn Garden City, 1964-73; prof., chmn. dept. pharmacology Univ. Coll., London, 1973-77; dir. therapeutic rsch. Wellcome Rsch. Labs., 1978-84; prof. analytical pharmacology King's Coll. Hosp. Med. Sch., U. London, 1984—; chancellor elect Dundee (Scotland) U., 1992—. Decorated Knight, 1981; recipient Nobel prize for medicine, 1988. Fellow Royal Coll. Physicians, Royal Soc. (Mullard award 1978); mem. Royal Coll. Vet. Surgeons (hon. assoc.). Office: U Dundee, Dundee DD1 4HN, Scotland*

BLACK, KAREN SHIPP, endocrinologist, educator; b. Ft. Worth, Nov. 6, 1959; d. Robert Lee and Joyce Rosalee (Castillo) Shipp; m. Quentin Robert Black, July 10, 1982. BS in Biology, Tex. A&M U., 1982, MD, 1986. Resident internal medicine Georgetown U. Hosp., Washington, 1986-89; fellow in endocrinology U. Tex. Sci. Ctr., San Antonio, 1989-92, instr. medicine, 1992-93, clin. asst. prof. medicine, 1993—; endocrinologist Endocrinology-Nuclear Medicine Assn., San Antonio, 1993—; mentor U. Tex. Health Sci. Ctr., 1993-96. Contbr. articles to profl. jours., chpts. to books. Mem. Citizens for Bonilla, San Antonio, 1993-96. Recipient Career Devel. award VA, 1991, Nat. Rsch. award NIH, 1991, Young Investigator award Am. Fedn. Clin. Rsch., 1991. Fellow Am. Assn. Clin. Endocrinologists; mem. AMA, Am. Coll. Physicians, Am. Soc. Bone andMineral Rsch., Nat. Osteoporosis Found., The Endocrine Soc. Republican. Roman Catholic. Home: PO Box 780967 San Antonio TX 78278 Office: Endocrinology-Nuclear Medicine Assn 1303 McCullough Ste 374 San Antonio TX 78212

BLACK, LOIS MAE, clinical psychologist, educator; b. Boston, Nov. 16, 1931; d. Lester and Lillian (Porter) B.; m. John Henning, June 23, 1956 (div. 1977); children: Paul, John, Thomas, Michael; m. Karl Barth, July 31, 1982. B.A., Brown U., 1953; M.A., Yale U., 1955; Ph.D., Cornell U., 1962. Diplomate: lic psychologist, N.Y. Lectr. Rutgers U., New Brunswick, N.J., 1960-62; asst. prof. SUNY, Cortland, 1963-64, Syracuse (N.Y.) U., 1967-68; assoc. prof. Onondaga Community Coll., Syracuse, 1971-74; research assoc. SUNY Coll. Medicine, Syracuse, 1965-78; clin. and research assoc. prof. pediatrics SUNY Coll. Medicine, 1984—; research assoc. prof. psychology and edn. Syracuse U., 1978-83, dir. affirmative action, 1974-82. Contbr. articles to profl. jours. Vestry mem. Grace Episcopal Ch., 1968-70; bd. dirs. Upstate Day Care Ctr., 1968-77, Central N.Y. council Girl Scouts U.S.A., 1981-84; co-chmn. council on women's issues United Way, Central N.Y., 1981-83, corp. bd. dirs., 1984-90; bd. dirs. Campfire Inc., 1986-89. Fulbright scholar, 1953-54; USPHS fellow, 1959-60; HEW grantee, 1977-80. Mem. Am. Psychol. Assn., Eastern Psychol. Assn., N.Y. State Psychology Assn., Soc. Rsch.in Child Devel., Am. Orthopsychiat. Assn., Ctrl. N.Y. Psychol. Assn., NOW, Sigma Xi. Home: 311 Berkley Dr Syracuse NY 13210-3041

BLACK, NICHOLAS ANDREW, health services researcher, educator, physician; b. Bristol, Eng., May 21, 1951; s. Joseph and Margaret Susan (Hewitt) B. MB, ChB, U. Birmingham, Eng., 1974, MD, 1983; diploma of child health, Royal Coll. Ob/Gyn. Registrar in cmty. medicine Oxfordshire Health Authority, Eng., 1978-80; sr. registrar U. Oxford, Eng., 1980-83; lectr. Open U., Eng., 1983-85; sr. lectr. in pub. health medicine London Sch. Health and Tropical Medicine, 1985-93, reader pub. health medicine, 1993-95, prof. health svcs. rsch., 1995—; hon. cons. in pub. health medicine North Thames Regional Health Authority, 1985-95, Kensington Chelsea and Westminster H.A., 1995—. Editor: Health and Disease: A Reader, 1985, Jour. Health Series Rsch. and Policy, 1995—. Fellow Faculty of Pub. Health Medicine; mem. Soc. Social Medicine (treas. 1994—). Office: London Sch Hygiene Tropical, Med Health Svcs Rsch Unit, Veppel St, London WC1E 7HT, England

BLACK, PATRICIA JEAN, medical technologist; b. Milw., Oct. 22, 1954; d. Dale B. and Geraldine L. (Milligan) Heywood; m. Robert S. Black, Oct. 14, 1978. BS, Millikin U., 1978; degree in med. tech., St. Mary's Hosp., 1978. Med. technologist Mercy Hosp., Urbana, Ill., 1978-85; biol. lab. technician No. Regional Rsch. Ctr., USDA Agrl. Rsch. Svc., Peoria, Ill., 1985-88; lab. mgr. Chapman Cancer Ctr., Joplin, Mo., 1989—. Patentee in field. Mem. AAUW, Am. Soc. Clin. Pathologists (cert., assoc.), Clin. Lab. Mgmt. Assn., Zeta Tau Alpha (scholar chmn. 1976, house mgr. 1977), Sigma Zeta.

BLACK, PAUL HENRY, medical educator, researcher; b. Boston, Mar. 11, 1930; s. Samuel Louis and May (Goldberg) B.; m. Sandra Merkin, June 2, 1962; children: Scott, Marc, Jeffrey. A.B., Dartmouth Coll., 1952; M.D., Columbia U., 1956. Diplomate Am. Bd. Internal Medicine. Intern Mass. Gen. Hosp., Boston, 1956-57, asst. resident in medicine, 1957-58, clin. and research fellow, 1958-60, resident in medicine, 1960-61; sr. asst. surgeon Lab. Infectious Diseases USPHS Nat. Inst. Allergy and Infectious Diseases, NIH, Bethesda, Md., 1961-63; sr. surgeon Lab. Infectious Diseases USPHS Nat. Inst. Allergy and Infectious Diseases, U. Glasgow Inst. Virology, Scotland, 1963-64, Nat. Inst. Allergy and Infectious Diseases, NIH, Bethesda, Md., 1964-67; asst. prof. medicine Harvard U. Med. Sch., Boston, 1967-70, assoc. prof. medicine, 1970-80; asst. physician Mass. Gen. Hosp., Boston, 1967-70; dir. Hubert H. Humphrey Cancer Research Ctr. Boston U., 1979-83; assoc. physician Mass. Gen. Hosp., Boston, 1970-80, hon. physician, 1980—; chmn., prof. microbiology, research prof. surgery, prof. medicine Boston U. Sch. Medicine, 1979-96, prof. emeritus, 1996—; cons. Roswell Park Meml. Inst., Buffalo, 1976-80, Monsanto Chem. Corp., St. Louis, 1976-82, Collaborative Research, Inc., Lexington, Mass., 1984—, Nat. Cancer Adv. Bd. Subcom. on the Evaluation of Cancer Ctrs., Bethesda, 1975-80 ; sci. cons. U.S.-Israel Binat. Sci. Found., Jerusalem, Israel, 1974—; mem. NIH Study Sect. Virology, 1968-72, Tumor Virus Detection Segment, Spl. Virus Cancer Program, Bethesda, 1972-76; mem. subcom. on environ. carcinogens, Am. Cancer Soc. Task Force on Cancer Prevention, 1975-82 , sci. adv. bd. Worcester Found. for Exptl. Biology, Mass., 1976-78, sci. adv. bd. Dartmouth-Hitchcock Med. Ctr., Hanover, N.H., 1976-80, Gov.'s Task Force on AIDS, Commonwealth of Mass., Boston, 1983—; chmn. spl. virus cancer program contract rev. com., Nat. Cancer Inst., 1977-79. Author monograph; contbr. articles to profl. jours., chpts. to books. Nat. Cancer Inst. grantee, 1967-87. Fellow AAAS; mem. Am. Soc. Clin. Investigation, Infectious Diseases Soc., Am. Soc. Microbiology, Am. Soc. Virology, Am. Assn. Med. Sch. Microbiology Chmn., Soc. Gen. Microbiology, Sigma Xi.

Democrat. Jewish. Home: 21 Dawes Rd Lexington MA 02173-5926 Office: Boston U Sch Medicine 80 E Concord St Boston MA 02118-2307

BLACK, PAUL WILLIAM, plastic and reconstructive surgeon; b. Quincy, Ill., Sept. 9, 1934; s. Orin Russell and Mary Louise (Staley) B.; divorced; children: Paul William II, Mary Elizabeth; m. Rebecca J. Schilling, July 5, 1985. BA, Knox Coll., 1956; MD, Washington U., 1960. Diplomate Am. Bd. Plastic and Reconstructive Surgery, Am. Bd. Surgery. Intern in surgery N.C. Meml. Hosp., U. N.C., 1960-61; resident in gen. surgery U. N.C., 1961-68; resident in plastic surgery U. N.C. and U. Fla., 1961-68; pres. Atlanta Plastic Surgery, 1969-95. Contbr. articles to profl. jours. Capt. U.S. Army, 82nd Airborne, 1961-63. Fellow Am. Coll. Surgeons, Am. Soc. Plastic and Reconstructive Surgeons, Am. Assn. Plastic and Reconstructive Surgeons, Am. Soc. Aesthetic Plastic Surgery and others. Office: Ctr for Plastic Surgery 5th and South Sts Highlands Profl Bldg Ste 1 Highlands NC 28741

BLACK, PERCY, psychology educator; b. Montreal, Que., Can., Jan. 6, 1922; s. Ovido and Rose (Vasilevsky) B.; m. Virginia Arne, June 21, 1951; children—Deborah, David, Elizabeth, Jonathan. B.S., Sir George Williams Coll., Montreal, 1944; M.Sc., McGill U., 1946; Ph.D., Harvard U., 1953. Instr. in Social Scis. U. Ky., 1948-49; rsch. asst. in Race Rels. U. Chgo., 1950-51; rsch. assoc. in Child Psychology U. Minn., 1949-50; Asst. prof. psychology U. N.B., Fredericton, 1951-53; vis. scholar Univ. Coll., London, 1953-54; dir. research Social Attitude Survey, Yonkers, N.Y., 1955-67; prof. emeritus in Psychology Pace U., Pleasantville, N.Y., 1967—; Contbg. author: Societies Around the World, 2 vols., 1953; author: The Mystique of Modern Monarchy, 1953; contbr. articles to profl. jours. Fellow AAAS; mem. APA, Am. Psychol. Soc., B'nai B'rith. Home: 29 Cross Hill Ave Yonkers NY 10703-1422 Office: Pace U Psychology Dept Pleasantville NY 10570-2799

BLACK, PERRY, neurological surgeon, educator; b. Montreal, Oct. 2, 1930; came to U.S., 1959, naturalized 1979; s. Ovido and Rose (Vasilevsky) B.; children: Daniel Ovid, Julie Miriam, Amy Rose. BSc, McGill U., Montreal, 1951, MD, CM, 1956. Intern, then asst. resident in medicine and gen. surgery Jewish Gen. Hosp., Montreal, 1956-58; asst. resident in neurology Montreal Neurol. Inst., 1958-59; resident in neurosurgery Johns Hopkins Hosp., Balt., 1959-63, neurosurgeon, 1964-79; NIH fellow in physiology Johns Hopkins U. Sch. Medicine, 1961-62, instr. neurol. surgery, 1964-67, asst. prof., 1967-69, assoc. prof., 1969-79, asst. prof. psychiatry, 1967-70, assoc. prof., 1970-79; prof. Hahnemann U. Sch. Medicine, Phila., 1979-94, chmn. dept. neurosurgery, dir. pain treatment program, 1979-94, dir. brain tumor program, 1983-94; prof. neurosurgery Med. Coll. Pa. and Hahnemann U., 1994—, dir. malignant brain tumor program, 1995—; dir. child head injury project dept. neurol. surgery Johns Hopkins Hosp., 1963-79; dir. lab. neurol. scis., chmn. ctrl. rsch. authority Friends Med. Sci. Rsch. Ctr., Balt., 1972-79, hon. dir., 1979—; mem. neurology study sect. NIH, 1973-77; coun. neurosurg. rep. Johns Hopkins Med. Sch., 1977-78, coun. vice chmn., 1978-79. Editor: Drugs and the Brain, 1969, Physiological Correlates of Emotion, 1970, Brain Dysfunction in Children: Etiology, Diagnosis, and Management, 1981; contbr. articles to profl. jours. Bd. dirs. Epilepsy Assn. Central Md., 1966-77, chmn. profl. adv. bd., 1973-75; mem. com. of fifty Epilepsy Found. Am., 1970-76, state coordinator for Md., 1973-76. Recipient Residents Paper award So. Neurosurg. Soc., 1963, Volvo award World Fedn. of Neurosurgical Socs., 1985. Mem. AAAS, Congress Neurol. Surgeons (chmn. sci. and edn. com. 1969-72, chmn. sci. program com. 1971-72, editor newsletter 1972-75, mem. exec. com. 1972-75, mem. nominating com. 1975-77, chmn. internat. com. 1975-81, assoc. editor jour. 1976-82, editor jour. internat. neurosurgery 1976-87, Disting. Svc. award 1977), AMA, AAUP, Am. Assn. Neurol. Surgeons (Harvey Cushing Soc., mem. subcom. on continuing edn. 1974-78), Am. Pain Soc., Soc. Neurol. Surgeons, Am. Soc. Stereotactic and Functional Neurosurgery, Soc. for Neurosci., Rsch. Soc. Neurol. Surgeons, Am. Epilepsy Soc., Am. Neurol. Assn., Internat. Assn. for Study of Pain, Philadelphia County Med. Soc., Phila. Neurol. Soc. (2nd v.p. 1982-83), Pa. Neurosurg. Soc. (mem. coun. 1989—, sec., treas. 1990, pres. 1992), Mid-Atlantic Neurosurg. Soc. Office: Hahnemann Univ Dept Neurosurgery Broad & Vine Mail Stop 407 Philadelphia PA 19102-1192

BLACK, ROBERT LINCOLN, pediatrician; b. Los Angeles, Aug. 25, 1930; s. Harold Alfred and Kathryn (Stone) B.; m. Jean Wilmott McGuire, June 27, 1953; children: Donald J., Douglas L., Margaret S. A.B., Stanford U., 1952, M.D., 1955. Diplomate: Am. Bd. Pediatrics. Intern Kings County Hosp., Bklyn., 1955-56; resident and fellow Stanford U. Hosp., 1958-62; practice medicine specializing in pediatrics Monterey, Calif., 1962—; Clin. prof. Stanford U., 1962—; cons. Calif. Dept. Health, Sacramento, 1962—; mem. Calif. State Maternal, Child, Adolescent Health Bd., 1984-93. Author: (with others) California Health Plan for Children, 1979. Bd. dirs. Lyceum of Monterey Peninsula, 1963—; mem. Monterey Peninsula Unified Sch., 1965-73, pres., 1968-70; mem. Mid-Coast Health System Agy., Salinas, Calif., 1975-80, pres., 1979-80; bd. dirs. Carmel Bach Festival, Calif., 1972-81. With USAF, 1956-58. Fellow Am. Acad. Pediatrics; mem. Calif. Med. Assn., Monterey County Med. Soc., Inst. Medicine Nat. Acad. Sci. Democrat. Home: 976 Mesa Rd Monterey CA 93940-4612 Office: 920 Cass St Monterey CA 93940-4507

BLACK, SAMUEL HAROLD, microbiology and immunology educator; b. Lebanon, Pa., May 1, 1930; s. Harold William and Beatrice Irene (Steckbeck) B.; m. Elisabeth Martha Zandveld, Aug. 16, 1961; children: Vicki Ann, Alisa Jo. Student, Hershey Jr. Coll., 1948-50; B.S., Lebanon Valley Coll., 1952; postgrad., U. Pa., 1952-54; M.S., U. Mich., 1958, Ph.D., 1961. NSF fellow Tech. U. Delft, The Netherlands, 1960-61; instr. U. Mich., Ann Arbor, 1961-62; asst. prof. Baylor Coll. Medicine, Houston, 1962-67, assoc. prof., 1967-71; assoc. prof. Mich. State U., East Lansing, 1971-73, prof., 1973-75; prof. microbiology and immunology Tex. A&M U., College Station, 1975—, head dept. med. microbiology and immunology, 1975-90, asst. dean for curriculum and undergrad. med. edn., 1985-87, interim dean Coll. Medicine, 1987-88, assoc. dean Coll. Medicine, 1988-91; lectr. U. Houston, 1964-66; vis. prof. Swiss Fed. Inst. Tech., Zurich, 1969-70. Served with M.C., U.S. Army, 1954-56. Recipient citation Lebanon Valley Coll. Alumni Assn., 1981. Fellow Am. Acad. Microbiology; mem. Am. Soc. Microbiology, Am. Soc. Cell Biology, Soc. Gen. Microbiology, Electron Microscope Soc. Am., Soc. Invertebrate Pathology. Home: 1205 King Arthur Cir College Station TX 77840-4827 Office: Tex A&M U Coll Medicine Dept Med Microbiology and Immunology College Station TX 77843

BLACK, THOMAS JOHN, hospital executive; b. Orange, N.J., July 29, 1943; s. Frank M. and Edith A. (Flanagan) B.; m. Gaetana M. Thomas, June 5, 1966; children: Ashley Ann, Tracy Ann, Thomas John. BS in Acctg., St. Peter's Coll., 1967. CPA, N.J. Staff asst. Main Hurdman, CPA's, N.Y.C., 1967-71; mgr. Fox & Co., CPA's, Paterson, N.J., 1971-74; dir. fin. St. Joseph's Hosp. and Med. Ctr., Paterson, 1974-75, asst. adminstr., 1975-80, v.p. fin. affairs, 1980-89, mem. pension plan com., 1984—, sr. v.p., chief fin. ofcr., 1989—; trustee V.H.S. Mgmt., Inc., 1987—, Qualcare PPO, 1993—, Seton Health Network Inc., Bayley Physicians' Svcs., Inc. Mem. AICPA, Healthcare Fin. Mgmt. Assn. (reimbursement com., CFO com.), N.J. Soc. CPAs, Fin. Com. BOT Hosp. Alliance N.J. Republican. Office: St Josephs Hosp and Med Ctr 703 Main St Paterson NJ 07503-2621

BLACKBURN, DAVID RALPH, psychologist; b. Houston, Dec. 23, 1955; s. Jack Armenious and Julia Maxine (Edwards) B.; 1 child, Joel; m. Leah Marlene Blackburn, Sept. 1996. BA, Okla. Christian Coll., 1978; ThM, Harding Grad. Sch. Religion, 1982; PhD, U. Houston, 1989. Lic. psychologist, Tex. Campus min. U. Houston, 1983-85; career counselor VGS Inc., Houston, 1985-88; intern in psychology VA Med. Ctr., Houston, 1988-89; psychologist Clear Lake Psychotherapy, Houston, 1989—; mem. dean's student adv. coun. U. Houston, 1985-86, adv. bd. VGS Inc., Houston, 1989—. Chief social actions officer Tex. Air N.G., Houston, 1984—. Mem. APA, Tex. Psychol. Assn., Houston Psychol. Assn., Clergy Subcommittee Mental Health Assn., Harris County Alliance for Mentally Ill., Psi Chi. Mem. Ch. of Christ. Home: 2213 Dublin Dr League City TX 77573-4955 Office: Clear Lake Psychotherapy 17625 El Camino Real #490 Houston TX 77058

BLACKBURN, ELIZABETH HELEN, molecular biologist; b. Hobart, Australia, Nov. 26, 1948; 1 child. BS, U. Melbourne, Australia, 1970, MS, 1971; PhD in Molecular Biology, Cambridge (Eng.) U., 1975; DSc (hon.), Yale U., 1991. Fellow in biology Yale U., New Haven, 1975-77; fellow in biochemistry U. Calif., San Francisco, 1977-78; from asst. prof. to prof. molecular biology U. Calif., Berkeley, 1978-90; prof. U. Calif., San Francisco, 1990—. Recipient Eli Lilly award in microbiology, 1988, NAS award in molecular biology, 1990. Mem. AAAS (elected 1991), NAS (fgn. assoc. 1993), Royal Soc. London. Office: U Calif Microbiology Biochemis San Francisco CA 94143

BLACKBURN, HENRY WEBSTER, JR., retired physician; b. Miami, Fla., Mar. 22, 1925; s. Henry Webster and Mary Frances (Smith) B.; m. Nelly Paula Trocme, Jan. 10, 1951 (div. 1984); children: John Keith, Katherine Ann, Heidi Elizabeth; m. Stacy Richardson, Sept. 1, 1991. Student, Fla. So. Coll., Lakeland, 1942-43; BS, U. Miami, 1947; MD, Tulane U., 1948; MS, U. Minn., 1957; Doctor Honoris Causa, U. Kuopio, Finland, 1988. Intern Chgo. Wesley Meml. Hosp., 1948-49; resident in medicine Am. Hosp. Paris, 1949-50; med. officer in charge USPHS, Austria, Fed. Republic Germany, 1950-53; med. fellow U. Minn., Mpls., 1953-56; retired Lab. Physiol. Hygiene, 1996; med. dir. Mut. Svc. Ins. Co., St. Paul, 1956; asst. prof. physiol. hygiene U. Minn., 1958-61, assoc. prof., 1961-68, prof., 1968—, lectr. medicine, 1956—, dir. lab. physiol. hygiene Sch. Pub. Health, 1972—, prof. medicine, 1972—, chmn. div. epidemiology, 1983-90, Mayo prof. pub. health, 1990-96; vis. prof. U. Geneva, 1970; mem. adv. coun. Nat. Heart, Lung and Blood Inst., 1989-93; mem. com. on diet and health NRC, 1986-89; Ancel Keys lectr., 1991; mem. food adv. com. FDA, 1995—. Author: Cardiovascular Survey Methods, 1968, On the Trail of Heart Attacks in Seven Countries, 1995; mem. editl. bd. numerous jours.; contbr. articles to profl. jours. Lt. (j.g.) USNR, 1942-50, capt. USPHS inactive res. Recipient Thomas Francis award in epidemiology, 1975, Naylor Dana award in preventive medicine, 1976, Louis Bishop award in cardiology, 1979, Gold Heart award Am. Heart Assn., 1990, Rsch. Achievement award Am. Heart Assn., 1992; Mayo chair in pub. health, 1988. Fellow APHA, Am. Coll. Cardiology, Am. Epidemiol. Soc.; mem. AAAS (chmn. med. sect.), Belgian Royal Acad. Medicine, Am. Heart Assn. (dir. 1971-74), Internat. Soc. Cardiology (coun. epidemiology 1971-74, chmn. 1986-91), Internat. Epidemiol. Soc., Alpha Omega Alpha, Phi Kappa Phi, Delta Omega. Home: 1525 Kaltern Ln Minneapolis MN 55416-3507 Office: U Minn Div Epidemiology 1300 S 2nd St Minneapolis MN 55454-1075

BLACKINGTON, SANDRA MARIE, pediatrics and neonatal nurse; b. Conn., Aug. 2, 1945; d. John C. and Marie (Nedwied) Zemek; m. Claude Blackington, May, 1968; children: Kenneth, Kevin, David. Diploma, Bellevue Hosp. Sch. Nursing, 1965; BS, Ea. Conn. State U., 1987; MSN, U. Conn., Storrs, 1991. Cert. Nat. Cert. Corp. for Obstetric, Gynecologic and Neonatal Nursing Specialties; cert. neonatal ICU nurse Am. Nurses Credentialing Ctr.; cert. nurse adminstr. Clin. II RN, neonatal ICU Hartford (Conn.) Hosp., 1979-88, critical care instr. neonatal and pediat. ICU, 1988-91, neonatal ICU nurse mgr., 1991-95, neonatal ICU unit dir., 1995-96; neonatal ICU/ PCN nurse mgr. Children's Hosp. Southwest Fla., Fort Myers, 1996—. Mem. ANA, Conn. Nurses Assn., Nat. Assn. Neonatal Nurses, Conn. Assn. Neonatal Nurses (treas. 1994-95), Sigma Theta Tau. Office: 9981 Health Park Cir Fort Myers FL 33908

BLACKLEDGE, MARY ANN, nursing educator; b. LaGrange, Tex., Aug. 3, 1943; d. Adolph Frank Sr. and Marie (Hajovsky) Ryza; m. John A. Blackledge, Sept. 2, 1967; children: Tomi Lynn, Todd Alan. BSN, Incarnate Word Coll., 1965; MSN, Cath. U. Am., 1970. Staff nurse Santa Rosa Med. Ctr., San Antonio, 1965-66; fee assigner Med. Svc. of D.C., Washington, 1969-70; asst. instr. geriatric nursing, clin. instr. Charles County Community Coll., LaPlata, Md., 1984, 86; insvc. coord. Calvert County Nursing Ctr., Prince Frederick, Md., 1982-90; adminstrn. pre-nursing program Launch Your Nursing Career, Prince Frederick, 1990-94; edn. counselor Project LINC, Md., 1994—. Mem. Nat. Student Nurses Assn., Sigma Theta Tau. Home: 5830 Shay Ln Huntingtown MD 20639-8548

BLACKLOW, ROBERT STANLEY, physician, medical college administrator; b. Cambridge, Mass., June 24, 1934; s. Leo Alfred and Clara Edna (Cumenes) B.; m. Winifred Young, Dec. 7, 1958; children: Stephen Charles, Kenneth Lawrence, David Alan. A.B. summa cum laude, Harvard U., 1955, M.D. cum laude, 1959. Intern Peter Bent Brigham Hosp., Boston, 1959-60; resident Peter Bent Brigham Hosp., 1960-61, 63-64, 67-68; instr. Harvard U., 1967-70, asst. prof. medicine, 1970-76, assoc. prof., 1976-78, asst. to dean faculty of medicine, 1969-73, asso. dean, 1973-78; prof., internal medicine Rush Med. Coll., 1978-85, dean, 1978-81; v.p. for med. affairs Rush-Presbyn.-St. Luke's Med. Center, Chgo., 1978-81; prof. medicine Jefferson Med. Coll., Phila., 1985-92, sr. assoc. dean, 1985-92; pres., dean Northeastern Ohio Univs. Coll. Medicine, 1992—, prof. community medicine, prof. medicine, 1992—; mem. sci. adv. com. Nat. Fund for Med. Edn., 1981-84, Nat. Cancer Inst., 1986—; bd. dirs. Nat. Resident Matching Program, pres.-elect, 1994-95, pres. 1995—. Editor: Signs and Symptoms, 1971, 6th edit., 1983. Trustee Chestnut Hill Sch., Newton, Mass., 1970-79, Belmont (Mass.) Hill Sch., 1973—, Chgo. chpt. ARC, 1979, Greater Akron Musical Assn., 1993—; mem. Ill. Health Svc. Corps Task Force, Ill. Dept. Pub. Health, 1980; corporator Belmont Hill Sch., 1978—. Served with USPHS, 1961-63. Fellow Inst. Medicine Chgo., ACP, Chgo. Soc. Internal Medicine; mem. N.Y. Acad. Scis., Assn. Am. Med. Colls., AAAS, Harvard Musical Assn., Phi Beta Kappa, Sigma Xi, Alpha Omega Alpha. Clubs: Longwood Cricket (Boston), Badminton and Tennis (Boston), Harvard (Boston); Harvard (N.Y.C.); Cliff Dwellers (Chgo.), Harvard (Chgo.) (bd. dirs.), Literary (Chgo.); Franklin Inn (Phila.); Germantown Cricket (Phila.), Twin Lakes Country Club. Home: 1150 Pin Oak Dr Sugar Bush Knolls OH 44240-6254 Office: Northeastern Ohio Us Coll Med 4209 State Rte 44 PO Box 95 Rootstown OH 44272

BLACKMAN, LIONEL HART, psychiatrist; b. N.Y.C., Apr. 26, 1923; s. Theodore Abraham and Bessie (Fishman) B.; m. Miriam Roder, Oct. 4, 1945; children: Jerome, Clifford, Daniel, Carol. BS, Tulane U., 1943, MD, 1946; postgrad., Columbia U. Psychiat. Inst., 1951-52, N.Y. Psychoanalytic Inst., 1951-53. Diplomate Am. Bd. Psychiatry and Neurology, Am. Bd. Forensic Psychiatry. Intern Maimonides Hosp., Bklyn., 1946-47; resident Bklyn. State Hosp., Bklyn., 1949-52, sr. psychiatrist, 1949-52; chief psychiatry McCornack Gen. Hosp., Pasadena, Calif., 1951-52; med. dir. Lake Hosp., Lake Worth, Fla., 1973-75; psychiatrist pvt. practice, N.Y.C., 1952-56, New Hyde Pk., N.Y., 1956-71, Palm Beach, Fla., 1971-75, West Palm Beach, 1975—; lectr. in field. Contbr. articles to profl. jours. Troop chmn. Boy Scouts Am., Roslyn, N.Y., 1960-65; mem. drug com. Mayor's Coun., Roslyn, 1969; physician Civil Def., Roslyn, 1968-70. Capt. AUS, 1947-49. Fellow Pan Am. Med. Soc., Am. Geriatric Soc., Am. Coll. Forensic Psychiatry, Am. Soc. Psychoanalytic Physicians, Am. Psychiat. Assn. (life); mem. AMA, Acad. Psychosomatic Medicine, Fla. Med. Assn. Fla. Psychiat. Soc., Palm Beach County Med. Soc., Palm Beach County Psychiat. Soc., Am. Acad. Psychiatry and Law, So. Psychiat. Assn., Marce Soc., Fla. Acad. Forensic Psychiatry, Internat. Psychiat. Assn. for Advancement Electrotherapy, Tulane Alumni Club. Jewish. Home: 2001 Embassy Dr West Palm Beach FL 33401-1004 Office: Presdl Med Pla 1501 Presidential Way Ste 6 West Palm Beach FL 33401-1852

BLACKMAN, MARC ROY, endocrinology educator, physician, scientist; b. Boston, Mar. 2, 1946; s. Max A. and Sue (Weiner) B.; m. Linda Ellen Richman, Aug. 8, 1971; children: David, Adam, Suzanne. AB, Northeastern U., 1968; MD, NYU, 1972. Diplomate Am. Bd. Internal Medicine, Am. Bd. Endocrinology and Metabolism. Asst. prof. medicine Sch. of Medicine Johns Hopkins U., Balt., 1978-86, assoc. prof. Sch. of Medicine, 1986—; clin. chief and chief endocrinology and metabolism Johns Hopkins Bayview Med. Ctr., Balt., 1993—, assoc. program dir. Gen. Clin. Rsch. Ctr., 1991—; cons. endocrinology Johns Hopkin's Hosp., 1985—. Contbr. chpts. to books, articles to profl. jours. Mem. AAAS, Am. Fedn. for Clin. Rsch., Gerontology Soc. Am., Endocrine Soc. Democrat. Jewish. Home: 7112 Fairfax Rd Bethesda MD 20814-1235 Office: Johns Hopkins Bayview Med C Gerontology Rsch Ctr Dept Medicine Baltimore MD 21224

BLACKSON, BENJAMIN F(RANKLIN), clinical social worker; b. Newark, Del., Nov. 4, 1933; s. Benjamin Franklin and Lulu Etta (Taylor) B.; m. Sirletta Fordelma Belcher, Feb. 28, 1957 (dec. Aug. 1990); children: Benita, Barbara. BS, Trenton State Coll., 1972; MSW, MBA, Rutgers U., 1975; MSW advanced cert., U. Pa., 1980; D of Human Service, The Fielding Inst., DHS, 1988. Bd. cert. diplomate in clin. social work; cert. social work. Commd. USAF, 1952, advanced through grades to maj., 1975, air traffic contr., 1952-59, multi engine pilot, 1957-65; clin. social worker USAFR, 1975-85, ret., 1985; mem. Blackson Enterprises, Bordentown, N.J., 1969-81; CEO B.E. Inc., Bordentown, 1975—. vice-chmn. Bordentown Recreation Com., 1973. Fellow Am. Orthopsychiat. Assn.; mem. Acad. Cert. Clin. Social Worker, Nat. Assn. Social Workers (clin. chmn. N.J. 1978-80), Nat. Fedn. Socs. for Clin. Social Work, Am. Assn. Sex Edn. Counselors and Therapists. Home and Office: 200 Mary St Bordentown NJ 08505-1816

BLADEK, THOMAS ROBERT, anesthesiologist; b. Middletown, Conn., July 19, 1956; s. Chester Henry and Violet Caroline Bladek; m. Marianne Calamari; 3 children. BS, John Carroll U., 1978; MD, St. Georges U., 1982. Intern Mt. Sinai Hosp., Hartford, Conn., 1982-84; resident St. Elizabeth Hosp., Boston, 1984-86; attending anesthesiologist St. Vincents Med. Ctr., Bridgeport, Conn., 1987—; anesthesiologist Southbury (Conn.) Tng. Sch., 1991—; bd. dirs. St. Vincents Med. Ctr.; ptnr. Med. Anesthesiology Assocs., Shelton, Conn., 1991—. Cardiac anesthesiology fellow Tufts-New England Med. Ctr., 1986-87. Mem. Exch. Club Easton. Republican. Roman Catholic. Office: Med Anesthesiology Assocs 4 Armstrong Rd Shelton CT 06484

BLAESS, DONNA ADELE, psychotherapist, counselor, educator; b. Detroit, Dec. 17, 1948; d. Marvin Julius and Mildred Catherine (Konka) B. BA, U. Tampa, Fla., 1970; MA, U. of South Fla., 1972; PhD, U. Iowa, 1976. Rsch. evaluator Boston U., 1976-77; project dir. Contract Rsch. Corp., Belmont, Mass., 1977-79; adj. prof. Peabody Coll. of Vanderbilt U., Oxford, 1980-81; clin. staff mem. Assocs. for Human Resources, Concord, Mass., 1982-84; program dir., asst. prof. St. Thomas U., Miami, Fla., 1985-91; assoc. prof. Barry U., Miami Shores, Fla., 1991-92; psychotherapist Ctr. for Family Learning, Ft. Lauderdale, Fla., 1986-88; pvt. practice psychotherapy, Miami, 1988-92, Ft. Lauderdale, 1992—; gov.'s appointee Fla. Dept. Profl. Regulation, 1991-92, expert witness, 1991—, chair probable cause panel, 1993—; adj. prof. Nova Southeastern U., 1992—; clin. cons. Children's Diagnostic and Treatment Ctr., Ft. Lauderdale, 1992-94. Edn. cons. homeless program New Horizons Mental Health Ctr., Miami, 1988; mem. adv. com. Parent to Parent, Miami, 1988-89; mem. Bd. Clin. Social Work Marriage and Family Therapy, and Mental Health Counseling, 1990-91. Mem. APA, AACD (media rev. bd. 1986-89), Am. Mental Health Counselors Assn., Fla. Mental Health Counselors Assn. (sec. 1988-89, treas. 1989-90, chmn. governance com. 1992-93). Home: West Lake Village 1155 Weeping Willow Way Hollywood FL 33019-4817

BLÁHA, VACLAV, physician, researcher; b. Velešín, Česky Krumlov, Czeck Republic, Mar. 17, 1931; s. Václav B. and Ludmila (Matušková) Bláhová; m. Alena Nápravníková Bláhová, June 14, 1958; children Adéla, Jitka Juřicová. Med. Univ. Dr., Charles U., Prague, 1949; PhD, Charles U., 1968. Physician dept. internal medicine Hosp. Č. Krzmlov, Czechoslovakia, 1955-60, Hosp. Č. Budějovice, Czechoslovakia, 1958-60, Inst. Railroad Health Cure, Czechoslovakia, 1960-64; researcher Inst. for Use of Radioisotopes in Medicine, Prague, 1964-68; tchr., researcher, asst. prof. dept. nuclear medicine Postgrad. Med. Sch., Prague, 1968-73; tchr., researcher Faculty of Medicine Charles U., Prague, 1973—, asst. prof. dept. nuclear medicine Faculty of Medicine, 1973-79, assoc. prof. dept. nuclear medicine Faculty of Medicine, 1979-90, prof. nuclear medicine, head dept. nuclear medicine Faculty of Medicine, 1979-90. Author: Nuclear Medici ne in Health Cure, 1973, Cholescintigraphy, 1987, (with L.G. Colombetti) Adverse Reactions to Radiotracers In: Principles of Radiopharmacology Vol. II, (textbook) Nuclear Medicine, 1980, 85, 90, 96. Basic mil. duty, 1958-60. Recipient Honor prize for extraordinary merit of devel. of nuclear medicine Czechoslovak Soc. Nuclear Medicine, 1972. Mem. European Assn. Nuclear Medicine (founding mem. 1976—), Internat. Assn. Radiopharmacology (founding mem. 1978—). Home: Hrusická 2520/16, 141 00 Prague 4, Czech Republic Office: Dept Nuclear Medicine Charles U, Srobárova 50, 100 34 Prague 10, Czech Republic

BLAHD, WILLIAM HENRY, physician; b. Cleve., May 11, 1921; s. Moses and Rae (Lichtenstader) B.; m. Miriam Weiss, Jan. 29, 1971; children—Andrea Margery, William Henry, Karen Ruth. Student, Western Res. U., 1939-40, U. Ariz., 1940-42; M.D., Tulane U., 1945. Diplomate Am. Bd. Nuclear Medicine (chmn. 1982, v.p. 1986—), Am. Bd. Internal Medicine (bd. govs. 1981). Resident in pathology and internal medicine VA Wadsworth Med. Center, 1948-52, ward officer metabolic research ward, 1951-52, asst. chief radioisotope service, 1952-56; chief nuclear medicine service VA Wadsworth Med. Center, Los Angeles, 1956—; prof. dept. medicine U. Calif., Los Angeles; mem. ACGME residency rev. com. for nuclear medicine, 1979—, chmn., 1991—; mem. Joint Rev. Com. on Ednl. Programs in Nuclear Medicine Tech., 1986-93; mem. subcom. on naturally occurring and accelerator produced radioactive materials Com. on Interagency Radiation Rsch. and Policy Coordination, 1988—; cons. nuclear medicine; mem. adv. com. on human uses radioisotopes Calif. Dept. Health Svcs.; mem. HEW Interagy. Task Force on Ionizing Radiation, 1978; dir. nuclear medicine Mt. Sinai Hosp., L.A., 1955-76, Valley Presbyn. Med. Ctr., Van Nuys, Calif., 1959-85, St. Joseph Hosp. Med. Ctr., Burbank, Calif., 1958-83. Author 3 textbooks on nuclear medicine. Contbr. numerous articles to med. jours. Served with U.S. Army, 1946-48. Grantee Muscular Dystrophy Assn. Am., 1965-69, Nat. Cancer Inst., 1973-76. Fellow ACP, Am. Coll. Nuclear Physicians (bd. regents 1974-80); mem. Soc. Nuc. Medicine (trustee 1966-74, pres. 1977-78, Disting. Scientist award No./So. Calif. chpts. 1975, Disting. Sci. award Western Regional chpts. 1995), Health Physics Soc. (pres. So. Calif. chpt. 1964-66), Calif. Med. Assn. (mem. sci. bd. 1975-81, chmn. adv. bd. nuclear medicine 1976-84), Am. Bd. Med. Spltys., COCERT, Soc. Exptl. Biology and Medicine, AMA, Los Angeles County, Calif. med. assns., Western Assn. Physicians, Am. Fedn. Clin. Research, Nat. Assn. VA Chiefs Nuclear Medicine (pres. 1985-87), Western Soc. Clin. Research, Alpha Omega Alpha. Office: Nuclear Med Svc West LA VA Med Ctr 691/W115 11301 Wilshire Blvd Los Angeles CA 90073

BLAIN, ALEXANDER, III, surgeon, educator; b. Detroit, Mar. 9, 1918; s. Alexander William and Ruby (Johnson) B.; m. Josephine Woodbury Bowen, May 3, 1941; children—Helen Bowen, Alexander IV, Bruce Scott Murray, Josephine Johnson; m. Mary E. Mains, 1968. B.A., Wayne U., 1940, M.D., 1943; M.S. in Surgery, U. Mich., 1948. Diplomate Am. Bd. Surgery. House officer, Halsted fellow in surgery Johns Hopkins U., 1943-46; resident surgeon U. Hosp., Ann Arbor, Mich., 1946-50; instr. surgery U. Mich., 1950-57; chief surgeon 14th Field Hosp., Bad Kreuznach, Fed. Republic Germany; clin. assoc. prof. surgery Wayne State U., 1962-87; surgeon-in-chief Alexander Blain Hosp., Detroit, 1953-78; cons. surgeon Highland Park Gen. Hosp, St. Joseph's Hosp., Blain Clinic, Ostego Meml. Hosp., Gaylord, Mich.; med. dir. The Budd Co., 1977-82; staff periop. St. John Hosp., 1988-92; med. cons. bd. 67 adjudication VA, 1990—; pres. Met. Detroit Family Svc. Assn., 1962-63, Detroit Mus. Soc., 1961-62; staff Harper Hosp., Detroit Deaconess Hosp.; surgeon Detroit Urban Indian Health Ctr., 1982-90. Author: (with F.A. Coller) Indications For and Results of Splenectomy, 1950, Prismatic Papers and an Ode, 1968, Prismatic Haiku Poems (Remembered Voices), 1973, (poems) Shu Shu Ga, 2d edit., 1983, Clackshant, 1982; contbr. numerous articles to surg. jours.; editorial bd. Rev. Surgery, 1959-79. Mem. Detroit Zool. Park Commn., 1974-82, pres., 1978-82; trustee Alexander Blain Hosp., 1942-67, Ostego Meml. Hosp. Found., Gaylord, Mich., 1976—; bd. dirs. Detroit Zool. Soc., 1972-75, 82—; pres. W.J. Stapleton Found. Health Edn., 1978-84. Served as lt. M.C., AUS, 1942-44, maj., 1955-57. Recipient Wayne State U. Med. Alumni award, 1968. Fellow ACS, N.Y. Acad. Scis.; mem. Internat. Cardiovascular Soc., F.A. Coller Surg. Soc., Am. Fedn. for Clin. Rsch., Cranbrook Inst. Sci., Soc. Vascular Surgery, Am. Thyroid Assn., Soc. Internat. de Chirugie, Mich. Med. Soc. (chmn. surg. sect. 1963), Assn. Clin. Surgery, Pan-Pacific Surg. Assn., Acad. Am. Poets, Am. Poetry Assn., Mich. Poetry Soc., Acad. of Surgery of Detroit, Coun. of Wayne County Med. Soc., Nu Sigma Nu, Phi Gamma Delta. Clubs: Grosse Pointe (fleet surgeon 1986-89), Otsego, Prismatic (pres. 1967), Detroit Racquet (pres. 1976-80), Cardio-Vascular Surgeons (pres. 1961-62), Acanthus, Waweatonong (pres. 1978), Circumnavigators, Witenagemote. Home: 8 Stratford Pl Grosse Pointe MI 48230-1907 Office: VA 477 Michigan Ave Detroit MI 48226-2523

BLAIN, DONALD GRAY, physician; b. Detroit, Feb. 27, 1924; s. Alexander and Ruby (Johnson) B.; ed. Princeton, 1946; M.D., Wayne State U., 1950; m. Grace Carpenter, June, 1954; children—Elizabeth, Ian, Patricia. Intern, Union Meml. Hosp., Balt., 1950-51; gen. surg. resident Ch. Home

Hosp., Balt., 1953-55, Henry Ford Hosp., Detroit, 1955-56, Alexander Blain Hosp., Detroit, 1956-58; staff Blain Hosp.; resident urology N.C. Bapt. Hosp. and instr. urology Bowman Gray Sch. Medicine, Winston-Salem, 1962-65; pvt. practice urology, Mount Clemens, Mich., 1965—; with staff St. Joseph and Henry Ford Hosp; pres. Oakland Macomb Profl. Standards Rev. Orgn., 1973-79. Mem. Gov.'s Conf. on Health Manpower, 1973; bd. dirs. Mich. MDPAC. Served to capt. USAF, 1951-53. Diplomate Am. Bd. Urology. Fellow A.C.S.; mem. Macomb County Med. Soc. (past pres.), Am. Assn. Clin. Urologists, Am. Urologic Assn., Societe Internationale d'Urologie, Detroit Surg. Soc. (council), St. Andrews Soc. Republican. Presbyterian. Clubs: Country of Detroit, Metamora Hunt, Sedgefield Hunt. Home: 14 Road 60R Cody WY 82414-8115

BLAINE, EDWARD H., health science administrator, educator; b. Farmington, Mo., Jan. 30, 1940; s. Theodore Warren and Tessa Ella (McClanahan) B.; m. Susan Irene Cring (div. 1992); children Jennifer, Marquis Edward. AB, U. Mo., 1962, MA, 1967, PhD, 1970, DSc (hon.), 1989. Player Green Bay Packers, Green Bay, Wisc., 1962-63, Phila. Eagles, Phila., Pa., 1963-67; asst. prof. physiology U. Pitts., 1973-77; dir. renal Pharmacology Merk Inst., West Point, Pa., 1977-86; sr. dir. G.D. Searle Rsch. & Devel., St. Louis, 1986-92; dir. Dalton Cardio-Vascular Rsch. Ctr., U. Mo., Columbia, Mo., 1992—; adv. com. NIH, Bethesda, Md., 1974-86; adv. bd. Global Interaction, Phoenix, Ariz., 1991-93. Contbr. to profl. jours. Deans adv. bd. grad. divsn. U. Mo., Columbia, 1988-92; chmn. Searle-St. Louis United Way, 1990; exec. com. U. Mo. Development Coun., 1993-94; bd. dirs. Mo. Found. for Med. Rsch., Columbia, Mo., 1993—; pres. Varsity M Assn. U. Mo., 1993-94. Named All Am. UPI/Look Mag., 1961; recipient Rsch. Career Development award NIH, 1975. Mem. Am. Soc. Hypertension (v.p. 1992-94), Am. Physiological Soc., Am. Soc. Pharm. Exptl. Therapeutics, Endocrine Soc. Home: 4 E Clarkson Rd Columbia MO 65203-3520 Office: Univ of Missouri Dalton Cardiovascular Rsch Ctr Columbia MO 65211

BLAINEY, CAROL GOHRKE, nursing educator; b. Bend, Oreg., June 1, 1939; d. George R. and Elizabeth (Brandon) Gohrke; m. John A. Blainey, Nov. 18, 1972; children: Joan, Paul. BSN, U. Oreg., 1962; MSN, U. Wash., 1968. Cert. diabetes educator. Staff nurse U. Oreg. Med. Sch. Hosp., Portland, 1962-63, asst. head nurse, 1963-65, supr., 1965-66; instr. U. Wash., Seattle, 1967-70, asst. prof., 1970-79, assoc. prof., 1979—. Contbr. articles to profl. jours., textbooks. Mem. Am. Assn. Diabetes Educators, Am. Diabetes Assn., Sigma Theta Tau. Office: Univ Wash Box 357266 Seattle WA 98195-7266

BLAIR, B(ALLARD) GLENN, podiatrist; b. Providence, Dec. 18, 1957; s. Ballard Glenn and C. Mafalda (Angelone) B.; m. Emily E. Tirpaeck, June 25, 1982; childen: Hillary Candice, Madeline Evelyn, Glenn Jr. BS in Microbiology, U. R.I., 1980; D of Podiatric Medicine, Coll. Podiatric Medicine & Surgery, 1986. Diplomate Am. Bd. Podiatric Surgery, Am. Bd. Podiatric Orthopedics. Podiatric surg. resident West Haven (Conn.) Veterans Hosp., 1986-88; pvt. practice Shelton, Conn., 1988—, Bridgeport, Conn., 1992—; clin. asst. instr. U. Osteopathic Medicine, Coll. Podiatric Medicine & Surgery, Des Moines, Iowa, 1986—. Fellow Am. Coll. Foot Surgeons. Republican. Roman Catholic. Office: 513 Howe Ave Shelton CT 06484-3157 also: 4920 Main St Bridgeport CT 06606-1300

BLAIR, CHARLES LEE, physician; b. Stamford, Conn., May 1, 1954; s. Charles Francis Jr. and Mae E. (Gallmoyer) B.; m. Ellen Jill Weiss; children: Eric Charles, Melanie Alison, Hayley Grace. BA, U. Vt., 1976; MD, U. Conn., 1981. Diplomate Am. Bd. Psychiatry and Neurology, Geriatric Psychiatry. Resident in psychiatry U. Conn. Sch. Medicine, Farmington, 1981-85, asst. clin. prof. psychiatry, 1985-93, assoc. clin. prof. psychiatry, 1993—; John C. Leonard fellow Hartford (Conn.) Hosp., 1985-86, dir. psychiat. edn., 1988-90; pvt. practice Hartford, 1985—; mem. psychiatry residency tng. com. U. Conn. Sch. Medicine, Farmington, 1983-84, 88-90. Rock Sleyster Meml. scholar AMA, 1980-81. Mem. APA, Conn. Psychiat. Soc., Hartford County Med. Assn., Hartford Psychiat. Soc. (treas. 1991-92, sec. 1992-93, program chair 1993-94, pres. 1994-95), Phi Beta Kappa. Home: 149 Steele Rd West Hartford CT 06119-1047 Office: 100 Retreat Ave Ste 612 Hartford CT 06106-2528

BLAIR, GEORGE STEWART, oral surgeon, educator; b. Greenock, Scotland, July 28, 1936; s. George and Wilhelmina (Montgomerie) B.; m. Ishbel Campbell Russell, Aug. 8, 1968; children: Alistair S., Andrew A. BDS, Glasgow (Scotland) U., 1958, DDS, 1980. House surgeon Glasgow Dental Hosp., 1958-60; gen. dental practitioner NHS, 1962-65; registrar Glasgow Dental Hosp., 1965-67; lectr. Glasgow U., 1968-73; sr. lectr., cons. Newcastle (Eng.) U., 1973—; chmn. Divsn. Dentistry, Newcastle, 1988-90, No. Regional Dental Com., 1988-92; chmn. panel of assessors Med. Ins. Agy./Brit. Dental Assn. Elective Awards Scheme, 1990-94. Reviewer, referee: Brit. Dental Jour., 1994-96, Brit. Jour. Plastic Surgery, 1995, 96. Capt. Brit. Army, 1960-61. Fellow Royal Coll. Physicians and Surgeons (Glasgow, Higher Dental Diploma, examiner postgrad. candidates 1976-95); mem. Fedn. Dentaire Internat., Brit. Dental Assn. (vice-chmn. rep. bd. 1985-91, coun. mem. 1979-93, nat. pres. 1996-97), Brit. Assn. Oral and Maxillofacial Surgeons. Mem. Ch. of Scotland. Home: 45 Cheviot View, Newcastle upon Tyne NE20 9BH, England

BLAIR, KAREN ELAINE, respiratory care practitioner; b. Arnold, Pa., Nov. 9, 1958; d. William Alpheus and Elizabeth Margaret (Koepp) Blair. AAS, Pa. State U., 1979; BS, Indiana U. of Pa., 1987; MEd, Pa. State U., 1991, doctoral student in health, 1995. Cert. pulmonary technologist; registered respiratory therapist. Coord. pulmonary rehab. dept., health club dir. Pa. State U., New Kensington; pulmonary rsch. technician U. Pitts.; gym supr. Pa. State U., New Kensington; respiratory therapist, instr., trainer CPR Western Pa. Hosp., Pitts.; level 1 coach U.S. Volleyball Assn.; spkr. in field. Mem. AAHPERD (chair cmty. health Pa. chpt.), NAFE, Pa. Sch. Health Assn., Health Educators Inst., Am. Assn. Respiratory Care, Pa. Soc. Critical Care Medicine, Nat. Soc. for Cardiopulmonary Tech., Pa. State U. Alumni Assn., Soc. for Clin. Data Mgmt. Sys., Biology Club. Home: 1907 Kenneth Ave New Kensington PA 15068-4224

BLAKE, GEORGE ALAN, JR., non-profit association executive; b. Niles, Mich., Jan. 8, 1956; s. George Alan Blake and Inez Edna (Ewert) Brock; m. Kathryn Jean Sanders, Mar. 2, 1979 (div. Nov. 1985); m. Audrey Ann Paxton, June 30, 1986; children: Amanda Sue Blake, Alexander Xavier Blake. BS, So. Ill. U., 1983; MS, U. So. Calif., 1988; PhD in Mgmt., Brighton U., 1996. Process cons., GM; cert. psyc. technician, AAPT. Commd. USMC, 1974, advanced through grades to staff sgt., 1984, resigned, 1984; sales trainer GM, Pontiac, Mich., 1985-86; systems engring. devel. profl. Electronic Data Systems, Pontiac, 1985-86; mktg. info. systems adminstr. Mastic Corp., South Bend, Ind., 1987-89; instr. Apollo Coll., Tucson, Ariz., 1989-90; mgmt. info. system mgr. Hutronix Mfg., Tucson, 1990; database mgr. Dames & Moore Environ. Cons., tucson, 1990-91; psychiatric technician Tucson Psychiatric Inst./Charter Hosp., Tucson, 1986-94; assoc. prof. Tucson U., 1993-94; pres. Am. Assn. Psychiatric Technicians, West Chicago, 1991—; reviewer Chronical Guidance Publs., Moravia, N.Y., 1994—; reviewer/writer NTC Pub. Group, Chgo., 1995—; interviewee Bus. Mktg. Mag., 1988. Editor: A Textbook for Psychiatric Technicians, 1995, Outline of Knowledge for Psychiatric Technicians, 1993; author: (curriculum) Social Research Methods/History of Psychology, 1993, (monograph) Occupational Report for Psychiatric Technicians, 1994. Chmn. behavioral health legis. com. Ariz. Coalition of Human Svcs., 1993-94, supervisory com., Mastic Employees Fed. Credit Union, South Bend, Ind., 1987-89. Staff Sgt. USMC, 1974-84. Mem. Mental Health Assn. (v.p. 1993-94, registered lobbiest, 1993-94), Tucson Pima County Job Club (bd. dirs. 1992-93), Tucson Assn. Vol. Adminstrs. Unitarian Universalist. Office: Am Assn Psychiat Tech 336 Johnson Rd Michigan City IN 46360

BLAKE, JAMES STEVEN, physician; b. Columbus, Miss., Jan. 9, 1958; s. Alfred Boyd Sr. and Irma Nell (Johnson) B.; m. Gwendolyn Ann Hicks, June 17, 1989 (div. Nov. 1991). BA, U. Miss., 1980; DO, Phila. Coll. Osteo. Medicine, 1989, MSc, 1994. Med. tech. North Miss. Med. Ctr., Tupelo, 1981-83, lab. supr., 1983-85; intern St. Joseph Hosp., Phila., 1989-90; resident Phila. Coll. Osteo. Medicine, 1991-92, fellow in gastroenterology, 1992-94; physician pvt. practice, Phila., 1994—; cons. in field. Mem. AMA, Am. Osteo. Assn., Nat. Osteo. Med. Assn., Pa. Osteo. Medicine Assn., MEd. Soc. Eastern Pa., Phila. County Med. Soc. (com. mem. 1995—). Office: The Nelton Med Group 1300 S 18yh St Philadelphia PA 19146

BLAKE, KATHLEEN, cardiologist; b. Washington, July 12, 1954. AB in Physics, U. N.C., 1976; MD, U. Chgo., 1980. Intern, resident in internal medicine Stanford (Calif.) Med. Ctr., 1980-83, fellow in cardiology, 1983-86, clin. asst. prof., 1986-87; clin. asst. prof. U. N.Mex., Albuquerque, 1989—; staff physician N.Mex. Heart Inst., Albuquerque, 1988—. Fellow Am. Coll. Cardiology; mem. Am. Heart Assn., Greater Albuquerque Med. Assn. (pres. 1995), N.Mex. Women and Heart Disease Coalition (chair 1989—). Office: NMex Heart Inst 1001 Coal SE Albuquerque NM 87106

BLAKE-INADA, LOUIS MICHAEL, cardiologist, researcher; b. Osaka, Japan, June 4, 1956; came to U.S., 1959; s. Edward Kneeland, Sr. and Setsuko (Inada) Blake. BA in Biochemistry and Molecular Biology, U. Calif., Santa Barbara, 1979; MD, Case Western Res. U., 1983. Diplomate Am. Bd. Internal Medicine, Am. Bd. Nuc. Medicine. Intern in gen. surgery Letterman Army Med. Ctr., San Francisco, 1983-84; resident in internal medicine Sch. Medicine Stanford U., Calif., 1988-90, resident in nuc. medicine, 1990-92, chief resident in nuc. medicine, 1991-92; fellow in cardiology Calif. Pacific Med. Ctr., San Francisco, 1992-93; fellow in cardiology, cardiac imaging U. Calif., San Francisco, 1993-95. Contbr. articles to med. jours. including Am. Jour. Radiology, Jour. Nuc. Medicine, others; contbr. editor Jour. Am. Coll. Cardiology, 1993-95. Capt. U.S. Army, 1979-88. Evelyn Neizer rsch. fellow Stanford U., 1992. Fellow Am. Coll. Angiology; mem. ACP, Am. Coll. Cardiology, Am. Coll. Nuc. Physicians, Am. Heart Assn. (coun. on cardiovascular radiology), Soc. Nuc. Medicine, Assn. Military Surgeons of the U.S. Republican. Roman Catholic. Home: 351 Durant Way Mill Valley CA 94941 Office: U Calif Med Ctr San Francisco CA 94110

BLALOCK, GEORGE ROBERT, JR., surgeon; b. Clinton, S.C., Mar. 4, 1939; s. George R. and Almena (Milling) B.; m. Essie Glenn Seter, Jan. 7, 1965; children: George R. III, Elizabeth T. BS, Davidson Coll., 1961; MD, Med. Coll. S.C., 1965. Intern Grady Meml. Hosp., Atlanta, 1965-66; resident Emory U. Affiliated Hosps., Atlanta, 1966-70; staff gen. surgeon Georgetown (S.C.) Meml. Hosp., 1972—. Maj. U.S. Army Med. Corps, 1970-72. Fellow Am. Coll. Surgeons; mem. SAGES. Office: 1101 Meml Ln Georgetown SC 29440

BLALOCK, RAYMOND BUSH, ophthalmologist, business executive; b. Huntsville, Tex., Oct. 19, 1927; s. William Ben and Minnie Sue Blalock; m. Winona M. Blalock, Aug. 15, 1948; children Raynona, Renee, Ray. MD, U. Tex., Galveston, 1950. Diplomate Am. Bd. Ophthalmology. Gen. practice medicine, 1951-62; practice medicine specializing in ophthalmology Huntsville, Tex., 1965—; clin. instr. dept. ophthalmology U. Tex. Med. Br., Galveston, 1965-75, clin. asst. prof., 1975-85, clin. assoc. prof., 1989-93; clinical prof., 1993—; bd. dirs. 1st Nat. Bank, vice chmn. bd., 1982-86, chmn. bd., 1987—; bd. dirs. 1st Huntsville Corp. Served with USN, 1956-57. Recipient Disting. Alumni award U. Tex., 1996. Mem. AMA, Tex. Med. Assn., Tri-County Med. Assn., Am. Acad. Opthalmology, Houston Opthal. Assn., Scotch Highlands Breeders Assn. (pres. 1984-87, chmn. bd. 1988-91), Am. Internat. Charolais Assn. Presbyterian. Home: 510 Riverside Dr Huntsville TX 77340-5421 Office: 1400 13th St Huntsville TX 77340-4422

BLALOCK, W(ILLIAM) STANFORD, plastic surgeon; b. St. Louis, Nov. 25, 1953. BS, Cornell U., 1976; MD, U. Louisville, 1980. Diplomate Am. Bd. Plastic Surgery. Resident in gen. surgery U. Ala. Hosps., Birmingham, 1980-83; resident in plastic surgery Med. Coll. Ohio, Toledo, 1983-85, fellow in hand surgery, 1986; pvt. practice plastic surgery Nashville, 1986—. Fellow Am. Coll. Surgeons; mem. Am. Soc. Plastic Surgeons, Am. Soc. Aesthetic Surgeons, Southeastern Soc. Plastic Surgeons. Office: Plastic Surgery Nashville 109 Kenner Ave #200 Nashville TN 37205

BLANCHARD, NORMAN HARRIS, retired pharmaceutical company executive; b. Pittsfield, Mass., Aug. 21, 1930; s. Norman Harris and Edna May (Perkins) B.; m. Margaret Eugenie Rahm, Apr. 10, 1954; children: Norman James, Michèle Blanchard Langstaff. BS in Geology, Tufts U., 1953; BS in Internat. Trade, Am. Grad. Sch. Internat. Mgmt., 1959. Geologist U.S. Geol. Survey, Harrisburg, Pa., 1957-58; internat. mgmt. trainee Upjohn Internat. Ops., Kalamazoo, 1959-60; adminstrv. dir. Sprout Waldron of France, Paris, 1961-66; european dir. Salsbury Labs., Charles City, Iowa, 1967-71; european dir. Smith Kline Animal Health, Phila., 1972-74, internat. dir., 1975-76, internat. v.p., 1977-81, pres., 1982-89; pres. Beecham Animal Health Products, London, 1989-92; corp. v.p. Smith Kline Beecham Corp., Phila., 1989-92; ret., 1992; chmn. Animal Health Inst., Alexandria, Va., 1988-89; mem. president's council Am. Grad. Sch. Internat. Mgmt., Phoenix, 1985-89. Chmn. Jr. Achievement of Del. Valley, Newtown Sq., Pa., 1986, 87; trustee Internat. House, Phila., 1984, 85. With CIC, U.S. Army, 1953-56. Home: 5 Half Hill Rd Spring City PA 19475-9507

BLANCHARD, ROBERT JOHNSTONE WEIR, surgeon; b. Winnipeg, Man., Can., Mar. 30, 1934; s. James Fleming and Thelma Rosilla (Weir) B.; m. Madeline Edith Elizabeth Blain, May 25, 1957; children: Elizabeth, James, Louise, Jonathan. BS in Medicine, U. Man., 1959, MD with honors, 1959; MS in Surgery, U. Minn., 1965. Med. license, cert. in surgery, Man. Intern St. Boniface Gen. Hosp., Winnipeg, 1959-60; resident Deer Lodge Vets. Hosp., Winnipeg, 1960-61, St. Paul Ramsay County Hosp., 1961-64; med. supt. Bach Christian Hosp., North-West Frontier Province, Pakistan, 1967-70, 71-73; clin. tutor Winnipeg Gen. Hosp., 1970-71; dir. intensive care Health Scis. Ctr., Winnipeg, 1973-77, svc. chief, gastrointestinal surgery, 1977-95, surgeon in chief, 1985-95; head dept. surgery U. Man., Winnipeg, 1985-95; cons. St. Boniface Hosp., Winnipeg, 1986—. Contbr. articles to profl. jours. Surg. rsch. fellow Winnipeg Gen. Hosp., 1965. Fellow Royal Coll. Surgeons Can. (Medal in Surgery 1965), ACS (past pres. Man. chpt.); mem. Soc. for Surgery of Alimentary Tract, Can. Assn. Gen. Surgeons, Christian Med. and Dental Soc. Anglican. Office: GF 318A Health Scis Ctr, 800 Sherbrook St, Winnipeg, MB Canada R3T 2N2

BLANCHARD, WILLIAM HENRY, psychologist; b. St. Paul, Mar. 25, 1922; s. Charles Edgar and Ethel Rachael (Gurney) B.; m. Martha Ida Lang, Aug. 11, 1947; children: Gregory Marcus, Mary Lisa. Diploma in Sci. Mason City Jr. Coll., 1942; BS in Chemistry, Iowa State U., 1944; PhD in Psychology, U. So. Calif., 1954. Lic. clin. psychologist, Calif. Shift chemist B.F. Goodrich Chem. Co., Port Neches, Tex., 1946-47; court psychologist L.A. County Gen. Hosp., 1954-55; psychologist, dir. rsch. So. Reception Ctr. and Clinic, Calif. Youth Authority, Norwalk, 1955-58; social scientist Rand Corp., 1958-60, System Devel. Corp., 1960-70; mem. faculty Calif. State U.-Northridge, L.A., 1970; assoc. prof. UCLA, 1971; faculty group leader urban semester U. So. Calif., L.A., 1971-75; sr. rsch. assoc. Office of Chancellor, Calif. State U., L.A., 1975-76; sr. fellow Planning Analysis and Rsch. Inst., Santa Monica, Calif., 1976-96; pvt. practice psychologist, Calif., 1976-96; clin. assoc. dept. psychology U. So. Calif., 1956-58. Author: Rousseau and the Spirit of Revolt, 1967; Aggression American Style, 1978; Revolutionary Morality, 1984; Neocolonialism American Style, 1996. Contbr. articles to profl. jours. Mem. com. on mental health West Area Welfare Planning Council, L.A., 1960-61; bd. dirs. L.A. County Psychol. Assn., 1969; commr. Bd. Med. Examiners, Psychology Exam. Com., State of Calif., 1969; v.p. Parents and Friends of Mentally Ill Children, 1968-69, pres., 1966-68, trustee, 1968-69. Mem. APA, AAAS, Internat. Soc. Polit. Psychology. Home: 4307 Rosario Rd Woodland Hills CA 91364-5546

BLANCK, GERTRUDE SACKS, psychologist; b. N.Y.C.; d. Irving and Elizabeth (Green) Sacks; m. Rubin Blanck, June 21, 1940; 1 child, Susan Blanck Franzen. BA, Hunter Coll., 1936; MS, Columbia U., 1943; PhD, NYU, 1963. Pvt. practice, supr. psychoanalysis N.Y.C., 1950-92; supr. Theodor Reik Clinic, N.Y.C., 1950-55; curriculum dir. Inst. for Study of Psychotherapy, N.Y.C., 1971-81; lectr. Smith Coll. Sch. Social Work, Northamton, Mass., 1982-92. Co-author: Marriage and Personal Development, 1968, Ego Psychology I, 1979, Ego Psychology II, 1984, Ego Psychology III, 1986; author: The Subtle Seductions, 1987. Recipient Margaret S. Mahler award Soc. for Advancement of Psychoanalytic Devel. Psychology, 1987; named Disting. Practitioner Nat. Acad. Practice, 1982; named to Hall of Fame, Hunter Coll., 1986. Mem. APA, N.C. Psychoanalytic Soc. (hon.). Home and Office: 10 West 66th St New York NY 10023

BLANCK, RONALD RAY, hospital administrator, internist, career officer; b. Lancaster, Pa., Oct. 8, 1941; s. Harvey Ray and Mildred Catherine (Smith) B.; m. Donna Rae Ault, Sept. 17, 1971; children: Jennifer, Susan. BS, Juniata Coll., 1963; DO, Phila. Coll. Osteo. Medicine, 1967; DSc in Osteopathy (hon.), New Eng. Coll. Osteo. Medicine, 1982; LLD (hon.), Phila. Coll. Osteo. Medicine, 1991. Diplomate Am. Bd. Internal Medicine. Intern Lancaster Osteo. Hosp., 1967-68; resident in internal medicine Walter Reed Army Gen. Med. Ctr., 1970-73; commd. capt. U.S. Army, 1968, advanced through grades to maj. gen., 1992; gen. med. officer U.S. Army, Vietnam, 1968-69, Ft. Myer, Va., 1969-70; asst. chief gen. med. svc. Walter Reed Army Med. Ctr., Washington, 1973-74, asst. chief dept. medicine, 1974-76; asst. dean student affairs Sch. Medicine Uniformed Svcs. U., Bethesda, Md., 1976-79; chief dept. medicine Brooke Army Med. Ctr., San Antonio, Tex., 1979-82; chief med. corps career activities office Army Med. Dept. Pers. Support Act, Washington, 1982-85; comdr. U.S. Army Hosp., Berlin, 1986-88, Army Regional Med. Ctr., Frankfurt, Germany, 1988-90; dir. prof. svcs., chief med. corps affairs Office of Surgeon Gen., Fall Church, Va., 1990-92; comdr. Walter Reed Army Med. Ctr., Washington, 1992—; asst. prof. clin. medicine Georgetown U., Washington, 1972-78; clin. instr. medicine Howard U., Washington, 1975-77; assoc. prof. medicine USUHS, Bethesda, 1976-79; clin. assoc. prof. medicine U. Tex., San Antonio, 1979-80, clin. prof. medicine, 1980-82. Guest editor Osteopathic Annals, 1981; mem. editorial adv. bd. History of Medicine in Vietnam, 1981. Trustee Assn. Mil. Osteo. Physicians and Surgeons, Boca Raton, Fla., 1992, U.S. Soldier's and Airmen's Home, Washington, 1992; advisor bd. regents Uniformed Svcs. U. Health Scis., Bethesda, 1992; bd. dirs. Nat. Med. Vets. Soc., Chgo., 1993. Decorated Bronze Star, Legion of Merit, Def. Superior Svc. medal; recipient Founder's award Tex. Coll. Osteo. Medicine, 1991. Fellow Am. Coll. Physicians (gov.); mem. AMA (alt. del.), Am. Acad. Physician Execs., Am. Osteo. Assn., Assn. Mil. Surgeons U.S. (John Shaw Billings award 1976), Berlin Internat. Med. Soc., Assn. Mil. Osteo. Physicians and Surgeons, Soc. Med. Cons. Armed Forces (assoc.). Episcopalian. Office: Walter Reed Army Med Ctr 7100 Georgia Ave NW Washington DC 20307-5000

BLANCO, PATRICIA SERAFINI, nurse; b. Paterson, N.J., Aug. 16, 1944; d. Louis and M. Eleanor (DiVito) Serafini; m. Camilo Blanco, Apr. 1978; children: Andrew, Maryellen. RN, St. Luke's Hosp. Sch. Nursing, 1965; BS with honors, Fairleigh Dickinson U., Teaneck, N.J., 1968; MPH, U. Hawaii, Honolulu, 1969; Assoc. in Risk Mgmt., Ins. Inst. Am., Malvern, Pa., 1987. Cert. health care risk mgr. Pres. Healthcare Risk Control, Coral Gables; pres., chief exec. officer, v.p., risk mgmt. cons. HASCO/Frank B. Hall, Coral Gables, Fla.; coord. patient edn. Jackson Meml. Hosp., Miami. Mem. Am. Soc. Health Care Risk Mgmt., Nat. Assn. Women Bus. Owners, Fla. Soc. Healthcare Risk, Am. Hosp. Assn., Fla. Hosp. Assn. Office: PO Box 140548 Coral Gables FL 33114-0548

BLAND, JOHN HARDESTY, physician, educator; b. Globe, Ariz., Nov. 7, 1917; s. Walter Perry and Clara Elliot (Hardesty) B.; m. Elizabeth Lowry Cornman, Sept. 22, 1944; children: John Hardesty, Walter Perry, Elizabeth Lowry, Linda Mendenhall. A.B., Earlham Coll., 1940; M.D., Jefferson Med. Coll., 1944; postgrad., U. Pa., 1945. Diplomate Am. Bd. Internal Medicine. Intern Bryn Mawr Hosp., Pa., 1944; resident in internal medicine Burlington County Hosp., Mt. Holly, N.J., and Pa. Hosp., Phila., 1944-46; mem. Clin. Lab., Ft. Hood Station Hosp., Tex, 1947-48; fellow in pharmacolgy U. Pa. Med. Sch., 1948, cardiovascular research U. Vt., Burlington, 1948-49, instr. medicine, 1949-52, 1952-55, assoc. prof., 1955-78, dir. rheumatism research unit, 1950-70, prof. medicine rheumatology, 1979—; co-ordinator teaching program DeGoesbriand Meml. Hosp., 1949-55, pres. med. staff, 1951-52; fellow in rheumatic diseases Mass. Gen. and New Eng. Ctr. Hosps., Boston, 1950-51; mem. staff Med. Ctr. Hosp. Vt., 1950—; hon. research fellow dept. rheumatology U. Manchester, Eng., 1958-59; vis. sci. worker Lab. Exptl. Pathology Sect. Rheumatic Diseases NIH, Bethesda, Md., 1972-73; yearly lectr. NIH, 1974-80; vis. prof. Hershey Med. Sch., Pa. U., 1976, Dalhousie U., Halifax, Nova Scotia, 1978; mem. med. supervisory team, U.S. Nordic Ski Team, 1977—; chief med. officer Nordic Div. XIII Winter Olympic Games, 1978-80; cons. NIH Inst. of Aging, 1980—, Arthritis Research Inst., 1986—. Author: Live Long, Die Fast: Strategies, 1993; author 10 textbooks. Contbr. numerous articles and sci. papers to profl. jours. and book chpts. Presenter TV pub. edn. spots on arthritis, 1977. Pres. Arthritis Found., Vt., 1965-68, pres., chmn. bd. trustees, 1970—. Served to capt. U.S. Army, 1946-48. Recipient Disting. Service award Arthritis Found. Vt. Chpt., 1970, Cert. Merit, U.S. Ski Assn., 1973, Karl Jefferson Thomson award, 1978, Silver and Bronze medal U.S. Master Cross Country Ski Championships, 1993, Gold and 2 Silver medals; named Tchr. of Yr. House Officers, 1976, Tchr. of Yr. Class of 1977; grantee New England Arthritis Rheumatism Soc., Nuffield Found., Commonwealth Found., NIH, Arthritis Found. Vt. chpt., Given Found., numerous private grants. Fellow ACP, Am. Coll. Sports Medicine; mem. AMA (cert. merit 1963-64), AAAS, Am. Fedn. Clin. Research, N.Y. Acad. Scis., Am. Coll. Rheumatology (master of rheumatology), Am. Rheumatism Assn. (mem. editorial bd. 1972—, fibrositis study com. 1975—, patient service com., program com. 1977-83), Can. Arthritis and Rheumatism Assn. (mem. study section to review grant applications), New England Rheumatism Soc. (pres. 1960-61), NIH Alumni Assn., Found. Advanced Edn. in Scis., AAUP, U.S. Combined Tng. Assn., Vt. State Med. Soc. (chmn. program com. 1950-54), Alpha Omega Alpha. Avocations: Competitive running; cross country skiing; equestrian sports. Office: U Vt Coll Medicine Vt Coll Medicine 1 S P # U Burlington VT 05405

BLAND, JOHN MARTIN, statistician, educator; b. Stockport, Cheshire, Eng., Mar. 6, 1947; s. Ernest and Phyllis (Lambert) B.; m. Pauline Cassy, Aug. 4, 1979; children: Nicholas David, Emily Sarah. BSc in Math., Imperial Coll., 1968, MSc in Stats., 1969; PhD of Epidemiology, U. London, 1980. Tech. officer Imperial Chem. Industries, Bracknell, Eng., 1969-72; lectr. St. Thomas's Hosp. Med. Sch., London, 1972-76; lectr. St. George's Hosp. Med. Sch., London, 1976-92, reader in med. stats., 1992-95, prof. med. stats., 1995—. Author: Introduction to Medical Statistics, 1987, 2d edit., 1995; contbr. numerous articles to profl. jours. Fellow Royal Statis. Soc.; mem. Biometric Soc., Royal Coll. Radiologists (hon.). Office: St Georges Hosp Med Sch, Cranmer Terr, London SW17 0RE, England

BLANE, HOWARD THOMAS, research institute administrator; b. De Land, Fla., May 10, 1926; s. Chesley Thomas and Olive Henrietta (Van Heest) B.; children: Benjamin, Eva. BA cum laude, Harvard U., 1950; MA, Clark U., 1951, PhD, 1957. Instr. Harvard Med. Sch., Cambridge, Mass., 1957-66, asst. clin. prof., 1966-70; assoc. prof. U. Pitts., 1970-72, prof., 1972-86; rsch. prof. SUNY, Buffalo, 1986—; dir. Rsch. Inst. Addictions, Buffalo, 1986—; cons. Nat. Inst. on Alcohol Abuse and Alcoholism, Washington, 1970—; v.p. Health Edn. Found., Washington, 1975—; bd. dirs. Rsch. Found. for Mental Hygiene, Albany, N.Y., 1986—; principal investigator numerous grants. Author: The Personality of the Alcoholic, 1968; editor: Frontiers of Alcoholism, 1970, Youth, Alcohol and Social Policy, 1979, Psychological Theories of Drinking and Alcoholism, 1987. Clark U. scholar, Worcester, Mass., 1950-51. Fellow APA, Am. Psychol. Soc.; mem. APHA, AAAS, Rsch. Soc. on Alcoholism. Office: Rsch Inst on Addictions 1021 Main St Buffalo NY 14203-1016

BLANK, BRUCE HENRY, physician; b. Portland, Oreg., Oct. 6, 1946. BA, Univ. Oreg., 1968, MD, 1972. Diplomate Am. Bd. Urology. Internship in surgery N.Y. Hosp. Cornell, 1972-73; residency in urology Univ. Oreg. Health Scis., 1975-79; pvt. practice, 1979—; clinical instr. urology Univ. Oreg., 1979-83, clinical asst. prof., 1983—; cancer com., Good Samaritan Hosp., 1979, cancer edn. subcom., 1979—, tissue com., 1991—, infectious disease com., 1990-93, chmn. tissue com., 1991-94. Contbr. articles to profl. jours.; cons. editor AUAA Jour., 1985-95. Medical dir. Cascade Run Off, 1986-94; medical adv. Robison Jewish Home for the Aging, 1990—; com. profl. edn. Am. Cancer Soc., 1982—, chmn. med. affairs com., 1994—. Fellow Am. Coll. Surgeons; mem. Oreg. Medical Assn., Oreg. Urological Soc., Northwest Urological Soc., Oreg. Assn. Transplant Surgeons, Am. Urological Assn. (western sect. exec. com. 1986-90, 94—), Portland Surgical Soc., Multnomah County Medical Soc., Portland Surgical Soc., Alpha Omega Alpha. Office: 1130 N W 22nd Ste 620 Portland OR 97210

BLANK, H. ROBERT, psychiatrist; b. Phila., Mar. 21, 1914; s. Jacob and Zina (Ettinzon) B.; m. Frieda Nurenburg, Apr. 16, 1938 (div. 1967); children: Emily J., Melanie R.; m. Virginia Sherwood, Sept. 8, 1968. BS,

Temple U., 1936, MD, 1939; Dipl., N.Y. Psychoanalytic Inst., N.Y.C., 1952. Diplomate Am. Bd. Psychiatry and Neurology in child psychiatry and psychiatry. Resident psychiatrist Springfield State Hosp., Sykesville, Md., 1940-42; psychiatrist Child Study Ctr. of Md., Balt., 1942-43, Mason Gen. Hosp., Brentwood, N.Y., 1943-46; pvt. practice psychiatry and psychoanalysis White Plaines, N.Y., 1947—; assoc. clin. prof. psychiatry Albert Einstein Med. Coll., Bronx, 1959-75; clin. prof. psychiatry Cornell U. Med. Coll., N.Y.C., 1975—. Assoc. editor the Psychoanalytic Quar., 1954-79; contbr. articles to profl. jours. Maj. U.S. Army, 1943-46. Fellow Am. Psychiat. Assn., Am. Acad. Child and Adolescent Psychiatry; mem. Am. Psychoanalytic Assn. Address: 53 Winslow Rd White Plains NY 10606-3715

BLANK, HOWARD STEVEN, physician, educator; b. Bklyn., Feb. 24, 1948; s. Carl and Bertha (Greenberg) B.; m. Jessica Beth Spielman, June 15, 1969; children: Evan Scott, Daniel Jason. BS, Bklyn. Coll., 1968; MD, Mt. Sinai Sch. Medicine, 1972. Diplomate Am. Bd. Internal Medicine, Am. Bd. Internal Medicine-Rheumatology. Intern internal medicine Mt. Sinai Hosp., 1972-73, resident, 1973-75, chief med. resident, 1975-76; physician Good Samaritan Hosp., Suffern, N.Y., 1977—; physician Nyack (N.Y.) Hosp., 1977—, chief divsn. rheumatology, 1990—; rehab. physician Helen Hayes Hosp., West Haverstraw, N.Y., 1977-91; fellow rheumatology Mt. Sinai Hosp., N.Y.C., 1975-77; asst. clin. prof. Columbia Presbyn. Med. Ctr., N.Y.C., 1991—; pvt. practice Suffern, 1977—; pres. med. staff Helen Hayes Hosp., 1981-83; co-chmn. pharmacy com. Good Samaritan Hosp., 1987—; chief, div. rheumatology Good Samaritan Hosp., 1989—. Fellow Am. Coll. Rheumatology; mem. Rockland County Med. Soc., N.Y. State Med. Soc., Alpha Omega Alpha. Jewish. Office: 222 Route 59 Suffern NY 10901-5204

BLANK, JONATHAN WILLIAM, anesthesiologist; b. Bloomington, Ind., May 17, 1960; s. Gordon Coleman and Joan Lee (Bevirt) B.; m. Lane Hoffman, Aug. 8, 1987. BA, Johns Hopkins U., 1981; MD, Cornell U., 1985. Diplomate Am. Bd. Med. Examiners, Am. Bd. Anesthesiology with added qualification in pain mgmt. Surg. intern U. N.C. Hosps., Chapel Hill, 1985-86, resident in orthopedic surgery, 1986-87, resident in anesthesiology, 1987-90; asst. prof. dept. anesthesiology Uniformed Svcs. U. of the Health Scis., Bethesda, Md., 1990-93; Longwood pain fellow Harvard U., 1993-94. Maj. M.C., USAFR. Cornell U. scholar, 1981-82, Johns Hopkins U. scholar, 1977. Mem. AMA, N.C. Med. Soc., Am. Soc. Anesthesiologists, Am. Soc. Regional Anesthesia, Internat. Anesthesia Rsch. Soc.

BLANK, MARION SUE, psychologist; b. N.Y.C., Dec. 20, 1933; d. Morris David and Tillie Jean (Sherman) Hersch; m. Martin Blank, July 3, 1955; children: Donna, Jonathan, Ari. B.A., CCNY, 1955, M.S. in Edn, 1956; Ph.D., Cambridge (Eng.) U., 1961. Asst. prof. Albert Einstein Coll. Medicine, 1965-70, asso. prof., 1970-73; prof. dept. psychiatry Rutgers Med. Sch., Piscataway, N.J., 1973-83; mem. adj. faculty dept. psychiatry Columbia Coll. Physicians and Surgeons, N.Y.C., 1980-83; dir. reading disabilities rsch. inst., pvt. practice, cons., 1983—; program dir. Read Net Found., 1995—. Author: Teaching Learning in the Preschool - A Dialogue Approach, Preschool Language Assessment Instrument, 1978, (with Rose and Berlin) The Language of Learning, 1978, (with Marquis) Directing Discourse, 1987, Sentence Master, 1990-92, (with Berlin) A Parent's Guide to Educational Software, 1991, (with Marquis and Klimovitch) Directing School Discourse, 1994, Directing Early Discourse with Marquis and Klimovitch, 1995. Pinsent-Darwin fellow, 1960; recipient award of commendation N.J. Speech and Hearing Assn., 1979, Spl. Edn. award Software Pubs. Am., 1990, N.J., USPHS Career Devel. award, 1965-73; named nominee Kleffner Lifetime Svc. award Am. Speech Hearing Assn., 1994, 95. Fellow Am. Psychol. Assn.; mem. Assn. for Children with Learning Disabilities, Coun. for Exceptional Children. Home: 157 Columbus Dr Tenafly NJ 07670-1635 Office: 116 E 63d St Ste 5D New York NY 10021

BLANKE, ROBERT VERNON, toxicologist, consultant; b. Leavenworth, Kans., Dec. 3, 1924; s. Henry and Irene (Meyer) B.; m. Lois Margaret Scholz, Sept. 9, 1950; children: Christine Louise, Steven Robert, Jonathan Andrew. BS, Northwestern U., 1949; PhD, U. Ill., 1958. Diplomate Am. Bd. Forensic Toxicology. Asst. toxicologist Md. Chief Med. Examiner Office, Balt., 1958-60; chief toxicologist Ill. State Health Dept., Chgo., 1960-63, Va. Chief Med. Examiner, Richmond, 1963-72; prof. pathology, pharmacology, and toxicology Med. Coll. Va., Richmond, 1972-87; dir. toxicology lab. Med. Coll. Va. Hosps., Richmond, 1972-87; cons. Richmond, 1987—; mem. toxicology study sect. div. rsch. grants. NIH, 1970-74; mem. peer review toxicology data bank Nat. Libr. Medicine, 1975-85; dir. Am. Bd. Forensic Toxicology, 1975-85, founder; participant First Symposium on Drugs of Abuse Testing, 1990; co-chmn. conf. on tech., sci., and procedural issues employee drug testing Nat. Inst. Drug Abuse. Author: (with others) Fundamentals of Clinical Chemistry, 1970, 76, 87, NIDA Resesearch Monograph 73, 1986, Environmental Toxicology-Taiwan, 1985; author (conf. report) NIDA Drug Testing Consensus Report, 1990; contbr. articles to profl. jours. With USAAF, 1943-46. Fellow AAAS, Am. Acad. Forensic Scis. (merit award 1973, 80, Harger award 1986, mem. exec. com. 1975-78); mem. Internat. Assn. Forensic Toxicologists (founder), Soc. Forensic Toxicologists (founder, v.p. 1977, pres. 1978). Lutheran. Office: Cons Toxicologist 4222 Croatan Rd Richmond VA 23235-1116

BLANK-REID, CYNTHIA ANNE, trauma and emergency nurse administrator; b. Camden, N.J., Sept. 27, 1961; d. Albert Edwin Jr. and Elizabeth Jane (DeNoé) B.; m. Paul C. Reid, Aug. 20, 1994. BSN, Villanova U., 1983; MSN, Widener U., Chester, Pa., 1988, postgrad., 1991—. Cert. emergency nurse, BLS, ACLS. Neurosurgery unit nurse Med. Coll. Pa. Hosp., Phila., 1983-86, emergency ctr. nurse, 1986-88, emergency med. svcs. coord., 1988-89, trauma nurse coord., 1989—; adj. faculty Widener U. Grad. Sch., 1989-91, Villanova U. Grad. Sch., 1990, Russell Sage Coll. Grad. Sch., Troy, N.Y., 1990, U. Va., 1992. Contbr. chpts. to books, articles to profl. jours. Recipient Pa. Gov.'s Safety award State of Pa., 1990. Mem. Phila. Emergency Nurses Assn. (treas. 1989-92), Phila. Neurol. Nurses Assn. (sec. 1987-89, pres. 1989-91), Am. Assn. Neurol. Nurses (Mid-Atlantic states del. 1990-95, bd. dirs. 1995—). Roman Catholic. Home: 3317 Bowman St Philadelphia PA 19129-1512 Office: Med Coll Pa Hosp 3300 Henry Ave Philadelphia PA 19129-1121

BLANKS, JAMES H., optometrist; b. Nashville, Mar. 15, 1963; s. James R. and Janice (Webb) B.; m. June-Ellen Schlimmer, Oct. 14, 1989; 1 child, J. Dean. OD, So. Coll. Optometry, Memphis, 1987. Pvt. practice McMinnville, Tenn., 1987-91; pvt. practice Tullahoma, Tenn., 1991—. Mem. Am. Optometric Assn., Tenn. Optometric Assn., South Ctrl. Tenn. Optometric Soc. (pres. 1994-95), Mid. Tenn. Orchid Soc., Lions Internat. Home: 408 N. Atlantic St Tullahoma TN 37388-3504 Office: 507 N Atlantic St Tullahoma TN 37388-3504

BLANKSON, MARY LARTEY, pediatrician; b. Tutu, Ghana, Mar. 16, 1946; came to U.S., 1977; d. Richard Emmanuel and Christiana Karl (Odei) L.; m. Joe Harry Blankson, Jan. 20, 1973; children: Kwamena Abaka Blankson, Kwabena Lattey Blankson, Amma Amene Blankson. Pre-med. degree, U. Ghana, West Africa, 1967, MD, 1972; MPH in Maternal and Child Health, U. Minn., 1982. Diplomate Am. Bd. Pediatrics; cert. PALS; cert. instr. nursing child assessment. Rotating intern to instr. interns Korle Bu Teaching Hosp., Accra, Ghana, 1972-74, instr. for interns, primary care physician, sr. med. officer, 1976-77; intern to resident in pediatrics Harlem Hosp. Ctr., Columbia U., 1980; fellowship ambulatory pediatrics U Minn., 1982; primary care physician, preceptor med. students and nurses Bur. Maternal and Child Health, Mpls. Health Dept., 1980-83; pediatrician, mentor for nurse practitioners Child Care Clinic, U. Minn., 1982-83; pediatrician Community Univ. Health Care Ctr., U. Minn., Mpls., 1983-84; clin. instr. in pediatrics Dept. Pediatrics, U. Minn., 1984—; asst. prof. maternal and child health tng. program Sch. Pub. Health, U. Ala., Birmingham, 1985—; primary care pediatrician Jefferson County Health Dept., 1985—; courtesy staff privileges The Children's Hosp. of Ala., 1985—; physician (part-time) Cancer Detection Ctr., U. Minn., 1981-83; pediatrician (part-time) Group Health Inc., Mpls., 1982-83; faculty advisor to African students orgn. U. Ala., 1987-90, mem. ednl. policy com. sch. pub. health, 1988-92, mem. admission com., 1993—; mem. Pub. Health Area 8 Perinatal Adv. Com., 1988—. Adv. coun. Child Care Resources, 1993—; Head Start Health Adv. Com., 1993—; chairperson med. adv. com. Healthy Start Project, co-chairperson needs assessment com., 1991, adolescent pregnancy prevention com., 1992; pediatric cons. Health Care for the Homeless, 1989—; mem. Hold Out the Lifeline com., 1990—; mem. program planning com. Reuben-Lindh, Child Devel. Ctr., Mpls., 1982-84; adv. bd. UAB Daycare, 1989—; mem. com. on AIDS and Child Welfare Svcs., 1988; bd. dirs. Planned Parenthood of Ala., 1987-90. Recipient Nestle's Pediatric Prize, 1971, Arrington award for Svc. Birmingham's Mayor, 1991; Ghana Cocoa Mktg. Bd. scholarship, 1959-66. Fellow Am. Acad. Pediatrics; mem. APHA, Soc. for Pediatric Epidemiol. Rsch., Ambulatory Pediatric Assn., Nat. Coun. for Internat. Health, Assn. of Tchrs. of Maternal and Child Health, Ghana Med. Assn. Home: 544 Iroquois Dr Birmingham AL 35214-3729 Office: Jefferson County Dep Health No Health Ctr 2817 30th Ave North Birmingham AL 35207

BLANKSTEIN, RONALD LARRY, cardiologist, consultant; b. Paterson, N.J., Mar. 15, 1946; s. Harold and Rachel (Suresky) B.; m. Monica H. Linderman, Dec. 28, 1991; children: Lauren, Danielle, Erin. BA, Franklin and Marshall Coll., 1968; MD, U. Miami, 1972. Diplomate in internal medicine and cardiology Am. Bd. Internal Medicine. Resident and fellow Montefiore Hosp./Albert Einstein Sch. Medicine, Bronx, N.Y., 1972-77; attending physician Miami Heart Inst., Miami Beach, Fla., 1977-91; assoc. clin. prof. medicine U. Miami, 1979-85; attending physician Boca Raton (Fla.) Cmty. Hosp., 1991—, Northridge Med. Ctr., Ft. Lauderdale, Fla., 1991—. Bd. dirs. Am. Heart Assn., Dade County, 1983-85. Fellow Am. Coll. Cardiology; mem. ACP, Am. Soc. Nuclear Cardiology, Am. Soc. Echocardiography. Office: Physicians Splty Group Ste 301 1905 Clint Moore Rd Boca Raton FL 33496

BLANPAIN, JAN EUGENE, physician, educator; b. Diest, Belgium, Feb. 24, 1930; s. Henri and Celine (Dochy) B.; m. Hedwig Van Landeghem, Apr. 7, 1958; children—Kristin, Marianne. M.D. summa cum laude, Leuven U., Belgium, 1956. Lectr., asso. adminstr. Leuven U. Hosp., 1958-61, asso. prof., dir., 1961-65, prof., dir. dept. hosp. adminstrn. and med. care orgn., 1965—; cons. WHO, W.K. Kellogg Found., Rockefeller Found., HEW; vis. prof. Ottawa U., 1968; mem. Nat. Research Council, 1967-76, Nat. Hosp. Council, 1963—, Nat. Health Planning Council, 1974—, WHO Expert Panel on Orgn. of Med. Care, 1974—. Author: Community Health Investment, 1976, National Health Insurance and Health Resources, 1978. WHO fellow, 1961-65; Council of Europe fellow, 1963. Fellow Am. Coll. Hosp. Adminstrs. (hon.); mem. Inst. Medicine, Nat. Acad. Scis., European Assn. Tng. Programs in Health Care Studies (pres. 1978—), Internat. Epidemiological Assn., Internat. Hosp. Fedn. Roman Catholic. Home: 61 Konijnenhoekstraat, 3044 Oud-Heverlee Belgium Office: 102 Vital Decosterstraat 3000 Louvain Belgium

BLANTON, CHRISTOPHER LEE, ophthalmologist, researcher; b. Sikeston, Mo., Sept. 14, 1960; s. Harry Augustine and Carol Marie (Page) B.; m. Bridget Ann Geegan, May 29, 1982; children: Robert, Lee, Rose. BS, U. Notre Dame, 1982; MD, Med. Coll. Ohio, 1986. Diplomate Am. Bd. Ophthalmology, Nat. Bd. Med. Examiners. Lt. comdr. USN, San Diego, 1982—; intern Naval Med. Ctr., San Diego, 1986-87, resident in ophthalmology, 1989-92; brigade surgeon 7th Marine Expdn., Twenty-nine Palms, Calif., 1987-89; fellow in cornea Wills Eye Hosp., Phila., 1992-93; dir. cornea svc., performance improvement coord., utilization rev. officer Naval Med. Ctr., San Diego, 1993—; dir. cornea svc. Inland Eye Inst., Loma Linda, Calif., 1995—; clin. asst. prof. Uniformed Svcs. U. Health Scis., Bethesda, Md., 1995—; prin. investigator Clin. Investigation Divsn., San Diego, 1994—. Contbr. articles to profl. jours. Com. chmn. Cub Scouts Am., Rockville, Md., 1992. Recipient Navy Achievement award, USN, San Diego, 1989, 92, 96. Mem. Am. Acad. Ophthalmology, Am. Soc. Cataract and Refractive Surgery, Assn. Rsch. Vision and Ophthalmology, Soc. Mil. Ophthalmologists, Alpha Omega Alpha, San Diego Eye Bank. Roman Catholic. Office: Inland Eye Inst 1900 E Washington St Colton CA 92324

BLASCHKE, TERRENCE FRANCIS, medicine and molecular pharmacology educator; b. Rochester, Minn., Oct. 4, 1942; s. Robert Elmer and Carmella Ann (Seeby) B.; m. Jeannette F. Martin, June 8, 1968; children: Anne, John. BS in Math. cum laude, U. Denver, 1964; MD, Columbia U., 1968. Diplomate Am. Bd. Internal Medicine, Nat. Bd. Med. Examiners. Intern in medicine UCLA Ctr. for Health Scis. 1968-69, asst. resident, 1969-70; clin. assoc. metabolism br. Nat. Cancer Inst., NIH, Bethesda, Md., 1970-72; clin. rsch fellow div. clin. pharmacology dept. medicine U. Calif. Med. Ctr., San Francisco, 1972-74; asst. prof. medicine (clin. pharmacology) Stanford (Calif.) U. Sch. Medicine, 1974-81, asst. prof. pharmacology, 1978-81, assoc. prof. medicine (clin. pharmacology) and pharmacology, 1981-91, prof. medicine (clin. pharmacology)-molecular pharmacology, 1991—; bd. govs. Am. Bd. Clin. Pharmacology, 1990-92; vis. worker div. molecular pharmacology Nat. Inst. for Med. Rsch., London, 1980-81, Ctr. for Biopharm. Scis., U. Leiden and dept. med. info. scis. Erasmus U., The Netherlands, 1990; mem. Medi-Cal drug use rev. bd. Calif. Dept. Health Svcs., 1993—; chmn. generic drugs adv. com. FDA, 1990-94; mem. bd. sci. advisors Merck Sharp and Dohme Rsch. Labs., Rahway, N.J., 1986-90; mem. pharmacology study sect. NIH, 1979-83. Mem. editl. bd. Drug Therapeutics: Concepts for Physicians, 1978-81, Rational Drug Therapy, 1984-85, Clin. Pharmacology and Therapeutics, 1981—, Drug Interaction Facts, 1983-87, Drug Metabolism and Disposition, 1994—; assoc. editor Ann. Rev. Pharmacology and Toxicology, 1989—. Officer USPHS, 1970-72. Recipient faculty devel. award in clin. pharmacology Pharm. Mfrs. Assn. Found.; Burroughs-Wellcome scholar. Mem. ACP, AAAS, Am. Soc. for Clin. Pharmacology and Therapeutics (chmn. liaison com. for clin. pharmacology 1985-89, sci. program com. 1986-87, pres. 1988-89, assoc. sec.-treas. 1990-92, chmn. long range planning com. 1992—), Am. Soc. Pharmacology and Exptl. Therapeutics (exec. com. clin. pharmacology divsn. 1986-89), Am. Fedn. Clin. Rsch., Western Soc. Clin. Investigation, Western Assn. Physicians, Western Pharmacology Soc., Phi Beta Kappa, Alpha Omega Alpha. Office: Stanford U Med Ctr Div Clin Pharmacology S-169 300 Pasteur Dr Palo Alto CA 94304-2203

BLASCO, CARMELO MARTINEZ, gastroenterologist; b. Asuncion, Paraguay, Aug. 13, 1950; m. Maria Fresco; children: Silvia, Enrique, Luis, Maria del Carmen. MD, Nat. U.; degree in gastroenterology, U. Autonoma Mex.; degree in endoscopy, Showa U.; degree in therapeutic endoscopy, Eppendortt U. Resident Hosp. Clinicas. Sch. Medicine, Asuncion, Paraguay, 1975-77; fellow Showa U. Fujigaoka Hosp., Tokyo, 1977-79; resident, chief of residents Gen. Hosp. I.M.S.S., Mexico City, 1980-81; staff mem. dept. gastroenterology Sch. Medicine, Asuncion, 1982-88; asst. prof. Catedra Semiologia Sch. Medicine, Asuncion, 1984-92, assoc. prof., 1993-95; co-chief dept. gastroenterology Catedra Semiologia Sch. Medicine, 1993—. Contbr. articles to profl. jours.; author: Gastroenterologia, 1995. Mem. Mex. Soc. Gastroenterology and Endoscopy, Colombian Soc. Gastroenterology, Chile Soc. Endoscopy, Argentine Soc. Gastroenterology, Japanese Soc. Endoscopy, Am. Coll. Gastroenterology. Roman Catholic. Home: Coronel Lopez 1445 Sajonia, Asuncion Paraguay Office: Eligio Ayala, 1026 Asuncion Paraguay

BLASEN, AMY VANHUSS, emergency medicine physician; b. Lansing, Mich., Dec. 5, 1961; d. Wayne Daniel and Edna W. (Goetzke) V.; m. Thomas James Blasen, June 20, 1987; children: Lindsay, Kylie, Lauren. BS in Med. Tech. cum laude, Mich. State U., 1986, BS in Chemistry, 1986, DO, 1990. Diplomate Am. Coll. Emergency Physicians. Resident emergency medicine Am. Coll. Emergency Physicians, Lansing, Mich., 1991-94; emergency medicine physician E.W. Sparrow Hosp., Lansing, 1994—; com. mem. Capital Area Health Alliance, Lansing, 1994—; core faculty mem. Emergency Medicine Residency, Lansing, 1994—; faculty mem. Mich State U. Coll. Osteo. Medicine, Lansing, 1995—; ccns., liaison to mayor of Lansing on health care, 1994-95. Author: Emergency Medicine, 1995, Neurologic Emergencies, 1996. Mem. AMA, Am. Osteo. Assn., Am. Coll. Emergency Physicians, Am. Coll. osteo. Emergency Physicians, Soc. Acad. Emergency Medicine. Office: E W Sparrow Hosp 1215 E Michigan Ave Lansing MI 48910

BLASER, KURT, medical research institute administrator; b. Thun, Berne, Switzerland, June 25, 1940; s. Gottfried and Alice (Aebischer) B.; m. Ruth Blaser-Blaser, Mar. 25, 1966; children: Eveline, Maya. Degree in chem. engring., State Engring. Sch., Berne, Switzerland, 1960; PhD, U. Berne, 1975, P.D., 1985; P.D., U. Zurich, Switzerland, 1991, prof., 1995. Postdoctoral fellow Ctr. for Cancer Rsch. MIT, Cambridge, Mass., 1975-77; sr. investigator Inst. for Protein Rsch. U. Berne, 1977-80, head Lab. of Molecular Immunology, 1980-88; dir. Swiss Inst. Allergy and Asthma Rsch., Davos, 1988—. Home: Obere Str 71, CH-7270 Davos Switzerland Office: Swiss Inst Allergy & Asthma Rsch, Obere Str 22, CH-7270 Davos Switzerland

BLASS, JOHN PAUL, medical educator, physician; b. Vienna, Austria, Feb. 21, 1937; s. Gustaf and Jolan (Wirth) B.; m. Birgit Annelise Knudsen, Dec. 20, 1960; children: Charles, Lisa. AB summa cum laude, Harvard U., 1958; PhD, U. London, 1960; MD, Columbia U., 1965. Postdoctoral fellow Am. Cancer Soc., Columbia U., 1962-63; intern Mass. Gen. Hosp., Boston, 1965-66; resident in medicine Mass. Gen. Hosp., 1966-67; research assoc. Nat. Heart and Lung Inst., Bethesda, Md., 1967-70; asst. prof. psychiatry and biol. chemistry UCLA, 1970-76, assoc. prof., 1976-78; mem. staff UCLA Hosps. Clinics, 1970-78; Winifred Masterson Burke prof. neurology, prof. medicine Cornell U. Med. Center, 1978—; attending neurologist N.Y. Hosp.; mem. NBS-1 rev. com. NIH, 1981-84; councilor Nat. Inst. Aging, 1986-89; chmn. Nat. Adv. Panel on Alzheimers's Disease U.S. Congress, 1987-91, mem., 1993-96. Editl. bd. Jour. Neurochemistry, 1981-86, Neurochem. Rsch., Neurochem. pathology, Neurobiol. Aging, Jour. Neurol. Scis.; assoc. editor Jour. Am. Geriatric Soc., 1982-87; co-editor: Caring for Alzheimer's Patients, 1990, Familial Alzheimer's Disease, 1989, Treatment of Alzheimer's Disease, 1989, Principles of Geriatrics and Gerontology, 2d edit. 1990, 3d edit. 1994; contbr. articles to profl. jours. Mem. sci. adv. bd. Will Rogers Inst., Allied Signal Aging Award Com. Served as asst. surgeon USPHS, 1967-70. Marshall scholar, 1958-60. Mem. Soc. Neurosci. (chmn. social issues com.), Biochem. Soc., Am. Soc. Biol. Chemists, Am. Soc. Neurochemistry (council, chmn. public policy com.), Internat. Soc. Neurochemistry (council, chmn. clin. com.), Am. Soc. Clin. Investigation, Am. Geriatrics Soc., Am. Fedn. Aging Rsch. (v.p., chmn. research com. 1982-87, pres. 1994-96), Assn. Alzheimers and Related Disease (sci. adv. bd. 1982-86), Am. Chem. Soc., Phi Beta Kappa, Sigma Xi, Alpha Omega Alpha. Jewish. Home: 1 Orchard Pl Bronxville NY 10708-2509 Office: Cornell U 785 Mamaroneck Ave White Plains NY 10605-2523

BLATT, SIDNEY JULES, psychology educator, psychoanalyst; b. Phila., Oct. 15, 1928; s. Harry and Fannie (Feld) B.; m. Ethel Shames, Feb. 1, 1951; children: Susan, Judith, David. B.S., Pa. State U., 1950, M.S., 1952; Ph.D., U. Chgo., 1957; postgrad., Western New Eng. Inst. for Psychoanalysis, 1972. Postdoctoral fellow Neuropsychiat. Inst. of U. Ill. Med. Ctr., Psychiat. and Psychosomatic Inst. of Michael Reese Hosp., New Eng., 1957-59; instr. Univ. Coll. U. Chgo., 1959-60; mem. faculty Yale U., New Haven, 1960—, prof. psychology and psychiatry, 1974—; mem. faculty Western New Eng. Inst. for Psychoanalysis, 1975—; Sigmund Freud prof. psychoanalysis, Ayala and Sam Zacks prof. of art history Hebrew U., 1988-89; Fulbright sr. rsch. fellow, 1988-89; mem. NIMH Rsch. Fellowship Rev. Panel, 1966-69, NIMH Psychology Tng. Rev. Panel, 1969-74. Author: (with J. Allison and C. Zimet) Interpretation of Psychological Tests, 1968, 2d edit., 1988, (with C. M. Wild) Schizophrenia: A Developmental Analysis, 1976, (with E.S. Blatt) Continuity and Change in Art: The Development of Modes of Representation, 1984, (with Z.V. Segal) The Self in Emotional Distress, 1993, (with R. Q. Ford) Therapeutic Change: An Object Relations Perspective, 1994. Recipient award for disting. contbns. to rsch. Assn. Med. Sch. Profs. Psychology; named Disting. Practitioner of Psychology, Nat. Acad. Practice, 1983; Found. Fund Rsch. in Psychiatry fellow, 1961-64. Mem. APA, AAAS, AAUP, Soc. Personality Assessment (pres. 1984-86, Bruno Klopfer and Marguerite R. Hertz awards for disting. contbns. to personality assessment). Office: Yale U 25 Park St New Haven CT 06519-1110

BLAU, GARY MICHAEL, social services administrator; b. Carbondale, Ill., Dec. 2, 1961; s. Burton Ira and Louise Irene (Wagman) B.; m. Gwenn Michelle Silver, Dec. 18, 1982; children: Jennifer, Andrew. BA magna cum laude, U. South Fla., 1983; MS, Auburn U., 1986, PhD, 1988. Lic. psychologist, Conn. Grad. teaching asst. Auburn (Ala.) U., 1983-84, grad. clinician psychol. svcs. ctr., 1983-85; grad. clinician East Cen. Mental Health-Charles Henderson Child Health Ctr., Troy, Ala., 1984-86, East Cen. Mental Health-Tuskegee, Ala., 1986-87; psychology intern Child and Family Svcs., Hartford, Conn., 1987-88, psychology resident, 1988-89, psychologist, 1989-90; dir. clin. svcs. Child and Family Agy., New London, Conn., 1990-93; dir. mental health Dept. Children and Families, State of Conn., Hartford, 1993—; clin. faculty Yale Child Study Ctr., 1995—; cons. Waterford (Conn.) Pub. Schs., 1990-93; mem. exec. com. State Mental Health Reps. for Children and Youth. Editorial bd., book rev. editor: Journal of Primary Prevention, 1990, rev. edit. 1996, Adolescent Dysfunctional Behavior: Causes, Intervention and Prevention. Named one of Outstanding Young Men Am., 1986, 88. Mem. APA, Southeastern Psychol. Assn. Democrat. Jewish. Office: State of Conn Dept Children and Families 505 Hudson St Hartford CT 06106

BLAU, JOHN, retired social worker; b. N.Y.C., Jan. 31, 1934; s. Alex Englander and Edith (Bachman) B. BBA, U. Ga., 1957; cert. of supervision Fordham U., 1971; MSW, Hunter Coll., 1974. Field supr. div. vol. and proprietary homes N.Y.C. Human Resource Adminstrn., 1962-95; ret.; former mem. N.Y.C. Interagy. Task Force on Mental Health. Dist. leader Dem. Party 65th Assembly Dist. Part B, 1987-91. Served with Intelligence Corps, U.S. Army, 1957-59, 61-62. Mem. Disabled Am. Vets. Assn., Acad. Cert. Social Workers, Nat. Assn. Social Workers, E 79th St Block Assn., Alumni Assn. U. Ga., Alumni Assn. Fordham U., Alumni Assn. Hunter Coll. Research on adult and family home industry, homeless men and women, alternate levels of care. Home and Office: 440 E 77th St New York NY 10021-2316

BLAU, ROBERT PHILIP, ophthalmologist; b. Detroit, 1942. BS, Wayne State U., 1965, MD, 1968. Intern Sinai Hosp. of Detroit, 1968-69, resident in ophthalmology, 1969-72; fellow in vitreo-retinal surgery U. Wis., Madison, 1972-73; ophthalmologist Franklin Eye Cons., Southfield, Mich., 1973—. Office: Franklin Eye Cons 29275 Northwestern Southfield MI 48034

BLAUFOX, MORTON DONALD, physician, educator; b. N.Y.C., July 19, 1934; s. Emanuel and Elizabeth (Rosenblum) B.; m. Paulette Goldberg, Dec. 20, 1958; children: Laurie Beth, Ellen Ruth, Andrew David. Student, Harvard U., 1952-55; M.D., SUNY, 1959; Ph.D., U. Minn., 1964. Diplomate Am. Bd. Internal Medicine, Am. Bd. Nuclear Medicine (bd. dirs. 1985-91). Intern Jewish Hosp. of Bklyn., N.Y.C., 1959-60; fellow in medicine Mayo Found. Med. Edn. and Research, Rochester, Minn., 1960-64; advanced research fellow Am. Heart Assn., 1964-66; research fellow in medicine Harvard Med. Sch., Boston, 1964-66; asst. in medicine and radiology Peter Bent Brigham Hosp., Boston, 1964-66; asst. prof. radiology, also assoc. in medicine Albert Einstein Coll. Medicine, Bronx, N.Y., 1966-71; dir. sect. nuclear medicine Albert Einstein Coll. Medicine, 1966-76, dir. unified dept., 1976-82, chmn. unified dept., 1982—, assoc. dir. clin. research center, 1968-72, assoc. prof. radiology, 1971-76, prof. radiology, 1976—, assoc. prof. medicine, 1972-78, prof. medicine, 1978—; asst. attending physician Bronx Mcpl. Hosp. Center, 1966-71, assoc. attending, 1972, attending physician, 1972—; dir. div. nuclear medicine Montefiore Med. Center, 1976-82, chmn. dept. nuclear medicine, 1982—; cons. kidney disease control program USPHS, 1967-72; me. adminstrv. coun. nuclear medicine VA, 1970-73; mem. panel on radiopharms. U.S. Pharmacopeia, 1970-85; mem. hypertension adv. com. N.Y.C. Dept. Health, 1975-76; treas. exec. com. Am. Bd. Nuclear Medicine, 1987-89, chmn., 1990; mem. clin. trials rev. com. Nat. Heart, Lung and Blood Inst., 1988-92, reviewer ready rsch., 1992—; mem. subcom. on non-pharmacologic therapy of Joint Nat. Com. on Detection Evaluation and Treatment of High Blood Pressure, 1991-92; mem. Brookhaven Linac Isotope Producer Users' adv. com. Brookhaven Nat. Lab., 1992—; mem. internat. liaison com. World Fedn. Nuclear Medicine and Biology, 1992-94; active Coun. Cardiovascular Radiology. Editor: (with others) Seminars in Nuclear Medicine, 1970—, Evaluation of Renal Function and Disease with Radionuclides, 1972, 2d edit., 1989, Procs. Internat. Symposium, 1972, 75, 80, 87, 90, PDR for Nuclear Medicine and Radiology, 1971-80, Unilateral Renal Function Studies, 1978, (with others) Secondary Hypertension: Current Diagnosis and Management, 1981, Non-Pharmacologic Therapy of Hypertension, 1987, Newer Diagnostic Methods in Nephrology and Urology, 1986; mem. editl. bd. Radionuclides in Nephrology, 1980, also editor: editl. bd. Jour. Nuclear Medicine, 1973-81, Nephron, Uroradiology, 1978—, Jour. Nuclear Medicine and Allied Sci., 1982—, Nuclear Medicine Comm., 1979—, Renal Failure, 1986-90, Am. Jour. Hypertension, 1987—; assoc. editor: Barnet's PEdiatrics; sect. editor for diagnostics and techniques Current Opinions in Nephrology and Hypertension, 1992—; contbr. The Merck

Manual, 14th, 15th and 16th edits., 1982-91; contbr. articles to profl. jours. Recipient Edward Nobel Found. award, Albert Lasker pub. health service award, 1980. Fellow ACP, Am. Coll. Nuclear Physicians, Coun. on High Blood Pressure Rsch., Coun. Cardiovascular Radiology, N.Y. Acad. Medicine (libr. com. 1986—, chmn. sect. on nuclear medicine 1993-95, chmn. ad hoc com. artifact collection, chmn. history of medicine adv. com. 1995); mem. AMA, Am. Heart Assn., Am. Physiol. Soc., Am. Fedn. Clin. Rsch., Am. Soc. Hypertension (membership com.), Soc. Nuclear Medicine (pres. Greater N.Y. chpt. 1976-77, chmn. acad. coun. 1976-77, exec. and sci. coms., chmn. publ. com. 1979-82, trustee, Berson-Yalow award 1989), Ind. Soc. Nuclear Medicine (Sarabhai Oration 1989), Internat. Soc. Nephrology, Internat. Hypertension Soc., Coun. on High Blood Pressure Rsch. (med. adv. bd.), N.Y. Med. Soc., N.Y. Nephrology Soc., Med. Collectors Assn. (pres. 1983—), Swiss Soc. Nuclear Medicine (hon., corr.), Sugma Xi. Home: 101 Drake Smith Ln Rye NY 10580-4316 Office: Montefiore Med Park 1695A Eastchester Rd Bronx NY 10461

BLAUSTEIN, ALVIN BERNARD, psychoanalyst; b. N.Y.C., Mar. 25, 1925; s. Lazarus and Adele (Quasha) B.; m. Florence Sybil Geiger, June 17, 1951. MD, Yale U., 1948. Diplomate Am. Bd Psychiatry and Neurology. Pvt. practice; asst. clin. prof. Mt. Sinai Med. Sch., N.Y.C., 1979—. Mem. Assn. for Psychoanalytic Medicine. Jewish. Office: 350 Central Park W New York NY 10025-6547

BLAUSTEIN, MORDECAI P., medical educator; b. N.Y.C., Oct. 19, 1935; s. Norman and Gertrude (Hellman) B.; m. Ellen Baron, June 21, 1959; children: Laura M., Marc B. BA in Zoology, Cornell U., 1957; MD, Washington U., St. Louis, 1962; postgrad., Cambridge (Eng.) U., 1966-68. Assoc. prof. physiology and biophysics Washington U. Sch. Medicine, 1968-75; prof. physiology and biophysics Washington U. Sch. of Medicine, 1975-80; NATO sr. fellow Phamacology Inst., Bern, Switzerland, 1971; guest scientist Marine Biol. Assn., Plymouth, Eng., 1973; prof., chmn. dept. physiology U. Md., Balt., 1979—, prof. medicine, 1983—; dir., chmn. exec. bd. Hypertension Ctr., U. Md., Balt., 1985—; mem. study sect. NIH, Bethesda, Md., 1982-84; mem. rsch. com. Am. Heart Assn., Dallas, 1984-89. Commr. Md. Commn. on High Blood Pressure and Related Cardiovascular Risk Factors, Balt., 1986-93. Lt. USN, 1963-66. Recipient Cardiovascular award Robert J. & Claire Pasarow Found., 1990, Humboldt Sr. U.S. Scientist award, 1993. Fellow AAAS; mem. Am. Physiol. Soc. (coun. 1992-95), Soc. Gen. Physiology (coun.), Physiol. Soc., Soc. for Neurosci., Biophys. Soc. Office: U Md Sch Medicine Dept Physiology 655 W Baltimore St Baltimore MD 21201-1509

BLAZAK, PAIGE GAYLE, psychotherapist, school counselor; b. Rochester, N.Y., Feb. 16, 1947; d. Morry and Diane (Jacobs) Storm; m. Robert S. Blazak, Apr. 22, 1967; children: Robin, Eric. BSW, Keuka Coll., Keuka Park, N.Y., 1978; MS, SUNY, Brockport, 1988. Cert. sch. counselor; nat. cert. mental health counselor; credentialed alcohol and addiction counselor, hypnotist. Realtor Sail Realty, Canandaigua, N.Y., 1975-89; weight counselor Nutri-Systems, Rochester, N.Y., 1986-87; dir. Cultured Concepts, Canandaigua, 1982-90; chem. dependency counselor Park Ridge Chem. Dependency, Canadaigua, 1987-89; sch. counselor Geneva (N.Y.) Middle Sch., 1989—; psychotherapist in pvt. practice Canandaigua, 1989—; cons. Cultural Concepts, Canandaigua, 1982-90; dir. Geneva Middle Sch. Theater Group, 1989—. Coord. Am. Cancer Soc., 1975. Breakfast Club grantee geneva Sch. Dist., 1990-91, GMS Theatre Group grantee, 1990—; Creative Works grantee Canandaigua Nat. Bank, 1985. Mem. Am. Assn. Counseling and Devel., N.Y. State Assn. Counseling & Devel., N.Y. State Tchrs. Assn. Home: 3694 W Lake Rd Canandaigua NY 14424-2449 Office: Geneva Middle Sch 63 Pulteney St Geneva NY 14456-2307

BLAZER, DAN GERMAN, psychiatrist, epidemiologist; b. Nashville, Feb. 23, 1944; s. Dan German and Mary Elizabeth (Owsley) B.; m. Sherrill Walls, Aug. 19, 1966; children: Dan German III, Natasha Leigh. BA, Vanderbilt U., 1965; MD, U. Tenn., 1969; MPH, U. N.C., 1979, PhD, 1980. Diplomate, Am. Bd. Psychiatry and Neurology. Fellow Montefiore Hosp. and Med. Ctr., N.Y.C., 1975-76; asst. prof., assoc. prof., then prof. psychiatry Duke U. Med. Ctr., Durham, N.C., 1976—, J.P. Gibbons prof. of psychiatry, 1990—; interim chair of psychiatry Duke U. Med. Ctr., 1990-93; dean of med. edn. Duke U., 1992—; prof. cmty. and family medicine Duke U. Med. Ctr., 1986—; chair, bd. dirs. Am. Geriatrics Soc., N.Y., 1983—; bd. dirs. ret. persons svcs. Am. Assn. Ret. Persons, Alexandria, Va., 1987-92, pres. Psychiat. Rsch. Soc., Salt Lake City, 1988; chmn. epidemiology and disease control study sect. NIH, Bethesda, Md., 1988—. Author: Depression in Late Life, 1993, Family Approach to Health Care in the Elderly, 1983, Life is Worth Living, 1987; editor: Handbook of Geriatric Psychiatry, 1980. Elder Brooks Ave. Ch. of Christ, Raleigh, N.C., 1982. Recipient Rsch. Career Devel. award, NIMH, 1977, Alex Haley award, East Tenn. Bapt. Hosp., Knoxville, 1986, Disting. Svc. award, U. N.C. Sch. Pub. Health, Chapel Hill, 1989. Fellow Am. Psychiat. Assn., Am. Coll. Psychiatrists, So. Psychiat. Assn., Gerontol. Soc. Am., Am. Psychopathol. Assn.; mem. Inst. of Medicine, Nat. Acad. Scis. Democrat. Office: Duke U Med Ctr PO Box 3005 Durham NC 27715-3005

BLAZER, JOHN ALLISON, marriage and family counselor; b. Nashville, Apr. 18, 1930; s. John Payne and Henryetta (Rowland) B.; B.S., Coll. William and Mary, 1959; M.S., Va. Commonwealth U., 1960; Ph.D., Free Protestant Episcopal U., 1962. Staff psychologist Mental Health Clinic, Bristol, Va., 1963-64; sr. clin. psychologist Mental Health Clinic, Savannah, Ga., 1964-74; dir. Savannah Testing Service, 1974-78; dir. Marriage and Family Counseling Center, Madison, Tenn., 1978—; cons. in field. Served with USMC, 1948-53. Decorated Purple Heart. Lic. profl. counselor, Va., social worker, Md.; cert. profl. marriage counselor; diplomate Am. Bd. Examiners in Psychotherapy. Mem. Am. Assn. Sex Educators, Counselors and Therapists, Am. Group Psychotherapy Assn., Am. Personnel and Guidance Assn., Am. Psychotherapy Assn., Nat. Psychol. Assn. Editor: Psychology, 1962-79; editorial advisor: Education, 1970—; cons. editor Educators and Psychologists Press, 1970—; editorial bd. Instructional Psychology, 1973—. Office: 1994 Gallatin Rd N Ste 301 Madison TN 37115-2025

BLAZING, MICHAEL AUGUST, internist; b. 1961. MD, U. Calif., San Francisco, 1987. Postdoctoral fellow Duke U. Med. Ctr. Recipient Clinician-Scientist award Am. Heart Assn., 1995-96. Office: Duke U Med Ctr 2113 Carriage Way Durham NC 27514-9466*

BLEACH, GAIL ANN, psychologist; b. Washington, Dec. 12, 1949; children: Greg Jeremy Reeker, Seth Simon Reeker. BA, U. Md., 1970, MA, 1972, PhD, 1974. Lic. psychologist. Dir. counseling svcs. Youth for Understanding, Washington, 1979-81; dir. Bleach and Assocs., Clinton, Md., 1975—. Mem. Am. Psychol. Assn., Md. Psychol. Assn. Office: Bleach and Assocs 9015 Woodyard Rd Ste 209 Clinton MD 20735-2508

BLECHER, CAROL STEIN, oncology clinical nurse specialist; b. Bronx, N.Y., July 5, 1947; d. Ludwig and Hedwig (Merkel) Stein; m. Niles Blecher, Mar. 20, 1971; children: Herbert B., Phillip J., Martin D. BSN, N.Y. Univ., 1969; MS, Rutgers Univ., 1989. Staff nurse asst. head nurse Mt. Sinai Hosp., N.Y.C., 1969-71; per diem nurse Orthopedic Surgeon, LIC, N.Y., 1972-77; staff nurse per diem Parkway Hosp., Forest Hills, N.Y., 1974-77; staff nurse Union (N.J.) Hosp., 1981-83, head nurse med./surg./oncology, 1983-88; patient care coord. D-7Oncology Newark (N.J.) Beth Israel Medical Ctr., 1988-89; oncology clinical coord. Union Hosp., 1989-96; spl. interest group com. ONS, Pitts., 1995—; cons. Disease Care Inc., 1996—. Mem. Am. Acad. Medical Adminstrs., Oncology Nursing Soc. (SIG coord. 1993-95, SIG com. 1995—), North Central N.J. Chpt. Oncology Nursing Soc. (treas. 1991-93), Upstate N.J. chpt. Oncology Nursing Soc., N.J. Nurses Assn. Democrat. Jewish. Home and Office: 615 Wyoming Ave Elizabeth NJ 07208

BLECHNER, MARK JACOB, psychologist; b. N.Y.C., Nov. 6, 1950; B.A., U. Chgo., 1972; M.S., Yale U., 1975, Ph.D., 1977; cert. in psychoanalysis William Alanson White Inst., 1983. Rsch. assoc. Haskins Labs., New Haven, 1974-77; pvt. practice clin. psychology, N.Y.C., 1977—; asst. clin. prof. med. psychology dept. psychiatry Columbia Coll. Physicians and Surgeons, 1981-94; dir., HIV- Clinical Svcs., teaching faculty, supr. William Alanson White Inst., 1984—; dir. curriculum Manhattan Inst. for Psychoanalysis, 1985—; asst. clin. prof. psychology postdoctoral program in psychoanalysis NYU, 1995—. NIMH trainee in clin. psychology, 1973-76. Mem. AAAS, APA, N.Y. Acad. Sci., Sigma Xi. Author book chpt.; contbr. articles to profl. jours. Address: 145 Central Park W New York NY 10023-2004

BLECHSCHMID, DANIEL HUDSON, health facility administrator; b. Garfield Heights, Ohio, Apr. 26, 1968; s. Thomas Alan and Susan (Reese) B.; m. Denise Christine Yaratch, Oct. 23, 1993. BS in Pre-Medicine and Zoology, Kent State U., 1991; MHA, Xavier U., 1993. Lic. nursing home adminstr., Ohio. Lab. asst. Kent (Ohio) State U., 1988; orderly Anna Maria of Aurora (Ohio) Nursing Facility, 1988-89; nursing asst. Marymount Hosp., Garfield Heights, Ohio, 1989-91; student asst. Med. Rsch. Labs., Cin., 1991-92; adminstrv. resident Providence Hosp., Sandusky, Ohio, 1993, quality resource mgmt. cons., 1993-94; adminstrv. resident Providence Care Ctr., Sandusky, Ohio, 1993; asst. adminstr. Middlebury Manor, Akron, Ohio, 1994-95, Ohio Extended Care Ctr., Lorain, Ohio, 1995—; mem. adv. com. O.W.A. Mem. cmty. bus. svc. com. United Way, Akron, 1994; vol. instr., cons. Jr. Achievement, Cin., 1992; fin. dir. Kent State U. Student Med. Assn., 1987-91. Recipient Cert. of Recognition VFW, 1984, Disting. Svc. award Solon Jaycees, 1984, Cert. Distinction State Bd. Edn., 1986. Mem. Am. Coll. Healthcare Execs. (assoc.), Am. Coll. Healthcare Adminstrs. (assoc.); mem. Ohio Healthcare Assn., Am. Soc. Quality Control, Healthcare Fin. Mgmt. Assn., Am. Hosp. Assn., Ohio Hosp. Assn. Methodist. Home: 1282 E Garfield Rd Aurora OH 44202 Office: Ohio Extended Care Ctr 3364 Kolbe Rd Lorain OH 44053

BLECK, PHYLLIS CLAIRE, surgeon, musician; b. Oak Park, Ill., Mar. 10, 1936; d. William Fred and Mildred A. (Jones) B. BS, U. Ill., 1958; MM, Northwestern U., 1968; DMA, U. So. Calif., 1970; postgrad., Autonoma U., Guadalajara, Mex., 1973-76; MD, Rush Med. Coll., 1979; MS in Surgery, U. Ill., 1983. Diplomate Am. Bd. Surgery, Am. Bd. Thoracic Surgery. Prin. trumpet Fla. Symphony Orch., 1960-66, Orch. Sinfonica Nat. de Peru, 1965; instr. Thornton Jr. Coll., 1966-68; lectr. U. So. Calif., 1969-73; asst. prof. Whittier Coll., 1973; intern Rush Presbyn. St. Luke's Med. Ctr., Chgo., 1979-80, resident, asst. in gen. surgery, 1980-82, instr. gen. surgery, 1982-84; resident in cardiothoracic surgery U. Medicine and Dentistry N.J., 1984-87; pvt. practice medicine specializing in cardiothoracic surgery, Aurora, Ill., 1987—; asst. prof. Rush U., 1996. Editor: Mozart Divertimento for Winds; research on vascular ischemia. Fellow ACS, Am. Coll. Chest Physicians, Ill. Thoracic Surg. Soc., Ill. Surg. Soc.; mem. AAAS, Soc. Thoracic Surgeons, Kappa Delta Pi, Pi Kappa Lambda, Sigma Alpha Iota. Office: 1315 N Highland Ave Aurora IL 60506-1400

BLEDSOE, BRYAN EDWARD, physician; b. Ft. Worth, Apr. 20, 1955; s. Buel Edward and Myrle Margareit (Clayton) B.; m. Emma Chavarria Ramirez, Mar. 11, 1978; children: Bryan Edward II, Andrea Lynn. BS, U. Tex., Arlington, 1981; DO, U. North Tex., 1987. Diplomate Am. Bd. Family Pracitce. Paramedic City of Ft. Worth, 1974-82; resident Tex. Tech. U., Odessa, 1987-88, Scott and White Hosp., Temple, Tex., 1988-90; med. dir., emergency physician Baylor Med. Ctr., Ellis County, Tex., 1990-91; emergency staff physician John Peter Smith Hosp., Ft. Worth, 1991—. Author: Prehospital Emergency Pharmacology, 1984, Atlas of Paramedic Skills, 1987, Paramedic Emergency Care, 1991, Manual of Emergency Drugs, 1991, Intermediate Emergency Care, 1994. Mem. AMA, Am. Coll. Emergency Physician, Tex. Med. Assn., Nat. Assn. Emergency Med. Svc. Physicians, Nat. Assn. EMT's, Tarran County Med. Soc., Sigma Sigma Phi. Republican.

BLEDSOE, MAYA BADACHHAPE, physician; b. Jalgaon, India, Mar. 24, 1959; came to U.S., 1963; d. Ramachandra B. and Saroj (Navgale) Badachhape; m. Murff F. Bledsoe IV, Aug. 11, 1984; children: Nathaniel, Grace. BA, Rice U., 1981; MD, Tex. A&M, 1986. Diplomate Am. Bd. Internal Medicine. Endocrinologist Austin Regional Clinic, Austin, 1992—. Mem. AMA, Am. Assn. Clin. Endocrinology, Tex. Med. Soc. (physician-patient advocacy com. 1992—), Travis County Med. Soc., Endocrine Soc. Office: Austin Regional Clinic 11111 Research Ste 475 Austin TX 78759

BLEDSOE-MELTZER, LAURA A., medical and surgical and pediatric nurse; b. Chgo., Sept. 26, 1959; d. Emmett C. and Elda A. (Antongiovanni) Ryan; m. Mark Meltzer, 1995; children: Ryan, Nathan. BSN, DePaul U., Chgo., 1981. Staff nurse Children's Meml. Hosp., Chgo., 1981-83, Shriners Hosp. for Crippled Children, Chgo., 1983-86; asst. dir. nursing Concerned Care Homehealth, Chgo., 1986-88; agy. nurse CM Health Resources, Arlington Hts., Ill., 1989-91; family care cons. Children's Meml. Hosp., Chgo., 1991—. Mem. ANA.

BLEIBERG, MARVIN JAY, pharmacologist, toxicologist; b. Bklyn., Feb. 19, 1928; s. Harold and Rena (Holzer) B.; m. Beulah Faye Matt, Jan. 17, 1960; children: Larry, Robert. BS, Coll. William & Mary, 1949; PhD in Pharmacology, Va. Commonwealth U., 1957. Cert. gen. toxicology Am. Bd. Toxicology. Postdoctoral trainee Worcester Exptl. Biology, Shrewsbury, Mass., 1957-58; instr., asst. prof. pharmacology Jefferson Med. Coll., Phila., 1958-61; pharmacologist FDA, Washington, 1961-62; rsch. scientist Melpar, Inc., Fairfax, Va., 1962-64; pharmacologist Woodard Rsch. Corp., Herndon, Va., 1964-75; pharmacologist, toxicology reviewer for food additive safety FDA, Washington, 1975—. Contbr. rsch. articles to profl. jours. Named Rohm and Haas fellow Med. Coll. Va., 1955. Mem. Am. Soc. Pharmacology and Exptl. Therapeutics, Soc. Toxicology, Am. Coll. Toxicology, Am. Chem. Soc., Biometrics Soc., Assn. Govt. Toxicologists (pres.-elect). Office: FDA CFSAN HFS-226 200 C St SW Washington DC 20204-0001

BLEICHER, JOEL N., plastic surgeon; b. N.Y.C., Dec. 7, 1945; s. Jerome and Freda (Scherman) B.; m. Sandy Bleicher, Feb. 25, 1989; children: Alison, Katie, Sarah, Aaron. BS in Biology, Creighton U., 1969, MD, 1973; postgrad., U. Neb. Omaha, 1968-69. Diplomate Am. Bd. Surgery, Plastic and Reconstructive Surgery. Intern Edward Sparrow Hosp., Lansing, Mich., 1973-74; resident Creighton U. Sch. Medicine, Omaha, 1974-77, Tulane U. Sch. Medicine, New Orleans, 1978-79; physician emergency dept. Creighton/St. Joseph Hosp., Omaha, Jennie Edmundson Hosp., Council Bluffs, Iowa, Touro Infirmary, New Orleans; chief plastic surgery divsn. Creighton U., Omaha; dir. burn program St. Joseph Hosp., Omaha; assoc. chief, surgery divsn. Creighton U./St. Joseph Hosp., Omaha, 1992; faculty surgery divsn. Creighton U., Omaha, 1976—. Patentee in field; presenter in field; contbr. numerous articles to profl. jours. Grantee Health Future Found., 1989-94, 93-95. Mem. ACS, Am. Burn Assn., Am. Soc. Plastic and Reconstructive Surgery, Assn. for Acad. Surgery, Internat. Coll. Surgeons (fellow, regent Nebr., v.p. U.S. sect.), Facial Plastic and Cosmetic Surgery (v.p.), Douglas County Med. Soc., Southwestern Surg. Soc., Nebr. Coll. Surgeons, Nebr. Med. Found., Midwest Assn. Plastic and Reconstructive Surgery, Surg. Infection Soc., Alpha Omega Alpha.

BLEICHER, SHELDON JOSEPH, endocrinologist, medical educator; b. N.Y.C., Apr. 9, 1931; s. Max and Fannie (Klieger) B.; m. Diane D. Cole, Aug., 1990; children from previous marriages: Erick Max, Phillip Thaddeus Samuel, Deborah Ann Cote, Sandra Lynn Gable, Jodie Lisa Cole. A.B., NYU, 1951; M.S., Western Ill. U., 1952; M.D., SUNY Downstate Med. Center, Bklyn., 1956. Intern L.I. Jewish Hosp. Ctr., New Hyde Park, N.Y., 1956-57; resident Boston City Hosp., 1959-60; chief rsch. fellow in medicine Harvard-Thorndike Meml. Lab., Boston, 1962-63; chief metabolic research unit Jewish Hosp. Med. Center, Bklyn., 1963-67, chief div. endocrinology and metabolism, 1967-77; pvt. practice specializing in endocrinology and diabetes Woodbury, N.Y., 1990—; prof. medicine SUNY Downstate Med. Center, 1975—; chmn. dept. internal medicine Bklyn.-Cumberland Med. Center, 1978-83, Bklyn.-Caledonian Med. Ctr., 1983-90; cons. IAEA, Vienna, Austria, 1966—; mem. attending staff North Shore Univ. Hosp. at syosset, North Shore Univ. Hosp. at Plainview, North Shore Univ. Hosp. at Manhasset. Mem. editorial bd. Diabetes in News, Practical Diabetes; contbr. articles to profl. jours. Vice pres. Locust Valley Central Sch. Bd., 1981-82, pres., 1982-85. Served to capt. M.C., USNR, 1957-92, ret. NIH fellow, 1960-63; NIH research career devel. award, 1970-75; recipient Torch of Liberty award Anti-Defamation League of B'nai Brith, 1982. Fellow ACP, Am. Coll. Endocrinology; mem. AMA, Am. Assn. Diabetes Educators, Am. Soc. Internal Medicine, Am. Diabetes Assn. (bd. dirs. 1979-85, Achievement award 1986, 90), N.Y. Diabetes Assn. (bd. dirs. 1965-93), pres. 1976-78), L.I. Diabetes Assn. (pres. 1978-81), N.Y. State Soc. Internal Medicine (state bd. dirs., treas. Bklyn. chpt., chmn. continuing edn. com.), Bklyn. Soc. Internal Medicine (treas. 1983-85, sec. 1985-87, pres. 1987-89), Endocrine Soc., Am. Assn. Clin. Endocrinologists, Am. Coll. Endocrinologists, Internat. Diabetes Fedn., Juvenile Diabetes Found. Internat., Sagamore Yacht Club (L.I., fleet surgeon 1983-86). Jewish. Office: 165 Froehlich Farm Blvd Woodbury NY 11797-2906

BLEIDT, BARRY ANTHONY, pharmacy educator; b. South Charleston, W.Va., Mar. 29, 1951; s. Robert Anthony and Mary Frances (Gash) B.; 1 child, Brittany Alice. B in Gen. Studies, BS, U. Ky., 1974; PhD, U. Fla., 1982; PharmD, Xavier U., 1994. Registered pharmacist, Fla., La., Ga. Owner Health Resources Cons., Boston and Houston, 1979—; asst. prof. pharmacy Northeastern U., Boston, 1983-86; asst. prof. pharm. U. Houston, 1986-89; assoc. prof. pharmacy adminstrn. Xavier U., 1989-94; med. information scientist Astra/Merck Group, 1994-95; prin. investigator Upjohn Pharmacy Econs. Grant, Houston, 1988; faculty dir. Practicing Pharmacists Inst., Boston, 1983-86; project dir., host William S. Apple Mem. Program in Pharm., Houston, 1988. Contbr. articles to profl. jours.; guest editor Jour. Pharm. Mktg. and Mgmt., 1988; mem. editorial bd. Clin. Rsch. Reg. Affairs, 1983—. Mem. Assn. Colls. Pharmacy (parliamentarian 1983—), Am. Inst. History of Pharmacy, Ind. Pharm. Assn., Nat. Pharm. Assn. (life), Am. Pub. Health Assn., Fla. Blue Key, U. Fla. Hall of Fame, Nat. Eagle Scout Assn., Sigma Xi, Rho Chi, Omicron Delta Kappa, Phi Lambda Sigma. Home: 2038 Thornton Pl South Charleston WV 25303 Office: Health Resources Cons 2038 Thornton Pl South Charleston WV 25303

BLEM, CHARLES ROBERT, biology educator; b. Dunkirk, Ohio, Apr. 18, 1943; s. Robert D. and Zola (Wykes) B.; m. Leann Borror Blem, Aug. 21, 1965; children: Karen, Robert. BS, Ohio U., 1965; MS, U. Ill., 1968, PhD, 1969. Asst. prof. Va. Commonwealth U., Richmond, 1969-75; assoc. prof. Va. Commonwealth U., 1975-80, prof., 1980—; editor Wilson Ornithological Soc. (The Wilson Bulletin), 1987—. Contbr. over 100 articles to profl. pubs. Office: Va Commonwealth Univ 816 Park Ave Richmond VA 23284-2012

BLENDON, ROBERT JAY, health policy educator; b. Dec. 19, 1942; s. Edward and Theresa B.; m. Marie C. McCormick, Dec. 31, 1977. BA, Marietta (Ohio) Coll., 1964; MBA, U. Chgo., 1966; MPH, Johns Hopkins U., 1967, DSc, 1969. Fellow Ind. U. Med. Ctr., Indpls., 1965-66; instr. dept. med. care and hosps. Johns Hopkins U. Sch. Hygiene and Pub. Health, Balt., 1969-70, also asst. to asso. dean for health care programs Sch. Medicine, 1969-70, asst. prof. dept. med. care and hosps., 1970-71; asst. dir. planning and devel. Office of Health Care Programs, Johns Hopkins Med. Instns., Balt., 1970-71; spl. asst. for health affairs to dep. undersec. for policy coordination HEW, Washington, 1971-72; and spl. asst. for policy devel. to asst. sec. to health and sci. affairs, 1971-72; sr. v.p. Robert Wood Johnson Found., Princeton, N.J., to 1987; prof. health policy and polit. analysis Harvard U. Sch. Pub. Health and Kennedy Sch. of Govt., Boston, 1987—; dep. dir. health policy Harvard U.; vis. lectr. Princeton U., 1972-87; sr. policy analyst com. on health svcs. industry Cost of Living Coun., Washington, 1971; bd. dirs. Johns Hopkins Hosp. and Health Sys. Mem. editorial bd. Jour. of Am. Med. Assn., 1992—. Mem. Council Fgn. Relations, Inst. Medicine, Nat. Acad. Scis. Home: 478 Quinobequin Rd Newton MA 02168-2127 Office: Harvard U Sch Pub Health 677 Huntington Ave Boston MA 02115-6028

BLENNER, JANET LYNN, nursing educator; b. Jersey City, N.J., June 24, 1948; m. Peter Suczek, May 31, 1982. BSN, L.I. U., 1973; MA, NYU, 1976, PhD, 1980; postdoctorate, U. Calif., San Francisco, 1984-86. Cert. clin. specialist in adult psychiat. and mental health nursing, ANA. Psychiat. nurse clin. specialist Bronx (N.Y.) VA Hosp., 1975-76; lectr. CUNY, N.Y.C., 1976-77; program and project dir. NIMH grant U. Calif., San Diego, 1978-84, assoc. prof., 1986-93, dir. rsch. and devel., 1986—, prof., 1993—; cons. Calif. Cmty. Alliance for Rsch. in Nursing, 1994—; mem. Expert Panel of Nursing Rsch. Cons., Calif. Nurses' Assn., 1990-95; COntent Expert on Infertility Treatment Cov.'s Office of Planning and Rsch., 1992—; cons. The Nursing Conceptual Models, San Diego VA Hosp., 1983-84; reviewer for various rsch. grants and rsch. profl. jours. Contbr. articles to profl. jours. and chpts. to books. Recipient Sigma Theta Tau award for excellence in rsch., Gamma Gamma, San Diego, 1991. Fellow ANA, Am. Acad. Nursing. Home: 11350 Grassy Trail Dr San Diego CA 92127 Office: San Diego State Univ School of Nursing College Ave San Diego CA 92182-0254

BLEYEN, LUC-JEAN, physician; b. Bree, Belgium, May 30, 1956; s. Jean and Romania (Ardans) B.; m. Mariane Franciska De Vriendt, Jan. 28, 1984; children: Liezelot, Bram. MD, Free U. Brussels, 1982; MSc, Tropical Medicine Inst., Antwerp, 1989. Med. officer Dept. Pub. Health, Shurugwi, Zimbabwe, 1984-85, dist. med. officer, 1985-88; project leader, researcher State U. Ghent, Belgium, 1989—. Fellow Belgian GpiO Breast Cancer Screening; mem. European Group Breast Cancer Screening, Flemish Adv. Com. Cancer Prevention. Office: U Hosp Block A, De Pinte Laan 185, Ghent B9000, Belgium

BLEYER, ANTHONY JOHN, epidemiologist; b. Providence, Jan. 17, 1962; s. John Michael and Jacqueline Marguerite (Massé) B.; m. Kimberly Bleyer; children: Anthony, John Jr., Michael Edwin. BSc in Chemistry, Rensselaer Poly. Inst., Troy, N.Y., 1982; postgrad., Swiss Fed. Inst. Tech., Zurich, 1983; MD, Baylor U., 1987; M Epidemiology, Wake Forest U., 1995. Intern, resident internal medicine Johns Hopkins U., Balt., 1987-90; fellow nephrology U. Pa. Sch. Medicine, Phila., 1990-92; instr. dept. medicine nephrology Bowman Gray Sch. Medicine, Winston-Salem, N.C., 1992-94, asst. prof. internal medicine/nephrology, 1994—. Reviewer Archives Family Medicine. Mem. European Dialysis and Transp. Assn., Internat. Soc. Nephrology, Polycystic Kidney Disease Found., Am. Soc. Nephrology, Am. Heart Assn. Home: 2837 Wesleyan Ln Winston Salem NC 27106 Office: Bowman Gray Sch Medicine Med Ctr Blvd Winston Salem NC 27157

BLICK, KENNETH EDWARD, clincial chemist, educator; b. Bluefield, W.Va., June 1, 1944; s. Isham Trotter II and Elinor (Wells) B.; m. Helen Veida Worthington, Mar. 15, 1969; children: David, Sharon, Brian. BS, Western Ky. U., 1966; PhD, U. Ky., 1970. Diplomate Am. Bd. Clin. Chemistry. Sr. rsch. assoc. dept. chemistry U. Ky., Lexington, 1971-75; chmn., asst. prof. phys. scis. U. Ky., Prestonsburg, 1971-75; asst. prof. allied health Midway Coll., Lexington, 1975-78; asst. prof. med. tech. Ind. State U., Evansville, 1978-82; asst. prof. pathology U. Okla., Okla. City, 1982-84, assoc. prof., 1984—; adj. asst. prof. dermatology U. Okla. Health Sci. Ctr., 1984—, med. technology, 1982—, assoc. prof. grad. program, 1984—; dir. Lab. Computer Systems, Okla. Med. Ctr., 1982—, sci. dir. endocrinology, 1982—. Co-author: Principles in Clinical Chemistry, 1985, 90. Regional dir. Metrication, Prestonburg, Ky., chmn. faculty senate U. Okla. Health Sci. Ctr., 1994-95. Mem. Am. Assn. for Clin. Chemistry (chmn. lab. info. systems div. 1983—, chmn.-elect Tex. sect. 1991), Okla. State Assn. Pathologists, Assn. Clin. Scientists, Medlab Users Group, Sigma Xi, Phi Kappa Phi. Presbyterian. Home: 3001 Broken Bow Rd Edmond OK 73013-7866 Office: U Okla Health Scis Ctr PO Box 26307 Oklahoma City OK 73126-0307

BLIM, RICHARD DON, pediatrician; b. Kansas City, Mo., Nov. 8, 1927; s. Miles G. and Latha Mae (Daniels) B.; m. Myrle Rae Blim, Apr. 12, 1952; children: Richard David, Carol Rae, John Miles. B.A., U. Kans., 1949, M.D., 1953. Diplomate: Am. Bd. Pediatrics. Intern U. Kans., 1953-54, resident in pediatrics, 1954-56; practice medicine specializing in pediatrics; pres. Pediatric Assocs., Kansas City, Mo., 1956-89; dir. med. affairs St. Lukes Hosp., Kansas City, 1989—; Peter T. Bohan lectr. U. Kans., Kansas City, 1978; Max Seham lectr. U. Minn., Mpls., 1982; mem. editorial bd. Mo. Medicine, 1978-92, Pediatric Annals, 1982-92, Pediatric News, 1983-92, Health Care Mgmt. Rev.; mem. VHA Phys. Leadership Coun. Bd. dirs. Marillac Spl. Sch. for Children, 1976-79 . Served to sgt. U.S. Army, 1946-48, PTO. Named Outstanding Med. Alumnus U. Kans. Sch. Medicine, 1978; recipient Clifford G. Grulee award, 1984. Fellow Am. Acad. Pediatrics (pres. 1980-81, exec. bd. 1973-80, chmn. Mo. chpt. 1964-67); mem. AMA, Inst. Medicine of NAS, Jackson County Med. Soc. (pres. 1976), S.W. Pediatric Assn. (pres. Kansas City 1963), Mo. Med. Assn., Coun. Med. Specialties Soc. (rep., exec. bd. 1974-80), Kans. U. Med. Alumni (pres. 1973), Loch Lloyd Club, Alpha Omega Alpha. Republican. Presbyterian. Home: 304 W 172d St Belton MO 64012-9758 Office: St Lukes Hosp 44th Wornall Kansas City MO 64111

BLINKS, JOHN ROGERS, physiology and biophysics educator; b. N.Y.C., Mar. 21, 1931; s. Lawrence Rogers and Anne Catherine (Hof) B.; m. Doris Marie Chambers, Dec. 28, 1953; children: Susan Mayo, Sarah Russell, Elizabeth Rogers. A.B., Stanford U., 1951; M.D., Harvard U., 1955. Med. house officer Peter Bent Brigham Hosp., Boston, 1955-56; research assoc. Nat. Heart Inst., Bethesda, Md., 1956-58; faculty Harvard Med. Sch., Boston, 1958-68; instr., 1958-61, assoc., 1961-64, asst. prof. pharmacology, 1964-68, John and Mary R. Markle Found. scholar, 1961-66; head dept. pharmacology Mayo Found., Rochester, Minn., 1968-88; assoc. prof. pharmacology Mayo Grad. Sch. Medicine, 1968-72; prof. dept. pharmacology Mayo Med. Sch., 1973-90, E.A. and M.F. Guggenheim prof., 1981-87, disting. investigator, 1985-90; prof. physiology/biophysics U. Wash. Sch. Medicine, Seattle, 1990—; hon. research asst. dept. physiology Univ. Coll., London, 1962-63; vis. lectr. dept. physiology U. Auckland, N.Z., 1974; established investigator Am. Heart Assn., 1965-70, mem. research com., 1975-79, chmn. research com., v.p. for research, 1979, sci. publs. com., 1983-87; mem. program projects com. Nat. Heart and Lung Inst., 1968-72, mem. cardiology adv. com., 1975-79; chmn. Gordon Research Conf. on Heart Muscle, 1970; mem. external adv. bd. Pa. Muscle Inst., 1975-77; mem. pharmacology test com. Nat. Bd. Med. Examiners, 1984-86. Field editor cellular pharmacology Jour. Pharmacology Exptl. Therapeutics, 1969-71; mem. editorial bd. Jour. Pharmacology Exptl. Therapeutics, 1965-80, Circulation Research, 1970-74. Served with USPHS, 1956-58. Recipient Rsch. Achievement award Am. Heart Assn., 1989. Fellow AAAS; Mem. Am. Soc. Pharmacology and Exptl. Therapeutics (Otto Krayer award 1987), Am. Physiol. Soc., Biophys. Soc., Cardiac Muscle Soc. (sec.-treas. 1977-79, pres. 1979-81), Soc. Gen. Physiologists. Office: U Wash Friday Harbor Labs 620 University Rd Friday Harbor WA 98250-9299

BLISS, MARY ROSE, geriatrician; b. Woking, England, May 6, 1935; d. Archibald Milne and Bettina Matraves (Collier) Hamilton; m. Anthony Rex Bliss; children: William Hamilton, Anthony James. MBBS, U. Coll., London, 1958. Sr. house officer pathology Radcliffe Infirmary, Oxford, England, 1959-61; rsch. registrar in geriatric medicine Whittington Hosp., London, 1962-64; registrar in geriatric medicine Eastern and Victoria Hosps., Edinburgh, Scotland, 1969-70, Bromley (Kent, England) Hosp., 1974-76; sr. registrar in geriatric medicine Kings Coll. Hosp., London, 1976-78; cons. geriatrician City and Hackney Health Authority, London, 1979-94, Hotherton Hosp., City and Hackney Cmty. Trust, London, 1995—. Contbr. articles to profl. jours. Rsch. grantee N.E. Thames Regional Hosp. Bd., 1990. Mem. Brit. Geriatric Soc., Tissue Viability Soc., Voluntary Euthanasia Soc. Home: 49 Groombridge Rd, London E97DP, England Office: Homerton Hosp, Dept Medicine for Edlerly, London E9 6SR, England

BLISSITT, PATRICIA ANN, nurse; b. Knoxville, Tenn., Sept. 23, 1953; d. Dewitt Talmadge and Imogene (Bailey) B. BSN with high honors, U. Tenn., 1976, MSN, 1985; postgrad., U. Wash., 1996—. RN; cert. in case mgmt.; cert. trauma nurse core course, ACLS, pediat. advanced life support. Staff nurse neurosci. unit City of Memphis Hosp., 1976-78, head nurse neurosci. unit, 1978-79; physician's asst. Dr. John D. Wilson, Columbus, Miss., 1979-81; staff nurse med.-surg.-trauma ICU U. Tenn. Meml. Hosp., Knoxville, 1982-83; staff nurse neurosci. ICU Bapt. Meml. Hosp., Memphis, 1985-86, clin. nurse specialist neurosci., 1986-94, trauma coord., 1991-93, neuro case mgr., 1993-94; staff nurse neurosurg. ICU Harborview Med. Ctr., Seattle, 1994—; nurse cons. neurosci. VA Hosp., Memphis, 1986; mem. adv. com. Tenn. Bd. Nursing Practice. Author: (with others) Critical Care Nursing in Clinics of North America, 1990, Jour. Neurosci. Nursing, 1986, 92, Guidelines for Critical Care Nursing; abstractor: Nursing SCAN in Critical Care, 1995—; contbr. articles to sci. jour., chpt. to book; mem. editl. cons. bd. Focus on Critical Care, 1990-92. Mem. ANA (mem. coun. med.-surg. nurses, mem. coun. clin. nurse specialists), Am. Assn. Neurosci. Nurses (cert. neurosci. nurse, pres. local chpt. 1989-90, treas. local chpt. 1987-89, mem. neurosci. nursing test devel. com. Am. Bd. Neurosci. Nursing 1996—, nat. lectr., mem. resource devel. com., mem. continuing edn./ann. sci. program com., program/seminar chairperson local chpt. 1990-93, mem. nurse practice com., chairperson patient edn. project 1991-92, mem. program/seminar com., program/seminar chairperson mid-South chpt. 1990-93, chairperson nat. resource devel. com. 1992-94, pres. local chpt. 1995—), AACN (life, cert. critical care nurse, lectr., mem. CCRN corp. exam. devel. com. 1989-92, NTI spkr. 1992, editl. cons. bd. 1990-92, pres.-elect Greater Memphis area chpt. 1989-90, pres. 1990-91, immediate past pres., chairperson nat. critical care awareness week 1990-93, chpt. cons. region II 1991-93, chpt of yr. com. chairperson 1992-94, chairperson-elect Puget Sound chpt. program 1995-96, chairperson program com. 1996-97), Am. Assn. Spinal Cord Injury Nurses, Wash. Nurses Assn., Tenn. Nurses Assn. (mem. com. on practice 1992-93), Tenn. Nursing Congress (pres. 1990-94), Sigma Theta Tau. Methodist. Avocation: music. Home: Apt 405 1105 Spring St Seattle WA 98104-3513

BLOCH, ANDREA LYNN, physical therapist; b. Cleve., Nov. 25, 1952; d. Sanford and Nadalane Lee (Benchell) B. BA in Zoology, Miami U., Oxford, Ohio, 1974; MA in Allied Health Scis., Kent State U., 1975; Cert. in Phys. Therapy, Ohio State U., 1977. Lic. phys. therapist, Ohio; bd. cert. orthopedic clin. specialist. Asst. dir. phys. therapy The Mt. Sinai Med. Ctr., Cleve., 1977-86; dir. rehab. therapy svcs. Marymount Hosp., Garfield Heights, Ohio, 1986-88; pres., owner Bloch Phys. Therapy, Inc., University Heights, Ohio, 1988—; speaker Arthritis Found.; speaker in field; mem. Ohio Occupl. Therapy, Phys. Therapy and Athletic Trainers Bd., 1994—. Editor newsletter Cleve. Phys. Therapy Orthopedic Study Group, 1989-91; contbr. articles to profl. jours. Chmn. essay-poster contest University Heights Meml. Day Parade, 1985-91; mem. coun.-at-large City of University Heights. Mem. AAPHERD, NAFE, Am. Phys. Therapy Assn. (reimbursement chmn. N.E. dist. Ohio 1992—), Am. Back Soc., Am. Soc. Profl. and Exec. Women, Ohio Phys. Therapy Assn., Delta Zeta Eastside Alumnae (program chmn. 1985-87, ways and means com. 1987-88, v.p. 1988-90, pres. 1990-92), Delta Zeta Province Alumnae (bd. dirs. Ohio V-N 1991-94, Outstanding Province V Alumna award 1992), Eta Sigma Gamma. Office: 2195 Warrensville Center Rd University Heights OH 44118-3155

BLOCH, ANTOINE, cardiologist; b. Lausanne, Switzerland, Aug. 9, 1938; s. Paul and Herta (Sonnenfeld) B.; MD, U. Lausanne, 1963; m. Josee Sánchez, Aug. 25, 1973. Intern, U. Lausanne Hosp., 1964-66; med. resident St. Antonius Hosp., Utrecht, Netherlands, 1966-67, univ. hosps., Lausanne and Geneva, 1967-70; chief resident Univ. Cardiac Center of Geneva, 1970-73, physician, 1975-80; cardiac fellow Mass. Gen. Hosp., Boston, 1973-75; privat-docent Geneva Med. Sch., 1975-80, charge de cours, 1980—; chief cardiac unit Hopital de la Tour, Geneva, 1981—. Swiss Nat. Fund grantee, 1977-79. Fellow Am. Coll. Cardiology, European Soc. Cardiology; mem. Am. Heart Assn., Am. Soc. Echocardiography, Swiss Med. Assn., Swiss Soc. Cardiology, French Soc. Cardiology, Swiss Soc. Intensive Care, Swiss Soc. Ultrasound, Internat. Soc. Cardiovascular Ultrasound. Contbr. more than 200 articles to profl. publs. Home: 33 Crêt-de-Choully, CH-1242 Choully Switzerland Office: Hosp de la Tour, Cardiac Unit, Geneva CH-1217, Switzerland

BLOCH, KONRAD EMIL, biochemist; b. Neisse, Germany, Jan. 12, 1912; came to U.S., 1936, naturalized, 1944; s. Frederick D. and Hedwig (Streimer) B.; m. Lore Teutsch, Feb. 15, 1941; children—Peter, Susan. Chem. Engr., Technische Hochschule, Munich, 1934; Ph.D., Columbia U., 1938. Asst. prof. biochemistry U. Chgo., 1946-50, prof., 1950-54; Higgins prof. chemistry Harvard U., Cambridge, Mass., 1954-82, prof. emeritus, 1982—. Recipient Nobel prize in physiology and medicine, 1964, Ernest Guenther award in chemistry of essential oils and related products, 1965, Nat. Medal of Sci., 1988. Fellow AAAS; mem. Am. Chemistry Soc. (Fritsche award 1964), Am. Soc. Biol. Chemists (pres. 1967), Nat. Acad. Scis., Am. Philos. Soc., Royal Sci. (fgn.). Office: Harvard U Dept Chemistry 12 Oxford St Cambridge MA 02138-2902*

BLOCH, KURT JULIUS, physician; b. Germany, Oct. 17, 1929; s. Max and Mathilde B.; m. Margot Bendit, June 25, 1953; children: Kenneth D., Donald B. BS, CCNY, 1951; MD, NYU, 1955. Diplomate Am. Bd. Internal Medicine, Am. Bd. Allergy and Immunology, subspecialties Rheumatology, Diagnostic Lab. Immunology. Intern, asst. resident Bellevue Hosp., N.Y.C., 1955-57; resident in medicine Mass. Gen. Hosp., Boston, 1960-61, physician, 1974—, chief clin. immunology and allergy units, 1976—; instr. medicine Harvard Med. Sch., Boston, 1965-68, asst. prof., 1968-70, assoc. prof., 1970-74, prof., 1974—; sr. investigator Arthritis Found., 1964-69. Contbr. articles to profl. jours. With USPHS, 1957-60. Mem. Am. Soc. Clin. Investigation, Am. Assn. Physicians. Office: Mass Gen Hosp Boston MA 02114

BLOCH, RAPHAEL S., ophthalmologist, educator; b. N.Y.C., Feb. 16, 1942; s. Abraham and Belle Bloch; m. Dorothy Richard, June 16, 1964; children: David, Joel. BA, Yeshiva U., 1963; MD, Albert Einstein Coll., 1967. Diplomate Am. Bd. Ophthalmology. Intern, resident Montefiore Med. Ctr., N.Y.C., 1967-71; asst. clin. prof. Albert Einstein Coll. Medicine, N.Y.C., 1974—; attending ophthalmologist No. Westchester Hosp. Ctr., Mount Kisco, N.Y., 1973—, chief, 1986-91; attending ophthalmologist Montefiore Med. Ctr., N.Y.C., 1974—. Contbr. chpts. in books. Maj. U.S. Army, 1971-73. Fellow ACS, Am. Acad. Ophthalmology; mem. N.Y. State Med. Soc., Westchester County Med. Soc. Office: 344 Main St Mount Kisco NY 10549

BLOCK, ALAN JAY, physician, educator; b. Balt., Apr. 11, 1938; s. Michael and Sylvia (Rosenberg) B.; m. Linda Ray Crone, May 25, 1961; children: Margo Dee, Allison Lee. BA, Johns Hopkins U., 1958, MD, 1962. Intern, then resident Johns Hopkins Hosp., Balt., 1962-67; attending physician Johns Hopkins Hosp., 1967-70; instr. in medicine Johns Hopkins Med. Sch., Balt., 1967-69, asst. prof. medicine Johns Hopkins Med. Sch., 1969-70; asst. prof. medicine U. Fla., Gainesville, 1970-73, asst. prof. anesthesiology, 1971-73, chief pulmonary div., 1973-95; chief pulmonary sect. VA Med. Ctr., Gainesville, 1995—; assoc. prof. medicine U. Fla., 1973-75, prof. medicine, 1975—. Mem. edit. bd. Am. Rev. Respiratory Disease 1981-87; contbr. over 180 articles to profl. jours. Mem. senate U. Fla., 1976-78. Fellow Am. Coll. Chest Physicians (pres. 1987-88, editorial bd. jour., editor-in-chief Chest, 1993—); mem. Fla. Thoracic Soc. (pres. 1977-79, bd. dirs. 1973-76), Am. Thoracic Soc. (chmn. com. 1975-76, chmn. scientific assembly), Am. Fedn. Clin. Research, Assn. Pulmonary Program Dirs. (sec., treas. 1987—). Democrat. Jewish. Home: 1520 NW 68th Ter Gainesville FL 32605-4133 Office: U Fla Coll of Medicine PO Box 100225 Gainesville FL 32610-0225

BLOCK, BARRY HERBERT, podiatrist, lawyer, educator, magazine editor; b. Scranton, Pa., Jan. 7, 1949; s. Jerome and Cherie (Gold) B.; m. Hermine Sudiker, Apr. 3, 1976; children: Steven, Julie, Michael. BA, Hunter Coll., 1971; DPM, N.Y. Coll. Podiatric Medicine, 1976; JD cum laude, N.Y. Law Sch., 1991. Diplomate Am. Bd. Podiatric Pub. Health (pres. 1993—). Gen. editor Jour. Am. Podiatric Med. Assn., Bethesda, Md., 1979-81; editor-in-chief Podiatry Mgmt., Upper Darby, Pa., 1982—; asst. prof. N.Y. Coll. Podiatric Medicine, 1989—; chief podiatry staff Cardinal Cooke Med. Ctr., N.Y.C., 1990—. Author: Foot Talk, 1984, Complications in Foot Surgery, 1984, Podiatric Marketing and Practice Management, 1988. Named Disting. Practitioner Nat. Acad. Eye Practitioners. Fellow Am. Assn. Hosp. Podiatrists; mem. Am. Podiatric Med. Assn., ABA, Am. Soc. Authors and Journalists, Am. Coll. Foot Surgeons (assoc.). Jewish. Office: PO Box 750129 Forest Hills NJ 11375

BLOCK, BARTLEY C., biologist; b. Chgo., Apr. 12, 1933; s. David and Anne (Been) B.; m. Janet Jacobs, May 26, 1963; children: Kenneth, Deborah, Steven. BS, Northwestern U., 1954, MS, 1955 student, Pa. State U., 1955-58. Entomologist USDA, Beltsville, Md., 1959; asst. prof. Lycoming Coll., Williamsport, Pa., 1959-63, Drexel Inst. Tech., Phila., 1964-65, So. Conn. State Coll., New Haven, 1965-67, U. Bridgeport, Conn., 1967-74; assoc. prof. biology U. Bridgeport, 1974-92; chief med. writer Pharmedica Comm., New Haven, Conn., 1992-96; sr. sci. editor PPS Europe Ltd., Greenwich, Conn., 1996—; cons. in field. Author: Man, Microbes and Matter, 1974; inventor in field. Chmn. Milford Conservation Commn., 1982-86; mem. Inland Wetland Agy., 1988-90. Grantee U.S. Atomic Energy Commn, 1960; U.S. Dept. Agriculture, 1960-62, NSF, 1962-63, Mellon Found., 1980; vis. fellow Yale U., 1988-89. Mem. AAAS, Am. Med. Writers Assn., Am. Inst. Biol. Sci., Am. Soc. Zool., Entomol. Soc. Am., Ecol. Soc. Am., Animal Behavior Soc. Democrat. Jewish. Home: 25 Lajoie Ln Milford CT 06460-2411 Office: Pharmedica Communications New Haven CT 06510

BLOCK, JAMES A., hospital administrator, pediatrician; b. Dayton, Ohio, 1940; married; 4 children. Grad., Haverford Coll., 1962; MD, NYU, 1966. Chief ambulatory svcs. Surgeon General's Comprhensive Health Planning office; assoc. dir. Community Health Svc. Health Svcs. and Mental Health Adminstrn. USPHS; intern pediatrics Strong Meml. Hosp., Rochester, N.Y., 1966-67; resident pediatrics and ambulatory medicine Strong Meml. Hosp. U. Rochester, 1969-71; pediatrician, head ambulatory svcs. Genesee Hosp., 1971-79; pres. Rochester Area Hosps. Corp., N.Y., 1979-85; asst. to pres., then pres., CEO U. Hosps. Cleve., 1985-86, 86-92; pres., CEO Johns Hopkins Hosp., Johns Hopkins Health System, Balt., 1992—; adj. prof. Health Policy Case Western Reserve U., 1991; faculty Hosp. Fin. Mgmt. Assn., Am. Assn. Med. Colls.; chmn. RHN bd. ops. com.; mem. gov's commn. ambulatory Care Cost Containment, N.Y. State, 1977—; HCFA Physician Discussion Group; adj. prof. pediatrics Johns Hopkins U. Sch. Medicine; adj. prof. health policy Johns Hopkins Sch. Hygiene and Pub. Health; cons. in field; speaker in field; bd. dirs. MMI Cos., Inc., Greater Balt. Com.; del. Coun. Teaching Hosps. Assn. Am. Med. Colls. Editorial adv. bd. Jour. Ambulatory Care Mgmt.; contbr. articles to profl. jours. Campaign cabinet United Way; mem. Lombardi Task Force Hosp.; bd dirs. Robert Wood Johnson Found. Community Hosp. Med. staff Primary Group Practice program (past), sr. program cons. 1974-82, Unicef, Mercantile Bankshares Inc., Soc. Med. Adminstrs.; trustee Johns Hopkins U., Johns Hopkins Health System/Johns Hopkins Hosp. Health fellow Nat. Urban Coalition, 1971-72. Mem. APHA, AMA, Am. Acad. Med. Dirs., United Way (corp. mem.), Ambulatory Pediatric Assn., Med. Adminstrs. Conf. Home: 928 Fell St Baltimore MD 21231-3504 Office: Johns Hopkins Hosp 600 N Wolfe St Baltimore MD 21205-2110*

BLOCK, JOHN HARVEY, medicinal chemistry educator; b. Yakima, Wash., May 11, 1938; s. Harvey Temple and Gladys Liddel (Spring) B.; m. Alice Lynn McCombe, Dec. 19, 1964; children: Alan, Bonnie, Charlotte. B Pharmacy, Wash. State U., 1961, MS in Pharm. Chemistry, 1963; PhD in Pharm. Chemistry, U. Wis., 1966. Registered pharmacist, Oreg. Asst. prof. Oreg. State U., Corvallis, 1966-72, assoc. prof., 1972-78, prof. medicinal chemistry, 1978—; vis. scholar Stanford U., 1972-73; cons. Bend (Oreg.) Rsch., 1975-78, Oreg. Bd. Pharmacy, Portland, 1977, 84, mem., 1990—, v.p., 1992-93, pres., 1993-94; sec.- treas. dist. 7 Nat. Assn. Bds. Pharmacy, 1995—. Author, co-editor: Inorganic and Pharmaceutical Chemistry, 1974, Solubility and Partition Coefficient, 1986, Probing Bioactive Mechanisms, 1989. Mem. adv. bd. Corvallis Youth Symphony, 1985-87; bd. dirs. Grace Ctr. for Adult Day Svcs., 1988-91, v.p., 1989-90, pres., 1990-91. Grantee in field. Mem. AAUP, Am. Chem. Soc., Sigma Xi, Phi Kappa Phi, Rho Chi (counselor 1968-70, v.p. 1975-77, pres. 1978-80). Lodge: Kiwanis. Home: 1310 NW 14th St Corvallis OR 97330-4658 Office: Coll Pharmacy Oreg State U Corvallis OR 97331

BLOCK, LAWRENCE HOWARD, pharmacist, educator; b. Balt., Nov. 24, 1941; s. Harry C. and Dina (Cooper) B.; m. Sharon Kelson, Aug. 4, 1974; children—Hal Zachary, Dana Elayne. B.S. in Pharmacy, U. Md., 1962, M.S., 1966, Ph.D., 1969. Asst. prof. pharmaceutics U. Pitts., 1968-70; asst. prof. pharm. chemistry and pharmaceutics Duquesne U., Pitts., 1970-71, assoc. prof., 1971-75, prof. pharmaceutics, 1975—, chmn. dept. pharm. chemistry and pharmaceutics, 1985—; cons. Thrift Drug Co. div. J.C. Penney Co., Upsher-Smith Labs. Inc., FMC Corp. Author numerous chpts. for sci. books, articles to profl. and sci. jours. Fellow Am. Found. Pharm. Edn.; mem. Acad. Pharm. Research Scis., Am. Pharm. Assn., Am. Assn. Colls. of Pharmacy (chmn. tchrs. of pharmaceutics sect 1989-90), Am. Assn. Adv. Sci., N.Y. Acad. Scis., Soc. Cosmetic Chemists, Am. Assn. Pharm. Scientists, Sigma Xi, Phi Kappa Phi, Rho Chi. Office: Duquesne U Sch Pharmacy 437 Mellon Hall of Sci Pittsburgh PA 15282

BLOCK, MARY ANN, osteopath; b. Oklahoma City, July 9, 1945; d. David Herman and Cecile Regina (Friedman) Ritzwoller; m. Stanley Byron Block, Mar. 30, 1969 (div. Dec. 1987); children: Michelle Lynn, Randall Douglas. BS, Tex. Christian U., 1981; DO, Tex. Coll. Osteo. Medicine, 1989. Computer programmer Gulf Oil Corp., Houston, 1967-71; rotating intern Osteo. Med. Ctr. Tex., Ft. Worth, 1989-90; pvt. practice The Block Ctr., Ft. Worth, 1990-91; asst. prof. Tex. Coll. Osteo. Medicine, Ft. Worth, 1991-93; staff physician Environ. Health Ctr., Dallas, 1994, The Block Ctr., Bedford, Tex., 1994—; clin. clerkship preceptor Tex. Coll. Osteo. Medicine, Ft. Worth, 1990—; mem. speakers bur. Osteo. Med. Ctr. Tex., Ft. Worth, 1990-95; Tex. statewide clin. preceptor, 1996—; mem. Tarrant County mental health, mental retardation instnl. review bd.; peer reviewer fed. guidlines for otitis media with effusion. Author: (book) No More Ritalin-Treating ADHD Without Drugs. Bd. dirs. Am. Cancer Soc., Ft. Worth, 1972—, Trinity Valley Coll. Prep. Sch., Ft. Worth, 1980-86; bd. dirs., v.p. Camp Fire Girls, Ft. Worth, 1978-80. Am. Acad. Osteopathy scholar, 1986, 87, 89. Mem. Am. Osteo. Assn., Am. Acad. Osteopathy (bd. govs.), Am. Acad. Environ. Medicine. Office: The Block Ctr 2509 Brown Trl Bedford TX 76021

BLOCK, MELVIN AUGUST, surgeon, educator; b. Evansville, Ind., July 2, 1921; s. August William and Alma (Klutey) B.; m. Marcia Jean Jacobs, May 28, 1955; children: Deborah Ann, Christopher Reed. B.S., Ind. U., 1942, M.D., 1944; Ph.D., U. Minn., 1953. Intern Ind. U. Med. Center, 1945; resident Mayo Clinic, Rochester, Minn., 1948-54; chmn. dept. surgery Henry Ford Hosp., Detroit, 1975-79, Scripps Clinic Med. Group, La Jolla, Calif., 1980-87; clin. prof. surgery U. Mich. Med. Sch., 1970-80, U. Calif., San Diego Med. Sch., 1980-93. Contbr. numerous articles to profl. jours. Served to capt. M.C. AUS, 1945-47. Fellow Royal Coll. Surgeons Can.; mem. ACS (past gov.), Am., Central, Western (past pres.) surg. assns., Am. Thyroid Assn., Am. Gastroenterology Assn., Soc. Surg. Alimentary Tract, Soc. Head and Neck Surgeons, Soc. Internationale de Chirurgie, AMA, Calif., San Diego County med. socs., Acad. Surg. Detroit (past pres.), Detroit Surg. Soc. (past pres.), Internat. Assn. Endocrine Surgeons, Am. Assn. Endocrine Surgeons, Sigma Xi, Alpha Omega Alpha. Home: 4575 Excalibur Way San Diego CA 92122-1513 Office: Scripps Clinic Med Group 10666 N Torrey Pines Rd La Jolla CA 92037-1027

BLOCK, ROBERT I., psychologist, researcher, educator; b. Newark, N.J., Jan. 30, 1951; s. Milton and Harriet (Safier) B. BA with honors, Shimer Coll., 1969; MS, Harvard U., 1972, Rutgers U., 1977; PhD, Rutgers U., 1981. Teaching asst. psychology dept. Rutgers U., New Brunswick, N.J., 1975-76; psychologist Lafayette Clinic, Detroit, 1982-84; rsch. assoc. psychiatry dept. Wayne State U., Detroit, 1982, instr., 1982-84; assoc. rsch. scientist dept. anesthesia U. Iowa, Iowa City, 1984-88, asst. prof. dept. anesthesia, 1988-94, assoc. prof. dept. anesthesia, 1994—; cons. State of Mich., Lafayette Clinic, Detroit, Hoffmann La-Roche, Inc.; reviewer Psychopharmacology and Anesthesiology; mem. faculty senate Sch. of Medicine, Wayne State U., Detroit, 1982-84. Contbr. articles to Anesthesiology, Brit. Jour. Anaesthesia, Psychopharmacology, Pharmacol. Biochem. Behavior. Fellow Rutgers U.; grantee Nat. Inst. on Drug Abuse, 1987-91, 93—. Mem. AAAS, Collegium Internat. Neuro-Psychopharmacologicum, Am. Psychol. Assn. Home: 2029 Waterford Dr Coralville IA 52241-2734 Office: U Iowa Dept Anesthesia Westlawn Bldg Iowa City IA 52242

BLOCK, ROBERT MICHAEL, endodontist, educator, researcher; b. Ann Arbor, Mich., Oct. 15, 1947; s. Walter David and Thelma Violet (Levine) B.; m. Anne Powell Marshall, Sept. 4, 1977. BA, DePauw U., 1969; DDS, U. Mich.-Ann Arbor, 1974; cert. in endodontics, Va. Commonwealth U., 1977; MS in Pathology, Va. Commonwealth U., 1978. Diplomate Am. Bd. Endodontics. Clin. instr. Va. Commonwealth U., 1975-77, instr. pathology, 1977-78; rsch. assoc. endodontics U. Conn.-Farmington, 1975—; vis. sr. scientist Nat. Med. Rsch. Inst., Bethesda, Md., 1976-78; rsch. assoc. McGuire Vets. Hosp., Richmond, Va., 1975-78; vis. rsch. scientist U. Conn.-Farmington, 1978—; lectr. endodontics Flint Community Schs.; bd. dirs. Republic Bancorp, S.E., Republic Bank-S.E. div. Republic Bancorp. Contbr. articles profl. jours., chpt. in book. Exec. mem. campaign com. candidate for U. Mich. Bd. Regents, 1980; candidate for Mich. State Bd. Edn., 1982. HEW and NIH summer research fellow, 1970-71; research grantee McGuire Vets. Hosp., 1976-78. Fellow Am. Coll. of Endodontics; mem. Internat. Assn. Dental Rsch. (Edward P. Hatton award 1977), Am. Assn. Dental Rsch., Am. Assn. Endodontists (Meml. Research award 1977), Lapeer Dental Study Club (treas. 1978-82), ADA (Preventive Dentistry award 1973), Loudoun County Dental Soc. (v.p.). Office: Loudoun Tech Ctr 21525 Ridgetop Cir Sterling VA 20166-6510

BLOCK, STANLEY HOYT, pediatrician, allergist; b. N.Y.C., Oct. 28, 1943; s. Julius and Zilla Augustus (Friedman) B. BA, U. Chgo., 1963; MD, Yale U., 1966. Diplomate Am. Bd. Pediatrics, Am. Bd. Allergy and Immunology. Intern Children's Hosp. of Phila., Lynn and Lowell, Mass., 1966-67; resident Babies Hosp., Columbia Presbyn. Med. Ctr., N.Y.C., 1967-69; pediatrician, allergist pvt. practice Lynn and Lowell, 1971-77; med. dir. Providence (R.I.) Ambulatory Health Care Found., 1977—; cons. Blue Cross/Blue Shield of R.I., Providence, 1985—. Major U.S. Army, 1969-71. Recipient Tchg. award in pediatrics R.I. Hosp. House Officers Assn., 1982, Dr. Charles L. Hill award for Pub. Svc., R.I. Med. Soc., 1995. Fellow Am. Acad. Pediatrics, Am. Acad. Allergy, Asthma and Immunology, R.I. Soc. of Allergy (past pres., sec.); mem. R.I. Med. Soc. Office: Providence Ambulatory Health Care Found 375 Allens Ave Providence RI 02905-5010

BLOCKER-BURNETTE, MAXINE PETERSON, social worker; b. Long Island, NY, Jan. 8, 1948; d. Yancy Billy Peterson and Priscilla Mae (Garrett) Smith; m. William Jerome Blocker, Feb. 8, 1964 (div. July 1975); m. Kenneth Tyrone Burnette, Nov. 8, 1980; children: Roslyn Michelle, William Jerome Jr. BA in Social Welfare, U. D.C., 1977; BS in Criminal Justice, Trinity Coll., 1977. Social worker DC Superior Ct., Washington, 1975-78; specialist mental health Alcohol and Drug Abuse Services, Washington, 1978-86, acting div. chief, 1986-90; equal employment counselor Addiction Prevention and Recovery Adminstrn., Washington, 1990—, chief personnel, 1990—. Chmn. community awareness, Operation PUSH, Washington 1974-76. Mem. Nat. Assn. Social Workers, Nat. Assn. Black Social Workers, Nat. Pol. Cong. Black Women. Democrat. Baptist. Home: 3114 Westover Dr SE Washington DC 20020-3720 Office: Addiction Prevention and Recovery Adminstrn 1300 1st St NE Washington DC 20002-1516

BLOEMENDAL, LEE CHARLES, surgeon; b. St. Paul, Jan. 16, 1943; s. Ernest Hendrick and Jeanette Edith (Larsen) B.; m. Marilyn Mays, Mar. 22, 1969; children: Lee Scott, Katherine. BA, U. Minn., 1965; MD, Baylor Coll. of Medicine, 1969. chief of surgery Harris Meth., Ft. Worth, 1992. Rotating intern Denver Gen. Hosp., 1969-70; surgery resident U. Colo., Denver, 1970-74; vascular surgery fellow Cedars-Sinai Med. Ctr., L.A., 1976-77; gen. surgeon, pvt. practice Ft. Worth, 1977—; chief of surgery Harris Meth., Ft. Worth, 1992—. Chmn. adminstrv. bd. First United Meth. Ch., Ft. Worth, 1994. Maj. USAF, 1974-76. Fellow ACS; mem. AMA, Tex. Med. Assn., Tex. Surg. Soc., Peripheral Vascular Surgery Soc. (pres. 1983-84), Ft. Worth Surg. Soc. (pres. 1996), Tarrant County Med. Assn. Office: 1325 Pennsylvania Ave Ste 610 Fort Worth TX 76104-2133

BLOEMKER, E. FREDRICK, physician, ophthalmologist; b. Indpls., Feb. 26, 1939; s. Albert W. and Kathleen (Cain) B.; m. Frances Ellen Hume, June 23, 1962; children: Anne, Kathleen, Jane. BS, St. Louis U., 1961; MD, Ind. U., 1965. Intern Meth. Hosp., Indpls., 1965-66; resident in ophthalmology Ind. U., Indpls., 1969-71; ophthalmologist Affiliated Eye Surgeons, Phoenix, 1971—; chmn. dept. ophthalmology St. Joseph's Hosp., Phoenix, 1975-85. Capt. USAF, 1966-68. Fellow ACS, Am. Acad. Ophthalmology. Republican. Home: 3500 E Lincoln Dr Phoenix AZ 85013 Office: Affiliated Eye Surgeons 222 W Thomas Rd Phoenix AZ 85013

BLOES, WALTER FRANKLIN, oral and maxillofacial surgeon; b. Wilkes-Barre, Pa., June 16, 1960; s. Walter Shaffer and Judith Anne (Wright) B.; m. Paige Windle, Jan. 22, 1964; 1 child, Corey Shaffer. BS, Tufts U., 1982, DMD, 1987. Diplomate Am. Bd. Oral and Maxillofacial Surgery. Intern, then resident Albert Einstein Coll. Medicine, N.Y.C., 1987-91; with Stamford (Conn.) Hosp., Montefiore Med. Ctr., N.Y.C., Albert Einstein Coll. Hosp., N.Y.C.; rsch. assoc. Harvard Med. Sch. and Brigham & Women's Hosp., Boston, 1982-83. Contbr. articles to profl. jours. Fellow Am. Assn. Oral and Maxillofacial Surgery, Am. Coll. Oral and Maxillofacial Surgery; mem. ADA, Greenwich Dental Soc., Young GOP Greenwich. Republican. Congregationalist. Home: 24 Talbot Ln Greenwich CT 06878 Office: 1171 E Putnam Ave Greenwich CT 06878

BLOM, GASTON EUGENE, psychiatrist; b. Bklyn., Mar. 29, 1920; s. Gaston Emanuel and Gunda (Engebretsen) B.; Dorothy Ruth Engstrand; children: Susan, Barbara, David, Douglas. BA summa cum laude, Colgate U., 1941; MD cum laude, Harvard U., 1944. Diplomate Am. Bd. Psychiatry and Child Psychiatry. Intern Columbia Presbyn. Hosp., N.Y.C., 1944-45; resident in gen. psychiatry USPHS Hosp., Ft. Worth, 1946-47, U. Mich. Hosp., Ann Arbor, 1947-48; resident in child psychiatry Mass. Gen. Hosp., Boston, 1948-49, Judge Baker Guidance Ctr., Boston, 1949-50; mem. staff, asst. dir., then dir. child psychiatry Mass. Gen. Hosp., Boston, 1950-58; adult analyst Boston Psychoanalytic Inst., 1956, child analyst, 1958; asst. instr. in psychiatry Harvard U. Med. Sch., Boston, 1951-58; faculty Smith Coll. Sch. Social Work, Northhampton, Mass., 1955-57; assoc. prof. to prof. dept. psychiatry, child psychiatry U. Colo. Med. Sch., Denver, 1958-75; tng. & supervisory analyst Denver Psychoanalytic Inst., U. Colo. Med. Sch., 1964-75; prof. edn. div. spl. edn. U. Colo., Boulder, 1966-75; prof. psychiatry & counseling ednl. psychology-spl. edn. Mich. State U., E. Lansing, 1975-84; staff psychiatrist South Shore Mental Health Ctr., Quincy, 1984-91; med. staff Charles River Hosp., Wellesley, Mass., 1984-89; prof. child devel. & child psychiatry Boston U. Med. Sch., 1985—; med. staff St. Elizabeth's Hosp., Brighton, Mass., 1991—; med. dir. Boston Childrens Svcs. Assn., 1991-95; analytic supr. Mass. Inst. Psychoanalysis, 1994—; cons. Mass. Families for Kids, Brookline, 1995—; lectr. Denver U. Sch. Social Work, 1962-66; adj. prof. psychology Mich. State U., East Lansing, 1980-84; vis. prof. edn. Boston U., 1967; cons. mental health study sect., divsn. rsch. grants NIMH, Bethesda, Md., 1960-64; acting chmn. dept. psychiatry U. Colo. Med. Sch., Denver, 1969-70, faculty coun., 1970-72; vis. staff psychiatrist Gentofte Hosp., U. Copenhagen, 1972-73; sr. rsch. assoc. U. Ctr. Internat. Rehab., Mich. State U., 1979-84; cons. Mass. Family for Kids, 1995—. Mem. editorial bd. Jour. Spl. Edn., 1960-75; jr. editor: Child Nurturance, 1984; sr. editor: Stress in Childhood, 1985; contbr. articles to profl. jours. Mem. Colo. Gov.'s Adv. Com. on Mental Health, Denver, 1966-71; mental health coun. West Interstate Com. on Higher Edn., Boulder, 1971-75; bd. dirs. Mich. Ptnrs. of Ams., Lansing, 1979-81; mem. spl. edn. adv. com. Mich. Dept. Edn., Lansing, 1981-84; mem. advisor, bd. dirs. Free Romania Found., 1990-93; mem. standing com. 1st and 2d Unitarian Ch. Boston, 1991-93. Lt. (j.g.) USNR, 1945-56; asst. surgeon UPSHS, 1946-47. Recipient commendation for disaster work Texas City fire, U.S. Surgeon Gen., USPHS, 1946. Fellow Am. Orthopsychiat. Assn., Am. Psychiat. Assn. (life), Am. Acad. Child and Adolescent Psychiatry (life, editorial bd. 1971-77), Am. Acad. Psychoanalysis; mem. Soc. for Rsch. in Child Devel., Coun. for Exceptional Children, Am. Assn. Psychiat. Svcs. for Children, Mass. Med. Soc., Phi Beta Kappa, Alpha Omega Alpha, Phi Delta Kappa. Democrat. Unitarian-Universalist. Home and Office: 11 Waverly St # 5 Brookline MA 02146-6818

BLOM, JOHANNES, oncologist/hematologist; b. Amsterdam, The Netherlands, Sept. 11, 1928; s. Johannes and Jannetje Blom; m. Bohen Ferrari, June 22, 1960; children: Hans, James, Robert. MD, U. Utrecht, The Netherlands, 1957. Intern Cen. Dispensary and Emergency Hosp., Washington, 1957-58; resident Washington Hosp. Ctr., 1958-61; internist Group Health Assn., Washington, 1961; fellow Walter Reed Army Med. Ctr., Washington, 1961-64, chief oncology sect., 1964-79; chief med. oncology Divine Providence Hosp., Williamsport, Pa., 1979—; prin. investigator Cancer and Acute Leukemia, Group B., Washington, 1962-79; clin. assoc. prof. Georgetown U. Med. Ctr., Washington, 1977-80. Author: Guide to Therapeutic Oncology, 1979. Recipient Jonathan Wainwright award Moses Taylor Hosp., Scranton, Pa., 1988. Fellow ACP; mem. Am. Soc. Clin. Oncology, Am. Soc. Hematology. Office: Cancer Treatment Assocs PC 1100 Grampian Blvd Williamsport PA 17701-1909

BLOMBERG, GORAN ERNST DANIEL, biologist; b. Tidaholm, Sweden, July 27, 1941; came to U.S., 1952; s. Ernst Harald Natan and Karin Josefina (Åsberg) B. BS, U. Minn., St. Paul, 1965; MS, Colo. State U., 1969; PhD, Mich. State U., 1990. Forester's aide No. Forest Inventory Div., Stockholm, 1962; lab. tech. asst. U. Minn., Mpls., 1965; biol. technician U.S. Fish and Wildlife Svc., Denver, 1969-71; crocodile biologist Peace Corps, Gaborone, Botswana, 1974-76; grad. teaching asst. Mich. State U., East Lansing, 1977-79; instr. biology Lansing (Mich.) Community Coll., 1979-87, tutor in biology, 1987-94, lab. technician, 1995—. Asst. mng. editor The Jack-Pine Warbler, 1987-90; contbr. The Atlas of Breeding Birds of Michigan, 1991, also articles to sci. jours., 10 book revs. Head children's nature program Capitol Area Audubon Soc., Lansing, 1981-93. Recipient faculty publ. recognition cert. Lansing Community Coll., 1989, 90. Mem. World Wildlife Fund, Wildlife Soc. (charter Mich. chpt.), Nature Conservancy, Nat. Audubon Soc. (Mich. chpt. bd. dirs. 1986-92). Pentecostal.

BLOMBERY, PETER ALEXANDER, medical practitioner; b. Sydney, NSW, Australia, Mar. 28, 1947; s. Alexander Morris and Marie Wilson (Jackson) B.; m. Angela Marie Childerhouse, Apr. 4, 1975; children: Emily, Piers, Oliver, Camilla. BSc in Medicine, U. Sydney, 1967, MBBS, 1970; PhD, Monash U., Melbourne, Victoria, Australia, 1980. Lic. med. practitioner. Intern, registrar Royal Prince Alfred Hosp., Sydney, 1971-74; rsch. officer Baker Med. Rsch. Inst., Melbourne, 1975-77; dir. vascular lab. Alfred Hosp., Melbourne, 1983—; sr. lectr. medicine Monash U., Melbourne, 1985—; dir. intensive care Ave Hosp., Melbourne, 1988—; vis. vascular physician Alfred Hosp., Melbourne, 1980—; steering com. Internat. Study into Prevention of Atherosclerotic Complications with Ketanserin, 1984-87. Contbr. articles to profl. jours. Vis. rsch. fellow NIH, Bethesda, Md., 1977-80. Fellow Royal Australian Coll. Physicians; mem. Australian Med. Assn., Australian Soc. Med. Rsch., Australian Soc. Clin. and Exptl. Pharmacology, Australian soc. Ultrasound Medicine. Office: Vascular Lab Alfred Hosp, Commercial Rd, Prahran VIC 3181, Australia

BLOME, ROBERT ARTHUR, retired surgeon; b. Iowa City, June 13, 1931; s. Glenn C. and Laura (Bolle) B.; m. Louann M. Nochtels, Mar. 25, 1958 (div. 1982); children: Elizabeth Ann, Jennifer Lynn, Lori Lynn; m. Dixie V. Kyoush, Apr. 26, 1984. BA, Grinnel Coll., 1952; MD, State U. Iowa, 1955. Diplomate Am. Bd. Surgeons. Intern Emanuel Hosp., Portland, Oreg., 1955-56; resident U. Iowa Hosp., Iowa City, 1956-60, staff physician, 1960-61; practice medicine specializiing in general and thoracic surgery Nampa, Idaho, 1963-94; ret., 1994; pres. med. staff, chief surgery Mercy Hosp., Nampa. Contbr. articles to profl. jours. Chmn. Nampa chpt. ARC; bd. dirs. United Way, Nampa. Capt. USAF 1961-63. Mem. Idaho State Med. Soc., SW Dist. Med. Soc. (sec., pres.), Nampa Aquatic Club (pres.), Kiwanis (bd. dirs. Nampa club). Republican. Methodist. Office: Med Ctr Physicians 215 E Hawaii Ave Nampa ID 83686-6011

BLOMQUIST, CARL GUNNAR, cardiologist; b. Båraryd, Sweden, Dec. 31, 1931; came to U.S., 1965, naturalized; s. Arvid Elias and Karin Johanna (Hullman) B.; m. Joan Barre Bakula, 1961; children: Mary Jennifer, Peter Carl. BM, U. Lund, 1954, MD, 1960; PhD, Karolinska Inst., Stockholm, 1967. Research fellow cardiovascular epidemiology U. Minn. Med. Center, Mpls., 1960-61; resident Karolinska Inst., 1962-65; mem. faculty U. Tex. Med. Ctr., Southwestern Med. Sch., Dallas, 1966—, prof. medicine and physiology, 1976—; dir. NASA Specialized Ctr. Rsch. and Tng. in Integrated Physiology, 1993—; mem. research study com. Am. Heart Assn., 1970-73; mem. applied physiology study sect. NIH, 1974-78; mem. space biology and medicine com. NAS, 1986-90. Author articles in field; mem. editorial bds. profl. jours. Grantee NIH; Grantee NASA; established investigator Am. Heart Assn. Fellow Am. Coll. Cardiology, Am. Coll. Sports Medicine; mem. Internat. Acad. Astronautics, Internat. Soc. Cardiology, Am. Heart Assn. (fellow coun. epidemiology), So. Soc. Clin. Rsch., Aerospace Med. Assn. (Luis H. Bauer Founders award 1995), Am. Physiol. Soc. Home: 4229 Willow Grove Rd Dallas TX 75220-1935 Office: Southwestern Med Sch Div Cardiology Dallas TX 75235

BLONDER, KAREN TOBY, medical/surgical and psychiatric nursing educator; b. N.Y.C., Nov. 29, 1942; d. Josef and Selma Einhorn; m. Jerry L. Toepfer, July 14, 1984; children: Lisa, David. AAS, Bklyn. Coll., 1963; BSN, NYU, 1965; MA, Columbia U., 1973, MEd, 1983, EdD, 1988. Prof. Dutchess Community Coll., Poughkeepsie, N.Y., 1991—. Bd. dirs. Dutchess-Ulster County Planned Parenthood; bd. dirs., v.p. SPCA. Mem. Advanced Nurse Practice Assn., Sigma Theta Tau, Kappa Delta Pi. Home: 9 Fair Way Poughkeepsie NY 12603-5014

BLONSKY, STEPHEN LAWRENCE, nephrologist; b. Elizabeth, N.J., May 9, 1955; s. Milford and Miriam (Landerman) B.; m. Susan Huza, Apr. 8, 1984; children: Daniel, Rebecca, Sarah, Joshua, Adam. BS, Union Coll., 1977; MD, U. of the East, Manila, 1981. Diplomate Am. Bd. Internal Medicine, Am. Bd. Nephrology. Resident Interfaith Med. Ctr., Bklyn., 1981-84, chief resident, 1984; fellow R.I. Hosp., Providence, 1984-86; physician Royce C. Lin MD. Svc. Corp., Greenbay, Wis., 1986-89, Nephrology Assocs., Watertown, N.Y., 1989—. Contbr. articles to profl. jours. Bd. dirs. Congregation Degel Israel, Watertown, 1991—. Fellow Am. Coll. Physicians; mem. AMA, Internat. Soc. Nephrology, Am. Soc. Nephrology. Office: Nephrology Assocs Watertown 218 Stone St Watertown NY 13601-3211

BLOODWORTH, EVERETT EARL, medical technologist; b. Anna, Ill., Apr. 11, 1950; s. Everett E. and Laura Jane (Boyer) B.; m. Vicki Rayban, Aug. 4, 1970 (div. Aug. 1986); children: Cherilyn, Laura; m. Kate DiNapoli, June 24, 1989; 1 child, Michael. Med. lab. tech., Mid State Med. Acad., 1969; BS, Murray State U., 1980. Technologist Western Bapt. Hosp., Paducah, Ky., 1969-70, 72-73, Houston-McDevitt Clinic, Murray, Ky., 1973-78; lab. mgr. Marshall County Hosp., Benton, Ky., 1978—. Editor The Bluegrass Technologist. With U.S. Army, 1970-72. Mem. Am. Med. Technologists (Disting. Achievement award 1988, Exceptional Merit award 1991), Ky. State Soc. Med. Technologists (treas. 1984-88, pres. 1988-92, 94—, Mem. of Yr. 1995). Baptist. Home: 930 Pine St Benton KY 42025 Office: Marshall County Hosp. 503 George McClain Dr Benton KY 42025

BLOODWORTH, J(AMES) M(ORGAN) BARTOW, JR., retired physician, educator; b. Atlanta, Feb. 21, 1925; s. J.M. Bartow and Elizabeth (Dimmock) B.; m. G. Jean Stone, Nov. 26, 1947; children: Lowell Ann, Joyce Lynn, Elizabeth Carol; m. Joan G. Wiltgen, July 8, 1972; children: Allison Joan, Ellen Lucy. Student, Emory U., 1942-43, 44-48, MD, 1948; student, Stanford U., 1944. Intern, then asst. resident pathology Columbia-Presbyn. Med. Ctr., N.Y.C., 1948-50; instr. pathology Columbia U., 1949-50; asst. resident medicine U. Iowa Hosp., 1950-51; mem. faculty Ohio State U. Coll. Medicine, 1951-62, prof. pathology, 1960-62; chief divsn. pathologic anatomy Ohio State U. Hosp., 1954-61; pathologist Columbus State Hosp., 1954-57; prof. pathology and lab. medicine U. Wis., Madison, 1962—; chief lab. svc. Madison VA Hosp., 1962-89, pathologist, 1989-95, ret., 1995. Editor: Endocrine Pathology, 1968, 3rd edit., 1996; contbr. numerous articles to publs. in field. Served with AUS, 1941-45. Recipient Fight for Sight citation Am. Assn. Rsch. in Ophthalmology, 1964. Mem. AMA, Wis. Med. Assn., Am. Assn. Clin. Endocrinologists (charter), Dane County Med. Soc., Wis. Soc. Pathologists (pres. 1977-79), Am. Soc. Investigative Pathologists, Histochem. Soc., Am. Diabetes Assn. (Lilly award 1963, Profl. Svc. award Wis. affiliate 1982), So. Wis. Diabetes Assn., Am. Heart Assn., Wis. Heart Assn., Soc. Exptl. Biology and Medicine, Internat. Acad. Pathology, Am. Soc. Clin. Pathology, Am. Assn. Neuropathologists, Nat. Soc. Med. Rsch., Am. Soc. Cell Biology, Gyro Internat. Club (pres. Columbus chpt. 1962, pres. Madison chpt. 1980, 95). Home: 4514 Crescent Rd Madison WI 53711-4721

BLOOM, BARRY MALCOLM, pharmaceutical consultant; b. Roxbury, Mass., Aug. 12, 1928; s. Morris and Ann (Levine) B.; m. Joan Martha Ensign, June 27, 1956; children: Catherine, Brian, Joanna. SB, MIT, 1948, PhD, 1951, postgrad., 1967; D of Humane Letters (hon.), Conn. Coll., 1992. Rsch. chemist Pfizer, Inc., Groton, Conn., 1952-63, dir. medicinal chems. and rsch., 1963-71, pres. cen. rsch. div., 1971-90, v.p. rsch., 1971-90, sr. v.p. R&D, 1990-92, exec. v.p. R & D, 1992-93; cons. pvt. practice, 1993—; bd. dirs. So. New Eng. Telecomm. Corp., Cubist Pharms., Inc., Neurogen Corp., Vertex Pharms., Inc., Incyte Pharms., Inc., Catalytica Fine Chems., Congl. Commn. on Fed. Drug Approval Process, PMA Commn. on Drugs for Rare Diseases; cons. U.S. Congress Office Tech. Assessment, 1976-77; mem. Conn. Tech. Adv. Bd., 1985-90. Mem. editorial bd. Ann. Reports in Medicinal Chemistry, 1968-70; patentee in field. Bd. mgrs. Lawrence and Meml. Hosp. NRC postdoctoral fellow U. Wis., 1952; Poly. Inst. Tech. fellow N.Y.C., 1980. Mem. Am. Chem. Soc. (chmn. div. medicinal chemistry 1967), Conn. Acad. Sci. and Engring., Pharm. Mfrs. Assn. (chmn. R&D sect. 1976). Home and Office: Mackintosh Rd Lyme CT 06371

BLOOM, BENJAMIN HARRIS, ophthalmologist; b. Boston, Mar. 25, 1946; s. Isadore Irving and Gertrude Ruth (Levine) B.; m. Esther Hannah Stern, Aug. 23, 1981; children: Chaim D.S., Nathan M. BSEE, Northeastern U., Boston, 1968; MD, Tufts U., 1974. Diplomate Am. Bd. Ophthalmology. Technologist NASA, Cambridge, Mass., 1968-70; intern Newton-Wellesley (Mass.) Hosp., 1974-75; resident in ophthalmology New Eng. Med. Ctr., Boston, 1975-79; retina fellow Cornell-N.Y. Hosp., N.Y.C., 1979-80, Manhattan Eye and Ear Hosp., N.Y.C., 1979-80; asst. prof. Hahnemann U., Phila., 1980—; staff ophthalmologist Germantown Hosp., Phila., 1983—; asst. surgeon Wills Eye Hosp., Phila., 1983—; attending surgeon Albert Einstein Hosp., Phila., 1984—. Contbr. articles to profl. jours. Fellow ACS, Am. Acad. Ophthalmology, Coll. of Physicians of Phila.; mem. AMA, Pa. Med. Soc., Phila. County Med. Soc., The Vitreous Soc., Pa. Acad. Ophthalmology, Ophthalmic Club of Phila., Beth Hillel Mens Club. Democrat. Jewish. Office: Germantown Hosp 2 Penn Blvd Ste 117 Philadelphia PA 19144-1480

BLOOM, CHERYL TUCHMAN, optometrist; b. Benton Harbor, Mich., Oct. 19, 1944; d. Nathanial S. and Florence (Guise) Tuchman; m. Murray A. Bloom, May 15, 1983; 1 child, Sandra Fay. BS, Mich. State U., 1966; MA, U. Tex., Galveston, 1974; OD, U. Houston, 1983. Intern Grant Hosp., 1983-84; optometrist Humana-Group Health, Annandale, Va., 1984—. Contbr. articles to profl. jours. Pres. PTO, Gesher Jewish Day Sch., Fairfax, Va., 1992-93. Tex. Assn. Optometry scholar, 1980, 81. Mem. Va. Optometric Assn., No. Va. Optometric Assn. (bd. dirs. 1986-88), B'nai B'rith. Jewish. Home: 8506 Bromley Ct Annandale VA 22003

BLOOM, DAVID ALAN, pediatric urology educator; b. Buffalo, July 26, 1945; m. Martha Lichty, June 8, 1980. BS, Rensselaer Poly. Inst., 1967; MD, SUNY, Buffalo, 1971. Diplomate Am. Bd. Surgery (exam. com. 1992-96), Am. Bd. Urology, Nat. Bd. Med. Examiners. Intern in surgery UCLA, 1971-72, resident, 1972-75, chief resident, 1975-76, resident in urology, 1976-77, sr. resident, 1978-79, chief resident, lectr., 1979-80; vis. fellow, registrar Inst. Urology and St. Peter's Hosp., U. London, 1977-78; asst. prof. surgery U. Mich., Ann Arbor, 1984-86, assoc. prof., 1986-93, prof., 1993—, chief pediatric urology, 1984-86, 93—; cons. in urology surgery br. Nat. Cancer Inst., NIH, Bethesda, Md., 1982, Naval Regional Med. Ctr., Portsmouth, Va., 1983, Walter Reed Army Med. Ctr., Washington, 1985; cons. in surgery (urology) VA Hosp., Ann Arbor, 1985; cons. in pediatric urology Henry Ford Hosp., Detroit, 1986; locum in urology Gt. Osmond Street Hosp. for Sick Children and Inst. Urology, Shaftesbury Hosp., London, 1986; asst. prof. surgery, then assoc. prof. Uniformed Svcs. U. Health Scis. Sch. Medicine, Bethesda, 1980-84, clin. assoc. prof., 1985, assoc. prof. pediat., 1984; numerous presentations in field; reviewer Jour. Endourology, 1992, 93, Jour. Pediatric Surgery, 1992, 93, Jour. Urolog, 1988-94, Surgery, 1992, So. Jour. Medicine, 1995, Clin. Pediat., 1995, Am. Jour. Managed Care; urology cons. Stedman's Med. Dictionary. Author: (with McGuire, Catalona and Lipshultz) Advances in Urology, 1995; mem. editl. bd. Urology, 1992—; contbr. numerous articles, abstracts and book revs. to med. jours. Lt. col. M.C., U.S. Army, 1980-84; mem. USAR, 1984-90. Fellow ACS; mem. AMA, Am. Acad. Pediat. (exec. com. sect. on urology 1989-93, historian 1993-98), Am. Assn. Clin. Urologists, Am. Assn. Gynecologic Laparoscopists, Am. Urol. Assn., Assn. Mil. Surgeons U.S, Halsted Soc. (photographer), Longmire Surg. Soc., N.Am. Soc. Pediatric and Adolescent Gynecology, Reed M. Nesbit Soc., Internat. Soc. for Pediatric Urology, Soc. Genitourinary Reconstructive Surgeons, Soc. Univ. Urologists, Uniformed Svcs. U. Surg. Assocs., Nat. Urologic Forum (treas. 1995), European Assn. Urology, European Soc. Pediatric Urology. Office: U Mich 1500 E Medical Center Dr Ann Arbor MI 48109-0330

BLOOM, DAVID MYRON, hospital administrator, neurosurgeon; b. Binghamton, N.Y., June 8, 1928; s. Myer Sol and Helene Ruth (Sheldon) B.; m. Naomi Muscatine, June 22, 1951; children—Peter Lawrence, Marcia Anne. B.A., Cornell U., 1950, M.D., 1953; M.B.A., SUNY-Binghamton, 1976. Diplomate Am. Bd. Neurol. Surgery. Intern, N.Y. Hosp.-Cornell U. Med. Ctr., N.Y.C., 1953-54; asst. resident gen. surgery SUNY Upstate Med. Ctr., Syracuse, 1954; clk. (neurology) Nat. Hosp. Nervous and Mental Diseases, London, 1957; jr. fellow in electroencephalography Montreal Neurol. Inst. (Que., Can.), 1957, asst. resident in neurosurgery, 1958-59; intermediate and sr. resident in neurosurgery U. Colo. Med. Ctr., Denver, 1959-60; practice medicine specializing in neurosurgery, Binghamton, N.Y., 1961-75; dir. med. affairs and continuing edn. Our Lady of Lourdes Meml. Hosp., Binghamton, 1975-78, v.p. med. affairs, 1978-89; v.p. med. affairs Sarasota (Fla.) Meml. Hosp., 1990-95. Capt. U.S. Army, 1955-57. Fellow Am. Coll. Physician Execs. (bd. dirs. 1979-82); mem. Am. Assn. Neurol. Surgeons, Am. Bd. Med. Mgmt. (bd. dirs. 1989-92), Congress Neurol. Surgeons. Democrat. Jewish. Office: 5361 Dominica Circle Sarasota FL 34233-3818

BLOOM, EUGENE CHARLES, gastroenterologist, educator; b. Tupelo, Miss., June 3, 1933; s. Robert Harold and Anna Esther (Kronick) B.; m. Joan Ellen Margoles, July 22, 1956; children: Marjorie Wynne Bloom Albert, Stacey Bloom Schlafstein, Robin Bloom Wolf. Student, Emory U., 1951-55, U. Fla., 1955-56; MD, U. Miami, 1960. Diplomate Am. Bd. Internal Medicine. Intern Cook County Hosp., Chgo., 1960-61; resident in internal medicine Jackson Meml. Hosp., Chgo., 1961-63; resident in gastroenterology Coral Gables VA Hosp., 1963-64; rsch. fellow dept. medicine, divsn. gastroenterology U. Miami (Fla.) Sch. Medicine, 1964-65, rsch. scientist, 1964-66, instr. medicine, 1964-74, clin. asst. prof. medicine, 1974—; gen. practice medicine Miami, 1966—; mem. staff Bapt. Hosp. Miami, sec.-treas. med. staff, 1979-80, chief of staff, 1980-82. Contbr. articles to profl. jours. Bd. dirs. Jewish Vocat. Svc.; active Greater Miami Jewish Fedn., chmn. physicians divsn., 1979-80. Capt. M.C., U.S. Army, 1963-67, Vietnam. Mem. AMA, AAAS, Fla. Med. Assn., Dade County Med. Assn. (alt. del. to Fla. Med. Assn. 1974), Am. Acad. Sci., Am. Coll. Gastroenterology, Am. Soc. Gastroent. Endoscopy, U. Miami Med. Alumni Assn. (chmn. Dade County chpt. 1972-75, nat. pres. 1975-77, v.p. pub. rels. 1987-89, v.p. 1987-90), Gen. Alumni U. Miami (bd. dirs. 1973-77, v.p. 1988-95, bd. overseers 1988—, sec. 1990, v.p. 1991), Fla. Gastroent. Soc., Greater Miami Jewish Fedn., Woodfield Country Club, Alpha Omega Alpha, Omicron Delta Kappa. Democrat. Office: 5599 N Dixie Hwy Oakland Park FL 33334

BLOOM, JACK, retired periodontist; b. Hartford, Conn., July 15, 1919; s. Louis and Esther (Nissenbaum) B.; m. Eleanor Ruth Berig, June 25, 1943; 1 child, Jane Ellen Bloom. BS, U. Vt., 1941; DDS, U. Md., Balt., 1944. Cert. periodontology, oral pathology. Asst. prof. oral pathology, chmn. sect. Boston U. Sch. Medicine, 1957-59, assoc. prof. oral pathology, chmn. sect., 1960-62; asst. vis. dental surgeon, asst. oral pathology Beth Israel Hosp., Boston, 1950-56, assoc. vis. dental surgeon, asst. oral pathology, 1957-62; head oral pathology slomatology clinic Mass. Meml. Hosp., Boston, 1961-62; asst. clin. prof. Tufts U. Sch. Dental Medicine, Boston, 1976-95; ret., 1995; past cons. VA Hops., Bedford, Mass., Manchester, N.H. Author: contbr. articles to profl. jours. Chmn. Fluoridation Com., Newton, Mass.; pres. UN Assn. of Greater Boston; bd. dirs. Pub. Health Mus. in Mass., Internat. Catacomb Soc.; Dem. ward committeeman, Newton. Lt. USN, 1944-45, 52-53. Fellow Am. Acad. Oral Pathology; mem. Am. Acad. Periodontology, N.Y. Acad. Scis., Internat. Assn. Dental Rsch. Democrat.

BLOOM, JANE MAGINNIS, emergency physician; b. Ithaca, N.Y., June 22, 1924; d. Ernest Victor and Miriam Rebecca (Mansfield) M.; m. William Lee Bloom, Mar. 31, 1944; children: David Lee, Jan Christopher, Carolyn Wells, Eric Paul, Joseph William, Robert Carl, Mary Catherine, Thomas Martin, Patrick Martin (dec.), Arthur Emerson. BS, U. Mich., 1968, MD, 1974. Diplomate Am. Bd. Internal Medicine, Am. Bd. Emergency Medicine. Rotating intern Wayne County Gen. Hosp., Eloise, Mich., 1974-75; resident in internal medicine St. Mary's Hosp., Rochester, 1975-77; emergency physician Emergency Physicians Med. Group, Ann Arbor. Fellow Am. Coll. Emergency Physicians (life); mem. AMA, Mich. State Med. Soc., Am. Coll. Medicine, Am. Med. Womens Assn., Am. Assn. Women Emergency Physicians, Washtenaw County Med. Soc. Home and Office: 537 Elm St Ann Arbor MI 48104

BLOOM, KERRY STEVEN, biology educator; b. Washington D.C., Dec. 28, 1953; s. Robert and Rita (Prince) B.; m. Elaine Ying Yeh, Aug. 5, 1983; 1 child, Rachael. BS, Tulane U., 1975; PhD, Purdue, 1980; postdoctoral, U. Calif., Santa Barbara, 1980-82. Asst. prof. U. N.C., Chapel Hill, 1982-86; assoc. prof. U. N.C., 1986-92, prof., 1992—. Recipient Hettlemen prize, Univ. N.C., 1990. Mem. Am. Soc. Cell Biology, Genetics Soc. of Am., Marine Biol. Lab. Democrat. Home: 115 Braswell Rd Chapel Hill NC 27516-9147 Office: U NC 623 Fordham Hall Chapel Hill NC 27599

BLOOM, PAUL, pediatrician; b. N.Y.C., Jan. 29, 1944; s. Marvin Lawrence and Rhoda (Kurz) B.; m. Rae Ellen Schmall, Aug. 30, 1967; children: Rebecca, Aaron. AB, Amherst Coll., 1966; MD, Albert Einstein Coll. Medicine, Bronx, 1970. Diplomate Am. Bd. Pediatrics. Pediatric resident Albert Einstein Coll. Medicine/Lincoln Hosp., Bronx, 1970-73, instr. pediatrics, 1973-75, asst. prof. pediatrics, 1975; pvt. practice, Haverstraw, N.Y., 1975—; attending physician Nyack Hosp., 1975—. Mem. Gay and Lesbian Med. Assn. Democrat. Jewish. Office: 48 New Main St Haverstraw NY 10927-1528

BLOOM, PETER BROWER, psychiatrist, educator; b. Phila., June 22, 1936; s. Herman Merle and Mary Bailey (Brower) B.; m. Marcia Arabelle Bloser, June 21, 1958; children: Kathleen Elizabeth, Diana Kimberly, David James. BA, Cornell U., 1958; MD, U. Pa., 1962. Diplomate Am. Bd. Psychiatry, Am. Bd. Med. Hypnosis, Nat. Bd. Med. Examiners. Rotating intern Hosp. of U. Pa., Phila., 1962-63, resident in internal medicine, 1965-67, fellow in gastroenterology, 1967-68, resident in psychiatry, 1968-69; resident in psychiatry Inst. of Pa. Hosp., Phila., 1969-71, assoc. attending, attending psychiatrist, 1971-82, sr. attending, 1982—, dir. continuing edn. program in psychiatry, 1971-88; instr., assoc. in psychiatry U. Pa. Sch. Medicine, Phila., 1971-76, clin. asst. prof., 1976-86, clin. assoc. prof., 1986-92, clin. prof., 1992—; vis. prof. dept. psychiatry U. Melbourne (Australia), 1987. Contbr. articles to med. jours. Lt. Med. Corps. USNR, 1963-65. Fellow Am. Psychiat. Assn., Am. Soc. Clin. Hypnosis, Coll. Physicians Phila., Soc. Clin. and Exptl. Hypnosis (Shirley R. Schneck award 1985, Bernard D. Rabinsky award 1990); mem. Internat. Soc. Hypnosis (sec.-treas. 1979-91, pres.-elect 1992-94, pres. 1994—), Rolling Green Golf Club. Republican. Presbyterian. Home: 416 Riverview Ave Swarthmore PA 19081 Office: Inst of Pa Hosp 111 N 49th St Philadelphia PA 19139-2718

BLOOM, RICHARD FREDRIC, psychologist, organizational consultant; b. Bklyn., Oct. 23, 1931; s. Morris and Mary (Schur) B.; m. Myra R. Thal, Dec. 27, 1956 (div.); children: Laura A.; David T.; m. Susan Davies, May 30, 1981 (div.); stepchildren: David Y. Redford II, Hugh T. Redford; m. Armelte Pitre, May 4, 1996; stepchildren: Jennifer Lyn WOmble, Paul Lamont Womble. BS, CUNY, Bklyn., 1953; AE, N.J. Inst. Tech., 1959, MS, 1962; PhD, NYU, 1969. Lic. psychologist, Conn. Physicist U.S. Nat. Bur. Standards, Washington, 1953; electronics engr. ITT Fed. Labs., Nutley, N.J., 1955-65; behavioral scientist Dunlap & Assocs., Inc., Stamford, Conn., 1965-89, dir., 1984-87; pvt. practice psychologist and indsl./orgnl. cons., Westport, Conn., 1970—; co-dir. Psychotherapy & Counseling Assocs., Westport, 1981—; co-founder ABA Assocs., Westport, Conn., 1996—; staff psychologist Summit Behavioral Health, LLC, 1996—. Author tech. reports and research papers. Bd. dirs. Am. Cancer Soc., Westport, Conn., 1981—. With U.S. Army, 1953-55; Korea. Fellow Soc. Clin. and Exptl. Hypnosis; mem. IEEE, Am. Psychol. Assn., Conn. Psychol. Assn. Jewish. Office: 292 Post Rd E Westport CT 06880-3614

BLOOM, SAMUEL MICHAEL, otolaryngologist; b. Portland, Maine, Dec. 27, 1908; s. Max Laib and Bessie Devorah (Baum) B.; m. Zita S. Greene, June 17, 1945; children: Lloyd Jay, Betty Ann. BS cum laude, NYU, 1932,

MD, 1935. Diplomate Am. Bd. Otolaryngology. Intern Mt. Sinai Hosp., N.Y.C., 1935-36; resident medicine and surgery Chesapeake & Ohio Hosp., Clifton Forge, Va., 1936-37; resident otolaryngology Mt. Sinai Hosp., N.Y.C., 1937-39, clin. asst., 1946-50, adj. attending, 1950-60; assoc. attending, 1960-72; cons. Mt. Sinai Hosp., N.Y.C., 1973-77; ret., 1977; staff ENT VA Med. Ctr., N.Y.C., 1980-90; assoc. clin. prof. Mt. Sinai Sch. Medicine, N.Y.C., 1965-77, assoc. clin. prof. emeritus, 1977—. Nat. comdr. Am. Defenders of Bataan and Corregidor, McKees Rocks, Pa., 1958-59; Dept. N.Y. surgeon Jewish War Vets. U.S.A., 1984-87. Maj. M.C., U.S. Army, 1941-46, PTO. Decorated Bronze Star. Fellow ACS, Am. Acad. Otolaryngology, Head and Neck Surgery, Am. Acad. Facial Plastic and Reconstructive Surgery (treas. 1969-74, guest of honor 1985), Am. Laryngologic, Rhinologic and Otologic Soc., N.Y. Acad. Medicine; mem. AMA, Med. Soc. State N.Y., New York County Med. Soc., Alpha Omega Alpha. Jewish. Home: 150 E 77th St Apt 4E New York NY 10021-1927 Office: 150 E 77th St Apt 4E New York NY 10021-1927

BLOOM, SHERMAN, pathologist, educator; b. Bklyn., Jan. 26, 1934; s. Philip and Sadie (Kaplan) B.; m. Miriam Fishman, Feb. 11, 1960; children: Naomi, Stephanie. BA, NYU, 1955, MD, 1960. Diplomate Am. Bd. Anat. Pathology. Intern in medicine Kings County Hosp., Bklyn., 1960-61; fellow in exptl. pathology, resident in anatomic and clin. pathology NYU Med. Ctr. and Bellevue Hosp., N.Y.C., 1961-65; instr. pathology NYU Sch. Medicine, 1965-66; asst. prof. U. Utah Coll. Medicine, Salt Lake City, 1966-70, assoc. prof., 1970-72; assoc. prof. U. South Fla. Coll. Medicine, Tampa, 1973-76, prof. pathology, 1976-77; prof. pathology George Washington U. Coll. Medicine, Washington, 1977-88; prof., chmn. dept. pathology U. Miss. Med. Ctr., Jackson, 1988—; cons. Sci. Rev., NIH; mem. cardiovascular study sect. NSF, FDA; bd. dirs. Scientists Ctr. Animal Welfare, pres. elect, 1987, pres., 1988. Mem. editorial bd. Jour. Am. Coll. Nutrition, 1982, Am. Jour. Cardiovascular Pathology, 1985; assoc. editor Cardiovascular Pathology, 1990; contbr. numerous articles to profl. publs. Del. Utah State Dem. Party, 1968. NIH fellow, 1962; Dilthey Found. fellow, 1982. Fellow Am. Coll. Nutrition; mem. Internat. Acad. Pathologists, Am. Physiol. Soc., Am. Assn. Pathologists, Internat. Soc. Heart Research, Soc. Cardiovascular Pathology (pres. 1986-87). Jewish. Home: 4433 Wedgewood St Jackson MS 39211-6219

BLOOM, STEPHEN EARL, cytogeneticist, educator; b. Bklyn., Oct. 18, 1941; s. Max and Miriam (Chansky) B. children: Lisa, Laura. BS, L.I.U., 1963; MS, Pa. State U., 1965, PhD, 1968. Asst. prof. Cornell U., Ithaca, N.Y., 1968-74, assoc. prof., 1974-82, prof. cytogenetics, 1982—; vis. prof. M. D. Anderson Hosp./Tumor Inst., Houston, 1974-75; staff scientist Worcester Found. Exptl. Biology, Shrewsbury, Mass., 1981; assoc. dir. Inst. Comparative Environ. toxicology, 1982—. Mem. P.T.A., Ithaca H.S., 1984-88. Inst. Environ. Health Sci. Health Sci. grantee, 1981—, Cornell Biotech. Inst. grantee. Mem. AAAS, Am. Assn. for Cancer Rsch., Mutagen Soc. Office: Cornell U C4111 Vet Med Ctr 105 Rice Hall Ithaca NY 14853-5601

BLOOM, WILLIAM H., neurosurgeon; b. Granville, N.Y., Jan. 18, 1926; s. Samuel William and Lillian Anna (Pinsker) B.; m. Barbara Renee Miller, Nov. 28, 1960; children: Deborah Jane, Jeffrey Martin, Sharon Ann, Jonathan Richard. Pvt. practice neurosurgeon Bay Shore, N.Y., 1961—; hon. clin. asst. faculty St. George Hosp., U. London, 1959-60; pres. Suffolk County med. Soc., Hauppauge, N.Y., 1976-77, Suffolk Acad. Medicine, Hauppauge, 1977-78, Nassau-Suffolk 2nd Dist. Br., M.S.S.N.Y., 1986-88; founder, pres. L.I. Neuroscis. Soc., Nassau-Suffolk, 1985-88. Collaborator: Atlas of Positive Contrast Myclography, 1961. Lt. USN, 1950-52. Mem. Am. Assn. Neurol. Surgeons, Congress Neurol. Surgeons, Sigma Xi. Republican. Jewish. Office: 270 E Main St Bay Shore NY 11706

BLOOMBERG, JOYCE ELAINE, nursing educator; b. Johnstown, Pa., July 2, 1939; d. James Elvin and Thelma Elvina (Causer) Colbert; m. Leon Bloomberg, Mar. 10, 1973; children: Lauri Anne, Douglas James. Diploma in nursing, Lankenau Hosp., Phila., 1960; B of Profl. Studies, Elizabethtown (Pa.) Coll., 1973; M in Gen. Edn., Temple U., 1980. Staff nurse obstetrics Lancaster (Pa.) Gen. Hosp.; operating room staff nurse St. Joseph's Hosp., Lancaster; charge nurse Lancashire Nursing Home, Neffsville, Pa.; instr., supr. practical nursing Lancaster County Area Vocat. Tech. Sch., Willow Street, Pa. Mem. Nat. League for Nursing, Lankenau Hosp. Sch. Nursing Alumni Assn.

BLOOME, MICHAEL A., ophthalmologist, vitreoretinal surgeon; b. Chgo., Oct. 3, 1943; s. Melvin B. and Bernice (Sidell) B.; m. Susan Lynn Delott, Au. 21, 1965; children: Denise, David, Jerrad. Student, U. Ill., 1960-64; MD, U. Ill., Chgo., 1967; MS in Ophthalmology, U. Iowa, 1972. Diplomate Am. Bd. Ophthalmology; lic. physician, Iowa, Ill., Calif., Ala., Tex. Intern U. Iowa Hosps., Iowa City, 1967-68, resident, 1968-72; clin. instr. ophthalmology U. Tex. Med. Ctr., Houston, 1972-76, asst. prof., 1976-85, assoc. prof., 1985-90, prof., 1990—; examiner Am. Bd. Ophthalmology, 1978-94. Author several books and numerous articles. Founder, v.p., pres. I. Weiner Secondary Sch., Houston, 1976-83; bd. dirs. Beth Teshurun Synagogue, 1990-93; mem. exec. bd. Houston Eye Assn. Found., 1991-95. Maj. USAF, 1972-74. Recipient Recognition award AMA, 1973, 78. Fellow ACS, Am. Acad. Ophthalmology (Cert. of Appreciation 1986, 89, Honor award 1986); mem. Vitreous Soc. (exec. com., v.p., pres.), Retinal Soc., So. Retinal Study Group (pres. 1989-90). Jewish. Home: 2121 Kiby Dr Houston TX 77019 Office: Houston Eye Assocs 2855 Gramercy Houston TX 77025

BLOOM-FESHBACH, JONATHAN STEPHEN, clinical psychologist; b. New Haven, Jan. 7, 1950; s. Seymour and Norma (Deitch) Feshbach; m. Sally Jan Bloom, Aug. 29, 1976; children: Alison, Kimberly. BA, U. Oreg., 1974; MS, Yale U., MPhil, PhD, 1980. Lic. clin. psychologist, D.C. Staff writer Yale Bush Ctr. Child Devel. and Social Policy, New Haven, 1979-80; sci. fellow U.S. Senate Com. Labor and Human Resources, Washington, 1980-81; coord. rsch. and evaluation Counseling and Psychiat. Svc./Georgetown U., Washington, 1981-84; cons., pvt. practice psychotherapy Washington, 1982—; assoc. clin. prof. dept. psychiatry, child health and devel. George Washington Sch. Medicine, Washington, 1981—; mem. faculty Wash. Sch. Psychiatry, 1992—. Co-editor: Psychology of Separation and Loss, 1987; contbr. articles to profl. jours., chpts. to books. Mem. Am. Psychol. Assn., Soc. Rsch. in Child Devel., Am. Orthopsychiat. Assn., Internat. Coun. Psychologists, D.C. Psychol. Assn., Washington Psychologists for Study of Psychoanalysis. Home: 2919 Garfield St NW Washington DC 20008-3504 Office: 1301 20th St NW Apt 608 Washington DC 20036-6016

BLOOM-FESHBACH, SALLY, psychologist; b. Balt., Feb. 11, 1953; d. Jordan and Carol (Wallerstein) Bloom; m. Jonathan Bloom-Feshbach, Aug. 29, 1976; children: Alison, Kimberly. AB, Brown U., 1975; MS, Yale U., 1977, MPhil, 1979, PhD, 1980. Lic. psychologist, Washington. Research cons. Nat. Acad. Scis.-NRC Com. on Child Devel., Washington, 1980-83; staff psychologist Am. U. Ctr. for Psychol. and Learning Services, Washington, 1980-84, dir. of postgrad. tng., 1982-84; psychotherapist in ind. practice, Washington, 1982—; asst. clin. prof. dept. of psychiatry and behavioral sci. George Washington U., Washington, 1985-94, assoc. clin. prof., 1994—. Contbr. articles to profl. jours., chpts. to profl. books. Coeditor Psychology of Separation and Loss, 1987. Yale U. fellow, 1975-77, NIMH fellow, 1977-80; travel grantee NATO, Am. Psychol. Assn., 1981, 82; research grantee, Sigma Xi, 1978. Mem. APA (bd. dirs. sect. on women/psychoanalysis), Phi Beta Kappa, Sigma Xi. Clubs: Brown U., Yale U. Home: 2919 Garfield St NW Washington DC 20008-3504 Office: 1301 20th St NW Apt 608 Washington DC 20036-6016

BLOOMGARDEN, GARY MICHAEL, neurosurgeon; b. N.Y.C., Apr. 12, 1954; s. Leonard J. and Annette B.; m. Jennifer Anne Frenzilli, Mar. 16, 1957; children: Jessica Ellen, Kara Elizabeth. BA summa cum laude, SUNY, Buffalo, 1976; MD, NYU, 1980. Diplomate Am. Bd. Neurosurgery. Surg. intern Parkland Meml. Hosp., Dallas, 1980-81; resident in neurosurgery Yale-New Haven Hosp., 1981-86, attending neurosurgeon, 1986—; attending neurosurgeon Hosp. of St. Raphael, New Haven, 1986—, Milford (Conn.) Hosp., 1986—, St. Mary's Hosp., Waterbury, Conn., 1995—; clin. asst. prof. in surgery Yale U. Sch. of Medicine, 1987—. Fellow ACS, Internat. Coll. Surgeons; mem. AMA, Am. Assn. Neurologic Surgeons, Congress of Neurologic Surgeons, Conn. State Med. Soc., Conn. State Neurol. Soc. Republican. Jewish. Office: Neurosurgical Assocs 60 Temple St New Haven CT 06510-2716

BLOSER, DIETER, radiologist; b. Yugoslavia, Aug. 17, 1944; came to U.S., 1947, naturalized, 1954; s. Peter and Eva Helen Bloser; A.B., Princeton U., 1966; M.D., Case Western Res. U., 1970; m. Deborah Pierce Forbes, Nov. 25, 1967; children—Peter Forbes, Timothy Philip. Intern dept. medicine U. Hosps. of Cleve., 1970-71, resident in radiology, 1971-72, 74-76, chief resident, 1975-76; practice medicine specializing in radiology, Parma, Ohio, 1976—; mem. staff Parma Community Gen. Hosp., 1976—, chief nuclear medicine, 1977—, chief radiology, 1984—; pres. Parma Radiologic Assocs, Inc., 1990—. Gen. Hosp. Bd. dirs. Cleve. chpt. Juvenile Diabetes Found., 1986-90; active Am. Diabetes Assn., 1985—; trustee Case Western Reserve U. Sch. Med Alumni Assn., 1985-89. Served to lt. comdr. USN, 1972-74. Diplomate Am. Bd. Radiology. Mem. Am. Coll. Radiology, Radiol. Soc. N. Am., Ohio Radiol. Soc., Cleve. Radiol. Soc. (pres.-elect 1986-87, pres. 1987-88), Am. Inst. Ultrasound in Medicine, Cleve. Acad. Medicine, AMA, Ohio Med. Assn., Princeton Alumni Assn. (schs. com.), Phi Beta Kappa, Alpha Omega Alpha. Lutheran. Office: Parma Community Hosps 7007 Powers Blvd Cleveland OH 44129-5437

BLOUKE, PETER, public health officer; b. Apr. 13, 1942; married; 2 children. BS, Livingston U., 1969; MA, U. Ala., 1970, PhD in Exptl. Psychology, 1972, postgrad., 1974-75. Coord. West Ala. Devel. Ctr., 1971-72; acting supt. Partlow State Sch. and Hosp., 1971-72; supt. Albert P. Brewer Devel. Ctr., 1972-74; clin. cons. N.W. Ala. Mental Health Ctr., 1974-75; intern VA, Bay Pines, Fla., 1975-76; program evaluator State of Mont. Dept. Instns., 1976-78; adminstr. Mental Health and Residential Svcs. Divsn., Dept. Instns., 1979-82, adminstrv. officer, 1982-84; sr. analyst Legis. Fiscal Analyst's Office, 1984-89; dep. dir. Dept. Social and Rehab. Svcs., 1989-91; asst. to dir. Dept. Health and Environ. Scis., 1991-93; dir. Dept. Social and Rehab. Svcs., 1993-95, Mont. Dept. Pub. Health and Human Svcs., Helena, 1995—; mem. exec. com. Ala. Assn. Retarded Children, 1973-75; exec. com. Ala. Spl. Olympics, 1973; chmn. policy bd. Mont. U. Affiliated Programs, 1982. Moderator, host series of 3 half-hour programs, Issues in Mental Health, KTVG, 1984; contbr articles to profl. jours. Bd. dirs. Gordon Smith Ctr., 1972-74, Group Aid for Retarded Children; mem. adv. com. Easter Seal Soc.; vice chmn. Gov.'s Interagy. Com. for Handicapped Children (vice-chmn. 1980-81); bd. dirs. St. Peter's Hosp., 1986—; mem. Mont. Petroleum Release Compensation Bd., 1992. Fellow mental retardation program U. Ala.; named Outstanding Alumnus Livingston U., 1974; recipient Resolution of Appreciation, Ala. Bd. Mental Health, 1975, Ann. Achievement award State Mental Health Programs, Mont., 1979; nominated Outstanding Hosp. Bd. Trustee, 1991. Coun. Exceptional Children, Mobile Psychol. Assn. (first pres. 1974). Home: 1500 Mt Helena Dr Helena MT 59601*

BLOUNT, CYNTHIA LOUISE, radiologist; b. Coldwater, Mich., June 16, 1963; d. Paul Edgar and Betty Louise (Gillette) Blount; m. Calvin Charles Sumrall, July 24, 1993. BA in Biology, Hillsdale (Mich.) Coll., 1985; DO, Kirksville Coll. Osteo. Med., 1990. Diplomate Am. Osteo. Bd. Radiology. Intern Flint (Mich.) Osteo. Hosp., 1990-91; resident in diagnostic radiology Mich. State U., 1991-95; fellow in nuclear medicine William Beaumont Hosp., Royal Oak, Mich., 1995-96. John M. Botts scholar, Scholl Found. scholar, State of Mich. grantee. Mem. Am. Osteo. Assn., Am. Osteo. Coll. Radiology, Am. Roentgen Ray Soc., Mich. Assn. Osteo. Physicians and Surgeons, Nat. Osteo. Women Physicians Assn., Radiol. Soc. N.Am., Soc. Nuclear Medicine, Beta Beta Beta, Delta Omega, Epsilon Delta Alpha, Iota Tau Sigma, Sigma Delta Pi, Sigma Zeta. Home: 1202 Woodlake Ln Pontiac MI 48340 Office: Beaumont Hosp 3601 W Thirteen Mile Rd Royal Oak MI 48073

BLOUNT, WILBUR CLANTON, ophthalmologist; b. Columbus, Ohio, Feb. 5, 1929; s. Percy Hammond and Bayetta (Dent) B.; m. Elsie M. Paradis; children: Angela Diane, Wilbur S., Elizabeth Rachel, Jacqueline Rebecca; 1 stepson, Michael C. Paradis. BSc in Bacteriology, Ohio State U., 1951, postgrad., 1951-52, MD, 1959. Intern, U. Ill. Rsch. and Ednl. Hosps., Chgo., 1959-60; gen. practice medicine, Williamson, W.Va., 1960-62; resident dept. ophthalmology Coll. Medicine, Ohio State U., Columbus, 1964-67, instr. ophthalmology 1970-71, clin. asst. prof., 1977—; spl. NIH fellow in retinal surgery U. Minn., 1967-69; practice medicine specializing in ophthalmology, especially surgery and diseases of retina; Lexington VA Hosp., 1971-77, attending staff Grant Hosp., 1977—; courtesy staff Mt. Carmel Med. Ctr., 1977—; asst. prof. surgery, dept. ophthalmology U. Ky. Med. Center, Lexington, 1971-77, dir. retinal svc.; nat. adv. coun. Nat. Eye Inst., NIH, 1991-93. Trustee Urbana U., 1994—, Ohio History of Flight Mus. Served to 1st lt. USAF, 1954-56; col. Air N.G., 1984—. Fellow ACS, Aerospace Med. Assn. (assoc.), Am. Soc. Laser Medicine and Surgery, Internat. Coll.; mem. AMA, Nat. Med. Assn., Ohio Med. Assn., Acad. Medicine Columbus and Franklin County, Soc. USAF Flight Surgeons, Am. Acad. Ophthalmology, Assn. Mil. Ophthalmologists, Columbus Ophthalmology/Otolantyngology Soc., Ohio Ophthalmol. Soc., Am. Soc. Cataract and Refractive Surgery, Ophthalmic Photographers Soc., Ohio State U. Alumni (life), Ohio State U. Coll. Medicine Alumni Assn. (life), Assn. Naval Aviation (life), Aerospace Med. Assn. (life), Exptl. Aircraft Assn. (aeromed. adv. coun. 1993), Civil Aviation Med. Assn., Tuskegee Airman, Inc., Air Force Assn. (life), Res. Officers Assn. (life), N.G. Assn. (life), Ohio State U. Pres.' Club, Lions. Home: 2820 E Broad St Columbus OH 43209-1866 Office: 300 E Town St Fl 15 Columbus OH 43215-4632

BLOW, JAMIE ANN, medical entomologist, medical technologist; b. Alma, Mich., Sept. 19, 1962; d. Donald Eugene and Jean Ann (Hicks) B. BS, Alma Coll., 1984; MS, Ctrl. Mich. U., 1991; postgrad., Mich. State U., 1995—. Lid. med. technologist, Mich. Commd. U.S. Army, 1984—, advanced thorugh grades to capt., 1993; med. lab. specialist 2d Gen. Hosp., Landstuhl, Germany, 1985-87; med. technologist Humana Hosp., Augusta, Ga., 1988; project mgr. U.S. Army Environ. Hygiene Agy., Ft. Meade, Md., 1991-92, 93-94; med. entomologist Joint Task Force Bravo, Honduras, 1992-93; instr. U.S. Army Med. Dept., Ft. Sam Houston, Tex., 1994-95, long-term health edn. tng. program student, 1995—.

BLUEMKE, DAVID A., radiologist; b. West Allis, Wis., Aug. 10, 1960; m. Bonnie Beavan. BSE, U. Wis., 1982; PhD, U. Chgo., 1987, MD, 1989. ACR; bd. cert. radiology. Rsch. asst. U. Wis., Madison, 1979-82, tchg. asst., 1982; tchg. asst. U. Chgo., 1985-86, rsch. asst., 1986-89; radiology resident Johns Hopkins Hosp., Balt., 1989-93, fellow and instr. radiology, 1993, asst. prof., 1994, acting clin. dir. MRI, 1996—. Mem. editl. bd. Jour. Computer Assisted Tomography; jour. reviewer Radiology, JMRI; contbr. articles to profl. jours. Mem. med. sch. coun. Johns Hopkins Hosp., Balt., 1993. Gatewood fellow Johns Hopkins Hosp., 1994. Mem. Am. Roentgen Ray Soc. (Exec. Coun. award 1993), Assn. U. Radiologists, Am. Coll. Radiology, Soc. Magnetic Resonance, Radiol. Soc. N.Am. (dep. editor radiology 1993—, Cum Laude award for poster presentation 1990, Seed grant 1995). Office: Johns Hopkins Hosp Dept Radiology 600 N Wolfe St Baltimore MD 21287

BLUESTEIN, VENUS WELLER, retired psychologist, educator; b. Milw., July 16, 1933; d. Richard T. and Hazel (Beard) Weller; m. Marvin Bluestein, Mar. 7, 1954. BS, U. Cin., 1956, MEd, 1959, EdD, 1966. Diplomate Am. Bd. Examiners in Profl. Psychology. Psychologist-in-tng. Longview State Hosp., Cin., 1956-58; sch. psychologist Cin. Pub. Schs., 1958-65; asst. prof. psychology U. Cin., 1965-70, assoc. prof., 1970-79, prof., 1979-93, prof. emerita, 1993—, dir. sch. psychology program, 1965-70, co-dir. sch. psychology program, 1970-75, dir. undergrad. studies, 1976-91, dir. undergrad. advising, 1991-93; cons. child psychologist. Sec., U.S. exec. com. rsch. Children's Internat. Summer Villages, 1964-68; chmn. Ohio Interuniv. Coun. Sch. Psychology, 1967-68. Editor Ohio Psychologist, 1961-68, co-editor, 1972-79; contbr. articles to profl. publs. Vol. Hamilton County Parks, 1982—, vol. naturalist, 1995—; vol. naturalist various ednl. programs Cin. Zoo, 1983—. Recipient George B. Barbour award, 1985. Fellow Am. Acad. Sch. Psychology; mem. AAUP, APA, Ohio Psychol. Assn. (citation 1972, Disting. Svc. award 1968), Cin. Psychol. Assn. (sec. 1961-62), Sch. Psychologists Ohio, Forum for Death Edn. and Counseling, Kappa Delta Pi, Sigma Delta Pi, Psi Chi (award for outstanding mentor 1985, award for outstanding contbns. to undergrad. psychology students 1994). Office: U Cin Dept Psychology ML 376 Cincinnati OH 45221

BLUESTONE, DAVID ALLAN, pediatrician; b. Pitts., Apr. 9, 1938; s. Sam Bluestone and Sarah Cohen Sager; m. John Sidlow, Oct. 12, 1957 (div. 1980); children: Daniel, Bradley, Deborah; m. Leslie Florence Widson Kaplan, May 26m 1983. BA, Hamilton Coll., 1959; MD, U. Pitts., 1963. Diplomate Am. Bd. Pediatrics. Pediatric intern Health Ctr. Hosps. U. Pitts., 1963-64; pediatric resident Children's Hosp., Pitts., 1964-65, L.A., 1967-68; pediatrician Med. Arts Pediatric Med. Group, Inc., L.A., 1968—. Lt. Med. Corps USNR, 1965-67. Mem. AMA, Calif. Med. Assn., Los Angeles County Med. Assn., L.A. Pediatric Soc., Phi Delta Epsilon (pres. 1982-83, assoc. regional gov. 1994—), Zeta Phi. Office: Med Arts Pediatric Med Group Inc 6221 Wilshire Blvd # 215 Los Angeles CA 90048

BLUETT, THOMAS BYRON, SR., child psychologist; b. Milw., May 29, 1931; s. Byron Walter and Ida Mae (Mineau) B.; m. Daina Lauretta Kubilius, Sept. 21, 1974; children: Thomas Jr., Elizabeth, William, Martha, Dorothea (dec.), Byron. BS, U. Wis., 1953, MS, 1955, PhD, 1971. Lic. psychologist, Wis.; nat. cert. sch. psychologist; listed Nat. Register Health Svc. Providers in Psychology. Counselor Appleton (Wis.) Pub. Schs., 1955-57; psychologist Green Bay (Wis.) Pub. Schs., 1957-65; exec. dir. United Cerebral Palsy, Green Bay, 1965-68; dir. pupil services Cooperative Edn. Service Agy., Wis., 1968-71; child psychologist Pediatrics Beaumont Clin., Green Bay, 1972—; sec.-treas. Tri-State Testing Svc., Inc., DePere, Wis., 1958—; child psychologist Sta. WTMJ-TV and Radio, Milw., 1981—, Sta. WOAI, San Antonio, 1986—, Sally Jessy Raphael Show, 1989, Montel Williams Show, 1993, Jerry Springer Show, 1993; lectr. child devel. U. Wis., Green Bay, 1968-73. Author, presenter (TV series) In-Charge Parenting, 1982, (book, audio tapes) In-Charge Parenting Kit, 1983; author: Conquering Low Impulse Control, 1984; co-author: Youth Tutoring Youth, 1970. Bd. dirs. United Cerebral Palsy, N.Y.C., 1957-65; exec. dir. Nat. Early Childhood Edn. Fund, Wis., 1971-80; mem. profl. and adv. bd. Wis. Assn. for Children with Learning Disabilities, 1989—; adult leader Kewaunee County 4-H Club, 1988—. With U.S. Army, 1953-55, Korea. Grantee Rural Pupil Services, HEW, Washington, D.C., 1969, Early Childhood Edn. , ESEA, Madison, 1970. Fellow Am. Assn. Mental Deficiency, Nat. Assn. Mental Deficiency; mem. Wis. Soc. Clin. Cons. Psychologists (charter, co-chmn. publicity com. 1986—), Nat. Gen. Psychol. Svcs. Corp., Nat. Assn. Sch. Psychologists (charter), Brown County Clin. Cons. Psychologists (treas. 1985-87), Children and Adults Attention Deficit Disorders S.E. Wis., Elks (handicapped children's chmn. 1958-68), Optimist (youth chmn. 1957-68), Phi Delta Kappa (pres. 1958-60). Roman Catholic. Office: Beaumont-Webster Med Clinic 1821 S Webster Ave Green Bay WI 54301-2253

BLUM, JACOB JOSEPH, physiologist, educator; b. Bklyn., Oct. 3, 1926; s. Paul and Anna (Brown) B.; m. Ruth Marsey, June 3, 1960; children: Mark, Douglas, lisa, Laura. BA, NYU, 1947; MS, U. Chgo., 1950, PhD, 1952. Mem. staff Naval Med. Rsch. Inst., Bethesda, Md., 1953-56; chief biophysics sect. gerontology br. NIH, Balt., 1958-62; prof. physiology Duke U., Durham, N.C., 1962—, James B. Duke prof., 1980—. With AUS, 1945-46. Merck postdoctoral fellow, 1952, Guggenheim fellow, 1969, Fogarty sr. internat. fellow, 1992. Mem. Am. Physiol. Soc., Soc. Protozoologists (pres. 1991). Home: 2525 Perkins Rd Durham NC 27706

BLUM, JON H., dermatologist; b. Detroit, Aug. 9, 1944; s. David and Hedwig B.; m. Rosie Jacobs, June 25, 1967; children: Michael, Steven, Suzanne. BS, Wayne State U., 1965, MD, 1969. Diplomate Am. Bd. Dermatology. Intern Beaumont Hosp., Royal Oak, Mich., 1969-70; med. resident Henry Ford Hosp., Detroit, 1970-71; dermatology resident Henry Ford Hosp., 1971-74; dermatologist Farmington Hills, Mich., 1974—; staff physician, William Beaumont Hosp.; cons., Internat. Hair Route, Mississauga, Ontario, Can., 1980—; clin. asst. prof. dermatology, Wayne State U., Detroit, 1976—. Author: (with others) Electrolysis, 1984. Mem. Am. Acad. Dermatology, Mich. Dermatology Soc., Mich. State Med. Soc., Oakland County Med. Soc. Office: Jon H Blum MD Ste 330 32905 W 12 Mile Rd Farmington Hills MI 48334-3345

BLUM, LAWRENCE DAVID, psychiatrist; b. July 31, 1955. MD, U. Pa., 1981; postgrad., Phila. Psychoanalytic Inst., 1985-91. Diploamte Am. Bd. Psychiatry and Neurology. Intern Pa. Hosp., Phila., 1981-82; resident in psychiatry Inst. of Pa. Hosp., Phila., 1982-85; dir. med. student edn. in psychiatry Cooper Hosp. U. Med. Ctr., Camden, N.J., 1985-87; pvt. practice psychiatry and psychoanalysis Phila. and Cherry Hill, N.J., 1987—; clin. asst. prof. psychiatry U. Medicine and Dentistry of N.J.-Robert Wood Johnson Med. Sch., 1987—; dir. Phila. Psychotherapy Tng. Program, Phila. Psychoanalytic Soc. and Inst. Mem. Am. Psychiat. Assn., Am. Psychoanalytic Assn., Phila. Psychoanalytic Soc. Office: 1 Cherry Hl Cherry Hill NJ 08002 also: Inst Pa Hosp 111 N 49th St Philadelphia PA 19139-2718

BLUM, RICHARD STEVEN, physician; b. N.Y.C., June 10, 1938; s. Irving and Mary Blum; m. Carole Sue Goodman, June 20, 1964; children: Michael, David. BS, Bethany Coll., 1959; MD, Chgo. Med. Coll., 1963. Diplomate Am. Bd. Med. Examiners. Intern L.I. Jewish Hosp., New Hyde Park, N.Y., 1963-64, asst. resident in internal medicine, 1966-68, chief resident in internal medicine, 1968-69; asstp. prof. clin. medicine SUNY, Stony Brook, N.Y.; med. dir. Methadone maintenance treatment ctr. L.I. Jewish Hosp., New Hyde Park, N.Y., 1970-78; pvt. practice New Hyde Park, 1969—; postdoctoral tng. in pharmacology St. Johns U., Jamaica, N.Y., 1972-77; sr. cons. com. for blind and visually handicapped, N.Y., 1969—; cons. in methadone Am. Pharm. Assn., Washington, 1973; physician to NBA, 1977-88; chmn. pharmacy and therapeutics com. St. Francis Hosp., Roslyn, N.Y., 1976—; mem. DUR panel of Com. of Revision of the USP, 1990-96; chmn. N.Y. State Drug Utilization Rev. Bd., 1993-94; adj. asst. prof. clin. pharmacy St. Johns U., Sch. Pharmacy; spl. govt. employee expert FDA. Author: Permaslim, 1981; inventor medication dispenser, 1987, telephone security device, 1987. Bd. dirs. Port Alert, Port Washington, N.Y., 1980-84; med. dir. L.I. (N.Y.) Marathon, 1980-88; adminstr. com. for physicians' health Med. Soc. State of N.Y. Capt. USAF, 1964-66. Fellow ACP, Am. Coll. of Clin. Pharmacology; mem. Am. Coll. of Utilization Physicians, Am. Soc. of Hosp. Pharmacists, Beta Beta Beta, Phi Delta Epsilon. Jewish. Home: 25 Spruce Dr Roslyn NY 11576-2331

BLUM, ROBERT ALLAN, psychiatrist; b. Phila., May 16, 1938; s. Frank Abraham and Sara (James) B.; m. Irene Harriet Segal, Aug. 2, 1959; children: Marc Daniel, Lisa Michelle, Lora Danielle, Amy Lynne. BS, MIT, 1959, MS, 1960; MD, U. Pa., 1964. Diplomate Nat. Bd. Med. Examiners, Am. Bd. Psychiatry and Neurology, Am. Bd. Psychoanalytic. Engr. Burroughs Corp., Paoli, Pa., 1956-57, Gen. Atronics Corp., Wyndmoor, Pa., 1958-61; rotating intern Meml. Hosp., Long Beach, Calif., 1964-65; teaching fellow Harvard U., Boston, 1965-67; staff assoc. NIMH, Washington, 1967-69, rsch. psychiatrist, 1969-71; rsch. psychiatrist NIAAA, Washington, 1971-74; pvt. practice Washington, 1968—; cons. U.S. Govt., Washington, 1974—; regional med. officer/psychiatry Am. Embassy, Singapore, 1995—; instr. Johns Hopkins U., Balt., 1969—; asst. prof. Georgetown U., Washington, 1972-92; assoc. prof. Uniformed Svcs. U. Health Scis., Bethesda, Md., 1987—; tchg. analyst Balt.-Washington Inst. Psychoanalysis, Laurel, Md., 1978—. Contbr. articles to profl. publs., sect. to book. Lt. comdr. USPHS, 1967-69. C. Mahlon Kline scholar, 1960-63, Mosby scholar, 1964; NSF fellow, 1959, 60. Fellow Am. Psychiat. Assn.; mem. Am. Psychoanalytic Assn., Am. Soc. Indsl. Security, Internat. Psychoanalytic Assn., Internat. Soc. Hypnosis, Soc. Clin. and Exptl. Hypnosis. Home: 9819 Hill St Kensington MD 20895-3136 Office: Regional Med Office Am Embassy Singapore PSC 470 RMO FPO AP 96534

BLUM, RONALD H., medical educator; b. Buffalo, June 19, 1944. AB in Biology, U. Rochester, 1966; MD with honors, SUNY, Buffalo, 1970. Diplomate Am. Bd. Internal Medicine, Am. Bd. Oncology. Intern Balt. City Hosp./Johns Hopkins Hosp., 1970-71; resident in internal medicine Boston City Hosp., 1973-74; from asst. to jr. assoc. in medicine Peter Bent Brigham Hosp., 1974-79; from instr. to asst. prof. medicine Sidney Farber Cancer Inst., 1975-79; from asst. prof. to assoc. prof. dept. medicine NYU, 1979-85, prof. dept. medicine, 1986—; chief sect. med. oncology dept. medicine West Roxbury VA Hosp., 1976-79; cons. med. oncology Boston Hosp. for Women, 1977-79; dir. divsn. oncology NYU, 1987—; assoc. dir. clin. programs Kaplan Cancer Comprehensive Ctr., 1979-92, dep. dir. for clin. oncology, 1993—; spl. asst. to assoc. dir. for cancer therapy evaluation divsn. cancer treatment Nat. Cancer Inst., Bethesda, Md., 1971-73, ad hoc reviewer, 1984—, cancer ctrs. support rev. com., 1989-93, chmn., 1992-93; chmn. human protection com. Sidney Farber Cancer Inst., 1976-79; chmn. oper. com. Nat. VA Coop. Study for Cancer Chemotherapy, 1978-85; chmn.

cancer edn. com. NYU Med. Sch., 1980-86. Mem. editl. bd. Am. Jour. Clin. Oncology, 1978—, Cancer Chemotherapy and Pharmacology, 1981-90, Jour. Psychosocial Oncology, 1983—, Jour. Clin. Oncology, 1989—, Cancer Prevention Internat., 1993—, Internat. Jour. Cancer Rsch. and Treatment Oncology, 1994—, Clin. Cancer Rsch., 1995—, Cancer Rsch., 1995—. Johns Hopkins U. Sch. Medicine fellow, 1970-71, clin. fellow Harvard Med. Sch., 1973-75, Sidney Farber Cancer Inst., 1974-75. Mem. ACP, Am. Cancer Soc. (clin. oncology com 1987-91, profl. edn. subcom. on clin. awards 1991—), Am. Cancer Insts (aging subcom. 1991—), Am. Soc. Clin. Oncology (publ. com. 1987—, chmn. publ. com. 1991-95, com. on cancer prevention and control, oncology tng. program com. 1993—), Am. Assn. for Cancer Rsch., Am. Assn. for Cancer Edn., N.Y. State Cancer Soc., N.Y. Soc. Med. Oncologists and Hematologists (exec. com. 1989—), Ea. Coop. Oncology Group (co-chmn. lung com. 1984-86, chmn. 1987-89, chmn. melanoma and sarcoma com., industry liaison, exec. com., 1989-93, chmn. sarcoma com. 1993—). Home: 2 E End Ave New York NY 10021

BLUM, SARAH LEE, nurse psychotherapist; b. Atlantic City, N.J., Dec. 5, 1939; d. David and Diana (Fedner) B.; m. Joseph J. McGoran, Aug. 24, 1970 (div. 1986); children: Lorna Hope Marie, Sean-David Justin. BSN, Seattle U., 1971; M in Nursing, U. Wash., 1976. Cert. clin. specialist. Nurse Atlantic City Hosp., 1960-62, Kaiser Found. Hosp., L.A., 1963-66; instr. nursing North Idaho Coll., Coeur D'Alene, 1972-74; pvt. practice Federal Way, Wash., 1977-85, Auburn, Wash., 1985—; nurse psychotherapist Christian Counselling Svc., Tacoma, 1977-83; founder The Found. for Planetary Healing; creator Drums, Dreams & Re-Membering; cons. in field; presenter workshops. Contbr. articles to profl. jours. Creator Healing Day, 1985. Capt. Nurse Corps, U.S. Army, 1966-71, Vietnam. Fellow Am. Orthopsychiatric Assn.; mem. ANA, Nat. Nursing Hon. Soc., Internat. Transactional Analysis Assn., Inst. Developmental Edn. and Psychotherapy (bd. dirs. 1989-93, chair profl. membership com. 1991-94), Vietnam Veterans of Am. (bd. dirs. 1983-85, 1st woman mem.). Home and Office: 303 O St NE Auburn WA 98002-4645

BLUMBERG, BARUCH SAMUEL, academic administrator, research scientist; b. N.Y.C., July 28, 1925; s. Meyer and Ida (Simonoff) B.; m. Jean Liebesman, Apr. 4, 1954; children: Anne, George, Jane, Noah. BS, Union Coll., Schenectady, 1946; MD, Columbia U., 1951; PhD, Oxford (Eng.) U., 1957; 20 hon. doctoral degrees. Intern, then resident Columbia div. Bellevue Hosp., N.Y.C., 1951-53; fellow in medicine Columbia-Presbyn. Med. Ctr., N.Y.C., 1953-55; chief geog. medicine and genetics sect. NIH, Bethesda, Md., 1957-64; assoc. dir. clin. rsch. Fox Chase Cancer Ctr., Phila., 1964-86, v.p. population oncology, 1984-89, Fox Chase disting. scientist, 1989—; sr. advisor to pres. Fox Chase Cancer Ctr.; univ. prof. medicine and anthropology U. Pa., 1977—; master Balliol Coll., Oxford (Eng.) U., England, 1989-94; George Eastman vis. prof. Oxford U., 1983-84; Raman vis. prof. Indian Inst. Scis., Bangalore, 1986; Ashland vis. prof. U. Ky., Lexington, 1986, 87; disting. vis. Nat. U. Singapore, 1992; vis. prof. U. Otago, Dunedin, New Zealand, 1994; sr. advisor to pres. Fox Chase Cancer Ctr., 1989—. Contbr. articles to profl. jours. Lt. USNR, 1943-46. Recipient Albion O. Berstein, M.D. award Med. Soc. State of N.Y., 1969, Grand Sci. award Phi Lambda Kappa, 1972, Ann. award Eastern Pa. br. Am. Soc. Microbiology, 1972, Passano award Williams & Wilkens Co., 1974, Modern Medicine Disting. Achievement award, 1975, Internat. award Gairdner Found., 1975, Karl Landsteiner Meml. award Am. Assn. Blood Banks, 1975, Nobel prize in physiology or medicine, 1976, Scopus award Am. Friends of Hebrew U., 1977, Strittmatter award Philadelphia County Med. Soc., 1980, Disting. Service award Pa. Med. Soc., 1982, Zubrow award Pa. Hosp., 1986, Achievement award Sammy Davis Jr. Nat. Liver Inst., 1987, John P. McGovern award Am. Med. Writers Assn., 1988, Gov.'s Award in the Scis. Commonwealth of Pa., 1989, John Blundell award Brit. Blood Transfusion Soc., 1989, Gold Medal award Can. Liver Found. and Can. Assn. Study of Liver, 1990, Showa Emperor Meml. award Japan, 1994; elected to Nat. Inventor Hall of Fame, 1993. Fellow ACP, Royal Coll. Physicians; mem. NAS, Assn. Am. Physicians, Am. Soc. Clin. Investigation, Am. Soc. Human Genetics,, Am. Assn. Phys. Anthropologists, Explorers Club N.Y., Athenaeum (London). Office: Fox Chase Cancer Ctr 7701 Burholme Ave Philadelphia PA 19111-2412

BLUMBERG, JOEL MYRON, cardiologist; b. N.Y.C., Oct. 17, 1940; s. Howard Godfrey and Lily Ruth (Goldberg) B.; B.A., DePauw U., 1962; M.D., N.Y. U., 1966; m. Judith Ellen Green, Aug. 23, 1964; children—Amy, Hillary, Michelle. Intern, N.Y. U.-Bellevue Med. Center, N.Y.C., 1966-67, resident in internal medicine, 1969-71; fellow in cardiology Cornell U.-N.Y. Hosp., 1971-73; pvt. practice internal medicine and cardiology, Greenwich, Conn., 1973—; attending staff Greenwich Hosp., 1973—, coronary care cons., 1973—; physician to out-patients N.Y. Hosp., 1973-77; clin. instr. Cornell U. Med. Coll., 1971-77; clin. asst. prof. Yale Sch. Medicine, 1975—; lectr. in preventive cardiology to civic groups. Trustee, Temple Sholom, Greenwich, Conn.; bd. visitors DePauw U., bd. incorporators Greenwich Hosp. Diplomate Am. Bd. Internal Medicine. Fellow A.C.P., Am. Coll. Cardiology, Am. Coll. Chest Physicians, Am. Heart Assn. (council on clin. cardiology); mem. Am. Soc. Internal Medicine, N.Y. Heart Assn., Greenwich, Fairfield County, Conn. State med. socs. Club: B'nai B'rith (Stamford, Conn.). Contbr. articles to profl. jours. Home: 59 Old Stone Bridge Rd Cos Cob CT 06807-1511 Office: 2 1/2 Dearfield Dr Greenwich CT 06831-5335

BLUMBERG, MARK STUART, health care researcher; b. N.Y.C., Nov. 16, 1924; s. Sydney N. and Mollie (Leshrowitz) B.; m. Luba Monasevitch, 1952; children: Bart David, Eve Luise; m. 2d Elizabeth R. Conner, 1974. Student, Johns Hopkins U., 1942-43, Harvard U., 1943-44; D.M.D., Harvard U., 1948, M.D., 1950, student Sch. Public Health, 1955. Intern, children's med. service Bellevue Hosp., N.Y.C., 1950-51; ops. analyst Johns Hopkins U. Ops. Research Office, Chevy Chase, Md., 1951-54; exchange analyst Army Ops. Research Group (U.K.), West Byfleet, Eng., 1953-54; staff Occupational Health Program, USPHS, Washington, 1954-56; asso. ops. analyst to dir. health econs. program Stanford (Calif.) Research Inst., 1956-66; asst. to v.p. adminstrn. to dir. health planning, office of the pres. U. Calif., Berkeley, 1966-70; corp. planning advisor to dir. spl. studies Kaiser Found. Health Plan, Inc., Oakland, Calif., 1970—; dir. Kaiser Found. Health Plan of Conn., Hartford, 1982—, Kaiser Found. Health Plan Mass., 1987—; various times cons. Pan Am. Health Orgn., Calif. State Dept. Mental Hygiene, Carnegie Commn. on Higher Edn., various agys. HHS. Contbr. writings to profl. pubs. Vol. Grenfell Med. Mission, Harrington Harbour, Que., Can., summer 1948; mem. tech. adv. com. AB 524 State of Calif., 1992—. Served with USNR, 1943-45; with USPHS, 1954-56. Mem. Ops. Research Soc. Am. (past mem. council, Health Applications sect.), Hosp. Mgmt. Systems Soc. (charter), Inst. of Medicine of Nat. Acad. Scis., Am. Public Health Assn., Soc. for Epidemiologic Research. Office: Kaiser Found Health Plan Inc 1 Kaiser Plz Oakland CA 94612-3610*

BLUMBERG, MICHAEL ZANGWILL, allergist; b. Phila., July 29, 1945; s. Jerome Blumberg and Vivian Rose (Liebman) Steiger; m. Barbara Sue Gurman, June 9, 1973; children: Jessica Lynn, Jason Mark. AB, Brandeis U., 1967; MD, Jefferson Med. Coll., 1971; postgrad., Med. Coll. Va., 1996—. Bd. cert. pediatrics, allergy and immunology. Fellow in allergy and immunology Nat. Jewish Hosp.-U. Colo. Med. Ctr., 1973-75; Chief allergy sect. major Scott Air Force Base, Ill., 1975-77; physician-ptnr. Va. Allergy, Asthma and Pulmonary Assn., Richmond, 1977—; intern, resident N.Y. Hosp.-Cornell U. Med. Ctr., 1971-73; asst. clin. prof. pediatrics Med. Coll. Va., Richmond, 1977—; chief of allergy Children's Hosp. of Richmond, 1987-96; med. advisor Rhone Poulenc Rorer, Allen Hansburys, Glaxo, Marion Merrell Dow Inc. Contbr. articles and abtracts to profl. jours.; contbg. editor: Review in Allergy, 1978; manuscript reviewer Asthma, 1995—. Bd. dirs. Jewish Cmty. Ctr., Richmond, 1984-87; exec. com. pres., bd. dirs., chmn. quality assurance bd. govs. Beth Shalom Home Va., Richmond, 1987—. Fellow Va. Allergy Soc. (program dir. 1989-90), Am. Coll. Allergy, Coll. Chest Physicians, Am. Acad. Pediatrics; mem. Am. Coll. Allergy Sports Medicine (practice stds. com. 1994-95), Am. Acad. Allergy, Am. Thoracic Soc., Friends of Brandeis Athletics, Masons. Jewish. Home: 1602 Swansbury Dr Richmond VA 23233-4628 Office: Va Allergy & Pulmonary Assocs 7605 Forest Ave Ste 102 Richmond VA 23229-4936

BLUMBERG, NEIL HOWARD, psychiatrist; b. Bklyn., Apr. 10, 1951. BA in Psychology, Emory U., 1973; MD, George Washington U., 1977. Lic. psychiatrist, Md.; Diplomate Am. Bd. Psychiatry and Neurology, Am. Bd. Forensic Psychiatry. Intern Sheppard & Enoch Pratt Hosp., Towson, Md., resident psychiatry, 1977-80; fellow in forensic psychiatry U. Md. Hosp., Inst. Psychiatry and Human Behavior, Balt., 1980-81; clin. instr. psychiatry U. Md. Sch. Medicine, Inst. Psychiatry and Human Behavior, Balt., 1981-91, clin. asst. prof., 1991—; pvt. practice gen. and forensic psychiatry Timonium, Md., 1981—; staff psychiatrist Clifton T. Perkins Hosp. Ctr., Jessup, Md., 1981-83; dir. forensic evaluation Clifton T. Perkins Hosp. Ctr., 1983-84, Spring Grove Hosp. Ctr., 1996—; retained as an expert in gen. and forensic psychiatry by many Md. state agys. and cts., fed. agys. and cts., NAACP Legal Defense Fund; qualified as an expert gen. and forensic psychiatry Md. cir. cts., Superior Ct. D.C., U.S. Dist. Ct. Balt., U.S. Dist. Ct. D.C., Pa. Ct. Common Pleas York County, N.J. Cir. Ct. Burlington County, Va. Cir. Ct. Fairfax County, Va. Alexandria Cir. Ct.; presenter and lectr. in field; mem. admissions com. U. Mo. Med. Sch. Contbr. articles to Jour. Rsch. in Personality, 1975, Bull. The Am. Acad. Psychiatry and the Law, 1981, 88, Ann. Rev. of Psychiatry and Law, 1991, Am. Jour. Psychiatry, 1992; editorial bd. Forensic Reports, 1987-92; reviewer Hosp. and Community Psychiatry, 1993—. Mem. Balt. County Med. Assn., Med. and Chirurgical Faculty of State Md., Am. Psychiat. Assn. (peer rev. com. 1983-87), Md. Psychiat. Soc. (legis. com. 1981-82), Am. Acad. Psychiatry and the Law (criminal behavior com. 1987-89, pub. info. com. 1987-89), Phi Beta Kappa. Office: 30 E Padonia Rd Ste 206 Lutherville Timonium MD 21093-2308

BLUME, SHEILA BIERMAN, psychiatrist; b. Bklyn., June 21, 1934; d. Benjamin and Rose (Lazar) Bierman; m. Martin Blume, June 12, 1955; children: Frederick, Janet. Student Cornell U., 1951-54; MD cum laude, Harvard U., 1958. Intern, Children's Hosp. Med. Ctr., Boston, 1958-59; Fulbright fellow to Tokyo U., 1959-60; resident in psychiatry Central Islip Psychiat. Center, 1962-65; dir. Charles K. Post Alcoholism Rehab. Center, Central Islip Psychiat. Ctr., 1964-79; dir. N.Y. State Div. Alcoholism and Alcohol Abuse, 1979-83; med. dir. Nat. Coun. on Alcoholism, 1983; med. dir. Alcoholism, Compulsive Gambling and Chem. Dependency Programs, South Oaks Hosp., 1984—; clin. assoc. prof. psychiatry Albany Med. Ctr., 1979-82; clin. prof. psychiatry SUNY-Stony Brook, 1984—; apptd. to Nat. Commn. Alcoholism and Other Alcohol Related Problems, 1980; mem. Nat. Commn. Confidentiality of Health Records, 1976-80, Nat. Coun. on Compulsive Gambling, adv. bd., 1972—; bd. dirs. Children of Alcoholics Found., 1983-95, mem. sci. adv. bd. 1995—. Recipient Dr. Milton Helpernbd. Disting. Physicians award for contbn. field of alcoholism, 1980, Harold Riegelman award for contbn. to field of alcohol policy, 1983, Disting. Svc. award Rutgers Sch. Alcohol Studies, 1993. Mem. Am. Psychiatric Assn. (coun. psychiatric svcs. 1987-90, coun. addiction psychiatry 1990-93, chmn. task force psychiatric svcs. to addicted patients 1992-95, chair com. on svcs. for addicted patients 1995—), Med. Soc. State of N.Y. (chmn. alcoholism com. 1990-95, com. physicians health 1983-88, 90—), L.I. Coun. Alcoholism and Other Drug Dependencies (dir. 1973-79), Am. Soc. Addiction Medicine (pres. 1979-80, bd. dirs. 1975—), Nat. Coun. Alcoholism, (dir. 1979-83, 86-91, chair task force on Addiction Medicine in the 21st Century, 1995—). Editor: (with S. Zimberg and J. Wallace) Practical Approaches to Alcoholism Psychotherapy, 1978; editor Bull. Suffolk County Med. Soc., 1969-76; contbr. articles profl. jours., chpts. in books.in books. Home and Office: 284 Greene Ave Sayville NY 11782-3003 also: South Oaks Hosp Amityville NY 11701

BLUMENAU, IRIS WARECH, nursing consultant; b. Newark, Dec. 12, 1928; m. William Blumenau, Aug. 20, 1949 (dec.); 1 child, Bonnie Kaplan. Diploma, Newark Beth Israel Hosp., 1949; BA, Jersey City State Coll., 1975. Office mgr., bus. adminstr. Ctr. for Dermatology, P.A., West Orange, N.J., 1952-89; ret., 1989; pvt. cons.

BLUMENBERG, ROBERT MURRAY, surgeon, educator; b. Rochester, N.Y., Jan. 5, 1934; s. Theodore Peter and Esther Frances (Sablowsky) B.; m. Linda Dibble, Dec. 13, 1962 (div. 1984); children: Andrew C., Dara R., Laura A.; m. Gayle Eastwood, Nov. 7, 1986. AB cum laude, Amherst Coll., 1955; MD, Albany Med. Coll., 1959. Diplomate Am. Bd. Surgery. Surg. intern Strong Meml. Hosp., Rochester, 1959-60; asst. resident in surgery Albany (N.Y.) Med. Ctr. Hosps., 1960-64, chief resident, 1964-65; instr. surgery Albany Med. Coll., 1967-68, asst. clin. prof., 1968—; pvt. practice Schenectady, 1968—; attending surgeon, chief divsn. vascular surgery Ellis Hosp., Schenectady, 1968—; attending surgeon St. Clare's Hosp., Schenectady, 1968—; cons. surgeon VA Hosp., Albany, Sunnyview Rehab. Hosp., Bellevue Maternity Hosp., Schenectady. Contbr. articles to med. jours., also chpts. to books. Fund raiser numerous local civic organs. and polit. causes. Capt. M.C., U.S. Army, 1965-67. USPHS grantee, 1963-65. Fellow ACS; mem. Soc. for Clin. Vascular Surgery (exec. com. 1978—, pres. 1981-82), Internat. Soc. for Cardiovascular Surgery, Ea. Vascular Soc. (founding), Upstate N.Y. Vascular Surg. Soc. (founding, pres. 1985-86), Am. Trauma Soc., Schenectady County Med. Soc., Vietnam Vascular Surg. Registry, Schuyler Meadows Club (Loudonville, N.Y.). Republican. Jewish. Home: 2259 Algonquin Rd Niskayuna NY 12309-4711 Office: 1201 Nott St Ste 202 Schenectady NY 12308

BLUMENFELD, SAMUEL, psychiatrist; b. Balt., Mar. 3, 1926; s. Max and Fanny (Yumkas) B.; m. Wilma Gruna Feinberg, Sept. 2, 1951; children: Sarah, Esther, Michael, Ruth. BA, U. Md., 1949, MD, 1953. Diplomate Am. Bd. Psychiatry. Intern and resident in internal medicine Sinai Hosp., Balt., Md., 1953-57; resident in psychiatry Sheppard & Enoch Pratt Hosp., Towson, Md., 1964-67, staff psychiatrist, 1967—; pvt. practice Balt., 1957-64; med. dir. No. Balt. Health Clinic, Cockeysville, Md., 1978—; dir. psychiat. edn. Greater Balt. Med. Ctr., Towson, 1968-81; psychiat. cons. Social Security Adminstrn., Woodlawn, Md., 1967—. Cpl. USAF, 1944-46. Mem. Am. Psychiatric Assn., Md. Chirurgical Soc. Office: Sheppard Pratt Hosp 6501 N Charles St Baltimore MD 21204-6819

BLUMENGOLD, JEFFREY GENE, health care financial and reimbursement expert; b. Bklyn., Dec. 25, 1950; s. Irving and Marjorie (Freeman) B.; BBA, Bernard M. Baruch Coll., CUNY, 1973, MBA, 1976; m. Vivienne Colletti, Oct. 15, 1972; children: Stacey, Craig. CPA, N.Y., N.J. Asst. mgr. royalty acctg. MacMillan Pub. Corp., N.Y.C., 1973-74; tchr. acctg. Port Richmond H.S., S.I., 1974-75; dir.-provider audit dept. Empire Blue Cross and Blue Shield, N.Y.C., 1976-77, 78-88; acct. Pannell, Kerr, Foster & Co., N.Y.C., 1977-78; dir. of fin. Cath. Med. Ctr. Bklyn. and Queens, Inc., 1988-91; ptnr. in charge of health care svcs. M.R. Weiser & Co. LLP, Certified Pub. Accountants and Cons., 1991—; vice chmn. bd. Ctr. for Home Health Devel.; adj. prof. acctg. Coll. S.I., CUNY, N.Y. Inst. Tech. Served with Mil. Police, USAR, 1972—. Mem. AICPA, Inst. Mgmt. Accountants, Hosp. Fin. Mgmt. Assn., Nat. Assn. Home Care-Fin. Mgrs. Forum (vice chmn. Ctr. for Home Health Devel.), N.Y. State Soc. CPA's (former chmn. health care instns. com.), Am. Acctg. Assn.

BLUMENKRANZ, MARK SCOTT, surgeon, researcher, educator; b. N.Y.C., Oct. 23, 1950; s. Edward and Helene (Cymberg) B.; m. Recia Kott, June 10, 1975. AB, Brown U., 1972, MD, 1975, MMS, 1976; postgrad., Stanford U., 1975-79, U. Miami, 1979-80. Intern, resident Stanford (Calif.) U. Med. Ctr., 1975-79; fellow Bascom Palmer Eye Inst. U. Miami, Fla., 1979-80; asst. prof. Bascom Palmer Eye Inst., Miami, 1980-85; assoc. prof. Wayne State U., Detroit, 1985-92; clin. prof. Stanford U., 1992—, dir. of retina, 1992—, dir. clin. programs, chief ophthalmology Stanford Health Svcs.; chmn. sci. adv. bd. Escalon Ophthalmics, 1990—; assoc. examiner Am. Bd. Ophthalmology; bd. dirs. OIS, Midlabs. Mem. editl. bd. Ophthalmology, Retina, Vitreoretinal Tech., Graefes Archives; contbr. chpts. to books and articles to profl. jours.; inventor ophthalmic devices. Mem. bd. overseers Brown U. Sch. Medicine. Recipient Visual Scis. medal in Visual Scis. Rosenthal Found., 1990, Heed award Heed Found., 1988, Manpower award Rsch. to Prevent Blindness. Mem. Am. Acad. Ophthalmology (mem. preferred practice com., others), Macula Soc. (chmn. rsch. com. 1986-90), Assn. Rsch. in Vision and Ophthalmology (chmn. retina sect. 1987-90), Retina Soc. (mem. membership com.), Maimonodes Soc. (mem. exec. com.). Office: Dept Ophthalmology Boswell A-157 Stanford CA 94305 Also: 1225 Crane St Menlo Park CA 94025

BLUMENTHAL, BRUCE, psychologist; b. Phila., June 11, 1952; s. Albert and Annette (Fink) B.; m. Eileen Saundra Lokyitch, June 9, 1974; children: Kim H., Alana J. BA in Psychology, Temple U., 1974; MS in Clin. Psychology, Hahnemann Med. Coll., 1976. Lic. psychologist, Pa. Rehab. counselor Gloucester County Jail, Woodbury, N.J., 1976-77; clin. coord. outpatient satellite Eagleville Hosp., Abington, Pa., 1977-81; sr. psychologist outreach drug and alcohol program Thomas Jefferson Univ. Hosp., Phila., 1981-86; psychotherapist Family and Community Svcs., Burlington, N.J., 1986—; staff clin. psychologist Trenton (N.J.) State Prison, 1986-87; sr. clin. psychologist N.J. Dept. Corrections, Trenton, 1987-96; acting dir. psychol. svcs. N.J. Dept. Corrections, 1991, quality assurance coord., 1996—; group psychotherapist Alcoholism/Addictions Program, Burlington, N.J., 1991—; cert. instr. N.J. Police Tng. Commn., 1992—; regional trainer for Project HOPE, 1993; surveyor Nat. Commn. on Correctional Health Care. Mem. Psi Chi (life). Democrat. Office: NJ Dept Corrections Stuyvesant Ave & Whittlesey Rd Trenton NJ 08625

BLUMENTHAL, GARY, federal commissioner. BA in Edn. and Social Studies, U. Kans., 1976; MA in Ednl. Adminstrn., U. Mo., Kansas City, 1992. Tchr. social studies Shawnee Mission Pub. Schs., Kans., 1976-87; dir. devel. Jewish Family and Children's Svcs., 1987-89; dir. managed care Charter Psychiatric Hosp., 1989-91; coord. Am. with Disabilities Act Human Resources Dept. Shawnee Mission Sch. Dist., Kans., 1991-92; tchr. Am. govt., coord. at risk svcs. Shawnee Mission North H.S., Kans., 1992-93; mem. dist. 23 Kans. Ho. of Reps., 1983-93; exec. dir., policy advisor to pres., policy advisor to asst. sec. for children and families, policy advisor to sec. for health and human svcs. Pres.'s Com. on Mental Retardation; chairperson Nat. Conf. State Legislatures Task Force on Devel. Disabilities. City councilman, precinct committeeman; del. Democratic Nat. Conv., 1976, 88, 92, alternate del. 1972; mem. B'Nai Brith Internat. Delegation, Germany, 1993; chair Nat. Conf. State Legislatures Task Force on Devel. Disabilities, mem. drafting com. report on devel. disabilities: policy directions for states, mem planning com., 1991, mem. U.S. delegation, Germany, 1993; nat. conf. state legislatures rep. Ctr. State Svcs. and Policy for Vulnerable Populations; mem. adv. panel Ctr. for Spl. Edn. Fin.; mem. B'Nai B'rith Internat. Delegation, Germany, 1993. Office: USDA 14th Independence Ave SW Washington DC 20500*

BLUMENTHAL, HERMAN THEODORE, physician, educator; b. N.Y.C., Apr. 8, 1913; s. Samuel and Jennie (Price) B.; m. Eleonore Gottlieb, Aug. 18, 1940 (dec. 1972); children: Daniels S., Frederic A.; m. Margaret B. Phillips, May 29, 1974; children: Edward P., Shana P. B.S., Rutgers U., 1934; M.S., U. Pa., 1936; Ph.D., Washington U., St. Louis, 1938, M.D., 1942. Resident in pathology Jewish Hosp., St. Louis, 1942-43; dir. labs of various hosps., 1945-65; asso. prof. pathology St. Louis U., 1947-52, adj. prof. community medicine, 1975—; mem. faculty Washington U., 1965—, research prof. gerontology, 1965—; dir. Midwest Med. Lab., 1965-82. Author: (with J.G. Probstein) Pancreatitis—A Clinical-Pathological Correlation, 1954; Editor: Cowdry's Arteriosclerosis—A Survey of the Problem, 2d edit, 1967, Medical Aspects of Gerontology, 1962, Interdisciplinary Topics in Gerontology, Vols. 1-8, 1968-71, Handbook of Diseases of Aging, 1981, Dilman's Elevational Hypothalmic Mechanisms in Aging and Disease, 1981; Contbr. articles on aging, transplanation, endocrinology, cancer, pathology to profl. jours.; editor Handbook of Diseases of Aging, 1983. Served to maj. M.C. AUS, 1942-45. Mem. Soc. Exptl. Biology and Medicine, Am. Heart Assn., Am. Diabetes Assn., Am. Assn. Cancer Research, Soc. Pathologists and Bacteriologists, Am. Soc. Exptl. Pathology, Gerontol. Soc., AAUP, Sigma Xi. Home: 6203 Washington Ave Saint Louis MO 63130-4847

BLUMENTHAL, SUSAN JANE, physician; b. N.Y.C., June 29, 1952; d. Stanley Robert and Eloyse Shirlee (Levine) B.; m. Edward John Markey, June 26, 1988. BA, Reed Coll., 1971; MD, U. Tenn., 1976; MPA, Harvard U., 1982; D (hon.), Trinity Coll., 1996. Diplomate Am. Bd. Psychiatry and Neurology. Intern. Stanford U. Sch. of Medicine, 1976-77, residency and fellowship, 1977-80; fellow NIMH, 1980-81, assoc. dir. Psychiatry Tng. Rev., head suicide rsch. unit and coord. of project depression, 1982-85, chief behavioral medicine program, 1985-93; clin. asst. prof. Tufts Med. Ctr., 1981-82; clin. asst. prof. psychiatry George Washington Sch. Medicine, 1982-86; clin. assoc. prof. psychiatry Georgetown Sch. Med., 1986-91; clin. prof. psychiatry Georgetown Sch. Medicine, Washington, 1991—; chief behavioral medicine Rsch. Br., NIMH, 1993-94; clin. prof. psychiatry Tufts Sch. Med., 1995—; chair NIH Coordinating Com. on Health and Behavior, 1991-94; co-chair NIH Reunion Task Force, 1992-94; dep. asst. sec. health, asst. surgeon gen. HHS, 1994—, chair fed. coordinating com. breast cancer, fed. coordinating com. women's health and the environ., co-chair nat. breast cancer action plan, coordinating com. women's health issues U.S. Public Health Svc.; mem. Pres.'s Interagy. Coun. on Women. Editor: Suicide Over the Life Cycle, 1989, Premenstrual Syndrome, 1985; mem. editl. bds. Jour. Women's Health, Depression; health columnist Elle Mag.; contbr. articles to sci. jours. Mem. Nat. Commn. on Sleep Disorders Rsch., workgroup on mental health Pres. Task Force on Health Care Reform, global commn. on Women's Health WHO. Capt. USPHS, 1992-94, rear adm., 1994—. Decorated Outstanding Svc. medal, Commendation medal, Meritorious Svc. medal USPHS. Mem. AMA, Nat. Women's Health Resource Ctr. (bd. dirs.), Am. Psychiat. Assn. (cons. Joint Coun. on Pub. Affairs), Am. Coll. Psychiatrists, Group for Advancement of Psychiatry, Am. Med. Women's Assn. (past chair com. on publicity and pub. rels., Pres.'s citation, 1996), Congl. Club, Internat. Club, Soc. Advancement Women's Health Rsch. (bd. dirs., v.p., scientific dir.), Am. Suicide Found. (bd. dirs. Washington divsn., pres.), Starlight Found. (chmn. sci. adv. bd.). Office: HHS Rm 712 E 200 Independence Ave SW Washington DC 20201-0004

BLUMTHAL, ROBERT JAMES, optometrist; b. Oak Park, Ill., June 16, 1950; s. Walter John and Rosemary Norine (O'Keefe) B.; m. Debra Louise Rhodes, Mar. 5, 1983; children by previous marriage: Matthew, Monica, Marc; 1 child by present marriage, Christina. BA, Loyola U., Chgo., 1972; BS cum laude, Northeastern Ill. U., Chgo., 1976; OD, Ill. Coll. Optometry, Chgo., 1981. Lic. optometrist, Ill. Optometrist Chittick Optometric Ctr., Paris, Ill., 1981-85, Bard Optical, Peoria, Ill., 1985-87; OD Dr. R.J. Blumthal & Assocs., Peoria, 1987-94; optometrist A. William G. Schubert, MD, Ltd., Charleston, Ill., 1994—. Vol. optometrist Heartland Clinic, Peoria, 1992-94; mem. Paris Union Sch. Dist. #95 Sch. Bd., 1983-85. Recipient Disting. Svc. award Paris Sch. Dist. #95, 1985. Mem. Am. Optometric Assn., Ill. Optometric Assn., Ea. Ill. Optometric Soc., Ill. Valley Optometric Soc. (sec. 1993-94), Charleston C. of C., Kiwanis, Gold Key. Roman Catholic. Home: 2005 S 92th St # E Charleston IL 61920 Office: A William G Schubert MD Ltd 1605 Reynolds Dr Charleston IL 61920

BLUTT, MITCHELL JONATHAN, physician; b. Windsor, Conn., Mar. 4, 1957; s. Herbert and Rose (Deckel) B. BA, U. Pa., 1978, MD, 1982, MBA, 1987. Diplomate Am. Bd. Internal Medicine. Intern, then resident N.Y. Hosp., Cornell Med. Ctr., N.Y.C., 1982-85; fellow clin. scholars program Robert Wood Johnson Program U. Pa., Phila., 1985-87; assoc. Chem. Venture Ptnrs. (now Chase Capital Ptnrs.), N.Y.C., 1987-88; v.p., gen. ptnr. Chem. Venture Ptnrs., N.Y.C., 1988-91, exec. ptnr., 1991—; adj. asst. prof. medicine N.Y. Hosp. Cornell Med. Ctr., 1987—. Contbr. articles to profl. jours. Recipient Kaiser Health Care award Kaiser Found., U. Pa., 1987, George Kirkham award Cornell Med. Coll., 1985. Fellow N.Y. Acad. Medicine; mem. AMA, ACP, Am. Acad. Med. Dirs., Soc. Gen. Internal Medicine, Sphinx Soc., Phi Beta Kappa, Beta Gamma Sigma.

BLYTHE, BRUCE KEITH, internist; b. Paris, Ill., June 5, 1958; s. Marion Keith and Marjorie Mae (Delap) B.; m. Kathryn Rose Schricker, Feb. 11, 1989; children: Garrett Keith, Andrew William. Student, Greenville Coll., 1976-78; BS magna cum laude, U. Ill., 1980; MD, U. Ill. Chgo., 1984. Diplomate Am. Bd. Internal Medicine, Geriatric Medicine. Resident Ind. U. Med. Ctr., Indpls., 1984-87; ptnr. Aspen Med. Group, Bloomington, Minn., 1987—. Mem. ACP, Christian Med. and Dental Soc., Minn. Physicians United for Life. Office: Aspen Med Group 7920 Cedar Ave S Bloomington MN 55425

BOAKE, CORWIN, III, psychologist, educator; b. Ft. Knox, Ky., Dec. 12, 1953; s. Corwin Jr. and Evelyn (Valldejuly) B.; m. Claudia Marie Harshner, Oct. 23, 1982; children: Caitlin Marie, Samuel James. BS, Pa. State U., 1975; MA, U. Louisville, 1980, PhD, 1982. Lic. psychologist, Tex.; diplomate Am. Bd. Clin. Neuropsychology, Am. Bd. Profl. Psychology. Neuropsychologist VA Med. Ctr., N.Y.C., 1984-85; treatment team coord. Transitional Learning Community, Galveston, Tex., 1985-87; clin. dir. behavioral medicine Dallas Rehab. Inst., 1988-89; clin. dir. challenge program Inst. for Rehab. and Rsch., Houston, 1989-90, dir. neuropsychology, 1990; neuropsychologist TIRR, Houston, 1991—; asst. prof. dept. phys. medicine and rehab. U. Tex.-Houston Med. Sch., 1995—. Author: (with others) Cognitive Rehabilitation for Persons with Traumatic Brain Injury, 1991; contbr. articles to profl. jours. Bd. dirs. Tex. Head Injury Assn., Austin, 1988-94, Brain Injury Assn. Tex., Austin, 1995—. Mem. APA, Soc. for Cognitive Rehab. (bd. dirs. 1989-90, adv. bd. 1993—), Internat. Neuropsychol. Soc., Houston Neuropsychol. Soc. (sec. 1992, pres. 1993). Home: 3519 Woodbine Pl Pearland TX 77584-4811 Office: TIRR 1333 Moursund St Houston TX 77030-3405

BOAL, BERNARD HARVEY, cardiologist, educator, author; b. Winnipeg, Man., Can., May 14, 1937; s. Charles and Bessie (Carr) B.; came to U.S., 1964; BS in Medicine, U. Man., 1962, MD, 1962; m. Pamela Sures Brownstone, Oct. 28, 1962; children: Steven, Jeremy, Hilary. Intern, Winnipeg Gen. Hosp., 1962-63, resident in medicine, 1963-64; resident in medicine U. Utah Hosps., Salt Lake City, 1964-66; USPHS trainee in cardiology NYU Med. Ctr., N.Y.C., 1966-68; practice medicine specializing in cardiology, Queens, N.Y., 1969—; chief sect. cardiology Booth Meml. Med. Ctr., 1969-87; chief cardiology Cath. Med. Ctr. of Bklyn. and Queens, N.Y., 1987—; cons. L.I. Jewish Hosp.; mem. staff NYU Hosp., Bellevue Hosp., 1968-81; instr. clin. medicine Sch. Medicine, NYU, 1968-81; clin. assoc. prof. medicine N.Y. Med. Coll., 1981-89; clin. assoc. prof. medicine Cornell U. Med. Coll., 1989-95; assoc. prof. medicine Albert Einstein Coll. Medicine, 1995—; lectr. Worldwide on cardiac pacing. Chmn. physicians divsn. Queens County Cabinet United Jewish Appeals of Greater N.Y., 1978-80; charter mem., founding treas. B'nai B'rith UN unit, 1984—; U.S. physician rep. pacemaker working group of the Internat. Standards Orgn., Geneva, 1988—, chmn., 1990—. Capt., M.C., USAR, 1970-73. Licenciate Med. Coun. Can.; diplomate Nat. Bd. Med. Examiners, Am. Bd. Internal Medicine in medicine and cardiology. Fellow N.Y. Cardiol. Soc., Am. Coll. Cardiology (chmn. med. devices com. Heart House campaign 1976-78, chmn. bequests and endowments com. 1980-85, pacemaker com. 1987-95, trustee 1985-90, mem. electrocardiology com. 1995—, mem. budget/fin./investment com. 1996—), ACP (treas. Queens chpt. 1976-78, sec. 1978-79, v.p. 1979-81, pres. 1981-85; govs. adv. coun. N.Y. State 1982-85); mem. AMA, Assn. Advancement of Med. Instrumentation (pacemaker com. 1976—, chmn. of pacemaker com. 1988—, bd. dirs. 1983-86, co-chmn. strategic planning com. 1983-85), Am. Heart Assn. (fellow coun. clin. cardiology), N.Y. Heart Assn., Am. Soc. Internal Medicine, Queens Soc. Internal Medicine, N.Am. Soc. Pacing and Electrophysiology (founding mem., mem. nat. adv. coun. 1984-85, mem. exec. com. 1985-88, chmn. fin. com. 1985-88, trustee 1987-91), U.S. divsn. Israeli Med. Assn. (founding mem.). Guest editor several major cardiology jours.; asst. editor: HeartNet; contbr. chpts. to books, articles to med. jours. Co-inventor Kolker-Boal Cardiac Pacemaker Electrode. Office: Cath Med Ctr Bklyn and Queens Jamaica NY 11432

BOAL, MARCIA ANNE RILEY, clinical social worker, administrator; b. Carthage, Mo., Sept. 29, 1944; d. William Joseph and Thelma P. (Simpson) Riley; m. David W. Boal, Aug. 12, 1967; children: Adam J. W., Aaron D. Boal. BA, U. Kans., 1966, MSW, 1981. Lic. clin. social worker. Child therapist Gillis Home for Children, Kansas City, Mo., 1981; social worker Leavenworth (Kans.) County Spl. Edn. Cooperative, 1981-84; sch. social worker, dir. health and social svcs. Kans. State Sch. for the Blind, Kansas City, Kans., 1984—; pvt. practice adoption counseling and workshops, 1981—; field instr. Sch. of Social Welfare, Kans. U., 1986—. Author: Surviving Kids, 1983, Teaching Social Skills to Blind and Visually Impaired Children, 1987. Nat. networking chmn. Jr. League Kansas City, 1977-81; bd. dirs. Wyandotte House Ind, 1973-81, Kans. Action For Children, Topeka, 1981, Gov.'s Commn. on Parent Edn., Topeka, 1984—, Lake of the Forest, 1994— (sec.). Named Kans. Sch. Social Worker of Yr., 1989. Mem. Council Exceptional Children, Nat. Assn. Social Workers, Kans. Assn. Sch. Social Workers, Am. Orthopsychiat. Assn., Kans. Conf. Social Welfare, R.P. Found., Phi Kappa Phi. Home: Lake Of The Forest Bonner Springs KS 66012 Office: Kans St Sch for Blind 1100 State Ave Kansas City KS 66102-4411

BOARDMAN, GREGORY DALE, environmental engineer, educator; b. Montpelier, Vt., Dec. 12, 1950; s. Theodore Robert and June Irene (Rogers) B.; m. Gail Cynthia Bedell, June 6, 1970 (div. Dec. 1986); children: Heather Eve, Kristina Marie, Jessica Anne; m. Shelley Ann Mitchell, Aug. 28, 1987; 1 child, Courtney Dale. MS, U. N.H., 1973; PhD, U. Maine, 1976. Registered profl. engr., Va. Asst. prof. civil engring. Va. Poly. Inst. and State U., Blacksburg, 1976-83, assoc. prof., 1983—; mem. bd. Dept. Commerce, Richmond, Va., 1987-94; cons. to numerous cos., 1976—. Author 2 manuals; contbr. numerous articles to profl. jours., chpts. to books. Chmn. Montgomery County Cmty. Shelter, Va., 1986-91, chmn. of program, 1990-91; mem. planning commn. Town of Blackburg, 1989-93. Rsch. grantee EPA, NIH, NOAA, Water Rsch., numerous others, 1976—. Mem. ASCE (coms.), Soc. Environ. Toxicology and Chemistry, Water Environ. Fedn., Internat. Assn. on Water Quality, Assn. Environ. Engring. Profs., Am. Assn. Textile Chemists and Colorists, Sigma Xi, Tau Beta Pi, Phi Kappa Phi. Office: Va Poly Inst and State U Dept Civil Engring 322 Norris Hall Blacksburg VA 24061

BOAS, NORMAN FRANCIS, consulting physician; b. N.Y.C., Aug. 4, 1922; s. Ernst Philip and Helen Boas; m. Doris Whitehead, Mar. 14, 1945; children: Deborah Howarth, Stephen, Barbara Johnson. Student, U. Wis., 1939-42; MD, Harvard U., 1945. Intern, then resident Michael Reese Hosp., Chgo., 1945-47; fellow Mt. Sinai Hosp., N.Y.C., 1947-51; investigator NIH, Bethesda, Md., 1951-55; sr. attending physician Norwalk (Conn.) Hosp., 1955-76; cons. Lawrence & Meml. Hosps., New London, Conn., 1976-85, ret., 1985; pres. Conn. chpt. Arthritis Found., Hartford; asst. clin. prof. Yale U. Sch. of Medicine, New Haven, 1975-80. Co-author books. Pres. Stonington Hist. Soc. Sr. surgeon USPHS, 1951-91. Fellow Manuscript Soc. (v.p. 1989-91). Home and Office: 6 Brandon Ln Mystic CT 06355-3103

BOAT, THOMAS FREDERICK, physician, educator, researcher; b. Pella, Iowa, Sept. 7, 1939; s. Bert Reuben and Anne Marie (Schoenbohm) B.; m. Barbara Mary Walling, June. 9, 1962; children: Sarah Elizabeth, Mary Barbara, Anne Christine. BA, Cen. Coll., Pella, 1961; MS, U. Iowa, 1965, MD, 1966. Diplomate Am. Bd. Pediatrics, Am. Bd. Pediatric Pulmonology. Pediatric resident U. Minn., Mpls., 1966-68; clin. assoc. NIH, Bethesda, Md., 1968-70; fellow in pediatric pulmonology Case Western Res. U., Cleve., 1970-72, instr. pediatrics, 1972-73, asst. prof. pediatrics, 1973-76, assoc. prof. pediatrics, 1976-81, prof. pediatrics, 1981-82; prof., chmn. dept. pediatrics U. N.C., Chapel Hill, 1982-93; chmn. dept. pediatrics U. Cin. Sch. Medicine, 1993—; dir. Cin. Children's Hosp. Rsch. Found., 1993—; prin. investigator Pediatric Pulmonary Specialized Ctr. Rsch., NIH, 1991-93; chmn. Am. Bd. Pediatrics, 1994. Editor Current Opinions in Pediatrics, 1990-93; mem. editorial bd. Lung Rsch. jour. Bd. dirs. Ronald McDonald House, Chapel Hill, 1985-88, Cystic Fibrosis Found., chmn. rsch. devel. program, 1983—; chmn. Am. Bd. Pediats., 1994. Lt. comdr. USPHS, 1968-70. Fellow Am. Acad. Pediatrics; mem. Am. Pediatric Soc. (coun.), Am. Thoracic Soc. (chmn. pediatric assembly 1983-84), Am. Soc. Pediatric Dept. Chairmen (pres.-elect 1994-95). Office: Children's Hosp Med Ctr 3333 Burnet Ave # 3301 Cincinnati OH 45229-3026

BOBRIN, YALE ROBERT, psychiatrist; b. Phila., Apr. 1, 1935; s. George Martin and Estelle (Lambert) B.; m. Barbara Ann Kahn (div. 1972); children: Elyse Lynn, Cindy Beth, Rona Ellen, Lori Elaine, Edward Matthew; m. Marlyn Waxler, 1975; one child, Joshua David. BA, Temple U., 1956; DO, Pa. Coll. Osteo. Medicine, 1961. Diplomate Am. Bd. Psychiatry and Neurology. Intern Del. Valley Hosp., Bristol, Pa., 1961-62; physician pvt. gen. practice, Phila., 1962-72; psychiatry resident Hahnemann Med. Coll., Phila., 1972-75; adult psychiatrist Friends Hosp., Phila., 1975—; dir. alcohol recovery program Frineds Hosp., Phila., 1980—; cons. in field; med. dir. alcohol recovery program Friends Hosp.; cons. M.C.P. Elkins Park, Jeans Hosp. Mem. Am. Med. Soc. on Addictions, Friends Hosp. Med. Staff, Am. Psychiat. Assn., Pa. Psychiat. Assn., Phila. County Psychiatric Soc., Bnai Brith Lodge. Democrat. Jewish. Home: 1567 Buck Hill Dr Huntingdon Valley PA 19006-7909 Office: Friends Hosp Roosevelt Boulevard Ave Philadelphia PA 19124

BOBRUFF, JEROME, physician; b. Hartford, Conn., June 18, 1930; s. Nathan and Mildred (Dobin) B.; m. Bernice S. Gendron, July 22, 1990; m. Carole Marks, June 20, 1954 (div. 1986); children: Ellen, Neal, Paul, Mark; stepchildren: Jeffrey Reynolds, Michael Reynolds. BA, Wesleyan U., 1952; MD, Yale U., 1955. Diplomate Am. Bd. Internal Medicine. Instr. Seton Hall Coll. Medicine, Jersey City, N.J., 1961-62; physician Lawrence Meml. Hosp., New London, Conn., 1962-95, chief gastroenterology, 1975-80; pres. Digestive Disease Assocs., New London, 1969-95; med. dir. MD Health Plan, New Haven, 1995—; bd. dirs. Colonial IPA, New London. Contbr. articles to profl. jours. Mem. Gov.'s Commn. on Reading, Conn., 1968, Charter Rev. Com., New London, 1970, Zoning Bd. Appeals, New London, 1986-91. Capt. USAF, 1957-59. Fellow Am. Soc. Gastrointestinal Endoscopy; mem. AMA (ho. of dels. 1989—), Conn. Med. Soc. (councillor 1979-88), New London County Med. Assn. (pres. 1979-80), Thames Club, Stonington County Club, Lions, Phi Beta Kappa. Democrat. Jewish. Home: 765 Pequot Ave New London CT 06320-4214 Office: Digestive Disease Assocs 268 Montauk Ave New London CT 06320-4712

BOC, STEVEN FRANCIS, podiatric surgeon, medical educator; b. Phila., Aug. 19, 1956; s. Stanley Frank and Genevieve Theresa (Szymanski) B.; m. Sara Gamble, Dec. 4, 1982; children: Steven Christopher, Allison Rebecca. BS in Biology, Albright Coll., 1978; DPM, Pa. Coll. Podiatric Medicine, Phila., 1983. Diplomate Am. Bd. Podiatric Surgery. Resident in surgery Met. Hosp., Phila., 1983-85; pvt. practice Phila., 1985-88; asst. prof. dept. surgery Pa. Coll. Podiatric Surgery, 1988—; pres. Phila. County Podiatric Med. Assocs., Phila., 1993-95; exec. bd. mem. Pa. Podiatric Med. Assn., Camp Hill, 1994—; chmn. divsn. podiatric surgery St. Agnes Med. Ctr., Phila., 1995—, dir. podiatric surgery residency tng., 1995—. Contbr. articles to profl. jours. Fellow Am. Coll. Foot and Ankle Surgeons; mem. Am Coll. Podiatric Sports Medicine (assoc.), Am. Coll. Podiatric Radiologists, Stirling Horford Hon. Anatomical Soc. Republican. Roman Catholic. Home: 1 Signal Hill Rd Cherry Hill NJ 08003 Office: Pa Coll Podiat Medicine Dept Surgery 8th and Race Sts Philadelphia PA 19107

BOCCIA, MARIA LIBORIA, psychobiologist; b. Bronx, Dec. 5, 1953; d. Silvio Mario and Emily (Russo) B. BA, SUNY, Geneseo, 1974; MS, U. Mass., 1979, PhD, 1981. Rsch. asst. dept. psychology U. Mass., Amherst, 1976-81; teaching asst. dept. zoology U. Mass., 1976-79, teaching assoc., 1979-81; postdoctoral fellow U. Denver, 1981-83; asst. prof. Okla. Bapt. U., Shawnee, 1983-86; rsch. assoc. psychiatry U. Colo. Health Scis. Ctr., Denver, 1986; asst. prof. psychiatry U. Colo. Health Scis. Ctr., 1986-93; assoc. prof. psychology U. N.C., Chapel Hill, 1993—, dir. observational methods core, 1993—; mem. spl. study sect. NIMH, Washington, 1988-89; outside reviewer NSF, 1988-90; reviewer various profl. jours. Editor Jour. Bibl. Equality, 1989-93; contbr. articles to profl. jours. Bd. dirs. Front Range Christians for Bibl. Equality, Denver, 1989-93. SUNY Regents scholar, 1971-74. Mem. AAAS, Am. Psychol. Assn., Animal Behavior Soc., Am. Soc. Primatologists (prog. com. 1986-90, R&D com. 1990—), Developmental Psychobiology Rsch. Group (exec. com. 1989-93). Office: U NC Frank Porter Graham Child Devel Ctr CB 8180 105 Smith Level Rd Chapel Hill NC 27599-8180

BOCCON-GIBOD, LAURENT MARIE, urologist; b. Salon de Provence, France, Sept. 4, 1940; s. Bertrand and Marie Jeanne (Lermoyez) B.-G.; m. Lialiane Arlette Friedmann, Oct. 23, 1964; children: Edouard, Isabelle, Bertrand, Jean Christophe. MD, Faculty of Medicine, Paris, 1968. From asst. prof. to assoc. prof. Hop Cochin, Paris, 1969-83, prof., 1983-87; prof., chmn. Chu Bichat, Paris, 1988—. Mem. French Assn. Urology, Am. Urological Assn. Home: 48 Rue de Grenelle, 75007 Paris France Office: Chu Bichat, 46 Rue Huchard, 75018 Paris France

BOCIAN, FRANKLIN LESLIE, ophthalmologist; b. N.Y.C., Mar. 23, 1938; s. Meyer Joseph and Ann (Singer) B.; m. Phyllis Rosen, Nov. 27, 1968; children: David A., Michael J. AB, Princeton (N.J.) U., 1960; MD, SUNY, 1964. Diplomate Am. Bd. Ophthalmology. Pvt. practice Eye Specialists of Westchester, New Rochelle, N.Y., 1969—; dir. dept. ophthalmology New Rochelle (N.Y.) Hosp. Med. Ctr., 1990—. Chmn. health adv. com. Scarsdale Sch. Bd. Fellow ACS, Am. Acad. Opthalmology. Office: 140 Lockwood Ave New Rochelle NY 10801

BOCK, BROOKS F., surgeon; b. Orange, N.J., Sept. 19, 1943. MD, Wayne State U., 1969. Intern Detroit Gen. Hosp., 1969-70; resident in surgery Wayne State U., 1970-71, resident in urology, 1971-73; surgeon Detroit Regional Hosp., Mich.; prof., chmn. dpet. emergency medicine Wayne State U.; pvt. practice. Mem. AMA, ACEP, MSMS, PFSR, WOMS. *

BOCK, TRACY ANNE, nurse; b. Pomona, Calif., Nov. 29, 1962; d. Kenneth David and Sherry Lee (DeVito) Ayers; m. Robert Charles Bock, Apr. 12, 1986; children: Kevin Albert, Alex Robert, David Kenneth. AS, San Bernardino Valley Coll., 1985; BSN, Calif. State U., San Bernardino, 1992. RN, Calif. ICU RN San Bernardino County Med. Ctr., 1985-90, transplant coord., 1988-90; transplant coord. Loma Linda (Calif.) U. Med. Ctr., 1990—. Mem. Internat. Transplant Nurses Soc., N.Am. Transplant Coords. Assn. Office: Loma Linda U Med Ctr 11234 Anderson St Rm 1405 Loma Linda CA 92354

BOCKSERMAN, ROBERT JULIAN, chemist; b. St. Louis, Dec. 20, 1929; s. Max Louis and Bertha Anna (Kremen) B.; m. Clarice K. Kreisman, June 9, 1957; children: Michael Jay, Joyce Ellen, Carol Beth. BSc, U. Mo., 1952, MSc, 1955. Chemist Sealtest Corp., Peoria, Ill, 1955-56; prodn. mgr. Allan Drug Co., St. Louis, 1957-59; rsch. chemist Monsanto Co., St. Louis, 1960-65; purchasing agt. Monsanto Co., Sauget, Ill., 1966-67; founder, pres. Pharma-Tech Industries, Inc., Union, Mo., 1967-84; tech. dir. Overlock-Howe Consulting Group, St. Louis, 1984-85; founder, pres. Conatech Consulting Group, Chesterfield, Mo., 1985—; sec., mem. industry packaging adv. com. Sch. of Engring., U. Mo., Rolla, 1979—; adj. prof. dept. food sci./nutrition U. Mo., Columbia; adj. prof. dept. engring. mgmt. U. Mo., Rolla; vis. lectr. U. Mo., Clayton, Northwestern U., Evanston, Ill., and various programs. Tech. reviewer Jour. Inst. of Packaging Profls., Jour. Packaging Tech., Mo. Waste Control Scholarship Grants and Research, Medical Device and Diagnostic Industry Jour., Medical Plastics and Biomaterials Publication. (editorial adv. bd.). Mem. Mo. Waste Control Coalition; mem. stormwater engring. com. City of Creve Coeur, Mo. With U.S. Army, 1952-54, Korea. SBIR grantee. Mem. ASTM, Cons. Packaging Engring. Coun., Inst. Packaging Profls., Am. Technion Soc., Inst. Food Technologists Arrangements (St. Louis), Nat. Forensic Ctr., Teltech Resource Network. Am. Chem. Soc., Am. Plastics Coun., Mo. Acad. Scis., N.Y. Acad. Sci., Sigma Xi. Home: 54 Morwood Ln Creve Coeur MO 63141-7621 Office: Conatech Cons Group 287 N Lindbergh Blvd Creve Coeur MO 63141-7849

BOCKWITZ, CYNTHIA LEE, psychologist, psychology/women's studies educator; b. Hallock, Minn., Apr. 11, 1954; d. Rodney Lee and Jeanette Yvonne (Vilen) B. AA in Arts and Scis., Richland Coll., 1983; BA in Psychology, U. Tex., Dallas, 1985; MA in Counseling Psychology, Tex. Woman's U., 1992. Lic. profl. counselor, Ga. Pers. adminstr. Automatic Data Processing, Miami, Fla., 1974-77; office mgr. G.A. Dexter Co., Atlanta, 1977-79; human resources mgr. No. Telecom, Atlanta and Dallas, 1979-84; mental health worker Timberlawn Psychiat. Hosp., Dallas, 1984-85; acct. NEC Am., Dallas, 1986-87; asst. program dir. Arbor Creek Hosp., Sherman, Tex., 1989; lic. profl. counselor Trinity Counseling Ctr., Carrollton, Tex., 1989-93, Atlanta, 1993—; adj. instr. psychology Tex. Woman's U., Denton, 1988-92; instr. psychology DeKalb Coll., Atlanta, 1993—; cons. The Resource Ctr., Atlanta, 1993-94, Laurel Heights Hosp., 1994—; mem. exec. com. Women Clinicians Network, Atlanta, 1994, 95. Mem. NOW (fin. contbr.), APA (assoc.), Am. Assn. for Marriage and Family Therapy (assoc.), Assn. for Women in Psychology, Ga. Marriage and Family Therapy Assn. (legis. com. 1993-94), Assn. for Play Therapy, Ga. Assn. for Play Therapy, Nat. Assn. of Masters in Psychology, Phi Kappa Phi, Psi Chi. Democrat. Home: 711 Tuxworth Cir Decatur GA 30033-5620 Office: Laurel Heights Hosp 934 Briarcliff Rd NE Atlanta GA 30306-2618

BOCOBO, CHRISTIAN REYES, rehabilitation medicine educator; b. Manila, May 28, 1954; s. Israel de Castro and Teresita Paz (Reyes) B. BS, U. Philippines, Manila, 1975, MD, 1979. Diplomate Am. Bd. Phys. Medicine and Rehab., Fed. Licensure Exams. Philippine Med. Bds. Intern Makati Med. Ctr., Manila, 1979-80; resident in family practice U. Mass. Med. Ctr., Worcester, 1982-83; chief resident in phys. medicine and rehab. Nassau County Med. Ctr., SUNY, Stony Brook, 1983-85; clin. instr. phys. medicine and rehab. U. Medicine and Dentistry N.J.-N.J. Med. Sch., Newark, 1986-89, assoc. dir. residency tng. program, 1987-89; clin. instr. rehab. medicine Stanford Med. Sch., Palo Alto, Calif., 1989-91, clin. asst. prof., 1991—; dir. phys. medicine and rehab. Elizabeth (N.J.) Gen. Med. Ctr., 1986-89; cons. Kessler Inst. for Rehab., West Orange, N.J., 1986-89; dir. outpatient clinics Rehab. Medicine Svc., Palo Alto, 1990-92. Contbr. articles to med. jours. Physician Zonta Internat., Manila, 198l. Fellow Am. Acad. Phys. Medicine and Rehab.; mem. Calif. Med. Assn., San Mateo County Med. Assn. Office: 101 S San Mateo Dr Ste 302 San Mateo CA 94401-3843

BODDIE, LEWIS FRANKLIN, obstetrics and gynecology educator; b. Forsyth, Ga., Apr. 4, 1913; s. William F. and Luetta T. (Sams) B.; m. Marian Bernice Claytor, Dec. 27, 1941; children: Roberta Boddie Miles, Lewis Jr., Bernice B. Jackson, Pamela, Kenneth, Fredda, Margaret. BA, Morehouse Coll., 1933; MD, Meharry Med. Sch., 1938. Diplomate Am. Bd. Ob-Gyn (proctor parti exam Los Angeles area 1955-63). Intern Homer-Phillips Hosp., St. Louis, 1938-39, resident in ob-gyn, 1939-42; mem. attending staff Grace Hosp., Detroit, 1944-48, Parkside Hosp., Detroit, 1944-48, Los Angeles County Gen. Hosp., 1952-79; sr. mem. attending staff Queen of Angels Hosp., Los Angeles, 1964-91, chmn. dept. ob-gyn, 1968-70; asst. clin. prof. U. So. Calif. Sch. Medicine, L.A., 1953-79, prof. emeritus, 1979—; assoc. clin. prof. U. Calif., Irvine, 1956-81; sec. Verndro Med. Corp., 1952-90. vice chmn. bd. mgrs. 28th St. YMCA, Los Angeles 1960-75; steward African Meth. Episc. Ch., Los Angeles, 1949—. Fellow ACS (life), Am. Coll. Ob-Gyn (life), Los Angeles Ob-Gyn Soc. (life): mem. Los Angeles United Way (priorities and allocations coms., 1985—, standards com. 1987—, new admission com. 1988—), Children's Home Soc. (bd. dirs. 1952-89, , trustee 1989—, v.p. 1963-68, pres. 1968-70), Child Welfare League Am. (bd. dirs. 1969-76). Republican.

BODE, ARTHUR PALFREY, pathology research scientist; b. Lima, Ohio, Oct. 12, 1953; s. Paul George and Marjorie Louise (Wellman) B.; children: Christopher, Scott, Joshua; m. Rhonda Kay Davenport, Feb. 28, 1993. BA, U. N.C., 1975, PhD, 1982. Postdoctoral fellow dept. pathology U. N.C., Chapel Hill, 1982-84, rsch. asst. prof. dept. pathology, 1984-86; asst. prof. dept. clin. pathology East Carolina U., Greenville, N.C., 1986-91, assoc. prof. dept. pathology and lab. medicine, 1991—; sci. dir. coagulation lab. Pitt County Meml. Hosp., Greenville, 1986—; lab. dir. platelet storage rsch. East Carolina U., Greenville, 1986—; acting co-dir. flow cytometry lab. Pitt County Meml. Hosp., Greenville, 1986-89; dir. ECU Core Facility in Flow Cytometry, 1992—; speaker on blood platelets at symposia, 1985—. Contbr. 30 articles and 40 abstracts to profl. jours. Judge Northeast Regional Sci. Fair, Elizabeth City, N.C., 1988; com. mem. Helms Rsch. award Sigma Xi Soc., Greenville, 1989—; cub scout asst. packmaster Boy Scouts Am.; asst. coach Little League. John Motley Morehead scholar Morehead Found., U. N.C., 1971; grantee N.C. affiliate Am. Heart Assn., 1988, Office of Naval Rsch., Bethesda, Md., 1989—, assoc. grantee U.S. Army Med. Rsch. Letterman Inst., San Francisco, 1986-88. Mem. AAAS, Am. Assn. Blood Bank, Am. Heart Assn. (coun. on thrombosis), Internat. Soc. Thrombosis and Hemostasis, Sigma Xi (pres. 1996). Republican. Office: Est Carolina U Sch Medicine Dept Pathology/Lab Medicine Diagnostic Medicine Greenville NC 27858

BODENHEIMER, HENRY CHARLES, JR., internal medicine and gastroenterology educator; b. Freeport, N.Y., Apr. 24, 1950; s. Henry Charles and Rosemary (Tierney) B.; m. Maureen Virginia Clarkin, June 23, 1973; children: Henry Charles III, Kevin Gerard, Alison Emily. AB, Holy Cross, 1971; MD, Tufts U., 1975; Ad eundem (hon.), Brown U., 1990. Cert. in internal medicine, gastroenterology. Intern medicine Mt. Sinai Med. Ctr., N.Y.C., 1975-76, resident in medicine, 1976-78, fellow liver disease, 1978-79; fellow in gastroenterology R.I. Hosp./Brown U., Providence, 1979-81; asst. prof. Brown U., Providence, 1981-90, assoc. prof., 1990-91; assoc. prof. medicine Mt. Sinai Sch. Medicine, N.Y.C., 1991-95, prof., 1995—; clin. dir. liver diseases Mt. Sinai Med. Ctr., N.Y.C., 1991—. Mem. editl. bd. Hepatology, 1990—, assoc. editor 1995—; sect. editor Bockus Gastroenterology, 1991; contbr. liver disease articles to profl. jours. Chmn. adv. com. Am. Liver Found., Providence, 1991. Fellow Am. Coll. Physicians; mem. Am. Assn. for Study of Liver Disease, Am. Gastroenterological Assn., Alpha Omega Alpha. Office: Mt Sinai Med Ctr #1039 1 Gustave L Levy Pl New York NY 10029-6504

BODEY, BELA, Hungarian-American immunomorphologist; b. Sofia, Bulgaria, Jan. 18, 1949; came to U.S., 1985, naturalized, 1994; s. Joseph and Rossitza (Derebeeva) B.; m. Victoria Psenko, Aug. 29, 1979; children: Bela Jr., Vivian. MD, Med. Acad., Sofia, 1973; PhD in Immuno-Biology, Inst. Morphology, Bulgarian Acad. Sci., Sofia, 1977. Lic. physician, exptl. pathologist, embryologist, immuno-morphologist, thymologist, exptl. oncologist. Asst. prof. Semmelweis Med. U., Budapest, 1977-80; prof. Inst. Hematology, Budapest, 1980-83; rsch. assoc. Tufts U., Boston, 1985; rsch. fellow immuno-pathology Mass. Gen. Hosp./Harvard U., Boston, 1986; rsch. fellow Childrens Hosp. L.A., 1987-90, rsch. scientist, 1991-92; asst. prof. rsch. pathology, Sch. of Medicine Univ. Southern Calif., 1992—; vis. prof. Alexander von Humboldt Found., Ulm, Fed. Republic Germany, 1984. Mem. Am. Assn. Cancer Rsch., Am. and Can. Acad. Pathology, French Soc. Cell Biology, French Soc. Electromicroscopy, Internat. Soc. Exptl. Hematology, Internat. Soc. Comparative Oncology, N.Y. Acad. Scis., Masons. Roman Catholic. Home: 15745 Saticoy St Van Nuys CA 91406-3155 Office: U So Calif Sch Medicine 2011 Zonal Ave Los Angeles CA 90033-1034

BODEY, GERALD PAUL, medical educator, physician; b. Hazelton, Pa., May 22, 1934; s. Allen Zartman and Marie Frances (Smith) B.; m. Nancy Louise Wiegner, Aug. 25, 1956; children: Robin Gayle Sparwasser, Gerald Paul Jr., Sharon Dawn Brantley. AB magna cum laude, Lafayette Coll., 1956; MD, Johns Hopkins U., 1960. Diplomate Nat. Bd. Med. Examiners; diplomate in internal medicine, med. oncology and infectious diseases Am. Bd. Internal Medicine. Intern Johns Hopkins U., Balt., 1960-61, resident, 1961-62; clin. assoc. Nat. Cancer Inst., Bethesda, Md., 1962-65; resident U. Wash., Seattle, 1965-66; internist, profl. U Tex. MDACC, Houston, 1975-95; prof. emeritus of medicine U. Tex.-M.D. Anderson Cancer Ctr., Houston, 1995—; chmn. dept. med. specialities U Tex. MDACC, Houston, 1987-95; emeritus prof. medicine U. Tex. MDACC, Houston, 1995—; chief sect. infectious diseases U Tex. MDACC, Houston, 1981-95, chief chemotherapy, 1975-83, med. dir. Cancer Clin. Rsch. Ctr., 1977-81; mem. lunar quartine ops. team Apollo 11-14, Manned Spacecraft Ctr., NASA. Contbr. more than 1000 articles to profl. jours. Dir. Korean Collaborative Program, 1985-95; past trustee Benevolence Found. Nat. AIDS Prevention Inst.; past bd. dirs. Christian Coalition Reconciliation. Recipient Am. Chem. Soc. prize, 1956, Merck award, 1956, Robert B. Youngman Greek prize, 1956, Eugene Yourassowsky award U. Libre de Bruxelles, Belgium, 1995; Henry Strong Denison fellow Johns Hopkins Sch. Medicine, Balt., 1958-60. Fellow ACP, Am. Coll. Chest Physicians, Am. Coll. Clin. Pharmacology, Royal Coll. Medicine, Royal Soc. Promotion Health; mem. AMA, AAAS, Am. Assn. Cancer Rsch., Am. Soc. Clin. Oncology, Am. Soc. Clin. Pharmacology and Therapeutics,, Tex. Med. Assn., Houston Acad. Medicine, Houston Soc. Internal Medicine, Academia Peruana de Cirugia (hon.), Mediterranean Med. Soc. (hon.), Phi Beta Kappa, Sigma Chi. Presbyterian. Office: U Tex MDACC 1515 Holcome Houston TX 77030

BODIN, JEROME I., pharmaceutical company executive, pharmaceutical chemist; b. N.Y.C., July 2, 1930; s. Sam and Martha (Warshofsky) B.; m. Jacqueline Sandra Kurlansky; children: Michelle Beth, Philip Louis. BS, Columbia U., 1952, MS, 1954; PhD, U. Wis., 1958. Cert. pharmacist, N.Y. Research analyst Pfizer, Inc., Bklyn., 1958-61; dir. Drug Standards Lab., Washington, 1962-63; chemist FDA, Washington, 1963-64; assoc. dir., pharmaceutical chemist Carter-Wallace, Inc., Cranbury, N.J., 1964—. Author: (with others) Pharmaceutical Analysis, 1961; contbr. articles to profl. jours. Trustee Citizens Organized for Med. Planning, Inc., East Windsor, N.J., 1971-74; chmn. East Windsor Bd. Health, 1972-74; mem. East Windsor Planning Bd., 1986, East Windsor Twp. Council, 1987. Fellow Am. Found. Pharm. Edn.; mem. Am. Chem. Soc., Am. Assn. Pharm. Scientists, Sigma Xi. Democrat. Jewish. Club: Democratic (East Windsor) (treas.). Lodge: Lions, B'nai B'rith. Home: 3 Wickham Ln Hightstown NJ 08520-1209 Office: Carter-Wallace Inc Half Acre Rd Cranbury NJ 08512

BODIS-WOLLNER, IVAN GYORGY, neurology and ophthalmology educator; b. Szeged, Hungary, Oct. 1, 1937; s. Lajos and Klara (Szabo) B.; children: Mara Julia, Stefanie Klara. MD, U. Vienna, Austria, 1965; DSc,

Hungarian Acad. Scis., 1994. Diplomate Am. Bd. Psychiatry and Neurology. Prof. neurology Mt. Sinai Sch. Medicine CUNY, 1982-92, prof. ophthalmology, 1982-92, mem. grad. sch. faculty, 1983-92; prof. neurology and ophthalmology U. Nebr. Med. Ctr., Omaha, 1992-93, SUNY Health Scis. Ctr., Bklyn., 1993—; adj. prof. SUNY Coll. Optometry. Editor: (books) Evoked Potentials, 1981, 87, Vision and the Brain, 1990, Dopaminergic Mechanisms in Vision, 1987; (jour.) Clin. Vision Scis., Vision Rsch., Clin. Neurosci. Recipient Humboldt prize, 1993; Thomas Chalmers fellow, 1985, Sr. Internat. Fogarty fellow, 1986-87. Fellow Am. Acad. Neurology, Am. EEG Soc., Am. Acad. Clin. Neurophysiology (past sec.), Ea. EEG Soc. (former pres.), Assn. Rsch. in Nervous and Mental Disorders (former sec.). Office: SUNY HSC/B Brooklyn NY 11203

BODMER, ROLF A., medical educator. MS in Natural Scis., U. Basel, Switzerland, 1980, PhD in Biochemistry and Neurobiology, 1983. Postdoctoral fellow Friedrich Miescher-Institut, Basel, 1983-84, Albert Einstein Coll. Medicine, Bronx, N.Y., 1984; rsch. assoc. Dept. Physiology and Biochemistry U. Calif., San Francisco, 1984-90; asst. prof. biology U. Mich., Ann Arbor, 1990—. Contbr. over 20 rsch. articles to profl. jours. Grantee NIH, Am. Heart Assn., Muscular Dystrophy Assn. Office: Dept Biology 830 N University Ann Arbor MI 48109-1048

BODNAR, LISA M., nurse practitioner; b. Buffalo, Oct. 22, 1959; d. Cyril S. and Theresa R. (Frydrych) B. BS in Psychology, Case Western Res. U., 1980; D Nursing, Frances Payne Bolton Sch. Nursing, Cleve., 1983; MS, U. Rochester, 1987. Cert. acute care nurse practitioner. Staff nurse SICU Allegheny Gen. Hosp., Pitts.; instr. nursing Stanley H. Kaplan Ednl. Ctr., Rochester, N.Y.; staff nurse SICU Rochester Gen. Hosp.; cardiothoracic clin. nurse specialist Cardiothoracic Group of Greater Rochester, 1988-92; cardiology nurse practitioner Buffalo Cardiology and Pulmonary Assocs., 1992-95; nurse practitioner, clin. coord. cardiothoracic surgery Buffalo Heart Surg. Assocs., 1995—; specialist in smoking cessation. Named one of Outstanding Young Women of Am., 1983; recipient Frances Payne Bolton Alumni award, Louise Wilson Haller award U. Rochester; N.Y. State Regents scholar.

BODNAR, PAUL ZOLTAN, pediatrician; b. N.Y.C., June 14, 1950; s. John and Edith (Schultz) B.; m. Sarah Anne Erwin, Jan. 18, 1975; children: Laura Elizabeth, Benjamin Erwin. BA, Johns Hopkins U., 1971; MD, Columbia U., 1975. Resident, teaching fellow Johns Hopkins Univ., Balt., 1975-80; academic fellow Sinai Hosp., Balt., 1978-80; pediatrician-in-chief Clinical Assoc., Balt., 1980—, med. dir., 1987—; com. mem. pediatrics dept. Sinai Hosp., Balt., 1985-90. Fellow Am. Acad. Pediatrics (chmn. Md. chpt. com. on pediatric ambulatory medicine 1992—, rsch. coord. 1988—, steering com. Pros Rsch. Group 1995—); mem. Alpha Omicron Alpha, Alpha Epsilon Delta. Democrat. Office: Clin Assocs 515 Fairmount Ave # 3401 Baltimore MD 21286-5466

BODZIN, JASON HOWARD, surgeon; b. Detroit, May 20, 1945; s. Harry Raymond and Dorothy (Zuckerbaum) B.; m. Pearlena N. Wilson, Aug. 9, 1966; children: Gordon, Beth. BS, Wayne State U., 1968, MD, 1970. Diplomate Am. Bd. Surgery. Intern Mt. Carmel Mercy Hosp., Detroit, 1970-71, resident, 1973-77, dir. surg. edn., 1977-91; dir. Inflammatory Bowel Disease Ctr. Sinai Hosp., Detroit, 1991—; pvt. practice Bingham Farms, Mich. Capt. USAF, 1971-73. Recipient Humanitarian award Nat. Found. for Ileitis and Colitis, 1987, Disting. (Physician) Leadership award Crohns and Colitis Found. of Am., 1995. Fellow ACS (sec. Mich. chpt. 1995-96); mem. AMA, Midwest Surg. Assn. (pres. Midwest region 1994-95), Detroit Surg. Assn. (pres. 1984-85), Detroit GI Soc. (pres. 1993-94). Jewish. Office: 31500 Telegraph Bingham Farms MI 48025

BODZINER, RICHARD ALLAN, physician; b. Savannah, Ga., Jan. 31, 1953; s. Lawrence S. and Dena (Yaschik) B.; m. Meredith Monsky, Dec. 20, 1975; children: Erica, Lisa. BA, Tulane U., 1975; MD, Med. Coll. Ga., 1979. Intern L.I. Jewish Hosp., New Hyde Park, N.Y., 1979-80; resident New Eng. Med. Ctr., Boston, 1980-83; fellow Columbia Presbyn. Med. Ctr., N.Y.C., 1983-84; physician Neurol. Inst. Savannah, 1984—. Pres. Savannah Jewish Fedn. Office: Neurol Inst Savannah 4 Jackson Blvd Savannah GA 31405

BOE, GERARD PATRICK, health science association administrator; b. Washington, Jan. 20, 1936; s. Harold David and Bernice Virginia (Lemon) B.; m. Irene Margaret Dazevedo, Oct. 24, 1959 (div. Jan. 1988); children: Steven Alan, Christine Ann; m. Charlotte Greene Hudson, Dec. 30, 1989. BS in Biology, W.Va. Wesleyan Coll., 1958; MS in Clin. Pathology, Ohio State U., 1969; PhD in Edn. and Mgmt., Tex. A&M U., 1976. Commd. 2d lt. U.S. Army, 1963, advanced through grades to lt. col.; health care adminstr., 1963-81, ret., 1981; adminstrv. dir. Ga. Radiation Therapy Ctr., Augusta, 1981-83; pres. Profl. Mgmt. Cons., Augusta, 1983-89; exec. dir. Am. Med. Technologists, Park Ridge, Ill., 1989—; faculty Webster U., So. Ill. U., 1980—. Contbr. articles to profl. jours. Recipient cert. of appreciation ARC, 1976, Pres.' award Augusta chpt. Internat. Mgmt. Coun., 1989. Mem. Soc. Armed Forces Med. Lab. Scientists (Pres.' award 1982), Nat. Clearing House for Licensure, Enforcement and Regulation, Clin. Lab. Mgmt. Assn., Inst. Cert. Profl. Mgrs. (cert., bd. regents 1990—), Am. Soc. Clin. Pathologist (cert.). Republican. Methodist. Office: Am Med Technologists 710 Higgins Rd Park Ridge IL 60068-5737

BOEDECKER, ANNE LOUISE, psychologist, business owner; b. Poughkeepsie, N.Y., Jan. 20, 1951; d. Ray F. and Elizabeth (Hutchinson) B.; m. Terrence P. Kimper, Aug. 19, 1979; 1 child, Wendy. Student, Dartmouth Coll., 1971-72; BA, Vassar Coll., 1973; MS, Pa. State U., 1975, PhD, 1978. Lic. psychologist, N.H. Adj. prof. Pa. State U., College Park, 1977-78; intern U. Tex. Counseling Ctr., Austin, 1978-80; staff psychologist Cen. N.H. Community Mental Health Svcs., 1980-81; prof. Grad. Sch. Antioch Coll., Keene, N.H., 1981-83; counselor, cons. Rundlett Jr. High Sch., Concord, N.H., 1983-85; adj. prof. New Eng. Coll., Henniker, N.H., 1985-86, Notre Dame Coll., Manchester, N.H., 1986-87; pvt. practice Concord, 1981—; exec. dir. Wellspring Ctr. for Human Devel., Concord, 1987—; mem. adv. coun. counseling program Notre Dame. Manchester, 1985-88; cons. Rape & Domestic Violence Crisis Ctr., Concord, 1986-88; mem. psychiatry dept. Concord Hosp., 1989—. Editor: Women Therapists Resource Directory New Hampshire Psychol. Orgn., 1986; contbr. articles to profl. jours. Founder, sec. Coalition Against Sexual Exploitation, Concord, 1987-89; mem. Bow (N.H.) PTA, 1989—. Rufus Choate scholar Dartmouth Coll., 1972. Fellow N.H. Psychol. Assn. (chair women and minorities com. 1986-89, editor Networker 1991-95, sec. 1992-94); mem. APA. Home: 4 One Stack Dr Bow NH 03304-4707 Office: Wellspring Ctr Human Devel 6A Hills Ave Concord NH 03301-4803

BOEDEKER, BEN HAROLD, anesthesiologist, educator; b. Jackson, Wyo., Mar. 17, 1953; s. Harold Steven and Eva Andra (Andrews) B.; m. Lisa Carol Mau, June 26, 1988; children: Kirsten, David. BS, Colo. State U., 1976, DVM, 1979; PhD, Georgetown U., 1988; MD, John Byrns Sch. Med., 1987. Diplomate Am. Bd. Anesthesiology, Am. Bd. Clin. Pharmacology, Nat. Bd. Med. Examiners. Advanced through ranks to maj. U.S. Army, 1979-96; resident in internal medicine Georgetown U., Washington, 1987-88; chief gen. med. Kirk Army Health Clin., Aberdeen Proving Ground, Md., 1988-90; resident in anesthesiology Walter Reed Army Med. Ctr., Washington, 1990-93, chief combat anesthesia, 1993-94, staff anesthesiologist, 1993—; adj. faculty Acad. Health Scis. Ft. Sam, Houston, Tex., 1995—; adj. asst. prof. Pa. State U., Hershey, 1994—; asst. prof. anesthesiology, Uniformed Svc. U., Bethesda, Md., 1994—; pres. Intellimed Biorsch., Wheatland, Wyo., 1992—. Student editor Med. Student, 1982-86; contbr. articles to profl. jours., chpts. to books. Pres. Casper (Wyo.) Coll. Young Reps., 1971-73; vol. fireman Dubois (Wyo.) Fire Dept., 1971-76; vol. ambulance attendent Dubois Vol. Ambulance, 1971-76; treas. students for Reagan, Honolulu, 1984. Mem. Am. Coll. Clin. Pharmacology, Am. Soc. Anesthesiology (cert. appreciation 1993, 94, Burroughs Welcome scholar 1992), Am. Pain Soc., Soc. Ambulatory Anesthesia, Am. Soc. Regional Anesthesiology, Wyo. Soc. Roman Catholic. Home: 3925 Dunes Way Burtonsville MD 20866 Office: Dept Surgery Walter Reed Army Med Ctr 6900 Georgia Ave NW Washington DC 20307

BOEHM, GÜNTHER, pediatrician; b. Gerstungen, Germany, Oct. 24, 1946; s. Heinz Werner and Ingeborg (Fräbel) B.; m. Margaret Kessner, Apr. 7, 1968 (div. 1980); children: Andreas, Steffen; m. Heidi Dippe, July 2, 1981; 1 child, Alexander. MD, U. Leipzig, Fed. Republic of Germany, 1972, Habil., 1986. Pediatrician U. Leipzig, Fed. Republic of Germany, 1972-86, sr. physician dept. neonatology, 1986-92; docent of pediatrics U. Leipzig, Germany, 1989-92; mem. rsch. dept. internat., head pediat. rsch. Milupa GmbHa Co. KG, Friedrichsdorf, 1994—; permanent cons. Centre for Infant Nutrition, Milan, Italy, 1994—; guest prof. Gondar (Ethiopia) Coll. Med. Scis., 1981-82; vis. prof. Nat. Rsch. Coun. Italy Inst. for Infant Nutrition, Milan, 1992-93; cons., chmn. working group postnatal devel. gastrointestinal tract Inst. Infact Nutrition, Milan, 1994—. Patentee in field; contbr. numerous articles to profl. jours. Recipient prize European Assn. Perinatal Medicine, 1986, Virchow prize, 1989; neonatology fellow U. Milan, 1987, 90, 91, 92; pediatrics fellow U. Lund, Sweden, 1984, 86-92; WHO fellow. Mem. Pediatric Soc. Germany, Soc. Perinatal Medicine of Germany, European Soc. Pediatric Gastroenterological Nutrition, German Soc. Pediatric Gastroenterological Nutrition, European Assn. Perinatal Medicine, N.Y. Acad. Scis. Office: Milupa AG Rsch Dept Internat, Bahnstr 14-30, D-61381 Friedrichsdorf Germany

BOEHM, WERNER WILLIAM, social work educator; b. Oberlangenstadt, Germany, June 19, 1913; came to U.S., 1937, naturalized, 1944; s. Karl and Bertha (Oppenheimer) B.; m. Bernice Roseburg Brower, June 5, 1948 (dec. Dec. 1983); 1 child, Andrew; m. Laurie Horn, Feb. 2, 1986. LL.B., U. Dijon, France, 1936, D.L., 1937; M.S.W., Tulane U., 1941, LHD (hon.), 1992. Prof. social work U. Minn., 1952-63, dir., coordinator U.S. and Canadian social work curriculum study, 1955-58; dean Grad. Sch. Social Work, Rutgers U., 1963-72, disting. prof., 1972-81, emeritus prof., 1981—; dir. Center for Internat. and Comparative Social Welfare, 1973-81; vis. Disting. prof. Seton Hall U., 1984-87; v.p. Minn. Welfare Conf., 1954-55; bd. dirs. U.S. Com. on Internat. Social Work, 1955-61, 76-92; vice chmn. commn. 10th Internat. Conf. Social Work, Italy, 1961; rep. 10th Internat. Conf. Social Work (11th Conf.), Brazil, 1962; mem. continuing edn. tng. rev. com. NIMH, 1969-72; chmn. Commn. I, XVth Internat. Conf., Manila, 1970; Sr. Fulbright travel grant Italo-U.S. Conf. on Ednl. Exchange in Social Welfare, Rome, 1969; sr. Fulbright appointment, Italy, 1971; vis. scholar Nat. Inst. Social Work Tng., London, 1972-73; U.S. rep. commn. on social devel. XVIII Internat. Conf. on Social Welfare, San Juan, 1976; lectr. internat. meetings Ger., France, 1975-80, 82, Australia, 83. Author: Objectives of the Social Work Curriculum of the Future, 1959, The Social Casework Method in Social Work Education, 1959; author U.S. report for, 19th and 20th Internat. Confs. on Social Welfare, 1978, 80, also seven monographs in field; adv. editor: Social Work Series, Harper & Row, Pubs., 1963-83; editor-in-chief: Internat. Social Work, 1975-81; contbr. articles to profl. jours., chpts. to books. Mem. Gov.'s Council on Aging, 1960; mem. N.J. Crime Commn., 1966-68; mem. nat. exec. council Am. Jewish Com., 1984—, mem. nat. affairs com., 1986—. Recipient Cassidy Meml. rsch. award U. Toronto, 1959, Disting. Alumnus award Tulane U., 1981, medal Rutgers U., 1983, Lifetime Achievement award Coun. Social Work Edn., 1995; named Social Worker of Yr., Nat. Assn. Social Workers, 1983. Mem. AAAS, NASW (chmn. commn. on edn. 1965-67, bd. dirs., exec. com. 1966-67), Internat. Coun. Social Welfare (bd. dirs. U.S. com. 1979-89), Coun. Social Work Edn. (exec. com. 1967-69, chmn. commn. on ednl. svcs. 1968-72, commn. internat. social work 1978-82, com. on inquiry N.J. chpt. 1986-92, del. 1986, Lifetime Achievement award 1995), Nat. Commn. Social Work Careers (bd. dirs.), Nat. Conf. Social Welfare (1st v.p. 1969-70), N.J. Welfare Coun. (exec. com. 1964-70), N.J. Assn. Social Workers (Social Work Pioneer 1992), Cosmos Club. Home: 21 Carpender Rd New Brunswick NJ 08901-1501 Office: Rutgers U Sch Social Work New Brunswick NJ 08903

BOEPPLE, ELIZABETH DELAPP, psychologist; b. Syracuse, July 12, 1950; d. Howard W. and Irene (Gratien) DeLapp; B.A. cum laude, SUNY, Buffalo, 1971, M.Ed., 1974, Ph.D., 1977; children—Karen Anne, Kathryn Marie. Instr., SUNY, Geneseo, 1974-75; research coordinator Research and Devel. Complex, State U. Coll., Buffalo, 1976; psychologist West Seneca Devel. Center, 1977-79; psychologist N.Y. State Div. for Youth, Masten Park Secure Ctr., Buffalo, 1979-90; pvt. practice, Snyder, N.Y., 1990—; cons. Families Adopting Need Support, 1996—; instr. Erie C.C., 1973-75, Bryant & Stratten Bus. Inst., 1976. Cert. psychologist, N.Y. Mem. Phi Beta Kappa. Roman Catholic. Office: 46 Washington Hwy Snyder NY 14226-4331

BOERINGA, J. ALEXANDER, psychologist; b. Oak Park, Ill., Feb. 26, 1940; s. Joseph S. and Alice (Van Stedum) B.; m. Karin Moreland, June 17, 1978; children: Michael Alexander, Matthew David. Student, Trinity Coll., 1961-63; BA, Hope Coll., 1965; PhD, U. Tex., 1979. Diplomate Am. Bd. Psychologists. V.p. Tex-Mex, Inc., Austin, 1968-73; psychology intern Va. Med. Ctr., Houston, 1977; asst. prof. psychology U. Tex., Galveston, 1978-82; clin. psychologist Peoria (Ill.) VA Outpatient Clinic, 1982-86; chief psychologist V.A. Med. Ctr., Boise, Idaho, 1986-91, VA Med. Ctr., Houston, 1991—. Contbr. articles to profl. jours. Served with U.S. Army, 1959-61. Woodrow Wilson fellow, 1965. Mem. APA, Tex. Psychol. Assn., Assn. VA Chiefs of Psychology (pres.), Phi Kappa Phi. Home: 3619 Yankee Ct Missouri City TX 77459-4819 Office: 2002 Holcombe Blvd Houston TX 77030-4211

BOËTHIUS, GERT JÖRGEN, neurosurgeon; b. Stockholm, Mar. 2, 1938; s. Gert Gunnar and Nora (Oelrich) B.; m. Siv Boalt, Apr. 8, 1968; children: Victoria, Ninna. Candidate Medicine, Karolinska Inst., Stockholm, 1960, PhD, 1970, MD, 1972. Neurosurg. intern Karolinska Inst., Stockholm, 1972-78, cons., 1978-88, sr. cons., 1988—; reader Karolinska Inst., Stockholm, 1971. Contbr. articles to profl. jours. Home: Lorensviksv 2, 18363 Täby Sweden Office: Karolinska Hosp, Dept Neurosurgery, Stockholm Sweden

BOGAN, MICHAEL L., radiologist, educator; b. Indpls., Apr. 14, 1957. MD, Ind. U. Indpls., 1983. Diplomate Am. Bd. Radiology. Asst. prof. Ind. U. Med. Ctr., Indpls., 1988-90; staff radiologist Irvington Radiologists, Indpls., 1990—. Mem. Am. Coll. Radiology, Radiol. Soc. N.Am., Ind. Roentgen Soc. Office: Irvington Radiologists PC 7205 Shadeland Sta Ste 150 Indianapolis IN 46256

BOGAN, STEPHEN J., ophthalmologist; b. Detroit, May 17, 1958; s. Robert F. and Dorothy (Lovell) B.; m. Linda MArie Pangburn, July 30, 1990. BS, U. Mich., 1980; MD, Wayne State U., 1984. Resident Albany Med. Ctr., 1984-88; ophthalmologist Shelby (N.C.) Eye Ctr., 1993—. Contbr. articles to profl. jours. Maj. USAF, 1990-93. Cornea fellow Emory U., Atlanta, 1988-90. Fellow Am. Acad. Ophthalmology, Am. Coll. Surgeons; mem. Phi Beta Kappa. Office: Shelby Eye Ctr 1413 N Lafayette St Shelby NC 28150

BOGARD, BRUCE NILS, pediatrician; b. Bklyn., July 1, 1942; s. George and Sherry (Felrice) B.; m. Susan Plenn, Dec. 29, 1963; children: Bennett, Meredith. BA, U. Pa., 1963; MD, SUNY, Buffalo, 1968. Diplomate Am. Bd. Pediatrics. Intern Albert Einstein Med. Ctr., Phila., 1968-69; resident in pediatrics Children's Hosp. of Phila., 1969-71; chief resident in pediatrics L.I. Jewish Med. Ctr., New Hyde Park, N.Y., 1971-72, physician-in-charge ambulatory pediatrics, 1974-86; asst. prof. pediatrics SUNY, Stony Brook, 1974-89; program dir. child protection team Schneider Children's Hosp., New Hyde Park, 1978—; head pediatrics clinics Schneider Children's Hosp., 1986—, unit chief med. 2, 1988-93; asst. prof. pediatrics Albert Einstein Coll. Medicine, Bronx, N.Y., 1989—; cons. in child abuse County Atty. Suffolk County, Hauppauge, N.Y., 1985—, Nassau County Child Protective Svcs., Mineola, N.Y., 1985—. Mem. Queens Borough Pres.'s Task Force on Child Abuse, Queens, N.Y., 1984—; pres. Queens Pediatric Soc., 1985-86. Maj. U.S. Army, 1972-74. Recipient Plaque of Honor, Queensboro Lung Assn., 1986. Fellow Am. Acad. Pediatrics (founding mem. sect. child abuse); mem. Internat. Soc. on the Abuse & Neglect, Am. Profl. Soc. on the Abuse Children. Democrat. Jewish. Office: Schneider Childrens Hosp New Hyde Park NY 11042

BOGART, KEITH CHARLES, neurologist; b. Lorain, Ohio, Apr. 12, 1936; s. Lloyd William and Evelyn (Overmyer) B.; m. B. Diane Seigel, June 8, 1967; children: Keith Charles Jr., Catherine Michelle; m. Alice Craib, July 21, 1976; 1 child, Matthew William. BA, Ohio State U., 1958, MD, 1961. Diplomate Am. Bd. Psychiatry and Neurology, Am. Bd. Qualification in EEG. Asst. prof. neurology U. Wis., Madison, 1968-69, Creighton U., Omaha, Nebr., 1975-78; chmn. neurology Gunderson Clinic, Lacrosse, Wis., 1969-75; clin. neurologist Mansfield (Ohio) Neurology, Inc., 1978—; med. dir. rehab. unit Mansfield Gen. Hosp., 1988-91; cons. neurology VA Hosp., Omaha, 1977-78. Bd. dirs. Boy Scouts Am., Mansfield, 1986. Served to lt. comdr. USPHS, 1963-65. Fellow Am. Acad. Neurology, Am. EEG Soc. (mem. lab. accreditation bd. 1984-87); mem. AMA (Physician's Recognition awad 1969, 72, 77, 82, 86, 87, 88, 91, 94), Cen. Assn. EEGers (pres. 1977-78), Nebr. Epilepsy League (pres. 1976-78), Wis. Med. Soc. (chmn. neurology sect. 1975), Wis. Neurol. Soc. (pres. 1973), Richland County Med. Soc. (pres. 1988, sec.-treas. 1986—), Knights of Magic (pres. 1986-87, Magician of Yr. 1984, 85, 86), Internat. Brotherhood Magicians (v.p. ter. 1986-91, Presdl. Citation 1988), Inner Magic Circle (assoc.), Internat. Platform Assn., Rotary. Home: 730 Woodhill Rd Mansfield OH 44907-1540 Office: Mansfield Neurology Inc 222 Marion Ave Mansfield OH 44903-2138

BOGDASARIAN, JOHN ROBERT, otolaryngologist; b. N.Y.C., Aug. 24, 1944; s. Robert Michael and Carol Cecile (Spahr) B.; m. Joellen Marie D'Esti, Aug. 15, 1970 (div. 1976); m. Sophia Despina Xenelis, Sept. 15, 1979; children: Robert Michael, Alexander John, Ronald Nicholas, Michael Andrew. BA cum laude, Harvard U., 1966; MD, Columbia U., 1970. Diplomate Am. Bd. Surgery, Am. Bd. Otolaryngology. Intern. Univ. Hosp., Boston, 1970-71, resident, gen. surgery, 1971-75, resident otolaryngology, 1975-78; pvt. practice otolaryngology Mont Head & Neck Surgery, Inc., Fitchburg, Mass., 1978-86, Cen. Mass. Otolaryngology, Fitchburg, 1986—; dir. speech and hearing dept. Burbank Hosp., Fitchburg, 1980-93, pres. med. and dental staff, 1986-87; vis. surgeon Boston VA Hosp., Jamaica Plains, Mass., 1982—; dir. speech and hearing dept. Nashoba Cmty. Hosp., Ayer, Mass., 1984-93; clin. asst. prof. Boston Sch. Medicine, 1987—, U. Mass. Med. Ctr., 1985—. Pres. Montachusett divsn. Am. Cancer Soc., Fitchburg, 1982-83; mem. Applewild Sch. Devel. Com., 1989-93, trustee, 1992—. Maj. Mass. N.G., 1971-77. Recipient Cert. Achievement Am. Cancer Soc., 1981, Burbank Hosp. Speech and Hearing Dept., Fitchburg, 1985. Fellow ACS; mem. AMA, Am. Acad. Otolaryngology-Head and Neck Surgery, New Eng. Otolaryngologic Soc., Mass. Med. Soc., Armenian Am. Med. Soc., N.Y. Rd. Runners' Club, Ctrl. Mass. Striders, Harvard Club (Boston), Fay Club, Oak Hill Country Club, Harvard Worcester Club, Columbia Club of New Eng., North Medford Track Club. Mem. Armenian Apostolic Ch. Home: Flat Rock Rd Fitchburg MA 01420-2204 Office: Cen Mass Otolaryngology 33 Electric Ave Fitchburg MA 01420-7954

BOGDEN, JOHN DENNIS, medical educator; b. Jersey City, N.J., Sept. 5, 1945; s. Paul Augustine and Anne (Stepanik) B.; m. Doreen Louise Southard, Aug. 16, 1945; children: Jennifer Lyn, Kimberly Ann. ScB in Chemistry, Brown U., 1967; MS in Chemistry, Seton Hall U., 1970, PhD in Chemistry, 1971. From postdoctoral fellow to prof. preventive medicine N.J. Med. Sch., Newark, 1971—. Mem. editorial bd. Jour. Nutritional Immunology, 1991-96, Jour. Nutritional and Environ. Medicine, 1995-96; cons. editor Nutrition Rsch., 1992; contbr. over 80 articles to profl. jours. Chmn. So. Plainfield (N.J.) Environ. Com., 1979-90; mem. Middlesex County (N.J.) Environ. Health Task Force, 1980-82, N.J. Drinking Water Quality Inst., Trenton, 1985-87; bd. dirs. Cen. N.J. Lung Assn., Clark, 1979-82; mem. pub. edn. com. Am. Cancer Soc. Grantee Am. Heart Assn., 1982, 89, 93, NIH, 1984, N.J. Commn. on Cancer Rsch., 1984, 88, Hoffmann-LaRoche Inc., 1989, 91, 93, March of Dimes, Birth Defects Found., 1992, Labcatal prize, 1991. Fellow Am. Coll. Nutrition; mem. Soc. Environ. Geochemistry and Health (bd. dirs. 1984-87), Am. Chem. Soc., AAUP, Am. Pub. Health Assn., Am. Inst. Nutrition, Am. Soc. Clin. Nutrition, Sigma Xi. Democratic. Roman Catholic. Office: UMDNJ NJ Med Sch Dept Preventive Medicine 185 S Orange Ave Newark NJ 07103-2714

BOGDON, GLENDON JOSEPH, orthodontist; b. Green Bay, Wis., Sept. 23, 1935; s. Joseph Frank and Anne Marie (Jacklin) B.; m. Susanne Ellen Daley, Aug. 8, 1959; 1 child, Amy Sue. BS, St. Norbert Coll., DePere, Wis., 1957; DDS, Marquette U., 1971, MS in Clin. Dentistry, 1973. Officer IRS, Chgo., 1958; social worker Cath. Welfare Bur., Milw., 1958-59; tchr. secondary sch. So. Door County Schs., Brussels, Wis., 1959-67; practice dentistry specializing in orthodontics Milw., 1973—. Writer fitness column Cath. Herald; contbr. articles to profl. jours.; patentee in field. Served with U.S. Army, 1957-58. Mem. Greater Milw. Dental Assn. (Continuing Edn. award 1971-73), Wis. Dental Assn. (Continuing Edn. award 1971-74, 79-81, ADA (Continuing Edn. award 1976-78), Royal Soc. Health, Wis. Soc. Orthodontists, Midwestern Soc. Orthodontists, Am. Assn. Orthodontists, Spitfire Soc., Am. Running and Fitness Assn. Democrat. Roman Catholic. Office: 3044 S 92nd St Milwaukee WI 53227-3678

BOGDONOFF, MAURICE LAMBERT, physician; b. Chgo., May 11, 1926; s. Harry A. and Mary Ivy (Grogan) B.; m. Diana Edith Rauschkolb, June 29, 1956; children: Vivian, Gregory, Audrey. BS, Tufts U., 1948; MD, Yale U., 1952. Intern U. Ill. Rsch. and Edn. Hosp., Chgo., 1952-53; resident in internal medicine Boston City Hosp., 1953-54; resident in radiology Columbia-Presbyn. Med. Ctr., N.Y., 1955-57; asst. prof. to assoc. prof. radiology to prof. U. Ill., Chgo., 1958-69; attending radiologist Rush-Presbyn.-St. Luke's Med. Ctr., Chgo., pres. med. staff, 1975-77; prof. radiology and medicine Rush Med. Coll., Chgo., 1970-88, 1969-88, prof. emeritus, 1988—; cons. Argonne (Ill.) Nat. Lab., 1963-88; cons., health dir. Canal Zone Panama, 1973-80; vis. lectr. nuclear power engring. Maine Maritime Acad., 1989. Contbr. articles to profl. jours. Pres. Wheaton (Ill.) Dist. 36 Sch. Bd.,1964-67; bd. visitors Coll. of DuPage Radio and TV Sys., Glen Ellyn, Ill., 1987-94. With USN, 1944-46. Fellow Am. Coll. Radiology, Inst. Medicine, also others; mem. Chgo. Lit. Club. Republican. Home: 203 W Willow Ave Wheaton IL 60187-5238

BOGGS, JOSEPH DODRIDGE, pediatric pathologist, educator; b. Bellefontaine, Ohio, Dec. 31, 1921; s. Walter C. and Birdella Z. (Coons) B.; m. Donna Lee Shoemaker, June 12, 1964; 1 son, Joseph Dodridge. A.B., Ohio U., 1941, Litt.D., 1966; M.D., Jefferson Med. Coll., 1945. Intern Jefferson Med. Coll. Hosp., Phila., 1945-46; resident Peter Bent Brigham Hosp., Boston, 1946-48; asso. pathologist Peter Bent Brigham Hosp., 1947-51; instr. pathology Harvard Med. Sch., Boston, 1948-51; with Children's Meml. Hosp., Chgo., 1951—; dir. labs. Children's Meml. Hosp., 1951—; prof. pathology Northwestern U., Chgo., 1952-92, prof. emeritus, 1992—; dir. BSP Ins. Co., Phoenix. Contbr. articles to profl. jours. Mem. med. adv. bd. Ill. Dept. Corrections, Springfield, 1971-77; bd. dirs. Blood Systems Inc., Phoenix, 1972-94, Community Hosp., Evanston, Ill., 1958-61, Lorretto Hosp., Chgo., 1971-72; chmn. Chgo. Regional Blood Program, 1978-80; bd. dirs. Ben Venue Labs., 1985—. Capt. M.C., U.S. Army, 1948-51. Mem. Am. Soc. Study of Liver Disease, N.Y. Acad. Scis., Midwest Soc. Pediatric Research, Inst. Medicine, Ill. Soc. Pathologists (pres. 1965), Ill. Assn. Blood Banks (pres. 1969-70). Office: 1448 N Lake Shore Dr Chicago IL 60610-1625

BOGGS, KATHLEEN R., neonatal nursing educator; b. Worcester, Mass., Oct. 1, 1946; d. Charles William and Ruth (Berger) Howard; m. Brian David Boggs, Aug. 16, 1975; 1 child, David Benjamin. Diploma, Mass. Gen. Hosp. Sch. Nursing, Boston, 1967; BSN, Calif. State U., Sacramento, 1976. RN, Calif.; cert. neonatal nurse. Staff nurse, neonatal intensive care nursery Stanford (Calif.) U. Med. Ctr., 1968-92; neonatal nurse educator Health Dimensions Inc., San Jose, Calif., 1991-93; per diem staff intermediate care nursery Packard Children's Hosp., Stanford, 1993—; neonatal nurse educator Kaiser Permanente Hosp., Santa Clara, Calif., 1993—; speaker on breastfeeding the premature infant. Pres. Springer Sch. PTA, Los Altos, 1987. Mem. Nat. Assn. Neonatal Nurses. Office: Kaiser Permanente Med Ctr 900 Kiely Blvd Santa Clara CA 95051

BOGGS, ROBERT W., healthcare administrator; b. St. Helena, Calif., Sept. 17, 1941; s. Wayne Cress Boggs and Ann (Stevenson) Isham; m. Donna F. Boggs, Nov. 24, 1967; children: Jacquelin, Ryan. BS, Fresno State U., 1964; PhD, U. Calif., Davis, 1970. Bd. cert. nutritionist. Staff mem. Procter & Gamble, Cin., 1970-73, sect. head, 1973-76, assoc. dir., 1976-83, dir., 1983—; mem. adv. bd. U. Cin., 1991-94, mem. pharm. sci. bd., 1987—; exec. sec. Procter Found., 1982-95. Mem. St. Xavier H.S. Athletic Bd., 1991-93; pres. Glendale Youth Sports, 1989, Christ Ch. Glendale, 1988; v.p. Team Cin., 1993; mem. adv. bd. Cin. Classics, 1995. Mem. Am. Inst. Nutrition (adv. bd. 1988-91), Nutrition Today Soc. Home: 725 Greenville Ave Cincinnati OH 45246

BOGRAD, MICHELE LOUISE, clinical psychologist; b. Denver, Mar. 12, 1952; d. Nathan Bograd and Ruth (Parker) Kaufman. BA, Colo. Coll., 1970-74; PhD, U. Chgo., 1983. Cons. Nat. Inst. of Mental Health, Northwestern U. and U. Chgo., 1978-79; psychology intern South Shore Mental Health Ctr., Quincy, Mass., 1979-80; child psychologist Harvard Community Health Plan, Cambridge, Mass., 1980-81; research ad tng. coordinator Family Svc. Unit of the Dist., Atty.'s Office, Quincy, Mass., 1980-82; rsch. assoc. Family Inst. Cambridge, 1983-84; assoc. faculty Family Inst. of Cambridge (Mass.), 1986-92; faculty Family Inst. Cambridge, Mass., 1992—; lectr. in psychiatry Harvard Med. Sch., Boston, 1985-87, 90; core faculty Kantor Family Inst., Somerville, Mass., 1985-90. Co-editor: Feminist Perspectives on Wife Abuse, 1988; editor: Feminist Approaches for Treating Men in Family Therapy, 1991; contbr. articles to profl. jours. Mem. APA, Mass. Psychol. Assn., Feminist Therapy Inst., Am. Assn. Marriage and Family Therapists, Am. Family Therapy Acad. Democrat. Jewish.

BOGRAKOS, WILLIAM LOUIS, osteopathic physician, army officer; b. Dover, N.H., Aug. 31, 1954; s. Louis and Evangeline (Pierrochakow) B.; m. Iris Michelle Monteith, May 25, 1985. BA, U. N.H., 1977; DO, New Eng. Coll. Osteo. Medicine, 1985; postgrad. study in tropical medicine, Walter Reed Army Inst. Rsch., 1995. Diplomate Am. Coll. Osteopathy; cert. sports medicine, family practice. Rsch. asst. in psychopharmacology Lenox Hill Hosp., N.Y.C., 1978-79; intern Bapt. Med. Ctr., N.Y.C., 1985-86; commd. capt. USAF, 1986; advanced through grades to lt. col. U.S. Army, 1991; emergency room physician 92d Strategic Hosp., Fairchild AFB, Wash., 1986-90, St. Elizabeth Hosp., Granite City, Ill., 1990-91; resident in physical medicine and rehab Walter Reed Army Med. Ctr., Washington, 1991-92; dep. commdr. clin. svcs. U.S. Army, Aberdeen Proving Ground, Md., 1993-94; bn. surgeon 115 MP Bn. Md., 1994—. Recipient physician recognition award AMA, 1988; Am. Heart Assn. fellow, 1984. Mem. Am. Osteo. Assn., Am. Coll. Family Practitioners in Osteo. Medicine and Surgery, Am. Osteo. Acad. Sports Medicine, Am. Osteo. Acad. Addictionology, Am. Soc. Tropical Medicine and Hygiene, Galen Soc., Spl. Ops. Med. Assn., Nat. Headache Found., U.S. Judo Assn., Am. Coll. Osteo. Emergency Physicians, World Assn. Disaster & Emergency Medicine, Assn. Emergency Phsyicians. Republican. Greek Orthodox.

BOGUSLAVSKY, GEORGE WILLIAM, psychologist, educator; b. Razdolnoye, Maritime, USSR, Oct. 17, 1911; came to U.S., 1930.; s. Vasilii P. and Anna (Lysenko) B.; m. Geneva K. Bowers, Jan. 8, 1943. BA, U. Wash., 1939, MS, 1941; PhD, Cornell U., 1953. Lic. psychologist, N.Y. Instr. U. Conn., Storrs, 1947-51; asst. prof. Cornell U., Ithaca, N.Y., 1953-57; prof., chmn. dept. psychology Rensselaer Poly. Inst., Troy, N.Y., 1957-77; cons. Am. Inst. Rsch., Pitts., 1952-77, Pergamon Inst., London, 1959-62; adv. N.Y. State Edn. Dept., Albany, 1957-59, Rensselaer Family Court, Troy, 1958-60. Contbg. author: Group Processes, 1957, Physiological Bases Psychiatry, 1958; also articles. Capt. Adjutant Gen.'s Dept., 1942-46, PTO. Rsch. grantee HEW, 1962-65. Mem. APA, Assn. N.Y. Acad. Scis., Pavlovian Soc., Sigma Xi.

BOGUSZ, MACIEJ JOZEF, forensic toxicology educator; b. Krakow, Poland, Apr. 11, 1940; s. Jozef and Janina Bogusz; m. Elzbieta Stradowska, June 15, 1963; children: Magdalena, Agata. Dr.med., Acad. Medicine, Krakow, 1967, Dr. habil.med., 1976. Rsch. assoc. Inst. Forensic Rsch., Krakow, 1964-74, chief toxicologist, 1974-86; toxicologist Inst. Forensic Medicine, Heidelberg, Fed. Republic Germany, 1987-91, Inst. Forensic Med., Aachen, Fed. Republic Germany, 1991—; privatdozent U. Heidelberg, Fed. Republic Germany, 1988, TU, Aachen, 1991; adviser WHO European Office, Copenhagen, 1978-81; cons. Toxicol. Clinic, Krakow, 1974-86. Contbr. articles to profl. jours. Home: Rommelweg 34, D-52159 Roetgen Germany Office: Inst Forensic Medicine, Pauwelsstr 30, D-52057 Aachen Germany

BOHAN, LINDA ANN, women's health nurse; b. Yonkers, N.Y., Mar. 4, 1943; d. Thomas and Elvira (Alonso) Obalde; m. John Bohan, Oct. 24, 1964; children: Thomas, David. Diploma, Grace-New Haven Sch. Nursing, 1964; BSN cum laude, Mercy Coll., 1980; MS in Nursing with distinction, Pace U., 1983. RN, N.Y. Staff nurse NIOR Columbia Presbyn. Hosp., N.Y.C., 1964-67; staff RN St. John's Riverside Hosp., Yonkers, 1975-79, head nurse, 1979-91, post-partum nurse, 1979-91, dir. maternal child nursing, 1991—. Mem. adv. com. March of Dimes. Mem. NAACOG (cert. inpatient obstetrics), Am. Soc. for Psychoprophylaxis in Obstetrics (cert. childbirth educator), Nat. Assn. Women's Health Profls., Assn. Law and Medicine, N.Y. State Perinatal Assn., Adolescent Pregnancy Prevention Program (planning com.). Home: 1 Pondview Ln Yonkers NY 10701-5227

BOHIGIAN, GEORGE MICHAEL, ophthalmologist; b. St. Louis, Jan. 21, 1940; s. Michael K. and Margaret (Kevoian) B.; m. Christie Shea, Dec. 24, 1968; children: David, Amy. BA, Washington U., 1961; MD, St. Louis U., 1965. Intern Milw. County Hosp., 1966; resident Barnes Hosp., St. Louis, 1966-69; asst. chief ophthalmology USNR, Camp LeJeune, 1970-72; prof. clin. ophthalmology Washington U. Sch. Medicine, St. Louis, 1972—; chmn. dept. ophthalmology Outpatient Surgery Ctr., St. Louis, 1992—. Author: Handbook of External Diseases of the Eye, 1987. Recipient Honor award Am. Acad. Ophthalmology, 1994. Mem. St. Louis Met. Med. Soc. (pres. 1979), Mo. State Med. Assn. (v.p. 1981). Office: 450 N New Ballas # 201 Saint Louis MO 63141

BOHMAN, HAROLD RAY, surgeon; b. Galesburg, Ill., Oct. 26, 1949; s. Raymond Harold and Eileen Angela (Calmer) B.; m. Cathleen Lynn Carlson, May 22, 1976; children: Eisha Lynn, Erik Raymond. BA magna cum laude, Bethany Coll., 1971; MD, U. Okla., 1975; cert. gen. surgery, Naval Med. Ctr., Oakland, Calif., 1980; cert. colon and rectal surgery, U. Medicine & Dentistry N.J., 1985. Diplomate Am. Bd. Surgery, Am. Bd. Colon and Rectal Surgery. Staff surgeon U.S. Naval Hosp., Guam, 1980-82, Nat. Naval Med. Ctr., Bethesda, Md., 1983-85; pvt. practice Sacramento, Calif., 1985-88; staff surgeon Naval Med. Ctr., Oakland, Calif., 1988-92; capt., chief profl. svcs. 1st Med. Bn. USN 1st Force Svc. Support Group, Camp Pendleton, Calif., 1992—; staff surgeon Naval Hosp., Camp Pendleton, 1992—; specialty advisor Bur. Medicine and Surgery USN, Washington, 1995—. Contbr. articles to profl. jours. Fellow ACS, Am. Soc. Colon and Rectal Surgeons; mem. Soc. Am. Gastrointestinal Endoscopic Surgeons. Lutheran. Office: Naval Hosp Dept Surgery Box 555191 Camp Pendleton CA 92055-5191

BOHN, PAUL BRADLEY, psychiatrist, psychoanalyst; b. Santa Monica, Calif., Apr. 11, 1957; m. Pamela Summit, Nov. 17, 1990. BA in Pharmacology, U. Calif., Santa Barbara, 1980; MD, U. Calif., Irvine, 1984; PsyD in Psychoanalysis, Inst. Contemporary Psychoanal., 1988-93; PsyD, Grad. Inst. Contemporary Psychoanaly, 1995. Diplomate Am. Bd. Psychiatry and Neurology. Psychiat. resident UCLA, 1984-88, assoc. dir. anxiety disorders clinic, 1989—, dir. social anxiety clinic, 1993—; fellow U. So. Calif., L.A., 1988-89; cons. in psychiatry Didi Hirsch Community Mental Health Ctr., Venice, Calif., 1986-88; substance abuse group co-leader Main St. Counseling Svcs., Venice, 1987-88; v.p. Pacific Psychopharmacology Rsch. Inst., Santa Monica, 1990—; pvt. practice psychiatry Santa Monica, 1988—; candidate L.A. Psychoanalytic Inst., 1988-93. Grantee Ciba-Geigy, Santa Monica, 1992. Mem. Am. Psychiat. Assn., So. Calif. Psychiat. Assn., Anxiety Disorders Assn. of Am., Obsessive Compulsive Found.. Office: 2730 Wilshire Blvd Ste 325 Santa Monica CA 90403-4747

BOHNKER, BRUCE K., military medical officer; b. Denison, Iowa, Apr. 8, 1951; s. Robert F. and Mary Lou (Webster) B.; m. Jacqueline P. Bohnker, Dec. 18, 1976; children: Suzanne, Robert, Christopher. BS, Iowa State U., 1973; MS, U. West Fla., 1976; MD, USUHS, 1982; MPH, Emory U., 1988. Commd. officer USN, 1984; advanced through grades to capt.; flight surgeon HSL-40, Jacksonville, Fla., 1984-87; sr. med. officer USS Forrestal, Jacksonville, 1990-92; asst. force med. officer Comnavairlant, Norfolk, Va., 1992-94; fleet surgeon Comsecondflt., Norfolk, 1994—; item writer Am. Bd. Preventive Medicine, Phila. Mem. editl. bd. Aviation, Space and Environmental Medicine, 1994—. Fellow Am. Coll. Preventive Medicine, Aerospace Med. Assn.; mem. AMA, Soc. USN Flight Surgeons (v.p.), Amsus.

BOHORQUEZ, FERNANDO AUGUSTO, surgeon; b. Bogota, Colombia, July 17, 1945; came to U.S., 1972; s. Saul and Graciela (Mahecha) B.; m. Olga Martinez, June 21, 1969; children: Fernando Jr., Alex, Mauricio, Michael. MD, U. Colombia, Bogota, 1970. Diplomate Am. Bd. Surgery. Intern Montfort Hosp., Villavicencio, Colombia, 1970-71; mem. staff St. Rafael Hosp., Ibague, Colombia, 1971-72; intern Community Hosp., Roanoke, Va., 1972-73; resident in gen. surgery St. Joseph Hosp., Towson, Md., 1973-78; mem. staff Provident Hosp., Balt., 1978-80; pvt. practice Balt., 1980—; chmn. nutritional support com. St. Joseph Hosp., Towson, 1986—, mem. surg, attending staff; mem. surg, attending staff Franklin Sq. Hosps., Balt. Mem. ACS, Balt. County Med. Assn. (bd. dirs. 1990-91), Am. Soc. Parenteral and Enteral Nutrition, U.S.A. Colombian Med. Assn. Office: 7505 Osler Dr Ste 503 Towson MD 21204-7740

BOINEAU, FRANKLIN GIRARD, pediatric nephrologist; b. Orangeburg, S.C., July 13, 1943; s. Franklin Girard Jr. and Rachel (Pratt) B.; m. Margaret Kizer, Aug. 14, 1965; children: Stephen Kizer, Girard Cullen. BS, Coll. Charleston, 1965; MD, Med. U. S.C., Charleston, 1969. Diplomate Am. Bd. Pediatrics, Am. Bd. Pediatric Nephrology. Intern Children's Hosp. Phila., 1969-70; asst. resident in pediatrics Strong Meml. Hosp., Rochester, N.Y., 1970-71, assoc. resident in pediatrics, 1971, chief resident in pediatrics, 1972; fellow in pediatric nephrology Cornell U. Med. Ctr.-N.Y. Hosp., N.Y.C., 1972-74; research fellow in physiology Cornell U. Med. Coll., N.Y.C., 1974-75; asst. prof. pediatrics U. Rochester, 1975-78; asst. prof. pediatrics Tulane U. Med. Ctr., New Orleans, 1978-83, assoc. prof., 1983-89, prof. pediatrics, 1989—; dir. pediatric nephrology Tulane U. Hosp., New Orleans, 1978—; invited cons. in nephrology U. South Ala. Sch. Medicine, Mobile, 1980-81; med. adv. com. La. High Blood Pressure Control Program, 1979-85. Contbr. numerous articles, papers to profl. and med. jours. Mem. adv. bd. Handicapped Children's Services Program State of La., 1984—. Fellow Am. Acad. Pediatrics (exec. com. nephrology sect. 1984—); mem. Am. Soc. Pediatric Nephrology, Am. Soc. Nephrology, Am. Soc. Transplant Physicians, Am. Council on Transplantation, Greater New Orleans Pediatric Soc., Internat. Soc. Nephrology, Nat. Kidney Found., Nat. Kidney Found. La., La. State Med. Soc. (subcom. on hypertension 1980-85), Orleans Parish Med. Soc., Southern Soc. for Pediatric Research, Southwest Pediatric Nephrology Study Group. Office: Tulane U Sch Medicine 1430 Tulane Ave New Orleans LA 70112-2699

BOKROS, JACK CHESTER, biomedical company executive, bioengineer; b. Park Falls, Wis., Feb. 24, 1931; s. John Chester and Clara Mae (Anderson) B.; m. Roberta Jean Capen, Nov. 3, 1958; children—Kathleen G., Carol L., Linda K. B.S., U. Wis.-Madison, 1954, M.S., 1955; Ph.D. in Metallurgy, U. Calif.-Berkeley, 1963; DEng (hon.), Rose-Hulman Inst. Tech., Terre Haute, Ind., 1986. Registered profl. engr., Calif. Sr. research engr. Atomics Internat., Canoga Park, Calif., 1955-58; sr. research engr. Gen. Atomic, San Diego, 1958-60, sr. staff mem., 1963-75, dir. med. products, 1975-79; pres. Carbomedics, Austin, Tex., 1979-89; pres. chmn. bd. Carbon Implants, Inc., 1989-94; pres., CEO Med. Carbon Rsch. Inst., 1994—; cons. in field, 1960-62. Contbr. articles to profl. jours. Patentee engring., materials, med. products. Recipient IR 100 award Indsl. Research Mag., 1971, Clemson award for contbn. to tech. lit. Clemson U., 1976, Citation for Disting. Service U. Wis., 1986. Mem. Am. Carbon Soc. (exec. com. 1974, Charles E. Pettinos award 1975), ASTM (com. surg. implants 1975), Assn. Advancement Med. Instrumentation (heart valve standing com. 1975), Soc. Biomaterials (council 1974), Am. Inst. Med. Biol. Engring. (founding mem.). Republican.

BOLAND, GERALD LEE, health facility financial executive; b. Harrisburg, Pa., Apr. 2, 1946; s. Vincent Harry and Alice Jane (Geiste) B.; 1 child, Peter Alexander. BS, Lebanon Valley Coll., 1968. Acctg. trainee Armstrong Cork Co., Millville, N.J., 1968; payroll supr., plant ops. acct., 1969-70; sr. fin. acct. Lancaster (Pa.) Gen. Hosp., 1970-71, mgr. gen. acctg., 1972; corp. acctg. mgr. HMW Industries, Inc., Lancaster, 1972; corp. controller Fleck-Marshall Co. subs. Gable Industries, Lancaster, 1973-74, sec.-treas., 1974-75; contr. Dominion Psychiat. Treatment Ctr., Falls Church, Va., 1975-76; contr., dir. fin. Miller & Byrne, Inc., Rockville, Md., 1976-79; v.p. internal auditing Medlantic Healthcare Group, 1979-88; v.p. ops. Kapner, Wolfberg & Assocs., Van Nuys, Calif., 1988-89; dir. acctg. Providence Hosp., 1989-95, asst. controller, 1995—. Mem. Am. Acctg. Assn., Nat. Assn. Accts., Hosp. Fin. Mgmt. Assn., Eastern Fin. Assn., Am. Hosp. Assn., Am. Mgmt. Assn., Fin. Mgmt. Assn., Inst. Internal Auditors. Home: 13021 Silver Maple Ct Bowie MD 20715-1933

BOLAND, JOSEPH PATRICK, psychologist; b. Johnsons AFB, Japan, Oct. 5, 1959; s. Joseph Frances and Marilyn (Tate) B.; m. Janet Updyke, June 28, 1986; children: Katherine Elizabeth, Jonathan Patrick. BA, U. No. Colo., 1981; PhD, U. S.C., 1987. Lic. clin. psychologist; cert. rational behavior therapist. Mental health worker U. Colo. Health Scis. Ctr., Denver, 1981-82; rsch. asst. psychology dept. U. S.C., Columbia, 1982-84, rsch. assoc. psychology dept., 1991-93; therapist Springdale Sch., Camden, S.C., 1984-85; family therapist Child and Family Ctr., Columbia, 1985-86; psychology intern Med. Coll. Ga., Augusta, 1986-87; staff psychologist G. Werber Bryan Psychiat. Hosp., Columbia, 1987-88, dir. Rational Behavior Therapy Ctr., 1988-91; lic. clin. psychologist Assessment and Counseling Svcs., Columbia, 1988—. Contbr. articles to profl. jours. Mem. Am. Psychol. Assn., Assn. Advancement of Psychology, S.C. Psychol. Assn. (chmn. membership com. 1989-90), S.C. Acad. Profl. Psychologists. Home: 140 Fishers Shore Rd Columbia SC 29223-5570 Office: Assessment & Counseling Svc 1 Harbison Way Ste 110 Columbia SC 29212-3406

BOLAND, MARK SHERIDAN, plastic surgeon; b. Harrisburg, Pa., Dec. 17, 1955; s. John Edward and Lillian Rose (Schmidt) B.; m. Susan Jane Kobler; children: Mark Sheridan II, Kyle Royce. BA summa cum laude, Dickinson Coll., 1978; DO, Phila. Coll. Osteo. Medicine, 1984. Diplomate Am. Osteo. Bd. Plastic Surgery. Resident gen. surgery Community Gen. Osteopathic Hosp., Harrisburg, 1984-86, chief resident gen. surgery, 1986-88; chief resident plastic and reconstructive surgery Holy Spirit Hosp., Harrisburg, 1988-89, Phila. Coll. Osteo. Medicine, 1989-90; pvt. practice plastic and reconstrv. surgery Harrisburg, Pa., 1990—; staff surgeon Dept. Plastic & Reconstructive Surgery Community Gen. Osteopathic Hosp., Harrisburg, Pa., 1990—; staff surgeon dept. plastic and reconstructive surgery Fulton County Med. Ctr., McConnellsburg, Pa., 1990—, Polyclinic Med. Ctr. and Harrisburg Hosps., 1995—. Mem. Am. Osteo. Assn., Am. Coll. Osteo. Surgeons, Pa. Osteo. Med. Assn., Phi Beta Kappa, Beta Theta Pi, Phi Sigma Gamma. Republican. Lutheran. Lodge: Masons. Home: 4736 Rock Ledge Dr Harrisburg PA 17110-3253

BOLASKI, JON ANDREW, director of counseling services; b. Springfield, Mass., Dec. 30, 1952; s. Walter and Eunice Eleanor (Gallerani) B.; m. Debra Joan Johnson, Oct. 4, 1975; children: Ashley Johnson, Chase Johnson. BA, U. New Eng., St. Francis Coll., 1975; MEd, Springfield Coll., 1976, CAS, 1978; EdD, Internat. Grad. Sch., 1984. Cert. clin. mental health counselor, Vt.; lic. mental health counselor, Mass. Psychotherapist, clin. case worker Franklin Med. Ctr., Greenfield, Mass., 1978-89; adj. faculty Community Coll. Vt., Brattleboro, 1984—; dir. counseling svcs. Landmark Coll., Putney, Vt., 1989—; bd. dirs. Inst. for Profl. Studies, St. Louis, 1990—; adj. faculty Norwich U., Montpelier, Vt., 1993—. Alumni coun. rep. St. Francis Coll., U. New Eng., Biddeford, Maine, 1988—. Named to Psi Chi. Mem. ACA, ACA of Mass., Vt. Mental Health Counselors Assn., Am. Coll. Counseling Assn., New Eng. Psychol. Assn., Vt. Counseling Assn. Home: 104 Bridge St Shelburne Falls MA 01370-1104 Office: Landmark Coll River Rd Putney VT 05346

BOLDEN, JACQUELYN ANDERSON, occupational therapist; b. Montgomery, Ala., Jan. 1, 1950; d. Clarence Burton and Luticia Virginia (Robinson) Anderson; m. Jerry L. Moore, July 11, 1970 (div. Dec. 1978); 1 child, Janee Tharese; m. Aljernon John Bolden, Aug. 14, 1982 (div. Aug. 1995); 1 child, Aljernon J. Jr. BS, U. Ala., 1972, MA, 1975; PhD in Sociology, Boston U., 1993. Cert. occupational therapist; lic. occupational therapist, Ga., Mass., Iowa. Dir. adjunctive therapy, mental health practitioner Hillcrest Hosp., Birmingham, Ala., 1973-76; dir. occupational therapy asst. program U. Ala., Birmingham, 1976-79; asst. prof. occupational therapy Sargent Coll., Boston U., 1979-82, coord. M.S. Occupational Therapy Program, 1980-82; liaison specialist Atlanta Bd. Edn., 1982-83; dir. occupational therapy Cen. Health Svcs., Atlanta, 1983-86; sr. asst. dir. grad. programs Boston U., 1982-89, chairperson dept. occupational therapy, 1989-90; cons. ednl. programs and human svcs. agys., 1982—; book reviewer Mosby Publs., 1989-90; mem. adv. bd. North Shore C.C., Beverly, Mass., 1989-90. Co-author, co-producer, actor instrn. videotapes Major Psychiatric Disorders, 1980 (Nat. Endl. Media award 1981). Mem. adv. bd. Ala. Sickle Cell Found., Birmingham, 1978-79, Ala. Cerebral Palsy Assn., Brimingham, 1978-79; bd. dirs. Emma Goldman Womens Health Clinic, Iowa City, 1992—, Domestic Violence Invervention Project, Iowa City, 1993-95, Nat. Black Women's Health Project, Iowa. Grantee HEW, 1977, Rehab. Svcs. Adminstrn., 1980, 89. Mem. NAACP, Am. Occupational Therapy Assn. (mem. criteria/topic com. competency assurance project 1978, role delineation study com. 1976-78, program adv. com. Commn. edn. 1979-82, chairperson clin. assessment devel. com. 1979-82, bd. dirs. 1995—), Am. Sociology Assn., Nat. Women's Polit. Leadership Caucus, New Eng. Assn. grad. Admissions Profls. (bd. mem. 1987-89), Mass. Occupational Therpay Assn., Ga. Occupational Therapy Assn. (chair legis. affairs com. 1985), Ala. Occupational Therpay Assn. (pres. 1977-79). Democrat. Methodist. Home: PO Box 3315 Iowa City IA 52244-3315 Office: U Iowa Sch Social Work 359 North Hall Iowa City IA 52242

BOLDREY, EDWIN EASTLAND, retinal surgeon, educator; b. San Francisco, Dec. 8, 1941; s. Edwin Barkley and Helen Burns (Eastland) B.; m. Catherine Rose Oliphant, Oct. 20, 1973; children: Jennifer Elizabeth, Melissa Jeanne. BA with honors, De Pauw U., 1963; MD, Northwestern U., Chgo., 1967. Diplomate Am. Bd. Ophthalmology. Rotating intern U. Wash., Seattle, 1967-68; resident in gen. surgery U. Minn., Mpls., 1968-69; resident in ophthalmology U. Calif., San Francisco, 1971-74; Heed Found. fellow in retinal and vitreous surgery Washington U., St. Louis, 1974-75; mem. staff dept. ophthalmology Palo Alto (Calif.) Med. Clinic, 1975-91; dept. chmn., 1989-91; pvt. practice, San Jose, Mountain View, Calif., 1991—; clin. instr. Stanford (Calif.) U. Med. Sch., 1975-79, asst. clin. prof., 1979-87, assoc. clin. prof., 1987—; cons. VA Hosp., Palo Alto, Calif., 1976—; vice chmn. dept. ophthalmology Good Samaritan Hosp., San Jose, 1993-95, chmn., 1995—. Contbr. articles to med. jours., chpt. to book. Lt. comdr. M.C., USNR, 1969-71. Recipient Asbury award dept. ophthalmology U. Calif., San Francisco, 1973. Fellow ACS, Am. Acad. Ophthalmology (honor award 1989); mem. AMA, Retina Soc., Vitreous Soc. (charter), Peninsula Eye Soc. (pres. 1987-88), Western Retina Study Club (charter, exec. sec.-treas. 1983-95), Cordes Eye Soc. (pres. 1995-96), also others. Office: Retina Vitreous Assocs Inc 2512 Samaritan Ct Ste A San Jose CA 95124-4002

BOLDT, DENNISE MARIE, nurse; b. Cuero, Tex., Nov. 23, 1951; d. August Joseph and Sophie Geneva (Hermes) Polasek; m. Michael Wayne Boldt, Feb. 19, 1977; children: Sarah, Steven. RN, Brackenridge Hosp. Sch. Nursing, Austin, 1973; postgrad., U. Tex., Austin, Victoria (Tex.) Coll. Staff nurse Brackenridge Hosp., Austin, Tex.; field nurse Coastal Bend Home Health, Victoria, Tex.; ICU-CCU supr. DeTar Hosp., Victoria; dir. patient svcs. Crossroads Home Health, Victoria; v.p. Crossroads Home Health; v.p. Crossroads Nursing Svc. Bd. dirs. Am. Cancer Soc.; mem. adv. com. Corpus Christi State U. Nursing Adv. Coun., Victorial Coll. Home Health Aide. Mem. ANA, Tex. Nurses Assn., Tex. Assn. Home Care (nominating com., clin. practice com.), Nat. Assn. Home Care. Home: 412 Sun Valley Dr Victoria TX 77904-9621 Office: 1501 E Mockingbird Ln Ste 403A Victoria TX 77904-2157

BOLDYS, HUBERT WALENTY, gastroenterologist, educator; b. Lędziny, Silesia, Poland, Jan. 14, 1955; s. Klemens and Aniela (Miśka) B.; m. Krystyna Józefa Rapacz, Apr. 19, 1980; children: Alexandra, Małgorzata, Lukas, Mateusz, Jakub. Degree in medicine, Silesian U., Katowice, Poland, 1980, MD, 1985, degree in internal medicine, 1986, degree in gastroenterology, 1993. Jr. asst. dept. gastroenterology Silesian U. Sch. Medicine, 1980-81, asst. dept. gastroenterology, 1981-84, asst. lectr., 1984-87, sr. lectr., 1987—. Contbr. articles to profl. jours. Recipient prize 3d United European Gastroenterology Week, 1994. Mem. N.Y. Acad. Scis., European Assn. Gastroenterology and Endoscopy. Mem. Solidarity Party. Roman Catholic. Office: SUSM Dept Gastroenterology, Medykow 14, 40-752 Katowice Poland

BOLE, GILES G., physician, researcher, medical educator; b. Battle Creek, Mich., July 28, 1928; s. Giles Gerald, Sr. and Kittie Belle B.; children—David Giles, Elizabeth Ann. B.S., U. Mich., Ann Arbor, 1949, M.D., 1953. Diplomate Am. Bd. Internal Medicine. Resident in internal medicine U. Mich., Ann Arbor, 1953-56, fellow rheumatology Rackham arthritis research unit, 1958-61, asst. prof. internal medicine, 1961-64, assoc. prof. internal medicine, 1964-70, prof. internal medicine, 1970—; physician-in-charge Rackham Arthritis Research Unit, Ann Arbor, 1971-86, chief rheumatology div., 1976-86; assoc. dean clin. affairs, sr. assoc. dean Med. Sch. U. Mich., Ann Arbor, 1986-88, exec. assoc. dean Med. Sch., 1988-90, interim dean Med. Sch., 1990-91, dean Med. Sch., 1991—; dir. U. Mich. Arthritis Ctr., Ann Arbor, 1977-86; bd. govs. Am. Bd. Internal Medicine, 1979-83, chmn. rheumatology com., 1979-83. dir. U. Mich. Arthritis Ctr., Ann Arbor, 1977-86; bd. govs. Am. Bd. Internal Medicine, 1979-83, chmn. rheumatology com., 1979-83; mem. physician payment rev. commn. Office Tech. Assessment, U.S. Congress. Capt. M.C., USAF, 1956-58. Recipient Borden Academic Achievement award U. Mich., 1953; Postdoctoral Research fellow Arthritis Found., 1961-63. Mem. Am. Fed. Clin. Rsch. (chmn. Midwest sect. 1967-68), Cen. Soc. Clin. Rsch. (pres. 1976-77), Am. Rheumatism Assn. (pres. 1980-81). Home: 6015 W Ellsworth Rd Ann Arbor MI 48103-9609 Office: U Mich Med Sch M7324 Med Sci I 1301 Catherine St Ann Arbor MI 48109-0624

BOLEN, TERRY LEE, optometrist; b. Newark, Ohio, Sept. 16, 1945; s. Robert Howard and Mildred Irene (Hoover) B.; BS, Ohio U., 1968; postgrad. Youngstown State U., 1973; O.D., Ohio State U., 1978; div. Quality control inspector ITT Grinnell Corp., Warren, Ohio, 1973, jr. quality control engr., 1974; pvt. practice optometry, El Paso, Tex., 1978-80, Dallas, 1980-81, Waco, Tex., 1981-85, Hewitt, Tex., 1983-89; comdr. U.S. Pub. Health Svc., 1989—; bd. dirs. Am. Optometric Found., 1975-77; nat. pres. Am. Optometric Student Assn., 1977-78; pres. El Paso Optometric Soc., 1980; adj. prof. clin. optometry Pacific U. Coll. Optometry, So. Calif. Coll. Optometry. Vol. visual examiner, Juarez, Mex., 1979—; chmn. Westside Recreation Ctr. Adv. Com., El Paso, 1979, Lions Internat. Sight Conservation and Work With the Blind Chmn. award, 1989 . Served to lt. USN, 1969-72; capt. USAIRNG, 1987-89. Recipient pub. svc. award, City of El Paso, 1980. Mem. Am. Optometric Assn., Tex. Optometric Assn., Assn. Mil. Surgeons of U.S. (life, USPHS HSO liaison 1990-94, edn. coord. optometry section, 1992), Res. Officers Assn. (sec. chpt. # 1 Nev. 1994-96, sr. v.p. Navy Nev. 1995-96, life), Ret. Officers Assn., Optometric Assn. (clin. assoc. Optometric Extension Program Found. 1978-89), Heart of Tex. Optometric Soc. (sec.-treas. 1984-85, pres.-elect 1986, pres. 1987), North Tex. Optometric Soc., USPHS (pres. No. Nev. chpt. Commd. Officers Assn. 1989-91), Epsilon Psi Epsilon (pres., 1977-78), Lions (3rd v.p. Coronado El Paso, svc. award, 1978, 79, Hewitt pres. 1985, v.p. W.Tex. Lions Eye Bank, 1980, 2d v.p. Cen. Tex. Lions Eye Bank, 1988, Hewitt Lion of Yr. 1987). Republican. Mem. Christian Ch. (Disciples of Christ). Home: 750 E Stillwater Ave Trlr 173 Fallon NV 89406-4063

BOLES, ROGER, otolaryngologist; b. Oakland, Calif., Jan. 13, 1928; s. Albert and Julia Boles; m. Marianna Reeves, June 16, 1956; children: Martin Reeves, Melissa. AB, Stanford U., 1949; postgrad., Denver U., 1950-52; MD with distinction, George Washington U., 1956. Diplomate Am. Bd. Otolaryngology, Am. Bd. Med. Specialties. Intern Fitzsimmons Army Hosp., Denver, 1956-57; asst. resident through sr. clin. instr. Mich. U. Hosp., Ann Arbor, 1959-63, faculty dept. otorhinolaryngology, 1963-74, prof., 1973-74; prof., chmn. otolaryngology U. Calif. San Francisco Sch. Medicine, 1974-89; pres. med. staff U. Calif., San Francisco, 1982-83; cons. for otolaryngology to Surgeon Gen., USAF, 1975-85; mem. staff San Francisco Gen. Hosp., 1984—, Childrens Hosp. San Francisco (bd. dirs. 1987-91); cons. in otolaryngology Va. Hosp., Ann Arbor, Wayne County Hosp., Eloise, Mich., So. Mich. Prison, Jackson, Fed. Penitentiary, Milan, Mich., 1963-74, Letterman Gen. Hosp., Presidio of San Francisco, U.S. Naval Hosp., Oakland, Calif., 1974-93, Kaiser Hosp., Oakland, 1975, Va. Hosp., San Francisco; bd. dirs. Council Med. Splty. Socs., 1981-82, sec., 1982-83; bd. dirs. Am. Acad. Otolaryngology-Head and Neck Surgery, 1981-88, coord. for continuing med. edn., 1980-83, pres., 1987; mem. Accreditation Coun. for Continuing Med. Edn., 1986-92, chmn., 1990; chmn. PEPP com., 1988-89, 90, vice chmn., 1989, residency rev. com. for otolaryngology; Marshall-Hale Hosp., San Francisco, 1975-83, bd. dirs., 1983-87; mem. Am. Bd. Med. Specialties, 1984-89, exec. com., 1988-89; vis. prof. various univs.; participant in confs., convs., workshops, seminars, insts. Contbr. chpts. to books, numerous revs., articles and abstracts to profl. lit. Served with M.C., AUS, 1956-59. Fellow ACS (chmn. adv. coun. for otolaryngology 1977-80, adv. com. for continuing med. edn. 1982-83), Am. Laryngol. Soc.; mem. AMA (ho. dels. 1975-82, bd. editors archives otolaryngology 1975-85, mem. reference com. on ins. and med. svc. 1978, adv. com. for continuing med. edn. 1981-87), Am. Acad. Opthalmology and Otolaryngology (assoc. sec. com. on continuing edn. 1974-80, chmn. manuals editorial com. 1977-80, mem. at large exec. com. div. otolaryngology 1977-78, mem. interspecialty cooperation com. med. specialty socs. 1978-88), Am. Acad. Facial Plastic and Reconstructive Surgery (co-chmn. standards com. 1977-80, med. edn. com. 1979-81—), Soc. Univ. Otolaryngologists (sec.-treas. 1973-80, chmn. com. on undergrad. curriculum 1969-74, mem. exec. council 1968-79, pres. 1978), Council Acad. Socs.-Assn. Am. Med. Colls., Assn. Acad. Depts. Otolaryngology (vice chmn. subcom. Nat. Cancer Inst. liaison com. 1977-81, chmn. edn. nominating coms. 1978-79), Am. Bronco-Esophagological Assn. (mem. council 1981-82), Am. Bd. Otolaryngology (bd. dirs. 1974-91, exec. com. 1981-88, mem. various coms. 1974-91, chmn. ad hoc com. for nomination process for membership on bd. dirs. 1976-77, pres. 1986-88), Am. Council Otolaryngology (mem. subcom. on hearing 1976-80, research adv. com. 1977-81, pres. 1978-79), Am. Laryngol., Rhinological and Otolaryn. Soc. (mem. editorial bds. transactions 1978-88, mem. council 1982-88, pres. 1986-87, historian 1994—), Am. Soc. for Neck and Head Surgery, Otosclerosis Study Group, Am. Tinnitus Assn. (sci. adv. bd. 1978-81), Pacific Coast Oto-Opthal. Soc., Soc. Med. Cons. to Armed Forces, Calif. Med. Assn. (program co-chmn. sects. on allergy and otolaryngology, neurology and otolaryngology 1977-78, chmn. adv. council of otolaryngology 1979-80), Calif. Otolaryn. Soc. (pres. 1978-80), U. Calif. San Francisco Sch. Medicine Alumni-Faculty Assn. (pres. 1978-79), Am. Otological Soc., Am. Laryngol. Assn. (council 1983-84), San Francisco Med. Soc. (bd. dirs. 1983-90, treas. 1989-90), Royal Coll. Surgeons in Ireland (hon.). U. Mich. Med. Ctr. Alumni Assn. (bd. govs. 1983). Office: Univ Calif San Francisco Dept Otolaryngology 400 Parnassus Ave # A-717 San Francisco CA 94122-2721 Home: PO Box 620203 Woodside CA062-0203

BOLHOFNER, BRETT ROBINSON, orthopedist; b. Monterey, Calif., Mar. 12, 1955. BS in Chemistry magna cum laude, Mercer U., 1977; MD, U. South Fla., 1980. Diplomate Am. Bd. Orthopaedic Surgery. Intern USPHS Hosp. and Tulane Affiliates, New Orleans, 1980-81; orthopaedic resident U. South Fla. Coll. Medicine, 1982-86; fellow Assn. for the Study of Internal Fixation Fellowship, Bern, Switzerland, 1986; physician All Fla. Orthopaedic Assocs., St. Petersburg, 1987—; physician Ctrl. Fla. Migrant and Cmty. Health Ctr., Sanford, Fla., 1981-82; clin. asst. prof. orthopaedic surgery U. South Fla. Coll. Medicine, 1986—; chief orthopaedic surgery Bayfront Med. Ctr., 1990—, mem. stds. and credentials com., 1992—; clin. asst. prof. family practice U. South Fla., 1990—; trustee AO Rsch. Inst. Bd. Dirs. AO/Assn. Study Internal Fixation Lab. for Exptl. Surgery, Davos, Switzerland, 1993. Contbr. articles to profl. jours. Staff orthopaedic surgeon Children's Med. Svcs., Pinellas County, Fla., 1987—, St. Petersburg Free Clinic, Pinellas County, 1989—. Commd. USPHS, 1980-81. Fellow Am. Acad. Orthopaedic Surgeons; mem. AMA, ACS (Fla. com. on trauma), Orthopaedic Rsch. and Edn. Found. (Fla. state devel. chmn., Order of Merit), Fla. Orthopaedic Soc. (exec. com. 1996—), Fla. Med. Assn., Orthopaedic Trauma Assn., Pinellas County Med. Soc., Gamma Sigma Epsilon, AO Alumni Assn. Office: All Fla Orthopaedic Assocs 4600 4th St North Saint Petersburg FL 33703

BOLHUIS, JOHAN JAN, zoologist, researcher; b. Groningen, The Netherlands, Feb. 18, 1958; s. Mintje and Hendrikje (Pastoor) B.; m. Zsuzsanna Ilona Varga, Oct. 25, 1995. BSc, U. Groningen, 1979, MSc, 1984, PhD cum laude, 1989. Rsch. assoc. U. Groningen, 1984-89; postdoctoral rsch. fellow U. Edinburgh, Scotland, 1989-90; postdoctoral rsch. assoc. U. Cambridge, Eng., 1990-91, postdoctoral rsch. fellow, 1991—. Editor: Causal Mechanisms of Behavioural Development, 1994; book revs. editor Quarterly Jour. of Exptl. Psychology, 1993; editl. bd. Behavioural Processes, 1995—; cons. editor Animal Behaviour, 1992—; contbr. articles to profl. publs. Mem. High Table, Sidney Sussex Coll., 1993—. Postdoctoral rsch. fellow Biotech. and Biol. Scis. Rsch. Coun., 1991-96; Twinning grantee European Sci. Found., 1985, 87. Mem. Assn. for Study of Animal Behaviour, European Neurosci. Assn. Office: U Cambridge Dept Zoology, Sub Dept Animal Behaviour, Madinglay Cambridge CB3 8AA, England

BOLIN, VERNON SPENCER, microbiologist, consultant; b. Parma, Idaho, July 9, 1913; s. Thadeus Howard Bolin and Jennie Bell Harm; m. Helen Epling, Jan. 5, 1948 (div. 1964); children: Rex, Janet, Mark; m. Barbara Sue Chase, Aug. 1965; children: Vladimir, Erik. BS, U. Wash., 1942; MS, U. Minn. 1949. Teaching asst. U. Minn.-Mpls., 1943-45; rsch. assoc. U. Utah, Salt Lake City, 1945-50, fellow in surgery, 1950-52; rsch. virologist Jensen-Salsbery Labs., Inc., Kansas City, Mo., 1952-57; rsch. assoc. Wistar Inst. U. Pa., 1957-58; rsch. virologist USPHS, 1958-61; founder Bolin Labs., , Phoenix, 1959—, also bd. dirs. Contbr. articles to profl. jours. Served with U.S. Army, 1931-33. Mem. N.Y. Acad. Scis., Phi Mu Chi. Home: 36629 N 19th Ave Phoenix AZ 85027

BOLLA, ROBERT IRVING, biology educator; b. Dansville, N.Y., Aug. 18, 1943; s. John A. and Thelma A. (Lawrence) B.; m. Terese F. Mandel, Sept. 4, 1966; children: Jennifer A., Stephen A. BS, SUNY, Buffalo, 1961; MS, U. Mass., 1965, PhD, 1970. Prof. biology U. Mo., St. Louis, 1976-88; prof., chmn. biology St. Louis U., 1988—; rsch. scientist Forestry & Forest Products Rsch. Inst., Tsukuba, Japan, 1988. Assoc. editor Jour. Nematology, 1988-94; contbr. more than 60 articles to profl. jours. Rsch. grantee USDA, 1986-93, Mo. Soybean Merchandising Coun., 1991-99. Mem. AAAS, Am. Aging Assn., Am. Soc. Microbiology, Japanese Soc. Nematologists (editorial bd.), European Soc. Nematologists, Russian Soc. Nematologists, Soc. Nematologists, Sigma Xi. Office: St Louis U Dept Biology Saint Louis MO 63103-2010

BOLLER, THOMAS PETER, plant physiologist, educator; b. Zurich, Switzerland, Dec. 10, 1949; s. Peter and Elisabeth (Merz) B.; m. Karin Elmer, Mar. 23, 1974; children: Christian, Regula, Stefan, Maya. Diploma with distinction, Swiss Fed. Inst. Tech., Zurich, 1973, PhD with distinction, 1977. Postdoctoral rsch. assoc. Plant Rsch. Lab. Mich. State U., East Lansing, 1977-78; asst. lectr. botany U. Basel, Switzerland, 1979-85, prof. botany, 1986—; group leader Friedrich Miescher Inst., Basel, 1987—. Mem. Swiss Soc. Plant Physiologists (pres. 1990—). Home: Im Thomasgarten 40, CH-4104 Oberwil Switzerland Office: Botanisches Inst, Hebelstrasse 1, CH-4056 Basel Switzerland

BOLLIGER, EUGENE FREDERICK, retired surgeon; b. Detroit, Sept. 19, 1923; s. Eugene Hans and Julia Frederick (Larson) B.; m. Lois Ann Doan, Dec. 16, 1946; children: Mark, Glen, Cynthia. MD, U. Mich., 1946. Diplomate Am. Bd. Surgery. Intern, then surg. resident Grace Hosp., Detroit, 1947-52; ward surgeon Madigan Army Hosp., Ft. Lewis, Wash., 1952-54; asst. chief surgery 2d Gen. Hosp., Munchweiler, Germany, 1954-55; chief surgery U.S. Army Hosp., Pirmasson, then Wurzburg, Germany, 1955-57; attending surgeon Northwestern Hosp., Mpls., 1957-58; chief of surgery Dickey County Meml. Hosp., Ellendale, N.D., 1958-82; surgeon SHARE HMO, Mpls., 1982-87; chief of surgery Mid-Dakota Hosp., Chamberlain, S.D., 1988-91, Gregory (S.D.) Community Hosp., 1991-94; retired, 1994; surg. cons. West Holt Hosp., Atkinson, Nebr., 1992-94, St. Anthony's Hosp., O.Neill, Nebr., 1992-94; real estate cons. Westin-Reid, Mpls., 1987-88. Major U.S. Army, M.C., 1949-57. Fellow ACS; mem. AMA. Republican. Lutheran.

BOLOKER, ROSE L., school psychologist; b. Bklyn., Mar. 18, 1951; d. Charles and Frances (Frey) B. BS in Psychology with honors, Bklyn. Coll., 1984; MS in Edn., Bklyn. Coll., CUNY, 1986. Cert. sch. psychologist, N.Y. Sch. psychologist N.Y.C. Bd. Edn., Bklyn., 1986—, field trainer, 1990—; co-dir. Biofeedback Tng. Inst., Bklyn., 1987-88. Bd. dirs., crew chief, tng. officer Flatlands Vol. Ambulance Corps, Bklyn., 1975-82. Mem. Nat. Assn. Sch. Psychologists, N.Y. Assn. Sch. Psychologists, Assn. Applied Psychophysiology and Biofeedback, Kappa Delta Pi. Home: 2163 E 23rd St Brooklyn NY 11229-3645 Office: NYC Bd Edn CSE Dist 19 301 Vermont St Brooklyn NY 11207-7004

BOLOOKI, HOOSHANG, cardiac surgeon; b. Langeh, Iran, Mar. 28, 1937; came to U.S., 1960, naturalized, 1976; s. Hossein and Fatima (Arjomand) B.; m. C. Joanne McDonald, Aug. 30, 1975; children: Hooshang Michael, Cyrus William, Andrew John. BS cum laude, Alborz Coll., Tehran, 1954; MD, Tehran U., 1960. Intern and resident in surgery Kings County Hosp.; asst. instr. SUNY Med. Center, Bklyn., 1961-67; resident in thoracic and cardiovascular surgery Jackson Meml. Hosp. and U. Miami Sch. Medicine, 1967-69; mem. faculty U. Miami (Fla.) Med. Sch., 1969—, prof. surgery, 1977—; attending surgeon, dir. adult cardiac surgery Jackson Meml. Hosp., 1969—; dir. Cardiopulmonary Transplant program U. Miami Jackson Meml. Hosp., 1986—; cons. VA Hosp., Miami, 1977-90; mem. adv. panel cardiovascular surgery Ethicon Inc., Davis & Geck Co., Inc. Author: Clinical Application of Intra-Aortic Balloon Pump, 1976, 2d edit., 1984, Medical Examination Review, Thoracic Surgery, 2d edit., 1972, 3d edit. Vol. 18, 1981, Cardiovascular Surgery, Vol. 38, 1981; contbr. articles to med. publs. Recipient Research Career Devel. award NIH, 1972-77, grantee, 1972-75; recipient Grand award U. Tex. Med. Br., 1968. Fellow ACS, Royal Coll. Surgeons Can., Am. Coll. Cardiology, Am. Coll. Chest Physicians; mem. AMA (cert. merit), Am. Surg. Assn., Am. Assn. Thoracic Surgery, Soc. Univ. Surgeons, Am. Heart Assn., Fla. Heart Assn. (cert. of merit), Fla. Thoracic Soc., Soc. for Thoracic Surgeons, So. Thoracic Surg. Assn. (membership com. 1985—, chmn. 1989, v.p. 1991), Soc. Internat. de Chirugie, Internat. Cardiovascular Soc., Soc. Vascular Surgery, Internat. Soc. Heart Transplantation, Soc. Acad. Surgeons, Hillcrest Racquet Club, Ski Club. Republican. Moslem. Office: U Miami Sch Med Thoracic Div Cardiovascular Surgery R-114 Miami FL 33101

BOLSTER, RICHARD EDWARD, laboratory administrator, educator; b. St. Paul, July 25, 1946; s. Robert Howard and Lucille Marion (Chase) B.; m. Charla Florine Bisbee, Nov. 7, 1968 (div. Nov. 1973); 1 child, Richard Edward Jr.; m. Patricia Joy Snyder, Jan. 19, 1974; children: Melinda, Amanda, Robert, Daniel, Naomi. Student, Lamar Jr. Coll., 1964-65; diploma, Brooke Army Med. Ctr., 1969; postgrad., Columbus Coll., 1978. Cert. clin. lab. scientist Nat. Cert. Agy. for Med. Lab. Personell, Inc. Specialist U.S. Army, 1965-74; lab. technician Lee County Hosp., Opelika, Ala., 1974-75; quality control mgr. Columbus (Ga.) Photo Svc., 1975-77; lab. technician Med. Ctr., 1977-80, med. technologist, 1980-82, supr., 1982—; adj. instr. Columbus Coll., 1982—. Mem. Am. Assn. for Clin. Chemistry, Abo Club. Office: Med Ctr 710 Center St Columbus OH 31902-0951

BOLTON, BARRETT HENRY, medical educator; b. Madrid, Spain, Oct. 30, 1932; s. Henry Ernest and Olive Laetitia (Barrett) B.; m. Mary Louise Hanna, July 16, 1955; children: Ann, Christopher, Kathryn J., Thomas, Susan V., Teresa M., Matthew H., David A., Michael J. AB, Stanford U., 1952; MD, Northwestern U., 1956. Resident Akron (Ohio) Gen. Hosp., 1956-58, VA Hosp., Iowa City, Iowa, 1961-64; physician VA Hosp., Dayton, Ohio, 1964-68, pvt. practice, Yellow Springs, Ohio, 1968; dir. edn. dept. medicine Miami Valley Hosp., Dayton, Ohio, 1969-84; chief med. svc. Dayton VA Med. Ctr., 1984-94; prof., vice chair medicine and pharm. Wright State Sch. Medicine, Dayton, 1984-94, prof. emeritus, 1994—. Contbr. articles to profl. jours. Pres. parish coun. Assumption Parish, Dayton, 1976. pres. Am. Cancer Soc., Montgomery County, Ohio, 1981. Capt. U.S. Army, 1959-61. Fellow Am. Coll. Physicians; mem. Am. Soc. Clin. Oncology, Am. Fed. Clin. Rsch., Montgomery County Med. Soc. (program chair 1969-75). Democrat. Roman Catholic. Home: 1608 Catapa Dr Dayton OH 45406

BOLTON, JOHN PHILIP, surgeon, consultant; b. Rochdale, Lancashire, Eng., Jan. 10, 1943; s. Seth and Selina (Barnes) B.; m. Mary Louise Patterson, June 8, 1968; children: Richard, Katherine James. BA, Cambridge (Eng.) U., 1964, M.B.B.Ch., 1967, MA, 1968; MSc, U. B.C., Can., 1977. House surgeon Middlesex Hosp., London, 1968, registrar, 1971-73, sr. registrar, 1973-80; registrar Cheltenham Gen. Hosp., 1969-71; rsch. fellow Vancouver (B.C.) Gen. Hosp., 1975-77; cons. surgeon Chase Farm Hosp., Enfield, 1980—; chmn. gen. surgery Practice Mgmt. Group, Enfield. Fellow Royal Coll. Surgeons Eng., Med. soc. London, Assn. Surgeons of Gt. Britain and Ireland.

BOLTON, JULIA GOODEN, hospital administrator; b. Wilmington, Del., Nov. 11, 1940; d. Merrill Harvey and Mary Rose (Amoroso) Gooden; m. Roger Edwin Bolton, June 27, 1964; children: Christopher Andrew, Jonathan Hughes. RN with honors, Johns Hopkins Hosp., Balt., 1961; BSN with honors, Case Western Res. U., Cleve., 1964; postgrad., Boston U., 1964-65; MS with honors, Russell Sage Coll., 1986. Lic. nurse, Vt. Staff nurse operating rm., clin. instr. Johns Hopkins Hosp., Balt., 1961-62; instr. practical nursing, acting coord. med. programs Charles H. McCann Vocat. Sch., North Adams, Mass., 1966, clin. instr. manpower devel. tng. act program, 1968, clin. instr. med., surg. and pediatric nursing, 1972-73; staff orientation and tour program for children North Adams Regional Hosp., 1973-74; health edn. coms. Williamstown (Mass.) Pub. Schs., 1978-81, Pine Cobble Sch., 1978-81; clin. cons. patient care stds. project North Adams Regional Hosp., 1985-86; dir. staff edn. and quality assurance Southwestern Vt. Med. Ctr., Bennington, 1986-87, asst. v.p. nursing, 1988, v.p. nursing, 1988-92, interim pres., 1991, sr. v.p., 1992—; dir. Vt. Ethics Network, 1995. Dir. United Way Bennington County, 1995; adv. com. Putnam Meml. Sch. Practical Nursing, 1989-94; profl. adv. com. Bennington Home Health Agy., 1988; alt. del. Diocesan Conv. No. Berkshire Deanery, Episc. Ch., 1987; dir. Vt. divsn. Bennington County unit Am. Cancer Soc., 1986-88; mem. Williamstown Betterment Study Com., 1985; adv. com. to plan for declining enrollments Mt. Greylock Reg. High Sch., 1985; bd. dirs. exec. com. Vt. Nursing Initiative Implementation Grant, Pew Charitable Trust Grant, 1992; vestry St. John's Episc. Ch., Williamstown, 1992; active many other civic and charitable orgns. in past. Recipient Hannah Karp award as outstanding student, Russell Sage Coll., 1985, traineeship, 1983-85, others. Mem. Am. Coll. Healthcare Execs., Am. Orgn. Nurse Execs., Nat. Forum Women Health Care Leaders, NLN, Vt. Orgn. Nurse Leaders (pres. 1995), New Eng. Healthcare Assembly (evaluation com.), Rotary, Phi Kappa Phi, Sigma Theta Tau.

BOMBARDIERI, MERLE ANN, psychotherapist; b. Atlanta, Mar. 16, 1949; d. Sol and Sadie (Drucker) Malkoff; m. Rocco Anthony Bombardieri, Jr., Aug. 22, 1971; children: Marcella, Vanessa. B.A. in Psychology, Mich. State U., 1971; M.S.W., San Diego State U., 1976. Cert. clin. social workers, Mass., clin. hypnosis Am. Soc. Clin. Hypnosis; Diplomate Nat. Assn. Social Workers, Am. Bd. Examiners in Clin. Social Work. Crisis intervention worker and trainer Listening Ear, East Lansing, Mich., 1969-71; tchr. English as 2d lang. Instituto Brasil Estados Unidos, Rio de Janeiro, 1971-73; supr. infant unit Married Student Day Care Ctr., Mich. State U., East Lansing, 1973-74; psychotherapist/family life educator Family Svc. Assocs., San Diego, 1975-77; psychotherapist Dade Wallace Mental Health Ctr., Nashville, 1977-78; psychotherapist/workshop leader Met. Beaverbrook Mental Health Ctr., Waltham, Mass., 1980-81; pvt. practice psychotherapy, Acton-Belmont, Mass., 1982—; clin. dir. Resolve, Inc., infertility orgn., Belmont, 1982-84; clin. cons., 1984—; cons. HealthData Internat., Westport, Conn., 1983—, Open Door Soc., Newton, Mass., 1983—, First Day Film Corp., 1985—, Mass. Dept. Social Svcs., 1987; sec. Boston Fertility Soc., 1995, others; psychology seminar leader; radio and TV appearances. Author: The Baby Decision, 1981; founder, editor, pub. Wellspring newsletter; contbr. articles to profl. and med. jours. N.Y. State Regents scholar, 1967; NIMH trainee, 1970. Mem. Acad. Cert. Social Workers, Phi Beta Kappa, Phi Kappa Phi. Home: 4 Broadview Rd Acton MA 01720-4202 Office: 33 Bedford St Lexington MA 02173-4430

BOMBERGER, JOHN HENRY AUGUSTUS, pediatrician; b. Wheeling, W.Va., June 12, 1929; s. John H.A. and Anna Laura (Gottwals) B.; div. 1975; children: Debra Ann, John H.A. IV. BS, Trinity Coll., Hartford, Conn., 1951; MD, Temple U., 1956. Diplomate Am. Bd. Pediatrics. Rotating intern U.S. Naval Hosp., Phila., 1956-57; resident in pediatrics U.S. Naval Hosp. and Children's Hosp. of Phila., 1957-59; Physician Phila. and Jacksonville (Fla.) Naval Hosp., 1956-62; staff physician Children's Hosp., Phila., 1962—, Delaware County Meml. Hosp., Drexel Hill, Pa., 1964—; pvt. practice pediatrics Drexel Hill, 1964-85; med. dir. Mirmont Rehab. Ctr., Lima, Pa., 1985-87, Alcoholism & Addiction Ctr., Delaware County Meml. Hosp., Drexel Hill, 1985-89. Lt. comdr. USN, 1955-62. Mem. Am. Med. Soc. on Alcoholism & Drug Dependencies (cert. 1987), Am. Acad. Family Physicians, Polyologists Med. Club (Phila. sec.-treas. 1968-88). Republican. Episcopalian. Home: 17-11 Valley Rd Drexel Hill PA 19026-5407

BOMMARITO, ANDREW, respiratory therapist; b. Albion, Mich., Nov. 23, 1964; s. Clement Patrick and Marjorie Elenore (Timmons) B.; m. Kimberly Gail Williams, June 11, 1988; 1 child, James Patrick. AD, Calif. Coll. Health Sci., National City, 1995. Cert. respiratory therapist, emergency med. technician. Ambulance driver, emergency med. technician Albion Area Ambulance Svc., 1980-91, CCEMS, Battle Creek, Mich., 1982-85; mental helth aide I Cmty. Mental Health, Albion, 1985; cardiopulmonary technician Albion Cmty. Hosp., 1985-95, respiratory therapist, 1995—; respiratory therapist Drs. Hosp., Jackson, Mich., 1996—; bd. dirs. Albion Area Ambulance Svc., 1985-88. Home: 916 N Monroe St Albion MI 49224

BOMMER, GERHARD, physician; b. Schmelz, Germany, Aug. 13, 1946; s. Erich and Katharina (Scherer) B. MD, U. Hamburg, 1972, Privatdozent Dr., 1981. specialist in pathology, 1981. Sci. asst. U. Hamburg (Germany) Dept. Pathology, 1974-81; dir. dept. pathology Gen. Hosp., Stade, Germany, 1982—; lectr. U. Hamburg, 1981—. Author, co-author books on morphology, biophysics, diabetology and endocrinology. Med. officer Navy, 1972-74, Germany. Recipient Martini award Martini foun., Hamburg, 1980. Home: Am Forstkamp 4, D-21683 Stade Germany Office: Krankenhaus Stade, Bremervorder Str 111, D-2160 Stade Germany

BONA, CHRISTIAN M., dentist, psychotherapist; b. Breslau, Schlesien, Germany, Apr. 24, 1937; arrived in Sweden, 1951; s. Humbert Serafin and Ingeborg Jenny (Holmgren) B.; m. Eva Tengblad, June 10, 1962 (div. 1980); children: Christian Georg, Richard Rolf, Henrik Nils; m. Monica Siv Karlsson, Jan. 26, 1982. DDS, Dental High Sch., Malmoe, Sweden, 1962; PhD in Acupuncture, U. Gothenburg, Sweden, 1986; cert. Traditional Chinese Medicine, U. Beijing, 1987. Asst. prof. Dental High Sch., Gothenburg, 1972-76; head dental health dept. Eriksbergs Mer. Verkstads AB, Gothenburg, 1972-78; head dental health and psychotherapy dept. Tandhalsovarden Mariaplan, Gothenburg, 1984—; sec. Swedish Dental Assn., Gothenburg, 1968-72, Swedish Soc. Clin. Hypnosis, Gothenburg, 1979-81, pres., 1981-84; cons. U. Computeraided Adminstrn., Gothenburg, 1972-78, U. Dental Practice Adminstrn., 1976-78. Author: Dental Psychotherapy and Hypnosis, 1986. Apptd. grand hospitaller, mem. high coun. Sovereign Order St. John in Denmark. Mem. German-Sweden Assn. (treas. 1968-71), Partille Sailing Club (founder 1976, pres. 1976-81), Fram Sailing and Yacht Club (bd. dirs. 1981-86), Knight of Sovereign Order Hosp. St. John Jerusalem in Denmark, St. Eskil of the Order of St. John (treas. 1995—). Office: Tandhalsovarden Mariaplan, Mariagatan 11 B, 41471 Goteborg Sweden

BONADONNA, GIANNI, oncologist; b. July 28, 1934. MD in Medicine and Surgery, Milan U., 1959; degree in Haematology, Ferrara U., 1973; degree in Oncology, Pavia U., 1973. Resident divsn. pathology Santa Cabrini Hosp., Montreal, 1960-61; postdoctoral rsch. fellow divsn. chemotherapy Sloan-Kettering Cancer Ctr., N.Y., 1963-64; rsch. fellow diagnostics divsn. Nat. Inst. Cancer, Milan, 1964-69; asst. Nat. Inst. Cancer, 1969-76, v.p., 1974-78; pres, Italian Assn. Med. Oncology, 1976—; researcher, head dept. cancer medicine Istituto Nazionale Tumori, Milan, Italy. Recipient ACS Medal of Honor Am. Cancer Soc., 1991; Unrestricted Cancer Research Grantees Program, Bristol-Myers Squibb, 1993; Internat. Soc. Chemotheraphy award, David A. Karnorsky Meml. award Am. Soc. Clinical Onocology; Josef Steiner Cancer Rsch. prize U. Bern Switzerland, Bristol-Meyers Squibb award, Gen. Motors Cancer Rsch. award, 1995, Fedn. European Cancer Socs. Clin. Rsch. award. Office: Istituto Nazionale Tumori, Via Venezian 1, 20133 Milan Italy

BONAVENTURA, LEO MARK, gynecologist, educator; b. East Chicago, Ill., Aug. 1, 1945; s. Angelo Peter and Wanda D. (Kelleher) B.; student Marquette U., 1963-66; M.D., Ind. U., 1970; married; children—Leo Mark, Dena Anne, Angela Lorena, Nicole Palmira, Leah Michelle, Adam Xavier. Intern in surgery, Cook County Hosp., Chgo., 1970-71; resident in ob-gyn., Ind. U. Hosps., 1973-76, fellow in reproductive endocrinology and infertility, 1976-78; asst. prof. ob-gyn., Ind. U., 1976—, asst. head sect. reproductive endocrinology and infertility, 1978-80, head sect., 1980-81. Served with USN attached to USMC, 1971-73. Named Intern of Yr., Cook County Hosp., 1971. Diplomate Am. Bd. Obstetrics and Gynecology, Am. Bd. Reproductive Endocrinology and Infertility. Mem. Central Assn. Ob-Gyn., Am. Coll. Obstetricians and Gynecologists, Am. Fertility Soc., Can. Fertility Soc., Soc. Reproductive Endocrinologists, Soc. Reproductive Surgeons. Roman Catholic. Contbr. articles to profl. jours. Office: 8091 Township Line Rd Indianapolis IN 46260-2495

BONCI, ANDREW S., chiropractor; b. Yonkers, N.Y., Apr. 27, 1963. BA, U. Denver, 1986; D Chiropractic, Cleveland Chiropractic Coll., Kansas City, Mo., 1989. Diplomate Am. Acad. Pain Mgmt. Pvt. practice N.Y.C., 1990-95; asst. prof. Cleveland Chiropractic Coll., 1995—. Office: Cleveland Chiropractic Coll 6401 Rockhill Rd Kansas City MO 64131

BONCZEK, MARY ELLEN, nursing administrator; b. S.I., N.Y., Dec. 30, 1955; d. Allen and Johanna (Mazza) Hooker; m. Joseph Bonczek, Apr. 14, 1984; children: Joseph, Jennifer, Michael. BSN, Wagner Coll., S.I., 1976; MPA, Fairliegh Dickinson U., 1992. RN, N.Y., N.J. V.p. patient svcs. Med. Ctr. of Ocean County Brick and Point Pleasant Hosps. Mem. ANA (cert. nurse adminnstr.), AACN, Orgn. Nurses Execs. N.J. (bd. dirs.), Sigma Theta Tau, Phi Alpha Alpha. Home: 51 Tremont Dr Neptune NJ 07753-5872

BOND, MARY LOU, health information management executive; b. Clarksburg, W.Va.; m. Philip Bond; 1 child, Laura. AA in Sci., Harford C.C., Bel Air, Md.; BS in Med. Record Sci., York Coll. of Pa. RRA, CCS. Dir. med. records Columbia (Pa.) Hosp., 1974-77, Fallston (Md.) Gen. Hosp., 1977-90; DRG mgr. Sinai Hosp., Balt., 1990—; cons., Columbia, 1974-83. Co-author, editor: Release of Information Guide, 1990. Bd. mem. Boy Scouts Am., Shrewsbury, Pa., 1983. Mem. Am. Health Info. Mgmt. Assn. Home: 35 Charles St New Freedom PA 17349

BOND, NELSON LEIGHTON, JR., health care executive; b. Glen Ridge, N.J., Apr. 17, 1935; s. Nelson Leighton and Dorothy Louise (Minsch) Hudson B.; m. Susan Priscilla McDonald, June 7, 1958 (div. May 1981); children: Sally Louise, Nelson Leighton III, Trevor Paul, Elizabeth Bond Brennan, Susan Bond Kearney; m. Gwendolen Nash Gorman, July 24, 1982. BA, Lehigh U., 1957; MBA, Harvard U., 1966. Dist. mgr. McGraw Hill, Inc., N.Y.C., 1957-64; assoc. McKinsey and Co., Inc., N.Y.C., 1966-68; fin. analyst Drexel Harriman Ripley, Inc., N.Y.C., 1968-69; instl. salesman Faulkner Dawkins and Sullivan, N.Y.C., 1969-70; v.p. Alex Brown and Sons, Balt., 1970-77; pres., dir. Blood Pressure Testing, Inc., Reisterstown, Md., 1977—; pres. Consumer Micrographics, Inc., Balt., 1980-83; pres. Medscreen, Inc., Balt., 1987-89, also bd. dirs.; mng. dir. Offutt Securities, Inc., 1987—, Bond & Assocs., Reisterstown, Md., 1991—; chmn., pres., chief exec. officer, bd. dirs. Power Source, Inc., Reisterstown, The Green Spring Group, Inc., Reisterstown. Pres. Parents' Club St. Paul's Sch., Brooklandville, Md., 1978-79. 1st lt. USAR, 1958-60. Foote, Cone and Belding fellow Harvard U., 1965. Republican. Episcopalian. Office: Bond & Assocs PO Box 1053 Reisterstown MD 21136-7053

BOND, ROBERT FRANKLIN, cardiovascular researcher, educator; b. Pullman, Wash., Apr. 9, 1937; s. William Ralph and Thelma Mae (Reigel) B.; m. Carol Helen Davis, Dec. 3, 1960; children: Susan Carol, Linda Marie, Brian Robert. BS, Ursinus Coll., 1959; MS, Temple U., 1961, PhD, 1964. Predoctoral cardiovascular trainee Temple U. Sch. of Medicine, Phila., 1959-64; assoc. physiology Bowman Gray Sch. of Medicine, Winston-Salem, N.C., 1964-65, instr. physiology, 1965-67, asst. prof. physiology, 1967-70, assoc. prof. physiology, 1970-73; prof., chmn. physiology Kirksville Coll. of Osteopathic Medicine, Kirksville, Mo., 1973-80, dir. Cardiovascular Rsch. Labs., 1974-80; prof., chmn. physiology Oral Roberts U., Schs. of Medicine and Dentistry, Tulsa, Okla., 1980-88; prof. physiology U. S.C., Columbia, 1988—; cons. Am. Jour. Physiology, 1973—, Am. Heart Jour., 1974-80, Circulation, 1990—, Carolina Med. Electronics, Inc., 1964—, Electromagnetic Probe Co., 1964-88; cons., rsch. grant reviewer Nat. Osteo. Found. Bur. Rsch., 1984-86; instl. rep. Am. Assn. for Lab. Animal Sci., 1973-75; mem. U.S. Army R&D Adv. Com. Trauma Group, 1984-86, Am. Inst. Biol. Scis., U.S. Army Rsch. Devel. Command Shock and Trauma Rev. Panel, 1985—; keynote spkr. Japanese Shock Soc., Osaka, 1990; vis. prof. and lectr. to various nat. and internat. univs. and confs. Author: (with others) Physiology Lab Manual, 1974, rev. edit., 1974-80; contbr. numerous articles to Am. Jour. Physiology, Jour. of Applied Physiology, Neurology, Jour. Occupational Medicine, Am. Heart Jour., Curculatory Shock, others; mem. editl. bd. Circulatory Shock, 1973-93, Shock, 1993—, Jour. Am. Osteo. Assn., 1974-80, Advances in Shock Rsch., 1982—. Adminstrv. bd. Boston Ave. United Meth. Ch., Tulsa, Okla., 1985-88, Shandon United Meth. Ch., Columbia, S.C., 1989-91, adult edn. coord. Commn. on Edn. James Schwinghamer Meml. lectr. Mich. State U., May, 1980; Am. Heart Assn. advanced rsch. fellow, 1968-70, Am. Heart Assn. Coun. on Circulation fellow, 1971, Am. Physiological Soc. Circulation Group fellow, 1974. Mem. AAAS, Am. Heart Assn. (bd. dirs. Mo. affiliate 1978-80, Tulsa chpt. 1981-88, Okla. affiliate 1981-88, S.C. affiliate 1989—, various offices and coms.), Am. Physiol. Soc., Microcirculation Soc., Shock Soc. (founding mem.), N.Y. Acad. Sics., Am. Inst. for Biol. Scis., Sigma Xi. Office: Univ of South Carolina Sch of Medicine Dept of Physiology Columbia SC 29208

BONDADA, SUBBARAO, immunology educator, researcher; b. Ambajipeta, India, June 1, 1948; came to U.S., 1976; s. Bhaskara Rao and Kausalya (Pulavarti) B.; m. Vimala Gadey, Aug. 30, 1980; children: Sandhya, Kavitha. BS, Andhra Loyola Coll., Vijavawada, India, 1968; MSc, Indian Inst. Tech., Kanpur, India, 1970; PhD, Tata Inst. Fundamental Rsch., Bombay, 1976. Fogarty vis. fellow NIH, Bethesda, Md., 1976-79; rsch. assoc. Foxchase Cancer Ctr., Phila., 1979-83; asst. prof. U. Ky., Lexington, 1983-89, assoc. prof., 1989-94, prof., 1994—, mem. staff Markey Cancer Ctr., 1988—, mem. grad. ctr. toxicology, 1993—; assoc. Ctr. on Aging, Lexington, 1988—; vis. scientist Basel (Switzerland) Inst. Immunology, 1981, 84; mem. allery and immunology com. NIAID/NIH. Reviewer Jour. Immunology, Jour. Leukocyte Biology, Cellular Immunology; contbr. articles to profl. publs.; contbr. chpts. to books. Organizer, tchr. WHO/ICRO courses in immunology, Bombay and Delhi, 1984, 88; dir. high sch. student rsch. fellowship program U. Ky., 1991-94, dir. minority coll. student fellowship program. NIH grantee; scholar Govt. of India, 1965-68, 68-70; recipient Rsch. Career Devel. award, 1988-93. Mem. AAAS, Am. Assn. Immunologists, Internat. Cell Rsch. Orgn. (UNESCO/WHO), N.Y. Acad. Scis., Immunocompromised Host Soc., Assn. Scientists of Indian Origin. Hindu. Office: Univ Ky 205 Sanders Brown Bldg Lexington KY 40536

BONDEMARK, LARS JOHAN, dental surgeon, orthodontist, consultant; b. Kristianstad, Skåne, Sweden, June 8, 1955; s. Yngve Karl and Siv Barbro (Larsson) B.; m. Inger Ann-Margret Palm, May 28, 1982; 1 child, Johan. Gen. cert. edn. advanced level, Coll. Kristianstad, Sweden, 1974; DDS, Ctr. for Oral Health Sci., Malmö, Sweden, 1979; specialist in orthodontics, Inst. Postgrad. Dental Edn., Jönköping, Sweden, 1990; D of Odontology, U. Lund, Sweden, 1994. Head Gen. Practice Clinic, Bjärnum, Sweden, 1979-88; asst. dept. orthodontics Inst. for Postgrad. Dental Edn., Jönköping, 1988-90; sr. cons., specialist in orthodontics Orthodontic Clinic, Hässleholm, Sweden, 1991—; referee, cons. Am. Jour. Orthodontics and Dentofacial Orthopedics, 1995—; assoc. cons. Dept. Oral Radiology, Kristianstad, 1988-91. Author: Orthodontic Magnets, 1994; contbr. articles to profl. jours. Sec. Dental Soc. Kristianstad County, 1991-96. Mem. European Orthodontic Soc., Swedish Assn. Orthodontists, Swedish Dental Soc. Home: Västerbogatan 5B, 281 47 Hässleholm Sweden Office: Orthodontic Clinic, Esplanadgatan 15, 281 38 Hassleholm Sweden

BONDS, JEAN FULTON, retired nurse; b. Harriston, Miss.; d. John Rivers and Ava Adine (Wade) Fulton; widowed; 1 child, John Christian. Diploma, Holy Name of Jesus Hosp. Sch. Nursing, Gadsden, Ala., 1956; BSN, Incarnate Word Coll., 1959; MSN, Tex. U., 1966. Draftsman Ill. Cen. R.R., Vicksburg, Miss., 1945-48; stenographer Child Welfare Dept., Fayette, Miss., 1951-53; clk. County Health Dept., Fayette, 1952-53; staff nurse VA Hosp., Jackson, Miss., 1956-57; asst. dir. nursing svcs. Grace Luth. Hosp., San Antonio, 1958-61, S.W. Tex. Meth. Hosp., San Antonio, 1962-65; edn./quality assurance coord. Holy Name of Jesus Med. Ctr., Gadsden, Ala., 1965-91, ret., 1991. Mem. Sigma Theta Tau (Alpha Delta chpt.). Roman Catholic.

BONDURANT, STUART, physician, educational administrator; b. Winston-Salem, N.C., Sept. 9, 1929; s. Stuart Osborne Bondurant; m. Susan Haughton Ehringhaus, May 5, 1991; children from previous marriage: Stuart, Margaret Lynn, Nancy Vance. B.S., Duke U., 1952, M.D., 1953; Sc.D. (hon.), Ind. U., 1980. Intern Duke Hosp., Durham, N.C., 1953-54; resident in internal medicine Duke Hosp., 1954-55; resident Peter Bent Brigham Hosp., Boston, 1958-59; asst. prof. medicine Ind. U. Sch. Medicine, Indpls., 1959-61; assoc. prof. Ind. U. Sch. Medicine, 1961-66, prof., 1966-67; assoc. dir. Ind. U. Cardiovascular Research Ctr., 1961-67; chief med. br. artificial heart-myocardial infarction program NIH, Bethesda, Md., 1966-67; prof. medicine, chmn. dept., physician in chief Albany Med. Ctr. Hosp., N.Y., 1967-74; pres., dean Albany Med. Coll., 1974-79; prof. medicine U. N.C., Chapel Hill, 1979—, dean Sch. Medicine, 1979-94; dir. Ctr. for Urban Epidemiology Studies N.Y. Acad. Medicine, N.Y.C., 1994-96. Contbr. articles to med. jours. Recipient Disting. Alumnus award Duke U. Sch. Medicine, 1974, Merit award Am. Heart Assn., 1975; Citizen Laureate U. Found., Albany, 1979. Master ACP (regent, pres. 1980); fellow Am. Soc. Clin. Investigation (v.p. 1974), Assn. Am. Physicians (pres. 1985-86), Inst. of Medicine, Assn. Am. Med. Colls. (exec. com. 1977, chmn. coun. deans 1979-81, chmn. 1993-94), Royal Coll. Physicians Edinburgh, Royal Coll. Physicians London. Office: U NC Sch Medicine Dept Medicine CB # 7005 Chapel Hill NC 27599-7005

BONEAU, C. ALAN, psychology educator, researcher; b. Cin., Feb. 2, 1926; s. Charles A. and Virginia Louise (Kircher) B.; m. Ann Mallin, Sept. 2, 1955; children: Denise Lynn, Jonathan Alan, Paul Charles. BA in Psychology with high honors, U. Cin., 1950, MA in Psychology, 1951; PhD in Exptl. Psychology, Duke U., 1957. Supr. employment testing aircraft gas turbine div. Gen. Electric Co., 1952-53; grad. asst., rsch. asst., univ. fellow Duke U., Durham, N.C., 1953-57, USPHS postdoctoral rsch. fellow, 1957-58, asst. prof., 1958-62, asst. to dean, 1962-64, assoc. prof., 1962-66; ednl. affairs officer Am. Psychol. Assn., 1966-71, dir. programs and planning, 1971-76, exec. officer, 1974-75; sr. assoc. Devel. Assocs., Inc., Arlington, Va., 1977-78; prgram mgr. Essex Corp., Alexandria, Va., 1978-80; prof. psychology George Mason U., Fairfax, Va., 1980—, chair psychology dept., 1980-82; mem. faculty senate Duke U., 1962-64; cons. in field, 1976-80; rsch. psychologist Army Rsch. Inst., 1980-89. Contbr. articles to profl. jours. Treas. Sci. Manpower Commn., 1976. With USN, 1944-46. USPHS spl. postdoctoral fellow Stanford U., 1965-66, citation classic recognition Current Contents, 1986. Fellow AAAS, APA (cons. editor Jour. Applied Psychology 1981-86, pres. div. gen. psychology 1987, exec. com. editor newsletter 1986—, rep. to Coun. Social Sci. Assns. 1975-76, liaison to Nat. Adv. Mental Health Coun.), Am. Psychol. Soc., Washington Acad. Sci.; mem. Psychonomic Soc., Soc. for Computers in Psychology, Soc. for Studying Unity Issues in Psychology (pres. 1987-88), Phi Beta Kappa, Sigma Xi. Office: Dept of Psychology George Mason U Fairfax VA 22030

BONFIGLIO, THOMAS ALBERT, pathologist, educator; b. Rochester, N.Y., Oct. 17, 1942; s. Charles P. and Minnie C. (Argentiere) B.; m. Mary Barat Rice, July 2, 1966; children: Susan Marie, Amy Elizabeth, Megan Lynn. BS magna cum laude, St. John Fisher Coll., 1964; MD, U. Rochester, 1969. Diplomate Am. Bd. Pathology; cert. Nat. Bd. Med. Examiners, Internat. Bd. Cytopathology, N.Y.S. lab. dir.; lic. Ohio, N.Y. Intern in pathology U. Hosps. Cleve., 1969-70, resident in pathology, 1969-71; tchg. fellow pathology Case Western Res. U., 1969-71; chief resident in pathology Strong Meml. Hosp., Rochester, N.Y., 1971-72; instr., pathology fellow U. Rochester Med. Ctr., 1971-72, asst. prof. pathology, 1972-76, assoc. dir. cytopathology lab., assoc. dir. sch. cytotech., 1973-76, acting dir. surg. pathology, divsn., dir. cytopathology lab., 1975-76; asst. prof. pathology Case Western Reserve U., 1976-77; asst. pathologist, chief divsns. cytopathology and surg. pathology Mt. Sinai Hosp., Cleve., 1976-77; assoc. prof. pathology U. Rochester Med. Ctr., 1977-84, prof. pathology, 1984-89, prof., acting chmn. dept. pathology and lab. medicine, 1989-90, prof., chair dept. pathology and lab. medicine, 1990—; cons. pathology Rochester Gen. Hosp., 1978—, Genesee Hosp., 1979—; attending pathologist, dir. surg./pathology unit, 1984-85, Strong Meml. Hosp., attending pathologist, dir. anatomic pathology divsn., 1985—, pathologist in chief, 1989: mem. sci. adv. bd. Cytyc Corp., Marlborough, Mass., 1994—; mem. Cytotechnologist Exam. Com., 1980-83, Biol. Stain Commn., 1981-91, cytopathology exam com. Am. Bd. Pathology, 1984-89, spl. ad hoc com. cytopathology N.Y. State Dept. Health, 1988, others; v.p. Intersoc. Pathology Coun., 1988, pres., 1989; bd. dirs. Univs. Assoc. Rsch. and Edn. in Pathology; presenter papers, abstracts; participant, invited spkr., dir., panelist numerous workshops, meetings, seminars, confs., teleconfs. in field; vis. prof., guest lectr. Med. Coll. Ohio, Toledo, 1980, Dartmouth-Hitchcock Med. Ctr., Hanover, N.H., 1982, William Beaumont Army Med. Ctr., El Paso, 1984, Med. U. N.J., Newark, 1984, New Eng. Deaconess Hosp., Boston, 1985, Henry Ford Hosp., Detroit, 1989, Loyola U. Sch. Medicine, Chgo., 1990, St. Francis Hosp., Hartford, Conn., 1991, Marshall U. Sch. Medicine, Huntington, W.Va., 1991, U. Iowa Sch. Medicine, Huntington, W.Va., 1991, U. Iowa Sch. Medicine, Iowa City, 1991, U. Mass. Sch. Medicine, 1994. Author: Cytopathologic Interpretation of Transthoracic Fine-Needle Biopsies, 1983, (with others) Histologic Typing of Female Genital Tract, 1994; mem. editl. bd. Human Pathology, 1982—, Am. Jour. Clin. Pathology, 1985—, Lab. Medicine, 1984-90; mem. N.Am. rev. bd., editl. adv. bd. ACTA Cytologica; contbr. articles to profl. jours.; author video Cytopathology of Fine Needle Biopsies of the Abdomen, 1985. Fellow Am. Soc. Clin. Pathologists (v.p. 1990-91, pres.-elect 1991-92, pres. 1992-93, clin. pathologists commn. on continuing edn., Disting. Svc. award 1988, bd. dirs. 1985-94, chmn. nominating com. 1988, 92, rsch. and devel. com. 1985-89, chmn. quality assurance steering com. 1987-92, dep. commr. commn. on continuing edn. 1984-90, chmn. coun. cytopathology 1983-84, coun. on cytopathology 1979-84), Coll. Am. Pathologists, Internat. Acad. Cytology (sci. program com. 1988-89, terminology com. 1992); mem. AMA, Am. Soc. Cytology (Cert. of Merit for outstanding svcs. 1987, Papanicolacu award 1991, v.p. 1984-85, pres.-elect 1985-86, pres. 1986-87, chmn. sci. program com. 1982-84, exec. com. 1980-88, numerous others), Am. Soc. Investigative Pathology, Arthur Purdy Stout Soc. Surg. Pathologists, Assn. Dirs. Anatomic and Surg. Pathology (coun. 1989-95), Assn. Pathology chmn., Internat. Soc. Gynecol. Pathologists, Monroe County Med. Soc., N.Y. State Soc. Pathologists, Rochester Area Assn. Pathologists (v.p. 1978-79, pres. 1979-80), U.S. and Can. Acad. Pathology, Alpha Omega Alpha. Roman Catholic. Home: 97 Stuyvesant Rd Pittsford NY 14534-3227 Office: U er Med Ctr Dept Pathology 601 Elmwood Ave Rochester NY 14642-0001

BONFORTE, RICHARD JAMES, pediatrician, educator; b. Newark Feb. 27, 1940; s. James Sebastian and Lillian Viola (Reiss) B.; m. Linda C. Berti, Dec. 29, 1979; children—Adrianna Marie, Philip Sebastian. A.B. cum laude, Seton Hall U., 1961; M.D. cum laude, Georgetown U., 1965. Diplomate: Am. Bd. Pediatrics. Intern Mt. Sinai Hosp., N.Y.C., 1965-66, pediatric resident, 1966-67, chief pediatric resident, 1967-68, ednl. fellow in pediatrics, 1970-72; dir. ambulatory pediatrics Mt. Sinai Med. Ctr., N.Y.C., 1972-82, dir. pediatric pulmonary and cystic fibrosis ctrs., 1972—; dir. pediatrics Beth Israel Med. Ctr., N.Y.C., 1982—, chmn. pediatrics, 1994—; prof. pediatrics Mt. Sinai Sch. Medicine, 1982—, adj. prof., 1994—; med. adv. council Cystic Fibrosis Found., 1976-80, 86-90; prof. pediatrics Albert Einstein Coll. Medicine, Bronx, N.Y., 1994—. Contbr. articles to profl. jours. Bd. dirs. N.Y. Lung Assn., 1984—, pres.-elect 1992-94, pres., 1994—. Decorated Army Commendation medal. Fellow Am. Acad. Pediatrics; mem. Am. Thoracic Soc., Am. Coll. Chest Physicians, N.Y. Acad. Sci., N.Y. Acad. Medicine, N.Y. Pediatric Soc., Am. Soc. Microbiology, Alpha Omega Aplha. Roman Catholic. Office: Beth Israel Med Ctr 1st Ave New York NY 10003

BONIEY, EMILY ANN, critical care nurse, anesthesist nurse; b. Weirton, W.Va., Mar. 27, 1965; d. Joseph and Mary (Kopa) B. ADN, W.Va. No. Community Coll., 1986; BSN, Duquesne U., 1988; MSN in Anesthesia, U. Pitts., 1991. RN, Pa. Staff nurse post-anesthesia ICU Presbyn. U. Hosp., Pitts., staff nurse anesthesist. Recipient U.S. Achievements Acad. award. Mem. Am. Assn. Nurse Anesthetists, Am. Assn. Critical Care Nurses, Phi Eta Sigma, Phi Theta Kappa.

BONIFAS, JANE MARIE, psychological assistant; b. Ottoville, Ohio. Jan. 18, 1935; d. George P. and Lucinda (Miller) Hilvers; m. Richard J. Bonifas, Nov. 28, 1953; children: James, Debra, Daniel, Linda, Carl, Darlene BA with high honors, Lourdes Coll., Sylvania, Ohio, 1989; MEd, U. Toledo, 1990; PhD in Clin. Psychology, Union Inst., 1994. Bookkeeper Ottoville Bank, 1953-55; seamstress Landeck, Ohio, 1960-76; dir. religious edn. St. John Ch., Landeck, 1976-85, Lima, Ohio, 1985-87; coord. regional programs Cath. Lay Ministry, Toledo, 1988-90; psychol. asst. Comprehensive Psychol. Svc. Inc., Lima, 1990—. Advisor 4-H, Landeck, 1964-78; den mother Cub Scouts, Boy Scouts Am., Landeck, 1964-78; organizer cmty. parade, Landeck, 1973; mem. AIDS Task Force, Lima, 1990-93. Mem. APA, ACA, Kappa Gamma Pi. Home: 13731 Converse Roselm Rd Venedocia OH 45894-9532 Office: Comprehensive Psychol Svc 1062 W Market St Lima OH 45805-2730

BONILLA-FELIX, MELVIN A., pediatrician, educator; b. San Juan, P.R., June 20, 1962. MD, U. Puerto Rico, 1986. Cert. pediat., pediat. nephrology, 1993. Intern U. San Juan Pediat. Hosp., 1986-87, resident in pediat., 1987-89; fellow in pediat. nephrology St. Louis Childrens, 1992; asst. prof. pediat. U. Tex., Houston, 1992—. Recipient Minority Scientist Devel. award Am. Heart Assn., 1995-96. Mem. Am. Assn. Pediat. Office: U Tex Health Sci Ctr 6431 Fannin St #3124 Houston TX 77030

BONIME, WALTER RAYMOND, psychiatrist, psychoanalyst, educator; b. Monteville, Conn., July 12, 1909; s. Ellis and Rebecca (Strongin) B.; m. Mary McGovern, Dec. 7, 1940 (div. 1953); children: Karen, Stephen; m. Florence Cummings, Sept. 5, 1953; stepchildren: Frank Cummings, Norma Lovins; children: Karen, Stephen. BA, U. Wis., 1933; MD, Columbia U., 1938. Intern Sinai Hosp., Balt., 1938-39; resident Cen. Islip State Hosp., L.I., N.Y., 1939-41; pvt. practice, N.Y.C., 1941—; clin. prof. psychiatry N.Y. Med. Coll., Valhalla, 1947—; tng. analyst Dept. Psychiatry, Inst. of Psychoanalysis of N.Y. Med. Coll. Author: (with Florence Bonime) The Clinical Use of Dreams, 1962; author: Collaborative Psychoanalysis, 1989. Passed asst. surgeon USPHS, 1943-46. Fellow Am. Psychiat. Assn., Am. Acad. Psychoanalysis (charter, editorial bd. jour. 1973—); mem. Soc. Med. Psychoanalysts (pres. 1963-64). Home and Office: 37 Washington Sq W New York NY 10011-9181

BONIN, JOHN DAVID, research biologist; b. New Haven, Dec. 28, 1951; s. Donald Francis and Helen (Mohla) B.; m. Corinne Yvette Davies, Junes 17, 1973; 1 child, David Frederick. BA, Salem State Coll., 1974; MA, SUNY-Buffalo, 1976. Fisheries rsch. biologist Ichthyological Assocs., Inc., Middletown, Del., 1976-77, sr. rsch. exptl. biologist 1977-78; rsch. asst. Tufts U.-New Eng. Med. Ctr. Hosp., Boston, 1979-82, sr. rsch. asst., 1982-84; fishery biologist Normandeau Assocs., Inc., 1984-87, tech. data processing supr., 1987-88; sr. program analyst EG&G/Dynatrend, Inc., Cambridge, Mass., 1989—; consulting sr. program anlayst Enlightened Software, Inc., Nashua, N.H., 1988-90; fisheries cons. Market Facts, Inc., Chgo., 1981-83. Contbr. articles to profl. jours. Mem. N.Y. Acad. Scis., Sigma Xi. Methodist. Home: 37 N Policy St Salem NH 03079-1949 Office: DTS-927 US DOT Transp Systems Ctr 55 Broadway Cambridge MA 02142-1001

BONK, ARNOLD E., dentist, consultant; b. Bklyn., Aug. 6, 1951; s. Jacob and Bernice Bonk; m. Helen Bonk, Aug. 29, 1972; children: Allison, Jason. BS, Bklyn. Coll., 1972; DMD, Tufts U., 1975. Resident Mt. Sinai Hosp., N.Y.C., 1975-76; pvt. practice Brookline, Mass., 1976-77, Boston, 1977-85, N.Y.C., 1986—; cons. Univ. Patents, Inc., Westport, Conn., 1985—, Howmedica/Pfizer, N.Y.C., 1988—; pres. Dental Techs., Westport, 1985-86. Fellow Acad. Gen. Dentistry; mem. ADA, Met. Dental Soc. (sec. 1982-85), lst Dist. Dental Soc. (peer rev. com. 1987—), Alpha Omega. Office: 2226 Black Rock Tpke Fairfield CT 06432-3240

BONKOVSKY, HERBERT LLOYD, gastroenterologist, educator; b. Cleve., Dec. 29, 1941; s. Otto Rudolph and Hanna (Ludwig) B.; m. Marilyn Louise Cahoon, June 3, 1967; children: Laura, Sarah, Erik. AB, Earlham Coll., 1963; MD, Case Western Res. U., 1967. Diplomate Am. Bd. Internal Medicine, Am. Bd. Gastroenterology, Nat. Bd. Med. Examiners. Intern Duke U. Med. Ctr., 1967-68; rsch. fellow, chief resident Dartmouth Med. Sch., Hanover, N.H., 1971-73, asst. prof., then assoc. prof., 1974-83; prof. Dartmouth Med. Sch., Hanover, 1983-85; rsch., clin. fellow Yale U. Sch. Medicine, New Haven, 1973-74; dir. digestive disease and liver rsch. lab. VA Med. Ctr., White River Junction, Vt., 1976-85; prof. medicine and biochem., dir. liver study unit Emory U., Atlanta, 1985-90; dir. hemochromatosis unit, dir. porphyria unit Emory U., 1985-90; dir. digestive disease lab. Emory Clinic, 1988-90; dir. div. digestive disease and nutrition U. Mass. Med. Ctr., 1990—, prof. medicine biochemistry and molecular biology, 1990—; dir. Liver-Biliary-Pancreatic Ctr., Ctr. for Study of Disorders of Iron and Porphyrin Metabolism, U. Mass. Med. Ctr. Author, editor ednl. materials, articles, papers, book chpts. Bd. deacons Evang. Congl. Ch., Harvard, Mass., 1994—; mem. adminstrv. bd. Oak Grove Meth. Ch., Decatur, Ga., 1989-90; trustee, chmn. bd. Norwich (Vt.) Congl. Ch., 1975-78, moderator, 1978-85, deacon, 1978-79; mem. Harvard Pro-Musica, 1990-93. Lt. comdr. USPHS, 1969—. Earlham merit scholar, 1959-63, Binz Meml. scholar, 1963-67. Fellow ACP, Am. Coll. Gastroenterology, Alpha Omega Alpha; mem. Am. Fedn. Clin. Rsch., Am. Soc. Clin. Investigation, Am. Gastroenterol. Assn., Iron Overload Diseases Assn. (sci. adv. bd.), Am. Porphyria Found. (chair profl. edn. com.), Am. Assn. for Study Liver Diseases (editorial bd., nominating com., assoc. editor Hepatology), AMA, Am. Soc. Biochemistry and Molecular Biology, Internat. Assn. Study Liver. Office: U Mass Med Ctr Worcester MA 01655

BONNER, DANIEL PATRICK, microbiologist, researcher; b. Bayonne, N.J., Oct. 9, 1945; s. Michael Francis and Agnes Margaret (Heeney) B.; m. Marianne Bernadette Walsh, June 3, 1972; children: Timothy, Mary Kate. BS, Fairleigh Dickinson U., 1967; MS, Rutgers U., 1969, PhD, 1972. Postdoctoral fellow Rutgers U., New Brunswick, N.J., 1972-76, asst. rsch. prof., 1977-78; rsch. investigator Squibb Inst. Med. Rsch., Princeton, N.J., 1978-79, sr. rsch. investigator, 1979-81, group leader, 1981-82, sect. head, 1982-83, asst. dept. dir., 1982-89; exec. dir. microbiology Bristol-Myers Squibb Co., Wallingford, Conn., 1989—. With U.S. Army, 1969-71. Fellow Am. Soc. Microbiology (divsn. chmn. 1989); mem. AAAS, N.Y. Acad. Scis., Japan Antibiotics Rsch. Assn., Sigma Xi. Office: Bristol Myers Squibb Co Microbiology 104 5 Research Pky Wallingford CT 06492-1927

BONNER, EILEEN M., occupational health physician; b. Phila., Apr. 8, 1955; d. Connell William and Dolores Marie (McManus) B.; m. James A. Kilgore, May 2, 1981 (div. 1985); 1 child, Susan Kilgore. BA in Biology, LaSalle U., 1977; MD, Temple U., 1981. Diplomate Am. Bd. Internal Medicine, Am. Bd. Geriat. Site physician occupl. health Rohm and Haas, Spring House, Pa., 1985—; staff physician Artman Home, Ambler, Pa., 1988—, mem. ethics com., 1993—; mem. adv. bd. Nursing Worldwide in-home RN care, Flourtown, Pa., 1995—. Mem. several coms. St. Anthony Ch., Ambler, 1989—. Mem. Am. Coll. Occupl. and Environ. Medicine, Pa. Med. Soc., Phila. Med. Soc. Republican. Roman Catholic. Office: Rohm and Haas Co PO Box 904 Spring House PA 19477

BONNER, JACK WILBUR, III, psychiatrist, educator, administrator; b. Corpus Christi, Tex., July 30, 1940; s. Jack Wilbur and Irldene (Turner) B.; m. Myra Lynn Taylor; children: Jack Wilbur, IV, Katherine Lynn, Shelley Bliss. AA, Del Mar Coll., Corpus Christi, 1960; BA with honors, U. Tex., Austin, 1961; MD, S.W. Med. Sch., U. Tex., Dallas, 1965. Diplomate Am. Bd. Psychiatry and Neurology. Intern U. Ark. Med. Center, 1965-66; resident Duke U. Med. Center, 1966-69; assoc. in psychiatry Highland Hosp. div. Duke U. Med. Center, Asheville, N.C., 1971, asst. prof. psychiatry, 1972-80, dir. outpatient services, 1972-75, med. dir., 1975-81; chmn. bd. dirs., chief exec. officer, med. dir. Highland Hosp., Asheville, N.C., 1981-92; med. dir. The Oaks Psychiat. Health Sys., Austin, Tex., 1992-93; exec. med. dir. The Oaks Psychiat. Health System, Austin, Tex., 1993-94; med. dir. Behavioral Health Svcs. Greenville (S.C.) Hosp. Sys., 1994—; asst. clin. prof. Duke U. Med. Ctr., Durham, N.C., 1982-87, asst. cons. prof. psychiatry, 1987—; clin. assoc. prof. U. N.C. Sch. Medicine, Chapel Hill, 1986-92, Quillen-Dishner Coll. Medicine, Johnson City, Tenn., 1989-92, U. Tex. Health Sci. Ctr., San Antonio, 1993-94, U. S.C. Sch. Medicine, Columbia, 1995—. Author: (with others) The Psychology of Discipline, 1983, Unmasking the Psychopath: Antisocial Personality and Related Syndromes, 1986; contbr. articles to profl. jours. Chmn. bd. dirs. The Highland Found., 1980-93; bd. dirs. Western N.C. Med. Peer Rev. Found., 1975-78; trustee La Amistad Found., Maitland, Fla., 1985-95, N.C. Symphony, 1987-92. Fellow Am. Psychiat. Assn., So. Psychiat. Assn. (v.p. 1984-85, chmn. bd. regents 1988-89, pres.-elect 1991-92, pres. 1992-93), Am. Coll. Psychiatrists (treas. 1992-95); mem. AMA, Nat. Assn. Psychiat. Health Sys. (trustee 1989-94, 1st v.p. 1990-91, pres.-elect 1991-92, pres. 1991-93), Am. Group Psychotherapy Assn., Nat. Acads. Practice, Buncombe County (N.C.) Med. Soc. (pres.-elect 1982, pres. 1983), N.C. Psychiat. Assn. (pres.-elect 1981-82, pres. 1982-83), Nat. Anorexic Aid Soc. (nat. anorexia adv. coun. 1979-86), So. Med. Assn. (sec. sect. on neurology, neurosurgery and psychiatry 1977-80, chmn.-elect 1980-81, chmn. 1981-82), Ctrl. Neuropsychiat. Hosp. Assn. (councillor 1981-85, pres.-elect 1982-83, pres. 1983-84), Group Advancement Psychiatry (treas. 1991—), U. Tex. Southwestern Med. Sch. Alumni Assn. (bd. dirs. 1988-95, pres. 1989-91), Benjamin Rush Soc., Phi Theta Kappa. Home: 4 Brookside Way Greenville SC 29605-1212 Office: Greenville Hosp Sys Behavioral Health Svcs 701 Grove Rd Greenville SC 29605-5601

BONNER, JOHN TYLER, biology educator; b. N.Y.C., May 12, 1920; s. Paul Hyde and Lilly Marguerite (Stehli) B.; m. Ruth Anna Graham, July 11, 1942; children: Rebecca, Jonathan Graham, Jeremy Tyndall, Andrew Duncan. Grad., Phillips Exeter Acad., 1937; BSc, Harvard U., 1941, MA, 1942, PhD (Jr. fellow 1942, 46-47), 1947; DSc (hon.), Middlebury Coll., 1970. Asst. to assoc. prof. Princeton U., 1947-58, prof., 1958-90, emeritus prof., 1990—, chmn. dept. biology, 1965-77, 83-84, 87-88; lectr. embryology Marine Biol. Lab., Woods Hole, Mass., 1951-52; spl. lectr. U. London, 1957, Bklyn. Coll., 1966; Arnold Bernhard vis. prof. Williams Coll., 1989; Raman prof. Indian Acad. Scis., 1990; trustee Biol. Abstracts, 1958-63; mem. bd. editors Princeton U. Press, 1965-68, 71, trustee, 1976-82. Author: Morphogenesis, 1952, Cells and Societies, 1955, The Evolution of Development, 1958 The Cellular Slime Molds, 1959, rev. edit., 1967, The Ideas of Biology, 1962, Size and Cycle, 1965, The Scale of Nature, 1969, On Development, 1974, The Evolution of Culture in Animals, 1980, (with T.A. McMahon) On Life and Size, 1983, The Evolution of Complexity, 1988, Researches on Cellular Slime Moulds, 1991, Life Cycles, 1993, Sixty Years of Biology, 1996; also sci. papers; editor: Growth and Form, 1961, Evolution and Development, 1981; assoc. editor Am. Scientist, 1961-69; mem. editl. bd. Am. Naturalist, 1958-60, 66-68, Jour. Gen. Physiology, 1962-69, Growth, 1955-89, Differentiation, 1976-90, Oxford Surveys in Evolutionary Biology, 1982-93. Pvt. to 1st lt. USAC, 1942-46; staff aero. med. lab. Wright Field, Dayton, Ohio. Sheldon traveling fellow Panama, 1941; Rockefeller traveling fellow France, 1953; Guggenheim fellow Scotland, 1958, 71-72; recipient Selman A. Waksman award for contbns. to microbiology Theobold Smith Soc.; NSF sr. postdoctoral fellow, 1963. Fellow Am. Acad. Arts and Scis., Indian Acad. Scis. (hon.); mem. NAS, Am. Soc. Naturalists, Soc. Growth and Devel., Am. Philos. Soc., Phi Beta Kappa, Sigma Xi.

BONNET, ANDRE, physician; b. St. Etienne, Loire, France, Jan. 28, 1953; s. Charles and Marcelle (Six) B.; m. Peillet Francoise, Sept. 13, 1975 (div. Feb. 1991); children: Geraldine, Alice, Juliette; m. Mariè-Josèphe Laneuw, Apr. 3, 1993; 1 child, Olivia. Mmed. Thesis, U. St. Etienne, France, 1981. With Assn. de Formation Practice in Manual Medicine, Paris, 1983-85; gen. practice medicine St. Etienne, 1981—. Fellow Assn. Formation Practice Manual Medicine.

BONNING, STEPHEN ARTHUR, physician assistant; b. Sayre, Pa., Oct. 16, 1952; s. Arthur L. Jr. and Betty Bonning; m. Julie A. Meriwether, Sept. 1, 1973; children: Matthew S., Katherine E. AAS in Bus. Adminstrn., SUNY Agrl. and Tech. Coll., Alfred, 1972; BSN, SUNY Coll. Arts and Scis., Brockport, 1981; AA in physician assistant, Essex C.C., Balt., 1986. RN, N.Y., Nev.; cert. physician asst., Md. Physician asst. bone marrow transplant Johns Hopkins Oncology Ctr., Balt., 1987-88; physician asst. Care First, Bel Air, Md., 1988-89; sr. physician asst. Johns Hopkins Oncology Ctr., Balt., 1995—; lectr. oncology Essex C.C., Balt., 1996—. Capt. USAF, USAFR, 1989-95. Fellow Am. Acad. Physician Assts., Md. Acad. Physician Assts., Nev. Acad. Physician Assts. (pres. 1991-92, sec. 1990-91). Home: 8657 Ridgely's Choice Dr Baltimore MD 21236

BONO-SNELL, BARBARA, nurse; b. Utica, N.Y., June 26, 1949; d. Joseph A. and Susan (Pricola) B.; m. James P. Snell, Oct. 16, 1976; children: Gregory, Meghan. Diploma, Utica Psychiat. Ctr., 1970; BSN, Syracuse U., 1974, MS, 1990. Head nurse Utica Psychiat. Ctr., N.Y.; community mental health nurse Hutchings Psychiat. Ctr., Syracuse, N.Y.; nurse, counselor Am. Heart Assn., Syracuse, N.Y., Benjamin Rush Ctr., Syracuse, N.Y.; clin. instr. psych nursing Crouse-Irving Meml. Hosp.; psychiat. instr. Crouse Irving Meml. Hosp. Sch. Nursing, Syracuse; instr. psych nursing Syracuse U.;

psychiat. clin. nurse specialist Home Health Care St. Joseph's Hosp., Syracuse; adult-mental health nurse Am. Nurses Credentialing Ctr., 1993. Contbr.: Understanding Basic Pharmacology: Practical Approaches for Effectice Application, 1994. Recipient award Syracuse Area Psychiat. Nurse Advanced Practice, 1993. Mem. N.Y. State Nurses Assn., Sigma Theta Tau.

BONOVITZ, JAY STUART, physician; b. Cleve., Feb. 16, 1943; s. Nathan and Fay (Belfer) B.; m. Jennifer Mary Caldwell, Jan. 27, 1973; children: Nathaniel John, Elizabeth Ann. BA with honors, U. Miami, Ohio, 1965; MD, U. Cin., 1969. Diplomate examiner Ab. Bd. Psychiatry and Neurology; lic. psychiatrist, Ohio, Pa., Md. Intern, then resident Cin. Gen. Hosp., Cin., 1969-71, fellow in adult psychiatry, 1971-73; asst. prof. U. Pa., Phila., 1975-81, clin. asst. prof., 1981-83, clin. assoc., 1992—; asst. chief psychiatry Phila. Gen. Hosp., Phila., 1976-77; dir. psychiatric svcs. Misericordia Hosp. Mercy Cath. Med. Ctr., Phila., 1977-81; dir. consultation and liaison psychiatry Graduate Hosp., Phila., 1981-83, dir. residency tng. dept. of psychiatry, 1982-83, acting dir. head injury program, 1983; pvt. practice Phila., 1983—; teaching cons. Phila. Veteran's Adminstrn. Hosp., Phila., 1980-83. Contbr. articles to profl. jours. With USN, 1973-75. Named Intern of the Year Cin. Gen. Hosp., 1970; recipient Maruice Levine Essay award, Univ. Cin., 1973. Mem. Physicians for Social Responsibility, Phila. Psychiat. Soc., Am. Psychiat. Assn., World Fedn. for Mental Health, Pa. Psychiatric Soc. Democrat. Jewish. Office: Medical Tower 255 S 17th St Ste 1605 Philadelphia PA 19103-6216 Office: Ste 111B 191 Presidential Blvd Bala Cynwyd PA 19004

BONOW, ROBERT O., cardiologist, educator; b. Camden, N.J., Mar. 11, 1947; s. S. Crawford and Sara Louise (Goden) B.; m. Patricia Hitchens, Sept. 12, 1982; children: Robert H., Samuel C. BSChemE, Lehigh U., 1969; MD, U. Pa., 1973. Diplomate Am. Bd. Internal Medicine, Am. Bd. Cardiovasc. Disease (examiner). Intern in medicine Hosp. of U. Pa., Phila., 1973-74, resident in medicine, 1974-76; commd. USPHS, 1976, advanced through grades to capt.; clin. assoc. cardiology br. Nat. Heart, Lung and Blood Inst., Bethesda, Md., 1976-79, sr. investigator, 1979-92, chief nuclear cardiology sect., 1989-92, dep. chief, 1989-92; ret., 1992; Goldberg prof. medicine Northwestern U. Med. Sch., Chgo., 1992—; chief div. cardiology Northwestern Meml. Hosp., 1992—; mem. ad hoc com. on tissue-type plasminogen activator (tPA) FDA, Bethesda, 1987; mem. working group on methods and techs. Nat. Heart Attack Alert Program, Bethesda, 1994—; mem. adv. com. vis. prof. program Pfizer, Inc., N.Y.C., 1993-96; vis. prof. 20 acad. med. ctrs.; invited lectr. over 400 nat. and internat. meetings, regional symposia and confs., acad. med. ctrs. Mem. editl. bd. 10 sci. jours.; contbr. over 400 articles and abstracts to med. jours., chpts. to books. Vol. leader Boy Scouts Am., Glencoe, Ill., 1995—. Fellow ACP, Am. Coll. Cardiology; mem. AMA (diagnostic and therapeutic assessment panel 1992-94), Am. Fedn. for Clin. Rsch., Am. Soc. for Clin. Investigation, Assn. m. Physicians, Am. Heart Assn. (chmn. program com. coun. on clin. cardiology 1994—), Soc. Nuclear Medicine (pres. cardiovasc. coun. 1991-92, mem. DuPont fellowship award com. 1991—), Am. Soc. Nuclear Cardiology (bd. dirs. 1994—), Assn. Profs. Cardiology (councilor 1994—), Assn. Univ. Cardiologists, Alpha Omega Alpha. Office: Northwestern U Med Sch 250 E Superior St Ste 524 Chicago IL 60611

BONTE, FREDERICK JAMES, radiology educator, physician; b. Bethlehem, Pa., Jan. 18, 1922; s. Frederick R. and Harriett (Stoudt) B.; m. Cecile Poetzel; children: Frederick W., Stephen J., John A., Therese A., Suzanne M., Ann E. BS, Western Res. U., 1942, MD, 1945. Diplomate: Am. Bd. Radiology (trustee 1969-75), Am. Bd. Nuclear Medicine. Intern Huntington Meml. Hosp., Pasadena, Cal., 1945-46; resident Univ. Hosp., Cleve., 1948-52; practice medicine, specializing in radiology and nuclear medicine Dallas, 1956—; mem. faculty Western Res. U. Sch. Medicine, 1952-56, asst. prof., 1952-56, chief radiotherapy and nuclear medicine, 1954-56; prof. U. Tex. Southwestern Med. Sch., Dallas, 1956—; chmn. dept. radiology U. Tex. Southwestern Med. Sch., 1956-73, dean, 1973-80; dir. Nuclear Medicine Research Center, 1980—, Effie and Wofford Cain disting. chair in diagnostic imaging; Dr. Jack Krohmer prof. in radiation physics; Mem. bd. Nat. Council Radiation Protection and Measurements, 1966-71; radiology tng. com. Nat. Insts. Gen. Med. Scis., USPHS, 1966-70, residency rev. com. radiology AMA, 1966-69, adv. and rev. coms. VA, 1972—; Founding trustee Am. Bd. Nuclear Medicine, 1971-73, chmn., 1977-80; internat. cons. on med. edn. Contbr. articles to profl. jours. Served to capt. USAAF, 1946-48. Fellow Am. Coll. Radiology, Am. Coll. Nuclear Physicians; mem. AMA (del., chmn. grad. med. edn. com., De Hevesy Nuclear Pioneer award 1995, Centennial Hartman medal 1995), Soc. Nuclear Medicine (bd. dirs.), Am. Roentgen Ray Soc. (exec. com.), Radiol. Soc. N.Am., Sigma Xi, Alpha Omega Alpha. Home: 11138 Wonderland Trl Dallas TX 75229-3943 Office: 5323 Harry Hines Blvd Dallas TX 75235-9061

BONUEL, JUAN JIMENEZ, nurse; b. Sorsogon, Philippines, Jan. 1, 1969; came to U.S., 1989; s. Justo Duazo and Virginia (Jimenez) B. BS in Med. Tech., Far Eastern U., Manila, 1989; ADN, Glendale (Calif.) C.C., 1993. RN, Calif.; cert. clin. lab. technologist, Calif.; cert. BLS, ACLS. Med. technologist Polymedic Gen. Hosp., Manila, 1989; staff nurse, telemetry unit Victor Valley Cmty. Hosp., Glendale, 1993—. Edvard Grieg Norwegian scholar, 1992; Dr. Griffin McKay scholar, 1992. Home: 12265 Four Winds Way Victorville CA 92392

BOODEN, THEODORE, dean; b. Chgo., Sept. 17, 1936; s. Hyman and Gertrude (Rubenzik) B.; m. Betty B. Katz, June 28, 1959; children: Michael R., Stewart K., Rebecca E. BS, Roosevelt U., 1960; MS, Northwestern U., 1962; DPhil, Fla. State U., 1968. From instr. to assoc. prof. The Chgo. Med. Sch., 1970-91, prof., 1991—; site sec. Liaison Com. Med. Edn., Chgo. and Washington. Office: FUHS/CMS 3333 Green Bay Rd North Chicago IL 60064*

BOOK, NANCY ANN WILEY, elementary school nurse; b. Waynesburg, Pa., Apr. 4, 1940; d. Asa Gordon and Mildred Louise (Fisher) Wiley; m. John R. Book, Dec. 4, 1965; children: Jennifer, Robert. RN, Presbyn. U. Hosp. Sch. Nursing, 1964; BS, Waynesburg Coll., 1965; cert. in sch. nursing, Slippery Rock (Pa.) U., 1975, postgrad.; M degree, Pa. State U. Staff pediatric nurse, pediatric nursing instr. Jameson Meml. Hosp., New Castle, Pa., 1964-66, blood bank nurse, 1972-76;, 1966-68, 76-78; sch. nurse Slippery Rock Area Schs. Mem. Nat. Assn. Sch. Nurses, Kappa Delta Pi, Sigma Theta Tau Internat.

BOOKER, JAMES AVERY, JR., surgeon; b. Richmond, Va., May 26, 1936; s. James Avery and Thelma Martha (Morton) B.; m. Rita M. Booker, Nov. 24, 1984; children: James A. III, Karla L., Michael J., Ja Rita B. BS, Hampton (Va.) U., 1957; DDS, Med. Coll. Va., 1961; MD, Howard U., Washington, 1968. Diplomate Am. Bd. Surgery, Am. Bd. Quality Assurance and UR Physicians (mem. fin. com. 1989-91). Pvt. practice gen. surgery Oakland, Calif., 1976-90, Torrance, Calif., 1991—; v.p., med. dir. Family Health Found., Alviso, Calif., 1989-90; pvt. practice Torrance, Calif., 1991—. With USAF, from 1962, col. Res. Decorated Air Force Commendation medal. Fellow ACS, Am. Coll. Med. Quality (membership and credentials com. 1990-91), Internat. Coll. Surgeons (exec. com. So. Calif. chpt. 1991—), Southwestern Surg. Congress; mem. Am. Coll. Physician Execs. Office: 3655 W Lomita Blvd #115 Torrance CA 90505

BOONE, CHARLES W., physician, pathologist; b. Berkeley, Calif., Dec. 21, 1925; s. Harmon Dunscomb and Florence Celia (Chandler) B.; m. Alexandra Weekes, Dec. 21, 1992. MD, U. Calif., San Francisco, 1951; PhD, U. Calif., L.A., 1964. Diplomate Am. Coll. Am. Pathologists. Intern gen. practice UCLA, 1954-56, resident pathology, 1956-60, PhD tng. Dept. Biochemistry, 1960-64; post doctoral tng. in Cell Biology Albert Einstein Coll. Medicine, Bronx, N.Y., 1964-65; chief cell biology sect. Nat. Cancer Inst., NIH, Bethesda, Md., 1965-80; chief pathology Al Hada Hosp., Taif, Saudi Arabia, 1980-84; program dir. chemoprevention branch, Divsn. of Cancer Prevention and Control Al Hada Hosp., Taif, 1984—. Author (book) Cancer Prevention, 1992; contbr. over 140 articles to sci. jours. Ensign USN, 1943-45. Home: 8011 Newdale Rd Bethesda MD 20814

BOONE, DANIEL RICHARD, speech disorders educator; b. Chgo., Oct. 30, 1927; s. Claude Benjamin and Pearl Lillian (Richardson) B.; m. Mary Augusta Mosenthal, Dec. 28, 1954; children: Mary P., James R., Robert T., Rebecca A. BA, U. Redlands, 1951; MA, Case Western Res. U., 1954, PhD, 1958. Chief speech pathology Highland View Hosp., Cleve., 1956-60; asst. prof. speech disorders Case Western Res. U., Cleve., 1960-63; assoc. prof. U. Kans. Med. Ctr., Kansas City, 1963-66; prof. U. Denver, 1966-73, U. Ariz., Tucson, 1973—; cons. U.S. Office Edn., Washington, 1967-75, NIH, Bethesda, Md., 1975-85, Prentice-Hall, Englewood Cliffs, N.J., 1973—. Author: The Voice and Voice Therapy, 1971, 5th rev. edit., 1994, Cerebral Palsy, 1973, Human Communication and Its Disorders, 1987, 2d rev. edit., 1993, Is Your Voice Telling on You?, 1991; contbr. articles to profl. jours. Served as cpl. U.S. Army, 1945-47, Korea. Recipient Disting. Service award U. Redlands, Calif., 1978. Fellow and honors Am. Speech Lang. and Hearing Assn. (v.p. 1969, pres. 1975-77); mem. Colo. Speech and Hearing Assn. (pres. 1971), Ariz. Speech and Hearing Assn., Acad. Aphasia (treas. 1969-72), Sigma Xi. Home: 5715 N Genematas Dr Tucson AZ 85704-5935

BOONE, FRANKLIN DELANOR ROOSEVELT, SR., cardiovascular perfusionist, realtor; b. Wake Forest, N.C., Aug. 19, 1942; s. John Henry and Beulah Bell (Massenburg) B.; m. Lois Mae Daye, July 20, 1962; children: Franklin Delanor Roosevelt Jr., Fredrick Louis (dec.). Student, N.C. Cen. U., 1960-62, U. N.C., 1968. Cert. cardiovascular perfusionist. Tech. trainee Dept. Cardiology Duke Med. Ctr., Durham, N.C., 1962-63, technician Hypobaric Surgery Dept., 1963-65; med. equipment specialist IV dept. cardiothoracic surgery N.C. Meml. Hosp., Chapel Hill, 1965-72, perfusionist, 1972—; chief cardiovascular perfusionist U. N.C. Hosps., Chapel Hill, 1991—; realtor Boone Realty Co., Durham, 1979—. Bd. dirs. Holy Cross Cath. Ch. Fellow Am. Soc. Extra-Corporeal Tech.; mem. State Employees' Assn., Durham Bd. Realtors, Holy Cross Men's Soc. Democrat. Home: 6136 Yellowstone Dr Durham NC 27713-9708 Office: NC Meml Hosp Dept Cardiothoracic Su Chapel Hill NC 27415

BOONE, MARSHALL NOLAN, JR., physician, educator; b. Langdale, Ala., Oct. 18, 1942; s. Marshall Nolan and Daisy (Zeiger) B.; m. Carla Wallace, Sept. 20, 1964; children: Jonathan Michael, Ashley Rebecca. BS, Samford U., 1964; PhD, U. Ala., Birmingham, 1972, MD cum laude, 1975. Diplomate Am. Bd. Family Practice, recert., 1991. Resident in family practice U. Ala., Huntsville, 1975-78; emergency room physician Shelby Med. Ctr., Alabaster, Ala., 1978-81, 83-85, Helena (Ala.) Clinic, 1982-83; med. dir. HealthAm./Maxicare, Montgomery, Ala., 1985-86; assoc. med. dir. Carraway Family Medicine, Birmingham, 1987-89, dir. residency program, 1989—. Recipient Mead Johnson award for grad. med edn., 1977. Fellow Am. Acad. Family Physicians; mem. AMA, Soc. Tchrs. Family Practice, Soc. Med. Assn., Jeferson County Acad. Family Physicians (pres. 1991-92), Alpha Omega Alpha. Republican. Baptist. Office: Carraway Family Medicine 3001 27th St N Birmingham AL 35207-4549

BOONE, ROBERT DAVID, healthcare executive; b. Newnan, Ga., Oct. 23, 1956; s. Daniel Walter Boone, Jr. and Winifred Trimble (Glover) Klein; m. Melissa Conklin, June 8, 1991; children: Callie Élise, Robert David Jr. BA in Chemistry, Wake Forest U., 1979; MBA, Ga. State U., 1985, MHA, 1986. Diplomate Am. Coll. Healthcare Execs. Adminstrv. resident Riverside Hosp., Newport News, Va., 1985-86; adminstrv. fellow Hamilton Healthcare Sys., Dalton, Ga., 1986-87; dir. profl. svcs. Moore Regional Hosp., Pinehurst, N.C., 1987-89, v.p. inpatient svcs., 1989-92, v.p. profl. svcs., 1992-95, v.p. bus. health svcs., 1996—; wellness/health promotion cons. RDB Enterprises, Pinehurst, 1990—; pres. Sandhills Healthcare Execs. Forum, Fayetteville, N.C., 1993-94, Pinehurst Bus. Guild, 1994. Explorer chmn. Boy Scouts of Am., Oconeechee Coun., So. Pines, N.C., 1988-94; bd. dirs. United Way of Moore County, So. Pines, 1989-95, Pinehurst Bus. Guild, 1991-94; deacon Bethesda Presbyn. Ch., Aberdeen, N.C., 1991-94. Capt. U.S. Army, 1979-86. Mem. Soc. for the Preservation and Encouragement of Barbershop Quartet Singing in Am., Ducks Unltd., Quail Unltd. Home: PO Box 1178 Pinehurst NC 28374 Office: Moore Regional Hosp PO Box 3000 Pinehurst NC 28374

BOONE, SEAN, physician; b. Hugo, Okla., Dec. 23, 1965; d. Douglas Ray and Alberta Gayle (Owens) Dawson; m. Larry Boone, Sept. 11, 1993. BA in Biology, U. North Tex., 1988; DO, U. North. Tex. Health Sci. Ctr, 1995. Rsch. tech. Southwestern Med. Sch., Dallas, 1989-91; resident U. Tex. Health Ctr., Tyler, 1995—. Mem. Am. Osteo. Assn., Am. Coll. Osteo. Family Practice, Tex. Med. Assn. Home: HC 69 Box 173 Hugo OK 74743

BOONE, STEPHEN CHRISTOPHER, neurosurgeon; b. Navasota, Tex., Mar. 18, 1938; s. Berrill Harrison and Joyce (Taylor) B.; m. Elizabeth Thompson, Apr. 9, 1960 (div. June 1979); children: Stephen, Michael, Laura; m. Susan Pate, Nov. 3, 1979; children: Christopher, Emily. BS, Duke U., 1960, MD, 1965, PhD, 1965. Diplomate Am. Bd. Neurological Surgery. Surg. intern Duke Hosp., Durham, N.C., 1965, resident in neurosurgery, 1967-72; chief neurosurgeon Brooke Army Med. Ctr., 1973-75; asst. chief neurosurgery Walter Reed Army Med. Ctr., Washington, 1975-77; from assoc. prof. to prof. neurosurgery U. N.C., 1977-82; neurosurgeon Raleigh Neurosurgery Clinic, N.C., 1982—. Brig. gen. U.S. Army, 1962-87. Republican. Episcopal. Office: Raleigh Neurosurgery Clinic 3009 New Bern Ave Raleigh NC 27620

BOOTH, ALLEN MICHAEL, cardiothoracic surgeon; b. Fulton, N.Y., Mar. 22, 1952; s. George Lawrence and Patricia (Goodman) B.; m. Sue Anne Newpher, June 15, 1974; children: Michelle, Philip, Matthew, Brian, Scott, Patrick, Kevin, David. BA, Jphns Hopkins U., 1974, MD, 1977; PhD, U. Minn., 1987. Resident U. Minn., Mpls., 1977-86, Albany Med. Ctr., 1986-88; cardiothoracic surgeon Heart and Lung Clinic, Bismarck, N.D., 1989—; clin. assoc. prof. surgery U. N.D. Med. Sch., Bismarck, 1989—; dir. Blue Cross Blue Shield N.D., Fargo, 1995—. Fellow Am. Coll. Surgeons (chpt. pres. 1993—), Am. Coll. Cardiology, Am. Coll. Chest Physicians; mem. AMA, Soc. Thoracic Surgeons. Office: Heart and Lund Clinic PO Box 2698 Bismark ND 58502

BOOTH, EDGAR JOHN, radiologist; b. San Diego, May 15, 1962; s. Edgar Kent and Mary Jean (Watts) B.; 1 child, James Edgar. BS in Biomed. Sci., U. Calif. Riverside, 1984; MD, UCLA, 1987. Diplomate Am. Bd. Radiology, Nuclear Medicine, Nat. Bd. Med. Examiners. Med. dir. nuclear medicine, radiologist LDS Hosp., Salt Lake City, 1994—. Mem. AMA, Am. Roentgen Ray Soc., Am. Coll. Radiology, Soc. Nuclear Medicine, Utah Med. Assn. Office: LDS Hosp Dept Radiology 8th Ave & C St Salt Lake City UT 84143

BOOTH, FRANK WEAVER, physiology educator, researcher; b. Akron, Ohio, July 3, 1943; s. Frank Weaver and Barbara Lou (Wilson) B. BS, Denison U., 1965; PhD, U. Iowa, 1970. Prof. integrative biology U. Tex. Med. Sch., Houston, 1975—. Contbr. articles to Am. Jour. Physiology, Jour. Applied Physiology, Physiology Rev. Office: U Tex Med Sch 6431 Fannin St 4.100 MSB Houston TX 77030-1501

BOOTH, FRANKLIN MILLER, plastic surgeon; b. Valley Park, Mo., Nov. 5, 1921; s. George William and Leila (Miller) B.; m. Janis A. Booth, Oct. 5, 1967; children: Adriann Miller, Briann Elizabeth. MD, St. Louis U., 1950. Diplomate Am. Bd. Plastic Surgery. Intern Mo. Bapt. Hosp., St. Louis, 1950-51; gen. surg. resident West Pa. Hosp., 1951-52, VA Hosp., St. Louis, 1952-55; plastic surg. resident Ind. U. Med. Ctr., 1955-57; pvt. practice South Bend, Ind., 1957—. With U.S. Army, 1942-45. Decorated Bronze Star medal. Fellow ACS; mem. Am. Soc. Plastic and Reconstructive Surgeons. Home: 3610 Northside Blvd South Bend IN 46615 Office: 2105 Valley Am Bank Bldg South Bend IN 46601

BOOTH, HILDA EARL FERGUSON, clinical psychologist, Spanish educator; b. Pinehurst, N.C., Aug. 14, 1943; d. Arthur C. and Edna Estelle (Henry) Ferguson; m. Thomas Gilbert Booth, Oct. 25, 1966 (dec. Apr. 1990). AA, Montreat-Anderson Coll., 1963; BA, Pembroke State U., 1965; MS, Valdosta State U., 1985; postgrad. U. S.C., 1991. Lic. profl. counselor, S.C., cert. counselor, hypnotherapist; Spanish instr. C.C., Lake City, Fla., 1983-86; clin. counselor Columbia Counseling, Lake City, Fla., 1985-87; children's psychologist I Coastal Empire Mental Health Ctr., Allendale, S.C., 1987; psychologist II, 1988; office mgr., 1987—; pvt. practice, Allendale, 1989-91; mem. assessment team, mutual health cons. Richland Meml. Hosp., Richland Springs; spl. svcs. coord., area coord. Allendale office, 1989; dir. women FORSPRO (Spain), Coral Gables, Fla., 1984-88; aquatics instr. Harbison Recreation Ctr., 1993; aquatics leader Nat. Arthritis Found., 1994; mem. mobile assessment team Richland Meml. Hosp., Richland Springs. 1994; emergency services staff Mental Health, Lake City, 1985-87; mem. Children at Risk team, Children's Advocacy team, 1987—. Mem. extension community planning com. City of Allendale, 1989-91, Shandon Presbyn. Ch.; pres. Protestant Women of Chapel, Nfld., Can., 1969, Church Women United, Lake City, 1976; deacon First Presby. Ch., Lake City, 1976-86, chmn. bd. deacons, 1982, elder 1985; elder Allendale Presby. Ch. 1988—, clk. of session, 1989—, tchr. Sunday sch., 1994; mem. LWV. Served to lt. (j.g.) USN, 1965-67. Fellow Internat. Biog. Assn.; Mem. NAFFE, AAUW, SEICUS, Inter-Am. Soc. of Psychology, Am. Legion (life), Nat. Beta Club, Soc. Noetic Scis., Robert Burns Soc. Republican. Avocations: painting, swimming, travel, reading, Spanish. Home and Office: 3134 Prentice Ave Columbia SC 29205-3940

BOOTH, RACHEL ZONELLE, nursing educator; b. Seneca, S.C., Feb. 10, 1936; m. Richard B. Booth, Feb. 13, 1957; 1 child, Kevin M. Student, Furman U., 1953-54; diploma in nursing, Greenville (S.C.) Gen. Hosp., 1956; student, U. Alaska, 1964-66; BS in Nursing, U. Md., Balt., 1968; MS in Nursing, U. Md., 1970, PhD in Adminstrn. Higher Edn., 1978. RN. Staff nurse VA Hosp., Murfreesboro, Tenn., 1957-58, U. Colo. Med. Ctr., Denver, 1957-58; nurse psychiatry dept. Patton State Hosp., Calif., 1958-59; staff nurse USAF Dispensary, Iraklion, Greece, 1959-60; charge nurse psychiatry Santa Rose Med. Ctr., San Antonio, 1961; staff nurse Shannon S.W. Tex. Meml. Hosp., San Angelo, 1962; supervisory clin. nurse, head nurse U.S. Dept. Health, Edn., and Welfare/USPHS/Indian Health Service, Anchorage, 1962-66; staff nurse U.S. Dept. Health, Edn., and Welfare/USPHS, Balt., 1966, 68; assoc. dir. dept. nursing U. Md. Hosp., 1970-76, dir. primary care nursing svc., 1976-81; asst. prof. Sch. Nursing U. Md., 1972-76, asst. prof. Sch. Pharmacy, 1972-80, acting assoc. dean Sch. Nursing, 1979-81, assoc. prof. Sch. Nursing, 1979, assoc. prof. clin. pharmacy, 1980-83, assoc. dean for undergrad. studies Sch. Nursing, 1981-83, co-dir. nurse practitioner program Sch. Nursing, 1972-76, chairperson grad. program dept. primary care, 1974-79; dean, Sch. of Nursing and asst. v.p. for health affairs Duke U., Durham, N.C., 1984-87; dean Sch. Nursing U. Ala. at Birmingham, University Station, 1987—; instr. Sch. Medicine U. Md., 1972-83, program dir. primary care nurse practitioner program continuing edn., 1976-82, project dir. Robert Wood Johnson Nurse Faculty Fellowship program, 1977-82; mem. joint practice com. Med. and Chirurg. Faculty Md., 1974-77, mem. tech. adv. com. for physician's assts. Bd. Med. Examiners Md., 1975-80; mem. adv. com. nursing program Community Coll. Balt., 1976-79; mem. Joint Commn. on Accreditation of Hosps., pres. Md. Council Dirs. of Assoc. Degree, Diploma, and Baccalaureate Programs, 1982-83; mem. adv. bd. nursing Essex Community Coll., 1983; mem. peer rev. panel advanced nurse edn. nursing div. U.S. Dept. Health and Human Services, 1987—. Editor (with others) Hospital Pharmacy, 1971-72; asst. editor Jour. Profl. Nursing, 1984-87; contbr. articles on nursing to profl. jours. Bd. dirs. Health and Welfare Coun. Ctrl. Md., Inc., 1974-78, v.p., 1975-78; mem. health adv. com. to Pres. of Pakistan, 1981—. Recipient numerous grants for nursing adminstrn., 1972—. Mem. ANA (mem. nat. rev. com. 1975-78, v.p. 1977, chair 1978), Internat. Coun. Nurses (observer conf. 1981), Nat. Acad. Practice for Nursing (vice chairperson 1984-89), Nat. Orgn. for Nurse Execs., Nat. League for Nursing, Coun. Nat. Acad. Practice, Am. Assn. Colls. in Nursing (dean's summer seminar com. 1984-85, edn. and credentialing com. 1985-86, nominating com. 1986-87, bd. dirs. 1989—, pres.-elect 1992-94, pres. 1994-96), N.C. Orgn. Nurse Execs. (bd. dirs. 1986-87), So. Coun. Collegiate Edn. for Nursing (exec. com. 1986-91, v.p., bd. dirs. 1991-94), Sigma Theta Tau (chairperson nominating com. 1974, mem. 1975, rec. sec. 1980-83). Home: 3112 Bradford Pl Birmingham AL 35242-4602

BOOTHMAN, DAVID ALLEN, molecular biologist, researcher; b. Detroit, Jan. 21, 1958; s. Raymond Joseph and Francis (Kazul) B.; m. Elizabeth M. Iglesias, June 21, 1989; 1 child, John Francis Iglesias-Boothman. BS, U. Mich., 1981; PhD, U. Miami, 1986. Postdoctoral fellow div. cell growth and regulation Harvard U. Dana Farber Cancer Inst., Boston, 1986-89; asst. prof. dept. radiation, oncology divsn. cancer biology U. Mich., Ann Arbor, 1989-93; asst. prof. dept. human oncology U. Wis., Madison, 1993-96, assoc. prof. dept. human oncology, 199—; bd. dirs. Ea. Student Rsch. Forum, Miami, 1984-86. Author: Pharmacol & Therap., 1989, Mutation Research, 1988; contbr. articles to profl. jours. Mem. Amnesty Internat., Ann Arbor, 1991. Recipient award Am. Assn. Cancer Rsch., 1985; grantee: Milheim Found. 1990, NIH, 1991-95 DOE, 1992, Breast Cancer Rsch. Fund, 1996, Breast Cancer Inspiration Fund, 1996. Mem. AAAS, Am. Soc. Microbiology, Am. Assn. Cancer Rsch., Radiation Rsch. Soc., Sigma Xi. Democrat. Roman Catholic.

BOOZ, BARBARA JEAN, critical care nurse; b. Doylestown, Pa., Sept. 3, 1953; d. Kenneth Stone and Doris (Cooper) B. Student, Ea. Coll., 1981; BSN, Widener U., 1983. Med. surgical nursing cert. Coronary care subacute nurse U. N.Mex. Hosp., Albuquerque. Mem. Am. Assn. Critical Care Nurses, Am. Nurses Assn., RNC.

BOOZE, THOMAS FRANKLIN, toxicologist; b. Denver, Mar. 4, 1955; s. Ralph Walker and Ann (McNatt) B.; children: Heather N., Ian T. BS, U. Calif., Davis, 1978; MS, Kans. State U., 1981, PhD, 1985. Registered environ assessor, Calif. Asst. instr. Kans. State U., Manhattan, 1979-85; sr. consulting toxicologist Chevron Corp., Sacramento, 1985-92; sr. toxicologist Radian Corp., Sacramento, 1992—; cons. in field, Manhattan, Kans., 1981-83. contbr. articles to profl. jours. Vol. Amigos de las Americas, Marin County, Calif., 1973, Hospice Care, Manhattan, 1985. Mem. N.Y. Acad. Sci., Soc. Toxicology, Soc. for Risk Analysis, Sigma Xi. Home: 8338 Titian Ridge Ct Antelope CA 95843-5627 Office: Radian Corp 10389 Old Placerville Rd Sacramento CA 95827-2506

BOOZER, CAROL SUE NEELY, nutrition researcher, educator; b. Jefferson, Iowa, Sept. 2, 1944; d. Frank E. and Mary Lucille (Worland) Neely; m. Allen H. Boozer, Aug. 10, 1968; children: Allen David, Anna L. BSc, Mich. State U., 1966; M in Nutrition Sci., Cornell U., 1968; MSc, Harvard U., 1973, DSc, 1976. Rsch. asst. Dunn Nutritional Lab., Cambridge, Eng., 1968-69; instr. biology Ithaca (N.Y.) Coll., 1969-70, Okaloosa-Walton Jr. Coll., Niceville, Fla., 1971; tchr. sci. Okaloosa County Sch. Bd., Ft. Walton Beach, Fla., 1970-71; instr./lectr. biology Princeton (N.J.) U., 1975-78; sys. nutritionist ComCater Internat., Skillman, N.J., 1983-85; postdoctoral fellow VA Med. Ctr., Hampton, Va., 1988-89, rsch. scientist, chief energy metabolism lab., 1989-94; instr. internal medicine Ea. Va. Med. Sch., Norfolk, 1988-89, asst. prof., 1989-94; insr. biology Gov.'s Sch. for Sci., Hampton, 1991-94; asst. prof. Coll. Physicians and Surgeons, Columbia U., 1994—; dir. Energy Metabolism Core Lab. Obesity Rsch. Ctr. St. Luke's-Roosevelt Hosp. Ctr., 1994—. Contbr. articles and abstracts to sci. jours. Pres. Coop. Nursery Sch., Rocky Hill, N.J., 1979-80; sec. Rocky Hill Cmty. Group, 1983-84; mem. Rocky Hill Sch. Bd., 1985-86. Rsch. grantee Ea. Va. Med. Sch., 1988-89, 90-91, Jeffress Meml. Trust, 1991-93, NIH, 1994—. Mem. N.Am. Assn. for Study Obesity, Am. Inst. Nutrition, Soc. for Study Ingestive Behavior, Am. Dietetic Assn. (Young Investigator award Va. chpt. 1988), Am. Diabetes Assn. (affiliate). Home: 450 Riverside Dr Apt 32 New York NY 10027-6821 Office: St Lukes-Roosevelt Hosp Ctr WH 1029 Obesity Rsch Ctr 1111 Amsterdam Ave New York NY 10025-1716

BOOZER, CHARLES HERBERT, dentist, educator; b. Port Neches, Tex., Sept. 19, 1933; s. Herbert and Mary E. (Tolle) B.; m. Marilyn Townsley, Mar. 28, 1959; children: Elizabeth, Douglas. BS, Lamar State Coll. Tech., Beaumont, Tex., 1954; DDS, U. Tex., Houston, 1957; MA, U. New Orleans, 1975. Diplomate Am. Bd. Oral Medicine. Pvt. practice Beaumont, Tex., 1957-70; prof., chmn. dept. oral diagnosis, medicine, radiology La. State U. Dental Sch., 1970; pres. Orgn. Tchrs. Oral Diagnosis, 1986-87; chmn. coun. dental therapeutics ADA, Chicago, 1980-85. Contbr. articles to profl. jours. Fellow Am. Coll. Dentists, Acad. Gen. Dentistry; mem. Acad. Oral Diagnosis, Medicine, Radiology (pres. 1986-88), Am. Assn. Stamatologists (sec., treas. 1995—). Baptist. Home: 4616 James Dr Metairie LA 70003 Office: La Stat Univ Dental Sch 1100 Fla Ave New Orleans LA 70119

BOPE, FRANK WILLIS, pharmacy educator; b. Thornville, Ohio, Oct. 30, 1918; s. Jesse Benton and Edna Blanche (Witmer) B.; m. Eleanor Parker, June 24, 1944 (dec. Nov. 1987); 1 child, Linda Bope Maeder; m. Mary Helser Ferguson, Sept. 2, 1992. BS in Pharmacy summa cum laude, Ohio State U., 1941; PhD in Pharm. Chemistry, U. Minn., 1948. Registered pharmacist, Ohio. Grad. teaching asst. U. Minn. Coll. Pharmacy, Mpls.,

1941-42; asst. prof. Ohio State U. Coll. Pharmacy, Columbus, 1948-52; assoc. prof. Ohio State U. Coll. Pharmacy, 1952-58, assoc. prof., coll. sec., 1958-60, prof., coll. sec., 1960-70, prof., asst. dean, coll. sec., 1970-81; prof., assoc. dean., coll. sec., 1981-84; assoc. dean., emeritus Ohio State U. Coll. Pharmacy, 1984—. Contbr. articles to Nat. Pharmacy Jour. Capt. U.S. Army, 1942-46. Mem. Am. Assn. Coll. Pharmacy, Am. Pharm. Assn., Ohio State U. Alumni Assn., Sigma Xi. Home: 177 Desantis Dr Columbus OH 43214-2738

BORAN, ROBERT PAUL, JR., orthopedic surgeon; b. Pottsville, Pa., May 21, 1952; s. Robert Paul Sr. and Ellen Elizabeth (Reisig) B.; m. Catherine Virginia Kling, Oct. 18, 1980; children: Catherine, Ellen, Mary. BS, St. Joseph U., 1974; MD, Jefferson Med. Coll., 1978. Diplomate Am. Bd. Orthopedic Surgery. Lab. technician Pottsville Hosp., 1972-74; disc jockey WPPA-AM and WAVT-FM, Pottsville, 1972-75; intern dept. sick and injured Pa. Hosp., Phila., 1978-79; resident in orthopedic surgery Thomas Jefferson U. Hosp., Phila., 1979-83; chief resident Alfred I. DuPont Inst. of Nemours Found. Crippled Children, Wilmington, Del., 1981, U.S. VA Hosp., Wilmington; pvt. practice Pottsville, 1983—; mem. clin. adj. faculty dept. allied health sci. Kings Coll., Wilkes Barre, Pa. Bd. dirs. Schuylkill Rehab. Ctr., 1987—, chmn. bd. dirs., 1988—. Fellow ACS, Am. Acad. Orthopaedic Surgeons; mem. AMA, Pa. Med. Soc., Schuylkill County Med. Soc., Am. Assn. Hip and Knee Surgeons, Assn. Arthritic Hip and Knee Surgeons, Ea. Orthopaedic Assn., Pa. Orthopaedic Soc., N.Am. Faculty of Swiss Assn. for Study of Internal Fixation of Fractures, AO Alumni N.Am., Jefferson Orthopaedic Soc., Alfred I. DuPont Inst. Alumni Assn., Thomas Bond Soc. of Pa. Hosp., Union League of Phila., Schuylkill Country Club, Vesper Club, Pottsville Club, Skytop Club, Ancient Order of Hibernians, Alpha Sigma Nu. Republican. Roman Catholic. Home: RD #5 Box 5857 Pottsville PA 17901 Office: 313 Washington St Pottsville PA 17901

BORAZ, ROBERT ALAN, dentist, surgery and pediatrics educator; b. St. Louis, Apr. 13, 1951; s. Herbert Sigmund and Pearl Yetta (Garber) B.; m. Janet Ruth Knie, Jan. 3, 1981; children: Jonathan Daniel, Katharine Elizabeth. Student, U. Mo., 1969-72, DDS, 1975, postgrad., 1975-77. Resident Children's Mercy Hosp., Kansas City, Mo., 1975-77; dir. dental svc. U. Kans. Med. Ctr., Kansas City, 1977—, prof. surgery, 1984—; assoc. prof. U. Mo. Dental Sch., Kansas City, 1977—, chief dentistry Children's Rehab. Unit, Kansas City, 1977—; assoc. dir. Sutherland Inst. Facial Rehab., Kansas City, 1984—; specialty examiner Mo. Dental Bd., Jefferson City, Mo., 1987-96. Contbr. articles to profl. jours. Mem. Gov.'s Task Force on Hemophilia, Topeka, 1984-86; mem. prof. edn. com. Am. Cancer Soc., Topeka, 1987-96; mem. regional bd. Easter Seal Soc., Greater Kansas City, 1979-82; trustee Am. Soc. of Dentistry for Children, 1989-96. Fellow Am. Coll. Dentists, Internat. Coll. Dentists, Am. Acad. Pediatric Dentistry (component pres. 1984-96, trustee 1991-94, parliamentarian 1994-96, sec.-treas. 1996—), Am. Soc. Dentistry for Children (Kans. pres. 1988—, bd. trustees 1989—, Cert. of Merit 1976), Am. Assn. Hosp. Dentists, Acad. Dentistry for the Handicapped; mem. ADA, S.W. Soc. Pediatric Dentistry (v.p. 1988-89, pres.-elect 1992, pres. 1992-93), Alpha Omega (local pres. 1973-75), Omicron Kappa Upsilon. Office: U Kans Med Ctr 3901 Rainbow Blvd Kansas City KS 66160-0001

BORDAGE, GEORGES, physician, medical education educator; b. St.-Louis-De-Kent, N.B., Can., May 30, 1947; came to U.S., 1992; s. Edmond and Rita (Gionet) B.; m. Joanne R. Fisher, Dec. 9, 1978; children: Anna, Daniel. BA, Coll. Bathurst, N.B., 1969; MD, U. Laval, Quebec City, Que., Can., 1973; MSc in Biometry, Case Western Res. U., 1976; PhD in Ednl. Psychology, Mich. State U., 1982. Intern Hotel Dieu de Que. Hosp., Quebec City, 1973-74; rsch. fellow dept. biometry Case Western Res. U., Cleve., 1974-76; rsch. fellow office med. edn. R&D Mich. State U., East Lansing, 1976-78; prof. U. Laval, 1978-92, founding dir. MA degree, 1984; prof., dir. grad. studies U. Ill., Chgo., 1992—; hon. cons. Greenwich Dist. Hosp., London, 1987-88; cons. WHO, Brussels, Karachi, 1982-83, 93, Eli Lilly, Awashima, Hacone, 1994. Recipient John P. Hubbard award Nat. Bd. Med. Examiners, 1994. Mem. Assn. Am. Med. Colls. (chmn. rsch. in med. edn. 1991, chmn. group on ednl. affairs 1995-96), Assn. for Surg. Edn., Assn. for Study Med. Edn., Soc. Tchrs. in Family Medicine, Friends of Osler Libr., Club Pedagogie Med. Que. (chmn., exec. sec. 1989-92). Office: U Ill Chgo Dept Med Edn 808 S Wood Chicago IL 60612-7309

BORDAN, DENNIS LAWRENCE, surgeon; b. Lynbrook, N.Y., Sept. 18, 1944; s. Harry and Sarah B.; m. Erika Aleese Pack, Apr. 25, 1981. BA, NYU, 1966; MD, SUNY, Buffalo, 1970. Diplomate Am. Bd. Surgery. Chief surg. svcs. USAF, Dover, Del., 1975-77; intern North Shore U. Hosp., Manhasset, N.Y., 1970-71, resident, 1971-75, asst. dir. surgery, program dir., 1977-82; assoc. chmn. dept. surgery North Shore Univ. Hosp., 1991—; chmn. dept. surgery St. Vincent's Med. Ctr., Bridgeport, Conn., 1982-90; pvt. practice Jameson Meml. Hosp., New Castle, Pa., 1990-91. Maj. USAF, 1975-77. Fellow ACS; mem. Assn. Program Dirs. in Surgery, Assn. Academic Surgery, Nassau Surg. Soc. (sci. program dir. 1980—), Soc. Crit. Care Med., Soc. Surg. Edn. Office: North Shore Univ Hosp 300 Community Dr Manhasset NY 11030-3801

BORDEN, SPENCER, IV, medical director; b. Boston, Jan. 26, 1941; s. Richard and Elizabeth (McGinley) B.; m. Dorothy B. Borden, June 23, 1963 (div. 1980); children: Jennifer L., Richard II, Rebecca B.; m. Elizabeth L. Clemens, June 6, 1981; children: Sarah Clemens Borden, Andrew Clemens Borden. AB, Harvard U., 1963; B Med. Sci., Dartmouth Coll., 1966; MD, Harvard U., 1968; MBA, U. Pa., Phila., 1986. Diplomate Am. Bd. Med. Mgmt., Am. bd. Radiology, Nat. Bd. Med. Examiners; cert. med. mgr. and quality assurance mgr. Intern in pediatrics Children's Hosp., Boston, 1968-69, fellowship, 1972-73; radiologist-in-chief Children's Hosp., Phila., 1978-88; resident in radiology Mass. Gen. Hosp., Boston, 1969-72, dir. pediat. radiology, 1975-78; med. dir. Aetna Life Ins. Co., Hartford, Conn., 1988-89, Mediqual Systems, Westboro, Mass., 1989-93; sr. med. cons. Wyatt Co., Wellesley Hills, Mass., 1993-95; medical dir. Value Health Scis., Santa Monica, Calif., 1995—. Asst. dir. United Way Aetna Life-EBD div., Middletown, Conn., 1988-89. Maj. USAF, 1973-75. Fellow ACP Execs., Am. Coll. Healthcare Execs., Am. Acad. Pediat., Am. Coll. Med. Quality, Am. Coll. Radiology. Home: 278 Hunters Ridge Rd Concord MA 01742-4718 Office: Value Health Scis 278 Hunters Ridge Rd Concord MA 01742-4718

BORDINI, ERNEST JOHN, psychologist; b. Boston, Oct. 16, 1957; s. Lorenzo and Anna (Del'Aversano) B. BA magna cum laude, Boston Coll., 1979; MA, U. Fla., 1983, PhD, 1988. Lic. psychologist, Fla. Psychology asst. North Fla. Evaluation and Treatment Ctr., Gainesville, 1982-85; psychology intern VA Med. Ctr., Gainesville, 1985-86; pvt. practice Behavioral Health Assocs., Gainesville and Ocala, Fla., 1987—; courtesy asst. prof. dept. psychiatry U. Fla., Gainesville, 1989—; cons., mem. allied med. staff Grant Ctr., Hosp. North Fla., Citra, 1987-92; mem. allied med. staff Charter Springs Hosp., Ocala, Fla., 1989—, North Fla. Regional Med. Ctr., Gainesville. Contbr. articles to profl. jours. Boston Coll. scholar, 1979; recipient Molly Harrower award U. Fla., 1985, Early Career Contbns. to FPA, 1995. Mem. APA, Internat. Neuropsychol. Soc., Am. Coll. Forensic Psychology, Southeastern Psychol. Assn., Fla. Psychol. Assn. (pres. North Ctrl. Fla. chpt. 1991, ins. chmn. 1993-96, pres. neuropsychology interest divsn. 1995-96), Nat. Acad. Neuropsychology. Democrat. Office: Behavioral Health Assocs 2631 NW 41st St Bldg D Ste1 Gainesville FL 32606-7470

BORECKY, MICHAEL, physician; b. Albuquerque, June 23, 1943; s. Antone and Elmira Clarina (Mehl) B.; m. Susan Yarnall Tucker, Aug. 5, 1974. BA cum laude, Wesleyan U., 1965; MD, Columbia U., 1969. Diplomate Am. Bd. Internal Medicine. Intern Roosevelt Hosp., N.Y.C., 1969-70, med. resident, 1970-72, fellow in cardiology, 1972-74; pvt. practice N.Y.C., 1974—; med. dir. Correctional Health Svcs., Inc., Montclair, N.J., 1996—. Fellow ACP, Am. Coll. Cardiology, N.Y. County Med. Soc. Office: 30 W 60th St New York NY 10023-7902

BOREL, GEORGES ANTOINE, gastroenterologist, consultant; b. Neuchatel, Switzerland, Oct. 13, 1936; s. Jean and Alice Marie (Perrenoud) B.; m. Beatrice de Przysiecki, Apr. 7, 1964 (div. 1980); children: Pascal, Sibylle, Fabienne. MD, U. Zürich, 1963; Privat Docent (hon.), U. Lausanne, Switzerland, 1977. Rsch. fellow Univ. Hosp., Ann Arbor, Mich., 1968-69; cons. physician Univ. Hosp., Geneva, 1975—; pvt. practice gastroenterologist Lausanne, 1976—. Author: Comprendre son appareil digestif, 1994; contbr. articles to profl. jours. Mem. Swiss Soc. Gastroenterology. Office: Blvd Grancy 7, 1006 Lausanne Vaud, Switzerland

BOREL, JAMES DAVID, anesthesiologist; b. Chgo., Nov. 15, 1951; s. James Albert and Nancy Ann (Sieverson) B. BS, U. Wis., 1973; MD, Med. Coll. of Wis., 1977. Diplomate Am. Bd. Anesthesiology, Nat. Bd. Med. Examiners, Am. Coll. Anesthesiologists. Research asst. McArdle Lab. for Cancer Research, Madison, Wis., 1972-73, Stanford U. and VA Hosp., Palo Alto, 1976-77; intern. The Cambridge (Mass.) Hosp., 1977-78; clin. fellow in medicine Harvard Med. Sch., Boston, 1977-78, clin. fellow in anesthesia, 1978-80, clin. instr. in anaesthesia, 1980; resident in anesthesiology Peter Bent Brigham Hosp., Boston, 1978-80; anesthesiologist Mt. Auburn Hosp., Cambridge, 1980; fellow in anesthesiology Ariz. Health Scis. Ctr., Tucson, 1980-81; research assoc. U. Ariz. Coll. Medicine, Tucson, 1980-81, assoc. in anesthesiology, 1981—; active staff Mesa (Ariz.) Luth. Hosp., 1981—; courtesy staff Scottsdale (Ariz.) Meml. Hosp., 1982—; vis. anaesthetist St. Joseph's Hosp., Kingston, Jamaica, 1980. Contbr. numerous articles to profl. jours. Mem. AMA, AAAS, Ariz. Anesthesia Alumni Assn., Ariz. Soc. Anesthesiologists, Am. Soc. Regional Anesthesia, Can. Anesthestists' Soc., Internat. Anesthesia Rsch. Soc., Am. Soc. Anesthesiologists. Office: Valley Anesthesia Cons 2950 N 7th St Phoenix AZ 85014-5404

BOREN, KENNETH RAY, endocrinologist; b. Evansville, Ind., Dec. 31, 1945; s. Doyle Clifford and Jeannette (Koerner) B.; m. Rebecca Lane Wallace, Aug. 25, 1967; children: Jennifer, James, Michael, Peter, Nicklas, Benjamin. BS, Ariz. State U., 1967; MD, Ind. U., Indpls., 1972; MA, Ind. U., Bloomington, 1974. Diplomate Am. Bd. Endocrinology, Am. Bd. Nephrology, Am. Bd. Internal Medicine. Intern in pathology Ind. U. Sch. Medicine, Indpls., 1972; intern in medicine Ind. U. Sch. Medicine, 1972-73, resident in medicine, 1975-77, fellow in endocrinology, 1977-79, fellow nephrology, 1979-80, instr., 1980; physician East Valley Nephrology, Mesa, Ariz., 1980—; chief medicine Mesa Luth Hosp., 1987-89, chief staff, 1990-91. Bd. dirs. Ariz. Kidney Found., Phoenix, 1984—, pres. 1993-94. Lt. USN, 1973-75. Fellow ACP, Am. Coll. of Clin. Endocrinology; mem. AMA, Maricopa County Med. Assn., Ariz. Med. Assn., Am. Soc. Nephrology, Internat. Soc. Nephrology, Am. Diabetes Assn. Republican. Latter Day Saints. Home: 4222 E Mclellan Rd Ste 10 Mesa AZ 85205-3119 Office: East Valley Nephrology 560 W Brown #3006 Mesa AZ 85201-3221

BORER, JEFFREY STEPHEN, cardiologist; b. Deland, Fla., Feb. 22, 1945; s. Lee Norton and Rita Doris (Feldt) B.; m. Brondi Beth Topchik, Sept. 16, 1978; children: Justine Isolde, Jon Andrew. BA in Govt., Harvard U., 1965; MD, Cornell U., 1969. Diplomate Am. Bd. Internal Medicine, Am. Bd. Cardiovascular Disease. Intern, then resident in medicine Mass. Gen. Hosp., Boston, 1969-71; clin. fellow in medicine Harvard U. Sch. Medicine, Boston, 1969-71; clin. assoc. in cardiology Nat. Heart, Lung and Blood Inst., NIH, Bethesda, Md., 1971-74, chief resident physician, 1973-74, sr. investigator, cardiology br., 1975-79; sr. Fulbright-Hays scholar, Glorney-Raisbeck fellow med. scis Guy's Hosp., U. London, 1974-75; assoc. prof. medicine Cornell U. Med. Coll., N.Y.C., 1979-82, prof., 1982—, Gladys and Roland Harriman prof. cardiovascular medicine, 1983—; prof. cardiovascular med. in radiology Cornell Univ. Med. Coll., N.Y.C., 1990—; chmn. cardiac and renal adv. com., U.S. FDA, Washngton, 1981-82, 83-87, cons., 1989—; mem. life scis. adv. com. NASA, Washington, 1984-88, mem. aero. med. adv. com., 1988-93, microgravity and life scis. adv. com. NASA, 1993—, chmn. NASA/Mir Peer Rev. adv. com. 1993—; chmn. NASA-NIH Biomec. and Behavioral Rsch. adv. com. 1995—; mem. NASA adv. coun., 1995—; vis. prof. Chinese Acad. Med. Scis., Beijing, 1993—; chief divsn. cardiovascular pathophysiology N.Y. Hosp.-Cornell Med. Ctr. 1996—. Mem. editl. bds. 10 med. jours.; contbr. more than 275 articles on cardiovascular disease to med. jours. Trustee N.Y.C. Historic Properties Fund, 1984-90; mem. steering com. Assocs. of the Jewish Bd. of Family and Children Svcs., 1989-91 pres. Am. Friends of Israel Nat. Heart to Heart Assn., 1991—. Sr. surgeon USPHS, 1971-79. Recipient Investigator's award prize European Cardiol. Soc., 1978, spl. award for contbns. to cardiology, Assn. Thoracic and Cardiovascular Surgeons of India, 1985, William A. Johnston award, Internat. Soc. Heart Rsch., 1986, spl. citation Israel Nat. Heart to Heart Assn., 1992; travelling fellow Am. Physicians Fellowship, 1981. Fellow ACP, Am. Soc. Clin. Investigation, Am. Coll. Cardiology (governing coun. N.Y. chpt. 1991-93, pres.-elect. N.Y. State chpt. 1995—, gov.-elect 1995—), Am. Heart Assn. (coun. clin. cardiology and circulation, established investigator 1979-84), Am. Coll. Chest Physicians (chmn. cardiology forum 1985-86, exec. com. clin. cardiology sect., 1991—), Am. Coll. Clin. Pharm., N.Y. Cardiol. Soc. (pres. 1990-91), Argentine Heart Assn. (hon.); mem. Soc. Nuclear Medicine (trustee cardiovascular coun. 1991-94), Soc. Cardiac Angiography and Interventions (gov. 1995—), Am. Soc. Nuclear Cardiology (fin com. 1993—), Credentialing Coun. Nuclear Cardiology (bd. dirs. 1996—), Harvard Club N.Y.C. Office: NY Hosp 525 E 68th St New York NY 10021-4873

BORG, RUTH I., home nursing care provider; b. Chgo., Mar. 29, 1934; d. Axel Gunner and Charlotte (Benston) B. Diploma, West Suburban Sch. Nursing, 1956; tchr.'s degree, Chgo. Conservatory, 1958; BSN, Alverno Coll., 1981. Staff nurse Boath Meml. Hosp., Chgo.; head nurse psychiatry, head nurse long-term medicine VA North Chgo. Med. Ctr.; staff nurse, night supr. intermediate care VA Clement Zabiocki Med. Ctr., Milw.; pool nurse, in-home nursing care provider Milw. County Mental Health Complex; in-home nursing care provider. Contbr. 2 articles to profl. jours.

BORGAONKAR, DIGAMBER SHANKARRAO, cytogeneticist, educator; b. Hyderabad, India, Sept. 24, 1932; came to U.S., 1959, naturalized, 1971; s. Shankarrao Apparao and Kumudinibai (Jatar) B.; m. Manda Purandare, Dec. 27, 1963; children: Rajendra, Sonya. BS in Agr., Osmania U. 1953; diploma, Indian Agrl. Rsch. Inst., 1955; PhD, Okla. State U., 1963. Rsch. asst. agr. dept. Hyderabad and Parbhani, 1955-59; lectr. Agrl. Coll., Parbhani, 1956-57; asst. prof. biology U. N.D., Grand Forks, 1963-64; faculty and head of chromosome lab. Johns Hopkins U., 1964-78, assoc. prof. medicine, 1972-78, lectr. dept. environ. health, 1975-78; prof. biol. scis., rsch. scientist, dir. rsch. Genetics Ctr. North Tex. State U., Denton, 1978-80; dir. Cytogenetics Lab., Med. Ctr. Del., Newark, 1980—; rsch. prof. pediatrics (med. genetics) Thomas Jefferson U., Phila.; adj. prof. life and health scis. U. Del. Author: Chromosomal Variation in Man: A Catalog of Chromosomal Variants and Anomalies, 7th edit., 1994; co-author: Repository of Human Chromosomal Variants and Anomalies: International Registry of Abnormal Karyotypes, 14th Listing, 1993; editor: (with Bergsma, McKusick, Scott) The First Conference on the Clinical Delineation of Birth Defects, vol. 5, 1969; (with Bergsma, Shah) Advances in Human Genetics and Their Impact on Society, Birth Defects, 1972 (with Applewhite and Busbee) Genetic Screening and Counseling: A Multidisciplinary Perspective, 1981. Hyderabad State Rsch. scholar Indian Agrl. Rsch. Inst., 1955; recipient Haldane award Soc. Bionaturalists, Bhopal, India, 1988. Fellow Indian Soc. Genetics, Am. Genetic Assn. (v.p. 1973), Hercules Country Club. Office: Cytogenetics Lab PO Box 6001 Newark DE 19718-0001

BORGER, MICHAEL HINTON IVERS, osteopathic physician, educator; b. Kirksville, Mo., Nov. 10, 1951; s. Donald L. Borger and Dorothy M. Hinton. BA in Sociology, U. Akron, 1974; DO, Coll. Osteo. Medicine and Surgery, Des Moines, 1977. Diplomate Nat. Bd. Examiners in Osteo. Medicine and Surgery; ordained elder Presbyn. Ch., 1969. Rotating extern Youngstown (Ohio) Osteo. Hosp., 1976; extern in family medicine Dietz Diagnostic Clinic, Des Moines, 1977; rotating intern South Bend (Ind.) Osteo. Hosp. (now Michiana Community Hosp), 1977-78, active staff, 1978-79, assoc. staff, 1979-82; pvt. practice Nappanee, Ind., 1978—; staff Elkhart (Ind.) Gen. Hosp., 1978—, Goshen Gen. Hosp., 1981—; clin. asst. prof. gen. practice Kirksville (Mo.) Coll. Osteo. Medicine, 1990-93; apptd. clin. preceptor Kansas City U. of Health Scis. Coll. of Osteo. Medicine, 1993—; asst. clin. prof. family practice Kansas City U. of Health Scis. Coll. of Osteo. Medicine, Kansas City, 1995—; Nappanee, Ind., 1993—; assoc. manuscript reviewer Jour. Respiratory Diseases, 1936-88, Jour. Musculoskeletal Medicine, 1989—; pres. Northwood Profl. Assocs., Inc., 1995—. Bd. dirs. Nappanee chpt. Families in Action, 1980-82; bd. dirs., chmn. Mission and Svcs. Commn., 1st Mennonite Ch., Nappanee, 1984-90, chmn. pastoral search com., 1989-90; mem. screening com. for elem. prin. Wa-Nee Sch. Dist., 1988; med. advisor United Presbyn. Ch. Nursery Sch., Nappanee, 1995—. Recipient Physician of Yr. award Ind. Assn. Emergency Med. Technicians, 1981, Good Citizens award Tower Savs., 1982, 1st degree black belt Tae Kwon Do, 1988, Tae Kwon Do Student of Yr. award, Hong's USA Tae Kwon Do, 1988; Burroughs-Wellcome Osteo rsch. fellow, 1980-81. Mem. Am. Osteo. Assn., Ind. Assn. Osteo. Physicians and Surgeons, Am. Acad. Applied Osteopathy, Nat. Honor Soc., Masons (3d degree), York Rite. Home: 353 N Hartman St Nappanee IN 46550-1417

BORGIA, CHARLES ANTHONY, orthopaedic surgeon; b. Rockford, Ill., Oct. 30, 1930; m. Patricia June Anderson, June 21, 1953; children: Scott, Ann Marie, Steven, Brian. BA, U. Calif., Berkeley, 1952; MD, U. Calif., San Francisco, 1955. Intern Santa Clara (Calif.) County Hosp., 1955; resident in gen. surgery USAF Hosp., Chanute AFB, Ill., 1956; resident Walter Reed Army Med. Ctr., Washington, 1957-60; chief orthopedic surgery USAF, Sacramento, 1960-64; pres. Samaritan Orthopedic and Med. Group, San Jose, Calif., 1964—; pres. Santa Clara Valley Orthopaedic Club, 1974. Maj. USAF, 1956-64. Decorated Air Force Commendation medal USAF, 1964. Fellow Am. Acad. Orthopedic Surgery, Am. Orthpaedic Foot and Ankle Soc.; mem. AMA, Calif. Med. Assn., Western Orthopaedic Assn. Office: 2505 Samaritan Dr #102 San Jose CA 95124

BORGSTAHL, KAYLENE DENISE, health facility administrator; b. Hampton, Iowa, May 21, 1951; d. Harry Dell and Berniece Irene (Muhlenbruck) Crabb; children: Elliot Michael, Brett Andrew. BS in Nursing, U. Iowa, 1973; MPA, Iowa State U., 1986. Asst. adminstr. Linn County Vis. Nurse Assn., Cedar Rapids, Iowa, 1975-85; v.p. program svcs. Voluntary Hosps. Iowa Home Health Care, Cedar Rapids, 1985-86; adminstr. Norell Home Health Svcs., Edina, Minn., 1986-87; case mgr. In Home Health Svcs., Mpls., 1987-88; adminstr. Sundance Med. Clinic Ltd., Shakopee, Minn., 1988-94, Apple Valley (Minn.) Med. Ctr., 1995—. Mem. Sigma Theta Tau. Republican.

BORIK, ANNE, osteopath; b. Pitts., Jan. 5, 1964; d. Nicolaus Charles and Norma (Budway) B. Student, Duquesne U., 1983-84; BS in Exercise Physiology, Temple U., 1987; DO, Phila. Coll. Osteo. Medicine, 1991. Rotating intern Grandview Hosp. and Med. Ctr., Dayton, Ohio, 1991-92; resident in internal medicine Allegheny Gen. Hosp., Pitts., 1992-95; internal medicine physician Casa Blanca Clinic, Apache Junction, Ariz., 1995—; emergency room physician Shadyside Hosp., Pitts., 1993, Urgicare of Pitts., 1993—, Mercy Providence Hosp., Pitts., 1993—; tchr. karate and self-defense Shitoryo Dotokushin Assn., Phila. Coll. Osteo. Medicine. Founder, tchr. Pitts. Blind Karate Club. Mem. AMA, ACP, Pa. Med. Assn., Allegheny County Med. Assn. Office: Casa Blanca Clinic 2050 W Southern Ave Apache Junction AZ 85020

BORINO, DOROTHY, nursing administrator; b. Bayonne, N.J., Apr. 8, 1945; d. Michael and Anne (Sissak) Bandur; m. Francis R. Borino, July 1, 1967; children: Mark, Eric. Diploma, Bayonne Hosp. Sch. Nursing, 1965; BA in Health Sci., Jersey City State Coll., 1981. RN, N.J.; cert. sch. nurse, cert. tchr. health edn. and practical nursing, N.J. Staff nurse, med.-surg. Bayonne Hosp., 1965-77; substitute sch. nurse Bayonne Bd. Edn., 1977-84; sch. nurse EIP/day care program ARC, Jersey City, 1984-89; occupational health nurse MSCLANT/Dept. of Navy, Bayonne, 1989-92; supr. sch. nurses Ind. Child Study Teams, Inc., Jersey City, 1992—. Mem. cmty. edn. coun. Bayonne Bd. Edn. Mem. Nat. Assn. Sch. Nurses, N.J. State Sch. Nurses Assn., Bayonne Hosp. Sch. Nursing Alumnae Assn. Roman Catholic. Office: Ind Child Study Teams Inc 377 Danforth Ave Jersey City NJ 07305-1904

BORLAND, JOHN SIMON, periodontist; b. Cape Town, South Africa, Apr. 12, 1966; s. Jonathan and Anjanette (Osmond) B. BChD, U. Pretoria, 1989; MDent, U. Witwatersrand, 1994. Pvt. practice Johannesburg, South Africa, 1995—. Lt. South African Mil. Svcs., 1989-90. Office: PO Box 97096, Petervale 2151, South Africa

BORMAN, KAREN RENEE, surgeon; b. Washington, Dec. 1, 1953; d. James G. and Caroline P. (Parrotta) B. BS in Chemistry with high honors, Ga. Inst. Tech., 1974; MD, Tulane U., 1978. Diplomate Am. Bd. Surgery. Intern U. Tex. Southwestern Affiliated Hosps., Dallas, 1978-79, resident, 1979-84; asst. prof. surgery U. Tex. Southwestern Med. Sch., Dallas, 1984-90, assoc. prof., 1990-94; attending surgeon Ochsner Clinic, New Orleans, 1994-95; assoc. chief trauma svcs. Fairfax Hosp., Falls Church, Va., 1995—; clin. assoc. prof. surgery Tulane U. Sch. Medicine, New Orleans, 1995. Contbr. articles to profl. jours. Fellow ACS (councillor North Tex. chpt. 1991-94, chmn. com. on applicants 1992-94, rep. to current procedural terminology adv. com 1995—); mem. AMA, Parkland Surg. Soc., Assn. for Acad. Surgery, So. Med. Assn. (sect. on surgery 1986—), Southwestern Surg. Congress, Soc. Critical Care Medicine, Am. Assn. for Surgery of Trauma, Am. Assn. Endocrine Surgeons, Am. Assn. Clin. Endocrinologists, Assn. for Surg. Edn. Office: Trauma Svcs Fairfax Hosp 3300 Gallows Rd Falls Church VA 22042

BORNMANN, ROBERT CLARE, physician, medical consultant; b. Pitts., June 29, 1931; s. John Arthur and Iona Ann (Flanegin) B.; children: Kristin L., Elizabeth A., Jennifer C., John W. AB, Harvard U., 1952; MD, U. Penna, 1956, MS in Pharmacology, 1963. Comdr. Cape Hallett Igy Station, Antarctica, 1958-59; med. officer Underwater Swimmers Sch., Key West, Fla., 1961-62, Deepseadivscol and Experimental Dvunit, Washington, 1963-68, Deep Submergence Systems Project, Navmat, Washington, 1968-70; exchange med. officer Royal Navy Inst. of Naval Med., Gosport, UK, 1970-73; staff med. officer, oceanographer U.S. Navy, Washington, 1973-81; staff dir. Defense Med. Standardization Board, Frederick, Md., 1981-85; prin. cons. Limetree Med. Cons., Reston, Va., 1985—; cons. Lawrence Livermore (Calif.) Nat. Lab., 1987-88, NOAA, 1987-88; mem. environ. rev. com. NASA, Houston, 1983-92. Contbr. articles and edited numerous med. jours. Fellow Aerospace Med. Assn., Royal Soc. Med.; mem. Undersea and Hyperbaric Med. Soc. (recipient C.W. Shilling award, 1988), Am. Coll. Occupational Med., Am. Assn. for Advancement of Sci., Harvard Club. Office: Limetree Med Cons 11569 Woodhollow Ct Reston VA 20191-4409

BORNSTEIN, HAROLD NELSON, physician; b. N.Y.C., Mar. 26, 1947; s. Jacob and Maria S. (Seltzer) B.; children: Robyn, Joseph, Alix. AB, Tufts U., 1968, MD, 1975. Resident in internal medicine Lenox Hill Hosp., N.Y.C., 1975-78; fellow in gastroenterology Bridgeport (Conn.) Hosp., 1978-80; physician pvt. practice, N.Y.C., 1980—; adj. physician Lenox Hill Hosp., N.Y.C., 1980—. With USAR, 1969-74. Mem. Am. Coll. Physicians, Am. Soc. Gastrointestinal Endoscopy, Am. Gastroenterologic Assn., N.Y. State Med. Soc., N.Y. County Med. Soc. Office: 101 E 78 St New York NY 10021

BORNSTEIN, MYER SIDNEY, obstetrician, gynecologist; b. Boston, Sept. 7, 1938; s. Abram and Celia (Stein) B.; B.S., Northeastern U., 1961; M.D., U. Vt., 1965; Grad. N.Y. Inst. Photography, 1988; m. Janet L. Difonzo, July 15, 1977; 2 children; 3 children by previous marriage. Intern, Rochester (N.Y.) Gen. Hosp., 1965-66, resident, 1966-69; practice medicine specializing in gyn, laparoscopy and infertility, 1969—, drug and alcohol treatment, 1984-87; chief ob-gyn Kinchloe AFB, Mich., 1969-71; asst. chief Weisbaden (Germany) Regional Hosp., 1971-74; attending physician Charleton Meml. Hosp., Fall River Mass., 1974-83, New London (N.H.) Hosp., 1983-87, Morton Hosp., 1987—, chief ob-gyn., 1991—, chair by laws com.; ed. dir. substance abuse treatment ctr. Seminole Point Hosp., N.E. Drug and Alcohol Svcs., 1984-87; med. dir. Greater Fall River Family Planning, 1981-83; owner Photography by BEE, Medichrome, Stock Shoppe Stock Agency; cons. ob-gyn Fall River Cmty. Devel. Ctr., 1976-83, Taunton State Hosp., 1988—, Stanley Street Alcohol Rehab. Ctr., Fall River, Mass ; guest lectr. dept. social work Providence Coll., 1980; vis. prof. Facility CMH Physician Tng. Ctr., Nashville; freelance nature photographer. Contbr. photographs to jours. and books. Bd. dirs. Kersang chpt. Am. Cancer Soc., Greater Fall River Children's Protective Services; Bd. of Greater Berkley; bd. dirs., coach, pres. Wattupa Youth Hockey Assn., 1978-81. Lt. col. USAF, 1969-74. Diplomate Am. Bd. Ob-Gyn. Mem. AMA, Fall River Med. Soc., Am. Soc. Gynecol. Laparascopy, Am. Soc. Colposcopy, Mass. Med. Soc. (tax support medicare com., managed care com., perinatal welfare com., vice chair nomination com. 1994-96, chair 1996—, bd. trustees), Bristol North Med. Soc. (v.p., pres.), Am. Coll. Obstetricians and Gynecologists, Southeastern New Eng. Ob-Gyn Soc., Am. Inst. Ultrasound in Medicine, Am. Fertility Soc., N.H. Med. Soc., Am. Coll. Physcian Execs., Merrimack County Med. Soc., N.H. Ob-Gyn Soc., Am. Legion. Lodge: Rotary (New London). Home:

13 Green St Berkley MA 02779-1510 Office: 72 Washington St Taunton MA 02780-2470

BORNSTEIN, MYRON PHILIP, psychiatrist; b. Milw., Jan. 9, 1935; s. Samuel and Sara Bornstein; widowed, 1994; children: Peter, Benjamin, Louisa. BS, Northwestern U., 1956, MD, 1959. Diplomate Am. Bd. Psychiatry and Neurology. Intern Mt. Sinai Hosp., Milw., 1959-60; resident in psychiatry Western Psychiat. Inst. and Clinic, Pitts., 1960-62; fellow in child psychiatry Inst. for Psychomatic Rsch. & Tng., 1964-66; chmn. dept. psychiatry Highland Park (Ill.) Hosp., 1985-94; pvt. practice Highland Park, 1966—. Lt. USMC, 1962-64. Office: 1971 Second St Ste 200 Highland Park IL 60035-3167

BOROS, LASZLO GEZA, medical researcher; b. Torokszentmiklos, Hungary, June 12, 1962; came to U.S., 1990; s. Ferenc Janos and Maria (Csanyi) B.; 1 child, Eva. MD, Szeged Sch. Medicine, 1987. Clinician, resident, house staff 1st dept. medicine Szeged (Hungary) Sch. Medicine, 1987-90; rsch. assoc. 2 Ohio State U., Columbus, 1990—; rsch. assoc. Hungarian Acad. Scis./Medicine, Budapest, 1987-90; students rsch. advisor Ohio State U., 1993—. Vis. scholar Essen Sch. Medicine, Germany, 1989-90. Office: Ohio State U 400 W 12th Ave DOAN Columbus OH 43210

BOROVOY, MARC ALLEN, podiatrist; b. Detroit, Oct. 22, 1960; s. Mathew and Joyce Francis (Weisman) B.; m. Michele Lynn Flusty, Oct. 23, 1983; children: Danielle, Brandon. Student, Wayne State U., 1978-81; D. Podiatric Medicine, Ohio Coll. Podiatric Medicine, 1985. Diplomate Am. Bd. Podiatric Sugery, Am. Bd. Quality Assurance and Utilization Rev. Resident Straith Hosp., Southfield, Mich., 1985-86; podiatrist Associated Podiatrists, Oak Park, Mich., 1986—; chief dept. podiatric surgery Providence Hosp., Southfield, Mich. Contbr. articles to profl. jours. Mem. exec. bd. Congregation Bnai Moshe, West Bloomfield, Mich., 1989—. Fellow Am. Coll. Foot Surgeons; mem. APHA, Am. Diabetes Assn., Mich. Podiatric Med. Assn. (exec. sec. 1986-89, chmn. pub. rels. 1988—, v.p. 1990-91, pres.-elect 1992-93, pres. 1993-95). Office: Associated Podiatrists 25725 Coolidge Hwy Oak Park MI 48237-1307 also: 47601 Grand River Ave Ste B-230 Novi MI 48374-1233

BOROVSKY, JURAJ, medical equipment manufacturing company executive; b. Bratislava, Slovakia, Feb. 24, 1940; s. Juraj Borovsky and Tamara (Rachmanova) Zlatohlávková; m. Anna Mitrova, Jan. 22, 1940; children: Andrea, Juraj. MSEE, Tech. U., Prague, Czechoslovakia, 1962; MBA, Econs. U., Bratislava, 1967. Asst. Tesla Orava/TV, Nižná, Czechoslovakia, 1963-66; fin. dir. Tesla Orava/TV, NiÜná, Czechoslovakia, 1966-70; mgr. R & D, Chirana Stará Turá, Czechoslovakia, 1971-89; fin. dir. Chirana-Prema a.s., Stará Turá, 1989-92; gen. dir. Chirana-Prema a.s., Stará Turá, Slovakia, 1992—; bd. dirs. Medimess CmbH, Aachen, Germany, Health Ins. Co. Perspective. Mem. Machinery Industry Assn. (v.p. 1991—), Comml. and Indsl. Chamber (bd. dirs. 1992—). Home: Hviezdoslavova 11, 916 01 Stará Turá Slovakia Office: Chirana-Prema as, Nám Dr A Schweitzera 194, 916 01 Stará Turá Slovakia

BOROWITZ, JOSEPH LEO, pharmacologist; b. Columbus, Ohio, Dec. 19, 1932; s. Joseph Peter and Anna Louise (Grundei) B.; divorced, 1985; children: Jon Joseph, Peter Joseph, Lynn Anne. BS in Pharmacy, Ohio State U., 1955; MS in Pharmacology, Purdue U., 1957; PhD in Pharmacology (NIH fellow), Northwestern U., 1960. Postdoctoral fellow dept. pharmacology Harvard U. Med. Sch., Boston, 1963-64; instr., then asst. prof. pharmacology Bowman Gray Sch. Medicine, 1964-69; assoc. prof. pharmacology and toxicology Purdue U., 1969-74, prof., 1974—; sabbatical leave to Cambridge, Eng., 1976, to Basel, Switzerland, 1984. Contbr. articles to profl. jours. Treas. Tippecanoe County (Ind.) Comprehensive Health Planning Coun., 1971-76. Capt. USAR, 1960. Recipient award for excellence in teaching Bowman Gray Sch. Medicine, 1969, Henry Heine award for excellence in teaching Purdue U. Coll. Pharmacy, 1983; named NIH postdoctoral fellow, 1962-64; grantee NSF, 1965-68, NIH, 1971-74, 86-89, 89-94, 94—. Mem. Am. Soc. Pharmacology and Exptl. Therapeutics, Rho Chi. Roman Catholic. Office: Purdue U Dept Pharmacology and Toxicology West Lafayette IN 47907

BORRESEN, THOR ERIK, neurologist; b. Larvik, Norway, Dec. 28, 1952; s. Thor H. and Liv (Carlsen) B.; m. Bonnie Weiner, Dec. 18, 1976; children: Cari, Michael. Student, U. Oslo, 1976; MD, N.J. Med. Sch., 1979. Intern Thomas Jefferson Hosp., Phila., 1979-80; neurology resident U. Pa., Phila., 1980-83; staff neurologist Culicchia Neurol., New Orleans, 1983—. Mem. Am. Acad. Neurology, Am. Assn. Electrodiagnosis and Electromyography, Am. Assn. for Study of Headache. Office: CNC Ste 750S 1111 Medical Center Blvd Marrero LA 70072-3064

BORRILL, DAVID RAYMOND, health services administrator; b. Queens, N.Y., Sept. 20, 1954; s. Boyd Raymond and Barbara Mary (Reden) B.; m. Donna Loray Newins, Sept. 29, 1984; children: Brittney Jane, Taylor Wray. BS in Biology, Southampton Coll., 1977; MBA, Dowling Coll., 1996. Cert. med. technologist. Med. technologist Nat. Health Labs., Plainview, N.Y., 1980-82, Eastern L.I. Hosp., Glenport, N.Y., 1983-87; med. technologist Southampton (N.Y.) Hosp., 1987-89, lab. supr., 1989-93, dir. extended svcs., 1993-94, dir. ambulatory care, 1994-96, dir. diagnostic svcs. mktg., 1996—. Named Citizen of the Yr. Suffolk County Life Underwriters Assn., 1994. Mem. Lions (pres. Club of the Moriches 1994-95), Potunk Masons (brother lodge 1071, master), Delta Mu Delta. Office: Southampton Hosp 240 Meeting House Ln Southampton NY 11968

BORRIS, ROBERT PATRICK, chemist, educator; b. Chgo., Nov. 12, 1952; s. Theodore J. and Leona C. (Godzich) B.; m. Kathryn Mary Liepold, Mar. 17, 1979; children: Anna Elizabeth, Christian Theodore. BS in Biology, Loyola U., Chgo., 1974; BS in Pharmacy with honors, U. Ill., Chgo., 1977, PhD in Pharmacognosy, 1981. Pharmacist Meyer Drugs, Chgo., 1979-80; postdoctoral rsch. fellow Inst. Organic Chemistry, U. Zurich-Irchel, Switzerland, 1981-82; asst. prof. pharmacognosy Rutgers U., Piscataway, N.J., 1982-83; sr. rsch. chemist Merck & Co., Rahway, N.J., 1983-87, rsch. fellow, 1987-93, sr. rsch. fellow, 1993—. Contbr. 20 articles to profl. jours. Dorothea H. Fleming rsch. fellow U. Ill., Chgo., 1980. Mem. AAAS, Am. Chem. Soc., Am. Soc. Pharmacognosy (exec. com. 1991—), Internat. Union of Pure and Applied Chemistry, Soc. Econ. Botany. Roman Catholic. Home: 211 Fox Hollow Rd Glen Gardner NJ 08826-3202 Office: Merck Sharp Dohme Rsch Labs PO Box 2000 Rahway NJ 07065-0900

BORROMEO, ROMANA GONZALEZ, obstetrician, gynecologist; b. Biñan, Laguna, The Philippines, May 19, 1940; d. Antonio Reyes and Basilia (Garcia) Gonzalez; m. Rafael Custodio Borromeo, Nov. 6, 1995; children: Rita, Ruth, Ricardo, Regina. AA, U. Santo Tomas, The Philippines, 1957, MD, 1962. Instr. ob-gyn. U. Santo Tomas, 1969-75; sr. cons. ob-gyn. Makati Med. Ctr., 1972—, tng. officer, 1994—. Fellow Am. Coll. Ob-Gyn. (affiliate), Philippines Ob-Gyn. Soc. Roman Catholic. Home: 21 Mercury St Bel Air Village, Makati 1209, The Philippines Office: Makati Med Ctr, de la Rosa St, Makati 1200, The Philippines

BORRUAT, FRANÇOIS-XAVIER, neuro-ophthamologist, consultant; b. Lausanne, Switzerland, Jan. 5, 1957; s. Jean-Pierre Borruat and Lucienne Berthoud; m. Joan Nicole Schwoerer, May 3, 1991; 1 child, Roxane Clara. Physician diploma, Lausanne Sch. Medicine, 1980, MD, 1993, FMN, 1994. Rsch. fellow Bascom Palmer Eye Inst., Miami, 1984-86, fellow, 1992; fellow Nat. Hosp. Neurology and Neurosurgery, London, 1991; resident Hosp. Jules Gonin, Lausanne, 1989-90, chief resident, 1989-90, médecin associé, 1993—; cons. neuro-ophthamologist CHUV, Lausanne, 1993—, Hosp. Jule Gonin, 1993—. Contbr. articles to profl. jours. Grantee Société Académique Vaudoise, Lausanne; recipient Prix Henri-Edouard de Cérenville, Lausanne, 1991. Mem. AAO, NANOS, SSO/SOG (Prix Poster 1993). Roman Catholic. Home: Ave des Bergieres 63, 1004 Lausanne Switzerland Office: Ctr Ophtalmologique dela Source, Ave des Bergieres 2, 1004 Lausanne Switzerland

BORSON, DANIEL BENJAMIN, physiology educator, inventor, researcher, lawyer; b. Berkeley, Calif., Mar. 24, 1946; s. Harry J. and Josephine F. (Esterly) B.; m. Margaret Ann Rheinschmidt, May 22, 1974; children: Alexander Nathan, Galen Michael. BA, San Francisco State Coll., 1969; MA, U. Calif., Riverside, 1973; PhD, U. Calif., San Francisco, 1982; JD, U. San Francisco, 1995. Lic. comml. pilot, flight instr. FAA. Musician Composer's Forum, Berkeley, San Francisco, 1961-70; flight instr. Buchanan Flying Club, Concord, Oakland, Calif., 1973-77, pres., 1975-77; lectr. dept. physiology U. Calif., San Francisco, 1984-92, asst. rsch. physiologist Cardiovascular Rsch. Inst., 1988-92; lectr. physiologist U. San Francisco, 1992-95; vis. scientist Genentech Inc., South San Francisco, Calif., 1990-92. Contbr. articles, rev. chpts. and abstracts to profl. jours., legal periodicals and law rev. Fellow NIH, 1976-84, grantee, 1988-93; fellow Cystic Fibrosis Found., 1985, grantee, 1989-91; fellow Parker B. Francis Found., 1985-87; grantee Am. Lung Assn., 1985-87. Mem. ABA, Am. Physiol. Soc. (editl. bd. Am. Jour. Physiology 1990-92), Am. Soc. Cell Biology, Am. Chem. Soc., Am. Intellectual Property Law Assn., San Francisco Intellectual Property Law Assn., Bay Flute Club (pres. 1978). Home: 146 San Aleso Ave San Francisco CA 94127-2531

BORSOS, ERIKA, cardiac care, medical/surgical nurse; b. Bakonycsernye, Hungary, May 8, 1952; d. John and Elizabeth (Nyevrikel) B. ADN, Thornton Community Coll., 1974, AS, 1979; BSN cum laude, U. S. Fla., 1984; candidate MSN, Andrews U., Berrien Springs, Mich., 1996—. RN Fla., Ind., Ill.;cert. BLS, ACLS Am. Heart Assn. Staff nurse, relief charge nurse, float nurse Ingalls Meml. Hosp., Harvey, Ill., 1974-79; staff nurse, team leader, float nurse Sarasota (Fla.) Meml. Hosp., 1979-84; staff nurse, clin. nurse I, cardiac catheter recovery nurse, preceptor Bon Secours Venice (Fla.) Hosp., 1985—. Editor, writer Cardiac Courier. Vol. pub. edn. Am. Cancer Soc., Sarasota Fla., 1983-90. Ill. State scholar, 1970. Mem. AACN, NLN (advocacy), Inst. Noetic Sci., Venice Hosp. Found., Folk Dance Coun., Sigma Theta Tau, Phi Theta Kappa (scholar). Home: 7416 Bounty Dr Sarasota FL 34231-7920

BORTNER, INGRID LAMBORN, nursing educator; b. Stockholm; d. Rolf K. and Florence Mary (Bouveng) Lamborn; m. Leigh N. Bortner, June 14, 1966; children: Birgitta Louise, Bret Stanley. BS in Nursing, Johns Hopkins U., 1966, MEd, 1976. RN, Md. Instr. team and med.-surg. nursing Union Meml. Hosp., Balt., 1966-70; home care field nurse Mt. Washington Pediatric Hosp., Balt., 1985-86; asst. prof. fundamentals of nursing, pediatric nursing Catonsville Community Coll., Balt., 1976-88; assoc. prof., coord. pediatric nursing Essex Community Hosp., Balt., 1988—. Mem. ANA, Md. Nurses Assn., Md. Orgn. for Advancement Assoc. Degree Nursing (treas.), Phi Delta Kappa. Home: 6442 Cloister Gate Dr Baltimore MD 21212

BORUCHOWITZ, STEPHEN ALAN, health policy analyst; b. Plainfield, N.J., Sept. 24, 1952; s. Robert and Earla Louise (Sloat) B.; m. Linda Susan Grant, Sept. 16, 1989; 1 child, Grant Stephen. BA in Internat. Affairs, George Washington U., Washington, 1974; MA in Sci., Tech. and Pub. Policy, George Washington U., 1981. Food prog. specialist U.S. Food & Nutrition Svc., Washington, 1978-81; internat. affairs specialist Office Internat. Cooperation & Devel., Washington, 1981-87; legis. analyst Wash. State Senate, Olympia, 1986-89; project dir. Wash. 2000 Project, Olympia, 1989-92; health policy analyst Wash. Dept. Health, Olympia, 1992—; mem. Pew Commn. task force on regulation of health professions, 1994-95. Editor newsletter: Project Update, 1990-92. Study team mem. Gov.'s Efficiency Commn., 1990-91; com. mem. Coun. of State Govts. Strategic Planning Subcom., Lexington, Ky., 1990-92; chmn. Montclair Divsn. IV Neighborhood Assn., 1989-92, Shadywood Homeowner's Assn., 1992-94; bd. dirs. Classical Music Supporters, Seattle, 1987-89. Recipient Superior Performance award, U.S. Dept. Agr., 1986. Mem. World Future Soc., Internat. Health Futures Network. Office: Wash Dept Health PO Box 47851 Olympia WA 98504-7851

BORUS, JONATHAN FREDERICK, psychiatrist, educator; b. Washington, May 4, 1941; s. Joseph B. and Rosalie (Bierman) B.; m. Dixie Lee Nelson, June 13, 1964; children: Joseph S., Joshua S., Daniel A. MD, U. Ill., 1965. Diplomate Am. Bd. Med. Examiners, Am. Bd. Psychiatry and Neurology. Rotating intern Cook County Hosp., Chgo., 1965-66; resident in psychiatry Neuropsychiat. Inst. U. Ill., Chgo., 1966-69; rsch. psychiatrist Walter Reed Army Inst. Rsch., Washington, 1969-72; cons. psychiatrist Henry Phipps Clinic Johns Hopkins Hosp., Balt., 1972; co-dir., sr. psychiatrist Freedom Trail Clinic Erich Lindemann Mental Health Ctr., Boston, 1972-76; chief psychiat. cons. North End Health Ctr., Boston, 1972-90; dir. tng. Erich Lindemann Mental Health Ctr., Boston, 1974-76; dir. social and community psychiatry Mass. Gen. Hosp., Boston, 1975-83, chmn. com. on teaching and edn., 1983-90, dir. residency and fellowship tng. in psychiatry, 1976-90; prof. psychiatry Harvard Med. Sch., Boston, 1994—; dir. psychiatry Brigham and Women's Hosp., Boston, 1990-92, psychiatrist in chief, 1992—; founding mem. steering com. psychiat. epidemiology Harvard U., 1979—, mem. mental health work group, 1982—; founding mem., sec. Nat. Psychiatry Match Rev. Bd., Washington, 1987-91; mem. appeals bd. Accreditation Coun. for Grad. Med. Edn., Chgo., 1989—; mem. adv. com. on mental health Nat. Acad. Scis., Inst. of Medicine, Washington, 1977-79; prin. investigator NIMH, 1975-90; vis. prof. U. Manitoba, 1978, Lettermen Med. Ctr., 1979, U. Conn., 1984, U. South Fla., 1987, USAF Med. Ctr., 1988, Calif. Pacific Med. Ctr., 1990, Tex. A&M, 1993; mem. exec. com. Harvard Consolidated dept. psychiatry, 1992—; steering com. Pertners Healthcare Psychiatry, 1995—. Assoc. editor Am. Jour. Psychiatry, 1982-90; editor Acad. Psychiatry, 1989-95; edn. editor Harvard Review Psychiatry, 1993—; contbr. numerous articles to profl. jours. Mem. Beacon Hill-West End Mental Health Com., Boston, 1972-76, Lt. Gov.'s Com. for Mental Health Ins., Commonwealth of Mass., 1977-78; disting. cons. Walter Reed Army Med. Ctr., Washington, 1986-89. Maj. U.S. Army, 1969-72. Named Outstanding Psychiat. Educator Assn. for Acad. Psychiatry, 1992. Fellow Am. Psychiat. Assn., Am. Coll. Psychiatrists; mem. Assn. Acad. Psychiatry (pres. 1986-88), Am. Assn. Dirs. Psychiat. Residency Tng. (treas. 1979-80, sec. 1981-82), Assn. Clin. Psychol. Rsch. Democrat. Jewish. Office: Brigham and Women's Hosp 75 Francis St Boston MA 02115-6110

BORUSIEWICZ, KAREN ANN, women's health nurse practitioner; b. Shamokin, Pa., Apr. 30, 1960; d. Michael Rex and Phyllis L. Daniels; m. Gary J. Borusiewicz, Sept. 12, 1981; 1 child, Alyssa. Diploma, Geisinger Med. Ctr., Danville, Pa., 1980; cert. ob/gyn. nurse practitioners program, U. Pa. Cert. ob-gyn. nurse practitioner, nurse colposcopist. Oper. rm. nurse Geisinger Med. Ctr., 1980-85, ob-gyn. clinic nurse, 1985-88; nurse practitioner, med. mgr. Family Planning Svcs. of Snyder, Union, Northumberland Counties, Lewisburg, Pa., 1988—. Mem. Am. Soc. Colposcopy and Cervical Pathology, Nat. Assn. Nurse Practitioners Reproductive Health, Assn. Reproductive Health Profls. Home: RR 2 Box 61 Shamokin PA 17872-9605

BORY, STEVEN J., health association executive; b. Nassau, N.Y., Jan. 22, 1956; s. Henry Charles and Joan Elizabeth (Keating) B.; m. Linda Ann Robb, oct. 21, 1979; children: Brian, Robert, Brittany. BS, L.I. U., 1979; M in Healthcare Adminstr., New Sch. for Social Rsch., 1987. Med. technologist North Shore Univ. Hosp., L.I., 1979-85; health care cons. Empire Blue Cross/Blue Shield, N.Y.C., 1986-87, contract adminstr., 1988-92; dir. of managed care Brookdale (N.Y.) Hosp. Med. Ctr., 1993-94; CEO Neighborhood Health Providers, N.Y.C., 1995—; prof. Hofstra U., L.I., 1990—; CEO Royal Healthcare LLC, N.Y.C., 1995—. Mem. Am. Coll. Healthcare Execs., N.Y. State HMO Coun. Office: Royal Healthcare LLC 630 3rd Ave New York NY 10017

BORYSKO, EMIL, biologist; b. Scranton, Pa., Sept. 24, 1918; s. Damyan and Katherine (Podgorno) B.; m. Gladys Lucille Roberts, May 30, 1955 (div. 1986); children: Katherine Z., Steven D. (twins), Robert A. BA in Biology, Bklyn. Coll., 1940; MA in Biology, George Washington U., 1951; PhD, Johns Hopkins U., Balt., 1955. Fibr technologist Nat. Bur. Stds., Washington, 1947-51; rsch. fellow, instr. Johns Hopkins U., Balt., 1951-56; rsch. assoc. NYU Dental Coll., N.Y.C., 1956-58; prin. rsch. scientist Ethicon, Inc., Bridgewater, N.J., 1958-91, ret., 1991. Recipient Disting. Analytical Chemist award, Johnson & Johnson, 1988, Phil B. Hoffman Rsch. award, 1985; Damien Runyon W. Winchell Cancer Soc. rsch. fellow, 1951-54. Fellow AAAS; mem. Electron Microscopy Soc. Am., N.Y. Acad. Sci., Am. Inst. Biol. Sci., Sigma Xi. Home: 211 Love Rd Bridgewater NJ 08807-1111

BOS, JAN DOSITHEUS, dermatology educator, academic administrator; b. Leiden, Netherlands, Sept. 13, 1951; s. Gerard J. Bos and Maria A.H. (Ruijs) Keppler; m. Anke Verrijp, Mar. 30, 1979; children: Sjoerd, Eelke. MD, Erasmus U., Rotterdam, Netherlands, 1976; PhD, U. Amsterdam, Netherlands, 1981. Resident in internal medicine Refaja Hosp., Dordrecht, Netherlands, 1976-78; resident in dermatology U. Amsterdam, 1979-83, from asst. to assoc. prof., 1983-88, prof., chmn. dept. dermatology, 1990—. Editor: Skin Immune System, 1990. Recipient local sci. awards. Mem. Netherlands Assn. Dermatology and Venereology, European Soc. Dermatological Rsch., European Immunodermatology Soc. (sec. 1990—), European Assn. Dermatology and Venereology. Office: U Amsterdam Acad Medi Sch, Centrun Dept Dermatology, Meibergdreef 9 1105 AZ Amsterdam The Netherlands

BOSACCO, DAVID N., orthopedic surgeon; b. Darby, Pa., Jan. 27, 1935; s. John and Mayre (Beattie) B.; m. Carol Bailey, June 18, 1960 (div. Aug. 1975); m. Priscilla Blue, July 17, 1982; children: Ann, Amy. BS, Lebanon Valley Coll., 1956; MD, Hahnemann Med. Coll., 1960. Diplomate Am. Bd. Orthopedic Surgery, Nat. Bd. Med. Examiners. Intern Bayfront Med. Ctr., St. Petersburg, Fla., 1960-61; resident in orthopedic surgery Hahnemann Med. Coll. and Hosp., Phila., 1961-64, State Hosp. Crippled Children, Elizabethtown, Pa., 1964-65; chief orthopedic surgery The Media (Pa.) Clinic, 1968-79; assoc. clin. prof. Med. Coll. Pa., Hahnemann U., 1968—; chief orthopedic surgery Riddle Meml. Hosp., Media, 1972—; pres. Eastern Orthopedic Inst., Media, 1979—. Capt. USAF, 1965-67. Mem. AMA, Am. Acad. Orthopedic Surgeons, Pa. Med. Soc., Phila. Orthopedic Soc., Delaware County Med. Soc. Hahnemann Alumni Orthopedic Soc., U. Pa. Orthopedic Assn. Roman Catholic. Home: 533 Darlington Rd Media PA 19063 Office: Riddle Health Care Ctr Ste 2302 1088 W Baltimore Pike Media PA 19063

BOSCH, E. PETER, physician, neurologist, educator; b. Linz, Austria, Apr. 26, 1945; came to U.S., 1971, naturalized, 1995; s. Erich and Gertrude (Blaschke) B.; m. Gundula Graziadei, Dec. 19, 1969; children: Patrick, Barbara, Julia. MD, U. Innsbruck, Austria, 1969. Diplomate in neurology Am. Bd. Psychiatry and Neurology. Intern Northwestern Hosp., Mpls., 1971-72; resident in neurology U. Iowa Coll. Medicine, Iowa City, 1972-75; neuromuscular fellow Tufts New Eng. Med. Ctr., Boston, 1977-78; attending neurologist U. Iowa Hosps. and Clinics, Iowa City, 1975-91, VA Med. Ctr., Iowa City, 1986-91; from asst. prof. to prof. U. Iowa Coll. Medicine, Iowa City, 1977-91; sr. assoc. cons. Mayo Clinic, Scottsdale, Ariz., 1991-94, cons. in neurology, 1995—; prof. Mayo Med. Sch., Rochester, Minn., 1992—; dir. MDA-Neuromuscular Clnic, Iowa City, 1982-91. Mem. editorial bd. Muscle and Nerve, 1988-91. Fellow ACP, Am. Acad. Neurology; mem. Am. Neurol. Assn., Ctrl. Soc. for Neurologic Rsch. Office: Mayo Clinic Scottsdale 13400 E Shea Blvd Scottsdale AZ 85259

BOSCH, JAIME, hepatologist, medical educator; b. Girona, Spain, Aug. 10, 1947; s. Carlos and Carmen (Genover) B.; m. Inmaculada Sansa; children: Carlos, Anna, Jaime, Alfonso. MD, U. Barcelona, 1970, PhD, 1982. Resident Hosp. Clin. Provincial, Barrcelona, 1970-73, assoc. doctor hepatology svc. intensive care unit gastroenterology and hepatology, 1975-85, chief hepatic hemodynamic lab., 1985—; from instr. to assoc. prof. sch. medicine U. Barcelona, 1971-85, prof. sch. medicine, 1985—; vis. asst. prof. sch. medicine Yale U., West Haven, Conn., 1980-82. Contbr. over 100 articles to profl. jours. Recipient grant NIH divsn. digestive and kidney diseases, Barcelona, 1993; recipient award for best communication, European Assn. Study of Liver, 1987. Mem. Am. Assn. Study of Liver Diseases, European Assn. Study of Liver, Catalan Soc. Digestology (pres. 1995—), Spanish Assn. for Study of Liver. Office: Hepatic Hemodyanic Lab, Villarroel 170 Hosp Clinic, 08036 Barcelona Spain

BOSCH, LORETTA ANN, social worker; b. Cambridge, Mass.; d. Arthur Richard and Loretta (Powers) Lavalle; m. Thomas T. Stewart; children: Ronald, Lisa, Darren, Lauren, Tammy, Thomas. BS, Old Dominion U., 1976; MSW, Norfolk State U., 1978. Cert. clin. social worker, master addiction therapist, criminal justice specialist; lic. clin. social worker, profl. geriatric care mgr. Sr. med. social worker Norfolk (Va.) Gen. Hosp., 1978-80, Temple U. Hosp., Phila., 1980-82; dir. group home for women Sanctuary of Tidewater, Va., 1983-84; social worker Cath. Family and Children's Svcs., Norfolk, 1984-86, Cath. Counseling Ctr., Cocoa, Fla., 1994—; pvt. practice psychotherapy, 1989—; faculty Phila. C.C., 1981-82, Med. Coll. Hampton Roads and Psychiat. Ctr., Norfolk, 1987-89; cons. Task Force on Adolescent Pregnancy, Va., 1978-80, Coord. Coun. for Human Svcs., Norfolk, 1980-81, Trico Home Health Care, Melbourne, Fla., 1990—, Devereaux Children's Hosp., Melbourne, 1990—. Mem. Brevard Art Ctr. and Mus. Active civilian, mil. sealift command, USN, 1982-83. Recipient scholarship NIMH, 1976-78. Mem. NASW, NAFE, ACSW, Nat. Register Clin. Social Workers, Nat. Register Bd. Cert. Diplomates, Women in Mil. Meml. Democrat. Office: Focus Ctr 2000 2000 Goff Pl Melbourne FL 32901

BOSCO, JAY WILLIAM, optometrist; b. Bay City, Mich., May 6, 1951; s. Frank Carl and Jeanette (Frontiera) B.; m. Mary Lou Roth, Jan. 22, 1972; children: Angela, Jason, Andrea. BS, Saginaw Valley State Coll., 1977; OD, Ill. Coll. Optometry, 1982. Pvt. practice optometry Bay City, Mich., 1982-83; dir. vision care services Blue Care Network of East Mich., Saginaw, 1983—. Served with USAF, 1969-73. Mem. Am. Optometric Assn., Mich. Optometric Assn., Beta Sigma Kappa. Roman Catholic. Lodge: Lions (chmn. Site-Mobile, Bay City, 1984—). Home: 1382 N Wagner Rd Essexville MI 48732-9532 Office: Blue Care Network East Mich 4200 Fashion Square Blvd Saginaw MI 48603-1247

BOSCO, LUIGI PAOLO, surgeon; b. Milan, Italy, June 21, 1929; s. Manfredo Francesco and Elvira Maria (Morelli de Castiglione) B.; m. Bianca Giacomina Reali, Feb. 5, 1958; children: Marcello, Annarosa. MD, U. Pavia, 1953. Specialist in surgery U. Milan, 1960, specialist in angiology, 1972, specialist in children's surgery, 1974; asst. Surg. Clinic. U. Milan, 1954-60, univ. asst., 1960-71; prof. surgical semeiotics Milan U., 1964—; vice chief Gen. Surgery Dept. Hosp. Vimercate, Milan, 1971-79; assoc. chief Gen. Surgery Dept. Hosp. Vimercate, 1979-80; chief gen. and vascular surgery dept. Hosp. Ivrea, 1980—; chmn. congress and workshop Ann. Internat. Surgery, Ivrea. Contbr. articles to profl. jours. Mayor, Mcpl. Adminstrn. Bareggio, 1964-72. Knight, Order of Italian Republic, 1970. Fellow Italian Soc. Surgery, Internat. Coll. Surgeons. Christian Democracy Party. Roman Catholic. Home: Via M Pagano 49, Via A da Giussano 11, Milan 20145, Italy Office: Hosp Dept Surgery, 2 Credenza Sq, Ivrea Italy 10015

BOSHES, LOUIS D., physician, scientist, educator; b. Chgo., Oct. 15, 1908; s. Jacob and Ethel (London) B.; children: Arlene Phyllis Boshes Hirschfelder, Judi Myrl; m. Natalie A. Boshes. BS, Northwestern U., 1931, MD, 1936; HHD (hon.), 1976. Diplomate neurology, psychiatry, and child neurology Am. Bd. Psychiatry and Neurology. Intern Michael Reese Hosp., Chgo., 1935-36, Cook County Hosp., 1936-37; fellow psychiatry Ill. Neuro-psychiat. Inst., Chgo., 1941-42, 46-47; sr. attending neurologist and psychiatrist, chief neurology clinic Michael Reese Med. Center, 1940—; prof. neurology and psychiatry Northwestern U., 1955-63; prof. neurology U. Ill. Coll. Medicine, Chgo., 1970-78, prof. emeritus, 1978—, historian and archivist in neurology; attending neurologist Ill. Research and Ednl. Hosps., 1963—, dir. consultation clinic for epilepsy, 1963-78; assoc. and attending neurologist, cons. neurology Cook County Hosp., 1947—; sr. cons. neurology Downey VA Hosp., 1952-60; prof. neurology Cook County Grad. Sch. Medicine, 1970—; practice medicine specializing in neurology and psychiatry, 1975—; mem. med. adv. com. Cook County chpt. Nat Found., 1947-55, March of Dimes, 1956—; mem. med. adv. com. Epilepsy Assn. Am., 1964—; bd. dirs., med. adv. com. Epilepsy Found. Am., 1964—; ambassador Internat. Bur. Epilepsy, 1969—; mem. profl. adv. com. Nat. Parkinson Found., 1960—, Nat. Myasthenia Gravis Found., 1972—, profl. adv. bd.; United Cerebral Palsy. Author, contbr. to books, med. jours.; assoc. editor Diseases of the Nervous System, 1962—; editor Chgo. Neurol. Soc. Bull., Behavioral Neuropsychiatry; mem. editorial bd. Excerpts Medica, Internat. Jour. Neurology and Neurosurgery. Historian, curator, archivist neurology U. Ill. Coll. Medicine at Chgo., 1990—. Lt. comdr. M.C., USNR, 1941-46. Fellow ACP, Am. Acad. Neurology, Am. Psychiat. Assn.; mem. AMA (cons. AMA Jour., bd. govs. 1991—), Inst. Medicine Chgo., Pan Am. Med. Assn. (pres. sect. neurology, 1973—, hon. D. of Humanities 1976), Cen. Neuropsychiat. Assn. (pres. 1973-74, historian, curator), Ill. Psychiat. Soc. (sec.-treas. 1949-50), Chgo. Neurol. Soc. (pres. 1965-66, historian, curator), Michael Reese Hosp. and Med. Center Alumni Assn. (pres. 1961-62), Assn. for Research in Nervous and Mental Diseases, Internat. League Against Epilepsy, Am. League Against Epilepsy, Ill. League Against Epilepsy (med. adv. com.), Ill. Med. Soc. (chmn. sect. neurology and psychiatry 1961—), Chgo. Med. Soc.,

World Fedn. Neurology, AAAS, Am. Med. Soc. of Vienna (life), Central Assn. Electroence-Phalographers, Sigma Xi, Phi Delta Epsilon, Alpha Omega Alpha (A). Home: 3150 N Lake Shore Dr Chicago IL 60657-4829

BOSHIER, MAUREEN LOUISE, health facilities administrator; b. Elizabeth, N.J., Oct. 1, 1946; d. John Henry and Mary Hanora (McGarry) B.; m. Robert Hall Rea, May 23, 1987. BSN, Coll. Misericordia, Dallas, Pa., 1968; MS in Psychiat. Nursing, U. Colo., 1973; MBA, U. Phoenix, 1987. Clin. specialist psychiat. nursing Denver Gen. Hosp., 1973-74; dir. rehab. services N.Mex. Cancer Control, Albuquerque, 1976-80; exec. dir. N.Mex. State Bd. Nursing, Albuquerque, 1980-84; exec. v.p. N.Mex. Hosp. Assn., Albuquerque, 1984-88; adminstr. surg. services, sr. nursing adminstr. U. N.Mex. Hosp., Albuquerque, 1988-94; CEO, pres. N.Mex. Hosps. and Health Systems Assn., Albuquerque, 1995—; dir. Profl. Seminar Cons., Inc., Albuquerque, 1982—; v.p. exec. bd. N.Mex. Health Resources, Albuquerque, 1981—, pres., 1989; vice chmn., bd. dirs. Hosp. Home Health Care, Albuquerque, 1978—; dir. Acad. Seminars, Inc., 1982—. Contbr. articles to profl. jours. Sec. N.Mex. Ballet Co., Albuquerque, 1982-87; vice chmn. Gov.'s Task Force on Nursing Issues, Albuquerque, 1982-88; adv. bd. Subarea Coun. Health Systems, Albuquerque, 1980-84. Capt. U.S. Army, 1967-71. Recipient Woman on the Move award YWCA, 1992, Wharton Sch. of Bus. fellowship for health care execs., 1993. Mem. Am. Orgn. Nurse Execs. (vice chmn. legis. advocacy com. 1992-94, chmn. 1993-94), N.Mex. Orgn. Nurse Execs. (treas. 1988-89, pres. 1990), N.Mex. League for Nursing, N.Mex. Nurses Assn. (Nurse Adminstr. award 1984), Rotary, Albuquerque C. of C. (quality of life com. 1994—), Sigma Theta Tau (pres.-elect 1994, pres. 1995—, Mentor award Gamma Sigma chpt. 1994). Democrat. Home: 9520 Kandace Dr NW Albuquerque NM 87114 Office: NMex Hosps and Health Sys Assn 2121 Osuna Rd NE Albuquerque NM 87113-1001

BOSIO, ANGELO, pharmacologist, psychiatrist, scientific advisor; b. Brescia, Italy, Jan. 18, 1955; s. Giulio and Teresa (Macetti) B. MD, Milan U., 1980, degree in pharmacology, 1982, degree in psychiatry, 1988. Intern Milan U. Med. Sch., 1984-88, cons. psychiatrist, 1988—; dir. pharmacological dept. St. Anne Clinic, Brescia, 1987—; dir. neurol. dept. St. Anne Clinic, Brescia, Italy, 1996—; cons. Internat. Pharm. Cos., 1983—, WHO, 1988, others; dir. A.A.N. Drug Monitoring Svc., N.Y.C., 1994—. Author: Handbook of Reaction Time Evaluation, 1991; editor Jour. Percorsi Sanitari, 1986—, Neuroscis. Collection, 1988, H & W in Medicine, 1992—; editor videotapes Neurotransmission, 1988, Axolytic Drugs: An Up to Date, 1989, The Metamorphosis, 1991, Mioclonus and Piracetam, 1991, The Living Proof, 1991, Video Minds Series, 1995, Depression, 1995, Epilepsy, 1996; journalist Sci. and Med. Press, 1982—; mng. dir. A.A.N., 1992—. Recipient Nutrition Found. award, Italy, 1982. Fellow AAAS, N.Y. Acad. Scis., Internat. Psychogeriatric Assn., Italian Psychiat. Soc.; mem. Assn. Advancement Neurosci. (pres. Brescia chpt. 1987-92, Internat. chpt. 1990—). Roman Catholic. Office: Assn Advancement Neurosci, Via Vivanti 9, Brescia 25133, Italy also: AAN 575 Madison Ave Ste 1006 New York NY 10022-2511

BOSKMA, ROMKE JELLE, pharmacist; b. The Netherlands, June 20, 1952. MS, PharmD, U. Groningen, 1979; BSc, U. Amsterdam, 1974. Pharmacist, 1980-84; clin. pharmacist Martini-Hosp., Groningen, 1984-88; dir. pharmacy Med. Ctr. Leeuwarden, The Netherlands, 1989—. Office: Medisch Centrum Leeuwarden, Henri Dunantweg 2, Postbus 888, Leeuwarden 8901, The Netherlands

BOSQUE, JESUS MANUEL, psychologist; b. Jaca, Huesca, Spain, Jan. 1, 1941; came to U.S., 1974; s. Manuel and Aquilina (Olivan) B.; m. Emily A. Giles, May 23, 1986. MA in Theology, U. Salamanca, Spain, 1966; MS in Psychology, U. Barcelona, Spain, 1973; MA in Edn., U. P.R., San Juan, 1979; PhD in Counseling Psychology, Clayton (Mo.) U., 1991. Cert. clin. psychologist, transactional analyst, P.R. Tchr. Latin and French Escuelas Pias, Soria, Spain, 1966-71; dir., counselor Colegio Calasanz, San Juan, P.R., 1974-85; clin. psychologist San Juan, 1985—; tchr. Cath. U., San Juan, 1976-78; lectr. Cath. Schs. Convs., San Juan, 1975, 78, 79; dir. Colegio Calasanz Parents Sch., San Juan, 1978-85. Mem. Internat. Transactional Analysis Assn., Am. Asns. Counseling and Devel., Am. Mental Health Counselors Assn., Nat. Acad. Cert. Clin. Mental Health Counselors, Fedn. Nat. P.R. Transactional Analysis, Assn. Psicologos P.R. Home: 23A St 2 11 Montecarlo Rio Piedras PR 00924 Office: Darlington Bldg Of 500 Rio Piedras PR 00925

BOSSEN, EDWARD HECHT, pathologist; b. Jacksonville, Fla., Aug. 9, 1939; s. Morris William and Sarah (Hecht) B.; m. Roxana Mack, Aug. 11, 1963; children: Deborah, Barbara, Rebecca. BS, U. Fla., 1961; MD, Duke U., 1965. Intern, resident Duke U., Durham, N.C., 1965-70; pathologist Duke U. Med. Ctr., Durham, N.C., 1972—. Maj. U.S. Army, 1970-72. Home: 2811 Wade Rd Durham NC 27705-5622 Office: Duke Univ Med Ctr Dept Pathology Durham NC 27710

BÖSTMAN, OLE MIKAEL, orthopedic surgeon; b. Helsinki, Finland, Dec. 12, 1950; s. Erik Willehard and Anita Margareta (Manner) B.; m. Leena A. Heikkonen, Feb. 24, 1986; children: Randolph, Beatrice, Manfred. M.D., Helsinki U., 1975, PhD, 1983; Cert. specialist in gen., orthopaedic and trauma surgery. Intern, Helsinki U. Central Hosp., 1974-75, resident in gen., thoracovascular, orthopaedic surgery, 1979-84, orthopaedic surgeon, 1984—; surgeon mem. Accident Bd. Helsinki, 1984—. Contbr. articles to profl. jours., chpts. to textbooks. Mem. Soc. Internat. de Chirurgie Orthop et de Traumatologie, Scandinavian Orthopaedic Assn. (regional sec. 1984—), Finnish Orthopaedic Assn. Office: Töölö Hosp Helsinki U, Topeliuksenkatu 5, Helsinki FIN-00260, Finland

BOSTWICK, JOHN, III, plastic surgeon, educator; b. Bostwick, Ga., Sept. 25, 1943. MD, U. Tenn., 1966. Diplomate Am. Bd. Surgery (bd. dirs. 1996—), Am. Bd. Plastic Surgery (bd. dirs. 1995—). Intern Emory U. Hosp., Atlanta, 1966-67, resident, 1970-73, resident, plastic surgery, 1973-74; staff Crawford Long Hosp., Atlanta, 1974—, Emory U. Hosp., Atlanta, 1974—; prof. surgery Emory U., Atlanta, 1982—, chmn. plastic surgery, 1992—. Fellow ACS; mem. AMA. Office: 1365 Clifton Rd Atlanta GA 30322

BOSWELL, DAN ALAN, health maintenance organization executive, health care consultant; b. Upland, Calif., July 25, 1947; s. Paul Leslie and Jana Delores (Thompson) B.; m. Lona Kathalene Bentley, Dec. 26, 1969; children: Bethanie Laurel, Daniel Alan II. Grad. in Mktg. and Sales Mgmt., UCLA. Mktg. dir. Maxicare Co., Los Angeles, 1974-78; v.p. Gen. Med, Santa Ana, Calif., 1978-81; exec. v.p. IMC Health Maintenance Orgn., Miami, Fla., 1981-83, Protective Health Providers, San Diego, 1981-83; CEO U.S. Health Plan, San Diego, 1982-84; pres., CEO Serra Health Plan, Sun Valley, Calif., 1984-85, Amerimed (formerly Serra Health Plan), Burbank, Calif., 1985; pres. The Wellstarr Group, Inc., Upland, Calif., 1986-89, pres., CEO, 1990-93; pres., CEO Humantics Managed Care Corp., 1989-92; pres. The Garvey Group, Calif., Upland, Calif., 1993—, Managed Care Specialists, Upland, 1993—; faculty fellow Nat. Health Maintenance Orgn. George Washington U., 1982-83; teaching asst. expert market devel., fed. reviewer health maintenance qualification HHS, Rockville, Md., 1982-84. Mem. governing body Healthsystems Agy., San Diego and Imperial Counties, Calif., 1981-85, pres. trauma task force, San Diego, 1984; mem. adv. bd. Calif. Med. Asst. Commn., San Fernando Valley, 1986; dist. dir. Pony Baseball, Inc.; mgr. Upland Black Am. Legion Baseball, 1992-94. Mem. Am. Mgmt. Assn., Am. Mktg. Assn., Group Health Assn. Am., Marine Corps Assn. Am., El Prado Men's Club (Chino, Calif.; bd. dirs. 1985-86), Sierra Laverne Country Club, Towns Club (Pomona, Calif.). Republican. Clubs: El Prado Men's (Chino, Calif.) (bd. dirs. 1985-86); Towns (Pomona, Calif.). Home: 851 Emerson St Upland CA 91784-1227 Office: The Garvey Group Calif 851 Emerson St Upland CA 91784-1227

BOSWELL, GEORGE MARION, JR., orthopedist, health care facility administrator; b. Dallas, May 12, 1920; s. George Marion and Viola (Scarbrough) B.; m. Veta M. Fuller, Oct. 30, 1958; children: Brianna Boswell Brown, Kama Boswell Koudelka, Maia Boswell. BS, Tex. Tech U., 1940; MD, U. Tex., Southwestern Dallas, 1950. Diplomate Am. Acad. Orthopaedic Surgery. Intern Parkland Hosp., Dallas, 1950-51; resident gen. surgeryand orthopedic surgery Parkland, Baylor and Scottish Rite Hosps., Dallas, 1951-55; practice medicine specializing in orthopedics Dallas, 1955—; v.p. med. affairs Baylor Health Care System, Dallas, 1982-86; dir. orthopaedic clin. studies Baylor U. Med. Ctr., 1995—; pres., owner Bee Aviation Inc., Dallas, 1968—, Boswell Realty Inc., Dallas, 1971—; lectr., cons. on health care delivery. Contbr. articles to profl. jours. Fellow ACS; mem. AMA, Am. Acad. Orthopaedic Surgery (Key Man U.S. Congress 1980—), Am. Hosp. Assn., Tex. Hosp. Assn. (Key Man Tex. Legislature 1980—, council on hosp. staffs), Flying Physicians (pres. Tex. 1960-64). Republican. Methodist. Club: Cresent (Dallas). Home: 7249 Wabash Ave Dallas TX 75214-3535 Office: Baylor U Med Ctr Dept Orthopaedic Surgery 3500 Gaston Ave Dallas TX 75246

BOSWELL, NATHALIE SPENCE, speech pathologist; b. Cleve., May 9, 1924; d. Harrison Morton and Nathalie Muriel (Clem) Spence; student Skidmore Coll, 1941-42; MusB in Edn., Northwestern U., 1945; MA, Western Res. U., 1961; m. June 15, 1946; children: Louis Keith, Donna Spence, Deborah Anne. Speech therapist Highland View Hosp., Cleve., 1961-64; speech pathologist Cleve. VA Hosp., 1964-87 ; chmn. Equal Employment Opportunity Counselors, 1969-74, Fed. Women Speakers Bur., 1968-87, Fed. Career Info. Program, 1970-72, Fed. Coll. Rels. Coun., 1970-74, Fed. Exec. Bd., 1972-73; adj. instr. Case Western Res. U., 1982-87; mem. adv. coun. sch. electromedicine scis., City U. Los Angeles, 1985; mem. adv. bd. Nat. Inst. Electromedicine Info., 1985; trustee, cons. Donna Spence Boswell Massther, 1992—. Mem. Cleve. Orch. Chorus, 1969-82; vol. Seamen's Svc., 1976—; patron Police Athletic League; mem. Citizen Adv. Com on Solid Waste, Cleveland Heights Ohio, 1989-94. Endowed Tuba Chair, Cleve. Orch., 1983. Recipient Performance award Equal Employment Opportunities, 1973; Quality Increase award, 1980; others; lic. speech pathologist, Ohio. Mem. Am. Speech and Hearing Assn. (cert. clin. competence), Ohio Speech and Hearing Assn., Aphasiology Assn. Ohio, Chi Omega Alumni Assn., Musical Arts Assn., Western Res. Hist. Soc., Cleve. Mus. Natural History (vol. 1988—), Cleve. Mus. Art, Smithsonian Assos., Nat. Wildlife Fedn., Audubon Soc., Nat. Trust Hist. Preservation, Am. Heritage Soc. Mem. Ch. Reorganized Latter-Day Saints. Author: Guidelines for EEO Counselors in their Training Program, 1973; prin. author: Laryngectomy-Orientation for Patients and Families, 1981; contbr., asst. editor: Am. Jour. Electromedicine, 1984. Home: 2946 Berkshire Rd Cleveland OH 44118-2444

BOSWORTH, WILLIAM POSEY, physician, physical education educator; b. Valdosta, Ga., Mar. 23, 1935; s. Paul Brooks and Myra Mae (Posey) B.; m. Wanda Marie Grimm; 1 child, Lynne Marie. BS, U. Tampa, 1957; MEd, Springfield (Mass.) Coll., 1961; postgrad., Orlando (Fla.) Jr. Coll., 1968; DO, U. Health Scis., Kansas City, Mo., 1972. Phys. edn. tchr., jr. high sch. tchr. Duval County Sch. Bd., Jacksonville, Fla., 1959-62; gen. practice, Jacksonville, 1974—; physician athletic team, 1975—. Mem. Duval County Sch. Bd., Jacksonville, 1986-90, Jacksonville Sports Com., 1981-86, Duval County Hosp. Authority, 1982-86, Fla. Gov.'s Coun. on Phys. Fitness and Sports, 1985-93, Fla. Sunshine State Games Found., 1990—. Capt. M.C. USNR, 1969—. Named Gen. Practitioner of Yr. Fla. Soc. Am. Coll. Family Physicians, 1982, Health Educator of Yr., Duval County Coalition Against Tobacco, 1991; recipient physician's recognition award AMA, 1988, 91, 94, vol. svc. 35-yr. gold pin award AAU/USA, 1988, Navy Commendation Medal, 1991. Mem. Fla. Med. Assn., Fla. Soc. Sons of Am. Revolution (pres. 1980, meritorious svc. medal Jacksonville chpt. 1986), Duval County Med. Soc., Duval County Acad. Family Physicians (treas., v.p., pres.), Assn. Mil. Surgeons U.S., Freedoms Found. at Valley Forge (pres. Jacksonville chpt. 1995—). Office: 9765 San Jose Blvd Jacksonville FL 32257

BOTERO-VELEZ, MAURICIO, physician; b. Cali, Colombia, Aug. 22, 1958; came to U.S., 1989; s. Josue and Marta (Belez) B. MD, U. Del Valle, 1984. Staff physician Vaughan Chilton Med. Ctr., Clanton, Ala.; mem. staff VA Hosp., Miami, Fla. Office: VA Hosp 1201 NW 16 St Miami FL 33125

BOTHWELL, ALFRED LESTER MEADOR, immunobiology educator; b. Springfield, Mo., Apr. 29, 1949; s. Wilber Clarence and Marcella Pearl (Lester) B.; m. Sallye Beth Fink, Dec. 29, 1974 (div. June 1983); children: Sara Gurley, Laura Elizabeth; m. Glenna Shirleen Roeder, Mar. 30, 1985. AB, Washington U., 1971; MPhil, Yale U., 1974, PhD, 1975. Postdoctoral fellow Cold Spring Harbor (N.Y.) Lab., 1975-76, MIT, Cambridge, Mass., 1976-82; asst. prof. pathology dept. Med. Sch. Yale U., New Haven, 1982-88; assoc. prof. immunobiology dept. Med. Sch. Yale Med. Sch., New Haven, 1988—. Author: (with Yancopoulos and Alt) Methods for Cloning and Analysis of Eukaryotic Genes, 1990; contbr. articles to profl. publs. Mem. Am. Soc. Microbiology, Am. Assn. Immunologists. Democrat. Office: Yale Med Sch Immunobiology Dept 310 Cedar St New Haven CT 06520-8011

BOTIMER, ALLEN RAY, retired surgeon, retirement center owner; b. Columbus, Miss., Jan. 30, 1930; s. Clare E. and Christel J. (Kalar) B.; m. Dorris LaJean, Aug. 17, 1950; children: Larry Alan, Gary David. BS, Walla Walla Coll., 1951; MD, Loma Linda U., 1955. Diplomate Am. Bd. Surgery. Intern U.S. Naval Hosp., San Diego, 1955-56, surg. resident, 1955-60; resident in surgery U.S. Naval Hosp., Guam, 1960-62; asst. chief surgery U.S. Naval Hosp., Bremerton, Wash., 1962-64; chief surgery Ballard Community Hosp., Seattle, 1970, chief of staff, 1972, chief surgery, 1986-87; pvt. practice Seattle, 1964-87; ret., 1987; ptnr. Heritage Retirement Ctr., Nampa, Idaho, 1972-82, owner, 1982—. Lt. comdr. USN, 1955-64. Fellow ACS, Seattle Surg. Soc.; mem. Wash. State Med. Soc., King County Med. Soc. Home and Office: 1319 Torrey Ln Nampa ID 83686

BOTNICK, ROBERT MARC, physician assistant; b. Long Branch, N.J., May 15, 1948; s. Howard Martin and Lila (Ferster) B.; m. Elisha Ian (div. Sept. 1984); m. Nancy Sneath, Aug. 8, 1992; children: Elisha Jordan, Ian Stuart. Student, Chadron (Nebr.) State Coll., 1966-67, U. Colo., 1973, U. Colo., Denver, 1973-74. Cert. physician asst. Pres. Physician Extender Svc., Denver, 1980—, Mountain View Med. Trans., Denver, 1981—; advisor para credential com. Columbia HCA, Denver, 1994—. Fellow Am. Acad. Physician Assts., Am. Assn. Surg. Assts. (bd. dirs. 1994-95), Nat. Assn. Physician Assts. Home: 725 Aegean Dr Lafayette CO 80026 Office: 9171 Grant St Thornton CO 80229

BOTSTEIN, DAVID, geneticist, educator; b. Zurich, Switzerland, Sept. 8, 1942; naturalized, 1954; A.B. cum laude in Biochem. Scis., Harvard U., 1963; Ph.D. in Human Genetics, U. Mich., 1967. Woodrow Wilson fellow, 1963; instr. dept. biology MIT, Cambridge, 1967-69; asst. prof. genetics MIT, 1969-73, assoc. prof. genetics dept. biology, 1973-78, prof., 1978-88; mem. sci. adv. bd. Collaborative Research, Inc., 1978-87. Editor in chief Molecular Biology of Cell, 1992—; mem. editorial bd. Virology, 1976-82, Jour. of Virology, 1976-85, Genetics, 1980—. NSF Study Sect. Genetic Biology, 1972-76, ACS Study Sect. Virology and Cell Biology, 1977-81; contbr. over 150 articles to profl. jours. Recipient Career Devel. award NIH, 1972-74; Eli Lilly and Co. award in Microbiology and Immunology, 1978, Rosenstiel award Brandeis U., 1992, Allen award Am. Soc. of Human Genetics, 1989, Inst. of Medicine, 1993. Mem. Nat. Acad. Scis., Genetics Soc. Am. (bd. dirs. 1984). Office: Stanford U Dept Genetics 300 Pasteur Dr Palo Alto CA 94304-2203

BOTT, KENNETH FRANCIS, JR., microbiology educator; b. Albany, N.Y., Dec. 19, 1936; s. Kenneth F. and Eva (Button) B.; m. Lacala Hall, July 8, 1990; m. Patricia Weiler, June 18, 1960; children: Allison Eva, Kenneth Alan. BS in Biology, St. Lawrence U., Canton, N.Y., 1958; MS in Microbiology, Syracuse (N.Y.) U., 1960, PhD in Microbiology, 1963; postgrad. virology, U. Chgo., 1963-64. Instr. dept. microbiology and The Coll. U. Chgo., 1964-67, asst. prof. dept. microbiology and The Coll., 1967-71; assoc. prof. dept. bacteriology and immunology U. N.C., Chapel Hill, 1971-80, prof. dept. microbiology and immunology, 1980—, mem. curriculum in genetics, 1972—, chmn. curriculum in genetics, 1985-91, mem. adminstrv. bd. Grad. Sch., 1985-92; Am. Soc. Engring. Edn.-NASA summer faculty fellow Stanford U., 1969; vis. prof., Fulbright grantee U. Paris XI, Orsay, France, 1971; CNRS sponsored Chercheur Associe Institut Pasteur, Paris, 1977; vis. researcher, Fulbright grantee Centre Genetique Moleculaire, CNRS Gif sur Yvette, France, 1982. Contbr. articles to profl. jours. Merck & Co. Found. grantee U. Chgo., 1969. Mem. AAAS, AAUP, Am. Soc. Microbiology (chmn. found. lectr. com. 1986-89, pres. N.C. br. 1978-79), Sigma Xi (sec. U. Chgo. chpt. 1967-68). Office: U NC Med Sch Dept Microbiology Chapel Hill NC 27599-7290

BOTTONE, JOANN, health services executive; b. Bklyn., June 20, 1943; d. Anthony and Claire (Bisesti) B.; m. William Recevuto, Feb. 12, 1989; children: Matthew, Sandra. RN, Kings County Hosp. Ctr., Bklyn., 1963; BS, St. Francis Coll., Bklyn., 1980; MPA, Russell Sage Coll., Albany, N.Y., 1986; PhD in Pub. Adminstrn. magna cum laude, Kensington U., 1995. From staff nurse, head nurse, quality assurance coord. Victory Meml. Hosp., Bklyn., 1961-81; instr. infection control Community Hosp. Bklyn., 1981-82; dir. quality assurance Profl. Stds. Rev. Orgn., Bklyn., 1982-85; devel. and coord. HIV post-test counseling program Greater N.Y. Blood Ctr., N.Y.C., 1985-88; dir. HIV/AIDS programs Health Sci. Ctr. SUNY, Bklyn., 1988—; tchr. SUNY Coll. Health Related Professions; mem. working group to develop statewide policies and procedures for health care workers involved in potential HIV exposures N.Y. State Health Commr., 1990; mem. tech. adv. group to develop guidelines for OSHA's bloodborne pathogen standard Greater N.Y. Hosp. Assn., 1992; lectr. in field. Contbr. articles to profl. jours. Mem. Am. Coll. Health Care Execs. (assoc.), Greater N.Y. Hosp. Assn. (tech. adv. group).

BOTVIN, GILBERT JOSEPH, psychologist, behavior scientist, educator; b. Trenton, N.J., Oct. 15, 1947; s. Gilbert J. and Dorothy L. (Kearney) B.; BA, Colgate U., 1969; MA, Columbia U., 1974, PhD, 1977; m. Elizabeth M. Koeppel, Jan. 2, 1982. Profl. musician, Boston, 1969-72, N.Y.C., 1972-74; lead trumpet Nat. Rock Opera Co. prodn. of Jesus Christ Superstar, 1971-72; rsch. assoc. Columbia U., N.Y.C., 1977; staff psychologist Am. Health Found., 1977-79; program dir. Child Health Behavior Rsch., 1979-80; sr. rsch. assoc. Cornell U. Med. Coll., N.Y.C., 1979-80, asst. prof. pub. health, 1980-85, assoc. prof. pub. health, 1985-91, prof., 1991—; clin. asst. prof. psychiatry, 1981-86, assoc. prof. psychiatry, 1986-91, prof. pub. health; asst. attending psychologist N.Y. Hosp., 1981-86, assoc. attending psychologist, 1986-91, attending psychologist, 1991—; bd. dir. Lab. of Health Behavior Research, Cornell U. Med. Coll., Inst. for Prevention Rsch. Cornell U. ; vis. assoc. prof. Columbia U., 1983-85; cons. Nat. Cancer Inst., Nat. Inst. Drug Abuse. Recipient Gov.'s Cert. of Merit for substance abuse prevention rsch. in N.Y. schs., 1984, FBI Cmty. leadership award. Mem. APA. Contbr. articles to profl. jours. Home: 19 Gorham Rd Scarsdale NY 10583-1153 Office: 411 E 69th St New York NY 10021-5603

BOUCHER, JOHN HENRI, medical technologist, bank officer; b. Buffalo, Dec. 28, 1956; s. Jean Henri and Helen (Fenato) B. AAS in Med. Tech., Alfred (N.Y.) State Coll., 1976; BS in Bus, SUNY, Buffalo, 1988. Cert. med. lab. technologist Am. Soc. Clin. Pathologists; cert. clin. lab. technologists HHS. Tech. sales rep. Baxter Healthcare Corp., West Sacramento, Calif., 1988-90; sales mgr. USA Jobseekers Directory, Hamburgh, N.Y., 1990; sales assoc. M.J. Peterson Real Estate, Buffalo, 1990-91, Grandview Devel. Group Inc., Buffalo, 1991-94; sr. med. technician Children's Hosp. Buffalo, 1978-88, med. technologist, 1990—; fin. sales assoc. Key Bank of N.Y., 1994—. Mem. Willow Ridge Civic Assn., Amherst, N.Y., 1982—; mem. games com. World U., Buffalo, 1991. Sarah Helen Kish Meml. scholar SUNY, 1985-86. Mem. NRA (life), U. Buffalo Alumni Assn., U. Buffalo Sch. Mgmt. Alumni Assn., Tonawanda Fitness Ctr., Alpha Sigma Lambda, Beta Gamma Sigma. Home: 378 Kaymar Dr Amherst NY 14228-3016

BOUCHIER, IAN ARTHUR, medical sciences educator; b. Cape Town, South Africa, Sept. 7, 1932; arrived in Eng. 1961; s. Edward Alfred and May (Simons) B.; m. Patricia Norma Henshilwood, Sept. 5, 1959; children: Anthony James, David Ian. MBChB, U. Cape Town, 1954, MD, 1960. Rsch. fellow Boston U. Sch. Medicine, 1963-65; sr. lectr. in medicine U. London, 1965-70, reader in medicine, 1970-73; prof. medicine U. Dundee, Scotland, 1973-86, U. Edinburgh, Scotland, 1986—; chmn. Health Svcs. Rsch. Com., Scotland, 1987-92; chief scientist for Scotland, 1992—. Author, editor textbooks in field, scientific publs. Vice chmn. Scottish AIDS Rsch. Appeal, Edinburgh, 1988. Comdr. Brit. Empire, 1990. Fellow Royal Coll. Physicians (London, Edinburgh), Inst. Biology, Royal Soc. Edinburgh, Royal Soc. Arts; mem. World Orgn. Gastroenterology (pres. 1990—), Brit. Soc. Gastroenterology (chmn. edn. com. 1987-90, pres. 1994-95), Med. Rsch. Coun., Am. Gastroenterol. Assn., Assn. Physicians Gt. Britain, Scottish Soc. Physicians, Scottish Soc. Exptl. Medicine, New Club. Liberal. Office: Royal Infirmary, Dept Medicine, Edinburgh EH39YW, Scotland

BOUCHILLON, BILL GENE, retired psychology educator; b. Louisville, Miss., Dec. 6, 1928; s. Caleb M. and Ora Belle (Robinson) B.; m. Pat Hall, Nov. 8, 1948; children: Cherie Bouchillon Bennett, Lynn Hall. BA, Samford U., 1950; EdD, U. Tenn., 1970. Pastor various So. Bapt. Chs., Miss., Tex., Calif., Nev., 1951-65; instr. psychology S.W. Bapt. Coll., Bolivar, Mo., 1966-67; acting dean students Carson Newman Coll., Jefferson City, Tenn., 1967-68; prof. psychology Union U., Jackson, Tenn., 1969-91, prof. emeritus, 1991—, dean sch. natural and behavioral scis., chair dept. psychology and div. social scis., 1969-89; mem. exec. bd. dirs. Calif. So. Bapt. Conv., Fresno, 1958-61; cons. Western State Hosp. Adolescent Unit, Bolivar, Tenn., 1970-74; interim pastor 26 Bapt. Chs. in Tenn., Ky., Miss., 1967-91; workshop conf. leader various community and ch. groups, Tex., Tenn., Miss., 1975-91. Contbr. article to profl. jours. Speaker high sch. commencements, community events, Tenn., Miss., Calif., 1959-91; cons. Jackson Boys Club, 1974-86. Recipient Ednl. Appreciation award Jackson Boys Club, 1982. Mem. APA, N.Am. Soc. Adlerian Psychologists, Kappa Delta Pi, Phi Delta Kappa. Republican. Home: 2197 Leisure World Mesa AZ 85206-5375

BOUDINOT, FRANK DOUGLAS, pharmaceutics educator; b. New Brunswick, N.J., Mar. 31, 1956; s. Frank Lins and Dorothy Jean (Libourel) B.; m. Sarah Garrett, Sept. 1992; 1 child, Frank Garrett. BS in Biology, Springfield Coll., 1978; PhD in Pharmaceutics, SUNY, Buffalo, 1986. Vet. technician Afton Animal Hosp., Williamsville, N.Y., 1978-79; rsch. technician SUNY-Millard Fillmore Hosp., Buffalo, 1979-80; grad. asst. SUNY, 1980-85; asst. prof. pharmaceutics U. Ga., Athens, 1986-90, assoc. prof., 1990—, head dept. pharm., 1992—; cons. Assn. Minority Profl. Health Schs., Drug Devel. Group for AIDS, Tex. So. U. Coll. Pharmacy and Health Scis., Oneida Rsch. Svcs., Inc. Mem. editl. bd. Jour. Pharmacy Tchg., 1989—, Biopharm. and Drug Disposition, Eng., 1994—; referee Jour. Pharm. Scis., 1988—, Jour. Pharm. Rsch., 1989—, Antimicrobial Agts. and Cehmotherapy, 1993—; contbr. over 80 articles to sci. jours. Bd. dirs. Oconee Animal Shelter, Watkinsville, Ga., 1986-88; vice chair govt. svcs. subcom. Oconee 2000, Waktinsville, 1986-87; del. Ga. State Rep. Conv., Atlanta, 1989, 91, 92. NIH grantee, 1987, 90, U.S. FDA grantee, 1989; named one of Outstanding Young Men of Am., 1987. Mem. Am. Assn. Pharm. Scientists, Am. Assn. Colls. Pharmacy (del. 1989-90, mem. profl. affairs com. 1990-91), Am. Soc. Microbiology, Rho Chi. Episcopalian. Office: U Ga Coll Pharmacy Brooks Dr Athens GA 30602

BOUDREAU CONOVER, MARY HELEN, nursing educator; b. Long Beach, Calif., June 16, 1931; d. Essel George Boudreau and Eleanor McPartlin; m. Edward Lee Conover, Oct 8, 1966; children: Edward Lee III, Catherine Marie. RN, St. Vincent's Coll Nursing, L.A., 1952; BSN, Univ. Coll., Dublin, Ireland, 1960. Dir. of edn. Sch. Nursing, Kabanya, Tanzania, 1962-63; insvc. dir., supr. critical care unit Queen of the Valley Hosp., West Covina, Calif., 1963-66; insvc. dir. Granada Hills (Calif.) Cmty. Hosp., 1967-68; dir. edn. Critical Care Cons., Santa Cruz, Calif., 1969—. Author: Exercises in Electrocardiography, 3d edit., 1984, Electrocardiography: A Home Study Course, 1984, Pocket Nurse Guide; Electrocardiography, 3d edit., 1993, Understanding Electrocardiography, 7th edit., 1996; co-author: (with H.J.L. Marriott) Advanced Concepts in Arrhythmias, 2d edit., 1989, (with H.J. Wellens) The ECG in Emergency Decision-making, 1992, (with A. Tilkian) Understanding Heart Sounds and Murmurs with an Introduction to Lung Sounds, 3d edit., 1993, (with S. Tilkian and A. Tilkian) Clinical Implications of Laboratory Tests, 5th edit., 1996; mem. editl. bd. Critical Care Quar., 1978-82, The Jour. of Cardiovascular Nursing, 1987-95; editl. cons. Critical Care Update, 1976-83; contbr. articles to profl. jours. Recipient Book of Yr. award Am. Jour. Nursing, 1981. Office: Critical Care Confs 33 Charles Dr Santa Cruz CA 95060

BOUDREAUX, GLORIA MARIE, nurse, educator; b. Lafayette, La., May 2, 1935; d. Simon Zepherin and Orta Marie (Pierret) B. Diploma, Charity Hosp. Sch. Nursing, 1962; BA maxima cum laude, St. Edward's U., 1974; MS in Psychiatric-Mental Health Nursing, Tex. Women's U., 1976. Head surg., med. nurse Lafayette (La.) Charity Hosp., 1962-65; commd. 1st lt. U.S. Army, 1965; advanced through grades to col. Nurse Corps, U.S. Army, 1983; ret. U.S. Army, 1995; psychiat. staff nurse VA Hosp., New Orleans,

1968-72; psychiatric nurse U.S. Army Nurse Corp., San Francisco and Augusta, Ga., 1966-67; instr. Tex. Woman's Univ. Sch. of Nursing, Houston, 1976-80; clin. specialist VA Med. Ctr., Houston, 1980-87; psychiat. nursing coord. Spring Shadows Glen, Houston, 1987-88; instr. assoc. degree nursing program Houston Community Coll., 1988-91; asst. prof. nursing La. State U., Eunice, 1992-96; with Circle of Support Home Health, 1996—; clin. specialist, cons. in psychiat.-mental health nursing. Recipient Nat. Def. Svc. medal, 1968, Army Res. Component medal, 1972, Armed Forces Res. medal, 1977 (10-yr. device 1988), Army Commendation medal, 1978, Army Meritorious Svc. medal, 1990, Presdl. Sports award, 1989, 90, 91. Mem. Am. Psychiatric Nurses Assn., Am. Orthopsychiatric Assn., Soc. for Edn. and Rsch. in Psychiatric-Mental Health Nursing, Res. Officers Assn. (chpt. pres. 1981-83), Assn. Mil. Surgeons of U.S., ANA (cert. in psychiat. mental health nursing), Vietnam Vets. Assn., Sigma Theta Tau, Retired Army Nurse Corps Assn., The Retired Officers Assn. Home: 307 Meadow Ln Lafayette LA 70506

BOUDREAUX, J. PHILIP, transplant surgeon, educator; b. Baton Rouge, Apr. 29, 1952; s. H. Bruce and Rosemae (Guidroz) B.; m. Deborah Lynne Malewicki B., Aug. 20, 1988. BS magna cum laude, La. State U., 1974, MD, 1978. Diplomate Am. Bd. Surgeons. Intern in pediats. St. Jude Children's Hosp., Memphis, 1978-79; resident in gen. surgery Charity Hosp., New Orleans, 1979-84; fellow in pediat. surgery Pitts. Children's Hosp., 1982; fellow in organ transplantation and immunlogy U. Minn. Hosp., Mpls., 1984-85; asst. prof. surgery, dir. pancreas-kidney and pediat. trans. U. Tex. Med. Br., 1986-90; dir. pancreas and liver transplantation Ocnsner Clinic, New Orleans, 1990-93; assoc. prof. surgery La. State U. Med. Ctr., 1993—; dir. liver and pancreas-kidney transplantation U. Hosp. and Mercy Bapt. Hosp., New Orleans, 1993—; dir. pediat. transplantation Children's Hosp., New Orleans, 1993—; med. dir. La. Organ Procurement Agy., New Orleans, 1993-96; bd. dirs., 1996—; 5 state rep. United Network Organ Sharing, Richmond, Va., 1994—; Tex. rep. End Stage Renal Network 14, Dallas, 1987-90. Contbr. over 30 articles to med. jours.; first to perform pancreas transplant in Tex., 1988, La., 1990, first liver-kidney transplant in La., 1990, first double transplant in La., 1990, first living-related liver transplant in La., 1992. Fellow ACS, Am. Soc. Transplant Surgeons (membership com. 1993—), Am. Soc. Transplant Physicians, Southeastern Surg. Congress.; mem. Am. Radio Relay League (Public Svc. award 1976). Office: La State U Sch Med Dept Sur 1542 Tulane Ave New Orleans LA 70112

BOUEY, ORA JAMES, nursing educator; b. Alamonte Springs, Fla., Nov. 23, 1931; d. Condor E. and Mary (James) Merritt; m. David L. Bouey, July 23, 1952; children: Daizzee Donaae Bouey-Noland, David L. II. Nursing diploma North Country Community Hosp., Glen Cove, N.Y., 1956; A.A.S., Suffolk Community Coll., 1969; M.A., NYU, 1977, nurse practitioner U. Stony Brook, 1978—. Charge emergency dept. Meadowbrook Hosp., East Meadow, N.Y., 1956-72; staff critical care Huntington (N.Y.) Hosp., 1957-80; instr. Bd. Coop. Ednl. Services, Dix Hills, N.Y., 1970-72; instr. SUNY-Stony Brook, 1972-77, asst. prof., 1977-82, assoc. prof., 1982—, chmn. dept. adult health nursing, 1982-89, dir. profl. resources devel., dir. acad. advancement, 1989—, asst. dean acad. advancement, 1993—; cons. in field. Contbg. author: Guide to Patient Evaluation, CGFNS Examination Review. Recipient Congl. award for meritorious service, 1980; Chancellors award SUNY, 1981, N.Y. State Black Faculty Staff award, 1982; Disting. Alumni award SUNY-Stony Brook, 1983. Bd. dirs. Youth Devel. Assn., Youth Devel. Ctr., Pederson Krag Ctr., 100 Black Women Inc., R.S.V.P. Suffolk County, Planned Parenthood Suffolk County. Mem. NAS, NAACP, United U. Profls. (N.Y. State legis. com., N.Y. State United Tchrs. Fed. of Nurses and Health Profls. laison Fed. of Nurses and Health Profls.), Am. Assn. Black Women in Higher Edn., Am. Assn. Critical Nurses, Am. Nurses Assn., N.Y. Acad. Sci., N.Y. State Nurses Assn., N.Y. State Conf. Aging, Am. Assn. Higher Edn., AAUP, AAUW, Assn. Black Nursing Faculty, Nat. League Nurses, Suffolk County Mental Health Assn., Chi Eta Phi, Sigma Theta Tau, Alpha Kappa Alpha. Presbyterian. Home: 158 Manor Rd Huntington NY 11743-5733 Office: SUNY-Stony Brook Health Scis Ctr 204 Stony Rm 233 Level 2 Stony Brook NY 11794-8240

BOUFFORD, JO IVEY, health and human services administrator; b. Durham, N.C., July 2, 1945. BA in Psychology magna cum laude, Wellesley Coll., 1965; MD with distinction, U. Mich., 1971; DSc(hon.), SUNY, Bklyn., 1992. Diplomate Nat. Bd. Med. Examiners, Am. Bd. Pediats. Resident in social pediats. medicine Montefiore Hosp. and Med. Ctr., Bronx, N.Y., 1971-74, asst. attending physician, 1975—, co-dir. Inst. for Health Team Devel., 1975-82, dir. residency program in social medicine, 1975-82; adminstrv. dir. Valentine Lane Family Practice, Yonkers, N.Y., 1975-82; v.p. med. ops. N.Y.C. Health and Hosps. Corp., 1982-83, v.p. med. and profl. affairs, 1983-85, exec. v.p., 1985, acting pres., 1985, pres., 1985-89; internat. fellow in comparative health sys. mgmt. King's Fund Coll., London, 1989-91, dir., 1991-93; prin. dep. asst. sec. for health Dept. Health and Human Svcs., Washington, 1993—; asst. prof. dept. pediats. Albert Einstein Coll. of Medicine, Bronx, N.Y., 1976-87, assoc. prof. dept. cmty. health, 1981-82, clin. assoc. prof. dept. pediats., 1987—, clin. assoc. prof. dept. epidemiology and social medicine, 1982—; adj. prof. Lehman Coll. Nursing, Bronx, 1974-80; mem. Nat. Adv. Coun. for Health Professions Edn. US-DHHS, 1976-80; mem. tech. panel on the ednl. environ. Grad. Med. Edn. Nat. Adv. Coun., 1979-80; cons. on manpower programs divsn. medicine bur. Health Professions Edn. HRSA-DHHS, 1980-88; mem. N.Y. State Coun. on Grad. med. Edn., 1987-89, N.Y. State Commn. on Grad. Med. Edn., 1985-86; mem. adv. bd. residency program in gen. preventive medicine and occupl. health Mt. Sinai coll. Medicine, 1986-89; mem. Nat. Vis. Coun. for the Health Scis. Faculty Columbia U., N.Y.C., 1988-90; mem. vis. faculty The New Sch. for Social Rsch., 1989; rep. of U.S. on exec. bd. WHO, 1994—; mem. joint coordinating com. for Radiation Health Effects Rsch., 1994—; U.S. staff dir. Gore-Chernomyrdin Commn. Health Com., 1994—; various consulting positions. Mem. editl. bd. Jour. Med. Edn., 1980-86; mem. editl. adv. bd. The New Physician, 1979-89; contbr. articles to profl. jours.; presenter in field. Fellow Am. Acad. Pediats.; mem. APHA, NAS Inst. Medicine (Robert Wood Johnson health policy fellow 1979-80), Am. Med. Women's Assn., Ambulatory Pediats. Assn., Soc. for Health and Human Values, Soc. Med. Adminstrs., Med. Adminstrs. Conf., Physician Leadership Network Healthcare Forum. Office: Dept Health & Human Svc Office Pub Health and Sci 200 Independence Ave SW Rm 716-G Washington DC 20201-0004*

BOUGHMAN, JOANN ASHLEY, dean; b. Kokomo, Ind., May 4, 1949; d. Robert George and Lydia Ann (Ashley) B. BS in Med. Tech., Ind. U., Indpls., 1972, PhD in Med. Genetics, 1978. Diplomate Am. Bd. Med. Genetics. Asst. prof. Med. Coll. Va., Richmond, 1979-82; assoc. prof. U. Md. Med. Sch., Balt., 1983-90, prof., 1990—; assoc. v.p. for rsch. U. Md. Balt. County, Balt., 1992-95, dean grad. sch., 1992—; v.p. for acad. affairs U. Md., Balt., 1995—; sec. Am. Bd. Med. Genetics, 1992-94, v.p., 1995-96; cons. NIH, Bethesda, Md., 1982—, Gallaudet U., Washington, 1977—. Contbr. articles to profl. jours., chpts. to 19 books; author ednl. materials. Bd. dirs., officer Har Sinai Congregation, Balt., 1987—; mem. exec. com. High Tech Coun., Balt., 1992—; com. chair Info. Tech. Bd., Balt., 1994—; mem. speaker bur. Jewish Family Svcs., Balt., 1987—. Grantee RP Genetics Registry Ctr., 1978-82, NIH, 1985-94, 90-94; Edwards fellow, 1976. Fellow Am. Coll. Med. Genetics; mem. Am. Soc. Human Genetics (cert., com. chair 1994), Am. Assn. Dental Rsch., Am. soc. Clin. Pathologists, Exec. Women's Network. Office: U Md Balt 520 W Lombard St Baltimore MD 21201

BOUJU, PHILIPPE PIERRE MICHEL, anesthesiologist; b. Bois-Colombes, France, Apr. 22, 1957; s. Pierre and Jacqueline (Landré) B.; m. Hélène Marie Francoise Henriette Dreux-Boucard; 1 child, Cyrielle. MD, Lariboisiere-St. Louis, Paris, 1983; Specialist Anesthesiology & CriticalCare, Faculte Rehe Descartes, Paris, 1989. Cert. d'etudes Speciales d'anesthesie reanimation. Anaesthesia tng. Hosp. Henri Mondro/Creteil Hosp. Tenon, Paris; medecin des hopitaux C.H. Robert Ballanger, Aulnay Sous Bois, France, 1991—, pres. Com. de Lutte Contre la Douleur, 1995—. Contbr. articles to profl. jours. Mem. Internat. Assn. for Study of Pain, European Soc. of Anaesthesiology, European Soc. Regional Anaesthesia, Soc. Francaise de la Douleur. Home: 32 Bld du General de Gaulle, 93250 Villemomble France Office: C H Robert Ballanger, Bld Robert Ballanger, 93602 Aulnay sous Bois France

BOULDIN, REGINA DIANE, speech and language specialist, elementary educator; b. McMinnville, Tenn., Oct. 11, 1964; d. Joe Ross and Charlotte Jean (Maynard) Clendenon; m. Dwight Lynn Bouldin, June 24, 1983; children: Courtney Tenai, Haley Lauren. BS, Mid. Tenn. State U., 1987, MEd in Adminstrn. and Supervision, 1995. Cert. speech/lang. and hearing specialist; cert. elem. tchr., Tenn. Substitute tchr. Warren County Sch. System, McMinnville, 1986-87, speech/lang. specialist, 1987-92; tchr. 5th grade Centertown Sch., 1992—; tutor for Japanese ESL Program, McMinnville, 1990. Named Outstanding Young Educator McMinnville Jaycees 1987. Mem. AAUW (corr. sec. 1988-90, Outstanding mem. 1989-90, chmn. baby show 1988-91), Jr. Aux. McMinnville. Mem. Ch. of Christ. Home: 76 Miriah Dr Mc Minnville TN 37110-5306

BOULPAEP, EMILE LOUIS J. B., physiology educator, foundation administrator; b. Aalst, East-Flanders, Belgium, Sept. 15, 1938; came to U.S., 1968; s. Henri Jules and Eulalie J. (de Croes) B.; m. Elisabeth J. Goris, July 25, 1964. BS, U. Leuven, Belgium, 1958, MD, 1962, Lic. Sc. Med., 1963; Doctor honoris causa, U. Louvain, Belgium, 1987; MA (hon.), Yale U., 1979. Asst. U. Louvain, Belgium, 1962-66, instr., chief asst., 1966-68; asst. prof. physiology Cornell U. Med. Coll., N.Y.C., 1968-69; asst. prof. physiology Yale U. Sch. Medicine, New Haven, 1969-72, assoc. prof. physiology, 1972-79, prof., 1979—, chmn. dept. physiology, 1979-87, chmn. dept. cellular and molecular physiology, 1987-89; mem. study sect., gen. medicine B, NIH, Bethesda, Md., 1976-80, chmn. spl. grants rev. subcom. on arthritis, diabetes and digestive and kidney diseases, 1985-87; overseas fellow Churchill Coll., Cambridge U., Eng., 1978—; fellow Branford Coll., Yale U, 1973—. Mem. editorial bd. Am. Jour. Physiology, 1976-78; assoc. editor Yale Jour. Biology and Medicine, 1976-84, dep. editor in chief, 1984—; editor Quar. Jour. Exptl. Physiology, 1985-89, Exptl. Physiology, 1990-91; contbr. numerous articles to sci. jours. Bd. dirs. Belgian Am. Ednl. Found., N.Y. and Brussels, 1971—, pres., New Haven, 1977—, chmn. bd. dirs., 1988—; bd. dirs. Fondation Universitaire, Brussels, 1977—, Fondation Francqui, Brussels, 1977—, Belgian Soc. Benevolence, N.Y.C., 1980—, Universitas, Ltd., N.Y.C., 1982—, v.p. 1987—; bd. dirs. Hoover Found. for Devel. U. Leuven-Louvain, 1988—, Hoover Found. for Devel. U. Brussels, 1990—. 1st lt. Belgian Air Force, 1966-68. Decorated Knight Order of Crown (Belgium) 1979, comdr. Order of Leopold II (Belgium) 1980; recipient spl. prize U. Louvain, 1962, Christophe Plantin award, 1993; John Polacheck Found. rsch. fellow, N.Y.C., 1965-66, Edgar Rickard fellow Belgian Am. Ednl. Found., N.Y.C., 1964-65; Prix des Alumni, Fondation Univ., Brussels, 1973. Mem. Am. Physiol. Soc. (internat. physiology com. 1992—), Am. Soc. Nephrology (Homer W. Smith joint award with N.Y. Heart Assn. 1986), Royal Acad. Medicine Belgium (fgn. corr. mem. 1983-90, fgn. hon. mem. 1990—), Biophys Soc., Am. Heart Assn. (coun. on kidney in cardiovascular disease 1973—), N.Y. Acad. Scis. Home: 96 Pond Meadow Rd Killingworth CT 06419-1143 Office: Yale U Sch Med 333 Cedar St New Haven CT 06510-8206

BOULTER, PATRICK STEWART, surgery educator; b. Annan, Dumfriesshire, Scotland, May 28, 1927; s. Frederick Charles and Flora Victoria (Black) B.; m. Patricia Mary Barlow, Mar. 7, 1946; children: Jennifer Mary Stewart Boulter Bond, Anne Margaret Stewart Boulter Wood. MB, BS with honors, U. London, 1955. Internat. master surgeon Internat. Coll. Surgeons. House surgeon Guy's Hosp., London, 1955-56, lectr. anatomy, 1956-57, sr. surg. registrar, 1959-62; surg. registrar Middlesex Hosp., London, 1957-59; cons. surgeon Regional Oncological Ctr. Royal Surrey (Eng.) Hosp., Guildford, 1962-91; prof. surg. sci. U. Surrey, Guildford, 1985—; examiner U. London, U. Edinburgh, Scotland, U. Newcastle, Eng., U. Nottingham, Eng., U. Glasgow, Scotland; vis. prof. U. Oreg., U. Nebr., U. Bombay, U. Pakistan, U. Queensland, U. Sydney, Australia, U. Auckland, New Zealand, U. Dunedin, New Zealand. Author book chpts. on surgery; contbr. articles to profl. jours. Trustee U.K. Thalidomide Trust. Fellow Royal Coll. Surgeons Edinburgh (pres. 1991-94, regent, 1995—), Royal Coll. Surgeons Eng. (Penrose-May tchr. 1985—), Royal Coll. Surgeons Glasgow, Royal Coll. Physicians Edinburgh, Acad. Med. Surgeons, Royal Australian Coll. Surgeons (hon.), Royal Soc. Medicine, Assn. Surgeons Gt. Britain and Ireland, Coll. Surgeons of South Africa (hon.), Coll. Surgeons of Sri Lanka (hon.), Coll. Surgeons Hong Kong (hon.), Acad. Medicine Singapore, Royal Coll. Surgeons Ireland (hon.), Soc. Surgeons Nepal; mem. Brit. Breast Group, Brit. Assn. Surg. Oncology (past v.p.), Surg. Rsch. Soc., Acad. Medicine Malaysia, Assn. Surgeons India, Alpine Club, Caledonian Club, New Club, Swiss Alpine Club, Yorkshire Fly Fishers Club. Home: Cairnsmore Merrow, Guildford Surrey GU1 2XN, Scotland Office: Royal Coll Surgeons, Nicolson St, Edinburgh EH8 9DW, Scotland also: Quarry Cottage, Salkeld Dykes, Penryth Cumbria England CA11 9LL

BOUMBULIAN, PAUL JERRY, health services administrator; b. Evanston, Ill., Jan. 8, 1943; s. Jerry Paul and Susan (Vidian) B.; m. Elizabeth B. Myers, May 30, 1970. BA, UCLA, 1966; M Health Svcs Adminstrn., U. Calif., Berkeley, 1974, MPH, 1970; DPA, U. Ga., 1985. Rsch. asst., coordinating asst. U. So. Calif., L.A., 1968-69; dir. rsch. and evaluation Athens (Ga.) Model Cities Program, 1970-73; dir comprehensive health planning Ga. Mountains Planning and Devel., Gainesville, 1974-76; exec. dir. Utah Health Sys. Agy., Salt Lake City, 1976-80; asst. adminstr., dir. strategic planning U. Calif., Sacramento, 1981-84; ind. cons., 1984-86; v.p. strategic planning and mktg. Parkland Meml. Hosp., Dallas, 1986-93, sr. v.p. strategic planning and population medicine dept., 1993—; asst. prof. Marjorie Webster Jr. Coll., Washington, 1973, U. Tex. Southwestern, Dallas, 1987—; clin. instr. U. Calif., Davis, U. Utah, Salt Lake City, 1977-80. Contbr. articles to profl. jours. Chmn. strategic planning com. Greater Dallas Healthy Cmty., 1995; bd. dirs. Homeward, Inc., 1993-95; tech. advisor Dallas Med. Resource, 1992-95; mem. City of Dallas Environ. Health Adv. Commn., 1990-91; mem. Dallas County Mental Health Planning Com., 1991-92. Acad. Rsch. Fund fellow UCLA, 1968, USPHS fellow, 1969-70, W. Ctr. for Healthcare Execs. fellow, 1980, Healthcare Forum fellow, 1993. Mem. Soc. for Ambulatory Care Profls. (chmn. strategic planning com. 1990-95), Med. Group Mgmt. Assn. (vice chmn. steering com. 1992-94). Home: 7654 Royal Ln Dallas TX 75230 Office: Parkland Meml Hosp 5201 Harry Hines Blvd Dallas TX 75235

BOUMEL, ARLENE RENEE GOREWITZ, family services administrator; b. Phila., Nov. 23, 1952; d. Solomon and Elaine Marilyn (Margolis) Gorewitz; m. Robert Charles Boumel, June 4, 1978; children: Joshua Michael, Adam Todd. BA in Social Welfare, Speech, Pa. State U., 1974; MSW, W.Va. U., 1975. Cert. ACSW; lic. ind. clin. social worker, Mass., Fla. Social worker Edn. Collaborative for Greater Boston, Inc., Brookline, Mass., 1977-78, South Shore Day Care Svcs. Inc., Braintree, 1978-81; program developer-trainer Mitterling Mgmt. and Tng. Consultants Inc., Winchester, Mass., 1982-85; family social worker, supr. family svcs. Fla. Sheriffs Youth Ranches Inc., Ft. Lauderdale, 1988—; clin. instr. Barry U., Miami, 1988—. Mem. NASW, Phi Beta Kappa. Home: 1750 NW 88th Way Coral Springs FL 33071-6173

BOUNDS, MARY LOU, nurse; b. Queens, N.Y., May 30, 1949; d. William Boykin and Ruth Elizabeth (Manning) Williams; m. Eldon Bounds; children: Wendy Rogers, Timothy Cagle; stepchildren: Vicki Rawls, Rita LeCompte. BSN, U. So. Miss., 1983. Med. asst. Dr. E.P. Reeves, Collins, Miss., 1968-79; med. sec. Dr. C.C. Tyler, Collins, 1968-79; subrural mail carrier U.S. Post Office, Seminary, Miss., 1979-90; RN Forrest Gen. Hosp., Hattiesburg, Miss., 1983-90, St. Luke's Episcopal Hosp., Houston, 1990-91, Clear Lake Regional Med. Ctr., Webster, Tex., 1991-95, Cypress Woods Care Ctr., Angleton, Tex., 1995-96; adminstr. in tng., RN, adminstrv. asst. Alvin Convalescent Ctr., Angleton, 1996—. Active PTA, Seminary, Miss., 1980-85. Mem. Am. Nursing Assn., Miss. Nursing Assn., Miss. Student Nursing Assn. (second v.p. 1981-82, first v.p. 1982-83, elected cons. 1983-84), Nat. Student Nurses Assn. (del. 1983), U.S. Rural Letter Carriers Assn., Athletic Booster Club (sec. 1983-85), Sigma Theta Tau. Republican. Roman Catholic. Home: RR 1 Box 133 Alvin TX 77511-9801 Office: Cypress Woods Care Ctr 135 1/2 Hospital Dr Angleton TX 77515

BOURDON, DINAH STEEL, nurse practitioner, health facility administrator; b. N.Y.C., Jan. 29, 1949; d. Erwin Michael and Gertrude Ruth (Glasser) Steel; m. Thomas E. Bourdon, Dec. 3, 1983; 1 child, Tessa Michelle. BFA, Syracuse U., 1970; AAS in Nursing, SUNY Upstate Med. Ctr., Syracuse, 1974; cert., SUNY Upstate Med. Ctr., 1977. RN, cert. nurse practitioner, advanced registered nurse practitioner. Nurse practitioner SUNY, Syracuse, 1977-79, Crouse Irving Meml. Hosp., Syracuse, 1979-80, Peliaon, Inc., Syracuse, 1980-86; pvt. practice Syracuse, 1986-94; dir. inpatient unit, mgmt., ARNP Guidance Clinic of the Middle Keys, Marathon, Fla., 1994—. Contbr. articles to profl. jours. Office: Guidance Clinic Middle Keys 3000 41st St Marathon FL 33050

BOURDON, FRANÇOIS, chemist; b. Saint-Lo, Manche, France, Mar. 28, 1966; s. Jean-Daniel and Odette (Fauvel) B. PhD in Chemistry, U. Caen, France, 1991. Analytical lab. mgr. Clintec, Montargis, France, 1993-95, quality control mgr., 1995—. Home: 32 Rue du Stade, 45700 Villemandeur France Office: Clintec, Z I D'Amilly BP 347, 45203 Montargis France

BOURGEAU, JEAN-PAUL LEONCE, pediatrician; b. Nouvelle Calédonie, France, Apr. 30, 1939; s. Jan and Lucienne (Beurnier) B. B, Mathematiques Elementaires, Versailles, 1957; MD, U. Paris, 1966. Externe Hosp. de Paris, 1961; specialist pediatrician Paris, 1969; attaché à la Consultation ds Adolescents Hosp. Necker Enfants Malades, Paris, 1988-94, 96—; pediatrician for children with behavioral disturbances Hosp. for the Deaf, Paris, 1985—. Mem. du Bur. de la Commn. Musicale de l'Assn. Culturelle de Larchant, 1983; pres. Assn. ds Proprietaires du Moulin à Vent à Larchant, 1986, Medecin de la Marine, 1966-67. Mem. Soc. Française Pediatrie. Office: 181 rue Legendre, 75017 Paris France

BOURGEOIS, JOHN ELLIOTT, ophthalmologist; b. Wiesbaden, Germany, Sept. 13, 1953; s. Harold John and Mary Wittenburg (Rion) B.; m. Emily Rumph, June 26, 1976; children: Townsend, John. BA, U. Va., 1975, MD, 1979. Diplomate Am. Bd. Ophthalmology. Resident Duke U. Eye Ctr., Durham, N.C., 1979-83, fellow in corneal external disease, 1983; ophthalmologist Charlotte Eye, Ear, Nose and Throat Assocs., 1984—; chmn. dept. ophthalmology Charlotte Eye, Ear, Nose and Throat Assocs., 1994—. Mem. Am. Acad. Ophthalmology, N.C. State Med. Soc., N.C. Soc. Ophthalmology, Mecklenburg County Med. Soc., Alpha Omega Alpha. Episcopalian. Home: 1944 Queens Rd W Charlotte NC 28207 Office: Charlotte EENT Assocs 1600 E 3d St Charlotte NC 28204

BOURGUIGNON, ERIKA EICHHORN, anthropologist, educator; b. Vienna, Austria, Feb. 18, 1924; d. Leopold H. and Charlotte (Rosenbaum) Eichhorn; m. Paul H. Bourguignon, Sept. 29, 1950. BA, Queens Coll., 1945; grad. study, U. Conn., 1945; PhD, Northwestern U., 1951. Field work Chippewa Indians, Wis., summer 1946; field work Haiti; anthropology Northwestern U., 1947-48; instr. Ohio State U., 1949-56, asst. prof., 1956-60, asso. prof., 1960-66, prof., 1966-90, acting chmn. dept. anthropology, 1971-72, chmn. dept., 1972-76, prof. emeritus, 1990—; dir. Cross-Cultural Study of Dissociational States, 1963-68; Bd. dirs. Human Relations Area Files, Inc., 1976-79. Author: Possession, 1976, rev. edit., 1991, Psychological Anthropology, 1979, Italian transl., 1983; editor, co-author: Religion, Altered States of Consciousness and Social Change, 1973, A World of Women, 1980; co-author: Diversity and Homogeneity in World Societies, 1973; adv. editor: Behavior Sci. Research, 1976-79; assoc. editor: Jour. Psychoanalytic Anthropology, 1977-87; editorial bd.: Ethos, 1979-89; editor: Margaret Mead: The Anthropologist in America—Occasional Papers in Anthropology, No. 2, Ohio State U. Dept. Anthropology, 1986; author articles. Fellow Am. Anthrop. Assn.; mem. Ctrl. State Anthrop. Soc. (treas. 1953-56, exec. com. 1995-98), Ohio Acad Sci., World Psychiat. Assn. (transcultural psychiatry sect.), Am. Ethnol. Soc., Current Anthropology (assoc.), Soc. for Psychol. Anthropology (nominations com. 1981-82, bd. dirs. 1991-93), Phi Beta Kappa, Sigma Xi. Office: Ohio State U Dept of Anthropology 124 W 17th Ave Columbus OH 43210-1316

BOURNE, CAROL ELIZABETH MULLIGAN, biology educator, phycologist; b. Rochester, N.Y., May 4, 1948; d. William Thomas and Ruth Townsend (Stevens) Mulligan; m. Godfrey Roderick Bourne, Dec. 21, 1968. BA in Botany/Bacteriology, Ohio Wesleyan U., 1970; MS in Botany, Miami University, Oxford, Ohio, 1978; PhD in Natural Resources, U. Mich., 1992. Lab. asst. Ohio Wesleyan U., Delaware, 1968-70; biol. lab. tech. USDA-Forest Svc., Delaware, 1970-73; grad. rsch. asst. botany dept. Miami U., Oxford, 1973-75; electron microscopist coll. medicine U. Cin., 1975-76; rsch. asst. sch. pub. health U. Mich., Ann Arbor, 1978-80, rsch. assoc. coll. medicine, 1981-83, grad. rsch. asst. sch. natural resources, 1983-86, grad. teaching asst. dept. biology, 1987; postdoctoral scientist U. Fla., Ft. Lauderdale, 1990-92; adj. instr. ecology Fla. Atlantic U. Coll. Liberal Arts, Davie, 1992-93; adj. asst. prof. dept. biology U. Mo., St. Louis, 1994—; adj. asst. prof. biology, Washington U., St. Louis, 1994—. Contbr. articles to scholarly jours. Grantee NSF, 1987-89. Mem. Am. Inst. Biolog. Scis., Am. Soc. Plant Taxonomists, Phycological Soc. Am., Internat. Soc. for Diatom Rsch., Internat. Soc. for Plant Molecular Biology, Brit. Phycological Soc., Soc. for Study of Evolution. Office: U Mo at St Louis Dept Biology 8001 Natural Bridge Rd Saint Louis MO 63121-4499

BOURNE, PETER GEOFFREY, physician, educator, author; b. Oxford, Eng., Aug. 6, 1939; s. Geoffrey Howard and Gwen (Jones) B.; m. Mary Elizabeth King, Nov. 9, 1974. M.D., Emory U., 1962; M.A. in Anthropology, Stanford U., 1969. Fellow dept. psychiatry Med. Sch.; co-dir. Alcoholism Project, Emory U., 1962-63; intern King County Hosp., Seattle, 1963-64; research psychiatrist Walter Reed Army Inst.; Research Washington, 1964-67; chief neuropsychiat. br. U.S. Army Med. Research Team, Vietnam, 1965-66; cons. S.E. Asia Health Br. (AID), Dept. State, 1966-67; resident dept. psychiatry, Stanford U. Med. Center, Palo Alto, Calif., 1967-69; dir. mental health unit Southside Comprehensive Health Center, Atlanta, 1969-71; founder, dir. Atlanta South Central Community Mental Health Center, 1970-71; dir. Ga. Office Drug Abuse, 1971-72; spl. adviser for health affairs to Gov. Jimmy Carter of Ga., 1971-73; asst. dir. White House Spl. Action Office for Drug Abuse Prevention, 1972-74; cons. Drug Abuse Council, Washington, 1974-76; pres. Found. for Internat. Resources, 1975-76; Mid-Atlantic coordinator, dep. campaign dir. Jimmy Carter Presdl. Campaign, 1975-76; spl. asst. for health issues to U.S. Pres., Washington, 1976-78; mem. U.S. del. to Exec. Council UNICEF, 1977; asst. sec. gen. UN, N.Y.C., 1979-81; pres. Global Water, 1981—; exec. v.p., pub. Devel. Internat., 1986-90; mem. U.S. Pres. Commn. on White House Fellows; head U.S. delegation UN Devel. Program Governing Council, 1978; emergency room physician Casualty Hosp., Washington, 1966-67, Kaiser Permanente Hosp., Santa Clara, Calif., 1967-69; psychiat. cons. Santa Clara County Hosp., 1968-69, San Mateo County Hosp., 1969; cons. WHO, Geneva, 1972, UN Div. on Narcotic Drugs, 1976; asst. prof. dept. psychiatry Emory U. Med. Sch., 1969-72, asst. prof. dept. preventive medicine and community health, 1969-72; vis. lectr. dept. psychiatry Harvard U. Med. Sch., 1974; v.p. Nat. Coordinating Council on Drug Abuse Edn., 1971-72; prof. psychiatry, chmn. dept. St. Georges Med. Sch., Grenada, 1979—; pres. Peter Bourne Assocs., Washington, 1985—. Author: Men, Stress and Viet Nam, 1970; editor: Psychology and Physiology of Stress, 1969, (with R. Fox) Alcoholism: Progress in Research and Treatment, 1973, Addiction, 1974, Acute Drug Abuse Emergencies, 1976, Water Resources: Social and Economic Aspects, 1983, Fidel, A Biography of Fidel Castro, 1986; mem. editorial bd. Psychiatry, 1968—, Am. Jour. Drug Alcohol Abuse, 1973—; contbr. articles to med. jours. and chpts. to books. Bd. dirs. Save the Children Fedn., Inst. for So. Studies, Hunger Project; chmn., bd. trustees Council on Hemispheric Affairs, 1986—; pres. Am. Assn. World Health, 1982—. Served to capt. U.S. Army, 1964-67. Decorated Bronze Star medal, Air medal, Combat Medics badge; recipient William C. Menninger award Central Neuropsychiat. Assn., 1967, Pub. Service award Nat. Assn. State Drug Abuse Program Coordinators, 1974, Pub. Service award Assn. Chinese Ams., 1978; named One of Five Outstanding Young Men, Atlanta Jaycees, 1971, One of Five Outstanding Young Men in Ga., Ga. Jaycees, 1972. Mem. AAAS, Am. Psychiat. Assn. (chmn. task force on drugs and drug abuse edn. 1969—), Ga. Psychiat. Assn., Washington Psychiat. Soc., Royal Soc. Medicine, Med. Assn. Ga., Soc. for Internat. Health (pres. 1988-92), Am. Med. Soc. on Alcoholism, Am. Anthrop. Assn., World Fedn. for Mental Health, Am. Assn. World Health (pres. 1984—). Democrat. Home and Office: 2119 Leroy Pl NW Washington DC 20008-1848

BOURQUE, LINDA ANNE BROOKOVER, public health educator; b. Indpls., Aug. 25, 1941; d. Wilbur Bone and Edna Mae (Eberhart) Brookover; m. Don Philippe Bourque, June 3, 1966 (div. Nov. 1974). BA, Ind. U., 1963; MA, Duke U., 1964, PhD, 1968. Postdoctoral researcher Duke U., Durham, N.C., 1968-69; asst. prof. sociology Calif. State U., Los Angeles, 1969-72; asst. prof. to assoc. prof. pub. health UCLA, 1972-86, prof. pub. health, 1986—, acting assoc. dir. Inst. for Social Sci. Research, 1981-82, vice chair dept. community health scis., 1991-94. Author: Defining Rape, 1989, (with Virginia Clark) Processing Data: The Survey Example, 1992, (with Eve

Fielder) How to Conduct Self-Administered and Mail Surveys, 1995; contbr. articles to profl. jours. Violoncellist with Santa Monica (Calif.) Symphony Orch., 1978—, Los Angeles Doctors' Symphony, 1981—. Mem. AAAS, Am. Sociol. Assn. (mem. med. sociology sect. council 1975-78, co-chmn. com. freedom research and teaching, 1975-78, cert. recognition 1980), Pacific Sociol. Assn. (co-chmn. program com. 1982, v.p. 1983), Am. Pub. Health Assn. (mem. standing com. on status of women 1974-76), Sociologists for Women in Society, Am. Assn. Pub. Opinion Rsch., Assn. Rsch. in Vision and Ophthalmology, Delta Omega, Phi Alpha Theta. Office: UCLA Sch Pub Health 10833 Le Conte Ave Los Angeles CA 90024-1772

BOUSKA, JENNIFER MARIE, cardiovascular nurse; b. Des Plaines, Ill., July 6, 1971; d. David Joseph and Mary Teresa (Novelli) B. BS, St. Mary's Coll., Notre Dame, Ind., 1993. RN, Ind. Rehab. nurse Methodist Hosp., Merrillville, Ind., 1993-94; cardiovascular nurse Methodist Hosp., Indpls., 1994—. Roman Catholic.

BOUTON, JANET LAURA, health care system executive; b. Pearl River, N.Y., Sept. 25, 1943; d. George Edward and Laura Grace (Hanna) B.; 1 child, Jessie McDade. BA, Tufts U., 1965; MS, London Sch. Econs., 1966; DSc, Johns Hopkins U., 1982. Rsch. asst. Boston U. Med. Sch., 1968-70, Harvard U. Med. Sch., Boston, 1970-71; grants mgr. Columbia Point Health Ctr., Boston, 1971-72; health plan analyst Kaiser Found. Health Plan, L.A., 1972-73; assoc. dir. Met. Atlanta Found. for Med. Care, 1973-74; staff asst. Inst. Medicine, Washington, 1977-78; sr. health planner Md. Health Planning Agy., Balt., 1978-79; dir. planning God Samaritan Hosp., Balt., 1979-84, v.p. for planning and mktg., 1984-94; sr. v.p. planning and mktg. Helix Health Sys., 1994—; sr. project cons. Policy Rsch., Inc., Balt., 1984; asst. prof. U. Balt., 1981; mem. Gov.'s Coun. Trauma Rehab., Balt., 1987-88; mem. Gov.'s Commn. on Local Health Svcs., 1993. Active Leadership Assn., Balt., 1988-96; v.p. planning Lupus Found. Am., Washington, 1988—; chmn. adv. bd. People's Comty. Health Ctr., 1989—; bd. dirs. Md. Lupus Found., Balt., 1982-88, 91-96, N.E. Comty. Orgn., Balt., 1978-82, Chesapeake and Potomac Blood region ARC, 1990—, Stella Maris Nursing Home, 1990-93; mem. exec. com. Md. Food Com., 1992—. Mem. APHA, Md. Hosp. Assn., Soc. for Hosp. Planning and Mgmt., Md. Soc. for Hosp. Planning (v.p. 1982-83). Office: Helix Health 2330 W Joppa Rd Lutherville MD 21093

BOVBJERG, DANA H., psychoneuroimmunologist, consultant; b. St. Louis, May 3, 1951; s. Richard V. and Dianna B. BA in Philosophy, Carleton Coll., 1973; BS in Psychology, U. Iowa, 1977; MA in Neuroscience, U. Rochester, 1983, PhD in Neuroscience, 1983. Instr. dept. medicine Cornell U. Med. Coll., N.Y.C., 1984-86, asst. prof., 1986—; asst. attending Meml. Sloan-Kettering Cancer Ctr., N.Y.C., 1989—. Author: The Joy of Cheesecake, 1980. Recipient Jr. Faculty award Am. Cancer Soc., 1990. Mem. Am. Assn. Immunologists, Am. Psychosomatic Soc., Soc. Behavioral Medicine, PsychoNeuroImmunology Rsch. Soc., Acad. Behavioral Medicine Rsch., N.Y. Acad. Scis. Office: Meml Sloan Kettering Cancer Ctr 1275 York Ave New York NY 10021-6007

BOVE, ALFRED ANTHONY, medical educator; b. Phila., Apr. 28, 1938; s. Alfred Anthony and Adeline Amelia (DeRose) B.; m. Sandra Ann Seltzer, June 25, 1966; children: Jacqueline, Christopher, Andrew. BSEE, Drexel U., 1962; MD, Temple U., 1966, PhD, 1970. Diplomate Am. Bd. Internal Medicine, Am. Bd. Cardiology. Med. intern Temple U. Hosp., Phila., 1966-67, med. resident, 1969-70, postdoctoral fellow, 1967-69, asst. prof. medicine, 1973-81, prof. medicine, 1986—; postdoctoral fellow Mayo Clinic, Rochester, Minn., 1970-71; prof. medicine Mayo Clinic, Rochester, 1981-86; chief of cardiology Temple U. Med. Sch., 1986—; team internist Phila. 76ers Basketball Team, Phila., 1987—. Co-author: Diving Medicine, 1990, Exercise Medicine, 1982; editor: (med. column) Skin Diver mag., 1981—; contbr. articles to profl. jours. Capt. USNR, 1971-73, 91. Recipient Established Investigator award Am. Heart Assn., 1975. Fellow ACP, Am. Coll. Cardiology (state gov. 1989-92); mem. Am. Physiologic Soc., IEEE, Undersea and Hyperbaric Med. Soc. (pres. 1983, Craig Hoffman award 1988, Stover-Link award 1974). Roman Catholic. Office: Temple Univ Hosp Cardiology Sect Philadelphia PA 19140

BOVE, SUSAN ELLEN, nurse practitioner; b. Salem, Mass., Oct. 26, 1965; d. Robert Haskins and Joanne Frances (Nangle) Bradley; m. Michael Bove, May 19, 1990. BSN, Boston Coll., 1987, MS, 1989. Formerly adult nurse practitioner internal medicine Med. Practice Assocs., Danvers, Mass.; adult nurse practitioner emergency medicine Physicians Urgent Care, Stoneham, Mass., adult nurse practitioner. Mem. ANA, Mass. Nurses Assn., Sigma Theta Tau.

BOVENMYER, DAN ALLEN, dermatologist; b. Beatrice, Nebr., May 22, 1931; s. Devoe Oakley and Margaret Jennette (Jenkins) B.; m. Helen Margaret Heinzen, Aug. 1, 1954; children: John, Anne. MD, State U. Iowa, 1956. Diplomate Am. Bd. Dermatology. Intern Hurley Hosp., Flint, Mich., 1956-57; resident U. Hosps., Iowa City, Iowa, 1959-62; pvt. practice Bovenmyer Dermatology, P.C., Davenport, Iowa, 1962—; clin. asst. prof. U. Iowa Coll. Medicine, Iowa City. Contbr. articles to profl. jours. Capt. U.S. Army, 1957-59. Mem. Am. Med. Soc., Am. Acad. Dermatology, N.Am. Clin. Dermatology Soc., Iowa Med. Soc., Iowa Dermatol. Soc., Scott County Med. Soc. (past treas.), Rotary, Alpha Omega Alpha. Office: Bovenmyer Dermatology PC 3319 Spring St #102 Davenport IA 52807

BOWDLER, ANTHONY JOHN, physician, educator; b. London, Eng., Oct. 16, 1928; came to U.S., 1967; s. Edward Thomas and Clara (Anthony) B.; m. Eleanor Madeleine Sladen, July 30, 1955; children: Noelle Clare, Jonathan Francis. B.Sc., U. Coll., London, 1949, M.B., B.S., 1952, M.D. (Bilton Pollard fellow), 1962, Ph.D., 1967; postgrad. (Buswell Sr. fellow), U. Rochester, 1962-64. Intern Univ. Coll. Hosp., London, 1952, Hammersmith Hosp., London, 1953, Brompton Hosp., London, 1956, Dorking Hosp., Surrey, Eng., 1957; registrar and research fellow U. Coll. Hosp., London, 1958-62; sr. instr. U. Rochester, N.Y., 1962-64; sr. lectr. U. Coll. Hosp. Med. Sch., London, 1964-67; assoc. prof. medicine Mich. State U., East Lansing, 1967-70; prof. medicine Mich. State U., 1971-80, Marshall U. Sch. Medicine, Huntington, W.Va., 1980—. Served as surgeon lt. Royal Navy, 1953-55. Fellow Royal Coll. Physicians, A.C.P., Royal Coll. Pathologists; mem. Am. Fedn. Clin. Research, Central Soc. Clin. Research, Am. Soc. Hematology, Am. Soc. Clin. Oncology, Med. Research Soc. London, Brit. Med. Assn. Home: Harmony Hills 2 Compton Ct Milton WV 25541-1135 Office: Marshall U Sch Medicine Dept Medicine 1542 Spring Valley Dr Huntington WV 25704-9388

BOWEN, ALMA THEODORA, medical technologist; b. Poblacion, Pampanga, The Philippines, Nov. 18, 1952; came to the U.S., 1983; d. Celestino Tabaday and Crispina Nila (Guda) Alcos; m. James Norman Bowen Jr., Dec. 2, 1984; children: Jacquelyn Nila, James Norman Celestino III. BS in Med. Tech., U. St. Tomas, Manila, 1976. Cert. Philippine Bd. Med. Tech.; licensed med. technologist, Tex. Med. records clk. United Doctor's Med. Ctr., Quezon City, The Philippines, 1979; lab. technologist Al Adan Hosp., Fahahed, Kuwait, 1980, Al Jahra Hosp., Jahra City, Kuwait, 1980-82, Refugio (Tex.) Meml. Hosp., 1983, Big Bend Meml. Hosp., Alpine, Tex., 1983; med. technologist Malone Hogan Hosp., Big Spring, Tex., 1983-86; head serology, parasitology, microbiology, blood bank Malone Hogan Clinic, Big Spring, 1986-88; med. technologist I Big Spring (Tex.) State Hosp., 1989-92; med. technologist Mitchell County Hosp., Colorado City, Tex., 1993-94. Girl Scout mem. Floridablanca Elem. Sch., Pampanga, The Philippines, 1962-68; comdr. sch. battalion St. Augustine Acad., Pampanga, 1968-72; ch. tchr. Legion of Mary, Children of Mary, Pampanga, 1968-72; choir mem. U. St. Tomas, Manila, 1972-76, Filipino Choir in Kuwait, 1979-82. Mem. Tex. State Soc. Am. Med. Technologists, Women's Aglow. Roman Catholic. Home: 1717 Purdue Ave Big Spring TX 79720

BOWEN, DONALD EYRE, psychiatrist; b. Newton, Mass., Sept. 22, 1912; s. Robert Sidney and Gertrude Margaret (Gammons) B.; m. Margaret Elizabeth Schrader, June 14, 1941; children: William Eyre, Lawrence Philip, Nancy Elizabeth. BS, Tufts Coll., Medford, Mass., 1935; MD, Tufts Med. Sch., Boston, 1939. Intern Hahnemann Hosp., Wochester, Mass., 1939-40; resident in psychiatry Boston U., 1951-53, Met. State Hosp., 1950-51, Boston U., Mass. Meml. Hosp., 1951-53; with indsl. medicine dept. Brown County Woods Dept. Medicine and Surgery, Megaloway Plantation, Maine, 1940-42; pvt. practice Newton-Wellesley Hosp., Newton Lower Falls, Mass., 1946-89, ret., 1989; chief psychiatry Newton-Wellesley Hosp., 1968-73; cons. in psychiatry, 1973—, chief psychiatry Waltham (Mass.) Hosp., 1954-64, sr. med. staff, 1964-89; asst. clin. prof. Tufts U. Med. Sch., Boston, 1973—; cons., founder Interfaith Counseling Svc., West Newton, Mass., 1953—. Cons. in psychiatry Commonwealth of Mass. Dept. of Welfare, Boston, 1956, United Ch.. of Christ Bd. of World Ministries, N.Y.C., 1965—; sch. physician City of Newton, 1947-50; lectr. Andover-Newton Theol. Sch., Newton Centre, Mass., 1956-58. Major USAAF, 1942-46. Recipient Legion of Honor, DeMolay, 1932, plaque Dept. Psychiatry, 1989, plaque Northeastern Regional Divsn. Am. Assn. Pastoral Counselors, 1995; MIT fellow, 1953-54. Fellow Am. Psychiat. Assn. (life); mem. AMA., New Eng. Soc. of Clin. Hypnosis (past pres.), Masons. Home and Office: 124 Country Dr Weston MA 02193-1136

BOWEN, JOHN CANADA, surgeon; b. Memphis, Mar. 8, 1941; s. John Canada Jr. and Laura Louise (McDaniel) B.; m. Mary Dupree Eldridge, Aug. 8, 1964 (div. Feb. 1972); children: Laura Bowen Wills, Eldridge; m. Myriam (Mimi) Robinson, Sept. 14, 1991. BA, Yale U., 1963; MD, Columbia Coll., 1967. Diplomate Am. Bd. Surgery, spl. qualifications in gen. vascular surgery. Intern Univ. Hosps. of Cleve., 1967-68, resident, 1968-69; resident, chief resident Case Western Res. U. Affil. Hosps., Cleve., 1971-73; asst. prof. surgery and physiology U. Tex. Med. Sch., Houston, 1974-76; surgeon Ochsner Clinic, New Orleans, 1976—; dir. surg. edn. and rsch., assoc. med. dir. Alton Ochner Med. Found., New Orleans, 1976-87; assoc. prof. surgery and physiology La. State U. Med. Sch., New Orleans, 1982—; program dir. gen. and vascular surgery Alton Ochsner Med. Found., New Orleans, 1993—; chmn. dept. surgery Ochsner Clnic anc Ochsner Found. Hosp., New Orleans, 1993—; bd. dirs., sec. South La. Med. Assocs., Houma, La., 1978—; Burroughs Wellcome vis. prof. Royal Soc. Medicine, Eng., 1992. Contbr. articles to profl. jours., chpts. to books. Bd. trustees Alton Ochsner Med. Found., New Orleans, 1988—; bd. govs. Ochsner Clinic, New Orleans, 1987-89, 93-94. Maj. U.S. Army, 1969-71. Decorated Bronze Star; rsch. grantee NIH, Washington, 1977-88. Fellow ACS; mem. Am. Physiol. Soc., So. Surg. Assn., Soc. Surgery Alimentary Tract, Soc. Surg. Oncology, Internat. Soc. Cardiovascular Surgery. Office: Ochsner Clinic Dept Surgery 1514 Jefferson Hwy New Orleans LA 70118

BOWEN, NEIL EDMUND, psychologist; b. Attleboro, Mass., Mar. 31, 1945; s. Charles Arthur and Miriam Julia (Claflin) B.; m. Carol Ann Cabana, Aug. 31, 1968; children: Nathaniel W., Moira C. BA, U. Notre Dame, 1967; MA, Boston U., 1969, PhD, 1974. Lic. psychologist, Mass. Chief psychologist New Bedford (Mass.) Area Mental Health Clinic, 1973-77; pvt. practice New Bedford, 1977—. Bd. dirs. Marion (Mass.) Ctr. for Human Svcs., 1982-85, pres. bd., 1985—. Lt. USNR, 1970-73. NIMH fellow, 1967-70; decorated Meritorious Unit Commendation. Mem. APA, Mass. Psychol. Assn. (adv. bd. 1994—, bd. dirs. 1995), Southeastern Mass. Psychol. Assn. (treas. 1984-86, bd. dirs. 1984-90, 93—, pres. 1992-94). Home: 28 Briggs Ln Marion MA 02738 Office: Southeastern Counseling Assocs 13 Welby Rd New Bedford MA 02745

BOWEN, RAFAEL LEE, dental materials researcher; b. Takoma Park, Md., Dec. 27, 1925; children: Cheryl, Heather. DDS, U. So. Calif., L.A., 1953; DSc (Hon.), Georgetown U., Washington, 1987. Cert. DDS D.C., Md., Calif. Rsch. assoc. ADA Health Found., Gaithersburg, Md., 1956—. Patentee (U.S. and fgn.) in field; contbr. over 200 articles in field to profl. jours. RecipientWilmer Souder award IADR Dental Materials Group, 1973, Hollenback Meml. prize Acad. Operative Dentistry, 1981, Mitch Nakayama Meml. award Japanese sect. Pierre Fauchard Acad., 1984, Merit award Nat. Inst. Dental Rsch., 1988. Mem. ADA, Am. Coll. Dentists, Internat. Assn. Dental Rsch., Md. Dental Soc., Fedn. Dentaire Internationale, Sigma Xi. Office: ADA Health Found NIST Bldg 224 A-153 Gaithersburg MD 20899

BOWEN, ROBIN JANINE, non-profit agency executive; b. N.Y.C., Mar. 1, 1956; d. Sheldon and Dorothy (Kashdan) Reich; m. Richard William Bowen, July 27, 1975; children: Rigel Steven, Maxwell James, Hannah Robin. BS in Psychology, Sonoma State U., Rohnert Park, Calif., 1978; MS in Health Svcs. Adminstrn., St. Mary's Coll., Moraga, Calif., 1988. Cert. childbirth instr. Childbirth educator Santa Rosa, Calif., 1979—; exec. dir. Calif. Parenting Inst., Santa Rosa, 1978—; tchr. Pacific Oaks Coll., Pasadena, 1990—. Chmn. Children's Network of Sonoma County, Santa Rosa, 1988-91; adv. mem. Foster Parent Tng. Prog., Santa Rosa, 1987-92; mem. Early Intervention Area Planning Com., Santa Rosa, 1990-95; mem. Sonoma County Family Action, 1994—. Recipient Commendation for work in child abuse prevention, State Dept. Social Svcs. and Social Svcs. Adv. Bd., 1987. Office: California Parenting Inst 3650 Standish Ave Santa Rosa CA 95407-8113

BOWER, BARBARA JEAN, nurse; b. Akron, Ohio, Aug. 25, 1942; d. William Howard and Maxine (Goodykoontz) Sturm; m. Howard Bower, Aug. 25, 1961 (dec. 1989); children: Nancy, Janet; m. Richard Chavez, Dec. 24, 1993. BA, Elmhurst Coll., 1974, postgrad., 1987—; diploma, Evang. Sch. Nursing, 1970; PhD, U. Chgo., 1993. RN. Supr. nursing Med. Ctr.; nurse critical care Loyola U., Maywood, Ill., 1970-78, Med. Staffing Services, Oak Park, Ill., 1978-84; pres. Heart Care Unltd., Oakbrook, Ill., 1982—; one of first ind. nurse contractors in Ill. Creator cdnl. programs for cardiac patients, families, 1971—. Stephen min. Christ Ch. of Oak Brook, Ill. Mem. AAUW, Am. Nurses Assn., Am. Assn. Critical Care Nurses, Am. Heart Assn., Elmhurst Coll. Alumni Assn. Home: 3203 York Rd Oak Brook IL 60521-2312 Office: Heart Care Unltd PC Oak Brook IL 60521

BOWER, DAVID HARRISON, dentist; b. Lafayette Hill, Pa., Jan. 18, 1947; s. Herbert Harrison and Helen Victoria (Swope) B.; m. Patrice Ann Campbell, July 31, 1984 (div. Mar. 1986). AB in English Lit., Syracuse U., 1968; DMD, U. Pa., 1973. High sch. tchr. Green Bank Pvt. Sch., Glenmoor, Pa., 1968-69; dental intern, resident Einstein No. Div., Phila., 1973; dentist Dr. Morris Saltz, Chester, Pa., 1975-77, Colonial Sch. System, Plymouth Meeting, Pa., 1975-78, Vis. Nurse Assn., Ambler, Pa., 1976-78; pvt. practice Lafayette Hill, Pa., 1976—. Contbr. articles to local newspapers. Pres. Whitemarsh Twp. Bus. Assn., Lafayette Hill, 1986-88, 90-91. 2d lt. USPHS, 1973-75. Bus. award Whitemarsh Twp. Bus. Assn., Lafayette Hill, 1988. Fellow Acad. Gen. Dentistry; mem. ADA, King of Prussia Study Club. Republican. Methodist. Home and Office: 3000 Joshua Rd Lafayette Hill PA 19444-2003

BOWER, DEBBY RAE, nursing administrator; b. Denver, Dec. 31, 1950; d. Lee Norwood and Wanda Jean (Winkelman) B. BSN, Augustana Coll., Sioux Falls, S.D., 1973. RN, Calif. Nurse paraplegic, urology unit Vets. Hosp., Long Beach, Calif., 1978-80; charge nurse, relief nurse supr. Midwood Cmty. Hosp., Anaheim, Calif., 1980-82; head nurse med., surg. unit, alcohol and drug rehab unit Costa Mesa (Calif.) Med. Ctr., 1982-85; asst. head nurse security unit Riverside (Calif.) Gen., 1985—. Active Special Olympics, Riverside, 1987-91; care provider for handicapped, Riverside, 1987— mem. adult advisory Ability Counts Sheltered Workshop, Riverside, 1990—. Lt. USN Nurse Corps., 1972-78.

BOWER, FAY LOUISE, academic administrator, nursing educator; b. San Francisco, Sept. 10, 1929; d. James Joseph and Emily Clare (Andrews) Saitta; BS with honors, San Jose State Coll., 1965; MSN, U. Calif., 1966, DNSc, 1978; children: R. David, Carol Bower Tomei, Dennis James, Thomas John. Office nurse Dr. William Grannis, Palo Alto, Calif., 1950-55; staff nurse Stanford Hosp., 1964-72; asst. prof. San Jose State U., 1966-70, assoc. prof., 1970-74, prof., 1974-82, coord. grad. program in nursing, 1977-78, chairperson dept. nursing, 1978-82; dean U. San Francisco, 1982-89, v.p. acad. affairs, 1988-89, dir. univ. planning and instl. rsch., 1989-91, pres. Clarkson Coll., 1991—; speaker; cons. univs.; vis. prof. Harding Coll., 1977, U. Miss., 1976; lectr. U. Calif., San Francisco, 1975. Cert. pub. health nurse, sch. nurse, Calif. Fellow Am. Acad. Nursing; mem. Nebr. Nurses Assn., Am. Pub. Health Assn. Calif., Nat. League Nursing (bd. dirs. 1993-95), Calif. League for Nursing (pres. 1989-92), Western Gerontol. Assn., Sigma Theta Tau (internat. pres. 1993-95), Jesuit Deans in Nursing (chair 1982-85). Democrat. Roman Catholic. Club: Rotary (Omaha). Author: (with Em O. Bevis) Fundamentals of Nursing Practice: Concepts, Roles and Functions, 1978; (with Margaret Jacobson) Community Health Nursing, 1978; The Process of Planning Nursing Care, 3d edit., 1982; author: Approaches to Teaching Primary Care, 1981, The Newman Systems Model: Application to Nursing Education and Practice, 1982, Managing a Nursing Shortage: A Guide to Recruitment and Retention, 1989, Cracking the Wall: Women in Higher Education Administration, 1993, (with Mae Timmons) Medical Surgical Nursing, 1995. Home: 1349 S 101st St # 303 Omaha NE 68124 Office: Clarkson Coll Office of Pres 101 S 42nd St Omaha NE 68131-2715

BOWER, PHILIP JEFFREY, cardiologist, administrator; b. Kenmore, N.Y., Nov. 23, 1935; s. Philip Graydon and Evelyn (McLoney) B.; m. Ann Bruce Weaver, Aug. 9, 1958; children: Elizabeth Ann, Susan Lynn. BA, U. Va., 1957; MD, Johns Hopkins U., 1961. Diplomate Am. Bd. Internal Medicine, subsplty. cardiology. Intern in medicine U. N.C., Chapel Hill, 1961-62; resident in medicine Johns Hopkins Hosp., Balt., 1962-63; resident in medicine Mayo Clinic, Rochester, Minn., 1965-66, resident in cardiology, 1966-68; staff physician cardiology Ochsner Clinic, New Orleans, La., 1968-78; dir. cardiology, dir. cardiac catheterization lab. East Jefferson Hosp., Metairie, La., 1978—; instr. medicine U. Ga. Sch. Medicine, 1963-65, Tulane U., New Orleans, 1970-74; clin. asst. prof. medicine La. State U., New Orleans, 1974—; clin. prof. medicine Tulane U., New Orleans, 1983—; bd. dirs. East Jefferson Gen. Hosp. Found.; faculty mem. Advanced Cardiac Life Support Affiliate; cons. Scimed., 1988—; adv. bd. Advanced Catheter Sys., 1988—; presenter in field. Contbr. articles to profl. jours. Capt. U.S. Army, 1963-65. Fellow ACP, Am. Coll. Chest Physicians, Am. Coll. Cardiology, Soc. Cardiac Angiography and Interventions; mem. AMA, Am. Heart Assn. (bd. dirs. 1979-83, fellow Coun. Clin. Cardiology), Am. Soc. Echocardiography, So. Med. Assn., La. Med. Soc., La. Heart Assn. (chmn. physician edn. com. pres.-elect 1976, pres. 1977), Jefferson Parish Med. Soc., Phi Kappa Psi, Phi Chi. Home: 199 Sauve Rd River Ridge LA 70123-1933 Office: East Jefferson Hosp Dept Cardiology 4200 Houma Blvd Metairie LA 70006-2970

BOWER, ROBERT HEWITT, surgeon, educator, researcher; b. Omaha, Aug. 20, 1949; s. John Walter and Dorothy May (Sibert) B.; m. Debra Lea Goettsche, July 4, 1980; children: Timothy Conrad, Michael Harvey, Emily Frances. BA, Grinnell Coll., 1971; MD, U. Nebr., 1975. Diplomate Nat. Bd. Med. Examiners, Am. Bd. Surgery (dir. 1995—). Intern, U. Nebr., 1975-76, resident in surgery, 1976-80, chief resident, 1979-80; clin. and rsch. fellow U. Cin., 1980-81; asst. prof. surgery, 1981-85; dir. dept. parenteral and enteral nutrition U. Hosp., 1981—, assoc. prof. surgery, 1985-95, prof. surgery, 1995—, dir. surg. residency, 1986—, vice chmn. edn., 1995—; chief surgery svc. Cin. VA Med. Ctr., 1994—; pres., trustee, chmn. bd. trustees Vocal Arts Ensemble of Cin. Fellow ACS; mem. Cen. Surg. Assn., Am. Coll. Nutrition, Soc. Am. Gastrointestinal Endoscopic Surgeons, Assn. Acad. Surgery, Am. Soc. Parenteral and Enteral Nutrition, Ohio Med. Assn., Surg. Infection Soc., Acad. Medicine Cin., Soc. Univ. Surgeons, Soc. Surgery of Alimentary Tract, Cin. Surg. Soc. Presbyterian, Surg. Infection Soc. Contbr. articles to profl. jours., chpts. to books. Office: Cin VA Med Ctr 3200 Vine St Cincinnati OH 45220-2213

BOWER, ROSE JANET, psychologist, educator; b. Pitts., Mar. 13, 1919; d. Alvin Lionel and Rose Clementina (Saller) B.; m. Albert E. Bachelet, 1993. BA, Waynesburg Coll., 1941; MA, U. Chgo., 1950, PhD, 1953. Rsch. assoc. U. Chgo., 1953-54; head dept. psychology Centenary Coll. for Women, Hackettstown, N.J., 1955-58; rsch. dir. Cath. Charities, Milw., 1958-59; rsch. assoc. Bank St. Coll. Edn., N.Y.C., 1959-61; assoc. prof. psychology and edn. Jersey City (N.J.) State Coll., 1961-68, prof., 1968-83, prof. emeritus, 1986—; vis. assoc. prof. grad. sch. edn. U. So. Calif., L.A., 1966-67, SUNY, New Paltz, 1965. Unitarian. Home: 35 Robert Gdns Queensbury NY 12804-1612

BOWER, ROY DONALD, minister, counselor; b. Pitts., June 20, 1939; s. Roy Clare and Evelyn June (Moorhead) B.; m. Sandra M. Daugherty, Mar. 16, 1963 (dec. 1976); children: Christine, Roy, Donald, Kathleen; m. Robin Jeanette Bird, Aug. 20, 1976; children: Daniel, Robin, William, Renée. Student, Indiana U. Pa., 1958, Geneva Coll., 1959-61; BS in Edn., Slippery Rock U., 1972; ThM, Am. Bible Coll., 1980; DD, Trinity Hall Sem., 1988. Ordained to ministry Ind. Christian Chs. Internat., 1970; cert. Christian counselor. Counselor La Casa Contenta, Colorado Springs, Colo., 1976-78; therapist Giles Inst., Colorado Springs, 1978-79; counselor Cheyenne Village, Manitou Springs, Colo., 1979-80, Tutoring and Counseling Svcs., Confluence, Pa., 1981—; resource counselor Family Rsch. Coun., Washington, 1985—; manuscript reviewer Nat. Coun. Social Studies, Washington, 1987; advisor Am. Pub. Welfare Assn., Chgo., 1970; rsch. theologian Ref. Faith Ctr., Confluence, Pa., 1986—, dir., 1986—; pres. Confluence Area Ministerium, 1986. Book reviewer Pastoral Counsel Newsletter, 1986—. Founder Yough Valley Symposium, Confluence, 1982—; mem. Western Pa. Conservancy, Pitts., 1980—; 1st lt. CAP, Scottdale, Pa., 1982—; state constable Somerset County Pa. Ct., 1988—. Recipient citation Dept. Social Svcs., El Paso County, Colo., 1975, Certs. of Merit ARC, Johnstown, Pa., 1987, Am. Cancer Soc., Somerset, Pa., 1990; Menninger Found. fellow, 1984—. Mem. United Assn. christian Counselors Internat., Am. Assn. Family Counselors, Nat. Christian Counselors Assn., Am. Assn. christian Counselors, Guild of Clergy Counselors (Award of Excellence 1991), Am. fedn. Police (state v.p. 1991—), Pa. State Constables Assn. Democrat. Home and Office: Tutoring and Counseling Svc 609 Oden St Confluence PA 15424-1033

BOWERMASTER, MICHAEL, psychologist; b. Canton, Ohio, Dec. 31, 1949; s. James Ralph and Irene Lucille (Franta) B.; m. Linda Beeson, Dec. 20, 1971 (div. Dec. 1979); m. Barbara Buckingham, June 25, 1983; children: Richard Jones, Thomas Jones. BA in Chemistry, U.N.C., 1971; MA in Psychology, Western Carolina U., 1977; Cert. Radiology Technician, Med. Field Svc. Sch., San Antonio, 1974; PhD in Psychology, Va. Commonwealth U., 1984. Lic. clin. psychologist, radiol. technologist. Radiol. technologist Duke Med. Ctr., Durham, N.C., 1974; rsch. chemist EPA, Research Triangle Park, N.C., 1974-75; radiol. technologist Med. Coll. of Va., Richmond, 1977-83; psychologist A, B Powhatan Reception Ctr., State Farm, Va., 1977-79; psychologist C Cen. Classification Bd., Richmond, Va., 1979-81; pscyhologist sr. Western State Hosp., Stanton, Va., 1984—; asst. prof. U. Va., Charlottesville, 1985—. With U.S. Army, 1971-74. Scholar NSF, U. Iowa, 1967. Mem. Am. Psychol. Assn. Home: 224 Fayette St Staunton VA 24401-4122 Office: Western State Hosp PO Box 2500 Staunton VA 24402-2500

BOWERS, JACK FREDERIC, ophthalmologist; b. Easton, Pa., Apr. 1, 1934; s. Charles Franklin and Helen Shell (Kantnor) B.; m. Edith Anna Hollmann, Oct. 8, 1960 (div. May 1990); children: Ailegra Ann, Charles Allston. AB, Lafayette Coll., Easton, Pa., 1955; MD, Yale U., 1959. Diplomate Am. Bd. Ophthalmology. Intern Lakenau Hosps., Phila., 1960; resident Washington Hosp. Ctr., 1960-63; ophthalmologist Hale Hosp., haverhill, Mass., 1965—; pres. med. staff Hale Hosp., Haverhill, Mass., 1976; dir. Mass. Eye & Ear Infirmary, Methuen Eye Ctr., 1992—; pres. Mass Eye & Ear Infirmary, 1976; mem. faculty Harvard Med. Sch., Boston, 1976—. Author: Games Womanship How to Win at Ladies Doubles, 1975; contbr. articles to profl. jours.; TV appearances include Good Morning Am., 1996, Evening News with Tom Brokow, 1996. Lt. comdr. USNR, 1963-65. Fellow Am. Acad. Ophthalmology; mem. Mass. Soc. Eye Physicians and Surgeons (pres. 1976), Essex No. Dist. Med. Soc. (pres. 1978), North Andover Country Club (treas. 1978-80). Home: 503 Main St # 1 Amesbury MA 01913 Office: Mass Eye & Ear Infirmary Methuen Eye Ctr 1 Branch St Metheun MA 01844

BOWERS, M. BLAIR, research biologist; b. Jackson, N.C., Apr. 2, 1930; d. Eugene Scott and Annie J. Bowers. BA, Duke U., 1952, MA, 1955; PhD, Radcliffe Coll., 1961. NIH post-doctoral fellow Harvard U., Cambridge, Mass., 1961-63, instr., 1963-66; staff fellow NIH, Bethesda, Md., 1966-69, rsch. biologist, 1969-95; mem. biotech. rev. com. NIH, 1980-84. Mem. editl. bd. Molecular and Cellular Biology, 1981-82, Jour. Eukaryotic Microbiology, 1994-96; contbr. 61 articles to profl. jours. Mem. Am. Soc. Cell Biology, Microscopy Soc. Am. (treas. 1983-87, bd. dirs. 1989-91), Histochem. Soc. (bd. dirs. 1988-92, treas. 1994-96), Chesapeake Soc. for Electron Microscopy (pres. 1975-76, 939-94, bd. dirs. 1968-82). Office: NIH Bldg 3 Rm B1-22 Bethesda MD 20892

BOWERS, THOMAS GLENN, clinical psychologist; b. Lincoln, Nebr., Nov. 3, 1950; s. Glenn Forrest and Shirley Belle (Parker) B. BS, U. Wash., Seattle, 1975; MA, U. B.C., Vancouver, 1979; PhD, Va. Poly. State U., 1984.

Lic. psychologist, Pa. Staff psychologist New River Valley Mental Helath Svcs., Radford, Va., 1984-86; dir. N.W. Counseling Ctr., Dyersburg, Tenn., 1986-87, Family Devel. Svcs., Harrisburg, Pa., 1988—; assoc. prof. Pa. State U., Middletown, 1987—. Contbr. articles to profl. jours. Mem. Am. Psychol. Assn., Pa. Psychol. Assn., Ea. Psychol. Assn. Office: Pa State U Dept Psycology Middletown PA 17057 also: Family Devel Svcs Harrisburg PA 17110

BOWKER, JOHN HALL, orthopedic surgeon; b. Springfield, Mass., Apr. 20, 1928; s. John Hall and Helen Frances (Rinck) B.; m. Alice Rhoda Martin, Dec. 13, 1969; 1 child, Thomas Hall. BS, SUNY, Albany, 1951; MD, Union U., 1956. Diplomate Am. Bd. Orthopedic Surgery. Resident in orthopedics U. Pitts., 1958-61; rsch. fellow Mass. Gen. Hosp.-Harvard U., Boston, 1961-63; from instr. to prof. orthopedic surgery Sch. Medicine U. Ark., Little Rock, 1963-82; prof. orthopedics and rehab. Sch. Medicine U. Miami, 1982—. Author: Amputation Surgery, 1996; editor, author: Atlas of Limb Prosthetics, 1992, The Diabetic Foot, 1993; editor Orthopedic Clinics of N.Am., 1978. Commr. State Spinal Cord Commn., Little Rock, 1975-78; councillor, mem. adv. coun. Dir. Vocat. Rehab., Tallahassee, 1985-93; mem. adv. bd. Nat. Ctr. for Med. Rehab. Rsch., Bethesda, Md., 1991-96. With USN, 1946-48. Recipient Ark. Traveler award Gov. and State of Ark., 1982, Key to City, Mayor and City of Tuskegee, Ala., 1985; named Disting. Alumnus SUNY, 1989. Fellow Am. Acad. Orthopedic Surgeons (com. membership 1967—), ACS, Internat. For for Prosthetics and Orthotics; mem. Am. Orthopedic Foot and Ankle Soc., Orthopedics Rehab. Assn. (pres. 1992-94), Am. Orthopedics Assn., Am. Acad. Orthotics and Prosthetics (hon.). Office: U Miami Sch Medicine 1611 NW 12th Ave Miami FL 33136

BOWLES, GROVER CLEVELAND, JR., pharmacist, educator; b. Piedmont, Mo., Feb. 15, 1920; s. Grover Clevel and Oca (Newton) B.; m. Mary Lois Van Inwagen, Dec. 23, 1947; children: Rebecca R., Deborah M. Student, S.E. Mo. State Coll., 1938-39; B.S. in Pharmacy, U. Tenn., 1942; D.Sc., Phila. Coll. Pharmacy and Sci., 1968. Intern hosp. pharmacy U. Mich. Hosp., 1946-47; instr. U. Tenn. Coll. Pharmacy, 1947-48; chief pharmacist Strong Meml. Hosp., also U. Rochester Sch. Medicine and Dentistry, 1948-55; assoc. adminstr. Meml. Hosp. Assn., Washington, 1955-56; dir. dept. pharmacy Bapt. Meml. Hosp., Memphis, 1956-85; prof. U. Tenn. Coll. Pharmacy, 1959-93, prof. emeritus, 1993—; mem. revision com. U.S. Pharmacopeia, 1960-70; mem. Tenn. Hosp. Licensing Bd., 1961-82. Bd. dirs. Memphis unit Am. Cancer Soc., Memphis Vis. Nurse Assn.; mem. Am. Coun. on Pharm. Ecn., 1978-86, pres., 1982-86; trustee Bapt. Meml. Coll. Health Scis., 1995—. Served with USNR, 1942-46. Recipient Remington Medal award, 1973, Meritorious Service citation Tenn. Hosp. Assn., 1976, Disting. Service award U. Tenn. Coll. Pharmacy, 1979, Outstanding Alumnus award U. Tenn. Coll. Pharmacy, 1989. Mem. AAAS, Am. Pharm. Assn. (pres. 1965-66, chmn. bd. trustees 1966-67, treas. 1967-78, Remington Honor medal 1973, Hugo H. Schaffer medal 1979, Practice Excellence award 1993), Am. Soc. Hosp. Pharmacists (pres. 1952, Harvey A.K. Whitney lectr. 1962), Am. Soc. Hosp. Pharmacists (hon.), Tenn. Soc. Hosp. Pharm. Edn. (pres. 1982-85), Phi Delta Chi. Home: 4997 Warwick Ave Memphis TN 38117-4203

BOWLES, JOHN T., social worker, therapist; b. London, Apr. 7, 1923; m. Pearl A. Dade; 1 child, Steven. BA, Howard U., 1950; MSW, Columbia U., 1952. Diplomate in clin. social work; lic. marriage counselor, lic. social worker, N.J. Psychiat. social worker Manhattan State Hosp., N.Y.C., 1952-53, VA, Newark, 1953-59, Clinic for Mental Health, Paterson, N.J., 1959-65; asst. dir. Fair Lawn (N.J.) Mental Health Ctr., 1965-69, exec. dir., 1969-79, clin. dir., 1979-89; part-time psychotherapist The Counseling Ctrs., Clifton, N.J., 1990-95; adj. prof. Essex County Coll., Newark, 1989-91; pvt. practice psychotherapy, Montclair, N.J., 1965—. Mem. Juvenile Conf. Com., Montclair, 1974-80; trustee ARC, Montclair, 1965-67. Staff sgt. U.S. Army, 1943-46. Mem. Omega Psi Phi. Home and Office: 7 Willowdale Ct Montclair NJ 07042-4426

BOWLES, L. THOMPSON, medical executive; b. Mineola, N.Y., Sept. 23, 1931; m. Judith E. Bowles, July 10, 1965; children: Julia, Amy, Lauren. AB, Duke U., 1953, MD, 1957; MS, NYU, 1964, PhD, 1971. Intern 4th surgery divsn. Bellevue Hosp., N.Y.C., 1957; acad. dean George Washington U. Med. Ctr., Washington, 1975-87, v.p., exec. dean, 1987-92; pres. Nat. Bd. Med. Examiners, Phila., 1992—; pres. Med. Licensing Bd., Washington, 1977-79. Founding editor: AAMC Curriculum Directory, 1973. Recipient Disting. Svc. award D.C. Med. Soc., 1981. Fellow ACS, Soc. Thoracic Surgeons, Am. Assn. for Thoracic Surgeons; mem. Alpha Omega Alpha. Office: Nat Bd Med Examiners 3750 Market St Philadelphia PA 19104

BOWLIN, STEVEN JAMES, physician, epidemiologist; b. Moses Lake, Wash., Aug. 22, 1957; s. Calvin Edward and Eldarene Jean (Hoff) B.; m. Ann Mary Faya, June 21, 1980; children: Andrew, Leah. BA in Chemistry, Cedarville (Ohio) Coll., 1979; DO in Medicine, Ohio U., 1983; M in Pub. Health, Columbia U., 1988, PhD in Epidemiology, 1994. Diplomate Am. Bd. of Preventive Medicine in Public Health and Preventive Medicine. Intern Richmond Heights (Ohio) Gen. Hosp., 1983-84, anesthesiologist resident, 1984-86; preventive medicine resident SUNY, Stony Brook, 1986-88; preventive cardiology rsch. fellow Mary Imogene Bassett Hosp., Cooperstown, N.Y., 1988-91; asst. prof. in epidemiology and biostatistics Case Western Res. U., Cleve., 1991—, asst. prof. in family medicine, 1992—, asst. prof. in oncology, 1995—; mem. Ohio Diabetes task force, Columbus, Ohio, 1992—, Ohio Cardiovascular Disease Adv. Com., Columbus, 1994—, Ohio Behavioral Risk Factor Surveillance adv. com., Columbus, 1994—. Contbr. articles to profl. jours. Mem. Am. Heart Assn. Republican. Office: Case Western Res U Dept Epidemology 10900 Euclid Ave Cleveland OH 44106

BOWLINE, DWAIN VIRGIL, rehabilitation consultant; b. Tulsa, June 3, 1957; s. Dwain Sr. and Nelva Hazel (York) B.; 1 child, Stephanie. BA, East Cen. Okla. State U., 1984; MA, N.E. Mo. State U., 1987; postgrad., Okla. State U., 1987—. Therapist Mid Am. Counseling, Columbia, Mo., 1986; dir. Ret. Sr. Vol. Program, Hannibal, Mo., 1987, Region III Devel. Disabilities Act Coun., Hannibal, 1988; pres. Affiliated Therapists Okla., Tulsa, 1988—; social worker III State Okla., Tulsa, 1989; instr. Rogers State Coll., Claremore, Okla., 1989-91, Okla. Jr. Coll., Tulsa, 1990; cons. Ability Consulting, Tulsa, 1991—. Vol. ARC, Tulsa, 1991. Office: Ability Consulting PO Box 1078 Bristow OK 74010-1078

BOWLING, JOHN ROBERT, osteopathic physician, educator; b. Columbus, Ohio, Feb. 18, 1943; s. Ardyce Saul and Wilma Garcia (Snider) B.; m. Janet Lou Bowman, July 10, 1965; children: Jack Robert, James Richard, Jason Russell. BS, Ohio U., 1965; DO, Kirksville (Mo.) Coll. Osteopathic Medicine, 1969. Cert. Am. Osteopathic Bd. Family Practice. Rotating intern Drs. Hosp., Columbus, 1969-70; gen. practice osteo. medicine Lancaster, Ohio, 1970-88; clin. assoc. prof. Ohio U. Coll. Osteo. Medicine, Athens, 1977-88; med. dir. Lancaster Health Care Ctr., 1980-88; assoc. prof. dept. family medicine U. N. Tex. Health Sci. Ctr. Coll. Osteopathic Medicine, Ft. Worth, 1988—, interim chmn. dept. family medicine, 1991, vice chmn. dept., 1991-95, course dir. core clin. clerkship in family practice, 1991—, mem. steering com. Catchum project, mem. exec. coun. of faculty, 1992, 96, mem. curriculum com., 1993-95; mem. admissions com. U. North Tex. Health Sci. Ctr. Coll. Osteo. Medicine, Ft. Worth, 1989—; mem. sr. attending staff Doctors Hosp., 1970-88, co-dir. family practice residency program, 1979, acting dir., 1980; chmn. dept. medicine Lancaster Fairfield Cmty. Hosp., 1975, sec. med. staff, 1982-83, pres., 1985; active staff Osteo. Med. Ctr. Tex., 1988—; team physician Bloom Carroll (Ohio) Sch., 1973-88. Pres., bd. dirs. Montessori Presch., Lancaster, 1975; chmn. youth basketball com. YMCA, Lancaster; former youth coord., tchr., mem. adminstrv. bd. United Meth. Ch., Lancaster. Named Outstanding Advisor, Tex. Coll. Osteo. Medicine, 1992. Mem. Am. Coll. Osteo. Family Physicians (com. on evaluation and edn. 1991Y, program chmn. nat. conv. 1995); mem. Am. Osteo. Assn., Ohio Osteo. Assn., Am. Acad. Osteopathy, Tex. Osteo. Med. Assn. (program chmn. state conv. 1994, 95), Tex. Med. Assn. (preventive medicine task force 1993-94). Methodist. Home: 6001 Lansford Ln Colleyville TX 76034-5230 Office: U North Tex Health Sci Ctr College Osteo Medicine 3500 Camp Bowie Blvd Fort Worth TX 76107-2644

BOWLING, JOHN SELBY, hospital administrator; b. Hattiesburg, Miss., Nov. 6, 1944; s. Selby Clark and Ochie Mae (Sumrall) B.; m. Rebecca Owens, Aug. 27, 1966; children: Amy L., John S. Jr., Emily R. BS, U. So. Miss., 1966; M in Hosp. Adminstrn., Med. Coll. Va., 1971. Adminstrv. resident Hamilton Meml. Hosp., Dalton, Ga., 1970-71; asst. adminstr. Kennestone Hosp., Marietta, Ga., 1971-75, assoc. adminstr., 1975-80; assoc. exec. dir. Kennestone Regional Healthcare System, Marietta, 1980-83; adminstr., chief exec. officer South Ga. Med. Ctr., Valdosta, 1984-94; pres. South Ga. Health Alliance, Inc., Valdosta, 1989—, Lanier Health Svcs., Inc., Valdosta, 1992—; pres., CEO South Ga. Med. Ctr., Valdosta, 1995—. Chmn. adminstrv. bd. 1st United Meth. Ch., Valdosta, 1989-90; chmn. bd. dirs. Valdosta Vocat./Tech. Sch., 1989-92; bd. dirs. United Way, Valdosta, 1985-89, campaign vice chmn., 1994, campaign chmn., 1995. 1st lt. U.S. Army, 1967-69. Decorated Commendation medal. Fellow Am. Coll. Healthcare Execs. (regent 1990-94); mem. Am. Hosp. Assn., Ga. Hosp. Assn. (pres. S.W. dist. 1988), Voluntary Hosps. Am. (chmn. elect 1989-92, chmn. 1992-95). Office: South Ga Med Ctr 2501 N Patterson St Valdosta GA 31602-1735

BOWLING, JOYCE BLANKENCHIP, retired critical care nurse; b. White Deer, Tex., Nov. 17, 1932; d. Roy Lee and Myrtle Dove (Milhoan) Blankenchip; m. J.C. Bowling, July 24, 1952. Diploma, Northwest Tex. Sch. Nursing, 1953; AS, Amarillo Coll., 1953; BSN, West Tex. State U., 1983. RN, Tex.; cert. med.-surg. nursing, gerontology, nursing adminstrn. AACN; cert. emergency nurse. Staff nurse emergency rm. Parkland Hosp., Dallas, 1960-62; staff nurse Meth. Hosp., Dallas, 1962-68; staff nurse medicine, then head nurse CCU St. Paul Hosp., Dallas, 1969-73; charge nurse, supr. Southwestern Dialysis Ctr., Dallas, 1973-74; dir. nurses Caruth Rehab. Inst., Dallas, 1974-75; staff nurse VA Med. Ctr., Dallas, 1976-79; staff nurse VA Med. Ctr., Amarillo, Tex., 1979-85, head nurse surg. unit, 1985-88, clin. coord., 1988-96, ret., 1996. Mem. AACN (cert.), Emergency Nurses Assn. (cert.), Tex. Nurses Assn., Am. Heart Assn., Nat. Kidney Found., Am. Cancer Soc., Sigma Theta Tau. Home: RR 1 Box 556a-10 Amarillo TX 79121-9754

BOWMAN, BARBARA ANN, nutritional biochemist; b. East Warwick, R.I., Dec. 12, 1954; d. Laverne William and Rosamond Frieda (Schafer) Brown. BS in Biology, Ill. Inst. Tech., 1974; MS in Clin. Nutrition, U. Chgo., 1979, PhD in Human Nutrition, 1986. Diplomate Am. Bd. Nutrition. Nutrition specialist U. Chgo., 1979-83; postdoctoral assoc., instr. Emory U., Atlanta, 1986-88; sr. nutritionist Coca-Cola Co., Atlanta, 1988-90; assoc. prof. dept. nutrition and dietetics Ga. State U., Atlanta, 1990-92; rsch. chemist, epidemiologist, chief U.S. Ctrs. for Disease Control and Prevention, Atlanta, 1992—. Contbg. editor Nutrition Revs., 1990—; contbr. articles to profl. jours. Pres. Ga. Nutrition Coun., 1990. Mem. APHA, Am. Inst. Nutrition, Am. Assn. Clin. Chemistry. Office: US Ctrs for Disease Control MS F18 4770 Buford Hwy NE Atlanta GA 30341-3717

BOWMAN, JEAN MARIE, nursing administrator; b. Danvers, Mass., Oct. 29, 1959; d. Henry J. and Dorothy A. (Letarte) Talbot; m. Gregory Scott Bowman, Apr. 1, 1989. BS, St. Anselm Coll., 1981; MS in Mgmt., Lesley Coll., 1987. Nurse, mgr. pediatric surgery New Eng. Med. ctr. Hosps., Boston, 1985-87, nurse, mgr. pediatric medicine, 1987-95; unit nursing dir. pediat. Johnston Willis Hosp., Richmond, Va., 1995—. Mem. Mass. Coun. Nurse Mgrs. (bd. dirs. 1991-94), Nat. Coun. Nurse Mgrs., Sigma Theta Tau. Home: 3620 Derby Ridge Way Midlothian VA 23113

BOWMAN, JEFFREY NEIL, podiatrist; b. Detroit, Apr. 25, 1957; s. Harry and Helen (London) B.; m. Carol Jane Bartlett, Apr. 12, 1986; 1 child, Dana. BS in Biology/Zoology, U. Mich., 1979; DPM, Ill. Coll. Podiatric Medicine, Chgo., 1983. Diplomate Am. Coun. Cert. Podiatric Physicians and Surgeons, Am. Acad. Pain Mgmt. Resident Harris County Podiatric Surg. Found., Houston, 1983-84; physician Houston Foot specialists, 1983-86, pres., CEO, 1986—; bd. dirs. West Houston Surgicare, 1994—, dept. chmn. surgery, 1995—; mem. residency selection com. Houston Podiatric Residency Found., 1990—. Mem. adv. bd. KTRH Radio Sta., Houston, 1994—; physician Houston Tenneco Marathon, 1984—; health care advisor Houston Ind. Sch. Dist., 1992-94. Recipient Cert. of Excellence, Disting. Physicians Am., 1994, 95, 96. Fellow Internat. Soc. Podiatric Laser Surgery, Acad. Ambulatory Foot Surgery; mem. Am. Podiatric Med. Assn., Tex. Podiatric Med. Assn., Harris county Podiatric Med. Assn. Republican. Jewish. Office: 8945 Long Point Rd #209 Houston TX 77055

BOWMAN, LOUIS L., emergency physician; b. Toledo, Nov. 1, 1953; s. Louis J. and JAcquelyn (PErkins) B.; m. Deborah Lynn Hayden, Sept. 30, 1977; children: Heather, Kara, Jason, Benjamin, Michelle. BA in Chemistry, U. Toledo, 1976; DO, Kirksville Coll. Osteo. Med., 1980. Intern Doctor's Hosp., Columbus, Ohio; emergency physician Scioto Emergency Physicians, Columbus, Ohio, 1981—; med. dir. emergency medicine Columbis Cmty. Hosp., 1987-92; med. dir. Mid-Ohio Sports Car Course, Lexington, 1988—; med. dir., chmn. dept. medicine Med. Ctr. Hosp., Chillicothe, Ohio, 1995. Fellow Am. Coll. Emergency Physicians; Am. Osteo. Assn., Ohio Osteo. Assn., Columbus Acad. Osteo Medicine, Internat. Coun. Motor Sports Scis. Republican. Methodist. Office: Ambulatory Care Affiliates PO Box 292642 Columbus OH 43229

BOWMAN, NED DAVID, medical administrator; b. Chattanooga, Tenn., July 15, 1948; s. Ned Turner and Ernie June (White) B. and Charlotte Bramblett B. (stepmother); m. Linda Carol Eggers, Sep. 18, 1970; children: Robert, Jean, Elizabeth, Scott, Benjamin. BS, U. Tenn., 1971; MBA, Vanderbilt U., 1982. Participant exec. program Managing Ambulatory Health Care Orgns., Harvard Sch. Pub. Health, 1987. Adminstr. Oak Ridge (Tenn.) Orthepedic Ctr., 1971-90, Nashville Orthopedic Assn., 1990-91, Charlotte (N.C.) Eye, Ear, Nose and Throat Assn., 1991—; pres. Anderson County Health Coun., Clinton, Tenn., 1976; v.p. Knoxville Soc. for Advancement of Mgmt., Knoxville, 1974; bd. dirs. Tng. and Tech. Ctr., Oak Ridge, Tenn., 1976-78. Bd. dirs. C. of C., Oak Ridge, 1972-76, Boys Club Am., Oak Ridge, 1982-86, ORI, Knoxville, 1982, Great Smoky Mtn. Coun. Boy Scouts Am., Knoxville, 1984-86, iedmont Health Care Preferred Provider Org., 1993; governing bd. dirs. Am. Soc. OphtAdminstrs., 1995; local exec. com. Ch. of Jesus Christ of Latter Day Saints, Charlotte, 1994; treas. UN com., Oak Ridge, 1980-86; trustee health plan Mechlenburg County Med. Soc., 1994—. Recipient Certs. of Appreciation Vocat. Edn. Dept., Oak Ridge High Sch., 1978, Anderson County Health Coun., Oak Ridge, 1980, Soc. for Advancement of Mgmt., Knoxville, 1976, Oak Ridge Human Resource Bd., 1975. Mem. AAAS, Am. Coll. Healthcare Execs., Am. Soc. Ophthalmic Adminstrs., Am. Coll. Med. Practice Execs., Med. Group Mgmt. Assn., Assn. Otolaryngology Adminstrs., Am. Acad. Med. Administrs., N.C. Med. Group Mgmt. Assn., Tenn. Med. Group Mgmt. Assn., Charlotte Area Med. Group Mgrs. Assn., Rotary. Office: Charlotte Eye Ear Nose Throat Assocs 1600 E 3rd St Charlotte NC 28204-3202

BOWMER, RICHARD GLENN, physiology educator; b. Spokane, Wash., Dec. 4, 1931; s. Glenn William Bowmer and Esther Mae (Shenefelt) Waymire; m. Leona Mae Willey, June 1, 1957; children: Mary, Linda, Richard, Edward, Theresa, James. BS, U. Idaho, 1953, MS, 1957; PhD, U. N.C., 1960. Asst. prof. plant physiology Lewis & Clark State Coll., Lewiston, Idaho, 1960-61; asst. prof. plant physiology Idaho State U., Pocatello, 1961-66, assoc. prof. plant physiology, 1966-75, prof. plant physiology, 1975—; asst. chair dept. biology Idaho State U. Cpl. U.S. Army, 1953-55, Korea. Home: 3747 Oriole Ave Pocatello ID 83201-5410 Office: Idaho State U Dept Of Biology Pocatello ID 83209

BOX, ROGER HAYWARD, healthcare products executive; b. Jonesboro, La., June 17, 1942; s. M.M. and Dorothy M. (Rogers) B.; m. Angela Phillips Pringos, Aug. 29, 1964; children: Laura Elizabeth, Andrea Marian. BS in Pharmacy, Northeast La. Univ., 1965. Registered pharmacist. Chief pharmacist Physicians and Surgeons Hosp., Shreveport, La., 1965-68; dir. pharmacy Jane Phillips Hosp., Bartlesville, Okla., 1968-72; pres. MedSource Corp., Bartlesville, 1972—. Contbr. articles to profl. jours. Bd. dirs., pres. Bartlesville Family YMCA, 1993-95, Bartlesville Civic Ballet, 1982-89, Green Conty Free Clinic; bd. dirs., chmn. Sunfest, Inc., Bartlesville, 1983-91; bd. dirs. Bartlesville Pub. Sch. Found., 1988-92. Mem. Okla. Soc. Hosp. Pharmacists (pres. 1972, Hosp. Pharmacist of Yr. 1972), Am. Soc. Hosp. Pharmacists, Am. Pharm. Assn., Assn. Healthcare Enterprises (bd. dirs. 1985), Rotary. Office: MedSource Corp PO Box 846 Bartlesville OK 74005-0846

BOXENBAUM, HAROLD GEORGE, pharmacokineticist; b. Phila., Dec. 26, 1942; s. Clifford Saul and Ray Irene (Ruttenberg) B.; m. Francine Marie Pivinski, Apr. 3, 1982; 1 child, Shelby Ariella. BS in Pharmacy, Temple U., 1965, PharmM, 1969; PhD in Pharm. Chemistry, U. Calif., San Francisco, 1972. Registered pharmacist, Pa., Calif., Ohio, Md. Asst. prof. Coll. Pharmacy Ohio State U., Columbus, 1972-74; sr. scientist Hoffman-La Roche Inc., Nutley, N.J., 1974-77; pharmacist various retail stores, San Francisco, 1977-80; assoc. prof. Sch. Pharmacy U. Conn., Storrs, 1980-85; rsch. assoc. Marion Merrell Dow Inc., Cin., 1985-92; dir. clin. pharmacokinetics Wyeth-Ayerst Rsch., Phila., 1992-94; disting. scientist pharmacokinetics Otsuka Am. Pharms., Inc., Rockville, Md., 1994—. Author or co-author of 70 sci. articles/book chpts.; mem. editl. bd. Internat. Jour. Pharmaceutics, Pharm. Rsch., Human and Ecol. Risk Assessment; co-editor Perspectives in Pharmacokinetics sect. Jour. Pharmacokinetics and Biopharmaceutics. Fellow AAAS, Am. Assn. Pharm. Scis. Home: 14621 Settlers Landing Way North Potomac MD 20878-4305 Office: Otsuka Am Pharm Inc 2440 Rsch Blvd Rockville MD 20850-3238

BOXER, MYRON CHARLES, medical educator; b. Bklyn., Mar. 20, 1937. BA, NYU, 1958, D of Podiatric Medicine, 1961. Diplomate Nat. Bd. Podiatry Examiners, Am. Bd. Podiatric Orthop. and Primary Podiatric Medicine, Am. Bd. Quality Assurance and Utilization Rev. Physicians; cert. podiatric orthopedics, primary podiatric medicine; lic. podiatric physician, Calif., Fla., N.Y. Prof. dept. medicine N.Y. Coll. Podiatric Medicine, 1965-81, dir. dept. medicine, 1971-80, assoc. prof. dept. surgery, 1976-81, dir. emeritus dept. medicine, 1980; aux. clin. prof. Dr. William M. Scholl Coll. Podiatric Medicine, 1985-88; clin. prof. Coll. Podiatric Medicine and Surgery U. Osteopathic Medicine and Health Scis., Des Moines, 1982—; clin. faculty Sch. Podiatric Medicine Barry U., 1986—; pvt. practice in podiatric medicine and surgery Woodmere, N.Y., 1964—; vis. lectr. Ohio Coll. Podiatric Medicine, 1980; adj. prof. Calif. Coll. Podiatric Medicine, 1982—; adj. clin. prof. N.Y. Coll. Podiatric Medicine, 1986—; adj. clin. faculty Pa. Coll. Podiatric Medicine, 1986—; dir. medicine clinic Foot Clinics of N.Y., N.Y.C., 1964-80; dir. dept. podiatry Peninsula Hosp. Ctr., Far Rockaway, N.Y., 1993—, Gouverneur Hosp., N.Y.C., 1965—; cons. VA, Franklin Delano Roosevelt Hosp., Montrose, N.Y., 1987—; mem. med. and sci. com. L.I. divsn. Arthritis Found., 1982; cons. med. staff Empire Blue Cross Blue Shield N.Y., N.Y.C., 1985—; presenter in field. Gen. editor: Jour. Am. Podiatric Med. Assn., 1974-79; mem. editl. rev. bd. rheumatology The Contemporary Podiatric Physician, 1991—; contbr. to numerous med. jours. Capt. USAF, 1961-64. Fellow Am. Coll. Foot and Ankle Orthopedics and Medicine, Am. Soc. Podiatric Medicine, Am. Coll. Podiatric Radiologists, Am. Assn. Hosp. Podiatrists, Am. Coll. Podiatric Med. Rev., Royal Soc. Health; mem. APHA (sec. podiatry sect.), Am. Coll. Foot and Ankle Surgeons (assoc., N.Y. divsn.), Am. Acad. Podiatric Sports Medicine (assoc.), N.Y. Acad. Sci., Am. Podiatric Med. Assn., Nassau County Podiatric Med. Assn., Pub. Health Assn. N.Y.C., Am. Physicians Fellowship, N.Y. State Pub. Health Assn., Assn. Mil. Surgeons of U.S., Am. Running and Fitness Assn. (clinic adv. bd. 1991—), Am. Podiatric Circulatory Soc., Acad. Clin. Electrodynography, Pi Delta. Office: 2 Woodmere Blvd S Woodmere NY 11598-1729

BOXLER, DOROTHY BACINO, dental hygienist; b. Del., Mar. 7, 1956; d. Evro James and Josephine (Camoirano) B.; m. Daniel Leo Boxler, June 22, 1955; 1 child, Anthony, Joseph. Cert. dental hygiene, Temple U., 1976; BS, West Chester U., 1981. Clin. dental hygienist Group Dental Assocs., Wilmington, Del., 1976-1987; dental health educator Avon Grove Sch. Dist., West Grove, Pa., 1984-90; clin. instr. Temple U., Sch. Dental Hygiene, Phila., 1982, Del. Tech. Community Coll., Sch. Dental Hygiene, Wilmington, 1982; implementor, coord. sch. fluoride tablets, cons., promoter Nat. Children's Dental Health month, Avon Grove Sch. Dist, West Grove, Pa., 1984-90. Mem. Am. Dental Hygiene Assn., New Castle County Dental Hygiene Assn., New Garden Art Assn. (pres., 1987-89), Sigma Phi Alpha, Kappa Delta Pi. Roman Catholic. Home: 141 Cold Springs Dr Kennett Square PA 19348-2647

BOXWILL, FRANK EGBERT, psychologist; b. Georgetown, Guyana, June 25, 1926; came to U.S., 1946, naturalized, 1960; s. Isaac and Stella (Bunbury) B.; m. Mary O. Boxwill; children: Frank E., Eric, Yvette, Francyne, André. Student, Howard U., 1947-48; BS, Wagner Coll., 1953; postgrad., New Sch. Social Rsch., 1954, L.I. U., 1956-58, U. Oreg., 1958-59; PhD, East Coast U., 1971. Fellow in psychology Bklyn. Psychiat. Ctr., 1959-61; clin. psychologist Kings County Hosp., Bklyn., 1961-65; psychotherapist Bklyn. Ctr. Psychotherapy, 1964-66, Bleuler Ctr. Psychotherapy, Forest Hills, N.Y., 1967-81; psychologist Brentwood (N.Y.) Pub. Schs., 1967-81, Amityville (N.Y.) Pub. Schs., 1967-84; founder Parent Adolescent Rels. Inst., Inc., 1980—; cons. cmty. mental health Bklyn., Queens, 1966, London, Paris, 1969; chmn. bd. Family Inst. for More Effective Living Inc., Wilmington, Del., 1985—; sr. rsch. assoc. Tng. Resources for Youth, Bklyn., 1965-66; coord. rsch. Harlem Psychiat. Rehab. Ctr., 1966-67; sr. rsch. assoc. Columbia U., N.Y.C.; dir. Family Inst. for More Effective Living, Westbury, 1973—; cons. Child Abuse Agy.; cons. in child devel., learning, marital and family therapy, tchr., trainer.; pres., bd. dirs. Orgn. Mgmt. Tng. Ednl. Conss. (OMTEC), 1986—, Cmty. Counseling & Mediation Ctrs., Bklyn., 1989—; stress mgmt. cons., trainer, program provider for fed., state, city funded programs; trainer supervisory mgmt. Headstart Agy. for Child Devel.; mem. N.Am. com. Policy and Planning in Kinship Care CWLA. Author: The Troubled Youngster in the Classroom, 1971, Understanding Ego Development of the Troubled Youngster, 1972, Learning Disabilities, A Multi-disciplinary Approach, 1973; rschr. child devel. parental discipline, behavior mgmt. child abuse, treatment, adolescent sexually abused and abusers, kinship care, prenatal exposure to drugs in children; relationship between ethnicity, social class and ability; early intervention with out of home placed children up to age 3; training biological parents to be responsible parents. Mem. Rep. Presdl. Task Force, 1983—; cons. nat. and state Foster Care programs. Fellow Royal Soc. Health (Eng.), Am. Orthopsychiat. Assn.; mem. ASTD, Nat. Assn. Sch. Psychologists, Nat. Coun. Family Rels., Am. Mgmt. Assn., Coun. on Exceptional Children, Am. Group Psychotherapy Assn., Assn. Sch. Psychologists Pa.

BOYAJIAN, MICHAEL JOHN, pediatric plastic surgeon; b. Boston, May 4, 1950; s. Harold M. and Leona (Kaprielian) B.; m. Andrea Lotze, Jan. 17, 1987; children: Alanna Julia, Michael Karl, Nicolas James. BA, Wesleyan U., Middletown, Conn., 1972; MD, NYU, 1976. Gen. surgery residency U. Colo., 1976-79; gen. surgery residency U. Cin., 1979-81; plastic surgery residency Brigham & Women's Hosp., Boston, 1981-83; craniofacial surgery fellowship The Children's Hosp., Boston, 1983; chmn. plastic surgery Children's Nat. Med. Ctr., Washington, 1983—. Mem. Am. Soc. Plastic and Reconstructive Surgeons. Office: Children's Nat Med Ctr 111 Michigan Ave NW Washington DC 20010

BOYAJIAN, TIMOTHY EDWARD, public health officer, educator, consultant; b. Fresno, Calif., Feb. 22, 1949; s. Ernest Adam and Marge (Medzian) B.; m. Tassanee Bootdeesri, Apr. 23, 1987. BS in Biology, U. Calif., Irvine, 1975; M of Pub. Health, UCLA, 1978. Registered environ. health specialist, Calif. Rsch. asst. UCLA, 1978-81; lectr. Chapman U., 29 Palms, Calif., 1982-84, 88-89; refugee relief vol. Cath. Relief Svcs., Surin, Thailand, 1985-86; lectr. Nat. Univ., L.A., 1989-91; environ. health specialist Riverside County Health Svcs. Agy., Palm Springs, Calif., 1991—; cons. parasitologist S. Pacific Commn., L.A., 1979; pub. health cons. several vets. groups, L.A., 1981-84, Assn. S.E. Asian Nations, Bangkok, Thailand, 1988. Veterans rights activist, Vietnam Vet. Groups, L.A., 1981-84. With USMC, Vietnam, 1969-71. Recipient U.S. Pub. Health Traineeship, U.S. Govt., L.A., 1977-81. Mem. VFW, Calif. Environ. Health Assn.,. Home: PO Box 740 Palm Springs CA 92263-0740

BOYCE, FRANKLIN DELANO, JR., family physician; b. London, Apr. 27, 1953; arrived in The Bahamas, 1985; s. Franklin Delano Sr. and Elizabeth Rose (Irvin) B.; m. Charlotte Helen Kenyon, Apr. 22, 1993; 1 child, Alysia Jane. BA, Vanderbilt U., 1975; MD, Med. Coll. Va., 1979. Bd. cert. Am. Bd. Family Practice. Intern dept. family practice Med. Coll. Va., Newport News, 1979-80, resident, 1980-85; locum tenens physician Comp Health, Salt Lake City, 1982-84; staff physician McMinnville (Tenn.) Family Practice, 1984-85; physician Blue Ridge Clinic, Marsh Harbour, Abaco, The Bahamas, 1985—; preceptor dept. family practice U. Calif. Sch. Medicine, Davis, 1995—, U. Mo., Columbia, 1996—. Mem. Am. Acad.

Family Practice, Med. Assn. of Bahamas. Home and Office: Box AB20459, Marsh Harbour Abaco, Bahamas

BOYCE, JAMES DANIEL, ophthalmologist; b. Rutland, Vt., Sept. 1, 1947; s. George Potter and Mary Emma (Bree) B.; m. Janet Muff, July 26, 1975. BA, Columbia Coll., 1969; MD, Columbia U., 1973. Diplomate Am. Bd. Ophthalmology. Intern medicine U. So. Calif., L.A., 1974-77; resident ophthalmology Columbia U., N.Y.C., 1977; pvt. practice L.A., 1977-78; ophthalmologist Orange County Ophthalmology Group, Garden Grove, Calif., 1978-79; pvt. practice Garden Grove, 1979-95; ptnr. Orange County Ophthalmology Group, Garden Grove, 1995—; instr. U. So. Calif. Doheny Eye Inst., L.A., 1983—; team ophthalmologist L.A. Rams Football Team, L.A., 1983-95. Pres. Rotary, Garden Grove, 1992-93. Recipient Cmty. Svc. award Sister City Assn., Garden Grove, 1993. Mem. L.A. Soc. Ophthalmology (program chair 1994-95, treas. 1995-96), Orange County Soc. Ophthalmology (program chair 1993-95). Republican. Office: Orange County Ophthalmology Med Group Ste 401 12665 Garden Grove Blvd Garden Grove CA 92643

BOYCE, THOMAS KENNETH, psychiatrist; b. Middletown, N.Y., Apr. 26, 1923; s. Thomas A. and Lillian (Hackett) B. Reg. profl. nurse, Middletown State Hosp., 1947; AB, Marietta (Ohio) Coll., 1951; MA, Tchrs. Coll. Columbia U., N.Y.C., 1953; MD, Cath. U. Louvain (Belgium), 1961. Diplomate Am. Bd. Psychiatry and Neurology. From supervisory psychiatrist to unit chief of svc. Middletown Psychiat. Ctr., 1966-82, chmn. hosp. forensic and spl. release com., 1980-83, 84—; cons. psychiatrist Mercy Cmty. Hosp., Port Jarvis, N.Y., 1966—, Social Security Bur. Disability Determination, Albany, N.Y., 1967—, St. Anthony's Cmty. Hosp., Warwick, N.Y., 1970—. Pharmacists mate USNR, 1943-46. Fellow Am. Coll. Phys.; mem. AMA, Am. Psychiat. Assn., Orange County Med. Soc. (chmn. mental health com. 1979-91). Roman Catholic. Home and Office: 150 N Beacon St Middletown NY 10940-3623

BOYD, ARTHUR BERNETTE, JR., surgeon, clergyman, beverage company executive; b. Durham, N.C., June 29, 1947; s. Arthur Bernette and Mammie Lee (Chalmers) B.; m. Delphine Victoria Huffman, Mar. 14, 1981; children: Arthur III, Vicki. BA, Fla. A&M Univ., 1969; postgrad., NYU, 1970; MD, Meharry Med. Coll., 1978. Cert. ATLS instr., PALS. Intern in surgery Howard Univ. Hosp., Washington, 1978-80; resident and chief resident in surgery St. Luke's Hosp., Cleve., 1981-84; fellow in liver transplant U. Pitts., 1984-85; chief adminstrv. fellow trauma/surg. critical care R.A. Cowley Shock Trauma Ctr., U. Md. Med. Sys., Cali, Colombia, 1993-94; clin. instr. surgery, sr. fellow, traumatologist R.A. Cowley Shock Trauma Ctr., U. Md. Med. Sys., Baltimore County, 1994—; co-traumatologist Prince George Cmty. Hosp., Cheverly, Md., 1994-95; chief surgeon, pres. Phoenix Med. Surgical Svc., Inc., Cleve., Carribean, 1986—; clin. instr. surgery, sr. trauma fellow Shock Trauma Ctr. U. Md. Med. Ctr., Balt., 1995-96; pres., CEO Motown Beverage Co. of Ohio, Cleve., 1988—, Towne Club Internat. of Ohio, Inc., Cleve., 1988—; chief adminstrv. fellow in trauma/crit. care R.A. Cowley Shock Trauma Ctr./U. Md. Med. Systems, 1993-94, clin. instr., sr. trauma rsch. fellow, 1994-95; sr. trauma fellow, clin. instr. Shock Trauma Ctr./U. Md., 1995; adj. prof. Anatomy and Physiology Cuyhoga C.C., Cleve., 1988—; cons. surgeon other hosps. and physicians, Cleve., 1988—. Inventor: wheelchair with mechanism to raise or lower left or right buttocks of person, hemostat that carries two sutures, synthetic covering with zipper to cover bowel when abdomen unable to be closed after surgery. Vol. Cleve. Community Action Against Addiction, 1987-88; mentor Case Western U. Inner City Program, Cleve., 1988—. Fellow ACS (assoc.), Internat. Coll. Surgeons; mem. AAAS, AMA, N.Y. Acad. Scis., Nat. Med. Assn. (mentor 1990—), Ohio State Med. Soc., Cleve. Surg. Soc., Nat. Assn. Small Bus. Owners, Internat. Assn. Small Bus. Owners, Greater Cleve. Urban League, Masons, Omega Psi Phi, Alpha Phi Omega. Democrat. Methodist. Home and Office: Motown Beverage Co 22462 Westchester Rd Shaker Heights OH 44122-4863

BOYD, BILLY WILLARD, internist; b. York, Ala., Jan. 21, 1948; s. Billy Morgan and Ruth Glover (Hutchinson) B.; m. Beverly Wallace, June 4, 1974; children: Elizabeth Wallace, Jessamyn Daniel. BA, Yale U., 1970; MD, U. Ala., 1975. Diplomate Am. Bd. Internal Medicine, Am. Bd. Pulmonary Disease. Tchr. Branford (Conn.) High Sch., 1970-71; intern in internal medicine U. South Ala. Med. Ctr., Mobile, 1975-76, resident in internal medicine, 1976-78, fellow in pulmonary disease, 1978-80; practice medicine specializing in internal medicine Montgomery, Ala., 1980—; mem. exec. com. Ala. TB Adv. Commn., 1980—; sec. med. staff Montgomery Bapt. Med. Ctr., 1985—; mem. utilization rev. com. South Haven Manor Nursing Home, Montgomery, 1980—. Contbr. articles to profl. jours. Bd. dirs. Capri Community Film Soc., Montgomery, 1984. Nat. Merit scholar, 1966, acad. scholar, 1966, W.B. Jackson Meml. scholar, 1969. Fellow ACP, Am. Coll. Chest Physicians; mem. Am. Soc. Internal Medicine, (pres. Ala. chpt. 1986-87), Med. Assn. Ala. Democrat. Presbyterian. Clubs: Montgomery Track, Capital City (Montgomery). Home: 3613 McCurdy St Montgomery AL 36111-2120 Office: Internal Medicine Assocs 2055 E South Blvd Montgomery AL 36116-2001

BOYD, CLARENCE ELMO, retired surgeon; b. Leesville, La., Nov. 2, 1911; s. Isaac Clarence and Ada Lee (Stakes) B.; m. Emma Kittredge Sims, Aug. 13, 1937; children: Charles Elmo, Marjorie Emily, Frances Ada, James E. B.A., U. Tex., 1932, M.D., 1935. Diplomate Am. Bd. Abdominal Surgeons (a founder 1959). Intern Charity Hosp., New Orleans, 1935-36; resident North La. Sanitarium (now Doctors Hosp.), Shreveport, 1936-37; vis. surgeon Doctor's Hosp., Shreveport, 1937-89, chmn. bd., 1959-80, founding dir., med. dir., 1959-89; gen. practice medicine, 1937-42; jr. vis. surgeon Charity Hosp., Shreveport, 1937-42; practice medicine specializing in surgery Shreveport, 1942-89; sr. vis. surgeon Confederate Meml. Hosp., 1942-77; 1st v.p. vis. staff, 1943-44; sr., founding mem. C. E. Boyd Clinic Ltd., 1942-89; clin. asst. prof. surgery La. State U., Shreveport, 1957-67; clin. asst. prof. surgery, co-founder La. State U. Sch. Medicine, Shreveport, 1967;; founding dir. Shreveport Bank & Trust Co., 1954, chmn. investment com., 1954-78, chmn. bd., 1961-87; spl. rsch. operative cholangiography, herniloplasty with local anesthesia and immediate ambulatio; keloids researcher. Author numerous articles; producer films in field. Bd. dirs. Volunteers Am., 1950-58, chmn. bd., 1955-57; trustee Pub. Affairs Research Council La., 1959-79; mem. nat. adv. bd. We, The People, 1964—; mem. sponsors com. Shreveport United Fund, 1962-66; Guest speaker Dean's lecture La. State Med. Sch., 1955, 57; founder, chmn. Student Loan Fund, 1942-87. hon. col. Gov. La. staff, 1964. Fellow ACS, Internat. Coll. Surgeons, Southeastern Surg. Congress, Am. Soc. Abdominal Surgeons a founder 1959, pres. 1966-67, 90-91, mem. teaching faculty 1962—, Gold medal 1962, Disting. Svc. award 1986); mem. AMA (chmn. surg. sect. 1965-66, 66-67, mem. surg. sect. 1969-71, alt. del. gen. surg. coun. 1972-78, surg. coun. 1972-78, del. 1978-79, Recognition award 1966-69, 70-72, 73-75, 76-78, 79-81, 82-84, 85-87), Assn. Am. Physicians and Surgeons (del. 1960-72, chmn. La. membership com. 1950-72, pres. La. chpt. 1972-73), Internat. Acad. Proctology, Surg. Assn. La., Am. Mastology Assn., La. State Med. Soc. (Ho. of Dels. 1945-49, chmn. pub. policy and legis. com. 1954-57, chmn. surg. sect. 1957, councilor 1959-66, 1st v.p. 1967-68, chmn. com. on hosps. 1968-71, vice chmn. socio-econs. 1970-71, 1st chmn. com. medicine and religion 1964-66), Shreveport Med. Soc. (Gold medal 1956-57, pres. 1956-57, 1st chmn. med. progress 1957-59), Am. Cancer Soc. (bd. dirs. Caddo br. 1952-59, vice chmn. bd. 1957-58), So. Med. assn. (asst. councilor 1959-68), Pan-Pacific surg. Assn. Episcopalian (vestryman 1966-69; Gold medal Bible Class 1965). Lodges: Masons (32 deg.), Shriners, Rotary (pres. South Shreveport Chpt. 1940-41, founder 1942, student loan com.). Home: 401 Delaware St Shreveport LA 71106-1633

BOYD, DEBORAH ANN, pediatrician; b. Urbana, Ohio, Jan. 30, 1955; d. John A. Sr. and Juanita Jean (Routt) B. BA cum laude, Wittenberg U., 1977; MD, U. Cin., 1982. Diplomate Am. Bd. Pediatrics, Nat. Bd. Med. Examiners. Intern Children's Hosp. Med. Ctr., Cin., 1982-83, pediatric resident, 1982-85; pediatrician Nat. Health Svc. Corps, Springfield, Ohio, 1985-89, Community Hosp. Health Care Ctr., Springfield, 1989—; mem. Continuing med. edn. com. Mercy Med. Ctr., Springfield, 1989—, infection control com., 1987—. Adv. com. Miami Valley Child Devl. Ctr., Springfield, 1985—, New Parents as Tchrs., 1986—. Democratic. Home: 2310 N Limestone St Apt 118 Springfield OH 45503-1144 Office: Community Hosp Health Care 144 W Pleasant St Springfield OH 45506-2206

BOYD, DONALD ALLEN, school psychologist, resource center director; b. Kingman, Kans., Apr. 27, 1945; s. Olen Finas and Lulu Carrie (Preston) B.; m. Sharon Lynn Craig, Nov. 23, 1985; children: LeeAnn Michelle, Preston Lawrence. B. Sacred Lit., Ozark Bible Coll., 1968; MS, Pittsburg State U., 1977, Edn. Specialist, 1980; PhD, Kans. State U., 1984. Nationally cert. sch. psychologist. Minister Norton (Va.) Christian Ch., 1971-75; sch. psychologist Marysville (Kans.) Sch. Dist., 1979-81, Geary County Pub. Schs., Junction City, Kans., 1983-88, Tri-County Spl. Edn Coop., Independence, Kans., 1988-91, Ark. spl. Edn. Resource Ctr., Little Rock, 1991—. Contbr. articles to profl. jours. Mem. Kans. Gov.'s Commn. on Edn. for Parenthood, Topeka, 1985—. Mem. Nat. Assn. Sch. Psychologists. Home: 14 Brook Ln Cabot AR 72023-9465 Office: Ark Spl Edn Resource Ctr 1401 N Pierce St Little Rock AR 72207-5365

BOYD, HERBERT REED, JR., dentist; b. Petersburg, Va., Sept. 15, 1925; s. Herbert Reed and Eula Jesse (Arnold) B.; m. Beverly Jane Lackey, Aug. 5, 1950; children: Herbert Reed III, Stuart Arnold, Amy Lewis. BA, U. Richmond, 1972; DDS, Med. Coll. Va., 1948. Dental intern in oral surgery Med. Coll. Va. Hosps., Richmond, 1948-49; instr. crown and bridge prosthodontics Med. Coll. Va., Richmond, 1951-53; asst. prof. Med. Coll. Va., 1953-56, assoc. prof., 1956-61, asst. clin. prof. periodontics, 1964-70; pvt. practice Petersburg, Va., 1961—. Capt. U.S. Army, 1949-51, lt. col. 1962. Fellow Va. Dental Assn.; mem. ADA, Southside Va. Dental Assn. (pres. 1977), Am. Coll. Dentists, Internat. Coll. Dentists, Am. Acad. Medicine, Pierre Fauchard Acad., Med. Coll. Va. Alumni Assn. (pres. 1977), U. Richmond Alumni Assn., Boatwright Soc. U Richmond, U.S. Lighthouse Soc. (adv. bd. Chesapeake chpt. 1992—), Petersburg C. of C., McKee Dental Study Club Richmond, Rotary (pres. 1976-77), Omicron Kappa Upsilon, Psi Omega, Phi Kappa Sigma. Home: 1200 Northampton Rd Petersburg VA 23805-1932 Office: 23 Goodrich Ave Petersburg VA 23805-2119

BOYD, JOHN HAMILTON, osteopath; b. Wharton County, Tex., Sept. 20, 1924; s. John Hamilton and Grace Laura (Smith) B.; m. Myrtle Juanita Ferguson, Feb. 21, 1970. BA, Tex. Tech U., 1949; DO, Kirksville (Tex.) Coll. Osteo. Medicine, 1955. Practice osteopathic medicine Louise, Tex., 1955-70, Silverton, Tex., 1971-74, Eden, Tex., 1974—; aviation med. examiner FAA, 1971—; clin. prof. Gen. and Family Practice Tex. Coll. Osteo Med.; clin. prof. health sci. ctr. U. North Tex., Ft. Worth, 1990—; mem. Tex. State Bd. Med. Examiners, 1987-93, sec., treas., 1989-93; health officer Wharton County, 1961-65, Briscoe County, 1971-74; health dir. City of Eden, 1974—; med. dir. Eden Detention Ctr., 1985-93; asst. adminstr. Concho County Hosp., 1987—; chmn. rev. com. Tex. Inst. Med. Assessment, 1979-81, pres., 1981-83. Mem. local SSS bd., 1967-70; bd. dirs. Concho County Hosp. Dist., 1975-84, Wharton County Jr. Coll., 1961-70, Tex. Med. Found., 1973-78, 82-91. Served with USAAF, 1942-46, ETO. Fellow Am. Coll. Utilization Rev. Physicians, Aerospace Med. Assn. (assoc.); mem. Am. Bd. Quality Assurance and Utilization Rev. Physicians (cert.), Am. Acad. Osteopathy, Tex. Osteo. Med. Assn. (pres. 1973-74, Disting. Svc. award 1994), Am. Osteo. Assn., Civil Aviation Med. Assn. (bd. dirs. 1978-80, v.p. 1980-84, 87—, pres. 1985-87), Am. Osteo. Coll. Preventive Medicine, Aerospace Med. Assn., Assn. Latinoam. de Aviación y del Espacio, Am. Med. Peer Rev. Assn. (chmn. by-laws com.), Nat. Rifle Assn. Home and Office: Drawer W Eden TX 76837

BOYD, LONNIE MARTIN, health facility administrator; b. Pocatello, Idaho, Aug. 31, 1948; s. Merlin O. and Norma L. (Ipock) B.; m. Martha P. Wallace, Jan. 10, 1970 (div. July 1987); 1 child, Jennifer L. Student, S.W. Mo. State U., 1966-70, S.W. Bapt. U., Bolivar, Mo., 1994-95. RN, Mo.; cert. hemodialysis nurse. Staff and charge nurse St. John's Regional Health Ctr., Springfield, Mo., 1976-79; head nurse/supr. U.S. Med. Ctr. for Fed. Prisoners, Springfield, 1979-82; adminstr. Ozarks Dialysis Svcs., Springfield, 1982-95; v.p. regional svc. Mid-Am. Transplant Svc., Springfield, 1995—; chmn. adv. coun. Mo. Kidney Program, Columbia, Mo., 1992-93, mem. network coord. coun., facility rep., Kansas City, Mo., 1982-95; bd. dirs. Bd. Nephrology Examiners, Boulder, Colo., 1985-86. Contbr. articles to profl. jours. Recipient Editl. Achievement award Dialysis and Transplantation, 1989. Mem. N.Am. Transplant Coords. Home: 185 Petunia Clever MO 65631 Office: Mid-America Transplant Svcs 2748 S Austin Springfield MO 65807

BOYD, ROBERT DAVID, pediatrician; b. Cambridge, Eng., May 14, 1938; s. J.D. and A.C. Boyd; m. Meriel Cornelia Talbot; children: Thomas, Diana, Lucy. MA, Cambridge U, 1959, MB, 1962, MSc (hon.), U. Manchester, Eng., 1981. Vis. prof. Oreg. Health Sci. U., 1988; prof. Manchester U., 1980-96; dean Manchester Med. Sch., 1989-93; chair Nat. Ctr. for R&D in Primary Care, 1994-96, Manchester Health Authority, 1994-96; prin.-elect St.. George's Hosp. Med. Sch., London, 1996—; asst. registrar Royal Coll. Physics, London, 1979-81; chair acad. bd. Brit. Pediatric Assn., 1987-90; mem. Nat. Standing Med. Adv. Com., 1989-92; mem. Med. Adv. Com., Higher Edn. Funding Couns. Author books in pediatrics and fetal physiology; editor Placenta, 1989-95; contbr. articles to profl. jours. Goldsmiths traveling fellow, 1972-73; grantee Med. Rsch Coun., Royal Soc., Wellcome Trust, Halley Stuart Trust. Fellow Royal Coll. Physicians. Office: St Georges Hosp Med Sch, Cranmer Ter, London SW17 0RE, England

BOYD, ROLAND L., osteopathic pediatrician; b. Savannah, Tenn., Aug. 5, 1964; s. Herman Leon and Norma Pauline (Moore) B.; m. Cynthia M. Schuetz, Apr. 13, 1995; children: Nicole D., Clayton R. AS, Jackson (Tenn.) State C.C., 1984; BS, Austin Peay State U., 1986; DO, W.Va. Sch. Medicine, 1990. Intern Ohio Valley Med. Ctr., Wheeling, W.Va., 1990-91; resident in pediatrics Phoenix Children's Hosp., 1991-94; locum tenens, Atlanta, 1994-95; pvt. practice, Mt. Airy, N.C., 1995—; mem. med. staff No. Surry Hosp., Mt. Airy, 1995—. Mem. AMA, Am. Osteo. Assn., Am. Acad. Pediat., Am. Coll. Osteo. Pediatricians. Republican. Office: No Pediat Ctr 708 S South St Mount Airy NC 17030

BOYD, TERESA DIANE, emergency medicine physician; b. San Augustine, Tex., Nov. 23, 1954; d. John Hamilton and Myrtle Juanita (Ferguson) Boyd; m. Peter Timothy Munson, Aug. 12, 1982 (div. Aug. 1989); m. Howard Harris Krantman, May 27, 1990; 1 child, Kayla Fay Krantman. DO, Tex. Coll. Osteo. Medicine, Ft. Worth, 1986. Active staff attending emergency rm. Brighton Med. Ctr., Portland, Maine, 1987-96, Brighton campus Maine Med. Ctr., Portland, 1996—; jr. ptnr. A.C.A., Portland, 1990-94; facilitator elder abuse workshops. Mem. Temple Beth El Sisterhood, Portland. Recipient awards Tex. Coll. Osteo. Medicine, 1986. Mem. Am. Coll. Emergency Physicians, Tex. Osteo. Med. Assn., Maine Osteo. Med. Assn., Maine Trauma Soc., So. Maine Women's Physicians Group, Mensa, Delta Omega. Republican. Jewish. Home: 21 Cape Woods Dr Cape Elizabeth ME 04107

BOYD, THOMPSON HENRY, III, physician, educator; b. Washington, June 8, 1952; s. Thompson Henry Jr. and Lore Esther (Wagner) B. BS in Engrng. Sci., Applied Math., U. Va., 1974, MD, 1979. Diplomate Am. Bd. Medicine. Intern Hahnemann U., Phila., 1979-80, resident, 1980-82, clin. instr., 1989—; chmn. utilization rev. com. Hahnemann U., 1995—. Mem. Am. Coll. Physicians, AMA (Physicians Recognition award 1989), Am. Soc. Internal Medicine, Phila. County Med. Assn. Office: 2126 Fairmount Ave Philadelphia PA 19130-2603

BOYER, CYNTHIA LOU, oncology nurse; b. Kingston, Pa., Feb. 21, 1955; d. Charles E. Jr. and Dorothy A. (Pickering) Boyer. BS, Pa. State U., 1977; MSN, U. Pa., 1983. Cert. med.-surg. clin. nurse specialist, nurse adminstr., advanced oncology nurse. Asst. head nurse, staff nurse Hosp. of the U. Pa., Phila., 1978-83; med. clin. nurse specialist Mercy Cath. Med. Ctr., Darby, Pa., 1983-86; clin. coord. Crozer Chester Med. Ctr., Chester-Upland, Pa., 1986—; lectr. to other health profls. on oncology and endocrine-metabolic emergency topics. Clin. editor: Oncologic Disorders Patient Teaching Manual 2, 1987. Mem. ANA, Del. Nurses Assn., Oncology Nursing Soc. (cert.). Home: 514 Ward Rd Brookhaven PA 19015-1419 Office: Crozer Chester Med Ctr Radiation Oncology One Medical Center Blvd Upland PA 19013

BOYER, FORD SYLVESTER, relationship consultant; b. Cadet, Mo., Jan. 12, 1934; s. Wilford Robert and Mary Elizabeth (DeClue) B.; m. Juelle-Ann Rupkalvis, May 2, 1970. BA in Psychology, USAF Inst., 1957; DD, Am. Bible Inst., Kansas City, Mo., 1977; MA, John F. Kennedy U., 1994. Cert. alcohol specialist. Adminstr. Getz Bros., San Francisco, 1969-73; supr. word processing U.S. Leasing Corp., San Francisco, 1977-82, dir. tng. and applications-word processing, 1982-84; computer cons Petaluma, Calif., 1984-87; massage therapist Petaluma, 1985-87; pvt. practice hypnotherapy Alameda, Calif., 1987—; cons. for chem. dependency Alameda, 1987—. Contbr. articles to profl. publs.; writer, pub.: (newsletter) Starfire, 1988—. With USAF, 1953-57, Korea. Mem. Am Coun. Hypnotist Examiners, Nat. Assn. Alcohol and Drug Abuse Counselors, Calif. Assn. Alcohol and Drug Abuse Counselors, Calif. Assn. Alcohol Recovery Homes. Home and Office: Spiritual Comm Sys 3327 Cook Ln Alameda CA 94502-6939

BOYER, JAMES LORENZEN, physician, educator; b. N.Y.C., Aug. 28, 1936; s. Ralph R. and Alice M. B.; m. Phoebe Bennet, Feb. 23, 1963; children: Phoebe Christine, Anna Birch. A.B., Haverford (Pa.) Coll., 1958; M.D., Johns Hopkins U., 1962. Diplomate: Am. Bd. Internal Medicine. Med. intern N.Y. Hosp., N.Y.C., 1962-63, resident in medicine, 1963-64; resident in medicine Yale-New Haven Hosp., 1966; postdoctoral fellow liver study unit Yale U., 1966-68; mem. faculty U. Chgo. Pritzker Sch. Medicine, 1972-78, prof. medicine, 1976-78, dir. liver study unit, 1972-78; prof. medicine, dir. liver study unit, chief div. digestive diseases Yale U. Med. Sch., 1978-96; dir. Yale Liver Ctr., 1984—; treas., bd. dirs. Am. Liver Found., 1976-85; dep. chmn. Nat. Digestive Disease Adv. Bd., 1981-84; council mem. NIDDK, 1985-90. Author papers, abstracts in field. Chmn. bd. trustees Mt. Desert Island Biol. Lab., Salsbury Cove, Maine, 1995—. Lt. comdr. USPHS, 1964-66. Josiah Macey faculty scholar, 1976. Mem. Am. Assn. Study Liver Disease (pres. 1980), Am. Fedn. Clin. Rsch., A.C.P., Am. Gastroenterol. Assn. (councillor 1983-86), Internat. Assn. Study Liver Diseases (v.p. 1982-84, pres.-elect 1986-88, pres. 1988-90), Am. Soc. Clin. Investigation, Assn. Am. Physicians, Soc. Clin. Rsch., Am. Clin. and Climatolgic Assn. Office: Yale U Sch of Medicine 333 Cedar St New Haven CT 06510-3206

BOYETTE, CHARLES OTIS, family physician; b. Chadbourn, N.C., Mar. 6, 1935. BA in History, U. N.C., Chapel Hill, 1957, MD, 1961. Pvt. practice family medicine Belhaven, N.C., 1964—; chief staff Pungo Dist. Hosp., 1977-96; mem. Gov's Commn. on Infant Mortality, 1989-95; med. dir. Hyde Home Health, 1990—; med. cons. Hyde County Health Dept., 1985—, supr., med. dir., 1989—; med. supr. Mattamuskeet Clinic, 1985-86; dir.-at-large Eastern AHEC, 1981-88, 90—; clin. asst. prof. Family Medicine East Carolina Sch. Medicine, 1983—. Pres. Beaufort County C.C. Found., 1985—; initial bd. dirs. Beaufort County Com. of 100, 1985—; mem. exec. com. Beaufort County Schs., 1986; co-chmn. Com. on Excellence in Edn., 1987; mayor Town of Belhaven, 1970-72, 75-78, 80-90, 92—; mem. Belhaven Dem. Precinct Com., 1964—, Beaufort County Dem. Exec. Com., 1980-81, 92-96; mem First Congl. Dist. Exec. Com., 1982-83; chmn. Beaufort County Dem. Systaining Fund Com., 1995-96; chmn. Trinity United Meth. Ch., Belhaven, 80-90; trustee Hebron Meth. Ch., 1994-96. Recipient Citizen of Yr. award C. of C., 1970, Physicians Recognition award AMA, 1973—, N.C. Physician of Yr. award N.C. Acad. Family Physicians, 1978, Cert. of Recognition, Family Health Found. Am., 1978, 82, 84-95, Disting. Svc. award U. N.C. Sch. Medicine, 1996. Fellow Am. Acad. Family Physicians; mem. AMA, N.C. Med. Soc. (dir. Dist. II 1979-83), N.C. Acad. Family Physicians (pres. 1986-87, chmn. legis. and pub. policy com. 1990-91), Pamlico Albemarle Med. Soc. (pres. 1978-79, del. to N.C. Med. Soc. 1978—). Office: Front and Haslin Sts Belhaven NC 27810

BOYKIN, CATHERINE MARIE, health care administrator; b. Phila., Dec. 25, 1944; d. William Lee (dec.) and Marie Eleanor (Hewson) B.; m. Walter Miller Morris Jr., Sept. 3, 1977; 1 child, William Martin Boykin-Morris. BSN, Villanova U., 1966; cert. PNP, U. Conn., 1973; postgrad., U. Vt. Cert. PNP, Vt. Pub. health nurse U.S. Peace Corps, Osorno, Chile, 1967-68; coronary care specialist Queen of the Angels Hosp., L.A., 1969-70; pub. health nurse Orthopaedic Hosp., L.A., 1970-72; PNP N.E. Kingdom Mental Health Svcs., Newport, Vt., 1973-75, The Child Health Ctr., St. Johnsbury, Vt., 1975-81; pvt. practice nurse practitioner New Directions in Health, St. Johnsbury, 1981-84; PNP The Burke Schs., Burke Hollow, Vt., 1983-84; dir. health Lyndon Inst., Lyndon Center, Vt., 1984—; chair Vt. Joint Practice Com.: Vt. State Nurses Assn., Vt. State Med. Soc., 1981-83; coord. Drug-Free Schs., Lyndon Inst., Lyndon Center, 1984—; bd. mem. Heart Healthy Vermonter Adv. Bd., St. Johnsbury, 1985-90; pediatric rep. Vt. State Bd. Nursing Nurse Practitioner Adv. Com., 1985—. Vice chairperson Caledonia County Dem. Com., St. Johnsbury, 1990-95, treas., 1995—; Justice of the Peace, Lyndonville, 1990—; chairperson Lyndon Town Dem. Com., Lyndonville, 1991—; mem. Lyndon Bd. Civil Authority, 1990—. Recipient Founding Assoc. award Club de Abstemios Nuevo Amanecer, Osorno, 1968. Mem. ANA, Vt. State Nurses Assn. (chairperson coun. of nursing practice 1975-77), Vt. State Sch. Nurses Assn., Vt. Pediatric Nurse Practitioners (treas. 1987-89, co-chair 1990—), Vt. Nurse Practitioners Inc., Am. Sch. Health Assn., Nat. Assn. Sch. Nurses, Nat. Family Life Edn. Network. Roman Catholic. Home: RR 2 Lyndonville VT 05851-9802 Office: Lyndon Institute Lyndon Center VT 05850

BOYLAN, ELIZABETH SHIPPEE, biology educator, academic administrator; b. Shanghai, Nov. 29, 1946; d. Nathan M. and Elizabeth (Little) Shippee; m. Robert J. Boylan, Oct. 2, 1971; children: Elizabeth B., Emily A. AB, Wellesley Coll., 1968; PhD, Cornell U., 1972. Lic. secondary biology tchr., N.Y. Postdoctoral fellow U. Rochester (N.Y.) Sch. Medicine, 1972-73; asst. prof. Queens Coll. CUNY, Flushing, 1973-78, assoc. prof., 1978-82, prof. biology, 1983-95, acting asst. provost, 1988-89, asst. provost, 1989-90, assoc. provost, 1990-92; acting provost Queens Coll. CUNY, Flushing, 1992-93; assoc. provost acad. programs and planning Queens Coll., Flushing, 1994-95; provost and dean of faculty Barnard Coll., N.Y.C., 1995—; prof. biology Barnard Coll., 1995—; chmn. Queens Coll. Acad. Senate, 1985-88; mem. grad. faculty Grad. Ctr. CUNY, N.Y.C., 1977-95; vis. investigator Sloan-Kettering Inst. Cancer Rsch., N.Y.C., 1979-80; trustee N.Y. Met. Reference and Rsch. Libr. Agy., Manhattan, 1989—, chair fin. com. 1991—; co-chair bd. trustees study com. on secondary edn. CUNY, 1987-88, co-chair vice chancellor's task force on sci., engring., tech. and math., 1988-89; panelist NSF grad. fellowship program, 1992-93; cons. to Nat. Cancer Inst., N.J. Commn. on Cancer Rsch., Endocrine Soc.; mem. breast cancer task force NCI, 1980-84; mem. adv. com. Am. Cancer Soc., 1981-85; Am. Coun. Edn. fellow Pace U., 1993-94. Contbr. and reviewer articles to profl. publs.; patentee in field. Grantee Nat. Cancer Inst., 1975-83, Am. Inst. Cancer Rsch., 1987-90, Am. Fedn. Aging Rsch., 1988-89. Mem. AAAS, AAHE, Endocrine Soc., Soc. Devel. Biology, Am. Assn. Cancer Rsch., Soc. Exptl. Biology and Medicine, Sigma Xi. Office: Barnard Coll Office of Provost 3009 Broadway New York NY 10027

BOYLAN, RICHARD JOHN, psychologist, researcher, educator, consultant; b. Hollywood, Calif., Oct. 15, 1939; s. John Alfred and Rowena Margaret (Devine) B.; m. Charnette Marie Blackburn, Oct. 26, 1968 (div. June 1984); children: Christopher J., Jennifer April, Stephanie August; m. Judith Lee Keast, Nov. 21, 1987; stepchildren: Darren Andrew, Matthew Grant. BA, St. John's Coll., 1961; MEd, Fordham U., 1966; MSW, U. Calif., Berkeley, 1971; PhD in Psychology, U. Calif., Davis, 1984. Lic. psychologist, Calif.; lic. clin. social worker, Calif.; lic. marriage, family and child counselor, Calif. Assoc. pastor Cath. Diocese of Fresno, 1965-68; asst. dir. Berkeley (Calif.) Free Ch., 1970-71; psychiat. social worker Marin Mental Health Dept., San Rafael, Calif., 1971-77; dir. Calaveras Mental Health Dept., San Andreas, Calif., 1977-85; prof., coord. Nat. U., Sacramento, 1985-86; instr. Calif. State U., Sacramento, 1985-90, U. Calif., Davis, 1984-88; dir. U.S. Behavioral Health, Sacramento, 1988-89; pvt. practice psychotherapy, Sacramento, 1974—. Author: Extraterrestrial Contact and Human Responses, 1992, Close Extraterrestrial Encounters, 1994. Bd. dirs. Marin Mcpl. Water Dist., 1975-77; cons. Calif. State Legis., Sacramento, 1979-80; chmn. Calaveras County Bd. Edn., Angels Camp, Calif., 1981-84. Recipient Geriatric Medicine Acad. award NIH, 1984, Experiment Station grant USDA, Calif., 1983. Mem. APA, ACA, Am. Assn. for Humanistic Edn. and Devel., Nat. Bd. Hypnotherapy and Med. Anaesthesiology, Calif. Psychol. Assn., Sacramento Valley Psychol. Assn. (past pres.), Sacramento Valley Psychol. Assn. (past pres.), Sacramento Soc. Profl. Psychologists (past pres.), Nat. Resources Def. Coun., Acad. Clin. Close-Encounter Therapists (founder, sec., treas.). Democrat. Office: 2826 O St Sacramento CA 95816-6400

BOYLE, BRIAN JOSEPH, gastroenterologist; b. Phila., Sept. 7, 1946; s. Bernard and Margaret (Meyer) B.; m. Elizabeth Cecelia Smith, June 9, 1973; children: Sarah Elizabeth, Brendan Joseph. BS, St. Joseph's U., Phila., 1968; DO, Phila. Coll. Osteo. Medicine, 1972. Diplomate Am. Bd. Internal Medicine, Gastroenterology. Intern Albany (N.Y.) Med. Ctr., 1972-73; resident internal medicine USPHS Hosp., S.I., N.Y., 1973-76; fellow gastroenterology U. Pa. Hosp., Phila., 1976-78; asst. chief medicine, dep. chief gastroenterology dept. USPHS Hosp., S.I., 1978-81; gastroenterologist Red Bank (N.J.) Med. Ctr., 1981—, Bayshore Med. Ctr., Holmdel, N.J., 1981—; asst. clin. prof. U. Medicine and Dentistry N.J. Office: Red Bank Med Ctr 365 Broad St Red Bank NJ 07701

BOYLE, DOROTHY ANN, medical and surgical nurse; b. Long Island, N.Y., Apr. 10, 1936; d. Frank and Emma Nutz; m. Francis Boyle, Sept. 16, 1961; children: Therese A., Peggy Ann. Diploma, Flushing Hosp. Sch. Nursing, 1957; BS in Hosp. Adminstrn., St Joseph's Coll., Patchoque, N.Y., 1992. RN, N.Y. Staff nurse John T. Mather Hosp., Port Jeff, N.Y.; head nurse operating room John T. Mather Hosp., Port Jeff; infertility nurse specialist L.I. Fertility and Endocrinology, 1993—. Mem. Assn. Operating Room Nurses (cert. ORN, del. to congress, 1985-91, pres. Suffolk County chpt. 1989-91). Home: 664 Route 25A Miller Place NY 11764-2628

BOYLE, JOSEPH, dermatologist, educator; b. Scotland, Apr. 24, 1954; s. Daniel and Mary Boyle; m. Monica Denise Devine, July 4, 1980; children: Marie-Claire, Christopher, Jamie. M.B.Ch.B., Glasgow U., 1977. Registrar dept. dermatology U. Glasgow, 1980-82; sr. registrar Bristol (Eng.) Royal Infirmary, 1982-86; cons. dermatologist Musgrove Park Hosp., Taunton, Eng., 1986—; clin. tutor U. Bristol, 1989—. Fellow Royal Coll. Physicians. Office: Musgrove Park Hosp, Dept Dermatology, Taunton/Somerset NHS Trust, Somerset England

BOYLE, MICHAEL DERMOT, medical educator; b. Belfast, Ireland, Jan. 4, 1949; naturalized citizen, 1990; s. Dermot Patterson and Joan Marjorie (West) B.; m. Carla Eileen Colville, Jan. 27, 1973; children: Kieron, Sarah. BSc in Biochemistry, U. Glasgow, Scotland, 1971; PhD, U. London, 1974. Expert Nat. Cancer Inst., Bethesda, Md., 1976-79, vis. scientist, 1980-81; assoc. prof. Coll. of Medicine U. Fla., Gainesville, 1981-84, prof. Coll. of Medicine, 1985-87; prof. Med. Coll. of Ohio, Toledo, 1988—; founder, pres. Gator Microbiols. Inc., 1986—. Assoc. editor: Molecular and Cellular Biochemistry, 1986-88; mem. editorial bd. Biotechniques, 1986—, Jour. Microbiol. Methods; contbr. over 150 articles to profl. jours. Mem. Am. Assn. Cancer Rsch., Am. Assn. Immunologists, Am. Soc. Microbiology, Sigma Xi (Sr. Rsch. award). Office: Med Coll of Ohio PO Box 10008 Toledo OH 43699

BOYLE, NANCY REYNOLDS, home health agency administrator; b. Rochester, N.H., Dec. 11, 1932; d. Robert Hodgkins and Helen Lee (Estey) Reynolds; R.N., New Eng. Baptist Hosp. Sch. Nursing, 1953; B.A., New Eng. Coll., 1977; m. John Emmanuel Boyle, Dec. 29, 1956. Pvt. duty nurse, Boston, 1953; neurosurg. nurse Lahey Clinic, Boston, 1953-56; staff nurse various hosps., N.H., Ky., 1956-58; staff nurse Dover Dist. Nursing Assn., 1959-62, supervising nurse, 1962-70, exec. dir., 1970-85; exec. dir. Squamscott Home Health, Inc., 1985-95, ret. 1995; dir. Strafford Hospice Care, 1982-89; mem. mgmt. team Wentworth-Douglass Hosp., 1994-95, ret. 1995; dir. S.E. Bank for Savs.; bd. dirs. Great Bay Bankshares, Inc., Constitution Trust Co.; mem. Gov.'s adv. com. Cancer and Chronic Diseases, 1985-95, Diaconate Bd., 1991-95. Home nursing instr. Dover Girl Scouts and Campfire Girls, 1960-70; dir. N.H. Soap Box Derby, 1962-72; mem. City Adv. Com. on Urban Renewal, 1964-70, chmn., 1967; dir. Dover United Way, 1962-74; dir. Dover 350th Anniversary Celebration, 1973; dir. Dover Tomorrow, Inc., 1975-82, mem. adv. com. Dover Adult Edn., 1962-76; bd. dirs. Strafford County unit Am. Cancer Soc., 1980-88, ABC of Dover, 1970—, Cocheco Chpt. ADA, 1985-89, Dover Day Care Learning Ctr., 1995—; mem. Friends of Cocheco Valley Humane Soc, 1988—, World Wildlife Fund, 1990—, Ch. World Svc., 1990—, The Housing Partnership, 1990—, Nat. Wildlife Fedn., 1992—, Dover Ready-to-Learn: Success By Six, 1992—, Nat. Mus. Women Arts, 1995—, N.H. Conf. UCC: Coun. on Mission Interpretation and Stewardship, 1996—. Mem. AAUW, APHA, Nat. Assn. Home Care, Nat., N.H. (dir. 1981-83) Leagues for Nursing, Mass. Diploma Nurses Assn., Cmty. Health Care Assn. N.H. (dir. 1981-85), Bus. and Profl. Women's Club (past pres.), N.H. Hist. Soc., Dover Rotary Club. Club: Dover Quota (sec. 1977-78). Republican. Congregationalist. Home: 4 Bellamy Rd Dover NH 03820-4302

BOYLSTON, ARTHUR WILLIAM, pathologist; b. Indpls., Nov. 16, 1942; arrived in U.K., 1972; s. George Arthur and Marie (Showers) B.; m. Authea Ethel Phelps, July 1, 1978; children: Thomas A., Nicholas J. BA, Yale U., 1964; MD, Harvard U., 1969. Intern Peter Bent Brigham Hosp., Boston, 1969-70; rsch. fellow NIH, Bethesda, Md., 1970-72; sr. registrar St. Mary's Hosp., London, 1972-78, hon. cons., sr. lectr., 1978-86, reader in pathology, 1986-88; prof. pathology Leeds (Eng.) U., 1988—. Contbr. articles to profl. jours. Sr. asst. surgeon USPHS, 1970-72. Grantee Med. Rsch. Coun. U.K., 1972—, Wellcome Trust, 1978—, Brit. Diabetic Assn., 1995—. Fellow Royal Coll. Pathologists; mem. Brit. Soc. for Immunology (meetings sec. 1996—), Pathol. Soc. Office: St James' Hosp, Molecular Medicine Unit, Leeds LS9 7TH, England

BOYNTON, GERALD WAYNE, psychologist; b. Madison, Tenn., Dec. 13, 1937; s. Gerald Willis and Evelyn Clair (Vaughn) B.;m. Marjorie Jane, Jan. 15, 1979; children: Colleen Michele, Rebecca Elizabeth, Andrew Wayne, Katherine Jane, Rachel Evelyn. BA, Columbia Union Coll., 1960; MSSW, U. Tenn., 1962; EdD, U. Ga., 1976; cert. human sexuality, U. Hawaii, 1976; cert. forensic evaluation, U. Va., 1994. Lic. clin. psychologist, Va. Asst. prof. U. Ga., Athens; assoc. prof., asst. dean W.Va. U., Charleston; assoc. prof. U. Houston GSSW; postdoctoral psychology intern U. Houston Counseling and Testing Ctr. Contbr. articles to profl. jours. Mem. APA, Nat. Social Sci. Assn. Home: 6295 Midnight Dr Mechanicsville VA 23111-9471

BOYSE, EDWARD ARTHUR, research physician; b. Worthing, Sussex, Eng., Aug. 11, 1923; came to U.S., 1960; s. Arthur and Dorothy Vera (Mellersh) B. MB, BS, U. London, 1952, MD, 1957. Mem. med. staff various hosps. Eng., 1952-57; researcher Guy's Hosp., London, 1957-60; researcher Sch. Medicine, NYU, 1960-71, adj. prof., 1971—; prof. Cornell Grad. Sch. Med. Sci., N.Y.C., 1969-89; assoc. scientist Meml. Sloan-Kettering Inst., N.Y.C., 1962-64, assoc. mem., 1964-67, mem., 1967-89; Disting. prof. U. Ariz., Tucson, 1989-94; prof. emeritus, 1994—; affiliated scientist Monell Chem. Senses Ctr., Phila. Contbr. articles to profl. jours. Served with RAF, 1941-46. Recipient Tumor Immunology award Cancer Research Inst., N.Y.C., 1975, Isaac Adler award Rockefeller U., Harvard U., 1976. Fellow Royal Soc., Am. Acad. Arts and Sci., Nat. Acad. Sci. Office: Univ Ariz Dept Microbiology Immunology 1501 N Campbell Ave Tucson AZ 85724-0001

BOYTIM, JAMES ALVIN, retired psychology educator; b. Tyrone, Pa., May 19, 1937; s. George Jr. and Nellie (Merritts) B.; m. Joan Lois Frey, Aug. 4, 1961. BS, Ind. U. of Pa., 1959, MEd, 1966; MS in Edn., Temple U., 1965; EdD, Ind. U., 1971. Lic. psychologist; nat. cert. counselor; cert. clin. mental health counselor, sch. counselor, gerontol. counselor. Tchr., math. Carlisle (Pa.) Area Sch. Dist., 1959-70, sch. counselor, 1970-75, counseling psychologist, 1975-80; asst. prof. psychology and edn. Dickinson Coll., Carlisle, 1980-85, asst. prof. psychology, 1985-93; counselor career svcs., 1993-94; v.p. Carlisle Exec. Search, 1994—; pvt. practice counseling psychology, Carlisle, 1971—; cons. Piezo Crystal Co., Carlisle, 1980-92. Contbr. articles to profl. jours. Mem. adv. bd. Program for Edn., Enrichment and Recreation, Carlisle, 1982—; bd. dirs. Meals on Wheels, Carlisle, 1982-85, Carlisle Day Care Ctr., 1981-83; trustee Bosler Free Libr., Carlisle, 1979-81. With U.S. Army, 1960. Recipient Ganoe award for Inspirational Teaching, Dickinson Coll., 1985-86. Fellow Pa. Psychol. Assn.; mem. ACA, APA, Pa. Assn. for Specialists in Group Work (pres. 1986-87, Outstanding Svc. award 1989), Pa. Counseling Assn. (Outstanding Counselor award 1985, Lifetime Achievement award 1992), Pa. Assn. for Adult Devel. and Aging (charter pres. 1989-90), Pa. Mental Health Counselors Assn. (pres. 1982-83, Leadership award 1984), Kiwanis (Legion of Honor award Carlisle club 1990). Republican. Methodist. Home: 160 Glendale St Carlisle PA 17013-2703 Office: Carlisle Exec Search 325 S Hanover St Carlisle PA 17013

BOZALIS, JOHN RUSSELL, physician; b. St. Louis, Sept. 19, 1939; s. George Sauter and Ruth (Russell) B.; m. Sharon Louise Sabo, June 21, 1963; children: John Jr., David L., Diana. BA, U. Okla., 1961, MD, 1965; MS, U. Mich., 1971. Diplomate Am. Bd. Internal Medicine, Am. Bd. Allergy and Immunology. Intern Henry Ford Hosp., Detroit, 1965-66, resident, 1966-68, chief resident, 1968-69; fellow in allergy-immunology U. Mich., Ann Arbor, 1969-71, instr., 1969-71; clin. asst. prof. U. Tex., San Antonio, 1972-73; pvt. practice Okla. Allergy Clinic, Oklahoma City, 1973—; clin. instr. Coll. Medicine, U. Okla., 1973, clin. asst. prof., 1977-83, clin. assoc. prof., 1983-89, clin. prof., 1989—; mem. courtesy staff Mercy Hosp., Bapt. Hosp., Deaconess Hosp., St. Anthony Hosp., Presbyn. Hosp., Children's Hosp., Okla. Tchg. Hosp., S.W. Med. Ctr. Trustee Casady Sch., 1977-85, United Way Okla. City, chmn. profl. divsn. 1983, Okla. Health Scis. Found.; bd. dirs. Infant Ctr., 1983-86, Allied Arts Okla. City, 1984-86, 92, Hosp. Hospitality House, 1983-86; vice chmn. health scis. ctr. U. Okla. Centennial Commn.; bd. trustees McGee Eye Inst., mem. search com. for chmn. dept. ophthalmology and dir., 1991; active Com. of 100, 1991; bd. trustees Okla. City Pub. Schs. Found., 1989—, Okla. Orthopedic and Arthritis Found., Inc., Bone and Joint Hosp., 1993. Maj. USAF, 1971-73. Recipient Regents' Alumni award U. Okla., 1992; named Physician of Yr.-Pvt. Practice, U. Okla. Coll. of Medicine Alumni Assn., 1993. Fellow ACP, Am. Coll. Chest Physicians, Am. Acad. Allergy; mem. AMA, Am. Thoracic Soc., Okla. State Med. Assn. (del. 1992), Okla. Lung Assn., Okla. Thoracic Soc. (pres. 1979), John M. Sheldon Soc., Okla. County Med. Soc. (editor Bull. 1978-83, chmn. orientation com. 1989—, pres. 1996), Osler Soc. (pres. 1984), Okla. City Acad. Medicine, Robert M. Bird Soc., U. Okla. Coll. Medicine Alumni Assn. (chmn. rsch. com., pres. 1983-85), Okla. City C. of C. (bd. dirs. 1988-90). Republican. Episcopal. Office: Okla Allergy Clin Inc PO Box 26827 Oklahoma City OK 73126-0827

BRAASCH, JOHN WILLIAM, surgeon, consultant; b. Rochester, Minn., Dec. 11, 1922; s. William Frederick and Nellie (Stinchfield) B.; m. Nancy Wheeler King, Mar. 21, 1946; children: William Frederick, Elizabeth King, Nancy Kathryn, Peggy Stinchfield. BS, Yale U., 1944; MD, Harvard U., 1946; MS in Physiology, U. Ill., 1948; PhD in Surgery, U. Minn., 1955. Diplomate Am. Bd. Surgery (bd. dirs. 1979-85). Intern St. Luke's Hosp., Chgo., 1946-47; resident in gen. surgery Mayo Clinic, Rochester, Minn., 1950-55; mem. attending staff Mpls. Gen. Hosp., 1955-57, Northwestern Hosp., Mpls., 1955-57; surg. staff New Eng. Bapt. Hosp., Boston, 1957-80, New Eng. Deaconess Hosp., Boston, 1957-80, Lahey Clinic Found., Boston, 1957—; sr. cons. dept. surgery Lahey Clinic, Burlington, Mass., 1983—; asst. clin. prof. surgery Harvard Med. Sch., Boston, 1975—. Author: 2 books, several book chpts.; also numerous articles. Capt. U.S. Army, 1948-50. Recipient Balfour award for rsch. Mayo Clinic Found., Rochester, 1955. Mem. Am. Surg. Assn., Soc. for Surgery Alimentary Tract (v.p. 1987-88), Internat. Soc. Surgery, So. Surg. Soc., New Eng. Surg. Soc. (pres. 1984-85), Boston Surg. Soc. (pres. 1982), Surgeons Travel Club. Republican. Office: Lahey Clinic Med Ctr 41 Mall Rd Burlington MA 01805-0001

BRABSON, MAX LAFAYETTE, health care executive; b. Otto, N.C., Dec. 9, 1926; s. John Miller and Mary Elizabeth (McDowell) B.; m. Kathryn Louise Rice, Sept. 22, 1951; children—Mary Kathryn, Max L. BS, U. Ga., 1950; MHA, Washington U., St. Louis, 1958. Adminstr., Middle Ga. Hosp., Macon, 1965-68, Americus-Sumter Co. Hosp., (Ga.), 1968-69; v.p. Charter Med. Corp., Macon, 1969-76; pres. Health Care Mgmt. Co., Columbus, Ga., 1976-77; pres., CEO Med. Ctr., Columbus, 1977-86; chmn., CEO Columbus Regional Healthcare System Inc., 1986-89; chmn., bd. dirs. Marion Community Hosp., Inc., 1987-92, Northside Psychiat. Svcs., Inc., Columbus, 1988-92; interim adminstr. Phoenix Med. Park Hosp., Phoenix City, Ala., 1993—; bd. dirs. Fedn. Am. Hosps., Inc., 1970-75, The Med. Ctr., Inc., Columbus, 1986-92, Columbus Ambulatory Healthcare Svcs., Inc., 1986-92, Columbus Regional Healthcare System, Inc., 1989-94; mem. hosp. adminstrs. devel. program Cornell U., Ithaca, N.Y., 1961. Mem. adv. bd. dirs. Ret. Sr. Vol. Program, Columbus, 1977-81; bd. dirs. United Way, Inc., Columbus, 1979-82, Blue Cross Blue Shield Ga.-Columbus, 1978-83. Lt. col. AUS, 1944-71, ret.; PTO. Fellow Am. Coll. Healthcare Execs. (life); mem. Ga. Hosp. Assn. (chmn. council on fin. Atlanta, 1982-83, chmn. bd. trustees 1987), Columbus C. of C. (bd. dirs. 1979-81), Harris County C. of C. (bd. dirs. 1990-92), Exec. of Columbus Club (pres. 1982-83), Kiwanis (Columbus). Recipient Entrepreneur of Yr. award Columbus, 1990. Office: 2854 Techwood Dr Columbus GA 31906-1260

BRABSTON, ROBERT JAMES, physician; b. New Brunswick, N.J., Apr. 9, 1938; s. James Henry and Celia (Pawlowski) B.; m. Louise Alice L'Herttier, Jan. 22, 1966; children: Robert, James, Timothy, Krista. BA, Seton Hall U., 1960; MD, N.J. Coll. Medicine, 1964. Diplomate Am. Bd. Internal Medicine, Am. Bd. Internal Medicine-Geriatrics. Intern & resident Jersey City (N.J.) Med. Ctr., 1964-65; resident Newark City Hosp., 1965-68; pvt. med. practice Med. Assocs. of North Jersey, P.A., Pompton Lakes, N.J., 1970—; med. dir. North Jersey Convalescent Ctr., Wayne, N.J., 1986—, Lakeland Health Care Ctr., Haskel, N.J., 1993—. Maj. U.S. Army Med. Corps, 1968-70. Mem. AMA, ACP, Med. Soc. N.J., Passaic County Med. Soc. Republican. Roman Catholic. Office: Med Assocs North Jersey PA 525 Wanaque Ave Pompton Lakes NJ 07442

BRACEWELL, RONALD NEWBOLD, electrical engineering educator; b. Sydney, Australia, July 22, 1921; s. Cecil Charles and Valerie Zilla (McGowan) B.; m. Helen Mary Lester Elliott; children: Catherine Wendy, Mark Cecil. BS in Math. and Physics, U. Sydney, 1941, B in Engring., 1943, M. in Engring. with 1st class honors, 1948; PhD, Cambridge (Eng.) U., 1951. Sr. rsch. officer Radiophysics Lab., Commonwealth Sci. and Indsl. Rsch. Orgn., Sydney, 1949-54; vis. asst. prof. radio astronomy U. Calif., Berkeley, 1954-55; mem. elec. engring. faculty Stanford U., 1955—, Lewis M. Terman prof. and fellow in elec. engring., 1974-79, now Terman prof. emeritus elec. engring.; Pollock Meml. lectr. U. Sydney, 1978; Tektronix Disting. Visitor, summer 1981; Christensen fellow St. Catherine's Coll., Oxford, autumn 1987; sr. vis. fellow Inst. Astronomy, Cambridge U., autumn 1988; Bunyan lectr. Stanford U., 1996; mem. adv. panels NSF, Naval Rsch. Lab., Office Naval Rsch., NAS, Nat. Radio Astronomy Obs., Jet Propulsion Lab. Adv. Group on Radio Experiments in Space, Advanced Rsch. Projects Agy. Author: The Fourier Transform and Its Applications, 1965, rev. edit., 1986, The Galactic Club: Intelligent Life in Outer Space, 1974, The Hartley Transform, 1986, Two-Dimension Imaging, 1995; co-author: Radio Astronomy, 1955; translator: Radio Astronomy (J.L. Steinberg and J. Lequeux); editor: Paris Symposium on Radio Astronomy, 1959; former mem. editl. bd. Internat. Jour. Imaging Sys. and Tech., Planetary and Space Sci., Proceedings of the Astron. Soc. Pacific, Cosmic Search, Jour. Computer Assisted Tomography; mem. bd. ann. rev. Astronomy and Astrophysics, 1961-68; contbr. articles and revs. to jours., chpts. to books; patentee in field. Recipient Duddell Premium, Instn. Elec. Engrs., London, 1952, Inaugural Alumni award Sydney U., 1992; Fulbright travel grantee, 1954, William Gurling Watson traveling fellow, 1978, 86. Fellow IEEE (life, Heinrich Hertz Gold medal 1994), AAAS, Royal Astron. Soc., Astron. Soc. Australia; mem. Inst. Medicine of NAS (fgn. assoc.), Astron. Soc. Pacific (life), Am. Astron. Soc. (past councilor), Internat. Astron. Union, Internat. Sci. Radion Union, Internat. Acad. Astronautics. Home: 836 Santa Fe Ave Stanford CA 94305-1023 Office: Stanford U 329A Durand Bldg Stanford CA 94305

BRACHMAN, PHILIP SIGMUND, public health educator, retired federal agency administrator; b. Milw., July 28, 1927; s. Sigmund and Helen (Mahler) B.; m. Susan Mary Ettenheim, June 15, 1950; children: Philip Sigmund, David Milton, Laura Helen, Sarah Susan. BS, U. Wis., 1950, MD, 1953. Intern U. Ill., Chgo., 1953-54; EIS officer ctrs. for disease control USPHS Wistar Inst., Phila., 1954-56, chief anthrax investigations unit, 1956-58; resident U. Pa., 1958-60; chief bacterial diseases br. CDC, USPHS, Atlanta, 1960-70, dep. dir. epidemiology program, 1967-70, dir. Bur. Epidemiology, 1970-81, dir. epidemiology program office, 1981-82, dir. Global Epidemic Intelligence Svc. program, 1982-86; prof. div. pub. health Emory U., Atlanta, 1986-90, prof. Sch. Pub. Health, 1990—; bd. dirs. Pub. Health Gen. Preventive Medicine. With USN, 1945-46. Mem. Am. Pub. Health Assn., Internat. Epidemiol. Assn., Am. Epidemiol. Soc., Infectious Diseases Soc., Soc. Epidemiol. Rsch., Assn. Practitioners in Infection Control, Soc. Hosp. Epidemiology. Home: 1111 Clifton Rd NE Atlanta GA 30307 Office: Emory U Rollins Sch Public Health 1518 Clifton Rd NE 7th Flr Atlanta GA 30322

BRACIALE, VIVIAN LAM, immunologist; b. N.Y.C., June 5, 1948; d. Wing Ching and Wai Ching (Li) Lam; m. Thomas J. Braciale Jr., Aug. 5, 1972; children: Kara, Michael Stephen, Laura. A.B., Cornell U., 1969; Ph.D., U. Pa., 1973. Postdoctoral fellow U. Pa., Phila., 1974-75, Washington U. Med. Sch., St. Louis, 1975-76, rsch. instr. pathology, 1978-83, rsch. asst. prof. pathology, 1983-89, asst. prof. pathology, 1989-91; assoc. prof. microbiology Beirne Carter Ctr. Immunology Rsch. U. Va. Health Scis. Ctr., Charlottesville, 1991—; mem. clin. scis. study sect. NIH, 1985-89, reviewers res., 1989-93. Assoc. editor Jour. of Immunology, 1989-94, sect. editor 1995—; contbr. articles in immunology to profl. jours. N.Y. State Regent scholar; NIH Rsch. Svc. awardee; vis. fellow Australian Nat. U., Canberra, 1976-78. Mem. Am. Assn. Immunologists, AAAS. Lutheran. Office: U Va Beirne Carter Ctr HSC Box MR4 4012 Charlottesville VA 22908

BRACKEN, KATHLEEN ANN, nurse; b. Chgo., Mar. 14, 1947; d. Thomas James and Catherine Anastasia (Cowal) B.; RN, CNA, Little Company of Mary Hosp., Evergreen Park, Ill., 1968; BSN, Lewis U., 1984, MBA, 1989. Mem. staff Little Company of Mary Hosp., Evergreen Park, 1968-69, 71-73, supr. ICUs, 1976-79, dir. ICUs, 1979-91; v.p. patient care svcs. South Chgo. Community Hosp., 1991-93; staff nurse coronary care unit Little Co. of Mary Hosp., Torrence, Calif., 1969-70; staff nurse Chgo. Lying-In Clinic, U. Chgo., 1970-71; nurse mgr. VA Westside Med. Ctr., Chgo., 1994—; bd. dirs., chmn. nursing cardiovascular com. South Cook Heart Assn., 1977-83, recipient Meritorious Service award, 1979, 81, 82, 83, 84, 85, 86. Mem. NAFE, Chgo. Heart Assn., Assn. Critical Care Nurses (pres. Southside Chgo., Area chpt. 1983-84, rec. sec. 1984-85), Am. Heart Assn. (cardiovascular nursing coun., Ill. Orgn. Nursing Execs., Brain Injury Assn. Ill., Inc. (facilitator family support group), Chgo. Healthcare Exec. Forum, Delta Epsilon Sigma, Sigma Theta Tau. Home: 10321 S Campbell Ave Chicago IL 60655-1016 Office: VA Westside Med Ctr 820 S Damen Ave Chicago IL 60612-3728

BRACKETT, BENJAMIN GAYLORD, physiology and pharmacology educator; b. Athens, Ga., Nov. 18, 1938; s. Ernest Marshall and Julia Claire (Cook) B.; m. Ann Thornton Crawford, Aug. 22, 1959; children: Laura Ellen, Jeffrey Crawford, David Gregory. DVM cum laude, U. Ga., 1962, PhD in Biochemistry, 1966; MA (hon.), U. Pa., 1971. Diplomate Am. Coll. Theriogenologists. Postdoctoral fellow dept. biochemistry U. Ga., Athens, 1962-66, prof. Coll. Vet. Med., 1983—, head dept. physiology/pharmacology, 1983-95; from assoc. to prof. dept. ob.-gyn. Sch. Medicine, U. Pa., Phila., 1966-74; prof. of animal reproduction Sch. Vet. Medicine U. Pa., Phila., 1974-83; also, prof. of rsch. ob.-gyn. Sch. Medicine; cons. on impacts of applied genetics Office of Tech. Assessment, U.S. Congress, 1979-80, to contraceptive R & D program Ea. Va. Sch. Medicine, Norfolk, 1986-91; pres., chmn. bd. dirs. Reproductive Biol. Assocs., Inc., Atlanta, 1983-88. Editor: New Technologies in Animal Breeding, 1981; contbr. over 200 articles to profl. publs. Grantee, NIH, USDA, others; Recipient Rsch. Career Devel. award USPHS/NIH, 1971-76. Mem. Internat. Embryo Transfer Soc. (pres. 1984-85), Am. Fertility Soc., Am. Soc. Andrology, Soc. for Study of Fertility, Soc. for Study of Reproduction (sec. 1982-86), Am. Vet. Med. Assn., Ga. Vet. Med. Assn., Am. Physiol. Soc., Four Chaplains Legion of Honor. Methodist. Office: U Ga Coll Vet Medicine Dept Physiol And Pharm Athens GA 30602

BRACKETT, EDWARD BOONE, III, orthopedic surgeon; b. Fort Worth, Jan. 5, 1936; s. Edward Boone and Bessie Lee (Hudgins) B.; student Tex. Tech. Coll., 1957; MD, Baylor U., 1961; JD, Ill. Inst. Tech., 1993; Bar: Ill. 1993; m. Jean Elliott, July 11, 1959; children: Bess E., Geoffrey, Elliott Mencken, Edward Boone IV, Anneke Gail; m. Andrea Inman, 1992; 1 child, Amelia. Intern, Cook County Hosp., Chgo., 1961-62; resident Northwestern U., Chgo., 1962-66; practice medicine specializing in orthopedic surgery, Oak Park, Ill., 1966—, Westgate Orthopaedics Ltd., Oak Park, 1969—; mem. staff Loyola U., Oak Park Hosp., Loretto Hosp., Hinsdale Hosp., Gottlieb Hosp., Westlake Hosp., Rush Med. Sch.; chmn. dept. orthopedics West Suburban Hosp., pres. med. staff, 1982-84 ; clin. assoc. prof. orthopedics Loyola U.; chmn. bd. Chgo. Loop Mediclinic, 1973-75; cons. orthopedic surgery City Svc. Oil Co., 1970. Guarantor, Lyric Opera Chgo., 1971-84; guest condr. Chgo. Symphony Orch., 1979 gov. mem. 1992, Chgo. Chamber Orch., 1980; trustee Music of the Baroque; nat. patron Met. Opera Co., N.Y.C.; mem. humanities adv. council Triton Coll., 1983-84; charter mem. vis. com. Northwestern U. Sch. Music, 1982—; chmn. Friends of WFMT, Inc. Served as lt. comdr. USNR, 1967-69; Vietnam. Recipient Outstanding Tchr. award Dept. Orthopedic Surgery, West Suburban Hosp., 1978, 79. Diplomate Am. Bd. Orthopedic Surgery, Am. Bd. Neurol. Orthopedic Surgeons. Fellow A.C.S., Am. Acad. Orthopedic Surgeons, Inst. of Medicine of Chgo., Am. Acad. Neurol. and Orthopedic Surgeons, Am. Assn. for Hand Surgery, Internat. Coll. Surgeons; mem. Am. Trauma Soc. (founder), Royal Soc. Medicine, Ill. Orthopedic Soc., Chgo. Orthopedic Soc., AMA, Chgo. Med. Soc. (alt. councilor, chmn. ethical rels. com., mem. book rev. panel), Clin. Orthopedic Soc. (chmn. membership com., libr. historian, 1994), Internat. Platform Assn., Civil War Round Table, Friends Chgo. Symphony Orch. (governing mem.), Chgo. Chamber Orch. Assn. (dir.v.p.), Symphonia Musicale (dir.), Sigma Alpha Epsilon, Phi Eta Sigma, Phi Chi, Alpha Epsilon Delta, Phi Alpha Delta. Cons. orthopedic editor Jour. Indsl. Medicine, 1966-67; mem. editl. bd. Jour. Clin. Orthopedics. Cert. flight instr. single and multi engine land, single engine sea and airline transport pilot, designated med. examiner, FAA. Home: 25333 W State Rte 60 Grayslake IL 60030-9542 Office: 1125 Westgate St Oak Park IL 60301-1007

BRADA, DONALD ROBERT, psychiatrist; b. Hutchinson, Kans., Oct. 11, 1939; s. Joseph Duane and Mary Elizabeth (Whitebread) B.; m. Carolyn Starr Cromb, Aug. 19, 1961; children: Donald Robert Jr., Stephen Andrew. AB, U. Kans., 1961, MD, 1965. Diplomate Am. Bd. Psychiatry and Neurology; Lic. Kans. State Bd. Healing Arts. Resident in psychiatry U. Kans., Kansas City, Kans., 1972; pvt. practice Hutchinson, 1976-77; med. dir., exec. dir. Horizons Mental Health Ctr., Hutchinson, 1977-87; med. dir. psychiatry St. Francis Regional Med. Ctr., Wichita, Kans., 1987—; bd. dirs. Kans. Found. Med. Care, Topeka, Wichita Preferred Providers Assn., Pschiat. Rsch. Inst., Wichita, 1989—; mem. Govs. Mental Health Svcs. Planning Coun., 1988-94. Contbr. articles to profl. jours. Elder First Presbyn. Ch., Hutchinson, 1984-86. Col. USAF, 1964-76. Fellow Am. Psychiat. Assn.; mem. Kans. Psychiat. Soc. (pres. 1988-90), Kans. Med. Soc. (treas. 1987-90, 2d v.p. 1991-92, 1st v.p. 1992-93, pres.-elect 1993-94, pres. 1994-95), Sedgwick County Psychiat. Assn. (chmn. 1990-92). Republican. Home: 52 Mission Rd Wichita KS 67207-1036 Office: St Francis Regional Med Ctr 1100 N Saint Francis St Ste 400 Wichita KS 67214-2878

BRADBURY, EILEEN THERESA, psychologist; b. London, Oct. 31, 1948; d. Patrick Joseph and Catherine Mary (O'Conner) Harnett; m. Stephen William Bradbury, July 31, 1971 (div. 1996); 2 children. B Social Sci., Birmingham (Eng.) U., 1970; PhD, Leeds (Eng.) U., 1995. Psychologist STUH, Leeds, 1988-93, SMHT, Manchester, Eng., 1993—; lectr. Manchester U., 1993—. Author: Counselling People with Disfigureuemtn, 1996; editor: Visibly Different, 1996; contbr. articles to profl. publs. Yorkshire Region grantee, 1990, 91; recipient Huddart medal, 1996. Mem. Brit. Psychol. Soc., Brit. Craniofacial Soc., Brit. and European Hand Soc. Office: Withington Hosp, Dept Plastic Surgery, Manchester M20 8LR, England

BRADDOCK, MARILYN EUGENIA, maxillofacial prosthodontist; b. Washington, Apr. 25, 1955; d. Ernest Lee and Rita Hazel Braddock. BS, Marquette U., 1977; DDS, Meharry Med. Coll., 1982; prosthodontic cert., U. N.C., 1992, MS, 1993. Commd. lt. USN, 1982, advanced through grades to comdr., 1995; hosp. dentistry resident Cook County Hosp., Chgo., 1982-83; gen. dentist USN Dental Corps., Washington, 1984-86, USN Portsmouth (Va.) Naval Hosp., 1983-84; prosthodontics instr. Howard U. Coll. Dentistry, Washington, 1986-89; pvt. practice Dr. A. Epstein & Assocs., P.C., Columbia, Md., 1986-89; grad. tchg. asst., resident U. N.C. Grad. Studies, Chapel Hill, 1989-92; grad. rschr. U. N.C. Sch. of Dentistry, Chapel Hill, 1990-92; asst. prof. Meharry Med. Coll., Nashville, 1992-95; prosthodontist USS John F. Kennedy, 1995—; cons. Head Start Program, Prince Georges County, Md., 1986-88. Troop leader Girl Scouts Am., Crofton, Md., 1985-89; walker Ann. March of Dimes Walk-A-Thon, 1984-94; food preparer, server So-Others-Might-Eat, Washington and Nashville, 1984—. Fellowship Patricia Roberts Harris Found., 1990; recipient Nat. Sci. award NIH, 1990. Mem. ADA, Am. Coll. of Prosthodontists, Fed. Dental Svcs., Omicron

Kappa Upsilon, Delta Sigma Theta. Office: USS John F Kennedy (CV-67) Dental Dept FPO AA 34095-2800

BRADDOM, RANDALL L., physician, medical educator; b. Monarch, Va., Oct. 29, 1942; s. Audy Lee and Ruth Janet Braddom; m. Carolyn Lentz; children: Eric C., Steven R., Karen L. BA, DePauw U., 1964; MD, Ohio State U., 1968, MS, 1971. Diplomate Am. Bd. Electrodiagnostic Medicine, Am. Bd. Phys. Medicine and Rehab. Rotating intern Mt. Carmel Hosp., Columbus, Ohio, 1968-69; resident in phys. medicine and rehab. Ohio State Univ. Hosps., Columbus, 1969-72; physiatrist, electromyographer Rancocas Valley Hosp., Willingboro, N.J., 1972-74, Phila. Naval Med. Ctr., 1972-74; asst. prof. phys. medicine and rehab. U. Cin., 1974-75, assoc. prof., dir. phys. medicine and rehab., 1975-81; med. dir. phys. med. and rehab. St. Francis-St. George Hosp., Cin., 1987-89, Providence Hosp., Cin., 1982-89; assoc. prof., dep. chmn. rehab. medicine Temple U., Phila., 1989-91; chmn. rehab. medicine Albert Einstein Hosp., Phila., 1989-91; v.p. med. affairs Moss Rehab. Hosp., Phila., 1989-91; practitioner Rehab. Assocs., Indpls., 1991—; med. dir. Hook Rehab. Ctr., Indpls., 1991—; prof., chmn. phys. medicine and rehab. Ind. U. Sch. Medicine, Indpls., 1991—; cons. physiatrist Albert Einstein Med. Ctr. N., Phila., 1973; clin. instr. rehab. medicine Thomas Jefferson Coll. Med., Phila., 1972-74; assoc. in medicine Jewish Hosp., Cin., 1974-89; cons. phys. medicine and rehab. VA Hosp., Cin., 1975-81; dir. phys. med. and rehab. U. Hosps., U. Cin., 1975-81; assoc. clin. prof. phys. med. Ohio State U., Columbus, 1984—; clin. assoc. prof. phys. medicine and rehab. U. Cin., Coll. Medicine, 1982-89; cons. St. Francis Hosp., Indpls., 1991—; phys. med. and rehab. svc. chief Wishard Meml. Hosp., Indpls., 1991—; dir. phys. medicine and rehab. svc. Richard Roudebush VA Hosp., Indpls., 1991—; presenter Internat. Rehab. Fedn., Montreal, 1968, U. Wash., Seattle, 1972, Thomas Jefferson U. Med. Coll., Phila., 1974, 75, 76, Santa Clara Valley Med. Ctr., San Jose, Calif., 1976, Ohio State U., 1976, Nat. Paraplegia Found., 1977, Am. Acad. Orthopaedic Surgery, New Orleans, 1977, Jewish Hosp., Cin., 1977, Rehab. Inst. Chgo., 1982, 84, Am. Assn. Electromyography and Electrodiagnosis, Toronto, 1984, Las Vegas, 1985, Pitts., 1985, Ky. Family Practice Assn. Symposium, Covington, 1984, Am. Heart Assn., Cin., 1984, Ohio State U. Coll. Medicine, Salt Fork, 1985, Am. Acad. Phys. Medicine and Rehab., Kansas City, 1985, Nat. Spinal Cord Injury Assn., Cin., 1985, Am. Rehab. Edn. Network, Pitts., 1985; presenter in field; vis. prof. Dept. Phys. Medicine and Rehab. U. Ark., 1992, U. Ky. Dept Phys. Medicine and Rehab., 1992, Dept. Internal Medicine Dvsn. Phys. Medicine & Rehab. La. State U. Sch. Medicine, New Orleans, La., 1994, Baylor Coll. Medicine Dept. Physical Medicine & Rehab., 1994, N.J. Sch. Medicine and Dentistry Dept. P.M. & R., lectr. in field; Licht lectr. Dept. Phys. Medicine & Rehab. U. Minn., 1993. Author: (with others) Physical Medicine & Rehabilitation Review, 1980; editor: Sports Medicine and Rehabilitation: A Sport-Scientific Approach, 1994; contbr. articles to profl. jours. Founder, med. dir. ECCO Family Health Ctr., Inc., Columbus, 1970-72; bd. dirs. Nat. Paraplegia Found., 1975-80; med. adviser Easter Seals Soc. Southwestern Ohio, 1980-82; asst. scoutmaster Troop 291, Boy Scouts Am., 1982-84; chmn. Citizens for Our Schs. Tax Levy Campaign, Forest Hills Sch. Dist., Cin., 1985; trustee Total Living Concepts, Inc., Cin., 1977-85, Disability Svcs. Group, Inc., Cin., 1985-89; bd. examiners The Henry B. Betts award, 1991—. Lt. comdr. USNR, 1972-74. Recipient Kiwanis Club Citizenship award, Dayton, 1960, Rsch. award Am. Paralyzed Vets. Assn., 1968, Am. Therapeutic Soc., 1968, Landacre Soc. award Ohio State U., 1978, Sidney Licht Lectureship Ohio State U., 1985, Alumni Achievement award Ohio State U., 1993, Sidney Licht Lectureship U. Minn., 1993, Randy Braddom award U. Cin. Coll. Medicine, 1989; named Man of Yr. Columbus Citizen-Jour., 1970, Landerwerlen award Muscular Dystrophy Found. Ind., 1m. Am. Coll. Phys. Execs., Indpls. Med. Soc., Ind. Soc. Phys. Med. and Rehab., Nat. Stroke Assn., Am. Kinesiotherapy Assn. (mem. adv. bd. 1993—), Am. Acad. Phys. Med. and Rehab. (med. edn. com. 1983-86, membership recruitment group 1987, career brochure devel. group 1987, joint annual meeting planning subcom. 1987-88, chairperson continuing med. edn. subcom. 1982-86, sci. program com. 1982-86, mktg. and comms. com. 1987—, chairperson med. edn. com. 1986-88, sec. bd. govs. 1988-90, third-mem.-at-large 1990-91, 2nd mem.-at-large 1991-92, 1st mem.-at-large 1992-93, chair awards com. 1992-93, v.p. 1994-95, fin. com. 1994-95, chair annual meeting task force 1994-95, pres. elect 1994-95), Am. Assn. Electrodiagnostic Medicine (com. on edn. 1974-76, exam. com. 1975-76, liaision to assn. of acad. physiatrists 1988, chairperson courses com. 1986-89, pres.-elect 1989-90, bd. dirs. 1989—, pres. 1990-91, immediate past pres.-chairperson long-range planning com. 1991-92, chmn. long range planning com. 1991-92, alt. del. AMA House of Dels. 1993-95, nominating com. 1993-94, chairperson 1994-95), Am. Congress of Rehab. Medicine, Am. Assn. Electrodiagnostic Medicine, Assn. Acad. Physiatrists, Ohio State Med. Alumni Assn., AMA, Am. Bd. Electrodiagnostic Medicine (bd. dirs. 1994, long-range planning com. 1994), Am. Kinesiotherapy Assn. (adv. bd. 1993—), Cin. Soc. of Phys. Medicine and Rehab. (pres., founder 1987-88), Internat. Med. Med. Assn. (U.S. counselor 1986-95). Office: Rehab Assocs 1400 N Ritter #351 Indianapolis IN 46219

BRADEMAS, MARY ELLEN, dermatologist; b. Detroit, Feb. 14, 1937. BA hons., Oakland U., 1975; MD, Georgetown U., 1979. Diplomate Am. Bd. Dermatology; lic. N.Y. Intern Providence Hosp., Washington, 1979-80; resident The Johns Hopkins Hosp., Balt., 1980-81, NYU Med. Ctr., N.Y.C., 1981-83; asst. attending physician NYU Med. Ctr. dept. dermatology; clin. asst. prof. of dermatology NYU Med. Ctr.; chief dermatology St. Vincent's Hosp., N.Y., 1985-93. Contbr. articles to profl. jours. lectr. Peking Med. Coll., 1985. Office: 11 Fifth Ave New York NY 10003-4342

BRADFORD, DAVID S., surgeon; b. Charlotte, N.C., Oct. 15, 1936; m. Helen Gray MacKay; children: David Mackay, Jennifer Sutherland, Tyler Speir. B.A., Davidson Coll., 1958; M.D., U. Pa., 1962. Diplomate: Am. Bd. Orthopaedic Surgeons. Intern in surgery Columbia-Presbyn. Med. Center, N.Y.C., 1962-63; resident in gen. surgery Columbia-Presbyn. Med. Center, 1965-66; resident in orthopaedic surgery N.Y. Orthopaedic Hosp., Columbia-Presbyn. Med. Center, N.Y.C., 1966-68; jr. Annie C. Kane fellow orthopaedic surgery Columbia-Presbyn. Med. Center, 1968-69; research trainee orthopaedics Nat. Inst. Arthritis and Metabolic Diseases, 1969-70; prof. orthopaedic surgery U. Minn. Hosps., Mpls.; prof. orthopaedic surgery Fairview Hosp., Twin Cities Scoliosis Center, Mpls.; mem. cons. staff Children's Health Center, Mpls. Mem. editorial bd.: Minn. Medicine; cons; editorial bd.: Jour. Bone and Joint Surgery; bd. editors: Spine; contbr. articles to profl. jours. Trustee Mpls. Soc. Fine Arts; reviewer grant and fellowship com. Orthopaedic Research and Edn. Found. Mem. Internat. Soc. Orthopaedic Surgery and Traumatology, Am. Acad. Orthopaedic Surgeons (dir.), A.C.S., AMA, Am. Orthopaedic Assn., Am. Spinal Injury Assn., Assn. Bone and Joint Surgeons (treas.), Orthopaedic Research Soc., Scoliosis Research Soc. (dir.), Frank E. Stinchfield Club, Pan-Pacific Surg. Assn., Minn. Orthopaedic Soc., Minn. Med. Soc., Western Trauma Assn., Hennepin County Med. Soc., Twin City Orthopaedic Soc. Office: U of Calif San Francisco Sch of Medicine 513 Parnassus Ave San Francisco CA 94122-2722

BRADFORD, JANE ELIZABETH, hospital administrator; b. Hong Kong, Apr. 26, 1958; d. Ian Halsey and Frances Sylvia (Kosta) B. Student, U. Calif., Davis, 1975-78; BS in Nursing with honors, U. Calif., San Francisco, 1980. Clin. RN III gen. surgery U. Calif. Med. Ctr., San Francisco, 1980-84; head nurse gen. medicine San Francisco Gen. Hosp., head nurse oncology infusion ctr., head nurse, utilization rev. coord./case mgmt. Author: (pamphlet) Enteral Feeding; editorial adv. bd. Williams and Wilkins Pubs. Editorial. Active San Francisco Symphony Vol. Coun., San Francisco Soc. Prevention Cruelty to Animals Jr. Bd., Edgewood Children's Home Aux., Jr. League San Francisco, Stern Grove Festival Assn., Susan Komen Found. for Breast Cancer Rsch.; fundraiser Salvation Army, Am. Diabetes Assn., St. Luke's Hosp. Jr. Aux. Recipient County Innovator award Calif. Assn. Pub. Hosps. Mem. San Francisco Nurse Mgrs. Network, U. Calif. Hosp. and Clinics Aux., U. Calif.-San Francisco Alumni Assn. Home: 123 Locust St San Francisco CA 94118-1813

BRADFORD, LOUISE MATHILDE, social services administrator; b. Alexandria, La., Aug. 3, 1925; d. Henry Aaron and Ruby (Pearson) B. BS, La. Poly. Inst., 1945; cert. in social work, La. State U., 1949; MS, Columbia U., 1953; postgrad., Tulane U., 1962, 64, La. State U., 1967; cert., U. Pa., 1966. Diplomate Am. Bd. Clin. Social Work; cert. social worker Acad. Cert. Social Workers. With La. Dept. Pub. Welfare, Alexandria, 1945-78; welfare caseworker La. Dept. Pub. Welfare, Alexandria, La., 1950-53; children's caseworker La. Dept. Pub. Welfare, Alexandria, 1957-59, child welfare cons., 1959-73, social svcs. cons., 1973-78, state cons. day care, 1963-66; dir. social svcs. St. Mary's Tng. Sch., Alexandria, 1978—; del. Nat. Day Care Conf., Washington, 1964; mem. early childhood edn. com. So. States Work Conf., Daytona Beach, Fla., 1968; mem. La. adv. com. 1970 White House Conf. on Children, also del.; mem. So. region planning com. Child Welfare League Am., 1970-73; mem. profl. adv. com. Cenla chpt. Parents Without Partners, 1970-95; adj. asst. prof. sociology La. Coll. Pineville, 1969-85; lectr. Kindergarten Workshop, 1970-72; mem. La. 4-C Steering Com.; social svcs. cons. La. Spl. Edn. Ctr., Alexandria, 1980-86; del. Internat. Conf. on Social Welfare, Nairobi, 1974, Jerusalem, 1978, Hong Kong, 1980, Brighton, 1982, Montreal, 1984. Bd. dirs. Cenla Cmty. Action Com., Alexandria, 1966-68; mem. kindergarten bd. Meth. Ch., 1967-87, ofel. bd., 1974-75, 77-81, 83-85, 96—). Recipient Social Worker of Yr. award Alexandria br. NASW La. Conf. Social Welfare, 1984, Hilda C. Simon award, 1987, George Freeman award, 1987. Mem. NASW, DAR, Acad. Cert. Social Workers, La. Bd. Cert. Social Workers, So. La. Assn. Children Under Six, La. Conf. Social Welfare (George Freeman award 1987, Hilda C. Simon award 1987), Internat. Coun. on Social Welfare, Am. Pub. Welfare Assn. (S.W. region planning com. 1965), Am. Assn. on Mental Retardation (La. social work chair 1989-94), DAR, Ctrl. La. Pre-Sch. Assn. (dir. 1967-70), Rapides Golf and Country Club. Home: 5807 Joyce St Alexandria LA 71302-2510 Office: PO Box 7768 Alexandria LA 71306-0768

BRADFORD, REAGAN HOWARD, JR., ophthalmology educator; b. Lawton, Okla., July 31, 1954; s. Reagan Howard Sr. and Conita Ann (Hargraves) B.; m. Cynthia Ann McGough, Apr. 22, 1988. BS, U. Okla., 1976; MD, U. Okla., Oklahoma City, 1980. Diplomate Am. Bd. Ophthalmology. Intern Bapt. Med. Ctr., Oklahoma City, 1980-81; resident Dean A. McGee Eye Inst. U. Okla., 1981-84; fellow in vitreo retina Bascom Palmer Eye Inst. U. Miami, Fla., 1984-85; assoc. clinical prof. Dean A. McGee Eye Inst., U. Okla., Oklahoma City, 1985—. Author: (with others) Basics of Neurophthalmology; contbr. articles to profl. jours. Fellow Am. Acad. Ophthalmology; mem. Okla. County Med. Soc., Okla. State Med. Assn., AMA, Okla. State Acad. Ophthalmology. Republican. Baptist. Office: Dean A McGee Eye Inst 608 Stanton L Young Blvd Oklahoma City OK 73104-5014

BRADHAM, DOUGLAS DONALDSON, health services researcher, educator; b. Roanoke, Va., June 20, 1950; s. Ingram Donaldson and Estelle Elizabeth (Huff) B.; m. Renee Lavern Ferree, June 5, 1971; (div. Aug. 1987); children—Douglas Page, Stefan Ryan. A.B., U. N.C., 1972, M.P.H., 1975, M.A. in Econs., 1982, Dr.P.H., 1981. With Office of Chief Med. Examiner, State Bd. Health, Chapel Hill, N.C., 1972-75; assoc. dir. Agassiz Health Systems, East Grand Forks, Minn., 1975-78; research asst. health adminstrn. dept. Sch. Pub. Health, U. N.C., Chapel Hill, 1978-81; asst. prof. Coll. Medicine and Coll. Pharmacy, U. Fla., Gainesville, 1981-85, asst. dir. Ctr. for Health Policy Research, 1983-85; asst. prof. Coll. Pub. Health, U. South Fla., Tampa, 1986-92; assoc. prof. Bowman-Gray Sch. Med., Wake Forest U., Winston-Salem, N.C., 1992—; assoc. prof. Babcock Grad. Sch. Mgmt.; assoc. prof., dir. sect. on med. outcomes and policy analysis U. Md. Med. Sch. Divsn. Gerontology, Balt., 1996—; cons. U.S. Dept. Vets. Affairs, 1983—, Blue Cross of Fla., 1983—. Contbr. articles to profl. jours. Elder, Grace Presbyterian Ch., Gainesville, 1982-85, v.p., 1982-84, pres., 1934-85; bd. dirs., sec. North Central Fla. Planned Parenthood, 1982-84. Research grantee Fla. Dept. Health and Rehab. Services, 1981-85, U.S. Dept. HHS, Blue Cross/Blue Shield of Fla., 1983-85, Fla. Hosp. Cost Containment Bd., 1984—, Robert Wood Johnson Found., 1985—, Nat. Inst. Aging, 1992, Nat. Tech. Info. Adminstrn., 1994-95, NSF, 1995—, Nat. Heart and Lung Inst., 1995—. Mem. Am. Econs. Assn., Am. Rural Health Assn., Am. Pub. Health Assn., Fla. Pub. Health Assn., U. N.C. Sch. Pub. Health Alumni Assn. Avocations: sailing, landscaping. Office: U Md Med Sch Divsn Gerontology Dept Medicine UAMC-GRECC (512/18) 10 N Greene St Baltimore MD 21201

BRADKOWSKI, KEITH A., patient services administrator; b. Chgo., July 18, 1956; s. Frank J. and Violet (Reshel) Bradkowski. BSN, Rush U., 1983; MS, U. Ill., Chgo., 1984. RN, Ill., Calif.; cert. nursing adminstrn. advanced ANCC. Tng. Nat. Inst. Mental Health, 1983-84; clin. nurse mgr. Northwestern Meml. Hosp., Chgo., 1986-90, clin. nurse mgr. II, 1990-92; clin. dir. surg. nursing Cedars-Sinai Med. Ctr., L.A., 1992-93; adminstrv. dir. patient care svcs. Santa Monica (Calif.) Hosp. Med. Ctr., 1993-95; assoc. dir. patient svcs. Santa Monica-UCLA Med. Ctr., 1995-96; sr. assoc. CurranCare, LLP, North Riverside, Ill., 1996—; mem. adv. bd. RN Times; instr. psychiat.-mental health nursing Lewis U., 1985-86; mem. adj. faculty med.-surg. nursing U. Ill., Chgo., 1986-92; adj. grad. clin. preceptor Rush U. Coll. Nursing, Chgo., 1986-88; mem. clin. specialist task force Calif. Bd. Registered Nursing, Sacramento, 1994. Mem. Am. Orgn. Nurse Execs. (exec. task force 1995), Calif. Orgn. Nurse Execs., Am. Coll. of Healthcare Execs., Sigma Theta Tau. Home: 6N351 Cloverdale Rd Roselle IL 60172-3222 Office: CurranCare LLP 7222 W Cermak #600 North Riverside IL 60546

BRADLEY, ANITA, nursing administrator; b. Memphis, Dec. 10, 1958; m. William Bradley, July 3, 1989; children: Antonio, William Christopher. A, Shelby State C.C., Memphis, 1981; BSN magna cum laude, Union U., Jackson, Tenn., 1989. cert. pediat. advanced life support, U. Tenn. Coll. Med. Charge nurse pediat. Lebonheur Children's Hosp., Memphis, 1981-88, asst. DON, 1989, RN pediat., 1990-95; coord. pediat. Housecall Health Care, Memphis, 1995; staff nurse Extendicare Home Health, Memphis, 1995—. Lt. Navy Res. Mem. NAFE, AACC Nurses, Am. Assn. Post Anesthesia Nurses, Nat. Assn. Physician Nurses, Tenn. Nurses Assn., Res. Officers Assn., Home Healthcare Nurses Assn., Alpha Chi. Baptist. Home: 2887 Signal ST Memphis TN 38127

BRADLEY, BERNARD LEO, physician; b. Lisburn, Antrim, Ireland, Apr. 19, 1956; s. John and Mary Ruth (Neeson) B. MB, BCh, BAo, Queens U., Belfast, Ireland, 1969; MD, U. Tex., 1975; MRCP, Royal Coll. Physicians, London, 1972; FACP, FCCP, Am. Coll. Physicians, 1976. Intern Royal Victoria Hosp., No. Ireland, 1969-70, resident, 1970-73; asst. prof., acting dir., pulmonary div. U. Tex. Med. Sch., Houston, 1975-82; asst. prof. clin. medicine Baylor Coll. Medicine, Houston, 1982—; asst. prof. occupational medicine Sch. of Pub. Health U. Tex., Houston, 1980—; asst. prof. respiratory therapy Sch. of Allied Health Sci. U. Tex., 1982—; med. dir. respiratory dept. San Jacinto Coll., Houston, 1986—; pres. Tex. Lung Ctrs., Houston, 1982—, Bayshore Med. Ctr., S.E. Harris County Med. Svc., Bayshore Physician Hosp. Orgn.; Diplomate Am. Bd. Internal Medicine, Can. Bd. Internal Medicine, U.K. Bd. Medicine. Mem. Citizens Adv. Com., Pasadena, Tex., 1990, emergency planning com., 1990. Fellow Am. Coll. Physicians, Am. Coll. Occupation Physicians, Am. Coll. Chest Physicians, Am. Coll. Preventive Physicians, Am. Acad. Disability Evaluating Physicians, Royal Coll. Physicians Can.; mem. Royal Coll. Physicians London. Office: Texas Lung Ctr 4003 Woodlawn Ave Pasadena TX 77504-1910

BRADLEY, CHARLES WILLIAM, podiatrist, educator; b. Fife, Tex., July 23, 1923; s. Tom and Mary Ada (Cheatham) B.; m. Marilyn A. Brown, Apr. 3, 1948 (dec. Mar. 1973); children: Steven, Gregory, Jeffrey, Elizabeth, Gerald. Student, Tex. Tech., 1940-42; D. Podiatric Medicine, Calif. Coll. Podiatric Medicine U. San Francisco, 1949, MPA, 1987, D.Sc. (hon.). Pvt. practice podiatry Beaumont, Tex., 1950-51, Brownwood, Tex., 1951-52, San Francisco, San Bruno, Calif., 1952—; assoc. clin. prof. Calif. Coll. Podiatric Medicine, 1992—; chief of staff Calif. Podiatry Hosp., San Francisco; mem. surg. staff Sequoia Hosp., Redwood City, Calif.; mem. med. staff Peninsula Hosp., Burlingame, Calif.; chief podiatry staff St. Luke's Hosp., San Francisco; chmn. bd. Podiatry Ins. Co. Am.; cons. VA; assoc. prof. podiatric medicine Calif. Coll. Podiatric Medicine. Mem. San Francisco Symphony Found.; mem. adv. com. Health Policy Agenda for the Am. People, AMA; chmn. trustees Calif. Coll. Podiatric Medicine, Calif. Podiatry Coll., Calif. Podiatry Hosp.; mem. San Mateo Grand Jury, 1989. Served with USNR, 1942-45. Mem. Am. Podiatric Med. Assn. (trustee, pres. 1983-84), Calif. Podiatry Assn. (pres. No. div. 1964-66, state bd. dirs., pres. 1975-76, Podiatrist of Yr. award 1983), Nat. Coun. Edn. (vice-chmn.), Nat. Acads. Practice (chmn. podiatric med. sect., sec. 1996), Am. Legion, San Bruno C. of C. (bd. dirs. 1978-91, v.p. 1992, bd. dir. grand jury assoc. 1990), Olympic Club, Commonwealth Club Calif., Elks, Lions. Home: 2965 Trousdale Dr Burlingame CA 94010-5708 Office: 560 Jenevein Ave San Bruno CA 94066-4408

BRADLEY, EDWARD BEHEN, physician; b. DuBois, Pa., Mar. 27, 1934; s. Thomas Bernard and Mary Angela (Behen) B.; m. Mary Lyons Durant, June 27, 1959; children: Mary Carney, Kathleen Sarah, Edward Behen, Elizabeth Durant. AB, Hamilton Coll., 1956; MD, Columbia U., 1960. Diplomate Am. Bd. Internal Medicine, Am. Bd. Geriat. Medicine; cert. med. dir. Intern SUNY, 1960-61, internal medicine resident, 1961-63; endocrinology fellow Peter Arnt Brigham Hosp., Boston, 1963-64; physician ptnr. Slocum Dickson Med. Group, Utica, N.Y., 1964-66, 68-86; med. dir. Masonic Home, Utica, N.Y., 1986—; chmn. Inst. Applied Ethics, Utica (N.Y.) Coll., 1987—. Reviewer Jour. Am. Geriatric Soc. Dir. Clin. Med. Network, Utica Coll., 1989-95. Capt. USAF, 1966-68. Recipient Scroll award Ctrl. N.Y. Acad. of Medicine, 1993, Hon. Alumnus award Utica Coll. Syracuse U., 1994. Fellow Am. Coll. Physicians, Am. Geriatric Assn.; mem. Am. Diabetes Assn. (pres. N.Y. State chpt. 1982-84, pres. Ctrl. N.Y. chpt. 1977-79), N.Y. Med. Dirs. Assn. (pres. 1992-94), Rotary (Paul Harris fellow). Office: Masonic Home 2150 Bleeker St Utica NY 13501

BRADLEY, GREGORY LEE, radiographer, educator; b. Portsmouth, Ohio, Apr. 25, 1958; s. Robert Harold and Mildred Louise (Dooley) B.; m. Lois Sue Frazier, Aug. 4, 1979; children: Jacob Lee, Abby Marie, Joshua Aaron. BS, AS in Radiol. Technology, Morehead State U., 1979; MEd, McNeese State U., 1987. Registered technologist radiography Am. Registry Radiol. Technologists. Radiographer Berger Hosp., Circleville, Ohio, 1979-80; instr. radiol. technology Morehead (Ky.) State U., 1980-81; dir. program, asst. prof. McNeese State U., Lake Charles, La., 1981-91, 94—; dir. radiol. technology program Kent State U., Salem, Ohio, 1991-93; site visitor joint review com. edn. radiol. technology, Chgo., 1992—. Editor: (jour.) Focal Spot Monitor-La. Soc. Radiologic Technologists, 1990-91, 95—. Mem. Am. Soc. Radiol. Technologists (edn. com. 1981—), La. Soc. Radiol. Technologists (Outstanding Radiol. Technologist of the Yr. 1995, apptd. exec. bd. 1989—), S.W. La. Soc. Radiol. Technologists (Outstanding Radiol. Technologists of the Yr. 1994, adv. bd. 1994—), Tri County Soc. Radiol. Technologists. Home: 804 University Dr Lake Charles LA 70605 Office: McNeese State U PO Box 92000 Lake Charles LA 70609

BRADLEY, JAMES P., orthopedist; b. Feb. 15, 1953. BS, Pa. State U., 1975; MS in Cell Biology, Fla. Inst. Tech., 1978; MD, Georgetown U., 1982. Diplomate Nat. Bd. Med. Examiners; cert. Am. Bd. Orthopaedic Surgery. Gen. surgery resident U. Tenn., Chattanooga, 1982-84; orthopaedic surgery resident U. Health Ctr. Pitts., 1984-87; sports medicine fellow Kerlan-Jobe Orthopaedic Clinic, Inglewood, Calif., 1987-88; orthopedist Oakland Orthopaedic Assocs., Pitts., 1988—; active staff U. Pitts. Med. Ctr., 1988—, Mercy-Providence Hosp., Pitts., 1992—, Passavant Hosp., Pitts., 1993—; asst. staff St. Margaret's Hosp., Pitts., 1988—; assoc. staff St. Francis Med. Ctr., Pitts., 1988—, Allegheny Valley Hosp., Natrona Heights, pa., 1988—; courtesy staff Shadyside Hosp., Pitts., 1988—, Citizens Gen. Hosp., New Kensington, Pa., 1988—; attending staff Allegheny Gen. Hosp., Pitts., 1994—; med. dir. Tennis Tng. and Mgmt. Group, 1993; chmn. Tutorials of the AOSSM, 1994; team physician Fox Chapel Area H.S. Football Team, 1990—, Dapper Dan Round Ball Classic, 1991—, Shadyside Acad. Football Team, 1991—, Pitts. Steelers Profl. Football Club, 1992—, Born 2 Run All Star Basketball Game, LaRoche Coll., 1995; dir. sports medicine dept. St. Margaret's Meml., Pitts., 1992—; clin. preceptor residency program St. Francis Med. Ctr., Pitts., 1992—; med. dir. Oakland Rehab., Pitts., 1993—; sports medicine fellowship program Tuckahoe Orthopaedic Assocs., Ltd., Richmond, Va., 1993—; clin. asst. prof. dept. orthopaedic surgery U. Pitts. Sch. Medicine, 1994—; presenter in field. Consulting reviewer Arthroscopy: The Journal of Arthroscopic and Related Surgery, 1991—, The Physician and Sports Medicine, 1992—; contbr. articles to profl. jours. Fellow Am. Acad. Orthopaedic Surgeons; mem. AMA, Am. Orthopedic Assn. Med. Honor Soc., Am. Orthopedic Soc. for Sports Medicine (edn. com.), Am. Shoulder and Elbow Surgeons, Arthroscopy Assn. N.Am., Ea. Orthpaedic Assn., Nat. Football League Physicians Soc., Pa. Med. Soc., Pa. Orthopaedic Soc., Pa. Athletic Trainers Soc., Allegheny County Med. Soc., Georgetown U. Alumni Assn., Alpha Omega Alpha. Home: 374 Fox Chapel Rd Pittsburgh PA 15238 Office: Oakland Orthopaedic Assocs 5820 Centre Ave Pittsburgh PA 15206

BRADLEY, JOHN, immunology educator, pathologist, physician; b. Bangor, North Wales, July 9, 1933; arrived in Australia, 1975; s. John and Doris (Whitehouse) B.; m. Brenda Mary Whitehouse, Apr. 27, 1961; children: Katherine A.L., Alexandra Lucy, David P.J. (dec.), Paul J.W. BS with honors, U. Birmingham, Eng., 1954, B of Surgery, B of Medicine, 1957, MD, 1967. Cert. med. specialist: internal medicine and pathology. Rsch. fellow dept. exptl. pathology U. Birmingham, 1964-67; USPHS internat. postdoctoral fellow Sch. Medicine U. Tex., Dallas, 1967-68; lectr., sr. lectr. dept. medicine U. Liverpool, Eng., 1969-73, dir. dept. immunology, 1973-75; prof., chmn. dept. immunology Flinders U., Adelaide, Australia, 1975—, dep. dean, 1979-81, 83-85; hon. prof. Clin. Immunology Centre Shanghai, 1991—; cons. internat. devel. program to Australian univs. Contbr. 140 sci. papers to profl. publs. Capt. Royal Army Med. Corps, 1961-62. Fellow Royal Coll. Physicians (London), Royal Coll. Physicians (Edinburgh, Scotland), Royal Australasian Coll. Physicians, Royal Coll. Pathologists of Australasia (chief examiner immunology 1988—, chmn. immunology quality assurance program 1988—). Home: 12 Balham Ave, Kingswood, Adelaide 5062, Australia Office: Flinders U, Bedford Pk PO Box 2100, Adelaide 5001, Australia

BRADLEY, JOHN ANDREW, hospital management company executive; b. Hammond, Ind., Aug. 3, 1930; s. Andrew C. and Florence (Wolfe) B.; m. Judith E. Salmi, June 1, 1955; children: John Michael, Kerry Kathleen, Kelly Ann. BS, Loras Coll., 1952; MHA, St. Louis U., 1955, PhD, 1962. Asst. adminstr. Incarnate Word Hosp., St. Louis, 1958-61; from assoc. adminstr. to administr. Santa Rosa Med. Ctr., San Antonio, 1961-69; from v.p. to sr. v.p. Am. Medicorp, Inc., San Antonio, 1969-78; with Am. Healthcare Mgmt., Dallas, 1978-89, pres., 1978-84, chmn., chief exec. officer, 1985-89; chmn., chief exec. officer Chancellor Health Systems Inc., Dallas, 1989—. Capt. AUS, 1953-57. Home: 4403 Westgrove Dr Dallas TX 75248-2412

BRADLEY, LAURENCE ALAN, clinical psychologist; b. Cleve., Sept. 13, 1949; s. Irving and Jeanne (Weil) B.; m. Gifford Weary, Dec. 28, 1974 (div. 1979); m. Elizabeth Wrenn, Oct. 3, 1981 (div. 1991). BA in Psychology, Vanderbilt U., 1971, PhD, 1975. Clin. intern Duke U. Med. Ctr., Durham, N.C., 1975-76; asst. prof. U. Tenn., Chattanooga, 1976-77, Fordham U., Bronx, N.Y., 1977-80; asst. prof. Bowman Gray Sch. Med., Winston-Salem, N.C., 1980-82, assoc. prof., 1982-89, adminstrv. head, sect. on med. psychology, 1981-89; adj. assoc. prof. U. N.C.-Greensboro, 1983-89, vis. behavorial scientist, Örebro Med. Ctr. Hosp., Örebro, Sweden, 1986-92; assoc. prof., dir. epidemiology, edn. and health svcs. rsch Multipurpose Arthritis & Musculoskeletal Diseases Rsch. Ctr. U. Ala., Birmingham, 1989-1992, prof., dir. epidemiology, edn. and health svcs. rsch., 1992—. Author: (with others) Health Psychology: Clinical Methods and Research, 1991; editor: (with others) Medical Psychology: Contributions to Behavioral Medicine, 1981, Coping with Chronic Disease: Research and Applications, 1983. Rsch. grantee Robert Wood Johnson Found., 1983-86, Am-Scandinavian Found., 1986, NIH, 1989—; recipient Disting. Scholar award Arthritis Health Professions Assn. Fellow APA, Soc. for Personality Assessment; mem. Internat. Assn. for Study of Pain, Am. Pain Soc., Sigma Xi, Phi Beta Kappa. Democrat. Achievements include research to determine that relaxation training and psychological therapy reduces pain behavior and number of painful joints among patients with rheumatoid arthritis, and that functional brain activity abnormalities are associated with chronic pain. Home: 3831 Clairmont Ave Birmingham AL 35222 Office: U Ala Divsn Clin Immunology & Rheumatology 429 Tinsley Harrison Tower Birmingham AL 35294

BRADLEY, MARIANNE GWIAZDA, nursing educator; b. Phila., Jan. 18, 1948; d. Stanley J. and Regina R. (Grzeskowiak) Gwiazda; m. Gary H. Bradley, Dec. 23, 1978. BSN, U. Del., 1970; MSN, U. Pa., 1986; BA, Wharton Sch., Phila., 1986. Special projects coord./quality assurance Norfolk (Va.) Gen. Hosp., 1982-84; staff nurse/critical care Cooper Hosp., Camden, N.J., 1975-76, 84-86; asst. dir. nursing Phila. Geriatric Ctr., 1987-89; asst. dir. quality assurance Grad. Hosp., Phila., 1989-92; mem. nursing faculty Holy Family Coll., Phila., 1992—. Mem. Nat. Gerontol. Nursing Assn., Am. Soc. Aging, Gerontol. Soc. Am., Am. Orgn. Nurse Execs., Phila. Area Coun. for Excellence, Sigma Theta Tau. Home: 1944 Sycamore St Haddon Heights NJ 08035-1004

BRADLEY, MARK EDMUND, physician, consultant; b. Balt., Nov. 29, 1936; s. J. Edmund and Kathryn (Strong) B.; m. Eileen Patricia Walkavich, Nov. 17, 1973 (div. Apr. 1977); 1 child, Meghan; m. Patricia Wynn Sullivan Paxton, July 12, 1987. BS, U. Notre Dame, 1958; MD, U. Md., 1962; MS, U. Pa., 1968; MPH, Harvard U., 1971. Diplomate Am. Bd. Occupational Medicine, Am. Bd. Preventive Medicine; cert. underseas medicine Am. Bd. Preventive Medicine. Intern. U. Va. Hosp., Charlottesville, 1962-63; commd. lt. USN, 1963, advanced through grades to capt., 1976; med. officer Polaris submarines, 1964-65, U.S. Submarine Base, Pearl Harbor, Hawaii, 1965-66; med. officer, Sealab aquanaut, Tech. Office Deep Submergence Systems Project, San Diego, 1967-70; resident, research fellow Sch. Pub. Health Harvard U., Boston, 1970-73; dep. dir. Environ. Bioscis. Dept. Naval Med. Research Inst., Bethesda, Md., 1973-76; dir. Hyperbaric Med. Program Ctr. Naval Med. Research Inst., Bethesda, 1976-84; ret., 1984; assoc. dir. hyperbaric medicine Md. Inst. for Emergency Med. Service Systems, Balt., 1985-86; cons. in field Potomac, Md., 1986—; mem. com. toxicology Nat. Acad. Scis. NRC, 1986—. Contbr. numerous articles to profl. jours.; inventor, patentee device for measuring respiration. Decorated Commendation medal, 1968, 2 Meritorious Service medals, 1980, 84, USN. Fellow ACP, Am. Coll. Preventive Medicine, Aerospace Med. Assn. (assoc., Environ. Sci. award 1987); mem. Undersea and Hyperbaric Med. Soc. (pres. 1985-86, Stover-Link award 1985, A. Behnke Jr. award 1990), Am. Physiol. Soc., Met. Washington Coll. Occupational and Environ. Medicine (pres. 1993—). Roman Catholic. Home and Office: 9316 Falls Bridge Ln Potomac MD 20854-3950

BRADLEY, NANCY LOVETT, medical and surgical nurse, administrator; b. Woonsocket, R.I., Jan. 30, 1937; d. Harold D. Sr. and Rena M. (Daigle) Gould; m. Joseph F. Bradley, Feb. 4, 1961; children: Joseph F., Naomiruth, Joellen, Johnna, Nobilee, Nannette, Nadine. Diploma, David Hale Fanning Sch., Worcester, Mass., 1978; ADN, Community Coll. R.I., Lincoln, 1983; BSN, Framingham State Coll., 1992. Cert. med.-surg. nurse, CPR instr., gerontol. nurse, diabetic instr. LPN, primary staff nurse Milford (Mass.)-Whitinsville Regional Hosp., 1978-83, RN, 1983-89; asst. nurse mgr. Landmark Med. Ctr., Woonsocket, 1989—. Chmn. profl. edn. Am. Cancer Soc. Mem. Nat. Gerontol. Nursing Assn., R.I. Coun. Nurse Mgrs. Home: 28 Maple St Mendon MA 01756-1247

BRADLEY, RICHARD EDWIN, retired college president; b. Omaha, Mar. 9, 1926; s. Louis J. and Betsy (Winterton) B.; m. Doris I. McGowan, June 8, 1946; children—Diane, Karen, David. Student, Creighton U., 1946-48; B.S.D., U. Nebr., 1950, D.D.S., 1952; M.S., State U. Iowa, 1958. Instr. State U. Iowa, 1957-58; asst. prof. Creighton U., 1958-59; asst. prof., chmn. dept. periodontics U. Nebr., 1959-62, assoc. prof., 1962-65, prof., 1965-67; assoc. dean Coll. Dentistry, 1967-68, dean, 1968-80; pres. Baylor Coll. Dentistry, 1980-90, pres., dean emeritus, 1990—; clin. prof. Coll. Dentistry U. Nebr. Med. Coll., Lincoln, 1990—; cons. dental edn., 199-93; mem. Commn. A, Coun. on Dental Edn., 1986-93; pres. Am. Assn. Dental Schs., 1977-78; mem. nat. adv. com. on health professions edn. Dept. Health and Human Resources, 1982-86; pres. Am. Fund for Dental Health, 1986-87. Editor: The New Dentist, 1992-94; contbg. editor Orban's Textbook of Periodontics, 1963; contbr. Clark's Clin., 1980. Served with USNR, 1944-46. Fellow AAAS, Internat. Coll. Dentists; mem. ADA, Am. Acad. Peridontology Found. (bd. dirs., pres. 1994-96), Am. Coll. Dentists (regent 1992-96, treas. 1996—), Internat. Assn. Dental Rsch., Sigma Xi, Omicron Kappa Upsilon. Home: 6424 Crooked Creek Dr Lincoln NE 68516-2955 Office: U Nebraska Coll Dentistry Lincoln NE 68583-0740

BRADLEY, RONALD JAMES, neuroscientist; b. Enniskillen, No. Ireland, Feb. 17, 1943; s. Samuel John and Mary Elizabeth (Irvine) B.; m. Doris Brown, Mar. 5, 1966; children—Nicola, Jason, Steven. B.Sc., Queens U., Belfast, No. Ireland, 1964; Ph.D., U. Edinburgh, Scotland, 1967. Mem. faculty Yale U., 1967-69, U. N.Mex., 1969-71, U. Ala., Birmingham, 1972-92; prof. psychiatry and neuroscis. U. Ala., 1976-92; prof. psychiatry and pharmacology La. State U. Med. Sch., Shreveport, La., 1992—; assoc. dean for instnl. devel., La. State U. Med. Sch.; guest prof. U. Saarlands, Fed. Republic of Germany, 1977-81. Editor: Internat. Rev. Neurobiology, 1974—. Recipient A. E. Bennett award Soc. Biol. Psychiatry, 1967. Mem. AAAS, Biophys. Soc., Neurosci. Soc., Soc. Biol. Psychiatry. Home: 2407 Lakecrest Dr Shreveport LA 71109-3003 Office: LSU Med Ctr Dept Psychiatry PO Box 33932 Shreveport LA 71130

BRADLEY, STERLING GAYLEN, microbiology and pharmacology educator; b. Springfield, Mo., Apr. 2, 1932; s. Benn and Lora (Brown) B.; m. Lois Evelyn Lee, May 13, 1951; children—Don, Evelyn, John, Phillip; m. Judith Bond, July 24, 1974; 1 son, Kevin. BA, BS, S.W. Mo. State Coll., 1950; MS, Northwestern U., 1952, PhD (NSF fellow), 1954; PhD certificate med. mycology, Duke U., 1957. Grad. teaching asst. Northwestern U., Evanston, Ill., 1950-51; Abbott research asst. Northwestern U., 1951-52, instr. biology, 1954; instr. dept. bacteriology and immunology U. Minn., 1956-57, asst. prof. dept. bacteriology, 1957-59, assoc. prof. dept. microbiology, 1959-63, grad. faculty genetics, 1961-68, prof., 1963-68, chmn. genetics faculty group, 1964; chmn. dept. microbiology Va. Commonwealth U., Richmond, 1968-82; prof. depts. pharmacology and microbiology Va. Commonwealth U., 1979-96, dean basic health scis., 1982-93; v.p. acad. affairs U. Md. Biotech Inst., College Park, 1996—; vis. worker in pharmacology Cambridge (Eng.) U., 1978; mem. bd. sci. counselors NIH, 1968-72, chmn., 1970-72; mem. Internat. Com. Bacteriol. Systematics, 1966-74, exec. bd., 1970-74; mem. U.S. Pharmacopeial Com. of Revision, 1980-85; coord. Project 3 U.S.-USSR Joint Working Group on Microbiology, 1979-82; v.p. Found. Immunotoxicology, 1985-91, pres., 1991—. Mem. editl. bd. Proc. Soc. Exptl. Biol. Medicine, 1966-72, Conf. on Anti-microbial Agts., 1960, Jour. Indsl. Microbiology, 1985-95; editor Jour. Bacteriology, 1970-78; contbr. articles to profl. jours. Trustee Southeastern U. Rsch. Assn., Inc., 1990-93; bd. dirs. Sci. Mus. Va. Found., 1993—. Recipient Charles Porter award, 1983; named S.W. Mo. State U. Outstanding Alumnus, 1991, Life Achievement award Sci. Mus. Va., 1996; Eli Lilly postdoctoral fellow U. Wis., 1954-55; NSF postdoctoral fellow dept. genetics, 1955-56; NIH Sr. Fogarty internat. fellow, 1978. Fellow AAAS (life), Va. Acad. Sci. (life, past mem. council, sec. 1976-77); mem. AAUP, Am. Assn. Immunology, Am. Acad. Microbiology, Am. Soc. Pharmacology and Exptl. Therapeutics, Am. Soc. Cell Biology, Am. Chem. Soc., Am. Soc. Microbiology (past mem. council, treas. 1985-91), Soc. Protozoologists, Soc. Indsl. Microbiology (past pres.), Am. Inst. Biol. Sci. (past dir., gen. chmn. 41st Meeting, 1989-90), Soc. Toxicology, U.S. Fedn. Culture Collections (pres. 1984-86), Internat. Union Microbiol. Socs. (treas. 1994—), Mycol. Soc. Am. (life), Soc. for Exptl. Biology and Medicine (past chmn. Minn. chpt.), Genetics Soc. Am., Torrey Bot. Club (life), N.Y. Acad. Scis. (life), Sigma Xi (life, pres. chpt. 1975-76, fin. com. 1991—). Home: 9015 Breezewood Terr Greenbelt MD 20770 Office: Univ Md Biotech Inst 4321 Hartwick Rd Ste 500 College Park MD 20740

BRADSHAW, DOROTHY ANN HOPKINS, health services administrator; b. Salisbury, Md., Jan. 22, 1939; d. Stephen Bunting and Dorothy Gene (Francis) Hopkins; m. Carlton Lee Bradshaw, Aug. 8, 1959; 1 child, Carlton Wrightson. Diploma in nursing, Peninsula Gen. Hosp. Sch., Salisbury, Md., 1960; AA, Chesapeake Coll., Wye Mills, Md., 1974; BS in Nursing, U. Md., 1975, MS in Nursing, 1980. RN, Md.; lic. nursing home adminstr., Md.; cert. nursing adminstrn. advanced. Staff nurse Ea. Shore Hosp. Ctr., Cambridge, Md., 1960-62, 69-70, instr. psychiat. nursing, 1970-78; staff nurse VA Hosp., Wilmington, Del., 1962-67; asst. DON Deers Head Ctr., Salisbury, 1978-85, DON, 1985-93, acting dir., 1993-95, dir., 1995—; founding mem. bd. dirs. Coastal Hospice, Salisbury, 1981-89; cons., instr. on Hospice, Eight Ea. Shore Counties, Md., 1980-85; mem., chair nursing adv. com. Wor Wic Tech. C.C., Cambridge, 1985—; mem., chair adv. com. Shore Up Adult Med. Day Care, Salisbury, 1986-93. Sunday sch. tchr. St. Paul's United Meth. Ch., Cambridge, 1990—. Mem. ANA (bd. dirs. MNA dist. 4 1991), Phi Kappa Phi, Sigma Theta Tau. Democrat. Office: Deers Head Ctr 351 Deer Head Hosp Rd Salisbury MD 21801

BRADSHAW, PETER HOLBROOK, surgeon, physician; b. Cleve., July 23, 1956; s. John S. and Laura H. (Crump) B.; m. Eloise L. DeLaney, Aug. 4, 1979; children: Kathleen DeLaney, John Andrew. BA in Chemistry, U. N.C., 1978, MD, 1982. Diplomate Am. Bd. Surgery. Intern, resident U. Ky., Lexington, 1982-87; physician Hickory (N.C.) Surg. Clinic, 1987—. Office: Hickory Surg Clinic 415 N Center St Hickory NC 28601

BRADSHAW, WILLIAM EMMONS, biology educator; b. Orange, N.J., May 16, 1942; s. John Hammond and Laura Francis (Ottis) B.; m. Christina Marie Holzapfel, May 10, 1971; 1 child, Pilar Antonia. AB, Princeton U., 1964; MS, U. Mich., 1965, PhD, 1969. Rsch. fellow Harvard U., Cambridge, Mass., 1969-71; asst. prof. U. Oreg., Eugene, 1971-77, assoc. prof., 1977-84, prof. biology, 1984—; rsch. assoc. Tall Timbers Rsch. Sta., Tallahassee, 1977-78; acad. visitorSilwood Park, Imperial Col., Ascot., U.K., 1986; panelist NSF Program in Population Biology and Physiol. Ecology, 1991-92, 94. Contbr. articles to Am. Naturalist, Evolution, Ecology, Sci., Nature, Biol. Bull., Oecologia, Can. Jour. Zoology, Jour. Med. Entomology, Nat. Geographic Rsch., Ecol. Entomology; contbr. 8 chpts. to symposium vols. Grantee NSF, 1973—, Tall Timbers Rsch., Inc., Fla., 1977-78, Nat. Geographic Soc., 1984, 86; John Simon Guggenheim Found. fellow, 1986; Fulbright fellow Internat. Exch. Scholars, 1986. Office: Univ Oreg Dept Biology Eugene OR 97403-1210

BRADY, ADRIAN JAMES, cardiologist; b. Edinburgh, Scotland, May 27, 1961. BSc, U. Edinburgh, 1982, MBChB, 1985. Intern Edinburgh Hosp., 1985-86; resident Hammersmith Hosp., London, 1986-89; fellow Nat. Heart and Lung Inst., London, 1991-93; sr. fellow Queen Elizabeth Hosp., Birmingham, U.K., 1993-96; cons., attending Glasgow Royal Infirmary, 1996—. Contbr. articles to profl. jours. Recipient Young Investigators award Am. Heart Assn., 1993, Young Rsch. Workers prize British Cardiac Soc., 1993. Mem. Royal Coll. Physicians, British Hypertension Rsch. Group (chmn.), British Cardiac Soc. Office: Dept Med Cardiology, Glasgow Royal Infirmary, Glasgow G4 0sF, United Kingdom

BRADY, JOHN PAUL, psychiatrist; b. Boston, June 23, 1928; s. James Henry and Evelyn Louise (Rice) B.; m. Christeen Nelson, Mar. 19, 1963; children—James Palmer, Pamela Eros, June Pamela, David Duncan. A.B., Boston U., 1951, M.D., 1955; M.A. (hon.), U. Pa., 1967. Rotating intern Gorgas Hosp., Panama, 1955-56; resident in psychiatry Inst. of Living, Hartford, 1956-59; research psychiatrist Ind. U. Med. Sch., Indpls., 1959-63; mem. faculty U. Pa. Med. Sch., Phila., 1963—; prof. psychiatry U. Pa. Med. Sch., 1968—, Kenneth Appel prof., 1974—, chmn. dept., 1974-82; co-founder, asso. editor Behavior Therapy, 1970—. Author: An Introduction to the Science of Human Behavior, 1963, Classics of American Psychiatry, 1975, Psychiatry: Areas of Promise and Achievement, 1977, Voyage to Inishneefa, 1987; co-editor: Controversy in Psychiatry, 1978, Behavioral Medicine; Theory and Practice, 1979, Psychiatry at the Crossroads, 1980, also articles. Recipient Research Scientist award NIMH, 1963-74; Strecker award Inst. of Pa. Hosp., 1972. Fellow Am. Psychiat. Assn., Indian Psychiat. Soc.; mem. Assn. Advancement Behavior Therapy (past pres.), Soc. Biol. Psychiatry (pres. 1979-80), Psychiat. Research Soc. (program chmn. 1973), Soc. Behavioral Medicine (dir. 1980-81), Soc. Interam. de Psicologia, Am. Psychosomatic Soc. Office: Inst Of Pa Hospital Philadelphia PA 19139

BRADY, LUTHER W., JR., physician, radiation oncology educator; b. Rocky Mount, N.C., Oct. 20, 1925; s. Luther W. and Gladys B. AA, George Washington U., 1944, AB, 1946, MD, 1948; DFA (hon.), Colgate U., 1988; DSc (hon.), Lehigh U., 1990; DSc (hon), Toyama U., Japan, 1996. Diplomate: Am. Bd. Radiology (treas. 1980-82, v.p. 1982-84, pres. 1984-86). Intern Jefferson Med. Coll. Hosp., Phila., 1948-50; resident in radiology Jefferson Med. Coll. Hosp., 1954-55; resident radiology Hosp. U. Pa., Phila., 1955-56; fellow Nat. Cancer Inst., 1953-57, 1957-59; practice medicine, specializing in radiation oncology Phila.; asst. instr. radiology Jefferson Med. Coll. Hosp., 1954-55, U. Pa., Phila., 1955, instr., 1956-57, assoc. radiology, 1957-59; asst. prof. radiology Coll. of Physicians and Surgeons, Columbia U., N.Y.C., summer, 1959; assoc. prof. radiology Hahnemann Med. Coll. and Hosp., Phila., 1959-62, prof., 1963—, chmn. dept. radiation oncology, 1970—; asst. prof. radiology Harvard Med. Sch., Boston, 1962-63; mem. med. radiation adv. com. Bur. Radiation Health, HEW, 1971-74; cons. radiation therapy various hosps.; mem. U.S. del. to Interam. Congress Radiology, 1975, Internat. Congress of Radiology, 1981; sec. gen. Internat. Congress Radiology, 1985; med. adv. radiation therapy, med. affairs com., 1984—; dir. Pa. Blue Shield, Camp Hill; chair Pa. Cancer Control Bd., 1989—. Author: Tumors of the Nervous System, 1975, Cancer of the Lung, Clinical Applications of the Electron Beam; editor Cancer Clin. Trials (Am. Jour. Clin. Oncology), (with C. Perez) Principles and Practice of Radiation Oncology; editorial bd. Cancer; assoc. editor: Gynecologic Oncology, Am. Jour. Roentgenology, Cancer Research; sr. editor: Internat. Jour. Radiol. Oncology; contbr. articles on radiation therapy to profl. jours. Bd. dirs. Assn. Artists Equity of Phila., Welcome House, 1974—, Settlement Music Sch., 1973—, Phila. Art Alliance, 1977-84; trustee Phila. Mus. Art, also mem. oriental art com., 1974—, chmn. exec. com., 1968-72, mem. print, contemporary art and Indian art coms., 1974—. Served to lt. M.C. USN, 1950-54. Recipient Grubbe award Chgo. Radiol. Soc., 1977, Disting. Alumni award George Washington U., 1991; Gold medal Gilbert Fletcher Soc., 1984, Albert Soiland Gold medal U. So. Calif., 1985, del Regato Gold medal, 1986, Padro Pio medal, 1993. Fellow Am. Coll. Radiology (chmn. commn. radiation therapy 1975-81, bd. chancellors 1975-81, Gold medal 1983), Royal Coll. Radiology (hon.), Deutsches Roetngengesellschaft (hon.), Italian Radiology Soc. (hon.); mem. Royal Soc. Med. Belgium (academician), Radiol. Soc. N.Am. (bd. dirs. 1977-84, chmn. bd. dirs. 1982-83, pres. 1984-85, chmn. refresher course com. 1971-75, Erksine lectr. 1979, Gold medal 1989), Pa. Radiol. Soc. (bd. dirs. 1970-77, councilor to Am. Coll. Radiology 1971-77), Am. Radium Soc. (pres. 1976-77, bd. dirs. Janeway medal 1979, Janeway lectr. 1980), Am. Cancer Soc. (pres. Phila. div. 1976-78, dir. 1968—, exec. com. 1976-78, mem. breast cancer task force 1974—, nat. dir. 1970-76), Am. Soc. Therapeutic Radiologists (pres. 1971-72, Gold medal 1987), Assn. U. Radiologists, Am. Roentgen Ray Soc., Am. Assn. for Cancer Rsch., Radiation Rsch. Soc., Am. Soc. Clin. Oncology, Phila. Roentgen Ray Soc. (pres. 1976-77, mem. exec. com. 1976-78), Am. Fedn. Clin. Rsch., Coll. Physicians Phila., James Ewing Soc., Assn. Pendergrass Fellows, Phila. County Med. Soc., AMA (chair residency rev. com. for radiology 1982-84, mem. 1988—, chair residency rev. com. radiation oncology 1992-94), Med. Soc. State Pa., Internat. Skeletal Soc., Coun. Acad. Socs., Soc. Chmn. Acad., Radiation Oncology Programs (pres. 1977-79), Soc. Chmn. Acad. Radiology Depts. (pres. 1974-75), Gynecologic Oncology Group (exec. com. 1971-85, assoc. chmn. 1971-85), Radiation Therapy Oncology Group (chmn. 1980-87), Am. Coll. Radiation Oncology (pres. 1989-92, chmn. 1992-93, gold medal 1996), Pa. Cancer Adv. bd.,(1989—, chm., 1990—), Internat. Club Radiotherapists, Nat. Cancer Inst. (bd. sci. counselors, com. for radiation therapy studies 1971-84, chmn. cancer clin. trails com.), Smith-Reed-Russell Soc., Alpha Omega Alpha, Phi Lambda Kappa. Clubs: Merion Cricket; Racquet, Union League (Phila.), Phila., Peale. Office: 230 N Broad St Philadelphia PA 19102-1121

BRADY, MARY SUE, nutrition and dietetics educator; b. Sedalia, Mo., Mar. 29, 1945; d. H. Wesley and K. Virginia (McGaw) Steele; m. Paul L. Brady, Sept. 2, 1967; 1 child, Chad W. BA, Marian Coll., Indpls., 1968; MS, Ind. U., Indpls., 1970, DMSc, 1987. Registered dietitian; cert. specialist in pediatric nutrition. Pediatric dietitian J.W. Riley Hosp. Children, Ind. U. Sch. Medicine, Indpls., 1970-75, acting dir. pediatric nutrition, 1975-78, 80-82, neonatal dietitian, 1978-80, dir. pediatric nutrition, 1982-96; asst. prof. Ind. U. Sch. Medicine, Indpls., 1975-88, assoc. prof., 1988-96, prof. 1996—. Contbr. articles to Jour. of Am. Dietetic Assn., Pediatric Pulmonology, Jour. of Pediatrics. Fellow Am. Dietetic Assn. (mem. jour. bd. 1988-94, Excellence in Practice of Clin. Nutrition award 1991, PNPG Outstanding Mem. of Yr. 1994); mem. Sigma Xi. Office: JW Riley Hosp for Children 702 Barnhill Dr Rm 3747 Indianapolis IN 46202-5200

BRADY, REBECCA ANN, pediatrics nurse; b. Rockford, Ill., Mar. 16, 1968; d. Dennis D. and Elizabeth Ann (Gorsuch) Lantz; m. Steven John Brady, Apr. 23, 1994. BSN, So. Ill. U., Edwardsville. RN, Ill. Staff nurse, neurology Meml. Med. Ctr., Springfield, Ill., 1993; pediat. nurse Naperville (Ill.) Pediat. Assocs., 1994—; office nurse Danada Family Medicine, 1995—. Vol. Rockford (Ill.) Meml. Hosp. emergency room, 1988, Habitat for Humanity, East Cooper, S.C., 1991; active children's ch. ministry Abundant Life Family Ch., Aurora, Ill., 1994—. Christian. Home: 3116 N Oakhurst Dr Aurora IL 60504-6627

BRADY, ROSCOE OWEN, neurogeneticist, educator; b. Phila., Oct. 11, 1923; s. Roscoe O. and Martha (Roberts) B.; m. Bennett Carden Manning, 1972; 2 sons. Student, Pa. State U., 1941-43; MD, Harvard U., 1947; post-grad., U. Pa., 1948-49. Intern Hosp. U. Pa., 1947-48; NRC fellow U. Pa., 1948-50, USPHS spl. fellow, 1950-52; sect. chief Nat. Inst. Neurol. Diseases and Blindness, NIH, 1954-67; asst. lab. chief neurochemistry Nat. Inst. Neurol. Diseases and Blindness, NIH, Bethesda, Md., 1967-72; chief developmental and metabolic neurology br. Nat. Inst. Neurol. Disorders and Stroke, 1972—; professorial lectr. George Washington U. Sch. Medicine, 1963-73; mem. faculty Georgetown U. Sch. Medicine, 1965—; mem. med. staff Children's Hosp. Washington, 1992—. Author: (with Donald B. Tower) Neurochemistry of Nucleotides and Amino Acids, 1960, Basic Neurosciences, 1975, (with John A. Barranger) Molecular Basis of Lysosomal Storage Disorders, 1984, also numerous articles. Recipient award Gairdner Found., 1973, Lasker Found., 1982, Passano Found., 1982, Warren Alpert Found. award, 1992, Myrtle Wreath award Hadassah, 1993, Exec. Excellence award Sr. Execs. Assn., 1993. Mem. NAS (J.S. Kovalenko medal 1991), Am. Soc. Biol. Chemists, Am. Acad. Neurology (Kotzias award 1980), Am. Acad. Mental Retardation, Am. Soc. Clin. Investigation, Am. Soc. Human Genetics, Inst. of Medicine. Home: 6026 Valerian Ln Rockville MD 20852-3410 Office: NIH 9000 Rockville Pike Bethesda MD 20892-1260

BRADY, SHANNON, neonatal nurse; b. Portland, Oreg., Nov. 9, 1955; d. Melvin L. and Jacqueline A. (Horne) B.; m. Kevin D. Harper, Febr. 23, 1985. AS in Nursing, Boise State U., 1976; cert. perinatal nurse clinician, U. Wash., 1979. Staff nurse Providence Hosp., Anchorage, 1976-78, Pendleton (Oreg.) Community Hosp., 1979-81; staff nurse III Fairbanks (Alaska) Meml. Hosp., 1981—, nurse, neonatal intensive care nursery. Mem. Shared Governance Nursing Affairs Coun. Mem. NAACOG (cert. neonatal intensive care, neonatal nurse clinician, practictioner). Home and Office: PO Box 81565 Fairbanks AK 99708-1565

BRADY, STEPHEN R.P.K., physician; b. New London, Conn., Oct. 13, 1955; s. Richard Harris and Jeanne Margaret (Halpin) B.; m. Marsha Anne Erickson, June 18, 1978 (div. Jan. 1993); 1 child, Ericka Anuhea; m. Elizabeth Ada Rewick, Dec. 27, 1994. AB cum laude, Harvard U., 1977; MPH, U. Hawaii, 1978, PhD, 1979; MD, U. Pa., 1982. Intern U. Hawaii, 1982-83, resident, 1983-85; physician Kaiser Clinics, Honolulu, 1985-86; physician, med. dir. Kokua Kalihi Valley, Honolulu, 1986-89; clin. instr. U. Hawaii. Sch. of Medicine, 1986—; physician Waianae (Hawaii) Coast Health Svc., 1989-94; asst. med. dir., physician Am. Hawaii Cruises, Honolulu, 1989—; physician Straub Clinic & Hosp., Honolulu, 1984—. Cubmaster Boy Scouts Am., Kailua, Hawaii, 1995—. Comdr. U.S. Merchant Marine, 1989—. Rsch. grantee Kuakini Med. Rsch. Inst., Honolulu, 1971, Pacific Health Rsch. Inst., Honolulu, 1972-78, Children's Hosp., Phila., 1979; Paul Harris fellow, 1995. Mem. AMA, Am. Coll. Physicians, Am. Soc. Internal Medicine, Am. Pub. Health Assn., Am. Statistical Assn., Hawaii Soc. Internal Medicine, Hawaii Med. Assn. (chair CME com. 1987—), Soc. Epidemiologic Rsch., Rotary, Soroptimist (v.p. 1993—). Congregationalist. Home: Ste A #731 2357 S Beretania St Honolulu HI 96826-1413 Office: Straub Clinic & Hosp 888 S King St Honolulu HI 96813

BRAEN, BERNARD BENJAMIN, psychology educator; b. Boston, Oct. 11, 1928; s. Simon Peter and Ethel (Davis) B.; m. Judith Krom; children: Philip, Eric, Benson. BA, U. Maine, 1949; MA, Boston U., 1950; PhD, Syracuse U., 1955. Diplomate clin. psychology Am. Bd. Examiners Profl. Psychology, 1962-93; lic. psychologist, N.Y. Chief clin. psychologist Onondaga County Child Guidance Ctr., Syracuse, N.Y., 1956-60; pvt. practice clin. psychology Syracuse, 1960-64; assoc. prof. psychology SUNY Upstate Med. Ctr., Syracuse, 1964-69, prof., 1969; prof. Syracuse U., 1969-92; ret.; dir. grad. program in clin. psychology, dir. psychology clinic Syracuse U., 1969-83; exec. dir. Nat. Alliance Concerned with School Age Parents, Syracuse, 1971-74, dir. research and publs., 1974-76. Contbr. articles to profl. publs., 1959—; guest editor Jour. Sch. Health, 1977. Recipient Disting. Service award Nat. Alliance Concerned with Sch. Age Parents, 1976. Fellow Am. Orthopsychiat. Assn.

BRAGG, DARRELL BRENT, nutritionist, consultant; b. Sutton, W.Va., May 24, 1933; s. William H. and Gertrude (Perrine) B.; m. Elizabeth Hosse, Dec. 28, 1957; children: Roger, Larry, Teresa. BSc, W.Va. U., 1959, MSc, 1960; PhD, U. Ark., 1966. Instr. dept. animal sci. U. Ark., Fayetteville, 1965-67; asst. prof. U. Man., Winnipeg, Can., 1967-68, assoc. prof., 1968-70; assoc. prof. dept. poultry sci. U. B.C., Vancouver, Can., 1970-74, prof., head dept., 1975-86; industry cons., Vancouver, 1986-89; nutritionist, dir. quality assurance Rangen Aquaculture Feeds, Buhl, Idaho, 1990-92; sr. rsch. scientist Rangen Aquaculture Rsch. Ctr., Hagerman, Idaho, 1991-92; indsl. biochem. cons. Deutrel Labs. Inc., Palmdale, Calif., 1991—. Contbr. numerous articles to sci. jours. With U.S. Army, 1954-56. Recipient numerous rsch. grants from industry, univs. and govts. Mem. Poultry Sci. Assn. (nat. bd. dirs., v.p., pres. 1978-84), World Poultry Sci. Assn. (bd. dirs., v.p. 1975-86), Sigma Xi, numerous others. Home: PO Box 38 Payette ID 83661-0038

BRAGG, DAVID GORDON, physician, radiology educator; b. Portland, Oreg., May 1, 1933; s. George Tully and Edith (Lee) B.; m. Marcia Robertson, Aug. 19, 1955; children: Eric Allan, Daniel Robert, James Tully, Anne Elizabeth. AB in History, Stanford U., 1955; MD, U. Oreg., 1959. Intern Phila. Gen. Hosp., 1959-60; resident in radiology Columbia-Presbyn. Med. Ctr., Coll. Physicians and Surgeons, N.Y.C., 1962-64, chief resident, 1964-65, instr., 1965-66; asst. prof. Cornell U. Med. Coll., N.Y.C., 1966-70, assoc. prof., 1970; chmn. diagnostic radiology Meml. Sloan-Kettering Cancer Ctr., N.Y.C., 1967-70; prof., chmn. dept. radiology U. Utah Med. Ctr., Salt Lake City, 1970-96; cons. Salt Lake City VA Hosp., Meml. Sloan-Kettering Cancer Soc., 1970—; mem. Nat. Cancer Adv. Bd., 1988-94; trustee Am. Bd. Radiology; mem. bd. sci. advisors Nat. Cancer Inst., 1996—. Editor: Oncologic Imaging ; mem. editorial bds. Internat. Jour. Radiation Oncology, Biol. Physics, Current Problems in Diagnostic Radiology, Postgrad. Radiology, Cancer. Mem. AMA, Assn. Univ. Radiologists (pres. 1980-81, Gold medal 1995), Soc. Chmn. Acad. Radiology Depts. (pres. 1979-80), Am. Soc. Therapeutic Therapists Radiology and Oncology (hon.), Radiol. Soc. N.Am., Soc. for Cancer Imaging (founder). Home: 4403 Covecrest Dr Salt Lake City UT 84124-4009 Office: U Utah Dept Radiology 1A-71 50 N Medical Dr Salt Lake City UT 84132-0001

BRAGGIO, JOHN THOMAS, psychologist; b. Italy, July 31, 1947; s. Battista and Joanne (Prandini) B.; m. Sherryll M. Baggio, Mar. 15, 1973. BA, Coe Coll., 1969; MA, Ga. State U., 1973, PhD, 1975; postgrad., Okla. U. Health Sci. Ctr., 1995—. Asst. prof. U. N.C., Asheville, 1974-82; sr. rsch. asst., postdoctoral fellow Okla. U. Health Scis. Ctr., Oklahoma City, 1983-84; adj. asst. prof. dept. psychiatry Okla. U. health Scis. Ctr., 1987-95; prin. investigator VA, Oklahoma City, 1987-92; epidemiologist Okla. State Dept. Health, 1992—; co-chair statewide psychology conf., 1987, 88, 91; postdoctoral fellow Okla. Health Scis. Ctr., 1983, U. Mich., 1992; chmn. social sci. degree program U. N.C., 1974-82; dir. Internat. Comparative Psychology Symposium, Italy, 1980, mem. faculty senate, 1980-82; adj. faculty U. Ctrl. Okla., 1983—. Contbr. articles to profl. jours., chpts. to books. Grantee NIH, NSF, VA, OCAST. Mem. Okla. Pub. Health Assn., Okla. Psychol. Assn. (pres. divsn. acad. and rsch. psychologists 1989-90), Rsch. Soc. on Alcoholism. Home: 504 NW 138th St Edmond OK 73013-1905

BRAHEN, LEONARD S., psychiatrist; b. Phila., Nov. 28, 1921; s. Nathan Brahen and Helen Berman; m. Roslyn Halin, Dec. 23, 1947; children: Ellyn, Norman, Cheryl. BS in Pharmacy, Temple U., 1949, MS in Pharmacy, 1951; PhD in Pharmacology, U. Md., 1954; MD in Medicine, U. Louisville, 1958. Diplomate Am. Bd. Med. Examiners; cert. Am. Bd. Psychiatry and Neurology, Am. Assn. Addiction Medicine. Med. dir. Chas. Pfizer-Divsn., N.Y.C., 1959-64; corp. med. dir. Endo (DuPont) Labs., N.Y.C., 1964-71; med. dir. Nassau County (N.Y.) Dept. Drug and Alcohol Addiction, 1971-91; cons., pvt. practice specializing in addiction medicine Durham, N.C., 1991—; clin. investigator medications to block addictive disorder cycles; spkr. in field. Contbr. numerous articles, papers, book chpts. to profl. publs. Recipient Award of Merit, Counties of U.S., 1982, Achievement award

Nassau County, 1983. Mem. N.Y. State Med. Soc. (mem. drug abuse com. 1983-95), Nassau County Med. Soc. (chmn. pub. health com. 1965-95, mem. comm. com., malpractice com. 1984-92, libr. com., Cert. of Merit 1993). Office: 7 Glenmore Dr Durham NC 27707

BRAIDFOOT, CYNTHIA LOUISE, medical technologist; b. Canon City, Colo., July 11, 1965; d. Delford William Crawford and Marjorie Kathleen (Weaver) Frost; m. Eddie Wayne Braidfoot; children: John Wayne, Matthew Del. Assoc. in Health Sci., Sayre (Okla.) Jr. Coll., 1985. Lab. and X Ray technologist Collingsworth Gen. Hosp., Wellington, Tex., 1985-88; lab. and mammography technologist Childress (Tex.) Regional Med. Ctr., 1988—. Home: 1410 J NW Childress TX 79201 Office: Childress Regional Med Ctr Hwy 83 N Childress TX 79201

BRAILLON, ALAIN L.H., health facility administrator; b. Amiens, Somme, France, Mar. 22, 1953; s. Philippe J.M. and Monique (Damade) B.; m. Brigitte M.T. Charrier, Sept. 9, 1978; children: Aymeric P.J., Aurore S.Y., Alexis R.H. MD, U. Amiens, France, 1982; MS, U. Paris, 1984, 86. Cert. in gastroenterology. Resident Amiens (France) U. Hosp., 1978-84, chief fellow in gastroenterology, 1984-86; postdoctoral fellow U. Iowa, 1986-87; assoc. dir. rsch. INSERM, Paris, 1987-90; biomed. rsch. adminstr. Paris Pub. Hosp. Authority, 1990—. Philippe Found. grantee, 1986, French Fgn. Office grantee, 1986. Office: AP-HP Rsch Clinic, 3 Ave Victoria, 75004 Paris France

BRAILSFORD, LUCIEN, physician, surgeon; b. Columbia, S.C., Aug. 21, 1934; s. Edward D. and Rosalie (Jones) B.; m. Evelyn Chandler, Aug. 26, 1956; children: Elizabeth, Charlotte, Robert, Mary. BS, U. of the South, Sewanee, Tenn., 1955; MD, Med. U. S.C., Charleston, 1959. Diplomate Am. Bd. Surgery, Am. Bd. Thoracic Surgery. Pvt. practice Wallace Wilson Brailsford Clinic, Spartanburg, S.C., 1965—; assoc. clin. prof. surgery Med. U. S.C., Spartanburg; mem. dir. St. Luke's Free Med. Clinic, Spartanburg, 1992—. Named Vol. of Yr., St. Luke's Free Med Clinic, Spartanburg, 1992-94, Health Person of Yr., Spartanburg County Health Planning Commn., Spartanburg, 1995; recipient Algernon Sydney Sullivan award Wofford Coll., 1994. Fellow ACS, Am. Coll. Chest Physicians; mem. AMA, Am. Thoracic Soc., S.C. Med. Assn., Piedmont Sertoma Club (pres. 1975-76). Episcopalian. Office: Wallace Wilson Brailsford Clinic 1776 Skyline Dr Spartanburg SC 29304

BRAIMAN, MARK STEPHEN, biomedical educator, researcher; b. Rochester, N.Y., Oct. 27, 1956; s. Alex and Pauline Dieter (Pommerenke) B. AB summa cum laude in Chemistry, Harvard U., 1977; PhD in Chemistry, U. Calif., Berkeley, 1983. Postdoctoral fellow dept. chemistry MIT, Cambridge, 1983-86; postdoctoral fellow dept. physics Boston U., 1986-87, rsch. asst. prof. dept. physics, 1987-88; asst. prof. dept. biochemistry U. Va., Charlottesville, 1988-94, assoc. prof., 1994—. Contbr. articles to profl. jours., chpts. to books. Mem. candidate selection com. All-Berkeley Coalition, 1981. NSF Grad. fellow, 1977, U. Calif. Regents fellow, 1980, Helen Hay Whitney fellow Helen Hay Whitney Found., 1983-86; Lucille P. Markey scholar Lucille P. Markey Charitable Trust, 1986-92. Mem. AAAS, Biophys. Soc., Am. Chem. Soc. Democrat. Unitarian. Office: U Va Health Scis Ctr Box 440 Charlottesville VA 22908

BRAIN, JOSEPH DAVID, biomedical scientist; b. Paterson, N.J., Jan. 20, 1940; married, 1961; 3 children. SM, Harvard U., 1962, SMHyg, 1963, SDHyg, 1966. Rsch. assoc. in physiology Harvard U., Boston, 1966-68, from asst. prof. to assoc. prof., 1968-78; prof. physiology Harvard Sch. Pub. Health, Cambridge, Mass., 1978—, Cecil K. and Philip Drinker prof. environ. physiology, dir. Harvard Pulmonary Specialized Ctr. Rsch., 1977-96; dir. respiratory biol. program Harvard Sch. Pub. Health, Cambridge, 1981-93; dir. physiology program Harvard Sch. Pub. Health, Cambridge, Mass., 1993—, chair dept. environ. health, 1990—; mem. com. Cardiovascular and Pulmonary Study Sect., NIH, 1975-79, program project rsch. rev. com. Nat. Heart, Lung and Blood Inst., 1980-83; bd. sci. counsellors Nat. Inst. Occupational Safety and Health, 1992—. Bd. trustees Taylor U., 1984—. Fellow AAAS, Am. Physiol. Soc., Am. Thoracic Soc., Reticuloendothelial Soc., Sigma Xi. Office: Harvard U Sch Pub Health 665 Huntington Ave Boston MA 02115-6021

BRAININ, CONSTANCE SPEARS, psychotherapist, educator, social worker, counselor; b. Princeton, N.J., Feb. 21, 1932; d. Alexander Joseph and Anna (Stuttman) Spears; m. Norman Herbert Brainin, May 29, 1955; children: Kenneth, Risa, Alissa. BA, Northeastern Ill. U., 1975, MA, 1979; PhD, Southeastern U., 1981. Lic. social worker, Ill.; cert. clin. mental health counselor; lic. clin. profl. counselor, Ill. Supr. counseling staff Park Med. Ctr., Chgo., 1980-83; pvt. practice psychotherapist Chgo., 1982—; mem. adj. faculty Oakton C.C., Des Plaines, Ill., 1982—, Northeastern Ill. U., 1984-88; mem. governing bd. Theatre 219, Skokie, Ill., 1984-88; v.p. Edgebrook/Sauganash chpt. Am. Cancer Soc., 1988-93; lectr. Edgebrook C. of C., Chgo., 1985, Am. Cancer Soc., Chgo., 1984. Workshop leader Hope Ctr., Long Grove, Ill., 1984. Mem. APA, ACA, Am. Orthopsychiat. Assn., Assn. for Humanistic Psychology, Nat. Acad. Cert. Clin. Mental Health Counselors, Ill. Psychol. Assn., Inst. for Logotherapy.

BRAKEBILL, JEAN NEWTON, naval officer, nurse, educator; b. Mobile, Ala., Sept. 4, 1953; d. James Harold and Eleanor (Mrotek) Newton; m. James Arden Brakebill, Dec. 15, 1985; 1 child, Justin James. BS in Nursing, West Tex. State U., 1975; MS, Corpus Christi U., 1982; MBA in Health Adminstrn., Nat. U., 1987. RN, Tex. Staff nurse Southwestern Gen. Hosp., El Paso, Tex., 1975-76; commd. ensign U.S. Navy, 1976, advanced through grades to comdr., 1992; staff nurse Naval Hosp. U.S. Navy, Charleston, S.C., 1976-78, Okinawa, Japan, 1978-80; head nurse ICU U.S. Navy, Corpus Christi, Tex., 1980-83; head nurse, clin. cons., program adminstr. Naval Hosp. U.S. Navy, San Diego, 1983-89; div. head med. surg. ward Naval Hosp., Long Beach, Calif., 1989-90, clin. nurse specialist inpatient nursing, 1990-91, head dept. inpatient nursing, 1991-92, head dept. command edn. and tng., 1992-93; command edn. and tng. program adminstr. Naval Med. Ctr., Portsmouth, Va., 1993-95; head dept. command staff edn. and tng. Twenty-Nine Palms Naval Hosp., Marine Corps Air Ground Ctr., Calif., 1995—; instr. trainer BLS Am. Heart Assn., various locations, 1985—; advanced trauma life support educator, San Diego, 1987-91; Red Cross nurse. Mem. Kappa Delta. Roman Catholic. Office: Naval Hosp MCAGICC Head Edn and Tng Twentynine Palms CA 92288

BRAKEL, WILLEM HENDRIK, scientist, diplomat; b. The Hague, Netherlands, Mar. 26, 1950; came to U.S., 1956, naturalized, 1985; s. Willem and Henriette (de Hoest) B. BA with high honors, Oberlin Coll., 1971; MPhil, Yale U., 1973, PhD, 1976. Lectr. zoology U. Nairobi, Kenya, 1977-81; asst. prof. biology Loyola Coll., Balt., 1982-87; with Fgn. Service, Dept. State, Am. Embassy Bangui, 1987-89, Embassy Paris, 1989-92, Oceans and Environment Bur., 1992, African Bur., 1993-95, Fgn. Svc. Inst., 1995-96, Embassy Brussels, 1996—. Office: PSC 82O Box 002 APO AE 09724

BRAKENBURY, PHILIP HEDLEY, accident and emergency medicine consultant; b. Near Reading, Berkshire, Eng., July 30, 1941; s. William Davie and Winefred Brenda (Ellis) B.; m. Rosemarie Erika Autenrieth, June 21, 1969; children: Ian Philip Autenrieth, Andrew Philip Autenrieth. BA in Nat. Scis., Cambridge (Eng.) U., 1963, MB BChir, 1966, MA, 1967. Specialist accreditation in accident and emergency medicine. Resident, surg. officer Warwick (U.K.) Hosp., 1971-76; med. supt. Ba (Fiji) Meth. Hosp., 1976-77; orthopaedic registrar West Midlands Regional Health Authority, Birmingham, Eng., 1977-80; sr. registrar in accident and emergency medicine South Tees (NHS) Trust, Middlesbrough, Cleveland, U.K., 1981-93, part-time cons., 1994-95, hon. cons. in accident and emergency medicine, 1996; founding fellow Faculty Accident and Emergency Medicine, 1994; chmn. Cleveland Paramedic Com., 1988-94; hon. asst. sec. Casualty Surgeons Assn., London, 1984-87; divisional surgeon St. John's Ambulance, Middlesbrough, 1980-85; rep. ann. Health Emergency Planning Officers Conf., 1989-94. Contbr. papers to med. jours. Vice-chmn. Cleveland Alcohol Abuse Ctr., Middlesbrough; mem. Gen. Nursing Coun., Sierra Leone, 1971-72; mem. Christian Med. Fellowship, U.K., 1980—. Fellow Royal Coll. Surgeons (Edinburgh); mem. Brit. Assn. Accident and Emergency Medicine, Brit. Med. Assn. Methodist. Home: Airdbreck Sta Great Ayton, Middlesbrough England

BRAME, MARILLYN A., hypnotherapist; b. Indpls., Sept. 17, 1928; d. David Schwalb and Hilda (Riley) Curtin; 1 child, Gary Mansour. Student, Meinzinger Art Sch., Detroit, 1946-47, U. N.Mex., 1963, Orlando (Fla.) Jr. Coll., 1964-65, El Camino Coll., Torrance, Calif., 1974-75; PhD in Hypnotherapy, Am. Inst. Hypnotherapy, 1989. Cert. and registered hypnotherapist. Color cons. Pitts. Plate Glass Co., Albuquerque, 1951-52; owner Signs by Marillyn, Albuquerque, 1952-53; design draftsman Sandia Corp., Albuquerque, 1953-56; designer The Martin Co., Orlando, 1957-65; pres. The Arts, Winter Park, Fla., 1964-66; supr. tech. publs. Gen. Instrument Corp., Hawthorne, Calif., 1967-76; pres. Camart Design, Westminster, Calif., 1977-86, Visual Arts, El Toro, Calif., 1978—; mgr. tech. publs. Archive Corp., Costa Mesa, Calif., 1986-90; adj. instr. Orange Coast Coll., Costa Mesa, 1985-90; hypnotherapist, Lake Forest, 1986—; bd. dirs. Orange County chpt. Am. Bd. Hypnotherapy. Author: Lemon and Lime Scented Herbs, 1994, (textbook) Folkdancing is for Everybody, 1974, Innovative Imagery, 1996; inventor, designer dance notation sys. MS Method. Mem. bd. govs. Lake Forest II Showboaters Theater Group, 1985-88, 90-95. Mem. Soc. Tech. Communication (v.p. programs, 1987, newsletter editor 1986-87, newsletter prodn. editor 1985-86).

BRAMMER, LAWRENCE MARTIN, psychology educator; b. Crookston, Minn., Aug. 20, 1922; s. Martin G. and Edna L. (Thiesen) B.; m. Marian S. Sjolin, Feb. 11, 1945; children: Karin Marie, Kristen Lenore. B.S., St. Cloud State U., 1943; M.A., Stanford U., 1948, Ph.D., 1950. Diplomate: Am. Bd. Prof. Psychology. Psychologist Stanford U. Counseling and Testing Ctr., 1948-50; assoc. dean students Sacramento State Coll., 1950-64; prof. ednl. psychology U. Wash., Seattle, 1964-88, prof. emeritus, 1988—. Author: Therapeutic Psuchology, 6th edit., 1993, Helping Relationships, 6th edit., 1996, Outplacement and Inplacement Counseling, 1984, How to Cope with Life Transitions, 1991. Lt. M.S.C. AUS, 1944-46. Fulbright fellow, 1951-62. Fellow APA; mem. ACA, Queen City Yacht Club, Elks. Democrat. Lutheran. Home: 7714 56th Pl NE Seattle WA 98115-6329 Office: U Wash Miller Dq # 12 Seattle WA 98155

BRAMWELL, MARVEL LYNNETTE, nurse, social worker; b. Durango, Colo., Aug. 13, 1947; d. Floyd Lewis and Virginia Jenny (Amyx) B. Diploma in lic. practical nursing, Durango Sch. Practical Nursing, 1968; AD in Nursing, Mt. Hood Community Coll., 1972; BS in Nursing, BS in Gen. Studies cum laude, So. Oreg. State Coll., 1980; cert. edn. grad. sch. social work, U. Utah, 1987, cert. counselor alcohol, drug abuse, 1988, MSW, 1992; M in Social Work, 1992. RN, Utah, Oreg., Ind.; cert. social worker, Utah, Ind.; cert. clin. social worker, Ind. Staff nurse Monument Valley (Utah) Seventh Day Adventist Mission Hosp., 1973-74, La Plata Community Hosp., 1974-75; health coordinator Tri County Head Start Program, 1974-75; nurse therapist, team leader Portland Adventist Med. Ctr., 1975-78; staff nurse Indian Health Service Hosp., 1980-81; coordinator village health services North Slope Borough Health and Social Service Agy., 1981-83; nurse, supr. aides Bonneville Health Care Agy., 1984-85; staff nurse Latter Day Saints Adolescent Psychiat. Unit, 1985-86; coordinator adolescent nursing CPC Olympus View Hosp., 1986-87, 91; charge and staff nurse adult psychiatry U. Utah, 1987-88; nurse MSW Community Nursing Svc., Salt Lake City, 1989-90; with Community Nursing Svc. and Hosp., Clearfield, Utah, 1993-94; med. social worker Meth. Home Health, Indpls., 1994—; assisted with design and constrn. 6 high tech. health clinics in Ala. Arctic, 1982-83; psychiat. nurse specialist Community Nursing Svc. Contbr. articles to profl. jours. Active Mothers Against Drunk Driving, Program U. Alaska Rural Edn., 1981-83. Recipient Cert. Appreciation Barrow (Alaska) Lion's Club, 1983, U.S. Census Bur., Colo., 1970. Mem. NOW, Nat. Assn. Social Workers, Assn. Women Sci. Home: 925 N Alabama St Indianapolis IN 46202-3318

BRANCACCIO, RONALD R., dermatologist; b. N.Y.C., Feb. 10, 1947; s. Ralph H. and Alma B.; B.S., Fairfield U., 1968; M.D., George Washington U., 1972. Intern, Lenox Hill Hosp., N.Y.C., 1972-73; resident in dermatology U. Oreg. Health Scis. Center, 1973-76; practice medicine specializing in dermatology, Bklyn. and N.Y.C.; assoc. clin. prof. dermatology Univ. Hosp., N.Y.C.; asst. attending physicians Bellevue Hosp., St. Vincent's Hosp., N.Y.C. Mem. Am. Acad. Dermatology, N.Y. State Dermatological Soc., Dermatologic Soc. Greater N.Y. (pres. 1981-82). Home: 67 Perry St New York NY 10014-3245 Office: 7901 4th Ave Brooklyn NY 11209

BRANCH, LAURENCE GEORGE, health policy researcher, educator, gerontologist; b. Cleve., Oct. 31, 1944; s. John Howard and Mercedes (Brachle) B.; m. Patricia Mary Skalski, June 24, 1967; children: Kathryn Helen, Carolyn Mercedes, Daniel Laurence. BA, Marquette U., 1967; MA, Loyola U., Chgo., 1969, PhD, 1971. Program dir. Ctr. Survey Rsch., Boston, 1973-79; Assoc. prof. Harvard Med. Sch., 1978-86, Harvard U. Sch. Pub. Health, 1980-86; exec. com. div. aging Harvard U. Med. Sch., 1979-86; assoc. dir. Geriatric Rsch. Edn. and Clin. Ctr. West Roxbury VA Outpatient Clinic, 1982-86; prof, chief health svcs., Boston U. Sch. Pub. Health, 1986-88; prof. Boston U. Sch. Medicine, 1986-95, Med. Sch. Duke U., 1995—; staff GRECC Bedford VA Hosp, 1986-89; trustee, pres. North Hill Life Care Community, Wellesley, Mass., 1980-89; trustee, pres. Mercy Svcs. for Aging, Farmington Hills, Mich., 1984-89; prins. Later Life Communities, Inc., 1988-92; dir. LTC Res. Abt Assoc., Cambridge, 1989-95; assoc. dir. VA Nat. Ctr. for Health and Promotion, 1995—; mem. prof. staff Brigham & Women's Hosp., Boston, 1981—; cons. Robert Wood Johnson Found., Princeton, N.J. Mem. editorial bd. Jour. Gerontology, 1981, Jour. Community Health, 1980, Gerontologist, 1982. Editor Jour. Aging and Health, 1988. Lt. col. USAR, 1968—. Fellow Gerontol. Soc. Am. (sect. chmn. 1989-90); Mem. AAAS, Am. Pub. Health Assn. (sect. chmn. 1983-84), Am. Psychol. Assn. Home: 3403 Medford Rd Durham NC 27705 Office: Duke U Aging Ctr Box 3003 Durham NC 27710

BRANCH, WILLIAM TERRELL, urologist, educator; b. Paragould, Ark., Dec. 7, 1937; s. William Owen and Mary Rose (Dempsey) B.; m. Mary Fletcher Cox, Dec. 11, 1965; children: Ashley Tucker, William T., Steven K. BS, Ark. State U., 1964; BS, U. Ark., 1966, MD, 1971. Diplomate Am. Bd. Urology. Adminstrv. asst. mental retardation planning project State of Ark., Little Rock, 1964-66; intern U. South Fla. Sch. Medicine Affiliated Hosps., Tampa, 1971-72, resident in surgery, 1972-73, resident in urology, 1973-75, chief resident in urology, 1975-76, clin. prof. urology, 1976—, mem. adv. bd. Suncoast Ednl. Telecommunications Systems, 1982; practice medicine specializing in urology, Tampa, 1976—; mem. staff, sec. urology Tampa Gen. Hosp., 1976-78, vice chief urology, 1978-80, chief urology, 1980-82; mem. staff, co-chief surgery Meml. Hosp. Tampa, 1978-80, vice chief med. staff, 1980-82, chief med. staff, 1982-84, trustee, 1983-88, also bd. dirs., vice chmn. bd. dirs. 1987-88; cons. in urology James A. Haley VA Hosp., Tampa, 1978—; mem. staff St. Joseph's Hosp., Tampa, 1976—, Tampa Gen. Hosp.; cons. staff Women's Hosp. Tampa; adv. bd. Glendale Fed. Savs., 1983-85, Beneficial Harbour Island Savs. Bank, 1985-87, South Trust Bank, 1988—, also bd. dirs., exec. com. chair audit com. Author: (with others) Mental Retardation in Arkansas 1964-66: A Demographic Study, 1966; cons. editor Jour. Fla. Med. Assn., 1978-93. Bd. dirs. Tampa Ballet, 1980, Tampa Charity Horse Show Bd. Dirs. Assn., 1985-87; United Way, Tampa, 1983-90, mem. exec. com., 1984-88; mem. med. adv. bd. Nat. Kidney Found. of Fla., Inc., 1983-90; mem. Tampa Bay Super Bowl Task Force; mem. adv. bd. dirs. Salvation Army; founding chmn. Kettle com., vice chmn. adv. bd. dirs. Recipient Disting. Alumnus award Ark. State U., 1986. Fellow ACS (credit com. Region IV, Fla. chpt. 1982—, exec. com. Fla. chpt. 1985—, sec./treas. 1987-88, pres.-elect 1989-90, pres. 1990-92); mem. ACS (gov. 1990-96, bd. gov. chpt. activities com. 1991-96, alt. 1993, chmn. nomination com. 1995, chmn. applications com. region IV), Am. Urol. Assn., Royal Soc. Medicine (affiliate), Fla. Med. Assn. (del. 1983, 88-96), Fla. Urol. Soc. (Milton Copeland award 1976, exec. com. 1978-82), Hillsborough County Med. Assn. (exec. com. 1978-81, treas. 1981-82, sec. 1983-84), Fla. Quality Med. Assurance, Inc. (bd. dirs., treas., chmn. exec. com. 1995, chmn. bd. govs.), Southeastern Surg. Congress, Greater Tampa C. of C. (dir. 1982-86, 87-90, chmn. med. meetings task force 1983-84, Super Star award 1983), Tampa Hist. Soc., Hillsborough County Med. Soc. (pres. polit. action com. 1986-87, 88-89). Clubs: Tampa Yacht and Country (gov. 1984-87), Centre of Tampa (founding mem. 1988-93, bd. dirs., chmn. membership com.), Univ., Ye Mystic Krewe of Gasparilla (bd. dirs. 1991—, 1st lt. 1988-89, lord chamberlain 1994-95, chmn. exec. com. 1995-96, capt. 1995—). Home: 909 S Golfview Ave Tampa FL 33629-5221 Office: 2919 W Swann Ave Ste 303 Tampa FL 33609-4051

BRANCO, MARY C., psychotherapist; b. Mass., Sept. 13, 1957; d. Norbert and Mary (Sardinha) B. AS with high honors, Bristol Community Coll., 1977; BA in Psychology, Southeastern Mass. U., 1979; MSW, Boston Coll., 1985. Lic. ind. clin. social worker; diplomate clin. social work Register of Clin. Social Work. Bilingual family therapist Family Svc. Assn., Fall River, Mass.; psychotherapist, coord. grad. student svcs.-tng. New Bedford (Mass.) Child and Family Svcs., dir. continuous quality improvement, asst. clinic dir.; field instr. Boston u. Mem. NASW (diplomate in clin. social work). Home: 305 Davis St Fall River MA 02720-5111

BRAND, JULIA MARIE, occupational health nurse; b. Paterson, N.J., Sept. 19, 1925; d. Winfield Aloysius and Julia (Donegan) Savage; m. Laurence Clifton Molloy Jr., Sept. 25, 1948 (div. 1971); children: Linda Jeanne, Laurence Clifton Jr., Lori Ann, Lance; m. Donald Edwin Brand, Oct. 27, 1978. Diploma in nursing, St. Joseph Sch. Nursing, Paterson, 1947; student, E. Tex. State U., 1975. RN, Tex.; cert. occupational health nurse, Tex. Office mgr., nurse Dr. Francis Brogan, Paterson, 1947-48; staff nurse Hackensack (N.J.) Hosp., 1948, St. Vincent Hosp., Little Rock, 1962-64; supr. Univ. Hosp., Albuquerque, 1964-66, Presbyn. Hosp., Dallas, 1966-75; occupational health nurse mgr. Tex. Instruments, Inc., Dallas, 1975-88; pvt. practice occupational health nurse cons. Dallas, 1988-95; ret., 1996. Vol. crisis counselor Truth House, Carrollton, Tex., 1974-75; nurse ARC Disaster Cadre, 1975-78; bd. dirs. Presbyn. Hosp. Credit Union, Dallas, 1972-75; health and fitness dir. Tex. Instruments, Dallas, 1984-88; vol. guardian Sr. Citizens Greater Dallas, 1996—. Named early pioneer of cardio-pulmonary resuscitation by the Southwestern Med. Sch. Dept. of Anesthesia, Tex., 1968. Mem. Am. Assn. Occupational Health Nurses, Tex. State Occupational Health Nurses, Dallas Area Occupational Health Nurses (chmn. fin. and edn. com. Dallas chpt. 1976-78), Employee Asst. Soc. N. Am., Bus. and Profl. Women's Assn. (past chmn. health and safety com. Dallas area chpt.). Republican. Roman Catholic. Home: 7614 Wellcrest Dr Dallas TX 75230-4857

BRAND, RICHARD DAVID, psychiatrist; b. N.Y.C., July 16, 1945; s. Nathan and Fay (Solomon) B.; m. Ann, July 3, 1968 (div. 1976); m. Jane Kelman, Apr. 6, 1980; children: Erica, Jonathan. BS in Psychology, CCNY, 1974; MD, N.Y. Med. Coll., 1977. Diplomate Am. Bd. Adolescent Psychiatry. Lead guitar player Left Banke, N.Y.C., 1966-68; intern in medicine and psychiatry N.Y. Med. Coll., Met. Hosp., 1977-78; resident Med. Coll. Cornell U., N.Y. Hosp., Westchester, 1978-81; health officer, staff psychiatrist Rockland County Community Mental Health Ctr., Pomona, N.Y., 1981-84; pvt. practice Bardonia, N.Y., 1982—. Mem. Am. Psychiat. Assn., Phi Beta Kappa. Home: 197 Waters Edge Valley Cottage NY 10989-1611 Office: 275 Route 304 Nanuet NY 10954-2049

BRAND, ROBERT L., orthopedic surgeon; b. Atlanta, Ga., July 8, 1942; s. Robert L. and Pauline (Vaughan) B.; m. Brenna Nipper; children: Alex, Robin. BA, Emory U., 1964; MD, Med. Coll. Ga., 1968. Diplomate Am. Bd. Orthopedic Surgery. Orthopedic surgeon U.S. Navy, Annapolis, Md., 1973-75, Augusta (Ga.) Orthopedic Specialists, 1975—; pres. med. staff Augusta Regional Med. Ctr., 1995, moderator bd. trustees, 1992; asst. clin. prof. surgery Med. Coll. Ga., Augusta. Deacon First Baptist Ch., Augusta; team physician Augusta Coll., 1968—, Westside H.S., Augusta, Ga., 1975—, Evans (Ga.) H.S., 1975—. Lt. cmdr. U.S. Navy, 1973-75. Fellow Am. Acad. Orthopedic Surgery, Am. Orthopedic Soc. Sports Medicine; mem. Med. Assn. Ga. (med. aspects of sports com.). Office: Augusta Orthopedic Spec Ste 210 3623 J Dewey Gray Cir Augusta GA 30909

BRANDEBERRY, CARL KENT, osteopathic physician; b. Bloomdale, Ohio, Jan. 16, 1928; s. Clyde Francis and Hilldred (Hartman) B.; m. Mary Louise Toro, Oct. 2, 1954; children: Kent C., Heather Ann, Todd Raymond. Student, Bowling Green State U., 1946-48; D.O., Kirksville Coll. Medicine, Mo., 1953. Pvt. practice ostepathic medicine Rock Creek, Ohio. Named Man of the Year, Orwell City, 1984. Mem. Ohio Osteopathic Assn., Nat. Osteopathic Assn., Rotary. Home: 7011 State Route 45 Orwell OH 44076-9777 Office: 3092 N Main St Rock Creek OH 44084

BRANDELL, JERROLD R., psychotherapist, educator; b. Chgo., Oct. 13, 1952; s. Jules and Edna B. (Honoroff) B.; m. Esther R. Teich, Aug. 30, 1980; children: Andrea Elizabeth, Joseph Wolf. BA, U. Ill., Chgo., 1975; MSSW, U. Wis., 1977; PhD, U. Chgo., 1982. Diplomate Am. Bd. Examiners in Social Work; lic. ind. social worker. Psychotherapist Bklyn. Psychiat. Ctrs., 1977-78, Youth and Family Counseling, Libertyville, Ill., 1981-83; Edith Abbott doctoral teaching fellow U. Chgo. Sch. Social Svc. Adminstrn., 1981-82; assoc. prof. Mich. State U. Sch. Social Work, East Lansing, 1983-88; assoc. prof. Boston U. Sch. Social Work, 1988-92, program coord. postgrad. program in advanced child and adolescent psychotherapy; assoc. prof. Sch. of Social Work, chmn. mental health prog. Wayne State U., Detroit, 1992—; clin. cons. Framingham (Mass.) Pub. Schs., 1989-91; sr. staff Grand Ledge (Mich.) Counseling Ctr., 1984-88. Editor: Jour. Analytic Social Work, 1990—, (books) Countertransference in Psychotherapy with Children and Adolescents, 1992, Narration and Therapeutic Action, 1996, Theory and Practice in Clinical Social Work, 1996; contbr. articles to profl. jours. Fellow Am. Orthopsychiat. Assn.; mem. Soc. for Clin. and Exptl. Hypnosis, Nat. Membership Com. on Psychoanalysis, Mich. Psychoanalytic Coun., Nat. Assn. Social Workers.

BRANDENBURG, DAVID SAUL, gastroenterologist, educator; b. Linz, Austria, Apr. 12, 1948; came to U.S., 1948; s. Mayer and Syda Brandenburg; m. Bette Ellen Hirschberg, Aug. 8, 1971; children: Stacey, Mark, Marci. BA, Rutgers U., 1968; MD, Georgetown U., 1972. Bd. cert. internal medicine; bd. cert. GI. Med. intern, resident R.I. Hosp.-Brown U. Affiliated, Providence, 1972-75; gastroenterology fellow Emory U., Atlanta, 1975-77; pvt. practice Atlanta Digestive Diseases and Internal Medicine, 1977-82, Brandenburg and Kramer M.D., P.C., Atlanta, 1983—; clin. asst. prof. medicine Emory U. Sch. Medicine, Atlanta, 1977—; med. dir. North Atlanta Endoscopy Ctr., Atlanta, 1986—; sec., v.p., pres. Ga. Soc. GI Endoscopy, Atlanta, 1980-86; chmn., med. adv. com. Ga. chpt. Crohn's and Colitis Found., Atlanta, 1995—. Bd. trustees Temple Emmanuel, Dunwoody, Ga., 1985-91, 95—, treas., v.p., 1985-91. Fellow Am. Coll. Gastroenterology (gov. 1991-95); mem. Am. Gastroenterol. Assn., Am. Soc. Gastrointestinal Endoscopy. Office: 5667 Peachtree-Dunwoody Rd Atlanta GA 30342

BRANDENBURG, MIYOKO ISHIGAKI, gerontology nurse; b. Japan, Mar. 2, 1932; came to U.S., 1958; d. Masaji Ishigaki and Sumi Murayama; m. Robert Brandenburg, Apr. 6, 1960; children: Michael, Dianne, Emily. RN with hons., Tokyo U. Hosp. Sch. Nursing, 1953; BS, Columbia U., 1960, MA, 1979, EdM, 1982. Staff nurse Tokyo U. Hosp., 1953-58; charge nurse Lenox Hill Hosp., N.Y.C., 1967-68; instr. N.Y.C. Sch. Practical Nursing, Bklyn., 1968-69; supr. Hiland Care Ctr., Jamaica, N.Y., 1985-87; instr., supr. Windsor Park Nursing Home, Queens, N.Y., 1987-88; head nurse Hempstead (N.Y.) Gen. Hosp. Med. Ctr., 1988-94, unit dir., 1994—. Fulbright Travel grantee; Parent in Career Edn. scholar. Mem. ANA, Nat. Gerontol. Nursing Assn., Nursing Edn. Alumni Assn., N.Y. State Soc. on Aging, Sigma Theta Tau, Kappa Delta Pi (historian reporter). Home: 2850 Chester St Oceanside NY 11572-1232

BRANDI, MARIA LUISA, endocrinologist, educator; b. Viterbo, Lazio, Italy, July 31, 1953; d. Domenico and Livia (Guadagni) B.; m. Vittorio de Leonardis, June 23, 1973; 1 child, Brando. MD, U. Florence (Italy), 1977, postgrad. in Endocrinology, 1980, PhD in Cell Biology, 1988. Cert. Italian Nat. Bd. Endocrinology. Rsch. fellow in Endocrinology U. Florence, 1977-84, rsch. assoc. Medicine, 1980-84, 88-92, assoc. prof. clin. pathophysiology dept., 1992—; vis. scientist metabolic diseases br. Nat. Inst. Diabetes Digestive and Kidney Diseases, NIH, Bethesda, Md., 1984-88. Recipient award Premio Roussel Italia, 1988, European Osteoporosis Found., 1989, Premio Schering della Società Italiana di Endocrinologia, 1990, Internat. Gerontol. award Sandoz Found. for Gerontol. Rsch., 1991. Mem. Am. Soc. Cell Biology, Am. Soc. Bone and Mineral Rsch., Endocrine Soc., Italian Endocrine Soc., Italian Osteo. Soc., Assn. of Women for Women's Health (pres.). Mem. Am. Soc. Cell Biology, Am. Soc. Bone and Mineral Rsch., Endocrine Soc., Italian Endocrine Soc., Italian Osteoporosis Soc. Home: Via Di Montalbano 3/G, 50135 Florence Italy Office: Dept Clin Pathophysiology, Viale Pieraccini 6, 50139 Florence Italy

BRANDON, ELIZABETH MARIE, osteopathic physician; b. Santa Barbara, Calif., May 6, 1951; d. A. Richard and Jacqueline Ann (Vercota) Bickmore; m. James Porter Brandon II, Feb. 14, 1971; children: James Porter III (dec.), Matthew Richard, Michael Patrick, Christopher Sean, Jeannine Marie. ADN, Grossmont Coll., El Cajon, Calif., 1975; BA in Molecular Biology, U. Calif., San Diego, 1990; DO, Chgo. Coll. Osteo. Medicine, 1994. RN, Calif. Staff nurse various hosps., San Diego, 1975-79; rsch. asst. Applied Mgmt. Scis., San Diego, 1979-81; intern Chgo. Osteo. Health Sys., 1994-95; resident U. Ill./Christ Hosp., Chgo., 1995—. Am. Med. Women's Assn. scholar, 1994. Mem. Am. Osteo. Assn., Am. Coll. Family Practice. Democrat. Roman Catholic. Home: 104 Country Ct Bolingbrook IL 60440 Office: U Ill Christ Hosp 1919 W Taylor St Chicago IL 60612-7248

BRANDON, GARY KENT, medical association administrator; b. Pueblo, Colo.; s. Vernon Charles and Eva M. (Hachey) B.; m. D.J. Harris, May 21, 1976; children: Terry, Belinda, John, Tracye, Sherry, Kimberly. BA, U. So. Colo., 1968; MS, N.Mex. Highlands U., 1969; DO, U. Health Scis., 1973; MPH, Johns Hopkins U., 1979; postgrad., Nat. War Coll., 1989-90. Diplomate Am. Bd. Preventive Medicine, Am. Bd. Med. Mgmt. Intern Lake Side Hosp., Kansas City, Mo., 1973-74; resident Johns Hopkins, 1978-79, USAF Sch. Aerospace Medicine, 1979-80; commd. capt. USAF, 1976, advanced through grades to col., 1986; hosp. comdr. Barksdale AFB, Shreveport, La., 1987-89, MacDill AFB, Tampa, Fla., 1990-93; dir. med. inspection USAF, Albuquerque, 1993-95; ret. USAF, 1995; med. dir. Valley Wide Health Svc., Alamosa, Colo., 1995—; sr. examiner Malcolm Baldridge Nat. Quality Award, Washington, 1993-96. Author: Aviation, Space and Environmental Medicine, 1980, co-author 2d edit., 1983. V.p. Rocky Mountain HMO, Grand Junction, Colo., 1975, Western Colo. Physicians, Inc., Grand Junction, 1975; pres. Mesa County Osteo. Assn., Grand Junction, 1976. Recipient Med. Leadership award Strategic Air Command USAF, Aboline, Tex., 1986, USAF award for profl. excellence, Washington, 1994. Fellow Am. Coll. Preventive Medicine; mem. APHA, Am. Coll. Occupl. and Environ. Medicine, Am. Soc. Quality Control, Nat. Assn. Managed Care Physicians. Home: 778 23rd Grand Junction CO 81505 Office: Valley Wide Health Svcs 204 Carson Ave Alamosa CO 81101

BRANDON, JEFFREY CAMPBELL, physician, interventional radiologist, educator; b. Reynoldsville, Pa., Dec. 5, 1953; s. Milton Boyd and Patricia Alfreda (Steele) B. BS, Allegheny Coll., 1975; MD, Jefferson Med. Coll., 1979. Diplomate Am. Bd. Radiology, Nat. Bd. Med. Examiners. Intern gen. surgery Bryn Mawr (Pa.) Hosp., 1979-80, resident gen. surgery, 1980-81; resident in diagnostic radiology Hahnemann U. Hosp., Phila., 1983-86; fellow interventional radiology, abdominal imaging Hahnemann U. Hosp., 1986-87; clin. instr. Hahnemann U. Hosp., Phila., 1987-88; asst. prof. U. Calif., Irvine, 1988-94, assoc. prof., chmn. radiol. scis., 1992-95; vice chmn. radiol. scis. U. South Ala., Mobile, 1995—; mem. adv. bd. Baxter Health Care Tech. and Ventures Divsn., Irvine, 1990-92, Laparomed Corp., Irvine, 1991-94, Visioneering, Fullerton, Calif., 1993-95. Author: (chpt.) Common Problems in Gastrointestinal Radiology, 1989, Critical Care Imaging, 1990, Textbook of Gastrointestinal Radiology, 1991, Textbook of Diagnostic Imaging, 1994; contbr. articles to books and profl. jours. Recipient S. Macuen Smith Otolaryngology award Jefferson Med. Coll., 1979, Baxter Healthcare grant Baxter Corp., 1990, Faculty Rsch. grant U. Calif., Irvine Coll. of Medicine, 1990. Mem. Am. Bd. Radiology (bd. examiner 1994—), Am. Coll. Radiology, Assn. Univ. Radiologists, Soc. Gastrointestinal Radiologists (lectr. 1989—), Am. Inst. Ultrasound in Medicine, Soc. Cardiovascular and Interventional Radiologists, Calif. Med. Assn. (bd. dirs., sci. adv. panel on radiology 1993—), Phi Beta Kappa. Office: U South Ala Mastin 301 Radiology 2451 Fillingim St Mobile AL 36617

BRANDON, JEFFREY EARL, health science educator, academic director; b. Herrin, Ill., Feb. 12, 1953; s. Virgil Ray and Wanda June (Cundiff) B.; m. Mary Teresa Chiu, Aug. 7, 1977; children: Christopher Earl, Vanessa Anne. BA, So. Ill. U., 1974, MA, 1978, PhD, 1982. Coord., work evaluation ctr. Highlands County Schs., Sebring, Fla., 1978-79; vocat. evaluator, rehab. inst. So. Ill. U., Carbondale, 1979-81; asst. prof. U. New Orleans, 1982-87, assoc. prof., 1987-89; acad. health sci. dept. head, prof. N.M. State U., Las Cruces, 1989—; assoc. dean Coll. Health and Social Svcs., 1996—; bd. dirs. Health Promotion and Rehab. Svcs., DeSoto, Ill., 1979-82. Contbr. articles to profl. jours., chpts. to books. V.P.-elect N.M. Alliance for Health and Physical Edn., 1990—. President's scholar So. Ill. U., 1974; Doctoral fellow, So. Ill. U., 1981. Mem. APHA, Am. Alliance for Health, Physical Edn., Recreation and Dance, Soc. Behavioral Medicine, Soc. Publ. Health Edn. United Methodist. Office: NM State U Health Sci Dept PO Box 3 HLS White Sands NM 88002-0019

BRANDON, JOHN MITCHELL, physician; b. Pitts., June 28, 1927; s. Albert Given and Adelaide Victoria (Mitchell) B.; m. Phyllis Katherine Wagner, June 22, 1966. BS, U. Pitts., 1952, MD, 1956. Diplomate in internal medicine and hematology Am. Bd. Internal Medicine; diplomate Am. Bd. Pathology. Intern Geisinger Meml. Hosp., Danville, Pa., 1956-57; resident in internal medicine Cleve. Clinic, 1957-60, renal fellow, 1960-61; pvt. practice internal medicine Allegheny Valley Hosp., Tarentum, Pa., 1961-66; resident in pathology VA Hosp. of Pitts., Oakland, Pa., 1966-70, resident in immunology, 1970-71; fellow in coagulation Ctrl. Blood Bank, Oakland, 1971-72; dir. lab. Monongahela Valley Hosp., Monongahela, Pa., 1972-94, part-time pathologist, 1994—; chmn. blood program Monessen (Pa.) Health Ctr., 1972-94; clin. asst. prof. pathology U. Pitts. Med. Sch., 1980—; prof. med. lab. tech. C.C. Allegheny County, Pitts., 1986—. Contbr. chpts. to books, articles to profl. jours. Cpl. USAAF, 1945-46. Recipient Sickman-Levin award for dimensions in medicine Monongahela Valley Hosp., 1993. Fellow ACP, Coll. Am. Pathologists, Am. Soc. Clin. Pathology, Internat. Pathology Soc.; mem. AMA, Pa. Med. Soc. Office: Monongahela Valley Hosp Rte 88 Monongahela PA 15063

BRANDON, KATHRYN ELIZABETH BECK, pediatrician; b. Salt Lake City, Sept. 10, 1916; d. Clarence M. and Hazel A. (Cutler) Beck; MD, U. Chgo., 1941; BA, U. Utah, 1937; MPH, U. Calif., Berkeley, 1957; children: John William, Kathleen Brandon McEnulty, Karen (dec.). Intern, Grace Hosp., Detroit, 1941-42; resident Children's Hosp. Med. Center No. Calif., Oakland, 1953-55, Children's Hosp., L.A., 1951-53; pvt. practice, La Crescentia, Calif., 1946-51, Salt Lake City, 1960-65, 86—; med. dir. Salt Lake City public schs., 1957-60; dir. Ogden City-Weber County (Utah) Health Dept., 1965-67; pediatrician Fitzsimmons Army Hosp., 1967-68; coll. health physician U. Colo., Boulder, 1968-71; student health physician U. Utah, Salt Lake City, 1971-81; occupational health physician Hill AFB, Utah, 1981-85; child health physician Salt Lake City-County Health Dept., 1971-82; cons. in field; clin. asst. U. Utah Coll. Medicine, Salt Lake City, 1958-64; clin. asst. pediatrics U. Colo. Coll. Medicine, Denver, 1958-72; active staff emeritus Primary Children's Hosp., LDS Hosp., and Cottonwood Hosp., 1960-67. Diplomate Am. Bd. Pediatrics. Fellow Am. Pediatric Acad., Am. Pub. Health Assn., Am. Sch. Health Assn.; mem. Utah Coll. Health Assn. (pres. 1978-80), Pacific Coast Coll. Health Assn., AMA, Utah Med. Assn., Salt Lake County Med. Soc., Utah Public Health Assn. (sec.-treas. 1960-66), Intermountain Pediatric Soc. Home and Office: PO Box 58482 Salt Lake City UT 84158-0482

BRANDON, RICHARD LEONARD, health care administrator; b. Winston Salem, N.C., Oct. 1, 1951; s. Richard Jack and Ruth Leola (Leonard) B.; m. Debra Marie Huffman, Aug. 11, 1973; children: Richard, Michael. B in Indsl. Engring., N.C. State U., 1974, M in Indsl. Engring., 1988. Registered profl. engr., N.C. Methods engr. Scovill Mfg., Wake Forest, N.C., 1973-74; plant engr. Sorensen-Christian Industries, Angier, N.C., 1974-77; mfg. engr. Stanadyne Corp., Sanford, N.C., 1977-82; mgmt. engr. II U. N.C. Hosps., Chapel Hill, 1982-89; dir. mgmt. engring. Mary Imogene Bassett Hosp., Cooperstown, N.Y., 1990-93; mgr., consulting svcs. Premier Healthcare Alliance, 1993—; MIT task force Vol. Hosps. Am., Syracuse, N.Y., 1990-93; cons. in field, 1986-89, 93—. Sr. warden St. Bartholomew's Episcopal Ch., Pittsboro, N.C., 1988. Mem. Inst. Indsl. Engrs. (sr.), Soc. Health Systems, Accreditation Bd. Engring. Tech., Health Info. Mgmt. Systems Soc. (sr.). Republican. Home: 2826 Winton Dr Hillsborough NC 27278-9632 Office: 122 S Churton St Hillsborough NC 27278

BRANDRETH, ELIZABETH ANNE, library director; b. N.Y.C., July 8, 1937; d. John Joseph and Edith M. (Mayer) B. AA, Mount Aloysius Jr. Coll., Cresson, Pa., 1957; BA, Coll. Misericordia, 1961; MS in Libr. Sci., Cath. U. Am., 1963; MS in Human Resources Adminstrn., U. Scranton, 1988. Mem. Sisters of Mercy. Asst. libr. Coll. Misericordia, Dallas, Pa., 1963-64; libr. Bishop McCort High Sch., Johnstown, Pa., 1964-67; reference libr. Mount Aloysius Jr. Coll., Cresson, Pa., 1967-71, libr. dir., 1971-79; dir. libr. svcs. Mercy Hosp., Scranton, Pa., 1979-95; regional dir. libr. svcs. Mercy Health Sys.-N.E. Region, Scranton, 1995—. Sec.-treas. bd. dirs. Catherine McAuley Ctr., Scranton, 1986-95; sec. bd. dirs. N.E. Pa. chpt. Susan G. Komen Breast Cancer Found., Scranton, 1989-93; bd. trustees Coll. Misericordia, Dallas, 1990-93. Mem. Med. Libr. Assn., Pa. Libr. Assn. (bd. mem. N.E. chpt. 1985-87), Beta Phi Mu. Roman Catholic. Office: Mercy Hosp 746 Jefferson Ave Scranton PA 18510-1624

BRANDRIET, LOIS MARIE, nurse educator, researcher; b. Watertown, S.D., Nov. 20, 1955; d. Elmer Louis and Lillian Mae (Wegner) Rogness; m. Randall Kent Brandriet, June 22, 1974; children: Jay Christopher, Justin Lee. ADN, Coll. St. Mary, Omaha, 1977; BS in Nursing, Westminster Coll., 1985; MS in Nursing, Brigham Young U., 1988; PhD in Nursing, U. Utah, 1993. Staff nurse Archbishop Bergen Mercy Hosp., Omaha, 1977-79, Holy Cross Hosp., Salt Lake City, 1979-80; staff nurse Pioneer Valley Hosp., West Valley City, Utah, 1980, discharge planning nurse, 1980-87; nursing instr. Weber State Coll., Salt Lake City, 1987-88; staff nurse LDS Hosp., Salt Lake City, 1988-93; pvt. geriat. care mgr. ElderCare Cons., Highland, Utah, 1995—; nursing instr. Brigham Young U., Provo, Utah, 1989-95; cons. ElderCare Cons., Highland, 1992-95. Contbr. articles to profl. jours. Utah Nurses Found. scholar, 1989. Mem. ANA, Nat. Assn. Profl. Geriat. Care Mgrs., Utah Nurses Assn. (editl. bd., bd. dirs. 1994—), Utah Dirs. Nursing Long-Term Care, Nat. Assn. Dirs. Nursing Long-Term Care, Nat. Gerontol. Nurses Assn. (rsch. com. 1993), Nat. Nurses in Bus. Assn., Sigma Theta Tau. Home: 11289 N Tamarack Dr Highland UT 84003 Office: ElderCare Cons 11289 N Tamarack Dr Highland UT 84003

BRANDS, JAMES EDWIN, medical products executive; b. Lebanon, Ind., July 5, 1937; s. Edwin Herman and Pearl Irene (Brown) B.; m. Gail Marian Knight, Sept. 12, 1959; children: Jeffrey, Scot, Alan, Susan. AB, Wesleyan U., Middletown, Conn., 1959; MBA, U. Chgo., 1961; JD, Kennedy-Western U., Boise, Idaho, 1992. CPA, Mo. Staff acct., mgr. Arthur Andersen & Co., Chgo., 1961-71; ptnr. Arthur Andersen & Co., St. Louis, 1971-82; sr. v.p. Scherer-Storz, Inc., St. Louis, 1982-86; exec. v.p. Scherer Sci. Ltd., Atlanta, 1986-95; bd. dirs., v.p. Ramco Fluid Svcs., Inc., Atlanta, BodyCare Inc., Atlanta, Maximum Benefits, LLC, Atlanta; bd. dirs., pres. Throwleigh Technologies LLC, Atlanta; bd. dirs. MicroCap Bridge Fund, N.Y.C., Ga. Am. Land Co., Atlanta, Creative Beverages, Inc., Evansville, Ind.; owner, mgr. Brands & Co., 1986—. Mem. AICPA, Mo. Soc. CPAs, Bellerive Country Club (St. Louis), Atlanta Nat. Golf Club. Republican. Presbyterian. Home: 4330 Bancroft Vly Alpharetta GA 30202-5175 Office: PO Box 767655 Roswell GA 30076-7655

BRANDSTATER, MURRAY EVERETT, physiatrist; b. Hobert, Australia, Apr. 21, 1935. BS, MD, U. Melbourne, Australia, 1957. Cert. in Phys. Med. Rehab. Intern Box Hill Dist. Hosp., Melbourne, 1958; resident in internal medicine Alfred Hosp., Melbourne, 1959, 61-62; resident Royal Children's Hosp., Melbourne, 1960; rsch. in phys. med. rehab. Mayo Clinic, Rochester, Minn., 1964-68; prof. phys. med. rehab. McMaster U., Hamilton, Ont., Can., 1968-84; mem. staff Loma Linda (Calif.) U. Med. Ctr., 1984—; prof. phys. med. rehab. Loma Linda U., 1981—. Mem. AMA, AAEM, MRCP, RCPC. Office: Loma Linda U Affil Hosps Dept Rehab Medicine Rm A237 Loma Linda CA 92354

BRANDT, BARBARA KINMAN, psychologist; b. Weisbaden, Fed. Republic Germany, Apr. 4, 1954; d. James G. and Ruth E. (Madaris) Caldwell; children: Charity, Jamie. AS, Okaloosa Walton Jr. Coll., Niceville, Fla., 1981; BS summa cum laude, Troy (Ala.) State U., 1984; MS, Ga. State U., 1986. Lic. profl. counselor. Mental health technician USAF, Eglin AFB, Fla., 1975-79; psychotherapist, owner Centacare, Columbus, Ga., 1985-91; psychologist specializing in early childhood trauma Martin Army Cmty. Hosp., Ft. Benning, Ga., 1991—. Recipient Meritorious Svc. Cert. USAF Hosp. Eglin, 1977, 78. Mem. Am. Mental Health Counselors, ACA, New Vision Bus. and Profl. Women (pres. 1987-88). Office: Martin Army Community Hosp Dept Of Psychiatry Fort Benning GA 31905

BRANDT, BLANCH MARIE, health care facility administrator; b. Dryden, Ont., Can., Apr. 12, 1937; came to U.S., 1964; d. Frederick William and Mary Elizabeth (Gamble) Morton; m. Les W. Brandt, Dec. 12, 1958. BA, Southwestern Bapt. Bible Coll., Tucson, 1983; MA in Psychology, Southwest U., 1991, PhD, 1993. Dir., proprietor SOI Learning Ctr., Riverside, Calif., 1991—; dir. SOI/Vision Clinic Twin Pines Ranch/Van Horn Youth Ctr., Riverside County Probation, 1994—; ednl. and career cons. Recipient Outstanding Project award Am. Pub. Health Assn., Nat. Jewel Young award, 1990, Outstanding Svc. award San Bernardino County Probation, 1995. Mem. Am. Correctional Health Svcs., Am. Probation and Parole Assn., Universal Ch. of the Master Mins. Home: 2686 W Mill St # 13 San Bernardino CA 92410-2019 Office: 5051 Canyon Crest Dr Ste 102 Riverside CA 92507-6035

BRANDT, CARL DAVID, research virologist; b. Bridgeport, Conn., Jan. 19, 1928; s. Carl August and Hildur (Wedberg) B.; m. Elsa Lund Erickson, Apr. 25, 1964; children—Karen, Erik. B.S., U. Conn., 1949; M.S., U. Mass., 1951; Ph.D., Harvard U., 1958. Rsearch instr. dept. vet. sci. U. Mass., Amherst, 1949-52, 54; research virologist Charles Pfizer & Co., Inc., Ind. and Conn., 1958-62; assoc., dept. epidemiology Pub. Health Research Inst. N.Y.C., 1962-66; research assoc. virology research Children's Nat. Med. Ctr., Washington, 1966-79, sr. research assoc., 1979-86, sr. scientist, 1986—; instr. Georgetown U. Med. Sch., Washington, 1966-69; asst. prof. pediatrics George Washington U. Med. Sch., Washington, 1969-74, assoc. prof., 1974-94, emeritus prof., 1994. Contbr. articles to profl. jours. Served to 1st lt. USAF, 1952-54. Fellow Am. Acad. Microbiology, Infectious Diseases Soc. Am., Am. Coll. Epidemiology; mem. AAAS, Am. Soc. Microbiology, Soc. Epidemiologic Research, Pan Am. Group Rapid Viral Diagnosis, Sigma Xi. Clubs: N.Y Color Slide (bd. dirs. 1965-66); Silver Spring Camera (pres. 1970-71); Rock Creek Amateur Radio Assn (pres. 1985-89). Avocations: photography; amateur radio. Home: 819 E Franklin Ave Silver Spring MD 20901-4709 Office: Childrens Nat Med Ctr Rm 189A 111 Michigan Ave NW Washington DC 20010

BRANDT, EDWARD NEWMAN, JR., physician, educator; b. Oklahoma City, July 3, 1933; s. Edward Newman and Myrtle (Brazil) B.; m. Patricia Ann Lawson, Aug. 29, 1953; children: Patrick James, Edward Newman III, Rex Carlin. BS, U. Okla., 1954, MD, 1960, PhD, 1963; MS, Okla. State U., 1955; LHD, Med. U. S.C., Rush U.; DSc, N.Y. Inst. Tech. Intern Oklahoma City VA Hosp., 1960-61; resident U. Okla. Hosps., 1961; from instr. to prof. preventive medicine and pub. health U. Okla. Med. Center, Oklahoma City, 1961-70; prof., chmn. dept. biostatistics U. Okla. Med. Center (Sch. Health), 1967-68; assoc. dean U. Okla. Med. Center (Sch. Medicine); assoc. dir. U. Okla. Med. Center (Med. Center), 1968-70; dean Grad. Sch., prof. preventive medicine and community health U. Tex. Med. Br., Galveston, 1970-72; acting dean U. Tex. Med. Br. (Grad. Sch.), 1972-74, assoc. dean clin. affairs, 1972-73, prof. preventive medicine and community health, 1970-84, acting dean medicine, 1973-74, prof. family medicine, 1973-84, dean medicine, 1974-76, exec. dean, 1976-77; vice chancellor health affairs U. Tex. System, Austin, 1977-81; asst. sec. health HHS, 1981-84; pres. U. Md.-Balt., 1985-89, also prof. epidemiology and preventive medicine, 1985-89; prof. internal medicine, exec. dean Coll. Medicine U. Okla., Oklahoma City, 1989-92; dir. Ctr. for Health Policy U. Okla., 1992—; prof. health adminstrn. Coll. Pub. Health, 1989—; mem. primate ctr. rev. com. NIH, 1975-79, chmn., 1978-79, mem. rsch. career devel. award com., 1968-72, mem. adv. com. on rsch. in women's health, 1995—; bd. regents Nat. Libr. Medicine, 1985-89, chmn., 1987-89; mem. exec. coun. WHO, 1982-84; chmn. adv. coun. on injury control CDC, 1988-93; chmn. adv. coun. on food FOA, 1992—. Editor, contbr. Proc. of Conf. at U. Okla. Med. Ctr., 1968; editor Continuing Education for the Family Physician, 1974-77, AIDS and Pub. Policy Jour., 1988-91. Recipient Superior Performance award VA Hosp. Oklahoma City, 1961; Lloyd M. Southwick Meml. award for med. writing, 1974, 75; Spl. Appreciation award Tex. Acad. Family Physicians, 1974; Leone award for adminstrv. excellence, 1976; Outstanding Alumni Svc. award U. Okla. Coll. Medicine, 1977; Disting. Svc. award U. Tex. Med. Br., 1977; 19th Ann. Stoneburner lectr. Med. Coll. Va., 1966, Disting. Leadership award HHS, 1984, Disting. Pub. Svc. award Dept. Def., 1986, Pub. Health award Am. Acad. Family Physicians. Fellow AAAS (chair med. scis. sect. 1992-93), Am. Coll. Cardiology (hon.); mem. AMA (chmn. sec. on med. schs. 1979-81, chmn. com. accreditation continuing med. edn. 1979-81), Assn. Am. Med. Colls. (exec. coun. 1986-89, Spl. Recognition award 1985), Okla. Med. Assn. (chmn. com. on family violence, 1993—, chmn. coun. on state legis. 1994—), Am. Acad. Family Physicians, Okla. Acad. Family Physicians, Philos. Soc. Tex., Inst. Medicine (governing coun. 1986-92), Sigma Xi, Alpha Omega Alpha, Phi Eta Sigma, Alpha Epsilon Delta, Phi Kappa Phi, Phi Sigma Pi, Mu Epsilon. Office: U Okla Health Scis Ctr PO Box 26901 Oklahoma City OK 73190

BRANDT, JOHN HENRY, physician; b. Cleve., July 30, 1940; s. Harold Paul and Dorothy Helen (Kern) B.; m. Jon Ellison, July 30, 1963 (div. 1971); children: Sylvia Ann, Laura Ann; m. Marilyn Ruth Brandt, July 25, 1980. BA, Yale U., 1962; postgrad., Cambridge (Eng.) U., 1962-64; MD, Harvard U., 1970. Asst. to dir. Harvard Ctr. for Community Health, Boston, 1968-69; clin. fellow Med. Sch. Harvard U., Boston, 1970-73, instr. in psychiatry Med. Sch., 1973-74, 74—; resident psychiatrist McLean Hosp., Belmont, Mass., 1970-73, dir. Waverley House, 1973-74, attending psychiatrist, 1974-90; attending psychiatrist Mass. Mental Health Ctr., 1991—; staff psychiatrist med. dept. MIT, Cambridge, 1979—. Mem. archives com. Trinity Ch., Boston, 1988—; active Mass. Hist. Soc., New Eng. Hist. Geneal. Soc. Mem. Am. Psychiat. Assn., Mass. Med. Soc., N.Y. Acad. Medicine, Internat. Inst., English Speaking Union, Boston Athenaeum, Yale Club of Boston (sec. 1988-90, dir. 1990-93), Harvard Club of Boston (chmn. Ho. com. 1989-91, v.p. 1991-93), Harvard Musical Assn. (dir. 1990-93), St. Botolph Club, Cosmos Club, Yale Elizabethan Club, Yale Mory's Assn., Bostonian Soc., Colonial Soc., Phi Beta Kappa. Republican. Episcopalian. Home: PO Box 530 Lincoln MA 01773-0530 Office: MIT Med Dept 77 Massachusetts Ave Cambridge MA 02139-4301

BRANDT, LAWRENCE JAY, gastroenterologist; b. Bronx, May 20, 1945. BS, CCNY, 1965; MD, SUNY, Brooklyn, 1964-68. Intern Mt. Sinai Hosp., NYC, 1968-69, resident in internal medicine, 1969-71; chief resident in internal medicine Mt. Sinai Hosp., NYC, 1972; fellow in gastroenterology Mt. Sinai Hosp., NYC; staff physician Montefiore Med. Ctr., Bronx, 1974—, prof., divsn. chief, 1985—. Author: Gastrointestinal Disorders of the Elderly, 1984; editor: Treating IBD: A Patient's Guide, 1989, Ischemic Disorders of the Intestinal Tract, 1992; patentee Brandt cytology balloon. Chmn. Scarsdale (N.Y.) Sch. Bd. Health Adv. Com., 1994-95. Maj. U.S. Army, 1966-74. Tchg. and rsch. scholar ACP, 1975-78, faculty initiate to AOA, 1990. Fellow Am. Acad. Physician and Patient; mem. Am. Coll. Gastroenterology (pres. 1 992-93, trustee 1984-95), Am. Gastroent. Assn. (disting. educator 1993), Am. Soc. Gastrointestinal Endoscopy, N.Y. Soc Gastrointestinal Endoscopy, N.Y. Acad. Gastroenterology, Phi Beta Kappa. Office: Montefiore Med Ctr 111 E 210th St Bronx NY 10467

BRANDT, PHILIP WILLIAMS, anatomy educator; b. Cleve., Sept. 23, 1930; s. Philip Francis and Ann (Williams) B.; m. Helene Blain, Oct. 27, 1954; children: David, Daniel. BA, Swarthmore Coll., 1952; PhD, Columbia U., 1960. Asst. instr. U. Pa., Phila., 1953-57; rsch. fellow Nat. Coun. to Combat Blindness, N.Y.C., 1958-60; instr. Columbia U., N.Y.C., 1960-61, asst. prof., 1961-68, assoc. prof., 1968-87, prof., 1988—. Contbr. articles to Exp. Cell Rsch., Jour. Biophys. and Biochem. Cytol., N.Y. Acad. Sci., Arch. Opth., Circulation, Jour. Cell Biology, Jour. Ultrastructure Rsch., Helv. Physiol. Acta, Jour. Gen. Physiology, Science, Jour. Colloid and Interface Sci., Am. Zoologist, Nature, Biophys. Jour., Jour. Membrane Biology, Am. Jour. Physiology, Proceedings NAS, Analytical Biochemistry, Jour. of Muscle Rsch. and Cell Motility, Jour. Molecular Biology. V.p. Bronx Orgn. for the Learning Disabled, Bronx, N.Y., 1970-76, chmn. fin. com., 1988—. Guggenheim fellow John Simon Guggenheim Mmel. Found., 1968, Hon. fellow Univ. Coll., London, 1975; recipient Career Devel. award NIH, 1968-73. Mem. Am. Assn. Anatomists, Am. Soc. Cell Biologists, Biophys. Soc., Soc. Gen. Physiologists, Sigma Xi. Office: Columbia U Coll Physicians & Surgeons 630 W 168th St New York NY 10032-3702

BRANDT-RAUF, PAUL WESLEY, preventive medicine educator, researcher; b. N.Y.C., Oct. 9, 1948; s. Charles Paul and Charlotte Elizabeth (Morton) R.; m. Sherry Iris Brandt, June 26, 1974; children: Elka, Joshua, Oren. BS, Columbia U., 1970, MS, 1973, ScD, 1974, MD, 1979, MPH, 1980, DPH, 1986. Diplomate Am. Bd. Internal Medicine, Am. Bd. Preventive Medicine in Occupl. Medicine. Asst. prof. Columbia U. Sch. Pub. Health, N.Y.C., 1985-89, assoc. prof., 1989-93, prof., 1993—. Editor-in-chief Jour. Occupl. and Environ. Medicine, 1992—. Fellow ACP, Am. Coll. Preventive Medicine, Am. Coll. Occupl. and Environ. Medicine (bd. dirs. 1994-97), Royal Soc. Medicine. Office: Columbia U Sch Pub Health 60 Haven Ave Ste B-1 New York NY 10032

BRANDWIN, LESLIE MARTIN, internist; b. N.Y.C., Mar. 22, 1946; s. Al and Yetta (Schindelman) B.; m. Linda Gale Kram, Aug. 24, 1969; children: Martin Lawrence, Emily Alisa. BS, CCNY, 1967; MD, St. Louis U., 1971. Diplomate Am. Bd. Internal Medicine, Am. Bd. Rheumatology. Pvt. practice, St. Louis, 1978—. Contbr. papers to profl. jours. Lt. M.C., USNR, 1972-74. Fellow Am. Coll. Rheumatology; mem. St. Louis Rheumatism Soc. (former v.p. and pres.), St. Louis Scleroderma Soc. (co-chair 1995), St. Louis Med. Soc. (councilor 1988-91). Republican. Jewish. Office: Med Assocs 8631 Delmar Ave Saint Louis MO 63124

BRANEA, IOAN DOREL, internal medicine and cardiology educator; b. Sibiu, Romania, Dec. 12, 1938; s. Ioan Ioan and Eugenia (Bălan) B.; m. Stela Simon, 1966 (div. 1986); children: Horea, Ioan; m. Felicia Munteanu, 1987; 1 child, Eugenia. Student, Inst. Medicine, Timosoara, Romania, 1957-63, PhD, 1973. Intern, then resident in internal medicine Clin. Hosp. #2, Timisoara, 1962-68, instr. internal medicine and cardiology, 1969-80; asst. prof. Inst. Medicine, Timisoara, 1971-80, prof., 1981—; prof. med. Polyclinic Inst. Medicine, Timisoara, 1981. Author: Medical Polyclinic, 1980, Chronic Myocardopathies, 1987, Ambulatory Medicine, 1993, Medical Emergencies, 1994; contbr. 149 articles in field to profl. jours. Sec. med. rev. Timisoara Medicală, 1978. Mem. Romanian Union Med. Scientists, Romanian Soc. Cardiology, Romanian Soc. Cardiovascular Rehab. (pres.), Balkanik Med. Union, Timisoara Commn. Cardiology (v.p. 1981), European Soc. Cardiology, European Assn. Cardiovasc. Rehab., French Soc. Cardiology (assoc.). Greek Orthodox. Avocations: travel, hunting. Home: Bd Cetatii 11, 1900 Timisoara Romania Office: Inst Medicine, Bd 23 August 12, 1900 Timisoara Romania

BRANNACK-EPPOLITE, LISA ANN, clinical forensic nurse, intensive care nurse; b. Pontiac, Mich., Mar. 14, 1967; d. Kenneth Ralph and Carol Ann (Scott) Schwark. BSN magna cum laude, No. Mich. U., 1992; postgrad., Clayton Sch. Natural Healing, Birmingham, Ala. RN; critical care RN; cert. emergency nurse; cert. BLS; cert. Pediatric Advanced Life Support; cert. flight RN.; cert. ACLS. ACLS instr. George Washington U., 1993—; emergency and intensive care nurse Md. Profl. Staffing Svcs., Bethesda, 1995—. Vol. Montgomery County Coalition for the Homeless, Gaithersburg, Md., 1995—. Ensign, USNR. No. Mich. U. Academic Achievement scholar, 1988-92, Am. Business Women's scholar, 1989-92, USN Nursing scholar, 1990. Mem. Jr. Mil. Nurse's Orgn. (sec. 1992-93). Lutheran. Home: 20454 Summer Song Ln Germantown MD 20874

BRANNAN, TIMOTHY S., neurologist, educator; b. Carlisle, Pa., Dec. 24, 1949; s. Martin C. and Margaret (Spangler) B.; m. Christine E. Parsch, June 30, 1971; children: Hilary, Meredith. BS, Elizabethtown (Pa.) Coll., 1971; MD, U. Pitts., 1975. Diplomate in neurology Am. Bd. Psychiatry and Neurology. Resident neurology Mt. Sinai Sch. Medicine, N.Y.C., 1976-79, fellow neurochemistry, 1979-80, instr. neurology, 1980-83, asst. prof. neurology, 1983-90, assoc. prof., 1990—. Contbr. articles to profl. jours., chpts. to books. Fellow Am. Acad. Neurology; mem. Movement Disorders Soc. Office: Mt Sinai Med Ctr 100th St & 5th Ave Box 1137 New York NY 07666

BRANNON, FRANCES JOAN, professor of exercise physiology; b. Parcoal, W.Va., Jan. 24, 1935; d. Doy Alton and Lona Margaret (Armstrong) B. BA, Berea Coll., 1956; MS, U. Tenn., 1961; PhD, U. Md., 1968.

Cert. tchr., Ky. Instr. Berea (Ky.) Coll., 1956-61, U. Md., College Park, 1965-68; asst. prof. Macalester Coll., St. Paul, Minn., 1968-69; prof. Slippery Rock (Pa.) U., 1969—; founder Brannon Health Resources Mgmt., Prospect, Pa., 1976—, founder, cons. Bio-Energetics Rehab., Prospect, 1976-89. Author: Exercise Physiology, 1978, 2d edit., 1994, (with others) Cardiac Rehabilitation, 1988, 2d edit., 1992 (pres. award 1988). Founder Tigger Neutering Fund, Butler Humane Soc., 1971. Recipient Commonwealth Disting. Teaching chair, State of Pa., 1974. Mem. Am. Coll. Sports Medicine, Tri-State Assn. Cardiac Rehab., Am. Assn. Cardiovascular and Pulmonary Rehab., Am. Assn. Health, Phys. Edn. and Recreation, Pa. Assn. Health, Phys. Edn. and Recreation, Phi Kappa Phi. Republican. Home: 223 Harmony Rd Prospect PA 16052-2209 Office: Slippery Rock U Field House Slippery Rock PA 16057

BRANNON, WILLIAM LESTER, JR., neurologist, educator; b. Olar, S.C., Jan. 11, 1936; s. William Lester and Lena Mae (Brigman) B.; m. Darrell Meeks, June 13, 1959; children: Debra Brannon DeMarco, William Bert, Victoria Brannon-Diaz. AB, U. S.C., 1957; MD, Med. U. S.C., 1961. Commd. ensign U.S. Navy, 1966, advanced through grades to capt., 1980; chmn. dept. neurology Nat. Naval Med. Ctr., Bethesda, Md., 1969-79; assoc. prof. neurology Georgetown U. Sch. medicine, Washington, 1969-79; prof. neurology Uniformed Svc. U. Health Scis., Bethesda, 1974-79, chmn. dept. neurology, 1978-79; dir. clin. svcs. Naval Regional Med. Ctr., Charleston, S.C., 1979-80; ret. U.S. Navy, 1980; clin. prof. neurology Med. U. S.C., Charleston, 1979-80; vice chair, dir. neurology U. S.C. Sch. Medicine, Columbia, 1980—; neurology cons. to attending physician U.S. Capitol and White House, 1970-79, to Surgeon Gen. U.S. Navy, 1970-79. Contbr. articles to sci. and med. reports. Fellow ACP, Am. Acad. Neurology, Am. Electroencephalography Soc. Democrat. Methodist. Office: U SC Sch Medicine 3555 Harden St Columbia SC 29203

BRANNON-PEPPAS, LISA, chemical engineer, researcher; b. Houston, Sept. 19, 1962; d. James Graham and Patricia Ann (Hightower) Brannon; m. Nicholas A. Peppas, Aug. 10, 1988. BS, Rice U., 1984; MS, Purdue U., 1986, PhD, 1988. Sr. formulations chemist Eli Lilly & Co., Indpls., 1988-91; pres., founder Biogel Tech., Indpls., 1991—. Author, editor: Absorbent Polymer Technology, 1990; mem. editorial bd. Jour. Applied Polymer Sci., 1995—; contbg. editor Polymer News, 1989—; contbr. articles to profl. jours. Vol. Indpls. Mus. Art, 1990—, Humane Soc. Indpls., 1990—, Indpls. Zoo, 1994—. Recipient Harold B. Lamport award Biomed. Engring. Soc., 1989. Mem. AIChE (exec. bd. programming coun., dir. materials divsn., chmn. subcom. biomaterials divsn. 1990-93, dir.-at-large food, pharm. and bioengring. divsn. 1992-94, 2d vice chair materials divsn. 1994-95, 1st vice chair materials divsn. 1995-96), Am. Chem. Soc. (membership com. 1990—), Controlled Release Soc. (treas. 1995—, internat. planning com. 1991, bd. govs. 1992-95), Jr. League Indpls. (bd. dirs. 1992-94). Office: Biogel Tech PO Box 681513 Indianapolis IN 46268-7513

BRANSCOM, JAMES JEFFERSON, radiologist; b. San Antonio, Oct. 11, 1939; s. James Jefferson and Margaret (Gillett) B.; m. Louise Watson, Jan. 28, 1967; 1 child, Sarah. BA in History, Stanford U., 1961; MD, Columbia U., 1965. Intern San Francisco Gen. Hosp., 1965-66; med. resident U. Calif., San Francisco, 1966-68, radiology resident, 1970-73; v.p. North Bay Radiology, Danville, Calif., 1973-89, pres., 1989—; pres. San Ramon (Calif.) Imaging, 1987—; mem. staff John Muir Hosp., Mt. Diablo Hosp.; pres. San Ramon Ully Imaging Assocs.; bd. dirs. Diablo Valley Radiology; dir. outpatient imaging Bay Imaging Cons. Lt. comdr. USNR, 1968-70. Mem. East Bay Radiol. Soc. (pres. 1978-79), Phi Beta Kappa. Office: San Ramon Imaging 3160 Crow Canyon Rd Ste 180 San Ramon CA 94583-1331

BRANSFIELD, JAMES JOSEPH, surgeon; b. Chgo., Nov. 8, 1932; s. James Joseph and Beatrice Catherine (Greene) B.; m. Virginia Kaye Paully, Dec. 17, 1967; 1 child, Helena Theresa. BS, Loyola U., 1955, MD, 1957. Diplomate Am. Bd. Emergency Medicine, Am. Bd. Surgery. Pvt. practice specializing in surgery Chgo., 1968—. Chief of police Chgo. Police Dept., 1983-94. Lt. comdr. USNR, 1960-63. Home: 6200 N Knox Chicago IL 60646-5030

BRANSFIELD, ROBERT CARROLL, psychiatrist; b. Wildwood, N.J., Sept. 17, 1946; s. Joseph Carroll and Dorothy Norma (Campbell) B.; m. Lynne Frances Kirkham, Nov. 11, 1982; children: Douglas, Craighton, Courtney. BA, Rutgers U., 1968; MD, George Washington U., 1972. Diplomate Am. Bd. Psychiatry and Neurology. Resident Sheppard & Enoch Pratt Hosp., Balt., 1972-75; cons. Eastern Shore Hosp. Ctr., Cambridge, Md., 1974-75; practice Psychiat. Assocs. Tidewater, Suffolk, Va., 1975-79; pvt. practice Freehold, N.J., 1979-81, Red Bank, N.J., 1979—; cons., Roanoke-Chowan Mental Health Svc., Ahoskie, N.C., 1975-77, Southhampton (Va.) Correction Farm, 1977; chmn. dept. psychiatry, Children's Psychiat. Ctr., Eatontown, N.J., 1983-85; assoc. dir. dept. psychiatry, chmn. quality assurance for dept. psychiatry, Riverview Med. Ctr., Red Bank, 1987—. Contbg. author: Psychiatric House Calls, 1988; contbr. articles to various publs.; spl. guest NBC Nightly News, 1994; presenter in field. Mem. rev. bd. Juvenile Conf. Com., Middletown, N.H., 1980-82; pres., bd. dirs. Navesink North Condominium Assn., Red Bank, 1987-89; bd. dirs. Monmouth County Mental Health Assn., 1990—. Mem. N.J. Psychiat. Assn. (pres. Monmouth-Ocean chpt. 1986-88), Monmouth County Mental Health Assn. (bd. dirs. 1990—), Mid-Atlantic Koi Club (no. region coord. 1987—). Office: 225 Highway 35 Red Bank NJ 07701-5919

BRANSON, BRANLEY ALLAN, biology educator; b. San Angelo, Tex., Feb. 11, 1929; s. Branley Allan and Era Elizabeth (Rogers) B.; m. Mary Louise Lewis, June 3, 1964; 1 son, Rogers McGowan. A.A., Northeastern Okla. A. and M. Coll., 1954; B.S., Okla. State U., 1956, M.S., 1957, Ph.D., 1960. Asst. prof. biology Kan. State Coll., Pittsburg, 1960-64; prof. biology Eastern Ky. U., Richmond, 1964—, found. prof., 1989-90. Contbr. articles to mags. Recipient Sci. award Okla. A. and M. Coll., 1953; named Disting. Scientist of Ky., 1984. Fellow Okla. Acad. Sci., AAAS; mem. Southwestern Assn. Naturalists (bd. govs. 1965—), Am. Malacological Union, Soc. for Study Evolution, Kan. Acad. Sci., Ky. Acad. Sci. (editor transactions), Soc. Systematic Zoologists, Am. Soc. Zoologists, Am. Soc. Ichthyologists and Herpetologists, Sigma Xi, Phi Theta Kappa, Phi Kappa Phi. Home: 100 Walnut Hill Dr Richmond KY 40475-3620 Office: Eastern Ky U Richmond KY 40475

BRANTIGAN, JOHN WILDER, orthopaedist, surgeon, educator; b. Balt., Mar. 16, 1945; s. Otto Charles and Edith B. BA, Cornell U., 1966; MD, Johns Hopkins U., 1970. Diplomate Am. Bd. Orthopaedic Surgery. Resident in orthopaedic surgery U. Wash., Seattle, 1974-78; pvt. practice Omaha, 1978-90, Cleve. Spine and Arthritis Ctr., 1990-92; orthopaedic cons. Cleve. Indians, 1991; assoc. prof. Creighton U., Omaha, 1992—; med. adv. panel AcroMed Corp., Cleve., 1989—. Author: Natural Consequences, 1995; patentee in field; contbr. over 50 articles to profl. jours. Capt. USAF, 1971-73. Henry Strong Dennison scholar Johns Hopkins U., Balt., 1969-70; recipient first prize Cecile Lehman Mayer Rsch. Forum Am. Coll. Chest Physicians, 1971. Mem. AMA, Am. Acad. Orthopaedic Surgeons, North Am. Spine Soc. Office: Dept Surgery Creighton U 601 N 30th St Omaha NE 68131

BRANTLEY, JEFFREY GARLAND, health science facility administrator; b. Rocky Mount, N.C., Nov. 4, 1949; s. Roy Garland and Irene (Cockrell) B.; m. Mary Mathews, Nov. 21, 1981. BA in History, Davidson Coll., 1971; MD, U. N.C., 1977. Diplomate Am. Bd. Psychiatry. Resident in psychiatry U. Calif., Irvine, 1981; pvt. practice psychiatry Laguna Niguel, Calif., 1981-82, Durham, N.C., 1985-87; med. dir. Hospice Orange County, Laguna Niguel, 1982; clin. dir. Durham County Mental Health Ctr., Durham, N.C., 1982-89; freelance cons., educator Durham, 1990—; clin. assoc. dept. psychiatry U. Calif., Irvine, 1981-82; consulting assoc. Dept. Psychiatry Duke U., 1983—. Mem. Am. Psychiat. Assn., N.C. Psychiat. Assn., Am. Soc. Clin. Hypnosis, Physicians for Social Responsibility. Democrat. Buddhist. Home: 1109 Huntsman Dr Durham NC 27713-2370 Office: 201 Providence Rd Chapel Hill NC 27514

BRASHER, GEORGE WALTER, physician; b. Jackson, Tenn., Dec. 7, 1936; s. George W. and Verla S. Brasher; m. Martha S. Brasher, Dec. 23, 1960; children: Suzanne Cheshier, George Brasher, John Brasher, David Brasher. BA, Lambuth U., 1959; MD, U. Tenn., 1961. Diplomate Am. Bd. Allergy and Immunology, Am. Bd. Pediatrics. Cons. Scott & White Clinic & Hosp., Temple, Tex., 1966—; dir. Allergy and Immunology Scott & White Clinic and Hosp., Temple. Tex., 1975—; prof. Medicine and Pediatrics Tex. A&M U. Coll. of Medicine, Temple, Tex., 1977—. Contbr. articles to profl. jours. Fellow Am. Acad. Allergy and Immunology, Am. Acad. Pediatrics, Am. Coll. Allergy and Immunology; mem. AMA, Tex. Med. Assn., Bell County Med. Soc., Tex. Allergy Soc. Office: Scott & White Clinic & Hosp 2401 S 31st St Temple TX 76508-0001

BRASHER, TERRY BRYAN, physician assistant; b. Seminole, Tex., Oct. 17, 1958; s. Floyd Howell and Mary Alice (Roberts) B.; children: Johnathan Michael, Christopher Lowell. BS, U. Tex., Galveston, 1986. Cert. physician asst. Nat. Commn. Certification of Physician Assts; cert. BCLS,ACLS. Medi-quick Dr. James Barbee, Beaumont, Tex., 1986-91; physicians asst. Bohman Clinic-Dr. Raymond Reese and Dr. Dan Dugi, Cuero, Tex., 1991-96, DeTar med. Ctr. Rural Health Clinic, Tex., 1996—. Team physician asst. West Brook H.s., Beaumont, Tex., 1986-91. Named Outstanding Young Men of Am., 1986. Fellow Am. Acad. Physician Assts., Tex. Acad. Physician Assts., Bexar County Physician Assts. Office: Detar Med Ctr Kenedy 113 W Main Kenedy TX 78119

BRASIC, JAMES ROBERT, psychiatrist; b. Chgo., Feb. 25, 1948; s. John James and Lillian Mathilda (Hilgart). BA, MD, Boston U., 1972; MA, Washington U., 1980; MPH, Columbia U., 1983, MS, 1984, MA, 1987. Med. diplomate in neurology, psychiatry, child and adolescent psychiatry. Assembler Welch Sci. Co., Skokie, Ill., 1966; straight med. intern Med Ctr. U. Ala., Birmingham, 1972-73; neurology resident Med. Ctr. L.A. County-U. So. Calif., 1973-75; psychiatry resident Barnes Hosp., St. Louis, 1975-77; psychiatrist USAF Med. Ctr., Wright Patterson AFB, Ohio, 1977-79; child psychiatry fellow Presbyn. Hosp., N.Y.C., 1980-82; psychiatrist I Rockland Children's Psychiat. Ctr., Orangeburg, N.Y., 1981-83; assoc. attending physician Harlem Hosp. Ctr., N.Y.C., 1983-87; faculty rsch. fellow Mt. Sinai Med. Ctr., N.Y.C., 1987-88; faculty rsch. fellow Med. Ctr. NYU, N.Y.C., 1988-89; faculty coord. devel. neurobiology unit div. child & adolescent psychiatry Bellevue Hosp. & NYU Med. Ctr., N.Y.C., 1989-95; attending psychiatrist comprehensive psychiat. program Bellevue Hosp. Ctr., 1995—; rsch. asst. prof. psychiatry NYU Sch. Medicine, N.Y.C., 1992—. Contbr. articles to profl. jours. Mem. Westside YMCA, N.Y.C. Maj. USAF, 1977-79. Decorated USAF Commendation medal; recipient Dept. Psychiatry Faculty Recognition award Wright State U., 1979. Fellow Am. Acad. Child and Adolescent Psychiatry; mem. Am. Psychiat. Assn., Am. Acad. Neurology, Am. Statis. Assn., Inst. Math. Statis., Mensa. Home: 35 W 64th St Apt 5G New York NY 10023-6553 Office: NYU Med Ctr 550 1st Ave New York NY 10016-6497

BRASIER, ALLAN R., medical educator. BA in Biomed. Engring., U. Calif., San Diego, 1979; MD, U. Calif., San Francisco, 1983. Diplomate Am. Bd. Internal Medicine. Intern, med. resident Brigham & Women's Hosp., Boston, 1983-86; endocrinology/ metabolism fellow Mass. Gen. Hosp., Boston, 1986-87, clin. & rsch. fellow dept. molecular endocrinology, 1987-89, rsch. assoc. Howard Hughes Med. Inst., 1988-91; assoc. prof. medicine Sealy Ctr. Molecular Sci. U. Tex. Med. Br., Galveston, 1991—, sr. scientist, 1996; instr. medicine Harvard Med. Sch., Boston, 1989-90, asst. prof., 1990-91; lectr. Nat. Coun. High Blood Pressure Rsch. Contbr. articles to profl. jours. Recipient Acad. Excellence award U. Calif. San Francisco Alumni Faculty Assn., 1983, Established Investigator award Am. Heart Assn., 1995. Mem. Phi Beta Kappa, Alpha Omega Alpha. Office: U Tex Med Br MRB 3 142 Divsn Endocrinology 301 University Blvd Galveston TX 77555-1060

BRASITUS, THOMAS ALBERT, gastroenterologist, educator; b. Bridgeport, Conn., Aug. 2, 1945; s. Albert Joseph and Mary Frances (Gazdowskas) B.; m. Christine Ann Legace, Aug. 19, 1967; children: Kristie, Thomas Jr. BA, U. Conn., 1963; MD, Jefferson Med. Sch., Phila., 1967. Asst. prof. Columbia U., N.Y.C., 1977-83; assoc. prof. U. Chgo., 1983-86, prof., 1986—, Walter Lincoln Palmer disting. sci. prof. of medicine, 1987—; dir. sect. of gastroenterology U. Chgo., 1985—. Contbr. numerous articles to profl. and sci. jours., 1973—. Bd. dirs. Gastrointestinal Rsch. Found., Chgo., 1985—. Maj. USAF, 1975-77. Recipient Merit award Nat. Cancer Inst./NIH, 1986—. Mem. Am. Assn. Physicians, Am. Soc. for Clin. Investigation, Am. Soc. for Biochemistry and Molecular Biology, Chgo. Soc. Gastrointestinal Endoscopy (pres. 1989-90), Chgo. Soc. Gastroenterology (pres. 1990-91). Office: U Chgo Kirsner Ctr Study Digestive Diseases 5341 S Maryland Ave Chicago IL 60637-1463*

BRASS, ERIC PAUL, internal medicine and pharmacology educator; b. Bklyn., Sept. 3, 1952; s. Edward A. and Barbara (Rosen) B.; m. Kathy E. Sietsema, Sept. 3, 1994; children: Carl, Courtney, Alexander. BS in Chem. Engring., Case Western Res. U., 1974, MS in Chem. Engring., 1975, PhD in Pharmacology, 1979, MD, 1980. Diplomate Am. Bd. Internal Medicine. Resident in internal medicine U. Wash., Seattle, 1980-82, fellow in clin. pharmacology, 1982-83; asst. prof. medicine and pharmacology U. Colo., Denver, 1983-89, assoc. prof., 1989-93; asst. dir. Calif. Clin Trials, 1993-94; prof., chair dept. medicine Harbor-UCLA Med. Ctr., 1994—. Contbr. articles to sci. jours. Recipient Faculty Devel. award Pharm. Mfrs. Assn. Found., 1985; NIH rsch. grantee, 1985, 88, 93. Mem. Am. Diabetes Assn. (rsch. grantee 1984), Am. Fedn. Clin. Rsch., Am. Soc. Pharmacology and Exptl. Therapeutics, Am. Soc. Clin. Pharmacology and Therapeutics (Young Investigator award 1987), Am. Soc. Clin. Investigation. Office: Harbor-UCLA Med Ctr 1000 W Carson St Torrance CA 90502-2004

BRASSARD, ROGER PAUL, physician; b. Ashland, N.H., Feb. 21, 1913; s. Edgar and Isabel (Savage) B.; m. Vivian Leonora Flanders, Apr. 12, 1950; children: Ann Louise, Deborah, Mary Jane. BS, U. N.H., 1935, MS, 1936; MD, Albany (N.Y.) Med. Coll., 1940. Intern Waterbury (Conn.) Hosp., 1940-41, resident, 1941-42; pvt. practice Laconia, N.H., 1946—. Maj. M.C., U.S. Army, 1942-46. Mem. Am. Acad. Family Practice, Am. Bd. Family Practitioners, N.H. Acad. Family Practice (Family Practitioner of the Yr. 1984). Republican. Roman Catholic. Home: 328 Union Ave Laconia NH 03246-2812 Office: 354 S Main St Laconia NH 03246-3722

BRASWELL, LAURA DAY, periodontist; b. Bowling Green, Ky., July 22, 1958; d. Lawson Moyers and Bettye (Wall) B.; m. DeFord Smith III; children: DeFord Lawson Smith, Ashley Smith, Alison Smith, Jeanette Smith. DDS, U. N.C., 1982; cert., Emory U., 1988. Diplomate Am. Acad. Periodontology. Staff dentist Sam Rudd DDS, Raleigh, N.C., 1982-83; mem. faculty Emory U., Atlanta, 1983-93; assoc. scientist Yerkes Regional Primate Ctr., Atlanta, 1984—; zoo dentist Zoo Atlanta, 1986—; pvt. practice Atlanta, 1988—. Vol. Healing for the Poor, Kingston, Jamaica, 1986, Ctrl. Presbyn. Health Ctr., Atlanta, 1986-91, Grant Park Family Health Ctr., 1989-93; 1st vice chmn. Arthritis Found., Ga. Mem. ADA, Internat. Assn. Dental Rsch., Am. Assn. Dental Rsch., Ga. Dental Assn., Acad. Laser Dentistry (charter), No. Dist. Dental Soc. (mem. exec. coun.), Psi Omega. Methodist. Home: 5064 Fields Pond Cv Marietta GA 30068-1572 Office: Yerkes Regional Primate Rsch Ctr at Emory U 954 Gatewood Rd Atlanta GA 30329-9999 also: 3312 Piedmont Rd NE # 270 Atlanta GA 30305-1706

BRATCHER, CARLA ELIZABETH, obstetrician-gynecologist; b. Wichita, Kans., Sept. 18, 1942; d. Carl E. and Armilda Elizabeth (Salmans) Dillon; m. Carl E. Bratcher III, Apr. 9, 1983. Student, U. Wash., 1960-62; BS, U. Fla., 1966; MD, U. Pa., 1979. Diplomate Am. Bd. Ob-Gyn. Rsch. technician Nat. Cancer Inst.-NIH, Bethesda, Md., 1967-73, Wistar Inst., Phila., 1973-75; ob-gyn intern Madigan Army Med. Ctr., Tacoma, 1979-80, resident in ob-gyn, 1980-83; chief ambulatory care svc. ob-gyn. 2d Gen. Hosp., Landstuhl, Fed. Republic Germany, 1984-87; pvt. practice, Grand Prairie, Tex., 1988-89; pvt. practice ob/gyn. Redmond, Oreg., 1990—; chief ob. dept. Ctrl. Oreg. Dist. Hosp., 1990—; vol. instr. dept. ob-gyn Dallas-Ft. Worth Med. Ctr., 1988-89. Maj. M.C., U.S. Army, 1979-87. Fellow Am. Coll. Obstetricians and Gynecologists; mem. AMA, AAUW, Oreg. Med. Assn., Am. Med. Women's Assn. Democrat. Office: Redmond Ob/Gyn 215 NW Kingwood Suite 150 Redmond OR 97756

BRATTER, THOMAS EDWARD, psychologist, educator; b. N.Y.C., May 18, 1939; s. Edward Maurice and Marjorie (Polikoff) B.; BA, Columbia Coll., 1961, MA, 1963, EdM, 1969; Columbia U., EdD, 1974; m. Carole Ann Jaffe, Aug. 25, 1963; children: Edward Philip, Barbara Ilyse. Instr. dept. health edn. Tchrs. Coll., Columbia U., N.Y.C., 1969-81; youth resources dir. Village Scarsdale (N.Y.), 1970-72; pvt. practice psychotherapy, 1970-84; dir. City Island Methadone Clinic, Bronx, N.Y., 1972-74; prof. Union Inst., Ohio, 1975-81; pres., founder John Dewey Acad., Gt. Barrington, Mass., 1984—, chmn. adv. bd., 1992—; adj. faculty continuing edn. divsn. dept. psychiatry Harvard U. Med. Sch., Boston, 1995—; cons. Dept. Probation City N.Y., 1973-77, Pan Am Commodities Corp., 1975-78, N. Castle Police Dept., 1978-88; adolescent group psychotherapy cons. Pelham (N.Y.) Guidance Council, 1973-79. Bd. dirs. Odyssey Inst., N.Y.C., 1975-77, Nat. Health Inst., Inc., 1974-76, Nat. Ind. Pvt. Schs. Assn., 1988-91; trustee Daytop Village, Inc., N.Y.C., 1972-84, Forest Inst. Profl. Psychology, Des Plaines, Ill., 1981-84, Gabelli Equity Trust (NYSE), N.Y.C., 1986—, Gabelli Multi-Media Trust, 1994—, Dewey Acad., 1991; chmn. adv. bd. John Dewey Found., 1992; troop master Boy Scouts Am., Scarsdale; varsity basketball coach Sarah Lawrence Coll., 1977-78. Served with NG, 1960-61. Mem. Am. Group Psychotherapy, Am. Psychol. Assn., Am. Assn. Marriage and Family Therapy, Am. Acad. Health Care Providers Addictive Disorders (mem. nat. adv. bd. 1992—), Small Boarding Schs. Assn. (v.p. 1992—), Kappa Delta Pi, Phi Delta Kappa. Author: (with A. Bassin and R.L. Rachin) Reality Therapy Reader, 1976; (with R. and N. Kolodny) How to Survive Your Adolescent's Adolescence, 1984, (with G. Forrest) Alcoholism and Substance Abuse: Strategies for Clinical Intervention, 1985, (with N. and R. Kolodny) Smart Choices, 1986; also over 175 articles on adolescent substance abuse and alcoholism treatment, individual and group psychotherapy and edn.; assoc. editor Jour. Drug Issues, 1970-78; mem. editorial bd. Jour. Corrective and Social Psychiatry, 1974-78, Addiction Therapist, 1975-78, Jour. Specialists in Group Work, 1975-78, Jour. of Mental Health Counseling Assn., 1979-82, Jour. Reality Therapy, 1980-85, Jour. Counseling and Devel., 1983-88, Jour. of Humanistic Education, 1989-93. Home: 53 Logan Rd Salisbury CT 06068-1513

BRATTLOF, BRIAN DANIEL, surgeon; b. St. Paul, May 3, 1951; s. Clifford and Grace Shirley (Fox) B.; m. Deborah Ann Smith, June 21, 1975; 1 child, Brent Daniel. BCE, U. Minn., 1973, MSCE, 1976; MD, W.Va. U., 1982. Bd. cert. Am. Bd. Surgery. Engr. Union Carbide Corp., South Charleston, W.Va., 1975-78; commd. officer U.S. Army, 1982, advanced through grades to maj.; resident U.S. Army, Ft. Lewis, Wash., 1982-87; surgeon U.S. Army, Ft. Leondard Wood, Mo., 1987-89, Dakota Clinic, Park Rapids, Minn., 1989—. Fellow ACS. Office: Dakota Clinic Hc 6 Box 36A Park Rapids MN 56470

BRAUDE, LAURENCE STANLEY, physician, surgeon, researcher; b. Johannesburg, South Africa, Mar. 5, 1953; came to U.S., 1978; s. Jakob and Sylvia (Binder) B. M.B.B.Ch., U. Witwatersrand, Johannesburg, 1976. Diplomate Am. Bd. Ophthalmology. Intern Johannesburg Gen. Hosp., 1977-78; resident U. Ill. Eye and Ear Infirmary, Chgo., 1978-81; corneal fellowship Swedish Hosps. Med. Ctr., Seattle, 1981-82; pvt. practice Laurence S. Braude, MD, PC, Highland Park, Ill., 1982—; clin. asst. prof. U. Ill., Chgo., 1982—; pres. Metro-Chgo. Eye Care Network, 1995—. Recipient grant Kroc Found., 1980, grant U. Ill., 1984-86. Fellow Am. Acad. Ophthalmology, Am. Coll. Surgeons, Royal Coll. Surgeons (Can.); mem. AMA, Chgo. Ophthal. Soc. (eye bank com. 1984—, program chmn. monthly meetings 1988-89). Office: Laurence S Braude MD PC 1971 Second St Ste 500 Highland Park IL 60035

BRAUDE, ROBERT MICHAEL, medical library administrator; b. L.A., Sept. 27, 1939; s. Aaron and Dorothy (Lishner) B.; m. Sharon Helene Katz, Dec. 16, 1961; children—Michael, Daniel, Julianne. BA, UCLA, 1962, MLS, MA, 1964; PhD, U. Nebr., 1987. Reference librarian Biomed Library Ctr. for Health Scis., UCLA, Los Angeles, 1964-65, head Medlars search sta., 1965-68; assoc. dir. U. Colo. Med. Library, Denver, 1968-75, dir., 1975-77; dir. U. Nebr. Med. Library, Omaha, 1978-86; asst. dean for info. resources, Frances and John Loeb librarian Cornell U. Med. Coll., 1986—; adj. faculty U. Denver, 1972-78; vis. assoc. prof. Sch. Libr. Sci., Pratt Inst., 1988—; del. White House Conf. on Libraries and Info. Services, 1979; mem. biomed. library rev. com. Nat. Library Medicine, Bethesda, Md., 1980-84, mem. panel on med. informatics long range planning project, 1985-86, mem. planning panel on outreach programs, 1988-89. Author: (continuing edn. syllabus) Planning: Strategic and Tactical, 1983, also articles and book chpts.; mem. editorial adv. bd. Bibliography of Bioethics; mem. editorial bd. ann. Statis. of Med. Sch. Librs. and U.S. and Can., 19887-93; mem. editorial bd. Jour. Am. Med. Informatics Assn. Sec.-treas. Children's Chorale, Denver, 1974-75, trustee, 1975-77. Fellow N.Y. Acad. Medicine, Med. Libr. Assn. (sec., bd. dirs. 1972-75, chmn. numerous coms. N.Y.-N.J. chpts., Outstanding Achievement award Midcontinental chpt. 1986); mem. ALA, Acad. Health Info. Profls. (disting.), N.Y. Acad. Medicine, Health Scis. Libr. Dirs. (stds. and practices com. 1980-83), Assn. Western Hosps. (chmn. hosp. librs. sect. 1976-77, membership com. 1976-77), Am. Med. Informatics Assn. (mem. editl. bd.). Home: 1320 York Ave Apt 34G New York NY 10021-4878 Office: Cornell U Med Coll CV Starr Biomedical Info Ctr 1300 York Ave New York NY 10021-4805

BRAUER, RAYMOND OLIVER, plastic surgeon; b. Fresno, Calif., Mar. 3, 1916; s. Oscar Leo and Anita (Graves) B.; m. Irene Kathryn Lien, Aug. 1939 (dec. May 1980); children: Kenneth W., Elizabeth K. Brauer Ziemba; m. Sylvia Schwartz Robertson, Nov. 1994. BS, Pacific Union U., 1939; MD, Loma Linda U., 1943. Diplomate Am. Bd. Plastic Surgery. Clin. prof. plastic surgery Baylor Coll. of Medicine, Houston, 1954—; acad. chmn. plastic surgery residency program St. Joseph Hosp., Houston, 1976-86; examiner Am. Bd. Plastic Surgery, 1974-80, sr. examiner, 1990—; vis. prof., lectr. in field. Contbr. articles to profl. jours. Maj. U.S. Med. Corps, 1944-48. Mem. Am. Assn. Plastic Surgeons, Am. Soc. Plastic and Reconstructive Surgeons, Am. Cleft Palate and Craniofacial Surgery, Plastic Surgery Edn. Found., Am. Soc. Maxillofacial Surgeons, Tex. Surg. Soc., Tex. Soc. Plastic Surgeons (founding mem., past pres.), Houston Soc. Plastic Surgeons (founding mem., past pres.), Houston Surg. Soc. (pres. 1978-79, Plaque of Recognition of Outstanding Leadership 1979, Surgeon of Yr. 1994), Plastic Surgery Rsch. (founding mem.), Doctors Club, Lakeside Country Club. Republican. Presbyterian. Home: 11 Pinewold Ct Houston TX 77056 Office: Cronin Brauer Smith Plast Surgery 1315 Calhoun # 940 Houston TX 77002

BRAULT, G(AYLE) LORAIN, healthcare executive; b. Chgo., Jan. 3, 1944; d. Theodore Frank and Victoria Jean (Pribyl) Hahn; m. Donald R. Brault, Apr. 29, 1971; 1 child, Kevin David. AA, Long Beach City Coll., 1963; BS, Calif. State U.-Long Beach, 1973, MS, 1977. RN, Calif; cert. nurse practitioner. Dir. nursing Canyon Gen. Hosp., Anaheim, Calif., 1973-76; dir. faculty critical care masters degree program Calif. State U., Long Beach, 1976-79; regional dir.. nursing and support svcs. Western region Am. Med. Internat., Anaheim, Calif., 1979-83; v.p. Hosp. Home Care Corp. Am., Santa Ana, Calif., 1983-85; pres. Hosp. Home Health Care Agy. Calif., Torrance, 1986-92; v.p. Hosp. Coun. So. Calif., L.A., 1993—; invited lectr. China Nurses Assn., 1983; cons. AMI, Inc., Saudi Arabia, 1983; advisor dept. grad. nursing Calif. State U., L.A., 1988, advisor Nursing Inst., 1990-91; guest lectr. dept. pub. health UCLA, 1986-87; assoc. clin. prof. U. So. Calif., 1988—; lectr. Calif. State U., Dominguez Hills, 1996-97; editl. advisor RN Times, Nurseweek, 1988—, chmn. editl. adv. bd. Contbr. articles to profl. jours., chpts. to books. Commr. HHS, Washington, 1988. HEW advanced nurse tng. grantee, 1978. Mem. Women in Health Adminstrn. (sec. 1989, v.p. 1990), Nat. Assn. Home Care, Am. Orgn. Nursing Execs., Calif. Assn. Health Svcs. at Home (task force chmn. 1988, bd. dirs. 1988-93, chmn. bd. dirs. 1990-93), Calif. League Nursing (bd. sec. 1983, program chmn. 1981-82), Am. Coll. Health Care Execs., ASAE, AONE, Phi Kappa Phi, Sigma Theta Tau. Republican. Methodist. Home: 1032 E Andrews Dr Long Beach CA 90807-2406

BRAUMAN, JOHN I., chemist, educator; b. Pitts., Sept. 7, 1937; s. Milton and Freda E. (Schlitt) B.; m. Sharon Lea Kruse, Aug. 22, 1964; 1 dau., Kate Andrea. B.S., Mass. Inst. Tech., 1959; Ph.D. (NSF fellow), U. Calif., Berkeley, 1963. NSF postdoctoral fellow U. Calif., Los Angeles, 1962-63; asst. prof. chemistry Stanford (Calif.) U., 1963-69, asso. prof., 1969-72, prof., 1972-80, J.G. Jackson-C.J. Wood prof. chemistry, 1980—, chmn. dept., 1979-83, 95-96; cons. in phys. organic chemistry; adv. panel chemistry divsn. NSF, 1974-78; adv. panel NASA, AEC, ERDA, Rsch. Corp., Office Chemistry and Chem. Tech., NRC; coun. Gordon Rsch. Confs., 1989-95, trustee, 1991-95. Mem. editl. adv. bd. Jour. Am. Chem. Soc., 1976-83, Jour. Organic Chemistry, 1974-78, Nouveau Jour. de Chimie, 1977-85, Chem.

Revs., 1978-80, Chem. Kinetics, 1987-89, Accts. Chem. Rsch., 1995—, Ann. Revs., 1995—; dep. editor for phys. scis. Sci., 1985—. Fellow Alfred P. Sloan, 1968-70, Guggenheim, 1978-79; Christensen, Oxford U., 1983-84. Fellow AAAS (chmn. sect. 1996—), Calif. Acad. Scis. (hon.); mem. NAS, Am. Acad. Arts and Scis., Am. Chem. Soc. (award in pure chemistry 1973, Harrison Howe award, 1976, R.C. Fuson award, 1986, James Flack Norris award 1986, Arthur C. Cope scholar, 1986, exec. com. phys. chemistry divsn., com. on sci. 1992—), Brit. Chem. Soc., Sigma Xi, Phi Lambda Upsilon. Home: 849 Tolman Dr Palo Alto CA 94305-1025 Office: Stanford U Dept Chemistry Stanford CA 94305-5080

BRAUN, JESSICA BROWN, women's health nurse; b. Cleve., Dec. 5, 1966; d. Frederick G. and Jean (Benfer) B. BSN, Pa. State U., 1988; MSN, U. Pa., 1994. Cert. trauma nurse, cert. RN inpatient obstetric nursing, NCC. Med.-surg. nurse clinician Hershey (Pa.) Med. Ctr., 1988-90, nurse clinician in obstetrics, 1990-94; perinatal nurse practitioner Sisters of Charity Hosp., Buffalo, N.Y., 1995—. Mem. N.Y. State Coalition of Nurse Pracitioners, Sigma Theta Tau. Office: Sisters of Charity Hosp 2157 Main St Buffalo NY 14214

BRAUN, PHILIP ROY, psychologist; b. N.Y.C., June 11, 1945; s. Jerome and Sylvia (Goldberg) B.; B.A., U. Mich., 1966; M.A., Temple U., 1967, Ph.D., 1971; m. Madelon Ostroff, June 12, 1966; children: Andrew Tobin, Jessica Suzanne. Sr. staff psychologist Diagnostic Rehab. Center, Phila., 1970-72; dir. drug rehab. unit Haverford (Pa.) State Hosp., 1972-74; adj. faculty Temple U., Chestnut Hill Coll., Villanova U., 1972-74; pvt. practice clin. psychology, Conshohocken, Pa., 1970—; dir. Partial Hosp., Lenape Valley Found., Doylestown, Pa., 1974-81, assoc. exec. dir., 1981—; adj. prof. Delaware Valley Coll., Doylestown, 1979—. Bd. dirs. personnel Whitemarsh Youth Program. Mem. Am. Assn. Partial Hospitalization (bd. dirs., pres.), Am. Psychol. Assn., Pa. Psychol. Assn., Phila. Soc. Clin. Psychologists, Eastern Psychol. Assn., Delaware Valley Partial Hospitalization Assn. (pres.). Democrat. Jewish. Home: 4 Vera Ln Conshohocken PA 19428-2134 Office: 500 N West St Doylestown PA 18901-2366

BRAUN, PHYLLIS CELLINI, biology educator; b. Bridgeport, Conn., Jan. 19, 1953; d. Rudolph V. and Rose B. (Nappi) Cellini; m. Kevin F. Braun, July 19, 1975; children: Ryan C., Jessica P. BS in Biology, Fairfield U., 1975; PhD in Microbiology, Georgetown U., 1978. Postdoctoral fellow NIH U. Conn. Health Ctr., Farmington, Conn., 1978-79; instr. biology Fairfield (Conn.) U., 1979-80, asst. prof. biology, 1980-84, assoc. prof. biology, 1984-89, prof. biology, 1989—, chair dept. biology, 1993—; cons. Miles Pharms., West Haven, Conn., 1984-90, Internat. Schoeffel Industries, N.J., 1984-86, Genetech, San Francisco, 1986; grant reviewer NIH, Bethesda, 1986—. Contbr. articles to scientific jours. Mem. AAAS, N.Y. Acad. Sci., Am. Soc. Microbiology, Am. Assn. for Women in Sci., Med. Mycology Assn. Am. Republican. Roman Catholic. Office: Fairfield U Dept Biology N Benson Rd Fairfield CT 06430-5152

BRAUN, ROBERT ALEXANDER, retired psychiatrist; b. Chemnitz, Germany, Dec. 14, 1910; came to U.S., 1939, naturalized, 1946; s. Leo and Bertha (Eisenschiml) B.; m. Gertrud E. Mittler, 1946; children: Eleanor, Ronald. MD, U. Vienna (Austria), 1937. Intern, William McKinley Meml. Hosp., Trenton, N.J., 1940-41; resident in psychiatry Rochester (Minn.) State Hosp., 1950-51, staff psychiatrist, 1951-56; resident in psychiatry Lafayette Clinic, Detroit, 1956-58; staff psychiatrist, clin. dir. Clinton Valley Center (formerly Pontiac State Hosp.), Pontiac, Mich., 1958-63, dir. Oakland Div., 1963-80; pvt. practice psychiatry, 1980-95; med. dir. Jensen Counseling Ctrs., Farmington Hills, Mich., 1984-95; ret. from practicing psychiatry, 1996; clin. assoc. prof. dept. psychiatry Mich. State U., 1969-80. Contbr. chpt. And So We Must Remember: Holocaust Memories, 1992. Life fellow Am. Psychiat. Assn.

BRAUN, ROBERT DANIEL, obstetrician; b. Toledo, Ohio, Jan. 19, 1939; s. Herbert Daniel and Una Margueite (Chapman) B.; m. Bonita S. Chapman, Dec. 30, 1961; children: Edythe Jane, James Daniel, Robert Oliver. BS, U. Toledo, 1960; MD, Baylor U., 1964. Diplomate Am. Bd. Ob-Gyn. Resident in ob-gyn. Ind. U., 1969; staff physician Scott & White Clinic, Temple, Tex., 1971-74; prof., chmn. ob-gyn. U. Tenn. RAHC, Chattanooga, 1974-79; prof. ob-gyn. U. N.D., Grand Forks, 1979-83, Tex. Tech. RAHC, Odessa, 1983-95, Ind. U. Med. Ctr., 1995—. Contbr. articles to profl. jours. Lay reader St. Thaddeus Episocpal Ch., Chattanooga, Tenn., stewardship chmn. 19778; fin. com. St. Paul's Episcopal Ch., Grand Forks, N.D., 1981-83, diocesan conv. del., 1981, 82, others; lay reader St. John's Episcopal Ch., 1983—, chalicist 1983—, vestryman, 1985-87; bd. dirs. Odessa chpt. March of Dimes, 1987—, Am. Diabetes Assn., 1987—. With USN, 1969-70. Mem. AMA, Tex. Med. Assn., Tex. Assn. Ob-Gyn., Am. Soc. Colposcopy and Cervical Pathology, Am. Coll. Ob-Gyn. (program dir. 1977, chmn. registration com. 1977, chmn. publicity com. 1977), Am. Assn. of Gyn. Laparoscopists, So. Perinatal Assn., Soc. for Obstetrical Anesthesia and Perinatology, Ob-Gyn. Ultrasound, Nat. Perinatal Assn. (com. on edn. 1980-84), Great Plains Orgn. for Perinatal Health Care (long range planing com. 1982-84, pres. N.D. chpt. 1981-82, bd. dirs. 1981-84). Office: 1001 W 10th St # F5 Indianapolis IN 46202-2859

BRAUN, STEPHEN HUGHES, psychologist; b. St. Louis, Nov. 20, 1942; s. William Lafon and Jane Louise B.; BA, Washington U., St. Louis, 1964, MA, 1965; PhD (USPHS fellow in Clin. Psychology), U. Mo., Columbia, 1970; 1 son, Damian Hughes. Asst. prof. psychology Calif. State U., Chico, 1970-71; dir. social learning div. Ariz. State Hosp., Phoenix, 1971-74; chief bur. planning and evaluation Ariz. Dept. Health Svcs., Phoenix, 1974-79; pres. Braun and Assocs., human svc. program cons.'s, Scottsdale, Ariz., 1979—; v.p. Ariz. Healthcare, 1991-95; dir. clin. svcs. Cmty. Partnership So. Ariz., 1995—; asst. prof. psychology Ariz. State U., 1971-79, vis. asst. prof. Ctr. of Criminal Justice, 1974-79, Ctr. for Pub. Affairs, 1979-81; cons. Law Enforcement Assistance Adminstrn., NIMH, Alcohol, Drug Abuse, and Mental Health Adminstrn., Ariz. Dept. Health Svcs., Ariz. Dept. Corrections, Ariz. Dept. Econ. Security, local and regional human svc. agys. NIMH rsch. grantee, 1971-74; State of Calif. rsch. grantee, 1971; lic. clin. psychologist, Ariz. Mem. Am. Psychol. Assn., Sigma Xi. Editorial cons.; contbr. articles to profl. publs. Office: 6655 N Canyon Crest Dr # 27103 Tucson AZ 85750

BRAUND, CAROL VIRTUE, critical care nurse; b. Guys Mills, Pa., Feb. 9, 1938; d. Ivan Archer and Frances (Williams) Virtue; m. Darwin G. Braund, July 22, 1934 (div. 1985); children: Michele, Wendy, Pamela (dec.). BS, Pa. State U., 1960; AAS, Onondaga Community Coll., Syracuse, N.Y., 1979; postgrad. studies Nursing, Syracuse U., 1995—, BSN, 1990, postgrad. CCRN; ACLS. Tchr. Cherokee Hts. Jr. High, Madison, Wis., 1960-61, Bd. of Edn., Auburn, N.Y., 1961-63; staff nurse CCU SUNY Health Sci. Ctr., Syracuse, 1979-88, clin. mgr. CCU, 1988-90, asst. DON, adminstrv. supr., co-chair total mgmt. adv. panel, 1990—. Mem. nurse edn. com. Am. Heart Assn. of Ctrl. N.Y., 1988—; mem. ethics com. Village of Fayetteville. Named Outstanding Alumna Onandaga C.C., 1996. Mem. ANA (Dist. 4 polit. action com. 1991-92), AACN (bd. adv. team for FY97), Think First Head/Spinal Cord Injury-Neurosurgery Group. Office: SUNY Health Sci Ctr 750 E Adams St Syracuse NY 13210-2306

BRAUNSTEIN, ETHAN MALCOLM, skeletal radiologist, paleopathologist; b. Chgo., June 16, 1945. BA, Dartmouth Coll., 1967; MD, Northwestern U., Chgo., 1970. Instr. radiology U. Mich., Ann Arbor, 1976-81, assoc. prof., 1983-87; asst. prof. radiology Harvard U., Cambridge, Mass., 1981-83; prof. Ind. U., Indpls., 1987—; adj. prof. anthropology Ind. U., Indpsl., 1990—. Contbr. numerous articles to profl. jours. and chpts. to books. Bd. dirs. Kelsey Mus. of Archeology, Ann Arbor, 1983-87. Mem. Internat. Skeletal Soc., Am. Assn. Physical Anthropologists, Radiologic Soc. N.Am., Assn. Univ. Radiologists. Office: Ind U Hosps Dept Radiology Indianapolis IN 46202

BRAUNSTEIN, GLENN DAVID, physician, educator; b. Greenville, Tex., Feb. 29, 1944; s. Mervin and Helen (Friedman) B.; m. Jacquelyn D. Moose, July 5, 1965; children: Scott M. Braunstein, Jeffrey T. Braunstein. BS summa cum laude, U. Calif. San Francisco, 1965, MD, 1968. Diplomate Am. Bd. Internal Medicine, subspecialty endocrinology, diabetes, metabolism. Intern, resident Peter Bent Brigham Hosp., Boston, 1968-70; clin. fellow in medicine Harvard U. Med. Sch., Boston, 1969-70; clin. assoc., reproduction rsch. br. NIH, Bethesda, Md., 1970-72; chief resident in endocrinology Harbor Gen. Hosp. UCLA, 1972-73; dir. endocrinology Cedars-Sinai Med. Ctr., L.A., 1973-86, chmn., dept. medicine, 1986—; asst. prof. medicine UCLA Sch. Medicine, 1973-77, assoc. prof., 1977-81, prof., 1981—, vice chair dept. medicine, 1986—; cons. for AMA drug evaluations, 1990—; mem. internat. adv. com. Second World Conf. on Implantation and Early Pregnancy in Human, 1994; mem. endocrinologic and metabolic drugs adv. com. FDA, 1991-95, chmn., 1994-95, spl. advisor, 1995—; bd. mem. Am. Bd. Internal Medicine Endocrinology, Diabetes, Metabolism Subspecialty, 1991—, chmn., 1995—, bd. dirs., 1995—. Editl. bd. Jour. Clin. Endocrinology & Metabolism, 1978-80, editor, 1980-83; editl. bd. Mt. Sinai Jour. Medicine, 1984-88, Early Pregnancy: Biology and Medicine, 1994—, Am. Family Physician, 1995—. Bd. dirs. Israel Cancer Rsch. Fund, 1991-94; mem. Jonsson Comprehensive Cancer Ctr., 1991—. Recipient Gold Headed Cane Soc. award U. Calif. San Francisco Med. Ctr., 1968, Merck scholarship, 1968, Mosby scholarship, 1968, Soc. of Hacham award Cedars-Sinai Med. Ctr., 1976, Morris Press Humanism award Cedars-Sinai Med. Ctr., 1984. Fellow ACP (mem. adv. com. to gov., So. Calif. region 1989—, credentials com. So. Calif. region 1993); mem. AAAS, Am. Diabetes Assn., Cross Town Endocrine Club (chmn. 1982-83), Endocrine Soc. (publs. com. 1983-89, long range planning com. 1986-87, recent progress hormone rsch. com. 1993—, ann. meeting steering com. 1993—), Pacific Coast Fertility Soc. (pres. 1988), Western Soc. for Clin. Rsch., Am. Fedn. for Clin. Rsch., Am. Fertility Soc., Western Assn. Physicians, Assn. Am. Physicians, Am. Soc. Clin. Investigations (mem. nominating com. 1989), USCF Sch. Medicine Alumni Faculty Assn. (regional v.p. so. Calif., mem. bd. dirs. Israel Cancer Rsch. Fund 1991-94, mem. Jonsson Comprehensive Cancer Ctr. 1991—), Phi Delta Epsilon, Alpha Omega Alpha. Office: Cedars Sinai Med Ctr Dept Med Pla Level B118 8700 Beverly Blvd Los Angeles CA 90048-1804

BRAUNWALD, EUGENE, physician, educator; b. Aug. 15, 1929; m. Nina H. Starr, 1952 (dec.); m. Elaine R. Smith, 1993; children: Karen G., Allison Jill. AB, NYU, 1949, MD, 1952; AM (hon.), Harvard U., 1972; MD (hon.), U. Lisbon, 1984, U. Lisbon, 1985; ScD (hon.), Mt. Sinai Med. Ctr., 1991; MD (hon.), U. Rome, 1991, U. Portg, 1992, U. Vienna, 1995, U. La Plata (Argentina), 1995. Diplomate Am. Bd. Internal Medicine, Am. Bd. Cardiovascular Disease. Intern, fellow Mt. Sinai Hosp., N.Y.C., 1952-54; research fellow Columbia U. Coll. Physicians and Surgeons, N.Y.C., 1954-55; clin. assoc. cardiovascular physiology lab. Nat. Heart Inst., Bethesda, Md., 1955-57; asst. resident Osler Med. Service, Johns Hopkins Hosp., Balt., 1957-58; chief cardiology sect., chief cardiology br., clin. dir. Nat. Heart and Lung Inst., Bethesda, 1958-68; prof., chmn. dept. medicine U. Calif.-San Diego, 1968-72; Hersey prof. of theory and practice of medicine Harvard U. Med. Sch., Boston, 1972—, Herrman Blumgart prof. Medicine, 1980-89; sr. cons. in medicine Mass. Gen. Hosp., 1994—; chmn. dept. medicine Brigham and Women's Hosp., 1972—, Beth Israel Hosp., 1980-89; lectr. physiology George Washington U., 1959-62; from asst. clin. prof. to clin. prof. Georgetown U. Sch. Medicine, 1960-68; lectr. medicine Johns Hopkins U., 1960-68; trustee Brigham and Women's and Mass. Gen. Hosps. Health Sys., 1993—; vis. prof. numerous U.S. and fgn. univs.; lectr. in field. Co-editor: Year Book of Cardiovascular and Renal Diseases, 1965-72, Year Book of Medicine, 1973-93, Harrison's Principles of Internal Medicine, 1967—; editor Heart Disease, 1980—; mem. editorial bds. Circulation, Jour. Clin. Investigation, 164-71, Jour. Cardiovascular Pharmacology, Am. Jour. Medicine, Am. Jour. Cardiology, New Eng. Jour. Medicine, numerous others. Bd. visitors Rockefeller U., 1978-82; mem. vis. com. MIT, 1979-85, Technion U., 1979. Recipient Arthur S. Fleming award, 1965, Superior Svc. award HEW, 1967, Disting. Achievement award Modern Medicine, 1968, Gustav Nylin award Swedish Med. Soc., 1970, Williams award Outstanding Chmn. and Medicine, 1987, Bristol Myers Squibb Excellence in Cardiovascular Rsch. award, 1993, J. Allyn Taylor Internat. prize Robarts Rsch. Inst., 1993. Fellow ACP (Phillips award 1991), Am. Acad. Arts and Scis., Am. Coll. Cardiology (v.p. 1967, trustee 1967, 70-75, Disting. Scientist award 1987); mem. Nat. Acad. Scis., Johns Hopkins Soc. Scholars, Assn. Profs. Medicine (pres. 1974-75), Assn. Am. Physicians, Western Assn. Physicians, Am. Soc. Clin. Investigation (pres. 1974-75), Am. Fedn. Clin. Research (pres. 1969-70), Western Soc. for Clin. Research (pres. 1971-72), Assn. Univ. Cardiologists, New England Cardiovascular Soc. (pres. 1987-88), Am. Physiol. Soc., Am. Soc. Pharmacology and Exptl. Therapeutics (John Jacob Abel award 1965), Am. Heart Assn. (bd. dirs. 1966-75, v.p. 1966-70, Research Achievement award 1972, Herrick award 1981), Harvey Soc., Royal Soc. Medicine, Internat. Soc. Cardiology, Alpha Omega Alpha. Office: Brigham and Women's Hosp 75 Francis St Boston MA 02115-6110

BRAUSE, BARRY DAVID, infectious diseases physician; b. N.Y.C., Apr. 15, 1945; s. Jack and Ruth (Heiman) B.; m. Geraldine Hersh, June 13, 1970; children: Juliet, Melissa, Jacqueline. BA, NYU, 1966; MD, U. Pitts., 1970. Diplomate Am. Bd. Internal Medicine, Infectious Diseases. Intern Boston City Hosp., 1970-71; resident N.Y. Hosp., 1971-73; fellow infectious diseases Cornell U. Med. Coll., N.Y.C., 1973-75, clin. assoc. prof. medicine, 1983-95, clin. prof. medicine, 1995—; assoc. attending physician Hosp. Spl. Surgery, N.Y.C., 1984-96, attending physician, 1996—; assoc. attending physician N.Y. Hosp., 1983-95, attending physician, 1995—. Editl. reviewer Jour. AMA, 1990—, Jour. Bone and Joint Surgery, 1989—; relevance reviewer Am. Bd. Internal Medicine, 1995—; contbr. chpts. in books. Bd. dirs. N.Y. County Soc. Internal Medicine. Recipient Andrew Mellon Tchr.-Scientist award Andrew W. Mellon Found., 1977-79, Frank Stinchfield award The Hip Soc., 1985. Fellow ACP; mem. Infectious Diseases Soc. Am., Am. Soc. Microbiology, Am. Soc. Internal Medicine. Office: 215 E 68th St New York NY 10021

BRAUTBAR, NACHMAN, physician, educator; b. Haifa, Israel, Oct. 22, 1943; came to U.S., 1975; s. Pinhas and Sabine (Lohite) B.; m. Ronit Aboutboul, Mar. 25, 1968; children: Sigalit, Shirley, Jaques. MD, Med. Sch. Jerusalem, 1968. Diplomate Am. Bd. Internal Medicine, Am. Bd. Nephrology. Intern, Rambam Hosp., Haifa, 1968-69; resident in internal medicine Hadassah Med. Center, Jerusalem, 1972-75; fellow in nephrology UCLA Med. Sch., 1975-77, asst. prof. medicine, 1977-78; asst. prof. medicine U. So. Calif., Los Angeles, 1978-80, assoc. prof. medicine, pharmacology and nutrition, 1980-87, clin. prof. medicine, 1987—, dir. Ctr. for Toxicology and Chem. Exposure; chmn. nephrology sect. Hollywood Presbyn. Med. Center, 1980—. Author: Cellular Bioenergetics, 1985; editor Internat. Jour. Occupl. Medicine and Toxicology; contbr. numerous articles, papers to scientific publs. Chmn. research com., pub. relations com. Kidney Foundation Los Angeles, 1980—. Named Hon. Citizen, Los Angeles City Council, 1984; Grantee Am. Heart Assn., 1980—, NIH, 1983. Mem. Am. Soc. Nephrology, Am. Soc. Bone and Mineral Rsch., Am. Physiol. Soc., Am. Chem. Soc., Am. Soc. Parenteral Nutrition, Am. Coll. Nutrition, Israeli Soc. Neprhology (hon.). Office: 2222 Ocean View Ave Los Angeles CA 90057-2757

BRAVER, MICHAEL BRUCE, clinical psychologist, educator; b. N.Y.C., Sept. 25, 1946; s. Solomon Wolf and Sylvia (Gruber) B.; m. Ricki Marsha Ellis, June 15, 1969 (div. Apr. 1973); m. Angela Robin Polansky, Sept. 9, 1979; children: Joshua Stanton, Andrew Emerson. AB, MA, UCLA, 1969; MSW, U. So. Calif., 1978; PhD, Calif. Sch. Profl. Psychology, 1983. Lic. clin. psychologist, clin. social worker, marriage and family counselor. Asst. prof. Cen. Wash. U., Ellensburg, 1969-71; field dir. Inst. Cultural N.Am., Puebla, Mex., 1970-71; psychiat. social worker, 1978-82; psychologist Comprehensive Care Adolescent Treatment Program, Glendale, Calif., 1983-84; program dir. Children's Home Soc., Los Angeles, 1984-85; pvt. practice clin. psychology Toluca Lake, Calif., 1980—; vis. prof. Ariz. State U., Tempe, 1974-75; bd. dirs. Valley Counseling Clinic, Sherman Oaks, Calif., 1984-86; health svcs. psychologist Mt. San Antonio Coll., Walnut, Calif., 1985-86; clin. supr. San Fernando Valley Counseling Ctr., Van Nuys, Calif., 1978-82, Calif. Family Studies Inst., 1986-92; dir., psychologist Consultation Bldg., Studio City, Calif., 1980—. Cons. Students for Dem. Soc., Ellensburg, Wash., 1971, E.L.F., Ellensburg, 1970. Recipient Meritorious Teaching award Cen. Wash. U., 1969. Mem. Am. Psychol. Assn., Calif. State Psychol. Assn., Los Angeles Psychol. Assn., San Fernando Valley Psychol. Assn., Nat. Assn. Social Workers, Phi Beta Kappa, Pi Gamma Mu. Office: 12854 Moorpark St Studio City CA 91604-1335

BRAWNER, THOMAS A., biology educator; b. Cleve., Dec. 8, 1945; s. Henry B. and Frances (L.) B.; m. Janet L. Brawner; children: David S., Michael J. BA, Albion Coll., 1961; PhD, U. Tex., Austin, 1972. Assoc. prof. U. Mo. Coll. Medicine, Columbia, 1973-81; sr. scientist Abbott Labs., North Chicago, Ill., 1981-89; prof. and chmn. biology Carthage Coll., Kenosha, Wis., 1989—, chmn. div. natural scis., 1990-93. Contbr. articles to profl. jours. Mem. AAAS, ASM, Sigma Xi, Phi Kappa Phi. Office: Carthage Coll 2001 Alford Dr Kenosha WI 53140-1929

BRAY, GEORGE AUGUST, physician, scientist, educator; b. Evanston, Ill., July 25, 1931; s. George A. and Mary H. B.; m. Martha, Aug. 8, 1959 (div. July 1983); children: George, Thomas, Susan, Nancy; m. Marilyn Rice, Jan. 1, 1984. BA summa cum laude, Brown U., 1953; MD magna cum laude, Harvard U., 1957. Diplomate Am. Bd. Internal Medicine; cert. Nat. Bd. Med. Examiners, Mass. Bd. Registration Medicine, Calif. Bd. Med. Examiners, La. Bd. Med. Examiners. Intern Johns Hopkins Hosp., Baltimore, Md., 1957-58; rsch. assoc. NIH, Bethesda, Md., 1958-60; resident U. Rochester, N.Y., 1960-61; rsch. assoc. Mill Hill Nat. Inst. Med. Rsch., London, 1961-62; asst. prof. medicine Tufts U., Boston, 1964-69, assoc. prof., 1969-70; assoc. prof. UCLA, 1970-72, prof., 1972-81; prof. U. So. Calif., Los Angeles, 1981-89, prof. medicine and physiology, 1983-89, chief of Diabetes and Nutrition Los Angeles County USC Med. Ctr., 1981-89; prof. medicine, vice chancellor Med. Ctr. La. State U., Baton Rouge, 1989—; exec. dir. Pennington Biomed. Rsch. Ctr., Baton Rouge, 1989—; vis. prof. U. Ill., 1981; cons. FDA, 1971, 95, Can. Dept. Health and Welfare, Ottawa, Ont., 1974, Nat. Inst. on Aging; mem. adv. coun. Nat. Inst. Diabetes, Digestive and Kidney Diseases, 1985-90. Author: Obese Patient, 1976; editor: Obesity in America, 1979, Obesity in Perspective, 1976, Treatment of Obesity, 1985, 89, Obesity: Basic Aspects and Clinical Applications, 1989; contbr. articles to profl. jours. Recipient Travel award Am. Thyroid Assn., 1970, Sam E. Roberts award Kans. Nutrition Soc., 1977, Wellcome Vis. Prof. award Mich. State U., 1978, U. Chgo., 1985, Alumni Day spkr. Harvard Med. Sch., Boston, 1982, Osborne and Mendel award Am. Inst. Nutrition, 1989, E.V. McCollum award Am. Soc. Clin. Nutrition, 1989, Joseph Goldberger award in Clin. Nutrition AMA, 1994; grantee NIH, 1965—, Weight Watchers Found., 1979-81, Kroc Found., 1980-81; fellow NSF, 1961-62, NIH, 1962-64. Master ACP (chmn.-elect coun. med. spltys. 1987-88, chmn. 1988-91, bd. regents 1987-91), Am. Coll. Endocrinology (pres. 1993-95, editor Endocrine Practice 1993-95); fellow AAAS (coun. del. for med. scis. 1985-88); mem. Am. Assn. Clin. Endocrinology (bd. dirs. 1990-96), Am. Soc. for Clin. Nutrition (councilor 1982-84, v.p. 1985-86, pres.-elect 1986-87, pres. 1987-88, McCollum award 1989), Assn. Am. Physicians (hon.), Endocrine Soc., Am. Diabetes Assn. (bd. dirs. So. Calif. 1984-87, 88-89), Am. Fedn. for Clin. Rsch., Peripatetic Club (hon.), Am. Soc. Clin. Investigation (hon.), Am. Inst. Nutrition (Osborne-Mendal award 1988), N.Am. Assn. for Study Obesity (chmn. organizing com. 1980-82, councilor 1984-88, pres.-elect 1988-89, pres. 1989-90, editor Internat. Jour. Obesity 1974-91, Obesity Rsch. 1991—), Internat. Assn. Study Obesity (pres.-elect 1990-94, pres. 1994—, Willendorf award 1980), Phi Beta Kappa, Sigma Xi, Alpha Omega Alpha. Office: Pennington Ctr 6400 Perkins Rd Baton Rouge LA 70808-4124

BRAY, GORDON LOUIS, medical association administrator; b. Bronx, N.Y., Sept. 29, 1953. BA summa cum laude, CUNY, 1975; MD, Yeshiva U., 1979. Diplomate Nat. Bd. Med. Examiners. Intern in pediatrics Children's Hosp. of Northern Calif., Oakland, 1979-80, resident in pediatrics, 1980-82; clin. fellow div. pediatric hematology/oncology Children's Orthopedic Hosp. and Med. Ctr., Seattle, 1982-83, jr. rsch. fellow div. hematology/oncology, 1983-84; sr. rsch. fellow div. hematology depts. pediatrics/medicine U. Wash., Seattle, 1984-85; asst. prof. dept. pediatrics George Washington U. Sch. Medicine, Washington, 1985-91, assoc. prof. dept. pediatrics, 1991-94; attending physician dept. hematology/oncology Children's Nat. Med. Ctr., Washington, 1985-94; dir. clin. devel., assoc. med. dir. Baxter Biotech Hyland Divsn., 1994—; regional liaison Nat. Resources and Consultation Ctr. for AIDS and HIV Infection, Nat. Hemophilia Found., 1987-88; regional project dir. HHS Region III Network of Federally Funded Hemophilia Treatment Ctrs.; cons. divsn. Blood diseases and resources, Nat. Hear, Lung and Blood Inst., NIH, 1990-94. Contbr. articles to profl. jours. Judith Graham Pool fellow Nat. Hemophilia Found., 1984, Poncin Fund fellow Seafirst corp., 1984; NIH grantee, 1987-94, Baxter Internat. grantee, 1990-94. Mem. Am. Soc. Hematology, World Fedn. Hemophilia, Internat. Soc. on Thrombosis and Haemostasis, Phi Beta Kappa. Home: 790 E California Blvd Apt 3 Pasadena CA 91106-3844 Office: Baxter Hyland Divsn Dept Med & Clin Affairs 550 N Brand Blvd Glendale CA 91225

BRAY, GRADY P., psychologist; b. Macon, Ga., Nov. 23, 1944; s. Sue Helen (Shiver) Brown; m. Marjorie Elizabeth Walker, Aug. 24, 1963; children: April, Scott. BA, David Lipscomb Coll., 1966; MEd, U. Ga., 1972, PhD, 1974. Diplomate Am. Bd. Sexology. Sci. tchr. Houston County Schs., Warner Robins, Ga., 1966-67; pyrotechnic chemist Maxon Electronics, Macon, Ga., 1967-68; sci. tchr. Bibb County Schs., Macon, 1968-70, spl. counselor, 1970-72; counseling psychologist U. Ga. Testing & Evaluation Ctr., Athens, Ga., 1973-74; dir. psychology dept., clin. psychologist Warm Springs (Ga.) Hosp., 1974-76; rsch. div. dir. Ga. Warm Springs Rehab. Ctr., 1976-77; asst. prof. rehab. medicine U. Rochester (N.Y.) Sch. Medicine, 1977-84; pres. Human Potentials, Rochester, 1984-91; pres., CEO Bray Assocs., 1991—; cons., adj. faculty Fed. Emergency Mgmt. Agy., Emmitsburg, Md., 1984—; adj. faculty Nat. Fire Acad., Emmitsburg, 1989—; behavioral scientist Nat. Disaster Med. Sys./Disaster Mortuary, 1994—. Co-author: Emergency Services Stress, 1990; author: A Stroke Family Guide, 1984; mem. editorial bd. Rehabilitation in the Aging, 1984; contbr. articles to profl. jours. EMT vol. N.Y. State. Mem. APA. Home: 131 E Lake Rd Penn Yan NY 14527-9581 Office: Bray Assocs Penn Yan NY 14527

BRAY, TIMOTHY CLARK, internist; b. Marlin, Tex., Jan. 23, 1961; s. Woodson Lee and Bobbie Lenore (Lane) B.; m. Cheryl Ann Richards, May 21, 1983; children: Aaron, Mason, Meredith. DO, U. North Tex. Health Sci. Ctr., 1990. Resident in internal medicine U. North Tex. Health Sci. Ctr., Ft. Worth; owner, internal medicine physician Lake Pointe Internal Medicine, Rockwell, Tex., 1993—; dir. quality assurance emer. rm. Lake Pointe Med. Ctr., Rowlett, Tex., 1993-95, chief internal medicine, dir. emer. rm., 1994—. Capt. U.S. Army, 1990-95. Mem. AMA, Am. Osteo. Assn., Tex. Osteo. Med. Assn., Am. Bd. Osteo. Internal Medicine. Office: Lake Pointe Internal Med 6701 Heritage Pkwy Ste 170 Rockwall TX 75087

BRAYLAN, RAUL CIPRIANO, pathologist, educator; b. Buenos Aires, Aug. 15, 1936; came to U.S., 1963; s. Susana Elena Cacedevant Braylan, Oct. 27, 1977; children: Alexander, Nicholas. BS, Avellaneda Coll., Buenos Aires, 1953; MD, Buenos Aires Med. Sch., 1960. Diplomate Am. Bd. Anatomic Pathology. Rotating intern Mount Sinai Hosp., Chgo., 1963-64, resident in pathology, 1964-65; resident in pathology Albert Einstein Coll. of Medicine, Bronx, 1965-67, Meml. Hosp. for Cancer Sloan Kettering Inst., N.Y.C., 1967-68; fellow pathologist Inst. of Hematologic Investigations, Buenos Aires, 1968-71; USPHS trainee in hematology, instr. Dept. Pathology, U. Chgo., 1971-73; sr. staff fellow Nat. Cancer Inst., NIH, Bethesda, 1973-77; assoc. prof. Dept. Pathology, U. Fla., Gainesville, 1977-80; prof. Dept. Pathology, U. Fla. Coll. Medicine, Gainesville, 1980—; dir. hematology course, med. students U. Fla. Coll. of Medicine, Gainesville; departmental exec. com. dept. pathology. Author: (with others) Pathology Annual, 1975, International Academy of Pathology Monographs No 16: The Reticuloendothelial System, 1975, Recent Results in Cancer Treatment Research, 1980, International Academy of Pathology Monographs: Techniques in Diagnostic Pathology, 1990, Lymphoid Malignancy, 1991, Manual of Clinical Laboratory Immunology, 4th edit., 1992, Flow Cytometry: Principles and Clinical Applications, 1992, Diagnostic Problems in Clinical Ophthalmology, 1994; contbr. numerous articles to profl. jours. Fellowship rsch. nat. coun. Inst. of Hematologic Investigations, 1968-71. Mem. Am. Assn. for Cancer Rsch. Am. Assn. of Pathologists, Am. Soc. of Hematology, Internat. Soc. for Analytical Cytology, Soc. for Hematopathology. Home: 9224 SW 43rd Ln Gainesville FL 32608 Office: U Fla Dept Pathology PO Box 100275 1600 SW Archer Rd Gainesville FL 32610

BRAYMAN, KENNETH LEWIS, surgeon; b. Boston, Mar. 3, 1955; s. Lawrence Joseph B. and Barbara (Lewis) Franklin; m. Kerrie Ann Lipsky, Oct. 4, 1987; children: Jonathan, Jacqueline, Lawrence, Madeline. BS in Biochemistry, U. Mass., 1977; MD, U. Pa., 1981, PhD, 1989. Diplomate Nat. Bd. Med. Examiners, Am. Bd. Surgery. Postdoctoral fellow Harrison Dept. Surg. Rsch., Phila., 1984-87; sr. resident Hosp. U. Pa., Phila., 1987-88, chief resident, 1988-89; fellow transplant surgery U. Minn. Hosp., Mpls., 1989-90; surgery instr. U. Minn. Med. Sch., Mpls., 1990-92; attending surgeon VA Hosp., Mpls., 1991-92; asst. prof. surgery, dir. pancreas and human islet transplant program U. Pa. Med. Ctr., Phila., 1992—; dir. renal transplantation Children's Hosp. Phila., 1995—. Manuscript reviewer Diabetes Jour., Cell Transplantation; contbr. articles to Surgery, Transplantation, Archives of Surgery. Measey Found. fellow, 1985-87, Pfizer Postdoctoral fellow, 1985-87, Daland fellow Am. Philos. Soc., 1986-87, 90-91, Sandoz Transplant fellow, 1990-92. Fellow ACS; mem. AMA, Am. Soc. Transplant Surgeons, Transplantation Soc., Am. Diabetes Assn., Sigma Xi. Office: Hosp U Pa 3400 Spruce St Philadelphia PA 19104

BRAZDA, FREDERICK WICKS, pathologist; b. New Orleans, Dec. 17, 1945; s. Fred George and Helen Josephine (Wicks) B.; student U. Chgo., 1962-64; B.S. cum laude, Tulane U., 1966; M.D., La. State U., 1970; m. Margaret Mary Hubbell, Sept. 8, 1973; children—Geoffrey Frederick, Gretchen Marie, Gregory Paul. Intern, then resident in pathology La. State U. div. Charity Hosp., New Orleans, 1970-75; pathologist Hotel Dieu Hosp., New Orleans, 1975-92, dir. Sch. Med. Tech., 1976-83; assoc. med. dir. Am. Bio-sci. Labs., New Orleans, 1983-84, Smith Kline Bio-sci. Labs., New Orleans, 1985-89; tech. dir. Smith Kline Beecham Clin. Labs., New Orleans, 1990-94; pathologist, tech. dir. Univ. Hosp. Lab., New Orleans, 1993-95, Med. Ctr. La. at New Orleans U. Campus Lab., 1995—; cons. St. Tammany Parish Hosp., Covington, La., Riverside Hosp., Franklinton, La, 1976-84; asst. prof. clin. pathology and med. tech. La. State U. Med. Center, New Orleans, 1976-93, prof. clin. pathology La. State U. Med. Ctr., New Orleans, 1994—. Diplomate Am. Bd. Pathology. Fellow Nat. Acad. Clin. Biochemistry; mem. AMA, Am. Soc. Clin. Pathologists, Coll. Am. Pathologists, Am. Assn. Clin. Chemistry, Nat. Acad. Clin. Biochemistry, So. Med. Assn., La. Med. Soc., La. Pathology Soc., Orleans Parish Med. Soc., Greater New Orleans Pathology Soc., Clin. Lab. Mgmt. Assn., La. Civil Service League, Friends of City Park, Friends of Zoo, Friends of Aquarium, Friends of Charity Hosp., New Orleans Mus. Art, Les Amis du Vin, Phi Beta Kappa, Alpha Omega Alpha, Phi Beta Pi. Democrat. Roman Catholic. Home: 422 Hector Ave Metairie LA 70005-4412 Office: 2025 Gravier St Ste 200 New Orleans LA 70112-2256

BRAZEAL, DONNA SMITH, psychologist; b. Greenville, S.C., Feb. 10, 1947; d. G.W. Hovey and Ollie Occena (Crane) Smith; m. Charles Lee Brazeal, June 27, 1970 (div. May 1980). BA, Clemson U., 1971, MEd, 1975; postgrad., Western Carolina U., 1974, Furman U., Greenville, 1977; PhD, Columbia Pacific U., 1994. Lic. sch. psychologist, S.C., N.C. Instr., head med. record dept. Greenville Tech. Coll., 1971-73; chief psychologist Greenville County Schs., 1975-80; coord. psychol. svcs. Union County Schs., Monroe, N.C., 1980—; pvt. practice psychology Monroe and Charlotte, N.C., 1986—; mem. learning disabilities com. Greenville County Schs., 1978-79; co-founder, bd. dirs. Ctr. for Spiritual Awareness of N.C., Monroe, 1982—. Co-author, co-editor: School Psychologist, 1980. Child find program coordinator Union County, 1980-85; mem. various coms. Assn. for Retarded Citizens, Monroe; mem. interagy. council Piedmont Mental Health, Monroe, 1983—. Catawba Bus. Women scholar, 1965; N.C. Dept. Pub. Instrn. Pre-Sch. Incentive grantee, 1984. Mem. Nat. Assn. Sch. Psychologists, N.C. Assn. Sch. Psychologist (mem. pub. relations com. 1984-85), Animal Protection Inst. Am., Greenpeace, Union County Humane Soc., River Hills Community Ch. (mem. adult edn. com. 1985-86), Delta. Libertarian. Unitarian. Home: PO Box 240173 Charlotte NC 28224-0173

BRAZER, SCOTT ROBERT, gastroenterologist; b. Dallas, Sept. 13, 1955; s. Robert Charles and Elaine (Ritz) B.; m. Barbara Ann Wells, July 23, 1983; children: Katherine Wells, Robert Charles II. BS in Zoology, Duke U., 1976; MD, Case Western Res. U., 1981; MHS, Duke U., 1990. Intern Duke U. Med. Ctr., Durham, N.C., 1981-82, resident, 1982-84, asst. med. dir. edn., 1984-85, chief resident, 1987-88, assoc., 1988-89, asst. prof. medicine, 1989-96, clin. dir. divsn. gastroenterology, 1996—. Gastroenterology fellow Duke U. Med. Ctr., 1985-87. Fellow Am. Coll. Gastroenterology; mem. Am. Coll. Physicians, Am. Gastroenterologic Assn., Am. Soc. Gastrointestinal Endscopy. Office: Duke U Med Ctr Box 3662 Durham NC 27710

BRECHENSER, DONN MARSH, psychotherapist, educator, administrator; b. Birmingham, Ala., May 28, 1940; s. Frank J. and Thelma (Gremp) B.; m. Karen Ann Askew, Oct. 9, 1963 (div. 1975); children: Lynn Payne, Jennifer Gabrenas; m. Sarena Beth Kaiser, Oct. 12, 1975; children: Jordan, Jillsen. BA in Sociology, W.Va. U., 1963; MS in Social Work, Va. Commonwealth U., 1967; PhD in Psychology, Saybrook Inst., San Francisco, 1983. Lic. ind. clin. social worker, Mass. Child welfare social worker Prince William County Welfare Office, Manassas, Va., 1963-65, supr., 1967-68; social work supr. Arlington County Human Resources Office, Arlington, Va., 1968-70; asst. prof. Greenfield (Mass.) Community Coll., 1972-75; psychiat. social worker Franklin Med. Ctr., Greenfield, 1970-72, clin. social worker, 1977-83, chief psychotherapist, 1983—; mgr. Outpatient Mental Health and Substance Abuse Svcs., 1990—; pvt. practice, Greenfield, 1970-86; cons. Northfield (Mass.)-Mt. Hermon Sch., 1984-86; clin. asst. prof. Smith Coll. Social Work Sch., Northampton, Mass., 1985—. Contbr. articles to profl. jours., chpt. to book. Mem. NASW, Acad. Cert. Social Workers, Internat. Assn. for Transactional Analysis. Home: Bascomb Rd Greenfield MA 01301 Office: Franklin Med Ctr 164 High St Greenfield MA 01301-2645

BREDESEN, DOROTHY LOUISE ANTIL, rehabilitation counselor, community activist; b. N.Y.C., July 20, 1929; d. Michael Charles and Mary (Holman) Antil; BA, Syracuse U., 1951, MA (scholar), 1956; postgrad. (scholar) U. Chgo., 1962-64; cert. advanced study, 1964; m. Nov. 1952 (div. Dec. 1972); children: Karen Louise, Mark Jon, Eric Tod. Social worker Maricopa County Welfare Dept., Phoenix, 1957; lectr. speech Ariz. State U., Tempe, 1957-59; instr. speech Memphis State U., 1960-62; vol. worker Christ Child Settlement House, 1964-65; rehab. counselor D.C. Rehab. Services Adminstrn., Washington, 1965-86. Chmn. working adv. com. New Brent Sch., 1967-68; mem. exec. com. Brent Elem. Sch., 1965-68. Panel chmn. Dist. Tng. Sch.'s 9th ann. conf. Mental Retardation, 1968; mem. internat. study tour profl. seminar, U.S.S.R., 1986. mem. counselor advisory com. Occupational and Tng. Center, 1971-75; mem. counselor adv. com. D.C. Evaluation Unit, 1972-73, Pres.'s com. on Employment of Handicapped, Washington, 1988; bd. dirs. Friends of Reston Community Center, 1981—, treas., 1982, 87, 88, 89, 90, Laison to RCC bd. govt. 1996, asst. treas., 1983, pres.; Recipient of the 1989-94. Recipient cert. of appreciation Help for Retarded Children, Inc., 1967, D.C. Dept. Vocat. Rehab., 1968, D.C. Rehab. Counseling Assn., 1977, 79, D.C. Assn. for Retarded Citizens, 1983, Very Spl. Arts, Reston, 1989; Betty L. Hardy Haney Meml. award, 1982; cert. of recognition D.C. Dept. Human Services, 1983, Cert. of award, 1984; United Black Fund Community Service award, 1986; cert. rehab. counselor, Recognition and Appreciation Plaque County of Fairfax, 1989. Mem. Adult Edn. Assn. Greater Washington (dir. 1967-68, rec. sec. 1968-69, 2d v.p. 1970-71, chmn. long-range planning 1974-75), Am. Sociol. Assn., Nat. Rehab. Assn. (program com. 1975, co-editor D.C. chpt. Newsletter 1976, bd. mem. nat. congress on rehab. of homeward bound and institutionalized persons 1977-78), Nat. Rehab. Counseling Assn. (dir. D.C. chpt. 1971-72, sec. 1978-80, Cert. of Award 1979), Am. Assn. Counseling and Devel., Capitol Hill Community Council (pres. 1968-69), AFSCME-AFL-CIO (treas. local affiliate D.C. Commn. Social Service Employees 1977-80, v.p., chief steward local affiliate 1980-81, steward local affiliate 1981-86, del. 26th internat. conv. San Francisco 1984), Delta Sigma Rho, Alpha Omicron Pi. Democrat. Roman Catholic. Home: 1951 Sagewood Ln Reston VA 22091-5409

BREECKER, STEVEN W., physician, educator. BA, Brandeis U., 1972; MD, Tufts U., 1982. Diplomate Am. Bd. Internal Medicine, Am. Bd. Cardiovascular Diseases. Intern in medicine New Eng. Deaconess Hosp., Boston, 1982-83, resident, 1984-86; resident in radiology Beth Israel Hosp., Boston, 1983-84; clin. fellow medicine Harvard Med. Sch., Boston, 1985-86; fellow in cardiology Thomas Jefferson Univ. Hosp., Phila., 1986-88, attending physician, 1988—; instr. medicine Jefferson Med. Coll., Phila., 1988—. Office: Thomas Jefferson U Hosp 111 S 11th St Ste G4280 Philadelphia PA 19107

BREEN, KATHERINE ANNE, speech and language pathologist; b. Chgo., Oct. 31, 1948; d. Robert Stephen and Gertrude Catherine (Bader) Breen; B.S., Northwestern U., 1970; M.A. (U.S. Rehab. Services trainee), U. Mo., Columbia, 1971. Speech/lang. pathologist Fulton (Mo.) pub. schs., 1971-73; co-dir. Easter Seal Speech Clinic, Jefferson City, Mo., summers 1972, 73; speech/lang. pathologist Shawnee Mission (Kans.) pub. schs., 1973-96; staff St. Joseph's Hosp., Kansas City, Mo., 1978-81, Midwest Rehab. Ctr., Kansas City, 1985; pvt. practice speech therapy; cons. East Central Mo. Mental Health Center; guest lectr. Fontbonne Coll., St. Louis. Clin. certification in speech pathology. Mem. Am., Kans. speech and hearing assns., NEA, Mo. State Tchrs. Assn., Kansas City Alumni Assn. of Northwestern U. (dir. alumni admissions council, Outstanding Leadership award for work on alumni admissions council 1981, Svc. award, 1991), Friends of Art Nelson/Atkins Art Gallery and Museum (vol.), Nat. Trust Hist. Preservation, Kansas City Hist. Found., Zeta Phi Eta. Methodist. Home: 6865 W 51st Ter Apt 1C Shawnee Mission KS 66202-1576

BREEN, ROY EUGENE, physician; b. Bethesda, Md., Mar. 18, 1952; s. Roy Eugene and Winifred (Legg) B.; m. Nancy Ann Nicklas, Jan. 8, 1956. BS, U. Calif., Davis, 1974; MD, U. Calif., Irvine, 1978. Diplomate Am. Bd. Colon and Rectal Surgery, Am. Bd. Surgery. Intern Good Samaritan Hosp., Portland, Oreg., 1978-79; resident in gen. surgery Oreg. Health Scis. U., Portland, 1979-84; fellow in colon and rectal surgery Sansum Med. Clinic, Inc., Santa Barbara, Calif., 1984-85; active staff Providence Med. Ctr.; courtesy staff Good Samaritan Hosp., St. Vincent Hosp. Coach baseball, basketball, soccer West Linn, Oreg. Fellow ACS, Am Soc. Colon and Rectal Surgeons; mem. AMA, Portland Surg. Soc., N.W. Soc. Colon and Rectal Surgeons, Oreg. Med. Assn., Multnomah County Med. Soc. Episcopalian. Office: 511 SW 10th St Ste 714 Portland OR 97205

BREFFEILH, LOUIS ANDREW, ophthalmologist, educator; b. Shreveport, La., Sept. 14, 1913; s. John Hypolite and Louise Claire (DeRichi(Marmouget)) B.; m. Marianna Franklin, Aug. 13, 1949; children—George Richard, Andrew Louis. Student, Loyola U. South, New Orleans, 1932-34; M.B., La. State U., 1938, M.D., 1939. Diplomate Am Bd. Ophthalmology, Am. Acad. Ophthalmology and Otolaryngology, A.C.S., Internat. Coll. Surgeons. Intern Shreveport Charity Hosp., 1938-39; practice medicine specializing in ophthalmology Shreveport, 1950-88; ret. from pvt. practice, 1988; prof. emeritus dept. ophthalmology La. State U., Shreveport, 1988—; staff Confederate Meml. Med. Center, 1950-94, pres., 1966-67; staff Schumpert Meml. Hosp., 1950—, pres., 1971-72; clin. instr. dept. ophthalmology Sch. Medicine, La. State U., New Orleans, 1946-50; asst. clin. prof. Sch. Medicine, La. State U., 1950-51; clin. prof. La. State U. Postgrad. Sch. Medicine, Shreveport, 1951-64; head dept., prof. Sch. Medicine, La. State U., Shreveport, 1970-92; prof. emeritus dept. ophthalmology La. State U. Sch. of Medicine, Shreveport, 1992—; sr. cons. USAF, 1950-55, VA Hosp., 1950-80. Contbr. articles to profl. jours. Pres. Breffeilh and Texada Med. Found., 1971-87. Maj. M.C. AUS, 1938-46; lt. col. USAFR ret. Mem. Am., So. med. assns., Pan Am. Ophthal. Soc., La., Miss., Ophthal. and Otol. Soc., Shreveport Med. Soc. (v.p. 1969-70). Club: Shreveport Yacht. Home: 439 Spring Lake Dr Shreveport LA 71106-4744

BREGER, BARBARA CAMILLE, ophthalmologist; b. San Francisco, May 9, 1938; d. Samuel and Frances Mary (Mordecai) B.; 1 child, Shimonah Eva. MD, U. Calif., San Francisco, 1963. Diplomate Am. Bd. Ophthalmology. Rotating intern Mount Sinai Hosp., N.Y.C., 1963-64, resident neurology, 1964-65, resident pathology, 1965-66, resident ophthalmology, 1966-69; pvt. practice, Beverly Hills, Calif., 1971—; med.-legal cons.; opthalmologist Vista Del Mar, Venice Family Clinic. Fellow ACS, Am. Acad. Ophthalmology; mem. Am. Med. Women's Assn., Contact Lens Assn. Ophthalmologists, Calif. Med. Assn., Women in Ophthalmology. Jewish. Office: 435 N Bedford Dr PHW Beverly Hills CA 90210

BREILLATT, JULIAN PAUL, JR., biochemist, biomedical engineer; b. Pensacola, Fla., Mar. 2, 1938; s. Julian Paul and Ruth (Walser) B.; m. Gaye Sorensen, Apr. 9, 1962; children: Elise, Adrienne, Alain, Andre. BA in Biochem., U. Calif., Berkeley, 1959; PhD in Biochem., U. Utah, 1967. Rsch. assoc. Oak Ridge (Tenn.) Nat. Lab., 1967-69, rsch. scientist, 1967-74, acting dir. molecular anatomy program, 1974-77; rsch. supr. E I DuPont, Wilmington, Del., 1977-78, sr. rsch. chemist, 1978-85. Baxter rsch. scientist Baxter Healthcare Corp., Round Lake, Ill., 1986-90, rsch. dir., 1990-94, sr. rsch. dir., 1994—. Contbr. articles to scientific jours.; patentee in field. Active Boy Scouts Am., 1949-96. Recipient IR-100 Indsl. Rsch. award, 1977. Mem. LDS Ch. Office: Baxter Healthcare Corp Baxter Tech Pk Round Lake IL 60073-0490

BREINDEL, JOSEPH H., obstetrician and gynecologist; b. Poland, May 24, 1909; came to U.S., 1938; s. Eliezer and Rachel (Benesch) B.; m. Sonia Weissenberg, May 24, 1953; children: Monique Breindel Oberman, Eric. MD, U. Rome, 1938. Diplomate Am. Bd. Ob-Gyn. Dir. ob-gyn. N.Y. Infirmary, N.Y.C., 1960-80; attending ob-gyn. Beth Israel Med. Ctr., N.Y.C., 1950-90. Fellow Am. Coll. Ob-Gyn.; mem. AMA. Home: 965 Fifth Ave New York NY 10021

BREINER, SANDER JAMES, psychiatry educator, psychoanalyst; b. Fiume, Italy, July 12, 1925; (parents Am. citizens); s. Alfred and Margaret (Steiner) B.; m. Beatrice Marsha Oboler, Mar. 18, 1951; children: Linda Marie, Myles Steven, Robert Ethan. BS, U. Ill., 1948; MB, MD, Chgo. Med. Sch., 1953. Diplomate Nat. Bd. Med. Examiners, Am. Bd. Psychiatry and Neurology, Nat. Bd. of Accreditation in Psychoanalysis. Asst. prof. psychiatry Wayne State U., Detroit, 1957—; assoc. prof. Mich. State U., East Lansing, 1970—; attending staff, mem. psychiatry dept. Harper Grace Hosp., Detroit, 1960—; attending psychiatry dept. William Beaumont Hosp., Royal Oak, Mich., 1968—; cons. depts. ob-gyn., surgery and medicine Harper Grace Hosp., 1960—; cons. dept. ob-gyn. William Beaumont Hosp., 1982—; cons. in marital/sexual problems; tng./supervising analyst Mich. Psychoanalytic Coun.; trustee Nat. Bd. Accreditation in Psychoanalysis. Author: Slaughter of the Innocents: Child Abuse Through the Ages and Today, 1990; contbr. more than 70 articles to profl. jours. Cons. Detroit Commn. on Children and Youth, 1957-62; cons. bd. edn. Detroit, Garden City and Bloomfield Hills, 1957-71. With inf. U.S. Army, 1943-45, ETO. Fellow Am. Psychiat. Assn., Am. Soc. Psychoanalytic Physicians; mem. AMA, AAAS, Psychosomatic Medicine, N.Y. Acad. Sci., Internat. Assn. for Psychohistory, Mich. Soc. for Psychoanalytic Psychology, Mich. Psychoanapytic Coun., Tng. and Supervising Psychoanalyst. Democrat. Home: 7410 Franklin Rd Bloomfield Hills MI 48301-3610 Office: 31811 Middlebelt Rd Ste 203 Farmington Hills MI 48334-2368

BREINES, ESTELLE BORGMAN, occupational therapy educator; b. Bklyn., Mar. 7, 1936; d. Sanford and Sylvia (Goldin) Borgman; m. Ira S. Breines, May 30, 1956; children: Roxanne Gail Breines Sukol, Eric Craig, Jacqueline Ruth Breines Danino. BS, NYU, 1957, PhD, 1986; MA, Kean Coll., 1976; postgrad., Rutgers, 1977-79. Cert. occupational therapist, occupational therapy tchr. Dir. occupational therapy Coney Island Hosp., Bklyn., 1957; sr. occupational therapist Meadowbrook Hosp., East Meadow, N.Y., 1965-67; dir. occupational therapy Brunswick Hosp. Ctr., Amityville, N.Y., 1967-69; pvt. practice N.J., 1971-80; coord. fieldwork Union Coll., Scotch Plains, N.J., 1975-78; pres. Geri-Rehab. Inc., Lebanon, N.J., 1987—; coord. fieldwork Dominican Coll., Blauvelt, N.Y., 1986-87; prof. NYU, 1987-95; chair occupational therapy programs, asst. to dean health sc Touro Coll., N.Y.C., 1995—; exec. dir. Devel. Rehab. Svcs., Lebanon, N.J., 1985-91. Author: Perception: Its Development and Recapitulation, 1981, Origins and Adaptations: A Philosophy of Practice, 1986, (assessment tool) Functional Assessment Scale, 1983, (monograph) Proprioceptive Schematic Orientation, 1990, Occupational Therapy Activities From Clay to Computers, 1995; Am. editor: Israeli Jour. Occupl. Therapy, 1991—; columnist OT Advance, 1994—; contbr. articles to profl. jours. Adminstrn. on Aging grantee, 1988. Fellow Am. Occupational Therapy Assn.; mem. N.J. Occupational Therapy Assn. (Merit award), World Fedn. Occupational Therapy (del.), Belgian Sheepdog Club Am. (treas. 1989-93), Raritan Belgian Sheepdog Club (pres. 1991). Democrat. Jewish. Home: 15 Hibbler Rd Lebanon NJ 08833-3016 Office: Touro Coll 27-33 W 23d St New York NY 10010

BREININ, GOODWIN M., physician; b. N.Y.C., Dec. 10, 1918; s. Louis and Mary (Mirsky) B.; m. Rose-Helen Kopelman, June 22, 1947; children: Bartley James, Constance. B.S., U. Fla., 1939; A.M., Emory U., 1940, M.D., 1943. Diplomate Am. Bd. Ophthalmology (dir., vice chmn., cons.). Intern U.S. Marine Hosp., Stapleton, N.Y., 1944; resident ophthalmology N.Y. U.-Bellevue Med. Center, 1947-51, sr. Heed fellow ophthalmology, 1954, Daniel B. Kirby prof. research ophthalmology, 1957, Daniel B. Kirby prof., chmn. dept. ophthalmology, 1959—, chmn. med. bd., 1975-77; dir. eye service Bellevue and U. Hosps., N.Y.C., 1959—; mem. vision commn. NRC, 1960-65; hon. assoc. U. Coll., London, 1966-67; chmn. vision research tng. com. Nat. Insts. Neurol. Diseases and Blindness, 1963-64; chief cons. Manhattan VA Hosp.; cons. Manhattan Eye, Ear and Throat, St. Vincent's, Beth Israel hosps., Lenox Hills Hosp.; surg. gen. USPHS; chmn. Nat. Res. Rev. Com., 1976-77; vis. prof., cons. Hailie Selassie I Univ. Found., Ethiopia, 1972; lectr. Mem. various adv. coms. relating to field, mem. med. adv. bd. Nat. Council to Combat Blindness; pres. Council for U.S./USSR Health Exchange, 1977; mem. Am. com. Internat. Agy. for Prevention of Blindness, 1980—; pres. 2d Internat. Symposium in Visual Optics, Tucson, 1982. Author: The Electrophysiology of Extraocular Muscle, 1962; editor: Advances in Diagnostic Visual Optics, 1983; mem. editorial bd. Investigative Ophthalmology, Archives of Ophthalmology; Contbr. articles to profl. jours. Mem. nat. coun. for medicine Emory U., Atlanta. Served as capt., M.C. AUS, 1944-46. Recipient Knapp medal for contbn. ophthalmology A.M.A., 1957, Edward Lorenzo Holmes lectr. citation and award for contbns. to med. sci. Inst. Medicine Chgo., 1959, Gifford lectr. and award Chgo. Ophthal. Soc., 1970, Heed Ophthalmic Found. award, 1968, Emory U. medal, 1993; Wright lectr. U. Toronto, 1972; Lloyd lectr. Bklyn. Opthal. Soc., 1971; May lectr. N.Y. Acad. Medicine, 1974; guest of honor Australian Coll. Ophthalmologists, 1974, Japanese Cong. Neuro-ophthalmalogy, 1979; Scobee lectr., 1977. Fellow Am. Acad. Ophthalmology and Otolaryngology (v.p. 1979, Sr. Honor award 1984), ACS, N.Y. Acad. Medicine (sec. sect. ophthalmology 1962-63, chmn. sect. 1967-68); mem. AMA (sec. sect. on ophthalmology 1966-69, chmn. 1970-71), Rsch. Ophthalmology, Am. Ophthal. Soc., N.Y. Ophthal. Soc. (pres. 1980), Harvey Soc., AAAS, Am. Commn. for Optics and Visual Physiology (chmn. 1970—), Am. Orthoptic Coun., Assn. Univ. Profs. Ophthalmology, Pan. Am. Assn. Ophthalmology, Sigma Xi, Alpha Omega Alpha. Clubs: Century Assn., Practitioners, Charaka (N.Y.C.). Home: 912 5th Ave New York NY 10021-4159 Office: NYU Med Ctr 550 1st Ave New York NY 10016-6481

BREIPOHL, GARY W., anesthesiologist; b. Albuquerque, Oct. 19, 1956; s. Arthur M. and Shirley A. (Otto) B.; m. Sandra K. Breipohl, May 7, 1983; 1 child, Adam Scott. BS in Engring., Kans. State U., 1978, MS in Engring., 1979; MD, U. Kans., 1983. Diplomate Am. Bd. Anesthesiology. Anesthesiologist St. John's Hosp., Joplin, Mo., 1986-88, Tulsa Anesthesiologist, Inc., 1988—. Mem. Am. Soc. Anesthesiologists. Office: Tulsa Anesthesiologists Inc 1145 S Utica Ste 465 Tulsa OK 74104

BREITBART, ROGER ERIC, pediatrician; b. N.Y.C., 1955. MD, Harvard Med. Sch., 1981. Diplomate Am. Bd. Pediatrics. Intern, resident in pediatrics Children's Hosp., Boston, 1981-84, fellow in pediatric cardiology, 1985, pediat. cardiologist, 1985—; Asst. prof. Harvard Med. Sch. Recipient Established Investigator award Am. Heart Assn., 1995. •

BREITENBACH, MARY LOUISE MCGRAW, psychologist, drug rehabilitation counselor; b. Pitts., Sept. 26, 1936; d. David Evans McGraw and Louise (Schoch) Neel; m. John Edgar Breitenbach, Apr. 15, 1960 (dec. 1963); m. Joseph George Piccoli III, Aug. 15, 1987; 1 dau. Kirstin Amethyst. Postgrad., Oreg. State Coll., 1960-61; BA, Russell Sage Coll., Troy, N.Y., 1958; MEd, Harvard U., 1983. Lic. profl. counselor, Wyo.; lic. chem. dependency specialist, Wyo.; cert. addiction specialist, level III; nat. cert. addiction counselor II. Paraprofessional psychologist St. John's Episc. Ch., Jackson, Wyo., 1963-94; pvt. practice Wilson, Wyo., 1983-94; counselor Curran/Seeley Found. Addiction Svcs., Jackson, 1989-91, Van Vleck House/Tri-County Group Home, Jackson, 1986-89, others. Trustee Teton Sci. Sch., Kelly, Wyo, 1960-76; pres. bd. govs. Teton County Mus. Bd., Jackson; vestry mem. St. John's Ch., Jackson. Mem. Am. Psychol. Assn., Wyo. Psychol. Assn., Wyo. Assn. Counseling and Devel., Wyo. Assn. Addiction Specialists. Democrat. Episcopalian. Home and Office: Star Rte Wilson WY 83014

BREITENSTEIN, BRYCE DIXON, JR., occupational medicine administrator, medical educator; b. Great Falls, Mont., June 5, 1930; s. Bryce Dixon and George Frances (Fuson) B.; m. Mikel Plummer, Sept. 17, 1984. BS in Pharmacy, U. Mont., 1952; MD, U. Oreg., 1958; MPH, U. Wash., 1973. Diplomate Am. Bd. Internal Medicine; diplomate in occupational medicine Am. Bd. Preventive Medicine. Pharmacist Missoula (Mont.) Drug, 1952-54; intern. L.A. County Hosp., 1958-59, resident in internal medicine, 1959-60, 62-64; med. corps officer U.S. Army, Würtzburg, Germany, 1960-62; pvt. practice in internal medicine Missoula, 1964-71; mem. staff occupl. medicine Hanford Environ. Health Found., Richland, Wash., 1974-79; CEO, med. dir. Hanford Environ. Health Found., 1979-89; dir. occupl. medicine Brookhaven Nat. Lab., Upton, N.Y., 1989—; clin. prof. Stony Brook (N.Y.) Med. Sch., 1989—; mem. extra-mural faculty REAC/TS ORISE, Oak Ridge, Tenn., 1985—; mem. environ. and radiation adv. com. Pa. Power and Light, Allentown, 1995—. Col. M.C., U.S. Army Res., ret. Fellow ACP, Am. Coll. Occupl. and Environ. Medicine, Am. Coll. Physician Execs.; mem. AMA, Am. Soc. Mil. Surgeons, Health Physics Soc. Home: 81 Oak Rd Bayport NY 11705

BREITMAN, JOSEPH B., prosthodontist, dental educator; b. Phila., Aug. 4, 1952; s. Abraham A. and Natalie (Ketchurin) B.; m. Barbara Susan Beitman, May 13, 1990; children: Ilana Michelle, Ariel Judah, Leela Sivie. B.A., LaSalle Coll., 1974; D.M.D., U. Pa., 1977; Cert. of Tng. in Prosthodontics, Temple U., 1979; Cert. of Tng. in Biomaterials, VA Hosp., Elsmere, Del., 1979. Gen. practice dentistry, Lafayette Hill, Pa., 1978-79; prosthodontist Raymond Hancock, Marlton, N.J., 1979-80; pvt. practice prosthodontics, Phila., 1980—; asst. prof. dental materials Temple U., Phila., 1978-84; assoc. in restorative dentistry U. Pa., Phila., 1985—; asst. prof. post-doctoral prosthodontics Temple U., 1990. Oral biology fellow Temple U., Phila., 1978. Fellow Internat. Congress of Oral Implantologists (elected 1994); mem. ADA, Am. Coll. Prosthodontics, N.E. Dental Soc. (pres. 1988-89), Ea. Dental Soc., Pa. Assn. Dental Surgeons (pres. 1984-85). Jewish. Lodge: Masons. Avocations: play bagpipes, tae kwon do. Office: 8021B Castor Ave Philadelphia PA 19152-2733

BREITSTEIN, ROBERT YALE, gynecologist; b. N.Y.C., Feb. 22, 1937; s. Louis and Hilda (Tanenbaum) B.; m. Dominique Rebecca Baechlé, Oct. 21, 1971; 1 child, Sandra Rachelle. BA, Bklyn. Coll., 1956; MD, SUNY, Bklyn., 1960. Diplomate Am. Bd. Ob-Gyn. Rotating intern Beth Israel Hosp., N.Y.C., 1960-61; residency in ob-gyn. Kings County Hosp. Ctr., Bklyn., 1961-65; asst. prof. ob-gyn. Bellevue Med. Ctr. NYU, N.Y.C., 1968—; assoc. attending physician ob-gyn. N.Y.-Beekman Downtown Hosp., N.Y.C., 1968—. Maj. USAF, 1966-68. Fellow ACS; mem. AMA, Am. Assn. Gynecologic Laporoscopists, Endometriosis Assn. N.Y. (adv. 1984—). Office: 333 E 5th St New York NY 10022-2950

BREITZER, GERARD MARTIN, pediatrics educator; b. Chgo., Oct. 27, 1948; s. Bernard and Dora (Margolis) B.; m. Susan J. Frank, Dec. 7, 1986; children: Joshua Aaron, Rebekah Ann. BS, U. Ill., 1970; DO, Chgo. Coll. Osteo. Medicine, 1975; MS in Adminstrv. Medicine, U. Wis., 1996. Diplomate Am. Bd. Pediatrics, Am. Bd. Osteo. Physicians, Am. Bd. Osteo. Pediatricians. Resident in pediatrics Fitzsimons Army Med. Ctr., Aurora, Colo., 1975-78; asst. prof. Mich. State U., East Lansing, 1980-84, assoc. prof., 1985-92, prof. pediats., 1992—, dir. pediatric clinic, 1983-93, dir. pediatric residence program, 1984—; chair dept. pediatrics Lansing Gen. Hosp., 1991-92; prof., 1992-96; chief divsn. ambulatory pediats. Sparrow Hosp.; cons. Mich. Peer Rev. Orgn., Lansing, 1989—, Mich. Dept. Social Svcs., Lansing, 1990. Contbr. articles to med. jours. Pres. Mich. Child Passenger Safety Assn., 1984. Maj. M.C., U.S. Army, 1975-80. Grantee USPHS, 1984-90; rsch. grantee Mich. State U., 1987. Fellow Am. Acad. Pediatrics (chmn. injury and poison prevention, sec. Mich. chpt., cert. merit 1982, pres.-elect Mich. chpt. 1995), Am. Coll. Osteo. Pediatricians (cert. merit 1984); mem. Am. Osteo. Assn., Ambulatory Pediatric Assn., Mich. Assn. Osteo Physicians. Jewish. Office: Mich State U Dept Pediatrics 545 W Fee Hall East Lansing MI 48824-1316

BREM, ANDREW SAMUEL, pediatric nephrologist, educator; b. Worcester, Mass., Nov. 7, 1948; s. Jacob and Martha (Herwitz) B.; m. Francine Steiner, Feb. 10, 1980; children: Matthew Benjamin, Douglas Jacob. BA, Case Western Reserve, 1970; MD, Tufts U., 1974; MA, Brown U., 1989. Intern Maine Med. Ctr., Portland, 1974-75; resident in pediatrics R.I. Hosp. Brown U., Providence, 1975-77; pediatric nephrology-renal physiology fellow Cornell Univ. N.Y. Hosp., N.Y.C., 1977-79; dir. div. pediatric nephrology R.I. Hosp., 1979—; assoc. prof. pediatrics Brown U., Providence, 1988-95, prof., 1995—; co-chmn. med. rev. bd. Network #1 End Stage Renal Disease, New Haven, 1989-92, bd. dirs., 1995—. Contbr. articles to profl. jours. Fellow Am. Acad. Pediatrics; mem. Am. Soc. Nephrology, Am. Fedn. Clin. Rsch., Am. Soc. Pediatric Nephrology (counselor 1991-95), Soc. Pediatric Rsch., Am. Pediatric Soc., Alpha Omega Alpha.

BREMER, KARL, physician; b. Limburg, Hessen, Germany, May 20, 1941; s. Bernhard and Hildegard (Hammes) B.; m. Gerda Schnell, Dec. 28, 1968; children: Monika, Joachim. MD, U. Ulm/Do, Germany, 1967; privat-dozent, U. Essen, Germany, 1980. Rschr. U. Ulm, Germany, 1967-72; asst. physician U. Essen, Germany, 1973-81; supervisory physician U. Bochum, Germany, 1981-82; head clinic hematology and oncology Augusta-Kranken-Anstalt, Bochum, 1982—; sec. Kiel Lymphoma Study Group, Essen, 1975-77; med. dir. Cancer Ctr., Bochum/Herne, 1990-93; chmn. Clin. Phase II/III Studies, 1980—. Co-author, editor book.j. With German Army, 1970-71. Mem. European Soc. Med. Oncology (cert.), German Cancer Soc., German Soc. Hematology and Oncology. Roman Catholic. Office: Augusta Kranken Anstalt, Berg Str 26, D-44791 Bochum NRW, Germany

BREMER, WILLIAM STEPHEN, physician; b. N.Y.C., July 18, 1950; s. Marvin Stephen and Patsy Virginia (Raskob) B.; m. Martha Jane Kirkpatrick, June 9, 1973; children: Matthew Stephen, Mark Patrick, Nicholas Ian. BS, Loyola Coll., 1972; MD, Georgetown U., 1976. Diplomate Am. Bd. Family Practice. Intern Fairfax Hosp., Falls Church, Va., 1976-77; resident in family practice Med. Coll. of Va., Fairfax, 1977-79; asst. dir. Fairfax (Va.) Family Practice Ctr., 1979-81; asst. clin. prof. Med. Coll. Va., Fairfax, 1979-81; pvt. family practice St. Michaels. Md., 1981-94; family physician, mgmt. com. Shore Clin. Found., Easton, Md., 1994—; med. dir. Easton Meml. Hosp. Detox Unit, 1982-86, Talbot County Hospice, Easton, 1987—, Talbot County Adult Day Care, Easton, 1995—, Shore Home Care and Hospice, Easton, 1996—; cons. Talbot County Dept. Addictions, Easton, 1982—, Talbot County Dept. Corrections, 1984-95. Author: Evaluation of Acute Knee Injuries, 1979, Beyond Survival, 1980. Pres. Chem. People, Easton, 1986-90; bd. dirs. Chesapeake Ctr.-Devel. Rehab., Easton, 1995—. Recipient Citation, Gov. of Md., 1990. Fellow Am. Acad. Family Physicians; mem. Acad. Hospice Physicians (founding mem.), Md. Acad. Family Physicians (bd. dirs. 1996), Nat. Congress of Parents and Tchrs. (hon. life). Home: PO Box I Saint Michaels MD 21663 Office: Shore Clin Found 800 S Talbot St Saint Michaels MD 21663

BREMNER, WILLIAM JOHN, physician; b. Bellingham, Wash., July 5, 1943; s. George Adelbert and Marian (Bay) B.; m. Jane Belden Stimpson, June 18, 1965; children: Jennifer, Andrew, Sara (dec.), Tim. BA, Harvard U., 1964; MD, U. Wash., 1969; PhD, Monash U., 1978. Diplomate Am. Bd. Internal Medicine; Nat. Bd. Med. Examiners. Med. intern Vanderbilt U. Hosp., Nashville, 1969-70; resident in internal medicine U. Wash., Seattle, 1970-72; sr. fellow in Endocrinology U. Wash. Sch. Medicine, Seattle, 1972-74; sr. research officer Australian Nat. Health and Med. Research Council, Melbourne, Australia, 1974-77; asst. prof. medicine U. Wash., Seattle, 1977-82; chief of endocrinology V.A. Med. Ctr., Seattle, 1979-87, chief. med. service, 1987—; assoc. prof. medicine U. Wash., Seattle, 1982-87, prof., vice chmn. dept. medicine, 1987—; mem. steering com. WHO, Geneva, 1984-87; cons. NIH, Bethesda, Md., 1985-88. Mem. editl. bd. Jour. Clin. Endocrinology and Metabolism, 1983-87; assoc. editor Internat. Jour. of Andrology, 1983-87; contbr. articles and book chpts. to numerous profl. jours. Mem. The Endocrine Soc., Am. Fedn. Clin. Rsch., Am. Soc. Clin. Investigation, Assn. Am. Physicians, Western Soc. Clin. Investigations (chmn. West Coast Endocrine Club Meeting 1982), The Am. Soc. Andrology (mem. coun. 1981-84, nominating com. 1983-86, program com. 1986-87), Soc. for Study Reproduction (publ. com. 1983-85, chmn. 1984-85), Pacific Coast Fertility Soc. (Wyeth award 1971), Am. Fertility Soc., Western Assn. Physicians, Alpha Omega Alpha. Office: Vet Adminstrn Med Ctr 1660 S Columbian Way Seattle WA 98108-1532

BREMS, CHRISTIANE, psychologist; b. Lampertheim, Germany, Jan. 17, 1961; d. Hand Bernhard and Rosemarie (Hilsheimer) B. BA, Okla. State U., 1982, MS, 1984, PhD, 1987. Asst. prof. U. Okla. Health Scis. Ctr., Oklahoma City, 1988-89; asst. prof. U. Alaska, Anchorage, 1989-92, assoc. prof., 1992—; sr. rsch. assoc. Alaska Psychiat. Inst., Anchorage, 1994—; assessment cons. South Ctrl. Counseling Ctr., Anchorage, 1994—. Author: Training Manual for a Self Psychologically Oriented Parent Education Series, 1990, A Comprehensive Guide to Child Psychotherapy, 1994; co-author: Between Two People: Exercises Toward Intimacy, 1993; contbr. articles to profl. jours., chpts. to books. Mem. APA, Soc. Personality Assessment, Alaska Psychol. Assn., Internat. Rorschach Soc., Western Psychol. Assn., Coun. Execs. Psychol. Assn. Office: U Alaska Anchorage Dept Psychology Anchorage AK 99508

BRENDER, ELLIOTT, surgeon; b. Bklyn., Feb. 25, 1946; s. Edward and Ruth Brender; m. Julie Ann Lee, Feb. 18, 1989; children: Jacob, Cady. BA, NYU, 1966; MD, U. Buffalo, 1970. Intern N.Y. Hosp.-Cornell Med. Ctr., N.Y.C., 1970-71, resident, 1971; resident Mount Zion Hosp. & Med. Ctr., San Francisco, 1973-77; pvt. practice San Francisco, 1977-85; instr. Saddleback Coll., 1985-87; med. dir. Charter Recovery Network, Fountain Valley, Calif., 1987—; pvt. practice Garden Grove, Calif., 1991—; asst. clin. prof. dept. surgery U. Calif., Irvine, 1991. Vol. Haight Ashbury Free Med. Clinic., 1983-85, 72-77. With U.S. Army, 1971-73. Fellow ACS; mem. S.W. Surg. Congress, SAGES, Orange County Med. Assn., Calif. Med. Assn. Home: 10661 Albany Circle Villa Park CA 92667 Office: 12665 Garden Grove Blvd #600 Garden Grove CA 92643

BRENDER, JEAN DIANE, epidemiologist, nurse; b. Bellingham, Wash., Nov. 23, 1951; d. Otto and Jennie Wilma Tolsma; m. Dennis Ray Brender, Aug. 30, 1975; 1 child, Valerie. BSN summa cum laude, Whitworth Coll., 1974; M of Nursing, U. Wash., 1979, PhD of Epidemiology, 1983. RN, Tex. Staff nurse, infection control Sacred Heart Med. Ctr., Spokane, Wash., 1974-80; instr. nursing Intercollegiate Ctr. for Nursing Edn., Spokane, 1979-80, asst. prof. nursing, 1982-84; teaching asst. epidemiology U. Wash., Seattle, 1981-82; rsch. health scientist Audie L. Murphy Vets. Hosp., San Antonio, 1984-85; staff epidemiologist bur. epidemiology Tex. Dept. Health, Austin, 1986-87, acting program dir. environ. epidemiology program, 1987, dir. environ. epidemiology program, 1987-93, dir. noncommunicable disease epidemiology and toxicology, 1993—, also state environ. epidemiologist; bd. dirs. Agriculture Resources Protection Authority; state environ. epidemiologist; adj. instr. allied health scis. and health adminstrn. S.W. Tex. State U., 1986-90; adj. asst. prof. epidemiology U. Tex. Health Sci. Ctr.-Houston Sch. Pub. Health, 1985-93, adj. assoc. prof., 1993—. Contbr. articles to profl. jours. Tchr., mem. adult choir St. Martin's Luth. Ch., Austin, 1991—. Recipient H.E.A.L.T.H. award, 1994; grantee in field. Mem. Soc. Epidemiologic Rsch., Coun. State and Territorial Epidemiologists, Exec. Women in Tex. Govt. Home: 6902 Alder Cv Austin TX 78750-8161 Office: Tex Dept Health 1100 W 49th St Austin TX 78756-3101

BRENEMAN, DEBRA LYNN, dermatologist, educator; b. Spirit Lake, Iowa, Jan. 17, 1955; d. Walter Edward and Mildred Mathilda (Bonde) Johnson; m. John Charles Breneman, May 30, 1981; children: Christopher John, Kevin Michael, Alyssa Nicole, Nathan Andrew. BS, Iowa State U., 1977; MD, U. Iowa, 1981. Intern, Butterworth Hosp., Grand Rapids, Mich., 1981-82; resident in dermatology U. Cin., 1982-85, instr. dermatology, 1985-86, asst. prof., 1986-91, assoc. prof. dermatology, 1991—, dir. div. dermatopharmacology, 1985—; staff physician U. Cin. Med. Ctr., 1985—; staff physician VA Med. Ctr., Cin., 1985-91, cons. physician, 1992—; cons. physician Children's Hosp. Med. Ctr., Cin., 1986—. Contbr. articles to profl. jours. Fellow Am. Acad. Dermatology; mem. Midwestern Congress Dermatol. Socs., Ohio Dermatol. Assn., Cin. Dermatol. Soc., Phi Beta Kappa, Phi Kappa Phi, Alpha Lambda Delta. Office: U Cin Dept Dermatology 234 Goodman St # 523 Cincinnati OH 45267-2364

BRENER, MAX DONALD, oral and maxillofacial surgeon; b. Chattanooga, Mar. 6, 1941; s. Robert and Helen (Barshay) B.; m. Susan Burke, Mar. 23, 1963; children: M. Scott, Robert M., Andrea E. Student, U. N.C., 1959-61; DDS, U. Tenn., Memphis, 1965. Diplomate Am. Bd. Oral & Maxillofacial Surgery. Resident U. Tenn. Meml. Hosp., Knoxville, 1967-70; pvt. practice Chattanooga, 1970—. Lt. USN, 1965-67. Fellow Am. Assn. Oral and Maxillofacial Surgeons, S.E. Soc. Oral and Maxillofacial Surgeons, Tenn. Soc. Oral and Maxillofacial Surgeons (pres. 1991-93); mem. ADA, Tenn. Dental Assn., 3d Dist. Dental Soc. (pres. 1991-92), Tenn. Valley Dental Study Group (pres. 1980-81). Office: 4110 Brainerd Rd Chattanooga TN 37411-3717

BRENER, WILLIAM, gastroenterologist; b. Chattanooga, Apr. 10, 1948; s. Robert and Helen (Barshay) B.; m. Christine Lloyd, June 11, 1973; children: Alexander, Andrew. BA with highest distinction, U. Va., 1970; MD, Johns Hopkins U., 1974. Diplomate Am. Bd. Internal Medicine, Am. Bd. Gastroenterology. Intern in internal medicine Johns Hopkins Hosp., Balt., 1974-75, sr. resident internal medicine, 1978-79, fellow gastroenterology and liver disease, 1979-81; resident in internal medicine U. Hosps., Cleve., 1975-76; surgeon USPHS, Barboursville, W.Va., 1976-78; asst. prof. medicine Med. U. of S.C., Charleston, 1981-84; pvt. practice Charleston, 1981—, Digestive Disease Assocs., Charleston, 1986—; staff physician Roper Hosp., Bon-Secours St. Francis Hosp., Baker Hosp., East Cooper Hosp., Charleston, 1981—. Soc. 1812 fellow Health Sci. Found., Med. U. of S.C., 1984; Miller scholar, 1970. Mem. ACP, Am. Gastroent. Assn., Crohns and Colitis Found., Phi Eta Sigma, Phi Beta Kappa, Alpha Omega Alpha. Jewish. Office: Digestive Disease Assocs 125 Doughty St Ste 300 Charleston SC 29403-5740

BRENNAN, BRIDGET ANNA, critical care nurse; b. Ireland, Aug. 1, 1943; arrived in U.S., 1967; d. Daniel and Mary (McDermott) B. RN, The Royal Alexandra Infirmary, Paisley, Scotland, 1965; Registered Midwife, Glasgow Royal Maternity, 1966; BS in Nursing, Herbert H. Lehman Coll., Bronx, N.Y., 1984; MS in Community Health, L.I. U., 1989. Cert. post anesthesia nurse. Staff nurse obstetrics Glasgow Royal Infirmary, 1966, Woking Maternity Hosp., Surrey, Eng., 1966; staff nurse ob-gyn. New Rochelle (N.Y.) Hosp. Med. Ctr., 1967-68; staff nurse Ob-Gyn United Hosp. Med. Ctr., Port Chester, N.Y., 1968-72, staff nurse med. surg. nursing, 1972-73, staff nurse CRCU, 1973-84, staff nurse post anesthesia care unit, 1984—. Recipient Dr. Thomas Watt Meml. prize in med. nursing practice, 1965. Mem. AACN, Am. Soc. Post Anesthesia Nurses, N.Y. State Nurses' Assn. Home: 55 N Broadway Apt 112 White Plains NY 10601-1640

BRENNAN, EDWARD NOEL, psychiatrist, psychoanalyst; b. N.Y.C., Dec. 28, 1929; s. Edward L. and Margaret A. (Fenelon) B.; B.S., Trinity Coll., 1951; M.D., Yale U., 1955; psychoanalytic tng. Columbia U. Psychoanalytic Clinic for Tng. and Research, 1964-69; m. Alice Ann MacHardy, Oct. 20, 1956; children: Alison Marie, Elizabeth Louise, Noel Edward McKenzie. Rotating intern Phila. Gen. Hosp., 1955-56; resident in psychiatry Boston Psychopathic Hosp., 1956-59; teaching fellow in psychiatry Harvard U., 1956-59; assoc. in medicine (psychiatry) Peter Bent Brigham Hosp., Boston, 1958-59; assoc. in psychiatry Tufts U., 1957-59; cons. Mcpl. Ct. Clinic, Cambridge, Mass., 1958-59 chief psychiat. in-patient service Reiss Mental Health Pavillion, St. Vincents Hosp., N.Y.C., 1961-64, asst. attending psychiatrist, 1961-64, assoc. attending psychiatrist, 1964-71, attending, 1972-91, supr. in psychotherapy psychiat. out-patient dept., 1964-91; collaborating psychoanalyst Columbia U. Psychoanalytic Center, N.Y.C., 1972-92, mem. faculty, 1992—, tng. and supervising analyst, 1993—; asst. attending psychiatrist Presbyterian Hosp., N.Y.C., 1976-93, assoc. attending psychiatrist, 1993—; assoc. attending psychiatrist Greenwich (Conn.) Hosp., 1979-92, honorary attending staff mem. dept. psychiatry, 1993—; asst. clin. prof. psychiatry Columbia U., 1976-93, assoc. clin. prof. psychiatry, 1993—. Served to capt. USAF, 1959-61. Diplomate Nat. Bd. Med. Examiners, Am. Bd. Psychiatry and Neurology; qualified psychiatrist N.Y. State Dept. Mental Hygiene. Fellow Am. Psychiat. Assn. (com. on pub. info., com. continuing med. edn. N.Y.C. br.); mem. Am. Assn. Gen. Hosp. Psychiatrists, Am. Psychoanalytic Assn. (chmn. continuing edn. com. 1982-91), Westchester Psychoanalytic Soc. (sec. 1978, pres. 1982), Soc. Liaison Psychiatry, Am. Acad. Psychoanalysis, Am. Coll. Psychoanalysts, AMA, N.Y. County Med. Soc., Fairfield County Med. Soc., Undersea Med. Soc., Assn. Psychoanalytic Medicine. Home and Office: Topping Rd Greenwich CT 06831 Office: 153 E 57th St New York NY 10022-2119

BRENNAN, HELEN BOBALICK, nurse administrator; b. Weirton, W.Va., Feb. 7, 1924; d. John and Anna (Urich) Bobalick; m. Thomas I. Brennan, Feb. 29, 1952; children: Matthew I., Faith I., Luke I., Hope I., Mark I. Diploma, Bellevue Hosp. Sch. Nursing, 1945; BS, NYU, 1948, MA, 1981. Cert. in nursing adminstrn. Vis. nurse Bklyn. Vis. Nurse Assn., 1945-48; pub. health nurse Dept. Health, Yonkers, N.Y., 1948-50, Jewish Child Care Assn., N.Y.C., 1950-54; nurse adminstr. Letchworth Village Devel. Ctr., Thiells, N.Y., 1971—. Mem. ANA, N.Y. State Nurses Assn., Bellevue Alumnae Assn., Soc. Rogerian Scholars, Nursing Alumni (NYU div.). Office: Letchworth Village Devel Thiells NY 10984

BRENNAN, JOHN JOSEPH, medical investigator; b. Cold Spring, N.Y., Oct. 2, 1951; s. Francis Joseph Brennan and Jean Margaret Marburger; m. Marsha Ann Schattner, June 9, 1973; children: Susan Catherine, John Francis. BA in Chemistry, Temple U., 1973; PhD in Pharm. Sci., Phila. Coll. Pharmacy, 1979. Postdoctoral fellow Ortho Pharms., Raritan, N.J., 1979-81; scientist, sr. scientist, asst. dir. Squibb Corp., Princeton, N.J., 1981-92; assoc. dir. Bristol Myers Squibb, Princeton, 1992; dir. Solvay Pharms., Marietta, Ga., 1992—. Bd. trustees Somerset (N.J.) Presbyn. Ch., 1984-92; session mem. Roswell (Ga.) Presbyn. Ch., 1995—. Samuel Sadtler fellow Phila. Coll. Pharmacy, 1977-79. Mem. Am. Assn. Pharm. Sci., Am. Coll. Clin. Pharmacy (pres. S.E. chpt. 1992—), Cedar Hill Club (bd. dirs. 1990-92). Home: 415 Holly Stream Trl Roswell GA 30075-1848

BRENNAN, JOHN LINDSAY, psychiatrist; b. Perth, Australia, Jan. 22, 1949; s. William Keith and Doreen Isabelle B.; m. Helen Louise, May 24, 1973. BS with honors, Sydney U., 1970, MB BS with honors, 1973. Resident Royal Prince Alfred Hosp., Sydney, Australia, 1973, resident in psychiatry, 1974-79; fellow in child psychiatry Westmead Ctr., Sydney, 1979, Austin Hosp., Melbourne, Australia, 1980; rsch. fellow U. Vt., Burlington, 1981-82; staff specialist Royal Alexandra Hosp., Sydney, 1982-89, dir. child psychiatry, 1985-88; rsch. fellow George Washington U., Washington, 1989; dir. adolescent svcs. Prince of Wales Hosp., Sydney, 1989—; lectr. U. New South Wales, 1989-94; dir. child and family/early intervention, Westmead Hosp.; cons. to Royal Far West Children's Health Sci. Contbr. articles to profl. jours. Active Community Aid Abroad. Mem. Royal Australian and New Zealand Coll. Psychiatrists (com. for tng. in child psychiatry 1985-94). Office: Redhawk House, High St, Westmead Hosp, Westmead/Sydney 2031, Australia

BRENNAN, NEIL JAMES, physician; b. Dublin, Ireland, July 8, 1947; s. Philip and Mary (Blayney) B.; m. Catriona O'Meara, Sept. 1, 1972; children: Suzanne, Aline, Mark. MB, BChir, U. Coll. Dublin, 1972. Med. sr. house officer Federated Dublin Hosps., 1974-75; house officer St. Vincent's Hosp., Dublin, 1972-74, med. registrar, 1975-77; med. registrar West Middlesex Hosp., London, 1977-78; rsch. registrar Brompton Hosp., London, 1978-79; post-doctoral fellow sch. hygiene Johns Hopkins U., Balt., 1979-80; lectr. medicine Univ. Coll. Dublin, 1980-83; cons. physician County Hosp., Clonmel, Ireland, 1983-84, Mercy Hosp., Cork, Ireland, 1984—; coun. mem. Irish Med. Orgn., 1988-90, v.p., 1989-90. Contbr. articles to profl. jours. Fellow Royal Coll. Physicians Ireland; mem. Irish Thoracic Soc., Brit. Thoracic Soc., European Respiratory Soc. Office: Mercy Hosp, Cork Ireland

BRENNEMAN, AUSTIN RUSSELL, dermatologist; b. Tulsa, Okla., Nov. 15, 1932; s. Everett Russell and Mary Teresa (Pishny) B.; m. N. Colleen Smith, June 3, 1977; children: Scott, Kevin, Robert, Dawn. Student, Coll. of Wooster, 1950-51; BS magna cum laude, Washington and Lee U., 1954; MD, Yale U., 1958. Diplomate Am. Bd. Internal Medicine, Am. Bd. Dermatology. Intern U. Va. Hosp., Charlottesville, 1958-59; resident Grace-New Haven (Conn.) Hosp., 1959-61; postdoctoral fellow NIH, Bethesda, Md., 1961-62; sr. asst. surgeon USPHS, Bethesda, 1962-64; postdoctoral fellow liver study unit Yale-New Haven Med. Ctr., 1964-66, resident in dermatology, 1966-68, physician ambulatory svc., clin. instr. dermatology, 1968-79; pvt. practice Hartford, 1968-79; active staff Muskogee (Okla.) Regional Med. Ctr., 1979-88, courtesy staff, 1988—; cons. Newington (Conn.) VA Hosp., 1968-77, VA Med. Ctr., Muskogee, 1979—; clin. asst. on staff Hartford (Conn.) Hosp., 1970-71, asst. to staff, Dept. of Medicine, 1971-79. Co-contbr. articles to profl. jours. Office: 2800 W Broadway St Muskogee OK 74401-2715

BRENNER, ALAN IRA, rheumatologist; b. Providence, Aug. 24, 1942; s. Louis Raymond and Jean (Poritsky) B.; m. Beverly Farber, Aug. 29, 1965 (div. 1983); m. Lynn Katoff, Jan. 8, 1984; children: Jessica, Adam, Richard, Cara. BA in Biology, Brown U., 1964; MD, U. Cin., 1968. Diplomate Am. Bd. Internal Medicine, Am. Bd. Rheumatology. Intern Northwestern U., Chgo., 1968-69; resident in medicine New Eng. Med. Ctr., Boston, 1969-70; fellow in rheumatology Boston U., 1972-74; pres. Rheumatol. Svcs., Framingham, Mass., 1974—; cons. immunology Metro West Med. Ctr., Framingham, 1978—; cons. rheumatology Milford Hosp., 1980—; cons. Lupus Found., Wellesley, Mass., 1991—. Bd. dirs. Marlboro Cultural Affairs, 1988—. Maj. USAF, 1970-72. Mem. AMA, ACP, Am. Acad. Sci., Am. Soc. Itnernal Medicine, New Eng. Rheumatism Soc., N.Y. Acad. Sci. Jewish. Office: Rheumatol Svcs 600 Worcester Rd Framingham MA 01701-5360

BRENNER, ANNE MANON, pediatrician, allergist; b. Jacksonville, Fla., Oct. 21, 1944. BA, Tex. Tech. U., 1966; MD, U. Tex., 1971. Diplomate Am. Bd. Allergy and Immunology, Am. Bd. Pediatrics. Intern in family practice John Sealy Hosp. U. Tex., Galveston, 1971-72, resident in pediatrics, 1972-74; pediatric practice Galveston, 1974-77; fellow in immunology and respiratory medicine Nat. Asthma Ctr., Denver, 1977-80; sr. staff physician Nat. Jewish Ctr., Denver, 1981—; assoc. prof. pediatrics U. Colo. Health Scis. Ctr., Denver. Contbr. articles to profl. jours. Mem. Am. Acad. Pediatrics, Am. Acad. Allergy and Immunology. Roman Catholic. Office: Nat Jewish Ctr Immunology and Respiratory Medicine 1400 Jackson St Denver CO 80206-2761

BRENNER, BETTY ESTHER BILGRAY, social worker; b. Providence, Feb. 13, 1943; d. Albert Theopore and Clara (Simon) Bilgray; m. Douglas Brenner, Sept. 1, 1968; children: Steven, Michael, Deborah. BA, U. Mich., 1965, MSW, 1967. Lic. clin. social worker, N.J. Social worker Peter Bent Brigham Hosp., Boston, 1967-69, Union County Psychiat. Clinic, Summit, N.J., 1969-71, Mental Health Resource Ctr., Montclair, N.J., 1977-83, Jewish Family Svc. N. Jersey, Wayne, N.J., 1983-91; pvt. practice Halepon and Liveingston, N.J., North Haledon and Livingston, 1991—. Home and Office: 61 E Sherbrooke Pky Livingston NJ 07039-3133 Office: 546 High Mountain RdN North Haledon NJ 07508-2606

BRENNER, DEAN ELLIOTT, medical oncology and pharmacology educator; b. Phila., Sept. 24, 1949. AB, U. Pa., 1971; MD, Hahnemann U., 1974. Diplomate Am. Bd. Internal Medicine, Am. Bd. Med. Oncology. Resident in medicine Pa. State U. Hershey Med. Ctr., 1974-77; clin. assoc. Nat. Cancer Inst. NIH and Balt. Cancer Rsch. Ctr., 1977-80, expert, 1980-81; asst. prof. medicine Vanderbilt U., Nashville, 1981-86; rsch. clinician Roswell Park Meml. Inst., Buffalo, 1986-89; assoc. prof. SUNY, Buffalo, 1987-89; assoc. prof. medicine and pharmacology U. Mich., Ann Arbor, 1989-92; chief sect. of hematology/oncology Dept. Veterans Affairs Medical Ctr., Ann Arbor, 1992-96; dir. Cancer Prevention Program, U. Mich. Cancer Ctr., 1996—; mem. adv. bd. on oncologics FDA, Rockville, Md., 1987-91; mem. Cancer Clin. Investigation Rev. Com., NCI, 1992—; reviewer jour. articles. Recipient Jr. Clin. Faculty award Am. Cancer Soc., 1982, Career Devel. award VA, 1984; rsch. grantee VA, 1984, 94, Nat. Cancer Inst., 1988, 92, 94, 95, 96, Am. Cancer Soc., 1993. Fellow ACP; mem. Am. Assn. for Cancer Rsch., Am. Soc. Clin. Oncology, Southwestern Oncology Group. Office: U Mich Med Sch 100 Simpson 102 Observatory Ann Arbor MI 48109-0724

BRENNER, FREDERIC JAMES, biology educator, ecological consultant; b. Warren, Ohio, Dec. 25, 1936; s. Frederick James and Katherine Louise (Newberry) B.; m. Patricia Elaine Gavin, Aug. 27, 1967; children: Elaine, Cheryl. BS, Thiel Coll., Greenville, Pa., 1958; MS, Pa. State U., 1960, PhD, 1964. Teaching intern Denison U., Granville, Ohio, 1964-65; asst. prof. biology Thiel Coll., 1965-69; asst. prof. biology Grove City (Pa.) Coll., 1969-70, assoc. prof., 1970-86, prof., 1986—; pres. Brenner Ecol. Svc., Grove City, 1974—. Editor: (with others) Species Spl. Concern Pa., 1985, Endangered and Threatened Species Program in Pa., 1986, Environ. Consequences of Energy Prodn., 1987, Westlands Ecology and Conservation Emphasis in Pa., 1989, Biological Diversity: Problems and Consequences, Environmental Contaminants, Ecosystems and Human Health, 1995, Forests: A Global Perspective; contbr. over 200 articles to profl. jours. Chmn. Mercer County Solid Waste Authority, 1988—; sec.-treas. Mercer County Conservation Dist., 1975—; treas., vice chmn., chmn. Mercer County Regional Planning Commn., 1989-93, sec., 1990; mem. exec. bd. Shenango Conservency; mem. exec. bd. French Creek Coun., Erie, 1972; dir. Woodbadge Course Boy Scouts Am., 1973-89 (Silver Beaver award 1973, Dist. award merit 1976). Recipient Nat. Conservation award DAR, 1989, Grove City United Way Cmty. Svc. award, 1993, Alpha Phi Omega Disting. Alumni Svc. award, 1994. Mem. Ecol. Soc. Am. (exec. coun. 1978-82), Pa. Acad. Sci. (editor newsletter PAS 1966, pres.-elect 1992-94, pres. 1994-96, exec. coun. 1986—), Nat. Assn. Acad. Scis. (sec. 1995—), Wildlife Soc. (pres. Pa. chpt. 1975-77), Beta Beta Beta (v.p. 1993—). Republican. Episcopalian. Office: Grove City Coll Dept Biol Grove City PA 16127

BRENNER, MICHAEL B., ophthalmologist; b. L.A., May 26, 1962; s. Sid and Marsha Brenner; m. Pamela Alcala, July 3, 1992; 1 child, Nicole. BS in Biomed. Scis., U. Calif., Riverside, 1984, BS in Psychology, 1984; MD, UCLA, 1987. Diplomate Am. Bd. Ophthalmology, Nat. Bd. Med. Examiners. Resident in internal medicine Huntington Meml. Hosp., Pasadena, Calif., 1987-88; resident in ophthalmology U. Ariz., Tucson, 1988-90, chief resident ophthalmology, 1991; eye physician/surgeon, cons. in cornea/refractive surgery Jules Mulach Eye Ctr., Long Beach, Calif., 1992; med. dir. Mulach-Brenner Eye Ctr., Long Beach, 1993—; vis. asst. prof. Jules Stein Eye Inst., UCLA, 1991-92; bd. dirs. Long Beach Health Sys.; clin. lectr., examiner Osler Inst., Terre Haute, Ind., 1994—; med. dirs. Vision Sculpting of Long Beach, 1995—. Contbr. articles to profl. jours.; co-inventor ophthalmic instrument. Contbg. surgeon Search for Sight Found., Long Beach, 1992-94; com. chmn. Found. for Ednl. Rsch., L.a., 1994, 96. Gunde Meml. scholar, 1984; Abe Meyer fellow Jules Stein Eye Inst., 1991; Fisons rsch. grantee Contact Lens Assn. of Ophthalmologists, 1992. Fellow Am. Acad. Ophthalmology; mem. AMA, Internat. Soc. Refractive Surgery, Am. Soc. Cataract and Refractive Surgery, Los Angeles County Med. Assn. (del. exec. com. 1993—), UCLA Dept. Ophthalmology Assn., Phi Gamma Delta (sec.-treas. 1980—), Lions. Office: Mulach-Brenner Eye Ctr Ste 200 3950 Long Beach Blvd Long Beach CA 90807

BRENNER, ROBERT SCOTT, physician; b. Cin., Oct. 23, 1943; s. Harry and Fanny Mildred (Leshner) B.; m. Barbara Michelle Engel; children: Jill H., Elin M. BS, Ohio State U., 1965, MD, 1969. Diplomate Am. Bd. Internal Medicine. Physician, pvt. practice Julius Filhmon, MD, Beechwood, Ohio, 1976-80, Drs. Markowitz Brenner & Assocs., Beechwood, 1980-91, Lyndhurst, Ohio, 1991—; chief clin. endocrinology Mt. Sinai Med. Ctr., Cleve., 1983—; asst. clin. prof. of medicine Case Western Res. U., 1995—. Trustee Diabetes Assn. of Greater Cleve., Beechwood, 1977-95, pres. 1990-93. Maj. U.S. Army, 1972-76. Fellow Am. Coll. Endocrinology; mem. Am. Assn. Clin. Endocardiologists. Office: 29001 Cedar Rd Lyndhurst OH 44124

BRENNER, RONALD JOHN, pharmaceutical industry executive; b. Bethlehem, Pa., June 9, 1933; s. Sam Ralph and Frieda V. E. (Buck) B.; m. Sally Gaskill, Oct. 24, 1964; children: Carol L., Nancy J., Katherine E., Richard J. BS in Pharmacy, U. Cin., 1955; MS in Pharm. Chemistry, U. Fla., 1957, PhD in Pharm. Chemistry, 1959. Rsch. scientist McNeil Labs., Ft. Washington, Pa., 1958-66, dir. devel. rsch., 1966-67, exec. dirs. new products, 1967-70, exec. v.p., 1974-78; v.p. Johnson & Johnson Internat., New Brunswick, N.J., 1970-74; pres. McNeil Pharm. Co., Ft. Washington, 1978; co. group chmn. Johnson & Johnson Co., New Brunswick, 1978-82, v.p., 1982-84; pres., chief exec. officer Cytogen Corp., 1984-88; ptnr. Hillman Med. Ventures, Inc., 1989—; trustee Phila. Coll. Pharmacy and Sci., 1976-88; mem. N.J. Gov.'s Commn. on Sci. and Tech., Task Force on Acad.-Indsl. Innovation; mem. adv. bd. Scripps Clinic and Rsch. Found. Bd. dirs. Am. Found. Pharm. Edn., 1983-95. Mem. Am. Pharm. Assn., AAAS, Acad. Pharm. Scis., Soc. Chem. Industry, Pharmacists Against Drug Abuse Found.

(v.p., trustee). Office: Hillman Med Ventures Inc 2 Walnut Grove Dr Ste 130 Horsham PA 19044-2219

BRENNESSEL, BARBARA ANNE, biology educator, researcher; b. Bklyn., Aug. 15, 1948; d. Warren William and Providence Rosalie (Cataldo) B.; m. Nicholas Francis Picariello, Sept. 17, 1977; children: Adriana, Gianina, Marisa, Nicholas. BS in Biology, Fordham U., 1970; PhD in Biochemistry, Cornell U., 1975. Rsch. fellow, instr. microbiology and immunology Med. Sch. Tulane U., New Orleans, 1975-77; rsch. fellow oral biology and pathophysiology Harvard Sch. Dental Medicine, Cambridge, Mass., 1977-78, Aid for Cancer Rsch. fellow, 1978-80; asst. prof. biology Wheaton Coll., Norton, Mass., 1980-86, assoc. prof., 1986-92, prof., 1992—; vis. lectr. oral biology and pathophysiology Harvard Sch. Dental Medicine, 1983-85. Author: (software) DNA Synthesis and Replication, 1986, DNA Sequence Analysis, 1989; contbr. articles to sci. jours. NIH grantee, 1970-74, Acad. Rsch. Enhancement award, 1987-89; Rsch. Corp. rsch. grantee, 1985-87. Mem. AAAS, N.Y. Acad. Scis., Am. Soc. Cell Biology, Coun. Undergrad. Rsch. Office: Wheaton Coll Dept Biol Norton MA 02766

BRENT, LAWRENCE BARRY, cardiologist; b. Pitts., July 26, 1929; s. George Francis and Margaret E. (Couch) B.; m. Gail Ziegler, Nov. 26, 1964; children—Gary, Holly, Kelly. B.S., U. Pitt., 1950; M.D., N.Y. Med. Coll., 1955. Diplomate Am. Bd. Internal Medicine, Am. Bd. Cardiovascular Disease. Intern, Allegheny Gen. Hosp., Pitts., 1955-56, resident, 1956-59, mem. staff, 1959—; resident U. Pitts., 1957-58, asstprof. medicine Med. Coll. of Pa., 1988—; mem. staff Allegheny Gen. Hosp., pres. med. staff, 1973-74; cons. St. Johns Hosp., Suburban Gen. Hosp. Contbr. articles to med. jours. Served to lt. comdr. USNR, 1959-61. Fellow ACP; mem. AMA, Am. Heart Assn., Western Pa. Heart Assn. (pres. 1973). Republican. Presbyterian. Clubs: Fox Chapel Golf, Duquesne (Pitts.). Home: RD 3 Wagner Rd Allison Park PA 15101-1215 Office: Carlton Cardiology Assocs Inc 490 E North Ave Pittsburgh PA 15212

BRENT, ROBERT LEONARD, radiology and pediatrics educator; b. Rochester, N.Y., Oct. 6, 1927; s. Charles and Rose (Katz) B.; m. Lillian H. Hoffman, Aug. 21, 1949; children: David A., James R., Lawrence H., Deborah A. AB, U. Rochester, 1948, MD with honors, 1953, PhD, 1955, DSc (hon.), 1988. Fellow Nat. Found., Strong Meml. Hosp., 1953-54; intern pediatrics Mass. Gen. Hosp., Boston, 1954-55; chief radiation biology Walter Reed Army Inst. Rsch., 1955-57; mem. faculty Jefferson Med. Coll., 1955—, prof. radiology, 1962—, also prof. pediatrics, Louis and Bess Stein prof. pediatrics, 1985—; apptd. Disting. prof. Thomas Jefferson U., 1989; hon. prof. Norman Bethume U. Med. Sci., People's Republic of China, 1992, West China U. Med. Scis., Chengdu, People's Republic of China, 1992; chmn. med. adv. bd. Nat. Found.; mem. fertility and maternal health com. FDA; mem. human embryology study sect. NIH, 1970-74; bd. trustees Health and Environ. Sci. Inst., 1991-94; pres. First Internat. Congress on Birth Defects, People's Republic of China, 1994. Editor in chief Teratology, 1976-93. Pres. Teratology Soc., 1968. Served with U.S. Army, 1955-57. Recipient Richie Meml. prize U. Rochester Med. Sch., 1953, Lindback Found. award for disting. tchg., 1968, Med. Sch. award Alpha Omega Alpha, 1952, Burlington Internat. award, 1990, Landauer award Health Physics Soc., 1995; travelling fellow Royal Soc. Medicine, 1971-72, vis. fellow FitzWilliam Coll., Cambridge, 1971-72; Lady Davis scholar Hadassah Med. Ctr., Jerusalem, 1983-84. Mem. AAAS, Teratology Soc. (pres. 1967-68), Internat. Life Sci. Inst., Radiation Rsch. Soc., Am. Soc. Exptl. Pathology, Soc. Pediat. Rsch., Am. Pediats. Soc., Am. Acad. Pediats., Soc. Exptl. Biology and Medicine, Phila. Coll. Physicians, Phila. Pediat. Soc., Am. Assn. Immunology (emeritus), Soc. Developmental Biology, Nat. Coun. Radiation Protection, Japan Teratology Soc., European Teratology Soc., Ambulatory Pediat. Assn., Sigma Xi.

BRESCH, CARSTEN JOHANNES, genetics educator; b. Berlin, Sept. 5, 1921; m. Mechthild Bresch. PhD in Physics, U. Berlin, 1948. Asst. MPI Physik-Chemie, Göttingen, Germany, 1949-55; assoc. prof. U. Cologne, Cologne, Germany, 1957-64; prof., head biology div. South-West Ctr. for Advanced Studies, Dallas, 1964-68, U. Freiburg (Germany), 1968—. Author: Klassische und Molekulare Genetik, 1964, 65, 68, 72, Zwischenstufe Leben, 1977, 80. Mem. AAAS, Genetics Soc. (pres. 1969-72). Office: Inst f Biologie III U Freiburg, Schaenzlestr 1, 7800 Freiburg Germany

BRESLIN, DONALD JOSEPH, internist; b. Toronto, Ont., Can., Mar. 16, 1929; s. R.H. Breslin and S.T. Breslin Dobkins; m. Evalynne Louise Wood, Jan. 30, 1954; children: Lisa, Mark, Paul. BA, Yale U., 1946; postgrad. Columbia U., 1947; BS, McGill U., 1950, MD, 1954 . Diplomate Am. Bd. Internal Medicine. Intern Cleve. Met. Gen. Hosp., 1954-55, resident in internal medicine, 1955-57; fellow in internal medicine Mayo Clinic, Rochester, Minn., 1957-60, 1st asst. internal medicine, 1960-61; pvt. practice internal medicine, Canton Ohio, 1961-66; mem. med. sch. faculty Case Western, 1962-66; mem. staff dept. internal medicine Lahey Clinic, Boston, 1966—, mng. editor Clinic Bull., 1975-83, head sect. vascular medicine, 1976-90, sr. cons. vascular medicine, 1990—; clin. instr. internal medicine Harvard Med. Sch., 1977-78, asst. clin. prof. medicine, 1979—. Active med. div. Northeastern sect. United Fund, 1968-70, chmn., 1970-71. Research fellow Royal Postgrad. Med. Sch., U. London, 1973-74. Editor: Vascular Disease in Elderly for Cardiology Clinics, 1991. Fellow ACP, Soc. for Vascular Medicine and Biology; mem. AMA, Mass. Med. Soc., Mass. Soc. Internal Medicine, Am. Heart Assn. (sci. councils clin. cardiology, hypertension), Mayo Alumni Assn., Yale Alumni Assn., Yale Alumni Greater N.Y., Yale Class of '46 Assn. Sr. editor Renovascular Hypertension (Williams and Wilkins), 1982; guest editor Cardiol. Clinics N.Am., 1991; contbr. articles on systemic hypertension and its med. and surg. aspects, idiopathic hypotension and vascular disease to profl. jours. Office: Lahey Clinic Found 41 Mall Rd Burlington MA 01805-0001

BRESLIN, EVALYNNE L. W., retired psychiatric nurse; b. Richmond, Ohio, July 7, 1931; d. Evan P. and Ada Augusta (Huscroft) Wood-Robertson; m. Donald Joseph Breslin, Jan. 30, 1954; children: Lisa Karen, Mark Nathaniel (dec.), Paul Andrew Scott. Diploma, Cleve. Met. Gen. Hosp., 1952; student, Case Western Res. U., Akron U.; HHD (hon.), London Inst. of Applied Rsch., 1973. Lic. RN, Ohio, Mass; RN, Ohio, Mass. Head nurse Cleve. Met. Gen. Hosp., Cleve. State Receiving Hosp.; cons. mental illness and addictions Mass.; ret. Bd. dirs. Triple Trouble; ret. vol. monitor state hosp. facilities Alliance for Mentally Ill; vol. nursing/psychiat. work with abandonded adolescents, 1968-89. Mem. ANA, Nat. League Nursing, Mass. Nurses Assn. (coun. on mental health).

BRESLIN, MARIANNE SONNENBRODT, psychiatrist, psychoanalyst; b. Buendheim, Fed. Republic of Germany, Dec. 10, 1918; came to U.S., 1951; d. Albert Robert Bernhard and Alice (Meyer) S.; m. Lou Eugene Breslin, Nov. 21, 1951 (dec. Aug. 1956); 1 child, Louanne Virginia. MD, Med. Acad, Duesseldorf, Fed. Republic of Germany, 1946. Diplomate Am. Bd. Psychiatry and Neurology. Rotating intern, surgery, ob-gyn., and internal medicine City Hosp. I and III, Hannover, Germany, 1946-47; resident in internal medicine City Hosp. I, Hannover, 1947-49; resident in surgery City Hosp. Bremen-Blumenthal, Germany, 1949-51; resident in psychiatry Dorothea Dix Hosp., Raleigh, N.C., 1955-59, N.C. Meml. Hosp., U. N.C., Chapel Hill, 1955-59; clin. instr. psychiatry Sch. of Medicine U. N.C., Chapel Hill, 1960-61, instr. psychiatry Sch. of Medicine, 1961-62, asst. prof. psychiatry Sch. of Medicine, 1962-68; assoc. prof. psychiatry Med. Sch. Duke U., Durham, N.C., 1968-85, assoc. prof. emeritus psychiatry Med. Sch., 1986; pvt. practice Chapel Hill, 1986—; cons. VA Hosp., Durham, 1968—; pres. N.C. Psychiat. Assn., 1980-81. Recipient Merit award N.C. Cancer Soc., 1957, Honored Tchr. award Psychiat. Residents Duke, Durham, 1977. Fellow Am. Psychiat. Assn. (life), Acad. Psychosomatic Medicine (life),So. Psychiat. Assn. (life); mem. Am. Psychoanalytic Assn., Am. Soc. Phys. Analysts (hon.). Office: 1704 Michaux Rd Chapel Hill NC 27514-7636

BRESLIN, NANCY ANN, psychiatrist, educator, researcher; b. Orange, N.J., Aug. 18, 1957; d. Alfred J. and Joyce L. (Deutcsh) B.; m. Peter J. Caws, Nov. 28, 1987; 1 child, Elisabeth Breslin Caws. BA, Rutgers U., 1979; MD, U. Pitts., 1983. Diplomate Am. Bd. Psychiatry and Neurology. Instr. in psychiatry George Washington U., Washington, 1986-87, asst. prof. psychiatry, 1987-96, assoc. clin. prof. psychiatry, 1996—, mem. grad. neurosci. program, 1992—; sr. staff fellow NIMH, Washington, 1989-90; mem. med. bd., NIMH Neuropsychiat. Rsch. Hosp., Washington, 1988-90, dep. med. dir., 1989-90. Editor (with Jerry Wiener): The Behavioral Sciences in Psychiatry, 1995. Laughlin fellow Am. Coll. Psychiatrists, 1987. Mem. AMA, Am. Psychiat. Assn. (chair APA/Lilly resident rsch. award com.), N.Y. Acad. Sci., Soc. for Neurosci., Med. Soc. of D.C. (sec. psychiat. sect. 1991-92, ho. dels. 1993), Alpha Omega Alpha. Home: 637 S St Asaph St Alexandria VA 22314-4118 Office: George Washington U Dept Psychiatry 2150 Pennsylvania Ave NW Fl 8 Washington DC 20037-2396

BRESLOW, ESTHER MAY GREENBERG, biochemistry educator, researcher; b. N.Y.C., Dec. 23, 1931; d. Harry Daniel and Lillian (Solomon) Greenberg; m. Ronald Charles David Breslow, Sept. 4, 1955; children: Stephanie Ruth, Karen Ann. BS with distinction, Cornell U., 1953; MS in Biochemistry, NYU, 1955, PhD in Biochemistry, 1959; postgrad., Radcliffe Coll., 1954-55. Postdoctoral fellow Cornell U. Med. Coll., N.Y.C., 1959-61, rsch. assoc., 1961-64, asst. prof., 1964-72, assoc. prof., 1972-78, prof. biochemistry, 1978—, acting chmn. dept. biochemistry, 1992-95; mem. rev. panels NIH, Bethesda, Md., 1973-77, 94—, NSF, Bethesda, 1981-84. Mem. editorial bd. Jour. Biol. Chemistry, 1982-87, Internat. Jour. Peptide and Protein Rsch., 1981; contbr. articles to profl. jours. Mem. Englewood (N.J.) Bd. Health, 1986-94; mem. Dem. Mcpl. Com., Englewood, 1985-91. Eli Lilly fellow, 1954-55; USPHS fellow, 1959-61; NIH grantee, 1961—. Fellow AAAS; mem. Am. Soc. for Biochemistry and Molecular Biology, Am. Chem. Soc. (sec. div. biol. chemistry 1972-76), Harvey Soc., Sigma Xi. Home: 275 Broad Ave Englewood NJ 07631-4350 Office: Cornell U Med Coll 1300 York Ave New York NY 10021-4805

BRESLOW, LESTER, physician, educator; b Bismarck, N.D., Mar. 17, 1915; s. Joseph and Mayme (Danziger) B.; children: Norman, Jack, Stephen; m. Devra J.R. Miller, 1967. BA, U. Minn., 1935, MD, 1938, MPH, 1941, DSc (hon.), 1988. Diplomate: Am. Bd. Preventive Medicine and Public Health. Intern USPHS Hosp., Stapleton, N.Y. 1938-40; dist. health officer Minn. Dept. Health, 1941-43; preventive medicine officer U.S. Army, 1943-45; chief bur. chronic diseases Calif. Dept. Public Health, Berkeley, 1946-60; chief div. preventive medicine Calif. Dept. Public Health, 1960-65, dir. dept., 1965-68; lectr. U. Calif. Sch. Pub. Health, Berkeley, 1950-68; prof. pub. health UCLA Sch. Pub. Health, 1968—, chmn. dept. preventive medicine and social medicine, 1969-72, dean, 1972-80, mem. div. cancer control, 1980—, dir. health promotion ctr., 1988-91; dir. study Pres.'s Commn. Health Needs of Nation, 1952; cons. Nat. Cancer Inst., 1981—, chmn. bd. sci. counsellors div. cancer prevention and control, 1982-84; cons. Office of Technology Assessment, Nat. Heart, Lung, Blood Inst., 1977; chmn. Nat. Com. on Vital and Health Stats., 1979-81; mem. U.S.-China Health Scis. Com., Dept. HHS, 1982. Author med. publs.; editor: Ann. Rev. Pub. Health, 1979-90; editorial cons. Preventive Medicine, other med. and pub. health jours. Served to capt. U.S. Army, 1943-45. Decorated Bronze Star; recipient Lasker award, Dana award, Sedgwick medal APHA, Healthtrac prize Healthtrac Found., 1995. Fellow ACP, AAAS, Am. Coll. Preventive Medicine (Disting. service award 1976); mem. Am. Heart Assn. (fellow epidemiology sect.), Am. Public Health Assn. (past pres.), Public Health Cancer Assn. (past pres.), Am. Epidemiol. Soc., Internat. Epidemiol. Assn. (past pres.), Am. Cancer Soc. (nat. dir., Calif. dir., chmn. adv. com. on research etiology), Assn. Schs. Public Health (pres. 1973-74), Inst. Medicine, Nat. Acad. Scis. (council 1978-80, chmn. bd. health promotion and disease prevention 1980-82). Home: 10926 Verano Rd Los Angeles CA 90077-2224

BRESLOW, NORMAN EDWARD, biostatistics educator, researcher; b. Mpls., Feb. 21, 1941; s. Lester and Alice Jane (Philp) B.; m. Gayle Marguerite Bramwell, Sept. 7, 1963; children: Lauren Louise, Sara Jo. BA, Reed Coll., 1962; PhD, Stanford U., 1967. Trainee Stanford U., 1965-67; vis. research worker London Sch. Hygiene, 1967-68; instr. U. Wash., Seattle, 1968-69, asst. prof., 1969-72, assoc. prof., 1972-76, prof., 1976—, chmn. dept. biostats., 1983-93; statistician Internat. Agy. Research Cancer, Lyon, France, 1972-74; mem. Hutchinson Cancer Ctr., Seattle, 1982—; statistician Nat. Wilms' Tumor Study, 1969—; cons. Internat. Agy. Research Cancer, Lyon, 1978-79, Stats. and Epidemiology Research Corp., Seattle, 1980—; assoc. prof. U. Geneva, 1994—. Recipient Spiegelman Gold medal APHA, 1978, Preventive Oncology Acad.award, NIH, 1978-83, Snedecor award Com. of Pres.'s on Statis. Socs., 1995, R.A. Fisher lectr. and award, 1995; rsch. grantee NIH, 1984—; sr. U.S. Scientist, Alexander Humboldt Found., Fed. Republic of Germany, 1982; sr. Internat. fellowship Fogarty Ctr., 1990. Fellow AAAS, Am. Statis Assn., Royal Statis. Soc.; mem. Internat. Statis. Inst., Inst. Medicine-Nat. Acad. Scis., Internat. Biometric Soc. (regional com. 1975-78, coun. 1994—). Office: Univ of Wash Dept Biostatistics Seattle WA 98195-7232

BRESNAHAN, JAMES FRANCIS, medical ethics educator; b. Springfield, Mass., Dec. 28, 1926; s. James Francis and Margaret Anna (Riley) B. AB, Coll. Holy Cross, 1947; MA, Weston Coll, 1953, STL, 1960; JD, Harvard U., 1954, LLM, 1955; PhD, Yale U., 1972. Bar: Mass. 1955, U.S. Dist. Ct. Mass. 1975. Joined S.J., Roman Catholic Ch., 1949; tchr. Cheverus High Sch., Portland, Maine, 1955-56; asst. prof. religious studies Fairfield U., 1962-66, 69-70; vis. prof. ethics Weston Coll., 1971-72; assoc. prof. religious studies and philosophy Regis U., 1972-74; prof. ethics Jesuit Sch. Theology in Chgo., 1975-81; vis. lectr. in med. ethics Northwestern U. Med. Sch., Chgo., 1978-80; vis. lectr. in legal ethics Northwestern U. Law Sch.. 1979; co-dir. ethics program Northwestern U. Med. Sch., 1980—, prof. med ethics and humanities, clin. medicine, 1989—; ethics cons. Northwestern Meml. Hosp., 1982—; treas. Chgo. Clin. Ethics Programs, 1989-90, pres.-elect, 1990-91, pres. 1991-92. Mem. adv. com. Jour. of Law and Religion. mem. editorial bd. Cambridge Quar. for Health Care Ethics, Annals of Health Law; contbr. articles to profl. jours. Mem. com. to draft code for profl. conduct Canon Law Soc. Am., 1978-79. Fellow Soc. Values in Higher Edn.; mem. AAUP (v.p. chpt. 1973-74), Soc. Christian Ethics (convenor ethics and law task force 1979-80, dir. 1981-85), Coun. on Religion and Law, Ill. Coalition Against Death Penalty, Soc. Health and Human Values, Am. Soc. Law, Medicine and Ethics, Soc. Bioethics Consultation, Inst. Medicine Chgo. (ethics adv. com. 1991—). Home: Jesuit Residence 2058 N Clark St Chicago IL 60614-4748 Office: Morton 1-658 Northwestern U Med Sch 303 E Chicago Ave Chicago IL 60611-3008

BRESTICKER, STANLEY, anesthesiologist, consultant; b. Hoboken, N.J., May 2, 1926; s. Hyman and Fannie (Faber) B.; m. Eileen Georgette Kandracs, Oct. 19, 1958; children: David, Michael, Julianne. BSc, Seton Hall U., 1949; MA, NYU, 1950; B in Med. Sci., U. Geneva, 1952, MD, 1956. Diplomate Am. Bd. Anethesiology. Intern St. Mary Hosp., Hoboken, 1956-57; resident in anesthesiology Bellevue Med. Ctr., N.Y.C., 1958-60; asst. chmn. anesthesiology dept. Middlesex Gen. Hosp., New Brunswick, N.J., 1960-72; chmn. anesthesiology dept. Robert Wood Johnson U. Hosp., New Brunswick, 1972-84; med. dir. Middlesex Same Day Surgery Ctr., East Brunswick, N.J., 1984-90; asst. clin. prof. anethesiology Robert Wood Johnson Med. Sch., New Brunswick, 1978—; Facility surveyor AAAHC, Skokie, Ill., 1991; anesthesia cons., N.J., 1990—. Recipient lifetime membership Am. Heart Assn., 1979. Mem. Am. Soc. Anesthesiologists (bd. dirs. 1960—), Soc. Ambulatory Anesthesia (bd. dirs. 1982—, Disting. Svc. award 1996), Acad. Medicine of N.J. (past pres.), N.J. Assn. Ambulatory Surgery Ctrs. (past pres.), N.J. State Soc. Anesthesiologists (past pres.), N.J. Assn. Med. Splty. Studies (past pres.), Somerset County Heart Assn. (past. pres.). Home: 1465 Easton Ave Somerset NJ 08873-1336 Office: Robert Wood Johnson Univ Hosp 1 Robert Wood Johnson Pl New Brunswick NJ 08901-1928

BRETAN, PETER NONENG, renal transplant surgeon, general surgeon; b. Ventura, Calif., May 6, 1954; s. Pedro Braza and Patria Grace (Guior) B.; m. Melanie Jean Mason, Sep. 13, 1981; children: Jonathan, Anna, Mason, Mark. BA in Physiology, U. Calif., Berkeley, 1976; MD, U. Calif., San Francisco, 1980. Resident in gen. surgery U. Calif., San Fransisco, 1980-82, resident in urology, 1982-84, chief resident in urology, 1984-85, fellow in radiology, 1985-86; surgical transplant fellow Cleve. Clinic Found., 1986-88; dir. transplants Cleve. Clinic Found. and St. Elizabeth Hosp., 1988-89, Harbor Med. Ctr.-UCLA, 1989-92, Kaiser Permanente, Oakland, Calif., 1994—; assoc. prof. surgery and urology U. Calif., Berkeley, 1992—; expert reviewer Med. Bd. Calif., Novato, Calif., 1996—; team physician Pan Am.Taekwondo. 2d lt. USPHS, 1980—. Fellow Am. Bd. Urology; mem. AMA, United Network Organ Sharing, Am. Urological Assn. (rsch. award 1986), Am. Soc. Transplant Surgeons, Am. Coll. Sports Medicine, Am. Soc. Transplant Physicians, Urology Soc. Transplant and Vascular Surgery (sci. chmn. 1994-96), Am. Taekwondo Assn. (cert. black belt instr.). Office: UCSF Renal Transplant SVC 505 Parnassuss Ave Box 0116 San Francisco CA 94143

BRETSCHNEIDER, ANN MARGERY, histotechnologist; b. Newton, Mass., May 11, 1934; d. Herman Frederick and Elizabeth Louise (Brady) B.; BS, Northeastern U., Boston, 1957; MS, Rutgers U., 1979. Histopathologic technician NIH, Bethesda, Md., 1957-58; chief histologic technician U. Ala. Med. Center, Birmingham, 1958-61; chief med. technologist in histology, instr. Muhlenberg Hosp., Plainfield, N.J., 1961-67; instr. anatomy Northeastern U., 1967-68; rsch.-teaching specialist U. Medicine and Dentistry-R. W. Johnson Med. Sch., 1968—; workshop leader, cons. in field. Mem. Am. Soc. Clin. Pathologists (affiliate), Nat. Soc. Histotech., Electron Microscopy Soc. Am., N.J. Soc. Histotech. Co-author: Thin Is In: Plastic Embedding of Tissue for Light Microscopy, 1981. Home: 96 Lenox Ct Piscataway NJ 08854-3169 Office: U Medicine and Dentistry NJ Teaching Labs R W Johnson Med Sch Piscataway NJ 08854

BREVE, FRANKLIN STEPHEN, pharmacist; b. Phila., Jan. 25, 1955; s. Albert Francis and Lillian Marie (Di Biase) B.; m. Linda Ruth Maedel, Mar. 16, 1985; children: Christina Lynn, Rebecca Anne, Allison Marie. BA in Psychology, Temple U., 1977, BS in Pharmacy, 1981. Registered Pharmacist. Oncology pharmacist Thomas Jefferson U., Phila., 1981-86, nuclear pharmacist, 1986-87; oncology pharmacist Rancocas Valley Hosp., Willingboro, N.J., 1987-88; night phramacy coord. West Jersey Hosp., Camden, N.J., 1988—; pres., CEO Pharmatech Cons. Group, Blackwood, N.J., 1992—; cons. and instr. in field. Mem. Am. Soc. Hosp. Pharmacists, Am. Pharm. Assn., N.J. Soc. Hosp. Pharmacists, N.Y. Acad. Scis., Am. Soc. Cons. Pharmacists, N.J. Pharm. Assn., N.J. Acad. Cons. Pharmacists. Republican. Roman Catholic. Home: 6 Briarwood Dr Blackwood NJ 08012 Office: West Jersey Health System 1000 Atlantic Ave Camden NJ 08104-1132

BREWER, CHERYL ANN, obstetrics-gynecology educator; b. New Rochelle, N.Y., Oct. 31, 1959; d. John Paul and Marie Elizabeth (Royance) B. BS, Miss. U. for Women, 1981; MD, Ind. U., Indpls., 1985. Resident in ob-gyn. SUNY Health Scis. Ctr., Syracuse, 1985-89, asst. prof. ob-gyn., 1989-91; asst. prof. dept. ob-gyn. Ind. U., Indpls., 1991-92; fellow in gynecologic oncology U. Calif., Irvine, 1992—. Fellow Am. Coll. Ob-Gyn. Home: 17632 Jordan Ave Apt 40B Irvine CA 92715-2976 Office: U Calif Med Ctr 101 The City Dr Irvine CA 92715

BREWER, ROBERT ALLEN, physician; b. Inpls., Jan. 29, 1927; s. Robert Dewayne and Viola Mae (Grant) B.; m. Mildred Noreen Barnett, Jan. 1, 1950; children: Robert A. Jr., Raymond, Richard, Brian, Andrew. AA, St. Petersburg Jr. Coll., Fla., 1949; AB, Ind. U., 1952; MD, Ind U., Inpls., 1955. Emergency dept. staff physician Mound Park Hosp., St. Petersburg, Fla., 1960; staff physician Pinellas Hosp., Largo, Fla., 1961-68; pvt. practice Logansport, Ind., 1969—. Mem. Cass County Republican Com., Logansport, Ind., candidate for city coun., 1995. Capt. U.S. Army, 1957-59. Mem. AMA, Am. Acad. Family Practitioner (bd. cert. diplomate), Ind. Med. Assn., Cass County Med. Assn. Republican. Office: PO Box 119 831 E Broadway Logansport IN 46947

BREWER, TIMOTHY FRANCIS, III, retired cardiologist; b. Hartford, Conn., Oct. 30, 1931; s. Timothy F. Jr. and Catherine Marie (Sullivan) B.; m. Norma Rae Flicker, June 14, 1954 (div. 1980); children: Raymond, Donna, Timothy, Kevin, William; m. Barbara Grace Bagdasarian, May 28, 1983. BA, Yale Coll., 1953; MD, N.Y. Med. Coll., 1957. Diplomate Am. Bd. Internal Medicine Cardiovascular Diseases. Intern St. Francis Hosp., Hartford, 1957-58; resident in internal medicine VA Ctr., L.A., 1958-60; spl. fellow in cardiovascular diseases Cleve. (Ohio) Clinic, 1960-62; pvt. practice St. Francis Hosp., Hartford, 1962-64; assoc. dir. clin. rsch. Pfizer Inc., Groton, Conn., 1964-71; dir. Clin. Pharmacology Miles Lab., West Haven, Conn., 1971-74; pvt. practice Middlesex Hosp., Middletown, Conn., 1974-96, ret., 1996; pres. med. staff Middlesex (Conn.) Hosp., 1981-83, chief sect. cardiology, 1988-95. Fellow ACP, Am. Coll. Cardiology (emeritus), Am. Coll. Chest Physicians, Coun. on Clin. Cardiology; mem. AMA (pres. South Ctrl. Conn. chpt. 1982, bd. dirs. 1980), Am. Heart Assn. (Conn. affiliate).

BREWERTON, TIMOTHY DAVID, psychiatrist; b. Baton Rouge, Mar. 26, 1953; s. John Lee and Helen (Bouy) B.; m. Therese Kathleen Killeen, June 16, 1990. BS, La. State U., 1974; MD, Tulane U., 1978. Diplomate Am. Bd. Psychiatry and Neurology. Intern, resident in psychiatry U. Calif., San Francisco, 1978-82; staff psychiatrist Hawaii State Hosp., Kaneohe, 1982-84; med. staff fellow NIMH, Bethesda, Md., 1984-87, guest rschr., 1987—; asst. prof. psychiatry and behavioral scis. Med. U. S.C., Charleston, 1987-90, assoc. prof., 1990—, fellow in child and adolescent psychiatry, 1994-96; dir. Eating Disorders Program, Inst. Psychiatry, Charleston, 1987—. Contbr. articles to profl. jours. Recipient Award for Creative Achievement Dept. Psychiatry U. Calif. San Francisco, 1982. Mem. Am. Psychiat. Assn., Soc. Biol. Psychiatry, AAAS, Am. Acad. Clin. Psychiatrists (Clin. Rsch. award 1989, bd. dirs. 1993—), N.Y. Acad. Sci. Office: Med U SC Inst Psychiatry 171 Ashley Ave Charleston SC 29425-0742

BREWNER, ERIC ARTHUR, family physician; b. Pontiac, Mich., Nov. 21, 1954; s. James M. and Ruth G. (Biesenthal) B.; m. Diane Marie Mitchell, Oct. 7, 1978; children: Sean, Hillary, Courtney, Kyle. BS, U.S. Mil. Acad., 1976; MD, U. Ill., Rockford, 1980. Diplomate Am. Bd. Family Medicine. Intern, resident in family practice DeWitt Army Cmty. Hosp., Fort Belvoir, Va., 1980-83; commd. 2d lt. U.S. Army, 1976, advanced through grades to lt. col., 1996; chief family practice Blanchfield Army Cmty. Hosp., Ft. Campbell, Ky., 1986-87, chief aviation medicine, 1987-90, chief family practice Keller Army Cmty. Hosp., West Point, N.Y., 1990-94, Evans Cmty. Hosp., Ft. Carson, Colo., 1994—; clin. isntr. family medicine N.Y. Med. Coll., Valhalla, 1991-94; asst. clin. prof. dept. family medicine U. Colo., Denver, 1994—. Fellow Am. Acad. Family Physicians; mem. Uniformed Svcs. Acad. Family Physicians. Methodist. Home: 15017 La Jolla Pl Colorado Springs CO 80921

BREWSTER, DONALD ELLIOTT, association executive; b. Paterson, N.J., Jan. 29, 1924; s. Benjamin John and Sarah Neille (Elliott) B.; student U. Ill., 1942; B.S., Bradley U., 1950; postgrad. Ind. U., 1968, Washington U., St. Louis, 1971; m. Jerre Owens, Nov. 1958; children: Stephanie, Barbara Jean, Dawn. V.p., sec., owner Brewster Assocs. dba Window Interiors, 1987—, with Am. Cancer Soc., 1960-87, exec. v.p. Mich. div., Lansing, 1970—; assoc. dir. Ketchum, Inc., Pitts., 1956-60; sr. fund raising cons. Benson & Co., Lakeland, Fla., 1988—. Chmn. fund raising campaign St. Paul Episcopal Ch., 1976, sr. warden vestry, 1978. Served with USN, 1943-46. Mem. Nat. Soc. Fund Raising Execs., Am. Soc. Assn. Execs., Mich. Soc. Assn. Execs., U.S. Power Squadron, U.S. Coast Guard Aux. Republican. Clubs: University, Muskegon Yacht, Lansing Racquet, Innisbrook Resort & Golf Club.

BREWSTER, LINDA JEAN, family nurse practitioner; b. Portland, Maine, Nov. 6, 1956; d. Thomas Stuart and Patricia Noreen (Dixon) Warden; m. James Ernest Brewster, Aug. 20, 1977; children: Ryan James, Seth Thomas. BS summa cum laude, U. So. Maine, 1987, MS, 1992; FNP, U. N.H., 1995. Cert. nurse clinician, cert. family nurse prctitioner; cert. ACLS. Staff nurse II Maine Med. Ctr., Portland, 1987-89, clin. level nurse III, 1989-91, case mgr., 1990-91, asst. head nurse, 1991-94; ICU and emergency rm. nurse So. Maine Med. Ctr., 1994-95; intravenous nurse clinician Homedco, Lewiston, Maine, 1994-95; instr. nursing So. Maine Tech. Coll., South Portland, 1994-95; FNP Family Care Assocs., PA, Cumberland, Maine, 1995—; site investigator Multisite Study Harvard Med. Sch., 1993-94; co-investigator Maine Med. Ctr., 1993. Author: Section Review Book for RNC Certification Examination, 1994; developer in field. Bd. dirs. Am. Heart Assn., 1989-93, programs chair, 1991-93. Mem. Am. Acad. Nurse Practitioners, Maine Nurse Practitioner Assn., Sigma Theta Tau (Kappa Zeta chpt.). Methodist. Home: 27 Old Gray Rd Cumberland Center ME 04021-9778

BREWSTER, LINDA ROUNDS, health services administrator; b. Providence, R.I., Sept. 26, 1943; d. Comer Armstrong and Doris Elizabeth (Sanders) Rounds; m. J. Alan Brewster, May 14, 1994; children: Christopher J., Evan C. BA, Beloit Coll., 1965; MBA, Harvard Grad. Sch., 1975. Bus. mgr. Mass. Half-Way Houses, Inc., Boston, 1969-73; fin. analyst Xerox

Corp., Stamford, 1975-76; dir. mgmt. sys. Commonwealth of Mass., Boston, 1976-78; from mgr. fin. svcs. to exec. dir. MIT Med. Dept., Cambridge, Mass., 1978-94; pres., ceo Suburban Physician Hosp. Orgn., Bethesda, Md., 1994—. Bd. dirs. Women's Action Nuclear Disarmament, 1980-83; adult literacy tutor Literacy Vols. Mass., Boston, 1992-94. Office: Suburban Physical Hosp 6430 Rockledge Dr Ste 501 Bethesda MD 20817

BREWTON, SAMUEL ALTON, JR., urologist; b. Jacksonville, Fla., Feb. 11, 1931; s. Samuel Alton Sr. and Estelle (Stephens) B.; m. Martha Mullins, Dec. 30, 1956; children: Martha Brewton Reddick, Samuel Alton III, Benjamin Howard. AB, Emory U., 1952; MD, Med. Coll. of Ga., 1956. Diplomate Am. Bd. Urology. Intern Duval Med. Ctr., Jacksonville, 1956-57; resident in gen. surgery Med. Coll. of Ga., Augusta, 1959-61, resident in urology, 1961-64; urologist, mem. staff Upson County Hosp., Thomaston, Ga., 1964—, Colisuem Pk. Hosp., Macon, Ga., 1964—; bd. dirs. Thomaston Fed. Savs. & Loan Assn. Councilman City of Thomaston, 1978-84, mayor pro tem, 1981-83; bd. dirs. Thomaston City Sch. Bd., 1971-78. Lt. comdr. USN, 1957-59. Mem. Med. Assn. Ga., Southeastern chpt. Am. Urol. Assn., Am. Urol. Assn. Baptist. Home: 100 Joyner Dr Thomaston GA 30286-3242 Office: 206 Cherokee Rd Thomaston GA 30286-2806

BREYSSE, PATRICK NOLAN, environmental health sciences educator; b. Helena, Mont., Aug. 15, 1956; s. Peter A. and Winifred C. (McCartan) B.; m. Jill V. Vollmerhausen, June 24, 1989; children: Patrick Conrad, Daniel Hayes. BS, Wash. State U., 1978; M of Health Scis., Johns Hoplkins U., 1980, PhD, 1986. Cert. indsl. hygienist. Asst. prof. Johns Hopkins U., Balt., 1986-92, assoc. prof., 1992—. Mem. editl. rev. bd. Applied Occupational and Environ. Hygiene, Cin., 1995—. Home: 11963 Harford Rd Glen Arm MD 21057 Office: Johns Hopkins U 615 N Wolfe St Baltimore MD 21205

BRIASCO, CATHERINE ANN, biochemical engineer; b. Framingham, Mass., Oct. 19, 1960; d. John Joseph and Catherine Rena (Tiramani) B.; m. Lawrence Colm Stewart, Oct. 26, 1991. SB in Chemistry, SB in Chem. Engring., MIT, 1982; MSChemE, Stanford U., 1983, PhD in Chem. Engring., 1988. NATO postdoctoral fellow in sci., rschr. Tech. U. Compiègne, France, 1988-89; prin. engr., lab. head Genetics Inst., Andover, Mass., 1989—. Contbr. articles to sci. jours. Grad. fellow NSF, 1983-86. Mem. Phi Beta Kappa, Tau Beta Pi. Home: 1 Arborwood Dr Burlington MA 01803 Office: Genetics Inst 1 Burtt Rd Andover MA 01810

BRICAUD, HENRI J., cardiologist, educator; b. Cenon, France, Sept. 18, 1925. Prof. cardiology Hosp. Cardiologique de Bordeaux, Pessac, France, 1958-94, prof. emeritus; dir. rsch. unit cardiology Hosp. Cardiologique de Bordeaux, 1962-85; chmn. French Del. for Sci. and Tech. Rsch., 1970-79; past expert, WHO; pres. U. Bordeaux II, 1970-75. Author, co-author over 450 publs. on cardiol. subjects. Decorated knight Legion of Honor, comdr. Merit Order (France). Fellow Am. Coll. Cardiology; mem. French Soc. Cardiology (pres. 1980-82), French Arterosclerosis Soc. (pres. 1983-92), Am. Heart Assn. Office: 12 place des Quinconces, 33000 Bordeaux France

BRICH, KAREN L, physician assistant, consultant; b. Pitts., Nov. 21, 1958; d. George R. and Mary J. (Perich) Thacker; m. John G. Brich, Jr., June 16, 1984; 1 child, Sarah Leigh. AS, Pitts., 1978; BS in Molecular Biology with honors, U. Pitts., 1980, MPH in Epidemiology with honors, 1996. Cert. Physician Asst., Nat. Cert. of Physician Assts. Supr. disabled children program Easter Seal Soc., Pa., 1981-85; rsch. asst. U. Pitts., 1987-92, rschr., 1987—, cons., 1995—; physicians asst. Drs. Baker and Singh, Pitts., 1994—; faculty cons. Chatham Coll., Pitts., 1995—, Duquesne U., Pitts., 1992-94; spokesperson Nat. Convention of Physician Assts. on Rsch., Las Vegas, 1995. Fellow Am. Acad. Physicians Assts., Pa. Soc. Physicians Assts. Republican. Presbyterian. Office: Drs. Baker and Singh 3601 McKnight East Dr Pittsburgh PA 15237

BRICK, JOHN, biopsychology educator, researcher; b. N.Y.C., Mar. 18, 1950; s. H.C. and V.A. (Carmella) B.; m. Laurie Stockton Krulish, May 1, 1976. BA, Queens Coll., CUNY, 1973; MA in Psychology, SUNY, Binghamton, 1979, PhD in Biological Psychology, 1981. Research asst. Rockefeller U., 1973-76; research assoc. Center Alcohol Studies Rutgers U., 1980-82, prof., 1982-94, lab. dir. Rutgers U. Alcohol Behavior Research Lab., 1984-88; chief of rsch. edn. tng. divsn., Ctr. Alcohol Studies Rutgers U., 1988-93, assoc. prof. Rutgers U., 1991—; pvt. practice Forensic Pharmacology, 1985-94; exec. dir. Intoxikon Internat., 1994—. cons. exec. office of the pres. The White House, Washington, D.C., 1992-93. Mem. editorial bd. Jour. Studies Alcohol; editor: Stress and Alcohol Use; contbr. articles to profl. jours. Fellow Am. Psychol. Assn.; mem. AAAS, Research Soc. on Alcoholism. Office: 1006 Floral Vale Morrisville PA 19067

BRICKEEN, JERRY WAYNE, health services administrator, naval officer; b. Lenoir City, Tenn., Mar. 30, 1946; s. William Jackson and Carrie Frances (Hagler) B.; m. Marsha Anne Little, July 3, 1966; children: Rebecca Jo Brickeen Williams, Paul Edward. BS in Healthcare Adminstrn., George Washington U., 1977. Cert. health care adminstr. Enlisted USN, 1965, advanced through grades to capt., 1988; patient adminstr. Naval Hosp. Memphis, Millington, Tenn., 1972-76; area med. program officer Navy Recrutiing ARea 4, Columbus, Ohio, 1976-80; officer-in-charge, CEO, COO Blanch Clinic Atlanta, Marietta, Ga., 1980-83; policy analyst Dir. of Naval Medicine, Washington, 1983-85; med. planner Comdr.-In-Chief U.S. Ctrl. Command, Tampa, Fla., 1985-88; dir. adminstr. Naval Hosp. Camp Lejeune, N.C., 1988-90; dep. fleet surgeon, fleed med. adminstr. U.S. Pacific Fleet, Pearl Harbor, Hawaii, 1990-93; COO Naval Hosp. Groton, Conn., 1993-95; commanding officer, CEO Naval Hosp. Lemoore, Calif., 1995—. Decorated Humanitarians Svc. medal Pres. of U.S., 1975, Navy Commendation medal, Meritorious Svc. medal. Mem. Am. Coll. Healthcare Adminstrn. Office: Naval Hosp Lemoore PO Box 5004 Lemoore CA 93246

BRICKER, ELLEN EDWARDS, mental health nurse; b. Pitts., June 17, 1956; d. George J. and Violet L. (Byrns) Edwards; m. Kenneth G. Bricker, Apr. 4, 1985; children: Michael P., Daniel R. ADN with honors, Community Coll. Allegheny Co., West Mifflin, Pa., 1984. Cert. psychiat./mental health nurse. Psychiat. nurse Mayview State Hosp., Bridgeville, Pa., 1984—. Mem. Pa. Nurses Assn. Home: 1894 Rt 519 S Canonsburg PA 15317-9607

BRICKER, NEAL S., physician, educator; b. Denver, Apr. 18, 1927; s. Eli D. and Rose (Quiat) B.; m. Miriam Thalenberg, June 24, 1951 (dec. 1974); children: Dusty, Cary, Susan, Dan Baker; m. Ruth T. Baker, Dec. 28, 1980. B.A., U. Colo., 1946, M.D., 1949. Diplomate Am. Bd. Internal Medicine (bd. govs. 1972-79, chmn. nephrology test com. 1973-76). Intern, resident Bellevue Hosp., N.Y.C., 1949-52; sr. asst. resident Peter Bent Brigham Hosp., Boston, 1954-55; asso. dir. cardio-renal lab. Peter Bent Brigham Hosp., 1955-56; instr. Harvard, 1955-56; fellow Howard Hughes Med. Inst., 1955-56; from asst. prof. to prof. Washington U., 1956-72, dir. renal div., 1956-72; Mem. sci. adv. bd. Nat. Kidney Found., 1962-69, chmn. research and fellowship grants com., 1964-65, mem. exec. com., 1968-71; prof. medicine, chmn. dept. Albert Einstein Coll. Medicine, 1972-76; prof. medicine U. Miami, Fla., 1976-78; vice chmn. dept. U. Miami, 1976-78; Disting. prof. medicine UCLA, 1978-86; Disting. prof. medicine, dir. sci. and tech. planning Loma Linda (Calif.) U., 1986-92; exec. v.p. Naturon Pharm., Riverside, Calif., 1992—; cons. NIH, 1964-68, chmn. gen. medicine study sect., 1966-68, chmn. renal disease and urology tng. grants com., 1969-71; vis. investigator Inst. Biol. Chemistry, Copenhagen, 1960-61; investigator Mt. Desert Island Biol. Labs.; advisor on health care delivery and biomed. research to Sen. Paul Simon, 1985; advisor on behalf Inst. Medicine to Sen. Lowell Weicker. Assoc. editor: Jour. Lab. and Clin. Medicine, 1961-67, Kidney Internat, 1972; editorial com.: Jour. Clin. Investigation, 1964-68, Physiol. Revs, 1970-76, Am. Heart Assn. Publs. Com., 1974-79, Calcified Tissue Internat., 1978-86, Proc. Soc. Exptl. Biology and Medicine, 1978-86; editor: Supplements, Circulation and Circulation Research, 1974-79; contbr. articles to profl. jours., chpts. to books. Served with USNR, 1944-45; Served with U.S. Army, 1952-54. Recipient Gold-Headed Cane award U. Colo., 1949, Silver and Gold Alumni award, 1975; USPHS Research Career award, 1964-72; Skylab Achievement award NASA, 1974; Pub. Service award, 1975; George Norlin Silver medal award U. Colo. 1982; citation Kidney Found. So. Calif., 1984. Fellow A.C.P.; mem. Am. Fedn. for Clin. Research, Central Soc. Clin. Research (council 1970-73), Assn. Am. Physicians, Am. Soc. for Clin. Investigation (pres. 1972-73, chmn. com. nat. med. policy 1973-77, Disting. Service award 1969), Internat. Soc. Nephrology (exec. com. 1966-81, v.p. 1966-69, treas. 1969-81), Internat. Congress Nephrology (pres. 1981-84), Am. Soc. Nephrology (1st pres., John Peters medal 1991), Am. Physiol. Soc., Soc. for Exptl. Biology and Medicine, Western Soc. Clin. Research, So. Soc. Clin. Investigation, Nat. Acad. Scis. (com. on space biology and medicine, ad hoc panel on renal and metabolic effects space flight 1971-72, mem. drug efficacy com. 1966-68, com. space biology, chmn. medicine in space sci. bd. 1972-81, com. chmn. 1978-81, chmn. com. renal and metabloic effects space flight 1972-74, chmn. study com. on life scis. 1976-81, mem. space sci. bd. 1977-81), Inst. of Medicine of Nat. Acad. Scis., Sigma Xi, Alpha Omega Alpha. Home: 2313 N 2d Ave Upland CA 91784

BRICKMAN, LAWRENCE HOWARD, surgeon; b. N.Y.C., June 17, 1943; s. Meyer Robert and Yette Mildred B.; B.S., Mich. State U., 1965; M.D., Free U. of Brussels, 1972; m. Linda Susan Samet, Mar. 20, 1970; children—Michal Alan, David Randall, Peter Scott. Intern, St. Peter's Hosp., Brussels, Belgium, 1971-72; intern Nassau County Med. Center, East Meadow, N.Y., 1972-73, resident, 1972-76, mem. staff, 1976—, attending in gen. and vascular surgery; pvt. practice medicine specializing in gen. and vascular surgery, Huntington, N.Y.; attending surgeon in gen. and vascular surgery and trauma surgery Huntington Hosp.; attending surgeon North Shore U. Hosp., Cornell U. Sch. Medicine; mem. staff VA Hosp., Northport, N.Y.; clin. instr. surgery Sch. of Medicine SUNY, Stony Brook, 1977—; clin. assoc. prof. surgery N.Y. Med. Coll. Capt. U.S. Army, until 1978. Diplomate Am. Bd. Surgery. Fellow Suffolk County Med. Soc., A.C.S., Suffolk Acad. Medicine, Internat. Coll. Surgeons, Soc. Abdominal Surgeons; mem. Med. Soc. N.Y. State. Office: 205 E Main St Huntington NY 11743-2923

BRICKMAN, MARC HOWARD, physician; b. Chgo., June 24, 1964; s. Daryl Lee and Diane Marilyn (Allen) B.; m. Mary Brickman. BA, North Park Coll., Chgo., 1986; DO, Chgo. Coll. Osteo. Medicine, 1990. Diplomate Am. Bd. Internal Medicine. Intern internal medicine Northwestern U., Chgo., 1990-91, resident, 1991-93; chief resident Evanston (Ill.) Hosp., 1993-94; pvt. practice Deerpath Med. Assocs., Deerfield & Lake Bluff, Ill., 1994—; aviation med. examiner FAA, Oklahoma City, Ill., 1994—; clin. instr. medicine Northwestern U., 1993—. Mem. ACP, Am. Soc. Internal Medicine. Office: Deerpath Med Assocs 707 Lake Cook Rd Ste 130 Deerfield IL 60015

BRICKNER, ROBERT JOSEPH, colon and rectal surgeon; b. Fostoria, Ohio, June 8, 1948; s. Robert Joseph and Anna Jane (Robenalt) B.; m. Patricia Kay Droll, June 30, 1972; children: Jonathan Frank, Matthew Robert. BS, Univ. Toledo, 1970; MD, Medical Coll. Ohio, 1973. Gen. surgeon Blodgett Meml. Medical Ctr., Grand Rapids, Mich., 1973-78; colon and rectal surgeon Ferguson Hosp., Grand Rapids, Mich., 1978-79; pvt. practice Lansing, Mich., 1979—. Fellow Am. Coll. Surgeons, Am. Coll. Colon & Rectal Surgeons; mem. Mich. State Medical Soc., Ingham County Medical Soc., Ferguson Surgical Soc., Mich. Soc. Colon & Rectal Surgeons (pers. 1985-86). Roman Catholic. Office: Robert J Brickner 737 N Grand Ave Lansing MI 48906

BRIDEAU, LEO PAUL, hospital administrator; b. Leominster, Mass., Mar. 1, 1947; s. Alfred Joseph and Marie Yvonne (Poulin) B.; m. Kathleen Margaret Quinlan, Oct. 5, 1968; children: Alexander, Elizabeth, Neil, Katherine, William. BS, Georgetown U., 1968; MHA, Med. Coll. of Va., 1980. Counselor vets. benefits VA, Togus, Maine, 1971-73; asst. dist. coord. VA, Richmond, Va., 1975-80; mgmt. analyst VA Med. Ctr., Togus, 1973-75; dep. dir. patient care services Strong Meml. Hosp., Rochester, N.Y., 1980-84; acting exec. dir. Strong Meml. Hosp., Rochester, 1984, dir. hosp. ops., 1984-89, exec. dir., 1990-94, gen. dir., CEO, 1995—; bd. dirs. Premier Hosps. Alliance, Inc.; preceptor dept. health svcs. Va. Commonwealth U., Richmond, 1985—; preceptor Washington U. Sch. Medicine, St. Louis; instr. health svcs. U. Rochester, 1985—. Author: chpt. Cost Containment in a University Hosp., 1987. Chmn. adv. bd. Lifeline, Rochester, 1982-85; bd. dirs. Monroe County Medicap Inc., Rochester, 1984-87, Finger Lakes Health Systems Agy., Rochester, 1985-92; bd. dirs. Rochester Regional Joint Ventures Corp., 1985—, chmn., 1987-89, bd. dirs. Rochester Area Health Maintenance Orgn., Inc., 1985-88. Fellow Am. Coll. Healthcare Execs.; mem. Am. Hosp. Assn., Healthcare Assn. N.Y. State (chmn. bd. dirs. 1996, chair govt. rels. com. 1985-86, trustee 1989—, chair strategic planning com. 1991—), Rochester Regional Hosp. Assn. (bd. dirs. 1985—, chmn. 1987-89) Assn. Univ. Programs in Health Adminstrn., Pi Sigma Alpha. Office: Strong Meml Hosp 601 Elmwood Ave # 612 Rochester NY 14642-0001

BRIDGE, CARL JAMES, psychiatrist; b. South Milwaukee, Wis., Feb. 14, 1922; s. Arthur and Anne Susan (Kuhls) B.; m. Ann Margaret Kilbourn, Feb. 17, 1951; children: Barbara Bridge Bassingthwaite, Kathryn Jane Bridge DeVine, Mary Elizabeth Bridge Lavine, John Kilbourn, Robert James. BS, U. Wis., 1947, MD, 1950. Diplomate Am. Bd. Psychiatry and Neurology. Intern Burbank Hosp., Fitchburg, Mass., 1951-52; pvt. practice gen. medicine Beresford, S.D., 1951-55; fellow in anatomy U. S.D., Vermillion, 1954-55; rsch. fellow Harvard U. Med. Sch. and Mass. Gen. Hosp., Boston, 1956-57; resident in gen. psychiatry Worcester (Mass.) State Hosp., 1960-63; psychiatrist and neurologist Keene (N.H.) Clin., 1963-87; clin. dir. Gardner (Mass.) State Hosp., 1963-64; forensic psychiatrist Probate Ct., Concord, N.H., 1982—. Author: Alcoholism and Driving, 1973; contbr. articles profl. jours. Capt. U.S. Army, 1958-59. Mem. Am. Psychiat. Assn., N.H. Psychiat. Soc., Monadnock Rails, New England Hist. Genealogic Soc., Masons. Episcopalian. Home and Office: 620 West St Keene NH 03431-2142

BRIDGERS, WILLIAM FRANK, physician, educator; b. Asheville, N.C., July 26, 1932; s. John Dixon and Ruth (Norberg) B.; m. Judith Ann Ware, Nov. 27, 1974; 1 child, Jana; children from previous marriage: Jeffrey, David, Daniel. BA, U. of the South, 1954; MD, Washington U., St. Louis, 1959, fellow in preventive medicine, 1963-65. Intern Barnes Hosp., Washington U., St. Louis, 1959-60, resident, 1962-63; assoc. prof. medicine U. Miami, Fla., 1968; prof., dir. neurosci. program U. Ala. - Birmingham, 1970-72, spl. asst. v.p. health affairs, 1976, chmn., prof. dept. pub. health, 1976-93; former dean U. Ala., Birmingham, 1981-89, prof., 1981-93, univ. scholar emeritus, 1993—; head Eutaw Health Policy Group, Birmingham, 1993—; staff mem. NAS, Washington, 1974; mem. governing bd. Nat. Coun. Internat. Health, Washington, 1979-87; dir. Lister Hill Ctr. for Health Policy, 1987-90; mem. com. on vital and health stats. HHS, USPHS, 1990-94. Co-editor (monthly feature) Policy Watch Am. Jour. Medicine and Am. Jour. Surgery, 1990—; contbr. articles to profl. jours. Mem. APHA, Assn. Schs. Pub. Health (pres., mem. exec. com.), Am. Men and Women of Sci., Am. Inst. Nutrition, Am. Soc. Biol. Chemistry, Phi Beta Kappa. Democrat. Home: 2221 English Village Ln Birmingham AL 35223-1730

BRIDGES, C(ECIL) DAVID, physiology educator, researcher; b. Northiam, E. Sussex, Eng., Jan. 16, 1933; came to U.S., 1961; PhD, U. London, 1956, DSc, 1983. Asst. prof. U. Miami, Fla., 1961-64; mem. staff Med. Rsch. Coun., London, 1964-67; asst. prof. NYU Med. Ctr., N.Y.C., 1967-69, assoc. prof., 1969-76, prof., 1976-77; prof. Baylor Coll. Medicine, Houston, 1977-87, Purdue U., West Lafayette, Ind., 1987—; mem. VISB study sect. NH, Bethesda, Md., 1975-79; distbg. editor Vision Rsch., Oxford, Eng., 1979-89; adj. prof. physiology & biophysics Ind. U. Sch. Medicine, Indpls., 1990—. Contbr. articles to Science, Jour. Biol. Chemistry, Vision Rsch., Nucleic Acids Rsch. Recipient Marjorie Margolin prize Retina Rsch. Found., Houston, 1982, Sam and Bertha Brochstein award, 1986; named Pfizer Travelling fellow, Clin. Inst., Montreal, 1983, MARC vis. scientist Fedn. Am. Soc. Exptl. Biology, Bethesda, Md., 1983-84. Mem. Assn. for Rsch. in Vision and Ophthalmology (v.p. 1986). Office: Purdue U Physiology Dept West Lafayette IN 47907

BRIDGES, GERALD JACKSON, social worker; b. Akron, Ohio, Feb. 25, 1928; s. John Richard and Olive Frances (Cliett) B.; m. Melda Lusk, Dec. 17, 1960; 1 child, Gerald Jackson. BS in Edn./Psychology, Carson-Newman Coll., Jefferson City, Tenn., 1958; MSW, U. Tenn., 1963. Caseworker Clover Bottom Hosp. & Sch., Nashville, 1963; social caseworker Nashville Mental Health Ctr., 1963-64; instr. U. Tenn., Knoxville, 1964-67; casework cons. Wesley House Day Care Ctr., Nashville, 1967-69; casework supr. Monroe Harding Children's Home, Nashville, 1967-69; pres. MacDonell United Meth. Children's Svcs., Inc., Houma, La., 1969—. With USN, 1950-54. Republican. Episcopalian. Office: MacDonell United Meth Svcs 1210 E Main St Houma LA 70363-4844

BRIDGES, JAMES GARY, anesthesiologist; b. Soperton, Ga., Aug. 9, 1961; m. Sandra G. Bridges. AS, Mid. Ga. Coll., 1981; BS in Pharmacy, U. Ga., 1984; DO, W.Va. Sch. Osteo. Medicine, 1992. Diplomate Nat. Bd. Med. Examiners; med. lic. Ala., Ga.; registered pharmacist, Ga.; cert. ACLS, ATLS. Resident Bapt. Med. Ctrs., Birmingham, Ala., 1992-93; resident in anesthesiology U. Ala., Birmingham, 1993-95, chief resident, 1995-96; profl. sales rep. Eli Lilly & co., Macon, Ga., 1985-88. Mem. AMA, Am. Osteo. Assn., Am. Soc. Anesthesiologists, Am. Soc. Regional Anesthesia, Internat. Anesthesia Rsch. Soc., Med. Assn. State of Ala., Ga. Osteo. Med. Assn., Ala. State Soc. Anesthesiologists, Jefferson County Med. Assn. Home: 2001 Inverness Cliffs Birmingham AL 35242 Office: Dept Anesthesiology JT9 Univ Alabama Birmingham AL 35233

BRIDGEWATER, NORA JANE, medical, surgical nurse; b. Rodgers, Tex., Feb. 27, 1924; d. Wiley Levi and Phoebajane (Owens) Shelgren; m. Joe Garland Bridgewater, Aug. 7, 1940; children: Garland, Janie William Clayton, Richard, Allen, Paula, Shewanna, Russell. AA in Psychology, Bakersfield Coll., 1970, BSN, 1978. Med. nurse Kern Med. Hosp., Bakersfield, Calif., 1964-68, Mercy Hosp., Bakersfield, 1969-78, Sherrif's Dept., Laredo, Calif., 1978-87; nurse Sheriff Facility, Bakersfield, 1986-87. Sgt. U.S. Army Nurses Corps, 1938-40. Mem. Calif. Nursing Assn. Democrat. Baptist.

BRIDGFORTH, WILLIAM A., JR., pediatrician; b. Johnson City, Tenn., July 16, 1948; s. William A. and Burgess Lowry (Kiser) B.; m. Elizabeth Mary Maddux, Apr. 8, 1972; children: Samantha Diane, William A. III. BS, E. Tenn. State U., 1970; MD, U. Tenn., Memphis, 1974. Diplomate Am. Bd. Pediatrics. Pvt. practice in pediatrics Johnson City Pediatrics, P.C., Tenn., 1978—; clin. asst. prof. East Tenn. State U. Coll. Medicine, Johnson City, 1980—; chmn. dept. pediatrics Johnson City Med. Ctr. Hosp., 1981-82, 88-90, mem. exec. com., 1988-90; staff Philmont Nat. Tng. Ctr., 1992. Bd. dirs. Johnson City Med. Ctr. Found., 1989—, pres., 1993; exec. com. Sequoyah coun. Boy Scouts Am., 1984—; S.E. region v.p. Nat. Assn. Presbyn. Scouters, St. Louis, 1987-91, nat. bd. dirs., 1987—; pres.'s trust East Tenn. State U., 1987—; bd. dirs. Nat. Commn. on Ch. and Youth Agy. Relationships, St. Louis, 1990—, Hands on Regional Mus., Johnson City, 1989-92. Recipient Silver Beaver award Boy Scouts Am., 1987, Wood Badge Beads award, 1983, Nat. Disting. Commr., 1989, Meritorious Svc. award Tenn. Hosp. Assn., 1989. Fellow Am. Acad. Pediatrics; mem. Tri-County Med. Assn., Tenn. Med. Assn., Tenn. Pediatric Soc., Tenn. Ornithol. Soc., Nat. Eagle Scout Assn., Phi Rho Sigma, Sons of the Am. Revolution, Huguenot Soc., Jamestowne Soc. Presbyterian. Office: Johnson City Pediatrics 615 N State Of Franklin Rd Johnson City TN 37604-8209

BRIEF, DONALD KERMIT, surgeon; b. Feb. 22, 1933; married; 4 children. AB cum laude, Dartmouth Coll., 1954; MD, Harvard U., 1957. Diplomate Am. Bd. Surgery; lic. physician, Mass., N.J., Pa. Intern surgery Peter Bent Brigham Hosp., Boston, 1957-58, resident, 1958-59, 60-63, chief resident, 1963-64; resident surgery Children's Med. Ctr., Boston, 1959-60; Arthur Tracy Cabot teaching fellow Harvard Med. Sch., 1963-64; clin. assoc. prof. surgery N.J. Coll. Medicine, 1965-68, clin. asst. prof., 1968-83; clin. prof. U. Medicine and Dentistry N.J., 1983—; pvt. practice gen. and vascular surgery Millburn, N.J.; attending in surgery St. Barnabas Hosp.; chief gen. surg. svc. Newark Beth Israel Med. Ctr., 1976-88, full attending surgeon, 1976, v.p. med. staff, 1980, pres. elect 1981, pres. 1982-85, chief divsn. gen. surgery, 1980-94, dir. surgery, 1994; attending surgeon East Orange VA Hosp.; cons. Irvington Gen. Hosp.; attending in gen. surgery St. Barnabas Med. Ctr., 1981; cons. vascular surgery Overlook Hosp., 1964, Bayonne Hosp., 1965, Greenville Hosp., 1965, St. Francis Hosp., Port Jervis, N.Y., 1975; lectr., presenter orgns., conventions, meetings. Contbr. articles to profl. jours. Bd. trustees Essex County divsn. Am. Cancer Soc., 1969-70, pres. N.J. divsn. Lt. col. U.S. Army, 1967-69. Decorated Bronze Star; recipient Maimonides award State of Israel Bonds, Edward Ill. awrd Nat. Acad. Medicine, 1996; Diamond Ball honoree Essex unit Am. Cancer Soc., 1992. Fellow ACS (liaison officer, credentials com. 1978, councilor N.J. chpt. 1979, state chmn. field liaison program of commn. on cancer, pres. elect N.J. chpt. 1988, pres. 1960, 90, gov.-at-large N.J. 1996—), Southeastern Surg. Assn.; mem. Am. Cancer Soc. (past pres. N.J. chpt. 1993-95), N.J. Med. Soc. (sec. surg. sect. 1969, chmn. 1970, bd. trustees, cancer com.), Acad. Medicine N.J. (bd. trustees 1980-82, Edmund, Ill. award 1996), N.J. Oncological Soc. (pres. elect 1980, pres. 1981), N.J. Vascular Soc. (pres. elect 1982, pres. 1983), Essex County Med. Soc., Internat. Cardiovascular Soc., Peter Bent Brigham Surg. Soc., N.J. Gastroent. Soc., Soc. Vascular Surgery, Harvard Med. Soc. N.Y., Am. Trauma Soc. (bd. trustees N.J. sect.), Soc. Surgeons N.J., Pan Pacific Surg. Soc., Acad. Medicine, Soc. Med. Cons. Armed Forces, Soc. Surg. Oncology. Home: 376 Beach Spring Rd South Orange NJ 07079 Office: 225 Millburn Ave Ste 104B Millburn NJ 07041

BRIEFSTEIN, RICHARD PETER, alcohol abuse counselor; b. Newark; s. Joseph M. and Edith (Gortz) B. BA in Sociology, Ohio State U., 1971; MSW, Rutgers U., 1985. Lic. clin. social worker, N.J. Acad. Cert. Social Workers; qualified clin. social worker; diplomate Clin. Social Work; cert. alcohol counselor, addictions counselor, master addictions counselor. Alcoholism counselor Salvation Army Rehab. Ctr., Paterson, N.J.; social worker Big Bros. and Big Sisters Passaic and Bergen County, Wayne, N.J.; alcoholism counselor State of N.J. Dept. of Health, Trenton; family alcohol counselor Cath. Charities, Flemington, N.J.; coord. outpatient dept. Ctr. for Addiction Illnesses, Morristown, N.J.; coord. alcohol and drug svcs. Wayne Gen. Hosp. Mental Health Svcs., Pompton Lakes and West Milford, N.J.; part time pvt. practice Clifton, N.J.; field instr. for grad. sch. of social work students, Rutgers U., NYU. Mem. NASW.

BRIEGER, GERT HENRY, medical historian, educator; b. Hamburg, Germany, Jan. 5, 1932; came to U.S., 1938, naturalized, 1943; s. Carl Helmuth and Ylse (Fuchs) B.; m. Katharine Crenshaw, July 2, 1955; children: Heidi E., William N., Benjamin C. A.B., U. Calif., Berkeley, 1953; M.D., UCLA, 1957; M.P.H., Harvard U., 1962; Ph.D., Johns Hopkins U., 1968. Intern UCLA Med. Center, 1957-58; asst. prof. history of medicine Johns Hopkins U. Sch. Medicine, Balt., 1966-70; assoc. prof. community health scis., assoc. prof. history Duke U., Durham, N.C., 1970-75; prof. history of health scis., chmn. dept. U. Calif., San Francisco, 1975-84; William H. Welch prof., dir. Inst. History of Medicine Johns Hopkins U., Balt., 1984—, chair dept. hist. sci. med. and tech., 1993—. Author: (with A.M. Harvey, S.L. Abrams and V.A. McKusick) A Model of Its Kind, A Centennial History of Johns Hopkins Medicine, 2 vols., 1989; editor: Medical America in the Nineteenth Century, 1972, Theory and Practice in American Medicine, 1976; co-editor Bull. of the History of Medicine, 1990—. Served to capt. U.S. Army, 1958-61. Mem. Am. Assn. History of Medicine (pres. 1980-82), History of Sci. Home: 107 W Lee St Baltimore MD 21201-2420 Office: 1900 E Monument St Baltimore MD 21205-2113*

BRIENING, EILEEN PATRICIA, nurse; b. Salem, N.J., Aug. 30, 1950; d. John Phillip and Catherine Elizabeth (Tyner) Toy; m. Jeffrey Alan Briening, Sept. 16, 1972; children: Michele Lynn, Matthew Alan, Andrew Phillip. BS in Nursing, U. Del., 1985; MS in Nursing, U. Pa., 1995. RN, Del.; CCRN; cert. pediatric critical care nurse practitioner. Nurse Med. Ctr. Del., Stanton, 1973-88, asst. head nurse, 1988-90, unit instr. in pediatric critical care and nursing, 1990—; staff nurse, transport team A.I. duPont Inst. Children's Hosp., Wilmington, Del., 1993-95; ped. critical care nurse practitioner Sinai Hosp. Balt., 1995—. Mem. AACN (unit base quality assurance chmn. Med. Ctr. Del. 1988-93). Home: 3 Canterbury Dr Pennsville NJ 08070-2303 Office: Sinai Hosp Baltimore MD 21215

BRIERLEY, GERALD P., physiological chemistry educator; b. Ogallala, Nebr., Aug. 14, 1931; s. Phillip and Myrtle (Shireman) B.; m. Miriam Grove, Apr. 17, 1971; children: David, Steven, Glenn, Lynn. B.S., U. Med.-Coll. Park, 1953, Ph.D., 1961. Asst. prof. U. Wis., Madison, 1962-64; faculty mem. Ohio State U., Columbus, 1964—; prof. physiol. chemistry Ohio State U., 1969—, chmn. dept., 1981-95, prof. emeritus, 1996—. Capt. USAF, 1953-56. USPHS grantee to study ion transport by heart mitochondria, 1965—; USPHS grantee to study pathology mitochondria in ischemia, 1977—. Mem. Am. Soc. Biol. Chemistry, Biophys. Soc., Am. Heart Assn. Office:

Dept of Medicine Biochemistry 333 Hamilton Hall 1645 Neil Ave Columbus OH 43210-1218*

BRIGGAMAN, ROBERT ALAN, dermatologist, medical educator; b. Hartford, Aug. 14, 1934; m. Irene Taluskie, Sept. 17, 1960; children: Kimberly Ann, John Scott. BS, Trinity Coll., Hartford, 1956; MD, NYU, 1960. Diplomate Am. Bd. Dermatology; cert. spl. competence in dermatopathology, Am. Bd. Pathology and Am. Bd. Dermatology, 1974. Med. intern U. Va. Hosp., Charlottesville, 1960-61, med. resident, 1961-62; resident in dermatology N.C. Meml. Hosp., Chapel Hill, 1964-65, dermatology fellow, 1965-67; instr. medicine and dermatology U. N.C. Sch. Medicine, Chapel Hill, 1967-68, asst. prof. medicine and dermatology, 1968-71, assoc. prof. medicine and dermatology, 1971-74, prof. medicine and dermatology, 1974—, chmn. dept. dermatology, 1987—. Contbr. numerous articles to med. and dermatology jours., chpts. to dermatology textbooks; dep. editor Jour. Investigative Dermatology, 1992—. N.C. State chmn. Leaders Soc., Dermatology Found., 1996—. Recipient J.N. Taub Internat. Meml. award for psoriasis rsch., 1983, Marion B. Sulzberger Meml. award, Am. Acad. Dermatology, 1985, MERIT award NIH, 1990, Clayton E. Wheeler Jr. Disting. professorship, 1992. Mem. AMA, Am. Acad. Dermatology, Am. Dermatologic Assn., Assn. Profs. Dermatology, Dermatology Found., Soc. for Investigative Dermatology. Office: UNC Sch Medicine Dept Derm CB #7287 3100 Thurston-Bowles Bldg Chapel Hill NC 27599-7287

BRIGGS, ARTHUR HAROLD, pharmacologist, educator; b. East Orange, N.J., Nov. 3, 1930; s. Arthur H. and Marie (Schoepf) B.; m. Elizabeth Jensen, June 6, 1953; children: Kimberlee, Norman A. BA, Johns Hopkins U., 1952, MD, 1956. Diplomate Am. Bd. Internal Medicine. Intern, resident in internal medicine Vanderbilt U. Hosp., Nashville, 1956-59; asst. prof. pharmacology and medicine U. Miss. Med. Ctr., Jackson, 1960-62, assoc. prof. pharmacology and medicine, 1962-67, prof. pharmacology and medicine, 1968—; prof. chmn. pharmacology U. Tex. Health Sci. Ctr., San Antonio, 1968-93, prof. emeritus, 1995—. Contbr. 60 articles to profl. jours. NIH Spl. fellow, 1968. Home: 3519 Hunters Sound St San Antonio TX 78230-2838 Office: U Tex Health Sci Ctr 7703 Floyd Curl Dr San Antonio TX 78284-6200

BRIGGS, BURTON A., medical educator; b. Orange, N.J., July 24, 1939; s. Carolyn Sue Briggs; 2 children. BS, Walla Walla Coll., 1961; MD, Loma Linda U., 1966; MA in Mgmt., Claremont Grad. Sch., 1990. Diplomate Am. Bd. Med. Examiners, Am. Bd. Anesthesiology; lic. physician, Calif., Mass. Intern Loma Linda (Calif.) U. Hosp., 1966-67; asst. resident in anesthesia Mass. Gen. Hosp., Boston, 1967-68, 69-70, clin. and rsch. fellow, 1968-69, chief resident, 1969, asst. in anesthesia, co-dir. recovery room/acute care unit, 1972-75; instr. anesthesia Harvard Med. Sch., Boston, 1972-75; asst. prof. anesthesia and surgery Loma Linda U., 1975-83, asst. prof. pediatrics, 1982-87, assoc. prof. anesthesiology and surgery, 1983-87, prof. anesthesiology, prof. surgery, 1987—; dir. surg. intensive care Loma Linda U. Med. Ctr., 1975-92, chief sect. critical care, 1983-92, med. dir. transport svcs., 1986—, med. dir. operating room svcs., 1991—, bd. trustees, 1986-90; dir. surg. intensive care J.L. Pettis Meml. VA Hosp., 1977-78; sec.-treas. Loma Linda Anesthesiology Med. Group, Inc., 1981-95, sec., 1995—, chmn. billing and reimbursement com., 1995—; chief anesthesiology svcs. Riverside Gen. Hosp., 1985-86;vis. prof. Socieda de Brasileira de Anestesiologia, 1980, Peking (China) Union Med. Coll., 1986; oral examiner Med. Bd. of Calif., 1990—; interviewer regional area Harvard/Radcliffe Colls., 1994—; bd. dirs. faculty physicians and surgeons Loma Linda U. Sch. Medicine, 1995—. Author: Principles of Critical Care, 1987; contbr. articles and abstracts to profl. jours., chpts. to books; article reviewer New Eng. Jour. Medicine, 1973-75, Jour. Critical Care Medicine, 1975-91; examiner Am. Bd. Anesthesiology, 1983-90. With U.S. Army, 1970-71. Fellow Am. Coll. Anesthesiology, Am. Coll. Critical Care Medicine; mem. Am. Soc. Anesthesiologists, Soc. Critical Care Medicine, San Bernardino County Med. Soc., Calif. Soc. Anesthesiology (alt. del. dist. 2 1983-86), Calif. Med. Assn., Loma Linda U. Sch. Medicine Alumni Assn. (bd. dirs. 1994—, CFO 1995—), Assn. Anesthesia Clin. Dirs. (bd. dirs. 1994—), Alpha Omega Alpha. Home: 10746 Winesap Ave Cherry Valley CA 92223*

BRIGGS, DICK DOWLING, JR., physician, educator; b. Electric Mills, Miss., Jan. 28, 1934; s. Dick Dowling and Anita (Carnathan) B.; m. Susan Hunt Davis, June 20, 1959; children—Adrienne Davis, Dick Dowling III, Daniel Roth. B.S. in Chemistry, U. of South, 1956; M.D., Washington U., 1960. Diplomate Am. Bd. Internal Medicine (pulmonary diseases). Intern, U. Ala. Hosp., Birmingham, 1960-62, resident in internal medicine, 1964-65, chief resident, 1965-66; mem. faculty U. Ala. Med. Sch., Birmingham, 1965—, prof. emeritus and eminent scholar chair in pulmonary diseases, 1995—, dir. div. pulmonary and critical care medicine, dept. medicine, 1971-94, vice-chmn. dept. medicine, 1981-94; dir. med. edn. pulmonary lab., also respiratory therapy Carraway Methodist Med. Ctr., Birmingham, 1968-71; cons. Birmingham VA Hosp. Chmn. claims com. U. Ala.-Birmingham Liability Ins. Trust; pres., CEO U. Ala. Health Svcs. Found., 1988-92; corp. med. dir. triton Health Sys., LLC. Served to capt. USAF, 1962-64. Baker scholar, 1952-56, Danforth scholar, 1956-60; grantee Nat. Heart, Lung and Blood Inst., 1972-77. Fellow ACP, Am. Coll. Chest Physicians (pres. 1984-85); mem. Am. Soc. Internal Medicine, Assn. Pulmonary Program Dirs. (pres. 1986-87), Am. Bd. Internal Medicine (pulmonary diseases), Am. Thoracic Soc., AMA, Assn. Am. Med. Colls., So. Med. Assn., Med. Assn. Ala., Jefferson County Med. Soc., Soc. Medica de Santiago (hon.), Phi Beta Kappa. Episcopalian. Clubs: Mt. Brook Swim and Tennis, The Club, The Summit Club, Ala. Tennis Assn. (pres. 1968-69). Author numerous papers in field. Office: U of Alabama Med Sch Divsn Pulmonary Crit Care Birmingham AL 35294-0012

BRIGGS, DONALD KNOWLES, hematologist, researcher; b. Northampton, Eng., Apr. 10, 1924; came to U.S., 1953; s. James Parker and Esther Mary (Reid) B.; m. June Nasseau, July 19, 1958; children: Lincoln Wiliam, Claudia Louise. BA, Cambridge U., Eng., 1946, MA, 1948; MB BChir, Cambridge U., 1947; MD, NYU, 1955. Registrar London U. King's Coll. Hosp., 1949-50; sr. resident Am. Hosp., Paris, 1951-53; prin. investigator USPHS, 1956-66; chief sect. hematology, dir. spl. hematology lab. Lenox Hill Hosp., N.Y.C., 1967-78; asst. prof. clin. medicine NYU, N.Y.C., 1956—; cons. physician James Lenox House, N.Y., 1988—. Author: Abnormalities of Leukocytes, 1963. Capt. Royal Army Med. Corps, 1947-49. Fellow ACP, Royal Soc. Medicine; mem. Listerian Soc. (life), St. George's Soc. (life). Home and Office: 170 E 79th St New York NY 10021-0436

BRIGGS, JANET MARIE LOUISE, nurse practitioner; b. Pitts., June 11, 1951. Cert. family med. nurse practitioner. Staff nurse neonatal ICU Univ. Hosps. Cleve., 1972-73; staff nurse gen pediatrics Mt. Sinai Hosp. Cleve., 1973-76; head nurse health svc. Mt. Sinai Med. Ctr., Cleve., 1976-82; grad. rsch. asst. Case Western Res. U., Cleve., 1983-84; dir. nursing Ashtabula County Health Dept., Jefferson, Ohio, 1984-85; staff nurse, dir. nursing insvc., coord., clin. nurse specialist, coord. infection control Meml. Hosp. Geneva, Ohio, 1985-87; nurse practitioner, unit mgr. Parkside Health Mgmt. Corp., Toledo, 1986-87; nurse practitioner ambulatory surgery. Met. Gen. Hosp., Cleve., 1987; nurse practitioner domiciliary homeless program VA Med. Ctr., Cleve., 1987-91, clin. nurse specialist, nurse practioner AIDS team, 1991—; project dir., chmn. Child and Family Health Svc. Grant, Ashtabula County, Ohio, 1984-85; cons. case mgmt. head injuries subcom. Gov.'s Task Force, Ohio, 1988; nurse practitioner Free Clinic, Cleve., 1988—; mem. ethics com. VA Med. Ctr., 1989—; adj. clin. faculty Kent. State U., 1993—; investigator multiple clinically based AIDS rsch. projects. Lectr., group leader Hitchcock House, Cleve., 1981-83. Recipient Fed. Exec. Bd. award, 1995, Hearts and Hands award, Sec. Vet. Affairs, 1995; grantee Fed. Facility Based HIV/AIDS Edn. Demonstration, 1991, Fed. Facility HIV/AIDS Edn. Rsch., 1992, 93, Dept. Vet. Affairs. Mem. Frances Payne Bolton Sch. Nursing Alumni Assn. (bd. dirs.), Sigma Theta Tau. Roman Catholic.

BRIGGS, JOHN JAMES, nuclear pharmacist, clinical specialist; b. Danvers, Mass., July 23, 1959; s. George Elmer and Betty Elizabeth (Abraham) B.; m. Martha Ann Stevenson, Oct. 18, 1985; children: John Charles, Jacqueline Elizabeth, James Stevenson. BS in Pharmacy, Northeastern U., 1982; cert. in radiology safety, U. So. Calif., 1986; grad., USAF Health Adminstrv. Sch., 1993. Cert. EMT. EMT Lyon's Ambulance Svc., Danvers, 1978-83; hosp. pharmacist Manatee (Fla.) Meml. Hosp., 1983-86; staff pharmacist Syncor Internat., Ft. Myers, Fla., 1986-88; facility mgr. Mallinckrodt Med. Inc., St. Petersberg, Fla., 1988-94; oncology clin. specialist Mallinckrodt Med. Inc., St. Louis, 1994—; designer positron pharmacy Mallinckrodt Med. Inc., St. Petersberg, Fla., 1989-90. Mem. Am. Pharmacy Assn., Soc. Nuclear Medicine, Fla. Pharmacy Assn., Res. Officers Assn. (past pres. local chpt., com. mem. Fla State chpt.), Am. Eagle Scout Soc. Office: Mallinkrodt Med Inc Box 5840 675 McDonnell Blvd Saint Louis MO 63134

BRIGGS, KENNETH RALPH, psychiatrist; b. Murtaugh, Idaho, Oct. 7, 1927; s. Glen Allen and Hazel (Menser) B.; m. Janet Keith Smith, Nov. 14, 1953; children: Carolyn Briggs Brafford, Keith Marshall. BS, U. Idaho, 1950; MD, Harvard U., 1954; MS, U. Minn., 1962. Diplomate Am. Bd. Internal Medicine, Am. Bd. Psychiatry and Neurology. Intern Salt Lake VA Hosp., Salt Lake City, 1954-55; resident physician Mpls. VA Hosp., 1955-58; internist USAF Hosp., Clark AFB, Philippines, 1958-60; resident physician Boston VA Hosp., 1960-63; pvt. practice Twin Falls, Idaho, 1963-80; staff psychiatrist East Boston Winthrop Counseling Ctr., Boston, 1980-83, med. dir., 1983-91; pvt. practice Durham, N.C., 1992-95; instr. in psychiatry Harvard Univ. Med. Sch., Boston, 1981-91; asst. in psychiatry Mass. Gen. Hosp., Boston, 1986-91, clin. assoc., 1981-86. Author: (with others) Yin & Yang Come Home, 1976. Capt. USAFR, 1958-60. Fellow Am. Psychiat. Assn.; mem. AMA. Methodist.

BRIGGS, ROBERT MERVYN, plastic and reconstructive surgeon; b. Rochester, N.Y., Jan. 12, 1939; s. Robert Mervyn and Gertrude Edna (Broadwell) B.; m. Christine Martha Horgen, Oct. 17, 1964; children: Kari H., Heidi A., Amy E. AB, Princeton U., 1960; MD, Yale U., 1964. Diplomate Am. Bd. of Surgery, Am. Bd. of Plastic and Reconstructive Surgery. Intern surgery U. Rochester-Strong Meml. Hosp., 1964-65; resident gen. surgery, plastic surgery Stanford U., Palo Alto, Calif., 1965-70; attending physician, reconstructive surgeon St. Barnabas Med. Ctr., Livingston, N.J., 1972—; pvt. practice Livingston, 1972—; chmn. dept. plastic surgery St. Barnabas Med. Ctr., Livingston, 1990-93; clin. asst. prof. surgery Rutgers-Robert Wood Johnson Med. Sch., Piscataway, N.J., 1975—. Contbr. chpts. to books, articles to profl. jours. Mem. Roseland (N.J.) Recreation Com., 1984-87; mem., v.p. West Essex Bd. of Edn., North Caldwell, N.J., 1987-92; bd. dirs. Emmanuel Cancer Found., 1983-87. Decorated Bronze Star. Fellow Am. Coll. Surgeons; mem. Am. Soc. Plastic and Reconstructive Surgery (com. mem.), Am. Assn. Plastic and Reconstructive Surgery, N.Y. Regional Soc. Plastic and Reconstructive Surgery (pres. and v.p.), N.J. Regional Soc. Plastic and Reconstructive Surgery (pres. 1985-86), Med. Soc. N.J. (chmn. plastic sect.), Essex County Med. Soc. (mem. com.), Kiwanis (pres. and officer 1980-88). Office: 349 E Northfield Rd Livingston NJ 07039-4802

BRIGHAM, ANNA JEAN MCALLISTER, nurse; b. Carbondale, Pa., Aug. 30, 1957; d. William and Mollie (Markley) McAllister; m. Arthur Brigham, June 8, 1986; 1 child, Sarah Diane. Diploma, Albany Med. Ctr. Sch. Nursing, 1978; BS cum laude, SUNY, New Paltz, 1986, M of Profl. Studies, 1991. Staff nurse Nyack Gen. Hosp., N.Y., 1978-79; head nurse Mid Hudson Psychiat. Ctr., New Hampton, N.Y., 1980-83; psychiat. nurse adminstr. I Middletown (N.Y.) Psychiat. Ctr., 1983-89, relief psychiat. nurse adminstr. I, 1989-93; cmty. mental health nurse Middletown Mental Health Clinic, 1992—. Office: Middletown Mental Health Bldg #54 141 Monhagen Ave Middletown NY 10940-6265

BRIGHAM, CHRISTOPHER ROY, occupational medicine physician; b. Guelph, Ontario, Can., Dec. 27, 1950; s. Kenneth Roy and Jean McCrea B.; m. Cathy Violet White, July 1, 1989; children: Melinda, Alison, Gina. BA, Rutgers Coll., 1972; MMS, Rutgers U., Piscataway, N.J., 1974; MD, Washington U., 1976. Diplomate Nat. Bd. Med. Examiners, Am. Bd. Preventive Medicine (occupational medicine), Am. Bd. Family Practice; lic. Maine, Mass; cert. ind. med. examiner Am.Bd. Ind. Med. Examiners. Resident in family practice Eastern Maine Med. Ctr., Bangor, 1976-79; ptnr. and family physician Med. Assocs. of Bar Harbor, Maine, 1979-85; pres. Marine Health Svcs., Bar Harbor, 1980-86; cons. med. dir. Emergency and Safety Programs, Inc., Media, Pa., 1983-86, 86-90; med. dir. St. Joseph Ambulatory Care, Inc., Bangor, Maine, 1985-86; occupational health cons. Envirologic Data, Portland, Maine, 1986-88; pres. and founder Occupational Health Excellence, Inc., Falmouth, Maine, 1988-94; med. dir. Seak, Inc., Falmouth, 1990—; sr. cons. Occupational Health Excellence of Maine, Falmouth, 1992—; v.p. med. affairs Occupational Health Resources, Inc., Falmouth, 1993-94; pres. Brigham and Assocs., Inc., Portland, 1994—; v.p. SEAK Inc., 1996—; dir. divsn. occupational health, Depts. Medicine and Family Practice, Maine Med. Contbr. articles to profl. jours., presenter at numerous confs., workshops and sci. meetings in field. Mem. Am. Coll. Occupational and Environ. Medicine (vice chmn. sect. on computers in occupational medicine, 1986-87, mem. 1986—, chmn. com. on occupational mental health, 1988-92, mem. 1988—, coun. on social issues 1988-92, com. on confs., 1995—, dir. 1996—, others), Am. Acad. Disability Evaluating Physicians, Am. Acad. Ins. Medicine, Am. Acad. Ind. Med. Examiners (founding dir., sr. cons.), Am. Pub. Health Assn. (sect. on occupational health), Humanities, Inc. (bd. dirs.), Maine Pub. Health Assn., New Eng. Occupational Med. Assn. (bd. dirs. 188-90). Home and Office: 31 Summer Pl Portland ME 04103

BRIGHAM, KENNETH LARRY, medical educator; b. Tenn., Oct. 29, 1939; m. Betty Brigham; 1 child, Heather. BA, David Lipscomb Coll., 1962; MD, Vanderbilt U., 1966. Intern Osler Med. Service, Johns Hopkins Hosp., Balt., 1966-67, asst. resident in medicine, 1967-68; with cholera research unit Johns Hopkins Ctr. for Med. Research and Tng., Calcutta, India, 1968; med. epidemiologist Ecol. Investigations program USPHS Nat. Communicable Disease Ctr., Phoenix, 1968-70; instr. in medicine, fellow in pulmonary diseases Vanderbilt U. Sch. Medicine, Nashville, 1970-71, dir. pulmonary research, 1973-76, asst. prof. medicine, 1973-74, assoc. prof., 1974-78, dir. Ctr. for Lung Research, 1976—, assoc. prof. biomed. engring., 1977-86, prof. of medicine, 1978—, dir. div. pulmonary medicine, 1978—, asst. prof. physiology, 1983-85, assoc. prof. molecular physiology and biophysics, 1985—, Joe and Morris Wethan prof. investigative medicine, 1984—, prof. biomed. engring., 1986—; research fellow Cardiovascular Research Inst., U. Calif. Med. Ctr., San Francisco, 1971-73; mem. council on cardiopulmonary disease Am. Heart Assn., investigator, 1975-80; mem. cardiovascular and pulmonary study sect. USPHS, Nat. Heart Lung Inst., 1975-79, mem. pulmonary nat. research service award group, 1975; mem. lung research rev. com. VA, 1976; mem. A program project rev. com. Nat. Heart Lung and Blood Inst., 1982-85, chmn., 1984-85, mem. pulmonary disease adv. com., 1986—; prin. investigator Specialized Ctr. Research in Pulmonary Vascular Disease, 1976—, Parker B. Francis Found. Fellowships in Pulmonary Research, 1977-83, Multidisciplinary Lung Research Tng. Grant, 1975—; mem. Am. Lung Assn./Am. Thoracic Soc. steering com., 1988-89; chmn. pulmonary diseases adv. com. NIH, 1988-90. Mem. editorial bd. Jour. Applied Physiology, 1978-84, Respiratory, Environ. and Exercise Physiology, 1978-84, Circulation Research, 1982—, Exptl. Lung Research, 1982—, Am. Jour. Med. Scis., 1983—, Am. Rev. Respiratory Diseases, 1984—, Jour. Clin. Investigation, 1985—, Intensive Care Medicine, 1985—; contbr. articles to profl. jours. Mem. planning com. Am. Lung Assn., 1983—; rep. Vanderbilt Univ. Senate, Nashville, 1986—. Grantee NIH, 1985—. Mem. Am. Physiol. Soc. (circulation and respiration groups), Am. Fedn. for Clin. Research (pres. So. sect. 1980-81), Am. Thoracic Soc. (pres.-elect pulmonary circulation sect. assembly on structure and function 1979-80, pres. pulmonary circulation sect. 1980-81, chmn.-elect assembly on respiratory structure function and metabolism 1981-82, chmn. assembly 1982-83, fed. lung program com. 1987—, pres.-elect 1988-89, bd. dirs. 1988-89, budget com. 1988-89), AAAS, Johns Hopkins Med. and Surg. Assn., Microcirculatory Soc., So. Soc. for Clin. Investigation (councilor 1988-89), Am. Soc. for Clin. Investigation, N.Y. Acad. Scis., Assn. Am. Physicians, ACP, Am. Soc. for Cell Biology, Nashville Soc. for Internal Medicine (v.p. 1985-86), Am. Lung Assn. (exec. com. 1988-89, planning com. 1988-89, program coordinating/program and budget com. 1988-89)). Home: 211 Printers Aly Nashville TN 37201-1414 Office: Vanderbilt U Sch MedicineT1217MCN 21st and Garland Nashville TN 37203*

BRIGHT, HARRY ANDREW, pharmacy manager; b. Elizabeth City, N.C., Nov. 17, 1947; s. Melvin Wellar and Marjorie Louise (James) B.; m. Jane Frances Jackson, June 11, 1972; children: Christi, Jackson, Leigh Ann and Elizabeth (twins). AB in Zoology, U. N.C., 1970, BS in Pharmacy, 1975; MS in Hosp. Pharmacy, Med. Coll. of Va., 1977; MBA, Old Dominion U., 1990. participant Drug Coun. Pharmacists. Pharmacist Maryview Hosp., Portsmouth, Va., 1977-80; asst. dir. Maryview Hosp., Portsmouth, 1980-84, pharmacy dir., 1984-90; pharmacist Farmco Pharmacy, 1990—. Mem. adopt-a-sch. com. Maryview Hosp., Portsmouth, 1986-87; del. Citizen Ambassador Program Trip to China, 1987. Served with U.S. Army, 1971-73. Mem. Am. Pharm. Assn., Va. Soc. Hosp. Pharmacists (v.p. region V 1983-84, state budget chmn. and bd. dirs. 1984-85), N.C. Soc. Hosp. Pharmacists, Am. Soc. Hosp. Pharmacists. Baptist. Club: Mended Hearts (Tidewater, Va.). Home: 4140 Weyanoke Dr Portsmouth VA 23703-1907 Office: 4018 W Mercury Blvd Hampton VA 23666

BRIGHTON, CARL THEODORE, orthopedic surgery educator; b. Pana, Ill., Aug. 20, 1931; s. Louis Frederick and Helen (Frinke) B.; m. Ruth Louise Krentz, July 27, 1954; children: David Carl, Susan Ruth, Andrew Paul, Joel Theodore. BA, Valparaiso U., 1953; MD, U. Pa., 1957; PhD, U. Ill., 1969. Diplomate: Am. Bd. Orthopedic Surgery. Intern U.S. Naval Hosp., Phila., 1957-58; resident orthopedics U.S. Naval Hosp., 1958-61; resident in orthopedics U. Pa., Phila., 1961-62; staff orthopedist U.S. Naval Hosp., Phila., 1962-63, Naval Hosp., Great Lakes, Ill., 1963-66, USS Sanctuary, South China Sea, 1966-67; asst. prof. orthopedic surgery U. Pa. Med. Sch., Phila., 1968-70; dir. orthopedic research U. Pa. Med. Sch., 1968-93, assoc. prof., 1970-73, prof., 1973—, chmn. dept. orthopedic surgery, 1977-93, Paul B. Magnuson prof. bone and joint surgery, 1977-96; attending staff VA Hosp., Phila., 1968-84; cons. orthopedic surgery U.S. Naval Hosp., Phila., 1968-78. Editor-in-Chief: Clinical Orthopaedics and Related Research, 1993—. Lt. comdr. (j.g.) USN, 1957-62. Recipient Kappa Delta award for outstanding research, 1974; spl. postdoctoral fellow NIH, 1967-68; Career devel. research award, 1971-76; Shands lectr. award, 1985, Merit award NIH, 1987, Bristol-Myers Squibb/Zimmer award for Disting. Achievement in Orthopaedic Rsch., 1992. Fellow ACS, Am. Acad. Orthopedic Surgeons; mem. Am. Orthopedic Assn., Orthopedic Rsch. Soc. (pres. 1977), Orthopedic Forum, Can. Orthopedic Rsch. Soc. (hon.), Bioelectric Repair and Growth Soc. (co-founder, pres. 1981, 82), Acad. Orthopaedic Soc., Assn. of Bone and Joint Surgeons. Lutheran. Home: 14 Flintshire Rd Malvern PA 19355-1108 Office: Hosp of the U of Pa 1224 Penn Tower 3400 Spruce St Philadelphia PA 19104

BRIGHTON, JOAN KATHLEEN, psychologist; b. Urbana, Ill., July 10, 1954; d. Gerald David and Lois (Robbins) B. BA in Sociology, So. Ill. U., 1974; MA in Psychology, U. Nev., 1982. VISTA vol. Oper. Life, Las Vegas, 1974-75; grad. asst. U. NEv., Las Vegas, 1978-80; psychologist So. Nev. Adult Mental Health Svcs., Las Vegas, 1984-92; vocational rehab. counselor State Indsl. Ins. System, Las Vegas, 1992—. Treas. Spiritual Assembly of Baha'is, North Las Vegas, 1977-92; vice chmn. Baha'is, Sunrise Manor, 1993—. Pres. scholar So. Ill. U., 1971-74. Mem. Nat. Alliance for Mentally Ill, Nat. Wildlife Fedn., World Wlidlife Fund, Nev. Alliance for Mentally Ill (liaison 1986-89), AAUW, Amnesty Internat., Sierra Club (Toiyabe chpt.), Habitat for Humanity, Phi Kappa Phi, Psi Chi. Home: 3648 Rochester Ave Las Vegas NV 89115-0229 Office: State Indsl Ins System 1700 W Charleston Blvd Las Vegas NV 89102-2335

BRIGHTWELL, DENNIS RICHARD, psychiatrist; b. Des Moines, Aug. 7, 1946; s. Harold W. and Margaret (Young) B. BS, Iowa State U., 1968; MD, U. Iowa, 1974. Diplomate Am. Bd. Psychiatry and Neurology. Internship The U. of Iowa Hosps. and Clinics, 1971-72; residency The U. of Iowa State Psychopathic Hosp., 1971-74; staff physician VA Med. Ctr., Lexington, Ky., 1974-75, chief behavioral psychiatry sect., 1975-78; chief psychiatry svc. VA Med. Ctr., Columbia, Mo., 1978-85, James A. Haley Vets. Hosp., Tampa, Fla., 1985-94; pvt. practice Daytona Beach, Fla., 1994—; asst. prof. psychiatry U. Ky., Lexington, 1974-78; assoc. prof. psychiatry U. Mo., Columbia, 1978-85; prof. psychiatry U. South Fla., Tampa, 1985-94; utilization rev. cons. Psychiatry Ctr., 1987-91, Merit Behavioral Care Corp., 1990—. Contbr. articles to profl. jours. Grantee, Pennwalt Corp., 1975-78, VA, 1976, 80. Fellow Am. Psychiat. Assn.; mem. Ctrl. Mo. Psychiat. Soc. (sec., treas. 1981-82), Mid-Continent Psychiat. Assn. (pres. 1982-83), Assn. Mil. Surgeons of U.s. (life), Soc. of U.S. Army Flight Surgeons (life), Nat. Assn. VA Chiefs of Psychiatry (sec., treas. 1989-90, pres. 1993-94), Sigma Xi (life). Episcopalian. Office: 1030 W Internat Speedway Ste 100 Daytona Beach FL 32118-3440

BRIGNONI, RENÉ AGUSTÍN, oral and maxillofacial prosthodontist; b. San Juan, P.R., July 5, 1961; s. René And Maria Emilia Brignoni. DMD, U. P.R., San Juan, 1987. Diplomate Am. Bd. Prosthodontics. Intern VA Med. Ctr., Dayton, Ohio, 1987-88; resident VA Med. Ctr., Maywood, Ill., 1988-90; fellow U. Tex., Houston, 1991; oral and maxillofacial prosthodontist, mem. coms. VA Med. Ctr., Gainesville, Fla., 1996—; clin. asst. prof. Loyola U., Maywood, Ill., 1988-90; clin. asst. prof., cons. Emory U., Atlanta, 1991-96; clin. assoc. prof. U. Fla., Gainesville, 1996. Contbr. articles to profl. jours. Named Outstanding Table Clinician, Am. Prosthodontic Soc., 1989, Outstanding Table Clinician, Thomas P. Hinman Annual Dental Meeting, 1993, 95. Fellow Am. Co.. Prosthodontics, Am. Acad. Maxillofacial Prosthetics (assoc.); mem. Acad. Gen. Dentistry. Home: 9640SW 54th Rd Gainesville FL 32608 Office: VA Med Ctr 1601 SW Archer Rd Gainesville FL 32608

BRILEY, MICHELLE STATON, operating room nurse; b. Mt. Vernon, Ky., Jan. 18, 1963; d. Charles Albert and Ruby Kathleen (Brown) Staton; m. William Keith Briley, May 18, 1985. Student, Berea Coll., 1981; BS in Indsl. Tech., East Carolina U., 1986, BSN, 1992. RN, N.C. ANA II Pitt County Meml. Hosp., Greenville, N.C., 1992; mem. nursing staff Pitt County Meml. Hosp., Greenville, 1993—. Mem. ANA, Assn. Operating Room Nurses (Coastal Cutters chpt.), N.C. Nurses Assn., East Carolina U. Sch. Nursing Profl. Alumni Soc. (nominating com. 1993-94). Republican. Mem. Ch. Christ. Home: Rt 1 Box 233-A Ayden NC 28513

BRILL, BONNIE, physical therapist, engineer, inventor; b. Charleston, S.C., Nov. 2, 1948; d. Harry Harris II and Virginia Brill. BS in Phys. Therapy cum laude, Ga. State U., 1972; MS, Ga. Inst. Tech., 1978. Pediatric phys. therapist Ga. State Health Agys., Atlanta, 1972-73; phys. therapist Peachtree Orthopedic Clinic, Atlanta, 1974; contractor Ga. Health Care Orgns., Atlanta, 1975-79; engr., cons. Medicas Systems Corp., Houston, 1979-81, Bay Area Hosps., San Francisco, 1981-82; chief phys. therapist San Francisco Gen. Hosp., 1982-83; dir. phys. therapy Ralph K. Davies Med. Ctr., San Francisco, 1983-84; contractor Calif. Health Care Orgns., San Francisco area, 1984—; founder Peak Relief, San Francisco, 1986—; cons. in field. Mem. Am. Phys. Therapy Assn. (Calif. chpt.), Eckankar, Bay Area Sea Kayakers.

BRILL, CHARLES B., child neurologist, educator; b. N.Y.C., July 9, 1937; s. D. Joseph and Gerda (Wasserman) B.; m. Paula Wolfe, Dec. 1960 (div. 1977); children: Stephen, Laura; m. Lynn Godmilow, June 1979; 1 child, Aaron. AB, Lafayette Coll., 1957; MD, Columbia U., 1961. Intern, resident Bronx (N.Y.) Hosp., 1961-63; resident Mt. Sinai Hosp., N.Y.C., 1965-69, fellow, 1969-72, asst. prof., 1972-77; from assoc. prof. to prof. Hahnemann U., Phila., 1978-87; clin. prof. Thomas Jefferson U., Phila., 1987—. Capt. USAF, 1963-65. Fellow Am. Acad. Pediats., Am. Acad. Neurology; mem. Child Neurology Soc., Internat. Child Neurol. Soc., Profs. Child Neurology. Office: Thomas Jefferson U 909 Walnut St Philadelphia PA 19107

BRILL, F. ARTHUR, psychologist, consultant; b. Delmar, Del., Dec. 19, 1930; s. Lewis Henry and Minnie Jane (Brumbley) B.; m. Dorothy Eleanor Williams, June 17, 1954; children: Vicki Allison Lawruk, Donald Williams. BS, Springfield (Mass.) Coll., 1952; MEd, U. Del., 1959; postgrad., Temple U., 1961-63. Certified sch. psychologist, tchr. spl. ed., social studies, Del. Sec. YMCA of Newcastle County, Wilmington, Del., 1952-54; tchr. Alfred I. DuPont Sch. Dist., Wilmington, 1954-55; rehab. counselor Del. Div. Vocational Rehab., Wilmington, 1956-61; psychologist and coordinator of spl. svcs. Alexis I. DuPont Sch. Dist., Greenville, Del., 1961-68; psychologist and tchr. Alexis I. DuPont Sch. Dist., Greenville, 1974-77; dir. Del. Vocational Rehab. Svc., Wilmington, 1968-72; psychologist Conrad Area Sch. Dist., Wilmington, 1972-74; dir. Jastak Assoc., Inc., Wilmington, 1977-80; psychologist and counselor Howard Career Ctr., Wilmington, 1980-95; counseling psychologist U. Del., Newark, summers 1965-68; pres. Brill

Assocs., Wilmington, 1980-95; owner A Small Wonder Bed and Breakfast, 1985-93. Chmn. Del. Chronic Renal Disease Adv. Com., 1971-72; mem. De. Manpower Adv. Com., 1974-75, Dover, Mt. Pleasant Sch. Bd. Edn., Wilmington, 1974-75, Del. Coun. on Crime and Justice, Dover, 1978-82. Mem. Am. Counseling Assn., Am. Rehab. Counseling Assn., Am. Fedn. Tchrs., Nat. Rehab. Assn., Del. Psychol. Assn. (pres. 1970-71), Del. State C. of C., Del. Conv. and Visitors Assn. Unitarian. Home: 213 W Crest Rd Wilmington DE 19803-4236

BRILL, NICHOLAS STEVEN, health care services executive; b. Washington, Dec. 5, 1946; s. Daniel Herbert and Charlotte (Lobel) B.; m. Margaret Rose Warshaw, May 10, 1970; children: Rachel Elizabeth, Jacob Andrew, Charlotte Danielle. BA, Colgate U., 1969; MBA, Harvard U., 1974. Urban affairs cons. Arthur D. Little, Inc., Cambridge, Mass., 1969-72; asst. commr. Mass. Pub. Health Dept., Boston, 1974-76; adminstr. Cambridge Ctr., 1976-80, v.p. mgmt. services, 1980-85, v.p. mktg., 1985-86; v.p. mktg. Harvard Cmty. Health Plan, Boston; chief ops. officer, bd. dirs. Dedicated Dental Systems, Wellesley, Mass., 1986-88; pres., founder Commonwealth Care, Inc., Newton, Mass., 1988-95; divsn. v.p. Quantum Health Resources, Newton, 1996—; trustee Boston University Med. Ctr., 1991—; v.p., bd. dirs. Health Planning Coun. Greater Boston, 1978-80. Democrat. Jewish. Home: 249 Lake Ave Newton MA 02161-1209

BRILL, WINSTON JONAS, microbiologist, educator, research director, publisher and management consultant; b. London, June 16, 1939; came to U.S., 1949; s. Walter and Irmgard (Levy) B.; m. Nancy Carol Weisburd, June 11, 1964; 1 child, Eric David. B.A., Rutgers U., 1961; Ph.D. in Microbiology, U. Ill., 1965. Postdoctoral fellow MIT, Cambridge, 1965-67; asst. prof. dept. bacteriology U. Wis., Madison, 1967-70, assoc. prof., 1970-74, prof., 1974-79, Vilas research prof., 1979-83, adj. prof., 1983—; v.p., dir. research Agracetus, 1981-89; pres. Winston J. Brill & Assocs., Madison, 1989—; panel mem. NSF, USDA, Pontifical Acad. Scis.; mem. recombinant DNA adv. com. NIH, 1979-83; mem. policy adv. com. USDA, 1985—; mem. genetic engring. adv. panel to U.S. sec. state, 1981; mem. exec. bd. Nat. Inst. Emerging Tech. Pub., editor: R&D Innovator, 1992—; mem. editl. bd. Jour. Biotech., Trends in Biotech., Critical Revs. in Biotech.; contbr. articles to profl. jours. Recipient Eli Lilly award in microbiology and immunology, 1979, Alexander von Humboldt Found. award, 1979, Award of Distinction U. Wis., 1990; Henry Rutgers fellow Rutgers U., 1961. Fellow AAAS, Am. Acad. Microbiology; mem. NAS, Am. Soc. Microbiology, Am. Soc. Plant Physiologists, Am. Soc. Biochemistry and Molecular Biology, Internat. Soc. Plant Molecular Biology.

BRILLIANT, ELEANOR LURIA, social work educator; b. Bklyn., Nov. 25, 1930; d. Joseph and Leah (Cohen) Luria; m. Richard Brilliant, June 24, 1951; children: Stephanie, Livia, Franca, Myron. BA, Smith Coll., Northampton, Mass., 1952; MS, Bryn Mawr (Pa.) Coll., 1969; DSW, Columbia U., 1974. Asst. in prodn. course Harvard Bus. Sch., Cambridge, Mass., 1952-54; instr. Bryn Mawr Coll., 1969-71; adminstr., dir. Lower East Side Family Union, N.Y.C., 1974-75; dir. planning/evaluation United Way of Westchester, White Plains, N.Y., 1975-78, assoc. exec. dir., 1978-80; asst. prof. Columbia U., N.Y.C., 1980-84, assoc. prof., 1984-85; assoc. prof. social work Rutgers U., New Brunswick, N.J., 1986-95, prof., 1995—; faculty mem. women's studies program, dir. BSW program Rutgers U., Livingston Coll., New Brunswick, 1987-89; chair, adminstr. policy and practice area MSW program Rutgers U., New Brunswick, 1992-95; cons. United Way of Westchester, White Plains, 1980, Family Info. and Referral Svc. Teams, Inc., White Plains, 1980-83, 87, James Bell Assoc., 1994—; mem. scholar's adv. coun. Ind. U. Ctr. on Philanthropy. Author: The Urban Development Corporation: Private Interests and Public Authority, 1975, The United Way: Dilemmas of Organized Charity, 1990. Mem. Westchester County Homeless Crisis Action Group, 1985-86, chair long range planning com., 1986; mem. Westchester Commn. on the Homeless, 1986-87; bd. dirs. Hudson Valley Health Sys. Agy., 1978-86, Nat. Ctr. for Social Policy and Practice, 1986-88; mem. Commn. on Mental Health and Children, Senator Nicholas Spano chair, N.Y. State, 1989-92; mem. ho. of dels. Coun. Social Work Edn., 1987-89; mem. Scholars Adv. Coun. of the Ind. U. Ctr. on Philanthropy, 1993—. U.S. Fulbright grantee, 1972-73, NIMH grantee 1968-69; fellow Douglass Coll., Rutgers U., 1992—. Mem. NASW (rep. to del. assembly 1987, 90, nat. treas. 1989-91), Assn. for Rsch. on Non-Profit Orgns., and Vol. Action, Nat. Coun. for Rsch. on Women, Assn. for Cmty. Orgn. and Social Adminstrn. Home: 10 Wayside Ln Scarsdale NY 10583-2908 Office: Rutgers U Sch Social Work 536 George St New Brunswick NJ 08901-1167

BRILLIANT, RICHARD LEWIS, optometrist, consultant, educator, researcher; b. Bklyn., Jan. 11, 1950; s. Seymour and Yvette (Silverman) B.; m. Karen Ann McNerney, aug. 11, 1974; children: Scott, Joshua. BS, SUNY, New Paltz, 1972; OD, Pa. Coll. Optometry, Phila., 1976. Diplomate in low vision Am. Acad. Optometry. Resident in low vision Pa. Coll. Optometry, Phila., 1976-77, assoc. prof., 1980—; clin. faculty Temple U. Hosp., Phila., 1980-90; chief low vision dept. Eye Inst./Pa. Coll. Optometry, Phila., 1980-90, sr. low vision clinician, 1990—; dir. Moore Low Vision Svc. Mercy Haverford Hosp., Havertown, Pa., 1994—; low vision cons. Ophthalmic Educators, Wyomissing, Pa., 1993—; mem. adv. bd. Dog Guide Users Network, Trevose, Pa., 1993—, Pa. Lions Sight Conservaton and Eye Rsch. Found., Feasterville, 1994—; optometric advisor Bur. Profl. and Occupational Affairs, Harrisburg, Pa., 1994—. Editor low vision sect. Rev. of Optometry, 1978; mem. editorial adv. bd. Jour. Vision Rehab., 1983; codeveloper Honeybee lens. Bd. dirs. Nat. Exhibits of Blind Artists, Pa., 1981-85; advisor Pa. Dept. Transp., Harrisburg, 1986—; mem. Coun. of Citizens with Low Vision, Phila., 1990—. Recipient Best Tech. Article award Optometric Editors Assn., 1983, Four Chaplains Legion of Honor award, 1982; grantee Am. Optometric Assn., 1978, Ben Franklin Found., 1988. Fellow Am. Acad. Optometry; mem. Am. Assn. Workers for the Blind. Office: The Eye Inst 1201 W Spencer St Philadelphia PA 19141

BRIM, ORVILLE GILBERT, JR., former foundation administrator, author; b. Elmira, N.Y., Apr. 7, 1923; s. Orville G(ilbert) and Helen (Whittier) B.; m. Kathleen J. Vigneron, May 30, 1944; children: John G., Scott W., Margaret L., Sarah M. B.A., Yale U., 1947, M.A., 1949, Ph.D. in Sociology, 1951. Instr. sociology U. Wis., 1952-53, asst. prof., 1953-55; sociologist Russell Sage Found., N.Y.C., 1955-64; asst. sec. Russell Sage Found., 1959-64, pres., 1964-72, trustee, 1964-72, cons., 1972-74; pres. Found. for Child Devel., 1974-85; mem. core study group MacArthur Found. Rsch. Program Successful Aging, 1985-89; dir. MacArthur Found. Rsch. Network on Successful Mid Life Devel., 1989—; pres. Life Trends, Inc., 1991—; vis. scholar Russell Sage Found., 1985-86; vice chmn. Am. Inst. for Research, 1971-88, chmn. 1988-91; chmn. bd. dirs. Automation Engring. Lab., 1959-67; dir. Consumer Behavior, Inc., 1957-61; chmn. environ. panel U.S. Office Edn., 1962-64; mem. drug research bd. Nat. Acad. Scis., 1964-66, adv. com. on child devel., 1971-76; mem. mental health tng. com. NIMH, 1959-62; chmn. commn. social scis. NSF, 1968-69; nat. adv. food and drug council HEW, 1967-69; chmn. com. on work and personality in middle years Social Sci. Research Council, 1972-79; trustee Found. for Child Devel., 1972-85, Center for Creative Leadership, 1972-78, Mental Health Law Project, 1973-77, William T. Grant Found., 1975-84, Greenwich Hosp., 1972-77. Author: Sociology and the Field of Education, 1958, Education for Child Rearing, 1959, Personality and Decision Processes, 1962, Intelligence: Perspectives 1965, 1966, Socialization after Childhood: Two Essays, 1966, American Beliefs and Attitudes Toward Intelligence, 1969, The Dying Patient, 1970, Learning to Be Parents, 1980, Ambition: How We Manage Success and Failure Throughout Our Lives, 1992; editor: Lifespan Development and Behavior, Vol. 2-6, 1979-83, Constancy and Change in Human Development, 1980; cons. editor: Child Devel., 1958-61, Sociology of Edn., 1963-69, Sociometry, 1959-62; mem. publ. com.: The Public Interest, 1967-75. Served as 1st lt. USAAF, 1943-46. Recipient Wilbur Lucius Cross medal Yale Grad. Sch. Assn., 1975; Kurt Lewin Meml. award Soc. Psychol. Study Social Issues, 1979. Fellow Am. Sociol. Assn., Am. Psychol. Assn., Am. Acad. Arts and Scis., AAAS, Am. Orthopsychiat. Assn. (pres. 1974-75), Eastern Sociol. Soc. (pres. 1971-72); mem. Inst. Medicine of Nat. Acad. Scis., Soc. Research Child Devel. (Disting. Sci. Contbns.award, 1985), Authors Guild. Club: Century.

BRINDIS, LEWIS W., physician assistant; b. Lawrence, Mass., Dec. 1, 1948; s. George J. and Phyllis B. (Baer) B.; 1 child, William C. BS, Johns Hopkins U., 1976, Syracuse (N.Y.) U., 1970. Registered physician asst.; cert. physician asst. Physician asst. Nat. Health Svc. Corp., USPHS, 1978-82; physician asst. correctional health State of N.Y. Dept. Corrections, 1988—; physician asst. Rural Health Samaritan Med. Ctr., Watertown, N.Y., 1982—; mem. adv. bd. County Health Dept., Syracuse, 1978-82. Mem. County Emergency Med. Svc., Clayton (N.Y.) Fire Dept., 1984-90; scoutmaster Boy Scouts Am., 1970-80. Fellow Am. Acad. Physician Assts. (del. 1976); mem. Pub. Health Svc. Acad. Physician Assts. (treas. 1978-82), N.Y. State Soc. Physician Assts. Home: 814 Riverside Dr Clayton NY 13624 Office: Samaritan Family Health Ctr 909 Strawberry Ln Clayton NY 13624

BRINE, JOHN ALFRED SEYMOUR, physician, consultant; b. Perth, Australia, Mar. 13, 1926; s. William Lane and Netta Gwendolyn (Wright) B.; m. Robyn Anne Santo; children: Lindesay, Christina, Jennifer. MB BS, Melbourne U., 1949; M.R.C., Physicians, London, 1955. Resident med. officer Royal Perth Hosp., Australia, 1949-52, cons. physician, 1962-91; resident med. officer Royal Postgrad. Med. Sch., London, 1953-55; med. officer Whittington Hosp., London, 1956-57; pvt. practice Perth, 1962—; emeritus cons. Royal Perth Hosp., Australia, 1992—. Author: Looking for Milligan, 1991. Fellow Royal Coll. Physicians; mem. Milligan Soc. (pres. 1980-89). Anglican. Office: 7 Richardson St, West Perth 6005, Australia

BRINER, WILLIAM H., radiologist, medical educator, researcher. With USPHS Commd. Corps, ret., 1970; with NIH; mem. faculty staff Duke U. Med. Sch., Durham, N.C., 1970—, now assoc. prof. dept. radiology; dir. of nuclear medicine lab. and radiopharmacy Duke U. Med. Ctr., Durham, N.C.; N.C. commr. to Southeast Compact for Low-Level Radioactive Waste Mgmt.; sec.-treas. Compact Commn., 1983—. Recipient Presdl. award Am. Coll. Nuclear Physicians, 1996. Office: Duke U Med Sch Radiology and Nuclear Med Dept Box 3304 Durham NC 27710*

BRINES, SEYMOUR, psychotherapist, consultant, educator; b. N.Y.C., July 9, 1927; s. Benjamin S. and Rose (Symbol) B. AB, Cornell U., 1951; postgrad., U. Ill., 1952-53, NYU Grad. Bus. Sch., 1964-66; MA in Psychology, NYU, 1979. Nat. cert. sch. psychologist. Rsch. asst. Inst. Communications Rsch., 1952-53; rsch. analyst NBC, N.Y.C., 1955-57; study dir. McCann-Erickson Inc., N.Y.C., 1958-62; pres. Brines Assocs., N.Y.C., 1962—; rsch. fellow N.Y. State Office Mental Health, 1976; cons., psychotherapist Office of Rel. Svcs. N.Y.C. Bd. Edn., 1991-93; mental health psychotherapist St. Vincent's Svcs. Outpatient Clinic, 1986-91; lectr. psychology Bloomfield (N.J.) Coll., 1987; vis. asst. prof. Pratt Inst., Bklyn., 1988-89; adj. lectr. Kingsborough C.C., CUNY, 1989—; adj. faculty in human svcs., Touro Coll., N.Y.C., 1994; adj. faculty Nassau C.C., SUNY, 1995; cons. N.Y. State Office Mental Health, 1981, Readership Rsch. Co., Tuckahoe, N.Y., 1973-76; dir. market rsch. Hayden Pub. Co., Rochelle Park, N.J., 1973. N.Y. tuition scholar Cornell U., 1948-51. Mem. Am. Psychol. Assn., Cornell Alumni Fedn., Cornell Club (N.Y.). Home: 2930 W 5th St Brooklyn NY 11224-4836

BRINEY, ALLAN KING, radiologist; b. Wilkinsburg, Pa., Nov. 17, 1921; s. Alonzo Tripp and Helen Marie (Hardman) B.; m. Gayle Diane Briney, July 4, 1986; children: Ronald A., Nancy E., Barbara A., Douglas C. BS summa cum laude, U. Pitts., 1943, MD, 1945; intern, Pitts. Hosp., 1945-46; fellow for Radiology, Hosp. U. for Pa., 1948-51. Diplomate Am. Bd. Radiology. Radiologist Topeka (Kans.) Med. Ctr., 1951-53, Murphy Meml. Hosp., Whittier, Calif., 1953-62, Whittier Radiology Med. Group, 1953-94, Memrad Med. Group, Whittier, 1995—; chief of staff Presbyn. Intercommunity Hosp., Whittier, 1979; chmn. risk mgmt. Presbyn. Intercommunity Hosp., 1981-91, radiologist, 1959—; chmn. bd. So. Calif. Physicians Ins. Exch., Beverly Hills, 1976—. Capt. USAF, 1946-48. fellow Am. Coll. Radiology, 1969. Libertarian. Mem. Deist Ch. Home: 14084 Bronte Dr Whittier CA 90602-2608

BRINK, ARTHUR M., hospital administrator; b. Madison, Wis., Sept. 20, 1943; s. Arthur M. and Shirlee (Quinn) B.; children: Damon J., Justin K., Sunny A.; m. Katharin R. Brink; children: Sean K. Riehl, Caroline M. Riehl, Katie K. Davis. BS in Edn., U. Vt., 1966, MAT in History, 1969. Cert. fin. planner. Alumni dir. U. Vt., Burlington, 1966-77, dir. ann. fund, 1977-78; dir. devel. U. Vt. and Med. Ctr. Hosp., Burlington, 1978-95; v.p. Vt. Health Found., Burlington, 1983-95; dir. devel. Fletcher Allen Health Care, 1995—; bd. dirs. Stratevest Group, Stratwest of Bank North Group, Inc., 1996—; chmn. dist. 1 Council for Advancement and Support Higher Edn., New Eng., 1982-83; chmn. Assn. Am. Med. Colls./Group on Pub. Affairs, Washington, 1986-87. Contbr. articles to profl. jours. Pres. Burlington Boys Club, 1986-88; bd. dirs. United Way, Burlington. Served to capt. F.A. U.S. Army, 1969-71, Vietnam. Decorated Bronze Star with Oak Leaf cluster, Air Medal with Oak Leaf cluster. Fellow Nat. Assn. Hosp. Devel.; mem. Rotary (pres. 1985-86). Home: 20 Hagan Dr Essex Junction VT 05452-3365 Office: Fletcher Allen Health Care Development Office 111 Colchester Ave Burlington VT 05401-1429

BRINK, MARION ALICE, employee assistance professional; b. Boston, Feb. 15, 1928; d. Martin Bernhard and Astrid Marie (Bjaastad) Windedal; m. A. Rudie Shobaken, Feb. 5, 1947 (div. 1963); children: Richard Michael, Ron Eric; m. James A Brink, Jan. 29, 1977. Student, Cambridge Jr. Coll., 1945-47, Framingham State Coll., 1967, Boston U., 1967-69; BA, U. N.H., 1983; M in Theol. Studies, Harvard U., 1987. From lab tech. to chemist Liberty Mut. Rsch., Hopkinton, Mass., 1963-77; asst. to mgr. Rec. Sec. Office Harvard U., 1977-79; sec. Sloan Sch. MIT, 1980-82; owner tech. typing svc. New Castle, N.H., 1982-84; counseling intern Green Pastures Counseling Ctr., Dover, N.H., 1984-85; alcohol educator Freedom From Chem. Dependency Found., Inc., Needham, Mass., 1985-87; dir. devel., editor News Bulletin Freedom From Chem. Dependency Found., Inc., Needham, 1987-88; ptnr. Palmerbrink, Charlestown, Mass., 1989-90; founder MB Assocs., Charlestown, 1991—. Counselor Women's Resource Ctr., Portsmouth, 1980; treas., bd. dirs. Friends of Metro Boston, Inc.; mem. canteen com. Lindemann Mental Health Ctr. Mem. Employee Assistance Profls. Assn., Am. Acad. of Health Care Providers in the Addictive Disorders, Ctr. for Process Studies. Democrat. Unitarian. Home: 86 Wentworth Rd New Castle NH 03854

BRINKHOUS, KENNETH MERLE, pathologist, educator; b. Clayton County, Iowa, May 29, 1908; s. William and Ida (Voss) B.; m. Frances E. Benton, Sept. 5, 1936; children: William Kenneth, John Robert. Student, U.S. Mil. Acad., 1925; AB, U. Iowa, 1929, MD, 1932; DSc, U. Chgo., 1967, U. N.C., 1995. Asst. in pathology U. Iowa, 1932-33, instr., 1933-35, assoc. in pathology, 1935-37, asst. prof., 1937-45, assoc. prof., 1945-46; prof. pathology U. N.C., Chapel Hill, 1946-61; alumni distinguished prof. U. N.C., 1961-80, emeritus, 1980—; Mem. Nat. Adv. Heart and Lung Council, 1969-74; chmn. med. adv. council Nat. Hemophilia Found., 1954-73; sec. gen. Internat. Com. Hemostasis and Thrombosis, 1966-78. Bd. editors Perspectives in Biol. Medicine, 1968—; editor Archives Pathology and Lab. Medicine, 1974-83, Yearbook Pathology Clin. Pathology, 1980-91. Served from capt. to lt. col. M.C. U.S. Army, 1941-46; col. Med. Res. Corps 1946—. Co-recipient Ward Burdick award Am. Soc. Clin. Pathologists, 1941, 63, O. Max Gardner award, 1961, N.C. award, 1969, Internat. Heart Rsch. award, 1969, Murray Thelin award Nat. Hemophilia Found., 1972, Disting. Achievement award Modern Medicine, 1973, Maude Abbott award Internat. Acad. Pathology, 1985, Disting. Svc. award AMA, 1986, 50th Yr. Rsch. award NIH, 1992, Landsteiner award Am. Assn. Blood Banks, 1994; named H.P. Smith lectr., 1974. Mem. Nat. Acad. Scis. Inst. of Medicine, Am. Acad. Arts and Scis., Assn. Am. Physicians, Internat. Soc. Thrombosis and Haemostasis (pres. 1971, Robert P. Grant award 1985), Am. Assn. Pathologists and Bacteriologists (sec., treas. 1968-71, pres. 1973, Goldheaded Cane award 1981), Am. Soc. Exptl. Pathology (pres. 1965-66), Fedn. Am. Socs. Exptl. Biology (pres. 1966-67), Univs. Assoc. Research and Edn. Pathology (pres. 1964-68), Assn. Pathology Chmn. (Disting. Svc. award 1989), Acad. Clin. Lab. Physicians and Scientists (Cotlove award 1991). Home: 524 Dogwood Dr Chapel Hill NC 27516-2884

BRINKLEY, GLENDA WILLIS, medical and surgical nurse, women's health nurse; b. Gore Springs, Miss., Dec. 23, 1961; d. Stark Willis and Loree Conley; m. Timothy L. Brinkley, Sept. 15, 1984; children: Victoria Celeste, Tia Danielle. BSN, Miss. U. for Women, 1987; BS in Biology, Miss. Valley U., 1984. RN, Miss.; cert. perinatal nurse. Edn. coord. Clay County Med. Ctr. Named to Outstanding Young Women of Am., 1987. Mem. Assn. Women's Health, Obstetrics, and Neonatal Nursing, Assn. Profls. in Infection Control.

BRINSON, RALPH ALAN, physician, pediatrician, neonatologist; b. Jackson, Miss., Dec. 31, 1954; s. Ralph C. and Catherine May (Shumaker) B.; m. Pamela Gail Barnett, Nov. 9, 1985; children: Rebecca Gail, Matthew Alan, Jessica Michelle. MD, U. Miss., Jackson, 1980. Diplomate Am. Bd. Pediatrics, sub-bd. Neonatal-Perinatal Medicine. Resident in pediatrics U. Ky., Lexington, 1980-83, fellow in neonatal-perinatal medicine, 1983-85; staff neonatologist Ochsner Clinic, New Orleans, 1985-87, Bapt. Hosp., Montgomery, Ala., 1987-89; pvt. practice neonatal-preinatal medicine, ptnr. North Miss. Neonatology, Tupelo, Miss., 1989-95; pvt. practice Methodist Hosp., Hattiesburg, Miss., 1995—; instr. Coll. Allied Health, U. Ky., 1982-84; instr. neonatal nurse practitioner program Ochsner Clinic, New Orleans, 1986-87; clin. instr. respiratory therapy Itawamba C.C., Tupelo, 1991, 92. Contbr. articles to profl. jours. Treas. First Evang. Ch., Tupelo, 1990-91. Fellow Am. Acad. Pediatrics; mem. AMA, Christian Med. and Dental Soc., So. Perinatal Assn. Office: 5003 Hardy St Ste 302 Hattiesburg MS 39402

BRINTON, GREGORY S., ophthalmologist, educator; b. Salt Lake City, Aug. 2, 1950; s. Sherman S. and Susan Bonna (Ashby) B.; m. Sally Jean Peterson, Apr. 7, 1976; children: Jonathan, Jason, Eric, Jessica, Stephanie, Lindsey, Samuel. Student, Stanford U., 1968-69; BA, U. Utah, 1973, MD, 1976, MBA, 1995. Diplomate Am. Bd. Ophthalmology; lic. Fla., Wis., Utah. Intern Beth Israel Hosp., Boston, 1976-77; resident Bascom Palmer Eye Inst., Miami, Fla., 1977-80; fellow Med. Coll. Wis., Milw., 1980-81, asst. prof., 1981-84; clin. assoc. prof. U. Utah, Salt Lake City, 1984-94, clin. prof., 1994—; staff physician Cottonwood Med. Ctr., LDS Hosp., Salt Lake Regional Hosp., U. Utah Med. Ctr., Primary Children's Med. Ctr., Utah Valley Regional Med. Ctr., Ogden Regional Hosp., Logan Regional Med. Ctr. Contbr. articles to profl. jours. Fellow Am. Acad. Ophthalmology; mem. Retina Soc., Vitreous Soc., Utah State Med. Assn., Utah Ophthalmol. Soc., Bascom Palmer Alumni Assn., Alpha Omega Alpha. Office: 5810 S 300 E Ste 210 Salt Lake City UT 84107 Also: 359 8th Ave Ste 210 Salt Lake City UT 84103

BRISOLARA, ASHTON, substance abuse and employee assistance programs consultant; b. New Orleans, Sept. 14, 1924; B.S. Maxima cum laude, Springhill (Ala.) Coll., 1952; M.Ed., Loyola U., New Orleans, 1960; certificate Yale, 1961, Columbia, 1961; m. Geri Martin, Mar. 12, 1961; children—Sharon, Anne Marie, Joanne, Janet. Tchr., St. Joseph's High Sch., Metuchen, N.J., 1943-46, St. Joseph's Novitiate, Metuchen, 1946-47, St. Willibrord High Sch., Montreal, Que., Can., 1947-48, McGill Inst., Mobile, Ala., 1948-50, St. Joseph High Sch., 1950-52, St. Stanislaus Coll., Bay St. Louis, Miss., 1952-54, St. Francis de Sales High Sch., Houma, La., 1954-55, Cor Jesu High Sch., New Orleans, 1954-55, St. Aloysius High Sch., Vicksburg, Miss., 1957-59, St. Aloysius High Sch., New Orleans, 1959-61; vocat. counselor high schs. and colls. in La., Miss., Ala. and Fla., 1955-57; exec. dir. Com. on Alcoholism and Drug Abuse for Greater New Orleans, Inc., 1961-91; cons. VA Hosp., New Orleans, 1978—, New Orleans Adolescent Hosp., 1982—, VA Med. Ctr. Aftercare Unit, 1981-90. Spl. lectr. dept. health and phys. edn. La. State U., New Orleans, 1961-74; pres. faculty La. Inst. Alcohol Studies, Baton Rouge, 1964-67, spl. lectr., 1966-81, faculty, 1972-81; faculty New Orleans Police Acad., 1961-74; lectr. So. U. of New Orleans, 1962-82, Charity Hosp. Sch. Nursing, 1963-91, Meth. Psychiat. Pavillion, 1985-93; staff Alcohol and Drug Unit, S.E. La. Hosp., Mandeville, 1965—; lectr., faculty Jefferson Parish (La.) Tng. Acad., Sheriff Dept., 1973-90; lectr. div. continuing edn. U. Miss., 1974; mem. exec. com. Blue Ridge (N.C.) Inst. So. Community Service Execs., 1964—, pres., 1975; lectr., group discussion leader Southeastern Alcoholism Clinic, 1965-73; faculty S.C. Sch. Alcohol Studies, 1975; faculty Fla. State Sch. Alcohol Studies, U. Miami, Fla. Technol. Inst., Orlando, 1965-73; hon. capt. New Orleans Police Dept., 1964, spl. officer, 1969-72; dep. sheriff Hancock County, Miss., 1969-72; faculty Southeastern Sch. Alcohol Studies, U. Ga., Athens, 1966-85; faculty dept. psychiatry and neurology Tulane U. Sch. Medicine, 1968—, adj. assoc. prof. dept. health services adminstrn., 1971-82; faculty, sect. leader Utah Sch. on Alcoholism and other Drug Dependencies, U. Utah, 1971-96; vis. prof., cons. U. So. Miss., 1973-85; faculty Southwestern Sch. Alcohol Studies, U. Ariz., 1975-84; vis. lectr. USAF Chaplain Sch., Maxwell AFB, Montgomery, Ala., 1975-90; assoc. dir., faculty Deep South Sch. Alcohol and Drug Studies, Centenary Coll., Shreveport, La., 1974, dir., 1975-80; cons. DePaul Community Mental Health Ctr., New Orleans, 1969-72, N.I.A.A.A. occupational br., 1972-73, N.W. Fla. Mental Health Ctr., Panama City, Fla., 1972-75, Gulf Coast Mental Health Ctr., Gulfport, Miss., 1973-82, S.W. La. Edn. and Referral Ctr., Inc., Lafayette, 1963; bd. mem. La. Inst. Alcohol Studies, 1964-67; staff La. State U. Exec. Program, 1972-93; cons., lectr. Ul Ga. Athletic Assn., 1995—; faculty Rutgers Advance Sch. Alcohol and Drug Studies, New Brunswick, N.J., 1993-95; mem. council of agencies bd. mgmt. Alcohol and Drug Problems Assn. N. Am.; community cons. Nat. Council on Alcoholism, N.Y.C.; mem. profl. advisory com. Social Welfare Planning Council, New Orleans; rep., contractor Anheuser-Busch Employee Assistance Program, 1980-96; EAP contractor Gulf Engring., 1990—, So. Eagle Sales and Svcs., 1996—, Hancock Bank, Miss. and La., 1990—; speaker, lectr. various univs. and orgns. Author: Handbook for Handling the Alcoholic Employee, 1978; co-author: House of Character(s), 1993; contbr. articles to profl. publs. Recipient Dr. Robert Lancaster De Paul Hosp. award for outstanding contbn. to mental health, 1987. Home: 4013 Cleary Ave Metairie LA 70002-4405 Office: PO Box 7321 Metairie LA 70010-7321

BRISTOL, RAYMOND CURTIS, psychiatrist, psychoanalyst, educator; b. Brawley, Calif., Dec. 18, 1932; s. Raymond Cecil and Amy (Ross) B.; m. Marie Drissel, June 2, 1979. BA, Stanford U., 1958; MD, U. So. Calif., 1962; cert. social psychiatry, Washington Sch. Psychiatry, 1970; grad., Balt.-Washington Inst. Psychoanalysis, 1980. Med. intern Univ. Hosp., Ann Arbor, Mich., 1962-63; postgrad. fellow N.Y. Hosp.-Cornell U., New York, 1963-64, Yale U., New Haven, 1964-65; postgrad. fellow Austen Riggs Ctr., Stockbridge, Mass., 1965-68, supr. psychiatry staff, 1968-69; psychiat. cons. Peace Corps, Brazil, 1969; chief psychiatrist Peace Corps, Washington, 1969-71, acting medical dir., 1970-71; asst. to assoc. clin. prof. Georgetown U., Washington, 1975-96, clin. prof., 1996—, co-dir. postgrad. edn., 1990—, codir. programs postgrad studies psychiatry, psychoanalysis, 1992—, founding mem. trauma study group, 1993; assoc. tchg. analyst faculty Balt.-Washington Inst. Psychoanalysis, Laurel, Md., 1982—, chair sci. program com., 1985-87; chmn. Forum Psychiatry, Psychoanalysis and the Humanities Georgetown U.; mem. faculty, co-chmn. Nat. Conf. on Romantic and Love, 1990—; co-chmn. confs. on romantic love Smithsonian Instn., 1992, 93; mem. Cloumbia Hosp. study group on psychoanalytic technique, Milw., 1982—; co-chmn. Nat. Conf. on Love Psychology, Washington Sch. Psychiatry, 1990, Georgetown U., 1991. Contbr. articles to profl. publs. Fellow Internat. Panetics Soc., Internat. Psychoanalytical Assn., Am. Psychiat. Assn. (chmn. task force on conflict resolution 1990-94), Washington Psychiat. Soc., Am. Psychoanalytic Assn.; mem. Balt.-Washington Psychoanalytic Soc., Am. Assn. Pvt. Practice Psychiatrists (founding), Wis. Psychoanalytic Soc. (corr.), Inst. Contemporary Psychotherapy (founder 1994). Episcopalian. Office: 1325 18th St NW Washington DC 20036-6515

BRISTOW, LONNIE ROBERT, physician; b. N.Y.C., Apr. 6, 1930; s. Lonnie Harlis and Vivian (Wines) B.; m. Margaret Jeter, June 1, 1957 (div. Aug. 1961); children: Mary, Mark; m. Marilyn Hingslage, Oct. 18, 1961; children: Robert, Elizabeth. B.S., CCNY, 1953; M.D., NYU, 1957. Diplomate: Am. Bd. Internal Medicine. Intern San Francisco City and County Hosp., 1957-58; resident VA Hosp., San Francisco, 1959-60, Francis Delafield Hosp., N.Y.C., 1960, VA Hosp., Bronx, N.Y., 1961; practice medicine specializing in internal medicine San Pablo, Calif., 1964—; mem. staff Brookside Hosp., San Pablo; cons. Calif. Dept. Health Care in Prisons, Sacramento, 1976-77, chmn. sickle cell com., 1976-79, mem. genetic disease com., 1977-79; mem. admissions com. U. Calif.-Berkeley, 1972-75; mem. Nat. Council Health Care Tech., Washington, 1980; mem. physician discussion group on physician payment Health Care Financing Adminstrn., Washington, 1983-86. Recipient ann. award of excellence Calif. Med. Polit. Action Com., 1977. Fellow ACP (master); mem. Inst. of Medicine of Nat. Acad. Scis., Am. Soc. Internal Medicine (trustee 1976-83, pres. 1981-82), AMA (coun. med. svc. 1976-85, trustee 1985-94, pres.-elect 1994-95, pres. 1995). Home: 3324 Ptarmigan Dr 3B Walnut Creek CA 94595-3157 Office: Brookside Hospital 2023 Vale Rd San Pablo CA 94806-3834*

BRISTOW, WILLIAM HARVEY, JR., psychiatrist; b. Harrisburg, Pa.; s. William H. and Rosa Leah (St. Clair) B.; m. Lillian H. Heise; children: Jill Virgina, Lisa Ann, William H. III. AB, Harvard U., 1949; MD, NYU, 1953. Diplomate Am. Bd. Psychiatry and Neurology. Intern 4th Med. div. Bellevue Hosp., N.Y.C., 1953-54, resident 4th Med. div., 1954-55; resident N.Y. VA Hosp. Dept. Psychiatry, N.Y.C., 1957-60; VA fellow Bellevue Psychiat. Hosp., N.Y.C., 1959-60; pvt. practice Ridgewood, N.J., 1960—; chmn. dept. psychiatry Bergen Pin County Hosp., Paramus, N.J., 1961; former chmn. dept. psychiatry Wayne Gen. Hosp., former pres. med. bd.; clin. dir. Ramapo Ridge Psychiat. Hosp., pres. med. staff. Fellow Am. Psychiat. Assn. (life); mem. AMA, Med. Soc. N.J., Bergen County Med. Soc., N.J. Psychiat. Assn., Assn. for Convulsive Therapy, NYU-Bellevue Psychiat. Soc. Congregationalist. Office: 10 Wilsey Sq Ridgewood NJ 07450-3729

BRITAIN, ARTHUR LEON, physician assistant; b. Balt.; s. Samuel Arthur and Anna Mae (Dawkins) B. BS, Morgan State U., 1971; BA, Johns Hopkins U., 1975; MS, Towson State U., 1987. Clk. typist Motor Vehicle Adminstrn., Balt., 1968-69; employee U.S. Post Office, Balt., 1969-70; caseworker assoc. Dept. Social Svcs., Balt., 1971-72; lab. tech. Balt. City Hosps., 1972-73; physician asst. Young People's Health Connection Balt. City Health Dept., 1975—; mem. West Balt. Adv. Bd., 1978-80; bd. dirs. Southwestern Family Day Care, Balt.; mem. Gov.'s Coun. on Adolescent Pregnancy Prevention, Balt., 1980—; creator, dir. Adolescent Clinic, West Balt. Cmty. Health Care Corp., 1983. Campaign vol. Dem. Senatorial Election, Balt., 1994. Recipient Other Race grant Minority Affairs Office, Towson State U., 1985-87. Fellow Am. Acad. Physician Assts. (cert.); mem. Physician Asst. Assn. for Ob/gyn. Baptist. Home: 3632 Templar Rd Randallstown MD 21133 Office: Balt City Health Dept Young Peoples Health 109 Mondawmin Mall Baltimore MD 21215

BRITSCH, DONNA K., personnel consultant; b. Ottawa, Ohio, Dec. 28, 1955; d. Donald A. and Phyllis M. (Kreinbrink) Hohenbrink; div.; children: Nathan M. Britsch, Tyson C. Britsch. AS in Psychology, Ohio State U., 1982; BS in Psychology with honors, Defiance Coll., 1984, BS in Social Work with honors, 1984. Cert. personnel cons. Exec. dir. Big Brothers/Big Sisters, Ottawa, 1978-83, Lima, Ohio, 1983-85; regional mgr. Cardinal Svcs., Lima, Ohio, 1985-88; cons. SP Assocs., Charlotte, N.C., 1991-96; cons. pharmaceuticals and biotech. SPA Assocs., Charlotte, N.C., 1991—; cons. Job Seekers Club, Charlotte, 1992—; mem. N.C. Quality Assurance Group, 1995—. Youth exch. coord. Lions club, Tega Cay, S.C., 1990—; youth leader Property Owners of Tega Cay, 1994—, pres., 1988—; cons. Jr. Achievement, Charlotte, 1995—; active Tega Cay Comty. Ch. (mem. worship com. 1994—, trainer 1995—, chair facilities use com. 1995). Mem. Tau Mu. Christian. Home: PO Box 3312 Tega Cay SC 29715-3312

BRIZZOLARA, MARY SUYDAM, psychologist; b. Plattsburgh, N.Y., Mar. 15, 1935; d. J. Bert and R. Elizabeth (Beardsley) Mace; m. E. Andrew Brizzolara, Sept. 8, 1973. B.S., St. Lawrence U., 1956; M.A., Mich. State U., 1959; Ph.D. (NIH fellow 1962-63), U. Mass., 1963. Research assoc. psychology U. Mass., Amherst, 1963-65, research coordinator, counseling ctr., 1965-66; assoc. prof. psychology Towson State U., Balt., 1966-70, prof., 1971—; psychologist II Balt. County Dept. Health, 1982-85; cons. North Charles Hosp., 1985-88; vis. prof. Lujiang U, Xiamen, Fujian, People's Republic of China, 1988-89. Mem. APA, Md. Psychol. Assn., Eastern Psychol. Assn., Internat. Soc. Hypnosis, Soc. Clin. and Exptl. Hypnosis, Sigma Xi. Club: Glenmar Sailing. Home: 8040 Forest Glen Dr Pasadena MD 21122-4805 Office: Towson State U Dept Psychology Baltimore MD 21252-7097

BROADBENT, DAVID N., physician; b. Heber City, Utah, July 24, 1939; s. Emer Elwood and Fern Ida (Huber) B.; m. Sally L. Tippetts, Aug. 31, 1965; children: Catherine Louise, David Emerson, Sara Elizabeth. BS in Zoology, U. Ill., 1963; MD, Duke U., 1967; MPH, U. Mich., 1973. Diplomate Am. Bd. Pediatrics, Am. Bd. Preventive Medicine. Intern Vanderbilt U., Nashville, 1968; resident Cin. Children's Hosp., 1969-73; dep. dir. Monroe County Health Dept., Rochester, N.Y., 1973-77; pediatrician The Genesee Health Svc./The Genesee Hosp., Rochester, 1977—; pediatrican in-patient group The Genesee Hosp., 1977—; dir. med. N.Y. State Div. Youth Monroe County Health Svcs., 1977—; cons. N.Y. State Div. for Youth, Albany, 1979—; dir., med. Hill Cumorah Pageant, Palmyra, N.Y., 1987—; mem. instl. rev. bd. Eastman Dental Ctr./U. Rochester, 1979—; attending physician Genesee Hosp./Strong Meml. Hosp., Rochester, 1977—; chmn. patient advocacy com. med./dental staff The Genesee Hosp., 1988—, treas. med. & dental staff, 1991-92; satellite dir. The Genesee Health Svc., Rochester, 1979-80; med. dir. Hilltop Group Home, Monroe Devel. Ctr., 1987-88, Hearing and Speech Ctr. of Rochester, 1987-91. Mem. med. adv. com. Alternatives for Battered Women; bd. dirs. Drug and Alcohol Coun., Rochester, 1970's, Am. Heart Assn., Rochester, 1970's; v.p. Arrowhead dist. Boy Scouts Am., Rochester. Maj. U.S. Army Med. Corps, 1969-71. Recipient award S.E. YMCA, 1981, Silver Beaver award Boy Scouts Am., 1991, fellowship Pub. Health Svc., 1972-73, and others. Mem. N.Y. Pub. Health Assn. (pres. 1977-79), Monroe County Med. Soc., Rochester Acad. Medicine. Republican. Mem. LDS Ch. Office: The Genesee Hosp The Genesee Health Svc 222 Alexander St Rochester NY 14607-4004

BROADNAX, WALTER D., federal official; b. Starcity, Ark., Oct. 21, 1944; s. Walter and Mary Lee (Cotton) B.; m. Angel LaVerne Wheelock; 1 child, Andrea Alyce. BA, Washburn U., 1967; MPA, Kans. U., 1969; PhD, Syracuse U., 1975. Dir. Svcs. Children, Youth and Adults, Kans., 1979-80; prin. dep. asst. sec. HHS, 1980-81; lectr. pub. mgmt. and pub. policy John F. Kennedy sch. govt. Harvard U., 1981-82, dir. innovations state and local govt., 1985-87; pres. N.Y. State Civil Svc. Commn., 1987-90; commr. N.Y. State Dept. Civil Svc., 1987-90; pres. Ctr. Govtl. Rsch., Inc., Rochester, N.Y., 1990-93; dep. sec. HHS, Washington, 1993-96; prof. school of pub affairs Univ of Md, College Park, MD, 1996. Contbr. articles to profl. jours. Whiting scholar Washburn U. Fellow Nat. Acad. Pub. Adminstrn.; mem. Am. Soc. Pub. Adminstrn. (Outstanding Pub. Svc. award Nat. Capital Area chpt.), Am. Polit. Sci. Assn. Home: 1612B Beekman Place NW Washington DC 20009 Office: Univ of Maryland School of Public Affairs College Park MD 20742

BROADWATER, JOHN RALPH, JR., surgeon; b. St. Louis, Sept. 29, 1955; s. John Ralph and Mauleene (Presley) B. BA in Chemistry, So. Meth. U., 1977; MD, U. Ark., 1981. Surg. intern U. Ark. for Med. Scis., Little Rock, 1981-82, resident in gen. surgery, 1982-85, chief resident in gen. surgery, 1985-86; fellow in surg. oncology U. Tex. M.D. Anderson Cancer Ctr., Houston, 1986-87, sr. fellow, teaching assoc., 1987-88; asst. prof. U. Ark. for Med. Scis., Little Rock, 1988—; assoc. prof. surgery, 1993—; vice chmn. for clin. affairs U. Ark. for Med. Scis., Little Rock, 1995—. Contbr. numerous articles and papers to profl. jours. Harold Jeskey scholar So. Meth. U., 1975. Fellow Am. Coll. Surgeons, Soc. Surg. Oncology; mem. ACS, Assn. for Acad. Surgery, Assn. for Surg. Edn., Am. Soc. Clin. Oncology, Am. Assn. for Cancer Edn., Southwestern Oncology Group, So. Oncology Assn., So. Med. Assn., M.D. Anderson Assocs., Nat. Surg. Adjuvant Breast Project, Soc. Surg. Oncology, Lambda Chi Alpha, Phi Beta Kappa. Methodist. Home: PO Box 7309 Little Rock AR 72217-7309 Office: U Ark Med Scis Dept Surgery Slot 725 4301 W Markham St Little Rock AR 72205-7101

BROADWELL, MILTON EDWARD, nurse, anesthetist, educator; b. Plattsburg, N.Y., Sept. 18, 1938; s. Russell Parrott and Carmen (Darrah) B.; m. Elizabeth Longsworth, July 12, 1986; children: Dwayne Scott (dec.), Renee Coleen Demitraszyk, James Russell, Mark Edward. AS in Nursing, Orange Community Community Coll., Middletown, N.Y., 1970; BS in Profl. Studies, Elizabethtown Coll., 1980; MEd, Temple U., 1983. RN anesthetist; cert. registered nurse anesthetist; LPN. Student anesthetist Albany (N.Y.) Med. Ctr., 1971-73; Cert. RN Anesthetist/CPR program coordinator Champlain Valley Physicians Hosp. & Med. Ctr., Plattsburg, 1973; staff CRNA, mem. product standard and evaluation com. Charles S. Wilson Hosp., Johnson City, N.Y., 1973-76; dept. head., chmn. air ambulance team Dakota Midland Hosp., Aberdeen, S.D., 1976-77; instr., trainer in BLS Hershey (Pa.) Med. Ctr., 1980; staff CRNA, instl. inservice programs, chmn. CPR com. Carlisle (Pa.) Hosp., 1977-80; research assoc. in arthroscopic surgery Johns Hopkins U., Balt., 1983; CRNA clin. instr. St. Joseph's Hosp., Sch. Nurse Anesthesia, Lancaster, 1980-87; asst. prof. nurse anesthesiology Med. Coll. Va., Sch. Nurse Anesthesiology, Richmond, 1987-88, asst. prof., dir. clin. edn., 1988-91; owner, operator surg. instrument repair svc. Inventor carbon dioxide intra-articular insufflator; contbr. articles to profl. jours. Treas. Cumberland County E.M.S. Coun., Harrisburg, Pa., 1978-80; emergency preparedness officer North Middletown Twp., Carlisle, Pa., 1980; instr. trainer BLS Am. Heart Assn., Hershey, 1980; instr. ACLS program Paramedic Tng. Inst., Lancaster, 1983. With USAF, 1956-60, maj. Nurse Corps, U.S. Army Res. Named Hon. Life Mem. USAF Air Defense Team, 1959; recipient Appreciation award Boy Scouts Am., 1979, Commendation Letter, SAC, 1957, Meritorious Achievement award U.S. Army, 1991. Mem. Am. Assn. Nurse Anesthetists, Masons, Shriners, Holy Cross Commandary, Elks.

BROADWELL, RICHARD DOW, neurocytologist, neuropathologist, researcher, educator; b. Oak Park, Ill., Nov. 4, 1945; s. Robert and Dorothy Jane (Dow) B. BA, Knox Coll., 1967; MS, U. Wis., Madison, 1971, D Phil, 1974. Staff fellow in neurocytology/neuropathology Nat. Inst. Neurol. and Communicable Diseases and Stroke, NIH, Bethesda, Md., 1974-80; full prof. pathology and neurol. surgery, head Lab. Exptl. Neuropathology and Labs. Neuro-Oncology and Cerebrovascular Studies (Neurol. Surgery), Brain Transplantation, U. Md. Sch. Medicine, 1980-93; sr. scientist, investigator Office of Rsch. Integrity, U.S. Pub. Health Svc., Rockville, Md., 1993—; dir. molecular and cellular neurobiology program NSF, Washington, 1987-89; coord. Decade of the Brain, Vets. Rsch. Adminstrn., Washington, 1991-92; cons. in field. Contbr. numerous articles, chpts. on brain and neurocytology to profl. publs.; mem. editorial bd. Jour. Neurocytology, Jour. Histochemistry and Cytochemistry, Exptl. Neurol.. Rstorative Neurology and Neurosci. Recipient Rsch. award NSF, 1966-67; Japanese Soc. for Promotion of Sci. fellow, 1980-81; NIH Nat. Inst. Neurol. and Communicable Diseases and Stroke grantee, 1982-93. Mem. Neurosci. Soc., Am. Soc. Cell Biology, Histochem. Soc., Chesapeake Electron Microscopy Soc. Republican. Presbyterian. Home: 10939 Brewer House Rd Rockville MD 20852-3456 Office: Office Rsch Integrity 5515 Security Ln Ste 700 Rockville MD 20852-5003

BROAS, DONALD SANFORD, hospital executive; b. Poughkeepsie, N.Y., July 30, 1940; s. Smith Wilton and Ethel Mae (Sanford) B.; m. Betty Jane Langer; children: Nancy Beth, Donald S. Jr., Kimberley Ann, Gregory Michael. BS cum laude, Springfield Coll., 1963; MHA, Med. Coll. Va., 1965. Resident Newton (Mass.) Wellesley Hosp., 1964-65; asst. dir. Malden (Mass.) Hosp., 1966, Norwood (Mass.) Hosp., 1966-69; asst. dir. Robert B. Brigham Hosp., Boston, 1969-72, dir., 1972-77; exec. dir. Hosp. for Spl. Surgery, N.Y.C., 1977-88, pres., 1988-93; pres. Health Care Devel. Internat. Inc., Tarrytown, N.Y., 1993-95; exec. v.p. InterFaith Med. Ctr., Bklyn., 1995—. bd. dirs. Hosp. Chaplaincy, Inc., N.Y.C., 1978-93; mem. exec. com., bd. dirs., sec. Medic Alert U.S., 1991—. Capt. USAR, 1965-73. Fellow Am. Coll. Health Care Execs.; mem. Greater N.Y. Hosp. Assn. (bd. dirs. 1978-82, 87-93), Hosp. Pres. Assn. (charter mem.), Hosp. Adminstrs. Club N.Y. (sec. 1979-81, pres. 1981-83). Home: 1 Larboard Dr Southampton NY 11968-1005 Home: 360 East 65th St New York NY 10021 Office: InterFaith Med Ctr 555 Prospect Pl Brooklyn NY 11238

BROBECK, JOHN RAYMOND, physiology educator; b. Steamboat Springs, Colo., Apr. 12, 1914; s. James Alexander and Ella (Johnson) B.; m. Dorothy Winifred Kellogg, Aug. 24, 1940; children: Stephen James, Priscilla Kimball, Elizabeth Martha, John Thomas. B.S., Wheaton Coll., 1936, LL.D., 1960; M.S., Northwestern U., 1937, Ph.D., 1939; M.D., Yale U., 1943. Instr. physiology Yale, 1943-45, asst. prof., 1945-48, asso. prof. physiology, 1948-52; prof. physiology, chmn. dept. U. Pa., Phila., 1952-70; Herbert C. Rorer prof. med. scis. U. Pa., 1970-82, prof. emeritus, 1982—. Editor: Yale Jour. Biology and Medicine, 1949-52; chmn. editorial bd.: Physiol. Revs, 1963-72. Fellow Am. Acad. Arts and Scis.; mem. Am. Physiol. Soc. (pres. 1971-72), Am. Inst. Nutrition, Nat. Acad. Scis., Am. Soc. Clin. Investigation, Halsted Soc., Phila. Coll. Physicians, Sigma Xi, Alpha Omega Alpha. Home: 224 Vassar Ave Swarthmore PA 19081-1634 Office: U Pa Dept Physiology Philadelphia PA 19104-6085

BROCHIER, JEAN G., immunologist; b. Chabottes, France, Feb. 28, 1940; s. Jean and Blandine Brochier; m. Nicole O. Rougeot, Aug. 30, 1969; children: Clarisse, Laetitia. Ingenieur, INSA, Lyon, France, 1962; PhD, Univ. I, Lyon, 1971. Cert. sci. dir. Researcher INSERM, Lyon, 1967-85; dir. rsch. INSERM, Montpellier, France, 1986—, bd. dirs. Contbr. articles to profl. jours. Recipient Bronze medal Nat. Edn., France, 1984. Mem. French Soc. for Immunology (v.p. 1980-84), British Soc. for Immunology, Am. Soc. Hematology, AAAS. Home: 91 Chemin La Monteille, 34820 Assas France Office: INSERM 291, 99 Rue Puech-Villa, 34090 Montpellier France

BROCK, BARRY JAMES, health services administrator, educator, consultant; b. Grove Hill, Ala., Oct. 1, 1953; s. Ben Jones and Doris (Forehand) B.; m. Denise Defant, Aug. 20, 1976; 1 child, Barry Jason. BS, U. Ala., 1976; MPA, U. W. Fla., 1982; EdD, U. Ctrl. Fla., 1993. Cert. healthcare exec. Dir. human resources Hosp. Corp. Am., Nashville, 1978-85, mktg. adminstr. Orlando (Fla.) Regl. Med. Ctr., 1985-88; adminstrv. dir. Rebound Rehab., Orlando and Nashville, 1988-89; v.p. Healthcare Rsch. & Resources, Orlando, 1989-93; acad. chair Barry U., Miami, Fla., 1993—; faculty U. Ctrl. Fla., Orlando, 1992—; coord. Health Profl. Inst., Seminole C.C., Sanford, Fla., 1992-93; adv. bd. Seminole C.C., Sanford, 1992-93, bd. dirs. HR & R, Mt. Dora, Fla., 1993—. Author: Analysis of Middle Manager Competencies, 1994. Chmn. United Way, Nashville, 1983-85; advisor Jr. Achievement, Orlando, 1986-87. Lt. Comdr. Med. Svc. Corps, USNR, 1992. Mem. Commerce Execs. Soc., Assn. Med. Svc. Corps Officers, Assn. Vocat. Edn. and Rsch., Toastmasters (pres., Nashville, 1984-85), Pi Kappa Phi. Home: 887 Bentley Green Cir Winter Springs FL 32708 Office: Barry U 1650 Sandlake Rd Orlando FL 32809

BROCK, BRIAN, nuclear medicine physician, radiologist; b. Mpls., July 28, 1940. BA, U. Minn., 1964; DO, Kirksville Coll. Osteo. Med., 1968. Diplomate Am. Bd. Nuclear Medicine, Am. Osteo. Bd. Nuclear Medicine, Am. Osteo. Bd. Radiology. Radiologist/nuclear medicine physician Diagnostic Radiol. group, Portland, Maine, 1974-95, Radiology Assocs., Portland, 1995—; chmn. diagnostic imaging U. New Eng., Biddeford, Maine, 1981—; clin. prof. U. New Eng. Coll., Biddeford, Maine, 1993—. Named Clin. Prof. of the Yr. U. New Eng. Coll. Osteo. Medicine Student Body, 1985, 89, 94. Office: 368 Blackstrap Rd Falmouth ME 04105-2411*

BROCK, HELEN RACHEL MCCOY, mental health and community health nurse; b. Cromwell, Okla., Dec. 10, 1924; d. Samuel Robert Lee and Ire Etta (Pounds) McCoy; m. Clois Lee Brock, Sept. 29, 1963; children: Dwayne, Joyce, Peggy, Ricki, Stacey. AS, Southwestern Union Coll., Keene, Tex., 1968; BS in Nursing, Union Coll., Lincoln, Nebr., 1970; postgrad., Vernon Regional Jr. Coll., Tex., 1972, 76; MPH, Loma Linda (Calif.) U., 1983. Cert. ARC nurse. Dir. nursing Chillicothe (Tex.) Clinic-Hosp., 1970-77, Pike County Hosp., Waverly, Ohio, 1977-79, Marion County Hosp., Jefferson, Tex., 1979-81; nurse III, nursing unit supr, patient health educator Vernon State Hosp., Maximum Security for Criminally Insane, 1981—; nurse, admissions and assessments Texhoma Community Health Svcs., 1987-94. Mem. Am. Nurses Assn., Tex. Nurses Assn. Home: PO Box 238 Chillicothe TX 79225-0238

BROCK, WILLIAM ALTON, pediatric urologist; b. Bklyn., Mar. 29, 1946; s. Charles Henry and Mary (Campisi) B.; m. Patricia Skelton, Dec. 8, 1983. BS, Fordham U., 1967; MD, Emory U., 1971. Diplomate Am. Bd. Urology. Intern surgery N.Y. Hosp., N.Y.C., 1971-72, resident surgery, 1972-73; resident urology U. Calif., San Diego, 1975-79; fellow pediatric urology U. Liverpool, Eng., 1979; chmn. dept. pediatric urology Children's Hosp., San Diego, 1984-85; prof. urology Albert Einstein Coll. Medicine, Bronx, N.Y., 1989—; ptnr. Pediatric Urologic Assocs., San Diego, 1979-85, Pediatric Urology Assn., N.Y., 1993—; chief pediatric urology L.I. Jewish Med. Ctr., New Hyde Park, N.Y., 1985—; assoc. prof. urology U. Calif., San Diego, 1980-85, SUNY, Stony Brook, 1985-89; sci. advisor Nat. Kidney Found., San Diego, 1981-85; chmn. quality assurance dept. urology L.I. Jewish Med. Ctr., New Hyde Park, N.Y., 1989-92; vis. prof. Wake Forest Sch. Medicine, Winston-Salem, N.C., 1988, Ohio State U. Sch. of Medicine, 1992; clin. adj. prof. urology Cornell U. Med. Coll., 1995—. Reviewer Jour. Urology, 1990-96; author med. textbooks; contbr. articles to profl. jours. Maj. USAF, 1973-75. Fellow ACS, Am. Acad. Pediatrics, N.Y. Acad. Medicine; mem. AMA, Soc. Pediatric Urology, Am. Urologic Assn., Pediatrics Soc. Dominican Republic (hon.). Roman Catholic. Office: Schneider Childrens Hosp 833 Northern Blvd Great Neck NY 11021

BROCKENBROUGH, EDWIN CHAMBERLAYNE, surgeon; b. Balt., July 24, 1930; s. Edwin Chamberlayne Sr. and Martha Davis (Coale) B.; m. Jean McClure, May 4, 1968; children: John, Martha, Andrew, Ann, Susan. BA, Coll. William & Mary, 1952; MD, Johns Hopkins U., 1956. Intern Johns Hopkins Hosp., Balt., 1956-57, resident, 1957-59; sr. asst. surgeon Nat. Heart Inst., Bethesda, Md., 1959-61; chief resident surgery U. Wash., Seattle, 1961-64, faculty mem. dept. surgery, 1964-75; pvt. practice Seattle, 1975—; clin. prof. surgery U. Wash., 1984—; pres. King County Med. Soc., Seattle, 1992; trustee Health Resources N.W., Seattle. Contbr. chpt. to book and articles to profl. jours. Sr. asst. surgeon USPHS, 1959-61. Fellow ACS (pres. Wash. State chpt. 1985), Seattle Surg. Soc. (sec. 1972); mem. North Pacific Surg. Assn. (pres. 1995), Pacific Coast Surg. Assn., Am. Rhododendron Soc. (pres. 1977-79, Silver medal 1985). Republican. Episcopalian. Home: 3630 Hunts Point Rd Bellevue WA 98004-1114 Office: 1560 N 115th St Seattle WA 98133-8414

BROCKMAN, LESLIE RICHARD, social worker; b. St. Paul, Aug. 10, 1940; s. Leslie Blair Brockman and Mary Emma (Miller) Hemenway; m. Rosemarie Lemus, Aug. 18, 1962; 1 child, Christopher Scott. BA, Loyola U. of L.A., 1963; MS, Troy (Ala.) State U., 1977; MS in Social Work, U. Tex., Arlington, 1984. Rational recovery specialist; lic. profl. counselor; lic. chem. dependency counselor, marriage and family therapist, master social worker; advanced clin. practitioner ACSW; diplomate clin. social work; cert. cognitive-behavioral therapist; cert. compulsive gambling counselor, criminal justice specialist; diplomate Am. Acad. Forensic Counseling. Exec. dir. Family Assessment Consultation Therapy Svc., Ft. Worth, 1984—; commd. 2d lt. USAF, 1963, advanced through grades to maj., retired, 1983. Fellow NASW (diplomate), Am. Bd. Med. Psychotherapists (diplomate); mem. ACA, Am. Assn. Marriage and Family Therapists, Am. Mental Health Counselors Assn., Am. Assn. Behavioral Therapists, Internat. Assn. Marriage and Family Therapists, Nat. Assn. Forensic Counseling. Home: 6400 Trail Lake Dr Fort Worth TX 76133-4810 Office: FACTS Inc 2821 Lackland Rd # 300A Fort Worth TX 76116

BROCKS, ERIC RANDY, ophthalmologist, surgeon; b. N.Y.C., Apr. 24, 1946; s. William Benjamin and Muriel (Welk) B.; m. Irene Loretta Kraut, Dec. 19, 1970; children: Jason Matthew, Daniel Charles. BA with high honors, U. Rochester, 1968, MD, 1972. Diplomate Am. Bd. Ophthalmology, Nat. Bd. Med. Examiners. Intern medicine NYU Sch. Medicine, N.Y.C., 1973, resident, chief resident ophthalmology, 1973-76; chief resident ophthalmology Bellevue Hosp., NYU Hosp., Manhattan VA Hosp., N.Y.C., 1975-76; attending physician St. Francis Hosp., Beacon, N.Y., 1976-89; asst./assoc. attending physician Vassar Bros. Hosp., Poughkeepsie, N.Y., 1976-80, attending physician, 1980—; clin. asst. ophthalmology Tisch (NYU) Hosp., N.Y.C., 1976—; clin. asst. attending physician Bellevue Hosp. Ctr., N.Y.C., 1976—; eye physician and surgeon Hudson Valley Eye Surgeons, P.C., Fishkill, N.Y., 1976—; med. dir. laservision correction Crystal Vision Assocs., Mt. Kisco, N.Y., 1996—; cons. ophthalmology Julia Butterfield Hosp., Cold Spring, N.Y., 1981-94, West Point (N.Y.) Mil. Acad., Keller Army Hosp., 1989—; chief surgery St. Francis Hosp., beacon, 1988-89, dir. ophthalmology sect., 1981-88, chief of staff, 1979-81; dir. dept. ophthalmology Vassar Bros. Hosp., 1992—; clin. asst. prof. ophthalmology NYU Sch. Medicine, N.Y.C., 1983—, course dir. ophthalmology elective, 1976-91; so. N.Y. coord. Nat. Eye Care Project, San Francisco, 1985—; adj. clin. asst. prof. ophthalmology Mt. Sinai Sch. Medicine, N.Y.C., 1993—. Contbr. articles to profl. jours. Vol. admissions network U. Rochester, 1986—, co-chmn. 25th reunion com., 1993. Fellow ACS, Am. Acad. Ophthalmology (media coord. N.Y. state Nat. Eye Care projects 1978—, pub. info. coun. 1985—); mem. AMA, Am. Soc. Cataract and Refractive Surgery, Med. Soc. State N.Y. (ho. of dels. 1984-89, 93—, subcom. officers and adminstrv. matters 1994, govt. affairs subcom. 1987, fed. legis. com. 1993—), Dutchess County Med. Soc. (exec. com. 1992—, chmn. legis. liaison com. 1990-92, pres. 1990-91), Boca West Club. Office: Hudson Valley Eye Surgeons So Dutchess Profl Park 335 State Route 52 Fishkill NY 12524-1515

BROD, ROY DAVID, ophthalmologist, educator; b. Phila., Oct. 8, 1957; s. Kenneth Lester and Carlene Marcy (Chalick) B.; m. Janice Hope Prossack, May 7, 1983; children: Jamie, Rebecca. BS in Biochemistry magna cum laude, Tulane U., 1979; MD with honors, Temple U., 1983. Diplomate Am. Bd. Ophthalmology. Intern in internal medicine Presbyn. U. Pa. Med. Ctr., Phila., 1983-84; resident in ophtholmology La. State U. Eye Ctr., New Orleans, 1984-87; fellow in vitreoretinal Bascom Palmer Eye Inst., Miami, Fla., 1987-88; assoc. vitreoretinal surgeon Geisinger Med. Ctr., Danville, Pa., 1988-91; pvt. practice, Lancaster, Pa., 1991—; asst. prof. Thomas Jefferson U. Sch. Medicine, Phila., 1991-92; clin. asst. prof. Pa. State U. Sch. Medicine-Hershey Med. Ctr., 1992-95, clin. assoc. prof., 1995—; presenter in field. Contbr. articles to med. jours., chpts. to books. Recipient Outstanding Tchr. award Geisinger Med. Ctr., 1990, 91; Tulane scholar, 1976, E.J. and Sarah Evans scholar, 1979, scholar Measy Found., 1982. Fellow Am. Acad. Ophthlmology; mem. AMA, Assn. for Rsch. in Vision and Ophthalmology, Vitreous Soc. (exec. com.), Retina Soc., Rsch. To Prevent Blindness, Soc. for Contemplation Fascinating Fluorescein Angiograms, Atlantic Coast Vitreoretinal Study Group, Atlantic Coast Fluorescein Angiography Club, Pa. Med. Soc., Pa. Acad. Ophthalmology, Phi Beta Kappa, Alpha Omega Alpha, Phi Eta Sigma, Alpha Epsilon Delta, Omicron Delta Kappa. Office: 2108 Med Office Ste 310 2100 Harrisburg Pike Lancaster PA 17604

BRODEHL, JOHANNES, pediatrician; b. Berlin, Oct. 20, 1931; s. Adalbert and Magdalena (Wallis) B.; m. Karin Diemke, Dec. 30, 1964; children: Raimund, Helmar, Marius, Nicoline. Abitur, Schadow-Schule, Berlin, 1949; med. grad., F.U., 1956, MD, 1956; priv. docent, U. Bonn, Fed. Republic Germany, 1967. Rotating intern various hosps., Berlin, Buffalo, 1956-58; rsch. fellow Path. Inst., Kiel, Fed. Republic Germany, 1958-60; resident Childrens Hosp. U., Bonn, 1960-64, chief resident, 1965-70; prof. Childrens Hosp. Med. Sch., Hannover, 1970-80, prof., head, 1981—; pres. Internat. Pediatric Nephrol. Assn., Hannover, 1980-83, German Soc. Pediatrics, Hannover, 1991-93. Fellow Royal Coll. Physicians (London); mem. Nat. Soc. Pediat., Nephrology & Rsch., Internat. Soc. Pediat. Baptist. Office: Childrens Hosp Med Sch, Konstanty Gutschow Str, D-30625 Hannover Germany

BRODELL, ROBERT T., internal medicine educator; b. Rochester, N.Y., Nov. 24, 1953; s. Harold Louis and Alma Jean (Moreland) B.; m. Linda P. Brodell, July 2, 1977; children: Lindsey Ann, Julie Lynn, David William, Erin Elizabeth, Nathan Thomas. BA, Washington and Jefferson Coll., 1975; MD, U. Rochester, 1979. Bd. cert. in dermatology and dermatopathology. Asst. prof. dermatology Washington U., St. Louis, 1984-85; asst. prof. internal medicine NEOUCOM, Rootstown, Ohio, 1986-90, 1990-94, prof. internal medicine, 1994—; asst. clin. prof. dermatology Case Western Res. U., Cleve., 1986-94, asst. clin. prof., 1994—; chmn. Midwest Congress Derm. Socs., Dayton, Ohio, 1995—. Trustee Ohio divsn. Am. Cancer Soc., Columbus, 1992—; bd. dirs. Warren (Ohio) Sports Hall of Fame, 1996. Fellow Am. Acad. Dermatology, Am. Soc. Dermatopathology; mem. AMA, Ohio State Med. Assn., Wilderness Med. Assn., Ohio Dermatol. Assn. (trustee 1994—), Masons (Master Old Erie # 3), Phi Beta Kappa, Alpha Omega Alpha. Home: 2660 E Market St Warren OH 44483 Office: Brodell Med Inc 2660 E Market St Warren OH 44483

BRODER, DAVID L., internist; b. Bklyn., Sept. 23, 1960; s. Howard and Elaine Shiela (Goldman) B. BA, U. Rochester, 1982; DO, N.Y. Coll. Osteopathic Med., 1987. Diplomate Am. Bd. Internal Medicine. Intern, resident Methodist Hosp., Bklyn., 1987-91; fellow in health policy Ohio University, Athens, 1994-95; asst. dean N.Y. Coll. Osteopathic Medicine, Old Westbury, 1995—. Coun. mem. Boy Scouts Am., Bklyn., 1989-91. Mem. ACP, Am. Osteo. Assn., Am. Coll. Osteo. Internists, Am. Osteo. Dirs. and Med. Educators, N.Y. State Osteo. Med. Soc. (bd. dirs. 1995—). Office: NY Coll Osteopathic Med NYIT Old Westbury NY 11568

BRODERICK, THOMAS ROBERT, orthodontist; b. Oshkosh, Wis., Nov. 14, 1952; s. Edward John and Marie Joan (Shea) B.; m. Linda Ann Ryan,

Nov. 26, 1977; children: Patrick Thomas, Alison Marie, Adele Lynn, Michael Kyle. BA, Hiram Coll., 1975; DDS, Case Western Res. U., 1979; MS, St. Louis U., 1986. Pvt. practice, orthodontist Savannah, 1984—; orthodontist Southeastern Ga. Cleft Lip and Palate Team, Savannah, 1987—. Mem. St. James Sch. Bd., Savannah, 1989-91; pres. Mayfair Swim Team, Savannah, 1990-94. Lt. USN, 1979-82, comdr. USNR, 1991—. Mem. ADA, Am. Assn. Orthodontists, Orthodontic Edn. and Rsch. Found., Ga. Dental Assn., Ga. Orthodontic Assn., Phi Beta Kappa, Delta Sigma Delta, Rotary Club (Savannah), KC (Savannah). Republican. Roman Catholic. Home: 7517 La Roche Ave Savannah GA 31406-6401 Office: 5010 Paulsen St Savannah GA 31405-4504

BRODEUR, ARMAND EDWARD, pediatric radiologist; b. Penacook, N.H., Jan. 8, 1922; s. Felix and Patronyne Antoinette (Lavoie) B.; m. Gloria Marie Thompson, June 4, 1947; children: Armand Paul, Garrett Michael, Mark Stephen, Mariette Therese, Michelle Bernadette, Paul Francis. AB, St. Anselm Coll., 1945; MD, St. Louis U., 1947, M.Rd., 1952; LLD (hon.), St Anselm Coll., 1974. Intern St. Louis U. Hosps., 1947-48, resident in pediat., 1948-49; resident in radiology St. Louis U. Hosps. and St. Louis U. Grad. Sch., 1949-52; instr. St. Louis U. Sch. Medicine, 1952-60, sr. instr., 1960-62, asst. prof., 1962-65, assoc. prof., 1965-70, prof. radiology, 1970—, chmn. dept. radiology, 1975-78, vice chmn. dept., 1978-88, prof. pediat., 1979—, prof. juvenile law, 1979—; pvt. practice specializing in pediat. radiology St. Louis, 1954-56; radiologist-in-chief Cardinal Glennon Meml. Hosp. for Children, St. Louis, 1956-88, Shriners Hosp. for Crippled Children, 1988—; assoc. v.p., bd. govs. Cardinal Glennon Children's Hosp., St. Louis; lectr. and cons. in field. Radio show host Doctor to Doctor, Sta. KMOX-CBS, St. Louis; host daily To Your Health; health reporter Sta. KMOV-TV, also Sta. WFUN-FM, Sta. KSIV-AM; TV host Sta. WCVB Channel 5, Boston; author: Radiologic Diagnosis in Infants and Children, 1965, Radiology of the Pediatric Elbow, 1980, Radiologic Pathology for Allied Health Professions, 1980, Child Maltreatment, 1993, also monographs; contbr. articles to profl. jours., numerous tchg. tapes. Bd. dirs. ARC, TB Soc., March of Dimes, 15 others. With U.S. Army, 1942-46, with USPHS, 1952-54. Decorated Knight Equestrian Order Holy Sepulchre Jerusalem; recipient Mo. Health Care Communicator of Yr. award, 1991, Welby award Nat. Acad. Radio and TV Health Communicators, Healthcare Leadership award Met. Hosp. St. Louis, 1994, Lifetime Achievement award Nat. Assn. Physician Broadcasters, numerous civic awards; Armand Brodeur Day proclaimed by City of St. Louis; named St. Paul Man of Yr., 1991. Fellow Am. Coll. Radiology, Am. Acad. Pediat.; mem. AMA (Bronze medal, Golden Apple), Soc. Pediat. Radiology, Radio. Soc. N.Am., Nat. Assn. Physician Broadcasters (charter, co-founder, pres. 1987-88), Sigma Xi, Alpha Omega Alpha, Alpha Sigma Nu, Rho Kappa Sigma. Roman Catholic. Home: 6 Huntleigh Trails Ln Huntleigh MO 63131-4801 Office: 2001 S Lindbergh Blvd Saint Louis MO 63131-3504

BRODHEAD, JOHN LYSTER, medical educator; b. Detroit, Feb. 4, 1953; s. John Lyster Sr. and Sarah Kathryn (Liebermann) B.; m. Jean Brady, Apr. 24, 1992. BS cum laude, U. So. Calif., 1976; MD with highest distinction, Autonomous U. Guadalajara, 1991. Diplomate Am. Bd. Internal Medicine. Clin. instr. medicine U. So. Calif., L.A., 1986-87, asst. prof. medicine, 1987-91, assoc. prof. medicine, 1991—. With USN, 1971-73. Mem. U.S. Naval Inst., Royal Soc. Medicine, Naval Acad. Alumni Assn. Office: U So Calif Dept Medicine 1355 San Pablo St Ste 137 Los Angeles CA 90033

BRODIE, HARLOW KEITH HAMMOND, psychiatrist, educator; b. Stamford, Conn., Aug. 24, 1939; s. Lawrence Sheldon and Elizabeth White (Hammond) B.; m. Brenda Ann Barrowclough, Jan. 26, 1967; children: Melissa Verduin, Cameron Keith, Tyler Hammond, Bryson Barrowclough. AB, Princeton U., 1961; MD, Columbia U., 1965; LLD hon., U. Richmond, 1987; LHD (hon.), High Point U., 1992. Diplomate Am. Bd. Psychiatry and Neurology. Intern Ochsner Found. Hosp., New Orleans, 1965-66; resident in psychiatry Columbia-Presbyn. Med. Center, N.Y.C., 1966-68; clin. assoc. intramural research program NIMH, 1968-70; asst. prof. psychiatry, dir. gen. clin. research center Stanford U. Med. Sch., 1970-74; prof. psychiatry, chmn. dept. Duke U. Med. Sch., 1974-82, James B. Duke prof. psychiatry and behavioral scis., 1981—, prof. dept. psychology, prof. law, 1980—; psychiatrist-in-chief Duke U. Med. Center, 1974-82; chancellor Duke U., 1982-85, pres., 1985-93, pres. emeritus, 1993—; mem. Pres. Biomed. Rsch. Panel, 1975; mem. Carnegie Coun. on Adolescent Devel., 1986—; bd. trustees Com. for Econ. Devel., 1987-90, mem. subcom. on edn. and child devel., 1990; bd. trustees Nat. Humanities Ctr., 1988-93; mem. nat. rev. and adv. panel for improving campus race rels. Ford Found., 1990—; mem. subcom. on Edn. on Child Devel. Com., 1990; bd. dirs. Inst. of Medicine, Mental Health and Behavioral Medicine, 1981-83, chmn., 1981-82; mem. Com. on Leadership Devel., Am. Coun. on Edn., 1990-93; chmn. Com. on Substance Abuse and Mental Health Issues in AIDS Rsch., 1992—. Co-author: The Importance of Mental Health Services to General Health Care, 1979, Modern Clinical Psychiatry, 1982; co-editor: American Handbook of Psychiatry, vols. 6, 7 and 8, 1975, 81, 86, Controversy in Psychiatry, 1978, Psychiatry at the Crossroads, 1980, Critical Problems in Psychiatry, 1982, Signs and Symptoms in Psychiatry, 1983, Consultation-Liaison Psychiatry and Behavioral Medicine, 1986, AIDS and Behavior: An Integrated Approach, 1994; assoc. editor: Am. Jour. Psychiatry. Recipient Disting. Med. Alumni award Columbia U., 1985, Disting. Alumnus award Ochsner Found. Hosp., 1984, Strecker award Inst. of Pa. Hosp., 1980. N.C. award for sci., 1990, William C. Menninger Meml. award ACP, 1994. Fellow Royal Soc. of Medicine; mem. Am. Psychiat. Assn. (sec. 1977-81, pres. 1982-83), Inst. Medicine, Royal Coll. Psychiatrists, Soc. Biol. Psychiatry (A.E. Bennet rsch. award 1970). Home: 63 Beverly Dr Durham NC 27707-2223 Office: Duke U Office of Pres Emeritus 205 E Duke Bldg Durham NC 27708

BRODIE, SHELDON J., physician; b. N.Y.C., Apr. 10, 1926; s. Barnet and Mildred (Maidman) B.; m. Charlotte Kaplan, Dec. 18, 1954; children: Martha Jane, Barnett. BS, L.I. U., 1946; MD, U. Lausanne, Switzerland, 1952; postgrad. med. degree, NYU, 1959. Diplomate Am. Bd. Dermatology, 1961. Intern Kings County Hosp., N.Y.C., 1953-54, resident specializing in Dermatology, 1954; base dermatologist Camp Lejeune, N.C., 1955-56; chief dermatology St. Albans Naval Hosp., N.Y.C., 1956; attending dermatologist NYU Hosp., N.Y.C., 1960—; prof. clin. dermatology NYU Med. Sch., 1961—; dermatologist Bellevue Med. Ctr., Vets. Adminstrn. Hosp., N.Y.C., Mid Island Hosp., Beth Page N.Y. Author: (with others) Archives of Dermatology, Yearbook of Dermatology. Served to lt. M.C., U.S. Navy, 1954-56. Fellow Am. Acad. Dermatology. Home: 12 Donald Dr Syosset NY 11791-5208 Office: Bethpage Med Ctr 4277 Hempstead Tpke Bethpage NY 11714-5706

BRODINE, CHARLES EDWARD, physician; b. Sioux City, Iowa, May 10, 1925; s. Ivar and Dorothy B.; m. Lois Bliss, June 26, 1949; children: Stephanie Kay, Jennifer Leah, Charles Edward. B.S., Iowa State U., Ames, 1948, research fellow malaria project, 1948-49; M.D., Washington U., St. Louis, 1953. Intern St. Louis County Hosp., 1953-54, resident in internal medicine, 1954-55; resident in internal medicine U.S. Naval Hosp., Oakland, Calif., 1957-59; fellow in hematology, clin. instr. medicine U. Cin. and Cin. Gen. Hosp., 1955-57; head hematology svc. U.S. Naval Hosp., Oakland, 1959-61, Bethesda, Md., 1961-62; cons. in hematology U.S. Naval Hosp., 1962-73; head divsn. rsch. hematology Naval Med. Rsch. Inst., Bethesda, 1962-66; chmn. dept. clin. investigation Naval Med. Rsch. Inst., 1966-70, exec. officer, 1970-73; program mgr. Navy frozen blood and trauma rsch. program research div. Bur. Medicine and Surgery U.S. Dept. Navy, Washington, 1962-71; dir. rsch. divsn. Bur. Medicine and Surgery U.S. Dept. Navy, 1973-74; spl. asst. med. rsch. and devel. to Surgeon Gen. U.S. Navy, 1974-77; comdg. officer Naval Med. Rsch. and Devel. Command, Nat. Naval Med. Center, Bethesda, 1974-77; asst. med. dir. environ. health and preventive medicine Office Med. Svcs. Dept. State, Washington, 1977-90; mem. Agt. Orange Working Group, 1982-90; exec. com. Nat. Council Internat. Health, 1982-90; Bd. dirs. Gorgas Meml. Inst. Tropical and Preventive Medicine, 1973-89; mem. Bur. Medicine and Surgery Policy Council, 1974-77; med. adviser ARC, 1975-79; adv. com. Nat. Sickle Cell Disease, NIH, 1974-77; mem. com. on biomed. rsch. U.S.-Egypt Joint Working Group, 1975-77; mem. White House Working Group on Internat. Health, 1977; clin. asso. prof. dept. medicine Georgetown U., Washington, 1971—; Dept. State mem. Nat. Council for Internat. Health, 1978-89. Contbr. articles in field to med. jours. Exec. com. Gorgas Meml. Inst., 1978-88. Decorated Legion of Merit for blood rsch. project, 1968; recipient Meritorious Service medal for work at Naval Med. Rsch. Inst. U.S. Dept. Navy, 1973; Robert Dexter Conrad award for outstanding sci. achievement Sec. of Navy, 1977. Mem. AMA, Assn. Mil. Surgeons (sustaining membership award 1967), Acad. Medicine of Washington (bd. dirs. 1992—), Soc. for Cryobiology (editorial bd. 1964-66), Soc. Fed. Med. Agys., Western Soc. Clin. Investigation, Soc. Med. Cons. Armed Forces. Home: 9213 Friars Rd Bethesda MD 20817-2313

BRODKIN, ADELE RUTH MEYER, psychologist; b. N.Y.C., July 8, 1934; d. Abraham J. and Helen (Honig) Meyer; m. Roger Harrison Brodkin, Jan. 26, 1957; children: Elizabeth Anne, Edward Stuart. BA, Sarah Lawrence Coll., 1956; MA, Columbia U., 1959; PhD, Rutgers U., 1977. Lic. psychologist, N.J. Sch. psychologist pub. schs., River Edge, Norwood, 1961-66, Morristown, Chatham, N.J., 1967-73; cons. psychologist United Hosp. Newark, 1973; assoc. dir. Infant Child Devel. Ctr. St. Barnabas Med. Ctr., Livingston, N.J., 1977-79; clin. asst. prof. dept. psychiatry U. Medicine and Dentistry N.J., Newark, 1979-90, clin. assoc. prof., 1990—; vis. scholar Hasting (N.Y.) Ctr. for Life Scis., 1979; mem. Essex County Mental Health Adv. Bd., Essex County, N.J., 1985-87; cons. Scholastic, Inc., 1988—; clin. assoc. prof. psychiatry UMDNJ-N.J. Med. Sch., 1990—. Author: Between Teacher and Parent, Supporting Young Children As They Grow, 1994, (with A.T. Jersild and E. Alina Lazar) The Meaning of Psychotherapy in the Teacher's Life and Work, 1962; author, prodr. (video documentary) Competing Commitments, 1984 (Best Ednl. Videotape award N.J. Cable); co-author, prodr. ednl. videotapes: Passage to Physicianhood, 1985, The Insidious Epidemic, 1986; columnist Between Tchr. and Parent, Pre-K Today mag., 1988-93, child devel. columnist, 1991-92; columnist You and Today's Child, Instr. mag., 1992-93, Kids in Crisis, Instr. mag., 1993-96; columnist Adolescent Devel., Mid. Yrs. mag., 1990-95; contbr. articles to profl. jours. Grantee Gannett Found., Cmty. Fund for N.J., Carter-Wallace, Inc., Schering Corp.; Adelaide M. Ayer fellow Columbia U., 1962-63, NIMH fellow, 1962, Louis Bevier fellow Rutgers U., 1976-77. Fellow Am. Orthopsychiat. Assn.; mem. APA, N.J. Psychol. Assn. (Psychol. Recognition award 1982, 86, 90), Am. Sociol. Assn. Home and Office: 2 Trevino Ct Florham Park NJ 07932-2724

BRODKIN, ROGER HARRISON, dermatologist, educator; b. Newark, July 31, 1932. A.B. Lafayette Coll., Easton, Pa., 1954; M.D., Jefferson Med. Coll., 1958; M.M.S. in Dermatology, NYU, 1967. Diplomate Am. Bd. Dermatology. Intern, Lenox Hill Hosp., N.Y.C., 1958-59; resident in dermatology NYU and Bellevue Hosp., N.Y.C., 1959-62; teaching asst. NYU, 1962-64, instr. dermatology, 1964-66; clin. asst. prof. U. N.J. Med. and Dental Sch., Newark, 1966-69, clin. assoc prof., 1969-79, clin. prof., 1979—. Fellow ACP, Am. Acad. Dermatology, Royal Soc. Medicine. Address: 101 Old Short Hills Rd West Orange NJ 07052-1023

BRODSKY, IVAN LOUIS, neurologist; b. Winnipeg, Manitoba, Can., Sept. 21, 1943; s. Joseph Brodsky and Edith (Gitterman) B.; m. Karen L. Steiman, June 5, 1945; children: Adam, Matthew. BS in Medicine, U. Manitoba, Winnipeg, 1967, MD, 1967. Lic. neurologist, Minn., Can. Resident then intern U. Minn., Mpls., 1968-72; pvt. practice Mpls. Clinic Neurology, Ltd., 1972—; mem. staff Meth. Hosp.; med. dir. rehab., chmn. biomed. ethics Com. North Meml. Med. Ctr.; clin. assoc. prof. U. Minn. Past pres. Beth El Synagogue; mem. Mpls. Inst. Art. Fellow Royal Coll. London, Royal Coll. Physicians; mem. AMA, Am. Spinal Cord Injury Assn., Am. Congress Rehab. Medicine, Am. Headache Assn., Am. Brain Tumor Assn., Am. Soc. Neurorehab., Minn. Specialty Physicians (governing coun.), Minn. Med. Soc., Minn. Soc. Neurol. Scis., Spinal Cord Injury Assn., Hennepin County Med. Soc., Spinal Cord Injury Assn., Ctrl. Neuroscis. Soc., Ctrl. EEG Soc. Home: 4505 Heathbrooke Cir Minneapolis MN 55422 Office: Mpls Clinic Neurology Ltd 4225 Golden Valley Rd Golden Valley MN 55422

BRODSKY, JOHN PUTNAM, internist; b. Bklyn., Mar. 11, 1930; s. John Charles and Dorothy Louise (Putnam) B.; B.A., Princeton U., 1952; M.D., Columbia U., 1956; m. Margaret Morse, June 27, 1953; children—John Charles, Carolyn Holmes, Robert Emery. Intern, Bellevue Hosp., N.Y.C., 1956-57; resident in internal medicine and pulmonary disease Bellevue Hosp., N.Y.C., 1957-59, Yale Med. Center, New Haven, 1960; practice medicine specializing in internal medicine and pulmonary disease, Rumson, N.J., 1963—; mem. staff Riverview Hosp., Red Bank, N.J., 1963—, dir. dept. medicine, 1976-78; instr. medicine Columbia U.-Bellevue Hosp., N.Y.C., 1963-68. Served as capt. M.C., U.S. Army, 1960-62. Diplomate Am. Bd. Internal Medicine. Fellow Am. Coll. Chest Physicians; mem. AMA, Med. Soc. N.J., Monmouth County Med. Soc. (exec. bd. 1968-78, v.p. 1978). Republican. Presbyterian. Clubs: Shrewsbury Sailing and Yacht, Sea Bright Beach, Rumson Country. Home and Office: 14 E River Rd Rumson NJ 07760-1515

BRODY, ARNOLD RALPH, research scientist, educator; b. Boston, Mar. 24, 1943; s. Sumner H. and Charlotte S. (Shuldiner) B.; m. Toby Pellman, Aug. 30, 1968; children: Janna Beth, Leah Meredith. BS, Colo. State U., 1965, PhD, 1969; MS, U. Ill., 1967. Postdoctoral fellow Ohio State U., Columbus, 1969-72; asst. prof. pathology U. Vt., Burlington, 1972-78; lab. dir. Nat. Inst. Environ. Health Scis., Research Triangle Park, N.C., 1978-93; prof. pathology Med. Ctr. Tulane U., New Orleans, 1993—, dir. lung biology Ctr. for Environ. Rsch., 1993—, prof. environ. health sci. Sch. Pub. Health, 1993—; Wellcome vis. prof. in basic med. scis. Burroughs Wellcome Fund, 1995; mem. adv. bd. Aspen (Colo.) Lung Conf., 1990—. Author more than 40 chpts. to books; assoc. editor Am. Jour. Respiratory Cell Molecular Biology, 1992—, Exptl. Lung Rsch., 1988—; mem. editl. bd. Jour. Environ. Pathology and Toxicology, 1990—; sect. editor pathology Jour. Lipid Mediators & Cell Signal, 1994—; contbr. more than 115 articles to profl. jours. Travel fellowship to Paris, U. Ky., 1986; grantee NIH, 1994—. Mem. AAAS, Am. Thoracic Soc., Internat. Wildlife Fedn., Nature Conservancy, Defenders of Wildlife, Wilderness Soc. Democrat. Jewish. Office: Tulane U Med Ctr Dept Pathology 1430 Tulane Ave New Orleans LA 70112

BRODY, DAVID HAROLD, internist, gastroenterologist; b. N.Y.C., June 19, 1946; s. Martin and Jeanette (Baum) B.; m. Frances Mary McKeon, July 16, 1972; children: Terrence Scott, Timothy Matthew. AB, Rutgers U., 1968; MD, N.J. Med. Sch., 1974. Diplomate Am. Bd. Internal Medicine, Am. Bd. Gastroenterology. With UMDNJ-N.J. Med. Sch., Newark, 1974-75, 1975-77, 1978-79; internist, gastroenterologist Tri-State Med. Assn., Port Jervis, N.J., 1979-82; pvt. practice Port Jervis, N.J., 1982—; bd. dirs. Franciscan Health Sys., Inc., 1995—. Mem. ACP, AMA, N.Y. State Med. Soc., Orange County N.Y. Med. Soc., Am. Soc. Gastrointestinal Endoscopy. Office: 56-58 Church St Port Jervis NJ 12771

BRODY, EUGENE B., psychiatrist, educator; b. Columbia, Mo., June 17, 1921; s. Samuel and Sophie B.; m. Marian Holen, Sept. 23, 1944; children: Julie Anne Brody d'Autremont, James Clarke, John Holen. AB, MA, U. Mo., 1941, DSc (hon.), 1991; MD, Harvard, 1944; grad., N.Y. Psychoanalytic Inst., 1957. Resident Yale Med. Sch., 1944-46, 48-49, from instr. to assoc. prof., 1949-57; prof. psychiatry U. Md. Sch. Medicine, Balt., 1957-76; chmn. dept., also dir. Inst. Psychiatry and Human Behavior, 1959-76, prof. psychiatry and human behavior, 1976-87, prof. emeritus, 1987—; sr. assoc. sch. of hygiene and pub. health Johns Hopkins U., 1986—; vis. prof. U. Brazil, 1968, U. W.I., Kingston, Jamaica, 1972, 73, James Cook U., No. Queensland, Australia, 1992; fellow Center for Advanced Studies in Behavioral Scis., Stanford, 1975-76, U. Otago (N.Z.), 1981, Inst. for Advanced Studies, Tel Aviv U., 1986; mem. adv. bd. Inst. Social Psychiatry, U. San Marcos, 1968-70; mem. nat. profl. adv. bd. psychiatry, psychology and neurology service VA, 1963-67; cons. WHO (Pan Am. Health Orgn. and Geneva, Switzerland), 1965—; program dir. Interam. Mental Health Studies Program, 1967-69; mem. exec. bd. World Fedn. Mental Health, 1969—, adminstrv. mem., 1972-74, mem.-at-large, 1979—, pres., 1981-83, sec. gen., 1983—; mem. epidemiol. studies rev. com. NIMH, 1975-79, cons. clin. infant devel. program, 1979-81, hosp. rev. com., 1979—, AIDS grant rev. com. 1987—; mem. internat. adv. bd. Peruvian Nat. Inst. Mental Health, 1984—, mem. editorial bd. jour., 1985—; mem. adv. coun. Hogg Found., 1986-89; mem. sci. com. Internat. Social Sci. Council, 1989, exec. com. 1989-91, 92—; cons. UNESCO, 1986—; sr. advisor in Refugee Trauma, Harvard Program, 1989—. Author: The Lost Ones, Social Forces and Mental Illness in Rio de Janeiro, 1973, Sex, Contraception and Motherhood in Jamaica, 1981, Psychoanalytic Knowledge, 1990, Biomedical Technology and Human Rights, 1993; editor: (with F.C. Redlich) Psychotherapy with Schizophrenics, 1952, (with R. Monroe and G. Klee) Psychiatric Epidemiology and Mental Health Planning, 1967, Minority Group Adolescents in the United States, 1968, Behavior in New Environments, 1970; cons. editor Jour. Nervous and Mental Disease, 1959-67, editor in chief, 1967—; adv. editor: Tice Med. Ency., 1967-80, Harper & Row Med. Ency., 1980-86; mem. editorial bd. Psychiatry Digest, 1967-71, Mental Hygiene, 1968-70, Social Psychiatry, 1970-81, Internat. Jour. Psychosomatic Obstetrics and Gynecology, 1984-92, Population and Environment, 1987-92; contbr. numerous articles to profl. jours. Chmn. adv. bd. Balt. chpt. Internat. Students Council, ARC, 1964-67; bd. dirs. Md. Partners of Alliance for Progress, 1965-66, Nat. Assn. Mental Health, 1964-66, mem. profl. adv. bd., 1967-71; mem. adv. bd. Inst. for Victims of Trauma, 1988—. Served to capt. M.C. AUS, 1946-48. Fellow Am. Psychiat. Assn. (life; chmn. com. transcultural psychiatry 1966-68, rep. interam. council 1965-71, trustee 1968-71, chmn. task force family planning 1973-75), Am. Coll. Psychiatrists (charter), Am. Coll. Psychoanalysts (charter); mem. Assn. Behavioral Sci. and Med. Edn. (pres. 1981), Am. Psychoanalytic Assn. (life), Internat. psychoanalytic assns., Internat. Coll. Pediatrics (senate 1978-86), Internat. Assn. Psychosomatic Ob-Gyn (exec. bd. 1977-86), Peruvian Psychiat. Assn. (hon.), Peruvian Assn. Psychiatry, Neurology and Neurosurgery (hon.). Club: Cosmos (Washington), West River Sailing Assn., 14 W. Hamilton St. Club (Balt.). Home: 70 Olmsted Green Ct Baltimore MD 21210-1508 Office: World Fedn Mental Health c/o Sheppard & Enoch Hosp PO Box 6815 Baltimore MD 21285-6815

BRODY, HAROLD, neuroanatomist, gerontologist; b. Cleve., May 15, 1923; s. Julius and Esther (Barowitz) B.; m. Anne Pertz, Mar. 24, 1951; children: David Andrew, Evan Barrett. Student, L.I. U., 1941-43; BS, Western Res. U., 1947; PhD, U. Minn., 1953; MD, U. Buffalo, 1961. Instr. anatomy U. Minn., Mpls., 1949-50; asst. prof. U. N.D., Grand Forks, 1950-54, U. Buffalo, 1954-59; assoc. prof. SUNY (merger with U. Buffalo 1961), 1959-63; prof. SUNY (merger with U. Buffalo 1961), Buffalo, 1963-95, disting. tchg. prof., 1995—; asst. dean SUNY, Buffalo, 1968-69; assoc. dean SUNY (merger with U. Buffalo 1961), 1969-70, Buswell rsch. fellow, 1970—, chmn. dept. anat. scis., 1971-92; acting dir. Ctr. for Study of Aging, SUNY, Buffalo, 1977-80, organizer, curator Mus. Neuroanatomy, 1994—; vis. prof. neurophthalmology St. Mary's Hosp., Rochester, N.Y., 1965-75, U. Copenhagen, 1987, 90, 91, 92, 93, 95; Anthes Wilson Abernathy disting. lectr. U. Toronto, Ont., Can., 1987; mem. com. on rsch. and demonstration White House Conf. on Aging, 1971; mem. biology coun. Canisius Coll., Buffalo, 1969; mem. sci. bd. Buffalo Otol. Found., 1968; mem. nat. adv. coun. Nat. Inst. on Aging, NIH, 1975-79. Abstractor, Excerpta Medica Sect. Gerontology and Geriat., 1959—; sci. referee Science, 1956—, Jour. Morphology, 1958—; sci. referee Jour. Gerontology, 1957-73, assoc. editor, 1973-75, editor-in-chief, 1975-80; editor Neurobiology of Aging, 1981—; mem. editl. bd. Gerontology and Geriat. Edn., 1980—, Exptl. Gerontology, 1984—. Trustee Erie County Meals on Wheels, Legal Svcs. for Elderly. With M.C., AUS, 1943-46. Recipient NSF travel award, 1957, Robert W. Kleemeier Rsch. award in gerontology Gerontol. Soc. Am., 1978; Fulbright sr. rsch. scholar, Copenhagen, 1963. Mem. AAAS, Roswell Park Med. Club (pres. 1978-79), Am. Assn. Anatomists, Am. Assn. Anatomy Chmn., Am. Geriat. Soc., Am. Aging Assn. (trustee 1970-77), Gerontol. Soc. Am. (mem. exec. com. 1961-63, 68-71, pres. 1974-75), Buffalo Neuropsychiat. Soc. (pres. 1967-68), Alpha Omega Alpha. Home: 144 Capen Blvd Amherst NY 14226-3053 Office: SUNY Buffalo Main St Campus Dept Anatomy & Cell Biology Rm 317 Farber Hall Buffalo NY 14214

BRODY, HAROLD JOSEPH, dermatologist; b. Sumter, S.C., Jan. 11, 1949; s. Abram and Sara B. BA in Chemistry, Duke U., 1970; MD, Med. U. S.C., 1974. Author: Chemical Peeling, 1992; sr. editor Jour. Dermatologic Surgery & Oncology, 1991. Bd. dirs. Theatre in the Square, Atlanta, 1986-89, Onstage Atlanta, 1987-90, Calibre Prodns., Atlanta, 1994; mem. Duke U. Nat. Drama Adv. Bd., Durham, N.C., 1994-96. Mem. Am. Soc. Dermatologic Surgery (sec. 1995—, bd. dirs. 1989-91), Atlanta Dermatological Assn. (pres. 1989). Office: Hailey & Brody 478 Peachtree St NE #711-A Atlanta GA 30308

BRODY, JEROME IRA, physician; b. N.Y.C., Jan. 24, 1928; s. Morris and Leah (Lewin) B.; m. Anita Jane Blumstein, Oct. 19, 1959; children: Lisa Ellen, Marion Beth, Timothy Alan. AB, NYU, 1947, AM, 1948; M.D., Jefferson Med. Coll., 1952. Diplomate Am. Bd. Internal Medicine, Am. Bd. Hematology. Rotating intern Phila. Gen. Hosp., 1952-53, resident in pathology, 1953-54, resident in cardiology, 1954-55; resident in internal medicine Grad. Hosp., Phila., 1957-58, dir. hematology, 1970-75; research fellow in hematology Yale U. Sch. Medicine, New Haven, 1958-60; asst. prof. U. Pa. Sch. Medicine, Phila., 1962-65, assoc. prof., 1965-75; prof. medicine Med. Coll. Pa., 1975—; dir. hematology lab Jefferson Park Hosp., Phila., 1981-94, chief hematology/oncology, 1989-94; prof. medicine Jefferson Med. Coll., 1989—. Contbr. articles to med. jours. Mem. Am. Soc. Clin. Investigation, Nat. Cancer Inst. (grantee 1962-75, RCDA award 1965-74), Sigma Xi. Office: Med Coll of Pa and Hosp 3300 Henry Ave Philadelphia PA 19129-1121

BRODY, LESLIE GARY, social worker, sociologist; b. Albany, N.Y., Aug. 30, 1944; s. Sanford and Cyrille L. (Kosatsky) B.; m. Marjorie A. Rubin, Feb. 1, 1970; children: Jennifer, Jonathan, David. AA, Corning Community Coll., 1966; BA, U. Maine, 1970; MSW, Ind. U., Indpls., 1972; PhD, Boston U., 1984. Lic. ind. clin. social worker, Mass. Dir. regional- statewide planning &devel. drug abuse div. Indpls., 1972-74; dep. dir. Iowa Drub Abuse Authority, Des Moines, 1974-76, dir., 1976-77; exec. dir. Eliot Community Mental Health Ctr., Concord, Mass., 1977-83; pres. Les Brody Assocs., Acton, Mass., 1983—. Author: Effective Fund Raising, 1994; contbr. chpt. to book and articles to profl. jours. Vice pres. Congregation Beth Elohim, Acton, 1979-81, pres., 1982-84; v.p. campaign Acton-Boxborough Cmty. Chest, 1986-87; pres. Acton-Boxborough United Way, 1990-93. With U.S. Army, 1964-67. Jewish. Office: PO Box 1121 Acton MA 01720-0014

BRODY, MICHELLE ELIZABETH, pediatrician; b. Syracuse, N.Y., Mar. 26, 1962; d. John Paul and Margaret Mary (Coyle) B.; m. Gregory Eugene Stump. BS in Biology, Coll. St. Elizabeth, Convent Station, N.J., 1983; MS, U.Md., 1987; DO, Phila. Coll. Osteo. Medicine, 1992. Intern, resident U. Medicine and Dentistry N.J., Stratford, 1992-93; pediatric resident Thomas Jefferson U., Phila., 1993-96, chief resident, 1996—. Fellow AAP. Home: 2620 Majestic Dr Wilmington DE 19810

BRODY, RONALD L., rehabilitation physician; b. Riverhead, N.Y., Dec. 18, 1957; s. Leon and Ruth (Gordon) B.; m. Beth Rosen, July 8, 1978; children: Eden, Jason, Benjamin. BA, George Washington U., 1975; MD, U. Autonoma de Guadaljara, Mex., 1979. Diplomate Am. Acad. Pain Mgmt.; lic. physician, Pa., N.J. Intern Albert Einstein Med. Ctr., Phila., 1981-82; resident Temple U./Moss Rehab. Hosp., Phila., 1982-85; pvt. practice Voorhees, N.J., 1985—; med. dir. Pavilions of Voorhees Therapy Ctr.; past med. dir. rehab. unit Cooper River Rehab. Ctr., Pennsauken, N.J., West Jersey Rehab. Ctr., Gibbsoboro, N.J.; staff West Jersey Health Sys., Voorhees, Berlin, Camden divsns., Garden State divsn., Bryn Mawr Rehab. Hosp., Malvern, Pa. Contbr. articles to profl. jours. Fellow Am. Acad. Phys. Medicine and Rehab.; mem. AMA, Am. Congress of rehab. Medicine, Assn. Acad. Physiatrists, Nat. Stroke Assn., N.J. Soc. Phys. Medicine and Rehab., Am. Assn. Electrodiagnostic Medicine, Internat. Rehab. soc. Office: 2301 Evesham Rd Voorhees NJ 08043

BRODY, THEODORE MEYER, pharmacologist, educator; b. Newark, May 10, 1920; s. Samuel and Lena (Hammer) B.; m. Ethel Vivian Drelich, Sept. 7, 1947; children—Steven Lewis, Debra Jane, Laura Kate, Elizabeth. B.S., Rutgers U., 1943; M.S., U. Ill., 1949, Ph.D., 1952. Mem. faculty U. Mich. Med. Sch., Ann Arbor, 1952-66; prof. pharmacology Coll. Medicine, Mich. State U., East Lansing, 1966-90, prof. emeritus, 1990—, chmn. dept., 1966-86; cons. NIH, 1969-73, NIDA, 1975-79, Internat. Soc. Heart Rsch., 1973—; mem. sci. adv. com. Pharm. Mfrs. Assn. Found., 1973—; U.S. rep. Internat. Union Pharmacology, 1973-76; mem. bd. Fedn. Am. Socs. for Exptl. Biology, 1973-76; mem. Com. Sci. Soc. Presidents; NSF Disting. scholar lectr. U. Hawaii, 1974. Mem. editl. bd. Jour. Pharmacology and Exptl. Therapeutics, 1965-80, specific field editor, 1981-92; mem. editl. bd. Rsch. Comm. in Chem. Pathology and Pharmacology, Molecular Pharmacology, 1972-90; co-editor: Human Pharmacology, 1991; editor: Human Pharmacology Molecular to Clinical, 1994; cons. Random House Dictionary of English Lang., 1964—; contbr. numerous articles to profl. jours. Served with AUS, 1943-46. Recipient Disting. Faculty award Mich.

State U., 1984. Mem. Soc. Pharmacology and Exptl. Therapeutics (John Jacob Abel award 1955, chmn. Abel award com. 1966, mem. council 1969-72, sec.-treas. 1970, pres. elect 1973, pres. 1974, Torald Sollmann award in pharmacology 1995), Internat. Soc. Biochem. Pharmacology, Am. Coll. Clin. Pharmacology, Assn. Med. Sch. Pharmacologists (sec. 1984-86), Soc. Toxicology, Soc. Neurosci., Japanese Pharmacology Soc., AAUP, Sigma Xi, Rho Chi, Phi Kappa Phi. Home: 842 Longfellow Dr East Lansing MI 48823-2444 Office: Mich State U Dept Pharmacology East Lansing MI 48824

BRODY, WILLIAM R., radiologist, educator; b. Stockton, Calif., Jan. 4, 1944. BS, MIT, 1965, MS, 1966; MD, Stanford U., 1970, PhD in Elect. Engring., 1972. With USPHS, 1973-75; tng. med. fellow cardiovascular surgery, diagnostic radiol. Stanford U., 1976, from assoc. prof. to prof. dept. radiology, 1977-84; founder, pres., CEO Resonex, Inc., 1984-87, chmn. bd., 1987-89; provost acad. health ctr. U. Minn., 1995—. Contbr. articles to profl. jours. Fellow Am. Coll. Radiologists, Am. Coll. Cardiology; mem. IEEE. Office: Johns Hopkins U/Sch Medicine Dept of Radiology & Radiolog Sci 720 Rutland Ave Baltimore MD 21205*

BROERING, LEO FREDRICK, dentist, prosthodontist; b. Bellevue, Ky., Oct. 18, 1940; s. Leo Joseph and Mary Louise (McLane) B.; m. Billie Jeanne Mooar, July 31, 1965; children: Dwight Andrew, Heather Lynn. D in Med. Dentistry, U. Louisville, 1965. Diplomate Am. Bd. Prosthodontics. Gen. dentist capt. Ft. Ord, Calif., 1966-67; gen. dentist, capt. Fort Benjamin Harrison, Indpls., 1968-71; removable prosthetic resident, major Tripler Army Med. Ctr., Honolulu, 1971-73, removable prosthetic officer, 1973-74; chief removable prosthetics, lt. col. USA DENTAC, Ft. Bliss, Tex., 1974-79; chief removable prosthetics USA DENTAC, Ft. Knox, Ky., 1979-83; comdr., col. 92nd Med. Detachment, Hanau, Germany, 1983-86; comdr. Area Dental lab., Ft. Sam Houston, Tex., 1986-90; comdr., col. USA DENTAC, Ft. Campbell, Ky., 1991-95; chief removable prosthetics USA DENTAC, Ft. Campbell, 1995-96; cons. to surgeon gen. U.S. Army, 1986-90; mentor gen. dentistry residency program, USA DENTAC; chief removable prosthetics mentor advanced gen. dentistry program, Ft. Campbell, Ky., 1995-96. Contbr. articles to profl. jours. Scoutmaster Boy Scouts Am., Ft. Knox, 1980-82; chmn. Panther Edn. Program, Hanau, 1983-86; coord. United Way, Ft. Sam Houston, 1986-90. Decorated Meritorious Svc. medal U.S. Army, 1979, 83, 86, Order of Mil. Merit, U.S. Army AMEDD Med. Dept., 1984, Legion of Merit 3 oak clusters U.S. Army, 1990, 95, 96. Fellow Am. Coll. Prosthodontists; mem. ADA, South Tex. Sect. Am. Coll. Prosthodontists (treas., v.p., pres. 1986-90). Home: 213 Chelsea Ct Clarksville TN 37043

BROGDON, BYRON GILLIAM, physician, radiology educator; b. Fort Smith, Ark., Jan. 22, 1929; s. Paul Preston and Lela Florence (Gilliam) B.; m. Barbara Walkow Schreiber, June 23, 1978; 1 child, David Pope; stepchildren: William and Diane Schreiber. BS, U. Ark., 1951, BS in Medicine, 1951, MD, 1952. Intern Univ. Hosp., Little Rock, 1952-53, resident, 1953-55; resident in radiology N.C. Bapt. Hosp., Winston-Salem, 1955-56; asst. prof. radiology U. Fla., 1960-63; assoc. prof. radiology and radiologist-in-charge diagnostic radiology div. Johns Hopkins U. and Hosp., 1963-67; prof., chmn. dept. radiology U. N.Mex., 1967-77; prof. radiology U. South Ala., Mobile, 1978-89, chmn. dept., 1985-92, univ. disting. prof. of radiology, 1989-96, emeritus univ. disting. prof., 1996—, asst. dean continuing med. edn., 1981-88; sabbatical leave Univ. Coll., Galway, Ireland, 1988. Author: Opinions, Comments and Reflections on Radiology, 1983; Contbr. articles to med. jours. Maj. USAF, 1953-60. Recipient Disting. Alumnus award U. Ark., 1978, Ark. Travelers Commn. award Gov. of Ark., 1985, Disting. Achievement award Wake Forest U. Med. Alumni Assn., 1990, medal from city of Brescia, Italy, 1991, Joint Resolution of Commendation for outstanding profl. achievement Ala. Legis., 1994. Fellow Am. Coll. Radiology (pres. 1978-79, gold medal 1987), Am. Acad. Forensic Scis. (John B. Hunt award 1995); mem. AMA (ho. of dels. 1988-95, Physician-Spkr. award 1979), Am. Roentgen Ray Soc. (exec. coun. 1974-75, 77-80, 84-90, 2d v.p. 1979-80, gold medal 1996), So. Radiol. Conf. (life hon., pres. 1967-68, sec. 1984-86, Eskridge lectr. 1994), Radiol. Soc. N.Am., Am. Assn. Acad. Chief Residents in Radiology (faculty adviso 1979—, nat. sponsor 1983-93, Malcolm Jones orator 1996), Soc. Pediat. Radiology, Assn. Univ. Radiologists (pres. 1973-74, gold medal 1985), Soc. Chmn. Acad. Radiol. Depts. (sec.-treas. 1969-70), Swiss Soc. Med. Radiology (hon., coord. internat. diagnostic course in Davos, Schinz medal 1992), Internat. Skeletal Soc., Country Club Mobile, Sigma Xi, Alpha Omega Alpha, Sigma Xi. Office: U South Ala Med Ctr Dept Radiology 2451 Fillingim St Mobile AL 36617-2238

BROGGER, ANTON WILHELM, geneticist; b. Capri, Italy, May 13, 1934; s. Waldemar and Elin Thon (Holst) B.; children: Lise, Lasse. Candidate Real., U. Oslo, 1958, PhD, 1967. Rsch. fellow U. Oslo, 1959-68, prof. II genetics, 1994—; scientist Norwegian Radium Hosp., Oslo, 1969-71, rsch. dir., 1972—. Author: Genetics, 1975, Radiation Accidents, 1986; contbr. articles to internat. jours. Mem. Nordic Environ. Mutagen Soc. (pres. 1994-95). Office: Norwegian Radium Hosp, Inst Cancer Rsch, Dept Genetics, Montebello, N-0310 Oslo Norway

BROGLE, RICHARD CHARLES, pharmaceutical company executive; b. Boston, July 12, 1927; s. Albert P. and Dorothy G. (Thompson) B.; m. Lucy F. Torrisi, Jan. 31, 1959; children—David, Nina, Kevin. S.B. in Biology, MIT, 1950, S.M. in Biochemistry, 1953, Ph.D. in Food Sci., 1960. Chemist, Am. Chicle Co., Long Island City, N.Y., 1960-66; dir. drug and cosmetic Warner-Lambert Co., Morris Plains, N.J., 1966-72, dir. clin. and regulatory, 1972-74, v.p. research services and quality assurance, 1974-77; v.p. lab ops. Block Drug Co., Inc., Jersey City, 1978-83, v.p., dir. R&D, 1983-87; ptnr. Fuld & Brogle, Cambridge, Mass., 1956-60; owner RCB Assocs., Montclair, N.J., 1987—. Contbr. articles to sci. jours. Mem. com. Boy Scouts Am., Montclair, 1977-82. Served to lt. US. Army, 1951-52; Japan. Mem. Am. Soc. Clin. Pharmacology and Therapeutics, Inst. Food Technologists, Nonprescription Drug Mfrs. Assn., MIT Alumni Club. Roman Catholic. Home: 8 Kenneth Rd Montclair NJ 07043-2542 Office: PO Box 43258 Montclair NJ 07043-7258

BROHAMMER, RICHARD FREDERIC, psychiatrist; b. Rockford, Ill., Nov. 9, 1934; s. Joseph C. and Marthe Marie (Ringuette) B.; m. Shirley Ruth Noble, June 22, 1956; children: Richard Frederic II, Renee Marie, Rory Christopher. PhB, U. Detroit, 1960; MD, U. Fla., 1964; postgrad. basic tng. diving medicine, Internat. Underwater Explorers Soc., 1973, advanced tng. diving medicine, 1974. Diplomate Am. Bd. Psychiatry and Neurology. Rsch. fellow tropical medicine La. State U., Costa Rica, 1963, Ctrl. Am., 1968; intern Duval Med. Ctr., Jacksonville, Fla., 1964-65; resident psychiatry U. Fla., 1965-68; practice medicine specializing in psychiatry, Ft. Lauderdale, Fla., 1968-93; mem. staff Broward Gen. Med. Ctr., 1968—, Imperial Point Med. Ctr.; chmn. dept. psychiatry Imperial Point Hosp., 1975-80, Holy Cross Hosp., 1981-83. Served with USAF, 1954-58, Korea. Mem. AMA (pres. student chpt. 1961-64), Broward County (Fla.) Med. Assn., Am. Psychiatr. Assn., Fla. Psychiat. Soc., Broward County Psychiat. Soc., Undersea Adventurers, Internat. Soc. Diving Medicine. Republican. Roman Catholic.

BROHMAN, MARK ALLEN, biologist, lawyer; b. McCook, Nebr., Oct. 12, 1963; s. Harold Horatio and Judy Louise (Neben) B.; m. Anessa Jo Schreiner, Aug. 1, 1987. BA in Biology and Chemistry, Chadron (Nebr.) State Coll., 1985; JD, U. Nebr., 1990, MS in Forestry, Fisheries and Wildlife, 1991. Bar: Nebr. 1990, U.S. Dist. Ct. Nebr. 1990. Rsch. biologist Chadron State Coll., 1981-85, Nebr. Game and Parks Commn., Lincoln, 1988-91; rsch. biologist U. Nebr., Lincoln, 1985-87, legal rschr., 1987-88; legis. asst. Nebr. Legislature, Lincoln, 1991; wetlands biologist Nebr. Dept. Roads, Lincoln, 1991-93; environ. analyst supr. Nebr. Game and Parks Commn., Lincoln, 1993—. Mem. ABA, Nebr. Bar Assn., Soc. Wetland Scientists, Lincoln Engrs. Club, Elks. Democrat. Home: 2637 Washington St Lincoln NE 68502-2955

BROITMAN, SELWYN ARTHUR, microbiologist, educator; b. Boston, Aug. 30, 1931; s. Julius Z. and Sara (Sallus) B.; m. Barbara Merle Shwartz, June 13, 1953; children: Caryn Beth, Jeffrey Z. B.S., U. Mass., 1952, M.S., 1953; Ph.D., Mich. State U., 1956. Dir. Biotech. Assocs., 1959-62; research instr. dept. pathology Boston U. Sch. Medicine, 1963-64, asst. prof. dept. microbiology, 1965-69, assoc. prof. dept. microbiology, 1969-75, prof., 1975—, prof. pathology and lab. medicine, 1983—, asst. dean med. sch. admissions, 1983—; assoc. prof. nutritional scis. Henry Goldman Sch. Grad. Dentistry Boston U., 1974—; assoc. medicine dept. medicine Harvard Med. Sch., 1969-74; research assoc. Mallory Inst. Pathology, Boston City Hosp., Gastro Intestinal Research Lab., 1956-71; assoc. in medicine Thorndike Meml. Lab., 1969-74. Contbr.: articles to profl. jours. Founding mem. Digestive Disease Found. Served with AUS, 1952-66. Recipient Outstanding Teaching award Boston U. Sch. Medicine 1st Yr. Class, 1976. Fellow Am. Coll. Gastroenterology; mem. AAAS, Soc. Exptl. Pathology, Am. Inst. Nutrition, Am. Assn. for Cancer Rsch., Fedn. for Clin. Rsch., Am. Soc. Microbiology, Soc. Applied Bacteriology (Eng.). Soc. Exptl. Biology and Medicine, Nutrition Today Soc. (founding), Am. Gastroent. Assn., Boston Gastroent. Soc., Nat. Acad. Scis. (com. diet, nutrition and cancer 1980-83), N.Y. Acad. Scis., Boston Bug Club (pres. 1976), Sigma Xi. Office: 80 E Concord St Boston MA 02118-2307

BROMBERG, ALBERT MARVIN, psychiatrist; b. Jersey City, May 6, 1932; s. Nathan and Anne (Yablon) B.; m. Adrienne Melba Cohen; children: Warren, Alison, Valerie. BS, Coll. William and Mary, 1953; MD, Duke U., 1957. Diplomate Am. Bd. Psychiatry and Neurology. Intern Montefiore Hosp., N.Y.C., 1958-59; resident in psychiatry Duke U. Hosp., Durham, N.C., 1959-61; fellow in child psychiatry Douglas A. Thom Clinic, Boston City Hosp, 1963-64; pvt. practice child and adolescent psychiatry Springfield, N.J., 1964—; staff child psychiatrist Union County Psychiat. Clinic, Plainfield, N.J., 1964-65; acting dir. tng. Union County Psychiat. Clinic, 1965-66, with adv. com., 1968-71, supr. child psychiat. residents, 1968-69; psychiat. cons. sch. systems, Elizabeth, N.J., 1965-70, Union County Regional H.S., 1966-75, Westfield, N.J., 1974-84; mem. child study team, Roselle Park, N.J., 1980—, Kenilworth, N.J., 1978-82, Garwood, N.J., 1989—; pres. N.J. Psychiat. Assn., 1985-86; chief dept. psychiatry Overlook Hosp., Summit, N.J., 1984-88, cons. Valerie Clinic, 1986-90. Capt. USAF, 1961-63. Fellow Am. Psychiat. Assn., Am. Soc. for Adolescent Psychiatry; mem. AMA, Am. Acad. Child Psychiatry, Med. Soc. N.J. (coun. on med. svcs. 1995—). Republican. Jewish. Home and office: 79 Green Hill Rd Springfield NJ 07081-3619

BROMLEY, GARY E., social worker; married; 1 child. BA, Ohio U., 1968; MSW, Washington U., 1975. Cert. clin. social worker Am. Bd. Examiners in Clin. Social Work; lic. ind. social worker, Mass., clin. social worker, Maine; cert. clin. social worker, N.H. Assoc. planner Maine Commn. on Drug Abuse, Augusta, 1973; mgr. alcohol info. and referral ctr. Dane County Mental Health Ctr., Madison, Wis., 1975-76; exec. dir. Washington County Coun. on Alcoholism, Inc., West Bend, Wis., 1976; program mgmt. specialist State. Bur. Alcohol and Other Drug Abuse, Madison, Wis., 1976-77; psychiat. social worker N.H. Program on Alcohol and Drug Abuse, Concord, N.H., 1977-78; asst. to town mgr. City of Exeter (N.H.), 1978-79; interim dir. Stafford County Welfare Dept., 1979-80; psychiat. social worker N.H. Hosp., Concord, 1980-83; ptnr. Seacoast Resource Assn., Portsmouth, N.H., 1981—; bd. dirs. Wis. Substance Abuse Clearinghouse U. Wis., Madison, 1976; instr. impaired driver intervention program N.H. Office Drug and Alcohol Abuse, Concord, 1989—. Grad. Rsch. scholar Washington U., St. Louis, 1973. Mem. NASW (bd. dirs. N.H. chpt. 1986-90, 91—), Acad. Cert. Social Workers. Office: Orchard Pk B3 875 Greenland Rd Portsmouth NH 03801-4164

BROMM, BURKHART F., physiology researcher; b. Wilhelmshaven, Germany, June 30, 1935; s. Franz and Herta (Weber) B.; m. Thussi Klemm; children: Karen, Boris. Student, U.'s Tübingen and Hamburg, Fed. Republic of Germany; MD, U. Kiel, Fed. Republic of Germany, 1965, PhD in medicine and physiology, 1968, Habilitation, 1969. Prof. physiology, dir. electrophysiology dept. U. Bochum, Fed. Republic of Germany, 1970-73; prof., dir. neurophysiology dept. U. Hamburg, 1974—, head Inst. of Physiology, 1977—. Editor: (book) Pain Measurement in Man., 1984, Pain and the Brain, 1995; contbr. articles to profl. jours. Mem. Internat. Assn. Study of Pain (local organizer world congress Hamburg 1987), European Assn. Neurosci. (co-organizer congress in Hamburg 1983), German Soc. Physiology and Pharmacology, Internat. Soc. Physiology and Pharmacology. Home: Jungmannstr 16, D-22605 Hamburg Germany Office: U Hamburg Inst Physiology, D-20246 Hamburg Eppendorf, Germany

BRONAUGH, DEANNE RAE, home health care administrator, consultant; b. Cameron, Mo., Feb. 3, 1952; d. Myron McMillin and Kathryn Marie (Ogden) Bell; m. Richard N. Bronaugh, July 18, 1987; 1 child, Elisabeth Catherine. BSN magna cum laude, Avila Coll., 1974. CNA, ANA. Staff nurse Bapt. Meml. Hosp., Kansas City, Mo., 1974-77; nurse clinician North Kansas City (Mo.) Meml. Hosp., 1977-78; asst. dir. Bethany Med. Ctr., Kansas City, 1978-79, spl. projects dir., 1979-80, dir. critical care, 1980-81; DON Lee's Summit (Mo.) Community Hosp., 1981-84; asst. adminstr. Muskogee (Okla.) Regional Med. Ctr., 1984-86; cons. Creative Nursing Mgmt., Mpls., 1986-87; pres. Liberty Cons., Muskogee, 1992-93; state liaison for accreditation affairs ABC Home Health, 1993-94; regional adminstr. 1st Am. Home Care (formerly ABC Home Health), 1994—; adv. bd. Am Heart Assn., Kansas City, Kans., 1979-81. Mem. Rep. Women's Club, Muskogee, 1988, P.E.O., Muskogee, 1992. Mem. Sigma Theta Tau. Home: 11502 W 127th Terr Overland Park KS 66213 Office: 7611 State Line Rd Ste 250 Kansas City MO 64114

BRONK, MARTIN IRWIN, surgeon; b. Buffalo, Oct. 13, 1952; s. Theodore Tobias and Dorothy (Freedman) B. BA in Biochemistry summa cum laude, Yale U., 1974; MD, Stanford U., 1978. Intern gen. surgery Stanford (Calif.) U., 1979-80, resident gen. surgery, 1980-84, chief resident, 1983-84; gen. surgeon Menlo Med. Clinic, Menlo Park, Calif., 1985—; clin. instr. dept. surgery Stanford U., 1985-92, clin. asst. prof. 1992-96. Chmn. Maimonides Soc. of Jewish Cmty. Fedn., South Peninsula, Palo Alto, Calif., 1993—. Fellow ACS; mem. AMA. Office: Menlo Med Clinic 1300 Crane St Menlo Park CA 94062

BRONLEY, GLENN I., psychologist; b. N.Y.C., Feb. 17, 1953; s. Frank and Bertha (Hyman) B.; m. Sarah Medak, Dec. 24,1976; children: Jonathan, Matthew, Jarred. BA, CUNY, Queens, 1976; MS, U. Utah, 1979, PhD, 1981. Assoc. psychologist Harlem Valley Psychiatric Ctr., Carmel, N.Y., 1981-83; chief psychologist Fishkill (N.Y.) Cons. Group, 1982-1986; clin. coord. Rockland Psychiat. Ctr., Peekskill, N.Y., 1983—; pvt. practice Peekskill, N.Y., 1983—. Fellow Am. Orthropsychiatric Assn., mem. APA, Am. Assn. Marriage and Family Therapy, Phi Beta Kappa, Phi Kappa Phi. Office: 2117 Crompond Rd Cortlandt Manor NY 10566

BRONN, LESLIE JOAN BOYLE MANOV See MANOV, LESLIE JOAN BOYLE BRONN

BRONSKI, BETTY JEAN, health care consultant; b. Chgo., Mar. 21, 1952; d. Joseph Jacob and Helen Margaret (Hruby) B. BS, Marquette U., Milw., 1974, MS, 1975; MS, Cardinal Stritch Coll., Milw., 1987. Speech pathologist Sch. Dist. BrownDeer, 1974-79; project analyst Eaton Corp., Milw., 1979-82; mktg. rsch. dir. SSM- Mgmt. Services, Milw., 1982-86; adminstr. asst. SSM-Ministry Corp., Milw., 1986-87; dir. planning & devel. St. Mary's Hill Hosp., Milw., 1987-89; pres. Carefinders, Inc., 1989—. Vol. Greater Milw. Area Spl. Olympics, 1979-82, Alzheimer's Assn. S.E. Wis., 1992-93; bd. dirs. St. Clare Mgmt., 1992-95. Roman Catholic. Home: 5150 N Berkeley Blvd Milwaukee WI 53217-5503 Office: Carefinders Inc PO Box 17900 # 146 Milwaukee WI 53217-0900

BROOK, DAVID WILLIAM, psychiatrist; b. N.Y.C., Sept. 19, 1936; s. Michael Marysson and Hilda Jeanette (Ascher) B.; BA, U. Rochester, 1958; MD, Yale, 1961 ; m. Judith Suzanne Muser, Dec. 15, 1962; children: Adam Michael, Jonathan Edward. Intern, U. Chgo. Hosps., 1961-62; resident Mt. Sinai Hosp., 1962-65, asst. attending psychiatrist, 1973-80, assoc. attending psychiatrist, 1980-90, attending psychiatrist (cmty. medicine), 1994—; practice medicine specializing in psychiatry, N.Y.C., 1965—; clin. asst. in psychiatry Hillside Hosp., 1965-67; sch. psychiatrist N.Y.C. Bur. Child Guidance, 1967-69; asst. clin. prof. psychiatry Mt. Sinai Sch. Medicine, 1977-88, assoc. clin. prof., 1988-90, adj. assoc. prof., 1990-92, prof. community medicine, 1994—; adj. asst. prof. psychiatry Fordham U. Sch. Social Work, 1970-73; med. dir. Washington Sq. Inst. Psychotherapy and Mental Health, 1977-82; assoc. attending psychiatrist Elmhurst Hosp., 1982-89; dir. group psychotherapy, 1982-90, attending psychiatrist, dir. dept. psychiatry Mt. Sinai Svcs., Elmhurst Hosp. Ctr., 1989-90; attending psychiatrist Westchester County Med. Ctr., 1990-94; dir. div. drug abuse rsch., prevention and treatment N.Y. Med. Coll., Valhalla, 1990-94, assoc. prof. psychiatry, 1990-92, prof. clin. psychiatry, 1992-94; adj. prof. psychiatry, 1994—. Diplomate Am. Bd. Psychiatry and Neurology. Fellow Am. Group Psychotherapy Assn. (bd. dirs. 1992-95), Am. Psychiat. Assn. (exec. coun. N.Y. County dist. br. 1988-91), N.Y. Acad. Medicine; mem. AAAS, Group Psychotherapy Found. (bd. dirs. 1992—), Am. Acad. Addiction Psychiatrists. Co-author, co-editor 4 books including Psychology of Adolescence, 1978; contbr. over 60 articles and book chpts. on group psychotherapy, adolescence, alcoholism and drug abuse to profl. jours. Office: 4 E 89th St New York NY 10128-0636

BROOK, JUDITH SUZANNE, psychiatry and psychology researcher and educator; b. N.Y.C., Dec. 31, 1939; d. Robert and Helen E. (Zimmerman) Muser; m. David W. Brook, Dec. 15, 1962; children: Adam, Jonathan. BA, Hunter Coll., 1961; MA in Psychology, Columbia U., 1962, EdD in Devel. and Ednl. Psychology, 1967. Lic. psychologist, N.Y. Asst. prof. psychology Queens Coll., CUNY, Flushing, 1967-69; rsch. assoc. Columbia U., N.Y.C., 1969-77, sr. rsch. assoc., 1977-80; assoc. prof. psychiatry Mt. Sinai Sch. Medicine, N.Y.C., 1980-90, adj. prof., 1990-94; prof. N.Y. Med. Coll., Valhalla, N.Y., 1990-94; prof. cmty. medicine Mt. Sinai Sch. Medicine, 1994—; rsch. scientist devel. Nat. Inst. on Drug Abuse, 1982-90, sr. rsch. scientist, 1992—, ad hoc reviewer, 1989—, chair study sect. epidemiology, prevention & rsch; ad hoc reviewer NIMH, NSF. Author: The Psychology of Adolescence, 1978, others; contbr. over 100 articles to profl. jours. Recipient 1st ann. Dean's Disting. Rsch. award N.Y. Med. Coll., 1992; grantee Nat. Inst. on Drug Abuse, 1979—. Fellow Am. Psychopathol. Assn.; mem. APA, Am. Psychol. Soc. (liaison officer 1989—), Assn. for Med. Edn. and Rsch. in Substance Abuse, N.Y. State Psychol. Assn. Office: Mt Sinai Sch Medicine Dept Cmty Medicine Box 1044 One Gustave Levy Pl New York NY 10029

BROOK, ROBERT HENRY, physician, educator, health services researcher; b. N.Y.C., July 3, 1943; s. Benjamin and Elizabeth (Berg) B.; m. Susan Jean Weiss, June 26, 1966 (div. 1980); children: Rebecca, Daniel; m. Jacqueline Barbara Kosecoff Plaut, Jan. 17, 1982; children—Rachel, Davida. B.S., U. Ariz., 1964; M.D., Johns Hopkins U., 1968, Sc.D., 1972. Diplomate: Am. Bd. Internal Medicine. Intern Balt. City Hosp., 1968-69, resident in medicine, 1969-72; project officer Nat. Ctr. Health Svcs. Rsch., HEW, Washington, 1972-74; vice chmn. medicine UCLA, 1990-92, dir. clin. scholar program, 1974—, prof. of medicine and pub. health, 1974—; dir. health program RAND Corp., Santa Monica, Calif., 1990—. Mem. editorial bd. Health Adminstrn. Press., 1986-92, Jour. Gen. Internal Medicine, 1987-89, Health Policy, 1986—; contbr. articles to profl. jours. Served as asst. surgeon USPHS, 1972-74. Lita Annenberg Biomed. fellow Inst. Humanistic Studies, Aspen, Colo., 1981; recipient Rsch. prize Baxter Found. Health Svcs., 1988, Glazer award Soc. Gen. Internal Medicine; selected as one of 75 pub. health heroes of Johns Hopkins, 1991. Fellow ACP (Rosenthal award); mem. Inst. Medicine, Am. Soc. Clin. Investigation, Assn. Health Svcs. Rsch. (bd. dirs. 1982-89, Disting. Health Svc. Researcher award), Assn. Am. Physicians, Johns Hopkins Soc. Scholars. Democrat. Jewish. Home: 1474 Bienveneda Ave Pacific Palisades CA 90272-2346 Office: Rand Corp 1700 Main St Santa Monica CA 90401-3208

BROOKBANK, JOHN W(ARREN), retired microbiology educator; b. Seattle, Apr. 3, 1927; s. Earl Bruce and Louise Sophia (Stoecker) B.; m. Marcia Ireland, Sept. 16, 1950 (div. 1978); children: Ursula Ireland, John W. Jr., Phoebe Bruce; m. Sally Satterberg Cahill, Aug. 6, 1983. BA, U. Wash., 1950, MS, 1953; PhD, Calif. Inst. Tech., 1955. Asst. prof. U. Fla., Gainesville, 1955-58, assoc. prof., 1958-68, prof. microbiology and cell sci., 1968-85, prof. emeritus, 1985—; vis. assoc. prof. U. Fla. Coll. Medicine, Gainesville, 1961-63, U. Wash., Seattle, 1965; cons. in field, Friday Harbor, Wash. 1986—. Author: Developmental Biology, 1978, (with W. Cunningham) Gerontology, 1988; editor: Improving Quality of Health Care of the Elderly, 1977, Biology of Aging, 1990; contbr. articles to profl. jours. Pres. Griffin Bay Preservation Com., Friday Harbor, 1985—, Bridge Council on Narcotics Addiction, Gainesville, 1974, Marine Environ. Consortium, 1986—; founding pres. Gainesville Regional Council on Alcoholism, 1976; mem devel. adv. bd. U. Wash. Friday Harbor Lab., 1995—. Research grantee NIH, 1957-80, NSF, 1972-73. Mem. Gerontol. Soc. Am., Seattle Tennis Club. Republican. Episcopalian. Home: PO Box 2688 Friday Harbor WA 98250-2688

BROOKE, MARVIN MCCLATCHEY, physical medicine and rehabilitation physician; b. Atlanta, Dec. 11, 1948. BA cum laude, BS cum laude, Washington and Lee U., 1971; MD, Emory U., 1975; MS in Phys. Medicine and Rehab., U. Wash., 1978. Diplomate Am. Bd. Phys. Medicine and Rehab., Am. Bd. Electrodiagnostic Medicine; lic. physician, Mass., Wash., Ga. Resident in internal medicine U. Fla. Coll. Medicine, Jacksonville, 1975-76; resident in phys. medicine and rehab. U. Wash., Seattle, 1976-78, chief resident dept. rehab. medicine, 1977; asst. prof. dept. rehab. medicine Emory U. Sch. Medicine, 1979-84, U. Wash., 1984-90; assoc. chief of svc. rehab. medicine Emory U. Hosp. Sch. Medicine, 1981-83, dir. Muscular Dystrophy Clinic, 1981-84; attending physician dept. rehab. medicine Harborview Med. Ctr., 1984-90, acting chief of svc. rehab. medicine, 1988; assoc. prof., chmn. dept. rehab. medicine Tufts U. Sch. Medicine, Boston, 1990—, chair dept. phys. medicine and rehab., 1996—; physiatrist-in-chief New Eng. Med. Ctr., Boston, New Eng. Sinai Hosp. and Rehab. Ctr.; instr. musculoskeletal sys., small group and gross group leader, 1986-87; dir. Outpatient clinic dept. rehab. medicine U. Wash. Harborview Med. Ctr., 1984-88; co-dir. Post-Polio Clinic, U. Wash., 1985-87, dir., 1987-90; attending physician dept. rehab. medicine Univ. Hosp., 1984-90; cons. physician rehab. medicine svc. VA Hosp., Seattle, 1984-90; courtesy staff Children's Orthopedic Hosp., 1984-90, Overlake Hosp., 1984-90;. Contbr. chpts. to books, procs. and software, articles to profl. jours. NIH Inst. Rsch. Training grant, 1993—. Mem. Am. Acad. Phys. Medicine and Rehab. (chmn. ad hoc. com. on acad. affairs 1985-86, chair rsch. com. 1993—), Am. Congress Rehab. Medicine Assn. of Acad. Physiatrists (ad hoc com. on acad. affairs 1985-87), Ga. Phys. Medicine and Rehab. Soc. (sec.-treas. 1981-84), Am. Assn. Electromyography and Electrodiagnosis, New Eng. Soc. Phys. Medicine and Rehab. (pres.). Office: Tufts U Sch Medicine Dept Rehab Medicine 136 Harrison Ave Boston MA 02111-1800

BROOKE, WALLACE SANDS, retired surgeon, educator; m. Josephine Critchlow, Nov. 3, 1943; children: Wallace Sands Jr. and Ann Terry Brooke Becker (twins), John. AB, Stanford U., 1936; PhD, Oxford (Eng.) U., 1940; MD, Johns Hopkins U., 1942. Diplomate Am. Bd. Surgeons. Intern, resident Johns Hopkins Hosp., Balt., 1942-44; resident U. Utah Hosps., 1946-48; pvt. practice Salt Lake City, 1949-85; clin. prof. surgery emeritus U. Utah Med. Coll., Salt Lake City; chmn. U. Utah Health Scis. Ctr., Salt Lake City, 1989-92; pres. Salt Lake County Med. Assn., 1957-58, Utah State Med. Assn., 1960-61; chmn. Utah Blue Shield, Salt Lake City, 1965-73; bd. dirs. Nat. Assn. Blue Shield Plans, Chgo., 1970-73; sec., chmn. Utah Rhodes Scholarship Commn., 1949-62; bd. dirs. Calif. Regional Rhodes Scholarship Commn., Pasadena, 1952-62. Contbr. some 25 articles to profl. jours. With M.C., USN, 1944-46, overseas. Recipient Disting. Svc. award Utah State Med. Assn., 1973, Nat. Assn. Blue Shield, 1974; named Disting. Hon. Alumnus, U. Utah, 1994; Rhodes scholar, 1937-40. Fellow ACS, Western Surg. Assn.; mem. Alta Club (pres. 1982-83), Phi Beta Kappa, Phi Kappa Phi. Home: 2260 Parleys Ter Salt Lake City UT 84109-1530

BROOKER, JEFF ZEIGLER, cardiologist; b. Columbia, S.C., Nov. 1, 1941; s. Jefferson Zeigler and Virginia (Ligon) B.; m. Rhoda Arrowsmith, June 12, 1966; children: Jeff III, John, Rhoda. BS, U. S.C., 1962; MD, Med. U. S.C., 1966. Cert. clin. cardiac electrophysiology, cardiovasc. disease and internal medicine Am. Bd. Internal Medicine. Intern, resident Hosp. U. Pa., Phila., 1966-68; resident internal medicine Stanford U. Med. Ctr., Palo Alto, Calif., 1970-71, rsch. fellow cardiology, 1971-73; staff cardiologist Tex. Heart Inst., Houston, 1973-74; assoc. dir. cardiology Providence Hosp., Columbia, S.C., 1974-81; pvt. practice cardiology Columbia, 1981—; cons. peer rev. Jour. AMA, Chgo., 1976-77; local and regional rsch. com. Am. Heart Assn., Dallas., 1977-86. Mem. editorial bd. Jour. S.C. Med. Assn., Columbia, 1991—; editorial reviewer: Essentials of Echocardiography, 1977. Legis. liaison S.C. Med. Assn., Columbia, 1991-92. Lt. comdr. USN, 1968-70. Recipient Best Sci. Article award Roe Found., Columbia, 1991. Fellow

ACP, Am. Coll. Cardiology, Am. Heart Assn. (coun. on clin. cardiology 1975—); mem. N.Am. Soc. Pacing and Electrophysiology, Phi Beta Kappa, Alpha Omega Alpha. Office: 1625 Brabham Ave Columbia SC 29204-2003

BROOKLER, KENNETH HASKELL, otolaryngologist, educator; b. Winnipeg, Man., Can., Sept. 28, 1938; s. Barney and Mary (Freedman) B.; m. Marcia A. Schuckett, Aug. 24, 1961; children: Richard, Jill, Brent. MD, U. Man., 1962, MS in Otolaryngology, U. Minn., 1968. Intern, Winnipeg Gen. Hosp., 1962-63; fellow Mayo Clinic, Rochester, Minn., 1964-67, fellow in neurotology, 1968; practice medicine specializing in otology and neurotology, N.Y.C., 1968—; pres. Rsch. Inst. for Hearing and Balance Disorders; mem. med. adv. bd. N.Y. State Athletic Commn. Bd. dirs. Hebrew Hosp. Author Dizziness, 1991; editorial bd. Ear, Nose Throat Jour., Jour. Vestibular Rsch.; contbr. chpts. to books, articles to profl. jours. Fellow ACS, Royal Coll. Surgeons (Can.); mem. N.Y. County Med. Soc., Am. Acad. Otolaryngology, N.Y. Otol. Soc., N.Y. Acad. Medicine, N.Y. Acad. Scis., Trilological Soc., Barany Soc., Am. Neurotology Soc., Internat. Vestibulometric Soc., Nat. Hearing Assn. (dir.). Office: Neurotologic Assocs PC 111 E 77th St New York NY 10021-1802

BROOKMAN, THOMAS JOHN, physician assistant; b. Bel Air, Md., May 2, 1948; s. Sherwood Wesley and Cynthia Ann (Jones) B.; m. Toni Anne Campanaro, June 13, 1970; children: Matthew Wesley, Katherine Anne. AS Physician Asst., Johns Hopkins U., 1977. Cert. physician asst. Staff physician asst. Ctrl. Med. Ctr., Balt., 1977-79; chief physician asst., radiologic technologist Balt. Indsl. Med. Ctr., 1979—; preceptor for physician asst. students Essex Cmty Coll. Physician Asst. program, 1980—. With USN, 1967-75. Fellow Am. Acad. Physician Assts., Md. Acad. Physician Assts., Am. Acad. Physician Assts. in Occupl. Medicine. Democrat. Roman Catholic. Office: Occusystems 1419 Knecht Ave Baltimore MD 21227

BROOKS, BENJAMIN RIX, neurologist, educator; b. Cambridge, Mass., Dec. 1, 1942; s. Frederic Manning and Miriam Adelaide (Rix) B.; m. Susan Jane Whitmore, May 31, 1970; children: Nathaniel Phillips, Alexander Whitmore, Joshua Cushing. AB cum laude, Harvard U., 1965, MD magna cum laude, 1970. Diplomate Am. Bd. Psychiatry and Neurology, Am. Bd. Internal Medicine. Intern, asst. resident Harvard Med. Svc., Boston City Hosp., 1970-72; resident in neurology Mass. Gen. Hosp., Boston, 1972-74; clin. assoc. med. neurology br. Nat. Inst. Neurolog. Diseases and Stroke, Bethesda, Md., 1974-76; rsch. fellow neurovirology div. Johns Hopkins Med. Sch., Balt., 1976-78, asst. prof. neurology dept., 1978-82; assoc. prof. neurology and med. microbiology U. Wis. Med. Sch., Madison, 1982-87, prof., 1987—; staff neurologist William S. Middleton Meml. VA Hosp., Madison, 1982-84, chief neurology svc., 1984—; examiner Am. Bd. Psychiatry and Neurology, Evanston, Ill., 1980—; chmn. neuropharmacologic drugs adv. com. FDA, Rockville, Md., 1982-85; vis. prof. various schs., U.S., Eng., Fed. Republic Germany, Japan, Spain. Editor: Amyotrophic Lateral Sclerosis, 1987, Brain Rsch. Bull., 1980-90; contbr. papers, revs., abstracts to profl. publs., chpts. to books. Mem. ushers com. Grace Episcopal Ch., Madison, 1983—; mem. talented and gifted evaluation com. Madison Sch. Bd., 1986; mem. com. on VA manpower of the Inst. of Medicine of the Nat. Acad. Scis. Lt. comdr. USPHS, 1974-76. Recipient Nat. Rsch. award Nat. Inst. Neurolog. and Communicative Disorders and Stroke, 1976-78, Tchr.-Investigator Devel. award, 1978-82. Mem. Am. Acad. Neurology (chair govt. svcs. sect. 1995—, mem. animal rsch. com. 1990-95), Am. Neurolog. Assn., Wis. Neurolog. Soc. (sec.-treas. 1985-87, v.p. 1988, pres.-elect 1989, pres. 1990), Soc. for Neurosci., N.Am. ALS Care Registry (adv. com.), Soc. Exptl. Neuropathology, Am. Soc. Microbiology, Internat. Soc. Neuroimmunology, Assn. VA Neurologists (pres. 1994-96, councilor 1996—), Soc. In Vitro Biology, Tissue Culture Assn., World Fedn. Neurology Rsch. Group on Neuromuscular Diseases—Motor Neuron Diseases (steering com.). Republican. Home: 4818 Fond Du Lac Trl Madison WI 53705-4815 Office: Wm S Middleton Meml VA Hosp 2500 Overlook Ter Madison WI 53705-2254

BROOKS, CLIFTON ROWLAND, pediatrician, environmental medicine specialist; b. Louisville, May 8, 1923; s. Herbert Berwick and Ella Tatum (Rowland) B.; m. Agnes Joan McVeigh, June 21, 1947 (dec. 1991); children: Clifton Rowland, Daniel R., Gordon B., Philip H.; m. Berverly Frances Thrower Persons, Feb. 14, 1993. BS, U. Wis., 1944, MD, 1946; MPH, UCLA, 1970. Diplomate Am. Bd. Pediat., Am. Bd. Environ. Medicine, Internat. Bd. Environ. Medicine. Pvt. practice Newark, 1950-60, Metro Washington, 1960-70, Orange County, Calif., 1970-83; clin. br. mgr. FAA, U.S. Dept. Transp., Oklahoma City, 1983-87; exec. dir. Am. Bd. Environ. Medicine, Norman, Okla., 1988-92, Internat. Bd. Environ. Medicine, Norman, Okla., 1988-93, Carl Albert Indian Health Facility, Ada, Okla., 1993; founder Am. and Internat. Accrediting Bd. Environ. Medicine, 1988, Harriet Lane Home 1954-60; instr. Epilepsy Clinic, Allergy Clinic, Johns Hopkins Hosp., Balt.; asst. prof. cmty. medicine Georgetown U., Washington; assoc. prof. pediat. U. Calif., Irvine; prof. oral surgery Loma Linda (Calif.) Dental Sch.; prof. health edn. Coll. Allied Health Scis., Health Scis. Ctr., Oklahoma City, 1987. Author: Audiovisual Training Programs, 1973; editor: Registers for the Boards, 1989-90; contbr. articles to profl. jours. Mem. Montgomery County (Md.) Safety Bd., 1962; mem. sci. adv. bd. U.S. EPA, Washington, 1976-80. Fellow APHA, AMA, Augustan Soc., Am. Coll. Allergy and Immunology, Am. Coll. Chest Physicians, Am. Coll. Preventive Medicine, Am. Coll. Occupl. and Environ. Medicine, Am. Acad. Environ. Medicine, Royal Soc. Medicine (U.K.), Am. Coll. Genealogy (cert.), Huguenot Soc. London, Soc. Antiquarians (Scot); mem. Manorial Soc. Gt. Britain. Presbyterian. Home: 10717 Sunset Blvd Oklahoma City OK 73120-2437

BROOKS, DAVID CHURCH, surgeon, educator; b. Boston, Nov. 9, 1946; s. John Robinson and Dorothy (Kalbfleisch) B.; m. Deborah Gannett, June 21, 1968; children: Margaret, Katharine, David Jr., Emily. AB, Harvard U., 1968; MD, Brown U., 1976. Diplomate Am. Bd. Surgery. Resident Brigham & Women's Hosp., Boston, 1976-83, surgeon, 1983—; asst. prof. surgery Harvard Med. Sch., Boston, 1986-96, assoc. prof., 1996—. Lt. (j.g.) USNR, 1968-71. Office: Brigham & Women's Hosp 75 Francis St Boston MA 02115

BROOKS, GERALD THOMAS, toxicology educator; b. Mansfield, Eng., Oct. 5, 1931; s. Harry and Edith Alberta (Beason) B.; m. Ann Weatherley, Mar. 29, 1958; children: Peter, Alan, Nicola. BSc, U. London, 1953, PhD, 1957, DSc, 1987. Chartered chemist and biologist, Eng. Civil svc. rsch. fellow Pest Infestation Lab., Slough, Eng., 1956-61, sr. sci. officer, 1961-64, prin. sci. officer, 1964-69; prin. sci. officer ARC Unit of Invertebrate Chemistry and Physiology, Sussex U., Brighton, Eng., 1969-76, sr. prin. sci. officer, 1976-82; head Agrl. and Food Rsch. coun. Insect Chemistry Group, Sussex U., 1982-87; vis. rsch. fellow biochemistry and physiology dept. U. Reading, Eng., 1987—; cons. Food and Agrl. Orgn. of U.N., Rome, Vienna, 1972—; bd. dirs. British Crop Protection Coun., Farnham, Eng., 1990—. Author: Chlorinated Insecticides, 1974; editor: Pesticide Science, 1990—. Fellow Royal Soc. Chemistry, Inst. Biology (coun. 1985-89); mem. Biochem. Soc., Brit. Toxicology Soc., Agrochem. Div. Am. Soc., Pesticide Sci. Soc. Japan, Soc. Chem. Industry London. Home: 40 Wykeham Way, Burgess Hill RH15 OHF, England

BROOKS, HARVEY, dentist; b. Newark, Mar. 15, 1931; s. Meyer and Fannie Brooks; m. Toby Englart, Dec. 16, 1956 (div. 1974); children: Joel, Judy; m. Marcia Hammer, Apr. 6, 1975. BA, Rutgers U., 1953; DDS, Temple U., 1957. Pvt. practice Hillside, N.J., 1957—; mem. dental staff Elizabeth Gen. Med. Ctr., 1983—; co-chmn. Hillside (N.J.) Health Fair, 1970-71, dental chmn. oral cancer screening, 1972—. Capt. U.S. Army, 1957-59. Fellow Acad. Gen. Dentistry; mem. Union County Dental soc. (pres. 1988-89), N.J. Dental Assn., ADA. Jewish. Office: 1156 Liberty Ave Hillside NJ 07205-2103

BROOKS, JOHN SAMUEL JOSEPH, pathologist, researcher; b. Phila., Feb. 2, 1948. BS in Biology, St. Joseph's Coll., Phila., 1970; MD, Thomas Jefferson U., 1974. Diplomate Am. Bd. Pathology. Resident in pathology U. Pa., Phila., 1974-78, chief resident, 1978, asst. prof., 1979-84, assoc. prof., 1984-88, prof., 1988-93; chmn. dept. pathology Roswell Pk. Cancer Inst., Buffalo, 1993—; prof., vice chmn. pathologymed. sch. SUNY, Buffalo, 1993—; vis. prof. Royal Marsden Hosp./Inst. Cancer Rsch., London, 1987; expert in immunohistochemistry. Author: Pathology, 1989; contbr. articles to New Eng. Jour. Medicine, Jour. of AMA, Jour. Urology, Internat. Jour. Ob.-Gyn. Pathology, Am. Jour. Pathology; editor Internat. Jour. Surg. Pathology, 1993—; mem. bd. editors: Jour. Modern Pathology, Jour. Surg. Pathology, and reviewer; contbr. over 140 articles to profl. jours. Mem. AAAS, Pathology Soc. Phila. (pres. 1988-90), Ea. Coop. Oncology Group (chmn. sarcoma pathology com. Madison chpt. 1988-95), Internat. Acad. Pathology (edn. com. Atlanta chpt. 1989—), U.S.-Can. Acad. Pathology (coun. mem. 1993—), Am. Soc. Clin. Pathologists (chair anatomical pathology coun. 1995—), Arthur Purdy Stout Soc. for Surg. Pathologists (coun. mem. 1994), Fedn. Am. Soc. for Exptl. Biology, Nat. Internat. Reputation in Diagnostic Surg. Pathology, Royal Coll. Pathology. Democrat. Roman Catholic. Home: 34 Deer Run Orchard Park NY 14127-3454 Office: Roswell Pk Cancer Inst Dept Pathology Elm & Carlton Sts Buffalo NY 14263

BROOKS, LARRY EDWARD, surgeon; b. Cynthiana, Ky., June 15, 1940; s. Edward H. and Esther Marie (Helmbrecht) B.; m. Ann Louise Miller, May 10, 1968; children: Esther Marie, Rachel Anna, Ronald Miller. BS in Indsl. Engring., Purdue U., 1963; MS in Chemistry, Ind. U., 1972, MD, 1976. Surgeon Jackson Cmty. Meml. Hosp., Seymour, Ind., 1981-82, Seymour, 1990—; surgeon Jennings Cmty. Hosp., North Vernon, Ind., 1985-90, Columbus (Ind.) Regional Hosp., 1985-90; mem. Jennings Cmty. Hosp. Found., North Vernon, 1985-89; mem. exec. bd. Jackson Cmty. Meml. Hosp., Seymour, 1993—, officer med. staff, 1993—. Coord. Jennings Cmty. United Fund, North Vernon. With USAF, 1963-69. Recipient Achievement cert. AMA, 1994. Fellow ACS; mem. Jackson County Med. Soc., Ind. State Med. Assn. Roman Catholic. Office: Larry Edward Brooks MD 1130 Med Pl Seymour IN 47274

BROOKS, LEWIS ALEXANDER, psychologist; b. Jersey City, Mar. 13, 1931; s. Joel Nathaniel and Louise (Tucker) B.; m. Lucille Hatchett, June 15, 1970 (div. 1983); m. Anna Erzsebet Toth, May 20, 1984. BA in English, Empire State Coll., 1979; MS in Edn., SUNY, New Paltz, 1983; MA in Psychology, CUNY, 1986, PhD in Psychology, 1992. Cert. spl. edn. tchr., N.Y. Residential aide Crystal Run Village, Fallsburg, N.Y., 1976-83, tchr., 1983-86, psychologist, 1986—; asst. prof. psychology Orange County C.C., Middleton, N.Y., 1991—; lectr. Janus Pannonius Egyetem, Pecs, Hungary, 1988; adj. instr. in psychology Marist Coll., Poughkeepsie, N.Y., 1990—. Mem. APA, Ea. Psychol. Assn., Soc. for Rsch. in Child Devel., Jean Piaget Soc., Coun. for Exceptional Children, N.Y. Acad. Scis., N.E. Ednl. Rsch. Assn. (presenter 1988-91, bd. dirs. 1990—), Sullivan County Assn. for Retarded Citizens, Assn. for Study Afro-Am. Life and History (pres. 1989), Nat. Rainbow Coalition. Democrat. Roman Catholic. Home: RR 4 Box 421 Middletown NY 10940-9510 Office: Crystal Run Village Box AA Fallsburg NY 12733 also: Orange County CC 115 South St SW #210 Middletown NY 10940-6441

BROOKS, LINDA BAXTER, social worker; b. Ypsilanti, Mich., Feb. 4, 1959; d. Glenn George and Lillian Joy (Clayton) B.; m. Joseph Edward Brooks, Sept. 4, 1983; children: Joseph A., Matthew G. AA, Brevard C.C., 1978; BS in Psychology, Fla. State U., 1980, BSW, 1980, MSW, 1990. Admissions dir. Devereux Fla. Treatment Network, Melbourne, 1984-84, 92—; crisis support specialist Human Resources Ctr., Orlando, Fla., 1985-89; quality assurance coord. Orange County Mental Health Ctr., Orlando, Fla., 1989-90; discharge/aftercare coord. Devereux Fla. Treatment Network, 1990-92. Mem. NASW (vice chair 1991-93). Office: Devereux Fla Treatment Network 8000 Devereux Dr Melbourne FL 32940

BROOKS, LLOYD WILLIAM, JR., osteopath, interventional cardiologist, educator; b. Amarillo, Tex., Nov. 4, 1949; s. Lloyd William and Tina Margaret (Roe) B.; m. Ann Nettleship, Apr. 3, 1987. BS, U. Tex., 1972; DO cum laude, Tex. Coll. Osteo. Medicine, 1985. Diplomate Am. Osteo. Bd. Internal Medicine; bd. cert. in internal medicine & cardiology. Intern Dallas-Ft. Worth Med. Ctr., 1985; resident in internal medicine Ft. Worth Osteo. Med. Ctr., 1986-88; fellow in cardiology Detroit Heart Inst.; fellow in angioplasty and interventional cardiology Riverside Meth. Hosp., Columbus, Ohio; pvt. practice Ft. Worth, 1990—; pvt. practice, pres. Ft. Worth Heart and Vascular Inst.; chief of medicine Osteo. Med. Ctr. of Tex.; clin. asst. prof. U. North Tex. Health Sci. Ctr., Ft. Worth, 1991—. Contbr. articles to med. jours. Fellow Am. Coll. Cardiology; mem. AMA, Am. Osteo. Assn., Am. Coll. Osteo. Internists (diplomate). Office: Ft Worth Heart & Vascular 1002 Montgomery St Ste 200 Fort Worth TX 76107-2693

BROOKS, MARION H., physician; b. Edwight, W.Va., May 30, 1936; s. Walter S. and Marion G. (Howard) B.; m. Betty Ann Brooks, June 6, 1959; children: Walter, Jeffrey, Michael. AB, W.Va. U., 1957, BS, 1959; MD, Northwestern U., 1961. Diplomate in internal medicine and endocrinology/metabolism Am. Bd. Internal Medicine. Intern Detroit Receiving Hosp., 1961-62; resident VA Rsch. Hosp., Chgo., 1962-64; fellow in endocrinology Cook County Hosp., Chgo., 1964-65; from asst. prof. to prof. Loyola U., Chgo., chmn. dept. medicine. Office: Loyola U Dept Medicine Stritch Sch Medicine 2600 S 1st Ave Maywood IL 60153-3304

BROOKS, MICHAEL LANE, biologist; b. Cleve., Sept. 4, 1963; s. Samuel Lane and Velma (McCalla) B. BS in Biology, Cen. State U., Wilberforce, Ohio, 1986. Rsch. asst. Cen. State U., 1981-86; electrophysiology rsch. tech. U. Hosps. Cleve., 1987-89; tech. info. specialist Corning (N.Y.) Inc., 1989-91; account mgr. Corning Costar Corp., N.Y.C. territory, 1991—. Office: Corning Costar Corp One Alewife Ctr Cambridge MA 02140

BROOKS, THOMAS EDWARD, podiatrist; b. Phila., Nov. 4, 1953; s. Thomas Edward and Julia Marie (Johnson) B.; m. Joni Marie Fiester, Mar. 5, 1977; children: Thomas, Jennifer, Heather, Daniel. BS, Wilkes Coll., 1984; DPM, Pa. Coll. Podiatric Medicine, 1984. Podiatrist U.S. Navy Hosps., 1972-85, USPHS, Rio Grande City, Tex., 1985-88; cons. Cmty. Action Coun. Southwest Tex., Rio Grande City, 1988—. Instr. CPR Am. Heart Assn., McAllen, Tex., 1985-86, adv. bd., 1986; team physician Rio Grande City Ind. Sch. Dist., 1984-88; mem. Rep. Nat. Com., 1994, senatorial com., 1994-96. Mem. Am. Podiatric Med. Assn., Tex. Podiatric Med. Assocs. Office: PO Box 98 Rio Grande City TX 78582-0098

BROOKS, THOMAS JOSEPH, JR., preventive medicine educator; b. Starkville, Miss., May 23, 1916; s. Thomas Joseph and Lelia Adeline (Perkins) B.; m. Mary Alice Pollard; children: Thomas Joseph III, Michael Pollard, Mary Browning, Melinda Anne. BS, U. Fla., 1937; MS, U. Tenn., 1939; PhD, U. N.C., 1942; MD, Wake Forest U., 1945. Diplomate Am. Bd. Med. Microbiology. Instr. bacteriology and parasitology Sch. Medicine Wake Forest U., Winston-Salem, N.C., 1942-45; intern Wake Forest U. and N.C. Bapt. Hosp., 1945-46; assoc. prof. pharmacology Sch. Medicine U. Miss., Oxford, 1947-48; med. officer assigned to VA Hosp. USNR, Lake City, Fla., 1946-47; officer-in-charge streptococcal diseases research unit U.S. Naval Tng. Ctr., Bainbridge, Md., 1953-55; prof., chmn. dept. preventive medicine U. Miss. Sch. Medicine, Jackson, 1952-81, prof. emeritus, 1981—; cons. Miss. State Dept. Health, 1981—; vis. prof. preventive medicine sch. medicine U. Costa Rica, San Jose, 1962-63, faculty medicine Keio U., Tokyo, 1968, faculty medicine Trinity Coll., U. Dublin, Ireland, 1979; vis. prof. pub. health faculty medicine Kyoto U., Japan, 1968-69; invited lectr. sch. medicine U. N.D., Grand Forks, 1971; physician-in-chief Univ. Hosp., Fla. State U., 1948-52; asst. dean in charge student affairs sch. medicine U. Miss., 1956-73; UN cons. in med. edn., India, 1966. Author: Essentials of Medical Parasitology, 1963; co-editor: Control of Communicable Diseases in Man, 11th edit., 1970, 12th edit., 1975; contbr. articles to profl. jours. Past pres. Jackson (Miss.) Photographic Soc., Jackson Amateur Radio Club; cons. to rector Universidad Industrial de Santander, Bucaramanga, Colombia, 1968; chmn. admissions com. Sch. Medicine, U. Miss., 1955-65. Gilchist Meml. scholar 1936-37, band scholar 1934-37 U. Fla.; teaching fellow parasitology dept. zoology U. Tenn., 1937-39, teaching fellow parasitology sch. medicine U. N.C., 1939-42, fellow in tropical medicine La. State U. 1956-60, Alan Gregg fellow in med. edn. China Med. Bd. N.Y., 1968-69; Assn. Am. Med. Colls. grantee sch. tropical medicine Tulane U., 1943, Assn. Am. Med. Colls. grantee for study tropical diseases Latin Am., 1944, Rockefeller Found. Travel grantee, 1952. Fellow Royal Soc. Health Eng.; mem. Am. Pub. Health Assn. (com. on communicable diseases 1968-75, nominating com. epidemiology sect. 1975, coun. internat. health div. 1978-81, chmn. nominating com. coun. internat. health div. 1981), Miss. Pub. Health Assn., U. Tenn. Hon. Biol. Soc. (pres. 1938-39), Omicron Delta Kappa, Sigma Xi. Presbyterian. Home: 750 Lenox Dr Jackson MS 39211-4105

BROOKS, WALTER S., dermatologist; b. Cleve., July 16, 1956; s. John R. and Christel W. (Plogsties) B.; m. Debra A. HArt, Aug. 29, 1981; children: Aaron S., David J.H., Arielle N. BA magna cum laude, U. Rochester, 1978, MD, 1982. Resident in internal medicine Rochester (N.Y.) Gen. Hosp., 1982-85; resident in dermatology U. Pitts., 1985-88; clin. instr. dermatology U. Rochester, 1989—; dermatologist pvt. practice, Rochester, 1988—. Bd. trustees Rochester Acad. Medicine, 1996—. Recipient Leadership award Dermatology Found. Soc., 1995. Fellow Am. Acad. Dermatology; mem. Nat. Bd. Med. Examiners, Buffalo-Rochester Dermatol. Assn. (pres. 1995-96), Rochester Dermatol. Soc. (pres. 1996—). Home: 22 Silver Fox Dr Fairport NY 14450 Office: 1561 Long Pond Rd Ste 408 Rochester NY 14626

BROOKSBY, GERALD ARMOND, ophthalmologist; b. Provo, Utah, Dec. 12, 1937; s. Wilford Armond and Myrna Mae (Thorson) B.; m. Linda Lee Larson, June 21, 1961; children: Scott, Alisa, Emily, Rachel, Craig, Anne, Ben. BS, Brigham Young U., 1960; PhD, U. Minn., 1971, MD, 1972. Diplomate Am. Bd. Ophthalmology. Rsch. scientist NASA, 1962-67; fellow Mayo Clinic, Rochester, Minn., 1967-71; instr. in physiology U. Minn. Med. Sch., Mpls., 1971-72; NIH fellow U. Oreg. Med. Sch., Portland, 1972-76, ophthalmology fellow, 1972-76, clin. asst. prof., 1976—; pvt. practice Portland, 1976—; cons. Alcon Rsch. Coun., Dallas, 1980-86; clin. asst. prof. U. Oreg. Med. Sch., Portland, 1983—. Contbr. articles to profl. jours. Rsch. grant U. Oreg. Med. Sch., 1972-76, spl. fellow, 1972-76. Fellow Am. Acad. Ophthalmology; mem. Oreg. Acad. Ophthalmology, Oreg. Med. Assn., Multnomah County Med. Soc., Oreg. Acad. Ophthalmology, Am. Physiol. Soc. Republican. Mem. Ch. LDS. Office: 1115 SW Taylor Portland OR 97205

BROOME, CLAIRE VERONICA, epidemiologist, researcher; b. Tunbridge Wells, Kent, England, Aug. 24, 1949; came to U.S., 1951; d. Kenneth R. and Heather C. (Platt) B.; m. John F. Head, Apr. 2, 1988; children: Gabriel K., Steven G. BA, Harvard U., 1970, MD, 1975. Diplomate Am. Bd. Internal Medicine. Dep. chief spl. pathogens br. Ctrs. for Disease Control, Atlanta, 1979-80, chief meningitis, spl. pathogens br., 1981-90, assoc. dir. sci., 1991-94, acting dir., nat. ctr. injury prevention and control, 1992-93, dep. dir., 1994—; cons. vaccine devel. AID, 1988—, WHO, NIH, various univs.; mem. steering com. on encapsulated bacterial vaccines, WHO, Geneva, 1989-91, chmn., 1992—; mem. adv. com. on vaccines FDA, Washington, 1990-94. Contbr. numerous articles to profl. jours. Recipient M. C. Rockefeller fellowship, 1970-71, Meritorious Svc. medal USPHS, 1986, rsch. grants NIH, FDA, Dept. of State. Fellow Infectious Diseases Soc. Am. (Bristol-Myers Squibb award 1993); mem. ACP, Am. Epidemiologic Soc., Am. Soc. Microbiology, Common Cause, Phi Beta Kappa, Alpha Omega Alpha. Office: Ctrs for Disease Control # D14 Atlanta GA 30333

BROOMES, EDWARD LOUIS, physician and surgeon; b. Morahwhanna, Guyana, Nov. 17, 1913; came to U.S., 1935; s. Charles Thomas Wesley and Sarah Rebecca (Hamilton) B.; m. Anna Leatha Brown, Dec. 4, 1946; children: Claude, Crystal. BS, Howard U., 1939, MD, 1942; LLD (hon.), Loyola, Chgo., 1981, Calumet Coll., Whiting, Ind., 1986. Intern Homer G. Phillips Hosp., St. Louis; resident St. Mary's Infirmity Hosp., St. Louis; practice gen. medicine East Chicago, Ind., 1945—; physician Lakeside Med. Clinic, East Chicago, 1957—; dep. coroner Lake County, Ind., 1968-76; mem. staff St. Catherin's Hosp.; mem. East Chicago Bd. Health, 1951-72, past pres., organizer 1st multi-zonal system of immunzation, 1963; mem. East Chicago Bd. Safety, 1973-77, pres., 1975-77, pres. N.W. Ind. Naval Adv. Coun., 1968; hon. consul Republic of Guyana, 1973-83, hon. consul gen., 1983-91. Patentee snoring prevention device. Scout master Boy Scouts Am., East Chicago, 1948-56; organizer East Chicago Jr. Police Patrol, 1968; founder No. Ind, Polit. Action Alliance, 1968, pres., 1968—; bd. dirs. Lake Area United Way, various other community orgns.; organizer East Chicago Combined Health Orgn., 1976. Recipient numerous awards for svc. including Prince Hall Freedom award for Jurisdiction of Ind., 1973, Humanitarian award East Chgo. Women's Club, 1974, Golden Arrow Achieement award Gov. of Guyana, 1979, Cachique Crown of honor Republic og Guyana, 1985. Fellow Internat. Coll. Surgeons; mem. NAACP, Am. West Indian (pres. 1950-60), Frontiers Club (pres. 1960, organizer 1st overseas chpt. Guyana), Masons (33 deg.), Shriners, Consistory (32 deg.), Alpha Phi Omega. Lodges: Masons (3d degree), Shriners, Consistory (32 degree). Home: 2301 Lithuanica Ave East Chicago IN 46312-3138 Office: Lakeside Med Clinic 2301 Lithuanica Ave East Chicago IN 46312-3138

BROOTEN, DOROTHY, nursing educator; b. Hazleton, Pa., Jan. 16, 1942; married; two children. BSN, U. Pa., 1966, MSN, 1970, PhD in Ednl. Adminstrn. Assoc. prof. nursing Thomas Jefferson U., 1972-77; from asst. to assoc. prof. nursing U. Pa., 1977-88, prof. nursing, chair Health Care of Women & Childbearing, 1988-90, dir. Ctr. for Low Birthweight, Sch. Nursing, 1990—, Overseers prof. perinatal nursing, 1990—; cons. Sch. Medicine, U. Utrecht, The Netherlands, 1989, Ministry of Health, Malawi, Africa, 1991. Recipient Contbrn. to Nursing Sci. award ANA, 1988. Mem. Inst. Medicine-NAS, Am. Acad. Nursing (mem. gov. coun. 1988-91). Office: U Pa Sch Nursing Low Birthweight Rsch Ctr Philadelphia PA 19104*

BROPHY, DENNIS RICHARD, psychology and philosophy educator, administrator, clergyman; b. Milw., Aug. 6, 1945; s. Floyd Herbert and Phyllis Marie (Ingram) B.; BA, Washington U., St. Louis, 1967, MA, 1968; M.Div., Pacific Sch. Religion, 1971; PhD in Indstrl. and Orgnl. Psychology, Texas A & M U., 1995. Cert. coll. tchr., Calif. Edn. rschr. IBM Corp., White Plains, N.Y., 1968-71; edn. minister Cmty. Congl. Ch., Port Huron, Mich., 1971-72, Bethlehem United Ch. of Christ, Ann Arbor, Mich., 1972-73, Cmty. Congl. Ch., Chula Vista, Calif., 1974; philosophy instr. Southwestern Coll., Chula Vista, 1975; assoc. prof. psychology and philosophy Northwest Coll., Powell, Wyo., 1975-96, prof., 1996—, chmn. social sci. divsn., 1992-95; religious edn. cons. Mont.-No. Wyo. Conf. United Ch. of Christ. Mem. APA (Daniel Berlyne award 1996), Wyo. Coun. for Humanities, Soc. Indsl. Orgnl. Psychology, Yellowstone Assn. of United Ch. of Christ, Phi Kappa Phi, Phi Beta Kappa, Sigma Xi, Omicron Delta Kappa, Theta Xi, Golden Key Nat. Honor Soc. Home: 533 Avenue C Powell WY 82435-2401 Office: Northwest Coll 231 W 6th St Powell WY 82435-1898

BROPHY, M. EILEEN, mental health and community health nurse; b. Nyack, N.Y., June 13, 1942; d. Martin J. and Mary Ellen (Gagan) B. AAS in Nursing, Rockland Community Coll., Suffern, N.Y., 1964; BSN, U. Rochester, 1969, MS in Community Svcs., 1984. Staff nurse, team leader Good Samaritan Hosp., Suffern, 1964-69; staff nurse Strong Meml. Hosp., Rochester, N.Y., 1969-70; community health nurse, sr. community health nurse Vis. Nurse Svc., Rochester, 1970-85; primary therapist DePaul Mental Health Svcs., Rochester, 1985-89, clin. team leader, 1989-92; clin. team leader St. Mary's Mental Health Ctr., Rochester, 1992—. Mem. ANA, N.Y. State Nurses Assn., Genesee Valley Nurses Assn. Office: St Mary's Mental Health Ctr 845 Main St W Rochester NY 14611-2335

BROPHY, MARY O'REILLY, industrial hygienist; b. N.Y.C., Aug. 3, 1948; d. Luke Edward and Regina (Mahoney) O'Reilly; children: Robert, Sara, Lena. Student, Fordham U., 1966-68; BS, U. Mich., 1970, MS, 1972, PhD, 1979. Rsch. asst. prof. Health Sci. Ctr., Syracuse, N.Y., 1979-84; environ. toxicologist Syracuse Rsch. Corp., 1984-86; pres. ARLS Cons., Inc., Syracuse, 1991—; sr. indsl. hygienist N.Y. State Dept. Labor, Syracuse, 1987—; adj. asst. prof. SUNY Sch. Pub. Health, Albany, 1990—; dir. Am. Bd. Indsl. Hygiene, Lansing, Mich., 1995—. Author: An Ergonomics Guide to VDTs, 1994, (with others) Occupational Ergonomics, 1996. Mem. Am. Indsl. Hygiene Assn. (treas. ctrl. N.Y. chpt. 1991-93), Am. Conf. Govtl. Indsl. Hygienists (ergonomic com. 1991-94, 95—, risk assessment com. 1996—). Home: 5954 Smith Rd North Syracuse NY 13212

BROSE, JOHN ADOLPH, medical educator; b. Teaneck, N.J., Oct. 6, 1950; s. Adolph Dahlke and Mary Wilhelmina (Quattlebaum) B.; m. Linda Diane Way, Aug. 20, 1972; children: Steven William, Christine Marie. DO, U. North Tex. Health Sci. Ctr., 1976; postdoc. fellow, Ohio State U., 1985-86. Diplomate Am. Bd. Family Practice. Resident Scott (AFB Ill.) Med. Ctr., 1979, resident faculty, 1979-82; prof. Ohio U., Athens, 1982—, head academic tng. program, dir. family medicine fellowship program, 1983—;

clin. assoc. prof. Ohio State U., Athens, 1985—, asst. dean clin. rsch.; mem. expert panel USP Family Medicine, 1990—. Served to maj. USAF, 1976-82. Named Outstanding Instr. Am. Med. Women's Assn., 1984, Family Medicine Club, 1984, Sigma Sigma Phi, 1983, 86, Family Practice Outstanding Instr., Ohio State U., 1990, Std. Excellence award, 1995. Fellow Am. Acad. Family Physicians; mem. Am. Osteo. Assn., Am. Coll. Gen. Practice (undergrad. com. 1982—), Ohio Acad. Family Physicians (pres. Hocking Valley chpt.). Home: 7277 Beechwood Dr Athens OH 45701-3544 Office: Ohio U Coll Osteo Med Athens OH 45701

BROSS, IRWIN DUDLEY JACKSON, biostatistician; b. Halloway, Ohio, Nov. 13, 1921; s. Samuel and Mina (Jackson) B.; m. Rida Singer, Aug. 6, 1949; children: Dean, Valerie, Neal. B.A. in Math, UCLA, 1942; M.A. in Exptl. Stats, N.C. State U., 1948, Ph.D. in Exptl. Stats, 1949. Research asso. dept. biostatistics Johns Hopkins U., 1949-52; asst. prof. public health and preventive medicine Cornell U., 1952-59; head research, design and analysis Sloan Kettering Inst., 1952-59; dir. biostatistics Roswell Park Meml. Inst., Buffalo, N.Y., 1959-83; pres. Biomed. Metatech., Inc., 1983—; research prof. biostatistics State U. N.Y. at Buffalo, 1961-83; asso. dept. epidemiology Johns Hopkins U., 1971-85. Author: Design for Decision, 1953, Scientific Strategies in Human Affairs: To Tell the Truth, 1975, Scientific Strategies to Save Your Life, 1981, Crimes of Official Science: A Casebook, 1988, Scientific Fraud vs. Scientific Truth, 1992, Fifty Years of Folly and Fraud in the Name of Science, 1994, (CD-ROM, 6 books) History of U.S. Science and Medicine in the Cold War, 1996; contbr. numerous articles in field to profl. jours. Served with U.S. Army, 1941-45. Mem. AAAS, Am. Statis. Assn., Biometric Soc., Am. Coll. Epidemiol. Home and Office: 109 Maynard Dr Buffalo NY 14226-3365

BROST, GERARD ROBERT, mental health counselor, addictions professional, educator; b. Evanston, Ill., Sept. 30, 1949; s. Andrew Joseph and Zoe Wilhelmena (Dreis) B. BS, Western Mich. U., 1975, MA, 1976. Cert. behavior analyst, Fla.; cert. math. tchr., Fla.; lic. mental health counselor, cert. addictions profl. Tchg. asst. U. Fla., Gainesville, 1979-85; clin. supr. Alcothon House, Gainesville, 1983-85; psychologist Sunland Ctr., Gainesville, 1985-88; rehab. therapist N.E. Fla. State Hosp., MacClenny, 1988; therapist Marion Citrus Mental Health, Ocala, Fla., 1988-89; lectr. Ctrl. Fla. C.C., Ocala, 1987-90; psychol. specialist Marion Correctional Inst., Lowell, Fla., 1989-90; psychologist N.E. Fla. State Hosp., Macclenny, 1989-90; behavior analyst Behaviortek, Gainesville, 1989-90; fin. cons. Corp. Securities Group Inc., Maitland, Fla., 1990-91; registered rep. Waddell & Reed Fin. Svcs., Winter Park, Fla., 1990-91; ind. mktg. rep. Excel Telecom., Orlando, Fla., 1991—; sr. therapist Lakeside Alternatives, Orlando, Fla., 1991-94; mental health counselor, addictions profl. Tampa Bay Consortium, Tampa, 1994-95; clin. assessment counselor Heart of Fla. Behavioral Ctr., Lakeland, 1993—; mental health counselor Daylight of West Fla. Inc., Lakeland, 1995—; mental health counselor, Daylight, Inc., Lakeland, Fla., 1995—; mental health counselor, addictions profl. Berit Behavioral Health, Tampa, Fla., 1996—; guest Sta. WCJB-TV, 1983; mental health counselor Continuum Behavioral Healthcare, Tampa, 1996. Mem. Food Bank, Gainesville, 1989-90; youth vol. Interface Youth Program, Gainesville, 1982-85; substance abuse vol. Corner Drugstore, Inc., Gainesville, 1983-84; crisis intervention vol. Alachua County Crisis Ctr., Gainesville, 1983. Recipient Outstanding Svc. award Transitions Substance Abuse Program, 1983, Interface Youth Program, 1985. Mem. Fla. Alcohol and Drug Abuse Assn., Dozenal Soc. Am., Dozenal Soc. Great Britain, Am. Literacy Coun., Affiliated Inventors Found., Math. Soc. Am., Am. Assn. Christian Counselors, Christian Assn. Psychol. Studies, World Future Soc., Nat. Assn. Masters in Psychology, Fla. Assn. Masters in Psychology. Home: 9631 Voyles Loop Polk City FL 33868-9732 Office: Heart of Fla Behavioral Ctr 2150 N Florida Ave Lakeland FL 33805-2919

BROSTROM, CHARLES OTTO, pharmacology educator, researcher; b. Downsville, Wis., Nov. 2, 1942; s. Carl Nicklas and Doris Estella (Decker) B.; m. Margaret Ann O'Brien, Dec. 18, 1965; 1 child, Arthur. BS, Wis. State U., 1964; PhD, U. Ill., Chgo., 1969. Postdoctoral fellow U. Calif., Davis, 1968-71; from asst. to full prof. pharmacology Robert Wood Johnson Med. Sch., Piscataway, N.J., 1971—, acting chmn. dept., 1989-92; mem. Instl. Rev. Bd. Janssen R&D, Piscataway, N.J., 1981-85; mem. grad. faculty Rutgers U., New Brunswick, N.J., 1972—; dir. program in Cellular and Molecular Pharmacology, 1995—. Mem. editorial bd. Molecular Pharmacology, 1982-95; contbr. over 70 articles to profl. jours. NIH Sci. Support grantee, 1972-94. Mem. AAUP, Am. Biol. Chemists and Molecular Biologists. Office: U Medicine & Dentistry NJ Robert Wood Johnson Med Sch 575 Hoes Ln Piscataway NJ 08854-5028

BROSZ, MARGARET HEADLEY, pediatrics nurse; b. Dover, N.J., Dec. 31, 1951; d. Charles E. and Carolyn (Cobb) H.; m. Walter J. Brosz, May 28, 1978. Student, Douglass Coll., New Brunswick, N.J., 1970-72; BS in Nursing, Cornell U., 1974; MS, Boston Coll., Chestnut Hill, Mass., 1978. Cert. trainer medication adminstrs. Nurse Vis. Nurse Assn. Boston, 1974-76; pediatric nurse practitioner Wrentham (Mass.) State Sch., Boston Children's Hosp., 1978-80; staff nurse pediatrics ICU Thomas Jefferson U. Hosp., Phila., 1980-81; employee health clinician Children's Hosp. Phila., 1981-83; unit nurse, campus relief nurse The Woods Svcs., Langhorne, Pa., 1983—. Vol. interpreter Pennsbury Manor, Morrisville, Pa., bd. dirs. Pennsbury Soc. Mem. Devel. Disabilities Nurses Assn.

BROTMAN, RICHARD DENNIS, counselor; Detroit, Nov. 2, 1952; s. Alfred David and Dorothy G. (Mansfield) B.; m. Debra Louise Hobold, Sept. 9, 1979. AA, E. L.A. Jr. Coll., 1972; AB, U. So. Calif., 1974, MS, 1976. Instructional media coord. Audio-Visual Div., Pub. Library, City of Alhambra, Calif., 1971-78; clin. supr. Hollywood-Sunset Community Clinic, L.A., 1976—; client program coord. N. L.A. County Regional Ctr. for Developmentally Disabled, 1978-81; sr. counselor Eastern L.A. Regional Ctr. for Developmentally Disabled, 1981-85; dir. community svcs. Almansor Edn. Ctr., 1985-87; tng. and resource devel. Children's Home Soc. Calif., 1987-90; program supr. Pacific Clinics-East, 1990-94; dir. clin. svcs. Alma Family Svcs., 1994—; intern student affairs div., U. So. Calif., 1976. Corp. dir. San Gabriel Mission Players, 1973-75. Lic. marriage, family and child counselor, Calif.; cert. counselor Calif. Community Coll. Bd. Mem. Am. Assn. For Marriage and Family Therapy (approved supr.), Calif. Personnel and Guidance Assn. (conv. participant, 1976, 77, 79), Calif. Rehab. Counselors Assn. (officer), San Fernando Valley Consortium of Agys. Serving Developmentally Disabled Citizens (chmn. recreation subcom.), L.A. Aquarium Soc. Democrat. Home: 3515 Brandon St Pasadena CA 91107-4542 Office: Alma Family Svcs 6505 Rosemead Blvd Ste 300 Pico Rivera CA 90660-3544

BROUGH, MICHAEL DAVID, plastic surgeon, consultant; b. London; s. Kenneth David and Frances Elizabeth (Davies) B.; m. Geraldine Moira Sleigh, June 8, 1974; children: Jonathan David, Charlotte Elizabeth, Veronica Mary, Nicholas Michael. MA MB BChir, Cambridge (Eng.) U., 1968; Fellow, Royal Coll. Surgeons, Eng., 1974. Consultant plastic surgeon N.E. Thames Regional Ctr., St. Andrews Hosp. Billericay, Essex, Eng., 1980-82, U. Coll. Hosps. London, 1982—, Royal Free Hosp., London, 1982—, Whittington Hosp., London, 1982—, King Edward VII's Hosp. for Officers, London, 1992—, St. Luke's Hosp. for Clergy, London, 1992—. Contbr. numerous articles to sci. jours. and chpts. to books. Mem. court of assts. The Worshipful Co. of Tin Plate Workers Alias Wire Workers, London, 1988—. Fellow Royal Coll. Surgeons; mem. Plastic Surgery Sect. Royal Soc. Medicine (pres. 1991-92), Brit. Assn. Plastic Surgeons (hon. treas. 1994-96), The Phoenix Appeal (founder, hon. sec. 1988-95), Hawks Club Cambridge. Office: The Consulting Ste, 82 Portland Pl, London W1N 3DH, England

BROUGHTON, JOHN MARCUS, psychology and cultural studies educator; b. Sutton, Surrey, Eng., Apr. 5, 1947; came to U.S., 1968; s. Ralph Leonard and Doris Edith (Willis) B. BA, MA, Cambridge U., Eng., 1968; PhD, Harvard U., 1975. Lic. psychologist, N.Y. Asst. prof. psychology Wayne State U., Detroit, 1974-76; asst. to assoc. prof. psychology and edn. Columbia U. Tchrs. Coll., N.Y.C., 1976—; visiting assoc. prof. edn. U. Rochester Grad. Sch. Edn., N.Y.C., 1986. Editor: The Cognitive Development Psychology of James Mark Baldwin, 1982, Critical Theories of Psychological Development, 1987; co-editor: New Ideas in Psychology Jour., 1982-91, PsychCritique: Internat. Jour. Critical Psychology & Psychoanalysis, 1985-87, Psychoculture: Review of Psychology and Cultural Studies, 1995—. Recipient Passingham prize Cambridge U., 1968; Choate fellow Harvard U., 1968-70; Rockefeller fellow Wesleyan U., 1987. Mem. Internat. Soc. Theoretical Psychology, Psychologists for Peace. Office: Tchrs Coll 525 W 120th St New York NY 10027-6625

BROUSSARD, CLIFFORD MICHAEL, health facility administrator; b. Crowley, La., May 29, 1953; s. Clifford Joseph and Dorothy (Trahan) B.; m. Sharlene Ann Broussard, May 30, 1981. BS, McNeese State U., 1980; MS, La. State U., 1985. Cert. clin. lab. scientist, La.; cert. med. technologist Am. Med. Technologists. Student team leader Lake Charles (La.) Charity Hosp., 1973-75; staff med. technologist, infection control officer St. Luke Gen. Hosp., Arnandville, La., 1976-78; med. technologist, 3-11 team leader West Calcasieu-Cameron Hosp., Sulphur, La., 1978-81; staff med. technologist Jo Ellen Smith Med. Ctr., New Orleans, 1981-91, clin. dir., 1991-93; adminstrv. dir. Our Lady of the Lake Regional Med. Ctr., Baton Rouge, 1993—. Mem. Phi Kappa Theta. Republican. Roman Catholic. Home: 11162 Paddock Ave Baton Rouge LA 70816

BROUSSEAU, JOANNE LYNN, occupational therapist, consultant; b. Manhasset, N.Y., Sept. 14, 1962; d. Kenneth Stewart Brousseau and Virginia Mary (Winstead) Lafer. BS in Occupl. Therapy, Med. Coll. Ga., 1990. Cert. OTR/L, Fla. Occupl. therapist Dept. Maternal and Child Health, V.I., 1990-93; traveling occupl. therapist Cross Country Healthcare, Jacksonville and environs, Fla., 1993-95; occupl. therapist, home health Interim Health-care, Marianna and environs, Fla., 1995—; occupl. therapist Rehab Mgmt. Outpatient Systems, Marianna and Chipley, Fla., 1995—; cons. Sunland Ctr., Cox Med. Ctr., Marianna, 1995, Jackson and Chipley Hosps., cmty. support/stroke clubs, 1996. Mem. Bus. and Profl. Women's Assn., Am. Soc. Hand Therapists, Am. Occupl. Therapy Assn., World Fedn. Occupl. Therapists, Fla. Occupl. Therapy Assn., World Wildlife Fedn., Audubon Soc., Moose. Democrat. Home: 3816 Bart Rd Marianna FL 32448 Office: Jackson Therapy Clinic 3015 Jefferson St Ste C Marianna FL 32448

BROWER, CORWIN LEE, pharmacy executive; b. Ludington, Mich., Feb. 11, 1956; s. Corwin Gordon Brower and Marilyn Irene (Petersen) Buchner; m. Nancy Magdalena Lueder, May 23, 1981; children: Timothy Lee, Steven William. BS in Pharmacy, Ferris State U., 1979; MBA, Radford U., 1989. Resident N.C. Meml. Hosp., Chapel Hill, 1979-81; staff pharmacist Holland (Mich.) Community Hosp., 1981-83; staff pharmacist Radford (Va.) Community Hosp., 1983-84, asst. dir. pharmacy, 1984-86, dir. pharmacy, 1986-91, dir. pharmacy and IV therapy, 1991-96; mgr. pharmacy svcs. Carilion Health Sys., 1996—; pharmacy exec. fellow SmithKline Beecham, 1992. Mem. Am. Soc. Hosp. Pharmacists (del. ann. meeting, 1991-93), Am. Pharm. Assn., Va. Soc. Hosp. Pharmacists (membership com. 1991, strategic planning com. 1988), Va. Pharm. Assn. Episcopalian. Home: 1010 Pendleton St Radford VA 24141-2228

BROWER, ROBERT CHARLES, rehabilitation counselor, small business owner; b. Allendale, N.J.; s. William P. and Adele (Braun) B.; m. Hilja Kristiansen, Dec. 21, 1963; children: Robert K., Kristine D. BA in Psychology, Rutgers U., 1963; MDiv, Luth. Theol. Sem., Phila., 1966; postgrad. in counseling, Princeton Theol. Sem., 1970-71; postgrad. in Bus. Adminstrn., N.Y. Inst. Tech., 1993—. Cert. rehab. counselor, disability mgmt. specialist, case mgr., N.Y., U.S. Dept. Labor; ordained to ministry Lutheran Ch., 1966. Pastor St. Paul Luth. Ch., E. Windsor, N.J., 1966-71; psychiatric rehab. counselor N.Y. State Office of Vocations, Cen. Islip, 1971-73; coord. Rehab. Inst., Mineola, St. James, N.Y., 1973-74; program dir. and mental health clinic adminstr. Skills Unlimited, Oakdale, N.Y., 1974-78; dist. mgr. Intracorp subs. CIGNA, Woodbury, White Plains, N.Y., 1978-83; mgr. disability mgmt. svcs. Nat. Ctr. Disability Svcs. (formerly Human Resources Ctr.), Albertson, N.Y., 1984-90; pres. Brower Rehab. Svcs., Inc., Medford, N.Y., 1990—; adj. prof. Sch. Counseling, Rsch., Spl. Edn. and Rehab., Hofstra U., Uniondale, N.Y., 1988—; speaker in field. Bd. dirs. Cert. Ins. Rehab. Specialist Commn., rep. to Found. for Rehab. Cert., Edn. and Rsch., 1993—, treas. found., treas. commn., 1993-94, vice chair, 1994-95, chair, 1995-96. Mem. AAUP, Nat. Rehab. Assn. (chmn. commn. for certification of disability mgmt. specialists commn.), Nat. Rehab. Profls. in Pvt. Sector, Profl. Rehab. Assn. L.I. and N.Y.C. (Rehab. Profl. of Yr. in Ancillary Care 1994), Delta Mu Delta. Home: 37 Crooked Pine Dr Medford NY 11763-4329

BROWN, ALBERT JACK, optometrists; b. Phila., July 26, 1941; s. Albert Joseph and Mildred Laverne (Mohler) B.; m. Rosalie Joan Carles, Sept. 16, 1959; children: Diane, Susan, Jacqueline. BS cum laude, Pa. State U., 1963; D Optometry cum laude, So. Coll. of Optometry, Memphis, 1966; ThD, Acad. Sch. of Theology, Harrisburg, Pa., 1979; D Ocular Medicine, Am. Coll. Optometric Physician, Memphis, 1987. Cert. eye laser physician N.E. State U./Phila. Light and Laser Inst. Rsch. asst. So. Coll. of Optometry, Memphis, 1964-65; pvt. practice Eye and Ear Aid Clinic, Andrews, N.C., 1966-68, Philipsburg, Pa., 1968—; theology tchr. Pa. State U., State College, 1972-76; dir., tchr. Acad. Sch. Theology, Harrisburg, 1977-79; TV co-host Rev. Dr. Brown Ministries, Harrisburg, 1985—; tchr. laser eye surgery Am. Coll. Optometric Physicians, North Miami Beach, Fla., 1994—, also bd. dirs. Fellow Am. Coll. Optometric Physicians (bd. dirs. 1987-96, award 1994); mem. Am. Pub. Health Assn., Pa. State U. Alumni Assn., Beta Sigma Kappa (hon. mem.), Sigma Alpha Sigma (hon.). Republican. Mem. Ch. of the Brethren. Office: Eye and Ear Aid Clinic Tyrone Pike Philipsburg PA 16866

BROWN, ARNOLD, health science facility administrator; b. Phila., July 20, 1939; s. Harry and Rita (Pearl) B.; m. Marguerite Sylvia Schlumpf, June 14, 1964; children: Daniel Stephan, Genevieve Cynthia, Dahvid Nathaniel. AB in Zoology, UCLA, 1960; MD, U. So. Calif., 1964. Diplomate Am. Bd. Internal Medicine, Am. Bd. Infectious Diseases. Intern in medicine Peter Bent Brigham Hosp., Boston, 1964-65, jr. resident in medicine, 1965-66; sr. resident in medicine Stanford (Calif.) U. Hosp., 1968-69; postdoctoral fellow Stanford U. Med. Ctr., 1969-72; instr. dept. moledcular biology U. Geneva, 1972-73; asst. prof. medicine U. Pitts., 1973-81, asst. prof. microbiology Grad. Sch. Pub. Health, 1975-81, assoc. prof. infectious diseases and microbiology, 1984-91; sect. chief, staff physician infectious diseases/microbiology VA Med. Ctr., Pitts., 1973-81; assoc. prof. medicine, microbiology/immunology Sch. Medicine, U. S.C., Columbia, 1981-84, prof. medicine and microbiology/immunology, 1984—; assoc. chief of staff for rsch. Dorn Vet.'s Hosp., Columbia, 1981—; acting dep. dir. med. rsch. VA Ctrl. Office, Washington, 1993-94; dep. chief of staff Dorn Veterans Hosp., Columbia, S.C., 1994—, interim coord. ambulatory care svcs., 1995—; coord. ambulatory care svc. Dorn Vets. Hosp., Columbia, 1995—; chief phys. exam. sect. 3270th U.S. Army Hosp., Ft. Jackson, S.C., 1985-92, dep. comdr., chief profl. svcs., 1992-94, comdr., 1994-96; chief preventive medicine svcs. U.S. Army Med. Activity, Ft. Jackson, 1991; comdr. Combat Support Hosp., Memphis, 1996—. Contbr. numerous articles to profl. jours. Lt. M.C., USNR, 1966-68; col. M.C., USAR. Fellow Infectious Disease Soc. Am.; mem. AAAS, Am. Fedn. Clin. Rsch., Soc. Exptl. Biology and Medicine, Am. Soc. Microbiology, Internat. Soc. of Travel Medicine, Alpha Omega Alpha. Office: Dorn Veterans Hosp Garners Ferry Rd Columbia SC 29201

BROWN, ARNOLD LANEHART, JR., pathologist, educator, university dean; b. Wooster, Ohio, Jan. 26, 1926; s. Arnold Lanehart and Wilda (Woods) B.; m. Betty Jane Simpson, Oct. 2, 1949; children—Arnold III, Anthony, Allen, Fletcher, Lisa. Student, U. Richmond, 1943-45; M.D., Med. Coll. Va., 1949. Diplomate: Am. Bd. Pathology. Intern Presbyn.-St. Luke's Hosp., Chgo., 1949-50; resident Presbyn.-St. Luke's Hosp., 1950-51, 53-56, asst. attending pathologist, 1957-59; practice medicine specializing in pathology Rochester, Minn., 1959-78; cons. exptl. pathology, anatomy Mayo Clinic, Rochester, 1959-78; also prof., chmn. dept. Mayo Clinic, 1968-78; prof. pathology U. Wis., Madison, 1978—, dean Med. Sch., 1978-91; mem. nat. cancer adv. council NIH, 1971-74, HEW, 1972-74; chmn. clearing house on environ. carcinogens Nat. Cancer Inst., 1976-80, chmn. com. to study carcinogenicity of cyclamate, 1975-76; mem. Nat. Com. on Heart Disease, Cancer and Stroke, 1975-79; mem. com. on safe drinking water NRC, 1976-77; mem. award assembly Gen. Motors Cancer Research Found., 1978-83, vice chmn., 1982-83; co-chmn. panel on geochemistry of fibrous materials related to health risks Nat. Acad. Scis.-NRC, 1978-80; chair working group Internat. Agy. for Research on Cancer, Lyon, France, 1979, 83, 87. Contbr. articles to profl. jours. Bd. sci. counselors Nat. Inst. Environ. Health Scis., NIH Nat. Toxicology Program, 1992—. With USNR, 1943-45, 51-53. Nat. Heart Inst. postdoctoral fellow, 1956-59. Mem. Am. Soc. Exptl. Pathology, Internat. Acad. Pathology, Am. Assn. Pathologists, Am. Gastroent. Assn., AMA, Assn. Am. Med. Colls. (chmn. council deans 1984-85). Home: 2822-8 Marshall Ct Madison WI 53705-2285 Office: 1300 University Ave Madison WI 53706-1510

BROWN, ARTHUR EDWARD, physician; b. Trenton, N.J., June 7, 1945; s. Milton Charles and Jeanne Ruth (Swern) B.; m. Jo Frances Meltzer, Nov. 24, 1985. BS, Bucknell U., 1967; MD, Jefferson Med. Coll., 1971. Intern, resident Roosevelt Hosp., N.Y.C., 1971-72, 74-76; trainee Nat. Cancer Inst., 1976-77; fellow infectious diseases Meml. Sloan-Kettering Cancer Ctr., N.Y.C., 1976-78, clin. asst. physician, 1978-82; asst. prof. medicine and pediatrics Cornell U. Med. Coll., N.Y.C., 1979-85, assoc. prof. clin. medicine and pediatrics, 1985-93, prof. clin. medicine and pediatrics, 1994—; asst. attending physician Meml. Hosp. for Cancer and Allied Diseases, N.Y.C., 1982-89, assoc. attending physician, 1989-93, attending physician, 1993—; assoc. attending pediatrician N.Y. Hosp., N.Y.C., 1985-94, attending pediatrician, 1994—; vis. assoc. physician The Rockefeller U. Hosp., N.Y.C., 1995—. Editor: Infectious Complications of Neoplastic Diseases Controversies in Management, 1985, Infections in Oncology, 1993—; mem. editl. bd. European Jour. clin. Microbiology and Infectious Diseases, 1993—, Infections in Medicine, 1995—, Microbial Drug Resistance, 1996—. Surgeon, USPHS, 1972-74. Recipient 2d pl. HeSCA Print Festival, 1985, Bronze Plaque award Film Coun. Columbus, 1985, Bronze medal Internat. Film & TV Festival, N.Y.C., 1985, Semi-Finalist Am. Jour. Nursing Media Festival, 1986. Fellow ACP, Infectious Diseases Soc. Am. (state and regional bd. dirs. 1995—); mem. AAAS, Am. Fedn. Clin. Rsch., N.Y. County Soc. Internal Medicine (pres. 1994-96) N.Y. State Soc. Internal Medicine (dir. 1995—), N.Y. Soc. Infectious Diseases (sec., treas. 1993—), Am. Soc. Internal Medicine, Am. Soc. Microbiology, N.Y. Acad. Scis., Am. Soc. Clin. Oncology, Soc. Health Care Epidemiology Am., Internat. Immunocompromised Host Soc. Office: Meml Sloan-Kettering Cancer Ctr 1275 York Ave New York NY 10021-6007

BROWN, ARTHUR S., plastic surgery educator; b. Phila., July 3, 1944; s. Leonard and Selma (Salkind) B.; m. Eileen Debby Telman, July 7, 1968; children: Ivy Robin, Chad Michael, Erik Lee. BA, U. Pa., 1966, MD, 1970. Diplomate Am. Bd. Surgery, Am. Bd. Plastic Surgery. Intern U. Pa., Phila., 1970-71, resident in surgery, 1971-76, resident in plastic surgery, 1976-78; from asst. prof. to prof. surgery U. Medicine and Dentistry N.J.-Robert Wood Johnson Med. Sch., Camden, 1978—, head dept. plastic surgery, 1978—, program dir. plastic surgery residency, 1993—, prof. pediatrics, 1987—; adj. assoc. prof. surgery U. Pa., Phila. Bd. dirs. Haddonfield (N.J.) Symphony, 1994—. Maj. USAR (ret.). Office: U Medicine and Dentistry NJ Robert Wood Johnson Med Sch 3 Cooper Plz Rm 411 Camden NJ 08103-1438

BROWN, BAILLIE RUSSELL, health services administrator; b. Olympia, Wash., Sept. 29, 1953; d. Montgomery and Patience (Baker) Russell; m. Harry Silsby Brown, Dec. 6, 1980. Student, St. Martin's Coll., 1970-75; cert. fin. planning for non-profits, U. Calif., Santa Barbara, 1992. Cert. charter optician Opticians Assn. Am., 1975; ophthalmic surg. technician Surg. Office Specialists, 1986. Lic. optician mgr. Cole Nat., Ann Arbor, Mich., 1973-74, Santa Barbara, 1975; lic. optician mgr. Geneau Optical, Santa Barbara, 1976, Robert Cibull, OD, Santa Barbara, 1977-81; med. pub. rels. program officer Direct Relief Internat., Santa Barbara, 1981-85; pub. rels. cons. Santa Barbara Bank & Trust, 1985-89; exec. dir., CFO S.E.E. Internat., Santa Barbara, 1985—. Author: Doctor, My Eyes Are Running, 1984; contbr. articles to profl. jours. Vol. visual aids cons. Braille Inst., Santa Barbara, 1988-91; vol. health care provider Santa Barbara Sch. Dist., 1990—. Fellow Nat. Acad. Ophthalmology; mem. Optician Assn. Am., Calif. Assn. Ophthalmology, Internat. Assn. Vol. Effort (cert. appreciation 1979), Am. Women for Internat. Understanding (v.p., sec., trustee 1979, cert. appreciation 1981). Republican. Anglican. Office: SEE Internat 27 C-2 East De La Guerra St Santa Barbara CA 93101

BROWN, BARBARA JUNE, hospital and nursing administrator; b. Milw., Aug. 17, 1933; d. Carl W. and Nora Anne (Damrow) Rydberg; children: Deborah, Robert, Andrea, Michael, Steven, Jeffrey. BSN, Marquette U., Milw., 1955, MSN, 1960, EdD, 1970. RN, Wash., Wis.; cert. nurse adminstr. advanced. Adminstr. patient care Family Hosp., Milw., 1973-78; assoc. clin. prof. U. Wash., Seattle, 1980-87; assoc. adminstr. nursing Virginia Mason Hosp., Seattle, 1980-87; assoc. exec. dir. King Faisal Specialist Hosp., Riyadh, Saudi Arabia, 1987-91; project dir. NIH, Sexual Assault Treatment Ctr., Milw., 1975-78; lectr., cons., 1974—. Founder, editor Nursing Administration Quarterly, 1976—. Vol. ski instr. for disabled, Winter Park, Colo. Fellow Am. Acad. Nursing (governing coun.), Nat. Acad. Practice; mem. ANA, Am. Orgn. Nurse Execs., Nat. League Nursing (bd. dirs.), Grand County Pub. Health and Emergency Svcs. (chmn. health adv. com. 1994—), Sigma Theta Tau.

BROWN, BENJAMIN THOMAS, urologist, educator; b. Beckley, W.Va., Sept. 30, 1948; s. Benjamin Porter Jr. and Nancy Jo (Ballengee) B.; m. Kimberlee Timbrook; children: Elizabeth Timbrook, James Schuyler. Student, Johns Hopkins U., 1966-69; MD, W.Va. U., 1973. Diplomate Am. Bd. Urology. Surg. intern W.Va. U., Morgantown, 1973-74, resident in medicine, 1974-75; resident in urology U. Miami (Fla.), 1975-78; pvt. practice Daytona Beach, Fla., 1978—; chief surgery Meml. Hosp. Ormond Beach, Fla., 1980-82, chief staff, 1986-87; chief urology Halifax Med. Ctr., Daytona Beach, 1982-84; clin. asst. prof. urology U. South Fla., Tampa, 1979—. Contbr. numerous articles to med. jours. Pres. I-Care, child abuse, Daytona Beach, 1988; vice chmn. adminstrv. bd. United Meth. Ch., 1990-91, pastor, mem. pastor-parish rels. com., 1990-94; bd. dirs. Am. Cancer Soc., 1993—, 2d v.p., 1994-97; bd. dirs. Ptnrs. for Cmty. Health, 1993—, v.p., 1996-97; bd. dirs. Volusia County Coop. Health Group, 1991—, vice chmn., 1993-94, chmn., 1994-96. Fellow ACS; mem. AMA, Am. Urol. Assn. (bd. dirs. Southeastern sect. 1994—, bd. rep. to exec. com. 1996—), Fla. Urol. Soc. (exec. com. 1990—, chmn. bylaws com. 1992-94, membership 1994-96), Underwater Med. Soc., Fla. Med. Assn. (Volusia County del. 1990—), Volusia County Med. Soc. (sec. 1990-91, pres.-elect 1991-92, pres. 1992-93, chmn. bd. govs. 1994-95), Daytona Beach Quarterback Club (team physician 1987), Univ. Club Volusia County (bd. dirs. 1986-89), Tiger Bay Club (2d v.p. 1995-97), Volusia County (bd. dirs.), Rotary, Masons. Republican. Home: 602 Riverside Dr Ormond Beach FL 32176-7714 Office: Atlantic Urol Assocs 545 Health Blvd Daytona Beach FL 32114-1493

BROWN, BRICE NORMAN, surgeon, educator; b. Chariton, Iowa, July 25, 1945; s. Brice Davis and Wilma (Bebout) B.; m. Esther McBride, May 18, 1996; children from previous marriage: Cherin Lynn, Peter Brice. BS in Chemistry, U. Iowa, 1967; MD, Stanford U., 1972. Diplomate Am. Bd. Surgery. Resident in surgery U. Calif., San Diego, 1972-78; pvt. practice Las Vegas, Nev., 1980—. Maj. M.C., U.S. Army, 1978-80. Fellow ACS (sec.-treas. Nev. chpt. 1988-90, pres. Nev. chpt. 1990-92, gov. 1991—), Southwestern Surg. Congress, Internat. Coll. Surgeons; mem. Nev. Med. Assn., Clark County Med. Soc. (trustee 1983-90). Office: Nev Surg Group Ste 204 3100 W Charleston Blvd Las Vegas NV 89102-1996

BROWN, BYRON WILLIAM, JR., biostatistician, educator; b. Chgo., Apr. 21, 1930; s. Byron William and Ruth (Munson) B.; m. Janet Louise Hyde, July 30, 1949; children: Byron William III, Eric Paul, Alan Thomas, Nancy Ellen, Mark Andrew, Lisa Anne. BA in Math., U. Minn., 1952, MS in Stats., 1955, PhD in Biostats., 1959. Asst. prof. biostats. Med. Sch. La. State U., New Orleans, 1956-57; from lectr. to prof. Sch. Pub. Health U. Minn., Mpls., 1957-65, prof., head dept. biostats., 1965-68; prof., head divsn. Stanford (Calif.) U., 1968—, chmn. dept. health rsch. and policy, 1988-96; cons. govt. and industry. Co-author: Statistics: A Biomedical Introduction, 1977; contbr. chpts. to books, articles to profl. jours. and encys. With USAF, 1949. Fellow AAAS, Am. Statis. Assn. (sect. pres., assoc. editor Jour.), Am. Heart Assn.; mem. Inst. Medicine of NAS (elected), Biometrics Soc. (pres. Western N.Am. region 1978), Inst. Math. Stats., Soc. for Clin. Trials (pres. 1988), Internat. Stats. Inst. (elected), Phi Beta Kappa, Sigma Xi. Home: 981 Cottrell Way Stanford CA 94305-1057

BROWN, CALVIN REED, family physician; b. Koosharem, Utah; m. Barbara Brown; 4 children. BA, U. Utah, 1948, MS in Health Scis., 1980, MD, 1951; JD, U. Chgo., 1963. Diplomate Nat. Bd. Med. Examiners, Am.

Bd. Preventive Medicine, Am. Bd. Occupl. Medicine, Am. Bd. Abdominal Surgery, Am. Bd. Family Practice, Internat. Bd. Proctology; lic. physician, Utah, Calif., Hawaii. Pvt. U.S. Army, 1944; advanced through the grades to col. U.S. Air Force, 1986; rotating intern USPHS, 1951-52; resident in surgery Salt Lake County Hosp., 1953-57; pvt. practice Salt Lake City; teaching asst. dept. anatomy U. Utah, 1955-56, 74-75, teaching staff health sci., 1978-81; instr. Calif. N.G.; surgeon gen. SAR, MOWN, VASAA. Contbr. articles to profl. jours. Bishop, High Coun. and missionary LDS Ch., 1953-70; mayor Charter Oak, Calif., 1975-1976; pres. Mt. Olympus Home Owners Assn., 1975-85; pres. Cmty. Coun. Recipient Bronze plaque Utah State Capitol. Mem. SAR (pres.), VFW, Disabled Am. Vets., Sons of Utah Pioneers, Descendents of Royalty of Europe, Mayflower Soc., Am. Coll. Occupl. and Environ. Medicine, Am. Coll. Acad. Surgeons, Am. Coll. Angiology, Am. Coll. Geriatrics, Am. Coll. Family Practice. Home: 4275 White Way Salt Lake City UT 84117

BROWN, CAROLYN BREWER, family nurse practitioner; b. DeKalb County, Ala., May 20, 1950; d. Thomas Cecil and Nancy Fay (Reed) Brewer; children: Daphne Luann, Charles Nathan. ADN, N.E. State Jr. Coll., 1982; BSN cum laude, U. Ala., Huntsville, 1990, MSN, 1994. RN, Ala.; cert. FNP. Nurse practitioner Jackson County Rural Health, Scottsboro, Ala., 96—; FNP Jackson County Rural Health Project, Scottsboro, Ala.; clin. nursing instr. N.E. St. C.C., Rainsville, Ala. Mem. ANA, ASNSA, Ala. Nurse Practitioners Coun., Sigma Theta Tau.

BROWN, CARY DOUGLAS, surgeon; b. Balt., Mar. 13, 1946; s. Paul Lucian and Eleanor June (Naugle) B.; m. Christine M. Nelka, May 1, 1978; 1 child, Phillip. BS, Capital U., 1968; Md, U. Md., Balt., 1972. Diplomate Am. Bd. Surgery. Chief surg. svcs. USAF Hosp., Patrick AFB, Cocoa Beach, Fla., 1977-84, USAF Hosp., Elmendorf AFB, Anchorage, 1984-89; emergency rm. physician Mercy Med. Ctr., Balt., 1989-90; surgeon Montgomery Med. Group, Rockville, Md., 1990—. Contbr. articles to profl. jours. Col. USAF, 1986-89. Fellow Am. Coll. Surgeons; mem. Soc. Air Force Clin. Surgeons, Undersea Med. and Hyperbaric Soc., Md. Med. and Chiurgical Faculty, Montgomery County Med. Soc. Office: 15225 Shady Grove Rd Ste 102 Rockville MD 20850-3234

BROWN, CHARLOTTE A., nurse; b. Salisbury, Md., Dec. 1, 1938; d. Clifford C. and Helen M. (Layton) Fitzgerald; m. James W. Brown, June 19, 1959. RN, Peninsula Regional Med. Ctr., Salisbury, 1959; AA, Wor Wic C.C., Salisbury, 1994. Cert. Cen. Svc. Mgr. Staff nurse Peninsula Regional Med. Ctr., Salisbury, 1959-60, asst. head nurse, 1960-64, head nurse ctrl. svc., 1964-68, supr. nursing svc., 1968-76, supr. ctrl. processing, 1976-91, clin. specialist materials mgmt., 1991—. Fellow Internat. Assn. Ctrl. Svc. Mgmt., Am. Soc. Ctrl. Svc. Mgmt., Delaware Valley Orgn. Ctrl. Svc. Pers., Del-Mar Assn. Ctrl. Svcs. Pers., AAMI, Salvation Army Nurse Fellowship, Alpha Nu Omicron. Home: 32499 Mt Hermon Rd Salisbury MD 21804

BROWN, CHRISTOPHER PATRICK, health care administrator, educator; b. Phoenix, June 7, 1951; s. Charles Francis and R. Patricia (Quinn) B.; m. Tracey Ann Wallenberg, May 23, 1987; 1 child, Ryan Matthew. AA in Biol. Scis., Shasta Coll., Redding, Calif., 1976; AS in Liberal Arts, SUNY, Albany, 1977; grad. Primary Care Assoc. Program, Stanford U., 1978; BA in Community Svcs. Adminstrn., Calif. State U., Chico, 1982; M. in Health Svcs., U. Calif., Davis, 1984. Gen. mgr. Pacific Ambulance Svc., El Cajon, Calif., 1974; primary care assoc. Family Practice, Oregon-Calif., 1978-82; cons. Calif. Health Profls., Chico, 1982-84; bus. ops. mgr. Nature's Arts, Inc., Seattle, 1985-86; instr. North Seattle C.C., 1984-89, program dir., 1986-89; asst. dir. Pacific Med. Clinic North, Seattle, 1990-92; dir. Pacific Med. Clinic Renton (Wash.), Pacific Med. Ctr., 1992-95; dir. ops./physician svcs. St. Luke's Regional Med. Ctr., Boise, Idaho, 1995—. Mem. Butte County Adult Day Care Health Coun., Chico, 1982-84; bd. dirs., pres. Innovative Health Care Svcs., Chico, 1982-84; bd. dirs. Highline W. Seattle Mental Health Ctr., 1985-90, v.p. 1988-90; tech. adv. com. North Seattle C.C., 1992-93, With U.S. Navy, 1970-74. Mem. Internat. Platform Assn., Soc. Ambulatory Care Profls., Med. Group Mgmt. Assn., Multispecialty Group Exec. Soc. Home: 2902 Crane Creek Rd Boise ID 83702 Office: St Lukes Regional Med Ctr 190 E Bannock Boise ID 83712

BROWN, CLAUDE LAMAR, JR., psychiatrist, educator; b. Mobile, Ala., Mar. 12, 1923; s. Claude Lamar and Pauline Johanna (Phifer) B.; m. Catherine McRaney, May 2, 1979; children by previous marriage—Claude Lamar, Paul William, Christianna Lori. B.S., Tulane U., 1943, M.D., 1945. Diplomate Am. Bd. Psychiatry and Neurology. Intern, City Hosp. Mobile, 1945-46; resident in psychiatry Menninger Found. Sch. Psychiatry, Topeka, 1948-51; practice medicine specializing in psychiatry, Mobile, 1951—; mem. staff Mobile Infirmary, Providence Hosp., Doctors Hosp., U. Med. Center Hosp., Southland Hosp., Mobile; clin. prof. psychiatry U. South Ala. Sch. Medicine, 1973—; mem. Ala. Mental Health Bd., 1959-71, chmn., 1967-69. Served to lt. USNR, 1946-48. Fellow Am. Psychiat. Assn.; mem. AMA, Ala. State Med. Assn., Ala. Dist. Br. Am. Psychiat. Assn. (pres. 1981), Mobile County Med. Soc. (pres. 1962). Methodist. Club: Mobile Yacht. Contbr. articles to profl. and popular publs. Office: 176 Louiselle St Mobile AL 36607

BROWN, DAVID ALAN, cardiothoracic surgeon; b. Iron Mountain, Mich., Jan. 23, 1959; s. Gerald F. and Colleen (Bess) B.; m. Elizabeth Ann Altenberger, June 17, 1995; 1 child, David Alan. BA, U. Calif., Berkeley, 1981; MD, U. Calif., Davis, 1985. Diplomate Am. Bd. Surgery, Am. Bd. Thoracic Surgery. Intern, resident in surgery Oreg. Health Scis. U., Portland, 1985-90; resident cardiothoracic surgery U. Calif., San Francisco, 1990-92; asst. prof. cardiothoracic surgery Ohio State U., Columbus, 1993—; mem. Leadership Coun. Clin. Value Enhancement Ohio State U., 1995—, mem. clin. quality assurance, 1994—. Fellow Am. Coll. Chest Physicians, Am. Coll. Surgeons; mem. Internat. Soc. for Heart and Lung Transplantation, Robert M. Zollinger Surg. Soc. Office: Ohio State U 410 W 10th Ave Columbus OH 43210

BROWN, DAVID M., physician, educator, dean; b. Chgo., Nov. 11, 1935; m. Sandra Miriam Brown. B.S., U. Ill., Urban, 1956; M.D., U. Ill., Chgo., 1960. Intern U. Ill. Research-Edn. Hosp., Chgo., 1960-61; resident in pediatrics U. Minn., Mpls., 1961-63; fellow in endocrinology and metabolism U. Minn., 1963-65; attending staff pediatric eoncrinology USAF Hosp., San Antonio, 1965-67; asst. prof. pediatrics, lab. medicine and pathology U. Minn., Mpls., 1967-70; assoc. prof. U. Minn., 1970-73, dir. clin. labs., 1970-84, prof. pediatrics, lab. medicine and pathology, 1974—, dean. Med. Sch., 1984-93; mem. adv. com. on rsch. on women's health NIH, 1995—; co-chair orgainzing com. 7th Internat. Symposium on Basement Membranes, 1995; mem. planning com. NIH 3d Internat. Symposium on Kidney Disease of Diabetes Mellitus, 1991. With USAF, 1965-67. Recipient USPHS Research Career Devel. award, 1968-73. Mem. AAAS, Acad. Clin. Lab. Physicians and Scientists, Am. Diabetes Assn., Am. Pediatric Soc., Am. Physiol. Soc., Am. Soc. Clin. Pathology, Am. Soc. Nephrology, Am. Soc. Pediatric Nephrology, Central Soc. for Clin. Research, Endocrine Soc., Internat. Soc. Nephrology, Lawson Wilkins Soc. Pediatric Endocrinology, Mpls. Pediatris Soc., Orthopaedic Research Soc., Soc. Pediatric Nephrology, Soc. Pediatric Research, Am. Assn. Pathologists, Am. Soc. Bone and Mineral Research, Internat. Acad. Pathology, Assn. Am. Med. Colls. (chmn. council acad. Socs.), Am. Assn. Pathologists, Am. Soc. Cell Biology, Minn. Soc. Clin. Pathology, Alpha Omega Alpha. Home: 2571 Abbey Hill Dr Hopkins MN 55305-2332 Office: Univ Minn Med Sch PO Box 404 420 Delaware St SE Minneapolis MN 55455

BROWN, DONALD DAVID, biology educator; b. Cin., Dec. 30, 1931; s. Albert Louis and Louise (Rauh) B.; m. Linda Jane Weil, July 2, 1957; children: Deborah Lin, Christopher Charles, Sharon Elizabeth. M.S., U. Chgo., 1956, M.D., 1956, D.Sc. (hon.), 1976; D.Sc. (hon.), U. Md., 1983; DSc (hon.), U. Cin., 1992. Staff mem. dept. embryology Carnegie Instn. of Washington, Balt., 1963—; dir. Carnegie Instn. of Washington, 1976-94; prof. dept. biology Johns Hopkins U., 1968—. Pres. Life Scis. Research Found. Served with USPHS, 1957-59. Recipient U.S. Steel Found. award for molecular biology, 1973; V.D. Mattia award Roche Inst., 1975; Boris Pregel award for biology N.Y. Acad. Scis., 1976; Ross G. Harrison award Internat. Soc. Developmental Biology, 1981; Bertner Found. award, 1982; Rosenstiel award for biomed. sci., 1985, Louisa Gross Horwitz award, 1985; Feodor Lynen award U. Miami Winter Symposium, 1987. Fellow Am. Acad. Arts and Scis., AAAS; mem. Nat. Acad. Scis. (mem. coun. 1994—), Soc. Devel. Biology (pres. 1975), Am. Soc. Biol. Chemists, Am. Soc. Cell Biology (pres. 1992), Am. Philos. Soc. Home: 5721 Oakshire Rd Baltimore MD 21209-4217 Office: Carnegie Instn Washington 115 W University Pky Baltimore MD 21210-3301

BROWN, DUDLEY EARL, JR., psychiatrist, educator, health executive, former federal agency administrator, former naval officer; b. Berryville, Va., Apr. 10, 1928; s. Dudley Earl and Rosa Lee (Costello) B.; m. Lelia Adrienne Motley, June 22, 1953; children—Lelia Brown Farr, David, Kevin. B.A., Washington and Lee U., 1949; M.D., Med. Coll. Va., 1953. Diplomate: Am. Bd. Psychiatry and Neurology. Commd. lt. (j.g.) M.C. U.S. Navy, 1953, advanced through grades to rear adm., 1974; intern Naval Hosp., Portsmouth, Va., 1953-54; resident in neuropsychiatry Naval Hosp., Bethesda, Md., 1957-60; service in Vietnam; comdg. officer Nat. Naval Med. Center, Bethesda, 1975-76, Naval Regional Med. Center, San Diego, 1976-78; fleet surgeon U.S. Pacific Fleet and staff surgeon, comdr.-in-chief U.S. Forces, Pacific, Pearl Harbor, Hawaii, 1978-80; ret., 1980; dep. asst. chief med. dir. for profl. services VA Central Office, Washington, 1980-82; assoc. dep. chief med. dir. VA, Washington, 1982-87; asst. prof. clin. psychiatry U. Pa. Med. Sch., 1967-70; prof. clin. psychiatry Uniformed Svcs. U. Health Scis., Bethesda, Md., 1981—, Med. Coll. Va., Va. Commonwealth U., Richmond, 1987—; dir. health policy studies, dir. Washington office Abt Assocs. Inc., 1987-93, v.p., 1992—, mng. v.p., 1993—. Contbr. to med. jours. Decorated Legion of Merit; recipient Meritorious Svc. medal, Navy Commendation medal, VA Disting. Svc. medal, Disting. Alumnus Med. Coll. Va., 1993. Fellow ACP, Am. Psychiat. Assn., Am. Coll. Psychiatrists; mem. Washington Psychiat. Soc., Nat. Health Coun. (bd. dirs. 1989-94), Assn. Mil. Surgeons U.S., Soc. Med. Cons. to Armed Forces (v.p. 1988-89, pres. 1989-90), Phi Gamma Delta, Alpha Epsilon Delta. Presbyterian. Home: 2415 Black Cap Ln Reston VA 22091-3027 Office: Abt Assocs Inc 4800 Montgomery Ln Ste 600 Bethesda MD 20814-5341

BROWN, EDITH, social worker; b. Milw., Nov. 25, 1935; d. Anton J. and Elizabeth K. (Kribitsch) Volk; m. Edward S. Brown. BS, U. Wis., 1958, MS in Social Work, 1964; MS in Mgmt., Cardinal Stritch Coll., Milw., 1985. Cert. ind. clin. social worker Wis., Dept. Pub. Instrn. sch. social work cert. Hosp. admissions worker, 1958-60; welfare worker, 1960-62; with Kiwanis Children's Ctr. and Children's Hosp. Psychiat. Clinic, Milw., 1962-64; social worker Lutheran Social Services, Milw., 1964-67; foster care supr. Milwaukee County Dept. Social Services, 1967-71, social services adminstr. child protection and parent services, comprehensive emergency services and a coordinated community edn. and support services, 1971-79; assoc. dir. Community Devel. Agy., City of Milw., 1979-89; med. social worker Children's Hosp. Wis.; tech. advisor for child abuse, neglect, woman abuse, domestic violence; grants writer, tchr., cons. in field. Mem. Summerfest Adv. Council, Mayor's Beautification Com.; chmn. Summerfest Planting, 1972—; chmn. Milwaukee County Child Abuse and Neglect Task force, 1976-78; chmn. adv. council Milw. Boy's Club, 1981-84; vice chmn. Internat. Yr. for Disabled Persons, 1982; liaison Nat. Yr. for Disabled Persons, City of Milw., 1982-83; asst. chairperson City of Milw. United Way Campaign, 1983; mem. Mayor's Youth Initiatives Task Force, 1984-85; mem. adv. panel M.P.A. degree program U. Wis., 1993—; mem. adv. coun. Arthritis Found. Office of Vocat. Rehab. scholar, 1962-64; Successful Women in Mgmt. award J. Wis., 1977; award Community Tchrs. Corps, 1977; Changemaker award Wis. Fed. Jr. Women's Clubs, 1978; Outstanding Community Services award Milwaukee County, 1979, Outstanding Services award, 1979, Exemplary Service award, 1982; Woman of Yr. award Mcpl. Women's Assn., 1981, Mem. of Yr. award Variety of Wis., 1991. Mem. Acad. Cert. Social Workers, Nat. Assn. Social Workers, Internat. Council on Social Welfare, Internat. Fedn. Social Welfare, Am. Soc. for Pub. Adminstrn. (pres. Milw. chpt., Outstanding Service and Dedication award 1984-85), Research Clearinghouse, Am. Bus. Women's Assn. (Woman of Yr. award 1975), Internat. Graphoanalysis Soc. (pres. Wis. chpt., 1988 Citation of Merit), Assn. Rheumatology Health Profls., Assn. for Care of Childrens Health, Variety of Wis. Tech. Club. Contbr. to profl., community, resource documents, 1971—; author print and broadcast programs. Office: Children's Hosp Wis 9000 W Wisconsin Ave Milwaukee WI 53226-3518

BROWN, EDWIN WILSON, JR., physician, educator; b. Youngstown, Ohio, Mar. 6, 1926; s. Edwin Wilson and Doris (McClellan) B.; m. Patricia Ann Currier, Aug. 9, 1952; children: Edwin Wilson, John Currier, Wende Patricia. Student, Carnegie Inst. Tech., 1943, Houghton Coll., 1946-47, Amherst Coll., 1943-44; M.D., Harvard U., 1953, M.P.H. (Nat. Found. fellow), 1957. Research fellow U. Buffalo, 1953-54; intern E.J. Meyer Meml. Hosp., Buffalo, 1954-55; resident pub. health Va. Dept. Health, 1955-56; tchr. medicine specializing in preventive medicine Boston, 1958-61, Hyderabad, India, 1961-63; assoc. med. dir. People-to-People Health Found., Washington, 1965-66; assoc. prof. medicine Ind. U.-Purdue U., Indpls., 1966-85, dir. div. internat. affairs, 1966-74, assoc. dean student services, dir. internat. services, 1979-85; pres. Global Health Svcs., Inc., Indpls., 1986—; med. dir. Ind. Dept. Correction, 1974-76; sr. med. edn. advisor King Faisal U., Dammam, Saudi Arabia, 1977-78; field dir. Harvard Epidemiol. Project, Egedesminde, Greenland, 1956-57; asst. prof. preventive medicine Sch. Medicine Tufts U., 1958-61; dep. chief staff Boston Dispensary, 1961; vis. prof. preventive medicine Osmania Med. Coll., Hyderabad, India, 1961-63; asst. dir. div. internat. med. edn., dir. AAMC-AID project internat. med. edn. Assn. Am. Med. Colls., Evanston, 1963-65; exec. sec. Study Group on Childhood Accidents, Boston, 1959-61; research asso. Sch. Pub. Health, Harvard U., 1959-60; dir. Curtis Pub. Co., Inc.; cons. Boston City Health Dept., 1959-60, WHO, 1973-74; chmn. bd. dirs. Med. Assistance Programs, Inc. Contbr. articles to profl. jours. Bd. dirs. Paul Carlson Found., Campus Teams, Iran Found., CARE/MEDICO, Internat. Students Inc. Served with AUS, 1944-46, ETO. Fellow Am. Pub. Health Assn.; mem. Assn. Tchrs. Preventive Medicine, Indian Assn. Advancement Med. Edn., Mass. Med. Soc., Internat. Policy Forum (bd. govs.), Nat. Policy Coun., Rotary Internat., Sigma Xi. Home: 8153 Oakland Rd Indianapolis IN 46240-2747 Office: PO Box 40951 Indianapolis IN 46240-0951

BROWN, ELISE ANN BRANDENBURGER, toxicologist; b. Jacksonville, Fla., Dec. 5, 1928; d. Oscar Louis and Inez Marie (Peterson) Brandenburger; m. Arthur Brickman Brown, June 14, 1952; children: Barron,Terrence Leon, Roderick Scott Kjelmyr. BS in Chemistry, George Washington U., 1949, MS in Biochemistry, 1950, PhD in Pharmacology, 1956. Diplomate toxicology Am. Bd. Toxicology. Rsch. asst. dept. pharmacology George Washington U., Washington, 1948-50; biochemist radioactivity U.S. Dept. Agr., 1950-52; asst. prof. pharmacology George Washington U., Washington, 1956-57; post-doctoral fellow McCollum-Pratt Inst., Johns Hopkins U., Sinai Hosp., 1957-59; rsch. pharmacologist lab. chem. pharmacology Nat. Inst. Heart, Lung, Blood NIH, Rockville, Md., 1962-73, rsch. pharmacologist pulmonary br. molecular pharmacology, 1973-75, 1975-79; toxicologist residue evaluation and planning div. Food Safety Inspection Svc., USDA, Washington, 1979—; chemist Naval Rsch. Lab., 1948; speaker 2d Conf. on Current Investigations Dealing with Elasmobranch Biology, Bar Harbor, Maine, 1971, Internat. Symposium on Hexachlorobenzene, Lyon, France, 1985, Am. Coll. Toxicology, 1986, 1st Internat. Congress on Toxicology in Developing Countries, Buenos Aires, 1987; participant Alpha Helix Expdn. to B.C., 1974; Food Safety Inspection Svc. rep. to EPA for residue rule making, 1989; mem. interagy. testing com. Toxic Substances Control Act, EPA, 1986-89. Contbr. articles and abstracts to profl. jours. Recording sec. Capt. John Smith chpt. NSDAR, 1967-69, vice regent, 1969-71, regent, 1971-73, registrar, 1976-77; active J.F. Cooper Intermediate Sch. PTA, chmn. landscape com., 1971-72; chairperson landscape com. McLean Community Ctr.; pres. Dolly Madison Stamp Club, 1980-82. Med. officer, 2nd lt. Civil Air Patrol, 1968—. Recipient Pres. award, 1981-88; predoctoral fellow NIH, Nat. Cancer Inst., 1955-59. Fellow Washington Acad. Scis. (sec. 1983-84), treas. 1984-85), Explorers Club; mem. Am. Chem. Soc. (chmn. by-laws com. Washington 1985, hospitality com. 1985-87, pres. 1988, chmn. pub. affairs nat. div. chem. health and safety 1980-82), Soc. Toxicology (chpt. councilor 1987-89), Soc. Exptl. Biology and Medicine (pres. 1979-80, 86-89), Am. Coll. Toxicology, Am. Soc. Pharmacology and Exptl. Therapeutics, Internat. Soc. Biochem. Pharmacology, Assn. Govt. Toxicologists (pres. 1991-92), Sigma Xi, Alpha Chi Sigma. Home: 6811 Nesbitt Pl Mc Lean VA 22101-2133 Office: USDA FSIS 300 12th St SW Washington DC 20024

BROWN, ELIZABETH RUTH, neonatologist; b. Washington, Sept. 29, 1946; d. Paul Ambrose and Helene Marie (Kiley) B.; m. William James Pyne, Sept. 28, 1990. BS, Coll. Mt. St. Vincent, Bronx, N.Y., 1968; MD, U. Md., 1972. Diplomate Am. Bd. Med. Examiners, Am. Bd. Pediatrics, sub-board neonatal-perinatal medicine; lic. physician, Mass. Pediatric intern McGill U., Montreal (Que., Can.) Children's Hosp., 1972-73, resident pediatrics, 1973-75; neonatal rsch. fellow dept. pediatrics Harvard Med. Sch. Joint Program in Neonatology, Boston, 1975-78; dir. Infant Follow-Up Program, med. dir. Project Welcome The Children's Hosp., Boston, 1979-85; dir. neonatology Newton (Mass.) Wellesley Hosp., 1984-85; dir. Neonatal Follow Up Clinic Boston City Hosp., 1985-88; co-dir. Boston Perinatal Ctr., 1985—; dir. neonatology Boston City Hosp., 1985—; clin. instr. pediatrics Tufts U. Sch. Medicine, Boston, 1987—; summer fellow tng. program in pub. health N.Y.C. Dept. Pub. Health, Met. Hosp., N.Y.C., 1969; mem. Kellogg Found. Nat. Fellowship Program, Battle Creek, Mich., 1988-91; assoc. prof. pediatrics Boston U. Sch. Medicine, 1987—, asst. prof. ob-gyn., 1985—; instr. pediatrics Harvard Med. Sch., 1979-85, tutor in medicine, 1980-82; lectr. Coll. Pharmacy and Allied Health Professions, Northeastern U., Boston, 1981—; assoc. neonatologist Joint Program in Neonatology, 1979-85. Contbr. articles to profl. jours., chpts. to books. Bd. dirs. Boston Inst. for Devel. of Infants and Parents, Inc., 1983—, NICU Parent Support, Inc., 1980—; mem. adv. bd. Children's Hosp. AIDS Program, 1988; bd. dirs. March of Dimes, Mass. chpt., 1989, Coalition on Addiction, Pregnancy and Parenting, 1990. Named Citizen of Yr. Mass. Assn. Retarded Citizens, 1984; recipient award of excellence Boston Inst. for Devel. Infants and Parents, Inc., 1988. Mem. AMA, Am. Acad. Pediatrics, Am. Med. Women's Assn., Nat. Assn. for Perinatal Addiction Rsch. and Edn., Mass. Perinatal Assn., Mass. Med. Soc., Aircraft Owners and Pilots Assn.

BROWN, ERIC JOEL, biomedical researcher; b. Ann Arbor, Mich., Sept. 27, 1950; s. Bernard and Shirley (Mark) B.; m. Marion Glynn Peters, Apr. 2, 1983; 1 child, Abigail. AB, Harvard Coll., 1971; MD, Harvard Med. Sch., 1975. Intern, then resident Beth Israel Hosp., Boston, 1975-77; clin. assoc. LCI/NIAID/NIH, Bethesda, Md., 1977-79, expert, 1979-81, sr. investigator, 1981-85; assoc. prof. Washington U., St. Louis, 1985-90, co-dir. divsn. infectious diseases, 1989—, prof., 1990—. With USPHS, 1981-85. Fellow Infectious Diseases Soc.; mem. Soc. for Clin. Investigation, Am. Assn. Physicians. Office: Washington U Divsn Infectious Diseases 660 S Euclid Ave Saint Louis MO 63110-1010

BROWN, FRANK REGINALD, III, pediatrician, educator; b. Kansas City, Mo., Oct. 15, 1943; s. Frank R. Jr. and Charlotte Elaine (Snider) B.; m. Martha Ann Wilson, Jan. 23, 1988; children: Frank R. IV, Riggs Wilson. BS in Chemistry, Stanford U., 1965, MS in Chemistry, 1967; PhD in Biol. Chemistry, Harvard U., 1971; MD, Washington U., 1975. Diplomate Am. Bd. Pediatrics. Rsch. assoc. Washington U. Sch. of Medicine, St. Louis, 1972-73; instr. pediatrics Johns Hopkins Med. Instns., Balt., 1980-81, asst. prof. pediatrics, 1981-84; assoc. prof. pediatrics Med. U. S.C., Charleston, 1984-88, prof. pediatrics, 1988-93; prof. pediatrics Baylor Coll. Medicine, 1993—; dir. Meyer Ctr for Devel. Pediatrics, Tex. Children's Hosp., Houston, 1993—; dir. div. devel. disabilities Med. U. S.C., also Vince Mosely Ctr. for Handicapped Children, Charleston. Author: Diagnosis and Management of Learning Disabilities, 1992, 96; editor Jour. of Learning Disabilities, Mental Retardation and Devel. Disabilities Rsch. Revs. Bd. dirs. S.C. Spl. Olympics, Columbia, 1987-90; advisor Joseph P. Kennedy Jr. Found. for Mental Retardation, Washington. Named Joseph P. Kennedy Jr. scholar for mental retardation, Joseph P. Kennedy Jr. Found., Washington, 1982, sr. fellow Nat. Multiple Sclerosis, N.Y., 1986, Jeffrey Edwin Gilliam Prof., Med. U. S.C., 1988-93. Fellow Am. Acad. Pediatrics; mem. Am. chem. Soc., Soc. for Devel. Pediatrics, Phi Beta Kappa, Sigma Xi, Alpha Omega Alpha. Home: 545 Begonia St Bellaire TX 77401-5005 Office: Texas Childrens Hosp Meyer Ctr 6621 Fannin St Houston TX 77030-2303

BROWN, FREDERICK LEE, health care executive; b. Clarksburg, W.Va., Oct. 22, 1940; s. Claude Raymond and Anne Elizabeth (Kiddy) B.; children: Gregory Lee, Michael Owen-Price. BA in Psychology, Northwestern U., 1962; MBA in Health Care Adminstrn., George Washington U., 1966. Vocat. counselor Cook County Dept. Pub. Aid, Chgo., 1962-64; adminstrv. resident Meth. Hosp. Ind., Inc., Indpls., 1965-66, adminstrv. asst., 1966, asst. adminstr., 1966-71, assoc. adminstr., 1971-72, v.p. ops., 1972-74; exec. v.p., chief operating officer Meml. Hosp. DuPage County, Elmhurst, Ill., 1974-82, Meml. Health Svcs., Elmhurst, 1980-82; pres., chief executive officer Christian Hosp. NW-NW, St. Louis, 1982-89; pres., chief exec. officer CH Health Techs., Inc., St. Louis, 1983-93, Christian Health Svcs., St. Louis, 1986-93, CH Allied Svcs., Inc., St. Louis, 1988-93; pres., CEO BJC Health System, St. Louis, 1993—; adj. instr. Washington U. Sch. Medicine, St. Louis, 1982—; mem. chancellor's coun. U. Mo., St. Louis, 1990—; bd. dirs. HealthLink, Inc., 1985-92, mem. exec. com., 1986-92, chmn. bd., 1989-91; pres., chief exec. officer Village North, Inc., 1986-93; bd. dirs. Am. Healthcare Systems, Inc., chmn. shareholder communications com., 1985-86, v. chmn. 1992; bd. dirs. Commerce Bank St. Louis, Am. Excess Ins. Ltd.; mem. corp. assembly Blue Cross Blue Shield Mo., 1991—. Contbr. articles to profl. jours. Co-chmn. hosp. div. United Way Greater St. Louis, 1983, chmn., 1984, chmn. health svcs. div., 1985-86, vice chmn. region, 1988—, bd. dirs., 1986, Kammergild Chamber Orch., 1984-88, v.p., 1985-88, Mo. Heart Inst., 1988-92, Alton Meml. Hosp., 1987-91, bd. dirs., 1987-91; mem. exec. bd. St. Louis Area coun. Boy Scouts Am. Northstar chpt., 1989, activities coun. chmn. 1993—, bd. trustees 1990-92, chmn. Friends of Scouting Campaign, 1991-92; communion steward Webster Hills Meth. Ch., 1987—; mem. medicaid budget task force Mo. Dept. Social Svcs., 1990; mem. emergency rm. svcs. task force St. Louis Regional Med. Ctr., 1985; mem. corp. assembly Blue Cross Blue Shield of Mo., 1991; bd. dirs. Sold on St. Louis, 1991-93; St. Louis Reg. Commerce & Growth Assn., 1993—; mem. St. Louis City and County Task Force, 1991—. Fellow Am. Coll. Healthcare Execs. (chmn. credentials com. 1978, task force governance and constituencies 1986-88; mem. Gold Medal award com. 1985, chmn. task force on governance and constituencies 1986-87, com. on ethics 1989-91, chmn. awards & testamonials com., 1992—, bd. regents 1991-93); gov. dist V, mem. Am. Acad. Med. Adminstrs. (life, state dir. 1988—, Health Care Exec. of Yr. 1990, Statesman in Healthcare, 1992), Hosp. Pres.'s Assn., Advt. Club Greater St. Louis, Am. Hosp. Assn. (coun. on mgmt. 1987, alt. del. for healthcare systems 1988-90, del. to ho. of dels. for health care systems 1991, fin. com. chair 1995), Am. Pub. Health Assn., George Washington U. Alumni Assn. for Health Svcs. Adminstrn. (preceptor 1975—, Alumnus of Yr. award 1981, Frederick Gibbs award, 1993), Hosp. Assn. Met. St. Louis (bd. dirs. 1984—, chmn. bd. 1988-89, sec. 1985-86, treas. 1987, chmn. coun. on pub. affairs and communications 1985, vice chmn. 1987, various coms.), Greater St. Louis Health Care Alliance (co-chair 1992—), Mo. Hosp. Assn. (mem. coun. on rsch. and policy devel. 1983-88, chmn. coun. on multi-instnl. hosps. 1986-88, mem. dist. coun. pres.'s 1986-89, bd. dirs. 1988-92, chmn. bd. trustees 1990), Cen. Ea. Profl. Rev. Orgn. (bd. dirs. 1982-85, various coms.), St. Louis Met. Med. Soc. (lay advisor 1990-92), Healthcare Execs. Study Soc., Internat. Health Policy and Mgmt. Inst. (bd. dirs. 1988—), Am. Protestant Health Assn. (bd. dirs. 1988-93, chmn. 1992-93), St. Louis Club, Algonquin Golf Club, Arena Club, Stadium Club (St. Louis), Rotary. Republican. Office: BJC Health System 4444 Forest Park Ave Saint Louis MO 63108

BROWN, GARY C., ophthalmologist; b. Mineola, N.Y., May 14, 1949; m. Melissa M. Brown; children: Heather, Heidi, Kathryn. BS, Colgate U., 1971; MD, SUNY Upstate Med. Ctr., Syracuse, 1975. Intern Grady Hosp./Emory U., Atlanta, 1975-76; resident Wills Eye Hosp., Phila., 1976-79, fellow, 1979-81; physician Retinovitreous Assocs., Wyndmoor, Pa.; pres., chmn. bd. dirs. Pa. Physician Health Plan, Inc., Harrisburg, 1994-96. Author medical texts, 3 novels, over 150 sci. papers in field; editor: Current Science in Ophthalmology, 1992-96. Mem. AMA, Am. Acad. Ophthalmology (sr. honor award 1994), Pa. Med. Soc., Pa. Acad. Ophthalmology (pres.-elect), Wills Eye Ex-Resident Soc. (pres. 1996), Ophthalmologic Club of Phila. (pres. 1985), Phi Beta Kappa, Alpha Omega Alpha. Office: Retinovitreous Assocs 910 E Willow Grove Ave Wyndmour PA 19038

BROWN, GAY WEST, school psychologist; b. L.A., Nov. 20, 1953; d. James Dale and Ola Maye (Daniels) West; m. Lorenzo Hubbard, Nov. 26, 1977 (dec. Feb. 1990); 1 child, Loren Rochelle; m. Fred Lyndle Brown, Jr., Dec. 28, 1992. BA, Calif. State U., Dominguez Hills, 1975; MS, U. So. Calif., 1976; PhD, UCLA, 1991. Lic. ednl. psychologist; cert. sch. psychologist. Student counselor Dignity Ctr. for Drug Abuse, L.A., 1974-76; community health worker Am. Indian Free Clinic, Compton, Calif.,

1974-76; student psychologist Martin Luther King Hosp., L.A., 1976-77; counselor aide Washington High Sch., L.A., 1974-77; vocat. counselor Skill Ctr., L.A., 1977-78; sch. psychologist L.A. Unified Sch. Dist., 1978—, tchr., advisor, 1988-90; psychol. asst. Verdugo Hills (Calif.) Mental Health, 1984-85; counselor, coord. Crenshaw High Sch., L.A., 1985-87; asst. behavior sci. cons. Coalition Mental Profls., L.A., 1992-93; psychol. asst. Martin Luther King Hosp., L.A., 1992-93; part-time prof. Calif. State U., L.A., 1994-95. Mem. APA, Nat. Assn. Sch. Psychologists, Calif. Assn. Sch. Psychologists, L.A. Assn. Sch. Psychologists, Assn. Black Psychologists (sec. 1992-93, historian 1995-96), Pan African Scholars Assn., United Tchrs. L.A., Delta Sigma Theta. Democrat. United Methodist. Office: Sch Mental Health Clinic 439 W 97th St Los Angeles CA 90003-3968

BROWN, GEORGE RICHARD, psychiatrist; b. Schenectady, Mar. 19, 1957; m. Sandra Dinwoodie. BS with high honors, U. Rochester, 1979, MD with honors, 1983. Diplomate Am. Bd. Psychiatry and Neurology. Commd. capt. USAF, advanced through grades to maj., 1991, retired, 1991; intern USAF Med. Ctr., Wright-Patterson AFB, Ohio, 1983-84; resident Wright State U., Dayton, Ohio, 1984-87; staff psychiatrist Wilford Hall USAF Med. Ctr., San Antonio, 1987-91; dir. psychiat. rsch. Wilford Hall USAF Med. Ctr., 1989-91; sr. rsch. scientist Henry M. Jackson Found., San Antonio, 1991-93; assoc. prof. psychiatry, vice-chmn. dept. psychiatry East Tenn. State U.; chief of psychiatry VA Med Ctr, Mountain Home, Tenn.; asst. clin. instr. Wright State U., 1983-87; cons. in field. Contbr. some 100 articles to profl. jours. Recipient Physicians Recognition award, AMA, 1986—, Pres.'s award, Ohio Psychiatric Assn., 1987, Acad. Psychosomatic Medicine 1990 Dlin Fischer award. Mem. Am. Psychiat. Assn., Harry Benjamin Internat. Gender Dysphoria Assn., Tenn. Psychiat. Assn., Alpha Omega Alpha, Phi Beta Kappa. Home: 175 Bill Jones Rd Jonesborough TN 37659-6520 Office: Dept Psychiatry VA Med Ctr 116A Mountain Home TN 37684

BROWN, GERALDINE, nurse, freelance writer; b. Clemson, S.C.; d. Isaac and Gladys (Patterson) B. AS in Nursing, U. D.C., Washington, 1973; real estate cert., Long and Foster Inst., College Park, Md., 1984; cert. in TV broadcasting, Columbia Sch., Bailey's Crossroads, Va., 1987; BS in Nursing, Bowie State U., 1989, MA in Communications, 1991; PhD, Howard U., 1994. RN, D.C., FCC Third Class License. Supr. staff nurse Walter Reed Hosp., Washington, 1970-76; supr. clin. nurse Dept. Human Svcs., Washington, 1976-78, community health nurse, 1978-84; nursing instr. Phillips Bus. Sch., Alexandria, Va., 1984-85; pvt. nurse Washington, 1973—; faculty Howard U. Coll. Nursing, 1994—; dir. pub. affairs Bible Way Chs. Worldwide, Inc., Washington, 1978-91; soc. columnist As It Happens, Charlotte (N.C.) Post, 1964-66; soc. editor Washington Cafe Soc. mag, 1971; contbr. feature stories Capital Spotlight newspaper, 1978—; mem. faculty Coll. Nursing, Howard U., 1994—. Asst. organizer DC Mayor's United Nations Day, 1980; vol. Met. Boys and Girls Clubs, Washington, 1980—; vol. Nursing Instr., The Washington Saturday Coll., 1982-84; Co. ARC, 1973—, Big Sisters of the Washington Met. Area, 1988—. Recipient certs. of excellence Govt. of D.C., 1978-84; cert. of appreciation Mayor of D.C., 1980, meritorious pub. svc. award, 1980; svc. trophy Washington Saturday Coll., 1984. Mem. ANA, NAACP, Nat. Coun. Negro Women, Smithsonian Inst. (assoc.), Nat. Black Nurses Assn., Washington Urban League, Chi Eta Phi, Sigma Theta Tau. Democrat.

BROWN, GLENDA BIRT, optometrist; b. Charlottetown, Can., Jan. 14, 1955; came to U.S., 1969, naturalized, 1972; d. Richard Mason and Reta Marie (McInnis) Birt; m. Alan David Brown, July 7, 1979; children: Meredith, Garrett, Mallory. BA, U. Ala., 1977; BS, U. Ala. Sch. Optometry, 1979, OD, 1981. Cert. optometrist, Ga. Pediatric optometrist Pediat. Eye Surgery of Atlanta, 1982—. Mem. Am. Optometric Assn., Atlanta 5th Dist. Optometry, Ga. Optometric Assn., Emory Vision Correction Group. Republican. Presbyn. Office: Pediatric Eye Surgery Ste 440 5671 Peachtree-Dunwoody Rd Atlanta GA 30342

BROWN, GORDON EARL, surgeon, consultant; b. Highland Park, Mich., Mar. 4, 1931; s. Cecil E. and Margaret Glenn (Thurston) B.; m. Christina Cordell Krauss, Feb. 1, 1990. AB, Kenyon Coll., 1953; MD, Columbia U., 1957; MPA, Pa. State U., 1995. Intern U. Va. Hosp., 1957-58; resident gen. surgery Cedars Sinai Hosp., L.A., 1963-66, L.A. County Harbor Gen. Hosp., 1966-68; surg. registrar Selly Oak Hosp., Birmingham, England, 1968-69; pvt. practice gen. surgery Bishop, Calif., 1971-82; gen. surgeon Whitaker Corp., 1982-84, Locum Tenens, 1984-86, Lancaster (Pa.) Cardiothoracic Surgeons, 1986-88; cons. Blue Shield of Pa., Camp Hill, 1988—; med. advisor QA and I Cmty. Gen. Hosp., Reading, Pa. Capt. USAF, 1959-62. Home and Office: 623 N Lime St Lancaster PA 17602-2217

BROWN, GRETCHEN MARCUM, health facility administrator; b. Lexington, Ky., May 25, 1948; d. Herbert Clay and June Catherine (Nall) Marcum; children: Gabriel, Andrew. BA, U. Ky., 1971, MSW, 1973. Mental health specialist Dept. Human Resources, Lexington, Ky., 1973-76; asst. dir. drug project Bluegrass East Comprehensive Care Ctr., Lexington, 1977-79; dir. substance abuse Bluegrass Mental Health/Mental Retardation Bd., Lexington, 1979-81; pres., CEO Hospice of the Bluegrass, Lexington, 1982—; bd. dirs. Nat. Hospice Orgn., Washington, Health Ky., Louisville, Bluegrass Mental Health, Lexington. Bd. dirs. Chrysalis House, Inc., Lexington. Named Outstanding Woman AAUW; recipient Creativity award Alpha Xi Delta. Mem. Ky. Assn. Hospices (legis. chair, former pres.), Ky. Women's Leadership Network. Home: 309 Desha Dr Lexington KY 40502 Office: Hospice of the Bluegrass 2312 Alexandria Dr Lexington KY 40504

BROWN, HARDIN, occupational health nurse; b. Memphis, July 6, 1955. ADN, Memphis State U., 1976; BSN, U. Neb. Med. Ctr., 1978; MPA, Portland (Oreg.) State U., 1984; MSN, Oreg. Health Scis. U., 1985. RN, Oreg., Tenn. DON svcs. Beverly Enterprises, Portland, 1981-82; instr. Meth. Sch. Nursing, Memphis, 1992-94, occupational health nurse, 1994—; rsch. assessment of staff turnover nursing assts. Oreg. Geriatric Nursing Homes. Mem. ARC. Lt. USN, 1985-90, USNR, 1990-92. Mem. Nat. Assn. Orthopaedic Nurses, Assn. Mil. Surgeons of U.S., Navy Nurse Corps Assn., Am. Assn. Occupational Health Nurses, Sigma Theta Tau.

BROWN, HENRY CHAPMAN, III, pharmacist; b. Lynchburg, Va., Aug. 14, 1959; s. Henry Chapman Jr. and Emily (Lindsay) B. Student, Lynchburg Coll., 1977-80; BS in Pharmacy, U. N.C., Chapel Hill, 1983. Registered pharmacist, Va. Pharmacist, v.p. Gretna (Va.) Drug Co., Inc., 1983—. Mem. Am. Pharm. Assn., Va. Pharm. Assn., Gretna Mchts. Assn., Chancellor's Club, Alumni Assn. Lynchburg Coll. Republican. Methodist. Home: PO Box 456 Gretna VA 24557-0456 Office: Gretna Drug Co Inc Henry At S Shelton St Gretna VA 24557

BROWN, HORACE JACK, surgeon; b. Oxford, Miss., Dec. 19, 1934; s. Horace Brightberry and Dorothy Pittman (Seale) B.; m. Suzanne Neill, Sept. 6, 1957 (dec. Nov. 1986); children—Camille Suzanne (dec.), Brandon Neill, Shannon Suzanne, Allison Elaine; m. Maribeth Potter, Mar. 14, 1987. B.S., U. Okla., 1956, M.D., 1959. Diplomate Am. Bd. Surgery. Intern Walter Reed Gen. Hosp., Washington, 1959-60; surgery resident Wilford Hall USAF Hosp., 1960-64; staff surgeon Mercy Hosp., Oklahoma City, 1969—, Edmond (Okla.) Meml. Hosp., 1974—; staff surgeon Presbyn. Hosp., Oklahoma City, 1969—, vice chmn. dept., 1975—; clin. instr. surgery U. Okla., 1969—; cons. Oklahoma City, Muskogee VA hosps., 1970—. Served to lt. col. USAF, 1958-69. Mem. ACS (sec.-treas. Okla. chpt. 1972), AMA, John Hunter Surg. Soc., Soc. Non-Invasive Vascular Technologists, Am. Soc. Bariatric Surgery, Southwestern Surg. Congress, Okla. Med. Assn., Okla. Surg. Assn., Oklahoma City Surg. Soc., Phi Sigma, Alpha Epsilon Delta, Alpha Omega Alpha, Phi Beta Pi, Beta Theta Pi. Republican. Methodist. Contbr. articles to profl. jours.

BROWN, J. MARTIN, oncologist, educator; b. Doncaster, Eng., Oct. 15, 1941; married; 2 children. BSc, U. Birmingham, 1963; MSc, U. London, 1965; DPhil in Radiation Biology, Oxford U., 1968. NIH fellow radiation biology Stanford U. Med. Ctr., Calif., 1968-70, rsch. assoc., 1970-71, from asst. prof. to assoc. prof., 1971-84, prof., dir. divsn. radiation biology, 1984—, dir. Cancer Biology Rsch. Lab., 1985—; sr. fellow Am. Cancer Soc. Dernham, 1971-74; mem. adv. com. biol. effects of ionizing radiations NAS, 1971—. Mem. AAAS, Am. Assn. Cancer Rsch., Am. Soc. Therapeutical Radiology & Oncology, Brit. Inst. Radiology, Brit. Assn. Cancer Rsch., Radiation Rsch. Soc. (9th Rsch. award 1980). Office: Stanford U Med Ctr Cancer Biology Rsch Lab Dept of Radiation & Oncology Stanford CA 94305-5468*

BROWN, JACK HAROLD UPTON, physiology educator, university official, biomedical engineer; b. Nixon, Tex., Nov. 16, 1918; s. Gilmer W. and Thelma (Patton) B.; m. Jessie Carolyn Schulz, Apr. 14, 1943. B.S., S.W. Tex. State U., 1939; postgrad., U. Tex., 1939-41; Ph.D., Rutgers U., 1948. Lectr. physics Southwest Tex. State U., San Marcos, 1943-44; instr. phys. chemistry Rutgers U., New Brunswick, N.J., 1944-45, rsch. assoc., 1944-48; lectr. U. Pitts., 1948-50; head biol. scis. Mellon Inst., Pitts., 1948-50; asst. prof. physiology U. N.C., Chapel Hill, 1950-52; scientist, prof. biology Oak Ridge Inst. Nuclear Studies, 1952; assoc. prof. physiology Emory U. Med. Sch., Atlanta, 1952-58, prof., 1959-60, acting chmn. dept. physiology, 1958-60; lectr. physiology George Washington U. and Georgetown U. med. schs., Washington, 1960-65; exec. sec. biomed. engring. and physiology tng. coms. Nat. Inst. Gen. Med. Scis., NIH, Bethesda, Md., 1960-62; chief spl. rsch. br. div. Rsch. Facilities and Resources NIH, 1962-63, acting chief gen. clin. rsch. ctrs. br., 1963-64, asst. dir. ops. Div. Research Facilities and Resources, 1964-65; acting program dir. pharmacology/toxicology program Nat. Inst. Gen. Med. Scis., NIH, 1966-70, asst. dir. ops., 1965-66, assoc. dir. sci. programs, 1967-70, acting dir., 1970; spl. asst. to adminstr. Health Services and Mental Health Adminstrn., USPHS, Rockville, Md., 1971-72; assoc. dep. adminstr. for devel. Health Svcs. and Mental Health Adminstrn., USPHS, 1972-73; spl. asst. to adminstr. Health Resources Adminstrn., 1973-78; coord. Southwest Rsch. Consortium, San Antonio, 1974-78; prof. physiology U. Tex. Med. Sch., San Antonio, 1974-78; prof. environ. scis. U. Tex. at San Antonio, 1974-78; adj. prof. health svcs. adminstrn. Trinity U., 1975-78; assoc. provost rsch. and advanced edn. U. Houston, 1978-80, prof. biology, 1980-89, prof. emeritus, 1990—; adj. prof. U. Tex. Sch. Public Health, 1978—; prof. public adminstrn. Tex. Women's U., 1978—; adj. prof. community medicine Baylor Coll. Medicine, Houston, 1986-89; vice-chmn. SCORE (Svc. Corps of Retired Execs.), 1993-96; chmn., 1996—; Fulbright lectr. U. Rangoon, 1950; cons. health systems WHO, Oak Ridge Inst. Nuclear Studies, Lockheed Aircraft Co., Drexel Inst. Tech., NASA, Vassar Coll., Va.; mem. adv. bd. Ctr. for Cancer Therapy, San Antonio, 1974—; bd. dirs. South Tex. Health Edn. Ctr.; mem. health adv. bd. Tel-Tech, cons., Univ. Tex. Health Sci. Ctr., Sumitomo, Tokyo. Author: Physiology of Man in Space, 1963, (with S.B. Barker) Basic Endocrinology, 1966, 2d edit., 1970, (with J.F. Dickson) Future Goals of Engineering in Biology and Medicine, 1968, Advances in Biomedical Engineering, vol II, 1972, vols. III, IV, 1973, vol. V, 1974, vol. VI, 1976, Vol. VII, 1978, (with J.E. Jacobs and L.E. Stark) Biomedical Engineering, 1972, (with D.E. Gann) Engineering Principles in Physiology, vols. I, II, 1973, The Health Care Dilemma, 1977, Integration and Control of Biol. Processes, 1978, Politics and Health Care, 1978, Telecommunications in Health Care, 1981, Management in Health Care Systems, 1983, A Laboratory Manual in Animal Physiology, 1984, 3d edit., 1988, High Cost of Healing, 1985, (with J. Comolo) Productivity in Health Care Systems, 1987, Guide to Collecting Fine Prints, 1989, (with J. Cumolo) Educating for Excellence, 1991, Footsteps in Sci., 1993, Starting and Running a Small Business, 1994, Records for Small Business, 1995; editor: (with Ferguson) Blood and Body Functions, 1966, (with Miller) Exercise Physiology, 1966, Life Into Space, (Wunder), 1968; contbr. numerous articles on biomed. engring. to sci. jours. Mem. adv. bd. San Antonio Mus. Assn.; mem. spl. effects com. Tex. Sesquicentennial, 1995-96; vice chmn. Svc. Corps Ret. Execs., 1995-96, chmn., 1996—; bd. dirs. Inst. for Health Policy, U. Tex. Health Sci. Ctr. Served with USNR, 1941. Recipient cert. appreciation NIH, 1969, 1st pl. award Atlanta Internat. Film Festival, 1970, spl. team award NASA, 1978, recognition awa Emergency Med. Care, 1980, Best Tchr. award Nat. Mortar Bd., 1986, Most Disting. Alumni award S.W. Tex. State U., 1986; Gerard Swope fellow Gen. Electric Co., 1946-48; Fulbright grantee, 1950; Dept. of Def. grantee, 1950-52; NIH grantee, 1950-60; Cancer Soc. grantee, 1958; Damon Runyon Cancer award grantee, 1959; Dept. Energy grantee, 1980-81; NASA grantee, 1987-89. Fellow AAAS, Nat. Acad. Engring., IEEE (joint com. engring. in medicine and biology 1966—); mem. Am. Chem. Soc. (sr.), Biomed. Engring. Soc. (pres. 1969-70, dir. 1968-69), Inst. Radio Engrs. (nat. sec. profl. group biomed. engring. 1962-64), N.Y. Acad. Scis., Endocrine Soc., Am. Physiol. Soc. (com. mem. 1959-63, nat. com. on animals in research 1985—), Tex. Print Soc. (founder, pres.), Soc. for Exptl. Biology and Medicine, Svc. Corps Ret. Execs. (vice chmn. 1994-95, chmn. 1995—), Exec. Svc. Corps, Sigma Xi (research award 1961, founder, pres. Alamo chpt. 1977-78), Council Biology Editors, Soc. Research Adminstrn., Pi Kappa Delta, Phi Lambda Upsilon, Alpha Chi. Club: Cosmos. Home: 2908 Whisper View St San Antonio TX 78230-3743 Office: U Houston 4800 Calhoun Rd Houston TX 77004-2610

BROWN, JAMES W., gastroenterologist; b. Detroit, May 20, 1938; s. Lisle Odel and Margaret Elizabeth (Kildal) B.; m. Lynn Elizabeth Wright, June 23, 1962; children: Steve, Dave, Kirsten. BS, U. Nebr., 1960; MD, Northwestern U., Chgo., 1964. Diplomate Am. Bd. Internal Medicine, Am. Bd. Internal Medicine in Gastroenterology. Gastroenterologist Wenatchee (Wash.) Valley Clinic, 1970—; chief gastroenterology U.S. Naval Hosp., San Diego; vice-chmn., bd. dirs. Wenatchee Valley Clinic, 1992-95, chmn., pres., 1995-96, chmn., CEO, 1996—. Contbr. articles to profl. jours. Chmn. bd. dirs. Mustard Seed Neighbor Ctr., Wenatchee, 1990-92, bd. dirs. 1989-95. Lt. comdr. USN, 1968-70. Fellow Am. Coll. Gastroenterology; mem. Alpha Omega Alpha. Methodist.

BROWN, JASON WALTER, neurologist, educator, researcher; b. N.Y.C., Apr. 14, 1938; s. Samuel Robert and Sylvia (Brown) B.; children: Jonathan Schilder, Jovana Millay. B.A., U. Calif.-Berkeley, 1959; M.D., U.S.C., 1963. Intern St. Elizabeth's Hosp., Washington, 1963-64; resident in neurology UCLA, 1964-67; practice medicine specializing in neurology N.Y.C., 1970—; instr. Boston U. Med. Sch., 1969-70; asst. clin. prof. Columbia-Presbyn. Hosp., N.Y.C., 1970-75; vis. asst. prof. neurology Albert Einstein Coll. Medicine, N.Y.C., 1972-75; vis. assoc. prof. Rockefeller U., N.Y.C., 1978-79; clin. assoc. prof. neurology NYU, 1975-79, clin. prof., 1979—; pres. Inst. Research in Behavioral Neurosci.; vis. scholar N.Y. Psychoanalytic Inst., 1993—. Author: Aphasia, Apraxia and Agnosia, 1972, Mind, Brain and Consciousness, 1977, Life of the Mind, 1988; editor: Jargonaphasia, 1982; English Translation of Aphasie by Arnold Pick (Aphasia), 1973, Neuropsychology of Visual Perception, 1989, Classics in Neuropsychology: Apraxia and Agnosia, Self and Process, 1991, Time, Will and Mental Process, 1996; contbr. numerous articles on neurology to med. jours.; mem. editl. bd. Jour. Nervous and Mental Disease, Aphasiology, Advances in Neurolinguistics. Grantee NIH; fellow Alexander von Humboldt Found., 1979—, World Rehab. Fund, 1982, Founds. Fund for Research in Psychiatry, 1974-75. Jewish. Home and Office: 66 E 79th St New York NY 10021-0217

BROWN, JAY CLARK, microbiology educator; b. Jersey City, June 23, 1942; s. John Robert and Vonna Lamme B.; m. Sallie Shepard Dietrich, June 26, 1965; children: Jeffrey F., Norman J., Michael E. BA, Johns Hopkins U., 1964; PhD, Harvard U., 1969. Postdoctoral fellow MRC Lab. Molecular Biology, Cambridge, Eng., 1969-71; asst. prof. microbiology U. Va. Med. Sch., Charlottesville, 1971-76, assoc. prof., 1976-87, prof., 1987—; mem. adv. com. personnel for research Am. Cancer Soc., 1979-86; instr. physiology Marine Biol. Lab., Woods Hole, Mass., 1977-80; study sect. mem. Calif. Tobacco-Related Disease Rsch. Program, 1990—. NATO fellow, 1969-70. Mem. Am. Soc. Microbiology, Am. Soc. Biochemistry and Molecular Biology. Democrat. Author: (with Flickinger) Medical Cell Biology, 1979, (with volk) Basic Microbiology, 1996. Office: Dept Microbiology U Va Med Center Charlottesville VA 22908

BROWN, JERRY MILFORD, medical company executive; b. Anderson, S.C., Apr. 30, 1938; s. James Milford and Jane Elizabeth (McCord) B.; m. Alice Alberta Thompson, July 30, 1960; children—John Milford, Allen Thompson. B.S., Furman U., 1960; M.A. in Biology, Wake Forest U., 1963, Temple U., 1967; Ph.D. in Physiology, Dental Sch., U. Md., 1972. Commd. lt. U.S. Army, 1960, advanced through grades to lt. col., 1980; research instr. Hahnemann Med. Coll., Phila., 1967-68; sect. leader, exptl. medicine div. Biomed. Lab., Edgewood Arsenal, Md., 1967-68; instr. anatomy Med. Sch., U. Md., Balt., 1970-77; sect. leader, exptl. medicine div. U.S. Army Research Inst. Environ. Medicine, Natick, Mass., 1973-76; dep. dir. U.S. Army Med. Intelligence and Info. Agy., Ft. Detrick, Md., 1976-80; dir. internat. health affairs Dept. Def., Washington, 1980-84; editor Mgmt. and Info. Study, Office of Surgeon Gen., 1984; chief plans ops. security, 2nd Gen. Hosp., Federal Republic of Germany, 1984-87; med. co-ordinator, Fed. Emergency Mgmt. Agy, Washington, 1987-90, nat. disaster med. system staff, bd. govs. Nat. Council Internat. Health, 1980-90; cons. and spl. asst. to the pres. Bio Technology Gen. Corp., Iselin, N.J., 1991—; pres., COO NeuroSurg. Internat., 1995—; v.p., chief oper. officer M/D Frontiers, Springfield, Va., 1990—; pres. Automated Med. Products, Inc., 1990—; v.p. Automated Systems, 1991—; assoc. dir. rsch. nat. study ctr. for trauma and emergency medicine U. Md.; U.S. mem. Internat. Com. of Mil. Medicine and Pharmacy, 1981-87; U.S. mil. mem. Joint Civil/Mil. Med. Working Group U.S., NATO, 1981—; mem. program planning com. Internat. Assembly on Emergency Med. Services, Balt., 1984; congress lobbyist; cons. in field. Contbr. articles to med. jours; pub. books in field of philately. Commr., Explorer Scouts, Natick, Mass., 1975-76; trustee Cardinal Spellman Philatlic Mus., Weston, Mass., 1980—. Decorated Meritorious Service medal with 3 oak leaf clusters, Legion of Merit; recipient gold medal Res. Officers Assn., 1960. Mem. Electron Microscopy Soc. Am., Am. Stamp Dealers Assn., Central Atlantic Stamp Dealers Assn. (pres. 1977-81), Research and Engring. Soc. Am., Balt. Philatelic Soc., Sigma Alpha Epsilon, Sigma Xi. Republican. Baptist.

BROWN, JERRY WILLIAM, cell biology and anatomy educator; b. Wichita, Kans., July 4, 1925; s. Jerry I. and Sarah Helen (Lowry) B.; m. Mary Mina MacNair, Aug. 12, 1950; children: Louise Hyde, Margaret Stewart Hildreth, Elizabeth Lowry Brown Bardo. AB, Wichita State U., 1946; MA, U. Kans., 1949, PhD, 1951. Instr. U. Pitts., 1951-56; asst. prof. U. Mo., Columbia, 1956-58, assoc. prof., 1958-64; assoc. prof. cell biology and anatomy U. Ala., Birmingham, 1964-70, prof., 1970-92, prof. emeritus, 1992—. Contbr. articles to profl. jours. NIH grantee, 1965-66, 68-71. Mem. AAAS, Am. Assn. Anatomists, Soc. for Neurosci., Am. Acad. Neurology, Ala. Acad. Sci., Sigma Xi. Republican. Episcopalian. Home: 177 Ross Dr Birmingham AL 35213-2547 Office: U Ala Dept Cell Biology Anat Birmingham AL 35294

BROWN, JOHN JEFFREY, general surgeon, educator; b. Gettysburg, Pa., June 27, 1948; s. John Calvin Brown and Corinne Elizabeth (Heiges) Reaver; m. Karen Lee Stafford, May 31, 1975; children: Douglas Joseph, Meredith Anne, Amy Elizabeth. BA, Duke U., 1970; MD, U. Pa., 1974. Diplomate Am. Bd. Surgery. Resident in surgery N.C. Bapt. Hosp., Winston-Salem, 1974-80; Bradshaw surg. rsch. fellow Bowman Gray Sch. Medicine, Winston-Salem, 1977-78; asst. prof. surgery U. S.C. Sch. Medicine, Columbia, 1980-88, assoc. prof., 1988—; chief surg. svc. Dorn VA Hosp., Columbia, 1994—. Fellow ACS; mem. Surg. Infection Soc., Assn. for Acad. Surgery, Assn. for Surg. Edn., Southeastern Surg. congress, Undersea and Hyperbaric Med. Soc., Phi Beta Kappa. Presbyterian. Home: 139 Springlawn Rd Columbia SC 29223 Office: U SC Dept Srugery Two Medical Park Ste 300 Columbia SC 29203

BROWN, JUNE GIBBS, government official; b. Cleve., Oct. 5, 1933; d. Thomas D. and Lorna M. Gibbs; children: Ellen Rosenthal, Linda Windsor, Victor Janezic, Carol Janezic. B.B.A. summa cum laude, Cleve. State U., 1971, M.B.A., 1972; postgrad., Cleve. Marshall Law Sch., 1973-74; J.D., U. Denver, 1978; postgrad. Advanced Mgmt. Program, Harvard U., 1983. Cert. govt. fin. mgr., 1995. Real estate broker, officer mgr. N.E. Realty, Cleve., 1963-68; staff acct. Frank T. Cicirelli, C.P.A., Cleve., 1970-71; asst. to comptroller S.M. Hexter Co., Cleve., 1971; grad. teaching fellow Cleve. State U., 1971-72; dir. internal audit Navy Fin. Ctr., Cleve., 1972-75; dir. fin. systems design Bureau of Land Mgmt., Denver, 1975-76; project mgr. Bureau of Reclamation, 1976-79; insp. gen. Dept. Interior, Washington, 1979-81, NASA, Washington, 1981-85; v.p. fin. and adminstrn. Systems Devel. Corp., a Burroughs Co., 1985-86; assoc. adminstr. for mgmt. NASA, 1986-87; insp. gen. U.S. Dept. Def., Arlington, Va., 1987-90; dep. insp. gen. USN-CINCPACFLT, 1990; insp. gen. USN Pacific Fleet, Pearl Harbor, Hawaii, 1991-93; inspector gen. HHS, Washington, 1993—, HHS, SSA, Washington, 1995-96; bd. dirs. Fed. Law Enforcement Tng. Ctr., 1984-85, Interag. Auditor Tng. program Dept. Agr. Grad. Sch., 1983-85; chmn. interag. com. on Info. Resource Mgmt., 1984-85; mem. bd. advisors Nat. Contract Mgmt. Assn., 1987-89; vice chair Pres.'s Coun. on Integrity and Efficiency, mem. audit com., rep. Nat. Intergovtl. Audit Forum; bd. dirs. Inspectors Gen. Auditor Tng. Inst. Mem. bd. advisors Howard U. Sch. Bus., 1987-89. Recipient award Am. Soc. Women Accts., 1969, 70, 71, Raulston award Cleve. State U., 1971, Pres.'s award Cleve. State U., 1971, Outstanding Achievement award U.S. Navy, 1973, Career Svc. award Chgo. region Fed. Exec. Bd., 1974, Outstanding Contbn. to Fin. Mgmt. award Denver region Fed. Exec. Bd., 1977, Donald L. Scantlebury award Joint Fin. Mgmt. Improvement Program, 1980, Outstanding Svc. award Nat. Assn. Minority CPA Firms, 1980, NASA Exceptional Svc. medal, 1985, Outstanding Achievement in Aerospace award, 1987, Woman of Yr. award, YWCA 1988, Bur. Land Mgmt., Dept. Interior, 1975, Disting. Pub. Svc. award Dept. Def., 1989, Meritorious Civilian Svc. award U.S. Navy, 1993, Nat. Capital Area chpt./Govt. Exec. Mag. award for leadership, 1994, George Washington U. Pi Alpha Alpha Pub. Svc. award, 1996; named Disting. Alumni Cleve. State U., 1990. Fellow Nat. Acad. Pub. Adminstrn. (standing panel exec. orgn. and mgmt.); mem. AICPAs, Assn. Govt. Accts. (nat. pres. 1985-86, nat. exec. com. 1977-87, vice chmn. nat. ethics com. 1978-80, 90, chmn. fin. mgmt. standards bd. 1981-82, service award 1973, 76, 93, outstanding achievement award 1979, Robert W. King Meml. award 1988, nat. ethics com. 1990, dir. Hawaii chpt. 1991-93), Hawaii Soc. CPAs (bd. dirs. 1991-93), Am. Accts. Assn., Nat. Contract Mgmt. Assn. (bd. advisors 1988-90), NASA Alumni Assn., Women in Aerospace, ASPA (at-large mem. nat. coun. 1994—, Profl. Responsibility Exemplary Practice award 1990, pres.-nat. capitol area chpt. 1989), Exec. Women in Govt., Beta Alpha Psi. Office: HHS Inspector Gen 330 Independence Ave SW Washington DC 20201-0001*

BROWN, KATHERINE KAY, clinical nurse specialist; b. Pitts., May 26, 1966; d. Wasyl and Luba (Nesterov) Kay; m. Edward Charles Brown, July 22, 1989. BSN magna cum laude, U. Pa., 1988, MSN in critical care, 1991. ACLS, CCRN. Staff nurse Hosp. of U. Pa., Phila., 1988-91, clin. nurse specialist cardiothoracic surg. ICU, 1991-92; clin. nurse specialist Allegheny Gen. Hosp., Pitts., 1992-95, clin. outcomes mgr., 1995—; asst. prof. critical care grad. nursing Laroche Coll., Pitts., 1993-95; asst. prof. grad. nursing Duquesne U., 1995—. Mem. AACN, Internat. Transplant Nurses Soc., ANA, Nat. League Nursing. Office: Allegheny Gen Hosp 320 E North Ave 17th Fl South Tower Pittsburgh PA 15212

BROWN, KENNETH ANDREW, cardiologist, educator; b. N.Y.C., Jan. 16, 1951; s. Gerry and Rita (Alpert) B.; m. Suzanne R. Braun, Aug. 8, 1976; children: Daniel Everest, David Abraham. AB, Rutgers U., 1973; MD, Cornell U., 1977. Cert. internal medicine and cardiovascular diseases Am. Bd. Internal Medicine. Intern Peter Bent Brigham Hosp.-Harvard U., Boston, 1977-78, resident, 1978-80; fellow in nuc. cardiology Mass. Gen. Hosp.-Harvard U., Boston, 1980-82; fellow in cardiology Beth Israel Hosp.-Harvard U., Boston, 1982-84; dir. nuclear cardiology, prof. medicine U. Vt. Coll. Medicine, Burlington, 1984—. Assoc. editor Jour. Nuclear Cardiology, 1994—; mem. editl. bd. Jour. Am. Coll. Cardiology 1995—; contbr. chpt. to book and articles to profl. jours. Mem. zoning bd. Town of Jericho, Vt., 1988-92. Recipient USPHS Nat. Rsch. award Mass. Gen. Hosp.-USPHS, Boston, 1980-82. Fellow Am. Coll. Cardiology, Am. Heart Assn., Soc. Nuc. Medicine; mem. Am. Soc. Nuc. Cardiology (treas. 1993-95, v.p. 1996—), Alpha Omega Alpha. Office: Med Ctr Hosp Vt Cardiology Unit Colchester Ave Burlington VT 05401

BROWN, KERRY MICHAEL, ophthalmologist; b. New Orleans, Sept. 29, 1956; s. Thomas Daniel and Gloria Juanita (Englehardt) B.; m. Mara Lissette Garcia, July 7, 1979; children: Kevin Michael, Elizabeth Marie, Eleanor Rene. BA in Biol. Scis., U. New Orleans, 1978; MD, La. State U., 1982. Diplomate Am. Bd. Ophthalmology. Intern Earl K. Long Meml. Hosp., Baton Rouge, 1982-83; resident La. State U., New Orleans, 1983-86; vitreoretinal fellow Hermann Eye Ctr., U. Tex. Med. Sch., Houston, 1986-87; ophthalmologist Young Eye Clinic, Abbeville, La. Mem. AMA, Am. Acad. Ophthalmology, So. Med. Assn., Vermilion Parish Med. Soc., La. State Med. Soc., La.-Miss. Ophthalmology and Otorhinolaryngology Soc., Vitreous Soc., So. Retina Study Group. Home: 8409 River Rd Abbeville LA 70510 Office: Young Eye Clinic 204 N Magdalen Sq Abbeville LA 70510

BROWN, LAWRENCE STEWART, JR., physician; b. Bklyn., Dec. 4, 1949; s. Lawrence S. and Mae Rose (Harris) B. BA, Bklyn. Coll., 1976; MD, NYU, 1979; MPH, Columbia U., 1979. Lic. physician, Calif., N.Y. Intern Harlem Hosp. Med. Ctr., N.Y.C., 1979-80, resident, 1980-82, chief resident, 1982-83; staff physician Addiction Rsch. and Treatment Corp., Bklyn., 1981-82, sr. med. coord., 1982-85, v.p. resch. and med. affairs Urban Resources Inst., 1986-88, sr. v.p. rsch. and med. affairs, 1988—; instr. clin. medicine Coll. Physicians and Surgeons Columbia U., N.Y.C., 1986-91; asst. clin. prof. medicine Coll. Physicians and Surgeons Columbia U., N.Y.C., 1991—; asst. attendint physician hosps. Columbia U., N.Y.C., 1986-90; vis. clin. fellow Columbia U., 1979-82, adj. prof., lectr. div. health adminstrn. and health policy, 1988—; mem. various com. NIH, 1986—. Pres. Greater Brownsville Athletic Coun., 1983-92. With U.S. Army, 1970-72, Vietnam. Decorated Bronze Star.; recipient Dr. Ralston R. Fillmore, Jr. award, 1976, Achievers award Alpha Upsilon chpt. Omega Psi Phi Fraternity, Inc., 1988; Sheldon E. Kalis Meml. scholar, 1967, N.Y. State Regents War Svc. scholar, 1973. Fellow N.Y. Acad. Scis.; mem. AAAS, APHA, Pub. Health Assn. N.Y.C. (bd. dirs. 1989—), Am. Soc. Addiction Medicine, Am. Soc. Internal Medicine, Am. Diabetes Assn. (profl. sect., N.Y. affiliate), Am. Coll. Physicians, Manhattan Cen. Med. Soc., Med. Soc. State N.Y.,. Office: Addiction Rsch & Treatment Corp 22 Chapel St Brooklyn NY 11201-1903

BROWN, LINDA JEAN, nursing administrator; b. Pana, Ill., Mar. 13, 1947; d. William H. and Meribah J. (Wardall) Laughlin; m. Robert W. Brown, Aug. 25, 1968; children: William H., Jeffrey A. RN, Decatur (Ill.) Meml. Hosp. Sch. Nursing, 1969; BS, Millikin U., 1969. RN, Colo.; cert. Profl. Healthcare Quality, Colo. Dir. quality assurance, utilization rev. St. Vincent Meml. Hosp., Taylorville, Ill., 1975-81. Cedar Springs Hosp., Colorado Springs, Colo., 1982-89; dir. quality assurance Ft. Morgan (Colo.) Community Hosp., 1989-90; dir. nursing Bethesda Care Ctr., Paonia, Colo., 1990-91; asst. adminstr. Mountain Crest Hosp., Ft. Collins, Colo., 1991-95; adminstr. First Am. Home Care, Denver, 1995—; PRN cons., Brim & Assocs., Portland, Oreg., 1989-90, conf. speaker, 1990; PRN cons. Horizon Mental Health Svcs., Denton, Tex., 1992; cons. Meritcare, Pitts., 1990. Author: (with others) Nurse Clinician Pocket Manual: Nursing Diagnosis, Care Planning and Documentation, 1989. Mem. Colo. Nurse Exec. Assn. Home: 12079 Forest St Denver CO 80241-3241

BROWN, LINDA JOAN, psychotherapist, psychoanalyst; b. Mineola, N.Y., Feb. 18, 1941; d. Charles Harold and Helen (Golbach) B. Student, Smith Coll., Northampton, Mass., 1958-60; BA, Barnard Coll., N.Y.C., 1962; MPS in Art Therapy, Pratt Inst., Bklyn., 1973; MSW, Hunter Coll., N.Y.C., 1976. Cert. social worker, psychoanalyst, N.Y.; lic. clin. social worker, Calif.; diplomate clin. social work Am. Bd. Examiners in Clin. Social Work. Singer, actress Broadway theatres, N.Y.C., 1962-65, pub. rels./community rels. specialist, real estate, publicist/editor, pub., edn. cons., 1965-71; art therapist Bronx (N.Y.) Psychiat. Ctr., 1972-74; clin. social worker North Richmond Community Mental Health Ctr., S.I., N.Y., 1977-79; staff therapist Lincoln Inst. Psychotherapy, N.Y.C., 1978-80; sr. staff therapist Ctr. for Study Anorexia and Bulimia, N.Y.C., 1983-85; staff therapist Inst. Contemporary Psychotherapy, N.Y.C., 1988—; pvt. practice psychotherapy N.Y.C., 1978—; mem. human svc. faculty Tristate Inst. Traditional Chinese Acupuncture, N.Y.C., 1986-89; mem. faculty N.Y. Open Ctr., N.Y.C., 1987—; adj. faculty Health Choices Ctr. for Healing Arts, Princeton, N.J., 1987-90; clin. cons. Personal Performance Cons., EAP, 1988; human resources cons. industry, N.Y.C., 1988—; workshop leader seminars on stress mgmt., assertiveness tng., comm. and counseling skills, intimate relationships skills, creative expression. Mem. NASW.

BROWN, LINDA LOCKETT, nutrition management executive, nutrition consultant; b. Jacksonville, Fla., Jan. 8, 1954; d. Willie James and Katie Lee (Taylor) Lockett; m. Thomas Lee Brown, Dec. 18, 1982; children: Ashanti, William, Timothy. BS in Agr., U. Fla., 1975, M of Agr., 1981. Lic. profl. nutritionist; cert. food svc. dir. III; registered dietitian. Chemist/microbiologist Green Giant Co., Alachua, Fla., 1975-77; lab. technologist II U. Fla., Gainesville, 1977-81, extension agt. I, Ft. Myers, 1981-85, extension agt. II, 1985-87, West Palm Beach, 1987-88; pres. CINET, Inc., 1985—; area supr. Palm Beach County Sch. Food Svc., 1988-90; adj. prof. Palm Beach Community coll., 1990, Fla. C.C., Jacksonville, 1993—; dir. sch. food svc. St. Johns County, 1990—; nutrition cons. Congregate Meals, Ft. Myers, 1984-87, Serenity House, Ft. Myers, 1985-87; cons. Performax, 1989—; treas. St. Augustine chpt. Internat. Food Svc. Execs. Assn., 1993—; apptd. by gov. Fla. Health and Human Svcs. Bd., elected vice chair, 1993-94, chair, 1994-96. Columnist Palm Beach Post, 1989—; contbr. articles to profl. jours. Mem. exec. bd. Community Coordinating Coun., Ft. Myers, 1985; Am. Heart Assn., Palm Beach, 1989-90; co-founder Friends of Hearing Impaired Youth, Gainesville, 1976; tutor-coord. Sampson, Gainesville, 1973; mem. Jr. League, Ft. Myers, 1987; mem. Jr. League, Palm Beach, Fla., 1987-90, mem. edn. tng. com., community rsch. com. 1989-90; mem. nutrition com. Am. Heart Assn., Palm Beach, 1989—. State U. System Bd. Regents grantee, 1980. Mem. NAFE, Soc. Nutrition Edn. (legis. network chmn.), Am. Dietetic Assn. (network of blacks in nutrition, chair legis. com. 1988-89, chair nominating 1989, sec. 1989-90, state profl. recruitment coord.), Fla. Dietetic Assn. (chair minority issues com., chair membership 1987-88, chair edn. and registration 1988-90, state profl. recruitment coord. rep. Fla. chpt., chair nominating com. 1994—), Palm Beach Dietetic Assn. (community nutrition chair 1988-89, chair legis. com. 1989-90), Caloosa Dietetic Assn. (sec.), Nat. Speakers Assn., Sch. Food Svcs. Assn. (1988—), Nat. Assn. Extension Home Econs. Agts., Internat. Platform Assn., Jacksonville Dietetic Assn., Nutrition Today Soc., Alpha Zeta, Epsilon Sigma Phi. Club: Greater Palm Beaches Bus. and Profl. Women (minority student mentor, role model mentor), Nat. Speakers Assn., N. Fla. Profl. Speakers Assn. Avocations: singing, violin. Office: 2234 George Wythe Rd Orange Park FL 32073-8507

BROWN, LORETTA ANN PORT, physician, geneticist; b. Kingston, N.Y., July 30, 1945; d. Frank and Sophie (Hormann) Port; m. Robert Don Brown, Aug. 22, 1970; 1 child, Adrian Robert. BS, SUNY, New Paltz, 1967; MS, U. Mich., 1968, postgrad., 1969; MD, Ea. Va. Med. Sch., Norfolk, 1981. Diplomate Am. Bd. Med. Examiners. Lab. tech. U. Mich., Ann Arbor, 1969-70; rsch. asst. M.D. Anderson Hosp. and Tumor Inst., Houston, 1970; rsch. instr. Baylor Coll. Medicine, Houston, 1971-76; resident internal medicine Ea. Va. Med. Sch., Norfolk, 1981-84; asst. prof. medicine Med. Coll. Hampton Rd, Norfolk, 1984—; physician Health America, Hampton, Va., 1984-87, Tidewater Pulmonary Assocs., Newport News, Va., 1987-88; chief, admitting and screening VA Med Ctr., Hampton, 1988-92, staff physician, 1988—; trainee genetics USPHS, Ann Arbor, Mich., 1967-69; rsch. participant NSF, Albion, Mich., 1966; cons. VA Med. Ctr., 1984-88. Contbr. articles to profl. jours. Recipient Achievement award Am. Med. Women's Assn., 1981, Am. Chem. Soc., 1966. Mem. Am. Morgan Horse Assn., Am. Horse Show Assn. (Morgan judge 1990—), Old Dominion Morgan Horse Assn. (v.p. 1987-89), Va. Carolina Morgan Horse Assn., Nu Pi Sigma. Roman Catholic. Office: VA Medical Ctr 590 170 Hampton VA 23667

BROWN, LOUISE L. SALLY, social services administrator; b. Mich., Feb. 3, 1917; d. Charles Samuel and Mabel Elina (Goodthrite) Langdon; m. Andrew W. L. Brown, nov. 1, 1941; children: Cameron Langdon Brown, Heather Langdon, Douglas Langdon, Grant Langdon. BA, Mich. State U., 1938; MSW, U. Mich., 1956. Cert. social worker. Faculty family studies Merrill-Palmer Inst., Detroit; dir. 4-C program Community Coordinate Child Care, Detroit; lectr. child care U. Mich., Ann Arbor; cons.-dir. coun. on early childhood Ctr. for Urban Studies, Wayne State U., Ann Arbor; founding adminstr. Skillman Ctr. for Children Wayne State U., Detroit, 1992—. Co-author: (with Sharon Elliott) An Interdisciplinary Model to Promote Family Development, 1978, (with Irving Sigel) The Value of Behavior Day Interviews on Diagnosis, 1956; author: The Children: Shapes of Child Care in Detroit, 1977. Recipient Eva Fillion award Grosse Pointe Human Rels. Coun., 1978, Merrill-Palmer citation, 1980, Child Care Advocate award Children's Chpt. and Cir. Cts. of Mich., 1979, Woman of Conscience award Nat. Coun. Women, 1968; named to Mich. Women's Hall of Fame, 1988. Mem. NASW, Internat. Coun. on Social Work Edn., Mich. Coun. on Social Work Edn., Nat. Assn. for Edn. Young Children. Home: 1111 N Gulfstream Ave Apt 2B Sarasota FL 34236-5531

BROWN, MARGARET REE, nurse; b. Sandersville, Ga., Mar. 1, 1949; d. Roger Lee Brown and Gladys Olee (Lawson) Arp; m. Bruce Edward Brown. BS, Northeastern U., 1975, MS, 1994. RN, Mass. Asst. team leader Mass. Rehab. Hosp., Boston, 1975-77; head nurse Jewish Meml. Hosp., Boston, 1977-81; med. nurse coordinator Roxbury (Mass.) Comprehensive Community Health Ctr., 1981-83; clin. nurse coordinator Mattapan (Mass.) Community Health Ctr., 1983-86; dir. staff devel. Fuller Men. Health Ctr., Boston, 1985-94; nurse clinician Mass. Mental Health Ctr., Boston, 1994—; nursing educator Concord Bapt. Ch. Nurses Unit, Boston, 1977—. Site coordinator Nat. Health for Vol. Orgns., Dorchester, Mass., 1981-84; bd. dirs. Am. Cancer Soc., Mattapan, 1981, Hawthorne Youth and Community Ctr., Roxbury, 1986. Mem. NAACP, Mass. Nurses Found., Mass. Nurses Assn., New Eng. Regional Black Nurses Assn. (sec. 1984-88, v.p. 1988-89, bd. dirs.), Nat. Black Nurses Assn. (nominating com. chair 1988-90, bd. dirs. 1991-94, 2nd v.p. 1994—). Democrat. Baptist. Home: 103 Homestead St Dorchester MA 02121-2301 Office: Mass Mental Health Ctr 74 Fenwood Rd Boston MA 02115-6113

BROWN, MARTIN HOWARD, physician; b. Bklyn., Feb. 21, 1953; s. Alan Aaron and Clarice (Steinberg) B.; m. Rebecca Jeanne Sarley; children: Meghan E., Elliott A. BS with honors, George Washington U., 1974, MD, 1978. Chief med. resident George Washington U. Hosp., Washington, 1981-82; staff physician Emergency Medicine Assocs., Bethesda, Md., 1982-83; asst. prof. medicine George Washington U. Med. Ctr., 1983—; aeromed. dir. Worldcare Travel Assistance Assn., Washington, 1985-88; vice chmn. dept. emergency medicine Nat. Hosp., Arlington, Va., 1985-87, chmn. dept., 1987-91; asst. prof. medicine Georgetown U. Hosp., Washington, 1988—; med. dir. USASSIST, Washington, 1988—; chmn. dept. emergency medicine Washington Adventist Hosp., 1991—; med. dir. Md. Ambulance Svc., 1995—; trauma ctr. site reviewer State of Va.; mem. adv. com. Emergency Med. Svcs. Curriculum, No. Va. Community Coll., 1990—; cons. in field. Trustee Nat. Hosp. Bd. Trustees, 1987—; mem. adv. com. emergency med. svcs. Arlington County Bd., 1987-91, chmn. adv. com., 1991. Fellow Am. Coll. Emergency Physicians, Am. Coll. Physician Execs., Alpha Omega Alpha. Jewish. Home: 10901 Cripplegate Rd Potomac MD 20854-1628 Office: Emergency Medicine Assocs 9210 Corporate Blvd Rockville MD 20850

BROWN, MARY JOANNE SKIDMORE, speech/language pathology services professional; b. Detroit, Jan. 17; d. Wesley LeRoy and Inez Elizabeth (Sackett) Skidmore; m. Irwin Brown, Nov. 11, 1956 (dec. Aug. 1982); children: Jennifer Elizabeth Hazelton, Jason LeRoy. Student, Ohio Wesleyan U., 1949-50, Wayne State U., 1951-53; BA in Speech Correction, U. Mich., 1955; MS in Speech Pathology, SUNY, Geneseo, 1976. Cert. tchr., N.Y.; lic. speech pathologist, ASHA, N.Y. Speech correctionist Dearborn (Mich.) Township #4 Pub. Sch., 1955-56; speech therpist City Sch. Dist., Rochester, N.Y., 1956-58, Monroe County Bd. of Coop. Ednl. Svcs. #2, Rochester, 1958-60; speech-lang. therapist Wayne-Finger Lakes Bd. Coop. Ednl. Svcs., Williamson, 1970-76, speech/lang. pathologist, 1977-91; pvt. prac. Rochester; adj. faculty Community Coll. of Finger Lakes, Williamson, 1983-85. Mem. Am. Speech Lang. Hearing Assn., N.Y. Speech Lang. Hearing Assn. (bd. dirs. 1978-79, 82-84), Wayne Finger Lakes Lang. Speech Hearing Assn. (pres. 1978-79, 82-84, v.p. 1980, com. chmn. 1985), Golden Link Folksing Soc. (bd. dirs., pres.), Rochester Eating Disorders Orgn. (group facilitator), Greater Rochester Attention Deficit Disorders Assn. (group facilitator). Home and Office: 3 Shelwood Dr Rochester NY 14618-3709

BROWN, MELISSA M., ophthalmologist; b. Memphis, Oct. 11, 1950; d. Roy Seeley and Muriel Jean (Cobb) Moore; m. Gary C. Brown, Aug. 16, 1973; children: Heather, Heidi, Katie. BSN, Keuka Coll., 1972; MSN, Emory U., 1976; postgrad., U. Pa., 1980-82, St. Joseph's U., 1980-82; MD, Jefferson Med. Coll., 1986. RN, Pa. Staff nurse Mass. Gen. Hosp., Boston, 1972-73; nurse educator Crouse Irving Meml. Hosp., Syracuse, N.Y., 1973-75; nursing instr., asst. prof. U. Pa., Phila., 1976-80, Thomas Jefferson U., Phila., 1979-80; transitional resident Chestnut Hill Hosp., Phila., 1986-87; resident in ophthalmology Wills Eye Hosp., Phila., 1987-90; pvt. practice ophthalmology Phila., 1990—; clin. instr. Wills Eye Hosp., 1990—; cons. Pa. Physician Health Care Plan, Harrisburg, 1994—. Contbr. articles to profl. jours. Trustee Keuka Coll., Keuka Park, N.Y., 1991—. Fellow Am. Acad. Ophthalmology; mem. AMA, Pa. Med. Soc. (mem. task force 1995—). Republican. Office: 1107 Bethlehem Pike Ste 209 Flourtown PA 19031

BROWN, MICHAEL DAVID, health care consultant; b. New Castle, Ind., July 2, 1951; s. David Seymour and Stella (Young) B.; m. Jacqueline Lee Dudley, Aug. 25, 1974; children: Christopher David, Nathaniel Patrick. BS, Ball State U., 1975. Supr. word process Blue Cross Blue Shield, Indpls., 1974-76, supr. customer svc., 1976-78; mgr. CHAMPUS Ind., Ky., Wis. Blue Shield, Madison, 1978, Blue Cross Blue Shield, Roanoke, Va.; pres. cons. Health Care Econs., Inc., Indpls., 1981—; cons. Internat. Cranio Mandibular Joint Dysfunction Orgn., 1985—, Med. Accts. Group, Inc., Indpl;s., 1986—, Allergan Corp., 1987, Assistex Corp., Storz Corp., 1991—, Ernst and Young, 1992-93, IOLAB, 1993; developed the 1st physician-owned HMO in Ind.; lectr., keynote speaker in field. Author: Health Care in the 80's, 1985, Techniques for Maximizing Medicare Reimbursement, 1987, Medical Economics Video, vol. 3, no. 1; contbg. editor Med. Econs. mag.; contbr. articles to profl. jours. Mem. Am. Coll. Gastroenterology, Nat. Assn. Health Care Cons., Med. Group Mgmt. Assn., Ind. State Med. Assn. (speaker 1989) Mich. State Med. Assn. (speaker 1989), Indpls. C. of C., Eye Found. (bd. dirs.), Westwood Country Club, Elks Lodge. Republican. Home: 2686 W 900 S Pendleton IN 46064-8916 Office: Health Care Econ Inc 6350 Shadeland Rd Ste 3 Indianapolis IN 46220-4300

BROWN, MICHAEL STUART, geneticist, educator, administrator; b. N.Y.C., N.Y., Apr. 13, 1941; s. Harvey and Evelyn (Katz) B.; m. Alice Lapin, June 21, 1964; children: Elizabeth Jane, Sara Ellen. BA, U. Pa., 1962, MD, 1966; DSc (hon.), Rensselaer Poly. Inst., 1982, U. Chgo., 1982, U. Pa., 1986, U. Buenos Aires, 1988, U. Paris, 1988, So. Meth. U., 1993. Intern, then resident in medicine Mass. Gen. Hosp., Boston, 1966-68; served with USPHS, 1968-70; clin. assoc. NIH, 1968-71; asst. prof. U. Tex. Southwestern Med. Sch., Dallas, 1971-74; Paul J. Thomas prof. genetics, dir. Ctr. Genetic Diseases, 1977—; mem. med. adv. bd. Howard Hughes Med. Inst., Scripps Inst., Salk Inst., Meml. Sloan-Kettering Hosp. Co-editor: The Metabolic Basis of Inherited Disease, 1983. Trustee U. Pa., Lamplighter Sch. Recipient Pfizer award Am. Chem. Soc., 1976, Passano award Passano Found., 1978, Lounsbery award U.S. Nat. Acad. Scis., 1979; Lita Annenberg Hazen award, 1982, Albert Lasker Med. Rsch. award, 1985, Horwitz prize, 1985, Nobel Prize in Medicine or Physiology, 1985, Nat. Medal of Sci. U.S., 1988. Mem. Nat. Acad. Scis., Am. Soc. Clin. Investigation, Assn. Am. Physicians, Harvey Soc., Royal Acad. Scis. (fgn. mem.). Office: U Tex Health Sci Ctr Dept Molecular Genetics 5323 Harry Hines Blvd Dallas TX 75235-7200*

BROWN, MORRIS, anesthesiologist; b. Richmond, Va., Feb. 2, 1951; s. Eli Matthew and Estelle Tamus (Neidish) B.; m. Rhonda Rosenberg, Mar. 5, 1977; children: Erica Claire, Jeremy Daniel. BA, U. Mich., 1972; MD, Wayne State U., 1976. Diplomate Am. Bd. Internal Medicine, Am. Bd. Anesthesiology, Am. Bd. Med. Specialties, Nat. Bd. Med. Examiners. Intern New Eng. Deaconess Hosp., Boston, 1976-77, resident, 1977-79; clin. fellow in medicine Med. Sch. Harvard U., Boston, 1976-79, clin. fellow in anesthesia, 1979-81; resident in anesthesia Mass. Gen. Hosp., Boston, 1979-81; instr. anesthesioloy Wayne State U., Detroit, 1982-84, asst. prof., 1984-88, assoc. prof., 1988-95, prof., 1995—; dir. critical care svcs. Sinai Hosp., Detroit, 1981-91, med. dir. respiratory care, Detroit, 1981-91, med. dir. surg. intensive care, Detroit, 1981—, dir. resident edn. dept. anesthesiology, Detroit, 1985—, chmn. dept. anesthesiology, 1991—; editorial bd. Internat. Anesthesia Clinics. Contbr. to profl. publs.; editor (jour.) Literature Scan: Anesthesiology, 1987. Mem. AMA (Physicians Recognition award 1984), Am. Soc. of Critical Care Anesthesiologists (founder, sec. 1985—, pres. 1990, chmn. sect. on clin. care, 1993-95), Wayne State Med. Assn. (pres. 1986-87), Mich. Soc. Critical Care Medicine (pres. 1987—), Am. Assn. Respiratory Care (chmn., bd. med. advs. 1989—), Am. Soc. of Anesthesiologists (chmn. com. acute medicine 1988—). Democrat. Jewish. Home: 29995 High Valley Rd Farmington MI 48331-2142 Office: Sinai Hosp Detroit 6767 W Outer Dr Detroit MI 48235-2893

BROWN, MYRTLE IRENE, nursing educator; b. East Peoria, Ill., Feb. 1, 1915; d. Clifford Richard and Sarah (Scoville) B. BA, Eureka Coll., 1939; BS, U. Minn., 1942, MS, 1947; PhD, NYU, 1961. Instr. supr. pediatric nursing Mont. State Coll., Great Falls, 1939-41; instr., supr. pediatric nursing U. Minn., 1942-46, instr. advanced pediatric nursing, 1947-49; nursing cons. maternal and child health team WHO, India, 1949-50; pub. health staff nurse Wayne County Health Dept., Eloise, Mich., 1950-52; asst. prof. maternal and child health Johns Hopkins, Balt., 1952-55; instr., then asso. prof. introductory epidemiology, sr. clin. nursing maternal and children's nursing NYU, 1955-61; rsch. cons. Am. Nurses' Found. N.Y.C., 1961-64; assoc. prof. community health and med. practice U. Mo. Sch. Medicine, Columbia, 1964-67; assoc., prof. Sch. Nursing, 1964-67; dean, prof. Sch. Nursing, Duke, 1967-70; prof., assoc. dean grad. studies Coll. Nursing, U. S.C., Columbia, 1970-80. Bd. dirs. Espicopal Housing Corp., 1975-93, Columbia; trustee Eureka Coll., Ill., 1985-92. Fellow APHA, Am. Acad. Nursing; mem. ANA, S.C. Nurses Assn., Am. Sociol. Assn., Trained Nurse Assn. India (life), Nat. League Nursing, N.C. League Nursing, Kappa Delta Pi. Home: 5400 Lakeshore Dr Columbia SC 29206-4911

BROWN, OLEN RAY, medical microbiology research educator; b. Hastings, Okla., Aug. 18, 1935; s. Willis Edward and Rosa Nell (Fulton) B.; m. Pollyana June King, Aug. 30, 1958; children: Barbara Kathryn, Diana Carol, David Gregory. BS in Lab. Tech., Okla. U., 1958, MS in Bacteriology, 1960, PhD in Microbiology, 1964. Diplomate Am. Bd. Toxicology, Am. Bd. Forensic Examiners. Instr. Sch. Medicine, U. Mo., Columbia, 1964-65, asst. prof., 1965-70, assoc. prof., 1970-77, prof. dept. molecular microbiology and immunology, 1981—; joint appointments, prof. depts. microbiology and biomed. scis. Coll. Vet. Medicine, U. Mo., 1977—, prof. biomed. scis., 1987—; guest lectr. Ross U., St. Kitts, W.I., 1984, 88; asst. dir. Dalton Rsch. Ctr., U. Mo., 1974-78, Dalton rsch. investigator grad. sch., 1968—; grant peer reviewer for program projects SCOR and Superfund grants NIH, 1979, Nat. Inst. Environ. Health Scis., Dept. Commerce, EPA, 1986, 90-96, Am. Inst. Biol. Scis. for Dept. Def.; cons. drug abuse policy office White House, 1982, Immunol. Vaccines, Inc., Columbia, 1984—, Lab. Support, Inc., Chgo., 1988-89, Ea. Rsch. Group, Lexington, Mass., 1991—, Teltech, Mpls., 1992—, Scis. Internat., Inc., Alexandria, Va.; judge top 100 products for 1996, Rsch. and Devel. Mag. Author: Laboratory Manual for Veterinary Microbiology, 1973, The Expert Witness: A Manual for Attorneys and Professionals Under Contract; co-author: elem. and advanced lab. manuals for med. microbiology, 2 vols., 1978, 79; contbr. Progress in Clinical Research, Vol. 21, 1978, 79, Oxygen, 5th Internat. Hyperbaric Conf., Vols. I, II, 1974, 79, numerous articles to profl. jours.; book and film critic AAAS, Washington, 1986—; item preparer Am. Coll. Test, Med. Coll. Admissions Test, 1981—; mem. editorial staff Biomed. Letters, 1981—; responder Sci. and Math. Helpline for Mus. Sci. Discovery, Harrisburg, Pa., 1996—, reviewer profl. jours. Track and field ofcl. U. Mo. and Big Eight Conf., Columbia, 1979-86. Investigative rsch. grantee Office Naval Rsch., Dept. Def., 1968-81, NIH, 1976-88, NIEHS, 1981-94, 95—, USAID, 1983-86, Nat. Inst. Dental Health Scis., 1989-92. Fellow Am. Inst. Chemists (cert. chemistry and chem engring., profl. program bd. 1989-90, sd com. chemistry and environ. concerns); mem. Top One Percent Soc., Soc. Toxicology, Internat. Soc. Study Xenobiotics, Am. Chem. Soc., Am. Heart Assn., Internat. Soc. Exposure Analysts, Nat. Space Soc., Oxygen Soc., Columbia Track Club (sec.-treas. 1979-82). Office: U Mo Dalton Rsch Ctr Columbia MO 65211

BROWN, OLLIE DAWKINS, marriage, family and child therapist, scientific researcher; b. Martin County, Tex., May 30, 1941; d. David G. and Wilma Loree (Turner) Dawkins; m. Robert Jerry Brown, Sept. 28, 1958 (div.); children: Mark Allen, James Russell. BS, Tex. Tech U., 1965; MEd, North Tex. State U., 1973; MS, East Tex. State U., 1983. Cert. tchr., Tex.; cert. hypnotherapist, Nat. Bd. Cert. Clin. Hynotherapists; lic. marriage and family therapists/supr., Tex.; cert. play therapist/supr., Am. Assn. Play Therapists; cert. group psychotherapist. Diagnostician Lillian Solomon, PhD, Dallas, 1972-82; with Environ. Health Ctr., Dallas, 1982-86; psychotherapist Pastoral Counseling and Edn. Ctr., Dallas, 1986-91, Alpha Counseling Ctr., Dallas, 1991-92; co-founder Agape Counseling Ctr., Dallas, 1992-93; dir., owner Aegis Ctr. North Tex., 1993—. Contbr. articles to profl. jours., chpts. to med. textbooks. Mem. Northrich Bapt. Ch., Richardson, 1967—. Mem. APA, ACA, Am. Assn. Marriage and Family Therapists, Tex. Counseling Assn., Tex. Psychol. Assn., Tex. Assn. Play Therapists, Am. Assn. Play Therapists (cert. supr., charter and founding mem. North Tex. chpt.), Am. Group Psychotherapy Soc. (cert. group psychotherapist), Southwestern Group Pscyhotherapy Soc., Dallas Group Psychotherapy Soc. (comms. chmn. Dallas chpt.), Am. Rose Soc., Collin County Rose Soc. (continuous rose show coord.). Republican. Home: 634 Williams Way Richardson TX 75080-3344 Office: Aegis Ctr N Tex 2007 N Collins Ste 509 Richardson TX 75080-2645

BROWN, OPAL DIANN, medical technologist, nurse; b. Gassaway, W.Va., Aug. 9, 1958; d. Albert Lee and Elizabeth Lee (Kidd) Persinger; m. Thomas David Brown, July 31,1993. BS in Med. Tech., W.Va. U., 1981; BSN, U. S.C., 1993. Med. technologist Biomed. Reference Labs., Fairmont, W.Va., 1981-82, Fairmont (W.Va.) Gen. Hosp., 1982, B.G. Thimmappa, M.D., Inc., Bridgeport, W.Va., 1982-83, Pocahontas Meml. Hosp., Marlinton, W.Va., 1984-87, Alexandria (Va.) Hosp., 1987-88, Richland Meml. Hosp., Columbia, S.C., 1988—; part-time RN Midlands Regional Ctr., S.C. Dept. of Disabilities and Spl. Needs, Columbia, 1994—. Mem. Am. Soc. Clin. Pathologists, Sigma Theta Tau. Democrat. Presbyterian. Home: 232 Laurel Meadows Dr West Columbia SC 29169-2361

BROWN, PAUL WOODROW, surgeon; b. N.Y.C., Dec. 28, 1919; s. La Verne C. and Mayme Catherine (DeClarke) B.; m. Patricia Ann Burris, May 24, 1986. BS, U. Mich., 1942, MD, 1950. Diplomate Am. Bd. Orthopaedic Surgery. Commd. pvt. U.S. Army, 1942, advanced through grades to col., ret., 1969; intern, resident Letterman Army Hosp., San Francisco, 1950-51, 51-54; resident Shriner's Hosp. for Crippled Children, San Francisco, 1954-55; prof. surgery U. Colo., Denver, 1969-72, U. Miami, Fla., 1972-74; chief surgery St. Vincent's Med. Ctr., Bridgeport, Conn., 1974-82; clin. prof. orthopaedic surgery Sch. Medicine, Yale U., New Haven, 1985—, clin. prof. plastic and reconstructive surgery, 1986—; pvt. practice surgeon Conn. Hand Surgery Ctr., Bridgeport, 1978—; fellowship hand surgery Walter Reed Army Hosp., Washington, 1962-63. Contbr. articles to profl. publs., chpts. to books. Home: 3071 North St Fairfield CT 06430-1627 Office: Conn Hand Surgery Ctr 3101 Main St Bridgeport CT 06606-4223

BROWN, RANDALL KEITH, orthodontist; b. Evansville, Ind., Aug. 10, 1955; s. Rodney Ferguson and Shirley Ann (Lane) B. Student, Ind. U., 1973-76, DDS, 1980; MS in Orthodontics, St. Louis U., 1982. Asst. instr. Ind. U. Sch. Dentistry, Indpls., 1979-80; orthodontist in pvt. practice Evansville, 1982—; exec. coun. First Dist. Dental Soc., Evansville, 1988-89. Mem. ADA, Am. Assn. Orthodontists, Orthodontic Edn. and Rsch. Found. (pres. 1996), Nat. Fedn. Ind. Businesses, Ind. Dental Assn., Gt. Lakes Soc. Orthodontists. Home: 5821 Woodridge Pl Evansville IN 47720 Office: 1330 First Ave Evansville IN 47710-2406

BROWN, REGINALD HARVEY, dental educator; b. Auckland, New Zealand, July 27, 1933; s. Andrew and Ivy O. (Belliss) B.; m. Janet Ann Brizzle, Mar. 11, 1961; children: Julie Ann Brown Cadzow, Jeffrey Andrew, Alison Mary, Sarah Margaret, Michael James. B. of Dental Surgery, U. Otago, Dunedin, New Zealand, 1956, DDS with distinction, 1972; cert. in pedodontics, U. Ill., Chgo., 1972. Sr. dental officer, prin. dental officer Div. Mental Health, New Zealand Dept. Health, Levin, 1957-70; from lectr. to sr. lectr. to assoc. prof. of dentistry U. Otago, 1970-93, chmn. dept. community dental health, 1985-93; hon. rsch. fellow Faculty of Dentistry, U. Otago, 1994—; editorial cons. Internat. Jour. Paediatric Dentistry, Bristol, U.K., 1985—. Editor New Zealand Dental Jour., 1973, 75—; contbr. numerous articles to profl. jours. Organist, choirmaster Wakari Union Ch., 1982—; asst. conductor So. Consort of Voices, 1980—; dep. conductor Schola Cantorum of Dunedin, 1978—; chair bd. trustees Logan Park High Sch., Dunedin, 1987—. Fellow New Zealand Dental Assn. (mem. coun. 1975—). Presbyterian. Office: U Otago Faculty Dentistry, PO Box 647 Great King St, Dunedin New Zealand

BROWN, RICHARD BRUCE, infectious disease physician; b. N.Y.C., May 22, 1944; s. Seymour Michael and Norma M. (Lipchansky) B.; m. Bonnie M. Morganstein, Oct. 11, 1970; children: Scott M., Robin D. BS, Tufts U., 1965; MD, George Washington U., 1969. Diplomate internal medicine and infectious diseases Am. Bd. Internal Medicine. Resident in medicine New Eng. Med. Ctr. Hosp., Boston, 1969-71, fellow infectious diseases, 1973-75; fellow infectious diseases Peter Bent Brigham Hosp., Boston, 1975-76; chief infectious disease divsn. Baystate Med. Ctr., Springfield, Mass., 1976—; health adv. bd. Smith Coll., Northampton, Mass., 1991—; interviewer Tufts

U., Medford, Mass., 1991—; prof. medicine Tufts U. Sch. Medicine, 1995; co-dir. Wound Healing and Hyperbaric Medicine Program Baystate Med. Ctr., Springfield, Mass., 1994—. Editor: Infections in Outpatient Practice, 1988, Clinical Problems in Infectious Diseases, 1994. Fellow ACP, Infectious Disease Soc. Am. Home: 20 Pinewood Dr Long Meadow MA 01106 Office: Infectious Disease Divsn Baystate Med Ctr Springfield MA 01199

BROWN, RICHARD DEAN, biology educator; b. Mansfield, Ohio, Feb. 6, 1941; s. Edward H. and Lydia (Reuss) B.; m. Judith W. Scoble, June 4, 1963; children: Richard D. Brown II, Kristin B. Stevenson. BA, Columbia Union Coll., 1964; MS, Ohio State U., 1970, PhD, 1975. Chmn., sci. instr. Garden State Acad., Tranquility, N.J., 1966-70; grad. teaching assoc. Dept. Zoology, Ohio State U., Columbus, 1970-75; curator Zool. Mus. U. N.C. Zool. Mus., Charlotte, 1975-81; asst. prof. biology U. N.C., Charlotte, 1976-83, lectr., 1987—; founder, exec. dir. Carolina Raptor Ctr., Inc., Charlotte, 1980-86; exec. dir. Carolina Raptor Ctr. Found., Inc., Charlotte, 1986-87; environ. cons. Brown Cons., Charlotte, 1987-95; adj. prof. biology U. N.C., Charlotte, 1987-95; biology lead instr. Brunswick C.C., 1993—; cons. in field; presenter workshops and ednl. programs. S.E. regional editor Hawk Migration Assn. N.Am.; contbr. articles to profl. jours. Recipient Svc. award Mecklenburg County Park and Recreation Commn., 1979; grantee U. N.C., 1976, 80. Mem. Raptor Rsch. Found., Ornithol. Soc. of N.Am., Ornithol. Soc. of the Carolinas (pres. 1982-84), Wilson Ornithol. Soc., Human Anatomy and Physiology Soc. Republican. Seventh-day Adventist. Home: PO Box 550 Supply NC 28462-0550 Office: Brunswick CC PO Box 30 Supply NC 28462-0030

BROWN, ROBERT GLENN, plastic surgeon; b. Norfolk, Va., Dec. 29, 1940; s. Charlie Glenn and Margaret Ella (Pridgen) B.; m. Betty Cletis Akers, Aug. 29, 1964; children: Glenn Christopher, Rebecca Aileen. BA, U. Va., 1962; MD, Duke U., 1966. Diplomate Am. Bd. Surgery, Am. Bd. Plastic Surgery. Intern U. Fla., Gainesville, 1966, resident in gen. surgery, 1967-68, 70-73; resident in plastic surgery Emory U., Atlanta, 1973-74; resident in head and neck surgery Roswell Park Meml. Inst., Buffalo, N.Y., 1975; asst. prof. surgery Emory U. Sch. Medicine, Atlanta, 1975-79; plastic surgeon Surg. Clinic Inc., Opelika, 1979—; chief surgery East Ala. Med. Ctr., Opelika, 1983, 95—, chief of staff, 1984, mem. exec. com., 1986. Contbr. numerous articles to profl. jours. Served with USNR, 1968-70. Fellow ACS; mem. Am. Soc. Plastic and Reconstructive Surgery, Soc. Head and Neck Surgeons, Am. Assn. Plastic Surgeons. Republican. Episcopalian. Home: 302 3rd Ave Opelika AL 36801-4202 Office: Surg Clinic Inc 121 N 20th St Opelika AL 36801-5449

BROWN, ROBERT HAINES, orthopedic surgeon; b. Atlantic City, N.J., June 9, 1938; s. J. Carlisle and Mary Elizabeth (Rosenberger) B.; m. Beverly Rennild Anderson, June 13, 1964; children: Joanne Elizabeth, Kristin Lee. BS, Northwestern U., 1960; MD, Temple U., 1964. Bd. cert. Am. Bd. Orthopedic Surgery. Intern Cooper Hosp./U. Med. Ctr., 1964-65, gen. surgery resident, 1967-68, orth. surg. resident, 1969-71; orth. surg. resident U. W.Va., 1968-69; pvt. practice orthopedic surgery Cherry Hill, N.J., 1972—. Capt. USAF, 1965-67. Office: 1210 Brace Rd Cherry Hill NJ 08034-3213 Also: PO Box 430 350 Front St Elmer NJ 08318-2143

BROWN, ROBERT HORATIO, SR., retired orthopedic surgeon; b. Dedham, Mass., Aug. 30, 1917; s. Walter Horatio and Harriet (Crocker) B.; m. Virginia Fales Lane, Dec. 26, 1943 (dec. Feb. 1994); children: Edith Persis, Robert Horatio Jr., Betsy; m. Vera Scott Townsend, Apr. 29, 1995. B.S., Tufts U., 1940; M.D., Harvard, 1943. Diplomate: Am. Bd. Orthopedic Surgery. Intern, surg. resident Mass. Gen. Hosp., 1944-45; surg. resident Cushing VA Hosp., 1946-47; orthopedic resident USN, Duke, 1952-56; commd. lt. (j.g.) USN, 1945; ret., 1946; commd. lt. USN, 1950, advanced through grades to capt., 1959; chief orthopedic service U.S. Naval Hosp., Nat. Naval Med. Center, Bethesda, Md., 1964-70; gen. practice medicine Sharon, Mass., 1947-50; course dir. orthopedic pathology Armed Forces Inst. Pathology, 1963-64; asst. clin. prof. orthopaedic surgery George Washington U. Sch. Medicine, 1968-70; hon. staff Eastern Maine Med. Center, 1970—; cons. rehab. service, 1971—; Navy liaison mem. musculoskeletal com. NRC, 1965-70; surg. study group B. NIH, 1968-70. Fellow A.C.S.; mem. AMA, Mass. Med. Soc., Am. Acad. Orthopedic Surgeons, Soc. Med. Cons. to Armed Forces, Maine Med. Assn., Phi Beta Kappa. Home: 23 Stoneybrook Rd Hampden ME 04444-1621

BROWN, ROBERT TINDALL, psychology educator; b. Greenwich, Conn., Jan. 3, 1940; s. Emerson Lee and Marguerite (Bangs) B.; m. Donna F. Ferris, June 25, 1964 (div. 1973); children: Ana Katherine, Julia Marguerite; m. 2d, Caryl Sue Lamb, Aug. 5, 1978. B.A., Hamilton Coll., 1961; Ph.D., Yale U., 1966; postgrad. U. Sussex, 1965-67. USPHS postdoctoral fellow U. Sussex, Brighton, Eng., 1965-67; vis. asst. prof. Coll. William and Mary, Williamsburg, Va., 1967-68; asst. prof. U. N.C., Chapel Hill, 1968-74, assoc. prof., Wilmington, 1974-79, prof. psychology, 1980—; cons. editor Ency. of Spl. Edn., 1987. Co-editor: (series) Plenum Perspectives on Individual Differences, 1982—, Perspectives on Bias in Mental Testing, 1984, Psychological Perspectives on Childhood Exceptionality: A Handbook, 1986; author: (booklet) Studying Psychology, 1991; sr. adv. bd. Ednl. Psychology Review, 1990—; contbr. Encyclopedia of Special Education, 1987, Encyclopedia of Psychology, 2d edit., 1994; contbr. numerous articles to profl. jours. USPHS grantee, 1974-77. Mem. Am. Psychol. Assn., Animal Behavior Soc., Psychonomic Soc., N.Y. Acad. Sci., Internat. Soc. Devel. Psychobiology, So. Soc. for Philosophy and Psychology, Southeastern Psychol., Phi Kappa Phi, Sigma Xi. Home: Route 4 1801 Futch Creek Rd Wilmington NC 28405 Office: Psychology Dept Univ NC Wilmington NC 28403

BROWN, RONNIE JEFFREY, biologist, researcher; b. Birmingham, Ala., Apr. 27, 1953; s. Eddie and Johnnie Mae (Pitts) B.; m. Fannie M. Garrett, Aug. 11, 1984. BS, U. Ala., 1975; student, Harvard U., 1974-75. Tutor in gross anatomy sch. dentistry U. Ala., Birmingham, 1976-77; biologist VA Med. Ctrs., Dallas, Oklahoma City, 1978-83; supervisory biologist USDA, El Reno, Okla., 1983-84; sr. mfg. supr. UTC Mostex, Carrollton, Tex., 1983-85; prodn. mgr. Kraft Inc., Garland, Tex., 1985-86; dir. surg. rsch. Baylor U. Med. Ctr., Dallas, 1986-90; instr. dept. surgery divsn. transplantation U. Ala., Birmingham, 1990—, lab. instr. human biology Sch. Natural Scis. and Math., 1996—; coord., lab. instr., laparoscopy program Dept. Vet. Affairs, Birmingham Regional Med. Edn. Ctr., 1996—; coord. metro. edn. Am. Assn. Lab. Animal Sci. Tex. Br., Dallas, 1987-90. Contbr. articles to profl. jours. including Jour. Ala. Acad. Sci., So. Med. Jour., Jour. Surg. Rsch., , Circulation, Jour. Thoracic and Cardiovascular Surgery, Annals of Thoracic Surgery and others. Named One of Outstanding Young Men of Am., 1979, 92. Mem. APHA, AAAS, Am. Assn. Lab. Animal Sci. (southeastern br.), Soc. Human Anatomy and Physiology, Am. Soc. Aesthetic Plastic Surgery (Bioskill lab. coord. 1994), Am. Soc. Surgery of the Hand (Bioskill lab. coord. 1994), Ala. Vet. Technicians Assn., Vet. Tech. Anesthetist Soc., U. Ala. at Birminghams Nat. Alumni Soc., Urban League, Young Men Rep. Club, Acad Surg. Rsch., Bread and Roses (bd. dirs.), Masons, Alpha Phi Alpha, Beta Beta Beta. Methodist. Hom: 1820 Forestdale Blvd Birmingham AL 35214-2028 Office: U Ala Dept Surgery Divsn Transpla Univ Sta Birmingham AL 35205

BROWN, SHIRLEY ANN, speech and language pathologist; b. Bklyn., Oct. 9, 1935; d. Hyman and Lillian (Fuhrer) Rubak; m. Ronald Wallace Brown, Sept. 29, 1956; children: Abbie Howard, Daniel Mark. BA, Bklyn. Coll., 1956, MA, 1961. Lic. speech/lang. pathologist, N.Y., N.J. Speech pathologist Richmond County CP Treatment Ctr., S.I., N.Y., 1956-59, Coney Island Hosp., Bklyn., 1959-61, Mendham Boro Schs. and Chatham Twp. Schs., 1962-67; pvt. practice home care speech pathologist various hosps. and med. facilities, 1967-79; dir. speech pathology dept. Englewood (N.J.) Hosp., 1974-92; speech pathologist Holy Name Hosp., Teaneck, N.J., 1992-96, chief speech-lang. pathology dept., 1996—; speech pathologist Home Health Care Agys., Bergen County, 1992—; clin. supr. comm. disorders grad. program Hunter Coll., N.Y.C., 1993—, Kean Coll., N.J., 1993—, Montclair State U., 1996—. Chair svc. and rehab. Am. Cancer Soc., Hackensack, N.J. Recipient Nat. Honor citation for Profl. Edn., Am. Cancer Soc., 1985, Crimson Sword award Am. Cancer Soc., 1989. Mem. Am. Speech. Lang. and Hearing Assn. (cert., congl. action com., state chair career info., Continuing Edn. award 1983—, Outstanding Clin. Achievement award 1985), N.J. Speech, Lang. and Hearing Assn. Home: 6 Sisson Ter Tenafly NJ 07670-1810 Office: Holy Name Hosp Speech-Lang Pathology Dept 718 Teaneck Rd Teaneck NJ 07666-4245

BROWN, STANLEY PAUL, medical educator; b. Plaquemine, La., Aug. 30, 1953; s. Joseph Harry and Vivian Cecilia (LeJeune) B.; m. Yvonne Zerangue, Dec. 8, 1984; children: Joanna Vivian, Elizabeth Yvette, Ruth Claire. BS in Gen. Studies, La. State U., 1980, MS in Cmty. Health and Cardiac Rehab., 1982; PhD in Exercise Physiology, U. So. Miss., 1989. Porgram dir. cardiac rehab. St. Francis Cabrini Hosp., Alexandria, La., 1983-84; dir. dept. cardiac rehab. River West Med. Ctr., Plaquemine, La., 1984-85; exercise physiologist Inst. for Wellness and Sports Medicine, Hattiesburg, Miss., 1985-86; dir. The Wellness Ctr. Jones County Cmty. Hosp., Laurel, Miss., 1986-87; instr. dept. health, phys. edn. and recreation U. Ark., Monticello, 1988-89; asst. prof. exercise sci. U. Miss., University, 1989-95, assoc. prof. exercise sci., 1995—, dir. Human Performance Lab., 1989—; spl. cons. diabetes Bapt. Med. Ctr., Little Rock, 1989; textbook reviewer Mosby-Year Book, Inc., St. Louis, 1993-94. Contbr. articles to profl. jours. Pres. Oxford-Lafayette County Right to Life, 1991-93. Fellow Am. Coll. Sports Medicine (cert. preventive rehab. exercise specialist, certification faculty mem. 1994, 95); mem. Am. Physiol. Soc., Am. Assn. for Cardiovascular and Pulmonary Rehab. Republican. Home: 214 Woodlawn Dr Oxford MS 38655 Office: Dept Exercise Sci Univ Miss University MS 38677

BROWN, STEPHEN LAWRENCE, environmental consultant; b. San Francisco, Feb. 16, 1937; s. Bonnar and Martha (Clendenin) B.; m. Ann Goldsberry, Aug. 13, 1961; children: Lisa, Travis, Meredith. BS in Engring. Sci., Stanford U., 1958, MS in Physics, 1961; PhD in Physics, Purdue U., 1963. Ops. analyst Stanford Rsch. Inst., Menlo Park, Calif., 1963-74, program mgr., 1974-77, dir. Ctr. Resource and Environ. Systems Studies, 1977-80, dir. Ctr. Health and Environ. Rsch., 1980-83; assoc. dir. Commn. on Life Scis. NAS, Washington, 1983-86; prin. Environ Corp., Arlington, Va., 1986-91; mgr. risk assessment ENSR Cons. and Engring., Alameda, Calif., 1992-93; dir. Risks of Radiation and Chem. Compounds (R2C2), Oakland, Calif., 1993—; mem. sci. adv. bd. EPA, Washington, 1991—; mem. coms. SAB, NAS, 1980-87. Contbr. over 20 articles to profl. jours., chpts. to books; author over 100 reports in field. Mem. AAAS, Internat. Soc. Exposure Assessment, Soc. for Risk Analysis, Phi Beta Kappa, Sigma Xi, Sigma Pi Sigma, Tau Beta Pi. Office: R2C2 4700 Grass Valley Rd Oakland CA 94605

BROWN, STEVEN BRIEN, radiologist; b. Ft. Collins, Colo., Jan. 18, 1952; s. Allen Jenkins and Shirley Irene (O'Brien) B.; m. Susan Jane DiTomaso, Sept. 10, 1983; children: Allison Grace, Laura Anne. BS, Colo. State U., 1974; MD, U. Calif., San Diego, 1978. Diplomate in radiology, vascular and interventional radiology Am. Bd. Radiology. Intern U. Wash., Seattle, 1978-79; resident in radiology Stanford (Calif.) U., 1979-82; fellow in interventional and neuro-radiology Wilford Hall, USAF Med Ctr., San Antonio, 1982-83; staff radiologist Wilford Hall, USAF Med Ctr., 1983-86, Luth. Med. Ctr., Wheat Ridge, Colo., 1986—; chief angiography and interventional radiology Luth. Med. Ctr., 1987-94, chief dept. med. imaging, 1994—; pres. Luth. Med. Ctr. Joint Venture, 1992-94; mem. bd. mgrs. Primera HealthCare LLC, 1995—; pres. HealthCare Select Inc., 1995-96. Contbr. articles to profl. jours. Mem. Rep. Nat. Com., Washington, 1984—, Nat. Rep. Senatorial Com., 1985—, Rep. Presdl. Task Force, 1986—; bd. dirs. The Health Care Initiative. Maj. USAF, 1982-86. Fellow Radiol. Soc. N.Am.; mem. Colo. Radiol. Soc. (pres. 1995-96), Rocky Mt. Radiol. Soc. (pres. 1994-95), Am. Coll. Radiology, Soc. Cardiovasc. and Interventional Radiology, Western Neuroradiol. Soc., Am. Soc. Neuroradiology, Colo. Preferred Physicians Orgn. (bd. dirs. 1987-89), World Wildlife Orgn., Colo. Angio Club. Republican. Presbyterian. Office: Luth Med Center 8300 W 38th Ave Wheat Ridge CO 80033-6005

BROWN, STUART I., ophthalmologist, educator; b. Chgo., Mar. 1, 1933; s. Leonard and Ann (Gladin) B.; m. Isabel Bodor; children: Sarah, Emily. B.M.S., U. Ill.-Chgo., 1955, M.D., 1957. Intern Jackson Meml. Hosp., Miami, Fla., 1957-58; resident in opthalmology, Eye, Ear, Nose and Throat Hosp., Tulane Med.Sch., New Orleans, 1961; fellow in cornea Mass. Eye and Ear Infirmary, Boston, 1962-66; clin. asst. prof. dept. opthalmology N.Y. Hosp.-Cornell Med. Ctr., N.Y.C., 1966, dir. cornea services cornea research lab, 1966-69, clin. assoc. prof., 1970-73; chmn., prof. dept. opthalmology U. Pitts. Sch. Medicine, 1974-82, U. Calif. Sch. Medicine-San Diego, 1983—; bd. dirs. nat. adv. commn. Nat. Eye Bank, Inc. Recipient Heed Ophthalmic Found. award, 1976. Mem. Am. Acad. Ophthalmology, AMA, Assn. Research in Vision and Ophthalmology, Assn. U. Profs. Ophthalmology, Internat. Soc. Eye Research, Internat. Corneal Soc. (pres.). Office: U Calif San Diego Ste 0946 Dept Opthalmology La Jolla CA 92093-0946

BROWN, THOMAS WILLIAM, osteopathic physician, obstetrician, gynecologist; b. Detroit, Oct. 10, 1946; s. William Floyd and Dorothy Fern (Skitch) Brown; m. Debra Lynne Dawson, Sept 29, 1984; children: Stephen Michael, Scott William. BA, Western Mich. U., 1968; DO, Coll. Osteopathic Medicine, Des Moines, Iowa, 1972. Diplomate Am. Bd. Ob.-Gynecologists. Chief ob.-gyn. USAF Hosp., Clovis, N. Mex., 1980-82; physician pvt. practice, Fairfield, Calif., 1982-90; staff physician Kaiser Permanente, Vallejo, Calif., 1990—. Mem. Am. Coll. Ob.-Gyn., Solano County Med. Soc., Rosicrucian Order, AMORC. Office: Kaiser Permanente 975 Sereno Dr Vallejo CA 94589

BROWN, VALERIE ANNE, psychiatric social worker, educator; b. Elizabeth, N.J., Feb. 28, 1951; d. William John and Adelaide Elizabeth (Krasa) B.; BA summa cum laude (fellow), C.W. Post Coll., 1972; MSW (Silberman scholar), Hunter Coll., 1975; Diplomate Am. Bd. Examiners, Am. Bd. Clin. Social Work, Nat. Assn. Soc. Work; cert. addictions specialist, cert. master hypnotherapist. Social work intern Greenwich House Counseling Center, N.Y.C., 1973-74, Metro Cons. Center, N.Y.C., 1974-75; sr. psychiat. social worker, co-adminstr. Saturday Clinic, Essex County Guidance Center, East Orange, N.J., 1975-80; pvt. practice psychiat. social work, psychotherapy, 1979—; sr. psychiat social worker John E. Runnells Hosp., Berkeley Heights, N.J., 1980-86; dir. social work Northfield Manor, West Orange, N.J., 1987; clin. coord. Project Portals East Orange Gen. Hosp., 1987-88; asst. dir. ARS/Century House Riverview Med. Ctr., Red Bank, N.J., 1988-93; sr. clin. case mgmt. specialist Prudential Ins. Co. Woodbridge, N.J., 1993-93; clin. dir. Greenhouse-KMC, Lakewood, N.J., 1994—; tech. advisor Nat. Comm. Network, 1988— instr. Brookdale Coll., 1991—; co-founder Women's Growth Ctr., Cedar Grove, N.J., 1979; counselor Passaic Drug Clinic, 1978-80; field instr. Fairleigh Dickinson U., Madison, N.J., 1981-86, Brookdale Coll., 1989-92; field supr. Union Coll., Cranford, N.J., 1986; instr. Sch. Social Work, NYU, N.Y.C., 1980-83, asst. prof., 1983-85; evaluator Intoxicated Driver Resource Ctr., Essex County, N.J., 1987-88. Alt. Monmouth County profl. adv. bd. Mem. NASW, Psi Chi, Pi Gamma Mu, Sigma Tau Delta. Office: 20 Ellsworth Ct Red Bank NJ 07701-5403

BROWN, W. VIRGIL, internal medicine educator; b. Royston, Ga., Sept. 25, 1938; m. Alice; 2 children. BA in Physics and Chemistry, Emory U., 1960; MD, Yale U., 1964. Diplomate Am. Bd. Internal Medicine, Am. Bd. Endocrinology. Intern, asst. resident Osler Med. Svc. Johns Hopkins Hosp., Balt., 1964-66; clin. assoc. Nat. Heart and Lung Inst., Bethesda, Md., 1966-69; fellow in endocrinology and metabolism Yale-New Haven Hosp., 1969-70; asst. prof. medicine U. Calif. Dept. Medicine, San Diego, 1970-74, assoc. prof. medicine, 1974-78, prof. medicine, 1978-87; dir. lipid rsch. clinic U. Calif., San Diego, 1972-78; prof. medicine Mt. Sinai Sch. Medicine, N.Y.C., dir. divsn. arteriosclerosis and metabolism, 1991—; pres., CEO Medlantic Rsch. Found., Washington, 1987-91; Charles Howard Candler prof. internal medicine, dir. divsn. arteriosclerosis and lipid metabolism Emory U., Atlanta, 1991—. Mem. editl. bd. Jour. Lipid Rsch., 1977-81, 91-95. Fellow ACP; mem. Am. Heart Assn. (mem. physiology study sect. 1978-80, mem. credentials com. arteriosclerosis coun. 1978-80, chmn. credentials com. arteriosclerosis coun. 1979-82, mem. nutrition com. 1981-86, mem. several rsch. coms., chmn. nutrition com. 1982-86, bd. dirs. 1983, vice-chmn. edn. and cmty. program com., pres.-elect 1990-91, pres. 1991-92, gold heart award 1996, fellow arteriosclerosis coun., fellow epidemiology and preventive cardiology coun., numerous others), Am. Fedn. Clin. Rsch., Am. Soc. Clin. Investigation, Am. Soc. Exptl. Biology, Southeastern Lipid Conf., Am. Bd. Bioanalysis (high-complexity clin. lab. dir.), Phi Beta Kappa, Alpha Omega Alpha. Office: Emory U Sch Med Divsn Arteriosclerosis & Lipid Metabolism Dept Med 1639 Pierce Dr 2001 WMB Atlanta GA 30322*

BROWN, WILLIAM MORRIS, JR., surgeon, educator; b. Macon, Ga., Dec. 13, 1926; s. W. Morris and Sarah Virginia (Turner) B.; m. Carmen Shaver, Oct. 17, 1953; children: Catherine Shaver, W. Morris III. BA, Mercer U., 1948; MD, U. Md., 1952. Diplomate Am. Bd. Surgery. Intern in surgery Grady Meml. Hosp., Emory U. Sch. Medicine, Atlanta, 1952-53, asst. resident in surgery, 1953-56, chief resident in surgery, 1956-57; pvt. practice Macon, 1957—; prof. surgery Mercer U. Sch. Medicine, Macon, 1982-92. Sr. warden Christ Episc. Ch., Macon, 1968-71, lay reader, 1964-76. Staff sgt. U.S. Army, 1944-46, PTO. Fellow ACS, Ga. Surg. Soc., Southeastern Surg. Congress. Office: 380 Hospital Dr Ste 430 Macon GA 31201-8001

BROWN, WILLIAM SAMUEL, JR., communication processes and disorders educator; b. Pottstown, Penn., Apr. 25, 1940; s. William Samuel and Elizabeth (Gallager) B.; m. Elaine Kay Whitehouse, Aug. 18, 1962; children: William Samuel III, Allen Reed. MA, SUNY, Buffalo, 1967, PhD, 1969. Speech therapist Crawford Cty. Schools, Meadville, Penn., 1962-65; rsch. asst. SUNY, Buffalo, N.Y., 1965-68; prof. U. Fla., Gainesville, Fla., 1970—; Contrib. numerous publications to scientific jours. Post-doctoral fellow U. Fla, Gainsville, 1968-70. Fellow Internat. Soc. Phonetic Sci. (coun. rep. 1980—), Am. Speech-Lang.-Hearing Assn., Acoustical Soc. Am.; mem. Am. Assn. Phonetic Sci. (exec. sec. 1980—). Republican. Presbyterian. Office: U Fla IASCP Dauer 63 Gainesville FL 32611

BROWN-CHRISTOPHER, CHERYL DENISE, physician; b. Washington, Dec. 4, 1954; d. Samuel and Cornelia Lela (Banks) Brown; m. Joseph William Christopher, Feb. 14, 1981; children: Jeremy, Callye Joelle. MD, Howard U., 1978. Intern Howard U., Washington, 1978-79, resident, 1982; physician pvt. practice, Annapolis, Md., 1982—; v.p. Bark Pain Assn., Pasadena, Md., 1995—. Tchr. jr. dept. Sunday Sch. Vt. Ave Bapt. Ch., 1990—choir mem., 1978—; ethics com. Md. State MEd. and Chirurgical Faculty, 1986, medicine and religion com., 1984-86. Washington Heart Assn. Summer rsch. fellow, 1970; recipient AMA Physicians Recognition award 1981, 84, 90, 93, Vt. Ave. Bapt. Ch. Health Fair award, Washington, 1985. Fellow Am. Acad. Family Physicians; mem. Am. Osteo. Acad. Sclerotherapy, Am. Acad. Pain Mgmt. (diplomate, bd. cert.), Am. Coll. Advancement of Medicine, Am. Soc. Clin. Hypnosis, So. Med. Assn., Order of Eastern Star. Office: Lifestyle Med Ctr 1419 Forest Dr Ste 202 Annapolis MD 21403

BROWNE, HOWARD STORM, orthopaedic surgeon; b. Ponca City, Okla., July 1, 1925; s. Howard Storm and Margaret May (Melvin) B.; m. Doris Mae Cox, Nov. 26, 1949; children: Stephen W., Catharine, Elizabeth, Alastair. Student, U. Okla., 1942-44; MB, Northwestern U., Chgo., 1948; MD, Northwestern U., 1949. Diplomate Am. Bd. Orthopaedic Surgery. Pvt. practice Newport, R.I., 1967-78; course dir. Harvard Orthopaedic Residency Program Faculty, Boston, 1979—; cons. orthopedic surgery RI Group Health/Harvard Community Health Plan, Providence, 1981-92; med. expert Social Security Hearings & Appeals, Providence, 1987—. Author: The Newport Hospital: A History, 1974; editor: So Few the Brave, 1976; editor Mil. Collector and Historian Jour., 1977-85; reviewer Jour. Bone and Joint Surgery, 1980—; contbr. articles to profl. jours. Bd. dirs., chmn. pubs. com. Newport Hist. Soc., 1985—; trustee Long Wharf Assn., Newport, 1985—; cons. Seaport '76, 1976—; sec. Newport & Old Colony R.R., Newport, 1980—. Capt. USN, 1943-67. Recipient Alan Weaver Hazleton award Mil. Order St. Lazarus of Jerusalem; knight Order of St. Michael the Archangel. Fellow Am. Acad. Orthopaedic Surgeons, Med. Soc. London; mem. R.I. Orthopaedic Soc. (pres. 1976-78), Venerable Order St. John of Jerusalem in the British Realm, Newport Reading Rm. (gov. 1979—), Savile Club (London), Army and Navy Club (Washington), N.Y. Yacht Club, Nat. Tennis Club (Newport). Episcopalian. Home and Office: 24 Kay St Newport RI 02840-2725

BROWNE, THOMAS REED, neurologist, researcher, educator; b. Lakewood, N.J., Aug. 10, 1943; s. Thomas Reed and Margaret (King) B.; m. Lynne Van Beuren, Mar. 27, 1969; children: Hilary Katherine, David Gerard. BA cum laude, Princeton U., 1965; MD with honors, U. Rochester, 1969. Diplomate Am. Bd. Psychiatry and Neurology, Am. Bd. Clin. Neurophysiology. Intern in medicine Cornell U. Med. Ctr., N.Y.C., 1969-70; staff assoc. epilepsy NIH, Bethesda, Md., 1970-72; resident in neurology Mass. Gen. Hosp., Boston, 1972-75; fellow in epilepsy Childrens Hosp., Boston, 1975-76; asst. prof. neurology Boston U. Sch. Medicine, Boston, 1976-80, assoc. prof. neurology, 1980-84, prof. neurology, 1984—, vice-chmn. dept. neurology, 1987—; clin. instr. in neurology Harvard Med. Sch., 1976-86; lectr. neurology Harvard Med. Sch., Boston, 1987—; assoc. chief neurology svc. VA Med. Ctr., Boston, 1987—. Editor: Epilepsy: Diagnosis and Management, 1983, 5th Frontiers of Pharmacology Symposium, Stable Isotopes in Pharm. Res., 1987; sect. editor Jour. Clin. Pharmacol., 1987—, Pharmacotherapy, 1982—, Am. Jour. Therapeutics, 1994—; contbr. 180 articles to profl. jours. Recipient Ciba Geigy award Internat. League Epilepsy, 1985. Fellow Am. Coll. Clin. Pharm. (regent 1985-90, McKeen Cattell award 1993), Am. Acad. Neurology, Am. EEG Soc.; mem. Am. soc. Clin. Pharmacol. Therapy, Mass. Epilepsy Soc. (profl. adv. bd.). Office: Boston U Sch Medicine Dept Neurology 80 E Concord St Boston MA 02118-2307

BROWNING, EDWARD TRACY, neurobiologist, pharmacologist; b. Cleve., July 15, 1939; s. Richard Lord and Charlotte (Tracy) B.; m. Carol Lynn Redfield, Aug. 3, 1968 (div.); children: Victor Redfield, Charlotte Elisabeth. BS, Purdue U., 1961; MS, U. Ill., 1964, PhD, 1966. Postdoctoral fellow U. Pa., Phila., 1966-68; asst. prof. Rutgers Med. Sch., Piscataway, N.J., 1968-74; assoc. prof. Rutgers Med. Sch., Piscataway, 1974-84; prof. Rutgers Med. Sch. (now Robert Wood Johnson Med. Sch.), Piscataway, 1984—. Mem., chmn. planning bd. Borough of Millstone, N.J. Mem. Am. Soc. for Neurochemistry, Internat. Soc. for Neurochemistry, Soc. for Neurosci., Am. Soc. for Pharmacology and Exptl. Therapeutics. Office: Robert Wood Johnson Med Sch Dept Pharmacology 675 Hoes Ln Piscataway NJ 08854

BROWNLEE, ROBERT CALVIN, pediatrician, educator; b. Due West, S.C., Mar. 13, 1922; s. Robert Calvin and Eleanor Louise (Pressly) B.; m. Judith Frances Irby; children: Eleanor Koets, Susan, Katherine Chambers, Jonathan, Robert Calvin. A.B., Erskine Coll., 1943; M.D., Vanderbilt U., 1945. Diplomate: Am. Bd. Pediatrics (pres. 1975), Am. Bd. Family Practice. Intern Vanderbilt U. Hosp., Nashville, 1945-46, resident, 1948-49; resident U. Va., Charlottesville, 1949-50; chief resident Vanderbilt U., 1950-51; practice medicine, specializing in pediatrics Christie Pediatric Group, Greenville, S.C., 1951-70; dir. pediatrics Greenville Hosp. System, 1970-75; asso. exec. sec. Am. Bd. Pediatrics, Chapel Hill, N.C., 1976, exec. sec., 1977-87, pres., 1987-92; clin. prof. pediatrics U. Pa., 1976-78; prof. pediatrics Med. U. S.C., 1971-75; clin. prof. pediatrics U. N.C., 1978—. Contbr. articles to med. jours. Served with AUS, 1943-45; with M.C. USAF, 1946-48, 53. Mem. Am. Acad. Pediatrics, Ambulatory PEdiatric Assn., So. Soc. Pediatric Rsch. Presbyterian. Home: 120 Sheffield Cir Chapel Hill NC 27514-6514

BROWNSON, KENNETH C., university dean; b. Hazleton, Pa., Apr. 16, 1945; s. Kenneth George and Mary Louise (Dennion) B. AAS in Nursing, Del. Tech. & Community Coll., 1978; BS in Profl. Arts, St. Joseph's Coll., Standish, Maine, 1984; MS in Mgmt., The Am. Coll., 1986; MS in Health Svc. Edn., Columbia Pacific U., 1987, PhD in Health Svc. Mgmt., 1988; MS in Psychology, Calif. Coast U., 1989; EdD in Adult and Nontraditional Edn., Newport U., 1991. RN, Del., Pa. Evening supr., asst. head nurse intensive/critical care unit Riverside Hosp., Wilmington, Del., 1980-83; staff RN, nurse/counselor crisis svc. unit Crozer-Chester Med. Ctr., Chester, Pa., 1983-94; pres. Adult Edn. Resource, Newark, Del., 1987—; dean undergrad. studies Greenwich U., Hilo, Hawaii, 1989—; mem. adj. faculty Newport U., Newport Beach, Calif., 1989—: provost Summit U., La., 1991—, New Orleans; mem. adv. bd. Insvc. Tng. Inst.. With USN, 1965-69, Vietnam. Supporting fellow The Alternative Edn. Assn.; mem. Nat. Assn. Pvt. Nontraditional Schs. and Colls. Home and Office: 2320 Milton Pl Newark DE 19702-4445

BROWN-STANDRIDGE, MARCIA DOROTHY, social worker, family therapist, educator; b. St. Louis, June 5, 1955; d. Gilbert Leon and Dorothy

Margaret (Hoffmann) Brown; m. Charles Robert Standridge, July 13, 1985. BSW, Valparaiso (Ind.) U., 1977; MSW, Tulane U., 1978; PhD, Purdue U., 1986. Clin. social worker Luth. Med. Ctr., St. Louis, 1979-82; cons. Luth. Child and Family Services, Indpls., 1984-85; asst. prof., dir. supervision tng. Tex. Tech U., Lubbock, 1985-89; assoc. prof. social work Fla. State U., Tallahassee, 1990—. Contbr. articles to profl. jours. Mem. Am. Assn. for Marriage and Family Therapy (clin. mem., approved supr.), Nat. Assn. Social Workers.

BROWNSTEIN, MARTIN HERBERT, dermatopathologist; b. N.Y.C., Aug. 20, 1935; s. Samuel C. and Florence (Sturm) B.; m. Ann Lehman, June 23, 1964 (div. Aug. 1993); children: Sara Leah, Michael Ari; m. Barbara Boltax, Sept. 19, 1993. AB, Harvard U., 1956; MD, Albert Einstein Coll. Medicine, 1961. Intern Lenox Hill Hosp., N.Y.C., 1961-62; resident in internal medicine VA Hosps., N.Y.C., 1962-65; resident in dermatology NYU, N.Y.C., 1965-66; pvt. practice medicine specializing in dermatopathology N.Y.C., 1970-72, Great Neck, N.Y., 1972-84, Port Washington, N.Y., 1984—; Osborne fellow Armed Forces Inst. Pathology, Washington, 1968-69; asst. clin. prof. dermatology N.Y. Med. Coll., N.Y.C., 1970-73, clin. assoc. prof. dermatology, 1973-78, clin. prof. dermatology, 1978-83, clin. asst. prof. pathology, 1971-83; clin. prof. dermatology Mt. Sinai Med. Ctr., N.Y.C., 1983—. Chief editor Jour. Cutaneous Pathology, 1984; contbr. articles to profl. jours. Trustee North Shore Hebrew Acad., Great Neck, N.Y., 1979-80; hon. trustee Great Neck Synagogue, 1986-88; sec. Ramot Shapira World Youth Ctr., bd. dirs., chmn. Chabad, Port Washington, N.Y., bd. dirs. Nat. Com. Futherance Jewish Edn., Nassau County. With M.C. U.S. Army, 1966-68. Recipient Pres.'s award Union Orthodox Jewish Congregations of Am., 1983. Mem. ACP, AMA, Am. Soc. Dermatopathology (pres. 1983-84), N.Y. State Soc. Dermatology, Am. Acad. Dermatology (chmn. com. on pathology 1980-82), Med. Soc. N.Y. State, Med. Soc. N.Y. County, Dermatol. Soc. Greater N.Y. (pres. 1978-79), L.I. Dermatology Soc. (pres. 1992-94), N.Y. Acad. Medicine. Home and Office: 2 N Plandome Rd Port Washington NY 11050-3443

BROWN-STIGGER, ALBERTA MAE, nurse; b. Columbus, Ohio, Nov. 11, 1932; d. Sylvester Clarence and Malinda (Mason) Angel; grad. Antelope Valley Coll., 1961; AA, L.A. Valley Coll., 1975; BS, Calif. State U., Dominguez Hills, 1981; m. Norman Brown, Dec. 29, 1967 (dec. Jan. 1989); children: Charon, Charles, Stevan, Carole; m. A.C. Stigger, June 14, 1992. RN, Calif.; lic. vocat. nurse. Nurses aid, vocat. nurse, respiratory therapist St. Bernardines Hosp., 1965-69, Good Samaritan Hosp., L.A., 1969-70, Midway Hosp., L.A., 1973-81; allergy nurse, instr. respiratory therapy VA Hosp., L.A., 1970-93, also acting dept. head; nurse, respiratory splty. unit Jerry L. Pettis Meml. Hosp., Loma Linda, Calif., 1984-93; with Wadley Regional Med. Ctr., Texarkana, Tex., 1993-94; rehab. nurse Robert H. Ballard Rehab. Hosp., San Bernardino, Calif., 1994—; instr. L.A. Valley Med. Technoogists Sch., Compton Coll. seminar instr., 1979. Active Arrowhead Allied Arts Coun. of San Bernardino; CPR instr. Am. Heart Assn. Mem. Am. Assn. Respiratory Therapy, Nat. Honor Soc., Eta Phi Beta. Democrat. Baptist. Clubs: Social-Lites, Inc. of San Bernardino, Order Ea. Star. Patentee disposable/replaceable tubing for stethoscope. Home: Orangewood Estates 1545 Hancock St San Bernardino CA 92411-1667

BROWNWOOD, JEFFREY O., physician; b. Walnut Creek, Calif., Sept. 8, 1956; s. David O. and Sigrid (Carlson) B.; m. Sara Jennifer Cooper, Sept. 9, 1995. BA in Biology, Reed Coll., 1980; DO, U. Health Scis., 1986. Diplomate Am. Bd. Family Practice. Resident in family practice Eastmoreland Hosp., Portland, Oreg., 1987-90, dir. Family Practice Residency Program, 1993—, dir. Family Practice Residency Clinic, 1993—, chmn. family practice dept., 1994—. Mem. ACFP (sec.-treas. Oreg. chpt. 1994—), Alpha Omega Alpha. Office: Family Care Med Clinic 17214 SE Division St Portland OR 97236

BROYLES, BONITA EILEEN, nursing educator; b. Ross County, Ohio, Sept. 29, 1948; d. Arthur Runnels and Mary Elizabeth (Page) Brookie; m. Roger F. Broyles, Dec. 29, 1984; children: Michael Richard Brown, Jeffrey Allen Brown. BSN, Ohio State U., 1970; MA with honors, N.C. Cen. U., Durham, 1988; EdD summa cum laude, LaSalle U., 1996. ADN instr., CPR instr. Piedmont C.C., Roxboro, N.C.; instr. nursing Watts Sch. Nursing, Durham; res. float staff nurse Durham County Gen. Hosp., Durham; dir. practical nursing edn., instr. Piedmont C.C., Roxboro, N.C.; maternity patient tchr. Mt. Carmel Med. Ctr., Columbus, Ohio; vice chmn. assoc. degree nursing faculty Piedmont Community Coll., 1990—. Contbr. articles to profl. jours. Named ADN Educator of Yr. N.C. Assoc. Degree Nursing Coun., 1993. Office: Piedmont CC Sch Nursing College St Roxboro NC 27573

BRUBAKER, CYNTHIA ANN, physician assistant; b. Lancaster, Pa., Nov. 7, 1955; d. George Charles and Audrey Lee (Barber) Kelec; m. Dale L. Brubaker, May 6, 1978; children: Laura Ashley, Shawn Andrew. Student, Hershey (Pa.) Med. Ctr., 1985; ADN with high distinction, Pa. State U., 1985. RN, cert. physician asst. Staff nurse Ephrata (Pa.) Cmty. Hosp., 1976-78; staff/charge nurse St. Joseph Hosp., Lancaster, Pa., 1978-85; physician assistant Gen. Internal Medicine, Lancaster, 1985-87, Ephrata Family Practice, 1987-88, Mastropietro & Assocs., Lancaster, 1988—. Tchr. Our Mother of Perpetual Help Ch., Ephrata, 1994—. Mem. Am. Acad. Physician Assts., Pa. Soc. Physician Assts. Roman Catholic. Office: Mastropietro & Assocs 322 N Arch St Lancaster PA 17603

BRUBAKER, LEONARD HATHAWAY, physician; b. Macon, Ga., July 14, 1934; s. Leonard Hathaway Sr. and Martha Frances (Bush) B.; m. Margaret Rowland Miles, June 22, 1957; children: Martha, Alice Elizabeth, Lenna. MS, MD, Emory U., 1964. Diplomate in hematology and med. oncology Am. Bd. Internal Medicine. Intern, then resident Emory U. Hosp./Atlanta VA, Atlanta, 1964-66; clin. assoc. NIH/Nat. Cancer Inst., Bethesda, Md., 1966-68; hematology fellow Sch. of Medicine Ohio State U., Columbus, 1968-69; asst. prof. Sch. of Medicine U. Mo., Columbia, 1969-74, assoc. prof. Sch. of Medicine, 1974-78; prof. Med. Coll. of Ga., Augusta, 1978-90; physician H&M Med. Clinic, Concord, N.C., 1990-91; Med. Oncology Assocs., Augusta, 1991—; mem. P. Vera Study Group, N.Y., 1969-84. Author chpts. in books; contbr. articles to profl. jours. Office: Med Oncology Assocs 818 Saint Sebastian Way Ste 205 Augusta GA 30901-2652

BRUCATO, ANTONIO, rheumatologist; b. Milan, Italy, Mar. 5, 1958; s. Giuseppe and Erminia (Vitali) B.; m. Giuseppina Guareschi, Apr. 15, 1959; children: Andrea, Alessandro. MD, U. Milan, 1983. From fellow to asst. head Niguarda Hosp., Milan, 1985—; liaison officer European Econ. Cmty., 1987-89. Served in Italian Army, 1980-81. Mem. Italian Soc. Immunology, Italian Soc. Rheumatology. Roman Catholic. Office: Niguarda Hosp, Piazza Ospedale Maggiore 3, 20162 Milan Italy

BRUCE, AMOS JERRY, JR., psychology educator; b. Rogersville, Ala., Feb. 24, 1942; s. Amos Jerry and Kathryn (Blakney) B.; m. Betty Bryant, June 24, 1963; children: Gregory Alan, Scott Blakney. BA, Anderson (Ind.) U., 1964; MS, U. Ga., 1968, PhD, 1972. Lic. psychologist, Tex. Vis. prof. Troy (Ala.) State U., 1970; asst. prof. psychology Sam Houston State U., Huntsville, Tex., 1970-75, assoc. prof. psychology, dept. chmn., 1975-80, prof., dept. chmn., 1980—, prof., chmn. dept. psychology and philosophy, 1981—. Mem. Am. Psychol. Assn., Southwestern Psychol. Assn., Tex. Psychol. Assn., Southwestern Soc. for Rsch. in Human Devel. Democrat. Methodist. Home: PO Box 1347 Huntsville TX 77342-1347 Office: Sam Houston State U Div Psychology And Phi Huntsville TX 77341

BRUCE, DAVID LIONEL, retired anesthesiologist, educator; b. Champaign, Ill., Oct. 27, 1933; s. Lionel Harry and Freda Eleanor (Tipsword) B.; m. Geraldine Zawasky, Nov. 24, 1956 (div. 1967); children: Ellen Marie, Brian David; m. Sharon Jean Wells, Jan. 18, 1985. Student, U. Ill., 1951-54, MD, 1960. Diplomate Am. Bd. Anesthesiology. Intern Ill. Rsch. and Ednl. Hosp., Chgo., 1960-61; resident U. Pa., Phila., 1961-64; asst. prof. anesthesiology U. Ky. Med. Ctr., Lexington, 1964-66; from asst. prof. to prof. Northwestern U. Med. Sch., Chgo., 1966-77; prof. U. Calif., Irvine, 1977-81; prof. anesthesiology NYU Med. Sch., 1981-84; prof. U. Miss. Med. Ctr., Jackson, 1984-90, chmn. dept., 1985-90; dir. outpatient surgery Athens (Ga.) Regional Med. Cr., 1990-92; prof. anesthesiology U. South Fla., Tampa Gen. Hosp., 1992-93; med. dir. surg. svcs. Tampa Gen. Hosp., 1993; med. dir. outpatient surgery ctr. Athens (Ga.) Regional Med. Ctr., 1993-95; cons. FDA, Rockville, Md., 1972-75, mem. adv. com., Bethesda, Md., 1973-77. Contbr. numerous articles to profl. jours. Cpl. U.S. Army, 1954-56. Recipient Rsch. Career Devel. award USPHS, 1967-72. Fellow Royal Soc. Medicine (Eng.) (travelling fellow 1975); mem. Am. Soc. Anesthesiologists. Republican. Home and Office: RR 1 Box 239F Moore Rd Tryon NC 28782-9719

BRUCE, MARIA ANTOINETTE, medical record technician; b. Houston, Feb. 17, 1944; d. Anthony Frederic Neugebauer and Tiny Frances (Rector) Carlson; m. Nick F. Lopez, Feb. 25, 1967 (div. Dec. 1969); 1 child: Dedra; m. Bill Warren Bruce, May 5, 1990. Accredited record technician, Med. Record Technician Sch., 1965. Med. record technician/asst. supr. MR dept. St. Mary's Hosp., Grand Junction, Colo., 1965-70; adminstrv. sec., med. record supr. St. Anthony Hosp. Systems, Denver and Westminster, Colo., 1970-86; med. record technician Aurora (Colo.) Cmty. Mental Health Ctr., 1986-87; med. record specialist Parkside Lodge of Colo., Thornton, 1988-90; dir. med. record dept. Mediplex Rehab.-Denver Hosp., Thornton, 1988-90, Charter Hosp. of Aurora, 1990; med. record technician Columbine Psychiat. Ctr., Englewood, Colo., 1991-92; health data supr. Denver Gen. Hosp., 1992-93; dir. med. record dept. Cherrelyn Health Care and Rehab. Ctr., Littleton, Colo., 1993—. Home: 17010 Walsh Ave Parker CO 80134 Office: Cherrelyn Healthcare Ctr 5555 S Elati Littleton CO 80120

BRUCE, MARTIN MARC, psychologist, publisher; b. N.Y.C., Mar. 28, 1923; s. David Isaac and Sarah Miriam (Rosen) B.; m. Betty Krassner, Aug. 16, 1942; children: Laurance David, Barbara Ann Elish. BSS, CCNY, 1946; MA, Columbia U., 1947; PhD, NYU, 1952. Psychologist, instr. Dept. Correction, N.Y.C., 1946; rsch. psychologist Office of Adj. Gen. War Dept., N.Y.C., 1946-47; chief psychologist Pers. Inst., N.Y.C., 1947-50; pub. Martin M. Bruce, PhD, Publishers, Larchmont, N.Y., 1949—; pvt. practice N.Y.C., New Rochelle, Larchmont N.Y., 1949—; psychologist Dunlap & Assocs., Inc., Stamford, Conn., 1950-58; psychologist, v.p. Clark Channel, Inc., Stamford, 1958. Author, editor numerous psychol. tests; editor 4 books; contbr. articles to profl. jours. County Dem. committeeman, N.Y.C., 1953. With USAAF, 1942-46. Fellow APA (treas. conv. 1955); mem. Ea. Psychol. Assn. (treas. 1956-62, bd. dirs. 1956-62), Am. Guidance and Pers. Assn., N.Y. Clin. Psychol. Assn., Soc. Projective Techniques. Home: 50 Larchwood Rd 22516 Caravelle Cir Boca Raton FL 33433 also: 22516 Caravelle Cir Boca Raton FL 33433 Office: Martin M Bruce PhD Pubs PO Box 248 50 Larchwood Rd Larchmont NY 10538

BRUCE-JUHLKE, DEBBIE, nursing consultant, social worker; b. Hughes Springs, Tex., Oct. 24, 1954; d. Norman L. and Arthur L. Bruce; m. Timothy Juhlke; children: Shay'La, Arthur II, Jonathan. AS, Tyler (Tex.) Jr. Coll., 1975; nursing diploma, Tex. Ea. Sch. Nursing, 1976; BS, Am. Tech. U., 1987. Emergency rm. nurse Mother Frances Hosp., Tyler, 1976-81; pub. health nurse Tyler (Tex.) Smith County Health Dept., 1981-84; nurse Girling Home Health, Temple, Tex., 1986-89; adult protective svcs. specialist Tex. Dept. Protective & Regulatory Svcs., Belton, 1988-94; dir. Am. Nat. Home Health, Killeen, Tex., 1994—; nursing dir. Advantage Adult Day Care and Health Svcs., Inc., Harker Heights, Tex., 1995—. Home: 1402 Wild Vine Cove Round Rock TX 78664

BRUCH, FRANK OSBORNE, sports medicine physician; b. Cleve., May 18, 1929; s. Karl Fredrich and Mildred M. (Osborne) B.; m. Sally Anne Rounds, Mar. 27, 1953; children: Jennifer, Matthew, Elizabeth, Amy, Sarah, Joshua. AB, Dartmouth Coll., 1952; MD, Case Western Res. U., 1956. Grop physician Kaiser Cmty. Health Ctr., Cleve., 1960-70; univ. physician U. Conn., Storrs, 1970-77; med. dir. Middlebury (Vt.) Coll., 1977-87, team physician, 1977—. Fellow Am. Coll. Sports Medicine. Presbyterian. Home: RR # 1 Box 64A Middlebury VT 05753 Office: Middlebury Coll Field House Middlebury VT 05753

BRUCKER, PAUL C., academic administrator, physician. Pres. Thomas Jefferson U., Phila. Office: Thomas Jefferson U Office of President 11th Walnut Philadelphia PA 19144*

BRUCKNER, HOWARD LEON, ophthalmologist; b. Bklyn., Mar. 4, 1941; s. S. David and Pauline (Penchina) B.; m. Ziva Rachel Najari, June 10, 1982; children: Seth, Jonathan, Adam. BS cum laude, Bklyn. Coll., N.Y.C., 1962; MD, N.Y. Med. Coll., N.Y.C., 1966. Diplomate Am. Bd. Ophthalmologists. Intern Brookdale Hosp. Ctr., Bklyn., 1966-67; resident, chief resident L.I. (N.Y.) Jewish Med. Ctr., 1967-70; fellow Bascom Palmer Eye Inst., Miami, Fla., 1972-73; pvt. practice Augusta, Ga., 1973—; asst. clin. prof. Med. Coll. Ga., Augusta, 1970-73; rotating faculty small incision cataract surgery courses and no-stitch cataract surgery courses, 1988—; med.-surg. dir. Acad. Cataract & Laser Surgery, 1990—; faculty Sarasota (Fla.) Cataract Ctr., 1990; preceptor oculoplastic laser skin resurfacing courses. Contbr. Cataract Surgery Thru Small Pupil, 1990. Maj. U.S. Army, 1970-72. Avocations: gourmet chef, canoeing, pilot. Fellow Am. Acad. Ophthalmology; mem. Team of Internat. Eye Surgeons, Kerato Refractive Soc., Internat. Soc. Radial Keratatomy, Am. Soc. Cataract and Refractive Surgeons, Med. Assn. Ga., Richmond County Med. Soc., Uptown Kiwanis Club of Augusta. Home: 137 Lakemont Dr Augusta GA 30904-6132 Office: 909 15th St Augusta GA 30901-2607

BRUCKSTEIN, ALEX HARRY, internist, gastroenterologist, geriatrician; b. Germany, Dec. 2, 1949; came to U.S., 1950; s. Jacob and Rose B., m. Dorothy Krausman, Mar. 23, 1973; children: Tammy, Sharon, Sarah, Michael. BS in Chemistry, CCNY, 1971; MD, Albert Einstein Coll. Medicine, 1975. Diplomate Am. Bd. Internal Medicine, Am. Bd. Gastroenterology, Am. Bd. Internal Medicine- Geriatrics. Intern in internal medicine Roosevelt Hosp., N.Y.C.; resident in internal medicine St. Luke's Hosp., N.Y.C.; resident in gastroenterology VA Hosp., N.Y.U., N.Y.C.; pvt. practice internal medicine, gastroenterology Staten Island, N.Y.; hosp. affiliations: Doctors' Hosp. Staten Island, N.Y., Staten Island U. Hosp. N., Staten Island U. Hosp. S., St. Vincent's Hosp., Staten Island; vis. clin. fellow Columbia U. Dept. Medicine, 1975-78, NYU Dept. Medicine, 1978-80; clin. asst. prof. medicine N.Y. Med. Coll., 1983-90, SUNY Health Sci. Ctr. at Bklyn., 1990—. Fellow Am. Coll. Physicians, Am. Coll. Gastroenterology; mem. AMA, Med. Soc. of the State of N.Y., Richmond County Med. Soc., Am. Gastroent. Assn., N.Y. Soc. Gastrointestinal Endoscopy, N.Y. Acad. Gastroenterology, Am. Geriatrics Assn. Office: 2627 Hylan Blvd Staten Island NY 10306

BRUECKNER, LAWRENCE TERENCE, orthopedic surgeon; b. Casper, Wyo., Jan. 24, 1945; s. Lawrence W. and Jayne Anne (Dennis) B.; m. Mary Ellen Coleman, May 11, 1974; children: Ellen, Amanda, Chris. MD, Creighton U., 1970. Diplomate Am. Bd. Orthop. Surgery. Intern S.I. Hosp., N.Y.C., 1974-77; resident Hosp. for Joint Disease, N.Y.C., 1977; orthop. surgeon Gwinnett Orthop. Ctr., Snellville, Ga., 1977—. Capt. U.S. Army, 1971-73. Fellow Am. Acad. Orthop. Surgeons; mem. AMA, Med. Assn. Ga., Atlanta Orthop. Soc., Orthop. Rsch. and Edn. Found., Alpha Omega Alpha. Office: Gwinnett Orthop Ctr 2121 Fountain Dr Ste E Snellville GA 30278

BRUEGGEMEYER, CARL DALE, nephrologist, educator; b. Cleve., Nov. 15, 1950; s. Carl William and Renee Ann (Molter) B.; m. Vilma Sylvia Canino-Rocher, AUg. 17, 1974; 1 child, Adrienne Karel. BS, Cleve. State U., 1973; MS, U. Rochester, 1975; MD, Ohio State U., 1978. Diplomate Am. Bd. Internal Medicine, Am. Bd. Nephrology. Asst. prof. U. South Fla., 1982-88; chief nephrology, medicine Cleve. Clinic Fla., 1988-92; chief nephrology Mayo Clinic, Jacksonville, Fla., 1992—; assoc. prof. nephrology Mayo Med., Jacksonville, Fla., 1992—; bd. dirs. Network 7, Fla., 1994—. Contbr. articles to profl. pubs. scholar U. Rochester, 1993-95. Fellow ACP; mem. AMA, Am. Soc. Nephrology, Renal Physicians Assocs., Internat. Soc. Nephrology, Fla. Soc. Nephrology. Office: Mayo Clinic 4500 San Pablo Rd Jacksonville FL 32224

BRUEL, IRIS BARBARA, psychologist; b. N.Y.C., June 10, 1933; d. Herman and Anna (Cohen) Goldstein; m. Robert Bruel, Apr. 1953 (div. 1957); adopted children: Michael Abraham, Russell Emanuel. BA in Psychology, CCNY, 1956, MS in Sch. Psychology, 1961; PhD in Clin. Psychology, U. Miami, Fla., 1972. Cert. profl. psychologist, Fla. Child supr. Linden Hill Sch., Hawthorne, N.Y., 1957-59; tchr., therapist The League Sch. for Severely Disturbed Children, Bklyn., 1959-61, Assn. for Mentally Ill Children, Yonkers, N.Y., 1961-63; asst. psychology rsch. U. Miami, Coral Gables, Fla., 1964-67; trainee VA Hosp., Miami, 1967-68; intern diagnostic testing and psychotherapy Henderson Clinic, Ft. Lauderdale, Fla., 1968-69; intern child psychol. svcs. San Fernando Valley Child Guidance Clinic, Van Nuys, Calif., 1970-71; cons. Sorensen Group, N.Y.C., 1972; clin. psychologist Dade County Dept. Youth and Family Devel., Miami, 1972-77; co-dir. Ctr. for the Whole Family, Inc., Coral Gables, 1976-79; pvt. practice clin. psychology, South Miami, Fla., 1979—; clin. psychologist Juvenile Ct. Assessment Ctr., Miami, 1989—; cons. Jewish Vocat. Svc., 1980-85; mem. affiliate staff Grant Ctr. Hosp., 1977—; med. staff Charter Hosp., 1991—; allied health staff Highland Park Hosp., 1988—; adj. prof. Nova U., Ft. Lauderdale, 1977; field supr. practicum students So. Fla. Sch. Profl. Psychology, Miami, 1978-80; cons. Guardian Ad Litem program, 1988—. Sec. Reform Dem. Club, N.Y.C., 1962-63. Mem. APA, Am. Soc. Clin. Hypnosis, Nat. Acad. Neuropsychology, Fla. Soc. Clin. Hypnosis (sec. editor newsletter), Dade County Mental Health Assn., Cousteau Soc., N.Y. Acad. Scis., Assn. for Play Therapy, Am. Bd. Profl. Disability Cons. (diplomate), Seaton Found., Amnesty Internat., Am. Bd. Assessment Psychology, Am. Coll. Forensic Examiners. Jewish. Home: 2869 Shipping Ave Miami FL 33133-4677 Office: 7800 S Red Rd Ste 310PH Miami FL 33143

BRUELS, MARK CHARLES, radiological physicist; b. Kansas City, Mo., Jan. 2, 1941; s. Clement B. and Florence R. (Collins) B.; m. Judith A. Fasnacht, Nov. 25, 1962 (div. 1976); children: Christine Bruels Powaser, Nicholas R.; m. Lucia R. Beacham, June 22, 1991. BA, Mankato State U., 1962; MS, U. Kans., Lawrence, 1965, PhD, 1969. Tchr. Durand (Ill.) Community Schs., 1962-63; asst. prof. physics Slippery Rock (Pa.) State Coll., 1969-72; presdl. intern Naval Aerospace Med. Rsch. Lab., New Orleans, 1972-73; fellow M.D. Anderson Hosp., Houston, 1973-75; radiol. physicist VA Hosp., Mpls., 1975-78; clin. asst. prof. Med. Sch. U. Minn., Mpls., 1975-78; radiol. physicist Radiology Cons., Inc., Omaha, 1978-83; clin. assoc. prof. Med. Sch. Creighton U., Omaha, 1978-83; dir. med. physics Greenville (S.C.) Hosp. Systems, 1983-96; pres. Bruels and Assocs., Ltd., Greenville, S.C., 1996—; pres. Interstate Radiol. Physics, Greenville, 1984—, Rad-Tec. System, Greenville, 1987—; rsch. affiliate, adj. prof. physics Clemson U., 1992-96. Contbr. articles to tech. publs. Mem. Am. Coll. Med. Physics (fin. com.), Am. Assn. Physicists in Medicine (various com.), Am. Coll. Radiology, N.Am. Hyperthermia Group, Radiation Rsch. Soc., Am. Phys. Soc. (S.C. chpt.), Am. Coll. Radiology, Am. Bd. Med. Phys. Exam Panels.

BRUESCHKE, ERICH EDWARD, physician, researcher, educator; b. nr. Eagle Butte, S.D., July 17, 1933; s. Erich Herman and Eva Johanna (Joens) B.; m. Frances Marie Bryan, Mar. 25, 1967; children: Erich Raymond, Jason Douglas, Tina Marie, Patricia Frances, Susan Eva. B.S. in Elec. Engring, S.D. Sch. Mines and Tech., 1956; postgrad., U. So. Calif., 1960-61; M.D., Temple U., 1965. Diplomate Am. Bd. Family Practice, also cert. in geriatrics. Intern Germantown Dispensary and Hosp., Phila., 1965-66; mem. tech. staff Hughes Research and Devel. Labs., Culver City, Calif., 1956-61; practiced gen. medicine Fullerton, Calif., 1968-69; dir. research Ill. Inst. Tech. Research Inst., Chgo., 1970-76; research asst. prof. Temple U. Sch. Medicine, 1965-69; mem. staff Mercy Hosp. and Med. Center, Chgo., 1970-76; vis. prof. Rush Med. Coll., Chgo., 1974-76, prof., chmn. dept. family practice, 1976—, program dir. Rush. Christ family practice residency, 1978-93, vice dean, 1992—, acting dean, 1993-94; dean, 1994—; trustee Anchor HMO, 1976—, v.p. med. and acad. affairs, 1981—; trustee Synergon Health Systems, 1993—; vice chmn., bd. dirs. Rush Presbyn. St. Lukes Health Assocs.; sr. attending Presbyn.-St. Luke's Hosp., Chgo., 1976—; med. dir. Chgo. Bd. of Health West Side Hypertension Center, 1974-78; Bd. dirs. Comprehensive Health Planning Met. Chgo., 1971-74. Assoc. editor Primary Cardiology, 1979-85; cons. editor for family practice Hosp. Medicine, 1986—; med. editor World Book/Rush Presbyn. St. Lukes/Med. Ency., 1987—; contbr. articles to profl. jours. Served with USAF, 1966-68. Named Physician Tchr. of Yr. Ill. Acad. Family Physicians, 1988. Fellow Am. Acad. Family Physicians, Inst. of Medicine of Chgo.; mem. IEEE (chmn. Chgo. sect. Engring. in Medicine and Biology group 1974-75), Internat. Soc. for Artificial Internal Organs, Am. Fertility Soc., Am. Occupational Med. Assn. (recipient Physician's recognition award 1969, 72, 75), Chgo. Med. Soc., Am. Heart Assn., Assn. for Advancement Med. Instrumentation, N.Y. Acad. Scis., Sigma Xi, Phi Rho Sigma, Eta Kappa Nu. Home: 319 N Lincoln St Hinsdale IL 60521-3442 Office: Rush Medical College of Rush Univ 600 South Paulina St Chicago IL 60612

BRUGAM, RICHARD BLAIR, biology educator; b. Phila., Dec. 23, 1946; s. Richard Jerrom and Margaret Suzanne (Blair) B.; m. Ella Suzanne Oren, Aug. 1, 1970; children: Amy Susann, Matthew Richard. BA in Biology, Lehigh U., 1968; M of Philosophy, Yale U., 1974, PhD in Biology, 1975. Rsch. assoc. Limnol. Rsch. Ctr. U. Minn., Mpls., 1975-78; asst. prof. So. Ill. U., Edwardsville, 1978-84, assoc. prof., 1984-90, prof., 1990—; vis. scholar U. Wash., Seattle, 1984-85. Contbr. articles to Ecology, Archiv fur Hydrobiologie. Sgt. U.S. Army, 1969-72. Recipient J. Willard Gibbs prize Yale U., 1968; grad. fellowship NSF, 1968. Mem. AAAS, Ecol. Soc. Am., Am. Soc. Limnology and Oceanography, Ill. Acad. Scis., Phi Beta Kappa, Sigma Xi (grant 1973). Home: 1400 Lantz Ct Edwardsville IL 62025-3901 Office: So Ill U PO Box 1651 Edwardsville IL 62026-1594

BRUGGEMAN, LEWIS LEROY, radiologist; b. N.Y.C., Sept. 9, 1941; s. Louis LeRoy and Edwina Jane (Mickel) B.; m. Ann Margaret Kayajan, May 28, 1966; children: Gretchen Ann, Kurt LeRoy. AB, Dartmouth Coll., 1963, B in Med. Sci., 1965; MD, Harvard U., 1968. Intern Los Angeles County Harbor Gen. Hosp., Torrence, Calif., 1968-69; resident in diagnostic radiology Columbia Presbyn. Med. Ctr., N.Y.C., 1969-72; chief dept. radiology Bremerton (Wash.) Naval Regional Med. Ctr., 1972-74; pvt. practice diagnostic radiology South Coast Med. Ctr., South Laguna, Calif., 1974—, dir. dept. radiology, 1983-95, hosp. bd. trustees, 1985-87; pvt. practice diagnostic radiology Saddleback Community Hosp., Laguna Hills, Calif., 1974—; pres., chmn. bd. dirs. South Coast Med. Group Inc., South Laguna, Calif., 1983-95; pres. So. Coast Radiol. Med. Group Inc., South Laguna, 1986-95; vice-chmn. and bd. trustees South Coast Med. Ctr. Found., 1993—. Lt. comdr. Med. Corps USN, 1972-74. Mem. Radiol. Soc. N.Am., Am. Coll. Radiology, Calif. Radiol. Soc., Dartmouth Club Orange County. Office: S Coast Radiol Med Group 28 Monarch Bay Plz Ste J Dana Point CA 92629-3455

BRUHN, ARNOLD RAHN, JR., clinical psychologist, personality theorist; b. Bklyn., Dec. 30, 1941; s. Arnold Rahn and Paula M.; m. Arlene Corinne Palmer, June 23, 1967 (div. Dec. 1986); children: Alexis Pamela, Erika Kerstin; m. Ellyn Kay, Dec. 24, 1991. BA in Psychology, U. Portland, 1963, MA in English, 1966; MS in Psychology, Portland State U., 1972; PhD in Clin. Psychology, Duke U., 1976. Diplomate Am. Bd. of Assessment Psychology. Intern in child clin. psychology, Duke U. Med. Ctr., Durham, N.C., 1975-76; asst. prof. psychology George Washington U., 1976-82; asst. rsch. prof. psychiatry and behavioral scis. George Washington Med. Ctr., 1980-83; staff psychologist Alexandria Community Mental Health Ctr., Va., 1977-85, Woodmont Psychiat. Assocs., Bethesda, Md., 1982-86; Arnold R. Bruhn & Assocs., 1986—. Fellow Soc. Personality Assessment; mem. Am. Psychol. Assn. USPHS fellow, 1972-76. Contbr. rsch. and theoretical papers on personality, personality assessment, autobiographical memory and earliest childhood memories to profl. pubs. Home: 4704 Hunt Ave Chevy Chase MD 20815 Office: Arnold R Bruhn & Assocs 4400 East West Hwy # 28 Bethesda MD 20814-3015

BRUIJNES, EDUARD, urologist; b. Amsterdam, The Netherlands, June 18, 1950; s. Antonie and Pietje (Stom) B.; m. Astrid Knaap, Sept. 30, 1977; children: Vincent Antonie Johan, Roderick Laurens Olivier. MD, U. Amsterdam, 1978. Scientist exptl. surgery U. Amsterdam Acad. Hosp., 1977—, asst. in surgery, 1978-83, asst. in urology, 1983-85; urologist Ziekenhuis Gooi Noord, Blaricum, The Netherlands, 1985—; dir. EB. Bruijnes B.V., Blaricum, 1989—; bd. dirs. Pro-Urologica Found., Blaricum, 1989—; contbr. articles to profl. jours. Mem. editorial bd. Urology Digest, The Netherlands, 1978—. Mem. European Urol. Assn., Dutch Soc. Urology, European Soc. Surg. Oncology, Dutch Soc. Surgery, European Soc. Paediatric Urology, Société Internat. D'Urologie, Genootschap ter Bevordering van natuurgenees-en heelkunde. Home: Drift 41, 1251 CB Larennh The Netherlands Office: Ziekenhuis Gooi Noord, Ryksstraatweg 1, 1261 AN Blaricum The Netherlands

BRUMBACK, CLARENCE LANDEN, physician; b. Denver, Apr. 19, 1914; s. Carl Alvin and Hildur Athelia (Landen) B.; m. Lucile Leslie Gillie, June 17, 1943; children—Richard, Carl. AB, U. Kans., 1936, MD, 1943; MPH, U. Mich., 1948. Diplomate: Am. Bd. Preventive Medicine. Intern U.S. Marine Hosp., San Francisco, 1943-44; dir. pub. health Laclede County, Mo., 1947, AEC, Oak Ridge, 1948-50; dir. Palm Beach County (Fla.) Health Dept., 1950-86; coord. grad. edn. Palm Beach County Health Dept., 1986—; clin. prof. U. Miami; adj. prof. Fla. Atlantic U., Boca Raton, Fla. Editorial bd.: Jour. Public Health Policy, 1981-88; contbr. articles to med. and public health jours. Bd. dirs. Palm Beach County chpt. A.R.C., Am. Lung Assn. S.E. Fla., Heart Assn. Palm Beach County, Community Mental Health Center Palm Beach County, Palm Beach County unit Am. Cancer Soc., Palm Beach County Mental Health Assn., Palm Beach County Health Dept., 1950-86; pres. YMCA of Palm Beaches, 1970. With AUS, 1944-47. Decorated Meritorious Svc. medal; recipient Meritorious Svc. award Fla. Public Health Assn., 1968; Merit award State of Fla., 1972; Physician of Yr. award Am. Assn. Public Health Physicians, 1975. Fellow APHA (Sedgwick Meml. medal 1989), Am. Coll. Preventive Medicine, Royal Soc. Health; mem. AMA (Dr. Nathan Davis award 1993), Fla. Med. Assn., Palm Beach County Med. Soc., Rotary, Elks. Democrat. Lutheran. Home: 7405 S Flagler Dr West Palm Beach FL 33405-4710 Office: 826 Evernia St West Palm Beach FL 33401-5708

BRUMBACK, GARY BRUCE, industrial and organizational psychologist; b. New Castle, Ind., July 23, 1935; s. Donald Clair and Doris Lydia (Utterberg) B.; m. Doris Anne Ast, June 15, 1958; children: Babette Anne, Lyndia Claire. BA, Ind. U., 1958; MA, Ohio State U., 1960, PhD, 1963. Rsch. asst. Ohio State U., Columbus, 1958-62; rsch. scientist N.Am. Aviation, Columbus, 1962-63; rsch. psychologist U.S. Dept. HEW, Washington, 1964-73; sr. rsch. scientist Am. Inst. for Rsch., Washington, 1973-79; psychologist pers. mgr. U.S. HHS, Washington, 1979-94. Mem. editorial bd. Pub. Pers. Mgmt. Jour., 1986, 91, 93; book reviewer Pers. Psychology; contbr. chpts. to books, articles to profl. jours. Sec. Banana Beach Assn., Ocean City, Md., 1978-84. Fellow APA, Am. Psychol. Soc. (charter); mem. Acad. Mgmt., Internat. Pers. Mgmt. Assn., Sigma Xi, Phi Beta Kappa. Home and Office: 10 Cottonwood Ct Palm Coast FL 32137

BRUMBACK, ROGER ALAN, neuropathologist, researcher; b. Washington, Feb. 15, 1948; s. Oscar Benjamin and Frances Elaine (Neufeld) B.; m. Mary Helen Skinner, Apr. 26, 1969; children: Darryl Wyatt, Audrey Christine, Owen Eliot. BS, Pa. State U., 1967; MD, Pa. State U., Hershey, 1971. Diplomate Nat. Bd. Med. Examiners, Am. Bd. Pediatrics, Am. Bd. Psychiatry and Neurology, Am. Bd. Pathology; cert. clin. electroencephalography. Pediatric intern Johns Hopkins Hosp., Balt., 1971-72, pediatric asst. resident, 1972-73; fellow in pediatrics Johns Hopkins U. Sch. Medicine, Balt., 1971-73; asst. resident neurology Barnes Hosp., St. Louis, 1973-74; fellow in pediatric neurology Washington U., St. Louis Children's Hosp., 1973-75; clin. assoc. neurology and exptl. neuropathology med. neurology br. Nat. Inst. Neurol. and Communicative Disorders and Stroke, Nat. Insts. of Health, Bethesda, Md., 1975-77; clin. instr. neurology and pediatrics U. Pitts., 1977-78; asst. prof. neurology U. N.D., Fargo, 1978-79, asst. prof. pediatrics, 1978-82, assoc. prof. neurology, 1980-82; resident/fellow anatomic pathology and neuropathology svcs. Strong Meml. Hosp., U. Rochester (N.Y.), 1982-86; assoc. prof. pathology U. Okla., Oklahoma City, 1986-89, prof. pathology, 1989—, chief neuropathology sect. Health Scis. Ctr., 1987—; chief neurology svc. V.A. Med. Ctr., Fargo, 1978-82; dir. Muscular Dystrophy Assn. Clinic, Fargo, 1978-82, co-dir., Oklahoma City, 1988-91; adj. assoc. prof. pediatrics U. Okla., 1986-90, adj. assoc. prof. psychiatry and behavioral scis., 1986-91, adj. prof. pediatrics, 1990—, adj. prof. psychiatry and behavioral sci., 1991—, adj. prof. neurology 1991—; clin. care cons. dermatology br. Nat. Cancer Inst., 1987—. Author: (with W.H. Olson, G. Gascon, L.A. Christoferson) Practical Neurology for the Primary Care Physician, 1981, (with J.W. Gerst) The Neuromuscular Junction, 1984, (with R.W. Leech) Color Atlas of Muscle Histochemistry, 1984, (with R.M. Herndon) The Cerebrospinal Fluid, 1989, (with M.H. Brumback) The Dietary Fiber Weight Control Handbook, 1989, (with R.W. Leech) Hydrocephalus: Current Clinical Concepts, 1991, Neurology and Clinical Neuroscience, 1993, (with W.H. Olson, G. Gascon, V. Iyer) Handbook of Symptom-Oriented Neurology, 2nd edit., 1994, (with R.W. Leech) Neuropathology and Basic Neuroscience, 1995; chief editor Jour. Child Neurology, 1986—; mem. editorial bd. Jour. Geriatric Psychiatry and Neurology, 1990—, Biomed. Rsch. India, 1990—, Neuropsychiatry, Neuropsychology and Behavioral Neurology, 1994—. With USPHS, 1975-77. Mem. Am. Acad. Neurology, Am. Assn. Electrodiagnostic Medicine, Am. Assn. Neuropathologists, Am. Neurol. Assn., Child Neurology Soc., Coun. Biology Editors, Internat. Child Neurology Assn., Soc. for Exptl. Neuropathology (sec.-treas. 1988-93, pres. 1995—), Behavioral Neurology Soc. (councillor 1990-91, sec.-treas. 1991-93, pres. 1993-95). Republican. Lutheran. Home: 4014 Hidden Hill Rd Norman OK 73072-3013 Office: Okla U Health Sci Ctr Dept Pathology BMSB Rm 451 940 S L Young Blvd PO Box 26901 Oklahoma City OK 73190

BRUMBACK PATTERSON, CATHY JEAN, psychologist; b. Birmingham, Ala., Oct. 15, 1953; d. Roy Clifton and Violet Lorraine (Wesley) Brumback; m. Louis Loomis Patterson, June 10, 1987; children: Catherine Elizabeth Patterson, Allyson Brumback Patterson. BA, U. Ala., Tuscaloosa, 1975; MA, U. Ala., Birmingham, 1977; EdS, Ga. State U., 1985, PhD, 1986. Diplomate Am. Bd. Profl. Psychology, Am. Bd. Forensic Examiners; lic. psychologist; cert. sch. psychologist. Tchr. Jefferson County Bd. Edn., Birmingham, 1975-76, Birmingham (Ala.) Bd. Edn., 1976-77, Baldwin County Bd. Edn., Bay Minette, Ala., 1977-79; psychometrist Regional Edn. Svc. Ctr., Bartlesville, Okla., 1979-81, Union Pub. Schs., Tulsa, 1981-82, Forsyth County Schs., 1982-84; sch. psychologist Atlanta (Ga.) Pub. Schs., 1984-87; pvt. practice psychologist Northport, Ala., 1987-94, Fairhope, Ala., 1994—; grad. rsch. asst. Ga. State U., Atlanta, 1982, 85, instr., 1986; instr. U. Ala., Tuscaloosa, 1988-90. Named Mrs. Ala., Mrs. Am. Assn., 1979, Outstanding Young Women of Am., 1982, 87, 89; recipient Outstanding Doctoral Student award Ga. Assn. Sch. Psychologists, 1987. Fellow Am. Acad. Sch. Psychology; mem. AAUW, APA, Ala. Psychol. Assn., Nat. Register Health Svc. Providers, Montrose Garden Club, Bayside Acad. Admirals Club (chair), Rock Creek Country Club, Rotary, Phi Delta Kappa, Kappa Delta Pi. Home: PO Box 687 Montrose AL 36559-0687 Office: 22787 Highway 98 Bldg A Fairhope AL 36532-3339

BRUMM, MARCIA COWLES, pharmacist; b. Cleve., Nov. 22, 1921; d. Forest Eugene and Vivian Curtis (Bonnallie) Cowles; m. Joseph Norris Brumm, Apr. 27, 1962 (dec.). BS, Case Western Res. U., 1944. Lic. pharmacist, Ohio, Calif., Ariz., Colo. Pharmacist Am. Pharm. Assn., Washington, 1944-70. Active United Meth. Women, Port St. Lucie; vol. U. Fla. Ext. Svc. Recipient Cert. 1000 Hours Vol. Work, U. Fla., Port St. Lucie, 1989. Mem. AAUW, Am. Assn. Hosp. Pharmacists in Ohio (treas. 1952-56), Gen. Fedn. Woman's Club (pres. St. Lucie chpt.). Democrat. Home: 1574 SE Colchester Cir Port Saint Lucie FL 34952-4279

BRUMMETT, ROBERT EDDIE, pharmacology educator; b. Concordia, Kans., Feb. 11, 1934; s. Gordon Legonia and Gladys Leona (Anderson) B.; m. Naomi Deen Weaver, Dec. 19, 1955; children: Randall, Wendy, Robin, Philip. BS, Oreg. State U., 1959, MS, 1960; PhD, U. Oreg., 1964. Registered pharmacist, Oreg. Asst. prof. pharmacology Oreg. State U., Corvallis, 1961-62; asst. prof. otolaryngology Oreg. Health Scis. U., Portland, 1964-70, assoc. prof. otolaryngology and pharmacology, 1970-80, prof. otolaryngology and Pharmacology, 1981—; mem. Oreg. Coun. on Alcohol and Drug Problems, Salem, 1979-85; instr. Am. Acad. Otolaryngology, Washington, 1964—; mem. adv. panel otorhinolaryngology U.S. Pharmacopeia, 1985—, mem. drug info. adv. panel, 1988—, mem. coun. on naturopathic physicians formulary, 1990—. Contbr. more than 100 articles to profl. jours.; patentee in field. Comdr. U.S. Power Squadron, Portland, 1988-89, adminstrv. officer, 1987, dist. ednl. officer, 1991-94, dist. adminstrv. officer, 1994-95, dist. exec. officer, 1995-96, dist. comdr. 1996—. Grantee NIH, 1969—, Deafness Research Found., 1970, Med. Research Found., 1979, 83. Mem. AAAS, Am. Acad. Otolaryngology (instr. 1964—), Head and Neck Surgery, Associated Rschrs. in Otolaryngology, Hayden Island Yacht Club, Elks, Sigma Xi. Republican. Home: 2366 N Menzies Ct Portland OR 97217-8219 Office: Oreg Health Scis U 3181 SW Sam Jackson Park Rd Portland OR 97201-3011

BRUNCK, BRIAN S., surgeon; b. Cin., July 29, 1958; s. James C. and Doris Ann Brunck; m. Debbie Brunck; children: Amanda, Nathan, Melinda. BS, U. Cin., 1980; MD, Ohio State U., 1984. Diplomate Am. Bd. Surgery. Gen. surgeon The Clinic, New Castle, Ind., 1989—. Mem. Ind. State Med. Assn. (pres. 1994). Home: 520 Edgewood Dr New Castle IN 47362 Office: The Clinic 1007 N 16th St New Castle IN 47362

BRUNDAGE, SCOTT REEDER, plastic surgeon; b. Medina, N.Y., Dec. 29, 1954; s. Joe R. and Joann (Swartz) B.; m. Jane Elizabeth Lingeman, Aug. 12, 1978; children: Kathleen, Joseph. BA, Ind. U., 1977, MD, 1981. Diplomate Am. Bd. Plastic Surgery. Resident in gen. surgery Butterworth Hosp., Grand Rapids, Mich., 1981-84; resident in plastic surgery Grand Rapids Area Med. Edn. Ctr., 1984-86; pvt. practice Centre for Plastic Surgery, Grand Rapids, 1987—; asst. program dir. plastic surgery residency St. Mary's Hosp., Grand Rapids, 1992—, chief divsn. plastic surgery, 1992—. Mem. Am. Soc. Plastic and Reconstructive Surgeons, Midwest Assn. Plastic Surgeons, Mich. Acad. Plastic Surgeons, Lipoplasty Soc. N.Am., Kent County Med. Soc., Mich. State Med. Soc. Office: Centre for Plastic Surgery 426 Michigan St Ste 300 Grand Rapids MI 48503

BRUNELL, PHILIP A., physician; b. N.Y.C., Feb. 1, 1931; s. Irving and Rose Brunell; children: Wayne, Robert, Rhonda. B.S., CCNY, 1950; postgrad., N.Y. U., 1950-51; M.S. in Physiology, U. Ill., 1952; M.D., U. Buffalo, 1957. Diplomate: Am. Bd. Pediatrics. Research asst. physiology U. Ill., 1951-52, teaching asst., 1952-53; intern E.J. Meyer Meml. Hosp., Buffalo, 1957-58; resident in pediatrics Children's Hosp., Buffalo, 1958-60; asst. in pediatrics Cornell U., 1960-61; instr. pediatrics Emory U., 1961-64; asst. prof. pediatrics N.Y. U. Sch. Medicine, 1964-71, assoc. prof., 1971-75; prof., chmn. dept. pediatrics U. Tex. Health Sci. Center, San Antonio, 1975-81; prof., head div. infectious diseases dept. pediatrics U. Tex. Health Sci. Center, 1981-87; attending physician Santa Rosa Children's Hosp., San Antonio, 1975-81; prof. pediatrics UCLA; chief pediatrics Bexar County Hosp. Dist. Teaching Hosps., San Antonio, 1975-81; vice chair Cedars Sinai Med. Ctr., L.A., 1987—; cons. Brooke Army Med. Ctr., Wilford Hall USAF Med. Ctr., 1977-81; mem. cons. group on vaccine devel., 1991-94; cons. FDA, 1994—; vis. rschr. Nat. Inst. Allergy and Infectious Diseases, 1995. Chief med. editor Infectious Diseases of Children, 1987—; contbr. chpts. to books; contbr. articles to med. jours. Chmn. Internat. Year of Child, San Antonio, 1979-80; bd. dirs. Santa Rosa Children's Hosp. Found. Served with USPHS, 1961-64. USPHS fellow, 1971-72. Fellow Infectious Diseases Soc. Am. (awards com. 1979, chmn. 1982); mem. Am. Acad. Pediatrics (chmn. com. pediatric research 1977-78, chmn. com. infectious diseases 1978-85), Am. Soc. Microbiology, Am. Acad. Microbiology, Am. Pediatric Soc., N.Y. Acad. Scis., Soc. Pediatric Infectious Diseases (council 1984, pres. 1987-89), Soc. Pediatric Research, San Antonio Pediatric Soc., Tex. Pediatrics Soc. (awards com.), Council Tex. Pediatric Dept. Chmn. (chmn. 1978-81), Tex. Med. Assn. (sec. treas. pediatric sect. 1979-80, pres. 1980-81), Bexar County Med. Soc., Tex. Infectious Disease Soc., Western Soc. Pediatric Rsch., L.A. Pediatric Soc. Home: 320 S Arnaz Dr Los Angeles CA 90048-2955 Office: Cedars Sinai Med Ctr 8700 Beverly Blvd Ste 4310 Los Angeles CA 90048-1804

BRUNER, DEBORAH WATKINS, oncological nurse, administrator, clinical nurse specialist; b. Chester, Pa., July 8, 1956; d. N. Charles and Mary Ann (Venditti) Watkins; m. Samuel Bruner, May 13, 1985; children: David, Jesse. BSN, West Chester (Pa.) U., 1978; MSN in Oncology, Widener U., MSN in Adminstrn., 1985; postgrad., U. Pa., 1994—. Cert. in oncology, coploscopy. Gynecol./oncol. clin. nurse specialist Albert Einstein Med. Ctr., Phila., 1985; nurse coord., clin. specialist dept. radiation oncology Fox Chase Cancer Ctr., Phila., 1989. Editor: Manual for Radiation Oncology Nursing Education & Practice; contbr. articles to profl. jours. Mem. Radiation Therapy Oncology Group (assoc., co-chair quality of life com., genitourinary com. and econ. impact com.), Am. Cancer Soc. (nurses edn. com., Doctoral Scholarship award, 1995), Oncology Nursing Soc. (Doctoral Scholarship award 1995), Am. Soc. Therapeutic Radiologists and Oncologists (assoc., chair quality of life com.), Gynecologic Oncology Group (mem. quality of life com.). Home: 422 Park Ave Swarthmore PA 19081-2015

BRUNER, ROBERT B., hospital consultant; b. N.Y.C., Aug. 4, 1933; s. Samuel Wolf and Pauline (Rothstein) B.; m. Janet Bergman, Aug. 26, 1956; children: Steven Wayne, Marc Richard. Student, NYU, 1950-53; B.A. cum laude, L.I. U., 1956; M.S., 1959. Adminstrv. asst., asst. adminstr. Bklyn. Hebrew Home and Hosp. for Aged, 1958-62; asst. adminstr. Montefiore Hosp., Bronx, N.Y., 1962-64, L.I. Jewish Hosp., New Hyde Park, N.Y., 1964-66; adminstr. L.I. Jewish Hosp., Queens, 1966-69, Univ. Hosp., SUNY, Stony Brook, 1969-71; exec. dir., pres. Mt. Sinai Hosp., Hartford, Conn., 1971-91; cons., 1990-93; prin. Healthcare Practice, The Futures Group, 1993; pres. Conn. Sinai Corp., 1984-90, Blueridge Health Svcs., 1984-91, Mt. Sinai Hosp. Found., 1984—; sr. cons. The Future Group, Signal Med. Svcs., Staff Builders, Cornerstone Health Svcs.; trustee People's Bank Holding Co., Bridgeport; adj. faculty U. Hartford; asst. prof. SUNY, 1969-71; prof NYU, 1973-75; preceptor Yale Sch. Pub. Health; commr. Conn. Commn. on Hosps. and Health Care, 1976-81; mem. Nat. Commr. on Certification of Physicians Assts., 1976-84, pres., 1981-84; cohmn. blud ribbon com. New Eng. Hosp. Assembly, 1979-91; pres. Combined Hosps. Alcoholism program, 1977-79; v.p. Capital Area Health Consortium, 1978-79, pres., 1982-84; vice chmn. Health Sys. Agy. Bd. dirs. Premier Health System, 1986-88. Recipient E. Clayton Gengras Humanitarian award Nat. Multiple Sclerosis Soc., 1987, Disting. Svc. award Capital Area Health Consortium, 1988; named Boss of Yr., Greater Hartford Jaycees, 1977. Fellow APHA, Am. Coll. Healthcare Adminstrn. (recert. 1989), Royal Soc. Health, Am. Acad. Med. Adminstrn.; mem. AAAS, N.Y. Acad. Sci. (coun. teaching hosps., del. to Assn. Am. Med. Colls.), Conn. Hosp. Assn. (trustee T.S. Hamilton Disting. Svc award, chmn.-elect 1985, chmn. 1986), Am. Hosp. Assn. (alt. del. regional planning bd. I, del. 1992), Am. Assn. Hosp. Planning, Greater Hartford C. of C. (futures com., bd. dirs.), Hosp. Execs., Healthcare Study Soc. Home: 141 Sunny Reach Dr West Hartford CT 06117-1534

BRUNER, THOMAS HAROLD, social services administrator, counselor; b. San Antonio, Apr. 24, 1961; s. Paul Harold and Doris Elizabeth (Holland) B. BS, Abilene Christian U., 1983; MA, Stephen F. Austin State U., 1985. Lic. profl. counselor, Tex. Therapist Tarrant County Mental Health-Mental Retardation, Ft. Worth, 1986-88; pvt. practice Profl. Alliance Counseling and Consultation Ctr., Ft. Worth, 1989-90; exec. dir. AIDS Outreach Ctr., Ft. Worth, 1988—. Bd. dirs. AIDS Coord. Coun. of Tarrant County, Ft. Worth, 1988-93, Tex. AIDS Network, 1988-91; chairperson Tarrant HIV Svcs. Consortium, 1991-93, bd. dirs. Tarrant County Cmty. AIDS Partnership, 1991-95; trustee Tarrant County Youth Collaboration, 1993-95; commr. Ft. Worth Human Rels. Commn., 1989-94; bd. dirs. Tarrant County Lesbian/Gay Alliance, Ft. Worth, 1988-91, Jubilee Theatre, 1992—; amb. Ft. Worth Mus. Sci. & History, 1994—; bd. dirs. Contemporary Dance, 1994—, Forum Ft. Worth, 1994—; mem. Leadership Ft. Worth, 1991-92; vol. camp counselor First Tex. Coun. Campfire, 1993-95; mem. class 1992-94 Harris Health Exch. Named Emerging Leader, Ft. Worth Star-Telegram, 1990, 40 Under 40, The Bus. Press, 1996. Indpendent. Office: AIDS Outreach Ctr 1125 W Peter Smith Fort Worth TX 76104-2115

BRUNETT, EMERY W., pharmacist, educator; b. Ovando, Mont., Dec. 3, 1927; s. Elbe James and Mary Katherine (Betzler) B.; m. Iris Eileen Brunett, Dec. 27, 1970; children: Emery Jr., Katherine, Stephenie, Barbara. BS in Pharmacy, U. Mont., 1953, MS in Pharmacy, 1956; PhD, U. Wash., 1966. Registered pharmacist, Mont., Wyo. Instr. U. Mont., Missoula, 1956-57, asst. prof., 1964-65; instr. U. Wash., Seattle, 1958-59; asst. prof. Drake U., Des Moines, 1966-69; asst. prof., assoc. prof. U. Wyo., Laramie, 1969-94, assoc. prof. emeritus, 1994—. Pres. Civitan Internat., Laramie, 1983, sec., 1985—. Sgt. U.S. Army, 1946-48. Mem. Elks, Laramie Sunrise Rotary (charter pres. 1996—), Rho Chi, Kappa Psi. Democrat. Lutheran.

BRUNI, RUDOLPH HANNEY, JR., dentist; b. Richmond, Va., Aug. 21, 1925; s. Rudolph Hanney and Laura (Gillam) B.; m. Sara Elizabeth Jones, Aug. 27, 1949; children: Frank Douglass, Elizabeth Anderson, Richard McNeil. Student, U. Richmond, 1943-47; DDS, Med. Coll. Va., 1951. Faculty mem. Med. Coll. of Va. Dental Sch., 1951-58; dentist pvt. practice Richmond. Lt. (j.g.) Dental Corps, USNR, 1952-53. Fellow Internat. Coll. Dentists (dep. regent 1981-84), Am. Coll. Dentists, Va. Dental Assn.; mem. Am. Dental Assn. (alt. del. 1972-78), Richmond Dental Soc. (treas. 1966-68, pres. 1971-72, medicaid adv. com. 1973-80, med. adv. com. to selective svc. 1972-76), Pierre Fauchard Acad., McKee Dental Study Club (v.p. 1982-83, pres. 1983-84), Psi Omega Dental Frat., Phi Gamma Delta.

BRUNJES, PETER CRAWFORD, neurobiology educator; b. Columbus, Ohio, June 19, 1953; s. Thomas Hilbert and Marie Elizabeth (Baker) B.; m. Victoria Lee Manning, July 31, 1976; children: Benjamin Manning, Lee Manning, Samuel Manning. BS, Mich. State U., 1974; PhD, Ind. U., 1979. Postdoctoral fellow U. Ill., Champaign, 1980; asst. prof. psychology U. Va., Charlottesville, 1980-86, assoc. prof. psychology, 1986-93; prof., 1993—. Contbr. articles to profl. jours. Recipient Takasago award Assn. for Chemoreception Scis., 1990, Outstanding faculty award U. Va., 1991. Mem. AAAS, Internat. Soc. for Devel. Psychobiology, Soc. for Neurosci., Assn. for Chemoreception Rsch. (Takasago award 1990), J.B. Johnston Club. Office: U Va Dept Psychology 102 Gilmer Hall Charlottesville VA 22903-2477

BRUNK, SAMUEL FREDERICK, oncologist; b. Harrisonburg, Va., Dec. 21, 1932; s. Harry Anthony and Lena Gertrude (Burkholder) B.; m. Mary Priscilla Bauman, June 24, 1976; children: Samuel, Jill, Geoffrey, Heather, Kirsten, Peter, Christopher, Andrew, Paul, Barbara. BS, Ea. Mennonite Coll., 1955; MD, U. Va., 1959; MS in Pharmacology, U. Iowa, 1967. Diplomate Am. Bd. Internal Medicine, Am. Bd. Internal Medicine in Med. Oncology. Straight med. intern U. Va., Charlottesville, 1959-60; resident in chest diseases Blue Ridge Sanatorium, Charlottesville, 1960-61; resident in internal medicine U. Iowa, Iowa City, 1962-64, fellow in clin. pharmacology (oncology), 1964-65, 66-67, asst. prof. internal medicine, 1967-72; assoc. prof. internal medicine, 1972-76; fellow in medicine (oncology) Johns Hopkins U., Balt., 1965-66; vis. physician bone marrow transplantation unit Fred Hutchinson Cancer Treatment Ctr., U. Wash., Seattle, 1975; practice medicine specializing in med. oncology Des Moines, 1976-94; attending physician Iowa Luth. Hosp., 1976-94, Iowa Meth. Med. Ctr., 1976-94, Charter Hosp., 1976-94, Mercy Hosp. Med. Ctr., 1976-94; dir. med. oncology Hahne Regional Cancer Ctr., DuBois, Pa., 1994; attending physician DuBois Regional Med. Ctr., 1994; dir. Pa. Cmty. Cancer Care, 1995; attending physician St. Mary's Regional Med. Ctr., 1994; med. oncologist Cancer Treatment Ctr., Tulsa, Okla., 1995—; attending physician Meml. Med. Ctr., Tulsa, Okla., 1995—; chief of staff Iowa Luth. Hosp., 1990, chmn. dept. internal medicine, 1988; cons. physician Des Moines Gen. Osteo. Hosp., 1976-94; prin. investigator Iowa Oncology Rsch. Assn. in assn. with N. Cen. Cancer Treatment Group and Ea. Coop. Oncology Group, 1978-83; prin. investigator Iowa Oncology Rsch. Assn. Comty. Clin. Oncology Program, 1983-84; mem. cancer care com. St. Mary's, Pa., 1995. Contbr. articles to profl. jours. Bd. dirs. Iowa div. Am. Cancer Soc., 1971-89, Johnson County chpt., 1968-72. Mosby scholar, U. Va., 1959. Fellow ACP, Am. Coll. Clin. Pharmacology; mem. AMA, Okla. Medical Soc., Tulsa County Medical Soc., Iowa Thoracic Soc., Am. Thoracic Soc., Iowa Clin. Med. Soc., Am. Fedn. Clin. Rsch., Iowa Heart Assn., Am. Assn. Cancer Edn., Am. Soc. Hematology, Am. Soc. Clin. Pharmacology and Therapeutics, Cen. Soc. Clin. Rsch., Raven Soc., Alpha Omega Alpha. Roman Catholic. Home: 2915 E 32d St Tulsa OK 74105-2425

BRUNKARD, KATHLEEN MARIE, biology educator; b. New Haven, June 21, 1953; d. David T. Peck and Jeanne Marie (Murray) Puziello; m. Michael Montaigne, 1973 (div. 1977); m. James Ross Brunkard, Dec. 30, 1983; children: Jacob Oliver, Molly Elizabeth. BS in Biology, So. Conn. State U., 1977; MS in Biology, Syracuse U., 1979; PhD in Plant and Soil Scis., U. Mass./Amherst, 1982. Postdoctoral rsch. assoc. Washington U., St. Louis, 1982-84; asst. prof. biology East Stroudsburg (Pa.) U., 1984-90, assoc. prof. biology, 1990—. Stewardship com. mem. Tannersville (Pa.) Cranberry Bog/Nature Conservancy, 1985—. Mem. Am. Soc. Plant Physiology, Bot. Soc. Am., Am. Inst. Biol. Scis., Sigma Xi. Democrat. Office: East Stroudsburg U Normal St East Stroudsburg PA 18301-2613

BRUNNER, KIRSTIN ELLEN, pediatrician, psychiatrist; b. Allentown, Pa., July 26, 1959; d. John Wilson and Ingrid Ulla Brita (Arvide) B. BS, Muhlenberg Coll., Allentown, Pa., 1981; DO, Phila. Coll. Osteo. Medicine, 1986. Diplomate Am. Bd. Pediatrics, Am. Bd. Psychiatry and Neurology in child and adolescent psychiatry and adult psychiatry. Resident U. Ky., 1992; dept. dir. Integra Health Family Devel. Ctr., Cedar Rapids, Iowa, 1993—. Fellow Am. Acad. Pediatrics; mem. AMA, Am. Acad. Child and Adolescent Psychiatry, Am. Psychiat. Assn. Office: Integra Health Family Devel 855 A Ave Ste 130 Cedar Rapids IA 52402

BRUNNER, LILLIAN SHOLTIS, nurse, author; b. Freeland, Pa.; d. Andrew J. and Anna (Tomasko) Sholtis; m. Mathias J. Brunner, Sept. 8, 1951; children: Janet Brunner Cramer, Carol Ann Brunner Burns, Douglas Mathias. RN, diploma, U. Pa., 1940, BS, 1945, LittD (hon.), 1985; MS in Nursing, Case-Western Res. U., 1947; ScD (hon.), Cedar Crest Coll., 1978. RN, Pa. Head nurse U. Pa. Hosp., Phila., 1940-42, operating room supr., 1942-44; head, fundamentals of nursing dept. U. Pa. Hosp., 1944-46; asst. prof. surgical nursing Yale U. Sch. Nursing, New Haven, Conn., 1947-51; surgical supr. Yale-New Haven Hosp., 1947-51; rsch. project dir. Sch. Nursing Bryn Mawr (Pa.) Hosp., 1973-77; co-founder History of Nursing Mus., Pa. Hosp., Phila., 1974; mem. bd. overseers Sch. Nursing U. Pa., 1982-88; bd. overseers emeritus, 1988—; chmn. nursing adv. Presbyn.-U. Pa. Med. Ctr., Phila., 1970-88, 90-93, trustee, 1976-88, 90-95, vice chmn. bd. trustees, 1985-88; bd. mem. Presbyn. Found. for Phila., 1995—. Author: Manual of Operating Room Technology, 1966, (with others) Lippincott Manual of Nursing Practice, 1974, 4th edit., 1986, Textbook of Medical and Surgical Nursing, 1964, 6th edit., 1988; editl. bd. Nursing Photobook Series, 1978-90. Recipient Disting. Alumnus award Frances Payne Bolton Sch. Nursing, Case Western Res. U., 1980, Alumni award for merit Soc. Alumni Assns., U. Pa., and Am. Dream Achievement award Class of '45, U. Pa., 1995. Fellow Am. Acad. Nursing; mem. ANA, Nat. League for Nursing (judge nat. writing contest 1982-84, Disting. Svc. award 1979), Nat. League Am. Pen Women (sec. Phila. chpt. 1972-76, nat. sec. 1984-86), Assn. Oper. Rm. Nurses, Nurses Alumni Assn. U. Pa. Hosp., Ben Franklin Soc., Internat. Old Lacers Soc., Sigma Theta Tau, Pi Gamma Mu, Pi Lambda Theta. Home and Office: 645 Willow Vly Sq J-411 Lancaster PA 17602-4871

BRUNNGRABER, LEE, psychiatric nurse; b. Dumont, N.J., June 8, 1954; d. Harold and Florence (Bieth) Stroessner; m. Rodric F. Brunngraber, June 19, 1976. BSN, U. Del., 1976; MSN, U. Colo., Denver, 1983. Cert. adult psychiat.-mental health clin. nurse specialist. Psychiat. staff nurse VA Med. Ctr., San Diego, 1976-77, psychiat. rsch. staff nurse, 1979; psychiat. staff nurse, team leader VA Med. Ctr., Palo Alto, Calif., 1977-79, psychiat. clin. nurse specialist, 1983-90; psychiat. clin. nurse specialist triage/crisis intervention Kaiser Permanente, Santa Clara, Calif., 1991-92; instr. nursing VA Med. Ctr., Palo Alto, Calif., 1983-84, psychotherapist, psychiat. clin.l nurse specialist, 1984—, psychiatric clin. nurse specialist, cons. geropsychiat. prog, 1989-90; nurse therapist Los Altos, Calif., 1989—; psychiat. nurse clinician partial hospitalization program Grossmont Hosp., La Mesa, Calif., 1979-80, acting coord., 1980-81; psychiat. clin. nurse specialist Kaiser Permanente Med. Group, Santa Clara, Calif., 1991; instr. nursing Cabrillo Coll., Aptos, Calif., 1991—. Mem. ANA (cert. adult psychiat.-mental health clin. nurse specialist), Am. Assn. Psychiat. Clin. Nurse Specialists, Am. Assn. Psychiat. Nursing, No. Calif. Assn. Clin. Nurse Specialists (v.p. 1987-90), Calif. Nurses Assn., Nat. Nursing Network Violence against Women and Children, Sigma Theta Tau, Phi Kappa Phi. Home: 19080 Brook Ln Saratoga CA 95070-3454

BRUNNING, RICHARD DALE, pathologist; b. Grand Forks, N.D., Mar. 5, 1932; s. William August and Mary Ellen (Hogan) B. BS in Medicine, U. N.D., 1957; MD, McGill U., 1959. Diplomate Am. Bd. Pathology, Am. Bd. Anatomic and Clin. Pathology. Asst. prof. U. Minn., Mpls., 1965-68, assoc. prof., 1968-73, prof., head hematopathology, 1973—, dep. chmn., dept. lab. medicine and pathology, 1988—; hematology panel FDA, Washington, 1978-81; clin. cancer investigation rev. com. Nat. Cancer Inst., Washington, 1988-91, cancer and acute leukemia group B, 1986—. Co-author: Tumors of the Bone Marrow, 1994; editl. bd. Am. Jour. of Clin. Pathology, Human Pathology, Hematological Oncology, Surgical Pathology, Jour. of Ultrastructural Pathology. Mem. Internat. Acad. Pathology (councillor 1986-89, edn. com. 1982-86, pres. 1987-89), Soc. for Hematopathology (pres. 1987-

89), U.S. and Can. Acad. Pathology (internat. councillor 1989-90), Arthur Purdy Stout Soc., Am. Soc. Clin. Oncology, Am. Soc. Hematology. Office: U Minn Hosp Box 609 420 Delaware St SE Minneapolis MN 55455

BRUNO, AUDREI ANN, nurse educator, administrator; b. Pitts., Oct. 31, 1946; d. Vincent Joseph and Julia Elizabeth (Karaffa) Mataya; m. Edward Orlando Bruno, Apr. 30, 1966; children: Brent Edward, Bradley Edward. AA, Community Coll. Alleghany County, 1976; BSN, Pa. State U., 1984; MSN, U. Pitts., 1988. Cert. nurse adminstr. Psychiat. nursing supr. Western Psychiat. Clinic and Inst., Pitts., 1976-81; staff charge nurse Magee Women's Hosp., Pitts., 1981-82; charge team leader Central Med. Pavillion, Pitts., 1982-84; clin. specialist Vis. Nurse Assn. of Alleghany County, Pitts., 1984-92; rschr. U. Pitts.; mem. speakers bur. Community Coll. Allegheny County; project developer WPIC Adolescent Module, 1980-81; CEO Psycho-Ednl. Cons., 1996; coord. grant Putting Cmty. Health into AD Curriculum, 1993-96. Chmn. North Huntington (Pa.) Suicide Awareness and Prevention Com., 1986-88; fieldworker Project Star, Pitts., 1986-88; mem. Pa. Task Force on Elder Abuse, Nurses Interest in Care of Elderly; mem. adv. com. Nat. Project DART. Mem. Nursing Quality Assurance (cons.), Sigma Theta Tau. Home: 14071 Ridge Rd North Huntingdon PA 15642

BRUNO, BARBARA ALTMAN, social worker; b. N.Y.C., May 26, 1947; m. Joseph Peter Bruno, Oct. 2, 1977. AB in English, Cornell U., 1969; MSW in Psychiat. Social Work, Calif. State U., Sacramento, 1974; PhD in Psychology, Columbia Pacific U., 1987. Diplomate clin. social work; cert. social worker, N.Y. Group facilitator San Francisco DWI Sch., 1975-76; social svc. coord. Kosher Nutrition Project, San Francisco, 1975-76; counselor SUNY, Purchase, 1980-81, Pace U. Counseling Ctr., N.Y.C., 1981-84; group leader No. Westchester YMHA/YWHA, Pleasantville, N.Y., 1981-91; pvt. practice psychotherapy Pleasantville, 1984—; adj. faculty Westchester Community Coll., Valhalla, N.Y., 1990—, COED program, Pleasantville, 1988-92; founder Weight Release Svcs., Pleasantville, 1989—, Thinside Out, Pleasantville, 1985-90. Author: Quakers, 1985, Worth Your Weight, 1996; editor Roundup, 1990—; columnist Dimensions mag.; contbr. articles to profl. jours. Fellow Soc. Clin. Social Work Psychotherapists (cert.), Nat. Assn. to Advance Fat Acceptance (chair Westchester-Rockland chpt. 1989-91, nat. bd. dirs. 1991—, mental health advisor 1991—); mem. Acad. Cert. Social Workers, Assn. for Health Enrichment of Large People (founding mem.).

BRUNO, CRAIG GEORGE, physician assistant, administrator; b. Port Chester, N.Y., Nov. 2, 1942; s. Joseph Aloysis and Gloria Ann (Novak) B.; m. Ellen Jackson, Feb. 14, 1976. Nursing Diploma, Nursing Sch., Kingston, N.Y.; cert., Duke U., Durham, N.C. Physician asst. Plymouth (N.C.) Clinic, 1968-86, 2CU SOM, Greenville, N.C., 1986-89; physician asst., administr. Greenville Health Care, 1989—; pres. Bru/Joy Mgmt. Inc., v.p. Greenville Health Care. With U.S. Navy. Fellow Am. Acad of Physician Assts. Home: 101 Christina Dr Greenville NC 27858

BRUNO, JUDYTH ANN, chiropractor; b. Eureka, Calif., Feb. 16, 1944; d. Harold Oscar and Shirley Alma (Farnsworth) Nelson; m. Thomas Glenn Bruno, June 1, 1968; 1 child, Christina Elizabeth. AS, Sierra Coll., 1982; D of Chiropractic, Palmer Coll. of Chiropractic West, Sunnyvale, Calif., 1986. Diplomate Nat. Bd. Chiropractic Examiners. Sec. Bank Am., San Jose, Calif., 1965-67; marketer Memorex, Santa Clara, Calif., 1967-74; order entry clk. John Deere, Milan, Ill., 1977; system analyst Four Phase, Cupertino, Calif., 1977-78; chiropractic asst. Dr. Thomas Bruno, Nevada City, Calif., 1978-81; chiropractor Chiropractic Health Care Ctr., Nevada City, 1987—; pvt. practice Cedar Ridge, Calif., 1991—. Area dir. Cultural Awareness Coun., Grass Valley, Calif., 1977—; vol. Nevada County Libr., Nevada City, 1987-88, Decide Team III, Nevada County, 1987-92, Active Parenting of Teen Facilitator Nev. Union H.S., 1989-93. Mem. Am. Chiropractic Assn., Women Health Practitioners of Nevada County (founder 1993—), Nevada County C. of C. (vol. task force health care 1993), Toastmasters (sec. 1988, pres. 1989, edn. v.p. 1990), Women's Forum, Noetic Scis. Republican. Office: Chiropractor Health Care PO Box 1718 Cedar Ridge CA 95924-1718

BRUNO, PETER JACKSON, counselor, consultant, pastor; b. White Plains, N.Y., Dec. 27, 1945; s. Charles Fredrick and Barbara (Jackson) B.; m. Barbara Suesens; 1 child, Linda; 2d m. Corky Jean Brown, July 3, 1976; children: Benjamin, Elizabeth. BA in Psychology, Brown U., 1968; MEd in Counseling, Mont. State U., 1978. Lic. min. Evangelical Ch.; lic. profl. counselor, Mont.; nat. cert. counselor; cert. clin. mental health counselor. Addictive disease counselor Mont. State Hosp., Galen, 1973-76; tchg. asst. Mont. State U., Bozeman, 1977-78; psychologist V Ea. Mont. Mental Health, Miles City, 1979-92; pvt. practice counselor Glendive, Mont., 1992—; clin. cons. Dept. Damily Svcs., Miles City, Home on the Range, Sentinel Butte, N.D., Pine Hills Sch., Miles City, all 1992-94; lead clin. staff Big Sky Ranch, Glendive, 1992—. Author: New Ways Workbook, 1992. Pres. Montanans for Children, Youth and Families, Inc.; leader, pastor, tchr. Evangelical Ch. Named Mont.'s Outstanding Direct Svc. Provider, Mental Health Assn. Mont., 1982. Mem. Am. Profl. Soc. on the Abuse of Children, Great Plains Counseling Assocs. (dir.), Toastmasters Internat. (Disting. Leadership award 1995). Office: Great Plains Counseling PO Box 684 513 N Merrill Ave Glendive MT 59330

BRUNO, RICHARD LOUIS, psychophysiologist, educator, researcher; b. Englewood, N.J., Nov. 19, 1954; s. Louis Sebastian and Linda (Rossi) B.; m. Nancy M. Frick, May 28, 1983. BA, Springfield, 1977; PhD, Yeshiva U., 1981. Clin. rsch. scientist dept. clin. psychopharmacology N.Y. State Psychiat. Inst., N.Y.C., 1978-81; fellow Columbia U., N.Y.C., 1981-84, clin. rsch. coord., assoc. rsch. scientist faculty of medicine, Coll. Physicians & Surgeons, 1984-88; dir. post-polio svc., clin. psychophysiologist & rehab. psychologist Kessler Inst. Rehab., Saddle Brook, N.J., 1988—; cons. N.Y. State Psychiat. Inst., N.Y.C., 1981-82, VA, Bklyn., 1982-84, Social Security Adminstrn., Balt., adv. 1985-86, N.J. Mfrs. Insurance Co., Trenton, N.J., 1990-93, Nat. Multiple Sclerosis Soc., 1991-95, ICN Pharm., 1995; organizer, chmn. Internat. Post-Polio Task Force, 1984—; assoc. prof. U. Medicine and Dentistry N.J., N.J. Med. Sch., 1989—. Manuscript peer rev. bd. Archives of Physical Medicine and Rehab, 1994—; contbg. editor New Mobility, 1995—; editor Jour. Orthopedics, 1985, 91; contbr. articles to profl. jours. Adviser N.J. Polio Network, 1991—; adviser disability affairs com. Ho. of Reps., 1993—; adviser labor and human resources com. U.S. Senate, 1984-85; mem. bd. dirs. N.Y. Neuropsychology Group, 1984-85. Recipient Excellence in Patient Edn. award Kessler Inst., 1992, Disting. Alumnus award Springfield Coll., 1993, N.J. Pride award in health, 1993, svc. award N.J. Polio Network, 1994, cert. of appreciation, 1995; grantee J.M. Found., 1982, Joel Leff Charitable Trust, 1983-84, 92, Deluxe Corp., 1993, George Ohl Jr. Infantile Paralysis Found., 1990, 91, 92, 93, 94, 95, 96, Sandoz Pharms., 1993. Mem. Am. Congress Rehab. Medicine (45th John Stanley Coulter Meml. award and lecture 1995). Office: Kessler Inst for Rehab Post-Polio Svc Saddle Brook NJ 07663

BRUNS, PETER JOHN, geneticist; b. Syracuse, N.Y., May 2, 1942; s. Hans J. and Ursula Margaret (Bahr) B.; m. Jennifer Hall Shea, Aug. 24, 1985; children: Christopher, Elizabeth, Nicholas. AB, Syracuse U., 1964; PhD, U. Ill., 1969. Asst. prof., then assoc. prof. genetics Cornell U., Ithaca, N.Y., 1969-82, chmn. sect. genetics and devel., 1980-85, prof. genetics, 1982—, assoc. dir. biotechnology program, 1984-88, faculty fellow, 1987-88, dir. div. biol. scis., 1987—, dir. Cornell Inst. Biology Tchrs., 1989—; vis. scientist Biol. Inst., Carlsberg Found., Copenhagen, 1977-78; mem. teaching staff European Molecular Biol. Orgn., Copenhagen, 1977; consulting examiner in genetics and biotechnology Charter Oak Coll., 1986-89; bd. dirs. Boyce Thompson Inst. Plant Rsch., Ithaca, Cornell Lab. Ornithology, Ithaca, Orgn. for Tropical Studies, Costa Rica, Cornell Ctr. Environ., Cornell High Energy Synchrotron Source. Assoc. editor: European Jour. of Protocology, 1996—; contbr. numerous articles to sci. jours. Grantee Rsch. Corp., 1970, NSF, 1971-81, 90-93, NIH, 1980-90, Howard Hughes Med. Inst., 1989—; John Simon Guggenheim Meml. Found. fellow, 1977-78. Mem. AAAS, Am. Soc. Protozoologists, Genetics Soc. Am., Ithaca Yacht Club. Home: 16 Wedgewood Dr Ithaca NY 14850-1063 Office: Cornell U Div Biol Scis 169 Biotechnology Bldg Ithaca NY 14853

BRUNSON, JOEL GARRETT, retired pathologist, educator; b. Greenville, S.C., Apr. 22, 1923; s. James Edwin and Leila (Ballenger) B. MD, SUNY, Buffalo, 1950. Diplomate Am. Bd. Med. Examiners, Am. Bd. Pathology. Internship U. Ala. Teaching Hosp., Birmingham, 1950-51; residency U. Minn. Hosp., Mpls., 1951-53; asst. prof. U. Minn. Med. Sch., Mpls., 1955-59; prof., chmn. dept. U. Miss. Med. Ctr., Jackson, 1959-77, Morehouse Med. Sch., Atlanta, 1978-80, U. Ife, Nigeria, 1980-81; prof. pathology St. George's (Grenada) U. Med. Sch., 1982-89, prof., chmn. dept., 1989-95, assoc dean Basic Scis.; dean Kingstown Med. Coll., St. Vincent, 1995; ret., 1995; asst. prof. pathology U. Minn., 1953-55; vis. prof. Am. U. Beirut, 1977-78; cons. rsch. grants award com. NIH, 1963-67, chmn. com., 1965-67, mem. internat. fellowship rev. panel, 1980; mem. instl. rsch. programs VA, 1965-70. Author, editor: (text) Concepts of Disease, 1971; mem. editorial bd. Am. Jour. Pathology, 1966-80; contbr. numerous rsch. articles to sci. publs. Am. Cancer Soc. fellow U. Minn., 1953-55, NIH sr. rsch., fellow, 1955-57; named to Internat. Parliament for Safety and Peace; named Knight of the Order of the Circulo Nobilario de los Caballeros Universates, Spain. Mem. AAAS, AMA, Coll. Am. Pathologists, Am. Assn. Pathology Chmn. (v.p. 19709-71, pres. 1972-72), Am. Soc. for Exptl. Pathology, Internat. Acad. Pathology, Am. Assn. Pathologists (editor symposia series 1973-76), Internat. Parliament for Safety and Peace, others. Home: AP 50 Nosara, Nicoya Costa Rica

BRUNSTING, LOUIS ALBERT, III, surgeon; b. Rochester, Minn., May 15, 1958; s. Louis Albert Jr. and Diane Bradford (Hacha) B.; m. Gina Elaine Ittner, July 21, 1979 (div. Aug. 5, 1989); 1 child, Nelson; m. Karyn Elaine Strauss, Sept. 30, 1989; children: Richard, Robert. BS, U. Calif., Irvine, 1984; MD, U. Calif., San Diego, 1985. Diplomate Am. Bd. Surgery, Am. Bd. Thoracic Surgery. Surg. intern U. Rochester (N.Y.), 1983-84, surg. resident, 1984-85, 87-89; rsch. fellow Duke U., Durham, N.C., 1985-87; thoracic fellow Duke U., 1989-91; asst. prof. U. Mich., Ann Arbor, 1991-94; cardiothoracic surgeon Cardiothoracic Surgery, Nashville, Tenn., 1994—. Recipient Am. Heart Assn. grant U. Mich., 1993. Assoc. fellow ACS; mem. Soc. Thoracic Surgeons. Office: Cardiothoracic Surgery Ste 523 2400 Patterson St Nashville TN 37203

BRUNSWICK, ANN FINKENBERG, social psychologist, health researcher; b. N.Y.C., July 1, 1926; d. Leo and Erna (Eiseman) Finkenberg; m. J. Peter Brunswick, Sept. 14, 1950 (div. June 1976); children: Debra, Naomi. AB, Hunter Coll., 1946; MA, Clark U., 1947; PhD, Columbia U., 1976. Asst. study dir. NORC U. Chgo., 1951-60, study dir., 1960-65; sr. rsch. assoc. CUNY, 1966; rsch. assoc., co-dir. adolescent health project Columbia U., 1966-71, prin. investigator, dir., 1972-73, sr. rsch. assoc., sociomed. area Ctr. Community Health Syste, 1973-74, sr. rsch. scientist, prin. investigator, dir. longitudinal Harlem health study, 1974—. Author book chpts. in field; contbr. numerous articles to profl. jours. Fellow APA, Am. Psychol. Soc.; mem. Soc. Psychologists in Substance Abuse, Am. Assn. Pub. Opinion Rsch., Soc. Psychol. Study of Social Issues, Am. Sociol. Assn., Soc. Study of Social Problems, Assn. Social Scis. in Health, Am. Pub. Health Assn., AAAS. Office: Columbia U Sch Pub Health 60 Haven Ave Box 394 New York NY 10032-2649

BRUNT, HARRY HERMAN, JR., psychiatrist; b. Phila., Jan. 22, 1921; s. Harry Herman and Ann (Zurbrugg) B.; m. Zoe M. Bower, July 2, 1944; children: Marianne Brunt Tallman, Margaret B. Griffin, Jane, Mary Lazar. B.S. with honors, Va. Poly. Inst., 1942; M.D., U. Pa., 1945. Diplomate: Am. Bd. Psychiatry and Neurology. Intern, Lankenau Hosp., 1946; resident psychiatry Trenton (N.J.) State Hosp., VA Hosp., Coatesville, 1948-52; practice medicine specializing in psychiatry Trenton, 1952, Princeton, N.J., 1952-54, Hammonton, N.J., 1954-69, Long Branch, N.J., 1969-74; acting asst. clin. dir. Trenton State Hosp., 1952; asst. supt. N.J. Neuropsychiat. Inst. Princeton, 1952-54; med. dir. Ancora State Hosp., 1954-69; dir. dept. psychiatry Monmouth Med. Center and Pollak Clinic, Long Branch, 1969-74; pvt. practice, 1974—; assoc. prof. psychiatry Jefferson Med. Coll., 1952-66; instr. psychiatry U. Pa., 1953-65; adj. asso. prof. psychiatry Temple Med. Sch., 1968-70; prof. psychiatry Hahneman Med. Coll., 1970-74; clin. prof. psychiatry Robert Wood Johnson Med. Sch., New Brunswick, N.J., 1971-96. Cons. bur. family services Dept. Health, Edn. and Welfare Dept., 1960-68. Served to capt. M.C. AUS, 1946-48. Fellow ACP, AAAS, Am. Psychiat. Assn. (life, chmn. future planning com. assembly dist. brs., mem. policy com. area III 1968, recorder 1969, speaker 1971-72, trustee 1972-73, 74-75), Am. Geriatric Soc., Am. Coll. Psychiatrists (founding); mem. AMA, Monmouth County Med. Soc. (exec. com.), N.J. Neuropsychiat. Assn. (past pres.), Med. Soc. N.J. (chmn. coun. mental health), Beach Haven Yacht Club (commodore 1992-93), Alpha Kappa Kappa, Phi Kappa Phi.

BRUNT, MANLY YATES, JR., psychiatrist; b. Winston-Salem, N.C., Nov. 7, 1926; s. Manly Yates and Jessie Corina (Evans) B.; M.D., Wake Forest U., 1948; m. Jacklyn Beatrice Bray, Dec. 2, 1961; children—Diane Strachan, William Bray, Douglas Evans, Kenneth Sherman. Intern, Grad. Hosp. U. Pa., 1949-50; exec. med. officer Inst. of Pa. Hosp., Phila., 1952-62, mem. sr. attending staff, 1968—, prin. investigator Behavior Research Lab., 1957-61; mem. faculty U. Pa., 1953-68; dir. emeritus dept. psychiatry Bryn Mawr (Pa.) Hosp., past pres. staff and chmn. exec. com. Pres. Community Nursing Bur. Met. Phila., 1961-64; bd. dirs. Main Line Health Care Group, Inc. Served with M.C., AUS, 1950-52. Diplomate Am. Bd. Psychiatry and Neurology. Mem. AMA, Am. Psychiat. Assn., Am. Psychoanalytic Assn., Phila. Coll. Physicians and Surgeons, Wake Forest U. Med. Alumni Assn. (pres. 1985), Alpha Omega Alpha. Republican. Presbyterian. Clubs: Merion Cricket, Phila. Skating and Humane Soc., Little Egg Harbor Yacht. Home: 633 Malin Rd Newtown Square PA 19073-2612 Office: 864 County Line Rd Bryn Mawr PA 19010-2516

BRUSCH, JOHN LYNCH, physician; b. Boston, Nov. 3, 1943; s. Charles and Margaret Agnes (Lynch) B.; m. Patricia Gahan, May 12, 1972; children: Amy Claire, Meaghan, Patrick. BS, Tufts U., 1965, MD, 1969. Diplomate Am. Bd. Internal Medicine, Am. Bd. Infectious Disease, Am. Bd. Geriatrics. Intern New England Med. Ctr., Boston, 1969-70, resident in medicine, 1970-71, resident in infectious disease, 1971-74; asst. chief medicine Brighton Pub. Health Svc. Hosp., Boston, 1974-76; pvt. practice physician Cambridge, Mass., 1976—; chief medicine Youville Hosp., Cambridge, 1991—, dir. cmty. medicine, 1995—; clin. assoc. medicine Mass. Gen. Hosp., Boston, 1996—. Co-author: Infective Endocardits, assoc. editor Infectious Disease Practice, 1984—; contbr. articles to med. jours. Dir. North Cambridge Coop Bank, 1980—. With USPHS, 1974-76. Fellow ACP; mem. Am. Soc. Microbiology, Longwood Cricket Club. Home: 52 Radcliffe Rd Belmont MA 02178-3340 Office: Cambridge Hosp 1493 Cambridge St Cambridge MA 02139-1047

BRUSKO, GREGORY, surgeon; b. Balt., Jan. 22, 1963; s. Michael and Vincentine (Carnfara) B.; m. Joann Nicole Brusko; 1 child, G. Damian. BS in Biology, Kutztown U. of Pa., 1984; DO, Phila. Coll. Osteo. Medicine, 1989. Diplomate Am. Bd. Osteopathic Medicine, Nat. Bd. Med. Examiners. Gen. surgeon Bethlehem, Pa. Mem. AMA, Pa. Osteo. Med. Assn., Northampton County Med. Soc., Alpha Omega Alpha. Office: Fry and Toselli Svc Assocs Ste 203 2597 Schoensville Rd Bethlehem PA 18017

BRUSTAD, ROBERT A., prosthodontist; b. Detroit, Feb. 27, 1945; s. Marvin Daniel and Sylvia Evelyn Brustad; m. Margaret Anne Brustad, Aug. 24, 1968; children: Carolyn, Thomas, James. BS, We. Mich. U., 1966; DDS, U. Mich., 1970, MS, 1972. Cert. dentist, prosthodontist, Mich. Tchg. asst., asst. prof. U. Mich. Sch. Dentistry, Ann Arbor, 1970-75; prosthodontist pvt. practice Ann Arbor, 1972—; bd. examiner State of Mich., Lansing, 1977-80, coun. splty. pres., 1979-81. Mem. ADA, Am. Coll. Prosthodontics, Acad. Osseointegration, Mich. Dental Soc., Mich. Soc. Prosthodontics (pres., 1976-96, charter), Washtenaw Dist. Dental Soc. (pres. 1969-96). Office: 1111 E Stadium Blvd Ann Arbor MI 48104

BRUUN, RUTH DOWLING, physician; b. N.Y.C., Sept. 13, 1937; d. Robert Whittle and Alice Bevier (Hall) D.; m. Lawrence W. Newman, June 18, 1958 (div. Feb. 1970); children: Timothy Dowling, Isabel Bettoney, Thomas Hitchcock; m. Bertel Bruun, Dec. 19, 1970; 1 child, Christian Bertel. AB, Radcliffe Coll., 1959; MD, Cornell U., 1968. Diplomate Am. Bd. Psychiatry & Neurology. Asst. psychiatrist Payne Whitney Clinic-N.Y. Hosp., N.Y.C., 1970-73; asst. adj. psychiatrist Lenox Hill Hosp., N.Y.C., 1973-75, adj. psychiatrist, 1975-79, assoc. psychiatrist, 1979-82; clin., instr. in psychiatry Cornell U. Med. Coll., N.Y.C., 1973-79; asst. attending psychiatrist N.Y. Hosp., N.Y.C., 1979-87, attending psychiatrist, 1987-90; attending psychiatrist North Shore Univ. Hosp., Manhasset, N.Y., 1990—; pvt. practice N.Y.C., 1973—, Westhampton Beach, N.Y., 1989—; clin. assoc. prof. psychiatry Cornell U. Med. Coll., N.Y.C., 1987—; adj. assoc. prof. psychiatry Med. Coll. NYU, 1996—. Co-author: Gilles de la Tourette Syndrome, 1978, The Human Body, 1982, Tourette's Syndrome & Tic Disorders, 1988, Your Brain, 1989, A Mind of Its Own: Tourette's Syndrome, A Story and a Guide, 1994; contbr. articles to profl. jours. Mem. Tourette Syndrome Assn. (med. adv. bd., chmn. med. com. 1983-89). Office: 969 Park Ave New York NY 10028-0322 also: 27B Old Riverhead Rd Westhampton Beach NY 11978-2020

BRYAN, BILLIE MARIE (MRS. JAMES A. MACKEY), biologist; b. Norfolk, Va., Dec. 30, 1932; d. William B. and Marie (Fortescue) Bryan; B.A. in Biology, U. Richmond, 1954; M.Ed., Am. U., 1966; m. James A. Mackey. Bacteriologist, Arlington County Health Dept., Arlington, Va., 1954-58; med. bacteriologist Walter Reed Army Inst. Research, Walter Reed Army Med. Center, Washington, 1959-62; tchr. Fairfax (Va.) High Sch., 1962-66; biologist NIH, Washington, 1966—. Mem. Am. Assn. for the Advancement of Sci., Soc. for Experimental Biology and Medicine, DAR. Contbr. articles to profl. jours. Home: 201 Quaint Acres Dr Silver Spring MD 20904-2715 Office: NIH-NIDDK Natcher Bldg Rm 6AS-19H Bethesda MD 20892

BRYAN, CYNTHIA JOAN, emergency medical science educator, special education educator; b. Kingman, Kans., Aug. 10, 1953. BE, Kans. Wesleyan U., 1978; M in ednl. psychol. with honors, Wichita (Kans.) State U., 1985; cert. in emergency mobile intensive care tech., Hutchinson Community Coll., 1987. Educator. Tchr. USD #331, Kingman, Kans., 1978-80; tchr. special edn. South Cen. Kans. Special Edn. Coop., Pratt, 1980-82; police dispatcher Kingman (Kans.) Police Dept., 1979-82; emergency medical technician Kingman Emergency Med. Svcs., 1980—; spl. edn. tchr. Three Lakes Spl. Edn. Coop., Burlington, Kans., 1982-83, South Cen. Kans. Spl. Edn. Coop., Iuka, Kans., 1983-89; paramedic Kingman Emergency Med. Svc., 1987—; emergency paramedic educator Hutchinson (Kans.) C.C., 1989-94; emergency mem. examiner Kans. Bd. Emergency Med. Svcs., Topeka, 1989—; established paramedic edn. program for Hutchinson C.C. on Wichita State U. Campus, 1991-94, establisher, lead instr. Iuka Alt. Sch., 1994—; presenter in field; EMS educator Pratt C.C., Kans., 1995—. Editor monthly newsletter. Mem. NEA, Kans. Instr./Coord. Soc. (pres.), Tchrs. Assn. Spl. Kids (pres.). Home: 827 N Spruce Kingman KS 67068-1012 Office: South Ctrl Kans Spl Edn Coop PO Box 177 Iuka KS 67066

BRYAN, FRANK LEON, microbiologist, consultant, researcher; b. Indpls., Aug. 29, 1930; s. Frank Leslie and Marie Georgia (Vogt) B.; m. Ruth Ann McDonald, Aug. 30, 1952; children: Steven Harris, Sharryl Ann. B.S., Ind. U., 1953; M.P.H., U. Mich., 1956; Ph.D., Iowa State U., 1965. Instr. U. Mass., Amherst, 1956-58, also tng. officer New Eng. Field Tng. Sta.; tng. officer in environ. health Communicable Disease Ctr., Atlanta, 1958-63, research in salmonella, Ames, 1963-65; chief foodborne disease activity and scientist dir. Ctrs. for Disease Control, Atlanta, 1965-85; cons. in food safety and tng., Lithoria, Ga., 1985—; mem. WHO adv. panel food safety, Internat. Commn. on Microbiol. Specifications for Foods, mem. com. Nat. Research Council, Nat. Acad. Scis.; lectr. foodborne disease epidemiology and control. Served to 1st lt. U.S. Army, 1953-55, to capt. USPHS, 1956-85. Recipient Norbert Sherman award, 1979, 82, 86, 91, Citation award Internat. Assn. Milk, Food and Environ. Sanitarians; Meritous Service medal USPHS, 1981. Mem. Am. Soc. Microbiology, Inst. Food Technologists, Internat. Assn. Milk, Food and Environ. Sanitarians, World Assn. Veterinary Food Hygienists (v.p.), Am. Pub. Health Assn., Nat. Assn. Sanitarians, Sigma Xi, Phi Tau Sigma, Gamma Sigma Delta. Author: (with Riemann) Foodborne Infections and Intoxications, 2d edit., 1979; (with others) Microorganisms in Foods 1, 1978, Microbiological Ecology for Foods, Vol. 1 and 2, 1980; Diseases Transmitted by Foods, 1982, Micoorganisms in Foods, 1986, Hazard Analysis Critical Control Point Evaluations; manuals or investigation of foodborne, waterborne and vector-borne illnesses, and hazard analyses cutical central point systems; contbr. articles to profl. jours.

BRYAN, GEORGE THOMAS, pediatrician, academic administrator; b. Sewanee, Tenn., Nov. 19, 1930; s. Lawton P. and Velma (Courtney) B.; m. Peggy Marie Graham, Dec. 19, 1952; children: Ralph T., Janice M. Student, Vanderbilt U., 1949-51; MD, U. Tenn., 1955. Intern D.C. Gen. Hosp., 1955-56; resident in pediatrics U. Iowa Hosp., Iowa City, 1956-58, fellow in pediatric endocrinology, 1958-59; clin. assoc. pediatrics, Lab. Clin. Investigation NIH, USPHS, Bethesda, Md., 1959-60, acting head pediatric svc., 1960-61, pediatrician clin. endocrinology br. Nat Heart Inst., 1961-63; asst. prof. pediatrics U. Tex. Med. Br., Galveston, 1963-67, assoc. prof., 1967-73, prof., 1973—, asst. dir. clin. study ctr., 1963-72, assoc. dir., 1972-75, assoc. dean curricular affairs, 1974-77, dean Sch. Medicine, 1977—. Contbr. articles to profl. jours. Lt. USNR, 1956-59. Markle scholar, 1967-72. Mem. Am. Pediatric Soc., Soc. Pediatric Rsch., Am. Acad. Pediatrics, Lawson Wilkins Soc. Pediatric Endocrinology, Endocrine Soc., Am. Fedn. Clin. Rsch., So. Soc. Pediatric Rsch., AMA, Tex. Med. Assn., Galveston County Med. Soc., Am. Assn. Med. Colls., Sigma Xi. Mem. Christian Ch. Office: U Tex Med Br Office Dean Sch Medici Galveston TX 77550*

BRYAN, KATHERINE BYRAM, health care executive; d. John Charles and Jane Ballew (Price) Byram; 1 child by previous marriage, George Gurley III; m. John Shelby Bryan, Mar. 12, 1982; children: Austin, Jack. BA, U. Mo., 1969, PhD in Counseling Psychology, 1979. With Corp. Health Examiners, N.Y.C., 1978—, v.p. mktg., 1980-84. Author articles in field. Jr. bd. dirs. Nelson Gallery, Kansas City, Mo., 1973-76; bd. dirs. Family Dynamics, N.Y., 1987-92. Mem. Am. Psychol. Assn., Biofeedback Soc. Am. Clubs: Maidstone (East Hampton, N.Y.); River (N.Y.C.). Home: 15 E 96th St New York NY 10128

BRYAN, NORMAN E., dentist; b. South Bend, Ind., Jan. 20, 1947; s. Norman E. and Frances (Kuhn) B.; m. Constance C. Cook, Feb. 23, 1974 (div. Apr. 1985); m. Linda Markley, Dec. 31, 1986; 1 child, Noelle. AB, Ind. U., 1969; DDS, Ind. U. Purdue U., Indpls., 1973. Sr. dentist Downtown Dental Svcs., Elkhart, Ind., 1973—; specialist Temporo-mandibular Joint Disfunction. Author: Canine Endodontics, 1982. Mem. ADA, Ind. Dental Assn., Elkhart Dental Assn. (pres. 1976-77, 84-86), Am. Acad. Head, Neck and Facial Pain, Great Lakes Cruising Club (Chgo.), Elcona Country Club, Great Lakes Cruising Club (Chgo.). Republican. Office: 505 Vistula St Elkhart IN 46516-2809

BRYAN, RICHARD ALAN, medical services administrator; b. Memphis, Dec. 29, 1956; s. Ernest W. Jr. and Margaret (Porter) B.; m. Karen Anderson Bryan, Dec. 24, 1979; children: Joseph, Kristopher. AAS in Nursing, Shelby State C.C., Memphis, 1983; BSN, Union U., Memphis, 1989. RN, Wash., Tenn. Staff nurse emergency dept. Profl. Health Care, Memphis; staff nurse Bapt. Meml. Hosp., Memphis, nursing supr. telemetry subacute unit; asst. head nurse critical care Madigan Army Med. Ctr., Tacoma, Wash.; cons., dir. med. svcs. Help Systems, Federal Way, Wash. With U.S. Army, 1989-92.

BRYAN, SANDRA HOWZE, medical/surgical nurse; b. San Angelo, Tex., Jan. 25, 1948; d. Herbert Hardy Jr. and Merle Evelyn (Edgington) Howze; m. Francis Steven Bryan, Sept. 2, 1972; children: Matthew Steven, Jacob Edgington. Diploma, Jackson Meml. Hosp., Miami, Fla., 1969; BS in Nursing with high honors, U. Md., 1987. RN, Md.; CPAN. Asst. head nurse CCU Jackson Meml. Hosp., Miami, 1970-71; ICU staff nurse Easton Meml. Hosp., 1972; clin. nurse III telemetry unit Meml. Hosp., Easton, 1986-90, staff nurse post-anesthesia care unit, 1990-93, clin. nurse III PACU, 1993—. Mem. ANA (cert. med.-surg. nurse, gen. nurse), Am. Heart Assn., Md. Nurses Assn., Jackson Meml. Hosp. Sch. Nursing Alumni Assn., U. Md. Sch. Nursing Alumni Assn., Talbot Coronary Club (co-founder), Am. Soc. Post Anesthesia Nurses, Sigma Theta Tau.

BRYANT, BERTHA ESTELLE, retired nurse; b. Va., Jan. 11, 1927; d. E.F. and Julia B. Diploma, Sibley Meml. Hosp., Washington, 1947; B.S., Am. U., 1948; M.A., Tchrs. Coll., Columbia U., 1962. Staff nurse, head nurse NIH, Bethesda, Md., 1954-59; asst. dir. nursing USPHS Alaska Native Hosp., Mt. Edgecumbe, 1959-61; instr. Sch. Nursing, U. Mich., 1962-64; chief div. clin. nursing Bur. Nursing, D.C. Dept. Public Health, Washington, 1964-65; commd. Nurse Corps, USPHS, 1965, nurse dir., capt., 1974—; nurse cons., hosp. facilities services br., div. hosps. and med. facilities Bur.

Health Services, HEW, Silver Spring; nurse cons., social analysis br., div. health services research and analysis Nat. Center Health Services Research, Health Resources Adminstrn., HEW, Rockville, Md.; nurse cons. div. extramural research Nat. Center Health Services Research, Office Asst. Sec. Health, HHS, Hyattsville, Md., 1977-81. Contbr. articles to profl. jours. Mem. AAUW, Assn. Mil. Surgeons U.S., Commd. Officers Assn. USPHS.

BRYANT, CHRIS HOUGHTON, forensic chemist, educator; b. Amityville, N.Y., July 6, 1955; d. Thorndike Whittmore and Beverly Ann (Heinrich) Houghton; m. Richard Louis Bryant, May 9, 1987. BA in Chemistry, Roanoke Coll., 1977. Cert. clin. chemist. Clin. chemist Lewis Gale Hosp., Salem, Va., 1976-80; forensic chemist State of Va., Roanoke, 1980-83, supr. forensic chemist, 1983—; instr. forensic sci. Va. We. C.C., Roanoke, 1981—, criminal justice adv. bd., 1992—. Bd. com. mem. Va. Combined Charitable Campaign, Roanoke, 1994—. Mem. Mid Atlantic Assn. Forensic Scientists. Office: Divsn Forensic Science 6600 Northside HS Rd Roanoke VA 24019

BRYANT, DOUGLAS E., public health service official. BS in Health Edn., U. S.C., 1976, MPH, 1981. Communicable disease investigator S.C. Dept. Health & Environ. Control, 1976-78, dist. dir. Upper Savannah Health Dist., 1982-85, dir. office primary care, 1986-87, asst. to commr., 1987-93, commr., 1993—; dir. specialized health care svcs. S.C. Dept. Corrections, 1978-81; asst. adminstr. State Pk. Health Ctr., 1981-82; interim exec. dir. Orangeburg Family Health Ctrs., Inc., 1985-86; adj. prof. dept. health adminstrn. U. S.C.; mem. AHEC Rural Physician adv. bd.; mem. adv. bd. Athletic Trainers. Mem. adv. bd., bd. visitors Lander Coll. Mem. Am. Coll. Hosp. Adminstrs., S.C. Pub. Health Assn., So. Health Assn., Delta Omega. Office: Dept Health & Environ Control 2600 Bull St Columbia SC 29201-1708

BRYANT, LESTER R., surgeon, educator; b. Louisville, Sept. 8, 1930; s. L.R. and Pearl Bryant; m. Linda H. Fletcher; children—Leslie Bond, Lance Bryant. B.S. with high distinction, U. Ky., 1951; M.D., U. Cin., 1955, D.Sc. in Surgery, 1962. Diplomate: Am. Bd. Surgery., Am. Bd. Thoracic Surgery. Intern Cin. Gen. Hosp., 1955-56, asst. resident in surgery, 1956-61, chief resident in surgery, 1961-62; fellow in physiology Baylor U. Coll. Medicine, 1961; mem. faculty U. Ky. Coll. Medicine, 1962-73, prof., 1969-73, chief div. cardiothoracic surgery, 1967-73, vice chmn. dept. surgery, 1972-73; prof. surgery, chief sect. thoracic and cardiovascular surgery La. State U., 1973-77; prof., chmn. dept. surgery East Tenn. State U. Coll. Medicine, Johnson City, 1977-85; cons. VA Hosp., Johnson City, 1977-85; attending staff Med. Center Hosp., Johnson City, 1978-85; v.p. health scis., dean Sch. Medicine, Marshall U., Huntington, WV, 1985-88; dean Med. Sch., U. Mo., 1989—; chmn. Surg. Merit Rev. Bd, VA, 1972-76; mem. anesthetic and life support drugs adv. com. HEW, Pub. Health Svc., FDA, Washington, 1975-80; mem. rsch. com. Tenn. affiliate Am. Heart Assn., 1978-80; vis. prof. U. Hong Kong, 1968; mem. spl. med. adv. group Dept. Vets. Affairs, 1993—. Contbr. articles to med. jours. Fellow A.C.S., Am. Heart Assn.; mem. Am. Assn. Thoracic Surgery, Am. Surg. Assn., Am. Coll. Chest Physicians, Central Surg. Assn., Soc. Thoracic Surgeons, Soc. Surg. Chmn., Soc. Univ. Surgeons, So. Surg. Assn., So. Thoracic Surg. Assn., U. Cin. Grad. Surg. Soc., Phi Beta Kappa, Alpha Omega Alpha, Pi Kappa Epsilon. Office: U Mo Columbia Sch Medicine MA 204 Medical Scis Bldg Columbia MO 65212

BRYANT, RICHARD MILES, retired clinical psychologist; b. Princeton, Ill., June 6, 1932; s. Miles William and Amanda (Kaar) B.; m. Patricia Ruth Patton, Aug. 20, 1955; children—Richard Miles, Jr., William Patton, Melissa Ruth. B.A., Washington U., St. Louis, 1954; student U. Iowa, 1954-55; Ph.D., U. Tex., 1958. Diplomate Am. Bd. Profl. Psychology. Chief clin. psychology sect. Mental Hygiene Consultation Service, Ft. Leonard Wood, Mo., 1958-60; supr. psychol. services Juvenile Residential Treatment Program, State Hosp., Fulton, Mo., 1960-63; part-time asst. prof. psychology Lincoln U., Jefferson City, Mo., 1960-63; spl. lectr. William Woods Coll., Fulton, Mo., 1960-63; sr. clin. psychologist Children's Med. Ctr., Tulsa, 1963-64, dir. psychol. services, 1964-75; pvt. practice clin. psychology, Tulsa, 1975-90; ret. 1990; past chmn. Okla. Bd. Examiners Psychologists. Mem. Am. Psychol. Assn., Midwestern Psychol. Assn., Southwestern Psychol. Assn., Okla. Psychol. Assn. (sec.-treas. 1969-71, pres. 1972-73), Am. Soc. Clin. Hypnosis, Tulsa Psychol. Assn. (past pres.), Sigma Xi, Kappa Alpha. Home: 5353 S Joplin Ave Tulsa OK 74135-7560

BRYANT, STEWART JAMES, pathologist; b. Maryborough, Queensland, Australia, June 3, 1939; s. James Dudley and Jean McVittee (Cunningham) B.; m. Lynette June Maskell, Sept. 7, 1963; children: Peter, Jonathan, Nicholas. MB, BS, Univ. Queensland, Brisbane, 1963. Intern Royal Brisbane Hosp., 1963-64, pathology registrar, 1965-69, chem. pathologist, 1970-72, dir. chem. pathology, 1973-82, dir. pathology svcs., 1982—, 1982-95; gen. mgr. Southpath St. George Hosp., Australia, 1995—; assoc. mem. commn. on quantites and units Internat. Union of Pure and Applied Chemistry., London, 1989—; del. commn. on world standards World Assn. Societies of Pathology., Northfield, Ill., 1990—. Contbr. articles to profl. jours. Fellow Royal Coll. Pathologists Australasia (bd. censors 1978-85, chmn. quality assurance and sci. edn. com. 1988—, rsch. grantee 1979); mem. Australian Assn. Clin. Biochemists, Am. Assn. Clin. Chemistry, Coll. Am. Pathologists (assoc.), Tattersal's Club, Untied Svcs. Club. Home: Hill-Side Smalls Rd, Highvale, Queensland 4520, Australia Office: Southpath, St George Hosp, Kogarah NSW 2217, Australia

BRYANT, THOMAS EDWARD, physician, lawyer; b. Bellamy, Ala., Jan. 17, 1936; s. Howard Edward and Alibel (Nettles) B.; m. Lucie Elizabeth Thrasher, July 9, 1961; children: Thomas Edward, Evelyn Thaxton. A.B., Emory U., 1958, M.D., 1962, J.D., 1967. Bar: Ga. 1967. Intern Grady Meml. Hosp., Atlanta, 1962-63; dir. health affairs OEO, Washington, 1969-71; pres. Nat. Drug Abuse Council, 1971-79; chmn., dir. Pres.'s Commn. Mental Health, 1977-79; chmn. Aspirin Found. of Am., 1987—. Pres. Friends of Nat. Library of Medicine, 1985—. Served with USAF, 1963-65. Recipient Exceptional Service award OEO, 1971. Mem. Ga. Bar Assn., D.C. Bar Assn., Nat. Acad. Scis., Inst. Medicine. Democrat. Clubs: Cosmos (Washington); Century Assn. (N.Y.C.). Office: Non Profit Mgmt Assocs Inc 1555 Connecticut Ave NW Ste 200 Washington DC 20036-1111

BRYK, DAVID, physician; b. N.Y.C., Nov. 23, 1929; s. Zorah and Bertha (Jacobson) B.; married; children: Eli Marc, Joel Daniel, Hillel Benjmin. B.S., CCNY, 1949; M.D., SUNY Downstate Med. Ctr., Buffalo, 1953. Intern, Maimonides Hosp., Bklyn., 1953-54; resident in radiology Mt. Sinai Hosp., N.Y.C., 1954, 1957-59; private practice specializing in radiology, Phila., 1959-61; clin. instr. to clin. prof. SUNY Downstate Med. Ctr., Bklyn., 1962-74, prof., 1974—; instr., asst. radiologist, Jefferson U., Phila., 1959-60; bd. dir. radiology Jewish Hosp., Bklyn., 1967-78; asst. dir. radiology Maimonides Hosp., Bklyn., 1961-67, bd. dir. radiology, 1979-94, chmn. radiology, 1995—. Lectr. in field. Contbr. 88 articles to profl. jours, 4 exhibits at nat. convs. Democrat. Jewish. Office: Mainmonides Hosp 4802 10th Ave Brooklyn NY 11219-2916

BRYT, ALBERT, psychiatrist; b. Marburg, Germany, Mar. 8, 1913; came to U.S., 1944; s. David Naftula and Rajzla (Malc) B.; m. Meta Sebag, June 17, 1935 (div. 1943); m. Natalie Lewy, April 19, 1957; children: Marguerite Maude, Allison Bartley. BS, Oberrealschule, Butzbach, Germany, 1932; PCN in Natural Sciences, Ecole de Plein Exercise, Tours, France, 1934; MD, U. de la Sorbonne, Paris, 1939; cert. in psychoanalysis, William Alanson White Inst., N.Y.C., 1950. Diplomate Am. Bd. Psychiatry and Neurology. Pvt. practice Tunisia, 1941-44; fellow, intern, resident, jr. psychiatrist Bellevue Hosp., N.Y.C., 1945-47; pvt. practice N.Y.C., 1947-95; psychiatrist in charge Adolescent Girls Ward Bellevue Hosp., 1949; chief Adolescent Outpatient Univ. Hosp., N.Y.C., 1951-57; supr., clin. dir. Northside Ctr. Child Devel., N.Y.C., 1957-60; psychiatrist in charge Adolescent Outpatient Bellevue Hosp., 1964-70; resident tng. Adolescent Psychiatry NYU-Bellevue Med Ctr., 1970-72; cons. psychiatrist Human Resource Adminstrn. City of N.Y., 1978-89; team psychiatrist Project Assist Manhattan Children's Psychiat. Ctr., N.Y.C., 1989; project assist Queens Children's Psychiatric Hosp., N.Y.C., 1995; mem. attending staff Univ. Hosp., N.Y.C., 1950; vis. neuro-psychiatrist Bellevue Hosp. Ctr., 1950; mem. exec. com., dir. of curriculum William Alanson White Inst., 1960, 62, 64-67, 69-71; cons. Luth. Community Svcs., 1954—; cons. The Salvation Army Social Svcs. for Children, 1975-90; cons. Dept. Mental Health, State of N.Y. Co-author: Facial Disfigurement and Plastic Surgery, 1953; contbr. to other books, scientific jours. With French Army Med. Corps, 1940. Named team psychiatrist USPH Rsch. Grant, NYU-Bellevue, 1948-51. Fellow Am. Psychiat. Assn. (life), N.Y. Soc. for Adolescent Psychiatry; mem. N.Y. Coun. on Child Psychiatry, William Alanson White Psychoanalytic Soc. (treas. 1954-56, com. on ethics 1989). Democrat. Jewish. Home and Office: 130 E 75th St New York NY 10021-3277

BUBRICK, MELVIN PHILLIP, surgeon; b. Chgo., June 2, 1944; m. Barbara Lynn Jacobs, Jan. 26, 1969; children: Jerome Bradley, Ellen Jeanne, Dena Beth. BA with honors, U. Ill., 1964, MD, 1968. Diplomate Am. Bd. Surgery, Am. Bd. Colon and Rectal Surgery; lic Minn. Intern in surgery Univ. Hosps., Madison, Wis., 1968-69; resident in gen. surgery Hennepin County Gen. Hosp., Mpls., 1969-74; postdoctoral fellow colon and rectal surgery U. Minn. Health Scis. Ctr., Mpls., 1974-75; clin. instr. div. colon and rectal surgery U. Minn., Mpls., 1975-77, clin. asst. prof., 1977-78, clin. asst. prof. dept. surgery, 1978-80, asst. prof., 1980-87, assoc. prof., 1987—; chief surgery, program dir. surg. residency Hennepin County Med. Ctr., 1988-94; pres., CEO Hennepin Faculty Assocs., 1995—; v.p. Mpls. Med. Rsch. Found., 1991-95; chmn. bd. dirs. Hennepin Faculty Assocs., 1991—, pres., CEO, 1995—. Author: (with others) Conn's Therapy, 1985, The Pancreas. Principles of Medical and Surgical Practice, 1985, Applied Therapeutics: The clinical use of drugs, 4th rev. edit., 1988; contbr. over 90 articles to Minn. Med. jour., Am. Surg. jour., Diseases of Colon and Rectum, Surgery, others. Bd. dirs. Mpls. Med. Rsch. Found., Inc., 1981-89. Mem. AMA, ACS, Am. Assn. Surgery of Trauma, Am. Soc. Colon and Rectal Surgeons (co-chair Self Assessment Exam. Com. 1984-85), Am. Soc. Microbiology, Assn. Program Dirs. of Surgery, Cen. Surg. Assn., Collegium Internat. Chirurgiae Digestivae, Soc. Surgery of Alimentary Tract, Minn. Assn. Pub. Teaching Hosps., Minn. Surg. Soc., Minn. Med. Assn., Mpls. Surg. Soc., Hennepin County Med. Soc. (mem. and chair various coms. 1975—, Hennepin faculty assoc. 1983—).

BUCAN, TERRY LYNN, emergency medicine physician; b. Salina, Kans., June 25, 1957; d. Donald John and Mary Barbara (Piper) Bodelin; m. Fredrick Michael Bucan, Dec. 27, 1953; children: Michael Fredrick, Casey Meredith. DO, Mich. State U., 1985. Cert. instr. advanced cardiac life support Am. Heart Assn., cert. in advanced cardiac life support, advanced pediatric life support. Intern Botsford Gen. Hosp., Farmington Hills, Mich., 1985-86; resident in emergency medicine Botsford Gen. Hosp., 1986-88; attending physician emergency medicine Elliott White Springs Meml. Hosp., Lancaster, S.C., 1988-89, Georgetown (S.C.) Meml. Hosp., 1989—. Mem. Am. Osteopathic Assn., Am. Coll. Osteopathic Emergency Physicians, So. Med. Assn. Office: Georgetown Meml Hosp 606 Black River Rd Georgetown SC 29442 Address: 5 Raintree Ln Pawleys Island SC 29585-6428

BUCCINI, FRANK JOHN, molecular geneticist; b. Jersey City, Mar. 28, 1959; s. Frank George and Catherine Mary (Kamrowski) B.; m. Judith Patricia Frazier, May 26, 1984; 1 child, Michelle Catherine. BS, Seton Hall U., 1981, MS, 1985. Cert. qualifications lab. technician and supr., N.Y.; cert. lab. supr., N.J. Med. rsch. technician VA Med. Ctr., East Orange, N.J., 1983-87; microbiology lab. mgr. Gen. Care Biomed. Rsch. Corp., Mountainside, N.J., 1987-88, supr. cancer immunology lab., 1988—; supr. molecular genetics lab. Gen. Care Biomed. Rsch. Corp., Mountainside, 1987-95; lab. supr. Bio-Reference Lab./GenCare Biomed., 1995—. Contbr. articles to sci. jours. Mem. Theobald Smith Soc., Am. Soc. for Microbiology, N.J. Acad. Sci., Sigma Xi. Office: Bio-Reference Labs Gen-Care Divsn 481 Edward H Ross Dr Elmwood Park NJ 07407

BUCETA, JOSEPH BENITO, psychiatrist; b. Pontevedra, Spain, Oct. 3, 1950; came to U.S., 1979; s. Jose and Peregrina (Santos) B.; m. Margarita Clavijo, Nov. 4, 1983. Cert. in English, Cambridge U., England, 1973; MD, U. Uruguay, 1978; PhD in Psychology, Inst. Psychology Uruguay, 1979. Intern PGY-I pediatrics Perth Amboy Gen. Hosp., Perth Amboy, N.J., 1981-82; PGY-I to IV psychiatry Brookdale Hosp., SUNY, Bklyn., 1982-86; child psychiatry fellow St. Luke's-N.Y. Psychiat. Inst., N.Y.C., 1986-88; fellow coll. physicians & surgeons Columbia U., N.Y.C., 1988; acad. appointee St. Luke's-Roosevelt Med. Ctr., N.Y.C., 1988, Coll. Physicians & Surgeons, N.Y.C., 1988; chief behavioral program Essex County Med. Ctr., Cedar Grove, N.J., 1988; pvt. practice psychiatry Cresskill, N.J., 1988—; asst. med. dir. Greystone Psychiat. Hosp., Greystone Park, N.J., 1989; chief outpatient dept. Lyons (N.J.) VA Hosp., 1990; outpatient psychiatrist Cath. Cmty. Charities, Newark, 1995—; expert witness appointee in child psychiatry N.J. Supreme Ct., 1988. Master Freemasonry, Uruguay, U.S., 1979; artisan Rosicrucian Order, San Jose, Calif., 1978. Grantee for outstanding med. studies Govt. of Spain, 1970-79; recipient scholarship to attend 1st Uruguayan Congress on Human Reproduction, Montevideo, 1977; named fellow nominee Group for the Advancemnt of Psychiatry, 1984. Fellow Coll. Physicians & Surgeons. Republican. Roman Catholic. Office: Greystone Pk Psychiat Hosp Main Building Fl 3 Greystone Park NJ 07950

BUCHALTER, PERRY M., health facility director; b. Cleve., Jan. 24, 1957. BS, Fla. Atlantic U., 1979. Dir. sales and mktg. Metpath, Deerfield Beach, Fla., 1979-93; dir. managed care Corning Clin. Labs., Deerfield Beach, Fla., 1993—. Office: Corning 1300 E Newport Ctr Dr Deerfield Beach FL 33442-7727

BUCHAN, RONALD FORBES, preventive medicine physician; b. Concord, N.H., Sept. 24, 1915; s. Robert and Mary Jean (Forbes) B.; m. Maureen O'Regan, June 17, 1940; children: Robert Bruce, Joan Dallas (Mrs. Fleming), Ian Forbes Morgan. A.B., U. N.H., 1936; M.D., C.M., McGill U., 1942; postgrad., Princeton U., 1958. Diplomate Nat. Bd. Med. Examiners, Am. Bd. Preventive Medicine. Reporter Concord Daily Monitor, 1936; asst. exec. sec. Unemployment Compensation Commn., N.H. Dept. Labor, 1937; sanitarian City of Concord and Eastern Health Dist. N.H., 1938; chief med. unit Bur. Indsl. Hygiene, Conn. Dept. Health, 1943-46; dir. Hartford Small Plant Indsl. Med. Svcs., 1946; clin. dir., asst. prof. indsl. medicine Yale U. Inst. Occupational Medicine and Hygiene, 1946-48; assoc. clin. prof. indsl. medicine N.Y.U. Bellevue Post Grad. Med. Sch., 1948-57; assoc. med. dir. Prudential Ins. Co. Am., 1948-49, dir. employee health, 1949-57; med. dir., v.p. med. svcs. Prudential Ins. Co. Am., Boston, 1957-74, cons. occupational medicine, environ. medicine, toxicology, 1974—; chief med. dir., v.p. Mediscreen, 1974-87; propr. Portsmouth (N.H.) Athenaeum; assoc. clin. prof. preventive medicine Tufts U. Sch. Medicine, 1958-74; vis. lectr. numerous med. schs., 1948-89. Narrator (audio hist. tour) The Freedom Trail, Boston, (audio visual hist. survey) Shipbuilding on the Kennebec-Maine Maritime Mus.; author: Industrial Toxicology; contbr. Oxford Medicine, Current Therapy, Occupational Medicine, Encyclopedia-Medico-Chirurgicale (Paris); also numerous articles to profl. and lit. jours. Chmn. rsch. adv. com. Brattleboro (Vt.) Retreat, 1960-70; mem. sci. adv. bd. Office Chief Staff USAF, chmn. life scis. human factors facilities, 1960-65, protocol rank, lt. gen.; cons. R.I. Group Health Assn., 1973-75 Harvard Community Health Plan, 1972-75; bd. dirs. Met. Boston chpt. ARC, 1971-73, chmn. com. on safety, 1972-74; founding mem. Challenger Space Ctr., 1987; trustee Miles Meml. Hosp., Damariscotta, Maine, 1988-91. Sr. asst. surg., USPHS, 1943-46; surgeon-lt. York (Maine) Militia-Gov.'s Footguard, 1971—. Recipient Honor award Wisdom Soc., 1970. Fellow Am. Coll. Occupl. and Environ. Medicine (past pres.), Am. Coll. Preventive Medicine (chmn. com. on clin. procedures 1972-74), Am. Acad. Occupl. Medicine (past pres.), Acad. Medicine N.J. (past pres.); mem. AAAS, Am. Indsl. Hygiene Assn., Am. Acad. Ins. Medicine, AMA (assoc. editor Archives Environ. Health), Assn. Internationale Pour La Medicine Du Travail (permanent commn. 1955-74), Mass. Med. Soc., Ramazzini Soc., Academie Europeene des Arts, Sciences et des Lettres, Am. Assn. Sr. Physicians, N.Y. Acad. Scis., Nat. Trust Hist. Preservation, Soc. for Preservation of New Eng. Antiquities, John Buchan Soc. (Edinburgh), Osler Libr. (patron McGill U., Montreal), Soc. for Protection of N.H. Forests, North Country Authors and Scientists League (past pres.), Newcomen Soc. N.Am., St. Andrew's Soc. of Maine, Can. Hist. Soc., Clan Buchan U.S.A., Clan Forbes U.S.A., U.N.H. Alumni Assn. (gen. awards com. 1987-90, sec. U.N.H. class of '36, 1981—), McGill U. Alumni Assn., Friends of Bowdoin Coll. Home: Hill Winds 1611 Clarry Hill Rd Union ME 04862-9500

BUCHANAN, JOHN DONALD, health physicist, radiochemist; b. Mesa, Ariz., Oct. 1, 1927; s. John Freeborn and Marguerite (Brimhall) B.; m. Donna Marie Smith, Aug. 27, 1955; children—Margaret MacNeil, John Michael, Andrew Tierney, David Brimhall. B.S. in Chemistry, U. Ariz., 1949. Diplomate: Am. Bd. Health Physics, Nat. Cert. Commn. in Chemistry and Chem. Engring. Sr. chemist Tracerlab, Inc., Richmond, Calif., 1950-59; staff asso. Gen. Atomic div. Gen. Dynamics Corp., San Diego, 1959-62; mgr. nuclear applications and measurements Teledyne-Isotopes Co., Palo Alto, Calif., 1962-71; mgr. applied research Internat. Nutronics Inc., Palo Alto, 1971-73; supr. radiol. monitoring programs NUS Corp., Rockville, Md., 1973-75; sr. health physicist, radiochemist U.S. Nuclear Regulatory Commn., Washington, 1975-94. Author papers on radiation protection, radioanalytical chemistry, radioactivity measurements, radioisotope applications. Served with USNR, 1945-46. Recipient Meritorious Service award U.S. Nuclear Regulatory Commn., 1981. Fellow AAAS, Am. Inst. Chemists, Health Physics Soc.; mem. Am. Nuclear Soc., Am. Chem. Soc., Soc. for Risk Analysis, Am. Acad. Health Physics, Phi Lambda Upsilon, Phi Delta Theta. Home: 7508 Dew Wood Dr Rockville MD 20855-1007

BUCHANAN, JOHN ROBERT, physician, educator; b. Newark, Mar. 8, 1928; s. John Hamilton and Elsie (Castles) B.; m. Susan Townsend Carver, Oct. 27, 1962; children: Ross, Allyn. A.B. cum laude, Amherst Coll., 1950; M.D., Cornell U., 1954; student, Inst. Arthritis and Metabolic Diseases, USPHS, 1956-57, 60-61. Diplomate: Am. Bd. Internal Medicine, Nat. Bd. Med. Examiners. Intern N.Y. Meml. Hosp., N.Y.C., 1954-55, resident physician, 1955-58; physician to outpatients N.Y. Meml. Hosp., 1960-62; from asst. to assoc. attending physician N.Y. Hosp., 1962-71, attending physician, 1971-76, assoc. dir. welfare med. care project, 1961-64; vis. asst. physician Rockefeller Inst. Hosp., N.Y.C., 1960-61; assoc. vis. physician Bellevue Hosp., N.Y.C., 1965-68; fellow Cornell U., 1956-57, instr. medicine, 1961-63, asst. prof. medicine, 1963-67, asst. dir. comprehensive care and teaching program, 1961-64, asst. to chmn. dept. medicine, 1964-65; assoc. dean Cornell U. (Med. Coll.), 1965-69, dean, 1969-76, clin. assoc. prof. medicine, 1967-69, assoc. prof., 1969-71, prof., 1971-76; pres. Michael Reese Hosp. and Med. Center, Chgo., 1977-82; prof. medicine Pritzker Sch. Medicine, U. Chgo., 1977-82, assoc. dean, 1978-82; gen. dir. Mass. Gen. Hosp., Boston, 1982-94, gen. dir. emeritus, 1994—; mem. com. on sci. policy Sloan-Kettering Inst., 1969-76, State of Ill. Med. Determination Bd., 1980-82, adminstrv. bd. Coun. Teaching Hosps., 1984-89; mem. composite com. of U.S. Med. Licensing Exam sponsored by Nat. Bd. Med. Examiners, Fedn. of State Bd. Med. Examiners, and Ednl. Coun. Fgn. Med. Grads.; sr. program cons. prepaid managed health care program Robert Wood Johnson Found., 1982-85; bd. dirs. Charles River Labs., AMI Holdings, Strategic Mgmt. Info. Inc., Hybridon, Well Care; chmn. Am. Telemedicine Internat.; trustee Ednl. Commn. Fgn. Med. Grads., 1989—, vice-chmn., 1929-93, chmn., 1994—. Chmn. nat. adv. coun. Children's TV Workshop, 1974-75; bd. dirs. Pub. Health Rsch. Inst. of N.Y.C., 1969-76, Winnifred Masterson Burke Relief Found., 1972-80, 82-88; trustee Cornell U., 1970-76; trustee China Med. Bd. of N.Y., Inc., 1970—, vice-chmn., chmn., 1989—; bd. mgrs. Meml. Hosp., 1969-76; mem. adv. com. Edwin L. Crosby and W.K. Kellogg Found. Fellowships, 1979-80; trustee Ctr. for Effective Philanthropy, 1981-85; trustee Aga Khan U., Karachi, Pakistan; mem. coordinating com. Boston Bus. Roundtable. Fellow ACP, Am. Pub. Health Assn.; mem. Harvey Soc., N.J. State Med. Soc., N.Y. County Med. Soc., N.Y. Acad. Sci. (coun. of deans 1969-76, exec. coun. 1971-76, chmn.-elect assembly 1990-91, chair assembly 1991-92), Assn. Am. Med. Colls. (vice chmn. liaison com. on med. edn. 1982-83, chmn., 1983, 91, chmn. elect coun. teaching hosps. 1987, chmn. 1988-89), Assn. Med. Schs. N.Y. N.J. (trustee 1970-76, pres. 1972-76), Inst. Medicine Nat. Acad. Scis., Ill. Hosp. Assn. (chmn. 1979-80), N.Y. Acad. Medicine, Mass. Hosp. Assn. (chmn.-elect 1989-90, chmn. 1990-91), Pvt. Industry Coun. Boston, Vol. Hosps. Am. (bd. dirs. 1990). Home: 19 Shipways Charlestown MA 02129 Office: RSTAR/ATI One Cambridge Ctr Cambridge MA 02138

BUCHANAN, PATRICIA R., geriatrics nurse; b. Johnstown, Pa., July 27, 1950; d. John and Mary M. (Everhart) Rachael; m. Randy W. Buchanan, July 23, 1977. Diploma in nursing, Mercy Hosp. Sch. Nursing, Johnstown, 1971; BSN cum laude, U. Pitts., 1985. RN, Pa. Staff nurse Lee Hosp., Johnstown, 1971-73; health facility quality examiner, divsn. nursing care Pa. Dept. Health, Ebensburg, 1973-84, supr., 1984—. Office: Pa Dept Health Divsn Nursing Care Facilities 650 Indsl Park Rd Ebensburg PA 15931-4108

BUCHANAN, WILLIAM LEE, psychologist; b. Atlanta, July 23, 1954; s. Taylor G. and Elizabeth (Chambliss) B.; m. Linda Paulk, Dec. 3, 1983. BA with honors, Emory U., 1976; MS, U. So. Miss., 1982; PhD, Ga. State U., 1987. Marital and family therapist Associated Counseling Svcs., Snellville, Ga., 1984-86; psychology intern U. Okla. Health Scis. Ctr., Oklahoma City, 1986-87; asst. dir. dept. clin. psychology and neuropsychology Northeast Ga. Med. Ctr., Gainesville, Ga., 1987-90; pvt. practice, psychologist Affiliated Psychol. and Med. Cons., Gainesville, 1990—; cons., supr. Eagle Ranch for Boys, Chestnut Mountain, Ga., 1985—, Family Rels. Prog., Gainesville, 1989-91; cons./behaviorist New Direction Weight Loss Prog./N.E. Ga. Med. Ctr., Gainesville, 1989-94. Co-author: Dictionary of Family Psychology and Family Therapy, 1991; contbg. author: Eating Disorder, 1991, Obesity, 1991. Mem. APA, Am. Assn. Marital and Family Therapy (clin. mem., approved supr.), Ga. Psychol. Assn. (chmn. for legal and legis. com. 1991—, past chmn. hosp. practice com., past treas. divsn. E), Internat. Neuropsychol. Soc., Nat. Acad. Neuropsychology, Assn. for Advancement of Behavior Therapy. Presbyterian. Office: Affiliated Psychol/Med Cons Ste 400 200 S Enota Dr NE Gainesville GA 30501-3466

BUCHBINDER, MAURICE, cardiologist; b. June 23, 1953; came to U.S., 1979; s. Jacob and Henriette (Jejati) B.; m. Lani Susan, May 5, 1956; children: Jaimie Lauren, Natalie Cara. BS, McGill U., 1974, MD, 1978. Cert. specialist in cardiovascular disease. Intern in internal medicine Montreal, 1980; resident in cardiology Stanford, Calif., 1981-83; asst. prof. of medicine/cardiology U. Calif. San Diego, 1985-95; dir. interventional cardiology Sharp Healthcare, San Diego, Calif., 1995—; founder Versaflex, Inc., San Diego, 1983-88; cons., chief of cardiology Scripps Hosp., San Diego, 1995-97. Fellow Am. Coll. Cardiology. Office: Found for Cardiovascular Medicine 7901 Frost St San Diego CA 92123

BUCHBINDER, SHARON BELL, health science educator; b. Washington, Nov. 27, 1951; d. James Wright and Effie Naomi (Rhodes) Bell; m. Dale Buchbinder, May 9, 1976; 1 child, Joshua Harlow. BA in Psychology, U. Conn., 1973; MA in Psychology, U. Hartford, 1976; AAS in Nursing, SUNY, Albany, 1981; PhD iin Pub. Health Scis., U. Ill., Chgo., 1992. RN, Md. Intravenous technician dept. intravenous therapy Hartford (Conn.) Hosp., 1974-76; supr. dept. intravenous therapy Albany Med. Ctr. Hosp., N.Y., 1976-80; asst. rsch. scientist N.Y. Dept. Mental Hygiene, Albany, 1980-81; staff specialist Nat. Commn. on Nursing, Chgo., 1982-83; staff specialist divsn. nursing Am. Hosp. Assn., Chgo., 1983-84; sr. rsch. assoc. divsn. evaluation and nomenclature med. terminology and nomenclature AMA, Chgo., 1984-86, exec. asst., 1986-88, mktg. exec., 1988-89, asst. dept. dir. dept. preventive medicine, 1989-90; dir. devel. Norbel Sch., 1990-91; postdoctoral fellow in children's mental health svcs. Sch. Hygiene and Pub. Health Johns Hopkins U., Balt., 1993-94, sr. staff rsch. coord. dept. pediats. Sch. Medicine, 1994-95, rsch. assoc. dept. pediats. Sch. Medicine, 1995-96; asst. prof. dept. health scis. Towson State U., Md., 1996—. Contbr. articles to profl. jours., chpts. to books; spkr. in field. Recipient rsch. grant Mut. Life Ins. Co. of N.Y., 1986. Mem. NAFE, AAUW, APA, APHA, Acad. of Mgmt., N.Y. Acad. Scis., Assn. for Health Svcs. Rsch., Phi Kappa Phi, Delta Omega (mem. Lambda chpt.). Democrat. Jewish.

BUCHHOLZ, JOHN NICHOLAS, pharmacology educator; b. Cahose, N.Y., Nov. 2, 1956; s. Walter Lawrence and Teresa Marie (Touzin) B.; m. Melisa Audrey Erick, June 22, 1981 (div. Apr. 1987); 1 child, Nickolaus Erick. BS, Loma Linda U., 1980, MS, 1983, PhD, 1988. Asst. prof., asst. rsch. Loma Linda U., U. Calif., Irvine, 1991—; cons. Allergan Pharms., Irvine, 1990—. Contbr. articles to profl. jours. Fellowship Am. Heart Assn., 1989, NIH, 1991; rsch. grant Am. Fedn. Aging Rsch. 1992. Mem. Soc. for Neurosci., Sigma Xi. Republican. Home: 12168 Mount Vernon Ave Apt 36 Grand Terrace CA 92313-5542 Office: U Calif Dept Pharmacology Irvine CA 92717

BUCHIN, JEAN, psychologist; b. N.Y.C.; d. Mac and Celia Jacobs; BA, CUNY, 1941; MA, Tchrs. Coll. Columbia U., 1948; PhD, NYU, 1965; m. May 18, 1941; children: Peter J., John D. Tchr., N.Y.C. Pub. Schs., 1946-59, part time 1959-62; counselor, asst. prof. CUNY, 1962—; Mem. Nat Bd. Cert. Counselors, Nat. Bd. of Cert. Career Counselors; asst. prof. coord.

Which Way With Women program Baruch Coll., 1980-82; vis. asst. prof. N.Y.U., 1969-72; cons. N.Y.C. Tchrs. Consortium, 1981-85; mgmt. tng. cons. Met. Life Ins. Co., N.Y.C., 1985—; cons. assessment programs N.Y.C. Div. of Pers., Sci. and Tech. Adv. Bd.; cons. N.J. Human Resources Div.; career cons. AARP; lectr., leader workshops 53d St. Y., NYU, Queens Coll., A.W.E.D.; mediator ABA; bd. dirs. Am. Coll. Forensic Examiners. Author: Singular Parent, 1982, Noah's Ark Minus One, 1989. Washington Sq. Coll. fellow, 1961-62. Mem. AAUP, APA (pres. Tri State chpt. Div. 35, 1977—), Am. Counseling Assn., Eastern Psychol. Assn., Met. N.Y. Assn. for Applied Psychology, Bus. and Profl. Women, Career Devel. Specialists Network.

BUCHIN, PETER JAY, physician; b. N.Y.C., Nov. 18, 1948; s. Irv D. and Jean J.; B.A., Williams Coll., 1970; M.D., Yale U., 1974. Diplomate Am. Bd. Internal Medicine, Am. Bd. Gastroenterology, Med. intern Columbia Presbyn. Med. Center, N.Y.C., 1974-75, resident in medicine, 1975-77; fellow in gastroenterology Yale-New Haven Med. Center, 1977-79; practice medicine specializing in internal medicine and gastroenterology, N.Y.C., 1979—; asst. attending physician Columbia Presbyn. Med. Center, 1979-92; asst. prof. Columbia U. Coll. Phys. and Surgs., N.Y.C., 1979-92; asst. attending physician Beth Israel North Divsn., N.Y.C., 1990-92, assoc. attending physician, 1992—; asst. clin. prof. medicine Mt. Sinai Sch. Medicine, N.Y.C., 1992—; asst. attending physician Mt. Sinai Hosp., N.Y.C., 1992—. Diplomate Am. Bd. Internal Medicine, Am. Bd. Gastroenterology. Contbr. articles to profl. jours. Fellow Am. Coll. Gastroenterology; mem. ACP, Williams Coll. Club, Phi Beta Kappa, Sigma Xi. Office: 133 E 73rd St New York NY 10021-3556

BUCHSBAUM, BETTY CYNTHIA, clinical psychologist; b. N.Y.C., May 27, 1927; d. Joseph and Kate (Havel) B.; m. William Weinstein; 1 child, Daniel James. BA, Cornell U., 1948; MA, U. Pa. 1950; PhD, Yeshiva U., 1965. Sch. psychologist N.Y.C. Bur. Child Guidance, 1954-57; staff psychologist Kings County Hosp., Bklyn., 1957-58; from instr. to asst. clin. prof. Jacobi Hosp.-Albert Einstein Coll. Medicine, Bronx, N.Y., 1958-67; chief psychology Ctr. for Preventive Psychiatry, White Plains, N.Y., 1967-68; asst. prof. Bellevue Hosp-N.Y. Med. Coll., N.Y.C., 1968-69; pvt. practice clin psychology Rye, N.Y., 1969-96; clin. asst. prof. N.Y. Hosp.-Cornell Med. Ctr., Westchester Div., White Plains, 1976-82, adj. clin. asst. prof., 1982—; asst. clin. prof. Albert Einstein Coll. Medicine, 1981-86; dir. psychology tng. program Ctr. for Preventive Psychiatry, 1986—. Contbr. chpts. to books and articles to jours.; researcher in parent loss in childhood. Mem. Am. Psychol. Assn., Westchester County Psychol. Assn., Phi Beta Kappa, Psi Chi, Phi Kappa Phi. Democrat. Address: 515 Greenhaven Rd Rye NY 10580-1016

BUCHSBAUM, DONALD JAY, immunology educator, researcher; b. N.Y.C., Mar. 27, 1945; s. Milton Buchsbaum and Estelle (Cerkos) Rapoport; children: Donelle, Lisa. BS, Carnegie Inst. Tech., 1967; MS, U. Rochester, 1970, PhD, 1972. Teaching asst. U. Rochester, N.Y., 1967-69; rsch. assoc. U. Minn., Mpls., 1972-74, instr., 1972-75, asst. prof., 1975-85, adj. asst. prof., 1985-90, adj. assoc. prof., 1990-95, adj. prof., 1995—; asst. prof. U. Mich., Ann Arbor, 1985-90; assoc. prof. radiation oncology U. Ala., Birmingham, 1990-95, prof., 1995—; adj. asst. prof. Emory U., Atlanta, 1983-90. Contbr. articles to sci. jours. Grantee Nat. Cancer Inst., NIH, 1975—. Mem. Am. Assn. for Cancer Rsch., Am. Assn. Immunologists, Am. Assn. Physicists in Medicine, Am. Soc. Therapeutic Radiology and Oncology, Soc. Nuclear Medicine. Jewish. Office: U Ala Dept Radiation Oncology 619 19th St S Birmingham AL 35233-1924

BUCHSBAUM, GERSHON, bioengineer, educator; b. Tel-Aviv, July 24, 1949; came to the U.S., 1979; m. Maya Y. Hecht, June 8, 1976; 3 children. BEE, Tel-Aviv U., 1974, MEE, 1975, PhD, 1978; MA (hon.), U. Pa., 1986. Asst. prof. bioengring. U. Pa., Phila., 1979-85, assoc. prof. bioengring., 1985-93, prof., 1993—, chair dept. bioengring., 1996—. Contbr. articles to profl. jours. Named Presdl. Young Investigator NSF, 1984. Fellow IEEE, Optical Soc. Am., Am. Inst. Med. and Biol. Engring. Office: U Pa Dept Bioengring 220 S 33rd St Philadelphia PA 19104-6315

BUCHSIEB, WALTER CHARLES, orthodontist; b. Columbus, Ohio, Aug. 30, 1929; s. Walter William and Emma Marie (Held) B.; BA, Ohio State U., 1951, DDS, 1955, MS, 1960; m. Betty Lou Risch, June 19, 1955; children: Walter Charles II, Christine Ann. Pvt. practice dentistry specializing in orthodontics, Dayton, Ohio, 1959-93; cons. orthodontist Miami Valley Hosp., Childrens Med. Ctr., Dayton; asst. prof. dept. orthodontics Ohio State U. Coll. Dentistry, 1984-93, clinic dir., 1993—. Mem. fin. and program com. United Health Found., 1971-73; mem. dean's adv. com. Ohio State U. Coll. Dentistry; bd. dirs. Hearing and Speech Ctr., 1968-82, 2d v.p., 1976-78, pres., 1978-79; orthodontic advisor Ohio Dept. Health Bur. Crippled Children's Services, 1983-84. Capt. AUS, 1955-58. Fellow Am. Coll. Dentists (pres. Ohio sect. 1988); mem. ADA (alt. del. 1968, del. 1991, coun. on ann. sessions and internat. rels. 1984-88), Am. Assn. Dental Schs., Am. Cleft Palate Assn., Am. Assn. Dental Schs., Internat. Assn. Dental Rsch., Ohio Dental Assn. (sec. coun. legis. 1969-78, v.p. 1978-79, pres.-elect 1979-80, pres. 1980-81, polit. action com. 1987—, Coun. on Constn. and Bi Laws 1988-92, Achievement award 1989), Am. Coll. Dentists (pres. Ohio sect. 1988), Dayton Dental Soc. (pres. 1970-71), Am. Bd. Orthodontics, Great Lakes Soc. Orthodontists (sec.-treas. 1972-75, pres. 1977-78), Internat. Coll. Dentists, Am. Assn. Orthodontists (chmn. council legis. 1976, speaker of house 1982-85, ad hoc com. to revise by-laws, coun. on govtl. affairs, 1988—, recipient James E. Brophy Dist. Svc. award 1992, bd. mem. political action com.), Pierre Fauchard Acad., Coll. of Diplomats Am. Bd. Orthodontics (pres. 1990-91), Ohio State U. Alumni Assn. (advocates group), Delta Upsilon, Psi Omega. Republican. Lutheran (elder 1965-68, v.p. 1974). Clubs: Masons, Rotary (pres. 1973-74, Paul Harris fellow). Home: 4145 Mumford Ct Columbus OH 43220-4435 Office: Ohio State U Orthodontics Dept 305 W 12th Ave Columbus OH 43210-1249

BUCHWALD, JED ZACHARY, environmental health researcher, science history educator; b. N.Y.C., June 25, 1949. BA, Princeton U., 1971; MA, Harvard, 1973, PhD, 1974. Instr., dir. Inst. History Philosophy Sci. and Tech. U. Toronto, 1974-92; prof., dir. Dibner Inst. History Sci. and Tech. MIT. Author: (book) The Creation of Scientific Effects, 1994. Named MacArthur fellow John D. and Katherine T. MacArthur Foundation, 1995; recipient award for excellence in environ. health rsch. Lovelance Inst., Albuquerque, 1995. Office: M I T Dibner Inst History of Science 77 Massachusetts Ave Cambridge MA 02139

BUCHWALD, MAX STANTON, dental surgeon; b. Richardson, Tex., May 7, 1956; s. Rudolph William and Betty Jo (Quickle) B.; m. Rosemary Anne Wichita, July 2, 1977; children: Blair Elizabeth, Maxey Stanton. Student, U. North Tex., 1974-77; DDS, U. Tex. Health Sci. Ctr., San Antonio, 1981. Assoc. dentist Fred Thompson DDS, Inc., Garland, Tex., 1981-82; staff dentist Dallas County Pub. Health, Dallas, 1982-83; owner, pres. Westgrove Dentistry, Addison, Tex., 1986-90, chief staff, 1986-90; owner, pres., dentist Max S. Buchwald, DDS, Richardson, 1981—; practice mgmt. cons. Westgrove Dental Partnerships, Addison, 1986-90. Bd. dirs., elder Messiah Luth. Ch., Richardson, 1988-90, mem. worship com., 1989—; vol. Richardson YMCA, 1984—. Recipient Quotabuster award Richardson YMCA, 1985, 86, 87. Mem. ADA (sustaining mem.), Dallas Orthodontic Study Club (pres. 1986-87), Tex. Dental Assn., Dallas County Dental Soc. (peer rev. com. 1988—), Internat. Assn. Orthodontics, S.W. Assn. Orthodontics (sec., dir. 1988-90), Richardson C. of C. Republican. Home: 1701 Old Course Dr Plano TX 75093-4933 Office: 1805 Promenade Ctr Richardson TX 75080-5489

BUCK, ALFRED ANDREAS, physician, epidemiologist; b. Hamburg, Germany, Mar. 9, 1921; came to U.S., 1958, naturalized, 1967; s. Heino C. and Antonie (Schwarz) B.; m. Kay A. Amann, Sept. 21, 1964; children: Suzanne Karen, Alfred Andreas. M.D. in Pharmacology, U. Hamburg, 1945; M.P.H., Johns Hopkins U., 1959, Dr.P.H., 1961. Med. resident Univ. Hosp., Hamburg, 1945-52; physician, cons. Gen. Govt. Hosp., Makassar, Celebes, Indonesia, 1952- 55; head physician Red Cross Hosp., Pusan, Korea, 1955-58; mem. faculty Johns Hopkins U., Balt., 1963—, prof. epidemiology and internat. health, 1968-92, prof. immunology and infectious diseases, 1986-92, dir. div. bacteriology and mycology Sch. Hygiene, 1967-72, chmn. tropical medicine council, 1973-74, also research dir., geog. epidemiology group; dep. dir. Vector-Borne Disease Project, Arlington, Va.; adj. prof. immunology and infectious diseases Johns Hopkins U., Balt.; cons. AID, Ethiopia, 1962-64, West and Ctrl. Africa, 1971; mem. sr. staff WHO, Geneva, 1971-73, chief med. officer divsn. malaria and other parasitic diseases, 1974-78, chief rsch. coordination, epidemiology and tng. and sec. sci. working group for epidemiology, spl. program rsch. and tng. in tropical diseases; tropical medicine adv. Office of Health, Dept. State, AID, Washington, 1978-88; adj. prof. Immunology and Infectious Diseases, Johns Hopkins U.; adj. prof. tropical medicine Tulane U., 1988—; vis. prof. Sch. of Medicine Ain Shams U., Cairo; vis. prof. Sch. of Medicine, Hannover, Germany, 1991—; expert tropical medicine NIH/NIAID; resident scientist, Cairo; mem. Steering Coms. of Sci. Working Groups "Fieldmal" and "Epidemiology" of WHO, Geneva. Author books; contbr. articles in field; asso. editor: Tropenmedizin und Parasitologie. Recipient Meritorious Honor award Dept. State, 1980, Bernhard Nocht medal in tropical medicine, 1981, Meritorious Svc. award USAID, 1985, Superior Unit citation, 1991, AID/Dept. State Meritorious Svc. award, 1986, Spl. award DHHS/NIH, 1991, Donald Mackay medal in tropical medicine jointly Am. Soc. Tropical Medicine and Hygiene and Royal Soc. Tropical Medicine, 1995; hon. fellow in tropical medicine Faculty Liverpool Sch. Tropical Medicine, 1982. Fellow APHA, Am. Coll. Epidemiology; mem. Epidemiol. Rsch. Assn., Am. Soc. Tropical Medicine, Internat. Epidemiologic Soc., Am. Epidemiol. Soc., Tropical Medicine Assn. D.C., Delta Omega. Lutheran. Home: 1603 East Ave Mc Lean VA 22101-4105

BUCK, DAVID S., physician; b. Houston, Dec. 12, 1960; s. Larry W. and Lois Bobbie (Kieters) B.; m. Valerie Howarth Ross, Oct. 8, 1994; 1 child, Molly Wells. MPH, U. Tex. Health Sci. Ctr., 1986; MD, Baylor Coll., 1990. Diplomate Am. Bd. Family Practice. Intern, residency U. Rochester (N.Y.) / Highland Hosp., 1990-93; staff physician La Familia Med. Ctr., Santa Fe, N.Mex., 1993-95; assoc. clin. faculty U. N.Mex. Dept. Family Medicine, Albuquerque, 1993-95; staff physician A.O. Fox Hosp.-Oneonta (N.Y.) Family Practice, 1995-96, Roaring Fork Family Practice, Carbondale, Colo., 1996—; cons. homeless shelter project Med. Coll. Ohio, Toledo, 1990. Developer, coord. Casa Juan Diego (free med. and dental clinics), Houston, 1985-90. Home: 85 Parkside Ln Carbondale CO 81623 Office: Roaring Fork Family Practice 1340 Hwy 133 Carbondale CO 81623

BUCK, PAULINE KOLKER, optometrist; b. St. Petersburg, Fla., Jan. 11, 1968; d. Abraham and Elena (Breiterman) Kolker; m. Evan Boyd Buck, June 19, 1994. BS, U. Fla., 1990; OD, New Eng. Coll. Optometry, 1994. Cert. in optometrics and therapeutics, Fla. Part-time adminstrv. asst. Office of Dr. Irwin Roth, OD, Miami, Fla., 1985-90; part-time optical technician Parrelli Optical, Boston, 1990; optometric technician Office of Alex Berenthal, OD, Hialeah, Fla., 1994; optometrist Perle Vision, Nashville, 1994-95; pvt. practice optometry Miami Beach, Fla., 1995—. Active Hadassah, 1980—. Mem. Am. Optometric Assn., Dade County Optometric Assn., Fla. Optometric Assn. Jewish. Home: 1735 Daytonia Rd Miami Beach FL 33141 Office: 230 71st St Miami Beach FL 33141

BUCKINGHAM, JOHN MICHAEL, surgeon; b. Melbourne, Victoria, Australia, July 19, 1947; s. Donald James and Joyce Olive (Craven) B.; m. Susan Margaret Mary Brady, June 10, 1972; children: James, Peter, Kathryn, Michael. MS BS, Sydney (Australia) U., 1971; MS in Surgery, U. Minn., 1977. Resident St. Vincent's Hosp., Sydney, 1971-72; fellow Mayo Clinic, Rochester, Minn., 1972-77; asst. prof. surgery Loyola U., Maywood, Ill., 1978; VMO gen. surgery Calvary Hosp., Bruce, ACT, Australia, 1979—; chmn. med. staff assn. Calvary Hosp., Bruce, Australia, 1986-88, 91-93. Fellow ACS, Royal Australian Coll. Surgeons (chmn. ACT com. 1993-95); mem. Royal Australian Coll. Med. Administrs. Roman Catholic. Office: State Bank Bldg, 161 London Ct, Canberra ACT 2601, Australia

BUCKLEY, JOHN JOSEPH, obstetrician, gynecologist; b. Youngstown, Ohio, Jan. 21, 1930; s. John Joseph and Rosalie Catherine (Singler) B.; m. Anne Theresa Finnerty, Apr. 24, 1954; children: John, Joy, Colleen, Mollie. BS in Biology cum laude, Holy Cross Coll., 1952; MD, Ohio State U., 1959. Staff St. Elizabeth Med. Ctr., Youngstown, Ohio, 1963—, chief ob-gyn., 1977-80, chief of staff, 1986—; practice medicine specializing in ob-gyn. Youngstown, Ohio, 1963—; asst. prof. Northeastern Ohio Coll. Medicine, Rootstown, 1980—. co-founder Right to Life, Youngstown, 1970. Served to lt. USN, 1952-55, with res. MC, 1959-63. Fellow Am. Coll. Ob-Gyn; mem. AMA, Ohio Med. Assn., Mahoning County Med. Assn., Youngstown Soc. Ob-Gyns., Alpha Omega Alpha. Democrat. Roman Catholic. Clubs: Youngstown Country, Cotillion. Home: 1337 Stonington Dr Youngstown OH 44505-1657 Office: 935 Trailwood Dr Youngstown OH 44512-5008

BUCKLEY, JOHN JOSEPH, JR., health care executive; b. Evanston, Ill., Oct. 5, 1944; s. John Joseph and Mary Ruth (Smith) B.; m. Sarah Amelia Puceloski, May 16, 1970; children—Ruth Mary, Patricia Kimberly, John Joseph III. A.B., Kenyon Coll., 1966; M.B.A., George Washington U., 1969. Asst. adminstr. Maricopa County Gen. Hosp., Phoenix, 1969-71; asst. adminstr. St. Joseph's Hosp. and Med. Ctr., Phoenix, 1971-74, assoc. adminstr., 1974-76, v.p., 1976-79, pres., 1984-88; pres. St. Anthony's Hosp., Amarillo, Tex., 1979-84, St. Anthony's Devel. Corp., Amarillo, 1982-84; chief operating officer Harrington Cancer Ctr., Amarillo, 1982-84; sr. v.p. Mercy Health System, Cin., 1988-91; pres. So. Ill. Healthcare Enterprises, Carbondale, Ill., 1992—. Active Amarillo Alliance of Cmty. Svc. Execs., Amarillo Area Acad. Health Ctr. Corp., Amarillo Area Hosp. Home Care, Amarillo Found. Health and Sci., Panhandle chpt. Tex. Soc. to Prevent Blindness, Amarillo Jr. League, Children's Oncology Svcs. of Tex. Panhandle; Amarillo diocesan coord. health affairs; mem. adminstrv. com. Amarillo; pres. Mercy Svcs. Corp., 1984-88; bd. dirs. Greater Phoenix Affordable Health Care Found., 1984-88; trustee Kenyon Coll., Gambier, Ohio, 1991-95. Fellow Am. Coll. Healthcare Execs. (regent Ariz. 1984-88); mem. Tex. Hosp. Assn. (trustee 1983-84), Ill. Hosp. & Health Sys. Assn. (trustee 1995—), Cath. Health Assn. U.S. (bd. dirs., svcs. com., trustee 1985-91), Ariz. Kidney Found., Ariz. Hosp. Assn. Republican. Roman Catholic. Office: So Ill Health Care Enterprises PO Box 3988 Carbondale IL 62902-3988

BUCKLEY, MARY ELIZABETH, clinical social worker; b. Providence, July 25, 1950; d. Cornelius Robert and Elizabeth Anna (Clarke) B. BA in Anthropology, U. R.I., 1972; MSW, R.I. Coll., Providence, 1985. Lic. ind. clin. social worker, R.I., Mass. Drug counselor City of Providence, 1975; sr. ctr. dir. The Salvation Army Corps. Community Ctr., Providence, 1976-79; field worker R.I. Dept. of Elderly Affairs, Providence, 1980-81; clinical social worker, geriatric specialist No. R.I. Cmty. Mental Health Ctr., Woonsocket, R.I., 1985-86; coord. elderly svcs. Providence Ctr. for Counseling and Psychiatric Svc., 1986-95; clin. social worker cons. Bayberry Commons Nursing Home, Pascoag, R.I., 1985-86, Gov.'s Commn. on Domestic Violence Against Elders, Providence, 1990; facilitator Family Care Givers of Frail Elders Support Groups, Woonsocket and Providence, 1985—; cіln. social worekr Counseling Resource Assocs., 1988-90, Human Resource Inst., Fall River, Mass., 1989-94, Roger Williams Hosp. Home Care Program, 1991-92, Outpatient Psychiatry Group Practice, 1993-94, Kent Meml. Hosp. Home Care, 1994—; chair Aging 2000 Health Care Reform Mental Health Task Force, 1992-94; mental health cons. R.I. Dept. Elderly Affairs, 1995-96. Officer Statewide Key Coun., R.I., 1986-95. Mem. NASW (R.I. chpt. Social Worker of Yr. for Aging Svcs. 1995), Acad. Cert. Social Workers, Am. Soc. on Aging, Geriat. Specialists Cmty. Mental Health Support Network.

BUCKLEY, MORTIMER JOSEPH, physician; b. Worcester, Mass., July 1, 1932; s. Mortimer Joseph and Kathleen Josephine (O'Sullivan) B.; m. Marilyn Scully, June 16, 1962; children—Kathleen, Deirdre, Kara, Mortimer. AB, Coll. Holy Cross, 1954; MD, Boston U., 1958; D in Medicine (hon.), Aristotlean U., Salonica, Greece; DSc, Assumption Coll., Worcester, Mass.; MA (hon.), 1989. Diplomate: Am. Bd. Surgery, Am. Bd. Thoracic Surgery. Intern in surgery Mass. Gen. Hosp., 1958-59, 3d asst. resident in surgery, 1959-60, 2d asst. resident, 1960-62, 1st asst. resident, 1964-65, resident in surgery, 1965-66, asst. in surgery, 1966-67; chief Vascular Clinic, 1967-69, asst. surgeon, 1968-71, asso. in surgery, 1968-69, chief cardiac surg. unit, 1970—, asso. vis. surgeon, 1972-76, vis. surgeon, 1977—; teaching fellow in anatomy Harvard Med. Sch., Boston, 1960-62, teaching fellow in surgery, 1965-66, instr. surgery, 1966-68, asso. in surgery, 1968-69, asst. prof. surgery, 1969-72, asso. prof. surgery, 1972-76, prof. surgery, 1977—; clin. asso. Clinic of Surgery, Nat. Heart Inst., Bethesda, Md., 1962-64. Decorated Knight Equestrian Order of Holy Sepulchre of Jerusalem, Knight Order of St. John (Knights of Malta). Mem. N.Y. Acad. Sci., AMA, Mass. Med. Soc., Am. Assn. Acad. Surgery, Am. Bd. Thoracic Surgery, Soc. Univ. Surgeons, A.C.S., Internat. Cardiovascular Soc., Soc. for Vascular Surgery, New Eng., Boston surg. socs., Am. Assn. Thoracic Surgeons (chmn. membership com. 1980, pres. 1995—), Soc. Thoracic Surgeons, Am. Heart Assn. (chmn. cardiovascular surg. council 1980), Mass. Heart Assn. (pres. 1991), Am. Soc. Artificial Internal Organs, Am. Coll. Cardiology, Am. Surg. Assn., Am. Coll. Chest Physicians. Office: Mass Gen Hosp 32 Fruit St Boston MA 02114-2620

BUCKLEY, REBECCA HATCHER, physician, educator; b. Hamlet, N.C., Apr. 1, 1933; d. Martin Armstead and Nora (Langston) Hatcher; m. Charles Edward Buckley III, July 9, 1955; children: Charles Edward IV, Elizabeth Ann, Rebecca Kathryn, Sarah Margaret. BA, Duke U., 1954; MD, U. N.C., 1958. Intern Duke U. Med. Ctr., Durham, N.C., 1958-59, resident, 1959-61, practice medicine, specializing in pediatric allergy and immunology, 1961—; dir. Am. Bd. Allergy and Immunology, Phila., 1971-73, chmn. exam. com., 1971-73, co-chmn. bd. dirs., 1982-84; chmn. Diagnostic Lab. Immunology, 1984-88; mem. staff Duke U. Med. Ctr.; asst. prof. pediatrics and immunology, 1968-72, assoc. prof. pediatrics, 1972-76, assoc. prof. immunology, 1972-79, prof. immunology, 1979—, J. Buren Sidbury prof. pediatrics, 1979—. Contbr. numerous articles to med. publs. Recipient Allergic Diseases Acad. award Nat. Inst. Allergy and Infectious Diseases, 1974-79, Merit Rsch. award NIH, 1990, Nat. Bd. award Med. Coll. Pa., 1991, Clemons von Pirquet award Georgetown, 1993, Disting. Tchr. award Duke U. Med. Alumni Assn., 1993, Outstanding Achievement award Immune Deficiency Found., 1994, Disting. Svc. award Am. Acad. Allergy and Immunology, 1996. Fellow Am. Acad. Allergy and Immunology (mem. exec. com. 1975-82, pres. 1979-80); mem. Am. Assn. Immunologists, Soc. Pediatric Rsch., Am. Acad. Pediatrics (Bret Ratner award 1992), Southeastern Allergy Assn. (pres. 1978-79), Am. Pediatric Soc. (coun. mem. 1991-97). Republican. Episcopalian. Home: 3621 Westover Rd Durham NC 27707-5032 Office: Duke U Med Ctr PO Box 2898 Durham NC 27715-2898

BUCKLEY, STANLEY JOSEPH, JR., nurse; b. Wilkes-Barre, Pa., Mar. 16, 1957; s. Stanley Joseph and Mary Agnes (Sakowski) B.; m. Theresa Marie Zuba, Aug. 4, 1979; children: David Joseph, Mary Frances, Nicholas Daniel. A in Applied Sci. in Nursing, Luzerne County Community Coll., 1980; BSN, Coll. Misericordia, Dallas, Pa., 1983; MS in Human Resources, U. Scranton, 1986. RN; cert. radiology, spl. studies. Nurse Wilkes-Barre Gen. Hosp., 1993—, relief charge cardiac cath. lab., 1993—; mem. communications com., Wilkes-Barre Gen. Hosp., 1985-87, quality assurance com., 1990, asst. nurse mgr. crit. care, 1987-89; adj. prof., nursing instr. Luzerne County Community Coll., 1990, mem. curriculum com. Author: (poetry) The Last Race, 1975; actor Fires in Paradise, 1991. Coach Boys and Girls Tee Ball. Mem. Sex Equity Commn. (bd. dirs., speaker 1987), Am. Assn. Critical Care Nurses, Am. Assembly for Men in Nursing, Sigma Theta Tau. Republican. Roman Catholic. Home: 518 N Pennsylvania Ave Wilkes Barre PA 18705-2420 Office: Wilkes-Barre Gen Hosp Auburn St Wilkes Barre PA 18702

BUCKLEY, THERESA MARIE RITA ZUBA, critical care nurse; b. Wilkes-Barre, Pa., Apr. 17, 1959; d. Frank and Mary (Brozena) Zuba; m. Stanley Joseph Buckley, Aug. 4, 1979; children: David Joseph, Mary Frances, Nicholas Daniel. ADN, Luzerne County C.C., 1980; BSN, Coll. Misericordia, Dallas, Pa., 1983; MS, U. Scranton, 1986. RN, Pa. Staff nurse Wilkes-Barre Gen. Hosp., 1980—, staff nurse surg. ICU, 1989, staff nurse CCU, 1989—. Mem. sex equity com. Luzerne County C.C.; vol. arts and crafts for children St. Mary's Sch., Wilkes-Barre, Pa. Mem. AACN, Sigma Theta Tau. Democrat. Roman Catholic. Home: 518 N Pennsylvania Ave Wilkes Barre PA 18705

BUCKLIN, ROBERT VAN ZANDT, forensic pathologist, lawyer; b. Chgo., June 25, 1916; s. James VanZandt and Lucy Monica (Dunderdale) B.; m. Patricia Lynch. BS in Medicine, Loyola U., Chgo., 1937, MD, 1941; JD, So. Tex. Coll. Law, 1969. Diplomate Am. Bd. Pathology, Am. Bd. Law In Medicine. Intern St. Joseph's Hosp., Tacoma, 1940-41; resident in pathology Tacoma Gen. Hosp., 1941-42, U.S. Army Hosps., 1942-45; dep. chief med. examiner Harris County (Tex.) Med. Examiner, Houston, 1964-69, 78-80; chief med. examiner Galveston County (Tex.) Med. Examiner, Galveston, 1969-71; dep. med. examiner L.A. County Med. Examiner, 1974-77, 80-83; chief med. examiner Travis County (Tex.) Med. Examiner, Austin, 1977-78; supervising pathologist San Diego County Coroner's Office, 1983-87; pvt. practice forensic pathology, 1987-95; med. examiner Clark County, Las Vegas, 1995—. Fellow ACP, Am. Coll. Legal Medicine, Am. Soc. Clin. Pathologists, Am. Acad. Forensic Scis. Republican. Home and Office: 3255 Lindell Rd Las Vegas NV 89102-6926

BUCKNALL, CLIFFORD ADRIAN, cardiologist; b. Sale, Eng., Feb. 25, 1956; s. Eric and Elsie Constance (Whittaker) B.; m. Sarah Anne Topp, July 30, 1983; children: Samuel Clifford, Thomas Adrian. Degree, Leamington (Eng.) Coll., 1967-74; MB BS, Westminster Med. Sch., London, 1979; MD, London U., 1987. House surgeon Warwick (Eng.) Hosp. Nat. Health Svc., 1979-80; house physician Westminster Hosp. Nat. Health Svc., London, 1980; sr. house physician Nottingham (Eng.) Hosp. Nat. Health Svc., 1980-82; rsch. fellow in cardiology Guys Hosp., London, 1982-84; sr. registrar Guy's Hosp., London, 1987-89, dir. cardiology, 1992-93; registrar Brighton (Eng.) Hosp., 1984-85, King's Coll. Hosp., London, 1985-86; sr. registrar King's Coll. Hosp., 1986-87, cons. cardiologist, 1989-92; dir. cardiology Guys & St. Thomas' Hosp. (NHS) Trust, 1993—; cons. cardiologist King's Coll., Dulwich Hosp., London Bridge Hosp., Cromwell Hosp., Sloane Hosp., Lister Hosp., all London, 1989—. Contbr. papers, chpts. to med. publs. Fellow Royal Soc. Medicine, Royal Coll. Physicians; mem. Royal Coll. Surgeons, Brit. Cardiac Soc., Brit. Med. Assn. Anglican. Office: Guy's Hosp, Cardiac Dept, Saint Thomas St, London SE1, England

BUCKNER-REITMAN, JOYCE, psychologist, educator; b. Benton, Ark., Sept. 25, 1937; d. Waymond Floyd Pannell and Willie Evelyn (Wright) Whitley; m. John W. Buckner, Aug. 29, 1958 (div. 1970); children: Cheryl, John, Chris; m. Sanford Reitman, Aug. 13, 1994. BA, Ouachita Bapt. Coll., 1959; MS in Edn., Henderson State U., 1964; PhD, North Tex. State U., 1970. Lic. psychologist, Tex., marriage and family therapist; cert. Nat. Registry Health Svc. Providers in Psychology; master trainer in imago relationship therapy. Assoc. prof. U. Tex., Arlington, 1970-80, chmn. dept. edn., 1976-78; pvt. practice psychology, Arlington, 1974—; dir., chief profl. officer Southwest Inst. Relationship Devel., Weatherford, Tex.; author, profl. speaker; appeared on internat. TV shows, including Oprah Winfrey Show. Mem. APA, Nat. Assn. for Imago Relationship Therapy (pres.), Nat. Speakers Assn., Am. Assn. Marital and Family Therapy. Home: 2208 Farmer Rd Weatherford TX 76087

BUCKWALTER, TERRY E., JR., osteopath; b. New Castle, Pa., Dec. 13, 1969; s. Terry E. Sr. and Florence M. (Toscano) B. BS in Biology, Allegheny Coll., 1992; DO, Phila. Coll. Osteo. Medicine, 1996. Mem. Beta Beta Beta, Lambda Sigma. Republican. Roman Catholic. Home: RD #1 New Wilmington PA 16142

BUCOVE, ARNOLD DAVID, psychiatrist; b. Toronto, Sept. 22, 1934. BA, Columbia U., 1956; MD, NYU, 1961. Diplomate Am. Bd. Psychiatry and Neurology. Intern Lenox Hill Hosp., N.Y.C., 1961-62; resident in psychiatry Bellevue Hosp., N.Y.C., 1962-63, St. Luke's Hosp., N.Y.C., 1963-65; chief psychiatry 36th Tactical Hosp., Bitburg, Germany, 1965-67; pvt. practice psychiatry Pleasant Valley, N.Y., 1967-92, Poughkeepsie, N.Y., 1992-93; pvt. practice Oneonta, N.Y., 1993—; attending staff Craig House, Beacon, N.Y., 1977-93; asst. dir. Dutchess County Mental Health Clinic, Poughkeepsie, N.Y., 1967-68; chief psychiatry Fox Meml. Hosp., Oneonta, 1993—; cons. psychiatrist Greer Children's Cmty., Millbrook, N.Y., 1968-77; mem. courtesy staff Sharon (Conn.) Hosp., 1967-90; cons. IBM, Poughkeepsie, 1968. Contbr. articles to profl. jours. Bd. dirs. Town of Washing Civic Assn., Millbrook, 1986-93, Millbrook Music Assn., 1986-92; mem. vestry Grace Ch., Millbrook, 1971-74, mem. vestry St. Peter's Ch., Millbrook, 1989-92. Capt. USAF, 1965-67. Fellow Am. Psychiat. Assn. (pres. Mid-Hudson chpt. 1977-79); mem. N.Y. State Med. Soc., Otsego County Med. Soc., Millbrook Hunt (bd. govs. 1968-71), Millbrook Golf and Tennis Club, Cooperstown Country Club. Office: Fox Hosp 1 Norton Ave Oneonta NY 13820-2629

BUCUR, JOHN CHARLES, neurological surgeon; b. Youngstown, Ohio, Mar. 5, 1925; s. John and Victoria (Marginean) B.; B.S., Ohio U., 1947; postgrad. U. Biarritz (France), 1946; M.D., U. Pitts., 1951, M.Surgery, 1952; m. Emily Leanne Elmore; children—John Ellsworth, Dean Charles, Victoria Ann, Michael Paul, Teri Leanne. Intern, Western Pa. Hosp., Pitts., 1951-52; resident in neurosurgery Long Beach (Calif.) VA Hosp., 1953-56, staff neurosurgeon, 1956-57; neurosurg. cons. Harbor Gen. Hosp., Torrance, Calif., 1956-57; practice medicine specializing in neurol. surgery, Falls Church, Va., 1957—; chief staff Nat. Orthopedic and Rehab. Hosp., Arlington, Va., 1973; chief neurol. surgery Fairfax Hosp., Falls Church, 1961-75, Nat. Orthopedic and Rehab. Hosp., Arlington, 1957-79, No. Va. Drs. Hosp., Arlington, 1963—, Arlington Hosp., 1977—; sr. attending neurosurgeon Alexandria Hosp., 1959—, Circle Terrace Hosp., Alexandria, Va., 1962—; sec., dir. 7 Corners Med. Bldgs., Inc., Falls Church, 1958—; partner Edward R. Lang, M.D., Falls Church, 1969—. Mem. Va. Gov.'s Com. for Regional Med. Program, dir. regional med. program, 1969-77; chmn. bd. dirs. Network Health Plan, 1984-87; bd. dirs. Nat. Hosp. for Orthopedics and Rehab. Served with U.S. Army, 1943-45; ETO. Diplomate Am. Bd. Neurol. Surgery. Fellow ACS; mem. Am. Assn. Neurol. Surgeons, Mid-Atlantic Neurosurgery Soc., Washington Acad. Neurosurgery, Neurosurg. Soc. Vas., No. Va. Acad. Surgery, Congress Neurol. Surgeons, Pan Am. Med. Assn., So. Med. Assn., Arlington County Med. Soc., Va. Health Assn. (pres.), Fairfax County Med. Soc., Am. Legion. Methodist. Club: Masons. Office: 6305 Castle Pl Falls Church VA 22044-1905

BUDD, ROBERT M., ophthalmologist; b. Pitts., Apr. 19, 1956; s. Theodore R. and Jane T. (Toutteny) B.; m. Diane C. Turscsanyi, Sept. 18, 1983; children: Christopher, Jeremy. MD, U. Pitts., 1983. Intern Mercy Hosp., Pitts., 1983-84; resident Eye & Ear Inst., Pitts., 1984-87, fellow in glaucoma, 1987-88; pvt. practice Altoona, Pa., 1988—. Bd. dirs. Ctrl. Pa. Diabetes Assn., Altoona, 1993. Mem. Pa. Med. Soc., Blair County Med. Soc., Am. Acad. Ophthalmology, Alpha Omega Alpha. Office: Altoona Ophthalmology Assoc 501 Howard Ave Altoona PA 16601

BUDINGER, THOMAS FRANCIS, radiologist, educator; b. Evanston, Ill., Oct. 25, 1932; married, 1965; 3 children. BS, Regis Coll., 1954; MS, U. Wash., 1957; MD, U. Calif. Berkeley, 1964, PhD, 1971. Asst. chemist Regis Coll., Colo., 1953-54; analytical chemist Indsl. Labs., 1954; sr. oceanographer U. Wash., 1961-66; physicist Lawrence Livermore Lab., U. Calif., 1966-67; resident physician Donner Lab. and Lawrence Berkeley Lab., 1967-76; H. Miller Prof. med. rsch. and group leader rsch. medicine Donner lab., prof. elec. engring. and computer sci. Donner Lab., U. Calif. Berkeley, 1976—; with Peter Bent Brigham Hosp., Boston, 1964; dir. med. svc. Lawrence Berkeley Lab., 1968-76, sr. staff scientist, 1980—; chmn. study sect. NIH, 1981-84; prof. radiology U. Calif. San Francisco, 1984—. Recipient Special award Am. Nuclear Soc., 1984. Mem. AAAS, Am. Geophysical Union, N.Y. Acad. Sci., Soc. Nuclear Medicine, Soc. Magnetic Rsch. Medicine (pres. 1984-85). Office: Lawrence Berkeley Lab Ctr for Functional Imaging 1 Cyclotron Rd Mail Stop 55-121 Berkeley CA 94720*

BUDMAN, CATHY LINDA, psychiatrist, physician; b. Bklyn., Mar. 15, 1957. ScB, Brown U., 1979; MD, SUNY, Buffalo, 1984. Diplomate Australian Med. Coun., Am. Bd. Neurology and Psychiatry. Intern, then resident in psychiatry U. Calif.-San Francisco Sch. Medicine, 1984-86; sr. resident in family medicine Royal Australian Coll. Family Medicine, St. Leonards, NSW, 1987-88; med. registrar drug and alcohol unit Royal Prince Alfred Hosp., Sydney, NSW, 1987-88; resident in psychiatry North Shore Hosp., Manhasset, N.Y., 1988-90, rsch. fellow neuropsychiatry, 1990-91, dir. med. student clerkship in psychiatry, 1994—; pvt. practice Manhasset, 1990—; dir. med. student edn. in psychiatry North Shore U. Hosp., Manhasset, 1994—; asst. prof. psychiatry and neurology Cornell U. Med. Coll., N.Y.C., 1993—; asst. prof. psychiatry NYU Sch. Medicine, N.Y.C., 1995; dir. Movement Disorder Clinic, 1990—; rsch. cons. dept. drug and alcohol Royal Prince Alfred Hosp., Westmead Hosp., 1986-88. Mem. APA, Nassau County Psychiat. Soc., Tourette Assn., Royal Australian Coll. Family Practitioners (assoc.). Office: North Shore Hosp Dept Psychiatry 400 Community Dr Manhasset NY 11030-3815

BUDNICK, THOMAS PETER, social worker; b. Ludlow, Mass., Feb. 16, 1947; s. Henry F. and Mildred Mary (Killian) B. BS, Am. Internat. Coll., 1972, MA, 1975. Lic. cert. profl. social worker. Mailhandler U.S. Postal Svc., Springfield, Mass., 1970-72; substitute tchr. Pub. Schs. Dept., Ludlow, Mass., 1973-74; social worker Mass. Dept. Pub. Welfare, Springfield, 1975—; pres. Am.'s Manifest Destiny Soc., Inc., West Harwich, Mass., 1979—; bd. dirs. Mass. Astronomy Club, Boston, 1988—. Contbr. numerous articles to jours. V.p. Local 509, Boston, 1989. Democrat. Home: 19 Harding Ave Ludlow MA 01056-2327

BUDOFF, PENNY WISE, physician, author, researcher; b. Albany, N.Y., July 7, 1939; d. Louis and Goldene Wise. B.A., Syracuse U., 1959; M.D., SUNY-Upstate Med. Sch., 1963. Intern, St. Luke's Meml. Hosp., Utica, N.Y., 1963-64; practice medicine specializing in family practice and women's health, Woodbury, N.Y., 1964-85; clin. assoc. prof. family medicine SUNY at Stony Brook, 1980—; founder, dir. emeritus Penny Wise Budoff Women's Health Svcs., Bethpage, N.Y., ground-breaking women's health care facility, 1985—; affiliated with North Shore U. Hosp.; attending dept. ob/gyn North Shore U. Hosp., 1992—; asst. prof. ob/gyn family practice Cornell U. Medical Coll., 1993—; prin. investigator pilot study to determine heavy metal pesticides in breast cancer tissue from patients residing on Long Island 10 years or more North Shore Hosp. and Brookhaven Nat. Lab, 1994; lectr., TV guest on women's medicine and health issues; mem. panel menopause NIH, 1993; clin. rsch. on menstrual pain, premenstrual syndrome, menopause, breast cancer and osteoporosis. Author: No More Menstrual Cramps and Other Good News, 1980, No More Hot Flashes and Other Good News, 1983; author: World Book Health & Medical Annual, 1994; Contbr. articles to profl. jours. Bd. dirs. Coalition Against Domestic Violence. Named Women of Yr. C.W. Post Coll., 1981; recipient Nat. Consumers League award, 1983, Max Cheplove award Erie chpt. N.Y. State Acad. Family Physicians, 1983, Women of Distinction award Soroptimist Internat. of Nassau County, L.I., 1990, honoree Nassau County Coalition Against Domestic Violence, 1992, Fellow Nassau County Med. Soc., Am. Acad. Family Physicians (nat. com. on pub. rels.); mem. NOW (Equality Award in Health 1988, Unsung Heroine award), Am. Med. Women's Assn. (co-chmn. nat. women's health com., liaison), Nassau Acad. Family Physicians (past pres.). Home: 3 Sea Crest Dr Huntington NY 11743-9765 Office: Penny W Budoff MD Womens Health Service North Shore U Hosp 4300 Hempstead Tpke Bethpage NY 11714-5704

BUDTZ-JØRGENSEN, EJVIND, dentist, gerodontology and prosthodontics educator; b. Aarhus, Denmark, May 21, 1938; arrived in Switzerland, 1989; s. Ejgil and Else (Jørgensen) B-J.; m. Annalise Griebe Knudsen, Dec. 31, 1972; children: Esben, Agnete. Cand. Odont, Royal Dental Coll., Aarhus, Denmark, 1962, D in Odont, 1974. Clin. instr. Dental Sch., Bergen, Norway, 1963-66; asst. prof. Royal Dental Coll., Aarhus, 1966-74, assoc. prof., 1974-84; prof. Royal Dental Coll., Copenhagen, Denmark, 1984-89, Sect. de Médecine Dentaire, Geneva, 1989—. Author: (sci. pub.) Prosthodontics, Mycology, 1970—; author (with others, textbooks) Prosthodontics, Mycology, 1974—; editor Nordic Clin. Odontology, 1986. Recipient Silver medal Ville de Paris, 1972. Mem. Danish Dental Assn., Internat. Assn. Dental Rsch. (Prosthodontics and Implants Rsch. award 1995), Scandinavian Soc. Prosthetic Dentistry (pres. 1986-88), European Prosthodontic Assn. (pres. 1990-91), Internat. Coll. Prosthodontics, European Coll. Gerodontology (pres. 1991-92), Swiss Dental Assn. Office: Sect Medéecine Dentaire, 19 rue Barthélemy-Menn, 1211 Geneva Switzerland

BUEHLER, SALLY SALMEN, clinical social worker; b. Newton, Mass., July 31, 1938; d. Stanley and Margaret (Green) Salmen; m. John A. Buehler, Aug. 24, 1971; 1 child, Daniel. AB, U. N.H., 1960; MSW, U. Calif., 1963. Lic. clin. social worker, Calif. Social worker psychiat. Child Guidance Clinic Children Hosp., San Francisco, 1965-69, supt. social worker psychiat., 1968-69; social worker psychiat. Family Service Agy., Pittsfield, Mass., 1970-71; social worker clin. Kentfield, Calif., 1971—; cons. Pacific Recovery Ctr., Larkspur, Calif., 1983—. Fellow Soc. Clin. Social Work (bd. cert. diplomate in Clin. Social Work). Home: 18 Turnagain Rd San Rafael CA 94904-2717

BUEHRENS, PAUL ERIC, family physician; b. Hackensack, N.J., Mar. 2, 1952; s. Clifford Arthur and L. Joan (Pikna) B.; m. Laetitia Ward, Sept. 3, 1977; children: Thomas Ward, Daniel Ward. BA cum laude, Harvard U., 1974; MD, Case Western Res. U., 1978. Intern then resident Dept. of Family Practice/Med. U. of S.C., Charleston, 1978-81; physician Lakeshore Clinic, Kirkland, Wash., 1981—, med. dir. for managed care, 1985—; med. dir. Lakevue Gardens Convalescent Ctr., Kirkland, 1986—; bd. dirs. Med. Ptnrs. N.W., Everett, Wash.; vice chmn. Wash. Med. Group Alliance, Seattle, 1995—. Fellow Am. Acad. Family Practice; mem. Am. Geriatrics Soc., Wash. State Med. Assn., Amnesty Internat. Democrat. Unitarian Universalist. Home: 1606 37th Ave Seattle WA 98122 Office: Lakeshore Clinic 515 State St Kirkland WA 98033

BUEHRING, PATRICIA LEE, marriage, family and child therapist; b. Ventura, Calif.; d. James Edgar and Ellolee (Welchhance) Wheat; m. George R. Buehring, Feb. 1989; children: James, Anna. Student, U. Calif., Santa Barbara, 1956-58; BA, San Jose State U., 1960, MA in Spl. Edn., 1968; MA in Marriage, Family, Child Therapy, Azusa Pacific U., Santa Clara, Calif., 1990. Lic. marriage, family, child therapist, Calif.; cert. tchr. spl. edn. K-adult. Tchr. Cupertino (Calif.) Sch. Dist., 1960-66; edn. cons. Behavioral Rsch. Labs., Palo Alto, Calif., 1968-69; tng. specialist, adminstr. Operation Share Santa Clara, San Jose, 1968-71; program specialist learning handicapped Spl. Edn. Svc., Santa Cruz, Calif., 1978-81; prin. Mid County Christian Sch., Aptos, Calif., 1986-88; cons./adminstr Calif. Office Edn., Santa Cruz, 1989-93; marriage, family, child therapist in pvt. practice Aptos, 1990—. Mem. Am. Assn. Marriage and Family Therapy, Calif. Assn. Marriage and Family Therapy, Christian Assn. for Psychol. Studies. Office: 3060 Valencia Ave #6 Aptos CA 95003

BUENAVENTURA, MILAGROS PAEZ, psychiatrist; b. Munoz, Nueva Ecija, Philippines, Oct. 28, 1943; came to U.S., 1974; s. Lupo P. and Pilar (Paez) B.; children: Robert, Melani. AA, U. Santo Tomas, Manila, 1962, MD, 1967. Clinic physician Dr. Jose R. Reyes Meml. Hosp., Manila, 1968-71, resident in neurology and psychiatry, 1971-74; resident dept. psychiatry Milton S. Hershey Med. Ctr., Hershey, Pa., 1975-78; staff psychiat. Holy Spirit Hosp., Camp Hill, Pa., 1978-82, Harrisburg (Pa.) State Hosp., 1982—; cons. Psychiatric Ctr., 1994—, Harrisburg, 1984—; mem. courtesy staff Harrisburg Hosp., 1987; med. dir. Helen Stevens Ctr., Carlisle, Pa. Mem. Am. Psychiat. Assn., Pa. Med. Soc., Pa. Psychiat. Soc., Cen. Pa. Psychiat. Soc. Republican. Roman Catholic.

BUENO, HECTOR, cardiologist; b. Pamplona, Navarra, Spain, June 10, 1964; s. Jesus and Esther (Zamora) B.; m. Maite Vidan, Oct. 20, 1990; children: Amaia, Itziar. Lic. in medicine, U. Navarra, Pamplona, Spain, 1988. Resident cardiology U. Hosp. Gregorio Marañon, Madrid, 1989-93, fellow on clin. cardiology rsch., 1994-95, staff mem. dept. cardiology, 1995—. Assoc. editor: Notes From the 8th Interventional Cardiology Course Theoretic Program, 1995; contbr. articles to profl. jours., chpts. to book. Mem. European Soc. Cardiology, Spanish Soc. Cardiology. Office: Hosp Univ Gregorio Maranon, Dept Cardiology, Dr Esquerdo 46, 28007 Madrid Spain

BUERK, DONALD GENE, medical educator, biomedical engineer; b. St. Louis, Jan. 28, 1946; s. Charles Albert and Virginia (Kirkpatrick) B.; m. Steffie Greif, July 7, 1968; children: Jesse Nathaniel, Daniel Joshua. BS, Case Western Res. U., 1969, MS, 1976; PhD, Northwestern U., 1980. Biomed. engr. St. Vincent Charity Hosp., Cleve., 1969-75; rsch. asst. Case Western Res. U., Cleve., 1976; rsch. fellow Evanston (Ill.) Hosp., Northwestern U., 1980-82; prof. La. Tech. U., Ruston, La., 1982-87; rsch. prof. Drexel U., Phila., 1987-90; rsch. prof. dept. physiology sch. medicine, bioengring. dept U. Pa., Phila., 1990—; vis. scientist Cath. U., Nijmegen, The Netherlands, 1988; vis. prof. Johns Hopkins U., Balt., 1986-92. Author: Biosensors--Theory and Applications, 1993; contbr. more than 50 articles to profl. jours. Recipient Travel award Internat. Soc. Oxygen Transport, Eng., 1978, Outstanding Rschr. award La. Tech. U., Ruston, 1984, New Investigator award NIH, 1986, Vis. Scientist award Dutch Govt., 1988, Ind. Investigator award NSF, 1990. Mem. IEEE, Am. Heart Assn., Am. Physiol. Soc., Biomed. Engring. Soc., Microcirculatory Soc., Sigma Xi. Office: U Pa Ifem 1 John Morgan Bldg Philadelphia PA 19104-6086

BUESCHEN, ANTON JOSLYN, physician, educator; b. Toledo, June 7, 1940; s. Robert F. and Mary J. (Joslyn) B.; m. Norma Jean McClanahan, Sept. 5, 1964; children—Anton, Elaine. Student, Va. Mil. Inst., 1958-61; M.D., U. Va., 1965. Diplomate: Am. Bd. Urology. Intern in surgery Vanderbilt U., 1965-66, asst. resident in surgery, 1966-67; resident in urology Ind. U., Indpls., 1969-72; practice medicine specializing in urology Birmingham, Ala., 1973—; instr. urology Tulane U. Sch. Medicine, 1972-73; asst. prof. div. urology dept. surgery U. Ala., Birmingham, 1973-75; assoc. prof. U. Ala., 1975-79, prof., 1979—, dir. div. urology, 1975-95; chief urology sect. Children's Hosp., Birmingham, 1978-86. Contbr. numerous articles on urology to profl. jours. Served with M.C. U.S. Army, 1967-69. Mem. ACS, AMA (Billings Gold medal 1978) AAUP, Am. Urol. Assn., Am. Assn. Clin. Urologists, Soc. Univ. Urologists, Birmingham Urology Club, Jefferson County Med. Soc., Soc. for Pediatric Urology, Soc. Urologic Oncology, So. Med. Assn. (chmn. urology sect. 1987), Soc. Nuclear Medicine, Med. Assn. Ala. Office: U Ala Div Urology University Sta Birmingham AL 35294

BUESSELER, JOHN AURE, ophthalmologist, management consultant; b. Madison, Wis., Sept. 30, 1919; s. John Xavier and Gerda Pernille (Aure) B.; m. Cathryn Anne Hansen, Dec. 26, 1959; 1 child, John McGlone. Ph.B., U. Wis., 1941, M.D., 1944; M.S. in Bus. Adminstrn., U. Mo., 1965. Intern Cleve. City Hosp., 1944-45; resident U. Pa. Hosp., 1948-51; practice medicine specializing in ophthalmology Madison, 1953-59; prof., founding chief ophthalmology U. Mo., Columbia, 1959-66; exec. officer Mo. Crippled Children's Service, 1967-70; exec. dir. Kansas City Gen. Hosp. and Med. Ctr., 1969-70; founding dean Tex. Tech U. Sch. Medicine, Lubbock, 1970-73, v.p. health affairs Univ. Complex, 1970-75, prof. dept. ophthalmology, prof. health orgn. mgmt., 1971—, chmn. dept. health orgn. mgmt., 1972-75, prof. grad. sch. faculty, 1972-80, chmn. dept. ophthalmology, 1973-75; adj. prof. bus. adminstrn. Coll. Bus. Tex. Tech., Lubbock, 1992—; Univ. prof. (disting. and multidisciplinary) Univ. Complex, 1973—; founding v.p. health scis., founding CEO Tex. Tech. Univ. Health Scis. Ctr., 1972-74; pres. Radiol. Testing Lab., Inc., Madison, 1956-59; dir. House of Vision, Inc., Chgo., 1973-82; v.p. Madison Radiation Ctr., Inc., 1956-59; cons. NASA, mem. space medicine adv. group on devel. Orbiting Space Lab., Washington, 1963-66; cons. AEC, mem. Assn. Midwestern Univs.-Argonne (Ill.) Nat. Lab. biology com., 1965-69; cons. to pres. Agronne Univs. Assn., Chgo., 1967-68; comdr. 94th Gen. Hosp., U.S. Army Res., Mesquite, Tex., 1973-75; co-founder, incorporator, bd. dirs., past pres. Joint Commn. on Allied Health Pers. in Ophthalmology, Inc.; mem. Residency Rev. Com. for Ophthalmology, 1974-80, chmn., 1978-80; sr. cons., CEO, founder Health Orgn. Mgmt. Sys. Internat., 1978—. Contbr. articles to profl. jours. Served to capt. AUS, World War II, ETO; to maj. USAF, Korea; to col. USAR, Vietnam. Decorated Air medal with cluster, Legion of Merit, Combat Medic badge, Sr. Flight Surgeon badge, Parachutist badge Spl. Forces; recipient Gold Medallion award for disting. achievement in ophthalmology Mo. Ophthal. Soc., 1967, Tex. Tech. U. Bd. Regents Resolution of Congratulations, 1973, Cert. of Citation Tex. Ho. of Reps., 1973, 87, Disting. Alumnus citation U. Wis. Sch. Medicine, 1987. Fellow ACS, Am. Acad. Ophthalmology (Disting. Svc. in Edn. award 1969); mem. AMA, Tex. Med. Assn., Mo. Ophthal. Soc. (founder, past sec.-treas., pres., dir.), Acad. Mgmt., Soc. Med. Cons. to Armed Froces, Sigma Xi, Alpha Omega Alpha. Home: 3305 59th St Lubbock TX 79413-5517

BUFFLER, PATRICIA ANN, dean; b. Doylestown, Pa., Aug. 1, 1938; d. Edward M. and Evelyn G. (Axenroth) Happ; m. Richard T. Buffler, Jan. 20, 1962; children: Martyn R., Monique L. BSN, Cath. U. Am., 1960; MPH, U. Calif., Berkeley, 1965, PhD in Epidemiology, 1973. Prof. epidemiology sch. pub. health U. Tex. Health Sci. Ctr., Houston, 1979-91; dean sch. pub. health, prof. U. Calif., Berkeley, 1991—; mem. expert adv. panel on occupl. health WHO, 1985-96; mem. environment, safety and health adv. com. U.S. DOE, 1992—; mem. bd. on water sci. and tech. Nat. Rsch. Coun., 1992-94; chair, bd. dirs. Mickey Leland Nat. Urban Air Toxics Rsch. Ctr., 1994—, Societal Inst. of Math. Scis.; mem. Nat. Commn. on Superfund, Keystone Ctr., 1992-94; mem. adv. panel on mng. nuclear materials from warheads U.S. Congress Office Tech. Assessment, 1992-93; bd. scientific counselors Nat. Inst. for Occupl. Safety and Health, 1991-93; mem. sci. adv. bd. radiation adv. com. subcom. on cancer risks associated with electric and magnetic fields U.S. EPA, 1990-93; mem. sci. adv. bd. USEPA, 1996—; mem. Nat. Adv. Coun. on Environ. Health Scis., 1995—; mem. Inst. Medicine, Nat. Coun. Radiation Protection. Contbr. articles to profl. jours. Fellow AAS, Am. Coll. Epidemiology (pres.-elect 1990-91, pres. 1991-92); mem. Soc. for Epidemiological Rsch. (pres.-elect, pres., past pres. 1984-88), Am. Pub. Health Assn. (epidemiology sect. 1964—), Am. Epidemiological Soc., Soc. for Occupl. and Environ. Health, Internat. Epidemiological Assn., Internat. Soc. for Environ. Epidemiology (pres.-elect 1989-91, pres. 1992-94), Internat. Soc. for Exposure Assessment (charter, bd. internat. councillors 1993—), Internat. Commn. on Occupl. Health, Collegium Ramazzini, Soc. of Toxicology. Office: U Calif Sch Pub Health 19 Earl Warren Hall Berkeley CA 94720

BUFFORD, RODGER KEITH, psychologist, educator; b. Santa Rosa, Calif., Dec. 23, 1944; s. John Samuel and Evelyn A. (Rude) B.; m. Kathleen A. Parson; children: Heather, Brett. BA, King's Coll., 1966; MA, U. Ill., 1970; PhD, 1971. Lic. psychologist, Oreg., Va. Psychologist, Adolph Meyer Zone Ctr., Decatur, Ill., 1969-70; asst. prof. psychology Am. U., Washington, 1971-76; asst. prof., chmn. dept. psychology Huntington (Ind.) Coll., 1976-77; assoc. prof. Psychol. Studies Inst., Atlanta, 1977-81; psychologist Atlanta Counseling Ctr., 1980-82; assoc. prof., chmn. dept. psychology Western Baptist Sem., Portland, Oreg., 1982-86, prof. and chmn., 1986-90; prof., chmn. Grad. Sch. Clin. Psychology George Fox Coll., 1990-95, prof., dir. rsch. and integration, 1995—; pvt. practice psychology, 1973—; allied health care prof. Portland Adventist Med. Ctr., 1982—, Cedar Hills Hosp., 1984-93, Woodland Park Hosp., 1988—; dir. Mental Health Assn., Huntington, Ind., 1976-77; acad. adv. bd. Family Rsch. Coun. of Am. V.p. Minirth and Meier Found., 1988-92, bd. dirs., 1986—; elder, Chapel Woods Presbyterian Ch., 1983. USPHS trainee, 1967-68, 70-71; Am. U. Faculty Research grantee, 1972. Mem. Am. Psychol. Assn., Western Psychol. Assn. (editor newsletter 1996—), Christian Assn. Psychol. Studies, Am. Sci. Affiliation, Oreg. Psychol. Assn. Author: The Human Reflex: Behavioral Psychology in Biblical Perspective, 1981, Counseling and the Demonic, 1988; contbg. editor Jour. Psychology and Theology, 1982—, Jour. Psychology and Christianity, 1982-87; contbr. chpts. to texts, numerous articles to profl. jours. Office: George Fox Coll 414 N Meridian St # 6146 Newberg OR 97132-2625

BUFFUM, WILLIAM ERWIN, social worker, educator; b. Grand Rapids, Mich., Dec. 11, 1944; s. Erwin Clair and Sena (Lucas) B.; m. Valerie Jane Regetz, Feb. 20, 1983; 1 child, Lindsay Louise. BA, Calvin Coll., 1966; MSW, U. Mich., 1970; PhD, Case Western Reserve U., 1981. ACSW, LMSW-ACP, Tex. Assoc. prof., assoc. dean U. Houston Grad. Sch. Social Work, 1981—. Mem. editorial bd. Jour. Sociology and Social Welfare, Jour. Community Practice. Bd. dirs. Refugee Svc. Alliance, Houston, 1988—. Mem. NASW, Coun. on Social Work Edn., Assn. Community Orgn. and Social Adminstrn. Democrat. Home: 2017 Catamaran Dr League City TX 77573-6933 Office: U Houston Grad Sch Social Work Houston TX 77204-4492

BUGBEE, ALAN CAMPBELL, JR., psychology educator, psychometric consultant; b. Allentown, Pa., Sept. 28, 1950; s. Alan Campbell and Patricia Pierce (Towle) B.; m. Pamela Jane Briney, Aug. 1, 1981. BA summa cum laude, U. Vt., 1973; MA in Edn., George Washington U., 1976, MPA, 1977; PhD, U. Pitts., 1983. Rehab. counselor Div. Vocat. Rehab., St. Louis, 1978-79; instr. in anesthesiology Sch. Medicine U. Pitts., 1983; quality and measurement specialist Data Gen. Corp., Woodstock, Conn., 1984-86; asst. prof. psychology Am. Coll., Bryn Mawr, Pa., 1986-91, assoc. prof., 1991—, dir. examination rsch., 1986-88, dir. edn. systems, 1988—; cons. Banyan Systems, Inc., Westboro, Mass., 1991, TRO Learning, Edina, Minn., 1992—, Profl. Examination Svc., N.Y.C., 1993—, Bur. Profl. & Fin. Regulation & Bur. Ins. State of Maine, 1993-94; psychometrist Columbia (Mo.) Pub. Schs., 1979-80; trainee NIMH, Washington, 1974-76. Book editor, 1996; contbr. articles, reports to profl. publs., chpt. to book. Judge Delaware Valley Sci. Fair, Phila., 1990, medals judge, 1991—. Mem. Am. Ednl. Rsch. Assn., Nat. Coun. on Measurement in Edn., Boulder Soc. Democrat. Congregationalist. Office: Am Coll 270 S Bryn Mawr Ave Bryn Mawr PA 19010-2110

BUHAIN, WILFRIDO JAVIER, medical educator; b. Bacoor, Cavite, Philippines, Oct. 12, 1940; m. Carlota Torres; children: Ronald, Edgar. AA, BS, U. Philippines, 1959, MD, 1964. Diplomate Am. Bd. Internal Medicine, Am. Bd. Pulmonary Diseases. Rsch. fellow in cardiology U. Philippines, Philippine Gen. Hosp., 1964-65; rotating intern Queens Hosp. Ctr., N.Y.C., 1965-66, resident in internal medicine, 1965-68; clin. fellow in pulmonary diseases Hosp. of U. Pa., 1968-69, chief pulmonary function lab. dept. medicine, 1971-72; rsch. fellow in pulmonary diseases Hosp. of U. Pa., VA Hosp., Phila., 1969-71; assoc. in medicine, cardiovascular-pulmonary div. med. dept. U. Pa. Sch. Medicine, 1971-72; assoc. in medicine, dept. medicine Mt. Sinai Sch. Medicine, CUNY, 1972-74; clin. instr. medicine Georgetown U., 1976-95; chief pulmonary function lab. dept. medicine Mt. Sinai Hosp. Svcs./City Hosp. Ctr. at Elmhurst, 1973-74; med. dir. respiratory therapy dept. Mt. Vernon Hosp., 1978—, chmn. dept. medicine, 1987-88, pres. med. staff, 1996—; mem. exec. com. Alexandria Hosp., 1983. Contbr. articles to profl. jours. Queensborough Soc. grantee; Pa. Thoracic Soc. grantee. Fellow ACP, Am. Coll. Chest Physicians; mem. AMA, Am. Soc. Internal Medicine, Am. Thoracic Soc., Am. Fedn. Clin. Rsch., Alexandria Med. Soc., Va. Med. Soc., Philippine Med. Assn. (exec. dir., past pres. Metro-Washington), Assn. Philippine Physicians in Am. Office: 6300 Stevenson Ave Apt B Alexandria VA 22304-3576

BUHAN, PAUL JOHN, biology educator; b. Bridgeport, Conn., Apr. 22, 1941; s. Paul and Helen Catherine (Goldembieski) B.; m. Bridgetta Ann Buhan; 1 child, David Arthur. BA, U. Bridgeport, 1963; MS, Va. Poly. Inst., 1966, PhD, 1970; postgrad. Pa. State U., 1978-79. Researcher NSF Mountain Lake Biol. Sta., Va., 1965; research asst. U. N.C., Morehead City, 1967; from asst. to assoc. prof. biology Shippensburg U., Pa., 1969—; cons. Gannett, Fleming, Cordory & Carpenter, Engrs., Harrisburg, Pa., 1976-77. Contbr. articles to profl. jours. on fish osteology. Mem. Sigma Xi, Phi Sigma. Avocations: painting, fishing, collecting miniatures.

BUHRER, D. PAUL, plastic surgeon. BS, Tulane U., 1977, MD, 1982. Diplomate Bd. Plastic Surgery. Pvt. practice plastic surgery Annapolis, Md., 1988—. Fellow ACS; mem. Am. Soc. Plastic and Reconstructive Surgeons, Am. Soc. Aesthetic Plastic Surgery. Office: 2448 Holly Ave Ste 400 Annapolis MD 21401

BUKOWSKI, ELAINE LOUISE, physical therapist; b. Phila., Feb. 18, 1949; d. Edward Eugene and Melanja Josephine (Przyborowski) B. BS in Phys. Therapy, St. Louis U., 1972; MS, U. Nebr., 1977. Lic. phys. therapist, N.J.; diplomate Am. Bd. Disabilities Analysts (sr. analyst, profl. adv. coun. 1995—). Clk. City of Phila., 1967; staff phys. therapist St. Louis Chronic Hosp., 1973, Cardinal Ritter Inst., St. Louis, 1973-74; dir. campus ministry musicals Creighton U., Omaha, 1974-75; tchg. asst. U. Nebr. Med. Ctr., Omaha, 1975-76; lectr. in anatomy U. Sci. and Tech., Kumasi, Ghana, 1977-78; chief phys. therapist Holy Family Hosp., Berekum, Ghana, 1978-79; coord. info. & guidance The Am. Cancer Soc., Phila., 1979-81; staff phys. therapist Holy Redeemer Vis. Nurse Assn., Phila., 1981-83; rehab. supr. Holy Redeemer Vis. Nurse Assn., Swainton, N.J., 1983-87; asst. prof. phys. therapy Richard Stockton Coll. N.J., Pomona, 1987-96, assoc. prof., 1996—; bd. dirs. The Bridge, Phila., 1979-80; vacation relief phys. therapist, N.J., summer 1988—; mem. profl. adv. coun. Holy Redeemer VNA, Swainton, N.J., 1982-93, chmn., 1985-91, mem. pers. com., cons. hospice program, 1985-87, rehab. cons., 1987-88; legis. adv. coun. subcom. on edn. and health care Cape May & Cumberland Counties, 1988-90; utilization rev. cons. rehab. svcs., 1990; mem. fitness screening team N.J. State Legislature, 1990; mem. geriatric rehab. del. Citizen Amb. Program, China, 1992. Co-author slide study program, 1976, (video) Going My Way? The Low Back Syndrome, 1976; contbr. articles to profl. jours. Vol. Am. Cancer Soc., Phila., 1979-82, Walk-a-Day-in-My Shoes prog. Girl Scouts Am., Cape May County, N.J., 1983-86; task force phys. therapy prog. Stockton State Coll., Pomona, N.J., 1985-88. U.S. Govt. trainee, 1971, 72; Physical Therapy Fund grantee, 1975, 76; recipient Vol. Achievement award Am. Cancer Soc., 1981. Mem. Am. Phys. Therapy Assn. (edn. sect., orthopedic sect., vice chair so.

sect. 1993-96, chair so. sect. 1996—, ho. of dels. 1994-96), N.J. Arthritis Health Professions Assn. (reader adv. network Arthritis Today, key contact voting dist. 1, legis. network State of N.J. 1989—, vice chair so. dist. 1994-96, chair so. dist. 1996—, bd. dirs. 1996—, ho. of dels.), Smithsonian Assn., Phys. Therapy Club (sec. 1971-72), N.J. Phys. Therapy Assn. (rsch. com. 1995—). Office: Richard Stockton Coll NJ Phys Therapy Program Jim Leeds Rd Pomona NJ 08240

BULAWA, BETH ANN, surgeon; b. Glens Falls, N.Y., June 13, 1962; d. Richard Cardy and Mary Jane (Murray) Merrill; m. Erick Charles Bulawa. BS, Sierra Coll., 1983; MD, SUNY, 1988. Resident in gen. surgery Albany (N.Y.) Med. Ctr., 1988-93; gen. surgeon Rome (N.Y.) City Hosp., 1993—. Office: 1614 N James St Rome NY 13440

BULGER, ROGER JAMES, academic health center executive; b. Bklyn., May 18, 1933; s. William Joseph and Florence Dorothy (Poggi) B.; m. Ruth Ellen Grouse, June 8, 1960; children: Faith Anne, Grace Ellen. AB, Harvard U., 1955, MD, 1960; postgrad., Emmanuel Coll., Cambridge (Eng.) U., 1955-56; hon. degree, Thomas Jefferson U., U. Md. Intern, resident internal medicine U. Wash. Hosps., 1960-62, 64-65; postgrad. trainee infectious disease and microbiology U. Wash., 1962-63, 65-66; renal and metabolic diseases Boston U., 1963-64; asst. prof., then assoc. prof. medicine U. Wash. Med. Sch., Seattle, 1966-70; med. dir. Univ. Hosp., Seattle, 1967-70; prof. community health scis., asso. dean allied health Duke U. Med. Ctr., 1970-72; exec. officer Inst. Medicine, Nat. Acad. Scis., 1972-76; prof. internal medicine George Washington U. Sch. Medicine, 1972-76; prof. internal medicine, family and community medicine, dean Med. Sch., chancellor Worcester campus U. Mass., 1976-78; pres. U. Tex. Health Sci. Ctr., Houston, 1978-88; pres., chief exec. officer Assn. Acad. Health Ctrs., 1988—; mem. report rev. com. Nat. Acad. Scis. Author: Hippocrates Revisited, 1973, In Search of Modern Hippocrates, 1987, Technology, Bureaucracy and Healing, 1988; also articles, chpts. in books; mem. editorial bds. various jours. Bd. dirs. Georgetown U. Lionel de Jersey Harvard fellow, 1955-56. Fellow A.C.P.; mem. Inst. Medicine, Am. Soc. Microbiology, Infectious Disease Soc. Am., Soc. Tchrs. Preventive Medicine, Am. Soc. Nephrology, Soc. Health and Human Values. Office: Assoc. Acad Health Ctrs # 720 1400 Sixteenth St NW Washington DC 20036

BULL, BRIAN STANLEY, pathology educator, medical consultant, business executive; b. Watford, Hertfordshire, Eng., Sept. 14, 1937; came to U.S., 1954, naturalized, 1960; s. Stanley and Agnes Mary (Murdoch) B.; m. Maureen Hannah Huse, June 3, 1963; children: Beverly Velda, Beryl Heather. B.S. in Zoology, Walla Walla Coll., 1957; M.D., Loma Linda (Calif.) U., 1961. Diplomate: Am. Bd. Pathology. Intern Yale U., 1961-62, resident in anat. pathology, 1962-63; resident in clin. pathology NIH, Bethesda, Md., 1963-65; fellow in hematology and electron microscopy NIH, 1965-66, staff hematologist, 1966-67; research asst. dept. anatomy Loma Linda U., 1958, dept. microbiology, 1959, asst. prof. pathology, 1968-71, assoc. prof., 1971-73, prof., 1973—, chmn. dept. pathology, 1973—, assoc. dean for acad. affairs sch. medicine, 1993-94, dean sch. medicine, 1994—; cons. to mfrs. of med. testing devices; mem. panel on hematology FDA; mem. Nat. Com. on Clin. Lab. Standards; mem. Internat. Commn. for Standardization in Hematology, pres., 1996-97. Mem. bd. editors Blood Cells, Molecules and Diseases, 1995—; contbr. chpts. to books, articles to med. jours.; patentee in field; editor-in-chief Blood Cells N.Y. Heidelberg, 1985-94. Served with USPHS, 1963-67. Nat. Inst. Arthritis and Metabolic Diseases fellow, 1967-68; recipient Daniel D. Comstock Meml. award Loma Linda U., 1961, Merck Manual award, 1961, Mosby Scholarship Book award, 1961; Ernest B. Cotlove Meml. lectr. Acad. Clin. Lab. Physicians and Scientists, 1972. Fellow Am. Soc. Clin. Pathologists, Am. Soc. Hematology, Coll. Am. Pathologists, FDA Panel on Hematology, Nat. Com. on Clin. Lab. Standards, Internat. Commn. for Standards in Hematology, N.Y. Acad. Scis.; mem. AMA, Calif. Soc. Pathologists, San Bernadino County Med. Soc., Acad. Clin. Lab. Physicians and Scientists, Am. Assn. Pathologists, Sigma Xi, Alpha Omega Alpha. Seventh-day Adventist. Office: Loma Linda U Sch Medicine 11234 Anderson St Loma Linda CA 92354-2804

BULLARD, KENNETH PENN, plastic surgeon; b. Chadbourn, N.C., Nov. 11, 1935; s. Jay Livingston Bullard and Hazel Irene (Burns) Barnitz; m. Nancy Jean Redding, Aug. 17, 1963; children: Steven Redding, Janine Elizabeth. BSEE, Ga. Tech., 1957; MD, Wake Forest U., 1966. Diplomate Am. Bd. Plastic Surgery. Engr. Md. Electric Mfg. Co., College Pk., 1957; comm. officer USAF, 1957-60; engr. Vitro Labs., Silver Spring, Md., 1960-62; intern Roanoke (Va.) Meml. Hosp., 1966-67; gen. surgery resident N.C. Bapt. Hosp./Bowman Gray Sch. Medicine, 1967-70; plastic surgeon resident Albany (N.Y.) Med. Ctr., 1971-73; pvt. practice physician Charlotte, N.C., 1973—; clin. asst. prof. dept. plastic surgery U. N.C. Sch. Medicine, Chapel Hill, 1990—; chief dept. plastic surgery Presbyn. Hosp., Charlotte, 1979-80. 1st lt. USAF, 1957-60. Republican. Baptist. Office: 201 Providence Rd Ste 103 Charlotte NC 28207

BULLARD, RAY ELVA, JR., retired psychiatrist, hospital administrator; b. Dallas, Jan. 25, 1927; s. Ray Elva and Beatrice (Taylor) B.; children by previous marriage: Suzanne, Ray Elva. BS, U. Wash., 1948; MD (Mead Johnson scholar), U. Tex. Med. Br., Galveston, 1953; BA, U. Tex., 1957. Diplomate Am. Bd. Psychiatry and Neurology. Intern Houston VA Hosp., 1953-54; resident in gen. practice U. Iowa, summer 1954, Nan Travis Meml. Hosp., Jacksonville, Tex., 1954-55; gen. practice medicine Normangee, Blanco and Austin, Tex., 1955-63; resident in psychiatry VA Hosp., Topeka, 1963-66; chief sect. psychiatry VA Hosp., 1966-71, chief svc., 1971-73; asso. prof. psychiatry U. Okla., 1971-73; supt. Hollidaysburg (Pa.) State Hosp., 1973-76, Torrance (Pa.) State Hosp., 1976-94; cons. Allegheny Valley Counseling Ctrs., 1994—; guest lectr. Pa. State U., U. Pitts.; adj. asst. prof. psychiatry U. Pitts. Sch. Medicine, 1978—; adj. asst. prof. St. Francis Coll., 1983-94. Served with U.S. Army, 1944-46. Menninger Found. fellow, 1963-66. Fellow APA (life); mem. AMA (Physicians Recognition award 1994), Am. Psychiat. Assn., Pa. Psychiat. Assn., Pa. Med. Assn., Masons. Episcopalian. Home: RR 1 Box 82A Vandergrift PA 15690-9652

BULLARD, RICKEY HOWARD, podiatric physician, surgeon; b. Corinth, Miss., Aug. 9, 1954; s. Herman A. and Bonnie Ruth (Gurley) B.; m. Carolyn Jean Strickland, June 6, 1981. BS in Biology, Millsaps Coll., Jackson, Miss., 1975; BS in Med. Sci., Ill. Coll. Podiatric Medicine, Chgo., 1980, DPM, 1980. Diplomate Am. Bd. Podiatric Orthopedics and Primary Podiatric Medicine. Courtesy med. staff Iuka (Miss.) Hosp., 1980—; assoc. med. staff North Miss. Med. Ctr., Tupelo, 1992—; pvt. practice Tupelo and Iuka, 1980—; cons. Miss. State Bd. Med. Licensure, Jackson, 1982—, Tighomingo Manor Health Ctr., Iuka, 1981—, Cedars Health Ctr., Tupelo, 1983—, Lee Manor Health Ctr., Tupelo, 1984—, Alcorn Care Inn, Corinth, 1985—; bd. dirs. Diabetes Treatment Ctr., Tupelo, 1994—. Watkins scholar Millsaps Coll., 1973. Fellow Am. Assn. Hosp. Podiatrists, Am. Coll. Foot and Ankle Orthopaedics and Medicine, Internat. Acad. Podiatric Medicine; mem. Am. Podiatric Med. Assn. (del. 1984, 87, 89), Miss. Podiatric Med. Assn. (pres. 1984-86, sec., treas. 1987—), SAR, Christian Med. Soc., Gen. Soc. War of 1812. Methodist. Home: 2381 Amelia Ln Tupelo MS 38801 Office: 1904 West Main St Tupelo MS 38801

BULLARD, ROBERT LEE, physician assistant; b. Muskogee, Okla., Jan. 24, 1947; s. Jack Lee and Ann Lee (Hamon) B.; m. DeAnn Marie Hoelscher; children: Robert, Josh, John. BS, Northeastern State U., 1971; B Health Scis. in Physician Asst., Wichita State U., 1979. Cert. physician asst., ACLS. Lab. dir. comparative anatomy Northeastern State U., Tahlequah, Okla., 1970-71; med. technologist Hillcrest Med. Ctr., Tulsa, 1972-77; physician asst. Dr. J. Lester, M.D., Mangum, Okla., 1979-80, Okemah (Okla.) Indian Hosp., 1980-85; assoc. prof. U. Okla. Coll. Medicine, Oklahoma City, 1980-85; physician asst. Latimer County Hosp., Wilburton, Okla., 1985-87, Dr. Max Alumbaugh D.O., Stigler, Okla., 1987—; instr. continuing med. edn. local hosp. and nursing homes, Stigler, 1979—; lab. dir. Alumbaugh Clinic, Inc., Stigler and Roland, Okla., 1987—. Mem. sch. bd. Stigler Pub. Sch., 1995—, v.p., 1996. Fellow Am. Soc. Clin. Pathologist (cert. med. technologist), Am. Acad. Physician Asst. (cert. physician asst.), Assn. Physician Asst. Program (cert. physician asst.); mem. Okla. Assn. Physician Asst. (cert. physician asst.). Democrat. Home: Rt 2 Box 2335 Stigler OK 74462 Office: Alumbaugh Clinic Inc 907 NW 6th Stigler OK 74462

BULLAS, LEONARD RAYMOND, microbiology educator; b. Lismore, New South Wales, Australia, Dec. 8, 1929; came to U.S., 1959; s. Raymond and Arum Adelaide (Semmens) B.; widowed; children: Roslyn, Graham. BSc, U. Adelaide, Australia, 1953, MSc, 1957; Phd, Mont. State U., 1963. Instr. bacteriology U. Adelaide, 1953-58; research asst. Mont. State U., Bozeman, 1959-62; instr. microbiology Loma Linda (Calif.) U., 1962-64, asst. prof., 1964-70, assoc. prof., 1970-80, prof. microbiology, 1980-96, ret., 1996; vis. prof. U. Louvain, Belgium, 1973-74, invited prof., 1989; vis. prof. European Molecular Biology Lab., Heidelberg, Fed. Republic Germany, 1981-82. Contbr. articles to sci. jours. Recipient Basic Sci. Investigator of Yr. award MacPherson Soc., 1975, 81; Basic Sci. fellow MacPherson Soc., 1981. Mem. Am. Soc. Microbiology, Genetics Soc. Am., Sigma Xi. Adventist.

BULLOCK, ERIC WAYNE, emergency and intensive care nurse, paramedic; b. Oceanside, Calif., July 16, 1967; s. Joe Charles Jr. and Carol Margrete (Lutener) B.; m. Maria Elizabeth Valles, May 11, 1991; 1 child, Eric Anthony. BSN, U. Tex., El Paso, 1992. RN, Tex.; cert. emergency nurse, cert. ICU nurse; cert. ACLS instr., PALS instr. Staff nurse, emergency Providence Meml. Hosp., El Paso, 1992-95; staff nurse ICU Sierra Med. Ctr., El Paso, 1995—; adminstr. Nurse Plus, Inc., 1996; 2d vice chmn. bd. dirs. ARC, El Paso, 1996. 2d lt. U.S. Army Res. Mem. AACCN, Am. Legion. Republican. Christian. Home: 1408 Oakdale El Paso TX 79925

BULLOCK, JAMES HOWARD, clinical psychologist; b. Washington, June 26, 1953; s. Howard Benjamin and Betty Maurine (Hasely) B.; m. Denise Lynn Ferree, Aug. 13, 1978; 1 child, Benjamin Richard. BS, Coll. William and Mary, Williamsburg, Va., 1975; MA, Wake Forest U., Winston-Salem, 1978; PsyD, Va. Consortium for Profl.Psych, Norfolk, Va., 1987. Lic. clin. psychologist, Va.; diplomate Am. Coll. Forensic Examiners. Clin. psychology intern Med. Coll. Va., Richmond, 1982-83; coord. Charles City/New Kent Mental Health Henrico Mental Health, Richmond, 1985-87; affiliate clin. prof. psychology Va. Commonwealth U., Richmond, 1989—; coord. outpatient svcs. Henrico Area Mental Health and Retardation Svcs., Richmond, 1987-92; clin. psychologist in pvt. practice Richmond, 1989-93; assoc. prof. dept. psychiatry Med. Coll. Va., Richmond, 1993—; chair Henrico County Case Cons. Com., Richmond, 1987-91; mem. Henrico County Multidiscipline Team, 1987-91; cons. Henrico Homicide Survivors Group, 1990-92; chair Charles City/New Kent Case Cons. Com., 1985-87. Mem. Am. Psychol. Assn., Va. Psychol. Assn., Va. Acad. Clin. Psychologists. Office: 7760 Parham Rd Ste 200 Richmond VA 23294

BULLOCK, JOSEPH DANIEL, pediatrician, educator; b. Cin., Jan. 23, 1942; s. Joseph Craven and Emilie (Woide) B.; m. Martha Foss, June 20, 1964; children: Jennifer Zane, Sarah Harrison. BA, Wittenberg U., 1963; MD, Ohio State U., 1967, degree in pediatrics, 1969; degree in immunology, allergy, U. Calif., San Francisco, 1971. Diplomate Am. Bd. Pediatrics, Am. Bd. Allergy and Immunology. Clin. prof. pediatrics Ohio State U., Columbus, 1971—; pres. Midwest Allergy Assocs., Inc., Worthington, Ohio, 1971—. Contbr. articles to profl. jours. Active fund raising Wittenberg U., Springfield, Ohio, 1980-83, Columbus Sch. for Girls, 1977-86. Served to capt. USAF, 1967-71. Recipient Mead Johnson award, 1965. Fellow Am. Acad. Pediatrics, Am. Acad. Allergy, Am. Coll. Allergists (Bd. Regents 1979-82, Clemens von Pirquet award 1968, 69, 70, 71), Am. Thoracic Soc., Interasma, Ohio Soc. Allergy and Immunology (pres. 1985-87). Republican. Lutheran. Clubs: Columbus Country; The Golf (New Albany, Ohio); Indian Creek Country (Miami Beach, Fla.), The Surf (Surfside, Fla.). Home: 189 N Parkview Ave Columbus OH 43209-1435 Office: Midwest Allergy Assocs Inc 85 E Wilson Bridge Rd Columbus OH 43085-2301

BULLOUGH, VERN LEROY, nursing educator, historian, sexologist, researcher; b. Salt Lake City, July 24, 1928; s. D. Vernon Bullough and Augusta Rueckert; m. Bonnie Uckerman, Aug. 2, 1947; children: David, James, Steven, Susan, Michael. BSN, Calif. State U., Long Beach, 1981; BS, U. Utah, 1951; MA, U. Chgo., 1951, PhD, 1954. Dean, faculty of nat. and social scis. SUNY, Buffalo, disting. prof. emeritus; vis. prof. U. So. Calif., 1994—. Author, co-author of more than 40 books; sr. editor Free Inquiry; contbr. more than 200 articles to profl. jours. With U.S. Army Security Agy., 1946-48. Named Oustanding Prof. Calif. State U. sys., Disting. Prof., SUNY; recipient Kinsey award. Fellow Am. Acad. Nursing, Soc. Sci. Study Sex (past pres.), Acad. Humanism (laureate); mem. Internat. Humanist and Ethical Union (pres.).

BULMER, GLENN STUART, medical mycologist, educator; b. Windsor, Ont., Can., May 3, 1931; s. Albert Frederick and Evelyn Mary (Simmers) B.; m. Amelia Castillo; children: Scott, Allison, Gary, Cindy, Ives, Mandy, Paz, Emilie. BS, Mich. State U., 1957, MS, 1960, PhD, 1960. Instr. U. Okla. Sch. Medicine, Oklahoma City, 1960-63, asst. prof., 1963-68, assoc. prof., 1968-73, prof., 1973-88, prof. emeritus, 1988—; professorial chair holder U. Santo Tomas Sch. Medicine and Surgery, Manila, 1989—, head mycology sect., 1989—; chargé de cours Univ. Geneva Sch. Medicine, 1972-73; assoc. prof. Univ. Saigon Sch. Medicine, Vietnam, 1974-75; vis. prof. Nat. Univ. Singapore, 1983; cons. WHO. Author: Fungus Diseases in the Orient, 1991, 93, 95, Medical Mycology Educational Text, 1991, others; contbr. over 50 articles on cryptococcosis to profl. jours. NIH grantee, 1962-81; postdoctoral fellow NIH, 1966-73. Mem. Internat. Soc. Human and Animal Mycology, Med. Mycology Soc. of Ams., Am. Soc. Microbiology, Am. Acad. Microbiology, Med. Mycology Soc. of Philippines (pres. 1995—). Office: Univ Santo Tomas Sch Med, Espana St Sampaloc, Manila 1100, The Philippines

BULMER, JUDITH NICOLA, pathology educator; b. York, Eng., Jan. 26, 1956; d. David and June (Gladders) B. MB ChB, U. Manchester (Eng.), 1978; PhD, U. Bristol (Eng.), 1985. House officer Sharoe Green Hosp., Preston, Eng., 1978-79; sr. house officer in pathology No. Gen. Hosp., Sheffield, Eng., 1979-80, registrar in pathology, 1980-81; lectr. pathology U. Bristol, 1981-82, Carey Coombs rsch. fellow dept. pathology, 1982-84; lectr. pathology U. Leeds, Eng., 1984-91; sr. lectr. pathology U. Newcastle upon Tyne, Eng., 1991—. Author (with others) books; contbr. articles in reproductive immunobiology to profl. jours. Rsch. grantee in field of reproductive immunology. Mem. Royal Coll. Pathologists, Brit. Med. Assn., Assn. Clin. Pathologists, Internat. Acad. Pathology, Path. Soc. Gt. Britain and Ireland, Brit. Soc. for Immunology, Soc. for the Study of Fertility, Internat. Soc. for Immunology of Reprodn. Office: U Newcastle upon Tyne, Sch of Pathol Scis, Royal Victoria Infirmary, Newcastle upon Tyne NE1 4LP, England

BULY, ROBERT LEON, orthopaedic surgeon, educator; b. New Castle, Pa., Sept. 13, 1956; s. Michael and Fedora (Gigli) B.; m. Lynne Schuette, July 19, 1980; children: Alexander, Jocelyn, Christopher. BS, Pa. State U., 1978, MS, 1982; MD, Cornell U., 1985. Bd. cert. Am. Bd. Orthopaedic Surgery. Intern gen. surgery N.Y. Hosp., N.Y.C., 1985-86; resident orthopaedic surgery Hosp. for Spl. Surgery, N.Y.C., 1986-90; fellow hip reconstruction Mueller Inst., Bern, Switzerland, 1990-91; fellow joint replacement Case Western Res. Sch. Medicine, Cleve., 1991, asst. prof. orthopaedic surgery, 1991-94; asst. prof. orthopaedic surgery Cornell U. Med. Coll., N.Y.C., 1994—; orthopaedic surgeon Hosp. for Spl. Surgery/The N.Y. Hosp., N.Y.C., 1994—. Fellow Am. Bd. Orthopaedic Surgery, Am. Acad. Orthopaedic Surgery. Republican. Episcopalian. Office: Hosp for Spl Surgery 535 E 70th St New York NY 10021

BUNAG, RUBEN DAVID, pharmacologist, researcher; b. Manila, The Philippines, June 3, 1931; came to U.S., 1960; s. Maximino G. and Angelina (David) B.; m. Pros Liongson, Apr. 7, 1956; children: Royce, Karen. MD, U. of The Philippines, 1955; MA, U. Kans., Kansas City, 1962. Instr. U. Philippines Med. Sch., 1955-60; rsch. fellow Western Res. U., Cleve., 1962-63, Cleve. Clinic, 1963-69; rsch. pharmacologist VA Hosp., Kansas City, Mo., 1970-72; assoc. prof. Med. Ctr. U. Kans., Kansas City, 1970-75, prof. pharmacology Med. Ctr., 1975—; mem. Kans. Drug Utilization Rev., Kansas City, 1981—, NIH Cardiovascular Study Sect., Bethesda, Md., 1983-87. NIH grantee, 1972—. Roman Catholic. Office: U Kans Med Ctr 39th & Rainbow 3901 Rainbow Blvd Kansas City KS 66160-0001

BUNCHMAN, HERBERT HARRY, II, plastic surgeon; b. Washington, Feb. 23, 1942; s. Herbert H. and Mary (Halleran) B.; m. Marguerite Fransioli, Mar. 21, 1963 (div. Jan. 1987); children: Herbert H. III., Angela K., Christopher. BA, Vanderbilt U., 1964; MD, U. Tenn., 1967. Diplomate Am. Bd. Surgery, Am. bd. Plastic Surgery. Resident in surgery U. Tex., Galveston, 1967-72, resident in plastic surgery, 1972-75; practice medicine specializing in plastic surgery Mesa, Ariz., 1975—; chief surgery Desert Samaritan Hosp., 1978-80. Contbr. articles to profl. jours. Eaton Clin. fellow, 1975. Mem. AMA, Am. Soc. Plastic and Reconstructive Surgery, Am. Soc. Aesthetic Plastic Surgery, Singleton Surgical Soc., Tex. Med. Assn., So. Med. Assn. (grantee 1974), Ariz. Med. Assn. Office: Plastic Surgery Cons PC 1520 S Dobson Rd Ste 314 Mesa AZ 85202-4727

BUNDICK, WILLIAM ROSS, dermatologist; b. Balt., Nov. 22, 1917; s. Percy Ross and Edith Ruth (Smith) B.; m. Katherine Harrison Epps, Apr. 22, 1945 (dec. Nov. 1986); children: Susan Bundick Sukeforth, Karen Lee Bundick Guth, Paul Ross. M.D., U. Md., 1941; postgrad., NYU, 1947-48. Diplomate Am. Bd. Dermatology. Intern Baroness Erlanger Hosp., Chattanooga, 1941-42; resident Ft. Howard (Md.) VA Hosp., 1946-47; practice medicine specializing in dermatology, 1947—; assoc. dermatologist Mercy Hosp., Balt., 1947-67; assoc. in dermatology U. Md. Sch. Medicine, 1952-58, Johns Hopkins U. Sch. Medicine, 1952-58; asst. dermatologist St. Joseph Hosp., Towson, Md., 1947-69, chief dermatology, 1970-84; pvt. practice medicine Timonium, Md., 1971—. Chess editor: Balt. Sunday Sun, 1963-74; compiler, editor Directory Internat. Assn. Jazz Record Collectors, 1979-88; contbr. articles to med. jours. Served to capt. M.C. AUS, 1942-46. Balt. amateur chess champion, 1973. Fellow Am. Acad. Dermatology; mem. AMA, Md. Dermatol. Soc. (pres. 1975), Med. and Chiurg. Faculty of Md., Md. Chess Assn. (pres. 1964), U.S. Chess Fedn. (del. 1959-64), Assn. Internat. de la Presse Echiqueene, Towson Chess Club (pres. 1959, 65), Timonium Rotary Club (pres. 1961-62). Home: 8800 Walther Blvd Apt 4114 Baltimore MD 21234 Office: 57 W Timonium Rd Lutherville Timonium MD 21093-3125

BUNDRED, NIGEL JAMES, surgeon; b. Sunderland, Durham, Eng., July 17, 1957; s. James and Georgina Bundred; m. Sara Michelle Prize, Mar. 18, 1969. MBBS, Newcastle U., Eng., 1980; MD, U. Newcastle-Upon-Tyne, Eng., 1990. Lectr. U. Edinburgh, Scotland, 1982-84, U. Birmingham, Eng., 1989-91; surg. registrar Leicester (Eng.) Area Health Authority, 1985-87; postfellowship registrar U. Hosp. of Wales, 1988-89; sr. lectr. U. Manchester, Eng., 1991—; cons. surgeon U. Hosp. South Manchester, 1991—, Christie Hosp., Manchester, 1991—; dir. Manchester Surg. Rsch. Fund, Eng., 1991—. Author: Wolfe Atlas of Breast Diseases, 1994. Fellow Royal Coll. Surgeons London (Hunterian prof. 1994), Royal Coll. Surgeons Edinburgh; mem. Surg. Rsch. Soc. (Patey prize 1991, 94), Brit. Assn. Surg. Oncology (mem. nat. com.). Office: U Hosp South Manchester, Dept Surgery, Nell Ln, Manchester M20 8LR, England

BUNDUKAMARA, MOSES ABRAM, pharmacologist; b. Freetown, West Africa, Mar. 20, 1921; s. Ibrahim Sori and Augusta Selina (Moriba) B.; m. Regina Joana Thompson, Sept. 14, 1957 (dec. June 5, 1990); children: Alafia Gloria, Moses Abraham, Francis Louis; m. Mary Sao, Jan. 31, 1991 (div. June 1995); m. Augusta Selina Moriba, Nov. 28, 1995. Cons. pharmacologist Psychiat. Inst. Md. Home: 10704 Francis Dr Silver Spring MD 20902

BUNGO, MICHAEL WILLIAM, physician, educator, science administrator; b. Passaic, N.J., July 18, 1950; s. John C. and Mary (Tabachuk) B.; children: Elise Nicole, Jonathan Michael. BS in Chemistry, Rensselaer Poly. Inst., 1971; MD, N.J. Med. Sch., 1975. Diplomate Am. Bd. Internal Medicine, Subsplty. Bd. Cardiovascular Diseases. Intern in internal medicine New Eng. Deaconess Hosp., Boston, 1975-76, resident, 1976-78; asst. in medicine Peter Bent Brigham Hosp., Boston, 1976-77; cardiology fellow New Eng. Deaconess Hosp., Harvard Med. Sch., Boston, 1978-80; head cardiovascular lab. NASA, Johnson Space Ctr., Houston, 1980-85; mem. Aerospace Medicine Bd., Houston, 1980-91; dir. Space Biomed. Rsch. Inst. NASA, Johnson Space Ctr., Houston, 1986-90; chief scientist med. scis. div. NASA, 1990-91; chmn. dept. medicine St. John Hosp., Houston, 1987-89; prof. medicine U. Tex., Galveston, med. dir. heart sta. divsn. cardiology, 1995—; fellowship advisor NRC, Washington, 1984-89. Editor: Results of Life Sciences Aboard the Space Shuttle, 1987; contbr. abstracts and articles to jours., chpts. to books; tech. reviewer Aviation, Space and environ. Medicine, 1989—. Recipient medal NASA, 1986. Fellow Am. Coll. Cardiology; mem. Am. Heart Assn., Aerospace Med. Assn. (Louis H. Bauer Founders award 1987), Tex. Med. Assn., Phi Lambda Upsilon. Office: Univ of Tex Med Br Divsn of Cardiology Galveston TX 77555

BUNKER, ANTHONY LOUIS, health science executive; b. Madison, Minn., Jan. 4, 1933; s. Anton and Christina (Schilmoeller) B.; m. Joan M. Stoick, Aug. 29, 1953; children: Denise Reilly, Debbie Schwartz, Tom, Paul, Diane Dwyer. BA in Acctg., St. Thomas Coll., St. Paul, 1954; MHA, St. Louis U., 1960. Acct. St. Joseph Hosp., St. Paul, 1952-54; adminstrv. resident City Hosp., St. Louis, 1959-60; rsch. assoc. Cath. Hosp. Assn., St. Louis, 1960-62; asst. adminstr. DePaul Hosp., St. Louis, 1962-65, adminstr., 1966-69; exec. dir. DePaul Health Ctr., St. Louis, 1969-85; chief exec. officer St. Paul Med. Ctr., Dallas, 1985—; Trsutee Tex. Conf. Cath. Health Care Facilities, 1989-93, Tex. Hosp. Assn., 1991-95; chair Tchg. Hosps., Consortium Assn., 1987-93; asst. prof. St. Louis U., 1965-85; bd. councillors U. Dallas, 1992—. Fundraiser Boy Scouts Am., Dallas, 1987-92; mem. adv. bd. Ronald McDonald House, Dallas, 1985—. Capt. USAF, 1955-58. Recipient Community Svc. award Dallas Hispanic C. of C., 1991. Fellow Am. Coll. Healthcare Execs.; mem. Am. Hosp. Assn. (ho. of dels. 1986-89), St. Louis U. Alumni Assn. (Disting. Alumni award 1991). Roman Catholic. Office: St Paul Med Ctr 5909 Harry Hines Blvd Dallas TX 75235-6209

BUNN, WILLIAM BERNICE, III, physician, lawyer, epidemiologist; b. Raleigh, N.C., June 28, 1952; s. William Bernice Jr. and Clara Eva (Ray) B.; m. Shirley Welch, July 31, 1982; children: Ashley Howell, Elizabeth Jordan. AB, Duke U., 1974, MD, JD, 1979; MPH, U. N.C., 1983. Diplomate Am. Bd. Internal and Occupational Medicine. Intern, then resident in internal medicine Duke U. Med. Ctr., 1981-83, fellow in occupational medicine dept. community medicine, 1983; asst. prof. Sch. of Medicine Duke U., Durham, N.C., 1984-86, dir. rsch. in occupational medicine Sch. of Medicine, 1985-86; dir. occupational health and environmental affairs Bristol Myers Co., Wallingford, Conn., 1986-87, sr. dir. occupational health and environ. affairs, 1987-88; asst. clin. prof. Yale U., New Haven, 1986—; clin. asst. prof. U. Colo., Boulder, 1989; assoc. clin. prof. U. Cin., 1989—; corp. med. dir. Manville Sales Corp., Denver, 1988, v.p., corp. med. dir., 1988-89, sr. dir. for health safety and environ., v.p., 1989-92; dir. internat. med. affairs Mobil Corp., Princeton, N.J., 1992—; dir. health, workers compensation, disability and safety Navistan Internat. Corp., Chgo.; cons. author, co-editor Dellacorte Publs., N.Y.C., 1984-87; sci. adv. bd. U.S. EPA, Washington, 1991—; chmn. radiation epidemiology com. NAS, Washington, 1991—. Author: (with others) Effects of Exposure to Toxic Gases, 1986; author, editor: Poisoning, 1986, Occupational Problems in Clinical Practice; editor: Occupational and Environmental Medicine. Bd. dirs. Colo. Safety Assn., Denver, 1988-90, Gaylord Hosp., Wallingford, 1987-88, Meriden-Wallingford Hosp., 1986-88, Chem. Industry Inst. Toxicology, 1989-91, Am. Coll. Occupational and Environ. Medicine, 1993—. NIOSH scholar, 1980; NIH fellow, 1982-83, Nat. Inst. Occupational Safety and Health fellow, 1983-84. Fellow Am. Occupl. Medicine Assn. (co-chmn. acad. affairs com. and publs. com. 1985-90, nat. affairs com. 1985-86, chmn. pubs. com. 1990, bd. dirs. 1993—, chair internat. coun. 1994), Am. Coll. Occupl. and Environ. Medicine; mem. ACP, AMA, APHA, Occupl. Medicine Assn. Conn. (sec., pres.-elect 1986-88), Internat. Coll. Occupl. Health, Phi Beta Kappa, Phi Eta Sigma. Home: 1907 N Cleveland St Chicago IL 60614-1648 Office: Mobil Corp PO Box 1038 Princeton NJ 08543-1038 also: Yale U Dept Epidemiology & Pub Health New Haven CT 06520 also: U Colo Sch Pharmacy Dept Toxicology Boulder CO 80309 also: U Cin Dept Occupational Medicine Cincinnati OH 45267

BUNNELL, BRENT EDWARD, osteopath; b. Columbus, Ohio, Nov. 11, 1963; s. Larry Larone and Donna Jean (Matthews) B.; m. Melody Ann Burton, Sept. 3, 1994. BS, Tex. Christian U., 1986; DO, Tex. Coll. Osteo. Medicine, 1990. Diplomate Am. Bd. Osteo. Family Physicians, Am. Bd. Family Practice. Intern Doctors Hosp. Stark County, Massillon, Ohio, 1990-91; family practice resident St. Elizabeth Med. Ctr., Edgewood, Ky., 1991-93; physician Family Medicine Assocs., Shepherdsville, Ky., 1993, Humana Health Care Plans, Louisville, 1994-95, Health First Med. Assocs., Arlington, Tex., 1995—. Mem. AMA, Am. Osteo. Assn., Am. Acad.

Family Practice, Am. Coll. Osteo. Family Physicians, Tex. Med. Assn., Tex. Osteo. Med. Assn., Tarrant County Med. Soc., Sigma Sigma Phi. Republican. Episcopalian. Office: Health First Med Assocs 515 W Mayfield Rd Ste 200 Arlington TX 76014

BUNNELL, JAMES BERT, biomedical engineer; b. Price, Utah, Apr. 28, 1947; s. Kay Leroy and Genevieve (Darrah) B.; m. Jacqueline Neilson, Mar. 1968 (div. June 1971); m. Kaltheen Marie Kovich, Dec. 21, 1981; 1 child, Keith Allen Lubsen. AS, Coll. Ea. Utah, 1967; BS, U. Utah, 1969; ScD, MIT, 1972. Pub. health trainee Mass. Gen. Hosp., Boston, 1970-72, rsch. fellow, 1972-75; assoc. pediatrics Harvard Med. Sch., Boston, 1972-75; biomed. rsch. engr. Air Products & Chems., Allentown, Pa., 1975-77; mgr. physiology lab. Hopal Med. Corp., Salt Lake City, 1977-79, mgr. respiratory product R & D, 1979-80; founder, CEO, chmn. Bunnell Inc., Salt Lake City, 1980-94, chmn., chief tech. officer, 1994—; vis. lectr. MIT, Cambridge, 1972-75; cons. Arthur D. Little, Inc., Cambridge, summer 1969; mem. indsl. adv. bd. U. Utah, Salt Lake City, 1994—; bd. dirs. MountainWest Venture Group, Salt Lake City. Author: (with others) Current Perinatology, 1990, Neonatology for The Clinician, 1993; contbr. articles to profl. jours.; patentee in field. Mem. Utah Gov.'s Task Force Biomed. Industry Devel., Salt Lake City, 1989-90, Utah Biomed. Industry Coun. Salt Lake City, 1991-95. Recipient Outstanding Alumnus award Coll. Ea. Utah, 1990; NSF grantee, 1969-72. Mem. Am. Assn. Respiratory Therapy, Am. Thoracic Soc., Soc. Critical Care Medicine. Home: 1720 Emigration Canyon Salt Lake City UT 84108 Office: Bunnell Incorp 436 Lawndale Dr Salt Lake City UT 84115

BUNNER, CHERYL SUE, nurse administrator; b. Cairo, W.Va., Apr. 5, 1944; d. Orvle A. and Una Pauline (Slocum) Ingram; m. Milton David Bunner, Oct. 18, 1969; children: Jason L., Cynthia Joan. BS, St. Joseph's, North Windham, Maine, 1987. RN, LNHA, W.Va. Pediat. nurse Dr. James Shaffer MD, Bloomington, Ind., 1966-68; med., surg. nurse St. Joseph's Hosp., Parkersburg, W.Va., 1968; pub. health nurse Pleasants County Health Dept., St. Marys, W.Va., 1968-72; surg. asst. Dr. M.G. Magno MD, Parkersburg, 1972-75; nurse mgr. Physical Measurements Inc., Parkersburg, 1976-77; asst. to DON The Willows, Parkersburg, 1980-82; owner, administr., DON Cedar Grove Personal Care, Parkersburg, 1982—; chairperson Political Action Com. W.Va. Health Care, Charleston, 1993-95; mem. Pub. Health Care Planning State W.Va., Charleston. Named Woman of Excellence in Bus. and Professions, Altrusa/YWCA, Parkersburg, 1995. Mem. W.V.A. Health Care Assn. (bd. dirs. 1985—), Am. Coll. Health Care Adminstr., Am. Health Care Assn., Parkersburg Woman's (pres. 1994-96), Christian Woman's Club (pres. 1979), C. of C. Democrat. Baptist. Office: Cedar Grove Personal Care PO Box 1142 Parkersburg WV 26102

BUNNEY, BENJAMIN STEPHENSON, psychiatrist; b. Lansing, Mich., Sept. 27, 1938; s. William E. and Nora Orpha (Null) B.; m. Marjorie Bunney, Oct. 6, 1984; children: Edward Bradshaw, Katherine Stephenson, Elizabeth Janice. BA, NYU, 1960, MD, 1964. Resident in internal medicine Bellevue Hosp. NYU, 1964-66; resident in psychiatry Yale U., New Haven, 1968-71; asst. prof. psychiatry Yale U., 1971-74, asst. prof. pharmacology, 1974-75, assoc. prof. psychiatry, 1975-84, assoc. prof. pharmacology, 1976-84, prof. psychiatry, 1984—, prof. pharmacology, 1984, vice chair dept. psychiatry, 1986-87, acting chair dept. psychiatry, 1987-88, chair dept. psychiatry, 1988—; mem. bd. sci. counselors NIMH; mem. Inst. Medicine NAS, 1993. Contbr. articles to profl. jours. Capt. USAF, 1966-68. Recipient Daniel H. Efron award for rsch. Am. Coll. Neuropsychopharmacology, 1983, Lieber prize for rsch. Nat. Alliance for Rsch. in Schizophrenia and Depression, 1987, MERIT award NIMH, 1990. Fellow Am. Coll. Neuropsychopharmacology; mem. ACNP (pres. 1996), AAAS, Am. Psychiat. Assn. Office: Yale U Dept Psychiatry 25 Park St New Haven CT 06519-1110*

BUNTEN, BRENDA ARLENE, geriatrics nurse; b. Paris, Ill., May 7, 1947; d. Arthur Ray Sr. and Maxine L. (Bacon) B. A in Arts and Scis., Lakeland Coll., Mattoon, Ill., 1968; ADN, Kapiolani C.C., Honolulu, 1992. Charge nurse Meml. Med. Ctr., Springfield, Ill., 1968-76, Mattoon Health Care Ctr., 1977-79; agy. nurse Kahu Malama, Inc., Honolulu, 1983; charge nurse, staff devel. coord., infection control officer Hale Nani Health Ctr., Honolulu, 1979-93, also nursing staff scheduler, supr., 1979-93; unit mgr. Randal Mill Manor, Arlington, Tex., 1994—; supr. Heritage Oaks, Arlington, Tex., 1994—; fundraiser Challenger Run Hawaii, Honolulu, 1986—; co-owner, cons. retail sales Sunset Enterprises, Honolulu, 1982—. Mem. USS Lancelot, Alpha Kappa Psi, Beta Sigma Phi (pres. 1985-86). Home: 2009 Newbury Dr Arlington TX 76014-3616

BUNTING, PETER DOUGLAS, plastic surgeon; b. Roanoke, Va., Oct. 9, 1944; s. Douglas Jr. and Martha Virginia (Clarke) B.; m. Derry Brice, July 10, 1971; children: Elisabeth Derry, Virginia Louise, Allen Brice, Mary Doug. BA, Birmingham So. Coll., 1966; MD, U. Ala., 1970. Intern, resident Mass. Gen. Hosp.-Harvard Med. Sch., Boston, 1970-76; pres. Bunting Plastic Surgery Clinic, Birmingham, 1978—. Maj. USAF, 1976-78. Clin. fellow HArvard U., 1976. Mem. ACS, Am. Soc. Aesthetic Plastic Surgery, Am. Soc. Plastic and Reconstructive Surgeons, Ala. Soc. Plastic and Reconstructive Surgeons (past pres.), Alpha Omega Alpha. Republican. Presbyterian. Home: 2950 Argyle Rd Birmingham AL 35213 Office: Bunting Plastic Surgery Clinic 860 Montclair Rd Ste 251 Birmingham AL 35213

BUONANNI, BRIAN FRANCIS, health care facility administrator, consultant; b. Pawtucket, R.I., Sept. 2, 1945; s. James and Roselle B.; m. Lynne Buonanni (div. 1982); children: Donna, Karen, Jamie; m. Diane Manenty, Feb. 23, 1985 (div. 1992); m. Gloria Berenguer, Sept. 2, 1995. BA, Providence Coll., 1967; EdM, Boston Coll., 1968; M in Health Adminstrn., St. Louis U., 1973. Lic. nursing home adminstr., N.J. Rehab. counselor, tchr. R.I. Assn. for Blind, Providence, 1968-71; adminstrv. resident Carney Hosp., Boston, 1972; asst. adminstr. Alton (Ill.) Meml. Hosp., 1973-77, Gnaden Huetten Meml. Hosp., Lehighton, Pa., 1977-80; v.p. ops. Burdette Tomlin Hosp., Cape May Ct. House, N.J., 1980-85; chief oper. officer St. Elizabeth's Hosp., Elizabeth, N.J., 1985—, exec. v.p., 1989—; pres. Health Care Practice Mgmt., Jenkinstown, Pa., 1984—; chmn., mem. adv. bd. Shifa, McFaul & Lyons, Morristown, N.J., 1987-95; mem. rev.com. N.J. Health Council, Trenton, 1987—. Fellow Am. Coll. Healthcare Execs.; mem. Nat. Assn. Purchasing Agts., Rotary (past pres.). Home: 42 W Henry Pl Iselin NJ 08830 Office: St Elizabeth Hosp 225 Williamson St Elizabeth NJ 07202-3625

BURACZEWSKI, MICHELE MARIE, emergency room nurse; b. Charleroi, Pa., Mar. 8, 1966; d. Michael and Joann (Galaski) B. RN, Mercy Hosp., 1986; BSN, Duquesne U., 1990, postgrad., 1993—. RN, Pa.; CEN; cert. ACLS, BLS. Staff nurse Mercy Hosp., Pitts., 1986-90, staff nurse dept. of emergency medicine, 1990—, CEN, 1992—, staff nurse III dept. emergency medicine, 1994—; casual CCU RN Mon Valley Hosp., 1991—; spkr. Mothers Against Drunk Driving, 1993—; coord. ENCARE, 1995—. Speaker Am. Cancer Soc., Pitts., 1991-92, HALT drunken driver class Mercy Hosp.,1991-92. Mem. Mercy Alumni Assn., Duquesne Alumni Assn., Sigma Theta Tau (Epsilon Phi chpt.). Roman Catholic.

BURAKOFF, STEVEN JAMES, immunologist, educator; b. N.Y.C., Oct. 13, 1942; s. Jack and Adelene (Van Praag) B.; m. Suzanne Weindling, Sept. 3, 1965; 1 child, Alexis. BA, Lehigh U., 1964; MA, Queens Coll., Flushing, N.Y., 1965; MD, Albany Med. Coll. Union U., 1970; MA (hon.), Harvard U., 1984. Diplomate Am. Bd. Internal Medicine. Intern, resident N.Y. Hosp., Cornell Med. Ctr., 1970-73.; instr. Harvard Med. Sch., Boston, 1976-77, asst. prof., 1977-80, assoc. prof., 1980-83, prof., 1983—; chief pediat. oncology Dana Farber Cancer Inst., Boston, 1985—. Contbr. over 300 articles to profl. jours. Recipient Sr. Faculty award Am. Cancer Soc., 1980-85. Mem. Am. Soc. Clin. Investigation, Am. Assn. Immunologists (head program com. 1985-86), Assn. Am. Physicians, Transplantation Soc. Office: Dana-Farber Cancer Inst Dept Pediatrics Harvard Med Sch 44 Binney St Boston MA 02115-6013

BURBANCK, WILLIAM DUDLEY, biology educator; b. Indpls., Aug. 20, 1913; s. George Graham and Flora Henrietta (Kokemiller) B.; m. Madeline Palmer, Sept. 7, 1940; children: Melinda Ann Miller, George Palmer. AB, Earlham Coll., 1935; MS, Haverford Coll., 1936; PhD, U. Chgo., 1941. Instr. Earlham Coll., Richmond, Ind., 1936-38, CCNY, N.Y.C., 1941-42; chmn., from asst. to prof. Drury Coll., Springfield, Mo., 1942-49; vis. prof. Emory U., Atlanta, 1949-50, prof., 1950-80; chmn. dept. biology Emory U., 1952-57, emeritus prof., 1980—; instr. marine zoology Marine Biol. Lab., Woods Hole, Mass., 1943-50. Author chpt. in books; mem. editorial bd. Jour. of Protzoology; past assoc. editor Estuaries. Grantee NSF, NIH, ONR, Ga. Power Co.; Haverford Coll. scholar, 1935-36. Mem. Soc. of Protozoologists (v.p. 1956-57), Assn. S.E. Biologists (pres. 1964-65), S.E. Estuarine Rsch. Soc. (pres. 1976-78). Home: 1164 Clifton Rd NE Atlanta GA 30307-1230

BURBAUM, JONATHAN JEFFREY, biochemist; b. Olean, N.Y., Sept. 29, 1959; s. William Allen and Ruth A. (Harbert) B.; m. Beverly Lynn Wolgast, May 16, 1981; children: Nicholas Chapman, Matthew Allen, Patricia Lynn. BS, Rensselaer Poly. Inst., 1981; PhD, Harvard U., 1988. Postdoctoral fellow MIT, Cambridge, Mass., 1989-91; sr. rsch. scientist Merck Rsch. Labs., Rahway, N.J., 1991-93; sr. rsch. fellow Pharmacopeia, Inc., Princeton, N.J., 1993—; sci. cons. Amira, Inc., Worcester, Mass., 1989-90. Contbr. articles to profl. jours.; patent in field. Mem. Am. Chem. Soc., Sigma Xi.

BURCH, DWAYNE LEE, chiropractor; b. Ft. Lauderdale, Fla., Feb. 17, 1946; s. Lawrence A. and Lillian M. (Boudreaux) B.; m. Carol Hebert, Sept. 2, 1989; 1 child, Candice Catherine; 2 stepchildren: Keri Elizabeth, Jason Scott. Student, U. So. Fla., 1974-77; dr. of chiropractic, Life Chiropractic Coll., Marietta, Ga., 1980. Diplomate Nat. Bd. Chiropractic Examiners (examiner, proctor, La. state del.). Assoc. Gideon Chiropractic Clinic, Hammond, La., 1980—; sec.-treas. La. Bd. Chiropractic Examiners; cons. Dept. Health, various hosps.; chmn. dist. 7 La. Chiropractic Peer Rev. Bd., Baton Rouge, 1984-87. League physician Ponchatoula (La.) Youth Football Conf., 1982-83; team physician Southwood Acad., Hammond, 1983-85; instr. Protect Your Back program ARC. Mem. Coun. on Diagnostic Imaging, Internat. Thermographic Soc., La. Thermographic Soc. (cert., charter bd. dirs., treas. 1988-93), Tangipahoa Parish Chiropractic Soc. (pres. 1991), Lions (charter, 1st v.p. Ponchatoula chpt. 1987-89, pres. Ponchatoula chpt. 1989-90, Leo chmn., zone chmn. dist. 8N, Melvin Jones fellow), La. Eye Found. (life), League for Crippled Children (life), Knight of Sight. Republican. Office: Gideon Chiropractic Clinic 1006 W Morris Ave Hammond LA 70403-3906

BURCH, HENRY BURDETTE, endocrinologist; b. Buffalo, Nov. 14, 1955; s. Ralph Stanton and Clare Lilian (Quenton) B.; m. Lily Wai-Ling Seah, Feb. 15, 1986; children: Daniel Q., David H., Alexander C., James. M. BS magna cum laude, UCLA, 1980; MD, Uniformed Svcs. U., 1984. Commd. 2d lt. U.S. Army, 1980, advanced through grades to lt. col., 1996; asst. chief endocrine svc. Walter Reed Army Med. Ctr., Washington, 1988—. Author: (chpts.) Principles & Practice of Endocrinology, 1995, The Thyroid, 1996. Mem. Am. Coll. Physicians, Am. Thyroid Assn., The Endocrine Soc. Home: 10309 Gainsborough Rd Potomac MD 20854

BURCH, JOHN TRAVIS, orthopaedic surgeon; b. Tampa, Aug. 25, 1958; s. John Travis Sr. and Betty Lee Burch; m. Marla Ann Gary, June 12, 1982; children: Travis, Taylor, Marissa. AA, Fla. Coll., 1978; BS, Western Ky. U., 1981; MD with high distinction, U. Ky., 1986. Diplomate Am. Bd. Orthopaedic Surgery. Physician ptnr. Western Ky. Orthopaedic Assocs., Bowling Green, Ky., 1991—; cons. Roche/Syntex Adv. Bd., San Francisco, 1993-95; chief of surgery Greenview Regional Medical Ctr., Bowling Green, 1994—. Nat. Audubon Soc. scholarship Nat. Audubon Soc., 1980, Ogden Coll. scholarship Western Ky. U., 1981. Fellow Am. Bd. Orthopaedic Surgery; mem. AMA, Warren County Med. Soc. (pres. 1992-95), Ky. Med. Assn. (del. 1991—, alt. trustee 1995-96), Ky. Orthopaedic Soc., Warren County/Bowling Green C. of C. Office: Western Ky Orthopaedic Assocs 1777 Ashley Circle Bowling Green KY 42104

BURCH, ROBERT EMMETT, physician, educator; b. St. Louis, Oct. 9, 1933; s. Robert A. and Virginia J. (Gresham) B.; m. Christina P. Efthim, Sept. 1, 1956; children: Robert M., Paula L. BS, St. Louis U., 1955, MD, 1959. Diplomate Am. Bd. Internal Medicine. Intern Jewish Hosp. St. Louis, 1959-60; resident Firmin Desloge Hosp of St. Louis U., 1960-62; postdoctoral fellow Case Western Res. U., Cleve., 1962-65; assoc. in medicine to asst. prof. Columbia U., N.Y.C., 1965-71; assoc. prof. to prof. medicine Creighton U., Omaha, 1971-77; prof. and assoc. chmn. dept. medicine Marshall U., Huntington, W.Va., 1977-80; Price Goldsmith prof. medicine Tulane U., New Orleans, 1980—. Editor: Trace Elements, 1976. Chmn. Mayor's Task Force on Nutrition, New Orleans, 1983-85; mem. Gov.'s Task Force on Sci. and Tech., Baton Rouge, 1985; mem. Office of Tech. Transfer, U. New Orleans, 1988-94; mem. rsch. com. La. br. Am. Heart Assn., 1991-95. Grantee, Nat. Heart Inst., 1965-72, Nat. Inst. Aging, 1977-80. Fellow ACP; mem. Cen. Soc. for Clin. Rsch., Am. Soc. for Clin. Nutrition, Am. Inst. Nutrition, Am. Physiol. Soc. Office: VA Hosp 1601 Perdido St New Orleans LA 70112-1207

BURCH, SHARRON LEE STEWART, woman's health nurse; b. Washington, Dec. 19, 1944; d. David A. Jr. and Ruthanna (Craig) Stewart; m. Donald Victor Burch, Aug. 27, 1966; children: Elizabeth Katherine, Craig Donald. BSN, Vanderbilt U., 1966; M in Nursing, U. Miss. Med. Ctr., Jackson, 1975. RN, Miss. Staff nurse Druid City Hosp., Tuscaloosa, Ala., 1966-69; instr. insvc. edn. U. Hosp., Jackson, Miss., 1969-71; specialized nurse cons. Miss. Bd. Health, Jackson, 1972-74; instr. ADN Miss. Gulf Coast Jr. Coll., Biloxi, Miss., 1975-81, Hinds Community Coll., Jackson, 1982-91; staff nurse Rankin Med. Ctr., 1987—. Contbr. articles to profl. jours. Mem. ANA, Orgn. for Advancement ADN (chmn. ad hoc competency validation com. 1983-91, 1st vice chmn. tech. com. on state of art curricula for vocat. and tech. programs for health and personal svcs. 1991—), Miss. Nurses Assn., Sigma Theta Tau. Home: 784 Benwick Dr Brandon MS 39042-8112

BURCHELL, ALBERT ROBERT, surgeon; b. N.Y.C., Dec. 26, 1932; s. Nicholas Anthony and Florence (Doscher) B. m. Barbara Jean Conway, Dec. 26, 1956; children: Theresa, Karen, Patricia, Susan, Maureen, Richard, Margaret, Donna, Amy, Kathleen. BA, Fordham U., 1954; MD, Cornell U., 1958. Intern, resident surgery St. Vincent's Hosp., N.Y.C., 1958-63, attending surgeon, 1963—; surg. rsch. fellow NIH, N.Y.C., 1963-65; instr. clin. surgery NYU Sch. Medicine, N.Y.C., 1962-70, asst. prof., 1970-81; assoc. prof. surgery N.Y. Med. Coll., Valhalla, N.Y., 1980—; mem. exec. com. med. staff St. Vincent's Hosp., N.Y.C., 1980-90; co-investigator NIH, Health Rsch. Coun., City N.Y., N.Y. Heart Assn., NIH, 1960-80; prin. investigator John A. Hartford Found., Inc., Irene Heinz and John Laporte Given Found., Irwin Strasburger Found., N.Y.C., 1966-73. Contbr. articles to profl. jours., chpts. to books. Trustee St. Vincent's Hosp., N.Y.C., 1985-89, mem. exec. com., 1988-89. Recipient Surg. Rsch. award Internat. Coll. Surgeons, 1962, Horace Aryes Surg. Rsch. award N.Y. State div. Internat. Coll. Surgeons, 1963. Fellow ACS; mem. Assn. Surg. Edn., N.Y. Surg. Soc., N.Y. Cancer Soc., N.Y. Soc. Cardiovascular Surgery, Surg. Soc. N.Y. Med. Coll., Internat. Soc. Chirurgie. Home: 120 Stacey Ct River Vale NJ 07675-6624 Office: 2 Fifth Ave New York NY 10011

BURCHIEL, SUSAN MARGUERITE, nurse educator; b. South Bend, Ind., Dec. 8, 1954; d. Robert Catlett and Josephine (Trygstad) Smith; m. Richard Earl Burchiel, Sept. 30, 1977; 1 child, Stephanie Evelyn. Diploma, U. So. Calif. Med. Ctr., L.A., 1976; BSN, Mount St. Mary's Coll., 1981; MSN, Consortium Calif. State U., 1988. Cert. med.-surg. nurse, ANA; CNA. Pediatric staff nurse St. Johns Hosp., Santa Monica, Calif.; ICU staff nurse UCLA Hosp. and Clinics, 1976-77; staff nurse ICU Valley Presbyn. Hosp., Van Nuys, Calif., 1978-81; staff nurse Sierra Vista Hosp., San Luis Obispo, Calif., 1981-93; staff nurse psychiat. ctr. French Hosp., San Luis Obispo, 1988-93; staff nurse med./surg. Twin Cities Cmty. Hosp., Templeton, Calif., 1994—; lectr. Calif. State U. Dominquez Hills; instr., asst. dir. nursing divsn. Cuesta Coll., San Luis Obispo, 1986—; CNA test site coord. San Luis Obispo County, 1992-94; reviewer Addison-Wesley Pub., 1993—. Contbg. author: Addison-Wesley Lab Manual for Nurses, 1996. Spkr. on health careers to teenagers Calif. Youth Authority, 1995—. Kellogg fellow; grantee Fed. Nurse Traineeship. Mem. ANA. Calif. Nurses Assn. (ADN-BSN articulation task force 1989-91), Nat. Coun. Licensing Examination for RNs (item writer 1989), Nightingale Honor Soc.

BURD, ROBERT MEYER, hematologist, oncologist, educator; b. N.Y.C., Aug. 25, 1937; s. David and Anne (Popkin) B.; m. Alice Stoller, May 30, 1964; children: Russell J., Stephen J. AB, Columbia U., 1959, MD, 1963. Diplomate Am. Bd. Internal Medicine, Am. Bd. Hematology and Oncology. Intern Albert Einstein Med. Sch., N.Y.C., 1963-64, resident in internal medicine, 1964-66; hematology fellow Montefiore Hosp., N.Y.C., 1966-67; pvt. practice medicine, specializing in hematology and oncology, Fairfield, Conn., 1969—; assoc. prof. medicine Yale U., New Haven, 1975; assoc. clin. prof. of medicine, 1975—; chief of hematology/oncology St. Vincent's Med. Ctr., 1980—, chmn. hosp. com. on cancer, mng. ptnr. Med. Specialists of Fairfield, LLC, 1995—; attending physician Yale Hosp., New Haven; mem. staff Yale-New Haven hosps., Bridgeport Hosp; adj. prof. medicine N.Y. Med. Coll. Editorial bd. Conn. Medicine, 1974-78; med. cons. U.S. News and World Report, 1990; dir. oncology fellowship Yale-St. Vincent, 1991—. Active Leukemia Soc. Am., Hemophilia Found.; chmn. profl. edn. com. Am. Cancer Soc. Lt. comdr. USN, 1967-69. Ettinger Meml. fellow Am. Cancer Soc., 1982. Fellow ACP; mem. AMA, AAAS, Am. Soc. Hematology, Am. Soc. Internal Medicine, Am. Soc. Clin. Oncology, N.Y. Acad. of Scis., Internat. Soc. Thrombosis and Hemostasis, Conn. Oncology Assn., Soc. Columbia Grads., Columbia U. Alumni Fedn. Coun., Columbia U. Alumni Club (pres. Fairfield County 1983-85, editor newsletter 1982-91), Bridgeport Medical Soc. (Physician of Yr. 1993). Office: 425 Post Rd Fairfield CT 06430-6232

BURDEN, ALFRED LIONEL, JR., ophthalmologist; b. Ballinger, Tex., Apr. 14, 1934; s. Alfred Lionel Sr. and Dovie (Armstrong) B.; m. Mary Elizabeth Smith, May 26, 1956; children: Shari Lynn, Cynthia Elizabeth; Susan Alane. Student, Abilene Christian Coll., 1951-54. Diplomate Am. Bd. Ophthalmology. Intern Hermann Hosp., Houston, 1958-59, resident in ophthalmology, 1959-62; pvt. practice San Antonio, 1965—; pres. hosp. staff Nix Meml. Hosp., San Antonio, 1978; pres. Eye Surg. Assocs., 1987-94. Capt. U.S. Army, 1962-65. Fellow ACS, Am. Acad. Ophthalmology; mem. AMA, Tex. Med. Assn., Tex. Soc. Ophthalmology and Otolaryngology, Tex. Ophthalmology Assn., Bexar County Med. Soc., San Antonio Soc. Ophthalmology, Am. Soc. Cataract and Refractive Surgery. Mem. Ch. of Christ. Home: 202 Sheffield San Antonio TX 78213-2627 Office: Ophthalmology Assocs San Antonio 400 Nix Profl Bldg San Antonio TX 78205

BURDEN, CHARLES EARLE, pediatrician; b. Bath, Maine, Aug. 25, 1933; s. Alexander A. and Evelyn O. (Redlon) B.; m. Jeanette Mott, Oct. 24, 1968 (div. 1976); children: Daniel M., Adam P., Christian C., Heidi P. Burden Sargent, Benjamin C.; m. Nancy E. Cornish, June 21, 1980 (div. 1994). BS, Yale U., 1955; MD, Harvard U., 1959. Diplomate Am. Bd. Pediatrics. Intern Children's Hosp., Boston, 1959-61, resident, 1961-62; resident Mass. Gen. Hosp., 1960-61; pvt. practice Bath, 1962—; pres. staff Bath Meml. Hosp., 1983-84; assoc. prof. U. Vt. Med. Sch., Burlington, 1982—; cons. Social Security Disability Determination Svcs.; lectr. numerous antiquarian subjects. Trustee Maine Maritime Mus., Bath., 1964—, Bath Meml. Hosp., 1989-91; dir. Bath Marine Mus., 1964-74; overseer Strawberry Banke, Portsmouth, N.H., 1987-93. Recipient Disting. Citizenship award Elks, 1975, Pres.' award Bath C. of C., 1980. Fellow Am. Acad. Pediatrics (v.p. Maine chpt. 1984-90); mem. County Med. Soc. (pres. 1972), Acad. Pediatrics (v.p. New Eng. dist. 1978-81), Am. Folk Art Soc. Republican. Office: Coastal Pediatrics 2 Davenport Cir Bath ME 04530-2880

BURDETTE, WALTER JAMES, surgeon, educator; b. Hillsboro, Tex., Feb. 5, 1915; s. James S. and Ovazene (Weatherred) B.; m. Kathryn Lynch, Apr. 9, 1947; children: Susan, William J. A.B., Baylor U., 1935; A.M., U. Tex., 1936, Ph.D., 1938; M.D., Yale, 1942. Diplomate: Am. Bd. Surgery, Am. Bd. Thoracic and Cardiovascular Surgery. Intern Johns Hopkins Hosp., 1942-43; Harvey Cushing fellow surgery Yale, 1943-44; resident staff surgery New Haven Hosp., 1944-46; instr., asst., assoc. prof. surgery La. State U., 1946-55; vis. surgeon Charity Hosp. of La., 1946-55; cons. Touro Infirmary and So. Baptist Hosp., 1952-55, Oak Ridge Inst. Nuclear Studies Hosp., 1953-59; vis. investigator Chester Beatty Inst. Cancer Research, Brompton, and Royal Cancer Hosp., London, 1953, Max Planck Institut Fuer Biochemie, Tuebingen, Germany, summer 1955; prof., chmn. dept. surgery U. Mo., 1955-56; prof. clin. surgery St. Louis U. Sch. Medicine, 1956-57; prof., head dept. surgery U. Utah, 1957-65; dir. lab. clin. biology, surgeon-in-chief Salt Lake Gen. Hosp., 1957-65; chief surg. cons. VA Hosps., Salt Lake City, 1957-65; prof. surgery, assoc. dir. U. Tex-M.D. Anderson Hosp. and Tumor Inst., Houston, 1965-72; prof. surgery U. Tex. Sch. Medicine at Houston, 1971-79; adj. prof. pharmacology U. Houston, 1975—; chief surgery Univ.Hosp., U. Mo., 1955-56, St. Louis U. Svc., John Cochran VA Hosp., 1956-57; chief thoracic and cardiovascular surgery Park Pla. Hosp., 1990—; pres. Nat. Biomed. Found., 1972—; cons. St. Luke's Hosp., 1975—, Park Plaza Hosp., 1976—, Meth. Hosp., 1976—; Gibson lectr. advanced surgery Oxford U., 1966; vis. prof. U. Oxford, spring 1965; ofcl. U. Congo, summer 1968. Editor, author: Etiology, Treatment of Leukemia, 1958, Methodology in Human Genetics, 1962, Methodology in Mammalian Genetics, 1962, Methodology in Basic Genetics, 1963, Primary Hepatoma, 1965, Carcinoma of the Alimentary Tract, 1965, Viruses Inducing Cancer, 1966, Carcinoma of the Colon and Antecedent Epithelium, 1970, Planning and Analysis of Clinical Studies, 1970, Invertebrate Endocrinology and Hormonal Heterophylly, 1974; editl. bd. Surg. Rounds, Yale Jour. Biology and Medicine, Cancer Rsch.; contbr. over 200 articles to med. and sci. jours. Chmn. genetics study sect., mem. morphology study sect. NIH; cons. Nat. Cancer Inst.; mem. Nat. Adv. Cancer Council, Nat. Adv. Heart Council, Surgeon General's Com. on Smoking and Health; chmn. U.S.A. nat. com. Internat. Union Against Cancer; mem. transplantation com. Nat. Acad. Scis.; chmn. working Cadre on cancer large intestine Nat. Cancer Inst.; elder, deacon Christian Ch. Rockefeller travel fellow USSR and Ea. Europe, summer 1957. Fellow ACS; mem. AAAS, Soc. Surgery Alimentary Tract, Am. Assn. Cancer Research (dir., v.p.), Am. Cancer Soc. (chmn. research adv. council, mem. council on analysis and projection), Am. Surg. Assn., Soc. Clin. Surgery (treas.), Soc. U. Surgeons, Soc. Exptl. Biology and Medicine, Genetics Soc. Am., Utah Genetics Soc. (pres.), Western Soc. Clin. Research, Am. Assn. Thoracic Surgery, Transplantation Soc., N.Y. Acad. Sci., Soc. Am. Naturalists, New Orleans, St. Louis, Salt Lake City, Houston surg. socs., Tex. Med. Soc., Harris County Med. Soc., So., Western surg. assns., So. Thoracic Surg. Soc., Peruvian Cancer Soc. (hon.), Soc. for Surgery Alimentary Tract, Am. Soc. Clin. Oncology, Am. Soc. for Cancer Edn., Tex. Surg. Soc., Assn. Yale Alumni in Medicine (exec. com. 1977), Soc. Internat. de Chirurg, Am. Guild Organists, Yale Club of Houston (pres. 1989—), Phi Beta Kappa, Sigma Xi, Alpha Omega Alpha. Home: 239 Chimney Rock Rd Houston TX 77024-5618 Office: Plaza Med Center 1200 Binz St Suite 740 Houston TX 77004

BURDICK, CLAUDE OWEN, pathologist; b. Oconomowoc, Wis.; s. Lawrence Theodore and Florence (Owens) B.; m. Margaret Huiskamp, June 22, 1955; children: Katherine, Roberta, Lawrence, Jack (dec.). BS in Med. Sci., U. Wis., 1955, MD, 1958. Diplomate Am. Bd. Pathology, Am. Bd. Dermatopathology. Intern Letterman Army Med. Ctr., San Francisco, 1958-59, resident, 1959-63; pathologist, chief hematology Berkshire Med. Ctr., Pittsfield, Mass., 1968-70; pathologist, dir. labs. Valley Care Health Sys., Livermore/Pleasanton, Calif., 1970—; chmn., bd. dirs. Valley Care Health Sys., 1993-96; med. dir., cons. Spectra Labs., Inc., Fremont, Calif., 1994-96; pres. Livermore Alameda Valley Med. Group, 1972-76. Lt. col. U.S. Army, 1957-68. Fellow Am. Soc. Clin. Pathology, Coll. Am. Pathologists; mem. AMA, Calif. Med. Assn., Calif. Soc. Pathologists (bd. dirs. 1983-86), Alameda Contra Costa Med. Soc., Am. Soc. Blood Banks, South Bay Pathology Soc. (pres. 1981). Democrat. Presbyterian. Office: Valley Care Hospital 5555 W Las Positas Blvd Pleasanton CA 94588

BURDICK, RALPH EDWARD, family practice physician; b. Buffalo, Sept. 23, 1947; s. Ernest Lavern and Catherine Lois (Reed) B.; m. Kim Rogers, Aug. 21, 1971; children: Robert, Elizabeth, Edward. BA in English Lit., Rice U., 1969; MS in Audiology, Ithaca Coll., 1972; DO in Family Practice, Phila. Coll. Osteo. Medicine, 1979. Audiologist, lectr. Phila. Coll. Osteo. Medicine, 1973-75; physician Michell Assocs., Wilmington, Del., 1980-87; primary care physician Delaware City, Del., 1987—; attending physican, mem. profl. activities com., house staff on edn. and civil disaster St. Francis Hosp., Wilmington, 1987—. Former elder Presbyn. Ch. of the Covenant, Wilmington; com. mem. troop 99 Boy Scouts Am., Bellefonte, Del., 1991—. Sgt. U.S. Army, 1969-71, Vietnam. Recipient Citation, Newark Emergency Rm., 1983; featured in Care Line periodical, 1990. Mem. Am. Osteo. Assn.

Republican. Home: 2420 Dorval Rd Wilmington DE 19810-3529 Office: 900 5th St Box 300 Delaware City DE 19706

BURDICK, WILLIAM MACDONALD, biomedical engineer; b. Providence, R.I., Apr. 24, 1952; s. Franklin Pierce and Lola Alice (Cook) B. BS, Ind. U. Pa., 1975; M of Engring., Tex. A&M U., 1981; postgrad., U. Tex., 1982-86. Engring. analyst FDA, Winchester, Mass., 1988-90; reviewer neurological devices FDA, Rockville, Md., 1990-94; reviewer, gen. hosp. and personal use devices FDA, Rockville, 1994—. Inventor in field; contbr. articles to profl. jours.; contbr. poem to: Dance on the Horizon (Editor's Choice award Nat. Libr. Poetry). Active Native Am. Rights Fund. With USAF, 1976-78. Mem. Internat. Platform Assn., Biomed. Engring. Soc., Nature Conservancy, Humane Soc. U.S., Nat. Multiple Sclerosis Soc., World Wildlife Fund, Greenpeace. Congregationalist. Office: HHS/PHS/FDA/ODE/GHDB 9200 Corporate Blvd Rockville MD 20850-4308

BURDINE, JOHN A., hospital administrator, nuclear medicine educator; b. Austin, Tex., Feb. 7, 1936; married; 3 children. BA, U. Tex., 1959; MD, U. Tex., Galveston, 1961. Diplomate Am. Be. Nuclear Medicine (orgnl. exam. com. 1971, bd. dirs. 1978—, chmn. certifyng exam. com. 1980-81, 81-82, editorial bd. Jour. Nuclear Medicine, 1973-81). Intern Med. Ctr. Ind. U., 1961-62; resident nuclear medicine, internal medicine U. Tex., Galveston, 1962-65; active med. staff St. Luke's Episcopal Hosp.-Tex. Children's Hosp., Houston, 1969-90; chief nuclear medicine svc. St. Luke's Episcopal Hosp.-Tex. Children's Hosp., Tex. Heart Inst., Houston, 1969-85; chief exec. officer, head adminstr. St. Luke's Episcopal Hosp., Houston, 1984-87, pres., chief exec. officer, 1986-91, vice chmn., chief exec. officer, 1991-95; also bd. dirs. St. Luke's Episcopal Hosp., 1991-94; cons. St. Luke's Hosp., 1991—; courtesy staff Tex. Children's Hosp., 1992—; asst. prof. dept. radiology Baylor Coll. Medicine, 1965-68, acting chmn. dept. radiology, 1968-71, chief nuclear medicine dept., 1965-95, assoc. prof. dept. radiology, 1968-74, prof. dept. radiology, 1974—, acting dir. sect. nuclear medicine dept. medicine, 1979-80, prof. dept. medicine, 1979—, mem. exec. faculty com., 1968-71, mem. com. human experimentation, 1969-71, chmn. radioisotope com., 1970-74, mem., 1966-82, other coms.; sec. Tex. Radiation Adv. Bd., 1981-86, exec. com., 1982-86, med. com., 1982-86, radioactive waste com., 1982-86, fee rules com., 1982-83; chmn. radioisotope com. Meth. Hosp., 1979-80, active med. staff, 1979-84, courtesy med. staff, 1984—, acting med. dir. radioisotope lab., 1979-80; chief nuclear medicine sect. Harris County Hosp. Dist., 1965-83; mem. forward planning com. Tex. Med. Ctr., 1986—; trustee Tex. Heart Inst., 1985—. Editorial bd. Cardiovascular Disease, 1974; contbr. book chpts., abstracts, papers. Bd. dirs. Houston Symphony Orch., 1987-88. Fellow Am. Coll. Nuclear Physicians (orgn. com. 1973-74, chmn. radioassay & radiopharmacy com. 1975-76, DOE speaker's bur. 1981-85), mem. AMA (rep. coun. nuclear medicine 1976-77), AAUP, Harris County Med. Assn., Tex. Med. Assn. (vice chmn. com. nuclear medicine 1968-71, chmn. 1971-78, others), Tex. Assn. Physicians in Nuclear Medicine, Soc. Nuclear Medicine (pres. 1982-83, southwestern chpt. trustee 1972-80, mem. numerous coms.), Phi Beta Kappa, Phi Eta Sigma, Alpha Epsilon Delta. Home: 347 Hunters Trail Houston TX 77024 Office: St Luke's Episcopal Hosp PO Box 20269 Houston TX 77225-0269

BURDOCK, GEORGE ALLAN, toxicologist, consultant; b. Oskaloosa, Iowa, July 31, 1945. BS in Biology, U. Miss., 1969, M in Combined Sci., 1973, PhD in Toxicology, 1980. Diplomate Am. Bd. Toxicology. Staff scientist Hazleton Labs. Inc., Vienna, Va., 1979-84; mgr. biol. svcs. Shulton Rsch. Div., Am. Cynnamid Corp., Clifton, N.J., 1984-86; dir. sci. affairs Flavor and Extract Mfrs. Assn., Washington, 1986-92; cons. in toxicology Burdock & Assocs., Reston, Va., 1986—. Mem. Am. Chem. Soc., Am. Coll. Toxicology, Soc. Toxicology (assoc.), Soc. for Regulatory Toxicology and Pharmacology. Office: Burdock & Associates PO Box 3705 Reston VA 20190-3705

BURDON, JONATHAN GARETH WILLIAM, respiratory physician, consultant; b. Simla, India, Mar. 9, 1946; s. Thomas Wilkinson and Barbara Josephine (Hobson) B.; m. Marilyn June Woodruff, Dec. 30, 1970; children: Rebecca Amanda, Natalie Justine, Nicholas Thomas. MB, BS with honors, U. Melbourne, Australia, 1971, MD, 1980. Resident med. officer Royal Melbourne Hosp., 1972-73, med. registrar, 1974-75, registrar hematology/oncology, 1976, registrar thoracic medicine/intensive care, 1977, rsch. fellow, vis. assoc., 1978-79; rsch. fellow cardio-respiratory unit, travelling fellow in applied health scis. McMaster U., Hamilton, Ont., 1980-82; hon. repsiratory physician Launceston Gen. Hosp., 1986—; respiratory physician, physician-in-charge Respiratory Function Lab. St. Vincent's Hosp., Fitzroy, Australia, 1983-90, dir. dept. respiratory medicine, 1990—; sr. assoc. dept. medicine St. Vincent's Hosp., U. Melbourne, 1983—; cons. respiratory physician St. George's Hosp., Kew, 1990—; mem. human rsch. ethics com. St. Vincent's Hosp., 1990-92, coord. advanced physician tng., 1984-89, mem. com. for med. grad. edn., 1984-89, mem. com. continuing edn., 1984-89, chmn. 1988-89. Fellow Royal Australasian Coll. Physicians, Am. Coll. Chest Physicians; mem. Thoracic Soc. Australia and New Zealand (mem. edn. subcom. 1986-90, chmn. fees subcom. 1987-96, convenor clin. spl. interest group 1991-93, chmn. ctrl. program com. 1996—), Am. Thoracic Soc., Australian Med. Assn., European Respiratory Soc., Asia Pacific Soc. Respirology. Office: 55 Victoria, Fitzroy 3065, Australia

BUREAU, MICHEL ANDRÉ, pediatrician, pulmonologist; b. Sherbrooke, Que., Can., Oct. 2, 1943; s. Jean Ernest and Julienne (Couture) B.; m. Renee Louise Bilodeau, May 20, 1967; children: Martin, Anne, Nicolas. MD, Laval (Que.) U., 1968; postgrad., McGill U., 1973. Intern and resident in pediatrics and pulmonology McGill U., Montreal, 1968-73; head newborn medicine Sherbrooke U., 1975-81, dean medicine, 1988-95; head respiratory medicine McGill-Montreal Children's Hosp., 1982-87; pres. Fonds de la recherche en santé du Que., 1995—; pres. Dean's Conf. Que., 1989, 93; chmn. numerous rsch. coms. Fonds de la recherche en santé du Que./Inst. de recherche en santé et sécurité au travail. Contbr. numerous articles to profl. publs.; external editor Jour. Applied Physiology, Pediatric Rsch., Am. Rev. Respiratory Diseases. Rsch. scholar Med. Rsch. Coun. Can.,1979—, Fonds de la recherche en santé du Que., 1980, Can. Cystic Fibrosis Found., 1981-86. Fellow Royal Coll. Physicians and Surgeons Can., Am. Coll. Chest Physician, Pediatric Rsch. Soc.; mem. Can. Thoracic Soc. (pres. 1987-88, chmn. various rsch. coms.), Can. Assn. Med. Schs. (treas.). Office: U Sherbrooke Faculty Med, 3001 12th Ave N, Sherbrooke, PQ Canada J1H 5N4

BURENING, GREGORY J., optometrist; b. Augusta, Ga., Feb. 25, 1964; s. Ronny J. and Judy K. (Cass) B.; m. Sue A Fiene, Apr. 15, 1989; children: Alexander Jay, Erik Gregory. BS, Dugne Coll., 1986; OD, New England Coll. Optometry, 1990. Cert. optometrist Nebr., Kans., Mo. Staff optometrist Humana, Kansas City, Mo., 1990-94, chief optometric svcs., 1994—. Recipient Am. Optometric Assn. Recognition award, 1993, 94, 95. Mem. Kansas City Soc. Optometry (bd. dirs. 1994—), Just Potters Investment Club (pres. 1993—). Office: Humana 9180 E 41st Terr Kansas City MO 64133

BURFORD, ALEXANDER MITCHELL, JR., physician; b. Memphis, Mar. 21, 1929; s. Alexander Mitchell and Mary Young (Tittle) B.; BS, Florence (Ala.) State Coll. (now U. North Ala.), 1951; MD, U. Tenn., Memphis, 1957. Intern, U. Tenn., Knoxville, 1957-58, resident in pathology, Memphis, 1958-62; assoc. pathologist Eliza Coffee Meml. Hosp., Florence, Ala., 1962-73, dir. lab., chief pathology, 1973-95, mem. med. staff, 1962—; practice medicine specializing in pathology, 1958—, Florence Pathology Svcs., 1983—. Active Florence Tree Commn., 1937-92, Am. Chestnut Found., 1985—, Mars Hill Bible Sch. Endowment Assn., 1985—, Nat. Arbor Day Found.; mem. pres. cabinet U. North Ala., 1992—; mem. alumni coun. Coll. Medicine U. Tenn. Mem. AMA, Ala. Urban Forestry Assn., Ala. Forest Owner's Assn., Tree City USA, Med. Assn. Ala., Ala. Assn. Pathologists (pres. 1974-75), Coll. Am. Pathologists (del. 1972-90), Am. Soc. Clin. Pathologists, Am. Assn. Blood Banks, Am. Forestry Assn., Am. Rifleman Assn., Nat. Wildlife Fedn., Lauderdale County Med. Assn., Shoals Symphony Assn. (bd. dirs. 1993—), Florence C. of C., Friends of Florence-Lauderdale Pub. Libr. (pres. 1993-95), Audubon Soc., Lions Club (past pres. local chpt. 1962-70, dep. dist. gov.), Alpha Kappa Kappa, Kappa Mu Epsilon, Alpha Psi Omega. Home: 652 Howell St Florence AL 35630-3537 Office: Eliza Coffee Meml Hosp PO Box 818 Florence AL 35631-0818

BURG, MAURICE BENJAMIN, renal physiologist, physician; b. Boston, Apr. 9, 1931; s. Charles and Augusta (Green) B.; m. Judith Anne Braverman (dec.); m. Ruth Cooper, Dec. 30, 1967; children: Elizabeth, Laurence, Joan, Robert. AB, Harvard U., 1952, MD, 1955. Investigator Lab. Kidney/Electrolyte Metabolism Nat. Heart Lung and Blood Inst., NIH, Bethesda, Md., 1956—, chief Lab. Kidney/Electrolyte Metabolism, 1975—. Contbr. over 145 articles to profl. jours. Mem. NAS. Office: Nat Heart Lung Blood Inst Bldg 10 Rm 6N307 Bethesda MD 20892*

BURGER, HENDRIK, surgeon, consultant; b. Alkmaar, Noord Holland, The Netherlands, Aug. 2, 1934; s. Hendrik and Johanna M.E. (Ophorst) B.; m. Jacoba P. Speelpenning, Sept. 4, 1965; children: Marjon, Kees, Hens, Pim. MD, Ryks U., Leiden, The Netherlands, 1961; PhD, Ryks U., Maastricht, The Netherlands, 1994. Asst. in surg. dept. Bergweg Ziekenhuis, Rotterdam, The Netherlands, 1961-69, chef de clinique, 1967-70; surgeon Drechtsteden Ziekenhuis, Dordrecht, The Netherlands, 1970—. Contbr. articles to profl. jours. Mem. Royal Netherlands Med. Assn. (del. 1986-91, chmn. 1987-91), Dutch Surg. Assn. (del. 1996—), Internat. Coll. Surgeons. Mem. Dutch Reformed Ch. Home: Gentiana 27, 3317 HH Dordrecht The Netherlands Office: Drechsteden Ziekenhuis, Postbus 444, 3300 AK Dordrecht The Netherlands

BURGER, JOANNA, environmental scientist, educator; b. Schenectady, N.Y., Jan. 18, 1941; d. E. Melvin and Janette Vivien (Male) B.; m. Michael Gochfeld, Aug. 18, 1981; stepchildren: Deborah, David. BS, SUNY, Albany, 1963; MS, Cornell U., 1064; PhD, U. Minn., 1972. Instr. SUNY, Buffalo, 1964-68; from asst. prof. to prof. Rutger's U., Piscataway, N.J., 1973-91, disting. prof., 1991—; liaison com. endangered Sea Turtles Bd. Environ. Sci. and Toxicology NAS, 1988-89, liaison com. Tuna-Porpoise Interactions, 1989-91; mem. U.S. nat. com. Scientific Com. for Problems of Environ. NAS, 1991—, co-chair coastal processes com., 1991-95, conf. on estuarine syntheses, 1995, mem. com. evaluate ecol. risk assessment NAS, Arlie, Va., 1991, com. endocrine disrupters NAS, 1995—, mem. life scis. panel, assoc. program NAS, 1995-96; mem. adv. bd. sustainable biosphere program Ecol. Soc. Am.-EPA; mem. harbor estuaries commn. EPA, 1989-95; mem. N.J. Endangered Species and Nongame Coun., 1980—; mem. task force Barnegat Bay, 1990-95, Jamaica Bay, 1993-94; peer rev. com. for Dept. Transp.; presenter, lectr. in field. Author: Before and After an Oil Spill: The Arthur Kill, 1994; editor: A Naturalist Along the Jersey Shore, 1996; co-editor: (with M. Gochfeld and D.N. Nettleship) Threats to Seabirds on Islandds, 1994; mem. editl. bd. Jour. Tioxicology and Environ. Health, 1993—, Archives Environ. Contamination and Toxicology, 1994—, Environ. Rsch., 1995—, Sci. and Total Environ., 1995—; contbr. 39 chpts. to books, 7 monographs, over 250 articles to profl. pubs. Recipient Rutger's Pres. award, 1994. Fellow Am. Ornithol. Union (mem. coun.); mem. Soc. Toxicologists, Wilson Ornitol. Club, Ecol. Soc. Am., Estuarine Soc., Colonial Waterbird Soc. (pres.). Office: Rutgers Univ Nelson Labs Piscataway NJ 08855-1059

BURGER, VALERIE ANN, oncology nurse; b. N.Y.C., July 15, 1965; d. Otto H. Barz and Barbara Schmidt Golser; m. Christopher Bishop, Mar. 5, 1988 (div. Nov. 1992); m. Leonard E. Burger, Jr., July 2, 1994. BS, Boston U., 1987; MS, MA, NYU, 1994. Cert. oncology nurse, cert. pediatric nurse. Staff nurse New Eng. Med. Ctr., Boston, 1987-89; home care nurse Staff Builders, Boston, 1988-89; clin. nurse III Meml. Sloan-Kettering Cancer Ctr., N.Y.C., 1990-93; nurse mgr. Phelps Meml. Hosp. Ctr., Tarrytown, N.Y., 1993-94; nursing care coord. New Rochelle (N.Y.) Hosp. Med. Ctr., 1994—. Mem. White City Cmty. Coun., Bellmore, N.Y., 1994. Mem. Assn. Pediatric Oncology Nurses, Oncology Nursing Soc., Sigma Theta Tau. Home: 414 Shore Rd Bellmore NY 11710-4819

BURGERMAN, ROBERT STEPHEN, neurologist; b. Washington, Aug. 21, 1958; s. Arthur and Marilyn (Purdy) B.; m. Linda Claire Ramatowski, May 21, 1989. BSEE, Washington U., St. Louis, 1979, MD, 1984. Diplomate Am. Bd. Clin. Neurophysiology, Am. Bd. Psychiatry and Neurology. Intern in gen. surgery Barnes Hosp./Washington U., St. Louis, 1984-85; resident in neurosurgery U. Md., Balt., 1985-87, resident in neurology, 1988-89, intern in internal medicine, 1989, fellow in neurology, 1990; fellow in epilepsy Grad. Hosp./U. Pa., Phila., 1990-92; dir. neurophysiology Sutter Cmty. Hosps., Sacramento, Calif., 1992—, dir. epilepsy monitoring unit, 1994—; med. dir. Sacramento Comprehensive Epilepsy Program, 1994—. Contbr. articles to profl. jours. John Hughlings Jackson fellow Epilepsy Found. Am., 1991. Mem. Am. EEG Soc., Am. Acad. Neurology, Am. Epilepsy Soc., Sutter Neurosci. Inst. Office: Sacramento Comprehensive Epilepsy Program 1020 29th St Ste 360 Sacramento CA 95816

BURGERT, E(RAN) OMER, JR., pediatrician, educator; b. Glasgow, Mo., Aug. 22, 1924; s. Eran Omer, Sr. and Dessie Fern (Beeler) B.; m. Helen Louise Eifert, Sept. 5, 1948; children: Mark Edmund, Stephen Louis, Carolyn Joy. MD, U. Okla., 1947; MS in Pediatrics, U. Minn., 1953. Asst. prof. pediatrics Creighton U. Med. Sch., Omaha, 1953-57; cons. Mayo Clinic, Rochester, Minn., 1957-92; prof. pediatrics Mayo Med. Sch., Rochester, Minn., 1974-92; prof. emeritus; pediatric oncologist Cancer and Leukemia, Group B, 1958-79, Intergroup Ewings Sarcoma Study, 1970-92, Children's Cancer Study Group, 1979-92; co-chair Nat. Intergroup Children's Cancer Studies. Contbr. numerous articles to profl. jours. Mem. med. adv. com. Minn. Dept. Welfare, St. Paul, 1980-88. Sigma Xi, 1950. Fellow AMA, Internat. Soc. Hematology, Am. Soc. Clin. Oncology, Am. Assn. Cancer Rsch., Am. Acad. Pediatrics, Am. Pediatrics Soc., Am. Soc. Hematology, Am. Soc. Pediatric Hematology-Oncology, Northwestern Pediatric Soc. Presbyterian.

BURGESON, NICHOLAS RUDOLPH, healthcare executive; b. Portland, Oreg., July 4, 1943; s. Rudolph Benjamin and Grace Ruth (Nimlos) B.; m. Donna Irene MacGlashan, Oct. 18, 1964; children: Tina Lynn, Robert Gene. AS in Nursing Sci., Pacific Union Coll., 1964; BS in Commerce, Golden Gate U., 1977; MBA in Mgmt., U. Beverly Hills, 1981. RN, Calif.; lic. nursing home adminstr. Staff nurse Napa (Calif.) State Hosp., 1964-68, nursing coord., 1968-70, assist to med. dir., 1970-71; assist. chief hosp. svc. sect. Calif. Dept. of Health, Sacramento, 1971-77; adminstr. Met. State Hosp., Norwalk, Calif., 1977-81; assoc. adminstr. Loma Linda (Calif.) Community Hosp., 1981-82; mgr., psychiat. hosp. devel. Am. Med. Internat., Inc., Beverly Hills, Calif., 1983-84; pres. NRB & Assocs., Sacramento, Calif., 1982—; dir. info. resources Atascadero (Calif.) State Hosp., 1984-90; spl. advisor-accreditation Calif. Dept. Mental Health, Sacramento, 1990-92, cons. on hosp. adminstn., 1992—. Appeared in TV documentary Cry Help, 1970; mem. editorial bd. dirs. Calif. Health Rev., 1981-83. With U.S. Army, 1966-68. Mem. Calif. Assn. Mgmt. (sec. 1975, pres. 1976-77), Forensic Mental Health Assn. Calif. (bd. dirs. 1988-92, pres. 1990-92), U.S. Judo Assn. (patron life). Republican. Home: 5612 Gitta Ria Ct Citrus Heights CA 95610-7915 Office: Calif Dept Mental Health 1600 9th St Rm 120 Sacramento CA 95814-6404

BURGESS, ANN WOLBERT, nursing educator. Van Ameringen prof. nursing U. Pa., Phila. Mem. NAS. Office: U Pa Sch Nursing Philadelphia PA 19104

BURGESS, CHARLES MONROE, JR., dentist; b. Montgomery, Ala., May 4, 1951; s. Charles Monroe Sr. and Jean (Hornsby) B.; m. Renee Steckley, Aug. 30, 1975; children: Charles Monroe III, Walter, Allen. BS, U. Ala., 1972; DMD, U. Ala., Birmingham, 1977. Lic. dentist. Pvt. practice Opp, Ala., 1977—; staff dentist Opp Head Start, 1979—. Coach Little League, Opp, 1989—, Youth Basketball League, 1990—; pres. Opp Babe Ruth Assn., 1994; mem. com. Opp Beautification, 1990—; pres. prin.'s adv. com. Opp H.S., 1995, 96; Sunday sch. tchr., deacon First Bapt. Ch., 1961—. Mem. ADA, Ala. Dental Assn. (trustee 1988-89), Third Dist. Dental Soc. (pres. 1988). Home: RR 3 Opp AL 36467-9803 Office: 104 E Gunter Ave Opp AL 36467-1604

BURGESS, GEORGE EVANS, III, anesthesiologist, director; b. New Orleans, July 21, 1946; s. George Evans Jr. and Olive Lenore (Williamson) B.; m. Marilyn Sue Hines, June 15, 1968; children: Ashley, Laura. BS in Zoology, La. State U., 1967; MD, Tulane Med. Sch., 1971. Diplomate Am. Bd. Anesthesiology. Intern and residence U. N.C. Meml. Hosp., Chapel Hill, 1971-74; clin. fellow Harvard Med. Sch. Beth Israel Hosp., Boston, 1974-75; instr. Harvard Med. Sch., Boston, 1975; staff anesthesiologist Ochsner Clinic, New Orleans, 1975-80, asst. med. dir., 1978-80, co-chmn. cardiac anesthesia, 1979-80, co-dir. intensive care unit, 1975-80; med. dir. Baton Rouge Ambulatory Surg. Svc., 1983-87; anesthesiologist Anesthesiology Group Assocs., Inc., Baton Rouge, 1980—; sr. v.p. med. affairs Our Lady of the Lake Regional Med. Ctr., Baton Rouge, 1995—; bd. dirs. Soc. Cardiovascular Anesthesiologists, Inc., Richmond, Va., 1978—, St. Charles Air Line Lands, Inc., New Orleans, 1980—, Anesthesiology Group Assocs., Inc., 1982—. Co-author: Applied Physiology of Respiratory Care, 1976, Assisted Ventilation of the Newborn, 1981; contbr. articles to profl. jours. Adminstrv. bd. dirs. First Meth. Ch., Baton Rouge, 1991, fin. com., 1991. Named Tchr. of Yr. Ochsner Med. Found., 1977-78. Fellow Am. Coll. Anesthesiologists; mem. Am. Soc. Anesthesiologists (del. 1990), Soc. Cardiovascular Anesthesiologists (pres. 1987-89), La. Soc. Anesthesiologists (pres. 1981-83), Baton Rouge Gen. Med. Staff (sec. 1991-93, pres. 1993-95), City Club Baton Rouge, Baton Rouge Country Club. Office: Our Lady of the Lake Hosp 5000 Hennessy Blvd Baton Rouge LA 70808

BURGESS, J. WESLEY, neuropsychiatrist; b. Mar. 5, 1952. BS, Purdue U., 1974; PhD, N.C. State U., 1979; MD, U. Miami, 1987. Diplomate Am. Bd. Med. Examiners,. Rsch. asst. N.C. Mental Health Dept., 1975-79; with Caribbean Primate Rsch., La Parquera, P.R.; instr. psychology U. Calif., Davis, 1979-81; mem. rsch. faculty UCLA, 1981-84; instr. Western Grad. Sch. Psychology, 1989-90; intern Stanford U., 1987-88, resident in psychiatry, 1988-91, staff psychiatrist geropsychiat. clinic, 1989-90, chief resident, 1990-91; teaching faculty Pacific Grad. Sch. Psychology, 1990-92; dir. adolescent div. Ctr. Mood Disorders, L.A., 1991-93; prof. Calif. Sch. Profl. Psychology, 1991-92; expert panel Superior Ct., Juvenile Ct., Mcpl. Ct. Calif., L.A.; chief investigator SmithKline Beecham/Chemtrials, 1992-94. Contbr. articles to profl. jours. Neuropsychiatric Inst. fellow UCLA, 1981-83, Stanford fellow, 1990-91; recipient Mead Johnson award Psychiatry, 1991. Mem. AMA (Physicians Recognition award), No. Calif. Psychiat. Soc. (Rsch. award 1991), Los Angeles County Med. Assn., So. Calif. Pediatric Assn., Am. Psychiat. Asns., Calif. Psychiat. Assn., So. Calif. Psychiat. Soc., Am. Assn. Advancement Psychotherapy, Internat. Soc. Adolescent Psychiatry, Am. Soc. Adolescent Psychiatry, Am. Soc. Clin. Psychopharmacology, Calif. Med. Assn., Acad. Magical Arts. Office: 11980 San Vicente Blvd Ste 620 Brentwood CA 90049-6604

BURGHARDT, GORDON M., biopsychology educator, researcher; b. Milw., Oct. 11, 1941; s. Elmer Ernest and Mildred Alice (Baumann) B.; m. Lorraine S. Hall, June 25, 1966 (div. 1977); 1 child, Niko L.; m. Sandra L. Twardosz, July 6, 1983; children: Karin T., Liana T. SB in Biopsychology, U. Chgo., 1963, PhD, 1966. Instr. biology U. Chgo., 1966-67; asst. prof. psychology U. Tenn., Knoxville, 1968-70, assoc. prof., 1970-74, prof., 1974—, prof. zoology, 1979—, dir. grad. program in ethology, 1981-91, disting. svc. prof., 1992—; vis. prof. Rockefeller U., N.Y.C., 1976-77; rsch. assoc. Smithsonian Tropical Inst., Washington, 1978-94; spkr. to profl. groups; rsch. proposal reviewer NSF, NIH, Nat. Geographic Soc. Editor: Foundations of Comparative Ethology, 1985, (with others) The Development of Behavior: Comparative and Evolutionary Aspects, 1978, Iguanas of the World: Their Behavior, Ecology, and Conservation, 1982, The Well-Being of Animals in Zoo and Aquarium Sponsored Research, 1996; contbr. numerous articles to profl. jours.; mem. editorial bd. Ethology, Jour. Chem. Ecology, Jour. Comparative Psychology. Recipient USPHS traineeship, 1963-66, NIMH rsch. grants, 1967-75, 71-73, rsch. grants NSF, 1975—, Chancellor's Rsch. Scholar award U. Tenn., 1983, Sci. Alliance award U. Tenn., 1984—, Nat. Inst. Child Health and Human Devel. tng. grant, 1986-92; named John Simon Guggenheim Found. fellow, 1976-77. Fellow APA, Am. Psychol. Soc., Animal Behavior Soc.; mem. AAAS, AAUP, Scientists Ctr. for Animal Welfare (trustee), Internat. Ethological conf. Com. (U.S. 1984-90), Internat. Soc. Chem. Ecology (charter, life), Internat. Soc. Devel. Psychobiology, Internat. Soc. Human Ethology (exec. com. 1981-83), Am. Soc. Ichthyologists and Herpetologists (life), Animal Behavior Soc. (del.-at-large 1980-83, pres. 1986-87), Herpetologists League, Soc. for Study of Amphibians and Reptiles (symposium coord. 1981-82), Human Behavior and Evolution Soc., Sigma Xi (admissions com. UTK chpt. 1981-83). Lutheran. Office: U Tenn Dept Psychology 303D Austin Peay Bldg Knoxville TN 37996

BURGIO, DAVID, nurse; b. Buffalo, July 16, 1959; s. John and Angeline (Lipomi) B.; m. Pamela Wright, June 4, 1988. BSN, D'Youville Coll., 1981, MS in Nursing, 1989; family nurse practitioner cert., U. Pitts., 1992. RN, N.Y., Fla. Staff nurse Lafayette Gen. Hosp., Buffalo, 1981-86; community health nurse VNA of Buffalo, 1986-88; admissions coord. Trico Home Care, Melbourne, Fla., 1988-89; nursing dir. Brevard Home Care, Merritt Island, Fla., 1989-90; family nurse practitioner Charles Cole Meml. Hosp., Coudersport, Pa., 1993-96, No. Nev. Med. Group, 1996—. Recipient D'Youville medal, St. Catherine of Alexandria medal. Mem. ANA, Pa. Nurses Assn., N.W. Pa. Coalition Nurse Practitioners, Sigma Theta Tau. Home: 110 Regier Springs Dr Sparks NV 89436

BURGIO, GIUSEPPE ROBERTO, pediatrician; b. Palermo, Italy, Apr. 30, 1919; s. Vito and Berta (Ahrens) B.; m. Rosano Francesca Paola, Oct. 11, 1950; children: Vito Lelio, Ernesto, Alberto. MD, U. Palermo, 1942; D honoris causa, U. Buenos Aires Med. Faculty, 1990. Intern Children's Hosp., Palermo, 1943-44, resident in pediatrics, 1945-48; prof. pediatrics, dir. pediatric dept. U. Perugia, Italy, 1962-65; dir. pediatric dept. U. Pavia, Italy, 1966-89. Author: Pediatria Essenziale, 1978; (with others) Current Therapy in Pediatrics, 1989, 92. Recipient Gold medal Ministry for Edn., Italy, 1974, Pub. Health Ministry Italy, 1990. Office: Clinica Pediatrica, Policlinico San Matteo, 27100 Pavia Italy

BURISH, THOMAS GERARD, psychology educator; b. Menominee, Mich., May 4, 1950; s. Bennie Charles and Donna Mae (Willkom) B.; m. Pamela Jean Zebrasky, June 19, 1976; children: Mark Joseph, Brent Christopher. AB summa cum laude, U. Notre Dame, 1972; MA, U. Kans., 1975, PhD, 1976. Lic. psychologist, Tenn. Asst. prof. psychology Vanderbilt U., Nashville, 1976-80, assoc. prof., 1980-86, prof., 1986—, dir. clin. tng., 1980-84, chair dept. psychology, 1984-86, assoc. provost, 1986-93; provost, 1993—; cons. VA Hosp., Tenn., 1978—; mem. cancer rsch. manpower rev. com. Nat. Cancer Inst., 1991-96; co-chair Bridge task force com., Am. Cancer Soc., 1994—; mem. breast cancer rsch. panel, U.S. Army Med. Rsch., 1995—. Co-editor: Coping with Chronic Disease, 1983, Cancer, Nutrition and Eating Behavior, 1985; co-author: Behavior Therapy, 1987, Health Psychology, 1991. Chmn. St. Mary's Sch. Bd., Nashville, 1982-83; participant Leadership Nashville, 1989-90; bd. dirs. Am. Cancer Soc. Fellow Am. Psychol. Assn., Am. Psychol. Soc.; mem. Acad. Behavioral Medicine Rsch., Phi Beta Kappa. Roman Catholic. Office: Vanderbilt Univ 221 Kirkland Hall Nashville TN 37240

BURK, JOHN ROBERT, pulmonary disease physician; b. Fort Worth, Feb. 19, 1944; s. Audis Nathan and Annie Carolyn (Wilson) B.; m. Sandra Newman (div. 1981); children: Tiffany Locket, Jennifer Lynn; m. Stephanie Steves, Sept. 25, 1982; children: Justin Rodes, Jonathan Sterling, James Thomas. BS, Washington & Lee U., 1966; MD, U. Va., 1970. Diplomate Am. Bd. Internal Medicine. Epidemic intelligence officer Ctr. for Disease Control, Ala., 1973-75; pres. Pulmonary Cons. of Tex., P.A., Fort Worth, Arlington, 1978—; intern Ochsner Found. Hosp., New Orleans, 1970-71, resident in internal medicine, 1971-73; fellow in pulmonary disease U. Tex. Health Sci. Ctr., Dallas, 1975-77; med. dir. cardiopulmonary dept. All Saints Hosp., Fort Worth, 1978—, med. dir. critical care, 1978—, co-med. dir. sleep disorder ctr., 1982—; co-dir. advanced cardiac life support Am. Heart Assn., Ft. Worth, 1987—; clin. instrn. dept. medicine U. Tex. Health Sci. Ctr., Dallas; adv. com. to sch. respiratory therapy Tarrant County Jr. Col., 1977—; bd. dirs. Am. Lung Assn. Tex., 1986-89, Trinity Health Network, chmn. credentials com., 1986-87; nat. med. adv. bd. CountDown USA, 1988-89. Contbr. numerous articles to profl. jours. Active All Saints Episc. Parish Day Sch., 1984-87. With USPHS, 1975-77. Mem. Am. Thoracic Soc., Am. Coll. Chest Physicians, ACS, Am. Soc. Internal Medicine, Soc. Epidemiologic Rsch., Am. Sleep Disorders Assn., Tarrant County Med. Soc., Tex. Med. Assn., AMA, Soc. for Health and Human Values, Nat. Assn. Med. Dirs. Respiratory Care.

BURK, NORMAN, oral surgeon; b. Dallas, Sept. 28, 1937; s. Rubin and Lena (Shodnisky) B.; m. Beverly Rae Hyken, Aug. 27, 1961; children: Ronald S., Steven J. BS, U. Okla., 1959; DDS, U. Mo., Kansas City, 1962. Diplomate Am. Bd. Oral and Maxillofacial Surgery. Resident in oral surgery

Kansas City (Mo.) Gen. Hosp., 1965; practice dentistry specializing in oral surgery Kansas City, Mo., 1965—; mem. staff Truman Med. Ctr., Independence Sanitarium and Hosp.; chief staff Bapt. Meml. Hosp., 1976-77, Menorah Med. Ctr., 1975-85; sec. med. staff St. Joseph Health Ctr., Kansas City, Mo., 1992-93; clin. assoc. prof. U. Mo., Kansas City, 1965085; appointed to Blue Cross/Blue Shield peer review com. for Greater Kansas City Oral Surgeons. Contbr. articles to profl. jours. Bd. dirs. Kehilath Israel Synagogue. Fellow Am. Coll. Oral and Maxillofacial Surgeons, Am. Assn. Oral and Maxillofacial Surgeons, Internat. Congress of Oral Implantologists, Acad. Osseointegration, Am. Coll. Oral and Maxillofacial Surgeons (founder); mem. Kansas City Soc. Oral Surgeons (pres. 1974), Mo. Soc. Oral Surgeons (pres. 1979), ADA, Midwestern Mo. and Kansas City Soc. Oral and Maxillofacial Surgeons, Delta Sigma Delta (advisor 1966-74), Univ. Study Club (pres. 1970), B'nai Brith Lodge. Home: 8400 Delmar Ln Shawnee Mission KS 66207-1824 Office: Burk Ennis & Allen 1010 Carondelet Dr Kansas City MO 64114-4859

BURK, RAYMOND FRANKLIN, JR., physician, educator, researcher; b. Kosciusko, Miss., Dec. 9, 1942; s. Raymond Franklin and Florence Annie (Davis) B.; m. Enikoe Vikor, June 17, 1967; children: Teresa Marie, Stephen Morrison. BA, U. Miss., 1963; MD, Vanderbilt U., 1968. Diplomate Am. Bd. Internal Medicine. Intern, Vanderbilt Hosp., Nashville, 1968-69, resident in medicine, 1969-70; asst. prof. medicine and biochemistry U. Tex. S.W. Med. Sch., Dallas, 1975-78; assoc. prof. medicine and biochemistry La. State U. Sch. Medicine, Shreveport, 1978-80; assoc. prof. medicine U. Tex. Health Sci. Ctr., San Antonio, 1980-82, prof., 1982-87; prof. medicine Vanderbilt U., 1987—; researcher in field; mem. staff Vanderbilt U. Hosp., Nashville. Served to maj. U.S. Army, 1970-73. NIH grantee, 1974—. Mem. Am. Soc. Biol. Chemists, Am. Soc. Clin. Investigation, Am. Inst. Nutrition. Contbr. articles to profl. jours. Office: Vanderbilt U Med Sch Div Gastroenterology Med Ctr N Nashville TN 37232

BURKE, ALFREDO EDMUNDO MARIO, physician, educator; b. Rio de Janeiro, Jan. 21, 1940; s. Nicolo E. and Selmira C. (Castro) B. Diploma, Santo Agostinho Coll., Rio de Janeiro, 1957; MD, Faculty Med. Scis., Rio de Janeiro, 1963. Diplomate Am. Bd. Internal Medicine. Intern Mt. Sinai Hosp., Chgo. Med. Sch., 1966-67; resident in internal medicine VA Hosp., George Washington U., Washington, 1967-68, 68-69, fellow in gastroenterology/liver disease, 1969-70, acad. fellow in medicine, 1970; pvt. practice Rio de Janeiro, 1971—; asst. prof. therapeutics Souza Marques U., Rio de Janeiro, 1972-76; asst. prof. medicine Gama Filho U., Rio de Janeiro, 1978-93, assoc. prof. medicine, 1993—; head physician 22nd Infirmary/Santa Casa Hosp., Rio de Janeiro, 1978—. Lt. Brazilian Army, 1963-64. Mem. ACP, N.Y. Acad. Scis. Roman Catholic. Home: Ave Delfim Moreira 350/901, 22441-000 Rio de Janeiro Brazil

BURKE, ARLENE L., osteopath, surgeon; b. Long Beach, Calif., Jan. 20, 1947; d. Luster B. and Margaret E. (Rives) Larch; children: David T. Burke, Christiene M. Burke, Sandra A. Hinsdale; m. Ronald H. Lloyd, Nov. 21, 1993. BA with honors, Loma Linda U., 1976; DO, U. Health Sci. Osteo. Medicine, Kansas City, Mo., 1981; MPH, The Johns Hopkins U., 1987. Commd. 2d lt. U.S. Army, 1977, advanced through grades to lt. col., 1993; resident in family practice Silas B. Hayes Army Cmty. Hosp., Fort Ord, Calif., 1981-83; family practice physician Weed Army Cmty. Hosp., Fort Irwin, Calif., 1983-85; med. dir. Med. Clinic, South Korea, 1985-86; resident in preventive medicine Madigan Army Med. Ctr., Tacoma, 1987-88; physician, occupl. health cons. Blanchfield Army Cmty. Hosp., Fort Campbell, Ky., 1988-91; preventive medicine physician Operation Desert Storm, 1990-91; occupl. health cons. Pueblo (Colo.) Health Clinic, 1991-93; physician, occupl. health cons. Evans Army Cmty. Hosp., Fort Carson, Colo., 1991-93; med. dir., staff physician several hosps., 1988-93; pvt. practice occupational medicine & adult primary care Colorado Springs, 1994-96; occpl. medicine clin. practice Peoria, Ill., 1996—. Contbr. articles to profl. jours. Mem. Am. Coll. Preventive Medicine, Colo. Soc. Osteo. Physicians, Colo. Pub. Health Assn., Colo. Med. Soc., El Paso County Med. Soc. Republican. Seventh Day Adventist. Office: 200 E Pennsylvania Ave Ste 101 Peoria IL 61603

BURKE, CHRISTINE ELEANOR, nurse, midwife, consultant; b. Washington, Nov. 12, 1948; d. Paul Joseph and Cynthia R. (Yates) B.; m. John M. Durrence, May 27 (dec. 1982); 1 child, Aubrey Burke Durrence. BS, Xavier Coll., Chgo., 1972; MS, Yale U., 1976; ABD, U. Colo., 1991, PhD, 1992. Nurse-midwife Georgetown U. HMO, Washington, 1976; mem. faculty Yale U., New Haven, 1977-83; pvt. practice nurse-midwifery County OB, P.C., New Haven, 1977-81; nurse-midwife Conn. Health Care Plan, New Haven, 1981-83; asst. prof. George Mason U., 1983-85; nurse-midwife, instr. Georgetown U., Washington, 1985-87; mem. faculty U. Colo., Denver, 1987-91; owner Pentmento Praxis, Denver, 1992—; cons. Joseph P. Kennedy Jr. Found., Washington, 1985—, Am. Bur. Cons., Colo. Trust Found., 1993—. Curriculum writer: Parenting for State of Colo., Teen Challenges and Choices for State of Colo., 1993, 94; contbr. articles to profl. jours. Docent, spkr. Nat. Mus. Women in the Arts; docent Denver Art Mus.; active Planned Parenthood of the Rocky Mountains. Mem. ANA, Clin. Nurse Rschrs., Am. Coll. Nurse-Midwife (site visitor accreditation divsn. 1984—, sec. found. 1985—), Sigma Theta Tau.

BURKE, DOROTHY DRECHSLER, acupuncturist, nurse; b. Balt., Nov. 9, 1949; d. William Edward and Helen Roberta (Kirkpatrick) Drechsler; m. Thomas R. Burke, Feb. 14, 1993. BA in Am. Studies, U. Md., 1971, BSN, 1974, MS in Nursing, 1983, M of Acupuncture, 1992. RN, Md.; cert. BLS instr.-trainer; nat. bd. cert. in acupuncture. Med. intensive care nurse U. Md. Hosp., Balt., 1974-77, Johns Hopkins Hosp., Balt., 1977-78; coronary care nurse clinician Frances Scott Key Med. Ctr., Balt., 1978-80; cardiac clin. specialist Greater Balt. Med. Ctr., 1980-82; instr., cardiac rehab. nurse Union Meml. Hosp., Balt., 1982-87; cardiac clin. specialist Harbor Hosp. Ctr., Balt., 1987-92; instr. Howard C.C., 1992—; pvt. practice acupuncture Frederick, Md., 1992—; staff in acupuncture and detox units Sheppard Pratt Hosp.; instr. RN Sch. Nursing-Harbor Hosp. Ctr., 1989. Author: (with others) Myocardial Infarction: A Guide to Patient Education, 1988. Mem. Am. Assn. Acupuncture and Oriental Medicine, Am. Holistic Nurses Assn., Sigma Theta Tau. Office: 176 Thomas Johnson Dr #203 Frederick MD 21702

BURKE, EDWARD NEWELL, radiologist; b. Wakefield, Mass., Apr. 28, 1916; s. Charles Edward and Laura Cecelia (Doherty) B.; BS, Holy Cross Coll., 1938; MD, CM, McGill U., 1942; postgrad. Brit. Postgrad. Med. Sch., 1946, Johns Hopkins Sch. Public Health, 1943; m. Mary A. Bryon, Nov. 26, 1949; children: Laureen, Martha, Newell, Laurence. Resident in pathology Mallory Inst., Boston City Hosp., 1942-43; intern Salem (Mass.) Hosp., 1946-47, resident in radiology, 1947-50; resident in supervoltage Therapy Lahey Clinic and MIT, 1949; assoc. radiologist Mass. Meml. Hosp., Boston, 1951-56; lectr. radiologic tech. Northeastern U., 1953-65; radiologist Lawrence Meml. Hosp., Medford, Mass., also Charles Choate Hosp., Woburn, Mass., 1956—; individual practice medicine specializing in radiology Medford, 1956—; radiologist St. Joseph's Hosp., Lowell, Mass., 1956-64, Hooper Infirmary, Tufts Coll., Medford, 1971-80; chmn., chief depts. radiology Lawrence Meml. Hosp., 1961-85, assoc. chief radiology, 1985—; chief dept. Charles Choate Meml. Hosp., 1963-82; assoc. prof. radiology Boston U., 1951-56; asst. clin. prof. radiology Tufts U., 1971-81, assoc. clin. prof., 1981—; pres. Charles Choate Hosp. med. staff, 1974-76, incorporator, trustee, 1974-81; incorporator Lawrence Meml. Hosp., 1972-96, pres. med. staff, 1980-82; dir. Carroll Ctr. for the Blind. Served to maj. M.C., U.S. Army, 1943-46. Diplomate Am. Coll. Radiology. Radiology wing dedicated in his honor Choate Hosp., 1982. Decorated Sovereign Mil. Order Malta. Fellow Am. Coll. Radiology; mem. AMA, Am. Roentgen Ray Soc., New Eng. Roentgen Ray Soc., Radiol. Soc. N.Am., N.Y. Acad. Scis., Mass. Radiol. Soc., Soc. Nuclear Medicine, Am. Inst. Ultrasound Medicine, New Eng. Ultrasound Soc., Mass. Med. Soc. Roman Catholic. Clubs: Clover Boston, Winchester Country. Contbr. articles to med. publs. Home: 40 Pine Ridge Rd Medford MA 02155-2135 Office: 170 Governors Ave Medford MA 02155-1643

BURKE, EUGENE FRANCIS, urologist; b. Orange, N.J., June 25, 1943; s. Eugene F. and Mary Eleanor (Connell) B.; m. Victoria L. Meinster; children: Deborah, Melanie. AB, Boston Coll., 1965; MD, U. Pa., 1969. Intern U. Wis., Madison, 1970, resident, 1970-74; mem. staff Naples (Fla.) Cmty. Hosp., 1974—. Office: Naples Med Ctr 400 8th St N Naples FL 33940

BURKE, HAROLD REYNOLDS, psychology educator, consultant; b. Sterling, Conn., May 17, 1915; s. Harold and Louise-Grace (Gallup) B.; m. Mary J. Burke, Nov. 3, 1956; children: Richard, Patricia, Sally, Harold, Laurence, Alysa. BS, Springfield (Mass.) Coll., 1940, MEd, 1942; EdD, Boston U., 1955. Dir. YMCA, Boston, 1941-43, Springfield, 1943-46; instr. group work Springfield Coll., Mass., 1946-52; counselor Boston U., 1952-53; dir. acad. advisement U. Conn., Storrs, 1954-65; dean students Western Conn. State U., Danbury, 1965-76, prof. psychology, 1976-84, prof. emeritus, 1985—; counselor educator Western Conn. State U., 1975—; workshop leader on multicultural edn., 1961-91; specialist career devel. workshops, 1970-91; cons. on orgn. devel., 1970-85. Mem. Storrs Town Com., 1962-64; justice of the peace Town of Storrs, 1963-65; pres., chmn. Greater Danbury Intercultural Assn., 1980—. Named Educator of the Yr., Phi Delta Kappa, 1970, 88. Mem. ACA, AAUP, ACES, Lions (dist. gov. Conn. 1964-65). Home: 21 Homestead Ave Danbury CT 06810-5108 Office: Western Conn State U 181 White St Danbury CT 06810-6845

BURKE, HARRY BRIAN, podiatrist; b. Pitts., Oct. 22, 1940; s. Harry Martin and Margaret Mae (Kelly) B.; m. Alice Rita Gurman, Aug. 15, 1965; children: Brian, Tracy. Grad., Duquesne U., 1967; D. of Podiatric Medicine, Ohio Coll. Podiatric Medicine, 1972. Diplomate Am. Bd. Podiatric Surgery, Am. Bd. Podiatric Medicine and Podiatric Orthopedics. Pvt. practice Monaca, Pa., 1972—; dir. Residency Program, Beaver, Pa. Contbr. articles to profl. jours. Mem. Am. Podiatric Med. Assn., Am. Coll. Foot Surgeons, Pa. Podiatric Med. Assn., Am. Coll. Foot and Ankle Orthopedics and Medicine, Coun. Podiatric Medicine. Roman Catholic. Office: 1256 Brodhead Rd Monaca PA 15061-2522

BURKE, JAMES B., health services administrator; b. Phila., Mar. 7, 1957; s. James Elwood Jr. and Carol (Robb) B.; m. Kathleen Olewnik, Nov 17, 1984; children: James Henry, Elizabeth Rose, Christopher Bradley. BA, U. Pa., 1979; MBA, Drexel U., 1984. Mgmt. engr. Frankford Hosp., Phila., 1981-85; corp. mgmt. engr. Universal Health Svc., Inc., King of Prussia, Pa., 1985-86; dir. program and ops. U. Pa. Hosp. Phila., 1986-94; v.p. ops. Lehigh Valley Hosp, Allentown, Pa., 1994—; bd. dirs. Wescott Steel Co. Treas. Am. Revolution Patriots Fund, Phila. 1993—; bd. dirs. Lehigh County Sr. Citizens' Ctr, Allentown, 1995—. Fellow Healthcare Info. and Mgmt. Sys. Soc. (bd. dirs. Delaware Valley chpt., treas. 1985-92, disting. svc. award, 1992); mem. Am. Coll. Healthcare Execs. (assoc.), Pa. Soc. S.R. (v.p., bd. dirs. 1995—), N.J. Soc. of Cincinnati (treas. 1994—). Office: Lehigh Valley Hosp PO Box 7017 17th and Chew Sts Allentown PA 18105

BURKE, JAMES FRANCIS, JR., nephrologist; b. Phila., May 8, 1940; s. James Francis and Margaret Mary (Bolger) B.; m. Diane Patricia Barrow, Feb. 12, 1966; childen: Laura, Jennifer, Dylan James. BS in Biology, St. Joseph's Coll., Phila., 1962; MD, Thomas Jefferson U., 1966. Diplomate Am. Bd. Internal Medicine in Internal Medicine and Nephrology. Intern Thomas Jefferson U. Hosp., Phila., 1966-67, resident in internal medicine, 1969-71, fellow in nephrology, 1971-72, instr. in medicine, 1972-74, clin. asst. prof. medicine, 1974-76, asst. prof. medicine, 1976-78, clin. assoc. prof. medicine, 1978-82, clin. prof. medicine, 1982—, from. attending physician to dir. divsn. nephrology, 1972-89, dir. divsn. nephrology, 1989—; mem. edtl. bd. Clin. Nephrology; reviewer Transplantation, Annals Internal Medicine, Kidney Internat., Am. Jour. Kidney Diseases; mem. Transplant Learning Ctr. Adv. Bd.; bd. dirs. Nat. Kidney Found. of Delaware Valley. Contbr. over 70 articles and abstracts to profl. jours. including Lancet, Am. Jour. Medicine, Archives Internal Medicine, New Eng. Jour. Medicine, Transplantation, Am. Jour. Kidney Diseases. Mem. Am. Soc. Nephrology, Internat. Soc. Nephrology, Am. Soc. Transplant Physicians, Internat. Soc. Peritoneal Dialysis. Democrat. Roman Catholic. Office: Thomas Jefferson U Hosp 111 S 11th St Ste 7320 Philadelphia PA 19107-5098

BURKE, JOHN CHARLES, social worker; b. N.Y.C., May 11, 1946; s. Charles John and Mary Rosalma (DeMott) B.; m. Kathleen Killough, Aug. 4, 1972; children: Eric John, Colleen Lee. BA in Sociology, Siena Coll., 1970; MS in Counseling, Laverne U., 1989; MBA, Chapman U., 1990. Owner, mgr. Burke's Apts., Saugerties, N.Y., 1973-76; owner, operator, tchr. Burke's Studio and Sch. Photography, Saugerties, 1973-76; outdoor recreation expert PM Mag., Channel 8 WFAA TV, Dallas, 1978; child placement worker Tex. Dept. Human Resources, Dallas, 1976-79; social worker State of Alaska Div. Family and Youth Svcs., Anchorage, 1979—; pres., CEO Internat. Bus. Devel. Corp., Anchorage, 1992; instr. Am. Inst. Banking, Am. Bankers Assn.; speaker in field. Contbr. articles to profl. publs. With U.S. Army, 1970-71. Roman Catholic. Home: 7500 Chalet Ct Anchorage AK 99516-1155

BURKE, JOHN F., health care administrator b. Bklyn., Dec. 10, 1942; s. Francis J. and Mary E. (Knight) B.; m. Geraldine Manning, Sept. 12, 1964; children: Timothy, Brendan, Sheila. BS, Siena Coll., Loudonville, N.Y., 1962; MPA, N.Y. State U., 1972; PhD, Clayton U., St. Louis, 1986. Cert. mental health adminstr.; cert. quality assurance profl. Systems analyst N.Y. State Dept. Health, Albany, 1968-72; accreditation specialist N.Y. State Office Mental Health, Albany, 1972-80; dir. quality assurance Capitol Dist. Psychiat. Ctr., Albany, 1980-86, adminstrv. dir., 1986-90, dep. dir., 1990-92; program dir. N.Y. State Office Mental Health, Albany, 1992—; surveyor Joint Commn., Chgo., 1978—; spkr. workshops on mental health adminstrn., N.Y.C., Chgo., L.A., Houston, Miami, Phila., 1986-94. Contbr. articles to profl. jours. Maj. U.S. Army, 1964-68. Decorated Bronze Star medal, Meritorious Svc. medal, Army Commendation medal. Mem. Res. Officers Assn., Am. Legion, Nat. Assn. Mental Health Adminstrs. (treas. N.Y. State chpt. 1990-94, pres. 1994-96, Chpt. of Yr. award 1994-95), Nat. Assn. Quality Assurance Profls. Democrat. Roman Catholic.

BURKE, KENNETH IBER, nutrition educator, food scientist, researcher; b. Covert, Mich., Aug. 21, 1933; s. Lloyd Ernest and Nora Francis (McNeal) B.; m. Theresa Ann Cunningham, Aug. 14, 1950; children: Thomas Edward, Sabrina Kay, Susan Marie, Daniel Gerald. BS in Chem., So. Missionary Coll., 1959; MEd in Natural Sci., Clemson U., 1963; PhD, Fla. State U., 1973. Assoc. prof. So. Missionary Coll., Collegedale, Tenn., 1972-74; chemist dept. agr. State of Fla., Tallahassee, 1968-72; instr. So. Missionary Coll., Collegedale, Tenn., 1963-66, assoc. prof., 1972-74; assoc. prof. Loma Linda (Calif.) U., 1974-83, prof. nutrition and dietetics, 1983—, assoc. chmn. dept. nutrition and dietetics, 1985—; cons. food industries, 1978—; chmn. mgmt. com. 1st Internat. Congress on Vegetarian Nutrition, Washington, 1987. Contbr. health and nutrition articles to profl. jours. Served as cpl. U.S. Army, 1953-55. Mem. Am. Dietetic Assn. (registered dietitian), Inst. Food Technologists (profl.), N.Y. Acad. Sci., Calif. Dietetic Assn. (treas. Inland dist. 1979-82, rep. 1981-82, 89-92, nominating com. 1982), Sigma Xi. Adventist. Office: Loma Linda U Dept Nutrition Dietetics Loma Linda CA 92350

BURKE, LEAH WEYERTS, physician; b. Richland, Wash., Jan. 29, 1954; d. Alfred Cornelius and Phyllis (Nietfeld) Weyerts; m. David Lew Burke, Oct. 15, 1994. BA, U. N.C., Chapel Hill, 1975; MAT, Duke U., Durham, N.C., 1978; MD, U. N.C. Sch. Medicine, Chapel Hill, 1987. Diplomate Am. Bd. Med. Genetics, Am. Bd. Pediatrics. Asst. prof. East Carolina U., Greenville, N.C., 1992-94, Allegheny U. Health Scis., Pitts., 1994—. Vol. Safe Summer Program, Pitts., 1995; vol. physician Little People of Am., Denver, 1995, Indpls., 1996. Recipient Resident Tchg. award UCSD Pediatric Residency, 1990, WSPR Travel award Ross Lab. and Genetech, 1993. Fellow Am. Coll. Med. Genetics, Am. Acad. Pediatrics; mem. Am. Cleft Palate-Craniofacial Assn., Am. Soc. for Human Genetics, Allegheny County Med. Soc., Pitts. Pediatrics Soc. Office: Allegheny-Singer Rsch Inst 320 E North Ave Pittsburgh PA 15212

BURKE, LILLIAN, physician; b. Lansing, Mich., Nov. 26, 1951. BA, Macalester Coll., 1974; BS, U. Minn., 1975, MD, 1979. Diplomate Am. Bd. Internal Medicine. Resident U. Ala., Birmingham, 1979-82; physician pvt. practice, Auburn, N.Y., 1983-90; med. reviewer FDA, Rockville, Md., 1995—; instr. medicine SUNY, Syracuse, 1984-87, asst. prof., 1988-90; clin. faculty Georgetown U., 1995—; adj. clin. asst. prof. dept. of medicine, Dartmouth U., 1996—. Contbr. articles to profl. jours. Leader Girl Scouts Am., St. Paul, 1969-72. Fellow rheumatology and microbiology U. Ala., 1982-83, rsch. fellow NIH, Bethesda, 1990-92, 92-95, Biotechnology fellow NCI, 1993-95; sr. award Nat. Rsch., 1990-92. Mem. Am. Coll. Physicians, Am. Fedn. Clin. Rsch. Mem. Soc. of Friends. Office: FDA 9B-45 Parklawn HFD-170 5600 Fishers Ln Rockville MD 20857

BURKE, MICHAEL DESMOND, pathologist; b. Galway, Ireland, May 25, 1935; came to U.S., 1959; s. James and Margaret (McKee) B.; m. Joan Long, June, 1960 (div. Apr. 1966); children: James Niall, Richard Joseph; m. Maria Sperazi, June 19, 1966: children: Marina, Claudia. MB, BCh., BAO, Nat. U. of Ireland, Galway, 1959. Diplomate Am. Bd. of Pathology in Clin., Chem. and Anatomical Pathology. Assoc. pathologist Mt. Sinai Hosp., Mpls., 1969-81; from asst. prof. to prof. pathology U. Minn., Mpls., 1971-81; prof. pathology and dir. clin. pathology U. Hosp. SUNY, Stony Brook, N.Y., 1981-95; prof. pathology, vice chmn. lab. medicine, dir. clin. labs. The N.Y. Hosp. Cornell Med. Ctr., N.Y.C., 1996—; Faculty of Pathology fellow Royal Coll. Physicians of Ireland, 1993; trustee Am. Bd. Pathology, Tampa, Fla., 1997; edtl. cons. clin. pathology Stedman's Med. Dictionary 25th edit., 1990. Editor Clinical Decisions and Laboratory Use, U. Minn. Press, 1982; adv. editor Lab. Medicine, 1985; assoc. editor Am. Jour. of Clin. Pathology, 1990. Capt. USAR, 1961-63. Fellow Am. Soc. Clin. Pathologists (pres. 1995-96, Disting. Svc. award 1984), Coll. of Am. Pathologists; mem. AAAS, AMA, Am. Assn. for Clin. Chemistry (Outstanding Speaker award 1991), Acad. Clin. Lab. Physicians and Scientists (pres. 1993-94). Office: NY Hosp Cornell Med Ctr 525 E 68th St New York NY 10021

BURKE, MICHELLE L., community outreach education nurse; b. Santa Monica, Calif., Apr. 13, 1961; d. Lois H. Hughes; m. Timothy J. Burke, Oct. 1, 1983; children: Shannon, Rachel. BS, Russell Sage Coll., Troy, N.Y., 1983. RN, N.Y.; breast cancer awareness and breast self-exam instr. Staff nurse Glens Falls (N.Y.) Hosp., 1989—, day surgery nurse, 1991-94, joint lead nurse postanesthesia care unit ambulatory surgery, cmty. outreach edn. nurse cancer prevention/early detection, 1994-96; quality assurance coord. for ambulatory surgery Glens Falls Hosp., 1986; co-chair, pub. edn. bd. dirs. Am. Cancer Soc. Clark nursing scholar, 1983. Mem. N.Y. State Fedn. Pub. Health Educators, Sigma Theta Tau.

BURKE, MILES JOSEPH, ophthalmologist; b. Coshocton, Ohio, Feb. 21, 1949; s. Mark Clark and Frances Edith (Moore) B.; m. Barbara Ellen Rosner, Feb. 9, 1974; children: Brian, Michael. BS, U. Ariz., 1970, MD, 1974; MS, U. Mich., 1978. Teaching asst. anatomy and physiology dept. biol. scis. U. Ariz., Tucson, 1970-72; intern med. edn. program Tucson Hosp., 1974-75; resident in ophthalmology U. Mich. Med. Ctr., Ann Arbor, 1975-78; fellow in pediatric ophthalmology and strabismus Wills Eye Hosp., Phila., 1978-79; asst. prof. dept. pediatrics U. Cin., 1979-85, asst. prof., chief pediatric ophthalmology and strabismus, 1979-85, acting dir. dept. ophthalmology, 1984-85, assoc. clin. prof. dept. pediatrics, 1986—, assoc. prof., chief pediatric ophthalmology and strabismus, 1986—; dir. dept. pediatric ophthalmology Children's Hosp. Med. Ctr., Cin., 1979—. Contbr. chpts. to books. Fellow ACS; mem. Am. Acad. Ophthalmology, AMA, Am. Acad. Pediatrics, Am. Assn. Pediatric Ophthalmology and Strabismus. Office: Childrens Hosp Med Ctr 3333 Burnet Ave Cincinnati OH 45229-3039

BURKE, PAUL M., JR., vascular surgeon; b. Munich, Germany, Oct. 20, 1952; came to U.S., 1953; s. Paul Mark and Dorothea Helen (Philbin) B.; m. Doris Hirsch, June 1, 1979; children: Paul, Andrew. BS, Bates Coll., 1974; MD, Boston U., 1979. Diplomate Am. Bd. Surgery. Intern in surgery U. Mass. Med. Ctr., Worcester, 1979-80, resident in surgery, 1980-83; gen. surgery fellow Lahey Clinic Med. Ctr., Burlington, Mass., 1983; chief resident in surgery U. Mass. Med. Ctr., Worcester, 1984, vascular surgeon fellow, 1985; staff Lowell (Mass.) Gen. Hosp., 1985—, St. Meml. Med. Ctr., Chelmsford, Mass., 1985—. Coach Andover Little League; vol. lectr. Lowell pub. schs. Fellow ACS; mem. Soc. Clin. Vascular Surgery, soc. of Peripheral Vascular Surgery, New Eng. Vascular Surg. Soc., Mass. Med. Soc., No. Middlesex Med. Soc., Vesper Country Club, Indian Ridge Country Club, Quechee Country Club, Coll. Club, Lanam Club, U.S. yacht Racing Union, U.S. Golf Assn., U.S. Ski Assn. Office: 43 Village Sq Chelmsford MA 01824

BURKE, PETER ARTHUR, microbiologist, chemist; b. Long Branch, N.J., Nov. 4, 1948; s. Edward S. and Dorothy M. (Jambore) B.; m. Joan Ann Schwenk, May 15, 1977; children: Kathleen Ann, Peter Arthur Jr. BA, Rutgers U., 1971; MS, Seton Hall U., 1976; PhD, St. John's U., 1985. Cert. Profl. Chemist. Pa. Supervisory microbiologist Booz, Allen & Hamilton, Florham Park, N.J., 1971-76; supr. disintectant devel. Am. Cyanamid Rsch. Ctr., Clifton, N.J., 1976-78; dir. R&D Kiwi Brands, Inc., Douglassville, Pa., 1978-88; dir. tech. affairs, Sara Lee/DE, Household and Personel Care div., Douglassville, 1988-90, v.p. R&D, 1990—; v.p. R&D Carter Products Divsn. Carter-Wallace, Inc., 1996—. Fellow Am. Inst. Chemists; mem. ASTM, Am. Soc. for Microbiology, Am. Chem. Soc., N.Y. Acad. Scis., Internat. Assn. Approved Basketball Ofcls., Eastern Coll. Football Ofcls. Assn., Sigma Xi. Roman Catholic. Home: 2 Surrey Ln Downingtown PA 19335-1508 Office: Carter-Wallace Inc Carter Products R&D Cranbury NJ 08512

BURKE, ROBERT HARRY, surgeon, educator; b. Cambridge, Mass., Dec. 22, 1945; s. Harry Clearfield and Joan Rosalyn (Spire) B.; m. Margaret Cauldwell Fisher, May 4, 1968; children: Christopher David, Catherine Cauldwell. Student, U. Mich. Coll. Pharmacy, 1964-67; DDS, U. Mich., 1971, MS, 1976; MD, Mich. State U., 1980. Diplomate Am. Bd. Oral and Maxillofacial Surgery, Am. Bd. Cosmetic Surgery. Pvt. practice cosmetic and reconstructive surgery Ann Arbor, Mich., 1976—; house officer oral and maxillofacial surgery U. Mich. Sch. Dentistry, U. Mich. Hosp., Ann Arbor, 1973-76; clin. asst. prof. dept. oral surgery U. Detroit Sch. Dentistry, 1976-77; adj. asst. rsch. scientist Ctr. Human Growth and Devel. U. Mich., 1976-77, adj. rsch. investigator, 1982-85; clin. asst. prof. Mich. State U., East Lansing, 1978-80, 1987—; house officer surg. emphasis St. Joseph Mercy Hosp., Ann Arbor, 1980-81; adj. rsch. investigator dept. anatomy U. Mich. Med. Sch., 1982-85; clin. asst. prof. oral and maxillofacial surgery U. Mich., 1984-86; lectr. U. Detroit Sch. Dentistry, 1986, assoc. clin. prof. oral and maxillofacial surgery, 1987-90; cons., lectr. dept. occlusion U. Mich. Sch. Dentistry, 1986; head sect. dentistry and oral surgery dept. gen. surgery St. Joseph Mercy Hosp., 1982-87, mem. exec. com. dept. gen. surgery, 1984-87; chmn. com. emergency care rev. Beyer Meml. Hosp., Ypsilanti, Mich., 1986, also active, 1987, 1990—; active staff St. Joseph Meml. Hosp.; courtesy staff Saline (Mich.) Community Hosp., 1978-88; Chelsea (Mich.) Med. Ctr., 1978-88, 90-92, McPherson Community Hosp., Howell, Mich., 1984-87. Mem. editl. bd. Topics in Pain Mgmt., 1985—; contbg. editor Am. Jours. Cosmetic surgery, 1990-91; sect. editor Internat. Jour. Aesthetic and Restorative Surgery, 1992-95, 96—. Campaign chmn. med. and dental sects. United Way Washtenaw County, Ann Arbor, 1982, dental sect. 1983; profl. adv. com. March of Dimes Genesee County Valley Chpt., Flint, 1979; pres. Huron Pkwy. Pla. Condominium, 1984—. Fellow ACS, Internat. Coll. Surgeons (bd. dirs. Mich. chpt., vice regent), Am. Coll. Oral and Maxillofacial Surgeons (v.p. 1987-88, pres.-elect 1989-90, pres. 1991-93), Am. Acad. Aesthetic and Restorative Surgery; mem. AMA, Am. Assn. Craniomaxillofacial Surgeons (pres. 1992—), Internat. Soc. Cosmetic Laser Surgeons (trustee 1992-93, sec. 1992), British Soc. for Oral and Maxillofacial Surgeons (assoc.), European Soc. Aesthetic Surgery and Liposuction, Chalmers Lyons Acad. Oral Surgery, European Assn. for Cranio-Maxillofacial Surgery (assoc.), Washtenaw County Med. Soc. (exec.com. sec. 1987-88, pres. 1990), Inst. Study Profl. Risk (bd. dirs. 1985-90), Victor's Club, Pres.'s Club, Omicron Kappa Upsilon. Congregationalist. Home: 4702 Mulberry Woods Cr Ann Arbor MI 48105 Office: 2260 S Huron Pky Ann Arbor MI 48104-5151

BURKE, THOMAS GEORGE, psychology educator; b. Bklyn., Mar. 16, 1947; s. George Joseph and Dorothy (Hohl) B.; m. Alice C. Heron, Aug. 29, 1976; children: George Albert, Jonathan Patrick. BA in Psychology, St. John's U., 1968, MA in Clin. Psychology, 1971; MA in Communication Arts, N.Y. Inst. Tech., 1989; postgrad. New Sch. Social Rsch., 1973—. Tchr., student drug counselor St. John's Prep. High Sch., Bklyn., 1969-72; psychologist New High Sch., Bklyn., 1972-73; adj. instr. dept. psychology St. John's U., Jamaica, N.Y., 1973-78, S.I. Community Coll. (N.Y.), 1973-78; dir. Human Resources Devel. Center, assoc. prof. psychology N.Y. Inst. Tech., Old Westbury, 1974—, v.p., 1983-86, sr. v.p., 1987—; psychotherapist Personal Awareness Center, 1977-78. Author: Contemporary Issues in Abnormal Psychology and Mental Illness, 1976; contbr. articles to profl. jours.; composer (with Charles Frazer): Jack in the Box, 1969. Vol.

psychologist Creedmoor State Mental Hosp., Queen's Village, N.Y., 1972-76. Mem. APA (assoc.), N.Y. State Psychol. Assn. (assoc.), N.Y. State Doctoral Assn. (v.p.), Delta Sigma Phi. Roman Catholic. Office: NY Inst Tech Tower House Old Westbury Campus Old Westbury NY 11568

BURKE, TIMOTHY ALAN, anesthesiologist; b. Robins AFB, Ga., Oct. 12, 1959; s. Robert Lester and Sara (Dingler) B.; m. Donna Marie Kaminski, Apr. 16, 1988; children: Joanna Elaine, Michael Patrick. BS, Emory U., 1981; MD, Vanderbilt U., 1985. Diplomate Am. Bd. Anesthesiology. Resident in anesthesia Georgetown U. Hosp., Washington, 1985-88, chief resident, 1988-89; staff anesthesiologist Pitt County Meml. Hosp., Greenville, N.C., 1993—. Maj. U.S. Army, 1989-93. Mem. AMA, Am. Soc. Anesthesiologists, N.C. Soc. Anesthesiologists. Office: Pitt County Anesthesia Asso Bldg F Physicians Quad Greenville NC 27834

BURKET, GEORGE EDWARD, JR., family physician; b. Kingman, Kans., Dec. 10, 1912; s. George Edward and Jessie May (Talbert) B.; m. Mary Elizabeth Wallace, Nov. 12, 1938; children: George Edward III, Carol Sue, Elizabeth Christine. Student, Wichita State U., 1930-33; MD, U. Kans., 1937. Diplomate Am. Bd. Family Practice (pres. 1975-77). Intern Santa Barbara (Calif.) Gen. Hosp., 1937-38, resident, 1938-39; grad. asst. in surgery Mass. Gen. Hosp., Boston, 1956-57; practice medicine Kingman, 1939-73; preceptor in medicine U. Kans. Med. Sch., 1950-73, assoc. prof., 1973-78, clin. prof., 1978-84; bd. dirs. Kingman Savings and Loan Assn. Contbr. articles to profl. jours. Mem. Kingman Bd. Edn., 1946-58; mem. Kans. State Bd. Health, 1960-66. Mem. AMA, Kans. Med. Soc. (pres. 1966-67), Am. Acad. Family Physicians (pres. 1967-68, John Walsh Founders award 1979), Inst. Medicine (sr.), Assn. Am. Med. Colls., Soc. Tchrs. Family Medicine, Alpha Omega Alpha. Republican. Episcopalian. Clubs: Garden of Gods (Colorado Springs, Colo.); Wichita Country, Wichita. Lodges: Masons, Shriners. Home: Spring Lake Rte 1 Kingman KS 67068

BURKET, JOHN MCVEY, dermatologist; b. Des Moines, Iowa, Oct. 4, 1935; s. George Austin and Elma (McVey) B.; m. Janice Lee Feilmeyer, Dec. 29, 1956; children: Denise, Bradley, Brent, Diana, Dawn, Brian. BA, U. Iowa, 1957, MD, 1960. Diplomate Am. Bd. Dermatology, Am. Bd. Pathology. Resident in dermatopathology U. Iowa Hosp., Iowa City, 1964; chief dermatology USAF, March AFB, 1964-66; pvt. practice dermatology Medford, Oreg., 1966—. Contbr. articles to profl. jours., chpts. to books. Office: 1000 E Main Medford OR 97504-7460

BURKET, ROGER CLAIR, child psychiatrist, educator; b. Phila., Feb. 19, 1948; s. L. Clair and Georgetta (Scheffer) B.; m. Cynthia Lynn Bryan, Aug. 20, 1977; 1 child, Bryan. BS in Aerospace Engring., Pa. State U., 1971; MD, George Washington U., 1981. Lic. psychiatrist, Fla., Ga. Resident in psychiatry and child psychiatry U. Fla., Gainesville, 1981-88, asst. prof. psychiatry, 1988-89, asst. prof. child and adolescent psychiatry, 1990-94; pvt. practice Lake Worth, Fla., 1989-90; assoc. prof. child and adolescent psychiatry Med. Coll. Ga., 1994—. Contbr. articles to profl. jours. Capt. U.S. Army, 1971-79, with Res. Mem. AMA, Am. Psychiat. Assn., Am. Acad. Child and Adolescent Psychiatry. Office: Med Coll Ga Dept Psychiatry 1515 Pope Ave Augusta GA 30904-5843

BURKET, WILLIAM R., health center financial executive; b. Roaring Spring, Pa., Sept. 23, 1948; s. Ralph L. and Martha J. (Benton) B.; BS in Acctg., Pa. State U., 1970; m. Connie L. Porta, Sept. 23, 1972; children: Mark A., Brian J., Christopher S., Patrick W.N. Staff auditor Ernst & Ernst, Pitts., 1970-73; asst. controller Altoona (Pa.) Hosp., 1973-75; dir. fin., 1975-78; chief fin. officer St. Joseph Mercy Hosp., Ann Arbor, Mich., 1978-79; v.p. fin. Catherine McAuley Health Ctr., Ann Arbor, 1979-86; CFO Hampton (Va.) Gen. Hosp., 1986-88; mgr. Mgmt. Con. Services Coopers & Lybrand, Harrisburg, Pa., 1988-94; asst. contr. Milton S. Hershey Med. Ctr., Hershey, Pa., 1994—; lectr. Sch. Pub. Health, U. Mich. CPA, Pa., Mich. Mem. Am. Inst. CPA's, Pa. Inst. CPA's, Mich. Assn. CPA's, Va. Soc. CPA's, Fin. Execs. Inst., Am. Hosp. Assn., Nat. Assn. Accts., Healthcare Fin. Mgmt. Assn. Office: Milton S. Hershey Med Ctr Pa State U PO Box 850 Hershey PA 17033

BURKETT, MARJORIE THERESA, nursing educator, gerontology nurse; b. Jamaica, West Indies, Mar. 21, 1931; d. David Cameron and Mabel Louise (McKenzie) Espeut; m. Leo A. Burkett, Apr. 4, 1962; 1 child, Catherine Ann. Diploma in Midwifery and Nursing, Kingston Sch. of Nursing, Kingston, Jamaica, 1953; diploma in Nursing Edn., U. Edinburgh (Scotland UK), 1963; diploma in Psychiat. Nursing, Royal Victoria Hosp., Montreal, Can., 1970; BA, U. West Indies, 1975; MSN Edn., U. Miami, 1977, PhD, 1990; adult health nurse practitioner, Fla. Internat. U., 1992. RN, Fla., Tenn., Eng. and Wales UK, Jamaica; cert. midwife, Jamaica. Assoc. prof. Fla. Internat. U., North Miami, 1988—, coord. adult med. and surg. nursing, 1990, coord. Childbearing Nursing, 1992—; faculty mem. numerous community colls. and profl. coms. Contbr. articles to profl. jours. Mem. ANA, Nat. League Nursing, Fla. League Nursing, Fla. Nurses Assn., Nat. Coun. on Aging, Golden Key Nat. Honor Soc., Sigma Theta Tau, Phi Lambda Pi, Phi Delta Kappa. Office: Fla Internat U Sch Nursing 3000 NE 145th St Miami FL 33181-3612

BURKHALTER, BARTON ROBERT, systems scientist; b. Toledo, July 22, 1938; s. Robert Richard and Mary Louise (Barton) B.; m. Nancy Ann Nasset, June 7, 1963 (div.); 1 child, Eric; m. Eliana Gabriela Godoy, Aug. 22, 1978; 1 child, Genevieve Divin. BS in Math. Engring. and Engring. Mechanics, U. Mich., 1961, MS in Indsl. Engring., 1962, PhD, 1964. Pres. Community System Found., Ann Arbor, Mich., 1963-72, sr. scientist, 1974—; chmn. Community Systems Found. Ltd., Ann Arbor, Mich., 1974-88; research prof. community medicine U. Ariz., Tuscon, 1979-88; pres. Winch Inst. Am., La Jolla, Calif., 1984-88; dir. Ctr. Inernat. Health Info., Washington, 1988-91; sr. program officer Acad. Ednl. Devel., Washington, 1991—; adj. prof. regional planning U. Mich., Ann Arbor, 1969-76. Author: (book) Case Studies in Systems Analyses in a University Library, 1968, An Investigation of Rapidly Changing Papago Tribal Health Programs, 1979; editor: Nutrition Planning, 1977-81. Pres Washtenaw County Planned Parenthood, Ann Arbor, 1973. Mem. Hosp. Mgmt. Systems Soc. Chgo. (pres. 1974). Home: 10310 Gary Rd Potomac MD 20854

BURKHARDT, ANN, occupational therapist, clinical educator; b. Providence, Dec. 21, 1954; d. Kenneth Ralph and Betty Jane (Neale) B. BA in Psychobiology, Wheaton Coll., 1976; MA in Occupational Therapy, NYU, 1979. Lic. occupational therapist, N.Y., R.I., Mass.; cert. neurorehab. therapist Am. Occupational Therapy Assn. Staff therapist Charlton Meml. Hosp., Fall River, Mass., 1979; staff therapist, sr. therapist Columbia U.-Harlem Hosp., N.Y.C., 1979-84; staff therapist, burn specialist Cornell Med. Ctr.-N.Y. Hosp., N.Y.C., 1984-86; dir. occupational therapy Greater Harlem Nursing Home, N.Y.C., 1986-87; chief occupational therapist Meml. Sloan-Kettering Cancer Ctr., N.Y.C., 1987-92; asst. dir. occupational therapy Columbia-Presbyn. Med. Ctr., N.Y.C., 1992—; clin. instr. Columbia U., N.Y.C., 1993—; pvt. practice N.Y.C., 1984—; del. Coll. of Occupl. Therapists, Edinburgh, Scotland, 1995, World Fedn. Occupl. Therapists, London, 1994; spkr. in field. Author: (chpt.) Occupational Therapy Intervention in Recreational Settings in Acute Care, 1993, (pamphlet) Lymphedema: Self-Care and Treatment, 1992; co-author: A Therapists Guide to Oncology, 1996; contbr. articles to profl. jours. Mem. Am. Occupl. Therapy Assn. (alt. rep. to rep. assembly 1992-94, polit. action com. 1994), N.Y. State Occupl. Therapy Assn. (Merit award 1990, alt. rep. 1992-94, pres.-elect. 1994-95, pres. 1995—), Metro N.Y. Dist. Occupl. Therapy Assn. (bd. dirs., sec. 1990-96), Am. Congress Rehab. Medicine, N. Am. Soc. Lymphology, Internat. Soc. Lymphology, Am. Phys. Medicine, Am. Soc. Assn. Execs., Am. Med. Writers Assn., Am. Burn Assn., Congress of Rehab. Medicine. Home: 160 E 91st St Apt 4B New York NY 10128-2458 Office: Milstein Hosp Bldg 8 Garden North 405 177 Fort Washington Ave New York NY 10032-3713

BURKHOLDER, PETER MILLER, physician, educator; b. Cambridge, Mass., May 7, 1933; s. Paul Rufus and Lillian Maud (Miller) B.; m. Barbara Beers, June 3, 1956; children: Kristen Ryner, Lisanne Ryner. B.S., Yale U., 1955; M.D., Cornell U., N.Y.C., 1959. Intern pathology N.Y. Hosp.-Cornell Med. Ctr., 1959-60; NIH trainee in pathology Cornell U., 1960-63, instr., 1963-64, asst. prof., 1964-65; asst. prof. Duke U., 1965-69, asso. prof., 1969-70; asso. prof. U. Wis.-Madison, 1970-72, acting chmn. dept. pathology, 1971-72, prof., 1972-79, chmn. dept. pathology, 1972-74; dir. Kidney Disease Inst., N.Y. State Dept. Health, 1979-80; dep. dir. div. labs. and research N.Y. State Dept. Health, 1980-81, dir. Ctr. Lab. Scis., 1981-82; chief of staff VA Med. Ctr., Ann Arbor, Mich., 1982-84, staff pathologist, 1984-89; prof. pathology U. Mich., Ann Arbor, 1982-89; chmn. dept. pathology Maricopa Med. Ctr., Phoenix, 1989-95, asst. med. dir., 1995; clin. prof. dept. pathology U. Ariz., Tucson, 1989—; adj. lectr. Southwestern Coll. Naturopathic Medicine, 1996—. Author: Atlas of Human Glomerular Pathology, 1974; contbg. author: Structural Basis of Renal Diseases, 1968, Pathobiology Annual, 1971, Tissue Typing and Transplantation, 1973, Glomerulonephritis Morphology Natural History and Treatment, 1973, Cornell Seminars in Nephrology, 1975; mem. editorial bd. Kidney Internat, 1970-76, Lab. Investigation, 1972-83, Exptl. Pathology, 1984-86, Clin. Nephrology, 1989—; contbr. numerous articles to profl. jours. NIH grantee, 1961-78. Mem. AMA, Am. Soc. Exptl. Pathology, Am. Assn. Pathology, Am. Soc. Immunology, Am. Soc. Nephrology, Internat. Acad. Pathology, Internat. Soc. Nephrology, Coll. Am. Pathology, Am. Soc. Clin. Pathologist, Am. Coll. Physician Execs., Renal Path. Soc., Pluto Soc. Home: 7248 N Red Ledge Dr Paradise Valley AZ 85253

BURKMAN, ALLAN MAURICE, pharmacology educator; b. Waterbury, Conn., Apr. 23, 1932; s. Leon Oscar and Anna (Deitcher) B.; m. Katherine Horween, Aug. 8, 1965; children: David Eric, Deborah Rae. BSc, U. Conn., 1954; MSc, Ohio State U., 1955, PhD, 1958. Registered pharmacist, Conn. Asst. prof. pharmacology U. Ill., Chgo., 1958-63; assoc. prof. Butler U., Indpls., 1963-66; assoc. prof. Ohio State U., Columbus, 1966-71, prof., 1971-95, prof. emeritus, 1995—, chmn. div., 1978-87, 94-95; vis. prof. U. Utah, Salt Lake City, 1981-82, Universidad Ctrl. de Venezuela, Carracas, 1994. Co-author: Introduction to Ocular Pharmacology and Toxicology, 1991; mem. editorial rev. bds., referee various profl. and sci. jours.; contbr. articles to profl. and sci. jours., chpts. to books. Recipient R.B. Allen Instructorship award U. Ill., 1963, award for rsch. direction Mead Johnson Co., 1965; grantee Am. Found. Pharm. Edn., 1957-58, NIH, Office Naval Rsch., industry, 1959-95. Mem. Am. Soc. Pharmacology and Exptl. Therapeutics, Soc. Exptl. Biology and Medicine, Am. Pharm. Assn. Home: 2990 Shadywood Rd Columbus OH 43221-2325 Office: Ohio State U Div Pharmacology 500 W 12th Ave Columbus OH 43210-1214

BURKMAN, SUE ANN, critical care nurse, educator; b. Bethlehem, Pa., May 20, 1946; d. Harold C. and Elmira (Weary) Erdman; m. John E. Burkman, Sept. 11, 1971; children: Jennifer Ann, Kathryn Michelle. Diploma, St. Luke's Hosp., Bethlehem, 1967; BSN, U. Hawaii, 1977, MSN, 1981. RN, Pa., Colo. Staff nurse St. Luke's Hosp., 1967-69; staff nurse, instr. Kaiser Hosp., Honolulu, 1971-82, Doctor's Hosp., Colorado Springs, Colo., 1983-89, Penrose Community Hosp., Colorado Springs, 1989—; mem. faculty Regis U., 1993—; mem. faculty AD nursing program Pikes Peak C.C., 1996—. Scholar Ladies Aide Soc., 1964, Ruth Bracken Hoffman scholar, 1967. Mem. AACN (cert.). Home: 4830 Montebello Dr Colorado Springs CO 80918-2722

BURKS, JACK SHELDON, neurologist; b. Charleston, W.Va., Nov. 28, 1943; s. Jack Sheldon Burks and Monica Louise (Long) Ghent; m. Susan Dawn Ayarbe, Aug. 19, 1989; children: Jonathan, Ryan, Jacqueline. BA, W.Va. U., 1965, MD with honors, 1969. Lic. physician, Colo. Intern U. Cin., 1969-70; resident in neurology U. Colo., Boulder, 1970-73; postdoctoral fellow in virology/immunology Johns Hopkins U., Balt., 1973-75, instr. neurology, 1974-75; asst. prof. neurology/microbiology/immunology U. Colo., Boulder, 1975-81, assoc. prof., 1981-88; pres. Rocky Mountain Multiple Sclerosis Ctr., Englewood, Colo., 1978—; lectr. in field; vis. prof. numerous med. schs., hosps., med. socs.; chief neurology Swedish Med. Ctr., 1993—. Contbr. numerous articles and abstracts to profl. jours.; editl. bd. Rehab Mgmt., 1994, Jour. Neurologic Rehab., 1986—; ad hoc reviewer various jours.; co-editor: Interdisciplinary Rehabilitation of Multiple Sclerosis and Neuromuscular Disorders, 1985. Bd. trustees Nat. Easter Seal Rsch. Found., 1990-91, mem. rsch. com., 1992—. Recipient Speedy award Paralyzed Vets. of Am., 1988; fellow Am. Cancer Soc., 1965, Nat. Multiple Sclerosis Soc., 1973. Fellow Am. Acad. Neurology (sec.-treas. sect. neurologic rehab. 1985-87, chmn./co-chmbn. various sci. sessions on neurologic rehab., vice chmn. sect. neurologic rehab. 1987-89, chmn. 1990-92, rep. to Am. Acad. Phys. Medicine and Rehab. 1993—, exec. com. 1985-94); mem. Am. Acad. Med. Dirs., Am. Congress Rehab. Medicine, Am. Neurol. Assn., Am. Soc. Neurorehab. (pres.-elect 1990-93, pres. 1994-96, bd. dirs. 1990—), Colo. Soc. Clin. Neurologists, Consortium of Multiple Sclerosis Ctrs. (co-chmn. com. on patient care 1986-92, exec. com. 1985-92, fin. com. 1987-91, membership rev. com. 1987-91, treas.), Multiple Sclerosis Soc. Colo. (med. dir. 1975-84, med. advisor 1988-91), Clin. Neurosci. Soc. (pres. 1979-80), Nat. Multiple Sclerosis Soc. (bd. dirs. Ctrl. Colo. chpt. 1976-78, med. adv. bd. 1985-89, com. on unitorm data base for multiple sclerosis 1986-89, clinic com., profl. adv. com. 1991-93, edn. com. 1991-94, med. adv. bd. 1991—), Colo. Neurol. Inst. (rsch. com. 1988—, edn. com. 1988—, sec. bd. dirs. 1990-94, chmn. clin. programs and outreach com. 1988-92), Arapahoe Med. Soc. (coun. mem.), Colo. Med. Soc. (ho. of dels. 1990—), Rotary, Alpha Omega Alpha. Office: Rocky Mountain MS Ctr Ste 420 701 E Hampden Ave Englewood CO 80110

BURLAND, J(OHN) ALEXIS, psychoanalyst; b. N.Y.C., Sept. 17, 1931; s. Elmer Granville and Catherine Alexander (Dobrushina) B.; m. Patricia Ruth Millar, Mar. 30, 1963. BA, Colgate U., 1952; MD, Columbia U., 1956; MSc, Temple U., 1962. Intern Mary Hitchcock Meml. Hosp., Hanover, N.H., 1956-57; resident in psychiatry Temple U. Hosp., Phila., 1957-58, 60-61; resident in child psychiatry St. Christopher's Hosp., Phila., 1961-63; candidate in gen. and child adolescent psychoanalysis Phila. Psychoanalytic Inst., 1963-72; pvt. practice Bala Cynwyd, Pa., 1963—; assoc. prof. psychiatry Temple U. Hosp., St. Christopehrs Hosp., Phila., 1963-79; clin. prof. Jefferson Med. Coll., Thomas Jefferson U., Phila., 1979—; tng.-supervising psychoanalyst Phila. Psychoanalytic Inst., 1983—, pres., 1991—; chmn. bd. dirs. Phila. Psychoanalytic Found., 1988—. Editor: Rapprochement: Critical Phase of Separation-Individuation, 1980, Self & Object Constancy, 1985. Lt. comdr. USNR, 1958-60. Fellow APA (life); mem. Am. Psychoanalytic Assn., Internat. Psychoanalytic Assn., Assn. Child Psychoanalysis, Phila. Psychoanalytic Soc. (pres. 1977-80), Union League, Phi Beta Kappa, Delta Upsilon. Home and Office: 15 Colwyn Ln Bala Cynwyd PA 19004-2308

BURLING, DANIEL JAMES, pharmacist, executive, county legislator; b. Batavia, N.Y., Jan. 11, 1947; s. James Edward and Joyce Mae (Crane) B.; m. Jean Marie Dunckel, July 10, 1970; children: Mary Jean, David Marc. Cert., Riverside Sch. Aeros., 1971; grad., Empire State Mil. Acad., 1976; Assoc. degree, Herkimer County Community Coll, 1977; BS in Pharmacy, SUNY, Buffalo, 1980. Aircraft mechanic Nellis Air Field, Ft. Plain, N.Y., 1972-75; commd. 2d lt. U.S. Army, 1976; project mgr., engr. Systems Rsch. Labs. Inc., Dayton, Ohio, 1975-77; mgr., pharmacist Wyo. Rexall Drug, Attica, N.Y., 1981-87; owner Medicine Man Charters, Lake Ontario, N.Y., 1985—; owner, chief exec. officer, pres. Burling Drug of Corfu (N.Y.) Inc., 1991—, Burling Drug Inc., Attica, 1987—; cons. pharmacist Genesee County Nursing Home, Batavia, N.Y., 1980-81; Genesee County legislator, 1993—. Bd. dirs. Jaycees, Ilion, N.Y., 1975; legislator dist. #6 Genesee County, 1994. Sgt. USMC, 1965-69, Vietnam, capt. USAR. Recipient FAA Approved Sch. Grad. award for excellence, 1972. Mem. VFW, Lions (bd. dirs., pres. 1990), Am. Legion, Aircraft Owners Assn., Elks. Republican. Roman Catholic. Home: 29 Main St Attica NY 14011-1038 Office: Burling Drug Inc 29-31 Main St Attica NY 14011

BURN, IAN JOHN, surgeon, oncologist; b. London, Feb. 19, 1927; s. Cyril and Margaret (Cawthorne) B.; m. Fiona May Allan, Sept. 22, 1951; children: Alastair, Hilary, Lindsay, Jonathan. MB BS, St. Bartholomew's Hosp., London, 1950. Surg. registrar St. Bartholomews and Hammersmith Hosps., 1955-65; travelling fellow Roswell Park Mem. Inst., Buffalo, 1961-62; cons. surgeon, asst. dir. surgical studies Royal Postgrad. Med. Sch. Hammersmith Hosp., London, 1965-73; cons. surgical oncologist Charing Cross Hosp., London, 1973-87; cons. surgeon, pvt. practice, med. dir. King Edward VII Hosp., Midhurst, Eng., 1987—. Author: Systematic Surgery, 1966; previous sr. editor European Jour. Surg. Oncology, 1986-94; co-editor: Understanding Cancer, 1977, European Handbook of Surgical Oncology, 1989, Operative Cancer Surgery, 1992. Mem. med. adv. com. Women's Nat. Cancer Campaign; former chmn. current treatment com. Internat. Union Against Cancer. Fellow Royal Coll. Surgeons (diplomate, Hunterian prof.), Royal Soc. Medicine (hon. sec. 1981-87, v.p. 1989-91; mem. U.I.C.C. Roll Honour, European Soc. Surg. Oncology (pres. 1987-91), World Fedn. Surg. Oncology Socs. (pres. 1992-95), Brit. Assn. Surg. Oncology (pres. 1980-83), Finnish Surg. Soc. (hon.), Belgian Assn. Surgeons (hon.), M.C.C., Barber-Surgeons Livery Co., Freeman. Office: King Edward VII Hosp, Midhurst, Sussex GU29 0BL, England

BURNE, MARYANN PAULA MCLAFFERTY, speech and language pathologist; b. Phila., Apr. 20, 1950; d. William S. and Beatrice E. (Baker) McLafferty; divorced; children: Amanda A., Brooke B. BA, Marywood Coll., 1972; MEd, Bloomsburg State U., 1974. Cert. communication disorders level II. Speech-lang. pathologist Northeastern Edn. Intermediate Unit #19, Mayfield, Pa., 1972-92, Valley View Schs., 1992—; pvt. practice speech-lang. pathology, Scranton, Pa., 1980—; co-operating pathologist for student Practicums Marywood Coll., Scranton, 1978—, East Stroudsberg (Pa.) Coll., 1978—, Emerson Coll., Boston, 1977. Homecoming chairperson Marywood Coll. Alumnae, Scranton, 1982; v.p. Ballet Theatre of Scranton, 1986-88. Home: 1010 Sunset St Scranton PA 18509-1936

BURNER, LAVERNE CAROLYN, retired nursing administrator; b. St. Louis, Apr. 15, 1923; d. Herman Frank and Caroline Mary (Spreckelmier) B.; R.N., DePaul Hosp. Sch. Nursing, 1948; B.S.N. (scholar 1948, 50), St. Louis U., 1952; M.S. in Hosp. Adminstrn., Northwestern U., 1957; postgrad. No. Ill. U., 1973. Instr., DePaul Hosp. Sch. Nursing, St. Louis, 1950-52; clin. coordinator St. Francis Sch. Nursing, Evanston, Ill., 1952-56; adminstr. Sandwich (Ill.) Community Hosp., 1957-61; bus. mgr. Victory Meml. Hosp., Waukegan, Ill., 1961-65; asst. adminstr. Rockford (Ill.) Meml. Hosp., 1966-74; v.p. Bergan-Mercy Hosp., Omaha, 1974-77; asst. adminstr. patient services St. Joseph's Hosp., Tucson, 1978-83; faculty No. Ill. U., DeKalb, 1972-74; clin. asso. U. Nebr., Omaha, 1974-77; guest lectr. U. Ariz., Tucson, 1979-81. Mem. task force Rockford Sch. Medicine, 1972-74, task force on nursing State of Ariz., 1980-83; steering com. Crusader's Clinic, Rockford, 1971-73; pres. Hidden Valley Townhomes Assn., 1980, 84-86. Recipient award for acad. and clin. performance Class of '48, DePaul Hosp., 1948. Mem. Ariz. Orgn. Nurse Execs. (hon.). Democrat. Roman Catholic. Home: 2650 W Camino Del Grijalva Tucson AZ 85742-9202

BURNETT, CLAY M., cardiac surgeon; b. Bethesda, Md., Oct. 26, 1954; m. Lori Burnett. BS, East Carolina U., Greenville, N.C., 1977, MD, 1984. Diplomate Am. Bd. Surgery, Am. Bd. Thoracic Surgeon. Rsch. asst. dept. surgery divsn. transplantation East Carolina U., 1980, asst. prof. surgery, chief thoracic transplantation, 1991-95; intern in gen. surgery U. South Fla., Tampa, 1984-85, resident, 1985-88, chief res., 1988-89; fellow in heart transplantation Tex. Heart Inst., Houston, 1989-90, resident in cardiovasc. and thoracic surgery, 1990-91; fellow in heart transplantation St. Luke's Episcopal Hosp. and Tex. Children's Hosp., Houston, 1990-91; pvt. practice, Savannah, Ga., 1995—; regional and nat. presenter in field; former mem. bd. Carolina Organ Procurement Agy. Former editor Cardiac Concepts newsletter; contbr. articles and abstracts to med. jours. Athletic scholar East Carolina U., 1972-77; grantee Am. Cancer Soc., 1981,. Fellow ACS; mem. Internat. Soc. for Heart and Lung Transplant, Soc. Critical Care, Am. Coll. Chest Physicians, Am. Coll. Cardiology, Denton A Cooley Cardiovasc. Surgery Soc., Alpha Omega Alpha. Office: Cardiovasc and Thoracic Surgery Assocs 2 Wheeler St Savannah GA 31405

BURNETT, ELIZABETH (BETSY), counselor; b. Columbus, Ohio, July 17, 1953; m. Gilbert C. Burnett, Jan. 2, 1973; children: Jeffrey, Stephanie. BS in Med. Tech. with honors, Rutgers U., 1976; MA in Counseling with honors, Denver Sem., 1992. Med. technologist various hosps., Denver and Plainfield, N.J., 1976-92; missions dir. Bear Creek Ch. and Family of Faith Ch., Denver, 1985-89; counseling dir. Providence Homes, Denver, 1989—; dir. Providence Counseling Ministry, Denver, 1993—; program cons. various urban counseling svcs. and rehabs., Denver, Colorado Springs, Mich., Calif., Australia, 1992—; urban ministry cons. Denver Sem., 1991-95; contract counselor So. Gables Ch., Littleton, Colo., 1992-96, presenter divorce recovery workshops, 1992-96; spkr. in field. Author: Handbook of Urban Christian Counseling, 1992. Children's dir. mothers of preschoolers, vacation Bible sch., and missions edn. program Bear Creek Ch., Denver, 1982-85; deaconess, lay leader So. Gables Ch., Littleton, 1992-96. Recipient med. tech. award Muhlenberg Hosp., 1976. Mem. Am. Counseling Assn., Am. Assn. Christian Counselors, Internat. Assn. Addictions & Offender Counselors, Assn. Multicultural Counseling and Devel., Christians for Bibl. Equality, Am. Soc. Clin. Pathologists. Office: Providence Homes 801 Logan St Denver CO 80203-3114

BURNETT, ELIZABETH M., critical care nurse, nursing educator; b. N.Y.C., Oct. 13, 1963; d. Charles Edward and Elizabeth Ann (McGrath) Driscoll; m. Robert James Burnett, Feb. 8, 1986; children: Kristen, Robert, Conor, Kyle. AAS, Pace U., 1982, BSN, 1984. RN, N.Y.; BLS. Med.-surg. nurse Bayley Seton Hosp., Staten Island, N.Y., 1982-84; med., surg. nurse, ICU/CCU nurse Staten Island U. Hosp. South, 1984-91; stepdown ICU Arden Hill Hosp., Goshen, N.Y., 1991—; per diem critical care nurse Westhchester County Med. Ctr., Valhalla, N.Y.; adj. faculty, clin. instr. Orange County C.C., Middletown, N.Y., 1991—; clin. supr. Horton Med. Ctr., Middletown, N.Y., 1996. Mem. AACN, NYSNA, Nat. Edn. Assn. of N.Y. Home: 11 Fleetwood Dr Goshen NY 10924

BURNETT, KELLEY ANNE, pediatrician; b. Palo Alto, Calif., May 26, 1962; d. Robert Wesley and Willow Nancy (Maxwell) B.; m. Alvin E. Crane, Mar. 17, 1995. BA, U. Calif., Santa Cruz, 1983; DO, Mich. State U., 1990. Diplomate Am. Bd. Pediatrics. Intern Muskegon (Mich.) Gen. Hosp., 1990-91; resident in pediatrics Butterworth Hosp., Grand Rapids, Mich., 1991-94; pvt. practice Blue Ridge Pediatrics, Staunton, Va., 1994-96, Grants Pass (Oreg.) Clinic, 1996—. Fellow Am. Acad. Pediatrics. Democrat. Mem. Soc. of Friends.

BURNETT, RITA MARLINE, dentist; b. Oswego, Kans., Apr. 29, 1954; d. Elizabeth Ann (Bassett) B.; m. Brett LaMarr Ferguson, Dec. 31, 1984; children: Brittny, Helene-Cole, Brett LaMarr Jr. Student, Blackburn Coll., 1972-73; BS, U. Kans., 1976; DDS, U. Mo., Kansas City, 1983. Diplomate Am. Bd. Dentistry. Jr. biologist Midwest Rsch. Inst., Kansas City, Mo., 1976-77; rsch. toxicologist Mobay Chem. Corp., Stillwell, Kans., 1977-79; assoc. in gen. dentistry Anne Johnson DDS, Kansas City, Mo., 1983-84; pvt. practice family dentistry Kansas City, Kans., 1984—. Vol. Wyandotte County chpt. ARC, 1984—, bd. dirs., 1986—; bd. dirs. Humane Soc. of Greater Kansas City, 1995—; mentor Digital Electronics for all area high schs., 1991—; mem. PTA bd. Shawnee Mission Sch. Dsit., 1994—. Named one of Kansas City Globe's 100 Most Influential African-Americans, 1995. Mem. ADA, Assn. Am. Women Dentists, Am. Soc. Dentistry for Children, Kans. Dental Soc., Mo. Dental Soc., Heart of Am. Dental Soc., Greater Kans. City (Mo.) Dental Soc., Wyandotte County Dental Soc., Am. Bus. Women's Assn. (pres. Women in Action chpt., Kans. City, Mo. 1986-87). Baptist. Home: 10195 Farley St Overland Park KS 66212-5433 Office: Ste 219 4631 Orville Ave Kansas City KS 66102-3647

BURNEY, DONALD PATRICK, cardiovascular surgeon; b. Corpus Christi, Tex., Mar. 31, 1945; s. James David and Lillian (Runyon) B.; m. Charlotte Wright, Dec. 26, 1967; children: James David, Joseph Patrick, Elizabeth Stacey. BS, Tex. A&M, 1967; MD, Washington U., St. Louis, 1970. Diplomate Am. Bd. Gen. Surgery, Am. Bd. Thoracic Surgery. Intern Vanderbilt U. Hosp., Nashville, 1970-71, resident in surgery, 1971-72, 74-76, chief resident, 1976-77, from jr. resident to chief resident cardiothoracic surgery, 1977-79; cardiothoracic surgeon Moses H. Cone Meml. Hosp., Greensboro, N.C., 1979—, Wesley Long Cmty. Hosp., Greensboro, N.C., 1979—. Contbr. articles to profl. jours. Pres. Am. Heart Assn., Chapel Hill, N.C., 1987, Greensboro, 1983. Maj. USAF, 1972-74, 1986, 88. Fellow ACS, Am. Coll. Chest Physicians, Am. Coll. Cardiology; mem. Soc. Thoracic Surgery, So. Thoracic Soc., So. Med. Assn., H. William Scott Jr. Soc., Phi Etta Sigma, Phi Kappa Phi. Office: Cardiovascular & Thoracic Surgeons Greensboro 1317 N Elm St Ste 1 Greensboro NC 27401

BURNHAM, ANN P., ophthalmologist; b. Lynnfield, Mass., Aug. 2, 1957; d. E.J. Pawlowski. BA in Biology, Harvard U., 1980; MD, Columbia U., 1984. Diplomate Am. Bd. Ophthalmology. Intern Virginia Mason Hosp., Seattle, 1984-85; resident New Eng. Med. Ctr., Boston, 1988-91; ophthalmologist Lexington (Mass.) Eye Assocs., 1991—; rsch. fellow Schepens Eye Inst., Boston, 1986-88. Rsch. fellow Fight-For-Sight, 1986;

glaucomal rsch. grantee NIH. Fellow Am. Acad. Ophthalmology; mem. AMA, Mass. Med. Soc., Mass. Soc. Eye Physicians and Surgeons, New Eng. Ophthalmology Soc. Office: Lexington Eye Assoc 281 Massachusetts Ave Arlington MA 02174

BURNHAM, DUANE LEE, pharmaceutical company executive; b. Excelsior, Minn., Jan. 22, 1942; s. Harold Lee and Hazel Evelyn (Johnson) B.; m. Susan Elizabeth Klinner, June 22, 1963; children—David Lee, Matthew Beckwith. BS, U. Minn., 1963, MBA, 1972. CPA, Wis. Sr. v.p. fin., chief financial officer Abbott Labs., North Chgo., 1982-84, exec. v.p., chief financial officer, dir., 1985-87, vice chmn., chief fin. officer, 1987-89, chmn., chief exec. officer, 1990—; bd. dirs. Sara Lee Corp., Evanston Hosp. Corp. Bd. dirs. Mus. Sci. and Industry, Chgo., Lyric Opera, Healthcare Leadership Coun.; trustee Northwestern U.; mem. adv. bd. J.L. Kellogg Grad. Sch. Mgmt.; chmn. Emergency Com. for Am. Trade. Office: Abbott Labs 100 Abbott Park Rd Abbott Park IL 60064-3500

BURNHAM, JANE ARLETTE, neurologist; b. Brighton, England, Aug. 26, 1955; came to the U.S., 1959; d. Thomas Keith Henry and Marie (McGenn) B.; m. Henry E. Raymundo, Dec. 23, 1983; children: Joanna Edith, Emily Katherine Agnes. BS, U. Mich., 1976; PhD, U. Wash., 1982, MD, 1985. Intern Jewish Hosp.-Washington U., St. Louis, 1985-86; resident in neurology Barnes Hosp.-Washington U., 1986-89; pvt. practice Denver, 1989—. Mem. Am. Acad. Neurology, Colo. Soc. Clin. Neurologists. Office: 701 E Hampden Englewood CO 80110

BURNHAM, LEM, psychologist; b. Winter Haven, Fla., Aug. 30, 1947; s. John L. and Lillie Belle B.; m. Barbara J. Mackin, Sept. 8, 1981; children: Shannon LeeAnne, Lewis, Kara, Bryan. Diploma N.Am. Sch. Conservation, Irvine, Calif., 1969; BA in Psychology, U.S. Internat. U., 1974; MS in Counseling Psychology, Minn. State U., 1978; PhD in Psychoednl. Processes, Temple U., 1984; Diplomat Am. Bd. Forensic Examiners; cert. employee assistance profl. Employee Assistance Certification Commn. Profl. football player World Football League, Honolulu, 1974-75, Can. Football League, Winnipeg, Can., 1976, NFL Phila. Eagles, 1977-80; cross-cultural community planner City and County of Honolulu, 1975; sr. counselor Pa. Prison Soc., Phila., 1982; pres. bd. Career Transition Inst., Inc., Phila., 1981-83; psychologist, health care adminstr. West Jersey Health System, 1984-87; pvt. practice cons., 1988—; pres., chief exec. officer Athletic Motivation, Inc., 1989—; team psychologist for Balt. Orioles, 1988—, Phila. Eagles, 1987—, Phila. 76ers, 1986—; lectr. in field; dir. player programs NFL, 1992—. Mem. President's Coun. on Violence Against Women, chmn. sports subcom., 1995—; bd. dirs. Corp. Alliance to End Ptnr. Violence, 1995—. Served with USMC, 1965-69, Vietnam. Decorated Vietnamese Service award, Vietnamese Commendation award; recipient cert. of appreciation Kiwanis Club, Ramona, Calif., 1979, Del. Valley Med. Ctr., Phila., 1980, Community Service award Chester, Pa., 1981, Community Service award Com. on Alcohol and Drug Abuse Crozer Chester Hosp., 1981. Mem. Am. Psychol. Assn., N.Y. Acad. Scis., Am. Coll. Forensic Examiners, World Fedn. Mental Health, NFL Players Assn., NFL Alumni Assn. (bd. dirs. Phila. Eagles chpt.), Maxwell Football Club (life, v.p. community rels., 1990—, bd. govs.).

BURNS, ALEXANDRA DARROW (SANDRA BURNS), health program administrator; b. West Point, Ky., Mar. 28, 1946; d. Eugene Alexander and Phyllis Anna (Kedroski) Darrow; m. Maurice Edward Burns Jr., Sept. 8, 1966 (div. May 1985); 1 child, Megan Alexandra. BS in Journalism, U. Colo., 1967, MA in Guidance and Counseling, 1974. Cert. rehab. counselor. Probation and parole officer Office of Probation and Parole, Olympia, Wash., 1969-70; employment counselor Div. Employment, Denver, 1971-73; rehab. counselor Colo. Div. Rehab.-Blind Svcs., Denver, 1973-77; rehab. supr. Colo. Div. Rehab., Denver, 1978-81, program supr. rehab. ins. svcs. for employment, 1981-91; program adminstr. Americans With Disabilities Act, Denver, 1991-94; supr. mktg. and resource acquisition Colo. Div. Rehab., Denver, 1994-95, tng. adminstr., 1995—. Vice chmn. Juvenile Parole Bd., Denver, 1982-91, acting chmn., 1987, chmn., 1988-91; del. Dem. County Caucus, Aurora, Colo., 1986; coun. del. Girl Scouts U.S.A., 1988-90, co-leader Brownie troop, 1988-9-, mem. area svc. team, 1989-90; mem. adv. bd. Indsl. Commn., 1983-86; mem. Jr. Symphony Guild, 1986-87; sec., bd. dirs. Mission Viejo Homeowners Assn., 1989-90. Mem. Nat. Rehab. Assn., Nat. Rehab. Adminstrn. Assn., Colo. Rehab. Adminstrn. Assn. (bd. dirs. 1988—, pres.-elect pvt. sector div. 1989, pres. 1990-91), Zonta (corr. sec. 1984-86). Mem. Ch. of Religious Science. Home: 15770 E Mercer Pl Aurora CO 80013-2559 Office: Colo Div Rehab 110 16th St Fl 2 Denver CO 80202-5202

BURNS, BARBARA JEAN, critical care nurse; b. May 3, 1943. AAS in Nursing, Ulster County C.C., 1976; BS, SUNY, 1980; MS, Syracuse U., 1986. RN, N.Y. Instr. St. Elizabeth Hosp., Utica, N.Y., 1982-89; clin. coord. critical care Faxton Hosp., Utica, 1989-92; asst. DON Cmty. Meml. Hosp., Hamilton, N.Y., 1992-93, DON, 1994—. Home: RR 1 Box 148K Poolville Rd Poolville NY 13432

BURNS, C(HARLES) PATRICK, hematologist-oncologist; b. Kansas City, Mo., Oct. 8, 1937; s. Charles Edgar and Ruth (Eastham) B.; m. Janet Sue Walsh, June 15, 1968; children—Charles Geoffrey, Scott Patrick. B.A., U. Kans., 1959, M.D., 1963. Diplomate Am. Bd. Internal Medicine, subsplty. bds. hematology, med. oncology. Intern Cleve. Met. Gen. Hosp., 1963-64; asst. resident in internal medicine Univ. Hosps., Cleve., 1966-68, sr. resident in hematology, 1968-69; instr. medicine Case Western Res. U., Cleve., 1970-71; asst. chief hematology Cleve. VA Hosp., 1970-71; asst. prof. medicine U. Iowa Hosps., Iowa City, 1971-75, assoc. prof. medicine, 1975-80, prof., 1980—, dir. sect. med. oncology, co-dir. divsn. hematatol./oncology, 1980-85, dir. div. hematology-oncology, 1985—; vis. scientist Imperial Cancer Rsch. Fund Labs., London, 1982-83; cons. U.S. VA Hosp.; mem. study sect. on exptl. therapeutics NIH, Cancer Ctr. Support Rev. Commn. Nat. Cancer Inst., NIH, NIH Cancer Clin. Investigation Rev. Com., VA Med. Rsch. Svc. Career Devel. Com.; mem. external adv. com. U. Oreg. Cancer Ctr., 1994—. Mem. bd. assoc. editors Cancer Rsch., 1988—; mem. editl. adv. bd. Life Sci. Advances, 1992—; rsch. and publs. on hematologic malignancies, tumor lipid biochemistry, leukemia and oncology. Served to capt. M.C., AUS, 1964-66. Am. Cancer Soc. fellow in hematology-oncology, 1968-69, USPHS fellow in medicine, 1969-70; USPHS career awardee, 1978. Fellow ACP; mem. AAAS, Am. Bd. Internal Medicine (Subsplty. bd. hematology 1992—), Am. Soc. Hematology, Am. Assn. Cancer Rsch., Internat. Soc. Hematology, Ctrl. Soc. Clin. Rsch., Am. Soc. Clin. Oncology, Soc. Exptl. Biology and Medicine, Oxygen Soc., Royal Soc. Medicine, Am. Fedn. Clin. Rsch., Internat. Soc. for the Study of Fatty Acids and Lipids, Phi Beta Pi, Lambda Chi Alpha, Alpha Omega Alpha. Home: 2046 Rochester Ct Iowa City IA 52245-3246 Office: U Iowa Univ Hosps Dept Medicine Iowa City IA 52242

BURNS, CONSTANCE MARY, nurse practitioner; b. N.Y.C., Feb. 4, 1941; d. Michael A. Sr. and Constance M. (Ryan) Triolo; children: James, Thomas, Jon, Deborah Jean, Kevin, Brian. Diploma, Vassar Bros. Hosp. Sch. of Nursing, 1961; AA, Orange County Community Coll., Middletown, N.Y., 1986; BSN, SUNY, New Paltz, 1988; MSN, Coll. of New Rochelle, N.Y., 1991; cert. in advanced grad. studies, Pace U., 1995. RN, N.Y.; clin. nurse specialist. Evening staff supr. Cornwall (N.Y.) Hosp., nurse, mgr. emergency rm.; nurse, office mgr. M.B. Grant, MD, New Windsor, N.Y. Mem. ANA, N.Y. State Nurse's Assn. (dist. 18 sec. 1991-92), Coalition of Nurse Practitioners, Sigma Theta Tau.

BURNS, DENNIS RAYMOND, hospital administrator; b. June 29, 1943; m. Joan Thomas, June 11, 1966; 3 children. BS in Liberal Arts, Alderson-Broaddus Coll., Philippi, W.Va., 1966; MS in Biology, Edinboro State Coll., 1971; postgrad., Pa. State U., 1974; MS in Health Svcs. Adminstrn., Gannon U., 1981. Adminstrv. asst. Hamot Med. Ctr.-Hamot Health Sys., Pa., 1971-75; dir. materials mgmt. Hamot Patient Svcs., 1975-87, asst. v.p., 1985-87; pres. Residential Patient Svcs., Inc., 1986-87, Ind. Profl. Svcs. Inc., 1988-90; v.p. Hamot Health Systems, Erie, 1987-93; pres. Ind. Profl. Svcs., Inc., Erie, 1988-90; CEO, Corry Meml. Hosp., 1991-92, Sonoma Valley Hosp., Sonoma, Calif., 1994—. Mem. numerous local healthcare related and civic orgns. Mem. Am. Coll. Healthcare Execs. (diplomate), Health Mgmt. Assn. Northwestern Pa. (past pres.), Cert. Profl. Healthcare Materials Mgmt., Internat. Materials Mgmt. Assn., Hosp. Coun. Western Pa., Purchasing Mgmt. Assn. Erie, Am. Hosp. Assn., Soc. Hosp. Purchasing and Materials Mgmt. Home: 4226 Kingsford Dr Napa CA 94558-1833

BURNS, JAMES F., social work therapist; b. Flushing, N.Y., Apr. 12, 1961. BA in Psychology, CUNY, 1984; MA in Family Counseling, Hofstra U., 1988; MSW, Adelphi U., 1994. Staff counselor ASPECTS Counseling Ctr. Family Devel., South Ozone Park, N.Y., 1988-89; social work therapist Madonna Heights Svcs., Dix Hills, N.Y., 1989-91, case work supr., 1991-92; coord. C.S.R. Youth and Family Svcs., Glen Cove, N.Y., 1992-96; social worker Devel. Evaln. Ctr., New Bern, N.C., 1996—.

BURNS, JOHN ALEXANDER, ophthalmologist; b. Delaware, Ohio, Sept. 17, 1938; s. Robert Edward and Margaret (Bing) B.; m. Suzanne L. Baber, June 13, 1961; children: Jennifer Ann, Robert Andrew. BA, Ohio Wesleyan U., 1960; MD, Ohio State U., 1964. Diplomate Am. Bd. Ophthalmology. Intern Grant Med. Ctr., Columbus, Ohio, 1964-65; resident Ohio State U., Columbus, 1965-68; pres. Ophthalmologic Surgeon and Cons. of Ohio, Inc., Columbus, 1968—; trustee Grant Med. Ctr., Columbus, 1982-88, U.S. Health Corp., Columbus; bd. dirs. U.S. Healthplan, Columbus; bd. dirs., chair U.S. Health Group, Columbus. Maj. USAF, 1965-74. Mem. Am. Acad. Ophthalmology (Honor award 1983), Ohio State Med. Assn., Am. Soc. Ophthalmic Plastic and Reconstructive Surgery (pres. 1992). Office: Ophthalmic Surgeons & Cons 340 E Town St # 8-200 Columbus OH 43215

BURNS, JOHN JOSEPH, pharmacology educator; b. Flushing, N.Y., Oct. 8, 1920; s. Thomas F. and Katherine (Kane) B. BS, Queens Coll., 1942; MA, Columbia U., 1948, PhD, 1950. With lab. chem. pharmacology Nat. Heart Inst., 1950-60, dep. chief lab., 1957-60; head sec. clin. pharmacology, also adj. asst. prof. biochemistry NYU research service Goldwater Meml. Hosp., Welfare Island, N.Y., 1950-57; dir. research pharmacodynamics div. Wellcome Research Labs., Burroughs Wellcome & Co. (U.S.A.) Inc., Tuckahoe, N.Y., 1960-66; v.p. for research Hoffmann-LaRoche Inc., Nutley, N.J., 1967-84; vis. prof. pharmacology Albert Einstein Coll. Medicine, 1966-68; adj. prof. Cornell U. Med. Coll., 1969-84, Rockefeller U., 1984-94; adj. mem. Roche Inst. Molecular Biology, 1984—; cons. pharmacology and toxicology programs NIH; chmn. com. problems drug safety Drug Rsch. Bd., 1965-72. Author articles metabolism drugs, vitamins and carbohydrates. Served with AUS, 1944-46. Fellow Am. Inst. Chemists; mem Inst. Medicine, Nat. Acad. Scis., N.Y. Acad. Scis. (v.p. 1964-65), Am. Soc. Pharmacology and Exptl. Therapeutics (pres. 1972-73), Am. Soc. Biol. Chemists, Am. Inst. Nutrition, Am. Coll. Neuropsychopharmacology, Internat. Union Pharmacology (pres. 1975-78). Home: 480 Catamount Rd Fairfield CT 06430-1604 Office: Roche Inst Molec Biology Nutley NJ 07110

BURNS, JOHN LAWRENCE, optometrist; b. Waterbury, Conn., June 24, 1964; s. John M. and Alanna (Martin) B.; m. Sandra Shock, Sept. 12, 1992; 1 child, Lindsay. BS, Widener U., 1986; OD, Pa. Coll. Optometry, 1989. Optometrist Eye Design, Clinton, Md., 1994—; mem. 20/20 Laser Ctrs., Bethesda, Md., 1994—. Mem. Am. Optometric Assn., Md. Optometric Assn. Roman Catholic. Office: Eye Design 7801 Old Branch Ave # 103 Clinton MD 20735

BURNS, JOHN LUTHER, psychologist; b. Walland, Tenn., May 25, 1932; s. John Luther and Hattie Leona (Hatcher) B.; m. Naomi Jean Staley, June 29, 1957; children: Martha Kay, Alan Scott. BS, U. Tenn., 1956, MS, 1957; PhD, U. Tex., 1969. Licensed psychologist, Ark. Asst. to dean students U. Tenn., Knoxville, 1957-66; asst. prof. of counselor edn. and psychology Ark. State U., Jonesboro, 1969-72, assoc. prof., 1972-78, prof., 1978-94, prof. emeritus, 1994—; pvt. practice Jonesboro, 1984-90. Contbr. articles to profl. jours. With USNR, 1952-54. University fellow U. Tex., 1966-69, Presidents fellow Ark. State U., 1984-85. Mem. APA, ACA, Southwestern Psychol. Assn., MidSouth Ednl. Rsch. Assn. (bd. dirs. 1991-93), MidSouth Ednl. Rsch. Found. (bd. dirs. 1992—), Sigma Xi, Phi Kappa Phi (chpt. pres. 1974-75). Baptist. Home: 212 University Dr Jonesboro AR 72401-8482 Office: Arkansas State Univ PO Box 987 State University AR 72467-0987

BURNS, JOHN RICHARD, chiropractor; b. Champaign, Ill., Sept. 30, 1951; s. Dale Eugene and Martha Ellen (Guy) B.; m. Vickie Lynn Rockwell, Mar. 9, 1974; children: Kelly, Keith. D of Chiropractic, Palmer Coll. of Chiropractic, 1973. Instr. Palmer Coll. Chiropractic, Davenport, Iowa, 1973-77, asst. prof., 1977-80, assoc. prof., 1980-85, prof., 1985—, chmn. technique, 1977—; practice chiropractic East Moline Chiropractic Clinic. Author: Extremities: Adjusting and Evaluation, 1983. Dir. Palmer Rugby Team, 1975-76. Fellow Internat. Chiropractors Assn., Gonstead Clin. Study Soc., Ill. Prairie State Chiropractic Assn. (bd. dirs. 1987—, Chiropractor of Yr. 1989). Office: East Moline Chiropractic 379 42nd St Moline IL 61265

BURNS, PADRAIC, physician, psychiatrist, psychoanalyst, educator; b. Des Moines, Aug. 31, 1929; s. Charles and Ethel P. (Bentz) B.; m. Ikuko Kawai, Oct. 19, 1959; children—Kenneth, Amelia, Margaret. B.A., U. Chgo., 1948; postgrad. NYU, 1949-51; M.D., Yale U., 1955. Diplomate Am. Bd. Psychiatry, Sub-Bd. Child Psychiatry. Asst. prof. psychiatry Boston U., 1969-72, assoc. prof. psychiatry, 1972—. Capt. U.S. Army, 1957-59. Fellow Am. Acad. Child Psychiatry; mem. Am. Psychiat. Assn., Mass. Psychiat. Soc., Boston Psychoanalytic Soc. and Inst. Home: 9 Downing Rd Brookline MA 02146-2114 Office: Boston U Med Ctr P-905 720 Harrison Ave Boston MA 02118-2334

BURNS, PATRICK OWEN, venture capital company executive; b. Yonkers, N.Y., Aug. 6, 1937; s. Edward Dermott and Anne L. (Gallagher) B.; A.B. (Class of '26 fellow), Dartmouth Coll., 1959; LL.B. cum laude, Harvard U., 1962; m. Barbara Hope Van Riper, Nov. 4, 1967; children—Patrick Owen, Elizabeth Willett. Admitted to N.Y. bar, 1964, U.S. Dist. Ct. (so. dist.) N.Y. bar, 1965; legal advisor Dept. Coops., Lesotho, 1962-63; assoc. firm Milbank, Tweed, Hadley & McCloy, N.Y.C., 1963-69; nat. dep. dir. Interracial Council for Bus. Opportunity, N.Y.C., 1969-75, acting nat. exec. dir., 1972-74; exec. v.p. Minority Equity Capital Co., Inc., N.Y.C., 1971-78, dir., 1974-85, pres., 1978-85; ptnr. Consumer Venture Group, 1985; v.p. R&D Funding Corp., 1986—, bd. dirs., 1989-92; v.p., 1st v.p., sr. v.p. Prudential Securities; bd. dirs. Creative Bio Molecules Inc., Ecogen Inc., Symbiotics Corp., Tex. Biotech. Corp.; cons. Warren Commn., 1964; mem. exec. com. SEC Govt.-Bus. Forum on Small Bus. Capital Formation, 1983-85, chmn. Task Force State Capital Formation, 1984. Bd. dirs. Cobble Hill Nursing Home, 1976—; regent L.I. Coll. Hosp., 1976—, vice chmn. bd., 1981—; dir. Resources for Children with Spl. Needs, Inc., 1990—, pres., 1994—; dir. Nat. Ctr. Social Entrepreneurs, 1985—; candidate for N.Y.C. City Council, 1969. Mem. Am. Assn. Minority Enterprise Small Bus. Investment Cos. (dir. 1979-85, chmn. bd. 1983-85), Council on Fgn. Relations, N.Y. Venture Capital Forum, Nat. Assn. Small Bus. Investment Cos. (gov. 1983-85). Democrat. Contbr. articles to profl. publs. Home: 22 Sidney Pl Brooklyn NY 11201-4607 Office: 199 Water St New York NY 10292

BURNS, RICHARD REECE, ophthalmologist; b. Peekskill, N.Y., Feb. 23, 1950; s. Robert M. and Mary E. (Jackson) B.; m. Jenny, July 23, 1976; children: Ashley, Alexandra. BA, So. Meth. U., 1974; MD, Mayo Med. Sch., 1980. Diplomate Am. Bd. Ophthalmology. Resident in ophthalmology U. Calif., San Diego, 1981-84; chief ophthalmology Harborview Hosp., San Diego, 1985-87, Sharp Cabrillo Hosp., San Diego, 1985-92; chmn. dept. ophthalmology and optometry Sharp Rees Stealy Med. Group, San Diego, 1985—, chmn. dept. surgery, 1995—; dir. Nat. Vision Rsch. Inst., San Diego, 1987-94, True Vision, San Diego, 1995—. Fellow Am. Acad. Ophthalmology. Office: 3555 Kenyon St Ste 101 San Diego CA 92110-5333

BURNS, ROSALIE ANNETTE, neurologist, educator; b. Phila., July 29, 1932; married. BA, Smith Coll., 1953; MD, Yale U., 1956. Intern in medicine Cornell Med. divsn. Bellevue Hosp., N.Y.C., 1956-57; resident in neurology Neurol. Inst. N.Y.-Columbia-Presbyn. Med. Ctr., 1957-60; asst. in neurology, fellow Nat. Cerebral Palsy Study, 1959-60; fellow in cerebral vascular disease NIH-dept. neurology Tufts U.-New Eng. Ctr. Hosp., Boston, 1960-61; asst. dir. 2d neurology divsn. Bellevue Hosp., N.Y.C., 1962-64; instr. neurology dept. medicine Cornell U. Sch. Medicine, 1962-64; asst. neurologist to outpatients N.Y. Hosp., N.Y.C., 1962-64; electroencephalographer The Inst. of Pa. Hosp., 1964-65; instr. in neurology Med. Coll. Pa., 1964-65, dir. neurology clinics 1965-74, assoc. in neurology, 1965-66, head sect. neurology, dept. psychiatry and neurology, 1965-71, asst. prof. neurology, 1966-70, assoc. prof. neurology, 1970-74, acting chmn. dept. neurology, 1971-74, prof. neurology, 1974-95, chmn. dept. neurology, 1975-95; univ. prof., exec. dir. Ctr. for Clin. Neurosci. Med. Coll. Pa./Hahnemann Univ., 1995—; program dir. NIH Devel. Grant Med. Coll. Pa., 1966-73; consulting physician in neurology Ea. Pa. Psychiat. Inst., 1965-76, Pathway Sch. for Learning Disorders, 1978-81, Phila. VA Med. Ctr., part-time staff, 1975-77, attending physician in neurology, 1967-68; cons. staff Inglis House, 1967-93, Phila. Geriatric Ctr., 1985; half-time rsch. asst. neuropathology lab. Walter E. Fernald State Sch. Mental Retardation, Waverly, Mass., 1961-62; adj. attending neurologist dept. neurology Sloan-Kettering Cancer Ctr., 1986; presenter in field. Contbr. chpts. to books, articles to profl. jours. Nat. Found. fellow, 1955. Fellow Am. Acad. Neurology (edn. com. 1975-78, practice com. 1990-92, del. to Coun. of Acad. Socs. 1987-91, nominating com. 1993, 2d v.p. 1983-85, women's liaison officer 1991); mem. Am. Bd. Med. Specialties, Am. Bd. Psychiatry and Neurology (bd. dirs. 1993-97, nominating com. 1993, rev. appeals com. 1992, credential com. 1992 and many other coms.), Am. Neurol. Assn. (annals of neurology oversight com. 1993), Assn. Univ. Profs. Neurology (sec.-treas. 1983-88, pres.-elect 1988-90, pres. 1990-92), Phila. Neurol. Soc. (1st v.p. 1971, 2nd v.p. 1977, pres. 1979-80, chmn. nominating com. 1981, and other coms.), Smith Coll. Club Phila., Alumnae Assn. Woman's Med. Coll. (assoc., Delaware Valley chpt.), Phi Beta Kappa, Sigma Xi, Alpha Omega Alpha (Delta chpt., chmn. membership com. 1980-81). Office: Hahnemann Univ Broad & Vine Philadelphia PA 19102

BURNS, SALLY ANN, medical association administrator; b. Findlay, Ohio, Dec. 13, 1959; d. Van Larson and Marian (Delia) B. Student, Findlay Coll., 1980-82, Bowling Green State U., 1982-83; AAS, Houston C.C., 1985. Lic. physical therapist asst., Tex. Intern in clin. studies various Hosps., Houston, 1984-85; patient care Spring Br. Meml. Hosp., Houston, 1985-86; pres. Burns Phys. Therapy Clinic, Inc., Houston, 1986—; pres., bd. dirs. Phys. Therapy Plus, Inc., Houston, 1988—; pres. FYI Med. Suppliers, Inc., 1991—, Pain Stop Inc., 1994—; pres. FYI Med. Suppliers, Inc., 1991—, FYI Med., Inc., 1991, Pain Stop, Inc., 1994—; mem. adv. com. Houston C.C. Sys. Physical Therapist Asst. Program. Author: Physical Therapy for Multiple Sclerosis. Mem. adv. com. Houston C.C. Sys. Phys. Therapist Asst. Program. Mem. Inst. for Profl. Health Svc. Administrs. (charter mem.), Am. Judicature Soc., Am. Phys. Therapy Assn., Tex. Phys. Therapy Assn., Community Health Administrn. Home: 1914 Potomac Dr Houston TX 77057-2922 Office: Phys Therapy Plus Inc 3303 Audley St Houston TX 77098-1921

BURNS, THEODORE WEBER, gastroenterologist; b. New Iberia, La., Apr. 15, 1944; s. James Patout and Mary T. (Weber) B.; m. Linda Ann Cox, Aug. 29, 1970; children: Theodore W. Jr., David D., William J., Jennifer L. DDS, Loyola U., New Orleans, 1968; MD, La. State U., 1972. Diplomate Am. Bd. Internal Medicine, Am. Bd. Gastroenterology. Intern, then resident U. Fla., Gainesville, 1972-75, fellow in gastroenterology, 1975-77; asst. prof. medicine Uniformed Svcs. Sch. Medicine, Bethesda, Md., 1977-79; staff physician, ptnr., dir. gastrointestinal rsch. Ochsner Clinic, New Orleans, 1979-86; ptnr., physician Digestive Disease Assocs., Gainesville, 1986—. Contbr. articles to profl. jours. Vol. United Way, Gainesville, 1990. Lt. comdr. USN, 1977-79. NIH rsch. svc. grantee U. Fla., 1976-77. Fellow ACP, Am. Coll. Gastroenterology; mem. Am. Gastroenterology Assn., Am. Soc. for Gastrointestinal Endoscopy, Am. Soc. for Internal Medicine, Alpha Omega Alpha. Roman Catholic. Office: Digestive Disease Assocs 7003 NW 11th Pl Gainesville FL 32605

BURNS, THOMAS PATRICK, orthopedic surgeon; b. Columbus, Ohio, Mar. 23, 1959; s. Paul Allan and Dorothy Ann (Eberly) B.; m. Phoebe Orr, July 14, 1984; children: Kendall Catherine, Peyton Thomas. BA in Biology, U. Tex., 1981; MD, Southwestern Med. Sch., Dallas, 1985. Lic. physician; diplomate Am. Bd. Orthopedic Surgeons. Resident in orthopedics U. Cin. Med. Ctr., 1985-90; fellow in sports medicine Steadman Hawkins Clin., Vail, Colo., 1990-91; orthopedic surgeon U. Cin. Med. Ctr., 1985-90; sports medicine fellow Steadman Hawkins Clinic, Vail, Colo., 1990-91; orthopedic surgeon Tex. Bone & Joint Inst., Austin, 1991—; team physician U.s. Olympic Ski Team, 1991—, vol. physician, 1991—; team physician St. Edwards U., Austin, 1992—. Contbr. articles to profl. jours., chpt. to book. Com. mem. Am. Cancer Soc., Austin, 1994. Named. Gold Club Mem. YMCA of Austin, 1993, Hon. Letterman St. Edward's U., Austin, 1994. Fellow Am. Acad. Orthopedic Surgeons; mem. Hawkins Shoulder Soc., Tex. Sports Medicine Soc. Roman Catholic. Office: Tex Bone & Joint Inst 711 W 38th Ste E-4 Austin TX 78705

BURNS, TODD PAUL, physician assistant; b. Saginaw, Mich., Dec. 6, 1949; s. Benjamin Urquhart and Muriel Edna (Henke) B. BS in Zoology, Mich. State U., 1974; BS in Medicine, Western Mich. U., 1979. Cert. physician asst., Mich. Physician asst., office mgr. Internal Medicine Assocs., Holland, Mich., 1979-93; physician asst. Mich. Med. Specialists, Holland, 1993-95, MMPC, Holland, 1995—. Fellow Am. Acad. Physician Assts., Mich. Acad. Physician Asst. Office: MMPC Ste 201 100 S Pine Ave Zeeland MI 49464

BURNSIDE, IRENE, nursing educator; b. Grove City, Minn., Oct. 4, 1923; d. Walter Hollyer and Rebecca (Wyckoff) Mortenson; m. Dean Burnside, Dec. 20, 1946; children: Mark, Tonya, Clark. Diploma, Ancker Hosp. Sch. Nursing, St. Paul, 1944; BFA, Denver U., 1957; MS, U. Calif., San Francisco, 1966; PhD, U. Tex., 1990. RN, Calif. Lectr. U. Calif.; coord. nursing edn. Andrus Gerontology Ctr., L.A.; assoc. prof. gerontol. nursing San Jose (Calif.) State U.; vis. fellow Phillip Inst., Melbourne, Australia. Author: Nursing and the Aged: A Self-Care Approach, 1976, 3d edit., 1988, Working with the Elderly: Group Process and Techniques, 1978, 3d edit., 1994, Psychosocial Nursing Care of the Aged, 1974, 2d edit., 1980. Recipient Long Term Care award Nat. League for Nursing, 1981, Gerontol. Profl. of Yr. award U. Tex. Health Scis. Ctr., 1988. Fellow Am. Acad. Nursing, Gerontol. Soc. Am.; mem. ANA (Gerontol. Nurse of Yr. award 1989), Internat. Congress Gerontology, Calif. Nurses Assn., Sigma Theta Tau (Excellence in Creativity award 1991).

BURNSIDE, JOHN WAYNE, medical educator, university official; b. Bryn Mawr, Pa., Jan. 15, 1941; s. Wayne D. and Catherine (Neamand) B.; m. Lynda Deanne Haskins, Mar. 21, 1964; children: Andrew, Matthew, Paul. M.D., U. Ill., 1966. Resident Mass. Gen. Hosp., Boston, 1966-72; instr. Harvard U., Cambridge, Mass., 1969-72; asst. prof. Hershey Med. Ctr., Pa. State U., 1972-74, prof. medicine, 1980-87, assoc. provost and dean for health affairs, 1982-84, assoc. sr. v.p. for health affairs, vice dean, 1984-87; prof. internal medicine, assoc. dean for profl. edn. U. Tex. Southwestern Med. Ctr., Dallas, 1987—. Author: Physical Diagnosis, 1972, Physical Diagnosis, 2d edit., 1978, Health and Human Values, 1982, Burnside's Medical Examination Review, 1985. Pres. Greater Dallas Coun. on Alcohol and Drug Abuse, 1995; bd. dirs. Ctrl. Pa. Arthritis Found., 1974-79, Health Sys. Agy., Camp Hill, 1978-80, Blue Shield, 1982-87; co-dir. Ctr. for Humanistic Medicine, 1979-87; legis. asst. to senator, Washington, 1979, to congressman, 1980. With USNR, 1968-74. Recipient Senear award U. Ill., 1968; Health Policy fellow Robert Wood Johnson Found., 1979-80. Fellow ACP; mem. AMA (del. 1994), Am. Soc. Internal Medicine, Tex. Med. Assn. (chmn. coun. sci. affairs 1993—), Soc. Health and Human Values, Dauphin County Med. Soc. (pres. 1982), Rotary, Alpha Omega Alpha. Republican. Episcopalian. Office: Southwestern Med Sch 5323 Harry Hines Blvd Dallas TX 75235-7200

BURO, EDWARD ANTHONY, podiatrist, educator; b. N.Y.C., May 20, 1956; s. Patrick J. and Rose E. (Lucibello) B.; m. Barbara L. Czeisler, Sept. 16, 1990. BS in Pharmacy, St. John's U., N.Y.C., 1979, MS in Pharmacology, 1981; D Podiatric Medicine, N.Y. Coll. Podiatric Medicine, 1985. Diplomate Am. Bd. Podiatric Surgery. Pvt. practice, Sunnyside, N.Y., 1987—, Commack, N.Y., 1995—; clin. assoc. prof. N.Y. Coll. podiatric Medicine, N.Y.C., 1993—. Contbr. articles to sci. jours. Mem. N.Y. State Podiatric Med. Assn. (pres. Queens divsn. 1995-97). Office: 45-13 Queens Blvd Sunnyside NY 11104

BURR, DAVID BENTLEY, anatomy educator; b. Findlay, Ohio, June 28, 1951; s. Willard Bentley and Dorothy Eleanor (Beiler) B.; m. Lisa Marie Pedigo; children: Kathryn Lise, Michael David. BA, Beloit Coll., 1973; MA, U. Colo., 1974, PhD, 1977. Instr. anatomy U. Kans. Med. Ctr., Kansas City, 1977-78, asst. prof. anatomy, 1978-80; asst. prof. anatomy and orthop. surgery W.Va. U., Morgantown, 1980-83, assoc. prof., 1983-86, prof., 1986-90; chmn. dept. anatomy, prof. anatomy and orthopedic surgery Ind. U.,

Indpls., 1990—; mem. adv. bd. dirs. Primate Found. Am., Tempe, Ariz., 1978—; cons. County Med. Examiner, Morgantown, 1983-89; mem. Adv. Group for the Treatment Human Remains, USDA, Monongahela Nat. Forest Svc., 1989; cons. NASA, 1990-91, Am. Inst. Biol. Sci., NAS, 1990—, U.S. Congress Office Tech. Assessment, 1990; mem. biochemistry study sect. Arthritis found., 1992-95. Author: Structure, Function & Adaptation of Compact Bone, 1989; mem. editl. bd. Bone, 1993—, Jour. Bone and Mineral Metabolism, 1994—; contbr. articles to profl. jours. Pres. First Ward Sch. PTA, Morgantown, 1987-88; sec. Cub Scout Pack Com., Morgantown, 1989; chmn. troop com. Boy Scouts Am., 1993-95; mem. adminstrv. bd. Epworth United Meth. Ch., Indpls., 1992-93; linesman Morgantown Soccer League, 1988. Rsch. grantee NIH, 1988—, Orthopedic Rsch. and Edn. Found., 1985-86. Mem. Orthop. Rsch. Assn., Am. Anatomy Assn., Assn. Anatomy, Cell Biology and Neurobiology Chairpersons, Sigma Xi. Office: Indiana U Sch Medicine Dept Anatomy 635 Barnhill Dr Indianapolis IN 46202-5126

BURR, ROBERT EATON, biomedical researcher, physician; b. Ithaca, N.Y., May 26, 1946; s. Malcolm Southack and Charlotte (Eaton) B.; m. Anne Christian, Sept. 1, 1968; children: Carolyn, Matthew. AB, Dartmouth Coll., 1968; MD, Hahnemann, 1973. Diplomate Am. Bd. Internal Medicine, Am. Bd. Nutrition, Am. Bd. Emergency Medicine; cert. internal medicine, endocrinology, clin. nutrition, emergency medicine. Intern Mayo Clinic, Rochester, Minn., 1973-74, resident, 1974-75; rsch. assoc., asst. physician Rockefeller U., N.Y.; clin. fellow in medicine Mass. Gen. Hosp., Boston, 1979-81, clin. fellow in childrens svc., 1980-81; rsch. fellow in medicine Harvard Med. Sch., Boston, 1979-81; prin. investigator Letterman Army Inst. Rsch., San Francisco, 1981-84; pvt. med. practice teaching Champaign-Urbana, Ill., 1984-90; med. advisor U.S. Army Rsch. Inst. Environ. Medicine, Natick, Mass., 1990—; environ. medicine cons. U.S. Army, 1991—; regulatory med. affairs dir., drug regulatory affairs ER Squibb and Sons, New Brunswick, N.J., 1987; asst. clin. prof. medicine U. Calif., San Francisco, 1982-84; clin. asst. prof..U. Ill. Coll. Medicine, Champaign, 1984-91, U. Mass. Med. Ctr., 1993—, attending physician, 1993—; attending physician Boston City Hosp., 1992—. Contbr. articles to profl. jours.; author tech. notes on heat illness, med. aspects cold weather mil. ops., preventive medicine for deployment to S.W. Asia, Somalia and Haiti; editor: (symposium) Current Practice Clinical Nutrition, 1986. Active Downstate Ill. affiliate Am. Diabetes Assn., 1984-87. Lt. col. U.S. Army. Fellow ACP, Am. Coll. Endocrinology, Am. Coll. Emergency Physicians, Am. Coll. Nutrition; mem. Assn. Mil. Surgeons U.S., Am. Diabetes Assn., Am. Coll. Sports Medicine, Endocrine Soc., Mass. Med. Soc., Wilderness Med. Soc., Aerospace Med. Assn. Office: USARIEM Kansas St Natick MA 01760

BURRELL, JOEL BRION, neuroimmunologist, researcher, clinician; b. Orange, N.J., Nov. 27, 1959; s. Robert and Barbara (Miller) B. BS in Biology, Rutgers U., 1982, grad. student, 1983; MD, Temple U., 1987. Diplomate Am. Bd. Med. Examiners. Intern Abington (Pa.) Meml. Hosp., 1987-88; neurology resident The Mt. Sinai Med. Ctr., N.Y.C., 1988-91; neuroimmunology fellow Cleve. Clin. Found., 1991-93; attending physician with pvt. clin. practice, 1993—; asst. clin. prof. Med. Coll. Ohio, 1993—. Presenter in field. Fellow Am. Stroke Coun. of Am. Heart Assn. Recipient Pinnacle award Being Single Mag., 1995. Fellow Stroke Coun. of Am. Heart Assn.; mem. AMA (Physician's Recognition award 1992—), Am. Acad. Clin. Neurophysiology, Internat. Cerebral Hemodynamics Soc., Am. Acad. Neurology, Nat. Med. Assn., Acad. Medicine Cleve., Cleve. Med. Assn., Ohio Acad. Sci., Ohio State Med. Assn., Med. Alumni Assn. Temple U., Temple U. Gen. Alumni Assn., Assoc. Alumni of Mt. Sinai Med. Ctr. of N.Y.C.; Huron County Medical Soc. (Treasurer/Secretary 1995—), New York Academy of Science. Office: Summit Profl Bldg 85 Benedict Ave Ste 103 Norwalk OH 44857-2112

BURRI, PETER HERMANN, anatomy, histology and embryology educator; b. Pfaeffikon, Zurich, Switzerland, July 18, 1938; s. Hermann Oskar and Clara (Gautschi) B.; m. Laurette Ida Barbey, Nov. 20, 1964; children: Christine, Anne-Françoise, Isabelle. Fed. diploma in medicine, U. Zurich and U. Paris, 1964; MD, U. Bern, Switzerland, 1968. Asst. Inst. Pathology, U. Zurich, 1965-66; asst. Inst. Anatomy U. Bern, 1966-68, grad. asst., 1968-73, lectr., 1969-73; rsch. fellow dept. pathology Royal Postgrad. Med. Sch.-Hammersmith Hosp., London, 1973-74; asst. prof. Inst. Anatomy U. Bern, 1974-78, prof., 1978—, head dept. devel. biology, 1974—, chmn. Inst. Anatomy, 1993—; vis. prof. medicine Boston U., 1987; Sam Stein Meml. lectr. L.I. Jewish Med. Sch., New Hyde Park, N.Y., 1988; pres. Com. for Reform of Med. Curriculum, 1990—. Contbr. numerous articles and revs. on lung devel., growth and regeneration and microvascular devel. and growth to med. jours., also chpts. to books. Recipient Degussa award, 1987. Mem. Swiss Soc. Anatomy, Histology and Embryology (bd. dirs. 1983-89, pres. 1986-89), Anat. Soc., Union Swiss Socs. Exptl. Biology (bd. dirs., v.p. 1987-90), Swiss Acad. Scis. (pres. biology sect. 1987-90), Am. Assn. Anatomists, Swiss Soc. Cell and Molecular Biology (bd. dirs. 1978-81), Swiss Soc. Optics and Electron Microscopy (bd. dirs. 1981-87). Home: Gurnigelstrasse 20, CH-3132 Riggisberg Switzerland Office: U Bern Inst Anatomy, Buehlstr 26, CH-3012 Bern Switzerland

BURRIER, GAIL WARREN, physician; b. Newark, Ohio, Apr. 6, 1927; s. Harold I. and Esther M. (Simpson) B.; m. Mary Lou Miller, June 12, 1948 (dec. 1982); children: Dale, Marie. BS, Ohio State U., 1950, MS, 1952, MD, 1956. Diplomate Am. Bd. Family Practice; cert. geriatrist. Intern Grant Hosp., Columbus, Ohio, 1956-57; pvt. practice Canal Winchester, Ohio, 1957-73; dir. family practice Grant Med. Ctr., Columbus, 1973-88; med. dir. Alum Crest Nursing Home, Columbus, 1988—; clin. instr. Ohio State U., Columbus, 1969-74, clin. asst. prof., 1974-81, clin. assoc. prof., 1981—; med. dir. Winchester Place Nursing Home, Canal Winchester, 1983—; med. tech. asst. State of Ohio, Columbus, 1988—. Trustee Columbus Area Mental Health, 1974-81; bd. dirs. Meth. Ch., Canal Winchester, 1959-63; team physician high sch. tournaments, Columbus, 1957—. Fellow Am. Acad. Family Physicians (local pres. 1973); mem. Am. Coll. Physician Execs., AMA, Am. Geriatric Soc., Am. Soc. on Aging, Ohio State U. Alumni Club (pres. Columbus chpt. 1985-86). Republican. Home and Office: 45 Trine St Canal Winchester OH 43110

BURRIGHT, RICHARD GEORGE, psychology educator; b. Freeport, Ill., Aug. 10, 1934; s. Willard Clarence and Emma Charlotte (Waller) B.; m. Shirley Louise Rock, Sept. 1, 1957; children: Lisa Ann, Scott Richard. BS, U. Ill., 1959, MA, 1962, PhD, 1966. Acting asst. prof. SUNY, Binghamton, 1963-66, asst. prof., 1966-69, assoc. prof., 1969-85, prof., 1985—, dir. grad. studies psychology, 1996—. Co-author chpt. in Genetics of the Brain, 1982, The Behavioral Biology of Early Brain Damage, 1984, Preoperative Events: Their Effects on Behavior Following Brain Damage, 1989, Rehabilitation of the Brain Injured: A Neuropsychological Perception, 1990; co-author cpt. in: The Vulnerable Brain: Nutrition and Toxins, 1992, Psychology Reports, 1995, Brain Injury, 1995, Physiology & Behavior, 1995, Brain Rsch. Bull., 1995. Coach Vestal (N.Y.) Jr. Baseball League, 1981, Vestal (N.Y.) Jr. Soccer League, 1983; webelo leader cub scouts Boy Scouts of Am., Vestal, 1980; mem. troop com. Boy Scouts of Am., Vestal, 1981-86. With U.S. Army, 1954-56. Grantee NIMH, 1969-72, NSF, 1974-76, 79-83, SUNY Rsch. Found., 1974-75, Nat. Inst. Childhood Devel., 1974-77. Mem. AAAS, Am. Psychol. Soc. (charter), N.Y. Acad. Sci., Behavior Genetics Assn., Twin Tier Mended Hearts, Sigma Xi. Home: 1201 Front St Vestal NY 13850-1221 Office: State Univ New York Vestal Pkwy Binghamton NY 13902-6000

BURRIS, HARRIET LOUISE, emergency physician; b. Alexandria Bay, N.Y., Apr. 7, 1949; d. Robert Barker and Harriet Louise (Dorman) Burtch; m. John Samuel Burris Jr., Nov. 30, 1974; children: Elizabeth Jane, Katherine Ann. SB, MIT, 1972; MD, SUNY, Syracuse, 1976. Diplomate Am. Bd. Family Practice, Am. Bd. Emergency Medicine, Nat. Bd. Med. Examiners; cert. added qualification in geriatrics. Resident in family practice St. Joseph's Hosp. Health Ctr., Syracuse, 1976-79; pvt. practice Cazenovia, N.Y., 1979-81; staff MD emergency dept. Middlesex Hosp., Middletown, Conn., 1982-83; staff MD family practice Cmty. Health Care Plan, Wallingford, Conn., 1983-84; staff MD emergency dept. Middlesex Med. Ctr.-Shoreline divsn. Middlesex Hosp., Essex, Conn., 1984—, acting med. dir., 1994. Fellow Am. Acad. Family Physicians, Am. Coll. Emergency Physicians; mem. Handweavers Guild Conn. (libr.). Home: 422 Westland Ave Cheshire CT 06410-3142 Office: Middlesex Med Ctr-Shoreline 260 Westbrook Rd Essex CT 06426-1513

BURROUGHS, JACK EUGENE, dentist, management consultant; b. Harlingen, Tex., Nov. 24, 1946; s. Jack Eugene and Virginia (Ayoub) B.; children by previous marriage—Brian A., Brad A.; m. Laura; children: Kyle, Tiffany. BS, U. Tex. Arlington, 1969, DDS, U. Tex. Dental Br. Houston, 1973. Practice dentistry, Houston, 1973—; seminar leader, cons. Quest, Dallas, 1983—. Contbr. articles to profl. jours. Recipient Speaker awards Aspen Med.-Dental Conf., 1982, 83, 84, N.Am. Med.-Dental Assn., 1984, Am. Internat. Seminars, 1984. Fellow Acad. Gen. Dentistry; mem. ADA, Tex. Dental Assn., Houston Dist. Dental Soc., Houston Northwest C. of C. (bd. dirs.). Republican. Mem. Christian Ch. Clubs: Exchange (bd. dirs.), Toastmasters (officer). Office: 17200 Red Oak Dr Houston TX 77090-2642

BURROW, GERARD NOEL, physician, educator; b. Boston, Jan. 9, 1933; s. William and Noelle Elvira (Money) B.; m. Ann Huntington Rademacher, June 22, 1956; children: Peter Noel, Elisabeth Huntington, Sarah Rogers. B.A., Brown U., 1954; M.D., Yale U., 1958. Diplomate: Am. Bd. Internal Medicine. Chief resident Yale-New Haven Med. Ctr., 1965-66; asst. prof. to prof. Yale U. Sch. Medicine, New Haven, 1966-76; prof. dept. medicine U. Toronto, Ont., Can., 1976-81, Sir John and Lady Eaton prof. medicine, 1981-88, chmn. dept., 1981-88; physician-in-chief Toronto Gen. Hosp., 1981-88; vice chancellor for health scis., dean sch. medicine U. Calif., San Diego, 1988-92, prof. dept. medicine, 1988-92; dean Sch. Medicine Yale U., New Haven, 1992—, prof. dept. medicine, 1992—; bd. dirs. Nat. Med. Fellowships. Author: The Thyroid Gland in Pregnancy, 1972; editor: (with Ferris) Medical Complications During Pregnancy, 1975, 82, 88, 94. With USPHS, 1959-61. Fellow ACP, Royal Coll. Physicians (Can.); mem. Am. Soc. Clin. Investigation, Assn. Am. Physicians, Am. Thyroid Assn. (pres. 1986), Inst. Medicine of NAS, Interurban Club. Office: Yale U School of Medicine 333 Cedar St New Haven CT 06520-8055

BURROW, WILLIAM HOLLIS, II, dermatologist; b. Walla Walla, Wash., Nov. 19, 1945; s. William Hollis and Patricia (Hoke) B.; m. Lafon Walcott, Jan. 29, 1967; children: William H. III, Kristina, Jamey. BA in Chemistry, Vanderbilt U., 1967; MD, U. Miss., 1973. Bd. cert. in dermatology. Dermatology resident U. Ala., Birmingham, 1974-77; pvt. practice Jackson, Miss., 1977—; clin. assoc. prof. medicine U. Miss. Med. Ctr., Jackson, 1977—. V.p. Young Life, Jackson, 1990, Downtown YMCA Bd., Jackson, 1991. Fellow AMA, Am. Acad. Dermatology, So. Med. Assn.; mem. Alpha Omega Alpha. Office: # 303 850 E River Pl Jackson MS 39202

BURROWS, ROBERT PAUL, optometrist; b. Chehalis, Wash., 1954; s. Fremont O. and Pauline A. (Kostick) B.; m. Marilyn Hermanson, Aug. 10, 1984. BS in Visual Sci., Pacific U., 1979, OD, 1981. Assoc. optometric physician L.E. Hedgen, O.D. & Assocs., Chehalis, 1981-86; ptnr. L.E. Hedgen, R.P. Burrows, O.D. & Assocs., Chehalis, 1986—. Mem. United Way, 1981—. PTU rsch. grantee, 1980. Mem. Am. Optometric Assn. (charter contact lens sect., Recognition award 1984-95), Wash. Assn. Optometric Physicians, Kiwanis (dir. 1984-85, 89-90), Twin City C. of C., Omega Epsilon Phi. Methodist. Office: 1179 S Market Rd Chehalis WA 98532

BURSTEIN, ALVIN C., physician; b. Bronx, N.Y., Sept. 14, 1950; s. Samuel and Rima (Sacks) B.; m. Lisa Fran Berger, July 14, 1974; children: Zachary, Adam. BS, Johns Hopkins U., 1972; MD, Wayne State U., 1976. Diplomate Am. Bd. Psychiatry and Neurology. Clin. instr. Harvard Med. Sch., Boston, 1980-85; asst. prof. psychiatry Tufts Med. Sch., Boston, 1980-84; attending psychiatrist Hampstead, N.H., 1985-91; med. dir. St. Luke's Behavioral Health, Phoenix, 1992-96, chief of staff, 1996—; med. dir. Ariz. Biodyne, Phoenix, 1994-96; psychiatrist Phoenix, 1992-96. Mem. Am. Psychiat. Assn., Am. Coll. Physicians Execs. Office: Well Being Systems #391 2701 E Camel Back Rd Phoenix AZ 85016

BURSTEIN, DAVID MICHAEL, nephrologist; b. Mpls., Jan. 11, 1962; s. Fred and Harriette Pearl (Goldstein) B.; m. Nancy Pollack, Aug. 12, 1995. BA summa cum laude, U. Minn., 1984, MD, 1988. Diplomate Am. Bd. Internal Medicine, Am. Bd. Nephrology. Internal medicine resident Rush Med. Coll., Chgo., 1988-91; nephrology fellow Rush Med. Coll., 1992-93, UCLA Med. Ctr., 1991-92; staff nephrologist Luth. Gen. Hosp., Park Ridge, Ill., 1993—; asst. prof. medicine U. Chgo., 1994—. Editor (newsletter) Family Focus, 1993—; contbr. articles to profl. jours. Mem. ACP, Internat. Soc. of Nephrology, Nat. Kidney Found., Am. Soc. of Nephrology. Office: Lutheran Gen Hosp 1775 Dempster St Park Ridge IL 60068

BURSTEIN, STEPHEN DAVID, neurosurgeon; b. Bklyn., Apr. 10, 1934; s. Moe and Anna (Bloch) B.; m. Ronnie Sue Deutsch, Oct. 8, 1972; 1 dau., Alissa Aimee. B.A. with distinction, U. Mich., 1954; M.D., SUNY-Bklyn., 1958; M.S. in Neurosurgery, U. Minn.-Rochester, 1965. Diplomate Am. Bd. Neurol. Surgery Surg. intern Johns Hopkins Hosp., Balt., 1958-59; neurosurgery fellow Mayo Clinic, Rochester, 1961-65; chief dept. neurosurgery South Nassau Community Hosp., Oceanside, N.Y., 1980—, pres. med. staff, 1980-82; chief dept. neurosurgery Franklin Gen. Hosp., Valley Stream, N.Y., 1980—; prin. Neurol. Surgery & Neurology, P.C., Freeport, N.Y., 1965—. Contbr. articles to med. jours. Bd. dirs. South Nassau Community Hosp., 1978—. Served to lt. USNR, 1959-61. Recipient Neurosurg. Travel award Mayo Found., 1966. Fellow ACS; mem. L.I. Hearing and Speech Soc. (bd. dirs.), N.Y. State Neurosurgeons Soc. (bd. dirs.), N.Y. State Neurosurg. Soc. (pres. 1981-82), Sigma Xi, Alpha Omega Alpha. Hebrew. Avocations: theatre; travel. Home: 19 Bridle Path Roslyn NY 11576-3115 Office: Neurol Surgery & Neurology 88 S Bergen Pl Freeport NY 11520

BURSTEIN, STUART SAMUEL, psychiatrist; b. Decatur, Ill., Jan. 9, 1936; s. Hyman J. and Edythe M. (Cohen) B.; m. Catherine D. Burstein, Aug. 7, 1960; children: Harold, Elizabeth, Suzanne. AB, Harvard U., 1957; MD, U. Ill., 1961; MBA, U. Chgo., 1982. Intern Michael Reese Hosp., Chgo., 1961-62, resident in psychiatry, 1962-65, attending psychiatrist, 1967-85; chief mental health svcs. Michael Reese Health Plan, Chgo., 1975-85; chief of psychiatry Woodville State Hosp., Carnegie, Pa., 1986-91; chair dept. psychiatry St. Clair Hosp., Pitts., 1996—; staff psychiatrist St. Francis Hosp., Pitts., 1986—, St. Clair Hosp., Pitts., 1986—, Allegheny Gen. Hosp., Pitts., 1993—; clin. asst. prof. psychiatry U. Chgo., 1974-84, U. Pitts., 1987—, Med. Coll. Pa., 1993—. Capt. USAF, 1965-67. Mem. AMA, Am. Psychiat. Assn., Pa. Psychiat. Soc., Pitts. Psychiat. Soc., Am. Acad. Psychiatry and Law, Pa. Med. Soc., Allegheny County Med. Soc. Home: 932 Old Hickory Rd Pittsburgh PA 15243-1114 Office: 1050 Bower Hill Rd Pittsburgh PA 15243-1868

BURSZTAJN, HAROLD JONAH, forensic psychiatrist, psychoanalyst; b. Lodz, Poland, Nov. 18, 1950; came to U.S., 1959; s. Abraham and Miriam (Briks) B. AB magna cum laude, Princeton U., 1972; MD cum laude, Harvard U., 1977. Diplomate Am. Bd. Psychiatry and Neurology; diplomate subspecialty of psychiatry with added qualifications in forensic psychiatry Am. Bd. Med. Specialties. Intern in pediatrics Children's Hosp., Boston, 1977-78; resident in psychiatry Mass. Mental Health Ctr., Boston, 1979-82; clin. instr. Harvard Med. Sch., Boston, 1979-86, asst. clin. prof., 1986-90, assoc. clin. prof., 1990—; co-dir. program psychiatry and the law Mass. Mental Health Ctr., Boston, 1982—; cons. ethics medicine and the law, 1987; book reviewer New Eng. Jour. Medicine, 1988—, Med. Decision Making, 1988—. Author: Medical Choices, Medical Chances: How Patients, Families and Physicians Can Cope with Uncertainty, 1981, rev. 1990, Divided Staffs, Divided Selves: A Case Approach to Mental Health Ethics, 1987; Decision Making in Psychiatry and the Law, 1991; contbr. articles to profl. jours. Mem. Am. Assn. Psychiatry and Law, Boston Psychoanalytic Inst., Phi Beta Kappa. Home and Office: 96 Larchwood Dr Cambridge MA 02138-4639

BURT, ALVIN MILLER, III, anatomist, cell biologist, educator, writer; b. Bridgeport, Conn., Aug. 14, 1935; s. Alvin Miller and Esther Louise (Carey) B.; m. Dorothy Hanlin, July 15, 1961 (div.); children: Constance Walker, Carolyn Marie; m. Judith Nath, July 13, 1991; 1 stepchild, Stephen Jacob Nath. B.A., Amherst Coll., 1957; Ph.D. (USPHS fellow 1960-61), U. Kans., 1962. Asst. prof. anatomy Med. Coll. Va., Richmond, 1962-63; instr. Yale U. Med. Sch., 1963-66; mem. faculty Vanderbilt U. Med. Sch., 1966—, prof. anatomy, 1974-85, prof. cell biology, 1985—; prof cell biology Nursing Sch. Vanderbilt U., Nashville, 1994—; vis. scientist Agrl. Research Council, Inst. Animal Physiology, Babraham, Cambridge, Eng., 1972-73. Author: Textbook of Neuroanatomy, 1993; contbr. articles to profl. jours. Vestryman Episcopal Ch. of Advent, Brentwood, Tenn., 1977-81, sr. warden, 1979-81, lay reader, chalice bearer, 1975-87, tchr. adult classes, mem. diocesan lay ministry com., 1981-85; lay reader, chalice bearer St. Philips Episcopal Ch., Donelson, Tenn., 1989-92, vestryman, 1991-92, mem. diocesan total ministry com., 1990-93; mem. Stephen Ministry Diocese of Tenn., 1991—; dir. pastoral care St. Ann's Episcopal Ch., Nashville, 1993—, lay reader, 1994—; mem. steering com. Interfaith AIDS Ministry, 1994—. Recipient Research Career Devel. award USPHS, 1968-73. Mem. Am. Assn. Anatomists, Am. Soc. Neurochemistry, Human Anatomy & Physiology Soc., Internat. Soc. Neurochemistry, Internat. Brain Rsch. Orgn., Soc. Neurosci., Tenn. Outdoor Writers Assn. (v.p. 1985-86, pres.-elect 1986-87, pres. 1987-88, chmn. bd. dirs. 1988-89), Southeastern Outdoor Press Assn., Bass Anglers Sportsmens Soc., Tenn. Spoonplugging Club (bd. dirs. 1980-88, editor newsletter 1980-85), Sigma Xi. Home: 317 McCoin Dr Goodlettsville TN 37072-1568 Office: Vanderbilt U Dept Cell Biology Nashville TN 37232

BURT, DAVID REED, pharmacology educator; b. East Orange, N.J., Oct. 28, 1943; s. Clifton Hersey and Ruth Elizabeth (Wurts) B.; m. Dorothy Ann Schick, June 21, 1968 (div. Dec. 1984); m. Mary Ellen Holmes, Dec. 19, 1991. AB in Biophysics, Amherst Coll., 1965; PhD in Biophysics, Johns Hopkins U., 1972. Assoc. rsch. scientist biophysics dept. Johns Hopkins U., Balt., 1972-73, postdoctoral fellow in pharmacology Sch. Medicine, 1973-76; asst. prof. U. Md. Sch. Medicine, Balt., 1976-82, assoc. prof., 1982-96; prof., 1996—; cons., reviewer NIH, VA, NSF, 1982—. Editl. bd. Life Scis., 1983-93; contbr. numerous articles to scientific jours. Nat. scholar GM, 1961-65; rsch. grantee Alcohol, Drug Abuse and Mental Health Adminstrn., NSF, NIH, 1977—; Fogarty sr. internat. fellow NIH, Cambridge (Eng.) U., 1985-86. Mem. Am. Soc. Pharmacology and Exptl. Therapeutics, Soc. for Neurosci., Am. Soc. Neurochemistry, Endocrine Soc., N.Y. Acad. Scis., Phi Beta Kappa, Sigma Xi. Office: U Md Sch Medicine Pharm 655 W Baltimore St Baltimore MD 21201-1509

BURTOFT, JOHN NELSON, JR., cardiovascular physician assistant; b. Pitts., Jan. 29, 1944; s. John Nelson Sr. and Elizabeth Louise (Lyons) B.; m. Jo Ann Stewart, Aug. 16, 1963 (div. Apr. 1966); 1 child, John Nelson III; m. Artie Ann Spilman, Sept. 19, 1966 (div. Dec. 1969); 1 child, Bonnie Beth; m. Sandra Ellen Bishop, Jan. 28, 1971; 1 child, Tracy Lynne. Grad., Sch. Health Care Sci., Sheppard AFB, 1975; grad. clin. preceptorship, Naval Hosp., 1976; BS, U. Nebr., Omaha, 1977. Physician asst. USN, 1961-80; retired chief warrant officer, 1980; surg. intern, resident Montefiore Hosp., Bronx, N.Y., 1980-82; cardiovascular physician asst. Cen. Ill. Cardiac Surgery Assocs., Peoria, Ill., 1982-83, Sanger Clinic, Charlotte, N.C., 1983-89, Dr. R. Carlton, Hickory, N.C., 1989-92, Mid-Atlantic Cardiothoracic Surgeons, Ltd., Norfolk, Va., 1992-93, C.V.T. Surgery, Baton Rouge, La., 1993—. Fellow Am. Acad. Physician Assts., Assn. Physician Assts. in Cardiovascular Surgery, L.A. Acad. Physician Assts. Office: 7777 Hennessy Blvd Ste 108 Baton Rouge LA 70808-4363

BURTON, JOHN LLOYD, dermatologist, author; b. Buxton, Derbyshire, Eng., Aug. 29, 1938; s. Lloyd and Dorothy (Pacey) B.; m. Patricia Anne Crankshaw, Sept. 12, 1964; children—Benjamin John, Jane Mary, Helena Catherine. B.Sc., Manchester U., 1961, M.B., Ch.B., 1964, M.D., 1970. Intern Manchester Royal Infirmary, 1964; resident Hammersmith Hosp., London, 1965, Edinburgh Royal Infirmary, 1966-68; sr. registrar Newcastle Royal Infirmary, Eng., 1969-73; sr. lectr. Bristol U., Eng., 1973-82, prof. dermatology, 1993. Author: Aids to Postgraduate Medicine, 6th edit., 1994, Aids to Undergraduate Medicine, 5th edit., 1989, Essential Medicine, 2d. edit. 1981, Essentials of Dermatology, 3rd edit., 1990; co-editor: Rook's Textbook of Dermatology (4 vols.), 1986, 5th edit. 1991; editor Brit. Jour. Dermatology, 1980-85; contbr. about 350 articles to profl. jours., chpts. to books. Recipient Dickson Research prize N.E. Regional Health Authority, 1971. Fellow Royal Coll. Physicians (Parkes-Weber lectr. and examiner 1988), Royal Soc. Medicine (pres. dermatology sect. 1994, Dowling Orator 1980); mem. Brit. Assn. Dermatologists (pres. elect, 1995), Brit. Soc. Investigative Dermatology, Swedish Dermatol. Assn. (corr.). Avocation: fine book binding. Home: Norland House, 33 Canynge Rd, Bristol BS8 3LD, England Office: Bristol Royal Infirmary Dermatology Dept, Maudlin St, Bristol BS3 8HW, England

BURTON, KATHLEEN T., mental health professional; b. Lynn, Mass., Jan. 29, 1962; d. Charles W. and Mary L. (Mayer) B. BA in Psychology/Comms., Notre Dame Coll., South Euclid, Ohio, 1985; MEd in Counseling, Cleve. State U., 1990, EdS in Counseling Psychology, 1991; postgrad., Saybrook Inst., San Francisco, 1992—. Cert. cognitive-behavioral therapist. Human rels. & devel. coord. Kaiser Permanente, Cleveland Heights, Ohio, 1984-87; counselor Cleve. Treatment Ctr., 1989-90; tchg. asst., counselor intern Cleve. State U., 1989-91; community trainer Woodland (Calif.) Community Options, 1991-95; mental health profl., psychologist intern Davis, Calif., 1992—; group facilitator for human sexuality course dept. psychiatry Davis Med. Sch., 1994—; group leader, facilitator anxiety, phobias and panic Woodland Sr. Ctr., 1993—; mental health cons., creator "Mental Health Matters" Pub. TV, 1995; founder Sr./Youth Fair, Woodland, 1995; mental health writer Davis Enterprise; lectr. anxiety, phobias, panic, drug addictions, Moscow, Kiev, 1994. Contbr. article to medical jour. 1st place winner Nat. Future Design competition, Washington, 1984. Mem. ACA, Internat. Assn. for Addictions & Offender Counselors, Ohi Counseling Assn. (past rep.), Am. Family Assn. Roman Catholic. Office: 14 Leisureville Cir Woodland CA 95776

BURTON, PAUL FLOYD, social worker; b. Seattle, May 24, 1939; s. Floyd James and Mary Teresa (Chovanak) B.; BA, U. Wash., 1961, MSW, 1967; m. Roxanne Maude Johnson, July 21, 1961; children: Russell Floyd, Joan Teresa. Juvenile parole counselor Div. Juvenile Rehab. State of Wash., 1961-66; social worker VA, Seattle, 1967-72, social worker, cons. Work Release program King County, Wash., 1967-72; supr., chief psychiatry sect. Social Work Svc. VA, Topeka, Kans., 1972-73; pvt. practice, Topeka and L.A., 1972—; chief social work svc. VA, Sepulveda, Calif., 1974—, EEO coord. Med. ctr., 1974-77. Mem. APHA, NASW (newsletter editor Puget Sound chpt. 1970-71), Acad. Cert. Social Workers, Ctr. for Studies in Social Functioning, Am. Sociol. Assn., Am. Hosp. Assn., Soc. Social Work Adminstrs. in Health Care, Assn. VA Social Work Chiefs (founder 1979, charter mem. and pres. 1980-81, newsletter editor 1982-83, 89-91, pres. elect 1993-95, pres. 1995—). Home: 14063 Remington St Arleta CA 91331-5359 Office: 16111 Plummer St Sepulveda CA 91343-2036

BURTON, RICHARD IRVING, orthopedist, educator; b. Providence, Sept. 18, 1936; s. Kenneth Gould and Edith Irving (Vayro) B.; m. Margaret Ann Leaman, Apr. 5, 1961; children: Thomas Kenneth, Douglas Leaman. BA, Amherst Coll., 1958; MD, Harvard U., 1962; Diplomate Am. Bd. Orthopaedic Surgery (examiner 1980—, bd. dirs. 1989—). Intern, U. Rochester, N.Y., 1962-63, resident in surgery, 1963-64; resident in orthopedic surgery Harvard U., 1966-70; fellow in hand surgery Roosevelt Hosp., N.Y.C., 1970-71; asst. prof. Cleve. Clinic Found., 1971-72, head sect. surgery of hand, 1971-74, assoc. prof., 1973-74; mem. faculty U. Rochester Med. Sch., 1974—, head sect. surgery of hand, 1974—, prof. orthopedics, 1979—, Marjorie Strong Wehle prof. of orthopedics, 1995—; assoc. chmn. dept. orthopedics, 1981-88, chmn., 1988—; sr. assoc. orthopedist Strong Meml. Hosp., Rochester, 1974-79, orthopedist, 1979—. Assoc. editor Jour. Hand Surgery, 1980-84; contbr. articles to profl. jours., chpts. to books. Dir. Am. Bd. Orthopaedic Surgery, 1989—, chair Certificate of Added Qualifications com., 1994—; mem. exec. com. Monroe County chpt. Am. Arthritis Found., 1983-86; elder Twelve Corners Presbyn. Ch., 1982-84, chmn. dept. Christian Edn., 1983-84. Buswell Disting. Service fellow U. Rochester, 1980-81; Exec. of Yr. award Profl. Secs. Internat., Flower City chpt., 1981. Mem. ACS, AAAS, Am. Acad. Orthopedic Surgeons (chmn. hand and wrist com. 1986-89, orthopaedic resources com. 1989-91), Am. Bd. Med. Specialties (rep.), Am. Soc. Surgery of the Hand (coordinator div. edn. 1982-85, council 1985-89, chmn. membership com. 1991, v.p. 1990, pres.-elect 1991, pres. 1992), Am. Orthopedic Assn. (exec. com. 1986, resident rsch. conf. com. 1987-89, chair 1989, membership com. 1989-92, chmn. 1992, exec. com. 1992), Interurban Orthopedic Soc., Am. Rheumatism Assn., Eastern Orthopedic Assn., Monroe County Med. Soc., N.Y. State Med. Soc., Rochester Acad. Medicine, Rochester Orthopedic Soc., Soc. N.Y. State Orthopedic Surgeons, J. William Littler Soc., Amherst Alumni Assn., Harvard Med. Sch. Alumni Assn., Am. Med. Joggers Assn. Home: 7869

Hidden Oak Pittsford NY 14534-9607 Office: U Rochester Med Ctr Dept Orthopedics 601 Elmwood Ave Rochester NY 14642-0001

BURTON, RICHARD MAX, management and healthcare educator; b. Rushville, Ill., Aug. 12, 1939; s. Arlie H. and Mabel E. (Hoyt) B.; m. Nadine Ferdman; 1 child, Aziel. BS, U. Ill., 1961, MBA, 1963, D in Bus. Administrn., 1967. Asst. prof. Naval Postgrad. Sch., Monterey, Calif., 1967-70; prof. Duke U., Durham, N.C., 1970—, program dir. health svcs. mgmt., 1991—; chmn. bd. trustees Durham County Hosp. Corp., 1987-89. Co-author: Designing Efficient Organizations, 1984, Innovation and Entrepreneurship in Organizations, 1986, Organizational Responses to the New Business Conditions, 1989, Strategic Organizational Diagnosis and Design: Developing the Ory for Application, 1995; editor: Mgmt. Sci., 1986—; contbr. articles to profl. jours. Exec. dir. LEAD Adv. Coun., Durham, 1985-93; chmn. acad. coun. Duke U., 1992-94. Office: Duke U Fuqua Sch Bus Durham NC 27706

BURTON, TRUDY CANDANA, nurse; b. Phila., Aug. 2, 1924; d. Edward and Pearl (Kagel) B.; children: David Haiby, Michael Haiby, Daniel Haiby. Diploma, Jewish Hosp., 1945; BSN, Calif. State Coll., 1970, MSN, 1971. RN; CRRN, cert. pub. health nurse. Sch. nurse L.A. Unified Sch. Dist.; instr. L.A. Valley Coll., Calif. State Coll., L.A.; staff nurse Betty Bacharach Rehab. Hosp., Pomona, N.J.; retired, 1994. Named Outstanding Grad. Student 1970. Mem. Assn. Rehab. Nursing, Theta Sigma Tau.

BURVILL, PETER WALTER, psychiatrist; b. Perth, Australia, Apr. 27, 1933; s. Alfred Joseph and Dorothy Alison (Tanner) B.; m. Marilyn Ann Hogan, June 5, 1961; children: Malcolm, Gordon, Stuart, Alastair, Fiona, Richard. MB BS, Adelaide (Australia) U., 1957; MD, U. Western Australia, 1970; DPM, U. Edinburgh, Scotland, 1963. Sr. lectr. U. Western Australia, Nedlands, 1965-73, assoc. prof., 1973-90, prof. psychiatry, 1990—; cons. psychiatrist Sir Charles Gawdne Hosp., Perth, Australia, 1990—, Royal Perth Hosp., 1966—. Contbr. articles to profl. jours., chpts. to books. Fellow RCP, Royal Australia and New Zealand Coll. Psychiatrists, Royal Coll. Psychiatry. Roman Catholic. Home: 35 Gardner St, Como WA 6152, Australia Office: U Western Australia, QE11 Med Center Verdean St, Nedlands WA 6152, Australia

BURZYNSKI, PETER RAYMOND, psychologist; b. Watertown, Wis., May 7, 1948; s. Eugene Edward and Helen Louise (Krieger) B.; m. M. Sue Case, July 14, 1979; children: Myka Danielle, Mara Louise. BA, Lawrence U., 1970; MS, Ind. State U., 1971, EdS, 1972, PhD, 1981. Cert. sch. psychologist, Ind.; lic. psychologist in pvt. practice, Ky. Psychologist Laporte (Ind.) Community Schs., 1972-74; asst. prof. Vincennes (Ind.) U., 1976-79, assoc. prof., 1979-83, chmn. psychology dept., 1983-86, prof., 1984-87; assoc. prof. U. So. Ind., Evansville, 1987-88, Evansville Rehab. Ctr., 1988-89; pvt. practice Henderson, Ky., 1991-93; consulting psychologist, 1993—. Author: Archeus and I, 1971, Days of ..., 1977, To Be A Child, 1979, (column) "Today's Parent" Evansville (Ind.) Courier; contbr. articles to profl. jours. Recipient rsch. award Blumberg Found., 1975, Ind. State U., 1975. Mem. Am. Psychol. Assn. (teaching award 1985), Internat. Sch. Psychology Assn., Nat. Assn. Sch. Psychologists, Midwestern Psychol. Assn., Ind. Psychol. Assn., Rotary (bd. dirs. Vincennes 1984-87). Home: 8688 Hillside Dr Newburgh IN 47630-2279 Office: Behavioral Healthcare Assocs 423 Main St Evansville IN 47719

BURZYNSKI, STANISLAW RAJMUND, internist; b. Lublin, Poland, Jan. 23, 1943; s. Grzegorz and Zofia Miroslawa (Radzikowski) B.; came to U.S., 1970; M.D. with distinction, Med. Acad., Lublin, 1967, Ph.D., 1968. Teaching asst. Med. Acad. Lublin, 1962-67; intern, resident in internal medicine, Med. Acad., 1967-70; research assoc. Baylor U., 1970-72, asst. prof., 1972-77; pvt. practice specializing in internal medicine, Houston, 1977—; dir. Burzynski Research Lab., 1977-83; pres. Burzynski Research Inst., Inc., 1983—. Nat. Cancer Inst. grantee, 1974 West Found. grantee, 1975. Mem. AAAS, Am. Assn. Cancer Research, AMA, Harris County Med. Soc., Polish Nat. Alliance (pres. Houston chpt. 1974-75), Soc. Neurosci., Tex. Med. Assn., Sigma Xi. Roman Catholic. Contbr. articles profl. jours. Discoverer of antineoplastons components of biochem. def. system against cancer; described structure of Ameletin, 1st substance known to be responsible for remembering sound in animal's brain; invented new treatment for cancer, AIDS, viral infections, autoimmune diseases, neurofibromatosis, and Parkinson's disease. Home: 20 W Rivercrest Dr Houston TX 77042-2127 Office: 12000 Richmond Ave Houston TX 77082-2431

BUS, JAMES STANLEY, toxicologist; b. Kalamazoo, June 27, 1949; s. Charles J. and Sena (Wolthuis) B.; m. Gerda W. Hekman, Apr. 20, 1974; children: Sara E., Timothy J., Brian M. BS in Medicinal Chemistry, U. Mich., 1971; PhD in Pharmacology, Mich. State U., 1975. Diplomate Am. Bd. Toxicology (v.p., pres. 1985-87). NIH predoctoral trainee Dept. Pharmacology, Mich. State U., East Lansing, 1971-75; asst. prof. environ. health U. Cin., 1975-76; scientist I (biochem. toxicologist) Chem. Industry Inst. Toxicology, Research Triangle Park, N.C., 1977-84, scientist II (biochem. toxicologist), 1984-86; assoc. dir. pathology/toxicology, dir. drug metabolism rsch. The Upjohn Co., Kalamazoo, 1986-89; toxicology rsch. lab. Dow Chem. Co., Midland, Mich., 1989-91, project mgr., 1992-93, rsch. mgr., tech. dir., 1994—; adj. assoc. prof. curriculum in toxicology U. N.C., Chapel Hill, 1984-88; adj. prof. pharmacology/toxicology Mich. State U. East Lansing, 1987—; toxicology expert Am. Conf. for Govtl. Indsl. Hygienists, Cin., 1993—; mem. safety assessment bd. advisors Merck, Sharp & Dohme Lab., West Point, Pa., 1985-86; mem. bd. sci. counselors EPA, 1996—. Co-editor: Patty's Industrial Hygiene and Toxicology, Vol. 3B, 1995; assoc. editor Toxicology and Applied Pharmacology, 1989-92; editl. bd. Reproductive Toxicology, 1986—; contbr. articles to profl. jours. Bd. trustees Covenant Coll., Lookout Mountain,. Ga., 1984-87. Mem. Soc. Toxicology (pres. 1996-97, Achievement award 1987), Am. Soc. for Pharmacology and Exptl. Therapeutics, Teratology Soc. Republican. Office: Dow Chemical Co Toxicology Rsch Lab 1803 Bldg Midland MI 48674

BUSACCO, DEBRA ANN, audiologist; b. Pittston, Pa., Oct. 2, 1958; d. Albert James and Lois Ann (Reddington) B.; m. Jerald Steven Pastro, 1996. AB in Spl. Edn., Marywood Coll., 1980; MS in Audiology, Columbia U., 1981, MPhil, 1986, PhD, 1988. Supr. audiology Tchrs. Coll. Columbia U., N.Y.C., 1983-84; instr. Marywood Coll., Scranton, Pa., 1983-85; rsch. assoc. Walter Reed Army Med. Ctr., Washington, 1985-87; coord. Lifelong Learning Inst. Gallaudet U., Washington, 1990-94; dir. audiology Sundance Rehab., Shelton, Conn., 1994—; asst. prof. Dept. of Speech-Lang. Hearing Scis., Hofstra U.; adj. asst. prof. Loyola Coll., Balt., 1988-91, Towson (Md.) State U., 1992; adj. assoc. prof. Howard U., Washington, 1993-94; audiology cons. Rsch. Corp., Rockville, Md., 1993-94, Gallaudet U., 1988-89, U.S. Dept. Edn., Rehab. Svcs., Washington, 1991-94. Author: Manual for Mental Health Professionals Providing Services to Hard of Hearing, 1991; contbr. articles to profl. jours. Grantee AARP; Jo-Ann Schwartz Doctoral scholar Columbia U., 1985-87; recipient VA Patient Care award, East Orange, N.J., 1990. Mem. Am. Speech-Lang.-Hearing Assn. (cert., New Clin. Investigator award 1987), Am. Acad. Audiology, Am. Coll. Allied Health Profls., Gerontol. Soc. Am., Interest Group on Aging. Democrat. Roman Catholic. Home: 21 Manor Ave Apt 105 Hempstead NY 11550 Office: Dept Speech Lang Hearing Scis Hofstra Univ Davison Hall Hempstead NY 11550

BÜSCH, ANNEMARIE, mental health nurse; d. Jurgen Julius and Anna (Stark) B. RN, Anschar Sch. Nursing, Kiel, Fed. Republic Germany, 1954; student, Traverse City State Hosp., Mich., 1959, Wayne State U., 1962, Colby-Sawyer Coll., New London, N.H., 1981. Lic. nurse, N.H., Vt., Fed. Republic Germany. Asst. head nurse Univ. Eye Inst., Kiel, 1954-56; nurse aide, grad. nurse Ontario Hosp., London, Can.; staff nurse, charge nurse Grace Hosp., Receiving Hosp., Detroit, 1962-67; coll. health nurse Wayne St. U., Detroit, 1967-70; staff nurse Mary Hitchcock Meml. Hosp., Hanover, 1970-71, nurse mental health dept., 1978-82; charge nurse Dartmouth Coll. Health Svc., Hanover, N.H., 1971-77; staff nurse, charge nurse Hanover Health Terrace; staff nurse Temporary Nurses, Inc., Hanover, Vis. Nurse Alliance of Vt. and N.H., White River Junction, Vt.; camp nurse Nat. Music Camp InterLochen, Mich.

BUSCH, CAROLE ANN MCGOVERN, psychotherapist, art therapist, nurse, consultant; b. Manhattan, N.Y., June 6, 1945; d. James Lenahan and Claire Beatrice (Murphy) McGovern; m. Joseph Jacob Busch Jr.; children: James McGovern, Angela Maureen, Caroline Claire. Diploma in nursing, St. Mary's Sch. Nursing, 1966; BA in Art magna cum laude, U. Tenn., Chattanooga, 1985, MEd in Guidance, 1988. RN, Tenn.; cert. clin. nurse specialist in adult psychiat. and mental health nursing; registered art therapist; lic. art therapist; cert. art therapist; nat. bd. cert. med. psychotherapist; fellow and diplomate Am. Bd. Med. Psychotherapists. Med. and surg. staff nurse St. Marys Hosp. Med. Ctr., Knoxville, Tenn., 1966-67; med. and surg. charge nurse William F. Bowld Hosp., Memphis, 1967-69; coronary care nurse Bapt. Meml. Hosp., Memphis, 1969-71; pvt. practice med. psychotherapist, art therapy cons. Signal Mountain, Tenn., 1988—; art therapy cons. Valley Psychiat. Hosp., Chattanooga, 1989-90; coord. art expressions group adaopt a parent Alexian Bros. Health Care Ctr., Signal Mountain, 1989-91; nat. and internat. presenter on arts and medicine, 1991—; profl. artist and photographer, 1975—. Numerous one-woman and group art exhbns. regionally, nationally, and internationally; works in pub. and pvt. collections in U.S., Ireland and China. Ann. workshop leader Very Spl. Arts Festival, Orange Grove Ctr., Chattanooga, 1981—; career beginning mentor U. Tenn. Ctr. for Community Career Edn., Chattanooga, 1988-89; vol. mental health counselor Signal Crest Meth. Ch., Signal Mountain, 1988—; amb. art therapy del. People to People, China, 1995. Recipient Disting. Leadership award in the mental health field, 1987. Mem. Tenn. Art Therapy Assn. (founder 1993, pres. 1995—), Golden Key Nat. Honor Soc., Kappa Delta Pi, Chi Sigma Iota, Alpha Soc., Girls Cotillion, Signal Mountain Tennis Club (bd. dirs. 1981). Roman Catholic. Office: Art Therapy Consults & Studio 715-B Mississippi Ave Signal Mountain TN 37377

BUSCH, DAVID TRUETT, psychologist educator, consultant, researcher; b. Port Arthur, Tex., May 14, 1954; s. John Claus and Lurlene Christel (Wiesen) B.; m. Cara Melissa Ferris, Dec. 18, 1983; children: Ukiah Jacob, Casey Montana, Sierra Dawn. BS in Psychology, Lamar U., 1976; MS in Psychology, East Tex. State U., 1984, PhD, 1986. Lic. psychologist; reg. play therapist, supr.; cert. EMDR therapist. Child therapist Ala.-Coushatta Indian Reservation, Livingston, Tex., 1977-78; child & adolescent therapist Mental Health/Mental Retardation of S.E. Tex., Beaumont, Tex., 1978-79; counselor Human Rels. Cons., Orange, Tex., 1980-81; instr. mktg. and distributive edn. Nederland High Sch., 1981-82; child & family therapist Wesley St. Clinic, Greenville, Tex., 1983-85; workshop leader Tex. Dept. Human Resources, 1985-86; head mental health unit Hunt County Family Svcs. Ctr., Greenville, 1986; asst. prof. psychology Columbia (Mo.) Coll., 1986-88; child & adolescent therapist Columbia Resource Ctr., 1987-88; asst. prof. psychology Valdosta (Ga.) State U., 1988-93, tenured assoc. prof., 1993—, mem. Grad. Faculty, 1994—; dir., psychologist Busch Clin., Valdosta, 1990—; cons. Ky. Dept. Edn., Frankfort, 1991; reviewer Harper Collins Pubs., N.Y.C., 1991. Originator Pragmatic Play Therapy (PPT), the Attention Deficit Hyperactivity Disorder Diagnotic and Prescriptive System (ADAPS), and The Test of Preferred Learning Style (TOPLS). Bd. dirs. Lowndes County Commn. on Children & Youth, Valdosta, 1990-91; mem. Child Abuse Coun., Valdosta, 1990-91; spokesperson Concerned Taxpayers for Sound Econ. Growth. Mem. AAUP, APA, Nat. Assn. for Edn. Young Children, Midwestern Psychol. Assn., Assn. for Childhood Edn. Internat., Internat. Assn. for Play Therapy, S.E. Psychol. Assn., S.W. Psychol. Assn., Assn. for Humanistic Psychology, Ga. Psychol. Assn., Ga. Coun. on Child Abuse, Lowndes County Mental Health Assn. Office: Valdosta State U Dept Psychology Valdosta GA 31698 also: Busch Clinic 305 University Dr Valdosta GA 31602-2538

BUSCHKE, HERMAN, neurologist; b. Berlin, Oct. 15, 1932; came to U.S., 1934, naturalized, 1945; s. Franz Julius and Ruth Helen (Minkowski) B.; children: Thomas, Katherine; m. Bertelle Selig, 1993. B.A., Reed Coll., 1954; M.D., Western Res. U., 1958. Diplomate: Am. Bd. Psychiatry and Neurology. Intern Bronx (N.Y.) Mcpl. Hosp. Center, 1958-59, resident in neurology, 1959-62; asst. instr. neurology Albert Einstein Coll. Medicine, Bronx, N.Y., 1961-62; asso. prof. Albert Einstein Coll. Medicine, 1969-74, prof., 1974—, prof. neurosci., 1974—; practice medicine specializing in neurology Bronx, N.Y., 1969—; staff mem., attending neurologist Hosp. of Albert Einstein Coll. of Medicine; instr. medicine Stanford U., 1962-63, asst. prof., 1963-69. Named Lena and Joseph Gluck Disting. Scholar in Neurology, 1973. Home: 50 E 89th St New York NY 10128-1225 Office: Albert Einstein Coll Medicine Saul R Korey Dept Neurology 1300 Morris Park Ave Bronx NY 10461-1926

BUSCHMANN, WILLIAM ROBERT, orthopaedic surgeon; b. Camden, N.J., Apr. 5, 1952. BA, Colgate Coll., 1974; MD, NYU, 1978. Resident M.S. Hershey Med. Ctr., 1978-83; assoc. prof. Albert Einstein Coll. Medicine, N.Y.C., 1993—. Foot & Ankle Surgery fellow Hosp. Joint Disorders, N.Y., 1990-91. Office: Westchester Bone & Joint Assocs 7 Reservoir Rd White Plains NY 10603

BUSH, ANDREW, pediatrician, consultant; b. London, Apr. 24, 1954; s. Geoffrey and Julie Kathleen (McKenna) B.; m. Susan Joan Crucefix, July 19, 1975; children: Matthew Curtin, Christopher Thomas, Naomi Kathleen, David Daniel. BA with honours, Cambridge (Eng.) U., 1975, MD, 1987; MB, BS with honours, London U., 1978. House officer Univ. Coll. Hosp., London, 1979, Taunton Hosp., Somerset, 1979-80, Brompton Hosp., London, 1981; registrar in renal medicine St. Mary's Hosp., London, 1981-82; registrar in medicine St. Charles Hosp., London, 1982-83; sr. house officer neonates dept. Univ. Coll. Hosp., London, 1988; registrar in pediatrics Hillingdon Hosp., London, 1988-89; sr. pediatric registrar Hammersmith Hosp., London, 1990-91, cons. pediatrician, 1992—; rsch. fellow Royal Brompton Hosp., London, 1983-88, registrar in pediatrics, 1989-90, cons. pediatrician, 1991—; cons. pediatrician Royal Marsden Hosp., London, 1991—, Pilgrims Sch., Sussex, Eng., 1993—; hon. med. adviser Cystic Fibrosis Rsch. Trust, 1991—. Contbr. articles to med. jours. Bd. govs. Burlington Danes Sch., London, 1993; hon. med. adviser Primary Ciliary Dyskinesia Support Group, 1992—; exec. com. mem. Brit. Lung Found., 1996—. Rsch. grantee Brit. Heart Found., 1984, 91, Respiratory Health Assn., 1988. Fellow Royal Coll. Physicians (dist. adviser in pediats. 1991-95). Office: Royal Brompton Hosp, Sydney St, London SW3 6NP, England

BUSH, DAVID FREDERIC, psychologist, educator; b. Watertown, N.Y., July 12, 1942; s. Frederic Ralph and Charlotte Mary (Ellingworth) B.; m. Joanne Arena; 1 child, Lara A. Butler; 1 stepchild, Ryan Tadeo. BA, U. South Fla., 1965; MA, U. Wyo., 1968; PhD, Purdue U., 1972. Cert. sr profl. in human resources. Instr. psychology Hiram Scott Coll., Scottsbluff, Nebr., 1967-69, Purdue U., West Lafayette, Ind., 1971-72; assoc. prof. psychology West Chester (Pa.) State Coll., 1972-73; asst. prof., chmn. grad. program psychology Villanova (Pa.) U., 1972-77, assoc. prof., 1978-84, prof., 1984—, assoc. dir. human resource devel., grad. program in human orgn. sci.; instr. seminar Am. Coll., Bryn Mawr, Pa., 1976-78; ptnr. Quality Mgmt. Group; cons. in field. Mem. coun. Unitarian fellowship Lafayette, Ind., 1970-72; bd. dirs. Ars Moriendi, Dennis Burton Day Care Ctr., 1971-72, Life Guidance Services, Inc., 1977-82; pres. Bush Assocs. NDEA fellow 1969-71, David Ross summer fellow, 1972; Villanova U. grantee, 1974, 77, 83. Mem. Am., Ea. psychol. assns., Am. Soc. Quality Control, Assn. of Mgmt., Internat. Human Resource Mgmt. Assn., Human Resources Profl. Assn. (pres 1991-93), Acad. Mgmt., Soc. for Human Resource Mgmt. (Pa. state coun., nat. editl. bd.), Assn. for Quality and Participation, Internat. Soc. Systems Improvement (co-founder), Sigma Xi, Psi Chi. Author: Human Development: The Psychology of the Life-Span, 1974; Canterbury Press Memory Improvement Course. Editor: Jour. Systems Improvement. Researcher work teams, orgn. behavior, orgn. devel., human resource mgmt., quality improvement programs, violence in the workplace. Home: 16 Pennswood Dr Glenmoore PA 19343-1425 Office: Villanova U Dept Psychology Villanova PA 19085

BUSH, DAVID SAMUEL, psychologist, neuropsychologist; b. Miami, Fla., Apr. 26, 1956; s. Louis B. and Elva (Kaplan) B.; m. Susan Ellen Wein; children: Eli Matthew, Lauren Anne. BA in Psychology, U. Colo., 1978; MA in Clin. Psychology, Washington U., 1980, PhD in Clin. Psychology, 1982. Diplomate Am. Bd. Clin. Neuropsychology, Am. Bd. Profl. Neuropsychology. Postdoctoral fellow Rehab. Inst. Chgo., 1983-84, staff psychologist, 1984-86; assoc. faculty Northwestern U. Med. Sch., Chgo., 1983-86; psychologist/neuropsychologist Palm Beach Neurol. Group, Palm Beach Gardens, Fla., 1986—. Mem. APA, Fla. Psychol. Assn., Nat. Acad. Neuropsychology, Internat. Neuropsychol. Soc., N.Y. Acad. Scis., Soc. for Personality Assessment. Office: Palm Beach Neurol Group 3355 Burns Rd Ste 201 Palm Beach Gardens FL 33410

BUSH, EUGENE NYLE, pharmacologist, research scientist; b. McKeesport, Pa., Apr. 14, 1952; s. Nyle E. and Rosalia M. (Merlino) B.; m. Janet Rosemary Ruscitto, May 7, 1977; children: Stephen Michael, Rebecca Renee, Timothy George. BS in Pharmacy, U. Pitts., 1977, PhD in Pharmacology, 1981. Registered pharmacist, Pa., Ill. Tchg. asst. U. Pitts., 1978-81; staff pharmacist Western Pa. Hosp., Pitts., 1977-81; pharmacologist II Abbott Labs., 1981-84, pharmacologist I, 1984-87; sr. rsch. sci. Abbott Labs., Abbott Park, Ill., 1986-88, rsch. investigator, 1988-89, group leader, endocrine pharmacol., 1989-91; sr. group leader endocrine pharmacol. Abbott Labs., 1991—, assoc. Volwiler rsch. fellow, 1996—. Co-author numerous publs.; contbr. articles to profl. jours. Asst. scoutmaster St. Joseph Ch. troop 60, Boy Scouts Am., Libertyville, Ill., 1994—. Assoc. Volwiler Rsch. fellow, 1996—. Mem. Endocrine Soc., Nat. Eagle Scout Assn., Sigma Xi, Am. Pharm. Assn. Republican, Roman Catholic. Home: 816 Bedford Ct Libertyville IL 60048-3002 Office: Abbott Labs 100 Abbott Park Rd Ap 10 Dept 46R Abbott Park IL 60064-3500

BUSH, HARRY LEONARD, JR., surgery educator; b. Auburn, Ala., July 11, 1942; m. Ellen Parker; children: Alexander, Charles, Scott. BS, Princeton U., 1964; MD, Columbia U., 1968. Diplomate Am. Bd. Surgery. Surgical intern Presbyn. Hosp., N.Y.C., 1968-69, fellow, dept. surgery, 1969-70, resident gen. surgery, 1973-76; instr. surgery Columbia U., N.Y.C., 1975-76, Boston U. Sch. Medicine, 1976-77; asst. prof. surgery Tufts U. Sch. Medicine, Boston, 1979-86, assoc. prof. surgery, 1986-87; assoc. prof. surgery Cornell U. Med. Coll., N.Y.C., 1987—; dir. surg. ICU Boston VA Med. Ctr, 1983-84, staff surgeon 1979-87, asst. dir. transplant svc. 1979-87, chmn. animal studies subcommittee 1980-85, chmn. R & D com. 1983-84; assoc. staff surgeon New Eng. Med. Ctr., Boston, 1979-83, staff surgeon 1983-87; asst. dir. organ preservation lab. New Eng. Organ Bank, Boston, 1979-87, trustee 1984-87; chief div. vascular surgery N.Y. Hosp., 1987—, assoc. attending surgeon 1987—, dir. non-invasive vascular lab 1987—; asst. dir. transplant svc. Tufts New Eng. Med. Ctr., Boston, 1979-87; chief surg. svc. Lemuel Shattuck Hosp., Boston, 1984-87; cons. med. rsch. svc. Va. Cen. Office, Washington, 1985-86. Author (with others): Complications of Thoracic and Cardiovascular Surgery, 1979, Peripheral Vascular Diseases, 1987, Common Problems in Vascular Surgery, 1989, Aortic Surgery, 1989, Current Critical Problems in Vascular Surgery, 1989, Current Therapy in Vascular Surgery, 1991; contbr. over 60 articles to profl. jours. Mem. Am. Heart Assn., 1976—. With U.S. Navy, 1970-73. Westchester Heart Assn. Rsch. fellow, 1969-70; co-prin. investigator VA Merit Rev. Program, 1980-82; prin. investigator, VA Merit Rev. Program, 1983-86, 86-89; co-investigator NIH, 1982-84; prin. investigator NIH, 1988-91, Wyeth-Ayerst Labs., 1989-90. Fellow Am. Coll. Surgeons; mem. Internat. Cardiovascular Soc., Internat. Soc. for Applied Cardiovascular Biology, New Eng. Soc. for Vascular Surgery, New Eng. Surg. Soc., N.Y. Soc. for Cardiovascular Surgery, N.Y. Surg. Soc., N.Y. Clin. Soc., Boston Surg. Soc., Ea. Vascular Soc., Assn. for Acad. Surgery, Soc. Critical Care Medicine, Soc. for Vascular Surgery, Coun. on Cardiovascular Surgery, Soc. Univ. Surgeons, Stroke Coun., Sigma Xi. Office: NY Hosp Cornell Med Ctr Dept Surgery 525 E 68th St # 2011F New York NY 10021-4873

BUSHER, PENELOPE CHACE-SQUIRE, school psychologist; b. Waterville, Maine, Aug. 29, 1943; d. Roger Chace and Geraldine Anne (Mosher) Squire; m. Eugene Lane Busher, June 27, 1970; children: Meredith Anne, Ellen Lane. BA, Northeastern U., 1966, MEd, 1968; postgrad. study, Bridgewater State Coll., 1975; MDiv, Andover Newton Theol. Sem., 1983. Ordained to ministry United Ch. Christ, 1985; lic. sch. psychologist and ednl. psychologist, Mass.; sch. adjustment counselor, Mass. Tchr. counselor Brookline (Mass.) High Sch., 1968-70, Portsmouth (R.I.) High Sch., 1971-73; minister East Rochester (Mass.) Congl. Ch., 1985-88; sch. psychologist Old Rochester Regional Sch. Dist., Mattapoisett, Mass., 1985—; part-time sch. psychologist Joseph Case H.S., 1975-84, pastoral counselor Lex King Souter Pastoral Counseling Ctr., Fall River, Mass., 1975-84. Dir. lead testing program Jr. League Fall River, Swansea, Mass., 1974; leader 4-H, Swansea, 1978-80; mem. fin. adv. bd. Tours of Swansea, 1986-88. Mem. NEA, Mass. Tchr.'s Assn., Nat. Assn. Sch. Psychologists, Mass. Sch. Psychologists Assn., Old Colony Min.'s Assn., Mass. Assn. Sch. Adjustment Counselors. Office: Old Rochester Regional High Sch 135 Marion Rd Mattapoisett MA 02739-1621

BUSHINSKY, DAVID ALLEN, nephrologist, educator, researcher; b. Elizabeth, N.J., Mar. 16, 1949; s. Morris and Frieda (Price) B.; m. Nancy Sue Krieger, Aug. 29, 1976; children: Joshua Mark, Seth Michael. B-SChemE magna cum laude, Lehigh U., 1971; MD, Tufts U., 1975. Instr. medicine Tufts U., Boston, 1979-80; asst. prof. medicine U. Chgo., 1980-87, assoc. prof. medicine, 1987-89, attending physician hosps., 1982-89; assoc. prof. physiology, assoc. prof. medicine U. Rochester, N.Y., 1989-92, prof. medicine, physiology, pharmacology, 1992—; attending physician Michael Reese Hosp. & Med. Ctr., Chgo., 1980-82; chief nephrology Strong Meml. Hosp., Rochester, 1989—, attending physician, 1989—. Contbr. 25 chpts. to books; contbr. over 75 articles to profl. jours. on calcium, protons and bone; editl. bd. Am. Jour. Physiology (Renal), Kidney, Jour. Bone and Mineral Rsch. Andrew Mellon fellow; grantee NIH, Am. Heart Assn., NSF, Michael Reese Rsch. Inst., Nat. Kidney Found. Mem. Am. Soc. Nephrology, Am. Heart Assn., Am. Fed. Clin. Rsch., Am. Soc. Bone and Mineral Rsch., Am. Soc. Clin. Investigation, Am. Physiol. Soc., Internat. Soc. Nephrology, Cen. Soc. Clin. Rsch. Home: 123 Heatherstone Ln Rochester NY 14618-4864 Office: U Rochester 601 Elmwood Ave Rochester NY 14642-0001

BUSHKIN, YURI, immunologist; b. Riga, Latvia, Oct. 22, 1949; s. Isser and Margarita (Skovronek) B.; m. Sandra Demaria, June 15, 1991. MS, Latvian State U., 1971; PhD, Weizmann Inst. Sci., 1978. Postdoctoral fellow Sloan-Kettering Inst. Cancer Rsch., N.Y.C., 1977-81, rsch. assoc., 1981-86; assoc. Pub. Health Rsch. Inst., N.Y.C., 1986-88, asst. mem., 1988-96, lab. head, 1988—, assoc. mem., 1996—; rsch. assoc. prof. pathology NYU Med. Ctr., N.Y.C., 1989—. Contbr. articles to profl. jours. Recipient Milberg Women's Cancer Rsch. Fund award, 1985, Nat. Cancer Cytology Ctr. award, 1986; grantee NIH, 1984-87, 87-91, Am. Cancer Soc., 1987-88, Coun. for Tobacco Rsch. U.S.A., 1992—. Office: Pub Health Rsch Inst 455 1st Ave New York NY 10016-9189

BUSHNELL, FRANCES KATHLEEN, nursing educator, family nurse practitioner; b. Albuquerque, Mar. 22, 1946; d. John Joseph and Elanor Kathleen (Marron) Lopez; m. Paul G. Bushnell, June 4, 1972; children: Kristen, Jonathan, Lisa, Tori, Whitney. BS in Nursing, U. N.Mex., 1969; MS in Nursing, Yale U., 1972, MPH, 1972; EdD, Boston U., 1982. Nurse Upman's Home Care, Boston; asst. prof. MGH-IHP, Boston; nurse practitioner Brigham & Women's Hosp., Boston; asst. prof. U. Lowell, Mass.; family nurse practitioner Vanderbilt U. Med. Ctr., Nashville, 1993—. Reviewer Nursing Rsch., Tri Svc. Nursing. Pres. Kids Care. Maj. U.S. Army, 1989. Grantee Mass. Med. Found., Emmanuel Coll., Boston U.; Tri-Svc. grantee COPC, 1992. Mem. ANA (chairperson; mem. Com. of Examiners), Mass. Nurses Assn. (v.p.), Sigma Theta Tau. Home: 2419 Valley Brook Rd Nashville TN 37240-0008

BUSHO, ELIZABETH MARY, nurse, consultant, educator; b. Ellendale, Minn., Feb. 26, 1927; d. Ruben Oscar and Lillian Katherine (Gahagan) B. RN, Kahler Hosps. Sch. of Nursing, 1948. RN, Minn. Oper. rm. staff nurse, Minn., Calif., Colo., 1948-53; oper. rm. head nurse, Mt. Sinai Hosp., Mpls., 1953-61; asst. supr. oper. rm. St. Barnabas Hosp., Mpls., 1961-71; asst. dir. surg. svcs. St. Mary's Hosp., Rochester, Minn., 1971-80, dir., 1980-90; sr. cons. oper. rms. Mayo Med. Ctr., Rochester, 1990-92; ind. cons. surg. svcs., 1992—; instr. Rochester Community Coll. Developer course in oper. rm. nursing. Mem. adv. bd. Rochester Area Vocat. Tech. Inst., Rochester Community Coll., Sigma Theta Tau. Republican. Methodist. Office: 2100 Valkyrie Dr NW Apt 415 Rochester MN 55901-2449

BUSINO, WILLIAM ANTHONY, JR., physician; b. Schenectady, June 15, 1949; s. William Anthony and Mary Helen (Rowley) B.; student Albany Coll. Pharmacy, 1967-69; B.S. summa cum laude, Union Coll., 1971; M.D. magna cum laude, Albany Med. Coll., 1975; m. Cheryl Ann Coppola, Mar.

10, 1979; 1 child, David William. Diplomate Am. Bd. Internal Medicine, Am. Bd. Geriatrics. Intern in medicine Albany (N.Y.) Med. Coll., 1975-76, resident in medicine, 1976-77, chief resident, 1977-78, asst. prof. medicine, 1979-86, assoc. prof. clin. med., 1986—; attending physician emergency room Ellis Hosp., Schenectady, 1978-79, attending physician in medicine, 1979—, assoc. dir. dept. medicine, 1979-82; attending physician St. Clare's Hosp., Schenectady; cons. physician in medicine Sunnyview Hosp. Bd. dirs. Schenectady County chpt. ARC, 1982-92, Capital dist. YMCA Camp Chiagachgock, 1994—. Robert Wood Johnson Found. grantee, 1980-85. Fellow ACP; mem. Med. Soc. State of N.Y., Schenectady County Med. Soc., Phi Beta Kappa, Alpha Omega Alpha. Roman Catholic. Home: 14 Sunnyside Rd Schenectady NY 12302-2409 Office: 2546 Balltown Rd Schenectady NY 12309-1079

BUSKIRK, ELSWORTH ROBERT, physiologist, educator; b. Beloit, Wis., Aug. 11, 1925; s. Ellsworth Fred and Laura Ellen (Parman) B.; m. Mable Heen, Aug. 28, 1948; children: Laurel Ann Buskirk Wiegand, Kristine Janet Buskirk Hallett. Student, U. Wis., 1943; BA, St. Olaf Coll., Northfield, Minn., 1950; MA, U. Minn., 1951, PhD, 1954. Lab. and teaching asst. Lab. Physiol. Hygiene, U. Minn., 1951-53; rsch. fellow Life Inst. Med. Rsch. Fund, 1953-54; physiologist Environ. Rsch. Ctr., Natick, Mass., 1954-57, Nat. Inst. for Arthritis, Metabolic and Digestive Diseases, NIH, Bethesda, Md., 1957-63; prof. applied physiology Pa. State U., University Park, 1963-92, dir. Lab. Human Performance Rsch., 1963-92; Marie Underhill Noll prof. Human Performance Pa. State U., 1988-92, emeritus, 1992—; mem. sci. adv. com. Pres.' Coun. on Phys. Fitness, 1959-61; mem. applied physiology study sect. divsn. rsch. grants NIH, 1964-68, 76-80; mem. com. on interplay of engrng. with biology and medicine NAS-NAE, 1968-74, 82-88; mem. rsch. com. Pa. Heart Assn., 1970-73, 82-86, 87-89, 90-95; mem. Pa. Gov.'s Coun. on Phys. Fitness and Sports, 1978-82; mem. com. on mil. nutrition rsch. NAS/NRC, 1982-90; mem. clin. scis. study sect. divsn. rsch. grants NIH, 1989-92; mem. Def. Women's Rsch. Com. IOM, NAS-NRC, 1995. Sect. editor Jour. Applied Physiology, 1974-78, assoc. editor, 1978-84; co-editor Sci. and Medicine in Sports and Exercise, 1974, editor, 1973-75; editor-in-chief, 1984-88, cons., editor, 1989—; mem. editl. bd. Physician and Sports Medicine, 1974-85, Jour. Cardiopulmonary Rehab., 1980—, Undersea and Hyperbaric Medicine, 1988-95, Am. Jour. Clin. Nutrition, 1982-92, Jour. Gerontology, 1982-92, Exptl. Gerontology, 1989—; aslo over 235 articles on physiology, revs. to sci. jours. Bd. visitors Sargent Coll., Boston U., 1976-92; bd. dirs. Ctr. Cmty. Hosp., Pa., 1966-70, sec., 1971-72, v.p., 1973, pres., 1974-75. Served with U.S. Army, ETO. Recipient Disting. Alumni award St. Olaf Coll., 1969; rsch. grantee NIH, 1963-92, U.S. Olympic Com., 1965-68, USAF, 1965-69, Pa. Dept. Health, 1966-67, Pa. Heart Assn., 1966, 76-80, NSF, 1968-70, Nat. Inst. Occupl. Safety and Health, 1969-74; NATO sr. fellow in sci., 1977. Mem. AAAS, AAPHERD, ASHRAE, Aerospace Med. Assn., Am. Acad. Phys. Edn., Am. Coll. Sports Medicine (citations 1973, 75, Honor award 1984, editl. award 1989, 93, Mid-Atlantic regional chpt. Svc. award 1991), Am. Inst. Nutrition, Am. Physiol. Soc. (pres. environ. and exercise sect. 1987-91, com. on coms. 1988-92, Honor award environ. exercise physiology sect. 1993), Am. Heart Assn. (coun. on epidemiology), N.Y. Acad. Scis., NIH Alumni Assn., Pa. Heart Assn. (rsch. com. 1988-94), Am. Diabetes Assn., Coun. Biology Editors (Healthy Am. Fitness Leaders award 1992). Lutheran. Club: Centre Hills Country. Home: 216 Hunter Ave State College PA 16801-6947 Office: Pa State U 119 Noll Lab University Park PA 16802-6900

BUSOWSKI, JOHN DENNIS, physician; b. Pitts., May 21, 1955; s. John and Patricia Ruth (Elliott) B.; m. Mary Theresa McCloskey, May 28, 1983; children: Katelyn Mary, Michael Patrick. BS, U. Pitts., 1976; MS, Bowman Gray Coll., Winston-Salem, N.C., 1980; MD, Hahnemann U., 1984. Diplomate Am. Bd. Ob/Gyn. Intern Aultman Hosp., Canton, Ohio, 1984-85, resident, 1984-88; dir. perinatal svcs. Pee Dee Health Svcs., Society Hills, S.C., 1988-91; physician So. Women's Clinic, Hartsville, S.C., 1991-92; with dept. ob-gyn. U. So Fla., Tampa, 1993-95; asst. prof. Dept. Ob-Gyn., U. So. Ala., 1995—. Author: Principles-Practices of Radiation Oncology, 1986, 2d edit., 1991. Mem. Alpha Omega Alpha. Home: 6827 Stonebrook Dr Mobile AL 36695-3053 Office: U So Ala Dept Ob-Gyn 2451 Fllingim St Mobile AL 36617

BUSS, JANE MOORE, infectious disease physician; b. Cin., Dec. 22, 1955; d. Ronald Edward and Wilma Lee (Easton) Moore; m. Leo William Buss, June 12, 1982; children: Evan Daniel, Blake William. AB in Biopsychology, Vassar Coll., 1978; M.T. (ASCP), MetPath Sch. Lab. Medicine, 1978-79; MD, N.Y. Med. Coll., 1987. Diplomate in internal medicine and infectious diseases Am. Bd. Internal Medicine. Resident internal medicine Hartford (Conn.) Hosp., 1987-90, fellow infectious diseases, 1990-92; staff physician infectious diseases Middlesex Hosp., Middletown, Conn., 1992—; cons. Profl. Home Care Svcs., Middletown, 1992-95. Mem. ACP, Am. Soc. Microbiology, Infectious Disease Soc. Am., Conn. Soc. Infectious Diseases, Alpha Omega Alpha. Office: Infectious Disease Assocs 80 S Main St Middletown CT 06457

BUSS, PATRICIA ARNOLD, plastic surgeon; b. Albany, N.Y., May 11, 1956; d. Edward Henry and Marion Gray (Griffing) Arnold; m. Donald Anderson Buss, May 21, 1983; children: Alison, Lindsey, Colin. ScB, Brown U., 1978, MD, 1981. Diplomate Am. Bd. Plastic Surgery. Commd. ens. USN, 1977, advanced through grades to comdr., 1992; intern U. Rochester, N.Y., 1981-82, resident in gen. surgery, 1981-83; gen. med. officer U.S. Naval Hosp., Phila., 1983-84; resident in gen. surgery Brown U., Providence, 1984-85, resident in plastic surgery, 1985-87; plastic surgeon U.S. Naval Hosp., Oakland, Calif., 1987-90; head dept. surgery U.S. Naval Hosp., Charleston, S.C., 1990-93; managed care analyst Navy Bur. Medicine and Surgery, Washington, 1993—; plastic surgeon DeWitt Army Cmty. Hosp., Ft. Belvoir, Va., 1994—; bd. dirs. My Image After Breast Cancer, Charleston, 1991-93. Fellow ACS; mem. Am. Assn. Plastic and Reconstructive Surgeons, Assn. Women Surgeons, Am. Coll. Physician Execs. Presbyterian. Office: Bur Medicine and Surgery Med-323 2300 E St NW Washington DC 20372

BUSSE, EWALD WILLIAM, psychiatrist, educator; b. St. Louis, Aug. 18, 1917; s. Frederick Ewald and Emily Louise (Stroh) B.; m. Ortrude Helen Schnaedelbach, July 18, 1941; children: Ortrude Susan Busse White, Barbara Ann, Ewald Richard, Deborah Emily Busse Bragg. A.B., Westminster Coll., 1938, Sc.D. (hon.), 1960; M.D., Washington U., St. Louis, 1942. Diplomate: Am. Bd. Psychiatry and Neurology, Am. Bd. Qualification in Electroencephalogy. Intern St. Louis City Hosp., 1942; resident in neuropsychiatry and psychiatry McCloskey Gen. Hosp., Temple, Tex., 1943-46, Colo. Psychiat. Hosp., Denver, 1946-48; mem. faculty, head dept. psychosomatic medicine U. Colo., Denver, 1950-53; prof. Duke U. Med. Ctr., Durham, N.C., 1953-65, J.P. Gibbons prof. psychiatry, 1965-87, chmn. dept., 1953-74, dir. Ctr. for Study Aging, 1957-70, assoc. provost, dean Sch. Medicine, 1974-82, dean emeritus, 1982—; pres., chief exec. officer N.C. Inst. Medicine, 1987-94, pres. emeritus, 1994—; mem. council Nat. Inst. on Aging, Bethesda, Md., 1979-83; chmn. geriatrics and gerontology adv. com. VA, 1981-86. Author, editor: Behavior and Adaptation in Late Life, 1969, 2d edit., 1977, Handbook of Geriatric Psychiatry, 1980, 2d edit., 1994, Part II, Vol. II-Psychiatry Update, 1983, The Duke Longitudinal Studies, 1985, Aging: The Universal Human Experience, 1987, Geriatric Psychiatry, 1989, (textbook) Geriatric Psychiatry, 1995; author: Cerebral Manifestations of Cardiac Dysrhythmias, 1979. Mem. N.C. State Commn. on Care of Elderly, Raleigh, 1968-73; mem. Durham County Commn. in Mental Health, 1971-74; sect. chmn. del. White Ho. Conf. on Aging, 1978-81; mem. sci. adv. bd. Alliance for Aging Rsch., 1986—; bd. dirs. Greater Durham United Way, 1987-92. Maj. U.S. Army, 1943-46. Recipient Brookdale Found. award, 1982, Alumni Achievement award Westminster Coll., 1984, Disting. Alumni award Washington U., 1992, Pioneer award Govs. Commn. on Reduction of Infant Mortality, 1993; Busse Bldg. named in his honor Duke U., 1985; Busse Rsch. award endowed, 1990; Wald Busse award created in his honor N.C. Dept. Human Resources, 1990; Busse Lecture endowment, 1995. Fellow Am. Psychiat. Assn. (pres. 1971-72, chmn. ethics com. 1981-85, Jack Weinberg Meml. award, Warren Williams award 1987, Disting. Service award 1988), Am. Geriatrics Soc. (pres. 1975-76 Allen Thewlis award), Gerontol. Soc. Am. (pres. 1967-68 Freeman award), ACP (Menninger award 1971), Southeastern Med. Dental Soc. (pres. 1978-80); mem. Internat. Assn. Gerontology (pres. 1983-89, Sandoz prize1983), World Psychiat. Assn. (ethics com.), N.Y. Acad. Medicine (Salmon award 1980). Clubs: Hope Valley; Beech Mountain (N.C.). Lodges: Rotary/Durham; Masons. Home: 1132 Woodburn Rd Durham NC 27705-5738 Office: Duke U Med Ctr PO Box 2948 Durham NC 27715-2948

BUSSELL, GLENDA FOWLER, mental health director; b. Louisville, Jan. 4, 1934; d. James Boxley and Clara Theresa (Ryan) Fowler; m. Harold Dean Bussell, Aug. 16, 1963 (div. 1973); 1 child, Scott Fowler. BA, Western Ky. U., 1955; MSW, U. Louisville, 1965. Asst. prof. social work Ohio State U., Columbus, 1970-74, adj. lectr., 1978-79; exec. dir. N. Cen. Mental Health Svcs., Columbus, 1974—; bd. dirs. Mental Health Corps. Am. Enterprises Inc., Tallahassee, Fla. Bd. dirs. Cen. Ohio Adolescent Ctr., Columbus, 1979, YWCA, 1979-81, Columbus Area Internat. Program, 1983-85. Mem. Nat. Assn. Social Workers (sec. 1980-81), Assn. Mental Health Adminstrs., Acad. Cert. Social Workers, Met. Columbus Club, Phi Kappa Phi. Democrat. Office: N Ctrl Mental Health Svcs 1301 N High St Columbus OH 43201

BUSSEY, GEORGE DAVIS, psychiatrist; b. Salta, Argentina, Apr. 14, 1949; s. William Harold and Helen (Wygant) B.; m. Moira Savage, July 26, 1975; children: Andrew Davis, Megan Elizabeth. BS, U. Denver, 1969; MD, Ea. Va. Med. Sch., 1977; JD, U. Hawaii, 1993. Intern Eastern Va. Grad. Sch. Medicine, 1977-78; resident Ea. Va. Grad. Sch. Medicine, 1978-79, Vanderbilt U. Hosp., Nashville, 1979-81; staff psychiatrist Hawaii State Hosp., Kaneohe, 1981-82; asst. prof. dept. psychiatry U. Hawaii, Honolulu, 1982-84; dir. adult svcs. Kahi Mohala Hosp., Ewa Beach, Hawaii, 1983-89; assoc. med. dir. Queens Healthcare Plan, Honolulu, 1988-94; med. dir. Managed Care Mgmt., Inc., 1994—; clin. assoc. prof. Dept. Psychiatry U. Hawaii, Honolulu, 1990—. Mem. U. Hawaii Law Rev., 1991-93; contbr. articles to profl. jours. Fellow Am. Psychiat. Assn., Hawaii Psychiat. Soc. (treas. 1982-83, pres. 1985-87).

BUSSLER, MARY L., podiatrist; b. Washington, Oct. 3, 1953; d. Robert B. and Evelyn L. (Murrell) B. BS in Biology, George Mason U., 1978; D in Podiatric Medicine, Pa. Coll. Podiatric Medicine, Phila., 1985. Diplomate Am. Bd. Foot and Ankle Surgery. Pvt. practice Alexandria, Va., 1986—; CEO, Common Sense Shoe Co., Ltd., Alexandria, 1996—; med. cons. Footware Industries of Am., Washington, 1996—. Designer ladies' shoe. Fellow Am. Coll. Foot and Ankle Surgery; mem. Am. Coll. Sports Medicine, Va. Podiatric Med. Assn. (chmn. ethics and greivance com. 1990—). Republican. Methodist. Office: 8407 B Richmond Hwy Alexandria VA 22309

BUSSMAN, JOHN WOOD, physician, health care administrator; b. Mankato, Minn., July 4, 1924; s. A.M. and Myrtle E. (Wood) B.; m. Muriel J. Koenck, June 17, 1950; children: David, John, Sarah, James, Rebecca, Penelope. BSc, U. Minn., 1946, MB, 1947, MD, 1948. Diplomate Am. Bd. Pediatrics, Am. Bd. Pediatric Cardiology. Intern Sioux Valley Hosp., Sioux Falls, S.D., 1948; residency in pediatrics U. Minn. Hosp., Mpls., 1949-50, pediatric cardiology fellow, 1951; gen. practice medicine The Children's Clinic-Sylvan Med. Svcs., Inc., Portland, Oreg., 1953-91; clin. prof. pediatrics U. Oreg. Md. Sch.; cons. in pediatric cardiology; chief pediatrics Emanuel Hosp., 1966-69, health maintenance orgn. com. 1972; bd. dirs. Health Choice, Inc., 1983-86; chmn. Physicians' Health Network, 1982-83; med. dir. Oreg. Med. Peer Rev., 1989—, Oreg. Med. Assistance Program, 1991—; bd. dirs. Am. Med. Peer Rev. Assn. Chmn. health services adv. com. Multnomah County Commrs., 1973-77; mem. Multnomah County Health Care Commn. 1977-82. Fellow Am. Acad. Pediatrics, Am. Coll. Chest Physicians (sec. com. myopathy in childhood 1976), Am. Coll. Cardiology (Oreg. gov. 1974-77); mem. Nat. Acad. Sci. (Inst. of Medicine), Portland Acad. Pediatrics (pres. 1963), Portland Acad. Medicine, Portland Heart Club, Oreg. Heart Assn. (chmn. 1976-77, exec. com., bd. dirs. 1960-81,89-92, chmn. community service com. 1972-74, chmn. rheumatic fever commn. 1954-77, del. Am. Heart Assn. regional heart com. 1973-80, budget com., chmn. program rev. council, 1985), Oreg. Thoracic Soc. (chmn. research com. 1966), Multnomah Found. Med. Care (pres. 1970-80, med. dir. 1972-83, treas. 1980-83), Multnomah County Med. Soc. (pres. 1970, trustee 1963-71, treas .1965, sec. 1966, v.p. 1967, pres.-elect 1969, chmn. bd. censors 1971, chmn. peer rev. commn. 1971, chmn. Portland Council Hosps. liaison com. 1971), Oreg. Med. Assn. (v.p. 1972, chmn. health manpower 1972, ad hoc com. peer rev. 1972, long-range planning com. 1972, trustee 1969-80), Oreg. Found. Med. Care (bd. dirs. 1972-77), Oreg. Comprehensive Health Planning Authority (health manpower com.), Comprehensive Health Planning Assn. (chmn. project rev. com., chmn. profl. health service com., bd. dirs. 1970-77, exec. com. 1970-74), N.W. Oreg. Health Systems (health planning com. 1978-80, diagnosis and treatment subcom. 1978-80, chmn. health care tech. assessment com. 1983), HEW (Exptl. Med. Care Rev. Orgns. 1972-73), Am. Assn. Profl. Standards Rev. Orgns. (pres. 1974-77), Nat. Prof. Standards Rev. Council (chmn. 1978-80), and others. Clubs: Portland City, Multnomah Athletic. Lodge: Rotary. Office: Sylvan Med Svc Inc 5415 SW Westgate Dr Portland OR 97221-2409*

BUSTAD, LEO KENNETH, veterinary educator, college administrator; b. Stanwood, Wash., Jan. 10, 1920; s. Rasmus and Thora (Larson) B.; m. Signe Elenor Byrd, June 13, 1942; children: Leo Byrd, Karen Ann (dec.), Rebecca Lee Bustad Henson. BS, Wash. State U., 1941, MS, 1948, DVM, 1949; PhD, U. Wash., 1960. Fellow NSF, 1958; component mgr. biology lab. Hanford Labs. GE, Richland, Wash., 1949-65; dir. radiobiology lab. and comparative oncology lab. U. Calif., Davis, 1965-73, prof. radiation biology and physiology, 1965-73; prof., dean Wash. State U., Pullman, 1973-83, prof. and dean emeritus, 1983—; cons. Surgeon Gen. USAF, 1975-91; mem. NAS/NRC Food Protection Com., Washington, 1967-75, NIH Adv. Rsch. Coun., Bethesda, Md. 1975-78; chmn. NAS/NRC Com. on Vet. Med. Sci., Washington, 1975-79; vis. prof. Murdoch U., Australia, 1983, U. Wash. Sch. Medicine, 1983, U. Ga., 1984, Pacific Luth. U., 1985, U. Tenn., 1986, 88, U. Ill., 1987, La. State U., 1988; Keynote address Japanese Ann. Hosp. Assn., Tokyo, 1988; lectr. Author: Animals, Aging, and the Aged, 1980, Compassion: Our Last Great Hope, 1990; co-author Learning and Living Together, 1986; co-editor Swine in Biomed. Rsch., 1965; contbr. numerous articles to profl. jours. Chmn. Sci. Adv. Com., Holden Village, Wash., 1975-85; mem. Pullman Coun. on Aging, Wash., 1973-90. With U.S. Army, 1941-46, col. Res., ret. Recipient Award of Merit Am. Animal Hosp. Assn. 1984, Regent's Disting. Alumnus award Wash. State U., 1987, Svc. to Profession award World Small Animal Vet. Assn., 1991, Waltham Veterinary award 1996; named Hon. Mem. Am. Coll. Lab. Animal Medicine, 1982; Battelle fellow, Battelle Meml. Inst., 1983. Mem. NAS (sr. mem. inst. medicine 1988—), Am. Physiol. Soc., Am. Soc. Animal Sci., Am. Soc. Vet. Physiologists, and Pharmacologists, AVMA (Bustad Companion Animal Vet. of Yr. award), Soc. Health and Human Values, Nat. Acads. Practice, Radiation Rsch. Soc., Vet. Acad. on Disaster Medicine, World Assn. Vet. Physiologists, Pharmacologists, Biochemists, Delta Soc. (pres. 1981-88, Disting Svc. award), Phi Kappa Phi, Sigma Xi. Lutheran. Office: Wash State Univ Coll of Vet Medicine Bustad Hall 110 Pullman WA 99164-7010

BUSTANI, NANCY KURTH, counselor; b. Alamogordo, N.Mex., Feb. 7, 1945; d. George John and Carmen Magdalena (DeLaRosa) Kurth; m. Joseph Leo Bustani Jr., Mar. 22, 1965; children: Leisa, Dina, Joseph III. Bachelor's summa cum laude, Palm Beach Community Coll.; postgrad. in counseling psychology, Palm Beach Atlantic Coll., BS in Human Resources Sci., 1994. Model Norton Art Gallery, West Palm Beach, Fla., 1972-74; art tchr. Lake Park (Fla.) Bapt. Sch., 1985-92; master chef, restaurant owner Safari and Polo Club, Palm Beach, Fla., 1990-91; counselor, pres., founder Comprehensive Counseling Ctr. (formerly H.O.P.E. Ctr.), West Palm Beach, Fla., 1987—. Contbr. recipes and poetry to publs. Past pres. Women's Ministries Palm Beach Cathedral, Lake Park, Fla.; vol. ARC. Named Mrs. Lake Worth, Lake Worth (Fla.) Exchange Club, 1972. Mem. Acad. Am. Poets, Kravis Ctr. for the Performing Arts, Palm Beach C. of C., Phi Theta Kappa. Republican. Mem. Ch. of God. Home: 11232 83rd Ln N West Palm Beach FL 33412-1503 office: Bustani's Ltd 350 S County Rd Palm Beach FL 33480

BUSUTTIL, ANTHONY, forensic medicine educator; b. Rabat, Malta, Dec. 30, 1945; s. Anthony and Maria (Vassallo) B.; m. Angela Bonello, Aug. 31, 1969; children: Godwin J., Christopher R., Joseph M. MD, Royal U. Malta, 1967; DMJ, Soc. Apothecaries, London, 1981. Intern St. Luke's Hosp., Malta, 1967-69; resident Western Infirmary, Glasgow, Scotland, 1969-71; lectr. U. Glasgow, Scotland, 1969-77; sr. lectr. U. Edinburgh, Scotland, 1977-88, regius prof. forensic medicine, 1988—; chmn. European Coun. for Legal Medicine. Contbr. chpts. to books, articles to profl. jours. Fellow Royal Soc. Medicine, Royal Coll. Physicians Edinburgh, Royal Coll. Pathologists, Royal Coll. Physicians and Surgeons Glasgow. Home: 78 Hill Park Ave, Edinburgh EH4 7AL, Scotland Office: Univ Edinburgh, Teviot Pla, Edinburgh EH8 9AG, Scotland

BUSZEWSKI, BOGUSLAW ANDRZEJ, chemistry educator; b. Wrocław, Silezien, Poland, Sept. 28, 1951; s. Antoni Jozef and Waleria (Trybula) B.; m. Tadeusza Pastuszak,Apr. 27, 1982; children: Marcin, Magdalena. MSc, U. Marie Curie Sklodovska, Lublin, Poland, 1982; PhD, Slovak Tech. U., Bratislava, Czechoslovakia, 1986, DSc, 1992. Lic. chem. engr. Asst. Marie Curie Sklodovska U., Lublin, 1974-83, adj., 1986-89; Humboldt fellow Tübingen U., 1989-91; vis. prof. Kent (Ohio) State U., 1992-94; head dept., prof. Nicholas Copernicus U., Torun, Poland, 1994—; Tempus fellow Eindhoven (Holland) U., 1991-92, Leeds U., Eng., 1994-95; head postgrad. study Marie Curie Sklodovska U., Lublin, 1989-94, Nicolas Copernicus, Torun, 1994—; chmn. symposium Nicolas Copernicus U., Torun, 1994—. Contbr. articles to internat. jours.; patentee in field. Recipient Gold Cross, Warsaw, Poland, 1986. Mem. Polish Chem. Soc., Polish Acad. Sci. (com. analytical chemistry 1996, award 1987), Chem. Soc. U.K. Roman Catholic. Office: Nicholas Copernicus U, Dept Environ Chemistry, PL-87100 Torun Poland

BUTKUS, DONALD EUGENE, nephrologist, medicine educator; b. Binghamton, N.Y., Oct. 9, 1934; s. John Geddy and Mary Margaret (Koval) B.; divorced; children: Allison, Brian, Christine; m. Nancy Ellen Romine, Sept. 14, 1984. BA, Cornell U., 1956; MD, Albany (N.Y.) Med. Coll., 1960. Diplomate Am. Bd. Internal Medicine, Am. Bd. Nephrology. Commd. 2d lt. U.S. Army, 1959, advanced through grades to col.; intern Brooke Army Med. Ctr. U.S. Army, San Antonio, 1960-61; resident Madigan Army Med. Ctr. U.S. Army, Tacoma, Wash., 1961-64; internist and chief nephrology various med. facilities U.S. Army, U.S. and Vietnam, 1964-81; dir. medicine Walter Reed Army Inst. Research U.S. Army, Washington, 1981-87; ret. U.S. Army, 1987; chief nephrology Jackson (Miss.) VA Med. Ctr., 1987-88; prof. medicine, med. dir. transplantation U. Miss. Med. Ctr., Jackson, 1988—; cons. nephrology U.S. Army Surgeon Gen., Washington, 1976-87; coord. nephrology Uniforme Svcs. Univ. Health Sci., Bethesda, Md., 1976-78. Contbr. numerous articles to profl. jours. Active on research com. Rocky Mountain Kidney Found., Denver, 1972-76. Recipient nephrology fellowship U. Colo. Med. Ctr., Denver, 1970-72. Fellow ACP; mem. Am. Soc. Nephrology, Internat. Soc. Nephrology, Am. Fedn. Clin. Rsch., Am. Physiol. Soc., Am. Soc. Transplant Physicians, Theta Chi (chaplain Cornell U. chpt. 1955-56). Republican. Mem. Christian Ch. (Disciples of Christ). Office: U Miss Med Ctr 2500 N State St Jackson MS 39216-4500

BUTLER, BRIAN, podiatric physician; b. N.Y.C., Mar. 30, 1949; s. William Leland and Mary Theresa (O'Leary) B.; m. Catherine Mary Collins; children: Irene, Matthew, Beth. BA, St. Francis Coll., Bklyn., 1970; MA, Manhattan Coll., Riverdale, N.Y., 1973; D in Podiatric Medicine, N.Y. Coll. Podiatric Medicine, 1981; fellow advanced mgmt. program for clinicians, NYU, 1987; postgrad., Columbia U., 1994—. Lic. podiatrist, N.Y., Va.; diplomate Am. Bd. Podiatric Orthopedics. Asst. to pres. govt. affairs N.Y. Coll. Podiatric Medicine, N.Y.C., 1979-82, assoc. prof. cmty. medicine, 1988—; resident in surgery Joint Diseases North Gen. Hosp., N.Y.C., 1982; chief sect. podiatry/foot surgery dept. surgery Bklyn. Hosp. Ctr., 1982—; adj. asst. prof. medicine N.Y. Med. Coll., Valhalla, 1984—; asst. clin. prof. surgery NYU Sch. Medicine, 1996—; chmn., pres. adv. bd. N.Y. Coll. Podiatric Medicine, 1991, chmn. curriculum reform commn., 1992. Author: Woodrow Wilson's Entry Upon the American Political Scene, 1973; contbr. articles to profl. jours. Pres., chmn. bd. U.S. Cath. Hist. Soc., N.Y.C., 1984—, EN EL Inc., Med. Mission to Guatemala, Roman Cath. Diocese of Bklyn., 1992—; bd. dirs. Rachmiel Levine Diabetes Found., Westchester County Med. Ctr., N.Y., 1984-90, Angel Guardian Home for Children, Bklyn., 1988—; bd. trustees Cath. Charities, Roman Cath. Diocese of Bklyn., 1991; past chmn. Bishop's Lay Com. for Charity. Named Outstanding Young Man in Am., U.S. Jaycees, Washington, 1981, Knight of Malta Sovereign, Mil. Order Malta, Rome, 1982; recipient The Franciscan Spirit award St. Francis Coll., Bklyn., 1990, Pub. Svc. award N.Y.C. Transit Police Dept./Police Benevolent Assn., 1994. Fellow Am. Coll. Foot Orthopedists; mem. Am. Podiatric Med. Assn., N.Y. State Podiatric Med. Assn. (peer rev. and pub. affairs and legis. coms., Disting. Svc. award student chpt. 1981), N.Y. Athletic Club, Pi Mu Delta (former nat. pres.). Democrat. Home: 77 Sagamore Rd Bronxville NY 10708-1506 Office: Bklyn Hosp Ctr Sect Podiatry/Foot Surgery 121 DeKalb Ave Brooklyn NY 11201

BUTLER, BYRON CLINTON, obstetrician, gynecologist; b. Carroll, Iowa, Aug. 10, 1918; s. Clinton John and Blance (Prall) B.; m. Jo Ann Nicolls; children: Marilyn, John Byron, Barbara, Denise; 1 stepdau., Marrianne. MD, Columbia Coll. Physicians and Surgeons, 1943; ScD, Columbia U., 1952; G.G. grad. gemologist, Gemol. Inst. Am., 1986. Diplomate Am. Bd. Ob/Gyn. Intern Columbia Presbyn. Med. Ctr.; resident Sloane Hosp. for Women; instr. Columbia Coll. Physicians and Surgeons, 1950-53; dir. Butler Rsch. Found., Phoenix, 1953-86, pres., 1970—; ret. as gyn. surgeon, 1989; pres. World Gems/G.S.G., Scottsdale, Ariz., 1979—, World Gems Software, 1988, World Gems Jewelry, 1990—; cosmologist, jewelry designer Extra-Terrestrial-Alien Jewelry & Powerful Personal Talismans, 1992—, 3rd Mellineum Line of Tektite Jewelry, 1994—. Patentee in field. Bd. dirs. Heard Mus., Phoenix, 1965-74; founder Dr. Byron C. Butler, G.G., Fund for Inclusion Research, Gemol. Inst. Am., Santa Monica, Calif., 1987. Served to capt. M.C. AUS, 1944-46. Grantee Am. Cancer Soc., 1946-50, NIH, 1946-50, 50-53. Fellow AAAS; mem. Am. Gemstones Trade Assn., Ariz. Jewelers Assn., Mufon, Mutual UFO Networks. Home: #20 77 E Missouri Phoenix AZ 85012-1380

BUTLER, CHARLES HENRY, hospital administrator; b. N.Y.C., Oct. 12, 1932; s. Charles Henry and Theresa Edith (Simmons) B.; m. Lois Evelyn Belle, Jan. 14, 1956; children: Charles Henry, Craig Aron. AAS, N.Y. City Community Coll., 1960; BS, L.I. U., 1962; MPA, NYU, 1970. Advt. claims adjuster N.Y. Times, N.Y.C., 1950-65; br. office mgr. Bklyn. Union Gas Co., 1965-67; corp. pers. specialist Endicott (N.Y.) Johnson Corp., 1967-69; sr. indsl. rels. rep. Kennecott Copper Corp., N.Y.C., 1969-70; dir. pers. N.Y.C. Health & Hosps. Corp., 1970-89, Greenpoint Hosp., 1970-75, Queens Hosp. Ctr., 1975-78, Cumberland Hosp., Bklyn., 1978-83; evening adminstr. Woodhull Med. and Mental Health Ctr., Bklyn., 1983-89; dep. commr. Dr. Robert L. Yeager Health Ctr., Pomona, N.Y., 1989-95; mem. faculty Marymount Coll., Tarrytown, N.Y., 1975-76. Contbr. article to profl. jours. Pres. PTA, N.Y.C., 1966-67; chmn. adv. com. Citizens Affirmative Action, N.Y.C., 1974-76; state adviser U.S. Congl. Adv. Bd.; lay reader St. Paul's Episcopal Ch., Spring Valley, N.Y. With USNR, 1953-55, USAFR, 1966-88, N.Y. Air NG, 1988-92., ret. Recipient Certificate of Appreciation N.Y.C. Bd. Edn., 1967, award N.Y. State Dept. Mental Hygiene, 1975. Mem. NAACP (life), Am. Mgmt. Assn., Res. Officers Assn., Soc. Advancement Mgmt., NYU Alumni Assn., 100 Black Men, Coun. Concerned Black Execs., N.Y. Orgn. Devel. Network, Assn. Mil. Surgeons U.S., Am. Soc. for Quality Control (chmn. Tappan-Zee br. 1993-95). Presbyterian. Home: 6 Foxcroft Dr Nanuet NY 10954-1211 Office: Ramapo Manor Nursing Ctr PO Box 248 Suffern NY 10901-0248

BUTLER, FREDERICK GEORGE, retired drug company executive; b. Greenwich, Conn., Mar. 25, 1919; s. Harold Nassau and Rosa (Rhinhart) B.; m. Sarah Lou Allred, Sept. 23, 1945; children: Pamela Sue, Frederick Houston. AB, Middlebury (Vt.) Coll., 1941; MBA, Columbia U., 1947. CPA, N.Y. With Price Waterhouse & Co. (C.P.A.'s), 1941-42, 47-49; with McKesson & Robbins, Inc., N.Y.C., 1949-63; asst. comptroller McKesson & Robbins, Inc., 1952-61, comptroller, 1961-63; controller Bristol-Myers Co., N.Y.C., 1963-66; v.p., controller Bristol-Myers Co., 1966-69, v.p. ops, 1970-76. Pioneered developement of bar code (compatible universal product code and nat. drug code) for supermarket automated checkout scanning and inventory control. Village mayor, Briarcliff Manor, N.Y., 1969-71. Served to comdr. USNR, 1942-46, 51-52. Mem. Fin. Execs. Inst. Golf Club at Marco (Fla.), Fairfield Mountains Club (Bald Mountain and Apple Valley, N.C.), Pres.'s Club, Hillsdale (Mich.) Coll., Chi Psi. Congregationalist. Home: 58 N Collier Blvd Apt 2103 Marco Island FL 34145

BUTLER, GRACE CAROLINE, medical administrator; b. Lima, Peru, Dec. 19, 1937; (parents Am. citizens); d. Everett Lyle and Mary Isabella (Sloatman) Gage; m. William Langdon Butler, Dec. 28, 1961; children: Mary Dyer, William Langdon Jr. AA, Stephens Coll., 1957; BS in Nursing,

Columbia U., 1960; postgrad., Union County Coll., 1984. Head nurse N.Y. State Psychiat. Inst., N.Y.C., 1960-61; clin. instr. Columbia U., N.Y.C., 1960-61; staff nurse, educator Vis. Nurse Service, Summit, N.J., 1962-63; health adminstr. Eagle Island Girl Scout Camp, Tupper Lake, N.Y., 1964; evening supr. Ashbrook Nursing Home, Scotch Plains, N.J., 1968-72; teaching asst. Scotch Plains-Fanwood (N.J.) Sch. System, 1975-78; staff nurse Westfield (N.J.) Med. Group, 1980-82, head nurse, 1982-83, supr., 1983-84; office adminstr. Harris S. Vernick, MD, PA, Westfield, 1984-86, corp. v.p., office adminstr., 1986-88; corp. v.p., office adminstr. Assocs. in Medicine, Westfield, 1988-90; pvt. researcher, 1990—; diabetes educator Boehringer Manneheim Diagnostics, 1984—, Eli Lilly and Co., Indpls., 1984—; microbiologist tester Med. Technol. Corp., Somerset, N.J., 1984—; computer advisor Cordis Corp., Miami, 1985—. Asst. leader Girl Scouts U.S., Fanwood, N.J., 1970-73; religious educator All Saints Episcopal Ch., Scotch Plains, 1967-82; bd. dirs. PTA, Scotch Plains and Fanwood, 1973-79; mem. altar guild All Saints Episcopal Ch., Scotch Plains, 1994—. Mem. League For Ednl. Advancement for Registered Nurses, Am. Soc. of Notaries, Columbia U./Presbyn. Hosp. Sch. of Nursing Alumni Assn. Republican. Episcopalian. Home: 125 Russell Rd Fanwood NJ 07023-1063

BUTLER, IAN JOHN, neurologist; b. Adelaide, Australia, Sept. 19, 1941; came to U.S., 1972; s. John Alfred and Susan Pearl (Matters) B.; m. Patricia Mary Gordon, Feb. 28, 1969; children: Sarah, Katherine, Philip. MBBS, U. Adelaide, 1964. Diplomate Am. Bd. Psychiatry and Neurology. Resident Adelaide (Australia) Childrens Hosp., 1966-67; med. registrar Royal Childrens Hosp., Victoria, Australia, 1968; fellow neurology U. Melbourne, Victoria, 1969; sr. house officer Hosp. for Sick Children, London, 1970; registrar U. Wales Hosp., Cardiff, 1971; resident neurology, asst. prof. Johns Hopkins Univ. Hosp., Balt., 1972-76; assoc. prof. neurology U. Tex., Houston, 1976-79, prof. neurology and pediatrics, 1979—; prof. pediatrics dept. M.D. Anderson Cancer Ctr., Houston, 1980—; assoc. prof. Grad. Sch. Biomed. Scis., U. Tex. Health Sci. Ctr., Houston, 1978—; cons., dir. neuromuscular clinic Shrine Hosp., Houston; lectr. in field. Mem. editl. bd. Jour. Child Neurology, 1987—, assoc. editor, 1990—; contbr. articles to profl. jours. Chmn. prof. adv. com. Ctr. for Retarded, Inc., 1981—, bd. govs. mem., 1981—. Grantee Huntington Chorea Found., 1977-79, NSF, 1978, March of Dimes, 1978-80, Am. Parkinson Disease Assn., 1980-83, Epilepsy Ctr. Baylor Coll. Medicine, 1984-86, 88-93, Brandt Family Found., 1986, Meadows Found., 1986-91, Muscular Dystrophy Assn., 1988-90, 90-91, 91-93, NIH, 1989-94, 91-94, Shriner Hosp. for Crippled Children, 1990-93, 93-94, 95-97, 96-99, NASA, 1991-93. Fellow Royal Soc. Medicine, Royal Australasian Coll. Physicians; mem. AAAS, Am. Neurol. Assn., Assn. Rsch. in Nervous and Mental Disease, Am. Acad. Neurology, Soc. Neurosci., Internat. Child Neurology Assn., Child Neurology Soc., N.Y. Acad. Scis., Tex. Med. Assn., Harris County Med. Soc., Houston Pediatric Soc., Houston Neurol. Soc., Alpha Omega Alpha. Episcopalian. Home: 2200 Glen Haven Blvd Houston TX 77030 Office: Univ Tex Dept Neurology 6431 Fannin St Ste 7044 Houston TX 77030-1501

BUTLER, JAVED, internist; b. Karachi, Sindh, Pakistan, Oct. 4, 1965; came to U.S., 1991; s. Abdur Rehman and Sharifa (Banu) B. Higher secondary cert. in Biology, Adamjee Sci. Coll., Karachi, Pakistan, 1983; MBBS in Medicine, Aga Khan U., Karachi, Pakistan, 1990. Diplomate Am. Bd. Internal Medicine; lic. MD, Conn. Intern dept. internal medicine/primary care Yale U. Sch. Medicine, New Haven, 1991-92, jr. asst. resident, 1992-93, sr. asst. resident, 1993-94, chief med. resident, instr. medicine, 1994-95; fellow in cardiovascular scis. Vanderbilt U., Nashville, 1995—; mem. residence rev. com. Yale Internal Medicine/Primary Care Residency, 1992-95. Recipient Pres.'s scholarship for Outstanding Performance in Med. Sch., 1989, Second award for Rsch. Presentation, Aga Khan U., 1990, Second award for Poster Presentations at Spring Sci. Session of Conn. Chpt. Am. Coll. Physician, 1993, First award for Assoc. Rsch., 1993. Mem. AMA, Am. Coll. Physicians (First award for assoc. rsch. Conn. chpt. 1994, chmn. Conn. chpt. scientific com. 1994-95). Home: 734 Shadowood Dr Nashville TN 37205

BUTLER, ROBERT ANDREWS, clinical psychologist; b. Lancaster, Calif., June 19, 1955; s. Robert Andrews and Ines Gertrude (Ottaviano) B.; m. Nadine Suzanne Pastor, Dec. 27, 1975; 1 child, Alex Robert. BA, Long Beach (Calif.) State U., 1977; MA, Dominguez Hills State U., 1979; PhD, Washington State U., 1983. Cert. Am Bd. Med. Psychotherapy; lic. psychologist, Wis. Dir. psychology Brown County Mental Health, Green Bay, Wis., 1983-89; pvt. practice psychology Green Bay, 1984-90; clin. dir. anxiety and affective disorders Fox Valley Hosp., Green Bay, 1989-90; dir. divsn. psychology Bellin Psychiat. Ctr., Green Bay, 1991-93; adj. prof. psychology U. Wis., Green Bay, 1983-86; cons. Family Violence Ctr., Green Bay, 1984, Whitman County (Wash.) Mental Health, 1981, St. Vincent Hosp. Sleep Disorders Ctr., 1989—. Contbr. articles to profl. jours. Fulbright fellow. Mem. Am. Psychol. Assn., Wis. Psychol. Assn., Syndicate Nat. Des Psychologues Francais (hon.). Home: 3740 Libal St Green Bay WI 54301-1253 Address: 2020 Riverside Dr Green Bay WI 54301-2300

BUTLER, ROBERT NEIL, gerontologist, psychiatrist, writer, educator; b. N.Y.C., Jan. 21, 1927; s. Fred and Easter (Dikeman) B.; m. Diane McLaughlin, Sept. 2, 1950; children: Ann Christine, Carole Melissa, Cynthia Lee; m. Myrna I. Lewis, May 17, 1975; 1 dau., Alexandra Nicole. BA, Columbia U., 1949, MD, 1953; hon. degree, U. So. Calif., U. Gothenburg, Sweden. Intern St. Lukes Hosp., N.Y.C., 1953-54; resident U. Calif. Langley Porter Clinic, 1954-55; resident NIMH, 1955-56, research psychiatrist, 1955-62; founder geriatric unit Chestnut Lodge, 1958, adminstr., 1958-59; research psychiatrist Washington Sch. Psychiatry, 1962-76; dir. Nat. Inst. on Aging, NIH, 1976-82; Brookdale prof. geriatics and adult devel. Mt. Sinai Sch. Medicine, N.Y.C., 1982—; dir. Internat. Longevity Ctr., 1990—; mem. faculty George Washington U. Med. Sch., Washington, 1962-82, Howard U. Sch. Medicine; cons. NIMH, 1967-76, U.S. Senate Spl. Com. on Aging. Author: (with others) Human Aging, 1963, (with Myrna I. Lewis) Aging and Mental Health, 1973, 4th edit., 1991, Why Survive? Being Old in America, 1975, Sex After Sixty, 1976, (with A. Bearn) The Aging Process, 1985, (with Herbert Gleason) Productive Aging, 1985, (with Myrna I. Lewis) Love and Sex After Forty, 1986, Modern Biological Theories of Aging, 1987, Human Aging Research, 1988, The Promise of Productive Aging, 1990, Who is Responsible for My Old Age?, 1993, (with Myrna I. Lewis) Love and Sex After Sixty, 3d edit., 1993, (with Jacob Brody) Delaying the Onset of Late-Life Dysfunction, 1995; editor: Geriatrics; mem. editl. bd. Jour. Geriatric Psychiatry. Sec. Nat. Ballet of Washington, 1962-75; chmn. D.C. Advisory Commn. on Aging, 1969-72; bd. dirs. Nat. Council on Aging, Mildred and Claude Pepper Found. Served with U.S. Maritime Service, 1945-47. Recipient Pulitzer prize for gen. nonfiction, 1976, Leo Laks award, 1976; McIntyre award, 1977, Allied-Signal award; others. Fellow Am. Psychiat. Assn., Am. Geriatrics Soc. (founding mem.); mem. Group for Advancement Psychiatry (trustee 1974-76), Gerontol. Soc., Forum for Profls. and Execs. (founding). Clubs: Cosmos (Washington); Century (N.Y.C.). Office: Mt Sinai Sch Medicine 1 Gustave L Levy Pl New York NY 10029-6504

BUTLER, STUART RAYMOND, neurophysiologist; b. Cambridge, Eng., June 17, 1941. MA, Cambridge U., 1963; PhD, London U., 1967. Rsch. fellow Calif. Inst. Tech., Pasadena, 1967-68; sr. lectr. Birmingham (Eng.) U., 1968-88; rsch. dir. Burden Inst., Bristol, Eng., 1988—; sec. 11th Internat. Congress EEG, London, 1985; vis. prof. U. Wales Eng., 1989, U. Ancana, Italy, 1993, inst. sci. and tech. U. Manchester, 1994; mng. dir. Burden Neurosci. Ltd., Bristol, Eng., 1991—. Editor various books on neurophysiology; contbr. articles on neurosci. rsch. topics to profl. jours. Mem. Anat. Soc., European Brain and Behaviour Soc., Brit. Soc. Clin. Neurophysiology (coun. mem. 1974-86, 90—, sec. 1979-85). Office: Burden Neurol Inst, Stoke Ln, Stapleton, Bristol BS16 1QT, England

BUTLER, VINCENT PAUL, JR., physician, educator; b. Jersey City, Feb. 16, 1929; s. Vincent Paul and Ruth Eilene (Lynch) B. A.B., St. Peter's Coll., 1949; M.D., Columbia U., 1954. Intern Presbyn. Hosp., N.Y.C., 1954-55; resident Presbyn. Hosp., 1955-56, 58-59, asst. physician, 1963-68, asst. attending physician, 1968-71, asso. attending physician, 1971-74, attending physician, 1974—; trainee clin. immunology U. Rochester Med. Center, 1959-61; research fellow immunochemistry dept. microbiology Columbia U., 1961-63, asst. prof. medicine, 1963-70, assoc. prof., 1970-74, prof., 1974—; asst. vis. physician 1st med. div. Bellevue Hosp., N.Y.C., 1963-68, Harlem Hosp., N.Y.C., 1968-88; mem. VA Merit Rev. Bd. in Immunology, 1974-77, chmn., 1976-77; mem. immunol. sci. study sect. NIH, 1979-83, chmn., 1980-83. Mem. rsch. com. Arthritis Found., 1986-91, chmn., 1989-91; bd. trustees St. Peter's Prep. Sch., Jersey City, 1985-93, chmn., 1991-93. Lt. M.C. USN, 1956-58. Helen Hay Whitney Found. fellow, 1960-63; Arthritis Found. investigator, 1963-68; Josiah Macy, Jr. Found. scholar dept. zoology Univ. Coll., London, 1979-80; recipient Research Career Devel. award NIH, 1968-73; Joseph Mather Smith prize Columbia U. Coll. Physicians and Surgeons, 1973; Irma T. Hirschl Charitable Trust Career Scientist, 1973-78. Fellow AAAS; mem. Assn. Am. Physicians, Am. Soc. Clin. Investigation, Am. Assn. Immunologists, Am. Soc. Pharmacology and Exptl. Therapeutics, Am. Heart Assn., N.Y. Heart Assn., Am. Fedn. Clin. Research, Harvey Soc. Roman Catholic. Home: 301 E 66th St Apt 6B New York NY 10021-6205 Office: 630 W 168th St New York NY 10032-3702

BUTLER, WILLIAM THOMAS, college chancellor, physician, educator; b. Boston, Aug. 10, 1932; s. Albert Quigg and Elizabeth West (Viskniskki) B.; m. Marilou Beutel, Apr. 26, 1957; children: Marilyn West, Thomas Charles, Robin Eileen; m. Carol Ann Pike, Nov. 23, 1977. A.B., Oberlin Coll., 1954; M.D., Western Res. U., 1958; grad. program for health systems mgmt., Harvard U., 1974, A.M.P., 1979. Intern and asst. resident in internal medicine Mass. Gen. Hosp., Boston, 1958-61; clin. fellow in medicine Mass. Gen. Hosp., 1960-61, resident in internal medicine, 1964-65; research fellow in bacteriology and immunology Harvard Med. Sch., 1960-61; clin. assoc. Lab. Clin. Investigations, Nat. Inst. Allergy and Infectious Diseases, NIH, Bethesda, Md., 1961-62; chief clin. assoc. Lab. Clin. Investigations, Nat. Inst. Allergy and Infectious Diseases, NIH, 1962-63, clin. investigator, 1963-64, acting head clin. immunology sect., 1965-56; asst. prof. Baylor Coll. Medicine, Houston, 1966-68; assoc. prof. Baylor Coll. Medicine, 1968-71, prof. microbiology and immunology, prof. internal medicine, 1971—, asso. dean, 1973-74, dean admissions, 1974-77, acting exec. v.p., 1976-77, exec. v.p., dean, 1977-79, pres., 1979-96, chancellor, 1996—; mem. spl. med. adv. group VA, 1981-91, chmn., 1984-91; bd. dirs. C.R. Bard Inc., Browning-Ferris Industries, Lyondell Petrochem. Co. Hon. trustee Gulf Coast Regional Blood Ctr.; mem. forward planning com. Tex. Med. Ctr., 1981-96; bd. dirs. South Main Ctr. Assn., exec. com., 1980-94, chmn., 1989-91, coun. advisors, 1995—; mem. nat. adv. bd. Amigos de las Americas; past assoc. chmn. key group United Way Campaign, Flagship Div., group chmn., 1990; mem. Houston Econ. Summit Host Com., 1990; bd. dirs. Blvd. Oaks Civic Assn., 1982-85, Sci. Engring. Fair of Houston, United Way Tex. Gulf Coast, trustee, 1994—; nat. bd. dirs. Points of Light Found., 1995—; mem. coordinating bd. Tex. Coll. and Univ. System, Health Professions Edn. Adv. Com., 1984-95, chmn., 1988-95; bd. govs. Houston Forum, 1996—; mem. Tex. Sesquicentennial Celebration Com., 1984-85; mem. bd. edn. blue ribbon com. Houston Ind. Sch. Dist., 1986; adv. bd. Covenant House Tex., 1987—; HISD City-Wide Com., 1987; vice-chmn. health svcs. U.S. Savs. Bond Program. Mem. AMA, Am. Assn. Immunologists, Am. Soc. Clin. Investigation, N.Y. Acad. Scis., Am. Soc. Microbiology, Soc. Exptl. Biology and Medicine, Infectious Diseases Soc. Am., So. Soc. Clin. Investigation, Transplantation Soc., Inst. Medicine of Nat. Acad. Scis., Assn. Acad. Health Ctrs., Assn. Am. Med. Colls. (chmn. coun. deans 1987-89, adminstrv. bd. 1983-90, exec. coun. 1984-92, mgmt. edn. programs planning com. 1986—, chmn.-elect 1989-90, chmn. 1990-91, project 3000x2000 implementation com. 1991—, chmn. 1992), Tex. Club Internists (hon.), Harris County Med. Soc., Houston Acad. Medicine, Tex. Med. Assn. (adv. coun. med. edn.), Houston C. of C. (bd. dirs. 1981-82, 83-89), Greater Houston Partnership, Inc. (bd. dirs. 1989, 92—), Points of Light Found., Houston Ptnrs. Com. (co-chmn. 1991-92), Houston Mus. Nat. Sci. (ex officio 1989—), Sigma Xi, Alpha Omega Alpha. Methodist. Clubs: River Oaks Country, Heritage, Doctors' (Houston) (bd. govs. 1980-84, pres. 1982), Harvard Bus. Sch. of Houston, Forum of Houston (bd. govs. 1983-92). Office: Baylor College of Medicine One Baylor Pl Houston TX 77030*

BUTNER, ROBERT WESTBROOK, ophthalmic surgeon, educator; b. Ft. Oglethorpe, Ga., July 5, 1942; s. Wendell Boise and Helen Salkeld (Taylor) B.; m. Mary Carol Steib, Aug. 20, 1966. BA cum laude, Rice U., 1964; MD, Johns Hopkins U., 1968. Diplomate Nat. Bd. Med. Examiners, Am. Bd. Ophthalmology. Intern Charity Hosp. (Tulane), New Orleans, 1968-69; resident ophthalmology Baylor Coll. Medicine, Houston, 1972-75, fellow in retinal surgery, 1975-76, clin. instr., 1977-83, clin. asst. prof., 1983-92, clin. assoc. prof., 1992—; pvt. practice ophthalmology Houston, 1977—. Contbr. articles to profl. jours. Col. U.S. Army, 1969-72, 91. Decorated parachutist badge Republic of China army, 1972, Italian army, 1986, master parachutist badge U.S. Army, 1986. Fellow ACS, Internat. Coll. Surgeons, Am. Acad. Ophthalmology; mem. AMA, Internat. Soc. Geog. Ophthalmology, Spl. Forces Assn., Tex. Ophthal. Assn., Tex. Med. Assn., Houston Ophthal. Soc., Harris County Med. Soc., Phi Beta Kappa. Office: McPherson Assocs 6560 Fannin St Ste 2200 Houston TX 77030-2707

BUTO, TIM TADASHI, orthodontist; b. L.A., June 25, 1956. BA in Biology, Williams Coll., 1978; DDS, U. So. Calif., L.A., 1982, cert. orthodontics, 1984. Ptnr. Redmond & Buto Orthodontic Dental Group, Oxnard and Thousand Oaks, Calif., 1984—. Mem. Omicron Kappa Upsilon. Office: 451 W Gonzales Rd #320 Oxnard CA 93030

BUTOUR, JEAN-LUC, molecular neuropharmacology researcher; b. Choisy-le-Roi, France, Nov. 17, 1946; s. Guy and Genevieve (Conche) B.; m. Odette Tardivel, Apr. 3, 1971; children: Caroline, Nathalie, Philippe. M., U. Orsay (France), 1969; PhD, U. Toulouse (France), 1980. Researcher Ctr. Nat. de la Recherche Scientifique, Toulouse, 1973—. Contbr. rsch. articles to profl. jours. With French mil., 1971-72. Mem. Am. Chem. Soc. Office: CNRS Inst. Pharmacologie, et de Biologie Structurale, 205 Rte de Narbonne, 31077 Toulouse France

BUTRIN, JOANN ELIZABETH, nurse; b. Canton, Ohio, Aug. 31, 1950; d. Geroge and Evelyn Winafred (Kuepfer) B. RN, Geisinger Sch. Nursing, 1971; BSN, Evangel Coll., 1975; MSN, Pa. State U., 1982; PhD, U. Minn., 1990. Supr. Allied Rehab. Ctr., Scranton, Pa., 1973-74; dir. med. svcs. Assemblies of God Fgn. Missions, Zaire, 1974-85; mem. adminstrv. staff Health Care Ministries, Lakeland, Fla., 1986—; cons. Health Care Ministries Internat., Lakeland, 1986—. Author: You Can Be Healthy, 1991; contbr. articles to profl. jours. Mem. Transcultural Nursing Soc., Bicultural Nursing Ci. Assn., Sigma Theta Tau. Republican. Assemblies of God. Home: 707 Carpenters Way Apt 38 Lakeland FL 33809-3913 Office: Health Care Ministries PO Box 90819 Lakeland FL 33804-0819

BUTROS, FRANK A., hospital laboratory administrator; b. Aug. 1, 1944; s. Aziz and Anyes (Youna) B.; m. Joyce D. Tripp, Nov. 19, 1972; 1 child, Heather K. BS, Detroit Inst. Tech., 1969; MS, Wayne State U., 1974; MBA, Fla. Inst. Tech., 1987. Cert. med. technologist. Chief med. technologist St. Joseph Hosp., Mount Clemens, Mich., 1969-75, adminstrv. dir., 1975-89; adminstr. Damon/Detroit Med. Ctr., 1990-95; divsn. adminstr. divsn. lab. medicine and pathology M.D. Anderson Cancer Ctr., Houston, 1995—; adj. faculty Cen. Mich. U., Mount Pleasant, 1987—, Macomb Community Coll., Mount Clemens, 1989—. Roman Catholic. Home: 3031 Bissonnet Houston TX 77005

BUTTERFIELD, PATRICK THOMAS, psychiatrist; b. Buffalo, Nov. 25, 1945; s. William John and Maybelle (Anderson) B. BA, Ohio State U., 1966, MD, 1969. Diplomate Am. Bd. Psychiatry and Neurology. Intern San Francisco Gen. Hosp., 1969-70; resident in psychiatry Dartmouth Med. Sch., Hanover, 1970-71, Letterman Army Med. Ctr., San Francisco, 1973-75; resident in child psychiatry Letterman Army Med. Ctr./Langley Porter Inst., San Francisco, 1975-77; chief dept. psychiatry Moncrief Army Hosp., Columbia, S.C., 1977-78; med. dir. McFarland Mental Health Ctr., Springfield, Ill., 1978-81; dir. residency tng. William S. Hall Psychiat. Inst., Columbia, 1981-82, dir. child psychiat. svc., 1982-86; pvt. practice psychiatry Columbia, 1986—; svc. chief W.S. Hall Psychiat. Inst., Columbia, 1995—; prof. psychiatry U. S.C., Columbia, 1981—. Fellow Am. Psychiat. Assn., Am. Acad. Child and Adolescent Psychiatry; mem. Am. Coll. Mental Health Adminstrn. Office: Ste 10B 1301 Taylor St Columbia SC 29201-2922

BUTTERWORTH, BYRON E., toxicologist; b. Salt Lake City, Dec. 9, 1941; s. Edwin J. and Dorothy (Leetham) B.; m. Amy Johnson; children: Jeffrey, Wendy, Kimberly, Chad. BS, Brigham Young U., 1968; PhD, U. Wis., 1972. Rsch. staff DuPont, Wilmington, Del., 1972-75; chief molecular biology DuPont's Haskell Lab., Newark, Del., 1975-77; head genetic toxicology CIIT, Research Triangle Park, N.C., 1977-88, sr. scientist, 1989—. Contbr. over 100 articles on chem. carcinogenesis to scientific publs.; editl. bd. Mutation Rsch., 1994—. Office: CIIT PO Box 12137 Research Triangle Park NC 27709

BUTTERWORTH, JANE ROGERS FITCH, physician; b. Louisville, Aug. 3, 1937; d. Howard Mercer and Jane Rogers (McCaw) Fitch; m. William Butterworth, Sept. 5, 1958 (div. Feb. 1968); children: Jane Rogers, William Stoddard, Robert Mercer, Benjamin Richard Mallory, Anne Lewis. BS, U. Louisville, 1971, MD, 1974. Rotating intern Humana Hosp. Audubon (formerly St. Joseph's Hosp.), Louisville, 1974-75, resident in radiology, 1975-76; resident in phys. medicine and rehab. Frasier Rehab. (formerly Inst. of Phys. Medicine and Rehab.), Louisville, 1976-80; staff physiatrist Rockford (Ill.) Meml. Hosp., 1980-83; clin. instr. Rockford Sch. Medicine, 1980-83; med. dir. phys. medicine and rehab. Western Res. Care System, Youngstown, Ohio, 1983-86, mem. teaching staff residency program, 1983-96; clin. instr. Northeastern Ohio U. Coll. of Medicine, Rootstown, 1983—, chairperson phys. medicine subcoun., mem. acad. rev. and promotions com., 1985-95; adj. faculty Youngstown State U., 1984—; regional med. advisor Rehab. div. Ohio Indsl. Commn., Youngstown, 1985—; mem. admissions com. Northeastern Ohio U. Coll. Medicine, 1988; cons. psychiatrist Vista Ctr., Lisbon, Ohio, 1994—. Mem. choir St. John's Episcopal Ch., Youngstown, vestrywoman, 1989-91; bd. dirs. Goodwill Industries, Youngstown, 1985-92, advisor rehab. divsn., 1986—, bd. advisors, 1993—; mem. med. rev. staff Hospice, Youngstown, 1984—; dir. med. svcs. Easter Seals Soc., Youngstown, 1987—; mem. med. bd. pub. TV, Youngstown, 1986—; violinist Youngstown State U. Cmty. Orch., 1985; mem. Youngstown Musica Sacra, 1989—; regional med. advisor Rehab. Divsn. Ohio Indsl. Commn., 1984-94, 95. Recipient Community Svc. award St. John's Episcopal Ch., 1988. Mem. AMA, Ohio Med. Assn., Mahoning County Med. Soc. (coun. 1989, alt. del to Ohio Med. Assn. 1990, pres. 1992), Ky. Med. Assn., Jefferson County Med. Soc., Am. Congress Rehab. Medicine, Colonial Dames Soc. Am., Phi Beta, Chi Delta Phi, Kappa Alpha Theta. Republican. Home: 186 Rockland Dr Boardman OH 44512-5921 Office: Western Res Care System Southside Hosp 345 Oak Ave Youngstown OH 44512-6124

BUTTERWORTH, ROBERT ROMAN, psychologist, researcher, media therapist; b. Pittsfield, Mass., June 24, 1946; s. John Leon and Martha Helen (Roman) B. BA, SUNY, 1972; MA, Marist Coll., 1975; PhD in Clin. Psychology, Calif. Grad. Inst., 1983. Asst. clin. psychologist N.Y. State Dept. Mental Hygiene, Wassaic, 1972-75; pres. Contemporary Psychology Assocs., Inc., L.A. and Downey, Calif., 1976—; cons. L.A. County Dept. Health Svc.; staff clinician San Bernardino County Dept. Mental Health, 1983-85; staff psychologist State of Calif. Dept. Mental Health, 1985—; media interviews include PA, L.A. Times, N.Y. Times, USA Today, Wall St Jour., Washington Post, Redbook mag., London Daily Mail and many others; TV and radio interviews include Larry King Live, CBA, NBA and ABC networks, Oprah Winfrey Show, CNN Newsnight, Can. Radio Network, Mut. Radio Network and many others. Served with USAF, 1965-69. Mem. Am. Psychol. Assn. for Media Psychology, Calif. Psychol. Assn., Nat. Accreditation Assn. Psychoanalysis. Office: Contemporary Psychology Assocs Inc PO Box 76477 Los Angeles CA 90076-0477

BUTTON, TIMOTHY L., physician assistant; b. Auburn, N.Y., Aug. 3, 1959; s. Howard and Eleanor (Lawrence) B.; m. Maureen O'Grady, Oct. 22, 1983; children: Katrina Marie, Ryan Nathaniel. B in Health Sci., U. Tex., Dallas, 1983. Nat. Comm. Cert. of Physician Assts. Emergency medicine postgrad. residency for physician assts. USC/L.A. County Med. Ctr., 1984-85; staff emergency dept. St. Al's Regional Med. Ctr., Boise, Idaho, 1986-89, Taylor Brown Hosp., Waterloo, N.Y., 1989-91; physician asst. Lifecare PA, Waterloo, 1991—. Basketball coach youth league Cath. Youth Orgn., Auburn, N.Y., 1995-96. Mem. Am. Coll. Sports Medicine (health and fitness instr. 1992—). Home: 19 Fairway Dr Auburn NY 13021

BUTTS, HERBERT CLELL, dentist, educator; b. Dover, Tenn., Aug. 24, 1924; s. Sidney Lewis and Georgia (Sawyer) B.; m. Quay Coker; children: Marla Lyce, April Chyrese, Dawn Denise, Sidney Coker. Student, U. Tenn. Jr. Coll., 1942-43, Memphis State U., 1946-47; DDS, U. Tenn., 1950; MS, U. Iowa, 1966. Pvt. practice dentistry Memphis, 1950-58; mem. faculty Coll. Dentistry, U. Tenn., Memphis, part-time 1950-58, 58-60, assoc. dean acad. affairs, 1978-81, spl. advisor to dean, 1986—; fgn. svc. officer, dental edn. advisor State Dept. Fgn. Aid program, San Salvador, El Salvador, 1960-64; assoc. prof. St. Louis U. Sch. Dentistry, 1966-67; prof., chmn. dept. operative dentistry Coll. Dental Medicine, Med. U. S.C., Charleston, 1967-70, asst. dean for admissions and student affairs, 1970, 72-74, acting dean, 1971; editor-in-chief ADA, Chgo., 1974-77; dean Sch. Dental Medicine So. Ill. U., Alton, 1981-86. With USNR, 1943-46. Recipient Outstanding Alumnus award U. Tenn. Coll. Dentistry, 1975. Mem. ADA, Tenn. Dental Assn. (fellowship award 1993), Memphis Dental Soc., Am. Coll. Dentists (pres. Tenn. sect. 1994, sec.-treas. Tenn. sect. 1995—), Internat. Coll. Dentists, Am. Assn. Dental Schs., Ala. Dental Assn. (hon.), Am. Assn. Women Dentists (hon.), Omicron Kappa Upsilon. Home: 1360 Peabody Ave Memphis TN 38104-3636 Office: U Tenn Coll Dentistry 875 Union Ave Memphis TN 38103-3513

BUTZ, ANDREW, biology educator; b. Perth Amboy, N.J., Feb. 15, 1931; s. John Andrew and Antoinette Catherine Butz. BS in Biology, St. Peter's Coll., Jersey City, 1952; MS, Fordham U., 1954, PhD, 1956. Teaching asst. Fordham U., N.Y.C., 1952-56, instr., 1956; asst. prof. biol. scis. U. Cin., 1956-64, assoc. prof., 1964—, coord. med. tech., 1962-73, chief health professions, 1976-83. Contbr. articles to Jour. N.Y. Entomol. Soc., Jour. Econ. Entomology, Annals Entomol. Soc. Am., Am. Zoologist, Comparative Immunology. With U.S. Army, 1956-58. Recipient Disting Svc. awrd U. Cin., Barbour award, 1990; grantee Am. Cancer Soc., 1967-68, Environ. Health Coun., 1967-68, Univ. Rsch. Coun., 1985-86. Mem. AAAS, Entomol. Soc. Am., Am. Soc. Zoology, N.Y. Acad. Scis., Sigma Xi (sec. U. Cin. chpt. 1965-78, v.p. 1979-80, pres. 1981-83, award 1966). Roman Catholic. Home: 882 Old Ludlow Ave Cincinnati OH 45220-1432 Office: U Cin Dept Biol Scis Cincinnati OH 45221

BUXBAUM, FREDERICK DAVID, podiatrist; b. Bklyn., Jan. 12, 1946; s. Irving and Beulah (Werner) B.; m. Elizabeth L. Stein, Aug 31, 1969; children: Joshua I., Julie R. BA cum laude, Long Island U., 1969; Dr. Podiatric Medicine, N.Y. Coll. Podiatric Medicine, 1973. Diplomate Am. Bd. Podiatric Surgery. Resident Kern Hosp. for Spl. Surgery, Warren, Mich., 1974; assoc. Allen Schor, DPM, Union City, N.J., 1975; v.p., podiatrist Robert A. Brody DPM & Frederick D Buxbaum DPM, P.C., Bklyn., 1976—; attending podiatrist Parkway Hosp., Forest Hills, N.Y., 1987—, Cmty. Hosp., Bklyn., 1987—, N.Y. Meth. Hosp., 1994. Fellow Am. Coll. Foot Surgeons, Am. Assn. of Hosp. Podiatrists. Jewish. Office: Brody DPM & Buxbaum DPM 1501 W 6th St Brooklyn NY 11204-4949

BUXER, CONSTANCE GERTRUDE, psychoanalyst, psychologist; b. N.Y.C., Oct. 5, 1923; d. Charles and Eva (Tucker) B.; m. Seymour D. Feinberg, Feb. 18, 1951; children: Andrew, Kenneth. BA, Hunter Coll., 1944; MA, Yeshiva U., 1973, PhD, 1974; postgrad., NYU, 1979. Lic. clin. psychologist, N.Y. Staff psychologist Bellevue Psychiat. Hosp., N.Y.C., 1974-75, Downstate Med. Sch., Bklyn., 1975-76; prof. psychology Baruch Coll., N.Y.C., 1976-77; pvt. practice N.Y.C., 1976—; cons. devel., self esteem adult issues, eating disorders. Office: 200 E 33rd St New York NY 10016-4874

BUXTON, DOUGLAS FRANCISCO, ophthalmologist; b. N.Y.C., Nov. 5, 1952; s. Jorge Norman and Amalia (Gonzalez) B. BA, Yale U., 1975; postgrad., Columbia U., 1977; MD, Cornell U., 1982. Diplomate Am. Bd. Med. Specialities, Am. Bd. Ophthalmology, Nat. Bd. Med. Examiners. Intern St. Vincent's Hosp. and Med. Ctr., N.Y.C., 1982-83; resident N.Y. Eye and Ear Infirmary, N.Y.C., 1983-86; fellowship Cornea and External Disease N.Y. Eye and Ear Infirmary, N.Y.C., 1986-88; assoc. attending staff N.Y. Eye and Ear Infirmary, 1986; clin. asst. Dept. Ophthalmology Manhattan Eye, Ear and Throat Hosp., 1988; clin. asst. prof. ophthalmology N.Y. Med. Coll., 1991; med. adv. bd. Eye-Bank for Sight Restoration, Inc., 1990; dir. edn. Crystal Vision Assocs., Inc., Laser Ctr. Contbr. articles to profl. jours. Fellow Am. Acad. Ophthalmology; mem. Am. Coll. Eye Surgeons, Am. Soc. Cataract and Refractive Surgeons, Castroviejo Cornea Soc., Internat. Soc. Refractive Keratoplasty, Eye Bank Assn. of Am., N.Y. County and State

Med. Soc., N.Y. Intra-Ocular Lens Implant Soc., N.Y. State Ophthalmol. Soc., Pan Am. Assn. Ophthalmology, N.Y. Keratorefractive Soc., Sociedad Medica Hispano-Am. de Neuva York, Inc. Office: NY Eye and Ear Infirmary 310 E 14th St New York NY 10003-4200

BUYNY, MARIANNE JO, eating disorders therapist, addictions counselor; b. Connellsville, Pa., Mar. 19, 1949; d. Marion Alyowich and Stella Louise (Sowinski) Marchewka; m. Jerome Michael Buyny, Oct. 21, 1972; children: Janean Estell, Jared Michael, Allison Victoria. BA in Psychology and Sociology, Alliance Coll., Cambridge Springs, Pa., 1971; MA in Psychology, Marywood Coll., Scranton, Pa., 1976; postgrad., C.C. Allegheny County, Pitts., 1985. Cert. allied addictions practitioner, criminal justice specialist. Med. social worker Schneider Home Health Care Agy., Inc., Pitts., 1985-87; mental health specialist Intercare, Hillside Psychiat. Ctr., McKeesport, Pa., 1987-91, Intercare, Lakewood Psychiat. Hosp., Canonsburg, Pa., 1991-95; psychol. specialist counselor II Med. Ctr. U. Pitts., 1995—; sr. rsch. assoc. Western Psychiat. Inst. and Clinic, Pitts., 1990—; therapist Willough at Naples, Naples, Fla., 1994—; asst. dir. in tng. of Group Psychotherapy and Psychodrama, Pitts., 1991—; reconstrn. therapist, Pitts., 1991—. Mem. Dance Therapy Assn., Pi Gamma Mu, Lambda Alpha. Home: 1712 Hathaway Ln Pittsburgh PA 15241-2706

BUZMINSKY, DAVID ANDREW, school psychologist; b. Colver, Pa., Sept. 19, 1954; s. Stephen Andrew and Susan Ann (Polenik) B. BS in Psychology, Juniata Coll., Huntingdon, Pa., 1977; MS in Sch. Psychology, Pa. State U., 1987, PhD in Sch. Psychology, 1988. Cert. sch. psychologist, Pa. Sch. psychologist Huntingdon (Pa.) Area Sch. Dist., 1987—; grad. asst. dept. ednl. psychology Pa. State U., University Park, 1984-86, instr. percussion, arranger Marching Blue Band, 1984—, adj. asst. prof. edn., 1991—. Mem. Nat. Assn. Sch. Psychologist, Assn. Sch. Psychologists Pa., Percussive Arts Soc., Pi Lambda Theta. Home: 283 Camelot Ln State College PA 16803-1339 Office: Huntingdon Area Sch Dist 2400 Cassady Ave Huntingdon PA 16652

BUZNEY, SHELDON MARC, retinal surgeon, researcher, ophthalmologist, educator; b. Cleve., Dec. 10, 1945; s. H.I. and D.P. Buzney. AB, Harvard U., 1968, MD, 1972. Diplomate Am. Bd. Ophthalmology, Am. Bd. Pediatrics. Intern, then resident Children's Hosp. Med. Ctr., Boston, 1972-74; resident in ophthalmology Mass. Eye and Ear Infirmary, Boston, 1976-79; rsch. assoc. NIH, Bethesda, Md., 1974-76; clin. asst. scientist Eye Rsch. Inst., Boston, 1976-95, clin. assoc. scientist, 1996—; clin. instr. ophthalmology Harvard U., Boston, 1981-92, clin. asst. prof., 1993—. Contbr. articles to profl. jours. Lt. comdr. USPHS, 1974-76. Recipient Honor award Am. Acad. Ophthalmology, 1989. Mem. Mass. Soc. Eye Physicians and Surgeons (pres. 1990-91), Mass. Med. Soc., New england Ophthal. Soc. (chmn. pub. health com. 1983-92, sec. 1993—), Assn. Rsch. Vision and Ophthalmology, Retina Soc. Office: Retina Specialists of Boston 4th Flr 100 Charles River Plz Boston MA 02114-2723

BYCK, ROBERT SAMUEL, psychiatrist, educator; b. Newark, Apr. 26, 1933; s. Louis and Lucy Ruth (Landau) B.; m. Therese Jaeger, May 4, 1963; children: Carl, Gillian, Lucas; 1 child, John Ivey. A.B., U. Pa., 1954, M.D., 1959; M.A. hon., Yale U., 1978. Intern U. Calif.-San Francisco, 1959-60; asst. prof. pharmacology and rehab. medicine Albert Einstein Coll. Medicine, Bronx, N.Y., 1964-69; resident in psychiatry Yale U., New Haven, 1969-72, lectr. in pharmacology, 1969-72, assoc. prof. psychiatry and pharmacology, 1972-77, prof. psychiatry and pharmacology, 1977—; dir. psychiat. cons. Yale New Haven Hosp., 1987-94; cons. N.Y. Zool. Soc., Bronx, 1968—, Nat. Inst. Drug Abuse, Bethesda, Md., 1976-80, West Haven VA Hosp., 1972—, Med. Letter on Drugs and Therapeutics, 1970-90. Editor: Cocaine Papers: Sigmund Freud, 1974; contbr. (articles to sci. publs.). Recipient Career Devel. award, 1967, H.L. Mencken award Free Press Assn., Apple Valley, Calif., 1988; Burroughs-Wellcome scholar in clin. pharmacology, Triangle Park, N.C., 1972-77. Mem. Am. Soc. Pharmacology and Exptl. Therapeutics, Am. Soc. Clin. Pharmacology and Therapeutics, Am. Coll. Neuropsychopharmacology, Sherlock Holmes Soc. Office: Yale U Sch Medicine 333 Cedar St New Haven CT 06510-3206

BYCZKOWSKI, JANUSZ ZBIGNIEW, toxicologist; b. Gdansk, Poland, May 29, 1947; came to U.S., 1979; s. Stanislaw and Halina (Osterczy) B.; m. Janina K. Slosarska, Aug. 6, 1977; children: Ian S., L. Peter. MSc in Toxicology, Acad. Medicine, Gdansk, 1970, PhD in Pharmacology, 1975, DSc in Biochem. Pharmacology, 1979. Cancer rsch. scientist dept. exptl. therapeutics Roswell Park Meml. Inst., Buffalo, 1979-80, 1985-87; adj. asst. prof. pharmacology Acad. Medicine Gdansk, 1980-83; pharmacologist and dir. of pharmacy Internat. Red Cross and Red Crescent, Tobruk, Libya, 1983-84; asst. prof. and rsch. scientist Coll. Pub. Health U. South Fla., Tampa, 1987-91; project scientist and study dir. ManTech. Environ. Tech., Inc., Dayton, Ohio, 1991—; editorial reviewer Bull. Environ. Contamination and Toxicology, Reno, Nev., 1989—, Free Radical Biology and Medicine, Baton Rouge, 1989—, Placenta, Manchester, Eng., 1991—. Contbr. articles to profl. publs., chpts. to books. Active mem. Solidarity, Poland, 1980-83. Recipient Rsch. award 1st degree Sci. Soc. Gdansk, 1975, Polish Pharmacol. Soc., 1977, Ministry Health and Social Welfare of Poland, 1977. Mem. AAAS, Soc. for Rsch. on Polyunsaturated Fatty Acids (pres. 6th sci. meeting 1992—, travel grantee 1992), N.Y. Acad. Scis., Oxygen Soc., Soc. Toxicology, Soc. for Risk Analysis (councilor Ohio chpt. 1994—). Home: 212 N Central Ave Fairborn OH 45324-5006 Office: ManTech Environ Tech Inc PO Box 31009 Dayton OH 45437-0009

BYDZOVSKY, VIKTOR, surgeon; b. Prague, Czechoslovakia, May 24, 1944; s. Viktor and Milada (Raus) B.; m. Anne Marie Berset, Feb. 26, 1977; children—Patricia, Pierre. Dr.Med., U. Prague, 1967. Hosp. asst., Kolin, Czechoslovakia, 1968-70, Montreux, Switzerland, 1970-71, Fribourg, Switzerland, 1971-73, Geneva, 1973-78; practice medicine specializing in gen. surgery, Fribourg, 1978—. Lt. M.C., Czechoslovakian Army. 1967-68, 1st lt. M.C., Swiss Army, 1990—. Mem. Internat. Soc. Surgery, Internat. Coll. Surgeons, Swiss Surg. Soc., Swiss Soc. Sports Medicine, Soc. Suisse Senologie. Avocations: sports, music. Home: Chemin de Primeveres 35, CH-1700 Fribourg Switzerland Office: Locarno 3, CH-1700 Fribourg Switzerland

BYEFF, PETER DAVID, hematologist, oncologist; b. Newark, Nov. 27, 1948; s. Herbert Isaac and Ruth Helen (Wolfe) B.; B.A., U. Pa., 1970; M.D., Johns Hopkins U., 1974; m. Gail Schneider, Apr. 2, 1982. Intern, Georgetown U. Hosp., Washington, 1974-75, resident in internal medicine, 1975-77; vis. fellow in hematology and oncology Columbia-Presbyn. Med. Center, N.Y.C., 1977-81, Damon Runyon-Walter Winchell oncology fellow, 1977-81; instr. Coll. Physicians and Surgeons, Columbia U., N.Y.C.; asst. prof., attending physician U. Conn.; attending physician Bradley Meml. Hosp., Southington, Conn., New Britain (Conn.) Gen. Hosp., med. dir. George Brug Cancer Ctr. Diplomate Am. Bd. Internal Medicine (subcert. in med. oncology and hematology), Nat. Bd. Med. Examiners. Office: Bradley Med Bldg 55 Meriden Ave Ste 1-a Southington CT 06489-3238 also: 40 Hart St New Britain CT 06052-1743

BYERLY, RONALD H., physician assistant; b. Harrisburg, Pa., July 27, 1954; s. Clyde Ronald and Mary-Frances (Leddy) B.; m. Luann Christine Surak, Sept. 26, 1981; children: Lauren K., Matthew G. BA, Bloomsburg U., 1976; AS in Clin. Health Scis., Pa. State U., 1980. Cert. physician asst. Physician asst. Selinsgrove (Pa.) Med. Ctr., 1980-83, Edgehill Newport, R.I., 1983-90, White Deer Run, Allenwood, Pa., 1990-92, Geisinger Med. Ctr., Danville, Pa., 1992—; faculty R.I. Coll., 1990; mem. admissions rev. com., physician asst. dept. Penn Coll., 1996. Adv. bd. Snyder County Children and Youth, Middleburg, Pa., 1983; chmn. Physician Extender Quality Improvement Com. Geisinger Med. Ctr., 1994-96; Big Brother Colombia County Children & Youth, Bloomsburg, 1975. Fellow Am. Acad. Physician Assts., Pa. Soc. Physician Assts. Roman Catholic. Office: Geisinger Med Ctr N Academy Ave Danville PA 17821

BYERLY, WESLEY GRIMES, JR., surgeon; b. Statesville, N.C., July 28, 1926; s. Wesley Grimes and Bessie (Hayes) B.; m. Katherine Jean Hurd, June 9, 1951; children: Wesley Grimes III, Katherine Hayes, Andrew Baxter. AB in Chemistry, U. N.C., 1948; MD, Harvard U., 1952. Diplomate Am. Bd. Surgery, Nat. Bd. Med. Examiners. Surg. intern First Div. Bellevue Hosp., N.Y.C., 1952; chief surg. resident Roosevelt Hosp., N.Y.C., 1953-57; pvt. practice Hickory, N.C., 1957-93; pres. Byerly Surg. Assocs./Med. Arts Clinic, Hickory, 1963-93; attending surgeon Richard Baker Hosp., Hickory, 1957-60; attending surgeon, chief Hickory Meml. Hosp., 1960-80, Catawba Meml. Hosp., Hickory, 1967-93, chief of surgery, 1968, 82, chief of staff, 1991-92; surgeon Vol. Physicians for Vietnam, 1967; mission pilot CAP, Hickory, 1976-86. Pres. Catawba County Red Cross, Hickory, 1962-64, Catawba County Cancer Soc., Hickory, 1966-68, U. N.C. Med. Alumni, 1989-90; chmn. Catawba County Rep. Party, N.C., 1988-90, 10th N.C. Congl. Dist. Rep. Party, 1995—; chmn. bd. trustees Catawba Valley C.C., Hickory, 1989—. Col. USAR, 1944-88, WWII, Vietnam. Decorated Legion of Merit with oak leaf cluster. Fellow ACS, Southeastern Surg. Congress; mem. AMA, Flying Physicians Assn., Mil. Surgeons, N.C. Med. Soc. (councilor, exec. com.), Catawba County Med. Soc. (pres. 1963), Kiwanis (pres. 1975-76, lt. gov. 1979-80), Mason. Republican. Episcopalian.

BYERS, JEROME LEON, retired ophthalmologist, educator; b. Dallas, Dec. 11, 1926; s. Abe and Eva (Feiner) B.; m. Hazel Manes Byers, Feb. 25, 1950; children: Marilyn, Joan, Marc. BS in Chemistry, So. Meth. U., 1948; MD, U. Tex., Galveston, 1952; postgrad. in ophthalmology, Tuland U. Sch. Medicine, 1954-55. Diplomate Am. Bd. Ophthalmology. Intern USPHS Hosp., New Orleans, 1952-53; Eye, Ear, Nose and Throat Hosp. physician USPHS Hosp., Carville, La., 1953-54; resident Eye, Ear, Nose and Throat Hosp., New Orleans, 1955-57, chief resident, 1956-57; instr. ophthalmology Tulane Med. Sch., New Orleans, 1957-58; pvt. practice med. and surg. diseases of the eye Dallas, 1958-94; mem. staff Parkland Memland; mem. staff Meth. Hosp. Dallas, chief ophthalmology dept., 1982-83; asst. prof. ophthalmology S.W. Med. Sch., Dallas, 1958-63, assoc. prof., 1962—; pres. med. staff Meth. Hosp. Dallas, 1980-81, bd. dirs. 1982-85; mem. med. adv. bd. Parkland Meml. Hosp., Dallas, 1971-74; pres. Dallas Acad. Ophthalmology, 1975; clin. assoc. prof. ophthalmology U. Tex. Health Sci. Ctr., Dallas, 1975—, ocular pathologist eye dept. Contbr. articles to profl. jours. Pres. Alliance for Mentally Ill Dallas, 1988-90, Planned Lifetime Assistance Network North Tex., Inc., 1991—. Lt. USPHS, 1952-54; bd. dirs., treas. Dallas Eye Bank, 1962-64; bd. dirs. Dallas chpt. Tex. br. Nat. Soc. Prevention of Blindness, 1969, vice med. dir., 1969-70; com. for Low Vision Clinic, Dallas Svcs. for Visually Impaired Children, 1981—. Recipient Pyramid award Dallas Mental Health Assn., 1991. Fellow Am. Acad. Ophthalmology and Otolaryngology; mem. AMA, Tex. Med. Assn., Dallas County Med. Soc., Tex. Ophthal. Assn., Tex. Soc. Ophthalmology and Otolaryngology, Am. Assn. Ophthalmology, Dallas Acad. Ophthalmology (bd. dirs. 1983-88), Internat. Eye Found., Am. Soc. Cataract and Refractive Surgeons, Internat. Soc. Refractive Keratoplasty, Pan Am. Assn. Ophthalmology, Soc. Israel Philatelists (pres. 1984-86). Hebrew.

BYERS, KARIN ELIZABETH, internist; b. Bellefonte, Pa., Oct. 9, 1965; d. Hal Kent and Sigrid (Fernelius) B. BS, Pa. State U., 1987; MD, Temple U., 1991; MS, U. Va., 1996. Diplomate Am. Bd. Internal Medicine. Intern in internal medicine Temple U. Hosp., Phila., 1991-92, resident, 1992-94; fellow in infectious disease U. Va. Health Scis. Ctr., Charlottesville, 1994—. Home: RR 21 Box 113 Charlottesville VA 22902-8721

BYERS, LOWELL J., physician, medical educator; b. Ulysses, Kans., July 6, 1955; s. Joseph and Wilma Byers; m. Martha S. Byers, Dec. 28, 1977. BSChemE, U. Kans., 1977; MD, U. Kans., Kansas City, 1980. Cert. Am. Bd. Ob-gyn., Am. Bd. Internal Medicine. Pvt. practice The Med. Ctr., Hutchinson, Kans., 1986-90; fellow in gynecologic oncology dept. ob-gyn. U. Minn., Mpls., 1990-93; asst. prof. ob-gyn. U. Mo., Kansas City, 1994—; mem. adv. bd. Dept. Chem. Engring., Lawrence, Kans., 1985-90. Contbr. chpt. to book and articles to profl. jours. Clin. oncology fellow Am. Cancer Soc., 1992-93. Fellow Am. Coll. Ob-Gyn.; mem. Western Assn. Gynecologists and Oncologists, Tau Beta Pi. Office: St Lukes Hosp Peet Outpatient Bldg 4323 Wornall Rd Kansas City MO 64111

BYERS, PETER H., geneticist; b. N.Y.C., May 31, 1943. MD, Case Western Reserve U., 1969. Diplomate Am. Bd. Molecular Genetics, clin. geneticist. Intern U. Calif., San Francisco, 1969, resident, 1969-70; fellow U. Wash., Seattle, 1974-77, asst. prof. pathology and medicine, 1979-82, assoc. prof., 1982-86, prof., 1986—. Office: U Wash Dept Pathology SM-30 Health Sci Bldg Rm E511 Seattle WA 98195-0001*

BYERS, SANDRA ROBERTS, health administrator; b. Rochester, N.Y., Nov. 18, 1937; d. Arthur Eugene and Janet Virginia (Ebert) Roberts; m. Thomas Jones Byers, Aug. 20, 1960; children: Stephen Arthur, Linda Byers Fontana. BSN, Cornell U., 1960; MS in Nursing Adminstrn., Ohio State U., 1972, PhD, 1990. Cert. nursing adminstrn. advanced. Staff nurse Hosp. of U. of Pa., Phila., 1960-61, instr., 1961-62; instr. Maturna Orgn., Washington, 1962-64; staff nurse St. Anthony Hosp., Columbus, Ohio, 1971-72; asst. dir., staff devel. Ohio State U. Hosp., Columbus, 1972-75; dir. med. nursing Riverside Meth. Hosp., Columbus, 1975-82; v.p. nursing Health Mgmt. Svcs. Inc., Columbus, 1982-86; sr. v.p. nursing Grant Med. Ctr., Columbus, 1982-86; dir. health policy Ohio Hosp. Assn., Columbus, 1990-94; v.p. corp. health affairs Peer Rev. Systems Inc., Westerville, Ohio, 1994-96; health care cons. Worthington, 1996—; adj. asst. prof. Coll. of Nursing Ohio State U., Columbus, 1993, 94; mem. editl. bd. Spl. Rschrs. Publ., JONA, 1994-95; mem. nat. adv. com. Ladders in Nursing Careers, 1992—; pres. adv. coun. Ashland (Ohio) Univ. Sch. Nursing, 1991—. Chair, bd. dirs. The Interprofl. Commn. of Ohio, Columbus, 1996; past pres., mem. Ohio Bd. of Nursing, Columbus, 1980-85; elder, mem. Worthington Presbyn. Ch. Tng. grant fellowship USPHS, 1971-73. Mem. ANA, Mid Ohio Dist. Nursing Assn., Nat. League for Nursing (mem. constituent league), Am. Orgn. Nurse Execs., Am. Soc. for Pub. Adminstrn., Midlands Rep. to Constitutional League (exec. com. 1993-95), Ohio League for Nursing (pres. 1992-94, bd. dirs. 1987-95), Sigma Theta Tau.

BYLECKIE, SCOTT ANDREW, SR., health facility coordinator; b. Plainfield, N.J., June 20, 1962; s. George Christopher and Barbara Ann Byleckie; m. Pamela Gasperini, Apr. 25, 1992; 1 child, Scott Andrew Jr.; 1 stepchild, Justin Michael Gasperini. BS in Health Edn., Ohio U., 1984; MS in Phys. Edn., West Chester U., 1987. Student trainer Ohio U., Athens, 1980-84; grad. asst. athletic trainer West Chester (Pa.) U., 1984-85, grad. asst. human performance rsch. lab., 1985-86; asst. athletic trainer Lafayette Coll., Easton, Pa., 1986, U. Nev., Las Vegas, 1986-90; coord. sports medicine svcs. St. Rose Dominican Hosp., Henderson, Nev., 1991—; co-clin. coord. Weigand Cardiac Rehab. Program St. Rose Dominican Hosp., Henderson, 1995-96. Mem. Nat. Athletic Trainers Assn. (cert., Nev. rep. secondary sch. athletic trainers com. Far West Athletic Trainers Assn. Dist. 8 1994—), Nev. Athletic Trainers Assn. (licensure com. 1992—, treas. 1996—, conv. com. 1996). Republican. Roman Catholic. Home: 810 Chimney Rock Dr Henderson NV 89015 office: St Rose Dominican Hosp 102 E Lake Mead Dr Henderson NV 89015

BYLUND, DAVID BRUCE, pharmacologist, educator; b. Spanish Fork, Utah, Apr. 16, 1946; s. H. Bruce and Rhea (Bowen) B.; m. Elaine C. Thurman, May 27, 1970; children: Carma, Eric, Michelle, Kevin, Jennie, Kristen, Emily. BS, Brigham Young U., 1970; PhD, U. Calif., Davis, 1974. Postdoctoral rsch. fellow Johns Hopkins Med. Sch., Balt., 1975-77; prof. med. sch. U. Mo., Columbia, 1977-89; prof., chmn. U. Nebr., 1989—. Series editor: The Receptors, 1988—. Mem. LDS Ch. Office: U Nebr Med Ctr Pharmacology 600 S 42nd St Omaha NE 68198-6260

BYNES, FRANK HOWARD, JR., physician; b. Savannah, Ga., Dec. 3, 1950; s. Frank Howard and Frenchye (Mason) B.; m. Janice Ratta, July 24, 1987; children: Patricia, Frenchye. BS, Savannah State Coll., 1972; MD, Meharry Med. Coll. Resident gen. surgery Staten Island (N.Y.) Hosp., 1978-82; resident internal medicine N.Y. infirmary Beekam Downtown Hosp., N.Y.C., 1983-86; dir. medicine USAF Sheppard Regional Hosp., Sheppard AFB, Tex., 1986-87; pvt. practice internal medicine N.Y.C., 1987-90; attending physician Bronx (N.Y.) Lebanon Hosp., 1990-93; pvt. practice intenal medicine Savannah, Ga., 1994—. Maj. USAF, 1986-87. Mem. AMA, AAAS, ACP, N.Y. Acad. Scis., Assn. Mil. Surgeons of U.S., Alpha Phi Alpha.

BYNUM, EDWARD BRUCE, clinical psychologist; b. Birmingham, Ala., Feb. 27, 1948; s. Bruce and Lillie (Grant) Bynum; m. Alyse Taub, June 6, 1981; children: Elijah, Ezra. BA, U. N.H., 1970; MS, Pa. State U., 1973, PhD, 1977. Lic. psychologist, Mass., Conn. Postdoctoral fellow Elmcrest Psychiatric Inst., Portland, Conn., 1976-77; program dir. adolescent unit Elmcrest Psychiatric Inst., 1977-79; dir. behavioral medicine U. Mass. Health Svcs., Amherst, 1979—. Author: The Family Unconsious, 1984, Transcending Psychoneurotic Disturbances, 1991, Families and the Interpretation of Dreams, 1993, The Dreaming Skull, 1996, Godzillananda, 1996. Mem. APA (pres. transpersonal psychology grp. 1990—), Nat. Assn. Black Psychologists, Assn. Transpersonal Psychology, Nat. Soc. Biofeedback. Office: Univ of Mass Health Svcs 127 Hills N Amherst MA 01003

BYRD, BENJAMIN FRANKLIN, JR., surgeon, educator; b. Nashville, May 18, 1918; s. Benjamin Franklin and Ida (Brister) B.; m. Allison Caldwell, Feb. 6, 1950; children: Benjamin Franklin, Barney Duncan, Damon Winston, Andrew Wayne, Evelyn Hope, John W. Thomas. A.B., Vanderbilt U., 1938, M.D., 1941. Intern, Nashville Gen. Hosp., 1941-42, asst. resident, 1942; asst. resident Vanderbilt U. Hosp., 1945-47, resident, 1947-48; practice medicine, specializing in surgery Nashville, 1948—; chief surgery St. Thomas Hosp., 1964-70, pres. staff, 1977-79; mem. staff Baptist Hosp.; instr. surgery Vanderbilt U., Nashville, 1947-54; assoc. clin. prof. surgery Vanderbilt U., 1954-71, clin. prof. surgery, 1971—; chmn. bd. of overseers Vanderbilt U. Cancer Ctr., 1993—; assoc. clin. prof. surgery Meharry Med. Coll., Nashville, 1951-69; prof. clin. surgery Meharry Med. Coll., 1969—; dir., mem. trust bd. Commerce Union Bank, 1974-80, 82-91; dir. NLT Corp. Pres. Tenn. divsn. Am. Cancer Soc., 1963, nat. bd. dirs., 1965—, natl. exec. com., 1970-80, chmn. med. and sci. exec. com., 1973—&, nat. pres., 1975-76; pres., mem. exec. bd. Tenn. Bot. Gardens and Fine Arts Ctr., 1971-73; trustee Sr. Citizens, Hermitage Assn.; bd. dirs. Cumberland Mus., Univ. Sch., 1985-91. Lt. col. M.C., AUS, 1941-45. Decorated Bronze Star with 2 oak leaf clusters, Silver Star, Purple Heart; named Nashvillian of Yr., Nashville Kiwanis, 1986; recipient Human Rels. award Nat. Fellow ACS (gov. 1973-79, chmn. commn. on cancer); mem. Am. Surg. Assn., So. Surg. Assn., Nashville Surg. Soc. (pres. 1962-63), Soc. Surg. Oncology, Tenn. Med. Assn. (mem. council, Disting. Service award, Physician of Yr. 1986), So. Med. Assn. (mem. council), Société International de Chirurgie, Southeastern Surg. Congress (mem. council, pres. 1968-69, Disting. Service award 1977), Nashville Acad. Medicine (pres. 1980, chmn. 1981), Nashville C. of C. (bd. govs. 1967-70, 82—, pres. 1985), Vanderbilt U. Med. Alumni (pres. 1979-81), Sigma Xi. Club: Nashville Exchange. Home: 400 Ellendale Ave Nashville TN 37205-3402 Office: 2611 West End Ave Ste 201 Nashville TN 37203-1446

BYRD, H. JOSEPH, pharmacy educator; b. Biloxi, Miss., Sept. 19, 1945; s. Herald N. and Marjorie (Alexander) B.; m. G. Jeanette McGuire, June 1, 1967; children: Angela Jean, Robert J. BS in Pharmacy, U. Miss., 1968, MS in Hosp. Pharmacy, 1970; D Pharmacy, Phila. Coll. of Pharmacy, 1971. Staff pharmacist Oxford-Lafayette Co. Hosp., Oxford, Miss., 1966-67; resident, pharmacy Jefferson Hosp., Philadelphia, 1970-71, investigational drug pharmacist, 1970-71; prof., chmn. dept. clin. pharmacy practice U. Miss. Med. Ctr., Jackson, 1971—; bd. dirs. Prime Nursing/Hospice, Greenville, Miss.; legal cons. in field, Jackson, Miss.; geriatric cons., St. Catherine's Village, madison, Miss., 1994-96. Reviewer Am. Jour. Hosp. Pharm., 1993—, Am. Jour. Pharmaceutical Edn., 1994-95. Pres. Huntcliff Homeowners, Clinton, Miss., 1971-72; program chmn. Lions Club, Clinton, 1974-76; pres. Miss. Soc. Hosp. Pharmacists, Jackson, 1990-91. Fellow Am. Soc. Health System Pharmacists; mem. Miss. Soc. Hosp. Pharmacists (pres. 1991), Am. Coll. Clin. Pharmacists, Phi Kappa Phi. Office: U Miss Med Ctr 2500 N State Jackson MS 39216

BYRD, JULIE ANDERSON, nurse; b. San Diego, Feb. 18, 1949; d. Asa Lee and Connie (Alderete) Anderson; m. Richard Allan Byrd, June 8, 1970. Diploma, Mercy Coll. Nursing, San Diego, 1970. RN; registered diagnostic cardiac sonographer; registered vascular technologist. Staff nurse Howard Meml. Hosp., Biloxi, Miss., 1971, Santa Rosa Med. Ctr., San Antonio, 1972; office nurse Dr. Mario Cardenas, Princeton, W.Va., 1973-74; acting head nurse Radford (Va.) Community Hosp., 1975; staff nurse Nurses Ctrl. Registry, Phoenix, 1976, Greenbrier Valley Med. Ctr., Ronceverte, W.Va., 1981-82; chief noninvasive cardiovascular lab. The Greenbrier Clinic, While Sulphur Springs, W.Va., 1976-91; nurse for adolescent child care agy. Davis-Stuart Inc., Lewisburg, W.Va., 1992—. Recipient Am. Legion Sch. award, 1964. Mem. Soc. Vascular Tech., Greenbrier Health Club, Calif. Scholarship Fedn. (life). Democrat. Roman Catholic. Home: PO Box 647 Lewisburg WV 24901-0647 Office: Davis-Stuart Rte 2 Box 188-A Lewisburg WV 24901

BYRD, KAREN S., nursing administrator; b. Fremont, Ohio, June 26, 1954; d. Robert Edward and Beverly Jane (Moyer) Andecover; divorced; children: Matthew David, John Marion, Michael Joseph. ADN, Ind. U., 1984; student, Spring Arbor Coll., 1990-91. RN, Ind., Ohio. Staff nurse ICU/CCU Reed Meml. Hosp., Richmond, Ind., 1984-87; supr. Cmty. Blood Bank, Dayton, Ohio, 1985-87; asst. DON Heritage House of Richmond, 1987-88; nursing supr. Cmty. Blood Bank, Richmond, 1988-90; staff nurse oncology St. Joseph Hosp., Flint, Mich., 1990-91; home care nurse Kimberly Quality Care, Flint, 1990-91; bone marrow transplant nurse Ind. U. Med. Ctr., Indpls., 1991-92; open heart recovery nurse St. Vincent Hosp., Toledo, Ohio, 1992; home care nurse Home Nutritional Svcs., Valley View, Ohio, 1992-93; DON Norrell/Nurses House Call, Toledo, 1993—. Vol. NOVA, Toledo, 1993-94. Mem. N.W. Ohio S.W. Mich. Case Mgrs. Assn. (v.p. 1995—). Democrat. Methodist. Home: 2751 Pinetrace Dr Maumee OH 43537 Office: Olsten Kimberly QualityCare 3450 W Central Toledo OH 43606

BYRD, LARRY DONALD, behavioral pharmacologist; b. Salisbury, N.C., July 14, 1936; s. Donald Thomas and Mildred (Gardner) B.; m. Corrinne Williams, Dec. 23, 1961; children: Kay, Lynn, Renee, Andrew. AB, E. Carolina U., Greenville, N.C., 1962; MA, E. Carolina U., 1964; PhD, U. N.C., 1968; postgrad., Harvard U., 1967-70. Faculty E. Carolina U., 1962-64; teaching and rsch. asst. exptl. psychology U. N.C., Chapel Hill, 1964-67; rsch. fellow pharmacology, instr. psychobiology Harvard Med. Sch., 1967-70; assoc. scientist Lab. Psychobiology New Eng. Reg. Primate Rsch. Ctr., 1969-74; psychobiologist, chmn. div. primate behavior Yerkes Primate Rsch. Ctr., Emory U., Atlanta, 1974-79, assoc. rsch. prof., chmn. div. primate behavior, 1979-80, lectr. dept. psychology, 1974-81, assoc. rsch. prof., chief div. behavioral biology, 1980-82; prof., chief divsn. behavioral biology Emory U., Atlanta, 1982—, Yerkes Primate Rsch. Ctr., Emory U., Atlanta, 1981-95;, 1982; prof. dept. pharmacology Yerkes Primate Rsch. Ctr., Emory U., Atlanta, 1995—; adj. prof. dept. psychology Emory U., 1981—; cons. Dept. Pharmacological and Physiol. Scis. U. Chgo., 1973, MIT Press, Cambridge, 1975, Nat. Ctr. for Toxicological Rsch. FDA, Jefferson, Ark., 1976-77, S.W. Found. for Rsch. and Edn., San Antonio, 1977, Naval Aerospace Med. Rsch. Lab. U.S. Naval Air Sta., Pensacola, Fla., 1977, G.D. Searle and Co., Skokie, Ill., 1986, Battelle Meml. Inst., Columbus, Ohio, 1989-94; mem. spl. rev. com. Contract Rev. Unit Nat. Inst. on Drug Abuse, Lexington, Ky., 1979-81, mem. spl. rev. com. biomed. rsch. rev. com., 1981-82, spl. rev. cons. clin., behavioral and psychosocial rsch. rev. com., 1981-82, mem., 1982-85, chmn., 1984-85, others; spl. rev. cons. dept. medicine and surgery VA, Washington, 1983, NSF, Washington, 1984, div. of rsch. resources NIH, Washington, 1983, mem. spl. study sect. div. rsch. grants, 1984, panel mem. Workshop on Implemenation of Pub. Health Svc. Policy on Humane Care and Use of Lab. Animals, 1989, others; panel mem. USPHS Animal Welfare Forum Alcohol, Drug Abuse and Mental Health Adminstrn., 1985; active numerous other career related orgns. Editorial bd. Jour. Exptl. Analysis of Behavior, 1969-79, 87-91; assoc. editor Jour. Exptl. Analysis of Behavior, 1970-76; cons. editor Am. Jour. Primatology, 1980-83; editor Psychopharmacology Newsletter, 1976-82; editorial advisor Jour. Pharmacology and Exptl. Therapeutics, Jour. Exptl. Analysis of Behavior, others; contbr. numerous articles to profl. jours. Mem. sci. adv. com. Nat. Families in Action, 1991—. Recipient Outstanding Alumnus award, E. Carolina U., 1977, Disting. Alumnus award, U. N.C., 1987. Fellow AAAS, Am. Psychol. Assn. (exec. com. psychopharmacology divsn. 1976-95, neurobehavioral toxicity test standards com. 1980—, coord. Young Psychopharmacologist award 1985-95, bd. sci. affairs com. on animals in rsch. and ethics 1990-93); mem. Am. Assn. Accreditation Lab. Animal Care (trustee 1990—, exec. com. 1991—, sec. 1993, vice chmn. 1994-95), Am. Soc. Pharmacology and Exptl. Therapeutics, Nat. Families in Action (sci. adv. com. 1991—), Am. Soc. Primatologist, Behavioral Pharmacology Soc. (pres. 1984-86), Soc. Exptl. Analysis of Behavior (v.p. 1975-76, bd. dirs. 1970-78), European Behavioral Pharmacology Soc., Southeastern Pharmacology Soc., Am Pub. Health Assn., Behavioral Toxicology Soc., Southeastern Assn. for Behavior Analysis, Internat. Study Group Investigating Drugs as

Reinforcers, Emory Neurosci. Group, Phi Sigma Pi. Home: 1026 Viking Dr Stone Mountain GA 30083-1707 Office: Yerkes Primate Rsch Ctr Emory U Atlanta GA 30322

BYRD, MALCOLM TODD, public health administrator; b. Phila., Mar. 22, 1956; s. Joseph Edward and Kathleen Jean (Quarterman) B. BA, Antioch U., Phila., 1984, MEd, 1986; cert. drug and alcohol counselor, Villanova U., 1991; M in Govtl. Adminstrn., U. Pa., 1993; grad. Phila. Urban League, Leadershp Inst., Phila., 1993; grad., Leadership Inc., 1994. Liaison Pa. Health Commr. Contbr. articles to profl. jours., column to newspaper; co-editor Network News and Peer Counselor, 1st Corinthian Bapt. Ch. Mem. hon. degree com. U. Pa., 1992-94; preceptor to grad. human svcs. program Lincoln U., 1991-92, 94—; mem. Juv. Justice Alliance, 1993—; v.p. bd. dirs. Phila. Tribune Charities, 1996; sec. bd. dirs. Philabundance, 1996; cmty. devel. fund allocation com. United Way, 1996; adv. coun. Thomas Jefferson U. Hosp. Cancer Ctr., 1996; mem. Health Promotions coun. southeastern Pa., 1996, Mng. Change Work group 21st Century League, 1996. Mem. First Corinthian Fellows (pres. 1990—). Democrat. Baptist. Home: 6027 Master St Philadelphia PA 19151-4207 Office: City of Philadelphia Dept of Pub Health 1600 Arch St 7th Flr Philadelphia PA 19103

BYRN, STEPHEN R., medical educator; b. New Albany, Ind., Oct. 7, 1944; m. Sarah Rushmore; children: Elizabeth, Andrew, John, Mary, David, Rebecca, Sarah, Daniel. BA, DePauw U., 1966; PhD, U. Ill., 1970; postdoctoral studies, UCLA, 1971-72. Asst. prof. medicinal chemistry and pharmacognosy Purdue U., West Lafayette, Ind., 1972-76, assoc. prof., 1976-81, prof., 1981-92, Charles B. Jordan prof., 1992—, assoc. dept. head, 1979-88, asst. dean grad. sch., 1984-89, dept. head, 1988-94, dir. ctr. AIDS rsch., 1988—, head Dept. Indsl. and Phys. Pharmacology, 1994—; cons. Mercke & Co., 1988-94, Parke-Davis/Warner Lambert, 1993-94. Mem. adv. bd. controlled substances State Ind., 1982—. Recipient Alumni citation DePauw U., 1991; Rector scholar, 1962-66; fellow Sinclair Oil Co., 1967-68, NSF, 1968-71, NIH, 1971-72. Fellow Am. Assn. Pharm. Scientists (mem. USP com. revision 1990—); mem. Am. Chem. Soc., Am. Crystallographic Assn., Am. Assn. Colls. Pharmacy, Phi Eta Sigma, Rho Chi, Phi Lambda Upsilon, Sigma Xi, Phi Kappa Phi. Home: 824 Barlow St West Lafayette IN 47906-1514 Office: Purdue Univ Dept Indsl and Phys Pharm West Lafayette IN 47907

BYRNE, DONN ERWIN, psychologist, educator; b. Austin, Tex., Dec. 19, 1931; s. Bernard Devine and Rebecca (Singleton) B.; m. Lois Ann Pugsley, Sept. 12, 1953 (div. 1978); children: Keven Singleton, Robin Lynn; m. Kathryn Kelley, Aug. 17, 1979 (div. 1996); children: Lindsey Kelley, Rebecka Byrne Kelley. BA, Calif. State U., Fresno, 1953, MA, 1956; PhD, Stanford U., 1958. Instr. psychology Calif. State U., San Francisco, 1957-59; asst. to assoc. prof. psychology U. Tex., Austin, 1959-66, prof. psychology, 1966-69, dir. exptl. personality program, 1963-69, asst. dept. chmn., 1964-66; prof. psychology Purdue U., West Lafayette, Ind., 1969-79, chmn. social personality program, 1972-78; prof. psychology SUNY, Albany, 1979-91, disting. prof., 1991—, chmn. social-personality program, 1980-84, 90—, chmn. dept., 1984-89; vis. prof. psychology Stanford U., Palo Alto, Calif., 1966-67, U. Hawaii, Honolulu, 1968; panel mem. NSF grad. fellowship program NRC, 1972; NIH participant Inst. Sex Research Summer Program, 1974; G. Stanley Hall lectr. Am. Psychol. Assn., 1981. Author: (with H.C. Lindgren) Psychology: An Introduction to the Study of Human Behavior, 1961, 4th edit., 1975, (with P. Worchel) Personality Change, 1964, An Introduction to Personality: A Research Approach, 1966, (with K. Kelley), 3d edit., 1981, (with M.L. Hamilton) Personality Research: A Book of Readings, 1966, The Attraction Paradigm, 1971, (with R.A. Baron and W. Griffitt) Social Psychology: Understanding Human Interaction, 1974, (with R.A. Baron) 8th edit., 1997, (with R.A. Baron, B.H. Kantowitz) Psychology: Understanding Behavior, 1977, 2d edit., 1980, (with L.A. Byrne) Exploring Human Sexuality, 1977, (with W.A. Fisher) Adolescents, Sex, and Contraception, 1983, (with K. Kelley) Alternative Approaches to the Study of Sexual Behavior, 1986, (with K. Kelley) Exploring Human Sexuality, 1992; contbr. numerous articles to psychol. jours. and chpts. to anthologies. Grantee NSF, NIMH, U. Tex. Rsch. Inst., USAF, others; recipient Disting Sci. Achievement award Soc. for Scientific Study of Sexuality, 1989. Mem. Midwestern Psychol. Assn. (pres. 1979-80), Soc. for Sci. Study Sexuality (pres. 1990-93). Home: 15 Indian Hill Rd Feura Bush NY 12067-2602

BYRNE, GEORGE MELVIN, physician; b. San Francisco, Aug. 1, 1933; s. Carlton and Esther (Smith) B.; BA, Occidental Coll., 1958; MD, U. So. Calif., 1962; m. Joan Stecher, July 14, 1956; children: Kathryne, Michael, David; m. Margaret C. Smith, Dec. 18, 1982. Diplomate Am. Bd. Family Practice, 1971-84. Intern, Huntington Meml. Hosp., Pasadena, Calif., 1962-63, resident, 1963-64; family practice So. Calif. Permanente Med. Group, 1964-81, physician-in-charge Pasadena Clinic, 1966-81; asst. dir. Family Practice residency Kaiser Found. Hosp., L.A., 1971-73; clin. instr. emergency medicine Sch. Medicine, U. So. Calif., 1973-80; v.p. East Ridge Co., 1983-84, sec., 1984; dir. Alan Johnson Porsche Audi, Inc., 1974-82, sec., 1974-77, v.p., 1978-82. Bd. dirs. Kaiser-Permante Mgmt. Assn., 1976-77; mem. regional mgmt. com. So. Calif. Lung Assn., 1976-77; mem. pres.'s circle Occidental Coll., L.A. Drs. Symphony Orch, 1975-80; mem. profl. sect. Am. Diabetes Assn. Fellow Am. Acad. Family Physicians (charter); mem. Am., Calif., L.A. County Med. Assns., Calif. Acad. Family Physicians, Internat. Horn Soc., Quarter Century Wireless Assn., Am. Radio Relay League (Pub. Service award), Sierra (life), So. Calif. Dx Club. Home: 528 Meadowview Dr Flintridge CA 91011

BYRNE, JEFFREY EDWARD, pharmacology researcher, educator, consultant; b. Mpls., July 15, 1939; s. Maurice Charles and Edna F. (Kinney) B.; m. Janice Grove, Feb. 1, 1960 (dec. Apr., 1976); children: Christopher, Maura; m. Margaret Ann Kaiser, June 17, 1978, 1 child, Jason. BA, U. N.D., 1962; MA, U. S.D., 1964, PhD, 1966. Sr. rsch. assoc. Bristol-Myers Co., Evansville, Ind., 1969-81, prin. rsch. scientist, 1981-87; sr. rsch. scientist II Bristol-Myers Squibb Co., Wallingford, Conn., 1987-91, Princeton, N.J., 1991-94; cons. in field, 1994—; adj. faculty Ind. U. Sch. Medicine, Evansville, 1972-81, Evansville U. Sch. Nursing, 1972-81. Contbr. articles to profl. jours.; author (with others) books. Mem. Am. Soc. for Pharmacology and Exptl. Therapeutics, Am. Heart Assn., Internat. Soc. for Heart Rsch., AAAS. Republican. Lutheran. Home: 590 Atkinson Ln Langhorne PA 19047-1462

BYRNE, MARY WOODS, pediatric nurse practitioner. BSN, Cornell U.-N.Y. Hosp., 1966; MPH, Columbia U., 1970; MS in Nursing, Adelphi U., 1986, PhD with highest honors, 1988. Diplomate in nursing sci. Faculty to dir., chief exec. officer Misericordia Hosp. Med. Ctr. Sch. Nursing, 1980-82; staff nurse, maternity White Plains (N.Y.) Hosp. Med. Ctr., 1984-85; asst. dir. Health Professions Inst. Herbert H. Lehman Coll., CUNY, 1985-86, from instr. to asst. prof. dept. nursing, 1985-88; assoc. prof. Coll. Mt. St. Vincent, 1988-91, coord. acad. affairs to chmn. undergrad. nursing program, 1988-91; rsch. faculty Columbia U. Sch. Nursing, N.Y.C., 1991—; cons. Am. Health Found., Ethics Ctr.; guest prof. Gothenburg U., Sweden, 1996. Contbr. chpts. to books, articles to profl. jours. Recipient numerous awards, scholarships, honors. Mem. ANA, So. N.Y. League Nursing, Nightingale Soc., N.Y. State Nurses Assn., Sigma Theta Tau. Home: 197 St Johns Ave Yonkers NY 10704-2913 Office: Columbia U Sch Nursing 630 W 168th St New York NY 10032-3702

BYRNE-FOX, BARBARA AGNES, mental health nurse; b. Pitts., Oct. 2, 1949; m. Arthur Berl Fox. BS in Psychology, U. Pitts., 1982, MSN in Psychiatric, Mental Health Nursing, 1990; BSN, Duquesne U., 1986. LPN; cert. adult mental health nurse, clin. nurse specialist. Staff nurse Western Pa. Hosp., Pitts., 1968-70; staff LPN York (Pa.) County Hosp., 1970-71, Magee Women's Hosp., Pitts., 1971-86; staff RN/clinician Western Psychiat. Inst. & Clinic, Pitts., 1986-90, asst. nurse clin. mgr., 1990-91; psychiat. clin. nurse specialist VA Med. Ctr., Pitts., 1991—; mem. deans search com. U. Pitts., 1990; psychiat. cons. Dept. of Probation, Pitts., 1991—; conductor seminars in field. Co-editor: Research Guidebook for Nursing Practice, 1995. Bd. dirs. Easter Seals Soc., Pitts., 1979-84. Mem. Assn. Clin. Nurse Specialists (Pitts. chpt.), Duquesne U. Alumni Assn., Sigma Theta Tau (archivist 1993—, author newsletter 1994). Democrat. Roman Catholic. Home: 2627 Broadway Ave Pittsburgh PA 15216

BYRNES, JO ANN, social work administrator; b. Paterson, N.J., Dec. 12, 1949; d. George J. and Josephine (Balady) Hajjar. BA, Douglas Coll., 1974; MSW, NYU, 1976. Cert. ACSW; lic. clin. social worker. Dir. social svcs. Vis. Homemakers, Jersey City; dir. social svcs. and admissions Summit Ridge, West Orange, N.J.; pvt. practice family counselor; dir. social svcs. Raritan Bay Med. Ctr. Home: 335 Turrell Ave South Orange NJ 07079-2331

BYRNES, JOHN FRANCIS, JR., physician assistant; b. Tokyo, Sept. 22, 1954; s. John Francis and Georgene Alice (Cowling) B.; m. Laura Jean Lyell, Jan. 7, 1984. BA in Pre-Medicine, Rollins Coll., 1976; BS in Medicine, U. Fla., 1979. Cert. physician's asst. Cardiovascular and thoracic physician's asst. Cardiovascular Surgeons, P.A., Orlando, Fla., 1979-92; pres. Southeastern Clin. Rsch. Cons., Inc., Orlando, 1983—; surg. physician asst. Southeastern Clin. Svcs., Orlando, 1992—; vol. med. asst. Bangkok (Thailand) Mission Hosp., 1975; vis. mem. profl. group, USSR, 1974; mem. staff Ctrl. Fla. Regional Hosp., Sanford, Columbia Park Med. Ctr., Orlando, Fla. Hosp. Med. Ctr., Orlando, Health Ctrl. Hosp., Orlando, Orlando Regional Med. Ctr., Princeton Hosp., Orlando, South Seminold Cmty. Hosp., Longwood, Fla., Winter Park (Fla.) Meml. Hosp.; mem. cardiothroacic surgery clin. practice expert panel Soc. Thoracic Surgeons/Health Care Fin. Adminstrn., 1995—; presenter in field. Contbr. articles to profl. pubIs. Fellow Am. Acad. Physician Assts. (vice chmn. surg. congress 1987-89, chmn. 1989-95, mem. task force on recertification 1990-91, del. to ho. of dels. 1990-95, task force on specialty physician assts. 1992-93, mem. pres.' adv. group on third-party coverage 1995—), Am. Assn. Surgeon Assts. (John W. Kirklin MD award for excellence in cardiovascular surgery 1989), Fla. Acad. Physician Assts. (Fla. del. to nat. ho. reps. 1988-89, 96, chmn. profl. reimbursement com. 1992, pres.-elect 1995-96, pres. 1996—), Soc. Critical Care Medicine; mem. Assn. Clin. Pharmacology, Am. Heart Assn., Assn. Physician Assts. in Cardiovascular Surgery (co-founder, pres. 1981-85, bd. dirs. 1981-94, panel advisor 1985-90, hon. fellow 1995), Wilderness Med. Soc., Fla. Citrus Sports Assn. (med. com., team selection com.), Undersea and Hyperbaric Med. Soc., Am. Heart Inst. Office: Southeastern Clin Rsch Cons 531 Versailles Dr Ste 210 Maitland FL 32751

BYSTRYN, JEAN-CLAUDE, dermatologist, educator; b. Paris, May 8, 1938; came to U.S., 1949, naturalized, 1958; s. Iser and Sara Bystryn; m. Marcia Hammill, May 14, 1972; children: Anne, Alexander. BS, U. Chgo., 1958; MD, NYU, 1962. Diplomate Am. Bd. Dermatology, Am. Bd. Immunodermatopathology. Intern Montefiore Hosp., N.Y.C., 1962-63, resident in medicine, 1963-64; resident in dermatology NYU Sch. Medicine, N.Y.C., 1966-69, USPHS postgrad. tng. fellow in immunology, 1968-72, asst. prof. clin. dermatology, 1971-72, assoc. prof., 1976-84, prof., 1984—; asst. dispensary physician Albany Med. Coll., 1964-66; asst. attending physician Univ. Hosp., N.Y.C., 1969—; asst. vis. dermatologist Bellevue Hosp. Ctr., N.Y.C., 1969—; dir. Melanoma Program and Melanoma Immunotherapy Clinic, NYU Kaplan Cancer Ctr., dir. Bullous Disease Clinic and Immunofluorescence Lab. NYU Med. Sch.; mem. adv. bd. Skin Cancer found., Vitiligo Found., Nat. Alepecia Areata Found. Contbr. articles to profl. jours. Lt. comdr. USPHS, 1964-66. Recipient Husik Prize, NYU Sch. Medicine, 1968; Irma T. Hirschl research career award AOA; Ford. Found. fellow, 1954-58; NIH grantee, 1970—. Mem. Am. Dermatology Assn., Am. Acad. Dermatology, Am. Assn. Immunologists, Am. Assn. Cancer Rsch., Soc. Investigative Dermatology, N.Y. Dermatol. Soc., Am. Soc. Cell Biology. Office: NYU Med Ctr U Hosp 530 1st Ave New York NY 10016-6402

BZOCH, KENNETH RUDOLPH, speech and language educator, department chairman; b. Chgo., Nov. 6, 1927; s. Rudolph and Mildred (Novotney) B.; m. Lorrayne M. Cali, Oct. 29, 1950; children: Kathlene Marie, Kevin Jude. BA, DePaul U., Chgo., 1951; MA, Northwestern U., 1952, PhD, 1956. Cert. clin. competence-speech pathology, CCC-audiology; lic. speech pathologist, Fla. Asst. prof. Loyola U., Chgo., 1953-57, Northwestern U., Chgo., 1957-59; assoc. prof. U. Fla., Gainesville, 1960-64, prof., chair, 1964—; program dir. Communicative Disorders and Craniofacial Ctr., Shands Hosp., U. Fla.; researcher in field. Author: Communicative Disorders Related to Cleft Lip and Palate, 4th edit., Emergent Language Development Craniofacial Disorders. Cpl. USMC, 1946-47. Fellow Am. Cleft Palate Assn. (past pres.), Fla. Cleft Palate Assn. (hon., past pres.), Fla. Speech Lang. and Hearing Assn. (hon., past pres.). Home: 640 NW 57th St Gainesville FL 32607-6103 Office: U Fla PO Box 100174 Gainesville FL 32610-0174

CABALLERO, BENJAMIN HUMBERTO, pediatrician, nutritionist; b. Paso de los Libres, Argentina, Feb. 4, 1948; came to U.S., 1982; s. Faustino Gerardo and Maria Esther (Villalba) C.; m. Linda Jane Wedmore, Jan. 3, 1982; children: Tania Maria, Martín Gerardo. M.D., U. Buenos Aires. 1975; M.Sc., Inst. Nutrition, Pan Am. Health Orgn., 1982; PhD MIT, 1987. Chief resident pediatrics Childrens Hosp., Buenos Aires, Argentina, 1979; rsch. scientist UN, Guatemala, 1980-82; rsch. fellow dept. nutrition MIT, Cambridge, 1982-84, asst. dir. clin. research ctr., 1985-90; dir. nutrition svc. Children's Hosp., Boston, 1988-90; asst. prof. pediatrics Harvard U. Med Sch, 1988-90; dir. Ctr. for Human Nutrition Johns Hopkins U., 1990—, assoc. prof. internat. health and pediatrics. Contbr. articles to profl. jours. Mem. Am. Inst. Nutrition, Am. Soc. Clin. Nutrition, N.Y. Acad. Scis., Latin Am. Soc. Nutrition, Sigma Xi. Home: 698 Budleigh Cir Lutherville Timonium MD 21093 Office: John Hopkins U 615 N Wolfe St Rm 2041 Baltimore MD 21205-2103

CABALLES, ROMEO LOPEZ, pathologist, bone tumor researcher; b. Pagsanjan, Laguna, The Philippines, Dec. 10, 1925; came to U.S., 1955; s. Eladio Luna and Ceferina (Lopez) C.; m. Lucia Rose Mercadante, June 29, 1958; children: Romeo Jr., Rose, Theresa, Nancy, James. AA, U Santo Tomas, 1946-48, MD, 1948-54. Diplomate Am. Bd. Pathology. Asst. pathologist St. Michael's Med. Ctr., Newark, N.J., 1960-68; assoc. pathologist United Hosp. Med. Ctr., Newark, 1968-74, attending pathologist, 1974-85, interim dir. labs., 1978-79; pathologist United Hosp. Orthopedic Ctr., Newark, 1968-85; clin. asst. prof. N.J. Med. Sch., Newark, 1971-81, clin. assoc. prof., 1981—; pro adv. panelist Med. Lab. Observer, Fairlawn, N.J., 1971-72; course dir. United Hosp. Orthopedic Ctr. Skeletal Symposium, Newark, 1977. Contbr. articles to profl. jours. Fellow Coll. Am. Pathologists, N.Y. Acad. Medicine; mem. N.Y. Acad. Scis., N.J. Soc. Pathologists, Philippine-Am. Med. Assn. (N.J. founding mem.), Practitioners Club N.J. Republican. Roman Catholic. Home: 2 Keystone Dr Livingston NJ 07039-1808

CABANAS, ELIZABETH ANN, nutritionist; b. Port Arthur, Tex., Oct. 27, 1948; d. William Rosser and Frances Merle (Block) Thornton. BS, U. Tex., 1971; MPH, U. Hawaii, 1973; postgrad., Tex. Woman's U., 1991—. Registered dietitian. Clin. nutritionist Family Planning Inst. Kapiolani Hosp., Honolulu, 1972-74; dietitian Kauikeolani Children's Hosp.-Pacific Inst. Rehab. Medicine, Honolulu, 1974-75; dietitian San Antonio Ind. Schs., 1975-84, asst. food service adminstr., 1984-89; coord. equipment and facilities Dallas Ind. Sch., 1990-91; dietitian SureQuest Solutions in Software, Richardson, Tex., 1990-91; nutritionist div. endocrinology, metabolism and hypertension, clin. studies unit rsch. nutritionist, asst. prof. dept. health related scis. U. Tex. Med. Br., Galveston, 1991—; lectr. nutrition U. Hawaii, Honolulu, 1974-75, St. Mary's U., San Antonio Coll., 1984-90; adj. faculty Tex. Woman's U., 1994—; cons. nutritionist, 1980—; presenter in field. Contbr. articles to profl. jours. Recipient diabetes educator recognition Eli Lilly & Co., 1994. Mem. Am. Dietetic Assn., Am. Assn. Diabetes Educators, Assn. Sch. Bus. Ofcls. Internat., Nutrition and Food Svc. Mgmt. Com., Am. Diabetes Assn. (adv. com. U. Tex. Med. Br. children's diabetes mgmt. program 1993—, mem. Galveston County diabetes support group 1991—, Disting. Svc. award 1995), Coun. Nutritional Scis. and Metabolism (profl. sect., non-peer rev. com. 1993-94), Tex. Sch. Food Svc. Assn. (dist. bd. dirs. 1977-78), Tex. Nutrition Coun. (nominating com. 1996-99, sports and cardiovasc. nutritionists practice group, Tex. gerontol. nutritionists practice group), Houston Area Dietetic Assn. (legis. network com. 1995—), San Antonio Sch. Food Svc. Assn. (com. chmn. 1975-89), Tex. Assn. Sch. Bus. Ofcls., Tex. Restaurant Assn., San Antonio Area Food Svc. Adminstrs. Assn. (pres. 1989-90), Assn. Profls. in Positions of Leadership in Edn., Dallas Dietetic Assn. (cons. nutritionists practice group, chmn. 1990-91), San Antonio Mus. Assn., Randolph C. of C., Grand Opera House, Galveston (patron), Galveston Hist. Found., Space City Ski Club, Sierra Club, Hawaii Club (chmn. entertainment com. 1983). Republican. Methodist. Home: 711 Holiday Dr Apt 75 Galveston TX 77550-5579 Office: Univ Tex Med Br Rte 1060 301 University Blvd Galveston TX 77555-1060

CABANSAG, VICENTE DACANAY, JR., medical association administrator; b. Solano, Neuva Vizcaya, Philippines, Jan. 20, 1942; Arrived in U.S., June 1968.; s. Vicente Pascua and Marcelina Espero (Dacanay) C.; m. Nieves Lalas, Dec. 6, 1970; children: Sharon Rose, Karen Mae, Vincent Walter. Student, Philippine Union Coll., Baesa, Caloocan City, 1962; postgrad., U. of the East RMMMC, Quezon City, Philippines, 1968. Surg. intern Christ Hosp., Cin., 1968-69; surg. resident Bapt. Hosp., Nashville, 1969-70, St. John's Hosp., Detroit, 1970-73; pvt. practice Sturgis, Mich., 1974—; chief of surgery Sturgis Hosp., 1976-86, v.p. med. staff, 1987—; pres. med. staff, trustee Sturgis Hosp., 1988-89; cons. gen. surgery LaGrance County Hosp., Ind., 1979-85; med. dir. Southwestern Mich. Laser Clinic, Sturgis, 1987—. Fellow Am. Soc. Abdominal Surgeons, Soc. Philippine Surgeons in Am., Am. Soc. Laser Medicine and Surgery; mem. AMA, Mich. Med. Soc., St. Joseph Med. Soc., Mich. Soc. Gen. Surgeons, N.Am. Soc. of Phlebology. Home: 439 Liberty Rd Sturgis MI 49091-9583

CABLE, DANA GERARD, psychologist; b. Sewickley, Pa., Aug. 27, 1943; s. Boyd and Jean (Clover) C.; m. Sylvia Kaufman, Mar. 19, 1977; children: David, Jennifer. AB, W.Va. Wesleyan Coll., 1965; MA, W.Va. U., 1971, PhD, 1972. Lic. psychologist; cert. grief counselor, death educator. Rsch. asst. W.Va. Wesleyan Coll., Buckhannon, 1965-68; instr. W.Va. U., Morgantown, 1968-71, vis. asst. prof., 1971-72; prof. psychology Hood Coll., Frederick, Md., 1972—; pvt. practice, 1974—. Author: Death and Dying, 1983; mem. editl. bd. Am. Jour. of Hospice and Palliative Care, 1988—. Mem. Md. Commn. on Aging, 1979-83; bd. dirs. Citizens Nursing Home, Frederick, 1977-82, 87-93, 94—, Daybreak Adult Day Care Ctr., Frederick, 1988-94, Hospice of Frederick County, 1991—, cons., 1981—. NDEA fellow, 1968-72; recipient Svc. award Assn. for Death Edn. and Counseling, 1982, Clin. Practice award Assn. for Death Edn. and Counseling, 1995. Mem. APA, Assn. Death Edn. (bd. dirs. 1981-87, 90-93), Gerontol. Soc., Internat. Platform Assn., Md. Gerontol. Assn. (bd. dirs. 1981-83), Capital Dist. Kiwanis (gov. 1990-91, Kiwanian of Yr.), Kiwanis Internat. (internat. chmn. tng. and leadership devel. 1993—), Elks. Republican. Home: 8605 Pinecliff Dr Frederick MD 21704-6619 Office: Hood Coll Frederick MD 21701

CABOT, JOSEPH, retired pedodontist; b. Detroit, Oct. 15, 1921; s. Benjamin and Ethel (Gutkovsky) C.; BS, Wayne State U., 1942; DDS, U. Mich., 1945, MS, 1947; m. Ruth Weiner, Aug. 19, 1945; children: Bonnie Cabot Kaufman, Gary Michael, Elizabeth Ann Cabot Stenvig, Jon Elliott. Mott fellow U. Mich., 1945-46; pedontic fellow Hurley Hosp., Flint, Mich., 1946-47; individual practice pedontics, Detroit, 1947-84, Lathrup Village, Mich., 1969-84; ret. 1984. Mem. bd. Delta Dental Plan Mich., 1959—, pres., 1963-66; pres., Detroit Dental Aid, 1952-55, pres. Profl. Planning Cons., 1985—. Local bd. chmn. Selective Svc., 1959-67, appeal bd. chmn., 1969—, dental adviser to state dir., 1968—; assemblyman United Community Svcs., 1971-77; pres. Nat. Found. Dentistry for the Handicapped; mem. dean's vis. com. U. Mich. Sch. Dentistry, 1983, hosting com., 1983-89; mem. Detroit Exec. Svc. Corps, 1989; dir. Nat. Found. Dental Handicapped; corp. mem. DELTA Dental Health Plan. Maj. Dental Corps, AUS, 1955-57. Recipient Disting. Svc. award U. Mich. Sch. Dentistry, 1993. Fellow Internat. Coll. Dentists, Am. Coll. Dentists, Am. Acad. Pedodontics; mem. ADA (ho. of dels. 1965-76, trustee 1977-83, 1st v.p. 1983-84), Mich. Dental Assn. (pres. 1975-76), Mich. Soc. Dentistry for Children (pres. 1953-54), Detroit Dist. Dental Soc. (Merit award 1964, pres. 1966-67), Kenneth A. Easlick Grad. Soc. (pres. 1973-75), Pierre Fauchard Acad., Wayne State U. Alumni Assn. (dir. 1989), Omicron Kappa Upsilon, Alpha Omega. Home: 3115 S Ocean Blvd Apt 501 Highland Bch FL 33487-2560 Office: 7459 Middlebelt Rd West Bloomfield MI 48322-4184

CACCAMO, MICHAEL, radiologist; b. Dearborn, Mich., July 26, 1963; s. Frank and Rosemary (Mileto) C.; m. Lisa Jean Herzog, June 11, 1988; children: Jimmy, Christina. BS in Chemistry and Biology, Wayne State U., 1986; DO, Mich. State U., 1990. Diplomate Am. Bd. Diagnostic Radiology. Chief intern Mich. Health Ctr., Detroit, 1990; chief resident in radiology Mich. Hosp. and Med. Ctr., Detroit, 1994-95; radiologist Greene Meml. Hosp., Xenia, Ohio, 1995—.

CACECI, THOMAS, biologist, anatomy educator; b. N.Y.C., Dec. 8, 1947; s. Thomas G. and Silvia J. (Buonocore) C.; m. Susan Ann Wolfe, June 28, 1975. AB, Kenyon Coll., 1969; PhD, Georgetown U., 1980. Program analyst Occupational Safety and Health Adminstrn. U.S. Dept. Labor, Washington, 1976-77; biologist FDA, Washington, 1977-80; rsch. associate George Washington U. Med. Ctr., Washington, 1980-82; instr. Prince Georges Community Coll., Largo, Md., 1982; asst. prof. vet. medicine Tex. A&M U., College Station, 1982-87; assoc. prof. Va./Md. Regional Coll. Vet. Medicine, Va. Poly. Inst. and State U., Blacksburg, 1987—. Author: (with authors) Biomaterials, 1986, Les Organes Lymphoides, 1990; contbr. over 50 articles to profl. jours. Staff sgt. USAF, 1970-74, Vietnam. Grantee NIH, 1983-84, 84-85, 85-86, 87-88, NAS, 1988-90, Am. Heart Assn., 1981-82, 1985-86, Nat. Oceanic and Atmoshperic Assn., 1989—, Alaska Dept. Wildlife, 1989-90, Arab Republic Egypt Peace Fellowship program, 1989-90, 92—, Va. Poly. Inst. and State U., 1987-88, 88-89, 89-90, numerous other grants in field; Georgetown U. fellow, 1975-79, Am. Heart Assn. Mamie D. Eisenhower Meml. fellow, 1981-82; N.Y. State Regents scholar, 1965. Mem. Am. Assn. Vet. Anatomists (corr. sec. 1988-90, pres. 1991-92), Am. Vet. Computer Soc., Electron Microscopy Soc. Am., Am. Fisheries Soc., Internat. Assn. Aquatic Animal Medicine, Am. Soc. of Icthyologists and Herpetologists, Tex. Soc. for Electron Microscopy, N.Y. Acad. Scis., Sigma Xi. Home: 1405 Westover Dr Blacksburg VA 24060-2650 Office: Va Poly Inst and State U Va/Md Regional Coll Vet Medicine Dept Biomed Scis Blacksburg VA 24061

CACERES, CESAR AUGUSTO, cardiologist; b. Puerto Cortes, Honduras, Apr. 9, 1927; s. Julian Rios and Mariana (Culotta) C. BS, Georgetown U., 1949, MD, 1953. Diplomate Nat. Bd. Med. Examiners. Intern, resident Boston City Hosp., 1953-55; resident New Eng. Med. Ctr., Boston, 1955-56; fellow in cardiology George Washington U. Hosp., Washington, 1957-60; from assoc. in medicine to clin. prof. cmty. & family med. Georgetown U. Med. Ctr., 1960—. Co-author: Electronic and Computer-Assisted Studies of Bio-Medical Problems, 1964, Diagnostic Computers, 1969, The Practice of Clinical Engineering, 1977; editor: Bio-Medical Telemetry, 1965, Management and Clinical Engineering, 1980, The Management of Technology in Health and Medical Care, 1980; co-editor: The Innocent Murmur, 1967, Clinical Electrocardiography and Computers, 1970, The Practice of Clinical Engineering, 1977, Medical Devices: Measurments, Quality Assurance, and Standards, 1983; contbr. articles to profl. jours.; editl. bd. Am. Jour. Electrocardiography, Computers in Biology & Medicine. Fellow Am. Heart Assn. Coun. Clin. Cardiology, Am. Heart Assn. Coun. Epidemiology, Am. Coll. Chest Physicians, Am. Coll. Med. Informatics; mem. Federal Profl. Assn., Soc. Advanced Med. Sys. (pres. 1969-70), ASTM, Internat. Health Evaluation Assn., Assn. for Advancement of Med. Instrumentation, Am. Soc. Internal Medicine. Roman Catholic. Home: 2500 Virginiana Ave NW Washington DC 20037 Office: 1759 Q Ste NW Washington DC 20009

CADDIGAN, MARY, health facility administrator; b. N.Y.C., June 25, 1943; d. John S. and Loretta (Zabicki) Budzinski; m. John F. Caddigan II, Sept. 5, 1964; children: Lisa Marie, Jacqueline Ann. Diploma, St. Clare's Hosp. Sch., N.Y.C., 1963; student, William Patterson Coll. RN, N.J.; Certified Rehab. RN. Nursing adminstr. Gen. Hosp., Passaic, N.J., head nurse, CCU; cardiac nurse practitioner pvt. office, Rutherford, N.J.; staff nurse Kessler Rehab. Hosp., Chester, N.J., 1990-91, unit coord., 1991—; pastoral minister in hospice program. Recipient recognition Passaic County Heart Assn., 1990. Home: 19 Rhone Rd Hopatcong NJ 07843-1822

CADDY, DEBORAH CAROL RUNYAN, social worker; b. Arkadelphia, Ark., Jan. 24, 1958; d. Dean and Marilyn (Yancey) Runyan; m. Rod Caddy, May 26, 1979; 1 child, Hallie Kaitlin. BA, Ouachita Bapt. U., 1980; MS Social Work, U. Tex., Arlington, 1986. Dir. rape crisis program Women's Ctr. Tarrant County, Ft. Worth, 1986—. Mem. NASW, Alpha Delta Mu. Office: Womens Ctr Tarrant County PO Box 11860 Fort Worth TX 76110-0860

CADE, TONI MARIE, medical educator; b. St. Martinville, La., Dec. 5, 1957; d. Dennis Peter and Susie Ann (Benoit) Hulin; m. Robert William Cade, June 9, 1978; children: Chelsea Lynn, Brittany Marie, Haley Elizabeth. BS, U. Southwestern La., 1979, MBA, 1991. Reg. record adminstr.; cert. coding specialist. Receptionist Surgery Ctr., Lafayette, La., 1976-77; supr. utilization review profl. stds. Rev. Orgn., Lafayette, La., 1979-80; coding supr. Our Lady of Lourdes Regional Med. Ctr., Lafayette, La., 1980-86, cons. health info. dept., 1987-88; cons. med. record OPTION Care, Lafayette, La., 1991; instr. med. record adminstrn. U. Southwestern La., Lafayette, 1987-92, instr. health info. mgmt., 1992-94, asst. prof. health info. mgmt., 1994—; cons. St. Anthony's Cons. Group, Reston, Va., 1995—; lectr. in field. Author: Medical Terminology Instructor's Resource and Activity Kit, 1994. Judge Jr. High Sch. Sci. Fair, Lafayette, 1995; vol. Lafayette Cmty. Health Care Clinic, 1993-94; participant United Way, Lafayette, 1987—. Mem. Am. Health Info. Mgmt. Assn. (del. 1992, 94, 95), Southwest Dist. Health Info. Mgmt. Assn. (dist. rep. 1993, treas. 1994-95), La. Health Info. Mgmt. Assn. (bylaws-strategy mgr. 1990-91, state convention project mgr. 1992-93, coding roundtable project mgr. 1995-96). Roman Catholic. Office: U So La PO Box 41007 Lafayette LA 70504

CADIEUX, ROGER JOSEPH, physician, mental health care executive; b. Bay Shore, N.Y., Feb. 7, 1945; children: Kevin, Kristin. BS, Northwestern State U., 1973; MD, La. State U., 1977. Cert. geriatric psychiatrist, RN anesthetist. Intern, then resident in psychiatry Coll. Medicine Pa. State U., Hershey, 1977-81, psychogeriatric fellow, instr. Coll. Medicine Milton S. Hershey Med. ctr., 1980-81, asst. prof. dept. psychiatry, 1981-93; assoc. prof. psychiatry, 1993—; dir. geriatric assessment program Pa. State U. Coll. Medicine, 1992—; psychiat. cons. Jewish Home of Harrisburg, 1985—, Homeland Ctr. of Harrisburg, 1993—; program dir. Pa. Dept. Aging, 1986—, physician cons., 1987—; pres. Commonwealth Affiliates, P.C., 1992—; assoc. dir. sleep rsch. and treatment ctr. Coll. Medicine Milton S. Hershey Med. Ctr., Pa. State U., 1981—. Contbr. articles to profl. jours. Fellow Am. Bd. Psychiatry and Neurology (diplomate); mem. Am. Psychiat. Assn., Am. Geriatric Soc., Am. Assn. for Geriatric Psychiatry, Acad. Sleep Disorders Medicine, Alpha Omega Alpha. Office: 2215 Forest Hills Dr Harrisburg PA 17112-1062

CADIGAN, ELISE, social worker; b. Topeka, Mar. 8, 1947; d. Grattan C. Huckabee and Virginia (Ross) Huckabee Specht; m. Glenn Koski, 1989; children: Kent, Matthew, Drew. BS, Washburn U., 1972; MSW, Kans. U., 1977. Bd. cert. diplomate clin. social work; lic. clin. social worker, Ill. Adj. prof. social work Ottawa (Kans.) U., 1977-78; social worker Lawrence (Kans.) Sch. Dist., 1978-79, Harlem Sch. Dist., Loves Park, Ill., 1979-82; pvt. practice Glenwood Evaluation & Treatment Ctr., Rockford, Ill., 1980—; mgr. adolescent svcs. Swedish Am. Hosp., Rockford, 1984-88; adj. faculty U. Ill., Rockford. Bd. dirs. Big Bros./Big Sisters, Rockford, 1980-85, Children's Devel. Ctr., 1986-94, pres., 1992-93. Mem. NASW (dist. chair 1983-85, Social Worker of Yr. award 1988), Rockford Area Substance Abuse Coun. (Cmty. Vol. of Yr. award 1988), Rockford Jr. League, Rockford Womans Club, Rotary (bd. dirs. Rockford club 1994-96), Phi Delta Kappa. Episcopalian. Office: Glenwood Ctr 2823 Glenwood Ave Rockford IL 61101-3542

CADORETTE, LISA ROBERTS, medical, surgical nurse; b. Johnson City, N.Y., June 12, 1966; d. John Lawrence and Dorothy Ellen (Ace) Roberts; m. Jeffrey Cadorette, May 31,1991; children: Jessica Renee, Jacqueline Elyse. BSN magna cum laude, Neumann Coll., 1989. RN, Pa.; cert. ACLS Am. Heart Assn. Commd. lt. USAF Nurse Corps., 1989; staff nurse USAF Nurse Corps., Andrews AFB, Md., 1989-90, Dover AFB, Del., 1990-91; asst. to chair divsn. nursing and health scis. Neumann Coll., Aston, Pa., 1992—; vol. emergency med. technician Lima (Pa.) Fire Co., 1988-91, Media (Pa.) Fire Co., 1988-91. Mem. Nightingale Soc., Sigma Theta Tau, Delta Epsilon Sigma. Office: Neumann Coll Divsn Nursing and Hlth Scis Aston PA 19014

CADWALDER, HUGH MAURICE, psychology educator; b. Mt. Ayer, Iowa, July 1, 1924; s. Hugh M. and Mary (Crouch) C.; m. Melba Atwood, May 22, 1944 (div. 1975); children: Mark M., Mindy M.; m. Dianna Renfro-Reeves, May 15, 1980. MA, Baylor U., Waco, Tex., 1955, PhD, 1962; DD, Houston Bible Coll., 1963; ArtsD (hon.), Inst. Applied Rsch., London, 1970. Lic. master social worker, Tex., chem. dependency counselor, Tex.; cert. compulsive gambling specialist, Tex., clin. assoc. Am. Bd. Med. Psychotherapists, cert. criminal justice specialist; master addictions counselor; ordained to ministry Bapt. Ch., 1944. Instr. psychology Baylor U., Waco, Tex., 1955-62; acad. dean Southwestern Agrl. Coll., Waxahachie, Tex., 1962-64; sr. minister Christian Life Community Ch., Dallas, 1964-69, 1st Assembly of God Ch., Corpus Christi, Tex., 1969-74; chmn. psychology dept. San Jacinto Coll., Pasadena, Tex., 1974—; seminar dir. Cadwalder Behavioral Ctr., Houston, 1982-90; staff psychologist Charter Hosp., Sugar Land, Tex., 1990-95; full staff mem. Bellaire (Tex.) Gen. Hosp., 1993—, Forest Springs Hosp., Houston, 1988-95; seminar dir. Sharpstown Christian Singles, Houston, 1975-92; v.p. 1st Colony Mcpl. Utility Dist. 6, Sugar Land, 1988-96; host radio talk show Sta. KTEK. Author: Some Psychological Determinants Involved in Religious Attitudes, 1965, The Spiritual Dimension of Recovery from Addiction, 1988, Emotional Adhesions and Their Cure, 1989, Some Current Trends in the Mental Health Field, Or What To Do until the Psychiatrist Arrives with the Paramedics, 1995. Pres. bd. Community Ednl. TV Network, 1989-92; bd. dirs. Cadwalder Behavioral Ctr.; mem. Rep. Presdl. Task Force. Mem. NASW, Am. Assn. Coll. Profs., Am. Pub. Health Assn., Community Coll. Humanities Assn., Am. Assn. Retired Persons, Tex. Jr. Coll. Tchrs. Assn., Am. Assn. Christian Counselors, Am. Bd. Med. Psychotherapy, Am. Coun. on Alcoholism, Am. Assn. Coll. Profs., Community Coll. Humanities Assn., Harris County Sheriff's Deputies Assn. (cert. hon. membership 1985), Nat. Mental Health Assn., N.Y. Acad. Sci., Tex. Assn. Social Workers, Nat. Asns. Ind. Bus., Forum Club Houston, Phi Delta Kappa. Office: Cadwalder Counseling 7324 Southwest Fwy Ste 850 Houston TX 77074-2037

CADWALLADER, DONALD ELTON, pharmacy educator; b. Buffalo, June 14, 1931; s. Donald E. and Catherine E. (Russell) C.; m. Cecelia Vidis, Feb. 13, 1961; children—Susan, Keith, Lynn. B.S. in Pharmacy, U. Buffalo, 1953; M.S. in Medicinal Chemistry, U. Ga., 1955; Ph.D. in Pharmaceutics, U. Fla., 1957. Research assoc. pharmacy dept. Sterling Winthrop Research Inst., Rensselaer, N.Y., 1958-60; sect. head pharmacy dept. White Labs., Kenilworth, N.J., 1960-61; asst. prof. Sch. Pharmacy U. Ga., 1961-64, assoc. prof., 1964-68, prof., 1968-77, prof., head dept. pharmacy, 1977-80, prof., 1980-90, head dept. pharmaceutics, 1991, part-time prof., prof. emeritus pharmaceutics. Author: Biopharmaceutics and Drug Interactions, 3d edit., 1983. Fellow AAAS, Am. Assn. Pharm. Scis., Acad. Pharm. Scis.; mem. Am. Pharm. Assn., Am. Assn. Colls. of Pharmacy, Sigma Xi. Home: 470 Brookwood Dr Athens GA 30605-3851 Office: U Ga Coll Pharmacy Athens GA 30602

CADY, PATRICIA ANN, critical care nurse; b. White Plains, N.Y., Oct. 6, 1956; d. George L. and Elizabeth A. (O'Neil) C. BSN, Georgetown U., 1978; MS, Boston Coll., 1984, PhD, 1991. Cert. critical care nurse. Clin. nurse surg. ICU Beth Israel Hosp., Boston, 1978—. Contbr. articles to profl. jours. Rose F. Kennedy fellow in nursing ethics. Mem. AACN, ANA, Mass. Nurses Assn., Sigma Theta Tau.

CAFFAREL, RANDAL CYRIL, psychiatrist, ophthalmologist; b. Baton Rouge, La., Sept. 29, 1948; s. Cyril Alonzo Jr. and Ann Lois (Thibodeaux) C. BA in Chemistry, La. State U., 1970; MD, La. State U. Medical Ctr., New Orleans, 1974. Diplomate Am. Bd. Ophthalmology, Am. Bd. Psychiatry and Neurology, Am. Bd. Adolescent Psychiatry. Intern Lake Charles (La.) Charity Hosp., 1974; ophthalmology resident La. State U. Med. Ctr., New Orleans, 1974-77, chief resident in ophthalmology, 1977, psychiatry resident, 1986-90, chief resident in psychiatry, 1989-90; ophthalmologist Ophthalmology Assocs., Baton Rouge, La., 1977-83; pvt. practice specializing in ophthalmology Baton Rouge, 1983-86; psychiatrist Davis Psychiat. Clinic, Harahan, La., 1990-91; staff psychiatrist adolescent unit S.E. La. Hosp., Mandeville, 1991-93, clin. dir. short stay adolescent program, 1993-96, vice chmn. med. staff, 1995-96; clin. asst. prof. psychiatry Tulane Med. Ctr., New Orleans, 1994—, U. South Ala., 1996—; vice chief ophthalmology Baton Rouge Gen. Med. Ctr., 1982, chief of staff chem. dependency unit, 1985-86; vice chief ophthalmology Our Lady of Lake Regional Med. Ctr., 1983, chief ophthalmology, 1984, mem. med. morals com., 1979-86; mem. adv. bd. Silkworth Ctr., 1984; adult and adolescent psychiatrist PrimeHealth, Mobile, Ala., 1996—; vis surgeon Charity Hosp. La., New Orleans, 1977-78. Bd. dirs. Lambda Ctr., Baton Rouge, 1985, Met. Community Ch., Baton Rouge, 1985. Recipient Physician's Recogniton award AMA, 1978, 83, 86, 89. Mem. Am. Psychiat. Assn. (continuing edn. award 1988), Am. Soc. Adolescent Psychiatry, So. Med. Assn., La. Psychiat. Medicine Assn. Democrat. Roman Catholic. Office: Prime Health 1400 University Blvd Ste K Mobile AL 36609-2999

CAFFERATA, RUTHANN, staff nurse; b. New Castle, Pa., Jan. 23, 1961; d. William John and Mary Jane (Bayuk) Zehner; m. Derek Keith Cafferata, Feb. 23, 1990. Diploma, James Hosp. Sch. Nursing, New Castle, 1982; BSN, Pa. State U., 1985; MSN, LaRoche Coll., Pitts., 1990. RN, Pa., Ohio, U.K.; cert. obstetric nurse Nat. Cert. Corp. Ob-gyn staff nurse Jameson Hosp., New Castle, 1982-87; NICU staff nurse West Pa. Hosp., Pitts., 1987-89; nursing instr. James Sch. Nursing, New Castle, 1990-94; staff nurse maternity St. Joseph Health Ctr., Warren, Ohio, 1994—. Mem. Sigma Theta Tau. Home: 3259 Overlook Dr NE Warren OH 44483-5621

CAFIERO, ANTHONY JOSEPH, financial analyst; b. Hartford, Conn., Mar. 14, 1968; s. Andrew John and Gloria Mary (Ponzillo) C. BS, Providence Coll., 1990; MS, U. New Haven, 1995. Internal auditor City West Haven, Conn., 1990-92; assoc. adminstr. Yale Sch. Medicine, New Haven, 1993-95; sr. fin. analyst Yale-New Haven Hosp., 1995—. Com. Am. Cancer Soc., Wallingford, Conn., 1995—. Mem. Assn. Acad. Surg. Adminstrs., Med. Group Mgmt. Assn., Healthcare Fin. Mgmt. Assn. Home: 28 Duncan St East Haven CT 06512 Office: Yale-New Haven Hosp 20 York St New Haven CT 06504

CAGE, JOHN MICHAEL, urologist; b. Monroe, La., May 8, 1936; s. Joseph Shelby and Virginia Fern (Ziegler) C.; m. Mary Virginia Stovall, June 18, 1960 (dec. 1979); children: Laura, Michael, Elizabeth, Sara; m. Lela Dianne King, Feb. 1989. BS, La. Tech. U., 1957; MD, La. State U., 1961. Diplomate Am. Bd. Urology. Resident urology La. State U., Shreveport, 1962-66; pvt. practice urology Monroe, 1966—. Fellow Am. Coll. Surgeons; mem. Am. Urol. Assn. Republican. Methodist. Office: 711 St John St Monroe LA 71201-8435

CAGGINS, RUTH PORTER, nurse, educator; b. Natchez, Miss., July 11, 1945; d. Henry Chapelle and Corinne Sadie (Baines) Porter; m. Don Randolph Caggins, July 1, 1978; children: Elva Rene, Don Randolph, Myles Thomas Chapelle. BS, Dillard U., New Orleans, 1967; MA, NYU, 1973; PhD Tex. Woman's U., 1992. Staff nurse Montefiore Hosp., Bronx, 1968-70, head nurse, 1970-72; nurse clinician Met. Hosp., N.Y.C., 1973-74, clin. supr., 1974-76; asst. prof. U. So. La., Lafayette, 1976-78; assoc. prof. Prairie View A&M U. Coll. Nursing, Houston, 1978—, apptd. project dir. LIFT Ctr. Active The Links Inc., Houston, 1982—, Cultural Arts Coun., Houston, Nat. Black Leadership Initiative on Cancer, Houston. Recipient Tchg. Excellence award Nat. Inst. Staff and Orgnl. Devel., 1992-93. Mem. ANA (clin. ethnic/racial minority fellow 1989-92, post doctoral proposal devel. program 1995), Nat. Black Nurses Assn., A.K. Rice Inst. (assoc. Ctrl. States Ctr., Tex. Ctr.), Assn. Black Nursing Faculty in Higher Edn. (Dissertation award 1990), Sigma Theta Tau, Delta Sigma Theta, Chi Eta Phi. Democrat. Baptist. Avocations: singing, sewing, traveling, aerobics, writing. Home: 5602 Goettee Cir Houston TX 77091-4523 Office: Prairie View A&M U Coll Nursing 6436 Fannin St Houston TX 77030-1519

CAGLE, PAULETTE BERNICE, mental health administrator and psychologist; b. Ft. Worth, July 14, 1944; d. James Frank and Cordelia Pauline (Bourke) C. BS, North Tex. State U., 1972; MA, So. Meth. U., 1976. Lic. chem. dependency counselor; cert. diagnostic and evaluation psychologist; qualified mental health profl. Part-time psychometrist Jack Waxler, Psychologist, Richardson, Tex., 1973-77; social worker Vernon (Tex.) State Hosp., 1977-78, psychologist, 1978-88; adminstr. tech. programs Wichita Falls (Tex.) State Hosp., 1988-91, assoc. dir. mgmt. and support, 1991—; cons. mem. quality improvement coun. Vernon State Hosp., 1992—. Co-founder and mem. Cmty. Svcs. Quality Assurance Dirs. of Tex., 1993—; designated contact Mental Health Disaster Assistance, Austin, 1994—; mem. Wichita County Mental Health Assn., 1992—. Named Sister of the Yr. Sisterhood of Freedom, 1991. Mem. Am. Counseling Assn., Am. Mental Health Counselors Assn., Tex. Assn. Alcoholism and Drug Abuse Counselors, Internat. Assn. of Marriage and Family Counselors. Office: Texas Dept Mental Health Wichita Falls State Hosp PO Box 300 Wichita Falls TX 76307-0300

CAGLIERO, ENRICO, endocrinologist; b. Torino, Italy, May 18, 1955; came to U.S., 1981; s. Giovanni Pietro and Teresa (Carminati) C.; m. Monica Galizzi, June 25, 1994. BS, Liceo Segre, Torino, 1973; MD, U. Torino, 1979. Rsch. fellow U. London, 1980; intern in medicine U. Torino, 1981; rsch. fellow, resident in medicine U. Calif., San Diego, 1982-87; fellow in medicine Mass. Gen. Hosp., Boston, 1987-90; vis. adj. prof. U. Genova, Italy, 1990-91; vis. scientist U. Uppsala, Sweden, 1991-92; asst. scientist Schepens Eye Rsch. Inst., Boston, 1992-94; asst. prof. medicine Harvard Med. Sch., 1995—. Mem. Am. Diabetes Assn. (rsch. award 1992), Juvenile Diabetes Found. (med. sci. reviewer 1995, rsch. award 1992), Mass. Med. Sci., European Assn. for the Study Diabetes. Office: Mass Gen Hosp Diabetes Unit Fruit St Boston MA 02114

CAGNEY, WILLIAM ROBERT, psychologist; b. Pitts., Oct. 7, 1937; s. Edward Patrick and Pearl Barbara (Sebastian) C.; m. Vivian Antoinette Tartaglia, June 26, 1965; children: Lori Anne, Julie Alissa, Melissa Beth. BS, Duquesne U., 1960, MA, 1965, PhD, 1968. Lic. psychologist, Pa.; cert. Nat. Register Health Svcs. Providers in Psychology. Psychology intern, staff psychologist Dixmont State Hosp., Glenfield, Pa., 1962-68; staff psychologist South Hills Child Guidance Ctr., Pitts., 1968-69; asst. dir., psychol. svcs. Woodville State Hosp., Carnegie, Pa., 1968-70; chief psychologist Counseling Ctr. of South Hills, Pitts., 1970-72; clin. dir. Chartiers MH/MR Ctr., Bridgeville, Pa., 1972-79; pvt. practice Pitts., 1971—; cons. Outreach South, Mt. Lebanon, Pa., 1976—, South Hills Interfaith Ministries, Bethel Park, Pa., 1969—, Crisis Addiction Recovery Edn., Inc., Washington, Pa., 1984-88, YMCA South Hills, Pitts., 1977-78; field supr. dept. psychology U. Pitts., 1970-73, W.Va. U., Morgantown, 1973-78; resident psychologist Sta. KDKA-TV Pitts. Today, 1978-79; presenter seminars and workshops to profl. and cmty. groups, 1972—. Cons. Twp. Upper St. Clair Adminstrn., Police, Schs., Family Resource Program, Upper St. Clair, Pa., 1986-89. Fellow Pa. Psychol. Assn.; mem. APA, Greater Pitts. Psychol. Assn. Office: 1725 Washington Rd Ste 509 Pittsburgh PA 15241-1207

CAHAN, LESLIE DARYLL, neurosurgeon, educator; b. Los Angeles, Oct. 12, 1946; s. Aaron and Ruth (Weiner) C.; m. Melinda Boobar; children: Benjamin, Molly. BS in Chemistry, UCLA, 1967, MD, 1971. Intern Mass. Gen. Hosp., Boston, 1971-72; resident UCLA Hosp., 1972-73, 75-80; clin. assoc. NIH, Bethesda, Md., 1973-75; house physician Nat. Hosp., London, 1976; asst. prof. UCLA Med. Sch., 1980-86; assoc. prof. surgery U. Calif., Irvine, 1986-91; clin. prof. neurosurgery U. So. Calif., L.A. and Irvine, Calif., 1992—. Served to surgeon USPHS, 1973-75. Fellow ACS; mem. Cong. Neurol. Surgeons, Am. Assn. Neurol. Surgeons, Phi Beta Kappa, Sigma Xi. Office: Neurosurgery 1505 N Edgemont St Los Angeles CA 90027-5209

CAHAN, WILLIAM GEORGE, surgeon, educator; b. N.Y.C., Aug. 2, 1914; s. Samuel George and Flora (Gomperts) C.; m. Mary Arnold Sykes, Dec. 26, 1952 (div.); children: Christopher, Anthony; m. Grace Mirabella, Nov. 24, 1974. B.S., Harvard U., 1935; M.D., Columbia U., 1939. Diplomate: Am. Bd. Surgery. Surg. pathology Presbyn. Hosp., N.Y.C., 1939; intern, house surgeon Hosp. Joint Diseases, N.Y.C., 1940-41; fellow cancer surgery Meml. Hosp., N.Y.C., 1942-48; thoracic cons. Strang Clinic, 1949-53, attending surg. staff thoracic service, 1949-85, cons. thoracic service, 1985—; asst. attending surgeon Manhattan Eye, Ear and Throat Hosp., 1950-58, cons. gen. surgeon, 1964—; asso. vis. surgeon James Ewing Hosp., N.Y.C., 1959-68; cons. tumor service Newark Beth Israel Hosp., 1968; instr. surgery Cornell U. Med. Coll., 1950-56, mem. faculty, 1956—, asso. prof. surgery, 1966-74, prof., 1974-84, prof. emeritus, 1984—; asst. clinician Sloan-Kettering Inst., 1953-68; co-chmn. Internat. Workshop on Multiple Primary Cancers, Meml. Sloan-Kettering Cancer Ctr., co-chmn. smoke free Am. awards, 1996; vis. scholar U. Ctr. Va., Richmond, 1967; mem. Lasker Award Jury, 1980-84; mem. nat. adv. bd. Look Good Feel Better Program, 1988—; bd. advisors Am. Coun. Sci. and Health; bd. dirs. Am.-Italian Found. Cancer Rsch. Author: No Stranger to Tears, 1992, (with Hans von Leden) Cryogenics in Surgery, 1971; editl. bd. (with Hans von Leden) Jour. Cryosurgery; contbr. numerous articles to med. jours. Pres. Treadwell Farm Hist. Dist., N.Y.C., 1966-69;; mem. overseers vis. com. music Harvard U., 1968-69, bd. advisors Sch. Pub. Health, 1995; chmn. People for a Smoke Free Indoors; adv. bd. Leeds Castle Found.; co-chair Smoke Free Am. Awards, 1996. Maj. M.C. USAAF, 1943-46. Recipient Disting. Svc. award Am. Cancer Soc., 1982, Life and Breath award N.Y. Lung Assn., 1990, Dynamic Duo Am. Cancer Soc., N.Y.C., 1994, 1st Pub. Svc. award Cancer Care, 1995. Fellow A.C.S.; mem. Am. Assn. Thoracic Surgery, Am. Cancer Soc., Am. Coll. Chest Physicians, A.M.A., Am. Radium Soc., Internat. Congress Smoking and Health (adv. bd.), N.Y. Cancer Soc. (sec. 1955-58), N.Y. County, N.Y. State med. socs., N.Y. Surg. Soc., N.Y. Soc. Thoracic Surgeons, Royal Soc. Medicine (affiliate), Soc. Cryobiology, Soc. Thoracic Surgeons. Office: 1275 York Ave New York NY 10021-6007

CAHILL, DAVID MORTON, surgeon; b. Bennington, Vt., Nov. 28, 1946; s. John James and Fedora (Morton) C.; m. Marjorie Louise George, Oct. 12, 1968; children: Daniel, Marcia, Kaitlin. BS, U. Calif., Davis, 1974; MD, Am. U. of the Caribbean, Montserrat, W.I., 1980. Intern, resident in surgery St. Lukes Hosp., Cleve., 1981-86; staff srugeon Soldiers and Sailors Meml. Hosp., Wellsboro, Pa., 1986—. Mem. AMA, Soc. Laparoendoscopic Surgeons. Roman Catholic. Office: 15 Meade St Wellsboro PA 16901

CAHILL, GEORGE FRANCIS, JR., physician, educator; b. N.Y.C., July 7, 1927; s. George Francis and Eva Marion (Wagner) C.; m. Sarah Townsend duPont, Dec. 20, 1949; children: Colleen Cahill Remley, Peter duPont, George Francis III, Sarah Rhett Cahill Zuckerman, Eva Wagner Cahill Georgaklis, Elizabeth Anglin Cahill Tiedemann. B.S., Yale, 1949; M.D., Columbia U., 1953; M.A., Harvard U., 1966. Intern Peter Bent Brigham Hosp., Boston, 1953-54; resident Peter Bent Brigham Hosp., 1954-55, 57-58; rsch. fellow biol. chemistry Harvard U. Med. Sch., 1955-57; asso. in medicine Peter Bent Brigham Hosp., 1962-65; practice medicine specializing in metabolism Boston, 1965-78; sr. physician Peter Bent Brigham Hosp., 1983—; prof. medicine Harvard U., 1970-90, prof. emeritus, 1990—; prof. biol. scis. Darmouth Coll., Hanover, N.H., 1990—; prin. cons. endocrinology, metabolism VA, 1972-75; investigator Howard Hughes Med. Inst., 1962-68, dir. rsch., 1978-85, v.p. sci. edn. and devel., 1985-89, sr. scientist, 1989-90, cons., 1991—; mem. rsch. tng. coms. NIH. Contbr. articles to profl. jours. Chmn. bd. dirs. Greenwall Found., 1992-96; v.p. trustees Hotchkiss Sch., 1992—; overseer Dartmouth Med. Sch. and the Everett C. Koop Inst., 1993—. With USNR, 1945-47. Recipient Banting medal U.S., 1971, Banting medal Eng., 1974, J.P. Hoet award Belgium, 1973, Gairdner Internat. award Can., 1979. Fellow AAAS, Am. Acad. Arts and Scis.; mem. Am. Diabetes Assn. (pres. 1975, Lilly award 1965), Endocrine Soc. (Oppenheimer award 1963), Nat. Commn. on Diabetes, Am. Soc. Clin. Investigation, Assn. Am. Physicians, Am. Clin. Climatol. Assn., Am. Physiol. Soc., Siasconset Casino Club. Home: Upton Pond Stoddard NH 03464 Office: Dartmouth Coll Dept Biol Scis 303 Gilman Hanover NH 03755

CAHINHINAN, NELIA AGBADA, retired public health nurse, administrator; b. Laguna, Philippines, Sept. 20, 1939; d. Manuel Navarro and Milagros Agbay (Adea) Agbada; m. Rodolfo DeGuia Cahinhinan, Jan. 29, 1967; children: Rodney Paul, Roel James, Renee Ann, Nelie Rose. Diploma, U. Philippines, 1961; BSN, U. Guam, 1985. RN; cert. in nursing adminstrn. Pub. health nurse Dept. Health, Laguna, 1962-67, Dept. Pub. Health and Social Svc., Agana, Guam, 1967-73; pub. health nurse supr., home care Dept. PHSS, Mangilao, Guam, 1974-82; cmty. health nurse supr. Regional Pub. Health Ctr., Dept. PHSS, Tamuning, Guam, 1982-86; nursing and program supr. maternal child health Family Planning Program, Dept. PHSS, Mangilao, 1986-89; asst. nursing adminstr. Bur. Family Health and Nursing Svcs., Dept. PHSS, Mangilao, 1990-94; mem. adv. coun. Coll. Nursing, U. Guam, Mangilao, 1994-95; mem. nursing asst. program adv. coun. Guam C.C., Mangilao, 1995-96; mem. profl. adv. bd. Clarke Home Nursing Svc., Tamuhning, 1995-96. Bd. dirs. Am. Cancer Soc., Agana, 1976-78; mem., sec., chair nursing and health svcs. com. ARC, Agana, 1980-83; mem. com. chair So. Tagalog Assn., Agana, 1980—. Recipient Centennial Leadership award Nat. League of Nursing, 1993; named Guam Top Ten Suprs., Gov. of Guam, 1990. Mem. Guam Nurses Assn. (pres. 1994-95, treas., dir. 1980, com. chair 1993, Svc. award 1983, Guam Nurse of Yr. 1985, Most Disting. Mem. award 1996), U. Philippines Alumni Assn. (pres. 1991-93, adviser 1994-96, treas., dir., Outstanding Svc. award 1993). Roman Catholic. Home: PO Box 11234 Tamuning GU 96931

CAHN, GLENN EVAN, psychologist; b. Washington, Jan. 10, 1953; s. Julius Norman and Ann (Foote) C.; m. Emily Zofnass, Sept. 2, 1990 (dec. June 1993). BA, Washington U., St. Louis, 1975; MA, Calif. Sch. Profl. Psychology, San Diego, 1978, PhD, 1980. Psychologist The Arbour, Boston, 1980-82, Stoughton Counseling Ctr., Mass., 1982, Mass. Rehab., Boston, 1982—, Fuller Meml. Hosp., S. Attleboro, Mass., 1985-90, Hurst Assocs., Boston, 1990—; pvt. practice psychology Newton, Mass., 1988—. Contbr. articles to profl. jours. Home and Office: 373 Massapoag Ave Sharon MA 02067

CAIACH, SIÂN MAIR, orthopaedic surgeon; b. Gelligaer, Wales, Aug. 9, 1957; d. Graham Walters and Joyce Edmonds; children: Arianwen, Lewys. MBBS, Charing Cross, London, 1981; FRCS, Royal Coll., Glasgow, 1987; Diploma in Forensic Medicine, U. Glasgow, 1990. House officer Devon Health Auth., 1981-82; sr. house officer South Glan Health Auth., Cardiff, Wales, 1983-86; registrar Mid Glan Health Auth., Church Village, 1986-88, Dundee Treating Hosps., 1988-72; sr. registrar No. Health Auth., Newcastle, 1988-92, Angus Health Bd., Stracathro, 1994; cons. orthopaedic surgeon Llanelli, Wales, 1994—. Contbr. articles to profl. jours. Fellow British Orthopaedic Assn.; mem. British Med. Assn. Office: Prince Philip Hosp, Dafen Rd, Bryngwynmawr Llanelli SA14 8QF, Wales

CAILLOUETTE, JAMES CLYDE, physician; b. L.A., June 2, 1927; s. Albert F. and Vera Helen C.; m. Joanne Thompson, Dec. 17, 1950; children: Laure, James Thompson, Anne. AB, Coll. Puget Sound, 1950; MD, U. Wash., 1954. Diplomate: Am. Bd. Ob-Gyn. Intern Los Angeles Gen. Hosp., 1954-56, resident in Ob-Gyn, 1956-59; instr. U. So. Calif. Sch. Medicine, 1959-64, asst. clin. prof., 1964-69, assoc. clin. prof., 1969-78, clin. prof., 1978—; mem. sr. attending staff Los Angeles County-U. So. Calif. Med. Center; sec. med. staff Huntington Meml. Hosp., Pasadena, Calif., 1973—. Contbr. articles to profl. jours.; inventor med. products. Bd. dirs. Pasadena Physicians United Crusade, 1961-63, chmn., 1964; v.p. Oak Knoll Property Owners Assn., 1965-75; chmn. ann. drive Nat. Found. March of Dimes, Pasadena, 1966, mem. med. adv. bd. 1966-76; bd. dirs., chmn. med. adv. bd. Pasadena Planned Parenthood World Population, 1970-75; trustee Poly. Sch. Pasadena, 1969-78, chmn. devel. com., 1970-76; bd. councilors U. So. Calif. Sch. Medicine, 1978-92; bd. dirs. Scripps Home, 1980-83, 88-94, Friends of Huntington Libr. With USNR, 1945-46. Fellow ACS, Am. Coll. Ob-Gyn. (mem. primary care task force 1991-92); mem. AMA, N.Y. Acad. Scis., Calif. Med. Assn. (past sec., chmn. ob-gyn. sect.), Pasadena Med. Soc., Pacific Coast Ob-Gyn. Soc. (bd. dirs. 1978—, pres. 1996—), L.A. Ob-Gyn. Soc. (pres. 1977-78), Ob-Gyn. Assembly So. Calif. (chmn. 1981-82), Los Angeles County-U. So. Calif. Med. Ctr. Profl. and Attending Staff Assn. (pres. 1988-90), Valley Hunt Club (bd. dirs. 1980-87, v.p. 10983-84, pres. 1984-85), Calif. Club, Alpha Omega Alpha, Nu Sigma Nu, Phi Sigma, Sigma Chi. Office: 50 Bellefontaine St Ste 401 Pasadena CA 91105-3132

CAIN, GEORGE DOUGLAS, biologist, parasitologist; b. Pitts., June 1, 1940; s. Ralph and Ettalou (McMaster) C.; m. Patricia Ann Thomas, June 5, 1966; children: Adam, Aaron. BS, Sterling Coll., 1962; MS, Purdue U., 1964, PhD, 1968. Postdoctoral fellow U. Mass., Amherst, 1968-70; asst. prof. U. Iowa, Iowa City, 1970-76, assoc. prof., 1976-83, prof., 1983—, chmn. dept. zoology, 1980-84, assoc. dean coll. liberal arts, 1984-87, chmn. dept. biological scis., 1991-94. Mem. Am. Soc. Parasitologists (sec., treas. 1997—), Am. Soc. Tropical Medicine and Hygiene, Sigma Xi. Office: U Iowa Dept Biol Scis Iowa City IA 52242

CAIN, NANCY NAPIER, psychiatrist; b. Zanesville, Ohio, Nov. 9, 1941; d. Paul A. and Laura (Golder) N.; m. Russell M. Cain, Oct. 23, 1965; children: Christine. BS, Muskingum Coll., New Concord, Ohio, 1963; MD, Ohio

State U., 1967. Diplomate Am. Bd. Psychiatry and Neurology. Intern, resident U. Wis., Madison, 1968-71; psychiatrist Eden Day Treatment Prog., San Leandro, Calif., 1972-73; med. dir. Day Treatment prog., Strong Meml. Hosp., Rochester, N.Y., 1973-81; clin. asst. prof. psychiatry U. Rochester, 1973-87, med. dir.; Assn. for Retarded Citizens, Monroe County Rochester, 1981-86; clin. assoc. prof. psychiatry U. Rochester, 1987—, clin. asst. prof. pediatrics, 1987—; med. dir. Family & Marriage Clinic, Rochester, 1989-91; dir. psychiat. clinic for developmentally disabled U. Rochester, 1986—, psychiat. supr. med. fellows, 1986-95; discipline coord. Strong Ctr. for Devel. Disabilities, 1986—; cons. in field. Contbr. articles to profl. jours. Recipient Med. Svcs. award, ARC of Monroe County, 1986. Fellow Am. Psychiat. Assn.; mem. Genesee Valley Psychiat. Assn., Nat. Assn. Dually Diagnosed. Office: 300 Crittenden Blvd Rochester NY 14642-0001

CAIN, RUSSELL M., psychiatrist; b. Pitts., Aug. 31, 1940; s. Ralph Harold and Lillian (Noon) C.; m. Nancy Napier, Oct. 23, 1965; 1 child, Christine Elizabeth. BS, Ohio State U., 1962; postgrad., Coll. de France, Paris, 1962-63, Inst. de Neurophysiologie Gen.; MD, Ohio State U., 1967. Cert. in psychiatry Am. Bd. Psychiatry & Neurology; med. lic., Calif., N.Y., Ohio, Wis. Intern U. Wis., Madison, 1967-68; resident psychiatry U. Wis., 1968-71, fellow family therapy, 1970-71; asst. prof. dept. psychiatry U. Rochester, Rochester, N.Y., 1973-77; attending psychiatrist Stong Meml. Hosp., Rochester, 1973—; clin. asst. prof. psychiatry U. Rochester, 1977-91, clin. assoc. prof., 1991—; pvt. practice psychiatry Rochester, 1973—; med. dir. Rochester Rehab. Ctr., Rochester, 1977-82; vice chmn. med. staff Strong Meml. Hosp., Rochester, 1975-77; cons. N.Y. Sch. Indsl. and Labor Rels., Cornell U., Ithaca, N.Y., 1978-80, Commn. on Accreditation Rehab. Facilities, Tucson, 1979-83, Samaritan Pastoral Counseling Ctr., Rochester, 1984—; examiner Am. Bd. Psychiatry & Neurology, Chgo., 1983—; chmn. psychiatry com. Rochester Cmty. Ind. Practice Assn., 1985-89; dep. rep. Assembly Am. Psychiat. Assn., 1989-91, rep., 1991—. Gen. Univ. scholar in medicine Ohio State U., 1963; NIMH fellow in psychiatry, 1968-71; recipient recognition award Commn. on Accreditation Rehab. Facilities. Fellow Am. Psychiat. Assn. (Falk fellow 1970); mem. Monroe County Med. Soc., N.Y. State Med. Soc., Rochester Acad. Medicine, Rochester Cmty. Ind. Practice Assn., Genesee Valley Psychiat. Assn., N.Y. State Psychiat. Assn., U.S. Naval Inst., Rochester Yacht Club, Gt. Lakes Cruising Club, Genesee Conservation League. Office: Univ Rochester Med Ctr Strong Ties Clin 1650 Elmwood Ave Rochester NY 14620

CAIN, WILLIAM STANLEY, psychologist, educator; b. N.Y.C., Sept. 7, 1941; s. William Henry and June Rose (Stanley) C.; m. Claire Murphy, Oct. 30, 1993; children: Justin, Alison, Michael, Jennifer, Courtney. BS, Fordham U., 1963; MSc, Brown U., 1966, PhD, 1968. From asst. fellow to fellow John B. Pierce Lab., New Haven, 1967-94; from instr. to assoc. prof. depts. Epidemiology, Pub. Health, and Psychology Yale U., New Haven, 1967-84, prof. dept. epidemiology, pub. health, psychology, 1984-94; prof. surgery (otolaryngology) U. Calif., San Diego, 1994—; mem. sensory disorders study sect. NIH, Bethesda, Md., 1991-95; mem. sci. adv. bd. Ctr. Indoor Air Rsch., Linthicum, Md., 1991—. Mem. editl. bd. Chem. Senses, 1985-94; editl. adv. bd. Indoor Air, 1990—, Physiology and Behavior, 1995—; editor 5 books, 1971—; contbr. over 185 articles to profl. jours. Recipient Crosby Field award ASHRAE, 1984, Jacob Javits/Claude Pepper award NIH, 1984, Sense of Smell award, Fragrance Rsch. Fund, 1986. Fellow APA, ASHRAE, Am. Psychol. Soc., Acad. Indoor Air Rsch.; mem. Assn. Chemoreception Scis. (exec. chmn. 1983-84), N.Y. Acad. Scis. (pres. 1986). Home: 4459 Nabal Dr La Mesa CA 91941-7168 Office: U Calif Dept Surgery MC0957 9500 Gilman Dr La Jolla CA 92093-0957

CAK, ROBERT JOHN, surgeon; b. East Chicago, Ind., Dec. 12, 1945; s. Julius and Marie (Prist) C.; m. Roberta Jean Wells, Aug. 24, 1968; children: Leslie Dianne, Robert John Jr., Steven Curtis. AB, Ind. U., 1967; MD, Ind. U., Indpls., 1971. Diplomate Am. Bd. Surgery. Intern West Pa. Hosp., Pitts., 1971-72, resident in surgery, 1972-76; gen. surgeon Cedar Valley Med. Clinic, Waterloo, Iowa, 1978—; chief surgery Allen Meml. Hosp., Waterloo, 1981-88, med. staff pres. to date; clin. asst. prof. surgery U. Iowa, Iowa City, 1993—. Named Tchr. of the Yr., Black Hawk Family Practice Residency Program, 1992. Fellow ACS. Roman Catholic. Office: Cedar Valley Medical Clinic 927 W 4th St Waterloo IA 50702

CAKEBREAD, STEVEN ROBERT, minister; b. Pittsburg, Calif., June 19, 1946; s. Robert Harold Cakebread and Mildred Irene (McQeen) Cowing; m. Margaret Anne Spandall, July 16, 1967; children: Robert, Scott, Andrew. ABS, Nazarene Bible Coll., Colorado Springs, Colo., 1977; BA, Mid. Am. Nazarene Coll., 1979; MDiv, Am. Bapt. Sem. of the West, Berkeley, Calif., 1983; postgrad., Calif. Culinary Acad. Ordained to ministry Ch. of the Nazarene, 1980, Am. Bapt. Ch., 1984. Pastor Ch. of the Nazarene, Brookfield, Md., 1978-80; hosp. chaplain VA Hosp., San Francisco, 1988—, Oakland (Calif.) Naval Hosp./Operation Desert Storm, 1990-91, Naval Reserves/Naval Base, San Francisco, 1985—; pastor 21st Ave Bapt. Ch., San Francisco, 1984-92, Yountville Community Ch., Yountville, Calif., 1992—; Coun. mem. Coun. of Chs., San Francisco, 1988. E-5 USN, 1966-70, Vietnam. Decorated Humanitarian Svc. medal USN, Navy Achievement medal (Desert Storm). Mem. Naval Res. Assn., ABA/USA Chaplains Coun., Am. Legion. Office: Am Baptist Personnel Svc 35 E 19th St Antioch CA 94509-2643

CALABRESE, ALPHONSE FRANCIS XAVIER, psychotherapist; b. Bklyn., Apr. 27, 1923; s. Charles Angelo and Josephine Maria (Ambrosino) C.; m. Florence E. Schumacher, Aug. 15, 1950 (div. Oct. 1979); children: Charles, Theresa, Thomas, Catherine, John, Bernardette, Eileen, James; m. Eleanor A. Wallace, July 13, 1980; children: William, Paul. BA, St. John's U., 1948; MSW, Cath. U. of Am., 1950; PhD, Fla. State Christian U., 1976. Cert. psychoanalyst; diplomate Am. Bd. Accreditation and Certification in Psychoanalysis, NASW. Psychiat. social worker Cath. Charities Psychiat. Clinic, Bklyn., 1950-53; psychiat. social worker Postgrad. Inst. for Psychotherapy, N.Y.C., 1953-55, fellow, psychoanalysis, 1955-58, fellow analytic group psychotherapy, 1958-60; pvt. practice psychotherapy N.Y.C., 1960—; exec. dir. Christian Inst. for Psycho-Therapeutic Studies, Hicksville, N.Y., 1975—. Author: The Christian Love Treatment, 1977; contbr. articles to profl. jours. Dir. edn. Vt. Right to Life, Montpelier, 1986. Recipient grant Postgrad. Inst. for Psychotherapy, N.Y.C., 1953, scholarship St. Vincent DePaul Soc., Bklyn., 1948. Fellow Nat. Assn. for Psychoanalysis; mem. AAAS, NASW, Assn. of Christian Therapists (pres. 1976-77), Christian Assn. for Psychol. Studies, KC, 3d Order St. Francis. Republican. Orthodox Ch. Home: 73 Godfrey Rd Ludlow VT 05149-9730 Office: Christian Inst for Psychotherapeutic Studies 183 S Broadway Hicksville NY 11801

CALABRESE, ANTHONY JOSEPH, gastroenterologist; b. Newark, Dec. 1, 1946; s. Arnold J. and Anna T. (Cicalese) C.; m. Nancy A. Meier, Aug. 8, 1970; children: Christopher, Michael. BS in Biology, St. Peter's Coll., 1968; MD cum laude, Jefferson Med. Coll., 1972. Intern and resident in internal medicine Temple U. Hosp., Phila.; fellow gastroenterology Thomas Jefferson U. Hosp., Phila.; gastroenterology cons. Calvert Meml. Hosp., Prince Frederick, Md., 1979-81; staff gastroenterologist Anne Arundel Gastroenterology Assocs., Annapolis, Md., 1979—; pres. med. staff Anne Arundel Med. Ctr., 1993-95, trustee, 1993—. Bd. trustees Archbishop H.S., Severn, Md., 1991-93. Maj. USAF, 1977-79. Fellow Am. COll. Gastroenterology; mem. AMA, Am. Gastroenterological Assn., Am. Liver Found., Crohn's & Colitis Found. Am., Ocean City Light Tackle Club, Alpha Omega Alpha. Republican. Roman Catholic. Office: Anne Arundel Gastroenterology Assocs 171 Defense Hwy Annapolis MD 21401

CALABRESI, PAUL, pharmacologist, oncologist, educator; b. Milan, Apr. 5, 1930; U.S. citizen; married; three children. BA, Yale U., 1951, MD, 1955. Diplomate Am. Bd. Internal Medicine. Intern Harvard Med. Svc., Boston City Hosp., 1955-56, asst. resident, 1958-59; project assoc. U. Wis., 1956-58; from instr. to assoc. prof. medicine and pharmacology Yale U., 1960-68; prof. med. sci. Brown U., 1968—, chmn. dept. medicine, 1974-93, Emer chmn. dept. medicine, 1993—; clin. prof. pharmacology Coll. Pharmacy, U. R.I., Kingston, 1977—; field investigator Nat. Cancer Inst., NIH, 1956-60, mem. cancer chemotherapy collaborative program rev. com., 1965-66, bd. sci. counselors, 1983-88; mem. Pharmacol.-Toxicol. Rev. Com., Nat. Inst. Genetic Med. Sci., 1967-70, exptl. therapeutic study sect., 1972-76, chmn., 1975-76; rsch. fellow dept. medicine Yale U., 1959-60, head divsn. clin. pharmacology and chemotherapy, dir. clin. pharmacol. rsch. ctr., 1965-67; vis. scientist U. Lausanne, Switzerland, 1966-67; physician-in-chief, chmn. dept. medicine Roger Williams Gen. Hosp., Providence, 1968-91, v.p. acad. affairs, 1977-91; mem. rsch. coun. and drug rsch. bd. NAS, 1968-75; mem. sci. group on evaluation and testing of drugs for mutagenicity, principles and problems WHO, 1971; cons. Study Group Hycanthone, 1971; counselor Environ. Mutagen Soc., 1971-74; chief medicine Women and Infants Hosp. R.I., 1974-80; cons. Miriam Hosp., Meml. Hosp., Providence VA MEd. Ctr., R.I. Hosp., St. Joseph's Hos., 1974—; mem. Sci. and Pub. Affairs Com., Am. Assn. Cancer Rsch., 1983—; vis. prof. numerous univs. Burroughs Wellcome scholar clin. pharmacology, 1964-68; Eleanor Roosevelt Internat. Cancer fellow Am. Cancer Soc., 1966-67. Master ACP (mem. sci. program com. 1975-78, clin. pharmacol. com. 1977-82, chmn. 1978-82); mem. Inst. Medicine-NAS, Am. Soc. Hematology, Am. Soc. Pharmacology and Exptl. Therapeutics, Am. Soc. Clin. Oncology (pres. 1969-70), Am. Fedn. Clin. Rsch., Am. Assn. Clin. Rsch., Am. Bd. Internal Medicine (sec.-treas. 1982-84), Am. Cancer Soc., Am. Soc. Clin. Pharmacology and Therapeutics. Office: Roger Williams Gen Hosp Clin Cancer Rsch Ctr 825 Chalkstone Ave Providence RI 02908-4728*

CALABRO, JOSEPH JOHN, III, physician; b. Carbondale, Pa., Sept. 4, 1955; s. Joseph J. and Judith A. (Fidati) C.; m. Anne Wroblewski Calabro, Jan 25, 1985; children: Lia Jude, J. John. IV. Secondary cert., Scranton Prep. Sch., 1973; BS in Biology cum laude, U. Scranton, 1977; DO, Phila. Coll. Osteo. Medicine, 1981. Commd. 2d lt. U.S. Army, 1977, advanced through grades to lt. col., 1993; intern Tripler Army Med. Ctr., Honolulu, 1981-82; resident in emergency medicine Madigan Army Med. ctr., Tacoma, Wash., 1984-86; chief dept. ambulatory care and emergency med. svcs. Letterman Army Med. Ctr., San Francisco, 1985-90; asst. clin. prof. Sch. Nursing U. Calif., San Francisco, 1987-89; attending physician San Francisco Gen. Hosp., 1987-91; asst. clin. prof. U. Calif. Sch. Medicine, San Francisco, 1987—; chmn. Dept. Emergency Medicine Jersey Shore Med. Ctr., Neptune, N.J., 1990-92; chmn. dept. emergency medicine Beth Israel Med. Ctr., Newark, 1992—; residency program dir. emergency medicine Beth Israel Med. Ctr., Newark, N.J., 1993—; asst. clin. prof. U. Medicine and Dentistry of N.J., 1991—; chmn. dept. emergency medicine West Hudson Hosp., Kearny, N.J., 1994—, St. Michael's Med. Ctr., Newark, 1995—; chmn. San Francisco City and County Emergency Med. Care Com., 1988-90; chmn. emergency med. care com. San Francisco chpt. Am. Heart Assn., 1989-90; pres. N.J. Inst. Med. Rsch., 1995—. Reviewer Jour. AMA, Jour. EMS, Annals of Emergency Medicine, Rescue, Acad. Emergency Medicine. Mem. AMA, Am. Coll. Emergency Physicians (N.J. chpt. bd. dirs., sec. 1995-96, treas. 1994-95, pres.-elect 1996—, chmn. EMS/trauma com., chmn. emergency medicine residency com., chmn. practice mgmt. com., nat. ACEP-EMS com. 1988—), Am. Coll. Osteo. Emergency Physicians (bd. dirs. 1993—, sec. 1995—), Am. Osteo. Assn., Assn. Mil. Surgeons U.S., Soc. Acad. Emergency Medicine, Nat. Assn. EMS Physicians, Phi Lambda Upsilon. Roman Catholic. Home: 18 Spier Ave Allenhurst NJ 07711-1117

CALAIS, JIMMY, critical care nurse, paramedic; b. Lafayette, La., June 7, 1966; s. Dalton and Genevieve (Babineaux) C. A in Emergency Health Sci., U. S.W. La., 1989; BSN, William Carey Coll., 1993. CCRN, La.; registered EMT, La. Paramedic Acadian Ambulance, Lafayette, La., 1989-91, Mobile Medic Ambulance, Gulfport, Mis., 1991-93; staff nurse ICU Lafayette (La.) Gen. Med. Ctr., 1993—. Mem. AACN. Mem. Ch. of Christ. Home: 283 Gayle St Breaux Bridge LA 70517

CALAMITA, KATHRYN ELIZABETH, nursing administrator; b. Portland, Maine, Oct. 12, 1943; d. Maurice Daniel and Eleanor Elizabeth (Sullivan) Casey; m. John Joseph Calamita, Jan. 9, 1965; children: Angela Marie, Carla Anne, Daniel John. RN, Mercy Hosp. Sch. Nursing, Springfield, Mass., 1964; student, Midwestern State U., Wichita Falls, Tex., 1979-86, Vernon Regional Coll., 1987; BS in Bus., St. Joseph's Coll., Windham, Maine, 1992. Staff nurse Mercy Hosp., Springfield, 1964; med/surg. nurse Wichita Gen. Hosp., Wichita Falls, Tex., 1976-77, nurse ICU, 1977-79, supr. dept. nursing, 1979-86, assoc. adminstr. nursing dept., 1986-92; health facility adminstr. Wichita Falls Rehab. Hosp., 1992; rehab. nurse Bay Convalescent and Rehab. Ctr., Panama City, Fla., 1993-94; asst. DON L.A. Wagner Nursing and Rehab. Ctr., Panama City, Fla., 1994—. Mem. ANA (cert. in mgmt., 1995), FNA. Democrat. Roman Catholic.

CALANDRA, JOSEPH CARL, medical educator; b. Chgo., Mar. 17, 1917; s. Domenic William and Angela (Palma) C.; m. Patricia June Mader, Sept. 9, 1944; children: Carolyn P. Selsor, Susan J. Sylvester, Joseph D., David B. BS, Lewis Inst., Chgo., 1938; PhD, Northwestern U., 1942, MD, 1950. Cert. Am. Bd. Clin. Chemistry, Am. Bd. Indsl. Hygiene. Asst. prof. chemistry Northwestern U. Med. Sch., Cago., 1942-50, assoc. prof. pathology, 1950-53, prof. pathology, 1954-83, prof. emeritus pathology, 1988—; pres. Indsl. Biotest Labs., Northbrook, Ill., 1954-78; med. dir. Nalco Chem. Co., Naperville, Ill., 1966-78; med. advisor Texaco, N.Y.C., 1954-86, PPG, Beaumont, Tex., 1968-88. Author: Pathologic Physiology of Oral Disease; contbr. articles to profl. jours. Pres. Evanston Golf Club, Skokie, Ill., 1975-76; bd. dirs. Cancer Detection Ctr., Chgo., 1960-68, Augustana Hosp., Chgo., Skokie Valley Hosp., Skokie, 1968-78, Nalco Chemical Co., 1970-78. Named Entrepreneur of Yr., Rsch. Dirs. Assn., Chgo., 1971. Mem. Am. Indsl. Hygiene Assn. (pres. Chgo. sect. 1970), Soc. of Toxicology (councilor 1969-71), Evanston Golf Club (bd. dirs. 1968-71). Roman Catholic. Home: 4630 Elm Ter Skokie IL 60076-2026 Office: Northwestern U 311 E Chicago Ave Chicago IL 60611-3008

CALDAMONE, ANTHONY ANGELO, pediatric urologist; b. Providence, May 16, 1950; s. Carmine Nicholas and Antonetta (Fargnoli) C.; m. Barbara Ward, July 22, 1973; children: Amy Lynn, Matthew Ward. AB, Brown U., 1972, MMS, 1975, MD, 1975. Diplomate Am. Bd. Urology. Resident U. Rochester, 1975-81; fellow Children's Hosp. of Phila., 1981-82; cons. pediatric urology, lectr. Hosp. for Sick Children, Inst. of Urology, London, 1982; asst. prof., dir. pediatric urology Case Western Res. U./Rainbow Babies & Children's Hosp., Cleve., 1983-86; prof., dir. pediatric urology Brown U./Hasbro Children's Hosp., Providence, 1986—; dir. urology residency Brown U., 1988—. Editor: Decision Making in Urology, 1990; Practice of Urology, 1991; contbr. articles to profl. jours., chpts. to books. Upjohn Achievement awardee, 1975, Lange Med. Pub. awardee, 1975, Med. Libr. award, Rochester Acad. Medicine, 1979, Walter S. Kerr First prize, Am. Urology Assn., 1981, First prize for sci. exhibit, 1982. Fellow Am. Acad. Pediatrics, ACS; mem. Am. Urol. Assn., Soc. Pediatric Urology, Soc. Univ. Urologists, Italian Pediatric Urology Soc. Roman Catholic. Office: 2 Dudley St Ste 185 Providence RI 02905-3247

CALDER, KENNETH THOMAS, psychiatrist, psychoanalyst, educator; b. Sault Ste. Marie, Mich., Apr. 15, 1918; s. Thomas Kenneth and Margaret Harkness (MacDonald) C.; m. Abbie Ingalls Knowlton, July 18, 1953; children: Thomas Kenneth, Mary Susannah. AB, U. Mich., 1941; MD, Columbia U., 1944. Diplomate Am. Bd. Psychiatry and Neurology. Intern Mass. Meml. Hosp., Boston, 1944-45; resident Cin. (Ohio) Gen. Hosp., 1945-46, N.Y. Psychiat. Inst., N.Y.C., 1948-49, Bellevue Hosp., N.Y.C., 1949-50; pvt. practice N.Y.C., 1950—; asst. clin. prof. NYU Med. Sch., N.Y.C., 1963—; mem. faculty N.Y. Psychoanalytic Inst., N.Y.C., 1963—, pres., 1982-84. Contbr. articles to med. jours. Capt. M.C., U.S. Army, 1946-48. Fellow Am. Psychiat. Assn.; mem. Am. Psychoanalytic Assn. (pres. 1977-78), Internat. Psychoanalytic Assn. (v.p. 1973-79). Democrat. Home and Office: 110 E 78th St New York NY 10021-0302

CALDERWOOD, WILLIAM ARTHUR, physician; b. Wichita, Kans., Feb. 3, 1941; s. Ralph Bailey and Janet Denise (Christ) C.; m. Nancy Jo Crawford, Mar. 31, 1979; children: Lisa Beth, William Arthur II. MD, U. Kans., 1968. Diplomate Am. Bd. Family Practice. Intern Wesley Med. Ctr., Wichita, 1968-69; gen. practice family medicine Salina, Kans., 1972-80, Peoria, Ariz., 1980—; med. dir. First Am. Home Care, 1994—, First Am. Homecare, 1995—; pres. staff St. John's Hosp., Salina, 1976; 28th jud. dist. coroner State of Kans., Wichita, 1978-80; cons. in addiction medicine VA Hosp., 1989-94; bd. dirs. Pelms House. Inventor, patentee lighter-than-air-furniture. Bd. dirs. Pelms House (For Chem. Dependence), 1995—, Gen. Health Medcare, 1995—. Fellow Am. Acad. Family Physicians; mem. AMA, Ariz. Med. Soc. (physicians med. health com., exec. com. 1988-92), Maricopa County Med. Soc., Ariz. Acad. Family Practice (med. dir. N.W. Orgn. Vol. alternatives 1988-91), Am. Med. Soc. on Alcoholism and Other Drug Dependencies (cert.), Shriners. Home: 7015 W Calavar Rd Peoria AZ 85381-4706 Office: 14300 W Granite Valley Dr Sun City West AZ 85375-5783

CALDWELL, ALLAN BLAIR, health services company executive; b. Independence, Iowa, June 13, 1929; s. Thomas James and Lola (Ensminger) C.; BA, Maryville Coll., 1952; BS, NYU, 1955; MS, Columbia U., 1957; MD, Stanford U., 1964; m. Elizabeth Jane Steinmetz, June 13, 1955; 1 child, Kim Allistair; m. Susan A. Koss, Feb. 12, 1984. Med. intern Henry Ford Hosp., Detroit, 1964-65; resident Jackson Meml. Hosp., Miami, Fla., 1956-57; admstr. Albert Schweitzer Hosp., Haiti, 1957-58; asst. admstr. Palo Alto-Stanford Hosp. Center, 1958-59; asso. dir. program in hosp. adminstrn. U. Calif. at Los Angeles, 1965-67; dir. bur. profl. service Am. Hosp. Assn., Chgo., 1967-69; v.p. Beverly Enterprises, Pasadena, Calif., 1969-71; exec. v.p., med. dir. Nat. Med. Enterprises, Beverly Hills, Calif., 1971-73; pres., chmn. bd. Emergency Physicians Internat., 1973—, Allan B. Caldwell, M.D., Inc., 1973—; dir. indsl. medicine Greater El Monte Cmty. Hosp., South El Monte, Calif., 1973-83; pres. Am. Indsl. Med. Svcs., 1978—; chmn. bd. dirs. Technicraft Internat., Inc., San Mateo, Calif., 1970-76; pres., med. dir. Shelton-Livingston Med. Group, 1984—; dir. Career Aids, Inc., Glendale, Calif., 1969-75; cons. TRW Corp., Redondo Beach, Calif., 1966-71; lectr. UCLA, 1965—, Calif. Inst. Tech., 1971—, Calif. State U., Northridge, 1980-85; examiner Civil Service Commn., L.A., 1966; adviser Western Center for Continuing Edn. in Hosps. and Related Health Facilities, 1965—; cons. L.A. Hosp. and Nursing and Pub. Health Dept., 1965—; adv. council Calif. Hosp. Commn., 1972-78; commr. Emergency Med. Services Commn. Bd. dirs. Comprehensive Health Planning Assn. Los Angeles County, 1972-76; vice chmn. Emergency Med. Care Commn., Los Angeles County, 1977-78, chmn., 1978-79. Recipient Geri award Los Angeles Nursing Home Assn., 1966, Outstanding Achievement award Health Care Educators, 1978; USPHS scholar, 1961-63. Diplomate Am. Bd. Med. Examiners. Mem. Am., United (pres. 1971-72) hosp. assns., Am. Coll. Hosp. Adminstrs., Am., Calif. med. assns., Los Angeles County Med. Assn., Am. Acad. Family Physicians, Am. Coll. Emergency Physicians (v.p. 1975-77 dir. continuing med. edn. for Western U.S., Hawaii, Australia, N.Z., 1976-84), Hosp. Fin. Mgmt. Assn., Am. Indsl. Hygiene Assn., Rolls Royce Owners' Club (dir. 1982—, vice chmn. 1982, chmn. 1983), Classic Car Club of Am. (life 1983), Antique Automobile Club Am., Model T Club Am. Home: 4405 Medley Pl Encino CA 91316-4344 Office: 1414 S Grand Ave Ste 123 Los Angeles CA 90015-3071

CALDWELL, GLYN GORDON, epidemiologist, physician; b. St. Louis, Jan. 14, 1934; s. Cecil Gordon and Zelma Mae (Peeler) C.; m. Mary Jean Pandolfo, Aug. 13, 1960; children: Michael Gordon, Elizabeth Ann, Thomas Gordon. BS, St. Louis U., 1960; MS, Mo. U., 1962, MD, 1966. Diplomate Nat. Bd. Med. Examiners. Intern, USPHS Hosp., Brighton, Mass., 1966-67; resident in internal medicine Cleve. Met. Gen. Hosp., 1969-71; grad. instr. microbiology U. Mo., 1960-62; with USPHS, 1966-85, med. virologist-epidemiologist Ecol. Investigations Program, Ctr. Disease Control, Kansas City, Kans., 1967-69, chief leukemia and oncogenic virus activities, 1968-69, acting chief virus disease sect., 1968-69, chief oncology and teratology activities, 1971-73, biohazards cons., 1972-73, asst. to chief leukemia sect. cancer and birth defects br. Bur. Epidemiology, Atlanta, 1973-74, dep. chief, 1974-77, chief cancer br. chronic diseases div., 1977-81, chief cancer br. chronic diseases div. Ctr. Environ. Health, 1981-82, dep. dir. chronic diseases div., 1982-85; asst. dir. disease prevention Ariz. Dept. Health Svcs., Phoenix, 1985-87, state epidemiologist, 1985-87, dep. dir., 1987-90; dir. Tulsa City-County Health Dept., 1990-94; assoc. clin. coord. Ind. Med. Rev. Organization, 1995—; asst. prof. microbiology U. Kans., 1968-70; docent Kansas City Gen. Hosp., 1972-73; clin. asst. prof. medicine U. Mo., Kansas City, 1972-73; clin. asst. prof. preventive medicine and cmty. health Emory U., Atlanta, 1975-85, asst. prof. cmty. medicine U. Ariz., 1986-90; dir. Atlanta Cancer Surveillance Ctr., 1976-77; mem. med. adv. bd. Ctr. for Disease Control, 1979-84; mem. subcom. on Three Mile Island, Interagy. Radiation Rsch. Com., 1980-84; mem. com. on health rsch. initiatives on radiation rsch. HHS, 1980-85; mem. fed. interagy. cen. coordinating com. for radiation planning and preparedness Fed. Emergency Mgmt. Agy., 1980-85, mem. subcom. on fed. response, 1982-85; mem. dosimetry assessment adv. com. Dept. Energy, 1980-87; chmn. Hanford Health Effects Radiation Rev. Panel, 1986; mem. Hanford Environ. Dose Reconstruction Tech. Steering Panel, 1988-95; bd. vis. Coll. Pub. Health, U. Okla., 1991-95; bd. dirs. Ariz. div. Am. Cancer Soc., 1988-90; chmn. HIV Resource Consortium, 1992-93, bd. dirs., 1992-95, sec. 1994; mem. Tulsa Community Aids Partnership, 1993-95; mem. fed. adv. com. Hanford Health Effects Subcom., 1995—. Served with Signal Corps, U.S. Army, 1954-60. St. Louis U. scholar, 1952-53; recipient McComas History of Medicine prize U. Mo., 1966, Commendation medal USPHS, 1980. Fellow Am. Coll. Epidemiology; mem. AMA, Internat. Assn. Comparative Research on Leukemia and Related Diseases, Am. Soc. Preventive Oncology, Am. Soc. Microbiology, Commd. Officers Assn. USPHS (pres. Atlanta br. 1976), Soc. Epidemiologic Research, N.Y. Acad. Scis., Tulsa Med. Soc., Okla. Med. Soc., Sigma Xi. Roman Catholic. Lodge: K.C. Contbg. editor Internat. Jour. Cancer Control and Prevention, 1979-84. Contbr. articles to profl. jours. Home: 3132 Woodlane Ct Indianapolis IN 46268

CALDWELL, JOHN, education educator, scientific consultant; b. Hillingdon, Middlesex, England, Apr. 4, 1947; s. Gilbert Reginald and Marian Elizabeth (Morgan) C.; m. Jill Gregory, Sept. 13, 1969; children: David George Mawdsley Caldwell, James Alexander Gregory Caldwell. B in Pharmacy, Chelsea Coll., London, 1969; PhD, St. Mary's Hosp. Med. Sch., 1972; DSc, U. London, 1987. Lectr. in Biochemistry St. Mary's Hosp. Med. Sch., London, 1972-78, sr. lectr. in pharmacology, 1978-82, reader in drug metabolism, 1982-88, prof. Biochemical Toxicology, 1988—, chmn. basic med. scis. div., 1991—, head dept. pharmacology and toxicology, 1992—; cons. various drug and chem. cos., Europe, U.S., Japan; vis. prof. U. Ariz., Tucson, 1987—; mem. steering group on food surveillance U.K. Ministry Agriculture, 1993—. Editor: Chirality; contbr. articles to profl jours. Chair of gov.'s., St. Matthew's Sch., Yiewsley, England, 1986—. Recipient Rsch. Grants, Health and Safety Exec., Flavor & Extract Mfg. Assn., 1983-93, Rsch. Inst. for Fragrance Materials; rsch. contracts Min. of Agr., 1987—. Mem. Internat. Soc. for Study of Xenobiotics (pres.). Office: St Marys Hosp Med School, Norfolk Pl, London W2 1PG, England

CALDWELL, LINDA M., nursing educator; b. Boston, Oct. 19, 1948; d. Edward W. and Marie V. (Hinchey) Leahy; m. Thomas Caldwell, May 1970; children: Christopher, Julie, Laura. AS, Northeastern U., 1969, BS, 1977; MS, Boston Coll., 1980; D of Nursing Sci., Boston U., 1989; CAGS, Mass. Gen. Inst. Health Profns, 1996. Cert. med./surg. nurse ANA. Asst. prof. nursing Laboure' Coll., Boston; instr. Boston State Coll., Boston Coll., Chestnut Hill, Mass.; prof. nursing Curry Coll., Milton, Mass. Mem. Sigma Theta Tau, Alpha Chi, Theta-at-Large (v.p. 1990—).

CALDWELL, MARY PERI, counseling psychologist, educator; b. Cleve., Aug. 21, 1935; d. Francesco and Gerlanda (Gagliano) Peri; m. Robert Joseph Caldwell, 1956 (div. 1962); children: Deborah Ann, Thomas Robert (dec.). BS in Edn., Kent State U., 1961; MA in Counseling Psychology, Alfred Adler Inst., Chgo., 1981. Cert. clin. mental health counselor; lic. mental health counselor, Fla., clin. counselor, Ohio. Tchr. various sch. systems Cleve., 1957-85; pvt. practice as counseling psychologist Brunswick, Ohio, 1980-87, Coral Springs, Fla., 1987—; mem. faculty, dir. Cleve. Inst. Adlerian Studies, 1983—, exec. sec., 1978-82, pres., 1982-84; mem. med. staff Care Unit, Coral Springs, FairOaks Hosp., Delray, Fla.; mem. mental health profl. staff Univ. Pavillion Hosp., Tamarac, Fla.; lectr. U.S. and Can. Author: Stress/Distress/Burnout: Resolving the Puzzle of Stress, 1983, also manual for advisors for Broward County Mental Health Assn.; editor: Adlerian Psychology Bull., 1983-86; contbr. articles to profl. jours. Leader various parent edn. groups, 1981—; bd. dirs. Kids In Distress, Inc.; bd. dirs., pres. Kids In Distress Aux. West. Jennings Found. grantee, 1979; recipient Disting. Service award N.E. Ohio Tchrs. Assn., 1983, Nat. Disting. Svc. award Registry Counseling and Devel., 1990, Woman of the Yr. award, 1995, 1000 Club award of the Am. Cancer Soc. Mem. AACD, N.Am. Soc. Adlerian Psychology (clin. mem., assembly del., Outstanding Woman award 1980), Am. Mental Health Counselors Assn., Fla. Assn. Counseling and Devel., Broward County Mental Health Assn. (adv. bd., bd. dirs. Kids in Distress Aux. West), Exec. Women Coral Springs, Am. Bus. Women's Assn., Fla. Speakers Assn., Broward County Assn. Counseling and Devel. (mem. exec. bd.), Coral Springs C. of C., Rotary, Gamma Phi Beta (pres. 1967-70).

Home: 8208 NW 100th Way Fort Lauderdale FL 33321-1291 Office: 3200 University Dr Ste 208 Coral Springs FL 33065

CALDWELL, PETER DEREK, pediatrician, pediatric cardiologist; b. Schenectady, N.Y., Apr. 16, 1940; s. Philip Graham and Mary Elizabeth (Glockler) C.; m. Olga Hoang Hai Miller, May 31, 1969. BA, Pomona Coll., 1961; MD, UCLA, 1965. Intern King County Hosp., Seattle, 1965-66; resident in pediatrics U. Wash., 1969-71, fellow in pediatric cardiology, 1971-73; pvt. practice Hawaii Permanente Med. Group, Honolulu, 1973—. Author: Bac-Si: A Doctor Remembers Vietnam, 1990, Adventurer's Hawaii, 1992; contbr. articles to profl. jours. Lt. comdr. USNR, 1966-69. Fellow Am. Acad. Pediatrics; mem. Am. Coll. Sports Medicine, Wilderness Med. Soc., Internat. Soc. Mountain Medicine. Office: Kaiser Punawai Clinic 94-235 Leoku St Waipahu HI 96797-1906

CALDWELL, STEVEN CLINE, marketing professional; b. Roanoke, Va., Nov. 13, 1957; s. Howard C. and Allie (Whitlow) C. BA in Psychology, Roanoke Coll., 1979. Sales rep. Huttig Sash and Door Co., Roanoke, 1980-81; customer sales agt. Piedmont Airlines, Charlotte, N.C., 1982-84; sales agt. L.S. Waldrop Realty Inc., Salem, Va., 1984-86; sr. territory mgr. Hoffmann-La Roche INc., Nutley, N.J., 1986-95; mktg. coord. Lewis-Gale Hosp., Salem, 1995—. Home: 2408 Avenham Ave Roanoke VA 24014 Office: Lewis-Gale Med Ctr 1902 Braeburn Dr Salem VA 24153

CALDWELL, SUSAN ELAINE, virologist; b. Knoxville, Feb. 4, 1952; d. Calvin Harold and Hope (Owen) C.; m. Michael Charles Cerrone, Nov. 27, 1981. BA in Biology, U. Tenn., 1978; PhD in Virology, Wake Forest U., 1985. Research assoc. Bowman Gray Sch. Medicine, Wake Forest U., Winston-Salem, N.C., 1983-87; assoc. scientist Genelabs Inc, Redwood City, Calif., 1987-88, scientist I, 1988-89; scientist II Genelabs Inc., 1989-91; sr. rsch. scientist Baxter Diagnostics, Inc., Miami, Fla., 1991-92, sr. clin. scientist, 1992-93; co-founder, ptnr. BioInformation Resources, Miami, 1993-95; assoc. dir. med. writing Berlex Labs., Richmond, Calif., 1995—. Contbr. articles to profl. jours. Mem. AAAS, NAFE, Am. Soc. Microbiology. Home: 195 Port Royal Ave Foster City CA 94404

CALDWELL, WILLARD E., psychologist, educator; b. Flushing L.I., N.Y., July 10, 1920; s. Howard Eugene and Lillian (Warner) C. AB in Psychology, U. Fla., 1940, MA in Psychology, 1941; PhD in Psychology, Cornell U., 1946; postgrad., Washington Sch. Psychiatry, 1948-53. Lic. psychologist, D.C. Grad. asst. psychology U. Fla., Gainesville, 1940-41; teaching asst. Psychology Dept. Cornell (N.Y.) U., 1943-46; prof. psychology, dept. chmn. Mary Baldwin Coll., Staunton, Va., 1947-48; asst. prof., assoc. prof., prof. psychology The George Washington U., Washington, 1948-85, prof. emeritus psychology, 1985—; psychotherapist. Editor, contbg. author: Principles of Comparative Psychology, 1960; contbr. over 50 articles to profl. jours. Pvt. U.S. Army, 1941-42. Mem. APA, D.C. Psychology Assn., Internat. Soc. Biometeorology. Republican. Episcopalian. Home: Apt 316 1101 New Hampshire Ave NW Washington DC 20037-1509

CALESCIBETTA, C.C., medical administrator, health law specialist; b. Auburn, N.Y., Oct. 1, 1932; s. Frank and Maria (Bauso) C.; m. Diane Marie Bunkers, Aug. 6, 1975; children: Christopher, Cara Mia. BA, Calif. State U., San Diego, 1956; MD, SUNY, Syracuse, 1960; JD, Pacific Coast U., Long Beach, Calif., 1988. Bar: Calif. 1989; diplomate Am. Bd. Internal Medicine, Sub-Bd. Nephrology. Intern Wishard Meml., Indpls., 1960-61; resident Kaiser Hosp., Oakland, Calif., 1961-62; resident L.A. County Harbor-UCLA, 1962-64, chief resident medicine, 1964-65, fellow in nephrology, 1969-70; dir. med. edn. St. Mary Med. Ctr., Long Beach, 1967-74, dir. Renal Ctr., 1971-95, med. dir. Renal Ctr., 1977-95; med.-legal cons., 1989—; clin. prof. medicine UCLA. Fellow ACP, Am. Coll. Legal Medicine; mem. Long Beach Med. Assn. (pres. 1994-95), Renal Disease Coun. So. Calif. (pres. bd. dirs. 1989-95). Home: 5500 E El Parque St Long Beach CA 90815-4127

CALHOUN, CHARLES LEWIS, ophthalmologist; b. Memphis, Oct. 22, 1943; s. John Critz and Camille (Bicknell) C.; m. Virginia Wilkins Carroll, Aug. 15, 1970; children: Marguerite Carroll, Virginia Camille, Charity Elizabeth. MD, U. Tenn., 1967. Diplomate Am. Bd. Ophthalmology. Intern City of Memphis Hosps., 1968-69; resident U. Tenn. Combined Program, 1973-76; pvt. practice West Ga. Eye Care Ctr., Columbus, 1976—; chief of staff Doctors Hosp., Columbus, 1988-89; bd. dirs. quality Health Ptnrs., Columbus. Com. chmn. Young Life, Columbus, 1982-87. Lt. comdr. USNR, 1969-72. Fellow Am. Acad. Ophthalmologists; mem. ACS, Ga. Soc. Ophthalmologists (legis. chmn. 1988-89), Am. Soc. Cataract and Refractive Surgery, Muscogee County Med. Soc. Office: West Georgia Eye Care Ctr 2000 10th Ave #400 Columbus GA 31901

CALHOUN, JASON HAROLD IRVING, orthopaedic surgeon, educator; b. Oriskany Falls, N.Y., May 4, 1950; s. Robert Paul and Florice Myrtle (Jeffrey) C.; m. Karen Hall, July 3, 1971; children: Zoey Abigail, Kenneth Paul. BA in Philosophy, Union Coll., Schenectady, N.Y., 1972; MEE, U. Louisville, 1975-76, MD, 1981. Diplomate Am. Bd. Orthopedic Surgery. Intern John Sealy Hosp., Galveston, Tex., 1981-82; resident U. Tex., Galveston, 1981-86; asst. prof. U. Tex. Med. Br., Galveston, 1986-91, chief, assoc. prof., 1992-94, med. dir., 1994—, prof., chief. chmn. dept., 1995—, adj. mem. Marine Biomed. Inst., 1986—, dir. foot and ankle fellowship, 1986—. Author: (with others) Foot and Ankle International, 1995; contbr. articles to profl. jours.; patentee in field. Parent organizer Trinity Episocpal Sch., Galveston, 1995. Recipient Ky. Cols. award, 1995. Fellow Academic Orthopaedic Soc. (grad. med. edn. com. 1995—), Am. Orthopaedic Foot and Ankle Soc. (chmn. rsch. tng. com. 1994—); mem. Assn. Study and Advancement of Methods of Ilizarov (pres. 1994), Tex. Orthopaedic Assn. (nominating com. 1995), Musculoskeletal Infection Soc. (pres. 1990-91). Office: U Tex Med Br Dept Ortho & Rehab 301 University Blvd Galveston TX 77555-0792

CALHOUN, KAREN HALL, otolaryngologist; b. Glen Cove, N.Y., Apr. 29, 1952; d. Kenneth Philip and Charlotte Joanne (Maley) Hall; m. Jason Harold Irving Calhoun, July 3, 1971; children: Zoey Abigail, Kenneth Paul. BA, U. Louisville, 1975, MD, 1979. Intern U. Louisville Hosps., 1979-80; emergency dept. physician Audoban Hosp., Louisville, 1980-81; resident in otolaryngology U. Tex. Med. Br., Galveston, 1981-85, head and neck fellow, 1985-87, asst. prof. dept. otolaryngology, 1987-90, assoc. prof., vice chair otolaryngology, 1990-94, prof., vice chair otolaryngology, 1994—. Author/editor: Surgery of the Lip, 1991; contbr. over 40 articles to profl. jours., chpts. to books. Fellow ACS, Am. Acad. Otolaryngology, Am. Acad. Facial Plastic and Reconstructive Surgery; mem. Am. Rhinology Soc., Soc. Univ. Otolaryngologists, So. Med. Assn. (chair sect. on otolaryngology 1991-92). Office: Univ Tex Med Br Dept Otolaryngology Galveston TX 77550

CALHOUN, LAWRENCE, psychology educator; b. Lavras, Brazil; came to U.S., 1963; BA, St. Andrews Presbyn. Coll., 1967; MA, Xavier U., Cin., 1969; PhD, U. Ga., 1973. Psychology educator Univ. N.C., Charlotte, 1973—. Author: Dealing With Crisis, 1976, Psychology and Human Reproduction, 1980; contbr. articles to profl. jours. Office: U NC Psychology Dept Charlotte NC 28223

CALHOUN, NOAH ROBERT, oral maxillofacial surgeon, educator; b. Clarendon, Ark., Mar. 23, 1921; s. Noah and Della (Sherman) C.; m. Cecelia Christopher, Oct. 19, 1950; children: Stephen Marc, Cecelia Noel. D.D.S., Dental Sch., Howard U., 1948; M.Dental Sci., Tufts Med. and Dental Sch., 1955. Oral surgeon VA Hosp., Tuskegee, Ala., 1950-52, Kessler AFB, Biloxi, Miss., 1952-53; chief dental service VA Hosp., Tuskegee, Ala., 1955-57; oral surgeon, asst. chief dental surgeon VA Hosp., Washington, 1964-74; chief dental service, oral surgeon VA Med. Center, Washington, 1974—; prof. oral surgery Dental Sch., Howard U., Washington, 1966—, Georgetown U., Washington, 1975—; prof. emeritus Dental Coll. Howard U.; Dir. Tuskegee (Ala.) Red Cross, 1962-64; chmn. Nat. Concerned VA Dentists, 1975, Inst. Medicine/Acad. Sci., 1975. Sect. editor Current Lit. in Internat. Oral/Maxillofacial Surgery, 1986; mem. editorial bd. Jour. Oral and Maxillo-facial Surveys, 1993; contbr. articles to profl. jours. Mem. ADA, Am. Soc. Oral and Maxillofacial Surgeons (Audio Visual award 1978), Internat. Coll. Dentistry, Am. Coll. Dentistry, NAACP (trustee D.C. chpt.), Omicron Kappa Upsilon (chpt. pres. 1974). Roman Catholic. Office: Dental Coll Howard U Washington DC 20001

CALIA, MARY ELIZABETH, microbiologist, business owner; b. Boston, May 23, 1954; d. Nicola and Christina (Liuzza) C. Cert. lab., Northeastern U., Boston, 1974. With Hinton course for cert. lab. technicians Ec. Bioran Med. Lab., Cambridge, Mass., 1969-72; clin. lab. technician Lawrence Meml. Hosp., Medford, Mass., 1974-82, clin. microbiologist, 1982—; owner Memories Preserved, Somerville, Mass., 1987—; presenter in field. Mem. Am. Soc. Clin. Pathologists, Am. Soc. Microbiology, N.E. Assn. for Clin. Microbiologist Infectious Disease, Reading (Mass.) Art Assn., Saugus Rotary (1st Pl. award 1981, 82, 83, 3d and 3d Pls. 1985). Roman Catholic. Office: Lawrence Meml Hosp 170 Governors Ave Medford MA 02155-1643

CALIANOS, THEODORE ARTHUR, II, plastic surgeon; b. Worcester, Mass., July 1, 1962; s. Theodore Arthur and Susan George (Eliopoulos) C.; m. Sheryl Ann Chalifoux, Oct. 31, 1992; 1 child, Zoe. BS, Boston Coll., 1983; MD, U. Tex., 1991. Resident in gen. surgery U. Mass. Med. Ctr., Worcester, 1991-94; fellow in hand surgery Rush-Presbyn.-St. Luke's Med. Ctr., Chgo., 1994-95; resident in plastic surgery U. Tex. Med. Br., Galveston, 1995—. Mem. AMA, Am. Coll. Surgeons (candidate group), Am. Heart Assn. (cardiovasc. disease com. 1990), Alpha Kappa Kappa (former dir. alumni affairs, fundraising). Greek Orthodox. Home: 206 E Seawall Blvd Galveston TX 77550 Office: U Tex Med Br Dept Plas Surg 301 University Blvd Galveston TX 75555

CALIENDO, THEODORE JOSEPH, pediatrician, neonatologist; b. Bklyn., Nov. 9, 1941; s. Leo J. and Anna C.; m. Arlene Mann, Jan. 7, 1970 (div. Aug. 1984); children: Michael, Robert, Barbra, David. BS, St. John's U., Bklyn., 1962; MD, N.Y. Med. Coll., 1966. Intern, resident Cedars Sinai Med. Ctr., L.A., 1966-69; pediatrician, neonatalogist Kaiser-Permanente, Mission Viejo, Calif., 1973—; attending physician Cedars Sinai Med. Ctr., L.A., 1971-81, Kaiser Hosp., Anaheim, Calif., 1979—; asst. prof. pediatrics UCLA Med. Sch., 1971-82. Lt. comdr. USN, 1969-71. Fellow Am. Acad. Pediatrics; mem. L.A. Pediatric Soc., Ritz Bros., Monarch Bay Club, Rancho Niquel Club, Ferarri Club Am. Office: Kaiser Permanente 23781 Maquina Mission Viejo CA 92691-2716

CALIO, ANTHONY JOSEPH, physician; b. Bklyn., Apr. 5, 1955; s. Joseph A. and Rose M. Calio; m. Maura Ann McCutcheon, July 22, 1989; children: Joseph, Conor, Caitlin. BS in Biology, SUNY, Stony Brook, 1977; MD, U. del Noreste, Tampico, Mex., 1982, SUNY, 1987. Diplomate Am. Bd. Internal Medicine. Intern Nassau Hosp. (now Winthrop U. Hosp.), Mineola, N.Y., 1983-84; resident in internal medicine Winthrop U. Hosp., Mineola, 1984-86; physician Winthrop Internal Medicine Assocs., Mineola, N.Y.; dir. employee health Winthrop U. Hosp., 1986-94, chmn. mortality com., 1989-95, dir. quality assurance, 1989-95; dir. clin. practice Winthrop Internal Medicine Assocs., 1995-96. Mem. AMA, Am. Coll. Physicians. Office: Winthrop Internal Medicine 222 Station Plaza N Mineola NY 11501

CALKIN, JOY DURFÉE, healthcare consultant, educator; b. Wolfville, N.S., Can., Apr. 7, 1938; came to U.S., 1970; d. Garth Longworth and Rena Coffin (Cox) C. BS in Nursing, U. Toronto, Ont., Can., 1960; MS in Nursing, U. Wis., 1968, PhD, 1980. Nurse various hosps., Toronto, N.S.and Aberdeen, Scotland, 1960-63; instr. U. N.B., Fredericton, Can., 1963-66, asst. prof., 1968-70; from asst. to assoc. to prof. Sch. Nursing, U. Wis., Madison, 1970-85; from asst. to assoc. to full prof. nursing Faculty Medicine, Dept. Preventive Medicine, 1980-85; dean, prof. sch. nursing U. Calgary, Alta., Can., 1985-89, assoc. acad. v.p., 1989-90—, acad. v.p., provost, 1990—; vis. prof. health scis. U. Oreg., Portland, 1980; cons. Troll Assocs., Madison, 1976-80, Thorne, Stevenson & Kellogg, Edmonton, 1985-86; mem. Premier's commn. on future health care for Alberta. Mem. editorial bd. Recent Advances in Nursing, U.K.; reviewer various nursing jours.; contbr. articles to profl. jours. Bd. dirs. Alberta Found. Nursing Rsch., 1988-91, Alberta Family Life and Substance Abuse Found., 1992-93, Muttart Found., 1993—, Extendicare, 1995—. Grantee in field. Mem. Am. Nurses Assn., Can. Nurses Assn. (various coms.). Office: U Calgary, 2500 University Dr NW, Calgary, AB Canada T2N 1N4

CALKINS, DAVID ROSS, physician, medical educator; b. Kansas City, Kans., May 27, 1948; s. Leroy Adelbert and Emily Virginia (Kyger) C.; m. Susan Spalding Rice, Sept. 22, 1989. AB, Princeton (N.J.) U., 1970; MD and MPP, Harvard U., 1975. Diplomate Am. Bd. Internal Medicine. Intern in medicine U. Wash., Seattle, 1975-76; resident in medicine Beth Israel Hosp., Boston, 1976-78, from asst. to assoc. in medicine, 1981-96; fellow The White House, Washington, 1978-79; spl. asst., dep. exec. sec. HHS, Washington, 1979-81; from instr. to asst. prof. dept. medicine Harvard U. Med. Sch., Boston, 1981-96; from instr. to asst. prof. Harvard Sch. Pub. Health, Boston, 1985-96, dir. profl. programs dept. health policy and mgmt., 1985-96; chief div. gen. internal medicine, med. dir. ambulatory svc. New Eng. Deaconess Hosp., Boston, 1991-96; assoc. dean for primary care, assoc. prof. internal medicine and preventive medicine U. Kans. Sch. Medicine, Kansas City, 1996—. W.K. Kellogg Found. fellow, 1987. Office: 3901 Rainbow Blvd Kansas City KS 66160-1825

CALKINS, EVAN, physician, educator; b. Newton, Mass., July 15, 1920; s. Grosvenor and Patty (Phillips) C.; m. Virginia McC. Brady, Sept. 9, 1946; children: Sarah Calkins Oxnard, Stephen, Lucy McCormick, Joan, Benjamin, Hugh, Ellen Rountree, Geoffrey, Timothy. Grad., Milton Acad., 1939; AB, Harvard U., 1942, MD, 1945. Intern, asst. resident medicine Johns Hopkins, 1946-47, 48-50; chief resident physician Mass. Gen. Hosp., 1951-52, mem. arthritis unit, 1952-61; NRC fellow med. scis. Harvard, 1950-51, instr., asst. prof. medicine, 1952-61; practice medicine, specializing in rheumatology Boston, 1951-61, Buffalo, 1961—; prof. medicine SUNY, Buffalo, 1961-94, prof. emeritus, 1994—; chmn. dept. SUNY, 1965-77; head dept. medicine Buffalo Gen. Hosp., 1961-68; dir. medicine E.J. Meyer Meml. Hosp., 1968-78; head gerontology sect. Buffalo VA Med. Ctr., 1978-90; head div. geriatrics/gerontology SUNY-Buffalo, 1978-90; founder, pres. Network in Aging of Western N.Y., Inc., 1980-83; cons. Nat. Inst. Arthritis and Metabolic Diseases Tng. Grants Com., 1958-62, Program Project Com., 1964-68, Nat. Instn. Spl. Study Sect. for Health Manpower, 1969-77, for Behavioral Medicine, 1978-79; mem. acad. awards com. Nat. Inst. on Aging, 1979-80, mem. nat. adv. coun., 1985-88; dir. Western N.Y. Geriatric Edn. Ctr., 1983-88, co-dir., 1988-90; dir. Multidisciplinary Ctr. on Aging SUNY-Buffalo, 1989-90, prof. family medicine, 1987-94; sr. physician and coord. geriatric programs Health Care Plan, 1990—. Editor: Handbook of Medical Emergencies, 1945, Geriatric Medicine, 1983, Practice of Geriatrics, 1986, 2nd edition 1991; mem. editl. bd. HMO Practice; contbr. articles to profl. jours. Pres. Nat. Assn. Geriatric Edn. Ctrs., 1992-93. Capt. M.C. AUS, 1943-45, 46-48. Recipient Presdl. citation for Community Service, 1983. Fellow ACP (master 1989), Am. Coll. Rheumatology (founder, pres. 1967-68, master 1986), Gerontol. Soc. Am. (chair clin. med. sect. 1989, Freeman award 1991), Am. Geriatrics Soc. (Milo D. Leavitt award 1986); mem. Am. Clin. and Climatological Assn. (v.p. 1987), Am. Soc. Clin. Investigation, Assn. Am. Physicians, Soc. Medicine Argentina (hon.), Argentine Soc. Gerontology and Geriatrics (hon.), Soc. Fellows John Hopkins U., Alpha Omega Alpha. Home: 3799 Windover Dr Hamburg NY 14075 Office: Mosher Med Bldg 899 Main St Buffalo NY 14203-1185

CALKINS, JAMES PHILLIP, ophthalmologist; b. Charlottesville, Va., July 7, 1925; s. LeRoy Adelbert and Mina Marie (Curry) C.; m. Roberta H. Fastje, July 6, 1926; children: Carol Sue, Kenneth, Janet, Robin. BS, U. Kans., 1945; MD, Kans. U., 1948; MS, U. Iowa, 1955. Diplomate Am. Bd. Ophthalmology. Intern Ohio State U. Hosp., Columbus, 1948-49; resident U. Pa., Phila., 1949-50, U. Iowa, Iowa City, 1950-51, 53-55; ophthalmologist pvt. practice, Tucson, Ariz., 1955—; clin. lectr. ophthalmology U. Ariz., Tucson, 1988—. Capt. USAF, 1951-53. Mem. Ariz. Ophthalmological Soc. (pres. 1967-68), Pima County Med. Assn. Office: 490 N Alvernon Tucson AZ 85711

CALKINS, JOANN RUBY, nursing administrator; b. Mich., June 28, 1934; d. William Russell and Imajean (Dunkle) Armentrout; m. James W. Calkins, 1952; children: Russell, Jill, Cindy; m. W. Arthur Brindle, May 7, 1983. AS, Delta Coll., 1964, BS, Cen. Mich. U., 1972, MA, 1977. Staff nurse, L.P.N. clin. instr., asst. dir. Sch. Nursing, Midland (Mich.) Hosp., 1964-71; dir. nursing, dir. substance abuse unit Gladwin (Mich.) Hosp., 1972-76; prin. Calkins Profl. Counseling & Cons., Harrison, Mich., 1976-78, part-time, 1978-83; dir. nursing svc. Ctrl. Mich. Cmty. Hosp., Mt. Pleasant, 1978-83; dir. nursing Oaklawn Hosp., Marshall, Mich., 1983-87; asst. adminstr. profl. svcs. DON Betsy Johnson Meml. Hosp., Dunn, N.C., 1987-93, v.p. profl. svcs., 1993-95, pub. rels., 1995—; part-time prin. W. Arthur and Assocs. Cons.; conducted workshops Mich. Dept. Pub. Health, Mich. Hosp. Assn.; exec. dir. Holistic Health Agy., 1977-82. Trustee Mid-Mich. C.C.; vol. counselor student nurses Cen. Carolina Coll., 1988-93; friends of the libr., 1995; mem. health task force for Harnett County HelpNet; adv. bd. to schs. of nursing Johnston C.C., Sampson C.C., Cen. Carolina C.C.; mem. adv. bd. St. Joseph of the Pines Home Health Agy., 1988-93; cert. layity spkr. Meth. Ch., 1994. Recipient Murial A. Grimmason Nursing Scholarship award, 1962; Cert. nursing adminstr. Mem. Mich. Soc. Hosp. Nursing Adminstrs. (mem. steering com. 1979-80, dir., 14 county rep. 1980-83, pres. 1983-84, chmn. devel. com.), Mich. Nurses Assn., Am. Orgn. Nurse Execs., N.C. Orgn. Nurse Execs. (exec. bd. dirs. 1990-93), Carolinas Healthcare Pub. Rels. and Mktg. Soc., Lioness Internat. (3d v.p. 1985). Office: 800 Tilghman Dr Dunn NC 28334-5510

CALLAGHAN, DANIEL PATRICK, family physician; b. Mineola, N.Y., June 9, 1961; s. Edward Patrick and Anne (Coleman) C.; m. Veronica Ann MacKay, Oct. 20, 1990; children: Sean, Kevin. B Chem. Engring., Manhattan Coll., 1982; MD, N.Y. Med. Coll., 1986. Diplomate Am. Bd. Family Practice. Intern Cath. Med. Ctr. of Bklyn. and Queens, Jamaica, N.Y., 1986-87, resident in family practice, 1987-89; family practice physician William W. Backus Hosp., Norwich, Conn., 1993-94; mem. family practice faculty Cath. Med. Ctr. Bklyn. and Queens, Jamaica, N.Y., 1994—. Maj. M.C., USAF, 1989-93. Roman Catholic. Office: Cath Med Ctr Bklyn-Queens Dept Family Practice 88-25 153d St Jamaica NY 11432

CALLAGHAN, SCOTT DANIEL, neurologist; b. Atlantic City, June 10, 1958; s. Peter John and Gloria M. (Klink) C.; m. Helen L. Callaghan, Aug. 14, 1982; 1 child, Emily Ann. DO, U. Medicine and Dentistry N.J., 1987. Diplomate Am. Bd. Psychiatry and Neurology, Am. Bd. Electrodiagnostic Medicine. Resident in neurology Med. Coll. Va., Richmond, 1988-91, fellow in neuromuscular disease, 1991-92; pvt. practice, Billings, Mont., 1992—. Fellow Am. Assn. Electrodiagnostic Medicine; mem. AMA, Am. Acad. Neurology, N.Am. Spine Soc. Roman Catholic. Office: Yellowstone Neurosci Ctr 1145 N 29th St Ste 304 Billings MT 59101

CALLAHAN, CHARLES WILLIS, pediatrician; b. Meriden, Conn., June 29, 1958; s. Charles Willis and Marjorie Anne (Floyd) C.; m. Linda Marie Callahan, Aug. 2, 1980; children: Jonathan, Timothy, Katherine, Christine, Bethany. BA, Rutgers U., 1979; DO, N.J. Sch. Osteo. Medicine, 1984. Diplomate Am. Bd. Pediatrics with subspecialty in pulmonology; lic. physician, N.J., Hawaii. Commd. U.S. Army, 1979—, advanced through grades to lt. col., 1996—; intern/resident Walter Reed Army Med. Ctr., Washington, 1984-87; staff pediatrician Darnall Army Hosp., Ft. Hood, Tex., 1987-90; fellow in pediatric pulmonology St. Christopher's Hosp. for Children, Phila., 1990-93; chief pediatric pulmonology Tripler Army Med. Ctr., Honolulu, 1993—; clin. instr. pediatrics Temple U. Sch. Medicine, Phila., 1991-93; clin. asst. prof. pediatrics J. Burns Sch. Medicine, Honolulu, 1993—, Univ Health Scis., Bethesda, Md., 1995—. Contbr. articles to profl. jours. Lay pastor Word Fellowship Ch., Stratford, N.J., 1990-93, New Life Christian Fellowship, Honolulu, 1993—; elder Killeen Evang. Free Ch., 1988-90; foster parent Phila. and Honolulu placement agencies, 1990—. Recipient Outstanding Teaching award Phase II Physician's Asst. Program, Ft. Hood, 1989, Angelo Digeorge Teaching award St. Christopher's Hosp. for Children, 1993, James Bass Teaching award Tripler Army Med. Ctr., 1995. Fellow Am. Acad. Pediatrics, Am. Coll. Chest Physicians; mem. Am. Coll. Osteo. Pediatrics, Christian Med. Dental Soc., Assn. Mil. Surgeons U.S., Am. Thoracic Soc. Home: 212A Hibiscus St Honolulu HI 96818 Office: Tripler Army Medical Ctr Dept Pediatrics Honolulu HI 96859

CALLAHAN, DANIEL JOHN, institute director; b. Washington, July 19, 1930; s. Vincent Francis and Anita (Hawkins) C.; m. Sidney Cornelia de Shazo, June 5, 1954; children: Mark Sidney, Stephen Daniel, John Vincent, Peter Thorn, Sarah Elisabeth, David Lee. B.A., Yale U., 1952; M.A., Georgetown U., 1957; Ph.D., Harvard U., 1965; D.Sc. (hon.), U. Medicine and Dentistry of N.J., 1981; DHL (hon.), U. Colo., 1990, Williams Coll., 1992. Exec. editor The Commonweal, N.Y.C., 1961-68; staff assoc. Population Council, 1969-70; pres. The Hastings Ctr., 1969—; resident scholar Aspen Inst. Humanistic Studies, 1975; vis. asst. prof. religion Temple U., 1064; vis. asst. prof. religious stuies Brown U., 1965; vis. prof. theology Marymount Coll., 1966; vis. prof. U. Pa., 1970; cons. med. ethics, jud. coun. AMA, 1972-82, ACP, 1979—; spl. cons. Commn. on Population Growth and Am. Future, 1970-71, NEH, 1979. Author: The Mind of the Catholic Layman, 1963, Honesty in the Church, 1965, The New Church, 1966, Abortion: Law, Choice and Morality, 1970, Ethics and Population Limitation, 1971, The Tyranny of Survival, 1973, The Teaching of Ethics in the Military, 1982, Setting Limits: Medical Goals in an Aging Society, 1987, What Kind of Life: The Limits of Medical Progress, 1990, The Troubled Dream of Life: Living with Mortality, 1993; also essays, articles; co-editor: Christianity Divided: Protestant and Roman Catholic Theological Issues, 1961, Ethical Issues in Human Genetics, 1973; editor: Federal Aid and Catholic Schools, 1964, Secular City Debate, 1966, The Catholic Case for Contraception, 1969, The American Population Debate, 1971, Science, Ethics and Medicine, 1976, Knowledge, Value and Belief, 1977, Morals, Science and Sociality, 1978, Knowing and Valuing, 1979, Ethics Teaching in Higher Education, 1980, Ethical Issues in Population Aid, 1980, The Roots of Ethics, 1981, Ethics in Hard Times, 1981, Ethics, the Social Sciences and Policy Analysis, 1983, Abortion: Understanding Differences, 1984, Applying the Humanities, 1985, Representation and Responsibility, 1985, A World Growing Old, 1995, What Price Mental Health?, 1995; mem. editl. adv. bd. Tech. in Soc., 1981—; mem. adv. bd. Ency. of Life Scis., 1982, Sci., Tech. and Human Values, 1979—, Bus. and Profl. Ethics, 1981, Criminal Justice Ethics, 1982, Environ. Ethics, 1982, Jour. Bioethics, 1985—. Mem. N.Y. Coun. for Humanities, 1975-79; mem. Nat. Book Award Com., 1975, N.Y. State Health Adv. Coun., 1975-76; selection com. Ford-Rockefeller Program in Population Policy, 1975-78, Rockefeller Found. Program in Humanities, 1980; elector Nat. Medal for Lit., 1979-83; pub. mem. Am. Bd. Med. Specialties, 1982-87, N.Y. Sci. Policy Assn., 1985-91; mem. N.Y. Task Force on Life and Law, 1985-87; mem. nat. adv. bd. Health Promotion Program, Henry J. Kaiser Family Found., 1987-91, N.Y. Panel and HIV Screening, 1987; trustee U. Pa. Med. Ctr., 1987-91; mem. adv. com. on sci. integrity HHS, 1991-93; adv. com. to dir. Ctr. for Disease Control, DHHS. Recipient Thomas More medal, 1970, Daryl J. Mase Disting. Leadership award, 1987, Book of Yr. award Am. Jour. Nursing, 1987, Henry Knowles Beecher award The Hastings Ctr., 1989, James H. Hamilton Book award Am. Coll. Health Care Execs., 1990, Pres. Cabinet award U. Tex., 1995, Scientific Freedom and Responsibility award AAAS, 1995; named one of 200 Outstanding Young Men Leaders Time mag., 1974, Tekolste scholar Ind. Hosp. Assn., 1986; nat. fellowship Bus. Enterprise Trust, 1989—. Fellow AAAS (Sci. Freedom and Responsibility award 1996); mem. Am. Assn. for Advancement Humanities, Inst. Medicine of NAS, Soc. for Study Social Biology (bd. dirs. 1987-95), Harvard Grad. Soc. (coun. 1989-92). Home: PO Box 178 Ardsley On Hudson NY 10503-7146 Office: The Hastings Ctr 255 Elm Rd Briarcliff Manor NY 10510-2207

CALLAHAN, DAVID MICHAEL, psychologist; b. Methuen, Mass., June 25, 1958; s. William John and Virginia Ann (Pageau) C.; m. Gretchen Stecher, July 31, 1982; children: Peter, Daniel. BS in Psychology, Fitchburg State Coll., 1980; MA in Clin. Psychology, U. Rochester, 1983, PhD in Clin. Psychology, 1985. Psychologist Herbert Lipton Mental Health, Fitchburg, Mass., 1985-86, Psychology Assocs., Plymouth, Mass., 1987-94; dir. Psychology Assocs., 1991-94, The Sandwich Ctr., 1995—; cons. psychologist Family Svc. Assn., Fall River, Mass., 1987—. Mem. Cult Awareness Network, 1986—. Mem. Am. Psychol. Assn. Democrat. Episcopalian. Office: Sandwich Ctr Inc 449 Rte 130 Ste 12 PO Box 1037 Sandwich MA 02563

CALLAHAN, JOHN J., federal official; b. Quincy, Mass., 1948; m. Susan Doherty; children: Kathleen, Erin, Sean. BA in Polit. Sci., Fordham U., 1965; MA in Regional Planning, Syracuse U., 1971, PhD in Social Sci., 1972. Staff mem. N.Y. Joint Legis. Com. to Revise & Simplify Edn. Law, 1968-69; cons. Syracuse Univ. Policy Rsch. Corp., 1969-70; sr. analyst U.S. Adv.

Commn. Intergovtl. Rels., 1969-74; asst. prof. edn. & planning U. Va., 1971-72; exec. dir. Legislators' Edn. Action Project, 1974-77; exec. dir. Nat. Conf. State Legislatures, 1974-77, dir. Fed.-State rels., 1977-79; staff dir. U.S. Senate Govtl. Affairs subcom. Intergovtl. Rels., Washington, 1979-83, minority staff dir., 1981-83; chief of staff U.S. Senator Jim Sasser, Washington, 1983-86, 93-95; dep. staff dir. U.S. Senate Budget com., Washington, 1987-93; asst. sec. mgmt. & budget HHS, Washington, 1995—. Office: HHS 200 Independence Ave SW Rm 514G Washington DC 20201*

CALLAHAN, LEEANN LUCILLE, psychologist; b. San Diego, Calif., Dec. 7, 1950; d. Charlie A. Olsen and Delores A. (Libke) Turner; m. Chuck Callahan, Oct. 31, 1970; children: Clint, Devin, Chet. BS/MS in Psychology, San Diego State U., 1983; PhD in Psychology, USIU, San Diego, 1990. Lic. clin. psychologist. Clin. dir. Sharp Cabrillo Hosp., San Diego, 1989-91, Charter Hosp., San Diego, 1991-93; psychologist San Diego, 1989—; preferred provider Charter Hosp., San Diego, 1990—, speakers bur., 1990—; staff psychologist Sharp Cabrillo Hosp., San Diego, 1989-92. Editor Parentteen Mag.; contbr. articles to profl. jours. Pres. PTA, San Diego, 1985; citizen adv./city coun. City of San Diego, 1987; vol. Poway Unified Sch. Dist., San Diego, 1975—; speaker Rotary, San Diego, 1994. Mem. APA, Calif. State Psychol. Assn. Office: 9320 Carmel Mountain Rd Ste D San Diego CA 92129-2159

CALLAHAN, MARILYN JOY, social worker; b. Portland, Oreg., Oct. 11, 1934; d. Douglas Q. and Anona Helen Maynard; m. Lynn J. Callahan, Feb. 27, 1960 (dec.); children: Barbara Callahan Baer, Susan Callahan Sewell, Jeffrey Lynn. BA, Mills Coll., 1955; MSW, Portland State U., 1971, secondary teaching cert., 1963. Bd. cert. diplomate in clin. social work. Developer, adminstr. ednl. program Oreg. Women's Correctional Ctr., Oreg. State Prison, Salem, 1966-67; mental health counselor Benton County Mental Health, Corvallis, Oreg., 1970-71; inst. tchr. Hillcrest Sch., Salem, Oreg., 1975-81; social worker protective svcs. Mid Willamette Valley Sr. Svcs. Agy., Salem, 1981-88; psychiat. social worker dept. forensics Oreg. State Hosp., 1988-93; pvt. practice treatment of adult male and female sexual offenders Salem, 1993—; pvt. practice in care/mgmt. of elderly, 1993—; panel mem. Surgeon Gen.'s N.W. Regional Conf. on Interpersonal Violence, 1987; speaker in field; planner, organizer Seminar on Age Discrimination, 1985. Mem. NASW (bd. dirs. Oreg. chpt.), Nat. Org. Forensic Social Work, Am. Acad. Forensic Scis., Acad. Cert. Social Workers (lic. clin. social worker), Oreg. Gerontol. Assn., Catalina 27 Nat. Sailing Assn. Office: Ste 304 780 Commercial St SE Salem OR 97301-3455

CALLAHAN-HUNT, ELEANOR MARJORIE, nursing user analyst; b. Concord, Mass., Oct. 5, 1966; d. Thomas T. and Eleanor Jean (Johnson) Callahan; m. Andrew W. Hunt, Apr. 16, 1989. BSN cum laude, U. Pa., 1988. RN, Conn. Pediatric nursing user analyst-CCSS project Yale-New Haven Hosp. Recipient computerized methods for ordering & administering chemotherapeutic agts. award MISA, ALLTEL Users Group, 1994. Mem. Sigma Theta Tau.

CALLAWAY, CLIFFORD WAYNE, physician; b. Easton, Md., May 28, 1941; s. Charles Herschel and Anna Agnes (Stradley) C.; m. Barbara Joann Boits (div.); 1 child, David Wayne; m. Marguerite Ethel Moore (div.); m. Jackie Cholkley. BA, U. Del., 1963; MD, Northwestern U., 1967. Diplomate Am. Bd. Internal Medicine, Am. Bd. Endocrinology and Metabolism, Am. Bd. Nutrition. Resident internal medicine Northwestern U. Med. Ctr., Chgo., 1967-69, Mayo Grad. Sch. Medicine, Rochester, Minn., 1971-73; advanced clin. resident endocrinology Mayo Grad. Sch. Medicine, 1973-75; assoc. cons. Mayo Clin., Rochester, 1975-78; cons. endocriminology Mayo Clin., 1978-85, dir. nutrition and lipid clins., 1980-85; rsch. assoc. Harvard Med. Sch., Boston, 1976-78; dir. ctr. clin. nutrition George Washington U., Washington, 1986-88; sr. sci. cons. Food & Ntrition Bd., NRC/NAS, Washington, 1987-88; pvt. practice Washington, 1988—. Author 3 books; contbr. articles to profl. jours. Acting exec. sec. nutrition coordinating office HHS, Washington, 1980. Mayo Found. scholar, 1976-78. Mem. Am. Soc. Clin. Nutrition (treas. 1988), Am. Bd. Nutrition (mem. bd. dirs. 1983-89, 95—, dir., sec.-treas. 1984-86, 82-88, v.p. 1986-88), Am. Inst. Nutrition (chair and various coms.), Am. Osler Soc. (bd. dirs.), Am. Assn. Clin. Endocrinologists (bd. dirs. 1992-95), Cen. European Ctr. for Health and Environment (bd. dirs. 1993—). Office: 2311 M St NW Ste 301 Washington DC 20037-1445

CALLAWAY, ENOCH, psychiatrist, educator; b. LaGrange, Ga., July 12, 1924; s. Enoch and Jennie L. (Crowell) C.; m. Dorothy Campbell, July 3, 1948; children: Rebecca, Deborah. AB, Columbia U., 1944, MD, 1947. Diplomate Am. Bd. Psychiatry and Neurology. Instr. U. Md., Balt., 1952-55, asst. prof., 1955-58; assoc. prof. U. Calif., San Francisco, 1958-65, prof., 1965-86, prof. emeritus, 1986—; founder, bd. dirs. Neurobiol. Techs. Inc., Richmond, Calif., 1995—; mem. rev. com. on psychopharmacology NIMH, 1963-67, rev. com. on alcohol, 1968-72, rev. com. on research scientists, 1975-76, adv. bd. EEG Systems Lab., San Francisco, 1985—. Author: Brain Electrical Potential and Individual Psychological Differences, 1975; editor: Event Related Brain Potentials in Man, 1978, Human Evoked Potentials, 1978, assoc. editor Biol. Psychiatry, 1983—, mem. editorial bd. AMA Archives Gen. Psychiatry, 1970-83; contbr. numerous articles to sci. jours. Served to comdr. USN, 1950-52. Recipient Career Devel. award NIMH, 1954-58; research prize Md. Assn. Pvt. Practicing Psychiatrists, 1956; Royer award U. Calif., San Francisco, 1981. Fellow Am. Coll. Neuropsychopharmacology; mem. Soc. Biol. Psychiatry (pres. 1982-83), Soc. Psychophysiol. Research (pres. 1982), Calif. Med. Assn. (exec. com. sci. bd. 1977-83)., Marin Recorder Soc. Democrat. Club: Tiburon Peninsula. Home: 1 Mt Tiburon Rd Belvedere Tiburon CA 94920-1511 Office: Neurobiol Techs Inc 1387 Marina Way S Richmond CA 94804

CALLAWAY, RICHARD EARL, dentist; b. Des Moines, Aug. 9, 1951; s. Grover Earl and Geraldine Anna (Dageforde) C.; m. Nancy Jean Clark, May 2, 1981; children: Scott, Jessica, Lindsey, Rachel. BA, Mo. Western State Coll., 1974; DDS, U. Mo., Kansas City, 1978. Gen. practice dentistry Fremont, Nebr., 1978—. Bd. dirs. Fremont Big Bros./Big Sisters, 1981-87. Named one of Outstanding Young Men of Am., Fremont Jaycees, 1985. Mem. ADA, Nebr. Dental Assn., Omaha Dist. Dental Assn., Tri Valley Dental Soc. (treas. 1980, v.p. 1981), Fremont Jaycees (bd. dirs. 1979-85, v.p. 1985-86, pres. 1986-87), Fremont Tennis Assn. Republican. Lutheran. Lodge: Optimists. Home: 545 N Platte Ave Fremont NE 68025-5273 Office: 1835 E Military Ave Fremont NE 68025-5465

CALLAWAY, WILLIAM JOSEPH, radiography educator; b. Moline, Ill., Jan. 15, 1951; m. Karen Callaway, Nov. 21, 1987; children: Amy, David, Kimberly. BA, Western Ill. U., 1979. Registered radiographer, Ill. Dir. edn., dept. radiology Luth. Hosp., Moline, 1977-86; sr. cons. Orgn. Dimensions, Inc., Wheeling, Ill., 1986-91; dir. edn. dept. radiology Meml. Med. Ctr., Springfield, Ill., 1989-92; dir. radiology edn. Lincoln Land Community Coll., Springfield, Ill., 1992—; lectr. various local, state, nat. and internat. orgns. Author: Introduction to Radiologic Technology, 1983, 4th edit., 1996, Mosby's Comprehensive Review of Radiography, 1996. Mem. Assn. Educators Radiol. Scis., Ill. Soc. Radiologic Technologists, Am. Soc. Radiologic Technologists. Home: 3612 Chelmsford Ct Springfield IL 62704-5500 Office: Lincoln Land Community Coll Shepherd Rd Springfield IL 62754-9256

CALLEN, JEFFREY PHILLIP, dermatologist, educator; b. Chgo., May 30, 1947; s. Irwin R. and Rose P. (Cohen) C.; m. Susan B. Manis, Dec. 21, 1968; children: Amy, David. BS, U. Wis., 1969; MD, U. Mich., 1972. Diplomate Am. Bd. Internal Medicine, 1975, Am. Bd. Dermatology, 1977. Intern/resident in internal medicine U. Mich., 1972-75, in dermatology, 1975-77; asst. clin. prof. U. Louisville Sch. Medicine, 1977-81, assoc. clin. prof., 1982-84, assoc. prof., dir. residency tng. program, 1984-88; chief dermatology service Louisville VA Hosp., 1984-93; prof., chief div. of dermatology, 1988—. Author: Manual of Dermatology, 1980, Cutaneous Aspects of Internal Disease, 1981; Neurology Clinics North America, 1987, Dermatologic Signs of Systemic Disease, 1988, 2nd edit., 1994, Color Atlas of Dermatology, 1993, Current Practice of Dermatology, 1995; editor: Clinics in Rheumatic Disease, 1982, Dermatologic Clinics, 1985, 89, Med. Clinics of N.Am., 1982, 84, 86, 89; editor in chief Dermavision video program; mem. editorial bd. Internat. Jour. Dermatology, 1980-87, Cutis, Jour. Am. Acad. Dermatology, 1990—, asst. editor, 1993—; editor spl. issues of jours. in field. Bd. dirs. Actor's Theatre of Louisville, 1982-91, 92—, sec., 1986-87, Ky. Arts and Crafts Found., 1991—; bd. govs. JB Speed Art Mus., 1995—. Fellow ACP, Am. Acad. Dermatology (chmn. audio/visual edn. com., task force therapeutic agts., internal medicine symposium 1978-83, chmn. sci. and tech. exhibits 1986-89, dir. symposium on cutaneous oncology 1984-87, symposium on diagnostic updates 1989-92, mem. coun. sci. assembly 1993—, bd. dirs. 1995—), Am. Coll. Rheumatology (founder); mem. Am. Fedn. Clin. Research, AMA, Am. Dermatol. Assn. Dermatology Found. (trustee 1984-90). Research on condition in which systemic disease has cutaneous manifestations, lupus erythematosus, psoriasis, dermatomyositis. Office: U Louisville Dept Dermatology 310 E Broadway St Ste 200 Louisville KY 40202-1745

CALLEN, LORY DEPAOLI, emergency room nurse; b. Wilmington, Del., July 22, 1953; d. Lino and Albina (Vittorelli) DePaoli; m. Kenneth J. Callen, Oct. 10, 1981; children: Christopher, Danielle. BSN, Our Lady of Angels Coll., Aston, Pa., 1975. Cert. ACLS. Primary care nurse Johns Hopkins Hosp., Balt., 1975-76; med.-surg., emergency rm. and intravenous nurse Riddle Meml. Hosp., Media, Pa., 1976-81; intravenous and recovery rm. nurse Providence Hosp., Anchorage, 1981-86; emergency rm. nurse Med. Ctr. Del., Wilmington, 1986—; clin. rsch. asst. PACT, Radnor, Pa., 1993-94. Mem. Emergency Nurses Assn.

CALLENBACH, JOHN CURRIE, neonatalogist; b. Bozeman, Mont., Apr. 10, 1947; s. John Anton and Lillian (Turek) C.; m. Leslie Largo, June 14, 1969; children: Corrie Patrick, Carlton Drew. BS, Washington State U., 1969; MD, U. Wash., 1973. Diplomate Am. Bd. Pediatrics, Am. Bd. Pediatrics and Neonatal Perinatal Medicine. Neonatologist Children's Mercy Hosp., Kansas City, Mo., 1977-91; assoc. prof. U. Mo., Kans. City, 1985—; dir. neonatal intensive care Unit Perinatal Pediatrics, Kansas City, Mo., 1991—; bd. dirs. Ronald McDonald, Kansas City, Mo., 1988-92, SIDS, Kansas City, Mo., 1990-94. Office: Perinatal Pediatrics 4400 Wornall Kansas City MO 64111

CALLENDER, CLIVE ORVILLE, surgeon; b. N.Y.C., Nov. 16, 1936; s. Joseph and Ida (Burke) C.; m. Fern Irene Marshall, May 25, 1968; children: Joseph, Ealena, Arianne. A.B., Hunter Coll., 1959; M.D., Meharry Med. Coll., 1963. Diplomate Am. Bd. Surgery, 1970. Intern U. Cin., 1963-64; asst. resident Harlem Hosp., N.Y.C., 1964-65, Howard U. and Freedmans Hosp., Washington, 1965-66, 67-68; chief resident Howard U. and Freedmans Hosp., 1968-69, instr. dept. surgery, 1969-71; asst. resident Meml. Hosp. for Cancer and Allied Diseases, N.Y.C., 1966-67; cons. surgery Port Harcourt Gen. Hosp., Nigeria, 1970, 71; med. officer D.C. Gen. Hosp., 1970-71; NIH postdoctoral rsch. and clin. transplant fellow U. Minn., 1971-73; asst. prof. surgery Howard U. Med. Coll., Washington, 1973-76; assoc. prof. Howard U. Med. Coll., 1976-81, prof. surgery, 1981—, vice-chmn. dept. surgery, 1980-95, chmn. dept. surgery, 1996—, LaSalle D. Sebball prof. surgery, 1996—, dir. transplant ctr., 1973—; transplantation cons., Bermuda, 1977, V.I., 1978, 82-86; cons. Ethiopian Surg., Amenity Med. Sch., 1984; G.P.A. Ford Meml. lectr., 1978; mem. task force on organ procurement and transplantation HEW, 1984; testifier com. on labor and human resources U.S. Senate, 1983; mem. end stage renal disease study com. Inst. Medicine, 1989-90, com. on xenograft transplantation: ethical issues and pub. policy Inst. of Medicine, 1995—, to the Sec. Health 1990-94; fellowship in liver transplantation Pitts. U., 1986-87. Mem. editl. adv. bd. New Directions, 1974-91, Contemporary Dialysis and Nephrology Jour., 1993-95; contbr. articles to med. jours. Testifier for Ho. of Reps. Com. on Appropriation, U.S. Congress, 1992; councillor Soc. Organ Sharing, 1993, sec., 1995; chmn. tissue com. D.C. chpt. ARC, 1993-95. Recipient Hoffman LaRoche award, 1961, Charles Nelson Gold medal, 1963, Hudson Meadows award, 1963, Charles R. Drew Rsch. award, 1969, Daniel Hale Williams award, 1969, William Alonzo Warfield award, 1977, Howard U. Faculty Outstanding Unit award, 1982, 1st Humanitarian award Cmty. of Caring Ctr., 1990, Disting. Svc. award Surg. Sect. Nat. Med. Assn., 1990, Howard U. Health Affairs Disting. Svc. award, 1984, Outstanding Svc. award Dialysis and Transplant Support, Inc., 1993, Howard U. Legacy of Leadership in Health award, 1995, 11th ann. Minds in Motion award Sci. Skills Ctr., 1993, Edler Garnet Hawkins Humanitarian award Bronx Urban League, 1993, Pearl Watson Meml. award Caribbean Am. Internat. Orgn., 1995; appreciation plaque for 1st renal transplant in V.I., Gov. St. Thomas, 1983, plaque for outstanding contbns. V.I. Legislature, 1984; named to Hunter Coll. Hall of Fame, 1989, Practitioner of Yr., Nat. Med. Assn., 1989, 1 of 10 Outstanding African Am. Male, WHMM-TV, Washington, 1994, 1 of 133 Gifts to the World Alumni Achievers, CUNY, 1995, Pearl Watson Meml. award for excellence in health care delivery Carribbean Am. Intercultural Orgn., Inc., 1995, Pioneer in Edn. award Inst. for Ind. Edn., 1995. Fellow ACS, Am. Cancer Soc.; mem. D.C. Med. Soc. (past vice chmn., chmn. surg. sect. 1994—, bd. trustees 1995), Soc. Acad. Surgeons Transplantation Soc., Am. Soc. Transplantation Surgeons (chmn. membership com. 1986, organ placement com. 1991), N.Y. Acad. Medicine, Nat. Kidney Found. (nat. bd. dirs. 1991-94, nat. capital area 1977-90), Am. Surg. Assn., Am. Coun. on Transplantation (bd. dirs.), Alpha Omega Alpha, Alpha Phi Omega, Alpha Phi Alpha. Home: 509 Kimblewick Dr Silver Spring MD 20904-6341 Office: 2041 Georgia Ave NW Washington DC 20060-0001

CALLIGARO, KEITH D., surgeon; b. Passaic, N.J., June 16, 1956; s. Mario V. and Ida (Battistus) C.; m. Ina Lee Stile, June 10, 1984. BS, Rutgers Coll., 1978; MD, U. Medicine and Dentistry N.J., 1982. Diplomate Am. Bd. Surgery. Vascular surgeon Pa. Hosp., Phila., 1989—, chief, sect. vascular surgery, 1994—; dir. vascular surgery fellowship, Pa. Hops., 1993—. Editor three books; co-author 50 articles. Office: 700 Spruce St Ste 101 Philadelphia PA 19106

CALLIGAS, GARY LAZAROS, home health care manager; b. Shreveport, La., Mar. 8, 1950; s. Lazaros G. and Pyra (Asimakis) C.; m. Tina Michelle Miaoulis, Apr. 28, 1974; children: Louis, Jason, Alexandra. BS, La. Tech. U., 1972. Communications engr. Tex. Ea. Gas Pipeline, Shreveport, La., 1973-77; exec. dir. N. La. Med. Rev., Shreveport, 1977-84; v.p. La. Med. Rev. Found., Shreveport, 1984-86; pres. Health Care Rev. Cons., Shreveport, 1986-93; br. dir. Olsten Kimberly QualityCare, 1993—. V.p. Byrd H.S. Football Booster Club; mem. Shreveport Regional Arts Coun.; bd. dirs., treas., choir dir. St. George Greek Orthodox Ch. of Shreveport; sect. chair So. Trace Homeowners Assn.; mem. March of Dimes Found. Named Outstanding Exec. Dir., Am. Peer Rev. Orgn., 1982, Outstanding Boss of Yr., Am. Bus. Women, Shreveport, 1985. Mem. APHA, Am. Med. Peer Rev. Assn., Am. Consulting League, Home Care Assn. of La., Nat. Assn. for Home Care, N.W. La. Soc. for Human Resource Mgmt., Sales and Mktg. Execs. of Shreveport-Bossier, Am. Hellenic Bus. Network, Health Care Inf. Mgrs. Assn., La. Hosp. Assn., Fedn. Ind. Bus., Shreveport C. of C., La. Tech. Alumni Assn., Shreveport Jaycees, Order of Ahepa, Southern Trace Country Club, Krewe of Gemini, Sigma Pi. Greek Orthodox. Home: 11220 Magnolia Gln Shreveport LA 71106-8374

CALLISON, NANCY FOWLER, nurse administrator; b. Milw., July 16, 1931; d. George Fenwick and Irma Esther (Wenzel) Fowler; m. B.G. Callison, Sept. 25, 1954 (dec. Feb. 1964); children: Robert, Leslie, Linda. Diploma, Evanston Hosp. Sch. Nursing, 1952; BS, Northwestern U., 1954. RN, Calif.; cert. case mgr. Staff nurse, psychiat. dept. Downey VA Hosp., 1954-55; staff nurse Camp Lejeune Naval Hosp., 1955, 59-61; obstet. supr. Tri-City Hosp., Oceanside, Calif., 1961-62; pub. health nurse San Diego County, 1962-66; sch. nurse Rich-Mar Union Sch. Dist., San Marcos, Calif., 1966-68; head nurse San Diego County Community Mental Health, 1968-73; dir. patient care services Southwood Mental Health Ctr., Chula Vista, Calif., 1973-75; program cons. Comprehensive Care Corp., Newport Beach, Calif., 1975-79; dir. Manpower Health Care, Culver City, Calif., 1979-80; dir. nursing services Peninsula Rehab. Ctr., Lomita, Calif., 1980-81; clinic supr., coordinator utilization and authorizations, acting dir. provider relations Hawthorne (Calif.) Community Med. Group, 1981-86; mgr. Health Care Delivery Physicians of Greater Long Beach, Calif., 1986-87; cons. Quality Rev. Assocs., West L.A., 1988-93; case mgr. Mercy Physicians Med. Group, 1992-93; rehab. nurse coord. network The Zenith Ins., 1993—; clin. coord., translator Flying Samaritans, 1965—, mem. internat. bd. dirs., 1975-77, 79-86, 89—, dir. San Quentin project, 1991-93, pres. South Bay chpt., 1975-81, v.p., 1982-85, bd. dirs. San Diego chpt., 1987-90, pres. San Diego chpt. 1991-92, adminstr. Clinica Esperanza de Infantil Rosarito Beach 1990-95. Mem. Rehab. Nurse Coord. Network, U.S.-Mex. Border Health Assn., Cruz Roja Mexicana (Delegacion Rosarito 1986-92).

CALLOWAY, DORIS HOWES, nutrition educator; b. Canton, Ohio, Feb. 14, 1923; d. Earl John and Lillian Ann (Roberts) Howes; m. Nathaniel O. Calloway, Feb. 14, 1946 (div. 1956); children: David Karl, Candace; m. Robert O. Nesheim, July 4, 1981. BS, Ohio State U., 1943; PhD, U. Chgo., 1947; DSc (Hon.), Tufts U., 1992. Head metabolism lab., nutritionist, chief div. QM Food and Container Inst., Chgo., 1951-61; chmn. dept. food sci. and nutrition Stanford Rsch. Inst., Menlo Park, Calif., 1961-63; prof. U. Calif., Berkeley, 1963-91, provost profl. schs. and colls., 1981-87; mem. expert adv. panel on nutrition WHO, Geneva, 1972-92, tech. adv. com. Consultative Group on Internat. Agrl. Rsch., 1989-93, Internat. Commn. on Health Rsch. for Devel., 1987-90, adv. coun. Nat. Inst. Arthritis, Metabolic and Digestive Diseases, Nat. Inst. Aging, NIH, Bethesda, Md., 1974-77, 78-82; trustee Internat. Maize and Wheat Improvement Ctr., 1983-88; trustee, bd. dirs. Winrock Internat. Inst.; cons. FAO, UN, Rome, 1971, 74-75, 81-83; lectr. Cooper Meml., 1983, Roberts Meml., 1985. Author: Nutrition and Health, 1981, Nutrition and Physical Fitness 11th edit., 1984; mem. editorial bd. Am. Dietetic Assn. Jour., 1974-77, Environmental Biology and Medicine, 1969-79. Recipient Meritorious Civilian Svc. Dept. Army, 1959, Disting. Achievement in Nutrition Rsch. award Bristol-Myers Squibb, 1994; named Disting. Alumna Ohio State U., 1974, Wellcome vis. prof. Fedn. Am. Soc. Exptl. Biol., U. Mo., 1980. Fellow Internat. Union of Nutritional Scis., Am. Inst. Nutrition (pres. 1982-83, sec. 1969-72, editorial bd. 1967-72, Conrad A. Elvehjem award 1986); mem. Inst. Medicine NAS, Sigma Xi. Office: U Calif Morgan Hall Berkeley CA 94720

CALSBEEK, FRANKLIN, health promotion educator; b. Rock Valley, Iowa, Dec. 20, 1931; s. August and Rena (Bakker) C.; m. Ula Kay Oosterbaan, June 8, 1963; children: Leslie Joan, Leah Rae, Laurel Beth. AA, Northwestern Coll., Orange City, Iowa, 1952; BS, Augustana Coll., 1956; MS, U. Ill., 1961; EdD, U. Oreg., 1969. Cert. health edn. specialist. Tchr., coach Illiana Christian High Sch., Lansing, Ill., 1956-62; prof. health sci. Dordt Coll., Sioux Center, Iowa, 1962-74; asst. dean Sch. Edn., S.W. Tex. State U., San Marcos, 1981-85; prof. health edn. Sch. Edn., S.W. Tex. State U., 1978—; assoc. dir. AIDS consortium Tex. Coll. and Univ.; cons. Tex. Edn. Agy. and Nat. Evaluation System, Inc., Amherst, Mass., 1985, 86, 89; researcher in field. Contbr. articles to profl. jours. Coun. mem. 1st Christian Reformed Ch., Sioux Ctr. With U.S. Army, 1953-55. Fellow Am. Sch. Health Assn., Tex. Pub. Health Assn., Tex. Sch. Health Assn. (bd. dirs. 1985-89); mem. Assn. for Advancement Health Edn., Tex. Assn. for Health, Phys. Edn., Recreation and Dance (v.p. 1974-78, pres. 1991-92).

CALTON, SANDRA JEANE, accountant; b. Portales, N.Mex., Feb. 3, 1945; d. Lloyd Paul and Nana Mae (Parris) Grant; m. Gary Jim Calton, Nov. 26, 1964; children: Deborah, April, Craig. BS, Ea. N.Mex. U., 1967, U. Md., 1984. CPA, Md. Comptr. Purification Engring. Inc., Columbia, Md., 1981-85, IBF Biotechnics Inc., Savage, Md., 1987-88; pres. Srchem, Inc., Elkridge, Md., 1988—; acct. Calton Rsch. Assocs., Elkridge, 1974—. Treas. Howard Coun. Extension Homemakers Coun., Ellicott City, Md., 1984. Mem. AICPA, Nat. Soc. Tax Profls., Md. Assn. CPAs. Home: 5331 Landing Rd Baltimore MD 21227-5717

CALTRIDER, PAUL GENE, pharmaceutical company executive, microbiologist; b. Mineral Wells, W.Va., Jan. 14, 1935; s. Caroll Lesta and Ora V. (Cooper) C.; m. Virginia D. Deem, Oct. 20, 1956; children: Jeffrey D., Steven P., Beth A. BS in Biology, Glenville State Coll., 1956; MS in Plant Pathology, W.Va. U., 1958; PhD in Plant Pathology, U. Ill., 1962. Sr. microbiologist Eli Lilly & Co., Indpls., 1962-66, mgr. tech. svcs., 1966-70; mgr. tech. svcs. Eli Lilly & Co., Clinton, Ind., 1970-76; mgr. fermentation devel. Eli Lilly & Co., Indpls., 1976-80, dir. biochem. devel. and tech. svc., 1980-94; cons. in fermentation tech. Zionsville, Ind., 1995—. Author: (with others) Antibiotics Vol. I, 1967; contbr. articles to scholarly and profl. jours. Mem. Zool. Soc., Indpls. Mem. Am. Soc. Microbiology, Am. Chem. Soc., Soc. Indsl. Microbiology, Optimists (pres. Zionsville, Ind. chpt. 1991), Sigma Xi. Republican.

CALVERLEY, JOHN ROBERT, physician, educator; b. Hot Springs, Ark., Jan. 14, 1932; s. John A. and Della (O'Neill) C.; m. Alice Mae Feller, Dec. 27, 1953; children: Mark (dec.), David. B.S., U. Oreg., 1953, M.D., 1955. Diplomate: neurology Am. Bd. Psychiatry and Neurology (dir. 1977-84, sec. 1981-83, v.p. 1983-84). Intern U. Iowa, Iowa City, 1955-56; resident in neurology U. Iowa, 1956; resident in internal medicine Mayo Found., Rochester, Minn., 1957; neurology resident Mayo Found., 1957-59; mem. faculty dept. neurology med. br. U. Tex., Galveston, 1964—; assoc. prof. med. br. U. Tex., 1966-70, prof. med. br., 1970—, chief div. neurology med. br., 1967-73, chmn. dept. neurology med. br., 1973—; interim chmn. dept. psychiatry U. Tex., Galveston, 1989-90; cons. neurology USAF, 1965-94, nat. cons. to surgeon gen., 1976-94. Capt. M.C. USAF, 1957-64. Served to capt. M.C. USAF, 1957-64. Mem. AMA (chmn. sect. coun. on neurology 1974-76), Tex. Med. Assn., Am. Acad. Neurology (exec. bd. 1983-86), Am. Neurol. Assn., Assn. Univ. Profs. of Neurology (pres. 1993-94). Home: 733 N Shore Dr Clear Lake Shores TX 77565-2387 Office: U Tex Dept Neurology Galveston TX 77550

CALVERT, BARBARA JEAN, healthcare company executive; b. Washington, Feb. 6, 1954; d. Charles M. and Jean D. (Bowman) C. BA in French summa cum laude, U. Md., 1976; cert. in Polish studies, Jagiellonian U., Cracow, Poland, 1978; MA in Internat. Rels., Johns Hopkins U., 1979. Economist Dept. Labor, Washington, 1976-77; intern Commn. of European Cmtys., Brussels, 1977-78; fgn. sales rep. Industrializzione Brevetti e Marchi, Bologna, Italy, 1978-79; internat. economist Dept. Treasury, Washington, 1979-81; sr. analyst pub. affairs Royal Dutch/Shell Corp., N.Y.C., 1981-84, mgr. internat. pub. affairs, 1984-86; pres. USA Copeland, Wickersham, Wiley Cons., Inc., N.Y.C., 1987; dir. internat. industry rels. Syntex Corp., Washington, 1988-92; pres. Calvert & Assocs., 1992-95; v.p. govt. rels. Integrated Health Svcs., Inc., Washington, 1995-96. Republican.

CALVERT, JON CHANNING, family practice physician; b. Sonora, Calif., May 17, 1941; s. Floyd Raymond and Aloha Jean (Fernandes) C.; m. Lynnette Laurene Jacobson, June 6, 1970; children: Joshua and Stephen (twins). A.B., Stanford U., 1963; M.S., Baylor U., 1968, M.D., 1968, Ph.D.; postdoctoral fellow in anatomy, 1970. Diplomate: Am. Bd. Family Practice. Intern Meth. Hosp., Houston, 1970-71; pvt. practice medicine Houston, 1971-73; asst. prof. anatomy and cell biology Baylor U., 1970-73; asst. prof. family practice Med. Coll. Ga., Augusta, 1973-75, assoc. prof., 1975-77, prof., 1977-82, chmn. dept., 1976-81; prof. family medicine Oral Roberts U. Sch. Medicine, Tulsa, 1982-88, chmn. dept., 1982-87, prof. dept. anatomy, 1982-88, assoc. dean clin. scis., 1984-87; chief dept. community and family medicine City of Faith Med. and Research Ctr., Tulsa, 1982-87; prof., chmn. dept. Family Medicine U. Okla., Coll. Medicine, Tulsa, 1988-92; prof. family medicine, ob-gyn. U. Okla. Coll. Medicine, Tulsa, 1995—; ob/gyn. residency U. Okla. Coll. Med., 1992-95; mem. Gov.'s Joint Bd. Family Practice, 1976-81; chmn. Ga. Fedn. Family Practice Residency Programs, 1976-77; mem. Ga. Dept. Human Resources Adv. Council on Phys. Health Needs of Children and Youth, 1977-78; med. dir. Tri-County Health System, Inc., 1981-82, H.M.O. of Okla., 1985-86; mem. family medicine del. to China, 1983. Bd. deacons Covenant Presbyn. Ch., 1979-81; chmn. bd. govs., chief operating officer City of Faith Med. and Research Ctr., Inc., 1987-88. Fellow Am. Acad. Family Physicians, Am. Coll. Ob-gyn. (jr.); mem. AMA, AAAS, Am. Assn. Med. Colls., So. Soc. Anatomists, So. Med. Assn. (chmn. family practice sect. 1977-78), Ga. Acad. Family Physicians (Disting. Svc. award 1975), Soc. Tchrs. Family Medicine, Sci. Rsch. Soc. N.Am., Christian Med. Soc., Tulsa County Med. Soc. Office: U Oklahoma Coll of Medicine Tulsa OK 74129

CALVERT, LINDA DARNELL, women's health nurse, educator; b. Huntsville, Tex., Nov. 5, 1960; d. Gary Mac and Jimmie Jo (Park) C. BSN, Harding U., Searcy, Ark., 1983; MS in Nursing, West Tex. State U., 1988. RN, Tex.; cert. in perinatal nursing, clin. nurse specialist in family nursing. Charge nurse, labor and delivery Huntsville (Tex.) Meml. Hosp., 1983-84; staff nurse, relief charge nurse in labor and delivery Scott and White Meml. Hosp., Temple, Tex., 1984-86; staff nurse, relief charge nurse Meth. Hosp. of Lubbock, Tex., 1986-88; jr. med.-surg. instr. Meth. Hosp. Sch. Nursing, Lubbock, 1988-91; instr. Abilene (Tex.) Intercollegiate Sch. Nursing, 1991-93, asst. prof., 1993—. Mem. health profl. adv. com. March of Dimes, Abilene; USPHS trainee, 1987-88. Named Outstanding Alumnae Harding U. Sch. Nursing, 1995, One of Outstanding Young Women of Am., 1987.

Mem. Assn. Women's Health Obstetrical Neonatal Nursing, Nat. League for Nursing, Tex. Perinatal Assn., Health Educators Resource Network Abilene, Sigma Theta Tau, Alpha Chi. Home: 3218 Winter Hawk Abilene TX 79606

CALVERT, LOIS PRINCE, geriatrics nurse; b. Lawrenceburg, Tenn., June 27, 1948; d. Virgil Miller and Beulah Mae (Fox) Prince; m. Albert Sidney Johnson, Sept. 26, 1970 (div. 1985); children: Kelley Nicole, Kristopher Scott; m. Malon Sherman Calvert, Oct. 19, 1990. Student, Bapt. Hosp. Sch. Nursing, 1966-67, Belmont Coll., 1966-67; ADN cum laude, Columbia State C.C., 1970; cert. in nursing home adminstrn., George Washington U., 1985. RN, Ala., Tenn. Psychiat. nurse, staff RN Bapt. Meml. Hosp., Memphis, 1970-71; staff RN, psychiat. staff nurse VA Hosp., Memphis, 1971-73; DON svc. Lawrenceburg (Tenn.) Health Care Ctr., 1975-80, nursing home adminstr., 1980-85; case mgr., aide supr., staff RN Lawrenceburg (Tenn.) Home Health Agy., 1985-86; staff RN, case mgr. home health patients, coord. home health Mid-South Home Health Agy., Florence, Ala., 1986-87; DON svcs. Lawrenceburg (Tenn.) Manor, Inc., 1987—; paramed. examiner ASB-Meditest, Nashville, 1989—; mem. NCLEX panel, item reviewer LPN State Bds., 1993. Sustaining membership chmn. Lawrence County coun. Girl Scouts U.S., 1977-78; pianist, dir. youth choir East Edn. Meth. Ch., 1985-94; vol. ARC, bd. dirs. Lawrence County chpt., 1995, also disaster health chmn. Fellow Am. Coll. Health Care Adminstrs. (profl. cert.); mem. Tenn. Employee Rels. Com., Nat. Assn. Dirs. Of Nursing Adminstrs. (founding mem. Tenn. chpt., corr. sec. 1995), Beta Sigma Phi (Girl of Yr. 1973, 76). Baptist. Home: 1613 Ann Rd Lawrenceburg TN 38464-3003 Office: Lawrenceburg Manor 3051 Buffalo Rd Lawrenceburg TN 38464-6189

CALVERT, WILLIAM PRESTON, radiologist; b. Warrensburg, Mo., July 2, 1934; s. William Geery and Elizabeth (Spaulding) C.; m. Mary Kay Kersh, Apr. 4, 1976. BS, MIT, 1956; MD, U. Pa., 1960. Diplomate Am. Bd. Nuclear Medicine, Am. Bd. Radiology. Intern Pa. Hosp., Phila., 1960-61, resident in medicine, 1961-62, 64-66, chief med. resident, chief resident physician, 1965-66; resident in gastroenterology U. Miami, 1966-67, NIH fellow in gastroenterology, 1967-68, resident in radiology, 1968-71; radiologist Meml. Hosp., Hollywood, Fla., 1971-72; chief dept. radiology Larkin Gen. Hosp., South Miami, Fla., 1972-80, radiologist, 1980-89; radiologist Jackson Meml. Hosp., U. Miami, 1989-93, Univ. Hosp., Tammarac, Fla., 1993-95; part-time radiologist Northern Navajo Med. Ctr., Shiprock, N.Mex., 1995—; clin. instr. radiology U. Miami Sch. Medicine, 1971-76, clin. asst. prof. radiology, 1984-88, clin. assoc. prof. radiology, 1988-94. Bd. dirs. Wediko Farms Children's Svcs., Carbondale, Ill. Served with M.C., USAF, 1962-64. Mem. AMA, Fla. Med. Assn., Fla., Greater Miami radiol. socs., Soc. Nuclear Medicine, Radiol. Soc. N.Am., Explorers Club. Home: PO Box 500157 #500 Marathon FL 33050

CALVIN, ALLEN DAVID, psychologist, educator; b. St. Paul, Feb. 17, 1928; s. Carl and Zelda (Engelson) C.; m. Dorothy VerStrate, Oct. 5, 1953; children—Jamie, Kris, David, Scott. B.A. in Psychology cum laude, U. Minn., 1950; M.A. in Psychology, U. Tex., 1951, Ph.D. in Exptl. Psychology, 1953. Instr. Mich. State U., East Lansing, 1953-55; asst. prof. Hollins Coll., 1955-59, assoc. prof., 1959-61; dir. Britannica Center for Studies in Learning and Motivation, Menlo Park, Calif., 1961; prin. investigator grant for automated teaching fgn. langs. Carnegie Found., 1960; USPHS grantee, 1960; pres. Behavioral Research Labs., 1962-74; prof., dean Sch. Edn., U. San Francisco, 1974-78; Henry Clay Hall prof. Orgn. and leadership, 1978—; pres. Pacific Grad. Sch. Psychology, 1984—. Author textbooks. Served with USNR, 1946-47. Mem. Am. Psychol. Assn., AAAS, Sigma Xi, Psi Chi. Home: 1645 15th Ave San Francisco CA 94122-3523 Office: U San Francisco Psychology Dept San Francisco CA 94117

CAMAYD-FREIXAS, YOEL, management, strategy & planning consultant; b. Holguin, Oriente, Cuba, Nov. 27, 1948; came to U.S., 1962; s. Alberto and Olga (Freixas) Camayd; m. Ana Maria Perez, Jan. 2, 1982; 1 child, Cristina de la Prat Camayd. BA summa cum laude, U. Mundial, San Juan, P.R., 1970; MEd, Northeastern U., 1972; MA, Boston Coll., 1978, PhD, 1982. Planner Multi-Svc. Ctr., New Bedford, Mass., 1971-74; psychologist Jamaica Plain Outreach Program, Boston, 1975-78, program dir., 1978-80, exec. dir., 1980-81; asst. prof. grad. sch. urban studies and planning MIT, Cambridge, 1982-86; sr. officer Office R & D Boston Pub. Schs., 1985-87; pres. Boston R & D, 1987-90; bd. chmn. Pavers & Tiles of Fla., Inc., Miami, 1987-91; exec. v.p. Health & Hosps. Corp., N.Y.C., 1990-91; bd. chmn., mng. dir. Nurse Referrals, Inc., N.Y.C., 1990-91; mng. ptnr. Camayd Cons., Miami, Fla., 1992—. Author: The Costs of Opportunity, 1983 (award Psi Chi 1983), Hispanics in Massachusetts, 1987, Effective Dropout Prevention, 1987, Crisis in Miami, 1988, Latino Health in New York City, 1992, Affordability Controls in Affordable Housing and Disaster Relief, 1995. Mem., co-chmn. Mass. Legislature Commn. on Hispanic Affairs, Boston, 1984-88; co-chmn. add-ons com. Mass. Dem. Com., Boston, 1985-90; bd. dirs. United Way Massachusetts Bay, Boston, 1986-90; pres. Mass. Coalition for Electoral Reform, Boston, 1987-90. Recipient nat. community svc. award Coalition Hispanic Human Svc. Orgns., 1980, gubernatorial citation State of Mass., 1988, 90, commendation Boston City Coun., 1990, legis. citation Mass. Ho. of Reps., 1990.

CAMBIAS, RONALD DUTRIEL, JR., psychologist; b. New Orleans, Feb. 14, 1963; s. Ronald Dutriel Sr. and Mary Ann (Boihem) C.; m. Bridget Karen McCarthy, Jan. 2, 1993. BA, Loyola U., 1985; MS, Nova Southeastern U., 1988, D of Psychology, 1991. Lic. clin. psychologist, La. Intern Children's Psychiat. Ctr., Miami, Fla., 1989-90; postdoctoral fellow Children's Hosp., New Orleans, 1990-91, staff psychologist, 1991-95; clin. psychologist Mercy Family Ctr., New Orleans, 1995—. Contbr. chpts. in books Test Critiques, 1992, 94, Innovations in Clinical Practice, 1994. Mem. APA (clin. divisn., family psychology divsn.), Assn. Play Therapy, Pediatric Oncology Group, La. Psychol. Assn. Roman Catholic. Office: Mercy Family Ctr Psychology Dept 3816 Bienville St New Orleans LA 70119

CAMENGA, DAVID LEROY, neurologist, educator; b. New Berlin, N.Y., Aug. 26, 1938; s. Kenneth Arnold and Evalyn Rosanna (Skaggs) C.; m. Mary Ruth Tilton, June 14, 1959 (div. Mar. 1986); children: Craig Steven, David Lloyd, James Kenneth; m. Joanna Lubicz Woyciechowska, Dec. 31, 1986 (div. Mar. 1993). BS in Quantitative Biology, MIT, 1960; MS in Neurophysiology, U. Wis., 1964, MD, 1965. Diplomate Am. Bd. Psychiatry and Neurology. Intern in internal medicine New England Ctr. Hosp., Boston, 1965-66; resident in neurology Barnes Hosp., Washington U., St. Louis, 1966-69; NINCDS fellow Johns Hopkins U. Sch. Hygiene and Pub. Health, Balt., 1971-73; asst. prof. neurology Emory U. Sch. Medicine, Atlanta, 1973-77; asst. prof. then assoc. prof. neurology U. Md. Sch. Medicine, Balt., 1977-87; neurologist The Duluth (Minn.) Clinic, Ltd., 1987—, chief sect. neurology, 1994—; clin. assoc. prof. U. Minn. Sch. Medicine, Duluth, 1988—; exch. scientist Fogarty Internat. Ctr., Polish Ministry of Health, Warsaw, 1986; assoc. med. dir. Duluth Comprehensive Multiple Sclerosis Ctr., 1988-93, med. dir., 1996; lectr. in field. Author: (with others) Neurologic Emergencies, 2d edit., 1990; contbr. articles to profl. jours. Surgeon USPHS, 1969-71. Recipient Borden Undergrad. Rsrch. award Borden Corp., 1965. Fellow Am. Acad. Neurology; mem. AMA, Minn. Med. Soc. Office: Duluth Clinic Ltd 400 E 3rd St Duluth MN 55805-1951

CAMER, STEPHEN JOSEPH, general surgeon; b. Boston, Sept. 16, 1938. BS in Biology, Boston Coll., 1961; MD, Tufts U., 1965. Diplomate Am. Bd. Surgery; lic. physician, Mass., N.Y., N.J. Intern St. Vincent's Hosp. and Med. Ctr. of N.Y., N.Y.C., 1965-66, resident, 1968-72; fellow in surgery Lahey Clinic Found., Boston, 1973-74; clinical fellow Am. Cancer Soc., N.Y.C. and Boston, 1971-72, 73-74; pvt. practice surgery Boston, 1974—; chief gen. surgery New Eng. Bapt. Hosp., Boston; attending surgeon Faulkner Hosp., Boston, New Eng. Deaconess Hosp., Boston, St. Elizabeth's Hosp., Brighton, Mass.; cons. surgeon Lemuel Shattuck Hosp., Boston; instr. surgery Harvard Med. Sch., Boston, 1978—; assoc. prof. clin. surgery Tufts U. Sch. Medicine, Boston, 1974—; clin. instr. surgery NYU Sch. Medicine, N.Y.C., 1971-72. Mem. ACS, Am. Assn. Clin. Anatomists, Internat. Soc. Hepatic Pancreatic and Biliary Surgery, New Eng. Cancer Soc., Mass. Med. Soc., Boston Surg. Soc., Boston Gastroen. Soc. Office: New Eng Bapt Hosp 125 Parker Hill Ave Boston MA 02120

CAMERANO, FRANKLIN, medical center administrator; b. Bklyn., Jan. 7, 1936; s. Anthony and Florence (Tucci) C.; m. Julia Marie Roche; children: Nicole, Douglas. BBA, St. John's U., N.Y.C., 1957; MA, U. Ill., 1965; MSHA, Columbia U., 1965. Assoc. adminstr. Mt. Auburn Hosp., Cambridge, Mass., 1965-68, St. Vincent's Hosp., N.Y.C., 1968-75; exec. dir. John E. Runnells Hosp., Berkeley Heights, N.J., 1975-80; sr. assoc. exec. dir. Booth Meml. Med. Ctr., Flushing, N.Y., 1980-94; 1st dep. commr., COO, Westchester County Med. Ctr., Valhalla, N.Y., 1994; COO The Mt. Vernon (N.Y.) Hosp., 1994—; adj. assoc. prof. St. John's U., 1984—; cons. in field; lectr. in field. Contbr. articles to profl. jours. With USAR, 1959-65. Recipient Meritorious 1st Ann. awd., Met. Health Care Assn.,1 989. Fellow Am. Coll. Healthcare Execs., Royal Soc. Health; mem. Internat. Hosp. Fedn., Met. Health Care Assn., Am. Scandinavian Found. (treas. 1960-61). Roman Catholic. Office: The Mt Vernon Hosp 12 N 7th Ave Mount Vernon NY 10550-2026

CAMERON, CHARLES METZ, JR., physician, medical educator; b. Morristown, Tenn., Dec. 20, 1923; s. Charles Metz and Mildred (Brown) C.; m. Vera L. Cheek, Nov. 25, 1948; children: Charles Metz III, Cheryl Lynn, David Alan. Student, U. Tenn., 1942, N.C. State Coll., 1943, U. Ky., 1944, U. Miss., 1945; MD, Vanderbilt U., 1948; MPH, U. N.C., 1955. Rotating intern U.S. Marine Hosp. System, 1949; dist. health officer Tenn. Dept. Pub. Health, 1949-52; physician USPHS, 1951-53; chief communicable disease control sect., accident prevention sect. N.C. Rd. Health, 1953-55; asso. prof., prof. U. N.C. Sch. Pub. Health, 1955-68, acting chmn. dept., 1960-61; dir. N.C. Office Comprehensive Health Planning, 1967-68; prof. dept. health adminstrn. U. Okla. Health Scis. Center, Oklahoma City, 1968-80; chmn. dept. U. Okla. Health Scis. Center, 1984-89, dean Coll. Pub. Health, 1984-89, dean emeritus, 1989—, adj. prof., 1980-82; dep. commr. Okla. State Dept. Health, 1980-82, chief preventive medicine, 1982-83; also dir. Mid-Continent Comprehensive Health Planning Ednl. Center and Health Resources Information Center. Contbr. papers to profl. lit. Served with AUS, 1943-45; med. dir. USPHS Res. Mem. Delta Omega (nat. pres. 1962). Home: 3132 Goshen St Oklahoma City OK 73120-2208

CAMERON, DUKE EDWARD, cardiac surgeon, educator; b. Miami, Fla., Mar. 9, 1952; s. Edward John and Joanne (Abbott) C.; m. Claudia Oppenheim; children: Danielle, Nicole. AB, Harvard Coll., 1974; MD, Yale U., 1978. Resident gen. surgery Yale-New Haven Hosp., 1978-84, resident cardiothoracic surgery, 1984-87; assoc. prof. surgery, dir. pediatric cardiac surgery Johns Hopkins Hosp., Balt. Fellow ACS; mem. Soc. Thoracic Surgeons, So. Thoracic Surg. Assn., Am. Assn. Thorac Surg. Home: 2209 South Rd Baltimore MD 21209-4437 Office: Johns Hopkins Hosp Blalock 618 600 N Wolfe St Baltimore MD 21287

CAMERON, JAMES ADAIR, physician; b. Erskine, Minn., Feb. 22, 1946; s. John Hugh and Annette Louise (Larson) C.; m. Sarah Bondurant, Sept. 13, 1975. BA, St. Olaf Coll., 1968; MD, McGill U., 1972. Diplomate Am. Bd. Internal Medicine, Am. Bd. Ophthalmology. Intern in internal medicine Emory U., Atlanta, 1972-75, resident in internal medicine, 1972-75; resident in ophthalmology U. Pa., Phila., Minn., 1975-78; pvt. practice Coon Rapids. Fellow Am. Acad. Ophthalmology. Home: 6 N Mallard Rd North Oaks MN 55127 Office: Anoka Eye Clinic 3960 Coon Rapids Blvd Coon Rapids MN 55433

CAMERON, JOHN LEMUEL, general surgeon; b. Howell, Mich., Sept. 29, 1936; m. Doris Mae Hood; children: Duncan, Heather, Shannon, Andrew. B.A., Harvard U., 1958; M.D., Johns Hopkins U., 1962. Asst. prof. surgery Johns Hopkins U., Balt., 1971-74; assoc. prof. Johns Hopkins U., 1974-78, prof. surgery, 1978—, chmn. dept. surgery, 1984—; chief surgery Johns Hopkins Hosp., 1984—. Editor: Current Surg. Therapy, 1984. Mem. Assn. Acad. Surgery, Soc. for Surgery of Alimentary Tract, Soc. Univ. Surgeons, Balt. Acad. Surgeons, Halsted Soc., So. Surg. Assn., Am. Surg. Assn., Pancreas Club, Surg. Biology Club II, Soc. Clin. Surgery. Home: 913 Rolandvue Ave Baltimore MD 21204-6814 Office: Johns Hopkins Sch of Medicine 720 Rutland Ave Baltimore MD 21205-2109

CAMERON, OLIVER GENE, psychiatrist, educator, psychobiology researcher; b. Evanston, Ill., Aug. 28, 1946; s. Gene Oliver and Elizabeth Marie (Burns) C.; m. Susan Linda Friedman, June 22, 1972; children—Leah Victoria, Peter Sean. B.A., U. Notre Dame, 1968; Ph.D., U. Chgo., 1972, M.D., 1974. Diplomate Am. Bd. psychiatry and Neurology. Med. intern U. Mich., Ann Arbor, 1974-75, psychiatry resident, 1975-78, psychiatry fellow, 1978-79, asst. prof. psychiatry, 1979-86, assoc. prof., 1986-92, prof., 1992—; dir. anxiety disorders program, dept. psychiatry, 1984-85, dir. adult psychiatry outpatient program, dept. psychiatry, 1985-90, Combined Mood & Anxiety Program, 1994—. Contbr. articles to profl. jours. Mem. Am. Psychiatric Assn., Am. Psychosomatic Soc., AAAS, Sigma Xi. Avocations: photography; travel; golf. Home: 1215 Southwood Ct Ann Arbor MI 48103-9735 Office: U Mich 1500 E Medical Center Dr Ann Arbor MI 48109-0722

CAMERON, ROBERT WILLIAM, ophthalmologist; b. San Francisco, Mar. 19, 1937; s. Dale C. and Irma Christine (Lippold) C.; m. Barbara Bridwell, Nov. 18, 1970; children: David, Susan. BA, Carleton Coll., 1959; MD, U. Minn., 1963. Diplomate Am. Bd. Ophthalmology. Pvt. practice Salt Lake City, 1969-74; fellow in intra ocular lens surgery Beach Cities Eye Med. Group, Long Beach, Calif., 1975; pvt. practice Abilene, Tex., 1976; pres. Abilene Eye Inst., 1977—; med. dir., chief exec. officer Abilene Cataract and Refractive Surgery Ctr., 1987—. Horn player Abilene Philharm. Orch., 1990—. Capt. USAF, 1964-66. Fellow ACS, Am. Acad. Ophthalmology; mem. Am. Soc. Cataract and Refractive Surgery, Internat. Horn Soc. Episcopalian. Office: Eye Med Assocs Abilene Eye Inst 2120 Antilley Rd Abilene TX 79606-5211

CAMESE, WANDA GREEN, nurse; b. New Orleans, Sept. 30, 1954; d. Elton Warren and Ida Mae (Smith) Lorio; m. Alton M. Green, June 4, 1977 (dec.); children: Nicole Uchenna, Ashley; m. Earl August Camese, Oct. 12, 1991. AS, La. State U., 1979, MSN, 1992; BS in Nursing, Dillard U., 1989. RN, La. Staff nurse Charity Hosp., New Orleans, 1979-80; nursing supr. St. Claude Gen. Hosp., New Orleans, 1980-82; unit supr. DePaul Hosp., New Orleans, 1981-82; dir. nursing Quality Care, New Orleans, 1981; head nurse Charity Hosp., New Orleans, 1982-83; unit patient mgr. New Orleans Gen. Hosp., 1984-86; charge nurse St. Charles Gen. Hosp., New Orleans, 1986-89; quality assurance coord. Charity Hosp., New Orleans, 1989-91; instr. Charity Sch. Nursing, New Orleans, 1991-95; adminstr. Family of Families Home Health Svcs. Inc., 1995—; cons. and instr. in field. Pres. Ladies Unltd. Civic, New Orleans, 1981-86; nurse vol. Health Fair, New Orleans, 1983-85; parent vol. PTA; bd. dirs. New Orleans East YMCA. Mem. NAACP, ANA, New Orleans Dist. Nursing Assn., Nat. Black Nurses Assn., Nat. League for Nurses, Nat. C. of C. for Women, Santa Filomena Nursing Assn., New Orleans Assn. Quality Assurance Professions, La. Pub. Health Assn., Gamma Phi Delta (first Anti-Basileum 1989, v.p. 1989, chpt. Basileus 1994). Democrat. Baptist. Home: 4401 Werner Dr New Orleans LA 70126-4545 Office: Delgado Community Coll Charity Sch Nursing 450 S Claiborne Ave New Orleans LA 70112-1310

CAMISHION, RUDOLPH CARMEN, physician; b. Riverside, N.J., July 16, 1927; m. Nancy Muzzarelli, June 28, 1952; children: Germain, Sandra, Lisa, Nancy, Janice. BS, St. Joseph's Coll., 1950; MD, Jefferson Med. Coll. of Phila., 1954. Cert. Am. Bd. Surgery, 1960, Bd. of Thoracic Surgery, 1961, Bd. Gen. Vascular Surgery, 1983. USNR Petty Officer, 1944-46; intern Cooper Hosp., Camden, N.J., 1954-55; resident in surgery Jefferson Med. Coll. Hosp., Phila., 1955-59; trainee Nat. Cancer Inst., 1958-59, 1959-62; asst. in surgery Jefferson Med. Coll., 1959-60, instr. in surgery, 1960-62, asst. prof. surgery, 1963-64; cons. thoracic surgery VA Hosp., Phila., 1963-66; assoc. prof. surgery Jefferson Med. Coll., 1964-67, prof. surgery, 1967-73; prof., head dept. surgery Robert Wood Johnson Med. Sch., Camden, 1973-91, prof. surgery, 1991—. Numerous medical presentations. Recipient Surgical Excellence award, 1991, rev. Clarence E. Shaffrey, S.J., award, 1991. Mem. Acad. Surgical Rsch., Am. Assn. Advancement of Sci., Am. Assn. for Thoracic Surgery, AAUP, Am. Coll. Chest Physicians, ACS, AHA, AMA, Am. Thoracic Soc., Am. Surgical Assn., Pa. Assn. for Thoracic Surgery, Phila. Acad. of Surgery, Camden County Med. Soc., Soc. of Univ. Surgeons, Soc. for Vascular Surgery, Vascular Soc. N.J., Eastern Vascular Soc., Soc. Clin. Vascular Surgery, Southeastern Surgical Cong., N.J. Chpt. Am. Coll. Surgeons, Alpha Omega Alpha. Office: R Wood Johnson Med Sch 3 Cooper Plz Rm 411 Camden NJ 08103-1438

CAMM, GERTRUDE ELIZABETH, physician, writer; b. Enid, Okla., Aug. 21, 1930; d. John Palmer and Gertrude (Hollis) C. AB, Duke U., 1951, postgrad., 1951-53; postgrad., Sarah Lawrence Coll., 1962-63, Columbia U., 1963-64, U. Okla, 1964-66; MD, U. Pa., 1968. Researcher in biochem. and biophys. Duke U. Sch. Medicine, Durham, N.C., 1953-55; intern and resident in internal medicine Royal Victoria Hosp., Montreal, Que., Can., 1968-70; resident in pediatrics U. Ill. Hosp., Chgo., 1970-71, Emory U. Affiliated Hosps., Atlanta, 1971-72; practice medicine specializing in pediatrics and family medicine Cen. Fla., 1973-75, Ala., 1975-76; practice medicine specializing in emergency medicine Chgo., 1976-84, Cen. Fla., Ala., Ga., 1984-89; practice medicine specializing in pub. health Fla., 1987-90; practice in internal & family medicine and pub. health svcs., 1990—; instr. pediatrics U. Ill., Chgo., 1970-71, ACLS, 1982-90, med. dir. clinic, 1994—; lectr. med. topics for cmty. groups, 1984—; dir. hosp. emergency depts., 1976-78, 84-87, cmty. emergency med. sys., 1984-86; chair profl. adv. bd. Epilepsy Assn. Ctr. Fla., 1995—; assoc. trustee Epilepsy Assn. Ctrl. Fla., 1995—; mem. cmty. adv. coun., mem. profl. adv. bd. two home health orgns., 1994—. Author: Atlanta Constitution, 1956-59, In the Deep Blue Sea, 1961; contbr. articles to profl. and popular jours.; sci. and med. writer, 1960-64. Musician amateur cmty. symphony orchs., chamber orchs. and choral groups, 1947—; trustee, mem. disability project Atlantic Ctr. for Arts, 1996—; patron, guild mem. Orlando Philharm., 1995—, Festival de Musica de Camara, San Miguel de Allende, Mex.; sec. Fla. Symphony Orch. affiliate bd. Lake County, 1985-86; mem. environ. groups, Orlando and Ormond Beach, Fla., 1984—; active John F. Lindsey for Mayor campaign, N.Y.C., 1960; vol. physician for Vietnam, AMA, 1972; vol. physician Boggy Creek Gang Camp for chronically ill, 1996—. Chemistry fellow Dept. Army Chem. Warfare Duke U. Grad. Sch., 1951-53, clin. fellow U. Pa. Sch. Medicine, 1967-68, NIH student fellow, 1964-66; preceptorship Columbia-Presbyn. Hosp., 1966. Mem. AAAS, AAUW (pres. Ormond Beach chpt. 1974-75), So. Med. Assn., Ctrl. Fla. Pediatric Soc., Flying Physicians Assn., Aircraft Owners and Pilots Assn., Atlantic Ctr. for Arts (bd. trustees and disability project 1996—), Fox Meadow Tennis Club, Halifax Club, Phi Beta Kappa. Presbyterian.

CAMMARATA, ANGELO, surgical oncologist; b. Italy, 1936; s. Giuseppe and Giuseppina (Ruggiero) C.; m. Diane M. Donner, Apr. 25, 1965; children: Joseph, Marisa, Michael, Christina. BA, Upsala Coll., 1958; MD, N.Y. Med. Coll., 1962. Diplomate Am. Bd. Surgery. Intern N.Y. Polyclin. Hosp., N.Y.C., 1962; resident, chief resident Met. Hosp. N.Y.C., 1963-67, asst. surgeon, 1968—; resident in surgery Meml. Hosp. Cancer and Allied Diseases, N.Y.C., 1967-68; assoc. surgeon, attending surgeon Cabrini Med. Ctr., N.Y.C.; attending surgeon Beth Israel North Hosp., N.Y.C.; instr. surgery N.Y. Med. Coll., N.Y.C., 1968-74, clin. asst. prof. surgery, 1974—; vis. attending surgeon Met. Hosp. Ctr., N.Y.C. Contbr. articles to profl. jours. Fellow ACS, Internat. Coll. Surgeons; mem. AMA, N.Y. Cancer Soc., N.Y. Met. Breast Cancer Group, N.Y. Acad. Scis., Meml. Alumni Soc., Alpha Club. Office: 55 E 87th St New York NY 10128-1043

CAMMERMEYER, MARGARETHE, nurse; b. Oslo, Mar. 24, 1942; came to U.S., 1951; d. Jan and Margrethe (Grimsgaard) C.; m. Harvey H. Hawken, Aug. 1965 (div. 1980); children: Matthew, David, Andrew, Thomas. BS, U. Md., 1963; MA, U. Wash., 1976, PhD, 1991. RN, Wash. Enlisted U.S. Army, 1961, advanced through grades to capt., 1965, resigned, 1968; staff nurse VA Hosp., Seattle, 1970-73, clin. nurse specialist in neurology, epilepsy, 1976-81; clin. nurse specialist in neuro-oncology VA Med. Ctr., San Francisco, 1981-86; clin. nurse specialist in neuroscis., nurse rschr. VA Med. Ctr., Tacoma, Wash., 1986-96; ret., 1996; capt. to col. USAR, 1972-88; asst. chief nurse, supr. Army Res. Hosp., Oakland, Calif., 1985-88; col. Wash. Army N.G. and N.G. Hosp., Tacoma, 1988-96. Coauthor: Neurological Assessment for Nursing Practice, 1984 (named Book of Yr. ANA), Serving in Silence, 1994; co-editor, contbg. author: Core Curriculum for Neuroscience Nursing, 1990, 93; contbr. articles to profl. jours. Decorated Bronze Star medal; recipient presdl. cert. for outstanding community achievement of Vietnam era vets., 1979, "A" Proficiency designation Office of Surgeon Gen. Dept. of Army, 1986, Woman of Power award NOW, 1993; named Woman of Yr. Woman's Army Corps Vets. Assn., 1984, Nurse of Yr. VA, 1985. Mem. Feminist Majority Found., Am. Assn. Neurosci. Nursing (chair core task force), Am. Nurses Assn. (hon. human rights award 1994), U. Wash. Nursing Assn. (Disting. Alumna 1995), Assn. Mil. Surgeons. of U.S., Sigma Theta Tau. Home and Office: 4632 Tompkins Rd Langley WA 98260

CAMMISA, FRANK P., JR., surgeon, educator; b. Waterbury, Conn., Jan. 18, 1956; m. Gail McGovern; children: Anne Katherine, Frank P. III, John Patrick. BS summa cum laude, Tufts U., 1978; MD, Columbia U., 1982. Diplomate Nat. Bd. Med. Examiners, Am. Bd. Orthopaedic Surgery. Resident in gen. surgery The Presbyn. Hosp., Columbia-Presbyn. Med. Ctr., N.Y.C., 1982-83; resident in orthopaedic surgery The Hosp. for Spl. Surgery, N.Y.C., 1983-87; fellow in spinal surgery U. Miami (Fla.)-Jackson Meml. Med. Ctr., 1987-88; asst. scientist rsch. divsn. The Hosp. for Spl. Surgery, N.Y.C., 1988—, asst. attending surgeon, 1988—, chief spine svc., 1995—; vis. clin. fellow surgery Coll. of Physicians and Surgeons, Columbia U., N.Y.C., 1982-83; clin. assoc. surgery Cornell U. Med. Coll., N.Y.C., 1983-87, instr. orthopaedic surgery, 1988-89, asst. prof. orthopaedic surgery, 1990—; attending surgeon VA Hosp., Miami, 1987-88; asst. attending surgeon The N.Y. Hosp., N.Y.C., 1988—; attending surgeon spinal cord injury svc. Burke Rehab. Ctr., White Plains, N.Y., 1988—; attending surgeon VA Hosp., Bronx, N.Y., 1988—; presenter in field; cons. Meml. Sloan Kettering Cancer Ctr., N.Y.C., 1988—; spinal cons. St. John's U. Athletic Teams, 1988—, N.Y. Knights World League of Am. Football, 1991-92, Phoenix Alliance, 1993, N.Y. Racing Assn., 1993. Editorial bd.: Orthopaedic Product News, 1990-91; contbr. chpts. to books and articles to profl. jours. Grantee The Hosp. for Spl. Surgery, 1986, Acromed Corp., 1988, Orthopaedic Rsch. and Edn. Found., 1991-92; recipient Harvard Book prize Harvard Club So. Conn., 1974, Tufts Psychology Soc. Rsch. award Tufts U., 1978, Resident award N.Y. Acad. Medicine, Sect. Orthopaedic Surgery, 1986, 87, Lewis Clark Wagner award Hosp. for Spl. Surgery, N.Y.C., 1986; N.Am. Traveling fellowship Am. Orthopaedic Assn., 1989; Ofcl. citation Gen. Assembly State of Conn., 1992. Mem. ACS, ACP, Am. Acad. Orthopaedic Surgeons, Internat. Coll. Surgeons; mem. AMA, N.Am. Spine Soc., Am. Spinal Injury Assn., Internat. Soc. for Study of Lumbar Spine, Cervical Spine Rsch. Soc., Scoliosis Rsch. Soc., Med. Soc. State N.Y., N.Y. State Soc. Orthop. Surgeons, N.Y. County Med. Soc., Alumni Assn. The Hosp. for Spl. Surgery, Assn. of the Alumni, Coll. Physicians and Surgeons, Columbia U., The Irish-Am. Orthop. Soc., Ea. Orthop. Assn. (Fellow scholar award 1988, Spinal Rsch. award 1989), Groupe Internat. Cotrel-Dubousset, N.Y. Athletic Club, Winged Foot Golf Club, Phi Beta Kappa, Psi Chi, Alpha Omega Alpha, Delta Tau Delta. Office: Hosp for Spl Surgery 535 E 70th St New York NY 10021-4892

CAMMOCK, EARL E., surgeon; b. Sheridan, Wyo., Jan. 18, 1926; s. Earl and Ruth (Elarth) C.; m. Iris Nordman, June 25, 1960; children: Christopher, Caryn, Craig. BA magna cum laude, U. Minn., 1950, BS, 1952, MD, 1953; MS in Surgery, U. Wash., 1962. Diplomate Am. Bd. Surgery. Intern King County Hosp. System, Seattle, 1953-54; resident gen. practice Sacramento (Calif.) County Hosp., 1954-55; resident in surgery U. Wash., 1955-62; chief resident surgery King County Hosp., Seattle, 1959, U. Wash. Hosp. and VA Hosp., 1960; rsch. fellow U. Wash., 1960-62; instr. U. Wash. Dept. Surgery, Seattle, 1960-62, clin. instr., 1962-85, clin. asst. prof., 1985—; practice gen., thoracic and cardiovascular surgery Mt. Vernon, Wash., 1962-93; practice proctology Mt. Vernon, 1993—; chief staff Skagit Valley Hosp., 1972; mem. exec. com. Skagit Valley Hosp., 1970-72, chief dept. surgery, 1969, mem. library and ethics coms., 1988—; med. advisor NW Ostomy Soc.; mem. endowment fund com. U. Wash. Co-author: Medicine for Mountaineering (4 edits.) 1993; contbr. articles to profl. jours. Bd. dirs. Lutherwood, Bellingham, Wash., 1974-76, v.p., 1976; council mem. Salem Luth. Ch., 1971-73, pres. 1973; troopmaster Cub Scout Boy Scouts Am., Mt. Vernon, 1977-78; mem. Physicians for Social Responsibility, 1982-86. With U.S. Army, 1944-47, PTO; USAR, 1947-50. Fellow ACS; mem. AMA, Am. Soc. Colon and Rectal Surgeons, N.W. Soc. Colon and Rectal Surgeons, Soc. Am. Gastrointestinal Endoscopic Surgeons, Am. Soc. Clin. Hypnosis, Wash. State Med. Assn., Henry Harkins Surg. Soc. (pres. 1983-84), Pan Pacific Surg. Assn., N.W. Ostomy Soc., Sigma Xi, Phi Beta Kappa. Lodge: Rotary (Paul Harris fellow), Vasa. Home: 1226 Madison Park Dr Mount Vernon WA 98273-2543 Office: 215 S 13th St Mount Vernon WA 98273-4107

CAMOUGIS, GEORGE, waste recycling company executive; b. Concord, Mass., May 10, 1930; s. Charles George and Angeliki (Georgekopoulou) C.; BS magna cum laude (Olmstead fellow), Tufts U., 1952; MA, Harvard U., 1957, PhD, 1958; m. Irene Andreson, Nov. 18, 1961; children—Caroline A., Elizabeth M., Sarah A. Asst. prof. physiology Clark U., 1958-62, assoc. prof., 1962-64, affiliate prof., 1964-79; sr. neurophysiologist Astra Pharm. Products, Inc., Worcester, Mass., 1964-66, head sect. neuropharmacology, 1966-68; pres., research dir., dir. New Eng. Research, Inc., Worcester, 1968-88; sr. cons. New Eng. Indsl. Waste, Inc., 1988-89; v.p., compliance officer Am. Reclamation Corp., 1989-96; cons. Bd. Radioactive Waste Mgmt. NAS, 1987-92, numerous state and fed. agys. including Army C.E., Fed. Hwy. Adminstrn., U.S. Dept. Interior, EPA; affiliate prof. Worcester Poly. Inst., 1970-82; adj. prof. toxicology Tufts U. Sch. Vet. Medicine, 1981-84; panelist NSF; mem. corp. Bermuda Biol. Sta. for Research, 1968-85; lectr. in field, U.S., Can.; mem. Worcester Sci. Center Planning Com., 1963. Bd. dirs. Worcester Children's Friend Soc., 1968-92, v.p., 1978-84, pres., 1984-87. Served with USNR, 1952-54; Korea. Virginia B. Gibbs scholar, 1954-55; E.L. Mark fellow, 1956; USPHS fellow, 1957-58; NIH grantee, 1962-64; Office Naval Research grantee, 1963-64; recipient Sci. Achievement award Worcester Engrng. Soc., 1985 . Mem. AAAS, Biophys. Soc., Am. Physiol. Soc., N.Y. Acad. Scis., ASTM, Soc. Environ. Toxicology and Chemistry, Phi Beta Kappa, Sigma Xi. Republican. Greek Orthodox. Clubs: Tatnuck Country (Worcester); Harvard (Boston). Author: Nerves, Muscles and Electricity, 1970; Environmental Biology for Engineers, 1981; contbr. numerous articles to profl. jours., 1959—; patentee drug; cons. editor Acad. Press, Inc., 1978; mem. editorial adv. bd. Hazardous Waste Mgmt., 1983-90. Home and Office: 7 Wheeler Ave Worcester MA 01609-1707

CAMP, FRANCES SPENCER, retired nurse; b. Lake Charles, La., Feb. 8, 1924; d. Henry Wesley and Annie Erle (Allen) S.; m. John Clayton Camp, Nov. 3, 1944; children: John C., Elizabeth C., Martha L., Charles H. Student, So. Meth. U., Dallas, 1943-44; BSRN, McNeese State U., Lake Charles, La., 1957. Surg. nurse St. Patrick's Hosp., Lake Charles, La., 1963-65; founder, dir. Home Health Svcs. Inc., Lake Charles, 1969-80; pres., mem. founding com. Hosp. Aux. for Charity Hosp., Lake Charles; mem. task group on ethical dilemmas caused by med. tech. George Washington U. Med. Ctr., Washington, 1991-95. Artist commd. oil paintings. Sustainer Jr. League of Am., 1957-94; mem. Hospitality and Info. Svcs. of Meridian House Internat. Ctr., Washington, 1980—, mem. steering com., 1992-93, 94-96, chmn. bridge svcs., 1995-96. Recipient Woman of Yr. award, Lake Charles, La., 1962. Mem. Nat. Presbyn. Ch. Women's Assn. (1st v.p. 1990-91, exec. bd. 1994, by-laws chmn., parliamentarian, 1996—), Congl. Country Club, Sigma Theta Tau. Home: 5450 Whitley Park Ter Apt 510 Bethesda MD 20814-2059

CAMP, JOHN FREDERICK, anesthesiologist; b. Westville, N.J., Apr. 27, 1952; s. Samuel Thomas and Helen Elizabeth (Seibert) C.; m. Amy Elaine Barbieri, Nov. 6, 1976; children: John F., Gregory A., Lauren N., Tiffany A. BA in Biology maxima cum laude, LaSalle U., Phila., 1974; MD, Jefferson Med. Coll., Phila., 1978. Diplomate Am. Bd. Anesthesiology, Am. Bd. Pain Mgmt. Intern Wilford Hall USAF Med. Ctr., 1978, resident in anesthesiology, 1978-81; asst. prof. anesthesiology Washington U., St. Louis, 1981-85, U. N.C. Sch. Medicine, Chapel Hill, 1986-91; dir. S.E. Pain Mgmt., Charlotte, N.C., 1986-91; anesthesiologist Carolinas Med. Ctr., Charlotte, 1985—; cons. to Surgeon Gen., USAF, 1981-85; mem. exec. com. S.E. Anesthesiology Assocs., Charlotte, 1988-96, pres., 1996; chmn. dept. emergency medicine Scott USAF Med. Ctr., dir. critical care medicine, 1981-85, chmn. dept. anesthesiology, 1983-85. Author: Handbook of Pain Management, 1989, 91, 93; contbr. numerous articles to profl. jours. Maj. USAF, 1974-85. Mem. AMA, Am. Soc. Anesthesiologists, N.C. Soc. Anesthesiologists, N.C. Med. Soc., Mecklenburg Med. Soc. Roman Catholic. Home: 6901 N Baltusrol Ln Charlotte NC 28210-7367 Office: SE Anesthesia Dept Anes/CMC PO Box 32861 Charlotte NC 28236

CAMPAGNA, JOHN A., ophthalmologist; b. Sharon, Pa., Apr. 25, 1962; s. Emilio and Carmela (Moschillo) C.; m. Gretchen A. Boggio, May 28, 1988; children: Giovanni A., Gabriella N. BS, U. Pitts., 1984, MD, 1988. Diplomate Am. Bd. Med. Examiners, Am. Bd. Ophthalmology. Chief glaucoma svd. Brooke Army Med. Ctr., San Antonio, 1993—. Fellow Am. Acad. Ophthalmology; mem. Soc. Mil. Ophthalmologists. Office: Brooke Army Med Ctr Ophthalmology Svc Fort Sam Houston TX 78234

CAMPAGNOLI, CARLO, endocrinologist, gynecologist; b. Ivrea, Turin, Italy, Sept. 4, 1940; s. Luigi and Maddalena Vittoria (Migone) C.; m. Paola Dagna; children: Giorgio, Maria Francesca. MD cum laude, U. Turin, 1965. Intern Sant Anna Gynecologic Hosp., Turin, 1970-78, asst. head dept. endocrinologic gynecology, 1978-89, head dept. endocrinologic gynecology, 1989—; prof. endocrinologic gynecology Postgrad. Sch. Ob-Gyn., Turin, 1971—. Contbr. articles to profl. jours. Chmn. sci. bd. Osteoporosis Found. Piemonte, Turin, 1995. Mem. Am. Fertility Soc., Italian Fertility-Sterility Soc. (vice chmn. 1983-88), Internat. Menopause Soc. Roman Catholic. Home: Via Principe Amendee 12, 10123 Turin Italy Office: St Anna Gynecology Hosp, Dept Endocrinol Gynecology, Via Buenos Aires 106, 10137 Turin Italy

CAMPBELL, ANDRE RENAY, physician, surgeon; b. N.Y.C., May 5, 1958; s. Ronald Ivan and Ether (Robinson) C.; m. Gillian Otway, May 11, 1991. AB, Harvard U., 1980; MD, U. Calif., San Francisco, 1985. Diplomate Am. Bd. Internal Medicine, Am. Bd. Surgery, Am. Bd. Surg. Crit. Care. Intern internal medicine Columbia Presbyn. Med. Ctr., N.Y.C., 1985-86, resident in internal medicine, 1986-88, resident in gen. surgery, 1988-91, chief resident in gen. surgery, 1991-92, fellow surg. critical care, 1992-93; clin. instr., attending surgeon U. Calif. San Francisco, 1993-94, asst. prof. surgery, 1994—; bd. dirs. Louis August Jonas Found., Rhinebeek, N.Y. Contbr. articles to profl. jours. Grantee NIH, 1994—. Mem. AMA, ACS, ACP, Soc. of Crit. Care Medicine, Howard Naffziger Surg. Soc., Nat. Med. Assn., Assn. for Acad. Surgery, Alpha Omega Alpha. Office: San Francisco Gen Hosp Dept Surgery 1001 Potrero Ave Ward 3A San Francisco CA 94110

CAMPBELL, ANDREW WILLIAM, immunotoxicology physician; b. Beirut, Apr. 3, 1948; s. William Alexander and Gisela (Landes) C.; m. Rosario Icenit Saenz, Dec. 19, 1969 (div. Sept., 1979); m. Sharon Venessa Micek, Sept. 1, 1984; children: Denia Giselle, MIchelle Elise, Colin Alexander, Ian William. BA in Pre-med., Psychology, Franklin Pierce Coll., Rindge, N.H., 1970; MD, U. Autonoma de Guadalajara, Mex., 1974. Diplomate Am. Bd. Family Practice, Am. Bd. Forensic Examiners, Am. Bd. Forensic Medicine. Intern Pediat. Hosp. Infantil, Ob-gyn., Clin. Santa Monica, Guadalajara, Mex., 1974-75, Pub. Health Dept., Guadalajara, Mex., 1975-76; resident gen. surgery Orlando (Fla.) Regional Med. Ctr., 1977-78; resident family practice Med. Coll. Ga., Augusta, 1978-81; pvt. practice family physician Two Physician Practice, Sarasota, Fla., 1981, with former chief surgeon Eisenhower Med. Ctr., Augusta, Ga.; pvt. practice Augusta, Wrens and Louisvlle, Ga., 1983-84, Houston, Tex., 1995—; med. dir. Ctr. for Immune, Environ. and Toxic Disorders, Houston, 1993—; staff mem. Meml. City Med. Ctr., West Houston Med. Ctr., Spring Branch Med. Ctr.; chmn. dept. family practice Sam Houston Meml.. Hosp., Houston, 1987, chmn. credentials com. 1988, mem. exec. com. 1987-89; internat. cons. and med. expert on artifical implants, toxic exposure and occupational medicine; lectr. and speaker at Artificial Implants and Toxic Exposure Symposia. Contbr. numerous articles to profl. jours.; made numerous presentations to sci. meetings; author: (with others) Health Effects of Toxic Chemicals, 1994, Textbook of Nephrology (2 vols.), 1995; co-editor Internat. Jour. Occupl. Medicine and Toxicology, 1985-95; mem. editl. bd. Internat. Jour. Toxicology and Indsl. Health, 1994—. Founder Clinic for the Indigent, St. John Vianney Ch., Houston, 1987; trustee Sam Houston Meml. Hosp., 1987-93. Recipient Consumer's Choice award Am. Nurses in Bus. Assn., Houston, 1994. Fellow Am. Acad. Family Physicians; mem. AAAS, Tex. Acad. Family Physicians, Am. Coll. of Occupational and Environ. Medicine, The Chronic Fatigue and Immune Dysfunction Syndrome Assn., Inc., Internat. Soc. Neuroimmunology, Soc. Mucosal Immunology, So. Med. Assn., Pan Am. Allergy Soc., Houston Med.-Legal Soc., Tex. Med. Assn., Tex. Med. Found., Harris County Med. Soc., Am. Bd. Forensic Examiners, Tex. Physicians Resource Coun. Republican. Office: Ctr Immune Environ & Toxic Disorders 14441 Memorial Dr Houston TX 77079

CAMPBELL, BARBARA ANN, podiatrist; b. Seattle, July 31, 1959; d. Mahlon Erb and Barbara Lee (Welch) C.; m. Allan Gray Dyer, Apr. 23, 1988. BS in Pre-medicine, Kans. State U., 1981; D of Podiatric Medicine, Calif. Coll. Podiatric Medicine, 1986. Diplomate Am. Bd. Podiatric Orthopedics and Primary Podiatric Medicine. Resident in podiatric surgery Cmty. Hosp. Med. Ctr., Phoenix, 1986-87; assoc. podiatrist Quinlan Foot and Ankle Ctr., Scottsdale, Ariz., 1987-95; pvt. practice podiatrist Barbar A. Campbell, DPM, Paradise Valley, Ariz., 1995—. Mem., vol. Internat. Soc. for Protection of Wild Mustangs and Burros-Bur. Land Mgmt., Scottsdale, 1991. Fellow Am. Coll. Foot and Ankle Orthopedics and Medicine; mem. Am. Coll. Foot and Ankle Surgeons (assoc.); mem. Am. Podiatric Med. Assn., Ariz. Podiatric Med. Assn. (sec. 1994-95, v.p. 1995-96), Am. Assn. for Women Podiatrists (regiona XIV rep. 1991-94, membership chair 1994—). Lutheran. Office: Barbara A Campbell DPM Ste C-123 10575 N Tatum Blvd Paradise Valley AZ 85253

CAMPBELL, BRUCE CRICHTON, hospital administrator; b. Balt., July 21, 1947; s. James Allen and Elda Shaffer (Crichton) C.; m. Linda Page Cottrell, June 28, 1969; children: Molly Shaffer, Andrew Crichton. B.A., Lake Forest Coll., 1969; M.H.A., Washington U., St. Louis, 1973; D.P.H., U. Ill., 1979. Adminstrv. asst. Passavant Meml. Hosp., Chgo., 1970-71; adminstrv. resident Albany (N.Y.) Med. Center Hosp., 1972-73; adminstrv. asst. Rush-Presbyn.-St. Luke's Med. Center, Chgo., 1973-75; asst. adminstr. Rush-Presbyn.-St. Luke's Med. Center, 1975-77, asst. v.p., 1977-79, v.p. adminstrv. affairs, 1979-83; chmn. dept. health systems mgmt. Rush U., Chgo., 1977-81, dean Coll. Health Scis., 1981-83; exec. dir. U. Chgo. Hosps. and Clinics, 1983-85; lectr. Grad. Sch. Bus., U. Chgo., 1983-85; pres. Campbell Assocs., Chgo., 1985-92; exec. v.p. Ill. Masonic Med. Ctr., Chgo., 1993, pres., 1993—. W.K. Kellogg Found. fellow, 1977; Leadership Greater Chgo. fellow, 1984-85. Fellow Am. Coll. Healthcare Execs.; mem. Young Adminstrs. Chgo. (pres. 1977), Assn. Univ. Programs in Health Adminstrn., Am. Hosp. Assn., Ill. Hosp. Assn., Chgo. Hosp. Council. Office: Ill Masonic Med Ctr 836 W Wellington Ave Chicago IL 60657-5147

CAMPBELL, CARLOS BOYD GODFREY, neurobiology educator, army officer; b. Chgo., July 27, 1934; s. Joseph Gattaz Bumzahem and Ruby Viola Brown Campbell; B.S., U. Ill., 1955, M.S., 1957, M.D., 1963, Ph.D., 1965; m. Deborah Ellen Stephens, June 28, 1958 (div. July 1971); m. 2d, Nydia Haydee Gonzalez, Feb. 3, 1979; children: Ellen, Gowan, Kenneth, Christopher; 1 stepdau., Zinnia. Surg. intern Presbyn.-St. Luke's Hosp., Chgo., 1963-64; resident in neurology U. So. Calif. Med. Center, L.A., 1973-74; resident in radiology U. Va., Charlottesville, 1974-75, U. Calif., Irvine, 1975-77; commd. 2d lt. U.S. Army, 1962, advanced through grades to capt., 1967, reentered in 1979, commd. lt. col., 1979, advanced to col., 1984; neuroanatomist Walter Reed Army Inst. Rsch., Washington, 1964-67, rsch. neurologist div. neuropsychiatry, 1979-94; chief microwave bioeffects br. U.S. Army Med. Rsch. Detachment, Brooks AFB, Tex., 1994-96, detachment comdr., 1995-96; prof. anatomy Southwest Coll. Naturopathic Medicine & Health Scis., Tempe, Ariz., 1996—; staff neurologist Walter Reed Gen. Hosp., 1983-87; asst. prof. neural scis. Ind. U., 1967-70, asso. prof., 1970-74; asso. clin. prof. anatomy U. Calif., Irvine, 1975-77; adj. prof. anatomy Georgetown U., Washington, 1980-94; adj. prof. psychology U. Md., 1989-94; vis. assoc. in biology Calif. Inst. Tech., 1976-77; prof. anatomy, chmn. dept. anatomy U. P.R., Rio Piedras, 1977-79; rsch. prof. neurology Uniformed Services U. Health Scis., 1983-94; collaborator div. mammals Smithsonian Inst., 1966-67. Decorated Sovereign Order Knights of St. John of Jerusalem Knights of Malta; USPHS fellow, 1959-61; NIH grantee, 1968-72; NSF grantee, 1969-70. Mem. AAAS, Soc. Neurosci., Am. Assn. Anatomists, Am. Soc. Primatologists, Soc. for Study of Mammalian Evolution, Internat. Primatol. Soc. Cajal Club, Am. Soc. Zoologists, Assn. Mil. Surgeons U.S., J.B. Johnston Club, Phi Rho Sigma. Episcopalian. Club: Mermaid Tavern. Home: 14827 Adios San Antonio TX 78248-0977 Office: SW Coll Naturopathic Med & Health Scis 2140 E Broadway Rd Tempe AZ 85282

CAMPBELL, CAROL SUE, sociology, social work, psychology, and criminal justice educator; b. Jacksonville, Fla., July 3, 1956; d. William Arthur and Juantia May (Vickery) C. BA, Valdosta State Coll., 1977, MS, 1979; PhD, La. State U., Baton Rouge, 1985, MSW, M. Criminal Justice, 1987. Cert. Acad. Cert. Social Workers, bd. cert. social worker, profl. counselor, La. Instr. La. State U., Eunice, 1982-88; asst. prof. Valdosta (Ga.) State Coll., 1988-89; asst.prof., coord. La. Coll., Pineville, 1989-92; asst. prof. McNeese State U., Lake Charles, La., 1992—; therapist Anglewood Clinic, Baton Rouge, 1985-88, Profl. Counseling Specialties, Inc., Lake Charles, 1996—; instr. La. State U., Eunice, 1990—; mem. Project Independence Adv. Com., Rapides Parish, La., 1991-92. Contbr. articles and revs. to profl. publs. Mem. NASW (pub. rels. 1991-92, chair 1994—). Alpha Kappa Delta (sponsor). Office: McNeese State Univ Dept Social Scis Lake Charles LA 70609

CAMPBELL, CLAIRE PATRICIA, nurse practitioner, educator; b. Jan. 10, 1933; d. Hugh Paul and Clara Louise (Bell) Campbell. Student So. Meth. U., 1956-57; BS in Nursing, U. Tex. Sch. Nursing-Galveston, 1959, Family Nurse Practitioner, 1979, cert., 1984, 89; MS in Nursing, Tex. Woman's U. Sch. Nursing, 1971. Staff nurse Parkland Meml. Hosp., Dallas County Hosp. Dist., 1955-70, head nurse gen. surgery, chest surgery, neurosurgery, orthopedics, and internal medicine, until 1970; instr. nursing Tex. Woman's U. Sch. Nursing, Dallas, 1971-72; rschr. nursing diagnosis, Dallas, 1972-77; FNP Otis Engring. Health Svc., Dallas, 1979-86, nurse practitioner pain mgmt. program Dallas Rehab. Inst., 1986-95, HealthSouth SubAcute Unit, 1995—; adj. asst. prof. U. Tex. Sch. Nursing, Arlington, 1976—; cons. nursing diagnosis. Author: Nursing Diagnosis and Intervention in Nursing Practice, 1st edit., 1978, 2d edit., 1984. Mem. ANA, Tex. Nurses Assn. - Dist. 4, North Am. Nursing Diagnosis Assn., Sigma Theta Tau. Roman Catholic.

CAMPBELL, CRAIG JOHN, podiatrist; b. S.I., N.Y., Feb. 12, 1963; s. John Joseph and Florence Elizabeth (Tromer) C.; 1 child, Catherine Judith. BA in Bus. Adminstrn., Muhlenberg Coll., 1985, BA in Psychology, 1985; D in Podiatric Medicine, N.Y. Coll. Podiatric Medicine, 1990. Diplomate Am. Bd. Podiatric Orthopedics, Am. Bd. Podiatric Surgery, bd. cert. in foot surgery. Resident N.Y. Cornell Med.-Wyckoff Heights Divsn., Bklyn., 1990-91; resident in podiatric surgery Little Neck Cmty. Hosp. divsn. Wyckoff Heights Med. Ctr., Bklyn., 1991-92, clin. asst., 1992—; clin. asst. Little Neck (N.Y.) Cmty. Hosp., 1992—, The Bklyn. Hosp. Ctr., 1993—, Doctors' Hosp. S.I., N.Y., 1993—, Bayley Seton Hosp., S.I., 1993—, St. Vincent's Med. Ctr., S.I., 1994—; founder Forest Foot Care Group, 1994—. Chmn. standing com. Ancient Order of Hiberians, S.I., 1996. Fellow Am. Coll. Foot Surgeons; mem. Am. Podiatric Med. Assn., N.Y. State Podiatric Med. Assn., Pi Mu Delta. Democrat. Roman Catholic. Office: Forest Foot Care Group 675 Forest Ave Staten Island NY 10310

CAMPBELL, DAVID C., ophthalmologist; b. Washington, Dec. 26, 1944; s. David Stephen and JoanAgnes (Crawford) C.; m. Ines S. Garcia, May 20, 1978; 1 child, Jennifer. AB, Cornell U., 1967; MD, U. Rochester, 1972. Diplomate Am. Bd. Internal Medicine, Am. Bd. Ophthalmology. Ophthalmologist Am. Samoa, 1978; pvt. practice San Diego, 1979—. Office: 3808 Front St Bldg A San Diego CA 92103-3041

CAMPBELL, DAVID NEIL, physician, educator; b. Peoria, Ill., Dec. 1, 1944; s. William Neil and Ullian May (Hunter) C.; m. Charlyn Harris, Nov. 16, 1968; children: Scott, Chris, Brad. BA, Northwestern U., 1966; MD, Rush Med. Sch., 1974. Resident in gen. and cardiothoracic surgery U. Colo. Health Sci. Ctr., Denver, from asst. prof. to prof. surgery, 1988-95, prof. surgery, 1995—; cons., Druner, Colo., 1986—. Lt. U.S. Army, 1966-67, Korea. Office: U Colo Health Sci Ctr 4200 E 9th Ave # C310 Denver CO 80242

CAMPBELL, EDWARD DUNNE, JR., orthopaedic surgeon; b. St. Louis, Jan. 1, 1942; s. Edward Dunn and Bernadean (Avis) C.; m. Kay Patsy Riddle, June 13, 1964 (div. Oct. 1986). Student, Washington U., St. Louis, 1960-61; BA, S.E. Mo. State U., 1964; MD, Tulane U., 1968. Diplomate Am. Bd. Orthopaedic Surgery. Intern Charity Hosp. La., New Orleans, 1968-69; resident in orthopaedics U. Tex., San Antonio, 1969-73; pvt. practice orthopaedic surgery and sports medicine, Phoenix, 1976—; cons., tchr. Baxter Internat. U.K.; mem. med. audit team Glendale Surgictr.; mem. med. and sci. com. Phoenix chpt. Arthritis Found.; numerous presentations in field. Contbr. articles to med. jours. Mem. Physicians for Phoenix Symphony. Maj. M.C., U.S. Army, 1973-76. Mem. AMA, ACS, Am. Acad. Orthopaedic Surgeons, Arthroscopy Assn. N.Am., Internat. Arthroscopy Assn. (complications com. S.W. dist.), Am. Orthopaedic Soc. Sports Medicine, Internat. Coll. Surgeons, Western Orthopaedic Assn., Far Western Med. Assn., Internat. Soc. of Knee, Ariz. Med. Assn., Maricopa County Med. Soc., Alamo Orthopaedic Soc., Anterior Cruciate Ligament Study Group. Republican. Methodist. Office: Instg Bone-Joint Disorders 3320 N 2d St Phoenix AZ 85012

CAMPBELL, EDWARD WALLACE, nutritionist; b. Elizabeth, N.J., June 29, 1939; s. Edward Wallace Sr. and Dorothy Mae (Fairchild) C.; m. Phyllis A. Vecere, Sept. 27, 1959 (div. 1985); children: Diane Theresa, Christina Marie. PhD, Am. Coll., 1988; DLitt, Wellington U., 1990; MD, Open Internat. U., 1991, DSc, 1992; diploma, Lyons Med. Lab. Sch. Diplomate Internat. Coll. Acupuncture, Am. Coll. Manipulation and Nutrition, Inst. for Human Biomechanics; bd. cert. diplomate in nutrition and clin. nutrition; cert. wellness counselor; Australian postgrad. cert. in acupuncture. Pvt. practice, 1974-94; dean of students Nat. Nutrition Inst., Oak Park, Ill., 1988-92; exec. dir. Am. Bd. Nutritional and Naturopathic Cert., Toms River, N.J., 1989-92; dir. R & D Vitagenics Rsch., Brick, N.J., 1990-95; dir. rsch. World AIDS Rsch. Inc., 1995—; featured speaker Nat. Health Fedn., 1987-93; prof. Open Internat. U. Author: Orthomolecular Protocol for Morbid Obesity with Adjunctive Congestive Heart Failure, 1987, Orthomolecular Protocols for the Physician, 1988, The Etiology of Hyperlipoproteinemia, 1990, Nutritional Management of Peripheral Vascular Diseases, 1991; contbg. editor: Am. Nutrition Cons. Assn. Jour., 1988-93. Assoc. mem. Am. Mus. Nat. History; mem. Lighthouse at Community Med. Ctr., Nat. Arbor Day Found., Rep. Nat. Com., Washington, 1980—; del. Rep. Party Platform Planning Com., Washington 1991, 92, Presdl. Trust, Washington, 1992; campaign trustee Rep. Presdl. Task Force, Washington, 1987, 93. Fellow Found. for Complementary Medicine, Commonwealth (U.K.) Inst. Natural Medicine, Medicina Alternativa Sci. Soc., The Homeopathic Found.; mem. AAARP (ret. tchrs. divsn.), Internat. Assn. Holistic Health and Medicine, Am. Nutrition Cons. Assn., Nat. Health Fedn., Am. Assn. of Nutritional Cons., Wilson Ctr. Assocs., Homeopathy and Homotoxicology Symposium, Ind. Order of Foresters, Am. Legion, Senators Club. Methodist. Home: PO Box 802 Ocean Gate NJ 08740-0802

CAMPBELL, EUGENE PAUL, physician, retired public health administrator; b. St. Paul, July 22, 1907; s. Eugene Paul and Fan (Berry) C.; B.A. in Zoology, UCLA, 1929; M.D., Johns Hopkins U., 1933; M.P.H., U. Pa., 1942; m. Reba Lowe, Oct. 3, 1936; 1 dau., Marilyn Joyce. Intern Balt. City Hosp., 1933-34, asst. resident in medicine, 1935; practice medicine specializing in preventive medicine, 1939—; ward officer Communicable Disease sect. Walter Reed Hosp., Washington, 1935-39; asst. prof. epidemiology U. Pa. Sch. Pub. Health, Phila., 1939-42; chief of Coop. Health Program, Guatemala, 1942; field dir. South Am. Coop. Health Programs, 1943-45; chief Coop. Health Program, Brazil, 1945-55; dep. chief pub. health div. ICA, Washington, 1955-57; dir. Office of Pub. Health, Washington, 1959-62; chief pub. health div. AID, New Delhi, India, 1962-65; health attache Am. embassy, India, 1962-65; chief pub. health div. AID, Brazil, 1966-70, ret., 1970, now cons.; v.p. Internat. Environ. Services, Inc., 1985—; mem. U.S. del. WHO Gen. Assembly, 1957, 58, 60. Bd. dirs. Am. Sch., Rio de Janeiro, Brazil, Strangers Hosp., Rio de Janeiro. Decorated grand ofcl. Order Med. Merit, Brazil, 1955; recipient Meritorious Service citation U.S. Govt., 1956, Merit citation Nat. Civil Service League, 1958. Fellow Am. Pub. Health Assn., ACP; mem. Royal Acad. Tropical Medicine and Hygiene, Am. Soc. Tropical Health and Hygiene, Indian Assn. Advancement Med. Edn., Royal Soc. Health, Brazilian Soc. Hygiene, Washington Soc. for History of Medicine (pres. 1979-80), Antarctican Soc. U.S.A. Home: 1001 Middleford Rd Seaford DE 19973-3638

CAMPBELL, GILBERT SADLER, surgery educator, surgeon; b. Toronto, Ont., Can., Jan. 4, 1924; s. Gilbert S. and Ellen (Thorson) C.; m. Dorothy Jean Nugent, Sept. 18, 1947 (div. 1960); children: Kathryn Ellen, Rebecca Sadler, Thomas Kim, William Riley; m. Joan Louise Hancock, Sept. 28, 1961; children: Susan Muffin, John Gilbert. Student, Hampden Sydney Coll., 1939-40; B.A., U. Va., 1943, M.D., 1946; M.S., U. Minn., 1949, Ph.D., 1954. Intern U. Minn. Hosps., Mpls., 1946-47, tchg. asst., 1947-49, researcher Am. Cancer Soc., 1951-53, sr. surgery resident, 1953-54; instr. physiology U. Minn., Mpls., 1948-49, instr. surgery, 1954-55, asst. prof., 1955-58; prof. surgery U. Okla., Oklahoma City, 1958-65; prof. surgery and thoracic surgery U. Okla. Med. Ctr., Oklahoma City, 1958-65; prof. surgery, chief thoracic surgery U. Ark. for Med. Scis., Little Rock, 1965-90; cons. surgery Little Rock VA Hosp, 1965-90, Ark. Children's Hosp., Little Rock, 1973-90; mem. courtesy staff Ark. Bapt. Med. Ctr., Little Rock, 1972-90; prof. emeritus, 1990—. Contbr. articles in field to med. jours. Served to capt. U.S. Army, 1949-51. Decorated Purple Heart, Bronze Star with oak leaf cluster, Silver Star with oak leaf cluster U.S. Army; Mary R. Markle scholar, 1954-59; recipient Horsley prize U. Va., 1954; named Surgery Alumnus of Yr. U. Minn., 1983. Mem. Am. Assn. Thoracic Surgery, AMA (ho. of dels. 1976-82), Am. Physiol. Soc., Am. Surg. Assn., Halsted Soc. (pres. 1978), Internat. Cardiovascular Soc. (v.p. N. Am. Chpt. 1973), Societe Internationale de Chirurgie, Soc. Thoracic Surgeons, Soc. Univ. Surgeons, Soc. Vascular Surgery, So. Surg. Assn. (1st v.p. 1981), Western Surg. Assn., S.W. Surg. Congress (pres. 1980), Raven Soc., Alpha Omega Alpha. Home: 66 River Ridge Rd Little Rock AR 72227-1526

CAMPBELL, GLENDA GAIL, medical and surgical nurse; b. Graham, Tex., July 28, 1953; d. Austin Bell and Margaret Louise (Ward) C. AA, Cisco (Tex.) Jr. Coll., 1974; BSN cum laude, Midwestern State U., 1992. Cert. NRP, PALS, TNCCP, ACLS. Asst. in lab. Graham Gen. Hosp., 1969-71; magnetic tape machine operator Graham Magnetics, 1972-73; sec./draftsman Dresser Atlas, 1974-84; sec. Campbell Rathole Drlg., Inc., 1984-91; clin. asst. Graham (Tex.) Gen. Hosp., 1991; grad. nurse, staff nurse RN Graham Gen. Hosp., 1992—. Recipient Nat. Collegiate Nursing award Midwestern State U., 1992. Mem. Nat. Student Nurses Assn., Midwestern State U. Nursing Honors Soc., Christian Broadcasting Network, Nat. Humane Edn. Soc., Nat. Bus. Assn., Sigma Theta Tau, Tex. Gamma Chpt. of Alpha Chi. Republican. Home: PO Box 52 Graham TX 76450-0052

CAMPBELL, JACK JAMES RAMSAY, microbiology educator; b. Vancouver, C., Can., Mar. 29, 1918; s. Murdoch and Margaret (Campbell) C.; m. Emily Ann Fraser, Sept. 4, 1942; children: Sheila, Merle, Ann, Ross. B.S.A., U. B.C., Vancouver, 1939; Ph.D., Cornell U., 1944. Research assoc. chem. warfare Dept. Def., Kingston, Ont., Can., 1944-46; mem. dairying dept. U. B.C., 1946-65, prof., head microbiology dept., 1965-82. Fellow Royal Soc. Can., AAAS; mem. Am., Can. socs. microbiology, Sigma Xi, Phi Kappa Phi, Alpha Delta, Sigma Tau Upsilon. Home: 3949 W 37th St, Vancouver, BC Canada V6N 2W4

CAMPBELL, JAMES DAVID, emergency physician; b. Grand Island, Nebr., Dec. 17, 1961; s. Donald Edward and Marla Kay (Pope) C.; m. Ramona Lynn Owens, July 11, 1986; children: Erynn Rachel, Brady Weston. BS, Northeastern State U., 1987; DO, Okla. State U., 1993. Patient care tech. emergency dept. Muskogee (Okla.) Regional Med. Ctr., 1980-87; med. examiner Portamedic Svcs., Tulsa, 1991-92; intern, resident Hillcrest Health Ctr., Oklahoma City, 1991-94; pvt. practice Gore, Okla., 1995—. Mem. Am. Heart Assn. Office: PO Box 449 Gore OK 74439

CAMPBELL, JUDITH LOWE, child psychiatrist; b. Indpls., Jan. 21, 1946; d. Albert St. Clair and Adele V. (Lobraico) Lowe; m. Robert Frank Campbell, Nov. 30, 1968; children: Christiaan Robert, Kevin Lowe, Geoffrey Ford. BS in Zoology, Butler U., 1967; MD, Ind. U., 1971. Resident in psychiatry Ind. U. Sch. Medicine, 1971-73, fellow in child psychiatry 1973-75; asst. dir. Riley Child Guidance Clinic, Indpls., 1975-79, dir. child psychiatry consultation, liaison svc. to pediatrics, 1975-79; dir. child psychiatry svcs. Riley Hosp. for Children, 1979-85; pvt. practice child psychiatry, Indpls., 1985—; child psychiatry cons. Ctr. for Mental Health of Madison County, Anderson, Ind., 1975-77, Lutheran Child Welfare Assn., Indpls., 1974—, Lutherwood Children's Home, Indpls., 1974—, Jewish Family and Children's Svcs., 1983-84, child and adolescent div. Midtown Cmty. Mental Health Ctr., 1983-85; assoc. med. dir. child and adolescent psychiat. svcs. Cmty. Hosps. of Indpls., Inc., 1989-90; med. dir. outreach svcs. Arbor Hosp. of Greater Indpls., 1990, med. dir. children's unit, 1990-92, pres. med. staff,

1990-92; med. dir. Arbor Hosp., 1992-94; child psychiatry cons. Charter Behavioral Health Sys., Lafayette, Ind., 1995—; instr. Ind. U. Sch. Medicine, Indpls., 1974-75, asst. prof. dept psychiatry, 1975-89, clin. assoc. prof., 1989—. Vice-precinct committeeman Rep. Party, 1990-94; mem. parent's adv. coun. Butler U., 1989-93, pres., 1990-93. Recipient Physician's Recognition award in Continuing Edn. AMA, 1974, 77; Helen McQuiston award in sci., 1967. Fellow Am. Psychiat. Assn., Ind. Psychiat. Soc. (councilor 1978-80, 90-91, sec. 1981-83, editor newsletter 1981-83, chmn. com. women 1983-92, mem. ethics com. 1992—), Am. Acad. Pediatrics (Ind. br.), Am. Acad. Child and Adolescent Psychiatry, Ind. Coun. Child and Adolescent Psychiatry (sec. 1986-87, pres.-elect 1987-88, pres. 1988-89, Smithsonian Assocs., Indpls. Mus. Art, Indpls. Zool. Soc., Pi Beta Phi. Clubs: Eastern Star, Woodland Country. Contbr. articles on child psychiatry to profl. jours. Research on emotional aspects of burns in children, craniofacial anomalies in children, also sex differences in child and adolescent population groups. Office: 1525 N Ritter Ave Indianapolis IN 46219

CAMPBELL, KATHLEEN CHARLOTTE MURPHEY, audiology educator and researcher; b. Sioux Falls, S.D., Mar. 20, 1952; d. Chester Humphrey and Ruth Maxine (Thompson) Murphey; m. Craig Anthony Campbell, Nov. 15, 1975. BA, S.D. State U., 1973; MA, U. S.D., 1977; PhD, U. Iowa, 1989. Cert. audiologist. Clin. grad. asst. dept. communication U. S.D., Vermillion, 1976-77; regional audiologist II British Columbia Ministry Health, Cranbrook, 1977-82; audiologist II dept. otolaryngology head and neck U. Iowa, Iowa City, 1983-88, rsch. asst. dept. speech, pathology and audiology, 1985; doctoral fellow Health Svcs. R&D, VA, Iowa City, 1987-88; assoc. prof. div. otolaryngology dept. surgery So. Ill. U. Sch. Medicine, 1989—; cons. Packer Engrng., Naperville, Ill., 1992—. Editorial cons. Am. Jour. Audiology, 1992; reviewer Annals of Otolaryngology, 1992; contbr. articles to profl. jours. Mem. Midamerica Playwrights Theatre, Springfield, Ill., 1989—, Sierra Club, Springfield, 1989—. Recipient Clin. Investigator Devel. Award grant NIH, 1990, Small Bus. Innovative Rsch. grant NIH, 1990, Ctrl. Rsch. Coun. grant So. Ill. U., 1991, Children's Miracle Network award So. Ill. U., 1991, 92, Alzheimer Disease Ctr. grant So. Ill. U. Sch. Medicine, 1992. Mem. Am. Speech-Lang.-Hearing Assn., Am. Acad. Audiology, Assn. Rsch. in Otolaryngology, Am. Acad. Otolaryngology-Head/Neck Surgery (assoc.), Mensa. Office: SIU Sch Medicine 301 N 8th St # 5B Springfield IL 62701-1041

CAMPBELL, LAURA CASTEEL, hematologist, oncologist, medical researcher; b. Paragould, Ark., Oct. 3, 1960; d. Charles Edwin and Helen Marie (Warren) Casteel; m. G. Douglas Campbell, July 29, 1989. BA, Hendrix Coll., 1982; MD, U. Ark., Little Rock, 1987. Diplomate Am. Bd. Internal Medicine, Am. Bd. Oncology. Chemist Ark. Dept. Hwy., Little Rock, 1982; intern, resident in internal medicine U. Ark. for Med. Scis., Little Rock, 1987-90; chief resident internal medicine La. State U. Med. Ctr., Shreveport, 1990-91, hematology/oncology fellow, 1991-94; instr. med. ethics La. State U. Med. Ctr., Shreveport, 1991-94, mem. emergency dept. jr. staff, 1991-95, instr. hematology/oncology, 1994—. Mem. AMA, Am. Soc. Clin. Oncologists, Am. Coll. Physicans. Methodist. Office: La State U Med Ctr Sect Hematology/Oncology 1501 E Kings Hwy Shreveport LA 71130-3392

CAMPBELL, LINDA ANN, healthcare administrator; b. Norristown, Pa., Apr. 11, 1958; d. Jerry Mitchell and Iva May (Raker) Beeson; m. Steven Campbell, May 14, 1983; children: Jessica Ann, Barbara Ann. Diploma, Sacred Heart Hosp., Norristown, 1980; AAS, Montgomery County Coll., 1982; BS in Nursing, Gwynedd Mercy Coll., 1987; MSA, West Chester U., 1992. Pediatrics nurse North Penn Hosp., Lansdale, Pa., Med. Coll Pa., Phila.; instr. med. programs Watterson Sch. Bus. & Technology, Phila.; dir. nursing svcs. Suburban ENT Group Ltd., Norristown; adminstr. Dr. Daniel W. Horner, Abington, Pa., Abington (Pa.) OB-GYN, Ltd.; cons., adminstr. MBA Group, Doylestown, Pa. Mem. Nat. Assn. Physicians Nurses, Am. Assn. Office Nurses, Med. Group Mgmt. Assn. Home: 1424 Marlyns Ln North Wales PA 19454-2220

CAMPBELL, LINDA SUE, guidance counselor; b. Carbondale, Pa., Oct. 9, 1960; d. Charles Frederick and Grace Elizabeth (Mackle) Koehler; m. Terrance Lee Campbell, May 5, 1984. BS in Social Work, Mansfield U., 1982; postgrad., U. Scranton, 1988-93. Student caseworker Children's Svcs. Tioga County, 1981; live-in resident advisor Dauphin Residences, Inc., Harrisburg, Pa., 1982-83; live-in resident mgr. Human Resources Ctr., Inc., 1983-84, evaluator, placement officer, 1984-86, program specialist, 1986-93; guidance counselor Veritas Therapeutic Community Inc., Barryville, N.Y., 1993—. Mem. adminstrv. coun. Bethany United Meth. Ch., Honesdale, Pa., 1993-95, 95—. Mem. ACA, Am. Sch. Counselor Assn., Social Work/Anthropol./Sociol. Club (v.p. 1981). Republican. Home: RR 3 Box 760 Honesdale PA 18431-9521

CAMPBELL, LINZY LEON, molecular biology researcher, educator; b. Panhandle, Tex., Feb. 10, 1927; s. Linzy Leon and Eula Irene (McSpadden) C.; m. Alice P. Dauksa, Feb. 7, 1953. B.A. in Bacteriology and Chemistry, U. Tex., 1949, M.A., 1950, Ph.D., 1952. Rsch. scientist U. Tex., 1947-51; predoctoral rsch. fellow NIH, 1951-52; postdoctoral rsch. fellow Nat. Microbiol. Inst., U. Calif. at Berkeley, 1952-54; asst. prof., then assoc. prof. Wash. State U., 1954-59; assoc. prof. Western Res. U. Sch. Medicine, 1959-62; sr. rsch. fellow USPHS, 1959-62; prof. microbiology U. Ill. at Urbana, 1962-72, head dept., 1963-71, dir. Sch. Life Scis., 1971-72; prof. microbiology, provost and v.p. acad. affairs U. Del., Newark, 1972-88, univ. rsch. prof. molecular bioscis., 1988-89, Hugh M. Morris rsch. prof. molecular bioscis., 1989—. Editorial bd.: Jour. Bacteriology, 1961-65; editor, 1964-65, editor-in-chief, 1965-77; Contbr. articles to profl. jours. Served with USNR, 1944-46. Fellow AAAS; mem. Am. Soc. Microbiology (chmn. publ. bd. 1965-80, councilor at large 1962-64, v.p. 1972-73, pres. 1973-74), Am. Soc. Biochemistry and Molecular Biology. Office: U Delaware Dept Biology 400 Morris Newark DE 19717

CAMPBELL, MARGARET M., social work educator; b. New Orleans, Dec. 1, 1928; d. Walter and Caroline Louise (Seither) C. BA, St. Mary's Dominican Coll., 1950; MSW, Boston Coll., 1952; 3d yr. cert. clin. practice, N.Y. Sch. Social Work, 1959; DSW, Columbia U., 1970. Caseworker Charity Hosp., New Orleans, 1951-53, Cath. Social Services, San Francisco, 1953-55; supr. Spl. Service Club sect. U.S. Army Europe, 1956-58; caseworker Children's Bur., New Orleans, 1959-60, Associated Cath. Charities, New Orleans, 1960-63; lectr. Dominican Coll., New Orleans, 1961-66; spl. projects worker Associated Cath. Charities, New Orleans, 1964-65; dir. Fla. Family Ctr., New Orleans, 1965-67; asst. prof. Tulane U. Sch. Social Work, New Orleans, 1968, assoc. prof., 1971; dir. continuing edn. programs Tulane U., New Orleans, 1976-80; dir. Child Welfare Svcs. Tng. Ctr. Region VI, New Orleans, 1979-82; dean Tulane U. Sch. Social Work, New Orleans, 1982-94, prof., 1986—; dir. Ctr. on Aging, 1993-96, ret., 1996; chmn. various coms. sch. social work including Advanced Programs Continuing Edn., Ednl. Policy, NASW Student Liaison, Priorities Com. Author numerous publications and articles in profl. jours. in field. Mem. Kingsley House Bd., 1985, Area Agy. on Aging, 1988; bd. dirs. Tulane Ctr. Aging Rsch. and Svcs., 1993. Recipient Alumnae award Dominican Coll., 1970, Dominican Coll. Torchbearer award, 1985. Mem. NASW (chpt. pres. 1973-75, bd. dirs., treas., program dir., membership com., 1955-85; social worker of yr. Southeastern La. chpt. 1976; La. chpt. award 1978, La. chpt. Lifetime Achievement award 1992), Acad. Cert. Social Workers, Internat. Conf. on Social Welfare, New Orleans Children's Council, Child Welfare Info. Exchange Panel for La., Task Force on Adolescent Treatment Ctr., New Orleans Collaborative Tng. Program, Child Welfare League (chmn. southeastern conf. 1980-83), Council on Social Work Edn. (steering com. 1980-81, coordinator 1985), La. State Med. Soc. (geriatics subcom. 1985-86), Nat. Council on Aging, Gerontological Soc. Am. (conf. com. 1985), Southern Gerontology Soc., Adult Protection Services Network, Coun. on Social Work Edn. (planning com. ann. meeting 1990-91), Am. Pub. Welfare Assn. (regional conf. com. 1989-90), Nat. Assn. Deans and Dirs. Schs. Social Work (chair 1991 meeting).

CAMPBELL, OLGA MARGARET, psychologist; b. Altrincham, Cheshire, Eng., June 20, 1943; came to U.S., 1968, naturalized, 1981; d. John Wilkinson and Margaret (Warmisham) Talbot; m. Phalguni Sekhar Roy, Sept. 5, 1964 (div. 1973); m. James Donald Campbell, Nov. 1, 1974 (div. 1980). B.S., Marywood Coll., 1972; M.A., Abilene Christian U., 1975; Ph.D., U. Tex., 1983. Lic. psychologist, Tex. Psychologist, Big Spring State Hosp., Tex., 1973-74, 80-84, Vernon State Hosp., Tex., 1974-76, Rusk State Hosp., Tex., 1975-77; pvt. practice psychology, Midland, Tex., 1985—. Mem. Am. Psychol. Assn., Soc. Personality Assessment, Tex. Psychol. Assn., Psychol. Assn. Greater West Tex., Mensa. Office: 2303 W Wall St Ste 220 Midland TX 79701-6348

CAMPBELL, PAUL THOMAS, cardiologist; b. Sept. 16, 1958; m. Margaret Lyn Campbell; children: Elizabeth Lynn, Thomas James II, Mary Margaret. BS in Pharmacy, Phila. Coll. Pharmacy and Sci., 1981; MD, Temple U., 1985. Diplomate Nat. Bd. Med. Examiners, Am. Bd. Internal Medicine, Am. Bd. Cardiovascular Disease; registered pharmacist, Pa.; ACLS instr., BLS provider. Intern Duke U. Med. Ctr., Durham, N.C., 1985-86, resident, 1986-88; fellow in cardiology Duke U. Med. Ctr., Durham, 1988-92; cardiologist Heart Group of the Carolinas, Concord, N.C., 1992—. Contbr. articles to profl. jours. Recipient William H. Rorer scholarship Phila. Coll. of Pharmacy and Sci., 1978, Samuel Juresco Meml. scholarship, 1979, Joseph W.E. Harrison award, 1981, Mahlon N. Kline Meml. prize, 1981, William B. Webb Meml. prize, 1981 and numerous others to Emanuel M. Weinberger prize, Temple U., 1985, others. Fellow Am. Coll. Cardiology; mem. Cabarrus County Med. Soc. Office: Heart Group of Carolinas 301 Medical Park Dr Concord NC 28025

CAMPBELL, RAYMOND W., surgical nurse; b. Orlando, Fla., Sept. 3, 1956; s. Frank Richard Sr. and Edythe Bertha (Voyles) C.; m. Brenda L. Campbell, May 8, 1978; children: Rachael D., Raymond W. II. AD, Kellogg Coll., Battle Creek, Mich., 1989. Cert. ACLS, emergency med. tech. Indsl. emergency med. technician Ingalls Shipbldg., Pascagoula, Miss., 1976-79; chief urodynamics technician Lucerne Gen. Hosp., Orlando, 1978-79; psychiat. nursing asst. U.S. VA Med. Ctr., Battle Creek, 1980-87; scrub and circulating nurse Battle Creek Health Sys., 1989-94, oper. rm. charge nurse, 1994; scrub and circulating nurse, neurosurg. svcs. coord. Borgess Med. Ctr., 1994—, clin. preceptor, 1994—; mem. oper. rm. safety and infection control policy and procedure com. Battle Creek Health Systems, chmn. oper. rm. product edn. com.; operating rm. reprocessing com. Borgess Med. Ctr., 1996—, neurosurgery preceptor, 1994—. Trustee Village of Augusta, Mich., fire marshall and police commr.; ward mission leader Ch. Jesus Christ of LDS, Kalamazoo, 1994-95. With USN, 1974-76. Office: Borgess Med Ctr Surgery Svc 1521 Gull Rd Kalamazoo MI 49001

CAMPBELL, ROBERT E., retired health care products company executive; b. Passaic, N.J., 1933. Grad., Fordham U., 1955, Rutgers U., 1962. Vice chmn., dir. Johnson & Johnson, New Brunswick, N.J.; ret., 1994. Chmn. bd. trustees Fordham U., 1992—; chmn. bd. dirs. Cancer Inst. N.J., 1995—. Home: 40 Lake Dr North Brunswick NJ 08902

CAMPBELL, ROBERT JOSEPH, pharmacologist; b. Bklyn., Mar. 26, 1943; s. Joseph Mortimer and Mary Melville (Garden) C.; m. Helen Agnes Muller, Aug. 11, 1966; children: Colin Matthew, Eric Scott. BS in Biology, Chemistry, CCNY, 1966; PhD in Pharmacology, SUNY, Bklyn., 1972. Postdoctoral/rsch. assoc. U. Mich., Ann Arbor, 1972-76; from instr. to asst. prof. U. So. Calif., L.A., 1976-80; program officer biology Office Naval Rsch., Arlington, Va., 1980-82; chief pharmacology Army Rsch. Office, Research Triangle Park, N.C., 1982-86; chief chemistry and biol. sci. U.S. Army European Rsch. Office, London, 1986-89, dir. rsch. div., 1988-89; chief biochemistry and neurosci. Army Rsch. Office, Research Triangle Park, 1989-95; assoc. dir., Chemistry and Biol. Scis. Divsn. Army Rsch. Office, 1995—. Author: (with others) Animal Models, 1983, Biomimetic Materials, 1995; contbr. articles to Biochem. Pharmacology, Physiology & Behavior. Predoctoral and postdoctoral fellow NIH. Mem. AAAS, Sigma Xi. Office: US Army Rsch Office PO Box 12211 Durham NC 27709-2211

CAMPBELL, ROSE MARIE, nurse; b. Colver, Pa., Dec. 14, 1961; d. Daniel Adair and June Drucilla (Russell) Keith; m. Terry Michael Campbell, June 3, 1978; children: Tabitha Rose, Joshua Daniel. BSN, St. Francis Coll., Loretto, Pa., MBA, 1995. RN, Pa. Staff nurse telemetry CVMH, Johnstown, Pa., 1986; staff nurse Altoona (Pa.) Hosp., 1985-86, staff nurse med. ICU-surg. ICU, 1986-88, charge nurse med. ICU-surg. ICU, 1988-90, nurse mgr. med. ICU, 1990—; chair Nurse Mgr.'s Conf. Group, Altoona, 1991-92. Mem. AACN (cert., publicity com. 1990-91, sec. 1990-91, pres.-elect 1991-92, pres. ctrl. Pa. chpt. 1992—), Sigma Theta Tau (Zeta Lambda chpt.).

CAMPBELL, WILLIAM ALEXANDER, laboratory assistant; b. Kingston, Jamaica, June 7, 1953; came to U.S., 1992; s. Uriel Jephtah and Ruby Dorret (Forrest) C.; m. Jenief Alyson Hylton, Dec. 1, 1979; children: Michanne Tanyke, Deborah Melanie Tamara. Cert. in med. tech., Caribbean Assn. Med. Technologists, Jamaica, 1974, diploma in bacteriology, 1979. Lab. asst. Govt. Med. Lab., Kingston, Jamaica, 1971-85, med. technologist, 1974-85; med. equipment sales rep. Facey Commodity Co., Ltd., Kingston, Jamaica, 1985-92; lab. asst. North Ctrl. Bronx Hosp., N.Y., 1993—; biomed. engr. Ministry of Health, Kingston, Jamaica, 1983-85. Mem. Am. Soc. Med. Technologists. Home: 3450 Boller Ave Bronx NY 10475

CAMPBELL, WILLIAM T., JR., cardiologist; b. Denver, Feb. 6, 1957; s. William T. and F. Louise (Coston) C.; m. Lisa A. Dowlen, Oct. 25, 1986; children: Justin William, Laura Ann. BA, U. Colo., 1979; MD, U. Tex. Med. Br., 1985. Fellow Am. Coll. Cardiography; mem. Victoria County Med. Soc., Tex. Med. Assn., AMA, Am. Soc. Echocardiography. Office: 2700 Citizens Plz # 206 Victoria TX 77901

CAMPBELL-FORSYTH, LINDSAY, nurse; b. St. Petersburg, Fla., Feb. 9, 1952; d. Robert Mathers and Mary Adele (Clark) Campbell; m. Bradley J. Forsyth, Oct. 30, 1987. BSN, U.Fla., 1974; MSN, U. South Fla. 1986. RN, Fla.; cert. gerontol. nurse practitioner; lic. radiologic technologist. Neuro/burn staff nurse Shands Teaching Hosp., Gainesville, Fla., 1974-75; staff nurse ICU/critical care unit North Fla. Regional Hosp., Gainesville, 1975-76, Univ. Community Hosp., Tampa, Fla., 1977-78; staff nurse radiation therapy St. Joseph's Hosp., Tampa, 1978-82; field nurse Forest Terr. Home Health Agy., Tampa, 1982-83; supr., quality assurance coord. Univ. Home Health Agy., Tampa, 1983-86; geriatric/psychiat. head nurse, James A. Haley VA Hosp., Tampa., 1986-87, cmty. nursing coord., 1987-88; cmty. nursing coord. Lake City (Fla.) VAMC, 1988-94, coord. hospice care program, 1991-94; nurse practitioner nursing home care unit, 1994—. Mem. ANA, Oncology Nursing Soc., Fla. Nurses Assn., Sigma Theta Tau, Phi Kappa Phi. Democrat. Home: 21756 120th St Live Oak FL 32060-9236

CAMPBELL-SMITH, ROSEMARY GILLES, retired dental science educator; b. Rapid City, S.D., Mar. 16, 1939; d. Albert Peter and Anna (Schmitz) Gilles; m. Richard Lee Smith, Aug. 6, 1978; 1 dau. by previous marriage, Christina Lynn Campbell. Cert., Eastman Sch. Dental Hygiene, 1960; B.S.H.E. with high honors, U. Fla., 1964; M.S., U. Miami, 1968, Dr.Arts, 1976. Registered dental hygienist, Fla. Dental hygienist in pvt. practice, Palm Beach County, Fla., 1960-63; chief lab. technician dept. physiology U. Fla., Gainesville, 1965-66; instr. dept. biology U. Miami, Coral Gables, 1968-70; asst. prof. dept. dental hygiene Miami-Dade Community Coll., 1974-77; lead instr. Dental Aux. Programs, Santa Fe Community Coll., 1977-81; cons. Campbell-Smith Cons., Gainesville, 1982-96, ret. Author: Head and Neck: What's It All About, 1976. Recipient Albert E. Sevenson award for art. sci. and service N.Y. Dental Soc., 1960; Sci. award Eastman Sch. Dental Hygiene, 1960; J. Hillis Miller award U. Fla., 1964; Cancer Assn. award, 1964; Merit Citation Am. Dental Assn. Commn. on Accreditation Report, 1979. Mem. Am. Dental Hygienists Assn. (Profl. Excellence in Dental Hygiene award 1988, Dist. IV trustee 1988-90), Fla. Dental Hygenists Assn. (Outstanding Svc. Merit award 1992), Internat. Assn. Dental Rsch., Sigma Xi, Phi Kappa Phi, Phi Lambda Pi. Democrat. Roman Catholic. Office: 3609 NW 30th Blvd Gainesville FL 32605-2669

CAMPEN, DAVID HOWARD, rheumatologist; b. San Jose, Calif., July 6, 1955; s. Alden Bernard and Tressie Campen; m. Christine Yuanchen Chang; 1 child, Natalie. BA, U. Calif., Berkeley, 1977; MD, Tulane U., 1983. Diplomate Am. Bd. Medicine, Am. Bd. Rheumatology. Intern L.A. County-U. So. Calif. Med. Ctr., 1983-84, resident in internal medicine, 1984-86, rheumatology fellow, 1986-89; staff rheumatologist Kaiser Santa Clara, Calif., 1989—; chair formulery com. Kaiser Permanente No. Calif., 1994—; pres. Kaiser Santa Clara Med. Staff Assn., 1994-95. Counselor Santa Clara County Med. Soc., 1993—. Fellow Am. Coll. Rheumatology; mem. ACP. Office: Kaiser Hosp 900 Kiely Blvd Santa Clara CA 95051

CAMPOS, EMILIO CARLO, ophthalmologist, educator; b. Trieste, Italy, Oct. 23, 1950; s. Raffaele and Styra (Goldstein) C. MD, U. Modena, Italy, 1974; MSc in Ophthalmology, U. Rome, 1979. Med. diplomate. Predoctoral fellow U. Eye Clinic, Tübingen, Germany, 1973-74; post-doctoral fellow U. Modena Eye Clinic, 1974-76; post-doctoral fellow dept. ophthalmology U. Fla., Gainesville, 1976-78; asst. prof. dept. ophthalmology La. State U., New Orleans, 1978-79; assoc. prof. dept. ophthalmology U. Modena, 1980-94; assoc. prof., chief orthoptic tng. program U. Bologna, Italy, 1994—; chmn. stds. com. Internat. Perimetric Soc., 1982-88. Co-author: (with G. Lennerstrand and G.K. Von Nooreen) Strabismus and Amblyopia, 1988; contbr. articles to profl. jours. Mem. European Strabismological Assn. (sec.-treas. 1987-95), Internat. Strabismological Assn. (pres. 1994—). Jewish. Office: Clinica Oculistica Dell U, via Massarenti 9, 40138 Bologna Italy

CAMPOS, PAULO CAMPANA, health services executive; b. Dasmarinas Cavite, Philippines, July 27, 1921; s. Jose Sayoto Campos and Luisa (Sayoto) Campana; m. Lourdes R. Espiritu, Dec. 9, 1951; children: Jose, Paulo, Enrique. AA, U. Philippines, 1940, MD, 1946, DSc (hon.), 1990; postgrad. various, including, Johns Hopkins Sch. of Medicine, 1951-53, 58; Nat. Scientist, 1989; MD, U. Philippines, 1990. Pres. Univ. Physicians' Svcs., Inc., 1967—; prof. medicine Coll. Medicine/Emilio Aguinaldo Coll., 1979-86; pres. Yaman Lahi Found., Inc., 1980-93; prof. Coll. of Medicine/Univ. Philippines, 1952-82, prof. emeritus, 1989; pres. emeritus De La Salle U./Emilio Aguinaldo Coll., 1991; fellow Third World Acad. Scis.; pres. emeritus Nat. Rsch. Coun. of Philippines, 1984—; mem. various governing couns. including Governing Coun. of Philippine Coun. for Health Rsch. and Devel., 1982-89, Governing Coun. of the Pacific Sci. Assn., 1983-89; pres. Nat. Acad. Sci. and Tech., 1978-89; mem. UNESCO Nat. Commn. of Philippine Tech. Group on Sci. and Tech., 1983-88; investigator various projects; mem. bd. of regents Univ. Philippines, 1995—; del. internat. confs. in field, other. Editorial bd.: The Medicial Jour. of Emilio Aguinaldo Coll., 1984-86, Acta Medica Philippines, 1961-73, Jour. of Philippine Med. Assn., 1963-71, The Family Physician, Asian Jour. of Medicine, others. Trustee Gota de Leche, 1963—, Joaquin P. Roces Found., Inc., 1989—; trustee Jose P. Rizal Meml. Found., Inc., 1967—, 1st v.p., 1987—. Fulbright grantee, 1952; recipient U.P. fellowship, 1958, Internat. Atomic Energy Agy. Travel grant, 1965, Rockefeller grant, 1966, IAEA fellowship, 1971, WHO travel grant, 1978, 79, NAST travel grant, 1982, ICSU travel grant, 1983, others. Fellow Am. Nuclear Soc., Philippine Assn. Advancement of Sci. (pres. 1966-68), Philippine Coll. Physicians, Philippine Heart Assn., Third World Acad. Scis.; mem. Philippine Med. Assn., N.Y. Acad. Scis., Ermita Sci. Community, WHO (expert adv. panel on health manpower 1980-83), Philippine Fulbright Assn., Philippine Music Found., Philippine Internat. Friendship Orgn., Am. Numismatic Soc., Manila Med. Soc., Philippine Diabetes Assn. (bd. dirs.), Rotary, Phi Kappa Phi, others. Home: Pasong Lawin, Dasmarinas, Cavite The Philippines Office: 1122 General Luna St, Ermita The Philippines

CAMPOS-ESTEVE, MIGUEL ANGEL, interventional cardiologist; b. Havana, Cuba, Oct. 16, 1959; came to U.S., 1960; s. Miguel A. Campos and Himilce Esteve; m. Esther I. Colberg, Dec. 18, 1985; children: Vanesa Esther, Miguel Angel. BS cum laude, Tufts U., 1981; MD, U. P.R., 1985. Diplomate Am. Bd. Internal Medicine, Am. Bd. Cardiovascular Diseases. Resident in internal medicine Baylor Coll. Medicine, Houston, 1985-88; staff internist Irwin Army Cmty. Hosp., Ft. Riley, Kans., 1988-90; fellow in cardiology Walter Reed Army Med. Ctr., Washington, 1990-93; staff cardiologist Brooke Army Med. Ctr., Ft. Sam Houston, Tex., 1993-95; fellow in interventional cardiology Med. Coll. Va., Richmond, 1995-96. Contbr. articles to profl. jours. Major U.S. Army, 1988-95. Decorated Army Commendation medal, 1990, Nat. Def. medal, 1992, Meritorious Svc. medal, 1995; recipient Superior Unit award U.S. Army, 1992. Fellow Am. Coll. Cardiology; mem. AMA, Am. Heart Assn. Home: Parque De Montebello C-4 Calle 4 Trujillo Alto PR 00976 Office: Edificio Centro Plz # 103 Santurce PR 00910

CAMRAS, CARL BRUCE, ophthalmologist, educator; b. Chgo., Nov. 23, 1953; s. Marvin and Isabelle Lillian (Pollack) C.; m. Nancy Louise Ross, June 3, 1979; children: Melanie, Lucinda. BA, Yale U., 1975; MD, Columbia U., 1979. Diplomate Am. Bd. Ophthalmology. Med. intern Los Angeles County Harbor-UCLA Med. Ctr., Torrance, Calif.; resident in ophthalomogy Jules Stein Eye Inst., UCLA Med. Ctr.; asst. prof. ophthalmology Mt. Sinai Med. Ctr., N.Y.C., 1983-87, assoc. prof., 1988-91; prof., vice chmn. dept. ophthalmology U. Nebr. Med. Ctr., Omaha, 1991—. Contbr. articles to Investigative Ophthalmology and Visual Sci., Exptl. Eye Rsch., Current Eye Rsch., Ophthalmology, Am. Jour. Ophthalmology, Archives of Ophthalmology, Ophthalmic Surgery. NIH grantee, 1988—; Heed Ophthalmic Found. fellow, 1983; recipient Travel Fellowship award Assn. for Rsch. in Vision, 1977, Sandoz award, 1979, Alvin Behrens Meml. Fund award, 1979. Fellow ACS, Am. Glaucoma Soc., Am. Acad. Ophthalmology, N.Y. Acad. Medicine, Assn. for Rsch. in Vision and Ophthalmology. Office: Univ Nebr Med Ctr Dept Ophthalmology 600 S 42nd St Omaha NE 68198-5540

CAMUNAS, CAROLINE, nursing consultant; b. Bklyn., July 13, 1944; d. Conrad and Gertrude (Becker) Emig; m. Jorge L. Camunas, Feb. 21, 1976. Diploma, Kingston Hosp. Sch. Nursing, 1965; BS, L.I. U., 1975; EdM, Columbia U., 1981, EdD, 1991. Staff nurse clin. rsch. ctr. Albany (N.Y.) Med. Ctr., 1965-66; staff nurse eye inst. Presbyn. Hosp., N.Y.C., 1966-68, staff nurse surg. metabolism unit, 1968-71, head nurse surg. metabolism unit, 1971-76, sr. supr. gen. clin. rsch. ctr., 1976-81, adminstrv. nurse clinician eye, medicine and surgery, 1981-83; assoc. Nurse Execs. Assocs., Inc., Washington, 1990—; presenter, lectr. in field; adj. assoc. prof. Columbia U. Tchrs. Coll., N.Y.C., 1994—; adj. faculty Adelphi U., Garden City, N.Y., 1996—; vis. fellow Joseph and Rose Kennedy Inst. Ethics, Georgetown U., Washington, 1994-95. Author: (with others) Handbook of Medical-Surgical Nursing, 1983, Political Action Handbook for Nurses, 1985, Manuel de Enfermeria Medicoquirurgica, 1986, The Nurse's Guide to Marketing, 1991 (Book of Yr. award Am. Jour. Nursing 1991); contbr. articles and revs. to profl. jouurs. mem. exec. com. alumni coun. Columbia U. Tchrs. Coll., 1985-86, 88-90, chmn. alumni day com., 1988-89, chmn. disting. alumni awards com., 1991-93. Mem. ANA, N.Y. State Nurses Assn., New York Counties RN Assn. (chmn. task force on mktg. dist. 13, 1986-88, com. on pub. rels. 1984-88, Amanda Silver Dist. Svc. award 1988), Found. New York Counties RN Assn., Nursing Edn. Alumni Assn. Columbia U. Tchrs. Coll. (chmn. subcom. on registration 1986-87, membership com. 1992-95, Stewart conf. on rsch. in nursing 1992-95, chair 1993-94), Nat. League for Nursing, Sigma Theta Tau. Home and Office: 309 W 105th St New York NY 10025-3418

CANADY, ALEXA IRENE, pediatric neurosurgeon; b. Lansing, Mich., Nov. 7, 1950; d. Clinton Jr. and Hortense (Golden) C.; m. George Davis, June 18, 1988. BS, U. Mich., 1971, MD cum laude, 1975; DHL (hon.), Marygrove Coll., 1994. Diplomate Am. Bd. Neurol. Surgery. Intern in surgery Yale U., New Haven, Conn., 1975-76; resident in neurosurgery U. Minn., Mpls., 1976-81; fellow in pediatric neurosurgery Children's Hosp. Pa., Phila., 1981-82; instr. neurosurgery U. Pa., Phila., 1981-82; staff neurosurgeon, instr. neurosurgery Henry Ford Hosp., Detroit, 1982-83; asst. dir. neurosurgery Children's Hosp. Mich., Detroit, 1986-87; chief of neurosurgery Children's Hosp. Mich., 1987-88; assoc. prof. neurosurgery Wayne State U., Detroit, 1988-91; vice chmn. neurosurgery Wayne State U., 1991—; clin. instr. neurosurgery Wayne State U. Sch. Medicine, 1985, mem. internal rev. com. dept. anatomy, 1988, chmn. search com. dept. neurosurgery, 1989, internal rev. com. dept. neurology, 1991-92, 125th anniversary celebration com., 1992, internal rev. com. dept. pediat., 1993, chmn. search com. dept. ophthalmology, 1992-93, internal rev. com. dept. neurosurgery, 1994; vis. prof. Med. Coll. S.C., 1990; cons. neurol. devices panel Med. Devices Adv. Com., FDA, 1994; mem. surg. com. Children's Hosp. Mich., chmn. operating room subcom. surg. com., intensive care unit com., med. record com., med. exec. com.; mem. med. staff Children's Hosp. Mich., William Beaumont Hosp, Royal Oak and Troy, Mich., Harper-Grace Hosps., Detroit, Hutzel Hosp., Detroit, Sinai Hosp., Detroit, Huron Valley Hosp., Milford, Mich., Crittenton Hosp., Rochester Hills, Mich., St. John Hosp. and Med. Ctr., Detroit; presenter various profl confs. in U.S. and internat. Contbr. chpts. to books. Mem. Mich. Head Injury Alliance, Mich. Myelodysplasia Assn.; bd. dirs. Inst. Am. Bus., 1986-88. Recipient Citation Women's Med. Assn., 1975, Candace award Nat. Coalition 100 Black Women, N.Y., 1986, Golden Heritage award, 1989, Leonard F. Sain Esteemed Alumni award U. Mich., 1990, Disting. Alumni award Everett H.S., Pres.'s award Am. Med. Women's Assn., 1993, Variety Heart award for Med., Sci. and Tech. Variety Club, 1994, Shining Star award Colgate-Palmolive Co./Starlight Found., 1994, Golden Apple award Roeper Sch., 1995, Athena award Alumni Assn. U. Mich., 1995; named Outstanding Young Woman in Am., 1977, Top 100 Bus. & Profl. Women of Am., 1985, Woman of Yr. Detroit Club Nat. Assn. Negro Bus. & Profl. Women's Club, Inc., 1986; named to Mich. Woman's Hall of Fame, 1989; grantee Am. Cancer Soc., 1979, Minn. Med. Found., 1979, Am. Cancer Soc., 1981-82, Widman Found. Early Intervention Treatment and Follow-Up of Infants with Post-hemorrhagic Hydrocephalus, 1984-85, Neuropsychol. Recovery and Family Adaptation to CHI Children's Hosp. Mich., 1987-88, Hydrocephalus Induced Endocrinopathies: Morphologic Correlates Children's Hosp. Mich., 1989, 91. Mem. AMA, ACS, Am. Assn. Neurol. Surgeons, Congress Neurol. Surgeons, Am. Soc. Pediatric Neurosurgery, Nat. Med. Assn. Detroit Med. Soc., Mich. Assn. Neurol. Surgeons (sec. 1992-93, v.p. 1994-95, pres. 1995-96), Transplantation Soc. Mich. (adv. bd. 1993-94), Mich. State Med. Soc. (child abuse and neglect divsn. 1986), Southeastern Mich. Surg. Soc. (sec. 1986-87), Soc. Crit. Care Medicine, Wayne County Med. Soc. (ethics com., pub. affairs com., law com.), U. Mich. Med. Ctr. Alumni Soc., Delta Sigma Theta. Office: The Neurosurgery Group 3901 Beaubien Detroit MI 48201

CANARINA, OPAL JEAN, nurse, administrator, educator, consultant, lecturer; b. Geneva County, Ala., Mar. 21, 1936; d. O. Lee and L. Ellen (Box) Peacock; m. Miles Steven Bajcar, June 27, 1953 (div.); children: Debra Lynn-Wilson; Wayne Steven; m. Arnold R. Canarina, June 19, 1965; children: Catherine Mary, Christopher John, Charles Benjamin. B.S.N. summa cum laude, George Mason U., Fairfax, Va., 1976, M.S.N., Vanderbilt U., 1981. R.N., Va., Tenn., Ky., Okla., Utah, Miss., Fla. Staff and charge nurse Georgetown U. Hosp., Washington, 1976; charge nurse ob-gyn Vanderbilt U. Hosp., Nashville, 1976-77; charge nurse labor and delivery svc. Baptist Hosp., Nashville, 1977-80; asst. prof. dept. baccalaureate nursing Austin Peay State U., Clarksville, Tenn., 1981-83; dir. nursing svcs. Meml. Hosp., Guymon, Okla., 1983-85; dir. Women's Ctr./Maternal-Child Nursing, McKay-Dee Hosp. Ctr., Ogden, Utah, 1985-87; dir. nursing Jeff Anderson Regional Med. ctr., Meridian, Miss., 1987-89, program mgr., dir. Women's Ctr. Univ. Community Hosp., Tampa, Fla., 1990-91; adminstrv. dir. women's health svcs. Scripps Meml. Hosp., La Jolla, Calif., 1991-92; asst. adminstr., prof. Hart County Hosp., Hartwell, Ga., 1992-94; cons. to middle Tenn. and No. Utah areas health and nursing issues; cons. quality assurance Al Hada Hosp, TAIF, Saudi Arabia, 1992, assoc. adminstr. nursing, 1992—.
Recipient cert. of excellence R.N.s on campus George Mason U., 1976. Mem. ANA (cert. in nursing adminstrn. 1989), NAFE, Am. Orgn. Nurse Execs., Am. Coll. Health Care Execs. (internat. assoc.), Tenn. Nurses Assn. (legis. chmn. dist. 13, 1982-83, pres. 1982), Va. Nurses Assn. (Student Nurse of Yr. award 1975), Sigma Theta Tau, Alpha Chi.

CANAVERO, SERGIO, neurosurgeon, researcher; b. Turin, Italy, Dec. 29, 1964; s. Stefano and Lina (Narducci) C. Cert. English proficiency, U. Mich., 1980; MD cum laude, U. Turin, 1989; cert., Edn. Commn. Fgn. Med. Grads., Phila., 1990. Intern Hopital Neurochirurg, Lyon, France, 1991; mem. attending staff Inst. Neurosurgery, Turin, 1993—. Contbr. articles to med. jours. Lt. Italian Army, 1990-91. Mem. N.Y. Acad. Scis. Home: Via Montemagno 46, 10132 Turin Italy Office: Inst Neurosurgery, Via Cherasco 15, 10126 Turin Italy

CANCALOSI, MARK FRANCIS, pharmacist; b. Scranton, Pa., Dec. 13, 1954; s. Joseph James and Dorothy Theresa (Calleo) C. BS in Pharmacy, Arnold and Marie Schwartz Coll. Pharmacy, Bklyn., 1978, MS in Biomed. Communications, 1986. Registered pharmacist, N.J., Fla. Pharmacist Hosp. Pharmacy, Paterson, N.J., 1980, Singac Pharmacy & Surg., Little Falls, N.J., 1980-81, Bergen Pharmacy, Englewood, N.J., 1984-86, Gateway Discount Drugs, Boynton Beach, Fla., 1986; staff pharmacist Englewood (Fla.) Hosp., 1980, 86, Holy Name Hosp., Teaneck, N.J., 1981-86; dir. pharmacy HCA Univ. Pavilion Hosp., Tamarac, Fla., 1988-93; sr. staff pharmacist West Boca Med. Ctr., Boca Raton, Fla., 1987-88, pharmacy dir., 1993-95, pharmacy mgr., 1995—. Mem. Am. Pharm. Assn., Am. Soc. Hosp. Pharmacists, Fla. Soc. Hosp. Pharmacists, Palm Beach Soc. Hosp. Pharmacists (pres. 1989-90), N.J. Soc. Hosp. Pharmacists (sec. North chpt. 1983-86), Boca Raton Hist. Soc., Met. Mus. Art, KC, Rho Chi. Republican. Roman Catholic. Home: 10262 Islander Dr Boca Raton FL 33498-6306 Office: West Boca Med Ctr 21644 State Road 7 Boca Raton FL 33428-1842

CANCIENNE, MICKIE, psychologist, counselor; b. N.Y.C., Jan. 16, 1937; s. Edward A. and Bertha (Inslicht) Rein; children: Shari, Glenn, Amy, Scott. BS, Park Coll., 1984; MA, Webster U., 1987. Lic. chem. dependency specialist, nat. cert. addictions counselor II; cert. supervisory cons., Tex.; cert. alcohol and drug abuse counselor, Tex.; cert. Army alcohol and drug abuse counselor. Personnel clk. Civilian Personnel Office, Ft. Bliss, Tex.; counselor William Beaumont Army Med. Ctr., El Paso, Tex. Mem. Nat. Assn. Alcoholism and Drug Abuse Counselors, Tex. Assn. Alcoholism and Drug Abuse Counselors. Home: 6016 Naples St El Paso TX 79924-4209

CANCILLA, ELIZABETH ANN, orthopedic, neurology/neurosurgery, urology nurse; b. Westfield, N.Y., Aug. 19, 1961; d. Richard C. and Alice S. Davis; m. Joseph James Cancilla, Oct. 4, 1986; children: Joseph Richard, Kayla Elizabeth. BSN, D'Youville Coll., Buffalo, 1983. RN, Pa.; cert. clin. nurse III Hamot Med. Ctr.; cert. trauma nurse Hamot Med. Ctr. Nurses aide Ball Pavilion Nursing Home, Harbor Creek, Pa.; nurses aide, unit. sec. Hamot Med. Ctr., Erie, Pa., 1984—, mem. primary nursing com., mem. infection control com., 1993—; primary nursing com. and infection control resource com. Hamot Med. Ctr. Home: 146 E Main St North East PA 16428-1329 Office: Hamot Med Ctr 201 State St Erie PA 16501

CANCRO, ROBERT, psychiatrist, educator; b. N.Y.C., Feb. 23, 1932; s. Joseph and Marie E. (Cicchetti) C.; m. Gloria Costanzo, Dec. 8, 1956; children: Robert, Carol. Student, Fordham U., 1948-51; M.D., SUNY, 1955. Intern Kings County Hosp., Bklyn., 1955-56; resident in psychiatry Kings County Hosp., 1956-59; attending staff Gracie Sq. Hosp., N.Y.C., 1959-66; clin. instr. SUNY Downstate Med. Ctr., Bklyn., 1959-66; staff psychiatrist Menninger Found., Topeka, Kans., 1966-69; cons. Topeka State and VA Hosps., 1967-69; prof. dept. psychiatry U. Conn. Health Ctr., Farmington, 1970-76; prof., chmn. dept. psychiatry NYU Med. Ctr., 1976—; dir. N.S. Kline Inst. Psychiat. Research, 1982—; cons. psychiat. edn. br. NIMH; biol. scis. sect. NIMH. Editor 10 books.; Contbr. articles on schizophrenia to profl. jours. Recipient Freida Fromm-Reichmann award, 1975, Strecker award, 1978, Dean award, 1981, Lehmann award, 1992. Fellow A.C.P., Am. Coll. Psychiatrists, Am. Psychiat. Assn.; mem. Am. Psychol. Assn., Assn. Am. Med. Colls., Am. Assn. Social Psychiatry (pres.-elect 1982-84), N.Y. Acad. Scis., AAAS, AMA. Home: 118 Mclain St Mount Kisco NY 10549 Office: NYU Med Ctr 550 1st Ave New York NY 10016-6481

CANDE, FREDERIC P., physician assistant, medical facility director; b. Bklyn., Oct. 4, 1917; s. Morris and Minerva (Rabeon) C.; m. Estelle N. Rapoport, Dec. 17, 1941; children: Stephen M., Susan G. AA, Bklyn. Coll., 1953; BS in Microbiology, Wagner Coll., 1969; DC, CUNY, 1951; postgrad., USPHS Hosp., Staten Island, N.Y., 1972-74, Wagner Coll., 1969-71. Cert. chiropractic physician N.Y., Fla., P.R., Vt. Instr. microbiology, clin. pathologist in parasitology CUNY, N.Y.C., 1953-67; lab. dir. M&M Labs., Bklyn., 1969-74; physician asst. Boro Med. Ctr., Bklyn., 1974-78; physician asst., dermatology VA Med. Ctr., Bklyn., 1987-905, VA UP OPC, Oakland Park, Fla., 1995—. Contbr. articles to profl. jours. With USN, 1939-45; with USNR, 1945-78. Fellow Am. Acad. Physician Assts., Fla. Assn. Physician Assts. Home: 9330 Sunrise Lks Blvd Sunrise FL 33322

CANDELARIA, LIONEL MICHAEL, military officer, dentist; b. Albuquerque, Dec. 17, 1958; s. John Julius and Agnus Victoria (Garcia) C.; m. Karil Rene Taylor, July 21, 1985. BS in Biology, U. N.Mex., 1981; DDS, U. Mo., Kansas City, 1985. Diplomate Am. Bd. Oral and Maxillofacial Surgery. Resident gen. practice Balboa Hosp., San Diego, 1986; commd. lt. USN, 1985; staff dentist 3d Dental Co. 3d FSSG USN, Okinawa, Japan, 1986-87; staff dentist 1st Dental Co. 1st. FSSG USN, Camp Pendelton, Calif., 1987-89; resident in oral and maxillofacial surgery U. Tenn., 1989-93; dept. head oral and maxillofacial surgery Naval Hosp., Arlington, Tenn., 1993-95; oral and maxillofacial surgeon USS Kitty Hawk, 1995-96; tchr. staff oral and maxillofacial surgery Balboa Naval Hosp., San Diego, 1996—; lectr. in field. Fellow Am. Assn. Hosp. Dentists, Am. Assn. Oral and Maxillofacial Surgeons; mem. Clinicians of ADA, Dive Club, Sigma Chi, Omicron Kappa Upsilon. Democrat. Roman Catholic. Home: 1722 Cannas Ct Carlsbad CA 92009 Office: USS Kitty Hawk (CU 63) FPO CA 96634-2700

CANDELL, BRIAN JOSEPH, internist; b. Oakland, Calif., Feb. 6, 1962; s. Cass and Marlene Ann (Schoenthal) C.; m. Susan Evelyn Plomgren, May 21, 1994. BA in Physiology, U. Calif., Santa Barbara, 1984; MD, St. Louis U., 1988. Bd. cert. internal medicine. Resident internal medicine Johns Hopkins U., Balt., 1988-91; pvt. practice internal medicine Orinda, Calif., 1991—. Mem. AMA, ACP, Am. Cancer Soc. (bd. dirs. Contra Costa county 1992—, chmn. tobbacco control group 1995—), Calif. Med. Assn., Alameda-Contra Costa County Med. Assn., Alpha Omega Alpha, Phi Beta Kappa, Sigma Alpha Epsilon (health edn. com. 1986-95). Home: 3200 Woodside Meadow Rd Pleasant Hill CA 94523

CANDER, LEON, physician, educator; b. Phila., Oct. 7, 1926; s. Joseph Harry and Anna (Glick) C.; m. Geraldine Piontkowski, Dec. 11, 1954; children—Alan Drew, Harris Scott. M.D., Temple U., 1951. Rsch. fellow in physiology Grad. Sch. Medicine, U. Pa., 1952-56; resident in medicine Beth Israel Hosp., Boston, 1956-58; asst. in medicine Harvard U. Med. Sch., Boston, 1957-58; practice medicine specializing in pulmonary medicine Boston, Phila. and San Antonio, 1958—; sr. instr. medicine Tufts U. Med. Sch., Boston, 1958-60; asst. prof. medicine Hahnemann Med. Coll., Phila., 1960-63, assoc. prof., 1963-66, clin. prof. medicine, 1985—; prof., chmn. dept. physiology and medicine U. Tex. Med. Sch., San Antonio, 1966-72; chmn. dept. medicine, dir. med. edn. Daroff div. Albert Einstein Med. Ctr., Phila., 1972-80, head sect. of chest diseases, dir. med. edn., 1980-88; head sect. of chest diseases Mt. Sinai Hosp., Phila., 1988-96; prof. medicine Jefferson Med. Coll., Phila., 1972-89; clin. prof. Hahnemann Med. Coll., Phila., 1985—; mem. Nat. Adv. Coun. on Black Lung; nat. cons. U.S. Dept. Labor Black Lung Program, 1978—. Soc. Editor: (with J. H. Moyer) Aging of the Lung, 1963. Research fellow Nat. Acad. Scis., 1954-55. Fellow ACP; mem. Am. Thoracic Soc., Am. Physiol. Soc. Home: 317 Cherry Ln Wynnewood PA 19096-1710 Office: Benjamin Franklin Clinic 6th & Chestnut St Philadelphia PA 19106

CANGEMI, JOSEPH PETER, psychologist, consultant, educator; b. Syracuse, N.Y., June 26, 1936; m. Amelia Elena Santaló, Oct. 6, 1962; children: Michelle, Lisa Ann. BS, SUNY, Oswego, 1959; MS, Syracuse U., 1964; EdD, Ind. U., 1974. Diplomate Am. Bd. Vocat. Experts, Am. Bd. Forensic Examiners; diplomate in profl. counseling Internat. Acad. Behavioral Medicine, Counseling and Psychotherapy; cert. sch. psychologist, counselor, N.Y. Instr. Syracuse Pub. Schs., 1959-60, vocat. rehab. coordinator, research assoc., 1961-65; asst. dir. Carol Morgan Sch., Santo Domingo, Dominican Republic, 1960-61; asst. head basketball coach SUNY Community Coll., Syracuse, 1962-63, lectr., chmn. dept. psychology evening-extension div., 1962-65, vis. lectr., 1966; supr. edn. Orinoco Mining div. U.S. Steel Corp., Ciudad Piar, Venezuela, 1965-66; supr. tng. and devel. Orinoco Mining div. U.S. Steel Corp., Puerto Ordaz and Ciudad Piar, Venezuela, 1966-68; asst. prof. psychology Western Ky. U., Bowling Green, 1968-75, assoc. prof., 1975-79, prof., 1979—; project dir. U. Los Andes, Merida, Venezuela, Inter-Am. Devel. Bank, Washington, Western Ky. U., 1975-77; cons. R.R. Donnelley & Sons, Coca Cola, Gould Corp., Eaton Corp., Firestone Corp., Uniroyal/Goodrich Tire and Rubber Co., Gen. Tire and Rubber Co., Jerrerson Smurfit, Standard Products, others; host Conversation program Western Ky. U. Div. Radio, TV Film, 1968-71; trustee William Woods U., 1987—, COCITE, Lisbon, Spain, 1996; mem. House of GOA, Lisbon, 1996. Author: Higher Education and the Development of Self-Actualizing Personalities, 1977, La Administracion Participativa, 1983, (with Casimir Kowalski) Perspectives in Higher Education, 1983, Higher Education in the United States and Latin America, 1983, (with George Guttschalk) Effective Management, 1980, (with Casimir Kowalski and Jeffrey Claypool) Participative Management: Employee Management Cooperation, 1985, Chinese edit., 1990, (with Mario Noronha) Marketing Y Venda, 1992 (with Casimir Kowalski) Andersonville Prison, Lessons in Organizational Failure, 1993, (with Carl Kreisler) Raymond C. Gibson-Distinguished Kentuckian, Renowned Educator and Statesman: An Anthology, 1996, (with Casimir Kowalski and Richard Miller) Developing Trust in Organizations, 1996, (with Mario Noronha, Casimir Kowalski, George Guttschalk) Falhas Organinaclones, 1996; editor: Educator's Svc. Bull., 1971-72, Psychology-A Quar. Jour. Human Behavior, 1977—, Jour. Human Behavior and Learning, 1983-90, Orgn. Devel. Jour., 1983-89; mem. editl. bd. Archivos Panamenos de Psicologia, 1968-88, Coll. Student Jour., 1973—, Faculty Rsch. Bull. of Western Ky. U., 1977-88, Jour. Instructional Psychology, 1977—, Counseling and Values, 1979-84, Technol. Horizons in Edn. Jour., 1979-92 Edn., 1976—; contbr. over 400 articles, chpts. to profl. publs. Mem. bd. trustees William Woods Univ., 1988—; bd. dirs. Cocite Technol. U., Lisbon; mem. Ho. of Gao, Lisbon, 1996—. Recipient certs. and awards U.S. Army Armor Sch., 1974; Eaton Corp., 1974, 76, Brazilian Acad. Humanities, 1975, Nat. Autonomous U. Nicaragua, 1976, ICETEX Colombia, 1977, Colombian Nat. Assn. Indsl. Engrs., 1977, City of Bucaramanga, Colombia, 1976, 77, Quality Control Assn., 1979, Decreto award State of Santander, Colombia, 1977, Excellence in Productive Teaching award Western Ky. U. Coll. Edn., 1979, 91, Firestone Tire and Rubber Co. award, 1978, 81, Profl.-Tech. Socs. award, 1983, Coll. Student Jour. and Models of Excellence award, 1983, Disting. Pub. Service award Western Ky. U. 1983, Excellence in Pub. Service award Coll. Edn., 1983, Disting. Alumnus award SUNY, Oswego, 1983; award from Uniroyal-Goodrich Tire and Rubber Co., 1986, Excellence in Research and Creativity award Coll. Edn., Weastern Ky. U., 1987, United Rubber Workers/Internat. Brotherhood Elec. Workers and Firestone Tire & Rubber Co. award, 1991; featured personality Organization Development Jour., 1989, Jour. Edn. award, Project Innovation, 1992 (featured on cover and in mer issue); Bridgestone-Firestone award Valencia, Venezuela, 1994, Outstanding Contbn. award Redman Industries southeastern divsn.. 1996. Mem. Am. Assn. Counseling and Devel. (regional chmn. com. internat. edn. 1976 life), Nat. Vocat. Guidance Assn. Profl., Internat. Council Psychologists (area chmn. Ky.), Assn. Specialists in Group Work (charter), Panamanian Psychol. Assn. (hon.), Southeastern Psychol. Assn., Ky. Acad. Arts and Scis. (life), Internat. Assn. Edn. and Vocat. Guidance, Nat. Assn. Gifted (bd. dirs. 1973), Colombian Nat. Soc. Indsl. Engrs. (hon.), Romanian Acad. Scis. (hon.), Internat. Registry Orgn. Devel. Profls. , RODC, InterAm. Soc. Psychology, Acad. Mgmt., Capitol Arts Assn., Alumni Assn. SUNY-Oswego, Ind. U. Alumni Assn. (life), Pi Kappa Delta, Psi Chi, Sigma Delta Psi, Sigma Tau Delta, Phi Delta Kappa. Club: Bowling Green Country. Home: 1409 Mt Ayr Cir Bowling Green KY 42103-4708 Office: Western Ky U Dept Psychology Bowling Green KY 42101

CANNARD, KEVIN ROBERTSON, neurologist; b. Balt., Nov. 12, 1959; s. John William and Ester Brooke (Robertson) C.; m. Anne Louise Whistler. BS in Chemistry and Physics cum laude, James Madison U., 1983; MD, Med. Coll. Va., 1987. Bd. cert. diplomate in neurology Am. Bd. Psychiatry and Neurology. Commd. officer U.S. Army, 1987, advanced through grades to maj.; resident in neurology Walter Reed Army Med. Ctr., Washington, 1991; chief neurology DeWitt Army Com. Hosp., Ft. Belvoir, Va., 1991-93; staff neurologist Tripler Army Med Ctr., Honolulu, 1993-95, asst. chief neurology, 1995—. Contbr. chpt. to book, articles to profl. jours. Mem. Am. Acad. Neurology (mem. subcom. on undergrad. med. edn. 1991—, exec. com. A.B. Baker edn. sect. sec. 1992—, subcom. on info. sys. and computers 1994—). Office: Neurolog Clinic MCHK-DMN Tripler AMC HI 96859-5000

CANNIZZARO, LINDA ANN, geneticist, researcher; b. S.I., N.Y., Aug. 4, 1953. BS, St. Peter's Coll., 1975; MS, Fordham U., 1977, PhD, 1981. Postdoctoral fellow Dartmouth U. Med. Sch., Hanover, N.H., 1981-83; fellow in human genetics Children's Hosp. Phila., 1983-84; co-dir. cytogenetics Milton S. Hershey (Pa.) Med. Ctr., 1984-86; dir. gene mapping S.W. Biomed. Rsch. Inst., Scottsdale, Ariz., 1986-89; asst. prof. Fels Inst. Temple U. Med. Sch., Phila., 1989-91; asst. prof. Jefferson Cancer Inst., Phila., 1991-93; assoc. prof. Albert Einstein Coll. Medicine, Bronx, N.Y., 1993—; dir. cancer and molecular cytogenetics Albert Einstein Coll. Medicine and Montefiore Hosp., Bronx, N.Y., 1993—. Editor-in-chief Cytogenetics Cell Genetics, 1995—; contbr. articles to profl. jours. Grantee Am. Cancer Soc., 1989-90, 94—. Mem. AAAS, AAUW, Am. Soc. Human Genetics. Office: Albert Einstein Coll Med Dept Pathology 1300 Morris Park Ave Bronx NY 10461-1926

CANNON, GERALDINE E., quality assurance nurse; b. Phila., Sept. 19, 1944; d. Charles and Florence (Klawiter) McKay; m. Joseph T. Cannon, Sept. 17, 1966; children: Kathy Cannon Van Deusen, Joseph J. BS in Profl. Arts, St. Joseph's Coll., Windham, Maine, 1984. Nursing supr. Northeastern Hosp., Phila., 1984; dir. nursing Geriatric-Med. Ctrs. Inc., Phila., 1986-92, quality assurance nurse, 1991; quality assurance nurse, cons. Hospicomm, Inc., Phila., 1992—; asst. adminstr. Delaire Nursing Home, Linden, N.J., 1994-95. Contbr. articles to profl. jours. Mem. Am. Soc. for Long Term Care Nurses (cert. nursing dir. in long term care), Pa. Dir. Nurses Assn. Home: 9415 Hilspach St Philadelphia PA 19115 Office: Hospicomm Inc 41 N 3d St Philadelphia PA 19106

CANNON, GRACE BERT, immunologist; b. Chambersburg, Pa., Jan. 29, 1937; d. Charles Wesley and Gladys (Raff) Bert; m. W. Dilworth Cannon, June 3, 1961 (div. 1972); children: Michael Quayle, Susan Radcliffe, Peter Bert Cannon. AB, Goucher Coll., 1958; PhD, Washington U., St. Louis, 1962. Fellow Columbia U., N.Y.C., 1962-64, Columbia U. Coll. Physicians and Surgeons, N.Y.C., 1964-65; staff fellow NIH Nat. Cancer Inst., Bethesda, Md., 1966-67; cell biologist Litton Bionetics, Inc., Kensington, Md., 1972-80, head immunology sect., 1980-85; dir. sci. ImmuQuest Labs., Inc., Rockville, Md., 1985-88; pres. Biomedical Analytics, Inc., Silver Spring, Md., 1988-94; mgr. ATLIS Fed. Svcs., Inc., Silver Spring, Md., 1991-95; dir. ATLIS Fed. Svcs., Inc., Rockville, Md., 1995—; Mem. contract rev. coms. Nat. Cancer Inst., 1983-87. Contbr. articles to profl. jours. Mem. Pub. Svc. Health Club, Bethesda, Md., 1984—, sec., 1990—; mem. bd. Cmty. Ministries Rockville. Grantee USPHS, 1959-65, NSF, 1959. Mem. AAAS, Am. Assn. for Cancer Rsch., N.Y. Acad. Sci., Sigma Xi. Home and Office: 4905 Ertter Dr Rockville MD 20852-2203

CANNON, STEPHEN CALDWELL, neurologist; b. Bryn Mawr, Pa., Mar. 6, 1958; s. James W. and Anne Ruth (Dufour) C.; m. Lisa Marie Halvorson, June 3, 1989; 1 child, Christopher. BS, Washington U., 1980, MS, 1980; MD, Johns Hopkins U., 1986, PhD, 1986. Resident in neurology Mass. Gen. Hosp., Boston, 1986-90, chief resident neurology, 1989-90; instr. neurology Harvard Med. Sch., Boston, 1990-94, asst. prof., 1995—. Contbr. articles to profl. jours. Klingenstein fellowship Klingenstein Found., 1995, Sloan fellowship Alfred P. Sloan Found., 1993, Postdoctoral fellowship Howard Hughes Med. Inst., 1991. Mem. Soc. for Neurosci., Biophys. Soc., Soc. for Gen. Physiologists. Office: Mass Gen Hosp Fruit St Boston MA 02114

CANNON, W. DILWORTH, orthopedic surgeion; b. N.Y.C., Apr. 1, 1937; m. Grace Bert, June 15, 1961; children: Michael, Susan, Peter; m. Helga Maass, Nov. 30, 1974; children: John, Robert. BS, Yale U., 1959; MD, Columbia Coll., 1963. Prof. clin. orthopedics, dir. sports medicine U. Calif., San Francisco. Co-editor: Knee Surgery—Current Practice, 1992; co-editor Sports Medicine and Arthroscopy Rev. Mem. Arthroscopy Assn. N.Am. (past pres.). Office: UCSF Sports Medicine Ctr 500 Parnassus Ave San Francisco CA 94143-1351

CANNON, WALTER B., general and thoracic surgeon; b. Cambridge, Mass., July 6, 1940; s. Bradford and Ellen (DeNormandie) C.; m. Irène Plattner, May 23, 1937; children: Lukas, Annatina, Barbara, Christopher. BA in Engring. and Physics, Harvard U., 1963, MD, 1969. Clin. prof. surgery Stanford Med. Sch., Palo Alto, Calif., 1975—. Fellow ACS; mem. Western Thoracic Surg. Assn., San Francisco Surg. Assn. Office: Palo Alto Med Clinic 300 Homer Ave Palo Alto CA 94301-2726

CANNON, WOODWARD, surgeon; b. Phila., Nov. 11, 1944; s. Bradford and Ellen (DeNormandie) C.; m. Helen Christy, June 7, 1969; children: Christy, Theresa, Colbert. BA, Harvard Coll., 1966, MD, 1970. Intern gen. surgery Mass. Gen. Hosp., Boston, 1970-71, resident, 1971-73, 76-77; staff surgeon Rex Hosp., 1978—, Wake County Hosp., 1978—, Raleigh (N.C.) Cmty. Hosp., 1978—. Lt. comdr. USPHS, 1973-76. Republican. Episcopalian. Office: 2800 Blue Ridge Blvd Raleigh NC 27607

CANTER, CHARLES EDWARD, medical educator; b. Independence, Mo., Sept. 25, 1952; s. Edward Harrison and Phyllis Maurine (Windrum) C.; m. Linda Faye Smith, Feb. 18, 1978; children: Timothy, Catherine, Stephen, Matthew. BS, Brown U., 1974, MSc, 1976; MD, St. Louis U., 1979. Diploamte Am. Bd. Pediatrics. Pvt. pracitce St. Louis, 1984-86; instr. pediatrics Washington U., St. Louis, 1987-89, asst. prof., 1989-93, assoc. prof., 1993—; med. dir. cardiac transplantation St. Louis Childrens Hosp., 1987—. Fellow Am. Acad. Pediatrics, Am. Coll. Cardiology. Home: 680 Oakwood Ave Webster Groves MO 63119 Office: St Louis Childrens Hosp 1 Childrens Pl Saint Louis MO 63110

CANTER, JEROME WOLF, surgeon, educator; b. Washington, Aug. 20, 1930; s. Edward Averill and Hattie Mary (Wolf) C.; m. Francine M. Carlie, June 1952 (div. 1956); 1 child, Douglas; m. Dorothy K. Aein, Aug. 30, 1964; children: David, Robert, Daniel. Student, Princeton U., 1948-51; MD, George Washington U., 1955. Diplomate, Am. Bd. Surgery. Resident in surgery Mt. Sinai Hosp., N.Y.C., 1955-60; pvt. practice Washington, 1962—; faculty George Washington U., 1962—; surgeon, pres. Canter Profl. Corp., Washington, 1974—; clin. prof. surgery, George Washington U., Washington. Contbr. numerous articles to med. jours. Trustee, Blue Cross/Shield of D.C., 1973-82, D.C. div. Am. Cancer Soc., 1974-78. Lt. Comdr. MC, USN, 1960-62. Fellow ACS; mem. Soc. Surg. Oncology, Soc. Surgery of Alimentary Tract, Assn. Acad. Surgery, Am. Fedn. Clin. Rsch., George Washington U. Med. Alumni Assn. (pres. 1970(, Woodmont Country Club, Army-Navy Club. Republican. Jewish. Office: 3 Washington Cir NW Washington DC 20037-2356

CANTO, DIANA CATHERINE, nurse practitioner; b. Antioch, Calif., Mar. 20, 1939; d. William Light and Emma Catherine (Disher) Clark; children: Paul Petroni, Peter Petroni, Patrick Canto, Alexander Canto. AS with honors, Contra Costa Coll., San Pablo, Calif., 1982; BSN summa cum laude, Holy Name Coll., Oakland, Calif., 1984; MS, U. Calif., San Francisco, 1987. RN, Calif.; cert. PNP, FNP, CPR. RN Children's Hosp. Oakland, Calif., 1984-86, Merrithew Meml. Hosp., Martinez, Calif., 1986-87; family nurse practitioner Contra Costa County Detention Facility, Martinez, Calif., 1987, Berkeley (Calif.) City Pub. Health Dept., West Berkeley (Calif.) Health Clin., 1987-88, Maxicare Health Svcs., Calif., 1988-90, Homeless Program Alameda, San Leandro, Calif., 1989-90; nurse practitioner, founder student health svcs. U. San Francisco, 1989-90; with San Francisco Pub. Health Dept., 1989-91; ind. nurse practitioner family, pediatrics, family planning, women's health care, 1991—; researcher Contra Costa County P.H.D., Pitts., 1984, Ctr. for New Americans, Concord, Calif., 1985, UCSF, 1986-87, edn. program developer, Children's Hosp. Oakland, 1984-85, other ctrs. Mem. Walnut Creek Com. on Aging. Mem. AAUW, LWV, NOWA, ANA, APHA, Calif. Nurses Assn., Calif. Coalition Nurse Practitioners, Wash. State Nurses Assn., Nat. Assn. Pediatric Nurse Practitioner Assn., Coun. Nursing and Anthropology, Intercultural Interest Group of the Bay Area, Kappa Gamma Pi, Sigma Theta Tau. Home: 618 Avenue A Snohomish WA 98290-2416 Office: Sky River Health Ctr 615 W Stevens Ste D Sultan WA 98294

CANTONI, LOUIS JOSEPH, psychologist, poet, sculptor; b. Detroit, May 22, 1919; s. Pietro and Stella (Puricelli) C.; m. Lucile Eudora Moses, Aug. 7, 1948; children: Christopher Louis, Sylvia Therese. AB, U. Calif., Berkeley, 1946; MSW, U. Mich., 1949, Ph.D., 1953. Personnel mgr. Johns-Manville Corp., Pittsburg, Calif., 1944-46; social caseworker Detroit Dept. Pub. Welfare, 1946-49; counselor Mich. Div. Vocat. Rehab., Detroit, 1949-50; conf. leader, tchr. psychology, coordinator family and community relations program Gen. Motors Inst., Flint, Mich., 1951-56; from assoc. prof. to prof., dir. rehab. counseling Wayne State U., Detroit, 1956-89. Author books and monographs including: The 1939-1943 Flint Michigan Guidance Demonstration, 1953, Marriage and Community Relations, 1954; (with Mrs. Cantoni) Counseling Your Friends, 1961, Supervised Practice in Rehabilitation Counseling, 1978, Writings of Louis J. Cantoni, 1981, Essays, Theses and Projects in Rehabilitation Counseling, 1989; (with Mrs. Cantoni) Theoretical Underpinnings of Practice in Family Service Agencies, 1990; (poetry) With Joy I Called to You, 1969, Gradually The Dreams Change, 1979, A Festival of Lanternes, 1994; editor: Placement of the Handicapped in Competitive Employment, 1957; co-editor: Preparation of Vocational Rehabilitation Counselors Through Field Instruction, 1985; prin. editor: (poetry) Golden Song Anthology, 1985; editor jours. Mich. Rehab. Assn. Digest, 1961-63, Grad. Comment, 1963-64, Cathedral Digest, 1973-75; contbr. articles, revs., poems and illustrations to jours. Judge Mich. regional and nat. essay and poetry contests, 1965-77; bd. dirs. Mich. Rehab. Assn., 1962-64, 78-79, Mich. Rehab. Conseling Assn., 1985-87. Served to 2d lt. AUS, 1942-44. Recipient award for leadership and service Mich. Rehab. Assn., 1964, Mich. Rehab. Counseling Assn., 1985, 87, 88, Outstanding Service award Mich. State Bd. Edn., 1989; South and West ann. poetry award, 1970; Award for Meritorious Service Wayne State U., 1971, 81, 86, 87, 89; Outstanding Service award Poetry Soc. Mich., 1984. Fellow AAAS; mem. AAUP, APA, Coun. of Rehab. Counselor Educators (sec. 1957-58, chmn. 1965-66), Nat. Rehab. Assn., Nat. Congress of Orgns. of the Physically Handicapped, Nat. Assn. of the Physically Handicapped, Nat. Alliance for the Mentally Ill, Am. Inst. Econ. Rsch., Poetry Soc. Am., Mich. Rehab. Assn. (pres. 1963-64), Detroit Rehab. Assn. (pres. 1958), Mich. Counseling Assn., Mich. Career Devel. Assn., Internat. Inst. Met. Detroit, World Poetry Soc. (Edwin A. Falkowski Meml. award 1990), Acad. Am. Poets, Detroit Inst. Arts, Friends of Detroit Pub. Libr., Friends of Marshall M. Fredericks Sculpture Gallery, Soc. for Study of Midwestern Lit., U.S. Hist. Soc., Italic Studies Inst., USN Meml., Internat. Sculpture Ctr., Nat. Sculpture Soc., Sculptors Guild Mich., Lladro Collectors Soc., Birmingham-Bloomfield Art Assn., Psychology and the Arts, Poetry Soc. Mich., Detroit Film Soc., Detroit Zool. Soc., Poetry Resource Ctr. Mich., Univ. Club, Scarab Club (Detroit), Phi Kappa Phi, Phi Delta Kappa. Democrat. Episcopalian. Home: 2591 Woodstock Dr Detroit MI 48203-1062

CANTOR, ELEANOR WESCHLER, medical association executive; b. N.Y.C., Dec. 30, 1913; d. Samuel Peter and Anna (Rauchwerger) W.; m. Alfred Joseph Cantor, June 9, 1938; children—Pamela Corliss, Alfred Jay. B.A., Hunter Coll., N.Y.C., 1938. Producer radio quiz show CBS, N.Y.C., 1936-41; exec. officer Internat. Acad. Proctology, N.Y.C., 1948—, Internat. Bd. Proctology, 1950—; co-founder Acad. Psychosomatic Medicine, 1954.

CANTOR, JEROME OWEN, surgical pathologist, educator, researcher; b. N.Y.C., Nov. 14, 1949; s. Morris and Helen (Resnick) C.; m. Linda Ellen Gultz, May 10, 1980. BA, Columbia U., 1971; MD, U. Pa., 1975. Diplomate Am. Bd. Pathology, Nat. Bd. Med. Examiners. Fellow Roche Inst. Molecular Biology, Nutley, N.J., 1975; intern Presbyn. Hosp., N.Y.C., 1975-76, resident, 1976-80; asst. prof. Coll. Physicians and Surgeons Columbia U., N.Y.C., 1980-95; rsch. assoc. St. Luke's/Roosevelt Inst. for Health Scis., N.Y.C., 1987—; attending pathologist Arden Hill Hosp., Goshen, N.Y., 1990-95, Horton Meml. Hosp., Middletown, N.Y., 1990-95, St. Joseph's Med. Ctr., Paterson, N.J., 1992-95, The Bklyn. Hosp. Ctr., 1995—; cons. dept. pediatrics U. Medicine & Dentistry of N.J., Newark, 1987-91. Editor: Handbook of Animal Models of Pulmonary Diseases, 1989; contbr. numerous articles to profl. jours. Grantee Measey Found., 1973, NIH, 1976-78, 80-86, 90-93, Am. Lung Assn., 1978-80, 87-90, Stony Wold-Hebert Fund, 1982-84; recipient Bausch and Lomb Sci. award, 1967; fellow Armed Forces Inst. Pathology, Washington, 1980. Fellow Coll. Am. Pathologists. Office: St Lukes/Roosevelt Hosp Ctr Antenucci Bldg 1000 10th Ave New York NY 10019-1056

CANTOR, MORTON B., psychiatrist; b. St. Louis, June 21, 1924; s. William and Sarah (Goldberg) C.; m. Cecilia Lola Gersch; children: Jonathan, David. BA in Chemistry, U. N.C., Chapel Hill, 1943; MD, St. Louis U., 1947. Diplomate Am. Bd. Psychiatry and Neurology, Nat. Bd. Med. Examiners. Intern Morrissania City Hosp., Bronx, N.Y., 1947-48, resident in neurology, 1948-49; resident psychiatrist Bklyn. State Hosp., 1949-52; lectr., supr. Karen Horney Inst. and Clinic, N.Y.C., 1955-59; faculty, asst. dean Postgrad. Ctr. Mental Health, N.Y.C., 1959-69; faculty supr. Westchester Ctr. For Study of Psychoanalysis and Psychotherapy, White Plains, N.Y., 1973—; faculty, clin. assoc. prof. N.Y. Med. Coll., Valhalla, N.Y., 1975—; assoc. attending psychiatrist Westchester County Med. Ctr., Valhalla, 1972—. Contbr. articles to profl. jours.; co-editor: Affect: Psychoanalytic Theory and Practice, 1983, Psychoanalysis and Severe Emotional Illness, 1990. Capt. U.S. Army, 1952-54. Fellow Am. Psychiat. Assn. (life), Am. Acad. Psychoanalysis (treas. 1967-72, jour. editor 1978-92); mem. Assn. Advancement Psychoanalysis (pres. 1965-67). Home and Office: 4 Tory Ln Scarsdale NY 10583-2315

CANTOR, PAMELA CORLISS, psychologist; b. N.Y.C., Apr. 23, 1944; d. Alfred Joseph and Eleanor (Weschler) C.; m. Howard Feldman, Sept. 11, 1969; children: Lauren Jaye, Jeffrey Lee. BS cum laude, Syracuse U., 1965; postgrad. in medicine, Johns Hopkins U., 1969-70; MA, Columbia U., 1967, PhD, 1972; postgrad., Harvard U.-Children's Hosp. Med. Ctr., 1973-74. Instr. Radcliffe Inst., Harvard U., 1977-78; assoc. prof. psychology Boston U., 1970-80; pvt. practice clin. psychology, Needham, Mass., 1980—; faculty Med. Sch., Harvard U.; lectr. in field, also TV and radio appearances. Author: Understanding A Child's World- Reading in Infancy through Adolescence, 1977; cons. editor: Suicide and Life-Threatening Behavior; columnist: For Parents Only; contbr. chpts. to handbooks and numerous articles to profl. jours. Apptd. mem. Mass. Gov.'s Office for Children Statewide Adv. Bd., 1980—; adv. bd. Samaritans of Boston; pres. Nat. Com. Youth Suicide Prevention; mem. HHS Presdl. Task Force on Youth Suicide. Mem. Am. Psychol. Assn., Am. Assn. Suicidology (pres. 1985-86), Am. Orthopsychiat. Assn., Mass. Psychol. Assn., Am. Assn. Suicidology (bd. dirs.). Home: 11 Parkman Way Needham MA 02192-2863

CANTOR, RICHARD IRA, physician, corporate health executive; b. N.Y.C., Jan. 25, 1944; s. Jacob Alvin and Sarah (Sanderow) C.; m. Patricia Ann Honeycutt, June 7, 1970. AB, NYU, 1965; MD, Med. Coll. Va., 1970; postgrad., Bellevue Hosp. Ctr., N.Y.C., 1970-73. Diplomate Am. Bd. Internal Medicine. Intern Bellevue Hosp. Ctr., N.Y.C., 1970-71, resident, 1971-73; practice medicine specializing in internal medicine N.Y. Med. Group, N.Y.C., 1973-76; asst. med. dir. substance abuse programs Bellevue Hosp., 1973-76, med. dir. substance abuse programs, 1976-79; med. dir. Med Plan, N.Y.C., 1979-84; employee health unit Equitable Life Assurance Soc. U.S., N.Y.C., 1984-87; v.p., dir. health and med. svcs. Citibank, N.Y.C., 1988-89, v.p., dir. health, med. and staff svcs., 1989-91, v.p., corp. med. dir., 1991—; teaching asst. in medicine N.Y.U. Med. Ctr., N.Y.C., 1970-73, asst. prof. clin. medicine, 1983—; attending physician Cabrini Med. Ctr., N.Y.C., 1973-76, Bellevue Hosp. Ctr., 1973—; chmn. policy adv. bd. N.Y.C. Methadone Maintenance Treatment Programs, 1976-77; med. cons. Am. Fedn. State, County, and Mcpl. Employees, N.Y.C., 1979-84. Columnist Ask Your Med Plan Doctor, Pub. Employee Press, 1980-84. NIH trainee in endocrinology Med. Coll. Va., 1968. Mem. ACP, AMA, Am. Coll. Occupational and Environ. Medicine, N.Y. Occupational Med. Assn., Med. Execs., Med. Soc. County N.Y., Med. Soc. State N.Y., Nat. Corp. Med. Assocs., Phi Beta Kappa, Alpha Omega Alpha, Sigma Zeta. Office: Citibank 399 Park Ave New York NY 10043-9999

CANTOR, STEPHEN AMHERST, physician; b. Melbourne, Victoria, Australia, Sept. 25, 1940; came to U.S., 1969; s. Cecil Nathanic Love and Shirley Harper (Gamble) C.; m. Patricia Jane McLoughlin; children: Christopher, Nicholas. MB, BS, U. Melbourne, 1963. Diplomate Am. Bd. Internal Medicine. Intern, then resident Alfred Hosp., Melbourne, Australia, 1963-68; asst. clin. prof. medicine U. Calif., San Francisco, 1975-86, assoc. clin. prof. medicine, 1986-95. Fellow Royal Australasian Coll. Physicians, Am. Coll. Cardiology. Episcopalian. Office: 1000 Willow Creek Rd # D Prescott AZ 86301

CANTRELL, LINDA MAXINE, counselor; b. Ann Arbor, Mich., June 20, 1938; d. Donald LaVerne and Lila Maxine (Crull) Katz; m. Douglas D. Cantrell, Dec. 28, 1963; children: Douglas David Jr., Warren Vincent, Bryan LaVerne. BA, U. Mich., 1960, MA, 1963, postgrad., 1963-65. Cert. secondary tchr., Mich. Caseworker Cook County Dept. Pub. Aid, Chgo., 1960; psychometrist Evanston (Ill.) Schs., 1960-61; rsch. assoc. U. Mich., Ann Arbor, 1961-64; guidance counselor Radcliff Mid. Sch., Garden City, Mich., 1964-66; dir. guidance and counseling St. Mary Acad., Monroe, Mich., 1985-87; counselor, head counselor, instr. Ypsilanti (Mich.) Adult Edn., 1987—; tchr. young adult program Ypsilanti Pub. Schs., 1995—. Rep. precinct leader Ann Arbor, 1971; clk., marker, rec. sec. Thrift Shop of Ann Arbor, 1981—; bd. dirs. Ypsilanti Adult/Cmty. Edn. Adv. Com., 1990—; treas. Burns Park Sch., Ann Arbor, 1978-79; rec. sec. Chapel of Love Ch., 1989—; co-chmn. benefits Ann Arbor Chamber Orch., 1981-82; chmn. ann. benefit Rudolf Steiner Sch. Ann Arbor, 1984-85; treas. Burns Park PTO, 1978-79; vol. Greenhills Schs., 1978-81, St. Paul's Luth. Sch., 1972-73, among others. Recipient Gil Bursley award Rep. Party, 1972, scholarship Chi Omega, 1957. Mem. AAUW (fellowship chmn. 1971-73), Mich. Assn. for Counseling and Devel. (membership chmn. Monroe County chpt. 1986-87), Ypsilanti Fedn. Tchrs. (rec. sec. 1989-91), Mich. Assn. for Acad. Advisors Community Edn., Washtenaw Counselors Assn., Monroe County Counselors Assn. (membership chmn. 1985-87), Ann Arbor Women's City Club (membership com. 1985-87), Ea. Mich. U. Coll. Bus. Wives (program chmn. 1974, pres. 1975), Phi Kappa Phi, Pi Lambda Theta. Office: Ypsilanti Adult Edn Ypsilanti Pub Schs Perry Sch Ypsilanti MI 48197

CANTRELL, ROBERT WENDELL, otolaryngologist, head and neck surgeon, educator; b. Neosho, Mo., Apr. 25, 1933; s. Lloyd L. and Ruby R. Moffett; m. Young Hi Lee, Feb. 6, 1964; children: Mark L., Elizabeth L., Victoria L., Robert Wendell. Student, U.S. Naval Acad., 1952-55; A.B., George Washington U., 1956, M.D., 1960. Diplomate Am. Bd. Otolaryngology. Intern N.Y. Hosp-Cornell U., 1960-61; resident in otolaryngology Nat. Naval Med. Center, Bethesda, Md., 1965-69; chmn. dept. otolaryngology Naval Regional Med. Center, San Diego, 1969-76; Fitz-Hugh prof. dept. otolaryngology-head and neck surgery U. Va., 1976—; acting v.p., provost U. Va. Health Scis. Ctr., Charlottesville, 1995-96, v.p., profost, 1996—; bd. dirs. Am. Bd. Otolaryngology, 1980—, exec. v.p., 1990—. Editorial bd.: Laryngoscope, 1976-88, Annals of Otology, Rhinology and Laryngology, 1977-88, Am. Jour. of Otolaryngology, 1978-82, Archives of Otolaryngology, 1979-88; Contbr. numerous articles in field to profl. jours. Mayor, Oakmont, Md., 1968-69. Capt. USN, 1961-76, USNR, 1976-91. Am. Heart Assn. fellow, 1959; recipient Huron W. Lawson prize, 1960. Mem. AMA, Am. Acad. Otolaryngology-Head and Neck Surgery (pres. 1987), Am. Acad. Facial Plastic and Reconstructive Surgery (v.p. So. sect. 1980-83), Triological Soc. (v.p. So. sect. 1989-90, Mosher award 1974), Am. Soc. Head and Neck Surgery (pres. 1985-86), Soc. Univ. Otolaryngologists (pres. 1982), Am. Broncho-Esophagological Assn. (pres. 1988-89), Am. Laryngbol. Assn. (coun. 1988-90, treas. 1990-95, pres.-elect 1995), Am. Otol. Soc., Alpha Omega Alpha. Home: 1925 Owensville Rd Charlottesville VA 22901-8824 Office: U Va Health Sci Ctr Office of VP and Provost PO Box 179 Charlottesville VA 22908-9999

CANTRELL, WILLIAM ALLEN, psychiatrist, educator; b. Everton, Ark., Nov. 6, 1920; s. William E. and Vida (Vinson) C.; m. Joyce Laree Hobbs, Jan. 17, 1945; children: Mary Elizabeth, William Robert. B.S., McMurry, 1940; M.D., U. Tex., 1943. Rotating intern U.S. Naval Hosp., Corona, Calif., 1943-44; resident neuropsychiatry U. Tex. Med. Br. Hosps., 1947-49; asst. prof. neuropsychiatry U. Tex. Med. Br., 1949-54; practice medicine specializing in psychiatry Houston, 1951-63; prof. psychiatry Baylor Coll. Medicine, Houston, 1963-90, prof. emeritus, 1990—; chief psychiatry service Meth. Hosp., Houston, 1966-73. Mem. med. adv. com. Tex. Bd. Mental Health and Mental Retardation, 1965-73, chmn., 1965-69, 72-73; bd. dirs. Tex. Assn. Mental Health, 1965-72. Served to lt. M.C. USNR, 1944-47. Fellow Am. Psychiat. Assn. (br. pres. 1958-59), Am. Coll. Psychiatrists; mem. Tex. Med. Assn., Tex. Neuropsychiat. Assn. (v.p. 1958-59), Central Neuropsychiat. Assn. (v.p. 1974-75), Central Neuropsychiat. Assn. (pres. 1976-77), Tex. Psychiat. Soc. (pres. 1980-81), Houston Psychiat. Soc. (pres. 1956). Home: 5018 Loch Lomond Dr Houston TX 77096-2724

CANTWELL, DENNIS PATRICK, psychiatrist, educator; b. Mar. 28, 1939; m. Susan Cantwell. BA, Notre Dame U., 1961; MD, Washington U., 1965. Intern U. Calif., San Francisco, 1966; resident in psychiatry Washington U., 1967; fellow in child psychiatry UCLA, 1970-71; rsch. fellow in child psychiatry Maudsley Hosp., London, 1971-72; dir. residency tng. in child psychiatry UCLA, 1972—, prof. child psychiatry, 1978-79, Joseph-Campbell prof. child psychiatry, 1980—; rsch. child psychiatrist Gateways Hosp., L.A.; coord. profl. edn. U. Affiliated Facility; mem. Task Force to develop DSM III, DEMIII-R and DSMIV. Contbr. articles to profl. jours. Recipient J. Franklin Robinson award for rsch. in child psychiatry, Norbert Reiger award AACAP, Lewis award, Agnes Purcell McGavin award, APA, Rsch. Psychiatry award,Blanche Ittleson prize APA, Edward A. Strecker award, Rosenberry award, C. Charles Burlingame award Inst. of the Living. Mem. NIMH, Am. Acad. of Child and Adolescent Psychiatry (ann. meeting program chmn., tng. dir. com. chmn.), Am. Assn. on Mental Deficiency Classification of Mental Retardation. Office: UCLA Neuropsychiat Inst 760 Westwood Plz Rm C8 867 Los Angeles CA 90024-8300

CANUP, LARRY DALE, data systems specialist; b. Cairo, Ill., Apr. 28, 1955; s. Micah C. and Alberta (Crockett) C.; m. Cheryl Darlene Mace, July 23, 1973; 1 child, Larry Dale Jr. Cert. programmer, Automation Machine Tng. Ctr., Kansas City, Mo., 1973. Cert. Novell engr., advanced AIX adminstr. Computer operator Phoenix Hecht, Geneva, Ill., 1973-74; lead computer operator Cessna Fluid Power, Hutchinson, Kans., 1974-75; systems programmer Tymshare, Wichita, Kans., 1975-77, Vickers Petroleum, Wichita, Kans., 1977-79, Beech Aircraft, Wichita, Kans., 1979-82; mgr. computer tech. BHP Petroleum, Wichita, Kans., 1982-87; supr. online systems Cessna Aircraft, Wichita, Kans., 1987-88; systems support mgr. St. Joseph Med. Ctr., Wichita, Kans., 1988-89; network svcs. mgr. Health Care Data Systems, Wichita, Kans., 1989—. Therapeutic foster parent Caring Connection, Wichita, 1989-90. Recipient Cert. of Merit Ill. State Scholarship Commn., 1973-74. Mem. Data Processing Mgmt. Assn. (publicity dir. 1984-85). Republican. Baptist. Home: 406 Peach Tree Ln Haysville KS 67060-1028

CANZONIER, WALTER JUDE, shellfish aquaculturist; b. New Brunswick, N.J., Feb. 6, 1936; s. Joseph V. and Mary M. (Patterson) C. BS, St. Peter's Coll., Jersey City, 1957; postgrad., Rutgers U., 1957-64. Teaching asst. dept. zoology Rutgers U., New Brunswick, N.J., 1958-59, rsch. asst. dept. oyster culture, 1960-67, rsch. assoc., 1968-71, 81-87; rsch. fellow Inst. Marine Biology, CNR, Venice, Italy, 1971-77; dir. Coastal Resources Applied Rsch. Lab., Venice, 1977-80; dir. R & D, Aquarius Assocs., Port Noris, N.J., 1987—; mem. tech. coms. Italian Ministry Sanita and Ministry Merchant Marine, 1974-80, Interstate Shellfish Sanitation Conf., 1980—; cons. on marine sci. UNESCO, France, 1978—. Contbr. over 45 articles to sci. jours. in N.Am., Europe and Asia. Organizer, treas. Point Pleasant Beach (N.J.) Taxpayers Assn., 1963-70; bd. dirs. N.E. Regional Aquaculture Ctr., 1992-96. Recipient numerous grants from pub. agys. in N.Am. and Europe, 1971—. Mem. Nat. Shellfisheries Assn., Soc. Invertebrate Pathology, World Aquaculture Soc. N.J. Aquaculture Assn. (trustee 1989—, pres. 1991-96). Home: 44 Cowart Ave Manasquan NJ 08736-3102 Office: Aquarius Assocs PO Box 662 Port Norris NJ 08349-0662

CAPALDO, GUY, obstetrician, gynecologist; b. Bisaccia, Italy, Jan. 1, 1950; came to U.S., 1958; s. Arturo Nunziante and Maria Carmela (Ciani) C.; m. Kathy Nicita, Apr. 20, 1985. BSEE magna cum laude, U. Dayton, 1972; MS, Ohio State U., Columbus, 1973; MD, Med. Coll. Ohio, 1978. Diplomate Am. Bd. Ob-Gyn. Research asst. Ohio State U., 1973-75; resident in ob-gyn Med. Coll. Ohio, Toledo, 1978-82; practice medicine specializing in ob-gyn Mansfield, Ohio, 1982—; chief ob-gyn. dept. Mansfield Gen. Hosp., 1985—; lab. dir. Mansfield (Ohio) Ob-Gyn Assocs. Contbr. articles to profl. jours. Clinic physician Plan Parenthood, Mansfield, 1982—. Pres. scholar U. Dayton, 1968-72, Univ. fellow Ohio State U., 1972-75. Fellow Am. Coll. Ob-Gyn; mem. AMA, Ohio State Med. Assn., Richland County Med. Soc. Office: Mansfield Ob-Gyn Assocs 500 S Trimble Rd Mansfield OH 44906-3452

CAPELLI, JOHN PLACIDO, nephrologist; b. Hammonton, N.J., May 23, 1936; s. John L. and Marie C.; m. Patricia Ann Verna, Nov. 4, 1961; children: John L., Elizabeth Ann, David S. BS in Biology, Villanova U., 1958; MD, Jefferson Med. Coll., 1962. Diplomate: Am. Bd. Internal Medicine (Nephrology). Intern Michael Reese Hosp., Chgo., 1962-63; resident Thomas Jefferson U. Hosp., 1963-65, NIH fellow in nephrology, 1965-67, Martin E. Rehfuss chief resident internal medicine, 1967-68; practice medicine specializing in nephrology Haddonfield, N.J., 1968—; clin. prof. medicine U. Medicine and Dentistry N.J., 1995—; pres. Lourdes Med. Assn., P.A. and Health Mgmt. Svcs. Orgn., Inc., 1995—, Nephrology Network for N.J., P.C., 1995—; dir. div. clin. pharmacology Jefferson Med. Coll., Phila., 1968-69; dir. hemodialysis unit Our Lady of Lourdes Med. Ctr., Camden, N.J., 1969—, dir. div. nephrology and transplantation, 1974—, chief of staff, 1980-86, v.p. med. affairs, 1987—; clin. prof. medicine Thomas Jefferson U., Phila., 1974—; mem. chronic renal disease adv. com. N.J. Dept. Health, 1969-79, chmn., 1971-73, 74-75. Discovered extra-renal source of renin in uterus, 1968; contbr. articles to med. jours. Named to Order of Knights St. Gregory, 1995. Mem. Am. Soc. Nephrology, Internat. Soc. Nephrology, Renal Physicians Assn. (pres. 1977-79), AMA, Med. Soc. N.J., Am. Soc. Artificial Internal Organs, Southeastern Organ Procurement Found., Nat. Kidney Found. Roman Catholic. Office: 35 Kings Hwy E Haddonfield NJ 08033-2009

CAPEN, CHARLES CHABERT, veterinary pathology educator, researcher; b. Tacoma, Sept. 3, 1936; s. Charles Kenneth and Ruth (Chabert) C.; m. Sharron Lee Martin, June 27, 1968. DVM, Wash. State U., 1960; MS, Ohio State U., 1961, PhD, 1965. Diplomate Am. Coll. Vet. Pathologists (pres. 1978-79, coun. 1975-81). Instr. dept. vet. pathology Ohio State U., Columbus, 1962-65, asst. prof. dept. vet. pathology, 1965-67, assoc. prof., 1967-70, prof., 1970—, prof. endocrinology Coll. Medicine, 1972—, acting chmn. dept. vet. pathobiology, 1981-82, chmn., 1982-94, interim chmn. dept. bioscis., 1994—; Israel Doniach Meml. lectr. Brit. Endocrine Soc. meeting, Manchester, 1989; plenary lectr. Italian Soc. Endocrinology Congress, Pisa, 1995. Editor: (series) Animal Models of Human Disease, 1979—; mem. editorial bd. Lab. Investigation, 1988—, Vet. Pathology, 1986-87, Am. Jour. Pathology, 1984-88, Exptl. and Toxicologic Pathology, 1990—, Food and Chem. Toxicology, 1993—, Drug and Chem. Toxicology, 1994—, Toxicology and Ecotoxicology News, 1993—, Handbook on Rat Tumor Pathology WHO/IARC, 1991—. Mem. Opera Columbus, 1982—, Columbus Symphony Assn., 1972—. Recipient Disting. scholar award Ohio State U., 1993, Dean's Tchg. Excellence award for grad. edn. Coll. Vet. Medicine, 1993. Mem. Inst. Medicine/NAS, AVMA (nat. Borden rsch. award 1975, small animal rsch. award 1984, Gaines rsch. award 1987, excellence in canine rsch. award 1995), U.S. Can. Acad. Pathology (coun. 1989-92), Soc. Toxicol. Pathologists (pres.-elect 1996-97). Office: Ohio State U Dept Vet Bioscis 1925 Coffey Rd Columbus OH 43210-1005

CAPISTRANT, TERRANCE DONALD, neurologist, consultant; b. St. Paul, Apr. 22, 1938; s. Roy Joseph and Anna Margaret (Solheid) C.; m. Jacqueline Jane Girard, Dec. 31, 1960; children: Timothy Girard, Theodore Mark, Todd Andrew. BA magna cum laude, BS, U. Minn., 1960, MD, 1963. Diplomate Am. Bd. Psychiatry and Neurology. Intern U. Oreg., Portland, 1963-64; resident, fellow in neurology U. Minn., Mpls., 1964-67, assoc. prof., 1969-70, clin. prof., 1996—; pvt. practice, St. Paul, 1970—; assoc. prof. Georgetown U., Washington, 1967-69; chief of staff Health East-Divine Redeemer Hosp., 1989-90. Contbr. articles to med. jours. Lt. comdr. USPHS, 1967-69. Fellow Am. Acad. Neurology; mem. Am. Assn. for Prevention Headache, Am. EEG Soc., Am. Heart Assn. (councilor stroke coun.), Minn. Neurol. Soc. (pres. 1978), Alpha Omega Alpha. Office: Neurol Assocs St Paul 280 N Smith Ave Saint Paul MN 55102

CAPITOSTI, SHEILA G., nursing administrator; b. Latrobe, Pa., Aug. 28, 1950; d. George and Dorothy (Miller) Sracic; m. Gary John Capitosti, Aug. 19, 1972; children: Gregory John, Scott Michael. Diploma RN, Latrobe Area Hosp., 1972; BSPA in Health Care Adminstrn., St. Joseph's Coll., North Windham, Maine, 1988, postgrad. Cert. gerontol. nurse ANA, pub. sch. nurse, Pa. Cons., instr. Coord. Coun. Long-Term Care Pa. State U., 1989-91; dir. staff devel., asst. adminstr. St. Andrew's Village, Indiana, Pa., 1992-88, dir. nursing svc., 1988-95; dir. clin. svcs. Presbyn. Homes, Inc., Camp Hill, Pa., 1995—; adminstr. Independence Ct. of Mount Lebanon, Pitts. Author: Nursing Assistant Orientation: Care of the Older Adult. Mem. Pa. Assn. Nonprofit Homes for Aging (reimbursement com.), Pres.' Club Presbyn. Homes Inc.

CAPIZZI, ROBERT LAWRENCE, physician; b. Phila., Nov. 20, 1938; s. Nunzio B. and Nancy (Gatto) C.; m. Barbara Ann Kain, July 10, 1965; children: Robert, Marc, Tara Ann, Mary Catherine. B.S., Temple U., Phila, 1960; M.D., Hahnemann Med. Coll., Phila., 1964. Asst. prof. medicine and pharmacology Yale U., New Haven, 1972-75, assoc. prof. medicine and pharmacology, 1975-77, acting chief sect. med. oncology, 1976-77; chief div. med. oncology U. N.C., Chapel Hill, 1977-79, co-dir. div. hematology and oncology, 1980-82; dir. Comprehensive Cancer Ctr., sect. head hematology and oncology Bowman Gray Sch. Medicine, Wake Forest U., Winston-Salem, N.C., 1982-91; exec. v.p. worldwide R&D U.S. Bioscience, West Conshohocken, Pa., 1991-96; Magee prof., chmn. dept. medicine Jefferson Med. Coll., Phila., 1996—; Mem. study sect. Cancer Clin. Investigation Rev. Com., NIH, 1982-85. Served to maj. U.S. Army, 1969-72. Investigator, Howard Hughes Med. Inst., Yale U., 1976-77; recipient Faculty Devel. award Pharm. Mfrs. Assn., Yale U., 1974-76. Mem. Am. Soc. Clin. Oncology (program com. 1983, membership com. 1983), Am. Fedn. Clin. Research (program com. 1983), Piedmont Oncology Assn. (bd. dirs. 1982-91, chmn. 1985-91), Am. Soc. Clin. Investigation. Roman Catholic. Office: Dept Medicine Rm 821 Jefferson Med Coll Philadelphia PA 19107

CAPLAN, LESTER, optometrist, educator; b. Balt., Mar. 27, 1924; s. Hyman and Jeannette (Frank) C.; m. Florence Shenker, Sept. 8, 1946 (dec. Jan. 1979); children: Bruce E., Eric Scott; m. Arlene Cohen, Jan. 10, 1981; children: Harriet Wilder (dec. Mar. 1994), Lori Hollander. Student, Wheaton Coll., 1943-44, U. Md., 1946-47; BS in Visual Optics, No. Ill. Coll. of Optometry, 1949, OD summa cum laude, 1949; MEd, Loyola Coll., Balt., 1967. Pvt. practice optometry, Balt., 1950-79; chief contact lens clinic Optometric Ctr. Md., 1975-76; vision cons. Prince George's County (Md.) public schs., 1968-70; optometric cons. and clinician Sinai-Druid Comprehensive Child Care Clinic, 1967-68; cons. and instr. optometric technician's program, Howard Community Coll., 1976-79; cons. to Indian Health Service, USPHS, 1969-85, FDA, 1985-90; adv. to dir. profl. service Fed. Health Programs Services, 1972-76; prof. Sch. of Optometry, U. Ala., Birmingham, 1979—, asst. dean for clin. services, 1987-93, dir. externship program, 1991—, chief div. contact lens services, 1982-86, assoc. prof. Sch. of Community and Allied Health, 1979-81, dir. optometric technician program, 1979-81, assoc. prof. dept. psychology Grad. Sch., 1985-88; guest lectr. various colls. and univs., 1970-79; mem. adv. council Md. Comprehensive Health Planning Agy., 1971-77; alt. mem. adv. group to Md. Statewide Profl. Standards Rev. Council, 1978-79; mem. Md. Bd. Examiners in Optometry, 1975-79. Contbr. author: Public Health and Community Optometry; contbr. articles to profl. jours. Pres. Beth Israel Congregation, Randallstown, Md., 1966-67; prof. adv. com. Optometric Ctr. Md., 1973-75, v.p., 1975. Served with Signal Corps, U.S. Army, World War II, PTO. Disting. Practitioner in Optometry, Nat. Acads. Practice. Fellow Am. Acad. Optometry; mem. Md. Optometric Assn. (hon., Optometrist of Yr. award 1974), Am. Optometric Assn. (Optometrist of Yr. 1975), Ala. Optometric Assn., Am. Pub. Health Assn. (gov. council 1981-88, vision care sect. chair 1993-94, intersectional coun. chair 1995-96), Assn. Clin. Dirs.-Adminstrs. Schs. and Colls. Optometry (pres. 1990-93), Assn. Schs. and Colls. Optometry (spl. cons., clin. affairs com. 1995—), Assn. Optometric Contact Lens Educators (treas. 1984-96), Optometric Hist. Soc. Home: 3708 Vicksburg Dr Birmingham AL 35213-1759 Office: U Ala at Birmingham Sch Optometry Birmingham AL 35294

CAPLAN, LOUIS ROBERT, neurology educator; b. Balt., Dec. 31, 1936; s. Carl Clarence and Bess Pauline (Cohen) C.; m. F. Brenda Fields, Nov. 28, 1963; children: Laura, Daniel, Jonathan, David, Jeremy, Benjamin. BA cum laude, Williams Coll., 1958; MD summa cum laude, U. Md., 1962. Diplomate Am. Bd. Internal Medicine, Am. Bd. Psychiatry and Neurology. Intern to jr. asst. resident Boston City Hosp., 1962-64; resident Harvard Neurol. Unit, Boston, 1966-69; cerebrovascular fellow Mass. Gen. Hosp., Boston, 1969-70; neurologist Beth Israel Hosp., Boston, 1970-78; asst. prof. Harvard Med. Sch., Boston, 1970-78; chief neurologist Michael Reese Hosp., Chgo., 1978-84; prof. neurology U. Chgo., 1980-84; chief neurologist New England Med. Ctr., Boston, 1984—; prof., chmn. dept. neurology Tufts U., Boston, 1984—, prof. medicine, 1989—. Author: Stroke: A Clinical Approach, 1986, 2d edit., 1993, Consultations in Neurology, 1987, The Effective Clinical Neurologist, 1990, Vertebrobasilar Arterial Disease, 1991, (with others) Cerebral Small Artery Disease, 1993, Management of Persons with

Stroke, 1993, Brainstem Localization and Function, 1993, Intercerebral Hemmorhage, 1994, Family Guide to Stroke, 1994, Brain Ischemia—Basic Concepts and Clinical Relevance, 1995, Stroke Syndromes, 1995, Posterior Circulation Disease, 1996; Neurologic Disorders: Course and Treatment, 1996; contbr. more than 350 articles to profl. jours. Bd. dirs. Solomon Schecter Day Sch., Boston, 1977-78, Chgo., 1983-85. Capt. U.S. Army, 1962-64. Recipient House Officer Teaching prize Michael Reese Hosp., 1980. Fellow Am. Acad. Neurology, Am. Neurol. Assn., Stroke Coun. Am. Heart Assn. (chmn. 1987-89, sci. adv. com. 1990—), Royal Soc. of Medicine; mem. Coun. Med. Specialties Socs. (rep. 1982-90), Chgo. Neurol. Soc. (chmn. 1984-85), Boston Soc. Neurology and Psychiatry (pres. 1988-89), Chgo. Heart Assn. (chmn. stroke com. 1979-84), Australian Neurol. Soc. (hon.), German Neurol. Assn. (hon.), Phi Beta Kappa, Alpha Omega Alpha. Democrat. Jewish. Office: New England Med Ctr Dept Neurology 750 Washington St Boston MA 02111-1533

CAPLINGER, PATRICIA E., family nurse practitioner; b. St. Louis, Oct. 6, 1956; d. Julius G. and Wanda L. (Guthrie) Kissel; child from previous marriage, Jeremy Michael Frederiksen; m. Ray E. Caplinger, Dec. 26, 1995. ADN, St. Louis C.C., 1977; BSN, U. State N.Y., 1982; FNP, U. Colo., Denver, 1985. RN, Colo.; CNOR, CNRN; cert. family nurse practitioner. Med. case mgmt. supr. Intracorp., Denver; clin. mgr. Rehab. Svcs. Corp., Eureka, Calif.; family nurse practitioner Burre Clinic, Eureka; pvt. practice Eureka; dir. PM&R Marian Health Ctr., Sioux City, Iowa; family nurse practitioner Lebanon (Mo.) Med. Ctr. Mem. ANA (nursing scholar), ARN, AANP. Home: 23241 Red Oak Dr Lebanon MO 65536

CAPLOVITZ, COLEMAN DAVID, retired physician; b. Liberty, Tex., Jan. 18, 1925; s. Harry and Rose Lillian (Friedenberg) C.; m. Marilyn Joy Grossberg, Aug. 12, 1950; children: Lori Rose Caplovitz Bohm, Karen Sue Caplovitz Barrett. BA, U. Tex., 1944; MD, U. Tex. Med. Br., Galveston, 1947. Diplomate Am. Bd. Internal Medicine. Intern St. Louis City Hosp., 1947-48, asst. resident medicine, 1948-49; resident medicine Jefferson Davis Hosp., Houston, 1949-51; clin. instr. medicine Baylor Coll. Medicine, Houston, 1953-54, clin. asst. prof. to clin. assoc. prof. medicine, 1954-73; clin. prof. medicine, 1973-94; sr. attending in medicine, Meth. Hosp., 1973-94, chief gen. med. sect., 1973-94. Capt. USAF, 1951-53, Japan. Recipient Kass Fellowship, 1947. Fellow ACP; mem. AM. Coll. Cardiology (assoc.), Am. Soc. Internal Medicine, Am. Heart Assn., Houston Soc. Internal Medicine (pres. 1992), Willow Fork Country Club, Alpha Epsilon Delta, Alpha Omega Alpha, Phi Eta Sigma. Jewish.

CAPODICE, JACK, JR., oral and maxillofacial surgeon; b. Blommington, Ill.; s. Jack and Betty Jean (Crews) C.; m. Joan Marie Beduette, Mar. 8, 1986; children: Sarah Elizabeth, Jack III, Michael Mariano. BS, Western Ill. U., 1981; DMD, Washington U., 1986; MD, U. Mo., Kansas City, 1990. Diplomate Am. Bd. Oral and Maxillofacial Surgery. Resident Truman Med. Ctr., Kansas City, 1986-91; pvt. practice Bloomington, Ill., 1992—. Author: (with others) National Medical Series Emergency Medicine, 1993. Fellow Am. Assn. Oral and Maxillofacial Surgeons, Am. Coll. Oral and Maxillofacial Surgeons, Am. Acad. Cosmetic Surgery; mem. ADA. Roman Catholic. Home: 1917 Haverhill Park Normal IL 61761 Office: Doran & Capodice 2103 E Washington St Bloomington IL 61701

CAPONE, ANTONIO, psychiatrist; b. Afragola, Naples, Italy, Feb. 18, 1926; came to U.S., 1954; s. Giulio and Giovanna (Fico) C.; m. Maria Morello, Mar. 21, 1957; children: Antonio Jr., John, Walter. MD, U. Naples, 1953. Diplomate Am. Bd. Med. Psychotherapists, Am. Bd. Psychiatry and Neurology, Internat. Acad. Behavioral Medicine, Am. Bd. Forensic Examiners. Intern Ospedale Incurabili, Naples, 1953-54, St. Francis Hosp., Jersey City, 1954-55; resident physician St. Clare's Hosp., Denville, N.J., 1955-56; hon. staff Butler Hosp., Providence, 1995—; chief psychiatry John E. Fogarty Meml. Hosp., North Smithfield, R.I., 1969-79, Pawtucket (R.I.) Meml. Hosp., 1971-80, St. Joseph Hosp., Providence, 1971-94; clin. asst. prof. psychiatry and human behavior Brown U. Med. Sch., Providence, 1980-95; med. dir. St. Joseph Ctr. for Psychiat. Svcs., Providence, 1987-94; hon. staff St. Joseph Hosp., Providence, 1995—, Pawtucket Meml. Hosp., 1995—; cons. John E. Fogarty Meml. Hosp., North Smithfield, 1995—; chief psychiat. cons. R.I. Divsn. Vocat. Rehab., Providence, 1967-72; med. advisor Dept. HEW, 1967-95; clin. elective course leader Brown Med. Sch., Providence, 1980-95. Contbr. articles to profl. jours. Various presentations on mental health and alcoholism, Lions Club, Kiwanis, TV, and radio. Fellow Am. Psychiat. Assn. (pres. R.I. dist. br. 1968-70, mem. peer rev. com. 1982-95, mem. fellowship com. 1984-95, mem. ad hoc on referral svc. 1987-88); mem. AMA, R.I. Med. Soc., Providence Med. Assn., Psychiatry and Neurology, Pan Am. Med. Assn., Am. Soc. Vienna. Roman Catholic. Office: PO Box 8988 Atlanta GA 30306-8988

CAPONE, RAYMOND A., JR., plastic surgeon; b. Pitts., Oct. 27, 1951; s. Raymond A. and Vivian I. (End) C.; m. Martha Randolph Clarice, May 7, 1977; children: Raymond, Avery. Home: 5727 Centre Ave Pittsburgh PA 15206-3707

CAPONETTI, JAMES DANTE, botany educator; b. Boston, Mar. 15, 1932; s. Michael Angelo and Maria Lucia (Cammarata) C.; m. Marilyn Joan Messieri, June 18, 1966; children: Ann Marie, James Michael. BS in Pharmacy, Mass. Coll. Pharmacy, 1954, MS in Pharmacy, 1956; AM in Biology, Harvard U., 1959, PhD in Biology, 1962. Registered pharmacist, Mass., Tenn. Grad. teaching asst. Mass. Coll. Pharmacy, Boston, 1954-56, Harvard U., Cambridge, Mass., 1956-61; asst. prof. U. Tenn., Knoxville, 1961-71, assoc. prof., 1971-84, prof. botany, 1984—, assoc. dept. head, 1986-92; exec. asst. to dept. head, 1992—. Grantee Knoxville Utilities Bd., 1988, Tenn. Wildlife Resources Agy., Nashville, 1990-91. Fellow AAAS, Tenn. Acad. Sci. (sec. 1966-77, pres. 1979, disting. svc. award 1989); mem. Am. Fern Soc. (treas. 1976—), KC. Roman Catholic. Office: U Tenn Dept Botany Knoxville TN 37996-1100

CAPP, MICHAEL PAUL, physician, educator; b. Yonkers, N.Y., July 1, 1930; s. Michael and Mary (Bybel) C.; children: Marianne, Michael, Steven, John; m. Constance Whitehead, Jan. 4, 1989. B.S., Roanoke Coll., Salem, Va., 1952; M.D., U. N.C., 1958. Diplomate: Am. Bd. Radiology (treas. 1982-85, v.p. 1985, pres. 1987-89, now exec. dir.). Lab. instr. physics Roanoke Coll., 1952; teaching asst. Grad. Sch. Physics, Duke, 1952-54; intern in pediatrics Duke Med. Center, 1958-59, resident in radiology, 1959-62, assoc. in radiology, 1962, asst. prof., 1963-66, assoc. prof., 1966-70, dir. diagnostic div., dept. radiology, 1967-70, asst. prof. pediatrics, 1968-70, radiologist in charge pediatric cardiology, 1962-70; dir. Duke Med. Center (Pediatric Radiology Program), 1965-70, Duke Med. Center (Med. Students Teaching Program Diagnostic Radiology), 1965-66; prof., chmn. dept. radiology U. Ariz. Coll. Medicine, Tucson, 1970-93; chief of staff Ariz. Med. Center, Univ. Hosp., 1971-73; mem. NRC com. on Radiology, James Picker Found., 1972; exec. dir. Am. Bd. Radiology, 1993—. Contbr. articles to profl. jours. Mem. AMA, Am. Coll. Radiology, Am. Roentgen Ray Soc. (pres. 1990), Am. Assn. U. Radiologists (exec. com. 1970, Gold medal 1988), Am. Heart Assn. (pres. coun. on cardiovascular radiology 1976-78), Am. Bd. Radiology (exec. dir. 1993—), Radiol. Soc. N. Am. (chmn. sci. exhibits com. 1976-79), N.Am. Soc. Cardiac Radiologists (pres. 1975), Nat. Acad. Scis., N. Y. Acad. Scis., Pima County Med. Soc., Ea. Radiol. Soc. (sci. program chmn. 1967, v.p. 1973—), Soc. for Pediatric Radiology, Soc. for Chmn. Acad. Radiology Depts. (pres. 1977), Inst. Medicine, Sigma Pi Sigma. Home: 5200 N Valley View Rd Tucson AZ 85718-6123 Office: 5255 E Williams Circle Ste 6800 Tucson AZ 85711

CAPPA, JOHN, podiatrist; b. White Plains, N.Y., Dec. 24, 1958; s. Carmine and Concetta (Alianiello) C.; m. Concetta L. Buccheri, June 3, 1984; children: Carmine, Nicholas. AS in Prepharmacy, Westchester C.C., Valhalla, N.Y., 1978; BS in Pharmacy, St. John's U., Jamaica, N.Y., 1981; DPM, N.Y. Coll. Podiatric Medicine, 1987. Diplomate Am. Bd. Podiatric Surgery. Resident N.Y. Coll. Podiatric Medicine, Affiliate Hosps. and Instns., 1987-88; asst. dir. pharmacy Burke Rehab. Ctr., White Plains, 1981-83; pvt. practice Valhalla, 1988—; chief podiatry Phelps Meml. Hosp. Tarrytown, N.Y., 1995—; cons. podiatrist N.Y. Hosp./Cornell Med. Ctr., White Plains, 1989—; adv. bd. Metrohealth Ins. Co., 1995—. Fellow Am. Coll. Foot Surgeons; mem. Am. Podiatric Med. Assn., Pi Delta. Office: 4 Broadway #103 Valhalla NY 10595

CAPPELLI, GIORGIO, nephrologist; b. Pavia. Italy, July 30, 1941; s. Egidio and Elena (Saglio) C.; m. Raffaella Giacchino, May 13, 1972; 1 child, Barbara. Degree in medicine, U. Genoa, Italy, 1967, postgrad., 1969-78. Intern Patologia Medica, Genoa, 1968-71; asst. divsn. internal medicine St. Martin Hosp., Genoa, 1971-75, asst. divsn. nephrology, 1975-89; asst. nephrology and dialysis unit Villa Scassi Hosp., Genoa, 1989-92, chief nephrology and dialysis unit, 1992—; dir. course on nephrology and dialysis for nurses, 1989-90. Mem. Am. Soc. Nephrology. European Dialysis Transplantation Assn., Italian Soc. Nephrology. Home: V Montallegro 13, 16145 Genoa Italy Office: Villa Scassi Hosp, C Scassi 1, 16149 Genoa Italy

CAPPER, PETER THOMAS, clinical social worker; b. St. Asaph, Clwyd, Wales, Dec. 29, 1948; came to U.S., 1976; s. Charles Frederick and Martha Turner (Ferguson) C.; m. Ann Beaupain Maebius, Mar. 8, 1980. MA with honors, Cambridge (Eng.) U., 1971; MSW, Sussex U., 1974. Lic. clin. social worker, Pa., Del., ACSW, A.A.M.F.T. Clin. social worker Children's Aid Soc. Pa., Phila., 1976-78; post masters trainee Phila. Child Guidance Clinic, Phila., 1978-79; sr. psychiat. social worker Woodberry Down Child Guidance Unit, London, 1980-81; sr. clinician, faculty mem. family therapy tng. ctr. Phila. Child Guidance Clinic, 1982-89; pvt. practice Plymouth Meeting, Pa., Wilmington, Del., 1989—; clin. cons. The Crefeld Sch., Phila., 1995—; social worker London Borough Lewisham Social Svcs. Dept., London, 1972-76. Mem. Am. Assn. Marriage and Family Therapists (clin.). Home: 7612 Mountain Ave Elkins Park PA 19027 Office: Schreiber and Assocs 4 E Germantown Pike Plymouth Meeting PA 19462-1533

CAPPO, REBECCA ANN, nursing educator; b. Braddock, Pa., Aug. 3, 1957; d. Emil and Ilan (Kossuth) Lavcek; m. Brian A. Cappo, May 8, 1982; children: Sarah Elizabeth, Phillip Michael. BSN, Indiana U. of Pa., 1979, MSN, 1987. RN, Pa. Staff nurse Allegheny Valley Hosp., Natrona Heights, Pa., 1979-81; instr. Lenape Sch. Practical Nursing, Ford City, Pa., 1981-89, asst. coord., 1989-90, coord., 1990—. Mem. Nat. League Nursing (coun. practical nursing), Pa. Nurses Assn., Pa. Assn. Practical Nursing Coords., Pa. Assn. Adult and Continuing Edn., Armstrong County Nurses Assn. Office: Lenape Sch Practical Nursing 2215 Chaplin Ave Ford City PA 16226-1608

CAPRANICO, GIOVANNI, molecular biologist; b. Popoli, Pescara, Italy, Mar. 15, 1959; s. Carmine Capranico and Elsa Ricci. PhD in Biochemistry, U. Perugia (Italy), 1982. Rsch. fellow Istituto Nazionale Tumori, Milan, 1983-86, assoc. researcher, 1986-88, sr. investigator, 1990—; guest researcher Nat. Cancer Inst., NIH, Bethesda, Md., 1988-90. Recipient Rsch. Tng. award Nat. Cancer Inst.-EORTC, 1988. Home: 9 Digione, 20144 Milan Italy Office: Istituto Nazionale Tumori, 1 Venezian, 20133 Milan Italy

CAPRIOLI, JOSEPH, ophthalmologist; b. Deer Park, N.Y., May 15, 1954; m. Tracey Caprioli, June 1993; 1 child, Isabella; children from previous marriage: Peter, Joseph, Jessica, Marie. BS, SUNY, Stony Brook, 1975; MD, SUNY, Buffalo, 1979; MA Privatum, Yale U., 1993. Diplomate Nat. Bd. Med. Examiners, Am. Bd. Ophthalmology; lic. physician, N.Y., Pa., Conn. Dir. Glaucoma Sect., 1984—; intern gen. surgery Yale U. Sch. Medicine, New Haven, 1979-80, resident ophthalmology, 1984-88, asst. prof. ophthalmology, dir. Glaucoma Svc., 1984—, assoc. prof. ophthalmology, 1988-93, prof. ophthalmology, 1993—; fellow glaucoma Wills Eye Hosp., Phila., 1983-84; acting chmn. Yale U. Sch. Medicine, New Haven, 1993-95; lectr. Ill. Soc. for Preservation of Blindness, 1992; mem. basic sci. and clin. glaucoma panels, planning subcom. Nat. Adv. Eye Coun., NIH, 1990, mem. visual scis. A study sect. NIH/Nat. Eye Inst., 1992-94, chmn., 1994—; mem. steering com. Advanced Glaucoma Intervention Study, NIH, 1988-91; lectr. various orgns. and symposiums. Book rev. editor Ophthalmic Surgery, 1984-89; mem. editl. bd. Ophthalmic Surgery, 1989—, Am. Jour Ophthalmology, 1991—, Investigative Ophthalmology and Visual Sci., 1992—, Jour. Glaucoma, 1991-94; editor: Ophthalmology Clinics of North America: Contemporary Issues in Glaucoma, 1991; contbr. articles to profl. jours., chpts. to books. Recipient award Alcon Rsch. Inst., 1992, Jules Francois prize, 1989; grantee Hoechst-Roussel Pharms., Inc., 1985-86, NIH/Nat. Eye Inst., 1987-89, 93—, New Haven Found., 1988-89, Merck Sharp & Dohme, 1989-90, 92-93, Alcon Pharms., 1989-90, Robert Leet and Clara Guthrie Patterson Trust, 1989-92, Alcon Rsch. Inst., 1992. Fellow ACS, Am. Acad. Ophthalmology (mem. quality of care com. glaucoma panel 1988—, chmn. 1991—); mem. Am. Ophthalmological Soc., Assn. for Rsch. in Vision and Ophthalmology, Internat. Soc. Eye Rsch., Am. Glaucoma Soc., Soc. Neurosci., Glaucoma Soc. of Internat. Gongress Ophahtlmology, New Eng. Ophthalmol. Soc. Office: Yale U Dept Ophthalmology and Visual Scis 330 Cedar St PO Box 208061 New Haven CT 06520-8061

CAPRIOLO, JOHN ANTHONY, dentist; b. N.Y.C., May 29, 1957; s. Sam Martin and Blanche Ann (Hopewood) C.; m. Angela Sue Grabiel, May 2, 1987; children: John Anthony II, Nicholas David, Christian Mark, Benjamin Samuel. BA in Psychology, U. Md., Balt., 1979, DDS, 1984. Resident VA, Martinsburg, W.Va., 1984-85; mem. staff, quality assurance coordinator, dir. dental student program VA, Martinsburg, 1986-90; gen. practice dentistry Balt., 1985; mem. staff Stockley Ctr. State of Del., Georgetown, 1985-86; asst. clin. prof. U. W.Va., Morgantown, 1986-90; pvt. practice gen. dentistry Glen Burnie, Md., 1990-92; regional dental dir. Balt. region/State of Md. Dept. Corrections, 1993—; staff dentist Dept. V.A., Columbus, Ohio, 1993—; mem. adv. bd. U. Md. Dental Sch., 1983-84. Campaigner Paul Capriolo for Md. Ho. of Dels., 1986; dir. youth ministry, mem. coun. Holy Family Cath. Ch., Randallstown, Md., 1979-84; lector St. Joseph's Cath. Ch., Martinsburg, 1986-90, coord. home svc. team min., 1989-90; pres. Pikeview West Homeowners Assn., 1989-90, Falcon Ridge Homeowners Assn., 1990-91, Summitview Woods Homeowner's Assn., 1993—, blockwatch capt. 1996—; coach Dublin Youth Athletics, 1996, soccer coach, 1995-96. Lt. USPHS, 1992-93. Mem. ADA, Acad. Gen. Dentistry, Moose. Democrat. Home: 8826 Worrell Ct Powell OH 43065-8690

CAPRON, ALEXANDER MORGAN, lawyer, educator; b. Hartford, Conn., Aug. 16, 1944; s. William Mosher and Margaret (Morgan) C.; m. Barbara A. Brown, Nov. 9, 1969 (div. Dec. 1985); m. Kathleen West, Mar. 4, 1989; children: Jared Capron-Brown, Charles Spencer West Capron, Christopher Gordon West Capron, Andrew Morgan West Capron. BA, Swarthmore Coll., 1966; LLB, Yale U., 1969; MA (hon.), U. Pa., 1975. Bar: D.C. 1970, Pa. 1978. Law clk. to presiding judge U.S. Ct. Appeals, Washington, 1969-70; lectr., research assoc. Yale U., 1970-72; asst. prof. law U. Pa., 1972-75, vice dean, 1976, assoc. prof., 1975-78, prof. law and human genetics, 1978-82; exec. dir. Pres.'s Commn. for Study of Ethical Problems in Med. and Biomed. and Behavioral Rsch., Washington, 1980-83; prof. law, ethics and pub. policy Law Ctr. Georgetown U., Washington, 1983-84, inst. fellow Kennedy Inst. Ethics, 1983-84; Topping prof. law, medicine and pub. policy U. So. Calif., L.A., 1985-89, Univ. prof. law and medicine, 1989—, Henry W. Bruce prof. law, 1991—; co-dir. Pacific Ctr. for Health Policy and Ethics, L.A., 1990—; mem. bd. advisors Am. Bd. Internal Medicine, 1985-95, chmn., 1991-95; cons. NIH, mem. recombinant DNA com., 1990-95, mem. subcom. on human gene therapy, 1984-92; chmn. Congl. Biomed. Ethics Adv. Commn., 1987-91; mem. Joint Commn. on Accreditation of Healthcare Orgns., 1994—, mem. ethics adv. com., 1984-85. Author: (with Katz) Catastrophic Diseases: Who Decides What?, 1976, (with others) Genetic Counseling: Facts, Values and Norms, 1979, Law, Science and Medicine, 1984, supplements, 1987, 89, (with others) Treatise on Health Care Law, 1991; contbr. articles to profl. jours. Bd. mgrs. Swarthmore Coll., 1982-85; bd. trustees Twentieth Century Fund. Fellow AAAS, Am. Coll. Legal Medicine (hon.), Hastings Ctr. (Inst. Society, Ethics and Life Scis., bd. dirs.); mem. Inst. Medicine NAS (bd. dirs. 1985-90), AAUP (exec. com. Pa. chpt.), Am. Soc. Law and Medicine (pres. 1988-89), Swarthmore Coll. Alumni Soc. (v.p. 1974-77). Office: U So Calif Law Ctr Univ Park Los Angeles CA 90089-0071

CAPUTI, MARIE ANTOINETTE, university official; b. Newport, R.I., Aug. 14, 1935; d. Saverio and Madeline (Esposito) C. AB, Barnard Coll., 1957; MS in Social Work, Columbia U., 1959; PhD, St. Louis U., 1978. Lic. social worker, Fla. Field instr. Columbia U. N.Y.C., 1962-64; social worker ob.-gyn. dept. Bronx (N.Y.) Mcpl. Hosp., 1964-65; generic supr. Maimonides Med. Ctr., Bklyn., 1965-75; asst. prof. Grad. Sch. of Social Work U. Wis., Madison, 1978-83; instr. dept. continuing edn. Edgewood Coll., Madison, Wis., 1982-85; asst. prof., dir. faculty svcs. region II Cardinal Stritch Coll., Milw., 1984-89; ptnr. Midwest Ctr. for Human Svcs., Madison, 1982-89; assoc. prof., dir. grad. and continuing edn. St. Thomas U., Miami, Fla., 1989-92, coord. Earth Literacy Programs, 1993-94; asst. to v.p. for acad. affairs Lynn U., Boca Raton, Fla., 1993, dir. Instnl. Rsch., Instnl. Effectiveness, 1994—; faculty mentor Walden U., 1993—; researcher, specialist U. Wis. Survey Rsch. Lab., Madison, 1982-84; rsch. cons. North Chicago VA Med. Ctr., 1984-89; cons. U. Wis. Hosp. & Clinics, Madison, 1987; adj. asst. prof. NYU Grad. Sch. Social Work, N.Y.C., 1967-69. Contbr. articles to profl. jours. Lavanburg Cornerhouse scholar, 1957-59; VA fellow, 1975-78. Mem. NASW, AAUW, Assn. of Institutional Rsch. Democrat. Home: 7120 SW 41st Pl Davie FL 33314-3182 Office: Lynn U 3601 N Military Trl Boca Raton FL 33431-5507

CAPUTO, DANIEL VINCENT, psychologist; b. N.Y.C.; s. Pasquale and Hortense C.; A.B., Bklyn. Coll., 1954; Ph.D., U. Ill., 1961. Prof. med. psychology Washington U., St. Louis, 1959-64; prof. psychology Queens Coll., CUNY, Flushing, 1964—, chair dept. psychology, 1974-77; research assoc. St. Vincent's Med. Center, S.I., N.Y.; pvt. practice clin. psychology, 1973—. Registered psychologist, Nat. Register of Health Providers in Psychology; cert. psychologist, N.Y.; research grantee NIMH, 1963. Fellow N.Y. Acad. of Sci.; mem. N.Y. Acad. Scis., Am. Psychol. Assn., Eastern Psychol. Assn., N.Y. State Psychol. Assn. (rep. exec. com. 1981-83), Biofeedback Soc. Am. (cert.). Roman Catholic. Contbr. to Infants Born at Risk, 1979, Pre-term Birth: Relevance to Optimal Psychological Development, 1981, Multivariate Analysis of the Type A Personality, 1981. Office: 16-07 150th St Whitestone NY 11357-2545 Office: Queens Coll Dept of Psychology Kissena Blvd Flushing NY 11367

CAPUTO, GARY RICHARD, radiology educator; b. Newark, Nov. 26, 1951. AB in Chemistry, Coll. of the Hoy Cross, 1973; MD, Mt. Sinai Sch. Medicine, 1977. Diplomate Am. Bd. Internal Medicine, Am. Bd. Nuclear Medicine. Intern in internal medicine Mt. Sinai Hosp., 1977-78, resident in internal medicine, 1978-79; fellow in cardiology U. Wash., Seattle, 1979-81, 82-83; resident in internal medicine St. Vincent's Hosp. & Med. Ctr., Portland, Ore., 1981-82; resident in nuclear medicine U. Wash., 1983-85; fellow in cardiovascular imaging U. Calif., San Francisco, 1985-86; asst. prof. U. Utah Sch. Medicine, Salt Lake City, 1986-89, U. Calif., San Francisco, 1989-92; assoc. prof. U. Calif., 1992—; clin. instr. U. Wash., 1982-83; adj. asst. prof. U. Utah 1987-89; dir. advanced cardiac imaging svc. LDS Hosp., Salt Lake City, 1986-89; clin. instr. U. Calif., San Francisco, 1985-86, supr. clin. cardiovascular magnetic resonance rsch. program and vis. fgn. scholars, 1989—; adminstr. NIH tng. grant, 1989—; coord. in-svc. tng. program, 1990-91; vis. fellow clin. magnetic resonance, 1990—; mem. com. on human rsch., 1991-93; lectr. Fla. Radiol. Soc., 1988—; cons. GE Med. Sys., Milw., 1991; dir. nuclear cardiology fellowship tng. program U. Utah Sch. of Medicine, 1987-89, mem. PhD candidate com. dept. med. informatics, 1987-91; apptd. bioengring. grad. group U. Calif., Berkeley, San Francisco, 1992—, staff scientist Lawrence Berkeley Lab., 1992—, U. Calif. San Francisco Lab. for Radiolog. Informatics, 1992—, U. Calif. San Francisco Magnetic Resonance Sci. Ctr., 1993-95, assoc. dir., 1993-95, U. Calif. San Francisco PET Ctr., 1993—, assoc. dir. 1993—. Grantee Deseret Found., 1987, Am. Heart Assn., 1988, Richards Meml. Med. Found., 1988, Merritt-Peralta Rsch. Found., 1990, NIH, 1986—, numerous others. Fellow Am. Heart Assn. Coun. Cardiovascular Radiology; mem. AAAS, Radiol. Soc. N.Am., N.Am. Soc. Cardiac Imaging, Soc. Nuclear Medicine, San Francisco Radiol. Soc. Office: U Calif Dept Radiology Box 0628 San Francisco CA 94143-0628

CAPUTO, RUGGERO, dermatologist; b. Milan, Italy, Jan. 2, 1938; s. Pietro and Teresa (Martino) C.; m. Evelina Avanzi, Feb. 10, 1966; children: Alberto, Nicoletta, Gioia, Federico. Degree in medicine and surgery, U. Milan, 1962, postgrad., 1964. Asst. U. Milan, 1966-72, assoc. prof., 1973-80, prof., 1981-84, head 1st dept. dermatology, 1984—. Author numerous pubs. Home: Via M Macchi 65, 20124 Milan Italy Office: Inst Sci Dermatologiche, Via Pace 9, 20122 Milan Italy also: Via Benedetto Marcello 36, 20124 Milan Italy

CAPUTO, WAYNE JAMES, surgeon, podiatrist; b. Newark, Feb. 18, 1956; s. James Vincent and Jennie (DeMaio) C.; m. Phyllis A. Grillo, Nov. 20, 1984; children: Karla, Stefanie. BS in Biology, Syracuse U., 1978; DPM, N.Y. Coll. Podiatric Medicine, 1982. Diplomate Am. Bd. Podiatric Surgery. Clin. asst. prof. N.Y. Coll. Podiatic Medicine, N.Y.C., 1984-89; chief dept. podiatric surgery Clara Maass Med. Ctr., Belleville, N.J., 1987—, Columbus Hosp., Newark, 1995—; dir. residency in podiatric surgery Union (N.J.) Hosp., 1990—. Contbr. articles to profl. jours. Fellow ACS, Am. Coll. Dermatologists. Office: Clara Maass Profl Med Ctr 5 Franklin Ave Belleville NJ 07109-3532

CARABASI, JANE MARKO, health educator, health education consultant; b. Bklyn., Feb. 3, 1954; d. Leon and Anna (Senyszyn) Marko; m. R. Anthony Carabasi III, May 15, 1976; children: Erik, Todd, Chloe. Student, Douglass Coll., 1971-73; BSN, Thomas Jefferson U., 1975; MS, St. Joseph's U., 1981; EdD, Temple U., 1989. RN; cert. health edn. specialist. Primary nurse Thomas Jefferson U. Hosp., Phila., 1975-76; asst. supr. Interstate Blood Bank, Inc., Phila., 1976-77; dialysis charge nurse Holy Name Hosp., Teaneck, N.J., 1977-78; dialysis nurse Dialysis Ctr. of Montgomery-Norristown, Pa., 1978-79; nursing educator Thomas Jefferson U., Phila., 1979-80, Del. County Community Coll., Media, Pa., 1980-81; ind. health edn. cons. Bryn Mawr, Pa., 1985—; adj. faculty St. Joseph's Univ., 1994—; chairwomen 5th reunion Coll. Allied Health Scis., Thomas Jefferson U., Phila., 1980, mem. dean's coun. of overseers, 1989—. Contbr. articles to profl. jours. Mem. Women's Bd. of Thomas Jefferson U. Hosp., Phila., 1976—, Spiritual Frontiers Fellowship Internat., Phila., 1980—; hon. mem. Jr. Svc. Bd., Pa., 1991—. Mem. Am. Alliance for Health, Phys. Edn., Recreation and Dance, Soc. for Pub. Health Edn., Am. Sch. Health Assn., Pa. Sch. Health Assn., Soc. for Pub. Health Edn. Home and Office: 818 Northwinds Dr Bryn Mawr PA 19010-2047

CARABELLO, BLASE ANTHONY, cardiology educator; b. Reading, Pa., Aug. 5, 1947; s. Charles Anthony and Fern June (Houck) C.; m. Susan Jane Beidman, Aug. 15, 1970 (div. June 1977); 1 child, Charles; m. Catherine Wheatley, Apr. 9, 1989; children: Nicholas, Blaise. BA, Gettsburg Coll., 1969; MD, Temple U., 1973. Diplomate Am. Bd. Internal Medicine, Am. Bd. Cardiology. Intern in Medicine Mass. Gen. Hosp., Boston, 1973-74, resident in Medicine Harvard Med. Sch., 1974-75, sr. resident in Medicine Harvard Med. Sch., 1975-76; fellow in Cardiology Peter Bent Brigham Hosp., Boston, 1976-78, cardiologist, 1978-79; asst. prof. Medicine U. Va. Hosp., Charlottesville, 1979-81; dir. Diagnostic Cardiology Temple U., Phila., 1981-85; prof. Medicine Med. U. S.C., Charleston, 1985-95, dir. clin. rsch., 1990—; Charles Ezra Daniel prof. medicine U. S.C., Charleston, 1995—. Author: Cardiology Pearls, 1993; contbr. articles to profl. jours. Beta-Blockade grantee Pub. Health Svc., 1988-89, Dept. Va. Pub. Health grantee, 1989-94. Fellow Am. Coll. Cardiology, Am. Heart Assn. (coun. on circulation, chmn. com. on cardiac catheterization); mem. Am. Soc. Clin. Investigation, Alpha Omega Alpha. Home: 528 Island Walk W Mount Pleasant SC 29464 Office: Dept Cardiology Med U SC 171 Ashley Ave Charleston SC 29425-0001

CARACCIO, BABETTE B., psychiatrist; b. N.Y.C., Feb. 11, 1957. BS summa cum laude, Coll. New Rochelle, 1978; MD, NYU, 1982. Intern N.Y. Hosp., 1982-83; resident Bellevue Hosp., N.Y.C., 1983-85, chief resident, 1985-86; fellow Westchester div. N.Y. Hosp., White Plains, 1986-88; attending psychiatrist Hall-Brooke Found., Westport, Conn., 1988-89; child psychiatrist Greenwich (Conn.) Hosp., 1989—. Mem. Am. Psychiat. Assn., Am. Acad. Child and Adolescent Psychiatry, Conn. State Psychiat. Soc., Alpha Omega Alpha. Republican. Home and Office: 23 Mianus View Ter Cos Cob CT 06807-2731

CARAUX, JEAN GÉRARD MARIE, medical director; b. Le Caire, Egypt, Apr. 28, 1951; s. André and Jacqueline (de Charnacé) C.; m. Danièle Garson-Pariente, Dec. 20, 1972; children: Baptiste, Anouk, Antoine. PhD, U. Paris-Montpellier, 1979, MD, 1980. Rsch. scientist molecular biology of viruses M. Girard, Villejuif, France, 1972-73; rsch. scientist transplantation immunology J. Hamburger, Paris, 1973; rsch. scientist Ctr. P. Lamarque, CNRS, Montpellier, 1975-81, 82-85; vis. scientist dept. immunopathology Scripps Clinic, La Jolla, 1981-82; head rsch. unit autoimmune diseases INSERM, Montpellier, 1985-86; head dept. immunology Pasteur-Merieux,

Marcy L'Etoile, France, 1986-88, head dept. blood deriv. and immunology, 1988-89, head med. dept. immunology div., 1989-92; chmn. bd., CEO Caraux Biomed. Internat. S.A., St Cyr Mont d'Or, France, 1992-95; med. dir. AMGEN S.A., Neuilly, France, 1996—. Contbr. articles to profl. publs. Recipient Laureate award Found. Vocation, Paris, 1976, Bronze medal Nat. Ctr. Sci. Rsch., 1985. Mem. AAAS, N.Y. Acad. Scis., Bris. Soc. Immunology, Soc. Française Immunologie, Internat. AIDS Soc. Office: AMGEN S A, 192 Ave Charles de Gaulle, 92523 Neuilly Cedex, France

CARAVATI, CHARLES MARTIN, dermatologist; b. Richmond, Va., May 9, 1937; s. Charles Martin and Mary Virginia (Dore) C.; m. Betty Noland, Aug. 31, 1963; children: Charles M. III, Elizabeth Caravati Butler, Nancy Caravati Johnson. BA, U. Va., 1959, MD, 1963. Diplomate Am. Bd. Dermatology. Resident in dermatology U. Va., Charlottesville, 1966-68, chief resident dermatology, 1968-69; founder, pres. Dermatology Assocs. Va., Richmond, 1969—; pres., chmn. bd. dirs. Richmond Acad. Medicine, 1980-82; bd. visitors U. Va., 1994—. Bd. dirs. Sheltering Arms Rehab. Hosp., 1990-95, St. Joseph's Villa, 1982-85. Fellow Am. Acad. Dermatology; mem. AMA, Va. Dermatol. Soc., Richmond Dermatol. Soc. Republican. Roman Catholic. Home: 931 Broad St Rd Manakin-Sabot VA 23103 Office: Dermatology Assocs Va 5600 Grove Ave Richmond VA 23226

CARBALLO, PEDRO PABLO, cardiologist; b. Artemisa, Cuba, Apr. 21, 1953; came to U.S., 1963; s. Pedro V. and Ofelia B. (Hernandez) C.; m. Maria T. Pol, Aug. 13, 1982; children: Suzanne E., Sarah A., Paul A. AA, Miami Dade Community Coll., 1974; BA, Northwestern U., 1976, MS, 1977; MD, U. Ill., Chgo., 1981. Diplomate Am. Bd. Internal Medicine, Am. Bd. Cardiovascular Medicine. Resident Ill. Masonic Med. Ctr., Chgo., 1981-84, fellow, 1984-86, dir., Intensive Care Units, 1986-92; pvt. practice Chgo., 1986-92; cardiologist PCA Family Med. Ctrs., Dade & Broward Counties, Fla., 1992—. Fellow Am. Coll. Cardiology, Am. Coll. Chest Physicians; mem. AMA, ACP, Ill. State Med. Soc., Chgo. Med. Soc., Alpha Omega Alpha, Beta Beta Beta. Roman Catholic. Office: 9732 SW 24th St Miami FL 33147-2114

CARBALLO, RICHARD, general and vascular surgeon; b. Chgo., Mar. 3, 1963; s. Fernando T. and Carmen (Llamas) C.; m. Mary Jill Castanoli, Dec. 27, 1986; children: Carla, Erica. BA, Ripon Coll., 1984; MD, U. Ill., Chgo., 1988. Diplomate Am. Bd. Surgery. Resident in general surgery Loyola U., Maywood, Ill., 1988-93; fellow in vascular surgery Med. Coll. Wis., Milw., 1993-95; staff surgeon St. Lukes Med. Ctr., Milw., 1995—. Republican. Catholic. Office: Southeast Surg SC Ste 485 2901 W Kinnickinnic River Milwaukee WI 53215

CARBALLO-DIEGUEZ, ALEX, research scientist behavioral studies; b. Buenos Aires, June 13, 1951; came to U.S., 1982; s. Ramon Carballo and Lilian Dieguez. Lic. in Psychology, Cath. U., Buenos Aires, 1975; PhD, New Sch., N.Y.C., 1986. Lic. psychologist, N.Y. Staff psychologist Ctr. for Mental Health, Interfaith Med. Ctr., Bklyn., 1982-85; unit chief spl. treatment unit Interfaith Med. Ctr., Bklyn., 1985-87; chief psychologist and AIDS mental health coord. Luth. Med. Ctr., Bklyn., 1987-88; dir. HIV/AIDS Mental Health Clinic Columbia Presbyn. Med. Ctr., N.Y.C., 1988-89; rsch. scientist HIV Ctr. for Clin. and Behavioral Studies, N.Y.C., 1988—; cons. Health Svc. Improvement Fund/Blue Cross Blue Shield, N.Y.C., 1989-90; Latino adv. bd. Gay Men's Health Crisis, N.Y.C.; supr. Inst. for Human Identity, N.Y.C., 1985-89. Recipient Scientific Achievement award 82nd Annual Scientific Assembly of So. Med. Assn., 1983. Mem. Am. Psychol. Assn. (disting. contbns. to ethnic minority psychology award 1995), N.Y. State Psychol. Assn., Internat. AIDS Soc. Home: 749 W End Ave Apt 12W New York NY 10025-6229 Office: HIV Ctr Clin & Behavioral Studies 722 W 168th St Fl 10 New York NY 10032-2603

CARBAUGH, BETH ANNE, private medical nurse; b. Chambersburg, Pa., Jan. 31, 1970; d. Terry Lee and Cynthia Ann (Martin) C. Student, Franklin County Vocat.-Tech., Chambersburg, Pa., 1992-93. Private duty nurse Chambersburg, 1993—, LPN, 1994—. Mem./EMT Chambersburg Fire Dept., 1988—. Recipient Emergency Med. Svcs. award Chambersburg Fire Dept., 1990, 91. Mem. LPN Assn. Pa., Goodwill Steam Engine and Hose Co. Republican. Home: 611 Lincoln Way W Apt E Chambersburg PA 17201

CARCAMO, MARIO IVAN, optometrist; b. Managua, Nicaragua, Apr. 15, 1962; came to U.S., 1981; s. Benjamin and Angela Rita (Garcia) C.; m. Maria Dolores Ayon, Feb. 21, 1982; children: Andrea Regina, Adriana Raquel, Mario. BS, DO, U. Calif., Berkeley, 1988. Pvt. practice, Palo Alto, CA, 1988-92, Miami, Fla., 1992—. Mentor Evergreen C.C., San Jose, Calif., 1989-90; leader trips to 3d. world countries to donate eyeglasses and free eyecare to indigents, 1988—. With USAR, 1983-89. Fellow V.O.S.H.; mem. Am. Optometric Assn. Roman Catholic. Office: Optical World 1455 NW 107th Ave Ste 654 Miami FL 33172

CARDEN, DAVID L., community health nurse; b. Phenix City, Ala., Feb. 27, 1958; s. William H. and Betty (Gillenwater) C.; m. Patty Odom, Aug. 15, 1981; children: Amy Louise, Benjamin David, Caroline Grace. BSN, Auburn U., 1981; MPH, Tulane U., 1988; postgrad., Baylor U. Commd. 2d lt. U.S. Army, 1982, advanced through grades to maj.; staff nurse U.S. Army, Ft. Irwin, Calif.; charge nurse ICU U.S. Army, Ft. Gordon, Ga., head nurse med./surg. ward; chief community health nursing U.S. Army, Ft. Rucker, Ala.; chief preventive medicine svc. U.S. Army, Camp Zama, Japan. Mem. ANA (cert. community health nurse), Nat. Coun. for Community Health Nurses, Assn. of the U.S. Army, Ala. State Nurses Assn.

CARDEN, ZACHARY FRANK, JR., dentist; b. Chattanooga, June 19, 1941; s. Zachary Frank and Mable (Torbett) C.; m. Anne Fowler, Jan. 28, 1967; children—Heather Anne, Zachary Frank III. B.S., Carson-Newman Coll., 1963; Med. Technologist, Erlanger Hosp., Chattanooga, 1964; D.D.S., U. Tenn., 1974. Med. technologist Erlanger Hosp., Chattanooga, 1964-65, 68-70; pvt. practice dentistry, Chattanooga, 1974—. Pres. Civic Art League, Chattanooga, 1980. Served to capt. U.S. Army, 1965-68. Decorated Army Commendation medal. Mem. ADA, Am. Acad. Oral Medicine (oral medicine award 1974), Tenn. Dental Assn. (del. 1983-85), Lookout Dental Study Group (pres. 1975), 3d Dist. Dental Soc. (chmn. peer rev. 1983-85), 3d Dist. Trustee for Hamilton County, 1996, Chattanooga Craniomandibular Study Group (pres. 1985-86). Republican. Methodist. Clubs: Tenn. Watercolor Soc., Ga. Watercolor Soc., Ky. Watercolor Soc. Avocations: watercolor and oil painting; golf. Office: Lake Hills Profl Bldg 4216 Cross St Chattanooga TN 37416-3334

CARDENALES-RODRIGUEZ, MARIA, medical record administrator; b. Santurce, P.R., Feb. 18, 1952; d. Gregorio Cardenales-Torres and Juana (Rodrigues) Rivera. BA, InterAm. U., San Juan, 1981; M in Med. Record Adminstrn. Sci., U. P.R., 1988. Adminstr. med. records Sys. & Computer Tech., San Juan, P.R., 1989-90; cons. Complejo Med./Social Antilla, Rio Piedras, P.R., 1990-93; dir. med. records Carolina (P.R.) Regional Hosp., 1993—. Mem. Am. Health Info. Mgmt. Assn., Asociacion de Profesionales en Manejo de Informacion de Salud de P.R., Asociacion de Calidad En Salud de Puerto Rico, Afiliada A La Naha Y Asqc. Home: Hermandad #18 Bo Amelia Catano PR 00965 Office: Carolina Regional Hosp PO Box 3869 Carolina PR 00984-3869

CARDENAS, DIANA DELIA, physician, educator; b. San Antonio, Tex., Apr. 10, 1947; d. Ralph Roman and Rosa (Garza) C.; m. Thomas McKenzie Hooton, Aug. 20, 1971; children: Angela, Jessica. BA with highest honors, U. Tex., 1969; MD, U. Tex., Dallas, 1973; MS, U. Wash., 1976. Diplomate Nat. Bd. Med. Examiners, Am. Bd. Phys. Medicine & Rehab., Am. Bd. Electrodiagnostic Medicine. Asst. prof. dept. rehab. medicine Emory U., Atlanta, 1976-81; instr. dept. rehab. medicine U. Wash., Seattle, 1981-82, asst. prof. dept. rehab. medicine, 1982-86, assoc. prof. dept. rehab. medicine, 1986-92, prof. rehab. medicine, 1992—; med. dir. rehab. medicine clinic U. Wash. Med. Ctr., Seattle, 1982; project dir. N.W. Regional Spinal Cord Injury System, Seattle, 1990—. Editor: Rehabilitation & The Chronic Renal Disease Patient, 1985, Maximizing Rehabilitation in Chronic Renal Disease, 1989; contbr. articles to profl. jours. Co-chairperson Lakeside Sch. Auction Student Vols., Seattle, 1991; bd. dirs. CONSEJO Counseling & Referral Svc., 1994. Mem. Am. Spinal Injury Assn. (chairperson rsch. com. 1991), Am. Acad. Phys. Medicine and Rehab., Am. Congress of Rehab. Medicine (chairperson rehab. practice com. 1980-84, Ann. Essay Contest winner 1976), Am. Assn. Electrodiagnostic Medicine. Office: Univ Wash Dept Rehab Med Box 356490 1959 NE Pacific St Seattle WA 98195-0004

CARDENAS, JUAN CARLOS, plastic surgeon, educator; b. Medellin, Antioquia, Colombia, July 3, 1964; s. Carlos Fidel and Lillian (Restrepo) C. MD, Medellin Coll., 1987. Physician SSSA, San Roque, Colombia, 1988-89; gen. physician CMSR, Envigado, Colombia, 188-89; resident in plastic surgery HUSVP, Medellin, 1991-95; plastic surgeon Medellin, 1996—, CMSR, Medellin, 1996—. Contbr. articles to profl. jours. Mem. Colombian Soc. Plastic Surgery, Colombian Med. Soc. Home: C1 46 sur #42-21, Envigado Autioqui, Colombia Office: San Roque Medical Ctr, CR 43A #32B/Sur 15, Envigado Autioqui, Colombia

CARDIFF, JOHN RODNEY, public health administrator; b. San Mateo, Calif., May 3, 1950; s. John Howard and Ruth Claire (Weaver) C.; m. Debra Truman, Sept. 1977 (div. 1981); m. Debra Marie Morganti, Jan. 9, 1982; 1 child, Nicole. BS, U. Nebr., 1972; MD, U. Nebr., Omaha, 1975; MPH, U. N.C., 1984; MPA, Fla. Atlantic U., 1992. Diplomte Am. Bd. Preventive Medicine, Am. Bd. Family Practice. Resident in family practice regional acad. program Tex. Tech U., Amarillo, 1975-78; family physician Moffat Family Clinic, Craig, Colo., 1978-80; physician Phelps Dodge Corp., Morenci, Ariz., 1980-81; emergency physician Coastal Emergency Svcs., Durham, N.C., 1982-83; pub. health resident Tex. Dept. Health, Austin, 1983-84; dir. Communicable Diseases Duval County Pub. Health Unit, Jacksonville, Fla., 1984-85; med. dir. Leon County Pub. Health Unit, Tallahassee, 1985-87; dir. St. Lucie County Pub. Health Unit, Ft. Pierce, Fla., 1987-95; pvt. practice family and preventive medicine, 1995—. Fellow Am. Coll. of Preventive Medicine; mem. APHA, Fla. Soc. Preventive Medicine (sec./treas. 1988—), Fla. Pub. Health Assn., St. Lucie Coun. Social Agys. (pres. 1990-91). Democrat. Methodist. Home: 1357 SW Cedar Cv Port Saint Lucie FL 34986-2001 Office: 170 S Enterada Ave Port St Lucie FL 34952

CARDIFF, ROBERT DARRELL, pathology educator; b. San Francisco, Dec. 5, 1935; s. George Darrell and Helen (Kohfield) C.; m. Sally Joan Bounds, June 23, 1962; children: Darrell, Todd, Shelley. BS, U. Calif., Berkeley, 1958, PhD, 1968; MD, U. Calif., San Francisco, 1962. Intern King's County Hosp., Bklyn., 1962-63; resident in pathology U. Oreg., Portland, 1963-66; NIH fellow U. Calif., Berkeley, 1966-68; mem. faculty med. sch. U. Calif., Davis, 1971—, prof. pathology med. sch., 1977—, chair dept. pathology, 1990—; mem. sci. adv. bd. Contra Costa Cancer Fund, Walnut Creek, Calif., 1985—; mem. Univ.-Wide AIDS Task Force, Berkeley, 1984-87; vis. prof. Sun-Yat Sen U. Med. Sci., Peoples Republic of China, 1985, 93. Mem. editorial bd. Human Pathology, 1992—, Tumor Markers, 1992—, Internat. Jour. Oncology, 1992—; contbr. articles to profl. jours. Lt. col. U.S. Army, 1968-71. Recipient Triton Rsch. award Triton Bioscis., Inc., 1985, Kaiser Found. Teaching award U. Calif. Med. Sch., Davis, 1985, Disting. Teaching award U. Calif., Davis, Sadusk award Peralta Cancer Inst., 1986, Faculty Rsch. award U. Calif. Med. Sch., 1988, Affirmative Action award U. Calif. Davis Med. Ctr., 1991, others. Mem. AAUP (exec. com. 1983-85), Pluto Soc., Internat. Acad. Pathology, Internat. Aassn. Breast Cancer (Bd. dirs. 1984—), Sacramento Pathology Soc. (bd. dirs. 1985—), No. Calif. Pathology Soc. (pres. 1990—), Coll. Am. Pathology, Sigma Xi. Office: U Calif Med Sch Dept Pathology MSIA Davis CA 95616

CARDIN, DENISE ANN, psychologist, researcher; b. Fall River, Mass., Dec. 20, 1955; d. Ernest Lucien and Theresa (Jusseaume) C. BS in Psychology, Providence Coll., 1977; MS in Edn., Purdue Univ., 1984; PhD in Counseling, Psychology, Auburn U., 1992. Lic. psychologist, Ala. Cardiology rsch. asst. R.I. Hosp., Providence, 1977-79, biopsychosocial rsch. asst., 1985-86; instr. ednl. psychology Purdue U., West Lafayette, Ind., 1980-81, Auburn U., Ala., 1982-87; psychology technician VA Med. Ctr., Tuskegee, Ala., 1987-90; psychology intern VA Med. Ctr., San Antonio, Tex., 1990-91; psychologist PCT VA Med. Ctr., Tuskegee, Ala., 1992-94; psychologist geriatrics VA Med. Ctr., Waco, Tex., 1994-95; psychologist PTSU VA Med. Ctr., Waco, 1995—; psychologist in geriatrics Cntl. Tex. Med. Ctr., Waco, 1995—; cons. to PTSD adv. com. Vietnam Vets. Am., Ala. State Coun., 1993-94. Contbr. articles to profl. jours. Charter mem. U.S. Holacaust Meml. Mus.; mem. Nat. Audubon Soc., Arthritis Found., Lupus Found., Nature Conservancy. Named Citizen of Yr. Vietnam Vets. of Am., Ala. State Coun., 1994. Mem. Am. Psychol. Assn. (counseling and psychology of women sects.), Internat. Soc. for Traumatic Stress Studies, Phi Delta Kappa. Home: 4720 Lake Shore Dr Apt 3 Waco TX 76710-1809

CARDINAL, BRADLEY JOHN, educational researcher; b. Everett, Wash., May 31, 1963; s. Vernon Clarence and Rosalie Anne (DeMatis) C.; m. Marita Katherine Brown, Dec. 10, 1988. BA in Education, Ea. Washington U., 1985, MS, 1987; PhD, Temple U., 1993. Grad. asst. Ea. Washington U., Cheney, 1985-87, asst. prof., 1987-90; grad. asst. Temple U., Phila., 1990-93; asst. prof. Wayne State U., Detroit, 1993—; instr. Joel E. Ferris High Sch., Spokane, Wash., 1985; asst. dir. Young Women's Christian Assn., Spokane, 1986. Author: Physical Fitness: The Hub of Wellness Wheel, 1989, The Complete Advanced First Aid Book, 1990; contbr. articles to profl. jours. Recipient Profl. Enrichment award Comprehensive Health Inst., 1988, Young Scholar award Western Coll. Physical Edn. Soc., 1990; numerous grants, 1988—. Mem. AAPHERD, Am. Coll. Sports Medicine, Am. Assn. Active Lifestyles and Fitness, Nat. Assn. Phys. Edn. in Higher Edn., Nat. Assn. for Sport and Phys. Edn., Assn. for Advancement of Applied Sport Psychology, Nat. Assn. Psychology of Sport and Phys. Activity, Eta Sigma Gamma.

CARDONI, ALEX ANTHONY, pharmacist, educator; b. Lackawanna, N.Y., May 23, 1943; s. Louis Alexander and Clementine Jenny (Miniri) C.; m. Judith Ann Baker, Oct. 15, 1966; children: Julianne, Christopher. BSc in Pharmacy, SUNY Buffalo, 1966; MSc in Hosp. Pharmacy, Ohio State U., 1969. Cert. pharmacist, N.Y., Ohio, Conn. Asst. dir. pharmacy Ohio State U. Hosps., Columbus, 1969-72; asst. prof., assoc. prof. U. Conn., Storrs, 1972—; asst., assoc. clin. prof. psychiatry U. Conn. Health Ctr., Farmington, 1980—, dir. drug. info., 1972-87, dir. poison ctr., 1976-84; cons. Hartford (Conn.) Hosp./Inst. of Living, 1987—. Snare drummer Sailing Masters of 1812 Fife and Drum Corps, Essex, Conn., 1980—. Recipient Lecture award Exerpta Medica, Inc., 1993, Cornelius Boelhoewer award Hartford Hosp. Dept. Psychiatry, 1994. Mem. Am. Assn. Colls. of Pharmacy, Conn. Soc. Hosp. Pharmacists (pres. 1983-84, Hosp. Pharmacist of Yr. 1987). Roman Catholic.

CARDULLO, MARIA ANN, secondary education educator; b. Boston, Apr. 11, 1942; d. Anthony Orlando and Rosina Margaret (Matthews) C. A.B. in Chemistry, Emmanuel Coll., 1963, A.B. in Biology, 1964; M.S. in Biology, Boston Coll., 1967, Ph.D. in Biology, 1971. Postdoctoral research assoc. in bacteriology and molecular biology, Boston Coll., 1971-77; chmn. sci. dept., tchr. biology and chemistry, Columbus High Sch., Boston, 1977-90; tchr. biology and chemistry Cath. Meml. High Sch., West Roxbury, Mass., 1990-94; tchr. biology, phys. sci., math. Savio Prep. H.S., East Boston, Mass., 1994—. Contbr. articles to scientific jours. Mem. Am. Soc. Microbiology, Nat. Assn. Biology Tchrs., Nat. Ednl. Assn., Nat. Catholic Ednl. Assn. (award for outstanding contbns. to secondary edn. 1984), Sigma Xi. Roman Catholic. Office: Savio Prep HS 145 Byron St East Boston MA 02128

CARDUS, DAVID, physician; b. Barcelona, Spain, Aug. 6, 1922; came to U.S., 1957, naturalized, 1969; s. Jaume and Ferranda (Pascual) C.; m. Francesca Ribas, July 19, 1951; children: Hellena, Silvia, Bettina, David. BA, BS, U. Montpellier (France), 1942; MD magna cum laude, U. Barcelona, 1949, diploma in cardiology, 1956; D honoris causa, Autonomous U. Barcelona, 1993. French Govt. fellow dept. cardiology Hosp. Boucicaut and Hosp. de la Pitié, Paris, 1953-54; fellow U. Manchester, 1957; rsch. assoc. Lovelace Found., Albuquerque, 1957-60; NIH trainee Summer Inst. Math. for Life Scientists U. Mich., 1966; mem. active med. staff Inst. for Rehab. and Rsch. Baylor Coll. Medicine, Houston, 1960—, prof. dept. rehab., 1969—, prof. dept. physiology, 1973—, dir. Biomath. Program, 1966-69, dir. biomath. com. Sch. Grad. Studies, 1968-69, head exercise lab., 1960—, head cardiopulmonary lab., 1969—; adj. prof. math. scis. Rice U., 1970—, adj. prof. stats., 1989—. Chmn. bd. dirs. Inst. Hispanic Culture, Houston; vice chmn. Gordon Conf. on Biomaths., 1970; pres. Am. Inst. Catalan Studies, 1980—. Recipient 1st prize for exhibit Am. Urol. Assn., 1967, 1st prize for sci. exhibit 5th Internat. Am. Cong. of Rehab. Medicine, 1968, Gold medal for demonstration use of computers and telecomm. in rehab. 6th Internat. Congress Phys. Medicine and Rehab., 1972, August Pi Sunyer prize Inst d' Estudis Catalans, 1968, Elisabeth and Sidney Licht award for sci. writing Am. Congress Phys. Med. and Rehab., 1980, Narcis Monturiol medal Generalitat de Catalunya, Spain, 1985, Catalunya Enfora prize Inst. Catalan de Cooperación Iberoamericana Fundación Bertran, 1987, Commendation of Isabel la Católica (Spain), 1980, Creu de Sant Jordi Generalitat de Catalunya, 1992, Joan d'Alos award Centre Cardiovascular Sant Jordi, Barcelona, Spain, 1996. Mem. Am. Coll. Cardiology, Am. Coll. Chest Physicians, Am. Coll. Sports Medicine, Am. Congress Rehab. Medicine, Am. Physiol. Soc., Am. Statis. Assn., Internat. Soc. for Gravitational Physiology (pres. 1993), Fedn. Am. Socs. Exptl. Biology, Spanish Profls. in Am. (pres. 1984-85), N.y. Acad. Scis., Societat Catalana Biologia, Sigma Xi. Home: 17207 Bonnard Cir Spring TX 77379-6275 Office: Baylor Coll Med 1333 Moursund St Houston TX 77030-3405

CAREK, DONALD J(OHN), child psychiatry educator; b. Sheboygan, Wis., Aug. 10, 1931; s. Peter and Rose (Gergisch) C.; m. Frances M. Schaefer, Jan. 28, 1956; children—Carla, Thomas, Therese, Peter, Mary Beth, Christopher. M.D., Marquette U., 1956. Diplomate Am. Bd. Psychiatry and Neurology (examiner in child psychiatry, psychiatry). Intern Walter Reed Army Hosp., 1956-57; resident U. Mich. Hosps., 1959-63; pediatrician Fort Meyer Dispensary, Arlington, Va., 1958-59; instr. psychiatry U. Mich., Ann Arbor, 1962-65, asst. prof., 1965-66; dir. day care Children's Psychiat. Hosp., Ann Arbor, 1965-66; assoc. prof. psychiatry and pediatrics Med. Coll. Wis., Milw., 1966-74, acting chmn. div. human behavior, 1970-73, prof. psychiatry, 1974-76; pres. med. staff Milw. Psychiat. Hosp., 1971-73; prof. psychiatry and pediatrics, chief youth div. Med. U. S.C., Charleston, 1976-96, prof. psychiatry, 1996—. Co-author: Guide to Psychotherapy, 1966; author: Principles of Child Psychotherapy, 1972; mem. editorial bd. Am. Jour. Child & Adolscent Psychiatry, 1988-93; contbr. articles to profl. publs. Bd. dirs. Cedarcrest Girls Residential Treatment Ctr., 1969-71. Served to capt. USAR, 1956-59. Fellow Am. Acad. Child Psychiatry (com. on adolescent psychiatry 1979-85, com. on psythotherapy 1986-90), Am. Psychiat. Assn., Am. Coll. Psychiatrists (membership com. 1991-94, 95—); mem. AMA, Am. Orthopsychiatry Assn., AAAS, Am. Psychisomatic Soc., Soc. Profs. Child Psychiatry, S.C. Med. Assn. (mental health com. 1992-93), S.C. Dist. Cr. Am. Psychiat. Assn., Charleston County Med. Soc., S.C. State Bd. Med. Examiners (med. disciplinary commn. 1992-95), Alpha Omega Alpha, Alpha Sigma Nu, Best Doctors in America Southeast Region, 1995. Fellow Am. Acad. Child Psychiatry (com. on adolscent psychiatry 1979-85, com. on psychotherapy 1986-90), Am. Psychiat. Assn., Am. Coll. Psychiatrists (membership com. 1991-94, 95—); mem. AMA, Am. Orthopsychiatry Assn., AAAS, Am. Psychosomatic Soc., Soc. Profs. Child Psychiatry, S.C. Med. Assn. (mental health com. 1992-93), S.C. Dist. Cr. Am. Psychiat. Assn., Charleston County Med. Soc., S.C. State Bd. Med. Examiners (med. disciplinary commn. 1992-95), Alpha Omega Alpha, Alpha Sigma Nu. Roman Catholic. Home: 51 Rebellion Rd Charleston SC 29407-7457 Office: Med Univ SC 171 Ashley Ave Charleston SC 29425-0001

CAREW, LYNDON BELMONT, JR., nutrition educator; b. Lynn, Mass., Nov. 27, 1932; s. Lyndon Belmont and Myrtle L. (Woodworth) C.; children: Leslie, Audre. Diploma, Essex Agrl. Inst., 1950; B.S., U. Mass., 1955; Ph.D., Cornell U., 1961. Rsch. assoc. Cornell U., Ithaca, N.Y., 1955-60; dir. Nat. Poultry Program and Animal Nutrition Lab., Rockefeller Found., Bogota, Colombia, 1961-65; head poultry rsch. Hess & Clark div. Richardson-Merrill, Ashland, Ohio, 1965-69; prof. animal and food scis. U. Vt., Burlington, 1969—, program mgr. Internat. Nutrition Project, 1980-83; lectr. in field; nutrition edn. cons. Vt. Info. System, Shelburne, 1982—. Contbr. articles to profl. jours. Mem. Vt. Nutrition Coun. (pres. 1975-77, 83-85), Animal Nutrition Rsch. Coun. (chmn. bd. trustees 1984-85), Endocrine Soc., Am. Inst. Nutrition, Poultry Sci. Assn., Nutrition Edn. Soc., Vt.-Honduras Ptnrs. Am. Home: 13 Collamer Cir Shelburne VT 05482-7229 Office: U Vt 207 Terrill Hall Burlington VT 05405-0148

CAREY, ASHER BURTON, III, plastic surgeon; b. Salisbury, Md., Mar. 25, 1952; s. Asher Burton and Pauline Bunting Carey; m. Cindy McNsour, Sept. 4, 1983; children: Adrienne, Asher, Ben, Amanda. BS, Duke U., 1974; MD, Jefferson Med. Coll., Phila., 1978. Diplomate Am. Bd. Sugery, Am. Bd. Plastic Surgery. Gen. surgery Tulane U., New Orleans, 1978-83; plastic surgery Vanderbilt U., Nashville, 1983-85. Contbr. articles to profl. jours. Fellow ACS, Am. Soc. Plastic and Reconstructive Surgeons. Office: 6445 Queen St Dover DE 19904

CAREY, JOHN C., pediatrician; b. Balt., 1946. MD, Georgetown, 1982. Diplomate Am. Bd. Molecular Genetics, Am. Bd. Pediatrics. Prof pediatrics U. Utah Med. Ctr., Salt Lake City. Office: U Utah Med Ctr Pediatrics 413 Med Edn Bldg 50 N Medical Dr Salt Lake City UT 84132-1001*

CAREY, MARTIN CONRAD, gastroenterologist, molecular biophysicist, educator; b. Clonmel, County Tipperary, Ireland, June 18, 1939; came to U.S., 1967; s. John Joseph and Alice (Broderick) C.; m. Gracia Antonieta Fernández, July 1, 1972 (div. 1987); children: Julian Albert, Dermot Martin. MB, BCh, BAO with 1st class honors, Nat. U. Ireland, 1962, MD, 1981, DSc, 1984; AM (hon.) Harvard U., 1989; LLD (hon.) Nat. U., Ireland, 1992. Intern, St. Vincent's Hosp., Dublin, Ireland, 1962-63, resident, 1965-67; resident Nat. Maternity Hosp., Dublin, 1963, St. Luke's Hosp., Dublin, 1964, Queen Charlotte's Hosp., London, 1964; postdoctoral fellow, rsch. assoc. Boston U. Sch. Medicine, 1968-73, asst. prof. medicine, 1973-75; asst. prof. medicine Harvard U. Med. Sch., Boston, 1975-79, assoc. prof., 1979-88, Lawrence J. Henderson assoc. prof. health sci. and tech., 1979-88; faculty mem. Grad. Sch. of Arts and Scis., assoc. mem. Dept. of Cellular and Molecular Physiology, Harvard U. Med. Sch., Boston, 1983—, prof. medicine 1988—, Lawrence J. Henderson prof. health sci. and tech., 1988-91, prof. health sci. and tech., 1991—; mem. staff Brigham and Women's Hosp., Boston, 1975—; cons. West Roxbury VA Hosp. and Dana-Faber Cancer Inst., Boston, 1975—, Calif. Biotech. Inc., Palo Alto, 1983-89, Gipharmex S.P.A., Milan, 1984-87, Dow Chem. Co., Midland, Mich., 1984-87, Merix Inc., Needham, 1986—, Oculon, Cambridge, 1987-95, Ciba-Geigy, Summit, N.J., 1988-93, Labs. Fournier, Dijon-Daix, 1992-93, Hoechst AG, Frankfurt, 1993—, Geltex Inc., 1993—; patentee in field. Author: Bile Salts and Gallstones, 1974, Hepatic Excretory Function, 1975; contbr. numerous articles to med. and sci. jours.; assoc. editor Jour. Lipid Rsch., 1978-81; mem. editorial bds. Am. Jour. Physiology, 1976-81, Gastroenterology, 1983-88, Hepatology, 1981-84. Recipient Acad. Career Devel. award NIH, 1976, also MERIT award, 1986, Adolf Windaus prize Falk Found., 1984, Fitzgerald medal Univ. Coll., 1993; Guggenheim Found. fellow, 1974; Fogarty internat. fellow NIH, 1968; McIlrath guest prof., Royal Prince Alfred Hosp., U. Sydney, Australia, 1987. Fellow Royal Coll. Physicians Ireland, AAAS; mem. Gastroenterology Rsch. Group (vice chmn., steering coms.), Am. Soc. Clin. Investigation, Am. Gastroent. Assn. (disting. achievement award 1990), Am. Oil Chemists Soc., Biophys. Soc., Interurban Clin. Club, Am. Assn. Physicians, Royal Irish Acad. (hon.), Wellesley (Mass.) Club. Democrat. Roman Catholic.

CAREY, ROBERT MUNSON, university dean, physician; b. Lexington, Ky., Aug. 13, 1940; s. Henry Ames and Eleanor Day (Munson) C.; m. Theodora Vann Hereford, Aug. 24, 1963; children: Adonice Ames, Alicia Vann, Robert Josiah Hereford. BS, U. Ky., 1962; MD, Vanderbilt U., 1965. Diplomate Am. Bd. Internal Medicine, Am. Bd. Endocrinology and Metabolism, Nat. Bd. Med. Examiners. Intern in medicine U. Va. Hosp., Charlottesville, 1966; jr. asst. resident in medicine N.Y. Hosp.-Cornell Med. Ctr., N.Y.C., 1968-69, sr. asst. resident, 1969-70; instr. endocrinology, dept. medicine Vanderbilt U. Sch. Medicine, Nashville, 1970-72; postdoctoral fellow in medicine St. Mary's Hosp. Med. Sch., London, 1972-73; asst. prof. internal medicine, endocrinology and metabolism U. Va. Sch. Medicine, Charlottesville, 1973-76, assoc. prof., 1976-80, prof., 1980—, James Carroll Flippin prof. medical sci. and dean, 1986—, assoc. dir. Clin. Rsch. Ctr., 1975-86, head. div. endocrinology and metabolism, dept. internal medicine, 1978-86, chmn. gen. faculty, chmn. med. adv. com., chmn. exec. com., 1986—; attending staff U. Va. Hosp., Charlottesville, 1973—, pres. clin. staff, 1977-79, vice chmn. med. policy com., 1986—, adv. bd. 1986—; mem. study sect. on exptl. cardiovascular scis. NIH, 1982-85; mem. cardiovascular and renal adv. com. USDA, 1988—; vis. prof. div. nephrology, U. Miami

Med. Sch., Fla., 1979, 83, 84, Hosp. das Clinicas da Univ., Fed. do Ceara, Forteleza, Brazil, 1981, hypertension div. Mt. Sinai Sch. Medicine, N.Y.C., 1981, div. pediatric endocrinology N.Y. Hosp.-Cornell Med. Ctr., 1981, dept. endocrinology St. Vincent's Hosp., Univ. Coll., Dublin, Ireland, 1982, depts. physiology and endocrinology Mayo Grad. Sch. Medicine, Rochester, Minn., 1984, div. rsch. Cleve. Clinic Found., 1984, Genentech, Inc., San Francisco, 1984, divs. endocrinology and metabolism U. Mass., U. Pa. Sch. Medicine, Boston U. Med. Sch., 1984, U. N.C. Sch. Medicine, 1985, Harvard Med. Sch., Boston, 1987, Jefferson Med. Coll., 1988; Bley Stein vis. prof. endocrinology U. So. Calif., 1987; Pfizer vis. prof. in pharmacology U. Chgo., 1988; co-organizer 3d Internat. Meeting on Peripheral Actions of Dopamine, Charlottesville, 1989; v.p. Va. Ambulatory Surgery, Inc., 1986—; speaker, presenter numerous nat. and internat. profl. meetings and congresses. Author: (with E.D. Vaughn) Adrenal Disorders, 1988; co-editor: Hypertension: An Endocrine Disease, 1985; mem. editorial bd. Jour. Clin. Endocronlogy and Metabolism, 1981-84, Hypertension jour., 1983-84, Am. Jour. Physiology: Heart and Circulatory Physiology, 1987-89, Am. Jour. Hypertension, 1987—; author over 150 articles, revs., papers for profl. jours., contbr. 19 chpts. to books. Mem. exec. com. and fin. com. U. Va. Health Services Found., 1986—; bd. dirs. Va. Kidney Stone Found., Inc., 1986—, The Harrison Found., Inc. U. Va., 1986—, Dyslexia Ctr., Charlottesville, 1986—. Surgeon (lt. comdr.) USPHS, 1966-68, res., 1968—. Recipient Attending Physician of Yr. awrd dept. internal medicine U. Va. Med. Ctr., 1983-84, Disting. Alumnus award and Founder's medal Vanderbilt U.; USPHS fellow Vanderbilt U., 1970-72; recipient numerous NIH grants as co-prin. and prin. investigator, 1972—. Fellow Am. Coll. Physicians (program com. regional meeting 1987), Coun. for High Blood Pressure Rsch. AMA (program com. 1984-86, exec. and long rang planning coms. 1992—); mem. Inst. Medicine of NAS, Am. Heart Assn. (established investigator 1975-80), Va. affiliate Am. Heart Assn. (bd. dirs. 1977-83, pres. 1979-80, Disting. Service award), The Endocrine Soc. (fin. com. 1988—, chair devel. com. 1991-92), Am. Fedn. Clin. Rsch. (so. sect. councilor 1978-81, nominating com. 1982), So. Soc. Clin. Investigation (nominating com. 1982, sec.-treas. 1985-86), Inter-Am. Soc. for Hypertension, Am. Soc. Clin. Investigation, Am. Clin. and Climatol. Assn., Am. Soc. Hypertension (intersocietal affairs com. 1986—), Internat. Soc. Hypertension, Assn. Am. Physicians, AMA, AlbeSoc., Med. Soc. Va., Assn. Am. Med. Coll.s Coun. of Deans, Inst. of Medicine, Nat. Acad. of Scis., The Raven Soc., Alpha Omega Alpha (Disting. Med. Alumnus award Vanderbilt U. 1994). Home: Pavilion Vi East Lawn Charlottesville VA 22903 Office: U of Va Sch Medicine Med Ctr Box 395 Makim Charlottesville VA 22908

CAREY, SHIRLEY ANNE, nursing consultant; b. Syracuse, N.Y., Sept. 27, 1939; d. John Crotty and Eva Mae (Pratt) Walsh; m. John Paul Carey, July 23, 1966; children: Jason Leo, Jonathan Paul, Jennifer Anne. BSN, Nazareth Coll., 1961. RN, Calif. Charge nurse surg. svcs. L.A. County Hosp., 1962-64; instr. nursing L.A. County-U. So. Calif. Med. Ctr. Sch. Nursing, 1964-70; rschr./developer nursing edn. films Concept Media, Irvine, Calif., 1971-78; cmty. health educator Huntington Beach (Calif.) Hosp. and Med. Ctr., 1983—; nursing cons., health educator, writer Huntington Beach, 1988—; dir. staff devel. Huntington Beach (Calif.) Hosp. and Med. Ctr., 1995—, Samaritan Med Ctr., San Clemente, Calif., 1995—; instr. basics of babysitting Huntington Beach Med. Ctr., 1986—; instr. basic life support Am. Heart Assn., Huntington Beach, 1986—; HIV/AIDS educator ARC, Tustin, Calif., 1991—; bd. dirs. West Orange County Consortium Spl. Edn., Huntington Beach, 1991-92, clk., 1992, alt., 1993; bd. trustees Huntington Beach City Sch. Dist., 1990-94, 94—, clk., 1992, pres., 1993. Author, rschr.: (film series) Impaired Mobility, 1993, Basic Patient Care, 1994, Infection Control, 1995; film coord.: (film series) Human Development: Conception to Neonate, 1992, Human Development: First 2 1/2 Years, 1992, Human Development 2 1/2 to 6 Years, 1993. Pres., bd. dirs. Harry W. Montague Basketball Meml. Scholarship Com., Huntington Beach, 1989—, sec., bd. dirs. Huntington Beach Sister City Assn., 1993-95; mem., past officer Orange County (Calif.) Adoptive Parents, 1975—; active Girl Scouts Am., Costa Mesa, 1984-96, PTA, Huntington Beach, 1976—; commr. Huntington Beach Comty. Svcs. Commn., 1994—; mem. Huntington Beach Children's Needs Task Force, 1995—, com. Orange County Sch. Orgn., 1994—; exec. bd. dirs. Huntington Beach PRIDE/DARE Found., 1995—. Recipient Hon. Svc. award PTA, 1989, 2nd Place award Am. Jour. Nursing Film Festival, 1996. Mem. AAUW (exec. bd. dirs. 1995—), Nat. Sch. Bd. Assn. (mem. fed. rels. network 1993—), Women in Leadership, Calif. Sch. Bd. Assn. (mem. legis. network 1990—, del. assembly 1993—). Home and Office: 21142 Brookhurst St Huntington Beach CA 92646-7407

CAREY, WILLIAM BACON, pediatrician, educator; b. Phila., Dec. 6, 1926; s. Henry Reginald and Margaret (Bacon) C.; m. Ann Lord McDougal, July 21, 1956; children: Katharine Blayney, Laura Bacon Carey-Annibalili, Elizabeth McDougal. BA, Yale U., 1950; MD, Harvard U., 1954. Diplomate Am. Bd. Pediatrics. Intern Phila. Gen. Hosp., 1954-55; resident in pediatrics Children's Hosp. of Phila., 1955-57, 59-60; practice medicine specializing in pediatrics Media, Pa., 1960-89; dir. sect. on behavioral pediatrics Children's Hosp. Phila., 1989—; instr. pediatrics U. Pa. Sch. Medicine and Children's Hosp. Phila., 1961-73, assoc. in pediatrics, 1973-79, clin. asst. prof., 1979-82, clin. assoc. prof., 1982-90, clin. prof., 1990—. Co-editor: Developmental-Behavioral Pediatrics, 1983, 2d edit., 1992, Clinical and Educational Applications of Temperament Research, 1989, Prevention and Early Intervention: Individual Differences as Risk Factors for the Mental Health of Children, 1994; co-author: (with S.C. McDevitt) Coping with Children's Temperament - A Guide for Professionals, 1995; mem. editl. bd. Pediatrics, Jour. Devel. and Behavior Pediatrics; contbr. articles to profl. jours.; developer Infant Temperament Questionnaire, 1970; co-developer Toddler Temperament Scale, 1978, Behavioral Style Questionnaire, 1976, Middle Childhood Temperament Questionnaire, 1980, Early Infancy Temperament Questionnaire, 1990. Bd. dirs. Benchmark Sch., Media, Pa., 1989—; pres. Friends of Wyck (House), Germantown, Phila. Capt. M.C., U.S. Army. 1957-59. Fellow Am. Acad. Pediat. (rsch. grantee 1975, 80, 85, Aldrich award 1991, Practitioner Rsch. award 1992); mem. Inst. Medicine of NAS, Am. Pediatic Soc., Soc. Rsch. in Child Devel., Ambulatory Pediatric Assn., Soc. for Devel. and Behavioral Pediatrics (exec. coun. 1983-85, pres.-elect 1989-90,pres. 1990-91), Phila. Pediatric Soc. (bd. dirs. 1969-71), Franklin Inn Club, Phi Beta Kappa. Home: 511 Walnut Ln Swarthmore PA 19081-1140

CARGILL, PAULA MARIE, social worker, gerontologist; b. Henrietta, N.C., Sept. 18, 1943; d. John Edwin and Mabel Anne (Bridges) C. BA in Sociology/French, Winthrop Coll., 1965; MSW, So. Bapt. Theo. Sem., 1973; MS in Social Work, U. Louisville, 1975; grad. in gerontology, U. Mich., 1983. Lic. ind. social worker, lic. nursing home adminstr. Social worker Connie Maxwell Children's Home, Greenwood, S.C., 1965, 70-71; tchr. French secondary pub. schs., N.C., S.C., 1965-70; instr. sociology and French North Greenville Coll., Tigerville, S.C., 1973-74; adj. assoc. instr. North Greenville Coll., Tigerville, 1973-85; clin. social worker S.C. Dept. Mental Health, Simpsonville, 1975-77; social work supr. J Health Care Ctr., Inc., Simpsonville, 1977-84, S.C. Dept. Corrections, Greenville, 1984-89, 90-91; exec. dir. Grady H. Hipp Nursing Ctr., Greenville, S.C., 1989-90; access and in-home program dir. Sr. Action, Greenville, 1991-92; social worker S.C. Dept. Health and Environ. Control, 1992; social work cons. Interim Healthcare, 1992-96; dir. social work Richard Michael Campbell Vets. Nursing Home, Anderson, S.C., 1993; social worker, nursing home and rehab. agy. cons. Aging Cons. Svcs., Greenville, 1982—; ctr. dir. Choice Cmty. Mental Health, 1996—. Contbr. articles to religious mag. Bd. dirs. Greenville County Alcohol/Drug Abuse Commn., 1981-84, Ch. Cmty. Ministries, Greenville Bapt. Assn., 1982—, Grady H. Hipp Nursing Ctr., 1985-89, Rolling Green Village Retirement Ctr., 1990-91, 97—, Upstate Alzheimer's Assn., 1990-92, 94—; mission action cons. So. Bapt. Conv., 1982-83; coun. mem. Bapt. Women, Greenville, 1979-81, 88-91. Mem. NASW (bd. dirs. S.C. chpt. 1976-77, 79-81, 83-85, 90-91), S.C. Health Care Assn., Alumni Leadership Greenville. Home and Office: 1 Kenilworth Dr Greenville SC 29615-2320

CARIFO, KAREN F., laboratory director; b. Rochester, Pa., June 24, 1948; d. Dominic E. and Olivia D. Carifo. BA in Biology, Seton Hill Coll., 1970; PhD in Med. Microbiology, Med. Coll. Wis., 1976; MS in Adminstrn., U. Notre Dame, 1982. Lab techologist West Side Hosp., Milw., 1972-75; divsn. mgr. microbiology/immunology/blood bank South Bend (Ind.) Med. Found., 1975-85; lab. cons. Cmty. Hosp. Bremen, Ind., 1986-93; lab. dir. South Bend Clinic, 1986—. Mem. South Ctrl. Assn. for Clin. Microbiology (area dir. 1983-85), Am. Soc. for Microbiology. Office: South Bend Clinic 211 N Eddy St South Bend IN 46617

CARITHERS, HUGH ALFRED, physician; b. Winder, Ga., July 21, 1913; s. Hugh A. and Starr (Blasingame) C.; m. Cornelia Davis Morse, July 27, 1942; children: Susan (Mrs. John F. Callender), Hugh Alfred, Starr (Mrs. Roy W. Waddell). A.B., Emory U., 1933, M.D., 1937. Diplomate: Am. Bd. Pediatrics. Intern Germantown Dispensary, Phila., 1937-39; resident St. Christophers Hosp. of Phila., 1939-40, Bellevue Hosp., N.Y.C., 1940-41; practice medicine specializing in pediatrics Jacksonville, Fla., 1945—; chief pediatrics Jacksonville Hosps. Edn. Program, 1953-69; chief dept. pediatrics St. Vincent's Hosp., 1952-64, staff pres., 1956-58; clin. prof. pediatrics U. Fla. Coll. Medicine, 1969—. Mem. editorial bd. Am. Jour. Deseases of Children, 1970-79. Served with M.C. AUS, 1941-45. Recipient award for rsch. Am. Acad. Pediatrics, 1994. Fellow Am. Pub. Health Assn.; mem. Fla. Pediatric Soc. (pres. 1949-50), Duval Med. Soc. (pres. 1963-64, Fla. Yacht Club, The River Club (Jacksonville), Phi Delta Theta, Alpha Kappa Kappa, Alpha Omega Alpha. Clubs: Fla. Yacht, The River (Jacksonville). Home: 3010 St Johns Ave Jacksonville FL 32205-9103 Office: 2121 Paris St Jacksonville FL 32204

CARL, ALLEN LAURENCE, surgery educator; b. Queens, N.Y., Apr. 14, 1953; s. O. Edward and Muriel (Lerner) C.; m. Susan A. Ross, Dec. 26, 1981; children: Alissa, Andrew, Scott, Danielle. BA with honors, SUNY, Binghamton, 1975; MD, SUNY, Buffalo, 1979. Diplomate Nat. Bd. Med. Examiners, Am. Bd. Orthopaedic Surgery; lic. surgeon, N.Y. Intern in gen. surgery Albert Einstein Hosp., Bronx, N.Y., 1979-80; resident in orthopaedic surgery, clin. instr. SUNY, Stony Brook, 1980-81; resident in orthopaedic surgery Bellevue Hosp., N.Y.C., 1981-85; fellow in spinal surgery Toronto (Ont.) Gen. Hosp., Can., 1985-86; asst. prof. orthopaedic surgery Albany (N.Y.) Med. Coll., 1986-91, assoc. prof. orthopaedic surgery, 1991—, vice chmn. orthopaedic surgery, 1993—, assoc. prof. pediatrics, 1994—; cons. and presenter in field. Contbr. articles to Head and Neck Surgery, Contemporary Orthopaedics, Foot and Ankle, Spine, Jour. of Bone Joint Surgery Am., Jour. Trauma, Med. Outlook for Orthopaedic Surgeons, Jour. Orthop Trauma, Current Opinions in Orthopaedics, Jour. Orthop Techniques. Fellow Am. Acad. Orthopaedic Surgeons, Acad. Pain Mgmt.; mem. Am. Spine Injury Assn., N.Am. Spine Soc. (profl. and tech. liaison com., subcom. materials and devices), New Eng. Spine Study Group, Ea. Orthopaedic Assn., Internat. Soc. Minimal Intervention in Spinal Surgery, Scoliosis Rsch. Soc. (instrumentation com.), Academic Orthopaedic Soc., Group Internat. Cotrel-Dubousset, Cervical Spine Rsch. Soc. Office: Albany Med Coll Divsn Orthopaedic Surgery A 61 OR Albany NY 12208

CARL, JUDITH LEE, psychologist; b. L.A., Aug. 26, 1944; d. Herbert Frank and June Pauline (Culler) Malone; m. Richard Allen Carl, Aug. 15, 1969 (div. Jan. 1989). BA, Calif. State U., L.A., 1968, MS, 1975; PhD, U. So. Calif., L.A., 1983. Lic. psychologist, Calif. Tchr. Hawaii Bd. of Edn., Honolulu, 1969-70; tchr. Torrance (Calif.) Unified Sch. Dist., 1970-75, counselor, 1975-82; pvt. practice marriage, family and child counselor Torrance, 1978-88; psychol. asst. dr. Melvyn Lewin, Palos Verdes Estate, Calif., 1980-88; pvt. practice Palos Verdes Estate, 1988—; clin. dir. Pev Mar Recovery, Torrance, 1984-85, Place in the Valley, Grants Pass, Oreg., 1989—; corp. cons. Internat. Law Ctr., Torrance, 1990—. Named Woman of the Yr., YWCA, 1981. Mem. APA, Calif. State Psychol. Assn., CAP-PAC, L.A. County Psychol. Assn. Office: 716 Yarmouth Rd Palos Verdes Peninsula CA 90274-2675

CARLE, HARRY LLOYD, social worker, career development specialist; b. Chgo., Oct. 26, 1927; s. Lloyd Benjamin and Clara Bell (Lee) C.; BSS, Seattle U., 1952; MSW, U. Wash., 1966; m. Elva Diana Ulrich, Dec 29, 1951 (div. 1966); adopted children: Joseph Francis, Catherine Marie; m. Karlen Elizabeth Howe, Oct. 14, 1967 (dec. Feb. 1991); children: Kristen Elizabeth and Sylvia Ann (twins), Eric Lloyd; m. Diane Wyland Gambs, May 23, 1993. Indsl. placement and employer rels. rep. State of Wash., Seattle, 1955-57, parole and probation officer, Seattle and Tacoma, 1957-61, parole employment specialist, 1961-63, vocat. rehab. officer, 1963-64; clin. social worker Western State Hosp., Ft. Steilacoom, Washington and U.S. Penitentiary, McNeil Island, Wash., 1964-66; exec. dir. Shohomish County Community Action Council/Social Planning Council, Everett, Wash., 1966-77; employment and edn. counselor Pierce County Jail Social Services, Tacoma, 1979-81; dir. employment devel. clinic, coord. vocat. program North Rehab. Facility, King County Div. Alccholism & Substance Abuse, Seattle, 1981-90; counselor Northgate Outpatient Ctr. Lakeside Recovery , Inc., Seattle, 1991; staff devel. cons. Counseling for Ind. Living, Newport, R.I., 1992; community orgn./agy. problems mgmt. cons., 1968—; mem. social service project staff Pacific Luth. U., Tacoma, 1979-81. Cons. to pres. Geneal. Inst., Salt Lake City, 1974-78. Served with USN, 1944-46. U.S. Office Vocat. Rehab. scholar, 1965-66, named First Honoree Hall of Success Iowa Tng. Sch. for Boys, 1969. Mem. NASW, Seattle Geneal. Soc. (pres. 1974-76), Soc. Advancement Mgmt. (chpt. exec. v.p. 1970-71), Acad. Cert. Social Workers, Pa. German Soc., Henckel Family Nat. Assn., various hist. and geneal. socs. in Cumberland, Perry and Lancaster counties, Pa., Peoria and Fulton Counties, Ill., Seattle Japanese Garden Soc. (v.p. 1993—), Hakone Found. (Saratoga, Calif.), Olympia-Yashiro Sister City Assn., Puget Sound Koi Soc., Dr. Sun Yat-sen Garden Soc. Vancouver (B.C., Can.), Kubota Garden Found. (Seattle), Bloedel Reserve (Banbridge Island, Wash.). Roman Catholic. Home: Karlensgarten Retreat 1425 10th Pl N Edmonds WA 98020-2629

CARLETON, RICHARD ALLYN, cardiologist; b. Providence, Mar. 15, 1931; s. Russell Francis and Margaret Rexford (Bristol) C.; m. April Michele Plumb, Jan. 29, 1975; children: Susan, Bradford, Margaret, Jennifer, Mary. A.B., Dartmouth Coll., 1952; M.D., Harvard U., 1955. Intern Harvard Service, Boston City Hosp., 1955-56, resident and fellow in cardiology, 1956-59; from asst. prof. to prof. medicine U. Ill., 1962-68; chief cardiology, prof. medicine Rush-Presbyn.-St. Luke's Med. Center, Chgo., 1968-72; chief med. service and cardiology San Diego VA Hosp., also prof. medicine U. Calif., San Diego, 1972-74; prof., chmn. dept. medicine Dartmouth Coll. Med. Sch., 1974-76; prof. med. sci., chief cardiology div. Meml. Hosp., Brown U. Med. Sch., Providence, 1976—; physician-in-chief Meml. Hosp., 1982-95; prin. investigator NIH heart disease prevention program, 1980—; chmn. R.I. Health Coord. Com., 1979-80, R.I. Health Edn. Study Com., 1978-81; mem. Nat. Heart, Lung and Blood Adv. Coun., HHS, 1984-88. Contbr. articles to med. pubis. Chmn. Population Panel, Nat. Cholesterol Edn. Program, 1988-90. Served to lt. comdr. M.C. USNR, 1960-62. Recipient Sci. award R.I. Gov., 1989. Mem. Am. Soc. Clin. Investigation, Assn. U. Cardiologists, Am. Coll. Cardiology, Am. Heart Assn. (recipient Gold Heart award 1993, coun. clin. cardiology and epidemiology), ACP, Soc. Behavioral Medicine. Club: Barrington (R.I.) Yacht. Office: Memorial Hosp Pawtucket RI 02860

CARLIER, JEAN JOACHIM, cardiologist, educator, administrator; b. Jemeppe-sur-Sambre, Belgium, July 31, 1926; s. Edouard-Georges and Hermance (Doucet) C.; m. Marie-Louise Barbier, Aug. 17, 1954; children: Pierre, Philippe. Specialist in internal medicine, U. Liège (Belgium), 1958, specialist in cardiology, 1961, Agrégé de l'Enseignement Supérieur, 1967, specialist in cardiac rehab., 1981. Asst., U. Liège, 1953-60, chef de travaux, 1960-67, agrégé de Faculté, 1967-68, chargé de cours associé, 1968-73, associated prof., 1973-91, prof. honor, 1991—, founder Unities of Cardiac Pharmacology and Cardiac Rehab. Contbr. numerous articles to med. jours. Recipient prix Masius U. Liège, 1958, prix Amis U. Lg, 1968; pres.'s Commn. Agreation Cardiologistes de Langue Française, Ministry of Pub. Health, 1972—. Fellow Internat. Coll. Angiology; mem. Belgian, European, French Socs. Cardiology, Belgian and European Socs. Hypertension, N.Y. Acad. Sci. Home: Rue Boulanger-Duhayon 23, B-5190 Jemeppe Belgium

CARLIN, MAURICE PATRICK, surgeon; b. Foley, Minn., July 3, 1924; s. John F. and Ida (Philomen) C.; m. Victoria L. Carlin; children: Brian, Barry, Thomas, Tama, Dierdra, Bonnie, Marci. MD, Marquette U., Milw., 1946. Diplomate Am. Bd. Neurol. Surgery, Am. Bd. Neurology. Intern Buffalo Gen. Hosp., 1947-48; fellow U. Minn. Grad. Sch., 1948-50; resident neurology Minn. VA Hosp. & Affiliated U. Minn. Hosps., 1948-50, resident, 1953-55; chief resident neurosurgery Ill. Neuropsy. Inst., 1954; pvt. practice neurology and neurol. surgery Santa Rosa, Calif., 1955—; mem. staff Santa Rosa Meml. Hosp; cons. neurol. and neurol. surgery Sonoma & Mendocino State Hosp, Sonoma Valley Hosp., St. Helena San; Neurol. Surgery Dept. San Diego USN Hosp., 1951-52; clin. ast. neurology and neurol. surgery U. Ill., 1953-55. Lt. USN, 1950-52. Mem. AMA, Am. Assn. Neurology, Am. Assn. Neurol. Surgery, Am. Assn. Physicians and Surgeons, Calif. Neurol. Soc. Office: 1120 Montgomery Dr Santa Rosa CA 95405

CARLIN, RICHARD, ophthalmologist; b. Chgo., Sept. 24, 1945; s. Thomas and Esther (Goodman) C.; m. Enid Susan Sullum, June 16, 1968; children: David, Erica. BS, Tufts U., 1967; MD, U. Ill., Chgo., 1971. Diplomate Am. Bd. Ophthalmology, Nat. Bd. Med. Examiners. Intern Michael Reese Hosp., Chgo., 1971-72; resident in ophthalmology U. Mich., Ann Arbor, 1972-75; pvt. practice, Snellville, Ga., 1977—. Contbr. articles to med. jours. Lt. comdr. M.C., USN, 1975-77. Student fellow Ill. Eye and Ear Infirmary, 1970; Bamberger scholar U. Ill., 1971. Fellow Am. Acad. Ophthalmology; mem. AMA (physician recognition award), Am. Soc. Cataract and Refractive Surgery, Am. Soc. Contemporary Ophthalmology, Internat. Assn. Ocular Surgeons, Ga. Soc. Ophthalmology, Med. Assn. Ga., Gwinett County Med. Assn., Atlanta Ophthal. Soc. Office: 2347 Lenora Church Rd Snellville GA 30278

CARLINE, JAN DANA, educational evaluator; b. Pontiac, Mich., Sept. 3, 1948; s. Stanley E. and Marjorie Jacquelyn (Walsh) C.; m. Carol Sue Ivory, Aug. 17, 1970. BA, U. Mich., 1970; MEd, U. Wash., 1976, PhD, 1979. Assoc. prof. dept. med. edn. U. Wash., Seattle, 1980—. Recipient Alumni award U. Mich., 1967. Mem. Am. Ednl. Research Assn., Am. Psychol. Assn., Pi Lambda Theta. Contbr. articles to profl. jours. Office: U Wash Med Edn SC-45 Seattle WA 98195

CARLING, PAUL JOSEPH, psychologist; b. N.Y.C., Nov. 2, 1945; s. James Andrew and Mary Amelia (Lorenzo) C.; m. Anne Lois Borker, Jan. 13, 1968 (div. Sept. 1989); children: Oliver Samuel, Nathaniel Philip; m. Cherise Ann Rowan, June 17, 1995. BA, U. Pa., 1971, MS, 1972, PhD, 1977. Lic. psychologist, Pa., Vt. Gen. contractor Carling & Keitt, Phila., 1970-72; lectr. U. Pa., Phila., 1972-75; dir. program devel. Horizon House, Phila., 1974-78; bur. chief N.J. Dept. Mental Health, Trenton, 1978-79; spl. asst. to dir. NIMH, Rockville, Md., 1979-81; dep. commnr. Vt. Dept. Mental Health, Waterbury, 1981-83; rsch. assoc. prof. of rehab. Boston U., 1984-87; rsch. assoc. prof. of psychology U. Vt., Burlington, 1981—; prof. of psychology Trinity Coll. of Vt., 1992—, dir. grad. program in cmty mental health, 1994—; exec. dir., pres. Ctr. for Community Change, Burlington, 1987—; adj. prof. Union of Experimenting Cons., Cin., 1986—; cons. internat., fed., state and local mental health agys., 1975—. Author: Community Integration in Mental Health, 1992, Return to Community, 1995; editor: Housing and Mental Health, 1981, Community Living with Disability, 1991,; contbr. chpts. in books, articles to profl. jours. and videotapes. Chair Vt. Advocacy Task Force, Waterbury, 1985. Recipient Switzer Scholar award Nat. Rehab. Assn. 1988; grantee fed. and state rsch. and dissemination 1975—. Fellow Am. Orthopsychiat. Assn.; mem. APA, Nat. Alliance for Mentally Ill, Nat. Mental Health Consumers Assn., Nat. Assn. Case Mgr. (bd. dirs.), Vt. Mental Health Assn. (bd. dirs.), Vt. Protection and Advocacy, Inc. (bd. dirs. Home: 70 Howard St Burlington VT 05401-4814 Office: Trinity Coll of Vt Ctr for Community Change 208 Colchester Ave Burlington VT 05401

CARLO, GEORGE LOUIS, epidemiologist; b. Jamestown, N.Y., Aug. 24, 1953; s. Louis Samuel and Josephine Lenora (Butera) C.; m. Patricia Herrgott; children: Jody, Doug, Matthew, Michael, Aaron, David, Kristen. BA in Biology cum laude, SUNY, Buffalo, 1975, MS in Epidemiology, 1977, PhD in Exptl. Pathology, 1979; JD in Environ. Law, George Washington U., 1988. Cert. Am. Coll. Epidemiology. Asst. prof. family and community medicine U. Ark. Med. Sci., Little Rock, 1979-81, asst. prof. pharmacology and interdisciplinary toxicology, 1980-81; rsch. leader in epidemiology Dow Chem. Co., Midland, Mich., 1981-84; chmn. Health and Environ. Scis. Group, Washington, 1984—; rsch. assoc. SUNY, Buffalo, 1985-86, clin. asst. prof., 1986—; advisor Ark. Hazard Waste Adv. Com., Little Rock, 1979-81, Office Tech. Assessment adv. panel U.S. Congress, Washington, 1982—; adj. prof. U. Ark. for Med. Sci., Little Rock, 1981-82; adj. faculty Roswell Park Meml. Inst./SUNY, Buffalo, 1982—; asst. professorial lectr. in medicine George Washington U., 1986—; chmn. Wireless Tech. Rsch. LLC; sci. advisor various industry and govts. groups; chmn. Inst. for Sci. and Pub. Policy; moderator Sci. at the Crossroads TV Show. Author more than 100 articles, reports, chpts. in books and commentaries; contbr. to numerous profl. jours. Named one of Outstanding Young Men Am., 1979; recipient Silver Anvil award Pub. Rels. Soc. Am., 1991, Toth award Pub. Rels. Soc. Am., 1991; N.Y. State Dept. Health fellow, 1977. Fellow Am. Coll. Epidemiology; mem. Soc. for Epidemiology Rsch., AAAS, N.Y. Acad. Scis., Soc. for Risk Analysis, Soc. Clin. Trials, Soc. for Risk Analysis Risk Commn. Specialty Group, Soc. Occupational and Environ. Health, Sigma Xi, Am. Pub. Health Assn. Soc. Epidemiological Rsch. Office: HES Group Ltd 1711 N St NW Ste 200 Washington DC 20036-2811

CARLOTTI, RONALD JOHN, food scientist; b. Martins Ferry, Ohio, Sept. 20, 1942; s. John Peter and Mary Rose (Pilla) C.; m. Eileen Theresa Dorsey, May 17, 1969; children: Lori Ann, Christina Maria, Jennifer Ann, Theresa Maria. Student, Wheeling (W.Va.) Jesuit Coll., 1960-63; BS, Ohio State U., 1964; MS, W.Va. U., 1966, PhD, 1970; MM, Aquinas Coll., 1996. Postdoctoral fellow Dept. Biochemistry, U. Iowa, Iowa City, 1971-72; asst. rsch. scientist Pediatrics Dept., U. Iowa, Iowa City, 1973-74; corp. nutritionist Kellogg Co., Battle Creek, Mich., 1974-77; mgr. nutrition/basic rsch. Frito Lay div. Pepsico, Dallas, 1977-82, prin. scientist new products, 1982-85; sr. rsch. scientist Amway Corp., Ada, Mich., 1985-89; dir. food sci. and tech. Country Home Bakers, Grand Rapids, Mich., 1990-93; pres. Carlotti and Assocs., Grand Rapids, 1994; pres., CEO Natura Inc., Lansing, Mich., 1995—; tech. rep. Snack Food Assn., Crystal City, Va., 1978-82, Grocery Mfrs. of Am., Washington, 1975-77; nutritionist Am. Frozen Food Assn., Washington, 1990-93. Contbr. articles to profl. jours. Pres. Mary Immaculate Sch. Bd., Dallas, 1981-83. Recipient Lovable Spud award, Nat. Potato Promotion Bd., Denver, 1981. Mem. Am. Chem. Soc., Am. Assn. Cereal Chemists, Inst. Food Tech. Roman Catholic. Home: 6921 Maplecrest Dr SE Grand Rapids MI 49546-9208 Office: Natura Inc Ste 1007 3900 Collins Rd Lansing MI 48910

CARLQUIST, SHERWIN, biology and botany educator; b. L.A., July 7, 1930; s. Robert William and Helen (Bauer) C. BA, U. Calif., Berkeley, 1952, PhD, 1956; postgrad, Harvard U., 1956. Assoc. prof. Claremont Grad. Sch., Calif., 1967-93, asst. prof. botany, 1956-61; prof. biology Pomona Coll., Claremont, 1976-93. Author: Japanese Festivals, 1965, Island Life, 1965 (Gleason award N.Y. Bot. Garden), Comparative Plant Anatomy, 1961, Hawaii: A Natural History, 1970, Island Biology, 1974, Ecological Strategies of Xylem Evolution, 1975, Comparative Wood Anatomy, 1988, Natural Man, 1991, Man Naturally, 1996, Outsiders, 1996; contbr. articles to profl. jours. Recipient career award Bot. Soc. Am., 1977, Allerton award, 1992, Asa Gray award Am. Soc. Plant Taxonomists, 1993.

CARLSMITH, LYN KUCKENBERG, psychologist, educator; b. Portland, Oreg., Oct. 7, 1932; d. Henry Andrew and Harriet Anne (Casey) Kuckenberg; m. James Merrill Carlsmith, July 27, 1963 (dec. 1984); children: Christopher, Kimberly, Kevin. BA in Internat. Relations, Stanford U., 1954, MA in Psychology, 1959; PhD in Psychology, Harvard U., 1963. Manuscript editor Mid-European Studies, N.Y.C., 1955-57; research assoc. Yale U., New Haven, 1963-64; research assoc. Stanford (Calif.) U., 1964-68, lectr. psychology, 1969-71, sr. lectr. psychology, 1978—; counseling psychologist Social Advocates for Youth, Mountain View, Calif., 1973-79; adv. bd. The Bridge Counseling Ctr., Stanford, 1983—, Action Research Liaison Office, Stanford, 1977-79. Bd. dirs. Ladera Community Assn., Portola Valley, Calif., 1975-78. Mem. Sierra Club. Office: Stanford U Dept Psychology Bldg 420 Stanford CA 94305

CARLSON, ALAN NEIL, ophthalmologist; b. Fairborn, Ohio, Mar. 7, 1956; s. H. Neil and Claunene (Sauter) C.; m. Patricia Ann Dalton, June 4, 1983. AB summa cum laude, Duke U., 1978, MD, 1981. Intern U. N.C., Chapel Hill, 1982-83; resident in ophthalmology Baylor Coll. Medicine, Houston, 1983-86, fellow in cornea/external disease, 1986-87; fellow in cornea/external disease Duke U., Durham, N.C., 1987-88, assoc. prof., 1988-96; attending physician Med. U. S.C., Charleston, 1989—; assoc. prof., dir. corneal svc., dir. refractive surgery Duke U. Eye Ctr., Durham, 1996—; med.

dir. S.C. Lions Eye Bank, 1989—. Editl. reviewer numerous profl. jours.; contbr. chpts. to books. Fellow Am. Acad. Ophthalmology; mem. AMA, Am. Soc. Cataract and Refractive Surgery, Assn. for Rsch. in Vision and Ophthalmology, Eye Bank Assn. Am., Ocular Microbiology Immunology Group,. Office: Duke U Eye Ctr Box 3802 Dume Durham NC 27710

CARLSON, BRIAN JAY, health facility executive; b. Mpls., Mar. 21, 1956; s. John Russell and Shirley Mae Joan (Warholm) C.; m. Ann Margaret Grabau, May 26, 1979; children: Daniel Jordan, Katja Mari, Anja Matia, Peder Christian. BA in Bus. and Hosp. Adminstrn., Concordia Coll., 1978; MSA in Instl. Adminstrn., U. Notre Dame, 1986. Dir. ops. St. Joseph's Med. Ctr., Brainerd, Minn., 1978-80, dir. research and devel., 1980-84, v.p. ops., 1984-95; adminstr. Lake View Meml. Hosp., Two Harbors, Minn., 1995—; engring. cons. St. Joseph's Med. Ctr., Brainerd, 1984-95. Mem. Am. Coll. Healthcare Execs., Am. Mgmt. Assn., Am. Hosp. Assn., Soc. for Hosp. Planning and Mktg., Brainerd C. of C. (mktg. expansion com. 1984-94). Democrat. Office: Lake View Meml Hosp 325 11th Ave Two Harbors MN 55616

CARLSON, CURTIS EUGENE, orthodontist, periodontist; b. Mar. 30, 1942; m. Dona M. Seely; children: Jennifer Ann, Gina Christine, Erik Alan. BA in Divisional Scis., Augustana Coll., 1965; BDS, DDS, U. Ill., 1969; cert. in periodontics, U. Wash., 1974, cert. in orthodontists, 1976. Dental intern Oak Knoll Navy Hosp., Oakland, Calif., 1969-70; dental officer USN, 1970-72; part-time dentist VA Hosp., Seattle, 1972-73; part-time periodontist Group Health Dental Coop., Seattle, 1973-76, part-time orthodontist, 1976-78; clin. instr. U. Wash., 1976; prin. Bellevue (Wash.) Orthodontic and Periodontic Clinic, 1976—; clin. instr., trainer Luxar Laser Corp., Bothell, Wash., 1992—; presenter in field. Master of ceremonies Auctioneer Friendship Fair, Augustana Coll., 1965, orientation group leader, 1965, mem. field svcs. com. for high sch. recruitment, 1965. Fellow Am. Coll. Dentists; mem. ADA, Am. Acad. Periodontology, Am. Assn. Orthodontics, Western Soc. Periodontology (bd. dirs. 1984-85, 86, program chmn. 1986, v.p. 1988, pres. elect 1989, pres. 1990), Seattle King County Dental Soc. (grievance, ethics and pub. info. coms.), Wash. State Dental Assn., Wash. State Soc. Periodontists (program chmn., pres. elect 1987, pres. 1988, 89), Wash. Assn. Dental Specialists (com. rep. 1987, 88, 89), Omicron Kappa Upsilon (dental hon. fraternity), Pi Upsilon Gamma (social chmn. 1964, pres. 1965). Home: 16730 Shore Dr NW Seattle WA 98155-5634 Office: Bellevue Orthodontic Periodontic Clinic 1248 112th Ave NE Bellevue WA 98004-3712

CARLSON, ERIC REINHOLD, surgeon; b. Newton, Mass., May 21, 1959; s. Reinhold Albert and Eleanor Fay (Leach) C.; m. Susan Marie Dougherty, Sept. 10, 1988; children: Katie Marie, Kristen Susan. BA, Conn. Coll., 1981; DMD, U. Pa., 1985. Resident in surgery Allegheny Gen. Hosp., Pitts., 1986-89; fellow in tumor surgery U. Miami, Fla., 1989-90, assoc. prof. surgery, 1993—; sr. staff surgery Henry Ford Hosp., Detroit, 1990-93; dir. maxillofacial tumor surgery U. Miami, 1993—. Editor: The Comprehensive Management of Salivary Gland Pathology, 1995; contbr. articles to profl. jours. Recipient St. George Oral Cancer award Am. Cancer Soc., 1985. Fellow Am. Assn. Oral and Maxillofacial Surgeons; mem. Am. Assn. Oral Pathology (Oral Pathology award 1985), Underseas and Hyperbaric Med. Soc. Republican. Lutheran. Home: 15622 SW 16 St Pembroke Pines FL 33027 Office: Drs Hosp 5000 University Dr Coral Gables FL 33146

CARLSON, HAROLD ERNEST, endocrinologist, educator; b. Staten Island, N.Y., May 17, 1943; s. Clarence Herbert and Edith Emilia (Anderson) C.; m. Gabrielle Arakelian, July 2, 1966; children: Gregory Allan, Jonathan Ernest. BS in Chemistry, Rensselaer Poly. Inst., 1964; MD, Cornell U., 1968. Diplomate Am. Bd. Med. Examiners, Am. Bd. Internal Medicine. Intern, then resident Barnes Hosp., St. Louis, 1968-70; clin. assoc. NIAMD, NIH, Bethesda, Md., 1970-72; fellow in metabolism Washington U. Sch. Medicine, St. Louis, 1972-74; asst. prof., then assoc. prof. medicine UCLA, 1974-82; assoc. prof., then prof. medicine U. Mo., Columbia, 1982-85; prof. medicine SUNY, Stony Brook, 1985—; chief endocrinology Northport (N.Y.) VA Med. Ctr., 1985—. Editor: Endocrinology, 1983; editorial bd. Jour. Clin. Endocrinology and Metabolism, 1979-82; contbr. articles to profl. jours. Lt. comdr. USPHS, 1970-72. Grantee VA, 1974—, March of Dimes, 1987-90. Fellow ACP; mem. Endocrine Soc., Western Soc. Clin. Investigation, Cen. Soc. Clin. Rsch. Office: Med Svc Northport VA Med Ctr Northport NY 11768

CARLSON, JANET FRANCES, psychologist, educator; b. Newport, R.I., Oct. 3, 1957; d. Robert Carl and Alice Marion (Orina) C.; m. Kurt Francis Geisinger, Sept. 22, 1984. BS summa cum laude, Union Coll., Schenectady, 1979; MA in Clin. Psychology, Fordham U., 1982, PhD in Clin. Psychology, 1987. Lic. psychologist, N.Y.; cert. sch. psychologist, N.Y., Conn. Clin. psychology intern Conn. Valley Hosp., Middletown, Conn., 1983-84; research fellow Schering-Plough Found., Bronx, N.Y., 1984-85; psychologist I Creedmoor Psychiat. Ctr., Queens Village, N.Y., 1985-86; psychologist Hallen Sch., Mamaroneck, N.Y., 1986-88; asst. prof. psychology Fordham U., Bronx, N.Y., 1988-89; asst. prof. sch. and applied psychology Fairfield (Conn.) U., 1989-93, dir. sch. and applied psychology programs, 1989-90; asst. prof. counseling and psychol. svcs. SUNY, Oswego, 1993-95, assoc. prof. counseling and psychol. svcs., 1995—; cons. N.Y.C. Bd. Edn. Office Rsch., Evaluation and Assessment, 1988-92; vis. asst. prof. psychology LeMoyne Coll., Syracuse, N.Y., 1992-93. Recipient Sugarfree scholarship, 1984-85, Sigma Xi Grant-in-Aid of Research, 1984-85. Mem. APA, Am. Ednl. Rsch. Assn., Nat. Assn. Sch. Psychologists, Ea. Psychol. Assn., N.Y. State Psychol. Assn., Northeastern Ednl. Rsch. Assn. (editor newsletter 1988-91, bd. dirs. 1990-93, pres. 1995-96), N.Y. Assn. Sch. Psychologists, Sigma Xi, Psi Chi (charter), Phi Kappa Phi (charter, pres. 1995-96).

CARLSON, JOHN CARL, surgeon; b. Chgo., Feb. 10, 1950; s. Elmer Roy and Jean Marie (Puyanic) C.; m. Mary Jo Henry, June 5, 1971; children: Erik John, Dana Beth, Ryan Matthew, Hope Elizabeth. BS, Loyola U., Chgo., 1972; MD, U. Chgo., 1975. Cert. Am. Bd. Surgery. Intern & resident St. Paul-Ramsey Med. Ctr., 1975-80; pvt. practice gen. surgery Hastings (Minn.) Surg. PA, 1980-88; staff surgeon River Valley Clinic, Hastings, 1988—; chief surgery Regina Med. Ctr., Hastings, 1980—. Fellow ACS; mem. Minn. Surg. Soc., St. Paul Surg. Soc. (adv. bd. mem. 1990-92). Home: 2410 Westview Dr Hastings MN 55033 Office: River Valley Clinic 1210 First St West Hastings MN 55033

CARLSON, JULIE NEI, optometrist; b. Chgo., Mar. 6, 1967; d. Gary E. and Priscilla (Waters) Nei; m. Lance K. Carlson, June 13, 1992. BS in Biology, U. Mich., 1989; OD, New Eng. Coll. Optometry, Boston, 1993. Assoc. Palozej & Palozej, Ellington/Stafford Spgs, Conn., 1993-94, Dr. Jeffrey Koziol, Arlington Heights, Ill., 1995—. Mem. Am. Optometric Assn., Ill. Optometric Assn. Home: 4744 Kingsway North Gurnee IL 60031

CARLSON, NANCY LYNN, psychologist; b. Kane, Pa., Dec. 15, 1936; d. Stanley H. and Elizabeth J. (Pratt) C. BS, Edinboro U., 1959; MA, Ohio U., 1964; PhD, U. Kans., 1970. Diplomate Am. Bd. Profl. Psychology. Asst. dean of women Edinboro (Pa.) U., 1959-64; program dir. U. Wis., Madison, 1964-66; counselor, instr. U. Kans., Lawrence, 1966-70; psychologist, asst. prof. U. Md., College Park, 1970-74; dir. counseling svcs. SUNY, New Paltz, 1975-78; dir. counseling and career svcs., assoc. prof. U. R.I., Kingston, 1978-86; psychologist U. Maine, Orono, 1986-88; pvt. practice Portland, Maine, 1987—. Co-author: Rape, Incest, Sexual Harassment, 1989; co-author: Handbook on Sexual Harassment, 1980; contbr. articles to profl. jours. and books. Danforth Found. grantee, 1961, 63. Mem. APA, Assn. for Psychol. Type.

CARLSON, SUSAN SPEVACK, hospital administrator, family physician; b. N.Y.C., July 20, 1945; d. Jerome S. and Ruth (Sporn) Spevack; m. Robert Howard Carlson, Dec. 27, 1970; 1 child, Christopher Randall. BA, Skidmore Coll., 1967; MD, Columbia U., 1973. Diplomate Am. Bd. Family Practice, Am. Bd. Quality Assurance and Utilization Rev. Physicians, Am. Bd. Med. Mgmt. Med. officer USPHS, Sitka, Alaska, 1973-86; med. dir. Mt. Edgecumbe Hosp., Sitka, 1986—. Contbr. articles to profl. jours. Pres. Alaska divsn. Am. Cancer Soc., 1984-86 (Vol. Leadership award 1988); bd. dirs. Sitka Summer Music Festival, 1985-94. Fellow Am. Acad. Family Physicians; mem. AAUW (treas. 1981-83), Commd. Officers Assn. Home: PO Box 1867 Sitka AK 99835-1867 Office: Mt Edgecumbe Hosp 222 Tongass Dr Sitka AK 99835-9416

CARLSON, TIM PAUL, physician assistant; b. Rockford, Ill., Jan. 17, 1956; s. C. Raymond and Dorothy E. Carlson; m. Marianne Carlson, Jan. 3, 1987; 1 child, Brittany Lyn. BS in Zoology, Butler U., 1978; EMT cert., Sante Fe C.C., Gainesville, Fla., 1980; GAS, U. Fla., 1980, BS in medicine, 1983. Lab. technician, phlebotomist Riverview Hosp., Noblesville, Ind., 1975-76; emergency rm., outpatient phlebotomist, technician North Fla. Regional Hosp., Gainesville, 1979-80; EMT Micanopy, Fla., 1979; physician asst. Downtown Med. and Diagnostic Ctr., St. Petersburg, Fla., 1983—; instr. anatomy dept. radiology Sch. Radiology Tech., Bayfront Med. Ctr., St. Petersburg; cons. State of Fla., Agy. for Health Care Adminstrn., Dept. Bus. and Profl. Regulation, 1995—; lectr. and presenter in field. Mem. Am. Acad. Physician Assts., Nat. Commn. on Certification Physician Assts., Fla. Acad. Physician Assts. (Tampa Bay area rep. 1989-95, mem. conf. planning com. 1994—, chmn. membership com. 1994—, chmn. endorsement com. 1995, legis. com., v.p. 1995, 96), Suncoast Corvette Assn. Home: 625 Quintana Pl NE Saint Petersburg FL 33703

CARLSON, TIMOTHY D., psychiatrist; b. Aug. 10, 1952. BA, Case Western Res. U., MD. Diplomate Am. Bd. Psychiatrists. Mem. Am. Psychiat. Assn., N.C. Psychiat. Assn. Office: 3717 National Dr Raleigh NC 27612-4878

CARLTON, CATHERINE KENNEY, osteopathic surgeon; b. Laredo, Tex., Oct. 20, 1915; d. Charles Francis and Helene (Larmoyeux) K.; m. Elbert P. Carlton, June 11, 1941 (dec. 1972); children: Cathy Carlton Landon, Helen McFall, Jane Carlton Toone; m. Eugene Hightower, May 23, 1974 (dec. 1992). Student, Incarnate Word Coll., San Antonio, 1933, U. Tex.-Arlington, 1934; DO, Kirksville Coll. Osteo. Medicine, Mo., 1938. Cert. Am. Acad. Osteopathy, Gen. Practice. Mem. staff Ft. Worth Osteo. Hosp., 1946—; practice medicine specializing in osteopathy, 1939—; prof. Tex. Coll. Osteo. Medicine, 1970-75, clin. prof., 1975-96; cons. and lectr. in field; lectr., demonstrator osteo. manipulative technique 1st Internat. Congress Osteo. Medicine, Brussels, 1984. Editor: A History of St. Mary of the Assumption Catholic Church 1908 to 1988, 1988; contbr. articles to profl. jours. Mem. NCCJ, Ft. Worth, 1984-93; eucharistic minister St. Mary Assumption, San Antonio, 1987, active in hist. places registration, 1984. Named Outstanding Alumnus, Kirksville Coll. Osteo. Medicine, 1965; recipient Meritorious Svc. award Tex. Coll. Osteo. Medicine, 1975, Outstanding Hosp. Staff Mem. award Osteopathis Med. Ctr., Texas, 1989, Edna Gladney Aux. Svc. award, Ft. Worth, 1978, Hist. Medallion award Tex. Hist. Commn., 1979, Founders medal Tex. Coll. Osteo. Medicine Bd. Regents, 1983, Profl. Woman award Ridglea Bus. & Profl. Women, 1984, Humanitarian Disting. Svc. award 4th degree KC, 1986. Mem. St. Mary's Parish Coun., Ft. Worth Diocese; pres. Nat. Coun. Cath. Women, 1952-53. Mem. Am. Acad. Osteopathy (pres. 1976-77), Kirksville Coll. Osteo. Medicine Alumni Assn. (sec. Tex. chpt. 1965-87, pres. 1979-80), Tex. Acad. Osteopathy (pres. 1969-88, sec.-treas. 1971-87), Tex. Coll. Osteo. Medicine Found. (sec. 1986-88). Republican. Lodges: Zonta (Outstanding Profl. Accomplishments award 1976), Rotary (1st v.p. Ft. Worth club 1986-87), Knights & Ladies of the Holy Sepulchre (lady commdr.), The Serra Internat. Avocations: swimming, walking, reading. Home: 2505 Ryan Place Dr Fort Worth TX 76110-2506 Office: 815 W Magnolia Ave Fort Worth TX 76104-4612

CARLTON, ROBERT L., clinical psychologist; b. Murray, Ky., June 1, 1918; s. Albert B. and Ophelia (Hughes) C.; m. Frances Suiter, July 10, 1946; children: Glenn R., Keith H. BS, Murray State U., 1948; MA, Ohio State U., 1950, PhD, 1953. Lic. psychologist, Ohio. Staff psychologist Children's Mental Health Ctr., Columbus, Ohio, 1952-55, chief psychologist, 1955-63, assoc. dir., 1963-82; pvt. practice Columbus, 1982—; clin. asst. prof. dept. psychiatry Ohio State U., Columbus, 1966-77, adj. assoc. prof. dept. psychology, 1972-81. 1st lt. USAF, 1942-46, PTO. Mem. Am. Psychol. Assn., Ohio Psychol. Assn. (spl. recognition award 1972), Cen. Ohio Psychol. Assn. Home: 27 Willow Brook Way Delaware OH 43015-3815

CARLTON, SARA BOEHLKE, rehabilitation services administrator; b. Black River Falls, Wis., July 1, 1937; d. Ralph William and Hazel Olive (Drecktrah) Boehlke; m. Mason Gant Carlton, Sept. 9, 1961 (dec.); children: Holly Gant, John Frederick. BS, U. Wis., 1959; MEd, Rutgers U., 1981, EdD, 1988. Occupl. therapist VA Hosp., Lyons, N.J., 1960-65; occupl. therapist Hunterdon Med. Ctr., Flemington, N.J., 1968-71, dir. occupl. therapy, 1971-73, dir. child evaluation & treatment, 1973-85, adminstrv. rehab. coord., 1985-88; asst. v.p. Mt. Washington Pediat. Hosp., Balt., 1988-96; rehab. program mgr. Johns Hopkins Bayview Med. Ctr., Balt., 1996—; mem. adj. faculty Rutgers U., 1981, Johns Hopkins U., Balt., 1991—; surveyor Commn. Accreditation Rehab. Facilities, 1993—; independent healthcare cons., 1995—. Mem. Holland Twp. Red. Fdn., Hunterdon County, N.J., 1972-78, v.p., 1974-78; trustee Hunterdon Occupational Tng. Ctr., Flemington, 1972-80, pres. 1978; trustee Hunterdon County Bd. Mental Health, 1975-77; mem. adv. bd. Inst. for Study of Exceptional Children, Ednl. Testing Svc., Princeton, N.J., 1978-80; trustee Upton Sch. Found., Balt., 1988—, sec. 1990—; trustee Shepherd's Clinic, Balt.; mem. Md. State Interagy. Coordinating Coun., 1989-95. Mem. Am. Coll. Healthcare Execs., Am. Occupational Therapy Assn., Md. Occupational Therapy Assn. Presbyterian (deacon 2d Presbyn Ch., Balt.). Home: 113 Fireside Cir Baltimore MD 21212-2417

CARLTON-ADAMS, DANA G.M., psychotherapist; b. Kansas City, Mo.; d. George Randolph Carlton and Harriett Marie (Smith) Carlton-Witt; m. John Adams; 1 child, J.J. II. Student, Kansas City (Mo.) Jr. Coll., Rockhill Coll., Trinity Coll., Dublin, Ireland, 1973, City U. of London (Eng.), 1978. Owner Pure White Electric Light and Magic, Lakewood, Calif., 1985—; dir., owner Trauma Buddy's, Lakewood, 1988—; clin. hypotherapist Inner Group Mgmt., Cerritos, Calif., 1989—; cons. Rockwell, McDonnell Douglas, Long Beach, Calif., 1987-90; owner In Print mag., 1990—; staff counselor FHP. Author: Who Calls on Pandora, 1969, Jupiter in Scorpio, 1974, Burma Route, 1989, Counterstrike: Dimitri Manulski, 1990, Kitty-Mophis, 1982, Mouse Tails, 1991, Bookish Miss Emma, 1993, A Little Trip Through the Universe, 1993, Handbook for the Living, 1990. Adv. Greater Attention Victims Violent Crimes; active Animal Rights Pet Protection Soc., Calif. Preventive Child Abuse Orgn., Sierra Club, Women's Abuse Shelters. Mem. Calif. Astronomy Assn., Acoustic Brain Rsch., Inner Group Mgmt., NLP Integration Soc. (pres. 1988-89), British Psychol. Assn., C. of C., Willmore Heritage Ctr. for Neighborhood Downtown Preservation. Home and Office: 243 W 8th St Long Beach CA 90813-4157

CARLUCCI, MARIE ANN, nursing administrator, nurse; b. N.Y.C., Apr. 22, 1953; d. Clarence Hugh and Anna Rebecca (Mills) McName; m. Paul Pasquale Carlucci, Aug. 18, 1973; children: Christine, Patricia. Diploma in nursing, Mt. Vernon Hosp. Sch. Nursing, N.Y., 1974; BS in Behavioral Sci. summa cum laude, Mercy Coll., 1991; postgrad., N.Y. Med. Coll., 1991—. Cert. emergency nurse; cert. nurse adminstr. Staff nurse Mt. Vernon (N.Y.) Hosp., 1974-82, Lawrence Hosp., Bronxville, N.Y., 1982-84; staff nurse No. Westchester Hosp., Mt. Kisco, N.Y., 1984-91, asst. dir. nursing, mem. nurse mgmt. and ethics coms., 1991-94; asst. DON svcs. Ferncliff Manor, Yonkers, N.Y., 1994-95, dir. nursing svcs., 1995—. Religious edn. tchr. St. John and St. Mary's Ch., Chappagua, N.Y., 1984-94; campaign mgr. Com. to Elect Paul P. Carlucci, Chappagua, 1990; mem. Surrogate Decision Making Com., N.Y. Commn. Quality Care for Mentally Disabled; mem. bd. trustees Field Home-Holy Comforter, 1995—; mem. Hastings Ctr. Mem. N.Y. Orgn. Nurse Execs., N.Y. State MR/DD Nurses Assn., St. John and St. Mary's Women's Assn., Psi Chi, Phi Gamma Mu. Roman Catholic. Home: 23 Pine View Rd #5 Mount Kisco NY 10549-3935 Office: Ferncliff Manor 1154 Saw Mill River Rd Yonkers NY 10710-3210

CARLUCCIO, SHEILA COOK, psychologist; b. Carbondale, Pa., Nov. 10, 1954; d. Harry Thomas and Elizabeth Mary Cook; m. Robert Carluccio, Feb. 28, 1987; 1 stepchild, Robert Jr. BA, Marywood Coll., 1982, MA, 1987. Lic. psychologist. Sign lang. interpreter for hearing-impaired Scranton (Pa.) State Sch. for Deaf, 1984-86, psychology intern, 1986; staff clin. psychologist Devereux Found., Chester, N.J., 1987-88; staff psychologist Hope House, Dover, N.J., 1989-94, U. Scranton, Pa., 1994-95; pvt. practice Carbondale, 1993—. One woman art shows include Sterling Hotel, Wilkes-Barre, Pa., Sol Hemma, Uniondale, Pa., 1980; exhibited at Suraci Gallery, Scranton, Pa., 1979; contbr. poems to lit. jours. Human svc. team mem. Morris County Human Svc. Orgn./Assn., Dover, 1992. Mem. Am. Psychol. Assn. (assoc.), Am. Deafness and Rehab. Assn. (assoc.), Pa. Psychol. Assn. Psi Chi. Roman Catholic. Office: 123 Huntington Dr Dickson City PA 18519

CARMACK, ROBERT WILLIAM, medical facility administrator; b. Fairmont, Minn., Oct. 29, 1940; s. Howard R. and Lois V. (Wilkerson) C.; 1 child, Christopher S. BBA, North Tex. State U., 1962; MBA, East Tex. State U., 1967. Regional rep. Med. Computer Sys., Inc., San Francisco, 1975-77; adminstr. Neurol. Assocs., Tucson, 1977-79, Hamilton Med. Group, Lafayette, La., 1979-85; dir. ops. MetLife HealthCare Network, Ft. Lauderdale, Fla., 1985-87; assoc. exec. dir. Humana Health Care Plans, Miami, Fla., 1987-89; v.p. for customer svc. Am. Express, Plantation, Fla., 1989-92; pres., CEO Dimension Physician-Hosp. Orgn., Miami Lakes, Fla., 1992—. Fellow Am. Coll. Med. Practice Execs., Am. Coll. Med. Group Adminstrs. (state pres., state treas. 1980-83). Episcopalian. Office: Dimension Health PHO 15500 New Barn Rd S-101 Miami Lakes FL 33014

CARMENA, THOMAS NEIL, internist; b. Baton Rouge, Mar. 11, 1932; s. Joseph William and Doris Anna (Ligon) C.; widowed 1980; children: Jane, Julie, Amy, Leslie. BS, La. State U., 1953; MD, La. State U., New Orleans, 1956. Intern Stanford svc. San Francisco Hosp., 1956-57; flight surgeon USAF, Itazuke AFB, Japan, 1957-59; resident internal medicine Charity Hosp., New Orleans, 1959-60, Henry Ford Hosp., Detroit, 1960-62; pvt. practice Las Vegas. Capt. M.C., USAF, 1957-59, Japan. Fellow ACP, Am. Coll. Cardiology, Am. Coll. Chest Physicians; mem. AMA, Am. Soc. Internal Medicine. Republican. Roman Catholic. Office: 2200 Rancho Dr Las Vegas NV 89102

CARMICHAEL, BRUCE FENTON, health facility administrator; b. Waterbury, Conn., Nov. 21, 1946; s. Thomas and Betty (Porzenheim) C.; married; 1 child, Ryan. BS, Rensselaer Poly. Inst., 1968, BArch, 1969; MArch, U. Mich., 1970; MS in Nursing, Yale U., 1982; MPA, U. New Haven, 1990, ScD, 1994. Registered architect, N.Y., Conn.; cert. Nat. Coun. Archtl. Registration Bd. Architect Atelier Assocs., Cheshire, Conn., 1972-79, Bruce F. Carmichael Architect, New Haven, 1982-83; head nurse Yale New Haven Hosp., New Haven, 1982-85; architect, 1985-89; assoc. dir. facilities planning Yale U. Sch. Medicine, New Haven, 1989-91, dir. project mgmt., 1991-95, exec. dir. facilities, 1995—; adjunct faculty U. New Haven, 1993-94; lectr. Yale U. Sch. Nursing, New Haven, 1982-87, clin. instr., 1983, asst. clin. prof., 1988—. Co-author: Housing, 1969, Discharge Teaching Manual for Cardiac Transplant Patients, 1981, Using College Facilities for Marketing, 1991, Small Can Be Beautiful, 1995. Fellow U. New Haven, 1988. Mem. AIA (New Eng. Regional Coun. Award of Merit 1976), Am. Soc. Hosp. Engrs., Conn. Soc. Architects, Nat. Fire Protection Assn., Sigma Beta Delta. Home: 672 Quinnipiac Ave New Haven CT 06513-4065 Office: Yale U Sch Medicine 37 College St New Haven CT 06510-3208

CARMICHAEL, DAVID BURTON, physician; b. Santa Ana, Calif., Sept. 12, 1923; s. David Burton and Phyllis (Adams) C.; m. Ava Louise Smith, Dec. 26, 1944; children: Catherine Ann, Heather Sue, Linda L., Ava L. Student, Graceland Coll., 1940-42; B.A., M.D., U. Iowa, 1946; postgrad., Harvard U., 1949-50; LL.D. (hon.), Graceland Coll., Iowa, 1985. Diplomate: Am. Bd. Internal Medicine. Clin. and research fellow medicine Mass. Gen. Hosp., Boston, 1949-50; cons. cardiovascular diseases U.S. Naval Hosp., San Diego, Camp Pendleton; cons. cardiovascular diseases U.S. VA; chief dept. medicine Scripps Meml. Hosp., La Jolla, Calif., 1961-63, 65-67; chief staff Scripps Meml. Hosp., 1970-71; clin. prof. medicine U. Calif. at San Diego, 1968—; pres. De Anza Lab. Corp., 1962-72, Carmichael-Carson Med.-Clin. Lab. Corp., 1962-75; sr. ptnr. Med. Clinic; med. dir. Cardiovascular Inst. Scripps Meml. Hosps., 1985—; pres. Orange County Pioneer Coun., 1993-94; trustee GDE Systems, Inc., 1992-94. Contbr. articles to profl. jours. Trustee Millicent Rogers Mus., Taos, N.Mex., 1986-90, Graceland Coll., Iowa, 1987—, Rancho de los Golondrinas Mus., Santa Fe, 1989—. Served to rear adm., med. insp. gen. USNR. Decorated Legion of Merit; recipient Alumni Disting. Service award Graceland Coll., 1967. Fellow ACP (gov. So. Calif. region III 1972-76, Laureate award 1991), Am. Coll. Cardiology (dir., sec. 1975, trustee 1979-85, Disting. Fellow award 1994), Am. Coll. Chest Physicians; mem. AMA (chmn. specialty soc. and service delegation 1985-87, 93—, mem. grad. med. edn. adv. com. 1983—89, chmn., 1985-87, chmn. sect. council on clin. cardiology), Am. Heart Assn., San Diego County Heart Assn. (pres. 1959-60), San Diego Biomed. Research Inst. (pres. 1958-59, 62-63, vice chmn. residency rev. com. internal medicine 1971-78), San Diego Soc. Internal Medicine (pres. 1959-61). Republican. Mem. Reorganized Ch. of Jesus Christ of Latter-day Saints (elder). Home: 8333 Calle Del Cielo La Jolla CA 92037-3033 Office: 9844 Genesee Suite 400 La Jolla CA 92037

CARMICHAEL, LYNN PAUL, family practice physician; b. Louisville, Sept. 15, 1928; s. Donald Palmer and Vivian Iris (Linler) C.; m. Joan Pauline Steinlight, June 26, 1954; children: John Kevin, Cynthia Gail, Jon Christian. Student, Ind. U., 1945-48; MD, U. Louisville, 1952. Diplomate Am. Bd. Family Practice. From intern to battalion surgeon U.S. Army, San Antonio, Korea, 1952-54; pvt. practice Mooresville, Ind., 1954-55; pvt. practice surgery Miami, 1955—; fellow Harvard Med. Sch., Boston, 1953-54; faculty U. Miami, 1965—; test com. Nat. Bd. Med. Examiners, 1976-79; residency rev. com. Accreditation Coun. for Grad. Med. Edn., Chgo., 1972-75; cons. Pub. Health Svc., Washington, 1976-90. Med. support ARC, Cuba, 1962, Medishare, Haiti, 1995. Decorated bronze star U.S. Army, 1953. Mem. AMA, Soc. Tchrs. Family Medicine (founding pres. 1967-70, founding editor 1978-83), Am. Acad. Gen. Practice, Inst. of Medicine Nat. Acad. Sci. (sr. membership 1995). Home: 5330 Banyan Dr Miami FL 33156 Office: U Miami Dept Family Med 600 Alton Rd #501 Miami Beach FL 33139

CARMICHAEL, PAUL LOUIS, ophthalmic surgeon; b. Phila., July 8, 1927; s. Louis and Christina Ciamaichela; B.S. in Biology, Villanova U., 1945; M.D., St. Louis U., 1949; M.S. in Medicine, U. Pa., 1954; m. Pauline Cecilia Lipsmire, Oct. 28, 1950; children—Paul Louis, Mary Catherine, John Michael, Kevin Anthony, Joseph William, Patricia Ann, Robert, Christopher. Rotating intern St. Joseph's Hosp., Phila., 1949-50; resident in ophthalmology Phila. Gen. Hosp., 1952-54; certified isotape methodology Hahnemann Med. Coll., Phila., 1960, asst. prof. ophthalmology, 1960-66, clin. assoc. prof. nuclear medicine, 1974-90; radioactive isotope dept. Wills Eye Hosp., Phila., 1956-61, sr. asst. surgeon, 1961-65, assoc. surgeon, 1966-72, assoc. surgeon retinal svc., 1972-90; attending ophthalmologist Holy Redeemer Hosp., Meadowbrook, Pa., 1963-65; assoc. ophthalmologist Grand View Hosp., Sellersville, Pa., 1958-75; instr. ophthalmology Grad. Sch. Medicine, U. Pa., Phila., 1956-63; clin. assoc. prof. ophthalmology Temple U., Phila., 1967-72; clin. assoc. prof. ophthalmology Thomas Jefferson U. Sch. Medicine, Phila., 1971-90; chief ophthalmology N. Pa. Hosp., Lansdale, 1959-90, pres. staff, 1959; pres. Ophthalmic Assocs., Lansdale, 1969-90. Pres. bd. dirs. N. Pa. Symphony, 1976-78. Capt., M.C., U.S. Army, 1950-51. Named Outstanding Young Man of Yr., Lansdale Jaycees, 1959, Outstanding Young Man State of Pa. Jaycees, 1960. Diplomate Am. Bd. Ophthalmology. Fellow A.C.S., Internat. Coll. Surgeons, Coll. Physicians Phila.; mem. AMA, Montgomery County Med. Soc., Pa. State Med. Soc., Am. Acad. Ophthalmology, Pa. Acad. Ophthalmology, Assn. Rsch. in Ophthalmology, Inter-County Ophthalmol. Soc. (co-founder, pres. 1975-78), Ophthalmic Club Phila. (pres. 1964), Delaware Valley Ophthalmol. Soc. (pres. 1985-89). Roman Catholic. Co-author: Nuclear Ophthalmology, 1976; contbr. chpts. to books, papers to profl. confs., articles to publs. in field. Home: Box 681426 2567 Columbine Ct Park City UT 84068

CARMICHAEL, ROBERT WILLIAM, medical group administrator; b. Lansdale, Pa., Dec. 22, 1958; s. Paul Louis and Pauline Cecilia (Lipsmire) C.; m. Ruth Maria Avendano, July 22, 1983; children: Diana Christina, Anna Maria. BS in Econs., U. Pa., 1980; MBA, U. Miami, 1987. Treas. AIESEC U.S., N.Y.C., 1980-81; asst. to contr. Comfamiliar Andi Fenalco, Barranquilla, Colombia, 1981-82; asst. to v.p. ops. ICN Pharms., Covina, Calif., 1982-83; fin. mgr. Paulmarc Systems, Lansdale, 1983-85; ops. mgr. Coopervision Info. Systems, Lansdale, 1985-86; bus. mgr. Ophthalmic Assocs., Lansdale, 1987-90; cons. Mass. Eye and Ear Infirmary, Boston, 1990-91, Carter Eye Ctr., Dallas, 1991-94, Fort Lauderdale (Fla.) Eye Inst., 1995—; ptnr. Poolside Cons., Lansdale, 1985—; founder, v.p. Profl.

Ophthalmic Adminstrs., Phila., 1989—; bd. advisors AIESEC, Long Beach, Calif., 1983. Acct. Mary Mother of Redeemer Ch., Montgomeryville, Pa., 1988—; bd. dirs. North Penn Symphony Orch., Lansdale, 1989. Named Outstanding Young Man of Yr., Lansdale Jaycees, 1990. Republican. Roman Catholic. Office: Fort Lauderdale Eye Inst 7800 W Oakland Park Blvd Ste B-206 Fort Lauderdale FL 33351

CARMICLE, LINDA HARPER, psychotherapist; b. Westmore, Tenn., Oct. 20, 1937; d. Noel Franklin and Mary Frank (Caldwell) Harper; m. Jerrel B. Carmicle, June 2, 1956; children: Roxanna Linn Carmicle Lynch, Jerry Noel. AA, St. Petersburg Jr. Coll., 1968; BSW with honors, Tex. Women's U., 1975, MA, 1977; PhD in Psychology, Fielding Inst., Santa Barbara, Calif., 1992. Lic. profl. counselor, marriage and family therapist; cert. eating disorder specialist, chem. dependency specialist; cert. group psychotherapist; supr. for LPCs. Dir. Galaxy Ctr., Garland, Tex., 1975-78; counselor Saudi Arabia Internat. Sch., Daharan, 1978, Dallas County Family Ct. Counselors, Dallas, 1979-83; pvt. practice psychotherapy Dallas and Plano, Tex., 1983—; mem. faculty S.W. Group Psychotherapy Inst., 1995; mem. adj. faculty Tex. Women's U., Denton, 1976-78, rep. Coun. on Social Work Edn., 1977. Contbr. articles to profl. jours. Active Custer Rd. United Meth. Ch. Mem. Am. Group Psychotherapy Assn., Am. Assn. Marriage and Family Therapy, Tex. Assn. Counseling Devel., Tex. Assn. Marriage and Family Therapy, Dallas Group Psychotherapy Soc. (chair program com.), Internat. Assn. Transactional Analysis, Internat. Assn. Eating Disorder Profls. Democrat. Methodist. Home: 3005 Saddlehead Dr Plano TX 75075-1529 Office: 2301 Ohio Dr Ste 215 Plano TX 75093-3902

CARMODY, JOHN L., surgeon; b. Worcester, Mass., Sept. 14, 1939; m. Judith Ann Botnick, Dec. 10, 1964; three children. BA, Yale U., 1961; MD, Harvard U., 1965. Cert. Nat. Bd. Med. Examiners, Am. Bd. Gen. Surgery. Intern in surgery Harvard Surg. Svc., Boston City Hosp., 1965-66, resident in surgery, 1966-68, chief resident surgeon, 1969-71; surg. registrar U. Aberdeen, Scotland, 1968-69; staff surgeon Brattleboro (Vt.) Meml. Hosp., 1974—; mem. Vt. State Bd. Med. Practice, 1976-83, chmn., 1981-83. Med. dir. Brattleboro (Vt.) Rescue Inc., 1984—. Maj. USAF, 1972-74. Fellow ACS; mem. Vt. State Med. Soc., New Eng. Surg. Soc. Office: 13 Belmont Ave Brattleboro VT 05301

CARNATHAN, GILBERT WILLIAM, pharmaceutical company executive, research scientist; b. Quincy, Mass., Nov. 1, 1951; s. Gilbert Caldwell and Regina Marie (Layden) C.; m. Jane Ellen Gabel, July 9, 1972; children: Paul Max, Jesse Gilbert. BS, Northeastern U., Boston, 1974; MS, U. Mass., 1979, PhD, 1982. Rsch. scientist G.D. Searle & Co., Skokie, Ill., 1980-85; sect. mgr. Rorer Cen. Rsch., King of Prussia, Pa., 1985-90; v.p. preclin. rsch. Cortech, Inc., Denver, 1990—. Contbr. 30 articles to profl. jours. Chairperson Rorer Blood Drive/ARC, King of Prussia, 1989-90; coach Hyland Hills (Colo.) Bantam B Hockey Team, 1991-93, 94-96. Mem. AAAS, Am. Assn. Pharm. Sci., Inflammation Rsch. Assn., Project Mgmt. Inst., Drug Info. Assn. Office: Cortech Inc 6850 N Broadway Denver CO 80221-2907

CARNEVAK, ROBERT A., cardiologist, educator; b. Providence, Jan. 6, 1951; s. A. Robert and Anna (Maccarone) C.; m. Joanne Neary, Mar. 10, 1979; children: Caroline, Jessica, Robert, Joseph. BSc, Providence Coll., 1972; MD, N.Y. Med. Sch., 1975. Diplomate Am. Bd. Internal Medicine. Cardiologist R.I. Hosp., Providence, 1980—; clin. asst. prof. Sch. Medicine Brown U., Providence, 1990—. Fellow ACP, Am. Coll. Cardiology; mem. Am. Soc. Echocardiology. Roman Catholic. Office: Coastal Med Inc-Elmhurst 1075 Smith St Providence RI 02908

CARNEY, DAVID LYNDEN, physician assistant; b. Sayre, Pa., Mar. 9, 1943; s. Byron George and Lillian Mae (Watson) C.; m. Sharon Louise Hubbard, Aug. 31, 1968; children: Jeffrey, Bryan, Phillip. AA in Music Edn., Mansfield State Coll., 1962; Cert. physician asst., Pa. State, 1975. Physician asst. Soldier & Sailors Meml. Hosp., Penn Yan, N.Y., 1976-80, J.C. Wilson Health Ctr., Rochester, N.Y., 1980-83, IMC, Miami, 1983-87, Prison Health Svcs., Bertow, Fla., 1987-94, Lake Wales (Fla.) Med. Ctrs., 1994—. Music dir. Shannan Ave. Bapt. Ch., Plant City, Fla., 1988—; bd. dirs. Am. Cancer Soc., Penn Yan, 1970-80, Nat. Kidney Found., Charlotte, N.C., 1979. With USN, 1964-68. Fellow Fla. Acad. Physicians Assts. (area rep. 1990—). Republican. Home: 2404 Twelve Pint Dr Lakeland FL 33811

CARNEY, JAMES CHRISTOPHER, internist; b. Detroit, Mar. 18, 1956. BS, U. Notre Dame, 1978; MD, Wayne State U., 1982. Diplomate Am. Bd. Internal Medicine; cert. ACLS. Intern in internal medicine Sinai Hosp., Detroit, 1983, resident, 1984-85, co-chief resident, 1985, asst. attending staff, 1985-87; pvt. practice, Southfield, Mich., 1985—; house physician St. Joseph Hosp., Mt. Clemens, Mich., 184-85; asst. med. dir. Select Care, 1994; assoc. staff William Beaumont Hosp., Royal Oak, Mich., 1986-92, attending staff, 1993—; active med. staff Mt. Carmel Mercy Hosp., Pontiac, Mich., 1992-93; mem. exec. com. Beaumont Physicians Group, Royal Oak, 1995; instr. preceptor program Wayne State U., Detroit, 1994-95, clin. asst. prof. dept. internal medicine, 1996—. Recipient award for contbn. to tchg. program CIBA-GEIGY, 1985.0. Fellow ACP; mem. AMA, Am. Soc. Internal Medicine, Oakland County Med. Soc. Office: 29210 Telegraph Rd Ste 404 Southfield MI 48034

CARNEY, JAMES MICHAEL, social services administrator, social worker; b. Berlin, Wis., May 12, 1944; s. John and Ethelyne M. (Fisher) C.; children: Aaron James, Amanda Mary; m. Lynn Carol Withers, May 12, 1982. BS in Psychology, U. Wis., Kenosha, 1973; MEd in Counseling, Marquette U., 1974, postgrad., 1974-80. Cert. ind. clin. social worker, Wis. Vocat. rehab. counselor Jewish Vocat. Svc., Milw., 1974-78, counseling supr., 1978-82, intake dir., 1982-83; med. social worker Sacred Heart Rehab Inst, Milw., 1983-87, med. social worker II, 1987-88, mgr. dept. social svc., 1988-91, mgr. head injury program, 1988-92; head injury program admissions coord. Sacred Heart Rehab Inst, 1992—. Mem. Nat. Head Injury Found., Brain Injury Assn. of Wis. (bd. dirs. 1989-93, treas. 1992-93), Wis. Assn. Rehab. Social Workers, Phi Beta Kappa (del. chpt. conv. 1980-81). Home: 4461 N Bartlett Ave Milwaukee WI 53211-1508 Office: Sacred Heart Rehab Inst 2350 N Lake Dr Milwaukee WI 53211

CARNEY, JEAN KATHRYN, psychologist; b. Ft. Dodge, Iowa, Nov. 10, 1948; d. Eugene James and Lucy (Devlin) C.; m. Mark Krupnick, Jan. 1, 1977; 1 child, Joseph Carney Krupnick. BA, Marquette U., Milw., 1970; MA, U. Chgo., Chgo., 1984; PhD, U. Chgo., 1986. Registered Clin. Psychologist, Ill. Reporter Milw. Jour., 1971-76, editorial writer, 1976-79; asst. prof. psychology St. Xavier Coll., Chgo., 1985-86; dir. Lincoln Park Clinic, Chgo., 1986-87; pvt. practice psychotherapist Chgo., 1987—; mem. sci. staff Michael Reese Hosp. Med. Ctr., Chgo., 1987—; instr. Northwestern U. Med. Sch., 1991—; lectr. U. Ill. Coll. Medicine, 1993—. Recipient Best Series Articles, 1975, Best Editorial, 1978, Milw. Press Club, William Allen White Nat. Award for Editorial Writing, 1978, Robert Kahn Meml. Award for Research on Aging, Univ. Chgo., 1985. Mem. APA, Ill. Psychol. Assn., Chgo. Assn. Psychoanalytic Psychology. Home: 915 Burns Ave Flossmoor IL 60422-1107 Office: 55 E Washington St Ste 1219 Chicago IL 60602-2108

CARNEY, PETER MALLISON, neurosurgeon; b. Cleve., Mar. 14, 1936; s. Richard Birchnal Westnedge and Dorothy (Mallison) C.; m. Gloria Smith, Apr. 11, 1970. BA, Williams Coll., 1958; MD, Western Reserve U., 1962. Intern in surgery Yale New Haven (Conn.) Hosp., 1962-63, resident in neurosurgery, 1963-68; neurosurgeon Tufts New Eng. Med. Ctr., Boston, 1968-71, Cape Cod Hosp., Hyannis, Mass., 1971-77, King Faisal Specialist Hosp., Riyadh, Saudi Arabia, 1977-83; Mellon fellow MIT, Cambridge, Mass., 1984-85; neurosurgeon Elkhart (Ind.) Gen. Hosp., 1985—; chmn. dept. surgery King Faisal Specialist Hosp., 1980-83, editor med. jour., 1980-83. Contbr. articles to profl. jours. Mem. AMA, Am. Assn. Neurologic Surgeons, Am. Soc. Law, Medicine, Ethics, Congress of Neurologic Surgeons, Internat. Assn. Study of Traumatic Brain Injuries, Ind. Med. Assn. Office: 238 Waterfall Dr Elkhart IN 46516

CARNEY, WILLIAM PATRICK, medical educator; b. Dillon, Mont., July 1, 1938; s. Thomas James and Helen Catherine (Ballard) C.; children: Christopher Patrick, Mark Daniel; m. Sharon Loreta Sonnek, Aug. 14, 1965. BA, St. Thomas U., Kenmore, Wash., 1960; BS, Western Mont. U., 1962; PhD, U. Mont., 1967; MPH, Johns Hopkins U., 1976. Cert. secondary tchr. in biol. scis. Rsch. assoc. Minot (N.D.) State U., 1967-69; commd. lt. USN, 1969, advanced through grades to capt., 1986; rsch. parasitologist Naval Med. Rsch. Inst., Bethesda, Md., 1969-70, 74-75; dir. parasitology dept. Naval Med. Rsch. Unit No. 2, Jakarta, Indonesia, 1970-74; dept. dir. Naval Med. Rsch. Unit No. 2, Taipei, Taiwan, 1976-79; lab. and scientific dir. Naval Med. Rsch. Unit No. 2, Jakarta, 1979-81; program mgr. Naval Med. Rsch. Devel. Command, Bethesda, 1981-84; lab. dir. Naval Bioscis. Lab., Oakland, Calif., 1984-87; prof., dir. grad. program Uniformed Svcs. U., Bethesda, 1987-91, ret., 1991; project mgr. schistosomasis rsch. project in Cairo Med. Svc. Corp. Internat., Arlington, Va., 1991-95; prof. Uniformed Svcs. U., Bethesda, Md., 1995—; exec. com. bd. dirs. Gorgas Meml. Inst., Bethesda; cons. Vector Biology and Control Project, Arlington, 1989-94, Am. Inst. Biol. Scis., Washington, 1987—. Contbr. articles to profl. jours. Adult leader Boy Scouts Am., Taipei, 1976-79. Decorated Legion of Merit. Mem. Am. Soc. Parasitologists, Am. Soc. Tropical Medicine and Hygiene, Helminthological Soc. Washington, Sigma Xi, Phi Sigma. Republican. Roman Catholic. Office: Uniformed Svcs U Dept Preventive Medicine 4301 Jones Bridge Rd Bethesda MD 20814-4799

CARNIOL, PAUL J., plastic and reconstructive surgeon, otolaryngologist; b. N.Y.C., Sept. 26, 1951; s. David A. and Diane (Hadler) C.; m. Renie Rich, Jan. 3, 1976; children: Michael P., Alan R., Eric T. BA, NYU, 1972; MD, U. Pa., 1976. Diplomate Am. Bd. Otolaryngology, Am. Bd. Cosmetic Surgery, Am. Bd. Med. Examiners, Am. Bd. Facial Plastic and Reconstructive Surgery. Surg. residency U. Pa., Phila., 1976-77, plastic and reconstructive surg. residency, 1981-83; surg. residency North Shore U. Hosp., Manhasset, N.Y., 1977-78; head and surg. residency, otolaryngology, clin. tchg. fellow Harvard Med. Sch., Boston, 1978-81; attending plastic surgeon, head and neck surgery Overlook Hosp., Summit, N.J., 1983—; clin. asst. prof. U. Medicine and Dentistry of N.J., Newark; cons. aesthetic, reconstructive and pediatric plastic surgery; pres. N.J. Acad. Otolaryngology, 1993-96; mem. bd. examiners Am. Bd. Cosmetic Surgery; numerous lectrs., TV presentations in field; chief sect. otolaryngology Overlook Hosp., Summit, N.J. Spl. editor Am. Jour. Cosmetic Surgery; contbr. articles to profl. jours. Interviewer for admissions com. U. Pa., Phila., 1987—. Recipient Community Svc. award Ciba-Geigy, Summit, 1978, Found. award NYU, 1972, Alumni Gold Med. award NYU, 1972. Fellow ACS, Am. Acad. Otolaryngoloy, Nead and Neck Surgery, Am. Acad. Cosmetic Surgery, Am. Acad. Facial Plastic and Reconstructive Surgery (dir. courses lasers in facial plastic surgery 1996, care com.), N.J. Acad. Medicine, Am. Rhinologic soc.; mem. AMA, N.J. State Med. Soc., Union County Med. Soc. (planning com. 1986-89, chmn. program com., exec. com.), Phi Beta Kappa. Office: Summit Med Group 120 Summit Ave Summit NJ 07901-2804

CARNOVALE, BENJAMIN VICTOR, health facility administrator; b. Timmins, Ont., Can., Dec. 14, 1935; came to U.S., 1982; s. John and Immacolata (Garritano) C.; m. Jane Elizabeth Sadler, Apr. 25, 1981; children: J. Christopher, R. Benjamin, Andrew A., Kenneth L. BA, Queen's U., Kingston, Ont., 1957, MD, 1962. Diplomate Am. Bd. Quality Assurance and Utilization Rev. Physicians. Intern Hotel Dieu Hosp., Kingston, Ont., 1962-63, resident in surgery, 1963-64; resident in surgery Kingston Gen. Hosp., 1964-65; resident in gen. surgery Plymouth (Eng.) Gen. Hosps., 1965-66; resident in gen. and surg. pathology St. Joseph's Hosp., Hamilton, Ont., 1966-67, emergency rm. physician, 1967-69; chief resident in gen. surgery Queen's U. Teaching Hosps., Kingston, Ont., Can., 1969-70; pvt. family practice Burlington, Ont., Can., 1970-81, Intracorp Med. Rev. Svcs., Dallas and Plano, Tex., 1982-92; physician advisor Intracorp Med. Rev. Svcs., Dallas, 1984-92, regional med. dir., 1989-91; assoc. med. dir. Blue Cross Blue Shield Tex., Dallas, 1992—. Mem. AMA, Am. Acad. Family Physicians, Am. Coll. Physician Execs., Am. Coll. Med. Quality, Tex. Acad. Family Physicians. Home: 1553 Sussex Dr Plano TX 75075-2718 Office: Blue Cross Blue Shield Tex 901 S Central Expressway Richardson TX 75080

CARNOW, BERTRAM WARREN, occupational and environmental health consultant; b. Phila., June 19, 1922; s. Louis H. and Helen (Warren) C.; m. Shirley Ann Conibear, Oct. 30, 1975; children: David Robert, Donald James, Tammi Jo, Rebecca Ann, Kalinka Rose, Tina Lisa. BS in Biology, NYU, 1947; MB, MD, Chgo. Med. Sch., 1951. Diplomate Am. Bd. Preventive Medicine. Intern Cook County Hosp., Chgo., 1951-52; basic sci. resident in cardiology Michael Reese Hosp., Chgo., 1952-53, clin. resident in internal medicine, 1953-55, attending physician internal medicine, cons. chest diseases, 1955-71; dir. Dept. Occupational and Environ. Medicine U. Ill Sch. Pub. Health, Chgo., 1972-78; dir. residency tng. in occupation medicine U. Ill. Hosp., Chgo., 1982-87, dir. programs in occupational medicine, 1977-87, dir. Great Lake Ctr. for Occupational Safety and Health, 1977-87; pres., sr. scientist Carnow, Conibear, and Assocs., Ltd., Chgo., 1974-88, exec. v.p., 1988—; pvt. practice in occupational and environ. medicine, Chgo.; prof. occupational medicine U. Ill., Chgo., 1966-92, dept. preventive medicine, 1987-92, environ. and occupational health scis., U.I. Sch. Pub. Health, 1972-92, ; dir. div. occupational medicine Cook County Hosp., 1976-80, Environ. Health Resource Ctr. State of Ill, 1969-77; chmn. com. for rev. of NIOSH criteria documents, Soc. for Occupational and Environ. Health, 1974-80; chmn. NRC panel on SO2, Nat. Acad. Scis., 1974, mem. panel on nonrenewable resources, 1974, mem. panel on polycyclic organic matter, 1974; cons. U.S. Congress Subcom. on Investigations and Oversight of the Pub. Works and Transp. Com. on Subcom. on Commerce, Transp. and Tourism of Energy and Commerce Com., Washington, Karolinska Inst., Sweden, NSF, EPA, NAS, City of El Paso, Tex., Minister of Environment City of Toronto, EPA, Senate Commerce Subcom. on Health Effects of Lead, AEC, Ill. Agent Orange Comm., Nat. Inst. Environ. Health Sci., State of Ill., Am. Pub. Health Assn., Acad. Pediatrics, Meat Packer's Union, AFL-CIO, Senate Subcom. on Environment, Sulfates and Intermittent Stack Tech., Pres. Coun. on Environ. Quality, State of Calif., State of Pa., State of N.Y., OSHA, Inst. on Man and Sci., Govt. of Can. B.C. (Can.) Coun. of Indian Chiefs, St. Regis Coun. Akwasame Indians. N Am. contbg. editor Am. Jour. Indsl. Medicine, assoc. editor, 1980; mem. editorial bd. Jour. Safety Rev., 1975—; contbr. articles to profl. jours. With USAF, 1942-46. Med. dir. Chgo. Lung Assn., 1970-78; mem. epidemiology com. Am. Heart Assn., 1976, mem. task force on heart disease in industry; mem. epidemiology and statistics task force, Ill. Cancer Coun., 1978. Grantee NIOSH, 1977-87, State of Ill., 1969-78, Kellogg Found., 1975-78, EPA, NIOSH, 1969-84. Master Am. Coll. Occupational and Environ. Medicine; fellow APHA, Am. Coll. Preventive Medicine, Am. Coll. Epidemiology, Royal Soc. Health, Chgo. Inst. Medicine; mem. AAAS, Am. Coll. Toxicology, Cen. States Occupational Medicine Assn., Am. Assn. Tchrs. Preventive Medicine, Am. Trudeau Soc., Am. Acad. Occupational Health, Ill. Coll. Chest Physicians, Nat. Thoracic Soc., N.Y. Acad. Scis. Office: Carnow Conibear & Assocs 333 W Wacker Dr Ste 1400 Chicago IL 60606-1225

CARNS, REBECCA SUSAN RAY, advanced clinical hypnotherapist; b. Franklin, Pa., Jan. 17, 1948; d. William Euan and Clarissa Rebecca (Davis) Ray; m. Lex Eugene Carns, May 13, 1967; children: Lex II, Douglas, Edward, Richard. Diploma, Clearfield Hosp. Sch. Nursing, 1968; student, U. Del., 1988; grad., Wellness Inst., 1994, 95, 95. Cert. CPR instr.; RN, Pa., Del., Fla. Staff nurse oper. rm. Clearfield (Pa.) Hosp., 1968-69, 70-73 part time; substitute sch. nurse Smyrna (Del.) Sch. Dist., 1988-89; staff nurse Vis. Nurse Assn., Milford, Del., 1988-93; community mental retardation nurse cons. Del. Dept. Mental Retardation, Dover, 1989-94; drug and alcohol rehab. staff nurse The Cloisters, Pineland, Fla., 1995; staff nurse Home Care, Ft. Myers, Fla., 1995—; pvt. practice hypnotherapy; staff nurse Profl. Nurses Registry, 1994—. Author curriculum in field.

CARO, JESUS JAIME, medical researcher; b. Bogota, Colombia, May 11, 1959; came to U.S., 1992; s. Jose Jaime and Graciela (de la Torre) C.; m. Heidi Ann Hunting, June 11, 1983; children: Elena, Anthony, Alexandra. Cert. and diploma, Bishop's Coll. Sch., Lennoxville, Que., Can., 1976; diploma health scis., Champlain Regional Coll., Lennoxville, Que., Can., 1978; MD CM, McGill U., Montreal, Que., Can., 1983. Asst. prof. McGill U., Montreal; sci. dir. Caro Rsch., Concord, Mass. Contbr. articles to profl. jours. Fellow ACP; mem. AMA, Mass. Med. Soc. Office: Caro Rsch 336 Baker Ave Concord MA 01770

CARON, ROXANNE, chiropractor; b. Rome, N.Y., Aug. 2, 1954. BS, Keene State Coll., 1976, MEd, 1981; D in Chiropractic, Tex. Chiropractic Coll., 1987. Pvt. practice chiropractic Nashua, N.H., 1988—; lectr. Keene (N.H.) State Coll., 1988-93. Mem. Nat. Athletic Trainers Assn., N.H. Athletic Trainers Assn. Office: 44 Archery Ln Nashua NH 03060

CARON, THERESA LYNN WHITE, health facility administrator, medical educator; b. Chgo., Dec. 10, 1958; d. Richard Irving and Anastasia Jane (Cronin) W.; m. Michael Joseph Caron, Nov. 9, 1991; children: Alexander, Sean Michael, Megan Anastasia. BSN, BS in Psychology, Elmhurst (Ill.) Coll., 1982; MS in Mgmt., MS in Human Resource Devel., Nat.-Louis U., 1990, postgrad., 1996—. RN, Ill. Staff nurse, vascular surgery Edward Hines, Jr. VA Med. Ctr., Hines, Ill., 1982-83, nat. vascular study nurse coord., 1983-89, med. quality mgmt. specialist, 1989-91; surg. quality mgmt. specialist West L.A. VA Med. Ctr., 1991-92, acting asst. dir. quality mgmt./clin. risk mgmt., 1992-93, quality mgmt. program dir., ambulatory care svcs., 1993-94; U.S. Congrl. adv. bd. mem. (invited), Chgo., 1983-84; adv. bd. mem. final exams. and critical care, Elmhurst Coll., 1988; cons. Dept. Vets. Affairs, West L.A., 1991-94. Mem. Nat. Assn. Health Care Quality, Soc. for Vascular Nursing, Am. Soc. Law Medicine and Ethics (invited), "Think First" Nat. Spinal Cord and Brain Injury Assn. (chpt. co-dir. 1993-96), Aesculapians UCLA Sch. Medicine, Pi Gamma Mu, Psi Chi, Sigma Kappa. Roman Catholic. Home: 822 S Monroe St Hinsdale IL 60521-4322

CARONE, FRANK, medical educator, pathologist; b. New Kensington, Pa., Nov. 28, 1927; married, 1952; 5 children. AB, W.Va. U., 1948; MD, Yale U., 1952. Cert. pathologist. Intern U. Pa. Hosp., 1952-53; instr. Yale U. Sch. Medicine, 1959-60; from asst. prof. to prof. Northwestern U. Sch. Medicine, 1960-69, Morrison prof. pathology, 1969—; dir. labs. Northwestern Meml. Hosp., Chgo., 1972-90. Editor yearbook of pathology, 1972-80. Mem. Nat. Adv. Bd. for Kidney and Urological Diseases, 1987-92. Capt. M.C. USAF, 1953-55. Life Inst. Med. Research Fund research fellow, 1957-59; Markle scholar, 1964-69. Mem. Am. Fedn. Clin. Research, Internat. Acad. Pathology, Am. Soc. Exptl. Pathologists. Office: Northwestern U Sch Medicine Dept Pathology 303 E Chicago Ave Chicago IL 60611-3008

CARP, RICHARD IRVIN, microbiologist; b. Phila., May 10, 1934; s. Maurice and Sara (Lee) C.; m. Sally E. Bennet, June 26, 1960; children—Daniel, Melissa, Joshua. B.A., U. Pa., 1955, V.M.D., 1958, Ph.D., 1962. Postdoctoral fellow Wistar Inst., Phila., 1958-62; asso. Wistar Inst., 1964-68; established virus and tissue culture labs. Baroda, India, 1963; vis. prof. Baylor U. Med. Coll., 1965; prin. research scientist dept. microbiology and animal experimentation N.Y. State Inst. Basic Research in Mental Retardation, S.I., 1968-71; research scientist VII dept. virology N.Y. State Inst. Basic Research in Devel. Disabilities, 1977—, head. dept. virology, 1987—; prof. SUNY-Downstate Med. Center, 1977—; faculty Richmond Coll., 1969-84, Wagner Coll., 1975-83; head animal care com. Research Facility and Research Found. Recipient award for outstanding contbns. in multiple sclerosis research Suffolk County chpt. Nat. Multiple Sclerosis Soc., 1976; Community Service award Tottenville Improvement Council, Inc., 1976. Mem. Am. Soc. Microbiologists, Am. Soc. Virology, AAAS, Phi Zeta. Home: 46 Duncan Rd Staten Island NY 10301-3809

CARPENETTI, STEFANO R., ophthalmologist; b. Phila., July 25, 1966; s. Aldo M. and Amina (Flocco) C.; m. Alison A. Botek, June 6, 1992. BS cum laude, Muhlenberg Coll., Allentown, Pa., 1988; DO, Phila. Coll. Osteo. Medicine, 1992. Intern Osteo. Med. Ctr., Phila., 1992-93; ophthalmology resident Phila. Coll. Osteo. Medicine, 1993—; jr. clin. faculty Phila. Coll. Osteo. Medicine, 1993-96. Mem. AMA, Am. Acad. Ophthalmology, Am. Osteo. Colls. of Ophthalmology and Otolaryngology, Head and Neck Surgery, Am. Soc. Cataract and Refractive Surgery, Am. Osteo. Assn. Home: 1812 Forrestal St Philadelphia PA 19145

CARPENTER, DIANE MARIE, nursing educator, health facility administrator; b. Allentown, Pa., Feb. 22, 1953; d. Bernard E. and Julia C. (Tkac) Spade; m. Peter Carpenter, June 27, 1981; children: Kaitlyn, Peter Tyler. BSN, Villanova U., 1975; MS, U. Scranton (Pa.), 1985. RN, Pa.; cert. facilitator for interactive mgmt., instr. in quality edn. system P.C. Cosby Assocs. Staff/temp. charge nurse med. ICU Hosp. of U. Pa., 1975-77; nurse acute coronary care Lehigh Valley Hosp., 1977-79, instr. critical care, 1979-83, asst. dir. nursing edn., 1983-88; dir. continuing edn. and orientation Lehigh Valley Hosp., Allentown, Pa., 1988-89, dir. human resource devel., 1989-95, dir. orgnl. devel., 1996—. Narrator (videotape) Nursing Liability. Mem. ASTD, Organl. Devel. Network, Sigma Theta Tau. Home: 161 Cook St Alburtis PA 18011 Office: Lehigh Valley Hosp 1200 S Cedar Crest Blvd PO Box 689 Allentown PA 18105

CARPENTER, JEANNINE NUTTALL, nurse; b. Safford, Ariz., Feb. 10, 1934; d. Joseph Heber and Alma (Woolsey) Nuttall; m. Jerry K. Carpenter, Apr. 1, 1953; children: Jeffrey, Joe, Jan, Jason, Julie. ADN, Mesa Community Coll., 1973; BSN, U. Phoenix, Tucson, Ariz., 1990. Cert. profl. health care quality, Ariz. Dental asst. Safford, Ariz., 1952-69; staff nurse Maricpa Med. Ctr., Phoenix, 1973, Mt. Graham Community Hosp., Safford, 1973-75; dance instr. Ea. Ariz. Coll., Thatcher, 1978-91, instr. cert. nursing asst., 1984-90; nurse supr. Mt. View Nursing Ctr., Safford, 1975-77; RN/EMT Caldwell's Ambulance, Safford, 1974-86; nurse supr. No. Cochise Hosp., Willcox, Ariz., 1977-79; dir. nurses Safford Care Ctr., 1986-87; swing bed coord. Mt. Graham County Hosp., Safford, 1987—; quality coord. nursing Mt. Graham Hosp., Safford, 1989—, interim dir. nursing, 1994, quality resources dept. dir., 1993—; v.p. Ariz. Bd. Adminstrs., Phoenix, 1987-90; clin. preceptor U. Phoenix, Tucson, 1990—; publ. bd. Ariz. Assn. Healthcare Quality, Tucson, 1990-93; coord. Joint Commn. Accreditation and State Dept. of Health Svcs. Licensure, 1991—. Actress mus. theater, 1974. Sec. Am. Heart Assn., Safford. Republican. Mormon. Office: Mt Graham Community Hosp 1600 S 20th Ave Safford AZ 85546-4011

CARPENTER, KENNETH JOHN, nutrition educator; b. London, May 17, 1923; came to U.S., 1977; s. James Frederick and Dorothy (George) C.; m. Daphne Holmes, June 22, 1944 (dec. 1974); 1 child, Roger Hugh; m. Antonina Pecoraro, June 18, 1977. BA, U. Cambridge, Eng., 1944, PhD, 1948, ScD, 1974. Mem. sci. staff Rowett Inst., Aberdeen, Scotland, 1948-56; lectr., then reader in nutrition U. Cambridge, 1956-77; prof. nutrition U. Calif., Berkeley, 1977-91. Author: History of Scurvy and Vitamin C, 1986, Protein and Energy, 1994; editor: Pellagra, 1982. Kellogg fellow Harvard U., 1955-56, Commonwealth fellow Cen. Food Tech. Rsch. Inst., Mysore, India, 1961, fellow Sidney Sussex Coll., U.K., 1961-77. Fellow Am. Inst. Nutrition (Atwater medal 1993, Hatch award 1993); mem. History of Sci. Soc.

CARPENTER, MALCOLM BRECKENRIDGE, retired neuroanatomist, educator; b. Montrose, Colo., July 7, 1921; s. Grover B. and Haidee (Moritz) C.; m. Carolyn I. Sloan, July 20, 1949; children—Duncan B., Gregory S., Rustin I. A.B., Columbia U., 1943; M.D., L.I. Coll. Medicine, 1947. Diplomate: Am. Bd. Psychiatry and Neurology. Intern Bellevue Hosp., N.Y.C., 1947-48; resident neurology Neurol. Inst. N.Y., 1950-53; fellow neurology Columbia Coll. Phys. and Surg., 1948-50, mem. faculty, 1953-76, prof. anatomy, 1962-76; prof. anatomy and medicine Pa. State U., Hershey, 1976-78; prof., chmn. dept. anatomy Uniformed Services U., Bethesda, Md., 1978-87, prof., 1987-90; retired, 1991; cons. NIH, 1962-66, 1968-72; adviser Parkinson Disease Found., 1962-65; mem. test com. Nat. Bd. Med. Examiners, 1977-81, edn. com. Fgn. Med. Grad., 1983-91. Author: (with R.C. Truex) Human Neuroanatomy, 1964, 6th edit., 1969, (with J.C. Madigan) Cerebellum of the Rhesus Monkey, 1971, Core Text of Neuroanatomy, 4th edit., 1991, Human Neuroanatomy, 1976, 8th edit., 1983; also articles; mem. editorial bd. Neurology, 1963-72, Neurobiology, 1970-76, Jour. Comparative Neurology, 1971-80; assoc. editor Am. Jour. Anatomy, 1968-74. Served with M.C. USNR, 1950- 52. Markle scholar, 1953-58. Mem. Internat. Basal Ganglia Soc. (pres. 1983-86, treas. 1986—). Home: 380 E Chocolate Ave Hershey PA 17033-1319

CARPENTER, PEGGY, medical technologist; b. Childress, Tex., Aug. 19, 1945; d. Eddie George and Lela Belle (Weedin) Bussey; m. Jimmy Ray Belyeu, June 7, 1961 (div. Sept. 1976); 1 child, Deborah Diane Belyeu; m. David Michael Carpenter, Aug. 4, 1989. Degree in med. tech., Amarillo, Tex., 1974. Chief med. tech. Univ. Hosp., Lubbock, Tex., 1974-79, Highland Med. Ctr., Lubbock, 1979—. Home: 4514 59th St Lubbock TX 79414 Office: Highland Med Ctr 2412 50th St Lubbock TX 79412

CARPENTER, THOMAS OLIVER, medical educator, pediatric endocrinologist; b. Ayer, Mass., June 26, 1952; s. William Bruce and Maria Laraine (Piermarini) C.; m. Caren Marie Gundberg, Oct. 18, 1981; 1 child, Matthew Thomas. BA with hons., U. Va., 1973; MD, U. Ala., 1977. Diplomate Am. Bd. Pediatrics. Intern U. Ala., Birmingham, 1977-78; resident in pediatrics U. Ala., 1978-80; fellow in pediatric endocrinology Harvard Med. Sch./Children's Hosp., Boston, 1980-83; instr. pediatrics Harvard Med. Sch./Children's Hosp., 1983-86; asst. prof. pediatrics Yale U. Sch. Medicine, New Haven, 1986-91, assoc. prof., 1991—; dir. pediatric endocrine fellowship tng. Yale U. Sch. Medicine, 1988—. Contbr. articles to profl. jours.; editl. bd. Magnesium Rsch. Jour., Paris, 1988—. NIH awardee, 1982, 87; Endocrinology Research awardee, Harvard Med. Sch., 1982. Mem. Lawson Wilkins Pediatric Endocrine Soc., Endocrine Soc., Am. Soc. Bone and Mineral Rsch., Am. Fedn. Clin. Rsch., Am. Physiol. Soc., Soc. for Pediatric Rsch. Episcopalian. Office: Yale U Sch Medicine PO Box 208064 New Haven CT 06520-8064

CARPER, BARBARA ANNE, nursing educator. BSN, Tex. Women's U., 1959; clin. cert. in anesthesia, U. Mich., 1962; MEd, Columbia U., 1966, EdD, 1975. Instr. U. N.Mex. Coll. Nursing, Alburquerque, 1966-69; assoc. prof. Tex. Women's U. Coll. Nursing, Denton, 1976-80, prof., coord. doctoral program, 1980-82; prof. grad. program U. So. Maine Sch. Nursing, Portland, 1982-84; prof., chairperson dept. nursing Colby-Sawyer Coll., New London, N.H., 1984-88; prof. Regents Coll., SUNY, Albany, 1985-89; assoc. prof., coord. undergrad. program U. N.C. Coll. Nursing, Charlotte, 1989-91, interim dean, 1991-92, prof., assoc. dean for acad. affairs, 1992—, prof., 1994—; vis. scholar Harvard U., 1981-82; mem. Nursing Theory Think Tank, 1982; mem. exec. bd., chmn. project com. New Eng. Orgn. Nursing, 1986-88; vis. prof. Marion A. Buckley Sch. Nursing, Adelphi U., 1989-90; Green Chair honor prof. Harris Coll. Nursing, Tex. Christian U., 1980-81; Margaret D. McLean lectr. Meml. U. Nfld., Can., 1990; numerous consultations, workshops, lectures, seminars and speeches in field. Mem. editorial bd. Jour. Advances in Nursing Sci., 1978—, Asian Jour. Nursing Studies, 1993-95; contbr. articles to profl. jours. Bd. dirs., mem. exec. com., mem. patient and cmty. svcs. com. Nat. Kidney Found. N.H., 1987-89; bd. dirs. Hospice at Charlotte, 1991—, co-chairperson ethics adv. com., 1995—, vice chair at large 1996—; bd. dirs. Cmty. Health Svcs., 1991-94. Fellow Am. Acad. Nursing (co-chair ethics/legal adv. com. 1983-86, mem. planning com. 1988, Ann. Sci. Sessions of Acad., mem. expert panel on ethics 1991—); mem. ANA (coun. nurse rschrs.), N.C. State Nursing Assn., Sigma Theta Tau (Disting. lectr. 1994-95), Phi Kappa Phi. Office: U NC Coll Nursing Charlotte NC 28223

CARR, ARTHUR CHARLES, psychologist, educator; b. Buffalo, Nov. 27, 1918; s. John E. and Katherine (Haas) C. B.S., Buffalo State Tchrs. Coll., 1941; M.A., Tchrs. Coll. Columbia U., 1946; Ph.D., U. Chgo., 1952; post-grad., William Alanson White Inst., 1953-54, Inst. Group Therapy, 1957-58, N.Y. Soc. Clin. Psychologists, 1954, 60. Diplomate Am. Bd. Examiners in Profl. Psychology, N.Y. State Edn. Dept. Trainee clin. psychology VA, 1947-52; sr. clin. psychologist Creedmoor State Hosp., Queens Village, N.Y., 1952-56; prin. clin. psychologist N.Y. State Psychiat. Inst., N.Y.C., 1956—; ret.; asst. prof. psychology Adelphi Coll., Garden City, N.Y., 1952-56; asso. prof. med. psychology, dept. psychiatry Coll. Physicians and Surgeons, Columbia U., 1956-71, prof., 1971-78, prof. emeritus, 1978—; prof. psychology in psychiatry Cornell U. Med. Coll., 1978—. Author: (with Shervert Frazier) Introduction to Psychopathology, 1964, (with Herbert Hendin, William Gaylin) Psychoanalysis and Social Research, 1965; author, editor: (with others) Loss and Grief, 1970, Psychosocial Aspects of Terminal Care, 1972, The Terminal Patient, 1973, Anticipatory Grief, 1974, Bereavement: Its Psychosocial Aspects, 1975, Grief, Selected Readings, 1975, The Mouth in Critical and Terminal Illness, 1980, Education of the Medical Student in Thanatology, 1981, Adolescent Marijuana Abusers and their Families, 1981, Bernard Schoenberg: Contributions to Psychiatry, Education of the Health Professional, Thanatology and Ethical Values, 1984, Principles of Thanatology, 1987, Psychodynamic Psychotherapy of Borderline Patients, 1989; editor-in-chief: Man and Medicine, 75-80; cons. editor, 1980—; editorial bd., cons. editor: Jour. Projective Techniques, 1967-73; asso. editor: Jour. Abnormal Psychology, 1966 70, Jour. Thanatology, 1971—; contbr. articles to profl. jours. Served to maj. AUS, 1941-46. Fellow Am. Psychol. Assn., Soc. Projective Techniques (dir. 1961-64, pres. 1971-72); mem. Eastern, N.Y. State psychol. assns., N.Y. Soc. Clin. Psychologists. Home: 560 Riverside Dr New York NY 10027-3202

CARR, CHARLES JELLEFF, pharmacologist, educator, toxicology consultant; b. Balt., Mar. 27, 1910; s. Joshua Barney and Pearl (Jelleff) C.; children: Daniel Jelleff, Noel Edward, Joseph Barney; m. Sallie D. Wenner, May 15, 1980. B.S. (Garvan scholar), U. Md., 1933, M.S., 1934, Ph.D. (Emerson fellow), 1937; D.Sc. (hon.), Purdue U., 1964. Teaching asst. pharmacology Sch. Medicine, U. Md., 1934-35, instr., 1935-37, asst. prof., 1937-39, assoc. prof., 1939-50, prof., 1950-55, adj. prof., 1957-91, prof. emeritus dept. pharmacology and exptl. therapeutics, 1991—; prof., chmn. dept. pharmacology Purdue U., 1955-57; chief pharmacology unit Psychopharmacology Service Center, NIMH, Bethesda, Md., 1957-63; chief sci. analysis br., life scis. div. Army Research Office, Office Chief Research and Devel. U.S. Army, Arlington, Va., 1963-67; dir. Life Scis. Research Office, Fedn. Am. Socs. for Exptl. Biology, Bethesda, 1967-77; exec. dir. Food Safety Council, Columbia, Md., 1977-80; sci. counsellor Food Safety Council, 1980-82; spl. lectr. Georgetown U. Sch. Medicine; instr. physicians course chem. warfare Emergency Med. Svc., Balt. Third Civilian Def. Region, 1943; cons. The Nutrition Found., 1982-84; exec. dir. Food Safety Coun., 1977-79, sci. counsellor, 1979-82; dir. life sci. rsch. Fedn. Am. Socs. for Exptl. Biology, 1967-77, dir. emeritus, 1977—; chief sci. analysis br. life scis. divsn. Army Rsch. Office, Office of Chief of Rsch. and Devel., Dept. Army, 1963-67; chief pharmacology unit Psychopharmacology Svc. Ctr., NIMH, 1957-63. Author: (with Krantz) Pharmacologic Principles of Medical Practice, 7th edit, 1969; also numerous sci. articles. Merit badge councilor for chemistry and pub. health Boy Scouts Am., 1957-67. Recipient U.S. Army Meritorious Civilian award, 1965, 68; U. Edinburgh fellow, 1986. Fellow N.Y. Acad. Scis., Am. Coll. Neuropsychopharmacology (life), Acad. Toxicological Scis.; mem. Am. Pharm. Assn. (life), Am. Chem. Soc. (life), Am. Assn. Pharm. Sci., Internat. Soc. Regulatory Toxicology and Pharmacology (sec., mng. editor Regulatory Toxicology and Pharmacology Jour., Internat. Achievement award 1993), Soc. Toxicology, Cosmos Club (Washington), Sigma Xi, Kappa Psi. Home and Office: U Md Dept Pharmacology Expt Ther 6546 Bellview Dr Columbia MD 21046-1054

CARR, DANIEL BARRY, anesthesiologist, endocrinologist, medical researcher; b. N.Y.C., Apr. 6, 1948; s. Andrew Joseph and Florence (Glassman) C.; m. Justine M. Meehan, Nov. 11, 1978; children: Nora, Rebecca, Andrew. BA, Columbia U., 1968, MA, 1970, MD, 1976. Diplomate Am. Bd. Internal Medicine (subsplty. bds. Endocrinology and Metabolism, Anesthesiology, Pain Mgmt.). Intern Columbia-Presbyn. Med. Ctr., N.Y.C., 1976-78; resident med. svc. Mass. Gen. Hosp., Boston, 1978-79, endocrine fellow, 1979-82, staff physician endocrine unit, 1982-94, clin. assoc. physician, clin. rsch. ctr., 1982-84, fellow in anesthesiology, 1984-86; dir. analgesic peptide research unit, 1986-94, staff physician anesthesia svc. and co-dir. anesthesia pain unit, 1986-91, dir. divsn. pain mgmt., 1991-94; anesthetist, 1992-94; instr. medicine Harvard U. Med. Sch., 1982-84, asst. prof., 1984-88; assoc. prof., 1988-94; rsch. staff Shriners Burns Inst., Boston, 1986-94; Saltonstall prof. Pain Rsch. in Anesthesia and Medicine Tufts-New England Med. Ctr., 1994—; co-chair acute and cancer pain mgmt. guideline panels, Agy. for Health Care Policy and Rsch., U.S. Dept. Health and Human Svcs., 1990-94; med. dir. Pain Mgmt. Program Tufts-New England Med. Ctr., 1995—; vice-chair rsch. Dept. Anesthesia, New England Med. Ctr., 1994—; mem. Gov. Mass. spl. commn. pain mgmt. Editor-in-chief IASP Pain: Clinical Updates, 1993—; mem. editl. bd. Clin. Jour. Pain, 1988—, Anesthesia and Analgesia, 1996—; contbr. articles, rsch. reports, essays, revs. to profl. lit. Daland fellow Am. Philos. Soc., 1980-83. Mem. Am. Pain Soc. (mem. bd. dirs. 1994—), Am. Acad. Pain Medicine (mem. bd. dirs. 1995—), France-Am. Pain Soc., Am. Soc. Anesthesiologists, Am. Burn Assn., Internat. Assn for Study Pain (coun. 1996—), Endocrine Soc., Soc. for Neurosci., Internat. Anesthesia Rsch. Soc., Assn. Univ. Anesthetists, Alpha Omega Alpha. Research on pain, analgesic peptides and stress responses; relationship between analgesia and clinical outcome; development of guidelines and regulatory policies for improved pain treatment in hospital, hospice, and home care settings. Office: New Eng Med Ctr-Dept Anesthesia 750 Washington St PO Box 298 Boston MA 02111-1533

CARR, DAVID TURNER, physician; b. Richmond, Va., Mar. 12, 1914; s. John Ernest and Mary Lela (King) C.; m. Rosemary Rudow, June 18, 1948 (div. 1953); 1 child, Jennifer Anne Carr Oderkirk; m. Christine Nadeau, Dec. 27, 1979. Student, U. Richmond, 1931-33; M.D., Med. Coll. Va., 1937; M.S. in Medicine, Mayo Grad. Sch. Medicine, 1947. Intern, then asst. resident Grady Hosp., Atlanta, 1937-39; resident chest diseases Bellevue Hosp., N.Y.C., 1940-41; fellow medicine Mayo Clinic, 1943-47, cons. medicine, 1947-79, chmn. dept. oncology, 1975; dir. Mayo Comprehensive Cancer Center, 1975; assoc. dir. Center for Cancer Control, 1976-79; prof. medicine Mayo Med. Sch., 1964-79, M.D. Anderson Hosp. and Tumor Inst., Tex. Med. Center, Houston, 1979-92. Mem.-at-large bd. dirs. Am. Lung Assn., 1959-74, v.p., 1971-72; bd. dirs. Rochester Civic Theatre, 1951-70, pres., 1965-67; bd. dirs. at large Am. Cancer Soc., 1967-74, pres. Minn. div., 1974-75. Fellow ACP, AAAS; mem. Central Soc. Clin. Research, Internat. Assn. for Study Lung Cancer (v.p. 1974-76, pres. 1976, treas. 1976-82), Am. Thoracic Soc. (v.p. 1963-64), Rochester C. of C. (pres. 1959-60); hon. mem. Peruvian Anti-Tb Assn. Home and Office: 103 Lockgreen Pl Richmond VA 23226-1744

CARR, DAWN ELIZABETH, nurse; b. Canton, Ohio, Sept. 7, 1954; d. Harry Russell and Majel Maxine (McConahey) Adams; m. Gregory Allen Carr, Aug. 16, 1975 (div.); 1 child, Christa Marie. RN, Aultman Hosp. Sch. Nursing, 1975. Staff RN operating room Aultman Hosp., Canton, 1975-79, asst. patient care coordinator, 1979-86, coordinator patient care, 1986-91, patient care specialist Ophthal. in the oper. rm., 1991—. Mem. Assn. Operating Room Nurses, Aultman Alumni Assn., Am. Soc. of Ophthal. RN. Mem. Christian Ch. Home: 116 1/2 Highland Ave Dover OH 44622-9533 Office: Aultman Hosp Operating Room 2600 Sixth St SW Canton OH 44710-1702

CARR, EDWARD GARY, psychology educator; b. Toronto, Aug. 20, 1947; came to U.S., 1969; s. Saul Isaac and Anne (Goldsmith) C.; m. Ilene Wasserman, Aug. 2, 1987; 1 child, Aaron. BA, U. Toronto, 1969; PhD, U. Calif., San Diego, 1973. Lic. psychologist, N.Y. Asst. prof. psychology SUNY, Stony Brook, 1976-81, assoc. prof., 1981-85, prof., 1985—; cons. Devel. Disabilities Inst., Smithtown, N.Y., 1976—, Maryhaven Ctr. of Hope, Port Jefferson, N.Y., 1996—. Author: In Response to Aggression, 1981, How to Teach Sign Language, 1982, Communication-Based Intervention for Problem Behavior, 1994; author monograph. Fellow Am. Psychol. Assn. Office: SUNY Dept Psychology Stony Brook NY 11794-2500

CARR, JACQUELYN B., psychologist, educator; b. Oakland, Calif., Feb. 22, 1923; d. Frank G. and Betty (Kreiss) Corker; children: Terry, John, Richard, Linda, Michael, David. BA, U. Calif., Berkeley, 1958; MA, Stanford U., 1961; PhD, U. So. Calif., 1973. Lic. psychologist, Calif; lic. secondary tchr., Calif. Tchr. Hillsdale High Sch., San Mateo, Calif., 1958-69, Foothill Coll., Los Altos Hills, Calif., 1969—; cons. Silicon Valley Companies, U.S. Air Force, Interpersonal Support Network, Santa Clara County Child Abuse Council, San Mateo County Suicide Prevention Inc.,Parental Stress Hotline, Hotel/Motel Owners Assn.; co-dir. Individual Study Ctr.; supr. Tchr. Edn.; administr. Peer Counseling Ctr.; led numerous workshops and confs. in field. Author: Learning is Living, 1970, Equal Partners: The Art of Creative Marriage, 1986, The Crisis in Intimacy, 1988, Communicating and Relating, 1984, 3d edit., 1991, Communicating with Myself: A Journal, 1984, 3d edit., 1991; contbr. articles to profl. jours. Mem. Mensa. Club: Commonwealth. Home: 4788 Raspberry Pl San Jose CA 95129 Office: Foothill College 12345 El Monte Ave Los Altos CA 94022-4504

CARR, JAMES ARTHUR, biologist, educator; b. Phila., Aug. 27, 1960; s. James Arthur and Frances Ruth (Cook) C.; m. Deborah Lynn Ditmore, Aug. 22, 1987; children: Jessica Lynn, Shannon Kelsy. BS with honors, Rutgers U., 1982; MA in Biology, U. Colo., 1986, PhD in Biology, 1988. Teaching asst. U. Colo., Boulder, 1982-88; NIH postdoctoral fellow U. N.Mex., Albuquerque, 1988-91; asst. prof. biology Tex. Tech U., Lubbock, 1991—. Contbr. articles to profl. jours. Grantee Tex. Tech U., 1991-93. Mem. Soc. for Neurosci., Am. Soc. Zoologists, Internat. Brain Rsch. Orgn. Democrat. Roman Catholic. Home: 5806 78th St Lubbock TX 79424-1722 Office: Tex Tech U Dept Biol Scis Box 4-3131 Lubbock TX 79409

CARR, JOANNE KLOPFER, optometrist, educator; b. Sept. 7, 1954; d. Leopold E. and Fujie (Matsuo) K. BA, Cornell U., 1975; OD, Pa. Coll. Optometry, 1979; MPH, Yale U. Sch. Medicine, 1985. Lic. optometrist, Pa., N.Y., N.J., Md., Del. Fellowship in primary care, The Eye Inst. Pa. Coll. Optometry, Phila., 1979-80, chief resident, The Eye Inst., 1980-81, instr. optometry, 1981-82, asst. prof. optometry and community health, 1983-86, chmn. dept. community health and behavioral sci., 1985-89, assoc. prof. optometry and community health, 1986—; fellowship in preventive ophthalmology Dana Ctr., Wilmer Inst. Johns Hopkins U. Hosp., Balt., 1990-92; faculty advisor Student Optometric Svc. to Humanity, Dominica, W.I., 1987, Lapenita, Mexico, 1990. Contbr. chpts. to books, articles to profl. jours. Faculty advisor Beta Sigma Kappa, Phila., 1985-90, 92—, Omega Epsilon Phi, Phila., 1984-88. Recipient Nat. Rsch. Svc. award NIH Nat. Eye Inst., 1992; rsch. grantee Am. Optometric Found., Washington, 1985, 86; Ezell fellow, 1982-83. Fellow Am. Acad. Optometry; mem. ASTM (F-31 com. 1987-89), APHA, Assn. Rsch. in Vision and Opthalmology, Am. Optometric Assn., Omega Epsilon Phi (Bro. of Yr. award 1978). Office: Pa Coll Optometry 1200 W Godfrey Ave Philadelphia PA 19141-3323

CARR, LES, psychologist, educator; b. Bklyn., Mar. 7, 1935; s. Samuel and Sarah (Berma) C.; m. Courtney Tall, June 2, 1967; children: Lincoln Damian, Sharon Rose, Lewis Wade, Faith.02579160Rice. BA, NYU, 1957; MA, New Sch. for Social Rsch., N.Y.C., 1959; Ph.D., Vanderbilt U., 1963. Diplomate Am. Bd. Med. Psychotherapists (fellow); lic. psychologist, Calif.; cert. psychologist R.I. Rsch. and clin. intern Rockland State Hosp., N.Y.C. Dept. Mental Hygiene, 1958-59; cons. clin. psychologist to sr. clin. psychologist Ctrl. State Hosp., Nashville, 1962-64; sr. coord. psychol. svcs. U. R.I., Providence, 1963-68; prof., chmn. psychology dept., dean Summer Sch., Salve Regina Coll., Newport, R.I., 1966-70, v.p. acad. affairs, 1969-71; project dir. Newport Hosp., 1967-71; pres. Lewis U., Lockport, Ill., 1971-76; chmn. bd., dean faculty Columbia Pacific U., San Rafael, Calif., 1977—; pres., chmn. bd. dirs. Elder 100 Plus, Inc., Petaluma, Calif.; chmn. bd. dirs. Sr. Univ., B.C., Can., 1994—; staff psychologist San Quentin State Prison, 1989—; former ednl. cons. to sultan and min. of edn., Oman. Past chmn. R.I. Gov.'s Task Force on Mental Health Rehab.; chmn. bd. dirs. Sr. U., Richmond, Can.; mem. nat. adv. coun. Profl. Children's Sch., N.Y.C.; past chmn. adv. bd. dirs. Comprehensive Mental Health Ctr., Newport; past bd. dirs. Regional Ballet Soc., Joliet, Ill., R.I. Rehab. Assn.; past chmn. bd. trustees St. Mary's Acad., Nauvoo, Ill.; past mem. exec. com. R.I. Gov.'s Commn. on Vocat. Rehab. With U.S. Army, 1958. Mem. APA, Calif. State Psychol. Assn., Am. Correctional Assn., Marin Psychol. Assn., Redwood Psychol. Assn., Nat. Register Assn., Assn. for Death Edn. and Counseling, Internat. Psychogeriatric Assn., Am. Assn. Higher Edn. Home: 148 Wilson Hill Rd Petaluma CA 94952-9430

CARR, MARJORIE BARNWELL, pediatrician; b. Kinston, N.C., Sept. 29, 1949; d. Robert Franklin and Marjorie (Rhodes) Barnwell; m. Robert Winston Carr Jr., June 7, 1975. BS in Zoology, U. N.C., 1971, MD, 1976; MTS, Duke U., 1992. Intern N.C. Meml. Hosp., Chapel Hill, 1976-77, resident, 1977-79, fellow, 1979-80; pediatrician Raleigh (N.C.) Children and Adolescent Medicine (formerly Fleming, Edwards, Goldman, Carr & Lehan,), 1980—; bd. dirs. Frankie Lemmon Developmental Presch., 1981—, v.p., 1982-83, 93—, sec., 1983-86; bd. dirs. Wake-Up for Children, Raleigh, 1981-83; mem. Wake County Task Force for Handicapped Children, 1982-86, chmn., 1985-86; mem. N.C. Project O-3, 1983-89; mem. steering com. Child Care for Wake County, Mem. Big Sister Program, Durham, 1976-78, Education for Ministry, 1985-89; mem. Christ Ch. Young Adults, Raleigh, 1982-86, Christ Ch. Altar Guild, 1984— (chmn. 1986-87, 92-93), coordinator library, 1986—; pres. Raleigh Area Masters Swim Team, 1980-82, W.Va. Mission Team, 1986, 1987; scholarship com., med. com. YMCA, camp com., bd. dirs. 1991-94; ethics com. Wake City Med. Ctr; mem. children's task force Wake County Hospice, 1993—. Fellow Am. Acad. Pediatrics; mem. AMA, N.C. Pediatric Soc. (office rsch. com.), N.C. Med. Soc., Wake County Med. Soc., Kappa Delta. Democrat. Episcopalian.

CARR, M(ARY) L(OIS), mental health professional; b. Quincy, Fla., May 13, 1948; d. J.T. and Clara Drucilla (Sexton) C.; m. Daniel L. Groothuis, Sept. 16, 1967 (div. Sept. 1977); children: Gregory David, Kristen Lea. AA, Pensacola (Fla.) Jr. Coll., 1969; BS, U. South Fla., 1981; MS, Nova U., 1988. Developer, dir. resource ctr. Girls Club of Sarasota, Fla., 1981-83, assoc. dir., 1983, exec. dir., 1983-86, also bd. dirs.; pvt. practice, 1989-95; bd. dirs. Girls Club of Sarasota County Found., 1983-86, Sarasota County Youth Related Services Assn., 1983-85; creator, co-developer various Girls Club Programs; lectr. in field; dir. Kids In Trauma, 1995—. Writer children's advice column, Kila, 1982; co-writer TV program Girls In Motion, 1982-83; writer local TV pub. service announcement for Girls Club of Sarasota County, Coast Update, 1985; Contbr. articles on children to popular mags. Active Sarasota County Drug Task Force, 1983; asst. dir. Community Health Edn. Council, 1982-83, Women's Support Group, Venice, Fla., 1982, Sarasota County Driving Under the Influence Panel, 1987; evaluator, program com. mem. Big Brothers, Big Sisters of Sarasota County, 1985; co-founder Venice chpt. Students Against Drunk Driving ,1984, fundraiser, 1986, advisor, 1987; mem. steering com. Resource co-chairperson project graduation Venice High Sch.; co-chmn. adv. bd. Make-A-Wish Found., Sarasota, 1988. Mem. Phi Kappa Phi. Republican. Roman Catholic. Home: 8088 E Via Del Valle Scottsdale AZ 85258-1825

CARR, RENÉE ANN, medical records director; b. Portland, Oreg., Apr. 12, 1961; d. Ronald Daniel and Ida Isabel (Joli) Helfrich; m. Robert Wayne Clem, Sept. 2, 1978 (div. Oct. 1984); children: Misty Nicole, Wendy Marie; m. Leonard Leroy Carr, July 15, 1989; 1 child, Jason Lee. AAS, Portland C. C., 1991. CNA. CNA Maryville Nursing Home, Beaverton, Oreg., 1978-79; activities dir. Hillhaven Care Ctr., Portland, 1979-81, Har Lyn Care Ctr., Portland, 1981-82; med. record clerk Portland Adventist Convalescent, 1982-91; utilization rev. asst. ETHIX Pacific, Beaverton, 1991-92; dir. med. records Adventist Rehab. & Extended Care, Portland, 1992—; BLS instr. Am. Heart Assn., Portland, 1988—; vol. adv. bd. Portland Adventist Convalescent, 1992, social com. chair, 1992-95. mem. cmty. roundtable Ptnrs. Caring Cmty., Portland, 1992-93; asst. coach grade sch. boys basketball. Named Disting. Student, Oreg. Med. Record Assn., 1991. Mem. Am. Health Info. Mgmt. Assn. (accredited record tech.), Oreg. Health Info. Mgmt. Assn. (dir. budget 1993-94, dir. pub. rels. 1994-95), Student Body Assn. (med. record tech., v.p. 1989-90, pres. 1990-91), Phi Theta Kappa. Office: Adventist Rehab & Extended Care 6040 SE Belmont Portland OR 97215

CARR, RONALD EDWARD, ophthalmologist, educator; b. Newark, N.J., Sept. 17, 1932; s. Frank Edward and Mildred (Sasso) C.; m. Nancy May Gould, June 8, 1957; children: Peter Richardson, Jacqueline Marie, Timothy Edward. A.B., Princeton U., 1954; M.D., Johns Hopkins U., 1958; M.Sc., NYU, 1963. Intern Bellevue Hosp., N.Y.C., 1958-59; resident NYU Med. Ctr., N.Y.C., 1959-63; clin. assoc. NIH, Bethesda, Md., 1963-64, assoc. ophthalmologist, 1964-65; asst. prof. ophthalmology NYU Med. Ctr., 1965-67, assoc. prof., 1967-71, prof., 1971—. Author: Visual Electrodiagnosis, 1981, Electrodiagnostic Testing of the Visual System, 1990. Served to lt. comdr. USPHS, 1963. Recipient Knapp award AMA, 1966. Fellow Am. Acad. Ophthalmology, ACS; mem. Am Ophthal. Soc., N.Y. Ophthal Soc., Assn. Research in Ophthalmology. Republican. Episcopalian. Clubs: Princeton, Stone Horse Yacht. Home: 130 E End Ave New York NY 10028-7553 Office: NYU Med Ctr 530 First Ave New York NY 10016-6402

CARR, WILEY NELSON, hospital administrator; b. Dayton, Ohio, Dec. 29, 1940; s. Russell Earl and Anna Lee (Stroud) C.; m. Grace Elizabeth Brown, June 4, 1960 (div.); children: Wiley Nelson, Alison Mary Ann, G. Elizabeth, Joshua William, Joy Kathleen. Student, Miami U., Oxford, Ohio, 1959-62; BSJ, Ohio U., 1963, MS, 1964; MBA, Xavier U., Cin., 1974. Lic. nursing home adminstr., Ky. Dir. pub. rels. Western Coll. for Women, Oxford, 1964-67, dir. devel., 1967-70; dir. devel. and community rels. St. Elizabeth Med. Ctr., Covington, Ky., 1970-74, asst. adminstr., 1974-83; v.p., chief operating officer St. Elizabeth Med. Ctr., Edgewood, Ky., 1983-90; pres., CEO, Porter Meml. Hosp., Valparaiso, Ind., 1990—; bd. dirs. Better-Care, Inc., Cin.; sec. Tri-State Healthcare Laundry, Edgewood, 1989-90. Pres. Tri-State Community Cancer Orgn., Cin., 1988—; bd. dirs. United Way Porter County, Community Devel. Corp., Valparaiso, N.W. Ind. Forum, YMCA Valparaiso. Fellow Am. Coll. Healthcare Execs.; mem. Ind. Hosp. Assn. Republican. Methodist. Home: 601 Stratford Ter Valparaiso IN 46383-2024 Office: Porter Memorial Hospital 814 Laporte Ave Valparaiso IN 46383-5860

CARRADINI, LAWRENCE, comparative biologist, science administrator; b. Astoria, N.Y., Apr. 18, 1953; s. George John and Florence (Camuti) C.; m. Susan Marie Peterson, Sept. 23, 1972 (divorced); 1 child, Daniel Lawrence. BS in Zoology, Columbia Pacific U., 1989, MS in Vertebrate Reproductive Physiology and Physiol. Ecology, 1992. Technician Charles River Labs., Wilmington, Mass., 1978, coord., tech. advisor, 1979, area supr., 1979, rsch. animal surgeon, 1980-87, coord., 1987-89, lab. supr., 1989-91, researcher, 1991; sr. scientist, mgr. Biol. Labs., Mass. Health Rsch. Inst., Boston, 1992—; co-chair Instnl. Animal Care and Use Com., State Lab. Inst./Mass. Pub. Health and Mass. Biologics Lab.; apptd. to State DPGS task force on procurement practices; mem. Lake Survey, U. N.H., Salem, 1982-83. Mem. adv. bd. Internat. Jour. Advances in Contraceptive Delivery Systems; contbr. articles to Jour. Lab. Animal Sci., Jour. Am. Vet. Med. Assn. Officer, selectman apptd. mem. 208 Water Quality Study Com., Salem, N.H., 1981-82, chmn., selectman apptd. mem., 1982-83; mem. adv. bd. Internat. M.C. Chang Meml. Festschrift. Recipient N.Y. State Regents Scholarship award, 1971. Mem. Soc. for Cryobiology, Nat. Am. Assn. Lab. Animal Sci., Am. Assn. Lab. Animal Sci. (New Eng. chpt., cert. nat. lab. animal technologist), Lab. Animal Mgmt. Assn., Internat. Platform Assn., Am. Mus. Natural History (assoc.), N.Y. Acad. Scis. Democrat. Home: 60 N Main St Apt 101 Natick MA 01760-3454 Office: 305 South St Boston MA 02130

CARRICO, C. JAMES, surgeon; b. Pasadena, Calif., Apr. 13, 1935; s. James Leon and Mary Lou (Jones) C.; m. Susanne Grace Stanwood, June 30, 1957; children: Ellen C. Telaneus, Christophe J., Amy Carrico Molloy. BS in Chemistry, U. North Tex., Denton, 1957; MD, U. Tex., Dallas, 1961. Diplomate Am. Bd. Surgery, sub-bd. Critical Care. Intern Parkland Meml. Hosp., Dallas, 1961-62, resident, 1962-67; fellow U. Tex. Southwestern Med. Sch., Dallas, 1952-63, from asst. prof. to assoc. prof., 1969-74, prof., chmn. dept. surgery, 1990—; assoc. prof. U. Wash. Sch. Medicine, Seattle, 1974-76, prof., 1976-90, chmn. dept., 1983-90; mem. Am. Bd. Surgery, vice chmn., 1990-91, chmn., 1991-92. Contbr. numerous chpts. to books, more than 75 articles to profl. jours. Lt. comdr. USN, 1967-69. Recipient Ho Din award Southwestern Med. Sch., 1961, Disting. Alumnus award U. North Tex., 1991. Fellow ACS (bd. regents 1992—, chmn. com. on emerging surg. tech. 1993—, bd. govs. 1987-90, chmn. bd. govs. 1989-90). Presbyterian. Home: 3629 Haynie Ave Dallas TX 75205 Office: U Tex SW Med Ctr 5323 Harry Hines Blvd Dallas TX 75235-9031

CARRICO, THOMAS JOSEPH, plastic surgeon; b. Washington, May 1, 1952; s. Lawrence Joseph and Margaret Virginia (Baker) C.; m. Ellen McLaughlin, Jan. 7, 1978; children: Thomas J. Jr., Robert J., Brian A., Elizabeth C. BS in Chemistry, Georgetown U., 1974; MD, Med. Coll. Va., 1978. Intern gen. surgery Med. Coll. Va., Richmond, 1978-79, gen. surgery resident, 1979-83, plastic & reconstructive surgery resident, 1983-85, instr. in surgery, 1984-85, assoc. clin. prof. plastic surgery, 1985—; cons. in plastic surgery McGuire VA Med. Ctr., Richmond, 1985-92; attending plastic surgeon Va. Bapt. Hosp., Lynchburg (Va.) Gen. Hosp., 1992—. Contbr. articles to profl. jours. and chpts. to books. Bd. deacons 1st Presbyn. Ch., 1995—. Fellow ACS; mem. Am. Soc. Plastic and Reconstructive Surgeons, Southeastern Soc. Plastic and Reconstructive Surgeons, Am. Assn. for Hand Surgery, Va. Surg. Soc., Med. Soc. Va., Lynchburg Acad. Medicine. Office: Plastic Surgery Assocs 1330 Oak Ln # 100 Lynchburg VA 24503

CARRICO, VIRGIL NORMAN, physician; b. Cumberland, Md., Aug. 28, 1940; s. Virgil Norman and Lucille E. (Gnagy) C.; m. Nina Lois Lemper, Aug. 17, 1963; children: Pamela Beth Carrico-Miller, Sandra Kelly (dec.). BA, Wabash Coll., 1962; MD, Ind. U., 1966. Diplomate Am. Bd. Family Practice. Intern Marion County Gen. Hosp., Indpls., 1966-67; resident in family practice Akron (Ohio) City Hosp., 1970-72, chief resident in family practice, 1972, assoc. dir. family practice residency, 1972; chief family practice Bryan Cmty. Hosp., past chmn. bd. dirs. home health care; past mem. undergrad. med. edn. subcom. Med. Coll. Ohio, Toledo, past preceptor cmty. medicine, clin. asst. prof. family medicine; past preceptor preventive medicine and family practice Ohio State U.; chief of staff Bryan Cmty. Hosp., 1977-78, preceptor Bryan Area Health Edn. Ctr., chmn. continuing med. edn. com.; past pres., bd. dirs. Bryan Med. Group, Inc. Contbr. articles to profl. jours. Trustee YWCA, Bryan, Ohio, v.p., 1990-92; bd. dirs. United Fund, pres., 1990-92; bd. dirs. Jr. Achievement, 1981-83, Bryan Area Found. Capt. USAF, 1967-70. Fellow Am. Acad. Family Physicians (bylaw coms. 1989, 90, 91, 92, nat. chmn. 1993, chmn. patient care svcs. commn. 1988-89, chmn. mem. svcs. commn. 1989-90); mem. Soc. Tchrs. Family Medicine, Ohio Acad. Family Medicine, Am. Acad. Family Medicine, Williams County Med. Soc. (rpes. 1976-79, sec.-treas., v.p. 1980-83), Ohio Acad. Family Physicians (del. to ho. of dels. 1972-85; pres. Fulton County chpt. 1973-85, chmn. resident affairs subcom., nominating com., student awards, fin. com., ref. com. of the ho. of dels.; treas. 1985-87, v.p. 1987-89, bd. dirs. 1983-92, pres.-elect 1990-91), Rotary Internat. Office: Bryan Med Group 442 W High St Bryan OH 43506

CARRIERE, SERGE, physiologist, physician, educator; b. Montreal, Que., Can., July 21, 1934; s. Virgile and Angelina (Malouin) C.; m. Irene Lafond, Dec., 1976; children: Sylvie, Brigitte, Alain, Francois. B.A., U. Montreal, 1954, M.D., 1959. Intern Notre Dame Hosp., Montreal, 1958-59; resident in internal medicine Notre Dame Hosp., 1959-62; practice medicine specializing in nephrology Montreal, 1964—; instr. physiology Harvard Med. Sch., Boston, 1962-64; asst. prof. dept. medicine U. Montreal, 1964-70, asso. prof., 1970-74, prof., 1974-80, prof., head dept. physiology, 1980-86, prof., head dept. medicine, 1986-88, dean med. sch., 1989-95; pres., COO Phoenix Internat., 1995—; mem. staff Maisonneuve-Rosemont Hosp. Contbr. numerous articles on research in physiology and nephrology to sci. and med. jours. Med. Rsch. Coun. Can. fellow, 1962-64, grantee, 1971—, career investigator, 1971-80. Fellow Royal Coll. Physicians; mem. Can. Soc. Physiology, Am. Soc. Physiology, Internat. Soc. Physiology, Am. Soc. Nephrology, Can. Soc. Nephrology, Am. Soc. Clin. Investigation, Can. Soc. Clin. Investigation. Home: 40 Du Chene Vandreuil, Sur Le Lac, PQ Canada J7V 8P3 Office: Phoenix Internat Life Scis, 2350 Cohen St, Saint Laurent, PQ Canada H4R 2N6

CARRIGAN, JOHN LIONEL, information specialist, library consultant; b. Leadville, Colo., Sept. 9, 1948; s. Lionel Ray and Helen Roberta (Plake) C.; children: Jeff, Patrick. BS, Tex. A&M U., College Station, 1970; MS, Calif. Inst. of Tech., Pasadena, 1973; MS in Library Sci., Calif. State U., Fullerton, 1979. Rsch. tech. City of Hope Nat. Med. Ctr., Duarte, Calif., 1973-74, asst. libr., 1974, chief libr., 1975, dir. of libr. svcs., 1976-86, info. specialist, 1986—. Bd. dirs. Am. Red Cross (IEW chapt.). N.Y. Acad. of Sci., Spl. Libr. Assn., Med. Libr. Assn., Am. Libr. Assn., Assn. Coll. Rsch. Librs., Calif. Acad. and Rsch. Librs., Am. Soc. for Info. Sci. Home: 4811 Orchard St Montclair CA 91763-3107 Office: City of Hope Nat Med Ctr 150 E Duarte Rd Duarte CA 91010

CARRINGTON, BETTY WATTS, nurse midwife, educator; b. W.Va., Mar. 14, 1936; d. James Henry and Odessa E. Watts; m. Homer S.I. Carrington, Aug. 17, 1958; children: Michael S., Lynn Ellen. BSN, U. Mich., 1958; MS, Columbia U., 1971, EdD, 1986. Cert. nurse-midwife. Dir. nurse-midwifery svc. Maternity-Infant Care Project/Brookdale Hosp. Affiliation, Bklyn., 1972-79; assoc. prof. nurse-midwifery SUNY Health Sci. Ctr., Bklyn., 1979-86; dir. grad. program in nurse-midwifery Columbia U. Sch. Nursing, N.Y.C., 1986-91; nurse-midwife rsch. assoc. dept. obstetrics and gynecology Harlem Hosp. Ctr., N.Y.C., 1989—; cons. minority recruitment and retention, 1981—. Contbr. articles to profl. jours. WHO fellow, Tanzania, 1983. Fellow Am. Coll. Nurse Midwives (nat. v.p. 1973-74); mem. NAUW (L.I. br. pres. 1986-90, chairperson nat. program standards com. 1994—), Sigma Theta Tau. Home: 11931 220th St Jamaica NY 11411-2010

CARROLL, BARBARA ANNE, radiologist, educator; b. Beaumont, Tex., Oct. 20, 1945; d. Theron Demp and Annette Ione (Anderson) C.; m. Olaf T. von Ramm. BA, U. Tex., 1967; MD, Stanford U., 1972. Intern, Stanford Hosp., Palo Alto, Calif., 1972, resident, 1973-76; research asst. Genetics Found., U. Tex., Austin, 1963-67; teaching asst. NSF Summer Biology Workshop, Austin, 1967; clinician Planned Parenthood, Santa Clara, Calif., 1973-76; instr. extension div. U. Calif.-Santa Cruz, 1972-76; asst. prof. radiology Stanford U. Med. Sch., Palo Alto, 1977-84, assoc. prof. radiology, 1984-85; chief diagnostic ultrasound, 1977-85; assoc. prof. radiology Duke U., Durham, N.C., 1985-92, prof. radiology, 1992—; cons. Searle, Santa Clara, 1977-78, Diasonics, Inc., Santa Clara, 1979-83, NIH, 1981-84, Acuson, 1984—. Contbr. articles to various publs.; reviewer numerous med. jours., 1982—; assoc. editor Radiology Jour., 1986—, Investigative Radiology, 1989-95, AJR, 1994—, Academic Radiology, 1995—, Jour. of Ultrasound in Medicine, 1990—. Bd. dirs. Planned Parenthood Santa Clara County, 1975-76. Agnes Axtell Moule Faculty scholar, 1979-84; recipient Cancer and Med. Rsch. Found. award, 1980. Fellow Am. Inst. Ultrasound in Medicine (bd. govs. 1987-90, Presdl. Recognition award 1988); mem. Soc. Radiologists in Ultrasound, Am. Coll. Radiology (commn. on ultrasound, 1989—, commn. on stds., 1994—), Radiologic Soc. N.Am. (sci. exhibits com.), sci. advisor rsch. and edn. fund), Am. Roentgen Ray Soc., Assn. Women Radiologists, Assn. Univ. Radiologists, Venezuelan Ultrasound Soc. (hon.), N.C. Ultrasound Soc. (faculty adv. 1986—), Phi Beta Kappa. Presbyterian. Office: Duke U Med Sch Dept Radiology PO Box 3808 Durham NC 27710-0001

CARROLL, GEORGE JOSEPH, pathologist, educator; b. Gardner, Mass., Oct. 14, 1917; s. George Joseph and Kathryn (O'Hearn) C. B.A., Clark U., Worcester, Mass., 1939; M.D., George Washington U., 1944. Diplomate: Am. Bd. Pathology. Intern Worchester City Hosp., 1944-45; resident in medicine Doctors Hosp., Washington, 1945-46; resident in pathology Sibley Hosp., Washington, 1948-49, VA Hosp., Washington, 1949-50; asst. pathologist D.C. Gen. Hosp., 1950-51, assoc. pathologist, 1951-52; pathologist Louise Obici Meml. Hosp., Suffolk, Va., 1952—; sec. med. staff Louise Obici Meml. Hosp., 1956-59, chief of staff, 1959-60, 67-69; pathologist Chowan Hosp., Edenton, N.C., 1952-71, Southampton Meml. Hosp., Franklin, Va., 1952—, Greensville Meml. Hosp., Emporia, Va., 1961—; instr. pathology Georgetown U. Sch. Medicine, 1950-52; instr. bacteriology Am. U., Washington, 1950-51; assoc. clin. prof. pathology Med. Coll. Va., Richmond, 1968-70; clin. prof. pathology Va. Commonwealth U., 1970—; prof. dept. pathology Eastern Va. Med. Sch., Norfolk, 1974—; sec.-treas. Va. Bd. Medicine, 1970-86. Contbr. articles to med. jours. Served with U.S. Army, 1946-48. Fellow ACP, Coll. Am. Pathologists, Am. Soc. Clin. Pathologists (bd. dirs. 1969—, pres. 1977—), Internat. Acad. Pathology; mem. AMA, So. Med. Assn. (Va. councilor 1965-70, pres. 1973-74), Med. Soc. Va., 4th dist. Med. Soc. (pres. 1968-70), Seaboard Med. Soc. (pres. 1957), George Washington Med. Soc., Tri-County Med. Soc. (pres. 1971-73), Am. Soc. Clin. Pharmacy Therapeutics, Va. Soc. Pathology (pres. 1973-74), Soc. Nuclear Medicine, Am. Assn. Blood Banks, Am. Cancer Soc. (bd. dirs. Va. div. 1955-62), Va. Med. Svc. Assn. (bd. dirs. 1960-71), Rotary. Home: 219 Northbrook Ave Suffolk VA 23434-6647 Office: Louise Obici Meml Hosp 1900 N Main St PO Box 1100 Suffolk VA 23434-4345

CARROLL, JAMES EDWIN, child neurologist, researcher; b. Joplin, Mo., May 15, 1945; s. George Henry and Sarah Frances (Montee) C.; m. Shirley Ann Carol Rohlander, July 1, 1967; children: John, Peter, Ruth, Rebecca, Timothy, Matthew, Lydia, Elizabeth. BS, U. Louisville, 1966, MD, 1969. Diplomate Nat. Bd. Med. Examiners, Am. Bd. Pediat., Am. Bd. Psychiatry and Neurology. Resident in pediat. Louisville (Ky.) Children's Hosp., 1969-71; resident in child neurology U. Colo., Denver, 1973-76; fellowship, faculty Washington U., St. Louis, 1976-84; chief child neurology, prof. Med. Coll. Ga., Augusta, 1984-88; prof., dir. pediat. tng. program Kuwait U., 1988-90; prof., dir. child neurology, vice chmn. neurology Med. Coll. Ga., Augusta, 1990—; co-dir. Jerry Lewis Neuromuscular Rsch. Ctr., Washington. U., 1982-84; dir. Muscular Dystrophy Clinic, Med. Coll. Ga., 1991—; mem. Ga. Myasthenia Gravis Med. Adv. Bd., 1985-88. Author book chpts.; contbr. over 60 articles to profl. jours. Mem. exec. bd. United Cerebral Palsy of Ctrl. Savannah River Area, Augusta, 1985-88. Served to lt. comdr. USN, 1971-73. Recipient Investigator award NIH, 1979-83, grant NIH, 1986-89, Meritorious Honor award for scv. in Embassy in Kuwait, U.S. Dept. State, 1990. Fellow Am. Acad. Pediat., Am. Acad. Neurology; mem. Soc. for Pediat. Rsch., Am. Neurol. Assn. Republican. Presbyterian. Home: 2711 Hunters Crossing Augusta GA 30907 Office: Med Coll Ga Child Neurology CJ2103 Augusta GA 30912

CARROLL, JOHN DOUGLAS, mathematical and statistical psychologist; b. Phila., Jan. 3, 1939; s. John Joseph and Nolie Fay (Godwin) C.; m. Sylvia Stevens Booma, Jan. 2, 1965; children: Gregory Alan, Steven Douglas. BS with honors, U. Fla., 1958; PhD, Princeton U., 1963. Research asst. dept. psychology Yale U., 1961-63; math.-statis. psychologist Bell Labs., Murray Hill, N.J., 1963-65, 66-89; bd. govs., prof. mgmt. and psychology Rutgers U., Newark, 1990—; asst. prof. indsl. engring. and ops. research NYU, 1965-66, adj. assoc. prof. stats., 1968-70; acting prof. psychology U. Calif.-San Diego, 1975-76; acting prof. social sci. U. Calif.-Irvine, 1975-76; adj. prof. stats. Baruch Coll., CUNY, 1971, adj. prof. mktg. U. Pa., 1978-79; Procter & Gamble adj. prof. of mktg. U. Pa., 1987-89; vis. rsch. prof. cognitive sci. U. Calif. Irvine, 1993. Contbr. numerous articles and chpts. to profl. publs.; author computer programs for multidimensional analysis of behavioral sci. data; assoc. editor: Psychometrika, 1973—, Jour. Exptl. Psychology, 1978-88; mem. editl. bd. Jour. Classification, 1984—, Jour. Mktg. Rsch., 1994—; editor Methodika, 1987—. Ednl. Testing Service psychometric fellow, 1958-61; NIMH fellow, 1959-61. Fellow AAAS, APA (active Div. 5, pres.-elect 1990-91, pres. 1991-92, APA Disting. Sci. Contbn. award 1989), Am. Psychol. Soc. (William James fellow 1989), Am. Statis. Assn. (program chair stats. in mktg. sect. 1992, chair stats. in mktg. sect. 1993-94, mem. exec. com. 1991—); mem. Psychometric Soc. (trustee 1971-77, 81-83, 84-87, 93—, pres. 1975-76, mem. editl. coun. 1975-81), Classification Soc. N.Am. (governing coun. 1974-77, pres. 1980-83, bd. dirs. 1984—), Internat. Fedn. Classification Socs. (rep. to coun. 1984—, v.p./pres.-elect 1995, pres. 1996—), Soc. Multivariate Exptl. Psychology (editl. adv. bd. 1980-81, pres. 1982-83), Ea. Psychol. assn., Psychonomic Soc., Soc. Math. Psychology, Am. Mktg. Assn., Assn. for Consumer Rsch., Soc. for Consumer Psychology, Inst. for Ops. Rsch. and Mgmt. Scis., Phi Beta Kappa, Sigma Xi, Beta Gamma Sigma. Home: 14 Forest Dr Warren NJ 07059-5802 Office: Rutgers U Grad Sch Mgmt Fac of Mgmt/Mgmt Edn Ctr 81 New St Rm 125 Newark NJ 07102-1895

CARROLL, JOHN E., JR., endocrinologist; b. Milw., Dec. 4, 1947; s. John E. Sr. and Madeline Vera (Wilcox) C.; m. Terry S. Smith Flynn, May 19, 1994; children: Kathleen A., Maureen S., John H. BS magna cum laude, Boston Coll., 1970; MD, U. Wis., 1974. Fellow endocrinology and metabolism Boston U. Med. Ctr., 1977-79; asst. prof. medicine U. Wis., Madison, 1979-85; chief endocrinology William S. Middleton VA Hosp., Madison, 1980-85; chief endocrinology sect. Indian River Meml. Hosp., Vero Beach, Fla., 1985—; endocrinologist Doctors' Clinic, Vero Beach, 1985—. Contbr. articles to profl. jours. Past mem. Rotary Club Vero Beach Sunrise. Col. USAFR. Cardiovascular Tng. grantee NIH, Boston U. Med. Ctr., Madison, 1978-79; rsch. grantee Nat. Heart, Lung & Blood Inst., Madison, 1985-88. Fellow ACP, Am. Coll. Endocrinology; mem. Endocrine Soc., Am. Diabetes Assn. (mem.-at-large 1986-89, bd. dirs. 1986-89). Office: Doctors Clinic 2300 Fifth Ave Vero Beach FL 32960

CARROLL, KIM MARIE, nurse; b. Ottawa, Ill., Feb. 13, 1958; d. John J. and Charin E. (Reilley) Marmion; m. Thomas Christopher Carroll, Aug. 25, 1979; children: Christopher John, Meaghan Elizabeth. BSN, U. Denver, 1983; diploma Copley Meml. Hosp. Sch. Nursing, Aurora, Ill., 1979. RN, Ill., Ind., Colo.; critical care practitioner. Staff nurse Penrose Hosp., Colorado Springs, Colo., 1979-83, asst. head nurse cardiac floor, 1983-84; asst. dir. nurses Big Meadows Nursing Home. Savanna, Ill., 1985-86, dir. nurses, 1986-88; clin. dir. Ind. Heart Physicians, Inc., Beech Grove, Ind., 1989-95; ambulatory care adminstr. The Gates Clinic, Denver, 1995—. Mem. Am. Orgn. Nurse Execs., Soc. Ambulatory Care Profls., Profls. In Workers' Compensation, Beta Sigma Phi (chpt. pres. 1988-89, rec. sec. 1991-92), Sigma Theta Tau. Roman Catholic. Avocation: skiing. Home: 5293 S Cathay Way Aurora CO 80015-4859 Office: The Gates Clinic 1000 S Broadway Denver CO 80209

CARROLL, PATRICIA L., nurse, respiratory therapist, educator; b. Mineola, N.Y., Mar. 17, 1958; d. George J. and Barbara (Fitzgerald) Fuchs; m. Robert B. Carroll, Sept. 15, 1984. AAS in Respiratory Therapy, SUNY, Syracuse, 1977; AS, Greater Hartford (Conn.) C.C., 1984; BS in Health Scis., Charter Oak Coll., Hartford, 1983; MS in Ednl. Techs., Ctrl. Conn. State U., New Britain, 1990; student, Regents Coll., Albany, N.Y. RN, Conn., Mass.; CEN; registered respiratory therapist; cert. gen. nurse, continuing edn. and staff devel. Asst. clin. instr., spl. cons. pediatric pulmonary care SUNY-Upstate Med. Ctr., Syracuse, N.Y., 1976-79; respiratory therapist dept. pediatrics SUNY-Upstate Med. Ctr., Syracuse. 1977-79; sr. critical care and pediatric respiratory therapist Hartford (Conn.) Hosp., 1979-83; instr. Faculty Allied Health Morse Sch. Bus., Hartford, 1984-86; home care nurse pvt. practice Hartford, Conn., 1984-85; AIDS grant coord. Conn. Nurses Assn., 1987-89, coord. continuing edn., 1987-90; owner, cons. Ednl Med. Cons., Middletown, Conn., 1986—; per diem staff nurse, emergency rm. Manchester (Conn.) Meml. Hosp., 1990—; tchr. respiratory therapy and allied health Manchester Cmty. Tech. Coll., 1993—; tchr. nursing re-entry program Capital City Cmty. Tech. Coll., Hartford, 1993—; tchr. respiratory therapy program Onondaga C.C., Syracuse, 1978-79; freelance producer/writer instrnl. videos. Recipient EDPRESS Disting. Achievement award, 1983, Freddie award, 1995, award of excellence Am. Med. Writers Assn. New England chpt., 1996. Mem. Middlesex County C. of C. Office: 87 Surrey Dr Meriden CT 06451

CARROLL, PETER ROBERT, physician; b. San Francisco, Dec. 30, 1950; s. William and Olga D. (Anderson) C.; m. Laura Presti Carroll; children: Lauren, Ryan, Savannah. BA in Zoology, U. Calif., Berkeley, 1974; MD cum laude, Georgetown U., 1979. Diplomate Am. Bd. Urology. Intern in surgery U. Calif., San Francisco, 1979-81, resident in urology, 1981-84; fellowship in urology dept. surgery Meml. Sloan-Kettering Cancer Ctr., N.Y.C., 1984-86; interim chief dept. urology U. Calif./Mt. Zion Cancer Ctr., San Francisco, 1986—, program leader urologic oncology program, —; assoc. prof. in residence dept. urology U. Calif., San Francisco, —, chmn. dept. urology, 1996—; dir. urology clinics U. Calif., San Francisco, 1986-90, med. sch. admissions com., 1987-90, quality assurance com., 1988-90, urology collaborative practice com., 1988-90, standing com. 1st year med. sch. screening com., 1990-95, laser com., 1988—, med. records com., 1989-94, physician aid com., 1990—, cancer center com., 1991—, transfusion com., 1994—, faculty coun., 1994—, bd. dirs. med. group, 1995—, budgetary task force, 1995; lectr. in field. Author books and periodicals; contbr. over 35 chpts. to books, over 125 articles to profl. jours. Recipient numerous rsch. grants. Mem. AAAS, AMA, Am. Assn. for Cancer Rsch., Am. Assn. for Surgery of Trauma, Am. Coll. Surgeons (com. on trauma), Am. Urol. Assn. (3d prize Joseph McCarthy Essay Contest 1989), Southwest Oncology Group (assoc.), Calif. Med. Assn., Nat. Urol. Forum, No. Calif. Urol. Assn., San Francisco Med. Soc., Internat. Soc. Urology, Soc. for Analytic Cytometry, Soc. for Basic Urologic Rsch., Soc. Urologic Oncology (exec. com.), Alpha Omega Alpha. Office: Univ Calif Dept Urology 533 Parrassus Ave U575 San Francisco CA 94143-0738

CARROLL, RICKY Z., health company executive; b. Stanton, Va., Oct. 23, 1958; m. Joyce Lynn Johnson, Oct. 16, 1981; children: Ricky Zane II, Curtis Jacob. Owner Bean Pot Restaurant, Roanoke, Va., 1986-88, Pizza King Restaurant, Roanoke, 1988-90; diagnostic imaging ops. mgr. Meritus Health, Roanoke, 1990—. Office: Meritus Health Sys 233 Hershberger Rd Roanoke VA 24012

CARROLL, ROBERT EUGENE, senior flight surgeon; b. St. Louis, Sept. 28, 1957; m. Melinda Lou Knab, Sept. 28, 1979; children: Diana Catherine, Paul Robert, Cullen Philip, William Douglas. BS summa cum laude, Houston Bapt. U., 1979; MD, Baylor Coll. Medicine, 1983; MPH, Harvard U., 1993. Diplomate Am. Bd. Occupl. Medicine, Am. Bd. Aerospace Medicine. Intern, then resident in gen. surgery New Britain (Conn.) Gen. Hosp., 1983-85; commd. 2d lt. USAF, 1979, advanced through grades to lt. col., 1983—; flight surgeon Aerospace Medicine Primary course Brooks AFB, San Antonio, 1985; flight surgeon USAF, Alexandria, La., 1985-89; resident in gen. surgery Wilford Hall Med. Ctr., San Antonio, 1989-90; flight surgeon, chief flight medicine Robert L. Thompson Strategic Hosp. Carswell AFB, Tex., 1990-92; resident in aerospace medicine Harvard Sch. Pub. Health, Boston, 1992-93, Sch. Aerospace Medicine, Brooks AFB, Tex., 1993-95; dep. chief aero. medicine Air Edn. Tng. Comd., Randolph AFB, Tex., 1995—. Mem. Aerospace Medicine Assn., Soc. USAF Flight Surgeons, Air Force Assn., Omicron Delta Kappa. Home: 11646 White Cross San Antonio TX 78253-6018 Office: HQ AETC/SGPA Randolph AFB TX 78150-4549

CARROLL, ROBERT GRAHAM, physiologist, educator; b. Lansdowne, Pa., Mar. 18, 1954; s. James Thomas Carroll Jr. and Jane Carroll (Graham) McCormack; m. Elizabeth Ann Butchart, May 19, 1984; children: R. Graham Jr., Anne Corinne, Elise Butchart. BS in Biology, U. Notre Dame, 1976; PhD in Physiology, U. Med. & Dentistry of N.J., 1981. Instr. U. Miss. Med. Ctr., Jackson, 1981-84; asst. prof. East Carolina U. Sch. Med., Greenville, N.C., 1984-90; assoc. prof. East Carolia U. Sch. Med., Greenville, NC, 1990-96; prof. East Carolina U. Sch. Med., Greenville, N.C., 1996—. Contbr. articles to profl. jours. Recipient Individual Nat. Rsch. Svc. award NIH, Bethesda, Md., 1981-84, Summer Faculty Rsch. award U.S. Army Rsch. Office, San Francisco, 1989. Mem. Am. Physiol. Soc. (counselor-teaching 1991-93, chair-teaching 1996—), N.C. Inst. Nutrition (bd. sci. dirs. 1991-94), Corp. of Mount Desert Island Biol. Lab., Sigma Xi. Republican. Roman Catholic. Home: 202 S Warren St Greenville NC 27858-2721 Office: East Carolina Univ Sch of Med Greenville NC 27858

CARROLL, ROBERT LLOYD, orthopaedic surgeon; b. L.A., Sept. 2, 1931; s. Robert Lide and Jean Livingston (Wilson) C.; m. Sally Britton Richardson, Aug. 28, 1954; children: John Fielding, Lynne Wilson Carroll Taylor. BS, UCLA, 1954; MD, U. So. Calif., 1958. Diplomate Am. Bd. Orthopaedic Surgery. Pvt. practice Orthop. Med. Group Pasadena (Calif.) Inc., 1965—. Capt. U.S. Army, 1959-61. Fellow Am. Orthop. Surgeons, Western Orthop. Surgeons Assn.; mem. AMA, Calif. Med. Assn., L.A. County Med. Assn. Republican. Episcopalian. Home: 1490 Charlton Rd San Marino CA 91108 Office: Orthop Med Grou Pasadena 50 Bellefontaine # 101 Pasadena CA 91105

CARROLL, ROBERT LYNN, biology educator, vertebrate paleontologist, museum curator; b. Kalamazoo, May 5, 1938; s. John Henry and Arvella Mae (Wickerham) C.; m. Helen Louise Swaim, June 22, 1961 (dec. Jan. 1972); 1 child, David Lynferd; m. Anna Di Turi, Sept. 26, 1987. BS, Mich. State U., 1959; MA, Harvard U., 1961, PhD, 1963. NRC postdoctoral fellow McGill U., Montreal, Que., Can., 1962-63, asst. prof. zoology, 1964-69, assoc. prof. biology, 1969-74, prof. biology, 1974—, Strathcona prof. zoology, 1987—; curator vertebrate paleontology Redpath Mus., McGill U., 1965—, dir., 1985-90, chmn. dept. biology, 1990-95; vis. prof. biology Sir George Williams U., Montreal, 1965-66. Author: Vertebrate Paleontology and Evolution, 1987; co-author: Paleontology-The History of Life, 1989; assoc. editor: Can. Jour. Earth Scis., 1984-93, Jour. Vertebrate Paleontology, 1989-92; cons. editor: Transactions of the Royal Soc. of Edinburgh: Earth Sciences, 1993—. Recipient Billings medal for contbns. to paleontology Geol. Assn. Can.; NSF postdoctoral fellow Brit Mus., London, 1963-64. Fellow Royal Soc. Can., Linnean Soc.; mem. Soc. Vertebrate Paleontology (pres. 1982-83), Soc. for Study Evolution, Paleontol. Soc. (Schuchert award 1978), Am. Soc. Zoologists, World Congress Herpetology (treas. 1989-94). Office: Redpath Mus/McGill Univ, 859 Sherbrooke St W, Montreal, PQ Canada H3A 2K6

CARRUTHERS, CLAUDELLE ANN, occupational and physical therapist; b. Chgo., Nov. 23; d. Veronica Josephine Walker. AA, Golden Valley Luth. Coll., Minn., 1981; BS in Occupational Therapy, U. Minn., 1984; M in Phys. Therapy, U. Iowa, 1991; PhD, U. Minn., 1995. Lic. occupational therapist, Iowa, phys. therapist, Iowa, Minn.; cert. occupational therapist, Minn. Dir., supr., occupational therapist Rehab. Specialists, Inc., Minnetonka, Minn., 1984-86; supr., occupational therapist St. Therese Home, Inc., Mpls., 1986-88; dir., supr., occupational therapist Allied Health Alternatives, Inc., Mpls., 1988-89; occupational therapist St. Luke's Hosp., Cedar Rapids, Iowa, 1989-91; occupational therapist, phys. therapist Fairview Riverside Med. Ctr., Mpls., 1991—; instr., rschr. U. Minn., 1992-95; prof. occupational and phys. therapy Coll. of St. Catherine, 1995—; research in field of virtual reality, neurology/kinesiology; mem. adv. bd. occupational therapy program Anoka Tech. Coll., 1992—; mentor for occupational and phys. therapy students Coll. of St. Catherine's, St. Paul, 1992; mentor for occupational and phys. therapy and women athlete's of color U. Minn. Author publs. in field. Human rights commr. City of Plymouth, 1994—; mem. allocation panel United Way Mpls., 1992; mem. Minn. Zoo, 1986—. Recipienvt Vol. Basketball award Courage Ctr., Golden Valley, Minn., 1987, 89. Mem. Am. Phys. Therapy Assn. (student rep. 1981-83), Iowa Occupational Therapy Assn., Minn. Occupational Therapy Assn., Am. Occupational Therapy Assn., Occupational Therapy Minn.-Dak Assn. (panel presentor 1992), Glende Ski Club (2d v.p. 1987), Martin Luther King Tennis Club, Alpha Kappa Alpha. Office: College Of St Catherine Dept of Physical Therapy Saint Paul MN 55105

CARRUTHERS, S. GEORGE, medical educator, physician; b. Londonderry, No. Ireland, Sept. 18, 1945; came to Can., 1977; s. Moses and Alice McKeague (Nicholl) C.; m. Gillian Margaret Devon, Oct. 4, 1969; children: Alison, David, Bruce, Michael. MB, BCh, Queen's U., Belfast, No. Ireland, 1969, MD, 1975. Diplomate Am. Bd. Internal Medicine, Am. Bd. Clin. Pharmacology (sec./treas. 1996—). Intern Royal Victoria Hosp., Belfast, 1969-70; various teaching positions Belfast City Hosp./Queen's U. Belfast, 1970-75; Fogarty Internat. fellow NIH Kans. U. Med. Ctr., Kansas City, 1975-77; asst. prof. U. Hosp./U. Western Ont., London, Can., 1977-82, assoc. prof., 1982-87, prof. dept. medicine, 1987-88, 95—, prof. dept. pharmacology and toxicology, 1987-88, 95—; Carnegie and Rockefeller prof., head dept. medicine Dalhousie U., Halifax, N.S., Can., 1988-95; physician-in-chief Victoria Gen. Hosp., Halifax, 1988-91, pres. med. staff, 1992-93; chief medicine London Health Scis. Ctr., St. Joseph's Hosp., 1995—; mem. bd. commrs. Victoria Gen. Hosp., 1992-93; rep. Brit. Med. Assn., London, 1973-75; Richard Ivey prof., chair dept. medicine U. Western Ont., 1995—; pres. Foyle Coll. OBA, 1993-94. Co-author: Handbook of Clinical Pharmacology, 1978, 2d edit., 1983. Fellow ACP, Royal Coll. Physicians Can., Royal Coll. Physicians (London), Am. Coll. Clin. Pharmacology; mem. Am. Soc. Clin. Pharmacology and Therapeutics (nominating com. 1989, v.p. 1991-92, awards com. 1992—, scientific program com. 1995—), Can. Soc. for Clin. Pharmacology (pres. 1984-86, Piafsky young investigator award 1982, disting. svc. award 1992), Can. Hypertension Soc. (pres. 1990-91, bd. dirs. 1988-92, disting. svc. award 1995), Can. Assn. Profs. Medicine (pres. 1994-95), Can. Inst. Acad. Med. (elected 1995), Br. Pharm. Soc. Mem. United Ch. of Can. Home: 2 Tobin Ct, London, ON Canada N6K 3Y3 Office: 5-OF5 London Health Scis Ctr, Univ Campus, London, ON Canada N6A 5A5

CARSIA, GENE VINCENT, physician; b. Hazelton, Pa., Nov. 10, 1961; s. Gene Vincent and Dolores Louise (Knelly) C. BS, U. Pitts., 1984; DO, U. Health Scis., Kansas City, Mo., 1988. Diplomate Am. Bd. Osteopathy; cert. Am. Osteopathic Bd. Family Practice. Resident family practice Dallas Family Hosp., 1988-91; pvt. practice Arlington, Tex., 1993—. Mem. Am. Osteopathic Assn., Am. Coll. Gen. Practitioners, Tex. Med. Assn., Tarrant County Med. Soc. Republican. Roman Catholic. Home: 2412 Jefferson Court Ln Arlington TX 76006 Office: 3295 S Cooper St Arlington TX 76015-2328

CARSKI, THEODORE ROBERT, physician, microbiologist; b. Balt., June 22, 1930; s. Theodore John and Katherine (Kocent) C.; m. Trudi Thau, July 10, 1954; children: Theodore Henry, Karen Anne, Christopher Robert, Gregory William. AB, Johns Hopkins U., 1952; MD, U. Md., 1956. Diplomate Am. Bd. Med. Microbiology; cert. med. and pub. health microbiology. Intern U. Md. Hosp., Balt., 1956-57; sr. asst. surgeon USPHS, Montgomery, Ala., 1957-60; dir. rsch. BBL Div., Balt., 1960-68; dir. microbiology Huntingdon Rsch. Ctr., Balt., 1968-69, asst. dir., 1970-72, dir., 1972-74; assoc. med. dir. Becton Dickinson & Co., Balt., 1974-76, corp. med. dir., 1976-94; pres. Niches Inc., Baldwin, Md., 1994—. Contbr. articles to profl. jours. Mem. Am. Soc. for Microbiology (com. policy com. 1976-79). Home: 14258 Baldwin Mill Rd Baldwin MD 21013-9003 Office: Niches Inc 14258 Baldwin Mill Rd Baldwin MD 21013-9003

CARSON, ANN KATHERINE, psychologist, nurse educator; b. San Diego, July 6, 1948; d. Merrel Arthur and Bette Lou (Roberts) Taylor; m. Michael Mather Carson, Aug. 6, 1970 (div. Jan. 1974); children: Ryan Michael, Sara Ann. BSN magna cum laude, San Diego State U., 1971; MS, U. Oreg., 1980; MN, Oreg. Health Sci. U., 1983; PhD, Calif. Sch. Profl. Psychology, San Diego, 1990. RN, nurse practitioner, Calif.; lic. psychologist, Calif.; cert. pub. health nurse. Sch. nurse practitioner San Diego City Schs., 1974-77, Eugene (Oreg.) Sch. Dist. 4J, 1977-80, 81-82; instr. Oreg. Health Scis. U., Portland, 1980-81, 82-83; health svcs. coord. Project IINTACT, San Diego, 1983-86; clin. psychology intern Halcyon Ctr., El Cajon, Calif., 1987-88,

Profl. Community Svcs., El Cajon, 1988-90, 90-91, Home Start, San Diego, 1989-90; psychol. asst. Kensington Psychology Assn., San Diego, 1989-90; lectr. San Diego State U., 1983-96; pvt. practice San Diego, 1991—. Author: (tng. guide) A Professional Challenge: Working With Multi Problem Families, 1986; contbr. articles to profl. jours. Vol. therapist U. Calif. San Diego Pediatric Hematology/Oncology Clinic, 1991; instr. ARC, San Diego, 1973-74; adv. com. Grossmont Coll. Nursing Program, El Cajon, Calif., 1986-91. Mem. APA, Assn. Humanistic Psychology, Calif. Psychol. Assn., San Diego Psychol. Assn. Office: 3921 Goldfinch St San Diego CA 92103-2926

CARSON, CULLEY CLYDE, III, urologist; b. Westerly, R.I., Feb. 25, 1945; s. Culley Clyde, Jr., and Dorothy (Scarborough) C.; B.S., Trinity Coll., 1967; M.D., George Washington U., 1971; m. Mary Jo McDonald, Aug. 10, 1970; children—Culley Clyde IV, Hilary. Intern, Dartmouth Med. Center, 1971-72, resident in surgery, 1971-73; fellow in urology Mayo Clinic, 1975-78; instr. urology U. Minn. Mayo Med. Sch., 1978; asst. prof. urology Duke U. Med. Center, Durham, N.C., 1978-84, assoc. prof., 1984-88, prof. 1988-93; prof. and chmn. urology U. N.C., 1993—; chief urology Durham VA Hosp. Served to maj. M.C., USAF, 1973-75. Am. Heart Assn. research fellow, 1969; O'Dea travel fellow, 1978; recipient Calvin Klopp research award, 1971, Friedman research prize, 1971, Cristol Mayo Alumni award, 1992; named Command Flight Surgeon of Yr., USAF, 1974. Diplomate Am. Bd. Urology. Fellow ACS; mem. AMA, Am. Urol. Assn., Internat. Sociétéd'Urologie, Am. Fertility Soc., Univ. Urol. Forum, AAAS, N.Y. Acad. Scis., Mayo Alumni Assn., Sigma Xi, Psi Chi, Alpha Omega Alpha. Clubs: Gov's., Carolina, Trinity (Hartford). Author: Endourology, 1985, Atlas of Urologic Endoscopy, 1986, Impotence, 1992, Complications of Invasive Procedures, 1995; contbr. chpts. in urol. texts. Home: 2719 Spencer St Durham NC 27705-5720 Office: Duke University Medical Center Durham NC 27710

CARSON, DAVID COSTLEY, psychologist, health care administrator; b. Dallas, Oct. 18, 1921; s. William Henry and Eula Lee (Costley) C.; BA, So. Meth. U., 1943; postgrad. U. Chgo., 1943-46; MA, U. Tex., 1950, postgrad., 1950-52; m. Barbara Dame, Aug. 22, 1946; children: Jonathan David, Laurel, Bruce Alan. Psychologist, Tex. State Youth Devel. Council, Austin, 1952-53; counselor, planner Tex. Edn. Agy., Austin, 1953-67; project dir. Planning Commn. for Vocat. Rehab., Olympia, Wash., 1967-70; exec. dir. Group Health Coop. S. Central Wis., Madison, 1972-76; pres. Austin Health Maintenance Orgn., Inc., 1978-84; cons. health care adminstrn., 1969—; pres. WindWatts, Inc., 1974—. Sec. Dane County Arts Commn., 1975-78; pres., bd. dirs. Austin Ballet Soc., 1955-67; pres. bd. trustees McDade Ind. Sch. Dist., 1986-89, pres. 1986-87. With M.C., U.S. Army, 1946-48. VA fellow, 1948-49. Mem. AAAS, Nat. Audubon Soc. (bd. dirs. 1991-94), Audubon Council Tex. (pres. 1986-88), Bastrop County Audubon Soc. (pres. 1986-87), Phi Delta Kappa, Psi Chi. Author: Satellite HMO, 1972; Rehabilitation Advance, 1969; co-author: Rehabilitation in Washington State, 1968. Home and Office: PO Box 4856 Mc Dade TX 78650-4856

CARSON, DENNIS LEE, toxicologist; b. Oklahoma City, Nov. 5; s. Herbert Lee and Rose Marie (Soderholm) C.; m. Mary Catherine Sneed, Sept. 6, 1987; children: Travis Lee, Hannah Claire. BS in Chemistry, U. Okla., 1980; PhD in Toxicology, U. Cin., 1987. Diplomate Am. Bd. Toxicology. Assoc. chemist Conoco, Inc., Ponca City, Okla., 1980-82; staff toxicologist Phillips Petroleum Co., Bartlesville, Okla., 1987-88; rsch. toxicologist Pfizer, Inc., Groton, Conn., 1988-90; sr. toxicologist Alcon Labs., Inc., Ft. Worth, 1990—. Mem. Soc. Toxicology (assoc.). Republican. Office: Alcon Labs Inc 6201 South Freeway Fort Worth TX 76134

CARSON, GORDON CUBBEDGE, III, physician; b. Savannah, Ga., Nov. 9, 1939; s. Gordon C. and Lucille Eleanor (Wilson) C. BS, Univ. Ga., 1960; MD, Medical Coll. Ga., 1965. Diplomate Am. Bd. Radiology, Diplomate Am. Bd. Nuclear Medicine. Chief resident in radiology Walter Reed Gen. Hosp., Washington, 1970-71; chief radiology svc. DeWitt Army Hosp., Ft. Belvoir, Va., 1971-73; chief nuclear medicine Bolton Road Hosp., Atlanta, 1974-75; chief nuclear medicine Candler Gen. Hosp., Savannah, 1976-77, dir. sch. radiologic tech., 1976-79, chmn. dept. radiology, 1977-82; chief emergency radiology Grady Meml. Hosp., Atlanta, 1983-88; chief dept. radiology LBJ Gen. Hosp., Houston, 1989-90; chief emergency radiology Grady Meml. Hosp., Atlanta, 1992-95; asst. prof. radiology Emory Univ. Medical Sch., Atlanta, 1983-88; assoc. prof. radiology Univ. Tex. Medical Sch., Houston, 1989-94; dir. radiology residency, 1990-91, dir. computer applications, 1989-91; radiology cons. Surgeon Gen. U.S. Army, 1972-73; radiology and nuclear med. cons. Surgeon Gen. USAF, 1984-85. Contbr. articles to profl. jours. Bd. dirs. Savannah Symphony, 1977-79; organizer, charter mem. Ga. Pub. Radio, 1980-82; bd. dirs. Choral Guild, Atlanta, 1986-88. With U.S. Army, USAFR, Ga. Air NG, brig. gen. ret. Recipient First prize Rocky Mountain Radiology Soc., 1987. Fellow Am. Soc. Emergency Radiology (v.p. 1992-94, sec.-treas. 1987-92, founder); mem. Am. Coll. Radiology, Am. Coll. Emergency Physicians, Rocky Mountain Radiology Soc., Rotary Club (dir. 1977-82). Episcopalian. Home: P O Box 80667 Conyers GA 30208

CARSON, HAMPTON LAWRENCE, geneticist, educator; b. Phila., Nov. 5, 1914; s. Joseph and Edith (Bruen) C.; m. Meredith Shelton, Aug. 14, 1937; children: Joseph II, Edward Bruen. A.B., U. Pa., 1936, Ph.D., 1943. Instr. U. Pa., 1938-42; mem. faculty Washington U., St. Louis, 1943-70; prof. biology Washington U., 1956-70; prof. genetics U. Hawaii, 1971-85, emeritus, 1985—; vis. prof. biology U. Sao Paulo, Brazil, 1951, 77. Author: Heredity and Human Life, 1963; Contbr. articles to profl. jours. on evolutionary genetics. Trustee B.P. Bishop Mus., Honolulu, 1982-88. Recipient medal for excellence in rsch. U. Hawaii, 1979, Leidy medal Acad. Natural Scis., Phila., 1985, Charles Reed Bishop medal Bishop Mus., Honolulu, 1992; Fulbright rsch. scholar zoology dept. U. Melbourne, Australia, 1961. Mem. Nat. Acad. Scis., Am. Acad. Arts and Scis., Genetics Soc. (pres. 1982), Soc. for Study Evolution (pres. 1971, George Gaylord Simpson award 1996), Am. Soc. Naturalists (pres. 1973), AAAS, Phi Beta Kappa, Sigma Xi. Address: Dept Genetics & Molecular Biology U Hawaii at Manoa Honolulu HI 96822

CARSON, JAMES HUBERT, surgeon; b. Waynesboro, Pa., Apr. 30, 1961; s. Harold John and Jean Elizabeth (Snyder) C.; m. Tonya Sue Shaffer, Jan. 14, 1989. BS, Dickinson Coll., 1983; MD, Johns Hopkins U., 1987. Resident Pa. State U. Coll. Medicine, Hershey, 1987-92; pvt. practice Lancaster, Pa., 1992—. Fellow Am. Acad. Orthopaedic Surgeons; mem. Phi Beta Kappa, Alpha Omega Alpha. Mem. Ch. of Brethren. Office: Orthopedic Assocs of Lancaster 2104 Harrisburg Pike Ste 100 Lancaster PA 17604-3200

CARSON, ROBERT CHARLES, psychology educator, writer; b. Providence, Jan. 6, 1930; s. Robert E. Carson and May (O'Bourne) Hamill; m. Mary Anne Mako, June 25, 1955 (div. 1977); children: David, Carolyn; m. Tracey Leigh Potts, Sept. 2, 1977; 1 child, Kelly. AB, Brown U., 1953; MA, Northwestern U., 1955; PhD, 1957. Diplomate Am. Bd. Profl. Psychology. Asst. prof. U. Chgo., 1957-60; from asst. prof. to prof. Duke U., Durham, N.C., 1960—, chmn. dept. psychology, 1981-85. Author: Interaction Concepts of Personality, 1969; co-author: Abnormal Psychology and Modern Life, 1980, 88, 92. With USN, 1948-49. NIMH fellow, 1967-68. Fellow Am. Psychol. Assn.; mem. Phi Beta Kappa. Avocations: woodworking, tennis. Home: 2007 Snowcrest Tr Durham NC 27707 Office: Duke U Dept Psychology Durham NC 27708

CARSON, WILLIAM GEORGE, JR., orthopaedic surgeon; b. Tampa, Fla., Mar. 15, 1952; s. William George and Dawn (Bowman) C.; m. Marguerite McGuinn, May 21, 1983; children: William George III, Kerry Lynn. BA in Chemistry, Emory U., 1974; MD, U. South Fla., 1977. Diplomate Am. Bd. Orthopaedic Surgery. Intern orthopedic medicine Emory U., Atlanta, 1977-78, resident orthopedic medicine, 1978-82; fellow sports medicine Orthopaedic & Fracture Clinic, Eugene, Oreg., 1982, Hughston Clinic, Columbus, Ga., 1983; pvt. practice orthopaedic surgeon Tampa, 1983—; asst. clin. prof. orthopaedic surgery U. South Fla., Tampa, 1983—; orthopaedic cons. Tamp Bay Bandits, 1984-85, U. Tampa, 1985-88, Tampa Bay Buccaneers, 1987—; spring tng. cons. Detroit Tigers, Lakeland, Fla., 1993—, N.Y. Yankees, Tampa, 1994—; developer Patellar Tendon Graft Guide, Linvatec Corp., Clearwater, Fla., 1988—. Mem. editl. bd. Jour. Arthroscopic Surgery, 1990-95; reviewer Am. Jour. Sports Medicine, 1993—; contbr. articles to profl. jours. Trustee Berkeley Prep. Sch., Tampa, 1995—. Recipient Best Paper award Fla. Orthopaedic Soc., 1991. Mem. AMA, Am. Acad. Orthopaedic Surgeons, Am. Orthopaedic Soc. for Sports Medicine, Arthroscopy Assn. N.Am., NFL Physicians Soc. (exec. com. 1995—), Fellowship of Christian Athletes (adv. bd. 1994—). Republican. Episcopalian. Office: Sports Medicine Clinic of Tampa 3006 Azeele St Tampa FL 33609

CARSTENSEN, EDWIN LORENZ, biomedical engineer, biophysicist; b. Oakdale, Nebr., Dec. 8, 1919; s. August Hans and Opal Lois (Norwood) C.; m. Pam McDonald, Aug. 1, 1947; children: Richard Lorenz, Allen Brent, Laura Lee, Loretta Dee, Christina Marie. B.S., Nebr. State Tchrs. Coll., 1941; M.S., Case Inst. Tech., 1947; Ph.D., U. Pa., 1955. Mem. sci. staff div. war rsch. Columbia U., 1942-45; head lab. sect. U.S. Navy Underwater Sound Reference Lab., Orlando, Fla., 1945-48; rsch. assoc. Moore Sch. Elec. Engring., U. Pa., 1948-55, asst. prof. elec. engring., 1955-56; prin. investigator U.S. Army Biol. Lab., Fort Detrick, Frederick, Md., 1956-61; assoc. prof. elec. engring. U. Rochester, 1961-73, prof., 1973-88, Arthur Gould Yates prof. engring., 1988-90, Arthur Gould Yates prof. engring. emeritus, 1990—, dir. biomed. engring., 1971-83, prof. biophysics, 1981-90, univ. mentor, 1982—, sr. scientist in elec. engring., 1990—; dir. Rochester Ctr. for Biomed. Ultrasound, 1986-90. Author: Biological Effects of Transmission Line Fields, 1987; contbr. numerous articles to profl. publs. Fellow Acoustical Soc. Am., IEEE, Am. Inst. Ultrasound in Medicine; mem. Biophys. Soc., Biomed. Engring. Soc., Nat. Acad. Engring. Democrat. Home: 103 Eastland Ave Rochester NY 14618-1027 Office: U Rochester Dept Elec Engring Rochester NY 14627

CARSWELL, ROBERT WAYNE, psychologist; b. Lincolnton, N.C., Sept. 25, 1933; s. Lester F. and Bryte (Wilson) C.; m. Elizabeth Cromer, Aug. 15, 1956; children: Sara Lynn, David Voigt. AB, Lenoir Rhyne, 1955; BD, Luth. So. Sem., 1958, STM, 1970; MEd, U. S.C., 1972, PhD, 1975. Ordained to ministry Luth. Ch., 1958. Pastor Faith Luth. Ch., Warner Robins, Ga., 1958-61, Shades Valley Luth. Ch., Birmingham, Ala., 1961-66, St. Andrew's Luth. Ch., Columbia, S.C., 1966-73; staff psychologist S.E. Psychol. Cons., Columbia, 1975-77; pres. Carswell & Assocs., Inc., Columbia, 1977—; adj. faculty U. S.C., Columbia, 1973-78; psychol. tester Nuclear Access Authorization, 1980—; teamwork specialist various orgns., 1978—. Author: Evaluation Dynamics, 1979, Basic Manual for Managers and Supervisors, 1989, Involvement and Response Teams: A Complete Teamwork System, 1991. Mem. bd. Luth. Social Svcs. Carolinas. Recipient award Ind. Soc. Privately Pub. Authors, 1980. Mem. APA, S.C. Psychol. Assn., Rotary Internat. Republican. Home: 2019 Riding Ridge Rd Columbia SC 29223-6732 Office: Carswell & Assocs Inc PO Box 23328 Columbia SC 29224-3328

CARTEE, LEANNE, pharmacologist, cancer researcher; b. Winston-Salem, N.C., June 26, 1962; d. Thomas Edward and Joanne (Todd) C. BS, Furman U., 1984; MS, U. N.C., 1993; postgrad., Sch. Medicine, Wake Forest U., 1993—. Sr. rsch. technician Duke U. Med. Ctr., Durham, N.C., 1984-87; clin. rsch. assoc. ICI Pharms. Group, Wilmington, Del., 1987-89, Xenon Vision Inc., Alachua, Fla., 1989-91. Mem. AAAS, League Am. Wheelmen, Am. Assn. Cancer Rsch., Women in Cancer Rsch., Piedmont Guitar Soc., Alpha Epsilon Delta, Omicron Delta Kappa.

CARTER, ANNE COHEN, physician; b. N.Y.C., Nov. 27, 1919; d. Arthur Joseph and Nellie (Zuckerman) Cohen; m. Charles Edward Carter, 1945 (div.); m. William Benjamin Heller, Nov. 4, 1947 (dec.); children: James Albert, Susan Klee. BA, Wellesley Coll., 1941; MD, Cornell U., 1944. Diplomate Am. Bd. Internal Medicine. Intern Bellevue Hosp., N.Y.C., 1944-45; resident in medicine N.Y. Hosp., N.Y.C., 1945-46; instr. in medicine Cornell U. Med. Coll., N.Y.C., 1948-52, asst. prof. medicine, 1952-55; rsch. fellow Russell Sage Inst. Pathology, N.Y.C., 1951-55; asst. prof. medicine SUNY-Downstate Med. Ctr., Bklyn., 1955-58, assoc. prof. medicine, 1958-68, chief div. endocrinology, 1958-82, prof. medicine, 1968-82; vis. scientist Bronx VA Hosp., Lab. Dr. Solomon A. Berson, Bronx, 1963-64; prof. medicine N.Y. Med. Coll., Valhalla, 1982—; vis. prof. medicine SUNY Health Sci. Ctr., Bklyn., 1982-95, prof. emeritus, 1995; asst. physician N.Y. Hosp., 1945-47, physician, 1947-55, asst. attending physician, 1953-55; asst. vis. physician Kings County Hosp. Ctr., Bklyn., 1955-59, vis. physician, 1959-72, active attending physician, 1972-84, cons., 1984-95; rsch. assoc. Jewish Chronic Disease Hosp., Bklyn., 1957-67; attending physician State U. Hosp., Bklyn., 1967-84, cons., 1984-95; cons. Bklyn. VA Hosp., 1971-84; attending physician Westchester County Med. Ctr., Valhalla, 1982—; dir. ambulatory cancer detection svcs., 1982—. Contbr. chpts. to books, articles to profl. jours. Bd. dirs. Am. Cancer Soc., Inc., N.Y.C., 1977—, Westchester div., 1985-91; trustee Wellesley Coll., 1971-89, trustee emerita, 1989—; trustee Dana Hall Sch., Wellesley, 1990—. Recipient Pub. Edn. award Am. Cancer Soc., Westchester div., 1988, Alumna Achievement award Dana Hall Sch., Wellesley, Mass., 1990, Alumnae Achievement award Wellesley Coll., 1994. Fellow AAAS, Westchester Acad. Medicine; mem. Am. Soc. Clin. Oncology, Am. Med. Assn., Endocrine Soc. (chmn. awards com. 1989-90), Soc. Exptl. Biology and Medicine, Am. Soc. Internal Medicine, Women's Med. Assn. N.Y.C. (v.p. 1990-92, fin. asst. fund treas. 1983—, pres. 1992—), Women's Med. Assn. Westchester (pres. 1988-90), AAUP, Am. Diabetes Assn., Am. Fedn. Clin. Research, Am. Med. Women's Assn., Inc., (dir. N.Y. State 1991—, Pres. Recognition award 1993), Am. Soc. Bone and Mineral Rsch., Assn. Community Cancer Ctrs., Assn. Women in Sci., Assn. Women in Sci. Ednl. Found. (bd. dirs. 1982—), Clin. Ligand Assay Soc., Harvey Soc., Internat. Soc. Preventive Oncology, Internat. Soc. Psychoneuroendocrinology, Nat. Hospice Orgn., Inc., N.Y. Acad. Sci., N.Y. Acad. Medicine, N.Y. State Med. Soc., N.Y. State Soc. Internal Medicine, Westchester County Med. Soc., N.Y. Met. Breast Cancer Group Inc., Cosmopolitan Club, Sigma Xi. Democrat. Jewish. Home: 33 E 70th St New York NY 10021-4946 Office: NY Med Coll Dept Medicine Munger Pavilion Valhalla NY 10595

CARTER, DALE M., neurologist, educator; b. Toronto, Apr. 15, 1951; came to U.S., 1967; naturalized, 1975; d. William Glendon and Margaret Berthe (Schudel) C. BS magna cum laude, SUNY, Brockport, 1973; MA summa cum laude European divsn., Ball State U., Muncie, Ill., 1979; MD, Union U., Albany, N.Y., 1984. Diplomate Am. Bd. Psychiatry and Neurology. Intern in internal medicine Albany Med. Ctr. Hosp., 1984-85, resident in neurology, 1985-88; staff physician Mich. Head Pain and Neurol. Inst., Ann Arbor, 1988-93; pvt. practice specializing in head pain, Ann Arbor, 1993—; staff physician Chelsea (Mich.) Cmty. Hosp., 1988—; instr. biology and nursing Washtenaw C.C., Ann Arbor, 1994—. Scholar Am. Heart Assn., 1982. Mem. AMA, Am. Assn. Neurology, Am. Assn. for Study Headache, S.E. Mich. Women Bus. Owners Assn. Office: 2345 S Huron Pkwy Ann Arbor MI 48104

CARTER, DALE WILLIAM, psychologist; b. Woodbury, N.J., Jan. 27, 1949; s. Charles Elmer and Dorothy Adele (Seibold) C. BS, Wake Forest U., 1971; MS, Radford U., 1976; PhD, U. Ga., 1982. Tchr. Gaston Day Sch., Gastonia, N.C., 1971-73, Charlotte (N.C.) Country Day Sch., 1973-74; psychologist Roanoke County Schs., Salem, Va., 1976-83; psychologist Gwinnett County Schs., Lawrenceville, Ga., 1983-94, coord. psychol. svcs., 1994—; pvt. practice Lilburn, Ga., 1985-93, Norcross, Ga., 1994—; adj. prof. Mercer U., Atlanta, 1984-85; cons. N.E. Consulting Ctr., Lawrenceville, 1985-92; intern supervision Gwinnett County Schs., Lawrenceville, 1985—. Mem. APA (div. sch. psychology), Ga. Assn. Sch. Psychologists, Nat. Assn. Sch. Psychologists, Beta Beta Beta, Kappa Delta Pi, Phi Kappa Phi. Home: 280 Sageglen Rd Lawrenceville GA 30244-5249 Office: Gwinnett County Schs 52 Gwinnett Dr SW Lawrenceville GA 30245-5624

CARTER, DAVID CRAIG, surgeon, educator; b. Penrith, Cumbria, U.K., Jan. 9, 1940; s. Horace Ramsay and Mary Florence (Lister) C.; m. Ilske Ursula Luth, Sept. 23, 1967; children: Adrian James, Ben Julian. Student, St. Andrew's U., Scotland, 1958-64, MB ChB, 1966; MD, Dundee U., Scotland, 1979. Lectr. clin. surgery Edinburgh U., Scotland, 1969-74, sr. lectr., 1974-77, regius prof. clin. surgery, 1988—; lectr. surgery Makerere U., Kampala, Uganda, Africa, 1972; vis. scientist UCLA, 1977; prof. surgery Glasgow U., U.K., 1979-88; exec. Brit. Jour. Surgery, London, 1991-95, coeditor, 1985-91; chmn. Scottish Coun. Postgrad. Med. Edn., 1990-96; vice chmn. Biomed. Rsch. Ctr., 1985-91; bd. dirs. Lotham Health Bd.; mem. coun. BBC, Scotland, 1989-94; active Med. Adv. Com. Higher Edn. Found. Coun. Co-author: Principles, Practice of Surgery, 1985, 3d edit., 1994, Pancreatitis, 1990, Surgery of Pancreas, 1993; editor: Peri-Operative Care, 1988, Operative Surgery, 1985—. Chmn. Scottish Found. for Surgery in Nepal, Edinburgh, 1988—. Created knight bachelor, 1996; recipient Moynihan prize Assn. Surgeons, 1973, William Leslie prize Edinburgh U., 1969, McKeown medal Royal Coll. Surgeons, 1982. Fellow ACS (hon.), Royal Coll. Surgeons Ireland (hon.), Royal Coll. Surgeons Edinburgh, Royal Coll. Physicians and Surgeons Glasgow, Royal Coll. Physicians Edinburgh, Royal Coll. Surgeons Eng., Royal Soc. Eng., Deutsche Gesellschart fur Chisurgie (hon), Soc. Surgeons Nepal (hon.); mem. Surg. Rsch. Soc. (pres. 1996—), Assn. Surgeons Gt. Britain and Ireland (pres. 1996—), Brit. Med. Assn. (pres.-elect). Home: 19 Buckingham, Edinburgh EH4 3AD, Scotland Office: Edinburgh Royal Infirmary, Lauriston Pl, Edinburgh EH3 9YW, Scotland

CARTER, DONALD CLAYTON, psychiatrist; b. Blair, Nebr., July 30, 1922; s. Earl Dion and Josephine Emma (Romanowski) C. Student S.E. Mo. State Tchrs. Coll., Cape Girardeau, 1943-45; M.D., U. Nebr., 1950; m. Selma Louise Smith, July 21, 1946; children—Gregory, Donna, Jeffrey, Theodore. Rotating intern Lincoln (Nebr.) Gen. Hosp., 1953-54; resident in internal medicine Riverside Hosp., Newport News, Va., 1950-51, in psychiatry Duke U. Med. Center, 1957-60; practice medicine specializing in family medicine, Beaver City, Nebr., 1954-57; asst. div. chief psychiatry VA Hosp., Durham, N.C., 1960-62; med. dir. Central Minn. Mental Health Center, St. Cloud, 1962-67; asst. prof. psychiatry U. Mo. Med. Sch., Columbia, 1967-68; practice medicine specializing in psychiatry, Morgantown, W.Va., 1968-87; mem. staff and faculty W.Va. Univ. Hosp. and Med. Sch., 1968-87, chief psychiatry outpatient dept., 1968-73, prof., chief psychosomatic consultative service, 1973-74, prof., dir. undergrad. edn. in psychiatry, 1974-82, chief of residency supervision, 1982-87, med. dir. AMHC, Elkins, W.Va., 1987-93 . Served to lt. (j.g.), USNR, 1942-46; as capt. M.C., U.S. Army, 1951-53. Decorated Bronze Star; recipient Outstanding Tchr. award W.Va. U., 1973-74, MacLachlin award, 1980, Psychiatry Resident Teaching award, 1986; diplomate Am. Bd. Psychiatry and Neurology. Fellow Am. Psychiat. Assn. (pres. W.Va. dist. br. 1977-78; assembly rep. 1977-87); mem. AMA, Tygert Valley County Med. Soc., W.Va. Med. Assn. (ho. of Dels.), Masons. Republican. Presbyterian. Address: RR 3 Box 600 Elkins WV 26241-9576

CARTER, FRANCES MONET, nursing educator; b. Mayfield, Ky., Aug. 6, 1923; d. Orlando Lee and Hattie Lois (Buckingham) C.; m. Carl Baker; Donald Matthies, Henry Evans. RN, Louisville Gen. Hosp., 1944; cert. advanced psychiat. nursing instrn., U. Minn., 1945; BS, UCLA, 1948; MA, San Francisco State U., 1957; EdD, U. San Francisco, 1978. RN, Calif. Supr., instr. Herrick Meml. Hosp., Berkeley, Calif.; instr. Compton (Calif.) Sanitarium; prof. U. San Francisco, prof. emerita. Author: The Role of the Nurse in Community Mental Health, 1968, Psychosocial Nursing: Theory and Practice in Hospital and Community Mental Health, 1971, 2d edit., 1976, 3d edit., 1981. First alumni fellow U. Louisville, 1990, World Health Orgn. fellow, 1961-62, 70. Fellow Am. Acad. Nursing; mem. ANA, Alliance for Mentally Ill, World Fedn. for Mental Health, Sigma Theta Tau, Alpha Sigma Nu.

CARTER, FRANK JAMES, retired obstetrician and gynecologist; b. Bklyn., June 30, 1923; s. Vincent James and Rose (Sanseviera) C.; m. Elizabeth Burrows, Jan. 8, 1977. AB, Columbia U., 1943; MD, NYU, 1947. Diplomate Am. Bd. Ob-Gyn. Intern Queens Gen. Hosp., 1947-49, intern in pathology, 1949-50; intern in ob/gyn. King County Hosp., 1955-56; intern Marmonides Hosp., 1956-59; v.p. Norwich (Conn.) Ob-Gyn. Group, 1959-87; ret., 1987. Capt. M.C., USAF, 1951-53. Home: 76 Briar Hill Rd Norwich CT 06360

CARTER, FRANK MOULTON, physician; b. Phila., Apr. 21, 1958; s. Frank Moulton and Esther Louise (Ruggiers) C.; m. Loretta Marie Volpe, Mar. 9, 1985; 1 child, Emma Elizabeth. BA, Univ. Va., 1980; MD, Temple Univ., 1994. Republican. Office: Berkshire Surgical Assoc 1075 Berkshire Blvd Wyomissing PA 19610

CARTER, JAMES HARVEY, JR., physician assistant; b. Jan. 17, 1960; s. James Harvey Sr. and Jettie Lucille (Strayhorn) C.; m. Brigit Maria Weaver, Sept. 11, 1993. BA in Psychology/Biology cum laude, Morehouse Coll., 1981; Cert. EMT, Forsyth Tech. Inst., 1981; B of Health Sci., Duke U., 1986, M of Health Sci., 1994. Registered U.S. Drug Enforcement Adminstr., Nat. Registry EMTs; cert. ACLS, BCLS, EMT, physician asst.; lic. N.C. Bd. Med. Examiners. EMT, dispatcher Southeastern Emergency Med. Svcs., East Point, Ga., 1980-81; EMT Fulton County Alcoholism Treatment Ctr., Atlanta, 1980-81, Tom Higgs Svc., Winston-Salem, N.C., 1981-82; physician asst. Duke U. Med. Ctr., Durham, N.C., 1986—, NES Govt. Svcs., Inc., Ft. Bragg, N.C., 1995—. Contbr. articles to profl. jours. mem. vocat. adv. bd. So. H.S., Durham, 1992—; Compassionate Tabernacle of Faith missionary Bapt. Ch., Raleigh, N.C., 1992—; mem. cultural diversity task force Am. Heart Assn., Durham County, 1993—; mem. health careers adv. bd. Ctr. for Employment Tng., Research Triangle Park, N.C., 1995—. With USNR and USMCR, 1989—. Named one of Outstanding Young Men of Am., 1983, 89; recipient Cert. of Appreciation, Am. Heart Assn., 1993, 94, Cert. of Recognition, Ch. of God of Prophecy, Sanford, N.C., 1995. Mem. NAACP, Am. Assn. Neurol. Surgeons, Nat. Assn. EMTs, Am. Acad. Physician Assts. (Cert. of Appreciation 1994), Assn. Med. Svc. Corps Officers of USN, Assn. Neurosurg. Physician Assts., U.S. Naval Inst., Res. Officers Assn. of U.S., Naval Res. Assn., Naval Assn. Physician Assts., Am. Assn. Surgeon Assts., Assn. Mil. Surgeons of U.S., N.C. Med. Soc., Triangle Area Physician Assts. (v.p. 1988-91, chmn. cmty. svc. com. 1988-91, pres. 1991-96), Duke U. Physician Asst. Soc., N.C. Acad. Physician Assts. (chmn. minority affairs com. 1990-96, trustee NCAPA endowment 1992—, bd. dirs. 1993-96, conf. planning com. 1993-96, Cert. of Appreciation 1994), Am. Legion. Home: 3 Mattie Ct Durham NC 27704

CARTER, JOHN ROBERT, physician; b. Buffalo, Apr. 21, 1917; s. John Harvey and Gertrude Ann (Buckpitt) C.; m. Adelaide Briggs, May 8, 1943; children—Marilyn Anne, Jeanne Catherine. B.S., Hamilton Coll., 1939; M.D., U. Rochester, 1943. Diplomate: Nat. Bd. Med. Examiners. Intern State U. Iowa, 1943-44, resident, 1944-48, asst. dept. pathology, 1944, from instr. to asso. prof., 1944-55, prof., 1955-59; prof., chmn. dept. pathology and oncology U. Kans. Med. Center, 1960-66; prof. pathology dept. orthopedics Case Western Res. U., Cleve., 1966—, dir. Inst. Pathology, chmn. dept. pathology, 1966-81; cons. VA Hosp., U.S. Army Hosp., U.S. Penitentiary, Watkins Meml. Hosp.; Past chmn. pathology study sect. NIH; mem. pathology tng. grant com. Nat. Inst. Gen. Med. Scis.; mem. pathology adv. council Central VA Office; mem. sci. adv. bd. Armed Forces Inst. Pathology.; Bd. dirs. Univs. Assoc. Research and Edn. Pathology; past pres. Mem. editorial bd.: Am. Jour. Pathology. Served to lt. USNR, 1946-48. Mem. AMA, AAAS, Cleve. Acad. Medicine, Path. Soc. Gt. Britain and Ireland, Am. Assn. Pathologists and Bacteriologists (past pres.), Internat. Acad. Pathology, Am. Soc. Clin. Pathology, Am. Soc. Exptl. Pathology, Coll. Am. Pathologists, Soc. Exptl. Biology, AAUP, Central Soc. Clin. Research, Phi Beta Kappa, Sigma Xi, Alpha Omega Alpha. Home: 36570 Ridge Rd Willoughby OH 44094-4106 Office: Inst Pathology Case Western Res U Cleveland OH 44106

CARTER, JOHN W., anatomy educator, researcher; b. Galveston, Tex., Dec. 19, 1945; s. Isham and Ellen F. (Barber) C.; m. Tess Penick, Aug. 25, 1967; children: Linzett Marie, Bryce Wayne. BS in Biology, So. Nazarene U., 1968; MS in Biology, Trinity U., 1972; PhD in Anatomy, U. Tex. Health Sci. Ctr., San Antonio, 1975. Asst. prof. biology Mid-Am. Nazarene Coll., Olathe, Kans., 1975-78; asst. prof. anatomy U. Kans. Med. Ctr., Kansas City, Kans., 1978-79; asst. prof. anatomy Sch. of Medicine Oral Roberts U., Tulsa, 1979-84, assoc. prof. anatomy Sch. of Medicine, 1984-89; assoc. prof. Wichita (Kans.) State U., 1990—. Contbr. articles to profl. jours. Pub. rels. officer U.S. Power Squadron, Tulsa, 1987-89. With USAF, 1969-72. Mem. AAAS, Am. Assn. Anatomists. Republican. Home: 8402 E Champions St Wichita KS 67226-3329

CARTER, L. PHILIP, neurosurgeon, consultant; b. St. Louis, Feb. 26, 1939; s. Russell G. and Dorothy Ruth (Zerwick) C.; m. Marcia L. Carlson, Aug. 26, 1960 (div. Apr., 1989); children: Kristin, Melinda, Chad Philip; m. Colleen L. Harrington, Oct. 20, 1990. MD, Washington U., St. Louis, 1964. Active staff Barrow Neurol. Inst., Phoenix, 1976-88, dir. microsurg. lab., 1978-88, chief cerebral vascular surgery, 1983-88; prof. neurosurgery, chief neurosurg. svcs. Coll. Medicine U. Ariz., Tucson, 1988-93; prof., chmn. dept.

neurosurgery U. Okla. Health Sci. Ctr., Oklahoma City, 1993—; med. cons. Flowtronics, Inc., Phoenix, 1980—; vis. prof. Japan Neurosurg. Soc., Kyoto, 1983. Editor: Neurovascular Surgery, 1994; co-editor: Cerebral Revascularization for Stroke, 1985; contbr. articles to profl. jours. Cons. Ariz. Head Injury Found., 1988-93, Ariz. Epilepsy Found., 1973-75. Capt. USAF, 1965-67. Recipient Internat. Coll. Surgeons fellowship, 1973, Ariz. Disease Control for the Study of Treatment of Stroke grant, 1986. Fellow ACS, Am. Heart Assn.; mem. Am. Assn. Neurol. Surgeons, Soc. Neurol. Surgeons, Rocky Mountain Neurosurg. Soc., Ariz. Neurol. Soc. (sec.-treas. 1985-91), We. Neurosurg. Soc. (program chmn. 1990, 95). Republican. Home: 21 Oakdale Farm Cir Edmond OK 73013-7453 Office: U Okla Health Scis Dept Neurosurgery PO Box 26901 Oklahoma City OK 73190

CARTER, MICHAEL ALLEN, college dean, nursing educator; b. Springfield, Mo., Feb. 13, 1947; s. William Franklin and Mable Belle (Buckner) C.; m. Sarah Ann Jennings, July 4, 1969; 1 child, Elizabeth Ruth. BS in Nursing, U. Ark., 1969, MS in Nursing, 1973; D of Nursing Sci., Boston U., 1979. Cert. family nurse practitioner. Instr. U. Ark., Little Rock, 1972-73; nurse practitioner VA Hosp., Bedford, Mass., 1974-75; asst. prof. Boston U., 1975-76; asst. prof. U. Colo., Denver, 1976-79, assoc. prof., 1979-82; prof., coll. dean U. Tenn., Memphis, 1982—; chmn. Vis. Nurses Assn., Memphis. 1st lt. Nurse Corps, U.S. Army, 1969-71. Named Vol. of Yr. Salvation Army, Denver, 1978; recipient Better Life award Tenn. Health Care Assn., 1988. Fellow Am. Acad. Nursing; mem. Nat. Acads. Practice (Disting. practitioner). Home: 2933 Robin Rd Memphis TN 38111-2521 Office: U Tenn Coll Nursing 877 Madison Ave Memphis TN 38103-3408

CARTER, REGINALD DENNY, medical educator; b. Newton, S.C., June 16, 1942. AA in Biology magna cum laude, Mars Hill (N.C.) Coll., 1960; BS in Biology cum laude, Wake Forest U., 1964, MS in Physiology and Biochemistry, 1969, PhD in Physiology and Pharmacology, 1970. Cert. physician asst., Duke U., 1978, nat. cert. physician asst. 1979. Sr. rsch. technician Wake Forest U. Sch. Medicine, Winston Salem, N.C., 1964-66, cardiovasc. trainee, 1966-70; NIH postdoctoral fellow, dept. physiology Duke U. Med. Ctr., Durham, N.C., 1970-71, asst. prof. physiology, 1971-72, clin. asst. prof.; assoc. dir. physician asst. program, 1972-84; clin. assoc. prof.; dir. physician asst. edn. divsn. Duke U. Med. Ctr. Dept. Cmty. and Family Medicine, Durham, N.C., 1984—. Co-editor: Alternatives in Health Care Delivery: Emerging Roles for Physician Assistants, 1984; contbr. articles to profl. jours., chpts. to books. *

CARTER, SARALEE LESSMAN, immunologist, microbiologist; b. Chgo., Feb. 19, 1951; d. Julius A. and Ida (Oiring) Lessman; B.A., National Coll., 1971; m. John B. Carter, Oct. 7, 1979; children: Robert Oiring, Mollie. Supr. lab. immunology Weiss Meml. Hosp., Chgo., 1973-80; lab. immunology supr. Henrotin Hosp., Chgo., 1980-84; tech. dir. Lexington Med. Labs., West Columbia, S.C., 1984—; mem. nat. workshop faculty Am. Soc. Clin. Pathologists; clin. instr. faculty Med. U. S.C. Mem. Am. Soc. Clin. Pathologists (subspecialty cert. in microbiology and immunology, cert. med. technologist). Researcher Legionnaires Disease and mycoplasma pneumonia World Soc. Pathologists, Jerusalem, Israel, 1980. Contbr. articles to profl. jours.; Mem. Rep. Senoritorial Inner Circle, co-chmn. S.C. Young Profls. for George Bush. Office: 110 Medical Ln E Ste 100 West Columbia SC 29169-4817

CARTER, THOMAS ROBERT, orthopedic surgeon; b. McKeesport, Pa., Aug. 5, 1957; s. Robert Dwuane and Nancy Ruth (Suckfiel) C.; m. Sheila Marie Collison, May 23, 1986; children: Garrett, Grady. BS, Allegheny Coll., 1979; MD, U. Pitts., 1983. Diplomate Am. Bd. Orthopedic Surgery. Resident in orthopedic surgery Ohio State U., Columbus, 1983-88; fellow in sports medicine Jackson Hole (Wyo.) Orthopedics, 1988, U. Western Ont., London, 1989; pvt. practice orthopedic surgery Phoenix, 1989—; cons. Ariz. State U., Tempe, 1991—, Phoenix Roadrunners Profl. Hockey Team, 1990-91, Phoenix Condors Profl. Soccer Team, 1990; med. dir. rehab. svc. Tempe St. Lukes Hosp., 1991—. Mem. Am. Acad. Orthopedic Surgeons, Arthroscopic Assn. N. Am., Western Orthopedic Soc., Maricopa County Med. Soc. Republican. Home: 5706 N Casa Blanca Dr Paradise Valley AZ 85283 Office: 2700 N 3d St #100 Phoenix AZ 85004

CARTHEW, PHILIP, toxicologic pathologist; b. Bristol, Eng., May 27, 1948; s. Albert Brinley and Joan Eileen (Rowe) C. BS in Chemistry with honors, Exeter (Eng.) U., 1969; PhD in Chemistry, Queen's U., Belfast, Northern Ireland, 1973; MS in Exptl. Pathology & Toxicology, Royal Postgrad. Med. Sch., London, 1979. Postdoctoral fellow Queen's U., Belfast, 1972-74, rsch. fellow, 1974-75; virologist Med. Rsch. Coun. Carshalton, Surrey, Surrey, Eng., 1975-81; pathologist Med. Rsch. Coun., Carshalton, Surrey, Eng., 1981-87, pathologist toxicology unit, 1987—; cons. Cambridge Antibody Tech., Huntingdon Life Scis. Contbr. more than 80 sci. papers to profl. publs. Grantee WHO, 1991. Mem. Royal Coll. Pathologists, Brit. Soc. Toxicological Pathologists (assoc.), Brit. Toxicology Soc. Office: U Leicester Med Rsch Coun Toxicology Unit, Hodgkin Bldg Lancaster Rd, Leicester LE1 9HN, England

CARTIER, CHARLES ERNEST, alcohol and drug abuse services professional; b. Chgo., Aug. 4, 1931; s. Charles E. and Kathryn (Hanlon) C.; m. JoAnne Murphy, July 12, 1958; children: Kevin, Julia, Theresa, Carol. BS in Commerce, DePaul U., 1953. Nat. cert. alcohol, drug and addictions counselor. Program asst. Alcoholism Svcs. of Cleve. (Ohio), Inc., 1983-84; community liaison coord. Merrick Hall Adolescent Chem. Dependency Program, Cleve., 1984-86; instr. D.W.I. Counter Attack Project Cleve. (Ohio) State Univ., 1984-92; clin. supr. Fresh Start, Inc., Cleve., 1986-91; rehab. therapist alcohol treatment program VA Med. Ctr., Brecksville, Ohio, 1991—; lectr. Cuya Hoga Community Coll., Sch. of Mental Health Tech., Cleve., 1987—; bd. mem., v.p. Exodus, Inc. Treatment Program, 1986-90. Sgt. U.S. Army, 1953-55. Mem. Nat. Assn. Alcoholism and Drug Abuse Counselors, Ohio Assn. Alcoholism and Drug Abuse Counselors (sec. 1986-91, Hinkle Meml. award for Outstanding Work in the Field of Alcoholism Counseling 1990). Roman Catholic. Home: 9049 Roosevelt Dr Northfield OH 44067-1222 Office: VA Med Ctr 10000 Brecksville Rd Cleveland OH 44141-3204

CARTON, ROBERT JOHN, environmental scientist; b. Ft. Monmouth, N.J., Nov. 23, 1943; s. John William and Ursula Juliet (Miller) C.; m. Christina Saunders, June 17, 1967; children: Sean Michael, Christina Noel. BA in Chemistry, LaSalle U., 1965; postgrad., Purdue U., 1965-66; MS in Environ. Sci., Drexel U., 1967; PhD in Environ. Sci., Rutgers U., 1974. Rsch. engr. E.I. DuPont, Wilmington, Del., 1967-69; chemist, environ. scientist U.S. EPA, Washington, 1972-92; environ. coord. U.S. Army Med. Rsch. and Materiel Command, Frederick, Md., 1992—; pres. Truth About Fluoride, Inc., Buckeystoen, Md., 1993-95. Editor: Fluoride Report, 1993-95. Pres. Nat. Fedn. Fed. Employees Local 2050/U.S. EPA, Washington, 1986-87, 89-90. Recipient Bronze medal U.S. EPA, 1973, 85. Mem. Internat. Acad. Oral Medicine & Toxicology, Internat. Soc. for Fluoride Rsch. Methodist. Office: US Army Med Rsch and Materiel Command Ft Detrick MRMC-RCQ-E Frederick MD 21702-5012

CART-ROGERS, KATHERINE COOPER, emergency nurse; b. Jacksonville, Tex., Aug. 7, 1948; d. Raymond Jesse and June (Walker) Cooper; m. Frank E. Rogers, Sept. 25, 1981; 1 child, Natalie Christine Cart. Med. Technologist, St. Mary's, Galveston, Tex., 1967; BS in Nursing, Stephen F. Austin U., Nacogdoches, Tex., 1989; MA in Mgmt., Regent U., Virginia Beach, Va., 1995. Cert. CPR, Emergency Nurse, ACLS, instr. trauma nurse core course. Pharmacology-toxicology researcher U. Tex. Med. Br., Galveston, 1967-68, Ohio State U., Columbus, 1968-72; physicians asst., lab. supr. Newborn Meml. Hosp., Jacksonville, 1975-78; lab. mgr. East Tex. Med. Ctr., Rusk, 1978-87; lab. supr. Nacogdoches Meml. Hosp., 1987-89, emergency rm. nurse, 1989-91; emergency rm. chrge nurse Kingwood (Tex.) Pla. Hosp., 1991-92; nursing cons. Thorstenson Eye Clinic, Nacogdoches, 1991-92; dir. surg. svcs. Thorstenson Ambulatory Surgery Ctr., Nacogdoches, 1992-93, dir. emergency svcs., trauma coord., 1992—, employee health dir., 1994, dir. admissions, 1995; dir. rural health clinic Nan Travis Meml. Hosp., 1996—. Mem. AACCN, Emergency Nurses Assn., Tex. Trauma Coords., Tex. Regional Adv. Coun. for Trauma Area G. Home: 310 N Mound St Nacogdoches TX 75961-5032

CARTWRIGHT, MARY LOU, laboratory scientist; b. Payette, Idaho, Apr. 5, 1923; d. Ray J. and Nellie Mae (Sherer) Decker; BS, U. Houston, 1958; MA, Ctrl. Mich. U., 1976; m. Chadwick Louis Cartwright, Sept. 13, 1947. Med. technologist Methodist Hosp., Houston, 1957-59, VA Hosp., Livermore, Calif., 1960-67, Kaiser Permanente Med. Ctr., Hayward, Calif., 1967-71, United Med. Lab., San Mateo, Calif., 1972-73; sr. med. technologist Oakland (Calif.) Hosp., 1974-86; cons. med. lab. tech. Oakland Public Schs. Chmn., Congressional Dist. 11 steering com. Common Cause, 1974-77; consumer mem. Alameda County (Calif.) Health Systems Agy., 1977-78. Served with USNR, 1945-53. Mem. Calif. Soc. Med. Tech., Calif. Assn. Med. Lab. Tech. (Technologist of Yr. award 1968, 78, Pres.'s award 1977, Svc. award chpt. 1978, 79), Am. Soc. Med. Tech. (by-laws chmn. 1981-83), Disabled Am. Vets. (adjutant treas. of chpt. 122, 1993-96), Am. Bus. Women's Assn., Nat. Assn. Female Execs. Democrat. Home and Office: 350 Bennett St Apt 9 Grass Valley CA 95945-6870

CARUANA, LOUIS BARTHOLOMEW, science educator; b. Norwich, N.Y., Mar. 5, 1937; s. V. James and Katherine (Sedoti) C.; m. Joyce Emogene Bowman, May 21, 1960; children: Louis M., Vincent J., Stephen D., Gregory J. BS, Midwestern State U., 1967, MS, 1978; PhD, Tex. A&M U., 1986. Program dir. Midwestern State U., Wichita Falls, Tex., 1972-75; asst. prof. S.W. Tex. State U., San Marcos, 1975-82, assoc. prof., 1982-88, prof., 1988—; site surveyor Nat. Accreditating Agy. of Clin. Lab. Scis., Chgo., 1982—. Editor Jour. Med. Tech., 1987; contbr. articles to profl. publs., chpt. to book. Mem. South Hays County Vol. Fire Dept., San Marcos, 1987—. Sgt. USAF, 1957-61. Mem. Am. Soc. Med. Tech. (1st Place State Publ. award 1980, cert. of recognition 1987), Tex. Soc. Med. Tech., Tex. Soc. Allied Health Profls. (bd. dirs. 1984-90), Sigma Xi, Beta Beta Beta. Home: 255 Pauls Dr San Marcos TX 78666-9326 Office: SW Tex State U Health Sci Ctr San Marcos TX 78666

CARUTHERS, MARILYNN LAIRD, health care consultant; b. Loomis, Calif., Dec. 7, 1922; d. Fenn Warner and Lorena May (Roberts) Laird; m. Ralph Rutland Caruthers, Nov. 16, 1946; children: Robert Lee, Laird David. Degree in nursing, Mt. Zion Hosp., San Francisco, 1944; BS summa cum laude, UCLA, 1960. RN. Nurse U.S. Army, 1944-46; clinic nurse Missionary Clinic, Morocco, 1954-56, 62-63; sch. nurse San Diego City Schs., 1956-58; supr. sch. health Placer County Schs., Auburn, Calif., 1960-62, supr. nurse head start, 1964-66; sch. nurse Roseville (Calif.) High Sch. Dist., 1967-69; coord. sch. health edn. El Dorado High Sch. Dist., Diamond Springs, Calif., 1969-81, cons. sch. health, health edn., 1981-86; field rep. Women in Mil. Svc. for Am. Found.; dir. Placer County Sch. Tutorial Program, Auburn, 1966-67; cons. Loomis Basin General Plan, Loomis, Calif., 1975. Vol. Placer County Immunization Clinic, Placer County Arthritis Support Group, Place County Office Edn. Mem. AAUW, Calif. Sch. Nurses Orgn., Calif. Coaches Assn., UCLA Alumni Assn., NORCAL Alumni Assn., Calif. Retired Tchrs. Assn., Calif. Sch. Adminstrs. Assn., UCLA Bruin Alumni Assn. (pres. 1959-60), Comstock Club. Democrat.

CARVAJAL, HUGO FRANCISCO, JR., pediatrics and surgery educator; b. Cartago, Costa Rica, Jan. 9, 1941; came to U.S., 1964; s. Hugo Francisco and Delia (Ulloa) C.; m. Konny Kay Salladay, Aug. 20, 1964 (div. 1977); children: Hugo Francisco III, Karina Kay; m. Susan Marie Carr, May 19, 1979; children: Krisana Marie, Eric Mitchell, Jessica Ann. MD, Nat. U. Mex., Mexico City, 1964. Intern San Juan de Dios Hosp., San Jose, Costa Rica, 1963; intern pediatrics Genessee Hosp., Rochester, N.Y., 1964-65; resident in pediatrics U. Tex. Med. Br., Galveston, 1965-67, from asst. prof. to assoc. prof. pediatrics, 1971-80, full prof. pediatrics, 1980-83; fellow NIH, 1968-69; instr. pediatrics U. Tex. Med. Sch., San Antonio, 1969-71; full prof. pediatrics and surgery U. Tex. Med. Sch. Houston, 1983—, dir. pediatric critical care, 1983—; chmn, Dept. of Pediatrics Humana Women's and Children's Hosp., San Antonio; clin. prof. pediatrics, Health Sci. Ctr. Univ. Tex., San Antonio; chmn., dir. pediatric ICU Women's and Children's Hosp., San Antonio, 1992—; clin. prof. of Pediatrics, Health Sci. Ctr. U. Tex., 1992—; chief pediatrics Shriners Bur. Inst., Galveston, 1975-83; dir. pediatric ICU Hermann Hosp., Houston, 1983-92. Editor: Burns in Children, 1988' contbr. articles to profl. jours. Pres. Minority Faculty Assn., 1990-91; exec. dir. Pediatric Burn Found. Houston, 1990-92. Maj. U.S. Army, 1969-71. Grantee Shriners of N.Am., 1971-82, faculty U. Tex., 1972-73, 83-87, Nat. Heart and Lung Inst. Project, 1973-76, Kiwanis Internat., 1989-90. Fellow Am. Acad. Pediatrics; mem. Am. Burn Assn., Am. Soc. Nephrology, Soc. Critical Care Medicine, Houston Yacht Club (flag surgeon 1989-90), Elmina Lodge. Roman Catholic. Home: 117 Ripple Creek St San Antonio TX 78231-1418 Office: 7922 Ewing Halsell Dr Ste 380 San Antonio TX 78229-3726

CARVAJAL, JORGE ARMANDO, endocrinologist, internist; b. Chiscas, Boyaca, Colombia, Dec. 20, 1935; came to U.S., 1963; s. Julio and Natividad (Caicedo) C.; m. Carlota Mellonunes Ribeiro, Sept. 5, 1965; children: Jorge Jr., Fernando, Eduardo. MD, U. Nacional Fac. Medicine, Bogota, Colombia, 1963. Diplomate Am. Bd. Internal Medicine with subspecialty in endocrinology. Resident Hosp. San Jose, Bogota, 1962-63; intern Meth. Hosp., Peoria, Ill., 1963-64; resident in medicine Meml. Hosp., Detroit, 1964-65, Mt. Sinai Hosp., Mpls., 1965-66, VA Med. Ctr., Long Beach, Calif., 1966-67; fellow in endocrinology VA Med. Ctr., L.A., 1967-69; asst. prof. U. Rosario, Bogota, 1969-72; fellow in metabolism U. Calif.-Davis, Sacramento, 1972-73; staff endocrinologist Kaiser-Permanente Hosp., Sacramento, 1973-75; staff physician VA Med. Ctr., Long Beach, Calif., 1975-76; pvt. practice Anaheim, Calif., 1976—; staff Anaheim Meml. Hosp., 1976—. Democrat. Roman Catholic. Home: 16562 Grimaud Ln Huntington Beach CA 92649 Office: 1211 W La Palma #702 Anaheim CA 92801

CARVER, DAVID HAROLD, physician, educator; b. Boston, Apr. 18, 1930; s. Elias and Lottie (Jaffe) C.; m. Patricia Jo Nair, Aug. 2, 1953; children: Randolph Nair, Rebecca Lynn, Leslie Allison. A.B. magna cum laude, Harvard U., 1951; M.D., Duke U., 1955. Intern Johns Hopkins Hosp., 1955-56; research fellow pediatrics Cleve. Met. Hosp., 1956-58; jr. asst. resident Children's Hosp. Med. Center, Boston, 1958-59; sr. asst. resident Children's Hosp. Med. Center, 1959-60 chief resident, 1960-61, USPHS spl. post doctoral research fellow, 1961-63; asst. prof. pediatrics Albert Einstein Coll. Medicine, 1963-66; assoc. prof., then prof. pediatrics Johns Hopkins U. Med. Sch., 1966-76; prof. pediatrics U. Toronto Med. Sch., 1976-88; physician-in-chief Hosp. Sick Children, Toronto, 1976-86; chmn. dept. pediatrics U. Toronto, 1976-86; prof., chmn. dept. pediatrics Robert Wood Johnson Med. Sch., 1988—; mem. study sect. USPHS Ctr. Disease Control, 1971-73; mem. provincial research grants rev. com. Ont. Ministry Health, 1977-83, chmn., 1981-83. Assoc. editor: Textbook of Pediatrics, 14th edit, 1968, 15th edit., 1972, 16th edit., 1977; editorial bd.: Pediatrics, 1973-79. Served with USPHS, 1956-58 Recipient Schaffer award clin. teaching Johns Hopkins U. Med. Sch., 1973, Bain award for clin. teaching Hosp. Sick Children, 1978, Kennedy sr. scholar, 1966-73. Mem. Am. Acad. Pediatrics (Com. on infectious diseases 1973-79), Infectious Disease Soc. Am., Am. Soc. Virology, Internat. Soc. Interferon Research, Canadian Infectious Disease Soc., Am. Soc. Microbiology, Soc. Pediatric Research, Am., Canadian pediatric socs., Harvard of Princeton Club. Home: 220 Sayre Dr Princeton NJ 08540-5852

CARY, FREEMAN HAMILTON, physician; b. LaGrange, Ga., Sept. 14, 1926; s. Ashton Hall and Edna Gwendolyn (Freeman) C.; m. Ruby I. Samples, July 26, 1951 (div.); children: Robin L., Freeman H., Emily A., Leslie L.; m. Sara Ellen Hunter, Nov. 15, 1971; children: Tim, Alex, Kippen, Eric. Student, Ga. Tech., 1943-45; B.S., Emory U., 1946, M.D., 1950. Diplomate: Am. Bd. Internal Medicine, Am. Bd. Cardiovascular Diseases. Intern, resident Grady Hosp., Atlanta, 1950-53; fellow cardiology Grady Hosp., 1953-54, instr., 1953-58, dir. cardiac clinic, 1957-60, dir. stroke rehab. clinic, 1958-60; dir. med. edn. Orange Meml. Hosp., Orlando, Fla., 1960-71; asst. attending physician Congress, Washington, 1971-72; attending physician Congress, 1973-86; assoc. in medicine Emory U. Med. Sch., 1958-60; clin. prof. med. edn. U.S. Fla., Tampa, 1968-71; clin. prof. allied health scis. Fla. Tech. U., Orlando, 1969-71; dir. Central Fla. Blood Bank, Orlando, 1963-71; prof. medicine U. Va. Sch. Medicine, 1987-90; ret., 1990. Served to rear adm. M.C. USNR, 1954-56, 71-86. Recipient Bronze medallion Ga. Heart Assn., 1961, Silver medallion Fla. Heart Assn., 1966. Fellow ACP, Am. Heart Assn. (coun. clin. cardiology, bd. dirs.), Am. Coll. Cardiology, Am. Coll. Chest Physicians; mem. Fla. Heart Assn. (pres. 1970-71), Ctrl. Fla. Heart Assn. (pres. 1968-69, bd. dirs. 1961-71), Washington Heart Assn. (bd. dirs. 1972), Burning Tree Club, Country Club of Orlando, Farmington Country Club. Home: 1101 Poinsettia Ave Orlando FL 32804-6337

CARY, GENE LEONARD, psychiatrist; b. Buffalo, Oct. 24, 1928; s. Leonard Albert and Margaret C.; m. Janice Frances McDonald, June 15, 1957; children: Phillip S., Brian C., Bruce L., Allison A., Meghan F. BA, U. Buffalo, 1952; MD, SUNY, Syracuse, 1957. Diplomate Am. Bd. Psychiatry and Neurology. Intern Buffalo Gen. Hosp., 1958; resident in psychiatry SUNY, Syracuse, 1958-61; clin. instr. dept. psychiatry SUNY, 1961-65, asst. prof. psychiatry, 1965-71, lectr. dept. psychology, 1966-67; lectr., cons. dept. spl. edn. Syracuse U., 1961-68, coordinator undergrad. edn., 1965-71; coordinator resident tng. prog. & outpatient psychiatric svc. Hershey Med. Ctr., Pa., 1971-73; asst. prof. psychiatry Hershey Med. Ctr., 1971-73; pvt. practice psychiatry Hershey Psychiatric Assocs., 1973—; Pa. Psychiatric Soc. rep. Dept. Pub. Welfare, Gov.'s Mental Health/Mental Retardation Adv. Com., Harrisburg, Pa., 1986—. Contbr. articles to profl. jours., chpts. to books. With U.S. Army, 1946-48. Fellow Am. Psychiat. Assn., Pa. Psychiat. Soc. (chmn. edn. com. 1976-93, councilor 1987-93, gov. rels. com. 1988—, treas. 1993-94, sec. 1994-95, v.p. 1995-96, pres.-elect 1996-97); mem. Pa. Soc. Adolescent Psychiatry (exec. com. councilor 1978-82), Cen. Pa. Psychiat. Soc. (coun. rep. to Pa. Psychiat. Soc. 1986), Pa. Med. Soc. (continuing edn. site surveyor 1987—, mem. com. edn. and sci. 1992—), Hershey Bus. Assn. (sec. 1971-72). Office: Hershey Psychiat Assocs 20 Briarcrest Sq Ste 205 Hershey PA 17033-2331

CARY, GEORGE R(IVES), JR., surgeon, educator; b. Atlanta, Nov. 20, 1930; s. George Rives Sr. and Mary (Kimbro) C.; m. Elizabeth Ann Stocker, June, 1954; children: Stocker, Ashley, George III, John. BA, Emory U., 1951; MD, Tulane U., 1955. Intern Charity Hosp., New Orleans, 1955-56; resident in orthopaedic surgery Tulane U., New Orleans, 1956-60; pvt. practice, New Orleans, 1965—; chief of staff Touro Infirmary, 1985-87; prof. orthopaedic surgery Tulane U., New Orleans, 1989—. Maj. M.C., USAF, 1960-65. Mem. La. Orthopaedic Assn. (pres. 1980), Greater New Orleans Orthopaedic Soc. (pres. 1982), Tulane Med. Alumni Assn. (pres. 1993-94). Home: 1411 Eleonore St New Orleans LA 70115-4317 Office: Orthopaedic Assocs 3525 Prytania St Ste 402 New Orleans LA 70115-3550

CARY, HUNSDON, III, health services administrator; b. Saundusky, Ohio, May 29, 1945; s. Hunsdon Jr. and Dorothy Elizabeth (Plummer) C.; m. Susan Holcombe Adams, June 14, 1968; children: Hunsdon IV, William Snead Adams, Virginia Adams. BS in Journalism, Ohio U., 1968; M in Hosp. Adminstrn., Med. Coll. of Va., 1970. Asst. adminstr. E.W. Springs Meml. Hosp., Lancaster, S.C., 1970; dir. physician svc. Charter Med. Corp., Macon, Ga., 1975-76; adminstr. Westminster-Canterbury, Lynchburg, Va., 1976-84, pres., chief exec. officer, 1984—. Vestryman St. John's Episcopal Ch., 1989, also sec.; bd. dirs. Lynchburg chpt. ARC, 1982-86. Capt. Med. Svc. Corps, USAF, 1971-75. Recipient Pub. Svc. award Va. Assn. Non-Profit Homes for Aging, 1988. Mem. Family Svc. of Ctrl. Va. (bd. dirs. 1987-89), Mental Health Assn. (bd. dirs. 1994-96), Va. Inland Sailing Assn., Rotary (bd. dirs. 1981-83, 94-96). Home: 3701 Manton Dr Lynchburg VA 24503-3015 Office: Westminster-Canterbury 501 Ves Rd Lynchburg VA 24503-4639

CASALE, THOMAS BRUCE, medical educator; b. Chgo., Apr. 21, 1951; m. Jean M. Casale; 1 son, Jeffrey G. BS cum laude, U. Ill., 1973; MD, Chgo. Med. Sch., 1977. Diplomate Am. Bd. Internal Medicine, Am. Bd. Allergy and Immunology. Resident in internal medicine Baylor Coll. Medicine, Houston, 1977-80; med. staff fellow lab. clin. investigation NIAID, NIH, Bethesda, Md., 1980-84; from asst. prof. to prof. internal medicine U. Iowa, Iowa City, 1984-94, prof. internal medicine, 1994-96; dir. Nebr. Med. Rsch. Inst., 1996—; clin. prof. pediatrics Coll. Medicine U. Nebr., 1996—; grad. asst. dept. microbiology U. Ill., 1974; chief med. staff fellow lab. clin. investigation, NIAID, NIH, Bethesda, 1982-83; attending physician VA Med. Ctr., Iowa City, 1984-96, staff physician, 1986-96, clin. investigator, 1991-96; asst. dir. tchg. allergy/immunology divsn. dept. internal medicine U. Iowa, Iowa City, 1989-92, acting dir., 1992, dir., 1993-96, faculty inerdisciplinary immunology grad. degree program, 1993-96; cons. panel minority biomed. rsch. support grants NIH, 1985; ad hoc grant reviewer Am. Lung Assn., 1986, VA, 1986-96, NIH, 1989; chmn. latex allergy com. U. Iowa Hosps., 1994-96; mem. rsch. devel. com. VA Med. Ctr., Iowa City, 1991-94. Contbr. over 175 articles to profl. publs.; mem. editl. bd. Jour. Allergy Clin. Immunology, 1988-93, clin. asthma revs., 1996—. Mem. asthma technical adv. group Am. Lung Assn., 1989-96. Lt. commdr. USPHS, 1980-83, USPHS Res., 1983—. Recipient Dr. John J. Sheinin Rsch. award Chgo. Med. Sch., 1977, Clin. Investigator VA, 1991-96, Am. Soc. clin. Investigation award, 1992; grantee Am. Acad. Allergy Immunology, 1981, Am. Coll. Allergy, 1984, Internat. Congress Allergology Clin. Immunology, 1985, 88, NIH, 1986-91, 87-90, 92-93, 93-94, VA Merit Rev., 1986-89, 89-92, 92-96, Environ. Health Sci. Core Ctr., 1990-96, CDC, 1994-95, Fisons Corp., 1994—, 95—, Sanofi Rsch., 1995—, Astra, U.S.A. Inc., 1995-96, ImmuLogic Pharm. Corp., 1995—, Zeneca Pharms., 1995-96, others. Fellow ACP, Am. Acad. Allergy Immunology (cutaneous allergy com. 1985-90, postgrad. edn. com. 1988-91, chmn. 1989-90, program com. dermatologic diseases sect. 1988-93, sec. 1989-90, vice chmn. 1990-91, chmn. 1991-92, edn. coun. 1989-90, sec. 1993-95, vice chair 1995—, chmn. bronchoalveolar lavage com. 1991-95, others), Am. Coll. Allergy Immunology (profl. allergy/immunology edn. com. 1989-94); mem. Am. Fedn. Clin. Rsch., Am. Thoracic Soc. (sec. allergy immunology and inflammation scientific assembly 1990-91, chair-elect 1991-93, chair program com. 1992-93, chair 1993-95, long-range planning and policy com. sci. assembly on allergy immunology and inflammation 1991-96, sci. conf. com. 1991-93, bd. dirs. 1993-95), Iowa Soc. Allergy Immunology (pres. 1987-89), Am. Assn. Immunologists, Midwest Sect. Am. Fedn. Clin. Rsch., Iowa Thoracic Soc., Ctrl. Soc. Clin. Rsch., Am. Soc. Clin. Invest. Office: Nebr Med Rsch Inst 401 E Gold Coast Rd Ste 124 Papillion NE 68046

CASALS-ARIET, JORDI, physician; b. Viladrau, Girona, Spain, May 15, 1911; came to U.S., 1936, naturalized, 1946; s. Martin and Margarida (Ariet) Casals-A.; m. Ellen Evelyn Brock, Dec. 6, 1941; 1 dau., Christina. B.Ciencias, Instituto Nacional, Barcelona, Spain, 1928; Licenciado en Medicina y Cirurgia con Grado, U. Barcelona, 1934. Intern Med. Sch. Hosp., Barcelona, 1934-36; research asso. Cornell U. Med. Coll., N.Y.C., 1936-38; asso. Rockefeller Inst. Med. Research, N.Y.C., 1938-52; mem. staff Rockefeller Found., N.Y.C., 1952-74; prof. epidemiology Yale U., 1964-81, prof. emeritus, 1981—; vis. prof. dept. neurology Mt. Sinai Sch. Medicine, N.Y.C., 1981-84; professorial lectr. dept. neurology Mt. Sinai Sch. Medicine, 1984—. Contbr. articles to profl. jours. Served with Spanish Army, 1933. Recipient Kimble Methodology award Am. Pub. Health Assn., 1969. Fellow Am. Soc. Tropical Medicine and Hygiene (Taylor award 1968), Royal Soc. Tropical Medicine and Hygiene (hon.); mem. Soc. Exptl. Biology and Medicine, Harvey Soc., AAAS, N.Y. Acad. Medicine, N.Y. Acad. Scis., French Soc. Microbiology (hon.). Home: 25 Claremont Ave New York NY 10027-6827 Office: One Gustave L Levy Pl New York NY 10029

CASANOVA, JAMES EDWARD, medical administrator; b. Watertown, Wis., Sept. 10, 1947; s. John Robert and Leanor Ann (White) C.; m. Jean Catherine Starr, May 3, 1975; children: Elizabeth Ann, Daniel Anthony. BA, Marquette U., 1970; MD, U. Wis., 1974. Diplomate Am. Bd. Internal Medicine. Intern Med. Coll. of Wisc./Affiliated Hosps., Milw., 1974-75; resident U. Wisc., 1975-77; instr. medicine U. Wis., Milw., 1977-78; pvt. practice Milw., 1978-86; asst. prof. medicine Med. Coll. Wis., Milw., 1986-93, assoc. prof. medicine, 1993—, asst. dean clin. affairs, 1996—, med. dir. managed care, 1996—; quality assurance com. Primecar Health Plan, Milw., 1983—; clin. guidelines com. Horizon Healthcare Inc., Milw., 1994—; chair credentials com. Med. Coll. Wis. Physicians and Clinics, Milw., 1995—. Contbr. chpt. to book and articles to profl. jours. Active Physicians for Social Responsibility, 1987-93, Milw. First in Quality, 1990—. Mem. ACP, Am. Coll. Physician Execs. (chair forum on guidelines 1994-95), Am. Soc. Internal Medicine, Soc. for Gen. Internal Medicine. Office: Med Coll Wis Froedtert East 9200 W Wisconsin Ave Milwaukee WI 53226

CASANOVA, MANUEL FERNANDO, physician, educator; b. San Juan, P.R., July 20, 1953; s. Manuel Fernando and Elisa (Soto) C.; m. Gisela Teresita Torres, Aug. 1, 1980; children: Cristina Gisela, Sabrina Priscila, Belinda Marie, Melina Aurora. BS, U. P.R., Rio Piedras, 1973, MD, 1979. Diplomate Nat. Bd. Med. Examiners, Am. Bd. Psychiatry and Neurology;

lic. physician, Ga. Med. intern U. Dist. Hosp., Rio Piedras, P.R., 1979-80, neurology resident, 1980-83; cons. Sinai Hosp., Balt., 1984-86, North Charles Hosp., Balt., 1985; rsch. assoc. Johns Hopkins Hosp., Balt., 1986-89; prof. psychiatry, neurology and pathology Med. Coll. Ga., Augusta, 1991—; dir. brain bank unit NIMH, Washington, 1987-91; dep. med. examiner Med. Examiners Office, Washington, 1990-91; neuropathologist D.C. Gen. Hosp., Washington, 1990-91; lectr. George Washington U., Washington, 1990-91; mem. staff VA Hosp., Augusta, 1991—; cons. Dwight D. Eisenhower Army Hosp., Augusta, 1992—. Contbr. articles to profl. jours. ALtd. comdr. USPHS, 1990-91. Recipient Mead and Johnson Co. award, 1982; Stanley scholar, 1994. Mem. AMA (Presdl. award 1981, Physicians Recognition award 1982), Armed Forces Inst. Pathology, others. Office: Downtown VA Med Ctr Rm 3B 121 116 A Psychiatry Svc Augusta GA 30911

CASARIEGO, JORGE ISAAC, psychiatrist, psychoanalyst, educator; b. Havana, Cuba, Apr. 25, 1945; came to U.S., 1960, naturalized, 1970; s. Isaac Alberto Casariego and Elena Mercedes Portela de Casariego. BS, U. New Orleans, 1967; MD, La. State U., 1969; postgrad., Balt.-Washington Psycho. Inst., 1983-90. Diplomate Am. Bd. Psychiatry and Neurology. Med. intern Jewish Hosp. Bklyn., N.Y.C., 1969-70; psychiat. resident N.Y. Med. Coll., N.Y.C., 1970-71, Walter Reed Army Hosp., Washington, 1971-73; chief psychiatry clinic U.S. Army Hosp., Heidelberg, Fed. Republic Germany, 1973-75; clin. instr. dept. psychiatry Sch. Medicine, U. Miami, Fla., 1976-78, asst. prof. psychiatry, 1978-82, clin. asst. prof., 1982-87, clin. assoc. prof., 1988—, chmn. continuing psychiat. edn. com., 1980-83; practice medicine specializing in psychiatry Miami, 1976—; mem. faculty Balt.-Washington Psychoanalytic Inst., 1991—, Fla. Psychoanalytic Inst., 1992—; med. dirs. drug dependence outpatient unit VA Med. Ctr., Miami, 1976, dir. crisis intervention program, 1976-87, attending psychiatrist, 1976—, dir. divsn. psycho-therapy, 1987-89; attending psychiatrist Jackson Meml. Hosp., U. Miami Hosps., 1976—, Mercy Hosp.; sr. attending South Miami Hosp., Larkin Hosp., Doctor's Hosp., Highland Park Hosp., others; chmn. continuing psychiat. edn. com. U. Miami, 1980-83, others. Reviewer, contbr. articles Am. Jour. Psychiatry, other profl. publs.; editor-in-chief The Tiger Rag (La. State U. Med Ctr.). Served with M.C., U.S. Army, 1971-75. NIH Tropical Medicine fellow, U. Recife, Brazil, 1968; recipient Physician's award AMA, 1977, 81, 87, 90. Fellow Am. Psychiat. Assn. (observer-cons. Coun. on Internal Orgn. 1979-81); mem. South Fla. Psychiat. Soc. (sec. 1988-89, chmn. membership com. 1978-80, chmn. Spanish speaking com. 1981-82, chmn. continuing med. edn. com. 1982-84, continuing edn. com. 1986-87, fellowship com. 1987, sec. 1988-89), Cuban Med. Assn. in Exile (mem. Fla. psychoanalytic tng. program faculty 1992—,, Fla. Psychoanalytic Assn. (libr. com. 1991—, clin. svcs. com. 1991—, chmn. com. on continuing med. edn. 1992—, sec. 1992—), Am. Psychoanalytic Assn. (mem. continuing edn. com. 1992—) Aesculapians. Home and Office: 1900 Coral Way Ste 202 Miami FL 33145-2661

CASARINO, JOHN PHILIP, psychiatrist; b. Bklyn., Oct. 19, 1940; s. John Joseph and Grace Emily (Esposito) C. BS, U. Notre Dame, 1961; MD, Med. Coll. Ala., 1965. Intern Meadowbrook Hosp., East Meadow, N.Y., 1965-66; pediatric resident Meadowbrook Hosp., 1966-67; psychiatric resident St. Vincent's Hosp. & Med. Ctr. N.Y., 1967-69, 71-72; staff psychiatrist Luth. Med. Ctr., Bklyn., 1971-72; chief partial hospitalization svc. St. Vincent's Hosp., N.Y.C., 1972-83, attending physician, 1983—; pvt. practice N.Y.C., 1983—; attending physician Cabrini Med. Ctr., 1985—; cons., Archdiocese of N.Y., 1973-83, Mary Manning Home, N.Y.C., 1987—; clin. asst. prof. psychiatry N.Y. Med. Coll., 1978. Maj. USAF, 1969-71, Vietnam. Fellow Am. Psychiat. Assn.; mem. AMA. Home: 115 Central Park W New York NY 10023-4153 Office: 51 Fifth Ave Ste 1C New York NY 10003

CASAS, CARMEN C., dermatologist; b. Bogota, Colombia, July 15, 1945; came to U.S., 1972; d. Pablo Emilio and Elvira (Molina) Casas; m. George D. Magel, Apr. 14, 1977; children: James, Gina, George. MD, Javeriana U., 1968. Diplomate Am. Bd. Dermatology. Intern Hosp. San Ignacio, Bogota, Colombia, 1968-69, Augustana Hosp., Chgo., 1972-73; resident Luth. Gen. Hosp., Park Ridge, Ill., 1973-74, U. Chgo., 1974-78; dermatologist Dermatology Assocs., Corpus Christi, Tex., 1978-87; pvt. practice Corpus Christi, 1987—; clin. asst. prof. U. Tex. Health Sci. Ctr., San Antonio, 1991-95; tchr. Meml. Med. Ctr., Corpus Christi, 1980-95. Fellow Am. Acad. Dermatology; mem. AMA, Am. Soc. Dermatol. Surgery, Tex. Med. Assn., Tex. Dermatol. Soc., Nueces County Med. Soc. (sec. 1990). Roman Catholic. Office: 5756 S Staples Ste J1 Corpus Christi TX 78413

CASCIANO, DANIEL ANTHONY, biologist; b. Buffalo, Mar. 1, 1941; s. Frederick James and Rose Ann C.; m. Gertrude Ann Tara, Aug. 22, 1964; children: Anne, Jonathan. B.S., Canisius Coll., 1962; Ph.D., Purdue U., 1971. Research asst. Roswell Park Meml. Inst., Buffalo, 1963-64; research asst. dept. biol. scis. Purdue U., Lafayette, Ind., 1965-66, teaching asst., 1969, research trainee, 1966-71; postdoctoral investigator U. Tenn., Oak Ridge Nat. Labs., 1971-73; research biologist Nat. Ctr. Toxicol. Research, Jefferson, Ark., 1973—, program dir. div. mutagenesis research, 1976-78, dir. divsn. genetic toxicology, 1979—; assoc. prof. dept. biochemistry and molecular biology U. Ark. for Med. Scis., Little Rock, 1974-90, prof. dept. biochemistry and molecular biology, 1990—; trainee NIH, 1966-71. Contbr. articles to profl. jours. Mem. Tissue Culture Assn., Environ. Mutagen Soc., AAAS, Beta Beta Beta. Home: 1921 Romine Rd Little Rock AR 72205-6723 Office: FDA Ctr Toxicological Rsch Jefferson AR 72079

CASDEN, ANDREW MICHAEL, orthopedist; b. Bklyn., June 13, 1957; s. Daniel D. and Hannah L. (Bernstein) C.; m. Jeri Casden, Aug. 3, 1981; children: Jared, Ryan. BA, Cornell U., 1979, MD, 1983. Bd. cert. Am. Bd. Orthopaedic Surgery; diplomate Nat. Bd. Med. Examiners. Intern gen. surgery The N.Y. Hosp., Cornell Med. Ctr., N.Y.C., 1983-84; resident orthopaedic surgery Hosp. for Joint Diseases, Orthopaedic Inst., N.Y.C., 1984-88; chief spine svc. dept. orthopaedics Mount Sinai Med. Ctr., N.Y.C., 1989—; asst. prof. orthopaedic surgery Mount Sinai Sch. Medicine, N.Y.C., 1989—, asst. prof. neurosurgery, 1994—; Chgo. Spine fellow Rush Presbyn.-St. Luke's Med. Ctr., Chgo., 1988-89; presenter in field. Contbr. articles to profl. jours. Mem. Am. Acad. Orthopaedic Surgeons (com. on evaluations 1995), Am. Spinal Injury Assn., N.Am. Spine Soc., Scoliosis Rsch. Soc. Office: Mt Sinai Med Ctr 5 East 98th New York NY 10029

CASE, DAVID BARTLETT, internist, educator; b. Plainfield, N.J., Mar. 17, 1942; s. George and Caroline (Bartlett) C.; m. Jean Brookhart, Aug. 2, 1969; children: Thayer Stimson, Nelson Chipman. A.B., Princeton U., 1964; M.D., Columbia U., 1968. Intern, then asst. resident Johns Hopkins Hosp., Balt., 1968-70; fellow Columbia Presbyn. Hosp., N.Y.C., 1972-75; asst., then assoc. prof. Cornell U. Med. Coll., N.Y.C., 1975-84, clin. assoc. prof., 1984—; mem. Council on High Blood Pressure Research, 1979—. Contbr. chpts. to books in field, also articles to profl. jours. Recipient Andrew Mellon Tchr. Scientist award Cornell U., 1978. Fellow Am. Soc. Internal Medicine, ACP, Am. Coll. Clin. Pharmacology; mem. Am. Soc. Nephrology, Am. Coll. Physicians (gov. downstate I), Internat. Soc. Hypertension. Office: 598 Madison Ave New York NY 10022

CASE, RONALD WILLIAM, ophthalmologist; b. Barberton, Ohio, June 18, 1939; m. Gayla Case; children: Craig, Christopher. BS, U. Ala., Tuscaloosa, 1961; MD, Med. Coll. Ala., Birmingham, 1965. Diplomate Am. Bd. Ophthalmology, Am. Bd. Eye Surgery; cert. med. risk mgmt. Ophthalmologist Ctrl. Fla. Eye Assocs., Lakeland, 1972—; asst. clin. prof. U. South Fla., Tampa, 1983—; MMI local physician adv. bd. Am. Cont. Ins., 1984—; case cons. ophthalmology Fla. Bd. Med. Exam., 1992—; physician advisor Peer Rev. Orgn., 1989—; aviation med. examiner FAA, 1990—, aircraft accident investigator, 1992—; flight surgeon Polk County Sheriff, 1990—. Maj. U.S. Army, 1968-69, Vietnam. Decorated Bronze Star, Air medal with 7 oak leaf clusters, Purple Heart. Fellow Am. Acad. Ophthalmology; mem. AMA, Fla. Med. Assn., Fla. Soc. Ophthalmology (pres.), Polk County Med. Assn. (pres.), Tampa Bay Soc. Ophthalmology (pres.). Office: Ctrl Fla Eye Assn 1247 Lakeland Hills Blvd Lakeland FL 33805

CASE, SHARON KAY, retired nurse, educator; b. Owosso, Mich., Aug. 15; d. Maurice R. and Thelma L. (Gurden) Goucher; m. Floyd E. Case, Feb. 5, 1966; stepchildren: F. Michael, M. David, Lynn M., Steven P. RN, Highland Park Gen. Hosp., Mich., 1958; BSN, U. Oreg., 1964. Cert. psychiat./mental health nurse. Geriatrics, obstetrics, med./surg. nurse various hosps., Oreg., 1960-69; psychiat. nurse I and II Harborview Devel. Ctr., Valdez, Alaska, 1969-72; substitute sch. nurse Anchorage Sch. Dist., 1975-79; nurse I and II Alaska Psychiat. Inst., Anchorage, 1981-95; ret., 1995.

CASELLI, RICHARD JOHN, neurologist; b. N.Y.C., Jan. 9, 1959; s. Frank and Martha (Garlando) C.; m. Maria M. Johnston, Oct. 25, 1957; children: Francesca, Derek, Lisa, Jason. AB, Columbia U., 1979, MD, 1983. Diplomate Am. Bd. Psychiatry and Neurology. Instr. Mayo Med. Sch., Rochester, Minn., 1987-91, asst. prof., 1991-95, assoc. prof., 1995—; cons. in neurology Mayo Clinic, Scottsdale, Ariz., 1992-95, chmn. behavioral/neurology divsn., 1995—, vice chmn. rsch. com., 1994—; mem. exec. bd. Phoenix chpt. Alzheimer's Assn., 1992—. Mem. editl. bd. Mayo Clinic Procs., 1991-95; contbr. articles to profl. publs. Mem. AMA, Am. Acad. Neurology, Behavioral Neurology Soc., Sigma Xi. Office: Mayo Clinic 13400 E Shea Blvd Scottsdale AZ 85259

CASENAVE, PIERRE, radiologist; b. Bayonne, Aquitaine, France, May 17, 1953; married; children: Julien, Marie-Anne, Arnaud. Intern CH Bordeaux (France), 1978-82, CCA, 1983-86; radiologist Clinic Lafourcade, France, 1986-96. Lt. physician, 1979-80. Mem. French Soc. Radiology, Soc. Med. Pays Basque. Home: 79 Ave Monseioneur Gieure, 64100 Bayonne Pays Basque, France Office: Clinic Lafourcade, Ave Docteur Lafourcade, 64100 Bayonne Pays Basque, France

CASE-PASFIELD, SUSAN JOY, emergency nurse; b. N.Y.C., Dec. 12, 1952; d. Truman Gordon and Peggy (Pappas) Case; m. Charles James Pasfield, Aug. 7, 1982; children: Krista Jean, Justin Lee. BS in Nursing, U. Bridgeport, 1976. Emergency nurse educator Univ. Hosp., Stony Brook, N.Y., 1979-88; emergency nurse St. Charles Hosp., Port Jefferson, N.Y., 1988. Recipient Emergency Nurse award Adelphi U. Home: 10 Barrett Ct Nesconset NY 11767-1543

CASERIO, MARIE, physician assistant; b. St. Angelo Limosano, Italy, Mar. 10, 1946; came to U.S., 1956; d. Vincent and Maria Rosa (Bozza) C.; m. Anthony Laurenzano, June 12, 1965 (div. July 1983); children: Danielle, Lisa, Georgette. AA, SUNY, Farmingdale, 1977; BA, SUNY, Stony Brook, 1979, MA, 1981, BS, 1983; postgrad., Calif. Coast U., 1995—. Lic. physician asst., Calif.; nat. cert. physician asst. Physician asst., house officer Southside Hosp., Bayshore, N.Y., 1983-86; physician asst. Ontario (Calif.) Indsl. Clinic, 1987-91, South Bay Med. Group, Gardena, Calif., 1991—. Fellow Am. Acad. for Physician Assts., Calif. Acad. for Physician Assts.; mem. Phi Epsilon Delta. Democrat. Roman Catholic. Home: 310 Lake St Apt 208 Huntington Beach CA 92648

CASERIO, REBECCA JOANN, dermatologist, educator; b. Pa., Aug. 2, 1949; d. James Joseph and Jolanda Marie (Denale) C.; m. Chris Max Allen, Apr. 15, 1978. BS summa cum laude, U. Pitts., 1971, MD cum laude, 1975. Intern Montefiore Hosp., Pitts., 1975-76, resident in internal medicine, 1976-78, chief resident, 1978; staff internist Penn Group Health Plan, Pitts., 1978-80; resident in dermatology U. Pitts., 1981-83, chief resident in dermatology, 1983, dir. hair clinic Falk Clinic, 1984-87, clin. asst. prof. dermatology, 1985-92, clin. assoc. prof. dermatology, 1992—. Mem. Pa. Med. Soc., Pitts. Acad. Dermatology, Pa. Acad. Dermatology, Am. Acad. Dermatology, Am. Soc. Dermatol. Surgeons, Allegheny County Med. Soc., Phi Beta Kappa, Kappa Kappa Gamma, Alpha Omega Alpha, Beta Beta Beta, Alpha Epsilon Delta. Roman Catholic. Home: 4142 Bigelow Blvd Pittsburgh PA 15213-1408

CASERTA, ROBERT ALLAN, physician, cardiologist; b. Bridgeport, Conn., Sept. 3, 1946; s. Victor Guido and Mafalda Rita (Veckerelli) C.; m. Susan Jane Mitchell, Jan. 5, 1974; children: Christine, Lisa, Kimberly. BA, U. Conn., 1969; MD, U. Zaragoza, Spain, 1975. Cert. Ednl. Coun. Fgn. Grads., AHA ALS; Diplomate Am. Bd. Internal Medicine, Am. Bd. Cardiovasc. Disease. Asst. resident, intern St. Vincent's Med. Ctr., Bridgeport, Conn., 1975-76, resident, 1976-77, chief resident, 1977-78, program dir. cardiology fellowship program, 1983-86, attending physician divsn. cardiology, 1980—, chmn. coronary care unit com., 1984-86; fellow in cardiology U. Mass. Med. Ctr., Worcester, 1978-80; researcher Pfizer Pharmaceutical, 1980-81. Fellow Am. Coll. Cardiology; mem. Conn. State Med. Soc., Fairfield County Med. Assn., U. Conn. Club. Roman Catholic. Office: Cardiac Assocs So Conn 2660 Main St Bridgeport CT 06606

CASEY, CATHERINE SUE, pediatrician, educator; b. Washington, Feb. 23, 1948; d. John Roland and Edna Hope (Batcheller) C.; m. J. Christopher Ryan, May 15, 1993. BS, Coll. William and Mary, 1970; MD, Med. Coll. Va., 1974. Diplomate Am. Bd. Pediatrics, Va. Bd. Medicine. Intern, Children's Hosp. Phila., 1974-75, resident, 1975-77; pvt. practice medicine specializing in pediatrics, Arlington, Va., 1977—; asst. clin. prof. pediatrics Georgetown U. Sch. Medicine, 1980—. Chmn. Project Santa Ana, humanitarian relief project, 1984-89 . Fellow Am. Acad. Pediatrics; mem. Am. Med. Women's Assn. (br. pres. 1983-84), Med. Soc. Va., No. Va. Pediatric Soc. (v.p. 1983-84, pres. 1984-85), Arlington County Med. Soc., Va. Bd. Medicine (pres. 1993-94). Democrat. Episcopalian. Office: 1715 N George Mason Dr Ste 205 Arlington VA 22205

CASEY, KATHERINE HELENE, nursing educator, adult nurse practitioner; b. Chgo., Mar. 17, 1957; d. David. L. Ruge; married. AA, Palomar Coll., 1981; BSN, Long Beach State U., 1984; M in Nursing, UCLA, 1987; adult nurse practitioner, U. Ariz., 1995. RN, Calif., Ariz.; CCRN. Staff nurse CCU Tri-City Med. Ctr., Oceanside, Calif., 1981-87, nurse educator critical care, 1987-91; clin. nurse specialist St. Joseph's Hosp. and Med. Ctr., Phoenix, 1991—; adult nurse practitioner Phoenix Cardiologists, P.C., 1996—. Mem. AACN, Sigma Theta Tau. Home: 16624 S 38th Pl Phoenix AZ 85044-7944 Office: St Josephs Hosp & Med Ctr 350 W Thomas Phoenix AZ 85013

CASEY, WILLIAM CARLETON, physician, urologist; b. Borton, Ill., Feb. 1, 1924; s. Albert O'Neil and Pauline Marjorie (Montoe) C.; m. Regina Rummel, Nov. 3, 1957 (div. Jan. 1963); children: Giselle Susan, David William; m. Susan Maureen Fowler, Oct. 2, 1965; 1 child, Patrick Sean McGahey. BSc, U. Ill., Champaign-Urbana, 1944; MD, U. Ill., Chgo., 1946. Diplomate Am. Bd. Urology; lic. physician, Calif., Ill. Clin. isntr. UCLA Sch. Medicine, 1955-67; clin. dir. Lakehead Psychiat. Hosp., Thunder Bay, Ont., Can., 1972-74; dir. children's and adolescents' svc. Dr. McKinnon Phillips Hosp., Owen Sound, Ont., 1974-76; clin. asst. prof. urology UCLA Sch. Medicine, 1977—. Capt. U.S. Army, 1948-50. Fellow Ryal Australian and New Zealand Coll. Psychiatrists; mem. Am. Urol. Assn. (1st prize sci. exhibit 1954, others), Am. Urol. Assn. Western Sect., Los Angeles County Med. Assn., Los Angeles County Urol. Soc., Royal Coll. Physicians (London), Royal Coll. Surgeons (Eng.), Royal Coll. Physicians and Surgeons Can., Brit. Royal Coll. Psychiatrists (found. mem.). Roman Catholic. Home: 2601 W Alameda Ave Ste 410 Burbank CA 91505

CASH, DEANNA GAIL, nursing educator; b. Coatesville, Pa., Nov. 28, 1940. Diploma, Jackson Meml. Hosp., 1961; BS, Fla. State U., 1964; MN, UCLA, 1968; EdD, Nova U., Ft. Lauderdale, Fla., 1983. Staff and relief charge nurse Naples (Fla.) Community Hosp., 1961-62; staff nurse Glendale (Calif.) Community Hosp., 1964-65; instr. Knapp Coll. Nursing, Santa Barbara, Calif., 1965-66; staff nurse, team leader Kaiser Found. Hosp., Bellflower, Calif., 1968-69; prof. nursing El Camino Coll., Torrance, Calif., 1969—; coord., instr. Internat. RN Rev. course, L.A., 1974-76; mentor statewide nursing program, Long Beach, Calif., 1981-88; clin. performance in nursing exam. evaluator Western Performance Assessment Ctr., Long Beach, 1981—. Mem. ANA.

CASHION, JOE MASON, home health care administrator; b. Lynchburg, Tenn., Jan. 24, 1938; s. C. Rufus Cashion and Mary (Mason) Templeton; m. Mary Soroka, July 31, 1973; children: Michael David, Steven Andrew. BS, U. Tenn., 1961; MBA, George Washington U., 1963; postgrad., Syracuse U., 1963, Cornell U., 1969. Adminstr. resident East Tenn. Baptist Hosp., Knoxville, 1962-63, asst. adminstr., 1965-66; Peace Corps hosp. adminstr. Dyer Maternity Ctr., Monrovia, Liberia, 1963-65; hosp. adminstr. Arabian Am. Oil Co., Dhahran, Saudi Arabia, 1966-73, Franklin County Hosp. & Nursing Home, Winchester, Tenn., 1973-75; pres. Mid. Tenn. Home Health Svc., Winchester, 1975—; health care cons. Trans World Airlines, Dubai, Hosp. Corp. Am., Saudi Arabia, Saudi Arabian Ministry of Health, Nat. Pub. Health Service, Liberia; mem. home health care profl. exchange to Republic of China with People-to-People program Spokane, Wash., 1987. Fellow Royal Soc. Health (London); mem. Nat. Assn. Home Care, Am. Coll. Healthcare Execs. Mem. Ch. of Christ. Lodge: Rotary (pres. Winchester 1979-80). Home: PO Box 399 Winchester TN 37398-0399 Office: Mid Tenn Home Health Svc PO Box 399 Winchester TN 37398-0399

CASIDA, JOHN EDWARD, entomology educator; b. Phoenix, Dec. 22, 1929; s. Lester Earl and Ruth (Barnes) C.; m. Katherine Faustine Monson, June 16, 1956; children: Mark Earl, Eric Gerhard. B.S., U. Wis., 1951, M.S., 1952, Ph.D., 1954. Research asst. U. Wis., 1951-53, mem. faculty, 1954-63, prof. entomology, 1959-63; prof. entomology, pesticide chemist and toxicologist U. Calif.-Berkeley, 1964—; scholar-in-residence Bellagio Study and Conf. Center, Rockefeller Found., Lake Como, Italy, 1978; Messenger lectr. Cornell U., 1985; Sterling B. Hendricks lectr. USDA and Am. Chem. Soc., 1992—. Author research publs. Served with USAF, 1953. Recipient medal 7th Internat. Congress Plant Protection, Paris, 1970, Disting. Svc. medal USDA, 1988, Wolf prize in agr., 1993; Haight traveling fellow, 1958-59, Guggenheim fellow, 1970-71, Founder's award Soc. Environ. Toxicology and Chemistry, 1994, Kôrô-sho prize Pesticide Sci. Soc. Japan, 1995; Jeffery lectr. U. NSW, Australia, 1983. Mem. NAS, Am. Chem. Soc. (Internat. award rsch. pesticide chemistry 1970, Spencer award in agrl. and food chemistry 1978), Entomol. Soc. Am. (Bussart Meml. award 1989, fellow 1989), Soc. Environ. Toxicology and Chemistry (Founder's award 1994). Home: 1570 La Vereda Rd Berkeley CA 94708-2036

CASIDA, LESTER EARL, JR., microbiologist, educator; b. Columbia, Mo., Aug. 25, 1928; s. Lester Earl and Ruth (Barnes) C.; B.S., U. Wis., 1950, M.S., 1951, Ph.D., 1953; m. Mardelle Elizabeth Baumgartner, Aug. 22, 1953; children—Nancy Ann, Sharon Ann. m. Veronica Guydos, May 29, 1993. Research asst. Abbott Labs., North Chicago, Ill., 1951; microbiologist Pabst Labs., Milw., 1953; fermentation biochemist Pfizer Corp., N.Y.C., 1954-57; asst. prof. microbiology Pa. State U., State College, 1957-62, assoc. prof., 1962-66, prof., 1966-93, emeritus prof. 1994—; chief scientific tech. officer Biotechnology Co., 1994—. cons. Recipient numerous research grants. Fellow Am. Acad. Microbiology; mem. Am. Soc. Microbiology, Am. Chem. Soc., Soc. Gen. Microbiology. Methodist. Author: Industrial Microbiology, 1968; contbr. articles on microbial ecology to profl. jours.; patentee indsl. fermentations. Home: 1364 Greenwood Cir State College PA 16803-3232 Office: Pa State U Dept Biochem & Molecular Biology Eberly College Sci University Park PA 16802-4500

CASKEY, CHARLES THOMAS, biology and genetics educator; b. Lancaster, S.C., Sept. 22, 1938; m. Peggy Ann Pearce, 1960; children: Clifton, Caroline. Student, U. S.C., 1956-58; MD, Duke U., 1963; DSc (hon.), U. S.C., 1993. Diplomate Am. Bd. Internal Medicine. Intern, resident dept. medicine Duke Med. Sch., 1963-65; rsch. assoc. Nat. Heart & Lung Inst., Bethesda, Md., 1965-67, head sect. med. genetics, 1970-71; sr. investigator Lab. Biomed. Genetics NIH, Bethesda, 1967-70; chief sect. med. genetics, prof. medicine, prof. biochemistry Baylor Coll. Medicine, Houston, 1971—, investigator Howard Hughes Med. Inst., 1976—, dir. Robert J. Kleberg, Jr. Ctr. for Human Genetics, 1980-94, dir. med. scientist tng. program, 1982-93, prof. cell biology, 1982-94, dir. and prof. molecular genetics Inst. Molecular Genetics, 1985-92, prof. molecular genetics Inst. Molecular Genetics, 1985-94, Henry and Emma Meyer chmn. molecular genetics, 1987-94, dir. Human Genome Ctr., 1991-94, chmn. dept. molecular and human genetics, 1994—; sr. v.p. rsch. Merck Rsch. Labs., 1995—; Josiah Macy, Jr. faculty scholar Med. Rsch. Coun. Cambridge (Eng.) U., 1979-80; dir. NATO ASI on Somatic Cell Genetics, 1980-81, NATO/EMBO/FEBS Spetsai European Molecular Biology Course, 1983, 87; Bernard Sachs lectr. Child Neurology Soc., 1993; Roy E. Moon disting. lectr. sci. Angelo State U., 1994; Samuel Rudin disting. vis. prof. Columbia U., N.Y.C., 1994; mem. biochem. test com. Nat. Bd. Med. Examiners, 1977-81, chmn. biochem. test com., 1981-84, mem. coord. com. for FLEX, 1984-86, mem.-at-large, 1984-88; chmn. sci. adv. bd. Xytronyx Inc., 1984-90; acad. assoc. Nichols Inst., 1987-92; liason mem. program adv. com. on human genome NIH, 1989-92; chair adv. panel forensic uses DNA tests U.S. Congress Office Tech. Assessment, 1989-90; mem. mapping the human genome adv. com. U.S. Dept. Energy, 1986-89; mem. adv. panel mapping the human genome U.S. Congress Office Tech. Assessment, 1987-88; mem. human genome coord. com. Dept. Energy, 1989-94. Author: Somatic Cell Genetics, 1982; author: (with others) Prebiotic and Biochemical Evolution, 1971, Frontiers of Biology: The Mechanism of Protein Synthesis and Its Regulation, 1972, The Enzymes, 1974, The Kidney in Systemic Disease, 1976, Protein Synthesis, 1976, Molecular Mechanisms of Protein Biosynthesis, 1977, Tay-Sachs Disease Screening and Prevention, 1977, Nonsense Mutations and tRNA Suppressors, 1979, Strauss and Welt Diseases of the Kidney, 3d edit., 1979, Gene Amplification, 1982, Internal Medicine, 1983, Advances in Gene Technology: Human Genetic Disorders, 1984, After Barney Clark: Reflections on the Utah Artificial Heart Program, 1984, Pediatric Neurology, 1986, Clinical Endocrinology, 1986, Gene Transfer, 1986, Molecular Biology of Homo Sapiens, 1986, Medical and Experimental Mammalian Genetics: A Perspective, 1987, Human Genetics, 1987, Molecular Neurobiology in Neurology and Psychiatry, 1987, Current Neurology, vol. 9, 1988, Textbook of Internal Medicine, 1988, Nucleic Acid Probes in Diagnosis of Human Genetic Diseases, 1988, Molecular Genetics of Brain, Nerve, and Muscle, 1989, Molecular Genetics of Diseases of Brain, Nerve, and Muscle, 1989, The Metabolic Basis of Inherited Disease, 6th edit., 1989, PCR Technology: Principles and Applications of DNA Amplification, 1989, The Polymerase Chain Reaction, 1989, PCR Protocols: A Guide to Methods and Applications, 1989, Genetic Engineering, Principles and Methods, vol. 11, 1989, The Science and Practice of Pediatric Cardiology, vol. 1, 1990, Ribosomes and Protein Synthesis: A Practical Approach, 1990, Etiology of Human Disease at the DNA Level, 1991, PCR: A Practical Approach, 1991, Neurodegenerative Disorders: Mechanisms and Prospects for Therapy, 1991, Reproductive Risks and Prenatal Diagnosis, 1991, Antisense RNA and DNA, 1991, Biomonitoring and Carcinogen Risk Assessment, 1991, Legal and Ethical Issues Raised by the Human Genome Project, 1991, Advances in Forensic Haemogenetics, 1992, Gene MappinUsing Law and Ethics as Guides, 1992, The Code of Codes, 1992, Antisense Strategies, 1992, Molecular Basis of Neurology, 1993, Genetic Engineering, Principles and Methods, 1993, Genetics and Society, 1993, numerous other chpts. to books; mem. editorial bd. Archives Biochemistry and Biophysics, 1975-78, Jour. Biol. Chemistry, 1978-83, Annals Intenal Medicine, 1980-83, Molecular Biology and Medicine, 1982-90, Somatic Cell and Molecular Genetics, 1983-94, Trends in Genetics, 1985-90, Genomics, 1987-90, Molecular and Cell Biology, 1988-90, Human Gene Therapy, 1990—, Jour. AMA, 1991-94, Genetic Epidemiology, 1992-94, Human Mutation, 1992—, Circulation, 1993—; mem. bd. reviewing editors Sci., 1991—. Mem. Human Genome Orgn., 1988—, pres., 1993—; mem. task force on genetics Muscular Dystrophy Assn., 1989-94. With USPHS, 1965-67. Recipient Borden Rsch. award, Disting. Alumnus award Duke U. Med. Sch., 1991, Wadsworth award N.Y. State Dept. Health, 1992, Svc. Merchandise Leadership award Muscular Dystrophy Assn., 1992, Basic Biomed. Rsch. prize Giovanni Lorenzini Med. Found., 1993, Lucy Wortham James Basic Rsch. award Soc. Surg. Oncology, 1994, Norberto Montalbetti Milan award, 1994, The Coriell medal Coriell Inst., 1995, 5th Milano award in memory of Norberto Montalbetti, 1995. Fellow AMA (founding), AAAS (sci. innovation program com. 1991-93), Am. Coll. Physicians, Am. Acad. Microbiology, Royal Soc. Medicine Found.; mem. Nat. Acad. Scis., Am. Fedn. Clin. Rsch., Am. Soc. Biochemistry and Molecular Biology, Am. Soc. Clin. Investigation, Am. Soc. Human Genetics, Am. Soc. Cell Biology, Am. Coll. Med. Genetics, Assn. Am. Physicians, Fedn. Am. Socs. for Exptl. Biology, N.Y. Acad. Scis., So. Soc. Clin. Investigation, Soc. Inherited Metabolic Disorders, Inst. Medicine Nat. Acad. Scis., Royal Soc. Medicine, Baylor Med. Alumni Assn. (disting. faculty mem. 1993), Alpha Omega Alpha. Home: 6402 Belmont St Houston TX 77005-3802 Office: Merck Rsch Labs Sumneytown Pike West Point PA 19486

CASKEY, OWEN LAVERNE, retired psychology educator; b. Corsicana, Tex., Mar. 10, 1925; s. Price Hamilton and Esma Eulysses (Lisman) C.; m. Shirley Jean Larned, Apr. 10, 1981; children: Leigh Ann, Deborah Jane. B.S., Tex. Tech U., 1947, M.Ed., 1948; Ed.D., U. Colo., 1952. Lic. psychologist, Tex.; lic. profl. counselor, Tex. Tchr. Lubbock (Tex.) Pub. Schs., 1941-43; instr. Tex. Tech U., Lubbock, 1947-50, prof. ednl. psychology, 1964-83, prof. emeritus, 1983—, v.p. student affairs, 1968-70, assoc. v.p. acad. affairs, 1970-73, dir. instructional research, 1974-81, assoc. dean. Coll. Edn., 1976-78; asst. prof. Colo. State U., 1950-53, assoc. prof.,

1954-58; counseling psychologist VA, Denver, 1954; cons. psychologist Rohrer, Hibler & Replogle, Dallas, 1958-63; assoc. prof. Okla. State U., 1963-64; psychologist El Paso (Tex.) Pub. Schs., 1981-87; cons. to state and govt. agys. including El Paso Police Dept., 1981-87. Chmn. Community Planning Council, 1973-75; Bd. dirs. United Way, 1973-75, mem. budget com., 1973-79, mem. long-range planning com., 1978-80; bd. dirs. South Plains Health System, 1976-81, mem. exec. com., 1978-81. Served to lt. (j.g.) USN, 1943-46; ETO. Fellow VA, 1954, U. Colo., 1954; recipient numerous research grants, 1966-86. Mem. Am. Psychol. Assn., Soc. for Accelerated Learning and Teaching . Methodist. Contbr. numerous articles to profl. jours. Home: 8201 Edgemere Blvd El Paso TX 79925-3840

CASLAVSKA, VERA BARBARA, chemist, researcher; b. Chrudim, Czechoslovakia, Jan. 18, 1934; came to U.S., 1966; d. Vilem and Vera (Kudrnkova) Novak; m. Jaroslav Ladislav Caslavsky, Dec. 25, 1952; 1 child, Veronika. MS, Charles U., Prague, Czechoslovakia, 1957, PhD, 1965. Rsch. assoc. Mining Inst., Prague, 1957-65; chemist Wiener Schwachstrom Werke, Vienna, 1965-66; rsch. assoc. materials rsch. lab. Pa. State U., University Park, 1966-69; asst. staff mem. Forsyth Dental Ctr., Boston, 1969-91; sr. scientist J. Gutenberg U., Mainz, 1992-94. Contbr. articles to profl jours. Patentee in field. Recipient Czechoslovak Acad. of Scis. award, 1965. Mem. Am. Assn. for Dental Rsch. (pres. Boston chpt. 1990), Internat. Assn. for Dental Rsch. (pres. mineralized tissue group 1990), Masaryk Club (pres. 1991), Sigma Delta Epsilon. Home: 244 East St Lexington MA 02173-2320

CASLOWITZ, JOEL, physician, educator; b. Woonsocket, R.I., Feb. 6, 1938; s. Himan M. and Gertrude (Golden) C.; m. Joyce Richard, June 29, 1986. AB, Brown U., 1959; MD, Tufts U., 1963. Diplomate Am. Bd. Internal Medicine. Intern Balt. City Hosp., 1963-64; resident Boston City Hosp., 1965-66; resident Boston VA Med. Ctr., 1964-65, 66-67, chief resident, 1969-70, program dir., 1970—; assoc. prof. medicine Boston U., 1978—. Capt. M.C., USAF, 1967-69. Recipient Robbins award Boston U. Sch. Medicine, 1991, Metcalf award Boston U., 1993. Democrat. Office: Boston VA Med Ctr 150 S Huntington Ave Boston MA 02130

CASPER, DANIEL S., ophthalmologist, medical illustrator, consultant; b. N.Y.C., Mar. 8, 1953; s. Sidney Joseph and Enid Ruth (Wagner) C.; m. Lauren Sass, May 31, 1981; children: Samuel, Nora. BS, Union Coll., Schenectady, N.Y., 1975; PhD, Tufts U., Boston, 1980; MD, Albany (N.Y.) Med. Coll., 1985. Diplomate Am. Acad. Ophthalmology. Ophthalmologist Columbia Presbyn. Med. Ctr., N.Y., 1991-93, Hudson Valley Eye Assocs., Tarrytown, N.Y., 1993—; med. illustrator, pres. Concept-Image, Hastings-On-Hudson, N.Y., 1990—; cons. Med. Publishers, N.Y.C., 1989—. Author, illustrator: (book) Orbital Disease: Imaging & Analysis, 1993. Office: Hudson Valley Eye Assocs 55 S Broadway Hastings On Hudson NY 10706

CASPER, MARY LEE, speech and language pathologist; b. Long Beach, Calif., Oct. 17, 1964; Lic. speech pathologist, Ind., Fla., Ohio, Ill., Minn. BA, U. Iowa, 1985; MA, Kans. State U., 1988. Lic. speech pathologist, Ind. Clin. fellow InSpeech, Inc., Merrillville, Ind., 1988-89; speech pathologist NovaCare, Inc., Mishawaka, Ind., 1989-90, clin. coord., 1990-92, sr. clin. coord., 1993, dist. mgr., 1994, clin. practice dir., 1994-95; corp. rehab. dir. Integrated Health Svcs., Elkhart, Ind., 1995—; pres. Heart City Health Ctr., Ind., Elkhart. Mem. Am. Speech-Lang.-Hearing Assn. (ACE 1990, cert. clin. comptence), Ind. Speech-Lang.-Hearing Assn. (continuying edn. com. 1990-93, convention program com. 1992-93, continuing edn. adminstr. 1994—), Michiana Speech-Lang.-Hearing Assn. (chair continuing edn. com. 1990-91, pres. 1993, pub. rels. dir. 1994, 95), Sigma Kappa Alumnia Assn. (pres. 1991). Presbyterian. Home: 116 S Vine St Elkhart IN 46514-2508 Office: Integrated Health Svcs 10065 Red Run Blvd Owings Mills MD 21117

CASS, GLEN ROWAN, environmental engineer; b. Pasadena, Calif., Apr. 18, 1947; s. Robert Mervin and Marie Vincent (Segner) C.; m. Jean Elizabeth Annis, Dec. 18, 1976; 1 child, Robert Covel. BSME, U. So. Calif., 1969; MSME, Stanford U., 1970; PhD, Calif. Inst. Tech., 1978. Officer USPHS, Atlanta, 1970-73; from instr. to prof. engring. Calif. Inst. Tech., Pasadena, 1978—; clean air scientific adv. com. U.S. EPA, Washington, 1991-92; com. on haze in nat. parks and wilderness areas Nat. Rsch. Coun., Washington, 1990-93; rsch. adv. com. Health Effects Inst., Cambridge, Mass., 1993—; cons. in field. Assoc. editor Aerosol Sci. and Tech., 1994—. Environ. goals com. L.A. 2000, 1987-88; clean air com., Pasadena Lung Assn., 1977-85. Mem. Am. Chem. Soc., Am. Assn. Aerosol Rsch., Air & Waste Mgmt. Assn. Office: Environ Engring Sci Dept Calif Inst Tech Pasadena CA 91125

CASS, ROGER M., allergist, educator; b. Madison, Wis., May 25, 1935; s. Milfred and Genevieve (Kelly) Justin; m. Carolyn Cass, Sept. 21, 1960 (separated); children: Daniel, Steven. MD, U. Wis., 1960. Chief allergy/rheumatology Genesee Hosp., Rochester, N.Y., 1967-87; prof. medicine U. Rochester, 1995—; pvt. practice. Founder Gen. Land Trust, Rochester, 1990, Fedn. Monroe County, 1987; mem. Town of Brighton Open Space Com. Capt. USAF, 1962-64. Home: 980 Highland Ave Rochester NY 14620-1861

CASSCELLS, SAMUEL WARD, III, cardiologist, educator; b. Wilmington, Del., Mar. 18, 1952; s. Samuel Ward and Oleda (Dyson) C.; m. Roxanne Bell, Feb. 10, 1990; children: Sam, Henry. BS cum laude, Yale U., 1974; MD magna cum laude, Harvard U., 1979. Intern then resident Beth Israel Hosp., Boston, 1979-82; cardiology fellow Mass. Gen. Hosp., Boston, 1982-85; Kaiser fellow clin. epidemiology Brigham and Women's Hosp. and Harvard Sch. Pub. Health, 1984-85; rsch. fellow Nat. Heart, Lung, and Blood Inst., Bethesda, Md., 1985-91; vis. scientist Scripps Inst. Medicine and Sci., LaJolla, Calif., 1991-92; chief cardiology, T.R. and M. O'Driscoll Levy prof. medicine U. Tex. Med. Sch., Houston, 1994—; chief cardiology Hermann Hosp., Houston, 1994—; assoc. dir. cardiol. rsch. Tex. Heart Inst. and St. Luke's Episc. Hosp., Houston, 1992—; med. dir. U. Tex. Telemedicine; founder Prizm Pharms., La Jolla, 1992—; cons. FDA, Advanced Rsch. Project Agy., NASA, NIH, VA. Mem. editl. bd. Circulation, 1992—, Am. Jour. Cardiology, 1992—, Tex. Heart Inst. Jour., 1992—, Vascular Medicine, 1995—, U.T. Lifetime Newsletter, 1996—; contbr. numerous articles to profl. jours. Mem. Am. Heart Assn. (Houston bd. dirs. 1992-96), Am. Fedn. Clin. Rsch., Am. Soc. Cell Biology, Soc. Vascular Biol. Medicine (bd. dirs.), Houston Cardiology Soc. (pres. 1995-96), Am. Coll. Cardiology, Assn. Univ. Cardiologists, Assn. Profs. of Cardiology, Chevy Chase (Md.) Club, Union Boat Club (Boston), Vicmead Hunt Club, Farmington Country Club (Charlottesville, Va.), City Tavern Club (Washington). Office: U Tex Med Sch 6431 Fannin St Houston TX 77030-1501

CASSEL, CHARLES THOMAS, orthopaedic surgeon; b. Algona, Iowa, June 22, 1953; s. Leo Joseph and Mary Helen (Neary) C.; m. Deborah Henningsen, June 12, 1976; children: Shannon, Owen, Anne. BA, Drake U., 1975; MD, U. Iowa, 1980. Resident U. Iowa, Iowa City, 1985; orthopaedic surgeon Orthopaedic Surgery Assocs., Davenport, Iowa, 1986—. Fellow Midwest Inst. Sports Medicine and Knee Surgery, Cin., 1986. Fellow Am. Acad. Orthopaedic Surgery. Office: Orthopaedic Surgery Assocs 1414 W Lombard St Davenport IA 52804

CASSEL, CHESTER, physician, health facility administrator; b. N.Y.C., Feb. 23, 1918; s. Lionel and Florence (Dannenberg) C.; m. Carol Isaacson, Dec. 27, 1947; children: Karen Cassel Carter, Laurie Cassel Libros, Claudia, Juliet Cassel Medoff. BS, U. Fla., 1939; MD, Columbia U., 1943. Diplomate Am. Bd. Internal Medicine, Am. Bd. Gastroenterology; cert. geriatrics. Intern Mt. Sinai Hosp., N.Y.C., 1943, resident, 1947-49; resident Bellevue Hosp., N.Y.C., 1946-47; fellow in gastroenterology Duke Hosp., Durham, N.C., 1949-51; pvt. practice Miami, Fla., 1951-90; clin. prof. medicine U. Miami Sch. Medicine, 1953-90; med. dir. Geriatric Ctr., Cedars Med. Ctr., Miami, 1990—. Contbr. 15 articles to profl. jours. Maj. U.S. Army, 1944-46, ETO. Chester Cassel Chair of Gerontology Rsch. named in his honor, U. Miami Sch. Medicine, 1989. Fellow ACP (fob. Fla. chpt. 1972-75, laureate 1991); mem. Am. Gastroenterologic Assn. (sr. mem., councillor 1975-78), Am. Soc. Gastrointestinal Endoscopy (sr. mem.), Dade County Med. Assn. (sr. mem.), Fla. Med. Assn. Home: 260 Shore Dr E Miami FL 33133-2622

CASSEL, JOHN MICHAEL, plastic surgeon; b. Miami, Mar. 25, 1948; m. Robyn Cassel, July 12, 1987; children: (twins) Adrienne and Brandon. BS, U. Miami, 1972, MD, 1978. Diplomate Am. Bd. Plastic Surgery. Gen. surg. intern U. Va., Charlottesville, 1978-79, gen. surg. resident, 1979-80; gen. surg. resident Cedars-Sinai Med. Ctr., L.A., 1980-81; jr. resident in plastic surgery U. Miami Sch. Medicine, 1981-82, sr. resident in plastic surgery, 1982-83; microsurgery and hand surgery fellow Ralph K. Davies Med. Ctr., San Francisco, 1984; pvt. practice plastic surgery Miami, 1985—; clin. assoc. prof. plastic surgery U. Miami Sch. Medicine, 1984—. Fellow Am. Coll. Surgeons; mem. Am. Soc. Plastic & Reconstructive Surgeons, Am. Soc. Aesthetic Plastic Surgeons. Office: 8950 N Kendall Dr #106 Miami FL 33176

CASSEL, WILLIAM ALWEIN, microbiology educator; b. Phila., Mar. 25, 1924; s. William Andrew and Bessie Shriver (Alwein) C.; m. Verne Madonna Finnell, June 18, 1949; children: William Stephen, Janet Lynn. BS, Phila. Coll. Pharmacy & Sci., 1946, MS, 1947; PhD, U. Pa., Phila., 1952. Bacteriologist Phila. Gen. Hosp., 1947-48; assoc. prof. Hahnemann Med. Coll., Phila., 1952-58; assoc. prof. microbiology, immunology Emory U., Atlanta, 1958-69, prof. microbiology, immunology, 1969-87, prof. emeritus, 1987—. Recipient USPHS Rsch. Career Devel. award, 1960-65; Girard Coll. Alumni award Merit, 1966; Phila. Lager Beer Brewers Assn. fellow, 1952. Fellow AAAS.

CASSELL, ERIC JONATHAN, physician; b. N.Y.C., Aug. 29, 1928; s. Hyman William and Anne (Lake) Goldstein; m. Joan M. Fishman; Oct. 17, 1957 (div. 1987); children: Justine, Stephen; m. Patricia M. Owens, May 26, 1990. BA, Queens Coll., 1950; MA, Columbia U., 1950; MD, NYU, 1954; DHL (hon.), Med. Coll. Pa., 1985. Intern 3d med. div. Bellevue Hosp., N.Y.C., 1954-55, asst. resident 3d med. div., 1955-56, 58-59, physician 3d, 4th med. div., 1965-66; USPHS trainee in infectious diseases Cornell U., N.Y.C., 1959-61, clin. prof. pub. health, 1971—; attending physician French Hosp., N.Y.C., 1961-74; assoc. attending physician Mt. Sinai (N.Y.) Hosp., 1966-71; assoc. dir. ambulatory care Community Med., Mt. Sinai, 1966-68; attending physician N.Y. Hosp., 1984—; clin. assoc. prof. medicine, NYU, 1965-66, Mt. Sinai Hosp., 1966-71; bd. dirs. Hasting's Ctr., Briar Cliff Manor, N.Y., 1975—; pres. Nat. Bioethics Adv. Commn. Author: Healer's Art, 1976, Place of Humanities in Medicine, 1984, Talking With Patients (2 vols.), 1985, The Nature of Suffering, 1991; editor: Changing Values in Medicine, 1979. Served to capt. M.C., U.S. Army, 1956-58. Master ACP; fellow N.Y. Acad. Medicine; mem. Inst. Medicine of NAS. Democrat. Jewish. Office: 1550 York Ave New York NY 10028-5970

CASSIDAY, KAREN LYNN, psychologist; b. Salina, Kans., Mar. 18, 1960; d. Donald Marion and Rosalie Jean (Yeoman) Cassiday; m. John Edward Calamari, May 26, 1989. BA, Wheaton Coll., 1982; PhD, Chgo. Med. Sch., 1990. Staff psychotherapist The Anxiety Clinic, Chgo., 1990-91; instr. dept. clin. psychology Chgo. Med. Sch., North Chicago, Ill., 1991—; program dir. Behavior Med, Inc., Lake Bluff, Ill., 1991-92; co-dir. Cognitive Behavioral Treatment Ctr., Arlington Heights, Ill., 1992-95; dir. Anxiety and Agoraphobia Treatment Ctr., Kenosha, Wis., 1995—; cons. Deborah's Place, Chgo., 1987-88. Contbr. articles to profl. jours.; author various manuals. Mem. Psi Chi. Episcopalian. Home: 141 Oak Knoll Dr Lake Villa IL 60046-8997 Office: Anxiety & Agoraphobia Treatment Ctr 10400 75th St #311 Kenosha WI 53142

CASSIDY, BARRY ALLEN, physician assistant, clinical medical ethicist; b. Chgo., Aug. 28, 1947; s. Frank Thomas and Ann Marie (Panek) C.; m. JoAnn DeRue (div.); m. Robin G. Lacher (div.); children: Colleen Osmond, Jason Lacher, Nathaniel Austin; m. Barbie A. Cassidy. Cert. physician assoc., Duke U., 1971; BS, Univ. State N.Y., Albany, 1992; PhD, Union Inst., 1995. Cert. physician asst. Physician assoc. Med. Offices of T.C. Rozema, MD, Waukegan, Ill., 1971-73; instr. in healthcare sci. Sch. Medicine George Washington U., Washington, 1973-75; med. cons. Medicolegal Rsch., Washington, 1975-79; CEO, dir. health svcs. Occucare, Inc., Research Triangle Park, N.C., 1979-81; v.p. Coastal Group, Inc., Durham, N.C., 1981-82; exec. v.p. So. Emergency Med. Assocs., Research Triangle Park, 1982-33; physician asst. Ariz. Heart Inst., Phoenix, 1983-86; pres. West Health Corp., Phoenix, 1986-87; thoracic and cardiovascular surgery asst. Mayo Clinic, Scottsdale, Ariz., 1987-96; assoc. prof., assoc. dir. physician asst. program Coll. Allied Health Scis. Midwestern U., Glendale, Ariz., 1996—; adj. faculty S.W. Ctr. for Osteo. Med. Edn. and Health Scis., 1995-96. Mem. editl. bd. Physician Assts. in Primary Care, 1985-88; inventor break-away catheter sys. Chmn. jud. affairs com. Am. Acad. Physician Assts., Arlington, Va., 1974, v.p., 1974; advisor on allied health Ill. Med. Soc., Chgo., 1972; advisor Gov.'s Health Licensure Commn., State of Ill., Chgo., 1972. Sgt. USAF, 1965-69. Mem. Ariz. Med. Assn., Ariz. Acad. Physician Assts., Hastings Ctr. for Med. Ethics (assoc.), Am. Soc. Law, Medicine and Ethics. Jewish. Home: 6630 E Lafayette Scottsdale AZ 85251 Office: Midwestern U Coll Allied Health Scis 19555 N 59th Ave Glendale AZ 85308

CASSIDY, CARL EUGENE, physician; b. Salineville, Ohio, Dec. 4, 1924; s. Clifford J. and Dortha (Lance) C.; m. Helen Ruth Skinner Collord, Dec. 21, 1961 (dec. 1975). AB, Kenyon Coll., 1946; MD, Western Res. U., 1948. Intern Youngstown (Ohio) Hosp. Assn., 1948-49; fellow in medicine Cleve. Clinic Found., 1951-54; rsch. fellow in endocrinology Pratt Clinic New Eng. Med. Ctr. Hosps., Boston, 1954-56, asst. physician, 1956-67, sr. physician, 1968-72; physician-in-chief Baystate Med. Ctr., 1972-76; dir. Postgrad. Med. Inst., Boston, 1978-94, New Eng. Jour. Medicine/Continuing Med. Edn., Waltham, Mass., 1994—; asst. in medicine Tufts U. Sch. Medicine, 1954-56, clin. instr. medicine, 1956-58, instr., 1958-59, sr. instr., 1959-62, asst. prof., 1962-68, assoc. prof., 1968-73, clin. prof., 1973—. Co-editor: Clinical Endocrinology II, 1968; contbr. articles to med. jours. Served with USNR, 1943-45; to lt. M.C. 1949-51. Mem. AMA, Mass. Med. Soc., Am. Thyroid Assn., Endocrine Soc., Am. Assn. Clin. Endocrinologists, Army-Navy Club (Washington), Longwood Cricket Club (Chestnut Hill, Mass.), Signing Beach Club, Manchester by the Sea (Mass.), Essex County Club. Office: 2 Boylston Plz Prudential Ctr Boston MA 02199

CASSIDY, EUGENE PATRICK, pathologist; b. N.Y.C., July 21, 1940; s. Eugene Zachary and Anita Hilda (Corsi) C.; m. Hollis Elizabeth Ward, Sept. 25, 1965; 1 child, Meredith. BA, Williams Coll., 1962; MD, Yale U., 1966. Diplomate Am. Bd. Pathology. Intern Yale-New Haven Hosp., Conn., 1966-67; resident then fellow in pathology and lab. medicine Yale U. Med. Ctr., 1967-70; dir. pathology Appalachian Lab. for Occupational Respitory Disease, Morgantown, Wis., 1970-72; pathologist Clarkson Hosp., Omaha, 1972-78, Scripps Hosp., Encinitas, Calif., 1978-84; dir. pathology Marshalltown (Iowa) Med. and Surgical Ctr., 1984—; asst. prof. W.Va. U. Sch. Medicine, Morgantown, 1970-72, U. Nebr. Sch. Medicine, Omaha, 1974-78. Contbr. articles to profl. jours. Served with USPHS, 1970-72. Fellow Internat. Acad. Pathology, Coll. Am. Pathologists, Am. Soc. Clin. Pathologists; mem. AMA, Am. Assn. Blood Banks. Republican. Home: Woodfield Rd Marshalltown IA 50158-3851 Office: Marshalltown Med & Surg Ctr 3 S Fouth Ave Marshalltown IA 50158-2924

CASSIDY, MAUREEN SMITH, gerontology advocate; b. N.Y.C., June 14, 1935; d. Adelbert Ward and Cathleen Veronica (Ryan) Smith; m. Harold E. Cassidy, July 14, 1954; children: Bruce Edward, Cynthia Maureen, Craig Smith. Student, SUNY, Albany, 1952-53; AAS with honors, Dutchess Community Coll., Poughkeepsie, N.Y., 1983; grad., Nat. Acad. Paralegal Studies, Middletown, N.Y., 1991-92; B in Profl. Studies, Empire State Coll., Saratoga Springs, N.Y., 1994; postgrad., Empire State Coll., 1996—. Pvt. duty RN Unique Nursing Svc., Poughkeepsie; patient care coord. Hudson Valley Home Care, Poughkeepsie; case mgr. Dutchess Manor Home for Adults, Poughkeepsie; sr. advocacy coord. Dutchess County Assn. for Sr. Citizens, Poughkeepsie; freelance writer. Mem. AARP, Dutchess County Mental Health Assn., Older Womens League, Dutchess C.C. Alumni Assn., Empire State Coll. Alumni Assn.

CASSILETH, PETER ANTHONY, internist; b. Bklyn., Aug. 16, 1937. MD, Columbia U., 1962. Diplomate Am. Bd. Internal Medicine, Am. Bd. Hematology, Am. Bd. Oncology. Intern Columbia Presbyn. Med. Ctr., N.Y.C., 1962-63, resident, 1963-65, fellow hematology-oncology, 1965-66, 68-69; prof. medicine U. Miami (Fla.) Sch. Medicine, 1975—. Mem. ACP, Am. Soc. Hematology, Am. Fedn. Cancer Rsch., ASCO. Office: U Miami Sch Med PO Box 016960 #D8-4 Miami FL 33101-6960 Office: U Miami Sch Medicine Hematology/Oncology Divsn 1475 NW 12th Ave Ste 3510 Miami FL 33136*

CASSIN, SIDNEY, physiologist, educator; b. Chelsea, Mass., June 8, 1928; s. Morris and Minnie (Cogan) C.; m. Barbara Elenore Covin, Sept. 4, 1950; children: Robin, Nancy, Lisa, Kim. BA, NYU, 1950; MA, U. Tex., 1954, PhD, 1957. Instr. physiology U. Fla. Coll. Medicine, Gainesville, 1957-60, asst. prof., 1960-66, assoc. prof., 1966-69, prof., 1969—, apptd. pediatrics, 1981—; vis. prof. U. Coll., U. London, 1979-80. Mem. editorial bd. Jour. Applied Physiololgy; reviewer Am. Jour. Physiol., Jour. Aplied Physiology. Fellow Hogg Found., 1955-57, NIH Spl. fellow Nuffield Inst. Med. Rsch., Oxford, England, 1962-63. Mem. A. Physiology Soc., Can. Physiology Soc. Home: 1405 NW 35th Way Gainesville FL 32605-4833

CASSMAN, MARVIN, biochemist; b. Chgo., Apr. 4, 1936; s. Harry and Anna (Singer) C.; m. Alice M. Baker, June 24, 1972. BA, U. Chgo., 1954, BS, 1957, MS, 1959; PhD, Albert Einstein Coll. Medicine, 1965. Postdoctoral fellow U. Calif., Berkeley, 1965-67; asst. prof. U. Calif., Santa Barbara, 1967-75; adminstr. Nat. Inst. Gen. Med. Sci. NIH, Bethesda, Md., 1975-78, sect. chief, 1978-84, program dir., 1984-89, dep. dir., 1989-93, acting dir., 1993—; mem. staff subcom. in sci., rsch. and tech. U.S Ho. of Reps., Washington, 1982-83; sr. policy analyst Office Sci. and Tech. Policy The White House, Washington, 1985-86. Recipient Sr. Exec. Svc. award USPHS, 1987, Pres. Meritorious award, 1991. Jewish. Home: 5608 Beam Ct Bethesda MD 20817-6303 Office: NIH Nat Inst Gen Med Sci 45 Center Dr MSC 6200 Bethesda MD 20892-6200*

CASTAGNARO, MARIE R., hospital executive; b. Bklyn., Dec. 23, 1944; d. Anthony and Frances Grace (Sagristano) C. BA, Nazareth Coll., 1971; MS in Curriculum Devel., Syracuse U., 1976; MS in Health Adminstrn., U. Notre Dame, 1984. Cert. tchr., N.Y. Tchr. elem. sch. Guardian Angels Sch., Rochester, N.Y., 1966-74, adminstrv. intern, 1972-73; prin. elem. sch. St. Paul's Acad., Oswego, N.Y., 1974-79; vice prin. St. Agnes H.S., Rochester, 1979-82; adminstrv. intern St. Joseph's Hosp., Elmira, N.Y., 1983; adminstrv. resident St. Joseph's Hosp., Augusta, Ga., 1984-85; planning asst. St. Joseph's Hosp., Elmira, 1985-86, v.p. clin. svcs., 1986-87, exec. v.p., COO, 1987-88, pres., CEO, 1988—. Chairperson United Way of Chemung and Steuben, Corning, N.Y., 1995; bd. dirs. Beecher Sch. Adv. Coun., Elmira, 1993—; mem. Gov. Pataki's Transition Team, Albany, N.Y., 1994. Recipient Employer of Yr. award N.G. and Res., 1989. Mem. Am. Coll. Health Execs. (assoc.), Rochester Regional Hosp. Assn., N.Y. State Cath. Health Coun. (pres. 1993-95), Seagate Alliance, So. Tier Health Mgmt., Finger Lakes Health Sys. Agy., Chemung C. of C. (bd. dirs. 1992—, Athena award 1994). Roman Catholic. Office: St Josephs Health Sys 555 E Market St Elmira NY 14901

CASTALDO, WENDY BETH, hospital executive; b. Toledo, Aug. 16, 1958; d. Robert Victor and Sylvia (Szymanski) Tossell; m. William Arthur Castaldo, Jan. 8, 1994; 1 child, Gabrielle Marie; stepchildren: Peter, Rafaela. BS in Health Care Adminstrn. cum laude, U. Toledo, 1990. Coord. physician devel. Mercy/St. Charles Hosp., Toledo, 1985-89, mgr. physician devel., 1989-92; dir. med. staff devel. Upper Valley Med. Ctr., Troy, Ohio, 1992—. Bd. dirs. Toledo Hearing & Speech Ctr., 1991, Miami County Abuse Shelter, Troy, 1993. Mem. Am. Hosp. Assn. (soc. health care planning and mktg.), Ohio Soc. Physician Svcs., Assn. Staff Physician Recruiters. Office: Upper Valley Med Ctrs 3130 N Dixie Hwy Troy OH 45373

CASTEEL, HELEN BUTLER, pediatric gastroenterologist; b. Tupelo, Ark., Feb. 21, 1953; d. John Calvin and Sue (Kimmons) Butler; m. John Anthony Casteel, Oct. 20, 1984; children: John Christopher, Sean Butler, Aaron Kyle. BA, U. Tex., 1973; MD, Tex. Tech. Sch. Medicine, 1976. Bd. cert. Am. Bd. Pediat., sub-bd. in pediat. gastroenterology and nutrition. Resident pediat. U. Ark. for Med. Sci., Little Rock, 1976-79, fellow pediat. gastroenterology, 1979-80; fellow pediat. gastroenterology U. Tex. Med. Br., Galveston, 1980-82; asst. prof. pediat. U. Ark. for Med. Sci., Little Rock, 1982-89, assoc. prof. pediat., 1989-91; pvt. practice Pediat. Gastroenterology Assocs., Little Rock, 1991—; chief pediat. gastroenterology U. Ark. for Med. Sci., Little Rock, 1983-91; lectr. Nat. Found. for Ileitis and Colitis, Little Rock, 1988, 91, 93; mem., treas. Women's Faculty Devel. Caucus, 1989-91. Author: Clinical Handbook of Pediatric Infectious Disease, 1994; contbr. articles to profl. jours. Med. adv. bd. Ark. chpt. Nat. Found. for Ileitis and Colitis, Little Rock, 1987-89; pres. parent's adv. com. Child Enrichment Ctr., Little Rock, 1990; bd. dirs. Ronald McDonald House, Little Rock, 1990-95. Rsch. grantee A.H. Robins, 1984, Ross Labs., 1987, 88, Nellcor, 1987, Ark. Sci. and Tech. Authority, 1987. Mem. Am. Acad. Pediat., So. Soc. for Pediat. Rsch., N.Am. Soc. for Pediat. Gastroenterology and Nutrition, Ark. Med. Soc., Pulaski County Med. Soc. Office: Pediat Gastroenterology Assocs 10220 W Markham Ste 120 Little Rock AR 72205

CASTEL, GÉRARD JOSEPH, physician; b. Gardanne, France, Nov. 16, 1934; s. Roger Alphonse and Marguerite Henriette (Bossy) C.; m. Maryse Tartaise (div. 1965); 1 child, Gilles; m. Charlotte Elisabeth Gaglio; 1 child, David. MD, U. Marseille, France, 1961; D of History, U. Aix en Provence, France, 1978. Extern, then resident Conception Hosp., Marseille, 1956-57, Timone Hosp., Marseille, 1957-58, Salvator Hosp., Marseille, 1958-59, Sainte-Marguerite Hosp., Marseille, 1959-60; gen. practice medicine Rognac, France, 1961—; historian, conferenceer History, Faculty Letters, Aix en Provence, 1978—, associated rschr., 1988; physician French Soc. Rys., 1966—; instr. physician French Red Cross, 1966-90. Author: Contribution a l'Etude Historique de Rognac, 1969, Rognac Depuis 3000 Ans, 1976, Raymond des Baux, Premier Seigneur de Berre, 1983, Histoire de la Paroisse de Rognac du XIo au XXo siècle, 1984, Histoire de Berre, 12 vols., 1983-96, Histoire de la Grande-Bastide de Rognac, 1986, Dictionnaire Archeologique de la Commune de Rognac, 1987, Musical Memories, 1987, Rognac un Antique Terroir, 1987, Souvenirs Musicaux, 1987, Réflexions sur l'Histoire, 1988; contbr. articles to profl. jours.; composer romantic piano works, also several records by internat. pianists. Recipient French League Instrn. medal, 1978. Mem. History Soc. Rognac (chmn. 1965—), Sci. and Culture Assn. Berre, Poetry and Music Assn. Rognac, Authors, Composers and Editors Music, Chopin Soc. Paris. Office: 4 Rue Lamartine, 13340 Rognac France

CASTELE, THEODORE JOHN, radiologist; b. New Castle, Pa., Feb. 1, 1928; s. Theodore Robert and Anne Mercedes (McNavish) C.; m. Jean Marie Willse, Oct. 20, 1951; children: Robert, Ann Marie, Richard, Mary Kathryn, Thomas, Daniel, John. BS, Case Western Res. U., 1951, MD, 1957. Diplomate Am. Bd. Radiology, 1962. Intern then resident U. Hosps. Cleve., 1957-61, fellow, 1961-62; dir. of radiology Luth. Med. Ctr., Cleve., 1968-75, 77-89; chief of staff Luth. Med. Ctr., 1975-81; pres. Med. Ctr. Radiologists, Inc., Cleve., 1978-95; v.p. med. and copr. devel. Health Cleve. Inc., 1989-91; chmn. Lakeshore Radiology Inc., Cleve., 1991—; med. editor sta. WEWS-TV-ABC, Cleve., 1975—; chmn. bd. Med. Cons. Imaging Co., Cleve., 1981—; asst. clin. prof. radiology Case Western Res. U. Chmn. Southwestern dist. Greater Cleve. coun. Boy Scouts Am., 1969, 73; mem. bd. med. cons. Cleve. Police Dept., pres., 1988-90; trustee Comty. Dialysis Ctr., Luth. Med. Ctr. Found., chmn. bd. trustees, 1969-75, pres., 1988-90; trustee Case Western Res. U., Blue Cross/Blue Shield Ohio, Greater Cleve. Hosp. Assn., Fairview Health, Luth. Med. Ctr., 1975-80, Fairview Hosp. Found., No. Ohio Lung Assn.; chmn. Health Mus. Cleve., 1996—, Humility of Mary Healthcare Sys., 1995—. With USN, 1946-47. Recipient Order of Merit award Boy Scouts Am., 1971, Silver Beaver award, 1972, Nat. Disting. Eagle Scout award, 1984, Frances Payne Bolton Sch. of Nursing Disting. Svc. award, 1990, Outstanding Philanthropist award Nat. Soc. of Fundraising Execs., 1991; named Knight of the Equestrian, Order of the Holy Sepulchre of Jerusalem, 1993—. Fellow Am. Coll. Radiology; mem. AMA (Physician Spkr. Gold award 1978, 90, Silver 1979, Bronze 1978, Benjamin Rush award 1989, Golden Achievement award 1996, chmn. Ohio del. 1988—), Ohio State Med. Assn. (5th dist. councilor 1977-79, Spl. award 1979), Cleve. Radiol. Soc. (pres. 1969-70), Cleve. Med. Libr. Assn. (pres. 1996), Case Western Res. U. Med. Alumni Assn. (pres. 1971-72, 91-92, Disting. Svc. award 1987), Cleve. Acad. Medicine (pres. 1974-75, Disting. Mem. award 1990, Disting. Svc. award 1984), Ohio State Radiol. Soc. (Silver award 1990). Home: 18869 Canyon Rd Cleveland OH 44126-1703 Office: 20325 Center Ridge Rd Rocky River OH 44116-3554

CASTELLA, XAVIER, critical care physician, researcher; b. Manresa, Catalonia, Spain, May 16, 1958; s. Josep Castella and Palmira Picas. MD, Autonomous U. Barcelona, Spain, 1982, Master in Statis. Methods Pub. Health, 1991. Resident in critical care medicine Hosp. Sant Pau, Barcelona, 1984-88; staff mem. ICU Ctr. Hosp. Manresa, Spain, 1988-90, Hosp. Sabadell, Spain, 1990-92; head critical care dept. Hosp. Gen. de Manresa, Spain, 1992—. Contbr. articles to profl. jours. Fellow Am. Coll. Chest Physicians; mem. European Soc. Intensive Care Medicine, European Diploma Intensive Care Medicine, European Med. Assn. Office: Hosp Gen de Manresa, La Culla Sin, 08240 Manresa Spain

CASTELLAN, ROBERT MICHAEL, epidemiologist; b. Wilmington, Del., July 11, 1950; s. Carl Albert and Mary Ellen (Mahoney) c.; m. Susan Eleanor Brandau, July 14, 1973; children: Allison Catherine, Erin Eleanor. AB, Brown U., 1975, Master Med. Sci., 1975, MD, 1975; MPH, U. Pitts., 1989. Diplomate Am. Bd. Internal Medicine, Am. Bd. Preventive Medicine. Capt. USPHS, 1978—; intern Rochester (N.Y.) Gen. Hosp., 1975-76, resident, 1976-78; epidemic intelligence svc. officer Ctrs. Disease Control, Atlanta, 1978-80; pulmonary medicine fellow W.Va. U. Sch. Med., Morgantown, 1980-83; resident in occupl. medicine Nat. Inst. Occupl. Safety and Health, Morgantown, 1983-84, chief clin. sect., 1983-88, acting chief epidemiological investigations br., 1989-91, chief epidemiological investigations br., 1991-94, sr. med. epidemiologist, 1994—; adj. assoc. prof. W.Va. Sch. Medicine, Morgantown, 1978—; cons. Nat. Inst. Occupl. Health, Ahmedebad, India, 1987, Inst. Occupl. Health and Safety Rsch., Montreal, Can., 1995. Contbr. over 70 articles to profl. pubs., chpts. to books. Mem. occupl. health com. Am. Lung Assn., N.Y.C., 1934-95; bd. dirs. Am. Lung Assn. W.Va., Charleston, 1991—; vol., coach, com. chair local schs., Monongalia County, W.Va., 1983-92; vol. ARC Blood Svcs., Morgantown, 1986—, W.Va. Adopt a Highway Litter Program, Monongalia County, 1991—; mem. leadership giving assn. United Way of Monongalia County, 1991—. Decorated Unit Commendations awards USPHS, 1991, 92, 93, Commendations medals, 1983, 91; recipient Future Leaders Pulmonary Medicine award Am. Coll. Chest Physicians, 1983, Outstanding Svc. award Am. Lung Assn. W.Va., 1995. Mem. Am. Pub. Health Assn., Am. Thoracic Soc., Brown Med. Alumni Assn., W.Va. Pub. Health Assn., W.Va. Thoracic Soc. (sec.), Sigma Xi. Office: NIOSH-CDC 1095 Willowdale Rd Morgantown WV 26505

CASTELLANOS GONZALEZ, JULIÁN, psychologist, consultant; b. Bogotá, Colombia, Oct. 18, 1939; s. Antonio Elias and Rosa María (González) Castellanos; m. Graciela Jiménez, Nov. 7, 1970; children: Javier, Julián Andrés, Sonia Patricia, Ricardo Augusto. Lic. in Philosophy, St. Buenaventura U., Bogotá, 1962; student, Nat. U. Colombia, Bogotá, 1964-65; grad. in Hispanoamerican lit., Caro y Cuervo Inst., Bogotá, 1970; postgrad., Javeriana U., Bogotá, 1975-78, M in Psychology, 1990. Dir. St. Buenaventura U. Libr., Bogotá, 1960-61; philosophy educator Pio XII Sch., Cali, Colombia, 1962-63; ethics and human devel. tchr. Servicio Nacinal de Apprendizaje, Bogotá, 1966-79, psychologist, 1979-86, selection mgr., 1986-89, profl. assessor, 1989—; profl. internal control office, 1990-95; prof. Jorge Tadeo Lozano U., Bogotá, 1970-74, Politecnico Trancolombiano U., 1993-96, U.M.B. U., 1995-96; mgr. of psychol. office, Bogotá, 1977-85; cons. numerous orgns., Bogotá, 1980-91. Mem. Javeriana Psychol. Assn., Behavior Analysis & Therapy Colombian Assn. Liberal. Roman Catholic. Home: Apartado Aereo 52134, Bogotá D.C. 2, Colombia

CASTELLINI, CLATEO, medical products manufacturing executive; b. 1935. BA in Econs., Bocconi U., Milan, Italy, 1958; MBA, Harvard U., 1973. With Lepetit, S.A. (became subs. Dow Chem. 1965), 1959-77; various mgmt. positions Becton Dickinson & Co., Franklin Lakes, N.J., 1978-89, pres. med. sector, 1989-94, chmn., pres., CEO, 1994—, also bd. dirs. Office: Becton Dickinson & Co 1 Becton Dr Franklin Lakes NJ 07417*

CASTELLINO, RONALD AUGUSTUS DIETRICH, radiologist; b. N.Y.C., Feb. 18, 1938; s. Leonard Vincent and Henrietta Wilhelmina (Geffken) C.; m. Joyce Cuneo, Jan. 26, 1963; children: Jeffrey Charles, Robin Leonard, Anthony James. Student, Creighton U., Omaha, 1955-58, M.D., 1962. Diplomate: Am. Bd. Radiology. Rotating intern Highland Alameda County Hosp., Oakland, Calif., 1962-63; USPHS/Peace Corps physician Brazil, 1963-65; resident in diagnostic radiology Stanford U. Hosp., 1965-68, chief resident, 1967-68; asst. prof. radiology Stanford U. Med. Sch., 1968-74, assoc. prof., 1974-81, prof., 1981-93, chief diagnostic oncologic radiology, 1970-89, chief CT body scanning, 1979-89, dir. div. diagnostic radiology and assoc. chmn. dept. radiology, 1981-86, acting chmn. dept. diagnostic radiology and nuclear medicine, 1986-89; chair dept. radiology, Carroll and Milton Petrie chair Meml. Sloan Kettering Cancer Ctr., N.Y.C., 1990—; prof. radiology Cornell Med. Sch., 1994—; mem. U.S. Cancer del., People's Republic China, 1977. Co-editor: Pediatric Oncologic Radiology, 1977; assoc. editor; Lymphology, 1973, Investigative Radiology, 1985-94, Academic Radiology, 1994—, Radiology, 1986-94, Postgrad. Radiology, 1986—; contbr. numerous rsch. papers to profl. jours., chpts. to books. Recipient T.F. Eckstrom Fund award, 1978; Guggenheim fellow, 1974-75. Mem. Internat. Soc. Lymphology (exec. com. 1975-85), Am. Coll. Radiology, Assn. Univ. Radiologists (exec. com. 1981-85), Radiol. Soc. N.Am., Soc. Cardiovascular and Interventional Radiology (charter), Am. Roentgen Ray Soc., Western Angiography Soc. (charter), Calif. Med. Assn. (adv. panel sect. radiology 1972-89), Calif. Radiol. Soc., Soc. Thoracic Radiology (charter), Soc. Cancer Imaging (charter), N.Am. Soc. Lymphology (charter, exec. com. 1982-86), Calif. Acad. Medicine, N.Y. Roentgen Soc., N.Y. Acad. Medicine, Am. Soc. Therapeutic Radiation Oncologists (hon.), Alpha Omega Alpha. Office: Meml Sloan Kettering Cancer Ctr Dept Radiology 1275 York Ave New York NY 10021-6007

CASTELLION, ALAN WILLIAM, pharmacologist, consultant; b. North Tonawanda, N.Y., May 1, 1934; s. Clarence George and Nora Agnus (Eick) C.; m. Judith Swaner, Aug. 17, 1961; children: Deena Manon, Jocelyn Sue. BS in Pharmacy, U. Buffalo, 1956; PhD in Pharmacology, U. Utah, 1964. Registered pharmacist, Utah. Tchg. asst. U. Utah, Salt Lake City, 1956-63, rsch. asst., 1963-64, postdoctoral fellow, 1964-66; sr. pharmacologist Smith Kline & French Labs., Phila., 1966-69; sect. chief pharmacology Norwich (N.Y.)-Eaton Pharm., 1970-77, dir. R&D compliance, 1977-82, dir. regulatory affairs, 1982-84, mgr. internat. product devel., 1984-93; pres. Global Pharma Assocs., Oxford, N.Y., 1993—. Contbr. articles to profl. jours. Recipient Lunsford Richardson Pharmacy award Richardson Vicks, U. Utah, 1961. Mem. Am. Pharm. Assn., Am. Soc. Pharmacology and Exptl. Therapeutics, Drug Info. Assn., Product Devel. and Mgmt. Assn., Regulatory Affairs Profl. Soc., Sigma Xi. Office: Global Pharma Assocs Bradley Hill Rd Oxford NY 13830-9533

CASTLE, GLORIA FARTHING, pediatrician; b. L.A., Mar. 10, 1931; d. James Edgar and Amy Leona (Huffman) Farthing; m. Richard Brister Castle, Sept. 13, 1959; children: Gregory F., Kelly A. Castle Dragojlovic, John R. Student, Pacific Union Coll., Angwin, Calif., 1947-50; BA in Chemistry, U. Pacific, Stockton, 1951; MD, U. So. Calif., L.A., 1958. Lab. asst. organic rsch. Dow Chem. Co., Pittsburgh, Calif., 1951-53; intern, resident pediatrics Children's Hosp. L.A., 1958-60, fellow adolescent medicine, 1967-69; sch. physician Montebello (Calif.) United Sch. Dist., 1960-67; attending physician divsn. adolescent medicine Teenage Health Ctr. Children's Hosp., L.A., 1970—; Teenage Health Ctr., Children's Hosp., L.A., 1979—, coord. community svcs., 1981—; dir. med. svcs. L.A. Job Corps, 1980—; asst. pediatrics U. So. Calif. Sch. Medicine, L.A., 1959-66, clin. instr. pediatrics, 1966-69, instr. pediatrics/adolescent medicine, 1969-75, asst. clin. prof. pediatrics, 1975-80, assoc. clin. prof. pediatrics, 1980-89, clin. prof. pediatrics, 1989—; cons. Florence Crittenton Ctr., L.A. Assoc. editor Jour. Adolescent Health Care, 1983-91, mem. editl. bd. 1991-93; contbr. articles to med. jours. Mem. Nat. Charity League, L.A. Zoo Assn. Recipient Youth Svc. award City Glendale, Glendale Sch. Dist., Calif., 1978, Hon Svc. award Calif. PTA, Glendale PTA, 1980, Cert. Appreciation & Commendation L.A. Job Corps, 1994; fellow Royal Soc. Health, 1969—. Mem. AMA, N.Am. Soc. Pediatric and Adolescent Gynecology, Soc. Adolescent Medicine, Royal Soc. Medicine, Calif. Med. Assn., L.A. County Med. Assn., L.A. Pediatric Soc., Salerni Collegium, Gamma Phi Beta. Office: Children's Hosp LA 4650 Sunset Blvd # 2 Los Angeles CA 90027

CASTLEBERRY, KAREN WITTLER, dental assisting educator; b. Chattanooga, Sept. 1, 1953; d. Ernest A. and Erlene L. Wittler; m. William Michael Castleberry, May 17, 1975; children: April, Jon. AS, Chattanooga State Tech. Coll., 1986; BS, Covenant Coll., 1995. Cert. dental asst., Tenn. Dental asst. to pvt. practice dentist Chattanooga, 1972-75, endodontic asst. to pvt. practice endodontist, 1975; instr. dental assisting Chattanooga State Tech. Community Coll., 1976—; speaker in field; mem. curriculum com. Tenn. Bd. Dentistry, Nashville; cons. in field; instr. community edn. courses. Inst. CPR, first aid, HIV/AIDS edn. ARC, 1980-90. Mem. Am. Dental Asst.'s Assn., Tenn. Dental Assts. Educators Consortium. Baptist. Home: 101 Tanforan Dr Rossville GA 30741-3232 Office: Chattanooga State Tech CC 4501 Amnicola Hwy Chattanooga TN 37406-1018

CASTLEBERRY, KIM ALAN, optometrist; b. Dalhart, Tex., Aug. 15, 1956; s. Onis Wilburn and Veta Bruce (Allison) C.; m. Gina Lea Meynig, May 21, 1956; children: Justin, Hunter. BS in Zoology and Chemistry, Tex. Tech. U., 1978; OD, U. Houston, 1983. Intern Carswell AFB, Plano, Tex., 1983; pvt. practice, sr. ptnr. Plano (Tex.) Eye Assocs., 1983—; Medicare rev. staff Blue Cross/Blue Shield of Tex., Dallas, 1991-96, physician adv. com. Medicare, 1992-96; adv. bd. Columbia-EyeCare Providers of Tex., 1993-95, Omega Health Network, Tex., 1995-96; adj. prof. U. Houston, Coll. Optometry, 1994-96. Author: Texas Optometric Association Insurance Manual, 1992; contbr. articles to profl. jours. Chmn. Tex. Optometry Polit. Action Com., Austin, 1990-96. Recipient Disting. Alumni award U. Houston, 1996. Mem. Am. Optometric Assn., Tex. Optometric Assn. (bd. mem. 1989-96, pres. 1994-95, Young Optometrist of Yr. 1989, Optometrist of Yr. 1994). Baptist. Office: Plano Eye Assocs 5509 Pleasant Valley Dr Plano TX 75023

CASTRANOVA, VINCENT, toxicologist, physiologist; b. Trenton, N.J., Mar. 18, 1949; s. Guy and Lillian (Rossi) C.; m. Bernadette Jean Nelson, June 20, 1970; 1 child, Melissa. BS, Mt. St. Mary's Coll., 1970; PhD, W.Va. U., 1974. NIH fellow Yale U., New Haven, 1974-76; mem. rsch. faculty Yale U., 1976-77; asst. prof. W.Va. U., Morgantown, 1977-81; assoc. prof. W.Va. U., 1981-85, prof. physiology, 1985—; prof. Sch. of Pharmacy W.Va. U., Morgantown, 1996—; rsch. physiologist Nat. Inst. Occupational Safety and Health, Morgantown, 1977-83; chief biochemistry sect. Occupl. Safety and Health, Morgantown, 1983-95; chief pathology sect. Nat. Inst. Occupational Safety and Health, Morgantown, 1989-95, chief pathology and physiology rsch. br., 1995—. Editor: Cellular Chemiluminescence, 1987, Silica and Silica-Induced Lung Diseases: Current Concepts, 1995; contbr. articles, abstracts to profl. publs. Mem. Am. Physiol. Soc., Soc. of Toxicology, Allegheny-Eris Soc. of Toxicology, Beta Beta Beta, Delta Epsi. Home: RR 7 Box 728 Morgantown WV 26505-9124 Office: WVa U Health Sci Ctr Dept Physiology Morgantown WV 26506

CASTRO, JOSEPH RONALD, physician, oncology researcher, educator; b. Chgo., Apr. 9, 1934; m. Barbara Ann Kauth, Oct. 12, 1957. B.S. in Natural Sci., Loyola U., Chgo., 1956, M.D., 1958. Diplomate: Am. Bd. Radiology, 1964. Intern Rockford (Ill.) Meml. Hosp.; resident U.S. Naval Hosp., San Diego; assoc. radiotherapist and assoc. prof. U. Tex.-M.D. Anderson Hosp. and Tumor Inst., 1967-71; prof. radiology/radiation oncology U. Calif. Sch. Medicine, San Francisco, 1971-94, prof. emeritus radiation oncology, 1994—; vice-chmn. dept. radiation oncology U. Calif. Sch. Medicine, 1980-94; dir. particle radiotherapy Lawrence Berkeley Lab., 1975—, faculty sr. scientist, 1991-94; mem. program project rev. com. NIH/Nat. Cancer Inst. Cancer Program, 1982-85. Author sci. articles. Past pres., chmn. bd. trustees No. Calif. Cancer Program, 1980-83. Served to lt. comdr., M.C. USN, 1956-66. Recipient Teaching award Mt. Zion Hosp. and Med. Center, San Francisco, 1972. Fellow Am. Coll. Radiology; mem. European Soc. Therapeutic Radiology and Oncology (hon.), Am. Soc. Therapeutic Radiology, Rocky Mountain Radiol. Soc. (hon.), Gilbert H. Fletcher Oncologic Soc. (past pres. 1988). Office: Lawrence Berkeley Lab Bldg 55 Berkeley CA 94720

CASTRO, MICHAEL DOMINIC, orthopaedic surgeon; b. Teaneck, N.J., July 15, 1962; s. Michael and Patricia Theresa C.; m. Lisa Lillian Gilbert, Feb. 25, 1996. BS, No. Ariz. U., 1985; DO, U. North Tex. Health Sci. Ctr., 1991. Lab. dir. No. Aris. U. Exercise Sci. Lab., Flagstaff, 1983-87; chief resident Mt. Clemens (Mich.) Gen. Hosp., 1995-96; orthopaedic surgeon Ctr. Sports Medicine and Orthopaedics, Phoenix, 1996—. U. North Tex. Dean's scholar, 1987-91. Mem. Am. Osteo. Assn., Am. Osteo Acad. Orthopaedics. Home: 780 Wellington Crescent Mount Clemens MI 48043 Office: Sports Medicine & Orthopedics 4220 N 19th Ave Phoenix AZ 85015

CASTRO, RAFAEL, pediatrician, hospital administrator; b. Santafé de Bogota, Colombia, Apr. 12, 1944; s. Rafael and Olga (Martinez) C.; m. Maria Mercedes Esguerra, Aug. 8, 1969; children: Juan P., Felipe, Santiago. MD, U. del Valle, Cali, Colombia, 1970. Diplomate Am. Bd. Pediatrics. Resident in pediatrics U. Tenn., Memphis, 1972-75; instr. pediatrics U. Javeriana, Bogota, 1975-77; asst. prof. pediatrics U. Militar Nueva Granada, Bogota, 1977-82, assoc. prof., 1982-87, titular prof. pediatrics, 1988—; chief pediatric svcs. Hosp. Militar Central, Bogota, 1988-91, head divsn. postgrad. med. edn., 1991—. Editor-in-chief Hosmil Medica, 1990—; contbr. articles to profl. jours., chpts. to books. Recipient Med. Merit award Hosp. Militar Central, 1993. Mem. Colombian Assn. Med. Schs. (coun. of pediatric edn. and curriculum 1980—), Colombian Pediatric Soc. (pres. 1995—), L.Am. Infectious Disease Soc., Colombian Soc. Infectious Diseases, Gun Club, Club Los Lagartos. Liberal Party. Roman Catholic. Home: Carrera 12 #79-07 (P-7), Bogota Colombia Office: Carrera 13 # 78-98, Bogota Colombia

CASTRO, ROBERT R., surgeon; b. Lima, Peru, Sept. 16, 1929; came to U.S., 1961; s. Hector and Eloise (Serrano) C.; m. Nicole Godin, Oct. 10, 1959; children: Isabelle, Michael. MD, U. Paris, 1957. Diplomate Am. Bd. Surgery. Intern Augustana Hosp., Chgo., 1957-58; resident in surgery McGill U. Hosp., Montreal, Que., Can., 1958-61, U. Wis. Hosp., Madison, 1961-66; surgeon Norwest Hosp., Chgo., 1966-67, Ottawa (Ill.) Cmty. Hosp., 1967-81, Friesbie Meml. Hosp., Rochester, N.H., 1985—; pvt. practice, Barrington, N.H., 1985—. Lt. col. USAF, 1981-85. Fellow ACS, Am. Coll. Chest Physicians, Internat. Coll. Surgeons. Republican. Roman Catholic. Home: 14 Hamilton St Dover NH 03820 Office: Barrington Profl Ctr Rt 125 and Century Pines Dr Barrington NH 03825

CASTRO-BRAUER, SYLVIA ELIZABETH, physician assistant; b. Phila., Aug. 22, 1953; d. Rene and Eva Kathe (Brauer) C.; m. Alan R. Dowling, July 15, 1972 (div. 1979); 1 child, Sean Lee Dowling. AS, San Antonio Coll., 1979; BS, U. Tex. Med. Branch, Galveston, 1982. Physician asst. Good Health Plus, San Antonio, 1982-84, Tex. Dept. Corrections, Huntsville, Tex., 1984-86, William Cannon Minor Emergency, Austin, Tex., 1986-87, Conifer Park, Scotia, N.Y., 1987-90, Wynantskill (N.Y.) Family Practice, 1990-92; with Albany (N.Y.) Med. Coll., 1992-94, East Tex. Cmty. Health Svc., Nacogdoches, 1994-96; lectr. Childs Nursing Home, 1992, Albany County Nursing Home, 1993, 94, Schenectady Family Health Svcs., 1993; participant ACTG (AIDS Clin. Trials Group), 1992-94. Author: (with others) Sexually Transmitted Disease, 1990; contbr. chpt. to Cocaine Workbook. Mem. adult edn. com. 1st United Meth. Ch., Schenectady, N.Y., 1989-90. Mem. Am. Acad. Physicians Assts., Tex. Assn. Physician Assts., East Tex. Mid-Level Practioners Assn. Office: Hill Country Med Assocs 711N Walnut St New Braunfels TX 78130

CASTRONOVO, FRANK PAUL, JR., radiopharmacologist, health physicist; b. Newark, Jan. 2, 1940; s. Frank Paul and Edna Viola (Weingartner) C.; B.S. in Pharmacy, Rutgers U., Newark, 1962, M.S. in Health Physics (USPHS fellow), New Brunswick, N.J., 1964; Ph.D. in Radiol. Scis., John Hopkins U., 1970; m. Judith Anne Belli, Apr. 3, 1977; children: Jessica Belli, Elizabeth Frances, Andrew David. Staff pharmacist Terry Drugs, Verona, N.J., 1962-63; research scientist Squibb Inst. Med. Research, New Brunswick, 1964-65; nuclear medicine technologist/pharmacist Johns Hopkins U. Hosp., 1965-70; asst. physicist Mass. Gen. Hosp., Boston, 1970-80, assoc. radiopharmacologist, radiation safety officer, 1980-89; instr. Harvard U. Med. Sch., Boston, 1970-76, asst. prof. radiology, 1976-86, assoc. prof., 1986—; adj. clin. assoc. prof. radiopharmacy Mass. Coll. Pharmacy, 1973—; dir. dept. health physics and radiopharmacology, radiation safety officer Brigham and Women's Hosp., Boston, 1989—, radiopharmacist, radiopharmacologist nuclear medicine div., 1989—. Recipient award for excellence in parenteral research Parenteral Drug Assn., 1969; USPHS research grantee, 1971-72, 75. Fellow Am. Soc. Healthcare Pharmacists; mem. Am. Pharm. Assn., Health Physics Soc., Soc. Nuclear Medicine, Am. Assn. Physicists in Medicine, AAAS, Am. Soc. Hosp. Pharmacists (chmn. spl. interest group in radiopharmacy 1976-77, fellow practice recognition program 1994), Ethnopharmacology Soc., Radiopharm. Sci. Council (dir. 1977-80, chmn. com. quality control 1978), Am. Coll. Radiology. Developer diagnostic bone imaging radiopharm., 1972, 82; patentee in field. Office: Brigham & Women's Hosp Radiology Carrie Hall Bldg 4 Boston MA 02115

CATALANO, JAMES ANTHONY, social worker; b. Lackawanna, N.Y., Nov. 5, 1954; s. George and Frances (McGowan) C. BA, Canisius Coll., 1977, Canisius Coll., 1992; MS, Columbia U., 1985; MDiv, Weston Jesuit Sch. Theology, Cambridge, Mass., 1994, ThM, 1995. Cert. social worker, N.Y.; diploma clin. social work NASW, 1991. Caseworker Neighborhood Info. Ctr., Buffalo, N.Y., 1975-79; dir. Youth Svcs. Program Lincoln Community Ctr., Buffalo, N.Y., 1979-80; psychiatric social worker, discharge planner Bry-Lin Hosp., Buffalo, N.Y., 1981; social worker Cath. Charities of Western N.Y., Buffalo, N.Y., 1987-89; asst. to the dir. Inst. of Faith and Justice Canisius Coll., Buffalo, N.Y., 1989-90; pvt. practice Buffalo, N.Y., 1989—; relief worker Jesuit Refugee Svcs., San Salvador, El Salvador, 1985; chmn. Site Selection Com. for Residential Care Facilities, Buffalo, 1979-81; adv. to chmn. Pub. Svc. Commn. of N.Y., 1979-81; speaker on San Salvador Diocese of Buffalo, 1990-91; workshop leader Buffalo Taditional High Sch., Buffalo City High Sch. East Campus, 1988-89; com. mem. Dem. Orgn. Erie County, Buffalo, 1978-81. Recipient Vol. Svc. award VA, Syracuse, N.Y., 1982. Mem. NASW. Home and Office: 30 W 16th St New York NY 10011

CATALANO, LOUIS WILLIAM, JR., neurologist; b. Bklyn., Apr. 20, 1942; s. Louis William and Aileen (Bobb) C.; children: Louis William III, Jamea Elizabeth. BS cum laude, U. Pitts., 1963, MD, 1967. Diplomate Am. Bd. Psychiatry and Neurology, Am. Bd. Electroencephalography, Am. Bd. Pain Medicine, Am. Bd. Med. Examiners. Intern Presbyn.-St. Luke's Hosp., Chgo., 1967-68; rsch. assoc. NIH, Bethesda, Md., 1968-70; fellow neurology The Neurol. Inst., N.Y.C., 1970-73; clin. asst., prof. neurology U. Pitts. Sch. Med., 1973—; pvt. practice Greensburg, Pa., 1973—; staff Latrobe (Pa.) Area Hosp., 1973—, Westmoreland Regional Hosp., Greensburg, 1973—, Torrance (Pa.) State Hosp., 1978—, Indiana (Pa.) Hosp., 1983—; cons. Jeannette (Pa.) Dist. Meml. Hosp., 1984—, Frick Cmty. Health Ctr., Mt. Pleasant, Pa., 1991—; lectr. in field. Contbr. articles to profl. jours. With USPHS, 1968-70. Spl. fellow Columbia U., NIH, 1970-73, epilepsy minifellow, Bowman Gray Sch. Medicine, Winston-Salem, N.C., 1988. Fellow Royal Soc. Medicine, Am. Acad. Neurology; mem. AMA, Am. Acad. Pain Mgmt., Am. Med. Electroencephalographic Assn., Am. Soc. Neuroimaging, Am. Acad. Clin. Neurophysiology, Am. Sleep Disorders Assn., Pa. Med. Soc., Westmoreland County Med. Soc., Latrobe Acad. Medicine, Pittsburgh Neurosci. Soc., Sigma Xi, Alpha Omega Alpha. Office: Pitts U Dept Neurology Greensburg PA 15601

CATALANO, PHILIP MARTIN, dermatologist; b. Pelham Bay, N.Y., Mar. 2, 1935; s. Philip Martin and Rose Regina Catalano; m. Nora Mace, May 26, 1962; children: Anne, Philip Mace, Margaret. AB in Chemistry magna cum laude, Harvard U., 1956; MD, U. Pa., 1960. Diplomate Am. Bd. Dermatology, Nat. Bd. Med. Examiners; lic. physician, Fla., N.C. Intern Tampa (Fla.) Gen. Hosp.; resident in dermatology U. Miami, Fla.; pvt. practice Bradenton, Fla., 1966—; instr. dermatology U. Miami, 1965-66, dir. out-patient clinic, 1965-66, clin. lectr., 1966-73, adj. assoc. prof., 1977-78, 78-95; active staff Manatee Meml. Hosp., Bradenton, Blake Meml. Hosp., Bradenton. Contbr. articles to profl. jours.; cons. editor Jour. Fla. Med. Assn., 1973-76; editor Selected Revs. of the Literature Archives of Dermatology, 1970-78; editl. adv. com. Index of Dermatology, Nat. Libr. Medicine, Bethesda, Md., 1973-80; editl. bd. Jour. Am. Acad. Dermatology, 1978-86. Chmn. Com. to Investigate Fla., Regional Med. Program in Manatee County, 1972-73; venereal disease control physician Manatee County Health Dept., Bradenton, Fla., 1966-68; med. and sci. com. Dermatology Found., 1980-82; med. adv. com. Blue Cross/Blue Shield, Fla., 1988-91. Mem. So. Med. Assn., Am. Soc. Dermatologic Surgery, Fla. Dermatol. Soc., Assn. Harvard Chemists, H.B. Dermatologic Soc., Manatee County Med. Assn., Fla. Med. Assn., Am. Acad. Dermatology, Soc. Investigative Dermatology, Am. Ctrl. Dermatologic Congress, South Ctrl. Dermatologic Congress, Coun. for Nail Disorders, Phi Beta Kappa, Alpha Omega Alpha. Methodist. Office: 1416 59th St W Bradenton FL 34209

CATALANO, RICHARD DANIEL, physician and surgeon; b. Loma Linda, Calif., Sept. 6, 1951; s. Donald Vincent and Anne-Marie (Guild) C.; m. Patti Lou Smith, June 27, 1976; children: Anthony Louis, Elisabeth Jane. BA magna cum laude, Pacific Union Coll., Angwin, Calif., 1973; MD, Loma Linda U., 1976. Diplomate Am. Bd. Surgery, sub.-bd. surg. critical care. Resident in surgery Loma Linda U. Med. Ctr., 1977-81; fellow in burn and trauma surgery U. Calif. San Francisco Med. Ctr., 1982-83; asst. prof. surgery Loma Linda U. Sch. Medicine, 1984-91, assoc. prof., 1991—; chief trauma surgery svc. Loma Linda U. Med. Ctr., 1984—. Contbr. chpts. to books, numerous articles to profl. jours. Fellow ACS; mem. Alpha Omega Alpha. Office: Loma Linda U Sch Medicine 11234 Anderson St Rm 2576 Loma Linda CA 92354

CATALANO, ROBERT ANTHONY, ophthalmologist, physician, hospital administrator, writer; b. Albany, N.Y., Nov. 24, 1956; s. Anthony Joseph and Ida Santa (Muscolino) C.; m. Madeline Faye Kalmer, Aug. 6, 1978; children: Christopher, Ruth, Thomas, Matthew. BS, Union Coll., Schenectady, 1978; MD, U. Va., 1982; MBA, Rensselaer Poly. Inst., 1992. Resident in ophthalmology Albany Med. Coll., 1983-86, vice-chmn. dept. ophthalmology, 1989-90, acting chmn., 1990-91; fellow in pediatric ophthalmology Wills Eye Hosp., Phila., 1986-87; v.p. med. affairs Olean (N.Y.) Gen. Hosp., 1991-93, COO, 1994-95, pres., CEO, 1995—; bd. dirs. Westlink Corp. Author: Atlas of Ocular Motility, 1989, Ocular Emergencies, 1992, Pediatric Ophthalmology: A Text/Atlas, 1994; contbr. articles to profl. jours. Recipient Nat. Found. award March of Dimes Found., 1978, Robert D. Reinecke award Albany Med. Coll., 1985, Shannon award U. Va., 1982; Heed Found. fellow, 1986, Forty Under Forty award, 1993. Fellow Am. Acad. Ophthalmology; mem. Am. Coll. Physician Execs., Am. Coll. Healthcare Execs., Western N.Y. Hosp. Assn. (bd. dirs. 1992-95), So. Tier Healthcare Network (bd. dirs. 1994—), Alpha Omega Alpha. Roman Catholic. Office: Olean Gen Hosp 515 Main St Olean NY 14760-1513

CATALDI, PATRICIA LEE, surgeon; b. Glastonbury, Conn., Sept. 7, 1945; d. George Anthony Cataldi and Frances Mary (Thurz) Scorso. MD, Hahnemann U., 1977. Joined Missionary Sisters of the Precious Blood; diplomate Am. Bd. Surgery. Gen. surgeon St. Jude's Hosp., St. Lucia, W.I., 1982-87, St. Anne's Hosp., Brunapeg, Zimbabwe, 1988—. Mem. Assn. of Sisters, Bros., Priests, Physicians, Surg. Soc. Zimbabwe, Assn. Women Surgeons. Roman Catholic. Home and Office: St Anne's Hosp Brunapeg, PO Bag T 5426, Bulawayo Zimbabwe

CATALFO, BETTY MARIE, health service executive, nutritionist; b. N.Y.C., Nov. 2, 1942; d. Lawrence Santo and Gemma (Patrone) Lorefice; children—Anthony, Lawrence, Donna Marie. Grad. Newtown High Sch., Elmhurst, N.Y., 1958. Sec., clk. ABC-TV, N.Y.C., 1957-60; founder, lectr., nutritionist Weight Watchers, Manhasset, N.Y., 1964-75; founder, pres. Every-Bodys Diet, Inc. dba Stay Slim, Queens, N.Y., 1976—; dir. in-home program N.Y. State Dept. Health, N.Y.C., 1985—; founder, pres. Delitegul Diet Foods, Inc., 1988—; lectr. in field. Author: 101 Stay-Slim Recipes, 1983, Get Slim and Stay Slim Diet Cook Book, rev. ed., 1987, Diet Revolution, 1991, Holiday Cookbook, 1992, Fat Counts in Fast Food Spots, 1992, Choose to Loose!, 1993, You Are Not Alone, 1993, Eating Out, 1994, Change or Select, 1994, Calories Do Count!, 1994, Fat Free Receipes, 1994; author, dir., producer: (video) Dancersize for Overweight, 1986, Get Slim and Stay Slim Diet Cook Book, Eating Right for Your Life, Hello It's Me and I'm Slim, (videos) Stay Slim Line Dancing, 1989, Stay Slim Food Facts, 1989, Help Me Before I Give In, 1990, A New Year A New You!, 1991, Relax and Meditate, 1991, Come Shop with Me, 1991, Change or Accept, 1993, The Bag Lady, 1993, Sneak Eater, 1993, Sins That Every Dieter Makes, 1994, Stay Slim from Start to Finish, 1994, Here's Some Helpful Diet Tips, 1994, What Every Smart Dieter Knows, 1994, Mirror Mirror on the Wall, 1994, Weight Management Techniques, 1995; author, editor: (video) Eating Right For Life, 1985, Isometric Techniques for Weight Reduction, Dance Your Calories A-Weigh; author, producer: (video) Eating Habits, 1986—; (video) Isometric Techniques for Weight Reduction, 1986, Patience

Is a Virtue When Weight Loss is the Goal, 1986, Slow Down you Eat to Fast, 1994, Always Giving Never Receiving, 1994, Relax and Don't You Worry, 1994; producer, dir.: (video) Positive and Negative Diet Forces, 1987, (video) Hello It's Me and I'm Thin, 1987, (video) Dance Your Calories A-Weigh, 1987, (video) Positive and Negative Diet Forces, 1987. Sponsor, lectr. St. Pauls Ctr., Bklyn., 1981—, Throgs Neck Assn. Retarded Children, Bronx, 1985—; active ARC, LWV, Am. Italian Assn., United Way Greenwich, Council Chs. and Synagogues, Heart Assn., N.Y. Meals on Wheels, 1985—, Health Assn. Fairfield County, Food Svcs. for Homeless People, 1993, 94, 95; chairperson, sponsor Battered Women, 1994—. Named Woman of Yr., Bayside Womens Club, N.Y., 1983, O, PK Woman of Yr., 1986—, Woman of Yr. Richmond Boys Club, 1987, Woman of Yr. Bronx Press Club Assn., 1987; recipient Merit award for Svc. Cath. Archdiocese of Bklyn., 1985, Merit award Svcs. Cath. Archdioces of Bklyn. and Queens, 1992, 93, 94, Community Service award Sr. Citizens Sacred Heart League Bklyn./Queens Archdiocese. N.Y. State Nutritional Guidance for Children Nat. Assn. Scis. Mem. Nat. C. of C. for Women (Woman of Yr. 1987, 90), Pres.'s Coun. on Nutrition, Roundtable for Women in Food Service, Bus. and Profl. Women's Club, Pres. Council for Phys. Fitness, Nat. Assn. Female Execs., Assn. for Fitness in Bus. Inc., Nat. Assn. Female Bus. Owners. Democrat. Roman Catholic. Club: Mothers Sacred Heart Sch. (chairperson 1979-82). Avocations: reading; travel, golf, family. Home: 21422 27th Ave Flushing NY 11360-2608 also: 58 Riverview Ct Greenwich CT 06831-4127 Office: 10005 101st Ave Ozone Park NY 11416-2610

CATALFOMO, PHILIP, university dean; b. Providence, Dec. 27, 1931; s. Antonio and Frances (Di Giuseppe) C.; m. Magdalena Wettstein, Jan. 8, 1962; children—Kristina, Anthony Werner. B.S., Providence Coll., 1953, U. Conn., 1958; M.S., U. Wash., Seattle, 1960, Ph.D., 1962. Mem. faculty Oreg. State U., 1963-75, prof. pharmacognosy, 1966-75, head dept., 1966-75; prof. pharmacognosy, dean Sch. Pharmacy, U. Mont., Missoula, 1975-86; dean coll. health scis. U. Wyo., Laramie, 1986-91; ret., 1991. Author research articles fungal metabolism. Served with AUS, 1953-55. Gustavus A. Pfeiffer Meml. research fellow, 1969-70. Home: 81800 Old Hwy # 93 Dayton MT 59914

CATANDELLA, KENNETH F., dentist, nutritionist; b. Bridgeport, Conn., May 21, 1936; s. Joseph Francis and Constance Marie (Florentino) C.; children: Kenneth M., Melinda A., Jolynn M., Gregg C. BS in Biology, Fairfield U., 1957; DDS, Fairleigh Dickinson U., 1962; MS in Nutrition, U. Bridgeport, 1981. Chief dental sci., capt. Ft. Lee (Va.) Army Hosp., 1962-64; chmn. alumni assn. Fairfield (Conn.) U., 1968-69; instr. U. of Bridgeport, Conn., 1970; asst. clin. prof. Fairleigh Dickinson Dental Sch., Teaneck, N.J., 1970-90; peer rev. com. Bridgeport, 1985-89; chmn. health dept. Trumbull, Conn., 1988-90; lectr. Cosmetic Dentistry Soc., 1980-91; cons. Trumbull Sr. Citizen Group. Contbr. articles to profl. jours. Named Fairfield U. Alumnus of Yr., U. of Bridgeport Disting. Alumnus. Fellow Acad. Gen. Dentistry; mem. Bridgeport Dental Assn., Conn. Dental Assn., Am. Dental Assn., Acad. Gen. Dentistry. Home and Office: 4746 Madison Ave Trumbull CT 06611-1717

CATANIA, A(NTHONY) CHARLES, psychology educator; b. N.Y.C., June 22, 1936; s. Charles John and Elizabeth (Lattarulo) C.; m. Constance J. Britt, Feb. 10, 1962; children: William John, Kenneth Charles. BA in Psychology with highest honors, Columbia U., 1957, MA, 1958; PhD (NSF fellow), Harvard U., 1961. Postdoctoral research fellow Harvard U., 1961-62; sr. pharmacologist Smith, Kline & French Labs., Phila., 1962-64; asst. prof. NYU, 1964-66, asso. prof., 1966-69, prof., chmn. dept. psychology, 1969-73; prof. dept. psychology U. Md. Baltimore County, Catonsville, 1973—; mem. psychobiology com. NSF, 1982-85; vis. prof. Keio U., Tokyo, 1992. Author: Learning, 1979, 2d edit., 1984, 3d edit., 1992; co-author: (with E. Shimoff and B.A. Matthews) Behavior on a Disk, 1989; editor: Contemporary Research in Operant Behavior, 1968; co-editor: (with T.A. Brigham) Handbook of Applied Behavior Analysis, 1978, (with S. Harnad) The Selection of Behavior: The Operant Behaviorism of B.F. Skinner, 1988, (with P.N. Hineline) Variations and Selections, 1996; editor: Jour. Exptl. Analysis Behavior, 1966-69, rev. editor, 1969-76, 83-91; assoc. editor: Behavioral and Brain Scis., 1980—; mem. bd. editors various jours.; contbr. articles to profl. jours.; contbr. chpts. to textbooks. Recipient James McKeen Cattell Sabbatical award, 1986-87, Outstanding Sci. Contbns. to Psychology award Md. Psychol. Assn., 1993, Outstanding Contbr. Behavior Analysis award No. Calif. Assn. Behavior Analysis, 1990; grantee NSF, 1965-67, 74-79, 82-88, USPHS grantee, 1967-73, 79-83; Fulbright sr. rsch. fellow U. Coll. North Wales, Bangor, 1986-87. Fellow Am. Psychol. Assn. (pres. of divsn. 25 1976-79, 96—); mem. Assn. Behavioral Analysis (pres. 1982-83, chairperson publ. bd. 1992-95), Ea. Psychol. Assn. (dir. 1979-82), Soc. Exptl. Analysis of Behavior (pres. 1966-67, 81-83), Phi Beta Kappa. Home: 10545 Rivulet Row Columbia MD 21044-2420 Office: U Md Balt County Dept Psychology 5401 Wilkens Ave Baltimore MD 21228-5329

CATANZARITI, ALAN R., podiatrist; b. McKees Rocks, Pa., May 3, 1956; s. Samuel Joseph and Ann Carmella Catanzariti; m. Tami Michelle Markoff; children: Gabrielle, Alan R. Jr. BS, U. Pitts., 1979; DPM, Calif. Coll. Podiatric Med., San Francisco, 1983. Diplomate Am. Bd. Podiatric Surgery. Resident in surgery Podiatry Hosp. Pitts., 1984, dir. residency tng., 1988—. Author: Comprehensive Textbook of Foot and Ankle Surgery, 1996; contbr. articles to profl. jours. Office: Podiatry Hosp of Pitts 215 S Negley Ave Pittsburgh PA 15206-3522

CATANZARO, DANIEL FRANK, molecular biologist, educator; b. Sydney, Apr. 4, 1957; came to U.S., 1990; m. Cathy L. Budman; two children. BA in Biol. Scis. with honors, Macquarie U., 1978; PhD in Physiology and Molecular Biology, U. Sydney, 1985. Rsch. asst. dept. physiology U. Sydney, 1982-85; vis. rsch. biochemist U. Calif., San Francisco, 1985; lectr. in eukaryotic molecular genetics U. Sydney, 1986-90; asst. prof. physiology in medicine Cornell U. Med. Coll., 1990-95, assoc. prof. physiology in medicine, 1995—. Contbr. articles and revs. to profl. jours. Postgrad. scholar U. Sydney Faculty of Medicine, 1979-81; recipient investigatorship award Am. Heart Assn., 1995. Fellow AHA High Blood Pressure Rsch. Coun.; mem. Endocrine Soc., Am. Soc. Hypertension (Young Scholars award 1993). Office: NY Hosp Cornell U Med Coll Cardiovascular Ctr 525 E 68th St New York NY 10021-4873

CATECHIS, SPYROS, psychologist; b. Port Arthur, Tex., Nov. 29, 1945; s. Anastosis Spyro and Grace (Manos) C.; m. Marian Elizabeth, May 19, 1979; children: Alexander, Steven; children by previous marriage: Christopher, Nicholas. BS, Stephen F. Austin U., Nacogdoches, Tex., 1968; MS, East Tex. State U., Commerce, 1969; EdD, U. Houston, 1978. Diplomate Am. Bd. Behavioral Medicine. Psychologist Briarwood Sch., Houston, 1973-74, Tex. Rsch. Inst., Houston, 1974-77, Houston Ednl. Cons., 1977—; exec. dir. Houston Learning Acad., 1986—; psychologist Ctr. for Retarded, Houston, 1985—. Bd. mem. Annunciation Orthodox Sch., Houston, 1985—. Office: Houston Learning Acad 2400 Augusta Dr Ste 255 Houston TX 77057-4911

CATENA, SALVATORE VINCENT, family physician; b. Bronx, N.Y., July 23, 1941; s. Vincent Salvatore and Eleonore (Mazzella) C.; m. June 5, 1966 (div. Apr., 1994); children: Janine, Vincent. BS, St. John's Coll., 1963; MD, N.Y. Med. Coll., 1967. Diplomate Am. Bd. Family Practice, cert. qualified practitiomer geriatrics. Med. intern N.Y. Med. Coll.-Met. Hosp. Ctr., Manhattan; pvt. practice family physician Nesconset, N.Y., 1970—; staff physician Ctrl. Islip (N.Y.) State Hosp., 1970-82, Kings Park (N.Y.) Psychiat. Ctr., 1982—. Lt. med. corps. USNR, 1968-70. Fellow Am. Acad. Family Practice; mem. Am. Acad Family Physicians. Home and Office: 9 Roy Dr Nesconset NY 11767

CATER, DAVID ANTHONY, psychologist, educator; b. Pasadena, Dec. 26, 1943; s. Wayland Hoyt and Ruth Louise (Mills) C.; m. Janet Kay Barnes, June 20, 1970; children: Jennifer Maire Cater Wilmoth, Kathleen Elizabeth. BA, Pasadena Coll., 1965; MA, Calif. State U., L.A., 1969, Fuller Theol. Sem., 1975; PhD, Fuller Theol. Sem., 1976. Intern San Fernando Valley Child Guidance Clinic, Van Nuys, Calif., 1971-72, Pasadena (Calif.) Cmty. Counseling Ctr., 1972-73; asst. prof., psychology dept. chmn. Simpson Coll., San Francisco, 1973-75; staff psychologist, clin. assoc prof. med. psychology Irvine Calif. Coll. Medicine, Orange, Calif., 1976-92; consulting psychologist Orange County Cmty. Hosp., Orange, Calif., 1992-93; assoc. prof. John Brown Univ., Siloam Springs, Ark., 1993—. Elder, trustee Presbyn. Ch. Mem. AAAS, Am. Psychol. Assn., N.Y. Acad. Scis., Nat. Register of Health Svc. Providers in Psychology Republican. Office: John Brown Univ 2000 W University Dr Siloam Springs AR 72761

CATLETT, JAMES C., JR., mental health administrator; b. Chattanooga, June 29, 1957; s. James C. and Mabel L. (Hinch) C.; m. Deborah Kaye Green, Oct. 13, 1983; 1 child, Rachel Loranne. BA in Psychology with honors, Lee Coll., 1978; MS in Clin. Psychology, U. Tenn., 1981. Lic. psychol. examiner, Tenn. Therapist Hiwassee Mental Health Ctr., Cleveland, Tenn., 1981-82, satellite dir., 1982-84, assoc. dir., 1984-90, dir. extended care, 1990-92; dir. adult svcs. Hiwassee Mental Health Ctr., Cleveland, 1992-95; mental health svcs. dir. Vol. Behavioral Health Care System, Chattanooga, 1995-96, regional dir., 1996—; program cons., workshop presenter to mental health agys. and convs. throughout Tenn., 1986—; cons. VISTA Cmty. Programs, Rossville, Ga., 1989-93; guest lectr. Lee Coll., Cleveland, 1987—, mem. adj. faculty, 1991; guest lectr. Cleveland State C.C., 1987. Profl. vocalist; composer; co-editor: Insane Jealousy, 1991. Democrat. Home: 3527 Brandon Ln NE Cleveland TN 37323 Office: Vol Behavioral Health Care c/o Hiwassee Mental Health 1855 Executive Park N Ste 1 Cleveland TN 37312

CATLIN, FRANCIS IRVING, physician; b. Hartford, Conn., Dec. 6, 1925; s. Robert Irving and Frances Rose (Maleski) C.; m. Rebecca Vaughan Graham, June 11, 1948; children: Robert, Andrew, Martha. AA, Princeton U., 1949; MD, Johns Hopkins U., 1948, DSc, 1959. Diplomate: Am. Bd. Otolaryngology. Intern Union Meml. Hosp., Balt., 1948-49; resident in otolaryngology Johns Hopkins Hosp., Balt., 1950, 52-54; from instr. to assoc. prof. Johns Hopkins U. Med. Sch., Balt., 1956-72; prof. otorhinolaryngology and communicative scis. Baylor U. Med. Sch., Houston, 1972-91, prof. emeritus, 1991—; chief otolaryngology svc. Tex. Children's Hosp., 1972-91, emeritus staff, 1991—. Contbr. articles to med. jours. Capt. M.C. USAF, 1950-52. Fellow Am. Otol. Soc.; mem. AMA, Tex. Med. Soc., Am. Acad. Otolaryngology (adv. com. 1972—), Am. Coun. Otolaryngology, Am. Laryngological, Rhinological and Otol. Soc., Med. and Chirurgical Faculty Md., Am. Speech and Hearing Assn. (life). Republican. Episcopalian. Home: 13307 Queensbury Ln Houston TX 77079-6013

CATLIN, RANDOLPH, JR., psychiatrist; b. N.Y.C., Nov. 17, 1925; s. Randolph and Hannah Hastings (White) C.; m. Marian Woolston, July 5, 1959; children: Laura, Jennifer, Randolph III. MD, U. Va., 1952; MPH, Harvard U., 1958. Cert. Am. Psychoanalytic Assn. Intern N.Y. Hosp., N.Y.C., 1952-53; resident Mass. Gen. Hosp., Boston, 1961-65; psychiatrist Harvard U. Health Svcs., Cambridge, Mass., 1966—; chief psychiat. svcs. Harvard U., Cambridge, 1983—; attending psychiatrist McLean Hosp., Belmont, Mass., 1980—; cons. MIT Health Svcs., Cambridge, 1989. Author: (with others) Counseling and the College Student, 1971; contbr. articles to profl. jours. Major USAF, 1953-61. Mem. Am. Psychiat. Assn., Am. Psychoanalytic Assn., Boston Psychoanalytic Soc. Republican. Office: Harvard U Health Svcs 75 Mt Auburn St Cambridge MA 02138-4901

CATLIN, SUSAN LYNN, alcohol and drug abuse psychotherapist; b. Chgo., Dec. 15, 1954; d. Charles Sexton and Dorothy Mary (Good) C. BA, U. Ill., 1977; postgrad., George Williams Coll., 1983; MA, Roosevelt U., 1995. Cert. alcohol and drug counselor. Psychiat. tech. Forest Hosp., Des Plaines, Ill., 1979-85; alcohol counselor Ptnrs. in Psychiatry, Des Plaines, 1985-90; dir., pres. S.L. Catlin and Assocs., Des Plaines, Schaumburg, Ill., 1990—; cons. Advanced Psychiat. Svcs., 1990-94. Fellow Div. of Ill. Addictions, Nat. Assn. Alcoholism and Drug Abuse Counselors. Republican. Methodist. Home: 258 Sierra Pass Dr Schaumburg IL 60194

CATOE, BETTE LORRINA, physician, health educator; b. Washington, Apr. 7, 1926; d. John Booker and Laura Beola (Adams) C.; BS cum laude, Howard U., 1948, MD, 1951; m. Warren J. Strudwick, Sept. 17, 1949; children: Laura Christina, Warren J., William J. Intern, Freedmen's Hosp., Washington, 1951-52; pediatric resident Howard U. Freedman's Hosp., 1952-55; practice medicine specializing in pediatrics, Washington, 1956—; instr. bacteriology Howard U., 1955-57; mem. staff Providence Hosp., Columbia Hosp., Howard U. Hosp., Washington Hosp. Center; sch. health officer Dept. Health, Washington, 1960-64; clin. instr. Howard U., 1956-58. Mem. D.C. Health Planning Adv. Council, 1967-77, chmn., 1973-77; chmn. D.C. Devel. Disabilities Adv. Council, 1970-74; mem. D.C. Mayor's Commn. on Food and Nutrition, 1971-72, Mayor's Commn. on Maternal and Child Health. 1978-84; mem. D.C. Commn. Jud. Tenure and Disabilities, 1977—, chair, 1984—; bd. dirs. United Way of Nat. Capital Area 1974-76, chmn. social planning com., 1974-75; bd. govs. St. Alban's Sch., 1978-84; bd. dirs. D.C. Health and Welfare Council, 1968-73, pres., 1973-74; del. Democratic Nat. Conv., 1976; bd. dirs. Met. Washington Health and Welfare Council, 1970-72, Parent Council of Washington, 1974-75, Met. Med. Founds., Inc., Silver Spring YMCA, 1977-80; mem. Mayor's Health Policy Coun.; chair emergency medicine com. Mem. AMA, D.C. Chirurg. Soc., D.C. Med. Soc. (bd. trustees 1996—), Nat. Med. Assn. (chmn. pediatric sect. 1981-83), Am. Med. Women's Assn., NAACP, Urban League, Assn Comprehensive Health Planners (dir. 1975-77), Women's Aux. Medico-Chirurg. Soc., Jack and Jill Am., Century Club of Nat. Assn. Negro Bus. and Profl. Women's Clubs (pres. 1985-89), Alpha Kappa Alpha. Baptist. Clubs: Links, Carrousels (nat. v.p. 1986-88, nat. pres. 1988-90), Women's Nat. Dem. Home: 1748 Sycamore St NW Washington DC 20012-1031 Office: 5505 Fifth St NW Washington DC 20011-6513

CATTANO, CHARLES JOSEPH, physician; b. N.Y.C., Mar. 30, 1955; s. Vincent Gaetano and Diana Theresa (Dimino) C.; m. Janice Michele Schnelling, June 18, 1989; 1 child, David Vincent. BA with honors, SUNY, Binghampton, 1976; MD, SUNY, Syracuse, 1982. Diplomate Am. Bd. Internal Medicine, Gastroenterology, Nat. Bd. Med. Examiners. Asst. prof. medicine U. Pitts. Med. Ctr., 1989-91, clin. asst. prof. of medicine, 1991-97; tchg. staff Mercy Hosp., Pitts., 1991-95; cons. residency rev. com. for internal medicine, Chgo., 1988-89; med. adv. bd. Intestine Diseases Found., Pitts., 1994-96; trustee SUNY Upstate Med. Ctr., Syracuse, N.Y., 1979-82. Contbr. articles to profl. jours. Chmn., founder Ann. Pitts. Gut Club awards, 1991-95; bd. dirs. Ocean Ridge Homeowners Assn., Bethany Beach, Del., 1994—, Greenshire Homeowners Assn., Phila., 1987-89, John Hancock Bldg. Condominium Assn., Chgo., 1983-86. Komoroff prize finalist Phila. G.I. Rsch. Forum, 1988, 89. Mem. AMA (house of dels. 1990-95), Am. Coll. Physicians, Am. Coll. Gastroenterology, Am. Gastroenterology Assn., Mensa, Phi Beta Kappa. Home: 5018 Quail Roost Rd South Boston VA 24592 Office: Fuller-Roberts Clinic 2212 Wilborn Ave South Boston VA 24592

CATTELL, HEATHER BIRKETT, psychologist; b. Carlisle, eng., Dec. 16, 1936; came to U.S., 1955; d. Wilfred B. and Anne Birkett; m. Russel B. Shields, June 10, 1953 (div. 1963); children: Vaughn, Gary, Heather Luanne; m. Raymond B. Cattell, May 9, 1981. BA. U. Hawaii, 1974, MA, 1977, PhD, 1979. Lic. clin. psychologist, Hawaii. Dir. rsch. Salvation Army, Honolulu, 1979-81; pvt. practice Honolulu, 1981—; lectr., workshop leader, U.S., Australia, Can., and United Kingdom, 1989—. Author: The 16PF: Personality in Depth, 1989. Mem. Phi Beta Kappa. Office: 1188 Bishop St Ste 1702 Honolulu HI 96813-3307

CATTERALL, WILLIAM A., pharmacology, neurobiology educator; b. Providence, Oct. 12, 1946; s. William V. and Alice (Aldred) C.; m. Nancy Sharples; children: W. Douglas, Elizabeth R. BA in Chemistry, Brown U., 1968; PhD in Physiol. Chemistry, Johns Hopkins U., 1972. Postdoctoral research fellow Lab. of Biochem. Genetics NIH, Bethesda, Md., 1972-76, staff scientist, 1976-77; assoc. prof. dept. pharmacology U. Wash., Seattle, 1977-82, prof., 1982—, chmn. dept. pharmacology, 1984—, chmn. interdisciplinaty com. on neurology, 1986—; Editor Molecular Pharmacology, 1986-90; contbr. numerous articles to profl. jours. and textbooks. Editor Molecular Pharmacology, 1986-90; contbr. numerous articles to profl. jours. and textbooks. Recipient Young Scientist award Passano Found., 1981, Jacob Javits Neurosci award, NIH, 1984, 91, Basic Sci. Prize award Am. Heart Assn., 1992; numerous grants. Mem. Nat. Acad. Sci., Am. Soc. Pharmacology and Exptl. Therapeutics, Soc. for Neurosci., Am. Soc. Biol. Chemists, Neurosci. Research Program. Office: Univ Wash Dept Pharmacology Sj # 30 Seattle WA 98195

CATTERTON, MARIANNE ROSE, occupational therapist; b. St. Paul, Feb. 3, 1922; d. Melvin Joseph and Katherine Marion (Bole) Maas; m. Elmer John Wood, Jan. 16, 1943 (dec.); m. Robert Lee Catterton, Nov. 20, 1951 (div. 1981); children: Jenifer Ann Dawson, Cynthia Lea Uthus. Student, Carleton Coll., 1939-41, U. Md., 1941-42; BA in English, U. Wis., 1944; MA in Counseling Psychology, Bowie State Coll., 1980; postgrad., No. Ariz. U., 1987-91. Registered occupational therapist, Occupational Therapy Cert. Bd. Occupational therapist VA, N.Y.C., 1946-50; cons. occupational therapist Fondo del Seguro del Estado, Puerto Rico, 1950-51; dir. rehab. therapies Spring Grove State Hosp., Catonsville, Md., 1953-56; occupational therapist Anne Arundel County Health Dept., Annapolis, Md., 1967-78; dir. occupational therapy Eastern Shore Hosp. Ctr., Cambridge, Md., 1979-85; cons. occupational therapist Kachina Point Health Ctr., Sedona, Ariz., 1986; regional chmn. Conf. on revising Psychiat. Occupational Therapy Edn., 1958-59; instr. report writing Anne Arundel Community Coll., Annapolis, 1974-78. Editor Am. Jour. Occupational Therapy, 1962-67. Active Md. Heart Assn., 1959-60; mem. task force on occupational therapy Md. Dept. of Health, 1971-72; chmn. Anne Arundel Gov. Com. on Employment of Handicapped, 1959-63; mem. gov.'s com. to study vocat. rehab., Md., 1960; com. mem. Annapolis Youth Ctr., 1976-78; mem. ministerial search com. Unitarian Ch. Anne Arundel County, 1962; curator Dorchester County Heritage Mus., Cambridge, 1982-83; v.p., officer Unitarian-Universalist Fellowship Flagstaff, 1988-93; co-moderator, founder Unitarian-Universalist Fellowship of Sedona, 1994—, respite care vol., 1994—; citizen interviewer Sedona Acad. Forum, 1993, 94. Mem. P.R. Occupl. Therapy Assn. (cofounder 1950), Am. Occupl. Therapy Assn. (chmn. history com. 1958-61), Md. Occupl. Therapy Assn. (del. 1953-59), Ariz. Occupl. Therapy Assn., Pathfinder Internat., Dorchester County Mental Health Assn. (pres. 1981-84), Internat. Platform Assn., Ret. Officers Assn., Air Force Assn. (Barry Goldwater chpt., sec. 1991-92, 94-96), Severn Town Club (treas. 1965, sec. 1971-72, 94-95), Internat. Club (Annapolis, publicity chmn. 1966), Toastmasters, Newcomers (Sedona, pres. 1986), Pathfinder, Zero Population Growth, Delta Delta Delta. Republican. Home: 415 Windsong Dr Sedona AZ 86336-3745

CATZ, BORIS, endocrinologist, educator; b. Troyanov, Russia, Feb. 15, 1923; s. Jacobo and Esther (Galbmilion) C.; came to U.S., 1950, naturalized, 1955; m. Rebecca Schechter; children: Judith, Dinah, Sarah Lea, Robert. BS, Nat. U. Mexico, 1941, MD, 1947; MS in Medicine, U. So. Calif., 1951. Intern, Gen. Hosp., Mexico City, 1945-46; prof. adj., sch. medicine U. Mexico, 1947-48; research fellow medicine U. So. Calif., 1949-51, instr. medicine, 1952-54, asst. clin. prof., 1954-59, assoc. clin. prof., 1959-83, clin. prof., 1983—; pvt. practice, Los Angeles, 1951-55, Beverly Hills, Calif., 1957—; chief Thyroid Clinic Los Angeles County Gen. Hosp., 1955-70; sr. cons. thyroid clin. U. So. Calif.-Los Angeles Med. Center, 1970—; clin. chief endocrinology Cedars-Sinai Med. Ctr., 1983-87. Served to capt. U.S. Army, 1955-57. Boris Catz lectureship named in his honor Thyroid Research Endowment Fund, Cedars Sinai Med. Ctr., 1985. Fellow ACP, Am. Coll. Nuclear Medicine (pres. elect 1982), Royal Soc. Medicine; mem. AMA, AAAS, Cedars Sinai Med. Ctr. Soc. for History of Medicine (chmn.), L.A. County Med. Assn., Calif. Med. Assn., Endocrine Soc., Am. Thyroid Assn., Soc. Exptl. Biology and Medicine, Western Soc. Clin. Research, Am. Fedn. Clin. Research, Soc. Nuclear Medicine, So. Calif. Soc. Nuclear Medicine, N.Y. Acad. Scis., L.A. Soc. Internal Medicine, Collegium Salerni, Cedar Sinai Soc. of History of Medicine, Beverly Hills C. of C., Phi Lambda Kappa. Jewish. Mem. B'nai B'rith. Club: The Profl. Man's (past pres.). Author: Thyroid Case Studies, 1975, 2d edit., 1981. Contbr. numerous articles on thyroidology to med. jours. Home: 300 S El Camino Dr Beverly Hills CA 90212-4212 Office: 435 N Roxbury Dr Beverly Hills CA 90210

CAUBLE, WILBUR GRIFFIN, retired surgeon, medical missionary; b. Benedict, Kans., Oct. 25, 1912; s. William Henry and Iva May (Griffin) C.; m. Daphayne Vivian Smith, Dec. 1942; children: Judy, Jack, Steve. Attended, Baker U., 1931-32; AB, Kans. U., 1934; MD, St. Louis U., 1939. Rotating intern Kansas City (Mo.) Gen. Hosp., 1939-40, tumor and cancer resident, 1940-41; resident in surgery Norton Meml. Infirmary, Louisville, 1941-42; gen. surgeon Snyder-Jones Clinic, Winfield, Kans., 1945-46; pvt. practice Wichita, Kans., 1946-86; ret., 1986; missionary work as surgeon Ch. of Brethren, Castaner, P.R., 1965, Montero, Bolivia, 1967, Evang. Gen. Hosp., Congo, 1970, Mennonite Gen. Hosp., Taiwan, 1972, Qualien, Guatemala, 1976, Bapt. Haiti Mission, Haiti, 1986. Contbr. articles to profl. jours. Organizer Walk for Mankind, Wichita, 1969; pres. bd. dirs. East Heights Meth. Ch., Wichita. Surgeon U.S. Army, 1942-45. Recipient Citizens award First Nat. Bank of Wichita, 1987, A. Price Woodward award NCCJ, 1990. Home: 155 S Belmont Wichita KS 67218

CAUDILL, LEROY, physician; b. Concord, Mich., Mar. 25, 1954; s. Isaac Jr. and Shirley Mae (Hackworth) C.; m. Gina Lee Pobst, Aug. 12, 1978; children: Allyson, Caleb, Stuart. AB, Stephens Coll., 1980; DO, Mich. State U., 1985. Cert. Am. Bd. Emergency Medicine. Chief intern Detroit Osteo. Hosp., 1985-86; resident emergency medicine Mt. Carmel Mercy Hosp., Detroit, 1986-89, chief resident emergency medicine, 1988-89; attending physician emergency dept. Winchester (Va.) Med. Ctr., 1989—, med. dir. emergency dept., 1991—; operational med. dir. Winchester-Frederick County EMS; chmn. med. control bd. Lord Fairfax EMS Coun., Winchester;. Med. dir. Winchester Fire & Rescue Dept., Frederick County Fire & Rescue Dept. With U.S. Army, 1973. Mem. Am. Coll. Emergency Physicians, (bd. dirs. Va. chpt. 1990-93), Nat. Assn. EMS Physicians, AMA, Disabled Am. Vets., Sons Confederate Vets. Home: 781 Johnston Ct Winchester VA 22601-6718 Office: Winchester Med Ctr 1840 Amherst St Winchester VA 22601-2808

CAUDLE, JEFFREY NELSON, nurse anesthetist; b. Wadesboro, N.C., Feb. 8, 1962; s. William Nelson and Cornelia Ann (Gaddy) C.; m. Michele Kristie Seawell, May 20, 1984; 1 child, Ashton Victoria. BS in Human Svcs., Wingate Coll., 1984; BSN, U. N.C., Charlotte, 1992; MSN, U. N.C., Greensboro, 1994. Nurse anesthesia resident N.C. Bapt. Hosp.-Bowman Gray, Winston-Salem, 1994; nurse anesthetist Catawba Meml. Hosp., Hickory, N.C., 1994—; freelance nurse anesthetist Alexander Cmty. Hosp., Taylorsville, N.C., 1995—, Southeastern Eye Ctr., Hickory, 1995—. Mem. N.C. Assn. Nurse Anesthetists, Am. Assn. Nurse Anesthetists. Republican. Office: Catawba Meml Hosp Dept Anesthesia 810 Fairgrove Ch Rd Hickory NC 28602

CAULFIELD, JAMES BENJAMIN, pathologist, educator; b. Mpls., Jan. 1, 1927; s. Linus Joseph and Olive Bell (Curtis) C.; m. Virginia Walsh, Jan. 28, 1950; children: Ann, John, Clare. BA, Miami U., Oxford, Ohio, 1947; BS, U. Ill., 1948, MD, 1950. Intern Henrotin Hosp., Chgo., 1950-51; resident U. N.C., Chapel Hill, 1951-52, U. Kans. Med. Ctr., Kansas City, 1954-55; vis. investigator Rockefeller Inst., N.Y.C., 1955-56; instr. pathology Harvard U., 1959-64, asst. prof., 1964-70, assoc. prof., 1970-75; asst. pathologist Mass. Gen. Hosp., Boston, 1960-64; assoc. pathologist Mass. Gen. Hosp., 1964-75; prof., chmn. dept. pathology U. S.C., 1975-85; prof. pathology U. Ala., Birmingham, 1985—; adj. prof. Med. U. S.C., Charleston, 1981-85; rsch. on collagen network of heart and changes associated with alterations in the network. Contbr. articles to profl. jours. Served with USN, 1944-46, 52-54. Mem. Am. Soc. Cell Biology, Am. Soc. Pathology, Internat. Acad. Pathology, Fedn. Exptl. Pathology, Electron Microscopy Soc., Internat. Study Group for Heart Research (treas. Am. sect. 1972-85), N.Y. Acad. Scis., Harvard Club, Boston Athenaeum Club, Sigma Xi, Phi Eta Sigma. Office: U Ala Dept Pathology 506 Kracke Bldg 619 S 19th St Birmingham AL 35233-6823

CAUSEY, G(EORGE) DONALD, medical educator; b. Balt., July 9, 1926; s. George Hopkins and Jessie Hitchens (Webster) C.; m. Alice Sherman Meredith, Mar., 1951 (div.); 1 child, Susan Victoria; m. Linda Marie McGranahan, Jan. 15, 1961; children: Christopher, Aimee, Julia. BA, U. Md., 1950, MA, 1951; PhD, Purdue U., 1954. Asst. clinic chief Dept. Pub. Health, Washington, 1954-55; audiology clinic chief VA Med. Ctr., Washington, 1955-68, dir. auditory rsch. lab., 1968-82; rsch. prof. U. Md., College Park, 1956-80; vis. prof. audiology Syracuse U., N.Y., summer 1968; affiliate prof. engring. Colo. State U., Fort Collins, 1975-78; clin. assoc. prof. surgery Georgetown U. Med. Ctr., Washington, 1976-82; rsch. prof. Cath. U. Am., Washington, 1980-91; pres. Causey Assocs., Chevy Chase, 1987-. Author 65 jour. publs., 6 book chpts; co-inventor: 5 U.S. patents, 1977-80, 1 Brit. patent, 1980. With USN, 1944-46, PTO. Recipient rsch. grants NIH, 1961-63, VA, 1967-79, Pub. Health Svc., 1971-72, EPA, 1979. Fellow Md. Speech and Hearing Assn. (pres. 1973-74), Am. Speech, Lang., Hearing Assn.; mem. IEEE (sr.), Acoustical Soc. Am., Am. Nat. Stds. Inst. (S-3-48 com.), Sigma Xi (hon.). Presbyterian. Home: 3504 Dunlop St Chevy Chase MD 20815-5932

CAUSHAJ, PHILIP FILLOR, surgeon; b. N.Y.C., Sept. 20, 1954; s. Sam A. and Virginia V. (Cakrane) C.; m. Angela S.H. Hodja, July 11, 1976; children: Katherine Emily, Samuel Robert. BA, NYU, 1975; MD, Johns Hopkins, 1979. Diplomate Am. Bd. Surgery, Am. Bd. Surg. Critical Care, Am. Bd. Colon and Rectal Surgery. Intern and resident in surgery Columbia-Presbyn. Med. Ctr., N.Y.C., 1979-84; fellow in colon and rectal surgery Lahey Clinic, Burlington, Mass., 1984-85; assoc. prof. surgery Med. Ctr. U. Mass., Worcester, 1989—; chmn. Med. Ctr. Ctrl. Mass., Worcester, Mass., 1992—. Mem. ACS, Am. Coll. Gastroenterology, Am. Soc. Colon and Rectal Surgeons, New Eng. Soc. Colon and Rectal Surgeons, Soc. Am. Gastrointestinal Endoscopy, Soc. Am. Endoscopic Surgeons, Soc. for Surgery of the Alimentary Tract.

CAUTHORNE-BURNETTE, TAMERA DIANNE, family nurse practitioner, healthcare consultant; b. Richmond, Va., Apr. 13, 1961; d. Robert Francis Cauthorne and Lois Avery (Lloyd) Cumashot; m. William Nichols Burnette, Dec. 3, 1983. BSN, U. Va., 1983; postgrad., Med. U. S.C., 1988; MSN, Old Dominion U., 1993, grad. cert. in women's studies, 1994; postgrad., Med. Coll. Va., 1994—. RN, Va.; family nurse practitioner. Staff nurse, charge nurse gynecology-oncology unit U. Va. Med. Ctr., Charlottesville, 1983, staff nurse, charge nurse high-risk labor and delivery, ICU, 1984-85; staff nurse, charge nurse, preceptor med. ICU Med. U. S.C., 1985-87, staff nurse ICU, 1988; staff nurse, charge nurse med.-surg. ICU, progressive care Stuart Cir. Hosp., Richmond, Va., 1988-90; staff nurse pediatric and neonatal ICU Childrens' Hosp. of the King's Dau., Norfolk, Va., 1990, staff nurse, team leader neonatal ICU, 1990-91; pvt. health care cons., 1993—; with Delmar Pub., 1994—; pres. The Foxmont Co., LLC, 1995—; with Sussex Ctrl. Health Ctr., 1995; men's responsibility clinic coord. Planned Parenthood, 1996; cons. Old Dominion U. Coll. Health Scis., Sch. Nursing, 1993—, undergrad. clin. facility, 1994—; condr. analysis of Russian and Ukrainian health care system; breast self-exam instr. Am. Cancer Soc., 1982—; presenter at profl. confs.; mng. mem. The Foxmont Co., L.L.C.; mem. adj. faculty Sch. Nursing U. Va., 1996. Contbg. author for med. texts Delmar Pub.; contbr. articles to profl. jours. Vol. Ronald McDonald House, 1980-83; docent Spoleto Festival USA, 1984-92, MacArthur Meml. Mus., 1991; vol. receptionist info. ctr. Gibbes Art Gallery, 1987-89; vol. ARC Blood Donation Ctr., 1986-92; mem. U. Va. Coll. of Health Scis. Coun. Fellow Internat. Pedagogical Acad./Moswoc. Order of Omega Nat. Honor Soc.; mem. AACN, DAR, AAUW, Va. Coalition for Nurse Practitioners, U. Va. Sch. Nursing Alumnae Assn. (pres., CEO 1994—), Jr. League Va. (chair state pub. affairs com.), Virginians Patient Choice Coalition, Jr. League Norfolk and Virginia Beach (state pub. affairs vice chmn./lobbyist 1995), Daus. of Confederacy, Carolina Art Assn., S.C. Hist. Soc., Confederate Meml. Lit. Soc., U. Va. Coll. Health Scis. Coun., Alpha Delta Pi (chmn. nat. panhellenic rels. com., nat. by-laws and resolutions com.), Sigma Theta Tau.

CAVA, THOMAS JOSEPH, rehabilitation physician; b. N.Y.C., July 12, 1959. BA, Columbia Coll., 1981; MD, U. Miami Sch. Medicine, 1987. Diplomate Am. Bd. Phys. Medicine and Rehab. Intern L.I. Jewish Med. Ctr., 1987-88; resident Mount Sinai Med. Ctr., N.Y., 1989-91; attending physician Columbia Presbyn. Med. Ctr., N.Y.C., 1991-93; asst. prof. rehab. medicine Columbia Coll. of Physicians and Surgeons, N.Y.C., 1991-93; assoc. dir. rehab. medicine Total Rehab. Ctr., Cedar Grove, N.J., 1993-95; dir. rehab. medicine PC Rehab., West Orange, N.J., 1995—; internat. and nat. lectr. on clin. use of botulinum toxin (botox) and muscle disorders; mem. pain mgmt. com. Montainside Hosp., Monclair, N.J., 1995-96. Fellow Am. Acad. of Phys. Med. and Rehab.; mem. Am. Acad. of Electrodiagnostic Medicine, N.J. Soc. Phys. Medicine and Rehab. Office: PC Rehab 960 Pleasant Valley Way West Orange NJ 07052

CAVALETTI, GUIDO, neurologist; b. Milan, Feb. 27, 1959; s. Roberto and Natalina (Malinverni) C.; m. Paola Marmiroli, Sept. 30, 1990; 1 child, Federica. MD, U. Statale, Milan, 1984, specialty in neurology, 1989. Fellow Inst. Anatomia U. Statale, Milan, 1984-90; asst. neurologist S. Gerardo Hosp., Monza, Italy, 1990—; cons. Univ.-Statale, Milan, 1990—; fellow U. Tampere, Finland, 1993. Contbr. articles to profl. jours. Mem. World Fedn. of Neurology, European Assn. for Neuro-Oncology, Peripheral Nerve Soc. Office: Clinica Neurologica, Ospedale S Gerardo, V Donizetti 106, 20052 Monza Italy

CAVALIERE, LUDWIG VINCENT, physician; b. San Francisco, June 15, 1954; s. Savino Cavaliere; 3 children. MD cum laude, U. Bologna, Italy, 1985. Diplomate Am. Bd. Internal Medicine, Am. Bd. Nephrology. Intern, then resident in internal medicine The Brookdale Hosp. Med. Ctr., N.Y.C., 1985-88, fellow in nephrology, 1988-90; med. dir. dialysis Renal Treatment Ctr., Macon, Ga., 1991—; chief med. dir. dialysis Med. Ctr. Ctrl. Ga., Macon, 1994—; assoc. prof. nephrology Mercer U. Sch. Med., Macon, 1993—; pvt. practice, Macon Med. Group, 1990—. Rsch. scholar Nat. Kidney Found. N.Y., 1989. Mem. ACP, AMA, Am. Soc. Internal Medicine. Office: Macon Medical Group 657 Hemlock St Ste 200 Macon GA 31201

CAVALLARO, JOSEPH JOHN, microbiologist; b. Lawrence, Mass., Mar. 18, 1932; s. John and Salvatrice (Zappala) C.; m. Kathleen Frances Kraus, Dec. 2, 1972; children: Theresa Margaret, Sandra Marie, Elizabeth Camille, Danielle Kay, Gina Kathleen. BS, Tufts U., 1952; MS, U. Mass., 1954; PhD, U. Mich., 1966. Pub. health sanitarian Hartford (Conn.) Health Dept., 1954-55, 57-61; teaching assoc. dept. microbiology U. Mass., Amherst, 1961-62; rsch. virologist Med. Rsch. Labs., Charles Pfizer & Co., Groton, Conn., 1966-67; rsch. assoc. dept. epidemiology Sch. Pub. Health, U. Mich., Ann Arbor, 1967-70; microbiologist, diagnostic immunology tng. br. Ctrs. for Disease Control, Atlanta, 1971-86, research microbiologist anaerobic bacteria br., Ctrs. for Disease Control, 1986—; lectr. resident pathologists Grady Meml. Hosp., Atlanta, 1975; asst. prof. pathology Morehouse Sch. Medicine, 1982-85, clin. assoc. prof., 1986—; adj. asst. prof. pathology and lab. medicine Emory U. Sch. of Medicine, 1985—; cons. Pan Am. Health Orgn., Colombia and Brazil, 1976, 77. Served with M.C., AUS, 1955-57. Registered specialist microbiologist Nat. Registry Microbiologist, Am. Acad. Microbiology. Fellow Am. Acad. Microbiology; mem. Am. Soc. Microbiology, Am. Assn. Immunologists, N.Y. Acad. Sci., KC, Sigma Xi. Democrat. Roman Catholic. Prin. author/co-author over 11 lab. manuals; contbr. articles to profl. jours., chpts. to books. Home: 1325 Balsam Dr Decatur GA 30033-2905 Office: 1600 Clifton Rd Atlanta GA 30333

CAVANAGH, PETER ROBERT, science educator, researcher; b. Wolverhampton, Staffordshire, Eng., July 31, 1947; came to U.S., 1972; s. John Joseph and Dorothy Ann (Stokes) C.; m. Magda Margalova, Dec. 21, 1968 (div. 1979); 1 child, Sasha; m. Ann Elizabeth Vandervelde, Apr. 18, 1981; children: Drew, Chris, Jennifer. BEd, U. Nottingham, Loughborough Coll., 1968; PhD, U. London, Royal Free Med. Sch., 1972. Rsch. asst. Royal Free Med. Sch., London, 1968-72; asst. prof. Pa. State U., University Park, 1972-75, assoc. prof., 1975-81, prof., 1981—, disting. prof. locomotion studies, kinesiology, biobehavioral health medicine, orthopaedics, 1994—, dir. Ctr. for Locomotion Studies, 1986—; cons. U.S. Olympic Com., Colorado Springs, Colo., 1984-90, NASA, Houston, 1986—, various athletic shoe cos., U.S., Japan, Germany, 1978—; expert witness; sec. Am. Gait Lab. Accreditation Bd., 1995—. Author: The Running Shoe Book, 1980; co-author: Biomechanics and Physiology of Cycling, 1978, The Biomechanics of Running, 1990, The Foot in Diabetes: A Bibliography, 1992, The Foot in Diabetes, 1994, Prevention, Protection and Recurrence Reduction of Diabetic Neuropathic Foot Ulcers, 1994; mem. editl. bd. Posture and Gait, Foot and Ankle Internat., 1994—. Fellow Am. Coll. Sports Medicine (trustee 1987, Wolffe lectr. 1987); mem. Internat. Soc. Biomechanics (pres. 1995-97), Am. Soc. Biomechanics (pres. 1986-87, Borelli award 1994), Am. Diabetes Assn. (chmn. rsch. com. of foot coun. 1992-94), Internat. Soc. Electrophysiol. Kinesiology, Brit. Diabetic Assn., European Assn. for Study Diabetes, Aerospace Med. Soc., Am. Soc. Gravitational and Space Biology, Am. Acad. Podiatric Sports Medicine (hon.), Orthopedic Rsch. Soc. Home: 1352 Deerfield Dr State College PA 16803-2208 Office: Pa State U Ctr for Locomotion Studies University Park PA 16802

CAVANAH, STEPHEN FREDERICK WADE, endocrinologist; b. Tucson, Dec. 7, 1954; s. Denzil E. and Joan M.H. (Betteridge) C.; m. Gail L. Harrison, Aug. 2, 1984; children: Justin W., Andrew T., Travis L., Allison G. BS, U. Ky., 1979; MD, U. Louisville, 1983. Diplomate Am. Bd. Internal Medicine; lic. physician, Ky. Intern U. Louisville, 1983-84, resident, 1983-86; commd. 2d lt. USAF, 1979, advanced through grades to lt. col., 1995; chief internal medicine, cir. critical care Air Univ. Regional Hosp., Montgomery, Ala., 1986-89; endocrinology fellow Wilford Hall Med. Ctr., San Antonio, 1989-91; chief endocrinology sect. Scott USAF Med. Sctr., Scott AFB, Ill., 1991-93; physician The White House, Washington, 1993-95; clin. instr./asst. prof. Uniformed Svcs. U. of Health Scis., Bethesda, Md., 1995—. Contbr. articles to profl. jours. Cubmaster Boy Scouts Am., Burke, Va., 1994. Fellow Am. Coll. endocrinology; mem. ACP, Soc. Air Force Physicians, Soc. Uniformed Endocrinologists, Am. Assn. Clin. Endocrinologists, Phi Beta Kappa. Mem. LDS Ch. Office: NNMC/Endocrinology Divsn 8901 Wisconsin Ave Bethesda MD 20889

CAVANAUGH, DAVID A., neurosurgeon; b. Alexandria, La., Aug. 10, 1956; s. Charles J. and Eloise Wise (Gill) C.; m. Donna Burnley, June 9, 1979. BS, La. Coll., 1977; MD, La. State U., 1981. Intern La. State U., Shreveport, 1982; resident neurosurgery U.T.H.S.C., San Antonio, 1987; pvt. practice Shreveport, 1987—. Bd. dirs. Shreveport Opera; bd. govs. Univ. Club, Shreveport, 1994-96; sec. La. Soc. Neurosurgery, 1995-97; chmn. phys. medicine com. Shreveport Med. Ctr., 1994-96. Named Outstanding Young Man of Yr. Shreveport Jaycees, 1990. Republican. Baptist. Home: 509 Loch Ridge Dr Shreveport LA 71106

CAVANAUGH, FRANCES MARIE, critical care nurse; b. Troy, N.Y., Dec. 10, 1958; d. Joseph J. and Helen J. (Soldo) C. BS, Russell Sage Coll., 1981, MS, 1990. RN, N.Y.; cert. critical care registered nurse, 1990. Med.-surg. nurse Samaritan Hosp., Troy, 1981-84, staff nurse ICU and CCU, 1984-87; staff nurse med. ICU Albany (N.Y.) Med. Ctr. Hosp., 1987-89; clin. nurse specialist critical care Samaritan Hosp., Troy, 1989—. Mem. Am. Heart Assn. Mem. AACN (past pres. Capital Dist. chpt.), N.Y. State Nurses Assn. (past chpt. treas., bd. dirs.). Home: 480 10th St Troy NY 12180-1418

CAVANAUGH, JAMES HENRY, medical corporate executive, former government official; b. Orange, N.J., Mar. 3, 1937; s. James H. and Madeline Rachel (McFerren) C.; m. Esther Sally Musselman, Jan. 20, 1962; children: Elizabeth Anne, Michael Patrick. BS, Fairleigh Dickinson U., 1959; MA, U. Iowa, 1961, PhD, 1964. Asst. adminstr. Princeton (N.J.) Hosp., 1961-62; asst. prof. hosp. and health care adminstrn. U. Iowa, 1964-66; spl. asst. to surgeon gen. USPHS, 1966-67, dir. office comprehensive health planning, 1967-68; dep. asst. sec. health and sci. affairs HEW, 1969-71; staff asst. for health affairs Pres. Nixon, The White House, 1971-73, asst. dir. domestic council, 1973-74, dep. dir., 1974-75; dep. chief White House staff for Pres. Ford, 1975-76; v.p. corp. devel. Allergan Pharms., Irvine, Calif., 1977-78, sr. v.p. sci. and planning, 1978-81; spl. cons. to Pres. Reagan, 1981; pres. Allergan Internat., 1981-82, SmithKline BioSci. Labs., 1983-85, Smith Kline & French Labs. US, Phila., 1985-88, HealthCare Investment Corp.; founding bd. dirs. Marine Nat. Bank, Santa Ana Calif.; bd. dirs. Nat. Ctr. for Genome Resources, Soc. for Women's Health Rsch., MedImmune, Inc., Human Genome Scis., Inc., Magainin Pharms., Inc., Procept, Inc. Mem. bd. councilors U. So. Calif. Sch. Pharmacy; mem. Pres.'s Export Council, 1981-85; bd. dirs. Proprietary Assn., 1980-82; trustee Nat. Com. for Quality Health Care, nat. chmn. 1988; trustee emeritus Calif. Coll. Medicine; mem. nat. adv. com. Am. Refugee Com. Recipient Disting. Alumnus award U. Iowa Coll. Medicine. Mem. Am. Coll. Healthcare Execs., Am. Hosp. Assn. (hon.), Pharm. Mfrs. Assn. (bd. dirs. 1986-88), Union League Club (Phila.). Episcopalian (vestryman). Home: 554 Dorset Rd Devon PA 19333-1845 Office: Health Care Investment Corp 379 Thornall St Edison NJ 08837-2225

CAVANAUGH, PAUL FRANCIS, JR., biochemical pharmacologist; b. Rochester, N.Y., Oct. 23, 1955; s. Paul Francis and Ann Marie Cavanaugh; m. Kathleen Anne Vastola, Apr. 9, 1983; children: Anthony, Samuel. BS in Chemistry, Boston Coll., 1977; PhD in Biochem. Pharmacology, SUNY, Buffalo, 1983. Cancer rsch. scientist Roswell Park Meml. Inst., Buffalo, 1982-86; sr. rsch. investigator Eastman Kodak Co./Sterling Winthrop Inc., Malvern, Pa., 1986-92, Health Care Divsn., Procter and Gamble Co., Cin., 1992-96; vol. assoc. prof. dept. otolaryngology head and neck surgery U. Cin. Coll. of Medicine, 1993—; sr. rsch. investigator Procter & Gamble Pharms., Cin., 1996—. Mem. Am. Assn. Cancer Rsch., Am. Chem. Soc., N.Y. Acad. Sci., Rho Chi. Office: Procert & Gamble Pharms Health Care Divsn 11450 Grooms Rd Cincinnati OH 45242

CAVASINA, MARY MAGDALENE, surgeon; b. Canonsburg, Pa., Dec. 26, 1927; d. Joseph Edward and Rose (Staffen) C. BS, U. Pitts., 1948; MD, Women's Med. Coll. of Pa., 1952. Diplomate Am. Bd. Surgery. Intern Mercy Hosp., Pitts., 1952-53, resident in gen. surgery, 1953-57; teaching fellow U. Pitts., 1953-57; sr. surg. staff mem. Canonsburg Gen. Hosp., 1957-92, chief surgery, 1962-75. Asst. chief and fire surgeon Canonsburg Vol. Fire Dept. Mem. Cath. Daus. of Am., Bus. and Profl. Women's Club, Pitts. Surg. Soc., Am. Coll. Surgeons. Republican. Roman Catholic. Office: 160 W Pike St Canonsburg PA 15317-1328

CAVE, ALICE REGINA SEVERN, medical and surgical nurse; b. Balt., Mar. 11, 1942; d. Harry Anthony Sr. and Eva Marie (Beierlein) Severn; m. Harry Harrison Cave, Feb. 11, 1984. Diploma, Mercy Hosp., 1963. RN, Md., N.J. Office nurse for pvt. physician Princeton, N.J., 1968-78; staff nurse Sinai Hosp., Balt., 1978-80, City Hosp./Kings Daughters, Martinsburg, W.Va., 1980-81; asst. head nurse Sinai Hosp., Balt., 1983-85; staff nurse Nurses' Inc., Towson, 1985-92; utilization rev. specialist Blue Cross Md., Balt., 1992—. Comdr. USNR, 1964-67, 90-91. Home: 3133 Willoughby Rd Baltimore MD 21234-4731

CAVE, DOUGLAS G., healthcare services executive; b. San Diego, Sept. 24, 1958. BS in Biol. Scis., Immunology, U. Calif., Irvine, 1981; MPH, UCLA, 1984, PhD, 1987. Sr. rsch. assoc. UCLA Sch. Medicine, 1983-86; adminstrv. cons. Maxicare Health Plans, 1986-88; cons. Mercer/Nat. Med. Audit, 1988-89; practice leader, sr. cons. Hewitt Assocs., 1989-95; found, CEO, chief sci. officer Practice Patterns Sci., Maryland Heights, Mo., 1995—; spkr. in field. Quarterly columnist Today's Managed Care Market; contbr. articles to profl. jours. Rsch. grantee Nat. Ctr. Health Svcs. Rsch.; UCI Alumni scholar; recipient Outstanding Student award UCLA Alumni Assn. Office: Practice Patterns Sci 14000 Riverport Dr Maryland Heights MO 63043

CAVE, MAC DONALD, anatomy educator; b. Phila., May 14, 1939; s. Edward Joseph and Adeline Roberta (MacDonald) C.; m. Donna Kay Brainard, Jan. 1, 1989; children from previous marriage: Eric MacDonald, Heidi Lee. B.A., Susquehanna U., 1961; M.S., U. Ill., 1963, Ph.D., 1965. Instr. dept. anatomy U. Ill. Coll. Medicine, Chgo., 1964-65; asst. prof. U. Pitts. Sch. Medicine, 1967-72; assoc. prof. anatomy U. Ark. Med. Ctr., Little Rock, 1972-79, prof. anatomy, 1979—. Contbr. numerous articles to profl. jours. Am. Cancer Soc.-Swedish Am. exchange fellow, 1966; USPHS postdoctoral fellow Max Planck Inst., Tubingen, W. Ger., 1966-67. Mem. AAAS, Am. Assn. Anatomists, Am. Soc. Cell Biology, Am. Soc. for Microbiology, Sigma Xi, Pi Gamma Mu. Home: 5220 Crestwood Dr Little Rock AR 72207-5404 Office: U Ark Med Scis Dept Anatomy 4301 W Markham St Little Rock AR 72205-7101

CAVETT, CLINTON MOORE, surgeon; b. Jackson, Miss., Aug. 8, 1948. MD, U. Miss., 1973. Intern Parkland Meml. Hosp., Dallas, 1973-74; surg. resident U. Miss. Med. Ctr., Jackson, 1974-78; fellow in pediat. surgery Childrens Hosp. Nat. Med. Ctr., Washington, 1978-80; dir. pediatric surgery Med. Ctr. for Children, Roanoke, Va., 1992—. Office: Med Ctr for Children 102 Highland Ave SE # 435 Roanoke VA 24013

CAVONIUS, CARL RICHARD, physiology educator; b. Santa Barbara, Calif., Dec. 23, 1932; came to W. Ger., 1977; s. Carl Volmar and Lillie (Vertti) C.; m. Rita Catherine Euerle, July 11, 1981; 1 child, Lillie. BA, Wesleyan U., 1953; MS, Brown U., 1960, PhD, 1961. Chartered psychologist, U.K. Sr. rsch. scientist Human Scis. Rsch., McLean, Va., 1962-64; dir. Eye Rsch. Found., Bethesda, Md., 1965-70; prof. U. Munich, Fed. Republic Germany, 1971-72; Cattell fellow U. Cambridge, Eng., 1972-73; sr. sci. officer U. Amsterdam, Netherlands, 1974-76; prof. physiology Inst. Arbeitsphysiologie, U. Dortmund, Fed. Republic Germany, 1977—; dir. Inst. Pedestrian Res., Grantchester, U.K., 1974—; contbr. numerous articles to sci. jours. Served to lt. comdr. 1954-59. USPHS fellow, 1961, Humboldt fellow, 1971, Cattell fellow, 1973; European Sci. Found. grantee, 1983. Fellow Am. Psychol. Soc., Optical Soc. Am.; mem. Exptl. Psychology Soc., European Brain and Behavior Soc., Human Factors Soc., Res. Officers Assn. (v.p. Europe 1983). Home: Altenderner Strasse 117, D-44329 Dortmund Germany Office: Inst Arbeitsphysiologie, Ardeystrasse 67, D-44139 Dortmund Germany

CAVUOTI, CLINTON PETER, JR., internist; b. Glen Cove, N.Y., May 17, 1953; s. Clinton Peter and Olga M. (Forlano) C.; m. Katherine Michiel Head, Aug. 21, 1982; 1 child, Whitney Ryan. BA in Biology, Johns Hopkins U., 1975; MD, Southwestern Med. Sch., 1979. Intern, then resident San Antonio, 1979-82; internist Abilene (Tex.) Diagnostic Clinic, 1982—. Office: Abilene Diagnostic Clinic 1150 N 18th # 300 Abilene TX 79601

CAWLEY, JAMES FRANCIS, physician assistant; b. Altoona, Pa., Sept. 11, 1948; s. Francis James and Anne (Jarkiewicz) C.; m. Roberta Mary Hall, Oct. 4, 1974 (dec. Feb. 1984); children: Patrick Benjamin, Andrea Beth; m. Suzanne Davidson, July 12, 1985; 1 child, Patti Gerhardt. BA in history, polit. sci., St. Francis Coll., 1970; BS, Touro Coll., 1974; MPH, Johns Hopkins U., 1979; postgrad., George Washington U. Cert. PA-C; lic. PA, Md. Asst. prof., clin. coord. PA Program Health Scis. Ctr. SUNY, Stony Brook, 1975-76; instr. Johns Hopkins U., Balt., 1976-79; assoc. prof. health care scis. George Washington U., Washington, 1981—; lectr. in medicine Yale U. Sch. Medicine, 1979-81; cons.Assn. Acad. Health Ctrs., Washington, 1993-95, Bur. Health Professions, Rockville, Md., 1992-95; mem. Coun. Grad. Med. Edn., Rockville, 1994—, Nat. Adv. Com. Nursing Edn. and Prodn. Author: (with G.E. Schaft) Physician Assistants in a Changing Health Care Environment, 1987; contbr. articles to profl. jours. Recipient Marriott/Charles Letourneau Student Rsch. Paper of Yr. award Am. Acad. Med. Adminstrs., 1992. Fellow. Am. Acad. Physician Assistants, Md. Acad. Physician Assts. (pres. 1989-91, chair legis. affairs com. 1992—, Physician Yr. award 1992); mem. Physician Asst. Found. (pres. 1987-91). Democrat. Roman Catholic. Office: George Washington U 2300 I St NW Washington DC 20037

CAWOOD, CHARLES DAVID, urologist; b. Lexington, Ky., May 22, 1937; s. Charles David and Helen Elizabeth (Rinke) C.; m. Susan Ruth O'Dell, June 10, 1962 (dec. July 1986); children: Todd Christopher, Amy Elizabeth; m. Charlotte Dee Barton, June 18, 1988; children: Elizabeth Ann Maddeaux, Scott Edward Maddeaux. BS cum laude, U. Ky., 1957; MD, U. Louisville, 1961. Diplomate Am. Bd. Urology. Intern St. Joseph's Infirmary, Louisville, 1961-62; urology resident Baylor Coll. of Medicine, 1964-68, instr. divsn. of urology, 1968-71, asst. clin. prof., 1971-83; assoc. chief of urology Ben Taub Gen. Hosp., 1968-72; chief or urology St. Luke's Episcopal Hosp., Tex. Med. Ctr., 1991-94; assoc. clin. prof., dept. urology Baylor Coll. of Medicine; active staff St. Luke's Episcopal Hosp., The Meth. Hosp.; cons. staff Tex. Children's Hosp., Ben Taub Gen. Hosp., VA Hosp.; presenter in field; cons. Am. Cystoscope Makers Inc./Baxter, 1981-84, Advanced Clin. Products, 1988-90, N.Am. Med., 1994—. Contbr. articles to profl. jours.; patentee in field. Mem. AMA, Harris County Med. Soc., Houston Urologic Soc., Am. Urol. Assn. (south ctrl. sect.), Tex. Assn. of Genitourinary Surgeons, Phi Beta Kappa. Office: Houston Urologic Assn 6560 Fannin Blvd Houston TX 77030

CAWTHON, AUBREY MARTIN, physician assistant; b. Nashville, Tenn., May 15, 1951; s. Aubrey Martin and Lillian (Dorris) C.; m. Rebecca Susan Potts, June 12, 1980; children: Rebecca Courtney, Aubrey Martin III. BS in Biology, Middle Tenn. State U., 1974; BS, physicians asst. cert., Trevecca Nazarene Coll., 1980. Cert. physicians asst., Tenn. Physicians asst., family medicine and gen. surgery Dr. John Derryberry and Dr. Henry Feldhaus, Shelbyville, Tenn., 1980-90; physicians asst., occupl. medicine Saturn Corp., Maury Regional Hosp., Springhill, Tenn., 1990-93, Clarksville Occupl. Health Specialist, 1993-95; physicians asst., ptnr. Northside Urgent Care Ctr., Shelbyville, 1995—; physicians asst. family and occupl. medicine Dr. Sam Sells, Occupl. and Corp. Health Svcs., Shelbyville, 1995—; bd. advisors Bedford Home Health Agy., Shelbyville, 1988; adv. bd. Trevecca Nazarene Coll. Physicians Asst. Program, Nashville, 1990-93. Fellow Tenn. Acad. of Physicians Assts. (pres. 1990, 92, bd. dirs. 1988-93, treas. polit. action com. 1991—), Am. Acad. of Physicians Assts.; mem. Am. Acad. of Physician Assts. in Occupl. Medicine. Home: 101 Tee Pee Ln Shelbyville TN 37160 Office: Occupl and Corp Health Svcs Dr Sam Sells 1701 N Main Ste A Shelbyville TN 37160

CAWTHON, DARLENE, laboratory director; b. Chgo., Mar. 4, 1956; d. Thomas and Gilda (Guido) DeMay; m. Philip Lee Cawthon, May 24, 1975; 1 child, Jeremy Lee. BS, Ea. Ill. U., 1977. Med. technologist, Ill., Ind. Med. technologist St. Francis, Litchfield, Ill., 1977-81; med. technologist Meml. Hosp., Carbondale, Ill., 1981-86, microbiology supr., 1983-86; med. technologist St. Vincent Hosp., Indpls., 1986-87; lab. supr. Westview Hosp., Indpls., 1987-89; lab. mgr. Margaret Mary Cmty. Hosp., Batesville, Ind., 1989-92; lab. dir. Anderson Hosp., Maryville, Ill., 1992—. Mem. Clin. Lab. Mgmt. Assn. Republican. Lutheran. Home: 514 Riggin Rd Troy IL 62294 Office: Anderson Hospital Rt 162 Maryville IL 62062

CAWTHORN, ROBERT ELSTON, health care executive; b. Masham, Eng., Sept. 28, 1935; came to U.S., 1982; s. Gerald P. and Gertrude E. (Longster) C.; m. H. Susan Marshall, Jan. 15, 1960; children: Amanda, Liza. BA in Agriculture, Cambridge U., 1959. Various exec. positions Pfizer, Inc., Can., Africa, Mid. East and Europe, 1961-79; pres. Biogen S.A., Geneva, 1979-82, Rorer Internat., Fort Washington, Pa., 1982-83; exec. v.p. Rorer Group, Inc., 1982-84, pres., 1985-85, pres., chief exec. officer, 1985-86, chmn., chief exec. officer, from 1986; CEO Rhône-Poulenc Rorer, Inc. (formerly Rorer Group, Inc.), Collegeville, Pa., 1988-95; chmn. Rhone-Poulenc Rorer, Inc. (formerly Rorer Group, Inc.), Collegeville, Pa., 1988-95, chmn. bd. dirs., 1995-96, chmn. emeritus, 1996—; bd. dirs. Sun Co. Inc., Vanguard Group Investment Cos., Westinghouse Elec. Corp.; chmn. Fisons plc. Bd. dirs. United Way Southeastern Pa., trustee, 1985; bd. dirs. Greater Phila. 1st. corp., 1986-95, World Affairs Coun. Pa., 1986-90, Internat. Bus. Forum, chmn., 1987-89; trustee The Baldwin Sch., 1984-86, U. Pa., 1992—; bd. trustees U. Pa. Med. Ctr. Sch. Medicine, mem. exec. com., bd. overseers. Mem. Pharm. Mfrs. Assn. (bd. dirs. 1985-94), Greater Phila. C. of C. (bd. dirs. 1987—). Home: 50 Crosby Brown Rd Gladwyne PA 19035-1513 Office: Rhone-Poulene Rorer Inc 500 Arcola Rd Collegeville PA 19426-3930

CAWVEY, CLARENCE EUGENE, physician; b. Du Quoin, Ill., May 16, 1929; s. Clarence Eli and Lois Jane (Matheny) C.; m. Paulina Isabel Hincke, Sept. 12, 1953 (dec. Apr. 1973); children: Janet Edna, William Clarence, Paulina Ann, Jean Hincke; m. Linda Mae Rice, Jan. 26, 1974. BA, Yale U., 1951; MD, U. Chgo., 1955. Diplomate Am. Bd. Family Practice. Intern Cook County Hosp., 1955-56; resident in psychology Brrok Army Hosp., 1956-57; ptnr. Pickneyville (Ill.) Med. Group, 1958—; clin. asst. prof. Med. Sch. So. Ill. U., Springfield, 1976—, mem. adv. com. continuing med. edn., 1977—; dir., mem. exec. com. Ctrl. Ill. Profl. Rev. Orgn., Champaign, 1988—; bd. dirs., chmn. First Nat. Bank, Pinckneyville. Founding mem., pres. Perry County Health Dept., Pinckneyville, 1970. Capt. U.S. Army, 1956-58. Fellow Am. Acad. Family Physicians; mem. AMA, Ill. State Med. Soc. (del. 1960-70), Perry County Med. Soc. Republican. Methodist. Home: 204 W Laurel St Pinckneyville IL 62274 Office: Pinckneyville Med Group 206 N Main St Pinckneyville IL 62274

CAYEN, MITCHELL NESS, biochemist; b. Montreal, Quebec, Can., Nov. 6, 1938; came to U.S., 1984; s. Benjamin and Herzelle (Ness) Cohen; m. Liliane Hoffman, Mar. 14, 1967 (div.); children: Ilene, Barry; m. Judy Rajczyk, Jan. 17, 1987; 1 child, Reuben. PhD, McGill U., 1965. Assoc. dir. drug metabolism Wyeth-Ayest Rsch., Princeton, N.J., 1984-89; sr. dir. drug metabolism and pharmacokinetics Schering-Plough Rsch. Inst., Kenilworth, N.J., 1989—; chmn. Gordon Rsch. Conf. on Drug Metabolism, 1985. Mem. editl. bd. Xenobiotica, 1985—, Chirality, 1993—, Drug Metabolism Revs., 1995—; contbr. over 100 articles to profl. jours. Fellow AAAS, Am. Assn. Pharm. Scientists, Coun. Arteriosclerosis, Am. Heart Assn.; mem. Internat. Soc. Study Xenobiotics (pres. 1992-93), Pharm. Mfrs. Assn. (exec. com.

1987-91, steering com. 1995-98). Home: 98 Autumn Ridge Rd Bedminster NJ 07921-1849 Office: 2015 Galloping Hill Rd Kenilworth NJ 07033-1310

CAYETANO, CECILIA LIM, physician; b. Batangas, Philippines, Nov. 22, 1941; d. Lim Hua Molina Bartolome and Maria (Torralba) Bago; m. Manuel Luna Cayetano, Apr. 22, 1962; children: Francisco, Cecille, Manuel, Jr., Juliana, Michael. Diploma in Medicine summa cum laude, Far Eastern Univ., Manila, Diploma in Medicine Proper with honors, 1965. Med. prof. Far Eastern U., Manila, 1965-68; med. dir. Cayetano Med. Clinic, Ipil, Philippines, 1968-71, Ibaan, 1971—; co. physician Phil Knitting Mills, Ibaan, 1971-91, Bestnet, Rosario, 1971-91, Monterey Farms, Quilo, Branches, 1971-90. Mem. United Way Philippines, Girl Scouts of the Philippines, Kapwa ko, Mahal ko. Mem. Philippine Med. Assn., Batangas Med. Assn. (councilor 1979-80), Philippine Hosp. Assn., Family Physicians of the Philippines. Home: 4230 Ibaan/Batangas The Philippines

CEASOR, AUGUSTA CASEY, medical technologist, microbiologist; b. Birmingham, Ala., Feb. 22, 1943; d. Augustus and Willie Mae (Stubbs) C. AS, SUNY, 1981; BS, So. Ill. U., 1981. Cert. clin. lab. scientist Nat. Cert. Agy. Lab. asst. Mt. Sinai Hosp., Miami Beach, Fla., 1967-68; lab. technician Coordinated Lab. Svcs., Jamaica, N.Y., 1969-71; med. technician Andrew Radar U.S. Army Health Clinic, Ft. Myer, Va., 1972-76; med. technologist Armed Forces Inst. Pathology, Washington, 1976-91, Dept. Army, Mil. Dist. Wash., Fort Myer, Va., 1991—; sci. fair judge Am. Soc. Microbiology, Washington, 1988—; high sch. sci. mentor Minority Women in Sci., 1989—; speaker to profl. groups. Mem. editorial bd. Metroscope Newsletter, 1985—, editor, 1989—; tech. asst. Mycobacteriology Rsch., 1985-90. Active minority alumni scholarship com. So. Ill. U., Carbondale, Ill., 1981—; mem. Montgomery Knolls Community Assn., Silver Spring, Md., 1983—, v.p., chairperson safety & environ. com., 1984-85. Recipient Cert. of Meritorious Svc., 1991, Performance award, 1987, 89, 93, 95. Fellow Alpha Mu Tau (scholarship com. 1995—); mem. Am. Soc. Clin. Lab. Sci. (minority forum sec. 1994-96), Am. Soc. Med. Tech. (mem. Region II Coun. 1986-93, Region II microbiology chair 1988-89, Region II mem. chair 1990-93, Cert. of Recognition 1990), D.C. Soc. Med. Tech. (profl. and pub. rels. chair 1985-86, 92-93, program com. chair 1986-87, pres. 1987-88, microbiology chair 1988-89, awards chair 1988—, Svc. award 1989, Mem. of Yr. 1989-90, Past Pres. award 1988, Disting. Svc. award 1991, Profl. Achievement award in Microbiology 1994), Capital Area Soc. for Clin. Lab. Sci. (pres.-elect 1995-96). Democrat. Roman Catholic. Home: 9114 September Ln Silver Spring MD 20901-3705

CEBRYNSKI, KEVIN BRIAN, dentist, prosthodontist; b. Anaheim, Calif., July 16, 1965; s. Stephen and Rose Violetta (Bursciuk) C.; m. Jane Elizabeth Chrisco, July 22, 1989; 1 child, Brian Christopher. BA in Biology, Calif. State U., Fullerton, 1988; DDS, U. Tenn., 1992; cert. prostodontics, Med. Coll. Ga., 1994. Resident Med. Coll. Ga., Augusta, 1992-94; pvt. practice Scottsdale, Ariz., 1994—; prosthodontic advisor Greater Scottsdale Dental Seminars, 1995-96; lectr. in field. Mem. ADA, Am. Coll. Prosthodontists (Undergrad. Achievement award 1992), Acad. Osseointegration, Am. Acad. Implant Dentistry, Acad. for Sports Dentistry, Ariz. State Dental Assn., Ctrl. Ariz. Dental Soc., Scottsdale Sunrise Rotary. Office: 10752 N 89th Pl Ste 214 Scottsdale AZ 85260

CECCARELLI, FRANK E., urologist; b. Bronx, Aug. 29, 1927; s. Frank E. and Agnes Fowler (Haddock) C.; m. Mary C., Oct. 4, 1930; children: Nance, Joan. BA, Bowdoin Coll., 1951; MD, NYU, 1951. Intern Yale U., New HAven, Conn., 1951-52, resident, 1952-53; resident Brooke Hosp., San Antonio, 1957-60; chief resident San Antonio Hosp.; urologist Castle Med. Ctr., Kailua, Hawaii, 1973-89; med. dir. Castle Med. Ctr., Hawaii, 1989—; vis. surgeon Kyungi-do Provincial Hosp., Inchon, Korea, 1954-55; vis. urologist Robert B. Green Meml. Hosp., San Antonio, 1960-63, Clinica Raymondo, R.P., 1963-66, Childrens Hosp., Honolulu, 1967-71, Kaiser Permanente Hosp., Honolulu, 1967-71, St. Francis Hosp., Honolulu, 1967-71; presenter, guest speaker and cons. in field. Contbr. articles to profl. jours. Col. U.S. Army, 1953-73. Decorated Purple Heart, Bronze Star, Meritorious Svc. medal, Legion of Merit. Mem. AMA, Am. Urological Assn. (south ctrl. sect., western sect.), Am. Acad. Pediatrics, Am. Coll. Physician Execs., Northwestern Urological Assn., Pan Pacific Surg. Assn., Hawaiian Urological Assn., Tri-County Urological Assn., San Antonio Urological Assn., San Antonio Surg. Assn., Soc. Internat. Urologists, Soc. Pediatric Urology, Isthmian Med. Soc., Urologists Corr. Club, Soc. Panama Urologists, Soc. Urologists Chile, Govt. Svcs. Urological Soc. Office: Castle Med Ctr Ulukahiki St Kailua HI 96734

CEFALO, ROBERT CHARLES, obstetrician, gynecologist; b. Boston, 1933. MD, Tufts U., 1959. Diplomate Am. Bd. Ob.-Gyn. Intern Chelsea Naval Hosp., Boston, 1959-60; resident in ob.-gyn. U.S. Naval Hosp., Oakland, Calif., 1961-64; prof. U. N.C. Med. Sch., Chapel Hill, N.C. Mem. ACOG, AMA, SGI. Office: U NC Med Sch 214 Macknider Chapel Hill NC 27514*

CEGLAREK, JOHN PETER, physician; b. Bay City, Mich., Apr. 10, 1947; s. Wallace John and Jeanette Agnes (Piotrowski) C.; divorced; children: Katherine Joan, John Alexander; divorced; 1 child, Jozsef Andrew. BA with high distinction, Wayne State U., 1974, MD, 1983; MPH, U. Mich., 1975. Diplomate Nat. Bd. Med. Examiners. Resident in family practice Providence Hosp., Southfield, Mich., 1987; staff physician emergency medicine North Detroit Gen. Hosp., 1987, med. dir., 1987-88; staff physician MED STOP, Sterling Heights, Mich., 1988-89; med. dir. North Detroit Gen. Hosp., 1987-88, Eleven Oaks Med. Ctr., Madison Heights, Mich., 1988-89; staff physician Madison Cmty. Hosp., Madison Heights, Mich., 1989; pvt. practice Madison Heights, Mich., 1989-91, Midland, Mich., 1991; pvt. practice Oakland County Dept. Helath, Warren, Mich., 1992—; cons. epidemiologist Oaklnad County Dept. Health, Pontiac, Mich., 1977. Maj. M.C., USAR, 1985—. Mem. AMA, Am. Acad. Family Practice, Mich. State Med. Soc., Macomb County Med. Soc., Assn. Mil. Surgeons U.S., Res. Officers Assn., Wayne State U. Alumni Assn., U. Mich. Alumni Assn., Detroit Zool. Soc.,Cranbrook Inst. Sci., Phi Beta Kappa. Home: 3924 Amherst Royal Oak MI 48073-6451 Office: 2539 12 Mile Rd Warren MI 48092-5648

CEKANSKI, ADAM ALEXANDER, obstetrician-gynecologist; b. Cracow, Poland, Oct. 22, 1921; s. Jacob and Hedwig (Kleczkowska) C.; m. Hedwig Malczyk, Feb. 20, 1950 (div. 1972); children: Katherine, Adam; m. Danuta Czekalowska, May 19, 1973; 1 child, Joanna Elizabeth. Diploma, Jagiellonian U., Cracow, 1949, MD, 1952; postgrad., U. Liverpool, Eng., 1965. Surgery asst. Mcpl. Hosp., Mikolow, Poland, 1949-51; gynecology asst. II dept. ob-gyn. Bytom Sch. Medicine, U. Katowice, Poland, 1951-68; asst. prof. Bytom Sch. Medicine, U. Katowice, Bytom, Poland, 1969; head dept. pregnancy pathology Bytom Sch. Medicine, U. Katowice, Poland, 1972-79, prof. extraordin, 1984, prof. ordin., 1987; head IV dept. ob-gyn. tech. sch. medicine Tychy, Sch. Medicine U. Katowice, 1979-92; cons. Miners Ctr. Hosp., Rwy. Regional Hosp., Katowice, Poland, 1993—; cons. Nat. Specialist Coun., Warsaw, Poland, 1985; lectr. Postgrad. Midwives Sch., Bytom, 1954-65, emeritus, 1993. Author: Obstetrical Nursing, 1961, Socioeconomical Factors, 1984; contbr. articles to profl. publs. Mem. Polish Underground Army, 1943-45. Recipient Polonia Restituta award, 1981, Nat. Edn. Medalion, 1982, Merit Tchr. award, 1983. Mem. Polish Acad. Medicine, Polish Gynecol. Soc. (v.p. 1991-94), Polish Family Planning Soc. (presidium mem.). Home: Estreicher Str 1/4, 41-902 Bytom Poland Office: Gornicze Centrum Medyczne, Dept Gynecology-Katowice, Ochojec ul Ziolowa 45, 40-100 Tychy Poland

CEKAUSKAS, CYNTHIA DANUTE, social worker; b. Detroit, Mar. 24, 1954; d. Vladas Algimantas and Isabel Gana (Stasiulis) C. BA in Sociology, Madonna Coll., Livonia, Mich., 1976; MSW, U. Mich., 1979. Bd. cert. social worker, La.; lic. clin. social worker, Fla. Psychiat. social worker Charity Hosp. New Orleans, 1982-84; social worker child and adolescent svc. DePaul Hosp., New Orleans, 1986-87; social worker, family advocacy programmgr. Army Cmty. Svcs., Friedberg, Fed. Republic Germany, 1988-89; social worker, mgr. family adv. program, chmn. family adv. case mgmt. team Cmty. Counseling Ctr., Camp Zama, Japan, 1989-90; social worker, exceptional family mem. program mgr. Army Cmty. Svcs., Bamberg, Germany, 1990-91; alt. family adv., on-call crisis counselor Desert Storm Army Cmty. Svcs., Bamberg, Fed. Republic Germany, 1990-91; social worker, family advocacy rep., head dept. family adv. Naval Med. Clinic, New Orleans, 1991-96; presenter child abuse prevention Bad Nauheim Elem. Sch., 1988-89. Contbr. articles to newspapers. Hosp. corpsman USN, 1979-82. Recipient Customer Svc. award Giessen Mil. Cmty., 1988-89, Friend Bad Nauheim Elem. Sch. award, 1989, commendation for exceptional svc. Cam Zama, 1990, Scroll of Appreciation for Desert Storm/Desert Shield, Bamberg, Germany, 1990-91, Outstanding Performance award, 1993, 94, Presdl. Sports Award for racewalking, 1996, for aerobic dance, 1996. Mem. NAFE, NASW, NOW, Acad. Cert. Social Workers, Federally Employed Women, New Orleans Track Club, Greater New Orleans Runners' Assn., Am. Racewalk Assn., Nat. Audubon Soc. Democrat. Roman Catholic. Home: 102 Amy Ln Sunny Hills FL 32428

CELESIA, GASTONE GUGLIELMO, neurologist, neurophysiologist, researcher; b. Genoa, Italy, Nov. 22, 1933; came to U.S., 1959, naturalized, 1970; s. Raffaele Amadeo and Ottavia (Tortrino) C.; m. Linda Irene Pike, Aug. 1, 1964; children—Gloria, Laura. M.D., U. Genoa, 1959; M.S., McGill U., Montreal, 1965. Diplomate Am. Bd. Psychiatry and Neurology in Neurology, Am. Bd. Psychiatry and Neurology in Clin. Neurophysiology. Intern Madison Gen. Hosp., Wis., 1960; fellow neurophysiology U. Wis., Madison, 1960-62, asst. prof. neurology, 1966-69, assoc. prof., 1970-73, prof., 1974-79, 1979-83; resident in neurology Montreal Neurol. Inst./McGill U., Montreal, Que., Can., 1962-66; chief neurology service VA Hosp., Madison, 1979-83; chmn. dept. neurology Loyola U., Chgo., 1983—. Editor in chief: Electroenceph. Clin. Neurophysiol.; contbr. articles to profl. jours. Fellow Am. Acad. Neurology; mem. AMA, Am. EEG Soc., Am. Acad. Clin. Neurophychol. (pres. 1993-95), Am. Neurol. Assn., Ctrl. Assn. EEG Wis. Neurol. Soc. Wis. Med. Alumni Assn., Wis. Neurol. Soc., Soc. Neurosci., Am. Epilepsy Soc., N.Y. Acad. Scis. AAAS, Sigma Xi. Office: Loyola Univ-Chgo Dept Neurology 2160 S First Ave Maywood IL 60153-3304

CELLI, BARTOLOME ROMULO, internist; b. Valencia, Venezuela. Dec. 17, 1946; came to U.S., 1970; s. Romulo and Dinorah (Croquer) C.; m. Doris Cruz; children: Doris Lucia, Natalia Dinorah Maria Gabriela, Romulo Alberto. BS, La Salle U., Caracas, Venezuela, 1964; MD, Cen. U., Caracas, 1971. Diplomate Am. Bd. Internal Medicine, Am. Bd. Pulmonary Diseases, Am. Bd. Critical Care Medicine. Intern St. Vincent Hosp., Worcester, Mass., 1971-72; resident Boston City Hosp., 1972-75; mem. pulmonary medicine staff Boston U. Med. Ctr., 1975-77; chief pulmonary and intensive care units Coromoto Hosp., Maracaibo, Venezuela, 1977-82; staff physician Boston City and Univ. Hosp., 1982—; adj. asst. prof. Boston U. Sch. Med., 1982, assoc. prof., 1988—; prof. medicine Tufts U., Boston, 1995—; dir. pulmonary physiology Boston City and Univ. Hosp., 1983—; chief pulmonary sect. Boston V.A. Med. Ctr., 1987-94; chief pulmonary/critical care sect. St. Elizabeth's Med. Ctr. Contbr. articles to med. jours. Recognition award AMA, 1983. Fellow Am. Coll. Chest Physicians; mem. Am. Thoracic Soc., Am. Fedn. Clin. Research, Am. Physiol. Soc. Roman Catholic. Office: 31 River Glen Rd Wellesley MA 02181-1626

CELMER, VIRGINIA, psychologist; b. Detroit, June 26, 1945; d. Charles and Stella (Kopicko) C. BA in English, Marygrove Coll., 1968; MA in Theological Studies, St. Louis U., 1977; PhD in Counseling Psychology, Tex. Tech. U., 1986. Lic. psychologist; lic. chem. dependency counselor; cert. diplomate in managed care; cert. alcoholism and drug abuse counselor; internat. cert. alcoholism and drug abuse counselor; cert. group psychotherapist. Chaplain Mercy Ctr. for Health Care Svcs., Aurora, Ill., 1977-81; grad. asst. counselor U. Counseling Ctr., Tex. Tech. U., Lubbock, 1982-86, pre-doctoral intern in counseling psychology, 1985-86; post-doctoral intern Consultation Ctr., San Antonio, 1986-89, staff psychologist, 1989-90; pvt. practice psychologist San Antonio, 1989—; instr. dept. psychology Tex. Tech. U., Lubbock, 1981-85, Oblate Sch. Theology, San Antonio, 1989-90. Contbr. articles to profl. jours. Mem. APA, Tex. Psychol. Assn. Bexar County Psychol. Assn., Am. Group Psychotherapy Assn., San Antonio Group Psychotherapy Assn., Nat. Assn. Alcoholism and Drug Abuse Counselors, Tex. Assn. Alcoholism and Drug Abuse Counselors, Leadership Conf. Women Religious (region XII), Intercongregational Leadership Group San Antonio. Office: 1603 Babcock Rd Ste 270 San Antonio TX 78229-4750

CEMAJ, SAMUEL, surgeon; b. Mexico City, Feb. 11, 1956; s. Jose and Rosa (Katz) C.; m. Shirley Cassab, June 16, 1985; children: Alexander Benjamin, Salomon Alan, Sophie Leyla. MD, Nat. Autonomous U. Mexico, Mexico City, 1980. Diplomate Am. Bd. Gen. Surgery. Pregrad. intern IMSS/Mexicali B.C., Baja, Calif., 1978; social worker Nutricion Hosp., Mexico City, 1979-80; postgrad. intern IMSS Social Security Hosp., Queretaro, 1980-81; resident gen. surgery Centro Medico La Raza, Mexico City, 1981-84; pvt. practice Clinica 26 IMSS, Mexico City, 1984-86; fellow transplant surgery U. Pitts., 1986-89; resident gen. surgery Cedars-Sinai Med. Ctr., L.A., 1989-90; resident gen. surgery Loma Linda (Calif.) U. Med. Ctr., 1990-93, fellow trauma critical care, 1993-94; pvt. practice ABC Hosp., Mexico City, 1994—. Fellow Internat. Coll. Surgeons; mem. Soc. Critical Care. Jewish. Office: 745-701, Avenida de las Palmas, Mexico City 11000, Mexico

CENSITS, RICHARD JOHN, healthcare company executive; b. Allentown, Pa., May 20, 1937; s. Stephen A. and Theresa M. Censits; m. Linda A. Malin, June 21, 1958; children: Debra, Mark, David. BS in Econs., U. Pa., 1958; MBA, Lehigh U., 1964. Sr. auditor Arthur Andersen & Co., 1958-62; mgr. acctg. Air Products & Chems., 1962-64; contr. Hamilton Watch Co., Lancaster, Pa., 1964-69; v.p., contr. IU Internat., Phila., 1969-75; v.p., CFO Campbell Soup Co., Camden, N.J., 1975-86; CEO, chmn. MedQuist Inc., Marlton, N.J., 1986-95, also bd. dirs.; bd. dirs. Checkpoint Sys., Inc., Energy North Inc., MedQuist Inc. Mem. undergrad. adv. bd. Wharton Sch., U. Pa.; health sys. trustee U. Pa.; trustee U. Pa. Mem. Atlantic City Country Club, The Club of Pelican Bay. Home and Office: 688 Annemore Ln Naples FL 34108

CENTURION, OSMAR ANTONIO, cardiologist; b. Asuncion, Paraguay, Dec. 2, 1958; s. Felipe Antonio and Aurora (Alcaraz) C.; m. Angelica Helga Neumann, Jan. 2, 1982; children: Gabriela, Elizabeth, Patricia Raquel, Karen Aurora, Veronica Arami. MD, Asuncion Univ. Sch. Medicine, 1983; PhD in Cardiology, Nagasaki U. Sch. Medicine, 1994. Med. diplomate. Resident in internal medicine Asuncion Univ. Hosp., Paraguay, 1984-87, chief of emergency duty guard, 1987-88; staff, dept. cardiology Asuncion Univ. Hosp., 1994—; staff ICU Sanatorio Migone-Battilana, Asuncion, 1987-89; postgrad. fellow in cardiology Nagasaki U. Hosp., Japan, 1989-94. Contbr. articles to profl. jours. F. Recipient scholarship AFS, 1976-77, Ministry of Edn. of Japan, 1989-94. Fellow Am. Coll. Angiology, European Soc. Cardiology; mem. AAAS, Japanese Circulation Soc., Am. Soc. Echocardiography. Roman Catholic. Home: Trejo y Sanabria 1657, Asuncion Paraguay Office: Sanatorio San Martin, Av Rca Argentina/Encarnacion, Asuncion Paraguay

CERAMI, ANTHONY, biochemistry educator; b. Newark, Oct. 3, 1940; s. Anthony and Hazel (Kirk) C.; m. Helen Vlassara, May 1, 1981; children: Carla, Ethan. B.S., Rutgers U., 1962; Ph.D., Rockefeller U., 1967. Asst. prof. biochemistry Rockefeller U., N.Y.C. 1969-72, assoc. prof., 1972-78, prof., 1978-91, head lab. med. biochemistry, 1972-91, dean grad. and postgrad. studies, 1986-91; pres. Picower Inst. for Med. Rsch., 1991—. Editor Jour. Exptl. Medicine, 1981-93. Recipient Abbott Laboratories award Am. Society for Microbiology, 1994. Mem. NAS, AAAS, Am. Soc. Pharmacology and Exptl. Therapeutics, Am. Soc. Biochemistry and Molecular Biology, Am. Diabetes Assn., Internat. Diabetes Fedn., N.Y. Acad. Sci., Clin. Immunology Soc., Am. Assn. for Cancer Rsch., N.Y. Biotech. Assn., Protein Soc., Juvenile Diabetes Found. Internat., Am. Aging Assn., Am. Assn. Immunologists, Am. Chem. Soc., Am. Fedn. for Aging Rsch., Internat. Cytokine Soc., Internat. Endotoxin Soc. Home: Ram Island Dr Shelter Island NY 11964*

CEREGHINO, JAMES JOSEPH, health facility administrator, neurologist; b. Portland, Oreg., Oct. 27, 1937; s. Joseph Thomas and Amelia E. (Arata) C. BS, Portland State Coll., 1959; MD, U. Oreg., 1964; MS in Neurophysiology, Linfield U., 1971. Intern Good Samaritan Hosp., Portland, 1964-65; resident Good Samaritan Hosp. and Med. Ctr., Portland, 1965-68; rotating resident in neuropathology Sch. of Medicine U. Wash., 1967; rotating resident in child neurology U. Calif. Med. Ctr., San Francisco, 1968; rotating resident in psychiatry Med. Sch. U. Oreg., 1968; neurol. cons. pub. health svc.-health svcs. and mental health adminstrn.-neurol. and sensory disease control program HEW, Rockville, Md., 1968-70; staff neuroglogist epilepsy br. NIH HEW, Bethesda, Md., 1970-85; chief epilepsy br. convulsive, devel. and neuromuscular disorders program Nat. Inst. Neurol. Disorders and Stroke, Bethesda, Md., 1985-93; dir. rsch. Epilepsy Ctr. Oreg. Health Scis. U., Portland, 1993—; prof. dept. neurology Oreg. Health Scis. U., 1993—; attending neurologist VA Med. Ctr., Portland, 1993—; speaker in field. Editor-in-chief Epilepsia, 1986-94, emeritus, 1994—, supplements editor, 1994—; contbr. numerous articles to profl. jours. Capt. USPHS, ret. Fellow Am. Electroencephalographi Soc. (pub. rels. com. 1980-81); mem. Am. Acad. Neurology, Am. Epilepsy Soc. (constn. com. 1970-74, chmn. 1975, membership com. 1975, chmn. 1976, 77 chmn. edn. com. 1978, 79, 80, dir. continuing med. edn. 1981-83, 1st v.p. 1982-83, pres. 1983-84, v.p. to ILAE 1985-86, coun. 1985-94), Am. Neurologic Assn., Epilepsy Found. of Am. (profl. adv. bd. Washington chpt. 1969-93, v.p. 1973-75, speaker's bur. 1972-93, Epilepsy Internat. (libr. devel. com. 1981, chmn. 1981-85), U. Oreg. Med. Sch. Alumni Assn., Internat. League Against Epilepsy (edn. com. 1985-94, coun. 1985-94), Med. Soc. D.C. (sect. neurology and neurol. surgery 1971-94), Uniformed Svcs. Orgn. Neurologists (chmn. awards com. 1984-85), Epilepsy Assn. Oreg. (sec. 1993—, region 9 rep. to Epilepsy Found. Am. 1996—), World Fedn. Neurology (epidemiology rsch group 1978—), Alzheimer's Rsch. Alliance Oreg. (exec. coun. 1994—, chmn. res. awards com. 1995—). Home: 525 SE 65th Ave Portland OR 97215-2038 Office: Oreg Health Scis Univ Epilepsy Ctr CDW-3 3181 SW Sam Jackson Park Rd Portland OR 97201-3011

CERIELLO, ANTONIO, physician; b. Naples, Italy, Sept. 13, 1953; s. Dohenico and Carmela (Cirillo) C.; m. Patrizia Dello Russo, Apr. 16, 1983; children: Fabio, Daniela. MD, U. Naples, 1979, specialty in metabolic disease, 1982. Asst. prof. U. Naples, 1983-90, U. Udine, Italy, 1990—. Author: (with others) International Textbook of Diabetes Mellitus, 2d edit., 1996. Recipient Nat. Award for Young Rschr. Italian Soc. Internal Medicine, 1984, Award Italian Soc. Study of Diabetes, Internat. Soc. Free Radic. Rsch. Office: U Udine Dept Int Med, Ple S Maria Misericordia, 33100 Udine Italy

CERIO, MILISSA BAUSCH, social worker; b. Binghamton, N.Y., July 10, 1959; d. Charles E. Bausch and Theresa M. (Benton) McKerrow); m. Charles P. Cerio, July 28, 1984; 1 child, Charles James. BSW, Lock Haven State Coll., 1981; MSW, Marywood Coll., Scranton, Pa., 1982. Cert. social worker. Child care worker Elmira (N.Y.) Glove House, Inc., 1982-83, asst. group home supr., 1983-84, sch. social worker, 1984-87; social worker alcohol rehab. unit New Dawn Alcohol Rehab. Unit, Elmira, 1987-90, clin. coord. alcohol rehab. unit, 1990-92; pvt. practice clin. social worker Clin. Social Work and Counseling Svcs. of The FingerLakes, Elmira, 1990—. Mem. coms. Jr. League Elmira, 1986-91. Mem. NASW. Home: 712 Pennsylvania Ave Elmira NY 14904-2243 Office: Clin Social Work and Counseling Svcs Finger Lakes 963 Walnut St Elmira NY 14901-1831

CERKLEWSKI, FLORIAN LEE, human nutrition educator, nutritional biochemistry researcher; b. Danville, Pa., May 28, 1949; s. Florian and Ruth C.; m. Irene Joan Farkas, June 9, 1973, children—Christopher Louis, James Andrew. B.S. in Nutritional Sci., Pa. State U., 1971; Ph.D., U. Ill., 1976. Postdoctoral fellow U. Cin., 1975-76; asst. prof. Marquette U., Milw., 1976-79; asst. prof. Oreg. State U., Corvallis, 1979-84, assoc. prof., 1984—. Contbr. articles to profl. jours. Recipient Nat. Inst. Dental Research New Investigator award, 1980-83, research investigator award, 1983-91; Oreg. Agrl. Experiment Sta. Research Investigator award, 1980—. Mem. Am. Inst. Nutrition. Office: Coll Home Econs and Edn Oreg State U Corvallis OR 97331

CERNADA, GEORGE PETER, community health educator; b. Somerville, Mass., Mar. 1, 1938; s. Peter George and Margaret Jane (Corbett) C.; m. Ching-Ching Chen, Oct. 26, 1961; children: Joseph, Isabel. BS, Boston Coll., 1959; MPH, U. Calif., Berkeley, 1965, D in Pub. Health, 1975. Pub. info. specialist N.Y. Dept. Mental Hygiene, Albany, 1962-64; USPHS trainee U. Calif., Berkeley, 1964-65; resident adv. E. Asia Office, The Population Coun., Taiwan, 1965-70; resident rep., chief adv. Population Coun., Taiwan, 1971-76; prof. pub. health U. Mass., Amherst, 1976-91, 95—; dir. Asia and Near East ops. rsch. The Population Coun., Islamabad, Pakistan, 1991-95; editor Internat. Quar. of Community Health Edn., 1979—; bd. dirs. Internat. Resource Devel. and Mgmt., Inc.; population program health svc. consultation abroad for World Bank and various U.S. and UN agys., Asian Devel. Bank, min. health & social welfare nat. govts. in Africa, Asia, L.Am., 1972—. Vice chmn. United Svcs. Orgn., Taiwan, 1970. With U.S. Army, 1961-62. Population Coun. fellow, 1965-66, 1970-71; recipient Population and Social Devel. Policy Study award, The Rockefeller-Ford Founds., 1979, Nat. Health medal Govt. Taiwan, 1994. Fellow Soc. for Health Edn., Am. Anthropol. Assn., Soc. Applied Anthropology; mem. Am. Pub. Health Assn., Soc. for Med. Anthropology, Internat. Union for Health Edn., Internat. Union Sci. Study Population. Roman Catholic. Author: Taiwan Family Planning Reader, 1970, Knowledge Into Action, 1982, Recommended Health Education Readings, 1985, contbr. articles to profl. jours. Office: U Mass Sch Pub Health Arnold House Amherst MA 01003

CERNAK, KEITH PATRICK, health care and financial consultant; b. Northampton, Mass., Mar. 17, 1954; s. Samuel and Geraldine (Dykstra) C.; m. Kristin Freedman, Sept. 10, 1983; children: Emily Samantha, Melanie Kristin. BA magna cum laude, U. Mass., 1976; MPH, U. Hawaii, 1980; MBA, UCLA, 1984. Healthcare researcher U. Hawaii, Honolulu, 1978; health planning cons. Guam Health Planning Agy., Agana, 1979; rsch. dir. Hawaii Dept. Health, Honolulu, 1980-81; grad. instr. UCLA Sch. Pub. Health, 1981; mgmt. cons. Am. Med. Internat., Beverly Hills, Calif., 1982; v.p. Crocker Bank, L.A., 1984-86; v.p. fin. Weyerhaeuser, San Francisco, 1986-91; cmty. partnership and outcome mgmt. dir. Evergreen Med. Ctr., Seattle, 1992—; health care cons.; nat. presenter in field. Author papers in field. Cabinet mem. Shepherd of the Hills Ch., Berkeley, Calif., 1988-90. Health Svc. scholar U. Hawaii, 1978. Mem. UCLA Sch. Mgmt., Beta Gamma Sigma. Home: 24503 SE 43d Pl Issaquah WA 98027-9518

CERNIGLIA, ELFREDA, home health nurse; b. Portsmouth, N.H., Aug. 26, 1940; d. William Lodge and Helen Elfreda (Wrigley) Courser; m. Michael Glowa, Apr. 9, 1962 (div. 1977); children: Robin Glowa, Michael Glowa; m. Joseph Cerniglia, May. 19, 1979. BSN, Castleton State, 1982; MEd, Antioch New Eng., 1983. RN, Vt., N.H. Med.-surg. charge nurse evenings Springfield (Vt.) Hosp., 1962-75; vis. nurse Springfield Regional Vis. Nurse Assn., 1976-87; supr. home health Mary Hitchcock Meml. Hosp., Hanover, N.H., 1991-92; regional mgr. Vis. Nurse Alliance of Vt. and N.H., Lebanon, N.H., 1992-94, quality improvement coord., 1994-96; case mgr. Healthworks Sringfield (Vt.) Hosp., 1996—; cons. Outcomes Unltd., Springfield, 1982-86. Pres. LWV, Springfield, 1974. Home: 335 River St Springfield VT 05156-2220 Office: Healthworks-Springfield Hosp 25 Ridgewood Rd Springfield VT 05156

CERNUDA, CHARLES EVELIO, physician; b. Tampa, Fla., June 19, 1941; s. Evelio Perez and Angelina (Leto) C.; B.A., Emory U., 1963, M.D., 1968; m. Mary Margaret McElory, Nov. 24, 1967; children: Mary Robin and Meredith Lynley (twins), Lindsey Elizabeth. Intern, Emory U. Affiliated Hosps., Atlanta, 1968-69, resident in internal medicine, 1969-70, fellow in pulmonary disease, 1970-72; practice medicine specializing in internal medicine and pulmonary disease, Tampa, 1974—; med. dir. ICU, pulmonary lab. and respiratory therapy depts. St. Joseph's Hosp., 1974—, sec. treas., 1977-81, pres.-elect med. staff, 1982, pres. med. staff, 1982-85; med. dir. pulmonary lab. and respiratory therapy depts. Centro Asturiano Hosp., 1974-87, vice chief med. staff, 1975-78, med. dir., 1991—, St. Joseph's Hosp. Home Health Agys., 1991— (chmn. bd. dirs. 1989-91); bd. dirs. Commerce Bank Tampa, 1985-87; v.p. St. Joseph's Physicians Healthcare Orgn., 1986-88, dir., 1986-96; pres., dir. St. Joseph's Physician Assocs., Inc., 1986-89, chmn. bd. dirs., 1989-91, exec. dir., 1991—; bd. dirs. Sun Health Plans-Gulf Coast, Inc., vice chmn., 1992—; dir. St. Joseph's Physician's Health Ctr. Orgn., 1986-96, pres. 1991-92, 93-94, chmn. bd. dirs. 1990-91, v.p. 1986-88; mem. bd. dirs. Bay Care Health Network, Inc., 1991—, vice chmn. 1992-93, chmn. 1994. Trustee Berkeley Prep. Sch., Tampa, 1985—. Served with M.C., USAF, 1972-73. Diplomate Am. Bd. Internal Medicine, also Sub-Bd. Pulmonary Disease. Fellow Am. Coll. Chest Physicians, ACP; mem. Am. Coll. Physician Execs., Nat. Assn. Med. Dirs. Respiratory Care, So. Med. Assn., Fla. Med. Assn., AMA, Am., Fla. thoracic socs., Fla. Soc. Internal

Medicine, Hillsborough County Med. Assn. (chmn. bd. censors 1981-82), West Coast Acad. Medicine (sec.-treas. 1981-83), Am. Soc. Internal Medicine, Med. Group Mgmt. Assn. Democrat. Episcopalian. Clubs: Univ. Tampa Yacht and Country, Rotary of Ybor City (Tampa). Home: 4930 Andros Dr Tampa FL 33629-4802 Office: 4900 N Habana Ave Tampa FL 33614

CERNY, JOSEPH CHARLES, urologist, educator; b. Oak Park, Ill., Apr. 20, 1930; s. Joseph James and Mary (Turek) C.; m. Patti Bobette Pickens, Nov. 10, 1962; children: Joseph Charles, Rebecca Anne. BA, Knox Coll., 1952; MD, Yale U., 1956. Diplomate Am. Bd. Urology. Intern U. Mich. Hosp., Ann Arbor, 1956-57, resident, 1957-62; practice medicine specializing in urology, Ann Arbor, and Detroit since 1962—; inst. surgery (urology) U. Mich., Ann Arbor, 1962-64, asst. prof., 1964-66, assoc. prof., 1966-71, clin. prof., 1971—; chmn. dept. urology Henry Ford Hosp., Detroit, 1971—; pres. Resistors, Inc., Chgo., 1960—; cons. St. Joseph Hosp., Ann Arbor, 1973—. Mem. editorial bd. Am. Jour. Kidney Diseases, 1988—; contbr. articles to profl. jours., chpts. in books. Bd. dirs., trustee Nat. Kidney Found. Mich., Ann Arbor, 1988—, chmn. urology council 1987—, exec. com. 1987—, pres. 1988—, disting. svc. award, 1993; bd. dirs. Ann Arbor Amateur Hockey Assn., 1980-83; pres. PTO, Ann Arbor Pub. Schs., 1980. Served to lt. USNR, 1956-76. Recipient Disting. Service award Transplantation Soc. Mich., 1982. Fellow ACS (pres.-elect Mich. br. 1984-85, pres. 1985—); mem. Am. Acad. Med. Dirs., Am. Coll. Physician Execs., Internat. Soc. Urology, Am. Urol. Assn. (pres. Mich. br. 1980-81, pres. North Cen. sec. 1985-86, Manpower com. 1987-88, Jud. Rev. com. 1987-91, tech. exhibits 1987-88, fiscal affairs rev. commn. 1985-89, manpower commn. 1990-92, audit commn. 1992-96, chmn. 1995, exec. commn. 1993—, bd. dirs. 1994—, work force com., publ. com., 1995—, Best Sci. Exhibit award 1978, Best Sci. Films award 1980, 82, audio-visual com., 1994—, program review com. 1994—, urology work force com. 1995—, publs. com. 1995—), Transplantation Soc. Mich. (pres. 1983-84), ACS (pres. Mich. chpt. 1985-86), Am. Assn. Transplant Surgeons, Endocrine Surgeons, Soc. Univ. Urologists, Am. Assn. Urologic Oncology, Am. Fertility Soc, Am. Coll. Physician Execs., Am. Acad. Med. Dirs., S.W. Oncology Group. Republican. Methodist. Clubs: Barton Hills Country; Ann Arbor Raquet . Avocations: tennis, fishing, Civil War. Home: 2800 Fairlane St Ann Arbor MI 48104-4110 Office: Henry Ford Hosp Dept Urology 2799 W Grand Blvd Detroit MI 48202-2608

CERRA, FRANK B., dean; b. Oneonta, N.Y., Feb. 13, 1943; m. Kathie Krieger; children: Josh, Christa, Nicole. BA in Biology, SUNY, Binghamton, 1965; MD, Northwestern U., 1969. Diplomate Nat. Bd. Med. Examiners, Am. Bd. Surgery. Intern, resident in surgery Buffalo Gen. Hosp., 1969-74; staff surgeon U. Minn. Hosp. Clinic, Mpls.; dean, prof. surgery U. Minn. Med. Sch., Mpls., 1995—; clin. asst. instr. surgery SUNY, Buffalo, 1969-75, asst. prof. 1975-80, assoc. prof. surgery and biophysics, 1980; interim head surgery U. Minn., 1994-95; rsch. asst. pharmacology Upstate Med. Ctr., 1963-64; rsch. asst. transplantation Northwestern U., 1967-69; rsch. assoc. immunology and cardiovascular rsch. labs. Buffalo Gen. Hosp., 1972-73, SUNY, Buffalo, 1974-75; dir. surg. critical care, dir. nutrition support svcs. U. Minn. Hosp. and Clinic; vis. lectr. in exptl. surgery Harvard U., 1991; vis. prof. Rush Presbyn.-St. Lukes Med. Ctr., 1991. Editor Perspective in Critical Care, 1988-91, Critical Care Outlook, 1988-90, Critical Care Medicine, 1990—; mem. editl. bd. Drug Intelligence & Clin. Pharmacy Panel onCritical Care, 1982-87, Nutrition, 1982—, Critical Care Medicine, 1983—, Circulatory Shock, 1987-93, Shock, 1993—, Jour. Parenteral and Enternal Nutrition, 1987-93, Am. Jour. Surgery, 1987—, Current Opinion in Gen. Surgery, 1992—, Jour. Critical Care Nutrition; contbr. articles to profl. jours.; patentee preparation for the prevention of catabolism, preparation for nutirtion support of immune function. Acute care com. Found. for Health Care Evaluation, 1983-86; adv. group Minn. Emerging Infections Program, 1995—. Clark Found. fellow, 1965-69, Kellogg Nutrition fellow, 1987-89, Surgical Infection Soc. Rsch. fellow, 1988-90, Soc. Critical Care Medicine Lilly Rsch. fellow, 1990-93, Svc. award fellow NIH, 1994-96; United Health Found. Rsch. Tng. grantee, 1972-73; recipient Owen Wangensteen award, 1987, Therapeutic Frontiers Rsch. award Am. Coll. Clin. Pharmacy, 1990, Disting. Investigator award Am. Coll. Critical Care Medicine, 1993. Fellow ACS (chmn. pre-postoperative care com. 1985-87), Am. Coll. Nutrition, Coll. Critical Care Medicine; mem. AMA, AAAS, Soc. Parenteral Alimentation, Soc. for Surgery the Alimentary Tract, Am. Soc. Parenteral and Enteral Nutrition (bd. govs. 1987-88), Soc. Critical Care Medicine (treas. 1990, pres. 1991-92), Assn. for Acad. Surgery, Assn. Internat. Anesthesistes-Reanimateurs D'Expression, Soc. Univ. Surgeons (exec. coun. 1984-85), Ctrl. Surg. Assn., Am. Assn. for the Surgery Trauma, Assn. for Surg. Edn., St. Paul Surg. Soc., Surg. Biology Club, Shock Soc., Soc. Internat. Surgery, Internat. Assn. for the the Surgery Trauma and Surg. Intensive Care, Am. Soc. for Artificial Internal Organs (membership com. 1994-95), Am. Soc. Home Care Physicisn, Hennepin County Med. Soc. Office: U Minn Hosps & Clinic Haward St at E River Rd Minneapolis MN 55455 Office: Univ Minn PO Box 293 420 Delaware St SE Minneapoiis MN 55455*

CERRETO, MARY CHRISTINE, psychologist, researcher; b. Putnam, Conn., Apr. 29, 1951; d. Sebastian S. and Viola (Bonneville) C.; m. David L. Coulter, Aug. 7, 1982. AB, Conn. Coll., 1973; PhD in Psychology, U. Wash., 1976. Lic. psychologist, Mass. Asst. prof. pediatrics U. Tex. Med. Br., Galveston, 1977-80, assoc. prof., 1980, 81-85; asst. prof. Vanderbilt U. Med. Sch., Nashville, 1980-81; chief exec. officer Accreditation Coun. Svcs. to People with Devel. Disabilities, Boston, 1985-88; dir. dept. psychology Franciscan Children's Hosp., Boston, 1988-91; asst. commr. Dept. Mental Retardation, Boston, 1991—; cons. Joseph P. Kennedy, Jr. Found., Washington, 1979-85. Editor Children's Health Care, 1980-84; contbr. articles to profl. jours., chpts. to books. Chmn. Natick (Mass.) Hist. Commn., 1988-90. HHS grantee, 1978-82, State of Tex. grantee, 1981-85. Fellow Am. Psychol. Assn., Am. Assn. on Mental Retardation (v.p. psychology 1981-84); mem. Soc. for Rsch. in Child Devel., Am. Acad. on Mental Retardation (bd. dirs. 1986-90), So. Soc. for Pediatric Rsch. Democrat. Roman Catholic. Office: Franciscan Children's Hosp Dept Mental Retardation 160 N Washington St Boston MA 02114-2120

CERSOSIMO, EUGENIO, medical educator; b. Laino Borgo Cosenza, Italy, Oct. 25, 1952. MD, Univ. Fed. Fluminense, Rio de Janeiro, 1974; PhD, Vanderbilt U., 1984. Diplomate Am. Bd. Internal Medicine. Intern, resident dept. internal medicine Hosp. Univ. Antonio Pedro, Rio de Janeiro, 1975-76, attending physician emergency rm., attending physician dialysis/renal ctr., 1976-79; fellow in clin. nutrition dept. internal medicine Univ. Fed. do Rio de Janeiro, 1978-80; instr. divsn. nephrology dept. internal medicine Univ. Fed. Fluminense, Rio de Janeiro, 1976-80, asst. prof. internal medicine, 1980-84, rsch. coord. internal medicine and pathology, 1985-86, assoc. prof. internal medicine, 1985—; rsch. fellow in surg. metabolism dept. surgery Meml. Sloan-Kettering Cancer Ctr., N.Y.C., 1986-88; intern, resident dept. internal medicine Mayo Grad. Sch. Medicine Mayo Clinic, Rochester, Minn., 1989-91, fellow in endocrinology and metabolism, clinician investigatorship program, 1991-94, instr. endocrinology and internal medicine, 1993-94; attending physician Fed. Med. Ctr. U.S. Dept. Justice, Rochester, Minn., 1992-94; attending physician SUNY Univ. Hosp., Stony Brook, 1994—, asst. prof. internal medicine, endcrinology, and diabetes, 1994—; attending physician VA Med. Ctr., Northport, N.Y., 1994—; vis. prof. grad. sch. Univ. Fed. do Rio de Janeiro, 1984-85; cons. in endocrinology and diabetes and metabolism SUNY, Stony Brook, 1994—. Scholarship Brazilain Nat. Rsch. Coun., 1980-84; recipient Trainee Investigator award Am. Soc. Clin. Investigation, 1994. Mem. ACP, AMA, Am. Diabetes Assn., Am. Soc. Renal Biochemistry and Metabolism, Union of Med. Doctors (Brazil), United Univ. Profs., Brazilian Soc. Medicine (vice sec. for Brazilian soc. of parenteral nutrition 1976-78). Office: SUNY Dept Medicine Divsn Endcrinology and Diabetes Health Sci Ctr T-15 Rm 060 Stony Brook NY 11794-8154

CERULLO-FRICK, KATHLEEN M., nursing administrator, computer professional; b. Pottsville, Pa., June 22, 1958; d. Anthony J. and Edith D. (Coleman) Cerullo; m. Michael S. Frick, Oct. 3, 1982. Diploma, Allentown Hosp. Sch. Nursing, 1979; BS, Lebanon Valley Coll., Annville, Pa., 1981; postgrad., Pa. State U. Cert. in play therapy. User info. mgr. Pa. State U., Hershey. Mem. Pa. Nurses Assn., Delaware Valley Nursing Computer Network, Am. Heart Assn., Am. Cancer Soc., Am. Psychology Assn. Home: 756 Pine Tree Rd Hummelstown PA 17036-8538

CERVANTES, DANIEL FELIPE, surgeon, consultant; b. Naga City, Camarines Sur, Philippines, June 13, 1958; s. Jose Dimaculangan and Carmen (Felipe) C.; m. Juliet Gopez, Jan. 10, 1993; children: Patricia, Paolo. BS in Zoology, U. Philippines, 1979; MD, Bicol Christian Coll. of Medicine, Philippines, 1985. Diplomate Philippine Bd. Surgery. Rural health physician Ministry of Health, Philippines, 1986, Dept. of Health, Philippines, 1988; med. officer III Rizal Med. Ctr., Philippines, 1989-92, Baliuag Dist. Hosp., Philippines, 1994; med. specialist I Mandaluyong Med. Ctr., Philippines, 1995-96; cons. St. Luke's Med. Ctr. , Quezon City, Philippines, 1995—, Cardinal Santos Meml. Hosp., Philippines, 1996. Fellow Philippine Coll. Surgeons; mem. Philippine Med. Assn. Roman Catholic. Home: 40-B T Gener St Kamuning, 1103 Quezon City Metro Manila, The Philippines Office: St Lukes Med Ctr, MAB Rm 302 E Rodriguez St, 1103 Quezon City Metro Manila, The Philippines

CERVANTES, EILEEN, medical equipment company executive; b. St. Louis, Aug. 16, 1961; d. Joe and Carol (Ellison) Meiners; m. Lucius Craig Cervantes, Sept. 18, 1994. BS, Regis Coll., Denver. Account exec. Cybertel, 1984-90; pres. NOA Med. Industries, Marthasville, Mo., 1990—. Mem. St. Louis Ambassadors, Ctrl. West End Alzheimers Assn., St. Louis; bd. dirs. YEO, St. Louis. Home: 5214 Washington Pl Saint Louis MO 63108 Office: NOA Medical 1601 Woodson Rd Saint Louis MO 63357-4000

CERVANTES, LUIS AUGUSTO, neurosurgeon; b. Torreon, Mexico, Mar. 5, 1953; came to the U.S., 1976; s. Luis Augusto and Gloria (Galindo) C.; m. Joann Frances Emanuele, Feb. 10, 1979; children: Luis III, Sara, Francis, Nicolas, Juan Carlos. MD, Nat. U. Mex., 1976. Intern Suburban Hosp., Bethesda, Md., 1977-78; surgery resident Washington Hosp. Ctr., 1978-79; neurology resident George Washington U., Washington, 1979-80, neurosurgery resident, 1980-84; chief neurosurgery sect. dept. surgery Meml. Hosp. Burlington County, Mount Holly, N.J., 1992—. Fellow ACS, Internat. Coll. Surgeons; mem. Am. Assn. Neurol. Surgeons, Congress Neurol. Surgeons. Roman Catholic. Office: 110 Marter Ave Moorestown NJ 08057

CERVENKA, JAROSLAV, geneticist; b. Prague, Czechoslovakia, Mar. 15, 1933; came to U.S., 1965; s. Jaroslav and Marta (Ciprova) C.; m. Alexandra Schrutz, Mar. 14, 1958; children: Vojta, Tereza. MD, Charles U. MEd. Sch., 1957; PhD, Czechoslovak Acad. Scis., 1967. Researcher Czechoslovakia Acad. Scis., Praque, 1961; asst. prof. U. Minn., Mpls., 1968-71; assoc. prof. U. Minn., 1971-77, prof., 1977—. Author: Chromosomes in Human Cancer, 1973, Mal d'Afrique, 1995. Mem. Am. Soc. Human Genetics, Omicron Kappa Upslion, Phi Beta Delta, Sigma Xi. Home: 4205 Beverly Ave Minneapolis MN 55422-5221 Office: U Minn 515 Delaware St SE Minneapolis MN 55455-0348

CERVIA, JOSEPH STEVEN, medical educator; b. N.Y.C., Apr. 10, 1959; s. Joseph T. and Margaret (Bleier) C.; m. Denise Laura Blumberg, Aug. 10, 1986; children: David Michael, Lisa Danielle, Michael Jason. BS in Biology summa cum laude, St. John's U., 1980; MD, N.Y. Med. Coll., 1984. Diplomate Nat. Bd. Med. Examiners, Am. Bd. Internal Medicine, Am. Bd. Pediatrics, Subspeciality Bd. Infectious Diseases Internal Medicine and Pediatric. Intern in medicine, pediatrics Brookdale Hosp. Med. Ctr., Bklyn., 1984-85, resident in medicine, pediatrics, 1985-88; fellow in infectious diseases N.Y. Hosp. Cornell Med. Ctr., N.Y.C., 1988-90; asst. prof. medicine, pediatrics SUNY Health Sci. Ctr., Stony Brook, 1990-92; attending physician Nassau County Med. Ctr., East Meadow, N.Y., 1990-92, dir. pediatric-maternal HIV svc., 1990-92; mem. pediatric AIDS grant adv. bd. Nassau-Suffolk Health Sys. Agy., Plainview, N.Y., 1991-92; dir. Program for Children with AIDS, The N.Y. Hosp. Cornell Med. Ctr., 1992—; asst. prof. pediatrics and medicine Cornell U. Med. Coll., 1992-95, assoc. prof. pediatrics and medicine, 1995—. Contbr. articles to profl. jours. Asst. scoutmaster Boy Scouts Am., Forest Hills, N.Y., 1977-80. Recipient Bausch and Lomb Hon. Sci. award, 1977, Harrison Scholarship award N.Y. Med. Coll., 1984, Henry Christian Meml. award Am. Fedn. Clin. Rsch., 1990; competitive and scholastic excellence scholarships, St. John's U., 1977-80. Fellow ACP, Am. Acad. Pediatrics, Pediatric Infectious Disease Soc.; mem. AAAS, AMA (physician's recognition award 1993—), Infectious Disease Soc. Am., Am. Soc. Microbiology, Am. Fedn. Clinic Rsch., AIDS Clin. Trials Group. Roman Catholic. Home: 9 Pine Dr N Roslyn NY 11576-2015 Office: NY Hosp.-Cornell Med Ctr 505 E 70th St Box 296 New York NY 10021-4873

CERVONI, PETER PAUL, pharmacologist; b. Jamaica, N.Y., Mar. 4, 1931; s. Louis and Domenica (Bernardi) C.; m. Antoinette Marie Angiolillo, Jan. 25, 1964; children: Peter Anthony, Christine Marie, Michael Francis. BS in Pharmacy cum laude, St. John's U., 1952; MS, U. Wash., 1955, PhD in Pharmacology, 1957. Rsch. asst. dept. pharmacology U. Wash., Seattle, 1952-57; postdoctoral fellow dept. pharmacology Downstate Med. Ctr., SUNY, Bklyn., 1959-60; asst. prof. dept. pharmacology U. Miss. Med. Ctr., Jackson, 1960-61, SUNY, Bklyn., 1961-66; sr. researcher phamacology Burroughs Wellcome, Tuckahoe, N.Y., 1966-70; dir. pharmacology USV Pharm. Co., Tuckahoe, 1970-79; head dept. cardiovascular pharmacology med. rsch. Am. Cyanamid Co., Pearl River, N.Y., 1979-94; dir. cardiac diseases Wyeth-Ayerst Rsch., Pearl River, 1994—; cons. Pharm/Tox, 1996—; adj. prof. St. John's U., Jamaica, N.Y., 1975-81, N.Y. Med. Coll., Valhalla, 1982—, U. Tenn. Med. Ctr., Memphis, 1984-89; adj. sr. rsch. scientist Coll. Physicians and Surgeons/Columbia U., 1994—; track dir. clin. rsch. adminstrn. N.Y. Med. Coll., 1995—. Author: Handbook Pharmacology of Aging, 1983, Biological Protection with Prostaglandins, 1985, Kirk-Othmer Encyclopedia Chemical Technology, 1984, 92; co-regional editor Pharm. Rsch., 1991—; editor Drug Devel. Rsch. Jour., 1990. 1st lt. MSC, 1957-64. Fellow N.Y. Acad. Scis., Coun. for High Blood Pressure Rsch. Am. Heart Assn.; mem. AAAS, Am. Soc. Pharmacology and Exptl. Therapeutics (membership com., Abel award com., Sollman award com., pharmacologists in industry com., councilor), Sigma Xi. Republican. Roman Catholic. Home and Office: 64 Sheldrake Pl New Rochelle NY 10804-1115

CESA, MICHAEL PETER, cardiologist, consultant; b. N.Y.C., Sept. 4, 1946; s. John J. and Catherine R. (Brunialti) C.; m. Barbara A. Perrelli, June 21, 1969; children: Christopher, Thomas, Gregory, Meredith. BS, Manhattan Coll., 1968; MD, SUNY, Bklyn., 1972. Diplomate Am. Bd. Internal Medicine, Am. Bd. Cardiovascular Disease. Intern dept. medicine Kings County Hosp., Bklyn., 1972-72, med. resident dept. medicine, 1973-75, cardiology fellow dept. medicine, 1975-77; pvt. practice Bruckstein & Lerner, Smithtown, N.Y., 1977-78, North Suffolk Cardiology Assocs., P.C., Stony Brook, N.Y., 1978—; clin. asst. prof. of medicine SUNY, Stony Brook, 1994—; pres., chief exec. officer North Suffolk Cardiology Assocs., Stony Brook, 1984—; pres. med. staff St. Johns Hosp., Smithtown, 1984. Fellow Am. Heart Assn. (Coun. on Clin. Cardiology), Am. Coll. Cardiology, Am. Coll. Chest Physicians. Roman Catholic. Office: North Suffolk Cardiology 2500-1 Nesconset Hwy Stony Brook NY 11790

CESARIO, NORMAJEAN DIERKING, nursing educator, medical/surgical nurse; b. S.I., N.Y., Dec. 21, 1946; d. James F. and Aida (Spadola) Dierking; m. Vincent Cesario, Oct. 19, 1968; children: Christopher, Daniel, Katherine. Diploma, Bellevue Hosp. Sch. Nursing, N.Y.C., 1967; BSN, CUNY, S.I., 1987; MS, Rutgers U., Newark, 1989. RN, N.Y., N.J.; cert. in nursing staff devel. and continuing edn. ANCC. Emergency rm. staff nurse Bellevue Hosp., N.Y.C., 1967-69; med.-surg. staff nurse St. Vincent's Med. Ctr. Richmond, S.I., 1969-83; home care nurse, 1978-89; instr. med.-surg. nursing Felician Coll., Lodi, N.J., 1989-90; nurse adminstr. South Beach Psychiat. Ctr., S.I., 1990, dir. nursing staff devel., 1990—; adj. instr. Kingsborough C.C., CUNY, Bklyn., 1989. Author: Health Teaching Modules, 1990. Else T. Marcus nursing scholar, 1986-87; Fed. Nurse trainee, 1987-89; recipient Saunders Frankel Meml. award, 1987. Mem. N.Y.C. RN Assn., Sigma Theta Tau. Home: 400 Heberton Ave Staten Island NY 10302-2135

CESARMAN, EDUARDO VITIS, cardiologist; b. Santiago, Chile, S. Am., Oct. 19, 1931; Mexican citizen; s. Carlos M. and Esther (Vitis) C.; BSc, Centro U. Mex., 1948; MD, U. Nacional Autonoma de Mex., 1955; m. Esther T. Kolteniuk, June 24, 1961; children: Carlos, Laura, Andrea, Paola. Intern, Univ. Hosp., U. Md., College Park, 1955-56; resident Mt. Sinai Hosp., N.Y.C., 1956-57, N.Y. Hosp.-Cornell U., 1957-59; fellow Instituto Nacional de Cardiologia de Mex., 1960-62, medico adjunto, 1962-73, chief dept. epidemiology, 1976-78; chief med. svcs. Comision Federal de Electricidad, 1976-77; dir. gen. Higiene Escolar y Programas de Salud, Secretaria de Educacion Publica, 1978-80; chief supervision and control med. svcs. Inst. Mexicano Seguro Social, 1980-83; assoc. prof. cardiology Facultad de Medicina, Universidad Nacional Autonoma de Mexico, 1961-74, prof. nosology, 1968-74, dir. gen. Servicios Escolares, U. Mex., 1965-67, Cooperación Técnica y Científica de la Secretaría de Relaciones Exteriores, 1993-94; pres. Mexican sci. coun. Weisman Inst., 1967-69; adv. Secretaria de Salubridad y Asistencia, 1967-70, U. Mex., 1973-76, Instituto Mexicano del Seguro Social, 1977-85, Fondo de Cultura Economica, 1973, Instituto de Seguridad Social al Servicio de los Trabajadores del Estado, 1989; dir. Colegio de Ciencias y Humanidades, U. Mex., 1970. Mem. steering com. Internat. Exec. Corps, 1976-85. Recipient Justo Sierra, U. Mex., 1955. Mem. Sociedad Mexicana de Cardiologia (sci. com. 1976-78), Am. Coll. Cardiology (chpt. gov. 1966-69), N.Y. Acad. Sci., Internat. Coll. Angiology, Am. Coll. Angiology, Israel Med. Assn., Am. Coll. Chest Physicians (chpt. gov. 1985—), Asociacion de Investigacion Pediatrica, Coun. on Epidemiology and Prevention of Internat. Soc. Cardiology, Sociedad Mexicana de Educacion para la Salud, Asociacion Mexicana de Periodismo Cientifico, Asociacion de Escritores Mexicanos, Acad. de. Ciencias Médicas, Sociedad Mexicana de Historia y Filosofía de la Medicina. Author: Parametros Cardiologicos, 1968, Aforismos Farmacologicos y Terapeuticos en Cardiologia, 1970, Hombre y Entropia, 1974, A Redefinition of the Resting State of the Myocardial Cell, 1976, La Vida es Riesgo, 1978, Orden y Caos, 1982, Fuera de Contexto, 1983, Cuarto Menguante, 1985, Dicho en México, 1986, Con alguna Intención, 1987, co-editor Fundamentos del Diagnóstico, 1976, Morrala, 1989 The Four Diastoles-A Cardiac Cycle Model, 1989, Trompa Talega, 1991, Ser Médico, 1991, A Theory of Heartbeat-Open Diastole and Closed Systole, 1991, The Origin of Diastole, 1992, Diastolic Uphill Organization, 1994, El Telar Encantado, 1995, Los Motivos de Sísifo, 1995, Thermodynamics of the Heart, 1996; contbr. articles to profl. jours. Home: 825 Sierra Ventana, 11000 Mexico City Mexico Office: 300-3 Paseo de la Reforma, 06600 Mexico City Mexico

CESARZ, PAUL MICHAEL, clinical pharmacist; b. Milw., Mar. 24, 1956; s. Jerome Edward and Carol Ann (Hendricks) C.; m. Colette Ann Chartier, Sept. 29, 1979; children: Claire Elizabeth, Kathryn Anne, Andrew Paul. B in Pharm. Sci., U. Wis., 1979. Intern Laabs Inc., Milw., 1977-79; staff pharmacist Snyder Pharmacy, Milw., 1979-82; prin. Cesarz Infusion Therapy Svc., Inc., Wauwatosa, Wis., 1982—; mem. faculty and staff U. Wis. Sch. Pharmacy, Madison, 1985—; preceptor Pharmacy Internship Bd., Madison, 1986—; lectr. in field. Mem. Am. Pharm. Assn., Am. Hosp. Pharmacists, Wis. Soc. Hosp. Pharmacists (adminstr. coun. 1986—, bd. dirs., pres. 1991—), Wis. Pharmacists Assn. (pres. 1992-93), Pharmacists Soc. Milwaukee County (bd. dirs. 1979-90, pres. 1984-85), U. Wis. Pharmacy Alumni Assn. (life, pres. 1990). Roman Catholic. Office: 11815 W Dearbourn Ave Milwaukee WI 53226-3910

CESSARIO, LYNDA F., nursing educator; b. Rochester, N.Y., May 21, 1947; d. Michael and Josephine Orrico; children: Danielle, Michael. BS, SUNY, Buffalo, 1969, PhD, 1995; MS, D'Youville Coll., 1986. RN, N.Y. Staff nurse, supr. Vis. Nursing Assn., Buffalo, 1974-76; asst. prof. Daemen Coll., Buffalo, 1987—. Mem. ANA, N.Y. State Nurses Assn., Assn. Community Health Educators, Sigma Theta Tau. Home: 153 Audubon Dr Buffalo NY 14226-4044 Office: 4380 Main St Buffalo NY 14226-3544

CHA, SE DO, internist; b. Seoul, Korea, Dec. 17, 1942; came to U.S., 1966, naturalized, 1977; s. Young Sun and Hee Joo (Chang) C.; m. Elsa Jane Greene, Dec. 21, 1974; 1 child, Elizabeth. M.D., Yon Sei U., 1966. Diplomate Am. Bd. Internal Medicine. Intern Presbyn.-U. Pa. Med. Ctr., Phila., 1966-67; resident in medicine Harrisburg (Pa.) Hosp., 1967-70; chief resident in medicine Roger Williams Gen. Hosp., Providence, 1970-71, cardiologist, 1973-75; fellow in cardiology Deborah Heart and Lung Center, Browns Mills, N.J., 1971-73, cardiologist, 1975—, asst. dir. adult cardiac catheterization lab., 1975-86, dir., 1987—; clin. asst. prof. U. Medicine and Dentistry N.J., 1987; instr. Brown U., Providence, 1973-75. Contbr. articles to profl. jours. Fellow ACP, Am. Coll. Angiology, Soc. for Cardiac Angiography; mem. AMA, Fedn. Clin. Rsch., Am. Heart Assn. Office: Deborah Heart and Lung Ctr Trenton Rd Browns Mills NJ 08015-3206

CHABALI, RAUL, pediatrician. BA, Ohio State U., 1974, MD, 1977. Diplomate Am. Bd. Pediatrics, Am. Bd. Pediatric Emergency Medicine. Resident in pediatrics Columbus (Ohio) Children's Hosp., 1977-79; resident in pediatrics Dayton (Ohio) Children's Med. Ctr., 1979-80, pediatric emergency dept. physician, 1980—, pediatric clinics physician, 1980-87, attending pediatrician, 1982-83; med. advisor Huber Heights (Ohio) Paramedic Squads, 1979-83. Contbr. articles to profl. jours.; reviewer Pediatrics Jour., 1982. Fellow Am. Acad. Pediatrics (pediatric rev. and edn. program award 1986, mem. pediatric emergency medicine sect.), Am. Coll. Emergency Physicians (pediatric emergency medicine sect.). Office: Dayton Childrens Med Ctr One Childrens Plz Dayton OH 45404

CHABALLOUT, AHMED, surgeon; b. Homs, Syria, Oct. 10, 1948; s. Mohamed Chaballout and Sara Marto; m. Amira Alturk, May 25, 1974; children: Hashem, Nada, Kenan, Omar, Mawada, Abdulla, Tasnem. MD, Damascus (Syria) U., 1973. Diplomate Am. Bd. Surgery. Surg. resident Detroit Macombe Hosp. Assn., 1974-79, attending surgeon, 1979-85; attending surgeon Riyadh (Saudi Arabia) Ctrl. Hosp., 1985-86, Saudi Am. Clinic, Jedda, Saudi Arabia, 1986-87; emergency rm. physician King Fahd Hosp., Riyadh, 1987-89, cons. transplant surgeon, 1990—; renal transplant fellow St. Vincent Hosp., L.A., 1989-90. Fellow ACS. Home and Office: King Fahd Hosp, PO Box 22490, Riyadh 11426, Saudi Arabia

CHABOT, GERRI LOUISE, counselor, nurse; b. Detroit, Oct. 2, 1949; d. Henry L. and Betty J. (Hale) Busuttil; m. Robert J. Chabot, Aug. 8, 1970 (div. Aug. 1975); 1 child, Michelle. AS in Arts and Nursing, L.A. Pierce Coll., 1980; B in Psychology cum laude, Calif. State U., Northridge, 1984; M in Counseling Psychology, Pepperdine U., 1986. RN, Calif. Chemotherapy cert., 1984, ONS cert., 1986, PICC cert., 1993, Medtronics Pain Mgmt. cert., 1995. Nurse Valley Presbyn. Hosp./Nursery, Van Nuys, Calif., 1978-80; staff nurse Med. Ctr. of Tarzana, Calif., 1980-82; staff nurse renal and surg. units Holy Cross Hosp., Mission Hills, Calif., 1982-84, staff nurse chem. dependency unit, 1984-85, nurse clin. level III oncology dept., 1986-91; clinician/case mgr. AIDS specific home healthcare. Critical Care Am., Van Nuys, 1991-94; owner, dir. Santa Clarita (Calif.) Counseling Ctr., 1989-96; infusion nurse Apria Healthcare, Chatsworth, Calif., 1995; infusion specialist Ctr. Infusions Homecare, Van Nuys, 1995—; cons. Holy Cross Med. Ctr., 1988; lectr. in field. Henry Mayo Hosp. Community Health Edn. Com. fellow, 1989—. Fellow Calif. Assn. Marriage and Family Therapists, Oncology Nursing Soc., Intravenous Nursing Soc. Roman Catholic. Home and Office: 5275 Colodny Dr #18 Agoura Hills CA 91301

CHACHQUES, JUAN CARLOS, cardiac surgeon, researcher; b. Godoy, Santa Fe, Argentina, Jan. 8, 1944; arrived in France, 1980; s. Manuel Ernesto and Sara (Vaintrub) C.; m. Paula Dardan, Oct. 15, 1983; children: Emmanuel, Valerie, Maria-Paula. MD, U. Med. Sch., Rosario, Argentina, 1970; MS, U. Paris, 1989, PhD, 1993. Diplomate Argentinian Bd. Surgery, French Bd. Cardiovasc. Surgery. Resident in gen. surgery U. Hosp., Buenos Aires, 1970-74, chief of residents, 1974-75; resident in cardiovasc. surgery Broussais Hosp., Paris, 1981-86, asst. prof. cardiac surgery, 1988-94, staff surgeon cardiovasc. surgery, 1988—, assoc. prof., 1994—; assoc. dir. for clin. rsch. Nat. Inst. Health, Paris, 1990—; sr. rsch. assoc. Lab. for the Study of Cardiac Grafts and Prostheses, U. Paris, 1983—. Editor, author: Cardiomyoplasty, 1991, Heart Failure, 1994, Cardiac-BioAssist, 1996; inventor method and apparatus for cardiac assistance (Cardiomyoplasty and Aortomyoplasty) and surgical device for muscular expansion and electrostimulation. Recipient prize French Acad. Surgery, 1985, French Acad. Scis. 1986, cardiology prize Acad. of Medicine of Argentina, 1988. Fellow Internat. Coll. Surgeons; mem. N.Y. Acad. Scis. (life), European Cir. of Cardiac Surgeons (founder 1991). Home: 116 rue de la Tour, 75116 Paris France Office: Broussais Hosp Dept Cardiovascular Surgery, 96 rue Didot, 75014 Paris France

CHADHA, KAILASH CHANDRA, cancer research scientist; b. Churu, Raj., India, July 1, 1943; came to U.S., 1969; s. Ralla Ram and Budhwanti (Kohli) C.; m. Anju Sabharwal, May 22, 1971; children: Sonia, Priya, Kunal. MSc, Indian Agrl. Rsch. Inst., Delhi, India, 1964; PhD, U. Guelph, Ont., Can., 1968. Cancer rsch. scientist Roswell Park Cancer Inst., Buffalo,

1969-76, cancer rsch. scientist III, 1976-81, cancer rsch. scientist IV, 1981—. Contbr. more than 80 rsch. publs. including book chpts. to peer rev. jours.; mem. editl. bd. Jour. Medicine. Mem. Am. Soc. Microbiology (v.p. western N.Y. chpt. 1988-90, pres. 1990-91), Am. Soc. Virology, Internat. Soc. for Interferon Rsch., N.Y. Acad. Scis., European Cancer Soc., Soc. for Exptl. Biology & Medicine. Home: 106 Summerview Rd Buffalo NY 14221-1344 Office: Roswell Park Cancer Inst Molecular Cellular Biology Dept Buffalo NY 14263

CHAET, DOUGLAS L., healthcare manager; b. Washington, Mar. 13, 1960; s. Alfred B. and Shirley R. Chaet. BA in Psychology, U. S. Fla., 1981, MS in Mgmt., 1983. Diplomate Am. Coll. Healthcare Execs. Ind. cons. N.Y.C., 1992—; asst. adminstr. HCA New Port Richey (Fla.) Hosp., 1981-84; dir. provider rels. Equicon/Tampa Bay Health Plan, St. Petersburg, Fla., 1984-86; regional dir. Pvt. Healthcare Systems, Atlanta, 1986-89, First Health, Atlanta, 1989-92; pres./CEO Piedmont Healthcare Orgn., Atlanta, 1992-94; pres., CEO Lenox Hill Physician-Hosp. Orgns., N.Y.C., 1994—. Author: Structuring Capitated Models for Integrated Delivery Systems, 1994. Mem. Am. Acad. Med. Adminstrs., Healthcare Fin. Mgmt. Assn., Am. Assn. Integrated Delivery Systems (chmn. bd. dirs. 1992—), Rotary. Home: 1775 York Ave Apt 33H New York NY 10128

CHAFETZ, LESTER, pharmaceutical educator, researcher, director; b. Providence, Sept. 21, 1929; s. Isaac and Dora (Gabrilowitz) C.; m. Jan Klapper, July 24, 1960; children: Jill Ellen, Glenn Richard. BS, R.I. Coll. Pharmacy, 1951; MS, U. Wis., 1953, PhD, 1955. Rsch. assoc. analytical chemistry Sterling Winthrop Rsch. Inst., Rensselaer, N.Y., 1959-61; chief analytical chemist Irwin Neislet & Co., Decatur, Ill., 1961-64; head devel. and control drug system rsch. U. Ark. Med. Ctr., Little Rock, 1964-65; dir. phys. and analytical rsch. Warner-Lambert Co., Morris Plains, N.J., 1965-84; pres. Chafetz Assoc. Pharm. Co., New Providence, N.J., 1984-87; prof., dir. pharm. tech. U. Mo., Kansas City, 1987—; cons. in field. Author: The Ill Tempered String Quartet, 1989; contbr. over 70 articles to profl. jours. Capt. USAF, 1955-59. Fellow AAAS, Am. Inst. Chemists, Am. Assn. Pharm. Scientists; mem. Am. Chem. Soc., Am. Pharm. Assn. Home: 4813 W 122nd Ter Overland Park KS 66209-1574 Office: U Mo Ctr Pharm Tech KPB 202 Kansas City MO 64110-2499

CHAFETZ, MICHAEL DAVID, psychologist, researcher; b. San Antonio, Apr. 8, 1953; s. Joseph David and Ruth (Phillips) C.; m. Marjorie Ruth Esman, May 25, 1979; 1 child, Hannah Esman Chafetz. BS, Tulane U., 1975, MS, 1978; PhD, Tex. Christian U., 1981; clin. respecialization student, U. So. Miss., 1992-94. Asst. prof. U. Southwestern La., Lafayette, 1981-84; vis. asst. prof. Tulane U., New Orleans, 1984-85; scientist Rockefeller U., N.Y.C., 1985-86; pvt. practice clin. asst. New Orleans, 1991-92; intern Baylor Coll. Medicine, 1994-95, clin. neuropsychology resident, 1995—; adj. asst. prof. U. New Orleans, 1986-91; expert witness fed. and state cts., La., 1987-89; referee, reviewer sci. jours. and books; sci. journalist local newspapers, La., 1983-84. Author: Nutrient Bases of Behavior, 1990, Smart for Life, 1992; co-editor spl. issue So. Psychologist, 1985; contbr. chpts. to books and articles to profl. jours. Recipient awards new play contest New Orleans Contemporary Arts Ctr., 1992, 93. Fellow Am. Psychol. Soc.; mem. APA, AAAS, Soc. for Neurosci., So. Soc. for Philosophy and Psychology (Richard M. Griffith Meml. award 1985), Nat. Acad. Neuropsychol. (assoc.), Sigma Xi.

CHAFKIN, RITA M., physician, dermatologist; b. N.Y.C., Apr. 11, 1929; d. Joseph and Dora (Winslow) Melnick; m. Samuel Chafkin, June 29, 1952; children: Elise Ceil Perkins, Marc David Chafkin (dec.). BA, NYU, 1949; MD, NYU Med. Sch., 1953; cert. in dermatology, NYU Postgrad. Med. Sch., 1957. Diplomate Am. Acad. Dermatology, 1959. Intern in internal medicine Kings County Hosp., Bklyn., 1953-54; dermatology resident Bellevue Hosp., N.Y.C., 1954-55; postgrad. trainee NYU Postgrad. Med. Sch., 1955-56, fellow in dermatology, 1956-57; preceptceship with Dr. Marion Sulzberger; pvt. practice dermatology Modesto, Calif., 1958-94; assoc. clin. peof. dermatology U. Calif., Davis, 1975—; clinic dir. dermatology Stanislaus County Med. Ctr., Modesto, 1958—. artist in mixed media. Mem. bd. dirs. Stanislaus County Med. Ctr. Found., 1982—, pres. 1984-85. Recipient Tchr. of the Yr. award Stanislaus County Med. Ctr., Modesto, 1988, Founder's Dinner honoree, 1992. Fellow Am. Acad. Dermatology; mem. AMA, Calif. Med. Soc., San Francisco Dermatology Soc., Stanislaus County Med. Soc. (pres. 1983-84), Pacific Dermatology Assn. (fin. com. 1959—). Hebrew.

CHAHINIAN, A(RAM) PHILIPPE, oncologist; b. Paris, June 21, 1942; came to U.S., 1974; m. Marjorie Ellen; 1 child, Michael J. B., Buffon Coll., Paris, 1960; MD, Paris U., 1969. Diplomate Am. Bd. Internal Medicine, Am. Bd. Med. Oncology. Intern, resident Paris Univ. Hosps., France, 1968-74; fellow noeplastic diseases Mt. Sinai Sch. Medicine, N.Y.C., 1974-76, asst. prof., 1976-79, assoc. prof., 1980-88; prof. clin. medicine Coll. Physicians and Surgeons Columbia U., N.Y.C., 1990-92; prof. dept. medicine Mt. Sinai Sch. Medicine, N.Y.C., 1995—, prof., 1995—; adj. prof. dept. neoplastic diseases Mt. Sinai Sch. Medicine, N.Y.C., 1992-95. Author: Lung Cancer, 1976; author (with others) of books; contbr. articles to profl. jours. Lt. Med. Corps, French Army, 1970. Rsch. grantee Nat. Cancer Inst., 1984. Fellow Am. Coll. Physicians; mem. Am. Soc. Clin. Oncology, Am. Assn. Cancer Rsch., Am. Fedn. Clin. Rsch., N.Y. Acad. Scis. Office: Mt Sinai Sch of Medicine Dept NeoPlastic 1 Gustave L Levy Pl New York NY 10029-6574

CHAI, CHEN KANG, geneticist, veterinarian; b. Hebei, People's Republic of China, Feb. 14, 1916; came to U.S., 1946; s. Yu Chie Chai and Manjung Wang; m. Ling Chi Mao, Feb. 3, 1952; children: Leon C., Jean J. DVM, Army Vet. Coll., Nanking, People's Republic of China, 1936; PhD, Mich. State U., 1951. Rsch. assoc. Jackson Lab., Bar Harbor, Maine, 1952-57, staff scientist, 1957-67, sr. staff scientist, 1967-83, sr. staff scientist emeritus; prof. Beijing Union Med. Coll., 1987; cons. Inst. Lab. Animal Sci., Pan Jin Yuan, Beijing, People's Republic of China, 1987—; vis. fellow MIT, Cambridge, 1952-53; vis. lectr. Inst. Animal Sci., Beijing, 1985, 87, Army Vet. Coll., Changchuen, People's Republic of China, 1985. Author: Taiwan Aborigines, 1967, Genetic Evolution, 1976. Maj. Chinese Army, 1940-46. Guggenheim fellow, 1962. Fellow AAAS. Office: Jackson Lab Bar Harbor ME 04609

CHAIKEN, BARRY PAUL, physician, health information company executive; b. Bklyn., July 17, 1956; s. Raymond and Estelle (Cohen) C. BA in Psychology, SUNY, Albany, 1977; MD, SUNY, Bklyn., 1981; MPH, Harvard U., 1981; student, SUNY, Stony Brook, 1973-74. Diplomate Am. Bd. Quality Assurance. Intern in internal medicine Brockton (Mass.) Hosp., 1981-82; epidemic intelligence svc. officer Ctrs. for Disease Control, Atlanta, 1982-84; resident N.J. Dept. Health, Trenton, 1984-85; med. dir. Newlevel Technology, Inc., Lawrence, Mass., 1985-86; staff physician Framingham (Mass.) Heart Study, 1986-88; med. dir., chief oper. officer Infomedics, Inc., 1988-90; cons. InterQual, Inc., Marlboro, Mass., 1990-91; v.p. med. planning and devel. Health Risk Mgmt., Inc., Mpls., 1992-93; v.p. clin. mktg. GMIS Inc., Mpls., 1993-95; med. dir. Access Health Inc., Boston, 1996—; physician cons. MediQual Systems, Inc., Westborough, Mass., 1986. Lt. USPHS, 1982-84. NIH grantee, 1987, 1989. Fellow Am. Coll. Preventive Medicine, Am. Bd. Quality Assurance and Utilization REv. Physicians (bd. dirs.); mem. AMA, APHA, NAMCP, Am. Coll. Med. Quality, Am. Coll. Physician Execs., Mass. Med. Soc. (editorial bd. Managed Care Medicine, Jour. of Clin. Outcomes). Home: 121 Saint Botolph St Boston MA 02115-4811 Office: Access Health Inc Prudential Ctr 13th Fl Boston MA 02199

CHAIKEN, BERNARD HENRY, internist, gastroenterologist; b. Bklyn., Oct. 14, 1927; s. Max and Esther (Golland) C.; m. Mildred Gilbert, Dec. 5, 1950; children: Barry Glenn, Caryl Joy Gordon. Student, NYU, 1944-45; MD, U. Tex., Dallas, 1949. Diplomate Am. Bd. Internal Medicine, subspecialty Bd. Gastroenterology. Intern Boston City Hosp., 1949-50; resident physician Cushing VA Hosp., Framingham, Mass., 1950-51, Phila. VA Hosp., 1953-54; staff physician VA Hosp. Dallas, 1954-55, VA Hosp., East Orange, N.J., 1955-56; attending physician Overlook Hosp., Summit, N.J., 1956—, St. Barnabas Med. Ctr., Livingston, N.J., 1956—; vis. fellow Hosp. of U. Pa., Phila., 1954; clin. instr. Southwestern Med. Sch., U. Tex., Dallas, 1954-55; clin. asst. prof. medicine Seton Hall Coll. Med. Sch., Jersey City, 1956-58. Contbr. articles to med. jours. Capt. U.S. Army M.C., 1951-53. Fellow ACP; mem. Am. Coll. Gastroenterology (Best Clin. Vignette Paper and Poster Presentation 1995), Am. Soc. Internal Medicine, Am. Gastroenterol. Assn., Med. Soc., N.J. Med. Soc., N.J. Gastroenterol. Soc. (pres. 1964-65). Home: 12 Taylor Rd Short Hills NJ 07078 Office: 58 Chatham Rd Short Hills NJ 07078

CHAIT, ARNOLD, radiologist; b. N.Y.C., Jan. 20, 1930; s. Irving and Tillie (Newman) C.; m. Joan Lois Oppenheim, Mar. 14, 1965; children: Andrea, Elizabeth, Caroline. B.A., N.Y. U., 1951; M.D., U. Utrecht, Netherlands, 1957; M.A. (hon.), U. Pa., 1971. Diplomate: Am. Bd. Radiology. Intern Kings County Hosp., Bklyn., 1958; resident in pathology Manhattan Vets. Hosp., N.Y.C., 1959; radiology Kings County Hosp., 1959-62; instr. radiology State U. N.Y., Bklyn., 1962-64; asst. prof. radiology State U. N.Y., 1964-67, asso. prof., 1967; asst. prof. radiology U. Pa., Phila., 1967-70; asso. prof. U. Pa., 1970-74, prof., 1974-76, clin. prof., 1976—; chief vascular radiology Hosp. U. Pa., 1969-76, dir. dept. radiology Grad. Hosp., 1976—, pres. med. staff, 1981-83; cons. radiology Bklyn. VA Hosp., 1962-67, Phila. VA Hosp., 1969-76, Phila. Naval Hosp., 1975-76. Contbr. articles to profl. jours. Fellow Coll. Physicians Phila., Am. Coll. Radiology; mem. Pa., Phila County med. socs., Am., Roentgen Ray Soc. Phila. Roentgen Ray Soc. (pres. 1983-84), Radiol. Soc. N. Am., N.Y. Roentgen Soc., AAAS, Assn. U. Radiologists, Soc. Cardiovascular Radiology Am. Heart Assn. (council on cardiovascular radiology), Soc. Uroradiology, Soc. Cardiovascular and Interventional Radiology. Home: 835 Chauncey Rd Narberth PA 19072-1303 Office: Univ Pa Grad Hosp Radiology Dept 19th And Spruce St Philadelphia PA 19142

CHAIT, MAXWELL MANI, physician; b. Linz, Austria, Nov. 7, 1947; Came to the U.S., 1953; s. Morris and Eva (Lederman) C.; m. Lynne Robin Milstein C.; children: Alanna Rose, Daniel Lawrence, Michael Paul. BA magna cum laude, U. Utah, Salt Lake City, 1969; BS cum laude, U. Calif., San Francisco, 1969, MD, 1972. Diplomate Am. Bd. Internal Medicine, 1975, Am. Bd. Gastroenterology, 1977; lic. N.Y., Utah. Intern st. medicine U. So. Calif. Med. Ctr., L.A. County, 1972-73; resident in medicine Cornell Coop. Hosps., North Shore U. Hosp., Manhasset, N.Y., 1973-75; fellow GI Cornell Coop. Hosps., Meml. Sloan-Kettering Cancer Ctr., N.Y.C., 1975-77; attending physician White Plains (N.Y.) Hosp., 1977—; asst. attending physician St. Agnes Hosp., White Plains, 1977—, Columbia Presbyn. Med. Ctr., N.Y., 1993—; asst. clin. prof. medicine Coll. Physicians & Surgeons of Columbia U., 1993—; Mem. MSO bd. dirs. Westchester Health Svcs. Network; lectr. in field. Mem. bd. dirs. United Synagogue of Conservative Judaism Commn. on Jewish Edn.; pres. Westchester Assn. of Hebrew Schs., 1992-94; former mem. bd. trustees Temple Israel of White Plains; coach baseball, softball, basketball Scarsdale Recreation Dept. Fellow Am. Coll. Gastroenterology, Am. Coll. Physicians; mem. Am. Gastroenterological Assn., Am. Soc. Gastrointestinal Study, N.Y. Acad. Gastroenterology, N.Y. Soc. Gastrointestinal Endoscopy, Westchester Acad. Medicine, Crohn and Colitis Found. of Am. (CMAC com.). Office: Hartsdale Med Group 180 E Hartsdale Ave Hartsdale NY 10530

CHAKOS, PETER S., pharmacist; b. Buffalo, June 7, 1956; s. Speros and Evangeline (Drepanoitis) C. BS in Pharmacy cum laude, SUNY, Buffalo, 1980, MBA, 1993. Registered pharmacist, N.Y. Pharmacy intern Children's Hosp., Buffalo, 1977-81; pharmacist Buffalo Gen. Hosp., 1981-82, Rochester (N.Y.) Gen. Hosp., 1982-88; clin. pharmacy coord. St. Mary's Hosp., Rochester, 1988—; lectr. L.A.H.E.C. Corp., Erie, Pa., 1991—; nursing home cons. PHARMAC Cons., Buffalo, 1991—; cons. pharmacist Western N.Y. Artificial Kidney Ctr., Buffalo, 1993—; adv. bd. HCR Home Health Care, Rochester, 1995—. Fellow Am. Soc. Cons. Pharmacists; mem. Am. Med. Writers Assn., Am. Soc. Hosp. Pharmacists, Nat. Strength and Conditioning Assn., N.Y. Soc. Hosp. Pharmacists. Office: St Marys Hospital 89 Genesee St Rochester NY 14623

CHALFIN, SUSAN ROSE, psychologist; b. Phila., Apr. 26, 1956; d. Harry Herbert and Arlene Sybil (Abrams) C.; m. Thomas Arthur Dughi, May 22, 1983. BA, Columbia U., 1978; postgrad., Wayne State U., 1978-79; MA, Clark U., 1982, PhD, 1990. Lic. psychologist, Fla. Rsch. asst. dept. psychology Barnard Coll., Columbia U., N.Y.C., 1976-78; grad. asst. Wayne State U., Detroit, 1978-79; psychometrician Spl. Edn. Program, Balt., 1984; family therapist, psychometrician Frederick County Spl. Edn. and Treatment Program, Frederick, Md., 1984-87; psychology assoc. Psychol. Counseling & Consultation Ctr., Glen Burnie, Md., 1987-88; behavioral specialist div. psychology Jackson Meml. Hosp., Miami, Fla., 1989-90; asst. prof. U. Miami, 1994—; cons. Hughes-Gaeda Ctr., Miami, 1989-90, Alliance for Psychol. Svcs., Miami, 1990-94. Contbr. articles to profl. jours. Univ. scholar Clark U., 1979-80, Univ. fellow, 1980-81, rsch. fellow, 1981-82; fellow NIMH, 1982-83. Mem. APA. Office: U Miami Dept Pediatrics D-820 1601 NW 12th Ave # 016820 Miami FL 33136-1005

CHALLELA, MARY SCAHILL, maternal, child health nurse; b. Hopedale, Mass., Nov. 30, 1927; d. James and Sarah Mary (Norton) Scahill; m. Charles V. Challela, May 29, 1976. BS, Boston U., 1954, MS, 1967, D in Nursing Sci., 1979. Staff nurse Mass. Gen. Hosp., Boston, 1949-51, U.S. Indian Svc., Ariz., 1951-52; sr. instr. Cleve. Met. Gen. Hosp. Sch. Nursing, 1954-66; asst. prof. Northeastern U., Boston, 1967-70; cons. Shriver Ctr., Waltham, Mass., 1970-72, dir. nursing univ. affiliated program, 1972-93; ret., 1993; mem. staff continuing edn. New Eng. Regional Genetics Group, 1990-92. Contbr. articles to profl. jours. Pres. Sacred heart Guild, Hopedale, 1972-74; chair Commn. on Disabilities, Hopedale, 1987-95; bd. dirs. Coun. on Aging, Hopedale, 1993—. Recipient Citizen Achievement award Mass. Assn. for Retarded Citizens, 1987, Excellence in Nursing award Sigma Theta Tau, 1987; Am. Assn. Mental Retardation fellow, 1988. Mem. ANA, Mass. Nurses Assn., Internat. Assn. Nurses in Genetics.

CHALLONER, DAVID REYNOLDS, university official, physician; b. Appleton, Wis., Jan. 31, 1935; s. Reynolds Ray and Marion (Below) C.; m. Jacklyn Davnes Anderson, Aug. 30, 1958; children: David Harvey, Laura Reynolds, Britt-Davnes. B.S. cum laude, Lawrence Coll., Appleton, 1956; postgrad., Cambridge (Eng.) U., 1958; M.D. cum laude, Harvard, 1961. Resident in internal medicine Columbia Presbyn. Hosp., N.Y.C., 1961-63; research assoc. Nat. Heart Inst., Bethesda, Md., 1963-65; chief med. resident and endocrinology research fellow U. Wash., Seattle, 1965-67; prof. medicine, asst. chmn. dept. Ind. U. Sch. Medicine, Indpls., 1967-75; vis. scholar Inst. Medicine, Nat. Acad. Sci., 1974; dean St. Louis U. Sch. Medicine, 1975-82; v.p. health affairs U. Fla., Gainesville, 1982—; chmn. pres.'s com. on nat. med. sci. NIH, 1988-91, mem. dirs. adv. com., 1990-96; mem. com. sci., engring. pub. policy NAS, 1993—; cons. Eli Lilly & co., NIH. Served to lt. comdr. USPHS, 1963-65. Recipient Harvard Med. Alumni award, 1961, Dr. William Beaumont award AMA, 1982, Disting. Alumnus award Lawrence U., 1987. Fellow AAAS; mem. Am. Fedn. Clin. Rsch. (pres. 1975), Inst. Medicine, Nat. Acad. Sci., Am. Soc. Clin. Investigation, Endocrine Soc., Am. Diabetes Assn., Assn. Am. Physicians, Boylston Soc., Am. Clin. and Climatol. Assn., Phi Beta Kappa, Alpha Omega Alpha, Beta Theta Pi. Clubs: Racquet (St. Louis); Cosmos (Washington). Home: 2715 NW 22nd Dr Gainesville FL 32605-2975 Office: U Fla PO Box 100014 Gainesville FL 32610-0014

CHALMERS, JOHN HOLBROOK, diagnostic radiologist; b. Monroe, La., Nov. 30, 1944; s. John Holbrook Sr. and Stella Mae (Blankenship) C.; m. Marilyn Dorris Tull, Dec. 31, 1970; children: Jennifer Lynn, Zachary Douglas. BA with honors, U. Tex., 1966; MD with high honors, Baylor Coll. of Medicine, 1970. Diplomate Am. Bd. Radiology, Am. Bd. Nuclear Medicine. Pvt. practice Brownwood, Tex., 1977-90, U. Tex. Health Ctr. at Tyler, 1991—. Maj. USAF, 1975-77. Mem. Am. Coll. Radiology, Tex. Radiol. Soc., Radiol. Soc. of N.Am., Am. Roentgen Ray Soc., Am. Coll. Nuclear Medicine, Tex. Med. Assn., Smith County Med. Soc., Alpha Omega Alpha, Alpha Epsilon Delta. Home: 18862 Big Timber Rd Tyler TX 75703 Office: U Tex Health Care Ctr PO Box 2003 Tyler TX 75710

CHALUPKA, STEPHANIE CHRZSIEWSKI, nurse educator; b. Worcester, Mass., Sept. 12, 1955; d. Laurence and Florence Dorothy (Haddad) Chrzsiewski; m. Norman Francis Chalupka Jr., Aug. 15, 1946; children: Anne, Andrew. BS, Worcester State Coll., 1980; MS, Boston Coll., Chestnut Hill, Mass., 1981; EdD Candidate, U. Mass., Amherst, 1991—. RN, Mass.; clin. specialist ANA; enterostomal therapist. Dir. infection control and patient edn. Hubbard Regional Hosp., Webster, Mass., 1976-78; dir. occupational health Lake View Farms, Grafton, Mass., 1978-80; post anesthesia care nurse U. Mass. Med. Ctr., Worcester, 1980-81; clin. specialist, dir. quality assurance Cert. Nursing Svcs. (St. Vincent Health Care), Worcester, 1982-89; dir. pub. health Town of Grafton, 1989—; instr. dept. nursing Worcester State Coll., 1991—; cons. infection control Millbury (Mass.) Dist. Nursing Soc., 1991—, Cert. Nursing Svc., Worcester, 1989—; mem. profl. adv. com. Mass. Easter Seal Soc., Worcester, 1993—, Cert. Nursing Svcs., Worcester, 1987—. Vol. Grafton Pub. Schs., 1989—, com. on sch. nursing practice, 1993—; first aid instr. 4-H Club, Grafton, 1990—; parent vol. coord. Grafton Intermediate Sch., 1990-92. Hiatt scholar Worcester State Coll., 1978. Mem. APHA, ANA, NEA, Mass. Pub. Health Assn., Mass. Nurses Assn., Mass. Edn. Assn., Sigma Theta Tau. Antiochian Orthodox. Home: 88 Merrian Rd Grafton MA 01519 Office: Worcester State Coll 486 Chandler St Worcester MA 01602

CHAMBERLAIN, BARBARA JEAN, nurse; b. Cambridge, May 15, 1949; d. Martin and Geraldine (Gonsalves) M.; m. Michael Hyman Goldberg, June 23, 1968 (dec. 1986); children: Caryn, Sheryl; m. Mark Munroe Chamberlain, Jan. 1, 1988. AAS, Gloucester County Coll., Sewell, N.J., 1981; BA, Glassboro (N.J.) State Coll., 1988; BSN, Stockton State Coll., 1990; MSN, U. Pa., 1992. RN, N.J., Pa., Del.; cert. CCRN, gerontology, clin. specialist in critical care and med.-surg. nursing, clin. specialist in gerontology. Nurse Kennedy Meml. Hosp., Turnersville, N.J., 1981—; nurse Mainland div. Atlantic City Med. Ctr., 1993—; nurse Kennedy Meml. Hosp., 1981—, Holy Redeemer Vis. Nurse Assn., 1995—; preceptor Kennedy Meml. Hosp., 1988; instr. nursing Gloucester County Coll., 1988-90; asst. prof. nursing Atlantic C.C., 1992—. Mem. AACN, N.J. State Nurses Assn. (com. mem.), Soc. Critical Care Medicine, Sigma Theta Tau, Kappa Delta Pi. Democrat. Episcopalian.

CHAMBERLAIN, DIANE, psychotherapist, author, clinical social worker; b. Plainfield, N.J., Mar. 18, 1950; d. John and Anna Delores (Chamberlain) Lopresti; m. Richard David Chmielewski, Apr. 14, 1973 (div. 1993). BSW, San Diego State U., 1975, MSW, 1978. Bd. cert. clin. social worker. Clin. social worker Social Advocates for Youth, San Diego, 1978-80; clin. social worker Sharp Meml. Hosp., San Diego, 1980-83, Children's Hosp. and Nat. Health Ctr., Washington, 1983-85; pvt. practice psychotherapy Alexandria, Va., 1985-92. Author: (novels) Private Relations, 1989, Lovers and Strangers, 1990, Secret Lives, 1991, Keeper of the Light, 1992, Fire and Rain, 1993, Brass Ring, 1994, Reflection, 1996; contbr. nonfiction articles to profl. jours. Mem. Novelists Inc. Democrat. Office: PO Box 1331 Vienna VA 22183-1331

CHAMBERLAIN, JOHN MEREDITH, health facility executive, consultant; b. Little Rock, Apr. 27, 1950; s. Charles Thomson and Frances (Goodlett) C.; m. Debra Lee McAden, May 21, 1981; children: Jason Meredith, Frances Elizabeth. BA, Westminster Coll., Fulton, Mo., 1972; M of Health Adm., Washington U., St. Louis, 1985. Group leader Mallinckrodt, Inc., St. Louis, 1972-76, ops. mgr., 1978-82; plant mgr. Mallinckrodt, Inc., Beaufort, N.C., 1976-78; mgr. customer compliance Sigma Chem. Co., St. Louis, 1982-83; cons. Warner Health Svcs., St. Louis, 1983-85; dir. mktg. St. Louis Children's Hosp., St. Louis, 1985-87; asst. adminstr. Lakeview Hosp., Bountiful, Utah, 1987, Drs. Hosp. of Sarasota, Sarasota, Fla., 1987-90; med. staff liaison, chief devel. officer Glenwood Regional Med. Ctr., West Monroe, La., 1990-93, sr. v.p., chief operating officer, 1993-95; assoc. adminstr. ops. Med. Ctr. Hosp., Odessa, Tex., 1995—; ptnr. Med. Devel. Svcs., Sarasota, 1989—. Active Leadership La., Leadership Ouachita, Leadership Odessa. Fellow Am. Coll. Healthcare Execs., Rotary; mem. Am. Hosp. Assn. Republican. Unitarian.

CHAMBERLAIN, STEVEN CRAIG, neuroanatomist, bioengineer, mineralogist; b. Everett, Pa., Dec. 13, 1946; s. Carl Eugene and D. Suzanne (Rearick) C.; m. Helen Haritou, Apr. 29, 1972. B.S. in Elec. Engring., MIT, 1968; Ph.D., Syracuse U., 1978. Elec. engr. U.S. Army CDAASG-EUR, Augsburg, Fed. Republic Germany, 1970-73; instr. Inst. Sensory Research, Syracuse U., N.Y., 1977-78, asst. prof., 1978-82, assoc. prof., 1982-88, assoc. dir., 1985-86, chmn. dept. bioengring., 1986-92, dean coll. of engring., 1992-95, prof., 1988—; cons. editor Rocks and Minerals, Washington, 1980—; Am. editor Jour of the Russell Soc., 1984—; curator minerals Hamilton Coll., Clinton, N.Y., 1981—. Cons. editor Visual Neurosci., 1991-93; contbr. articles to profl. jours. Served with U.S. Army, 1970-73. Decorated Army Commendation medal, Meritorious Svc. medal; Grass Found. fellow, 1977; recipient Pres. Award for Teaching by Sharing, Eastern Fed. Mineral Lapidary Soc., 1978; Best Paper award, Friends of Mineralogy, 1984. Fellow Rochester Acad. Sci.; mem. Soc. Neurosci., Assn. for Rsch. in Vision and Ophthalmology, Mineralogical Assn. Can., Sigma Xi (Faculty Rsch. award 1993), Tau Beta Pi. Avocations: photography; opera; collecting minerals and hostas. Home: 105 Academy St Manlius NY 13104-1901 Office: Syracuse Univ Inst Sensory Rsch Syracuse NY 13244-5290

CHAMBERS, DAVID L., retired adult educator; b. Picton, Ont., Can., Apr. 28, 1920; s. David Lyall and Ruth (Farrington) C.; m. Patricia Anne Chambers; children: Katherine Anne, David William, Sharon Patricia, Michelle Laverne, Scott Alexander. Diploma, Rochester Inst. Tech., 1965. Tool and die maker Xerox Corp., Webster, N.Y., foreman indsl. components, ret., tchr. machine use, adult evening classes; now ret. With U.S. Army, 1939-43 WW II.

CHAMBERS, DONALD ARTHUR, biochemistry and molecular medicine educator; b. N.Y.C., Sept. 24, 1936. AB, Columbia U., 1959, PhD, 1972. Rsch. biochemist dept. surgery Harvard Med. Sch./Mass. Gen. Hosp., Boston, 1961-66; rsch. fellow in hematology dept. surgery Harvard Med. Sch./Beth Israel Hosp., Boston, 1967-68; faculty fellow in chem. biology Columbia U., N.Y.C., 1969-71; asst. rsch. biochemist Ctr. for Med. Genetics Dept. Medicine U. Calif. Med. Ctr., San Francisco, 1972-74, lectr. in biochemistry and biophysics Dept. Biochemistry, 1972-74, asst. prof. molecular biology and biochemistry, 1974-75; asst. prof. biol. chemistry and dermatology U. Mich., Ann Arbor, 1975-79, assoc. prof. biol. chemistry, 1979; prof. molecular biology U. Ill., Chgo., 1979—, prof. biol. chemistry, 1980—, rsch. prof. dermatology, 1981—; assoc. mem. Dental Rsch. Inst. U. Mich., 1978-79, adj. rsch. investigator Dept. Biol. Chemistry, 1979—; dir. Ctr. for Molecular Biology of Oral Disease, U. Ill., Chgo., 1979—, interim head dept. biochemistry, 1985, head dept. biochemistry, 1986—; vis. scholar Green Coll., Oxford U., 1989-93, hon. vis. fellow, 1993—; fellow Honors Coll., 1985—, hi Kappa Phi lectr., 1991, mem. rsch. adv. bd. Coll. Dentistry, 1979—, co-dir. MD/PhD program Coll. Medicine, 1988-93, mem. exec. com. Coll. Medicine, 1990—, others; vis. prof. Oxford U., 1989—; mem. nat. action com. Am. Assn. Dental Rsch., 1981—. Editorial reviewer Analytical Biochemistry, Archives Biochemistry and Biophysics, Archives Dermatology, Biochemica Acta, Biophysica Acta, Biochem. Jour., Blood, Cell, Endocrinology, Jour. Investigative Dermatology, Jour. Dental Rsch., Jour. Clin. Investigation, Jour. Biol. Chemistry, Molecular and Cell Biology, Nature, New Eng. Jour. Medicine, Procs. NAS, Sci., Thrombosis Rsch.; contbr. numerous articles to profl. jours. including Archives Oral Biology, Jour. Periodontal Rsch., Jour. Investigative Dermatology, Procs. NAS, Jour. Experimental Medicine, Cell, Archives Biochemistry and Biophysics, Nature. Recipient James Howard McGregor prize Columbia U., 1971; named Inventor of Yr., U. Ill., 1990; fellow in hematology NIH, 1967-68; fellow in chem. biology, 1969-71; rsch. grantee NIH-NIAMDD, 1975-79, 75-85, 79-80, 84—, NIH-NIDR, 1975-79, 78-79, Mich.-Phoenix Project, 1975-76, Am. Cancer Soc., 1977-78, 78, The Upjohn Co., 1982-87, Xytronyx, Inc., 1984—, Office of Naval Rsch., 1986—, Helene Curtis, Inc., 1988—; tng. grantee NIH-NIGMS, 1975-79, NIH-NIAMDD, 1976-79, 77-80, NIH-NIDR-NIAMDD, 1980—, NIH-NCI, 1982-88. Mem. AAAS, Am. Assn. Med. Colls., Am. Chem. Soc., Am. Fedn. Clin. Rsch., Am. Soc. Biol. Chemistry, Am. Soc. Cell Biology, Am. Soc. Microbiology, Internat. Assn. Dental Rsch. (com. on rsch. progress 1982-85, chmn. 1984-85, chmn. grad. tng. forum com. exptl. pathology sect. 1983), Assn. Dept. Chmn. Biol. Chemistry, Chgo. Assn. Immunologists, Chgo. Cancer Assn., N.Y. Acad. Scis. (organizer meeting The Double Helix, 40 Yrs. 1993), Royal Soc. Medicine, Soc. Investigative Dermatology, Phi Kappa Phi, Sigma Xi. Office: U Ill Coll Med Dept Biochemistry 1819 W Polk St # C 536 Chicago IL 60612-7331 Office: Ctr Molecular Biol Oral Diseases 801 S Paulina St # C 860 Chicago IL 60612-7210

CHAMBERS, EVA, retired gerontology nurse; b. Ft. Smith, Ark., Sept. 29, 1928; d. Ernest H. and Winnie (Williams) McLellan; m. James E. Chambers, July 23, 1952 (dec.); children: Linda, Hal, Mildred. Diploma, Ark. Bapt.

Hosp., 1950; BSN, U. Cen. Ark., 1976. RN, Ark. Charge nurse emergency dept. Bapt. Hosp., Little Rock; supr. Meml. Hosp., North Little Rock, Ark.; asst. dir. nurses Doctor's Hosp., Little Rock; charge nurse VA Hosp., Little Rock.

CHAMBERS, FLOYD ALLEN, counselor; b. Shreve, Ohio, Oct. 3, 1928; s. Roscoe Coral and Myra Elizabeth (Wright) C.; m. Lyndall Lee Wooley, Feb. 1, 1953; children: Mark Allen, Debra Lynn, Norman Kent, Sheryl Yvonne, Jon Scott. BA, Coll. Wooster, 1950; MDiv, McCormick Seminary, Chgo., 1953; MEd, Coll. William and Mary, 1980, EdD, 1986. Lic. profl. counselor, Va. Min. Presbyn. Ch., Ky., Canada, 1953-56; chaplain, 1st lt. USAF, 1956, advanced through grades to lt. col., 1971, ret., 1978; pastoral counselor Tidewater Pastoral Counseling Svcs., Norfolk, Va., 1979—. Fellow Am. Assn. Pastoral Counselors; mem. Am. Assn. for Marriage and Family Therapy (clin.). Office: Tidewater Pastoral Counseling Svcs 800 Colonial Ave Norfolk VA 23507-1810

CHAMBERS, HENRY GEORGE, orthopedic surgeon; b. Portsmouth, Va., June 22, 1956; s. Walter Charles and Teresa Frances (Fernandez) C.; m. Jill Annette Swanson, June 10, 1978; children: Sean Michael, Reid Christopher. BA summa cum laude in Biochemistry, U. Colo., 1978; MD, Tulane U. Sch. Medicine, 1982. Diplomate Am. Bd. Orthopaedic Surgery. Commd. 2d lt. U.S. Army, 1978; advanced through grades to maj.; intern Fitzsimmons Army Med. Ctr., Aurora, Colo., 1982-83; orthopaedic surgery resident Brooke Army Med. Ctr., Ft. Sam Houston, Tex., 1983-87, chief resident, 1986-87, staff orthopaedic surgeon to asst. residency program dir., 1987-89, asst. chief surgeon orthopaedic surgery svc., 1990-92; staff orthopaedic surgeon DeWitt Army Hosp., Ft. Belvoir, Va., 1987; pediatric orthopaedic fellow San Diego Children's Hosp., 1989-90; adj. prof. natural scis. Incarnate Word Coll., San Antonio, 1986—; asst. prof. surgery Uniformed Svcs. U. Health Scis., Bethesda, Md., 1987—; asst. program dir. Brooke Army Med. Ctr. Orthopaedic Surgery, 1987-92; asst. prof. U. Calif. San Diego Med. Ctr., 1989—. Co-author: Long Distance Runner's Guide to Training, 1983; contbr. various articles to profl. jours. Physician St. Vincent de Paul Clinic for Homeless, San Diego, 1989—; v.p. United Cerebral Palsy. Recipient Comdrs. award for oustanding rsch. Brooke Army Med. Ctr., 1987. Fellow Acad. Cerebral Palsy Devel. Medicine, Pediatric Orthopedic Soc. N.Am., Am. Acad. Pediatrics, Acad. Orthopedic Soc., Orthopedic Rsch. Soc., Am. Acad. Orthopedic Surgeons, Physicians for Social Responsibility, Physicians Coun. for Responsible Medicine, We. Orthopedic Soc., Earth Island Inst., World Wildlife Fedn., Wilderness Soc., Union Concerned Scientists, Friends of Earth, Handgun Control, Phi Beta Kappa. Democrat. Unitarian. Home: 5458 Sandburg Ave San Diego CA 92122-4128

CHAMBERS, JAY LEE, clinical psychologist; b. Providence, Ky., Apr. 7, 1923; s. Jay Lee and Anna Royston (Griggs) C.; m. Willa Marie Browning, June 1, 1952 (dec. Aug. 1994); children: Ann Marie, Carol Louise; m. Elizabeth T. Burnette, Dec. 29, 1995. BA, George Washington U., 1948; MA, U. Ky., 1952, PhD, 1954. Chmn. psychology dept. Muskingum Coll., New Concord, Ohio, 1954-56; dir. psychol. svcs. Eastern State Hosp., Williamsburg, Va., 1956-58; dir. Charles L. Mix Meml. Fund, Inc., Americus, Ga., 1958-64; dir. psychol. svcs. Ky. State Hosp., Danville, 1964-66; clin. psychologist Student Health Svcs., Fla. State U., Tallahassee, 1966-70; dir. Ctr. for Psychol. Svcs., Coll. William and Mary, Williamsburg, 1970-90; pres. Motivation Analysis, Fairfield, Va., 1991—. Served with USMCR, 1942-46. Mem. Am. Psychol. Assn., Southeastern Psychol. Assn., So. Soc. for Philosophy and Psychology. Democrat. Contbr. articles to profl. jours. Home and Office: 258 Mackeys Ln Fairfield VA 24435-9801

CHAMBERS, ROBERT TULLY, surgeon; b. Chandler, Que., Can., July 28, 1941; s. Robert John and Catherine Clara (Tully) C.; m. Julian Patricia Irwin, Sept. 21, 1968 (div. May 1994); children: Alexandra Katherine, Elizabeth Margaret, Rebecca Victoria, Robert Andrew David. MD, Queens U., 1966; MSc in Exptl. Surgery, McGill U., 1969. Diplomate Am. Bd. Surgery. Rotating intern Montreal Gen. Hosp., 1966-67, resident I, II, III, 1967-70, chief resident, 1971-72; resident IV U. Colo. Med. Ctr., 1970-71; surg. staff, cons. in surgery Prince George Regional Hosp., Prince George, B.C., Can., 1972-78; active staff dept. surgery Saint Joseph's Med. Ctr., Joliet, 1978-95; active staff AmSurg Inc., Joliet, 1981-95, Silver Cross Hosp., Joliet, 1978-95; surgeon MeritCare Clinic, Wahpeton, 1995—; assoc. staff Saint Francis Med. Ctr., Breckenridge, Minn., 1995—; chmn. strategic planning Glenwood Med. Group, Ltd., 1987-89, chmn. fin. com., 1989-95, corp. sec.-treas., 1991-92, corp. treas. 1985-95, corp. sec. 1982-83; surgery com. Saint Joseph's Med. Ctr., Joliet, 1986-89, 90-95, chmn. 1988-89, 90-91, cancer com. 1982-85, 86-88, 90-95, chmn. 1983-85, 93-95, tumor bd. 1991-95, exec. com. 1985-86, 88-89, 90-91, utilization rev. com. 1982-86, 91-92, chmn. 1985-86, formulary com. 1979-81, blood transfusion com. 1979-85, orthopedic com. 1982-85, endoscopy com., 1993-95, chmn. 1994-94. Exec. prodr. Joliet Jaguar TV, 1991-95. Biship's com. Trinity Episcopalian Ch., Wahpeton, 1996—; bd. dirs. Joliet Vol. TV, 1990-95, v.p. 1993-94, Joliet Jaguar Youth Hockey Club, Inc., 1988-92, dir. pub. rels., 1990-92; citizen adv. panel Joliet Plant Amoco Chem. Co., 1992-95. Fellow Royal Coll. Surgeons of Can.; mem. ACS, Soc. of Am. Gastroenterol. Endoscopic Surgeons, Am. Soc. of Parenteral and Enteral Nutrition, Am. Coll. of Occupl. and Environ. Medicine, Am. Cancer Soc. (v.p. Will county unit 1985-87, pres. Greater Joliet unit 1987-89, dir. Ill. divsn. 1987-89, pub. edn. com. 1987-89, incidence and end-stage reporting com. 1987-89. Office: MeritCare Clinic-Wahpeton 332 Second Ave North Wahpeton ND 58075-4528

CHAMBERS, VINZUELLA, critical care nurse; b. Bklyn., May 27, 1961; d. Harvey and Thelma (Folks) Williams; 1 child, Nathaniel. AAS, Borough of Manhattan Coll., N.Y.C., 1987; BSN, SUNY, Bklyn., 1989. RN. Staff nurse Kings County Hosp. Ctr., Bklyn.; staff nurse post-anesthesia and surg. ICU Woodhull Hosp., Bklyn. Lincoln scholar; recipient B.M.C.C. Peer Tutor award. Mem. AACCN, N.Y. State Nurses Assn., Phi Theta Kappa.

CHAMBERS, WILLIAM ELDRIDGE, surgeon; b. Miami, Fla., Oct. 12, 1931; s. Silas Eldridge and Helen Patricia (Hughes) C.; m. Judith Lee Johnson, Dec. 28, 1952; children: William Eldridge Jr., Elizabeth Ann (dec.), Michael M., Howard N., Susan H. Peeler. BA, U. Va., 1951; MD, U. Pa., Phila., 1955. Diplomate Am. Bd. Surgery. Mem. staff Munroe Regional Med. Ctr., Ocala, Fla., 1962—; mem. staff Marion Community Hosp., Ocala, 1973—, pres. staff, 1975-77. Bd. dirs. Ocala Civic Theatre, 1985-91, chmn. devel. com., planning com., long-range planning com., search com., 1985-91, pres., 1991-92; trustee Marion Cmty. Hosp., 1979-81. Lt. comdr. USNR, 1960-62. Named Most Outstanding Bd. Mem., Ocala Civic Theatre, 1989. Fellow ACS (chmn. com. on applicants Ctrl Fla. chpt.); mem. AMA, Fla. Med. ASsn., Marion County Med. Soc. (pres. 1973). Republican. Home: 14350 SE 108th Ter Summerfield FL 34491-3780 Office: 220 SW 15th St Ocala FL 34474-4027

CHAMPE, PAMELA CHAMBERS, biochemistry educator, writer; b. Oakland, Calif., Aug. 29, 1945; d. Robert Leroy and Leah June (Musser) Chambers; m. Sewell Preston Champe, June 28, 1969; stepchildren: Mark Adrian, Sewell Peter. BA, Stanford U., 1967; MS, Purdue U., 1969; PhD, Rutgers U., 1974. Instr. Rutgers Med. Sch., Piscataway, N.J., 1974-76; asst. prof. Robert Wood Johnson Med. Sch. (formerly Rutgers Med. Sch.) U. Medicine and Dentistry N.J., Piscataway, 1977-84, assoc. prof. Robert Wood Johnson Med. Sch., 1984—; lectr. several med. schs. and tng. programs. Coeditor: Gene Families of Collagen and Other Proteins, 1980; co-author: Biochemistry (Lippincott's Illus. Revs.), 1987, 2d edit., 1994; co-author, coeditor: Pharmacology (Lippincott's Illus. Revs.), 1992. Health and Human Svcs. grantee, 1988-94; recipient Nat. award Basic Sci. Educator of the Year, 1995. Mem. AAAS, Assn. Am. Med. Colls., N.Y. Acad. Scis. Office: U Medicine and Dentistry NJ Robert Wood Johnson Med Sch 675 Hoes Ln Piscataway NJ 08854-5635*

CHAMPE, SEWELL PRESTON, molecular and microbiology educator; b. Montgomery, W.Va., Nov. 24, 1932; s. Sewell Jackson and Janice (Montgomery) C.; m. Pamela Chambers, June 28, 1969. BS, MIT, 1954; PhD, Purdue U., 1959. Asst. prof. Purdue U., West Lafayette, Ind., 1962-65, assoc. prof., 1966-69; prof. microbiology and molecular biology Rutgers U., New Brunswick, N.J., 1969—. Rsch. grantee NIH and NSF, 1962-92. Home: 308 6th Ave Montgomery WV 25136 Office: Rutgers U Waksman Inst New Brunswick NJ 08903

CHAMPION, MICHAEL EDWARD, physician assistant, clinical perfusionist; b. Oroville, Calif., Jan. 30, 1954; s. Robert Joseph and Shirley Anne (Rowland) C.; m. Marie S. Sittner, Oct. 8. 1990; children: Erin Kelly, Meghan Kathleen. AS, Cuyahoga C.C., 1980; BS, SUNY, Albany, 1983; MEd, Boston U., 1986; M of Med. Sci., St. Francis Coll., 1996. Cert. physician asst., NCCPA, clin. perfusionist ABCVP. Enlisted U.S. Army, 1972, advanced through grades to maj., 1994; ret., 1994, aviation medicine physician asst., 1980-87; chief physician asst./perfusionist Letterman Army Med. Ctr., 1989-91; founding physician asst./perfusionist Madigan Army Med. Ctr., 1991-94; cardiac surgery mgr., chief physician asst/perfusionist Mercy Med. Ctr., Janesville, Wis., 1994-96; dir. cardiac svcs. Hutchinson (Kans.) Hosp., 1996—; clin. instr. U.S. Army Physician Asst. Program, 1981-84, U.S. Army Adult Nurse Practitioner Program, 1982; EMS instr. Fayetteville Tech. Inst., 1983; instr. MEDEX program U. Washington, 1992-95, MMS programs St. Francis Coll., Loretto, Pa., 1996—; CEO Champion and Assocs., LLC; organizer Surg. Physician Asst. course, Jamaica, 1995. Contbr. articles to profl. jours. Treas. Rock County Rep. Party, Janesville, 1994; mem. Red Cross, Am. Cancer Soc., EAA Young Eagles Program. Mem. Am. Acad. Physician Assts. (rsch. rev. com. 1984, profl. and continuing edn. com. 1988, vets. caucus bd. dirs. 1989-91, vets. caucus pres. 1991-92, chmn. pilots assn. 1995, chmn. vets. caucus awards 1992-95, jud. affairs com. 1994, vice chmn. surg. congress 1994-96, chmn. 1996—, Outstanding Svc. award 1989), Wis. Acad. Physician Assts. (chair legis. com., sec. 1995, pres.-elect 1996), Soc. Army Physician Assts. (life, chief del. 1983-84, v.p. 1984-85, pres. 1985-86), Assn. Physician Assts. in Cardiovascular Surgery, Assn. Mil. Surgeons of U.S. (life, Physician Asst. ot Yr. 1992), Am. Soc. Extracorporeal Tech., Am. Heart Assn. Republican. Roman Catholic. Home: c/o 2237 Forest Park Derby KS 67037

CHAMPLIN, WILLIAM GLEN, clinical microbiologist-immunologist; b. Rogers, Ark., Sept. 10, 1923; s. Glen and Anna Champlin; m. Helen Elizabeth Garner, Feb. 2, 1951; 1 child, Steven. BS, N.E. Okla. State U., 1948; MS, U. Ark., 1965, PhD, 1971. Lab. dir. VA Med. Ctr., Fayetteville, Ark., 1955-65, clin. microbiologist, lab. dir., 1965-80; cons. ANL Med. Lab. Wash. Regional Med. Ctr. VA Med. Ctr., 1965-90; edn. coord. Antaeus Inst. Sch. Med. Tech., 1980-90; vis. prof. microbiology U. Ark., 1978-85. With U.S. Army, 1943-45. Mem. Am. Acad. Microbiology (specialist), Am. Soc. Clin. Pathologists (specialist), Sigma Xi.

CHAN, CARLYLE HUNG-LUN, psychiatrist, educator; b. Clarksdale, Miss., July 4, 1949; s. Henry Howe and Jennie (Wong) C.; m. Patricia Meyer, June 18, 1977; children: Christopher, Diana. BS, U. Wis., 1971; MD, Med. Coll. Wis., 1975. Diplomate Am. Bd. Psychiatry and Neurology. Resident in psychiatry U. Chgo., 1975-78; asst. prof. Med. Coll. Wis., Milw., 1980-86, assoc. prof., 1986—, dir. residency edn., 1987—; dir. catchment area Milw. County Mental Health Complex, 1981-82; dir. continuing med. edn., 1990; chief psychiatrist Psychiatrist Ctr., Columbia Hosp., Milw., 1982-87; dir. continuing med. edn. Med. Coll. Wis., Milw., 1990—, Soc. Tchg. Scholars, 1994; dir. course annual psychiat. conf., 1982—; dir. Door County (Wis.) Summer Inst., 1987—. Asst. editor Asian-Am. Psychiatry Newsletter, Washington, 1983-84; assoc. editor Acad. Psychiatry Newsletter, 1991-94; contbr. articles to profl. jours. Bd. dirs. Planning Council for Mental Health and Social Service, 1983—. Robert Wood Johnson clin. scholar Yale U., 1978-80; jr. Faculty Devel. award NIMH, 1983-85; Community Devel. award Apple Computer Co., Milw., 1984. Fellow Am. Psychiat. Assn.; mem. Wis. Psychiat. Assn. (pres. Milw. chpt. 1990-91), Assn. Acad. Psychiatry (regional coord. 1987—, regional coord. dir. 1993-96, treas. 1996—), Am. Assn. Dirs. Psychiat. Residency Tng. (sec. 1994-95, pres.-elect 1995, pres. 1996, treas. 1990-92, program com. chair 1993-94), Wis. State Med. Soc., Milw. County Med. Soc. Med. Coll. of Wis., Soc. Teaching Scholars. Office: Med Coll Wis Dept Psychiatry 8701 W Watertown Plank Rd Milwaukee WI 53226-3548

CHAN, CLARA SUET-PHANG, physician; b. Swatow, Guandong, People's Republic of China, Sept. 23, 1949; came to U.S., 1969; d. Hon-Kwong and Suet-Hing (Wong) C. BS, Mary Manse Coll., 1972; MD, George Washington U., 1976. Diplomate Am. Bd. Internal Medicine, Am. Bd. Hematology, Am. Bd. Oncology. Intern U. Miami (Fla.) Hosp., 1976-77, med. resident, 1977-79; fellow hematology, oncology George Washington U., 1979-81; fellow oncoloy research City of Hope Med. Ctr., Duarte, Calif., 1981-83, instr. medicine, 1982-83; asst. chief hematology VA Med. Ctr., Washington, 1983-91; with Hematology/Oncology Cons., Greenbelt, Md., 1991—; asst. prof. medicine George Washington U., 1983-88, assoc. prof., 1988—; prin. investigator stem cell lab. VA Med. Ctr., Washington, 1983-91; physician Hematology Oncology Cons., Greenbelt, Md., 1991—; project chmn. S.E. Cancer Study Group, Birmingham, Ala., 1982-85; mem. med. staff George Washington U., 1983—. Contbr. articles to profl. jours. Del. cancer update Citizen Ambassador program People to People Internat., 1986. Recipient Internat. Peace scholarship George Washington U. 1972-76; Med. Student Research grantee Pan Am. Health Orgn., 1974; Reader's Digest Internat. fellow United Christian Hosp., Hong Kong, 1976; research fellow VA Career Devel. program, Washington, 1981. Fellow ACP; mem. Am. Soc. Clin. Oncology, Am. Soc. Hematology, N.Y. Acad. Sci., William Beaumort Med. Soc. Home: 7001 Bybrook Ln Bethesda MD 20815-3166 Office: Hematology Oncology Cons 7525 Greenway Center Dr Ste 20 Greenbelt MD 20770-3509

CHAN, DANIEL SIU-KWONG, psychologist; b. Swatow, China, June 6, 1952; came to U.S., 1973; s. Hon-Kwong and Suet-Hing (Wong) C.; m. Rosario Arroyo, Dec. 14, 1985; children: Nathaniel Arroyo, Jennifer Arroyo. BA, Buena Vista Coll., 1977; MS, U. La Verne, 1980; PhD, U.S. Internat. U., 1984. Lic. psychologist Calif. Dir. outreach program Chinese Cmty. Ch., San Diego, 1980-81; exec. dir. Chinese Social Svc. Ctr., San Diego, 1981-82; rehab. counselor Asian Rehab. Svcs., Inc., L.A., 1982-84; program dir. Hawthorne (Calif.) Cmty. Group Home, 1984-86; psychologist Pacific Clinics, Pasadena, Calif., 1986-89, Fairview Devel. Ctr., Costa Mesa, Calif., 1989—; pvt. practice, Monterey Park, Calif., 1989—; cons. psychologist Ingleside Hosp., Rosemead, Calif., 1991—, Garfield Med. Ctr., Monterey Park, 1993—, Asian Youth Ctr., Rosemead, 1993—, Allied Physicians of Calif., San Gabriel, 1993—, Project SHINE, Inc., Downey, Calif., 1982-88. Mem. APA, Am. Soc. Clin. Hypnosis, Calif. Psychol. Assn., Fairview Psychol. Assn. Republican. Presbyn. Home: 11107 McVine Ave Sunland CA 91040 Office: ACRO Cons 943 S Atlantic Blvd Ste 221 Monterey Park CA 91754

CHAN, DANIEL TAK MAO, nephrologist; b. Hong Kong, Aug. 14, 1961; s. S.C. and Y.S. (Yeung) C. M.B.B.S., U. Hong Kong, 1985, MD, 1995. Med. officer Queen Mary Hosp. Medicine, Hong Kong, 1986-91, sr. med. officer, 1991-93; lectr. U. Hong Kong/Queen Mary Hosp., 1994-96, chief divsn. nephrology, 1996—. Fellow Hong Kong Coll. Physicians, Hong Kong Acad. Medicine; mem. Royal Coll. Physicians (U.K.), Am. Soc. Nephrology, Hong Kong Soc. Nephrology (coun. 1992—). Office: Univ of Hong Kong, Queen Mary Hospital, Dept Medicine, Pokfulam Hong Kong

CHAN, DONALD PIN-KWAN, orthopaedic surgeon, educator; b. Rangoon, Burma, Jan. 21, 1937; s. Charles Y.C. and Josephine (Golamco) C.; m. Dorothy Chan, July 31, 1966; children: Joanne, Elaine. BS, U. Rangoon, Burma, 1955, MD, 1960. Intern medicine U. Hong Kong, 1960-61, resident surgery and orthopaedics, 1961-68; resident orthopaedic surgery U. Vt., 1968-71; assoc. orthopaedist Strong Meml. Hosp., Rochester, N.Y., 1972-80, sr. assoc. orthopaedist, 1980-86, attending orthopaedist, 1986—; asst. prof. U. Rochester, 1972-80, assoc. prof., 1980-87, prof., 1987-93; prof., head of divsn. spine surgery U. Va., Charlottesville, 1994—; dir. Goldstein Fellowship, Rochester, Orthopaedic Clin. Svcs., Rochester; chief sect. spine surgery dept. orthopaedics, Rochester, 1993. Contbr. articles on clin. rsch. related to the spine. Bd. dirs. Rochester Chinese Assn., 1991. Traveling fellow Scoliosis Rsch. Soc. Fellow ACS, Am. Acad. Orthopaedic Surgeons, Am. Orthopaedic Assn., Scoliosis Rsch. Soc. (1st v.p. 1995); mem. AMA, N.Am. Spine Soc., Am. Spinal Injury Assn., Ea. Orthopaedic Assn. Office: Univ Va Health Scis Ctr PO Box 159 Charlottesville VA 22902-0159

CHAN, JAMES CHUNG-YU, virologist, educator; b. Hongkong, Nov. 20, 1937; came to U.S., 1961; s. Yuk-Chien and Betty (Kwok) C.; m. Grace Yap, Aug. 28, 1964. BS, Internation Christian U., Tokyo, 1961; PhD, U. Rochester Sch. Medicine, 1966. Sr. rsch. scientist Squibb Inst. Med. Rsch., New Brunswick, N.J., 1966-68; asst. prof. Ind. U. Med. Sch., Indpls., 1968-71, Baylor Coll. Medicine, Houston, 1971-72; asst. prof virology U. Tex. M.D. Anderson Cancer Ctr., Houston, 1972-82, assoc. prof. virology, 1982—. Contbr. chpts. to books, some 150 arcticles to sci. jours. Grantee Coun. for Tobacco Rsch., Inc., 1988-91, Nat. Cancer Inst., Bethesda, 1990-95. Mem. Am. Assn. Cancer Rsch., Am. Soc. for Microbiology, Am. Soc. Virology, Internat. Leukemia Soc.

CHAN, MICHAEL CHIU-HON, chiropractor; b. Hong Kong, Aug. 31, 1961; came to U.S., 1979; s. Fuk Yum and Chun Wai (Ma) C. D of Chiropractic, Western States Chiropractic Coll., 1985; fellow, Internat. Acad. Clin. Acupuncture, 1986. Assoc. doctor Widoff Chiropractic Clinic, Phoenix, 1986, Horizon Chiropractic Clinic, Glendale, Ariz., 1986-88; dir. North Ranch Chiropractic Assoc., Scottsdale, Ariz., 1988-91; pvt. practice Phoenix, 1991—; dir. Neighborhood Chiropractic, Phoenix, 1988-89. Contbr. articles to profl. jours. Mem. Am. Chiropractic Assoc., Internat. Platform Assn., Coun. on Diagnostic Imaging, Paradise Valley Toastmaster Club. Office: 6544 W Thomas Rd Ste 37 Phoenix AZ 85033-5741 also: 3109 E Cactus Rd Phoenix AZ 85030

CHAN, PAUL, cardiologist, consultant; b. Hong Kong, July 14, 1958; arrived in Taiwan, 1978; s. Man Yin Chan and Choi Wan Lee; m. Ling Chen, June 9, 1984; children: Yu-Shin, Yu-Fung. MD, Taipei Med. Sch., 1984; PhD, Nat. Yang-Ming U., Taiwan, 1996. Cert. internal medicine, cardiology, critical care, Taiwan. Resident in internal medicine Chang Gung Meml. Hosp., Taiwan, 1984-87; fellow cardiology Chang Gung Meml. Hosp., 1987-89; attending physician Taipei Mcpl. Chung Hsaio Hosp., 1989—; dir. clin. pharmacology and therapeutics unit Taipei Chung Hsaio Hosp., 1995—; assoc. prof. Beijing Med. U., 1996—; hon. assoc. prof. Nat. Cheng Kung U., Taiwan, 1994—. Contbr. articles and papers to profl. jours. Mem. Am. Soc. Hypertension. Home: 6-1 Ln 9 Nan Chang Rd Sec 2, 107 Taipei Taiwan Office: Taipei Mcpl Chung Hsaio Hos, # 87 Tung Teh Rd Nan Kang, 115 Taipei Taiwan

CHAN, PETER PAK-FAI, osteopathic physician; b. Hong Kong, Sept. 3, 1954; s. Sick-Kee and Hong-King (Leung) C.; m. Betty Chi-Mee Jew, May 24, 1992; 1 child, Christopher Gai-Jun. AS, Vincennes U., 1975; BS in Pharmacy, U. Okla., 1978; DO, Okla. State U., 1983. Diplomate Am. Osteo. Bd., Am. Osteo. Bd. Family Physicians. Intern Hillcrest Health Ctr., Oklahoma City, 1983-84; pvt. practice Oklahoma City, 1984—; physician advisor Okla. Found. for Med. Quality, 1988-96; adj. clin. prof. family practice Coll. Osteo. Medicine Okla. State U., 1994-96; mem. med. records com. Hillcrest Health Ctr., 1986-89, chmn. pharmacy and thereaputics com., 1987-89, sec. gen. practice dept., 1987-89, chmn. instrnl. rev. com., 1987-89, other coms. Mem. Am. Osteo. Assn., Am. Coll. Osteo. Family Physicians, Okla. Osteo. Assn., Sigma Sigma Phi, Rho Chi. Office: 4901 S Pennsylvania Oklahoma City OK 73119

CHAN, PETER WING KWONG, pharmacist; b. L.A., Feb. 3, 1949; s. Sherwin T.S. and Shirley W. (Lee) C.; m. Patricia Jean Uyeno, June 8, 1974; children: Kristina Dionne, Kelly Alison, David Shoichi. BS, U. So. Calif., 1970, D in Pharmacy, 1974. Lic. pharmacist, Calif. Clin. instr. U. So. Calif., 1974-76; staff clin. pharmacist Cedars-Sinai Med. Ctr., L.A., 1974-76; 1st clin. pharmacist in ophthalmology Alcon Labs., Inc., Ft. Worth, 1977—, formerly in Phila. monitoring patient drug therapy, teaching residents, nurses, pharmacy students, then assigned to Tumu Tumu Hosp., Karatina, Kenya, also lectr. clin. ocular pharmacology tng. course, Nairobi, Cairo, Athens, formerly dist. sales mgr. Alcon/BP, ophthal. products div. Alcon Labs., Inc., Denver; v.p., gen. mgr. Optikem Internat., Sereine Products Div., Optacryl, Inc., Denver, 1980-91; product mgr. hosp. pharmacy products Am. McGaw div. Am. Hosp. Supply Corp., 1981-83; internat. market mgr. IOLAB subs. Johnson & Johnson, 1983-86, dir. new bus. devel. Iolab Pharms., 1986-87, dir. Internat. Mktg., 1987-89, dir. new products mktg., 1989; bus. and mktg. strategies cons. to pharm. and med. device cos. Chan & Assocs., Northridge, Calif., 1989—; ptnr., chmn., CEO PreFree Techs., Inc., 1992-96; med. dir., comml. ops. liaison Nexstar Pharms., Inc., Boulder, 1996—; ptnr. Vitamin Specialties Corp., 1993-95, JSP Ptnrs., Ltd., 1992—; bd. dirs. SUDCO Internat., L.A. Del. Am. Pharm. Assn. House of Dels., 1976-78, Calif. Youth Theatre at Paramount Studios, Hollywood 1986-87, 91-96; bd. councillors U. So. Calif. Sch. Pharmacy, 1995—. Recipient Hollywood-Wilshire Pharm. Assn. spl. award for outstanding svc., 1974. Mem. Chinese Am. Pharm. Assn., Am. Pharm. Assn., Calif. Pharm. Assn., Hollywood-Wilshire Pharm. Assn. (bd. dirs. 1972-76), Am. Soc. Hosp. Pharmacists, Am. Pharm. Assn. Acad. of Pharmacy Practice, U. So. Calif. Assocs. (life), U. So. Calif. Gen. Alumni Assn., U. So. Calif. (steering com. lifescis. info. networking coun.), Granada Hills H.S. Highlanders Booster Club (bd. dirs. 1991, 92, 93, chmn.-Project 2000), QSAD Centurions, U. So. Calif. Lifetime Assocs., Gamma Epsilon Omega Alumni Assn. (bd. dirs.), Phi Delta Chi, NRA (life), Golden Eagle, Calif. Rifle and Pistol Assn. (life mem.). Republican. Home: 10251 Vanalden Ave Northridge CA 91324-1240 Office: Nexstar Pharms Inc 2860 Wilderness Pl Boulder CO 80013

CHAN, PHILIP, dermatologist; b. Oceanside, N.Y., Oct. 14, 1946. BA, Harvard U., 1968; MD, Columbia Physicians & Surg., 1972. Diplomate Am. Bd. Dermatology. Resident in dermatology Walter Reed Army Med. Ctr., Washington, 1979; col. U.S. Army; dermatologist Martin ACH, Ft. Benning, Ga., 1995—. Office: Martin ACH Dermatology Svc PO Box 56100 Fort Benning GA 31905-6100

CHAN, PHILIP J., medical educator; b. Malaysia, May 11, 1956; m. Hilda Chan, 1981; 3 children. BA cum laude in biology, Kalamazoo Coll., 1979; MS in Physiology, Mich. State U., 1981, PhD in Physiology, 1983. Diplomate Am. Bd. Bioanalysis. Dir. sperm processing & IVF and embryo transfer lab. Kennedy Meml. Hosps./U. Med. Ctr., Cherry Hill, N.J., 1983-87; dir. labs. Hillcrest Fertility Ctr., Tulsa, 1987-89; dir. andrology/male reproduction and molecular biology labs. Loma Linda (Calif.) U. Obstetrics Med. Group, 1989—; mgr. info. sys. lab. computers and network Loma Linda U. Ob-Gyn. Med. Group, Inc., 1991—; from instr. to asst. prof. U. Medicine and Dentistry of N.J. Sch. Osteopathic Medicine, 1983-87; assoc. prof. Oral Roberts U. Sch. Medicine, 1987-89; from assoc. prof. to prof. Loma Linda U. Sch. Medicine, 1989—; mem. comparative medicine study sect. NIH, 1994—; insp. Coll. Am. Pathologists, 1993—. Mem. AAAS, Am. Soc. Reproductive Medicine, Am. Soc. Andrology, Am. Soc. Primatologists, Am. Assn. Bioanalysts. Office: Loma Linda U Fac Med Office Dept Ob-Gyn Ste 3950 11370 Anderson St Loma Linda CA 92354

CHAN, PO CHUEN, toxicologist; b. Hupeh, China, May 13, 1935; came to the U.S., 1960; s. Tin Wa and Pui Wa (Ho) C.; m. Lillian Mak, Oct. 16, 1961; children: Yola, Vella. BA, Internat. Christian U., Tokyo, 1960; MA, Columbia U., 1963; PhD, NYU, 1967. Rsch. assoc. Sloan-Kettering Inst. Cancer Rsch., N.Y.C., 1967-70; assoc. mem. Am. Health Found., Valhalla, N.Y., 1970-78; cancer rsch. scientist IV Roswell Park Meml. Inst., Buffalo, 1978-83; project leader Nat. Inst. Environ. Health Sci., Research Triangle Park, N.C., 1983—. Contbr. more than 100 papers to profl. jours. Active Gov.'s Task Force on Racial, Religious and Ethnic Violence and Intimidation, N.C., 1989—. USPHS grantee. Fellow AAAS; mem. Am. Assn. for Cancer Rsch., Am. Physiol. Soc., N.Y. Acad. Scis. Office: Nat Inst Environ Health Sci Research Triangle Park NC 27709

CHAN, W. Y., pharmacologist, educator; b. Shanghai, China, Dec. 1, 1932; came to U.S., 1952, naturalized, 1968; m. Beatrice Ho Chan, June 11, 1961; children—Mina, Jennifer. B.A., U. Wis., 1956; Ph.D. in Pharmacology, Columbia, U., 1961. Rsch. assoc., then asst. prof. biochemistry Cornell U. Med. Coll., N.Y.C., 1960-67, asst. prof., then assoc. prof. pharmacology, 1966-76, prof., 1976—, acting chmn., 1983-91; mem. basic pharmacology adv. com. Pharm. Mfrs. Assn. Found., 1973-80; mem. study sect. NIH, 1977, cons., 1981. Contbr. articles to profl. jours. Recipient NIH research career devel. award, 1968-73; Irma T. Hirschl Career Scientist award 1973-77; NIH grantee, 1965—. Mem. Am. Soc. Pharmacology and Exptl. Therapeutics, Soc. for Study of Reprodn., Soc. Exptl. Biology and Medicine, Harvey Soc., N.Y. Acad. Scis., AAAS. Research on pharmacology of neurohypophys hormones and polypeptides, uterine and renal actions of oxytocin and prostaglandins, pathophysiology and pharmacology of dysmenorrhea. Office: Cornell U Med Coll 1300 York Ave New York NY 10021-4805

CHAN, WAI-YEE, molecular geneticist; b. Canton, China, Apr. 28, 1950; came to U.S., 1974; s. Kui and Fung-Hing (Wong) C.; BSc with first class honors, Chinese U. of Hong Kong, 1974; PhD, U. Fla., 1977; m. May-Fong Sheung, Sept. 3, 1976; children: Connie Hai-Yee, Joanne Hai-Wei, Victor Hai-Yue, Amanda Hai-Pui, Bessie Hai-Lui. Teaching asst. dept. biochemistry and molecular biology U. Fla., Gainesville, 1974-77; rsch. assoc. U. Okla., Oklahoma City, 1978-79, asst. prof. dept. pediatrics, 1979-82, assoc. prof., 1982-89, asst. prof. dept. biochemistry and molecular biology, 1979-82, assoc. prof., 1982-89; staff affiliate Pediatric Endocrine Metabolism & Genetic Svc., Okla. Children's Meml. Hosp., Oklahoma City, 1979-89, dir. Clin. Trace Metal Diagnostic Lab., 1979-85, asst. sci. dir. Biochem. Genetics and Metabolic Screening Lab., 1980-87; cons. VA Med. Center, Oklahoma City, 1981-87; co-sci. dir. State of Okla. Teaching Hosp., 1982-87; prof. dept. pediatrics, biochemistry and molecular biology and cell biology, mem. Vincent T. Lombardi Cancer Rsch. Ctr., sci. dir. Molecular Genetics Diagnostic Lab. Georgetown U., Washington, 1989—. Assoc. mem. Okla. Med. Res. Found., Oklahoma City, 1987-89. Chinese U. Hong Kong scholar, 1972-74, 73-74; NATO fellow, 1979; recipient Okla. Med. Rsch. Found. Merrick award 1988. Mem. Am. Inst. Nutrition, Am. Soc. Biochem. Molecular Biology, Am. Soc. Human Genetics, Am. Chem. Soc., Biochem. Soc. (U.K.), Internat. Assn. BioInorganic Scientists, N.Y. Acad. Sci., Am. Soc. Cell Biology Soc. Pediatric Rsch., Am. Assn. Immunology, Endocrinology Soc., Am. Genetic Assn., Am. Coll. Nutrition, Sigma Xi. Editor 2 books and monograph; editor Jour. of Am. Coll. Nutrition; contbr. articles to profl. jours. Achievements include patent on application of pregnancy specific glycoproteins and development of in vitro diagnostic method for Wilson's disease. Home: 10708 Butterfly Ct North Potomac MD 20878-4209 Office: Georgetown U Childrens Med Ctr Dept Pediatrics 3800 Reservoir Rd NW Washington DC 20007-2196

CHAN, WAYNE LYMAN, dermatologist; b. San Francisco, Aug. 14, 1938; s. Shau Wing and Anna Mae (Chan) C.; m. Elizabeth Han-Sun Lee, May 27, 1967; children: Lisa Anne, Christopher Wayne. BA in Biology, Stanford U., 1960; MD, George Washington U., 1967. Diplomate Am. Bd. Dermatology. Intern Santa Clara Valley Med. Ctr., San Jose, Calif., 1967-68; resident in dermatology Stanford (Calif.) Med., 1970-73; pvt. practice San Jose, 1973—; clin. assoc. prof. dermatology Stanford Hosp., 1973—. Capt. USAF, 1968-70. Fellow Am. Acad. Dermatology; mem. San Francisco Dermatol. Soc., Pacific Dermatol. Assn., Calif. Med. Assn. Office: 2323 Montpelier Dr Ste C San Jose CA 95116

CHAN, YUN LAI, medical educator, physiologist; b. Taichung, Taiwan, China, Dec. 3, 1941; came to U.S. 1968, naturalized, 1977; s. Yunn-Perng and Tsai-Mei C.; m. Vicky Chiu, June 18, 1968; children: Jason, Grace. BS, Kaohsiung Med. Coll., 1965; MS, Nat. Taiwan U., 1967; PhD U. Louisville, 1971. Instr. U. Louisville, 1971, 73; fellow Max Planck Inst., Frankfurt, Germany, 1972-73; instr. Yale U., New Haven, 1974-76; asst. prof. U. Ill.-Chgo., 1976-81, assoc. prof., 1981-88, prof. 1988—; vis. prof. Nat. Yang Ming Med. Coll., Taipei, Taiwan, 1982, 84; vis. specialist Nat. Sci. Council, Taipei, 1982-84; prin. investigator NIH, Bethesda, Md., 1981—. Contbr. articles to profl. jours. Active Chgo. Heart Assn. Recipient Golden Apple award U. Ill., 1980; grantee Pharm. Mfrs. Assn., 1972, Am. and Chgo. Heart Assn., 1977. Mem. Am. Physiol. Soc., Am. Soc. Nephrology, Internat. Soc. Nephrology, Am. Fedn. Clin. Rsch., Am. Heart Assn. (mem. coun.), Chinese Acad. and Profl. Assn. Mid-Am. (pres. 1995-96). Achievements include discovered adenergic receptors in renal tubule, cellular mechanism of renal reabsorption of bicarbonate.

CHANATRY, FRANCIS, surgeon; b. Utica, N.Y.; s. Raymond and Bahia Margaret (Gharibа) C. AB, Hamilton Coll., 1946; MD, Albany Med. Coll., 1948. Diplomate Am. Bd. Surgery, Am. Bd. Medical Examiners. Intern USPHS, Staten Island, N.Y., 1948-49; sr. surgeon USPHS, Washington, 1949-50; surg. resident Upstate Med. Ctr., Syracuse, N.Y., 1950-55, chief resident in surgery, instr., 1954-55; attending surgeon St. Luke's Meml. Hosp., Utica, N.Y., 1955—, St. Elizabeth Hosp., Utica, N.Y., 1955—, Faxton Hosp., Utica, N.Y., 1955—. Fellow Am. Coll. Surgeons (gov. 1989—); mem. AMA, N.Y. State Med. Soc., N.Y. Acad. Medicine, Oneida County Med. Soc. (pres. 1981-82), Cen. N.Y. Surgical Soc. (pres. 1984-86). Roman Catholic. Home: 1109 Parkway E Utica NY 13501-5523 Office: Francis Chanatry MD PC 103 Pleasant St Utica NY 13501-4854

CHANCE, KENNETH BERNARD, endodontist, educator, university official; b. N.Y.C., Dec. 8, 1953; s. George E. and Janie L. (Bolles) C.; m. Sharon Lee Lewis, July 11, 1981; children: Kenneth Bernard, Dana Marie, Christopher, Jacquelyn. BS, Fordham U., 1975; DDS, Case Western Res. U., 1979; cert. Endodontics U. Medicine and Dentistry of N.J., Newark, 1982. Asst. attending Jamaica Hosp., Queens, N.Y., 1981-87; chief endodontics Kings County Med. Ctr., Bklyn., 1982-91; assoc. prof. endodontics U. Medicine and Dentistry of N.J., 1987, also dir. external affairs N.J. Dental Sch.; asst. attending North Ctrl. Bronx Hosp. (N.Y.), 1983-91, Kingsbrook Jewish Med. Ctr., 1986-92; asst. dean for external affairs and urban resource devel. N.J. Dental Sch., 1989; cons. Harlem Hosp., N.Y.C., 1982-90; health policy advisor to U.S. Senator Frank Lautenberg of N.J., 1991—; dir. health policy program The Joint Ctr. Polit. and Econ. Studies, 1993-94; acting chmn., dept. endodontics N.J. Dental Sch., 1994—; fed. rels. adv. U. Medicine and Dentistry of N.J., 1994—. Min. of music, sr. organist Sharon Bapt. Ch., Bronx, 1983; health care taskforce mem. Congressional Black Caucus, 1994—. Recipient Dr. Paul F. Sherwood award for excellence in endodontics Case Western Res. U. Dental Sch., 1979; Found. Grant award U. Medicine and Dentistry of N.J., 1984, Exceptional Merit award, 1985, Excellence award, 1990; fellow Nat. Dental Leadership Devel. PEW, 1991, Robert Wood Johnson Health Policy, 1991, Pierre Fauchard Acad., 1996. Fellow Am. Coll. Dentists, Internat. Coll. Dentists; mem. ADA, Internat. Assn. Dental Research, Am. Assn. Dental Schs., Nat. Dental Assn., Am. Assn. Endodontists, Greater Met. Dental Soc. N.Y. (pres.-elect 1986-87, v.p. 1984-86), Omicron Kappa Upsilon. Office: N J Dental Sch U Medicine and Dentistry N J 110 Bergen St Newark NJ 07103-2400

CHAND, DEEP, radiologist, consultant; b. Sardarshahr, Rajasthan, India, Sept. 19, 1945; arrived in U.K., 1977; s. Nathmal and Sugani (Gangparia) Prajapat; m. Sushma Vashishtha, Jan. 21, 1975; children: Sudeep, Sourabh. MB BChir, S.P. Med. Coll., India, 1972; MD, Postgrad. Inst. Med. Edn. and Rsch., Chandigarh, India, 1976. Gen. medicine accreditation Royal Coll. Radiologists. House officer S.P. Med. Coll., 1972-73; resident sr. house officer neurology and radiotherapy All India Inst. Med. Scis., Delhi, 1973; resident sr. house officer medicine and surgery Safdarjung Hosp., New Delhi, 1974; resident in radiology Postgrad. Inst. of Med. Edn. and Rsch., Chandigarh, 1975-77; registrar, sr. registrar Northstaff Med. Ctr., Stoke-on-Trent, Eng., 1977-81; cons. radiologist Sandwell DGH, West Bromwich, Eng., 1982—; chmn. dept. radiology Sandwell DGH, 1983-87. Contbr. articles and rsch. papers to profl. publs. Maj. Royal Army M.C., 1989—. Recipient Distinction Merit award Nat. Health Svc., 1989. Fellow Faculty of Radiologists, Royal Coll. Surgeons in Ireland, Royal Soc. Medicine; mem. Internat. Soc. Magnetic Resonance, Soc. Magnetic Resonance in Medicine and Biology, Royal Coll. Surgeons and Physicians, Brit. Med. Assn. (chmn. Sandwell divsn. 1987-89), Am. Assn. Ultrasound (sr. mem.). Office: Sandwell Gen Hosp, Lyndon, West Bromwich B714HJ, England

CHANDA, JYOTIRMAY, cardiovascular surgeon, researcher; b. Jessore, Bangladesh, Jan. 1, 1961; s. Naresh and Reba (Sarker) C.; m. Anuradha Das, Jan. 22, 1995; 1 child, Anindita Chanda. MD, Patrice Lumuba Peoples' Friendship U., Moscow, 1986, postgrad. in surgery, 1988; PhD, Akita (Japan) U. Sch. Medicine, 1996. Pvt. practice in gen. surgery Jessore, Bangladesh, 1989-92; postgrad. rsch. fellow dept. cardiovasc. surgery Sree Chitra Tirunal Inst. Med. Scis. and Technology, Trivandrum, India, 1992-93; fellow Inst. Cardiovascular Diseases, dept. surgery Madras Med. Mission, Madras, India, 1993; fellow dept. cardiovasc. surgery Akita U. Sch. Medicine, 1994-96. Contbr. articles to profl. jours. Mem. Internat. Soc. Cardiothoracic Surgeons. Home: Sreedhar Tank Rd, Bejpara Jessore 7400, Bangladesh Office: Akita U Sch Medicine, Dept Cardiovasc Surgery, Akita 010, Japan

CHANDLER, ARTHUR BLEAKLEY, pathologist, educator; b. Augusta, Ga., Sept. 11, 1926; s. Clemmons Quillian and Mary Isabella (Bleakley) C.; m. Jane Stoughton Downing, Sept. 2, 1953; children—Arthur Bleakley, John Downing. Student, U. Ga., 1943-44; M.D., Med. Coll. Ga., Augusta, 1948. Diplomate: Am. Bd. Pathology. Intern Baylor U. Hosp., Dallas, 1948-49; resident in pathology, NIH trainee in cancer dept. pathology Med. Coll. Ga., 1950-51, asst. in pathology, 1949-50, mem. faculty, 1949—, prof. pathology, 1962—, chmn. dept., 1975—; mem. coms. Nat. Heart, Lung and Blood Inst., 1969-93. Author papers in field, chpts. in books; mem. editorial bd.: Haemostasis, 1975-83, Pathology Research and Practice, 1987—. Trustee Young Mens Library Assn. Fund, 1962-72, Historic Augusta, Inc., 1966-69; Trustee Augusta-Richmond County Mus., 1955-87, Dan Printup Meml. Trust, 1985—, trustee Acad. Richmond County, 1984—. Served as officer M.C. AUS, 1951-53. Commonwealth Fund fellow Norway, 1963-64. Mem. AMA, Internat. Acad. Pathology, Internat. Soc. Thrombosis and Haemostasis,;Am. Assn. History Medicine, Coll. Am. Pathologists, Am. Assn. Pathologists, Am. Soc. Hematology, Am. Heart Assn. (fellow coun. arteriosclerosis, chmn. coun. on thrombosis 1979-80, chmn. com. on coronary lesions and myocardial infractions 1980-82), Ga. Assn. Pathologists (pres. 1984-85), Ga. Heart Assn., Med. Assn. Ga., Richmond County Med. Soc. (trustee 1984—, sec. 1987, v.p. 1988), Sch. Medicine Alumni Assn. Med. Coll. Ga. (pres. 1996-97), Alpha Omega Alpha. Episcopalian. Home: 803 Milledge Rd Augusta GA 30904-4351 Office: Med Coll Ga Dept Pathology Augusta GA 30912

CHANDLER, BRUCE FREDERICK, internist; b. Bohemia, Pa., Mar. 26, 1926; s. Frederick Arthur and Minnie Flora (Burkhardt) C.; m. Janice Evelyn Piper, Aug. 14, 1954; children: Barbara, Betty, Karen, Paul, June. Student, Pa. State U., 1942-44; MD, Temple U., 1948. Diplomate Am. Bd. Internal Medicine. Commd. med. officer U.S. Army, 1948, advanced through grades to col., 1967; intern Temple U. Hosp., Phila., 1948-49; chief psychiatry 7th Field Hosp., Trieste, Italy, 1950; resident Walter Reed Gen. Hosp., Washington, 1949-53; battalion surgeon 2d Div. Artillery, Korea, 1953-54; chief renal dialysis unit 45th Evacuation Hosp. and Tokyo Army Hosp., Korea, Japan, 1954-55; various assignments Walter Reed Gen. Hosp., Fitzsimons Gen. Hosp., Letterman Gen. Hosp., 1955-70; comdg. officer 45th Field Hosp., Vicenza, Italy, 1958-62; pvt. practice internist Ridgecrest (Calif.) Med. Clinic, 1970-76; chief med. svc. and out-patients VA Hosps., Walla Walla, Spokane, Wash., 1976-82; med. cons. Social Security Adminstrn., Spokane, Wash., 1983-87; ret. Panel mem. TV shows, 1954-70; lectr.; contbr. numerous articles to med. profl. jours. Decorated Legion of Merit. Fellow ACP, Am. Coll. Chest Physicians; mem. AMA, Am. Thoracic Soc., N.Y. Acad. Scis., So. European Task Force U.S. Army Med. Dental Soc. (pres., founder 1958-62). Republican. Methodist. Home: 6496 N Callisch Ave Fresno CA 93710-3902

CHANDLER, JAMES JOHN, surgeon; b. Dayton, Ohio, Nov. 13, 1932; s. James Kapp and Margaret Bertha (Paulson) C.; m. Fleur Elizabeth Varney, July 23, 1955; 1 child, Jennifer Hauge. A.B., Dartmouth Coll., 1954, diploma in medicine, 1955; M.D. cum laude, U. Mich., 1957. Diplomate in surg., critical care Am. Bd. Surgery. Intern Harvard Surg. Service, Boston City Hosp., 1957-58, jr. asst. resident, 1953; resident, chief resident in surgery, clin. fellow Am. Cancer Soc. U. Oreg. Hosps., Portland, 1961-64; instr. surgery U. Oreg. Hosps., 1964; sr. attending staff, chmn. surgery Med. Ctr. at Princeton, N.J., 1972-92; pres. med. and dental staff Med. Ctr. at Princeton, 1993-94; clin. prof. surgery Coll. Medicine and Dentistry N.J.-Robert Wood Johnson Med. Sch., Piscataway, 1976—; cons. in surgery Princeton U., Robert Wood Johnson U. Hosp.; bd. trustees Med. Ctr. of Princeton, 1993-94. Contbr. chpt. to book, articles to profl. jours. Bd. dirs. Trinity Counseling Svc., 1968—, chmn., 1968-72, 79-81; pres. Princeton Day Sch. PTA, 1976-78, trustee, 1976-81; active All Saints Episcopal Ch., Princeton, 1965—; mem. alumni coun. Dartmouth Med. Sch., 1981-86, Dartmouth Coll., 1983-86. Lt. USN, 1958-60; to lt. comdr. USNR, 1960-61. Fellow ACS (pres. N.J. chpt. 1976-77, gov. 1981-87), Am. Coll. Chest Physicians, Soc. Surg. Oncology; mem. Am. Soc. Clin. Oncology, Soc. Surgeons N.J., Med. Soc. N.J. (sec., chmn. surgery sect. 1967-69), Mercer County Med. Soc., Collegium Internationale Chirurgiae Digestivae, Soc. Surg. Alimentary Tract, Soc. Internat. Surgery, Alpha Omega Alpha. Home: 95 Russell Rd Princeton NJ 08540-6729 Office: 281 Witherspoon St Princeton NJ 08540-3210

CHANDLER, JANICE VANSTON, cardiac pacing nurse specialist; b. Passaic, N.J., Nov. 9, 1950. Diploma, Presbyn. Sch. Nursing, 1971. BSN, Rutgers U., 1983, MS, 1985; postgrad., NYU, 1986—. RN; cert. basic life support, clin. specialist med.-surg. nursing, intravenous therapy, coronary care nursing; advanced practice lic., N.J. Staff nurse, relief charge nurse ICU Albert Einstein Med. Ctr., Phila., 1971-73; staff nurse, rotating charge nurse ICU Upstate Med. Ctr., Syracuse, N.Y., 1973-75; staff nurse ICU and CCU, Dover (N.J.) Gen. Hosp., 1975-76; clinic nurse Planned Parenthood N.W. N.J., Newton, 1975-83; staff nurse ICU and CCU adult med.-surg. unit Newton Meml. Hosp., 1979-81, pacemaker nurse clinician, clin nurse specialist, 1982—; clin. asst. prof. dept. nursing edn. and svcs. U. Medicine and Dentistry N.J., Newark, 1987—. Contbr. numerous articles to profl. jours. Recipient Ladies Aid Soc. award for Outstanding Citizenship Presbyn. Hosp., 1971, Nat. Disting. Svc. Registry in Nursing, 1988; alternate doctoral scholar Nurses Ednl. Funds, Inc. Mem. AACN, ANA, Am. Heart Assn. (bd. dirs. 1987-88), Nat. Space Soc., N.J. Nurses Assn., Nat. Alopecia Areata Found., Presbyn. Sch. Nursing Alumni Assn., Rutgers U. Coll. Nursing Alumni Assn., Sigma Theta Tau. Home: 141 Frank Chandler Rd Newton NJ 07860-6915

CHANDLER, MICHAEL DAVID, pharmaceutical company executive; b. Austin, Tex., Dec. 24, 1959; s. Ronald Royce and Jeannette Elizabeth (Wilson) C.; m. Hildy Zenor Harrell, May 22 1981; children: Kegan Alan, Corrie Ann. BA with honors, U. Tex., 1981. Sales rep. Roche Pharms., Austin, 1985-86, profl. products rep., 1986-87; mgr. intern Roche Pharms., Tex., 1987; divsn. sales mgr. Roche Pharms., Houston, 1987-95; sr. territory mgr. Roche Pharms, Houston, 1995—. Pulpit preacher, officer New Life Ministries Am. Fellow NIH 1982; recipient Pres.'s Achievement award 1986. Mem. Phi Eta Sigma, Alpha Epsilon Delta (pres. 1978-81). Home and Office: 4106 Brook Shadow Dr Humble TX 77345-1266

CHANDLER, PAUL TIVIS, physician; b. Jamestown, Ky., Oct. 11, 1942; s. Henry Tivis and Etta (Knuckles) C.; m. Sharon Ann Dennett; children: Mark David, Michael Andrew, Matthew Paul. BS, Western Ky. U., Bowling Green, 1964; MD, Emory U., Atlanta, Ga., 1968. Diplomate Am. Bd. Internal Medicine. Flight surgeon U.S. Army, Ft. Knox, Ky., 1970-72; chief resident Dept. Medicine Tulane U., New Orleans, 1974-75; fellow in endocrinology U. Cin., Ohio, 1975-77, pvt. practice in endocrinology, 1977—. Capt. U.S. Army, 1970-72. Mem. AMA, Am. Coll. Physicians, Am. Diabetes Assn., Am. Assn. Diabetes Educators, Ohio State Med. Assn. Methodist. Address: 6694 Apache Circle Cincinnati OH 45243

CHANDLER, PEGGY JAN, surgeon; b. Millen, Ga., Apr. 9, 1954. d. Billy Evans and Peggy Jean (Mallard) C. BS, Ga. So. Coll., 1975; MD, Med. Coll. Ga., 1979. Diplomate Am. Bd. Surgery, Am. Bd. Colon and Rectal Surgery. Intern then resident in gen. surgery Greenville (S.C.) Hosp. System, 1979-84; commd. lt. USN, 1983, advanced through grades to comdr.; gen. surgeon Portsmouth (Va.) Naval Hosp., 1984-86, Pensacola (Fla.) Naval Hosp., 1986-91, Nat. Naval Med. Ctr., Bethesda, Md., 1991-93, 94—; fellow in colo-rectal surgery U. Tex. Health Sci. Ctr., Houston, 1993-94. Mem. ACS, AMA, So. Med. Assn., Am. Mil. Surgeons of the U.S. Republican. Methodist. Home: 9322 Elmhirst Dr Bethesda MD 20814-3953 Office: Nat Naval Med Ctr Bethesda MD 20814

CHANDLER, WILLIAM KNOX, physiologist; b. Chgo., Oct. 13 1933; s. William Knox and Margaret Belle (Colston) C.; m. Caroline Hardee Teague, June 6, 1957; children—William Knox, Janet Colston, Caroline Louise, Margaret Teague. A.B., U. Louisville, 1955, M.D., 1959. Postdoctoral fellow Physiol. Lab., Cambridge, Eng., 1962-65; staff asso. Lab. Biophysics, Nat. Inst. Neurol. Diseases and Blindness, Bethesda, Md., 1965-66; asso. prof. physiology Yale U. Sch. Medicine, 1966-72, prof., 1973—. Editor Physiol. Revs, 1968-74, Jour. Physiology, 1974-81, Jour. Gen. Physiology, 1990—. Served with USPHS, 1959-61, 65-66. Mem. NAS, Biophys. Soc., Physiol. Soc., Soc. Gen. Physiologists. Democrat. Home: 594 County Rd Guilford CT 06437-1035 Office: 333 Cedar St New Haven CT 06510-3206

CHANDRAN, V. RAVI, scientist, pharmaceutical executive; b. K. Puram, Tamil Nadu, India, May 3, 1955; came to U.S., 1981; s. T. R. V. Subrahmanyan and Vasanta (Lakshmi) Krishnamurthy; m. Judith Ann Reichenthal, Sept. 14, 1991 (div. July 1996) MS, U. Fla., 1983, PhD, 1986. Scientist Lister Labs., Bombay, 1979-81, Sterling Drug Co., Rensselaer, N.Y., 1986-89; pres., chief exec. officer Am. Generics, Inc., West Sand Lake, N.Y., 1989-91, Signature Pharms., Inc., Ballston Lake, N.Y., 1991—; cons. Harvard U., Cambridge, 1989—. Mem. Am. Pharm. Assn. (assoc.), Am. Assn. Pharm. Scientists, Rho Chi. Office: Signature Pharms Inc 48 Woodstead Rd Ballston Lake NY 12019-1630

CHANDRASHEKAR, RAMASWAMY, immunoparasitologist, researcher; b. Madras, India, Aug. 27, 1957; came to U.S., 1988; s. Krishnaswamy and Visalakshi R.; m. Bhagya Chandrashekar, June 19, 1994. MS, U. Madras, 1980; PhD, U. Bombay, India, 1987. Rsch. asst. Ciba-Geigy Ltd., Bombay, 1980-88; postdoctoral rsch. assoc. Washington U. Jewish Hosp., St. Louis, 1988-91; rsch. instr. dept. medicine and dept. molecular microbiology Washington U., 1991-95, rsch. asst. prof. dept. medicine and molecular biology, 1995; sr. scientist Heska Corp., Ft. Collins, Colo., 1995—; cons. NIAD-USAID Regional Project on the Epidemiology and Control of Vector Borne Diseases, Egypt and Israel, spl. program tropical diseases WHO. Contbr. articles to profl. jours. including Jour. Infectious Diseases, Jour. Parasitology, Internat. Jour. Parasitology, Parasitology Rsch., Jour. Clin. Investigation, Molecular and Biochem. Parasitology, Jour. Immunology, Jour. Clin. Microbiol., Tropical Medicine and Internat. Health, Internat. Jour. Biochem. Recipient Nat. Sci. Talent award NCERT, New Delhi, India, 1975, Gold-Medals U. Madras, 1978, 80. Mem. AAAS, Am. Soc. Troptical Medicine and Hygiene, Am. Soc. Parasitologists, Am. Soc. Microbiology, N.Y. Acad. Scis. Home: 2212 Vermont Dr F 104 Fort Collins CO 80525 Office: Heska Corp 1825 Sharp Point Dr Fort Collins CO 80525

CHANG, CHAE HAN JOSEPH, radiologist, educator; b. Seoul, Korea, July 7, 1929; came to the U.S., 1954; s. Byong Il and We Duck (Min) Chang; m. C.S. Chun, Nov. 24, 1956; children: Paul, Marian, Deborah, Linda. MD, Yonsei U., Seoul, 1953; PhD, Nagoya (Japan) U., 1966. Cert. Am. Bd. Radiology. Intern St. Joseph's Hosp., Phoenix, Ariz., 1954-55; resident Emory U. Hosp., Atlanta, Ga., 1955-58; prof. radiology, acting chmn. dept. radiology W.Va. U. Sch. Medicine, Morgantown, 1969-70; prof. radiology, head roentgen divsn. U. Kans. Med. Ctr., Kansas City, 1970—; presenter in field. Contbr. chpts. to books and articles to profl. jours. Recipient Cum Laude award for sci. exhibits Radiol. Soc. N.Am., Chgo., 1973. Fellow Am. Coll. Radiologists; mem. Kans. Radiol. Soc. (pres. 1979-81), Greater Kansas City Radiol. Soc. (pres. 1992-93). Office: Univ Kans Med Ctr Dept Radiology 3901 Rainbow Blvd Kansas City KS 66160-7234

CHANG, CHI-SEN, gastroenterologist; b. Taichung, Taiwan, Aug. 30, 1957; s. Te-Jung and Su-Ping (Tsai) C.; m. Chuan-Huei Hsiung, Sept. 3, 1984; children: Yun-Hsuan, Yun-Tsui, Yun-Fang. MB, Kaoshiung (Taiwan) Med. Coll., 1982. Intern Chang-Gung Meml. Hosp., Taipei, 1981-82; med. officer Chinese Army Field Hosp., 1982-84; resident Taichung (Taiwan) Vets. Gen. Hosp., 1984-87, fellow gastroenterology, 1987-89, attending physician, 1989—; cons. Nutrition Support Team Taichung, Vets. Gen. Hosp., 1994—, cons. Hospice Care Taichung, 1995—. Recipient Award of Outstanding Dr., Bur. Health, 1994. Mem. Med. Dr. Soc. Republic of China, Gastroenterology Soc. Republic of China, Chinese Soc. Parenteral and Enteral Nutrition. Home: 66-20 Sec 1 Nan-Tun Rd, 403 Taichung Taiwan Office: Taichung Vets Gen Hosp, 160 Sec 3 Chung-Kang Rd, 407 Taichung Taiwan

CHANG, CHRIS C.N., physician, pediatric surgeon; b. Taiwan, China, June 20, 1943; s. Shu-Ming and Yu-Bow (Chow) C.; m. Rose Lee Chang, Mar. 4, 1972; children: Lynda, Steven. MD, Nat. Taiwan U., 1969. Dir. pediat. surgery Lehigh Valley Hosp., Allentown, Pa., 1993—. Fellow ACS, Internat. Coll. Surgeons, Am. Acad. Pediats.; mem. Am. Pediat. Surg. Assn. Office: Lehigh Valley Hosp 401 N 17th St Ste 206 Allentown PA 17104

CHANG, CHUNG-HO, pathologist, diagnostic electronmicroscopist; b. Taiwan, Dec. 19, 1937; came to U.S., 1965; s. Sen-Zu and Ching-Chee (Kuo) C.; m. June 20, 1968; children: Christine, Vivian, Sandra. MD, Kaohsiung Med. Coll., Taiwan, 1964. Diplomate Am. Bd. Pathology. Rotating intern Grace Hosp., Detroit, 1965-66, resident in internal medicine, 1966-67, resident in pathology, 1967-68; resident in pathology Albert Einstein Coll. Medicine, Bronx, N.Y., 1968-71; staff pathologist Children's Hosp. Mich., Detroit, 1971-91, dir. surg. pathology, 1983—; assoc. prof. pathology Wayne State U., Detroit, 1986—; staff pathologist William Beaumont Hosp., Royal Oak, Mich., 1991—. Mem. Christian Ch. Office: William Beaumont Hosp 3601 W 13 Mile Rd Royal Oak MI 48073-6712

CHANG, CHUN-HSING, psychologist, educator; b. Changlo, Shantung, China, Nov. 18, 1927; s. Hwa-Yun Chang and Yu (Yun) Kau; m. Chou Hwei-Chiang, Dec. 27, 1958; children: Hsiu-Jan, Jieh-Jan, Yi-Jan. BEd, Taiwan Normal U., Taipei, 1955, MEd, 1959; MA, U. Hawaii, 1962; PhD, U. Oregon, 1972. Prof. psychology Taiwan Normal U., Taipei, 1966-72, chmn. psychology dept., 1972-77; vis. prof. Purdue U., West Lafayette, Ind., 1977-78, Taiwan Normal U., Taipei, 1978—; cons. Ministry Edn., Taipei, 1987—. Author: Principles of Psychology, 1977, Educational Psychology, 1980, Series in Today's Youth and Education (6 vols.), 1985-89, Modern Psychology, 1990; editor: Chang's Dictionary of Psychology, 1988, Perspectives in Educaitonal Psychology: Pedagogical, Holistic, and Cultural, 1993; chief editor Tunghua Psychology Series, 20 vols. Mem. Chinese Psychol. Assn. (pres. 1983-85), Chinese Ednl. Soc., Chinese Mental Health Assn., Chinese Guidance Assn. Office: Taiwan Normal U Ednl Psycho, 162 Hoping Rd E Sec 2, Taipei Taiwan

CHANG, FRANK MINTO, pediatric orthopaedic surgeon, educator; b. San Francisco, Feb. 10, 1949; m. Nancy Chang, Aug. 19, 1978; children: Luke, Nicole. BS in Biology, Calif. State U., Chico, 1971; MD, St. Louis U., 1975. Intern St. Louis U., 1975-76, resident in orthopaedic surgery, 1976-80; pvt. practice, Denver, 1980—; dir. orthopaedics Children's Hosp., Denver, 1981—; asst. clin. prof. U. Colo., Denver, 1981—; med. dir. Adam's Camp, Denver, 1984—. Vol. instr. handicapped ski team, Winter Park, Colo.; physician, vol. U.S. freestyle ski team, Salt Lake City. Fellow Am. Acad. Orthopaedic Surgeons; mem. Am. Acad. Pediat., Pediatric Orthopaedic Surgeons N.Am. Office: Children's Orthopaedics 1056 E 19th Ave Ste B060 Denver CO 80218

CHANG, JAE CHAN, internist, educator; b. Chong An, Korea, Aug. 29, 1941; s. Tae Whan and Kap Hee (Lee) C.; came to U.S., 1965, naturalized, 1976; M.D., Seoul (Korea) Nat. U., 1965; m. Sue Young Chung, Dec. 4, 1965; children: Sung-Jin, Sung-Ju, Sung-Hoon. Intern, Ellis Hosp., Schenectady, 1965-66; resident in medicine Harrisburg (Pa.) Hosp., 1966-69, fellow in nuclear medicine, 1969-70; fellow in hematology and oncology, instr. in medicine U. Rochester, N.Y., 1970-72; chief hematology sect. VA Hosp., Dayton, Ohio, 1972-75; hematopathologist Good Samaritan Hosp., Dayton, 1975—, dir. oncology unit, 1976—, coord. of med. edn., 1976-77, chief oncology-hematology sect., 1976—; co-dir. hematology lab., 1988—; asst. clin. prof. medicine Ohio State U., Columbus, 1972-75; assoc. clin. prof. medicine Wright State U., Dayton, 1975-80, clin. prof., 1980—, co-dir. hematology and med. oncology fellowship program Wright State U. Sch. Medicine, 1993—; staff Kettering Med. Ctr., St. Elizabeth Med. Ctr., Dayton, Miami Valley Hosp., Dayton; cons. in hematology VA Hosp. Mem. med. adv. com. Greater Dayton Area chpt. Leukemia Soc. Am., 1977; trustee Montgomery County Soc. for Cancer Control, Dayton, 1976-85, Dayton Area Cancer Assn., 1985-88, Community Blood Ctr., 1982-86; bd. dirs. Samaritan Health Found., 1992. Recipient Wright State U. Acad. Medicine award, 1985, Med. Econ. Essay Competition award, 1990. Nat. Cancer Inst. fellow in hematology and oncology, 1970-72; diplomate Am. Bd. Internal Medicine, Am. Bd. Pathology (hematology). Fellow ACP, Am. Soc. Clin. Pathologists; mem. AAAS, Am. Soc. Hematology, Am. Fedn. Clin. Research, Am. Soc. Clin. Oncologists, Am. Assn. Cancer Research, Dayton Oncology Club, Dayton Soc. Internal Medicine (pres. 1989), Montgomery County Med. Soc. (dir. 1990-93). Contbr. articles to profl. med. jours., essays to newspaper columns, mags. and periodicals. Home: 1905 Kresswood Cir Kettering OH 45429-1152 Office: Good Samaritan Hosp & Health Ctr 2222 Philadelphia Dr Dayton OH 45406-1813 also: 2661 Salem Ave Ste 232 Dayton OH 45406-2933

CHANG, JOSEPH YOON, health products company executive; b. Ipoh, Perak, Malaysia, Oct. 22, 1952; came to U.S., 1978; s. Chee Kong and Philomena (Wong) C.; m. Wan Ping Wong, Oct. 16, 1974; children: Colin, Christopher. BSc with honors, Sch. of Pharmacy, Portsmouth, Eng., 1974; PhD, U. London, 1978. Postdoctoral fellow Johns Hopkins U., Balt., 1978-

80, rsch. assoc., 1980-81; sr. rsch. scientist Wyeth Labs., Radnor, Pa., 1981-85, assoc. dir., 1985-87; dir. Wyeth-Ayerst Rsch., Princeton, N.J., 1988-91; OsteoArthritis Scis., Inc. Osteoarthritis Scis. Inc., Boston, 1991-94, also bd. dirs.; dir. Binary Therapeutics, Inc., Boston, 1994—. Editor: Pharmacological Methods in the Control of Inflammation, 1990; inventee in field; contbr. numerous articles to profl. jours. Board dirs. The Arthritis Found., Md., 1979. Bain Meml. fellow Brit. Pharmacology Soc., 1976; Med. Rsch. Coun. scholar, 1974-77. Mem. AAAS, Am. Coll. Rheumatology, Am. Soc. Pharmacology and Exptl. Therapeutics, Am. Thoracic Soc., N.Y. Acad. Scis., Inflammation Rsch. Assn., Reticuloendothelial Soc.

CHANG, MOSES SHUNG, pharmacist, hospital material administrator, consultant; b. Taipei, Republic of China, July 24, 1956; came to U.S., 1983; s. Ying (Woo) Chang; m. Katherine Y. Hsu, Dec. 5, 1992. BS in Pharmacy, Taipei Med. Coll., 1979; postgrad., U. So. Calif., 1985. Lic. pharmacist, Calif. Dir. pharmacy L.A. Cmty. Hosp., 1985-88; clin. pharmacist Bay Harbor Hosp., Harbor City, Calif., 1988-93; dir. pharm. and material Long Beach (Calif.) Doctors, 1993-95; pres. Rigel Co., Lomita, Calif., 1992—; dir. ops. Moses Trading Co., Lomita, 1989-92; cons. Daniel Lab., Danville, Calif., 1987-90. Editor Vitamin Formula jour., 1978. Mem. South Bay Pharmacists. Office: Rigel Co 2375 W 246th St Lomita CA 90717

CHANG, PETER, interventional radiologist; b. Kansas City, Kans., June 25, 1953; s. Jeffrey Peh-I and Jeannette (Klemola) C.; m. Gloria Craven, Mar. 22, 1980; children: Jeffrey Paul, Amy Leela. BA with high honors, U. Tex., Austin, 1975; MD, U. Tex., San Antonio, 1979. With Lantern Lane Art Gallery, Houston, 1970; jr. rsch. technician M.D. Anderson Hosp., 1971; with Houston Mus. of Natural Sci., 1972; med. illustrator dept. zoology U. Tex., Austin, 1975; med. illustrator dept. anatomy U. Tex. Health Sci. Ctr., San Antonio, 1977, pediatrics intern, 1979-80, resident, 1981-82, resident in radiology, 1984-85, fellow dept. radiology, 1985-86; radiologist Palm Beach Gardens (Fla.) Med. Ctr., 1986-87, Everglades Meml. Hosp., Pahokee, Fla., 1986-87, North Ridge Med. Ctr., Ft. Lauderdale, Fla., 1987-89, Austin Diagnostic Clinic, 1989—. Author: (bibliography, with others) Expandable Intrahepatic Portocaval Stents in Dogs with Chronic Portal Hypertension, 1986. Rhodes scholar U. Tex., 1975, scholar Carl Geis Sch. Judo (Brown Belt), 1967, Houston Ballet Found., 1968; recipient 1st place for sculpture Tex. Med. Soc. Annual Art Show, 1990. Mem. AMA, Tex. Med. Assn., Am. Coll. Radiology, Radiol. Soc. N.Am., Soc. Cardiovascular and Interventional Radiology, Travis County Med. Soc., Tex. Radiol. Soc., Phi Beta Kappa. Home: 1103 Sprague Ln Austin TX 78746-4309 Office: ADMC Radiology 12221 Mopac N Austin TX 78758-2401

CHANG, PHYLLIS, physician, surgeon; b. N.Y.C., July 27, 1954; d. Paul and Eleanor (Ho) C. BA in Biochemistry, Vassar Coll., 1976; MD, Albany Med. Coll., Union U., 1980. Diplomate Am. Bd. Surgery, Am. Bd. Plastic Surgery, sub.-bd. hand surgery. Resident in surgery Albany Med. Ctr. Hosp., 1980-86; resident in plastic surgery U. Chgo. Hosp., 1986-88; fellow in hand surgery NYU-Bellevue Hosp., N.Y.C., 1988-89; assoc. dept. surgery U. Iowa Hosp. and Clinics, Iowa City, 1989-90, asst. prof. dept. surgery, 1990—. Fellow ACS; mem. Am. Soc. Plastic and Reconstructive Surgeons, Am. Soc. Surgery of the Hand, Am. Assn. Hand Surgeons, Am. Soc. Reconstructive Microsurgeons, Assn. Women Surgeons. Office: U Iowa Hosps and Clinics Divsn Plastic Surgery JPP 2960 Iowa City IA 52242

CHANG, ROBERT SHIHMAN, virology educator; b. Quangdong, China, July 26, 1922; came to U.S., 1947; m. Yinette Yangsen Yu, June 12, 1951; children: Jeffrey, Holly, Charlene, Garrick. BS, St. John's U., Shanghai, China, 1943, MD, 1946; DSc, Harvard U., 1952. Rsch. assoc. Harvard U. Sch. of Pub. Health, Boston, 1952-54, asst. prof., 1954-60, assoc. prof., 1960-68; prof. U. Calif., Davis, 1968—. Recipient Presdl. award 4th Internat. Polio Congress, 1957, Excellence in Teaching award Kaiser Found. Hosps., 1975, 93. Fellow Am. Acad. Microbiology, Am. Coll. Preventive Medicine. Home: 1620 Holly Ln Davis CA 95616-1010 Office: U Calif Med Microbiology Dept Davis CA 95616

CHANG, SYLVIA TAN, health facility administrator, educator; b. Bandung, Indonesia, Dec. 18, 1940; came to U.S., 1963; d. Philip Harry and Lydia Shui-Yu (Ou) Tan; m. Belden Shiu-Wah Chang, Aug. 30, 1964; children: Donald Steven, Janice May. Diploma in nursing, Rumah Sakit Advent, Indonesia, 1960; BS, Philippine Union Coll., 1962; MS, Loma Linda (Calif.) U., 1967; PhD, Columbia Pacific U., 1987. Cert. RN, PHN, ACLS, BLS instr., cmty. first aid instr., IV, TPN, blood withdrawal/. Head nurse Rumah Sakit Advent, Bandung, Indonesia, 1960-61; critical care, spl. duty and medicine nurse, team leader White Meml. Med. Ctr., L.A., 1963-64; nursing coord. Loma Linda U. Med. Ctr., 1964-66; team leader, critical care nurse, relief head nurse Pomona (Calif.) Valley Hosp. Med. Ctr., 1966-67; evening supr. Loma Linda U. Med. Ctr., 1967-69, night supr., 1969-79, adminstrv. supr., 1979-94; sr. faculty Columbia Pacific U., San Rafael, Calif., 1986-94; dir. health svc. La Sierra U., Riverside, Calif., 1988—; site coord. Health Fair Expo La Sierra U., 1988-89; adv. coun. Family Planning Clinic, Riverside, 1988-94; blood drive coord. La Sierra U., 1988—. Counselor Pathfinder Club Campus Hill Ch., Loma Linda, 1979-85, crafts instr., 1979-85, music dir., 1979-85; asst. organist U. Ch., 1982-88. Named one of Women of Achievement YWCA, Greater Riverside C. of C., The Press Enterprise, 1991, Safety Coord. of Yr. La Sierra U., 1995. Mem. Am. Coll. Health Assn., Assn. Seventh-day Adventist Nurses, Pacific Coast Coll. Health Assn., Adventist Student Pers. Assn., Loma Linda U. Sch. Nursing Alumni Assn. (bd. dirs.), Sigma Theta Tau. Republican. Seventh-day Adventist. Home: 11466 Richmont Rd Loma Linda CA 92354-3523 Office: La Sierra U Health Svc 4700 Pierce St Riverside CA 92505-3331

CHANG, THOMAS MING SWI, medical scientist, biotechnologist; b. Swatow, Kwantang, China, Apr. 8, 1933; arrived in Can., 1952; m. Lancy Yuk Lan, June 21, 1958; children: Harvey, Victor, Christine, Sandra. BSc, McGill U., Montreal, Que., Can., 1957, MD, CM, 1961, PhD, 1965. Intern Montreal Gen. Hosp., 1961-62; rsch. fellow depts. physiology and chemistry McGill U., 1962-65, asst. prof. physiology, 1966-69, assoc. prof., 1969-72; prof. physiology McGill U., Montreal, 1972—; dir. artificial organs rsch. unit McGill U., 1975-79; prof. medicine, 1975—; dir. artificial cells and organs rsch. ctr. McGill U., 1979—, assoc. dept. chem. engring., 1985—, assoc. dept. chemistry, 1986—, prof. biomed. engring., 1990—; lab. and clin. researcher med. scis., biotech. and biomed. engring. Montreal, 1962—; mem. staff Royal Victoria Hosp.; hon. mem. staff Montreal Chinese Hosp., 1970—; cons. Montreal Children's Hosp., 1979—, Med. Rsch. Coun. fellow, 1962-65, scholar, 1965-68, career investigator, 1968—; hon. prof. Nankai U., 1983—. Inventor artificial cells and blood substitutes; author: Artificial Cells, 1972, Biomedical Application of Immobilized Enzymes and Proteins, Vols. I and II, 1977, Artificial Kidney, Artificial Liver and Artificial Cells, 1978, Hemoperfusion-Kidney and Liver Supports and Detoxification, 1980, Hemoperfusion, 1981, Past, Present and Future of Artificial Organs, 1983, Microencapsulation and Artificial Cells, 1984, Hemoperfusion and Artificial Ogans, 1985, Blood Substitutes, 1988, Blood Substitutes and Oxygen Carriers, 1993; editor-in-chief Jour. Artificial Cells, Blood Substitutes and Immobilization Biotechs.; sect. editor Internat. Jour. Artificial Organs, 1977—, Trans. Am. Soc. Artificial Organs, 1987—; assoc. editor Jour. Artificial Organs, 1977-92; mem. editl. bd. Jour. Biomaterial Med. Devel. and Orgn., 1972-87, Jour. Membrane Sci., 1975-92, Jour. Bioengring., 1975-79, Jour. Enzyme and Microbial Tech., 1978-86. Decorated officer Order of Can., 1992—. Fellow Royal Coll. Physicians Can.; mem. Internat. Soc. Artificial Organs (trustee 1982-87, 89-92, congress pres. 1991, pres. 1994—), Can. Soc. Artificial Organs (pres. 1980-82), Internat. Soc. Artificial Cells, Blood Substitutes and Immobilization Biotech. (hon. pres. 1990—, hon. congress pres. 1994-96, immediate past pres. 1996—), Internat. Soc. Microencapsulations (hon.). Office: Artificial Cells & Organs Rsch Ctr, 3655 Drummond St Rm 1005, Montreal, PQ Canada H3G 1Y6

CHANG, WILLIAM WEI-LIEN, pathologist, histologist; b. Taipei, Taiwan, China, Feb. 7, 1933; came to U.S., 1970.; s. Symonds Tung-Lan and Grace Yun-Huei (Chen) C.; m. Delphine Li-Fen Yang, Oct. 23, 1965; children: Phyllis, Bernice, Albert. MD, Nat. Taiwan U., 1958; MS, Ohio State U., 1966; PhD, McGill U., Montreal, Can., 1970. Lic. Medical, N.J., W.Va.; cert. Am. Bd. of Pathology. Resident in pathology Ohio State U. Hosp., 1962-66; rsch. fellow in pathology Queen's U., Kingston, Ont., Can., 1966-67; rsch. fellow anatomy McGill U., Montreal, Que., 1967-70; from asst. prof anatomy to assoc. prof. anatomy Mt. Sinai Sch. Medicine, N.Y.C., 1970-79; from assoc. prof. pathology to prof. W.Va. U., Morgantown, 1979—, vice chmn. pathology, 1989-93; pathologist W.Va. U. Hosps., 1979—; cons. Chief Med. Examiner's Office of W.Va., Charleston, 1979-93. Contbr. articles to Am. Jour. Anatomy, Jour. Nat. Cancer Inst., Virchows Archiv B. Cell Pathology, Scandinavian Jour. Gastroenterology, Archives of Pathology and Lab. Medicine, Am. Jour. Pathology, others. Mem. AAAS, Am. Soc. Investigative Pathology, U.S. and Can. Acad. Pathology, Am. Assn. Anatomists, Am. Soc. for Cell Biology. Home: 117 Bakers Dr Morgantown WV 26505-2501 Office: West Virginia U Univ Health Sci Ctr Dept Pathology Morgantown WV 26506-9203

CHANNING, ALAN HAROLD, hospital administrator; b. Sayre, Pa., Feb. 6, 1945. BS, U. Cin., 1968; MS, Ohio State U., 1971. With Ohio State U. Hosps., Columbus, 1970, adminstrn. asst., 1971-72, asst. adminstr., 1972-74, assoc. adminstr., 1975-80; v.p. ops. Washington County Hosp. Assn., Hagerstown, Md., 1981-84; adminstr. William N. Wishard Meml. Hosp., Indpls., 1985-86; CEO Elmhurst Hosp. Ctr., Flushing, N.Y., 1986-89, Bellevue Hosp. Ctr., N.Y.C., 1989-91; pres., CEO N.Y. Downtown Hosp., N.Y.C., 1991—; asst. prof. Ohio State U., 1972—. Office: NY Downtown Hosp 170 William St New York NY 10038-2612

CHANOCK, ROBERT MERRITT, pediatrician; b. Chgo., July 8, 1924; married; two children. BS, U. Chgo., 1945, MD, 1947, DSc (hon.), 1977. NRC fellow Children's Hosp., Cin., 1950-52; asst. prof. rsch. pediat. Coll. Medicine, U. Cin., 1954-56; asst. prof. epidemiology Sch. Hygiene and Pub. Health, Johns Hopkins U., 1956-57; surgeon USPHS, 1957-59, head respiratory viruses sect., 1959-61; chief lab. infectious diseases Nat. Inst. Allergy and Infectious Diseases, NIH, Bethesda, Md., 1968—; Nat. Found. Infantile Paralysis fellow, 1951-52; sr. rsch. fellow USPHS, 1956-57; virologist Children's Hosp. D.C., 1957—; mem. Internat. Nomenclature Com. Myxoviruses, 7th and 8th Internat. Microbiol. Congress; mem. Armed Forces Epidemiology Bd., Com. Acute Respiratory Disease, 1960-62; assoc. mem. Com. Influenza, 1963-74; dir. Internat. Ref. Ctr. Lab. Mycoplasms, WHO, 1962; mem. Internat. Com. Nomenclature Bacteria, 1966; clin. prof. Georgetown U., 1970-71; mem. nominating com. NAS, 1979-80; mem. sci. rev. com. Scripps Clin. and Rsch. Found., 1986-89. Recipient E. Mead Johnson award pediat. rsch., 1964, Squibb Gorgas medal Assn. Mil. Surgeons, 1972, Robert Koch medal Fed. Republic Germany, 1981, Virol prize ICT INternat., 1990. Mem. NAS, Soc. Pediat. Rsch., Am. Soc. Microbiology, Am. Epidemiol. Soc., Am. Epidemiology, Am. Pediat. Soc., Am. Soc. Clin. Investigation, Soc. Exptl. Biology and Medicine, Assn. Am. Physicians, Royal Danish Acad. Scis. (fgn. mem.). *

CHANT, ANTHONY DAVID, vascular surgeon, educator; b. Eng., Feb. 21, 1938; s. Percival James and Ethel Helen (Quick) C.; m. Ann Nadia Venning, Mar. 21, 1959; children—Ben, Harvey, Thomas. B.Sc. in Physiology with honors, U. London, 1961, M.B., 1964, M.S., 1971. House surgeon St. Bartholomew Hosp., London, 1965-66; research asst. Welsh Nat. Sch. Medicine, Cardiff, 1968-69; lectr. U. Soton, Southampton, Eng., 1971-74; cons. vascular surgeon Royal South Hants Hosp., Southampton, 1975—; hon. sr. lectr. U. Southampton, 1975—. Contbr. articles to profl. jours. Mem. Amnesty Internat. Fellow Royal Coll. Surgeons (Eng.), Royal Soc. Medicine; mem. Royal Inst. Philosophy. Avocation: fishing. Office: Royal Hants Hosp, Dept Surgery, Graham Rd, Southampton SO9 4PE, England

CHANY, CHARLES, microbiology educator; b. Budapest, Sept. 1, 1920; s. Nicolas and Irene (Lobl) Csanyi; m. Francoise Fournier, Dec. 18, 1975. MD, U. Paris, 1957. Rockefeller fellow Rockefeller Inst., N.Y.C., 1957-58; rsch. asst. NIH Inst. Pasteur, Paris and Bethesda, Md., 1954-60; assoc. idr. Inserm, Paris, 1960-66; dir. U-43 Inserm, Paris, 1966-86; prof. Univ. Paris V, 1966-88; dir. Virus Diagnosis Unit, Hosp. St. Vincent de Paul, Paris, 1954-86. Officer Order of Nat. Merite, France, 1980. Mem. Internat. Soc. Interferon Rsch. (hon.), Rapid Viral Diagnosis Assn. (hon.), Rsch. Assn. A.D.B.E.A. (pres. Paris br. 1986—). Home: 34 Rue Du Docteur Blanche, 75016 Paris France

CHAO, YOU-CHEN, gastroenterologist, researcher; b. Keelung, Taiwan, Jan. 27, 1956; s. Bin Chao and Sue-Ming Chang; m. Kuei-Fang Wang, Mar. 14, 1982; children: Victor W., Yi. MD, Nat. Def. Med. Ctr., Taipei, 1981. Cert. Nat. Bd. Med. Examiners; cert. ednl. commn. for fgn. med. grads. Instr. Nat. Def. Med. Ctr., Taipei, 1987-88; rsch. assoc. U. So. Calif., L.A., 1988-90; assoc. prof. Nat. Def. Med. Ctr., Taipei, 1991—; dir. divsn. phys. check-up Tri-Svc. Gen. Hosp., Taipei, 1991-95. Contbr. articles to profl. jours. Recipient Prof. Juei-Low Sung award for rsch. in hepatology Prof. Juei-Low Sung Med. Found., 1994, Best Tchr. award Ministry Nat. Def., 1993, 95. Mem. Soc. Gastroenterology Taiwan (Best Poster award 1991), Soc. Med. Ultrasound Taiwan, 1991—. Home: # 51, Alley 4 Ln 154 Yung-Chun St, Taipei Taiwan Office: Tri-Svc Gen Hosp, Divsn Gastroenterology, POX90055 Taipei Taiwan

CHAPDELAINE, JOAN MURPHY, health services administrator, nursing educator; b. Newport, R.I., July 25, 1936; d. Quentin Leo and Helen (Hamilton) Murphy; m. Armand Joseph Chapdelaine, July 23, 1960. BSN, Salve Regina U., Newport, 1957, MS in Health Svcs. Adminstrn., 1985; MS in Nursing Adminstrn., Boston U., 1972; PhD, Walden U., Mpls., 1991. RN, R.I., Mass.; cert. nurse adminstr. advanced. Coord. nursing program Newport Hosp. Sch. Nursing, 1957-71; resident in adminstrn. St. Luke's Hosp., New Bedford, Mass., 1971-72; dir. nursing Truesdale Hosp., Fall River, Mass., 1972-77; dir. nursing component R.I. Cancer Control Program, Providence, 1977-79; assoc. dir. nursing svcs. St. Luke's Hosp., New Bedford, Mass., 1979-81; asst. prof. nursing Salve Regina U., 1981-85, assoc. prof. nursing and health svc. adminstrn., 1985-93, prof. health svcs. adminstrn., 1993—, dir. grad. program in health svcs. adminstrn., 1985—; cons. nursing dept. St. Luke's Hosp., New Bedford, Mass., 1982-86; cons. Nat. Cancer Inst., 1979; guest speaker on nursing mgmt. and bioethics, 1983—. Mem. evaluation com. United Way, Providence, 1986-91, chmn. Southeastern Mass. chpt. evaluation task force, 1988-90; vol. Am. Cancer Soc., Providence, 1986—. Mem. Am. Hosp. Assn., Am. Orgn. Nurse Execs., Salve Regina U. Alumni Assn., Boston U. Alumni Assn., Sigma Theta Tau. Roman Catholic. Home: 47 Harrison Ave Newport RI 02840-3883 Office: Salve Regina U Ochre Point Ave Newport RI 02840

CHAPIN, ROBERT ELLIOT, reproductive toxicologist; b. Providence, R.I., May 13, 1953; s. Richard M. and Eve (Schoch) C.; m. Diane Cole; children: Hannah Cole, Elaine Lorin. BA, Earlham Coll., 1975; PhD, U. N.C., 1980. With Chem. Industry Inst. Toxicology, Research Triangle Park, N.C., 1980-82; staff fellow Nat. Toxicology program Nat. Inst. Environ. Health Scis., Research Triangle Park, 1982-83, sr. staff fellow, 1983-87, toxicologist, 1987—; head environ. awareness adv. com. Nat. Inst. Environ. Health Scis., 1990—. Contbr./co-contbr. chpts. to books, articles to sci. publs., 1980—. Recipient Young Andrologist of Yr. award Am. Soc. Andrology, 1993, NIH Dir.'s award for outstanding rsch., 1995. Mem. Soc. Toxicology (sec./treas. N.C. chpt. 1990-92, councillor reproduction/devel. toxicology specialty sect. 1988-90, v.p., pres. 1993-95). Office: Nat Inst Environ Health Sci MD A2-02 PO Box 12233 Research Triangle Park NC 27709-2233

CHAPIN, SUZANNE PHILLIPS, retired psychologist; b. Syracuse, N.Y., Aug. 9, 1930; d. Harold Bridge and Charlotte Virginia (Warner) Phillips; m. Richard Hilton Chapin, June 13, 1953 (div. 1964); children: Bruce Phillips Chapin, Linda Chapin Fry. BA, Syracuse U., 1952; MA, Columbia U., 1965. Statis. asst. Syracuse Bd. of Edn., 1952-53; psychol. examiner Stamford (Conn.) Pub. Schs., 1965-68, psychologist Head Start program, 1967-68; psychologist Southbury (Conn.) Tng. Sch., 1968-74, Onondaga Assn. for the Retarded, Syracuse, 1974, Harlem Valley Psychiatric Ctr., Wingdale, N.Y., 1974-93, Mid-Hudson Psychiat. Ctr., New Hampton, 1993; ret., 1993. Mem. LWV, Audubon Soc., Sierra Club. Democrat. Home: 10 S Bearwood Dr Palmyra VA 22963

CHAPLEAU, MARK WILLIAM, physiologist, educator; b. Hartford City, Ind., Feb. 27, 1955; s. Craig William and Florene Helen (Gibbons) C.; m. Colleen Reardon, Aug. 21, 1982; children: Gina Marie, Nicole Calia, Riley Craig. BS, U. Wis., Whitewater, 1977; PhD, La. State U. Med. Ctr., 1985. Postdoctoral rsch. fellow dept. internal medicine U. Iowa, Iowa City, 1985-87, asst. rsch. scientist dept. internal medicine, 1987-89; rsch. health sci. specialist VA Med. Ctr., Iowa City, 1988—; asst. prof. cardiovascular diseases, dept. internal medicine U. Iowa, Iowa City, 1989—; reviewer profl. jours., 1988—. Mem. editl. bd. Hypertension, 1991-96, Primary Sensory Neuron, 1995—; contbr. articles to profl. jours. Fellow Am. Physiol. Soc. (cardiovascular sect.), Am. Heart Assn. (coun. high blood pressure rsch., coun. on circulation); mem. Soc. Neurosci., Am. Fed. Clin. Rsch., N.Y. Acad. Sci. Roman Catholic. Office: U Iowa Coll Medicine E327 General Hosp Iowa City IA 52242

CHAPLIN, DAVID DUNBAR, medical research specialist, medical educator; b. London, Aug. 28, 1952; came to U.S., 1952; s. Hugh Jr. and Alice Elizabeth (Dougherty) C.; m. Jane Ellen Bryant; children: Vernon H., Rosalind K., Daniel B. AB, Harvard U., 1973; MD, PhD, Washington U., St. Louis, 1980. Intern, then resident Parkland Meml. Hosp., Dallas, 1980-82; post-doctoral fellow dept. genetics Harvard U. Med. Sch., Boston, 1982-84; asst. prof. medicine Washington U. Sch. Medicine, St. Louis, 1984-91, prof. medicine, 1995—; assoc. investigator Howard Hughes Med. Inst., St. Louis, 1984—. Assoc. editor: The New Biologist, 1990-92, Diabetes, 1992-96; contbr. articles to profl. jours. Mem. grants com. Arthritis Found., Atlanta, 1989-92. Scholar Harvard U., 1972, 73; Jane Coffin Childs Fund for Med. Rsch. fellow, 1982-84. Mem. Am. Soc. Clin. Investigation, Am. Fedn. Clin. Rsch., Am. Assn. Immunologists, Am. Soc. Human Genetics, Alpha Omega Alpha. Democrat. Roman Catholic. Office: Howard Hughes Med Inst 4566 Scott Ave PO Box 8022 Saint Louis MO 63110

CHAPMAN, ALBERT LEE, anatomy educator, university dean; b. Anderson, Mo., Nov. 5, 1933; s. Coleman V. and Lorena (Farley) C.; m. Patsy Joan Pickett, Aug. 31, 1958; children: Gregory Paul, Robin Annette, Janette Lee, Jeffrey Coleman. AA, Joplin Jr. Coll., 1954; BA, U. Mo., 1956, U. Mo., 1959; PhD, U. Nebr., Omaha, 1962. Instr. U. Kans., Kansas City, 1962-64, asst. prof. med. ctr., 1964-69, assoc. prof. dept. anatomy, 1969-74, dir. Electron Microscopy Rsch. Ctr., 1973-91, prof., 1974—, acting dean grad. studies med. ctr., 1983-85, dean. grad. studies and research med. ctr., 1985-93, assoc. vice chancellor for rsch. adminstrn., dean, 1993-96; acting exec. vice chancellor U. Kans., 1995, vice chancellor acad. affairs, dean grad. studies & rsch., 1996—; pres. U. Kans. Med. Ctr. Rsch. Inst., Inc., 1992—. Mem. Am. Assn. Anatomists, Am. Soc. Cell Biology, Cen. States Electron Microscopy Soc. (pres. 1979-80, 85-86), Electron Microscopy Soc. Am., Sigma Xi (pres. 1978-79). Office: U Kans Med Ctr Office Grad Studies and Rsch 3901 Rainbow Blvd Kansas City KS 66160-0001

CHAPMAN, ANTHONY BRADLEY, psychiatrist; b. Salem, Mass., Aug. 22, 1938; s. Anthony Bredick and Gladys Gwendolyn (Poole) C.; m. Ella Mueller, Aug. 30, 1963; children: Bradley, Jeffrey. BS with honors, Northeastern U., 1961; MD, Stanford U., 1966. Diplomate Am. Bd. Psychiatry and Neurology. Rsch. asst. Harvard Med. Sch., Boston, 1957-61; intern Case-Western Res. U., Cleve., 1966-67; resident Johns Hopkins Hosp., Balt., 1967-69, fellow in behavioral medicine, 1969-71; fellow in child psychiatry U. Pa., Phila., 1969-71; pvt. practice Alexandria, Va., 1973—; dir. Attention Disorder Ctr. No. Va., Alexandria, 1991—; guest lectr. Children and Adults with Attention Deficit Disorder, Arlington, Va., 1990-96. Editor Hyperactive Child Newsletter, 1974-78. Maj. U.S. Army, 1971-73. Recipient Outstanding Tchr. award Am. Acad. Family Practice, 1976-81. Mem. Am. Med. Soc., Am. Psychiat. Electrophysiology Assn., Va. Med. Soc., Alexandria Med. Soc., Attention Deficit Disorders Profls. No. Va. (pres. 1990-92). Office: 2059 Huntington Ave Ste 108 Alexandria VA 22303

CHAPMAN, ANTONY JOHN, psychology educator; b. Canterbury, Kent, Eng., Apr. 21, 1947; s. Arthur Charles and Joan Muriel Chapman; m. Siriol Sophia Jones David, June 1, 1985; children: David, Luke, Harriet, Madeleine. BSc, U. Leicester (Eng.), 1968, PhD, 1972. Lectr. UWIST, Cardiff, Wales, 1971-78; sr. lectr. U. Wist, Cardiff, Wales, 1978-83; prof. U. Leeds, Eng., 1983—, dean of sci., 1992-94, pro-vice chancellor, 1994—; founding dir. Centre for Applied Psychol. Studies, 1987-90; auditor, vice-chancellors' and prins.' Acad. Audit Unit, Higher Edn. Quality Coun., 1990-93; chair U.K. dean's sci. 1993-94. Editor: Brit. Jour. Psychology, 1989-95; co-editor Current Psychology: Rsch. & Revs., 1984—; contbr. articles to 14 books, profl. jours. Fellow Brit. Psychol. Soc. (chartered psychologist, pres. 1988-89, fellowship award 1978); mem. Assn. Learned Socs. in the Social Scis. (pres. 1995—), Brit. Assn. Advancement of Sci. (pres. psychology sect. 1993-94). Home: Home Farm House, 9 Breary Ln, Bramhope LS16 9AD, England Office: U Leeds, Leeds LS2 9JT, England

CHAPMAN, BARBARA, pediatric nurse practitioner; b. Ft. Belvoir, Va., Apr. 5, 1954; d. Howard Clark and Margaret Jean (Kerr) C.; children: Antonia Michelle, Jessica Lynn. BSN, U. Md., Balt., 1977; MS, SUNY, Stony Brook, 1989. Cert. pediatric nurse practitioner. Sch. nurse practitioner Brookdale Hosp. Med. Ctr., Bklyn.; pediatric clinician, hemodialysis nurse Univ. Hosp., Stony Brook; nurse physician's office, East Setauket, N.Y.; pediatric nurse practitioner Nassau County Med. Ctr., East Meadow, N.Y. With U.S. Army, 1972-75. Walter Reed Army Inst. Nursing scholar. Mem. Nat. Assn. Neonatal Nurses, Nat. Assn. Pediatric Nurse Assocs. and Practitioners, N.Y. State Coalition Nurse Practitioners, Sigma Theta Tau.

CHAPMAN, CHRISTINE ROSE, biomedical scientist; b. Hounslow, Middlesex, Eng., May 17, 1957; d. Brian and Lena (Grech) C.; m. David Spratt, Mar. 3, 1989. Nat. Cert. Scis., Paddington Coll., London, 1975, Diploma Med. Lab. Mgmt., 1984; Higher Nat. Cert. Microbiology, NESCOT, Surrey, Eng., 1977; Cert., Diploma in Mktg., Harrow Coll., 1990. Jr. med. lab. sci. officer Ashford Hosp., 1973-75, med. lab. sci. officer, 1975-77; med. lab. sci. officer St. Heliers Hosp., Carshalton, 1977-80; pub. health analyst Bermuda Govt., 1980-81; sr. med. lab. sci. officer Cen. Pub. Health Lab., Colindale, 1981-85, St. Thomas Hosp., London, 1985-86, Wellington Hosp., London, 1986-89; mktg. mgr. Clin-lab Svcs., Mill Hill, 1989-90; bus. devel. mgr. Ravenscourt Labs., London, 1990-92; bus. mgr. for pathology Derriford Hosp., Plymouth, Eng., 1992-95; immunologist Kings Coll. Hosp., London, 1995—; mem. bd. studies PCL, London 1988; locum biomed. scientist, mgmt. cons., 1986—. Fellow Ins. Med. Lab. Scis. Coun. (covenor mgmt. discussion group, spl. exam. in immunology 1981); mem. Brit. Inst. Mgmt., Chartered Inst. Mktg., Henry Doubleday Rsch. Assn.

CHAPMAN, GEORGE BUNKER, biology educator; b. Bayonne, N.J., June 10, 1925; s. George Bunker and Ella (Greer) C. AB magna cum laude, Princeton U., 1950, AM, 1952, PhD, 1953. Asst. instr. dept. biology Princeton (N.J.) U., 1950-52, asst. rsch. dept. biology, 1952-53, rsch. asst. dept. biology, 1953-54, rsch. assoc. dept. biology, 1954-56; rsch. biologist RCA Labs., Princeton, 1953-56; asst. prof. dept. biology Harvard U., Cambridge, Mass., 1956-60; assoc. prof. anatomy Cornell U. Med. Coll., N.Y.C., 1960-63; prof., chmn. dept. biology Georgetown U., Washington, 1963-90, prof. dept. biology, 1990—; editorial bd. Jour. Bacteriology, Washington, 1960-69. Contbr. over 100 articles to profl. jours. With USNR, 1944-46. Fellow Am. Acad. Microbiology; mem. Am. Soc. Microbiology, Am. Microscopical Soc. (bd. reviewers 1966-94), Sigma Xi (pres. chpt. 1967-68, historian 1968—), Phi Beta Kappa (pres. chpt. 1988-90). Republican. Office: Georgetown U Biology 37th and O Sts NW Washington DC 20057-1229

CHAPMAN, HOPE HORAN, psychologist; b. Chgo., Feb. 13, 1954; d. Theodore George and Idelle (Poll) H.; m. Stuart G. Chapman, Dec. 4, 1983. BS, U. Ill., Champaign-Urbana, 1976; MA, No. Ill. U., 1979; student lawyer's asst. program Roosevelt U., Chgo. 1996. Lic. counselor, Ill. Psychologist Glenwood (Iowa) State Hosp. Sch., 1979-83, Gov. Samuel H. Shapiro Devel. Ctr., Kankakee, Ill., 1985-86; dir. staff tng. and devel. Glenkirk, 1988-90; clin. assoc. Bennett & Assoc., 1990-91; psychologist Singer Mental Health & Devel. Ctr., Rockford, Ill., 1992-93; forensic psychologist Elgin (Ill.) Mental Health Ctr., 1993-94; Scholar State of Ill. Active Omaha Symphonic Chorus, 1981-83; mem. Omaha Public Schs. Citizens Adv. Com., 1980-81; mem. edn. com. Anti-Defamation League, 1980-85, chmn. com. anti-Semitism and Jewish youth, 1981-84; commr. youth commn. Village of Hoffman Estates, Ill., 1988-94; vice-chmn. oversight com. Vogelei Teen. Ctr., 1988-94; commr. Environ. Commn., Village of Hoffman Estates, 1994—, chmn. Schaumburg Twp. Mental Health Bd., 1993-94. Mem. APA, Midwest Psychol. Assn., Am. Assn. on Mental Retardation, Am. Psychology-Law Soc., Am Coll. Forensic Examiners, Phi Kappa Phi, Psi Chi. Jewish. Contbr. papers to profl. confs., articles to jours.

CHAPMAN, JOHN EDMON, university dean, pharmacologist, physician; b. Springfield, Mo., July 5, 1931; s. Loran Edmon and Bertha Gay (Duncan) C.; m. Judy Jean Cox, Mar. 9, 1968. BEd, BS in Biology and Chemistry, Southwest Mo. State Coll., 1954; MD, U. Kans., Kansas City, Kans., 1958; MD (hon.), Karolinska Med. Inst., Stockholm, 1987. Diplomate Nat. Bd. Med. Examiners (mem.-at-large, 1988—, fin. com. 1989—, bylaws com. exec. bd.). Intern Kans. Med. Ctr., 1958-59; asst. chief med. staff U. Ariz., Tucson, 1959-60; resident and fellow in internal medicine and clin. pharmacology U. Kans. Med. Ctr., 1960-63; instr. medicine and pharmacology Sch. Medicine U. Kans., 1961-62, asst. to assoc. prof. pharmacology, 1962-67, asst. dean to assoc. dean student affairs, 1963-67, coordinator med. edn. for nat. def., 1963-67; assoc. dean for edn. Sch. Medicine Vanderbilt U., Nashville, 1967-75, dean Sch. Medicine, 1975—; co-chmn. Liaison Com. on Med. Edn., 1988; fgn. adj. prof. Karolinska Inst., Stockholm. Mem. steering com. Health Policy Agenda for Am. People, 1982-87; mem. exec. bd. Mid. Tenn. couns. Boy Scouts Am., Nashville, 1984—; active Leadership Nashville, 1985—; bd. dirs. Health Edn. Media Assn., Washington, 1973-84. Recipient Medal of Achievement, 1979, Crystal Gavel award in Internat. Medicine, 1986 Karolinska Med. Inst., Medal of Merit Rene Descartes Sch. of Medicine, Paris; named Winthrop Sterlin Disting. Lectr. U. Kans. Med. Ctr., 1982, William Root Prof. Med. Edn. U. Kans. Med. Ctr., 1982, William Root Prof. Med. Edn. U. Kans. Med. Ctr., 1985, Disting. Alumnus of Yr. U. Kansas Med. Ctr. Sch. of Medicine, 1988. Fellow ACP; mem. AMA (chmn. sect. on med. schs. 1981-83, founding mem. sect. on med. schs., del. ho. of dels., coun. on med. edn. 1989—, accreditation coun. for grad. med. edn.), Am. Coll. Clin. Pharmacology (life, regent 1972-82, 89—), Am. Soc. Clin. Pharmacology and Therpaeutics, Am. Acad. Mgmt., Am. Acad. Med. Adminstrn., Assn. Am. Med. Colls. (coun. deans, adminstrv. bd. coun. deans 1977-84, exec. coun. 1977-84), Soc. Med. Cons. to Armed Forces, Alpha Omega Alpha. Office: Vanderbilt U Sch Medicine D-3300 Med Ctr North 21st Ave S at Garland Ave Nashville TN 37232-2104*

CHAPMAN, LORING, psychology educator, neuroscientist; b. L.A., Oct. 4, 1929; s. Lee E. and Elinore E. (Gundry) Scott; children: Robert, Antony, Pandora (dec.). BS, U. Nev., 1950; PhD, U. Chgo., 1955. Lic. psychologist, Oreg., N.Y., Calif. Rsch. fellow U. Chgo., 1952-54; rsch. assoc., asst. prof. Cornell U. Med. Coll., N.Y.C., 1957-61; rsch. dir. Music Rsch. Found., N.Y.C., 1958-61; assoc. prof. in residence Neuropsychiat. Inst., UCLA, 1961-65; rsch. prof. U. Oreg., Portland, 1965; br. chief NIH, Bethesda, Md., 1966-67; prof., chmn. dept. behavioral biology, joint prof. human physiology Sch. Medicine U. Calif., Davis, 1967-81, prof. psychiatry and head Divsn. of Clin. Psychology, 1977-91; prof. emeritus Sch. Medicine U. Calif., 1991—, prof. neurology, 1977-81, prof. human physiology, 1977-81; asst. dean, rsch. affairs Sch. Medicine U. Calif., Davis, 1972-74; vice chmn. div. of sci. basic to medicine, 1976-79; Lic. psychologist, Calif. Author: Pain and Suffering, 3 vols, 1967, Head and Brain 3 vols, 1971, (with E.A. Dunlap) The Eye, 1981; assoc. editor courtroom medicine series updates, 1965—; contbr. sci. articles to publs. Fogarty Sr. Internat. fellow, 1980; grantee NASA, 1969-80; grantee NIH, 1956-91; grantee Nat. Inst. Drug Abuse, 1971-80; recipient Thorton Wilson prize, 1958, Career award USPHS, 1964, Commonwealth Fund award, 1970. Mem. Am. Acad. Neurology, Am. Physiol. Soc., Am. Psychol. Assn., Royal Soc. Medicine (London)., Am. Neurol. Assn., Am. Assn. Mental Deficiency, Aerospace Med. Assn., Soc. for Neurosci. Home: 205 Country Pl Apt 188 Sacramento CA 95831-2076 Office: U Calif Med Ctr Dept Psychiatry 2315 Stockton Blvd Sacramento CA 95817-2201

CHAPMAN, MARVIN JOHN, psychiatric administration consultant; b. Milw., Dec. 31, 1935; s. George Matthew and Martha (Baehr) C.; m. Marie Louise Olson, May 9, 1959; children: Nancy, Michael, Eric. BS in Zoology summa cum laude, U. Wis., Madison, 1955, MD, 1959, MS in Preventive Medicine, 1985. Cert. profl. in healthcare quality. Sr. med. officer U.S. Naval Disciplinary Command, Portsmouth, N.H., 1965-67; asst. clin. dir., clin. dir. C. State Hosp., Wis., 1967-72; dir. adult svcs. M. Mental Health Inst., Madison, Wis., 1972-75; med. dir. Rock County Cmty. Mental Health Bd., Wis., 1975-85; dir. forensic svcs. Wis. Divsn. Mental Hygiene, Madison, 1976-93; physician, cons. Wis. Divsn. Treatment Facilities, Madison, 1993-96; clin. instr. Dept. Psychiatry U. Wis. Med. Sch., Madison, 1973-77, clin. asst. prof., 1977-83; surveyor Joint Com. Accreditation Healthcare Facilities, 1979-96; cons. in field. Contbr. chpts. to books in field, articles to profl. jours. Lt. comdr. USN, 1959-67. Recipient Spl. Recognition award Nat. Assn. State Forensic Dirs., 1987. Mem. Wis. Med. Alumni Assn., Nat. Assn. Health Quality, State Mental Health Forensic Dirs. (1st program dir., nat. exec. 1979—), Divsn. Nat. Assn. State Mental Health Dirs. (exec. coun. 1979-89). Home: 7320 Cedar Creek Trail Madison WI 53717

CHAPMAN, MICHAEL WILLIAM, orthopedist, educator; b. Newberry, Mich., Nov. 29, 1937; m. Elizabeth Casady; adopted sons: Mark, Craig. AA, Am. River Coll., Sacramento, Calif., 1957; postgrad., U. Calif., Davis, 1957-58; BS, U. Calif., San Francisco, 1959, MD, 1962. Diplomate Am. Bd. Orthopaedic Surgery (ad hoc appeal com. 1986, site visitor 1986, certification renewal com. 1985-88, certification renewal com. chmn. 1986-88). Intern San Francisco Gen. Hosp., 1962-63, resident in orthopedic surgery, 1966, asst. chief orthopaedic surgery svc., 1971-79, acting chief orthopaedic surgery svc., 1972-73; resident in orthopaedic surgery U. Calif., San Francisco, 1963-67, asst. prof. dept. orthopaedic surgery, Sch. Medicine, 1971-76, assoc. prof. dept. orthopaedic surgery, Sch. Medicine, 1976-79; resident in orthopaedic surgery U. Calif. Hosps., San Francisco, 1963-64, Samuel Merritt Hosp., Oakland, Calif., 1964, Highland-Alameda County Hosp., Oakland, 1965, Children's Hosp. of the East Bay, Oakland, 1966, Shriners Hosp., Honolulu, 1966-67; fellow Nat. Orthopaedic Hosp., London, 1967-68; chmn. dept. orthopaedic surgery U. Calif., Davis, Sacramento, 1979—, prof. dept. orthopaedic surgery, 1981—; panelist Calif. Crippled Children Svcs. Panel in Orthopaedic Surgery; cons. VA Hospital, Martinez, Calif.; cons. staff Sutter Gen. Hosp., Sacramento, California; co-chmn. Zimmer Trauma Panel, 1983-84; vis. prof. Fresno Valley Med. Ctr., 1975, Dept. Orthopaedics, U. Calif., Davis, 1976, U. Hawaii, Honolulu, 1977; vis. prof., cons. to Surgeon Gen. U.S. Army, Europe, 1978; vis. prof. U. Basel, Switzerland, 1979, Phoenix Orthopaedic Residency Program, 1979, Stanford U., 1981, U. Hawaii, 1982, U. So. Calif., L.A., 1984, SUNY, Buffalo, 1985, U. Utah, 1985, U. Iowa Coll. Medicine, 1987, Duke U. Sch. Medicine, 1988, U. Calif. Irvine, Div. Orthopaedics, 1990, U. S.C., 1990, Mass. Gen. Hosp., Harvard U., 1990; also guest lectr. numerous instns.; insp. for residency rev. com. ad hoc appeal com. Accreditation coun. for Grad. Med. Specialist Site, 1983-86. Editor: (with M. Madison) Operative Orthopaedics, 1988 (Best New Book in Clin. Medicine Assn. Am. Pubs.); contbr. 128 articles, 54 abstracts to profl. jours.; presenter 9 exhibits, 22 audiovisual programs, 476 other presentations; cons. editor Skiing Mag., 1973-77; mem. bd. assoc. editors Clin. Orthopaedics and Related Rsch., 1982-85, Internat. Med. Soc. Paraplegia, 1972-80; reviewer Jour. Bone and Joint Surgery, 1980-95, New Eng. Jour. Medicine. With U.S. Army, 1968-70. Decorated Army Commendation medal; recipient Outstanding Tchg. award U. Calif., San Francisco, 1972, Outstanding Tchr. award U. Calif., Davis, 1984, 93; named One of Best 100 Doctors Am., Good Housekeeping Mag.; Fogarty Sr. Internat. fellow NIH, 1978-79, 80-81; grantee Johnson & Johnson, 1983-84, Zimmer Inc., 1983-85, 85-86, 87-90, Interpore Internat., 1985-86, 89-90, Collagen Inc., 1985-86, 88-89, Upjohn Inc., 1985-86, Orthopaedic Rsch. and Edn. Found., 1988-89. Mem. AMA (Physicians Recognition award 1989-92), ACS, ASTM, Am. Acad. Orthopaedic Surgeons (bd. dirs. 1982-83, numerous coms.), Am. Orthopaedic Assn. (bd. dirs. 1985-86, pres. 1990-91, various coms.), Internat. Orthopaedic Assn., Assn. for Study of Internal Fixation (N.Am. chpt.), Internat. Soc. Orthopaedic Surgery and Traumatology, Internat. Soc. for Fracture Repair, Internat. Soc. for Skiing Safety, Pan-Pacific Surg. Assn., Brit. Orthopaedic Assn., South African Orthopaedic Assn. (hon.), Pres.'s Coun. English Speaking Orthopaedic Assns., Internat. Coun. on Edn., Acad. Orthopaedic Soc. (previously Assn. Orthopaedic Chmn.), Am. Acad. Orthopaedic Surgeons, Am. Assn. for Surgery of Trauma, Am. Bd. Med. Spltys., Am. Bd. Orthopaedic Surgery, Am. Orthopaedic Soc. for Sports Medicine, Am. Trauma Soc., Assn. Am. Med. Colls., Assn. Bone and Joint Surgeons, Leroy C. Abbott Orthopaedic Soc., Austrian Trauma Assn., Paul R. Lipscomb Soc., Northwestern Med. Assn., Orthopaedic Rsch. Soc., Orthopaedic Trauma Assn., Srra Club, U.S. Ski Assn., U.S. Ski Coaches Assn., U. Calif. San Francisco Alumni Assn., Western Orthopaedic Assn., Houston Orthopaedic Assn. (hon.), Calif. Med. Assn., Calif. Orthopaedic Assn., Sacramento-El Dorado Med. Soc., Wilson Interurban Orthopaedic Soc., Alpha Omega Alpha. Office: U Calif-Davis Sch Med Dept Orthopedics 2230 Stockton Blvd Sacramento CA 95817-1419

CHAPMAN, ROBERT GALBRAITH, retired hematologist, administrator; b. Colorado Springs, Colo., Sept. 29, 1926; s. Edward Northrop and Janet Galbraith (Johnson) c.; m. Virginia Irene Potts, July 6, 1956; childen: Lucia Tully Chapman Chatzky, Sarah Northrop Chapman Bohrer, Robert Bostwick. Student, Westminster Coll., 1944-45; BA, Yale U., 1947; MD, Harvard U., 1951; MS, U. Colo., 1958. Diplomate Am. Bd. Internal Medicine and Pathology; lic. physician, Colo., Calif. Intern Hartford (Conn.) Hosp., 1951-52; resident in medicine U. Colo. Med. Ctr., Denver, 1955-58; fellow in hematology U. Wash., Seattle, 1958-60; chief resident in medicine U. Colo., Denver, 1957-58, instr. medicine, 1960-62, asst. prof. medicine, 1962-68, assoc. prof., 1968-91; chief staff VA Hosp., Denver, 1968-70; dir. Belle Bonfils Meml. Blood Ctr., Denver, 1977-91; mem. regionalization com. Am. Blood Commn., Washington, 1985-87, Colo.sickle cell com., Denver, 1978-91, gov.'s AIDS Coun., 1987-88; trustee Coun. Community Blood Ctrs., v.p., 1979-81, pres., 1989-91, mem. rsch. inst. bd. Palo Alto Med. Found., 1991—. Contbr. articles to profl. jours. Served as capt. USAF, 1953-55. USPHS fellow, 1958-60. Fellow ACP; mem. Am. Assn. Blood Banks, Mayflower Soc., Denver Med. Soc., Colo. Med. Soc., Western Soc. Clin. Rsch., Am. Radio Relay League. Mem. United Ch. Christ. Home: 47 La Rancheria Carmel Valley CA 93924-9424

CHAPMAN, ROBERT JAMES, dentist; b. Clinton, Mass., Oct. 9, 1941; s. James Alexander and Grace (Brown) C. BS, Tufts U., 1963, MD, 1967, cert. in prosthodontics, 1974. Instr. Tufts U. Sch. Dentistry Medicine, Boston, 1974-75, asst. prof., 1975-81, assoc. clin. prof., 1981-90, clin. prof., 1981-90, head fixed and removeable parcial prostheodontics, 1983—; cons. Tekscan Corp., Boston, 1985-93. Author: (with others) Removeable Partial Prosthodontics, 1980, Implant Prosthodontics, 1985; contbr. articles to profl. jours. With USN, 1967-72. Fellow Internat. Coll. of Dentists, Am. Coll. Dentists, Am. Coll. of Prosthodontics (assoc.), Am. Coll. of Implant Prosthodontics (mastership 1995). Office: Lewis Wharf Dental Assocs 237 Lewis Wharf Boston MA 02110

CHAPNICK, ROBERT IAN, physician; b. N.Y.C., Oct. 23, 1951; s. Seymour and Laura Helene (Wilk) C.; m. Henny Gurewich, Dec. 8, 1979; 1 child, Daniel. BA, CUNY, 1972; MD, SUNY, Bklyn., 1976. Diplomate Am. Bd. Internal Medicine. Internal medicine intern Brookdale Med. Ctr., Bklyn., 1976-77, internal medicine resident, 1977-79; pvt. practice San Leandro, Calif., 1979-88; med. dir. City/County San Francisco Homeless Programs, 1988-95, Cmty. Med. Ctrs. Inc., Stockton, Calif., 1995—; asst. clin. prof. U. Calif., San Francisco, 1990—; co-chair San Francisco Dept. Pub. Health Joint Pharmacy & Therapeutics Com., 1994-95; mem. San Francisco Gen. Hosp. Pharmacy & Therapeutics Com., 1992-95; mem. San Francisco Dept. Pub. Health AIDS Com., 1990-95; med. expert, cons. State of Calif., Sacramento, 1995—. Mem. AMA, San Joaquin Med. Soc., Calif. Med. Assn. Home: 26551 Durham Way Hayward CA 94542 Office: Cmty Med Ctrs Inc 701 E Channel St Stockton CA 95202

CHAPPEN, EDWARD PETER, physician; b. Carbondale, Pa., July 8, 1925; s. Peter E. and Amelia E. (Kouloumpy) C. BS, Pa. State U., 1946; MD, Jefferson Med. Coll., 1952. Diplomate Am. Bd. Psychiatry and Neurology. Intern Jefferson Med. Coll. Hosp., Phila., 1953; fellow Menninger Sch. Psychology; practice gen. psychiatry, Trenton, N.J., 1955—; resident in psychiatry Menninger Sch. Psychiatry, Topeka, Kans., 1967-70; staff psychiatrist Cen. Santa Clara County Mental Health Ctr., San Jose, Calif., 1970-71; mem., then chmn. staff St. Francis Hosp.; cons. in psychiatry Hamilton Hosp., Union Indsl. Home, Trenton. Mem. Trenton Mayor's Com. for Selection of Trenton Sister City, 1961, Trenton Landmarks Commn. for Hist. Preservation, Trenton Civic Improvements Com.; mem. spl. groups div. Del. Valley United Fund, 1958; treas. local chpt. Am. Assn. UN, 1960-61; mem. exec. bd. Greater Trenton chpt. People to People; exec. council, chmn. pub. relations com. Parnassos Greek Cultural Soc. of N.Y. Inc., 1963; mem. adv. com. for study sociology, death and dying Mercer County; mem. fine arts com. Anglican Cathedral of the Trinity, Trenton; bd. govs. Greater Trenton Symphony Assn., 1966-67; trustee Friends of Trenton Free Pub. Library, Vis. Nurse Assn. Trenton bd. mgrs. Donnelly Meml. Hosp.; trustee Greek Orthodox Ch., 1962-64. Served to lt. (j.g.) USMC, 1954. Menninger Sch. Psychiatry fellow, 1970. Mem. N.Y. Acad. Scis., AMA, Am. Psychiat. Assn., Santa Clara-Monterey Counties Psychiat. Soc., Mercer County Med. Soc. (chmn. physician placement service com.), Navy League U.S., Internat. Platform Assn., Byzantine Fellowship, Pa. Soc., Assn. Mil. Surgeons U.S., UN Assn. U.S.A. (chpt pres. 1966), Alumni Assn. Menninger Sch. Psychiatry, Princeton Soc. Archeol. Inst. Am., Trenton Mus. Soc., State House Dist. Assn., Douglass House Commn., Archeol. Inst. Am., Nat. Hist. Soc., Trenton Hist. Soc., Hist. Soc. Hamilton Twp., Nat. Trust Hist. Preservation, Trent House Assn., Symposium Soc. Trenton, Met. Mus. Art, Friends of Art Mus. Princeton U., Phi Alpha Sigma. Clubs: Architectoniki (Athens, Greece); Commd. Officers U.S. Naval Base (Phila.). Lodges: Rotary, Soc. of Mary, Masons (32 deg.), Shriners. Office: 476 Hamilton Ave Trenton NJ 08609-2711

CHAPUT, ANDRE NMN, anesthesiologist; b. Montreal, Que., Can., June 12, 1947; came to the U.S., 1987; B. ès Arts, Coll. L'Assomption, Que., 1967; MD, U. Montreal, Que., 1971; lic. from conseil, Med. de Can., Montreal, 1972. Diplomate Am. Bd. Anesthesiology. Founder, chief Family Medicine Dept. Hotel-Dieu de Gaspe Hosp., 1972-80; anestnesiology resident Centre Hospitalier Universitaire de Sherbrooke, Sherbrooke, Que., Que., 1981-82; staff anesthesiology Sherbrooke Hosp., 1982-87, interim chief of anesthesiology dept., 1985-87; resident U. Miami Sch. Medicine, 1987-89; staff anesthesiologist Meadville (Pa.) Med. Ctr., 1989-91, Samaritan Med. Ctr., Watertown, N.Y., 1991—; pres. Jefferson Anesthesiologist Svcs., 1993-95, v.p., 1995-96, treas., 1996—. Mem. AMA, ASA, Am. Soc. Regional Anesthesiology, N.Y. State Soc. Anesthesiology, Meyers Aircraft Owners Assn., Watertown Racquet Club. Office: Jefferson AnesthesiologistSvcs 830 Washington St Watertown NY 13601

CHARET, ROBERT LANCE, ophthalmologist; b. N.Y.C., Aug. 23, 1959; s. Richard and Annette (Silver) C. BA, NYU, 1981; MD, SUNY, N.Y.C., 1985. Diplomate Am. Bd. Ophthalmology. Resident SUNY, N.Y.C., 1986-89; ophthalmologist pvt. practice, Hawthorne, Calif., 1992—. Ophthalmology fellow SUNY, N.Y.C., 1989-90. Fellow Am. Acad. Ophthalmology; mem. Phi Beta Kappa. Office: Robert F Kennedy Eye Med Group 11726 Grevillea Ave Hawthorne CA 90250-2223

CHARIF, PIJA MOHAMMAD-HOSSEIN, pediatrician; b. Paris, June 20, 1930; s. Yadollah and Sedigheh (Sorour) C.; m. Fereshteh Fathi, July 27, 1964; children: Shahrzad, Lila. MD, Geneva U., 1958. Diplomate Am. Bd. Pediatrics. Chief dept. pediatrics NIOC, Tehran, Iran, 1964-76, Pars Hosp., Tehran, 1975—; pvt. practice Tehran; cons. physician Iran-Air, 1984—. Contbr. articles to profl. jours. Fellow Am. Acad. Pediatrics; mem. Iranian Soc. Pediatrics.

CHARKINS, HOPE ELLEN, social worker. MSW, San Diego State U., 1986. Med. social worker Children with Spl. Health Needs, White River Junction, Vt., 1994—; exec. dir. Treacher Collins Found., Norwich, Vt., 1988—. Author: Children with Facial Difference: A Parents' Guide, 1996. Office: Treacher Collins Found PO Box 683 Norwich VT 05055

CHARLES, LEROY RICHARD, health facility administrator; b. Flushing, N.Y., Apr. 18, 1953; s. Joseph and Joyce (Munroe) C. BA, Tufts U., 1976; MBA, CUNY, 1979. Health planner Mid.-La. Health Sys. Agy. Baton Rouge, 1978-79; asst. dir. N.Y.C. Health Sys. Agy., 1979-80; sr. project review and data analyst Houston/Galveston Health Sys. Agy., Houston, 1981-82; hosp. planner Lifemark Corp., Houston, 1982-84; mgmt. cons. L.F. Laster & Assocs., Houston, 1984-85; planning/mktg. cons. Hosp. Corp. Am., Nashville, 1985-86; asst. hosp. adminstr George Washington U Hosp., Washington, 1986-90, sr. asst. hosp. adminstr., 1990-93, asst. v.p., 1993—; coord. vol. activities George Washington Med. Ctr., 1992—. Chmn. DC/PRO-Am. Summer Classic, Washington, 1990—. Mem. Nat. Assn. Health Svcs. Execs., Am. Health Planning Assn., Am. Pub. Health Assn. Democrat. Roman Catholic. Office: George Washington Med Ctr 2300 I St Ste 713 Washington DC 20037

CHARLES, NORMAN C., ophthalmologist; b. Schenectady, N.Y., June 4, 1937; s. Milton and Ann Charlotte (Appelbaum) Chodikoff; m. Barbara Jane Breinin, June 29, 1969; 1 child, Lauren Allegra. AB, Yale Coll., 1959; MD, NYU, 1963. Intern NYU-Bellevue Med. Ctr., N.Y.C., 1963-64; resident in ophthalmology NYU Med. Ctr., N.Y.C., 1966-70; Assoc. attending surgeon N.Y. Eye and Ear Infirmary, N.Y.C., 1972-85, attending surgeon, 1985—; instr. ophthamology N.Y. Med. Ctr., N.Y.C., 1970-73, dir. ophthalmic pathology, 1973—, clin. asst. prof., 1973-78, clin. assoc. prof., 1978-83; clin. prof. NYU Med. Ctr., N.Y.C., 1983—; cons. Manhattan VA Med. Ctr., N.Y.C., 1981—; assoc. adj. ophthalmologist Lenox Hill Hosp., N.Y.C., 1995—. Contbr. articles to profl. jours. Mem. nat. program com., bd. dirs. N.Y. Assn. for Blind, 1989—. Lt. USNR, 1964-66. Fellow ACS, Am. Acad. Ophthalmology; mem. Am. Assn. Ophthalmic Pathologists, Ea. Ophthalmic pathology Soc., Theobald Ophthalmic Pathology Soc., N.Y. Ophthal. Soc., N.Y. Soc. Clin. Ophthalmology, Med. Socs. of N.Y. County and N.Y. State, Soc. Alumni of Bellevue Hosp., Phi Beta Kappa, Alpha Omega Alpha. Home: 180 W 58th St New York NY 10019-2131 Office: 620 Park Ave New York NY 10021-6591

CHARLES, STEVEN THOMAS, vitreoretinal surgeon; b. Raleigh, N.C., Dec. 26, 1942; s. Clayton Henry and Modene Johnson Charles; m. Shiree Charles, Aug. 6, 1966 (div. 1989); children: Kelli Charles-Ross, Kerri, Marci; m. Janie Marie Pardue, Feb. 2, 1991. MD, U. Miami, 1969. Diplomate Am. Bd. Ophthalmology, Am. Bd. Med. Examiners. Intern Jackson Meml. Hosp., Miami, 1969-70; ophthalmology resident Bascom Palmer Eye Inst., Miami, 1970-73; clin. assoc. Nat. Ey Inst., NIH, Bethesda, 1973-75; pvt. practice Charles Retina Inst., Memphis, 1975—; clin. prof. ophthalmology U. Tenn. Coll. Medicine, Memphis; adj. assoc. prof. dept. biomed. engring. U. Tenn., Memphis, 1992; adj. faculty mem. in biomed. engring. dept. Memphis State U., 1988-89; chmn. bd., founder InnoVision Med., 1986-91; tech. application bd. Ballistic Missile Def. Orgn., 1987—; scientific adv. bd. Ioptex Rsch., Inc., 1987-91; CEO, founder MicroDexterity Systems, 1991—, Pinnacle Imaging, 1991—; chief tech. officer HC3, 1992—; adv. bd. MicroVision, 1994—, VirtualVision, 1994—. Editl. bd. Retina: The Jour. of Retinal and Vitreous Disease, 1982, Ophthalmic Laser Therapy, 1984, Video Jour. of Ophthalmology, 1984, EyeCare Tech., 1993, Rev. of Ophthalmology, 1994; patentee in field. Mem. Helen Keller Eye Rsch. Found., Biomed. Rsch. Zone, 1987-89; med. adv. bd. Project Orbis, 1989, South Tex. Eye Found., 1984-85. Active USPHS, 1973-75. Fellow ACS; mem. Mid-South Med. Assn., Am. Acad. of Ophthalmology, Am. Soc. of Mech. Engrs., Laser Electro Optic Soc., Soc. of Photo Instrumentation Engrs. Office: Charles Retina Inst Ste 190 6401 Poplar Ave Memphis TN 38119

CHARLTON, JOHN KIPP, pediatrician; b. Omaha, Jan. 26, 1937; s. George Paul and Mildred (Kipp) C. A.B., Amherst Coll., 1958; M.D., Cornell U., 1962; m. Susan S. Young, Aug. 15, 1959; children: Paul, Cynthia, Daphne, Gregory. Intern, Ohio State U. Hosp., Columbus, 1962-63; resident in pediatrics Children's Hosp., Dallas, 1966-68, chief pediatric resident, 1968-69; nephrology fellow U. Tex. Southwestern Med. Sch., Dallas, 1969-70; pvt. practice medicine specializing in pediatrics, Phoenix, 1970; chmn. dept. pediatrics Maricopa Med. Ctr., Phoenix, 1971-78, 84-93, assoc. chmn. dept. pediatrics, 1979-84, med. staff pres., 1991; med. dir., bd. dirs. Crisis Nursery, Inc., 1977—; dir. Phoenix Pediatric Residency, 1983-85, Phoenix Hosps. affiliated pediatric program, 1985-88; clin. assoc. prof. pediatrics U. Ariz. Coll Medicine. Pres. Maricopa County Child Abuse Coun., 1977-81; bd. dirs. Florence Critenton Svcs., 1980-83, Ariz. Children's Found, 1987-91; mem. Gov.'s Coun. on Children, Youth and Families, 1984-86. Officer M.C., USAF, 1963-65. Recipient Hon Kachina award for volunteerism, 1980, Jefferson award for volunteerism, 1980, Horace Steel Child Advocacy award, 1993. Mem. Am. Acad. Pediatrics, Ariz. Pediatric Soc., Maricopa County Pediatric Soc. (past pres.). Author articles, book rev. in field. Home: 6230 E Exeter Blvd Scottsdale AZ 85251-3060 Office: Maricopa Med Ctr 2601 E Roosevelt St Phoenix AZ 85008-4973

CHARLTON, RANDOLPH SEVILLE, psychiatrist, educator; b. Salt Lake City, Nov. 16, 1944; s. Randolph Seville and Patricia Joy (Jensen) C.; m. Louise Bryden Buck, Feb. 14, 1975; children: Genevieve, Blake. BA, Wesleyan U., 1966; MD, Cornell U., 1970. Diplomate Am. Acad. Psychoanalysis. Intern U. Calif., San Francisco, 1970-71; resident psychiatry Stanford U., 1971-74; clin. faculty Standford Med. Sch., Palo Alto, Calif., 1974—; prof. clin. psychiatry Stanford (Calif.) U. Med. Ctr., 1990—; pvt. practice psychiatrist Palo Alto, 1974—. Editor: Treating Sexual Disorders, 1996; contbr. chpt. to book, articles to profl. jours. Bd. trustees Castilleja Sch., Palo Alto, 1992-96; bioethics com. Recovery Inn, Menlo Park, Calif., 1994—. Fellow Am. Acad. Psychoanalysis; mem. C.G. Jung Inst. (tng. analyst 1978—). Democrat. Office: 690 Waverley St Palo Alto CA 94301-2549

CHARNEY, EVAN, pediatrician, educator; b. N.Y.C., Feb. 24, 1933. BA, Cornell U., 1954; MD, Albert Einstein Coll. Medicine, 1960. Intern, resident Strong Meml. Hosp, N.Y.S., 1960-63; from asst. to assoc. prof. pediatrics Strong Meml Hosp., U. Rochester, N.Y., 1963-75; prof. pediatrics, chief pediatrics dept. Sinai Hosp. Balt., Johns Hopkins U., 1975-87; prof., chmn. dept. pediatrics U. Mass. Med. Ctr., Worcester, 1987—; Active Resident Rev. Com. in Pediatrics. 1st lt. Ordinance Corps, U.S. Army, 1954-56. Recipient Armstrong award Ambulatory Pediatric Assn., 1982; Markle scholar Acad. Medicine, 1968-73. Fellow Inst. Medicine NAS; mem. Am. Acad. Pediatrics (assoc. editor Pediatrics in Rev. 1994—). Home: 146 Stiles Rd Boylston MA 01505-1504 Office: U Mass Med Ctr Dept Pediatrics 55 Lake Ave N Worcester MA 01655-0002

CHARNEY, JONATHAN ZACHARY, neurologist; b. Bklyn., Dec. 20, 1942; s. Morris and Nettie Charney; m. Ellen Dryer, June 24, 1973; children: Samuel, Aaron. BA, Franklin and Marshall Coll., 1963; MD, N.Y. Med. Coll., 1969. Diplomate Am. Bd. Psychiatry and Neurology, Nat. Bd. Med. Examiners. Intern Meth. Hosp., Houston, 1969-70; resident in neurology Baylor Coll. Medicine, Houston, 1970-71, Neurol. Inst., Presbyn. Hosp., N.Y.C., 1971-73; pvt. practice N.Y.C., 1975—; asst. attending Mt. Sinai Hosp., N.Y.C., 1975—; lectr. neurology Cath. Med. Coll., Seoul, Korea, 1973-74; instr. neurology U. Hawaii, Honolulu, 1974-75; asst. prof. neurology Mt. Sinai Coll. Medicine, N.Y.C., 1975-77, asst. clin. prof. neurology, 1977—. Contbr. articles to profl. jours. With U.S. Army, 1973-75. Fellow N.Y. Acad. Medicine, Am. Heart Assn. (stroke coun.); mem. AMA, Acad. Neurology, N.Y. State Med. Soc., N.Y. County Med. Soc., Assn. Rsch. in Nervous and Mental Disorders. Office: 1111 Park Ave #1H New York NY 10128-1234

CHARNEY, MICHAEL, science laboratory administrator; b. N.Y.C., Aug. 6, 1911; s. Jacob Louis and Sonja (Barnhard) C.; m. Helen Ricci, Mar. 2, 1941 (div. 1963); children: Elena Diane, Danielle; m. Jean Ellen Ormsbee, Sept. 7, 1966; children: Jacob Mattson, Alexandra Ormsbee, Jared Kirk. BA, U. Tex., 1934; postgrad., Columbia U., 1950-55; PhD, U. Colo., 1969. Diplomate Am. Bd. Forensic Anthropology. Forensic scientist Tex. State Police, Austin, 1938-39; bioassayist Hormone Prodn., N.Y.C., 1941-42; chief bacteriologist Longevity Research, N.Y.C., 1946-47; dir. Bio-chem. Lab., Hackensack, N.J., 1947-65; prof. anthropology Colo. State U., Ft. Collins, 1971-77, prof. emeritus, affiliate prof. biology, dir. forensic sci. lab., 1973—; dep. coroner Larimer County, Colo., 1974—; spl. investigator forensic scis., Larimer County Sheriff Ft. Collins and Colo. State U. Police, 1976—; vis. honors prof. Brookhaven Coll., Farmers Ranch, Tex., 1988; cons. Gen. Hosp., Saddle Brook, N.J., 1947-65, Colo. Bur. Investigation, Denver, 1976—; researcher Shoshone Reservation, Pocatello, Idaho, 1969-71. Author: Forensic Anthropology, 1973, Skulls and Faces, 1995; contbr. chpts. to books, articles to profl. jours. Mem. Victims Compensation Bd., Ft. Collins, 1986—. Served to maj. U.S. Army, 1942-46, ETO. Recipient Letter of Appreciation Gov. Colo., Ft. Collins, 1976; named Adm. Great Navy of Nebr. Gov. of Nebr., 1987. Fellow Am. Acad. Forensic Scis (Cert. Appreciation, 1977); mem. Sigma Xi. Mem. Soc. Friends. Home: 635 Peterson St Fort Collins CO 80524-3135 Office: Forensic Sci Lab Colo State U Fort Collins CO 80523

CHARNEY, PHILIP, dermatologist; b. N.Y.C., Dec. 15, 1939; s. Louis and Rose (Shay) C. BA cum laude, CUNY, Bklyn., 1960; MD, SUNY, Bklyn., 1964. Diplomate Am. Bd. Dermatology; lic. physician, N.Y., D.C., N.J., Calif., Nev., Ariz. Intern Interfaith Med. Ctr., Bklyn., 1964-65; resident dermatology USPHS Hosp., S.I., N.Y., 1965-67; vis. fellow dermatology Columbia-Presbyn. Med. Ctr., N.Y.C., 1967-68; asst. chief medicine dermatology outpatient clinic USPHS, Washington, 1968-70; asst. dir. clin.

rsch. Schering Corp., Bloomfield, N.J., 1970-73, assoc. dir. clin. rsch., 1973; pvt. practice dermatology South Lake Tahoe, Calif., 1973-76, Lake Tahoe, Carson City, Nev., 1976-84, Phoenix, 1984-87, Castro Valley, Calif., 1987-94; career physician The Permanente Med. Group, Vallejo, Calif., 1994—; attending staff dept. dermatology Howard U. Washington, 1968-70; clinic asst. St. Luke's Hosp. Ctr., N.Y.C., 1971-73; attending staff Barton Meml. Hosp., South Lake Tahoe, 1973-84; courtesy staff Carson Tahoe Hosp., Carson City, 1978-84; active staff Chandler (Ari.) Regional Hosp., 1985-87, Eden Hosp. Ctr., Castro Valley, Calif., 1987-94, Kaiser Hosp., Vallejo, 1994—. Contbr. articles to profl. jours. Mem. AMA, Am. Acad. Dermatology, Am. Soc. Dermatologic Surgery, Internat. Soc. Dermatology, Pacific Dermatological Assn., San Francisco Dermatological Soc., Sacramento Valley Dermatological Soc., Alameda/Contra Costa County Med. Assn., Calif. Med. Assn., N.Y. Acad. Sci., ACLU, Sierra Club. Democrat. Jewish. Office: 975 Sereno Dr Vallejo CA 94589

CHARNEY, RICHARD, cardiologist; b. N.Y.C., Oct. 19, 1962; s. Sol and Maxine (Gurvitch) C.; m. Stacy Sperling. BS magna cum laude, CCNY, 1984; MD, Mt. Sinai Sch. Medicine, 1986. Diplomate Am. Bd. Internal Medicine, Nat. Bd. Med. Examiners. Resident in internal medicine Mt. Sinai Hosp., N.Y.C., 1986-89; fellow in cardiology Montefiore Med. Ctr., Bronx, 1989-93, interventional cardiologist, 1993-94; interventional cardiologist Sound Shore Cardiology P.C., New Rochelle, N.Y., 1994—; asst. prof. clin. medicine N.Y. Med. Coll., 1995—; attending cardiologist Westchester County Med. Ctr., New Rochelle Hosp., United Hosp., all 1994—; cons. Med. Advisors, Inc., Phila., 1993—. Contbr. articles to profl. jours. Recipient Mosby Book award for excellence in clin. medicine Mt. Sinai Sch. Medicine, 1986. Fellow Am. Coll. Cardiology; mem. Am. Heart Assn., N.Y. Heart Assn. Office: Sound Shore Cardiology 175 Memorial Hwy New Rochelle NY 10801

CHARNSANGAVEJ, CHUSILP, radiologist; b. Nakhon Sawan, Thailand, Sept. 24, 1948; arrived in U.S., 1973; BSc, Mahidol Univ., Bangkok, Thailand, 1970; MD, Ramathiboid Sch. Medicine, Bangkok, Thailand, 1972. Internship Albert Einstein Medical Ctr., Phila., 1973-74; fellowship UT M.D. Anderson Cancer Ctr., Houston, 1980-81; prof. radiology UT MDA Cancer Ctr., Houston, 1990—, chief abdominal imaging & Computed Tomography, 1990—, deputy chmn. acad. affairs, 1990—, Weiss chair in diagnostic radiology, 1990—; adj. prof. dept. radiology Baylor Coll. Medicine, 1992—; lectr. in field. Contbr. articles to profl. jours. Fellow The Soc. Cardiovascular & Interventional Radiology; mem. Am. Coll. Radiology, Am. Roentgen Ray Soc., Radiological Soc. N.Am., AMA, Radiology Soc. Thailand & Royal Coll. Radiologists (hon.). Home: 8806 Ferris Houston TX 77096 Office: UTMD Anderson Cancer Ctr 1515 Holcombe Blvd Houston TX 77030

CHARROW, JOEL, physician, genetics consultant; b. N.Y.C., May 24, 1951; s. Saul David and Doris Elaine (Yates) C.; m. Martha K. McClintock, Oct. 23, 1982; children: Benjamin Whitmore, Julia Rachel. BS in Chemistry and Psychology, Antioch Coll., 1972; MD, Mt. Sinai Sch. Medicine, 1976. Diplomate Nat. Bd. Med. Examiners, Am. Bd. Pediatrics; diplomate in clin. genetics and biochem. genetics. Am. Bd. Med. Genetics. Pediatric intern Children's Meml. Hosp./Northwestern U. Med. Sch., Chgo., 1976-77, resident in pediatrics, 1977-79, fellow in clin. and biochem. genetics, 1979-81; attending physician Children's Meml. Hosp., Chgo., 1981; from asst. prof. to assoc. prof. pediatrics Northwestern U. Med. Ctr., Chgo., 1981-94; dir. Genetics Lab., head sect. clin. genetics Children's Meml. Hosp., Chgo., 1991—. Contbr. chpts. to books, more than 40 articles to profl. jours. Regional coord. Internat. Collaborative Gaucher Group, 1994—; mem. health profl. adv. com. March of Dimes, Chgo., 1986—; mem. sci. adv. com. Nat. Tay-Sachs and Allied Diseases Assn., 1984—; mem. State of Ill. Genetic and Metabolic Diseases Adv. Com., 1989—; mem. Genetics Task Force of Ill., 1982—, v.p., 1990-91, pres., 1991-93. Recipient Bela Schick Pediatric Soc. award Mt. Sinai Sch. Medicine, 1976. Fellow Am. Coll. Med. Genetics (founding), Am. Acad. Pediatrics; mem. Midwest Soc. for Pediatric Rsch., Soc. for Inherited Metabolic Disorders, Bone Dysplasia Soc., Internat. Neurofibromatosis Assn., Alpha Omega Alpha. Office: Children's Meml Hosp Sect Clin Genetics 2300 Children's Plz Chicago IL 60614

CHARTERS, KAREN ANN ELLIOTT, critical care nurse, health facility administrator; b. Chelsea, Mass., Apr. 3, 1946; d. Albert Charles and Hazelle Marie (Kraus) Elliott; m. Byron James Charters, Feb. 4, 1972. Diploma, Grace New Haven Sch. Nursing, New Haven, Conn., 1967; student, So. Conn. State Coll., 1968, U. New Haven, 1974, St. Leo Coll., 1988—. Cert. CCRN. Asst. head nurse Yale New Haven (Conn.) Hosp., 1972-76; staff nurse critical care unit Hosp. Corp. Am., 1982—; relief clin. coord. Columbia New Port Richey (Fla.) Hosp., 1987—. Mem. AACN (bd. dirs. Gulf Coast chpt. 1990-91, treas. 1991-93), Am. Heart Assn. (past bd. dirs.). Home: 13318 Hillwood Cir Hudson FL 34667-1421 Office: Col New Port Richey Hosp 5637 Marine Pkwy New Port Richey FL 34653

CHASE, HARRY EUGENE, IV, family therapist, minister; b. Balt., July 5, 1919; s. Harry Eugene and Lena Gray (Fowler) C.; m. Mary Ellen Connor, July 13, 1940; children: Mary Ellen Chase Link, Alice Chase-Hassan. AB, San Diego State U., 1948; MDiv, Princeton Theol. Sem., 1951; EdS, Seton Hall U., 1983. Lic. therapist, N.J.; ordained minister Presbyn. Ch. Resident chaplain Rensselaer Poly. Inst., Troy, N.Y., 1951-55; univ. pastor Calif. State U., Long Beach, 1955-61; assoc. pastor 1st Presbyn. Ch., Englewood, N.J., 1961-68; sr. pastor Presbyn. Ch., Tenafly, N.J., 1968-88; pvt. practice family therapy Haworth, N.J., 1988—; bd. dirs. Family Counseling Svcs., Hackensack, N.J., 1960-80. Author: Eden in Winter, 1978, Gold I Have Given Away, 1983, also edn. materials. Advisor Bergen County Med. Soc., Hackensack, 1960-80, Mayor's Adv. Com., Tenafly, 1970-80. Warrant officer USN, 1936-46. Recipient awards Freedoms Found., 1965-75. Fellow Am. Orthopsychiatric Assn.; mem. ACA, Am. Assn. Marriage and Family Therapists (clin.), Assn. for Advancement of Family Therapy, Am. Assn. Family Counselors and Mediators (clin.), Am. Bd. Med. Psychotherapists, Nat. Acad. Counselors and Family Therapists, Nat. Coun. on Family Rels., Internat. Assn. Marriage and Family Counselors, N.J. Assn. for Marriage and Family Therapy, N.J. Profl. Counselors Assn., Navy League, Knickerbocker Country Club, Masons. Office: 160 Terrace St Haworth NJ 07641-1842

CHASE, JEFFREY LAKE, clinical psychologist, educator; b. Summit, N.J., Nov. 8, 1954; s. Henry Hughes and Joanna (Barineau) C.; m. Anna Maria Csaky, June 11, 1983. BA summa cum laude, St. Louis U., 1978; PhD, U. S.C., 1988. Rsch. asst. Baylor Coll., Houston, 1982; clin. psychology intern Va. Treatment Ctr. For Children, Richmond, 1983-84; fellow neuropsycholgy Med. Coll. Va., Richmond, 1984-86; psychologist Children's Hosp., Richmond, 1986-89; assoc. prof. Radford (Va.) U., 1989—; pvt. practice Blacksburg, Va., 1990—; supr. Va. Bd. of Medicine. Contbr. articles to profl. jours. Grantee Nat. Inst. Mental Health, 1979. Mem. Am. Psychol. Assn., Va. Head Injury Found. Office: Radford U Dept of Psychology Radford VA 24142

CHASE, JOHN DAVID, university dean, physician; b. Detroit, Sept. 24, 1920; s. Clyde Harrison and Bonnie Lucille (Fogas) C.; m. Edwarda I. Walther (Layne), June 18, 1985; 1 child from previous marriage, Robert Winslow. A.B., Wabash (Ind.) Coll., 1942; M.D., Western Res. U., 1945. Diplomate: Am. Bd. Internal Medicine. Intern Detroit Receiving Hosp., 1945-46; resident in internal medicine Wayne State U. Hosp., 1948-52; teaching fellow Nat. Heart Inst., 1952; with VA, 1952-78; dep. asso. chief med. dir. academic affairs VA, Washington, 1970-73; chief med. service VA Hosp., Tacoma, 1973-74; chief med. dir. VA Central Office, Washington, 1974-78; assoc. dean clin. affairs U. Wash. Sch. Med., Seattle, 1978-81, dean Sch. Medicine, 1981-82, dean emeritus, 1983—; mem. nat. adv. council Heart and Lung Inst., 1968-70, Regional Med. Programs, 1970-73, Nat. Library Medicine, 1972-73; mem. Nat. Adv. Council VA Edn., 1973, Nat. Adv. Council Health Services Planning and Resources, 1976, Fed. Coordinating Council Sci., Engring. and Tech., 1976-78, Nat. Adv. Council Health Planning and Devel., 1976—; bd. govs. Armed Forces Inst. Pathology, 1976-78. Mem. Inst. Medicine, 1982—. Served with M.C. USNR, 1946-48. Recipient Distinguished Service award Wayne State U. Med. Sch., 1976. Fellow ACP, Am. Coll. Chest Physicians; mem. Assn. Mil. Surgeons U.S., AMA (ho. dels.), Am. Hosp. Assn. (trustee 1976-78). Home: 1356 E Eight Steet Port Angeles WA 98362-6610

CHASE, LINDA ANN, social worker, psychotherapist; b. Bklyn., Sept. 25, 1943; d. Albert A. and Frances (Rosenstein) Lessner; m. Alan Chase, Sept. 14, 1968 (div. June 1976); children: Nicole Shana, Isaac Lessner. MS in Criminal Justice, SUNY, Buffalo, 1965; BA in Sociology, U. New Haven, 1976; MSW, U. Conn., 1983. Cert. ind. social worker. Caseworker Suffolk County Child Welfare, Bayshore, N.Y., 1966-67; social worker Montefiore Hosp., Bronx, N.Y., 1967-68, Dept. Child Welfare, New Haven, Conn., 1968-70, Dept. of Children and Youth Svcs., New Haven, Conn., 1976-77; supr. parent-aides Coord. Coun. for Children in Crisis, New Haven, Conn., 1978-84; dir. bereavement svcs. Conn. Hospice, Branford, 1984-92, social worker, 1985-88; pvt. practice Orange and Branford, 1985—. Mem. NASW, Conn. Soc. Clin. Social Workers. Home: 506 Alps Rd Branford CT 06405-4726 Office: 2 Summit Pl Ste 2C Branford CT 06405-4100

CHASE, MERRILL WALLACE, immunologist, educator; b. Providence, Sept. 17, 1905; s. John Whitman and Bertha H. (Wallace) C.; m. Edith Steele Bowen, Sept. 5, 1931 (dec. 1961); children: Nancy Steele (Mrs. William W. Cowles), John Wallace, Susan Elizabeth (dec. 1985); m. Cynthia Hambury Pierce, July 8, 1961. AB, Brown U., 1927, ScM, 1929, PhD, 1931, ScD honoris causa, 1977; ScD honoris causa, Rockefeller U., 1988; MD honoris causa, U. Münster, Fed. Republic Germany, 1974. Instr. biology Brown U., 1931-32; staff mem. Rockefeller Inst. Med. Research, 1932-79; prof. immunology and microbiology, head lab. immunology and hypersensitivity Rockefeller U., 1956-79; med. adv. council Profl. Ednl. and Research Task Force, Asthma and Allergy Found. Am., 1955-83. Editor: (with C.A. Williams) Methods in Immunology and Immunochemistry, Vol. 1, 1967, Vol. 11, 1968, Vol. III, 1970, vols. IV, 1977, and V, 1976. Fellow Am. Acad. Allergy (hon., Disting. Svc. award 1969), Am. Coll. Allergists (hon.), Am. Acad. Arts and Scis.; mem. AAAS, Am. Assn. Immunologists (pres. 1956-57), Am. Soc. Microbiology (program chmn. 1959-61), Harvey Soc., N.Y. Acad. Scis., N.Y. Allergy Soc. (hon.), Nat. Acad. Sci. Republican. Universalist-Unitarian. Office: Rockefeller U 1230 York Ave New York NY 10021-6399

CHASE, PAUL JOEL, radiologist; b. Bronx, N.Y., July 29, 1939; s. Albert and Ethel (Weinman) C.; m. Linda Mae Goodman, June 23, 1963; children: Jodi, Jeffrey, Mark. DO, Kirksville (Mo.) Coll. Osteo., 1960-64. Diplomate Am. Osteo. Bd. Radiology, Am. Osteo. Bd. Nuc. Medicine, Am. Bd. Nuc. Medicine. Intern Brentwood Hosp., Cleve., 1964-65; resident in radiology Cherry Hill (N.J.) Med. Ctr., 1965-69; Mead Johnson fellow in radiol. therapy Hahnemann U., Phila., 1972-74; attending radiologist Del. Valley Hosp., Bristol, Pa., 1969-70; vice chmn. dept. radiology Kennedy Meml. Hosp., Stratford, N.J., 1970-93; chmn. dept. radiology South Jersey Hosp. Sys., Bridgeton, 1993—; dir. radiology residency U. Medicine and Dentistry/Kennedy Meml. Hosp., 1978-93. Fellow Am. Osteo. Coll. Radiology (pres. 1994-95); mem. Am. Coll. Radiology, Am. Coll. Nuc. Medicine, Am. Osteo. Assn., Am. Osteo. Coll. Nuc. Medicine (pres. 1991-92), Am. Osteo. Edn. Found., N.J. Soc. Radiology, Phila. Roentgen Ray Soc., Rotary. Home: 1029 Dell Dr Cherry Hill NJ 08003

CHASE, ROBERT ARTHUR, surgeon, educator; b. Keene, N.H., Jan. 6, 1923; s. Albert Henry and Georgia Beulah (Bump) C.; m. Ann Crosby Parker, Feb. 3, 1946; children: Deborah Lee, Nancy Jo, Robert N. B.S. cum laude, U. N.H., 1945, DSC (hon.), 1993; M.D., Yale, 1947. Diplomate: Am. Bd. Surgery, Am. Bd. Plastic Surgery. Intern New Haven Hosp., 1947-48, asst. resident, 1949-50, sr. resident surgery, 1952-53, chief resident surgeon, 1953-54; mem. faculty Yale Sch. Medicine, 1948-54, 59-62, asst. prof. surgery, 1959-62; mem. faculty U. Pitts., 1957-59, resident plastic surgeon, also teaching fellow, 1957-59; attending surgeon VA Hosp., W. Haven, Conn., 1959-62, Grace New Haven Community Hosp., 1959-63; prof., chmn. dept. surgery Stanford Sch. Medicine, 1963-74, Emile Holman prof. surgery, 1972—; prof. surgery U. Pa., 1974-77; attending surgeon Pa. Hosp., Hosp. U. Pa., Grad. Hosp., Phila., 1974-77; pres., dir. Nat. Bd. Med. Examiners, Phila., 1974-77; prof. anatomy Stanford (Calif.) U., 1977—; Cons. plastic surgery Christian Med. Coll. and Hosp., Vellore, S. India, 1962; cons. to surgeon gen. USAF, 1970—; Benjamin K. Rank prof. Australasian Coll. Surgeons, 1974. Author: Atlas of Hand Surgery; Editor: Videosurgery, 1974—; editorial bd.: Med. Alert Communication; Contbr. articles to profl. jours. Served to maj. M.C. AUS, 1949-57. Recipient Francis Gilman Blake award Yale Sch. Medicine, 1962, Henry J. Kaiser award Stanford U. Sch. Medicine, 1978, 79, 84, 86, 90, 93, Calif. Golden Apple award 1991, Albion William Hewlett award, 1992. Fellow ACS, Australasian Coll. Surgeons (hon.); mem. NAS, Am. Assn. Plastic Surgeons (hon.), Calif. Acad. Medicine (pres.), San Francisco Surg. Soc., Am. Surg. Assn., Santa Clara County Med. Soc., Conn. Med. Soc., Am. Soc. Surgery Hand (pres.), Am. Assn. Clin. Anatomists (hon., pres.), Am. Soc. Cleft Palate Rehab., Am. Assn. Surgery Trauma, Plastic Surgery Rsch. Coun., AMA, Soc. Clin. Surgery, Western Surg. Assn., Pacific Coast Surg. Soc., Am. Assn. Plastic Surgery (hon.), James IV Assn. Surgeons, Am. Cancer Soc. (clin. fellowship com.), Found. Am. Soc. Plastic and Reconstructive Surgery (dir.), Soc. Univ. Surgeons, Inst. Medicine (exec. com. 1976, coun. 1986—), Am. Soc. Most Venerable Order Hosp., St. John of Jerusalem, Halsted Soc., South African Soc. Surgery Hand (hon.), South African Soc. Plastic and Reconstructive Surgery (hon.), Am. Soc. Clin. Anatomists (hon., pres.)Phi Beta Kappa, Sigma Xi. Home: 1215 Welch Rd Stanford CA 94305-1045 Office: Stanford U Div Anatomy 1215 Welch Rd Palo Alto CA 94305

CHASE, SANDRA LEE, pharmacist, consultant; b. Oak Park, Ill., July 31, 1959; d. William Warren and Charlene Lois (Johnson) C.; m. Christopher Paul Bloch, Sept. 8, 1984; children: Kyle Thaddeus, Matthew William. Student, Mich. State U., 1977-80; BS in Pharmacy, U. Mich., 1983, PharmD, 1984. Lic. pharmacist, Del., Mich., Pa. Rsch. asst. U. Mich., Ann Arbor, 1980-81; pharmacy intern Three Rivers (Mich.) Hosp., 1981, Cmty. Pharmacy, Ann Arbor, 1980-83; pharmacy intern, grad. intern St. Francis Hosp., Wilmington, Del., 1982-83; resident in hosp. pharmacy Thomas Jefferson U. Hosp., Phila., 1984-85, clin. pharmacist in cardiopulmonary medicine, 1985-89; sr. med. info. coord. ICI Pharms. Group, Wilmington, Del., 1989-92; clin. pharmacist Thomas Jefferson U. Hosp., Phila., 1989-93, clin. pharmacist drug use policy Med. Info. Svc., 1993—; clin. instr. in pharmacy practice Phila. Coll. Pharmacy and Sci., Phila., 1985-87, clin. asst. prof., 1987-88, clin. assoc. prof., 1988—; instr. critical care cardiopulmonary medicine in nursing Episcopal Hosp., Phila., 1986-88, Thomas Jefferson U. Hosp., Phila., 1985-91, Our Lady of Lourdes Med. Ctr., Camden, N.J., 1988-91; coord., prof. pharmacology and drug therapeutic for advanced nursing practice course Sch. Nursing, Ctr. for Profl. Devel., U. Pa., Phila., 1994—; presenter in field. Mem. editl. bd. RN, Med. Econs.; referee AHFS Drug Info., Am. Druggist, Am. Jour. Hosp. Pharmacy, Nursing 96 Drug Handbook, Nursing 97 Drug Handbook, Pharmacotherapy, RN Mag., Annals of Pharmacotherapy, U. Hosp. Consortium Monographs; contbg. editor RN Mag., mem. editl. bd.; contbr. numerous articles to profl. jours. Mem. adv. bd. Nursing Mothers Network; bd. dirs. Coll. Pharmacy Alumni Soc., 1991—. Mem. Am. Coll. Clin. Pharmacy, Mid-Atlantic Coll. Clin. Pharmacy, Am. Soc. Health Sys. Pharmacists, Pa. Soc. Health Sys. Pharmacists, Del. Valley Soc. Health Sys. Pharmacists, Am. Pharm. Assn., Del. Pharm. Soc. (conv. com. 1990-94, ACPE com. 1990-94), Rho Chi Pharm. Soc. Republican. Lutheran. Office: Thomas Jefferson U Hosp 111 S 11th St Philadelphia PA 19107

CHASE, SUSAN KRIENKE, nursing educator; b. Wausau, Wis., May 1, 1948; m. Randall Chase, Jr., Jan. 23, 1976; children: Peter, Andrew. BS, Columbia Presbyn., 1972; BA in Chemistry, Vanderbilt U., 1970; MA, NYU, 1975; EdD, Harvard U., 1990; postgrad., U. Wis., 1996. With NYU Hosp., 1971-75, Manatee Community Coll., Bradenton, Fla., 1975-77, Miami (Fla.) Dade Community Coll., 1979, Broward Community Coll., Ft. Lauderdale, Fla., 1981-84, Fla. Atlantic U., Boca Raton, 1984; asst. prof. Grad. Sch. of Nursing U. Mass., Worcester, 1985-90; staff devel. specialist Mass. Gen. Hosp., Boston, 1990-92, clin. nurse specialist, 1992; asst. prof. adult health Boston (Mass.) Coll., 1992—. Mem. ANA, AACN (chpt. pres.), Eastern Nursing Rsch. Soc., North Am. Nursing Diagnosis Assn. (diagnosis rev. com.), Soc. for Vascular Nurses, Sigma Theta Tau. Home: 26 Longfellow Rd Sudbury MA 01776-1254

CHASIS, HERBERT, physician, educator; b. N.Y.C., Nov. 9, 1905; s. Joel Morris and Annie (Kutner) C.; m. Barbara Ann Parker, Jan. 19, 1943; children: Joel Anne, Sarah. B.A., Syracuse U., (N.Y.), 1926; M.D., NYU, 1930, D.Sc. in Medicine, 1937. Am. Bd. Internal Medicine. Intern Bellevue Hosp., N.Y.C., 1930-31, resident, 1931-32; instr. dept. medicine NYU, 1934-39, asst. prof., 1939-49, assoc. prof., 1949-64, prof., 1964—; cons. Phelps Meml. Hosp., North Tarrytown, N.Y., 1962—, VA Hosp., N.Y.C., 1951—. Author: Three Worlds of Medicine, 1995, (with William Goldring) Hypertension and Hypertensive Disease, 1944, Homer William Smith, His Scientific and Literary Achievements, 1965. Recipient Responsible Investigator award USPHS Nat. Heart Inst., 1957-72; recipient Sci. Achievement award NYU Sch. Medicine Alumni Assn., 1965. Mem. N.Y. Heart Assn. (pres. 1963-65), Am. Heart Assn. (chmn. sect. on circulation 1959-61), Am. Physiol Soc., Am. Soc. Clin. Investigation, N.Y. Acad. Medicine (chmn. sect. medicine 1959-60), Sigma Xi, Alpha Omega Alpha. Home: 465 W 23rd St New York NY 10011-2104 Office: NYU Med Center 550 First Ave New York NY 10016-6481

CHASKELSON, MARSHA INA, neuropsychologist; b. Brookline, Mass., Jan. 6, 1950; d. Hyman and Doris (Sacks) C.; m. Allen Noah Elgart, July 8, 1973; children: Jonah Elgart, Benjamin Elgart, Sarah Elgart. BA in Psychology, U. Mass., 1971; MEd in Spl. Edn., Boston Coll., 1972, PhD Counseling Psychology, 1985. Lic. psychologist; cert. sch. psychologist; cert. provider. Resource room specialist for emotionally disturbed Acton-Boxborough Regional Jr. High Sch., Acton, Mass., 1972-76; faculty mem., on-site facilitator Boston Coll., Chestnut Hill, Mass., 1976-77; in-patient coord., out-patient staff psychologist Kennedy Meml. Hosp., Brighton, Mass., 1977-80; contracted sch. psychologist Beverly (Mass.) Pub. Schs., 1981; contracted staff psychologist Human Resource Inst., Franklin, Mass., 1980-82; mental retardation coord. Human Resource Inst., 1982-83; clin. specialist Alternatives, Unltd., Whitinsville, Mass., 1981-87; dir. Lexington Psychol. & Ednl. Resources, Lexington, Mass., 1987—; psychology intern psychology dept. Kennedy Meml. Hosp., Brighton, 1976-77, post-doctoral psychologist Children's Hosp. Med. Ctr., Boston, 1984-85; post-doctoral neuropsychologist New Eng. Rehab. Hosp., Woburn, Mass., 1985-86; co-chairperson Lexington A.D.D. Parent Group, 1987-88. Mem. Am. Psychol. Assn., Internat. Neuropsychol. Soc., Mass. Neuropsychol. Soc., Coun. for Exceptional Children, Mass. Psychol. Assn., Mass. Assn. for Children with Learning Disabilities. Democrat. Jewish. Office: Lexington Psychol & Ednl Resources 76 Bedford St Ste 26 Lexington MA 02173-4441

CHASTAIN, LORI LYNN, medical and surgical nurse; b. Cordell, Okla., Nov. 11, 1961; d. Richard Noel Drummond and Bettie DeWitt Horan; m. Layne Elzie Chastain, Mar. 11, 1979 (div. Aug. 1992); children: Jessica Lynn, Jonathan Layne. ASN, North Ark. C.C., Harrison/Mountain Home. In data processing First Nat. Bank & Trust, Mountain Home, 1984-89; with Pine Lane Health Care, Mountain Home, 1991-93; various positions Baxter County Regional Hosp., Mountain Home, 1992-96; infection control/wound and skin supr. Good Samaritan Village, Mountain Home, 1994-95; with Twin Lakes Med. SPecialists, 1994-96; adminstr. HomeBound Med. No. Ark., 1996—; aerobic instr. Seventh Heaven, Mountain Home, 1987-91. Home: PO Box 27 Mountain Home AR 72653

CHATELIER, PAUL RICHARD, aviation psychologist, training company officer; b. St. Petersburg, Fla., Oct. 1, 1938; s. Paul Andrew and Mary (Knecht) C.; m. Mary Lu Moss, Sept. 26, 1964; children: Michael Andrew, Suzanne Margaret. BS in Biology, Chemistry, Psychology, U. Fla., 1960; MA in Psychology, U. Miss., 1962; postgrad., U. N.Mex., 1967-69. Commd. ensign USN, 1962, advanced through grades to capt., 1986; sr. v.p. strategic planning Perceptronics, Inc., Washington, 1986-93; with Office Sci. and Tech. Policy Exec. Office of President U.S., Washington, 1993—; U.S. rep. on human factors NATO, Brussels, 1978-86; mem. task force tng. and wargaming Def. Sci. Bd., 1986-88; U.S. rep. on tng. The Tech. Cooperation Panel, Washington, 1987-86; mem. indsl. adv. com. U. Cen. Fla. Inst. for Simulation and Tng.; edn. and tng. cons. Office Sci. and Tech. White Ho., 1993—; workshop dir. internat. tng. and human factors. Author: (chpt.) Psychology of Reality, 1985; editor: Manprint & System Integ, 1988, International Human Factors, 1991, Advanced Technology for Training Design, NATO, 1993, Opening the Classroom Doors...Distance Learning, 1995. Career advisor Fairfax County Pub. Sch., 1982-88. Mem. Nat. Human Factors Soc. (exec. coun. 1982-85), Va. Human Factors Soc. (pres. 1982-83), Nat. Security Indsl. Assn. (chmn. manpower pers. tng. 1986-89). Home: 8021 W Point Dr Springfield VA 22153-3023 Office: Exec Office of Pres US Office Sci and Tech Policy 1901 N Beauregard Ste 510 Alexandria VA 22311

CHATER, SHIRLEY SEARS, former vice chancellor, federal commissioner; b. Shamokin, Pa., July 30, 1932; d. Raymond and Edna Sears; m. Norman Chater, Dec. 5, 1959 (dec. Dec. 1993); children: Cris, Geoffrey. BS, U. Pa., 1956; MS, U. Calif., San Francisco, 1960; PhD, U. Calif., Berkeley, 1964. Asst., assoc., prof. dept. social and behavioral scis. Sch. Nursing U. Calif.-San Francisco, Sch. Edn.-Berkeley, 1964-86; asst. vice chancellor acad. affairs U. Calif., San Francisco, 1974-77, vice chancellor acad. affairs, 1977-82; council assoc. Am. Council Edn., Washington, 1982-84; sr. assoc. Presdl. Search Consultation Svc. Assn. Governing Bds., Washington, 1984-86; pres. Tex. Woman's U., Denton, 1986-93; chair Gov's health policy task force State of Texas, 1992; commr. Social Security Adminstrn., Washington, 1993—. Bd. dirs. Carnegie Found. for Advancement of Teaching, United Educators Ins. Risk Retention Group, Denton United Way, 1986-93; mem. commn. on women Am. Coun. on Edn. Mem. Inst. Medicine, NAS, Dallas Forum, Charter 100 of Dallas, Internat. Alliance, Nat. Acad. Pub. Adminstrn., Nat. Acad. Social Ins. Home: 5175 Macomb St NW Washington DC 20016-2611 Office: Social Security Adminstrn Altmeyer Bldg 6401 Security Blvd Baltimore MD 21235-0001

CHATOOR-KOCH, IRENE, child psychiatrist; b. Kassel, Hessen, Fed. Republic of Germany, Nov. 10, 1937; came to U.S., 1969; d.Hugo and Marie (Wetterau) Koch; m. Ramcoomair Chatoor, Mar. 18, 1968. MD, Ruperto Carola U., Heidelberg, Fed. Republic of Germany, 1965. Diplomate Am. Bd. Pediatrics, Am. Bd. Psychiatry and Neurology in Psychiatry, Am. Bd. Psychiatry and Neurology in Child Psychiatry. Intern City Hosps. Kassel and Amberg, Fed. Republic of Germany, 1965-67; resident pediatrics City Hosp. Amberg, Fed. Republic of Germany, 1967-68; intern Providence Hosp., Washington, 1969-70; resident pediatrics Children's Hosp., Washington, 1970-72; resident adult psychiatry George Washington U. Med. Ctr., Washington, 1972-74; fellow child psychiatry Children's Hosp., Washington, 1974-76; part-time pvt. practice College Park, Md., 1976-86; part-time faculty Children's Hosp. Nat. Med. Ctr., Washington, 1978-86, full time faculty, 1986-94; assoc. prof. psychiatry and child health and devel. George Washington U. Med. Sch., Washington, 1985-94, prof. psychiatry & behavioral scis., 1994—. Fellow Am. Acad. Child and Adolescent Psychiatry; mem. Am. Orthopsychiat. Assn., Am. Psychiat. Assn., World Assn. Infant Mental Health. Office: Children's Hosp Nat Med Ctr 3800 Reservoir Rd NW Bldg 2phc Washington DC 20007-2196

CHATTERJEE, DEBABRATA, surgeon; b. Chandernagore, India, Dec. 1, 1937; s. Debendranath and Nandarani (Mukherjee) C.; m. Adele Patricia Powell, Sept. 17, 1971; children: Crispin Dara, Justin Sanjay. MB BS, Calcutta (India) U., 1960; ChM, Liverpool (Eng.) U., 1973. House surgeon medicine, surgery, gynae, ortho, urology Calcutta and Kent, Eng., 1960-64; univ. rsch. fellow, 1965-67; surg. registrar London, Liverpool & Leeds, Eng., 1965-70; surg. registrar, tutor, asst. gen. surgeon Univ. Coll. Cork, Northern Ireland, 1970-74; lectr., cons. gen. surgeon Univ. Hosp. W.I., Jamaica, 1974-77; cons. surgeon N.W. Thames Regional Authority London & Plymouth Gen. & Royal Infirmary, Edingubrh, Scotland, 1977-81; cons. gen. surgeon Dauburgh Hosp., South Uist, Scotland, 1982—; tching, rsch. and svc. adminstr. London, Leeds, Liverpool, Cork, Jamaica and Edinburgh, 1965—, univ. undergrad. and postgrad. tchr., 1965-81; rschr. in field; examiner U. W.I., 1974-77. Contbr. articles to profl. jours. Rsch. fellow/grantee Medica Rsch. Com., Liverpool U., 1966, 67, rsch. and publs. grantee U. W.I., Jamaica, 1974, 75, 76, grantee Med. Rsch. Coun. Eire, 1971, Med. Edn. & Rsch. Coun., Belfast, 1972, 73. Fellow Royal Coll. Surgeons, Royal Soc. Medicine, Internat. Coll. Surgeons, Assn. Surgeons Gt. Britain; Brit. Assn. Surg. Oncologists (founding mem.), Assn. Endoscopic Surgeons (founding mem.), Soc. Laparoscopic Surgeons U.S.A., Brit. Med. Assn., Hosp. Cons. Specialists Assn. Home: 26 Aldwickbury Crescent, Harpendent AL5 5RR, England Office: Doctors House, Luchboisdale, South Uist H58 5TH, Scotland

CHATTERTON, ROBERT TREAT, JR., reproductive endocrinology educator; b. Catskill, N.Y., Aug. 9, 1935; s. Robert Treat and Irene (Spoor) C.;

m. Patricia A. Holland, June 24, 1956 (div. 1965); children: Ruth Ellen, William Matthew, James Daniel; m. Astrida J. Vanags, June 4, 1966 (div. 1977); 1 child, Derek Scott; m. Carol J. Lewis, May 24, 1985. BS, Cornell U., 1958, PhD, 1963; MS, U. Conn., 1959. Postdoctoral fellow Med. Sch. Harvard U., 1963-65; rsch. assoc. div. oncology Inst. Steroid Rsch. Montefiore Hosp. and Med. Ctr., N.Y.C., 1965-70; asst. prof. Coll. Medicine U. Ill., 1970-72, assoc. prof. Coll. Medicine, 1972-79; prof. Med. Sch. Northwestern U., Chgo., 1979—; mem. sci. adv. com. AID; chairperson Instl. Review Bd. Northwestern U., 1982-83, Intellectual Properties Com., Northwestern U., 1987-95. Contbr. numerous articles to sci. jours.; patents: method of totally suppressing ovarian follicular devel. and method of ovulation detection. Grantee NIH, 1972-90, 95—, NSF, 1975, 95—, AID, 1971-86, Army Office Rsch., 1987-94. Mem. AAAS, N.Y. Acad. Scis., Am. Chem. Soc., Endocrine Soc., Soc. Gynecologic Investigation, Soc. Study Reprodn., Chgo. Assn. Reproductive Endocrinologists (pres. 1987-88), Sigma Xi, Phi Kappa Phi. Presbyterian (deacon). Home: 6001 N Knox Ave Chicago IL 60646-5821 Office: Northwestern U Prentice 1516 333 E Superio Chicago IL 60611

CHAU, BENJAMIN J., ophthalmologist; b. Hong Kong, Aug. 18, 1940; came to U.S., 1942; s. Sham Tai and Kitty (Chan) C.; m. Anita Leong, June 25, 1975; children: Melissa, Kimberly. BME, CCNY, 1963; MD, SUNY, Buffalo, 1969. Diplomate Am. Bd. Ophthalmology. Resident in ophthalmology White Med. Hosp., L.A., 1970-73; pvt. practice Torrance, Calif., 1973—; clin. instr. ophthalmology U. So. Calif./White Meml. Hosp.-Loma Linda, L.A., 1973-78. Fellow ACS, Am. Acad. Ophthalmology. Office: 3655 Lomita Blvd Ste 301 Torrance CA 90505-3934

CHAUDHRY, ABDUL GHAFOOR, surgeon; b. Punjab, Pakistan, Dec. 12, 1947; came to U.S., 1974; s. Sardar Ali and Sardar Begum Chaudhry; m. Fauzia Jabeen, Jan. 16, 1982; children: Sulemon, Saba. FSC, Govt. Inter-Coll., Jhelum, Pakistan, 1965; MD, King Edward Med. Coll., Lahore, Pakistan, 1970. Diplomate Am. Bd. Surgery, Am. Bd. Thoracic Surgery. Rotating intern Perth Amboy (N.J.) Gen. Hosp., 1974-75; resident gen. surgery The Meth. Hosp., Bklyn., 1975-79; resident cardiothoracic surgery Boston U. Med. Ctr., 1979-81, The Children's Hosp. Med. Ctr., Boston, 1981; attending physician Raleigh (N.C.) Cardiovascular and Thoracic Inst., Inc., 1982—. Fellow ACS; mem. AMA, Mass. Med. Soc., N.C. Med. Soc., Wake County Med. Soc. Republican. Home: 4009 John S Raboteau Wynd Raleigh NC 27612-5330 Office: Raleigh Cardiovasc Thoracic Inst Inc 2800 Blue Ridge Rd Raleigh NC 27607-6478

CHAVEZ, CESAR T., ophthalmologist, surgeon; b. Mexicali, Mexico, Aug. 3, 1952; s. Felipe and Norbertha Chavez; m. Teresa Cardenas, June 1977; children: Elena, Esteban. BA, UCLA, 1973; MD, U. Wash., 1977, MPH, 1977. Diplomate Nat. Board of Med. Examiners, Am. Board Ophthalmology. Intern Kaiser Permanente Hosp., Fontana, Calif., 1977-78; resident Jules Stein Eye Inst.-UCLA Med. Ctr., 1983-85; div. chief Comprehensive Ophthalmology, UCLA, 1985-88; med. dir. Jules Stein Eye Inst. OPD, UCLA, 1985-88, U. Ophthalmology Assocs., Los Angeles, 1986-88; asst. prof. ophthalmology UCLA, 1985-88; med. dir. Camino Coastline Eye Surgeons, Encinitas, Calif., 1988—; assoc. examiner Am. Bd. Ophthalmology. Contbr. articles to profl. jours. Bd. dirs. Calif. State U., San Marcos Found. Lt. USPHS, 1978-81. Fellow Am. Acad. Ophthalmology; mem. Med. Group Mgmt. Assn., San Diego County Med. Soc., Calif. Assn. of Ophthalmologists, Calif. Med. Assn. Roman Catholic. Office: Camino Coastline Eye Surgeons 477 N El Camino Real Ste C200 Encinitas CA 92024-1332

CHAVEZ, MARY ANN, osteopathic family physician; b. York, Pa., Dec. 6, 1942; d. Henry David Gross and Mary Ellen (Ness) Rhoads; m. Richard L. Ziegler, Dec. 24, 1965 (div. Jan. 1983); children: Richard L. Ziegler Jr., Mara L. Tammaro, Brian L. Ziegler. BS, Alvernia Coll., 1983; DO, Coll. Osteopathic Medicine, Phila., 1992. Legal sec. Louis Sager, Esquire, Pottstown, Pa., 1962-67; homemaker, tailor in pvt. practice Pottstown, 1967-85; intern Riverside Hosp., Wilmington, Del., 1992-93, resident in family practice, 1993-95; osteo. family physician Spring Grove (Pa.) Family Medicine, 1995—. Pell grantee, Beog grantee Alvernia Coll., 1979-83. Mem. AMA, Am. Osteo. Assn., Am. Coll. Osteo. Family Physicians, Am. Acad. Osteopathy, Pa. Osteo. Med. Assn., York County Osteo. Med. Assn, Nat. Osteo. Women's Physicians Assn. United Methodist. Office: Mary Ann Chavez DO PO Box 184 Wrightsville PA 17368-0184

CHAVIN, WALTER, biological science educator and researcher; b. N.Y.C., Dec. 6, 1925; s. Isidor and Fanny (Kesch) C. BS, CCNY, 1946; MS, NYU, 1949, PhD, 1954. Research asst. N.Y. Aquarium, N.Y.C., 1947-48; instr. dept. zoology U. Ariz., Tucson, 1949-51; research specialist dept. fishes Am. Mus. Natural History, N.Y.C., 1951-53; prof. biol. scis. Wayne State U., Detroit, 1953-90, prof. emeritus, 1990—, prof. radiology, med. sch., 1975-80, dir. Radiation Biology Inst., 1959-71; research assoc. Argonne (Ill.) Nat. Lab., 1955-58. Contbr. 225 articles to profl. jours. NSF Sr. Postdoctoral fellow, 1960-61; Rsch. grantee NSF, AEC, NIH; named Pres. scholar Acad. Scholars Wayne State U., 1980. Fellow AAAS (sec. 1978-85), N.Y. Acad. Scis.; mem. Am. Physiol. Soc., Am. Soc. Zoologists (treas., sec.), Soc. Exptl. Biology and Medicine (com. 1986-90), Endocrine Soc., Am. Orchid Soc., South Fla. Orchid Soc., Boca Raton Orchid Soc., PanAm Orchid Soc. Independent. Home: 16484 Bridlewood Cir Delray Beach FL 33445-6678

CHAWNER, THOMAS J., administrator, consultant; b. Bklyn., Sept. 24, 1949; s. John K.; m. Linda Farina, Aug. 6, 1972; 1 child, Stephen T. BBA, Bernard M. Baruch Coll., 1971, M in Community Planning, 1974. Asst. project mgr. Office of Multi-Svc. Systems Planning, N.Y.C, 1973-74; asst. exec. dir. Suffolk Community Council, Smithtown, N.Y., 1974-86; program developer Breakthrough Concepts at Gracie Square Hosp., N.Y.C., 1982-86; adminstr. Steps Psychiatric Svcs., N.Y.C., 1987-88; dir. Residential Treatment Ctr., Staten Island, N.Y., 1988-90, Adolescent Diagnostic Ctr., Queens, N.Y., 1990-91. Exec. dir. L.I. Adolescent and Family Svcs., Inc., 1991.

CHEAH, KEONG-CHYE, psychiatrist; b. Georgetown, Penang, West Malaysia, Mar. 15, 1939; came to U.S., 1959; s. Thean Hoe and Hun Kin (Keong) C.; m. Sandra Massey, June 10, 1968; children: Chylynn, Maylynn. BA in Psychology, U. Ark., 1962; MD, U. Ark., Little Rock, 1967, MS in Microbiology, 1968. Diplomate Am. Bd. Psychiatry and Neurology (examiner 1982, 85); cert. Ark. State Sci. Bd., Ark. State Med. Bd. Intern U. Ark. Med. Ctr., 1967-68; resident VA Med. Ctr. and U. Ark. Med. Ctr., Little Rock, 1968-72; chief addiction sect. Little Rock (Ark.) VA Med. Ctr., 1972-73, staff psychiatrist, 1975-80; chief psychiatry Am. Lake VA Med. Ctr., Tacoma, Wash., 1981-86; chief consultation, liason Am. Lake VA Med. Ctr., Tacoma, 1986-94; asst. prof. medicine, psychiatry U. Ark., Little Rock, 1975-81; asst. prof. psychiatry and behavioral scis. U. Wash., Seattle, 1981-86, clin. assoc. prof., 1987—; mem. dist. br. com. The CHAMPUS, 1977-91; site visitor AMA Continuing Med. Edn., 1979-83; book reviewer Jour. Am. Geriatrics Soc., 1984-85; mem. task force alcohol abuse VA Med. Dist. 27, 1984, survey mem. Sytematic External Rev. Process, 1985; mem. mental health plan adv. com. State of Ark., 1976-81, chmn. 1979-81, chmn. steering com., 1979; mem. Vietnamese Resettlement Program, 1979; many coms. Am. Lake VA Med. Ctr. including chmn. mental health coun. 1981-84, utilization rev. com., 1981-86. Contbr. articles and abstracts to profl. jours.; presenter to confs. and meetings of profl. socs. Mem. Parents Adv. Com., Lakes H.S., Wash., 1987-91; mem. Mayor's Budget and Fin. Foresight Com., 1992—, chmn. 1990-92; sch. cons. Child Study Ctr. U. Ark., 1972-74; bd. dirs. Crisis Ctr. Ark., 1974-79, chmn. pub. rels. com., 1975-79, mem. pers. com. 1974, vice chmn. bd. 1977; pres. Chinese Assn. Ctrl. Ark., 1977; mem. gifted edn. adv. coun. Clover Park Sch. Dist. 400, Wash., 1983-85, Parent Tchr. Student Orgn. Recipient U.S. Govt. scholarship 1959, cert. merit State of Ark., 1973, Leadership award, Mental Health Svcs. Divsn., State of Ark., 1980. Fellow Am. Psychiat. Assn. (sec. treas. Asian Am. caucus 1985-87, pres. 1987-94); mem. Assn. Mil. Surgeons U.S., Wash. State Psychiat. Assn. (mem. peer rev. com. 1982-92, chmn. pub. psychiatry com. 1985-93, exec. coun. 1985-93), N. Pacific Soc. Neurology and Psychiatry Assn. (sec.-treas. 1986—, pres. 1993), S. Puget Sound Psychiat. Assn., Assn. Chinese-Am. Psychiatrists, Ark. Caduceus Club, Alpha Epsilon Delta, Psi Chi, Phi Beta Kappa. Office: VA Med Ctr Am Lake Tacoma WA 98493

CHEATHAM, MARY ANN, auditory physiologist, educator, researcher; b. Rockford, Ill., June 1, 1944; d. George Marvin and Edna (Givens) C. BA, U. Kans., 1966; MA, Northwestern U., 1967, PhD, 1983. Rsch. assoc. Northwestern U., Evanston, Ill., 1967-73, instr., 1973-77, rsch. assoc., 1978-81, 84-87, sr. rsch. assoc., 1987-89, rsch. assoc. prof., 1990—. Editl. bd. Audiology and Neuro-Otology, 1995—; contbr. articles to profl. jours. Grantee Deafness Rsch. Found., 1985-87, 90-92; Hugh Knowles Ctr. fellow, 1989—. Fellow Acoustical Soc. Am. (psychol. and physiol. acoutics tech com. 1995—); mem. AAAS, Assn. for Rsch. in Otolaryngology (long-range planning com. 1996—), Sigma Xi. Office: Northwestern U 2-240 Frances Searle Bldg 2299 N Campus Dr Evanston IL 60208-3550

CHEATHAM, VALERIE MEADOR, clinical dietitian; b. Huntington, W.Va., June 17, 1957; d. Phillip Jarrell and Anna Lee (Law) Meador; m. Edward Lee McCallum, May 13, 1978 (div. 1990); children: Shaun Jeffrey, Briana Marie; m. Miles W. Cheatham III, Oct. 26, 1990. BS in Biology, James Madison U., 1979; MS in Nutrition, Clemson U., 1986. Registered dietitian, 1987. Cytotechnologist Roanoke (Va.) Meml. Hosp., 1979-80; greenhouse mgr. Greenwood Nurseries, Princeton, W.Va., 1980-81; vet. technician Lewisburg (W.Va.) Animal Hosp., 1981-82; rsch. asst. Clemson (S.C.) U., 1984-86; clin. dietician Anderson (S.C.) Meml. Hosp., 1986-87, asst. food svc. dir., 1987-91, nutritionist III dept. health and environ. control, 1994—; nutritionist Dept. Health and Environ. Control Anderson County (S.C.) Health Dept., 1994—; dir. maternal and child health programs Anderson County Appalachia I Health Dist., 1996—. Mem. Am. Dietetic Assn., Am. Soc. Hosp. Food Svc. Adminstrs. (pres. Palmetto chpt. 1991—), Piedmont Dist. Dietetics Assn. (sec.), S.C. Dietetics Assn., S.C. Pub. Health Assn. Home: 111 Yorkshire Dr Anderson SC 29625-2521 Office: Dept Health Environ Control 200 McGee Rd Anderson SC 29625-2104

CHECHUCK, BETTY JEAN, critical care nurse; b. Harriman, Tenn., Feb. 28, 1955; d. Charles E. and Elizabeth Jane (Crump) R. Student, State Vo-Tech, Harriman, 1982, Roane State Community Coll., Harriman. Staff nurse ICU, CCU, cardiac rehab. Chamberlain Meml. Hosp., Rockwood, Tenn.; charge nurse Spring City (Tenn.) Health Care; staff nurse intensive care-coronary care unit Loudon (Tenn.) County Meml. Hosp.; charge nurse Marshall Voss Health Care, Harriman, Tenn.; staff nurse Roane County Ambulance Svc., staff nurse with pediat. nursing specialists, Nashville, 1992, Elk Valley Health Svcs., Fayetteville, Tenn., 1994. Home: PO Box 483 Harriman TN 37748-0483

CHECK, JEROME HARVEY, reproductive endocrinologist; b. Phila., May 11, 1946; s. Harry and Freida (Scheinfeld) C.; m. Deena Check, June 6, 1971; children: Matthew L., Darren J. BA in Biology, U. Pa., 1967; MD, Hahnemann Med. Coll., 1971. Diplomate Am. Bd. Internal Medicine, sub-bd. Endocrinology and Metabolism. Straight med. intern Lankenau Hosp., Phila., 1971-72, resident in internal medicine, 1972-74; fellow in gynecologic endocrinology Jefferson Med. Coll. and Hosp., Phila., 1974-75; practice med. and gynecologic endocrinology, infertility Phila., 1975—; mem. staff dept. ob-gyn. Meth. Hosp., Jeanes Hosp., 1977—; prof. clin. ob-gyn. U. Medicine and Dentistry, N.J., 1989—; dir. Cooper Ctr. for IVF; assoc. prof. ob-gyn. Thomas Jefferson U., 1975-89. mem. editorial staffs various jours.; contbr. 300 articles to profl. jours. Capt. U.S. Army Res., 1971-77. Recipient Charles Ebberhardt award for cancer rsch., 25 Yr. Profl. Achievement award Hahnemann Med. Sch.; U. Pa. scholar; Hahnemann Med. Coll. scholar. Fellow ACP, ACE, Am. Coll. Ob-gyn. (assoc.), Am. Coll. Clin. Endocrinology; mem. AAAS, Am. Soc. Reproductive Medicine, Endocrine Soc., Assn. Profs. Gynecology and Obstetrics, Am. Soc. for Bone and Mineral Rsch., Am. Soc. Andrology, N.Y. Acad. Scis., Internat. Soc. Gynecol. Endocrinology, Am. Assn. Gynecologic Laparoscopists, European Soc. Human Reprodn. and Embryology, Internat. Soc. for Immunology of Reprodn., Montgomery County Med. Soc., Phi Beta Kappa, Alpha Omega Alpha. Home: 1205 Gordon Rd Jenkintown PA 19046-3908 Office: Repro and Med Endocrin Asso 7447 Old York Rd Elkins Park PA 19027-3006

CHECKO, CAROLYN MARIE, nurse; b. Scranton, Pa., Feb. 23, 1968; d. Robert Checko and Marie Alimenti. Diploma, Cmty. Med. Ctr., 1989; student, Pa. State U., Worthington, 1989, Marywood Coll., 1989; BSN, Thomas Jefferson U., 1996. RN, Pa.; clin. RN II. Nurses aide Taylor Nursing Home, Pa., Quality Care, Wilkes Barre, Pa., VNA Home Health Svcs., Scranton, Pa.; staff nurse Thomas Jefferson U. Hosp., Phila., 1996; traveling nurse Med. Express Co., 1996—; staff nurse Columbia JFK Meml. Hosp., Atlantis, Fla., 1996—; part-time nurse Protocall; co-chair neurosensory care program profl. practice com. Thomas Jefferson Univ. Hosp., unit chair profl. practice com., active Design Team 2000, 1996. Recipient Clin. Excellence award, Excellence in Intensive Care award, Nat. Nurse's Day award, 1990, Profl. Practice award Nat. Nurse's Week, 1991. Home: 5241 Cedar Lake Rd #4-27 Boynton Beach FL 33437

CHECTON, JOHN BURT, cardiologist; b. Jersey City, Feb. 6, 1952; s. John Bert and Margaret Mary (Donahue) C.; m. Maria Geiger; children: Meghan Farrell, Stephanie Margaret, Tara Maria, John Geiger. BS in Biology, Rensselaer Poly. Inst., 1974; MD, UMDNJ-N.J. Med. Sch., 1978. Diplomate Am. Bd. Internal Medicine. Intern Monmouth Med. Ctr., Long Branch, N.J., 1978-79, resident, 1979-80, chief resident, 1980-81; pres., ptnr., prin. Monmouth Cardiovascular Cons., Long Branch, N.J., 1984—; co-dir. cardiology Monmouth Med. Ctr., Long Branch, 1987—. Cardiovascular disease fellow U. Louisville Sch. of Medicine, 1981-83, chief fellow, 1982-83. Fellow Am. Coll. Cardiology, Am. Heart Assn., Am. Coll. Chest Physicians; mem. ACP, AMA, Am. Soc. Nuclear Medicine, Monmouth Beach Club, Skytop Club, Navesink Country Club, Am. Soc. of Enchocardiography, Monmouth County Med. Soc., N.J. Med. Soc. Republican. Roman Catholic. Home: 26 Ward Ave Rumson NJ 07760-1914 Office: Monmouth Cardiovascular Cons PA 215 Brighton Ave Long Branch NJ 07740-5219

CHEE, PERCIVAL HON YIN, ophthalmologist; b. Honolulu, Aug. 29, 1936; s. Young Sing and Den Kyau (Ching) C.; m. Carolyn Tong, Jan. 27, 1966; children: Lara Wai Lung, Shera Wai Sum. BA, U. Hawaii, 1958; MD, U. Rochester, 1962. Intern Travis AFB Hosp., Fairfield, Calif., 1962-63; resident Bascom Palmer Eye Inst., Miami, Fla., 1965-68, Jackson Meml. Hosp., Miami, 1965-68; partner Straub Clinic, Inc., Honolulu, 1968-71; practice medicine specializing in ophthalmology, Honolulu, 1972—; mem. staffs Queen's Med. Center, St. Francis Hosp., Kapiolani Children's Med. Center, Honolulu; clin. assoc. prof. surgery U. Hawaii Sch. Medicine, 1971—; cons. Tripler Army Med. Center. Mem. adv. bd. Services to Blind; bd. dirs. Lions Eye Bank and Makana Found. (organ bank), Multiple Sclerosis Soc. Served to capt. USAF, 1962-65. Fellow Am. Acad. Ophthalmology, ACS; mem. AMA, Pan Am. Med. Assn., Pan Pacific Surg. Assn., Am. Assn. Ophthalmology, Soc. Eye Surgeons, Hawaii Ophthal. Soc. Pacific Coast Ophthal. Soc., Am. Assn. for Study Headache, Pan Am. Ophthal. Found. Contbr. articles to profl. pubs. Home: 3755 Poka Pl Honolulu HI 96816-4409 Office: Kukui Pla 50 S Beretania St Ste C116 Honolulu HI 96813-2222

CHEEK, SHERYL RAULSTON, occupational health nurse; b. Carlisle, Pa., May 17, 1955; d. John Allen and Mary Ann (Riley) Raulston; m. William Kane Cheek, May 21, 1983; children: Megan, Jonathan, Rebecca. AAS in Nursing, Coll. of the Mainland, 1981; BS, Tex. Woman's U., 1990. RN, Tex.; cert. occupl. nurse specialist, occupl. hearing conservationist. Staff nurse II NBN U. Tex. Med. Branch, Galveston, 1981-83, staff nurse II recovery room, 1983-85, staff nurse II neonatal ICU, 1988-91; home health nurse Mainland Home Health Svcs., League City, Tex., 1986; clinic nurse pulmonary-allergy Diagnostic Clin. of Houston, 1986-87; occupl. health nurse Amoco Corp., Tex. City, Tex., 1991-95; coord. first aid Amoco Torch Classic, Tex. City, 1994. Inventor emergency Benzene exposure kit. Perry scholar Tex. Woman's U., 1990. Mem. Am. Assn. Occupl. Health Nurses, Tex. State Assn. Occupl. Health Nurses, Houston Tex. Assn. Occupl. Health Nurses, Houston Fedn. Profl. Women. Methodist. Home: 12331 Hammond Ln Santa Fe TX 77510 Office: Amoco Petroleum Products PO Box 401 Texas City TX 77592

CHEEMA, MOHAN KRISHAN SINGH, internist; b. Lassoi, Punjab, India, Jan. 13, 1936; came to U.S. 1964; s. Anokh Singh Cheema and Jagir Kaur Tawana; m. Sheila Fairlie, Sept. 9, 1966; children: Ariana, Ranji. FSc, Mahandra Coll., India, 1955; MD, Med. Coll. Patiala, India, 1960. Diplomate Am. Bd. Internal Medicine and Pulmonary Disease and Geriatric Medicine. Intern Fordham Hosp., Bronx, N.Y., 1964-65, resident in internal medicine, 1965-66; resident in internal medicine L.I. (N.Y.) Coll. Hosp., 1966-67, VA Hosp., Bklyn., 1967-69; pvt. practice New Rochelle, N.Y.; Chief pulmonary sect. New Rochelle Hosp. Med. Ctr. Fellow Am. Coll. Chest Physicians, Am. Coll. Cardiology (assoc.); mem. AMA. Office: 158 Lockwood Ave New Rochelle NY 10801-4902

CHEITLIN, MELVIN DONALD, physician, educator; b. Wilmington, Del., Mar. 25, 1929; s. James Cheitlin and Mollie Budman; m. Hella Hochschild, Aug. 4, 1952; children: Roger, Kenneth, Julie. AB, Temple U., 1950, MD, 1954. Intern, resident internal medicine Walter Reed Army Med. Ctr., Washington, 1954-59, cardiology fellow, 1959-60, chief cardiology, 1971-74; chief cardiology Madigan Army Med. Ctr., Tacoma, Wash., 1960-64, Tripler Army Med. Ctr., Honolulu, 1964-68, Letterman Army Med. Ctr., San Francisco, 1968-71; assoc. chief cardiology San Francisco Gen. Hosp., 1974-91, chief cardiology, 1991—; prof. medicine U. Calif., San Francisco, 1974—. Author: Clinical Cardiology, 1994; assoc. editor: Cardiology, 1988, rev. edit., 1993. Mem. ACP, Am. Coll. Cardiology. Democrat. Jewish. Home: 224 Castenada Ave San Francisco CA 94116 Office: San Francisco Gen Hosp 1001 Potrero Avee San Francisco CA 94110

CHEN, BARBARA MARIE, anesthesiologist; b. Youngstown, Ohio, May 17, 1960; d. Ching Chi and Kim Lian Chen. BS summa cum laude, Youngstown State U., 1981; MD, St. Louis U., 1985. Diplomate Am. Soc. Anesthesiologists. Resident in surgery Bklyn.-Caledonian Hosp., Bklyn., 1985-88; resident in anesthesia Georgetown U. Hosp., Washington, 1989-92; staff anesthesiologist NIH, Bethesda, Md., 1992-93; staff anesthesiologist, researcher Georgetown U. Hosp., Washington, 1992-95; staff anesthesiologist Providence Hosp., Anchorage, Alaska, 1996—. Vol. Spl. Olympics, Arlington, Va., 1992, Cmty. for a Creative Nonviolence, Washington, 1989-95, Holiday Project, 1989-95, Martha's Table, 1994-95. Recipient Robert Dripps Meml. award Janssen Pharm., 1991. Mem. AMA, Am. Soc. Anesthesiologists, Am. Regional Soc. Anesthesiologists, Am. Heart Assn., Am. Med. Women's Assn., Soc. Cardiovascular Anesthesiologists. Office: Providence Hosp 3300 Providence Dr Ste 107 Anchorage AK 99508-4619

CHEN, CHONG-MAW, molecular biology educator; b. Tauyuan, Taiwan, Republic of China; came to U.S., 1962; s. Jen-Ho and Jao-chu Chen; m. Gong-rong (Jo Ann) Chen, Jan. 29, 1967; children: Sharon, Alice, Howard. BS, Nat. Taiwan Normal U., Taipei, China, 1959; PhD, Kans. U., 1967. Postdoctoral fellow in biochemistry McMaster U., Ont., 1967-69; postdoctoral fellow Roche Inst. Molecular Biology, Nutley, N.J., 1969-71; from asst. to assoc. prof. U. Wis., Parkside, 1971-73; prof. U. Wis., Kenosha, 1977—; disting. prof. U. Wis. System, 1988—; vis. prof. U. Wis., Madison, 1982. Contbr. over 90 articles to profl. jours. Pres. Racine/Kenosha Chinese Assn., 1981—. Office: U Wis at Parkside Wood Rd Kenosha WI 53141

CHEN, EDWARD CHIH-HUNG, physician; b. Taiwan, Aug. 21, 1954; came to U.S. 1980; MD, Taipei (Taiwan) Med. Coll. 1980; MPH, Harvard U., 1981. Diplomate Am. Bd. Internal Medicine, Am. Bd. Gastroenterology. Intern North Gen. Hosp., N.Y.C., 1982-83; resident in internal medicine St. Luke's Hosp., Chesterfield, Mo., 1983-85; fellow in gastroenterology William Beaumont Hosp., Royal Oak, Mich., 1985-87. Mem. AMA, Am. Coll. Gastroenterology, Am. Gastroenterological Assn. Office: 701 Ostrum St Ste 301 Bethlehem PA 18015-1152

CHEN, JAMES PAI-FUN, biology educator, researcher; b. Fengyuan, Taichung, Taiwan, May 1, 1929; came to U.S., 1952; s. Chuan and Su-wuo (Lin) C.; m. Metis Hsiu-chun Lin, Dec. 19, 1964; children: Mark Hsin-tzu, Eunice Hsin-yi, Jeremy Hsin-tao. BS, Houghton (N.Y.) Coll., 1955; MS, St. Lawrence U., 1957; PhD, Pa. State U., 1961. From instr. to assoc. prof. Houghton Coll., 1960-64; rsch. assoc. Coll. of Medicine U. Vt., Burlington, 1964-65; rsch. assoc. Sch. of Medicine SUNY, Buffalo, 1965-68; asst. prof. U. Tex. Med. Br., Galveston, 1968-75; sr. rsch. assoc. NASA/Johnson Space Ctr., Houston, 1975-76; rsch. assoc. prof. U. Tenn. Meml. Rsch. Ctr., Knoxville, 1976-78; assoc. prof. Coll. of Medicine U. Tenn., Knoxville, 1978-84, prof. Grad. Sch. of Medicine, 1984—; mem. rsch. rev. com. Tex. affiliate Am. Heart Assn., Austin, 1974-76; co-investigator Spacelab I project, Johnson Space Ctr., Houston, 1976-83; vis. prof. Trnovo Hosp. Internal Medicine, Ljubljana, Yugoslavia, 1985. Contbr. more than 40 articles to profl. jours. including Thrombosis and Haemostasis. Grantee Robert Welch Found., 1970-74, Ortho Rsch. Found., 1971-75, NIH, 1975-82, Am. Heart Assn. Tex. affiliate, 1969-72, 74-75, Am. Heart Assn. Tenn. affiliate, 1984-85, 89-90, U.S. Army Med. Rsch., 1988-91. Fellow Internat. Soc. Hematology; mem. Am. Assn. Immunologists, Am. Soc. Biochemistry and Molecular Biology, Internat. Soc. Thrombosis and Haemostasis, Internat. Fibrinogen Rsch. Soc., Internat. Soc. Fibrinolysis Thrombolysis, Am. Bd. Bioanalysis (clin. lab. dir.). Office: U Tenn Med Ctr 1924 Alcoa Hwy Knoxville TN 37920-6999

CHEN, JANET, ophthalmologist; b. San Francisco, June 10, 1964. AB, Harvard U., 1984; MD, Columbia U., 1989. Diplomate Am. Bd. Ophthalmology. Med. intern U. Calif., San Francisco, 1989-90, ophthalmology resident, 1990-93, glaucoma fellow, 1993-94, asst. prof., co-dir. glaucoma dept. ophthalmology, 1994—; dir. glaucoma San Francisco VA Hosp. Heed Ophthalmic Found. fellow, 1993-94. Fellow Am. Acad. Ophthalmology; mem. Assn. for Rsch. in Vision and Ophthalmology. Office: Univ of California Dept Ophthalmology 10 Kirkham St San Francisco CA 94143

CHEN, JOHN CALVIN, child and adolescent psychiatrist; b. Augusta, Ga., Apr. 30, 1949; s. Calvin Henry Chen and Lois (Lee) Liu. BA, Pacific Union Coll., 1971; MD, Loma Linda U., 1974; PhD in Philosophy, Claremont Grad. Sch., 1984; JD, UCLA, 1987. Bar: Calif. 1987, U.S. Dist. Ct. (ctrl. dist.) Calif. 1988; diplomate Am. Bd. Psychiatry and Neurology, Child and Adolescent Psychiatry. Gen. resident in psychiatry Loma Linda U. Med. Ctr., 1975-77; fellow in child and family psychiatry Cedars-Sinai Med. Ctr., L.A., 1977-78; psychiat. cons. San Bernardino (Calif.) County Mental Health Dept., 1979-83; pvt. practice psychiatry Claremont, Calif., 1980-84; fellow in child and adolescent psychiatry U. So. Calif., L.A., 1983-84; law clk. to Hon. William P. Gray U.S. Dist. Ct., L.A., 1987-88; mental health psychiatrist L.A. County Mental Health Dept., L.A., 1988-94, Alameda County Health Care Svcs. Agy., Fremont, Calif., 1994—; adj. instr. philosophy Fullerton (Calif.) Coll., 1989-90. Recipient Cert. Recognition Pub. Svc. L.A. County Mental Health Dept., 1993; univ. fellow Claremont Grad. Sch., 1980-81. Mem. ABA, Am. Philos. Assn., Chinese for Affirmative Action, Soc. for Exploration of Psychotherapy Integration, Chinese Hist. Soc. Am., Calif. Hist. Soc. Office: 39270 Paseo Padre Pky # 346 Fremont CA 94538-1616

CHEN, JOUNG-HUEI, pediatrician; b. Chang-Hwa, Taiwan, Oct. 15, 1948; s. Chia-Cheng Chen and Chen-Se Wang; m. Lilly Wu, Oct. 11, 1950; children: Maison, Robert, Jenny. MD, Taipei Med. Coll., 1973. Cert. Am. Bd. Pediats., Am. Bd. Pediats. sub-bd.; cert. neonatal-perinatal medicine. Intern Mackay Meml. Hosp., Taipei, 1972-73, pediat. resident, 1974-76; pediat. asst. resident The Jewish Hosp. and Med. Ctr. Bklyn., 1976-77; pediat. chief resident Jewish Meml. Hosp., N.Y.C., 1977-78; instr., fellow pediats. (neonatology) Rochester (N.Y.) U., Strong Meml. Hosp., 1978-80; attending physician pediats. Chang Gung Meml. Hosp., Taipei, 1980-81; pvt. practice specializing in pediats. Taipei, 1981—; asst. prof. Taipei Med. Coll., 1980-86; cons. Chang Gung Meml. Hosp., Taipei, 1994—, Mackay Meml. Hosp., Taipei, 1993—. Mil. physician Taiwanese Air Force, 1973-74. Home and Office: 103 Min-Sheng E Rd Sect 2, Taipei Taiwan

CHEN, KUEN HAI, physician; b. Tachia, Taiwan, May 23, 1937; came to U.S., 1966, naturalized 1976; s. Jon Bei and Yeh (Liang) C.; M.D., Nat. Taiwan U. Med. Coll., 1964; m. Fu Mei Lai, Jan. 1, 1966; children—Richard, Humphrey, Christopher. Intern, Ill. Central Hosp., Chgo., 1966-67; resident in gen. surgery Sisters Hosp., Buffalo, 1967-69, C & O Hosp., Huntington, W.Va., 1970-71; fellow spinal cord injury service VA Hosp., East Orange, N.J., 1971-72, chief, 1972-76; mem. staff First Ave. Med. Center, N.Y.C.; mem. physicians' coun. Heritage Found., 1994—; dir. K.F.C. Corp. Founding prodr. GOP-TV, 1994—. Active Taiwan Union Presbyn. Ch. in N.Y., chmn. exec. com., 1983, pres. Parents' Assn., 1980-84; mem. Presdl. Adv. Commn., 1992, Presdl. Commn. Am., 1992; del. Presdl. Trust, 1992; adv. mem. Rep. Nat. Commn. Am. Agenda, 1992—; del. N.J. Rep. Presdl. Task Force, 1994—; mem., chmn. adv. bd. Rep. Nat. Com.,

1994—; founding mem. Rep. Campaign Coun., 1994—, nat. campaign advisor, 1995—. Served with Taiwan Air Force, 1965. Recipient physician recognition award AMA, 1969, 72, 75, 78, 81, 84, 87, 90, 93; Disting. Service and Leadership award Nat. Taiwan U.; Patriotic award medal Pres. of U.S. Diplomate Am. Bd. Family Practice. Fellow Am. Acad. Family Physicians, Am. Geriatric Soc.; mem. N.Y. Acad. Sci., Am. Coll. Emergency Physicians, AMA, N.Y. County Med. Soc. (com. health care agy.), Internat. Soc. Paraplegia, Heritage Found., Taita Jing-Fu Med. Found. (hon. dir.), Nat. Taiwan U. Med. Coll. Alumni Assn. (exec. dir. 1979-81, pres. 1981-83, permanent bd. dirs. 1984, chmn. edn. com. 1987—, chmn. fund campaign com. 1988—, N.Y. chpt. bd. dirs. and bd. trustees 1985-88, chmn. by-law com. 1994—), Am. Spinal Injury Assn., W.Va. Med. Inst., N. Am. Taiwanese Med. Assn. (bd. dirs. greater N.Y. chpt. 1985—, pres. 1987-89, chmn. edn. com. 1989—), Nat. Taiwan U. Alumni Assn. (bd. dirs. 1981—, chmn. edn. com. 1984-94, chmn. by-law com. 1994—, treas. 1991—). Presbyterian. Author: American Spoken English.

CHEN, LINDA LI-YUEH HUANG, nutritional biochemistry educator, program director; b. Tokyo, Mar. 22, 1937; d. Chun-mu and Chiung-tein (Lin) Huang; m. Boris Yuen-jien, Dec. 23, 1961; children: Audrey Huey-wen, Lisa Min-yi. BS in Pharmacy, Nat. Taiwan U., Taipei, 1959; PhD In Biochemistry, U. Louisville, 1964. Rsch. assoc. U. Louisville, 1964-66; asst. prof. U. Ky., Lexington, 1967-72, assoc. prof., 1972-79, prof., 1979—, assoc. dean for rsch. and grad. edn., 1979-81, chmn., 1983-87, dir. multidisciplinary PhD program in nutritional scis., 1989—. Author: Nutritional Biochemistry Laboratory Methods, Experiments and Exercises, 1972; editor: Nutritional Aspects of Aging, Vol. I, Vol. II, 1986; contbr. articles to profl. jours. Mem. Am. Soc. for Clin. Nutrition, Am. Inst. Nutrition, Am. Aging Assn. Home: 531 Southbend Dr Lexington KY 40503-1231 Office: U Ky 204 Funkhouser Bldg Lexington KY 40506

CHEN, PETER WEI-TEH, mental health services administrator; b. Fuchow, Fukien, Republic of China, July 20, 1942; came to U.S., 1966; s. Mao-Chuang and Sheu-Lin (Wang) C.; m. Lai-Wah Mui, Nov. 8, 1969; children: Ophelia Mei-Chuang, Audrey Mei-Hui. BA, Nat. Chung Hsing U., Taipei, Taiwan, Republic of China, 1964; MSW, Calif. State U., Fresno, 1968; D of Social Work, U. So. Calif., 1976. Case worker Cath. Welfare Bur., L.A., 1968-69; psychiat. social worker L.A. County Mental Health Svcs., 1969-78, mental health svcs. coordinator, 1978; sr. rsch. analyst Jud. and Legis. Bur. L.A. County Dept. Mental Health, 1978-79; Forensic In-Patient Program dir. L.A. County Dept. Mental Health, 1979-86, chief Jail Mental Health Svcs., 1986-89, asst. dep. dir. Adult Svc. Bur., 1989, dir. specialized commnunity programs, 1989—; pres. Orient Social and Health Soc., Los Angeles, 1973-75; bd. dirs. Am. Correctional Health Assn., 1986-87. Author: Chinese-Americans View Their Mental Health, 1976. Bd. dirs. San Marino (Calif.) Cmty. Chest, 1986-87; trustee San Marino Schs. Found., 1987-90; advisor San Marino United Way, 1989-92, AIDS Commn. L.A. County, 1993; bd. dirs. Chinese Am. Profl. Soc., 1984. 2d lt. Chinese Marine Corps, Taiwan, Republic of China, 1964-65. Recipient several cmty. svc. awards, 3 spl. awards Nat. Assn. County Orgn. Mem. Nat. Assn. Social Workers (bd. dirs. Calif. chpt. 1979-80), Nat. Correctional Health Assn., Forensic Mental Health Assn. Calif., L.A. World Affairs Coun. Clubs: Chinese of San Marino (pres. 1987-88), San Marino City. Home: 2161 E California Blvd San Marino CA 91108-1348 Office: LA County Dept Mental Health 505 S Virgil Ave Los Angeles CA 90020-1403

CHEN, PHIL YUAN-CHUNG, osteopath; b. Keelung, China, Nov. 6, 1961; came to U.S., 1986; s. Chi-Hua and Ching-Fang C. BS, U. Calif., Irvine, 1992; degree in osteo. medicine, Coll. Osteo. Medicine Pacific, 1995. Med. team mem. Taipei (Taiwan) Med. Coll., 1986; lab. asst. Inst. Zoology/Acad. Sinica, Taipei, 1985-86; tchg. asst. Coll. Osteo. Medicine Pacific, Pomona, Calif., 1993-94; intern Bi-county Comty. Hosp., Warren, Mich., 1995-96, family medicine resident, 1996—. Contbr. articles to profl. jours. Asian-Am. scholar Coll. Osteo. Medicine Pacific, 1994. Mem. Am. Osteo. Assn., Am. Acad. Family Physicians, Am. Coll. Osteo. Family Physicians, Calif. Med. assn., Mich. Assn. Osteo. Physicians & Surgeons, Wayne County Osteo. Assn. Home: Apt 101 30789 Ouinkert St Bldg 4 Roseville MI 48066 Office: Bi-County Cmty Hosp 13355 E Ten Mile Rd Warren MI 48066

CHEN, SHIUM ANDREW, psychologist, educator; b. Tsunjiang, Jaingsu, China, Sept. 17, 1931; came to U.S., 1954; s. Ten and Quison (Hu) C.; m. Veronica Ling Koo, Aug. 28, 1964; children: Thomas, Herald, Andrea. BEd, Nat. Taiwan Normal U., Taipei, 1953; MEd, U. Oreg., 1956; MA, Columbia U., 1962; PhD, U. Pitts., 1970. Lic. psychologist, Pa. Rsch. asst. Bur. Applied Social Rsch. Columbia U., N.Y.C., 1956-61; instr. dept. edn. Hofstra U., New Hemstead, N.Y., 1961-62; asst. prof. psychology Emporia (Kans.) State U., 1963-66; prof. dept. counseling and ednl. psychology Slippery Rock (Pa.) U., 1966—, chair dept., 1980-87; ednl. specialist Tainjiang U., 1990; vis. prof. Oxford (Eng.) U., summer, 1986, Nat. Taiwan Norman U., 1973-74. Mem. steering com. Enlish Plus Info. Clearinghouse, 1988—; chair Asian Am. adv. coun. Pa. Heritage Affairs Commn., Harrisburg, 1988-95; participant First Asian Pacific Am. Leadership Health Summit, San Francisco, 1995. Recipient Heritage Achievement award Chinese Assn. of Fairfield County, Conn., 1986. Fellow APA (mem. commn. on violence and youth 1990-93); mem. Asian Am. Psychologists Assn. (bd. dirs. 1983-91, pres. 1993-95, Outstanding Contbn. award 1992), Orgn. Chinese Ams. (pres. 1985-86, chair anti-Asian violence task force, 1989-95, Disting. Leadership award 1986). Home: 107 Mohawk Dr Butler PA 16001-1249 Office: Slippery Rock U Dept Counseling Ednl P Slippery Rock PA 16057

CHEN, SOW-YEH, pathology educator; b. Zhang-Hua, Taiwan, Aug. 28, 1939; came to U.S., 1966.; s. Chung and Sue (Shieh) C.; m. Ming-Ming Hsu, Sept. 9, 1972; children: Howard K., Hubert M. BMD, Nat. Taiwan U., Taipei, 1965; MS, U. Ill., Chgo., 1970, PhD, 1972. Diplomate Am. Bd. of Oral Pathology; cert. Dentist Dental Bd. of Commonwealth of Pa. Rsch. asst. U. Ill., Chgo., 1966-71, nat. inst. health fellow, 1971-73; from asst. prof. to prof. Temple U., Phila., 1973—; cons. Hunan Med. U., Chengsha, Hunan, China, 1990. Contbr. 2 book chpts., 37 articles to profl. jours. Mem. AAAS, Am. Acad. Oral Pathology, Sigma Xi, Omicron Kappa Upsilon. Office: Temple University 3223 N Broad St Philadelphia PA 19140-5096

CHEN, STEPHEN SHAU-TSI, psychiatrist, physiologist; b. Tou-Nan, Yun-Lin, Taiwan, Aug. 18, 1934; s. R-Yue and Pi-Yu (Huang) C.; m. Clara Chin-Chin Liu, Sept. 7, 1936; children: David, Timothy, Hubert. MD, Nat. Taiwan U., Taipei, 1959; PhD, U. Wis., 1968. Diplomate Am. Bd. Psychiatry and Neurology, also sub. bd. Geriatric Psychiatry. Intern Nat. Taiwan U. Hosp., 1959; instr. dept. physiology U. Wis., Madison, 1968-71, asst. prof., 1971-75; resident in psychiatry SUNY, Stony Brook, 1975-78; asst. prof. psychiatry dept. psychiatry U. Pitts., 1978-80; asst. prof. psychiatry dept. psychiatry and behavioral sci. U. Wash., Seattle, 1981-86, clin. asst. prof. psychiatry, 1986—; chief mental health clinic VA Med. Ctr., Tacoma, 1981-85. Contbr. articles to Am. Jour. Physiol., Jour. Physiology, Can. Jour. Physiology and Pharmacology, Acta Physiol. Fellow Wis. Heart Assn., 1966-68. Mem. APA, North Pacific Soc. Neurology and Psychiatry, Formosan Assn. for Pub. Affairs (pres. Seattle chpt. 1986-88, bd. dir. Washington chpt. 1988-89). Presbyterian. Office: VA Med Ctr Psychiatry Svc Tacoma WA 98493

CHEN, STEPHEN SHI-HUA, pathologist, biochemist; b. Taipei, Taiwan, Republic of China, Dec. 25, 1939; came to U.S., 1965; s. Ah-wen and Shun (Pan) C.; m. Hsin-Hsin Yu, July 5, 1969; children: Peter T., Margaret T. MD, Nat. Taiwan U., 1964; PhD, U. Pitts, 1972. Diplomate Am. Bd. of Pathology. Asst. prof. pathology U. Pitts., 1972-76; staff pathologist Presbyn. Hosp., Pitts., 1973-76; asst. prof. pathology dept. Stanford U., Palo Alto, Calif., 1976-80, clin. assoc. prof. pathology dept., 1980-96, clin. prof., 1996—; staff pathologist Veterans Affairs Med. Ctr., Palo Alto, 1976—. Contbr. articles to Jour. Cellular Physiology, Jour. Chromatography, Clinica Chimca Acta. Fellow Coll. Am. Pathologists; mem. Am. Soc. Investigative Pathology, U.S. and Can. Acad. Pathology Inc., Am. Soc. Clin. Pathologists. Office: Vets Affairs Med Ctr (113) 3801 Miranda Ave Palo Alto CA 94304-1207

CHENELL, LILLIAN, community health and pediatrics nurse; b. Boston, Apr. 16, 1941. Student, McLean Hosp. Sch. Nursing, Belmont, Mass., Assumption Coll., Worcester, Mass. Cert. family nurse practitioner, pediatric nurse practitioner. Pediatric nurse Mass. Gen. Hosp., Boston; pediatric nurse practitioner City of Cambridge, Mass.; family nurse practitioner Med. Ctr. Hahnamann, Worcester; pediatric and family nurse practitioner Family Health and Social Svc. Ctr., Worcester. Recipient Wetherill award, 1966. Mem. ANA, Mass. Coalition of Nurse Practitioners, Nat. Assn. of Pediatric Nurse Assocs. and Practitioners. Home: 261 Berlin Rd Marlborough MA 01752-1195

CHENEY, BRIGHAM VERNON, physical chemist; b. Salt Lake City, June 11, 1936; s. Silas Lavell and Klara (Young) C.; m. Marsali McAllister, Aug. 20, 1964; children—Jill, Mark Vernon, Heather, Karin, Brigham McAllister, John David. B.A., U. Utah, 1961, Ph.D., 1966. Research asst. U. Utah, 1964-66; research scientist Upjohn Co., Kalamazoo, 1966-71, scientist, 1971-75, sr. research scientist, 1975—, vis. scientist, Oxford U., 1986-87. Missionary, Ch. Jesus Ch. Latter-day Saints, Germany, 1956-59; high councilor, Lansing, Mich., 1969-75, Grand Rapids, Mich., 1975-78; bishop, Kalamazoo, 1978-84; leader Boy Scouts Am., 1972—. Served with Army N.G., 1959-67. Mem. Am. Chem. Soc., Sigma Xi, Phi Eta Sigma, Sigma Pi Sigma. Contbr. articles to profl. jours. Home: 3507 Runnymede Dr Kalamazoo MI 49004-3153 Office: Pharmacia and Upjohn Inc Kalamazoo MI 49001

CHENEY, CARL DOUGAL, behaviorologist, researcher; b. Buhl, Idaho, Feb. 19, 1934; s. Dougal Marles and Mary Ann (Dolana) C.; m. LaDawn Rae Rigby, June 2, 1955 (div. 1970); children—Scott Dolana, Taya Christine; m. Debra Ann Black, Dec. 15, 1973 (div. 1990); children—Carter Dougal, Mary Ann. BS, Utah State U., 1956; MA, Ariz. State U., 1962, PhD, 1966. Asst. prof. Eastern Wash. State U., Cheney, 1965-68; prof. dept. psychology Utah State U., Logan, 1968—, faculty interdeptl. program in toxicology, 1978—; dir. Basic Behavior Lab., Logan, 1968—. Author: Analysis of Behavior, 1982. Contbr. articles to profl. jours. Served to capt. USAF, 1956-59. NSF Sci. for Citizens grantee, 1980. Mem. Internat. Behaviorol. Assn., Assn. Behavior Analysis, B.F. Skinner Found. Office: Dept Psychology Utah State U UMC 28 Logan UT 84322

CHENEY, FREDERICK W., anesthesiologist; b. Ayer, Mass., Jan. 17, 1935; s. Frederick and Laura (Lynch) C.; m. Pi, June 13, 1959; children: Pamela, Brenda. BS, Tufts Coll., 1956, MD, 1960. Diplomate Am. Bd. Anesthesiology. Intern, resident Maine Med. Ctr., Portland, 1960-64; from instr. to prof. U. Wash. Sch. Medicine, Seattle, 1964—; dir. respiratory care svcs. Univ. Hosp., Seattle, 1967-94, dir. critical care ctr., 1982-87, acting dir. cardiac anesthesia, 1987-90, chair dept. anesthesiology, 1994—. Mem. AMA, Assn. Univ. Anesthetists, Am. Soc. Anesthesiologists, Anesthesia Patient Safety Found. Office: U Wash Dept Anesthesiology Box 356540 Seattle WA 98195-6540

CHENEY, LOIS SWEET, infection control nurse; b. Clifton Springs, N.Y., Oct. 26, 1933; d. Merton E. Sr. (dec.) and Jennie M. (Smith) S. (dec.); divorced; children: Linda Cheney Thorpe, Susan Cheney Post, Douglas A. Cheney. Diploma in nursing, Rochester (N.Y.) Gen. Hosp., 1954; BS in Edn. with high honors, Mansfield (Pa.) State Coll., 1973; MS, Columbia Pacific U., Mill Valley, Calif., 1982. RN, N.Y. With Meml. Hosp., Towanda, Pa., 1974-82; coord. infection control and employee health Clifton Springs Hosp. and Clinic, 1982-87; now infection control officer Monroe Cmty. Hosp., Rochester, 1987—; spkr. on mgmt. AIDS in long term care, 1987, 88, 89, 92; spkr. and cons. in infection control. Contbr. articles to profl. jours. Mem. Assn. Profls. in Infection Control and Epidemiology (cert., Rochester-Finger Lakes chpt.), Bus. and Profls. Women's Club, Toastmasters Internat. Intravenous Nurses Soc., N.Y. State Pub. Health Assn.

CHENG, ALEXANDER LIM, internist; b. Dipolog City, The Philippines, Mar. 28, 1957; s. Cheng Tin and Maria Soriano (Lim) C. BS, U. of the East, Manila, The Philippines, 1976; MD, Far Eastern U., Manila, The Philippines, 1980. Diplomate Am. Bd. Internal Medicine. Post-grad tng. Rural Health Practice, Katipunan, Z. D Norte, The Philippines, 1981; resident internal medicine Our Lady of Lourdes Hosp., Manila, The Philippines, 1982-85; fellow Adult Cardiology Philippine Heart Ctr., Quezon City, The Philippines, 1985-88; resident Elmhurst (N.Y.) Hosp. Ctr., 1991-94; family internist HIP-Queens Long Island Med. Group, P.C., Elmhurst, N.Y., 1994—. Mem. AMA, Am. Coll. Physicians, Am. Soc. Internal Medicine. Home: 8425 Elmhurst Ave Ste 2 W Flushing NY 11373-3359 Office: James Rudel Ctr Queens Long Island Med Grp 86-15 Queens Blvd Elmhurst NY 11373

CHENG, CHARLES, physician; b. Taipei, Taiwan, Mar. 20, 1967; came to U.S., 1978; s. Henry and Judy Cheng; m. Karen Cheng, July 1, 1993; 1 child, Geoffrey. BA in Biophysics, U. Calif., Berkeley, 1989; MD, U. So. Calif., 1994. Resident Med. Coll. Pa., Phila., 1994-95, U. Buffalo, 1995—. Mem. AMA. Home: 2011 Northwood Dr Williamsville NY 14221

CHENG, CHE PING, cardiology, physiology and pharmacology educator; b. People's Republic of China, Jan. 24, 1950; came to U.S., 1982; d. Ji and Yu Zhi (Pan) C.; m. Ping Tan, Feb. 23, 1951; 1 child, Xiao Tan. MD, Nanjing (People's Republic of China) Railway Med. U., 1976; PhD, Wayne State U., 1986. Diplomate Am. Bd. Internal Medicine. Attending physician dept. cardiology First Hosp. of Harbin (People's Republic of China) Med. Sch., 1977-81; rsch. assoc. Harbin Cardiovascular Rsch. Inst., 1980-81; teaching asst. dept. pathology Wayne State U., Detroit, 1982-83, teaching asst. dept. physiology, 1983-86; postdoctoral fellow cardiology rsch. Bowman Gray Sch. Medicine, Winston-Salem, N.C., 1986-88, rsch. instr. medicine dept. internal medicine, 1989-91, asst. prof. medicine dept. internal medicine, 1991-95, assoc. prof. medicine dept. internal medicine, 1995—, assoc. physiology and pharmacology, 1991, mem. grad. faculty Ctr. Neurobiol. Investigation Drug Abuse, 1993—; lectr. in field. Author: Novel Pharmacological Interventions for Alcoholism, 1992, Diastolic Relaxation of the Heart: Modulation of Diastolic Dysfunction in the Intact Heart, 1994, Effect of Felodipine on Left Ventricular Performance in Conscious Dogs: Assessment by Left Ventricular Pressure-Volume Analysis, 1994, Left Ventricular Systolic and Diastolic Performance, 1995, Altered Ventricular and Myoyte Response to Antiotensic II in Pacing-induced Heart Failure, 1996, Response of Left Ventricular Filling to Exercise Before and After Heart Failure, 1996; contbr. articles to profl. jours. Travel grantee Internat. Soc. for Biomed. Rsch., Rsch. Soc. on Alcoholism, 1990, grantee Am. Heart Assn., 1988-94, 95-97, NIH, 1986-95, Hassle Pharm., Sweden, 1991-94, travel grantee Nat. Inst. Alcohol Abuse and Alcoholism, 1994; recipient Exptl. Biology Losartan Travel award, 1996. Mem. Am. Heart Assn. (coun.), Am. Fedn. Clin. Rsch., Am. Physiol. Soc., Internat. Soc. Biomed. Rsch. on Alcoholism, Internat. Soc. for Heart Rsch. Home: 651 Dover Dr Winston Salem NC 27104-1529 Office: Bowman Gray Sch Medicine Cardiology Dept Medical Center Blvd Winston Salem NC 27157-1045

CHENG, EDWARD HSIN-YI, gastroenterologist, researcher, educator; b. Tokyo, Feb. 28, 1955; came to U.S., 1959; s. Charles Kang and Shirley Sui-Lan (Lau) C.; m. Sue-Fong Leong, Sept. 19, 1981; 1 child, Wesley. BS, SUNY, Stony Brook, 1976; MD, NYU, 1980. Diplomate Am. Bd. Internal Medicine, Bd. Gastroenterology. Resident in medicine U. Calif., San Diego, 1980-83; gastroenterology fellow SUNY, Stony Brook, 1983-85; attending physician SUNY/VA Hosp. Northport, Stony Brook, 1985—; asst. prof. medicine SUNY, Stony Brook, 1989—. Contbr. articles to profl. jours. Named Assoc. Investigator, VA Career Devel., 1983-85. Fellow ACP; mem. Am. Gastroent. Assn. Office: VA Med Ctr Northport 79 Middleville Rd Northport NY 11768-2200

CHENG, HSUEH CHING, physician; b. Taikang, Henan, Republic of China, Jan. 26, 1927; arrived in U.S., 1961; s. Chih-kuo and Noong (Hou) C.; m. Meio Chien, May 19, 1956; childen: Wen, Julie, Ken, Gene. MD, Nat. Def. Med. Ctr., Taipei, 1952. Diplomate Am. Bd. Internal Medicine, Am. Bd. Cardiovascular Diseases. Intern Buffalo (N.Y.) Gen. Hosp., 1961-62, St. Boniface (Can.) Gen. Hosp., 1962-63; resident physician in medicine Passavant Meml. Hosp., Chgo., 1963-65; fellow in cardiology Maine Med. Ctr., Portland, 1965-66; resident in physician in medicine Hamilton (Ont.) Civic Hosps., 1966-67; physician Mt. Sinai Hosp., Ste-Agathe-des-Monts, 1967-71; chief divsn. of medicine Augusta (Maine) State Hosp., 1971-72, chmn. dept. medicine, 1976-77; attending physician Kennebec Valley Med. Ctr., Augusta, 1972—. Maj. Chinese Nationalist Army, 1952-61. Fellow Royal Coll. of Physicians and Surgeons of Can., Am. Coll. Cardiology; mem. AMA, Maine Med. Assn., Am. Soc. Internal Medicine, Chinese Med. Assn. (Taiwan). Office: 6 Middle St Augusta ME 04330-5211

CHENG, KENNETH, family practice physician; b. Covina, Calif., Apr. 17, 1962; s. Robert and Kathleen (Tam) C.; m. Lisa G. Santell, Nov. 26, 1988; children Jason Alexander, Katherine Lauren. BS, Calif. Poly. U., Pomona, 1986; DO, Coll. Osteo. Med. Pacific, Pomona, 1990. Diplomate Am. Bd. Family Practice. Intern U. Calif., Irvine, 1990-91, resident in family medicine, 1991-93; ptnr. Newport Family Medicine, Newport Beach, Calif., 1993—; mem. adv. bd. Orange Coast Coll., Costa Mesa, Calif., 1994—; vol. instr. diving medicine Nat. Assn. Underwater Instrs./Sport Chalet, Huntington Beach, Calif., 1994—; asst. clin. prof. U. Calif., Irvine, 1993—. mem. bd. dirs., Greater Newport Physicians, Inc., 1996—. Office: Newport Family Medicine 360 San Miguel Dr #501 Newport Beach CA 92660

CHENG, KENNETH TAT-CHIU, pharmacy educator; b. Hong Kong, Feb. 24, 1954; came to U.S., 1972; s. Shiu Fun and Alice Shiu-Wing (Leung) C.; m. Ying Hsu, Aug. 11, 1984; children: Jonathan Yee-Hang, Hannah Yee-Shing. BS in Pharmacy, SUNY, Buffalo, 1977; PhD, Purdue U., 1985. Lic. pharmacist N.Y., Ind., Kans., N.Mex., S.C.; diplomate Am. Bd. Sci. in Nuclear Scis.; cert. expert nuclear medicine tng.; cert. nuclear pharmacist. Resident in hosp. pharmacy U. Kans. Med. Ctr., Kansas City, 1978-79; research/teaching asst. Purdue U., West Lafayette, Ind., 1980-84; research fellow Harvard U. Med. Sch., Boston, 1984-85; assoc. prof. U. N.Mex., Albuquerque, 1985-88; dir. nuclear pharmacy and radiology rsch., assoc. prof. Med. U. S.C., Charleston, 1988—, assoc. prof., 1992—, tenured assoc. prof., 1995—; bd. dirs. Am. Bd. of Sci. in Nuclear Medicine. Recipient Donald E. Francke award Drug Info. Assn., 1981, Glenn E. Jenkins Qualifying Research award Purdue U., 1984; named one of Outstanding Young Men of Am., 1986; David Ross fellow Purdue U., 1982-83, research fellow Am. Cancer Soc., 1984-85. Mem. AAAS, Soc. Nuclear Medicine, Am. Soc. Hosp. Pharmacists, Am. Chem. Soc., Soc. Magnetic Resonance Imaging, Internat. Assn. Radiopharmacology, Health Physics Soc., Sigma Xi, Rho Chi, Eta Sigma Gamma. Office: Med U SC Nuclear Pharmacy Charleston SC 29425

CHENG, THOMAS CLEMENT, parasitologist, immunologist, educator, author; b. Nov. 5, 1930; came to U.S., 1946; s. James Tsu-Mook and Dorothy (Lee) C.; m. Barbara Ann Schimmel, May 31, 1957 (div. 1982); children: Thomas C., J. Bradford, Allison E.; m. Anne Foos Whitelaw, June 19, 1982 (div. 1985). A.B., Wayne State U., 1952; M.S., U. Va., 1956, Ph.D., 1958. Asst. prof. U. Md. Med. Sch., Balt., 1958-59; from asst. prof. to assoc. prof. Lafayette Coll., Easton, Pa., 1959-64; chief immunology and parasitology Northeast Marine Health Sci. Lab USPHS, Narragansett, R.I., 1964-65; from assoc. prof. to prof. U. Hawaii, Honolulu, 1965-69; prof., dir. Ctr. for Health Sci., Lehigh U., Bethlehem, Pa., 1969-80; sr. prof. cell biology Med. U. S.C., Charleston, S.C., 1980-83, dir. Marine Biomed. Research, 1980-91, sr. prof., 1991-92; sr. sci. cons. Atlantic Clam Farms, Folly Beach, S.C., 1993—; dir. Shellfish Rsch. Inst., Charleston, 1993—; cons. Acad. Press, San Diego, 1969—, Univ. Park Press, Balt., 1969—, Divsn. Microbiology FDA, Washington, 1968-72, biomed. rsch. Internat. Copper Rsch. Assn., Inc., N.Y.C., 1970-92, Sandoz Pharm. Co., Winter Park, Fla., 1979—, Xytronyx, Inc., San Diego, 1984—, Atlantic Clamfarms, Folly Beach, S.C., 1993—; mem. USPHS Commn. on Food Protection, Washington, 1965-66, environ. biology and chemistry study sect. NIH, Bethesda, Md., 1969-71, spl. study sect. Marine Environ. Health, Bethesda, 1973-75, planning com. FDA-HHS, Washington, 1969-71; mem. adv. bd. Ctr. for Pathobiology U. Calif.-Irvine, 1969—; mem. rev. panel Div. Ocean Scis., Office of Internat. Decade of Ocean Exploration NSF, Washington, 1977-78, divsn. cell physiology, 1980-83; chmn. molecular biology Office Naval Rsch., Arlington, Va., 1983-92; dir. WHO Collaborative Lab. of Vector Biology, Charleston, S.C., 1982-92, rsch. Centre Nationale de la Recherche, France, 1986-87; prin. lectr. Internat. Soc. Comparative Physiology, Switzerland, 1989; co-chmn. Internat. Congress Parasitology, Paris, 1990; mem. sci. directorate Internat. Orgn. Pathology Marine Aquaculture; adj. marine scientist Marine Resources Rsch. Inst., S.C. Wildlife and Marine Resources Dept., 1993—. Author: The Biology of Animal Parasites (1st prize Phila. Book Show), 1964, 65, Marine Molluscs as Hosts for Symbiosis, 1967, Symbiosis: Organisms Living Together, 1970, General Parasitology, 1973, 2d edit. 1986, Human Parasitology, 1990; editor, contbr. Some Biochemical and Immunological Aspects of Host-Parasite Relationships, 1963, Aspects of the Biology of Symbiosis, 1971, Molluscicides in Schistosomiasis Control, 1974, Invertebrate Immune Responses, 1977, Invertebrate Models for Biomedical Research, 1978, Structure of Membranes and Receptors, 1984, Invertebrate Blood: Functions of Serum Factors and Cells, 1984; editor: Pathogens of Invertebrates: Application in Biological Control and Transmission Mechanisms, 1984; co-author: Medical and Economic Malacology, 1974, Biology of Microsporidia, 1976, Systematics of the Microsporidia, 1977, Pathology in Marine Science, 1990; editor Jour. Invertebrate Pathology, 1969-91, Exptl. Parasitology jour., 1969-88, Comparative Pathobiology jour., 1975-84; contbr. numerous articles to profl. jours. and revs. Mem. Mayor's Marine Mus. Project, Charleston, 1984—; regional coord. Nat. Disaster Med. System, Charleston, 1987-94. Capt. USPHS, U.S. Army, 1952-54, 64-65, Korea. Recipient George C. Wheeler Disting. Lectureship award U. N.D., Grand Forks, 1973, Disting. Lectr. Southwestern Assn. Parsitologists, 1973, Disting. Lectureship award Tulane Med. Sch., New Orleans, 1977; Parasitology prin. lectr. award Coll. of Physicians of Phila., 1980; Andrew Felming Rsch. award U. Va., Charlottesville, 1958, Roy and Ira Jones Superior Tchg. award Lafayette Coll., Easton, Pa., 1962, Disting. Alumnus award Wayne State U., Detroit, 1975, Medal of Honor U. Montpellier, 1992; Fulbright Rsch scholar, France, 1986-87; grantee AEC, 1958-59, 60-62, NSF, 1959-61, 78-83, 82-85, 95-96, NIH 1-76, 75-78, 77-79, Am. Cancer Soc., 1966-69, FDA, 1973-75, Internat. Copper Rsch. Assn., 1971-76, 75-77, 81-84, Nat. Marine Fisheries, NOAA, 1991-93, 95-96, Dept. Agrl. 1995-96, Dept. Commerce, Dept. Energy, WHO, USDA, Am. Cyanamid Co.; Disting Stoll lectr. Rutgers U., 1988; named to Hon. Citizen City of Montpellier, France, 1992. Fellow Royal Soc. Tropical Medicine and Hygiene, AAAS; mem. Am. Microscopical Soc. (pres. 1980-81), Am. Physiol. Soc., Jefferson Soc. U. Va., Am. Soc. Zoologists (rep. pub. affairs 1982-88), Am. Soc. Parasitologists (exec. council 1974-78), Soc. for Exptl. Biology and Medicine, Soc. Protozoologists, Reticuloendothelial Soc., N.Y. Acad. Scis., Helminthological Soc. Washington, Soc. for Invertebrate Pathology (chmn. publs. bd. 1969-84), N.Y. Soc. Tropical Medicine (sec.-treas. 1975-76), Council of Biology Editors, N.J. Soc. Parasitology (pres. 1977-78), Sigma Xi, Tau Kappa Epsilon. Democrat. Episcopalian. Home and Office: 8 Queen St Charleston SC 29401-2111 also: Shellfish Rsch Inst PO Box 12139 Charleston SC 29422-2139

CHENG, TSUNG O., cardiologist, educator; b. Shanghai, Mar. 30, 1925; came to U.S., 1950, naturalized, 1960; s. Keith S. and Fanny (Wang) C.; m. Marie Ellen Roe, June 18, 1955; children: Mark Dudley, Yvonne Joyce. BS, St. John's U., China, 1945; MD, U. Pa., 1950, MS in Medicine, 1956. Diplomate Am. Bd. Internal Medicine (subsplty. cardiovascular disease), Nat. Bd. Med. Examiners. Intern St. Barnabas Hosp., Newark, 1950-51; resident Cook County Hosp., Chgo., 1952-55; fellow in cardiovascular disease George Washington U., D.C. Gen. Hosp., Washington, 1955-56; instr. cardiology Harvard Med. Sch. Mass. Gen. Hosp., Boston, 1956-57; fellow in cardiorespiratory physiology Johns Hopkins U. Sch. Medicine and Hosp., 1957-59; practice medicine specializing in cardiology Washington, 1970—; asst. prof. medicine SUNY Downstate, 1959-70; asso. prof. medicine George Washington U., 1970-72, prof., 1972—; chief cardiology D.C. Gen. Hosp., 1971-72; dir. cardiac catheterization lab. George Washington U. Med. Center, 1972-78, assoc. dir. cardiology, 1972-75; asst. physician Cardiac Clinic, Johns Hopkins Hosp., 1957-59, mem. staff cardiac catheterization lab., 1957-59; dir. cardiopulmonary lab. Bklyn. Hosp., 1959-66; co-chief Pediatric Cardiac Clinic, 1959-66; chief Adolescent Cardiac Clinic, 1961-66; attending physician Adult Cardiac Clinic, 1959-66; chief Pediatric Cardiac Clinic Cumberland Hosp., Bkly., 1963-66; asst. chief cardiology VA Hosp., Bklyn., 1966-69; chief Cardiovascular Lab., 1966-70, chief cardiology, 1969-70; asst. vis. physician Kings County Hosp. Med. Center, Bklyn., 1964-70; attending physician Univ. Hosp., SUNY, Bklyn., 1967-70; cons. Beth Israel Med. Ctr., N.Y.C., 1970-82; guest lectr. Chinese Med. Assn., 1972, 73, 75, 77, 79, 83, 86, 89, 92, Chinese Ministry Health, 1990; hon. prof. Shanghai 2d Med. Univ. 1986—, Qingdao Med. Coll., 1989—, Binzhou Med. Coll., 1992—, Taishan Med. Coll., 1992—, Tongji Med. U., Wuhan, China, 1993—, Jiujiang Med. Coll., Jiangxi, China 1994—, U. Cape Town, South Africa, 1995—; hon. dir. Qingdao Cardiovascular Rsch. Inst., 1989—,

Guangdong Provincial Cardiovascular Inst., 1990—; hon. pres. Dandong 1st Hosp., Dandong, Liaoning Province, People's Republic of China 1988—, Shanghai St. Luke's Hosp., 1990—, Binzhou Med. Coll. Affiliated Hosp., 1992—, Taishan Med. Coll. Affiliated Hosp., 1992—, Jiujiang Med. Coll. Affiliated Hosp., Jiujiang, Jiangxi, China, 1994—, Second People's Hosp., Jin De Zhen, Jiangxi, 1994—; vis. prof., Peking Union Med. Coll., 1986—; hon. cons. Beijing Hosp., 1989—; vis. prof. Sun Yatsen Med. U., Canton, 1992—, Cairo U., Egypt, 1994—, U. Oxford, Eng., 1995—, U. Witwatersrand Med. Sch., Johannesburg, South Africa, 1995—, U. Paris Hosp., Tenon, France, 1995—, U. Natal, Durban, South Africa, 1995—, Cath. U. Inst. Cardiology, Rome, 1996—, Inst. Clin. Physiology, Nat. Rsch. Coun., Pisa, Italy, 1996—, Inst. Pathol. Anatomy med. Sch. U. Milan, 1996—; v.p. Am. Ctr. for Chinese Med. Sci., 1982-91; pres. Friends St. Luke's Hosp. Shanghai, 1991—, chmn. bd., 1992—; hon. dir. Inst. Invasive Therapy PLA 150th Ctrl. Hosp., Luoyang, China 1994—; disting. sr. visitor Royal Brompton Hosp./ Nat. Heart and Lung Inst., London, 1995—; hon. advisor Guangdong Soc. Interventional Cardiology, Guangzhou, China, 1996—. Sr. editor Vascular Medicine, 1983-88, Angiology, 1986—; editor: The International Textbook of Cardiology, 1986, 87, Percutaneous Balloon Valvuloplasty, 1992; mem. editl. bd. Catheterization and Cardiovasc. Diagnosis, 1991—, Jour. Noninvasive Cardiology, 1996—; co-editor: Congestive Heart Failure, 1991, Modern Cardiology, 1994, Genetics of Cardiovascular Diseases, 1995; contbr. numerous articles to sci. and med. jours. Fellow ACP, Am. Coll. Chest Physicians, Am. Coll. Cardiology (ofcl. rep. to standards com. on catheters Assn. Advancement Med. Instrumentation 1971—), Am. Heart Assn., Coun. Clin. Cardiology, Soc. Cardiac Angiography and Interventions, Internat. Coll. Ang Geriatric Cardiology (founding); mem. AAAS, Am. Fedn. Clin. Rsch., Am. Heart Assn., Washington Heart Assn. Home: 7508 Cayuga Ave Bethesda MD 20817-4822 Office: George Washington U Med Ctr 2150 Pennsylvania Ave NW Washington DC 20037-2396

CHENG, WILFRED DAVID, clinical psychologist, psychoanalyst, educator; b. Hong Kong, Sept. 10, 1948; came to U.S., 1968; s. Wo and Ching-Sum (Ngan) C. BA magna cum laude, Lafayette Coll., 1971; MS, Rutgers U., 1973, PhD, 1976; cert. in psychotherapy and psychoanalysis, Postgrad. Ctr. Mental Health, N.Y.C., 1980. Staff mem. Community Guidance Svc., N.Y.C., 1977-81; clin. psychologist N.Y.C. Police Dept., 1981-85; prof. Baruch Coll. CUNY, N.Y.C., 1985—; pvt. practice psychotherapy N.Y.C., 1977—; adj. clin. supr. Yeshiva U., N.Y.C., 1980-82; chmn. China com. Sch. Liberal Arts and Scis., Baruch Coll., CUNY, 1989—, dir. counseling and psychol. svcs., 1989—, head coach men's tennis team; dir. Asian Students Workshop Series, 1987—; guest spkr. documentary ABC-TV, 1988. Mem. Am. Psychol. Assn., Asian Am. Psychol Assn., Am. Coll. Pers. Assn., Phi Beta Kappa. Home: 315 Central Park W New York NY 10025-7664 Office: Baruch Coll 17 Lexington Ave Box 304 New York NY 10010

CHENGAPPA, KADIAMADA NANAIAH, physician; b. Bangalore, Karnataka, India, Sept. 26, 1955; came to U.S., 1989; s. Nanaiah K. and Leela (Aiyappa) Kadiamada; m. Dara Ann Davis, Aug. 6, 1988; children: Leela Beck, Lara Ann. MD, Kasturba Med. Coll., Manipal, India, 1981. Diplomate Am. Bd. Psychiatry and Neurology; cert. in psychiatry and geriatric psychiatry. Intern Kasturda Med. Coll. Hosp., India, 1980-81; resident Ediburgh U., 1983-86, Dalhousie U., Halifax, Can., 1986-88; NIMH rsch. fellow U. Pitts., 1989-90, asst. prof. psychiatry dept. psychiatry, 1991—; dir. clin. trials of new psychotropic medications U. Pitts., 1991—. Fellow Royal Coll. Physicians and Surgeons Can.; mem. Royal Coll. Psychiatry (U.K.), Soc. Biol. Psychiatrists, Am. Soc. Clin. Psychopharmacology. Office: Western Psychiat Inst & Clinic 3811 O'Hara St Pittsburgh PA 19213-2593

CHENGOT, MATHEW THOMAS, cardiologist; b. Kottayam, Kerela, India, Feb. 2, 1951; came to U.S., 1978; s. Thomas and Mary (Francis) C.; m. Binny George Pottant, Apr. 9, 1978; children: Thomas, Marilyn. Pre-Med., Deva Matha Coll., India, 1968, BS, 1971; MD, Govt. Med., Kottayam, India, 1976. Intern Govt. Med. Coll., Kottayam, 1977-78; fellow internal medicine Lincoln Hosp., Bronx, N.Y., 1979-82; cardiology fellow Mt. Sinai Med. Ctr., Miami Beach, Fla., 1982-84; cardiologist Amityville, N.Y., 1984—; clin. instr. North Shore Univ. Hosp., Manhasset, N.Y., 1984—; co-dir. CCU, Brunswick HCS Ctr., Amityville, 1989—, dir. cardiac rehab., 1994—. Contbr. articles to profl. jours. Mem. AMA, Am. Heart Assn., Am. Coll. Cardiology, Am. Coll. of Chest Physicians, Suffolk Acad. of Medicine, Med. Soc. N.Y. Roman Catholic. Office: 129 Broadway Amityville NY 11701

CHENHALLS, ANNE MARIE, nurse, educator; b. Detroit, May 26, 1929; d. Peter and Beatrice Mary (Elliston) McLeod; m. Horacio Chenhalls, 1953 (dec.); children: Mark, Anne Marie Chenhalls Delamater. Student Detroit Conservatory Music, 1946-47; grad. Grace Hosp. Sch. Nursing, 1951; B. Vocat. Edn., Calif. State U.-Los Angeles, 1967, B.S. in Nursing, 1968; M.A., Calif. State U.-Long Beach, 1985. R.N., Calif. Nurse, Grace Hosp., Detroit, 1951-52; pvt. duty nurse, Mexico City, 1953-54; nurse St. Francis Hosp., Lynwood, Calif., 1957-63; assoc. prof. nursing Compton Coll. (Calif.), 1964-72; health educator, sch. nurse Santa Ana Unified Sch. Dist. (Calif.), 1972-76, 79—; med. coord., internat. health cons. Agape Movement, San Bernardino, Calif., 1976-79; instr. community health, Uganda, 1982; med. evaluator Athletes in Action, 1979; pub. health nurse Orange County Health Dept., Calif., 1990-95 . Assoc. staff mem. Campus Crusade for Christ. Solo vocalist, Santa Ana, Orange, Seal Beach, Dinner Theater, Calif., Civic Light Opera, Buena Park, Calif.; acting Master's Repertory Theater, 1990—, Santa Ana. U.S. govt. grantee, 1968. Mem. Calif. Sch. Nurses Assn., Nat. Educators Assn., Calif. Tchrs. Assn. Democrat. Home: 30802 S Coast Hwy Trlr A2 Laguna Beach CA 92651-4207 Office: Santa Ana Unified Sch Dist 1405 French St Santa Ana CA 92701-2414

CHENKIN, THEODORE, physician; b. Bklyn., Oct. 1, 1921; s. Meyer and Jennie (Rosen) C.; A.B., Cornell U., 1943; MD, NYU, 1949; m. Freda Goldstein, June 11, 1948; childrenDavid, Michael, Harriet. Rotating intern Queens Gen. Hosp., Bklyn., 1949-51; resident in medicine NYU med. rsch. svc. Goldwater Meml. Hosp., 1951-52, rsch. fellow, 1952-54; resident in medicine VA Hosp., Bklyn., 1954-55; practice medicine specializing in internal medicine, Carteret, N.J., 1955-95; emeritus staff dept. medicine Rahway (N.J.) Hosp., 1971-78, instr. emeritus Robert Wood Johnson Med. Sch.; clin. asst. prof. medicine Rutgers U. Med. Sch., 1978—, Robert Wood Johnson Med. Sch., 1978—; mem. Carteret Bd. Health, 1975-77, v.p., 1978, pres., 1979-95. Served with USPHS, 1951-54. Recipient OSRD citation, 1945. Fellow Am. Geriatric Soc., N.J. Acad. Medicine; mem. Med. Soc. N.J., Union County Med. Soc., Sigma Xi. Contbr. articles to profl. publs.; rsch. in blood clotting. Home: 29 Oak St Carteret NJ 07008-2232

CHERENZIA, BRADLEY JAMES, radiologist; b. Niagara Falls, N.Y., Aug. 22, 1931; s. Peter and Myrna (Bradley) C.; m. Paula Joyce, Mar. 9, 1978; children: Kevin, Lori, David, Robert, Lisa. BS in Pharmacy cum laude, U. Buffalo, 1953; MD, SUNY Upstate Med. Ctr., Syracuse, 1957. Cert. Am. Bd. Radiology, Am. Bd. Nuclear Medicine. Intern SUNY Upstate Med. Ctr. Hosps., Syracuse, 1957-58; resident in radiology Wayne State U. Sch. Medicine Hosps., Detroit, 1960-63; practice medicine specializing in radiology Diagnostic Radiology Cons., P.C., Warren, Mich., 1965—, also chmn. bd. dirs.; sr. attending radiologist Detroit-Macomb Hosp. Corp., chmn. divsn. diagnostic radiol. quality improvement com., med. care and evaluation com., chmn. radiation safety com.; med. dir. dept. diagnostic radiology Macomb Hosp. Ctr., mem. med. exec. com. Served to capt. M.C., U.S. Army, 1958-60. Mem. AMA, Am. Soc. Nuc. Cardiology, Wayne County Med. Soc., Mich. State Med. Soc., Radiol. Soc. N.Am., Mich. Radiol. Soc., Am. Coll. Radiology, Soc. Nuclear Medicine, Am. Coll. Nuclear Medicine, Am. Coll. Physician Execs., Soc. Radiologists in Ultrasound, Am. Heart Assn., Am. Med. Tennis Assn. Republican. Roman Catholic.

CHERKASKY, MARTIN, physician; b. Phila., Oct. 6, 1911; s. Samuel and Sarah (Kosharsky) C.; m. Sarah Griffin, Feb. 3, 1941; children: Marny, Michael, Karl. M.D., Temple U., 1936. Pvt. med. practice Phila., 1939-40; exec. home care dept. Montefiore Hosp., 1947; dir. Med. Group, 1948-51, chief div. social medicine, 1950; dir. Montefiore Hosp. and Med. Center, 1951-75, pres., 1975-81, cons. to hosp. and to bd. trustees, 1981—; Atran prof. dept. community health Albert Einstein Coll. Medicine, 1967-77; cons. N.Y. State Joint Hosp. Rev. and Planning Council; cons. to commr. hosps. N.Y.C. Dept. Hosps., 1961-62; exec. com. Health Research Council of N.Y.C., 1968-74; regional health adv. bd. Region II, Dept. Health, Edn. and Welfare, 1970-72; chmn. profl. adv. com. Joint Distbn. Com., N.Y.C., 1969-78; com. of 100 for Nat. Health Ins., 1969—; dir. Asso. Hosp. Service, 1969—; mem. Gov.'s Steering Com. Social Problems, 1970-72. Editorial bd. jour.: Chronic Diseases, 1957—, Commonwealth and Internat. Library Sci. Tech. and Engring; Contbr. articles to various publs.; Lectr. Served as lt. col. M.C. AUS, 1940-46. Fellow N.Y. Acad. Medicine (chmn. bd. trustees 1990); mem. NAS (sr. mem. inst. medicine 1971—, coun. inst. 1972-74), Am. Pub. Health Assn., Am. Hosp. Assn., Greater N.Y. Hosp. Assn. (past pres.), Assn. Am. Med. Colls. Office: 111 E 210th St Bronx NY 10467-2490

CHERLIN, RICHARD STANLEY, endocrinologist; b. Bklyn., Sept. 28, 1947; s. Leonard and Violet (Gross) C.; m. Patricia Bloom, Aug. 20, 1970 (div. June 1986); 1 child, Marcus; m. Claudia E. Fitzmaurice, Sept. 10, 1994. BS summa cum laude, Bklyn. Coll., 1968; MD, Albert Einstein Coll. Medicine, 1972. Diplomate Am. Bd. Internal Medicine with subspecialty in endocrinology and metabolism. Intern Bronx Mcpl. Hosp. Ctr., 1972-73, jr. resident, 1973-74; sr. resident Stanford U., Palo Alto, Calif., 1974-75; fellow in endocrinology Mass. Gen. Hosp., Boston 1975-77; pvt. practice Los Gatos, Calif., 1977—; clin. assoc. prof. Stanford Med. Ctr., 1985—; chief of staff Valley West Hosp., Los Gatos, 1981-82; dir. diabetes svcs. Los Gatos Cmty. Hosp., 1991—; clin. instr. Harvard Med. Sch., Boston, 1975-77; chmn. dept. medicine Good Samaritan Hosp., 1996—. USPHS grantee, 1976. Mme. Calif. Med. Assn., Santa Clara County Med. Soc., Diabetes Soc. (chpt. pres. 1985), Endocrine Soc., Phi Beta Kappa, Alpha Omega Alpha. Office: Ste 12 15899 Los Gatos-Almaden Rd Los Gatos CA 95032

CHERMANN, JEAN CLAUDE, virologist; b. Paris, Mar. 23, 1939; s. Camille Andre and Benbeneda (Montoya) C.; m. Pearron Daniele, Dec. 22, 1962; children: Jean Francois, Olivier. Bachelor, Michelet, 1959; Maitrise Biochemistry, Paris U., 1963, PhD, 1967. Rsch. asst. Pasteur Inst., Paris, 1963-77, head lab., 1977-87; chief viral oncology lab., Pasteur Inst., Paris; rsch. dir. Insti. Nat. de le Recherche Medicale, Marseille, France, 1988—; vis. scientist Nat. Cancer Inst., Bethesda, Md., 1971. Decorated Ordre Nat. du Merite Pres. de la Republique (France), Ordre Nat. Legion d'Honneur(France); co-recipient King Faisal Internat. prize Medicine, 1993. Developer with Francoise Barre-Sinoussi and Luc Montagnier isolation of HIV-the causative agt. of AIDS. Office: Campus Univ Luminy Bt INSERM, Laboratoire de Recherches, F-13273 Marseilles 9, France other: care Inst Pasteur, 25-28 rue du Dr Roux, 75015 Paris France

CHERN, JI-WANG, pharmacy educator; b. Tainan County, Taiwan, Republic of China, Sept. 6, 1953; s. Yuan-Chun and Shih-Shia (Shiau) C.; m. Mei-Ying Kuo, Sept. 4, 1978; children: Ting-Rong, Ting-Zhao. BS in Pharmacy, Nat. Def. Med. Ctr., Taipei, Taiwan, 1977; MS in Medicinal Chemistry, U. Mich., 1982, PhD in Medicinal Chemistry, 1985. Registered pharmacist, Taiwan. Teaching asst. Nat. Def. Med. Ctr., Taipei, 1977-80; postdoctoral fellow Coll. Pharmacy U. Mich., Ann Arbor, 1985; assoc. prof. Nat. Def. Med. Ctr., Taipei, 1985-89, prof. Inst. Pharmacy, 1989—, dir med. labs., 1995—; prof. Sch. Pharmacy Nat. Taiwan U., 1995—; adj. prof. sch. pharmacy Nat. Taiwan U., 1993—, prof., 1995—; dir. med. lab. Nat. Def. Med. Ctr., 1995—. Mem. editorial bd. Chinese Pharm. Jour., 1988—, sr. editor, 1994—; asst. editor Jour. Med. Scis., 1988-89. Patentee in field. Col. Taiwan mil., 1994. Recipient Best Rch. Scientist award Nat. Sci. Coun., Taipei, 1988, 89, 93-94, Outstanding Rsch. Scientist award, 1992; named One of 10 Outstanding Young Persons in Republic of China, 1991. Mem. AAAS, Am. Chem. Soc., Internat. Soc. Heterocyclic Chemistry, Am. Cancer Rsch. Assn., N.Y. Acad. Scis., Chinese Chem. Soc. Mem. Nationalist Party. Home: 9F 108 77Ln Sect 4, Hsin-Hai Rd, Taipei 100, Taiwan Taiwan Office: Nat Taiwan U Sch Pharmacy, Coll of Medicine, No 1 Sect 1 Jen-Ai Rd Taipei 100, Taiwan

CHERNIACK, NEIL STANLEY, physician, medical educator; b. Bklyn., May 28, 1931; s. Max and Rebecca (Roulnik) C.; m. Sandra Lebowitz, Dec. 31, 1954; children: Evan, Andrew, Emily. AB with honors, Columbia U., 1952; MD, SUNY, 1956; MA, U. Pa., 1972; hon. degree, Karolinska U., 1991. Intern U. Ill., Chgo., 1956-57, resident, 1957-58, 60-62; resident, fellow Columbia Presbyn. Hosp., N.Y.C., 1962-64; practice medicine specializing in pulmonary disease Chgo., 1964-69, Phila., 1969-77, Cleve., 1977—; asst. prof. medicine U. Ill., Chgo., 1964-68, assoc. prof., 1968-69; assoc. prof. U. Pa., Phila., 1969-73, prof., 1973-77; prof. Case Western Res. U., 1977—, chief pulmonary svc., 1977-89, prof. physiology, 1982—, assoc. dean, 1983-90, dean sch. medicine, v.p. med. affairs, 1990—, vice chmn. div. gen. med. sci., 1986-90, vice chmn. dept. medicine, 1987-90; chief pulmonary svc., sr. attending physician Phila. Gen. Hosp., 1969-77; assoc. dir. pulmonary svc., attending physician U. Pa. Hosp., 1973-77, U. Hosps. of Cleve., Cleve. VA Med. Ctr.; vis. prof. Karolinska U., Stockholm, 1976-77; dir. of clin. svcs., acting chmn. dept. physiology & pharmacology U. Medicine & Dentistry N.J., Newark, 1995—. Mem. editorial bd. Circulation Research, Am. Rev. Respiratory Disease; editor: Jour. Applied Physiology, Handbook of Physiology; assoc. editor Jour. Lab. Clin. Medicine, Handbooks of Physiology. Served to capt. USAF, 1958-60. Mem. Am. Assn. Physicians, Am. Soc. Clin. Investigation, Am. Thoracic Soc., Am. Lung Assn., Am. Physiol. Soc., Bioengring. Soc., Biomed. Engring. Soc. (bd. dirs. 1984-87), Central Soc. Clin. Research, Neurosci. Soc., Phi Beta Kappa, Alpha Omega Alpha, Beta Sigma Rho. Home: 11 Wood Dr Morris Plains NJ 07950 Office: Univ Med Dental NJ Newark NJ 07103-2714

CHERNICOFF, DAVID PAUL, osteopathic physician, educator; b. N.Y.C., Aug. 3, 1947; s. Harry and Lillian (Dobkin) C. AB, U. Rochester, 1969; DO, Phila. Coll. Osteo. Medicine, 1973. Rotating intern Rocky Mountain Hosp., Denver, 1973-74; resident in internal medicine Community Gen. Osteo. Hosp., Harrisburg, Pa., 1974-76; fell in hematology and med. oncology Cleve. Clinic, 1976-78; asst. prof. medicine sect. hematology-oncology Chgo. Coll. Osteo. Medicine, 1978-82, assoc. prof., 1982-89 ; co-chmn. tumor task force Chgo. Osteo. Med. Center, 1978-89 , dir. clin. cancer edn., 1978-89 , hematology and oncology; asst. clin. prof medicine Pa. State U. Coll. Medicine, 1993—; chmn. tumor task force Olympia Fields (Ill.) Osteo. Med. Center. Trustee, mem. clin. exec. com. Ill. Cancer Coun., 1982-89; bd. dir. Chgo. unit Am. Cancer Soc., 1981-86, chief sec. of Hematology-Oncology Hosp. of Chgo. Coll. Osteo Medicine, 1981-89. Diplomate Nat. Bd. Osteo. Examiners, Am. Osteo. Bd. Internal Medicine, also in Hematology-Oncology. Fellow Am. Coll. Osteo. Internists, Pa. Osteo. Med. Soc., Eastern Coop. Oncology Group (sr. investigator 1981-89), Am. Soc. Clin. Oncology; mem. Am. Osteo. Assn. Contbr. articles to med. jours. Office: 4830 Londonderry Rd Harrisburg PA 17109-5240

CHERNOFF, AMOZ IMMANUEL, hematologist, consultant; b. Malden, Mass., Mar. 17, 1923; s. Isaiah and Celia (Margolin) C.; m. Renate R. Fisher, Jan. 25, 1953; children: David F., Susan N., Judith A. BS in Chemistry with honors, Yale U., 1944, MD cum laude, 1947. Diplomate Am. Bd. Internal Medicine. Med. intern Mass. Gen. Hosp., Boston, 1947-48; asst. resident in medicine Barnes Hosp., St. Louis, 1948-49; fellow in hematology Michael Reese Hosp., Chgo., 1949-51; asst. dir. hematology research lab. Michael Reese Hosp., 1950-51; A.C.P. fellow Washington U. Sch. Medicine, St. Louis, 1951-52; USPHS spl. research fellow, 1952-53, instr. in medicine, 1952-54, asst. prof., 1954-56; assoc. prof. medicine Duke U., 1956-58; chief sect. hematology VA Hosp., Durham, N.C., 1956-58; rsch. prof. U. Tenn. Meml. Rsch. Ctr., Knoxville, 1958-79, dir., 1964-77; assoc. vice chancellor for acad. affairs Ctr. Health Scis., 1977-79; prof. medicine Coll. Medicine, Memphis, 1966-79; med. dir. Cystic Fibrosis Found., Atlanta, 1975-77; dir. div. blood diseases and resources Nat. Heart Lung and Blood Inst., NIH, Bethesda, Md., 1979-88; assoc. exec. dir. sci. affairs Am. Assn. Blood Banks, Arlington, Va., 1988-90; cons. transfusion medicine programs. Contbr. articles to profl. jours. Served with U.S. Army, 1943-45. Recipient Campbell award Yale U. Sch. Medicine, 1947, Research Career award USPHS, 1962-77. Fellow ACP; mem. Am. Soc. Clin. Investigation, Am. Soc. Hematology, Internat. Soc. Hematology, Cen. Soc. Clin. Rsch., So. Soc. Clin. Investigation, Soc. Exptl. Biology and Medicine, Am. Fedn. Clin. Rsch., Am. Assn. Blood Banks, Sigma Xi, Alpha Omega Alpha.

CHERNOW, BART, critical care physician; b. N.Y.C., June 26, 1947. BA, Queens Coll., 1968; MD, SUNY, N.Y.C., 1976. Internal medicine intern Nat. Naval Med. Ctr., Bethesda, Md., 1976-77, internal medicine resident, 1977-79; dir. rsch. dept. critical care medicine Bethesda Naval Hosp., 1981-85, head acad. affairs, 1985-86; assoc. prof. anesthesia Harvard Med. Sch., Boston, 1986-90; assoc. dir. SICU Mass. Gen. Hosp., Boston, 1986-90; prof. medicine, anesthesia and critical care Johns Hopkins U. Sch. Medicine, Balt., 1990—; physician-in-chief Sinai Hosp., Balt., 1990—; program dir. John Hopkins U./Sinai Hosp. Program in Internal Medicine, 1990—. Editor: Pharmacologic Approach to the Critically Ill Patient, 1983, 88, 94; editor-in-chief: Critical Care Medicine, 1990-97. Comdr. med. corps USNR, 1969-86. Recipient Lifetime Achievement award Am. Coll. Nutrition, 1995. Fellow ACP, Am. Coll. Critical Care Medicine; mem. Soc. Critical Care Medicine, Am. Coll. Chest Physicians (regent 1990—, pres.-elect 1995-96, pres. 1996-97). Office: Sinai Hosp Dept Medicine 2401 W Belvedere Ave Baltimore MD 21215

CHERRICK, HENRY MORTON, oral and maxillofacial surgery educator, college administrator; b. Bklyn., Dec. 4, 1939; s. Nathan and Rhoda (Karmiol) C.; m. Naomi Strichard, June 11, 1961; 1 son, Andrew. A.A., U. Fla.-Gainesville, 1961; D.D.S., Med. Coll. Va., 1965; cert. oral and maxillofacial surgery, U. Cin. Med. Ctr., 1968; M.S.D., Ind. U.-Indpls., 1970. Am. Bd. Oral Pathology. Asst. Prof. oral pathology Washington U., St. Louis, 1970-71; asst. prof. oral pathology UCLA, 1971-72, assoc. prof., 1973-77, prof., 1977-78; dean, prof. Sch. Dentistry-So. Ill. U., Edwardsville, 1978-81; dean Coll. Dentistry-U. Nebr., Lincoln, 1981-88; dean, prof. UCLA Sch. Dentistry, 1988—; cons. VA Hosp., Lincoln, 1981-88, U.S. Surgeon Gen.-USAF, Washington, 1982—. Assoc. editor: Jour. Oral Medicine, 1976—; mem. editorial bd.: Colo. Oral Cancer Bull., 1978—; contbr. chpts. to books. Advisor Los Angeles City Coll., 1977-78; com. chmn. Am. Heart Assn., Lincoln, 1983. Grantee NIH, 1979; recipient Alumni Disting. Teaching Award UCLA, 1977; Kellogg Found. fellow in internat. devel., 1984-87. Fellow Am. Coll. Dentists, Am. Soc. Oral and Maxillofacial Surgery, Am. Acad. Oral Pathology (Samuel Charles Miller Meml. award 1981), Am. Dental Assn., Internat. Coll. Dentists. Office: UCLA Sch Dentistry Los Angeles CA 90024-1668*

CHERRY, ANDREW LAWRENCE, JR., social work educator, researcher; b. Dothan, Ala., Nov. 11, 1943; s. Andrew L. Cherry and Wyalene Cain; m. Mary Elizabeth Dillon, July 16, 1988. MSW, U. Ala., Tuscaloosa, 1974; D Social Work, Columbia U., 1986. Child welfare worker Escambia County Dept. Pensions and Securities, Brewton, Ala., 1968-72; psychiat. social worker Bryce State Hosp., Tuscaloosa, 1974-79; instr. Salisbury (Md.) State Coll., 1981-85; asst. prof. Marywood Coll. Sch. Social Work, Scranton, Pa., 1986-87; prof. Barry U. Sch. Social Work, Miami, Fla., 1987—; conf. Informed Families Dade County, Miami, 1990-94, Miami Coalition for Care to Homeless, 1991-93; with drug abuse prevention program Cath. Social Svcs., Miami, 1991—, Broward Children's Svc., Ft. Lauderdale, 1992-94, The Biscayne Inst., 1994—, St. Luke's Addiction Recovery Ctr., 1996—. Author: the Socializating Instinct: Individual, Family and Social Bonds, 1994; contbr. articles to profl. jours. Scholar NIMH, 1979. Fellow Am. Orthopsychiat. Assn.; mem. NASW, Conf. Social Work Edn., N.Y. Acad. Scis. Democrat. Office: Barry U Sch Social Work 11300 NE 2nd Ave Miami FL 33161-6628

CHERRY, BARBARA WATERMAN, speech and language pathologist, physical therapist; b. Norfolk, Va., June 25, 1949; d. Robert Bullock and Dorothy Estelle (Walsh) Waterman; m. Albert Glen Cherry, Sept. 17, 1977; 1 child, Dorothy Louise. BS in Phys. Therapy, U. Fla., 1972, MA in Speech-Lang. Pathology, 1982. Lic. phys. therapist, speech and lang. pathologist, Fla.; cert. tchr., Fla. Staff phys. therapist Retreat for the Sick Hosp., Richmond, Va., 1973-75; clin. instr. in phys. therapy Sch. of Rehab. Scis., Tehran, Iran, 1975-76; staff phys. therapist Sulmaniya Hosp., Manama, Bahrain, 1976-77, Cathedral Rehab. Ctr., Jacksonville, Fla., 1978-80; staff speech-lang. pathologist S. Allen Smith Clinic, Jacksonville, 1982-87, Mt. Herman Exceptional Child Ctr., Jacksonville, 1987-91, Duval County Sch. System, Jacksonville, 1991—. Mem. Am. Speech, Lang., and Hearing Assn., Am. Phys. Therapy Assn., Phi Kappa Phi. Episcopalian. Home: 8821 Ivey Rd Jacksonville FL 32216-3369 Office: Moncrief Elem Sch 5443 Moncrief Rd Jacksonville FL 32209-3160

CHERRY, JOEL M., physician, urologist; b. Balt., June 23, 1942; s. Bernard and Dora (Summers) C.; m. Harriet Beth Sapperstein; children: Jill, Stuart. BS in Biology, George Washington U., 1964; MD cum laude, U. Md., 1968. Diplomate Am. Bd. Urology. Intern U. Md. Hosp., Balt., 1968-69; resident in surgery Sinai Hosp., Balt., 1969-70, resident in urology, 1970-73; pvt. practice Balt., 1975—; asst. dep. med. examiner State of Md., 1991-95; peer review, physician advisor DelMarVa Found.; mem. exec. com. Chesapeake Lithotripsy, 1992-94; med. dir. ContinenceCare, 1995. Contbr. articles to profl. jours. Maj. USAF, 1973-75. Mem. Am. Coll. Physician Execs., Am. Urol. Assn. (Mid-Atlantic sect.), Am. Coll. Surgeons, Md. Urologic Soc., Balt. City Med. Soc., Alpha Omega Alpha. Home: 2205 Shefflin Ct Baltimore MD 21209 Office: Ste 210 6609 Reisterstown Rd Baltimore MD 21215

CHERRY, WILLIAM BAILEY, microbiologist; b. Bowling Green, Ky., Apr. 27, 1916; s. William Bailey and Cora Belle (Gott) C.; m. Kathryn Challinor, June 17, 1944; children: Anne Carter, William Bailey II. BS in Chemistry, Western Ky. State Tchrs. Coll., 1937; MS in Bacteriology, U. Ky., 1942; PhD in Microbiology, U. Wis., 1949. Diplomate Am. Bd. Med. Microbiology. Tech., teaching asst. U. Ky., Lexington, 1939-41; bacteriologist U. Ky. Agrl. Experimental Sta., Lexington, 1941-43; teaching and rsch. asst. U. Wis., Madison, 1946-47, rsch. fellow, 1947-49; asst. prof. U. Tenn., Knoxville, 1949-51; commd. officer USPHS, Atlanta, 1951-81; retired USPHS, 1981, with rsch. tng. and diagnosis depts. Ctr. Disease Control, 1951-81; cons. clin. microbiology St. Mary's Hosp., Knoxville, Tenn., 1950-51; adj. prof. Ga. State U., Atlanta, 1970-81. Contbr. numerous articles to profl. jours. Lt. USNR, 1943-46. Decorated D.S.M., USPHS; recipient Kimble award State Lab. Dirs., 1967. Fellow Am. Acad. Microbiology; mem. APHA (lab. sect.), AAAS, Am. Soc. Microbiology (sec., vice chmn., chmn. divsn. med. microbiology and immunology 1967-70, Becton-Dickinson award 1982), Sigma Xi. Democrat. Unitarian. Home: 1484 Brianwood Rd Decatur GA 30033-1741

CHERVENAK, FRANCIS ANTHONY, obstetrician and gynecologist; b. Newark, Dec. 20, 1953; s. Francis and Jody (DiGiacomo) C.; B.S. with highest distinction, Pa. State U., 1974; M.D., Jefferson Med. Coll., 1976. Intern, N.Y. Med. Coll., 1976-77; resident ob-gyn N.Y. Med. Coll., 1977-79, St. Luke's Med. Center, N.Y.C., 1979-81; fellow maternal-fetal medicine Yale U., 1981-83, also instr. ob-gyn Yale-New Haven Hosp., 1981-83; asst. prof. Mt. Sinai Sch. Medicine, N.Y.C., 1983-86; assoc. prof. Cornell Med. Ctr., 1987-92, prof. 1993—. Fellow Am. Coll. Obstetricians and Gynecologists (jr.); mem. AMA, Soc. Perinatal Obstetricians (asso.), Am. Inst. Ultrasound in Medicine, Alpha Omega Alpha. Roman Catholic. Contbr. articles and abstracts to profl. jours., including New Eng. Jour. Medicine, Lancet. Home: 82 Park Pl South Orange NJ 07079-2303 Office: NY Hosp Cornell Med Ctr 525 E 68th St New York NY 10021-4873

CHERVIN, PAUL NIESEN, neurologist; b. Boston, Oct. 11, 1941; s. Albert and Eva (Hurwitch) C.; children: Bradford, Amy. BA, U. Vt., 1963; MD, Duke U., 1967. Diplomate Am. Bd. Pediat., Am. Bd. Psychiatry and Neurology (examiner 1989—). Intern Strong Meml. Hosp. of U. Rochester, 1967-68; resident in pediatrics Children's Hosp. Med. Ctr., Boston, 1968-70; resident in neurology Peter B. Brigham Hosp., Children's Hosp., Beth Israel Hosp., Boston, 1970-73; clin. fellow in neurology Harvard Med. Sch., Boston, 1970-73; pvt. practice specializing in neurology Woburn, Mass., 1973—; attending physician Univ. Hosp. of San Diego, 1973-76; child neurologist Children's & Adolescent's Unit, San Diego County Mental Hlth, 1975-76; attending physician VA Hosp., LaJolla, Calif., 1975-76; tchg. fellow in pediat. Harvard Med. Sch., Boston, 1968-70, instr. neurology, 1976—; clin. asst. prof. neurosci. U. Calif., San Diego, 1973-76; mem. staff Children's Hosp., Boston, Winchester Hosp., Lawrence Meml. Hosp., Medford. Lt. comdr. M.C., USNR, 1973-76. Mem. AMA, Mass. Med. Soc., Am. Acad. Neurology, Child Neurology Soc., Mass. Neurol. Assn. (pres. 1986-87). Office: 604 Main St Woburn MA 01801-2982

CHESHIRE, WILLIAM POLK, JR., neurologist; b. Richmond, Va., May 2, 1960; s. William Polk and Lucile (Geoghegan) C.; m. Doris Elisabeth Schmidt, Aug. 7, 1982; children: Elisabeth Ashley, William Polk III. AB cum laude, Princeton U., 1982; MD, W.Va. U., 1987. Diplomate Am. Bd. Psychiatry & Neurology, Nat. Bd. Med. Examiners. Intern in internal medicine W.Va. U., Morgantown, 1987-88; resident in neurology, then fellow in pain U. N.C., Chapel Hill, 1988-92; asst. prof. neurology Mayo Med. Sch., Jacksonville, Fla., 1992—; cons. in neurology Mayo Clinic Jacksonville, 1992—; vis. lectr. Wake Med. Ctr., Raleigh, N.C., 1992; faculty Neurology for the Non-neurologist, Jacksonville, 1992-95. Mem. AMA, Internat. Assn. Study of Pain (data base task force 1991), Am. Pain Soc., Am. Autonomic Soc., Am. Acad. Neurology (edn. com. 1994). Episcopal. Office: Mayo Clinic Jacksonville 4500 San Pablo Rd Jacksonville FL 32224

CHESLEY, MARTHA, nurse, nursing home administrator; b. Hanover, N.H., June 17, 1954; d. Stewart James and Velma Edith (Emerson) McConnell. Grad., N.H. Vocat. Tech., Claremont, N.H. LPN, N.H.; cert. nursing home adminstr. Nurse Hanover Terrace Health Care, Hanover, 1974-83, social worker, 1983-88; adminstr. Springfield (Vt.) Health and Rehab. Ctr., 1988—. Fellow Am. Coll. Health Care Adminstrs. (pres. Vt. chpt. 1994—, chmn. facility standards). Office: Springfield Health & Rehab Ctr 105 Chester Rd Springfield VT 05156

CHESNA-SERINO, EDNA MAE, nurse; b. Chelsea, Mass.; d. John 1st and Edna Winifred (Daly) Chesna; m. Robert E. Serino Sr., May 1, 1960; children: Robert Jr., Marie Elena, Susan Olivia. Assoc. Nursing, North Shore C.C., 1977; BSN, Salem State Coll., 1995. RN. Med./surg. nurse Mass. Soldiers Home, Chelsea, 1973-82; allergy nurse cons. Respiratory Care Physicians, Lynn, Mass., 1983-88, Allergy Assocs., Lynn, 1983-88; sch. nurse Abraham Lincoln Elem. Sch., Revere, Mass., 1988-89; adult day health nurse Cmty. Family Adult Care, Everett, Mass., 1990-91; assessment/evaluation nurse Chelsea, Revere, Winthrop Home Care, 1992-93; founder, CEO The Vital View Corp., Revere, 1983-88; clin. instr. Essex Agrl. & Tech. Inst., Danvers, Mass., 1996—; substitute sch. nurse, Winthrop and Revere, Mass. Mem. Rep. Presdl. Task Force, Washington, 1985—; treas. Friends of Revere Pub. Libr., 1993-94. Mem. Mass. Nurses Assn. (bd. dirs. 1985-86), Rotarian, Rotary (disting. svc. award 1991-94, nurse and women rep., London and Paris 1989). Roman Catholic. Office: PO Box 92 Revere MA 02151-0001

CHESNEY, CHARLES FREDERIC, biomedical executive, pathologist, toxicologist; b. Kew Gardens, N.Y., Oct. 16, 1942; s. Morris H. and Esther S. (Storch) C.; m. Patricia A. Staffeld, June 12, 1965; children: Holly Beth, Jason Alan, Amy Marie. BS, U. Wis., 1965, PhD in Med. Pathology, 1973; BS in Med. Scis. cum laude, U. Minn., Mpls., 1968; DVM cum laude, U. Minn., St. Paul, 1970. Bd. eligible Am. Bd. Vet. Pathology and Gen. Toxicology; bd. cert. in regulatory affairs R.A. Profls. Soc. Assoc. dir. drug safety Hoechst-Roussel Pharms., Bridgewater, N.J., 1974-77; dept. head toxicology rsch. Lederle Labs./Am. Cyanamid, Pearl River, N.Y., 1977-79; pres., owner P-T Cons. Assocs., Sunfish Lake, Minn., 1976—; founder, v.p., tech. dir. Xybion Med. Systems Corp., Cedar Knolls, N.J., 1979-83; mgr. rsch. and devel. Riker Pharms./3M Co., St. Paul, 1984-87; pres., chief exec. officer, corp. sec., bd. dirs. Hypertension Diagnostics, Inc., South St. Paul, Minn., 1988-95; v.p., chief ops. officer M-T Venture Capital Funds., Inc., Mpls., 1989-91; also bd. dirs., exec. v.p. and chief technology officer, 1996—; bd. dirs. Enteric Products., Inc., Westbury, N.Y. Contbr. numerous sci. articles, reports, abstracts to profl. publs. and meetings. Mem. troop com., merit badge counselor Boy Scouts Am., Bridgewater, 1978-84. NIH postdoctoral rsch. fellow NIEHS, USPHS, 1970-73; Minn. Vet. Med. Assn. alumni scholar, 1966-69. Mem. Soc. Toxicology, Soc. Toxicologic Pathologists, Am. Soc. Clin. Pathologists, Am. Assn. Pathologists, Internat. Acad. Pathology, Am. Vet. Med. Assn., Am. Heart Assn., Am. Soc. Hypertension, Am. Coll. Toxicology (charter), Regulatory Affairs Profs. Soc., Internat. Soc. for Study of Xenobiotics (charter), Nat. Soc. Histotech. (charter), Gamma Sigma Delta, Phi Zeta, numerous others. Home and Office: 5 Acorn Dr Sunfish Lake MN 55077-1420

CHESSICK, RICHARD D., psychiatrist; b. Chgo., June 2, 1931; m. Marcia Chessick, Sept. 3, 1953; three children. BS, U. Chgo., 1950, MD, 1954; PhD, Calif. Coast U., L.A., 1977. Diplomate in psychiatry Am. Bd. Psychiatry and Neurology; diplomate in psychoanalysis Am. Acad. Psychoanalysis. Intern Cook County Hosp., Chgo., 1954-55; resident in psychiatry U. Ill. Rsch. and Ednl. Hosp., Chgo., 1955-58; prof. psychiatry Northwestern U., Chgo., 1960—; adj. prof. philosophy Loyola U., Chgo., 1980-87; sr. attending psychiatrist Evanston (Ill.) Hosp., 1972—; examiner Am. Bd. Psychiatry and Neurology, 1974, 76, 79, 82, 88. Author 13 books on psychoanalysis, intensive psychotherapy and philosophy; mem. editl. bd. Am. Jour. Psychotherapy, 1980—, Jour. Am. Acad. Psychoanalysis, 1992—; editor Bull. Am. Soc. Psychoanalytic Physicians, 1993—; contbr. some 200 articles to profl. jours. Surgeon USPHS, 1958-60. Fellow Am. Acad. Psychoanalysis, Am. Psychiat. Assn., Acad. Psychosomatic Medicine, Am. Orthopsychiat. Assn., Am. Soc. for Adolscent Psychiatry; mem. Am. Soc. Psychoanalytic Physicians (sec. 1993-95, pres. 1996—, German Psychoanalytical Soc. (corr.). Office: 9400 Drake Ave Evanston IL 60203-1106

CHESSIE, EVELYN JANET, women's health nurse; b. Ft. Monmouth, N.J., Apr. 2, 1963; d. David C. Sr. and Janet E. (Jussen) Quintero; m. James C. Chessie, Sept. 5, 1988. BSN, Molloy Coll., Rockville Centre, N.Y., 1985. Cert. flight nurse. Staff nurse USAF, Rome, N.Y., 1985-90; staff nurse CN III St. Francis Hosp., Roslyn, N.Y., 1990-92; perinatal nurse Healthdyne, 1992—. Capt. USAFR, 1991-92, Desert Storm.

CHESSLER, RICHARD KENNETH, gastroenterologist, endoscopist; b. N.Y.C., Apr. 6, 1944. BS, Fairleigh Dickinson U., Rutherford, N.J., 1965; MD, Chgo. Med. Sch., 1969. Diplomate Am. Bd. Internal Medicine and Gastroenterology. Asst. chief gastroenterology Englewood Hosp., N.J., 1982—, chief endoscopy, 1992-96. Author: Chemical Technicians Ready Reference Book, 1996; mem. editl. bd. Practical Gastroenterology, 1977—. Fellow Am. Coll. Gastroenterology (bd. govs. 1989). Office: 1555 Center Ave Fort Lee NJ 07024

CHESTER, ALEXANDER CAMPBELL, III, physician; b. N.Y.C., Dec. 21, 1947; s. Alexander C. II and Gladys (Edelhauser) C.; m. Kimberly Robinson Chester, Dec. 20, 1970; children: Kristin Elizabeth, Alexander C. IV. BS cum laude, Georgetown U., 1969; MD, Columbia U., 1973. Diplomate Am. Bd. Internal Medicine, Nat. Bd. Med. Examiners. Intern Georgetown U., Washington, 1973-74, resident in medicine, 1974-76; clin. fellow in nephrology Georgetown U., 1976-77, research fellow in nephrology, 1977-78, clin. instr. medicine, 1978-80, clin. asst. prof. medicine, 1980-84, clin. assoc. prof. medicine, 1985-89, clin. prof. medicine, 1990—; govs. com. for coll. affairs Am. Coll. Physicians, 1980-90; clin. prof. medicine Georgetown U. Med. Ctr.; researcher in unexplained chronic fatigue. Contbr. articles to profl. jours. and publs. Mem. AMA, Am. Soc. Internal Medicine (alt. del. Nat. Meeting 1980), Am. Soc. Nephrology, Am. Fedn. Clin. Rsch., Hippocrates-Galen Med. Soc. (sec., treas. 1991-92, pres. 1993-94), Osler Soc. (sec., treas. 1986-88, pres. 1989-90), Nat. Kidney Found. (coun. on clin. nephrology, dialysis and tranplantation, profl. adv. bd. 1983-86, program com. ann. kidney symposium 1983-86), N.Y. Acad. Sci., Am. Soc. Hypertension, Soc. Rsch. and Edn. in Primary Care Internal Medicine, Am. Heart Assn. (coun. on kidney 1988-90), Clinico-Pathol. Soc., Am. Rhinologic Soc., Soc. Gen. Internal Medicine, Am. Soc. Tropical Medicine & Hygiene, Am. Coll. of Physicians (mem. gov.'s nominating com.), N.Y. Acad. of Scis., Soc. for the Study of Human Behavior and Evolution, Am. Acad. of Otolaryngic Allergy, Southern Med. Assn., Clinico-Path. Soc., Pavlovian Soc. N.Am., Am. Med. Writers Assn., Internat. Corres. Soc. Allergists, Assn. Medicine and Psychiatry, Phi Beta Kappa. Home: 4618 Laverock Pl NW Washington DC 20007 Office: 3301 New Mexico Ave NW Ste 348 Washington DC 20016-3622

CHESTER, THOMAS J., physician; b. Bklyn., Apr. 20, 1947; s. Benjamin J. and Helen (Weltman) C.; m. Dawn C. Bryden, June 2, 1969; children: Janet A., Joyce E. BS in Life Science, MIT, Cambridge, 1968; MD, Stanford U., Palo Alto, Calif., 1973; MPH in Epidemiology, U. Wash., Seattle, 1978. Diplomate Am. Bd. Preventive Medicine. Lt. comdr. USPHS, 1972-78; med. epidemiologist Ctrs. for Disease Control and Prevention, Atlanta, Ga., 1975-78; chief state epidemiologist Ala. Dept. Pub. Health, Montgomery, 1978-81; dir. health svcs. Conoco, Inc., Houston, 1981-88; v.p. health systems ENSR Health Scis., Alameda, Calif., 1988-90; assoc. prof., acting chmn. Pub. Health & Prevention Medicine U. North Tex. Health Science Ctr., Fort Worth, 1993-95; med. dir. preventive health Mutual of Omaha, Nebr., 1995—. chmn. editl. com. (CD-ROM) ACOEM Physician's Silver Platter-Occupational Medicine, 1994—. Fellow Am. Coll. Preventive Medicine, Am. Coll. Occupational and Environmentall Medicine, Am. Coll. Epidemiology, Am. Coll. Physicians; mem. Okla. Occupational Medicine Assn. (pres. 1986-87), Ala. Pub. Health Assn. Office: Mutual of Omaha Mutual of Omaha Plaza Omaha NE 68175

CHEUNG, AMBROSE LIN-YAU, microbiologist, researcher; b. Hong Kong, Nov. 21, 1951; came to U.S., 1972; s. Shui Leung and Shuk Ping (Cheng) C.; m. Yvonne Y., Jan. 8, 1983; children: Christopher, Hoi Wan, Ken Wan. BA, Colby Coll., 1976; MD, Northwestern U., 1980. Diplomate Am. Bd. Internal Medicine. Intern UCLA Med. Ctr., Torrance, 1980-81, residency, 1981-83, fellow, 1983-85, instr., 1985-86; rsch. assoc. The Rockefeller U., N.Y.C., 1986-89, asst. prof., 1990-95, assoc. prof., 1996—. Mem. editorial bd. Jour. Infection and Immunity, 1991—. Recipient Nat. Rsch. Svc. award NIH, 1985-86; N.Y. Heart Assn. investigator, 1990-93, Am. Heart Assn. established investigator, 1994. Mem. Am. Soc. for Microbiology. Office: Rockefeller U 1230 York Ave New York NY 10021-6307

CHEUNG, LAURENCE YUN-NIN, surgeon. MD, Nat. Defense Med. Ctr., Taipei, Taiwan, 1974. Diplomate Am. Bd. Surgery. Intern Holy Cross Hosp., 1968-69; resident in surgery Utah Med. Ctr., Omaha, 1969-73; staff Bell Meml. Hosp., Kansas City, Kans., 1973—; prof. surgery, chmn. dept. surgery U. Kans. Med. Ctr., Kansas City, Kans., 1973—. Mem. AMA. Office: U Kansas Med Ctr Dept Surg Rm 5008 Sudler 3901 Rainbow Blvd Kansas City KS 66103-7583*

CHEVALIER, ROBERT LOUIS, pediatric nephrologist, educator, researcher; b. Chgo., Oct. 25, 1946; s. Frank Charles and Marion Helen (Jahnke) C.; m. Janis Julia Slezak, Dec. 23, 1970; 1 child, Juline Arianne. BS, U. Chgo., 1968, MD, 1972. Diplomate Am. Bd. Pediatrics, Bd. Pediatric Nephrology. Pediatric resident U. N.C., Chapel Hill, 1972-75, postdoctoral fellow, 1975-77; nephrology fellow U. Colo., Denver, 1977-78; asst. prof. U. Va., Charlottesville, 1978-83, assoc. prof., 1983-88, prof., 1988—, chief pediatric nephrology, 1978-91, vice chmn. pediatrics, 1988—, Genentech prof., 1993—; established investigator Am. Heart Assn., 1983-88. Mem. editl. bd. Renal Failure, 1988—, Pediatric Nephrology, 1995—; contbr. numerous articles to profl. jours., chpts. to books. Chmn. med. adv. bd. Nat. Kidney Found. Va., Richmond, 1986-89. Fellow Am. Acad. Pediatrics; mem. Am. Pediatric Soc., Am. Physiol. Soc., Am. Soc. Nephrology, Am. Soc. Pediatric Nephrology (pres. 1991-92), Am. Bd. Pediatrics, Soc. Pediatric Rsch., So. Soc. Pediatric Rsch. (pres. 1990-91). Office: Univ Va Dept Pediatrics Box 386 Charlottesville VA 22908

CHEVES, HARRY LANGDON, JR., physician; b. Birmingham, Ala., Oct. 17, 1924; s. Harry Langdon and Myrtle (Churchill) C.; A.B., Mercer U., 1949; M.D., Med. Coll. Ga., 1953; m. Lois Rebecca Corry, Dec. 25, 1949; children: Rebecca Churchill, Harry Langdon III; m. 2d, Mary Agnes Moon; 1 son, Harry Michael. Intern, Univ. Hosp., Augusta, Ga., 1953-54; practice medicine, East Point, Ga.; mem. staff S. Fulton Hosp., chief of staff, 1980-81; bd. dirs. South Fulton Med. Ctr. Served with USAAF, 1942-46. Fellow Internat., Am. colls. angiology; mem. Royal Soc. Health, AMA, So. Med. Assn., Med. Assn. Atlanta, Atlanta, So. Dist. (past pres.) med. socs., Am. Geriatric Soc., Med. Assn. Ga., Ga. Heart Assn., Phi Delta Theta. Clubs: Am. Antique Automobile, Classic Car Club Am., Packard Automobile Classics, Rolls-Royce Am., Rolls-Royce Owners, Model A, Chrysler Restorers. Home: 333 Plantation Cir Riverdale GA 30296-1106 Office: 1136 Cleveland Ave Ste 400 East Point GA 30344-3618

CHEVRIER, JEAN-MARC, psychologist, publisher, author; b. Chénéville, Que., Can., Mar. 2, 1916; s. Joseph H. and Olevina (Mallette) C.; m. Madeleine Bourassa, Jan. 4, 1941; children: Marie-Paule Chevrier, Marcel, Claudette Chevrier Quintal, Madeleine Chevrier Taylor, Robert. B.A., U. Montreal, 1938, high sch. tchr. diploma, 1939, lic. sc. ped., 1942, Ph.D. (Psychology), 1949; Didactic psychoanalysis, 1958; post doctoral studies, U. Iowa Hosp. Sch. for Severely Handicapped Children, 1953, U. Calif. Lawrence Hall of Sci., Berkeley, 1970, U. Minn., 1986. Diplomate in counselling psychology (bd. dirs.) Am. Bd. Examiners in Profl. Psychology; lic. psychologist. Tchr. Noranda (Que.) High Sch., 1940-42; prof., dir. studies Arts and Crafts Sch., Octave-Cassegrain, 1942-47; founder and dir. guidance Provincial Govt. Que., 1947-53; prof. U. Montreal, 1950-62; dir. psychology dept. Rehab. Inst. Montreal, 1953-62; dir. guidance Montreal Cath. Sch. Bd. Commn., 1962-64; pres., dir. gen. Inst. Psychol. Rsch., inc., Montreal, 1964—; exec. dir. U. Montréal, Montreal, 1968—; v.p. Centre de Psychologie et de Pédagogie, 1945-47. Author numerous sci. papers, textbooks and psychol. tests. Recipient Silver medal Surintendant l'Instruction publique, 1939, Bronze medal for svc. to graphic arts Province of Que., 1958, award Edn. Coun. of Graphic Arts Md., U.S., 1960, Cert. of Honor Assn. of Hong Kong Overseas Psychologists, 1979, Corp. award Profl. Corp. of Guidance Counsellors of Que., 1990, Distinction in psychometry from psychology profs. of U. Montreal, 1992. Mem. APA (life), NSTA (life), ACFAS l'Assn. des Psychologues de Que. (past pres.), Order Psychologists Province Que., Can. Psychol. Assn. (life), Am. Bd. Examiners in Profl. Psychology (emeritus), Psychologists Interested in Religious Issues, Nat. Coun. on Psychol. Aspects of Disability, Order Guidance CFounsellors Que., Can. Guidance and Counseling Assn. (life, Resources and Tng. Material award 1991), Ont. Sch. Counselors Assn. (Frank Clute award 1991), Ont. Psychologists Assn. (hon. life), Union des Écrivans Québécois. Home: 524 De Marigny, Laval-des-Rapides, Ville de Laval, PQ Canada H7N 5A3 Office: 34 Fleury St W, Montreal, PQ Canada H3L 1S9

CHEW, KEITH ELVIN, health facility administrator; b. Webb City, Mo., Jan. 1, 1957; s. David Elvin and Melinda Lou (Barker) C. BS in Physiology with distinction, U. Ill., 1979, MS in Biol. Sci., 1981, postgrad., 1981-83; MA in Health Svc. Adminstrn., Sangamon State U., Springfield, Ill., 1986. Instr. Sangamon State U., 1985-86; program dir. So. Ill. U. Sch. Medicine, Springfield, 1984-86; dir. bus. and clin. affairs Tex. Tech Health Sci. Ctr., Lubbock, 1986-88; cons. Profl. Cons. Svcs., Long Grove, Ill., 1988-90; adminstr. Primary Care Family Ctr., Libertyville, Ill., 1988-90; instr. Coll. St. Francis, Joliet, Ill., 1991; adminstr. North Suburban Clinic, Skokie, Ill., 1990-91; cons. KEC Healthcare Mgmt. Cons., Forest Lake, Ill., 1991-92; dir. practice mgmt. Contemporary Mgmt. Assocs., Inc., Portsmouth, N.H., 1992-95; exec. dir. Network, Health Mgmt. Ltd. Partnership-Drs. Hosp., Springfield, 1995—. Author reports and articles. Mem. Am. Coll. Med. Group Adminstrs. (cert. med. practice exec. 1994), Med. Group Mgmt. Assn., Healthcare Fin. Mgmt. Assn., Chgo. Health Exec. Forum. Home: 235 Eagle Ridge Chatham IL 62629

CHEW, THERESA TAI NGOR, optometrist; b. Hong Kong, Apr. 12, 1964; came to the U.S., 1968; d. Pui Wan and Shun Chuk (Chan) C. BA, U. Calif., Berkeley, 1986; D in Optometry, Pacific U., 1991. Registered optometrist. Optometric asst. West County Optometry, Richmond, Calif., 1991-92; optometrist Visioncare Calif., Antioch, 1992-93, Eyexam 2000, San Francisco, 1992—, East Bay Vision Ctr., Oakland, Calif., 1992-95; owner, optometrist Crystal Clear Vision Ctr., San Francisco, 1995—. Mem. Am. Optometric Assn. (contact lens sect.), Calif. Optometric Assn., San Francisco Optometric Assn., Bay Area Optometric Assn. Office: Crystal Clear Vision Ctr 781 Vallejo St San Francisco CA 94133

CHEY, WILLIAM YOON, physician; b. Ki Jang, Korea, Jan. 21, 1930; s. Kee Bok and Myungkwon (Lee) C.; m. Fan K. Tang, May 21, 1959; children: William D., Donna C., Richard D., Laura C. M.D., Seoul (Korea) Nat. U., 1953; M.Sc., U. Pa., 1962, D.Sc., 1966. Intern, N.Y.C. Hosp., 1954-55, resident, 1955-56; resident in pathology Mount Sinai Hosp., N.Y.C., 1956-57; fellow Seton Hall Med Coll., Jersey City, 1957-58; practice medicine specializing in gastroenterology Phila., 1967-71; attending physician Temple U. Med Center, Phila., 1963—; rsch. fellow Samuel S. Fels Rsch. Inst., 1959-60; rsch. assoc. Samuel S. Fells Rsch. Inst., 1961, instr. medicine, 1961, assoc., 1963, asst. prof., 1965-68, assoc. prof., 1968-71; prof. medicine U. Rochester, N.Y., 1971-77; clin. prof. U. Rochester, 1977-88, prof. medicine, 1988—; sr. attending physician, founding dir. Isaac Gordon Ctr. for Digestive Diseases and Nutrition, The Genesee Hosp., 1971-91; dir. divsn. gastroenterology and hepatology U. Rochester Sch. Medicine and Dentistry, 1992—; physician Strong Meml. Hosp., Rochester, 1992—; founding dir. William B. and Sheila Konar Ctr. for Digestive Liver Disease, Rochester, 1995—; cons. gastroenterologist Canandaigua (N.Y.) VA Hosp., 1977—; hon. prof. Catholic U. Med. Coll., Seoul, Korea, 1983; clin. prof. medicine Yunsei U. Sch. Medicine, Seoul, Korea, 1984; vis. prof. Peking Union Med. Coll., Beijing, Chinese Acad. Med. Scis., Beijing, 1985, Hallym U. Coll. of Medicine, Choonchun, Korea, 1986, Shanghai (People's Rep. China) Med. U., 1987, Korea U. Coll. Medicine, Seoul, 1991; mem. surgery and bioengring. study sect. Nat. Inst. of Diabetes, Digestive and Kidney Diseases, NIH, Bethesda, Md., 1982-86. Contbr. articles to profl. and sci. jours and textbooks; mem. editorial bd. The Pancreas, Internat. Jour. Pancreatology. Fellow Am. Coll. Gastroent.; mem. AAAS, Am. Fedn. Clin. Rsch., Am. Gastroent. Assn., Am. Physiol. Soc., Am. Assn. Study Liver Disease, Am. Pancreatic Assn., Am. Motility Soc., Am. Soc. Gastrointestinal Endoscopy, Am. Soc. Acupuncture, Am. Coll. Acupuncture, Sigma Xi. Office: 601 Elmwood Ave Rochester NY 14642-0001

CHEZ, NANCY LYNN, critical care and emergency nurse; b. L.A., Sept. 30, 1957; d. Ronald August Chez and Doris Suzanne (Feder) Walsh. BSN, Georgetown U., 1979; MA, NYU, 1985, ANP, 1996. RN, N.Y.; cert. instr. ACLS, cert. provider pediatric advanced life support, cert. instr. trainer BCLS, Am. Heart Assn.; cert. instr. trauma nurse core curriculum. Staff nurse med.-surg. unit N.Y. Hosp., N.Y.C., 1979-82, staff nurse med. special care unit, 1983-87, clin. instr. emergency dept., 1987-96; critical care and emergency nurse Project Samaritan, Bronx, 1996—. Mem. AACN (CCRN), Emergency Nurses Assn. (cert.), Nat. Nursing Staff Devel. Assn. Office: Project Samaritan NY Hosp Dept Nursing Edn 1401 University Ave Bronx NY 10452

CHEZMAR, JUDITH LYNN, physician; b. Plainfield, N.J., Feb. 18, 1955; d. William Michael and Elizabeth (Onder) C.; m. Stephen Clyde Redd, May 2, 1987; 1 child, William Chezmar Redd. AB in Biology, Princeton U., 1977; MD, U. Cin., 1981. Diplomate Am. Bd. Radiology. Asst. prof. Emory U. Sch. Medicine, Atlanta, 1988-94, assoc. prof., 1994—. Office: Emory Univ Hosp Dept Radiology 1364 Clifton Rd Atlanta GA 30322

CHI, MYUNG SUN, nutritional biochemist; b. Ik-San, Cheon Buk, Republic of Korea, Sept. 28, 1940; came to U.S., 1969; s. Won K. and Soon R. (Lee) C.; m. Eun J. Kim, June 13, 1970; children: Linda, Carolyn. BS, Kon Kuk U., Seoul, Republic of Korea, 1966; PhD, U. Minn., 1975. Rsch. assoc. U. Minn., Mpls., 1974-77; asst. prof. Alcorn State U., Lorman, Miss., 1977-81; assoc. prof. Lincoln U., Jefferson City, Mo., 1981-88, prof., 1988—; panelist AID gen. agrl. tng. program S.E. Consortium for Internat. Devel., Jefferson City, 1990—. Consulting editor Nutrition Rsch., 1986—; contbr. over 34 articles to profl. publs. Dir. Korean Inst. of Minn., Mpls., 1976-78, Mid-Mo. Korean Inst., Columbia, 1982-89; lay leader Minn. Korean Meth. Ch., Mpls., 1976-78; mem. adminstrv. bd. 1st United Meth. Ch., Jefferson City, 1985—. Recipient Outstanding Rsch. Paper awards 3d Biennial Rsch. Symposium, Atlanta, 1980, 4th Biennial Rsch. Symposium, Orlando, Fla., 1982; grantee FDA, Washington, 1974-79, USDA, Washington, 1978-83, 82-87, 87-90, 87-92, 92-97, 94-97. Mem. Am. Inst. Nutrition, Am. Heart Assn., Am. Assn. Clin. Chemistry, Internat. Soc. Study Fatty Acid Lipid. Home: 917 Airview Dr Jefferson City MO 65109-0626 Office: Lincoln U Human Nutrition Lab Jefferson City MO 65101

CHIACCHIERINI, RICHARD PHILIP, healthcare consultant; b. Elmira, N.Y., Mar. 21, 1943; s. Frank Andrew and Grace Rose (Spallone) C.; m. Kathleen Doris O'Grady, Aug. 14, 1965; children: Paul Thomas, Lisa Marie. BS, St. Bonaventure U., 1965; MES, N.C. State U., 1967; PhD, Va. Tech. Inst., 1973. Jr. statistician bioeffects div. Nat. Ctr. Radiol. Health, Rockville, Md., 1967-72; chief stats. sect. Office Radiation Programs EPA, Washington, 1972-73; sr. statistician epidemiol. studies br. BRH Bur. Radiol. Health-FDA, Rockville, Md., 1973-79, chief stats. sect., 1979-83; chief ionizing rad. and statis. br. FDA, Rockville, Md., 1982-84, chief stats. br. Ctr. Devices and Radiol. Health, 1984-85, dir. biometric sci. divsn., 1985-94; v.p. for statis. svcs. C.L. McIntosh and Assocs., Inc., 1994—; chief scientist USPHS Commd. Corps, Rockville, 1987-91; chair UPSHS Epidemiol. Tng. Commn., Bethesda, Md., 1989-92. Mem. editl. bd. Statistics in Medicine, 1991-96. Chmn., bd. dirs. Bennington, Gaithersburg, Md., 1978. Capt. USPHS, 1967—. Recipient Exemplary Svc. medal Surgeon Gen. USPHS, 1990, Outstanding Svc. medal, 1987, Commendation medal, 1987, 91, Citation, 1985, 87. Mem. AAAS, Am Statis. Assn., Biometrics Soc., Commd. Officer Assn. (bd. dirs., chmn. 1991—), Phi Kappa Phi. Roman Catholic. Office: C L McIntosh and Assocs Inc Ste 625 12300 Twinbrook Pky Rockville MD 20852

CHIAFFITELLI, JOHN J., osteopath, chiropractor; b. Bklyn., Dec. 10, 1960. BA in Psychology, U. Okla., Norman, 1987; DO, U. Okla., Tulsa, 1995; D Chiropractic, Palmer Coll. Chiropractic, Davenport, Iowa, 1991. Pvt. practice, Oklahoma City, 1995—. Mem. Okla. Chiropractic Assn. Office: Total Health Care Clinic 5835 S Pennsylvania Oklahoma City OK 73119

CHIANG, CHENG-WEN, internal medicine educator, physician; b. I-Lan, Taiwan, Oct. 24, 1943; s. Are-Jee (Yuh) C.; m. Yang Mei-Yu Chiang, Nov. 8, 1972; children: Chiang Yih-Shien, Chiang Yih-Tsung. MD, Nat. Taiwan U., Taipei, 1971. Intern Nat. Taiwan U. Hosp., 1970-71, resident dept. internal medicine, 1972-75; lectr. Chang Gung Meml. Hosp., Taiwan, 1979-82, assoc. prof., 1982-88, dir. CCU, 1987-92; prof. internal medicine Chang Gung Coll. of Medicine and Tech., Taiwan, 1989—; dir. 1st cardiovascular divsn. Chang Gung Med. Coll., Taiwan, 1992—; vis. physician Case Western Reserve U., Cleve., 1981. Editor Jour. of Ultrasound in Medicine of the Republic of China, 1987-92, Acta Cardiologica Sinica, 1987-93; chief editor Chang Gung Medical Jour., 1990—. Recipient Cheng-Hsing Med. award Med. Assn. Taiwan, 1979; Internat. scholar Cleve. Clinic, 1982; rsch. fellow Johns Hopkins Hosp., Balt., 1982. Fellow Sci. Coun. Internat. Coll. Angiology, Am. Coll. Chest Physicians; mem. Soc. Ultrasound in Medicine Republic of China (standing supr. 1992-94, chmn. med. consultation com. 1992-94, pres. 1994—), Western Pacific Assn. Critical Care Medicine Taiwan (bd. dirs., chmn. edn. com. 1992-94), Republic of China Soc. Cardiology (bd. dirs., chmn. Preventive Cardiology com. 1993-95, v.p. 1995—). Office: Chang Gung Coll Medicine & Tech, Taipei 10591, Taiwan

CHIAPELLA, ANNE PAGE, epidemiologist; b. Oakland, Calif., Oct. 12, 1942; d. Karl Josef and Anne Elizabeth (Gorrill) C. BA in Polit. Sci., Stanford U., 1964, PhD in Neurosci., 1982, MS in Stats., 1985; MPH in Epidemiology, Johns Hopkins U., 1986. Med. rschr. Stanford (Calif.) U., 1966-75, postdoctoral fellow, 1983-85; postdoctoral fellow Johns Hopkins U., Balt., 1986-88; program officer Inst. Medicine NAS, Washington, 1989-91; sr. analyst Nat. Inst. on Alcohol and Alcohol Abuse, Rockville, Md., 1991—; statis. and intellectual property cons. various orgns., Washington, 1983—. Writer humorous, tech. and travel speeches, 1985—; reviewer grants and sci. jours., 1992—; contbr. articles to sci. jours. Pres. Nebr. Ave. Neighborhood Assn., Washington, 1987-91; assoc. Smithsonian Instn., Washington, 1987—; active in Friends of Kennedy Ctr., Washington, 1987—, Friends of Nat. Zoo, Washington, 1987—, Textile Mus., Washington, 1986—. Grantee and fellow NIH, 1975, 77, 83, 86; grantee Environ. Health Sci. Ctr., 1986. AAAS, APHA, Soc. Epidemiologic Rsch., Toastmasters Internat. (officer 1987-89). Home: 5126 Nebraska Ave NW Washington DC 20008-2047

CHIAPPONE, ROBERT CARL, orthodontist; b. Fresno, Calif., May 4, 1938; s. Carlo Paul and Clotilda Elena (Gaiato) C.; children: Tracy, Christopher, Cary, Craig. BA, U. Calif., Berkeley, 1960; DDS, U. Calif., San Francisco, 1966. Pvt. practice Concord, Calif., 1966—. Contbr. articles to profl. jours. Republican. Home: 1266 Panorama Dr Lafayette CA 94549 Office: 1003 Willow Pass Rd Ste 201 Concord CA 94520-5817

CHIARAMONTE, JOSEPH SALVATORE, allergist, educator; b. Bklyn., Mar. 30, 1938; s. Joseph I. and Concetta (Tuttolomondo) C.; m. Lucy Conte, Sept. 3, 1961; children: Joseph Vincent, Andrea Concetta. BS, L.I. U., 1960; MD, U. Padua, Italy, 1965. Diplomate Am. Bd. Pediatrics, Am. Bd. Allergy and Immunology. Intern Bklyn.-Cumberland Med. Ctr., 1966; resident Brookdale Hosp. and Med. Ctr., 1967-68; fellow in allergy and clin. immunology L.I. Coll. Hosp., Bklyn., 1970-71; practice medicine specializing in allergy and clin. immunology Bay Shore, N.Y., 1971—; mem. staff Good Samaritan Hosp., also co-dir. Cystic Fibrosis Ctr., dir. Chronic Childhood Asthma Ctr., Pediatric Ambulatory Svcs., Family Asthma/Allergy Ctr.; asst. prof. clin. pediatrics Stony Brook U., N.Y.C., 1975—; adj. assoc. prof. pediatrics N.Y. Med. Coll. Osteo. Medicine. Capt. USAF, 1969-70. Fellow

Am. Assn. Cert. Allergists, Am. Acad. Allergy, Am. Acad. Pediatrics, Am. Coll. Chest Physicians, Am. Coll. Allergists; mem. AMA, Suffolk County Med. Soc., Nassau-Suffolk County Med. Soc., Nassau-Suffolk Allergy Soc., Suffolk County Pediatric Soc., N.Y. Trudeau Soc., Phi Sigma. Home: 2 Southwood Ct Bay Shore NY 11706-7738 Office: 649 W Montauk Hwy Bay Shore NY 11706-8222

CHIASSON, GABE MICHAEL, health care management consultant; b. Washington, Dec. 30, 1953; s. Wilfred Gabe and Olive Cecilia (Smith) C.; m. Sheryl Ann Cohn, Nov. 1, 1986; children: Basil Gabriel, Avery Raphael. BA, U. Md., 1975; MBA, Temple U., 1977, JD, 1989. Bar: Pa. Chief application and award sect. Nat. Health Svc. Corps Scholarship Program, Hyattsville, Md., 1978-80; asst. to the assoc. hosp. dir. USPHS Hosp., Staten Island, N.Y., 1980-81; mgr. dental health ctr. Thomas Jefferson Univ. Hosp., Phila., 1982-85; exec. v.p. DataMed Mgmt. Systems, Inc., Vienna, Va., 1985-86; dir. fin. and ops. Health Ptnrs. of Phila., 1986-91; sr. assoc. McManis Assocs., Inc., Washington, 1992—. Home: 11206 Bybee St Silver Spring MD 20902-3206 Office: McManis Assocs Inc 2000 K St NW Ste 300 Washington DC 20006-1809

CHIAZZE, LEONARD, JR., biostatistician, epidemiologist, educator; b. Falconer, N.Y., June 19, 1934; s. Leonard and Jennie (Bondi) C.; m. Ellen Anne Bergman, June 12, 1954; children: Kathleen, Caroline, Michael, Ellen. A.A. SUNY, SUNY, Jamestown, 1953; B.S., U. Buffalo, 1955, M.B.A., 1957; Sc.D., U. Pitts., 1964. Instr. stats. U. Buffalo, 1955-57; biostatistician Nat. Cancer Inst., Bethesda, Md., 1957-66, acting chief biometry br., 1975-76, dir. div. occupl. health studies, 1994—; dir. div. biostats. and epidemiology Georgetown U. Sch. Medicine, Washington, 1955-94, asst. prof., 1966-69, assoc. prof., 1969-77, prof., 1977—, dir. grad. program in biostats., 1970-94, dir. divsn. occupational health studies, 1994—. Contbr. articles to profl. jours. Served with USPHS, 1957-66. Fellow Am. Coll. Epidemiology, Am. Pub. Health Assn.; mem. Am. Statis. Assn., Soc. Occupational and Environ. Health (past pres. governing coun.), Soc. Epidemiologic Rsch., Internat. Epidemiol. Assn., Internat. Assn. Sci. Study Population, Population Assn. Am., Assn. Tchrs. Preventive Medicine, Sigma Xi; mem. Beta Gamma Sigma. Home: 11237 Waycross Way Kensington MD 20895-1034 Office: Georgetown U 3750 Reservoir Rd NW Washington DC 20007-2111

CHICKADONZ, GRACE HARLOW, dean, nursing educator. BSN, U. Kans., 1958; MS, U. Md., 1968, PhD, 1974; attended, Inst. Edn. Mgmt., Harvard U., 1985. Staff nurse U. Kans. Med. Ctr., Kansas City, 1958-59; instr. Enid (Okla.) Gen. Hosp. Sch. Nursing, 1959-61; staff nurse grants N.Mex. State Health Dept., 1961-63; staff nurse Arlington (Va.) County Health Dept., 1963-64; asst. prof. nursing Georgetown U., Washington, 1967-78; Robert Wood Johnson nurse faculty fellow in primary care U. Md., Balt., 1978-79, dir. nursing practice, psychophysiology clinic, dept. psychiatry, 1979-80; dean, prof. nursing Med. Coll. Ohio, Toledo, 1979-87, Syracuse (N.Y.) U., 1987—; designer plan Ohio Commn. on Nursing Implementation Project, 1981-82; vice chancellor for health affairs' com. Deans and Dirs. of Baccalaureate Programs Rev. Com., 1981-86; pres. Ohio Coun. of Deans and Dirs. of Baccalaureate Programs and Grad. Programs, 1986-87; mem. N.Y. State Health Task Force, 1988; mem. statewide planning com. N.Y. State Legis. Nurse of Distinction Program, 1988-93; accreditation site visitor Calif. State U., Dominguez Hills, 1989; presenter in field. Contbr. articles to profl. jours. Mem. Cradle-to-Kindergarten Health Subcom., 1988-89, mem. task force and steering com., 1989-90; chair health care adv. com. Loretto Geriatric Ctr., 1989—, also mem. med. adv. com., bd. trustees; mem. long term care task force Ctrl. N.Y. Health Sys. Agy., 1989—, mem. capital investment com., 1989-92, mem. regional maternal and newborn svc. adv. com., 1990-92; mem. infant mortality coalition Women's Commn., Syracuse, 1990-94, mem. health task force, 1990-94; bd. dirs. Boys and Girl's Club of Syracuse, 1990—, mem. pers. com., 1991—, mem. pub. rels. com., 1991, mem. exec. dir. search, 1993, mem. devel. officer search, 1994; organizer, co-chair Ctrl. N.Y. Com. to Establish Nurse-Midwifery Ednl. Program, 1991—. Spl. Nurse fellow NIH, 1972-74; recipient Leadership award Ohio Nurses Assn., 1984, Program Excellence award Ohio Bd. Regents, 1986-87, Disting. Alumnus award U. Kans., 1990, Martha M. Borlick award U. Md., 1990. Fellow Am. Acad. Nursing; mem. ANA, Nat. League Nursing (mem. nat. rsch. com. 1981-83, accreditation visitor 1982-89, bd. rev. 1990-93), Am. Assn. Colls. Nursing (mem. membership com. 1980-81, mem. rsch. com. 1984-86, mem. edn. and credentialing com. 1989-91), N.Y. State Nurses' Assn. (chair coun. on nursing edn. 1992—, mem. ad hoc com. on recredentialing 1993—), N.Y. State Deans and Dirs. Colls. Nursing (treas. 1990-94), Sigma Theta Tau (mem. nat. rsch. com. 1979-83, Omicron chpt. 1987—). Home: 15 Arnold Park Rochester NY 14607 also: 917 Madison Apt 2 Syracuse NY 13210 Office: Syracuse U Coll Nursing 426 Ostrom Ave Syracuse NY 13244-3240*

CHIECO, PASQUALE, research oncologist, toxicology educator; b. Bologna, Italy, Aug. 23, 1948; s. Angelo and Paola (Gentilini) C.; m. Luciana Vicini, Jan. 19, 1974; children: Angelo, Camilla, Benedetta. PhD in Biology, U. Bologna, 1974; Specialist in Histochemistry, U. Pavia (Italy), 1983. Postdoctoral scientist dept. pathology U. Tex. Med. Bd., Galveston, 1978-80; rsch. assoc. Inst. Oncology, Bologna, 1972-74, staff instr., 1974-78, rsch. scientist, 1980-85, sr. rsch. scientist, head Lab. Histochemistry, 1985—; prof. toxicology U. Bologna, 1988—; mem. Italian Bd. Biologists, 1975—. Mem. Tech. Med. Com., Emilia Region, Italy, 1986-94; v.p. Pharm. Mcpl. Co., Bologna, 1985-91; bd. dirs. Am. Cancer Co., Tex., 1979-80, Mcpl. Water and Gas Co., Bologna, 1991-94. Mem. Soc. Toxicology, Histochem. Soc., Italian Soc. Cytology (bd. dirs. 1990—). Roman Catholic. Office: Inst Oncology, Viale Ercolani 4, 40138 Bologna Italy

CHIEN, SHU, physiology and bioengineering educator; b. Beijing, June 23, 1931; came to U.S., 1954; s. Shih-liang and Wan-tu (Chang) C.; m. Kuang-Chung Hu, Apr. 7, 1957; children: May Chien Busch, Ann Chien Guider-a. MB, Nat. Taiwan U., Taipei, Republic of China, 1953; PhD, Columbia U., 1957. Instr. physiology Columbia U. Coll. Physicians & Surgeons, N.Y.C., 1956-58, asst. prof. physiology, 1958-64, assoc. prof. physiology, 1964-69, prof. physiology, 1969-88, dir. div. circulatory physiology and biophysics, 1973-88; dir. Inst. Biomed. Scis. Academia Sinica, Taipei, 1987-88; prof. bioengring and medicine U. Calif.-San Diego, La Jolla, 1988—, bioengring. group coord., 1989-94, dir. Inst. Biomed. Engring., 1991—, chmn. dept. bioengring., 1994—; chmn. adv. com. Am. Bur. for Med. Advancement in China, N.Y.C., 1991—, Inst. Biomed. Scis., Academia Sinica, Taipei, 1991—, Nat. Health Rsch. Inst., Taipei, 1991—. Editor: Vascular Endothelium in Health and Disease, 1988, Molecular Biology in Physiology, 1989, Molecular Biology of Cardiovascular System, 1990; co-editor: Nuclear Magnetic Resonance in Biology and Medicine, 1986, Handbook of Bioengineering, 1986, Clinical Hemorheology, Applications in Cardiovascular and Hematological Disease, Diabetes, Surgery and Gynecology, 1987, Fibrinogen, Thrombosis, Coagulation and Fibrinolysis, 1990, Biochemical and Structural Dynamics of the Cell Nucleus, 1990, others; contbr. more than 300 sci. articles on physiology, bioengring. and related biomed. rsch. to profl. jours. Recipient Fahraeus award European Soc. for Clin. Haemorheology, London, 1981, Melville award ASME, 1990, Zweifach award World Congress of Microcirculation, Louisville, 1991, Spl. Creativity Grant award NSF, 1985-88, Merit Grant award NIH, 1989-99. Mem. Am. Physiol. Soc. (pres. 1990-91), Biomed. Engring. Soc. (sr., ALZA award 1993), Internat. Soc. Biorheology (v.p. 1983-89), Microcirculatory Soc. (pres. 1990-91, Landis award 1983), N.Am. Soc. Biorheology (chmn. steering com. 1985-86), Fedn. Am. Socs. for Exptl. Biology (pres. 1992-93), Am. Inst. for Med. and Biol. Engring., Inst. of Medicine, U.S. Nat. Acad. Sci. Office: U Calif San Diego Dept Bioengring Mail Code 0412 La Jolla CA 92093

CHIEN, YIE W., pharmaceutics educator; b. Keelung, Taiwan, Oct. 20, 1938; came to U.S., 1967; s. Chou-lin and Ai-wen (Chen) C.; m. Margaret C. Chuang, Apr. 23, 1964; children: Steven, Linda. BSc in Pharmacy, Kaohsiung Med. Sch., Taiwan, 1963; PhD in Pharmaceutics, Ohio State U., 1972. Group leader, rsch. scientist G.D. Searle and Co., Skokie, Ill., 1972-78; sect. head Endo Lab. The Dupont Co., Garden City, N.Y., 1978-81; prof. pharmaceutics Coll. Pharmacy Rutgers U., Piscataway, N.J., 1981-86, prof. II, 1986-89, dept. chmn., 1982-88, Parke-Davis chair, 1989—; dir., founder Controlled Drug-Delivery Rsch. Ctr. Rutgers U., Piscataway, 1982—; cons. WHO, UN, 1988—; mem. editl. bd. several sci. jour., U.S., Spain, France, Taiwan, 1983—; com. of revision U.S. Pharmcopeial Conv., 1995—. Author: Novel Drug Delivery Systems, 1982, 2d rev. edit., 1992, Nasal Systemic Drug Delivery, 1989; editor: Transdermal Controlled Systemic Medications, 1987; contbr. more than 306 articles to profl. jours. Recipient Sci. and Tech. Achievement award, Bd. of Trustees award for rsch. excellence, Disting. Lecture Chair Parke-Davis Endowed chair. Fellow Acad. Pharm. Sci. Rsch./Am. Pharm. Assn., Am. Assn. Pharm. Scientists, Am. Inst. Chemists; mem. AAAS, Controlled Release Soc. (bd. dirs. 1984-87), Acad. Pharm. Rsch. and Sci., Parenteral Drug Assn., Fed. Internationale Pharmaceutique, Am. Chem. Soc. (polymeric materials scis. and engring. divsn.), Am. Assn. Coll. of Pharmacy, Am. Found. for Pharm. Edn., N.Y. Acad. Scis., Sigma Xi, Rho Chi. Office: Rutgers Univ Controlled Drug-Delivery Rsch Ctr 41-D Gordon Rd Piscataway NJ 08854-5945

CHILA, ANTHONY GEORGE, osteopathic educator; b. Youngstown, Ohio, Dec. 14, 1937; s. Paul and Anne (Jurenko) C.; m. Helen Paulick, Oct. 9, 1965; 1 child, Anne Elizabeth. BA, Youngstown State U., 1960; DO, Kansas City Coll. Osteopathy and Surgery, 1965. Assoc. prof. family medicine Mich. State U. Coll. Medicine, East Lansing, 1977-78; assoc. prof. family medicine Ohio U. Coll. Medicine, Athens, 1978-83, prof. family medicine, 1983, chief clin. research, 1982; chmn. instl. rev. bd. Ohio U., Athens, 1986-88; George C. Kozma Meml. lectr. Cleve. Acad. Osteo Medicine, 1979, Andrew Taylor Still Meml. lectr., Chgo., 1990, Sutherland Meml. Lectr., San Francisco, 1992. Contbr. numerous articles to profl. jours. Trustee Saint Vladimir's Orthodox Theol. Sem., Tuckahoe, N.Y., 1975-89; active Kootaga Area coun. Boy Scouts Am. Mem. AAAS, Am. Osteo. Assn. (Louisa M. Burns lectr. Clearwater, Fla. 1987), Am. Coll. Gen. Practitioners, Am. Acad. OSteopathy (pres. 1983-84, 85-86, Scott Meml. lectr. Kirksville, Mo. 1984, Thomas L. Northup lectr. Las Vegas 1986, Gutensohn-Denslow award 1995), Cranial Acad., N.Y. Acad. Scis., Am. Assn. Orthopaedic Medicine, Gen. Charles Grosvenor Civil War Round Table. Republican. Office: Ohio U Coll Osteo Medicine Grosvenor Hall Athens OH 45701

CHILCOTE, DALE JAMES, nursing home administrator; b. Jackson, Mich., Aug. 8, 1964; s. Paul E. and Cheryl G. (Schoettle) C. AA, Jackson Cmty. Coll., 1985; BS, Mich. State U., 1990. Lic. nursing home adminstr. Mich. Asst. adminstr. Capitol View Care Ctr., Lansing, Mich., 1992-93; adminstr. Tex. Health Enterprises, Lansing, McBain, Mich., 1993—. Mem. Am. Coll. Healthcare Adminstrs., Health Care Assn. Mich., Downtown Devel. Assn. McBain C. of C. (pres.). Office: Autumnwood of McBain 220 S Hughston St McBain MI 49657

CHILCOTE, ROBERT RALPH, pediatrician, educator; b. Cleve., Oct. 8, 1941; s. Ralph E. and Margaret A. (Fisher) C.; m. Denise Buckley; children: Kelly, Krista, Ryan, Andrew. AB, Cornell U., 1963; MD, U. Rochester, 1969. Diplomate Am. Bd. Pediatrics. Intern in pediatrics Strong Meml. Hosp. U. Rochester, N.Y., 1969-70, resident in pediatrics, 1970-71, chief resident in pediatrics, 1971-72; fellow in pediatric hematology James Whitcomb Riley Hosp. for Children Ind. U. Sch. Medicine, Indpls., 1972-75; practice medicine specializing in pediatric hematology and oncology Chgo., 1975-84; dir. div. pediatric hematology Michael Reese Hosp. and Med. Ctr., Chgo., 1975-77; co-dir. div. pediatric hematology-oncology Wyler Children's Hosp., Chgo., 1977-84; asst. prof. dept. pediatrics Pritzker Sch. Medicine U. Chgo., 1975-85; assoc. prof. pediatric hematology-oncology U. So. Calif., L.A., 1985-87; pediatric oncologist and hematologist U. Calif., Irvine, 1987-91; sect. chief hematology-oncology City of Hope Hosp., Duarte, Calif., 1991-96. Contbr. articles to profl. jours. Mem. Am. Acad. Pediatrics (sect. on oncology-hematology), Am. Cancer Soc., Am. Soc. Clin. Oncology, Am. Soc. Hematology. Home: 10 Thompson Ct Irvine CA 92612-4044

CHILD, CARROLL CADELL, research nursing administrator; b. Vicksburg, Miss., Nov. 10, 1949; s. John Clifton and Marie Adelaide (Gerwig) C.; m. Nicole Louise Child, Feb. 11, 1984; children: Dylan Christopher, Brendan Thomas. BA in Philosophy, So. Ill. U., 1972; BSN with honors, U. Calif., San Francisco, 1980; MSc with honors, San Francisco State U., 1994. RN, Calif. Nurse supr. USDA/U. Calif., Berkeley; clin. rsch. supr. drug studies unit U. Calif., San Francisco; rsch. nurse educator Stanford (Calif.) U.; clin. trials coord. Community Consortium U. Calif., San Francisco; participant, co-presenter V Internat. Conf. on AIDS, Montreal, Que., Can., 1989, VI Internat. Conf. on AIDS, San Francisco, 1990, VIII Internat. Conf. on AIDS, Amsterdam, 1992; co-presenter univ.-wide task force on AIDS conf. U. Calif., Berkeley, 1990. Contbr. to profl. jours. Mem. Internat. AIDS Soc., Assn. Nurses in AIDS Care, Assn. Rsch. Nurses.

CHILD, IRVIN LONG, psychologist, educator; b. Deming, N.Mex., Mar. 11, 1915; s. Arthur Henry and Martina Avila (Long) C.; m. Alice Dukes Blyth, Mar. 29, 1941; children: Richard Blyth, Pamela Colman (dec.). B.A., UCLA, 1935; Ph.D., Yale U., 1939. Instr. psychology Harvard U. and Radcliffe Coll., 1939-41; with Yale U., 1941—, successively Latin-Am. research fellow, asst. prof., asso. prof., prof. psychology, 1954-85, prof. emeritus, 1985—. Author: Italian or American? The Second Generation in Conflict, 1943, (with J.W.M. Whiting) Child Training and Personality: A Cross-Cultural Study, 1953, Humanistic Psychology and the Research Tradition: Their Several Virtues, 1973, (with Alice B. Child) Religion and Magic in the Life of Traditional Peoples, 1993. Mem. APA, Parapsychol. Assn., Am. Psychol. Soc., Phi Beta Kappa, Sigma Xi. Home: 2 Cooper Rd North Haven CT 06473-3001 Office: 2 Hillhouse Ave New Haven CT 06511-6814

CHILDERS, MARTIN K., osteopathic, rehabilitation physician, educator; b. Anchorage, Apr. 11, 1958. BA, Seattle Pacific U., 1980; DO, Coll. Osteo. Med. Pacific, Pomona, Calif., 1990. Diplomate Am. Bd. Phys. Medicine and Rehab. Intern Sun Coast Hosp., Largo, Fla., 1990-91; resident in phys. medicine and rehab. U. Mo., Columbia, 1991-94, asst. prof., 1994—. Office: Rusk Rehab Ctr One Hospital Dr Columbia MO 65212

CHILDERS, PERRY ROBERT, psychology educator; b. Monticello, Ky., July 17, 1932; s. Charles T. and Leva M. (Spradlin) C.; children: William Charles, Richard Calvin, Linda Louise, Leva Catherine; m. Joyce Carolyn Irby Murray, May 14, 1988. BA, U. Ky., 1958; MA (Grad. fellow), U. Ga., 1961, EdD, 1963, PhD, 1966; JD, Woodrow Wilson Coll. Law (now Ga. State U.), 1978. Lic. psychologist, Wis. Asst. prof. psychology U. Ky., 1963-65; mgmt. psychologist Rohrer, Hibler & Replogle, Atlanta, 1966-67; assoc. prof. psychology U. Fla., 1967-68, U. Wis., 1968-73; dep. supt. edn. State of La., 1973; dir. evaluation and monitoring, social and rehab. service HEW, Atlanta, after 1974; dir. quality control Social Security Adminstrn., after 1977, state program officer, 1980-88, dep. commr. Tenn. Dept. Human Services, 1979-80; dir. work programs, refugee resettlement, spl. initiatives HHS, 1988-95; prof. psychology Gulf Coast Coll., Panama City, Fla., 1995—; psychol. cons. to bus. mgmt. Commd. Ky. col., 1988. Recipient Spl. Achievement award HEW, 1976, Outstanding Performance award, 1977, 81. Mem. Am. Mem and Women Sic., N.Y. Acad. Sci., Greater Atlanta U. Ky. Alumni Assn. (pres. 1989-91), Psi Chi, Phi Delta Kappa (founding, charter mem. Jacksonville U. chpt. 1965), Phi Kappa Phi. Author publs. in field. Office: 2905 Kings Dr Panama City FL 32405-1615

CHILDRESS, BARRY LEE, child psychoanalyst; b. Chgo., Apr. 19, 1941; s. Affie Sylvester and Dorothy Mildred (Rein) C.; m. Gene Ziupsnys, June 29, 1963; children: Brett Lee, Brian Lee. BS with honors, U. Ill., 1961, MD, 1965; grad. Inst. for Psychoanalysis, Chgo., 1983. Diplomate Am. Bd. Psychiatry and Neurology. Intern Ill. Masonic Hosp., Chgo., 1965-66; resident in adult psychiatry Presbyn.-St. Lukes Hosp., Chgo., 1966-69, fellow in child psychiatry, 1971-72; dir. child psychiatry sect. Rush-Presbyn.-St Lukes Hosp., Chgo., 1975-76; mem. faculty child and adolescent psychotherapy tng. program Inst. Psychoanalysis, Chgo., 1980—, dir., 1985—, core faculty, 1985—, chmn. child and adolescent psychoanalysis program, 1987-91, dir. child clinic, 1990—, dir. clin. svcs., 1994—, Chgo. Inst. Psychoanalysis, 1991—, Barr-Harris Ctr. Study of Parent Loss, 1994—; leader clin. case conf. child psychiatry fellwos Rush Presbyn. St. Lukes Med. Ctr., 1992-95; cons. Hephzibah Children's Home Assn., Oak Park, Ill., 1984-89, adminstrv. sch. Francis W. Parker Sch. Chgo., 1993-95; lecturer Dept. Psychiarty U. Chgo., 1992—. Editor: (with Jacquelyn Sanders) Psychoanalytic Approaches to the Very Troubled Child, 1989, Severely Disturbed Youngsters-Alliances Between Therapists and Parents, 1992. Capt. USAF, 1969-71. Mem. Am. Psychoanalytic Assn., Ill. Coun. Child Psychiatry, Ill. Soc. Adolescent Psychiatry, Chgo Psychoanalytic Soc., Assn. Child Psychoanalyst, Chgo. Child Psychoanalytic Fourm. Avocations: camping, hiking, running, computer applications to psychoanalytic practice and the devel. of therapeutic nurseries. Home: 1221 N East Ave Oak Park IL 60302-1231 Office: 520 N Michigan Ave Ste 1420 Chicago IL 60611-3705

CHILDS, BARTON, retired, physician, educator; b. Chgo., Feb. 29, 1916; s. Robert William and Katherine Sayles (Barton) C.; m. Eloise L.B. MacKie, Mar. 29, 1950 (dec. 1980); children—Anne Lloyd, Lucy Barton; m. Ann E. Pulver, Dec. 1986. A.B., Williams Coll., 1938; M.D., Johns Hopkins, 1942. Successively intern, asst. resident, resident pediatrics Johns Hopkins Hosp., 1942-43, 46-48; research fellow Children's Hosp., Boston, 1948-49; Commonwealth Fund fellow Univ. Coll., London, Eng., 1952-53; mem. faculty Johns Hopkins Sch. Medicine, 1949—, prof. pediatrics, 1962—; Mem. NIH Cons. Coms., 1959-63, 63-67, 67-69, 70-74, 78—. Served to capt., M.C. AUS, 1943-46. John and Mary Markle scholar, 1953-58; Grover F. Powers Distinguished scholar, 1960-62; recipient Research Career award NIH, 1962, Meade Johnson award pediatrics, 1959, Allen award human genetics, 1974, Howland award pedicatrics, 1989. Mem. Am. Pediatric Soc., Soc. Pediatric Research, Am. Acad. Pediatrics, Am. Soc. Human Genetics, Genetics Soc. Am., Inst. Medicine, Am. Acad. Arts and Scis. Home: 1019 Winding Way Baltimore MD 21210-1232

CHILDS, DONALD RICHARD, pediatric endocrinologist; b. Chgo., Sept. 14, 1945; s. Robert Henry Edward and Doroth Jane (Mills) C.; m. Diane E. Martin, Apr. 28, 1972 (div. 1981); 1 child, Elena M.; m. Jacquelynne Celeste Bostrom, Aug. 29, 1989; stepchildren: Brandon R. Alexander, Eric T. Alexander. MD, U. Mich., 1970. Diplomate Am. Bd. Pediatrics. Intern Children's Hosp., L.A., 1970-71; resident William Beaumont Hosp., Royal Oak, Mich., 1973-75; fellow U. Calif., Davis, 1975-77; pvt. practice Riverside, Calif., 1977—. Capt. U.S. Army, 1971-73. Fellow Am. Acad. Pediatrics; mem. Am. Diabetes Assn., Calif. Perinatal Assn., Calif. Med. Assn., Endocrine Soc., Juvenile Diabetes Found. Office: Riverside Med Clinic 9041 Magnolia Ave Riverside CA 92503

CHILDS, ELAINE JARCZYNSKI, nurse educator; b. Rockledge, Fla., Aug. 14, 1957; d. Joseph Francis Jarczynski and Patricia Ann Sturrock; m. Stephen Mark Childs, Jan. 26, 1980. RN, Brevard Community Coll. Nursing, 1977; BSN, U. Cen. Fla., 1985; postgrad., U. Fla., 1991—. RN, Fla. Mgr. clin. svcs. HILL-ROM Co., Batesville, Ind., 1987—; lectr./educator on wound mgmt. and issues related to immobility. Author: (with Oscar Alvarez) Pressure Ulcers: Physical, Supportive and Local Aspects of Management, 1991. Mem. AACN, Am. Assn. Geriatric Nursing, Wound Healing Soc. (assoc.), Wound, Ostomy and Continence Nurses Soc., Sigma Theta Tau.

CHILDS, MARY ELLEN CRABTREE, occupational health nurse; b. Mobile, Ala., Oct. 11, 1940; d. Edward Beauregard and Annie Irene (Barton) O'Rourke; divorced; children: Claude Vincent, Marley Barton, Milissa Mayrene Crabtree, Mary Angelique Smith. Student, 20th Century Bus. Coll., 1960, Southwest State Coll., 1970, George Wallace Coll., 1975, U. Auburn, 1978. RN, Ala., Calif.; ACLS. Staff nurse, ICN, NBN, CCU U. South Ala., Mobile; nurse Home Health Svcs., Enterprisee, Ala.; relief house supr. Crenshaw County Hosp., Luverne, Ala.; vocat. educator practical nursing Trenholm Tech. Coll., Montgomery, Ala.; dir. insvc. edn. Wiregrass Hosp. & Nursing Home, Geneva, Ala.; psychiatric house supr. Charter Woods Hosp., Dothan, Ala.; nurse emergency rm. Edge Meml. Hosp., Troy, Ala.; nurse coronary care Flower Hosp., Dothan, Ala.; charge nurse, quality assurance Lyster Army Hosp, Ft. Rucker, Ala.; insvc. educator, house supr. Linda Vista Hosp., L.A.; supr. Edgemont Psychiat. Hosp., L.A., 1991-92; charge nurse Naval Clinic, Port Hueneme, Calif., 1992—; occupational health nurse specialist U.S. Naval Clinic, 1992-93, Woodland Community Hosp., 1993-94; occupational health nurse specialist, workers comp. claims specialist Wrangler, Inc., Oneonta, Ala., 1994—. Author: A Babe in the Woods, 1989. Instr. ARC. Mem. Ala. Nurses Assn., Am. Heart Assn. (BLS-C instr.), Tri-State Quality Assurance Assn., Ala. Safety Coun., Occpl. Health Nurse Assn., NAFE, Kiwanis Club of Ala. Home: PO Box 842 Hanceville AL 35077-0842

CHILES, ROSS PERSHING, physician; b. Aberdeen, S.D., Sept. 7, 1939; s. Albert B. and Mabel Lee (Pershing) C.; m. Sharon Kathleen Zumm, June 23, 1962; children: Bethany Kristin, Lesley Anne. Student, S.D. State U., 1957-60; BS in Medicine, U. S.D., 1962; MD, U. Mich., 1964. Diplomate Am. Bd. Internal Medicine. Resident in internal medicine Ohio State U. Hosps., Columbus, 1964-67,, 1967-69, fellow in endocrinology; pvt. practice, Austin, Tex., 1972—. Major USAF, 1969-71. Mem. AMA, Am. Assn. Clin. Endocrinologists, Tex. Med. Assn., Travis County Med. Soc., Alpha Omega Alpha. Republican. Methodist. Office: Austin Diagnostic Clinic 12221 Mopac Expwy N Austin TX 78758-2401

CHIMOSKEY, JOHN EDWARD, physiologist; b. Traverse City, Mich., Apr. 15, 1937; s. Edward John and Jane Marie (Langworthy) C.; m. Dianne Marie Dailey, June 1962 (div. 1973); children: Stefan John, David Clifford. Student, U. N.Mex., 1955-56, Cen. Mich. U., 1956-58; MD, U. Mich., 1963. Intern dept. medicine U. Calif., San Francisco, 1963-64; rsch. fellow in physiology Harvard Med. Sch., Boston, 1964-66; rsch. fellow in muscle rsch. Retina Found., Boston, 1966-67; assoc. prof. in physiology Hahnemann U., Phila., 1969-70; resident, rsch. fellow in dermatology Stanford U., Palo Alto, Calif., 1970-71; asst. prof. in bioengring. U. Wash., Seattle, 1971-74; assoc. prof. in physiology and surgery Baylor Med. Coll., Houston, 1974-78; prof. Mich. State U., East Lansing, 1978—, chairperson dept. physiology, 1989-93; adj. assoc. prof. in bioengring. Rice U., Houston, 1974-78; physiology cons. Stedman's Med. Dictionary, 1990—. Contbr. articles to Sci., Am. Jour. Physiology. Lt. comdr. USNR, 1967-69. Fulbright fellow, Brazil, 1990. Mem. Am. Physiol. Soc. Home: 643 Spartan Ave East Lansing MI 48823-3624 Office: Mich State U Dept Physiology East Lansing MI 48824

CHIN, ANGELA MERICI AUDREY, dentist; b. Mandeville, Jamaica; came to U.S., 1973; d. Lester Aubrey Donald and Jean Evelyn C. BS in Biology, Ga. Tech. Inst., 1977; DMD magna cum laude, Tufts U., 1981. Resident in gen. dentistry Queen's Med. Ctr., Honolulu, 1981-82; pvt. practice Aiea, Hawaii, 1982—; mem. Bd. of Dental Examiners State of Hawaii, 1990—; staff Queens Med. Ctr., 1982—. Mem. Aiea Pearl City Bus. Assn. Fellow Acad. Gen. Dentistry (sec. Hawaii chpt. 1984-85); mem. ADA, Hawaii Dental Assn., Honolulu County Dental Soc. (sec. 1989-90), South Shore Dental Soc., Anak, Omicron Kappa Upsilon, Omicron Delta Kappa. Office: 98-1247 Kaahumanu St Ste 103 Aiea HI 96701-5300

CHIN, CONWAY, physician; b. N.Y.C., Nov. 3, 1966; m. Kimberly Chin, June 12, 1993. BS in Engring., U. Pa., Phila., 1988; DO, U. Osteo. Medicine, Des Moines, 1992. Diplomate Am. Bd. Hypnotherapy. Intern Firelands Cmty. Hosp., Sandusky, Ohio, 1992-93; phys. medicine and rehab. resident Rusk Inst., NYU Med. Ctr., N.Y.C., 1993-96. Mem. Am. Acad. Phys. Medicine and Rehab., Am. Osteo. Coll. Rehab. Medicine, Am. Osteo. Assn., Am. Acad. Osteo., Cranial Acad.

CHIN, DAVID LEE, preventive medicine physician, air force officer; b. Pullman, Wash., May 22, 1962; s. Gat Ming and Wan Gee (Lee) C.; m. Kimnie Lee, Mar. 2, 1991; 1 child, Judah Lee. BS in Psychobiology, U. So. Calif., 1984; med. asst. diploma, Calif. Coll. Med.-Dental Careers, 1985; MD, U. Tex., Galveston, 1989; MS in Pub. Health, Meharry Med. Coll., 1993. Diplomate Am. Bd. Preventive Medicine in Pub. Health and Gen. Preventive Medicine. Lab. asst., computer data entry person Profl. Labs. Svcs., Fullerton, Calif., 1985; med. ins. examiner Meditest, Calif., 1985; commd. 2d lt. USAF, 1986, advanced through grades to maj., 1995; resident in preventive medicine Meharry Med. Coll., 1990-93; preventive medicine staff physician Wilford Hall USAF Med. Ctr., Lackland AFB, Tex., 1993—; instr. preventive medicine Trevecca Nazarene Coll., Nashville, 1992. Mem. AMA (physician's recognition award), Aerospace Med. Assn., Am. Coll. Preventive Medicine, Christian Med. and Dental Soc., U.S. Chess Fedn.

CHIN, JENNIFER YOUNG, public health educator; b. Honolulu, June 22, 1946; d. Michael W.T. and Sylvia (Ching) Young; BA, San Francisco State Coll., 1969; M.P.H., U. Calif., Berkeley, 1971; m. Benny Chin, Nov. 16, 1975; children: Kenneth Michael, Lauren Marie, Catherine Rose. Edn. asst. Am. Cancer Soc., San Francisco, 1969-70; intern Lutheran Med. Ctr., Bklyn., 1971; community health educator Md. Dept. Health and Mental

Hygiene, Balt., 1971-74; community health educator Northeast Med. Svcs., San Francisco, 1975; pub. health educator Child Health and Disability Prevention, San Francisco Public Health Dept., 1975-83; health educator maternal and child health, 1991—. USPHS grantee, 1970-71. Mem. Soc. No. Calif. Pub. Health Edn. (treas. 1976, 77), Am. Public Health Assn. Office: 680 8th St Ste 200 San Francisco CA 94103-4942

CHIN, KENNETH PAUL, optometrist; b. Kingston, Jamaica; s. Kenneth Chin. Student, U. Miami, 1986; OD, So. Coll. Optometry, 1990. Cert. AOA, HOA, FOA. Office: Ste A 1066 Alakea St Honolulu HI 96813

CHIN, LINDA G., research nurse; b. N.Y.C., July 13, 1958; d. Sing Quon and So Keen (Yee) C. BS, NYU, 1980, MA, 1982. RN, N.Y. Staff nurse, urology NYU Med. Ctr., N.Y.C., 1980, staff nurse, neurosurgery, 1982-83, sr, staff nurse neurosurgery ICU, 1983-84, sr. rsch. nurse, neurology, 1984—, study coord. neurology, 1989—, coord. Am. Parkinson's Disease Info. and Referral Ctr., 1994—. Contbr. chpt. to book, articles to profl. jours. Active Tiananmen N=Meml. Found., Chinese Festival/Garden State Arts Ctr., N.J., 1989—, sec. Concert for Democracy in China, 1990, treas., trustee, 1989—; mem. Newtown Civic Assn., Elmhurst, N.Y., 1995—; Parkinson's Disease Support Group Leader. USPHS scholar, 1980-81, SEHNAP scholar, 1978-80, Martin Luther King Jr. scholar, 1976-78, Regents scholar, 1976-80. Mem. ANA, N.Y. State Nurses Assn., Am. Parkinson Disease Assn. (coord. Walk-A-Thon 1994—, coord. nat. symposium 1995—), Assocs. of Clin. Pharmacology, Am. Assn. Neuroscience Nurses, Nat. Assn. Physician Nurses. Republican. Home: 51-31 Simonson St Elmhurst NY 11373 Office: NYU Med Ctr 530 First Ave Ste 9Q New York NY 10016

CHIN, NEE OO WONG, reproductive endocrinologist; b. Hong Kong, Nov. 27, 1955; came to U.S., 1958; s. Bing Leong and Din Sui (Gee) C.; m. Shelly Loraine Crumrine, June 25, 1977; children: Jason Lei, Taryn Mae. BA, U. Cin., 1977; MD, Ohio State U., 1981. Diplomate Am. Bd. Ob-Gyn. Resident Duke U. Med. Ctr., Durham, N.C., 1981-84; chief resident Duke U. Med. Ctr., Durham, 1984-85; fellow Ohio State U. Coll. Medicine, Columbus, Ohio, 1985-87; teaching staff Good Samaritan Hosp., Cin., 1987—; clin. asst. prof. U. Cin. Med. Ctr., 1987—; dir. assisted reproductive techs. The Christ Hosp., Cin., 1992—; mem. High Sch. for the Health Profl. subcom., Cin., 1989—. Author: (with others) Current Therapy in Obstetrics, 1988; contbr. articles to profl. jours. Named to Honorable Order of Ky. Cols., Gov. Martha Collins of Ky., 1987. Fellow Am. Coll. Ob-Gyn.; mem. AAAS, Am. Fertility Soc., Soc. Assisted Reproductive Tech., Soc. for Immunology Repro., Cin. Ob-Gyn. Soc. (med. malpractice com. 1989—), Acad. Medicine Cin. Office: The Christ Hosp 2123 Auburn Ave Ste 044 Cincinnati OH 45219

CHIN, WILLIAM WAIMAN, biomedical research scientist, physician; b. N.Y.C., Nov. 20, 1947; s. James Gampoy and Yoke Ting (Chu) C.; m. Denise Jean-Claude, Mar. 28, 1981; children: Samantha, Daniel. AB, Columbia U., 1968; MD, Harvard U., 1972. Assoc. investigator Howard Hughes Med. Inst., Boston, 1979-84, investigator, 1984-95; asst. prof. Med. Sch., Harvard U., Boston, 1981-84, assoc. prof., 1984-93; prof. Harvard U., Boston, 1993—; chief div. genetics Brigham & Women's Hosp., Boston, 1987—, sr. physician, 1991—. Lt. comdr. USPHS, 1974-76. Mem. Am. Soc. Biochemistry and Molecular Biology, Am. Physiol. Soc. (Bowditch lecture 1984), Am. Thyroid Assn. (Van Meter-USV award 1986, Ingbar award 1992, coun. mem. 1992—), Am. Soc. Clin. Investigation (coun. mem. 1988-92, v.p. 1991-92), Am. Assn. Physicians, Endocrine Soc. (coun. mem. 1989-92, Boots award 1993), Am. Fedn. Clin. Rsch. (award for clin. rsch. 1988), Interurban Clin. Club. Office: Brigham & Womens Hosp 75 Francis St Boston MA 02115-6195

CHINN, PEGGY LOIS, nursing educator, editor; b. Columbia, S.C., Feb. 25, 1941; d. Hubert R. and Margaret (Gasteiger) Tatum; m. Philip C. Chinn, June 15, 1964 (div. 1974); children: Kelleth Roger, Jonathan Mark (dec.). AA, Mars Hill Coll., 1960; BS, U. Hawaii, 1964; MS, U. Utah, 1970, PhD, 1971. From instr. to asst. prof. U. Utah, Salt Lake City, 1971-74; assoc. dir., prof. Tex. Woman's U., Denton, 1974-78; prof. Wright State U., Dayton, Ohio, 1978-81, SUNY, Buffalo, 1981-90, U. Colo., Denver, 1990—; founder, editor Advances in Nursing Sci., Rockville, Md., 1978—; cons., lectr. in field. Author: Child Health Maintenance, 1974, 2d edit., 1978, Theory in Nursing, 1983, 4th edit., 1995, Peace and Power, 3d edit., 1991; contbr. articles to profl. jours. Co-founder Cassandra: Radical Feminist Nurses Network, nationwide 1982, Margaret Daughters Inc., Buffalo, 1984. Fellow Am. Acad. Nursing (governing coun. 1987-90); mem. Am. Nurses Assn., Nat. League for Nursing, Sigma Theta Tau. Office: U Conn Nursing Health Sci Ctr 231 Glenbrook Rd. Storrs CT 06269-2026

CHIORAZZI, MARY LORRAINE, psychiatrist; b. New York. BS, Marymount Manhattan Coll., 1966; MD, Georgetown U., 1970. Diplomate Am. Bd. Psychiatry. Pvt. practice child, adolescent, adult psychiatry Englewood, N.J., 1975—. Office: 163 Engle St Englewood NJ 07631-2530

CHIOTELLIS, PHILIP NICOS, cardiologist; b. Kyrenia, Cyprus, May 31, 1942; s. Nicos Philip and Maria (Constantinides) C.; m. Lavinia Conroy; children: Nicos, Peter, Fiona. MD, Athens U., 1966. Resident in medicine N.J. Med. Sch., Newark, 1968-71; fellow in cardiology Mass. Gen. Hosp./Harvard Med. Sch., Boston, 1972-74; instr medicine Harvard Med. Sch., Boston, 1974-75; practice cardiology Boston/Cape Cod Area, 1974—; cardiologist Heart Ctr., Hyannis, Mass. Fellow Am. Coll. Cardiology, Paul Dudley Med. Soc., Algonquin Club (Boston). Office: Heart Ctr 52 Park St Hyannis MA 02601-5206

CHIRBAN, JOHN THOMAS, psychologist, theologian, educator; b. Chgo., June 24, 1951; s. Thomas Angelo and Georgia (Kappos) C.; m. Sharon Stefanov, 1992. BA, Hellenic Coll., Brookline, Mass., 1973; MDiv, Holy Cros Sch. Theology, 1975; ThM, Harvard U., 1976, ThD, 1980; PhD, Boston U., 1990. Lic. psychologist, Mass.; diplomate and fellow Am. Bd. Med. Psychotherapists. Researcher Harvard U., Cambridge, Mass., 1974-75; geriatric tng. specialist Dept. Mental Health, Boston, 1978-79; cons. Mass. Disabilities Commn., Boston, 1979-84; psychologist Andover (Mass.) Psychol. Svcs., 1986-89, Mass. Corrections Inst., Shirley, 1986-88; sr. lectr. Northeastern U., Boston, 1979—; cons. Mass. Rehab. Commn., Boston, 1980—; founder, co-dir. Cambridge Counseling Assocs., 1983—; assoc. Harvard U., Cambridge, 1980-91; co-dir. counseling and spiritual devel. Hellenic Coll. Holy Cross, 1978-95, prof., 1975—; psychologist behavioral medicine program The Cambridge Hosp. Harvard Med. Sch., 1993—; co-dir. Carlisle Counseling Assn., 1995—; prof. Hellenic Coll. Holy Cross, 1975—. Mem. APA, Mass. Psychol. Assn., Orthodox Christian Assn. Medicine, Psychology and Religion (pres.). Greek Orthodox. Home: 137 E Riding Dr Carlisle MA 01741 Office: 1105 Massachusetts Ave Apt 3E Cambridge MA 02138-5207

CHIRIBOGA, DAVID ANTHONY, pyschology educator; b. Boston, Mar. 10, 1941; s. Segundo Virgilio Vicente Chiriboga and June Lillian (Rowson) Squarebrigs; m. Kikue Suzuki, Mar. 15, 1980 (div. 1985); m. Barbara Wai-Kinn Yee, Mar. 25, 1986; children: Carlos Daniel, David Anthony II. AB, Boston U., 1964; PhD, U. Chgo., 1972. Asst. to assoc. prof. U. Calif., San Francisco, 1974-85; vis. prof. U. Calif., Davis, 1983-85; dir. for research Ctr. on Aging Univ. Calif., Davis, 1983-85; dir. Gerontology Ctr. San Jose (Calif.) State U., 1985-86; assoc. prof. to prof. U. Tex., Galveston, 1986—, chair dept. health promotion and gerontology Med. Br., 1988—; cons. dept. cmty. health, U. Calif., Davis, 1985-88; bd. dirs. Coordinating Ctr. on Aging, Med. Br., U. Tex., Galveston, 1987-91, assoc. dir., 1993—. Author: (with M. Fiske) Change and Continuity in Adult Life, 1990, (with others) Four Stages of Life, 1975, Divorce: Crisis, Challenge or Relief?, 1991; mem. editl. bd. Generation, 1983-93, Jour. Aging and Health, 1988—; contbr. articles to profl. jours. Bd. dirs. Outreach & Escort, San Jose, 1985-86, Coalition on Aging, Galveston, 1986—; exec. coun. Galveston Sr. Citizens Ctr., 1988—. Grantee NIH, 1976-91, John Sealy Found., 1988-91, Henry A. Murray Ctr., 1991-95, Bur. Health Professions, 1992—. Fellow Gerontol. Soc. Am., Am. Psychol. Assn. (pres. div. 20 1988-89); mem. Am. Soc. on Aging, Asociacion Nacional Pro Personas Mayores, Phi Beta Kappa. Democrat. Episcopalian. Home: 23 Lakeview Dr Galveston TX 77551-1563 Office: U Tex Med Br Dept Health Promotion/Geron SAHS Galveston TX 77555

CHIRICO-POST, JEANNETTE A., health facility administrator; b. N.Y.C., May 14, 1943; m. James Edward Post; children: Christopher, Margaret, Jonathan. BS in Chemistry, St. John's U., 1964; MD, Med. Coll. Pa., 1968. Diplomate Am. Bd. Electrodiagnostic Medicine, Psychiatry and Neurology, Nat. Bd. Med. Examiners. Chief electromyographic lab., asst. chief of staff VA Med. Ctr., Boston, 1974-95; chief of staff VA Med. Ctr., Providence, R.I., 1995—; mem. jr. affinity group Brown U., Providence, 1995—. Mem. Am. Acad. Neurology, Am. Acad. Clin. Neurophysiology, Am. Med. Women's Assn., Internat. Soc. Quality Assurance, N.Y. Acad. Sci. Office: VA Medical Center 830 Chalkstone Ave Providence RI 02908

CHIRIGOS, MICHAEL ANTHONY, immunopharmacologist; b. Wierton, W.Va., Sept. 14, 1924; s. Anthony and Marianthi (Michallos) C.; m. Mary Lazopoulos, Sept. 19, 1954; children: Ferronia, Michael Jr., Melanie. BS, Western Md. Coll., 1952; MS, U. Del., 1954; PhD, Rutgers U., 1957; DSc (hon.), Western Md. Coll., 1972. Section chief Nat. Cancer Inst., Bethesda, Md., 1957-84; v.p. rsch. and devel. Newport Pharmaceuticals, Inc., Newport Beach, Calif., 1984-86; dep. for sci. USA Med. Rsch. Inst., Frederick, Md., 1986-91; pvt. cons. Rockville, Md., 1991—; sci. adv. bd. Am. Cancer Soc., N.Y.C., 1978-82, Newport Pharmaceuticals, Newport Beach, Calif., 1986-88. Editor Jour. Immunu Pharmacology, 1984—, rsch. books (10); assoc. editor sci. jours. (8); contbr. rsch. publs. (260). Bd. dirs. Greek Orthodox Ch., Bethesda, 1967-80, pres., bd. dirs., 1978. With USN, 1943-46, ETO. Fellow Soc. Biol. Resp. Modifiers; mem. Am. Assn. Cancer Rsch., N.Y. Acad. Sci. Home: 4 Cold Spring Ct Rockville MD 20854-2425

CHIRKINIAN, GEORGE WILLIAM, chiropractic physician; b. Richmond, Va., Sept. 21, 1947; s. George William and Frances Carolyn (Box) C.; m. Sharon Juanita Mason, June 18, 1968; children: Tara Lynn, Amanda Kay, Melanie Ann, George William. AAS, John Tyler C.C., Richmond, 1972-74; student Va. Commonwealth U., 1974-75; BS in Biology, Logan Coll., 1976, DChiropractic, 1978, cert. applied acupuncture, 1980; D.Homeopathy, Brandon (Fla.) Med. Inst., 1981-82. Physician's asst. Commonwealth of Va., 1972-75; clinic dir., instr. Logan Coll. Chiropractic, St. Louis, 1978-80; gen. practice chiropractic medicine, Richmond, 1980—; originator World Nat. Bodybuilding Fedn. Am. Chiropractic Cup. Served in M.C., USAF, 1967-71. Recipient Instr. of Yr. award Logan Coll. Chiropractic, 1980. Mem. Am. Chiropractic Assn., Va. Chiropractic Assn. (sec. 1985—, pres. 1986—, Chiropractor of Yr. 1986, lobyist to Va. Gen. Assembly), Med. Soc. Va. (mem. impaired physicians com.), Va. Bd. Medicine (mem. chiropractic test com.), Ctrl. Va. Chiropractic Soc. (pres. 1986-87), Southeastern Chiropractic Fedn., Richmond C. of C., Chi Rho Sigma. Author: Kinesiology Memory Book, 1978; editor student newspaper, 1976-78, Sherwood Forest lit. mag., 1974; contbg. author, cons. Natural Physique Mag.; contbr. articles to news jour., 1981, 82. Office: 3509 Jefferson Davis Hwy Richmond VA 23234-2146

CHISHOLM, GEORGE NICKOLAUS, dentist; b. Pullman, Wash., Sept, 21, 1936; s. Leslie L. and Lila Rene (Cates) C.; D.D.S., U. Nebr., 1960; 1 son, Andrew M. Practice dentistry, Lincoln, Nebr., 1963-83; clin. instr. Coll. Dentistry, U. Nebr., 1976-83. Mem. S.E. Nebr. Health Planning Agy., 1976-82. Served to capt. Dental Corps, USAF, 1960-63. Mem. ADA (del. 1980), Nebr. Dental Assn. (del. 1974-80, trustee 1980-83), Lincoln Dist. Dental Assn. (pres. 1979-80), Sigma Alpha Epsilon, Xi Psi Phi. Mason (32 deg., Shriner). Asst. editor Nebr. State Dental Jour., 1967-69. Home: 1735 S 38th St Lincoln NE 68506-5253

CHISHTI, ATHAR H., biochemist; b. Aligarh, India, Dec. 25, 1957; s. M. Tahir and Naim (Akhtar) Husain; m. Yasmin Qadiri, July 25, 1987; 1 child, Imran H. MSc, A.M.U., Aligarh, India, 1980, MPhil, 1980; PHD, U. Melbourne, Victoria, Australia, 1984. Postdoctoral fellow, rsch. lab. Biol. Labs. Harvard U., Cambridge, Mass., 1984-88, teaching fellow, 1986-88; asst. prof., assoc. investigator St. Elizabeth's Hosp./Tufts U. Sch. Medicine, Boston, 1988—; sci. advisor Immunetics, Inc., Cambridge, 1991—. Contbr. articles to profl. publs. Am. Heart Assn. fellow, 1987; grantee Am. Cancer Soc., 1991, NIH, 1992. Office: St Elizabeth's Hosp 736 Cambridge St Boston MA 02135-2997*

CHISOLM, JACK TAYLOR, physician; b. Birmingham, Ala., July 27, 1923; s. Joseph James and Lillie Tom (Thomasson) C.; student Samford U., 1941-43; Stanford U., 1944; M.D., U. Ala., Birmingham, 1947; m. Martha Lee Hatcher, Feb. 7, 1953; children—James Edward, John Craig, Patrick Taylor. Intern, St. Louis City Hosp., 1947-48; resident in surgery Hackensack (N.J.) Hosp., 1948-49, Scott & White Clinic, Temple, Tex., 1949-50, 53-55; pvt. practice medicine, specializing in surgery, Dallas, 1955—; mem. med. staff St. Paul Hosp., Dallas, pres. 1969; mem. med. staff, Presbyn. Hosp., Dallas, pres., 1981 . Served with AUS, 1943-45, USNR, 1951-53. Diplomate Am. Bd. Surgery. Mem. Am., Tex., So. med. assns., Dallas County Med. Soc. (pres. 1972), A.C.S., Dallas Soc. Gen. Surgeons (pres. 1983-84). Baptist. Home: 6126 Averill Way Apt 205W Dallas TX 75225-3326 Office: 8230 Walnut Hill Ln Ste 814 Dallas TX 75231-4405

CHISWICK, NANCY ROSE, psychologist; b. East Orange, N.J., May 8, 1945; d. Haim Hershel and Beatrice May (Levinson) C.; m. Arthur Howard Patterson, Aug. 5, 1973; children: Michael Chiswick-Patterson, Emily Chiswick-Patterson. AB, Smith Coll., 1966; MA, U. Ill., Chgo., 1970; PhD, U. Ill., 1973. Lic. psychologist, Pa. Intern Northwestern U. Med. Sch., Chgo., 1973; mental retardation specialist The Counseling Svc., Bellefonte, Pa., 1973-75; clin. staff psychologist Pa. State U., 1975-80; dir. clin. psychologist Child, Adult and Family Psychol. Ctr., State College, Pa., 1980—; adj. prof. psychology and human devel. Pa. State U., 1974—; mem. allied staff Ctr. Cmty. Hosp., State College, 1985—; staff Meadows Psychiat. Hosp., Centre Hall, Pa., 1985—. Creator, co-host pub. TV Series About Women, 1979-80. Del. White House Conf. Families, 1980, bd. dirs. Meadows Psychiat. Hosp., 1983-85, Jewish Cmty. Ctr., 1989-96. Named Guest in Residence W. Marlin Butts Com. Oberlin (Ohio) Coll., 1978. Fellow Ctrl. Pa. Psychol. Assn. (sec. 1987-89); mem. APA, Pa. Psychol. Assn. Home: 2443 Hickory Hill Dr State College PA 16803-3361 Office: Child Adult & Family Psychol Ctr 315 S Allen St Ste 218 State College PA 16801-4850

CHITRE, SHARADCHANDRA RAGHUNANDAN, physician; b. Pune, India, Apr. 11, 1936; came to U.S., 1968; s. Raghunandan Ballal and Sarojini C.; M.B., B.S., M.S. U., Baroda, India, 1961, M.S., 1966; m. Rekha Balkrishna Chitnis, May 6, 1961; children—Nanda, Priya, Yash. Resident in orthopedic surgery Royal Sea Bathing Hosp., Margate, Eng., 1967-68; resident in surgery Beverly (Mass.) Hosp., 1968-70, emergency physician, 1971—, chief emergency and outpatient dept., 1975-85; fellow in plastic surgery Meth. Hosp., Bklyn., 1970-71; instr. North Shore Community Coll., Beverly; former mem. state adv. bd. on emergency med. Services. Fellow Royal Soc. Health (London); mem. Mass. Med. Soc., Essex South Dist. Med. Soc., Indian Med. Assn. New Eng. (trustee), Am. Coll. Emergency Physicians, Baroda Med. Coll. Alumni Assn. (pres. 1987-90). Home: 901 Bay Rd Hamilton MA 01936-0327 Office: Parkhurst Med Bldg 75 Herrick St Beverly MA 01915-2772

CHIU, MICHAEL JOSEPH, internist; b. Midland, Mich., July 31, 1964. BS, U. Mich., 1986, MD, 1988. Diplomate Am. Bd. Internal Medicine. Intern in internal medicine U. Tex. Southwestern Med. Ctr., Dallas, 1988-89, resident in internal medicine, 1989-91, asst. prof. internal medicine, 1991—; med. dir. ambulatory care clinic Parkland Meml. Hosp., Dallas, 1991—. Author: (with others) Infectious Diseases-Hoeprich, 1994, Atlas of Infectious Diseases, 1995, Textbook of Internal Medicine, 1996. Nat. Merit scholar 1981. Fellow ACP; mem. Dallas County Med. Soc., Tex. Med. Assn. Office: Univ Tex Southwestern Med Ctr 5323 Harry Hines Blvd Dallas TX 75235-8889

CHIU, PETER YEE-CHEW, physician; b. China, May 12, 1948; came to U.S., 1965; naturalized, 1973; s. Man Chee and Yiu Ying (Cheng) C. BS, U. Calif., Berkeley, 1969, MPH, 1970, DrPH, 1975; MD, Stanford U., 1983. Diplomate Am. Bd. Family Practice; registered profl. engr., Calif.; registered environ. health specialist, Calif. Asst. civil engr. City of Oakland, Calif., 1970-72; assoc. water quality engr. Bay Area Sewage Services Agy., Berkeley, 1974-76; prin. environ. engr. Assn. Bay Area Govts., Berkeley, 1976-79; intern San Jose (Calif.) Hosp., 1983-84, resident physician, 1984-86; ptnr. Chiu and Crawford, San Jose, 1986-89, Good Samaritan Med. Group, San Jose, 1989-90, The Permanente Med. Group, 1991—; adj. prof. U. San Francisco, 1979-83; clin. asst. prof. Stanford U. Med. Sch., 1987—. Contbr. articles to profl. publs.; co-authored one of the first comprehensive regional environ. mgmt. plans in U.S.; composer, pub. various popular songs Southeast Asia, U.S. mem. Chinese for Affirmative Action, San Francisco, 1975—; bd. dirs. Calif. Regional Water Quality Control Bd.,Oakland, 1979-84, Bay Area Comprehensive Health Planning Coun., San Francisco, 1972-76; mem. Santa Clara County Ctrl. Dem. Com., 1987—; mem. exec. bd. Calif. State Dem. Ctrl. Com.; commr. U.S. Presdl. Commn. on Risk Assessment and Risk Mgmt., Washington, 1993—. Recipient Resident Tchr. award Soc. Tchrs. Family Medicine, 1986, Resolution of Appreciation award Calif. Regional Water Quality Control Bd., 1985. Fellow Am. Acad. Family Physicians; mem. Am. Pub. Health Assn., Chi Epsilon, Tau Beta Pi. Democrat. Office: The Permanente Med Group 770 E Calaveras Blvd Milpitas CA 95035-5491

CHIU, YANEK SIN-YEUNG, surgeon; b. Hong Kong, 1945. MD, Boston U., 1971. Intern Boston City Hosp., 1971-72, resident gen. surgery, 1972-76; fellowship Mayo Clinic, Rochester, Minn., 1977-78; with Childrens Hosp., San Francisco, Calif. Pacific Med. Ctr., San Francisco; asst. clin. prof. surgery U. Calif., San Francisco; pvt. practice. Office: 3838 California St #616 San Francisco CA 94118

CHIVIAN, ERIC SETH, psychiatrist, educator; b. Newark, June 10, 1942; children: Cybele, Dylan C., Judah B. AB, Harvard U., 1964, MD, 1968. Staff psychiatrist MIT, 1980—; asst. clin. prof. psychiatry Harvard Med. Sch., 1987—, dir. Ctr. for Health and the Global Environment, 1996—. Recipient Nobel Peace prize, 1985. Mem. Physicians Social Responsibility, Internat. Physicians Prevent Nuclear War (co-founder, treas. 1980-85). Home: 136 Carter Pond Rd Petersham MA 01366

CHLUBNA, DAVID JOHN, psychotherapist; b. Detroit, Mar. 18, 1953; s. John and Vonda Cleone (DeGeer) C.; m. Sandra Lynne Jacobs, Aug. 14, 1982 (dec. June 1996). BA, Oakland U., Rochester, Mich., 1975; MS, Ea. Mich. U., 1982. Resident mgr. Renaissance House, Inc., Ypsilanti, Mich., 1979-80; resource coord. psychology dept. Ea. Mich. U., Ypsilanti, 1980-82; psychologist intern Huron Valley Child Guidance Ctr., Ypsilanti, 1981-82; career counselor JTPA Kankakee (Ill.) C.C., 1983-84; staff psychotherapist Mental Health Ctr. Kankakee County, Kankakee, 1984-87; mental health coord. Kewaunee County Cmty. Programs, Algoma, Wis., 1987-89; psychotherapist Door County Counseling Svc., Sturgeon Bay, Wis., 1987-93; staff psychotherapist Cath. Social Svc., Green Bay, Wis., 1992-96. Editor Single Child Rev., 1991; editorial bd. Jour. of Mental Health Counseling, 1993; contbr. articles to profl. jours. Mem. ACA, APA (assoc.), Am. Psychol. Soc., Am. Mental Health Counselors, Assn. for Behavior Analysis, Am. Assn. Applied and Preventive Psychology, Am. Ortho-Psychiat. Assn. Home: 1522 Memorial Dr Sturgeon Bay WI 54235-1502 Office: Cath Social Svcs 1825 Riverside Dr Green Bay WI 54305-5825

CHMELIK, CHRISTINE DIANE, intensive care nurse; b. Youngstown, Ohio, Mar. 31, 1964; d. Charles William and Margaret Lucille (Neider) C. AAS, Youngstown (Ohio) State U., 1985, BSN, 1993. RN, Ohio.

CHMELL, SAMUEL JAY, orthopedic surgeon; b. Chgo., Aug. 21, 1952; s. Samuel and Elsie (Wauterlek) C.; m. Nancy Jean Aumiller, June 22, 1974; children: Jessica, Carson, Alexis, Lesley, Samuel Jayson. BS, U. Notre Dame, 1974; MD, Loyola U., 1977. Diplomate Am. Bd. Orthop. Surgery. Intern Loyola U. Med. Ctr., Maywood, Ill., 1977-78, resident in orthop. surgery, 1980-84; emergency rm. physician USPHS Indian Health Svc., Chinle, Ariz., 1978-80; attending orthop. surgeon Hines (Ill.) VA Hosp., 1984-88, Shriners Hosp. for Crippled Children, Chgo., 1985-89, Gallup (N.Mex.) Indian Hosp., 1988-89, Humana-Michael Reese Hosp. and Health Plan, Chgo., 1989—; chmn. sect. orthopaedic surgery Humana-Michael Reese HMO, Chgo., 1991—; asst. prof. dept. orthopaedic surgery U. Ill., Chgo., 1991—; clin. instr. in orthop. surgery Loyola U. Med. Ctr., Maywood, 1985-88; asst. prof. dept. orthop. surgery U. Ill., Chgo. Contbr. articles in field to profl. jours. Active Olmsted Hist. Soc. Riverside, Ill. Sofield travelling fellow Orthop. Rsch. Soc. Gt. Britain, 1985. Fellow ACS, Am. Acad. Orthop. Surgeons; mem. AMA, Ill. State Med. Soc., Ill. Orthop. Soc., Chgo. Med. Soc., Notre Dame Orthop. Soc., Founders' Cir. of Sorin Soc. U. Notre Dame, Alpha Omega Alpha. Office: Humana-Michael Reese Health Plan 2545 S King Dr Chicago IL 60616-2419

CHMIELEWSKI, RICHARD ANTHONY, physician; b. Youngstown, Ohio, Sept. 26, 1952; s. Steve and Genevieve (Starr) C.; m. Sharon Kathleen Berger, May 23, 1980; children: Amy Elizabeth, Eric Stephen, Mark David. BA, Youngstown State U., 1973; MD, U. Pa., 1977. Diplomate Am. Bd. Infectious Diseases, Am. Bd. Internal Medicine. Intern U. Hosps. of Cleve., 1977-78, resident, 1978-80; chief infectious disease dept. St. Vincent Charity Hosp., Cleve., 1982—; med. dir. Hospice of No. Ohio, Cleve., 1988-90. Contbr. articles to Jour. of Clin. Investigation, Chest, Medicine. Mem. Am. Soc. Microbiology. Office: St Vincent Charity Hosp 2322 E 22nd St Ste 200 Cleveland OH 44115-3176

CHMURA, LANCE KENNETH, physician assistant; b. Lincoln Park, Mich., Nov. 7, 1969; s. Joseph Stanley and Linda Jean (Baldwin) C. BS in Biology, U. Mich., 1991, BS in Biochemistry, 1991; BS in Physician Asst. Studies, U. Tex., Galveston, 1993. Lic. physician asst., Pa., Wis.; cert. ATLS, ACLS, PALS. Physician asst. Lufkin (Tex.) Heart Ctr., 1993-94, U. Tex. Med. Br., Galveston, 1994-95, Hermann Hosp., Houston, 1991-96, Ben Taub Gen. Hosp., Houston, 1991-96; physician asst. in emergency medicine Preferred Emergency Physicians, Mequon, Wis., 1996—. Fellow Am. Acad. Physician Assts., Tex. Acad. Physician Assts., Wis. Acad. Physician Assts., Am. Assn. for Surgery of Trauma; mem. Am. Heart Assn. Roman Catholic. Home: 7200 W Marine Dr Milwaukee WI 53223-2012 Office: Preferred Emergency Phys SC 1251 Glen Oaks Ln Ste 102 Mequon WI 53092-3356

CHO, BYUNG CHAE, medical educator; b. Taegu, Korea, Feb. 26, 1959; s. Jun Seung Cho and Jung Duck Kim; m. Suk Hee Kim; 2 children. Bachelor's degree, Kyungpook Nat. U., Taegu, 1984, Master's degree, 1990; Doctoral degree, Kyungpook Nat. U., 1992. Bd. cert. plastic and reconstructive surgery, Korea. Instr. Kyungpook Nat. U., Taegu, 1994-95, asst. prof., 1996—. Capt. Korean Mil. Med. Ctr., 1985-87. Mem. Plastic and Reconstructive Surgeons Korea, Hand Surgery of Korea, Aesthetic Surgery of Korea. Home: Durhyu 3 dong 487-35, Dalsuhgu Taegu 704-063, Korea Office: Kyungpook U Hosp, Samduk 2 ga 50, Dept Plastic/Recon Surgery, Taegu 700-412, Korea

CHO, JAI HANG, internist, hematologist, educator; b. Busan, Republic of Korea, May 1, 1942; came to U.S., 1972; s. Neung Whan and Heo Jai (Min) C.; m. Jawon Nam, Oct. 8, 1971; children: Karen, Austin. M.D., Catholic Med. Coll., Seoul, Republic of Korea, 1968. Diplomate Am. Bd. Internal Medicine. Intern, White Plains Hosp., N.Y., 1972-73; resident in internal medicine Nassau Hosp., Mineola, N.Y., 1973-76, fellow in hematology, 1976-77; fellow in hematology and oncology U. South Fla. Med. Coll., Tampa, 1977-79; practice medicine specializing in internal medicine and hematology, Tampa, 1979—; mem. staff Univ. Community Hosp.; clin. asst. prof. medicine U. South Fla. Med. Coll., 1985-92. Served to capt. Korean Army, 1968-71. Mem. AMA, ACP, Fla. Med. Assn., Hillsborough County Med. Assn. Avocation: art, antiques. Home: 16114 Ancroft Ct Tampa FL 33647-1040 Office: Ste 105 13701 Bruce B Downs Blvd Tampa FL 33613-4606

CHO, WONHWA, medical educator; b. Seoul, Korea, Apr. 27, 1958. BS in Chemistry, Seoul Nat. U., 1980, MS in Chemistry, 1982; PhD in Chemistry, U. Chgo., 1988. Postdoctoral fellow Calif. Inst. Tech., Pasadena, 1989-90; asst. prof. chemistry U. Ill., Chgo., 1990—. Mem. Am. Soc. Biochemistry & Molecular Biology, Am. Chem. Soc. Office: U Ill Chgo Dept Chemistry 845 W Taylor St M/C 111 Chicago IL 60607-7061*

CHOATE, LEWIS DUANE, health care company executive; b. Baytown, Tex., Feb. 26, 1959; s. Walter Lewis and Lavora (Jackson) C.; m. Betsy Ann Sebesta, July 9, 1983. AA in Math. with hons., Lee Jr. Coll., Baytown, 1979; BBA in Acctg. cum laude, U. Houston, 1981. CPA, Tex. Supervising sr. auditor Peat, Marwick, Main, Houston, 1981-84; asst. contr. HMSS, Inc., Houston, 1984-88, contr., 1988-90; pres. Discovery Group Inc., Houston, 1991-92; contr. Am. Oncology Resources, Inc., Houston, 1992-93, dir. fin.,

1994-96. Participant Easters and March of Dimes, Houston, Habitat for Humanity, Houston Hunger Walk. Mem. AICPA, Tex. Soc. CPA's, Houston chpt. of Tex. Soc. CPA's, Healthcare Fin. Mgmt. Assn., Med. Group Mgmt. Assn. Home: 202 S Cochrans Green Cir The Woodlands TX 77381-6207

CHOBANIAN, ARAM VAN, medical school dean, cardiologist; b. Pawtucket, R.I., Aug. 10, 1929; s. Van and Marina (Arsenian) C.; m. Jasmine Goorigian, June 5, 1955; children: Karin, Lisa, Aram. B.A., Brown U., 1951; M.D., Harvard U., 1955. Intern, resident Univ. Hosp., Boston, 1955-59, cardiovascular research fellow, 1959-62; asst. prof. Boston U. Sch. Medicine, 1964-67, assoc. prof., 1967-70, prof. medicine, 1970—, prof. pharmacology, 1975—, John Sandson disting. prof. health scis., 1992—, dir. U.A. Whitaker Labs. for Blood Vessel Rsch., 1973-88, dir. Hypertension Specialized Ctr. Rsch., 1975-95, dir. Cardiovascular Inst., 1975-92, dean, 1988—, provost Med. Ctr., 1996—; dir. Nat. Rsch. and Demonstration Ctr. in Hypertension, 1985-90; chmn. FDA Cardiovascular and Renal Adv. Com., 1978-80, NIH Hypertension and Arteriosclerosis adv. com., 1977-78; chmn. Cardiovascular Study Sect. B. NIH, 1982-84; chmn. 4th Joint Nat. Com. on Hypertension NIH, 1990-91; Sandoz lectr. Royal Coll. Physicians and Surgeons Can., 1989; mem. NIH Nat. Heart, Lung and Blood Adv. Coun., 1993—. Author: Heart Risk Book, 1982; mem. editorial bd. New Eng. Jour. Medicine, Hypertension, Jour. Hypertension, Jour. Vascular Biology, Hypertension Rsch., Cardiovascular Pharmacology. Pres. Am. Heart Assn., Boston, 1974-75; bd. dirs. Armenian Culture Soc., 1976—; fellow trustee Armenian Assembly of Am. Capt. USAF, 1956-57. Recipient Community Edn. and Disting. Svc. award Am. Heart Assn., Boston, 1975, 78, Eastman Kodak award Nat. Acad. Clin. Biochemistry, 1987, Abbott award Am. Soc. Hypertension. Fellow ACP, Am. Heart Assn. (chmn. coun. high blood pressure rsch. 1984-86, Corcoran lectr. 1989, award of merit 1990, Modern Medicine award 1990, Lifetime Achievement award in hypertension Bristol-Myers Squibb), Am. Soc. of Hypertension (Abbott award 1993), Soc. Clin. Investigation, Assn. Am. Physicians, Am. Physiol. Soc., New Eng. Cardiovascular Soc. (pres. 1985-86), Phi Beta Kappa, Sigma Xi, Alpha Omega Alpha. Home: 5 Rathburn Rd Natick MA 01760-1011 Office: Boston U Sch Medicine 80 E Concord St Boston MA 02118-2307

CHOCK, CLIFFORD YET-CHONG, family practice physician; b. Chgo., Oct. 15, 1951; s. Wah Tim and Leatrice (Wong) C. BS in Biology, Purdue U., 1973; MD, U. Hawaii, 1978. Intern in internal medicine Loma Linda (Calif.) Med. Ctr., 1978-79, resident in internal medicine, 1979; resident in internal medicine U. So. Calif.-L.A. County Med. Ctr., L.A., 1980; physician Pettis VA Clinic, Loma Linda, Calif., 1980; pvt. practice Honolulu, 1981—; physician reviewer St. Francis Med. Ctr., Honolulu, 1985—, chmn. peer/credentials family practice care, 1990-93, 95—, chmn. utilization rev., 1990-91, 95-96, acting chmn. credentials com., 1992; physician reviewer Peer Rev. Orgn. Hawaii, Honolulu, 1987-93; mem. Hawaii Claims Conciliation panel, 1990, 96; chmn. dept. family practice St. Francis Med. Ctr., Liliha, 1994—. Fellow Am. Acad. Family Physicians, King James Bible Study. Office: 321 N Kuakini St Ste 513 Honolulu HI 96817-2361

CHODAK, GERALD WALTER, urologist; b. N.Y.C., Mar. 13, 1947; s. Roslyn Chodak; m. Ruth Chodak; 1 child, David. BA in Chemistry, U. Rochester, 1969; MA in Chemistry, SUNY, Buffalo, 1971, MD, 1975. Lic. physician, Ill. Rsch. assoc. in surgery Children's Hosp. and Med. Ctr., Boston, 1977-79, 81-82; sr./chief resident in urology U. Chgo., 1979-81, rsch. assoc. sect. of urology, 1981-82, asst. prof. urology, 1982-85, assoc. prof., 1985-90, dir. prostate and urology ctr., 1990—, prof. surgery/urology, 1990—. Contbr. articles to profl. jours. Mem. physician's profl. edn. com. Am. Cancer Soc., Chgo. unit, 1983-84, early detection and prevention com., 1983-86. NIH grantee, 1994—. Mem. ACS, Am. Urol. Assn. (North Ctrl. chpt.), Soc. Urol. Oncology, Soc. Univ. Urologists, Am. Assn. Clin. Urologists. Home: 1041 W Montana Chicago IL 60614 Office: Louis A Weiss Meml Hosp 4646 N Marine Dr Chicago IL 60640

CHODOROW, JOAN, psychoanalyst, dance therapist; b. N.Y.C., May 29, 1937; d. Eugene Aaronovitch and Lillian (Kleidman) C.; m. Louis H. Stewart, June 23, 1985; step-children: Daniel Stewart, Sarah Stewart Hawklyn. MA in Psychology, Dance Therapy, Goddard Coll., 1972; Diploma in Analytical Psychology, C. G. Jung Inst. Los Angeles, 1983; PhD in Psychology, Union Grad. Sch., 1988. Registered dance therapist; lic. MFCC, Calif. Founder, tchr. Community Dance Studio, Los Angeles, 1957-64; dance therapist Child Psychiat. County Hosp., Los Angeles, 1964-66, Lawrence Sch., Van Nuys, Calif., 1965-67; dance therapist, psychotherapist Psychiat. Med. Group, Santa Barbara, Calif., 1968-73; lectr. U. Calif., Santa Barbara, 1967-79, Community Coll., Santa Barbara, 1967-79; dance therapist Psychiat. Dept. Cottage Hosp., Santa Barbara, 1968-83; practicing psychotherapist Santa Barbara, 1973-83; practicing Jungian analyst Fairfax, Calif., 1983—; tchr. C.G. Jung Inst., San Francisco, 1983—; visiting faculty Insts. Los Angeles, Houston,Israel 1976—; dir., tchr. Dance Therapy, Santa Barbara 1975-83; faculty Active Imagination course Geneva, 1984, 90, 95, Zurich 1985-86. Author: Dance Therapy and Depth Psychology, 1990; editor: What is Dance Therapy, Really?, 1973, Jung on Active Imagination, 1996; keynote speaker Internat. Dance Therapy Conf. in Berlin, 1994; contbr. articles to profl. jours. Mem. Am. Dance Therapy Assn. (pres. 1974-76, keynote speaker 1983, 91), Internat. Assn. Analytical Psychol., Am. Psychol. Assn., Calif. Assn. Marriage and Family Therapists, C.G. Jung Inst. San Francisco. Jewish.

CHODOS, WESLEY S(TANLEY), physician; b. Bklyn., Nov. 15, 1949; s. Harold and Lisa (Gershon) C.; m. Cynthia Ann Sacks, July 23, 1952; 1 child, Nicole Jennifer. BS in Biology, L.I. U., 1972; DO, Coll. Osteo. Medicine, Des Moines, 1978. Diplomate Am. Bd. Ob/Gyn. Intern Drs. Hosp., Columbus, Ohio, 1977-78; resident in ob/gyn. Met. Hosp., Phila., 1978-82, fellow reproductive endocrinology, 1982-83; pvt. practice Bala Cynwyd, Pa. and Cherry Hill, N.J., 1983—; sci. tchr. N.Y.C. Bd. Edn., Bklyn., 1972-74; clin. asst. prof. ob/gyn. U. Medicine & Dentistry, Stratford, N.J., 1984—, N.J. Sch. Osteo. Medicine, 1984—, Phila. Coll. Osteo. Medicine, 1983—; lectr. in field. Contbr. articles to profl. jours. Advisor Planned Parenthood Greater Camden (N.J.) Area, 1982; tchr. sex edn. Cherry Hill (N.J.) Bd. Edn., 1990-95; asst. coach Girls Softball, Cherry Hill, 1995. With USAFR, 1971-77. Recipient Presdl. Citation, 1972. Mem. Am. Coll. Osteo. Ob/Gyn., Am. Fertility Soc., Am. Osteo. Soc., Am. Coll. Gynecol. Laparoscopic, Camden County Soc. Osteo. Physicians, Phila. Area Reproductive Endocrine Soc. (sec.-treas.). Office: Reproductive Gynecologists PC 1 Belmont Ave GSB Bldg Ste 825 Bala Cynwyd PA 19004

CHOI, YONG SUNG, immunologist; b. Seoul, Korea, Sept. 11, 1936; came to U.S. 1962; s. Kap Soo and Soon-Ok (Lee) C.; m. Ilze Anna Zemjanis, Aug. 26, 1966. BMS, Seoul Nat. U., Korea, 1957, MD, 1961; MS, U Minn., 1964, PhD, 1965. Rsch. assoc. Salk Inst., LaJolla, Calif., 1967-69; asst. prof. U. Minn. Med. Sch., Mpls., 1969-73; mem. and prof. immunology Sloan-Kettering Inst./Cornell U. Med. Sch., N.Y.C., 1973-85; disting. investigator Ochsner Med. Found., New Orleans, 1985—. Contbr. articles to profl. jours. including Jour. Molecular Biology, Biochemistry, Jour. Immunology, Jour. Exptl. Medicine. NIH spl. rsch. fellow, 1969; recipient Faculty Rsch. award ACS, 1971; rsch. grantee NCI, NIH, 1970—. Mem. Am. Assn. Immunologists, Am. Assn. Pathologists, Harvey Soc. Office: Oschsner Med Found 1516 Jefferson Hwy New Orleans LA 70121-2429

CHOJNACKI, PAUL ERVIN, pharmacist, pharmaceutical company official; b. Chgo., Dec. 29, 1950; s. Ervin Edward and Monica (Jablonski) C.; m. Doris Warenberg, May 26, 1979; children: Brittany, James. BS in Bus., Chgo. State U., 1975; BS in Pharmacy, St. Louis Coll., 1977; MA in Mktg., Webster U., 1982. RPh, Mo., N.C., Ind. Clk. Filmanowicz Drug, Chgo., 1968-70; stock clk. Sears, Roebuck & Co., Chgo., 1974-75; sales rep. Chgo. Motor Club, 1975-76; pharmacist Family Pharmacy, St. Louis, 1977; sales assoc. Eli Lilly & Co., St. Louis, 1977-84; regional mgr. Hosp. Pharmacies Inc., St. Louis, 1984-85; hosp. rep. Glaxo Inc., St. Louis, 1985-91; State of Ind. dist. mgr. Allen & Hanburys/Glaxo Pharms., Fishers, 1991—; assoc. product mgr. Oral Cephaloporins Glaxo, Inc., 1989. Local campaign worker, St. Louis, 1985. Mem. Am. Pharm. Assn., St. Louis Pharmacists Assn., St. Louis Hosp. Pharmacists Assn., Ind. Pharm. Assn., Ind. Pharmacists Assn., St. Joseph County Pharmacist Assn. (officer 1995, continuing edn. coord.), Alpha Zeta Omega (treas. St. Louis 1977-78, pres. 1978-79). Home and Office: 10110 Bent Tree Ln Fishers IN 46038

CHOJNOWSKI, DONNA A., cardiac transplant nurse, administrator; m. John Chojnowski. BSN, Trenton (N.J.) State Coll., 1979; postgrad., Temple U. RN, Pa.; cert. critical care nurse; cert. ACLS. Staff nurse ICU, asst. head nurse Albert Einstein Med. Ctr., Phila.; nurse mgr. cardiothoracic surg. ICU, Temple U. Hosp., Phila.; cardiac transplant clin. nurse coord./administr. Hahneman U. Hosp., Phila.; lectr., rschr. on cardiac transplantation. Mem. AACN (bd. dirs. S.E. Pa. chpt., coord. monthly edn. program, Mgr. of Yr. award 1989).

CHOLE, RICHARD ARTHUR, otolaryngologist, educator; b. Madison, Wis., Oct. 12, 1944; s. Arthur Steven and Wendy Elveyn (Danielczyk) C.; m. Cynthia Beiseker, Dec. 27, 1969; children: Joseph Michael, Timothy Thomas, Katharine, Melinda. Student, U. Calif., Berkeley, 1962-65; MD, U. So. Calif., 1969; PhD in Otolaryngology, U. Minn., 1977. Diplomate Am. Bd. Otolaryngology (alt. bd. examiner). Rotating intern U. So. Calif. Med. Ctr., 1969-70; med. fellow dept. surgery Sch. Medicine, U. Minn., 1972-73, med. fellow dept. otolaryngology, 1973-77; asst. prof. dept. otolaryngology-head and neck surgery Davis Sch. Medicine, U. Calif., 1977-81, assoc. prof., 1981-84, prof., 1984—, acting chmn. dept., 1985, chmn., 1985—; mem. sci. rev. com. Deafness Rsch. Found., 1986—; mem. communicative disorders rev. com. Nat. Inst. Deafness and Communication Disorders, 1989—; staff cons. Dept. Air Force, David Grant USAF Med. Ctr., Travis AFB, Calif., 1981—; keynote speaker 92d Japan Oto-Rhino-Laryngol. Soc. Meeting, Fukuoka City, 1990; faculty mem. 4th Internat. Cholesteatoma Conf., Niigata City, Japan, 1992; lectr. in field. Mem. editorial bd. Laryngoscope, 1985-87; mem. exec. editorial bd. Otolaryngology-Head and Neck Surgery, 1990—; contbr. numerous articles to profl. jours., book chpts., revs.; patentee in field. Mem. profl. edn. com. Am. Cancer Soc., 1977-78, Sacramento Noise Control Hearing Bd., 1977—, Greater Sacramento Profl. Standards Rev. Orgn., 1978-79; deacon 1st Bapt. Ch., Davis, 1979-82, elder, 1983-88. Recipient 1st pl. award Am. Acad. Ophthalmology and Otolaryngology, 1977, care recognition awards U. Calif., Davis, 1988-91; rsch. grantee NIH, Nat. Inst. Aging, Nat. Inst. Neurol. and Communicative Disorders and Stroke, Nat. Inst. on Deafness and Other Communication Disorders, Deafness Rsch. Found., Am. Otol. Soc., U. Calif., 1978-91. Mem. Collegeum Otorhinolaryngologicum Amicitiae Sacrum (U.S. group), Am. Acad. Otolaryngology-Head and Neck Surgery (Honors award 1984, com. on rsch. 1987—, rsch. coordinating coun. 1987—, continuing edn. com. 1991—), Am. Otol. Soc. (trustee rsch. fund 1986—, sec.-treas. 1989—), Assn. for Rsch. in Otolaryngology (award of merit com. 1988—), Am. Laryngol., Rhinol. and Otol. Soc., Am. Soc. for Bone and Mineral Rsch., Assn. Acad. Depts. Otolaryngology-Head and Neck Surgery (coun. 1986—), Calif. Med. Assn. (sci. adv. panel, sect. on otolaryngology-head and neck surgery 1986—), Sacramento Soc. Otolaryngology and Maxillofacial Surgery, Soc. Univ. Otolaryngologists-Head and Neck Surgeons. Office: U Calif-Davis Sch Medicine Dept Otorhinolaryngology 2521 Stockton Blvd Rm 7200 Sacramento CA 95817-2208

CHOMA, NATHAN DAVID, physician; b. Somerville, N.J., Aug. 29, 1957; s. David and Alice (Kuzmick) C.; m. Susan Elizabeth Tuma; children: David Jonathan, Amy Elizabeth. BS in Chemistry, U. South Fla., 1978, MD, 1981. Resident in gen. surgery Cleve. Clinic Found., 1981-83, resident in internal medicine, 1984-86, clin. assoc. dept. preventive medicine, 1986-89; pvt. practice North Royalton, Ohio, 1989-95; clin. instr. Univ. Hosps., Cleve., 1995—. Mem. AMA, Ohio State Med. Assn., Cleve. Acad. Medicine. Office: 7171 Royalton Rd Ste 203 North Royalton OH 44133

CHOMSKY, AVRAM NOAM, linguistics and philosophy educator; b. Phila., Dec. 7, 1928; s. William and Elsie (Simonofsky) C.; m. Carol Doris Schatz, Dec. 24, 1949; children: Aviva, Diane, Harry Alan. BA, U. Pa., 1949, MA, 1951, PhD, 1955, DHL (hon.), 1984; DHL (hon.), U. Chgo., 1967, Loyola U., Chgo., 1970, Swarthmore Coll., 1970, Bard Coll., 1971, U. Mass., 1973, U. Maine, 1992, Gettysburg Coll., 1992, Amherst Coll., 1995; LittD (hon.), U. London, 1967, Delhi (India) U., 1972, Visva-Bharati U., Santiniketan, West Bengal, 1980, Cambridge (Eng.) U., 1995. Mem. faculty MIT, 1955—, prof. modern langs., 1961—, Ferrari P. Ward prof. modern lang. and linguistics, 1966—, Inst. prof., 1976—; vis. prof. Columbia U., N.Y.C., 1957-58; mem. Inst. Advanced Study Princeton U., 1958-59, Am. U. of Cairo, 1993; Linguistic Soc. Am. prof. UCLA, summer 1966; Beckman prof. U. Calif.-Berkeley, 1966-67; John Locke lectr. Oxford U., 1969; Bertrand Russell Meml. lectr., Cambridge, 1971; Nehru Meml. lectr. New Delhi, 1972; Huizinga lectr. U. Leiden, 1977; Woodbridge lectr. Columbia U., 1978; Kant lectr. Stanford U., 1979; Jeanette K. Watson disting. vis. prof. Syracuse U., 1982; Pauling Meml. lectr. Oreg. State U., 1995. Author: Syntactic Structures, 1957, Current Issues in Linguistic Theory, 1964, Aspects of the Theory of Syntax, 1965, Cartesian Linguistics, 1966, Topics in the Theory of Generative Grammar, 1966, (with Morris Halle) Sound Pattern of English, 1968, Language and Mind, 1968, American Power and the New Mandarins, 1969, At War with Asia, 1970, Problems of Knowledge and Freedom, 1971, Studies on Semantics in Generative Grammar, 1972, For Reasons of State, 1973, (with Edward Herman) Counterrevolutionary Violence, 1973, Peace in The Middle East, 1974, Logical Structure of Linguistic Theory, 1975, Reflections on Language, 1975, Essays on Form and Interpretation, 1977, Human Rights and American Foreign Policy, 1978, (with Edward Herman) The Political Economy of Human Rights, 2 vols., 1979, Language and Responsibility, 1979, Rules and Representations, 1980, Lectures on Government and Binding, 1981, Concepts and Consequences of the Theory of Government and Binding, 1982, Towards a New Cold War, 1982, Radical Priorities, 1982, Fateful Triangle, 1983, Turning the Tide, 1985, Barriers, 1986, Knowledge of Language, 1986, Pirates and Emperors, 1986, On Power and Ideology, 1987, Language and Problems of Knowledge, 1987, Language in a Psychological Setting, 1987, Generative Grammar, 1987, Culture of Terrorism, 1988, (with Edward Herman) Manufacturing Consent, 1988, Language and Politics, 1988, Necessary Illusions, 1989, Deterring Democracy, 1991, Chronicles of Dissent, 1992, What Uncle Sam Really Wants, 1992, Year 501, 1993, Rethinking Camelot, 1993, Letters from Lexington, 1993, The Prosperous Few and the Restless Many, 1993, Language and Thought, 1994, World Orders, Old and New, 1994, The Minimalist Program, 1995, Powers and Prospects, 1996. Recipient Disting. Sci. Contbn. award APA, 1984, Kyoto prize, 1988, George Orwell award Nat. Coun. Tchrs. English, 1987, 89, James Killian faculty award MIT, 1992, Lannan Lit. award for nonfiction, 1992, Joel Seldin Peace award Psychologists for Social Responsibility, 1993, Homer Smith award NYU Sch. Medicine, 1994, Loyola Mellon Humanities award Loyola U., Chgo., 1994; jr. fellow Soc. Fellows, Harvard U., 1951-55, rsch. fellow Harvard Cognitive Studies Ctr., 1964-67. Fellow AAAS, Brit. Acad. (corr.), Brit. Psychol. Soc. (hon.), Royal Anthrop. Inst. Gt. Britain, Royal Anthrop. Inst. of Ireland, Utrecht Soc. Arts and Scis. (hon.), Gesellschaft für Sprachwissenschaft (hon.), Am. Acad. Philosophy; mem. APA (William James fellow 1990), NAS, Am. Acad. Arts and Scis., Linguistic Soc. Am., Deutsche Akademie der Naturforscher Leopoldina, Assn. for Edn. in Journalism and Mass Comm. (Profl. Excellence award 1991). Home: 15 Suzanne Rd Lexington MA 02173-1837 Office: MIT 77 Massachusetts Ave Cambridge MA 02139-4301

CHONG, CHRISTOPHER KIAN, obstetrician, gynecologist; b. Tawau, Malaysia, June 29, 1948; came to U.S., 1976; w. Kyam Kee and Siew Kyau (Ng) C.; m. Janely Rusly, Oct. 10, 1975; children: Samuel, Christina, Jessica. MB, Med. Coll., Nat. Taiwan U., Taipei, 1975. Diplomate Am. Bd. Obstetrics/Gynecology. Urology resident U. Hosp., Nat. Taiwan U., 1975-76; intern dept. ob-gyn Coney Island Hosp., Bklyn., 1976-77; resident in ob-gyn Maimonides Med. Ctr., Bklyn., 1977-81; assoc. Coastal Ob-Gyn Assocs., Pomona, N.J., 1984-87; ptnr. Perkins & Chong, P.A., Absecon, N.J., 1987—; chief attending physician, assoc. chmn. dept. ob-gyn Atlantic City Med. Ctr. Mem., bd. dirs. Caring Inc., 1992; deacon Seaview Bapt. Ch., Linwood, N.J., 1989-95, bd. trustees, 1995—. Maj. USAF, 1981-84. Fellow Am. Coll. Ob-Gyn.; mem. AMA, Am. Soc. Reproductive Medicine, Soc. Study Breast Disease, N.J. Med. Soc., Atlantic County Med. Soc. Republican. Office: Perkin's & Chong MDs PA 634 E Lost Pineway Rd Absecon NJ 08201-9603 also: Linwood Commons 2106 New Rd Ste D-5 Linwood NJ 08221-1046

CHONG, DENNIS KHIN-HEUNG, physical medicine and rehabilitation specialist; b. Petaling Jaya, Selangor, Malaysia, June 12, 1965; s. Seong-Hin and Tang-Lay (Siak) C.; m. Sweelin Alicia Wong, June 29, 1991. 1 chld, Samuel. MD, U. Calgary, 1988. Diplomate Am. Bd. Phys. Medicine and Rehab. Resident Meml. U. Nfld., 1988-90, McMaster U., Hamilton, Ont., Can., 1990-93; staff physician Rehab. Inst. of Mich., Detroit, 1993—, md. dir., 1994—; asst. prof., assoc. grad. faculty Wayne State U., Detroit, 1994—; clin. asst. prof. Oakland U., Rochester, Mich., 1995—; cons. physician Grace Hosp., Detroit Receiving Hosp., Univ. Health Ctr., Harper Hosp., Hutzel Hosp., all Detroit, 1994—; mem. adv. bd. Rsch. Ctr., Kessler Inst. for Rehab., West Orange, N.J., 1994—; liaison to Am. Acad. Family Practice, Am. Acd. Phys. Medicine and Rehab., Chgo., 1996—. Contbr. articles to profl. jours. Deacon Free Meth. Ch., Troy, Mich., 1994. Fellow Am. Acad. Phys. Medicine and Rehab., Royal Coll. Physicians (Can.); mem. AMA (organized med. staff sect. 1994—, Physician's Recognition award 1993-99), Am. Acad. Family Physicians, Assn. Acad. Physiatrists, Am. Coll. Occupl. and Environ. Medicine, Coll. of Family Physicians (cert.), Med. Coun. of Can. Office: Rehab Inst of Mich 261 Mack Blvd Detroit MI 48201

CHONG, FRANK K., physician, pathologist; b. Seoul, Korea, Mar. 24, 1938; s. Peter I. and Tae-Boon (Choi) C.; m. Maria C. Lee, Nov. 23, 19676; children: Cathy, Vivian. MD, Pusan (Korea) Nat. U., 1962. Diplomate Am. Bd. Pathology. Pathologist St. Elizabeth's Med. Ctr., Boston, 1974—; assoc. clin. prof. Tufts U. Med. Sch., Boston, 1976—. Lt. comdr. Korean Navy, 1962-69. Fellow Am. Soc. Clin. Pathologists, Korean Med. Assn.; mem. Mass. Med. Soc., New Eng. Soc. Pathologists. Democrat. Roman Catholic. Office: St Elizabeth's Med Ctr 736 Cambridge St Brighton MA 02135

CHONMAITREE, TASNEE, pediatrician, educator, infectious disease specialist; b. Bangkok, Thailand, Dec. 9, 1949; came to U.S., 1975; d. Surajit and Arporn (Maitong) C.; m. Somkiat Laungthaleong Pong, June 27, 1981; children: Ann L. Pong, Dan L. Pong. BS, Mahidol U., Bangkok, 1971; MD, Siriraj Med. Sch., Bangkok, 1973. Diplomate Am. Bd. Pediatrics, Am. Bd. Pediatric Infectious Diseases. Rotating intern Siriraj Hosp., Bangkok, 1973-74, resident in pediatrics, 1974-75; resident in pediatrics Lloyd Noland Hosp., U. Ala., Birmingham, 1975-78; fellow infectious disease U. Rochester (N.Y.), 1978-81; asst. prof. pediatrics U. Tex. Med. Br., Galveston, 1981-87, asst. prof. pathology, 1985-87, assoc. prof. pediatrics and pathology, 1987-94; prof. pediatrics and pathology, 1994—; assoc. dir. clin. virology lab. U. Tex. Med. Br., Galveston, 1985-92, dir. divsn. pediatric infectious disease, 1985-92. Contbr. 50 articles to profl. jours. Grantee NIH, 1994-99. Fellow Am. Acad. Pediatrics, Pediatric Infectious Diseases Soc., Infectious Diseases Soc. Am.; mem. Soc. Pediatric Rsch., European Soc. for Pediatric Rsch., Tex. Infectious Disease Soc. Buddhist. Home: 1906 Cherrytree Park Cir Houston TX 77062-2327 Office: U Tex Dept Pediatrics Med Br Ninth Street & Market Galveston TX 77555-0371

CHOPPIN, PURNELL WHITTINGTON, research administrator, virology researcher, educator; b. Baton Rouge, July 4, 1929; s. Arthur Richard and Eunice Dolores (Bolin) C.; m. Joan Harriet Macdonald, Oct. 17, 1959; 1 dau., Kathleen Marie. MD, La. State U., 1953; DSc (hon.), Emory U., 1988, La. State U., 1988, Tulane U., 1989, Washington U., 1991, Med. U. S.C., 1995, U. Md., Baltimore County, 1995; D Medicine (hon.), U. Cologne, 1988; DHL (hon.), Mt. Sinai Sch. Medicine, 1996. Diplomate: Am. Bd. Internal Medicine. Intern Barnes Hosp., St. Louis, 1953-54, asst. resident, 1956-57; postdoctoral fellow, rsch. assoc. Rockefeller U., N.Y.C., 1957-60, asst. prof., 1960-64, assoc. prof., 1957-60, prof., sr. physician, 1970-85, Leon Hess prof. virology, 1980-85, v.p. acad. programs, 1983-85; dean grad. studies Rockefeller U., 1985; v.p., chief sci. officer Howard Hughes Med. Inst., 1985-87, pres., 1987—; chmn. sect. 43 microbiology and immunology NAS, 1989-92, chmn. class IV med. scis., 1983-86, mem. com. on reorganization structure, 1985-86; coun. Inst. Medicine, 1987-92, exec. com., 1988-91; mem. virology study sect. NIH, 1968-72, chmn. virology study sect., 1975-78; bd. dirs. Royal Soc. Medicine Found. Inc., N.Y.C., 1978-93; mem. adv. com. fundamental rsch. Nat. Multiple Sclerosis Soc., 1979-84; chmn. adv. com. fundamental rsch., 1983-84; mem. adv. coun. Nat. Inst. Allergy and Infectious Diseases, 1980-83; mem. bd. scis., cons. Meml. Sloan-Kettering Cancer Ctr., N.Y.C., 1981-86; chmn. bd. scis., 1983-84; mem. commn. on life scis. NRC, Washington, 1982-87; mem. sci. rev. com. Scripps Clinic and Rsch. Found., La Jolla, Calif., 1983-85, chmn. sci. rev. com., La Jolla, Calif., 1984; mem. coun. for rsch. and clin. investigation Am. Cancer Soc., N.Y.C., 1983-85; mem. com. priorities for vaccine devel. Inst. Medicine, Washington; mem. governing bd. NRC, 1990-92. Contbr. numerous articles to profl. pubs., chpts. on virology, cell biology, infectious diseases to profl. publs., 1958—; editor: Procs. Soc. Exptl. Biology and Medicine, 1966-69; assoc. editor Virology, 1969-72, editor, 1973-86; assoc. editor: Jour. Immunology, 1968-72, Jour. Supramolecular Structure, 1972-75; mem. editorial bd. Jour. Virology, 1972-85, Comprehensive Virology, 1972; mem. overseas adv. panel Biochem. Jour., 1973-77. Served as capt. USAF, 1954-56, Japan. Recipient Howard Taylor Ricketts award U. Chgo., 1978; Waksman award for excellence in microbiology Nat. Acad. Scis., 1984; named to alumni Hall of Distinction La. State U., Baton Rouge, 1983. Fellow AAAS; mem. NAS, Am. Acad. Arts and Scis., Am. Philos. Soc., Assn. Am. Physicians, Am. Soc. Clin. Investigation, Am. Soc. Microbiology (chmn. virology div. 1977-79, div. group councilor 1983-85), Harvey Soc., Am. Assn. Immunologists, Soc. Cell Biology, Infectious Diseases Soc. Am., Practitioners Soc. N.Y., Am. Clin. and Climatological Assn., Am. Soc. Virology (pres. 1985-86), Sigma Xi (chpt. pres. 1980-81), Alpha Omega Alpha. Office: Howard Hughes Med Inst 4000 Jones Bridge Rd Chevy Chase MD 20815-6720

CHOPRA, RAJ P., urologic surgeon; b. India, Aug. 29, 1932; came to U.S., 1963; s. Roshanlal and Savitri Devi C.; m. Rani, Feb. 6, 1960; children: Bipin, Atul, Anuj. MD, Grant Med. Coll., 1957. Fellow Am. Coll. Surgeons, Internat. Coll. Surgeons; mem. AMA, Am. Urological Assn., Pa. Med. Soc., Columbia Med. Soc. Republican. Hindu.

CHOPRA, RAJPAL, physician; b. Bombay, Apr. 26, 1958; came to U.S., 1984; s. Prabjot and Jaswant (Gujral) C.; m. Ravinder Chopra; children: Mehak, Neha. MBBS, Tepiwala Nat. U., Bombay, 1982; MD, North Gen. Hosp., N.Y.C., 1986. Diplomate in internal medicine, endocrinology, metabolism and diabetes, also geriatrics Am. Bd. Internal Medicine. Resident North Gen. Hosp., 1986-89; fellow Mt. Sinai Hosp., N.Y.C., 1989-91; mem. staff North Gen. Hosp., N.Y.C., 1989—, Parkway Hosp., N.Y.C., 1989—, Cath. Med. Ctr., N.Y.C., 1991—. Mem. AMA, ACP, Am. Diabetes Assn., Endocrine Soc. Home: 601 N Fifth Street New Hyde Park NY 11040

CHORPENNING, FRANK WINSLOW, immunology educator, researcher; b. Marietta, Ohio, Aug. 17, 1913; s. Roy Albert and Laura Leola (Klintworth) C.; m. Annie Laurie Kay; children: Anne Kay, Jonathan Edward, Kathleen, Janie Cecelia. AB, Marietta Coll., 1939; MSc, Ohio State U., 1950, PhD, 1963. Immunologist USAREUR Med. Lab./U.S. Army, Germany, 1952-55; chief clin. pathology Brooke Gen. Hosp., Ft. Sam Houston, Tex., 1955-61; cons. Nationalist Chinese Army, Taiwan, 1960; from lectr. to prof. Ohio State U., Columbus, 1961-81, prof. emeritus, 1981—; me. coop. study group WHO, 1953-55. Div. editor Ohio Jour. Sci., 1974-83; editor: Clinical Pathology Procedures, 1959; author: (chpt.) Regulation of Immune Response Dynamics, 1982, Immunology of Bacterial Cell Envelope, 1983; author: The Man from Somerset, 1993; contbr. articles to profl. jours. Mem. Epidemiol. Com., San Antonio, 1949; mem. Rep. Nat. Com., Delaware, Ohio, 1979-96, Rep. Presdl. Task Force, Delaware, 1983. Lt. col. U.S. Army, 1941-61. Recipient Commendation, Chinese Surgeon Gen., 1960, C.G. Brooke Gen. Hosp., 1960. Fellow Am. Acad. Microbiology, Ohio Acad. Sci.; mem. Am. Assn. Immunologists, Ohio Acad. Sci., Assn. for Gnotobiotics, Ohio Hist. Soc. Roman Catholic.

CHOTE, CARLA JANE, nurse; b. Hot Springs, Ark., Sept. 9, 1961; d. Carl E. and Carrie Lucille (Reynolds) C. BSN, U. Ark. Med. Scis., 1983. RN, Ark. Shift nursing supr. Nat. Park Med. Ctr., Hot Springs, 1988—.

CHOU, CHING-CHUNG, physiology and medical educator; b. Taipei, Taiwan, June 25, 1932; came to U.S., 1960; m. Lucy Ai-shu Tzen Chou, Nov. 15, 1962; children: Jane, Belinda, Michael. MD, Nat. Taiwan U., Taipei, 1958; PhD, U. Okla., Oklahoma City, 1966. Instr. physiology U. Okla., Oklahoma City, 1965-66; asst. prof. physiology and medicine Mich. State U., East Lansing, 1966-69, assoc. prof. physiology and medicine, 1969-73, prof. physiology and medicine, 1973—, assoc. chairperson physiology, 1992—; pres. Splanchnic Circulation Group, 1978-83, exec. sec., 1983—. Author: (book) Physiology of Gastrointestinal Tract, 1968, (book chpt.) Intestinal Motility and Blood Flow, 1989; contbr. numerous articles to profl. jours. Fulbright scholar, Brazil, 1987; recipient Disting. Faculty awards Coll. Medicine Mich. State U., 1988, 89. Fellow Am. Heart Assn.; mem. Am. Physiol. Soc., Am. Gastroent. Assn., Cen. Soc. Clin. Rsch., N.Am.

Tiawanese Med. Assn. (bd. dirs. 1990-92), N.Am. Taiwanese Prof. Assn. (bd. dirs. 1993—). Home: 4845 Mohican Ln Okemos MI 48864-1406

CHOU, JAMES CHING-YUNG, psychiatrist; b. Phila., June 4, 1959; s. Pei Chi and Rosalind (Chen) C.; m. Emily Yi-Min Chen, July 18, 1981; children: Stephanie Shao-Tsi, Valerie Shao-Hsin. AB, Harvard Coll., Cambridge, Mass., 1979; MD, Tulane U., 1983. Diplomate Am. Bd. Psychiatry and Neurology. Intern then resident psychiatry NYU Med. Ctr., N.Y.C., 1983-87; psychiatrist Asian Bicultural Clinic/Gouverneur Hosp., N.Y.C., 1985—; rsch. psychiatrist Nathan Kline Inst., Orangeburg, N.Y., 1987—; pvt. practice psychiatry White Plains, N.Y., 1988—; rsch. asst. prof. psychiatry NYU Sch. Medicine, N.Y.C., 1987-89; asst. prof. psychiatry NYU, 1991—. Author: (videotape psychiatry rev. course) Pass the Boards!, 1992; contbr. articles to profl. jours. Pres. N.Y. Coalition for Asian-Am. Mental Health, N.Y.C., 1989. Mem. Am. Psychiat. Assn. (assembly rep.-caucus of Asian-Psychiatrists 1995—, Resident Rsch. award N.Y. County dist. br. 1986, Am. Psychiat. Assn./NIMH fellow 1985-88). Office: Nathan Kline Inst Research Psy Orangeburg NY 10962

CHOU, SHELLEY NIEN-CHUN, neurosurgeon, university official, educator; b. Chekiang, China, Feb. 6, 1924; s. Shelley P. and Tse-tsun (Chao) C.; m. Jolene Johnson, Nov. 24, 1956 (div. 1977); children: Shelley T., Dana, Kerry; remarried, 1979. B.S., St. John's U., Shanghai, China, 1946; M.D., U. Utah, 1949; M.S., U. Minn., 1954, Ph.D., 1964. Diplomate: Am. Bd. Neurol. Surgery (mem. bd.). Resident U. Minn. Hosps., 1950-55; practice medicine, specializing in neurosurgery Salt Lake City, 1955-58, Bethesda, Md., 1959, Mpls., 1960—; clin. asst. Coll. Medicine U. Utah, 1956-58; vis. scientist Nat. Insts. Neurol. Diseases and Blindness NIH, 1959; mem. faculty U. Minn., 1960—, assoc. prof. neurosurgery, 1965-68, prof. neurosurgery, 1968-92, head dept. neurosurgery, 1974-89, prof. emeritus, 1992, interim dean med. sch., dep. v.p. med. affairs, 1993-95; mem. Am. Bd. Neurol Surg., 1974-79; mem. residency rev. com. ACGME, 1984-90, chmn., 1987-89. Contbr. numerous articles to profl. jours.; Publs. on studies of intracranial lesions using radioactive angiography techniques; malformations of cerebral vasculature; neurol. dysfunctions of urinary bladder. Mem. AMA, A.C.S. (mem. adv. council neurosurgery 1981-87, mem. grad. Med. edn. com. 1984—), Congress Neurol. Surgery, Soc. Neurol. Surgeons (pres. 1978-79), Am. Acad. Neurol. Surgery (pres. elect 1985-86, pres. 1986-87), Soc. Nuclear Medicine, Am. Assn. Neurol. Surgeons (bd. dirs. 1980-83, v.p. 1984-85), Neurosurg. Soc. N.Am. (pres. 1977-78), N.Y. Acad. Medicine, Forum Univ. Neurosurgeons (pres. 1968-69), AAAS, Phi Rho Sigma. Home: 183 Galtier Pl Shoreview MN 55126-2113 Office: Box 96 UMHC 420 Delaware St SE Minneapolis MN 54455-0392*

CHOU, SHYAN-YIH, nephrologist, internist, researcher; b. Taipei, Taiwan, Aug. 7, 1941; came to U.S., 1968, naturalized, 1980; s. En-Truen and Lin-Oh (Lin) C.; m. Wanda Louie, Dec. 7, 1974; children—Janet, Denise. M.D., Nat. Taiwan U., Taipei, 1966. Diplomate Am. Bd. Internal Medicine. Intern Brookdale Hosp. Med. Ctr., Bklyn., 1968-69, resident in medicine, 1969-70; Nat. Kidney Found. fellow, 1970-73, asst. attending physician, 1973-74, assoc. attending physician, 1974-77, attending physician, 1977—, chief sect. nephrology lab., 1977—; asst. prof. medicine SUNY Health Sci. Ctr. at Bklyn., 1978-84, assoc. prof., 1984-93; prof. of medicine, 1993—. Contbr. sci. articles to profl. publs. N.Y. State Health Research Council grantee; NIH grantee. Fellow ACP, Am. Coll. Clin. Pharmacology; mem. Am. Soc. Nephrology, Internat. Soc. Nephrology, Am. Fedn. Clin. Research, Am. Heart Assn., AAAS, Am. Physiol. Soc. Research on hormonal factors regulating medullary blood flow; role of medullary hemodynamics in regulating renal sodium excretion. Office: Brookdale U Hosp & Med Ctr Divsn Nephrology & Hypertension 1 Brookdale Plz Brooklyn NY 11212-3198

CHOU, TING-CHAO, pharmacology educator; b. Taiwan, Sept. 9, 1938, came to U.S., 1965, naturalized, 1976; s. Chao-Yun and Sheng-Mei (Chen) C.; m. Dorothy Tsui-chin Tseng, June 26, 1965; children: Joseph Hsin-I, Julia Hsin-Ya. BS, Kaohsiung Med. Coll., Taiwan, 1961; MS, Nat. Taiwan U., 1965; PhD, Yale U., 1970. Teaching asst. pharmacology Nat. Taiwan U., 1964-65; rsch. asst. pharmacology Yale U., 1969; postdoctoral fellow Johns Hopkins U., Balt., 1969-72; assoc. Sloan-Kettering Inst. Cancer Rsch., N.Y.C., 1972-78, assoc. mem., 1978-88, mem., 1988-95, head lab. biochmn. pharmacology, 1988—, dir. preclin. pharmacology core facility, 1995—; asst. prof. Grad. Sch. of Med. Sci. Cornell U., 1972-78, assoc. prof., 1978-88, prof. pharmacology, 1988—; cons. Biogen, 1989, Boehringer Ingelheim Pharm., Inc., 1990-96, Hoffman-La Roche, Inc., 1990-91, U. Tex., Houston, 1991—, Sphinx Pharms., 1992-94, Synaptic Pharms., 1993-95; vis. prof. Chinese Second Mil. Med. U., Shanghai, 1992—, Tonji Med. U., 1993—; hon. prof. Chinese Acad. Med. Scis., Beijing, 1993—, Nanjing Med. U., 1994—. Author (with J. Chou) Dose Effect Analysis with Microcomputers, 1986; Coeditor Synergism and Antogonism in Chemotherapy, Acad. Press, 1991; mem. edit. adv. bd. Cancer Biochemistry Biophysics, 1984—, Jour. of the Nat. Cancer Inst., 1988-92, Kaohisung Jour. Med. Scis., 1992—; chmn. pub. bd. Bio/Pharma Quarterly, 1995—; contbr. articles on cancer, and AIDS chemotherapy and theoretical biology to profl. jours. Rsch. grantee Nat. Cancer Inst., Nat. Inst. of Allergy and Infectious Diseases, Elsa U. Pardee Found. and Am. Cancer Soc., 1975—. Mem. AAAS, Am. Assn. Cancer Rsch., Am. Soc. Pharmacology and Exptl. Therapeutics, Am. Soc. Preventive Oncology (founding mem.), Am. Soc. for Biochem. and Molecular Biol., Am. Bur. Med. Advancement in China (bd. dirs. 1990—, v.p. 1994—), N.Y. Acad. Sci., Kaohsiung Med. Coll. Alumni Assn. Am. (bd. dir. 1968-91, pres. 1972), Harvey Soc., Sigma Xi. Office: 1275 York Ave New York NY 10021-6007

CHOUCAIR, RAMSEY JOE, surgeon, educator; b. Knox City, Tex., May 28, 1957; s. Joseph and Selma (Salem) C.; m. Ginger Mariani, Nov. 14, 1987; children: Christine, Jacqueline. BA, Rice U., 1979; MD, Southwestern Med. Sch., Tex., 1983. Diplomate Am. Bd. Surgery, Am. Bd. Plastic Surgery, Am. Bd. Hand Surgery. Extern Parkland Meml. Hosp., Dallas, 1981-83; intern gen. surgery St. Paul Med. Ctr., Dallas, 1983-84, resident in gen. surgery, 1984-87, chief resident in gen. surgery, 1987-88; resident in plastic and reconstructive surgery Ohio State U., Columbus, 1988-89, chief resident in plastic and reconstructive surgery, 1989-90, instr. surgery, 1988-90; aesthetic plastic surgeon, Bruce F. Connell clin. prof. surgery Med. Sch. U. Calif.-Irvine, Santa Ana, 1990; aesthetic plastic surgeon, Eugene H. Courtiss clin. prof. surgery Harvard Med. Sch., Newton, Mass., 1990-91; clin. fellow in surgery Harvard Med. Sch., 1991, instr. surgery, 1991—; reconstructive plastic surgeon Shriners Burns Inst., Mass. Gen. Hosp., Harvard Med. Sch., Boston, 1991; plastic surgery and gen. surgery residency tng. instr. Shriners Burns Inst., Mass. Gen. Hosp., Harvard Med. Sch., 1991—; asst. in surgery, lectr. Mass. Gen. Hosp., 1991—; active staff surgeon, lectr. Newton Wellesley Hosp., 1991—; lectr. Shriners Burns Inst., 1991—; active staff surgeon Waltham Weston Hosp., 1991—; mem. affialiated staff Southwood Cmty. Hosp., 1995—, Norwood Hosp., 1995—; cons. in surgery Shriners Burns Inst., 1991—; mem. cons. staff Nantucket Cottage Hosp., 1994—. Contbr. articles to profl. jours. and chpts. to book. Recipient Noenthal scholar Rice U., 1977-78. Fellow Am. Coll. Surgeons (assoc.); mem. AMA, Am. Burn Assn., Am. Assn. for Hand Surgery, Am. Assn. Clin. Anatomy, Am. Soc. Aesthetic Plastic Surgery, Am. Soc. Plastic and Reconstructive Surgeons, Mass. Med. Soc., Mass. Soc. Plastic Surgery, New Eng. Assn. for Hand Surgery, Northeastern Soc. Plastic Surgery, Charles River Dist. Med. Soc., Robert M. Zollinger Ohio State U. Surg. Soc. Home: 79 Leighton Rd Wellesley MA 02181 Office: Shriners Burns Inst 51 Blossom St Boston MA 02114

CHOUKROUN, GABRIEL, nephrologist; b. Fez, Marocco, Aug. 26, 1961; arrived in France, 1965; s. Simon and Messody (Belelty) C.; m. Sylvie Joncour, Nov. 14, 1995; children: Laurie, Alice. BS, U. Paris, 1979, MD, 1991. Resident Hosp. Paris, 1986-90; asst. prof. Hosp. Necker, Paris, 1992-95; rsch. fellow Mass. Gen. Hosp., Boston, 1995—. Author: Désordres Hydroelectrolytiques, 1995. Lt. French Navy, 1990-91. Grantee Found. Fed. Rsch., 1990, Lilly Inst. Internat. Rsch., 1995, Ministry Fgn. Affairs, 1995. Mem. Internat. Soc. Nephrology, Soc. French Nephrology. Home: 11 Howard St Arlington MA 02174 Office: Mass Gen Hosp E 149 13th St Charlestown MA 02129-2060

CHOVAN, JOHN DAVID, biomedical engineer; b. Canton, Ohio, Sept. 14, 1958; s. John Jr. and Esther Lee (Baker) C. BS, Ohio State U., 1980, BS in Audio Recording, 1980, BSEE, 1982, MS, 1984, PhD, 1990. Registered profl. engr., Ohio. Evaluation programs assoc. Nat. Bd. Med. Examiners, Phila., 1985-87; rsch. scientist Battelle Meml. Inst., Columbus, 1991-95; grad. rsch. assoc. Ohio State U., Columbus, 1982-84, lead programmer-analyst, 1984-85, grad. rsch. assoc., 1987-90, postdoctoral researcher, 1990-91, sr. tech. specialist, 1995—. Author: Educom Selected Academic Software, 1990; editor: Preprints of the 1991 IFIP Working Group on Intelligent CAD, 1991; author conf. papers, tech. reports. Mem. Columbus AIDS Task Force, 1985; mem. Ohio State U. AIDS Edn. and Rsch. Com., Columbus, 1987-90, Am. Rose Soc. Recipient numerous baking and cooking state level competitions. Mem. Engring. in Medicine and Biology Soc. of IEEE, Biomed. Engring. Soc., Internat. Neural Networks Soc., Mensa, Knitting Guild Am., Sigma Xi. Home: 135 Arden Rd Columbus OH 43214-3719 Office: Ohio State U JL Camera Ctr 2050 Kenny Rd Columbus OH 43221

CHOW, CHUN-CHUNG, physician, researcher; b. Hong Kong, Hong Kong, June 7, 1958; s. Kwai-Chau and Muk-Ying (Ng) C. MBBS, U. Hong Kong, 1983; MRCP, Royal Coll. Physicians of the United Kingdom, 1986. Med. officer Princess Margaret Hosp., Hong Kong, 1984-85; med. officer Medicine, Prince of Wales Hosp., Hong Kong, 1985-88, 89-91, sr. med. officer, 1991—; rsch. fellow U. Wales Coll. Medicine, Cardiff, 1988-89; hon. lectr. Faculty of Medicine Chinese U. of Hong Kong, 1991-95, hon. assoc. prof. 1996—. Editor: (book) The Prince of Wales Hospital Manual for Management of Diabetes Mellitus, 1996, (in Chinese) Living Positively With Diabetes, 1995; contbr. articles to profl. jours. Recipient Commonwealth Med. scholarship Assn. Commonwealth Univs., 1988-89. Fellow Hong Kong Acad. Medicine, Hong Kong Coll. Physicians, Royal Coll. Physicians of Edinburgh. Office: Dept Medicine-Prince of Wales Hosp, Chinese U Hong Kong, Shatin NT, Hong Kong

CHOW, FRANKLIN SZU-CHIEN, obstetrician, gynecologist; b. Hong Kong, Apr. 15, 1956; came to U.S., 1967; s. Walter Wen-Tsao and Jane Ju-Hsien (Tang) C. BS, CCNY, 1977; MD, U. Rochester, 1979. Diplomate Am. Bd. Ob-Gyn. Intern Wilmington (Del.) Med. Ctr., 1979-80, resident in ob-gyn, 1980-83; practice medicine specializing in ob-gyn Vail (Colo.) Valley Med. Ctr., 1983—, chmn. obstetrics com., 1984-85, 86-87, chmn. surg. com., 1987-88, vice chief of staff, 1989-91, chief of staff, 1991-92. Named to Athletic Hall of Fame, CCNY, 1983. Fellow Am. Coll. Ob-Gyn's; mem. AMA, Colo. Med. Soc., Intermountain Med. Soc. (pres. 1985-86), Internat. Fedn. Gynecol. Endoscopists, Am. Assn. Gynecol. Laparoscopists, Gynecologic Laser Soc., Am. Soc. Colposcopy and Cervical Pathology. Home: Box 5657 401 Winslow Rd Vail CO 81688-5657 Office: Vail Valley Med Ctr 181 W Meadow Dr Ste 600 Vail CO 81657-5058

CHOW, GEORGE, physician; b. Nov. 22, 1958; m. Marie Kwok; 1 child, Phillip Alexander. BS with honors, Stanford U., 1980; MD with honors, U. Calif., San Diego, 1985. Diplomate Am. Bd. Psychiatry and Neurology. Intern in medicine St. Mary's Hosp. Med. Ctr., San Francisco, 1985-86; resident in neurology U. Calif., Los Angeles, 1986-89; neurologist San Fernando Valley Neurol. Group, Tarzana, Calif., 1989—. Mem. AMA, Am. Soc. Neurorehab., Am. Acad. Neurology, Calif. Med. Assn., L.A. Med. Soc. Office: San Fernando Valley Neurol Med Group 18370 Burbank Blvd # 107 Tarzana CA 91356

CHOW, KAO LIANG, neurobiologist, educator; b. Tientsin, China, Apr. 21, 1918; came to U.S., 1946, naturalized, 1963; s. Su Tau and Tau Yu (Tsau) C.; m. Margaret W.C. Zee, May 2, 1964. B.S., Yenching U., China, 1943; Ph.D., Harvard, 1950. Staff Yerkes Lab. Primate Biology, Orange Park, Fla., 1947-54; research asso. Yerkes Lab. Primate Biology, 1947-54; faculty U. Chgo., 1954-61; mem. faculty Stanford Med. Sch., Palo Alto, Calif., 1961—; prof. neurology Stanford Med. Sch., 1965-84, prof. emeritus, 1984—. Contbr. articles profl. jours. Mem. Internat. Brain Rsch. Orgn., Am. Physiol. Assn., AAAS, Soc. for Neuroscience, Sigma Xi. Home: 101 Alma St Apt 805 Palo Alto CA 94301-1009

CHOW, RITA KATHLEEN, nurse consultant; b. San Francisco, Aug. 19, 1926; d. Peter and May (Chan) C. BS, Stanford U., 1950, nursing diploma, 1950; MS, Case Western Res. U., 1955; profl. diploma in nursing edn. adminstrn, Columbia U., 1961, EdD, 1968; B of Individualized Studies, George Mason U., 1983. Asst. in teaching Stanford U., Calif., 1951-52; instr., dir. student health Fresno (Calif.) Gen. Hosp. Sch. Nursing, 1952-54; instr. Wayne State U. Coll. Nursing, Detroit, 1957-58; rsch. assoc., project dir. cardiovascular nursing rsch. Ohio State U., Columbus, 1965-68; commd. officer USPHS, 1968, advanced through grades to nurse dir., capt., 1974; spl. asst. to dep. dir. Nat. Ctr. Health Svcs. Rsch., Health Svcs. and Mental Health Adminstrn., HEW, Rockville, Md., 1969-73; dep. dir. manpower utilization br., 1970-73; dep. dir. Office Long Term Care; dep. chief nurse officer USPHS, Rockville, 1973-77; chief quality assurance br. div. long-term care Office of Standards and Certification, Health Standards and Quality Bur., Health Care Fin. Adminstrn., HHS, 1977-82; supervisory clin. nurse and spl. asst. to health systems adminstr. USPHS Indian Hosp., HRSA, HHS, Rosebud, S.D., 1982-83; dir. patient edn., asst. dir. nursing G.W. Long Hansen's Disease Ctr., USPHS, Carville, La., 1984-89; dir. nursing Fed. Med. Ctr., Ft. Worth, 1989-95; now pvt. cons. Author: Identifying Nursing Action with the Care of Cardiovascular Patients, 1967, Cardiosurgical Nursing Care: Understandings, Concepts, and Principles for Practice, 1975; mem. editorial bd. Nursing and Health Care, 1983-95; contbr. to publs. in field. Served with Nurse Corps U.S. Army, 1954-57. Recipient Nursing Svc. award Assn. Mil. Surgeons U.S., 1969, Commendation medal USPHS, 1972, citation for outstanding contbn. to cardiovasc. nursing Am. Heart Assn., 1972-79, Nursing Edn. Alumni Assn. award for disting. achievement in nursing rsch. Columbia U. Tchrs. Coll., 1973, Meritorious Svc. medal USPHS, 1977, Disting. Alumnus award Case Western Res. U. Sch. Nursing, 1979, Disting. Svc. medal USPHS, 1987, Artist of Life award Internat. Women's Writing Guild, 1987, Women's Honors in Pub. Svcs. award ANA, 1988, Commendable Svc. medal U.S. Dept. Justice, Bur. Prisons, 1995; AAUW scholar, Nat. League Nursing fellow, 1959-61; rsch. grantee Sigma Theta Tau, 1966.

CHOWHAN, NAVEED MAHFOOZ, oncologist; b. Pakistan, Oct. 19, 1960; came to U.S., 1979; Student, Mao and Forman Christian Coll., Pakistan, 1979; MD cum laude, U Cetec, Dominican Republic, 1982. Bd. cert. internal medicine, 1986, hematology, 1992, oncology, 1993. Resident internal medicine Georgetown U. Svc., D.C. Gen. Hosp., Washington, 1983-86; fellowship oncology-hematology SUNY, Stony Brook, 1988-91, clin. asst. prof. dept. medicine divsn. oncology, 1992-94; pvt. practice New Albany, Ind., 1994—; pvt. practice, South Bend, Ind., 1986-88; attending physician Meml. Hosp. and St. Joseph Med. Ctr., South Bend, 1987-88, Floyd Meml. Hosp., New Albany, 1994—, Clark Meml. Hosp., Jeffersonville, Ind., 1994—; mem. Com. on Rsch. Involving Human Subjects, 1993-94; physician pioneer bone marrow transplant program SUNY, Stony Brook, 1994; chair cancer conf., mem. cancer com. and cont. med. edn. com. Floyd Meml. Hosp., 1995—; mem. cancer com. and blood transfusion com. Clark Meml. Hosp., 1995—; investigator, rschrs. and presenter in field. Contbr. articles to profl. jours. Fellow ACP; mem. Am. Soc. Clin. Oncology, Am. Soc. Hematology. Office: Ste 440 1919 State St New Albany IN 47150

CHOWNING, ORR-LYDA BROWN, dietitian; b. Cottage Grove, Oreg., Nov. 30, 1920; d. Fred Harrison and Mary Ann (Bartels) Brown; m. Kenneth Bassett Williams, Oct. 23, 1944 (dec. Mar. 1945); m. Eldon Wayne Chowning, Dec. 31, 1959. BS, Oreg. State Coll., 1943; MA, Columbia U., 1950. Dietetic intern Scripps Metabolic Clinic, LaJolla, Calif., 1944; sr. asst. dietitian Providence Hosp., Portland, Oreg., 1945-49; contact dietitian St. Lukes Hosp., N.Y.C., summer 1949; cafeteria food svc. supr. Met. Life Ins. Co., N.Y.C., 1950-52; set up food svc. and head dietitian McKenzie-Willamette Meml. Hosp., Springfield, Oreg., 1955-59; foods dir. Erb Meml. Student Union, Eugene, Oreg., 1960-63; set up food svc. and head dietitian Cascade Manor Retirement Home, Eugene, 1967-68; owner, operator Veranda Kafe, Inc., Albany, Oreg., 1971-80; owner, operator, sec.-treas. Chownings Adult Foster Home, Albany, 1984—. Contbr. articles to profl. jours. Lin County Women's chmn. Hatfield for Senator Spaghetti Rally, Albany H.S., 1966; food preparation chmn. Yi for You, Mae Yih for State Senate, Albany Lebanon, Sweet Home, 1982; Silver Clover Club sponsor Oreg. 4-H Found., Oreg. State U., Corvallis, 1994, 95. Recipient coll. scholarship Nat. 4-H Food Preparation Contest, Chgo., 1939. Mem. Am. Dietetic Assn. (registered dietitian, gerontol. nutritionist dietetic practice group 1988—), Oreg. Dietetic Assn. (diet therapy chairperson, newsletter editor 1963-64), Willamette Dietetic Assn., Kappa Delta Pi (Kappa chpt.), Mu Beta Beta. Republican. Mem. Disciples of Christ. Home and Office: Chownings Adult Foster Home 4440 Woods Rd NE Albany OR 97321-7353

CHOY, JENNIFER HOW MUN, internist, pharmacist; b. Hong Kong, Aug. 24, 1964; d. John Choy and Jane (Shum) Chow. D Pharmacy, U. of the Pacific, 1990; DO magna cum laude, U. of Health Scis., 1995. Pharmacist Carteron and Co., Marina Del Rey, Calif., 1991, Rx Relief, Inc., Fallbrook, Calif., 1991; resident in internal medicine Tucson Gen. Hosp., 1995—; tutor in osteo. manipulation U. of Health Scis., Kansas City, Mo., 1992-93. Recipient award for osteo. manipulation Pfizer Co., 1995. Mem. Am. Coll. Internists, Am. Osteo. Assn., Psi Sigma Alpha. Home: 1507-A E Prince Rd Tucson AZ 85719

CHOY, WAI NANG, toxicologist, geneticist; b. Canton, China, Nov. 23, 1946; came to U.S., 1970; s. Kim Ball and Shue (Young) Tsai. BSc with honor, Chinese U. Hong Kong, 1969; PhD, Rutgers U., 1976. Diplomate Am. Bd. Toxicology. Postdoctoral fellow dept. pediatrics Sch. Medicine, Johns Hopkins U., Balt., 1975-79, instr. div. biophysics Sch. Hygiene and Pub. Health and Dept. Environ. Health Scis., 1979-82; rsch. geneticist Western Regional Rsch. Ctr., USDA, Berkeley, Calif., 1982-84; specialist Sch. Pub. Health, U. Calif., Berkeley, 1982; rsch. genetic toxicologist Haskell Lab. Toxicology, E.I. Du Pont de Nemours and Co., Newark, Del., 1984-86; staff toxicologist Calif. Dept. Health Svcs., Berkeley, 1986-91; sr. prin. scientist Schering-Plough Corp., Lafayette, N.J., 1991-95, drug safety and metabolism fellow, 1995—. Contbr. articles to sci. jours., chpts. to books. Scholar Yale-in-China Assn., 1967, Lee's scholar, 1968; recipient Nat. Rsch. Svc. Award NIH, 1975-79. Mem. ASTM (com. 1985-86), AAAS, Soc. Toxicology, Am. Soc. Human Genetics, Environ. Mutagen Soc. Office: Schering-Plough Rsch Inst Safety Evaluation Ctr PO Box 32 Lafayette NJ 07848-0032

CHRISLER, JOAN C., psychologist, educator; b. Teaneck, N.J., Jan. 1, 1953; d. Eugene Reed and Anna Mary (Whalen) C.; m. Christopher Bishop, Nov. 20, 1976. BS in Psychology, Fordham U., 1975; MA, PhD in Exptl. Psychology, Yeshiva U., 1986; cert. in behavior therapy, L.I. U. Adj. instr. Mercy Coll., Dobbs Ferry, N.Y., 1979-85, Coll. of Mt. St. Vincent, Riverdale, N.Y., 1979, Monroe Bus. Inst., Bronx, N.Y., 1980, Iona Coll., New Rochelle, N.Y., 1980, Ramapo Coll., Mahwah, N.J., 1980-84, Upsala Coll., East Orange, N.J., 1981-85, St. Thomas Acquinas Coll., Sparkill, N.Y., 1984, SUNY, Purchase, 1984-87, Coll. New Rochelle, N.Y., 1984-85, Bergen Community Coll., Paramus, N.J., 1984-85; asst. prof. Conn. Coll., New London, 1987-93, assoc. prof., 1993—; vis. scholar The Stone Ctr., Wellesley Coll., 1994; asst. to dir. Internat. English Lang. Inst. Hunter Coll., N.Y.C., 1978-80; asst. to coord. Media Ctr. Payne Whitney Psychiat. Clinic, N.Y.C., 1980-82; fieldwork in behavior therapy Creedmoor Psychiat. Ctr., Queens Village, N.Y., 1982; group therapist Health Improvement Sys., Cin., 1982-84. Author: (with others) New Directions in Feminist Psychology, Variations on a Theme: Diversity and the Psychology of Women, Lectures on the Psychology of Women, Menstruation, Health and Illness, Feminist Perspectives on Addictions, Overcoming Fear of Fat; contbr. numerous articles to profl. jours. Dist. leader New Rochelle Dem. Com., N.Y., 1985-87; mem. Westchester County Dem. Com., White Plains, N.Y., 1985-87; v.p. Westchester NOW, White Plains, 1985-87; state bd. mem. Conn. NOW, 1988—; mem. exec. com. Westchester Women's Polit. Caucus, Mt. Vernon, N.Y., 1985-87. Named Woman of Yr., Westchester County, N.Y., 1987; recipient Susan B. Anthony award Westchester NOW, 1987, Christine Ladd-Franklin award AWP, 1996. Mem. APA, AAUP (Conn. v.p. 1993-95), Assn. Women in Psychology (spokesperson 1985-88, conf. coord. 1990, nat. coord. 1992-95), Soc. Menstrual Cycle Rsch., New Eng. Psychol. Assn. (steering com. 1991—, treas. 1992-94, pres. 1996), New Eng. Women's Studies Assn., Psi Chi. Home: 116 Fifth Ave Milford CT 06460 Office: Conn Coll Dept Of Psychology New London CT 06320

CHRISMAN, NOEL JUDSON, nursing educator; b. Visalia, Calif., July 30, 1940; s. Elmer Judson and Margaret Jensine (Jacobsen) C.; m. Judith Beeber, Aug. 4, 1989; children: Michael Chrisman, Christian Beeber, Robert Linsky. AB in Anthropology, U. Calif., Riverside, 1962; PhD in Anthropology, U. Calif., Berkeley, 1966, MPH, 1967. Asst. prof. anthropology Pomona Coll., Claremont, Calif., 1967-73; prof. Sch. Nursing U. Wash., Seattle, 1973—, coord. grad. program in cross-cultural nursing. Contbr. articles to profl. publs. Grantee NSF, 1979-82. Fellow Soc. Applied Anthropology (exec. com. 1988-91), Am. Anthropol. Assn.; mem. Coun. on Nursing and Anthropology (treas. 1988-90), Transcultural Nursing Soc., Delta Omega. Office: U Washington Dept Pschosocial and Cmty Health Sch Nursing PO Box 357263 Seattle WA 98195-7263

CHRIST, JACOB, psychiatrist; b. Langenbruck, Baselland, Switzerland, Feb. 10, 1926; s. Anton Leonard and Anna Alice (Kambli) C.; m. Cornelia A. van der Horst, Sept. 30, 1950 (dec. May 1952); 1 child, Frans; m. Barbara R. Fierke, Sept. 15, 1956 (dec. Nov. 1968); children: Charlotte, Martin, Catherine; m. Jane Lippincott Smith, Jan. 6, 1979; children: Heidi, Jonathan. MD, U. Lausanne (Switzerland), 1951, U. Amsterdam (the Netherlands), 1952; MD (Thesis), U. Zürich (Switzerland), 1952. Diplomate Am. Bd. Psychiatry and Neurology; cert. Specialty Bd. Psychiatry, Switzerland. Intern U. Amsterdam Hosps., 1949-52; resident Med. Coll. Va., Richmond, 1952-53, N.Y. Hosp., Cornell Med. Ctr., 1953-54, Yale Psychiatric Inst., New Haven, Conn., 1954-55; asst. instr., clin. assoc. psychiatrist Harvard U. Med. Sch., McLean Hosp., Boston, 1956-70; assoc. prof. Emory U. Med. Sch., Atlanta, 1970-79; cons. staff Northside Community Mental Health Ctr., Atlanta, 1973-79; psychiatrist in chief External Psychiat. Svcs. of Canton Baselland, Liestal, Switzerland, 1979-91; pvt. practice psychiatry Basel, Switzerland, 1991—; vis. instr. Med. U. of S.C., Charleston, 1970-77; instr. Sch. for Social Work, Basel, 1979—. Co-editor: Contemporary Marriage, 1976. Lt. USN, 1955-57. Rsch. grantee NIMH, 1967-69. Fellow Am. Psychiat. Assn., Am. Group Psychotherapy Assn. Home and Office: Sevogelplatz 2, 4052 Basel Switzerland

CHRIST, PHILIP WILLIAM, orthopaedic surgeon, osteopath; b. Sellersville, Pa., Feb. 27, 1955; s. William Clifford and Dorothy (George) C. BS in Chemistry, Ursinus Coll., Collegeville, Pa., 1978; DO, Phila. Coll. Osteo. Medicine, 1982. Diplomate Am. Bd. Orthopaedic Surgery, Am. Osteo. Bd. Orthopaedic Surgery. Intern Delaware Valley Med. Ctr., Bristol, Pa., 1982-83; resident in orthopaedic surgery Southeastern Med. Ctr., Miami, Fla., 1983-87; pvt. practice, Miami, 1987-91, Seminole, Fla., 1992—; vice chmn. dept. surgery Univ. Gen. Hosp., Seminole, 1995—, Seminole Hosp., 1995—, Pinellas Cmty. Hosp., Pinellas Park, Fla., 1995—. Mem. Am. Osteo. Assn., Am. Osteo. Acad. Orthopaedics, Pinellas Osteo. Med. Soc. Republican. Methodist. Office: Seminole Orthopedics & Sports Medicine 10099 Seminole Blvd Seminole FL 34642

CHRISTENSEN, BRENT J., surgeon; b. Salt Lake City, Apr. 21, 1954; s. James D. and Betty M. (Schoenfeld) C.; m. Sharon K. Lewis, June 29, 1979; children: Kelci, Jamie, Jordan, Chase, Dayne. BS, U. Utah, 1978, MD, 1984. Diplomate Am. Bd. Surgery. Intern St. Joseph Hosp., Denver, 1984-85, surg. resident, 1984-89; gen. surgeon Bryner Clinic, Salt Lake City, 1989—; dir. intermountain endosurg. inst. LDS Hosp., Salt Lake City, 1991—, chair divsn. gen. surgery, 1994—, vice chair dept. surgery, 1994—; asst. clin. prof. U. Utah, Salt Lake City, 1994—. Fellow ACS; mem. AMA, Utah Med. Assn., Salt Lake County Med. Soc., Southwestern Surg. Congress, Soc. Am. Gastrointestinal Endoscopic Surgery, Soc. of Lapasoendoscopic Surgeons. Mormon. Office: Bryner Clinic 745 E 300 S Salt Lake City UT 84102

CHRISTENSEN, CARL J., hospital administrator; b. Creston, Iowa, Aug. 21, 1951; s. Carl R. Christensen and Gladys H. (Olson) Maasson; m. Susan G. Huedepohl, Dec. 31, 1971; children: Anjeanette, Lesley Ann, Holly Ann, Leanna. AA, U. San Diego Health Sci., 1976; AS, Calif. Coll. for Health Sci, 1976; BA, Ottawa U., 1990, MA, 1991. Cert. health care exec. Chief respiratory therapist Mercy Hosp., Oelnein, Iowa, 1976-85; assoc. dir. St. Francis Hosp., Waterloo, Iowa, 1985-87; adminstr. Grundy County Hosp., Grundy Ctr., Iowa, 1987-89; pres. Mercy Hosp., Oelnein, Iowa, 1989-92; CEO De Witt (Iowa) Cmty. Hosp., 1992—; cons. B. Haynes & Assocs., Kansas City, Kans., 1990—. Bd. dirs. De Witt Referral Ctr, 1993, Health Svcs. Credit Union, Clinton, Iowa, 1993—. With U.S. Air Force, 1970-74, Vietnam. Mem. Iowa Hosp. Assn. (fin. com. 1990-95), De Witt C. of C.

(ambassador), Lions Club (program chmn. 1993-94, 3rd v.p.). Methodist. Office: De Witt Cmty Hosp 1118 11th St De Witt IA 52742

CHRISTENSEN, FINN NORRING, executive; b. Copenhagen, June 8, 1956; s. Svend Erik and Grethe Norring (Andersen) C. MS in Chem. Engring., Tech. U. Denmark, 1980; PhD in Indsl. Rsch., Danish Acad. Tech. Scis., 1984. Indsl. rsch., edn. A/S Alfred Benzon, Copenhagen, 1981-83, lab. head, 1983-85, dir. rsch. & devel. pharms., 1985-89; dir. Repro-Dose drug delivery systems Benzon Pharm. A/S, Copenhagen, 1989—; asst. prof. Royal Danish Sch. Pharmacy, Copenhagen, 1989—. Contbr. articles to profl. jours.; inventor in field. Served with Danish Army, 1975-76. Mem. Controlles Release Soc. Office: Benzon Pharm A/S, Helseholmen 1, DK-2650 Hvidovre Denmark

CHRISTENSEN, HANNE, physiologist; b. Copenhagen, Oct. 2, 1950; d. John Thomas Alfred and Karen (Jørgensen) Willumsen; m. Tom Howy Christensen, Sept. 1, 1973 (div. Feb. 1988); children: Julie, Jesper, Rasmus. MSc, U. Copenhagen, 1981, PhD, 1988. Researcher Nat. Inst. Occupational Health, Copenhagen, 1987-91, sr. researcher, 1991—; leader nat. governmental program concerning repetitive work, 1994-98. Contbr. articles to profl. jours. Grantee The League of Polio- Traffic- and Accident Injuries, Copenhagen, 1986, Found. of Workers Protections, Copenhagen, 1987, Danish Assn. Manual Medicine, Copenhagen, 1988. Mem. Danish Assn. Neurophysiology, Internat. Engring. in Medicine and Biology Soc. Home: Borups Allé 22, Ved Vigen 4, DK 2400 Copenhagen Denmark Office: Nat Inst Occupational, Health Lerso Parkalle 105, DK 2100 Copenhagen Denmark

CHRISTENSEN, JULIEN MARTIN, psychologist, educator; b. Capron, Ill., Sept. 3, 1918; s. Peter Martin and Lucile Marie (Edson) C.; m. Imogene E. Willis, Mar. 27, 1954; children: Kim, Kyle, Karen. BS, U. Ill., 1940; MA, Ohio State U., 1952, PhD, 1959; ScD (hon.), U. Dayton, 1989. Diplomate Am. Bd. Forensic Psychology; lic. psychologist, Ohio, lic. scuba diver, pilot. Statis. clk., personnel technician U.S. Air Force Tng. Command, Ft. Worth, 1941-43; research scientist Aerospace Med. Research Lab., Wright-Patterson AFB, Ohio, 1946-56; dir. human engring. div. Aerospace Med. Research Lab., 1956-74; prof. dept. indsl. engring. and ops. research Coll. Engring. Wayne State U., Detroit, 1974-78; dept. chmn. Wayne State U., 1974-77; dir. human factors div. Stevens, Scheidler, Stevens, Vossler Inc., Dayton, Ohio, 1978-80; chief scientist human factors Gen. Physics Corp., Dayton, 1980-83; chief scientist Ergonomics Div. Universal Energy Systems, Inc., 1983-96; chief scientist Ergonomics Div. UES, Inc. (formerly Universal Energy Systems, Inc.), 1983-96, sr. cons., 1996—; vis. lectr. U. Mich., Ann Arbor, 1959-95; chmn. NASA Behavior/Tech. Com., 1976; vis. lectr. USPHS Sch. Medicine, 1977-81; adj. prof. Wright State U., U. Dayton, Wittenberg U., Sinclair Coll., Ohio State U.; vis. lectr. Air Force Inst. Tech.; cons. and lectr. in field; one of six experts on govt./industry adv. group for NASA man-systems integration standards, 1986-87. Mem. editorial bd. Jour. Systems Engring., 1969, Jour. Safety Research, 1969. Contbr. chpts. to books and articles to profl. jours. Cons. and mem. of numerous editorial bds. of profl. jours. Chmn. human performance sci. adv. com. for Manned Orbiting Lab. Developer of methods for gathering in-flight activity data. Served with USAF, 1943-46. NSF fellow, 1957; named Outstanding Scientist Engring. and Sci. Found., Dayton, Ohio, 1986; recipient AF Assn. Citation of Honor, 1966, AF Decoration of Exceptional Civilian Svc., 1966, Pres. disting. svc. award Human Factors Soc., 1992. Fellow Human Factors Soc. (pres. 1964-65, 86-87), APA (Franklin V. Taylor award 1969); mem. NAS/NRC (naval studies bd. future carrier study 1990), Explorers Club, Am. Soc. Safety Engrs. (acad. accreditation coun. 1979-85), Am. Soc. Safety Rsch. (bd. govs. 1975-79), Soc. Automotive Engrs. (chmn. human factors com. 1975-77, exec. com.), Soc. Engring. Psychologists (past pres., past chmn. exec. coun.), Can. Human Factors Assn. (Julien M. Christensen award), Internat. Ergonomics Rsch. Soc., Miami Valley Psychol. Assn. (past pres.), Soc. Logistics Engrs., S.E. Mich. Human Factors Soc. (past pres.), Systems Safety Soc., Inst. Nuclear Power Ops. (adv. coun. 1989-95), Alpha Kappa Psi, Pi Mu Epsilon, Psi Chi, Tau Beta Pi. Home: 5950 Little Sugar Creek Rd Dayton OH 45440-4005 Office: UES, Inc. 4401 Dayton Xenia Rd Dayton OH 45432-1805

CHRISTENSEN, MARGARET ANNA, nursing educator, consultant; b. San Francisco, Nov. 10, 1938; d. John Bernard and Catherine (Scott) Thielen; m. Robert Edwin Christensen, June 24, 1961; children: Marthe Elizabeth Christensen Groves, Katrina Marie Christensen Head, Andrea Susan Christensen Clark. B.S., Wichita State U., 1978; Ed.M., U. Central Okla., 1984; EdD Okla. State U., 1986. Staff devel. supr. St. Joseph Med. Ctr., Wichita, Kans., 1972-79; head nurse Baptist Med. Ctr., Oklahoma City, 1979-80; clin. supr. Mercy Health Ctr., Oklahoma City, 1980-81, staff devel. coordinator, 1981-84; pres., sr. cons. Human Resource Cons., Inc., Edmond, Okla., 1982-90 ; dir. planning and devel. Allied Nursing Care, Inc., Oklahoma City, 1984-85; rehab. specialist LDH Cons., Oklahoma City, 1985-90; pres., CEO Christensen Mgmt. Co., Portsmouth, 1990—; adj. faculty U. Ctrl. Okla., Edmond, Okla., 1986-90, asst. prof., coord. health scis. grad. programs, Ohio U., 1990-94, coord. health sci. grad. program, 1994-96; coord. health care mgmt. program Dept. of Bus. Shawnee State U., Portsmouth, Ohio, 1996—; author performance enhancement plans for long-term care employees, 1995, mgrs. and supr. Health Care, 1992; performance enhancement plans for profl., tech. workers in Health Care, 1992, performance enhancement plans for office/clerical svc. and maintenance workers Health Care, 1992. Author human resource devel. process, 1984; (booklet) Live-In Companion Guide, 1984, report on hosp. appraisal system impact, 1986. Bd. dirs. Dr.'s Hosp. Nelsonville. Mem. Am. Coll. Health Care Execs., Am. Coll. Health Care Adminstrs., Assn. Univ. Programs in Health Adminstrn., Alpha Chi, Kappa Delta Pi, Sigma Kappa. Republican. Roman Catholic. Home: 13535A US Hwy 52 Portsmouth OH 45663 also: 208 Bus Bldg SSU Portsmouth OH 45662

CHRISTENSEN, MARI ALICE, nursing auditor, medicolegal analyst, consultant; b. Omaha, June 13, 1934; d. Benjamin Marion and Alice Minnie (Thompson) Voelte; m. Gerald H. Christensen, Mar. 17, 1956; 1 child, Amy Michaela. Diploma, Nebr. Meth. Coll. Nursing, Omaha, 1955; BSN, U. Nebr., Omaha, 1961; postgrad., Pitts. State U., Ins. Inst. Am., 1992. RN, Nebr.; rehab. nurse certificate, Ga. Nurses Assn. Charge nurse Nebr. Meth. Hosp., Omaha, 1955-56; office nurse Geo. Robertson, M.D., Omaha, 1956-57; surgeon's asst., office nurse Physicians Clinic, Omaha, 1957-74; medicolegal analyst Turner & Boisseau, Chartered, Great Bend, Kans., 1975-82, Schmid, Mooney & Frederick, P.C., Omaha, 1984-89; cons. Mutual of Omaha Ins. Co., 1989-91; nurse auditor, workers compensation case mgr., analyst Mid-Am. Med. Mgmt., Omaha, 1991-92; pvt. nurse auditor, case mgr., medicolegal analyst Omaha, 1992; ret., 1992; rehab. cons. Crawford Rehab., Omaha, 1982. Mem. ANA (exec. com.), Nat. Assn. Legal Assts. (continuing edn. com. 1988), Nebr. Nurses Assn. (sec., bd. dirs. com. mem.), Assn. Oper. Rm. Nurses (sec.), Nat. Disting. Svc. Registry Nursing, Sigma Theta Tau, Gamma Pi Sigma. Home: 11315 Castelar Cir Omaha NE 68144-3085

CHRISTENSEN, OLE, general practitioner; b. Copenhagen, May 12, 1944; s. Gunnar and Rigmor (Sørensen) C.; m. Mariann Drasbek Jensen, Nov. 5, 1945; children: Mette, Søren. Cand. med., U. Copenhagen, 1971. Mem staff dept. surgery Amtssygehuset Nakskov, Denmark, 1971-73, mem. staff dept. medicine, 1973-74; pvt. practice Nakskov, 1974—; cons. Egeborg addict treatment ctr., Copenhagen ministry of health, 1990—, Nakskov alcohol abuse clinic, 1974—, County Coun., Storstrøm, 1986-92, 94—. Contbr. articles to profl. jours. Recipient Town of Yr. prize of Initiative, 1993, Lion's prize of Initiative, 1993. Mem. Danish Med. Assn., Danish Assn. Gen. Practitioners, Rotary. Office: Krøyers Gaard 1, DK 4900 Nakskov Denmark

CHRISTENSEN, ROBERT WAYNE, oral maxillofacial surgeon, minister; b. N.Y.C., Apr. 6, 1925; s. Charles Joseph Brophy and Eva Sutherland (Hart) Christensen; m. Ann Forsyth (div.); children: Robert, Joan, Elizabeth, Peter, Mary, Colleen, Patricia, Michelle; m. Lynne Blindbury; children: Andrew, Matthew. DDS, NYU, 1948. Oral surgery tng. L.A. County Gen. Hosp., 1950; oral maxillofacial surgeon, 1950-88; pres. TMJ Implants, Inc., Golden, Colo., 1988—; minister, founder Covenant Marriages Ministry, Golden, 1988—; pres. Design Dynamics Internat., Golden, 1994—; R&D med. adv. bd. mem. Sch. Medicine LLU, Loma Linda, Calif.; pres.'s cabinet mem. Jerry Savelle Ministry, Ft. Worth, 1994—; bd. dirs. RBFLC, Denver. Inventor of 5 U.S. patents. Lt. USNR. Republican. Office: TMJ Implants Inc 17301 W Colfax Ave # 135 Golden CO 80401

CHRISTENSEN, THOMAS GASH, biomedical scientist, experimental pathologist; b. Richmond, Va., Sept. 16, 1944; s. Thomas and Carolyn E. Christensen; m. Lora Lou Durett, Aug. 2, 1969; children: Wendy, David. BS, Rutgers U., 1966; PhD, U. Vt., 1971. Postdoctoral rsch. assoc. Med. Sch. U. Vt., Burlington, 1971-74; rsch. assoc. Sch. of Medicine Boston U., 1974-77, asst. rsch. prof. Sch. of Medicine, 1977-80, asst. prof. pathology Sch. of Medicine, 1980-88, assoc. prof. Sch. of Medicine, 1988—; rsch. assoc. Mallory Inst. of Pathology, Boston, 1974-85, sr. rsch. assoc., 1985—; vis. lectr. U. Vt., Burlington, 1971-74, Sargent Coll., Boston U., 1979-82, Northeastern U., Boston, 1980; prin. investigator rsch. grants NIH. Contbr. numerous articles to profl. jours. Mem. AAAS, Am. Soc. for Cell Biology, Am. Thoracic Soc., Microscopy Soc. Am., Alpha Zeta, Sigma Xi. Office: Boston U Sch of Medicine Mallory Inst Pathology 784 Massachusetts Ave Boston MA 02118-2336

CHRISTENSON, EILEEN ELAINE, geriatrics nurse; b. Fosston, Minn., July 26, 1950; d. Arthur L. and Gertrude E. (Jaworsky) Maruska; m. Leonard Dale Christenson, Mar. 16, 1968; children: Kristy, Dale, Melissa, Alicia. Grad., Thief River Fall Tech. Inst., Minn., 1996. LPN, Ill., N.Mex., Minn. Staff nurse Beltram (Minn.) Nursing Home, 1990—, Clearwater County Meml. Hosp., Bagley, Minn. Troop leader Land O'Lakes coun. Girl Scouts U.S., 1974-89. 1st lt. USAF, 1968-76, Vietnam. Decorated Purple Heart, Silver Cross, Bronze Star (2). Mem. VFW, Am. Legion, Eagles 351. Home: RR 5 Box 330A Bemidji MN 56601-8531

CHRISTENSON, PAUL J., surgeon; b. L.A., Jan. 16, 1953; s. Luther B. and Velda Ruth (Johnson) C.; m. Melissa L. Rosado, May 23, 1980; children: E. Jon, Jennifer Ruth, Heather Kathleen. BS magna cum laude, Brigham Young U., 1972; MD, U. Utah, 1976. Cert. Nat. Bd. Med. Examiners, Am. Bd. Urology. Commd. ensign USN, 1972, advanced through grades to capt.; intern Naval Regional Med. Ctr., Portsmouth, Va., 1976-77; battalion surgeon 1st Div. 9th Marines, Okinawa, Japan, 1977-78; urology resident Nat. Naval Med. Ctr., Bethesda, Md., 1978-82, staff urologist, 1982-84; dir. surg. svcs., chief urology 13th Air Force Med. Ctr., Clark AFB, Philippines, 1984-88; chief urology div. USNS Comfort, Persian Gulf, 1990-91; asst. chief urology Nat. Naval Med. Ctr., Bethesda, 1988-93, chief of urology, 1993—; assoc. prof. surgery Uniformed Svcs. Univ. of Health Scis., Bethesda, 1988—. Contbr. urology articles to profl. jours.; co-producer 4 films in the fields of urology and wound ballistics. Fellow ACS; mem. Am. Urol. Assn., Am. Assn. Clin. Urologists, Phi Kappa Phi. Republican. Mem. LDS Church. Office: Nat Naval Med Ctr Urology Bethesda MD 20814

CHRISTENSON, RICHARD HARRY, physician; b. Milw., Feb. 22, 1943; s. Ray T. and Dorothy E. (Oakland) C.; m. Karen E. Brindley, Aug. 13, 1966; children: Nathan G., Rachel A. BS, U. Wis., 1965, MD, 1969. Diplomate Am. Bd. Radiology. Intern L.A. County-U. So. Calif. Med. Ctr., L.A., 1970-71; med. officer USPHS-Indian Health Svc., Phoenix, 1971-72, Anchorage, 1972-73; resident Vanderbilt U. Hosp., Nashville, 1973-76; radiologist Mt. Sinai Med. Ctr., Milw., 1976-88; med. dir. Mt. Sinai IPA, Milw., 1986-88, pres., 1987-88; chief radiology Mt. Sinai Med. Ctr., Milw., 1987-88; pres. Precision Health Systems, Milw., 1989-92; corp. med. dir. United Wis. Svcs. Inc. (Blue Cross/Blue Shield Compcare), Milw., 1989—. Office: United Wis Svcs Inc 401 W Michigan St Milwaukee WI 53203-2896

CHRISTIAN, JOE CLARK, medical genetics researcher, educator; b. Marshall, Okla., Sept. 12, 1934; s. Roy John and Katherine Elizabeth (Beeby) C.; m. Shirley Ann Yancey, June 5, 1960; children: Roy Clark, Charles David. BS, Okla. State U., 1956; MS, U. Ky., 1959, PhD, 1960, MD, 1964. Cert. clin. geneticist, Am. Bd. Med. Genetics. Resident internal medicine Vanderbilt U., Nashville, 1964-66; asst. prof. med. genetics Ind. U., Indpls., 1966-69, assoc. prof., 1969-74, prof., 1974—, assoc. dean basic scis. & regional ctrs., 1996—. Served with USAR, 1953-60. Mem. AMA, Am. Soc. Human Genetics. Democrat. Methodist. Office: Ind U Dept Med/ Molecular Genetics 975 W Walnut St Indianapolis IN 46202-5251

CHRISTIAN, JOHN JERMYN, biologist; b. Scranton, Pa., Apr. 12, 1917; s. John Oren and Margaret Adams (Jermyn) C.; m. Constance O. Koons, June 26, 1942 (div. Sept. 1958); 1 child, John J. Jr.; m. Patricia Hart, Nov. 6, 1958; 1 child, Patricia Jean. AB, Princeton U., 1939; ScD, Johns Hopkins U., 1954. Rsch. pharmacologist Wyeth Inc. Rsch. Labs., Phila., 1947-51; physiologist Naval Med. Rsch. Inst., Bethesda, Md., 1951-59; rsch. assoc. Johns Hopkins Sch. Hygiene and Pub. Health, Balt., 1954-59; assoc. dir. Phila. Zool. Soc., Penrose Rsch. Lab., Phila., 1959-62; mem. Albert Einstein Med. Ctr. Rsch. Labs., Phila., 1962-70; prof. biology SUNY, Binghamton, 1970-87, prof. emeritus, 1987—; sec. Endocrine Study, NIH, Bethesda, 1958-63. Author (book chpt.) Physiological Mammalogy, 1959; contbr. papers and rsch. to profl. jours. Life mem. Nature Conservancy, 1989. Lt. USNR, 1942-46. Recipient Mercer award Ecol. Soc. Am., 1957, Honors, Armed Forces Inst. Pathology, 1962. Mem. Am. Soc. Mammalogists, Am. Ornithologists Union, Am. Assn. Pathologists, Endocrine Soc., AAAS, N.Y. Acad. Sci., Wildlife Soc. Home: PO Box 24 Starlight PA 18461-0024 Office: SUNY Dept Biol Scis Binghamton NY 13902-6000

CHRISTIANSEN, JOHN, surgeon, consultant; b. Jyderup, Denmark, Nov. 17, 1934; s. Einar and Grethe (Jensen) C.; m. Inge Brydensholt, Sept. 5, 1959; children: Merete, Anette. M.D., U. Copenhagen, 1961, Ph.D., 1972. Chief surgeon Glostrup Hosp., Copenhagen, 1976-92; chmn. dept. surgery Herlev Univ. Hosp., Copenhagen, 1992—; sr. lectr. U. Copenhagen, 1985—; cons. in surgery Danish Nat. Bd. Health, Copenhagen, 1979—; gen. sec. Danish Surg. Soc., Copenhagen, 1980-83; mem. sci. com. Danish Cancer Soc., 1989; pres. European Bd. Surgery Qualification in Coloproctology, 1996. Editor Danish Med. Jour., 1980—; corr. editorial mem. Annales de Chirurgie, Paris, 1987—; editorial mem. Internat. Jour. Colorect Disease. Fellow Royal Soc. Medicine (London), Soc. Surgery Alimentary Tract, U.S.A., Am. Soc. Colon and Rectal Surgeons; mem. Internat. Soc Univ. Colon and Rectal Surgeons (v.p. northern Europe 1988). Home: 24 Bregentved Alle, 2820 Gentofte, Copenhagen Denmark Office: Herlev Hosp, Dept Surgery, DK-2730 Copenhagen Denmark

CHRISTIANSEN, MARJORIE MINER, nutrition educator; b. Canton, Ill., Feb. 28, 1922; d. John Ernest and Margaret Ellen (Wilson) Miner; m. Theodore Leo Christiansen, Aug. 10, 1951; 1 dau., Karen Lee. Student Joliet Jr. Coll., 1939-41, Iowa State U., 1941-42; B.S., U. N.Mex., 1949, M.A., 1955; Ph.D., Utah State U., 1967. Instr. sci. and nutrition Regina Sch. Nursing, Albuquerque, 1950-64, project dir., 1966-69; project dir., adj. prof. U. Albuquerque, 1969; prof. home econs. James Madison U., Harrisonburg, Va., 1969-84, prof. emeritus, 1984—; nutrition cons. Mental Devel. Ctr., Albuquerque, 1968-69; project dir. Dietary Mgmt. Seminars, VA Regional Med. Program, 1973-76. Mem. adv. Com. on spl. edn. Harrisonburg (Va.) pub. schs., 1972-84. Utah State U. fellow, 1963-67; grantee Corn Products Co., 1965, Nurse Tng. Act Pub. Health Service, 1966-69. Mem. Am. Dietetic Assn., N.Mex. Dietetic Assn., Va. Dietetic Assn. (pres., 1974-75, chmn. of dels., 1978-79). Methodist. Contbr. articles to profl. jours. Home: 10008 Wellington NE Albuquerque NM 87111-7401

CHRISTIANSEN, XENIA ANNETTE, medical and surgical nurse, pediatric nurse, educator; b. San Nicholas, Aruba, Feb. 28, 1932; d. John L. and Beatrice V. (Serrão) De Abreu; m. Johan S. Christiansen, Sept. 8, 1962; children: John F., Peter A. BSN magna cum laude, Adelphi U., 1954; MA in Nursing Edn., Columbia U., N.Y.C., 1959. RN, N.Y., Mass. Asst. dir. nursing N.Y.U. Med. Ctr., N.Y.C., 1959-62; nursing instr. St. Luke's Hosp., New Bedford, Mass., 1962-63, Cape Cod Hosp., Hyannis, Mass., 1964-71; prof. Cape Cod C.C., West Barnstable, Mass., 1971—. Mem. Am. Heart Assn., Mass. Nurses Assn., Mass. Tchrs. Assn. Home: 569 Crowell Rd North Chatham MA 02650-1117

CHRISTIANSON, CECELIA L., health information professional; b. Eldora, Iowa, Jan. 6, 1955; d. George Bernard and Virginia (Rule) Meimann; m. Kevin L. Christianson, Oct. 12, 1974; children: Tara Ann, Keith Blaine. AA, Des Moines Area C.C., Ankeny, Iowa, 1974; Med. Records Technician, AHIMA, Chgo., 1977. Accredited records technician. Health info. dir. Clarke County Hosp., Osceola, Iowa, 1986-90, Charter Community Hosp., Des Moines, 1990-91, Story County Hosp., Nevada, Iowa, 1991-93, 95-96, Ellsworth mcpl. Hosp., Iowa Falls, Iowa, 1993-94; adminstrv. asst. I Iowa Vets. Home, Marshalltown, Iowa, 1994-95; cons. State Ctr., 1990-96; speaker/instr. Nevada Community Sch., 1995—; monitor/instr. AHIMA Ind. Study Program, Chgo., 1992—. Mem. Am. Health Info. Mgmt. Assn., Iowa Health Info. Mgmt. Assn. (mem. budget com., mem. credential com.). Democrat. Roman Catholic. Home: 108 3rd Ave NW State Center IA 50247

CHRISTIE, DONALD MELVIN, JR., physician; b. Lewiston, Maine, May 5, 1942; s. Donald Melvin and Dorothy Carolyn (Doble) C. AB, U. Rochester, 1964, MD, 1968; DLFC, U. Paris, 1963. Diplomate Am. Bd. Internal Medicine, CAQ in Sports Medicine. Med. intern U. Iowa Hosps. and Clinics, Iowa City, 1968-69, resident, 1969-70, 73, chief med. resident, 1973-74; asst. prof. preventive medicine and medicine Sch. Medicine, U. Rochester (N.Y.), 1974-77; univ. physician, dir. clin. services Princeton (N.J.) U. Health Services, 1977-83; clin. instr. family medicine U. Med. and Dentistry N.J., Rutgers U., 1978-83; internist Cmty. Health Plan, Poughkeepsie, N.Y., 1983—; contract escort-interpreter (French), U.S. Dept. State, 1964-70; coord. Robert Wood Johnson Found. grant, primary care tng. evaluation U. Rochester, 1974-77. Trustee Gould Acad., Bethel, Maine, 1984—; coord. internal medicine Hudson Valley Family Practice Residency St. Francis Hosp., Poughkeepsie, 1989-93, teaching attending, 1990—; dir. dept. internal medicine Vassar Bros. Hosp., Poughkeepsie, 1992—. Served with M.C., U.S. Army, 1970-72. Fellow ACP, Am. Coll. Sports Medicine; mem. Am. Pub. Health Assn., Am. Med. Soc. Sports Medicine. Democrat. Home: 15 S Clover St Apt 1 Poughkeepsie NY 12601-3004 Office: 160 Union St Poughkeepsie NY 12601-3014

CHRISTIE, LAURENCE GLENN, JR., surgeon; b. Houston, May 13, 1930; s. Laurence Glenn and Tommie Katherine (Myers) C.; m. Constance Graham Kelsey, Sept. 15, 1973; 1 child, Susan Elizabeth. BS, Washington and Lee U., 1953; MD, Med. Coll. Va., 1957. Diplomate Am. Bd. Surgery. Intern surgery Med. Coll. Va., Richmond, 1957-58, resident surgery, 1957-62, clin. instr., 1963—; practice medicine specializing in gen. and vascular surgery, Ft. Smith, Ark., 1962-63, Richmond, Va., 1963—; mem. active staff Henrico Doctors Hosp.; mem. courtesy staff Johnston-Willis Hosp., Stuart Circle Hosp., St. Mary's Hosp., Richmond Meml. Hosp., St. Luke's Hosp., Retreat Hosp.; chmn. dept. surgery chmn. med. exec. com., med. dir. Henrico Doctors Hosp., also vice chmn. bd. trustees, 1981—, chief staff, 1982—; courtesy staff Richmond Met. Hosp., Johnston-Willis Hosp.; pres. Med. Planning Corp.; mem. sci. adv. bd. Richmond chpt. Nat. Found. for Ileitis and Colitis, Inc. Contbr. articles to profl. jours. Fellow ACS; mem. Southeastern Surg. Congress, So. Med. Assn., Richmond Acad. Medicine, Richmond Surg. and Gynecol. Soc., Med. Soc. Va., AMA, Humera Soc. Episcopalian. Clubs: Bull and Bear, Irish Setter of Greater Richmond, Irish Setter of Am. Home: PO Box 130 1224 The Forest Crozier VA 23039-0130 Office: 7605 Forest Ave Ste 402 Richmond VA 23229-4936

CHRISTMAN, EDWARD ARTHUR, physicist; b. Lakewood, Ohio, Aug. 3, 1943; s. John N.H. and Mary Elizabeth (Fuller) C.; m. Florence T. Cua, July 21, 1979. MS, Rutgers U., 1975, PhD, 1977. Mech. engr. missile systems div. AVCO Corp., Wilmington, Mass., 1966-72; instr. Rutgers U., New Brunswick, N.J., 1975-77, radiol. physicist, 1977-89, assoc. dir., 1989-91; dir. environ. health and safety Columbia U., N.Y.C., 1991—; cons. in field, North Brunswick, N.J., 1977—; assoc. faculty Rutgers U., 1978—; faculty Columbia U., 1991—. Mem. Health Physics Soc. N.J. (pres. 1989-90), Health Physics Soc. Home: PO Box 59 Eleanor Dr Kendall Park NJ 08824 Office: Columbia U Health Scis 630 W 168th St New York NY 10032-3702

CHRISTMAN, LUTHER PARMALEE, retired university dean, consultant; b. Summit Hill, Pa., Feb. 26, 1915; s. Elmer and Elizabeth (Barnicoat) C.; m. Dorothy Mary Black, Dec. 5, 1939; children: Gary, Judith, Lillian. Grad., Pa. Hosp. Sch. Nursing for Men, 1939; BS, Temple U., 1948, EdM, 1952; PhD, Mich. State U., 1965; LHD (hon.), Thomas Jefferson U., 1980. Cons. Mich. Dept. Mental Health, Lansing, 1956-63; assoc. prof. psychiat. nursing U. Mich., 1963-67; rsch. assoc. Inst. Social Rsch., U. Mich., 1963-67; prof. nursing and sociology, dean nursing Vanderbilt U., 1967-72; DON Vanderbilt U. Med. Ctr. Hosp., 1967-72; prof. sociology Rush Coll. Health Scis., Chgo.; sr. scientist Rush-Presbyn.-St. Luke's Med. Center; prof. nursing, v.p. nursing affairs Coll. Nursing Rush U., 1972-87; dean Coll. Nursing Rush U., 1972-87; dean emeritus Coll. Nursing, Rush U., 1987—; sr. advisor to pres. Ctr. of Nursing, Am. Hosp. Assn., 1989; pvt. cons., 1989—; pres. Christman-Cornesky & Assocs., 1990-94; adj. prof. Vanderbilt U., 1991—; cons. cmty. svcs. and rsch. br. NIMH, 1963-66; psychiat. rsch. project So. Regional Edn. Bd., 1964-67; chmn. planning com. 1st Midwest Conf. Psychiat. Nursing, Mpls., 1956; mem. team to survey mental health facilities of Colo. NIMH, 1992, of Ga., 1964; mem., workshop leader White House Conf. on Children, 1970; mem. nursing panel Nat. Commn. for Study Nursing and Nursing Edn., 1968-70; mem. regional med. programs rev. com. Health Svcs. and Mental Health Adminstrn., HEW, 1968-72; cons. dept. medicine and surgery VA Ctrl. Office, 1968-71, 74-77; mem. panel nurse cons. to com. on nursing AMA, 1968-71; mem. health svcs. adv. com. Am. Assn. Med. Colls., 1968-71; mem. acting com. pub. health Am. Health Found, 1970-72; mem. membership com. Inst. Medicine, NAS, 1972-76, mem. com. on edn. in health professions, 1973-75; participant numerous confs. in field; mem. S.D. Bd. Nursing, Tenn. Bd. Nursing; cons. to programs in 16 fgn. countries. Contbr. numerous articles to profl. jours. Recipient Disting. Practitioner award Nat. Acads. of Practice, 1985, Old Master Purdue U., 1985, Coun. of Specialists in Psychiat. and Mental Health Nursing award, 1980, Hon. Recognition award Ill. Nurses Assn., 1987, Edith Copeland Founders award for Creativity, 1981, History Makers in Nursing award Ctr. for Advancement of Nursing Practice, Beth Israel Hosp./Mass. Gen. Hosp., 1992, Lifetime Achievement award Sigma Theta Tau, 1992, Disting. Alumnus award Temple U., 1992. Fellow AAAS, Am. Acad. Nursing (Living Legend award 1995), Inst. Medicine Chgo., Soc. Applied Anthropology; mem. ANA (3d v.p., Jesse M. Scott award 1985), Mich. Nurses' Assn. (pres. 1961-65), Am. Sociol. Assn., Soc. Gen. Sys. Rsch., Inst. Medicine, N.Y. Acad. Scis., Biomed. Engring. Soc., Nat. Acad. Practice (chmn. acad. nursing 1985-92, sec. 1992-96), Alpha Omega Alpha (hon.), Alpha Kappa Delta. Home and Office: 5535 Nashville Hwy Chapel Hill TN 37034-2074

CHRISTODOULOU, ARIS PETER, pharmaceutical executive, investment banker; b. Athens, Greece, Feb. 23, 1939; came to U.S., 1945; s. Peter and Angeline (Magafas) C.; m. Marilena Lyratzakis, Aug. 23, 1975; 1 child, Peter. B.S. in Chem. Engring., MIT, 1960; M.S. in Nuclear Engring., Columbia U., 1963, Indsl. Engr., 1965; Ph.D. in Chem. Engring., CUNY, 1967. Sr. scientist Booz, Allen and Hamilton, N.Y.C. and Washington, 1967-70; sr. chem. analyst Lehman Bros. Inc., N.Y.C., 1970-72; sr. chem. analyst Blyth Eastman Dillon, N.Y.C., 1972-74, 1st. v.p., 1976-80; industry specialist Merrill Lynch, N.Y.C., 1974-76; pres., chief exec. officer Mayfair Capital Ptnrs. Inc., N.Y.C., 1980—; chmn., pres., chief exec. officer Penick Corp., Newark, 1988—. Contbr. numerous articles to profl. jours. Mem. AIChE, N.Y. Acad. Scis., Comml. Devel. Assn., Chem. Mktg. Rsch. Assn., N.Y. Soc. Security Analysts, Am. Chem. Soc., Inst. Cert. Fin. Analysts, MIT Club. Home: 137 E 66th St New York NY 10021-6130 Office: Penick Corp 158 Mount Olivet Ave Newark NJ 07114-2114

CHRISTOPH, SUSAN SHIPLEY, nurse, consultant; b. Phila., Jan. 13, 1946; d. Fred Stanley and Lorraine Freda (Timmer) Bertsch; children: Philip Brian, Gail Marie. BSN, Mich. State U., 1967; MSN, U. Ariz., 1975; D of Nursing Sci., Cath. U. of Am., 1985. RN. Charge nurse Holland (Mich.) City Hosp., 1967; enlisted U.S. Army, 1967—, advanced through grades to col.; staff nurse U.S. Army, Ft. Benjamin Franklin Harrison Hosp., Ind., 1967-68; head nurse, emergency U.S. Army, 36th Evacuation Hosp., Vietnam, 1968-69; staff nurse U.S. Army, various, 1969-71; supr. emergency services U.S. Army, Ft. Rucker, Ala., 1971-72; head nurse coronary care U.S. Army, William Beaumont Med. Ctr., El Paso, Tex., 1972-75; supr., head nurse emergency services U.S. Army, Ft. Carson, Colo., 1975-78; researcher nursing research service Walter Reed Army Med. Ctr., Washington, 1978-81; chief nurse U.S. Army Med. Research and Devel. Comd., Frederick, Md., 1984-88; chief army nurse corps div. U.S. Army Recruiting Command, Ft. Sheridan, Ill., 1988; chief dept. nursing Ireland Army Community Hosp., Ft. Knox, Ky., 1991-93; research cons. Soc. Post Anesthesia

Nurses, Richmond, Va., 1987—. Co-author: The Recovery Room, 1979, 87, AACN's Education Standards, 1986; contbr. author AACN's Clinical Reference, 1988; rsch. dept. editor Critical Care Nurse, Bridgewater, N.J., 1987-89; contbr. articles to profl. jours.; mem. editl. bd. Current Revs. for Post Anesthesia Nurses, Miami, 1981—. Decorated Meritorious Svc. medal U.S. Army, 1978, 81, 86, 88, Legion of Merit, 1991, 93. Mem. ANA, AACCN, Am. Soc. Post Anesthesia Nurses, Assn. Operating Rm. Nurses (ediorial bd. Jour., Denver, 1981-84), Sigma Theta Tau. Republican. Methodist. Home: 805 Clifford Dr Elizabethtown KY 42701-2880 Office: PO Box 2006 Elizabethtown KY 42702-2006

CHRISTOPHER, JAMES LEE, family physician, educator; b. Baton Rouge, Jan. 7, 1932; s. Warren Niel and Dorothy (Converse) C.; m. Dianne Mayeaux, May 29, 1969; children: James Warren, Leslie Dianne, Regan Alene. BA, U. Tex., 1956; MD, La. State U., 1960. Diplomate Am. Bd. Family Practice. Intern Confederate Meml. Med. Ctr., Shreveport, La., 1960-61, gen. surgery resident, 1961-63; pvt. practice, New Roads, La., 1964—; assoc. clin. prof. medicine La. State U. Sch. Medicine, New Orleans, 1968—. Mem., chmn. New Roads Zoning and Planning Commn., 1978-86. With USN, 1949-53. Mem. Am. Acad. Family Practice, La. Med. Soc., La. Acad. Family Practice, Lions (Mardi Gras king 1966-95), Masons (master), Shriners (pres., sec.-treas.), Alpha Omega Alpha. Republican. Episcopalian. Office: PO Box 430 New Roads LA 70760

CHRISTOPHER, ROBERT PAUL, physician; b. Cleve., Apr. 27, 1932; s. Walter Matthews and Charity Marie (Roberts) C.; m. Doreen Mary O'Leary, Apr. 28, 1962; children: Robert Jr., Judith, Mark. BS, Northwestern U., 1954; MD, St. Louis U., 1959. Diplomate Am. Bd. Physical Medicine and Rehab. Chief rehab. medicine V.A. Hosp., Ann Arbor, Mich., 1963-67; asst. prof. rehab. medicine U. Mich., Ann Arbor, 1964-67; assoc. prof. rehab. medicine U. Tenn., Memphis, 1967-71, prof. rehab. medicine, 1971—; med. dirs. Les Passees Children's Rehab. Ctr., Memphis, 1976—, Le Bonheur Hosp. Rehab. Svcs., Memphis, 1981—, Regional Med. Ctr. Rehab. Svcs., Memphis, 1967—, assoc. med. dir. St. Joseph Rehab. Ctr., Memphis, 1981—. Contbg. author: Seating the Cerebral Palsey Child, 1983; author: sound/slide program Systems of Physical Therapy in Cerebral Palsy, 1971; contbr. articles to profl. jours. Pres. Mid-South Health Systems Agy., Memphis, 1980; mem. Mayor's Adv. Council for Disabled, Memphis, 1977—. Recipient Disting. Svc. Commn. on Accredited Rehab. Facilities, 1982. Fellow Am. Acad. Phys. Medicine and Rehab. (sec. 1982-88, v.p. 1992—, pres. elect 1993, pres. 1994), Am. Acad. Cerebral Palsy (pres. 1987); mem. AMA, Am. Congress Rehab. Medicine, So. Soc. Phys. Medicine and Rsch. (sec. 1976—), Am. Bd. of Phys. Medicine and Rsch. (vice chmn. 1992—), East Memphis Cath. (bd. dirs. 1969-80), K.C. (Grand Knight 1969-70). Home: 506 Thorn Ridge Cv Memphis TN 38117-3651 Office: U Tenn Coll Med 800 Madison Ave Memphis TN 38163-0002

CHRISTOPHERSON, WILLIAM MARTIN, physician; b. Salt Lake City, July 2, 1916; s. George Walter and Myrtle (Jack) C.; m. Kathryn Donley, July 24, 1943; 1 son, George Walter. Student, U. Utah, 1938; M.D., U. Louisville, 1942. Intern Akron (Ohio) City Hosp., 1942-43, resident, 1946-48; resident U. Louisville Hosp., 1948-49; fellow pathology Meml. Hosp., N.Y.C., 1949-50; mem. faculty U. Louisville Grad. Sch., 1950—, prof. pathology, 1956—, chmn. dept., 1956-74; spl. cons. Nat. Cancer Inst., bur. state service USPHS, adv. com. cancer control program, 1963-67; cons. Oak Ridge Inst. Nuclear Studies, 1956-68, Louisville VA Hosp.; mem. panel experts on cancer WHO.; Pres., bd. dirs. Ky. div. Am. Cancer Soc., 1970—; mem.-at-large bd. dirs. Nat. Am. Cancer Soc., 1967-72, exec. com., 1968-70; mem. council on pathology AMA, 1970-77. Mem. editorial bd. Am. Jour. Surg. Pathology, Am. Jour. Clin. Pathology, Internat. Jour. Anti-Cancer Research, Internat. Jour. Gynecologic Pathology and Cancer; assoc. editor: Acta Cytologica. Served to capt. AUS., 1943-46. Mem. Am. Soc. Cytology (pres. 1966-67), Am. Assn. Cancer Edn. (pres. 1967-68), Soc. Exptl. Pathology, Internat. Acad. Pathology (pres. 1971-72), Arthur Purdy Stout Soc. Surg. Pathology (pres. 1981-82), Internat. Acad. Cytology, Pathol. Soc. Gt. Britain and Ireland, European Soc. Pathology, Am. Soc. Clin. Pathology, Sigma Xi, Alpha Omega Alpha. Home: 2211 Cherokee Pky Louisville KY 40204-2214

CHRISTY, NICHOLAS PIERSON, physician; b. Morristown, N.J., June 18, 1923; s. Leroy and Elizabeth (Baker) C.; m. Beverly Vairin Morris, June 21, 1947; children—Nicholas Pierson, Martha Vairin. A.B., Yale, 1945; M.D., Columbia, 1951. Diplomate: Am. Bd. Internal Medicine. Asst. vis. physician Delafield Hosp., N.Y.C., 1955-66; vis. physician Delafield Hosp., 1966-75; asst. vis. physician 1st med. div. Bellevue Hosp., N.Y.C., 1958-66; assoc. attending physician Presbyn. Hosp., N.Y.C., 1962-78; attending physician Presbyn. Hosp., 1978-93; dir. med. svc. Roosevelt Hosp., N.Y.C., 1965-79; faculty Columbia Coll. Phys. and Surg., N.Y.C., 1956—, assoc. prof. medicine, 1962-65, assoc. clin. prof., 1965-67, clin. prof. medicine, 1967-71, prof. medicine, 1971-79, lectr. in medicine, 1979-88, sr. lectr. medicine, 1988-93, spl. lectr. in medicine, 1993—; mem. Columbia U. Health Scis. adv. coun., 1993—; prof. medicine, assoc. dean vets. affairs Health Sci. Ctr. at Bklyn., SUNY, 1979-88, prof. emeritus, 1988—; chief staff Bklyn. VA Med. Ctr., 1979-88; writer-in-residence, alumni writer Coll. Physicians and Surgeons, Columbia U., 1988—; assoc. Nat. Humanities Ctr., Research Triangle Park, N.C., 1979; cons. FDA, 1966, Bd. of Health, N.Y.C., 1965—, NIH Nat. Inst. Diabetes, Digestive and Kidney Diseases tng. grants divsn., 1969-72, endocrinology study sect., 1975-79; cons., bd. dirs. Royal Soc. Medicine Found., 1984-93. Editor, co-author: The Human Adrenal Cortex, 1971; editor-in-chief: Jour. Clin. Endocrinology and Metabolism, 1963-67; assoc. editor: Beeson-McDermott Textbook of Medicine, 1968-75; cons. editor, 1975-79; cons. Med. Dictionary (Dorland), 1988; adv. editor and contbr. Internat. Dictionary of Medicine and Biology (Endocrinology), 1986; mem. adv. bd.: Am. Jour. Medicine, 1971-88; contbr. numerous papers to profl. publs. Served to lt. (j.g.) USNR, 1943-46, PTO. Recipient Borden award, Joseph Mather Smith prize Columbia; John and Mary R. Markle scholar; NIH tng. grantee, 1959-65, endocrinology study sect. grantee, 1958-69. Fellow Am. Med. Writers Assn. (hon., Swanberg award 1989); mem. Harvey Soc., AAAS, Soc. Exptl. Biology and Medicine, Am. Soc. Clin. Investigation, Am. Fedn. Clin. Rsch., A.C.P., N.Y. Acad. Medicine, Laurentian Hormone Conf., Am. Physiol. Soc., N.Y. State Med. Soc., N.Y. County Med. Soc., Am. Clin. and Climatol. Assn. (recorder 1977-88, pres. 1990), Am. Assn. Study Liver Diseases, Endocrine Soc. (sec.-treas. 1978-89, Ayerst award 1986), N.Y. Clin. Soc., N.Y. Med. and Surg. Soc., Assn. Am. Physicians, Interurban Clin. Club, Hosp. Grads. Club, Peripatetic Soc., Practitioners Soc., Elizabethan (Yale), Colony (Yale), Century Assn. (pres. 1987-90, hon. 1995—). Home: 1260 Palmetto Ct # 105 Vero Beach FL 32963-4008

CHRONISTER, VIRGINIA ANN, school nurse, educator; b. York, Pa., Sept. 25, 1940; d. Ernest B. and Mary L. (Anderson) Stokes; m. Burton F. Chronister, June 13, 1964; children: Scott E., Karen A. Student, York Jr. Coll., Millersville (Pa.) Coll.; diploma, Harrisburg (Pa.) Hosp., 1961; BS in Profl. Arts, St. Joseph's Coll., North Windham, Maine, 1985; M. (equivalency), Pa. State U., 1989; postgrad., St. Joseph's Coll., North windham, Maine. RN, Pa.; cert. sch. nurse (edn. specialist II), Pa. Charge nurse Harrisburg Hosp., 1961-64; instr., practical nurses York City Sch. Dist., 1964-68; instr., med. secs. Yorktowne Bus. Inst., York, 1985; sch. nurse West York Sch. Dist., York, 1985—; substitute sch. nurse, 1972-85. Recipient Cardiac Nursing award. Mem. NEA, AAUW, Pa. State Edn. Assn. (sch. nurse sect.), Pa. Sch. Health Assn., Nat. Assn. Sch. Nurses, Harrisburg Hosp. Alumnae Assn., York County Sch. Nurse Assn. (pres. 1991-92), United Ostomy Assn. (charter mem.), West York Area Edn. Assn. (pres. 1991—), York County Coord. Coun., Beta Sigma Phi. Home: 2090 Loman Ave York PA 17404-4214

CHRYMKO, MARGARET MARY, pharmacist; b. N. Tonawanda, N.Y., Aug. 25, 1955; d. Horace O. and Gertrude M. (Murtagh) C. AS, Erie Community Coll., Buffalo, 1975; BS, SUNY, Buffalo, 1978, PharmD, 1979. Registered pharmacist. Clin. pharmacist Erie County Med. Ctr., Buffalo, 1979-85, clin. pharmacy coord., 1985-87, asst. dir. clin. pharmacy, 1987-88; clin. instr. medicine SUNY, Buffalo, 1980-88, clin. asst. prof. pharmacy, 1981-88; asst. dir. clin. pharmacy svcs. and rsch. Hamot Med. Ctr., Erie, Pa., 1988-92, assoc. dir. pharmacy for patient care svcs., 1992—; adj. asst. prof. U. Pitts., 1990—; mem. con. panel Upjohn Co., Inc., Kalamazoo, 1988-91; reviewer Am. Soc. Hosp. Pharmacists meetings, 1987—. Reviewer Hosp. Pharmacy, 1990—; contbr. articles to profl. jours. mem. Erie Cursillo Movement, 1990—; mem. choir St. George Ch., 1990-94, mem. parish coun. 1992-95; assoc. Sisters of St. Joseph, Erie, 1991—; vol., bd. dirs. St. Patrick's Haven Homeless Shelter, 1992—; active Greater Erie Area Habitat for Humanity, 1992-95. Roche Hosp. Pharmacy grantee, 1988. Mem. Fellow Am. Soc. Hosp. Pharmacists (pharmacy practice mgmt. adv. group 1995-96); mem. Am. Pharm. Assn., Am. Assn. Colls. Pharmacy, Pa. Soc. Hosp. Pharmacists (bd. dirs. 1991-96, pres. 1994-96, N.Y. State Coun. Hosp. Pharmacists (bd. dirs. 1985-88), Western N.Y. Soc. Hosp. Pharmacists (pres. 1982-83). Roman Catholic. Office: Hamot Med Ctr 201 State St Erie PA 16550-0002

CHRZANOWSKI, FRANK ALAN, research pharmacist; b. Camden, N.J., Feb. 1, 1945; s. Frank Stanley and Mary (Krowicki) C.; m. Eileen Marie Kennedy, June 1, 1968; children: Frank Jr., Jeff, Dave. BS, Phila. Coll. Pharmacy Sci., 1968, MS, 1972, PhD, 1975. Registered pharmacist, N.J. Grad. trainee NSF, 1970-71; asst. prof. pharmacy Mass. Coll. Pharmacy, Boston, 1974-75, Northeastern U. Coll. of Pharmacy, Boston, 1975-76; rsch. scientist, sr. scientist McNeil Labs., Fort Washington, Pa., 1976, 77-79; prin. scientist McNeil Pharm., Spring House, Pa., 1980-86; group leader McNeil/R.W. Johnson Pharm., Spring House, 1986-90; rsch. mgr. The R.W. Johnson Pharm. Rsch. Inst., Spring House, 1991—; mem. drug delivery subcom., assoc. mem., ann. meeting co-chairperson Johnson & Johnson Corp., 1988-93; adj. asst. prof. Coll. Pharmacy U. Cin., 1983-93; presenter in field. Contbr. articles to Biochem. Medicine, Jour. Pharm. Sci., Clin. Pharm. Therapy, Jour. Med. Chemistry, Acta Pharm. Tech., Drug Devel., Indsl. Pharmacy. Mem. Cherokee H.S. Drama Guild, Marlton, N.J., 1989-92; coach youth basketball league Marlton Recreation Coun., 1988-92; adult advisor WINGS Youth Group, Marlton, 1987-92; eucharistic min. area Roman Cath. ch., 1992-96. Fellow Am. Found. Pharm. Edn., 1972-75. Mem. Am. Assn. Pharm. Scientists (chmn. membership com. 1988-89, sec., treas. pharm. techs. sect. 1991—), Am. Pharm. Assn., KC, Rho Chi. Office: R W Johnson Pharm Rsch Inst Spring House PA 19477

CHU, CHUNG-BIN, physician; b. Tchungnam, Korea, Sept. 3, 1923; s. Seoung-no and Manrye (Whang) C.; m. Manwon Kim, Apr. 6, 1945 (dec. 1951); children: Tchoontak, Soontak; m. Hee-Suk Yang, June 24, 1957; children: Yongtak, Intak, Euitak. MD, Yonsei U., Seoul, Korea, 1944; MS, Yonsei U., 1959, D.M.Sc., 1961. Prof. orthopedics Yonsei U. Med. Coll., Seoul, 1957-64; dir. Severance Rehab. Ctr., Seoul, 1963-64; cons. Dept. Nat. Def., Seoul, 1957-65; pvt. practice orthopedic surgery Seoul, 1964—; founder, chmn. Manrye Found., Seoul, 19754-84; chmn. Seoul Congress Western Pacific Orthopedic Assn., 1972, charter mem., 1962—, mem. editorial bd., 1962-88. Bd. trustees Korea Rehab. Fund, 1988—. Lt. col. Korean Army, 1949-55. Fellow Internat. Coll. Surgeons (chmn. 1983-87); mem. Korean Orthopedic Assn. (bd. advisors, pres. 1975-76), Korean Med. Assn., Korean Soc. for Rehab. (pres. 1961-64), Korean Soc. Spinal Surgery (chmn. 1986-87), Societe Internationale de Chirurgie Orthopedique et de Traumatologie (nat. del. 1975-84, councillor 1981-84, pres. 1991-93 Seoul congress), Seoul Country Club (bd. trustees 1978-83). Home: 1-65 Sungbuk-dong, Sungbuk-ku Seoul Korea Office: 17 Daeshin-Dong, Seodaemoon-ku, Seoul Republic of Korea

CHU, FOO, physician; b. N.Y.C., Feb. 3, 1921; s. Fook Chu and Jan Hong; m. Nannie Marguerite Hainje, Mar. 27, 1948; children: Janice, David, Carol. BA, Oberlin Coll., 1942; MD, Cornell U., 1945. Diplomate Nat. Bd. Med. Examiners, Am. Bd. Pathology, Am. Bd. Quality Assurance and Utilization Rev. Physicians. Intern Bellevue Hosp. Cornell div., N.Y.C., 1945-46; resident in medicine Lincoln Hosp., Bronx, N.Y., 1948-50; pvt. practice N.Y.C., 1950-96; personnel health asst. N.Y. Hosp., N.Y.C., 1950-51; asst. pathologist Lincoln Hosp., Bronx, 1951-64, pathologist, 1964-81, physician cons. dept. quality assurance, 1987—; assoc. med. dir. Comprehensive Med. Review, Inc., Bronx, 1982-87; instr. in medicine Cornell Med. Coll., N.Y.C., 1950-62; clin. instr. Albert Einstein Coll. of Medicine, Bronx, 1967-74, asst. clin. prof. pathology, 1974-76; mem. Minority Adv. Com. N.Y. State Dept. Mental Health, 1979-91. Contbr. articles to profl. jours. Chmn. Chinatown Health Coun., N.Y.C., 1969-73, Asian-Am. Mental Health, 1979-91; trustee Chinatown Community Health Ctr., 1979-91, Community Family Planning COun., 1982-93; trustee Hamilton Madison House, 1988—; mem. adv. bd. Asian Am. Mental Health Project, 1983—. WiTh U.S. Army, 1946-48. Recipient Community Service award Hamilton Madison House, 1985. Mem. AMA, N.Y. State Med. Soc., N.Y. County Med. Soc. Home: 116 Altamont Ave Tarrytown NY 10591-4203

CHU, GEOFFREY, physician, gastroenterologist, consultant; b. Sydney, Australia, Jan. 2, 1961; m. Karen Chu; 1 child, Justin. MBBS, U. New South Wales, Australia, 1984. FRACP 1991. cons. physician O.B. Hosp., 1993—. Office: PO Box 2172, 2800 Orange New South Wales Australia

CHU, JOHNSON CHIN SHENG, physician; b. Peiping, China, Sept. 25, 1918; came to U.S., 1948, naturalized, 1957; s. Harry S.P. and Florence (Young) C.; m. Sylvia Cheng, June 11, 1949; children—Stephen, Timothy. M.D., St. John's U., 1945. Intern Univ. Hosp., Shanghai, 1944-45; resident, research fellow NYU Hosp., 1948-50; resident physician in charge State Hosp. and Med. Ctr., Weston, W.Va., 1951-56; chief services, clin. dir. State Hosp., Logansport, Ind., 1957-84; active mem. Meml. Hosp., Logansport, Ind., 1968—. Research in cardiology and pharmacology; contbr. articles to profl. jours. Fellow Am. Psychiat. Assn., Am. Coll. Chest Physicians; mem. AMA, Ind. Med. Assn., Cass County Med. Soc., AAAS. Home: 36 E Lake Shafer Monticello IN 47960 Office: Southeastern Med Ctr Walton IN 46994

CHU, MON-LI HSIUNG, molecular biologist, educator; b. Kwangtung, China, July 27, 1948; came to U.S. 1970; d. Tsun-Shiang and Ah-Wha (Yang) Hsiung; m. Shaw-Chang Chu, Nov. 10, 1972; children: Emily, Andy. BS, Nat. Taiwan U., 1970; PhD, U. Fla., 1975. Adj. asst. prof. U. Med./Dentistry N.J.-Rutgers Med. Sch., Piscataway, N.J., 1979-84, adj. assoc. prof., 1984-86; assoc. prof. Thomas Jefferson U., Phila., 1986-90, prof. molecular biology, 1990—. Contbr. over 100 articles to profl. jours. NIH grantee, 1986—. Mem. AAAS, Am. Soc. Biochemistry and Molecular Biology. Office: Thomas Jefferson U 233 S 10th St Philadelphia PA 19107-5566

CHU, TSANN MING, immunochemist, educator; b. Kaohsiung, Taiwan, Apr. 18, 1938; came to U.S., 1963, naturalized, 1971; s. Tsi Fa and Su Lian (Sun) C.; m. Bonnie Diane Covert, Sept. 28, 1967; children: Nancy, Daniel. BS, Nat. Taiwan U., 1961; MS, N.C. State U., 1965; PhD, Pa. State U., 1967. Fellow Med. Found. Buffalo, 1967-69, Buffalo Gen. Hosp., 1969-70; assoc. chief cancer rsch. scientist, dir. diagnostic immunology and clin. chemistry Roswell Park Meml. Inst., Buffalo, 1970-76, dir. cancer rsch. in diagnostic immunology research and biochemistry, 1976—; asst. prof. exptl. pathology SUNY, Buffalo, 1970-74, assoc. prof., 1974-77, prof., 1977—; cons. nat. prostatic cancer project Nat. Cancer Inst., NIH, 1973-84, mem. com. cancer immunodiagnosis, 1978-79, mem. tumor immunology com., 1979-81; mem. immunology and immunotherapy com. Am. Cancer Soc., 1979-81; rsch. cons. Nat. Sci. Coun., Taiwan, 1976-94, vis. prof., 1986; adv. coun. Internat. Soc. Oncodevel. Biology and Medicine, 1978-94; mem. sci. rev. panel N.J. Commn. on Cancer Rsch., 1983-85, 87—; cons. Merit Rev. Bd., VA, 1980-85, 94, 95; mem. cancer therapeutic program rev. com. Nat. Cancer Inst., 1985-88; reviewers reserve NIH, 1988-92, 94; mem. scientific adv. coun. Internat. Acad. Tumor Marker Oncology, 1986—; mem. sci. coun. Swedish Cancer Found., 1988—; adv. com. Nat. Def. Med. Ctr. Cancer Rsch. Group, 1993—. Mem. editorial bd. Tumor Biology, 1983-92, Jour. Clin. Lab. Analysis, 1985—, Jour. Tumor Marker Oncology, 1988—, Cancer Investigation, 1989—; contbr. articles to profl. jours. United Health Found. Western N.Y. fellow, 1968-69; recipient Presdl. Citation award Am. Urol. Assn., 1993, Am. Found. for Urologic Disease, 1993, Dornier Innovative Rsch. award, 1993, Roswell Park Cancer Inst. and Geritourinary Cancer Symposium award, 1993, Disting. Alumni award Pa. State U., 1994, N.C. State U., 1995. Mem. Am. Chem. Soc., Am. Assn. Clin. Chemists, Am. Assn. Cancer Rsch., Am. Assn. Immunologists, Am. Soc. Biochem. and Molecular Biology, Am. Assn. Investigative Pathology, Phi Lambda Upsilon. Home: 117 Old Orchard St Buffalo NY 14221-2136 Office: Roswell Park Mem Inst 666 Elm St Buffalo NY 14263-0001

CHUA LEE, ANTONIO A., pharmacologist; b. Manila, Philippines, Mar. 20, 1944; came to U.S., 1970; m. Margie, June 12, 1969; children: Margaret, Maribel, Anthony, Anne. BS, U. St. Thomas, 1964, MD, 1969. Med. dir. Libertyville (Ill.) Manor, Riverside Found., Mundelein, Ill.; chmn. dept. medicine, active staff Condell Med. Ctr., Libertyville, Ill.; staff St. Therese Med. Ctr., Waukegan, Ill. Mem. AMA, Am. Geriatric Soc., Ill. Med. Soc., Lake County Med. Soc. Office: 1105 W Park Ste 2 Libertyville IL 60048

CHUANG, HANSON YII-KUAN, biochemist, experimental pathologist; b. Nanking, China, Sept. 24, 1935; came to U.S., 1963; s. Wei-Ching and Yei-Feng (Chang) C.; m. Lucy W. Tai, Apr. 2, 1966; children: Philip Duen-Ho, Helen Duen-Feng. BS, Nat. Taiwan U., 1958; PhD, U. N.C., 1968. Rsch. asst. Academia Sinica, Taipei, Taiwan, 1960-63; instr. to asst. prof. U. N.C., Chapel Hill, 1971-75; asst. prof. Brown U., Providence, 1975-77; asst. prof. U. S. Fla., Tampa, 1977-79; rsch. assoc. prof. U. Utah, Salt Lake City, 1979-88; sr. rsch. scientist Hyland divsn. Baxter Biotech Group, 1988—. Author: (with R.G. Mason, S.F. Mohammad) Hemostasis & Thrombosis, 1982, Replacement of Renal Function by Dialysis, 1983; (with R.G. Mason, S.F. Mohammad, H.I. Saba) The Thromboembolic Disorders, 1983; Blood Compatibility, 1987; contbr. articles to profl. jours. NIH grantee, 1979-85, 78-86, NIH postdoctoral fellow, 1968-71. Mem. Am. Chem. Soc., Soc. Investigative Pathology, Am. Assn. Blood Banks. Republican. Achievements include 1 patent; research in development and manufacture of pharmaceuticals such as blood substitutes and monoclonal antibodies recombinant plasma components for human use. Home: 19192 Salt Lake Pl Northridge CA 91326-2343 Office: 1710 Flower Ave Duarte CA 91010-2923

CHUBB, HENDON, psychologist; b. N.Y.C., Mar. 1, 1933; s. Percy and Corinne Roosevelt (Alsop) C.; m. Nita Colgate, 1958 (div. 1981); children: Amber, Oliver; m. Phyllis Lancaster Nauts, June 12, 1982. BA, Yale U., 1954; MA, Adelphi U., 1976, PhD, 1978. CFO Chubb Corp./Chubb & Son, Inc., N.Y.C., 1957-74; sr. psychologist Kings County Med. Ctr., Bklyn., 1977-80; psychologist Kaiser Permanente, Martinez & Pleasanton, Calif., 1980-88; pvt. practice Torrington and Cornwall, San Francisco, Conn., 1988-89, Winsted, Torrington, Cornwall, Conn., 1989—; dir. Brief Therapy Inst., West Cornwall, Conn., 1986—; clin. asst. prof. dept. psychiatry U. Conn., Farmington. Translator: If You Love Me, Don't Leave Me, 1990; mem. editl. bd. Jour. Systemic Therapies; contbr. articles to profl. jours. Pres. Lexington Dem. Club, N.Y.C., 1970-72; mem. Bd. Fin., Cornwall, Conn., 1991—. With U.S. Army, 1954-56. Mem. Coun. on Fgn. Rels., Am. Family Therapy Acad., Internat. Family Therapy Assn., Conn. Psychol. Assn. Democrat. Home and Office: 65 Johnson Rd West Cornwall CT 06796-1623

CHUBB, STEPHEN DARROW, medical corporation executive; b. Newton, Mass., Mar. 16, 1944; s. Phillip Darrow and Clarissa Stoddard (Nye) C.; m. Kathleen Alice Zimmerman, 1973. BS, U.S. Naval Acad., 1965; MBA, Northwestern U., 1974. CPA, Ill. With Am. Can Co., 1970-73, Baxter Travenol Labs., Deerfield, Ill., 1974-81; pres. Hyland Diagnostics, 1978-81; pres., chief exec. officer, dir. Cytogen Corp., 1981-84, T Cell Scis., Inc., 1984-86, Matritech Inc., 1987—; dir. Charles River Labs., 1994—, Compucyte, Cambridge, Mass., 1992—; mem. adv. bd. Phila. Ventures, 1987—, Kellogg Grad. Sch. Mgmt.; alumni adv. bd. Northwestern U., 1993—. Bd. dirs. Sherwood Cmty. Assn., 1978-79, v.p., 1979-80; trustee Huntington Theatre Co., Boston, 1991-95, treas., 1992-95; trustee Mt. Auburn Hosp., Cambridge, 1995—; mem. Literacy Vols. Mass. With USN, 1965-70; capt., USNR (ret.). Recipient Meritorious Svc. medal, Combat Action Ribbon, U.S. Navy. Mem. AICPA, John Evans Club Northwestern U., U.S. Naval Acad. Alumni Assn. Home: 282 Beacon St # 9 Boston MA 02116-1152 Office: Matritech Inc 330 Nevada St Newton MA 02160-9999

CHUKSORJI, JEAN CAULFIELD, nursing educator; b. New Orleans, Feb. 23; d. Benjamin Caulfield and Alma (Crenshaw) Caulfield Adams; m. Ejimofor Chuksorji; children: Nneze, Blessed. BS, Dillard U.; MSN, U. Wash., 1967; school nurse program, U. Calif., San Francisco; cert. in gerontology, U. So. Calif., L.A.; postgrad., U. Calif., San Francisco. Cert. psychiat. nurse ANA. Clin. instr. Dillard U., New Orleans; supr. Flint Goodridge Hosp.; psychiatric nurse Neuro-Psychiatric Inst., UCLA; staff devel. Mount Zion Hosp., San Francisco, 1969-70; asst. prof./lectr. U. Calif., San Francisco, 1970-77; sch. nurse L.A. Unified Sch. Dist., 1977-78; prof. nursing East L.A. Coll., 1979—; asst. chmn. nursing dept. East L.A. Coll., 1978—; instr. Calif. State U., San Fransisco Skill Ctr., 1977. Vol. ARC, chaplain Pan Hellanic coun.; mem. ladies aux. St. Peter Claver chpt. KC; bd. dirs. L.A. chpt. Jack and Jill Am., Inc.; active YMCA. Mem. AAUS, AAUP, APHA, LWV, NAACP, Nat. League for Nursing, Calif. Nurses Assn., Calif. Maternal Child Health Assn., Am. Assn. Women in Cmty. Jr. Colls., Am. Health Assn. (past sec., treas.), Sigma Theta Tau. Home: PO Box 76536 Los Angeles CA 90076-0536

CHULIK, JOHN D., urologist; b. Lorain, Ohio, Jan. 5, 1946; s. John Joseph and Margaret Frances (Bozik) C.; m. Beverly Joyce Johnson, Aug. 28, 1970 (div. June 1995); children: Laura, Amy, John. BA, Coll. Wooster, 1967; MD, Loyola U., 1971. Bd. cert. Am. Bd. Urology. Intern Akron (Ohio) City Hosp., 1971-72, resident, 1972-73; resident Akron Gen. Med. Ctr., 1973-76; urologist Akron Clinic, 1976-94, Akron Urologic Surgery, 1994—; asst. prof. urology Northeast Ohio Univs. Coll. Medicine, Rootstown, 1979—. Capt. U.S. Army, 1971-81. Office: Advanced Urology Assocs 201 W Cedar St Akron OH 44307

CHUNG, DOUGLAS CHU, pharmacist, consultant; b. N.Y.C., Jan. 20, 1951; s. Gook Wah and Yot Woy (Chin) C. BS, NYU, 1974; BS in Pharmacy, L.I. U., 1979; PharmD, Mercer U., 1981; postgrad., Harvard U., 1984. Lic. pharmacist, N.Y., Fla., Ala., Mass., Conn.; cert. in CPR and emergency cardiac care; bd. cert. nutrition specialist Am. Coll. Nutrition. Design engr. Jaros, Baum and Bolles, Cons. Engrs., N.Y.C., 1972-75; staff amd emergency disaster medications pharmacist Hosp for Joint Disease North Gen., N.Y.C., 1979, 80; postdoctoral splty. clin. resident in parenteral and enteral nutrition/metabolic care Bapt. Med. Ctr., Gadsden, Ala., 1981-83, Mercer U., Atlanta, 1981-83; clin. dir. Metabolic Support Pharmacy, Suffield, Conn., 1983-86; founder, pres., chmn., chief exec. officer Metabolic Homecare, Inc., Suffield, 1986-92; pres. Metabolic Support Inc., Advanced Infusion Care, Manchester, Conn., 1993—; clin. cons. Caremark, Inc., Deerfield, Ill., 1985, 86; adj. prof. clin. pharmacy Mercer U., 1984-86; mem. med. staff Park City Hosp., Bridgeport, Conn., 1984—, Noble Hosp., Westfield, Mass., 1986—; lectr. in field, 1980—. Contbr. articles to Jour. Toxicology: Clin. Toxicology. Vol. health screener Asian Ams. for Community Health, N.Y.C., 1977-79. Fellow Am. Coll. Nutrition (cert.); mem. Am. Soc. for Parenteral and Enteral Nutrition, Am. Soc. Nutrition Support Svcs. (bd. dirs. 1984-86), Am. Pharm. Assn., Am. Soc. Hosp. Pharmacists, Soc. Critical Care Medicine, Atlanta Soc. Instnl. Pharmacists, Ala. Soc. Hosp. Pharmacists, N.Y. Acad. Scis., N.Y. State Coun. Hosp. Pharmacists, N.Y.C. Soc. Hosp. Pharmacists, European Soc. Parenteral and Enteral Nutrition, Conn. Soc. Parenteral and Enteral Nutrition (pres. 1993—), Marie Schwartz Coll. Pharmacy Alumni Assn., Mercer U. Pharmacy Alumni Assn., NYU Alumni Assn. Office: Metabolic Support Inc Advance Infusion 44 Purnell Pl Manchester CT 06040-5412

CHUNG, ED B(AIK), pathologist, educator; b. Kilchoo, Korea, Mar. 16, 1928; came to U.S. 1954; s. Hi Sam and Ok Bong (Lee) C.; m. Ok Hyung Kang, Nov. 9, 1958; children: Sophia M., Jeanne M., Theodore D., Virginia M., Esther K. MD, Severance Union Med. Coll., Seoul, Korea, 1951; MS in Pathology, Georgetown U., 1956, PhD in Pathology, 1958. Diplomate Am. Bd. Pathology in Anatomic Pathology and Clin. Pathology. Resident in pathology Georgetown U. Med. Ctr., Washington, 1954-58; instr. in pathology Georgetown U., Washington, 1958-61, asst. prof. pathology, 1961-63; assoc. prof. pathology Howard U., Washington, 1964-70, prof. pathology, 1970—; attending pathologist Howard U. Hosp., Washington, 1964—, dir. surg. pathology, 1968—; cons. Glen Dale (Md.) Hosp., 1968-74, Coroner's Office, Washington, 1969-71; vis. prof. soft tissue pathology, Padua (Italy) U. Inst. Anatomic and Histologic Pathology, 1989. Contbr. numerous articles to profl. jours. Bd. dirs. Washington Korean Community Svc. Ctr., 1974—, vice chmn. 1974-81, chmn. 1981-86; trustee the Korean Sch., Washington, 1971-73; chmn. bd. deacons Washington Korean Bapt. Ch., 1959-69; elder Full Gospel (Assembly of God) First Ch., Washington, 1979—. Capt. Republic of Korea Army Med. Corps, 1952-54. Fellow Am. Soc. Clin. Pathologists, Coll. Am. Pathologists; mem. Internat. Acad.

Pathology, Washington Soc. Pathologists. Office: Howard U Coll Medicine Dept Pathology 520 W St NW Washington DC 20001-2337

CHUNG, HACK RYANA, psychiatrist; b. Korea, July 23, 1937; came to U.S., 1965.; s. Gene H. and Hyun-Kyung (Lee) C.; m. Apr. 28, 1965; children: John, Mike. BS, Seoul (Republic of Korea) U., 1960, MPH, 1961; MD, Yonsei U., Seoul, 1965. Diplomate Am. Bd. Psychiatry and Neurology. Intern Mercy Hosp., Wilkes-Barre, Pa., 1965-66; resident Phila. Gen. Hosp., 1966-69; fellow Phila. Psychiat. Ctr., 1969-70, unit med. dir., 1971-80; unit med. dir. Northwestern Inst., Ft. Washington, Pa., 1980—; v.p. med. staff Northwestern Inst., 1977-79; med. dir. Philip Jaison Med. Ctr., Phila., 1987—. Pres. lay orgn. Korean Cath. Cmty., Phila., 1989; trustee Germantown Acad., Ambler, Pa., 1988—; chmn. bd. dirs. Nationalities Svc. Ctr., Phila., 1995—. Decorated Legion of Honor. Mem. AMA, Am. Psychiat. Assn., Montgomery County Med. Soc., Korean-Am. Assn. of Phila. (pres. 1980, 87—). Home: 1250 Fairland Dr Ambler PA 19002 Office: 450 S Bethlehem Pike Fort Washington PA 19034-2312

CHUNG, HWAN YUNG, neurosurgeon; b. Seoul, Korea, June 16, 1927; s. Yoon Sik and Bok Hyun (Bak) C. MD, Junnam U., 1949; PhD, Korea U., 1966. Diplomate Korean Neurosurgery Specialty, Korean Gen. Surgery Specialty. Bd.; m. Jong Sun Kim; children: Hyo Min, Hyo Sook, Hyo Sun, Chun Kee, Hyo Gyung, Soon Gi. Commd. lt. Republic of Korea Army, 1951, advanced through grades to col., 1965, discharged, 1965; intern Junnam Univ. Hosp., Gwangju, Korea, 1949-50; gen. surg. resident Gwangju Mil. Gen. Hosp., 1952-56; neurosurg. resident Korea Univ. Hosp., Seoul, 1956-60; neurosurgeon Korea U. Hosp., Seoul, 1956-60, 121st Evacuation Hosp., U.S. Army in Korea, 1960-61, Letterman Gen. Hosp., San Francisco, 1961-62; chief neurosurgeon 1st Korean Army Hosp., Daegu, Chung-Ang Gil Hosp., Inchun, 1993—; clin. asst. prof. Gyungbook U., Daegu, 1963-65; asst. prof. Korea U., 1965-66; asst. prof. Yonsei U., Seoul, 1966-68, assoc. prof., 1968-73, prof., 1973; prof. and chmn. neurosurgery Hanyang U., Seoul, 1973-92, emeritus prof. 1992—, hosp. dir. Joong-Ang Gen. Hosp., 1992-93, Hanyang U. Hosp., 1986-87. Decorated Bronze Star (U.S.A.), Hwarang Medal of Hon., Korea, 1952; Recipient Citation of Merit Ministry Def., Republic of Korea, 1964, Citation of Merit, Ministry Health and Welfare, 1987. Mem. Korean Neurosurg. Soc. (pres. 1978-79), Korean Microsurg. Soc. (pres. 1984-85), Korean Vascular Surg. Soc. (adviser 1984-92), Pan-Pacific Surg. Assn. (pres. Korean chpt. 1984—, v.p. hdqrs. 1984—), Spinal Neurosurgery Rsch. Soc. (pres. 1987-91, hon. pres. 1991—). Home: 80-102 Hyundai-Apt, Abgoojung Gangnam, Seoul 135-110, Republic of Korea

CHUNG, KIAN FAN, thoracic physician, educator, researcher; b. Rose-Belle, Mauritius, Feb. 12, 1951; arrived in Eng., 1970; s. Young Cheong and Ah-Line (How) S.; m. Soop Chin Ng-Kee-Kwong, July 9, 1977; children: Joanne, Katie, Annabelle. MB, B Surgery, U. London, 1975, MD, 1983. Intern Addenbrookes Hosp., Cambridge, 1975-76; resident Middlesex Hosp., London, 1976, Radcliffe Infirmary, Oxford, 1977, Hammersmith Hosp., 1978; chef-de-clinique Geneva Med. Sch., 1978-79; lectr. medicine Med. Sch., Charing Cross Hosp., London, 1979-82; vis. scientist Cardiovascular Rsch. Inst., U. Calif., San Francisco, 1983-85; sr. lectr., cons. physician Nat. Heart and Lung Inst. and Royal Brompton Hosp., London, 1986—; reader in thoracic medicine Imperial Coll. Sci., Tech. & Medicine U. London, 1994—. Author: Therapeutics of Respiratory Disease, 1994; editor: Pharmacology of Respiratory Tract, 1993; mem. editorial bd. Pulmonary Pharmacology, London, 1989-94, European Respiratory Jour., 1995—, Am. Jour. Respiratory Critical Care Medicine, 1996—; contbr. articles to profl. jours. Dorothy Temple-Cross travelling fellow Med. Rsch. Coun. U.K., 1983-84, rsch. program grantee, 1992—; Harold Boldero scholar Middlesex Hosp. Med. Sch., London, 1975. Fellow Royal Coll. Physicians (London); mem. Am. Thoracic Soc., Brit. Pharmacological Soc. Office: Nat Heart and Lung Inst, Dovehouse St, London SW3 6LY, England

CHUNG, KING-THOM, microbiologist, educator; b. Tou Fen, Taiwan, Apr. 25, 1943; came to U.S., 1966; s. Aa-Yuan and Yi-Ing (Buu) C.; m. Lan-Seng Fang, Oct. 27, 1973; children: Theodore, Serena. MA, U. Calif., Santa Cruz, 1967; PhD, U. Calif., Davis, 1972. Scientist Frederick (Md.) Cancer Rsch. Ctr., 1972-77; vis. asst. prof. Food Sci. Inst. Purdue U., West Lafayette, Ind., 1977-78; assoc. prof. Tunghai U., Taichung, Taiwan, 1978-80; prof., chmn. dept. Soochow U., Taipei, Taiwan, 1980-87, dean, 1983-87; vis. scientist U.S. Meat Animal Rsch. Ctr., Clay Center, Nebr., 1987-88; assoc. prof. biology U. Memphis, 1988-93, prof., 1993—; mem. adv. bd. Dept. Agr. and Forestry, Taiwan Provincial Govt., Taichung, 1982-87; exec. sec. Internat. Symposium on Biogas, Microalgae and Livestock Wastes, Taipei, 1980. Author: (in Chinese) Environment and Pollution, 1987, Intellectuals and Academic Education, 1987; contbr. articles to profl. jours. Grantee Am. Inst. Cancer Rsch., 1992. Fellow Am. Acad. Microbiology; mem. Am. Soc. Microbiology, Am. Acad. Microbiology, Inst. Food Technologists, Sigma Xi. Office: U Memphis Dept Biology Memphis TN 38152

CHUNG, SOPHIA MIHE, ophthalmology; b. Arlington, Va., Sept. 16, 1959; d. Ed Baik and Ok Hyung (Kang) C.; m. John Bryan Holds, Nov. 9, 1991; children: John Harrison. BA, Duke U., 1981, MD, 1985. Diplomate Am. Bd. Ophthalmology. Internal medicine intern St. Luke's Episc. Hosp., Houston, 1985-86; ophthalmology resident Cullen Eye Inst. Baylor Coll. Medicine, Houston, 1986-89; neuro-ophthalmology fellow Baylor Coll. Medicine, 1989-90; from instr. to asst. prof. ophthalmology Anheuser-Busch Eye Inst., St. Louis U., 1990—. Mem. AMA, Am. Acad. Ophthalmology, Nat. Multiple Sclerosis Soc., Nat. Neurofibromatosis Soc., N. Am. Neuro-ophthalmol. Soc. Office: Anheuser-Busch Eye Inst 1755 S Grand Saint Louis MO 63104

CHUNG, TAE-SOO, physician; b. Tae-Gu, Korea, Feb. 1, 1937; came to U.S., 1964, naturalized, 1978; s. Sang-Taik and Chuwan (Ha) C.; m. Kwangja Park, Apr. 3, 1965; children: Peter, Alexander. MD, Yonsei U., Seoul, 1963. Chief resident rehab. medicine N.Y.U. Med. Ctr., 1967; fellow in rehab. medicine N.Y. Med. Coll., 1968; clin. dir. Children's Rehab. Ctr., St. John's, Nfld., Can., 1969-71; chief spinal cord injury svc., chief children's rehab. unit N.Y. Med. Coll., 1971-75, clin. asst. prof., 1971-80; dir. phys. medicine and rehab. dept. Northwest Covenant Med. Ctr., N.J., 1975—; dir. rehab. unit Newton (N.J.) Meml. Hosp., 1981—; clin. asst. prof. U. Medicine and Dentisty N.J., Newark, 1976—; mem. N.J. State Phys. Therapy Bd., 1995—; cons. to Sussex County Edn. Commn., 1980—. Mem. N.J. Soc. Phys. Medicine and Rehab. (sec. 1979-80, pres. 1983-84), Am. Korean Med. Soc. (v.p. N.Y. met. area 1979-80, news editor 1989-90), Am. Acad. Phys. Medicine and Rehab., N.J. Acad. Medicine, N.J. State Physical Therapy Bd. Office: Dover Gen Hosp Dover NJ 07801

CHUNG-WELCH, NANCY YUEN MING, biologist; b. N.Y.C., July 28, 1960; d. Thomas Richard and Jennie Kan Fee (Lew) Semler; m. James Michael Welch, June 29, 1985. BS, Northea. U., Boston, 1982; PhD, Boston U., 1990. Rsch. technician Dept. Biology, Boston U., 1983-85, tchg. fellow, 1987-89; rsch. fellow surgery Mass. Gen. Hosp., Harvard Med. Sch., Boston, 1989-94, instr. surgery, 1994-95; instr. in surgery Harvard Med. Sci., 1994-95; rsch. assoc. prof. Boston U., 1996—. Contbr. articles to profl. jours. including Jour. Cellular Physiology, Differentiation, Analytical Biochemistry, Surg. Forum. Boston U. Grad. Sch. grad. rsch. award, 1987, Biology Dept. grad. travel award, 1988, 89, Grega-Zacharkow Young Investigator award Microcirculatory Soc., 1988; named Outstanding Young Woman of Mass., 1988; Repligen Corp fellow, 1993-95. Mem. AAAS, Am. Soc. Cell Biology, N.Y. Acad. Scis., Tissue Culture Assn. Office: Boston U Biology Dept 5 Cunnington St Boston MA 02215

CHURCH, JAY KAY, psychologist, educator; b. Wichita, Kans., Jan. 18, 1927; s. Kay Iverson and Gertrude (Parrish) C.; BA, David Lipscomb Coll., 1948; MA, Ball State U., 1961; PhD, Purdue U., 1963; m. Dorothy Agnes Fellerhoff, May 21, 1976; children: Karen Patrice Turnbull, Caryn Annice Church Casey, Rex Warren, Max Roger. Chemist, Auburn Rubber Corp., 1948-49; salesman Midwestern United Life Ins. Co., 1949-52; owner, operator Tour-Rest Motel, Waterloo, Ind., 1952-66; tchr., guidance dir., public schs., Hamilton, Ind., 1955-61; counselor Washington Twp. (Ind.) Schs., Indpls., 1961-62; asst. prof. psychology Ball State U., 1963-67, assoc. prof., 1967-71, prof., 1971-88, prof. emeritus, 1988—, chmn. dept. ednl. psychology, 1970-74, dir. advanced grad. programs in ednl. psychology, 1978-81; pvt. practice psychology, 1963—. Mem. Am. Psychol. Assn., Nat. Assn. Sch. Psychologists. Home: 8501 N Ravenwood Dr Muncie IN 47303-9313

CHURCH, RUSSELL MILLER, psychology educator; b. N.Y.C., Dec. 24, 1930; s. Donald E. and Dee (Friedman) C.; m. Ruth Kutz, Apr. 4, 1954; children—Kenneth, Emily. B.A., U. Mich., 1952; M.A., Harvard U., 1954, Ph.D., 1956. Mem. faculty Brown U., 1955—, prof. psychology, 1965—, chmn. dept. psychology, 1980-83; chair faculty exec. com. Borwn U., 1995—. Editor: (with E.E. Boe) Punishment: Issues and Experiments, 1968; editor (with B.A. Campbell) Punishment and Aversive Behavior, 1969. Fellow AAAS, Am. Psychol. Assn. (pres. div. exptl. psychology 1987-88, comparative and physiol. psychology 1991-92); mem. Ea. Psychol. Assn. (pres. 1991-92). Office: Brown U Dept of Psychology 89 Waterman St Providence RI 02912-9079

CHURCHILL, LARRY RAYMOND, ethics educator; b. Russellville, Ark., June 24, 1945; s. Olen Raymond and Mary Josephine (Cheek) C.; m. Sandra Wade; children: Shelley, Blair Naylor. BA, Rhodes Coll., 1967; MDiv, Duke U., 1970, PhD, 1973. Asst. prof. U. N.C., Chapel Hill, 1976-82, assoc. prof., 1982-88, prof., 1988—, chmn. dept. social medicine, 1990—; cons. med. schs. and orgns. in bioethics, 1976—. Author: Rationing Health Care in America, 1987; co-author: Professional Ethics of Primary Care, 1986, The Physician As Captain of the Ship, 1988. Charles E. Culpeper scholar in med. humanities, 1991—. Mem. Soc. for Health and Human Values (pres. 1980-81), Inst. of Medicine, Soc. for Values in Higher Edn., The Hastings Ctr. Office: Univ of NC Dept Soc Medicine Campus Box 7240 Wing D Chapel Hill NC 27599*

CHURCHILL, MAIR ELISA ANNABELLE, medical educator; b. Liverpool, Eng., Nov. 28, 1959. BA in Chemistry, Swarthmore (Pa.) Coll., 1981; PhD in Chemistry, Johns Hopkins U., 1987. Lab. asst. Swarthmore Coll., 1979-81; teaching asst. Johns Hopkins U., Balt., 1981-83; non-clin. sci. staff grade I MRC Lab. Molecular Biology, Cambridge, Eng., 1987-93; asst. prof. biophysics U. Ill., Urbana, 1993—. Contbr. numerous articles to profl. jours. Am. Cancer Soc. fellow, 1987-89, Cambridge U. fellow, 1988-91. Mem. Am. Chem. Soc., Sigma Xi (assoc.). Office: U Ill 506 Morrill Hall 505 S Goodwin Ave Urbana IL 61801

CHURG, JACOB, pathologist; b. Dolhinow, Poland, July 16, 1910; came to U.S., 1936, naturalized, 1943; s. Wolf and Gita (Ravich) C.; m. Vivian Gelb, Oct. 18, 1942; children: Andrew Marc, Warren Bernard. M.D., U. Wilno, Poland, 1933; M.D. in pathology, 1936. Diplomate: Am. Bd. Pathology. Intern City Hosp., Wilno and State Hosp., Wilejka, Poland, 1933-34; asst. in gen. and exptl. pathology U. Wilno, 1934-36; asst. in bacteriology Mt. Sinai Hosp., N.Y.C., 1938; fellow in pathology Mt. Sinai Hosp., 1941-43, rsch. assoc., 1946-91, attending physician, 1962-81, cons., 1982—; resident in pathology Beth Israel Hosp., Newark, 1939-40; pathologist Barnert Meml. Hosp., Paterson, N.J., 1946—; prof. pathology and community med. Mt. Sinai Sch. Med., N.Y.C., 1966-81, prof. emeritus, 1982—; cons. pathologist VA Hosp., Bronx, N.Y., Nassau County Med. Ctr., East Meadow, N.Y., St. Barnabas Med. Ctr., Livingston, N.J., Valley Hosp., Ridgewood, N.J., St. Joseph's Hosp., Paterson, Englewood Hosp.; chmn. mesothelioma reference panel Internat. Union Against Cancer, 1965-81, mem., 1982—; chmn. com. for histologic classification renal diseases WHO, 1975—; Lady Davis vis. prof. pathology, Jerusalem, 1975; past mem. sci. adv. group NIH, Bethesda, Md.; clin. prof. pathology U. Medicine and Dentistry N.J. Author: Histological Classification of Renal Diseases, Renal Disease—Present Status, Glomerular Diseases (2 edits.), Tubulo-Interstitial Diseases (2 edits.), Tumors of Serosal Surfaces, Vascular Diseases of the Kidney (2 edits.), Developmental and Hereditary Diseases of the Kidney, Infections and Tropical Diseases of the Kindey, Systemic Vasculitides, Urinary Tract Pathology, The Kidney on Collagen-Vascular Diseases; mem. editl. bd. Nephron., Contbns. to Nephrology, Histopathology (formerly Lab Investigation), Modern Pathology; contbr. numerous articles to sci. jours.; discovered Churg-Strauss Syndrome, 1951. Served to capt., M.C. AUS, 1943-46. Mem. Am. Assn. Pathologists, Am. Soc. Nephrology (John P. Peters award 1987), N.Y. Acad. Medicine, Internat. Acad. Pathology, Harvey Soc., Internat. Soc. Nephrology, Alpha Omega Alpha. Address: 711 Ogden Ave Teaneck NJ 07666-2203

CHUTKOW, LEE ROBINSON, physician; b. Denver, Feb. 10, 1927; s. Samuel and Yvette (Robinson) C.; m. Mary Lou Murdock, June 1957 (div.); 1 child, John; m. Betty Miller Hanish, June 3, 1973; children: Jennifer Hanish Chutkow Baldwin, Jonathan Hanish. Ph.B., U. Chgo., 1948; M.D., U. Colo., 1954; Diplomate Am. Bd. Psychiatry and Neurology. Intern, Strong Meml. Hosp., Rochester, N.Y., 1954-56; resident in psychiatry U. Colo. Med. Ctr., Denver, 1956-59; pvt. practice psychiatry, Newark, 1959-64, Los Alamos, N.Mex., 1964-68, Louisville, 1969—; clin. dir. Central State Hosp., Louisville, 1982-89; staff psychiatrist Seven Countries Svcs., Inc., Louisville, 1990-95; clin. faculty dept. psychiatry U. Louisville. Served with USN, 1945-46. Mem. AMA, Am. Psychiat. Assn. Democrat. Jewish. Home: 3019 Colonial Hill Rd Louisville KY 40205-2705

CHUTORIAN, ABE M., pediatrician, educator; b. Winnipeg, Man., Can., Feb. 8, 1929; s. Morris and Rose (Cohen) C.; m. Helen Carol Olasker, Sept. 2, 1951; children: Leslie, Sandra, Tracy. MA, U. Man., 1952, MD, 1957, BSc (hon.), 1957. Diplomate Am. Bd. Pediatrics, Neurology. Intern Winnipeg Gen. Hosp., 1957-58; resident L.A. Children's Hosp., 1958-60; from fellow of neurology to prof. pediatrics and neurology Columbia U., N.Y.C., 1960-90; prof. pediats. and neurology, chief dept. pediat. neurology Cornel U., N.Y. Hosp., 1990—; adv. bd. Riverdale (N.Y.) Mental Health, 1985—. Mem. editl. bd. Pediatric Neurology Jour., 1992—; assoc. editor ACTA Neuropediatrica, 1996—; contbr. chpts. in books, articles and abstracts to profl. jours. Fellow Am. Acad. Pediatrics, Am. Acad. Neurology; mem. AMA, Am. Neurol. Assn., Internat. Chile Neurol. Soc., Child Neurology Soc., N.Y. State Med. Soc., N.Y. County Med. Soc. Office: NY Hosp/Cornell Univ Divsn Pediatric Neurology 525 E 68th St New York NY 10021

CHYTIL, FRANK, biochemist; b. Prague, Czechoslovakia, Aug. 28, 1924; came to U.S., 1965, naturalized, 1971; s. Frantisek and Ruzena (Vitouskova) C.; m. Lucie Scheinost, Nov. 26, 1949; children: Frank, Anna, Helena. M.S., Sch. Chem. Tech., Prague, 1949, Ph.D., 1952; C.Sc., Czechoslovak Acad. Sci., Prague, 1956. Research biochemist Charles U., Prague, 1949-51; research fellow Inst. Human Research, Prague, 1952-63; sr. scientist Czechoslovak Acad. Sci., Prague, 1956-64; sr. research fellow Brandeis U., Waltham, Mass., 1964; sr. research assoc. Brandeis U., 1965-66; head sect. enzymology S.W. Found. Research and Edn., San Antonio, 1966-69; mem. faculty Vanderbilt U., 1969—, prof. biochemistry, 1975—, Gen. Foods Disting. prof. of nutrition, 1984-89, Harrie Branscomb disting. prof., 1993-94; adj. assoc. prof. U. Tex., San Antonio, 1968-69. Editor: Vitamins and Hormones, 1983; mem. editl. bd. Analytical Biochemistry, 1980-87, Jour. Biol. Chemistry, 1982-88, 96—, Am. Jour. Clin. Nutrition, 1993-95; contbr. articles to profl. jours. Recipient Osborne-Mendel and Lederle awards; USPHS grantee, 1967-95. Fellow Am. Soc. Nutritional Scis.; mem. Am. Soc. Biochemistry and Molecular Biology, Endocrine Soc., Sigma Xi. Address: 914 Lynnwood Blvd Nashville TN 37205-4527 Office: Vanderbilt U Sch Medicine Nashville TN 37232

CIAK, ANN D., nursing educator; b. Erie, Pa., Apr. 6, 1951; d. Harry S. and Sophie (Sulecki) Dombrowski; m. John F. Ciak, Apr. 11, 1987; children: Jeffrey, Brian (twins). BSN, Pa. State U., 1972; MSN, U. Pitts., 1976, PhD in Higher Edn., 1985. Staff nurse emergency room Children's Hosp., Pitts., 1972-73; pub. health nurse Vis. Nurse Assn., Erie, Pa., 1973-74; pediatric nurse Tufts New Eng. Med. Ctr., Boston, 1974-75; faculty Duquesne U., Pitts., 1976-78; supr. Allegheny Gen. Hosp., Pitts., 1978-79; instr. St. Margaret Meml. Hosp. Sch. Nursing, Pitts., 1979-90; dir. sch. nursing St. Margaret Meml. Hosp., Pitts., 1990—. Lt. col. Nurse Corps, USAR, 1974—. Mem. Nat. League Nursing, Pa. League for Nursing (past treas. area 6), Univ. Pitts. Sch. Nursing Alumni Assn. (2nd v.p. 1984-85), Sigma Theta Tau. Roman Catholic. Office: St Margeret Meml Hosp Sch Nursing 815 Freeport Rd Pittsburgh PA 15215

CIAK, BRENDA SUSAN, nurse; b. Springfield, Mass., Jan. 29, 1955; d. Stanley Peter and Jessica Evelyn (Jorkowski) Ciak; divorced, 1989. BS in Pub. Health, U. Mass., 1976, BSN, 1979, RN, 1979; MSN, Boston U., 1986. RN, Mass.; cert. in infection control; cert. gerontological nurse. Staff nurse Miriam Hosp., Providence, 1979-80; head nurse Western Mass. Kidney Ctr., Springfield, 1980-85; nurse epidemiologist Providence Hosp., Holyoke, Mass., 1985-86; infection control program mgr. VA Med. Ctr., Northampton, Mass., 1986-94; clin. nurse supr. infection control, quality & case mgmt. Mercy Hosp., Springfield, Mass., 1995—; presenter at profl. confs. Contbr. to profl. publs. Co-founder, co-chair AIDS/HIV Positive Support Group VA Med. Ctr., Northampton, 1989-92. Featured in article in Women Unltd. mag., 1991; contbr. articles to profl. jours. Mem. NAFE, Assn. Practitioners in Infection Control (elected mem. New England chpt. nominating com. 1993-94), Advanced Nursing Practice Group of Western Mass. (chairperson 1989-94), Zonta Club Internat. (bd. dirs. 1992-94), Springfield Mus. and Libr. Assn., Sigma Theta Tau (chpt. archivist 1990-92). Home: 102 Wolcott St Springfield MA 01104-2418 Office: Mercy Hosp Dept Quality & Case Mgmt 271 Carew St Springfield MA 01104

CIANCIO, SEBASTIAN GENE, periodontist, educator; b. Jamestown, N.Y., June 21, 1937; m. Marilyn Bonfiglio; children: Michele Ann, Sebastian. D.D.S., SUNY-Buffalo, 1961. Diplomate: Am. Bd. Periodontology; cert. periodontist, 1965. Postdoctoral fellow depts. pharmacology and periodontology SUNY-Buffalo, 1963-65, instr., 1964-65, asst. clin. prof. pharmacology, asst. prof. periodontology, 1966, acting co-chmn. dept. periodontology, 1967-68, acting chmn., 1968, chmn. dept. periodontology, 1969-72, prof., chmn. dept. periodontics-endodontics, 1972-80, chmn. dept. periodontics, 1980—, clin. prof. dept. pharmacology, 1973—; vis. faculty Sch. Dentistry, U. Zurich, Switzerland, 1976; dental chmn. com. on revision U.S. Pharmacopeia, 1981—. Author: Clinical Pharmacology for Dental Professionals, 1980, 3rd edit., 1989; editor Biological Therapies in Dentistry; editor Peridontal Insights; contbr. numerous articles to profl. jours., chpts. to books. Served to capt. U.S. Army Dental Corps, 1961-63. Recipient George B. Snow prize in Prosthetic dentistry, 1961, hon. citation U. Chile, 1980, Gies. Found. award in Periodontics, 1988, Sch. of Dental Medicine Dean's award, 1992; named Alpha Omega Dental Educator of Yr., 1971, Buffalo Dental Man of Yr., 1987. Fellow Internat. Coll. Dentist, Am. Acad. Periodontology (exec. com. 1981—, spl. citation 1983, v.p. 1989-90, pres. 1991-92); mem. ADA (chmn., cons. coun. on dental therapeutics, 1976-78, cons. coun. on dental edn. 1982—, coun. on scientific affairs 1995—), Internat. Assn. Dental Rsch., Nat. Soc. Dental Rsch. (bd. dirs. 1981-84), Royal Soc. Health (London), 8th Dist. Dental Soc., Erie County Dental Soc., Fedn. Dentaire Internationale, Omicron Kappa Upsilon. Office: SUNY at Buffalo Dept of Pharmacology Buffalo NY 14214

CIANFICHI, ANNE LOUISE, medical and surgical nurse; b. Scranton, Pa., Oct. 30, 1948; d. Francis A. and Helen M. (Sandrowicz) Kane; m. James L. Cianfichi, June 29, 1968; children: James, Michael. Diploma, Mercy Hosp. Sch. Nursing, Scranton, 1969. Staff nurse Maryvale Hosp., Phoenix, 1970-71, Allied Rehab. Inst., Scranton, 1979-81, Mercy Hosp., Scranton, 1985-86; per diem float nurse Moses Taylor Hosp., Scranton, 1986-91; staff nurse Interim Health Care, 1991-95; home health aide supr. Cmty. Vis. Nurses Inc., Avoca, Pa., 1995—.

CIARDULLO, ROBERT CARL, plastic surgeon; b. N.Y.C., Oct. 2, 1950; s. Sam and Amy (Bonicoro) C.; m. Kira A. Geraci; children: Jean-Paul, Christina. BA, Vassar Coll., 1972; MD, Johns Hopkins U., 1976. Diplomate Am. Bd. Plastic Surgery. Intern Columbia-Presbyterian Hosp., resident in gen. surgery; resident in plastic surgery N.Y. Hosp.-Cornell; pvt. practice, White Plains, N.Y., 1981—; plastic surgeon White Plains Hosp., 1981—. Contbr. articles to med. jours. Mem. AMA, Am. Soc. Plastic and Reconstructive Surgeons (govt. rels. com. 1985—), N.Y. State Med. Soc., Westchester County Med. Soc. (pub. rels. com. 1994—). Office: 170 Maple Ave White Plains NY 10601

CIBIS, GERHARD WOLFGANG, physician; b. Heidelberg, Germany, Nov. 5, 1942; s. Paul Anton and Lisa Magdalena C.; m. Melanie Ann Crandall; children: Paul, Ilah. BA, Washington U., St. Louis, 1963, MD, 1968. Diplomat. Am. Bd. Ophthalmology. Intern Baylor U. Sch. Medicine, Houston, 1968-69; fellow U. Iowa, 1969-70; fellow in pediatric ophthalmology U. Miami Bascom Palmer Eye Inst., 1976-77; clin. prof. ophthalmology U. Mo. Kansas City - Children's Mercy Hosp., 1977—, assoc. prof. ophthalmology, dir. pediatric ophthalmology, 1979-83, chief ophthalmologist, 1981—, pres. med. staff, 1986-88. Author: Decision Making in Pediatric Ophthalmology; patentee in field. Mem. cen. gov. bd. Children's Ctr. for Visually Impaired, Kansas City, 1980, Children's Mercy Hosp., Kansas City, Mo., 1993—. Lt. comdr. USN, 1970. Fellow Am. Ophthalmology Soc., German Ophthalmol. Soc.; mem. Mo. Ophthal. Soc., Am. Soc. Pediatric Ophthal. and Strab., Internat. Soc. of Clin. and Exptl. Electro-ophthalmology, Assn. for Rsch. in Ophthalmology, Internat. Soc. Ophthal Genetics. Office: Gerhard W Cibis MD Ste 421 4620 JC Nichols Pkwy Kansas City MO 64112

CIBOROWSKI, PAUL JOHN, counseling psychology educator; b. N.Y.C., Jan. 15, 1943; s. Paul J. and Mary (Deptuch) C.; m. Doris E. Carlo, June 24, 1973; children: Philip Alan, Kevin Michael. BA, U. Dayton, 1965; MA, NYU, 1969; PhD, Fordham U., 1979. Cert. counselor. Counselor Christ the King High Sch., Queens, N.Y., 1967-70; coordinator drug edn. Sachem Sch. Dist., Holbrook, N.Y., 1971-73, sr. counselor/grant coordinator Sachem Schs., 1973-89; mental health counselor, 1980—; assoc. prof. counseling and psychology L.I. U., 1989—; pres. Stratmar Ednl. Systems; pvt. practice marriage and family therapy; cons., trainer Family Life Bur., Diocese of Rockville Centre. Author: The Changing Family I, 1984, 2d edit., 1986, Survival Skills for Single Parents, 1987; contbr. articles to profl. jours. Mem. parish council St. Mark's Roman Cath. Ch., also chmn. fin. com.; bd. dirs. Soundview Civic Assn.; fellow Ctr. for Study of the Changing Family, Port Chester, N.Y.; chair Brookhaven; mem. Brookhaven Anti-Bias Coalition; chair N.Y. Youth Bd., Western Suffolk Coalition on child Abuse & Neglect. Grantee in field. Mem. N.Y. State Assn. for Counseling and Devel. (legis. chmn. 1989—, v.p., state curriculum com. 1981-82), Am. Assn. Counseling and Devel. (com. on children, youth and families), Am. Mental Health Counselors Assn. (chmn. spl. interest network on children and adolescents, coord. Child Adv. Network, exec. bd., nat. com. for the rights of children 1992—), Western Suffolk Counselors Assn. (past treas., past v.p.), Phi Delta Kappa. Home: 38 Mary Pitkin Path PO Box 284 Shoreham NY 11786

CICACCI, MOLLIE ANN, director of information management; b. Pitts., July 9, 1969; d. William Lee and Frances Marie (Mazur) Edwards; m. Mark Cicacci, May 29, 1993. BS, U. Pitts., 1992. Registered record adminstr. Supr. med. records Scranton (Pa.) Cmty. Med. Ctr., 1992-94; dir. health info. mgmt. Intercare/Southwood & Lakewood Hosps., Pitts., 1994—. Mem. Am. Health Info. Mgmt. Assn. Republican. Roman Catholic.

CICALA, ROGER STEPHEN, physician, educator; b. Parkersburg, W.Va., Aug. 21, 1956; s. Edmond D. and Ann (Pettit) C.; m. Shari Lee Miller, Mar. 17, 1982 (div. Dec. 1989); children: Kristin Pettit, Paul Andrew. BS in Biology, Christian Bros. Coll., Memphis, 1978; MD, U. Tenn., Memphis, 1982. Diploamte Am. Bd. Anesthesiology, Am. Bd. Med. Examiners. Intern dept. surgery U. Tenn., 1982-83, chief resident, 1985, from instr. to asst. prof., 1987-90, assoc. prof. anesthesiology, 1990-94, dir. pain ctr., 1988-94; pvt. practice Memphis, 1986-87; med. author, illustrator, 1994—; anesthesiology staff Memphis Neuroscis. Ctr., 1986-87; dir. trauma anesthesia Elvis Presley Trauma Ctr., Memphis, 1988-92, mem. staff, 1987-94; mem. staff Meth. Hosp. Memphis, 1986-94, Eastwood Med. Ctr., Memphis, 1991-94; presenter in field. Author: (with others) Courtroom Medicine: Pain and Suffering, 1991, Geriatric Anesthesiology, 1992, Textbook of Trauma Anesthesia and Critical Care, 1992, Headache: Diagnosis and Interdisciplinary Treatment, 1992, Refresher Course in Anesthesiology, vol. 20, 1992, Handbook of Trauma Surgery, 1993, Manual of Trauma Anesthesia, 1993, The Heart Disease Handbook, 1996; editor: (with others) Textbook of Trauma Anesthesia and Critical Care, 1992, and others. Mem. AAAS, AMA, Am. Soc. Anesthesiologists, Am. Pain Soc., Internat. Soc. Study of Pain, Internat. Trauma Anesthesia and Critical Care Soc. (co-chmn. task force 1991-93), Internat. Anesthesia Rsch. Soc., Tenn. Med. Assn., Tenn. Soc. Anesthesiologists, Shelby County Med. Soc., Shelby County Anesthesia Soc., Soc. Cardiovascular Anesthesiologists, Soc. Pain Practice Mgmt. (bd. dirs. 1991-94), Assn. U. Anesthesists. Home: 3080 Walnut Grove Rd Apt 401 Memphis TN 38111-3521

CICCIARELLI, JAMES CARL, immunology educator; b. Toluca, Ill., May 26, 1947; s. Maurice Cicciarelli and Helen Ippolito; m. Patricia Cook, Feb. 17, 1996; 1 child, Nicola. BS, Tulane U., 1969; PhD, So. Ill. U., 1977. Lic. clin. lab. dir., Calif. Postdoctoral fellow dept. surgery UCLA, 1977-79, asst. prof. immunology, 1980-87, assoc. prof., 1987-91; prof. urology and microbiology U. So. Calif., L.A., 1992—; lab. dir. Metic Transplant Lab., Inc., L.A., 1984—; bd. dirs.. So. Calif. Organ Procurement Agy., 1987—; clin. lab. dir. Am. Bd. Bioanalysis, 1991—; mem. histocompatibility com. United Network Organ Sharing, 1991-94. Contbr. articles to sci. jours., chpts. to books. NIH rsch. grantee, 1985-88. Mem. Am. SOc. Histocompatibility and Immunogenetics, Internat. Transplant Soc., Am. Soc. Transplant Physicians, Internat. Soc. Heart Lung Transplantation. Libertarian. Roman Catholic. Home: 2524 Manhattan Ave Hermosa Beach CA 90254-2543 Office: USC Dept Urology Metic Transplant Lab 2100 W 3rd St Ste 280 Los Angeles CA 90057-1922

CICCOCIOPPO, MICHAEL VICTOR, health services administrator; b. Mechanicsburg, Pa., Nov. 14, 1952; s. Michael Victor and Blanche Olive (Martin) C.; m. Margaret Mary O'Grady, Feb. 9, 1974; children: Mary Margaret, David William, Melinda Marie, Melissa Marie. BA, McKendree Coll., 1977; M Health Adminstrn., Baylor U., 1983. Commd. USAF, advanced through ranks to maj.; adminstrv. clk. USAF Clinic Ramstein, Germany, 1971-74; ops. supr. 57th Aeromed. Evacuation Square, Belleville, Ill., 1974-77; asst. adminstr. USAF Hosp., Dover, Del., 1977-81; adminstrv. resident USAF Acad. Hosp., Colorado Springs, 1982-83; asst. adminstr. USAF Hosp. Seymour-Johnson, Goldsboro, N.C., 1983-85; adminstr. USAF Clinic Comiso, Italy, 1985-86; staff officer Air Force Surgeon Gen. Office, Washington, 1986-91; ret. USAF, 1991; v.p. Holy Spirit Hosp., Camp Hill, Pa., 1991—. Mem. Gov.'s Club, Cumberland County, Pa., 1993—, Capital Region C. of C., Harrisburg, Pa., 1992—, Leadership Harrisburg Area, 1994—; lector Ch. of the Good Shepherd, Camp Hill, 1991—. Decorated Meritorious Svc. medal USAF, Commitment to Svc. Silver medal, Chief of the Med. Svc. Corps/USAF. Fellow Am. Coll. Healthcare Execs. (regent 1995-99); mem. Healthcare Execs. Forum of Cen. Pa. (sec. 1995-96). Republican. Roman Catholic. Home: 12 Victoria Way Camp Hill PA 17011 Office: Holy Spirit Hosp 503 N 21st St Camp Hill PA 17011

CICCOTTI, MICHAEL GERARD, orthopaedic surgeon; b. Scranton, Pa., Nov. 3, 1960; s. Angelo Michael and Mary Louise (McGraw) C.; m. Patricia Ann McDade, June 22, 1984; children: Michael, Matthew, Emily, Caroline. B. Arts and Scis. summa cum laude, Coll. of Holy Cross, Worcester, Mass., 1978-82; MD summa cum laude, Georgetown U., 1986. Diplomate Am. Bd. Orthopaedic Surgery; lic. physician, Pa. Resident in orthop. surgery Thomas Jefferson U., Phila., 1986-91; sports medicine fellow Kerlan-Jobe Clinic, U. So. Calif., L.A., 1991-92; asst. clin. prof. dept. orthop. Thomas Jefferson U. and Pa. Hosp., Phila., 1992—; co-dir. sports medicine and sports medicine rsch. Pa. Hosp., 1995—; team physician asst. L.A. Lakers, Rams, Dodgers, Kings, Calif. Angels profl. sports teams, 1991-92; assoc. team orthop. cons. U.S. Women's Nat. Soccer Team, 1994-96; orthop. cons. Phila. Flyers Hockey Team, 1995-96, Phila. Eagles Football Team, 1995-96; coord. alliance Pa. Hosp., 1993-94, mem. Team 2000, 1995-96; lectr. in field. Author: The Knee, 1994, Upper Extremity Injuries in Sports, 1995; contbr. articles to profl. jours. Fellow Am. Acad. Orthop. Surgeons (Outstanding Audiovisual award 1993), Am. Orthop. Soc. for Sports Medicine; mem. Phila. Coll. Physicians, Phila. Orthop. Soc. for Sports Medicine, Jefferson Orthop. Soc. (Philip Syng Physick award for outstanding rsch. 1990), Pa. Orthop. Soc. (fellowship rsch. award 1995), Alpha Omega Alpha. Office: Rothman Inst Thomas Jefferson Univ 800 Spruce St Philadelphia PA 19107

CICHOKE, ANTHONY JOSEPH, JR., chiropractor, writer, health consultant; b. Peoria, Ill., Nov. 23, 1931; s. Anthony Joseph Sr. and Margaret Mary (Conwell) C.; m. Margaret A. Kovner, Feb. 24, 1962; children: Anthony Joseph III, Michael David, William F., Margaret Kathleen. BS in Social Sci., John Carroll U., 1954; student, Army Lang. Sch., Monterey, Calif., 1955; MA in Speech and Theater, St. Louis U., 1964; MA in Speech Sci. Pathology and Audiology, U. Minn., 1967; postgrad., Case Western Res. U., 1969; D. Chiropractic, Nat. Coll. Chiropractic, Lombard, Ill., 1973; postgrad., Western States Chiropractic Coll., 1975. Diplomate Am. Chiropractic Bd. Nutrition. Actor, promoter Schubert Orgn., N.Y.C., 1960-61; entertainment dir., producer U.S. Army and 2d Army, Ft. Eustis, Va., 1961-62; actor, tchr. radio announcer U. Minn., Mpls., 1964-67; tchr., researcher Eastman Dental Ctr., Rochester, N.Y., 1967-68; team physician Portland State U. Amateur Athletic Union, 1975-84; instr. and lectr. on sports medicine, nutrition, and chiropractic medicine at seminars, convs. and various colls. and univs; researcher. Contbr. over 100 articles to profl. journals; editor Nutritional Prospectives mag, 1979; producer Blockheads, London, 1984-85, This was Burlesque, L.A., 1985. Chmn. sports medicine com. Amateur Athletic Union, 1975—; mem. postgrad. faculty numerous chiropractic colls. 1st lt. U.S. Army, 1955-59. Grantee U.S. Office Edn., 1965-67, Case We. Res. U., 1968-69, U. Minn., 1965-67, NIH, 1968-69. Fellow Internat. Assn. Study of Pain (diplomate), Internat. Coll. Chiropractic; mem. Am. Chiropractic Assn. (coun. orthopedics, 3 man posture com., coun. sports injuries, past pres. and v.p. coun. nutrition), N.Y. Acad. Scis., Orthomolecular Med. Soc., Acad. Orthomolecular Psychiatry, Acad. Sports Medicine, U.S. Sports Acad., Found. Chiropractic Edn. and Rsch., Metabolic Rsch. Found. Republican. Roman Catholic. Office: PO Box 16189 Portland OR 97216-0189

CIFU, DAVID XAVIER, physician, physical medicine and rehabilitation specialist; b. N.Y.C., July 17, 1962; s. John Lewis and Rosa (Shwartz) C.; m. Ingrid Anne Marie Prosser, June 22, 1986; 1 child: Gabriella Nicole. BS, Boston U., 1986, MD, 1986. Intern Baylor Coll. Medicine, 1986-87, resident in phys. medicine and rehab., 1987-90; asst. prof. Baylor Coll. Medicine, Houston, 1990-91; asst. prof. Med. Coll. Va., Richmond, 1991-96, assoc. prof., 1996—; med. dir. Rehab. and Rsch. Ctr., Richmond, Va., 1991—; dir. Rehab. Consultation Svcs.-Med. Coll. Va., 1991—. Author chpts. to books; editor: (series) Manual of PM&R, 1996—. Nat. Inst. Disability and Rehab. Rsch. grantee, 1992—. Mem. Am. Assn. Phys. Medicine and Rehab. (mem. liaison activities com. 1993-96, study guide com. 1992-96). Office: Med Coll Va MCV Box 980661 Richmond VA 23298-0661

CIMINO, JAMES ERNEST, physician; b. N.Y.C., July 7, 1928; s. Ernest S. and Rose (Gorga) C.; m. Dorothy Hilary Naperkoski, June 5, 1954; children: James, Ernest, Christopher, Peter, Paul, Maria. Student, Syracuse U., 1946-48; AB, NYU, 1950, MD, 1954. Diplomate Am. Bd. Internal Medicine, Am. Bd. Nephrology. Intern, then resident E.J. Meyer Meml. Hosp., Buffalo, 1954-58; rsch. fellow in physiology U. Buffalo, 1957-58; internal medicine physician, dir. renal svc. VA Hosp., Bronx, N.Y., 1960-68; attending physician Calvary Hosp., Bronx, N.Y., 1961—, chief medicine, med. dir., 1963-80, co-med. dir., 1994, dir. Palliative Care Inst., 1994—; cons. medicine St. Joseph's Hosp., Yonkers, N.Y., Holy Name Hosp., Teaneck, N.J., cons. medicine VA Hosp., Bronx, 1970-77, dir. hemodialysis unit, 1960-70; asst. clin. prof. medicine Mt. Sinai Sch. Medicine, N.Y.C., 1970-73; clin. prof. medicine N.Y. Med. Coll., 1980—; adj. prof., cons. nutrition NYU, 1972-93; cons. internal medicine N.Y.C. Dept. Health, 1971-74, also chmn. con. advanced cancer, 1971-74; mem. instnl. biohazards com. Albert Einstein Coll. Medicine, 1980-92. Mem. edit. bd. N.Y. Med. Quar.; mem. edit. review bd. Am. Jour. of Hospice and Palliative Care; contbr. articles to med. jours. Bd. dirs. N.Y.C. chpt. Am. Cancer Soc. With USAF, 1958-60. Recipient commendation VA, 1968, Ann. Merit award N.Y.C. Pub. Health Assn., 1979, 1st ann. Catherine McParlan Humanitarian award, 1980, Dialysis Pioneering award Nat. Kidney Disease Found., 1982, Il Leone di San Marco award in medicine, 1991; co-recipient Good Samaritan award Nat. Cath. Devel. Conf., 1981. Fellow ACP (Laureate award 1992); mem. AMA, Am. Heart Assn., Internat. Soc. Nephrology, Am. Soc. Nephrology, Am. Dietetic Assn. (Hon. Membership award 1995). Office: 174070 Eastchester Rd Bronx NY 10461-2248

CIMINO, JOSEPH ANTHONY, physician, educator; b. N.Y.C., Jan. 1, 1934; m. Margaret Langan; children—Andrea, Laura, Lisa, Joseph, Linda, Margaret, John. B.A. in Am. History, Harvard U., 1956, M.I.H., 1964, M.P.H., 1965; M.S. in Biology, Fordham U., 1958; M.D., U. Buffalo, 1962. Diplomate: Am. Bd. Preventive Medicine. Intern Grasslands Hosp., Valhalla, N.Y., 1962-63; AEC fellow in environ. medicine Harvard U. Sch. Public Health, 1963-65; research asso., health officer N.Y.C. Dept. Health, 1965-66; dir. Bur. Community Safety and Occupational Health, 1968-71, dep. commr. health, 1971-72, commr. health, 1972-74; chief med. officer N.Y.C. Dept. Sanitation, 1966-69; med. dir. N.Y.C. Poison Control Center, 1966-72; dir. health and safety N.Y.C. Environ. Protection Adminstrn., 1968-71; commr. hosps. Westchester County, N.Y., 1974-78; pres., chief exec. officer N.Y. Med. Coll., 1978-81, prof. preventive medicine, 1976—, chmn. dept. preventive medicine, 1980—; pres. Occupational Medicine Assocs., 1978—; assoc. prof. environ. medicine and pub. health NYU, 1971-76; prof. comty. dynamics Pace U., 1977-78; adj. prof. pub. health and tropical medicine Tulane U., 1972-76; lectr. in pub. health Columbia U., 1973-76; vis. prof. comty. health Albert Einstein Coll. Medicine, 1973-76, N.Y. State Pub. Health Coun.; pres. bd. Dominican Sisters Family Health Svcs., Inc.; bd. dirs. Westchester Artificial Kidney Ctr. Author: Safety: Protection from Injury, 1969, Medical Service Manual, 1971, Drug Abuse Treatment Agencies in New York City, 1972; author numerous profl. monographs; contbr. articles to profl. publs. Chmn. Cath. Interracial Coun. of Westchester County; chief med. cons. N.Y.C. CSC, 1966-71. With U.S. Army, 1964-65. Fellow Am. Coll. Preventive Medicine, N.Y. Acad. Medicine, Am. Coll. Occupational Medicine, N.Y. Acad. Sci.; mem. Am. Pub. Health Assn., N.Y.C. Pub. Health Assn., Indsl. Med. Assn., Assn. Govtl. Hygienists, Aerospace Med. Assn., Westchester County Med. Soc., N.Y. State Med. Assn., AMA, Am. Soc. Clin. Nutrition. Home: 50 Willard Ave Tarrytown NY 10591-1210 Office: NY Med Coll Dept Preventive Med Valhalla NY 10595

CIMOCH, PAUL JOSEPH, II, medical facility administrator, researcher; b. Scranton, Pa., July 16, 1957; s. Paul J. Sr. and Malvina A. (Ardziejewski) C.; m. Cathy Ann, Feb. 11, 1995. BA, U. Tex., 1979; MD, U. Tex., Galveston, 1983. Diplomate Am. Bd. Internal Medicine. Intern U. Miami/Jackson Meml. Hosp., 1983-84, rresident in internal medicine, 1984-86; pvt. practice Ft. Lauderdale, Fla., 1983-86; dir. med. svcs. Ctr. Spl. Immunology, Irvine, Calif., 1986—; pres. Physicians Assn. for AIDS Care, Chgo., 1994-95. Fellow ACP. Office: Ctr Spl Immunology 100 Pacifica # 100 Irvine CA 92718

CINO, PAUL MICHAEL, microbiologist; b. N.Y.C., Dec. 8, 1946; s. Salvatore Joseph and Pauline Mary (Raimondo) C.; m. Julia Pepe, Sept. 29, 1973; 1 child, Paula Marie. BS in Botany, Hunter Coll., 1967; MS in Microbiology, Rutgers U., 1970, PhD in Microbiology, 1973. Postdoctoral rsch. fellow dept. microbial biochemistry Rutgers U., 1973-75; sr. rsch. scientist E. R. Squibb & Sons, New Brunswick, N.J., 1981-87; rsch. group leader E. R. Squibb & Sons, New Brunswick, 1987-92; assoc. dir. Bristol-Myers Squibb, New Brunswick, 1992—; guest lectr. dept. bacteriology Rutgers U. Contbr. articles to profl. jours. Chmn. Bridgewater (N.J.) Bd. Adjustment, 1979—; Bridgewater mem. Dem. Com., 1973—. Charles and Joanna Busch postdoctoral fellow, 1973-75. Mem. Am Soc. Microbiology, Theobald Smith SOc. (pres. 1981-82), Soc. Indsl. Microbiology, N.J. Roman Catholic. Home: 4 Crest Dr Bound Brook NJ 08805-1227 Office: Bristol-Myers-Squibb One Squibb Dr New Brunswick NJ 08903

CINOTTI, ALFONSE ANTHONY, ophthalmologist, educator; b. Jersey City, Jan. 1, 1923; s. William John Cinotti and Carrie Ilaria; m. Kathleen Dolores Higgins, June 26, 1948; children: Donald, Kathleen, Lawrence, Carol Ann, William. BS, Fordham U., 1943; MD, SUNY, Bklyn., 1946. Diplomate Am. Bd. Ophthalmology. Dir. resident tng. N.Y. Eye and Ear Infirmary, N.Y.C., 1955-59, assoc. dir. Postgrad. Inst., 1956-63; assoc. prof., dir. div. of Ophthalmology N.J. Med. Sch., 1963-72, prof., dir., 1972-74, chmn. faculty, 1974-75; prof., chmn. dept. ophthalmology U. Medicine & Dentistry N.J. Med. Sch., 1974-93; prof., chmn. emeritus U. Medicine & Dentistry, 1993—; med. dir. Eye Inst. N.J., Newark, 1970-93; trustee N.J. State Commn. for the Blind and Visually Impaired, Newark, 1971-76, 80—, chmn., 1992; founder, mem. Eye Bank of N.J., 1970—. Contbr. articles to profl. jours. Founder Joint Commn. on Allied Health Ophthalmology; mem. adv. bd. Essex County Div. on Aging, Newark, 1984; chmn. med. adv. com., mem. exec. com. Nat. Soc. to Prevent Blindness, N.J. Recipient Outstanding Citizens award Lions 16A, Disting. Alumnus award N.Y. Eye and Ear Infirmary, N.Y.C., Visionary Yr. Eye Inst., N.J., Lions Eyebank, N.J., 1991, Sr. Honors award Am. Acad. Oph., 1991, Master Teaching award Ophth. Alumni Assn. SUNY, Disting. Svc. Award Peter Rodino Law Soc. Seton Hall U. Fellow Am. Coll. Surgeons, Am. Acad. Ophthalmology (bd. councillors 1981-84); mem. AMA (alt. del. 1978-89), Am. Assn. Ophthalmology (pres. 1978, 79), Hudson County Med. Soc. (pres. 1978), N.J. Acad. Ophthalmology and Otolaryngology (pres. 1974). Republican. Roman Catholic. Lodge: Knights of Malta. Home: 82 Winsor Pl Glen Ridge NJ 07028-2137 Office: U Md-NJ Med Sch Eye Inst NJ 90 Bergen St Newark NJ 07103-2425

CINQUE, THOMAS J., dean. Dean Creighton U. Sch. Medicine. Office: Creighton U Sch Medicine 2500 California Plz Omaha NE 68178*

CINQUEGRANI, MICHAEL PETER, cardiologist; b. Chgo., Feb. 28, 1953; s. Peter Michael and Helen Ann (Marine) C.; m. Carol Marie Callahan, Sept. 23, 1994. BA, Knox Coll., Galesburg, Ill., 1975; MD, Loyola U., Chgo., 1978. Diplomate in cardiology Am. Bd. Internal Medicine. Resident in internal medicine So. Ill. U. Sch. Medicine, Springfield, 1978-81; fellow in cardiology U. Rochester (N.Y.) Med. Ctr., 1982-85, instr. medicine, 1982-85; instr. medicine Med. Coll. Wis., Milw., 1985-86, asst. prof., 1986-91, assoc. prof., 1991—; mem. staff. Froedtert Meml. Luth. Hosp., Milw., 1985—. Contbr. articles to profl. jours. Am. Chem. Soc. scholar, 1975. Fellow ACP, Am. Coll. Cardiology (chair pvt. sector com. Wis. chpt. 1994); mem. Am. Fedn. for Clin. Rsch., State Med. Soc. Wis. (govtl. affairs com. 1994), Phi Beta Kappa. Roman Catholic. Home: 2401 E Jarvis Shorewood WI 53211 Office: Med Coll Wis Divsn Cardiology 9200 W Wisconsin Ave Milwaukee WI 53226

CIOCZEK, HENRYK ANTONI, internist; b. Lublin, Poland, May 27, 1961; came to U.S., 1987; s. Jan and Marianna (Szyszkowska) C.; m. Anna Wlaz, June 11, 1988. MD, Med. Acad., Lublin, 1985. Surgical intern Teaching Hosp. nr 1, Lublin, 1985-86, resident in neurosurgery, 1986-87; rsch. worker NYU Med. Ctr., N.Y.C., 1987-89, intern in surgery, 1991-92; intern in medicine Flushing (N.Y.) Hosp. Med. Ctr., 1992-93, resident in medicine, 1993-95; fellow in oncology Albert Einstein Cancer Ctr./Montefiore Med. Ctr., 1995—; rsch. coord. Flushing Hosp., 1992-93, del. com. interns and residents, 1993-94; rsch. coord. Harvard U., 1993-94. Author: (in Polish) Intern of Bellevue Hospital N.Y., 1994; contbr. articles to profl. jours. Active Student Orgn. Solidarity, Lublin, 1980-85. Recipient Rectors award and Sci. scholar Med. Acad., Lublin, 1982, 84, 85. Mem. AMA, Polish Med. Soc. Club.

CIOFFI, ALBERT FRANCIS, psychiatrist; b. N.Y.C.; s. Vincenzo and Rafaela (Russo) C.; m. Margaret Mary Herlihy, Sept. 29, 1963; children: Vincent, Mary, Theresa, Margaret P. BA, NYU, 1953; MD, U. Bologna, 1967. Diplomate Am. Coll. Forensic Examiners. Intern U. Hosp. Bologna, 1968, St. Francis Hosp., Jersey City, N.Y., 1969-70; resident NYU-Bellevue, N.Y.C., 1970-72; resident Kirby-Pavillion, Ward's Island, N.Y., 1972-73, attending psychiatrist, 1973-74; dir. Bernstein Meth. Program, N.Y.C., 1974-78, Westchester Psychiatry Group, Yorktown, N.Y., 1980-96; dir. psychiatry EMSA, Vallhala, N.Y., 1996—; cons. psychiatry Opengate, Somers, N.Y., 1978-80; psychiatrist Bur. of Child Guidance, N.Y.C., 1978-79; pres. Western Diet and Nutrition Ctr., Yorktown, 1990-94; staff psychiatrist Westchester County Jail, Valhalla, N.Y. Del. Dem. Party, Westchester, 1992. Scholarship Ea. Biologicals, 1960-67. Mem. Am. Coll. of Forensic Examiners, Am. Coll. of Forensic Examiners, Am. Psychiat. Assn., K.C. Office: Westchester Psychiat Group 305 Hill Blvd #10598 Westchester NY 10598

CIONGOLI, ALFRED KENNETH, neurologist; b. Phila., Jan. 11, 1943; s. Alfred Anthony and Antoinette Marie (Ragano) C.; m. Barbara, Nov. 22, 1966; children: Adam, Happy, Gregory, Alessandra, Antonio. AB, U. Pa., 1964; DO, Phila. Coll. Osteopathic Med., 1968. Diplomate Am. Bd. Psychiatry & Neurology. Fellow in neuroimmunology U. Pa. Med. Sch., Phila., 1968-74; rsch. fellow in neuroimmunology Danish Muscular Sclerosis Soc., Copenhagen, 1974-75, Hosp. U. Pa., Phila., 1975-77; pres. Neurol. Assocs. Vt., Burlington, 1977—; attending neurologist Hosp. U. Pa. Med. Sch., 1975-77; clin. asst. prof. neurology U. Vt. Coll. Medicine, Burlington, 1977-87, clin. assoc. prof., 1987—; pres. Bd. Alumni Dirs. Phila. Coll. Osteopathic Med., 1994—, chmn. internat. fellowship com., 1990—; chmn. com. NIH, 1990—. Apptd. boxing commr. State of Vt., 1982; sr. med. officer U.S. Olympics team, 1986. Mem. AMA, Am. Assn. Neurology, Phila. Neurol. Soc., Ethan Allan Club (bd. govs.), Nat. Italian-Am. Found. (sr. v.p. 1992-95, pres. 1996—). Office: Neurol Assn Vt 89 S Williams St Burlington VT 05401

CIOROIU, MICHAEL GELU, surgeon; b. Brasov, Romania, July 27, 1947; came to U.S., 1978; s. Marin and Margareta (Juranescu) C.; m. Monica Moca, Aug. 4, 1978; 1 child, Monica Comana. BS, Nr 1 Liceum, Romania, 1965; MD, Faculty of Medicine, Romania, 1971. Diplomate Am. Bd. Surgery. Instr. clin. surgery Inst. Medicine & Pharmacy, Cluj, Romania, 1971-77; resident in surgery Cabrini Med. Ctr., N.Y.C., 1980-85, attending physician, surgeon, coordinator nutrition support services, 1985—; dir. surg. residency tng. program N.Y. Med. Ctr. Manhattan Divsn., N.Y.C., 1987—; dir. residency tng. program N.Y. Med. Coll., Manhattan, 1994—; med. dir. Cabrini Wound Care Ctr., 1995; assoc. prof. clin. surgery N.Y. Med. Coll., Valhalla, 1985—. Contbr. articles to profl. jours. Recipient cert. appreciation Bayley Seton Hosp., 1984. Fellow ACS, Internat. Coll. Surgeons, Am. Soc. Abominal Surgeons; mem. AMA (award 1987, 90), Soc. Am. Gastrointestinal Endoscopic Surgeons, Soc. Laparoendoscopic Surgeons, Surg. Soc. N.Y. Med. Coll. Republican. Office: 247 3rd Ave # L-3 New York NY 10010-7457

CIOSEK, NANCY CAROL, dietitian, educator; b. Chgo., May 4, 1942; d. Bruno George and Ann Barbara (Krawiec) C. BA in Home Econs., Rosary Coll., 1964; MS in Foods and Nutrition, No. Ill. U., 1972; postgrad., Depaul U. Law Sch., 1975-76. Registered and lic. dietitian; cert. nutrition specialist. Dietitian Chgo. State Hosp., 1965-66; dietary mgr. Read-Chgo. State Mental Health Ctr., Chgo., 1966-69; instr. Wesley-Passavant Sch. Nursing, Chgo., 1969-79; dir. health and nutrition svcs. Community and Econ. Devel. Assn. Cook County, Inc., Chgo., 1980-84; dir. dietetic programs Chgo. State U., 1985-91, assoc. prof., 1985—; mem. adv. com. Ill. Dept. Pub. Health Nutrition Svc., Springfield, 1982-95; mem. Chgo. Area Dietetic Edn. Programs Coun., 1986-90; mem. interdisciplinary faculty Gt. Lakes Geriatric Ctr., Chgo., 1987-90. Author: (with others) Manual of Clinical Dietetics, 3d edit., 1988, The Hunger Handbook, 5th edit., 1988, 7th edit., 1993. Co-founder, mem. Healthy Mothers and Babies Coalition, Chgo., 1982-88; mem. Ill. Caucus on Teenage Pregnancy, Chgo., 1981-88, Ill. Hunger Action Coalition, Chgo., 1985, 88, Ill. Citizens for Better Care, Chgo., 1987-88, Chgo. Hospitality/Food Svc. Careers for Youth Speakers Forum, 1989—; bd. dirs. Suburban Cook County-DuPage County Health Systems Agy., 1983-87, exec. bd., 1985-87; bd. dirs. Health and Medicine Policy Rsch. Group, 1983-90, Suburban Health Planning Assn., 1987-88; mem. dietetic tech. adv. bd. Malcolm X Coll., 1985-92, Wm. Rainey Harper Coll., 1988-93. Named honoree Spl. Supplemental Food Program for Women, Infants and Children 10th Anniversary awards Ceremony Ill. Dept. Pub. Health Region VIII, 1984. Mem. Am. Dietetic Assn. (renal dietetics practice group), Ill. Dietetic Assn. (chair dietetic educators of practitioners 1988-91, co-chair 1992-93), Chgo. Dietetic Assn., Chgo. Nutrition Assn., Ill. Pub. Health Assn., Ill. Assn. Allied Health Profls. (bd. dirs. 1992—). Roman Catholic. Office: Chgo State U 95th and King Dr Chicago IL 60628

CIOTOLA, THOMAS J., internist, cardiologist; b. Hazelton, Pa.. BS in Gen. Arts and Scis., Pa. State U., 1972; MD, Hahnemann Med. Coll., Phila., 1976. Resident Geisinger Med. Ctr., Danville, Pa., 1976-79; fellow in cardiology Hershey (Pa.) Med. Ctr., 1979-82; cardiologist Cariology Assocs. of Greater Hazelton, Pa., 1982—. Office: Med Arts Bldg 1730 E Broad St Hazelton PA 18201

CIPANI, ENNIO CIRO, psychologist; b. N.Y.C., Mar. 26, 1952; s. Ennio Leo and Elvira (Portante) C.; m. Lucinda Suzanne Gerasch, June 27, 1981; children: Lorenzo Vittorio, Vanessa Lynn, Alessandra Lynn. BS in Psychology, Fla. Technol. U., 1973, MS in Clin. Psychology, 1975; Ph.D in Ednl. Psychology, Fla. State U., 1979. Lic. psychologist, Calif. Behavioral program specialist, ward supr. Sunland Tng. Ctr., Orlando, Fla., 1973-75; grad. rsch. asst. Fla. State U., Tallahassee, 1978-79; ad hoc asst. prof. U. Wis., Kenosha, 1980; psychologist III So. and No. Wis. Ctr., Union Grove & Eau Claire, 1979-81; asst. prof. edn. U. Pacific, Stockton, Calif., 1981-92, dept. chmn., 1989-92; full prof. Calfi. Sch. Profl. Psychology, 1993—. Author: (with A.F. Rotatori) Behavior Modification in Special Education, Vols. 7a and b, 1990; editor: The Treatment of Severe Behavior Disorders: Behavior Analysis Approaches, 1989, Curriculur and Instructional Approaches for Persons with Severe Disabilities, 1994; reviewer profl. jours.; contbr. articles to profl. jours., chpts. to books. Spl. Edn. grantee U. Pacific, 1981, 83—. Home: 15650 Mills Dr Visalia CA 93292-9150

CIPOLLONE, LEANORE MARIE, adult nurse practitioner; b. Phila., Oct. 31, 1965; d. James Joseph McCabe and Leanore Marie (Tumolo) Schlueter; m. Steven Joseph Cipollone, May 11, 1991. Diploma in nursing, Our Lady of Lourdes Hosp., 1985; AS, Camden County Coll., 1985; grad., LaSalle U., 1993; MSN, U. Pa., 1995. Staff nurse med./surg. unit Our Lady Lourdes Hosp., Camden, N.J., 1986-88, asst. nurse mgr., 1988, staff nurse ICU/critical care unit, 1988-91, staff nurse catheterization lab., 1991-92, care mgr., asst. edn. coord. CCU, 1991-95; cardiology nurse practitioner Cardiovascular Assocs. of the Delaware Valley, 1995—. Mem. AACN (CCRN), Am. Heart Assn., Sigma Theta Tau. Roman Catholic. Office: Heart House 210 W Atlantic Ave Haddon Heights NJ 08035

CIPRANDI, GLORGIO FEDERICO, allergist; b. Milan, Italy, Oct. 26, 1957; s. Giuseppe and Maria Camilla (Nicolini) C.; m. Maria Angela Tosca, Sept. 30, 1989; 1 child, Riccardo. MD, Genoa (Italy) U., 1981, postgrad., 1986-93. Asst. dept. internal medicine Genoa U., 1988-93, prof., 1988—, sr. asst. dept. internal medicine, 1993—. Contbr. articles to profl. publs. Recipient award Italian Soc. Ophthalmology, 1986, Italian Soc. Allergy, 1989, Internat. Acad. for Biomed. and Drug Rsch., 1992. Mem. European Acad. Allergy, Heliou Soc. Allergy. Home: Via Casshi 6/9, 16131 Genoa Italy Office: Dept Internal Medicine, Viale Benedetto XV n6, 16132 Genoa Italy

CIRAULO, STEPHEN JOSEPH, nurse, anesthetist; b. Danville, Pa., Feb. 25, 1960; s. Leonard Joseph and Mary Louise (Purpuri) C. Diploma, Geisinger Med. Ctr. Sch. Nursing, Danville, 1980; cert., Sch of Anesthesia for Nurses Univ. Health Ctr. Pitts., 1983; student, Ottawa U., 1986—. Nursing asst. Geisinger Med. Ctr., Danville, 1978-80; staff RN, part time charge RN cardiac care unit Williamsport (Pa.) Hosp., 1980-81; asst. gastroenterology research group Presbyn. Univ. Hosp., Pitts., 1982-83; staff nurse anesthetist dept. anesthesia Duke U. Med. Ctr., Durham, N.C., 1983-90; with Anesthesia Anytime, Winston-Salem, N.C., 1990, Nash Gen. Hosp., Rocky Mount, N.C., 1991-92; staff nurse anesthetist, mem. epidural analgesia svc. Nash Gen. Hosp., 1991-92; staff nurse anesthetist Wake Anesthesiology Assocs., Inc., Raleigh, N.C., 1992—; mem. coun. for nurse anesthetists dept. anesthesia Duke U. Med. Ctr., Durham, 1985-89; staff nurse anesthetist Epidural Analgesia Svc., Rocky Mount, 1991-92, Wake Anesthesiology Assocs., Inc., 1992—. Charter mem. Outstanding Young Ams., 1988; mem. Duke U. Artists Series Adv. Bd., 1994—. Mem. Am. Assn. Nurse Anesthetists, N.C. Assn. Nurse Anesthetists (bylaws com. 1984-86, chmn. fin. com. 1986-88, mem. fin. com. 1988-95, fall program com. 1988, spring program speaker 1990, treas. 1991-93, pres. 1994-95), Triangle Transplant Recipient Internat. Orgn. (charter), Internat. Platform Assn. Republican. Home and Office: 1710 Falls Church Rd Raleigh NC 27609-3531

CIRIACY, EDWARD WALTER, physician, educator; b. Phila., Feb. 12, 1924; s. William Frederick and Elizabeth Jane (McGettigan) C. B.S., Pa. State Coll., 1948; M.D., Temple U., 1952. Diplomate: Nat. Bd. Med. Examiners, Am. Bd. Family Practice (chmn. recertification com. 1972-76). Intern Frankford Hosp., Phila., 1952-53; surg. resident Frankford Hosp., 1953-54, Temple Hosp., Phila., 1953-54; practice medicine specializing in family practice Ely, Minn., 1954-57, 58-71, Miami, Fla., 1957-58; mem. staffs Ely-Bloomenson Community Hosp.; prof. U. Minn., 1971—, head dept. family practice, 1971-95; mem. adv. panel for subcom. on patient care Cancer Coordinating Com. for Health Scis. Contbr. articles to med. jours. Served with USAAF, 1944-46. Recipient Merit award Minn. Acad. Gen. Practice, 1963. Fellow Am. Acad. Family Physicians (charter); mem. Minn. Acad. Family Physicians (pres. 1975), Minn. Med. Assn. (mem. com. med. services 1970), Range Med. Soc. (pres. 1961), Babcock Surg. Soc., Assn. Am. Med. Colls., Alpha Omega Alpha. Club: Mason. Office: Phillip Wagensteen Bldg

U Minn Minneapolis MN 55455 also: U Minn Med Sch 420 Delaware St SE Minneapolis MN 55455-0374

CIRILLO, PATTI ANN, mental health and geriatrics nurse; b. Utica, N.Y., Nov. 8, 1952; d. Arthur Anthony and Helen Laura (Karolowicz) Rodzinka; m. Mark L. Wengert, Oct. 30, 1976 (div. Oct. 1982); m. Nicholas Cirillo, Sept. 6, 1985; 1 child, Andrew. BSN, SUNY, Utica, 1984. Cert. N.Y. Staff, head nurse female med.-surg. unit Mohawk Valley Psychiat. Ctr., Utica, 1973-84, nurse practitioner, 1984—, gen. hosp. liason, 1990—; nurse practitioner York St. Clinic, 1994—. Fellow Nurse Practitioners of Mohawk Valley, Mohawk Valley Psychiat. Ctr. Nurse Practitioner Group (v.p. 1988-90, rec. sec. 1991-93), Task Force of Nurse Practitioners and Physicians' Assts. in N.Y. State Svc. (rec. sec. 1986—). Democrat. Roman Catholic. Home: 627 French Rd New Hartford NY 13413-1013

CIROCCO, WILLIAM CARMEN, physician; b. Detroit, Dec. 27, 1958; s. Louis and Nancy (Paliaroli) C.; m. Susan Kay Brickner, Sept. 18, 1987; children: Amy, Andrew, Claire, Kay, Peter. BS in Biology, Wayne State U., 1981, MD, 1985. Diplomate Am. Bd. Surgery, Am. Bd. Colon and Rectal Surgery. Asst. prof. surgery SUNY, Bklyn., 1991-94; pvt. practice colon and rectal surgeon Colon and Rectal Surgeons of Kansas City, 1994—. Contbg. author: Surgery of the Colon, Rectum and Anus, 1995; contbr. articles to profl. jours. Recipient Merit scholarship Wayne State U., 1977-81, Charles G. Johnston award Detroit Surg. Assn., 1989. Fellow ACS, Am. Soc. Colon and Rectal Surgeons (young surgeons com. 1992—, self-assessment com. 1992—), Pa. Soc. Colon and Rectal Surgeons; mem. Am. Soc. for Gastrointestinal Endoscopy, Soc. Am. Gastrointestinal Endoscopic Surgeons, Assn. for Acad. Surgery, Midwest Surg. Assn., Nat. Honor Soc. Roman Catholic. Office: Colon and Rectal Surgeons of Kansas City 8901 W 74th St Ste 149 Shawnee Mission KS 66204

CISAR, CRAIG JAMES, physiologist; b. Vermillion, S.D., May 22, 1950; s. Richard Walter and Mary Lorraine (Sogge) C.; m. Rebecca Ann Barrett, Sept. 3, 1988; 1 child, Jamie Ann; 1 stepchild, Ryan Thomas Bellevue. BSBA, U. S.D., 1972; postgrad., U. Ill., 1979-80; M in Phys. Edn., U. Nebr., Lincoln, 1984, PhD in Exercise Physiology, 1986. CPA; cert. exercise test technologist, strength and conditioning specialist, cert. personal trainer. Acct. Coopers & Lybrand, Omaha, 1972-73, Henry Scholten & Co., Sioux Falls, S.D., 1973-79; grad. asst., faculty U. Nebr., Lincoln, 1980-86; asst. prof. San Jose (Calif.) State U., 1986-89, assoc. prof., 1989-93, prof., 1993—, HUP dept. grad. coord., 1990—; presenter, author in field. Reviewer articles to profl. jours. Fellow Am. Coll. Sports Medicine; mem. Nat. Strength and Conditioning Assn. (No. Calif. state dir. 1991—), Am. Coll. Sports Medicine (S.W. chpt.), Beta Gamma Sigma. Home: 144 Laumer Ave San Jose CA 95127-2430 Office: San Jose State U Human Performance Dept One Washington Sq San Jose CA 95192-0054

CITAK, KENNETH ANTON, neurologist; b. N.Y.C., Feb. 4, 1960; s. Burton and Audrey (Kahn) C.; m. Shari Fabrikant, Mar. 1, 1986; children: Jennifer Sara, Matthew William. BA, Brown U., 1982; MD, NYU, 1986. Diplomate Am. Bd. Psychiatry and Neurology. Neurology resident Mt. Sinai Med. Ctr., N.Y.C., 1986-90, fellow dept. neurology, 1990-91; attending physician Neurology Group of Bergen County, Ridgewood, N.J., 1991—; edn. chmn. neurosci. dept. Valley Hosp., Ridgewood, 1992-96. Trustee Englewood Cliffs (N.J.) Bd. Edn., 1995—. Mem. AMA, Am. Acad. Neurology, Am. Acad. Pain Mgmt., Am. Soc. Neuroimaging, Am. Acad. Electrodiagnostic Medicine, N.J. Med. Soc. Office: Neurology Group Bergen Cty 106 Prospect St Ridgewood NJ 07450

CITRON, DAVID SANFORD, physician; b. Atlanta, Jan. 8, 1920; s. Morris and Ida (Levine) C.; m. Doris Berman, Feb. 14, 1946; children: Michael, Dennis, Lynn, Steven. A.B., U.N.C.-Chapel Hill, 1941, cert. in medicine, 1943; M.D., Washington U., St. Louis, 1944. Lic. physician, N.C. cert. Am. Bd. Internal Medicine, Am. Bd. Family Practice. Intern Barnes Hosp., St. Louis, 1944-45; resident Barnes Hosp, St. Louis, 1945-46, 48-49, USPHS Hosp, Boston, 1949-50; gen. practice medicine Charlotte, N.C., 1952—; dir. family practice residency Charlotte Meml. Hosp. & Med. Ctr., 1973-84, dir. med. edn., 1984-87; mem. N.C. Bd. Med. Examiners, 1974-81, 1984-87; bd. dirs. Nat. Bd. Med. Examiners, 1981—. Served with USPHS., 1946-52. Recipient Disting. Service award U.N.C. Sch. Medicine, 1975. Fellow ACP; mem. Nat. Acad. Sci., Inst. Medicine, AMA, N.C. Med. Soc., Mecklenburg County Med. Soc. (pres. 1972-73). Democrat. Jewish. Club: Raintree (Charlotte). Home: 8117 Rising Meadow Rd Charlotte NC 28277-8612

CIULLO, ROSEMARY, psychologist; b. Chgo.. BA, U. Ill., Chgo., 1974; MA, Gov.'s State U., University Park, Ill., 1977; PsyD with high distinction, Forest Inst. Profl. Psychology, 1986. Pvt. practice clin. psychologist North Shore Counseling & Consulting, Lake Zurich, Ill., 1995—. Mem. APA, Ill. Psychol. Assn., Orthopsychiatry. Office: 830 Main St Lake Zurich IL 60047

CIVAN, MORTIMER M., physiology investigator, educator; b. N.Y.C., Nov. 13, 1934. AB, Columbia Coll., 1955; MD, Columbia U., 1959. Diplomate Am. Bd. Internal Medicine. Med. intern, then resident in internal medicine Presbyn. Hosp., N.Y.C., 1959-62; staff assoc. Nat. Inst. Arthritis and Metabolic Diseases/NIH, 1962-64; clin. and rsch. fellow in medicine Mass. Gen. Hosp./Harvard U. Med. Sch., 1964-65; instr. in medicine Med. Sch. Harvard U., 1965-68, asst. prof. physiology Med. Sch., 1969-72; assoc. prof. physiology U. Pa., Phila., 1972-77, prof. physiology, 1977—; assoc. prof. medicine U. Pa. Sch. Medicine, Phila., 1972-88; prof. of medicine U Pa. Sch. Medicine, Phila., 1988—; vis. scientist dept. polymer rsch. Weizmann Inst. of Sci., 1970-71, Imperial Cancer Rsch. Fund Labs., London, 1984-85, 91-92; vis. prof. zoology U. Cambridge, Eng., 1978-79; established investigator Am. Heart Assn.; faculty scholar Josiah Macy Jr. Found., 1978-79; cons. NIH/NSF, 1972—; Harold Chaffer Meml. lectr. faculty medicine U. Otago, Dunedin, New Zealand, 1990. USPHS fellow, 1964-65, 70-71. Fellow AAAS; mem. Am. Physiol. Soc. (steering com. cell and gen. physiology sect. 1981-83, chmn. steering com. cell and gen. physiology sect. 1982-83), Am. Soc. Clin. Investigation, Am. Soc. Nephrology, Assn. for Rsch. in Vision & Ophthalmology, Internat. Soc. Nephrology, Soc. Gen. Physiologists (sec. 1981 1981-84), John Morgan Soc., Biophys. Soc., Nat. Kidney Found., Salt and Water Club, Phi Beta Kappa, Alpha Omega Alpha. Office: U Pa Dept Physiology Richards Bldg A-303 Philadelphia PA 19104-6085

CIVANTOS, FRANCISCO, pathologist, educator; b. June 25, 1935; m. Elsa Gonzalez, Dec. 20, 1959; children: Francisco, Marlene, Joseph, Gloria, John, Christine. BS, U. Havana, 1957; MD, Tulane U., 1961. Lic. physician, Fla. Intern Detroit Receiving Hosp., 1961-62; resident in pathology, then chief resident in pathology Mass. Gen. Hosp., Boston, 1962-66; pathologist Mt. Sinai Hosp., Miami Beach, Fla., 1968-73; dir. clin. lab. St. Francis Hosp., Miami Beach, 1973-78; anatomic and clin. pathologist Jackson Meml. Hosp., Miami, Fla., 1978—; prof. pathology Med. Sch., U. Miami, 1985-95, dir. J.B. Miale Coagulation Lab., 1985—; dir. urologic and hepatic pathology U. Miami at Cedars Med. Ctr., 1989—. Contbr. numerous articles to sci. publs. Chmn. adv. coun. on clin. labs. to gov. State of Fla., Tallahassee, 1989-92. Capt. M.C., USAF, 1966-68. Fellow Am. Soc. Clin. Pathology (dir./lectr. workshops on endocrine pathology and coagulation), Coll. Pathology; mem. Internat. Acad. Pathology, Fla. Soc. Pathology (pres. 1990-92), Peruvian Soc. Pathology (hon.), Internat. Randonneurs (Paris-Brest-Paris medal 1991, 95), Everglades Bicycle Club. Democrat. Roman Catholic. Office: U Miami Med Sch D-33 Pathology PO Box 16960 Miami FL 33101-6960

CIVISH, GAYLE ANN, psychologist; b. Lynnwood, Calif., Sept. 29, 1948; d. Leland and Arline (Frazer) Civish; children: Nathan Morrow, Shane Morrow. BA, U. Nev., Reno, 1970; MA, U. Colo., 1973, PhD, 1983. Lic. psychologist, Colo.; cert. sch. psychologist, Colo. Sch. psychologist Jefferson County (Colo.) Schs., 1983-89; psychologist in pvt. practice Lakewood, Colo., 1983—. Contbr. articles to profl. jours. Mem. APA, Colo. Psychol. Assn. (bd. dirs. 1990-93), Colo. Women Psychologists (past external liaison), Am. Soc. Clin. Hypnosis, Feminist Therapy Inst. (steering com. 1994—), Assn. for Women in Psychology, Phi Kappa Phi, Phi Delta Kappa. Democrat. Office: PO Box 713 Easton PA 18044

CLAES, DANIEL JOHN, physician; b. Glendale, Calif., Dec. 3, 1931; s. John Vernon and Claribel (Fleming) C.; AB magna cum laude, Harvard U., 1953, MD cum laude, 1957; m. Gayla Christine Blasdel, Jan. 19, 1974. Intern, UCLA, 1957-58; Bowyer Found. fellow for rsch. in medicine, L.A., 1958-61; pvt. practice specializing in diabetes, L.A., 1962—; v.p. Am. Eye Bank Found., 1978-83, pres., 1983—, dir. rsch., 1980—; pres. Heuristic Corp., 1981—. Mem. L.A. Mus. Art, 1960—. Mem. AMA, Calif. Med. Assn., L.A. County Med. Assn., Am. Diabetes Assn., Internat. Diabetes Fedn., Internat. Pancreas & Islet Transplant Assn. Clubs: Harvard and Harvard Med. Sch. of So. Calif.; Royal Commonwealth (London). Contbr. papers on diabetes mellitus, computers in medicine to profl. lit. Office: Am Eyebank Found 15327 W Sunset Blvd Ste 236 Pacific Palisades CA 90272-3674

CLAFFEY, THOMAS F., internist, educator; b. Hartford, Conn., July 26, 1944; s. Joseph Michael and M. Carol (Fox) C.; m. Peggy Anne Calahan, Sept. 13, 1969; children: Elizabeth, Theresa, Amy. BS, Boston Coll.; MD, U. Vt. Diplomate Am. Bd. Internal Medicine. Resident in internal medicine Hartford Hosp., 1970-72; resident in internal medicine U. Iowa, Iowa City, 1972-73, fellow in infectious disease, 1973-75; pvt. practice, South Portland, Maine, 1975—; active staff Maine Med. Ctr., Portland, Maine, 1975—, dir. divsn. infectious disease, 1984—; clin. assoc. prof. medicine U. Vt., Burlington, 1988—; bd. dirs., treas. Med. Network, Portland, 1985—. Maj. M.C., USAR, 1970-76. Fellow ACP; mem. Infectious Diseases Soc. Am., Am. Soc. for Microbiology, Maine Soc. Internal Medicine (pres. 1988-90), Cumberland County Med. Soc. (pres. 1986-88), Ocean Reef Club (Key Largo, Fla.), Woodlands Club (Falmouth, Maine), Portland Country Club. Republican. Roman Catholic. Office: Intermed 238 Western Ave South Portland ME 04106

CLAFLIN, ROBERT MALDEN, veterinary educator, university dean b. Flint, Mich., Nov. 11, 1921; s. Robert Hugh and Kathryn Elizabeth (Ruhl) C.; m. Barbara Ellen Garrison, June 21, 1957; children—Deborah Ann, Elair Lawrence, Kathryn Elizabeth. D.V.M., Mich. State U., 1952; M.S., Purdue U., 1956, Ph.D., 1958. Mem. faculty Purdue U., Lafayette, Ind., 1952—, prof. vet. pathology Sch. Vet. Sci. and Medicine, 1959—; prof. emeritus Purdue U., 1988—; head dept. vet. microbiology, pathology and pub. health Purdue U., Lafayette, Ind., 1959-86, assoc. dean Sch. Vet. Medicine, 1986-88; assoc. dean emeritus Purdue U., 1988—. Mem. AVMA, Internat. Acad. Pathology, Conf. Research Workers Animal Diseases N.A., Sigma Xi, Phi Zeta, Phi Kappa Phi. Home: 601 N Lakeshore Dr Ludington MI 49431-1327 Office: Purdue U Dean Sch Vet Med Lafayette IN 47907

CLAIR, THEODORE NAT, educational psychologist; b. Stockton, Calif., Apr. 19, 1929; s. Peter David and Sara Renee (Silverman) C.; A.A., U. Calif. at Berkeley, 1949, A.B., 1950; M.S., U. So. Calif., 1953, M.Ed., 1963, Ed.D., 1969; m. Laura Gold, June 19, 1961; children: Shari, Judith. Tchr., counselor Los Angeles City Schs., 1957-63; psychologist Alamitos Sch. Dist., Garden Grove, Calif., 1963-64, Arcadia (Calif.) Unified Sch. Dist., 1964-65; head psychologist Wiseburn Sch. Dist., Hawthorne, Calif., 1966-69; asst. prof. spl. edn., coordinator sch. psychology program U. Iowa, Iowa City, 1969-72; dir. pupil personnel services Orcutt (Calif.) Union Sch. Dist., 1972-73; adminstr. Mt. Diablo Unified Sch. Dist., 1973-77; program dir., psychologist San Mateo County Office of Edn., Redwood City, 1977-91; assoc. prof. John F. Kennedy U. Sch. Mgmt., 1975-77; pvt. practice as ednl. psychologist and marriage and family counselor, Menlo Park, Calif., 1978—, Menlo Park, Calif., 1977-93, dir. Peninsula Vocat. Rehab. Inst., 1978—; psychologist Coll. Counseling Svc., Menlo Pk., 1992—, Calif. Pacific Hosp., San Francisco, 1993—. Served with USNR, 1952-54. Mem. APA, Nat. Assn. Sch. Psychologists, Calif. Assn. Marriage and Family Counselors, Nat. Rehab. Assn, Palo Alto B'nai B'rith Club (pres.). Author: Phenylketonuria and Some Other Inborn Errors of Amino Acid Metabolism, 1971; editor Jour. Calif. Ednl. Psychologists, 1992-94; contbr. articles to profl. jours. Home and Office: 56 Willow Rd Menlo Park CA 94025-3654

CLAMAR, APHRODITE J., psychologist; b. Hartford, Conn.; d. James John and Georgia (Panas) Clamar; m. Richard Cohen, June 24, 1973. BA, CCNY, 1953; MA, Columbia U., 1955; PhD, NYU, 1978; student, Stella Adler Conservatory of Acting and Playwrights Horizon Thetare Sch., 1987-91. Mgmt. cons., psychologist Milla Alihan Assocs., N.Y.C., 1957-62; rsch. psychologist coord. Inst. Devel. Studies N.Y. Med. Coll., N.Y.C., 1964; intern psychologist Bellevue Psychiat. Hosp., N.Y.C., 1964-66; assoc. prof. Fashion Inst. Tech., N.Y.C., 1966-69; supervising psychologist Lifeline Ctr. Child Devel., N.Y.C., 1966-67; chief psychologist I Spy Health Program Beth Israel Med. Ctr., N.Y.C., 1967-70; dir. community-sch. mental health programs Soundview Community Svcs., Albert Einstein Coll. Medicine Yeshiva U., N.Y.C., 1970-73; dir. treatment program court-related children, dept. child psychiatry Harlem Hosp.; mem. faculty dept. psychiatry Coll. Physicians and Surgeons Columbia U., N.Y.C., 1973-76; pvt. practice psychotherapy N.Y.C., 1976-95; pres. Richard Cohen Assocs. Pub. Rels., N.Y.C., 1995—; cons. to pub. health and mental health agys., N.Y.C., 1976-91; mem. faculty Lenox Hill Hosp. Psychoanalytic and Psychotherapy Tng. Program, 1982-88; theater producer, artistic dir. Tom Cat Cohen Prodns. Inc., 1990—. Author: (with Budd Hopkins) Missing Time, 1981; contbr. articles to profl. jours. Fellow AAAS; mem. APA, Dramatists Guild, Authors Guild. Democrat. Greek Orthodox. Home: 162 E 80th St New York NY 10021-0439 Office: 40 W 55th St New York NY 10019

CLAMPITT, OTIS CLINTON, JR., health agency executive; b. Burlington, N.C., Nov. 17, 1947; s. Otis Clinton and Audrey Mae (Brafford) C.; m. Martha Jane Redding, Apr. 3, 1971. BA in English, Guilford Coll., 1971. Unit exec. dir. N.C. div. Am. Cancer Soc., Winston-Salem, 1972-73, area rep., 1973-74, met. area dir., 1974-75; dir. pub. edn./info. S.C. div. Am. Cancer Soc., Columbia, 1976-78, dir. devel., 1978-79, dep. exec. v.p., 1979-81; exec. v.p. Miss. div. Am. Cancer Soc., Jackson, 1981-89; nat. v.p. Am. Cancer Soc., Washington, 1989—; faculty, cons. Am. Cancer Soc. Acad., Atlanta, 1989—. Co-founder, pres. Forsyth County Interagy. Health Coun., Winston-Salem, 1975; chmn. Miss. Combined Fed. Campaign, Jackson, 1987-89, Miss. Com. on Indigent Patient Care, Jackson, 1989; appointed Govs. Task Force on Agy. Registration, Jackson, 1989; bd. dirs. Miss. Seatbelt Coalition, Jackson, 1986-90, Nat. Vol. Health Agency Capital Area, 1994—. Mem. Miss. Soc. Assn. Execs., Nat. Soc. of Fund Raising Execs. Home: 1712 Woodlore Rd Annapolis MD 21401-6568 Office: Am Cancer Soc PO Box 6640 Annapolis MD 21401-0640

CLANCEY, JEANNE KATHERINE, neurosurgical nurse; b. Erie, Pa., Dec. 31, 1948; d. Albert E. and Ruth A. (Gillespie) C. RN, St. Vincent Hosp. Sch. Nursing, 1969; BSN, Pa. State U., State College, 1983; MSN, U. Pitts., 1987. RN, Pa. Staff nurse med./surg. unit St. Vincent Hosp., Erie, 1969-71; staff nurse neurosurgery unit Presbyn. U. Hosp., Pitts., 1971-77, staff nurse recovery rm., 1977-78; neurosurg. clin. coord. Montefiore Hosp., Pitts., 1978-90; neurosurg. clin. nurse specialist West Penn Neurosurgery/West Penn Hosp., Pitts., 1990—; bd. dirs. Oncology Nursing Certification Corp. Mem. Am. Assn. Neurosci. Nurses (bd. dirs. 1987-89, pres.-elect 1990, pres. 1991) Home: 622 Whitney Ave # 5 Pittsburgh PA 15221-3353 Office: 4800 Friendship Ave Pittsburgh PA 15224-1722

CLANCY, MARGARET M., psychiatrist; b. N.Y.C., July 15, 1948; d. Harry F. and Catherine (Connors) C.; m. Wayne T. Rose, Apr. 30; children: Victoria, Christopher. BS, Fordham U., 1969; MD, Georgetown U., 1973. Diplomate Am. Bd. Psychiatry and Neurology, Nat. Bd. Med. Examiners; lic. psychiatrist, D.C. Resident in psychiatry Georgetown Hosp., Washington, 1973-76; staff psychiatrist Washington VA Hosp., 1976-78; pvt. practice Washington, 1976—; cons. Washington Met. Transit Authority, 1978-80, Upjohn Physicians Adv. Bd., Washington, 1988—. Contbr. articles to profl. jours. Mem. Nat. Coalition for Cancer Survivorship, Washington, 1989—. Recipient Physicians Recognition award AMA, 1990. Mem. Am. Psychiat. Assn., Am. Assn. Psychosomatic Medicine, Am. Soc. Psychiat. Oncology, N.Y. Acad. Scis. Office: 1015 33rd St NW Washington DC 20007-3523

CLANON, THOMAS LAWRENCE, retired hospital administrator; b. Detroit, Sept. 17, 1929; s. William John and Wilhelmina T. (Francis) C.; m. Esther Theresa Giffin, June 11, 1955; children: John P., Kathleen A. Paul A., David L., Daniel J. BS, U. Detroit, 1951; MD, U. Mich., 1955. Diplomate: Am. Bd. Psychiatry and Neurology. Intern St. Mary s Hosp., Grand Rapids, Mich., 1955-56; grad. tng. Menninger Sch. Psychiatry, Topeka, 1956-59; resident psychiatrist in tng. Kans. Boys Indsl. Sch., Topeka, 1953-59; psychiatrist U.S. Med. Ctr. for Prisoners, Springfield, Mo., 1959-61; mem. staff Calif. Med. Facility, Vacaville, 1961-66, 72—, asst. supt. psychiat. svcs., 1972, supt., 1972-80; med. asst. Broadmoor Spl. Security Hosp., Crowthorne, Eng., 1971-72; med. dir. mental health program St. Luke's Hosp., San Francisco, 1986-94; cons. on clin. and adminstrv. hosp. problems, 1994—; staff psychiatrist San Francisco Parole Outpatient Clinic; asst. clin. prof. U. Calif. Med. Sch., Davis, 1969-81. Contbr. articles to med. jours. Former mem. community adv. bd. dept. psychiatry San Francisco Gen. Hosp. Served with USPHS, 1958-61. Fellow Am. Psychiat. Assn.; mem. Am. Correctional Assn., San Francisco Med. Soc., No. Calif. Psychiat. Soc., Vacaville Kiwanis Club (past pres.).

CLAPP, NEAL KEITH, experimental pathologist; b. Waldron, Ind., Oct. 14, 1928; s. Worrill Groven and Dora M. (Hurst) C.; m. Dorothy Louise Stockwell, Dec. 19, 1953; children: Cheryl Lynne, Mark Allen, Stephen Neal. BS, Purdue U., 1950; DVM, Ohio State U., 1960; MS, Colo. State U., 1962, PhD, 1964. NIH postdoctoral fellow Colo. State Univ., Ft. Collins, 1961-64; experimental pathologist Oak Ridge (Tenn.) Nat. Lab., 1964-81; dir. Marmoset Rsch. Ctr. Oak Ridge (Tenn.) Assoc. U., 1981-92; dir. MARCOR U. Tenn. Med. Ctr., Oak Ridge, 1992—. Editor: A Model for Colon Diseases, 1993; contbr. over 150 articles to profl. jours. Min. Clinton (Tenn.) Christian Ch., 1972-94. With USAF, 1951-55. Mem. Am. Assn. Cancer Rsch., Am. Vet. Med. Assn., Inflammation Rsch. Assn., Am. Assn. Lab. Animal Sci., Am. Primatology Assn., Radiation Rsch. Soc., Optimist Club, Masons. Republican. Home: PO Box 88 628 Riverbend Rd Clinton TN 37716 Office: U Tenn Marmoset Rsch Ctr 110 Badger Ave Oak Ridge TN 37830

CLARK, ALAN JAMES, ophthalmologist; b. Malden, Mass., Nov. 24, 1946; s. Lloyd James Clark and Barbara (Ramsdell) Clark Tesch; m. Claudia Beatrice Horning; children: Corinne Kimberly, Kylene Lindsay. BA, Yale U., 1968, MD, 1972. Diplomate Am. Bd. Ophthalmology. Pediatric-med. intern Maine Med. Ctr., Portland, 1972-73; resident in ophthalmology Albany (N.Y.) Med. Ctr., 1973-76; assoc. S.M. Sorrel, MD, Somerville, Mass., 1977-79; solo practice Cable Meml. Hosp., Ipswich, Mass., 1976-77, Ormond Meml. Hosp., Ormond Beach, Fla., 1979-81; staff ophthalmologist Fla. Health Care HMO, Daytona Beach, 1980-81; solo practice Pascagoula, Miss., 1981-93; assoc. Thomas Edwards MD, Jacksonville, Fla., 1992-93; subcontractor Humana HMO/Century Optical, Daytona Beach, 1993-95; solo practice Cigna/Health Options, Daytona Beach, 1995—. Contbr. articles to med. and geneal. jours. Mem. SAR, Sons Colonial Wars, Sons of Patriots and Founders of Am., United Empire Loyalists, U.S. Polo Assn., Am. Acad. Ophthalmology. Republican. Office: Cenetury Optical 104 N Nova Rd Daytona Beach FL 32214

CLARK, ALVIN JOHN, educator, molecular biologist; b. Oak Park, Ill., Apr. 13, 1933; s. Alvin John and Marion C.; m. Mary Claire King, Sept., 1969 (div. 1973). B.S., U. Rochester, 1955; Ph.D., Harvard U., 1959. Asst. prof. bacteriology U. Calif., Berkeley, 1962-67, assoc. prof. molecular biology, 1967-72, prof. molecular biology, 1972-89, prof. genetics, 1989-91, prof. genetics emeritus, 1991—. Guggenheim fellow, 1969. Mem. Am. Soc. Microbiology, Genetics Soc. Am., Sigma Xi. Democrat. Siddha Yoga. Office: Univ Calif-Barker Hall Dept Molecular and Cell Biology Berkeley CA 94720-3202

CLARK, CHARLENE ELIZABETH, nursing educator; b. Spokane, Wash., Jan. 8, 1941; d. Carl G. and Anna E. (Miller) Miller; m. Robert S. Clark, Apr. 14, 1962; children: Robert S. Jr., Jeffrey C. Diploma in nursing, Sacred Heart Sch. Nursing, Spokane, 1962; BS, Whitworth Coll., 1965, MEd, 1974. RN, Wash. Instr Sacred Heart Sch. Nursing, Spokane, 1962-66; instr. RN refresher course Spokane Community Coll., 1968; from instr. to prof. Intercollegiate Ctr. for Nursing Edn. Wash. State U., Spokane, 1969-94, dir. learning resource Intercollegiate Ctr. for Nursing Edn., 1981-95, asst. dean for instrnl. resources, 1995—; cons. in field. Contbr. articles to profl. jours. Recipient nurse excellence award: edn. Mem. ANA, Assn. Ednl. Comm./Tech. (continuing edn. com.), Am. Acad. Nursing, Sigma Theta Tau. Office: Wash State U W 2917 Fort George Wright Spokane WA 99204

CLARK, CONSTANCE MARY, hospital administrator; b. Rochester, N.Y., Apr. 19, 1946; d. Charles N. and Mary Jane (Winter) C. BS in Nursing, Med. Coll. Va., Richmond, 1968; MS in Nursing, U. Mich., Ann Arbor, 1971; MS in Indsl. Rels., Loyola U., Chgo. Cert. nursing adminstr. advanced. Clin. specialist St. Joseph Mercy Hosp., Ann Arbor, 1971-76; unit leader Rush-Presbyn.-St. Luke's Med. Ctr., Chgo., 1976-85; asst. dir. nursing Gottlieb Meml. Hosp., Melrose Park, Ill., 1985-89, v.p. nursing, 1989—. Mem. Sigma Theta Tau. Home: 1749 N Wells St Apt 1311 Chicago IL 60614-5827

CLARK, DANNY MILES, obstetrician, gynecologist; b. Paris, Ky., July 8, 1937; s. Daniel P. and Lela (Whittington) C.; m. Wanda Joyce Carew; children: Joyce Ann, Michael, Mark, Patrick, Miles. AB, Transylvania U., 1958; MD, U. Cin., 1962. Intern L.A. County Gen. Hosp., 1962-63; resident in ob-gyn. L.A., 1963-67; pvt. practice Somerset, Ky., 1969—; bd. dirs. Ky. Med. Ins. Co., Louisville; mem. Ky. Bd. Med. Licensure, Louisville, 1987—. Active Somerset Ind. Sch. Bd., 1979-87; chmn. official bd. 1st Christian Ch., Somerset, 1984-87. Capt. USAF, 1967-69. Mem. AMA, ACOG, Pulaski County Med. Soc., Ky. Med. Assn. (trustee 1978-86, vice spkr. ho. of dels. 1986-89, spkr. 1990-95, pres. 1995-96), Eagles Nest Country Club. Republican. Home: 4055 Barnesburg Rd Somerset KY 42501-5060 Office: 349 Bogle St Somerset KY 42503-2895

CLARK, DONALD GRAHAM CAMPBELL, surgeon, gynecologic oncologist; b. Airdrie, Scotland, May 9, 1920; came to U.S., 1945; s. Archibald Campbell and Alice Graham (Smillie) C.; m. Ann Beveridge Kiersted; children: Donald Graham Campbell, Michael Archibald Campbell, Alison Clark Zorman, Peter Fraser Campbell. BS, St. Andrews (Scotland) U., 1941, MB CHB, 1944; MD, Yale U., 1943. Diplomate Am. Bd. Surgery. Clin. attending surgeon N.Y. Med. Coll., N.Y.C.; dir. gynecol.-oncology Met. Hosp., N.Y.C.; pres. Meml. Hosp. Gen. Staff, N.Y.C., 1985-87; attending surgeon emeritus Meml. Sloan Kettering Cancer Ctr. Author: (with others) Gynecologic Oncology, 1982; contbr. articles to profl. jours. Pres. Greenville Community Coun., Scarsdale, N.Y., PTA Edgemont Sch. Dist., Scarsdale. Surgeon Merchant Marine, 1944-45. Mem. Soc. Pelvic Surgeons, Soc. Surg. Oncology, N.Y. Athletic Club, Scarsdale Golf Club. Home: 145 Old Army Rd Scarsdale NY 10583-2612 Office: Met Hosp New York NY 10028

CLARK, DUNCAN WILLIAM, physician, educator; b. N.Y.C., Aug. 31, 1910; s. William H. and Lillian (Keating) C.; m. Carol Dooley, Jan. 30, 1943 (dec. 1971); children: Carol Ann, Duncan William, James Fenton (dec.).; m. Ida O'Grady, June 10, 1972. A.B., Fordham U., 1932. Diplomate: Am. Bd. Internal Medicine, Am. Bd. Preventive Medicine. Intern Bklyn. Hosp., 1936-38; resident in medicine coll. div. Kings County (N.Y.) Hosp., 1938-40; fellow in medicine Yale U., 1940-41; dir. student health L.I. Coll. Medicine, 1941-49, dean, 1948-50, asst. prof. medicine, 1948-50; prof., chmn. dept. environ. medicine and community health SUNY Health Sci. Ctr., Bklyn., 1951-78; prof. preventive medicine State U. Coll. Medicine at N.Y.C., 1978-82, prof. emeritus, 1982—; cons. USPHS, 1961-81; cons. NIH, 1961-65, NRC, 1965-68; chmn. health services research tng. com. USPHS, 1965-69, mem. health services research study sect., 1961-65, 73-77; WHO traveling fellow, 1952; vis. prof. Med. Sch., U. Birmingham, Eng., 1961. Co-editor, co-author: Textbook of Preventive Medicine, 1967, 2d edit., 1981; Contbr. articles on med. edn., pub. health and medicine. Bd. dirs. Health Ins. Plan, N.Y.C., 1953-71; chmn. N.Y. Study Com. Rsch. Accident Prevention in Children, 1958-60, Assn. Aid Crippled Children; bd. dirs. Health Sys. Agy., N.Y.C., 1980-88, Kings County Health Care Rev. Orgn., 1980-84; mem. AIDS Adv. Coun. to N.Y. State Health Dept., 1984—; chmn. Nat. Adv. Com. on Local Health Depts., 1960-61; mem. N.Y. State Commn. on Grad. Med. Edn., 1985; mem. distbn. com. N.Y. Cmty. Trust, 1983-85; bd. dirs. Med. and Health Rsch. Assn., N.Y.C., 1963—. Recipient Health Education award AMA/Edn. Rsch. Found., 1995. Fellow ACP, Am. Pub. Health Assn., N.Y. Acad. Medicine (trustee 1975, 85-89, v.p. 1976-78, coun. 1975-89, pres. 1983-84, Disting. Svc. plaque 1986), Am. Coll. Preventive Medicine; mem. AMA (alt. del. 1983-88, 92-96, del 1989-91), AAAS, N.Y. Pub. Health Assn. (bd. dirs. 1951-55, 86-88, pres. 1954-55), N.Y. State Med. Soc., (chmn. preventive medicine com. 1982-96, pres.'s citizenship award, 1993), Conf.

Profs. Preventive Medicine (chmn. 1953-54), Assn. Tchrs. Preventive Medicine (pres. 1954-56, editor Newsletter 1959-70), Com. to Protect Our Children's Teeth (pres. 1957-60), N.Y. State Med. Soc. (del. 1978—), Kings County Med. Soc. (chmn. cmty. medicine com. 1975-83, pres. 1983-84, trustee 1978-94, hon. trustee 1994—, v.p. 1981-82, censor 1991-92, chmn. pub. health com. 1990-94), Harvey Soc., N.Y. Acad. Sci., Internat. Epidemiological Assn., Alpha Omega Alpha (faculty councillor 1948-76). Roman Catholic. Home: 35 Prospect Park W Brooklyn NY 11215-2370 Office: 450 Clarkson Ave Brooklyn NY 11203-2012

CLARK, GORDON HOSTETTER, JR., physician; b. New Haven, Aug. 5, 1947; s. Gordon Hostetter and Elizabeth Master (Mapes) C.; m. Gail Marie Theroux, July 23, 1988; children from previous marriage: Emily Blakeslee Clark, Christopher Robert. BA, Yale U., 1970; MDiv, Pacific Sch. Religion, 1973; MD, George Washington U., 1977. Diplomate Am. Bd. Psychiatry and Neurology; cert. in adminstrv. psychiatry, APA, 1992. Intern, then resident, then fellow Dartmouth-Hitchcock Med. Ctr., Hanover, N.H., 1977-81; staff psychiatrist Lakes Region Med. Health Ctr., Laconia, N.H., 1981-82, med. dir., 1982-86; dir. psychiat. unit Lakes Region Gen. Hosp., Laconia, 1986-89; med. dir. behavioral svcs. St. Vincent Health Ctr., Erie, Pa., 1990-93; dir. med./profl. adminstrn. Deerfield Mgmt. Group, Erie, Pa., 1991-94; pres. Deerfield Profl. Assocs., 1992-94; med. advisor Deerfield Behavioral Health Network, 1994-95; sr. psychiat. cons. Med. Groups Divsn. Maine Harvard Cmty. Health Plan, Portland, Maine, 1994—; pres., med. dir. Integrated Behavioral Health Svcs., Portland, Maine, 1995—; med. dir. Behavioral Health Network of Maine, 1995—, Augusta (Maine) Mental Health Inst., 1995-96; assoc. med. dir. Maine Dept. Mental Health and Mental Retardation, Augusta, 1995-96; adj. asst. prof. clin. psychiatry Dartmouth Med. Sch., Hanover, 1983-90; clin. asst. prof. psychiatry U. Pitts. Sch. Medicine, 1990-95; clin. assoc. prof. psychiatry U. Vt. Med. Sch., 1996—; chmn. com. psychiatrists in N.H. Cmty. Mental Health Ctrs., Concord, 1982-86; med. liason to Pa. Office of Mental Health and Mental Retardation and Erie County Office of Mental Health and Mental Retardation, 1991-94. Exec. v.p. Erie Phiharm., 1991-92. Recipient Exemplary Psychiatrist award Nat. Alliance for Mentally Ill, 1992; recipient Benjamin Manchester award George Washington U., 1977. Fellow Am. Psychiat. Assn. (task force to develop guidelines for psychiat. practice in community mental health ctrs., com. on state and community psychiatry systems, com. chronically mentally ill, Falk fellow 1979-81, examiner oral part of examinations cert. adminstrn. psychiatry 1993—), Am. Coll. Mental Health Adminstrn., Am. Assn. Social Psychiatry (mem. coun.); mem. AMA, Am. Assn. Community Psychiatrists (com. to develop guidelines for psychiat. practice in community mental health ctrs., founding pres. 1984-90, Disting. Svc. award 1990), Am. Assn. Psychiat. Adminstrs., Am. Assn. Gen. Hosp. Psychiatrists, Am. Coll. Physician Execs., Am. Coll. Psychiatrists, Nat. Psychiatric Alliance (chmn. med. staff com. 1992-94, exec. com. 1992-95), Psychiat. Physicians Pa. (coun., govt. rels. com., fed. legis. rep. pub. psychiatry com. 1993-94, treas. 1994), Western Pa. Psychiat. Soc. (pres. elect. 1992-94). Home: 1 Park St Yarmouth ME 04096-1124 Office: Integrated Behavioral Health Svcs 100 Commercial St Ste 108 Portland ME 04101-4724

CLARK, GRAEME MILBOURNE, otolaryngologist, educator; b. Sydney, Australia, Aug. 16, 1935; s. C.M. Clark; m. Margaret Clark, Dec. 27, 1961; 5 children. BM and BS, U. Sydney, 1957, PhD, 1969, MD (hon.), 1989; MD (hon.), Med. Hochschule, Hanover, Fed. Republic of Germany, 1988. Prof. otolaryngology U. Melbourne, Australia, 1970—, head cochlear implant program, 1970—, dir. Bionic Ear Inst., 1974—, dir. Human Comm. Rsch. Ctr., 1988—, dir. Coop. Rsch. Ctr. Cochlear Implant, Speech/Hearing Rsch., 1992—. Author: Science and God, 1979. Recipient Vocat. Svc. award Rotary Club, Melbourne, 1986, Advance Australia award, 1986, Award for Pursuit of Excellence in Sci. and Tech., B.H.P., 1984, Sudholz prize in otolaryngology, 1970, Fletcher award in tech. application, 1988, James Cook medal Royal Soc. NSW, 1992, Clunies Ross Nat. Sci. and Tech. award Ian Clunies Ross Meml. Found., 1992, Volta award Cochlear Implant Club Internat., 1993; named first hon. fellow Audiol. Soc. Australia, 1992; decorated Office of Order of Australia, 1983. Fellow Royal Australian Coll. Surgeons (John Mitchell Crouch fellow 1985), Royal Coll. Surgeons (Edinburgh, Scotland), Royal Coll. Surgeons (Eng.); mem. Internat. Fedn. Otorhinolaryngological Socs., Collegium Oto-Rhino-Laryngoligicum Amicitiae Sacrum, Royal Soc. Medicine (hon. mem. sect. otology). Office: U Melbourne Dept Otolaryngology, 32 Gisbourne St, Melbourne Victoria 3002, Australia

CLARK, HARRY EDGAR, pharmacist; b. Canton, N.Y., Apr. 12, 1925; s. Harold Safford and Edgarita (Blankman) C.; B.S., Union U., 1949. Pharmacist, Brooks Pharmacy, Ithaca, N.Y., 1949-51; partner, pharmacist Clark Pharmacy, Waverly, N.Y., 1951-71, owner, sr. pharmacist, 1971—; staff pharmacist VA Outpatient Clinic, Sayre, Pa., 1984-89. Bd. dirs. Tioga County unit Am. Cancer Soc., 1970—, pres., 1973-74. Served with USNR, 1943-46. Am. Cancer Soc. fellow, Strong Meml. Hosp., Rochester, N.Y., 1980. Mem. Nat. Assn. Retail Druggists, Am. Pharm. Assn., N.Y. State Pharm. Soc., Acad. Gen. Practice, Am. Legion, VFW. Mem. Ch. of Jesus Christ of Latter-day Saints. Clubs: Masons (32 deg.), Rotary (dir. 1963-79, pres. 1967-68, sec. 1964-79). Home: 444 Clark St Waverly NY 14892-1309 Office: 330 Broad St Waverly NY 14892-1326

CLARK, IRA C., hospital association administrator, educator. BA Gen. Sci., U. Iowa, 1959, MA honors Health and Hosp. Adminstrn., 1966; grad. Bus. Adminstrn., Rider Coll., 1963. Adminstrv. asst. divsn. Hosps. Iowa State Dept. Health, Des Moines, 1964; spl. asst. dir. planning and devel. Montefiore Hosp. and Med. Ctr., Bronx, N.Y., 1970; asst. dir. Montefiore Hosp. and Med. Ctr., Bronx, 1965-70; assoc. dir. Jersey City Med. Ctr., 1970-71, exec. dir., 1971-75; CEO Woodhull Hosp. and Mental Health Ctr., 1982-84; exec. dir. Bellevue Hosp. Ctr., 1984-85; CEO, regional adminstr. Kings County Hosp. Ctr., Bklyn., 1976-87; pres. & ceo Pub. Health Trust Jackson Meml. Hosp., 1987—; bd. dirs. Fla. Hosp. Assn., So. Fla. Hosp. Assn.; panelist Robert Wood Johnson Found. Symposium, Princeton, N.J., 1986; chmn. Coun. Exec. dirs. N.Y.C. Health and Hosps. Corp., 1978-82; chmn. com. strategic planning Coun. Exec. dirs. Counterpart com. bd. dirs.; spl. adv. panel Emergency Svcs. Act, Advanced Para-medic Tng. N.J.; adj. faculty, lectr. various Univs.; spkr. in field. Author: The History and Development of Continuing Physical Education, 1966. Recipient Disting. Svc. award Commr. Mental Health, N.Y., 1981. Mem. Am. Hosp. Assn. (house dels., charter mem. pub. gen. hosps. sect., com. nominations bd. trustees pub.-gen. hosp. sect.), Assn. Am. Med. Colls. (gen. assembly coun. teaching hosps.), N.J. Hosp. Assn. (vice chmn., chmn. coun. govt. ops. of bd. trustees, spl. com. polit. strategy). Office: Jackson Meml Hosp 1611 NW 12th Ave Miami FL 33136-1005

CLARK, JACOB A., ophthalmologist; b. San Juan, P.R., Aug. 6, 1958; s. Samuel and Carmen (Cruz) C. BS, U. P.R., 1977, MD, 1981. Resident in ophthalmology U. P.R., San Juan, 1981-85; fellow glaucoma, cataract Hartford (Conn.) Hosp., 1986-87; ophthalmologist David K. Chow MD, P.C., Alexandria, Va., 1987-89, Capital Eye Physicians & Surgeons, Washington, 1989-92, Alexandria Ophthalmic Assoc., 1993—. Fellow Am. Acad. Ophthalmology; mem. AMA, No. Va. Acad. Ophthalmology, French Ophthal. Soc. Office: Alexandria Ophthalmic Assoc 428 S Washington St Alexandria VA 22314

CLARK, JAMES HENRY, cell biology educator; b. Earlington, Ky., June 17, 1932; s. Henry H. and Louise (Peyton) C.; m. Janis L. Hendrix, May 31, 1957; children: Gregory, Tricia. BS, We. Ky. U., 1959; MS, Purdue U., 1966, PhD, 1968. Asst. prof. Purdue U., West Lafayette, Ind., 1970-73; prof. cell biology Baylor Coll. Medicine, Houston, 1973—; adv. bd. NIH, Bethesda, Md., 1974-84; pres. Laurentian Hormone Conf., 1985-88. Author: Sex Steroids: Receptous and Function, 1979; editor: Regular Sex Hormone Action, 3 vols., 1982-87, Recent Progress Hormone Research, 4 vols., 1985-88. Grantee Am. Cancer Soc., 1974-80, NIH, 1972—. Office: Baylor Coll Medicine Dept Cell Biology Houston TX 77030

CLARK, JAMES LEWIS, JR., pharmacist; b. Elmira, N.Y., Aug. 14, 1951; s. James Lewis and Esther Mae (Strock) C.; m. Jean Marie Winchell, June 7, 1975; children: Richard Hastings, Juliet Elizabeth. BS in Pharmacy, Albany (N.Y.) Coll. Pharmacy, 1975; MBA, Syracuse U., 1981. Registered pharmacist, N.Y. Sr. rsch. pharmacist clin. packaging Sterling Winthrop Pharm. Rsch. Divsn., Collegeville, Pa., 1983-87, mgr. clin. packaging and warehousing, 1987-92, mgr. clin. supply planning, 1992-93; mgr. clin. supply unit Janssen Pharmaceutica, Titusville, N.J., 1993—; founder, chairperson Almedica Drug Label System Users Group, Rensselaer, N.Y., 1985-86; workshop leader, discussion panel mem. various nat. meetings relating to clin. supplies. Mem. Internat. Soc. Pharm. Engring. (clin. materials adv. group), Investigational Materials Discussion Group. Home: 6 Steeplechase Dr Doylestown PA 18901 Office: Janssen Rsch Found PO Box 200 11257 Trenton-Harbourton Rd Titusville NJ 08560

CLARK, JAMES RANDOLPH, clinical psychologist; b. Shreveport, La., Sept. 1, 1950; s. John Patrick and Helen Marie (Scavnicky) C.; m. Victoria Finney, Feb. 7, 1976; children: Michael Patrick, Richard Andrew. BA, Pomona Coll., 1972; MA, U. Ariz., 1976, PhD, 1977. Lic. psychologist, N.Y. Chief psychologist Monroe County Mental Health Clinic, Rochester, N.Y., 1979-83, dir., 1983—; pvt. practice psychology Rochester, N.Y., 1984—; cons. various state and county agencies, Rochester, 1979—. Capt. U.S. Army, 1977-79. Recipient Linda Mills Meml. award N.Y. State, 1995. Mem. APA, N.Y. State Psychol. Assn. Roman Catholic. Office: Mental Health Clinic 65 W Broad St Rochester NY 14614

CLARK, JANE ANGELA, medical group administrator, educator; b. Linton, Ind., Sept. 18, 1955; d. Frank William and Doris Louise (French) Barlich; m. William H. Clark, June 4, 1977; children: William Daniel, Stephanie Lynne. BA, Purdue U., 1976; postgrad., U. Wis., 1978-79, U. Pa., 1985-90. Cert. employee benefits specialist. Rsch. asst. Purdue U., West Lafayette, Ind., 1977; pers. specialist Sentry Ins., Stevens Point, Wis., 1977-81; adminstr. Indianhead Med. Group, Rice Lake, Wis., 1981-88, Emergency Room Physicians Group, Rice Lake, 1985—; instr. mgmt. Wis. Indianhead Tech. Coll., Rice Lake, 1985—; cert. instr. Zenger-Miller courses; mem. suprs. mgmt. adv. com. Wis. Indianhead Tech. Coll., 1985-87. Chairperson Am. Heart Assn., Shell Lake, Wis., 1989; bd. dirs. United Way, Rice Lake, 1987-88. Mem. After Five Club (bd. dirs.), Alpha Lambda Delta, Phi Alpha Theta, Kappa Delta Pi. Republican. Baptist. Home: RR 1 Box 267A Shell Lake WI 54871-9780

CLARK, JANET, retired health services executive; b. Detroit, Oct. 3, 1941; d. John Francis Bullock and Martha Barbara (Bauer) Clark; m. Donald Bruce Tyson, Feb. 29, 1964; children: William John, Barbara June; m. Herman John Husmann, Nov. 11, 1988. AAS in Dental Hygiene, Broome C.C., 1961; BS in Health Edn., SUNY, Cortland, 1963; MPA in Mgmt., SUNY, Albany, 1993. Dental hygiene tchr. West Genessee Ctrl. Schs., Camillus, N.Y., 1964-65; health educator N.Y. State Dept. of Health, Syracuse, 1965-70; sr. sanitarian N.Y. State Dept. of Health, Monticello, 1977-80; prin. sanitarian N.Y. State Dept. of Health, N.Y.C., 1980-86; field ops. rep. N.Y. State Dept. of Health, Albany, 1986-89, mgr. Indian health, 1990-95, ret., 1995; sanitarian, health educator Onondaga County Health Dept., Syracuse, 1970-77; chmn., CEO Hažawi Found. for Econ. Deve. in Indigenous Nations, 1994—. Mem. Nat. Environ. Health Assn., N.Y. Soc. Profl. Sanitarians (sec. 1970-84), N.Y. State Registry of Sanitarians (treas. 1987-90, pres. 1990-95, Meritorious Svc. award 1986). Home: 355 Manning Blvd Albany NY 12206-1815 Office: PO Box 2033 Albany NY 12220

CLARK, JEANNE MARIE, physician assistant; b. Brookville, Pa., July 7, 1953; d. Richard Emerson and Noreen Joan (Shofestall) Clark; m. Tim Clark, Apr. 27, 1979; children: Mackenzie, Meredith. Diploma, Buffalo Gen. Hosp., 1974; student, U. Wash., 1982. RN, N.Y.; cert. physician asst. Nurse ICU Buffalo Gen. Hosp., 1974-76; supr. cardiovasc. svcs. Marquette (Mich.) Hosp., 1976-78; staff nurse Clarion (Pa.) Hosp., 1978; ICU nurse Fairbanks (Alaska) Meml. Hosp., 1978-79; internal medicine nurse Tanana Valley Med. Ctr., Fairbanks, 1979-81; physician asst. Tarara Valley Med. Ctr., Fairbanks, 1982-88, pvt. physician, Fairbanks, 1988—. Active Suzuki Music Group, Fairbanks, 1993—. AAPA Burroughs Wellcome fellow, 1995-96. Mem. Am. Acad. Physician Assts., Alaska Acad. Physician Assts. (sec.-treas. 1991-93, pres. 1996). Lutheran. Home: 479 Slater Dr Fairbanks AK 99701

CLARK, JOHN D., optometrist; b. Geneva, N.Y., Aug. 19, 1952; s. John and Jane (Passalacqua) C.; m. Francesca Marie Berretta Clark, June 29, 1974; children: John Joseph, Annjeannette. AAS, Finger Lakes C.C., 1976; BS, SUNY, Brockport, 1989, Pa. Coll. Optometry, 1990; DO, Pa. Coll. Optometry, 1993. RN N.Y. State Dept. of Mental Hygiene, Geneva, 1976-85; pvt. practice Clark Eye Care Ctr., Geneva, 1995—. Mem. Rochester Optometric Soc., N.Y. State Optometric Assn., Am. Optometric Assn. Office: Clark Eye Care Ctr 81 North St Geneva NY 14456

CLARK, JOYCE NAOMI JOHNSON, nurse; b. Corpus Christi, Tex., Oct. 4, 1936; d. Chester Fletcher and Ermal Olita (Bailey) Johnson; m. William Boyd Clark, Jan. 4, 1958; (div. 1967); 1 child, Sherene Joyce. Student, Corpus Christi State U., 1975-77. RN, CNOR, ACLS; cert. instrument flight instr., oper. rm. nurse. Staff nurse Van Nuys (Calif.) Community Hosp., 1963-64, U.S. Naval Hosp., Corpus Christi, 1964-68; patient care coord. Meml. Med. Ctr., Corpus Christi, 1968—. Leader Paisano Coun. Girl Scouts U.S.A., Corpus Christi, 1968-74; past comdr. 3rd group USAF Aux., CAP Air Search and Rescue, wing chief pilot, ret. lt. col. 1993. Recipient Charles A. Mella award Meml. Med. ctr., 1981, Paul E. Garbert award CAP, 1986, cert. of appreciation in recognition of Support Child Guard Missing Children Edn. Program Nat. Assn. Chiefs of Police, Washington, 1987, Charles E. Yeager Aerospace Edn. Achievement award, 1985, Grover Loenig Aerospace award, 1986, Cert. of World Leadership Internat. Biographical Ctr., Cambridge, Eng., 1987, Gill Robb Wilson award #1021, 1988, Merit award Drug Free Am. Through Enforcement, Edn., Intelligence Nat. Assn. Chiefs of Police, Sr. Mem. of Yr. USAF Aux., CAP Air Search and Rescue, 1986. Mem. USAF Aux., CAP Air Search and Rescue (past comdr. 3rd group, wing chief pilot, Sr. Mem. of Yr. 1986), Am. Assn. Oper. Rm. Nurses (v.p. 1969), Am. Fed. Police, Aircraft Owners and Pilots Assn. Home: 1001 Carmel Pky Apt 33 Corpus Christi TX 78411-2152 Office: Meml Med Ctr 4606 Hospital Blvd Corpus Christi TX 78405-1818

CLARK, DAME JUNE, nurse, educator; b. Sheffield, Yorkshire, Eng., May 31, 1941; d. Ernest Harold and Marion Louise (Walter) Hickery; m. Roger Michael Geoffrey Clark, July 23, 1966; children: Andrew, Gillian. BA with honors, U. London, 1962; MPhil, U. Reading, 1972; PhD, South Bank U., London, 1985. Health visitor and sr. rsch. nurse West Berkshire Health Dist., Reading, 1981-85; spl. projects coord. Lewisham & North Southwark Health Authority, London, 1985-86; dir. community nursing svcs. West Lambeth Health Authority, London, 1986-88; chief nursing advisor Harrow Health Authority, London, 1988-90; prof. nursing Middlesex U., London, 1990—. Author: A Family Visitor, 1973, What Do Health Visitors Do?, 1977, others; contbr. articles to profl. jours. Nurse mem. Berkshire Area Health Authority, Reading, 1973-82, Oxfordshire Dist. Health Authority, 1983-85. Named Dame Comdr. Order of the British Empire Queen Elizabeth, 1995; recipient Winston Churchill fellow, 1996. Fellow Royal Coll. Nursing of U.K. (chmn. congress 1978-82, dep. pres. 1986-90, pres. 1990-94). Office: Middlesex Univ, Queensway, Enfield England EN4 3SF

CLARK, KENNETH JOHN, medical facility administrator; b. Marblehead, Mass., Feb. 24, 1950; married. B Health Care Adminstrn., Ithaca Coll., 1972; M Health Care Adminstrn., George Washington U., 1975; DS, Loyola U. of L.A., 1982. Adminstrv. resident VA Med. Ctr., Martinez, Calif., 1974-75, mgmt. analyst trainee, 1975-76; mgmt. analyst VA Med. Ctr., Roseburg, Oreg., 1976-77, New orleans, 1977-79; sr. mgmt. analyst VA Med. Ctr., Long Beach, Calif., 1979-81; asst.dir. tng. VA Wadsworth Med. Ctr., L.A., 1981-82; asst. dir. VA Med. Ctr., Palo Alto, Calif., 1982-84; assoc. dir. Jerry L. Pettis Meml. Vet. Hosp., Loma Linda, Calif., 1984-86; dep. regional dir. Dept. Vets/ Affairs, Washington, 1986-89; med. ctr. dir. VA Med. Ctr., Reno, Nev., 1989-92, L.A., 1992—. Active cmty. orgns. Fellow Am. Coll. Health Care Execs. Office: VA Med Ctr West LA 11301 Wilshire Blvd Los Angeles CA 90073-0275*

CLARK, LAURA MARY, women's health nurse; b. Phila., Jan. 18, 1964; d. Richard T. and Veronica Ann (Dormer) Rickards; m. John W. Clark, Nov. 29, 1986; children: Amanda Marie, Lisa Jean. ASN, Hahnemann U., 1985. Staff RN Atlantic City (N.J.) Med. Ctr., Meth. Hosp., Phila., Underwood Meml. Hosp., Woodbury, N.J.; perental therapist Meth. Hosp., Phila.; staff nursemed. oncology Presbyn. Med. Ctr., Phila.; IV therapist Underwood Meml. Hosp., Woodbury, N.J.

CLARK, LEONOR ANDRACA, social worker; b. Habanai, Cuba, Jan. 26, 1943; came to U.S., 1961; d. Jose and Esther (Lamadriz) Andraca; m. Jose B. Clark, June 27, 1961; children: Leonor, Ana, Jose Jr., Eddie. B Social Work, Fla. Internat. U., 1987, MSW, 1991. Student advisor MDCC, Miami, Fla.; social worker, clinic asst. Epilepsy Found., Miami, 1988; clin. social worker Coral Gables Hosp., Miami, 1993, South Miami Hosp., 1996—. William McKnight scholar. Mem. Nat. Assn. Social Workers. Home: 2379 SW 12th St Miami FL 33135-5018

CLARK, NOREEN MORRISON, behavioral science educator, researcher; b. Glasgow, Scotland, Jan. 12, 1943; came to U.S., 1948; d. Angus Watt and Anne (Murphy) Morrison; m. George Robert Pitt, Dec. 3, 1982; 1 child, Alexander Robert. BS, U. Utah, 1965; MA, Columbia U., 1972, M.Phil., 1975, PhD, 1976. Rsch. coord. World Edn. Inc., N.Y.C., 1972-73; asst. prof. Sch. Pub. Health Columbia U., N.Y.C., 1973-80, assoc. prof., 1980-81; assoc. prof. Sch. Pub. Health U. Mich., Ann Arbor, 1981-85, prof., chmn. dept. health behavior and health edn., 1985-95, Marshall H. Becker prof. of pub. health, 1995—, dean, 1995—; adj. prof. health adminstrn. Sch. Pub. Health Columbia U., 1988—; prin. investigator NIH, 1977—; mem. adv. com. pulmonary diseases Nat. Heart, Lung & Blood Inst., Rockville, Md., 1983-87, mem. adv. com. for prevention, edn. and control, 1987-91, coordinating com. Nat. Asthma Edn. Program, 1991—; assoc. Synergos Inst., N.Y.C., 1987—. Author: (monograph) Education for Development, 1980; co-author: Evaluation of Health Promotion, 1984; contbr. articles on disease self-management to profl. jours.; editor Health Edn. Quarterly, 1985—; mem. editorial bd. Women in Health, Advances in Health Edn. and Promotion, Home Health Care Services Quarterly. Hon. dir. Freedom from Hunger Found., Davis, Calif., 1980—; bd. dirs. Aaron Diamond Found., 1990—, Family Care Internat., N.Y.C., 1987—, Am. Lung Assn., N.Y.C., 1988—, chair govt. rels., 1994—. Fellow Soc. Pub. Health Edn. (pres. 1985-86, Disting. Fellow award 1987); mem. APHA (chair health edn. sect. 1982-83, Derryberry award in behavioral sci. 1985, Disting. Career award 1994), Am. Thoracic Soc. (Health Edn. Rsch. award Nat. Asthma Edn. Program 1992), Internat. Union Health Edn., Soc. Behavioral Medicine, Coun. Fgn. Rels., Overseas Devel. Coun., Pi Sigma Alpha. Office: U Mich Sch Pub Health 109 S Observatory St Ann Arbor MI 48109-2029

CLARK, OLIVER CARL, optometrist; b. Lakeland, Fla., June 27, 1926; s. Olive K. Gurdeau Clark; m. Jacqueline Turner, June 30, 1949; 1 child. OD, Ill. Coll. Optometry, 1948. Cert. Occular Therapeutics. Pvt. practice optometry Jacksonville Beach, Fla., 1948—; cons. in field. Contbr. articles to profl. jours. Recipient 2nd Optometrist of the Decade award Fla. Optometric Assn. Democrat. Episcopalian. Office: 303 N 3rd St Jacksonville Beach FL 32250

CLARK, ORVILLE MAYO, JR., optometric physician; b. Pikeville, Ky., Sept. 3, 1925; s. Orville Mayo and Kathleen (Coleman) C.; m. Betty Jo Greer; children: Orville Mayo III, Gina Lyn, Alicia Ann. BS, So. Coll., 1956, OD, 1956. Pvt. practice Pikeville, Ky., 1956—; pres. Ea. Ky. Optometric Assn., 1974-75, Ky. Optometric Assn., Frankfort, Ky., 1976-77; trustee So. Coun. Optometry, Atlanta, 1976-78. Mem. Pikeville (Ky.) Rotary Club, 1960-64; pres. Pikeville Coll. Alumni Assn., 1976-79; dir. 1st Fed. Savs. and Loan, 1975-80. Recipient Presdl. award, Wiliam C. Leadingham award, Ky. Optometric Assn., Frankfort, Ky. Mem. Pikeville Jr. C. of C. (past pres.), Am. Optometric Assn., Am. Radio Relay League, El Hasa Shrine Temple. Democrat. Baptist. Home: 501 3rd St Pikeville KY 41501-1246 Office: Drs Clark & Clark, PSC 2nd And Caroline Pikeville KY 41502

CLARK, PATRICIA, molecular biologist; b. Lake Village, Ark., Mar. 21, 1928; d. Cleburn Clem and Helen Miller (Baker) C. BA, Washington U., St. Louis, 1950, MA, 1955; PhD, Purdue U., 1962. Microanalyst Washington U., St. Louis, 1950-51; rsch. chemist The Chemstrand Corp., Decatur, Ala., 1953-55; assoc. chemist So. Rsch. Inst., Birmingham, Ala., 1955-56; grad. asst. Purdue U., West Lafayette, Ind., 1956-61; biochemist Gerontology Rsch. Ctr. Child Health and Human Devel. NIH, Balt., 1961-78, Nat. Inst. on Aging NIH, Balt., 1978-96; ret. Fellow Am. Inst. Chemists; mem. AAAS, Am. Chem. Soc., Gerontol. Soc., N.Y. Acad. Scis., Sigma Xi, Pi Mu Epsilon, Alpha Lambda Delta. Home: Dulaney Towers 1 Smeton Pl Unit 1206 Baltimore MD 21204-2734

CLARK, PATRICIA ANN, community health and mental health nurse; b. Washington, Feb. 23, 1933; m. Thomas H. Clark, 1957; children: Norman, Letitia, Andrew, Lisa. BSN, Adelphi U., 1955; MS in Nursing, Boston U., 1959. Cert. adult psychiat./mental health clin. specialist. Asst. dir. VNA S. Shore, Braintree, Mass., 1983-86; pvt. practice psychotherapist Norwell, Mass., 1986-89; exec. dir. Hingham (Mass.) Visiting Nurse Assn., 1990—; treas. Affiliated Cmty. Vis. Nurse Assn., Inc., 1996. Mem. ANA, Mass. Nurses Assn., Home and Health Care Assn. Mass., Vis. Nurse Assn. New Eng., Inc. (bd. dirs.), Sigma Theta Tau (Theta chpt.). Office: 10 Downer Ave Hingham MA 02043

CLARK, PAUL THOMAS, healthcare executive; b. Ironton, Ohio, Oct. 13, 1943; s. Charles Nelson and Lucille May (Dudley) C.; m. Janice M. Merrill, Oct. 16, 1965; children: Colin, Sean. BA in Journalism, Ohio State U., 1969, postgrad., 1971-73. Editor, Ohio Petroleum Marketers Assn., Columbus, 1969; dir. pub. relations Otterbein Coll., Westerville, Ohio, 1970-72, Riverside Meth. Hosp., Columbus, 1972-77, Bronson Meth. Hosp., Kalamazoo, Mich., 1977-84; sr. v.p. Deaconess Hosp., Cin., 1984-86; healthcare mktg. cons., Cin., 1986-87; v.p. corp. devel. Southside Health Care Systems, Pitts., 1987; with Healthcare Mktg. Group, Cin., 1987-89; prin. Paul Clark Group, 1989-93; mgr. mktg. Mercy Heart Inst., 1993-95; exec. dir. Washington (Pa.) Physician Hosp. Orgn., 1995—. Spl. events chmn. Kalamazoo United Way, 1978. Served with AUS, 1961-64. Recipient McEachern award Am. Hosp. Assn., 1974, Ohio Hosp. Assn. award, 1974-76, Columbus Advt. Fedn. awards, 1975-76. Mem. Pub. Rels. Soc. Am. (Silver Anvil award 1981), Am. Coll. Healthcare Execs., Am. Acad. Med. Adminstrs., Kalamazoo County C. of C. (mem. pub. affairs com. 1977). Lodge: Rotary. Home: 1773 Clearview Dr Pittsburgh PA 15241-2014 Office: 155 Wilson Ave Washington PA 15301

CLARK, RICHARD LEE, radiologist; b. Mt. Vernon, N.Y., June 1, 1940; s. Kenneth Fenton and Gertrude Lathrop (Dezendorf) C.; m. Linda Lenore Horne, Aug. 27, 1963; children: Jonathan Kenneth, Jennifer Lee. BA magna cum laude, Oberlin Coll., 1962; MD, Johns Hopkins U., 1966; grad., Mgr. Leadership Inst. N.C. Meml. Hosp. U. N.C. Sch. Bus. Adminstrn., 1987. Diplomate Am. Bd. Radiology. Intern U. Ky. Med. Ctr., Lexington, 1966-67; resident in radiology Johns Hopkins Hosp., Balt., 1967-70, chief resident, instr., 1970-71; assoc. prof. radiology U. N.C., Chapel Hill, 1973-83, prof., 1983—; dir. diagnostic radiol. rsch., 1973-79, adv. to med. class of 1981; cons. to Chief Med. Examiner, N.C., 1973—; dir. div. gen. radiology N.C. Meml. Hosp., 1979-86, acting chair dept. radiology, 1987, assoc. chair, 1987-91, vice chmn. rsch., 1991—; sci. integrity officer U. N.C. Sch. Medicine, 1993—. Co-author: Renal Microvascular Disease, 1980; assoc. editor Academic Radiology; contbr. numerous articles to profl. jours. and textbook chpts. Bd. dirs. Chapel Hill Village Orch.; past trustee, past pres. Eno River Unitarian-Universalist Fellowship. Served with USPHS, 1971-73. Recipient Henry Strong Denison award Johns Hopkins U., 1965-66; faculty research grantee N.C., 1974-75, NIH research grantee, 1976-94; James Picker Found. scholar 1975-79. Fellow Am. Coll. Radiology; mem. Assn. Univ. Radiologists, Soc. Uroradiology (pres.-elect), Am. Coll. Radiology (past pres., councilor NCC-ACR), Am. Roentgen Ray Soc., Radiol. Soc. N.Am., N.C. Med. Soc., Johns Hopkins Med. Assn., Johns Hopkins U. Alumni Assn., Durham Orange County Med. Soc., Sigma Xi. Unitarian-Universalist. Clubs: Oberlin Alumni of N.C. (co-pres. 1975-77), Chapel Hill Chamber Players, Doctoral Themes Chamber Music Group. Home: 901 Phils Creek Rd Chapel Hill NC 27516-5443 Office: U NC Sch Medicine Dept Radiology Chapel Hill NC 27599

CLARK, RICK GENE, radiologist, osteopath; b. Sharon, Pa., Nov. 7, 1947; s. Kenneth Leroy and Mary Rosellen (Faller) C.; divorced; children: Jason Howard, Bradley Kenneth. BS, Youngstown State U., 1974; DO, Phila. Coll. Osteo. Medicine, 1978. Diplomate Nat. Bd. Osteo. Med. Examiners. Intern Warren (Ohio) Gen. Hosp., 1978-79; with USPHS, 1979-80; resident in pathology Southeastern Med. Ctr., North Miami Beach, Fla., 1981-82; pvt. practice emergency medicine, Bradenton, Fla., 1982-88; resident in radiology Phila. Coll. Osteo. Medicine, 1988-91; radiology fellow Lehigh Valley Hosp., Allentown, Pa., 1994-95; locum tenens radiologist various locations, 1995—. Maj. M.C., USAF, 1991-93. Mem. Am. Osteo. Assn. Republican. Baptist.

CLARK, ROBERT ALFRED, psychiatrist; b. Boston, Oct. 26, 1908; s. Alfred Pugh and Annie (Gibson) C.; m. Braxton Guilbeau, May 11, 1908; children: Allen M., Mary C. Mayo, John R. AB, Harvard U., 1930, MD, 1934. Resident Boston City Hosp., 1934-35; intern Lakeside Hosp., Cleve., 1935-37; resident Boston Psychiat. Hosp., 1937-39; staff psychiatrist R.I. Hosp., Providence, 1939-41; clin. dir. Western Psychiat. Inst., Pitts., 1943-53, Friends Hosp., Phila., 1955; med. dir. Northeast Cmty. Mental Health Ctr., Phila., 1955-78. Author: Six Talks on Jung's Psychology, 1953, Mental Illness in Perspective, 1973, Talking With God, 1992. Fellow Am. Psychiat. Assn. Democrat. Mem. LDS Ch. Home: 8301 Forest Ave Elkins Park PA 19027

CLARK, ROBERT DWIGHT, nurse; b. Yakima, Wash., Aug. 19, 1963; s. Robert Dwight and Carol Lois (Kopp) C.; m. Carolyn Sue Tyus, Oct. 9, 1993. BA in Chemistry, Tabor Coll., 1986; BSN, Wichita State U., 1990. Staff nurse Wesely Med. Ctr., Wichita, Kans., 1990, Harris Meth. HEB, Bedford, Tex., 1991—.

CLARK, RONALD GEORGE, surgery educator; b. Aberdeen, Scotland, Sept. 8, 1928; s. Goerge and Gladys (Taylor) C.; m. Tamar Welsh Harvie, Dec. 9, 1960; children: Tamar Taylor, Deborah Harvie. MB ChB, U. Aberdeen, 1956; MD (hon.), U. Sheffield, 1996. Registrar Western Infirmary, Glasgow, Scotland, 1957-59; rsch. fellow Harvard U., Boston, 1960-61; lectr. surgery U. Glasgow, 1961-65; sr. lectr. surgery U. Sheffield (Eng.), 1966-71, prof. surgery, 1971-93; pro-vice chancellor U. Sheffield, 1988-93, dean faculty of medicine and dentistry, 1982-85; mem. Gen. Med. Coun., U.K., 1983-93, Gen. Dental Coun., 1990-93. Founder editor Clin. Nutrition, 1980-85; contbr. articles to profl. jours. Fellow Royal Coll. Surgeons (Edinburgh), Royal Coll. Surgeons (Eng.); mem. Surg. Rsch. Soc., Assn. Surgeons Gt. Britain and Ireland, European Soc. Parenteral and Enteral Nutrition (hon. mem., chmn. 1983-88, pres. 1993-94), The Nutrition Soc. (hon.), Internat. Soc. Surgeons, Royal Soc. Medicine, Royal Commonwealth Soc. Home: 2 Chesterwood Dr, Sheffield S10 5DU, England Office: Univ Surg Unit No Gen Hosp, Sheffield S5 7AU, England

CLARK, SANDRA ANN, clinical social worker; b. Long Branch, N.J., Dec. 4, 1942; d. Richard Marshall and Margaret (Novak) C.; m. John Jacob Hoffman, May 4, 1969 (div. 1987); children: Rebecca L., Benjamin C., Rachael A.; m. William E. Wilbur, June 25, 1989. BA, Valparaiso U., 1966; MSW, SUNY, Albany, 1968. Lic. clin. social worker. Pvt. practice psychotherapy Kittery, Maine, 1982—; asst. exec. dir., coord. children's program N.H. Parents Anonymous, Portsmouth, 1985-86; mental health cons. Strafford County Head Start, Somersworth, N.H., 1985-88; interim exec. dir. N.H. Parents Anonymous, Portsmouth, 1986-87; home sch. coord. Portsmouth Sch. System, 1986-87; clin. social worker Rackingham Counseling Ctr., Exeter, N.H., 1986-89, York County Counseling Svcs., Kittery, 1989-90; exec. dir. Growing Consciousness Assn., Saco, Maine, 1995—; mem. faculty U. Conn., Concord, N.H., 1987. Mem. Nat Assn. Social Workers, Acad. Cert. Social Workers. Democrat. Home: 25 Old Ferry Ln Kittery ME 03904-1305 Office: 110 Main St Ste 1508 5th fl Saco ME 04072

CLARK, SUSAN MATTHEWS, psychologist; b. Newton, Kans., Aug. 5, 1950; d. Glenn Wesley Matthews and Jane Buckles; m. S. Bruce Clark, Aug. 14, 1971; children: Casandra Jane, Ryan Matthews. BME, Wichita State U., 1971, MME, 1975, MA, 1982; PhD, North Tex. State U., 1985. Elem. tchr. Derby (Kans.) Pub. Schs., 1972-74; profl. musician Amarillo (Tex.) Symphony, 1974-77; psychol. cons. Achenbach Ctr., Hardtner, Kans., 1983-85; psychologist VA Med. Ctr., Wichita, Kans., 1984-85, St. Francis Acad., Inc., Salina, Kans., 1986-89, Psychiat. Clinic Wichita, 1989-93; gen. mgr. Affiliated Psychiat. Svcs., Wichita, 1993-95; psychologist Charter Clinic, Wichita, Kans., 1995—; bd. dirs. Salina Coalition for the Prevention of Child Abuse, 1986-87. Author: Grant, 1987. Bd. deacons Plymouth Congl. Ch., Wichita, 1989-92, mem. bd. Christian Edn., 1993. Recipient: Phi Kappa Phi, Mu Phi Epsilon, Psi Chi. Mem. APA, Nat. Acad. Neuropsychology, Southwestern Psychol. Assn., Kans. Psychol. Assn., Wichita Area Psychol. Assn., Kans. Assn. Profl. Psychologists. Republican. Congregationalist. Office: Charter Clinic 8911 E Orme Ste C Wichita KS 67207

CLARK, TERESA WATKINS, psychotherapist, clinical counselor; b. Hobart, Okla., Dec. 18, 1953; d. Aaron Jack Watkins and Patricia Ann (Flurry) Greer and Ralph Gordon Greer; m. Philip Winston Clark, Dec. 29, 1979; children: Philip Aaron, Alisa Lauren. BA in Psychology, U. N.Mex., 1979, MA in Counseling and Family Studies, 1989. Lic. profl. clin. counselor, N.Mex. Child care worker social svcs. divsn. Family Resource Ctr., Albuquerque, 1978-79; head tchr., asst. dir. Kinder Care Learning Ctr., Albuquerque, 1979-80; psychiat. asst. Vista Sandia Psychiat. Hosp., Albuquerque, 1980-87; psychotherapist outpatient clinic Bernalillo County Mental Health Ctr.-Heights, 1989-91; therapist adolescent program Charter/Heights Behavioral Health Sys., Albuquerque, 1991—. Mem. ACA, Am. Assn. Multicultural Counseling and Devel., N.Mex. Health Counselors Assn. (former cen. regional rep. bd. dirs., ethics chairperson, bd. dirs.), Mental Health Coundelor's Assn., Phi Kappa Phi, "Billy The Kid Outlaw Gang" Hist. Soc. Democrat. Office: Charter/Hlth Behav Hlth Sys 103 Hospital Loop Albuquerque NM 87109

CLARK, THOMAS ROLFE, clinical psychologist; b. Detroit, Oct. 30, 1941; s. Edward Rolfe and Ruth Ann (Spurr) C.; m. Mary Franzen, July 15, 1972. AB cum laude, Greenville Coll., 1963; MA, Wayne State U.; PhD, U. Windsor, Can., 1972. Intern Wayne County Psychiat. Hosp., Detroit, mem. staff, 1972-77; chief psychologist Heritage Hosp., 1978-81; dir. mental health, program dir. Marian Manor Med. Ctr., exec. and clin. dir. Alpha Psychol. Svcs.s, Livonia, Mich.; pvt. practice clin. and police psychology and psychotherapy, Detroit, 1972—; exec. dir. Alpha Psychol. Svcs., 1982—; faculty Henry Ford Community Coll., Dearborn, Mich., 1972-76; dir. clin. svcs. Met. Guidance Ctr., Livonia, Mich., 1978-82; mental health cons. People's Community Hosp. Authority, various police depts. Organist First United Meth. Ch., Dearborn, 1965-83, Grace Chapel, 1983—; concert organist, 1975—; bd. dirs. Meth. Children's Home Soc., Livonia, Mich., 1974-78. NIMH-Va fellow Wayne State U., Robards doctoral fellow U. Windsor, teaching fellow Grad. Theol. Found. Fellow Am. Orthopsychiat. Assn., Am. Coll. Psychology, Masters and Johnson Inst., Christian Assn. Psychol. Studies, Acad. Family Psychology; mem. Am. Guild Organists, Assn. Fraternal Order Police (assoc.), Christian Assn. Psychol. Studies (nat. bd. dirs.). Contbr. articles to profl. jours.; rec. artist. Recipient awards in music, psychology. Office: 39209 6 Mile Rd Ste 207 Livonia MI 48152-2681

CLARK, THREESE ANNE, occupational therapist, disability analyst; b. Bath, N.Y., Jan. 16, 1946; d. Frank George and Beulah Irene (Harris) Brown; m. Jacob Clark, Mar. 11, 1966 (div. Mar. 1977); 1 child, Jayson Todd. BS in Occupational Therapy, U. N.D., 1967, MS in Counseling and Guidance, 1977. Lic. occupational therapist, Pa., Md.; diplomate Am. Bd. Disability Analysts (charter adv. bd. mem. 1995—). Occupational therapist U. N.D. Med. Ctr., 1968; chief occupational therapist, program developer Corning (N.Y.) Hosp., 1968-69, Arnot-Ogden Hosp., Elmira, N.Y., 1969-71; staff occupational therapist VA Ctr., Bath, N.Y., 1971-74; instr. occupational therapy U. N.D., Grand Forks, 1974-77; prin. investigator occupational therapy Ohio State U., 1977-79; occupational therapist Regional Ednl. Assessment and Cons. Team, Hillsboro, Ohio, 1979-81; occupational therapist, phys. medicine and rehab. Saint Mary's Hosp., West Palm Beach, Fla., 1981-82; chief occupational therapist Mercy Med. Ctr., Oshkosh, Wis., 1982-87; dir. occupational/recreational therapy HealthSouth Rehab. Hosp., Altoona, 1987-95, clin. dir. spinal injury program, 1987-95; pres. and owner Life Care Planning and Mgmt. Inc., Altoona, 1993—; assoc. prof., program chair profl. occupl. therapy program Mt. Aloysius Coll., Cresson, Pa., 1995—; cons. Founders Pavillion, Corning, 1969, Grafton (N.D.) State Sch. for the Retarded, 1975-76, Heart of Am. Rehab. Ctr., Rugby, N.D., 1976-77, Andrea Clifford program, 1978; guest lectr. support groups, community groups, ednl. programs, 1987—; presented numerous papers on occupational therapy. Contbr. articles to profl. jours. Charter mem. profl. adv. coun. Am. Bd. Disability Analysts; pres. adv. bd. Occupational Therapy Asst. Program, Mt. Aloysius Jr. Coll., 1988-92, 94-96; mem. adv. profl. com. Home Nursing Agy., Altoona, 1988-93; mem. Com. Health Care Adv. Com., 1994—; bd. dirs. Ctr. for Internat. Living of South Cen. Pa., 1992—; mem. med. svc. com. Evergreen Manor, Oshkosh, 1985-87; chair home/family life and human rels. Northtowne Elem. Sch. PTA, Columbus, Ohio, 1978, others. Mem. Am. Occupational Therapy Assn. (coun. edn. 1974-76, coun. affiliate pres. 1976), Nat. Rehab. Assn., Ohio Occupational Therapy Assn., Columbus Dist. Occupational Therapy Assn., Pa. Occupational Therapy Assn., Am. Assn. Hand Therapists. Baptist. Home: 5300 5th Ave Altoona PA 16602-1312 also: Life Care Planning Mgmt Inc 5300 5th Ave Altoona PA 16602-1312 Office: Mt Aloysius Coll 7373 Adm Peary Hwy Cresson PA 16630

CLARK, WESLEY GLEASON, pharmacologist, educator; b. Wadsworth, Ohio, July 1, 1933; s. Alfred William and Mary June (Starn) C.; m. Yvonne Lee Stanfield, Apr. 16, 1965; children: David Lee, Rebecca Lynne Clark Catlett, Roger Dale. BA, U. Colo., 1955, MS, 1958; PhD, U. Utah, 1962. Instr. U. Tex. Southwestern Med. Ctr., Dallas, 1962-63, asst. prof., 1963-72, assoc. prof., 1972—. Editor: (textbook) Goth's Medical Pharmacology, 13th rev. edit., 1992; contbr. over 50 rsch. articles and over 20 rev. articles to profl. jours. Grantee NIH, 1964-66, 70-78, Nat. Inst. on Drug Abuse, 1979-81. Mem. Am. Soc. Pharmacology and Exptl. Therapeutics. Home: 1334 Carriage Dr Irving TX 75062-5303 Office: U Tex Southwestern Med Ctr 5323 Harry Hines Blvd Dallas TX 75235-9041

CLARK, WILDER CRAWFORD, medical psychologist; b. Timmins, Ont., Can., Oct. 15, 1926; came to U.S., 1953; s. Wilder Crawford and Vera Ellen (Nordenstierna) C.; m. Susanne Loewe, Oct. 18, 1965. BA, Queen's U., Kingston, Ont., 1952, MA, 1953; PhD, U. Mich., 1958. Analytical chemist Atomic Energy Commn., Port Hope, Ont., 1948-50; instr. U. Mich., Ann Arbor, 1957-59; sr. rsch. assoc. Courtney & Co. Phila., 1959-60; mem. tech. staff AT&T Bell Labs., Holmdel, N.J., 1967-68; hon. prof. CUNY, 1960—; prof. Coll. of Physicians and Surgeons Columbia U., N.Y.C., 1960—; rsch. scientist VI N.Y. State Psychiat. Inst., 1960—; scientific advisor Reflex Sympathetic Dystrophy Assn., Cherry Hill, N.J., 1984—; ad hoc cons. NIH, Washington, 1976—; cons. Cygnus Inc., Patterson, N.J., 1986—. Author: (with others) Marihuana: Biological Effects, 1979, Stress Induced Analgesia, 1987, Encyclopedia of Neuroscience, 1987, Handbook of Chronic Pain Management, 1987, Issues in Pain Measurement, 1989. Grantee NIH, 1970, 86, 92. Fellow AAAS, N.Y. Acad. Scis., Am. Psychol. Assn.; mem. Eastern Pain Assn. (bd. dirs.), Am. Pain Soc. (exec.), Internat. Assn. for the Study of Pain (founder). Office: Columbia U Dept Psychiatry 722 W 168th St New York NY 10032-2603

CLARK, WILLIAM HILTON, biology educator, water and ecological scientist; b. Caldwell, Idaho, Dec. 17, 1944; s. Hilton Montrose and Margret Lucille (Bales) C.; m. Mary Elizabeth Clark, June 8, 1968; children: Ellen Mary, Cynthia Jane, Karen Diana. BS in Biology, Coll. Idaho, 1967; MS in Biology, U. Nev., 1971; leader 27 expdns. Cert. sr. ecologist; cert. fisheries scientist. Research asst. U. Nev., Reno, 1968, 72-73; research asst. Coll. Idaho, Caldwell, 1967, 76, expdn. leader, 1977—, asst. dir. Orma J. Smith Mus. Natural History, 1978—; adj. prof. biology Albertson Coll. of Idaho, Caldwell, 1979—; affiliate prof. entomology U. Idaho, Moscow; sr. water quality specialist Div. Environ. Quality Idaho Dept. Health and Welfare, Boise, 1974-85; sr. water quality analyst Rock Creek Rural Clean Water, 1985-89; sr. surface water quality analyst Div. Environ. Quality Idaho Dept. Health and Welfare, Boise, 1989—; nonpoint source monitoring coord. Div. Environ. Quality Idaho Dept. Health and Welfar; cons. Nev. Archeol. Survey, Reno, 1972; bd. dirs. Coll. Idaho Alumni Assn. Contbr. articles to profl. jours. Served with U.S. Army, 1969-71, Vietnam. Decorated Bronze Star; recipient Disting. Alumni award Coll. Idaho, 1985; named Employee of Yr., Idaho Divsn. Environment, Boise, 1984; grantee Earthwatch, Am. Philos. Soc., Environ. Sci. and Rsch. Found. Mem. Ecol. Soc. Am., Idaho Acad. Sci. (rep. to Nat. Acad. Sci. and AAAS 1984—, pres. 1991-92), Am. Fisheries Soc., Idaho Entomology Group (pres., editor 1976-79, pres.-elect 1987, pres. 1988), Boise State U. Club Sigma Xi (pres. 1988-90). Home: 6305 Kirkwood Rd Boise ID 83709-2928 Office: Idaho Dept Health Welfare Div Environ Quality 1410 N Hilton St Boise ID 83706-1255

CLARK, WILLIAM STRATTON, physician; b. Dayton, Ohio, Nov. 24, 1914; s. Clyde Melvin and Hazel Marie (Walker) C.; m. Vivien Ranschburg, June 25, 1971; children: William Stratton, Judith Ann, Robin Walker, James Pennell. BS, U. Dayton, 1934; MD, St. Louis U., 1938. Diplomate Am. Bd. Internal Medicine. Intern Miami Valley Hosp., Dayton, 1938-39; gen. practice medicine Dayton, 1939-44; asst. in pathology Tulane U., 1944-45; clin. fellow medicine Mass. Gen. Hosp., 1945-48; rsch., tchr. Mass. Gen. Hosp., Med. Sch. Harvard, 1948-53; asst. prof. medicine Western Res. U., 1953-56, assoc. prof. medicine, 1956-58; dir. med. dept. Nat. Found., 1958-64; pres., chief exec. officer Arthritis Found., N.Y.C., 1964-70; assoc. attending physician St. Luke's Hosp., 1971-74, attending physician, 1974-80, cons. physician, 1980—, acting dir. dept. medicine, 1975-76, dir. dept. medicine, 1977-79, chief div. rheumatic diseases, 1979-85; prof. clin. medicine Columbia U. Coll. Physicians and Surgeons, 1975-84, lectr., 1985—. Former editor-in-chief: Arthritis and Rheumatism (ofcl. jour. Am. Rheumatism Assn.); contbr. articles to profl. jours. Master Am. Coll. Rheumatology; fellow ACP; mem. AMA, Century Assn. Episcopalian. Address: 1349 Lexington Ave New York NY 10128-1511

CLARKE, BARBARA ANN BARDO REIFF, community health nurse; b. Williamsport, Pa., Sept. 7, 1940; d. Willard C. and Charlotte C. (Livingston) Bardo; m. Frank X. Clarke, Aug. 19, 1988; children: Christopher Reiff, Stephen Reiff. Diploma, Harrisburg Polyclinic, 1961. Cert. CEN. Staff nurse Harrisburg (Pa.) Polyclinic, 1961-63; office nurse Dr. C.A. Lehman, Williamsport, Pa., 1970-76; staff nurse emergency rm. Williamsport Hosp., 1963-69, 71-87, head nurse emergency rm., 1982-87; staff nurse emergency rm. Divine Providence Hosp., Williamsport, 1987-88; staff nurse Liberty Health System, Springfield, Pa., 1989—. Mem. com. on pre-hosp. transp. Pa. Dept. of Health, 1975-76. Mem. EDNA (past pres. Tiadahton chpt.), Harrisburg Polyclinic Alumni Assn.

CLARKE, KIT HANSEN, radiologist; b. Louisville, May 24, 1944; d. Hans Peter and Katie (Bird) Hansen; AB, Randolph-Macon Woman's Coll., 1966; MD, U. Louisville, 1969; m. John M. Clarke, Feb. 14, 1976; children: Brett Bonnett, Blair Hansen, Brandon Chamberlain; stepchildren: Gray Campbell, Jeffrey William John M. Intern, Louisville Gen. Hosp., 1969-70; resident in internal medicine and radiology U. Tenn., Knoxville, 1970-73; resident in radiology U.S. Fla., Tampa, 1973-74; staff radiologist, chief spl. procedures Palms of Pasadena, St. Petersburg, Fla., 1974—, chmn. radiology dept., 1992—. Active Fla. Competitive Swim Assn. of AAU. Diplomate Am. Bd. Radiology. Fellow Am. Coll. Radiology; mem. AMA, Fla. West Coast Radiology Soc., Radiol. Soc. N.Am., Fla. Med. Assn., Pinellas County Med. Soc., Fla. Radiology Soc., Am. Horse Show Assn. (hunter, jumper divsn). Episcopalian. Home: 7171 9th St S Saint Petersburg FL 33705-6218 Office: 1609 Pasadena Ave S Saint Petersburg FL 33707-4565

CLARKE, OSCAR WITHERS, physician; b. Petersburg, Va., Jan. 29, 1919; s. Oscar Withers and Mary (Reese) C.; m. Susan Frances King, June 18, 1949; children—Susan Frances, Mary Elizabeth, Jennifer Ann. B.S., Randolph Macon Coll., 1941; MD, Med. Coll. Va., 1944. Intern Boston City Hosp., 1944-45; resident internal medicine Med. Coll. Va., 1945-46, 48-49, fellow in cardiology, 1949-50; pvt. practice specializing in internal medicine and cardiology Gallipolis Holzer Med. Ctr., Ohio, 1950—; pres., bd. dirs. Holzer Clinic Inc., 1981-89; bd. dirs. Ohio Valley Devel. Co., Gallipolis, Cmty. Improvement Corp.; pres. Ohio State Med. Bd.; chmn. Ohio Med. Edn. and Rsch. Found., Commn. Heart Attack Alert Program NIH, 1995-96; pres. Gallipolis City Bd. Helath, 1955—, Gallia County Heart Coun., 1955—. Contbr. articles to med. jours. V.p. Tri-State Regional coun. Boy Scouts Am., 1957; pres. Tri-State Community Concert Assn., 1957-59; trustee Med. Meml. Found., Holzer Hosp. Found. Capt. M.C., AUS, 1946-48, ETO. Recipient John Stewart Bryant pathology award Med. Coll. Va., 1943. Fellow ACP, Royal Soc. Medicine; mem. AMA (chmn. coun. on ethics and jud. affairs 1991—), Am. Heart Assn., Gallia County Med. Soc. (pres. 1953), Cen. Ohio Heart Assn. (Merit medal 1960, trustee), Ohio Med. Assn. (pres. 1973-74, Disting. Svc. citation 1988, Physician of Century 1996), Am. Soc. Internal Medicine (Disting. Internist award 1992), Alpha Omega Alpha, Sigma Zeta, Chi Beta Phi. Presbyterian. Club: Rotary (pres. 1953-54). Home: 108 Spruce Knls Gallipolis OH 45631-1066 Office: Holzer Med Clinic PO Box 344 Gallipolis OH 45631-0344

CLARKE, RICHARD LEWIS, health science association administrator; b. Indpls., Sept. 9, 1948; s. John Richard and Opal (Emmons) C.; m. Linda DeMattia, Aug. 12, 1972; children: John, Laura, R. Bradley. BS, Bradley U., 1971; MBA, U. Miami, 1972. Bus. mgr. Jackson Meml. Hosp., Miami, 1973-76; controller Palmetto Gen. Hosp., Hialeah, Fla., 1976-80; sr. v.p. fin. Swedish Med. Ctr., Englewood, Colo., 1980-86; pres. Healthcare Fin. Mgmt. Assn., Westchester, Ill., 1986—; bd. dirs., treas. Colo. Hosp. Assn. Trust, Denver. Fellow Healthcare Fin. Mgmt. Assn.; mem. Am. Soc. Assn. Execs., Econ. Club of Chgo. Office: Healthcare Fin Mgmt Assn 2 Westbrook Corp Ctr Ste 700 Westchester IL 60154

CLARKE, ROBERTA NANCY, health care marketing educator; b. Boston, Nov. 4, 1948; d. Joel Leon and Rhoda Eleanor (Coppleman) C.; m. Allen Jeffrey Michel, June 26, 1977; children: Aaron, Alexandra. BS magna cum laude, Tufts U., 1970; MBA, Harvard U., 1972, DBA, 1978. Rsch. asst. mktg. mgmt. Harvard Grad. Sch. Bus. Adminstrn., 1972-73; lectr. Boston U. Sch. Mgmt., 1974-78, asst. prof., 1978-84, assoc. prof., 1984—; lectr. health care mktg. Harvard Sch. Pub. Health, 1976-90, lectr. master's program health policy and mgmt., 1979-87; asst. prof. Boston U. Sch. Pub. Health, Sch. Medicine, 1981-84, assoc. prof., 1984—; mem. exec. edn. faculty Harvard Grad. Sch. Edn., 1991-94; chmn. dept. Boston U., 1988-91; cons., rschr. Prudential Ctr. Health Rsch., Atlanta, 1995-96; cons. Kaiser Family Found., Project HOPE East European Health Mgmt. Project, Am. Coll. Healthcare Execs., Am. Coll. Rheumatology, Maine Atty. Gen.'s Office, Found. for Informed Med. Decision Making, Hebrew Rehab. Ctr. for Aged, Curative Technologies, GTE. Co-author: Marketing for Health Care Organization, 1987; mem. editl. bd. Health Svcs. Mgmt. Rsch., Strategies for Healthcare Excellence; contbr. numerous articles to profl. jours. Mem. Fin. Com. New Eng. Organ Bank, Newton, Mass., 1995—; mem. faculty Project HOPE, Millwood, Va., 1995—; bd. dirs. Temple Beth Elohim, Wellesley, Mass., 1992-94; bd. mem. Acad. Ednl. Devel., 1990—; pro-bono cons. to bd. dirs. Jewish Cmty. Ctr., Newton, 1984—. Customer svc. award named for her, Jewish Cmty. Ctr., Newton; recipient Philip Kotler award for excellence in health care mktg. Am. Mktg. Assn., 1995; named Health Care Marketer of Yr., Am. Coll. Health Care Mktg., 1985. Mem. Soc. Health Care Planning and Mktg. Am. Hosp. Assn. (bd. dirs. 1985-87, pres.-elect 1987-88, pres. 1988-89). Home: 68 Bay State Rd Weston MA 02193 Office: Boston U 595 Commonwealth Ave Boston MA 02215

CLARKE, SUE ELLIN GRIER, women's health and neonatal nurse; b. Hagerstown, Md., Nov. 13, 1958; d. Jack B. and Audrey (Sprecher) Grier; m. Robert A. Clarke, Sept. 29, 1984; children: Robert Ryan, Lindsay Kathryn. Student, Hood Coll., 1977; AA with honors, Hagerstown Jr. Coll., 1978; BSN with honors, U. Md., Balt., 1980. Internat. cert. lactation cons. Clin. nurse neonatal ICU, perinatal researcher Meml. Med. Ctr.-Children's Hosp., Long Beach, Calif., 1981-85; sr. staff nurse, charge nurse neonatal ICU/newborn nursery George Washington U. Hosp., Washington, 1985-87; staff and charge nurse spl. care nursery Shady Grove Adventist Hosp., Rockville, Md., 1987-88; sr. clin. nurse II, quality assurance rep. Sibley Meml. Hosp., Washington, 1988-93; vis. nurse Adventist Home Health Svc. Inc., 1991-95; patient care coord. HomeCall Inc., 1994-96; advice nurse supr. Kaiser Permanente, Fair Oaks, VA. With USPHS, 1979. Recipient 1993 Hagerstown Jr. Coll. Alumni Assn. Citation Award for Community Svc. Mem. Nat. Assn. Neonatal Nurses,Washington Met. Assn. Neonatal Nurses, Assn. Women's Health, Obstetrics and Neonatal Nurses, Sigma Theta Tau, Phi Theta Kappa. Home: 17121 Whites Rd Poolesville MD 20837-2236

CLARKE, THOMAS PASCHAL, III, psychiatrist; b. Birmingham, Ala., May 4, 1923; s. Thomas Paschal Jr. and Mary Francis (White) C.; m. Lucille Musgrave; children: William Paschal, Craig Musgrave, Lisa Clarke Bonner. BA, Rice U., 1947; MD, U. Tex., Galveston, 1947. Diplomate Am. Bd. Psychiatry and Neurology. Intern Hermann Hosp. of Tex. Med. Ctr., Houston, 1947-48; resident Colo. Psychopathic Hosp., Denver, 1948-50; pvt. practice psychiatry Houston, 1954—; cons. Hermann Hosp., Methodist Hosp.; mem. med. staff St. Luke's Episcopal Hosp., Heights Hosp., Rosewood Hosp.; assoc. clin. prof. psychiatry Baylor U., U. Tex. at Houston. Mem. founding bd. trustees Houston/Galveston Psychoanalytic Found.; bd. trustees, pres. Mus. Med. Sci., Houston, 1977—, pres., 1978-80; bd. trustees Found. for Houston Psychiatric Soc., 1989—; mem. dist. rev. com. Tex. Bd. Med. Examiners. Capt. U.S. Army, 1949-53, Korea. Fellow So. Psychiat. Soc. (life), Am. Acad. Child Psychiatry, Am. Psychiat. Assn. (life), Nat. Inst. Mental Health; mem. Cen. Neuro-Psychiat. Assn., Houston Psychiat. Soc. (pres.), Tex. Soc. Psychiat. Physicians (v.p.), Houston Adolescent Psychiatry (pres.), Tex. Med. Assn. (cons. to coms.), Houston Acad. Medicine (past pres.), Harris County Med. Soc. (past officer), Doctors Club (v.p. bd. dirs.), April Sound Club. Republican. Methodist. Office: # 475 952 Echo Ln Houston TX 77024

CLARKIN, JOHN FRANCIS, health care management executive; b. Atlantic City, Dec. 30, 1936; s. John Francis and Agnes (Winterholer) C.; B.S. in Bus. Adminstrn., Rider Coll., 1959; postgrad. Temple U.; m. Dorothy Louise Piffath; 1 son, John F. Mktg. rep. Scott Paper Co., Indpls., 1960-62; systems and mktg. rep. Burroughs Corp., Phila., 1962-67; dir. Mid-Atlantic health care ops. mgmt. practice Coopers & Lybrand, Phila., 1967-92; v.p. corp. fin. svcs. Crozer-Keystone Health System, Upland, Pa., 1992—; lead instr. speaker numerous meetings and seminars. Mem. Grand Oak Run Civic Assn., 1970—. With U.S. Army, 1959. Rotary Club grantee, 1955-59; cert. mgmt. cons. Mem. Inst. Mgmt. Cons., Hosp. Mgmt. Systems Soc., Hosp. Fin. Mgmt. Assn., Med. Group Mgmt. Assn., Am. Hosp. Assn. Republican. Roman Catholic. Clubs: Vesper, Pickering Racquet. Author: Topics in Health Care Financing, 1982; (with others) Handbook of Health Care Accounting and Finance, 1982, 89, Billing Systems, 2 vols., 1982, 89, Managing Accounts Receivable, 1990; contbr. articles to profl. jours. Home: 1421 Grand Oak Ln West Chester PA 19380-5951 Office: Crozer-Keystone Health Sys 1 Med Ctr Blvd Chester PA 19013-3995

CLARK-RUBIN, LORNA JAYNE, psychiatrist. MD, Case Western Res. U., 1981. Diplomate in psychiatry, child and adolescent psychiatry Am. Bd. Psychiatry and Neurology. Intern Crozer Chester Med. Ctr., Upland, Pa., 1981-82; resident in psychiatry Hahnemann U., Phila., 1982-86, fellowship in child and adolescent psychiatry, 1986-88; psychiat. cons. Devereux Found., Malvern, Pa., 1988-90; pvt. practice psychiatrist Champlain Valley Psychiat. Assocs., Plattsburgh, N.Y., 1990—; med. staff, attending staff Champlain Valley Physicians Hosp. Med. Ctr., Plattsburgh. Mem. Am. Psychiat. Assn., Am. Assn. for Child and Adolescent Psychiatry. Office: 11 Hammond Ln Ste A Plattsburgh NY 12901

CLARKSON, JOCELYN ADRENE, medical technologist; b. Bennettsville, S.C., July 9, 1952; d. Henry Louis and Frankie Allene (Carter) C. BA in Biology, Columbia (S.C.) Coll., 1973; cert. med. tech., Presbyn. Hosp., Charlotte, N.C., 1975. Coll. tutor of Germanic language Columbia Coll., 1970-73, switchboard operator, 1972-73; lab aide Richland Meml. Hosp., Columbia, 1974, now, med. technologist; profl. model. Appeared (TV comms.) Back Porch Restaurant and Meat Market, 1992, (film) The Chasers; author: poems, compilation, short stories, Messages from Hijac, 1989. Mem. Am. Soc. Clin. Pathologists (assoc.), Assn. for Studies of Classical African Civilization, African Am. Resource Inst. Roman Catholic. Home: 201 H L Clarkson Rd Hopkins SC 29061-9723

CLARKSON, JOHN G., academic administrator, ophthalmologist; m. Diana Teasdale; children: Paige Black, David. BS, Princeton U.; MD, Miami Sch. Medicine, 1968. Intern U. Hosp., Boston; resident ophthalmology U. Miami/Jackson Meml. Med. Ctr., Fla.; opthalmic pathology, reginal and vitreous surgery fellow Johns Hopkins U., Balt.; chmn. dept. ophthalmology, dir. Bascom Palmer Eye Inst.; sr. v.p. med. affairs, dean Sch. Medicine U. Miami, 1995—. Mem. Am. Bd. Ophthalmology (bd. dirs.), Am. Acad. Ophthalmology, Retina Soc., Club Jules Gonin, Macula Soc. Office: U Miami Sch Medicine PO Box 016099 (R699) 1600 NW 10th Ave Miami FL 33101*

CLARKSON, JOHN J., dentist, dental association administrator; b. Mullingar, Ireland, Oct. 23, 1941; m. Marie Bannon; children; Ruth, Robert, Alan. B Dental Surgery, Nat. U. Ireland, Dublin, 1964; PhD, Nat. U. Ireland, Cork, 1987. Asst. in gen. dental practice Dartford, Kent, Eng., 1964, London, Eng., 1964-65; dental surgeon in gen. dental practice Armagh,

No. Ireland, 1965-67; dental surgeon Dublin Health Auth./Eastern Health Bd., Ireland, 1968-79; acting. sr. dental surgeon Crumlin Area, Dublin, 1979-80; dental officer Dept. Health, Dublin, 1980-82, dep. chief dental officer, 1982-90; exec. dir. Internat. Assn. for Dental Rsch./Am. Assn. for Dental Rsch., Washington, 1990—; hon. lectr. in community dental health and preventive dentistry Trinity Coll., Dublin, 1983-90; mem. WHO Collaborating Ctr. for Health Svcs. Rsch., U. Coll., Cork, Ireland, 1987-90; mem. steering coms. Nat. Survey Children's Dental Health, Ireland, 1984, Nat. Survey Adult Dental Health, Ireland, 1988; sci. advisor Dental Health Found., Ireland; mem. radiation adv. com. Nuclear Energy Bd., Ireland, 1987-90; cons. European Community, France, Britain, Ireland. 1989-90, WHO, 1989—. Contbr. articles to Jour. Irish Dentistry, Jour. Dental Rsch., others; presenter papers in field. Sec. Oatlands Coll. Parents Coun., 1987-90. Coun. Europe fellow, 1981. Fellow Royal Acad. Medicine (Ireland); mem. ADA, AAAS, Am. Soc. Assn. Execs., Greater Washington Soc. Assn. Execs., Internat. Assn. for Dental Rsch., European Orgn. for Caries Rsch., Irish Dental Assn. (pub. dental officers com., sci. com., rep. staff negotiations bd. on conciliation and arbitration), Irish Soc. Dentistry for Children (pres. 1989), Brit. Assn. for Study Community Dentistry, Brit. Dental Assn., Fedn. Dentaire Internat. (cons. 1988-90), Local Govt. and Pub. Svcs. Union (sec. dental br.), Blainroe Golf Club, St. Mary's Lawn Tennis Club, Carderok Swim and Tennis Club. Home: 12400 Bobbink Ct Potomac MD 20854-3005 Office: American Assoc for Dental Rsch 1619 Duke St Alexandria VA 22314

CLARKSON, NANCY ELAINE, nursing educator; b. Rochester, N.Y., Mar. 13, 1949; d. Irvin E. and Lucille O. (Weigert) Peitscher; m. Stanley Clarkson, June 29, 1974; children: Jeffrey, Lindsey. BS in Nursing, Keuka Coll., 1971; MEd in Nursing, Columbia U., 1979. Instr. nursing Highland Hosp. Sch. Nursing, Rochester, N.Y., 1974-77; dir. staff devel. Community Gen. Hosp. of Sullivan County, Liberty, N.Y., 1977-79; instr. nursing Keuka Coll., Keuka Park, N.Y., 1981-82; adj. prof. nursing Community Coll. of the Finger Lakes, Canandaigua, N.Y., 1983—; asst. prof. nursing Finger Lakes C.C., Canandigua, N.Y., 1992—. Contbr. NSNA NCLEX-RN Rev., 1992. Vocat. Edn. Act grantee. Mem. Genesee Valley Nurses Assn. Office: Finger Lakes Community Coll 4355 Lakeshore Dr Canandaigua NY 14424-8347

CLARKSON, THOMAS BOSTON, comparative medicine educator; b. Decatur, Ga., June 13, 1931. DVM, U. Ga., 1954; Diploma, Am. Coll. Lab. Animal Medicine, 1963. Rsch. assoc. pharmacology and exptl. therapeutics sect. S. E. Massengill Co., 1954-57; from asst. to assoc. prof. exptl. medicine, dir. vivarium Wake Forest U., Winston-Salem, N.C., 1957-64, assoc. prof. lab. animal medicine, head dept., 1964-65, prof., chmn. dept. Bowman Gray sch. medicine, 1965—, dir. arteriosclerosis rsch. ctr., 1971-91, dir. comparative medicine clin. rsch. ctr., 1989—; mem. sci. adv. com. regional primate rsch. ctr. U. Wash., 1971—; mem. adv. com. Cerbrovascular Rsch. Ctr., 1973—; mem. com. vet. med. sci. NAS-Nat. Rsch. Coun., 1975—; chmn. arteriosclerosis, hypertension and lipid metabolism adv. com. Nat. Heart Lung & Blood Inst., 1983-85. Recipient Griffin award Am. Assn. Lab. Animal Sci., 1977, Albion O. Bernstein award N.Y. State Med. Soc., 1992; Duphar lectr. British Menopause Soc., 1993; Joseph Price orator Am. Ob-Gyn. Soc., 1993. Fellow Am. Soc. Primatology, Acad. Behavioral Med. Rsch., Soc. Behavioral Medicine; mem. NAS (mem. clin. sci. panel study nat. needs biomedical and behavioral rsch. pers. com. and task force animal models atherosclerosis 1976—), Am. Heart Assn. (mem. com. coronary artery lesions and myocardial infarctions 1970—, chmn. task force rsch. animal use, vice-chmn. coun. arteriosclerosis 1979-81, chmn. 1981-83, G. Lyman Duff Meml. lectr. 1985, Award of Merit 1987, Lewis A. Conner Meml. lectr. 1991), Am. Assn. Advancement Lab. Animal Sci., Am. Assn. Pathologists, Am. Soc. Exptl. Pathology, Am. Vet. Medicine Assn. (Charles River prize 1978), Sigma Xi. Office: Wake Forest U Dept Comparative Medicine Medical Center Blvd Winston Salem NC 27157*

CLARKSON, THOMAS WILLIAM, toxicologist, educator; b. Eng., Aug. 1, 1932; came to U.S., 1957; s. William and Olive (Jackson) C.; m. Winifred Browne, Mar. 4, 1957; children: Ian, Jean, Ann. BSc, U. Manchester, 1953, PhD, 1956; Dr Medicine (hon.), U. Umea, Sweden, 1986. Sci. officer tox research unit Med. Research Council U.K., Carshalton, Surrey, 1962-64; sr. fellow polymer sci. Weizmann Inst. Sci., Rehovot, Israel, 1964-65; mem. faculty U. Rochester (N.Y.) Med. Sch., 1958—, prof. toxicology, 1971—, head div., 1980-86, J. Lowell Orbison Disting. Svc. Alumni prof., 1983—, dir. Environ. Health Scis. Ctr., 1986—; chmn. Dept. Environ. Medicine, 1992—; dir. NASA Ctr. Rsch. and Tng. in Space Environ. Health, 1991—. Mem. editorial bds. profl. jours.; author articles in field. Mem. Inst. Medicine of NAS, Permanent Commn. Internat. Assn. Occupational Health, Soc. Toxicology (Arnold J. Lehman award 1993), Brit. Pharm. Soc., Am. Soc. Pharmacology and Exptl. Therapeutics, Internat. Soc. for Trace Element Rsch. in Humans, Ramazzini Collegium, Polish Toxicology Soc. (hon.), La Academia Nacional de Medicina de Buenos Aires (hon. mem.). Office: Dept Environ Medicine U Rochester Med Sch Rochester NY 14642

CLARREN, STERLING KEITH, pediatrician; b. Mpls., Mar. 12, 1947; s. David Bernard and Lila (Reifel) C.; m. Sandra Gayle Bernstein, June 8, 1970; children: Rebecca Pia, Jonathan Seth. BA, Yale U., 1969; MD, U. Minn., 1973. Pediatric intern U. Wash. Sch. Medicine, Seattle, 1973-74, resident in pediatrics, 1974-77, asst. prof. dept. pediatrics, 1979-83, assoc. prof., 1983-88, prof., 1988, Robert A. Aldrich chair in pediatrics, 1989—; head divsn. congenital defects U. Wash. Sch. Medicine, 1987-95; dir. dept. congenital defects Children's Hosp. and Med. Ctr., Seattle, 1987-96, dir. fetal alcohol syndrome clinic Child Devel. and Mental Retardation Ctr. U. Wash., 1992—, dir. Fetal Alcohol Syndrome Network, 1995—; dir. infant inpatient svcs. Children's Hosp. & Med. Ctr., Seattle, 1996—. Contbr. articles to profl. jours.; patentee for orthosis to alter cranial shape. Cons. pediatrician Maxillofacial Rev. Bd., State of Wash., Seattle, 1984—, chmn. Health-Birth Defects Adv. Com., Olympia, 1980—; mem. gov.'s task force on FAS State of Wash., 1994-95; mem. fetal alcohol adv. com. Children's Trust Found., Seattle, 1988—; mem. adv. bd. Nat. Orgn. on Fetal Alcohol Syndrome; mem. fetal alcohol com. Inst. Medicine, NAS, 1994-95. Rsch. grantee Nat. Inst. Alcohol Abuse & Alcoholism, 1982—, Ctrs. for Disease Control, 1992—. Fellow AAAS; mem. Am. Acad. Pediatrics, Soc. for Pediatric Rsch., Teratology Soc., Rsch. Soc. on Alcoholism (pres. fetal alcohol study group 1993), Am. Cleft Palate Assn., N.Y. Acad. Scis. Home: 8515 Paisley Dr NE Seattle WA 98115-3944 Office: Children's Hosp and Med Ctr Divsn Congenital Defects PO Box C-5371 Seattle WA 98105

CLARYSSE, ALBERT MAR, oncologist; b. Izegem, Belgium, July 13, 1936; m. Brigitte Caubergs, Oct. 27, 1978; children: Nathalie, Barbara. MD, U. Louvain, Belgium, 1962; postgrad., U. Paris, 1969. Diplomate Am. Bd. Internal Medicine. Intern U. Manitoba, Winnipeg, Can., 1961-62; resident in internal medicine U. Wis., Madison, 1963-64, U. Minn., Mpls., 1964-66; fellow hematology U. Utah, Salt Lake City, 1966-68; fellow oncology Inst. Cancerologie, Villejuif, France, 1968-69; rsch. assoc. oncology U. Toronto, Can., 1969-71; asst. prof. oncology U. Utah, Salt Lake City, 1971-73; chief div. med. oncology St. Jans Hosp., Brugge, Belgium, 1974—; prof. St. Jans Sch. Nursing, Brugge, 1985—. Author: (Dutch) Breast Cancer, 1992, 2d edit. 1996; co-author: Cancer Chemotherapy, 1976; contbr. articles to profl. jours. Active Regional Cancer Ctr. West Flanders, Belgium, 1985—. Fellow ACP; mem. Am. Soc. Clin. Oncology, European Soc. Med. Oncology, Dutch Soc. Oncology, Belgian Soc. Med. Oncology (founding pres. 1977), Belgian Soc. Senology, Belgian Soc. Cancer Rsch., European Orgn. Cancer Rsch., European Soc. Senology,. Home: Augustijnenrei 3, Brugge 8000, Belgium Office: St Jan Hospital, Rudders Hove 10, Brugge 8000, Belgium

CLAUSE, HARRY PAUL, thoracic surgeon; b. Lynchburg, Va., May 2, 1930; s. Harry Paul and Mayme Ruth (Slaughter) C.; m. Mary Anne Harris, Mar. 14, 1992; children: H. Paul III, Sandra Lee, William Carey. AA, Mars Hill (N.C.) Coll., 1949; BS, Wake Forest U., 1951; MD, Johns Hopkins U., 1955. Diplomate Am. Bd. Thoracic Surgery, Am. Bd. Surgery. Intern Jefferson Davis Hosp., Houston, 1955-56; surg. resident Baylor Coll. Medicine, Houston, 1956-57, 59-61; chief thoracic surg. resident Charlotte (N.C.) Meml. Hosp., 1961-63; pvt. practice thoracic surgery Roanoke, Va., 1963-94; med. dir. Alliant Techsystems, Radford, Va., 1994—. Founding mem. Bapt. Med.-Dental Fellowship, Memphis; vol. missionary surgeon So. Bapt. Hosps., Gaza, 1974, 80, Yemen Arab Republic, 1980; mem. ch. choir, deacon Bapt. Ch. With USPHS, 1957-59; capt. U.S. Navy, 1985-94. Fellow ACS; mem. Am. Coll. Occupl. and Environ. Medicine, So. Thoracic Surg. Assn., Johns Hopkins Med.-Surg. Assn., Michael E. DeBakey Internat. Cardiovascular Soc., Elks, Phi Beta Kappa. Home: 1709 Kingston Cir Bedford VA 24523 Office: Alliant Techsystems Box 1 Radford VA 24141-0100

CLAUSEN, JANET M(AXINE), women's health nurse; b. Cherokee, Iowa, Sept. 16, 1959; d. Ervin A. and Florence M. (Bumann) Miesner; 1 child, Chase James. Grad., St. Lukes Sch. Nursing, Sioux City, Iowa, 1981. RN, Iowa, Colo.; cert. BLS, neonatal resuscitation, inpatient obstetrics. Float RN Horn Meml. Hosp., Ida Grove, Iowa, 1981-83; nurse ob. Sioux Valley Meml. Hosp., Cherokee, 1983-85; coord. ob. St. Thomas Moore Hosp., Canon City, Colo., 1985-91; staff nurse labor and delivery St. Mary's Hosp., Grand Junction, Colo., 1991-93; charge nurse, surg. asst. Colorado West Woman Care, Grand Junction, Colo., 1993—.

CLAUSEN, JERRY LEE, psychiatrist; b. Wausau, Wis., Nov. 5, 1939; s. Douglas William and Florence Jean (Amidon) C.; m. Nancy Eileen Longdon, Aug. 3, 1962; children: Keith Russell, Pamela Dawn. BA, Wesleyan U., Middletown, Conn., 1961; MD, Albany Med. Coll., N.Y., 1965. Dilomate Am. Bd. Psychiatry and Neurology with qualification in Addiction Psychiatry; cert. Am. Soc. Addiction Medicine, N.Y. State Alcoholism Counselor. Psychiatry intern Upstate Med. Ctr., Syracuse, N.Y., 1965-66; psychiatric resident Upstate Med. Ctr., 1966-67, 69-71, asst. attending, 1971-72, attending, 1972-80; staff psychiatrist Onondaga Mental Health Clinic, Syracuse, 1971-72; courtesy staff Benjamin Rush Psychiatric Ctr., Syracuse, 1971-84, active staff, 1984—; pvt. practice psychiatry Syracuse, 1971—; clin. asst. prof. SUNY, 1972—; staff psychiatrist Onondaga Pastoral Counseling Ctr., Syracuse, 1971-73, 81—, psychiatric dir., 1973-81; cons. psychiatrist Loretto Rest Geriatric Ctr., Syracuse, 1972-74. Tchr. First Universalist Ch., Syracuse, 1966—. Lt. comdr. USN, 1967-69. Fellow Am. Psychiat. Assn. (chmn. ins. mktg. com. 1979-88); mem. Onondaga County Med. Soc., N.Y. State Med. Soc. Universalist-Unitarian. Office: 300 Burnet Ave Syracuse NY 13203-2302

CLAUSEN, ROBERT WILLIAM, allergist, immunologist, internist; b. Englewood, N.J., June 18, 1947; s. Richard William and Elsie Bertha (Kramer) C.; m. Barbara Ann Kraemer, Aug. 3, 1975; 1 child, Amalie Kaye. BS, Valparaiso (Ind.) U., 1969; MedB, B in Surgery, Kasturba Med. Coll., Manipal, South India, 1974; fifth pathway cert., Rutgers U., 1975. Diplomate Am. Bd. Internal Medicine, Am. Bd. Allergy and Immunology. Intern, then resident in internal medicine Henry Ford Hosp., Detroit, 1975-78, fellow in allergy and clin. immunology, 1978-80, sr. staff physician, instr., 1978-82; ptnr., physician The South Bend (Ind.) Clinic, 1982—; teaching attending physician family practice residency program Meml. Hosp., South Bend, 1983—, St. Joseph's Med. Ctr., South Bend, 1983—; clin. instr. dept. medicine U. Mich., Ann Arbor, 1980-83; guest asst. prof. dept. biol. scis. U. Notre Dame, Ind., 1984—; clin. asst. prof. dept. medicine Ind. U. Sch. Medicine, 1986—, course dir., South Bend, 1987—; mem. Speaker's Bur., Vellore Christian Med. Coll. and Hosp., 1988—. Contbr. articles to profl. jours. Bd. dirs. North Cen. Ind. chpt. Am. Lung Assn., South Bend, 1984—, chmn. program work com., 1988; bd. dirs. Fischoff Chamber Music Assn., South Bend, 1986-88, vol. 1988—; mem. president's adv. coun. Valparaiso U., 1984—, chmn. med. alumni assn., 1983—; mem. AIDS Task Force St. Joseph County, South Bend, 1985—; active internat. student host family program U. Notre Dame. Recipient Disting. Alumni award Kasturba Med. Coll., 1989; grantee NSF. Fellow Am. Coll. Physicians (gov.'s adv. council Ind. chpt. 1985-87, program com. 1985-86, 89-90), Am. Acad. Allergy and Immunology (insect allergy com, Hymenoptera Sting Fatality com.), Am. Coll. Allergy and Immunology (stinging insect com.); mem. AMA, Ind. Med. Soc., Mich. Allergy Soc. (program com. 1985—), Nat. Hospice Orgns., Clin. Immunology Soc., Lutheran Acad. Scholarship, Phi Delta Epsilon. Home: 51194 Lilac Rd South Bend IN 46628-9384 Office: The South Bend Clinic 211 N Eddy St South Bend IN 46617-2808

CLAUSER, ANGELA FRANCES, medical surgical, pediatrics and geriatrics nurse; b. Leavenworth, Kans., June 25, 1955; d. Donald F. Sr. and Agnes Angela (Forge) C. AA, Kansas City (Kans.) Jr. Coll., 1984; BSN, Pitts. State U., 1986. RN, Kans.; cert. provider CPR, Am. Heart Assn. Sec. U.S. Army, Ft. Leavenworth, Kans., 1978, 79-80, USAF Acad., Colorado Springs, Colo., 1981-82, VA, Leavenworth, 1982-84; staff nurse St. John's Hosp., Leavenworth, 1989—, unit edn. coord., 1995—. Mem. Nurses Svc. Orgn., Pitts. State U. Alumni Assn., Kans. City Jr. Coll. Alumni Assn.

CLAUSMAN, GILBERT JOSEPH, medical librarian; b. Los Angeles, Nov. 8, 1921; s. Peter Joseph and Lila (Mason) C. A.B., Willamette U., 1947; B.S., Columbia U., 1948, M.S., 1952. Med. librarian N.Y. Acad. Medicine, N.Y.C., 1948-55; med. librarian NYU Med. Ctr., N.Y.C., 1955-86, librarian emeritus, 1987—; cons. Milton Helpern Library Legal Medicine, 1963-88. Served with USN, 1942-45. Mem. Med. Libr. Assn. (pres. 1977-78), Archons of Colophon, N.Y. Acad. Medicine, Acad. Health Info. Profls. (Disting. mem. emeritus). Home: 6 Cobble Hill Rd Westport CT 06880-2915

CLAUSSEN, LELA MAY, hospital program administrator, educator; b. Kearney, Nebr., June 20, 1935; d. Carl John Sr. and Anna May (Crow) Cornelius; m. Dwayne N. Claussen, Sr., June 3, 1960 (dec. June 1990); children: Joseph, John, Le Ann, Jay, Sarah. Diploma, Good Samaritan Sch. Practical Nursing, 1954; cert. in practical nursing, U. Wyo., 1961, BSN, 1964. RN, Kans., Calif.; cert. pub. health nurse, Calif. Gen. practical nurse, staff nurse DePaul Hosp., Cheyenne, Wyo., 1956-64; staff nurse, head nurse, house supr., DON Ivinson Meml. Hosp., Laramie, Wyo., 1961-69; instr. in nursing U. Wyo. Coll. Nursing, Laramie, 1964-66; emergency rm. nurse St. John Hosp., Salina, Kans., 1970-71; ICU, obstet. nurse St. Vincent Hosp., Santa Fe, 1971-73; staff nurse, continuing edn. developer, DON Alpine Meadows Hosp., Steamboat Springs, Colo., 1974-78; DON Routt County Meml. Hosp., Steamboat Springs, Colo., 1974-78; staff nurse, infection control, DON Warnerview Convalescent Hosp., Alturas, Calif., 1978-83; charge nurse Modoc County Med. Ctrs., Cedarville, Calif., 1978-83; head nurse adolescents Larned (Kans.) State Hosp., 1986; lead nurse geropsych., asst. dir. nursing edn., charge nurse Osawatomie (Kans.) State Hosp., 1988, 89; psychiat. nurse, counselor, case mgr., partial hospitalization program nurse Franklin County Mental Health Ctr., Ottawa, Kans., 1991; program dir., Transitions Ctr. Geropsychiatry Cushing Hosp., Leavenworth, Kans., 1993—; writer ann. and quar. MDS Mental Health-Long Term Care, Bedford Nursing Ctr., Gardner, Kans., 1993; mem. state adv. com. Osawatomie State Hosp., 1995-96; faculty advisor Nu Upsilon Omega, U. Wyo., Laramie, 1964, 65, 66; mem. adv. bd. Sch. Practical Nursing, Laramie, 1966-69, Ottawa Retirement Plaza, 1992-93; co-founder Coun. Cmty. Health Agys., Laramie, 1968, Hap Crawford Nurses Assn., Alturas, 1981, 82, 83; lectr. in field. Mem., sec., pres. Modoc Joint Unified Sch. Dist., Alturas, 1980-83; mem. Calif. Sch. Bds., 1980-83; mem. adv. bd. Rainbow for Girls, Alturas, 1981, 82; organist numerous chs., 1950—. Grantee, USPH/Children's Bur., 1965, Grad. Sch. Nursing, N.Y. Med. Coll.; recipient Outstanding Svc. award Modoc Joint Unified Sch. Dist., 1984. Mem. U. Wyo. Alumni Assn., Kearney H.S. Alumni Assn., Skilton Music Club (pres. 1991-92), Order Ea. Star, Sigma Theta Tau. Republican. Home: 2707 Broadway Ter Leavenworth KS 66048

CLAVIEN, PIERRE-ALAIN, physician, researcher; b. Geneva, Switzerland, Nov. 23, 1957; came to U.S., 1994; s. Pierre and Georgette (Perrochon) C.; m. Sylvie M. Buchs, Oct. 16, 1988; children: Aurelie, Caroline. MD, Geneva U., 1982; PhD, U. Toronto, 1991. Resident dept. surgery Basel (Switzerland) U., 1982-87; fellow divsn. hepatosiliary surgery & liver transplantation U. Toronto, Can., 1991-93; resident dept. surgery Basel (Switzerland) U., Durham, N.C., 1982-87; fellow divsn. hepatobiliary surgery & liver transplantation U. Toronto, Durham, N.C., Can., 1991-93; asst. prof. surgery Duke U. Med. Ctr., Durham, N.C., 1994-95, assoc. prof. surgery, 1995—, dir. liver transplant program, 1994—, chief hepatobiliary surgery, 1996—. Editor: Medical Care of the Liver Transplant Patient, 1996; contbr. more than 60 articles to profl. jours. Grantee NIH, 1990-95. Fellow ACS; mem. numerous med. socs. in U.S. and Europe. Office: Duke U Med Ctr Dept Surgery PO Box 3247 Durham NC 27710

CLAY, LUCIUS DUBIGNON, III, surgeon, educator; b. Tampa, Fla., Oct. 11, 1948; s. Lucius Dubignon Jr. and Betty Rose (Commander) C.; m. Kathryn Ann Nay, Sept. 10, 1981; children: Lucius Dubignon IV, Geraldine Margaret. BA in History, Washington and Lee U., 1971; MD, U. Va., 1979. Surg. intern NYU/Bellevue Hosp., N.Y.C., 1979-80; surg. resident St. Luke's Hosp., N.Y.C., 1980-84; surg. fellow Ochsner Clinic, New Orleans, 1984-85; attending physician Princeton (N.J.) Med. Ctr., 1985—; clin. asst. prof. surgery Robert Wood Johnson Med. Sch., New Brunswick, N.J., 1985—; pvt. practice Princeton Surg. Assocs., 1985—. Office: Princeton Surg Assocs 281 Witherspoon St Princeton NJ 08540

CLAY, MARGARET LEONE, community psychologist, consultant; b. St. Joseph, Mo., Oct. 23, 1923. BS with distinction, U. Mich., 1956, MS, 1958, PhD, 1962. Teaching fellow psychology dept. U. Mich., Ann Arbor, 1958-59, lectr., 1963-71, rsch. asst., 1956-60, asst. rsch. psychologist, 1960-62, assoc. rsch. psychologist Mental Health Rsch. Inst., 1962-82, asst. dir., 1965-68, asst. prof. psychiatry dept. Med. Sch., 1975-82, asst. prof. emeritus, 1982—; pvt. practice human svcs. cons. Hillman, Mich., 1982—; mem. faculty extension svc. U. Mich. Sch. Pub. Health, Ann Arbor, 1969-72; mem. vis. faculty Rutgers U. Summer Sch. Alcohol Studies, New Brunswick, N.J., 1972-76; mem. bd. rsch. advisors Walden U., Naples, Fla., 1979—; bd. dirs. Thunder Bay Cmty. Health Svcs., 1983—, chmn. bd., 1993-95. Contbr. articles to profl. jours. Mem. Gov.'s Sect. 20 Rev. Com., Lansing, Mich., 1976; mem. Gov.'s Task Force on Drinking Drive Problem, Lansing, 1970-74; bd. mem. Gov.'s Adv. Commn. on Substance Abuse, Lansing, 1976-83; coun. mem. Statewide Health Coord. Coun., Lansing, 1977-83; mem. Mich. Coun. on Crime and Delinquency, Lansing, 1979—, pres., 1981-83; bd. mem. Mich. Coalition on Substance Abuse, 1986—, Shelter, Inc., 1989-92, N.E. Mich. Cmty. Partnership for Prevention, 1991—, No. Regional Acad./Cmty. Health System, 1993—; bd. dirs. Northeast Mich. Comm. Mental Health Bd., 1993—, chmn., 1996—. Recipient Disting. Svc. award Mich. Alcohol and Addiction Assn., 1977, Outstanding Svc. award Mich. Prevention Assn., 1993, Award for Outstanding Svc. in Prevention, 1993; named Vol. of Yr. Nat. Coun. on Alcoholism, Mich., 1985. Mem. APHA, APA (vis. psychologist 1976-78), Am. Assn. Correctional Psychologists (sec.-treas. 1975-77), N.Am. Assn. Alcohol Problems (program chmn. 1970-72), Alcohol and Drug Problems Assn. N.Am. (chmn. rsch. com. 1973-75, program chmn. 1976-78, bd. dirs. 1980-82, Outstanding Svc. award 1978), Mich. Pub. Health Assn. (hon. life, chmn. mental health div. 1969-70). Office: PO Box 251 Hillman MI 49746-0251

CLAYCOMB, CECIL KEITH, biochemist, educator; b. Twin Falls, Idaho, Oct. 19, 1920; s. Cecil R. and Frilla E. (Reams) C.; m. Elizabeth Jane Gregg, Mar. 10, 1943; children: John K., Mary E. B.S., U. Oreg., 1947, M.S., 1948, Ph.D., 1951. Prof., head dept. biochemistry Dental Sch. U. Oreg., Portland, 1951-82, dir. minority recruitment, 1971-74, asst. to pres./dir. minority student affairs, 1974-84, coordinator basic sci. curriculum, 1951-77, chmn. admissions com., 1959-69, emeritus, 1985—; emeritus prof. biochemistry Oreg. Health Scis. U., 1986—. Contbr. articles to sci. jours. Served to 1st lt. AUS, 1943-46. Scholar dental bd. New South Wales, Sydney, Australia, 1970. Mem. Am. Chem. Soc., Internat. Assn. Dental Research, AAAS, Res. Officers Assn., Sigma Xi. Home: 3326 SW 13th Ave Portland OR 97201-2922

CLAYDON, CHARLES THOMAS, physician; b. Mt. Vernon, N.Y., Apr. 25, 1935; s. Frank Joseph and Ethel Catherine (Wynne) C. BA, Coll. Holy Cross, 1956; MD, Johns Hopkins Med. Sch., 1956-60. Diplomate Am. Bd. Surgery. Intern Johns Hopkins Hosp., Balt., 1960-61; resident Grady Meml. Hosp., Atlanta, 1963-67; chief of surgery Martha's Vineyard Hosp., Oak Bluffs, Mass., 1967—; clin. assoc. Mass. Gen. Hosp., Boston, 1969—, Harvard Med. Sch., Boston, 1969—; trustee, dir. Martha's Vineyard Hosp. Found., Oak Bluffs, Mass., 1986—. Capt. U.S. Army, 1962-63. Home: 54 Cooke St Edgartown MA 02539 Office: PO Box 1166 Oak Bluffs MA 02557-1166

CLAYPOOL, NANCY, social worker; b. Monterey, Calif., Aug. 6, 1957; d. Harold Herbert and Nancy Jeanne (Klohe) C.; 1 child, James Paul. BA in Social Welfare cum laude, San Francisco State U., 1980; M Social Work, U. Calif., Berkeley, 1985. Program developer Women's Found., San Francisco, 1984-85; foster care coord., house supr. Charila Svcs. for Girls, San Francisco, 1985-87; therapist Sierra Clinic, San Francisco, 1987-88; clin. social worker Youth Homes, Inc., Walnut Creek, Calif., 1988-90; homebased early childhood devel. tchr. Thurgood Marshall Family Resource Ctr., Oakland, Calif., 1990-92; psychiat. social worker Eden Med. Ctr., Castro Valley, Calif., 1992-94; chief clinician, primary therapist Transitions Geropsychiatry Alameda (Calif.) Hosp., 1994-96; program dir. Transitions Geopsychiatry Alameda (Calif) Hosp., 1996—. Contbr. articles to profl. publs. Mem. Alameda County Mental Health Bd., 1992—, chair, 1993-94, vice chair, 1994-95. Named Regional Clinician of Yr., Horizon Mental Health Svcs., 1994; Health-Social Networking grantee, 1984. Mem. Nat. Assn. Social Workers, Internat. Platform Assn. (appointee 1995). Home: 3946 35th Ave Oakland CA 94619-1435

CLAYTON, FRANCES ELIZABETH, cytologist, scientist, educator; b. Texarkana, Tex., Nov. 6, 1922; d. Carl C. and Louise (Heath) C. AA, Texarkana Coll., 1942; BA, Tex. Womens U., 1944; MA, U. Tex., 1947, PhD, 1951. Instr. U. Ark., Fayetteville, 1950-51, mem. faculty, 1954—, prof. zoology, 1961-87, prof. emeritus, 1987—; instr. U. Tex., Austin, 1951-52; Rosalie B. Hite Postdoctoral fellow U. Tex., 1952-53, research scientist, 1953-54; vis. colleague in genetics U. Hawaii, 1963-64; researcher cytology species of Drosophila; prin. investigator grants Atomic Energy Commn., 1955-60, NIH, 1961-66, NSF, 1980-82. Contrbr. to Handbook of Genetics, vol. 3, 1975, Genetics and Biology of Drosphila, vol. 3E, 1986, also articles to tech. jours. Mem. Evolution Soc. Home: 1923 E Joyce St Apt 362 Fayetteville AR 72703-5174 Office: Univ Ark Dept Biol Scis Scen # 601 Fayetteville AR 72701

CLAYTON, LAWRENCE OTTO, marriage and family therapist; b. Fallon, Nev., Mar. 24, 1945; s. Lawrence Otto and Nathalie E. (Gow) C.. BS summa cum laude, Tex. Wesleyan Coll., Ft. Worth, Tex., 1976; postgrad., Emory U., Atlanta, 1976-77; MDiv, Tex. Christian U., 1978; PhD, Tex. Woman's U., 1983. Cert. alcohol and drug counselor, clin. supr. group psychotherapist, program dir. Pastor First United Meth. Ch., Maypearl, Tex., 1977-78, Godley United Meth. Ch., Tex., 1978-79, United Meth. Ch., Belton, 1979-80, Edge Park United Meth. Ch., Ft. Worth, 1980-81; exec. dir. Johnson County Mental Health Clinic, Cleburne, Tex., 1981-83; adminstr. United Meth. Counseling Svcs., 1983-88; cons. Roserock Med. Network, Oklahoma City, 1987-88; prog. coord. The Greenleaf Ctr., Oklahoma City, 1989-90; clin. dir. Fountainview Ctr., El Reno, Okla., 1990; exec. dir. Systemic Orgnl. Learning Through Vital Edn., Oklahoma City, 1989-94; with Systematic Orgnl. Learning Through Vital Edn., Piedmont, Okla., 1994-96; ret., 1996; cons. Great Plains Correctional Facility, Hinton, Okla., 1993—; adj. prof. Mid-Am. Bible Coll., Oklahoma city, 1991—, Bacone Coll., Muskogee, Okla., 1992-94. Author: Assessment and Management of the Suicidal Adolescent, 1990, Coping with Depression, 1990, Coping with a Drug Abusing Parent, 1991, Coping with Being Gifted, 1991, Coping with a Learning Disability, 1992, Careers in Psychology, 1992, Coping with Sports Injuries, 1992, Designer Drugs, 1993, Barbiturates and Other Depressants, 1994, Amphetamines and Other Stimulants, 1994, The Professional Alcohol and Drug Counselor Supervisor's Handbook, 1993, All You Need to Know About Sports Injuries, 1994, Steroids, 1995, Drug Testing, 1996, Coping With Drug Testing, 1996, Tranquilizers, 1996, Working Together Against Drug Addiction, 1996, Drugs & Drug Testing, 1996, others; assoc. editor Family Perspective, 1987-95; columnist Woman's Weekly, 1991-93, Growthline, 1992-95. Sec., Okla. Coun. on Family Rels., Oklahoma City, 1985-86. With U.S. Army, 1962-68. Named Okla. Drug and Alcohol Counselor of the Yr. Mem. Okla. Inst. Adult Children of Alcoholics (pres. 1987-91), Okla. Soc. for Sci. Study of Sex (pres. 1986-88), Okla. Drug and Alcohol Profl. Counselors Cert. Bd. (vice chmn. 1988-90, pres. 1990-95, counselor of yr., 1994). Republican.

CLAYTON, PAULA JEAN, psychiatry educator; b. St. Louis, Dec. 1, 1934; 3 children. B.S., U. Mich., 1956; M.D., Washington U., St. Louis, 1960. Intern St. Luke's Hosp., St. Louis, 1960-61; asst. resident and chief resident psychiatry Barnes and Renard Hosp., St. Louis, 1961-65; from instr. to assoc. prof. psychiatry Sch. Medicine Washington U., 1965-74, prof., 1974—; prof., head dept. psychiatry U. Minn. Med. Sch., Mpls., 1980—; dir. tng. and rsch., 1975; dir. psychiat. inpatient svc. Barnes and Renard Hosp., 1975-81. Author 4 books; contbr. numerous articles to profl. pubs. Fellow Am. Psychiat. Assn.; mem. Psychiat. Rsch. Soc., Assn. Rsch. in Nervous and

Mental Diseases, Am. Psychopath. Assn., Soc. Biol. Psychiatry, Am. Coll. Neuropsypharm. Office: U Minn Hosps & Clinic Box 77 Minneapolis MN 55455 also: U Minn Med Sch 420 Delaware St SE Minneapolis MN 55455-0374

CLAYTON, THOMAS STANFORD, IV, health facility administrator; b. Highland Park, Mich., Sept. 19, 1944; s. Thomas Stanford III and Betty Lou (Richardson) C.; m. Jean Arnolda Wyndham, Oct. 9, 1970 (div. July 1995); 1 child, Lynda Katheryn. AA, Santa Monica Coll., 1966; BS in Medicine, U. Nebr., 1976; DS (hon.), USN, 1983. Enlisted USN, 1966, advanced through ranks, 1966-86; physician asst., substance abuse counselor Seaborne Hosp., Dover, N.H., 1986-89; mgr. occupl. medicine clinic Ctr. Occupl. and Environ. Mental Health, Seabrook, N.H., 1990-94, Bus. Health Mgmt., Seabrook, 1994—. Contbr. short stories and poems to mags. Fellow Am. Acad. Physician Assts. (cert., bd. dirs. 1977-79, publ. com. 1980-81, editl. adv. bd. 1978-80), N.H. Soc. Physician Assts. (impairment contact com. chair 1994—), United Bikers Maine (York County dir. 1995-97). Shamanist. Home: 36 Tideview Dr Dover NH 03820 Office: Bus Health Mgmt PO Box 599 Hampton Falls NH 03844

CLAYTON, WINN R., medical technologist; b. Erwin, N.C., Oct. 11, 1950; s. Clearence Thomas and Ollie (Denning) C.; m. Donna Adams, Nov. 22, 1973; 1 child, Windy. BS, Barton Coll., 1975. Med. technologist Edgecombe Gen. Hosp., Tarboro, N.C., 1973-76, Warren Gen., Warrenton, N.C., 1976-77; tchr. Franklin County Schs., Louisburg, N.C., 1977-85; med. technologist, lab. sch. adminstr. Maria Parham Hosp., Henderson, N.C., 1989-95; tchr. Franklin County Schs., 1995—. Mem. Am. Med. Technologists, Am. Soc. Clin. Pathologists. Methodist. Home: 719 S Chestnut St Henderson NC 27536

CLEARFIELD, HARRIS REYNOLD, physician; b. Phila., Aug. 8, 1933; s. Samuel and Rae (Lewis) C.; m. Louise Libby, June 30, 1957; children: Andrea, Jonathan. BS, Franklin and Marshall Coll., 1955; MD, Jefferson Med. Coll., 1959. Intern Grad. Hosp. U. Pa., Phila., 1959-60, resident in internal medicine, 1960-62, resident in gastroenterology, 1962-63, mem. staff, 1963-72; mem. staff Episcopalian Hosp., Phila., 1967-72, head sect. gastroenterology, until 1972; sr. attending physician Phila. Gen Hosp., 1972-77; mem. faculty U. Pa. Med. Sch., Phila., 1963-72; clin. asst. prof. medicine Temple U. Med. Sch., Phila., 1967-72; dir. div. gastroenterology Hahnemann Hosp., Phila., 1972—, prof. medicine, 1972—; lectr., cons. Naval Regional Med. Ctr., Phila., 1976-78; sr. cons. Phila. Gen. Hosp., 1972-74; mem. gov.'s adv. com. of ACP, 1980-88; dir. Krancer Ctr. for Inflamatory Bowel Disease Rsch., 1985—. Author: (with Dinoso) Gastrointestinal Emergencies, 1979, (with Borowsky) Case Studies in Gastroenterology, 1989; editorial cons. Am. Jour. Proctology, 1976-86; contbr. articles to profl. jours. Chmn. sci. adv. bd. Nat. Found. Ileitis and Colitis, 1976-80, trustee, 1990—. Recipient Lindback award for excellence in teaching Phila. chpt. Nat. Found. Ileitis and Colitis, 1979, named Physician of Yr., 1980. Fellow ACP, Phila. Coll. Physicians; mem. Am. Gastroenterologic Assn., Bockus Internat. Soc. Gastroenterology (trustee, v.p., pres. 1993-95), Phila. Gastroenterology Group (pres. 1974-75), Am. Soc. Gastrointestinal Endoscopy, Am. Coll. Gastroenterology (gov. Ea. Pa. 1990-92, bd. trustees 1992—), Pa. Soc. Gastroenterology (pres. 1993-95), Delaware Valley Soc. Gastrointestinal Rsch. Forum, Pa. Med. Soc. (commn. on accreditation 1986-92), Phila. Med. Soc. (bd. dirs. 1996—). Home: 720 Oxford Rd Bala Cynwyd PA 19004-2112 Office: 230 N Broad St Philadelphia PA 19102-1121

CLEARY, BERYL BOARDMAN, nurse; b. Sayre, Pa., May 7, 1926; d. Erwin W. and Mildred (Haight) Boardman; m. James G. Cleary, Aug. 15, 1954; 1 child, Michael. Diploma, Robert Packer Hosp. Sch. Nursing, 1947; BS in Nursing Edn., U. Pa., 1951, MEd, 1953. Staff nurse Robert Packer Hosp., Sayre, 1947-48, nursing sch. instr., 1972-89; retired Robert Packer Hosp. Sch. of Nursing, Sayre, 1989; instr. U. Pa. Hosp., Phila., 1951-58; nursing sch. instr. U. Pa., Phila., 1966-72. Author: Robert Packer Hospital School of Nursing: A History, 1901-1989, 1994. Mem. Am. Nurses Assn., Sigma Theta Tau. Republican. Roman Catholic. Home: PO Box 276 107 West St Sayre PA 18840-0276

CLEARY, PAUL DAVID, sociomedical educator; b. Toronto, Can., May 14, 1948; s. Frank C. and Janet E. (Sweeney) C.; m. Cynthia F. Barnett, May 20, 1981; children: Janet A., Barnett D. BS in Physics, U. Wis., 1970, MS in Sociology, 1973, PhD in Sociology, 1980. Lectr. dept. sociology U. Wis., 1976-77; asst. rsch. prof. grad. sch. of social work Rutgers U., 1979-81, assoc. rsch. prof., 1981-82; asst. prof. dept. social medicine and health policy Harvard Med. Sch., 1982-87, assoc. prof. dept. health care policy and social medicine, 1988-92, prof. dept. health care policy and social medicine, 1993—; lectr., prof. dept. behavioral scis. Harvard Sch. of Pub. Health, 1983—; vis. assoc. prof. dept. sociomed. scis. Columbia U. Sch. of Pub. Health, 1988—; rsch. assoc. dept. medicine Beth Israel Hosp., Boston, 1982—; assoc. epidemiologist dept. medicine, Brigham and Women's Hosp., Boston, 1987—; cons. Marshfield Rsch. Found., 1978-80, Hershey Med. Sch., Nat. Heart, Lung, and Blood Inst., Bundesgesundheitsamt, West Berlin, 1983-85, Harvard Inst. for Internat. Devel. Applied Diarrheal Disease Rsch. Project; mem. study sect. NIMH, 1980, 81, 85-89; study sect. sci. adv. com. Am. Found. AIDS Rsch., 1987-92; mem. program rev. panel Mass. AIDS Office, 1988-91; local adv. com. VIII Internat. Conf. on AIDS, 1989-92, co-chair social sci., policy, and law track, 1990-92; mem. faculty coun. Harvard Med. Sch., 1991-93, com. promotions, reappointments and appointments, 1993—; vis. prof. Dept. Sociology, U. Stockholm, Sweden, 1982. Author: The Three Mile Island Nuclear Accident, 1988, (with others) Heart Disease and Rehabilitation, 1979, Handbook of Health, Health Care and the Health Professions, 1983, Heart Disease and Rehabilitation, 1986, Illness Behavior: A Multidisciplinary Model, 1986, Taking Care: Understanding and Encouraging Self-Protective Behavior, 1987; Gender and Stress, 1987, AIDS: The Safety of Blood and Blood Products, 1987, Evaluating Family Programs, 1988, The Future of Mental Health Services Research, 1989, AIDS and The Health Care System, 1990, Depression in Primary Care: Screening and Detection, 1990, Effectiveness and Outcomes in Health Care, 1990, International Law and AIDS: International Responses, Current Issues, and Future Directions, 1992; assoc. editor: Jour. of Health and Social Behavior, 1983-86, 89-92; editor The Milbank Quar., 1992—. Mem. AAAS, Am. Sociol. Assn. (med. sociology sect. nominations com. 1985-86, 89-90), APHA, Am. Assn. of Health Svcs. Rsch., Inst. of Medicine. Home: 25 Old Orchard Rd Newton MA 02167-1213

CLEARY, ROBERT EMMET, gynecologist, infertility specialist; b. Evanston, Ill., July 17, 1937; s. John J. and Brigid (O'Grady) C.; M.D., U. Ill., 1962; m. June 10, 1961; children—William Joseph, Theresa Marie, John Thomas. Intern, St. Francis Hosp., Evanston, 1962-63, resident, 1963-66; practice medicine specializing in gynecology and infertility, Indpls., 1970—; head Sect. of Reproductive Endocrinology and Infertility, Chgo. Lying-In Hosp., U. Chgo., 1968-70; head Sect. of Reproductive Endocrinology and Infertility, Ind. U. Med. Center, Indpls., 1970-80; prof. ob-gyn Ind. U., Indpls., 1976-80, clin. prof. ob-gyn, 1980—. Recipient Meml. award Pacific Coast Obstetrical and Gynecol. Soc., 1968; diplomate Am. Bd. Ob-Gyn, Am. Bd. Reproductive Endocrinology and Infertility. Fellow Am. Coll. Ob-Gyn, Am. Fertility Soc.; mem. Endocrine Soc.,Soc. Gynecol. Investigation, Pacific Coast Fertility Soc., Soc. Reproductive Endocrinologists, Soc. Reproductive Surgeons, N.Y. Acad. Scis., Sigma Xi. Roman Catholic. Contbr. articles in field to med. jours. Home: 7036 Dubonnet Ct Indianapolis IN 46278-1541 Office: 8091 Township Line Rd Indianapolis IN 46260-2495

CLEGG, JOHN FAWCETT, surgeon; b. Manchester, U.K., May 24, 1939; s. Henry Fawcett and Vera (Fricker) C.; m. Hilary Mary Crabtree, Oct. 18, 1969; children: Alison, Fiona, Charlotte. MA, St. Johns Cambridge, 1960, MB BChin, 1963. William Clarke rsch. fellow Hammersmith Hosp. Dept. of Urology, 1965-66; registrar in surgery Davyhulme Hosp., Manchester, 1968-69, Manchester Royal Infirmary, 1969-73; cons. in surgery Leighton Hosp., Crewe, 1973—; mem. specialist adv. coun. gen. surgery Royal Coll. of Surgeons, 1990-95; examiner in surgery Royal Coll. Surgeons, Edinburgh, 1985—. Mem. Royal Soc. of Medicine, Vascular Soc. of Great Britain and Ireland, Assn. of Surgeons Great Britain and Ireland, Sandway Golf Club (capt. 1989), Blasters Golf Soc. (capt. 1994). Office: Leighton Hosp, Crewe England

CLEGHORN, CHEREE BRIGGS, healthcare executive; b. Phoenix, June 25, 1945; d. Dale Sheaffer and Jeannetta Jeanne (Sebaugh) Briggs; m. George Reese Cleghorn, Mar. 15, 1975; stepchildren: Nona Elizabeth, John Michael. BA, Newcomb Coll., 1966; BJ, U. Mo., 1969. Reporter The Charlotte (N.C.) Observer, 1969-72; dir. pub. affairs Sch. Medicine U. N.C., Chapel Hill, 1972-75; spl. asst. to pres. Queens Coll., Charlotte, 1975-76 dir. pub. affairs WSU Health Care Inst., Detroit, 1976-79; cons. pub. affairs Detroit Med. Ctr. Corp., 1979-81, Johns Hopkins Med. Instns. Office of Pub. Affairs, Balt., 1982-83; v.p. pub. affairs Washington Healthcare Corp., 1983-86; pres. Cleghorn Health Communications, Bethesda, Md., 1985-88; pres. pub. rels. div. Rosenthal, Greene & Campbell, Bethesda, 1988-90; pres. Cleghorn & Assocs., Bethesda, 1990-94; sr. v.p. corporate affairs Loudoun Healthcare, Inc., Leesburg, Va., 1994—. Mem. communications com. Greater Washington Bd. Trade, 1988-90. Healthcare Forum fellow, 1996. Mem. Soc. Profl. Journalists, Am. News Women's Club, Pub. Rels. Soc. Am., Assn. Am. Med. Coll.'s Group on Pub. Affairs. Democrat. Presbyterian. Office: Loudoun Healthcare Inc 224 Cornwall St NW Leesburg VA 22075-2701

CLELAND, CHARLES CARR, psychologist, educator; b. Murphysboro, Ill., May 15, 1924; s. Homer W. and Stella (Carr) C.; m. Betty Lou Woodburn, July 18, 1948. B.S., So. Ill. U., 1950, M.S., 1951; Ph.D., U. Tex., 1957. Lic. psychologist, Tex. Chief psychologist Lincoln State Sch., Ill., 1956-57; chief psychologist Austin State Sch., 1957-59; supt. Abilene State Sch. Tex., 1959-63; prof. spl. edn. and ednl. psychology U. Tex.-Austin, 1963—. Author: Mental Retardation, 1969, 2d edit., 1978; Profound Retardation, 1979; Exceptionalities, 1982. Contbr. articles to profl. jours. Patentee in field. Bd. dirs. Child Guidance Ctr., Austin, 1966-67. Served with USAAF, 1943-46, PTO. Recipient Disting. Psychologist award Tex. Psychol. Assn., 1980, Edn. award Am. Assn Mental Deficiency, 1978. Fellow AAAS, Am. Psychol. Assn., Am. Assn. for Mental Deficiency (v.p. psychology div. 1973); mem. Tex. Psychol. Assn. (pres. 1962-63). Republican. Presbyterian. Office: U Tex E Db408A Austin TX 78712

CLEMENCE, BONNIE J., pediatrics nurse; b. McKeesport, Pa., Jan. 8, 1953; d. Lester Jack Sr. and Betty Ann (Carrberry) Arthur; m. Ronald D. Clemence, Oct. 12, 1974. Diploma, Butler County Meml. Hosp. Sch. Nursing, Butler, Pa., 1971-73; cert. enterostomal therapist, Harrisburg (Pa.) Sch. Enterostomal Therapy, 1977; BSN, Pa. State U., 1980; MS in Nursing, U. Pitts., 1983. RN, Pa. Pediatric staff nurse Allegheny Valley Hosp., Natrona Heights, Pa., 1973-75, asst. head nurse pediatrics, staff devel. instr., 1978-80, head nurse pediatrics, 1980-82, staff nurse med./surg. unit, 1983-84; office nurse Freeport (Pa.) Med. Assn., 1982-83; asst. prof. nursing Community Coll. Allegheny County, Monroeville, Pa., 1984; pvt. duty nurse Pitts. Nursing Specialists, 1984-86; pvt. duty nurse, cons. pediatric patients Norelle Nursing Agy., Mars, Pa., 1987-88; head nurse pediatric/adult orthopedic unit, cons. enterostomal therapy Butler (Pa.) Meml. Hosp., 1985-88; emergency rm. staff nurse Children's Hosp. Pitts., 1988-90, asst. head nurse emergency rm., 1990—. Contbr. articles to profl. jours. (writing award for article 1980). Mem. Pa. State U. Alumnae Assn., U. Pitts. Alumnae Assn., Butler County Alumnae Assn. Home: 371 Collins Dr Pittsburgh PA 15235-3839 Office: Children's Hosp Pitts 1 Childrens Way Pittsburgh PA 15212-5250

CLEMENDOR, ANTHONY ARNOLD, obstetrician, gynecologist, educator; b. Port-of-Spain, Trinidad, West Indies, Nov. 8, 1933; s. Anthony Arnold and Beatrice Helen (Stewart) C.; came to U.S., 1954, naturalized, 1959; A.B., NYU, 1959; M.D., Howard U., 1963; m. Elaine Browne, May 31, 1958 (dec. May, 1991); children: Anthony Arnold, David Alan; m. Janet Jenkins, Sept. 23, 1993. Intern, USPHS, S.I., N.Y., 1963-64; resident Met. Hosp. Ctr., N.Y.C., 1964-68, chief outpatient dept. ob-gyn, 1969-73 med. dir. family planning Human Resources Adminstrn., N.Y.C., 1973-74; assoc. dean student affairs, dir. office of minority affairs N.Y. Med. Coll., Valhalla, N.Y., 1974—, assoc. clin. prof. dept. ob-gyn., 1978-90, prof. clin. ob-gyn, 1990—. Bd. dirs. Elmcor, Caribbean-Am. Ctr. N.Y.C., Nat. Assn. of Minority Med. Educators, Inc., 1978-88, Empire State Med. Sci. and Ednl. Found., Inc., Caribbean Am. Ctr. of N.Y., 1988-91; mem. Nat. Urban League, N.Y. Urban League; life mem. NAACP. Diplomate Am. Bd. Ob-Gyn. Fellow Am. Coll. Ob-Gyn, Am. Pub. Health Assn.; mem. Royal Soc. Medicine, Nat. Med. Assn., N.Y. State Med. Soc., N.Y. County Med. Soc. (sec. 1989, v.p. 1990, pres. elect 1991, pres. 1992-93, bd. trustees)), N.Y. Acad. Medicine, N.Y. Gynecol. Soc. (v.p. 1986, pres. 1988), N.Y. Acad. Medicine.

CLEMENS, MARY, quality improvement professional; b. Lebanon, Ind., Feb. 2, 1958; d. Herschel W. and Ethel D. (Birchfield) Swisher; m. Michael W. Cummins; 1 child, Michael Scott. BBA, Ind. Vocat. Tech. Sch., 1980. Mem. svcs. rep. Maxicare Ind., Inc., Indpls., grievance analyst, quality improvement supr.; mem. svcs. rep. Metro Health, Indpls., mem. svcs. supr.; ednl. assistance specialist Meth. Hosp., Indpls. Mem. Nat. Assn. for Healthcare Quality, Ind. Assn. for Healthcare Quality. Office: Maxicare Ind Inc 9480 Priority Way W Dr Indianapolis IN 46240

CLEMENT, KATHERINE ROBINSON, social worker; b. Balt., Dec. 19, 1918; d. Alphonso Pitts and Sue Seymour (Ashby) Robinson; m. Harry George Clement, 1941 (dec. 1992). BA, Coll. of Wooster, Wooster, Ohio, 1940; MS in Social Work, Smith Coll., 1953; post grad., Washington Sch. of Psychiatry, 1951. Lic. clin. social worker, Calif. Social worker Family Svc., Cin., 1953-55, Hamilton, Ohio, 1955-57; social worker Orange County, Calif., 1957-60; counselor pvt. practice, Fullerton, Calif., 1959-63; social worker Family Svc., Long Beach, Calif., 1961-1963; child welfare worker San Mateo (Calif.) County Welfare Dept., 1963-1967; supr. child protection Yolo County Dept. Social Svcs., Woodland, Calif., 1967-79; pvt. practice Woodland, Calif., 1980—; cons. psychiatric social svc. State Dept. Social Svcs., Sacramento, 1984—. Active Yolo County Dem. Ctrl. Com.; treas. Feminist Legal Svcs.; founding bd. dirs. Yolo County Ct. Apptd. Spl. Advocates; bd. dirs. Yolo County ARC; mem. Yolo County Health Coun. Mem. NASW, NOW, LWV, Mensa, Toastmasters, Soroptimist Internat. Democrat. Unitarian. Home: 205 Modoc Pl Woodland CA 95695-6662

CLEMENTE, CARMINE DOMENIC, anatomist, educator; b. Penns Grove, N.J., Apr. 29, 1928; s. Ermanno and Caroline (Friozzi) C.; m. Juliette Vance, Sept. 19, 1968. A.B., U. Pa., 1948, M.S., 1950, Ph.D., 1952; postdoctoral fellow, U. London, 1953-54. Asst. instr. anatomy U. Pa., 1950-52; mem. faculty UCLA, 1952—, prof., 1963—, chmn. dept. anatomy, 1963-73, dir. brain research inst., 1976-87; prof. surg. anatomy Charles R. Drew U. Medicine and Sci., L.A., 1974—; hon. rsch. assoc. Univ. Coll., U. London, 1953-54; vis. scientist Nat. Inst. Med. Rsch., Mill Hill, London, 1988-89, 91; cons. VA Hosp., Sepulveda, Calif., NIH; mem. med. adv. panel Bank Am.-Giannini Found.; chmn. sci. adv. com., bd. dirs. Nat. Paraplegia Found.; bd. dirs. Charles R. Drew U., 1985-94. Author: Aggression and Defense: Neurol Mechanisms and Social Patterns, 1967, Physiological Correlates of Dreaming, 1967, Sleep and the Maturing Nervous System, 1972, Anatomy, An Atlas of the Human Body, 1975, 3d edit., 1987; editor: Gray's Anatomy, 1973—, 30th Am. edit., 1985, also Exptl. Neurology; assc. editor: Neurol. Research; contbr. articles to sci. jours. Recipient award for merit in sci. Nat. Paraplegia Found., 1973; 23d Ann. Rehfuss Lectr. and recipient Rehfuss medal Jefferson Med. Coll., 1986; John Simon Guggenheim Meml. Found. fellow, 1988-89. Mem. Pavlovian Soc. N.Am. (Ann. award 1968, pres. 1972), Brain Research Inst. (dir. 1976-87), Am. Physiol. Soc., Am. Assn. Anatomists (v.p. 1970-72, pres. 1976-77, Henry Gray award 1993), Am. Acad. Neurology, Am. Assn. Clin. Anatomists (Honored Mem. of Yr. 1993), Am. Acad. Cerebral Palsy (hon.), Am. Neurol. Assn., Assn. Am. Med. Colls. (exec. com. 1978-81, disting. service mem. 1982), Council Acad. Socs. (adminstrv. bd. 1973-81, chmn. 1979-80), Assn. Anatomy Chairmen (pres. 1972), Biol. Stain Commn., Inst. Medicine of Nat. Acad. Scis. (sci. adv. bd.), Internat. Brain Research Orgn., AMA-Assn. Am. Med. Colls. (liaison com. on med. edn. 1981-87), Med. Research Assn. Calif. (dir. 1976—), N.Y. Acad. Sci., Nat. Bd. Med. Examiners, Nat. Acad. Sci. (mem. com. neuropathology, BEAR coms.), Japan Soc. Promotion of Sci. (Research award 1978), Soc. for Neurosci., Sigma Xi. Democrat. Home: 11737 Bellagio Rd Los Angeles CA 90049-2158 Office: Dept Neurobiolgoy UCLA Sch Medicine Los Angeles CA 90024

CLEMENTE, CELESTINO, physician, surgeon; b. Penns Grove, N.J., June 11, 1922; s. Ermanno and Caroline (Friozzi) C.; m. Marie Ann Strangio, Nov. 16, 1946; children: Jeffrey, Roderick, Mark, Laurie Ann, Jonathan. BS, Rutgers U., 1942; MD, U. Pa., 1945. Diplomate Am. Bd. Surgery. Intern Jersey City Med. Ctr., 1945-46; resident in gen. surgery Martland Med. Ctr., 1950-53; practice medicine specializing in gen. surgery Newark, 1953—; dir. surgery Children's Hosp., Newark, 1962-70, St. Vincent's Hosp., Montclair, N.J., 1972-83; trustee United Hosps. Med. Ctr., Newark, 1972-88, v.p. med. affairs, 1975-88; assoc. clinic prof. surgery N.J. Med. Sch., Newark, 1975—; dir. surgery Roseland (N.J) Surg. Ctr., 1983—, also chmn. bd. Rep. candidate for U.S. Ho. of Reps, N.J., 1968; active Nat. Ad Council/HEW, 1970-74. Served to lt. USNR, 1946-48. Fellow ACS, Internat. Coll. Surgeons; mem. AMA, AAAS. Club: Essex (Newark). Home and Office: 364 Ridgewood Ave Glen Ridge NJ 07028-1513 Office: 556 Eagle Rock Ave Roseland NJ 07068-1500

CLEMENTS, JAMES DAVID, retired psychiatry educator, physician; b. Pineview, Ga., May 7, 1931; s. Marcus Monroe and Dewey Thelma (Gammage) C.; m. Janet Collier Swan, Aug. 25, 1952; children—Leiliar Ann, David Marcus. B.A., Emory U., 1952; M.D., Med. Coll. Ga., 1956. Intern Temple U., Phila., 1956-57; resident in pediatrics Temple U., 1957-59; fellow mental retardation Sch. Medicine, Yale U., 1959-60; med. dir. Gracewood (Ga.) State Sch. Hosp., 1960-62, asst. supt., 1963-64; dir. planning mental retardation Ga. Dept. Pub. Health, Atlanta, 1964-65; dir. Ga. Retardation Center, Atlanta, 1964-79; med. cons. mental retardation Ga. Dept. Human Resources, 1979-81; resident in psychiatry Emory U., Sch. Medicine, Atlanta, 1983-86; clin. asst. prof. pediatrics and psychiatry Emory U. Sch. Medicine, Atlanta, from 1964, asst. prof. psychiatry, 1985-95; ret., 1995; assoc. clin. prof. neurology, asst. clin. prof. pediatrics Med. Coll. Ga., Augusta, 1970—; spl. cons. neurology mental retardation dept. pediatrics Ga. Bapt. Hosp., 1965—; mem. adv. com. program exceptional children Ga. Dept. Edn., 1968-70; mem. adv. bd. Sch. Allied Health Sci., Ga. State U., 1971-76; mem. accreditation council mental retardation council Joint Commn. on Accreditation Hosps., Chgo., 1975-79; del. White House conf. Ga. com. children youth, 1970; mem. Pres.'s Com. on Mental Retardation, 1975-78; chmn. Willowbrook rev. panel Fed. Ct. Eastern Dist. N.Y.; reviewer NSF; cons. Inst. Society, Ethics and Life Scis., Hastings Center; commr. Am. Bar Assn., 1976-80. Contbr. articles to profl. jours., anthologies, seminars. Mem. adv. bd. Arbor Acad., DeKalb County (Ga.) Dept. Edn., 1973-75; mem. bd. founders, adv. com. Ashdun Hall, 1965-70; trustee Gatchell Sch., Mental Health Law Project (now Bazelon Ctr. for Mental Health Law); adv. com. Kennedy Center, Johns Hopkins U. Recipient Leadership award Am. Assn. Mental Deficiency, 1980. Fellow Am. Acad. Pediatrics (cons. head start med. cons. service), Am. Assn. Mental Deficiency (pres. 1974-75), Pan Am. Med. Assn., Am. Geriatrics Soc.; mem. Ga. Pediatric Soc., Nat. Assn. Supts. Pub. Residential Facilities Mentally Retarded, Nat. Assn. Retarded Citizens (legal advocacy adv. com. 1975), Internat. Assn. Sci. Study Mental Deficiency (chmn. local organizing com. 4th internat. congress, mem. council 1976-78), Am. Psychiatric Assocs. Home: 475 Grant St SE Atlanta GA 30312-3154

CLEMENTS, JOHN ALLEN, physiologist; b. Auburn, N.Y., Mar. 16, 1923; s. Harry Vernon and May (Porter) C.; m. Margot Sloan Power, Nov. 19, 1949; children: Christine, Carolyn. MD, Cornell U., 1947; MD (honoris causa), U. Berne, Switzerland, 1990, Philipps U., Marburg, Germany, 1992; ScD (honoris causa), U. Manitoba, 1993. Rsch. asst. dept. physiology Med. Coll. N.Y., Cornell U., Ithaca, 1947-49; commd. 1st lt. U.S. Army, 1949, advanced through grades to capt., 1951; asst. chief clin. investigation br. Army Chem. Ctr., 1951-61; assoc. rsch. physiologist U. Calif., San Francisco, 1961-64, prof. pediat., 1964—, Julius H. Comroe Jr. prof. pulmonary biology, 1987—; mem. staff Cardiovascular Research Inst. Cardiovasc. Rsch. Inst., San Francisco, 1961—, mem. grad. group in biophysics, 1987—; career investigator Am. Heart Assn., 1964-93; mem. group in biophysics and med. physics U. Calif., Berkeley, 1969-87; cons. Surgeon Gen. USPHS, 1964-68, Surgeon Gen. U.S. Army, 1972-79; sci. counselor Nat. Heart and Lung Inst., 1972-75; Bowditch lectr. Am. Physiol. Soc., 1961; 2d ann. lectr. Neonatal Soc., London, 1965; Distinguished lectr. Can. Soc. Clin. Investigation, 1973; mem. Nat. Heart Lung and Blood Adv. Coun., 1990-93; Ulf von Euler Meml. lectr. Karolinska Inst., 1996. Mem. editorial bd.: Jour. Applied Physiology, 1961-65, Am. Jour. Physiology, 1965-72, Physiol. Reviews, 1965-72, Jour. Developmental Physiology, 1979-85; assoc. editor: Am. Rev. Respiratory Diseases, 1973-79; chmn. publs. policy com.: Am. Thoracic Soc., 1982-86; assoc. editor: Ann. Rev. Physiology, 1988-93, Am. Jour. Physiology: Lung Cellular and Molecular Physiology, 1988-94. Recipient Dept. Army R & D Achievement award, 1961, Modern Medicine Disting. Achievement award, 1973, Howard Taylor Ricketts medal and award U. Chgo., 1975, Mellon award U. Pitts., 1976, Calif. medal Am. Lung Assn. Calif., 1981, Trudeau medal Am. Lung Assn., 1982, Internat. award Gairdner Found., 1983, J. Burns Amberson lecture award Am. Thoracic Soc. and Am. Lung Assn., 1991, Christopher Columbus Discovery award NIH, 1992, Albert Lasker Clin. Med. award, 1994, Virginia Apgar award Am. Acad. Pediat., 1994, Warren Alpert Found. award, 1995; named Mayo Clinic Disting. Lectr. in Med. Sci., 1993. Fellow AAAS, Am. Coll. Chest Physicians (hon.), Royal Coll. Physicians (London); mem. NAS, Western Assn. Physicians, Western Soc. Clin. Rsch., Perinatal Rsch. Soc. (councillor 1973-75), Am. Lung Assn. (hon., life). Office: U Calif Sch Medicine Cardiovascular Rsch Inst 3rd and Parnassus Ave San Francisco CA 94143

CLEMENTS, KENNETH BRESEE, family therapist; b. Scott, Ga., July 30, 1933; s. Willie Marvin and Ruby Lee (Foskey) C.; m. G. Elaine Reed, Aug. 14, 1953; children: Lori Susan, Lisa Shawn. BA, Trevecca Nazarene Coll., Nashville, 1955; BD, Nazarene Theol. Sem., Kansas City, Mo., 1962; MA, L.I. U., 1973, Azusa-Pac U., 1978. Lic. marriage and family therapist, mental health counselor; ordained to ministry Nazarene Ch., 1961. Pastor Ch. of the Nazarene, Carrollton, Mo., 1958-62, Smyrna, Ga., 1962-64, Manhattan, Kans., 1964-65, Fayetteville, N.C., 1990-93; commd. chaplain U.S. Army, various locations worldwide, 1965-87; advanced through grades to lt. col. U.S. Army, 1979, ret., 1987; exec. dir. Samaritan Counseling Ctr., Lincoln, Nebr., 1987-90; family therapist Fayetteville (N.C.) Family Life Ctr., 1992-94, Cedarwood Ctrs., Hendersonville, Tenn., 1994—; adj. prof. marriage and family therapy U. Louisville, 1985-86, Kans. State U., Manhattan, 1986-87. Decorated Bronze Star, 1971. Mem. Am. Assn. Marriage and Family Therapists, Am. Mental Health Counselors Assn., Assn. Counseling and Devel. Republican. Home: 109 Winding Way Dr Hendersonville TN 37075 Office: Cedarwood Ctrs 109 Hazel Path Ste 6 Hendersonville TN 37075

CLEMENTS, LYNNE FLEMING, family therapist, programmer; b. Bklyn., Aug. 8, 1945; d. Daniel Gillies and Dorothy Frances (Zitzmann) Fleming; m. Louis Myrick Clements, Feb. 19, 1972; children: Ryan Louis, Glenn Fleming. BA in Sociology, Bradley U., 1967; MSW, Fordham U., 1973; postgrad. studies, Columbia U., 1970-71; cert. family therapy, Inst. for Mental Health Edn., 1990. Lic. clin. social worker, N.J., 1994—. Computer programmer Employer's Comml. Union Group Ins. Cos., Boston, 1967-69, Harvard Bus. Sch., Cambridge, Mass., 1969-70, Volkswagon of Am., Englewood Cliffs, N.J., 1971; psychiatric social worker Associated Cath. Charities Family and Children's Svcs., Paramus, N.J., 1973-74, Christian Health Ctr., Wyckoff, N.J., 1976; owner, mgr. Wicker Wagon, Bergenfield, N.J., 1977-85; psychotherapist The Psychotherapy Counseling Ctr., Bergenfield, N.J., 1982-89; programmer analyst Atlas Computing Svcs., Secaucus, N.J., 1984-86; program coord., family therapist Div. of Family Guidance, Hackensack, N.J., 1986-91; pres. Corp. Family Resources, Ridgewood, N.J., 1989—; family therapist cons. Family Recovery of Valley View, White Plains, N.Y., 1992-94, Furman Clinic, Fair Lawn, N.J., 1995-96, Van Ost Inst. for Family Living, Englewood, N.J., 1996—; part-time family therapist N.J. Ctr. for Psychotherapy Inc., Ridgefield Park, 1990; family therapist cons. Family Recovery of Valley View, White Plains, N.Y., 1992-94; family therapist, cons. Furman Clinic, Fair Lawn, N.J., 1995—. Sunday sch. tchr. All Saints Ch., 1982-89, 94—, chmn. bd. community play ctr., 1977-78; mem. Twin-Boro Youth Ministry Coun., 1989—, Bergen County Family Day Care Coalition, 1989—; apptd. sec. Mayor's Beautify Bergenfield Com., 1991-95; chmn. entertainment Bergen County Children's Festival, 1993; apptd. chmn., designer Bergenfield's Coun. for Arts, 1993—; chmn. curriculum enhancement com. Bergen County Acad. for Advancement of Sci. and Tech., 1992—. Recipient 1st and 2nd pl. awards Bergenfield 1980 Art Contest; NIMH grantee, 1973. Mem. AAUW, Gifted Child Soc. (parent workshop coord. 1989—, bd. dirs. 1991—), Nat. Assn. Social Workers, Acad. Cert. Social Workers, Am. Orthopsychiat. Assn., Fordham U. Alumni Assn., N.J. Commerce and Industry Assn. (child care com.

1990—, human resources com. 1990—), N.J. Soc. Clin. Social Workers, Zonta (Amelia Earhart chmn. 1987-88, literacy com. 1995—, status of women in China com. chmn. 1993-94), Women of Accomplishment (founder, pres. 1990—, chmn. women's coalition conf. 1993—). Episcopalian. Home: 148 Harcourt Ave Bergenfield NJ 07621-1917 Office: Corp Family Resources 15 Godwin Ave Ste 1 Ridgewood NJ 07450-3817

CLEMENTS, MICHAEL CRAIG, health services consulting executive, retired renal dialysis technician; b. Cin., Sept. 17, 1945; s. Marvin Hubert and Mildred Helen (Rabe) C.; m. Minnie Faye Pospisil, Dec. 1, 1972; children: Melissa Ayn, Michael Aaron. Student, U. Cin., 1968-70; EMT/paramedic, Good Samaritan Health Ctr., 1980. Cert. renal dialysis technician. Hemodialysis technician Christ Hosp., Cin., 1968-79; tech. svcs. dir. Dialysis Clinic, Inc., Cin., 1980-91; pres. Critical Care Svcs., Inc., Mason, Ohio, 1987—; firefighter/paramedic Mason Vol. Fire Co., 1978-85, EMS tng. officer, 1984, EMS capt., 1985. Contbr. articles to profl. jours. Mem. Mason Environ. Adv. Commn., 1990—, vice chmn., 1992-93, bus. and parent curriculum review com. Mason City Schs., 1992; employer advisor coop. program Cin. Tech. Coll. Biomed. Engring. Tech., 1986-91. With USN, 1964-70. Mem. AAMS, Assn. for Advancement of Med. Instrumentation, Ohio Acad. Sci. Mem. Ch. of Christ. Office: Critical Care Svcs Inc PO Box 252 1083A Reading Rd Mason OH 45040

CLEMENTS, PAUL GREGORY, psychologist; b. Augusta, Ga., Jan. 5, 1955; s. Grady Paul and Myrtis Barbara (Farr) C.; m. Stephanie Kaye Matthews, July 29, 1989; children: Robert Grady, Matthew Taylor. BA in Psychology-English, Mercer U., 1977; MS in Psychology, Miss. State U., 1981, PhD, 1986. Lic. psychologist. Counselor Augusta Diversion Ctr., 1977-79; grad. asst. psychology dept. Miss. State U., Mississippi State, 1979-81, rsch. asst. Rehab. Rsch. & Tng. Ctr. Blindness & Low Vision, 1981-86; adj. instr. behavioral scis. Brenau Coll., Ft. Gordon, Ga., 1987—, 1987-91; chpt. I chmn. Wrens (Ga.) Elem. Sch., 1987-93; sch. psychologist/chpt. I tchr. Jefferson County Sch. System, Wrens, 1991—; psychologist Hancock County Sch. Sys., 1993-95, dir. spl. edn., psychologist, 1995—; pvt. practice; item writer tchr. cert. test Ga. Dept. Edn., Atlanta, 1990; mem. Ogeechee Area Interagy. Coord. Coun. on Early Childhood Intervention. Co-author: The Application of Motivational Theories to Business and Industry, 1983; jr. author: Training Opportunity Profiles for Visually Impaired Persons, 1986. Mem. APA, Ga. Psychol. Assn. (continuing edn. com. mem.), Ga. Assn. Sch. Psychologists, North Jefferson-Wrens Optimist Club (pres. 1990-91, Community Svc. award 1986, Svc. award 1987, Outstanding Svc. award 1988, Optimist of Yr. 1989). Home: PO Box 113 Wrens GA 30833-0113 Office: Hancock County Bd Edn PO Box 488 Sparta GA 31087-0488

CLEMENTS, RICHARD, radiologist, consultant; b. Abergavenny, U.K., Apr. 22, 1951. BA with 1st class honors, U. Oxford, Eng., 1972, MA, 1976, BM BChir, 1975. Accredited radiologist, U.K. Cons. radiologist Royal Gwent Hosp., Newport, U.K., 1991—; chmn., clin. dir. Radiology Directorate, Glan Hafren NHS Trust, Newport, 1994—; clin. tchr. U. Wales Coll. Medicine, Cardiff, 1994. Contbr. book chpt.: Questions and Uncertainties about Prostate Cancer, 1996; contbr. articles to med. jours. Univ. entrance exhbn. scholar St. Thomas' Hosp. Med. Sch., 1972-75. Fellow Royal Coll. Surgeons Eng., Royal Coll. Radiologists (Ellis Barnet prize 1987, Graham Hodgsen scholar 1989); mem. European Soc. Uroradiology, Brit. Med. Soc., Brit. Prostate Group. Office: Royal Gwent Hosp, Dept Clin Radiology, Newport NP9 2UB, England

CLEMETSON, CHARLES ALAN BLAKE, physician; b. Canterbury, Eng., Oct. 31, 1923; came to U.S., 1961, naturalized, 1972; s. Charles Harold and Gwendoline Maude Winefred (Blake) C.; m. Helen Cowan Forster, Mar. 29, 1947; children: Claudia, Charles, David, Andrew. B.M.,B.Ch., Oxford (Eng.) U., 1948. Lic. physician, La., U.K. Research asst. Obstetric Hosp., Univ. Coll. Hosp., London, 1950-52; Nichols research fellow Royal Soc. Medicine, 1951-52; house surgeon obstetrics W. Middlesex Hosp., 1952-53; resident med. officer obstetrics Queen Charlotte's Hosp., 1953; house surgeon gynecology Hammersmith Hosp., 1953-54; obstetric and gynecol. registrar Lake Hosp., Ashton-under-Lyne, Lancashire, Eng., 1954-56; lectr. ob-gyn. Univ. Coll. Hosp., London, 1956-58; asst. prof. Univ. Hosp., Saskatoon, Sask., Can., 1958-61, U. Calif., San Francisco, 1961-67; dir. dept. ob-gyn. Meth. Hosp., Bklyn., 1967-81, Huey P. Long Meml. Hosp., Pineville, La., 1981-91; assoc. prof. SUNY, Bklyn., 1967-72; prof. Downstate Med. Ctr., SUNY, 1972-81; prof. Tulane U., 1981-91, prof. emeritus, 1991; mem. obstetric adv. com. N.Y.C. Dept. Health, 1968; cons. in field; mem. med. adv. com. Planned Parenthood N.Y.C., Inc., 1971; mem. physicians rev. com. Blue Cross-Blue Shield N.Y.C., 1975; lectr. maternal health U. Calif., Berkeley, 1964-65. Author: Vitamin C, 3 vols., 1989; contbr. articles to med. jours. Served in RAF, 1948-50. Recipient Rsch. Career Devel. award NIH, 1965-67. Fellow ACOG, Royal Coll. Obstetricians and Gynecologists, Royal Coll. Physicians and Surgeons Can.; mem. Bklyn. Gynecol. Soc. (pres. 1977-78).

CLEMMONS, DAVID ROBERT, internist, educator; b. Nashville, May 19, 1947; s. Robert Starr and Beatrice (Winter) C.; m. Kathy Silverman, Nov. 27, 1971; children: Amy Elizabeth, Anna Katherine. Student, Vanderbilt U., 1965-66; BS, Davidson Coll., 1969; MD, U. N.C., 1974. Diplomate Am. Bd. Internal Medicine. Intern in medicine Mass. Gen. Hosp., Boston, 1974-75, jr. and sr. resident in medicine, 1975-77; fellow in endocrinology Harvard U., Boston, 1977-79; asst. prof. medicine U. N.C., Chapel Hill, 1979-83, assoc. prof., 1983-87, prof., 1987—, div. chief endocrinology and metabolism, 1990—; assoc. dir. clin. rsch. unit N.C. Meml. Hosp., Chapel Hill, 1979—; cons. Monsanto Inc., St. Louis, 1982—, Celltrix Inc., Santa Clara, Calif., 1991—, Genentech, Inc., San Francisco, 1991—; mem. cell biology and Physiology study sect. NIH, 1986-90. Contbr. articles to profl. jours. Chmn. adminstrv. bd. Univ. Meth. Ch., Chapel Hill, 1986, lay leader, 1987. Research grantee Nat. Inst. Aging, 1980, 83, 87, Nat. Heart, Lung and Blood Inst., 1980, 84, 86, Am. Heart Assn. Fellow ACP; mem. Am. Soc. Clin. Investigation, Am. Fedn. Clin. Research, So. Soc. Clin. Investigation (young investigator award 1986), Endocrine Soc. Democrat. Office: U NC Dept Medicine Cb # 7170 Chapel Hill NC 27599

CLENDENNING, WILLIAM EDMUND, dermatologist; b. Waynesburg, Pa., June 23, 1931; s. William Burdette and Anna Marie (Schellhase) C.; m. Elizabeth Woodbury Bennett, Sept. 6, 1958; children—William Alan, Joy Marie, Bruce Bennett, Sarah Elizabeth. B.S., Allegheny Coll., Meadville, Pa., 1952; M.D., Jefferson Med. Coll., Phila., 1956. Diplomate Am. Bd. Dermatology, Am. Bd. Dermatopathology. Intern St. Luke's Hosp., Cleve., 1956-57; resident in dermatology Univ. Hosps. of Cleve., 1957-60; sr. investigator dermatology br. Nat. Cancer Inst., USPHS, 1961-63; asst. prof. dermatology Western Res. U. Med. Sch., 1963-67; prof. medicine (dermatology) Dartmouth Coll. Med.; prof. emeritus, 1996—; also mem. staff Mary Hitchcock Meml. Hosp., Hitchcock Clinic, 1967-94; mem. Nat. Mycosis Fungoides Coop. Group, N.Am. Contact Dermatitis Group; Prosser White Orator St. John's Hosp. Dermatol. Soc., London, 1985. Author articles in field, chpts. in books. Nat. Cancer Inst. grantee, 1963-67. Mem. Am. Acad. Dermatology, Soc. Investigative Dermatology, Am. Dermatol. Assn., Am. Soc. Dermatopathology, New Eng. Dermatol. Soc., Am. Fedn. Clin. Research, N.H. Med. Assn., AMA. Home: 7 Pleasant St Hanover NH 03755-2008 Office: 1 Medical Center Dr Lebanon NH 03756-0001

CLERKIN, EUGENE PATRICK, physician; b. N.Y.C., Feb. 22, 1931; s. Eugene and Nance (Fitzsimmons) C.; m. Nancy Lucille Oshirak, Aug. 16, 1958; children: Eugene J., Brian A., Lucille A., Kathryn M. BS, Manhattan Coll., 1952; MD, NYU, 1956. Diplomate Am. Bd. Internal Medicine. Physician Lahey Clinic Found., Burlington, Mass., 1963—, chmn. dept. internal medicine, 1970-91, also bd. govs., 1981-91; asst. clin. prof. medicine Harvard Med. Sch., Boston, 1976—; mem. corp. N.E. Deaconess Hosp., 1980-93. Lt. USNR, 1958-60. Fellow ACP; mem. Endocrine Soc., Am. Diabetes Assn. Roman Catholic. Office: Lahey Clinic Med Ctr 41 Mall Rd Box 541 Burlington MA 01805

CLERMONT, YVES WILFRID, anatomy educator, researcher; b. Montreal, Que., Can., Aug. 14, 1926; s. Rodolphe and Fernande (Primeau) C.; m. Madeleine Bonneau, June 30, 1950; children—Suzanne, Martin, Stephane. B.Sc., U. Montreal, 1949; Ph.D., McGill U., 1953. Lectr. anatomy McGill U., Montreal, 1953-56, asst. prof., 1956-60, assoc. prof., 1960-63, prof., 1963—, chmn. dept., 1975-85; mem. Nat. Bd. Med. Examiners, Phila., 1979-82; mem. rsch. grant com. Med. Rsch. Coun., Ottawa, 1970—; cons. WHO, NIH, Ford Found., Fonds pour la formation de chercheurs et l'aide à la recherché, Quebec; sec. Artur Lucian Award Com. for Rsch. in Circulatory Diseases, 1983—. Contbr. chpts. to books, numerous articles to profl. jours. Recipient Ortho prize Can. Soc. Study Fertility, 1958, Prix Scientifique Govt. of Que., 1963, S.L. Siegler award Am. Soc. Study Fertility, 1966, Van Campenhout award Can. Fertility and Andrology Soc., 1986, Osler Teaching award McGill U., 1990. Fellow Royal Soc. Can.; mem. Am. Assn. Anatomists (v.p. 1970-73), Soc. Study of Reprodn., Am. Assn. Andrology (Disting. Andrologist award 1988, Serono award lectureship 1992), Can. Assn. Anatomists (J.C.B. Grant award 1986), Can. Assn. Microscopy (v.p. 1982-83). Home: 567 Townshend St, Saint Lambert, PQ Canada J4R 1M4 Office: McGill U Dept Anatomy Cell Biol, 3640 University St, Montreal, PQ Canada H3A 2B2

CLETSOWAY, RICHARD WILLIAM, urologist; b. Las Vegas, June 3, 1924; s. Eric and Ruth Hemans (Schlott) C.; m. Emily Gertrude Coons, Dec. 19, 1949; children: Deborah Ruth, Eric Lloyd. MD, Southwestern Med. Coll., 1948. Intern Kans. City (Mo.) Gen. Hosp., 1948-49, resident in urology, 1949-53; pvt. practice San Luis Obispo, Calif., 1956-95, ret., 1995; mem. urol. surg. staff Sierra Vista Hosp., San Luis Obispo, 1956-96, French Hosp., San Luis Obispo, 1956-90, San Luis Obispo Gen. Hosp., 1956-90, chief of staff, 1968, French Hosp., 1971. Capt. U.S. Army, 1953-56. Home: 1528 Fredericks St San Luis Obispo CA 93405

CLEVELAND, CHARLENE S., community health nurse; b. Haverhill, N.H., Aug. 20, 1945; d. Thomas D. and Willie E. (Smith) Sargent; children: Laura, Mary Ann. Diploma, Sylacauga Hosp. Sch. Nursing, 1967; student, Gadsden State Jr. C.C., 1979-82; BSN magna cum laude, Jacksonville State U., 1995. Staff nurse Sylacauga (Ala.) Hosp.; pub. health nurse Ala. Dept. Pub. Health, Sylacauga; staff nurse TCRC Child Devel. Ctr., Talladega, Ala.; homebound nurse Ala. Dept. Rehab., Anniston. Mem. Ala. State Nurses Assn., ARA, ASEA.

CLEVELAND, JOSEPH CORNELIUS, heart surgeon; b. Birmingham, Ala.; s. Edward Farrell and Lula Gladys (Moore) C.; m. Esther Georgienne Burow, June 22, 1958; children: Joseph C. Jr., Jonathan B. BA, DePauw U., 1957; MD, Case Western Res. U., 1961. Diplomate Am. Bd. Thoracic Surgery, Am. Bd. Surgery. Intern Univ. Hosps., Cleve., 1961-62, resident in gen. surgery, 1962-64; resident in gen. surgery Hahnemann Hosp., Phila., 1964-66; asst. prof. surgery Yale U., New Haven, 1966-69; pvt. practice gen. surgery Danville, Ill., 1969-72; fellow cardiothoracic surgery Tufts U.-New Eng. Med. Ctr., Boston, 1973-75; chief cardiothoracic surgery Carle Clinic, Urbana, Ill., 1975-82; founder, pres., pvt. practice Missoula, Mont., 1982—; surgeon Internat. Heart Inst. Mont., Missoula, 1996—. Contbr. articles to profl. jours. Mem. ACS, Soc. Thoracic Sureons. Office: 554 W Broadway Missoula MT 59802

CLEVELAND, PEGGY ROSE RICHEY, cytotechnologist; b. Cannelton, Ind., Dec. 9, 1929; d. "Pat" Clarence Francis and Alice Marie (Hall) Richey; cert. U. Louisville, 1956; B. Health Sci., U. Louisville, 1984; m. Peter Leslie Cleveland, Nov. 25, 1948 (dec. 1973); children: Pamela Cleveland Litch, Paula Cleveland Bertloff, Peter L. Cytotechnologist cancer survey project NIH, Louisville, 1956-59; chief cytotechnologist Parker Cytology Lab., Inc., Louisville, 1959-75; mgr. cytology dept. Am. Biomed. Corp., 1976-78, Nat. Health Labs., Inc., Louisville, 1978-89; clin. instr. cytology Sch. Allied Health U. Louisville, 1989—; leader cytotechnologist del. to People's Republic of China, 1986; with various hosps. and labs., 1990—; ptnr. Sham Star Stable thoroughbred horse breeding and racing. Mem. Am. Soc. Clin. Pathologist (cert. cytotechnologist), Internat. Acad. Cytology (cert. cytotechnologist), Am. Soc. Cytology (del.-person to person cytology delegation, amb. USSR, 1990), Kentuckiana Cytology Soc., Cytology Soc. Ind., Horseman's Benevolent and Protective Assn. Democrat. Roman Catholic. Home: 8774 Lieber Hausz Rd NE Lanesville IN 47136-8522

CLEVENGER, CYNTHIA GREENE, community health nurse; b. Ashland, Ky., May 12, 1967; d. Robert Lester and Gracie Jean (Horton) Greene; m. Kyle Wayne Clevenger, Aug. 25, 1984; children: Zachery Kyle, Kevin Garrett. AAS in Nursing, Morehead State U., 1993. RN, Ky. Staff nurse, ACLS provider Our Lady of Bellefonte Hosp., Ashland, Ky., 1993-94; cmty. health nurse Morgan County Health Dept., West Liberty, Ky., 1994—. Democrat. Baptist. Home: HC-81 Box 425 Sandy Hook KY 41171-9402 Office: Morgan County Health Dept 493 Riverside Dr West Liberty KY 41472

CLEVER, LINDA HAWES, physician; b. Seattle; d. Nathan Harrison and Evelyn Lorraine (Johnson) Hawes; m. James Alexander Clever, Aug. 20, 1960; 1 child, Sarah Lou. AB with distinction, Stanford U., 1962, MD, 1965. Diplomate Am. Bd. Internal Medicine, Am. Bd. Preventive Medicine in Occupational Medicine. Intern Stanford U. Hosp., Palo Alto, Calif., 1965-66; resident Stanford U. Hosp., Palo Alto, 1966-67, fellow in infectious disease, 1967-68; fellow in community medicine U. Calif., San Francisco, 1968-69, resident, 1969-70; med. dir. Sister Mary Philippa Diagonostic and Treatment Ctr. St. Mary's Hosp., San Francisco, 1970-77; chmn. dept. occupational health Calif. Pacific Med. Ctr., San Francisco, 1977—; clin. prof. medicine Med. Sch., U. Calif., San Francisco; NIH rsch. fellow Sch. Medicine, Stanford U., 1967-68; mem. San Francisco Comprehensive Health Planning Coun., 1971-76, bd. dirs.; mem. Calif.-OSHA Adv. Com. on Hazard Evaluation System and Info. Svc., 1979-85, Calif. Statewide Profl. Stds. Rev. Coun., 1977-81, San Francisco Regional Commn. on White House Fellows, 1979-81, 83-89, 92, 95, chmn., 1979-81, bd. scientific counselors Nat. Inst. of Occupl. Safety and Health, 1995—. Editor Western Jour. Medicine, 1990—; contbr. articles to profl. jours. Trustee Stanford U., 1972-76, 81-91, v.p. 1985-91; trustee Marin Country Day Sch., 1978-85; bd. dirs. Sta. KQED, 1976-83, chmn., 1979-81; bd. dirs. Ind. Sector, 1980-86, vice chmn. 1985-86; bd. dirs. San Francisco U. H.S., 1983-90, chmn. 1987-88; active Womens Forum West, 1980—, bd. dirs. 1992, 93; mem. Lucile Packard Children's Hosp. Bd., 1993—; mem., co-chair U. Calif. Berkeley Sch. of Pub. Health Dean's Policy Adv. Coun.; mem. Nat. Inst. Occupl. Safety and Health Bd. of Scientific Counselors, 1995—. Fellow ACP (gov. No. Calif. region 1984-89, chmn. bd. govs. 1989-90, regent 1990-96, vice chair bd. regents 1994-95), Am. Coll. Occupl. and Environ. Medicine; mem. Inst. Medicine NAS, Calif. Med. Assn., Calif. Acad. Medicine, Am. Pub. Health Assn., Western Occupl. Medicine Assn., Western Assn. Physicians, Stanford U. Women's Club (bd. dirs. 1971-80), Chi Omega. Office: 2351 Clay St San Francisco CA 94115-1931

CLIFFORD, JOHN ROBERT, neurosurgeon; b. Pitts., June 4, 1941; m. Paula B. King. MD, Tulane U., 1966; BS, U. Miami, 1962. Cert. Am. Bd. Neurol. Surgery. Intern mixed medicine Charity Hosp., New Orleans, 1966-67, resident gen. surgery, 1971; resident neurol. surgery Ochsner, VA and Charity Hosps., New Orleans, 1971-75; physician The NeuroMed. Ctr., Baton Rouge, 1976—; trustee Gen. Health, Baton Rouge, 1989-95; past pres. La. Neurosurg. Soc., La. Head Injury Found. Contbr. articles to profl. jours. Lt. comdr. USNR, 1967-70. Fellow ACS; mem. Am. Assn. Neurol. Surgeons, La. State Med. Soc., East Baton Rouge Parish Med. Soc. (past pres.), Rotary Internat. Home: 423 Woodleigh Dr Baton Rouge LA 70810 Office: The NeuroMed Ctr Ste 10000 7777 Hennessy Blvd Baton Rouge LA 70808

CLIFFORD, JOHN STEPHEN, psychologist; b. Hackensack, N.J., Dec. 27, 1951; s. John Patrick and Elizabeth Dorothy (Hanson) C.; m. Terry Janette Griswold, Oct. 6, 1979; children: Sean Michael, Tracy Elizabeth. BA, Skidmore Coll., 1973; MEd, Northeastern Univ., 1976; PhD, N.Mex. State U., 1983. Lic. psychologist, R.I., Mass. Rsch. asst. McLean Hosp., Belmont, Mass., 1974-76; clin. specialist Sangre De Cristo Community Mental Health Ctr., Santa Fe, N.Mex., 1977-80; psychology intern North Charles Gen. Hosp., Balt., 1982-83; sr. assoc. Social Sci. Cons., Inc., New Orleans, 1983-85; chief psychologist Edgehill Newport, Inc., Newport, R.I., 1985—; dir. Sakonnet Psychol. Assocs., Tiverton, R.I., 1990—; clin. cons. Bristol Community Coll., Fall River, Mass., 1986-89, Stanley St. Treatment and Resource Ctr., Fall River, 1990—; book reviewer Jour. of Substance Abuse Treatment, N.Y., 1985-90. Author: Dual Diagnosis, 1989, Cocaine Addiction, 1989. Clin. adv. com. Counseling for Ind. Living, Middletown, R.I., 1990—. Mem. Am. Psychol. Assn., Nat. Acad. Neuropsychology, R.I. Psychol. Assn., Mass. Psychol. Assn., New Eng. Psychol. Assn. Office: Sakonnet Psychol Assocs 1061 Fish Rd Tiverton RI 02878-3103

CLIFFORD, MAURICE CECIL, physician, former college president, foundation executive; b. Washington, Aug. 9, 1920; s. Maurice C. and Rosa P. (Linberry) C.; m. Patricia Marie Johnson, June 15, 1945; children: Maurice Cecil III, Jay P.L., Rosemary Clifford McDaniel. AB, Hamilton Coll., 1941, ScD, 1982; AM, U. Chgo., 1942; MD, Meharry Med. Coll., 1947; LHD, LaSalle Coll., 1981, Hamilton Coll., 1982, Hahnemann U., 1985, Meharry Med. Coll., 1992; LLD, Med. Coll. Pa., 1986. Diplomate Am. Bd. Ob-Gyn. Intern Phila. Gen. Hosp., 1947-48, resident in ob-gyn, 1948-51, asst. chief service ob-gyn, 1951-60; mem. faculty Med. Coll. Pa., Phila., 1955—, prof. ob-gyn., 1975-91, prof. emeritus, 1992—, v.p. for med. affairs, 1978-80, pres., 1980-86, bd. dirs., 1980—, pres. emeritus, 1992—; commr. pub. health City of Phila., 1986-92; chmn. HMA Found., Phila., 1991-93; exec. v.p. The Lomax Cos., Chalfont, Pa., 1993-96; pres. The Lomax Companies, Chalfont, Pa., 1996—. Contbr. articles to profl. jours. Former trustee Phila. Award, Phila. Art Mus., 1982-93; hon. trustee Phila. Coll. Textiles and Sci., 1982-94; trustee emeritus Phila. Acad. Natural Scis.; life trustee Meharry Med. Coll.; trustee Allegheny U. Health Scis., 1996—; former alumnus trustee Hamilton Coll.; mem. nat. med. com. Planned Parenthood, 1975-78; mem. adv. com. on arts John F. Kennedy Ctr. for Performing Arts, 1978-80. Capt. M.C., U.S. Army, 1952-54. Recipient Dr. Martin Luther King, Jr. award PUSH, 1981, Dr. William H. Gray, Jr. award Educators Roundtable Assn., 1981, Ann. award Phila. Tribune Charities, 1981, Disting. Am. award Edn. and Rsch. Fund Am. Found. for Negro Affairs, 1980, Outstanding Svc. award Phila. br. NAACP, 1965, others. Fellow Am. Coll. Obstetricians and Gynecologists (life); mem. Nat. Med. Assn., Pa. Med. Soc., Med. Soc. Eastern Pa., Philadelphia County Med. Soc., Phi Beta Kappa, Alpha Omega Alpha. Office: 200 Highpoint Dr Chalfont PA 18914-3925

CLIFT, ROBERT CHANDLER, urologist; b. L.A., July 4, 1939; s. J. Robert and Olive (Chandler) C.; m. Linda Smith, June 30, 1984; children: Amy A., Jill E. Mathur, W. Charles. BA, U. Wash., 1961; MD, U. Kans., 1965. Diplomate Am. Bd. Urology. Intern St. Joseph Hosp., Ann Arbor, Mich., 1965-66; resident St. Mary's Hosp., Grand Rapids, Mich., 1966-67; resident in urology U. Kans., Kansas City, 1967-70; urologist Reno Carson Urology, 1970—; assoc. clin. prof. U. Nev., Reno, 1972—. Fellow ACS; mem. AMA, Washoe County Med. Soc. (pres. 1981), Nev. State Med. Soc., Am. Urol. Assn., Reno Surg. Soc. Office: Reno Carson Urology 343 Elm St # 305 Reno NV 89503

CLIFTON, JAMES ALBERT, physician, educator; b. Fayetteville, N.C., Sept. 18, 1923; s. James Albert, Jr. and Flora M. (McNair) C.; m. Katherine Rathe, June 25, 1949; children—Susan M. (dec.), Katherine Y., Caroline M. B.A., Vanderbilt U., 1944, M.D., 1947. Diplomate: Am. Bd. Internal Medicine (mem. 1972-81, mem. subsplty. bd. gastroenterology 1968-75, chmn. 1972-75, mem. exec. com. 1978-81, chmn. 1980-81). Intern U. Hosps., Iowa City, Iowa, 1947-48; resident dept. medicine U. Hosps., 1948-51; staff dept. medicine Thayer VA Hosp., Nashville, 1952-53; asst. clin. medicine Vanderbilt Hosp., Nashville, 1952-53; cons. physician VA Hosp., Iowa City, 1965-93; assoc. medicine dept. internal medicine Coll. Medicine, U. Iowa, 1953-54, chief div. gastroenterology, 1953-71, asst. prof. medicine, 1954-58, assoc. prof., 1958-63, prof., 1963-91, prof. emeritus, 1991—, traveling fellow, 1964, vis. prof. dept. physiology, 1964, vice chmn. dept. medicine, 1967-70, chmn. dept. medicine Coll. Medicine, 1970-76, Roy J. Carver prof. medicine, 1974-91, Roy J. Carver prof. emeritus, 1991—, dir. James A. Clifton Ctr. Digestive Diseases, 1985-90, interim dean, 1991-93; investigator Mt. Desert Isle Biol. Lab., Salisbury Cove, Maine, 1964; vis. faculty mem. Mayo Found. and Mayo Clinic, 1966; vis. prof. dept. medicine U. N.C., Chapel Hill, 1970; cons. gastroenterology and nutrition tng. grants com. Nat. Inst. Arthritis and Metabolic Diseases, NIH, 1964-68, chmn., 1965-68; mem. Nat. Adv. Arthritis and Metabolic Diseases Coun., 1970-73; mem. gastroenterology tng. com. VA, Washington, 1967-71, chmn. tng. grants com., 1971-73; mem. med. adv. bd. Digestive Disease Found., 1969-73; vis. prof. gastroenterology U. London (St. Marks Hosp.), 1984-85; mem. sci. adv. com. Ludwig Inst. Cancer Rsch., Zurich, Switzerland, 1984-95. Mem. internat. editorial bd.: Italian Jour. Gastroenterology, 1970-90, Gastroenterology, 1964-68. Recipient Disting. Alumnus of Yr. award Vanderbilt U. Sch. Medicine, 1984; Phi Connell scholar Vanderbilt U., 1943-44; spl. rsch. fellow NIH, USPHS, 1955-56, fellow in medicine Evans Meml. Hosp., Mass. Meml. Hosps., also Boston U. Sch. Medicine, 1955-56. Fellow ACP (bd. regents 1972-79, pres. 1977-78 Alfred Stengel award 1984, Laureate award 1989); mem. Inst. Medicine of Nat. Acad. Scis., Am. Gastroent. Assn. (pres. 1970-71), AMA (liaison com. grad. med. edn. 1976-77), Am. Heart Assn., Am. Assn. Study Liver Disease, Am. Soc. Internal Medicine (Internist of Yr. award Iowa chpt. 1986), AAAS, Am. Fedn. Clin. Research, Am. Clin. and Climatol. Assn. (v.p. 1984), Assn. Am. Physicians, AAUP, Soc. Exptl. Biology and Medicine, Am. Physiol. Soc., Assn. Am. Med. Colls., Assn. Profs. Medicine (councillor 1972-73, sec.-treas. 1973-75), Internat. Soc. Internal Medicine (exec. com. 1978-80). Home: 2620 Newport Rd NE Iowa City IA 52240-7852 Office: U Iowa Hosp and Clinics 4 JCP Hawkins Dr Iowa City IA 52242

CLIFTON, KELLY HARDENBROOK, biology educator; b. Spokane, Wash., July 22, 1927; s. John Minton and Nora Marie (Toole) C.; m. Mayre-Lee Harris, Aug. 27, 1949; children: Kelly H. Jr., William H., Brice M. BA honors, U. Mont., 1950; MS, U. Wis., 1951, PhD, 1955. Postdoctoral fellow Children's Cancer Rsch. Found., Boston, 1955-56, rsch. assoc., 1956-59; from asst. prof. to prof. radiology U. Wis., Madison, 1959-67, prof. human oncology and radiology, 1975-95, prof. emeritus human oncology, 1995—; spl. rsch. fellow Nat. Cancer Inst. at Karolinska Inst., Stockholm, 1970-71; chief of rsch., bd. dirs. Radiation Effects Rsch. Found., Hiroshima and Nagasaki, Japan, 1980-82. Contbr. over 100 articles to profl. jours. Bd. dirs. Madison Gen. Hosp. Med. Surg. Found., 1984-91. With USCG, 1945-46. Grantee Am. Cancer Soc., U. Wis., 1960-83, U.S. Nat. Cancer Inst., U. Wis., 1972—, Dept. of Energy, U. Wis., 1984-95; named Disting. Alumnus U. Mont., 1995. Mem. Am. Assn. for Cancer Rsch., Soc. for Exptl. Biology and Medicine (chmn. Wis. sect. 1963-64), Radiation Rsch. Soc., Sigma Xi (nat. lectr. 1990-92). Home: 1218 University Bay Dr Madison WI 53705-2253 Office: U Wis K4 330 Comprehensive Cancer Ctr 600 Highland Ave Madison WI 53792-0001

CLIFTON, RACHEL KEEN, psychology educator; b. Burkesville, Ky., Oct. 5, 1937; d. James Em and Regina Elizabeth (Simpson) Keen; m. James Bertram Hickman, Aug. 22, 1961 (div. 1963); m. Charles Egolf Clifton, Jr., Aug. 20, 1965; children: Ramona, Catherine. BA, Berea (Ky.) Coll., 1959; MA, U. Minn., 1960, PhD, 1963. Fellow U. Wis., Madison, 1963-65; rsch. assoc. U. Iowa, Iowa City, 1966-68; from asst. prof. to assoc. prof. U. Mass., Amherst, 1968-76, prof., 1976—; vis. prof. Stanford U., Palo Alto, Calif., 1975-76, U. Sussex, Brighton, Eng., 1981-82, U. Cambridge, Eng., 1989-90; mem. rsch. rev. com. NIMH, 1983-87; mem. human devel. study sect. NIH, 1990-94. NIMH fellow U. Minn., 1961-63; grantee NIMH, NIH, NSF, 1968—; named Disting. Alumna Berea Coll., 1994. Fellow APA, AAAS; mem. Soc. Rsch. Child Devel. (sec. 1979-85, assoc. editor jour. 1977-79, editor Monographs 1993—), Fedn. Behavioral, Psychol. and Cognitive Scis. (sec. 1987-90), Soc. Psychophysiol. Rsch. (bd. dirs. 1975-78, assoc. editor jour. 1972-75), Internat. Soc. Infant Studies (pres. elect 1996—). Democrat. Congregationalist. Office: U Mass Dept Psychology Amherst MA 01003

CLIMO, LAWRENCE HANON, physician; b. New Haven, Jan. 5, 1938; s. Samuel and Esther (Levitin) C.; m. Diane June Schwartz, July 16, 1967; children: Alison Heather, Amy Catherine, Elana Dawn. BA, Yale U., 1959; MD, Albert Einstein Coll. Medicine, 1964. Diplomate Am. Bd. Psychiatry and Neurology. Dir. edn. Austen Riggs Ctr., Stockbridge, Mass., 1977-80; cons. and supervising psychiatrist Mass. Dept. Mental Health, Lawrence, 1980-91, Mass. Dept. Pub. Health, Tewksbury, 1988-90; sr. assoc. psychiatry Beth Israel Hosp., Boston, 1982—; mem. teaching faculty Harvard U. Med. Sch., Boston, 1985—, Psychopharmacology Clinic, Consulting Forensic; emergency svcs. psychiatrist Greater Lawrence Mental health Ctr. Capt. U.S. Army, 1965-67. Decorated Bronze Star. Mem. Am. Psychiat. Assn., Am. Acad. Psychiatry and the Law. Office: PO Box 405 Andover MA 01810-0007

CLINE, CAROLYN JOAN, plastic and reconstructive surgeon; b. Boston; d. Paul S. and Elizabeth (Flom) Cline. BA, Wellesley Coll., 1962; MA, U. Cin., 1966; PhD, Washington U., 1970; diploma Washington Sch. Psychiatry, 1972; MD, U. Miami (Fla.) 1975. Diplomate Am. Bd. Plastic and Reconstructive Surgery. Rsch. asst. Harvard Dental Sch., Boston, 1962-64; rsch. asst. physiology Laser Lab., Children's Hosp. Research Found., Cin., 1964, psychology dept. U. Cin., 1964-65; intern in clin. psychology St. Elizabeth's Hosp., Washington, 1966-67; psychologist Alexandria (Va.) Community Mental Health Ctr., 1967-68; research fellow NIH, Washington, 1968-69; chief psychologist Kingsbury Ctr. for Children, Washington, 1969-73; sole practice clin. psychology, Washington, 1970-73; intern internal medicine U. Wis. Hosps., Ctr. for Health Sci., Madison, 1975-76; resident in surgery Stanford U. Med. Ctr., 1976-78; fellow microvascular surgery dept. surgery U. Calif.-San Francisco, 1978-79; resident in plastic surgery St. Francis Hosp., San Francisco, 1979-82; practice medicine, specializing in plastic and reconstructive surgery, San Francisco, 1982—. Contbr. chpt. to plastic surgery textbook, articles to profl. jours. Mem. Am. Soc. Plastic and Reconstructive Surgeons, Royal Soc. Medicine, Calif. Medicine Assn., Calif. Soc. Plastic and Reconstructive Surgeons, San Francisco Med. Soc. Address: 490 Post St Ste 735 San Francisco CA 94102-1408

CLINE, FRANKIE KAY, social worker; b. Monongalia County, W.Va., Jan. 14, 1952; d. Wayne Franklin and Mary Kathleen (Parker) C. BSW cum laude, W.Va. U., 1974, MSW, 1986. Lic. social worker, W.Va., Pa.; cert. practitioner gerontology, W.Va. Geriatric social worker Family Svc. Assn., Morgantown, W.Va., 1976-80; social svc. dir. Sr. Monongalians, Inc., Morgantown, 1980-88; social worker/discharge planner Greene County Meml. Hosp., Waynesburg, Pa., 1988-92; case mgr. Mountainview Regional Rehab. Hosp., 1992-95; home health social worker Monongalia Gen. Hosp., Morgantown, 1995—; cons. Franklin Care Ctr.; govs. task force on long-term care, W.Va.; bd. dirs. Am. Cancer Soc.; co-facilitator Cancer Support Group; mem. Greene County Health and Welfare Coun.; adv. bd. Southwestern Home Health Agy., Inc., Waynesburg, 1995; field faculty W.Va. U. Sch. Social Work, 1980-95. Bd. dirs. Meals on Wheels, 1988. Mem. NASW, Monongalia County Coun. Social Agys., Am. Acad. Cert. Social Workers, Nat. Assn. Case Mgrs.

CLINE, JOHN CARROLL, clinical psychologist; b. Staunton, Va., Sept. 6, 1955; s. Carroll Hubert and Naomi Edith (Hevener) C.; m. Diane Jeannette Goudreau, May 21, 1983; 1 child, Virginia Goudreau Cline. BA, U. Va., 1977; PhD, U. Toledo, 1984. Lic. psychologist, Conn.; cert. biofeedback; clin. assoc. Am. Bd. Med. Psychotherapists; diplomate Am. Acad. Pain Mgmt. Psychology intern U. Toledo, 1980-81; predoctoral intern VA Med. Ctr., West Haven, Conn., 1981-82, attending psychologist, 1984-85; clinician Alcohol Svcs. Orgn., New Haven, 1982-85; team leader, staff psychologist Elmcrest Hosp., Portland, Conn., 1985-86, asst. unit chief, 1986, dir. behavioral medicine svc., 1986-90; pvt. practice psychologist Hamden, Conn., 1986-94; dir. adult outpatient svcs. Inst. of Living, Hartford, Conn., 1990-93; psychol. svcs. cons. Hamden, Conn., 1994—; clin. dir. dept. counseling and psychiat. svcs. Grove Hill Med. Ctr., New Britain, Conn., 1994—, chair quality assurance & outcomes mgmt. dept. psychiat. svcs., 1995—; clin. affiliate Yale Psychol. Svcs. Clinic, Yale U., New Haven, 1985—; cons. psychologist VA Med. Ctr., West Haven, 1985-91; asst. prof. clin. psychiatry U. Conn. Med. Sch., Farmington, Conn., 1991-94; instr. orthopaedic phys. therapy program Sch. Grad. and Continuing Edn. Quinnipiac Coll., Hamden, Conn., 1992—; sr. cons. network devel. Inst. Living, Hartford, 1993-94. Mem. mission study com. 1st Presbyn. Ch., New Haven, 1990-91; mem. Conn. Coun. Mental Health Providers, 1993-96, chair, 1993-94. Mem. AAAS, APA, Conn. Psychol. Assn. (chair hosp. practice com. 1990-92, practice directorate coord. 1993, pres.-elect 1994, pres. 1995-96), Conn. Behavior Therapy Assn. (mem. exec. com. 1992—), N.Y. Acad. Scis., Soc. for Psychotherapy Rsch., Assn. Psychiat. Clinics of Conn. (mem. polit. com. 1993-94, mem. edn. com. 1993-94), Assn. for Applied Psychophysiology and Biofeedback, Soc. Behavioral Medicine. Home: 4 Lamkin St Hamden CT 06517-3309 Office: Grove Hill Med Ctr 300 Kensington Ave New Britain CT 06051-3916

CLINE, ROBERT EDWARD, cardiothoracic surgeon; b. Newton, Iowa, Aug. 25, 1938; s. John Edward and Iro (Campbell) C. MD, Duke U., 1964. Diplomate Am. Bd. Surgery, Am. Bd. Thoracic Surgery. Resident in cardiothoracic surgery Duke U. Med. Ctr., Durham, N.C., 1964-70, tchg. scholar, 1970-71; pvt. practice, Ft. Lauderdale, Fla., 1975—; clin. prof. surgery U. Tex., San Antonio, 1971-74; cardiothoracic surgeon Northridge Hosp., Ft. Lauderdale, 1975—. Lt. col. M.C., USAF, 1971-74. Fellow ACS, Am. Coll. Cardiology (young investigator award 1965); mem. Soc. Thoracic Surgeons, Internat. Soc. Vascular Surgeons, So. Thoracic Surg. Assn., Fla. Med. Assn. (chmn. coun. sci. affairs 1991-95, bd. govs. 1995—), Broward County Med. Assn. (pres. 1994-95, editor Record 1994—), Ft. Lauderdale Surg. Soc., Caducean Soc. (pres. 1990-91). Republican. Presbyterian. Home: 31 Seneca Rd Fort Lauderdale FL 33308 Office: Heart Surgery Assocs 5601 N Dixie Hwy Fort Lauderdale FL 33334

CLINTON, LAWRENCE PAUL, psychiatrist; b. Lubbock, Tex., Apr. 27, 1945; s. Lewis Paul Clinton and Dorothy E. (Higgins) Clinton-Billingslea; m. Bonnie Gail Orenstein, June 22, 1969; children: Kerry Elizabeth, Andrew James, Alexander Geoffrey, Kaylin Lee. BA with honors, So. Conn. State Coll., 1966; postgrad., Ohio State U., 1966-68; MD, Hahnemann U., 1972. Diplomate Am. Bd. Psychiatry and Neurology. Teaching asst. Ohio State U., Columbus, 1966-68, research fellow, 1966-68; clin. instr. psychiatry Hahnemann U., Phila., 1975-82, asst. clin. prof., 1982—; chief exec. officer Bldg. Mgmt. Group, Vineland, N.J., 1986—; psychiat. dir. James Guiffre Med. Ctr., Phila., 1976-79; med. dir. PSI Group, 1990—; cons. Superior Ct. N.J., 1975—, Ranch Hope, Alloway, N.J., 1989-92. Contbr. articles to profl. jours. Mem. Am. Security Coun., 1975—, Rep. Senatorial Com., 1978—, Rep. Nat. Com., 1978, The Pres.'s Club, 1990—. Recipient awards Am. Security Coun., 1982, Buena Regional Sch. Dist., N.J., 1983, Vineland Parent Support and Adv. Group, 1990, Rep. Presdl. Legion of Merit medal, 1992; decorated Chevalier Comdr. Ordre Souverain et Militaire de la Milice du Saint Sepulcre, 1990—. Mem. AMA, Am. Psychiat. Assn., Internat. Assn. Group Psychotherapy, N.J. Psychiat. Soc., Phila. Coll. Physicians and Surgeons, Internat. Platform Soc., Med. Club Phila., World Fedn. Mental Health, InterAm. Coll. Physicians and Surgeons, Hahnemann Undergrad. Rsch. Soc. (treas. 1971-72), Confedn. of Chivalry, Am. Chem. Soc., Phi Lambda Kappa (v.p. 1972), Societe d'Chemie (pres. 1965-66), South Jersey Psychiat. Soc. (sec.-treas. 1994—), SPQR Club (pres. 1961-62) (Milford, Conn.). Office: 1138 E Chestnut Ave Bldg 6 Vineland NJ 08360-5053

CLISHAM, FAYE FLYE, retired pediatrics nurse; b. Brooklin, Maine, Feb. 24, 1926; d. Leonell Alberto and Laura Mae (Joyce) Flye; m. William J. Clisham, Nov. 3, 1956 (dec.); children: Andrew M., Peggy F. Clisham Brown. Diploma, Ea. Maine Gen. Hosp., 1948. Cert. CPR, IV's. Staff nurse Ea. Maine Med. Ctr., Bangor, 1948-59, 69-91, St. Joseph's Hosp., Bangor, Maine, 1969; ret., 1995. Mem. ANA, Maine State Nurses Assn. Home: 120 Old County Rd Hampden ME 04444-1718

CLOCHESY, JOHN MICHAEL, nursing educator, critical care nurse; b. Fond Du Lac, Wis., May 27, 1954; s. Ralph E. and Lillian M. (Miller) C. BSN, Marian Coll., Fond Du Lac, 1976; MS, U. Wis., 1981; PhD, Case Western Res. U., Cleve., 1993. RN, Ohio, Mich., Pa., Ariz., Wis. Assoc. dir. nursing U. Med. Ctr., Tucson; clin. nurse specialist Dept. Vets. Affairs Med. Ctr., L.A.; instr. critical care nursing Case Western Res. U., 1989-93; asst. dean U. Pitts., 1993-96, assoc. dean, 1996—; lectr. and researcher in field. Contbr. articles to profl. jours. Fellow Am. Coll. Critical Care Medicine, Am. Acad. Nursing; mem. AACN (founding editor in chief AACN Clin. Issues jour.), Soc. Critical Care Medicine, Sigma Theta Tau. Home: 3001 Marshall Rd #108 Pittsburgh PA 15214-2655

CLONINGER, CLAUDE ROBERT, psychiatric researcher, educator, genetic epidemiologist; b. Beaumont, Tex., Apr. 4, 1944; s. Morris Sheppard and Marie Concetta (Mazzagatti) C.; m. Sharon Lee Rogan, July 11, 1969; children: Bryan Joseph, Kevin Michael. BA U. Tex., 1966; MD, Washington U., St. Louis, 1970, (hon.) U. Umea, Sweden, 1983. Diplomate Am. Bd. Psychiatry and Neurology. Instr. psychiatry Washington U., St. Louis, 1973-74, asst. prof. 1974-78, assoc. prof., 1978-81, prof., 1981—, prof. genetics, 1978—, prof. psychology, 1989—, Wallace Renard prof. psychiatry, 1991—, head dept. psychiatry, 1989-94, dir. ctr. psychobiology personality, 1994—; psychiatrist-in-chief Barnes and Renard Hosps., St. Louis, 1989-94; vis. prof. U. Hawaii, Honolulu, 1978-79, U. Umea, Sweden, 1980; chmn. NIMH psychopathology Review Com., Washington, 1930-84; cons. WHO, Geneva, 1981—, Am. Psychiatric Assn., Washington, 1978—, Nat. Inst. on Alcohol Abuse and Alcoholism, 1984—, Inst. Medicine, 1986; chmn. genetics initiative schizophrenia NIMH, 1989—; mental health commr. State of Mo., 1990-95. Author 6 books; editor: Jour. Behavior Genetics, 1980-86, Am. Jour. Human Genetics, 1980-83; assoc. editor Genetic Epidemiology, 1983-92, Human Heredity, 1989—; mem. editl. bd. Arch. Gen. Psychiatry, Comprehensive Psychiatry, Neuropsychopharmacology, Jour. Comprehensive Psychiatry, Jour. Psychiat. Rsch., Jour. Med. Genetics; contbr. articles to profl. jours. Recipient Rsch. Scientist award NIMH, 1975, 80, 85, Strecker award Inst. Pa. Hosp., 1988, James B. Isaacson award, ISBRA, 1992. Fellow AAAS, Am. Psychiat. Assn. (Adolph Meyer award, 1993), Am. Psychopathol. Assn. (treas. 1984-89, v.p. 1990, pres. 1991-93, sec. 1994—, Samuel Hamilton award 1993); mem. Am. Soc. Human Genetics (editl. bd. 1980-83), Behavior Genetics Assn. (editl. bd. 1980—), Inst. Medicine of NAS, Rsch. Soc. Alcoholism (bd. dirs. 1987-90). Avocations: gardening, reading, travel. Home: 7100 Delmar Blvd University Heights MO 63130-4303 Office: Washington U 4940 Children's Pl Saint Louis MO 63110-1002

CLOSE, BENJAMIN BUELL, allergist; b. Travis AFB, Calif., Feb. 1, 1961; s. Carl Buell Jr. and Betty Anne (Reeves) C.; m. Karen Ann Nicaols, Aug. 13, 1983; children: Victoria Ann, Kyle Benjamin, Jackson Reeves. BS, La. State U., 1983, MD, 1987. Physician, pres. La. Allergy/Asthma Specialists, Alexandria, 1992—. Fellow Am. Coll. Allergy, Asthma & Immunology (com. mem. 1994—), Am. Coll. Chest Physicians; mem. AMA, Am. Coll. Physicians, Am. Acad. Allergy, Asthma & Immunology (com. mem. 1993—), La. State Med. Soc., Kiwanis (bd. dirs. 1993-95, chmn. 1995). Office: La Allergy/Asthma Spl 3311 Prescott Rd Ste 210 Alexandria LA 71301

CLOSE, LANNY GARTH, otolaryngologist, educator; b. San Antonio, Aug. 13, 1946; s. James Garth and Nona Lee (Galbraith) C.; m. Sharron Maredith Smith, Nov. 22, 1980; children: Hunter, Maredith. BA summa cum laude, Tex. Tech. U., 1968; MD cum laude, Baylor Coll. Medicine, 1972. Diplomate Am. Bd. Otolaryngology. Resident in surgery Johns Hopkins Hosp., Balt., 1972-74; resident in otolaryngology Baylor Affiliated Hosps., Houston, 1974-77; asst/assoc. prof. otolaryngology U. Tex., Houston, 1977-82; asst. surgeon dept. head & neck surgery M.D. Anderson Hosp., Houston, 1978-79; from assoc. prof. to prof. otolaryngology U. Tex. Southwestern Med. Sch., Dallas, 1982-94; prof., chmn. dept. otolaryngology/head and neck surgery Columbia U., N.Y.C., 1994—; guest examiner Am. Bd. Otolaryngology, 1993, 94, 96. Contbr. 80 articles to profl. jours. Fellow ACS, Am. Laryngological Assn., The Triological Soc., Am. Rhinological Assn., Am. Broncho Esophageal Assn., Am. Soc. for Head & Neck Surgery, Soc. of Head and Neck Surgery; mem. Alpha Omega Alpha. Office: Coll Physicians & Surgeons Columbia U 630 W 168th New York NY 10032

CLOUD, MARINA TAYLOR, mental health counselor; b. Buawang, La Union, The Philippines, Dec. 2, 1945; came to U.S., 1947; d. Clyde and Emilia (Mazon) Blount; m. Gregory Doy Cloud, June 20, 1975 (div.). BA, U. N.C., 1978; MA, U. Fla., 1984; MEd, U. North Fla., 1989. Lic. mental health counselor, Fla. Mental health technician I Dorothea Dix Hosp., Raleigh, N.C., 1973-75; nurse's aide Wesley Long Community Hosp., Greensboro, N.C., 1976-77; community planner Guilford Native Am. Assn., Greensboro, 1979; researcher U. Fla., Gainesville, 1983-84, fin. aid evaluator Office Student Fin. Aid, 1984-85; counselor in tng. personal counsel and career devel. U. North Fla., Jacksonville, 1985-90; student aid advisor Fla. Community Coll., Jacksonville, 1986-87; employment primary counselor in stabilization unit Mental Health Ctr. Jacksonville, 1990-93, inpatient clin. svcs. mgr.; emergency svcs./inpatient clin. svcs. mgr., 1993-95; stabilization adult clin. program mgr. Mental Health Ctr., Jacksonville, 1995-96; dir. at large N.C. State U. Student Union, Raleigh, 1974; sec. U. Fla., Gainesville, 1983. Mem. ACA, Am. Mental Health Counselors Assn. Democrat. Presbyterian.

CLOUD, WENDY MICHELLE, home health nurse; b. Atlanta, Sept. 27, 1969; d. William Jessie and Patricia Lee (Stuart) Wilder; m. John David Cloud, May 24, 1991. AAS in Nursing, Chattanooga (Tenn.) State Tech. C.C., 1993. RN, Tenn. Home health aide ResCare, Chattanooga, Tenn., 1990-92, 1990-92; staff RN Parkridge Hosp., Chattanooga, Tenn., 1993-94; home health care nurse Housecall Home Health Agy. Instr. CPR ARC, Chattanooga, 1988-95; beginners ch. tchr. Calvary Bapt. Ch., Chattanooga, 1987-94. Republican.

CLOUSE, MELVIN E., radiologist; b. Vinita, Okla., June 6, 1934; s. Clifford Powell and Agnes Elizabeth (Betcher) C.; m. Marian Upton, Feb. 16, 1966; children: Graydon Melville, Thomas Philip. BS, Tex. Christian U., 1967; MD, U. Tex., 1960. Diplomate Am. Bd. Radiology; lic. physician, Mass., Tex. Intern Phila. Gen. Hosp., 1960-61; resident in radiology Mass. Gen. Hosp., Boston, 1962-64, fellow radiology, 1964-65, radiologist, 1966-69; fellow radiology Armed Forces Inst. Pathology, Washington, 1965; from asst. in radiology to prof. Harvard Med. Sch., 1966-87; radiologist New Eng. Deaconess Hosp., Boston, 1969—; chmn. dept. radiology Deaconess Hosp., Boston, 1975—; vis. prof. radiology U. Conn. Med. Sch., 1980, U. Va. Med. Sch., 1980, Loyola U., Maywood, Ill., 1981; examiner Am. Bd. Radiology, various yrs., question devel. written exam., 1994; staff dept. radiology Dana Farber Cancer Inst., 1989—; mem. various coms. New Eng. Deaconess Hosp., 1975—, ex-officio mem. bd. dirs., 1979-81; clin. assoc. Cancer Rsch. Inst./New Eng. Deaconess Hosp., 1978-90; chief radiology svc. Quigley meml. Hosp./Soldiers Home, 1985-87; pres. Deaconess Profl. Practice Group/New Eng. Deaconess Hosp. Mem. editl. bd. Cardiovascular and Interventional Radiology, 1980—, Transplantation, 1981—, Radiology, 1982—, Radiographics, 1988—, Investigative Radiology, 1990—, Liver Transplantation and Surgery, 1994—, Gastroenterology, 1994—; contbr. articles to profl. jours. Trustee Beaver Country Day Sch., Chestnut Hill, Mass., 1988-91, v.p., trustee, 1991. Grantee Nat. Inst. Arthritis, Diabetes, Digestive and Kidney Diseases, Nat. Inst. Neurol. Diseases and Blindness, Am. Cancer Soc., USPH; U. Tex. fellow, 1958; recipient 4th Pl. award Soc. Nuclear Medicine, 1983; named Hon. Prof. Xi'an Med. U., China, 1989. Fellow Am. Coll. Radiology (councillor 1971-75), Soc. Cardiovascular and Interventional Radiology; mem. AMA, Am. Roentgen Ray Soc., Radiol. Soc. N.Am. (councillor, program com. cardiovascular radiology 1983), Mass. Radiologic Soc. (exec. com. 1971-75, councillor 1973-76, tribunal com. 1980, com. on standards in radiol. practice 1984-85, standards on radiologistical practice com., others, 1992), Mass. Med. Soc., New Eng. Roentgen Ray Soc. (sec. 1974-77, pres. 1980-81, exec. com. 1981-82, chmn. exec. com. 1983-84, nominating com., profl. ethics com. 1984-85, chmn. nominating com. 1986-87), New Eng. Cardiovascular and Interventional Roentgen Soc. (pres. 1982-83), Soc. for Magnetic Resonance in Medicine, Assn. Univ. Radiologists (membership com. 1985-87), Am. Heart Assn. Home: 53 Seaver St Brookline MA 02146

CLOUSE, VICKIE RAE, biology and paleontology educator; b. Havre, Mont., Mar. 28, 1956; d. Olaf Raymond and Betty Lou (Reed) Nelson; m. Gregory Scott Clouse, Mar. 22, 1980; 1 child, Kristopher Nelson. BS in Secondary Sci. Edn., Mont. State U. No., Havre, 1989; postgrad., Mont. State U., Bozeman, 1991-94. Teaching asst. biology and paleontology Mont. State U.-No., Havre, 1986-90; rsch. asst. dinosaur eggs and embryos Mus. of the Rockies, Bozeman, 1992-95; instr. biology and paleontology Mont. State U.-No., Havre, 1990—. Bd. trustees H.E. Clack Mus., Havre, 1991-97, H.E. Clack Mus. Found., Havre, 1991-97, Mont. Bd. Regents of Higher Edn., Helena, 1989-90, Mont. Higher Edn. Student Fin. Assistance Corp., Helena, 1989-90; mem. Ea. Mont. Hist. Soc., 1993—. Named Young Career Woman of Yr., Bus. and Profl. Woman's Club, 1986 Mem. Soc. Vertebrate Paleontologists, Mont. Geol. Soc. Office: Mont State U-No Hagener Sci Ctr Havre MT 59501

CLOVIS, WILLIAM LEROY, psychiatrist, educator; b. Waynesburg, Pa., Nov. 20, 1932; s. Leroy William and May (Phillips) C.; m. Oct. 17, 1965 (div. 1982); 1 child, Brian W. BS, Dickinson Coll., 1953; MD, U. Pa., 1957. Diplomate Am. Bd. Psychiatry and Neurology. Resident in psychiatry Inst. of Pa. Hosp., 1958, Phila. Gen. Hosp., 1962-64; pvt. practice, Phila., 1964—; instr. psychiatry U. Pa., Phila., 1965-69; sr. clin. instr. psychiatry Hahnemann U., Phila., 1969-71, asst. clin. prof., 1971—. Mem. Am. Psychiat. Assn., Pa. Psychiat. Soc., Phi Beta Kappa, Alpha Omega Alpha. Democrat. Mem. Soc. of Friends. Office: 1930 Chestnut St Philadelphia PA 10103

CLOWARD, REBECCA KNIGHT, medical and surgical nurse; b. Salt Lake City, June 17, 1954; d. Jo Lewis and Janette Mae (Chapman) Knight; m. Paul J. Cloward, June 22, 1985; children: Casey Lewis, Katie, Kelly Paul, Cory J. AD, Brigham Young U., 1979, BSN, 1982. RN, Utah. Staff nurse Payson (Utah) Hosp., 1979-81; staff nurse ICU, LDS Hosp. Salt Lake City, Utah, 1981-82; nurse practitioner Office Donald N. Marquardt, Ticaboo, Utah, 1982-83; head nurse, staff nurse Mountain View Hosp., Payson, Utah, 1984-87; adult nurse practitioner Office Lowell M. Jones, Provo, Utah, 1987-94, Utah Valley State Coll., Provo, 1994—. Mem. ANA (cert. adult nurse practitioner). Home: 241 N 1200 E Mapleton UT 84664-3928

CLOWERS, DEBRA CHERIE, medical records technician; b. Kansas City, Mo., June 3, 1963; d. Churby Conrad and Hazel Marie-Elizabeth (Hendrix) C.; m. Jarvis Edwards (div.); 1 child, Taylor Marie-Elizabeth. AS, Cin. Tech. Coll. Cert. accredited records technician. With Jewish Hosp., Cin., 1986-87; dir. med. records Walnut Hills/Evanston Family Practice, Cin., 1987-96, ctr. dir., 1996—. Mem. Am. Health Info. Mgmt. Assn., Ohio Health Info. Mgmt. Assn. Office: Walnut Hills-Evanston Med Corp 4531 Reading Rd Cincinnati OH 45229

CLOWES, ALEXANDER WHITEHILL, surgeon, educator; b. Boston, Oct. 9, 1946; s. George H.A. Jr. and Margaret Gracey (Jackson) C.; m. Monika Meyer. AB, Harvard U., 1968, MD, 1972. Resident in surgery Case Western Reserve, Cleve., 1972-74, 76-79; rsch. fellow in pathology Harvard Med. Sch., Boston, 1974-76; fellow in vascular surgery Brigham and Womens Hosp. Harvard Med. Sch., 1979-80; asst. prof. surgery U. Wash., Seattle, 1980-85, assoc. prof., 1985-90, prof., 1990—, assoc. chmn. dept., 1989-91, acting chmn. dept., 1992-93, adj. prof. pathology, 1992, chief divsn. vascular surgery, 1995—, dept. vice chmn., 1995—. Contbr. chpts. to books; author numerous sci. papers. Trustee Marine Biol. Labs., Woods Hole, Mass., 1989—, Seattle Symphony, 1994—; bd. dirs. Seattle Chamber Music Festival, 1990. Recipient NIH Rsch. Career Devel. award, 1982-87; NIH Tng. fellow, 1974-77; Loyal Davis Traveling Surg. scholar ACS, 1987. Mem. Am. Surg. Assn., Am. Assn. Pathologists, Am. Heart Assn. (coun. on arteriosclerosis), Am. Soc. Cell Biology, Internat. Soc. Applied Cardiovasc. Biology, Seattle Surg. Soc., Soc. Vascular Surgery, Cruising Club Am., Quisset Yacht Club, Sigma Xi. Episcopalian. Home: 702 Fullerton Ave Seattle WA 98122-6432 Office: U Wash Dept Surgery Box 356410 Seattle WA 98195

CLOYD, JAMES COKELY, pharmacy educator; b. Louisville, July 1, 1948; s. James Cokely and Helen (Burrichter) C.; m. Therese Elizabeth Bowman, July 24, 1982; children: Elizabeth, Thomas. BS in Pharmacy, Purdue U., 1971; PharmD, U. Ky., 1976. Asst. prof. pharmacy U. Minn., Mpls., 1976-81, assoc. prof., 1981-93, prof., 1993—, head dept. pharmacy practice, 1982-96; adv. panel USP Neurology, 1985—. Contbr. articles to profl. and sci. jours. Fellow Am. Coll. Clin. Pharmacy; mem. Am. Pharm. Assn. (acad. rep. 1991—), Am. Epilepsy Soc. (chair subcom. on elderly, 1991—), Epilepsy Found. Am. (profl. adv. bd. 1989—). Office: U Minn Coll Pharmacy 308 Harvard St SE Minneapolis MN 55455-0353

CLUETT, HELEN CATHERINE, nursing educator; b. Quincy, Mass., Mar. 31, 1935; d. William Patrick and Mary Louise (Foley) C. Diploma in nursing, Whidden Meml. Hosp. Sch., Everett, Mass., 1956; BSN, Boston Coll., 1975; MSN, Boston U., 1979. Staff nurse med.-surg. unit Milton (Mass.) Hosp., 1956-57, asst. head nurse med.-surg. unit, 1957-58; pvt. duty nurse Mass. State Nurses Registry, Boston, 1958-60; intravenous nurse Mass. Gen. Hosp., Boston, 1961-66; staff nurse oper. rm. Boston Floating Hosp., Tufts New Eng. Med. Ctr., 1966-67; instr. oper. rm. nursing Peter Bent Brigham Hosp. Sch. Nursing, Boston, 1967-73, instr. med.-surg. nursing, 1975-85; perioperative nurse educator Brigham and Women's Hosp., Boston, 1985—; facilitator, lectr. Cmty. High Schs., Boston; provider lecture to nursing students from Simmons Coll., Quincy Coll., Roxbury C.C., Bunker Hill C.C., Boston and Quincy, Mass., U. Mass., Boston, 1989—; coord. clin. experience cardiopulmonary vascular sci. dept. Northeastern U., Boston, 1986—; clin. assoc. U. Mass. Coll. Nursing, Boston, 1990—; presenter in field. Contbg. author (textbook) Comprehensive Perioperative Nursing, vol. 2, 1995. Treas. Nursing Rsch. Network Boston, 1988-92; mem. capital devel. campaign Sacred Heart Parish, Weymouth, Mass., 1992. Mem. ANA, Mass. Nurses Assn., Brigham and Women's Nursing Orgn. (coord. nursing ground rounds 1986—), Assn. Oper. Rm. Nurses (chair awards com. Mass. chpt. I 1995-96, chair project Alpha com. Mass. chpt. I 1988-95, mem. project Alpha com. 1995-96, nominating com. 1991-92, chair 1992-93, editorial com. 1987-88, del. 1987-92, 95, mem. nurse educator/cln. nurse specialty 1994—, Excellence in Perioperative Nursing award 1992, bd. dirs. 1994-96), Sigma Theta Tau. Home: 466 Front St Weymouth MA 02188-2804 Office: Brigham and Women's Hosp 75 Francis St Boston MA 02115-6110

CLUFF, LEIGHTON EGGERTSEN, physician; b. Salt Lake City, June 10, 1923; s. Lehi Eggertsen and Lottie (Brain) C.; m. Beth Allen, Aug. 19, 1944; children: Claudia Beth, Patricia Leigh. BS, U. Utah, 1944, ScD (hon.), 1989; MD with distinction, George Washington U., 1949; ScD (hon.), Hahnemann Med. Sch., 1979, L.I. U., 1988, St. Louis U., George Washington U., 1990, U. Utah, 1990. Intern Johns Hopkins Hosp., Balt., 1949-50, asst. resident, 1951-52; asst. resident physician Duke Hosp., Durham, N.C., 1950-51; vis. investigator, asst. physician Rockefeller Inst. Med. Research, 1952-54; fellow Nat. Found. Infantile Paralysis, 1952-54; mem. faculty Johns Hopkins Sch. Medicine, Balt.; staff Johns Hopkins Hosp., Balt., 1954-66, prof. medicine, 1964-66, physician, head div. clin. immunology, allergy and infectious diseases, 1958-66; prof., chmn. dept. medicine U. Fla., Gainesville, 1966-76; VA disting. physician U. Fla., 1990-95, prof. dept. medicine, 1990—; exec. v.p. Robert Wood Johnson Found., Princeton, N.J., 1976-86, pres., 1986-90, trustee emeritus, 1990—; U.S. del. U.S.-Japan Coop. Med. Sci. Program, 1972-81; mem. council drugs AMA, 1965-67; mem. NRC-NAS Drug Research Bd., 1965-71; mem. expert adv. panel bacterial diseases (coccal infection) WHO; mem. council Nat. Inst. Allergy and Infectious Diseases, 1968-72; cons. FDA; mem. tng. grant com. NIH, 1964-68. Author, editor books on internal medicine, infectious diseases, clin. pharmacology, long-term care; contbr. articles to profl. jours. Bd. dirs. Nat. Coun. on Aging, 1995—. Recipient Ordronaux award for med. scholarship, 1959, Career Rsch. award NIH, 1962, Edward Jill award Acad. Medicine N.J., 1990, Disting. Alumnus award Duke U. Sch. Medicine, 1978, Disting. Alumnus award Johns Hopkins Sch. Med., 1992, Theobald Smith award Albany Med. Coll., 1988; Markle scholar, 1955; Maed-Johnson Postgrad. scholar, 1954-55. Mem. ACP (master, Fla. gov. 1975-76, Mead-Johnson postgrad. scholar 1954-55, Ordronaux award for med. scholarship 1949), Inst. Medicine of NAS, Assembly Life Scis. of NAS, Am. Soc. Clin. Investigation, Assn. Am. Physicians, Soc. Exptl. Biology and Medicine, Am. Assn. Immunologists, Am. Fedn. Clin. Rsch., Harvey Soc., Infectious Diseases Soc. Am. (pres. 1975-76), N.Y. Acad. Scis., So. Soc. Clin. Investigation, Am. Clin. and Climatol. Assn., Am. Social Health Assn. (bd. dirs. 1990—), Johns Hopkins U. Soc. Scholars, Alpha Omega Alpha. Home: 8851 SW 45th Blvd Gainesville FL 32608-4138

CLUFF, MARIELLEN SMITH, gerontology and rehabilitation nurse; b. Greenfield, Ohio, Dec. 21, 1945; d. William DeWitt and Elizabeth Belle (Hamilton) Smith; m. James Edward Cluff, Jan. 23, 1970; children: James Edward Jr., Jerry R., Jennifer Diane. Diploma, Community Hosp Sch. Nursing, Springfield, Ohio, 1983; AA, AS, So. State Community Coll., Hillsboro, Ohio, 1980; BSN, Ohio U., 1990. RN, Ohio; cert. gerontology nurse. Med.-surg. staff nurse Greenfield Area Med. Ctr., dir. rehab.; staff nurse VA Med. Ctr., Chillicothe, Ohio, 1992—. Mem. ANA, Ohio Nurses Assn., Assn. Rehab. Nurses. Named Employee of Yr., Greenfield Area Med. Ctr., 1989. Home: 7766 Keplinger Rd Hillsboro OH 45133-9790

CLYDE, WALLACE ALEXANDER, JR., pediatrics and microbiology educator; b. Birmingham, Ala., Nov. 7, 1929; s. Wallace Alexander and Martha Louise (Pou) C.; m. Barbara Jean McClain, Aug. 21, 1953; children: Martha Elizabeth, Susan Ann, Kevin Alexander. BA, Vanderbilt U., 1951, MD, 1954. Intern in pediatrics Vanderbilt Hosp., Nashville, 1954-55, resident, 1956-57; resident Bapt. Hosp., Winston-Salem, N.C., 1955-56; chief pediatrician U.S. Naval Hosp., Millington, Tenn., 1957-59; fellow in preventive medicine Case Western Res. U., Cleve., 1959-61; instr. in pediatrics U.

N.C., Chapel Hill, 1961-62, asst. prof., 1963-67, assoc. prof., 1967-71, prof. pediatrics and microbiology, 1972—; vis. assoc. prof. dept. pathology Yale U., New Haven, 1971-72; assoc. mem. Armed Forces Epidemiol. Bd., Washington, 1981—; mem. bacteriology-mycology study sect. NIH, Bethesda, Md., 1966-70; dir. Pediatric Pulmonary Specialized Ctr. Rsch., Chapel Hill, 1976-91. Mem. editorial bd. to several sci. jours.; contbr. articles to sci. publs., chpts. to books. Lt. USN, 1957-59. Recipient bronze medal City of Bordeaux (France), 1983, career devel. award NIH, 1964, 69, citation classics award Inst. Sci. Info., 1984, key of City of Birmingham, 1986. Fellow Infectious Diseases Soc. Am.; mem. Internat. Orgn. for Mycoplasmology (sec.-gen. 1980-82, chmn. 1984-86, Presdl. Citation 1990, Kliene-berger Nobel award 1992), Soc. Pediatric Rsch., Am. Soc. Clin. Investigation. Democrat. Baptist. Office: U NC 535 Burnett Womack Bldg CB#7200 Chapel Hill NC 27599-7220

CLYMER, ELLEN SAXE, health professions education educator; b. Indiana, Pa., Mar. 17, 1930; d. Foster Charles and Mary Louise (Woods) Johnson; m. Charles Lee Saxe, Dec. 22, 1951 (div. 1984); 1 child, Charles Lee Saxe III; m. John Francis Clymer, July 15, 1989. BSN, Ariz. State U., 1974; MA in Sch. and Community Health Edn., Sam Houston State, 1976; postgrad., Nova Southeastern U., 1992-95. Nursing position Yuma County Health Dept., Yuma, Ariz., 1965-70, Kofa High Sch., Yuma, 1970-74; coord. community health edn. U. Tex. Med. Br., Galveston, 1976-78; dir. nursing edn. Cochise Coll., Douglas, Ariz., 1978-81, Imperial Valley Coll., Imperial, Calif., 1981-90; asst. prof., coord. MS in health professions edn. Coll. Osteo. Medicine of the Pacific, Pomona, Calif., 1991-94, dir. Ctr. for Faculty Devel. in Health Professions; presenter workshops in nursing. Contbr. articles to profl. jours. Past v.p. bd. dirs. Imperial Valley Womenhaven; past. mem. Health Systems Agy. CHC; past sec. bd. dirs. Clinicas de Salud del Pueblo, Inc.; past bd. dirs. Cochise County Bd. Health. Mem. AAUW, Am. Vocat. Assn., Delta Kappa Gamma. Mem. Ch. of Religious Science. Home: 4529 Central Ave Riverside CA 92506-2385 Office: Coll of Osteo Medicine of the Pacific College Plz Pomona CA 91766-1853

COADY, MARIE ROSE, physical therapist; b. Tampa, Fla., Feb. 13, 1954; d. James Michael and Marie Vincentia (Relihan) Paleveda, m. Leo Dean Coady Jr., Mar. 21, 1986. AS in Phys. Therapy with honors, St. Petersburg (Fla.) Jr. Coll., 1989; BS in Phys. Therapy summa cum laude, Fla. A&M Univ., 1993. Physical therapist asst. Bay Area Rehab., Inc., Tampa, Fla., 1989-91; physical therapist TGH Sports Medicine Ctr., Tampa, Fla., 1993—; clinical instr. PT and PTA students, Tampa Gen. Healthcare Sports Medicine Ctr., 1993—. Vol. Am. Lung Assn., 1996, Gasparilla Distance Classic, 1996, vol. h.s., jr. h.s. athletic physical Tampa Gen. Healthcare, 1994-96. Mem. Am. Physical Therapy Assn. Roman Catholic. Office: Tampa Gen Healthcare Sports Medicine Ctr 4 Columbia Dr Ste 250 Tampa FL 33629

COATES, DIANNE KAY, social worker; b. Adrian, Mich., Jan. 4, 1945. Student Jackson Bus. U., Mich., 1962-63; AA with honors, Macomb Community Coll., Warren, Mich., 1977; BA with high distinction, Madonna Coll., Livonia, Mich., 1979; MSW, Wayne State U., 1982; postgrad. Internat. Grad. Sch., St. Louis, 1984, Eastern Mich. U., 1989; cert. devel. disabilities Wayne State U., 1996. Cert. social worker, Mich. Nat. service officer Mil. Order of the Purple Heart, Detroit, 1973-80; psychology technician VA Med. Ctr., Allen Park, Mich., 1980-84; clin. cons. HOMEBASE, Detroit, 1983-85; clin. social worker Community Counseling Assocs., Adrian, Mich., 1983, Roseville, Mich., 1983-87; clin. social worker Ypsilanti (Mich.) Regional Psychiat. Hosp., Mich., 1987-90, Southgate (Mich.) Regional Ctr. for the Developmentally Disabled, 1990-92, 92-96, Lafayette Clinic, 1992; intake/admissions/discharge coord. Southgate (Mich.) Ctr., 1996—; field instr. Wayne State U., 1988—; internat. exch. counselor Edn. Found. Fgn. Study, 1987-92; area rep. Ednl. Resource Devel. Trust, 1991-94; ind. contract therapist Renaissance West Community Mental Health Services Clinic, Detroit, 1988-89; Caknipe-Kovach Assocs., 1988-92; vol. HAVEN, Pontiac, Mich., 1986-87; group counselor Survivors of Homicide Detroit, 1981-82. Recipient LA MOPH Dept. of Mich. ann. disting. svc. award, 1992. Mem. NASW (bd. cert. diplomate), Nat. Acad. Cert. Social Workers, Assn. State Employed Mental Social Work (v.p. 1991-93), Mich. Mental Health Assn., Mich. Assn. Mental Health Profls., Social Work Assn. Madonna Coll. (co-founder), Mich. Alcohol and Addiction Assn., Wayne State U. Alumni Assn., Bus. and Profl. Women, Vietnam Vets. Am. (hon. life assoc. mem.), Met. Svc. Officers Assn. (pres. 1990-92). Lodges: Ladies Aux. Mil. Order of Purple Heart (region 2 v.p. 1985-86, nat. membership officer 1995), Ladies Aux. VFW, DAV Aux. Home: 1502 Elias St Westland MI 48186-4919

COATES, PATRICIA ANNE, nursing administrator, community health nurse, college health nurse; b. Boston, Apr. 7, 1936; d. Thomas F. and Mary F. (Folan) Oates; m. Paul F. Coates, June 21, 1958; children: Elizabeth, Catherine, Paul F. Jr., Roy, Thomas, Mary, Michael. RN, St. Elizabeth Hosp. Sch. Nursing, 1956; BS, Roger Williams Coll., 1979. RN, Mass.; cert. in coll. health nursing. RN operating rm. St. Elizabeth Hosp., Boston, Malden (Mass.) Hosp.; asst. coord. health svcs. Regis Coll., Weston, Mass.; dir. health svc. Emerson Coll., Boston. Recipient Svc. award ARC, Louise Gazzara award for excellence in Coll. Health Nursing, 1993. Mem. Coll. Health Assn. Nurse Dirs. (pres.), Am. Coll. Health Assn. (sec. nursing sect.), ANA, Mass. Nurse's Assn. Home: 40 Robinson Rd Medford MA 02155-1519

COATS, ANDREW JUSTIN STEWART, physician; b. Melbourne, Australia, Feb. 1, 1958; s. Douglas Alan and Pamela Julie (Edwards) C.; m. Susan Jane Clark, June 21, 1986; children: Thomas, Alexander, Edward. BA, St. Catherines Coll., Oxford, U.K., 1976-79; MA, 1981; MBChir, Clare Coll., Cambridge, U.K., 1981. Registrar St. Vincent's Hosp., Melbourne, Australia, 1984-86; rsch. fellow Oxford (Eng.) U., 1986-89; sr. lectr. in cardiology Nat. Heart and Lung Inst., London, 1991-96; Viscount Royston prof. clin. cardiology Imperial Coll., London, 1996—; hon. cons. cardiologist Royal Brompton Hosp., London, 1991—. Contbr. articles to profl. jours. Fellow Royal Australian Coll. Physicians, European Soc. Cardiology, Circulation Soc., Am. Heart Assn., Am. Coll. Cardiology. Home: 105 Cadogan Gardens, London SW3 2RF, England Office: Nat Heart and Lung Inst, Dovehouse St, London SW3 6LY, England

COATS, JOEL ROBERT, toxicology educator; b. Kenton, Ohio, Apr. 24, 1948; s. William Gilbert and Catherine Elizabeth (Dodds) C.; m. Susan Anne Orkins, June 12, 1971 (div. 1987); children: Sarah, Jesse, Aaron; m. Rebecca Jane Fisher, July 9, 1988; stepchildren: Beth, Annie. BS, Ariz. State U., 1970; MS, U. Ill., 1972, PhD, 1974. Rsch. assoc. U. Ill., Urbana-Champaign, 1974-76; vis. prof. U. Guelph, Ont., Can., 1976-78; asst. prof. Iowa State U., Ames, 1978-81, assoc. prof., 1981-86, prof., 1986—; sci. rev. panel U.S. EPA, Washington, 1986-95; rev. team U.S. Nat. Inst. Environ. Health Sci., Washington, 1986-87; cons. Battelle Inst., Richland, Wash., 1988-89, Continental Grain, N.Y., TelTech, Mpls., Ea. Rsch. Group, Lexington, Mass. Co-author: Pyrethroids: Their Effects on Aquatic and Terrestrial Ecosystems; editor: Insecticide Mode of Action, 1982, Enhanced Biodegradation of Pesticides, 1990, Pesticide Transformation Products, 1991, Bioremediation through Rhizosphere Technology, 1994; contbr. 20 book chpts. and 75 articles to profl. jours. Coach Ames Little League Baseball, 1984-89. Fellow AAAS, Am. Chem. Soc. (chmn. agrochem divsn. 1992); mem. Entomol. Soc. Am., Soc. Toxicology (pres. ctrl. state chpt. 1988), Soc. Environ. Toxicology and Chemistry, Pesticides Sci. Soc. Japan, Quantitative Structure Activity Relations hip Soc., Assn. Official Analytical Chemists. Methodist. Office: Iowa State Univ Dept Entomology Ames IA 50011

COATS, STEPHEN H., general surgeon; b. Gallipolis, Ohio, Nov. 26, 1939; s. Robert Lee and Edna Maxine (Hayes) Gaskill; m. Mary Elizabeth Conley, Nov. 12, 1966; children: Robert Sean, Lloyd Wayne, Laura Beth, Stephen Andrew, Douglas Scott, Walter Christopher. Student, Rio Grande Coll., 1959, U. Denver, 1959-61, Cin. Coll. Mortuary Sci., 1961-62; BS in Biology, Miami U., 1964; DO, Kirksville Coll. Osteopathy, 1968. Diplomate Am. Bd. Osteo. Surgeons. Intern Dr.'s Hosp., Columbus, Ohio, 1968-69; resident Flint (Mich.) Osteo. Hosp., 1971-75; pvt. practice West Plains, Mo., 1975—; med. dir. Ozarks Med. Ctr. Trauma Ctr., West Plains, 1993-95, mem. credentials com., 1991—, chmn. dept. surgery, 1978-82. Bd. chmn. Howell County Rural Fire Dept., West Plains, 1982-89; Eagle scout adult advisor, expdn. leader Boy Scouts Am., West Plains, 1978—; chmn. pastor-parish rels. 1st United Meth. Ch., West Plains, 1984-86. Capt. U.S. Army, 1969-71, Vietnam. Fellow Am. Coll. Osteo. Surgeons (ethics com. 1983-90, chmn. young surgeons com. 1982-84); mem. Am. Osteo. Assn., Mo. Assn. Osteo. Physicians and Surgeons, South Ctrl. Ozarks Osteo. Assn. (sec.-treas. 1976—), West Plains C. of C. Home: PO Box 749 West Plains MO 65775 Office: 1115 Alaska Ste 214 West Plains MO 65775

COBB, ALTON B., healthcare foundation administrator, physician; b. Madison County, Miss., Oct. 19, 1928; s. Joseph Harrison and Winnie Ora (Mabry) C.; m. Mary O'Connor, Sept. 26, 1954; children: Mary Alene, Tommy, Susan. BA, U. Miss., 1950; MD, Johns Hopkins U., 1954; MPH, Tulane U., 1960. Diplomate Am. Bd. Preventive Medicine and Pub. Health. Rotating intern Charity Hosp., New Orleans, 1954-55; resident in pub. health Miss. State Bd. Health, Indianola, 1960-62, county health officer, 1957-59; dir. health planning Miss. Exec. Dept., Jackson, 1968-69; dir. Miss. Medicaid Commn., Jackson, 1969-73; state health officer Miss. Dept. Health, Jackson, 1973-93; coord. quality improvement Miss. Found. for Med. Care, Jackson; clin. prof. preventive medicine U. Miss. Sch. Medicine, Jackson. Col. Miss. N.G. Recipient Alumnus of Yr. award Tulane Sch. Pub. Health, 1982; named Pub. Adminstr. of Yr., Miss. Soc. for Pub. Adminstrn., 1981. Fellow Am. Coll. Preventive Medicine; mem. Ctrl. Med. Soc., Miss. State Med. Assn., Assn. State Territorial Health Ofcls. (pres. 1979-80, McCormack award 1984), APHA (award of Excellence 1992), Rotary, Delta Omega. Presbyterian. Home: 5476 River Thames Rd Jackson MS 39211-4133 Office: Miss Found for Med Care PO Box 4665 Jackson MS 39296-4665

COBB, HENRY VAN ZANDT, psychologist; b. East Orange, N.J., Feb. 22, 1909; s. Sanford Ellsworth and Margaret Brown (Macleish) C.; m. Florence Ruth Crozier, Aug. 3, 1932; children: Margaret Alice, Judith Helen, Catherine Macleish, Peter Van Zandt, David Crozier. A.B., Pomona Coll., 1930; Ph.D., Yale, 1936. Acting prof. psychology and philosophy Furman U., Greenville, S.C., 1934-35; instr. philosophy Carleton Coll., Northfield, Minn., 1936-41; asst. prof. Carleton Coll., 1941-44; prof. philosophy and psychology, head dept. U. S.D., 1946-58, prof., chmn. dept. psychology, 1958-67; dean U. S.D. (Coll. Arts and Scis.), 1967-69; v.p. acad. affairs, acting dean U. S.D. (Grad. Sch.), 1969-74, prof. emeritus, 1975—; vis. prof. edn. Tchrs. Coll. Columbia U., 1964-65; vis. scholar U. N.C., 1974-76, clin. prof., 1977-81; with Florence R. Cobb (weekly radio program Our Children), 1952-53; faculty study fellowship Ford Found., 1953; cons. Peace Corps, Kenya, 1977-78; Mem. Gov.'s Com. on Mental Health, S.D., 1954; mem. S.D. Gov.'s Com. Mental Retardation, 1962; councilor Internat. League Socs. for Mentally Handicapped, 1963- 65, pres., 1966-70; bd. dirs. Joint Commn. on Mental Health of Children, 1966-70; chmn. Joint Commn. Internat. Aspects Mental Retardation, 1970-73; chmn. tech. adv. com. Joint Commn. Accreditation of Hosps., 1971-73; Mem. Pres.'s Com. on Mental Retardation, 1973-79, vice chmn., 1977-79. Author: Man's Way, 1942, Forecast of Fulfillment, 1972; editor, prin. author: Mental Retardation: A Report to the President, 1976, Mental Retardation, Past and Present, 1977, (poetry) Images of Goose Cove, 1992, Covenant: Life and Times of a Late-Coming Pilgrim, 1995; contbr. articles and revs. to profl. jours. Served with USNR, 1944-45; assigned duty on U.S.S. Wichita at Okinawa, Nagasaki. Mem. AAAS, Am. Assn. U. Profs., Am. Philos. Assn., Am. Psychol. Assn., Soc. Religion in Higher Edn., Nat. Assn. Retarded Citizens (pres. 1964-65), S.D. Assn. Retarded Citizens (pres. 1954), Am. Assn. Mental Deficiency, Sigma Xi, Phi Beta Kappa. Home: Apt 4201 750 Weaver Dairy Rd Chapel Hill NC 27514-1442

COBB, JEWEL PLUMMER, former college president, educator; b. Chgo., Jan. 17, 1924; divorced; 1 child. A.B., Talladega Coll., 1944; M.S., N.Y. U., 1947, Ph.D. in Biology, 1950. Fellow Nat. Cancer Inst., 1950-52; instr. anatomy U. Ill. Coll. Medicine, 1952-54; mem. rsch. surgery staff Postgrad. Med. Coll., N.Y. U., 1955, asst. prof., 1955-60; Cancer Rsch. Found. prof. biology Sarah Lawrence Coll., 1960-69; prof. zoology, dean Conn. Coll., 1969-76; prof. biology, dean Douglass Coll., Rutgers U., 1976-81; pres. Calif. State U., Fullerton, 1981-90, pres. emerita, prof. emerita, 1990—; Calif. State U. Trustee prof. Calif. State U., L.A., 1990—; mem. Nat. Inst. Medicine; b. dirs. 21st Century Found., CPC Internat., Inc., Allied Sigmal Corp., First Interstate Bancorp, Ga. Pacific. Trustee Drew U. Medicine and Sci., Calif. Inst. Tech. Recipient Alumnae Woman of Yr. award N.Y. U., 1979. Fellow N.Y. Acad. Scis., Tissue Culture Assn.; mem. AAUW, Sigma Xi. Office: Calif State U Off of Pres Los Angeles CA 90032-8500*

COBB, MARGARET MARY, research physician; b. Binghamton, N.Y., Nov. 7, 1948; d. John William and Margaret Mary (Jones) Menta; m. Fredrick Donald Cobb, June 5, 1971; 1 child, Heather Edith. MS, Syracuse U., 1977; PhD, Cornell U., 1981; MD, N.Y. Med. Coll., 1985; MPH with distinction, Yale U., 1990. Diplomate Nat. Bd. Med. Examiners. Rsch. assoc. E.R. Squibb & Sons, Princeton, N.J., 1970-73; rsch. asst. Syracuse (N.Y.) U., 1973-77; sr. rsch. assoc. Cornell U., Ithaca, N.Y., 1977-79; postdoctoral fellow Upstate Med. Ctr., Syracuse, 1980-81; med. intern Yale U. Affiliate, New Haven, Conn., 1985-86, postdoctoral fellow, resident pub. health, 1986-87; rsch. assoc., physician Rockefeller U., N.Y.C., 1987-90; assoc. dir. profl. med. svcs. Am. Cyanamid Corp., Pearl River, N.Y., 1990-93; sr. assoc. med. dir. Pfizer Inc., N.Y.C., 1993-94; pvt. practice N.Y.C.; sr. med. dir. Warner Lambert Co., N.J., 1994—. Eucharistic minister St. Catherine's Ch., Riverside, Conn. Mem. AAAS, AMA, APHA, N.Y. Lipid Club, Sigma Xi. Roman Catholic. Home: 9 Rosewood Ln Denville NJ 07834-3801 Office: 170 Tabor Rd Bldg 3 Morris Plains NJ 07950-2536

COBB, RONALD DAVID, pharmacist, educator; b. Louisville, May 10, 1945; s. Harry D. and Ruth (Roberts) C.; m. Patricia Lee Carroll, Sept. 4, 1964; children: Joy Ruth, Tracy Renee. BS in Pharmacy, U. Ky., 1968, PharmD, 1973. Staff pharmacist Kettering (Ohio) Meml. Hosp., 1968; pharmacist mgr. Lawrence Drugs, Inc., Lexington, Ky., 1969-70; asst. prof. Coll. Pharmacy U. Ky., Lexington, 1973-79, assoc. prof. Coll. Pharmacy, 1980—; pharmacist cons. Blue Cross/Blue Shield of Ky., Louisville, 1976-90, Market Measures, Inc., West Orange, N.J., 1976-94. Contbr. numerous articles to profl. jours. Bd. dirs. Am. Found. for Pharm. Edn., 1991—; trustee Am. Pharm. Assn. Found., 1990-93. Fellow Am. Coll. Apothecaries (assoc.); mem. Blue Grass Pharmacists Assn. (treas. 1969, exec. com. 1969-76, pres.-elect 1970, pres. 1971), Ky. Pharmacists Assn. (bd. dirs. 1972-79, chmn. 1977-78, pres.-elect 1975-76, pres. 1976-77), Am. Inst. History Pharmacy (bd. dirs. 1994—), Am. Pharm. Assn. (chmn. bd. 1989, pres. 1990, trustee 1985-91), Acad. Pharmacy Practice (pres.-elect 1982-83, pres. 1983-84, bd. dirs. 1980-86). Democrat. Baptist. Home: 1516 Pine Meadow Ct Lexington KY 40504-2310 Office: U Ky Coll Pharmacy Lexington KY 40536-0082

COBB, TIMOTHY LEE, physician assistant, military officer; b. Indpls., Nov. 20, 1948; s. John and Norma Alice (Lacey) C.; m. Sandra Lynn Sleeper, May 10, 1975; children: Elizabeth Anne Cobb, Sarah Ann Cobb. AA, St. Petersburg (Fla.) Jr. Coll., 1972; B of Health Scis. magna cum laude, Duke U., 1977. Cert. physican asst.; cert. orthopedic physician asst. Physician asst. emergency medicine Carteret Gen. Hosp., Morehead City, N.C., 1977-80; commd. 2d lt. USAF, 1980, advanced through grades to major, 1989; physician asst. emergency medicine USAF Hosp., Robins AFB, 1980-83; physician asst. dept. medicine David Grant USAF Med. Ctr., Travis AFB, Calif., 1983-86, resident in othropedic surgery, 1986-87; instr. in surgery Uniformed Svcs. U. of Health Scis., Bethesda, Md., 1988—; orthopedic physician asst. Malcolm Grow USAF Med. Ctr., Andrews AFB, Md., 1987-89, 11th Air Force Regional Hosp., Elmendorf AFB, Anchorage, 1989-93; physician asst. Calallen Orthopaedics, Corpus Christi, Tex., 1994—; officer-in-charge dept orthopedic surgery Malcolm Grow USAF Med. Ctr., Andrews AFB, 1987-89. Contbr. articles to profl. jours. Decorated Purple Heart, Vietnamese Cross of Gallantry. Fellow Am. Acad. Physician Assts., Am. Coll. Sports Medicine, Soc. Air Force Physician Assts.; mem. Am. Acad. Pain Mgmt. (clin.), Assn. Mil. Surgeons U.S. Home: 14034 River Rock Dr Corpus Christi TX 78410 Office: Calallen Orthopaedics LLP 13725 F M 624 Corpus Christi TX 78410

COBURN, MARJORIE FOSTER, psychologist, educator; b. Salt Lake City, Feb. 28, 1939; d. Harlan A. and Alma (Ballinger) Polk; m. Robert Byron Coburn, July 2, 1977; children: Polly Klea Foster, Matthew Ryan Foster, Robert Scott Coburn, Kelly Anne Coburn. B.A. in Sociology, UCLA, 1960; Montessori Internat. Diploma honor grad. Washington Montessori Inst., 1968; M.A. in Psychology, U. No. Colo., 1979; Ph.D. in Counseling Psychology, U. Denver, 1983. Licensed clin. psychologist. Probation officer Alameda County (Calif.), Oakland, 1960-62, Contra Costa County (Calif.), El Cerrito, 1966, Fairfax County (Va.), Fairfax, 1967; dir. Friendship Club, Orlando, Fla., 1963-65; tchr. Va. Montessori Sch., Fairfax, 1968-70; spl. edn. tchr. Leary Sch., Falls Church, Va., 1970-72, sch. administr., 1973-76; tchr. Aseltine Sch., San Diego, 1976-77, Coburn Montessori Sch., Colorado Springs, Colo., 1977-79; pvt. practice psychotherapy, Colorado Springs, 1979-82, San Diego, 1982—; cons. spl. edn., agoraphobia, women in transition. Mem. Am. Psychol. Assn., Am. Orthopsychiat. Assn., Phobia Soc., Council Exceptional Children, Calif. Psychol. Assn., San Diego Psychological Assn., The Charter 100, Mensa. Episcopalian. Lodge: Rotary. Contbr. articles to profl. jours.; author: (with R.C. Orem) Montessori: Prescription for Children with Learning Disabilities, 1977. Office: 826 Prospect St Ste 101 La Jolla CA 92037-4206

COBURN, RONALD MURRAY, ophthalmic surgeon, researcher; b. Detroit, Aug. 25, 1943; s. Sidney and Jean (Goldberg) C.; m. Barbara Joan Levy, Feb. 21, 1969; children: Nicholas Scott, Lauren Joy. BS, Wayne State U., 1965, MD, 1969. Diplomate Am. Bd. Ophthalmology, Am. Bd. Eye Surgery (surg. examiner). Dir. The Coburn Clinic, Dearborn, Mich., 1976—; chief ophthalmology Straith Hosp. for Spl. Surgery, Southfield, Mich., 1985—; cons. CooperVision, Inc., Bellevue, Wash., 1985-88, Alcon Surg., Inc., Ft. Worth, 1988—. Co-author: Lens-Stat Intraocular Lens Modeling System; editorial advisor Phaco and Foldables, 1990. Trustee Straith Hosp. for Spl. Surgery, 1986—. Capt. Mich. N.G., 1969-76. Fellow ACS, Internat. Coll. Surgeons, Soc. Eye Surgeons, Royal Soc. Medicine (London), Leadership Soc. ACS; mem. AAAS, Am. Soc. Cataract and Refractive Surgery, Am. Diabetes Assn., Mich. Ophthal. Soc., Wayne County Med. Soc., Rsch. To Prevent Blindness, N.Y. Acad. Scis., Internat. Assn. Ocular Surgeons, Internat. Eye Found., Soc. Geriatric Ophthalmology, Soc. for Excellence in Eye Cre, Internat. Glaucoma Congress, Phi Beta Kappa. Home: 1490 W Long Lake Rd Bloomfield Hills MI 48302-1340 Office: The Coburn Clinic 19855 Outer Dr Dearborn MI 48124-2037

COCANOUR, BARBARA ANN, anatomy educator; b. Mansfield, Ohio, June 17, 1942; d. Milo Charles and Helen Pauline (Mawhorr) C.; m. Don Hilton, Aug. 23, 1969; children: Kirsten Ann, Eric James. PhD, U. Maine, 1969. Asst. prof. Lowell (Mass.) Tech. Inst., 1969-70, vis. prof., 1971-73; vis. prof. U. Lowell, 1976-81, asst. prof., 1981-86, assoc. prof., 1986-91, prof., 1991—. Co-author: Activities Manual for Anatomy and Physiology, 1990; Laboratory Manual for Human Anatomy and Physiology, 1990; author: Flashcards for Human Anatomy and Physiology, 1990, Photographic Atlas, 1995, A Videodisc Index for Slice of Life VI, 1995, Photographic Atlas, 1995. Mem. AAAS, Nat. Sci. Tchrs. Assn., Human Anatomy and Physiology Soc.,. Home: 175 Massachusetts Ave Harvard MA 01451 Office: U Mass Lowell Dept Phys Therapy Lowell MA 01854

COCANOUR, CHRISTINE SUSAN, surgery educator, researcher; b. Mansfield, Ohio, Nov. 13, 1955; d. Milo Charles and Helen Pauline (Mawhorr) C. BA in Chemistry, BS in Biology, U. Toledo, 1977; MD, U. Cin., 1982. Diplomate Am. Bd. Surgery. Intern Case Western Res. U., 1982-83, resident in integrated surgery, 1983-85, 86-88, Dudley P. Allen surg. rsch. fellow, 1985-86; trauma/critical care fellow U. Tex. Health Sci. Ctr., Houston, 1988-89; clin. instr. surgery U. Tex. Med. Sch., Houston, 1988, asst. prof., 1989—. Mem. Assn. for Acad. Surgery. Office: U Tex Med Sch 6431 Fannin St # 164 Houston TX 77030-1501

COCANOUR HILTON, BARBARA ANN, anatomist, educator; b. Mansfield, Ohio, June 17, 1942; d. Milo Charles and Helen Pauline (Mawhorr) Cocanour; m. Donald Bertram Hilton, Aug. 23, 1969; children: Kirsten Ann Hilton, Eric James Hilton. AB, Defiance Coll., 1964; MS, U. Maine, 1966, PhD, 1969. Asst. prof., then vis. lectr. Lowell (Mass.) Technol. Inst., 1969-74; from vis. lectr. to asst. prof. U. Lowell, 1976-86; from assoc. prof. to prof. physical therapy U. Mass., Lowell, 1986—. Author: Activities Manual for Anatomy & Physiology, 1990, Photographic Atlas, 1995. Mem. AAAS, Nat. Sci. Tchrs. Assn., Soc. Coll. Sci. Tchrs., Human Anatomy and Physiology Soc., Sigma Xi. Office: U Mass Lowell Lowell MA 01854

COCCARO, MAUREEN, health facility administrator; b. Jersey City, Jan. 15, 1950; d. Philip A. and Winifred Reilly; m. Frank N. Coccaro, May 10, 1975; children: Courtney, Frankie, Brianne. Diploma, St. Francis Hosp., Jersey City, 1971; BA, Jersey City State Coll., 1975, MS, 1987. Cert. tchr., N.J., sch. nurse; RN, N.J.; cert. quality mgmt. profl. Staff nurse critical care unit St. Francis Hosp.; staff nurse emergency room Jersey City Med. Ctr., critical care coord., supr., asst. dir. nursing. Mem. ANA, EDNA. Home: 91 Ottawa Ave Hasbrouck Heights NJ 07604-1410

COCHÉ, JUDITH, psychologist, educator; b. Phila., Sept. 2, 1942; d. Louis and Miriam (Nerenberg) Milner; m. Erich Coché, Oct. 16, 1966 (dec.); 1 child, Juliette Laura; m. John Anderson, Jan. 1, 1994. BA, Colby Coll., 1964; MA, Temple U., 1966; PhD, Bryn Mawr Coll., 1975. Diplomate Am. Bd. Profl. Psychology. Rsch. asst. Jefferson Med. Coll., 1965-66; diagnostician Law Ct., Aachen, Germany, 1967-68; staff psychologist N.E. Community Mental Health Ctr., Phila., 1969-74; family clinician Inst. Pa. Hosp., 1974-76; instr. psychology Drexel U., 1976-77; lectr. Med. Coll. Pa., 1977-78; asst. clin. prof. Hahnemann Med. Coll., Phila., 1979—; pvt. practice Phila., 1974—, N.J., 1985—; assoc. prof. psychiatry U. Pa., 1985—; mem. faculty Family Inst. of Phila., 1990—; sr. cons. Phila. Child Guidance Clinic, 1992—; clin. cons. Hilltop Prep Sch., 1977-86; clin. supr. Am. Assn. Marriage and Family Therapy. Co-author: Couples Group Psychotherapy, A Clinical Practice Model, 1990; contbr. chpts. to books, articles to profl. jours. Bd. dirs. Whitemarsh Art Ctr., 1977-78, Please Touch Museum, 1982-89; mem. prof. adv. bd. Parents Without Ptnrs., 1977-86; mem. adv. com. Pa. Ballet/Shirley Rock. Grantee Del. Children's Bur. Bryn Mawr Coll., 1974-75, Pa. Hosp., 1975-77. Fellow Am. Group Psychotherapy Assn.; mem. APA, Am. Assn. Marriage and Family Therapy (approved supr.), Am. Family Therapy Assn., Phila. Soc. Clin. Psychologists (pres. 1980-81), Family Inst. Phila., Pa. Psychol. Assn. (chmn. legis. com. 1982), Soc. Rsch. in Psychotherapy. Address: 210 W Rittenhouse Sq Ste 404 Philadelphia PA 19103

COCHIN, ARNOLD MITCHELL, dentist; b. N.Y.C., Feb. 9, 1951; s. Henry and Fannie (Osherowitz) C.; m. Laurie Anne Chizever; 1 child, Hillary Fayth. BA, Queens Coll., 1972; DDS, Columbia U., 1977. Lic. dentist, N.Y. Gen. practice resident USPHS, San Francisco, 1977-78; staff USPHS, 1978-79; pvt. practice N.Y.C., 1979—; asst. prof. prosthodontics Columbia U. Sch. Dental and Oral Surgery, N.Y.C., 1979—; cons. Lithghouse Child Devel. Ctr., 1982—. Vol., N.Y. Assn. for Blind, 1982—. Lt. USPHS, 1977-79. Recipient Fraternal Achievement award Psi Omega, 1977; Acad. Gen. Dentistry fellow, 1983. Fellow N.Y. Acad. Dentistry; mem. Dental Soc. N.Y., ADA, Acad. Gen. Dentistry, Am. Golf Club, Oku Honor Soc. Jewish. Home: 420 E 72nd St # 4J New York NY 10021-4615 Office: 47 E 64th St New York NY 10021-7044

COCHRAN, KENNETH WILLIAM, toxicologist; b. Chgo., Nov. 2, 1923; m. Martha Louise Wells, May 10, 1945; children: Kenneth W. III, Kimberley W. Cochran Nelson. SB, U. Chgo., 1947, PhD, 1950. Rsch. asst. to instr., toxicity lab. and dept. pharmacology U. Chgo., 1946-52; from rsch. assoc., instr. to prof. emeritus U. Mich., Ann Arbor, 1952—. Contbr. articles to profl. jours. 1st lt. U.S. Army, 1943-46. Fellow AAAS; mem. Am. Soc. for Microbiology, Soc. for Exptl. Biology and Medicine, Am. Soc. for Pharmacology and Exptl. Therapeutics, Mycol. Soc. of Am., N.Am. Mycol. Assn. (exec. sec. 1988—). Home: 3556 Oakwood St Ann Arbor MI 48104-5213 Office: N Am Mycol Assn 3556 Oakwood St Ann Arbor MI 48104-5213

COCHRAN, MARY ANN, nurse educator; b. Chgo., Dec. 12, 1951; d. Lawrence Donovan and Mary Gracz (Capizzi) Lee; m. Thomas Lee Cochran, Mar. 12, 1971; 1 child, Nathan Edgar. Diploma in nursing, St. Joseph's Hosp., Joliet, Ill., 1973. RN, Ill.; cert. post anesthesia nurse; cert. ambulatory perianesthesia. Staff nurse Silver Cross Hosp., Joliet, 1973—, stafff nurse ICU, 1979—, in-svc. educator post anesthesia care unit, 1987-92, BLS instr., 1987—, postanesthesia care unit charge nurse, 1994—. Mem. AACN, Am. Soc. Post Anesthesia Nurses, Ill. Soc. Post Anesthesia Nurses (membership chair 1990-92, ways & means chair 1992-95, Ill. dist. 1 dir. 1995—). Office: Silver Cross Hosp 1200 Maple Rd Joliet IL 60432-1439

COCHRAN, ROBERT CARTER, surgical educator; b. Newton, Mass., Oct. 9, 1932; s. Williams and Mary Faith (Williams) C.; m. Norma Rae Creighton, Aug. 27, 1958 (div. Aug. 1986); children: Barbara, Gwen, William; m. Rebecca Anne Fain, Feb. 3, 1990. BA, Princeton (N.J.) U., 1955; MD, Boston U., 1960. Diplomate Am. Bd. Surgery. Intern Mass. Meml. Hosp., Boston, 1960-61; resident Bethesda (Md.) Naval Hosp., 1963-67; commd. ensign USN, 1956, advanced through grades to capt.; intern Mass. Gen. Hosp.; resident in surgery N.H. Bethesda Hosp.; mem. surg. staff USN, Bethesda, Md., 1961-80; chief of surgery USN Hosp., Bethesda, 1980-83; pvt. practice Hygeia Med. Specialist Group, Charleston, W.Va., 1983-86; prof. Med. Sch. W.Va. U., Charleston, 1986; asst. prof. surgery Uniformed Svcs. Univ. of Health Scis. Decorated Cross of Gallantry (Vietnam), Meritorious Svc. medal USN. Episcopalian. Office: U Health Assocs 3110 MacCorkle Ave SE Charleston WV 25304

COCHRAN, SAMUEL WARREN, psychology educator; b. Wayne County, Miss., Aug. 1, 1921; s. Samuel Wilburn and Bessie Irene (Robinson) C.; m. Pauline Wingo, Feb. 17, 1945; children: Thomas Wilburn, Rebecca Suzanne. BA, Miss. Coll., 1947; MA, George Peabody Coll. Tchrs., 1948; PhD, Ohio State U., 1963. Lic. psychologist, Tex. Assoc. prof. Miss. Coll., Clinton, 1949-52; human factors engr. Air Force Flight Test Ctr., Calif., 1959-60; assoc. prof. USAF Acad., Colo., 1960-66; prof. psychology East Tex. State U., Commerce, Tex., 1969-85; sr. Fulbright lectr. Turkey, 1982-83; adj. prof. U. Tex., San Antonio, 1986—. Co-author: Long Range Planning by the Delphi Method, 1972; contbr. articles to profl. jours. Lt. col. USAF ret., 1940-45, 53-69. Decorated Disting. Flying Cross. Mem. APA, S.W. Psychol. Assn. Baptist. Home: 5100 John D Ryan Blvd Apt 635 San Antonio TX 78245-3535 Office: U Tex San Antonio San Antonio TX 78285

COCHRAN, TERENCE A., general, vascular and chest surgeon; b. Marion, Ohio, July 8, 1944; s. William Dean and Marian Eleanor (Marks) C.; m. Regina Ellen Denault, May 1, 1985; children: Jason, Nathan, Joshua. BS, Ohio State U., 1966, MD, 1970. Diplomate Am. Bd. Surgery. Resident in surgery Univ. Hosp.-Ohio State U., Columbus, 1970-71, Thomas Jefferson U. Hosp., Phila., 1973-76; pvt. practice, Scranton, Pa., 1976—; v.p. Moses Taylor Hosp., Scranton, 1992-94, pres., 1994-95; pres. Vascular Diagnostic Ctr., Scranton, 1994—. Capt. M.C., U.S. Army, 1971-73, Vietnam. Fellow ACS; mem. Pa. Thoracic Surgery Soc. Office: Integrated Surg Assocs 1054 Oak St Scranton PA 18508

COCHRANE, ROBERT LOWE, biologist; b. Morgantown, W.Va., Feb. 10, 1931; s. Thomas Joseph and Isabelle Durston (Lowe) C. BA, W.Va. U., 1953; MS, U. Wis., 1954, PhD, 1961. Rsch. asst. genetics U. Wis., Madison, 1953-55, rsch. asst. zoology, 1957-60; agt. in animal husbandry U.S. Dept. Agr., Madison, Wis., 1955-61; biologist FDA, Washington, 1961-62; sr. research fellow dept. anatomy U. Birmingham (Eng.), 1962-65; project assoc. dept. physiology U. Pitts., 1965-66; sr. endocrinologist Eli Lilly & Co., Indpls., 1966-80; rsch. assoc. G.D. Searle & Co., Skokie, Ill., 1980-81; with Short's Fur Farm, Granton, Wis., 1981-83; rsch. assoc. Marshfield (Wis.) Med. Found., 1983-84; biologist Northwood Fur Farms, Inc., Cary, Ill., 1984; cons. for FAO to Wildlife Inst. India, Dehra Dun, 1985; adj. prof. div. animal and vet. sci., W.Va. U., Morgantown, 1987—; ad hoc reviewer various sci. jours.; ad hoc reviewer U.S. Dept. of Agr. Competitive Rsch. Grants. Contbr. numerous research articles and abstracts on reproduction to profl. jours.; participant Internat. Mink Show, Madison, Wis., 1976-96, W.Va. State Fox Show, Morgantown, 1989; rsch. bd. of advisors The Am. Biog. Inst., 1988-96; mem. adv. coun. Internat. Biog. Centre, 1989-96. Recipient Knight of Golden Horse Shoe award W.Va. Pub. Sch. System, 1945, W.Va. Boy's State, 1948; U. Birmingham (Eng.) sr. rsch. fellow, 1962-65. Mem. AAAS, Am. Inst. Biol. Scis., Soc. Exptl. Biology and Medicine, Soc. for Study of Fertility, Soc. Study of Reproduction, Am. Soc. Animal Sci., Endocrine Soc., N.Y. Acad. Sci., Soc. Endocrinology, Coun. Agrl. Sci. and Tech., Internat. Platform Assn., NRA (life), Sigma Xi, Pi Kappa Alpha. Achievements include major contributions to the establishment of the hormonal requirements for ova-implantation and embryonic diapause in the rat, the elucidation of the role played by prostaglandins in corpus luteum function, parturition and ductus arteriosus closure in the rat; the development of steroid synthesis inhibitors for controlling reproduction in mammals; the documentation of the timing, duration and pattern of reproductive cycles in martens; the dissemination of scientific information on fur farming to the commercial fur trade and public. Presbyterian. Home: 404 Junior Ave Morgantown WV 26505-2208

COCKE, WILLIAM MARVIN, JR., plastic surgeon, educator; b. Balt., Aug. 2, 1934; s. William M. and Clara E. (Bosley) C.; m. Sue Ann Harris, Apr. 25, 1981; children: Gregory William, Laura Marie, Julie Ann; children by previous marriage: William Marvin III, Catherine Lynn, Deborah Kay, Brian Thomas. B.S. with honors in Biology, Tex. A&M U., 1956; M.D., Baylor U., 1960. Diplomate: Am. Bd. Plastic Surgery (guest examiner 1978). Intern surgery Vanderbilt U. Hosp., Nashville, 1960-61; fellow gen. surgery Ochsner Clinic and Found. Hosp., New Orleans, 1961-64; chief resident surgery Monroe (La.) Charity Hosp., 1963-64; resident reconstructive surgery Roswell Park Meml. Inst., Buffalo, 1965-66; chief resident plastic surgery VA Hosp., Bronx, N.Y., 1966; practice medicine specializing in plastic surgery Nashville, 1968-75, Sacramento, 1976-79; pvt. practice medicine specializing in plastic surgery Bryan, Tex., 1980-92; prof. surgery, head div. plastic/reconstructive surgery Marshall U. Sch. of Medicine, Huntington, W.Va., 1992—; mem. staff St. Mary's Hosp., Cabell-Huntington Hosp., Huntington Vets. Med. Ctr.; asst. prof. plastic surgery Vanderbilt U. Sch. Medicine, Nashville, 1968-69, asst. clin. prof. plastic surgery, 1969-75; assoc. prof. plastic surgery Ind. U. Sch. Medicine, Indpls., 1975-76; chief plastic surgery service Wishard Meml. Hosp., Ind. U., 1975-76; assoc. prof. surgery U. Calif. Sch. Medicine, Davis, 1976-79, chmn. dept. plastic surgery, 1976-79; prof. surgery, chief div. plastic surgery Tex. Tech. U. Sch. Medicine, Lubbock, 1979-80, dir. Microsurg. Research Lab., 1979-80; clin. prof. surgery Tex. A&M U. Sch. Medicine, 1983-92; prof. plastic surgery, 1986-89; chief plastic surgery svc., dept. surgery, Olin Teague VA Med. Ctr., Temple, Tex., 1986-92; prof. head surgery divsn. plastic and reconstruction Marshall U. Sch. Medicine, 1992—. Author textbooks on plastic surgery; contbr. articles to profl. jours. Served with M.C. USAF, 1966-68. Recipient Dean Echols award Ochsner Hosp. Found., 1963. Mem. ACS, Am. Assn. Plastic Surgeons, Soc. Head and Neck Surgeons, Assn. for Acad. Surgery, Alton Ochsner Surg. Soc. Episcopalian. Home: 45 Olde Farm Rd Ona WV 25545-9747 Office: Marshall U Sch Medicine Dept Surgery 1801 6th Ave Huntington WV 25703-1585

COCKEFAIR, DOROTHY ANN, nurse, educator; b. Hackensack, N.J., July 7, 1949; d. Richard Charles and Dorothea Margaret (Bastow) Thomas; m. James Arthur Cockefair, Apr. 28, 1973; 1 child, Cheryl Lynn. Diploma, Englewood (N.J.) Hosp. Sch. Nursing, 1969; cert. tchr., Montclair (N.J.) State Coll., 1975; BSN, Jersey City State Coll., 1981. RN, N.J.; cert. tchr., N.J. Staff nurse cen. CCU, ICU Hackensack Hosp., 1969-70; head nurse Holy Name Hosp., Teaneck, N.J., 1970-72; nursing instr. Bergen County Vocat. Bd. Edn., Hackensack, 1972-82; staff nurse Hackensack Med. Ctr., 1981-82, nurse educator, 1982—; rehab. nurse cons. Alternatives for Growth, Inc., Elmwood Park, N.J., 1986—; instr. CPR Bergen County Heart Assn., 1983—. Chairperson Bogota High Sch. Reunion Com., 1986—. Nursing scholar Am. Legion, 1967, Women's Club, 1967, Altrusia Club Am., 1967. Mem. Am. Heart Assn., Sigma Teta Tau (chair. nominating com. 1986—). Office: Hackensack University Medical Ctr 30 Prospect Ave Hackensack NJ 07601-1915

COCKERHAM, COLUMBUS CLARK, retired geneticist, educator; b. Mountain Park, N.C., Dec. 12, 1921; s. Corbett C. and Nellie Bruce (McCann) C.; m. Joyce Evelyn Allen, Feb. 26, 1944; children: Columbus Clark Jr., Jean Allen, Bruce Allen. B.S., N.C. State Coll., 1943, M.S., 1949; Ph.D., Iowa State Coll., 1952. Asst. prof. biostats. U. N.C., Chapel Hill, 1952-53; mem. faculty N.C. State U., Raleigh, 1953—, prof. stats., 1959-72, William Neal Reynolds prof. stats. and genetics, 1972—, disting. univ. prof., 1988—, prof. emeritus, 1991—; mem. genetics study sect. NIH, 1965-69; cons. adv. com. protocols for safety evaluation FDA, 1967-69. Author papers population and quantitative genetics, plant and animal breeding; editor, assoc. editor: Theoretical Population Biology, 1975-85; editl. bd.: Genetics, 1969-72, Genetic Epidemiology, 1984-90; assoc. editor: Am. Jour. Human Genetics, 1978-80. Served with USMCR, 1943-46. Recipient N.C. award in sci., 1976, Oliver Max Gardner award, 1980, D.D. Mason faculty award, 1983, N.C. State U. Alumni Assn. award, 1986, Superior Svc. award (group award) USDA, 1990, Alexander Quarles Holladay medal, 1994; grantee Nat. Inst. Gen. Med. Scis., 1960-95. Fellow AAAS, Am. Soc. Agronomy, Crop Sci. Soc. Am.; mem. NAS, Am. Soc. Animal Sci., Biometric Soc., Genetics Soc. Am., Genetics Soc. Japan (fgn. hon. mem.), Sigma Xi, Gamma Sigma Delta (award merit 1954), Phi Kappa Phi. Office: NC State U Dept Stats Box 8203 Raleigh NC 27695

COCKERHAM, LORRIS G., radiation toxicologist; b. Denham Springs, La., Sept. 27, 1935; s. Warren Conrad and Leda Frances (Scivicque) C.; BA, La. Coll., 1957; MS, Colo. State U., 1973, PhD, 1979; m. Patricia Ann Stagg, Aug. 16, 1957; children: Michael B., Richard L., Ann E., Joseph D. Commd. 2d lt. USAF, 1961, advanced through grades to lt. col., 1977; instr. James Connelly AFB, Tex., 1963-66; squadron electronic warfare officer, Fairchild AFB, Wash., 1966-71; asst. prof. dept. chemistry and biology USAF Acad., Colo., 1973-77; wing electronic warfare officer Griffiss AFB, N.Y., 1977-78, comdr. 416 Munitions Maintenance Squadron, 1978-80, Armed Forces Radiobiology Rsch. Inst., Def. Nuclear Agy., Bethesda, Md., 1980-86; Air Force Office of Sci. Rsch., Bolling AFB, D.C., 1986-87, ret., 1987; exec. dir. NCTR-Associated Univs., Little Rock, 1988-89; pres. The Delta Agy., Little Rock, 1989-93, Phenix Cons. and Svcs. Corp, Little Rock, 1993—; dir. Product Safety Labs., East Brunswick, N.J., 1994-95; asst. prof. physiology Sch. Medicine, Uniformed Svcs. U. Health Scis., 1981-87; assoc. prof. U. Ark. for Med. Scis., 1988-89. Troop com. chmn. Iroquois council Boy Scouts Am., 1978-80. Decorated D.F.C. (2), Airman's medal, Air medal (12), Air Force Commendation medal; Air Force Logistics Command Dioxin Research grantee, 1974-79; recipient Order of Arrow, Boy Scouts Am.; named Disting. Alumnus La. Coll., 1989. Mem. Soc. Neurosci., Internat. Brain Research Orgn., World Fedn. Neuroscientists, Soc. Toxicology, Am. Physiol. Soc., Am. Coll. Toxicology, Sigma Xi, Phi Kappa Phi. Republican. Southern Baptist.

COCKERHAM, MICHAEL BRET, pharmacist, educator; b. Sacramento, Calif., Aug. 4, 1962; s. Lorris G. and Patricia A. (Stagg) C. BS, La. Coll., 1984, N.E. La. U., 1989; MS, N.E. La. U., 1986. Biol. lab. technician Armed Forces Radiobiology Rsch. Inst., Bethesda, Md., 1981-83; biology lab. asst. La. Coll., Pineville, La., 1982-84; vet. asst. Rapides Annual Med. Ctr., Alexandria, La., 1983-84; grad. teaching asst. N.E. La. U., Monroe, 1984-86, dialysis technician, 1985-86, adj. asst. prof. clin. pharmacy, 1994—; chemistry tchr. West Monroe (La.) High Sch., 1986-87; grad. teaching asst. N.E. La. U., Monroe, 1988-89; chief pharmacist, asst. mgr. Revco Drug Stores, Haughton, La., 1989-90; staff pharmacist VA Med. Ctr., Shreveport, La., 1990—, clin. pharmacy specialist in oncology, 1992-95; asst. prof clin. pharmacy practice Notheast La. U., Monroe, 1995—; clin. pharmacy specialist hematology, oncology La. State Univ. Med. Ctr., Shreveport, 1995—. Mem. Am. Soc. Hosp. Health System Pharmacists, La. Soc. Hosp. Health System Pharmacists, No. La. Soc. Hosp Pharmacists, La. Soc. Hosp. Pharmacists. Republican. Baptist. Home: 9017 Cedar Hill Ln Shreveport LA 71118-2322 Office: NE La U Sch of Pharmacy 700 University Ave Monroe LA 71209

COCKETT, ABRAHAM T. K., urologist; b. Maui, Hawaii, Sept. 4, 1928. BS, Brigham Young U., 1950; MD, U. Utah, 1954. Diplomate Am. Bd. of Urology. Intern VA Hosp., L.A., 1954-55; gen. surgery resident VA Hosp., Los Angeles, 1955-56; urology resident UCLA Sch. of Med., 1956-60; chief experimental surgery dept. USAF Aerospace Div., Brooks AFB, Tex., 1961-62; chief urology service Harbor Gen. Hosp., Torrance, Calif., 1962-69; Winfield W. Scott prof., chmn. dept. urology U. Rochester, N.Y., 1969-95; pres. Internat. Consultation on BPH, Paris, 1991, 92, 95. Author: Manual of Urologic Surgery, 1979; co-author: Colora Atlas of UrologicSurgery, 1996; editor: Male Infertility, 1976; contbr. more than 300 articles to profl. jours. Mem. Am. Urol. Assn. (sec. 1987-92, pres.-elect 1992, 93, pres. 1993-94, editor AUA Today 1992—), Am. Assn. Genitourinary Surgeons, Clin. Soc. Genitourinary Surgeons. Office: Strong Meml Hosp 601 Elmwood Ave Rochester NY 14642-0001

COCKING, ROBERTA ELAINE, health educator, training specialist; b. Las Vegas, Dec. 19, 1949; d. Robert D. and Carmen C. (Gallegos) Geoffrion; m. Steven A. Cocking, June 6, 1969; children: Steven, Brian, Matthew. BS, Eastern N.M. U., 1972; cert. health, U. N.M., 1985. Health educator Los Alamos (N.M.) Middle Schs., 1977—; tng. specialist Los Alamos Nat. Lab., 1990—. Named Outstanding Cmty. Health Educator Dept. Health and Environment, Washington, 1988, Tchr. of Yr., Apple Macintosh Computers, Washington, 1991, Outstanding N.M. Woman, Gov. N.M., Santa Fe, 1994; recipient N.M. State Legis. award for tchg. excellence, Santa Fe, 1995. Roman Catholic. Home: 318 Garver Ln Los Alamos NM 87544 Office: Los Alamos Middle Schs 2101 Cumbres Dr Los Alamos NM 87544

COCORES, JAMES ALEXANDER, psychiatrist; b. Newark, Nov. 29, 1953; s. Stephen and Helen (Genakos) C.; m. Mary Christina Syris, Nov. 1, 1981; children: Eleni, Alexa, Stephanie. AA, County Coll. Morris, Randolph, N.J., 1973; BA, Rutgers U., 1975; MD, SanPedro, Dominican Republic, 1980. Intern Bergen Pines County Hosp., Paramas, N.J. 1981; resident Bergen Pines County Hosp., Paramas, 1982-84; rsch. psychiatrist Fair Oaks Hosp., Summit, N.J., 1984-92; inpatient substance abuse unit dir. Fair Oaks Hosp., 1985-87, med. dir. outpatient recovery ctrs., 1985-93; dir. Spruce Hill Treatment Ctr., Henryville, Pa., 1993-94; editor The Clin. Mgmt. of Nicotine Dependence. Author: 800 Cocaine Book of Drug and Alcohol Recovery, 1990; contbr. articles to profl. jours. Recipient Menninger award Cen. Neuropsychiat. Assn., 1983. Republican. Christian Orthodox. Office: 66 Maple Ave Morristown NJ 07960 also: 95 Summit Ave Summit NJ 07902

CODA, LESLIE ANNE, community health nurse, pediatrics nurse; b. Erie, Pa., May 17, 1952; d. Nello and Gene (Hendrickson) C. BSN, U. Pitts., 1974; MSN, U. Va., 1979. RN, Pa.; cert. registered nurse practitioner. Staff nurse Children's Hosp., Pitts., 1974-76, staff devel. instr., 1976-77; PNP West Pa. Hosp., Pitts., 1979—. Mem. NAPNAP (sec. Three Rivers). Home: 322 Edgewood Rd Pittsburgh PA 15221-4424

CODERRE, CAROLE A., pediatrics nurse; b. Boston, Jan. 16, 1969; d. Ferdinand Andrew and Esther Anne (Peterson) C. BS, Northeastern U., 1993. RN, Mass. Staff nurse in charge of pediat. New England Med. Ctr., Boston, 1993—. Vol., Mission Tour to Dominican Republic, 1991-93, Main Springhouse, Brockton, Mass., 1990—; youth leader TABCOM, Boston/Dedham, 1992—; chair, missions com., Hanover, 1993—. Recipient award for outstanding cmty. svc., Northeastern U., 1993. Mem. Mass. Nursing Assn., Northeastern Nursing Alumni Assn. (mem. ethics com. 1993—). Republican. Baptist.

CODISPOTI, ANDRE JOHN, allergist, immunologist; b. Bklyn., Apr. 27, 1938; s. Bruno Mario and Antoinette (Savarese) C.; m. Miranda Babini, June 14, 1967; children: Rita, Elisa, Andrew. BA, Coll. of Holy Cross, 1959; MD, U. Bologna, Italy, 1965. Diplomate Am. Bd. Pediatrics, Am. Bd. Allergy and Immunology. Pvt. practice medicine Suffern, N.Y., 1972—; rotating intern. Long Island Coll. Hosp., Brooklyn, N.Y., 1966, resident ped., 1967-69, fellow Allergy and Immunology, 1971-73. Maj. Med. Corps U.S. Army, 1969-71. Fellow Am. Coll. Allergy, Asthma and Immunology, Am. Acad. Allergy, Asthma and Immunology. Republican. Roman Catholic. Office: 7 Hemion Rd Suffern NY 10901

COE, FREDRIC L., physician, educator, researcher; b. Chgo., Dec. 25, 1936; s. Lester J. and Lillian (Chaitlen) C.; m. Eleanor Joyce Brodny, May 5, 1965; children: Brian, Laura. A.B., U. Chgo., 1955; M.S., U. Chgo., 1957; M.D., U. Chgo., 1961. Diplomate Am. Bd. Internal Medicine. Intern Michael Reese Hosp., Chgo., 1961-62, resident, 1962-65; resident U. Tex. S.W. Med. Sch., 1967-69; chmn. nephrology Michael Reese Hosp., 1972-82; prof. medicine U. Chgo., 1977—, prof. physiology, 1979—; chmn. nephrology A.M. Billings Hosp., Chgo., 1982—; founder, pres. Litholink Corp. Author: Nephrolithiasis, 1978, 2d edit. (with J. Parks), 1987, (with B. Brenner and F.C. Rector) Renal Physiology, 1986, Clinical Nephrology; editor: Renal Therapeutics, 1978, Nephrolithiasis, 1980, Hypercalciuric States, 1983, (with M. Favus) Disorders of Bone and Mineral Metabolism, 1993; editor-in-chief Yearbook of Nephrology; editor: (with others) Kidney Stones: Medical and Surgical Management, 1996. Served to capt. USAF, 1961-67. Grantee NIH, 1977—. Fellow ACP; mem. Am. Soc. Clin. Investigation, Am. Physiol. Soc., Assn. Am. Physicians. Jewish. Home: 5490 S South Shore Dr Chicago IL 60615-5920 Office: U Chgo Med Ctr 5841 S Maryland Ave Chicago IL 60637-1463

COELHO, ALÍPIO D'OLIVEIRA, health facility director, education educator; b. Pelotas, R.S., Brazil, July 1, 1945; s. Paulo Soares and Yolanda (D'Oliveira) C.; m. Elizabeth Roth, July 18, 1970; children: Cristiane, Luciano, Rogério. Degree in medicine, U. Fed. Pelotas, 1969. Asst prof. U. Fed. Paraná, Curitiba, Brazil, 1971-77, Pelotas, Brazil, 1984—; asst prof. U. Católica Pelotas, 1977—; pres. dir. Clin. Doencas Renais, Pelotas, 1984—; clin. dir. Hemodialysis Unit Santa Casa, Pelotas, 1977—, Transplantation Unit Santa Casa, Pelotas, 1981—; clin. dir. Santa Casa Misericordia, Pelotas, 1990—. Mem. ACP, Internat. Soc. Nephrology, Soc. Medicina Pelotas (sci. dir. 1991-93), Soc. Brasileira Nefrologia. Home: Rua Alexandre Gastaud 01, 96020 Pelotas RS, Brazil Office: Clinica Doenças Renais, Praça Piratinino Almeida 53, 96015-730 Pelotas RS, Brazil

COELHO, ANTHONY MENDES, JR., health science administrator; b. Danbury, Conn., May 26, 1947; s. Anthony Mendes and Angela (Fernandes) C.; m. Linda Straw, Jan. 12, 1974. BS in Social Scis., Western Conn. State U., 1970; MA in Phys.-Biol. Anthropology, U. Tex., 1973, PhD in Phys.-Biol. Anthropology, 1975. Cert. social scis. secondary tchr., Conn. Asst. prof. anthropology Tex. Tech U., Lubbock, 1974-75; instr. social-cultural anthropology U. Tex., Austin, 1971-72, teaching asst. phys.-biol. anthropology, 1972-74; asst. scientist S.W. Found. for Biomed. Rsch., San Antonio, 1975-76, assoc. scientist, 1976-86, scientist, 1986-92, head Behavioral Medicine Lab., 1975-92; health sci. and sci. rev. adminstr., leader clin. studies NIH, Bethesda, Md., 1992—; adj. asst. prof. pediatrics U. Tex. Health Scis. Ctr., San Antonio, 1976-84, adj. assoc. prof., 1984-92, adj. assoc. prof. dental diagnostic scis., 1984-90, adj. prof. surgery and neurosurgery, 1989-92; lectr. social and behavioral scis. U. Tex., San Antonio, 1977-82; mem. rsch. manpower rev. com. NIH, Bethesda, Md., 1988-92; grant reviewer NSF, Nat. Geog. Soc., NIMH, Alcohol Drug Abuse and Mental Health Adminstrn., Nat. Scis. and Engring. Rsch. Coun., Can. Wenner-Gren Found. for Anthrop. Rsch.; leader Clin. Studies and Tng. Sci. Review Group; reviewer various sci. jours. Contbr. articles to sci. jours.. Active Am. Heart Assn. Scholar Command Security Corp., 1970, U. Tex., 1972-74; grantee NIH, 1983, 85, 89. Mem. Am. Soc. Primatologists (exec. sec., bd. dirs. 1982-84, cons. editor Am. Jour. Primatol., 1986—, editor book reviews 1989-91), Am. Assn. Phys. Anthropologists, Soc. Behavioral Medicine, Nat. Coun. U. Rsch. Adminstrs., Animal Behavior Soc., Human Biology Coun., Inst. for Advancement Health, Internat. Primatol. Soc., Latin Am. Soc. Primatology, Soc. Rsch. Adminstrs., Sigma Xi, Phi Kappa Phi, Delta Tau Kappa. Home: 6 Canterfield Ct Germantown MD 20876-4374 Office: NIH-NHLBI Rev Br 6701 Rockledge Dr Bethesda MD 20892-7294

COEN, STANLEY JEROME, psychiatrist; b. N.Y.C., July 17, 1937; s. Abraham and Helen (Gershick) C.; m. Ruth Imber, June 30, 1972; children: Gwendolyn, Jennifer, Michael, Deborah, David. AB summa cum laude, Columbia Coll., 1958, MD, 1962; cert. psychoanalysis, Columbia U., 1973. Intern and resident Johns Hospkins Hosp., Balt., 1962-66; svc. chief NIMH Clin. Rsch. Ctr., Lexington, Ky., 1966-68; asst. attending psychiatrist Presbyn. Hosp., N.Y.C., 1968-73, N.Y. Hosp., 1977-78; staff psychoanalyst Columbia U. Psychoanalytic Ctr., N.Y.C., 1976—, tng. and supervising analyst, 1991—, faculty, 1973—; mem. faculty Columbia U. Coll. Physicians and Surgeons, N.Y.C., 1968—, assoc. clin. prof. psychiatry, 1985-90, clin. prof., 1990—; manuscript reviewer numerous jours. and univ. presses. Author: The Misuse of Persons: Analyzing Pathological Dependency, 1992, Between Author and Reader: A Psychoanalytic Approach to Writing and Reading, 1994; contbr. articles to profl. jours. Surgeon USPHS, 1966-68. Recipient Alexander Beller Meml. Prize Columbia U. Psychoanalytic Ctr., 1982. Fellow Am. Psychiat. Assn.; mem. Am. Psychoanalytic Assn. (editl. bd. Jour. 1990-93, 1995—), Internat. Psychoanalytic Assn., Assn. for Psychoanalytic Medicine (sec. 1981-85).

COFFELT, TERRY ALAN, research geneticist; b. South Bend, Ind., Nov. 7, 1947; s. Theo Laverne and Eilene (Brant) C.; m. Shirley Marie Armstrong, Sept. 9, 1972; children: Charles, Thomas. BS, Purdue U., 1969; MS, U. Ga., 1971, PhD, 1973. NDEA fellow U. Ga., Athens, 1970-73; rsch. geneticist Agrl. Rsch. Svc., USDA, Suffolk, Va., 1973-94, Phoenix, 1994—. Contbr. articles and abstracts to Arachis hypogaea Linnaeus, Jour. Am. Peanut Rsch. and Edn. Assn., Ga. Agron. Abstracts, Jour. Heredity, Oleagineaux, Peanut Sci., Procs. Am. Peanut Rsch. and Edn. Assn., Plant Disease Reporter, Agronomy Jour., Va.-Carolina Peanut News, Plant Disease, Crop Sci., Va. Jour. Sci., Va. Agrl. Exptl. Sta. Bull., Indsl. Crops and Products, Horticultural Sci.; author: (with others) Peanut Science and Technology, 1982, Oil Crops of the World, 1989. Sec., v.p., then pres. Holland Ruritan Club, Suffolk, 1974-80. Fellow Am. Peanut Rsch. and Edn. Soc. (mem. several coms.); mem. Am. Soc. Agronomy, Crop Sci. Soc. Am., Am. Assn. Indsl. Crops, Am. Genetic Assn., Sigma Xi, Gamma Sigma Delta. Lutheran. Home: 1330 W Broadway Rd Apt A216 Tempe AZ 85282-1202 Office: USDA Agrl Rsch Svc US Water Conservation Lab 4331 E Broadway Rd Phoenix AZ 85040-8807

COFFIN, JOHN MILLER, molecular biologist, educator; b. Boston, Apr. 20, 1944; s. Louis Fussell and Mary Elizabeth (McCarthy) C.; m. Marion Clair Szurek, June 22, 1968; children: Erica Mary, Heather Rachel. BA, Wesleyan U., 1967; PhD, U. Wis., 1972. Fellow U. Zurich (Switzerland), 1972-75; asst. prof. molecular biology Tufts U., Boston, 1975-78, assoc. prof., 1978-82, prof., 1982—; mem. virology study sect. NIH, Bethesda, Md., 1980-84; mem. scientific adv. bd. Viagene, Inc., San Diego, 1988; Am. Cancer Soc. rsch. prof., 1994. Editor: RNA Tumor Viruses, 2 vols., 1985; mem. editorial bd. Jour. Virol, Virology, Oncogene, Oncogene Res., Leukemia; editor Jour. Virol, 1991—; contbr. over 80 articles to profl. jours. Trustee Leukemia Soc. Am., N.Y., 1987. Recipient Outstanding Investigator award Nat. Cancer Inst., 1987; Am. Cancer Soc. Rsch. Professorship, 1994. Mem. AAAS, Am. Soc. Microbiology. Office: Tufts Med Sch 136 Harrison Ave Boston MA 02111-1800

COFFMAN, JAY DENTON, physician, educator; b. Quincy, Mass., Nov. 17, 1928; s. Frank David and Etta (Kline) C.; m. Louise G. Peters, June 29, 1955; children: Geoffrey J., Joanne K., Linda J., Robert B. A.B., Harvard U., 1950; M.D., Boston U., 1954. Med. intern Univ. Hosp., Boston, 1954-55; asst. resident in medicine Univ. Hosp., 1955-56, chief resident in medicine, 1957-58, fellow in cardiovascular disease, 1956-57, sect. head peripheral vascular dept., 1960—; asso. in medicine Boston U. Med. Sch., 1960-65, mem. faculty, 1965—, prof. medicine, 1970—. Author: Raynaud's Phenomenon, 1989; co-author: Ischemic Limbs, 1973. Trustee Solomon Carter Fuller Mental Health Center, Boston, 1975-81. Served to capt. M.C. USAR, 1958-60. Diplomate Am. Bd. Internal Medicine.; Mem. Am. Soc. Clin. Investigation, Am. Fedn. Clin. Research, Am. Physiol. Soc., Am. Heart Assn., A.C.P., Begg's Soc., Phi Beta Kappa, Alpha Omega Alpha. Office: 88 E Newton St Boston MA 02118-2308

COFFMAN, WILLIAM BRENT, dentist; b. Wytheville, Va., Nov. 6, 1945; m. William Henry and and Esther Virginia (Brent) C.; m. Patricia McGhee, 1982; children: William Brent, Amy Louise. BA, Columbia Union Coll., 1969; MA, Andrews U., 1971; DDS, Loma Linda (Calif.) U., 1983. Ordained to ministry Seventh-Day Adventist Ch., 1974. Pastor Ohio Conf. SDA Ch., Kettering, 1969-73, SE Calif. Conf. U. Ch., Loma Linda, 1974-80; pvt. practice Yucaipa, Calif., 1983—. Pres. Neal C. Wilson Southeastern Calif. Conf. Mem. ADA (ho. of dels., internat. svc. award 1983), Calif. Dental Assn., Tri-County Dental Soc. (bd. dirs. 1996—), Columbia Union Coll. Alumni Assn., Assn. Adventist Forums, Andrew Soc. for Religious Studies. Home: 613 E Sunset Dr N Redlands CA 92373-6404 Office: Bryant Profl Ctr 11834 Bryant St Ste 101 Yucaipa CA 92399-3848

COFIELD, ROBERT HAHN, physician, orthopedic surgeon; b. Cin., Oct. 24, 1943; s. Robert Hedrick and Virginia (Hahn) C.; m. Pamela Joyce Haarbauer, Aug. 12, 1967; children: Robert, Stacey, Virginia. BA, Washington and Lee U., 1965; MD, U. Ky., 1969; MS, Mayo Grad. Sch. Medicine, 1976. Diplomate Am. Bd. Orthopedic Surgery. Intern Charity Hosp./Tulane U., New Orleans, 1970; cons. Mayo Clinic, Rochester, Minn., 1975—; from instr. to assoc. prof. Mayo Med. Sch., Rochester, 1975-88, prof., 1988—; vice chair dept. orthopedics Mayo Clinic, Rochester, 1992—, Frank R. and Shari Caywood prof. orthopedic surgery, 1993; assoc. dean Mayo Grad. Sch., Rochester, 1992-94, dean, 1994—. Editor-in-chief Jour.

Shoulder and Elbow Surgery, 1990—; contbr. chpts. to books, more than 100 articles to profl. jours.; co-inventor humeral resect. guide; co-designer Cofield total shoulder sys. Lt. comdr. USNR. Mem. ACS, AMA, Am. Acad. Orthopedic Surgery (dir. 1994—), Am. Orthopedic Assn., Am. Shoulder and Elbow Surgeons (founding sec.-treas. 1982-87, pres. 1988-89, chair planning and devel. com.). Republican. Presbyterian. Office: Mayo Clinic 200 1st St NW Rochester MN 55905

COFRANCESCO, DONALD GEORGE, health facility administrator; b. New Haven, May 29, 1953; s. George William and Marie Teresa (Marra) C. BS with distinction in Chemistry and Life Scis., Worcester Poly. Inst., 1975; MA in Gerontology, U. New Haven, 1979; MPH, Yale U., 1992. Lic. nursing home adminstr., Conn. Dir. biostats. and health planning Dept. of Health, New Haven, 1980; adminstr. Golden Manor Convalescent Home, New Haven, 1980-81, West Haven (Conn.) Nursing Ctr., 1981-85, Independence Manor, Meriden, Conn., 1986-87, Hillside Manor, Hartford, Conn., 1987-88; asst. in rsch. Sch. Medicine, Yale U., New Haven, 1975-77, asst. adminstr., fin. analyst, lectr., reimbursement mgr., 1990—; cons. Hospice: Project Care, Inc., Watertown, Conn., 1989-90; v.p., CFO Environ. Health Corp., Hamden, Conn., 1991—. Bd. dirs. Partnerships Ctr. for Adult Day Care, Inc., Hamden, 1991—; mem. Health Systems Agy. South Cen. Conn., Inc., Woodbridge, 1982-87. Named one of Outstanding Young Men of Am., 1983. Mem. APHA, NRA (cert. firearms instr., light rifle expert, air pistol sharpshooter), Am. Chem. Soc., Conn. Pub. Health Assn., Planetary Soc. Roman Catholic. Home: 104 Hillfield Rd Hamden CT 06518-1852 Office: Yale U Sch Medicine PO Box 208041 333 Cedar St New Haven CT 06520-8041

COFRANCESCO, SIMON ROBERT, gastroenterologist; b. New Haven, Conn., Feb. 20, 1960; s. Simon Ronald and Mary Cofrancesco. BS in Biology cum laude, Springfield Coll., 1985; DO, U. Health Scis. Coll. Osteo. Medicine, Kansas City, Mo., 1989. Diplomate Am. Bd. Internal Medicine, Am. Bd. Gastroenterology. Intern, resident Baystate Med. Ctr., Tufts U., Springfield, 1989-92; fellow in gastroenterology L.I. Coll. Hosp., Bklyn., 1991-94; attending physician S.W. Miss. Regional Med. Ctr., McComb, 1994—; spkr. Mercke, 1995-96, Jannsen, 1995-96. Mem. AMA, Am. Gastroent. Assn., Am. Coll. Gastroenterology, Am. Soc. Gastrointestinal Endoscopy, Am. Coll. Physicians, Crohn Colitis Found. Assn., Tri Bet, Psi Sigma Alpha. Office: Gastroenterology Assocs 300 Rawls Dr Ste 1200 McComb MS 39648

COGAN, ANN MARIE, quality management specialist and gerontological nurse. Diploma, St. Vincent Hosp., 1960; BSN in Edn., St. John's U., 1964; MA, NYU, 1984; cert. in geriatric edn., CUNY-Mt. Sinai Hosp., 1992. Instr. Coll. S.I., N.Y., 1976-78; staff devel. instr. St. Vincent's Med. Ctr., S.I., 1973-85; asst. DON New Vanderbilt NH, S.I., 1985-89; geriatric cons., 1989-91; asst. to dir. quality mgmt. Kateri Residence, N.Y.C., 1991—; nurse reviewer Profl. Stds. Rev. Coun. Am., Inc., 1995—. Mem. N.Y. City Nurses Assn. (gerontology spl. interest group), N.Y. Nurses Network for Health Care Quality, Archdiocesan Coun. Cath. Nurses (sec. Manhattan chpt.), Sigma Theta Tau. Office: Kateri Residence 150 Riverside Dr New York NY 10024-2298

COGAN, MYLES IRVING COURTENAY, oral and maxillofacial surgeon, medical director; b. Tampico, Mex., June 3, 1929; came to U.S., 1940; s. Myles Honohan Ressugan and Ruth Lillian (Sessoms) C.; m. Felicia Lee Henderson, Oct. 15, 1960; 1 child, Courtenay Cogan Diederich. DDS, U. Tex., 1953; MPH, U. Mich., 1958; MSD, Baylor Coll. Dentistry, 1966. Diplomate Am. Bd. Oral and Maxillofacial Surgery, Am. Assn. Hosp. Dentists. Clin. instr. U. Tex. Dental Br., Houston, 1956-57; pvt. practice Pasadena, Tex., 1958-62; intern, resident in oral surgery U. Tex., So. Tex. Med. Sch., San Antonio, 1962-64; rsch. assoc. in dentistry VA Hosp., Dallas, 1966-67, staff dentist, 1967-70; oral and maxillofacial surgeon VA Hosp., Martinsburg, W.Va., 1970-73, chief, dental svc., 1973—; asst. prof. oral surgery Baylor Coll. Dentistry, Dallas, 1967-70; adjunct instr. oral hygiene Allegany Cmty. Coll., Cumberland, Md., 1976—; clin. prof. oral surgery W.Va. U. Sch. of Dentistry, Morgantown, 1986—, vis. clinician, 1984—. Contbr. articles to profl. jours. V.p. Ea. Panhandle Dental Soc., Martinsburg, 1973; chmn. VA Dental Chiefs, dist. 6, Washington, 1974; vice-chmn. adv. com. Dental Programs, Cumberland, Md., 1975; chmn. W.Va. sect. Am. Assn. Hosps. of Dentistry, Morgantown, 1980. To capt. USAF, 1953-55. Recipient Pub. Health Trainee award USPHS, Washington, 1957; fellow Am. Coll. Dentists, 1975. Fellow Internat. Assn. Oral and Maxillofacial Surgeons, Royal Soc. Health; mem. ADA, Am. Assn. Oral and Maxillofacial Surgeons, Rotary Internat. (Paul Harris fellow 1984), Omicron Kappa Upsilon, Sigma Xi. Home: PO Box K/105 Shepherd Lane Shepherdstown WV 25443 Office: VA Med Ctr Dental Svc Route 9 Martinsburg WV 25401

COGEN, ROBERTA, nursing administrator, medical and surgical nurse; b. Bklyn., Feb. 2, 1929; d. Dewey and Sarah (Taylor) Gottlieb; m. Sanford Cogen, Nov. 14, 1949; children: Ellen Rose, Jerald Leslie, Richard Mark. Diploma in nursing, Jewish Hosp. and Med. Ctr., Bklyn., 1950. RN, N.Y. Staff nurse, instr. Sch. Nursing, Jewish Hosp. Bklyn., 1950-51; staff nurse surg. unit L.I. Jewish Med. Ctr., New Hyde Park, N.Y., 1966-69; coord. nursing care adult cardiology-catheterization unit L.I. Jewish-Hillside Med. Ctr., New Hyde Park, 1969-94; ret., 1994; guest lectr. Adelphi U.; clin. instr. SUNY, Stony Brook; presenter 10th World Congress Cardiology, Washington, 1986. Contbr. articles and book rev. to nursing jours. Mem. Am. Heart Assn. (past bd. dirs. Nassau chpt.), L.I. Heart Coun. (past bd. dirs.).

COGEN, STEPHEN THOMAS, gastroenterologist; b. N.Y.C., Mar. 19, 1933; s. Alexander Max and Lillian (Yelon) C.; m. Helene Ruth Josephs, July 3, 1960;children: Jeffrey Scott, Mitchell Jay. BA, Cornell U., 1954; MD, N.Y. Med. Ctr., 1959. Intern Montefiore Hosp., Bronx, N.Y., 1959-60; resident Montefiore Hosp. and VA Hosp., Bronx, 1960-65; internist, gastroenterologist Miami Beach, 1965—. Capt. USAMC, 1961-63, Germany. Mem. Am. Soc. Internal Medicine, Fla. Gastroenterology Soc. Office: 1680 Meridian Ave Miami Beach FL 33139

COGER, RICK, health science facility administrator, educator; b. Pineland, S.C., June 30, 1940; s. Martin and Mary (Brantley) C.; m. Lillian Annette Beasley, July 28, 1964; children: Brenton Raval, Tiffany Ashelia. BS, Savannah State U., 1962; MA, Ball State U., 1965; PhD, Ohio State U., 1972. Cert. secondary tchr., S.C. Asst. prof. Miss. Valley State U., Itta Bena, Miss., 1965-67, Cen. State U., Wilberforce, Ohio, 1967-70; adminstrv. assoc. Ohio State U., Columbus, 1970-72; prof. Wilberforce U., 1972-75; asst. dir. instructional design South Cen. Regional Med. Edn. Ctr. VA Med. Ctr., St. Louis, 1975-91; program dir. Continuing Edn. Ctr. Dept. Vets. Affairs, St. Louis, 1991—; adj. prof. Concordia U. Wis., St. Louis, Mo., 1993—; arbitrator BBB, St. Louis, 1984—; edni. evaluator Nat. Accrediting Commn. of Cosmetology Arts and Scis., Washington, 1983—; instrnl. designer Am. Med. Record Assn., Chgo., 1978-81. Author: (book) Developing Effective IS, 1975; editor Jour. Allied Health, 1977, Jour. Bio-Communications, 1982; designer various video programs (Gold award 1985). Vol. Peace Corps, Belize City, Belize, 1962-64; bd. dirs. PTO Oakville Elem. Sch., St. Louis, 1980-84; pres. Cross of Christ Luth. Ch., 1984-86; mem. sch. improvement leadership team, mem. tech. task force for Mehlville Sch. System,; mem. parents adv. com. Oakville Sr. High Sch. Named Disting. Leader, Am. Leadership Coun., 1984-85; recipient various awards VA, 1979, 82, 84, 85, Tng. Officers award U.S. Govt., 1979, Disting. Leadership award, 1989, Internat. Leaders in Achievement award, 1990. Mem. Am. Tech. Assn., Health Edn. Media Assn., Am. Counc. Comparative Edn., Health Scis. Communication Assn. (program mem. 1987), Phi Delta Kappa. Home: 2781 Brandenberg Ln Saint Louis MO 63129-4009 Office: Continuing Edn Ctr Dept Vets Affairs Jefferson Barracks Saint Louis MO 63129

COGGIN, CHARLOTTE JOAN, cardiologist, educator; b. Takoma Park, Md., Aug. 6, 1928; d. Charles Benjamin and Nanette (McDonald) Coggin; BA, Columbia Union Coll., 1948; MD, Loma Linda U., 1952, MPH, 1987; DSc (hon.), Andrews U., 1994. Intern, L.A. County Gen. Hosp., L.A., 1952-53, resident in medicine, 1953-55; fellow in cardiology Children's Hosp., L.A., 1955-56, White Meml. Hosp., L.A., 1955-56; rsch. assoc. in cardiology, house physician Hammersmith Hosp., London, 1956-57; resident in pediatrics and pediatric cardiology Hosp. for Sick Children, Toronto, Ont., Can., 1965-67; cardiologist, co-dir. heart surgery team Loma Linda (Calif.) U., asst. prof. medicine , 1961-73, assoc. prof., 1973-91, prof. medicine, 1991—, asst. dean Sch. Medicine Internat. Programs, 1973-75, assoc. dean, 1975—, spl. asst. to univ. pres. for internat. affairs, 1991, co-dir., cardiologist heart surgery team missions to Pakistan and Asia, 1963, Greece, 67, 69, Saigon, Vietnam, 1974, 75, to Saudi Arabia, 1976-87, People's Republic China, 1984, 89-91, Hong Kong, 1985, Zimbabwe, 1988, Kenya, 1988, Nepal, 1992, 93, China, 1992, Zimbabwe, 1993; mem. Pres's. Advisory Panel on Heart Disease, 1972—; hon. prof. U. Manchuria, Harbin, People's Republic China, 1989, hon. dir. 1st People's Hosp. of Mundanjiang, Heilongjiang Province, 1989. Apptd. mem. Med. Quality Rev. Com.-Dist. 12, 1976-80. Recipient award for service to people of Pakistan City of Karachi, 1963, Medallion award Evangelismos Hosp., Athens, Greece, 1967, Gold medal of health South Vietnam Ministry of Health, 1974, Charles Elliott Weinger award for excellence, 1976, Wall Street Jour. Achievement award, 1987, Disting. Univ. Svc. award Loma Linda U., 1990; named Honored Alumnus Loma Linda U. Sch. Medicine, 1973, Outstanding Women in Gen. Conf. Seventh-day Adventists, 1975, Alumnus of Yr., Columbia Union Coll., 1984. Diplomate Am. Bd. Pediatrics. Mem. Am. Coll. Cardiology, AMA (physicians adv. com. 1969—) Calif. Med. Assn. (com. on med. schs., com. on member services), San Bernardino County Med. Soc. (chmn. communications com. 1975-77, mem. communications com. 1987-88, editor bull. 1975-76, William L. Cover, M.D. Outstanding Contbn. to Medicine award 1995), Am. Heart Assn., AAUP, Med. Research Assn. Calif., Calif. Heart Assn., AAUW, Am. Acad. Pediatrics, World Affairs Council, Internat. Platform Assn., Calif. Museum Sci. and Industry MUSES (Outstanding Woman of Year in Sci. 1969), Am. Med. Women's Assn., Loma Linda Sch. Medicine Alumni Assn. (pres. 1978), Alpha Omega Alpha, Delta Omega. Author: Atrial Septal Defects, motion picture (Golden Eagle Cine award and 1st prize Venice Film Festival 1964); contbr. articles to med. jours. Democrat. Home: 11495 Benton St Loma Linda CA 92354-3682 Office: Loma Linda U Magan Hall Rm 105 11060 Anderson St Loma Linda CA 92350

COGGINS, LOUISE WEEKS, psychotherapist; b. Rocky Mount, N.C., Sept. 29, 1953; d. James Leggett and Carolyn Hayes (Gaither) Weeks; m. Stephen Dalton Coggins, May 18, 1974. BA in Psychology, U. N.C., 1974, MSW, 1980. Cert. social worker, N.C. Houseparent, primary therapist Children's Treatment Ctr., Southern Pines, N.C., 1974-75; ctr. dir. N.W. Child Devel. Ctr., Winston-Salem, N.C., 1975-76; social worker adolescent and drug abuse unit Forsyth Mental Health Ctr., 1976-79; psychotherapist C.D. Wallace, M.D., Raleigh, N.C., 1980-90; pvt. practice psychotherapist Chris Heaton, M.D.P.A., Raleigh, 1991—; employee assistance counselor various pvt. corps., Raleigh, 1980—; clin. supr. Pvt. Practitioners, Raleigh, 1982—. Mem. Nat. Assn. Social Workers, N.C. Clin. Social Work Soc. (treas. 1985-86), N.C. Soc. for Study of Multiple Personality Disorder and Dissociation (treas. 1988, pres. 1989), Internat. Soc. for Study of Multiple Personality Disorder and Dissociation, Acad. Cert. Social Workers. Democrat. Episcopalian. Office: Chris Heaton MD 3809 Computer Dr Raleigh NC 27609-6518

COGGINS, WILMER JESSE, physician, medical school administrator; b. Madison, Fla., Feb. 20, 1925; s. Wilmer Jesse and Audrey (Walker) C.; m. Deborah Ferne Reed, Apr. 16, 1949; children: Pamela, Deborah, Wilmer Jesse, Audrey Ann, Christopher. M.D., Duke U., 1951. Intern Georgetown U. Med. Ctr., Washington, 1951-52; resident U. Fla. Coll. Medicine, Gainesville, 1960-62, instr. internal medicine, 1962-63, asst. prof., 1963-67, assoc. prof., 1967-73, prof., 1975-80; prof. U. Md., College Park, 1974-75; dean Coll. Community Health Scis. U. Ala., Tuscaloosa, 1980-91, dean emeritus, 1991—. Recipient Fla. Blue Key, 1971; recipient Hon. Physicians Asst. award U. Fla. Coll. Medicine, 1976. Fellow ACP (councillor Ala. chpt. 1993—), Am. Coll. Health Assn. (pres. 1974-75 Ruth C. Boynton award); mem. Med. Assn. State Ala. (Disting. Svc. award 1989), AMA, Tuscaloosa County Med. Soc., Nat. Rural Care Assn. (exec. com. 1978-81). Democrat. Presbyterian. Club: North River Yacht (Tuscaloosa). Home: 9010 Admiralty Ln Tuscaloosa AL 35406 Office: U Ala Coll Community Health Scis PO Box 870326 Tuscaloosa AL 35487-0326

COGLIANESE, CAROL LYNN, internist, pediatrician; b. Chgo., Jan. 24, 1960; d. Glen William Coglianese and Barbara Marie Rezmer. BS in Agr., U. Ill., 1982, MS, 1984, MD, 1991. Instr. dept. life scis. Parkland Coll., Champaign, Ill., 1985-87; resident U. Tenn., Memphis, 1991-95; pvt. practice internist, pediatrician Kankakee, Ill., 1995—. Mem. AMA, ACP, Am. Acad. Pediat. Roman Catholic. Home: 911 Thomas Dr Momence IL 60954 Office: Med Peds Assocs 122 E Washington St Momence IL 60954

COGNETTO, ANNA MARIE, social worker; b. Herkimer, N.Y., May 25, 1957; d. Anthony N. and Margaret J. (Williams) C. AS with honors, Herkimer County C.C., 1977; BS with honors, Cornell U., 1979; MSW, Syracuse U., 1981. Cert. social worker, N.Y.; cognitive behavioral therapist; diplomate in clin. social work. Social worker The Ctr. for Youth Svcs., Rochester, N.Y., 1981-82; psychiat. social worker Rockland Children's Psychiat. Ctr., Newburgh, N.Y., 1982-88; pvt. practice Poughkeepsie, N.Y., 1983—; social worker CHP Alcohol Clinic, Poughkeepsie, 1988-90; social worker II Dutchess City Dept. Mental Hygiene Alcohol Clin., Poughkeepsie, 1990-92; adj. lectr. Dutchess C.C., Poughkeepsie, 1985—; social worker, evaluator N.Y. State DWI Program, Poughkeepsie, 1991—; guest lectr. Sanctuary/N.Y. State Spl. Edn. Tng. Resource Ctr., Poughkeepsie, 1993—; cons. Hudson Valley Counseling, Poughkeepsie, 1993—; cons. Spectrum Behavioral Health, 1994—. Mem. NASW (N.Y. State chpt., mem. gay and lesbian issues com., Hudson Valley divsn. steering com., chair various coms.), Am. Bd. Clin. Social Workers (diplomate), Chronic Fatigue and Immune Dysfunction Syndrome Assn. Office: 24 Davis Ave Poughkeepsie NY 12603-2408

COHEN, ALAN SEYMOUR, internist; b. Boston, Apr. 9, 1926; s. George I. and Jennie (Laskin) C.; m. Joan Elizabeth Prince, Sept. 12, 1954; children: Evan Bruce, Andrew Hollis, Robert Adam. AB magna cum laude, Harvard Coll., 1947; MD magna cum laude, Boston U., 1952. Intern Harvard Med. Svc., Boston City Hosp., 1952-53, resident, 1953-55; exch. registrar in medicine Dundee Royal Infirmary and U. St. Andrews, Scotland, 1955-56; rsch. and clin. fellow in rheumatology Mass. Gen. Hosp., Boston, 1956-58; instr. Med. Sch. Harvard Coll. and Mass. Gen. Hosp., 1958-60; head arthritis and connective tissue disease sect. Evans dept. clin. rsch. Mass. U. Hosp., Boston, 1960-72; Conrad Wesselhoeft prof. medicine Sch. Medicine Boston U., 1972-93, prof. pharmacology, 1974—, disting. prof. medicine in rheumatology, 1993—; dir. Arthritis Ctr., 1977—; dir. divsn. medicine Boston City Hosp., 1973-93; dir. Thorndike Meml. lab., 1973-93. Editor: Laboratory Diagnostic Procedures in the Rheumatic Diseases, 1967, rev. edit., 1975, 3d edit., 1985, (with others) Symposium on Amyloidosis, 1968, (With R. Friedin and M. Samuels) Medical Emergencies: Diagnostic and Management Procedures from Boston City Hospital, 1977, (with J. Combes and H. Koh) 2d edit., 1983, Rheumatology and Immunology, 1979, (with J.C. Bennett) 2d edit., 1986, Progress in Clinical Rheumatology, 1984, (with D. Goldenberg) Drugs in the Rheumatic Diseases, 1986, Amyloidosis, 1986, Clinical Problems in Acute Care Medicine (J.J. Heffernan, R.A. Witzburg, A.S. Cohen), 1989; founder, editor-in-chief Amyloid: The Internat. Jour. of Exptl. and Clin. Investigation, 1994—; contbr. over 700 articles to profl. jours. Trustee Arthritis Found., Atlanta, 1976-82, trustee Mass. chpt., 1966-85, vice chmn., 1971-84, pres., 1981-94; vice sec. for N.Am., mem. exec. com. Pan Am. League Against Rheumatism, 1982-85; chmn. Boston City Hosp. Physician Alumni Reunion Com., 1992; pres. Boston City Hosp. Fund for Excellence, 1992. Served to surg. USPHS, 1953-55. Recipient Outstanding Alumnus award Boston U. Sch. Medicine, 1975, Purdue Frederic Arthritis award, 1979, James H. Fairclough Jr. award for disting. svc. to Mass. chpt. Arthritis Found., 1981, Alumni award for spl. distinction Boston U., 1981, Jan Van Bremeen Gold medal Dutch Rheumatism Soc., 1990, Commrs. Disting. Physician award Boston City Hosp., 1991, Gold medal Am. Coll. Rheumatology, 1994, Dr. Marian Ropes award Arthritis Found., 1995. Master Am. Coll. Rheumatology; fellow ACP; mem. Am. Coll. Rheumatology (pres. 1978-79), Am. Soc. Clin. Investigation, Assn. Am. Physicians, Am. Fedn. Clin. Research, Am. Soc. Exptl. Pathology, Interurban Clin. Club, Soc. Exptl. Biology and Medicine, Electron Microscopy Soc. Am., New Eng. Soc. for Electron Microscopy, Am. Soc. Cell Biology, N.Y. Acad. Sci., AMA, Mass. Med. Soc., New Eng. Rheumatism Assn. (past pres.), Italian Rheumatism Soc. (hon.), Spanish Rheumatism Soc. (hon.), Finnish Rheumatism Soc. (hon.), Brazilian Rheumatism Soc. (hon.), Irish Soc. Rheumatism and Rehab. (hon.), Italian Soc. Amyloidosis (hon.), Boston U. Sch. Medicine Alumni Assn. (past pres.), Phi Beta Kappa, Alpha Omega Alpha. Jewish. Clubs: Harvard (Boston); Wightman Tennis Center (Weston, Mass.). Office: Boston U Sch Medicine Amyloid Program 80 E Concord St F-113 Boston MA 02118

COHEN, ALBERTO, cardiologist; b. Rio de Janeiro, Aug. 12, 1932; came to U.S., 1959; s. Nessim and Anneta (Rabischoffsky) C.; m. Bertha Kalichztein, Dec. 27, 1958; children: Deborah Cohen Stein, Annabel, Miriam Cohen Disner. BS, Edn. Rui Barboza, Rio de Janero, 1952; MD, Brazil U., Rio de Janero, 1958. Diplomate Am. Bd. Internal Medicine, Am. Bd. Cardiovascular Disease, Am. Coll. Cardiology in Electrocardiography; cert. bd. med. examiners, Ariz., Fla., Tex., Calif. Intern Robert Wood Johnson Med. Ctr., New Brunswick, N.J., 1959-60; resident Detroit-Macomb Hosp., 1960-61; fellow cardiology medicine Harper Hosp., Detroit, 1961, Detroit Gen. Hosp., 1963-65; practice medicine specializing in cardiology and internal medicine Mt. Clements and Clinton Twp., Mt. Clements, Mich., 1966—; attending staff St. Joseph's Mercy Hosp.; mem. attending cardiology staff Sinai Hosp., Detroit, 1995—, cardiologist, 1995—; instr. medicine Wayne State U., Detroit, 1964-65, asst. prof. medicine, 1965-67, clin. asst. prof. medicine, 1967-87. Contbr. numerous articles to profl. jours. Pres. Macomb County Heart Unit, 1974-77. Fellow ACP, Am. Coll. Chest Physicians, Am. Coll. Angiology, Am. Coll. Internat. Physicians, Am. Coll. Cardiology, Internat. Coll. Angiology; mem. AMA, Brazilian Soc. Medicine, Brazilian Soc. Cardiology, Am. Soc. Internal Medicine, Mich. Soc. Internal Medicine (trustee 1974-77), Mich. State Med. Soc., Wayne County Med. Soc., Macomb County Med. Soc., Am. Heart Assn. (fellow sci. coun. clin. cardiology), Detroit Heart Club (pres. 1989-90). Jewish. Home: 1477 Lochridge Rd Bloomfield Hills MI 48302-0734

COHEN, ALFRED MARTIN, surgical oncologist, cancer researcher; b. N.Y.C., Nov. 3, 1941; s. Milton and Ethel (Haines) C.; m. Patricia Seaver, Aug. 27, 1963 (div. 1983); children: Julie Diana, Daniel Jared; m. Constance Hurley, Sept. 11, 1983. BA, Cornell U., 1963; MD, Johns Hopkins U., 1967. Diplomate Am. Bd. Surgery. Resident, then chief resident in surgery Mass. Gen. Hosp., Boston, 1967-69, 72-75; surg. oncology fellow Nat. Cancer Inst., Bethesda, Md., 1969-71; instr. surgery Harvard Med. Sch., Boston, 1976-77, asst. prof., 1977-82, assoc. prof., 1983-86; assoc. prof. surgery Cornell U. Med. Coll., N.Y.C., 1987-89; chief colorectal surgery, vice chmn. dept. surgery Meml. Sloan-Kettering Cancer Ctr., N.Y.C., 1986—; prof. surgery Cornell U. Med. Coll., N.Y.C., 1990—; full mem. Meml. Sloan-Kettering Cancer Ctr., N.Y.C., 1989—; co-dir. surg. oncology Mass. Gen. Hosp., Boston, 1980-86. Contbr. numerous articles to profl. jours.; also book chpts. and revs. Jr. Faculty Clin. fellow Am. Cancer Soc., 1976-79; Henry Strong Denison scholar Johns Hopkins U. Sch. Medicine, 1966, Ira Nathanson scholar Mass. div. Am. Cancer Soc., 1976-86. Fellow Am. Coll. Surgeons; mem. Am. Soc. Clin. Oncology, Soc. Surg. Oncology, Assn. Acad. Surgery, Am. Assn. Cancer Rsch., Am. Assn. Immunologists, AMA, AAAS, Soc. Surgery Alimentary Tract, Soc. Univ. Surgeons, Am. Soc. Colorectal Surgery, Am. Surg. Assn., Physician's Sci. Soc., N.Y. Acad. Scis., N.Y. Soc. Colorectal Surgeons, New Eng. Surg. Soc., Boston Surg. Soc., New Eng. Cancer Soc., Mass. Med. Soc., World Assn. Hepato-Pancreato-Biliary Surgery, Johns Hopkins Med. and Surg. Soc., Soc. Internat. de Chirurgie, N.Y. Acad. Sci., N.Y. Surgical Soc., N.Y. Clin. Soc. Office: Meml Sloan-Kettering Cancer Ctr 1275 York Ave New York NY 10021-6007

COHEN, ALLAN, gastroenterologist; b. N.Y.C., Mar. 11, 1953; s. Benjamin and Alice Cohen; married, July 7, 1976. BS, Bklyn. Med. Coll., 1975; MD, Downstate Med. Ctr., 1979. Diplomate Am. Bd. Internal Medicine, sub-bd. gastroenterology. Intern Kings County Hosp., Bklyn., 1979-80, resident, 1980-82, gastrointestinal fellow, 1982-84; mem. staff Community Med. Ctr., Toms River, N.J., 1984—; asst. mem. staff Kimbak Med. Ctr., Lakewood, N.J., 1984—. Office: 477 Lakehurst Rd Toms River NJ 08755-6342

COHEN, AMY JANE, psychiatrist; b. Flushing, N.Y., Sept. 9, 1950; d. Sidney Mortimer and Grace Sheryl (Fishman) C.; m. A. Patrick McCaughey, May 30, 1988; 1 child, Benjamin. BSN summa cum laude, Boston U., 1976; MD, U. Pa., 1984. Rn, Mass.; cert. nurse practitioner. Nurse practitioner behavioral pediatrics Children's Hosp., Boston, 1978-88; fellow in child psychiatry McLean Hosp., Belmont, Wash., 1987-89, asst. psychiatrist in charge Hall Mercer Children's Ctr., 1990-91; cons. psychiatrist Family Svc. of Greater Boston, 1991-95; pvt. practice Cambridge, Mass., 1990—; clin. instr. Harvard Med. Sch., Boston, 1984—; pre-med. tutor Harvard U., Cambridge, 1984-88, resident advisor; clin. supr. and child therapy cons. Family Svc. Greater Boston, Malden, Mass., 1991-95. Tchr. composition workshop Atrium Sch., Watertown, Mass., 1995—. Office: 127 Mt Auburn St Cambridge MA 02138

COHEN, ARNOLD NORMAN, gastroenterologist; b. N.Y.C., Nov. 5, 1949; s. Norman and Edna Clara (Arnold) C.; m. Colleen Ruth Carey; children: Eric Arnold, Leslie Carey. BA summa cum laude, Hobart Coll., 1971; MD, Harvard U., 1975. Diplomate Am. Bd. Internal Medicine, Am. Bd. Gastroenterology. Resident internal medicine U. Pa., Phila., 1975-78, asst. instr. medicine, 1977-78; fellow gastroenterology, instr. medicine Northwestern U., Chgo., 1978-80; asst. clin. prof. medicine U. Wash. Med. Sch., Seattle, 1980—; mem. faculty Spokane (Wash.) Family Medicine Residency, 1980—; pvt. practice gastroenterology Spokane, 1980—; mem. various coms. St. Lukes-Deaconess Hosp., Spokane, 1980—; pres. med. staff St. Lukes Hosp., 1985-86. Contbr. articles to profl. jours. and textbooks. Fellow ACP, Am. Coll. Gastroenterology; mem. Am. Soc. Gastrointestinal Endoscopy, Am. Gastroent. Soc., Wash. Med. Soc., Spokane Internal Med. Soc., Phi Beta Kappa, Alpha Omega Alpha. Home: 3514 S Jefferson St Spokane WA 99203-1441 Office: Spokane Gastroenterology PS 801 W 5th Ave Spokane WA 99204-2823

COHEN, ARNOLD ROBERT, psychiatrist; b. Jersey City, Aug. 12, 1938; s. Godfrey G. and Lilyan (Levine) C.; m. Sue Teitelbaum, July 4, 1966; children: Daniel, Jennifer. BA, Rutgers U., 1959; MD, SUNY, Syracuse, 1963. Diplomate Am. Bd. Psychiatry and Neurology. Cons. N.Y.C. Dept. Social Svcs., 1970-74; instr. psychiatry Mt. Sinai Med. Sch., N.Y.C., 1970-75, clin. asst. prof. psychiatry, 1975—; clin. dir. Children's House, N.Y.C., 1978-92; med. dir. Assoc. in Manhattan for Autistic Children, 1993—; mem. adv. com. to bd. dirs. Children's Aid Soc., 1989-92. Capt. USAF, 1967-69. Mem. Am. Psychiat. Assn., Am. Acad. Children's Adolescent Psychiatry, N.Y. Coun. on Child and Adolescent Psychiatry (bd. dirs. 1977—, treas. 1989-92, pres. 1993-94). Democrat. Jewish. Office: 64 E 94th St New York NY 10128-0773

COHEN, B. STANLEY, physician; b. Balt., Sept. 12, 1923; s. Louis James and Anna Sara (Cohen) C.; m. Margery Joy Germain, Oct. 30, 1949; children: Ellen , Lori B., Evan M. M.D., U. Md., 1947. Diplomate Am. Bd. Internal Medicine, Am. Bd. Phys. Medicine and Rehab. Rotating intern Sinai Hosp., Balt., 1947-48, resident in internal medicine, 1950-51; resident in internal medicine Bronx VA Hosp., N.Y., 1948-50; practice medicine specializing in internal medicine Balt., 1953-63; fellow phys. medicine and rehab. Baylor U. Med. Ctr., Dallas, 1963-65; chief dept. rehab. medicine Sinai Hosp. Balt., 1965-86; pres. Sinai Hosp. of Balt., 1986-91; prof. rehab. medicine U. Md., Balt., 1972-87, clin. prof. neurology, from 1987; sr. assoc. epidemiology Johns Hopkins U., Balt., from 1981; chief med. cons. Md. State Div. Vocat. Rehab., Balt., 1980-91; cons. rehabilitation Med. Sinai Hosp., 1991—. Contbr. articles to profl. jours. Mem. Gov. Commn. Employment Handicapped, Balt., 1968-70, Balt. Commn. Problems of Aging, 1968-73; citizens adv. Regional Planning Coun., Balt., 1970-71; exec. coun. Md. Hosp. Assn., 1986-92. 1st lt. U.S. Army, 1951-53. Recipient award of merit Gov.'s Commn. Employment Handicapped, 1972; citation for meritorius service Pres.' Com. on Employment Handicapped, 1972. Fellow Am. Acad. Phys. Medicine and Rehab. (Disting. Clinician award 1992), ACP; mem. Am. Bd. Physical Medicine and Rehab. (dir. 1976-88, chmn. 1984-88, residency rev. com. 1982-88), Md. Soc. Rehab. Medicine (pres. 1971-73), Md. Rehab. Assn. (pres. 1971-72), Washington-Balt. Soc. Phys. Medicine (pres. 1968-69). Jewish.

COHEN, BEN ZANE, ophthalmologist; b. N.Y.C., Sept. 7, 1948; s. Sidney Meyer and Shirley (Kleinman) C.; m. Barbara Lukash, June 18, 1978; children: David, Jesse. MD, N.Y. Med. Coll., 1976. Pvt. practice Retina Assocs. of New York, N.Y.C., 1983—; pres. Retina Rsch. Found., N.Y.C., 1993—. Named fellow Head Found. Fellow Am. Coll. Ophthalmology;

mem. N.Y. State Med. Soc. Office: Retina Assocs of NY 140 E 80th St New York NY 10021

COHEN, BERTRAM DAVID, psychologist, educator; b. Bklyn., Jan. 16, 1923; s. Irving and Rose (Rabinowitz) C.; m. Helen Elizabeth Swartley, Aug. 8, 1946; children: Philip S., Sarah L., Matthew A., Michael B., Aaron M., Andrew S. B.A., Bklyn. Coll., 1944; M.A., U. Ia., 1945, Ph.D., 1949. Asst. prof. Ind. U., 1949-52; chief psychologist Iowa City VA Hosp., 1952-56; dir. psychology Lafayette Clinic, Detroit, 1956-62; dir. clin. tng. Rutgers U., 1962-69, chmn. grad. psychology, 1970-74, adj. prof. Grad. Sch. Applied and Profl. Psychology, 1974—; prof. psychiatry U. Medicine and Dentistry N.J.-Rutgers Med. Sch., 1965-93; prof. emeritus Dept. Psychiatry Robert Wood Johnson Med. Sch., 1993—; cons. NIMH, VA, Rutgers Mgmt. Services; mem. certification commn. for psychology state Mich., 1960-62; Mem. bd. profl. advisers Coll. Profl. Psychology, Maplewood, N.J., 1971-74. Assoc. editor: Jour. Exptl. Research in Personality, 1964-72; adv. editor: Jour. Cons. and Clin. Psychology, 1964-73; cons. editor: Jour. Abnormal Psychology, 1973-79, assoc. editor, 1979-82. Trustee Warren Twp. Library Assn., 1964-66, N.J. Acad. Psychology, 1978-80. NSF grantee, 1963-74; NIMH grantee, 1963-69; Fulbright scholar Denmark, 1975-76. Fellow Am. Psychol. Soc., Am. Psychol. Assn. (chmn. sect. 3 div. clin. psychology 1969-70), Am. Coll. Neuropsychopharmacology; mem. N.J. Group Psychotherapy Soc. (pres. 1976-77), Soc. Rsch. Psychopathology, Sigma Xi. Home: 9 Rockage Rd Warren NJ 07059-5506

COHEN, BRIAN JEFFREY, internist, nephrologist, educator; b. N.Y.C., July 29, 1953; s. Franklyn Woodrow and Dee Miriam (Green) C.; m. Lynn Murphy. AB, Harvard U., 1974; MD, U. N.C., 1978; SM in Pub. Health, Harvard U., 1991. Diplomate Am. Bd. Internal Medicine, Am. Bd. Nephrology. Resident in internal medicine U. N.C., 1978-81; postdoctoral fellow dept. physiology Sch. of Medicine Yale U., 1981-83; clin. fellow renal unit Mass. Gen. Hosp., 1983-84; instr. medicine Harvard U. Med. Sch., Boston, 1984-90; staff physician Beth Israel Hosp., Boston, 1984-88, New Eng. Deaconess Hosp., Boston, 1988-90; fellow Div. Clin. Decision-Making New England Med. Ctr., Boston, 1991-93; asst. prof. medicine Tufts U. Sch. Medicine, 1993—. Contbr. articles to med. jours. NIH grantee, 1984-87. Mem. Am. Soc. Nephrology, Soc. for Med. Decision Making, Soc. Gen. Internal Medicine. Office: New England Med Ctr Box 302 750 Washington St Boston MA 02111-1526

COHEN, BRUCE ARNOLD, nuerologist; b. Chgo., Nov. 6, 1949; s. Norman and Frances (Fisher) C.; m. Susan Sackheim, Aug. 18, 1974; children: Danielle, Michael, Benjamin. BA in psychology, Univ. Ill., 1971, MD, 1978. Diplomate Am. Bd. Psychiatry & Neurology, Am. Bd. Internal Medicine. Resident in internal medicine Lutheran Gen. Hosp., Park Ridge, Ill., 1978-81; resident in neurology Northwestern Univ. Medical Ctr., Chgo., 1981-84; instr. neurology Northwestern Univ. Medical Sch., 1984-88, asst. prof. neurology, 1988-92, assoc. prof. neurology, 1992—; attending neurologist Northwestern Meml. Hosp., Chgo., 1984—; cons. neurologist Rehabilitation Inst. Chgo., 1987—; cons. neurology AMA, 1991—, neurology bd. examiner Am. Bd Psychologu & Neurology, 1993, 94, reviewer Neurology, 1993, 94; clinical practice dir. dept. neurology Northwestern Medical Faculty Found., 1990-95. Contbr. articles to profl. jours. Spl. review com. AIDS grant NIMH, Washington, 1987-89; profl. adv. com. Chgo-Ill. MS Soc., 1991—. Recipient Edmund James scholar Univ. Ill., 1967-71. Fellow ACP, Am. Heart Assn. (stroke coun.), Am. Acad. Neurology; mem. Am. Neurologic Assn., Phi Beta Kappa. Office: Northwestern Univ Dept Neurology 645 N Michigan Ave # 1058 Chicago IL 60611

COHEN, CAROL NAOMI, infectious disease, critical care nurse; b. Bklyn., Apr. 22, 1950; d. Jerome and Rita (Rosenberg) Tillis; m. Donald Cohen, Feb. 11, 1971; children: Jackie, Saul. AAS, Queensborough C.C., Bayside, N.Y., 1971; BS, St. John's U., Jamaica, N.Y., 1986. Nursing care coord., case mgr. AIDS unit Luth. Med. Ctr., Bklyn., 1976—. Mem. Assn. for Nurses in AIDS Care, Oncology Nursing Soc.

COHEN, D. ASHLEY, clinical neuropsychologist; b. Omaha, Oct. 2, 1952; d. Cenek and Dorothy A. (Bilek) Hrabik; m. Donald I. Cohen, 1968 (div. 1976); m. Lyn J. Mangiameli, June 12, 1985. BA in Psychology, U. Nebr., Omaha, 1975, MA in Psychology, 1979; PhD in Clin. Psychology, Calif. Coast U., 1988. Lic. psychologist, Calif.; lic. marriage and family therapist, Nev. Family specialist Ea. Nebr. Human Svcs. Agy. Consultation & Edn., 1979-80; psychotherapist Washoe Tribe, Gardnerville, Nev., 1980; therapist Family Counseling Svc., Carson City, Nev., 1980-93; psychotherapist Alpine County Mental Health, Markleeville, Calif., 1981-89, dir., 1990-93; psychologist Golden Gate Med. Examiners, San Francisco, San Jose, Calif., 1993—; conf. presenter and spkr. in field; presenter rsch. findings 7th European Conf. Personality, Madrid, 1994, Oxford (Eng.) U. ISSID Conf., 1991; site coord. nat. standardization Kaufmann brief intelligence test A.G.S., 1988-90. Vol. EMT, Alpine County, 1983-93. Recipient Svc. to Youth award Office Edn., 1991. Mem. APA, Internat. Neuropsychol. Soc., Internat. Soc. Study Individual Differences, Am. Psychol. Soc., Nat. Acad. Neuropsychology. Office: 127 Carson Ct Sunnyvale CA 94086

COHEN, DAVID B., optical company executive; b. Bklyn., Apr. 22, 1943; s. Noah and Sylvia (Naimark) C.; 1 child, Ronald; m. Madeleine Goldman, Dec. 21, 1975; children: Lawrence, Louis, Linda. BA in Philosophy, SUNY, Buffalo, 1960-64; student, CUNY, Long Island U., Bklyn. Coll., St. John's U., Hofstra U., 1964-70; AS in Opticianry, Interboro Inst., 1972-74. Lic. ophthalmic dispenser, N.Y.; cert. optician. Educator N.Y.C. Bd. Edn., 1966-90; v.p. dir. ops. London Optical, Long Island, 1990—; pres. Quick 'n Easy Convenience Stores, L.I., 1972-74, Eyesite, L.I., 1982—; chmn. Optical Adv. Bd. Coun. to Interboro Inst., N.Y., 1993-96; mem. NYSSO Conv. Com., N.Y., 1993-96, dir. L.I. chpt., 1994-96, sec. 1995—. Trustee, pres. Temple Beth El Men's Club, Cedarhurst, N.Y., 1992-94; trustee, L.I. regional Met. N.Y. Fedn. Jewish Men's Clubs, 1995—; pres. Cedarhurst Bus. Assn., 1993—; mem. Cmty. Chest Fair Com., Cedarhurst, 1992—; Ann. CBA Mayoral Program Golf and Tennis Charity Tournament, 1993-95; bd. govs. North Woodmere Civic Assn.; mem. 5 Towns Jewish Cmty. Coun. Mem. Kiwanis Internat., Rep. Club. Republican. Jewish. Home: 33 Captains Rd N Woodmere NY 11581-2806 Office: London Optical 494 Central Ave Cedarhurst NY 11516-2007

COHEN, DAVID JOEL, medical educator; b. New Haven, Conn., Nov. 2, 1960. AB summa cum laude, Harvard U., 1982, MD, 1986, MSc, 1994. Diplomate Am. Bd. Internal Medicine; lic. physician, Mass. Intern then resident Brigham and Women's Hosp., Boston, 1986-89; clin. rsch. fellow Beth Israel Hosp., Boston, 1989-94; fellow Harvard Sch. Pub. Health, Boston, 1992-94, instr. health policy and mgmt., 1995—; instr. medicine Harvard Med. Sch., Boston, 1993—; asst. dir. invasive cardiology sect. Beth Israel Hosp., 1994—. Contbr. chpts. to books and numerous articles to profl. jours. Grantee Johnson and Johnson, 1993-94, Am. Heart Assn., 1995—. Mem. Phi Beta Kappa. Home: 2D Brewer St Jamaica Plain MA 02130

COHEN, DAVID JOHN, cardiothoracic surgeon; b. San Antonio, Jan. 13, 1947; s. Melvin David and Betty (Brown) C.; m. Deborah Milton, May 29, 1976; children: John, Christopher, Scott, Joshua, Benjamin. BA in Biochemistry, Rice U., 1968; MD, Washington U., 1972. Intern Johns Hopkins Hosp., Balt., 1972-73, resident in gen. surgery, 1973-74; resident in gen. surgery U. Wash. Affiliated Hosps., Seattle, 1976-79; resident in cardiothoracic surgery Hosp. of U. Pa., Phila., 1979-81; chief dept. cardiovasc. physiology Walter Reed Army Inst. of Rsch., Washington, 1981-83; staff Brooke Army Med. Ctr., Ft. Sam Houston, Tex., 1983-84, U. Wis. Hosp., Madison, 1984-87; staff William S. Middleton VA Hosp., Madison, 1984-87, chief thoracic surgery svc., 1986-87; staff Med. Ctr. Hosp., San Antonio, 1987-92; staff Audie L. Murphy VA Hosp., San Antonio, 1987-92, chief cardiothoracic surgery, 1991-92, dir. surg. ICU, 1988-92; asst. chief cardiothoracic surgery Brooke Army Med. Ctr., San Antonio, 1992-93, chief cardiothroacic surgery, 1993—; bd. dirs. South Tex. Orgn. Bank, San Antonio. Asst scoutmaster Boy Scouts Am., San Antonio, 1990—, Weblos den leader, 1988-90. Col. U.S. Army. Decorated Bronze Star, Meritorious Svc. medal (2), Army Commendation medal (4), Order fo Mil. Med. Merit; cardiac transplant fellow Tex. Heart Inst., Houston, 1993. Fellow Am. Coll. Surgeons, Am. Coll. Cardiology, Am. Coll. Chest Physicians; mem. Am. Assn. Thoracic Surgeons, Soc. Thoracic Surgeons, Soc. Univ. Surgeons. Jewish. Home: 15638 Dawn Crest San Antonio TX 78248 Office: Cardiothoracic Surgery Svc BAMC 3851 Roger Brooke Dr Fort Sam Houston TX 78234

COHEN, DAVID JONATHAN, transplant nephrologist, educator; b. Mt. Vernon, N.Y., Aug. 24, 1948; s. Samuel Jacob and Minnie (Mayer) C.; m. Lois Ellen Draegin, Jan. 20, 1991 (div.); 1 child, Rafael. BA, U. Mich., 1970; MA, N.Y. U., 1972; MD, Albert Einstein Coll. Med., Bronx, N.Y., 1977. Intern Mt. Sinai Med. Ctr., N.Y.C., 1987-88, resident, 1988-90; assoc. prof. Columbia U., 1983—, med. dir. renal transplant, 1988—. Mem. Am. Soc. Transplant Physicians, Am. Soc. Nephrology. Office: Columbia Presbyn Med Ctr 622 W 168 St New York NY 10032

COHEN, DAVID LEON, physician; b. St. Louis, Feb. 2, 1947; s. Benjamin David and Hannah (Firfer) C.; m. Sheila Zeisel, July 2, 1974; children: Robin, Lori, Jonathan, Jennifer. BS, Roosevelt U., 1963; MS, Chgo. Med. Sch., 1972; MD, Mt. Sinai Sch. Medicine, 1976. Diplomate Am. Bd. Dermatology. Intern in internal medicine Michael Reese Hosp., Chgo., 1976-77; resident Mt. Sinai Hosp., N.Y.C., 1977-80; pvt. practice Hewlett and Jamaica, N.Y., 1980—. Office: 1800 Rockaway Ave # 208 Hewlett NY 11557

COHEN, DAVID WALTER, academic administrator, periodontist, educator; b. Phila., Dec. 15, 1926; s. Abram and Goldie (Schlein) C.; m. Betty Axelrod, Dec. 19, 1948 (dec. Mar. 1992); children: Jane Ellen, Amy Sue, Joanne Louise. DDS, U. Pa., 1950; DSc (hon.), Boston U., 1975; FhD (hon.), Hebrew U., Jerusalem, 1977, U. Athens, 1979; Dr Honoris Causa U. Louis Pasteur, Strasbourg, France, 1986; DHL (hon.), U. Detroit, 1989. Diplomate: Am. Bd. Periodontology (chmn. 1972). Research fellow pathology and periodontia Beth Israel Hosp., Boston, 1950-51; mem. faculty U. Pa. Sch. Dentistry, Phila., 1951—, prof. periodontics, 1962-86, chmn. dept., 1962-73; dean Sch. Dental Medicine U. Pa., Phila., 1972-83; dean emeritus U. Pa. Sch. Dentistry, Phila., 1983—; pres. Med. Coll. Pa., 1986-93; chancellor Allegheny U. of Health Scis., 1996—; mem. staff Albert Einstein Med. Center, Phila., Children's Hosp., Phila.; pres. Jewish Publ. Soc., 1993-96; vis. prof. Boston U. Sch. Grad Dentistry, 1972—; nat. cons. periodontics USAF, 1965-70; bd. govs. Hebrew U., Jerusalem, Betty and Walter Cohen chair in periodontal rsch., 1986; D. Walter Cohen endowed chair in periodontics U. Pa., 1995. Author: (with H.M. Goldman) Periodontia, 1957, (with others) An Introduction to Periodontia, 1959, Periodontal Therapy, 1960, (with R. Genco and Goldman) Contemporary Periodontics, 1990; also numerous articles and chpts. V.p. Jewish Publ. Soc., 1985-89, pres., 1993. Served with USN, 1944-45. First Presdl. scholar U. Calif., San Francisco, 1985-86; named for him Hebrew U. Betty and D. Walter Cohen Chair in Periodontal Rsch., 1986, U. Pa. D. Walter Cohen Endowed Chair in Periodontics, 1995. Fellow AAAS, Am. Acad. Oral Pathology, Am. Acad. Periodontology, Inst. of Medicine of Nat. Acad. Scis.; mem. Am. Soc. Periodontists (pres. 1967). Office: Med Coll Pa 3300 Henry Ave Philadelphia PA 19129-1121

COHEN, DIANA LOUISE, mental health administrator, psychology, educator, psychotherapist; b. Phila., Apr. 8, 1942; d. Nathan and Dorothy (Rubin) Blasberg; m. Jules L. Frankel, July 3, 1987; 1 child, Jennifer. BA, Temple U., 1964, MEd, 1969; PhD, Temple Univ., 1996. Lic. psychologist, Pa., N.J.; nat. cert. mental health counselor. Caseworker Phila. Gen. Hosp., 1964-69, staff psychologist, 1969-70; staff psychologist Atlantic Mental Health Ctr., McKee City, N.J., 1970-80, unit dir., 1980-87, v.p. profl. svcs., 1987-91; pvt. practice Pa., N.J., 1991—; mem. adj. faculty Glassboro (N.J.) State Coll., 1988—; cmty. & family mediator Cmty. Justice Inst., Atlantic County, N.J., 1990—. Com. chmn. Atlantic County Commn. for Missing and Abused Children, 1984-89. Grantee N.J. Dept. Edn., 1988-89, N.J. Job Tng. Partnership Act, 1990. Mem. APA (assoc.), NJCA, N.J. Mental Health Counselors Assn. (pres.-elect 1996), South Shore Region Mental Health Counselors Assn. (sec. 1994—). Home: 569 Gravelly Run Rd Mays Landing NJ 08330-1654 Office: 2106 New Rd Linwood NJ 08221-1046 also: 1718 Welsh Rd Philadelphia PA 19115-4213

COHEN, DONALD JAY, pediatrics, psychiatry and psychology educator, administrator; b. Chgo., Sept. 5, 1940; m. Phyllis Cohen, 1964; children—Matthew, Rebecca, Rachel, Joseph. B.A. in Philosophy and Psychology summa cum laude, Brandeis U., 1961; Student in philosophy and psychology, U. Cambridge, 1961-62; M.D., Yale U., 1966. Diplomate Am. Bd. Psychiatry and Neurology, Am. Bd. Child Psychiatry. Intern in pediatric medicine Children's Hosp. Med. Ctr., Boston, 1966-67; resident in child psychiatry Judge Baker Guidance Ctr., Children's Hosp. Med. Ctr., Boston, 1969-70; resident in psychiatry Mass. Mental Health Ctr., Boston, 1967-69; fellow in child psychiatry Hillcrest Children's Ctr. and Children's Hosp., Washington, 1970-72; asst. in medicine Children's Hosp., Boston, 1967-69; asst. to dir. child devel. Dept. Health, Washington, 1970-72; assoc. prof. pediatrics, psychiatry, and psychology Yale U., New Haven, Conn., 1972-79; prof. pediatrics, psychiatry, psychology Yale U., New Haven, 1979—; Irving B. Harris prof. child psychiatry, pediatrics and psychology Yale U., New Haven, Conn., 1987—, dir. Child Study Ctr., 1983—; clin. assoc. adult psychiatry bd. NIMH Sect. on Twin and Sibling Studies, 1970-72; vis. prof. Hebrew U. Hadassah Med. Ctr., summer 1982; mem. Nat. Commn. on Children, 1988; tng. and supervising analyst Western New Eng. Psychoanalytic Inst., 1992—; trustee Anna Freud Ctr., London, 1992; pres. pubsls. com. Yale U. Press, 1995—. Contbr. numerous articles to profl. jours., chpts. to books; author monographs: Serving Sch. Age Children, 1972, Serving Presch. Children, 1974; editor monographs: Schizophrenia Bul., Vol. 8, No. 2, 1982, Jour. Autism and Devel. Disorders, 1982; co-editor monographs: (with A. Donnellan) Handbook of Autism and Pervasive Developmental Disorders, 1985; (with A.J. Solnit, J.E. Schowalter) Psychiatry, 1985, 91; author of book revs.; mem. editl. bd. Jour. Am. Acad. of Child Psychiatry, 1972-76, 80—, Israel Jour. Psychiatry, 1983—, Am. Jour. Psychiatry, 1996—; mem. adv. bd. Jour. Child Psychology and Psychiatry, 1977. Chmn. profl. adv. bd. Nat. Soc. for Autistic Children, 1981—; mem. med. adv. bd. Tourette Syndrome Assn., 1980—, mem. profl. adv. bd. Benhaven, New Haven, Conn., 1972—; bd. dirs. NIMH Treatment Devel. and Assessment Study Sect., 1979-82, Psychoanalytic Research and Devel. Fund, 1982—, Found.'s Fund for Research in Psychiatry, 1977-81, Spl. Citizens, Futures Unlimited, Inc., 1983—, Ounce of Prevention Fund Nat. Adv. Com., 1983—, B'nai B'rith Hillel Found., Yale U., 1984—; trustee Brandeis U., 1982—, Western New Eng. Inst. for Psychoanalysis, 1984—. Served with USPHS, 1970-72. Recipient Ann. Pub. Svc. award Nat. Soc. for Autistic Children, 1972, Spl. Recognition, Hofheimer prize Am. Psychiatric Assn., 1977, Ittleson award Am. Psychiat. Assn., 1981, Strecker award Inst. of Pa. Hosp., U. Pa., 1990; Woodrow Wilson fellow, 1961, Falk fellow Am. Psychiat. Assn., 1970-71; Fulbright scholar Trinity Coll., U. Cambridge, 1961-62. Fellow Am. Acad. Child Psychiatry (chmn. com. on rsch. 1975-81), Am. Pediatric Soc., Am. Acad. Pediatrics; mem. Inst. Medicine of NAS, Soc. for Rsch. in Child Devel., Internat. Assn. Child and Adolescent Psychiatry and Allied Professions (pres. 1992—), Internat. Psychoanalytic Soc., Am. Psychoanalytic Assn., Israel Psychoanalytic Soc. (corr.), Western New Eng. Psychoanalytic Soc., Phi Beta Kappa, Sigma Xi, Alpha Omega Alpha. Office: Yale Child Study Ctr PO Box 207900 New Haven CT 06520-7900

COHEN, DONNA, program director, educator; b. Balt., Apr. 3, 1947. BS in Zoology, Duke U., 1969; MA in Psychology, U. So. Calif., L.A., 1973, PhD in Psychology, 1975. Social sci. analyst Brentwood VA Hosp., UCLA, 1971-74, rsch. psychologist psychogenetics unit, 1974-76; asst. prof. dept. psychiatry and behavioral scis. Sch. Medicine, U. Wash., Seattle, 1976-79, assoc. prof., 1980, co-dir. geriatric psychiatry postgrad. fellowship program, 1978-80; dir. rsch. and tng. Beth Abraham Hosp., Bronx, N.Y., 1981-84; head unified divsn. aging and geriatric psychiatry Montefiore Med. Ctr., Albert Einstein Coll. Medicine, Bronx, 1981-85; dir. geriatric psychiatry postgrad. fellowship program Montefiore Med. Ctr., Albert Einstein Coll. Medicine, Bronx, N.Y., 1981-85; assoc. prof. dept. psychiatry Montefiore Med. Ctr., Albert Einstein Coll. Medicine, Bronx, 1981-85; dep. dir. Gerontology Ctr. U. Ill., Chgo., 1986-91, prof. Sch. Pub. Health, 1986-92; prof. dept. psychiatry U. South Fla., Tampa, 1992—, prof. dept. gerontology Coll. Arts and Scis., 1992—; prof. dept. aging and mental health U. South Fla., Fla. Mental Health Inst., Tampa, 1992—, chmn. dept. aging and mental health, 1992—; dir. Aging Studies Initiative U. South Fla., Tampa, 1993-94, dir. Inst. on Aging, 1994—; prin. investigator behavioral biology unit, Geriatric Rsch. Ednl. and Clin. Ctr., Seattle (Wash.)/Am. Lake VA Hosps., 1976-78; mem. study sect. psychopathology and clin. biology, NIHM, 1979-82, bd. sci. counselors, 1983-88; dir. rsch. and tng. Beth Abraham Hosp., Bronx, 1981-84; vis. prof. Shaare Zedek Hosp., Jerusalem, 1982; adv. bd. Ctr. for Aging and Devel., Med. Coll. Wis., Milw., 1991—; tech. adv. com. Nat. Nutrition Screeing Initiative, 1990—; com. for phys. thought U. Ill. Sch. Architecture and Gerontology Ctr., 1989—; blue ribbon adv. bd. Alzheimer's Disease Alliance Western Pa., Pitts., 1988—; cons. VA Merit Rev. Bd., 1980, Saing Petersburg Times, ABC's 20/20, numerous others. Author: (with others) Conceptual Bases of Psychopathology, 1980, Psychopathology of Aging, 1981, Mental Health Care of the Aging: A Multi-Disciplinary Curriculum, 1982, A Handbook for Families Caring for a Relative with Dementia, 1982, The Loss of Self: A Family Resource for Alzheimer's Disease and Related Disorders, 1986, Caring for Your Aging Parents: A Planning and Action Guide for Adult Children with Aging Parents, 1993; mem. editl. bd. Experimental Aging Rsch., 1977-86, Generations, 1977-84, Am. Jour. Alzheimer's Care, 1986—; book rev. editor Behavior, Health and Aging, 1990—; ad hoc rev. numerous jours.; editor-in-chief Jour. Mental Health & Aging; contbr. articles to profl. jours. Recipient Nat. Inst. Child & Human Devel. Traineeship, 1971-74, Founders award Alzheimer's Disease and Related Disorders Assn., 1987, Met. Chgo.'s Health Care Coun. award for health care mgmt., 1988, Spl. citation The 39th Annual Progressive Architecture awards, 1991-92; named One of 100 Women Shaping Chgo.'s Future, Today's Chgo. Woman, 1988. Office: U South Fla Dept Aging Mental Health 13301 Bruce B Downs Blvd Tampa FL 33612-3807

COHEN, ELIE JOSEPH, orthopaedic surgeon; b. Cairo, Sept. 29, 1931; came to U.S., 1957; s. Joseph and Rachel (El-Gamil) C.; m. Marcia Cohn, July 29, 1961; children: Renee Elaine Cohen Dworman, Audrey Jacqueline, Lawrence Howard. Grad., Ein Shams U., Cairo, 1955. Diplomate Am. Bd. Orthopaedic Surgeons, Am. Bd. Forensic Examiners. Rotating intern Miriam Hosp., Providence, 1958-59; resident in surgery Washington Hosp. Ctr., 1959-60; resident in orthopaedics U. Md., Balt., 1960-63, Kernan Hosp., Balt., 1962-63; pvt. practice, Newport, R.I., 1963—; mem. Workers' Compensation Adv. Bd. R.I., 1987—, R.I. Med. Examiners Commn., 1987—. Fellow ACS, Am. Acad. Cerebral Palsy and Devel. Medicine, Internat. Coll. Surgeons, Nat. Acad. Forensic Examiners, Am. Acad. Orthopaedic Surgeons; mem. AMA, R.I. Orthopaedic Soc., Ea. Orthopaedic Soc., R.I. Med. Soc., U. Md. Surg. Soc., Newport County Med. Soc. (past pres.), Boston Orthopaedic Club. Jewish. Office: 136 Rhode Island Ave Newport RI 02840

COHEN, ELLEN DANK, education program director; b. N.Y.C., Nov. 21, 1950; d. Irving and Harriet (Miller) Dank; m. Jeffrey Leonard Cohen, Dec. 23, 1978 (dec. Feb. 1983). BS, CUNY, 1971, MS, 1974; MBA, Adelphi U., 1986. Patient accounts coord. French and Polyclinic Med. Sch. and Health Ctr., N.Y.C., 1971-75; mgr. in-patient billing Roosevelt Hosp., N.Y.C., 1975-76; adminstr. L.I. Jewish-Hillside Med. Ctr., New Hyde Park, N.Y., 1976-78; exec. dir. faculty practice plan SUNY Clin. Practice Mgmt. Plan, Stony Brook, N.Y., 1979—. Mem. Am. Coll. Med. Group Adminstrs., Am. Coll. Healthcare Execs., Assn. Am. Med. Colls. (group on faculty practice), Centralized Practice Plan Dirs. Roundtable, Med. Group Mgmt. Assn., Healthcare Fin. Mgmt. Assn. (guest spkr., com. co-chairperson, Follmer award 1991). Home: 12 Beaumont Dr Melville NY 11747 Office: Clin Practice Mgmt Plan PO Box 1554 Stony Brook NY 11790-0988

COHEN, EMANUEL MALCOLM, retired physician; b. Jan. 24, 1912. BA, Columbia Coll., 1933; MD, NYU, 1939. Intern Sydenham Hosp., 1940-42, clin. asst. in medicine, 1943-44, asst. adj. physician, 1944-56, assoc. attending physician, 1956-73, attending physician, 1973—; pvt. practice, 1945-91; clin. asst. attending physician Mt. Sinai Hosp., 1955-57, sr. clin. asst. physician, 1957-73, physician Hypertension Clinic, 1973. Mem. AMA, N.Y. State Med. Soc. (life), N.Y. County Med. Soc. (life). Home: 310 West End Ave #8C New York NY 10023-8146

COHEN, FELISSA L., nursing educator, researcher; b. N.Y.C., Apr. 6, 1941; d. Jack and Ruth (Dorbin) Lashley; divorced; children: Peter, Heather, Neal. BSN, Adelphi Coll., 1961; MA, NYU, 1965; PhD, Ill. State U., 1973. Cert. Am. Bd. Med. Genetics., Am. Coll. Med. Genetics. Dean Sch. of Nursing So. Ill. U., Edwardsville, Ill. Editor: The Person with AIDS: Nursing Perspectives, 1987 (Book of Yr. award), Tuberculosis: A Sourcebook for Nursing Practice and Women, Children and HIV/AIDS (Book of Yr. award 1993). Mem. ANA (coun. nurse researchers), AAAS, Am. Soc. Human Genetics, Am. Acad. Nursing, Am. Sleep Disorders Assn., Nat. League Nursing, Midwest Nursing Rsch. Soc., N.Y. Acad. Scis., Ill. Nurses Assn., Sleep Rsch. Soc., Sigma Xi, Sigma Theta Tau, Alpha Tau Delta, Pi Lambda Theta, Phi Sigma.

COHEN, GARY P., physician; b. Newark, Jan. 24, 1942; s. Leonard Elliot and Ruth (Levine) C.; m. Jeannine M. Izard, Apr. 10, 1971; children: Stephanie, Melanie. MD, U. Montpellier, France, 1976. Pvt. practice Cohen, Henr, Jafer, Szobo Med. Assocs., Bloomfield, Conn., 1979—; bd. dirs. St. Francis-Mt. Sinai Hosp., Hartford, Conn. Mem. ACP. Office: 701 E Cottage Grove Rd Bloomfield CT 06002

COHEN, GRAZYNA B., emergency room nurse; b. Warsaw, Poland, June 4, 1965; d. Bernard and Maria M. (Golec) Kozikowski; m. Frederick Cohen, Aug. 3, 1986; 1 child, Jessica Danielle. BSN, SUNY, Bklyn., 1989. Cert. IV therapy, coronary care, BCLS, ACLS. Kings Hwy. Hosp. (name changed to Beth Israel Med. Ctr.) Beth Israel Med. Ctr.-King's Hwy. divsn., Bklyn.; staff nurse Downstate Med. Ctr., Bklyn. Mem. Downstate Nursing Honor Soc. Home: 1402 E 100th St Ph Brooklyn NY 11236-5521

COHEN, HARRIS L., diagnostic radiologist, consultant; b. Bklyn., Sept. 18, 1951; s. Samuel G. and Lola Estera (Altman) C.; m. Sandra Wilensky, Oct. 18, 1979; children: David Matthew, Lauren Elizabeth, Benjamin Adam. BA, CUNY, Bklyn., 1973; MD, SUNY, Bklyn., 1976. Diplomate Am. Bd. Radiology, Nat. Bd. Med. Examiners; cert. added qualifications in pediatric radiology Am. Bd. Radiology. Asst. prof. radiology SUNY Health Sci. Ctr., Bklyn., 1981-88, prof. radiology, 1993—, med. dir. radiol. sci. and tech. program, 1985-88, 94—; asst. chief of imaging Brookdale Hosp. Med. Ctr., Bklyn., 1983-85; assoc. prof. radiology Cornell U. Med. Coll., N.Y.C., 1988-93; chief pediatric CT and ultrasound North Shore U. Hosp.-Cornell, Manhasset, N.Y., 1988-93, assoc. dir. divsn. CT/ultrasound/magnetic resonance imaging, 1988-93; assoc. dir. radiology Kings County Hosp., Bklyn., 1993—; dir. divsn. ultrasound U. and Kings County Hosps., Bklyn., 1985-88, 93—; cons. ultrasound and pediatric imaging Brookdale Hosp. Med. Ctr., Bklyn., 1988—; cons. diagnostic radiology Med. Mut. Liability, N.Y.C., 1992—. Article reviewer: Am. Jour. Roentgenology, 1988—, Radiographics, 1991— (Editor's Recognitiion award); co-editor: (textbook) Fetal and Neonatal Sonography; mem. editl. bd. Jour. Diagnostic Med. Sonography, 1985—; contbr. articles to sci. jours. and chpt. to med. texts. Fellow Soc. Radiologists in Ultrasound, 1993. Fellow Soc. Radiologists in Ultrasound, 1993; recipient Master Tchr. award in radiology SUNY-HSC/B Alumni Assn., 1996. Home: 78 Grove Ave Cedarhurst NY 11516-2311

COHEN, HARVEY JAY, physician, educator; b. Bklyn., Oct. 21, 1940; s. Joseph and Anne (Margolin) C.; m. Sandra Helen Levine, June 1964; children: Ian Mitchell, Pamela Robin. BS, Bklyn. Coll., 1961; MD, Downstate Med. Coll., Bklyn., 1965. Diplomate Am. Bd. Internal Medicine, Am. Bd. Hematology. Intern, then resident internal medicine Duke U. Med. Ctr., Durham, N.C., 1965-67, fellow hematology and oncology, 1969-71; chief hematology-oncology VA Med. Ctr., Durham, N.C., 1975-76, chief med. service, 1976-82, assoc. chief of staff-edn., 1982-84, now dir. geriatric research, edn. and clin. ctr.; assoc. prof. medicine Duke U. Med. Ctr., Durham, 1976-80, now prof. medicine, chief geriatric div., also dir. Ctr. for Study of Aging. Author: Medical Immunology, 1977; editor: Cancer I and II, 1987; editor Jour. Gerontology: Med. Scis., 1988-92; contbr. numerous articles to profl. jours. Served as surgeon USPHS, 1967-69. Fellow ACP, Am. Geriatrics Soc. (bd. dirs. 1987—, sec. 1991-93, ethics com. 1992—, pres. 1994-95), Gerontology Soc. Am. (clin. sect., rsch. com. 1987-92, chair 1993-94, publs. com. 1992—, program chair 1994—); mem. Am. Soc. Clin. Oncology, Am. Soc. Hematology, Am. Assn. Cancer Rsch. Home: 2811

Friendship Cir Durham NC 27705-5521 Office: Duke U Med Ctr for Study Aging & Human Devel Box 3003 Durham NC 27710-3003

COHEN, HARVEY JOEL, pediatric hematology and oncology educator; b. N.Y.C., July 4, 1943; s. Phillip and Ida (Teitel) C.; m. Ilene Verne Bookseger, Aug. 15, 1965; children: Philip Jason, Jonathan Todd. BS, CUNY, 1964; MD, PhD, Duke U., 1970. Intern Children's Hosp., Boston, 1970-71, resident, 1973-74; instr. pediatrics Harvard U. Med. Sch., Boston, 1974-76, asst. prof., 1976-79, assoc. prof., 1979-81; assoc. prof. pediatrics U. Rochester (N.Y.) Med. Ctr., 1981-84, prof., 1984-93, assoc. chmn. dept., 1987-93, chief pediatric hematology and oncology, 1981-93; prof., chmn. dept. pediatrics Stanford (Calif.) U. Sch. Medicine, 1993—; chief staff Lucile Salter Packard Children's Hosp. at Stanford, 1993—; med. advisor Montgomery Med. Ventures, San Francisco, 1984—; sci. advisor St. Jude Children's Rsch. Hosp., Memphis, 1985-90; chmn. hematology study sect. NIH, Washington, 1986-88. Editor: Hematology: Basic Principles and Practice, 1991. Med. dir. Camp Good Days and Spl. Times, Rochester, 1981-93, Monroe County chpt. Am. Cancer Soc., Rochester, 1983-93, Rochester br. Cooley's Anemia Found., 1984-93. Surgeon USPHS, 1971-73. Tng. grantee Nat. Inst. Gen. Med. Scis., 1983-90, Nat. Inst. Child Health and Human Devel., 1990-94. Mem. Soc. for Pediatric Rsch. (pres. 1988-89), Am. Soc. for Clin. Investigation, Am. Pediatric Soc. Democrat. Jewish. Office: Stanford U Sch Medicine Dept Pediatrics Rm H-310 Stanford CA 94305

COHEN, HERBERT JESSE, physician, educator; b. N.Y.C., Apr. 27, 1935; s. Barnet and Edith (Lepolstat) C.; m. Marion E. Finger, Aug. 29, 1960; children—Linda Elizabeth, Gerald Daniel, Seth Michael. B.A. (Ford Found. scholar), Columbia, 1955; M.D., State U. N.Y., 1959. Intern Bellevue Hosp., N.Y.C., 1959-60; resident N.Y. Hosp., N.Y.C., 1960-62; asst. instr. Cornell Med. Sch., 1961-62; instr. Tulane Med. Sch., 1962-64; NIH fellow Albert Einstein Coll. Medicine, 1964-66, asst. prof. pediatrics and rehab. medicine, 1966-71, assoc. prof., 1971-76, prof., 1976—; dir. Children's Evaluation and Rehab. Ctr., Rose F. Kennedy Center for Mental Retardation and Human Devel., Bronx, N.Y., 1968-74, 78—, Bronx Developmental Services, N.Y. State Dept. Mental Hygiene, 1971-80; dir. Rose F. Kennedy Univ. Affiliated Facility Program, 1974—, dir. div. child devel. and devel. disabilities, dept. pediatrics, 1981—; vice chmn. Pres.'s Com. on Mental Retardation, 1978-81; mem. study sect. human devel. NIH, 1978-82; mem. profl. adv. bd. various founds. and profl. orgns. Author 4 books; also contbr. over 70 articles to profl. pubs. Served with USPHS, 1962-64. Recipient Disting. Humanitarian Research and Devel. awards Mental Retardation Service Orgns.; United Cerebral Palsy Research and Edn. Found. fellow, 1966-68. Fellow Am. Acad. Pediatrics (chmn. child devel. sect., chmn. com. on children with disabilities); mem. AAAS, Am. Acad. Cerebral Palsy, Am. Assn. Univ. Affiliated Facilities (pres. 1980-81, dir. 1977-84), Am. Assn. Mental Retardation (Leadership award 1996). Office: R F Kennedy Center 1410 Pelham Pky S Bronx NY 10461-1101

COHEN, JEFFREY, neurologist; b. Bklyn., Dec. 16, 1955; s. Julian and Sylvia (Funt) C.; m. Linda Lee Gunderman, May 28, 1989; children: Jordan, Max. BA in Psychology, Brandeis U., 1976; PhD in Psychobiology, Rutgers U., 1981; MD, SUNY, Bklyn., 1987. Diplomate in neurology Am. Bd. Psychiatry and Neurology; diplomate Am. Bd. Clin. Neurophysiology. Intern Beth Israel Med. Ctr., N.Y.C., 1987-88; resident Columbia-Presbyn. Med. Ctr., N.Y.C., 1988-91, fellow, 1991-92; asst. clin. prof. neurology U. Calif. Irvine Med. Ctr., Orange, 1992-94; asst. prof. neurology Albert Einstein Coll. Medicine, Bronx, 1994—; dir. epilepsy program and clin. neurophysiology Beth Israel Med. Ctr., N.Y.C., 1994—. Contbr. articles to profl. jours., chpts. to books. Recipient Abraham Rabinen Neurology award, 1987, SUNY Alumni Assn. award for rsch., 1987, Rutgers Grad. Student Govt. award for rsch., 1980; N.Y. State Regents scholar, 1972. Mem. Am. Acad. Neurology, Esatern Electroencephalographic Soc. (bus. com. 1994—), Soc. for Neurosci., Am. Epilepsy Soc., Am. Clin. Neurophysiology Soc., Epilepsy Soc. of N.Y.C. (bd. dirs. 1995—, chmn. bd. dirs. 1996—, profl. adv. com. 1994—), Alpha Omega Alpha. Office: Beth Israel Med Ctr First Ave at 16th St New York NY 10003

COHEN, JEFFREY STEVEN, psychologist; b. Hartford, Conn., Dec. 29, 1952; s. Thomas and Marion S. (Reisner) C.; m. Lisa Koval, June 28, 1987. BA, Cen. Conn. State Coll., 1975; PhD, U.S. Internat. U., 1981. Mental health worker Elmcrest Psychiat. Inst., Portland, Conn., 1974-76; rsch. asst. dept. psychiatry U. Calif., San Diego, La Jolla, 1977-78; psychology intern Conn. Valley Hosp., Middletown, 1980-81; staff clin. psychologist Day Hosp.-Hall-Brooke Found., Inc., Westport, Conn., 1981-82; psychologist Greenwich (Conn.) Family Ctr., 1983—, chief psychologist, 1986—; pvt. practice psychology, Stamford, Conn., 1983—; prof. psychology Norwalk Community Coll., Conn., U. Conn., Stamford, 1988—; cons. Conn. Cts. Diagnostic Clinic, Conn. Div. Vocat. Rehab., Conn. Bur. Disability, Industry and Bus, The Personnel Lab. Mem. AAAS, Am. Psychol. Assn., Conn. Psychol. Assn. (bd. dirs. 1995—), Mid-Hudson Inst Bioenergetic Analysis, Toastmasters Internat. Psi Chi. Jewish. Home: 108 Fawn Ridge Ln Norwalk CT 06851-1140 Office: 833 Summer St Apt 1-a Stamford CT 06901-1024

COHEN, JOEL RALPH, microbiologist, health science educator; b. Chelsea, Mass., Oct. 20, 1926; s. Julius Meyer and Pearl (Mankin) C.; m. Marilyn R. Lezar, Sept. 7, 1947; children: Robert Neil, Deborah Ellen, Peter Alan. BS magna cum laude, U. Mass., Amherst, 1949, MS, 1950, PhD, 1975. Registered and specialist microbiologist. Microbiologist Baystate Med. Ctr., Springfield, Mass., 1950-68, chief clin. labs., 1954-68, cons., 1968—; assoc. prof. biosci. Springfield Coll., Mass., 1968-75, chmn. biology dept., 1969-81, prof. biosci., 1979-83, prof. biology and health sci., 1983-92; coord. Health Related Programs, 1982-92; cons. Health-Related Affairs, 1992—; cons. microbiology VA Med. Ctr., Northampton, Mass., 1963-86; cons. lab. Mcpl. Hosp., Springfield, 1960—. Contbr. articles to profl. jours. Col. USAR, 1943-86. Fellow AAAS, Am. Acad. Microbiology, Am. Pub. Health Assn. (sect. lab. sec. 1979-82), Royal Soc. Health; mem. Am. Soc. Microbiology, N.Y. Acad. Scis., Am. Inst. Biol. Scis., Am. Assn. Blood Banks, Am. Soc. Allied Health Profs., Sigma Xi, Phi Kappa Phi. Jewish. Office: Springfield Coll 263 Alden St Springfield MA 01109-3797

COHEN, JOHN S., ophthalmologist; b. Ellenville, N.Y., Nov. 5, 1942; s. Herman and Renee (Hartman) C.; m. Julie S. Shavzin, Oct. 14, 1972; children: Howard, Bradley. BS, U. R.I., Kingston, 1964; MD, U. Louisville, 1968. Diplomate Am. Bd. Ophthalmology. Intern Balt. City Hosps., 1969; resident in ophthalmology U. Cin., 1974; fellow in glaucoma U. Calif., San Francisco, 1975; asst. prof. dept. ophthalmology U. South Fla., 1975-77; assoc. clin. prof. dept. ophthalmology U. Cin., 1977—; ophthalmologist, chief glaucoma svc. Cin. Eye Inst., 1977—; instr. Am. Acad. Ophthalmology, 1976—; examiner Am. Bd. Ophthalmology, 1983-90; vol. ophthalmologist Orbis Mission, Yugoslavia, Costa Rica, Philippines, India, China, Bulgaria, 1989—; med. cons. Wyoming City Schs., 1984. Contbr. articles to profl. jours., chpt. to book. Capt. USAF, 1969-71. Mem. Am. Acad. Ophthalmology (honor award 1985), Am. Glaucoma Soc., Shaffer Fellows Soc., Cin. Soc. Ophthalmology, Ohio State Soc. Ophtahlmology, Phi Kappa Phi. Office: Cin Eye Inst 10494 Montgomery Rd Cincinnati OH 45242

COHEN, JONATHAN BREWER, molecular neurobiologist, biochemist; b. Akron, Ohio, Dec. 17, 1944; s. Saul G. and Doris E. (Brewer) C.; m. Victoria Ann Rhoden, July 20, 1981; children: Deborah Karen, Samuel Max. AB, Harvard U., 1966, MA, 1967, PhD, 1972. Postdoctoral fellow Pasteur Inst., Paris, 1971-74; asst. prof. pharmacology Harvard Med. Sch., Boston, 1975-80, assoc. prof., 1980-82; prof. neurobiology Washington U. Med. Sch., St. Louis, 1982-92, prof. biol. chemistry, 1982-92; prof. neurobiology Harvard Med. Sch., Boston, 1992—; head neurosci. grad. program Washington U., 1987-92, Harvard Med. Sch., 1993—; mem. pharm. scis. rev. com. NIH, 1988-92. Mem. editorial bd. Jour. Biol. Chemistry, 1986-91, 94—. Mem. Am. Chem. Soc., Soc. Neurosci., Am. Soc. Pharmacology and Exptl. Therapeutics, Am. Soc. Biochemistry and Molecular Biology, Phi Beta Kappa. Office: Harvard Med Sch Dept Neurobiology 220 Longwood Ave Boston MA 02115-5701

COHEN, JORDAN JAY, medical association executive; b. St. Louis, June 18, 1934; s. Bernard and Gladys (Brauer) C.; m. Carole Goldstein, Aug. 26, 1956; children: Deborah, Joel, David. BA, Yale U., 1956; MD, Harvard U., 1960; DSc, George Washington U. Sch. Med., and Health Scis., 1995, SUNY Health Sci. Ctr., Syracuse, 1996. Diplomate Am. Bd. Internal Medicine (mem. critical care medicine test and policy com. 1985-87, chmn. 1987-89, mem. subspecialty com. on nephrology 1981-86, chmn. 1986-88, chmn. com. on evaluation of clin. competency 1987-92, bd. dirs. 1986-94, mem. exec. com. 1990-94, chmn. 1993-94). Intern, asst. resident Boston City Hosp., 1960-62, sr. resident, 1964-65; rsch. fellow in renal medicine New Eng. Med. Ctr. Hosp., Boston, 1962-64; tchg. fellow Harvard U. Med. Sch., Boston, 1964-65, instr. in medicine, 1968-74, lectr. in medicine, 1974-82; asst. prof. med. scis. Brown U., Providence, 1965-68, assoc. prof. med. scis., 1968-71; assoc. prof. medicine Tufts U. Sch. Medicine, Boston, 1971-75, prof. medicine, 1976-82; prof., assoc. chmn. medicine Pritzker Sch. Medicine, U. Chgo., 1982-88; dean sch. medicine, prof. medicine SUNY, Stony Brook, 1988-94; dir. Univ. Med. Ctr., Stony Brook, 1993-94; pres. Assn. Am. Med. Colls., Washington, 1994—; dir. divsn. renal disease R.I. Hosp., Providence, 1965-71; chief renal svc. New Eng. Med. Ctr. Hosp., Boston, 1971-82, pres. med. staff, 1975-76, physician-in-chief and chmn., dept. medicine Michael Reese Hosp. and Med. Ctr., Chgo., 1982-88; pres. med. staff Univ. Hosp., Stony Brook, N.Y., 1988-94. Co-author: (textbooks) Acid-Base, 1982, Nephrology Forum, 1983, Repairing Bodily Fluids, 1989; author chpts. to books; editor Nephrology Forum, 1978—, Tufts Family Health Guides, 1979-82; manuscript reviewer Am. Jour. Physiology, Annals Internal Medicine, Jour. Clin. Investigation, Kidney Internat., New England Jour. Medicine; contbr. articles to profl. jours. Lt. col. M.C., U.S. Army, 1969-71. Master ACP (mem. coun. on subsplty. socs. 1979-84, chmn. edn. policy com. 1983-89, bd. regents 1983-89, chmn. search com. for assoc. exec. v.p. for edn., mem. nephrology com. med. knowledge self-assessment program, chmn., com., rep. to Coun. Med. Splty. Socs. 1991-94, vice chmn. 1988-89), Dept. Vet. Affairs, Spl. Med. Adv. Group, 1995-98; fellow Royal Soc. Medicine; mem. Inst. Medicine of NAS, Am. Clin. and Climatol. Assn., Am. Fedn. Clin. Rsch. (chmn. Ea. sect. 1975), Am. Geriat. Soc. (mem. program com. 1985-88), Am. Heart Assn., Am. Soc. Clin. Investigation, Am. Soc. Nephrology (rep. to CSS 1978-82, chmn. manpower task force 1980), Nat. Kidney Found. (mem. task force on nephrology manpower 1987-89), Soc. Med. Adminstrs., Assn. Am. Physicians, Assn. Program Dirs. in Internal Medicine (mem. coun. 1984-90, pres. 1988-89), Ctrl. Soc. Clin. Rsch., Internat. Soc. Nephrology, Midwest Salt and Water Club, Cosmos Club, Phi Beta Kappa, Sigma Xi. Home: 1211 28th St NW Washington DC 20007-3316 Office: Assn Am Med Colls 2450 N St NW Washington DC 20037-1127

COHEN, KENNETH BRUCE, health agency director; b. Springfield, Mass., Jan. 19, 1950; s. Samuel A. and Shirley F. (Austin) C.; m. Deborah F. Roberts, Aug. 3, 1975; children: Kimberly A., Lauren B., Meredith L. BS, Ithaca Coll., 1971; M in Hosp. Adminstrn., George Washington U., 1975. Budget dir. Meml. Hosp., Hollywood, Fla., 1976-77; asst. adminstr. Meml. Hosp., Hollywood, 1977-78, sr. asst. adminstr., 1978-83; chief ops. officer Hollywood (Fla.) Med. Ctr., 1983-85; adminstr. Riverside (Calif.) Gen. Hosp., 1985-91; health agy. dir. Riverside (Calif.) Health Svcs. Agy., 1991—. Mem. Health Planning and Devel Council, Fla., 1985, bd. Nursing Home Adminstrs., Fla., 1981-84. Named one of Top 25 Turnaround CEO's, Health Week, 1989; recipient 3d Ann. County Hosp. Innovators award, 1990. Mem. Health Care Fin. Mgmt. Assn., Am. Hosp. Assn., Calif. Hosp. Assn., Calif. Assn. Pub. Hosps. (County Hosp. Innovators award 1989), Nat. Assn. Pub. Hosps. (1st Ann. Safety Net Devel. award 1990), Am. Coll. Health Care Execs. Office: Riverside County Health 4065 County Circle Dr Riverside CA 92503-3420

COHEN, KENNETH DAVID, psychiatrist, psychoanalyst; b. Phila., Mar. 16, 1928; s. Joseph S. and Sylvia (Levy) C.; m. Ann Ruth Fedorka, Mar. 13, 1955; children: Stuart Lloyd, Richard Ira, Paul Seth. MD, U. Health Scis./ Chgo. Med. Sch, 1953; BA, U. Pa., 1949. Cert. in psychiatry, psychoanalysis, adminstrv. psychiatry. Intern Albert Einstein Med. Ctr.So. Div., Phila., 1953-54, resident, 1956-57; resident Phila. Psychiat. Ctr., 1954-56; chief mental hygiene consultation svc. U.S. Army, Ft. George G. Meade, Md., 1957-59; sr. staff psychiatrist Phila. Psychiat. Ctr., 1959-62; with NIMH drug rsch. team dept. psychiatry U. Pa., Phila., 1963-67; assoc. dir. adult psychiatry northern div. Albert Einstein Med. Ctr., Phila., 1968-69, cons. renal dialysis and transplant team northern div., 1968-69; chief psychiat. consultation Vets. Hosp., Phila., 1970-72; clin. dir., dir. profl. edn. Phila. Psychiat. Ctr., 1973-80; assoc. chief psychiatry ASSD Ctr., Presbyn. U. of Pa., Phila., 1980-83; dir. adult div. Inst.-Phila. Assn. for Psychoanalysis, 1984-90; supervising and tng. analyst Inst.-Phila. Assn. for Psychoanalysis; clin. prof. dept. psychiatry U. Pa., Phila., 1981—; adj. clin. assoc. prof. dept. psychiatry Thomas Jefferson U., Phila., 1983-91. Contbr. sci. papers to profl. jours. Pres., Bala Cynwyd (Pa.) Jr. High Home and Sch. Assn., 1971-72. Capt. U.S. Army, 1957-59. Recipient Cert. Appreciation U.S. Army, 1959, Disting. Svc. award Phila. Psychiat. Ctr. Med. Staff, 1981; featured in Phila. mag. Top Docs publ., 1996. Fellow Am. Psychiat. Assn. (life), Coll. of Physicians of Phila., Phila. Psychiat. Soc. (Practitioner of Yr. 1992), Pa. Psychiat. Soc.; mem. AMA, Phila. County Med. Soc., Pa. Med. Soc., Phila. Assn. for Psychoanalysts (treas. 1972-76, v.p. 1978-80, 82-84), Am. Psychoanalytical Assn., Internat. Psychoanalytical Assn. Jewish. Home: 37 E Princeton Rd Bala Cynwyd PA 19004-2242 Office: Ste 116 191 Presidential Blvd Bala Cynwyd PA 19004

COHEN, KENT I., emergency physician; b. Macon, Ga., Apr. 9, 1960; s. Marvin Bertram and Sandra (Bresler) C.; m. Lisa Robyn Singer, Dec. 13, 1992; children: Lindsey, Miles. BS, U. Ga., 1982; MD, Emory U., 1986. Diplomate Am. Bd. Emergency Medicine. clin. instr. Washington U., St. Louis, 1991-93; asst. prof. Emery U., Atlanta, 1994-96. Maj. USAF, 1989-93. Fellow Am. Coll. Emergency Physicians; mem. AMA, So. Med. Assn. (chmn. emergency medicine sect. 1995—).

COHEN, LARRY KENNETH, dermatologist, educator; b. Greensburg, Pa., June 1, 1948; s. Harold Samuel and Libbye (Leibovitz) C.; B.S. in Chemistry summa cum laude, U. Pitts., 1970; M.D., Albert Einstein Coll. Medicine, 1974; m. Arlene Dale Rabinovitch, Feb. 3, 1974; children—Warren, Erik, Ryan. Intern, Presbyn. U. Hosp., Pitts., 1974-75; resident in dermatology UCLA Hosp. and Clinics, 1975-78; staff dermatologist Kaiser Permante Hosp., Panorama City, Calif., 1978; tng. in chemosurgery, Los Angeles and Madison, Wis., 1977-78; with Dermatol. Assocs., McKeesport, Pa., 1978-79, Allegheny Dermatology Assocs., Tarentum, Pa., 1979—; clin. assoc. prof., dermatologist U. Pitt. Sch. Medicine, 1979—; cons. dermatologist Allegheny Valley Hosp., Natrona Heights, Pa., Citizens Gen. Hosp., New Kensington, Pa., Forbes Health System, Monroeville, Pa. Named Alpha Epsilon Delta Man of Yr., 1970; Beta Phi scholar, 1969-70. Diplomate Am. Bd. Dermatology. Mem. Am. Acad. Dermatology, Pa. Acad. Dermatology (v.p. 1986, pres. 1987), Pitts. Acad. Dermatology (pres. 1987), Pa. Dermatology Soc., Pitts. Dermatology Soc., Soc. for Investigative Dermatology, Soc. for Dermatol. Surgery, AMA, Allegheny County Med. Soc., Pa. Med. Soc., Phi Beta Kappa. Jewish. Club: Racquet, Green Oaks Country. Office: 215 1st Ave Tarentum PA 15084 Address: 2571 Mosside Blvd Suite 1 Monroeville PA 15146

COHEN, LAUREL, case manager; b. Chgo., Dec. 1, 1943; d. Carl Eugene and Joan Adele (Arenz) Patterson; m. Sidney Henry Cohen, June 29, 1968 (div. Nov. 1981); children: Elizabeth Ann Cohen Jonsson, David Arthur Patterson, Douglas Edward, Deborah Sue; m. Frederick Joseph Foti, Jan. 19, 1985 (div. June 1994). Diploma in nursing, Swedish Covenant, 1967; BS, Moody Bible Inst., 1976. RN, N.J. Staff nurse Overlook Hosp., Summit, N.J., 1980-82; pub. health nurse Patient Care Svc., West Orange, N.J., 1982-83; hospice nurse The Hospice, Inc., Montclair, N.J., 1984-92; fin. svc. rep. Primerica Fin. Svcs., Duluth, Ga., 1985-89; coord. home care Vis. Nurse Assn. Essex Valley, East Orange, N.J., 1993-96; Medicare case mgr. U.S. Healthcare, Fairfield, N.J., 1996—. State coord. La Leche League, N.J., 1976-78; hospice vol. The Hospice, Inc., 1992—; mem. MADD, Rep. Presdl. Task Force, 1989. Lt. (j.g.) USNR, 1967-69. Mem. Adoptees Liberty Movement Assn. (spokesman 1977-83), DAR. Republican. Lutheran. Home: 79 Broad St Summit NJ 07901-4044 Office: US Healthcare 55 Lane Rd Fairfield NJ 07004

COHEN, LAWRENCE N., health care company executive; b. Woodmere, N.Y., June 30, 1932; s. Irving and Helen (Spiegel) C.; m. Ilene R. Lang, Nov. 1968; children by previous marriage: Randall, Douglas, Pamela. BA in Econs., Cornell U., 1954, PhD (hon.) in Commercial Sci., Dowling Coll, 1993. With Lumex, Inc., Bay Shore, N.Y., 1966-94, contr., 1966-72, treas., 1972-81, sec., 1975-81, pres. div., 1981-86, v.p., 1975-86, chmn., pres., chief exec. officer, 1986-94; mem. exec. com., past chmn. Medmarc; mem. adv. bd. Liberty Mut. N.Y.; chmn., gen. chairperson Southside Hosp. annual ball, 1990; former mem. bd. dirs., former vice chmn. L.I. Assn. former co-chair Helen Keller Svcs. Sound and Light Ball; hon. bd. dirs. Community Program Ctr. of L.I.; bd. dirs. L.I. Edn. Conf. Bd.; hon. co-chair Alzheimers Assn. 3d ann. Memory Walk; vice chmn. fin. leadership com. L.I. chpt. NCCJ; trustee, dep. police commr. Village of Brookville, rd. commr.; former mem. Pres. Coun. Dowling Coll. Lt. (j.g.) USNR, 1954-56. Decorated Korean Svc., medal; recipient Disting. Citizen award Dowling Coll., 1993; honoree United Cerebral Palsy, 1991. Avocation: piloting. Home: 9 Hemlock Dr Brookville NY 11545-3324 Office: LN Cohen & Assocs 9 Hemlock Dr Brookville NY 11545

COHEN, LAWRENCE SOREL, physician, educator; b. N.Y.C., Mar. 27, 1933; s. Max and Fannie (Cooper) C.; m. Jane Abramson, Aug. 5, 1961; children: Melanie, Wendy. A.B., Harvard U., 1954; M.D., N.Y. U., 1958; M.A. (hon.), Yale U., 1970. Diplomate: Am. Bd. Internal Medicine, Sub Bd. Cardiovascular Diseases. Intern, then resident in medicine Yale-New Haven Hosp., 1958-60, 64-65; asst. in medicine Harvard U. Med. Sch., 1962-64; sr. investigator Nat. Heart, Lung and Blood Inst., 1965-68, mem. task force on arteriosclerosis, 1978-80, chmn. clin. trials rev. com., 1984-85, 87-89; assoc. prof. medicine U. Tex. Med. Sch., Dallas, 1968-70; prof. medicine Yale U. Med. Sch., 1970-81, Ebenezer K. Hunt prof. medicine, 1981—, dep. dean, 1991-95, spl. advisor to dean, 1995—. Mem. editorial bd. Circulation, Am. Jour. Cardiology, Am. Heart Jour.; contbr. over 160 articles to med. jours. Active Am. Heart Assn., chpt. pres., 1980-81, affiliate pres. Conn. chpt., 1984-86. With USPHS, 1960-62. Recipient Francis Gilman Blake award for Teaching of Med. Scis., 1973. Fellow ACP, Am. Coll. Cardiology (trustee 1978-83, mem. editorial bd. jour.); mem. Assn. Univ. Cardiologists (pres.-elect 1990, pres. 1991), Interurban Clin. Club (pres. 1988), Alpha Omega Alpha. Home: 149 E Rock Rd New Haven CT 06511-1325 Office: Yale U Sch Medicine 333 Cedar St New Haven CT 06510-3206

COHEN, LEE STEVEN, psychiatrist; b. Bklyn., June 22, 1959; s. Seymour and Carol (Krinsky) C.; m. Correy Hope Kustin, Aug. 19, 1984; children: Spencer Ari, Hayden Lev. BS in Biomed. Scis., CUNY, 1980; MD, SUNY, Stony Brook, 1982. Lic. psychiatrist, N.Y.; diplomate Am. Bd. Psychiatry and Neurology, Nat. Bd. Med. Examiners. Resident in pediatrics Mt. Sinai Hosp., N.Y.C., 1982-83, resident in psychiatry, 1983-85; fellow Columbia U., N.Y.C., 1985-86, chief fellow Coll. physicians and Surgeons, 1986-87, rsch. psychiatrist Coll. Physicians and Surgeons, 1987—, instr. clin. psychiatry Coll. Physicians and Surgeons, 1987—, asst. clin. prof. psychiat. Coll. Physicians and Surgeons, 1992—; team leader The Holliswood (N.Y.) Hosp., 1987-90, dir. rsch., 1990—; lectr. N.Y.C. Bd. Edn., 1989—, SUNY Sch. Medicine, Queens, N.Y., 1989—. Contbr. articles to profl. jours. Mem. AMA, Am. Psychiat. Assn., N.Y. County Psychiat. Assn., N.Y. State Psychiat. Assn. Office: 623 Washington Ave Hastings NY 10706

COHEN, MARCUS, allergist; b. Appleton, Wis., June 8, 1937; s. Frank and Hannah (Weinstein) C.; m. Sheila Terman, July 14, 1963; children: Kimberly Ellyn, Louis Jeffrey. BA, U. Wis., Madison, 1959, MD, 1962. Rotating intern San Francisco Gen. Hosp., U. Calif. San Francisco, 1962-63; intern, resident pediatrics U. Calif., San Francisco, 1962-65; fellow in allergy & immunology U. Wis., Madison, 1965-66; pvt. practice allergy & immunology Madison, 1966—; pres. Madison Gen. Hosp. Med.-Surg. Found., 1986-91, 1986-91; pres. Quisling Clinic S.C., 1973-86; vice chair Physicans Plus Med. Group, 1987; vice chair, mem. exec. com. Physicians Plus Ins. Co., 1993-96, bd. chair, 1995—; chair dept. pediatrics Madison Gen. Hosp. Meriter Found., 1994-95; mng. ptnr. Quisling Clinic Real Estate Partnership; clin. asst. prof. dept. pediat. U. Wis. Med. Sch. Fellow Am. Acad. Pediatrics, Am. Acad. Allergy, Asthma & Immunology, Am. Coll. Allergy, Asthma and Immunology, Wis. Allergy Soc. (pres. 1993-95), Bascom Hill Soc., Univ. Wis. Found. Jewish. Office: 1 S Park St Ste 440 Madison WI 53715

COHEN, MARJORIE KAREN, nursing educator; b. N.Y.C., Nov. 27, 1953; d. Meyer and Marion (Garrick) Weisberg; m. Bruce A. Cohen, Aug. 24, 1980; children: Melissa, Samantha, Marlo. BS, SUNY, Bklyn., 1974; MA, NYU, 1979. RN. Asst. prof.; instr. nursing SUNY, Bklyn., Alvernia Coll., Reading, Pa.; asst. prof. Reading Area C.C., 1988-93; faculty Durham (N.C.) Tech. C.C., 1995-96; dir. cmty. edn. Home Health Profls., Roxboro, N.C., 1996—; cons. Avalon Nurses Registry, N.Y.C., 1980-81. Bd. dirs. Berks County chpt. ARC, Reading, 1985-91; mem. Jr. League, Reading, 1988-91. Mem. AAUW, Sigma Theta Tau. Home: 12 Ludwell Pl Durham NC 27705-5460

COHEN, MARK STEVEN, dentist; b. N.Y.C., Dec. 10, 1948; s. Lawrence and Yetta (Grossman) C.; m. Arlene Debbie Deutsch, Aug. 23, 1970 (div. May 1984); 1 child, Aaron Philip; m. Donna Lynn Poissonnier, Nov. 27, 1985. BS, CCNY, 1971; DDS, Columbia U., 1975, cert. in Pedodontics, 1976. Practice dentistry Yonkers, N.Y., 1975-76, Bristol, Conn., 1976-79, Brookfield, Conn., 1977—; dir. dental service N.Y. Inst. for the Edn. Blind, Bronx, 1976-78; assoc. attending dentist Danbury (Conn.) Hosp., 1976-82, Blythdale Children's Hosp., Valhalla, N.Y., 1986-87; assoc. clin. prof. dentistry Columbia U., N.Y.C., 1976—, mem. quality assurance com., 1982-85. Patentee in field. Active Dental Guidance Council for Cerebral Palsy, N.Y.C., 1976-81. Chemistry fellow NSF, Washington, 1969-71, research fellow NIH, 1971, United Cerebral Palsy, 1975-76. Mem. ADA, Conn. State Dental Assn., Greater Danbury Dental Soc., Am. Dental Vols. for Israel, OKU Dental Honor Soc. Democrat. Jewish. Home: 4 Yale Dr New Fairfield CT 06812-3617 Office: Cohen Metcalf 304 Federal Rd Brookfield CT 06804-2418

COHEN, MARTIN BRUCE, physician; b. Bayshore, N.Y., Nov. 2, 1954. BA, Brandeis Univ., 1976; MD, SUNY, 1980. Diplomate Am. Bd. Internal Medicine, Am. Bd. Cardiovasc. Disease. Attending physician Westchester County Medical Ctr., Valhalla, N.Y., 1985—. Fellow Am. Coll. Cardiology, mem. Medical Soc. State N.Y. Office: Cardiology Cons Westchester Westchester County Med Ctr Valhalla NY 10595

COHEN, MARTIN DAVID, psychologist, educator; b. Bklyn., Jan. 24, 1947; s. Norman D. and Millicent (Rome) C.; m. Sara Jane Reisman, Aug. 18, 1968; children: Daniel Adam, Gillian Elizabeth. BA, Lehigh U., 1968; PhD, Temple U., 1976. Mem. psychol. staff Hillsborough Community Mental Health Ctr., Tampa, Fla., 1973-77, dir. community oriented svcs., 1977-80, chief psychologist, 1979-80; gen. practice in psychology, Tampa, 1977—; co-founder, dir. Suncoast Ctr. Consultation, Edn. and Growth, Tampa, 1980—; clin. dir. The LIFE Ctr., Tampa, 1981—; co-founder, dir. Suncoast Ctr. for Attitudinal Healing, Tampa, 1981-84, co-founder, dir. Health Profiles, Inc., 1987, Divorce Accord, Inc., 1987; clin. dir. Tampa Bay Critical Incident Stress Debriefing Team, 1989—; mem. clin. faculty dept. psychiatry U. South Fla. Coll. Medicine, Tampa, 1977-79, mem. adj. faculty dept. psychology, 1980-85; mem. adj. faculty Hillsborough Community Coll. Human Svcs. Program, Tampa, 1980-85; mem. adj. faculty Goddard Grad. program Vt. Coll., Montpelier, 1982—; mem. adj. faculty Union Inst., Cin., 1986—; cons. in field. Mem. health adv. com. Head Start Program, Hillsborough County (Fla.) Policy Coun., 1977-82; bd. dirs. Community Council on Child Abuse and Neglect, 1978-83, v.p., 1981-82; mem. adv. bd., tng. cons. Rape Crisis Ctr., 1979-87; mem. Hillsborough-Manatee (Fla.) Dist. Human Rights Advocacy Com., 1982-84. Recipient Outstanding Svc. award Hillsborough County Head Start Program, 1980, Victim's Voice award, 1994; NIMH fellow Temple U., 1972. Mem. Am. Psychol. Assn., Fla. Psychol. Assn. (exec. council 1978-84, pres. pub. svc. div. 1980-84). Lectr. to profl. confs., seminars and workshops; developer: model program in mental health prevention, 1979; prepared parenthood course, Tampa, 1981; co-producer Options for Living, TV programs, Tampa, 1981-82. Home: 510 Crestover Dr Tampa FL 33617-3852 Office: 3450 E Fletcher Ave Ste 300 Tampa FL 33613-4603

COHEN, MARVIN WILLIAM, periodontist; b. N.Y.C., Mar. 16, 1936; s. Abe O. and Sadie (Faust) C.; M. Honi Carol Prybutok, June 18, 1961; children: Rachelle Ruth, Alisa Beth, Sara Perle. BS, L.I. U., 1956; DDS, Temple U. Sch. Dentistry, 1961; postgrad., Georgetown U. Grad. Sch., 1970. Commd. mil. dental officer U.S. Army, 1961, advanced through grades to capt., 1964; comdr. dental svc. U.S. Army R & D Ctr., Ft. Belvoir and Camp Tuto, Va. and Greenland, 1964-67; chief Stone Dental Clinic, Ft. Ord,

Calif., 1967-68; periodontal resident Fitzsimons Gen. Hosp., Denver, 1971; chief of periodontics 768th Dental Detachment, Augsburg, Federal Republic of Germany, 1971-74; mentor in periodontics Eisenhower Army Med. Ctr., Ft. Gordon, Ga., 1974-78; chief of periodontics Saloman Dental Clinic, Ft. Benning, Ga., 1978-81; pvt. practice in periodontics Utica, N.Y., 1981—; spl. lectr. U. Ga. Dental Sch., Augusta, 1974-78; attendee in periodontics St. Luke's Meml. Hosp., Utica, 1982—; lectr. in field. Bd. dirs. Bd. Edn., Temple Beth El, Utica, 1985, bd. trustees, 1994—; bd. dirs. United Jewish Fedn. Utica, 1988-89. Recipient cert. of achievement U.S. Army Materiel Command, 1967, Army Commendation medal, 1978, Meritorious Svc. award U.S. Army, 1981. Mem. ADA, Am. Acad. Periodontology, N.Y. Dental Soc. (appreciation award 1985, Bronze cert. 1986), Oneida-Herkimer County Dental Soc. (program chmn. 1984), Ret. Officers Assn. (Rome, N.Y.), KP, Alpha Omega (pres. Augusta chpt. 1976-78, treas. Syracuse chpt. 1994—). Jewish. Home: 6 The Hills Dr Utica NY 13501-5514 Office: 286 Genesee St Utica NY 13502-4639

COHEN, MARY ANN ADLER, psychiatrist; b. N.Y.C., July 2, 1941; d. Carl and Rose Adler; m. Richard Cohen, June 11, 1960; 1 child, Steven Clifford. AB, NYU, 1962; MD, The Med. Coll. Pa., 1966. Diplomate Nat. Bd. Med. Examiners, Am. Bd. Psychiatry and Neurology added certification in Geriatric Psychiatry. Dir., consultation-liaison psychiatry Fordham Hosp., Bronx, N.Y., 1975-76; fellow, consultation-liaison psychiatry Montefiore Hosp. and Med. Ctr., Bronx, 1976-77, attending, consultation-liaision psychiatry, 1977-81; dir., consultation-liaison psychiatry Met. Hosp. Ctr., N.Y.C., 1981-95; psychiatrist Rivington House Health Care Facility, 1995—; attending psychiatrist St. Vincent's Hosp. and Med. Ctr., N.Y.C., 1995—; prof. clin. psychiatry N.Y. Med. Coll., Valhalla, N.Y., 1990—, assoc. prof., 1986-90, asst. prof. clin. medicine, 1986-92, prof. clin. medicine, 1992—; pres. med. bd. Met. Hosp. Ctr., 1989-92. Recipient Nancy C.A. Roeske APA Award for outstanding teaching N.Y. Med. Coll., 1992. Fellow Am. Coll. Physicians, Acad. Psychosomatic Medicine (Best Jour. Paper award 1986); mem. Am. Coll. Psychiatrists, Soc. Liaison Psychiatry (pres. 1987-88). Office: 350 Central Park W Apt 62 New York NY 10025-6504

COHEN, MAURICE, gynecologist; b. Winnipeg, Man., Can., Dec. 26, 1931; s. Max and Thelma (Slawsky) C.; came to U.S., 1958, naturalized, 1962; M.D., U. Man., 1957; div. 1986, children: Adam, Alec, Nel; m. Marcia R. Micay, Nov. 29, 1991; stepchildren: Kevin, Lindsay. Faculty of Arts Scis., U. Manitoba, Can. Intern, St. Boniface Hosp. (Man.), 1956-57; resident in pathology Albert Einstein Coll. Medicine, 1957-58, instr. ob-gyn, 1962-64; resident in ob-gyn L.I. Jewish-Hillside Med. Center, New Hyde Park, N.Y., 1958-61; fellow in gynecology Columbia-Presbyn. Med. Ctr., N.Y.C., 1961-62; practice medicine specializing in gynecology and gynecol. endocrinology, New Hyde Park, N.Y., 1964—; attending physician L.I. Jewish Med. Ctr., New Hyde Park, Queens Hosp. Center, Jamaica, N.Y.; asst. prof. clin. ob-gyn Albert Einstein Coll. Medicine; dir. women's health program North Shore Diabetes and Endocrine Assocs., New Hyde Park; spkr. in field. Diplomate Am. Bd. Ob-Gyn. Fellow ACS, Am. Coll. Ob-Gyn; mem. Am. Assn. Clin. Endocrinologists, Am. Soc. Reproductive Medicine, Soc. Clin. Dentistometry, Soc. Study Reprodn., Queens Gynecol. Soc., N.Am. Menopause Soc., The Endocrine Soc. Office: 3003 New Hyde Park Rd Ste 201 New Hyde Park NY 11042-1214

COHEN, MAX HARRY, surgeon; b. Macon, Ga., June 8, 1940; s. Harry M. and Rena C. (Cain) C.; AB with honors, Columbia U., 1961; MD with honors, Harvard U., 1965; PhD with honors, George Washington U., 1970; m. Leslie G. Krupsaw, Mar. 23, 1969; children: Adam, Heather, Robyn. Intern, Mass. Gen. Hosp., Boston, 1965-66, resident in surgery, 1966-67, resident in surgery, 1970-72; practice medicine specializing in surgery, oncology, head and neck surgery and cancer immunotherapy, Bethesda, Md. and Washington, 1977—; asst. prof. dept. microbiology George Washington U. Sch. Medicine, Washington, 1968-70; surg. scientist designee Mass. Gen. Hosp., 1970-72; rsch. assoc., Nat. Cancer Inst., NIH Bethesda, 1967-70, sr. staff, surgery branch, 1973-77; clin. prof. surgery George Washington U. and sr. attending surgeon Washington Hosp. Center, 1977—; mem. staff Washington Hosp. Center, residency review com., 1984-92, attending surgeon team leader, 1990-94; surgical oncologist, cons. Pigmented Lesion Clinic, Washington Cancer Inst., 1994—; mem. staff George Washington Univ., Suburban, Holy Cross, Sibley and Shady Grove Adventist hosps., mem. exec. com. divsn. surg. services Nat. Rehab Hosp., mem. skin cancer prevention and detection com. D.C. Med. Soc., 1990; cons. in surgery Nat. Cancer Inst., Bethesda, 1977-79. Author: Beginning Chemistry: A Programmed Instruction Textbook, 1975. Pres., Fox Den Civic Assn., 1976-78; co-chmn. mid-Atlantic melanoma protocol com., 1987-92. With USPHS, 1967-69, 73-77. Recipient Nat. Health Found. award, 1957; ann. award for excellence in teaching dept. surgery Washington Hosp. Center, 1979. Diplomate Am. Bd. Surgery. Fellow ACS; mem. Montgomery County, D.C. med. socs., Am. Fedn. Clin. Research, Am. Soc. Microbiology, AMA, Boylston Med. Soc., Dean Van Amringe Hon. Soc., Am. Soc. Clin. Oncology, Soc. Surg. Oncology, Phi Beta Kappa, Sigma Xi, Phi Delta Epsilon. Author: Beginning Chemistry: A Programmed Instruction Textbook; contbr. numerous articles on clin. and exptl. cancer treatment, immunology and immunotherapy to profl. jours.; author film on surg. treatment of malignant melanoma. Home: 8812 Twin Creek Ct Potomac MD 20854-4472 Office: 10215 Fernwood Rd Ste 402 Bethesda MD 20817-1106 also: 106 Irving St NW Ste 301 Washington DC 20010-2927

COHEN, MAX MARK, surgeon; b. Glasgow, Scotland, Feb. 11, 1939; came to U.S., 1987; s. Harry and Rachel (Goldstein) C.; children: Simon, Talya; m. Marilyn Silverstein. MB ChB, U. Glasgow, 1963. Intern U. Glasgow Hosps., 1963-64, resident surgery, 1964-69; surgical rsch. fellow U. B.C., 1969-70, Harvard U., Cambridge, Mass., 1970-71; chief resident surgery Vancouver Gen. Hosp., 1971-72; asst. prof. surgery, then assoc. prof. surgery U. B.C., Vancouver, Can., 1972-80; assoc. prof. surgery, then prof. surgery U. Toronto, Ont., Can., 1980-87; prof. surgery U. Pa., Phila., 1987-94, U. Colo., Denver, 1989-94; chmn. surgery Grad. Hosp., Phila., 1987-89; prof. surgery Wayne State U., Detroit, 1994—; chmn. surgery Rose Med. Ctr., Denver, 1989-94; dir. Rose Videoscopic Surgery Ctr., Denver, 1991-94; chief surgery Grace Hosp., 1994—. Editor: Biological Protection with Prostaglandins (2d vols.), 1985; editorial bd. Can. Jour. Surgery, 1983-87, Jour. Laparoendoscopic Surgery, 1992—; assoc. editor Clin. and Investigative Medicine, 1985-89; contbr. articles to profl. jours. Grantee Med. Rsch. Coun. Can., 1974-86. Fellow ACS, Royal Coll. Surgeons Edinburgh, Royal Coll. Surgeons Can.; mem. Soc. Am. Gastrointestinal Endoscopic Surgeons, Soc. Univ. Surgeons, Undersea Med. Soc., Am. Gastroenterology Assn., Am. Coll. Physician Execs., Can. Assn. Gen. Surgeons (chmn. rsch. com. 1984-87), Anti Def. League (bd. dirs. 1992). Office: Grace Hosp 6071 W Outer Dr Detroit MI 48235

COHEN, MEL, computer programmer; b. Toronto, Ont., Can., Jan. 3, 1952; came to the U.S., 1987; s. Harry and Martha Cohen; m. Ann Louise Judith Bradley, May 27, 1973; children: Erin, Stephanie. BSc, U. Guelph, Ont., 1977. Transplant coord. M.O.R.E., Toronto, 1977-83; exec. v.p. RSMC Computers Svcs., Toronto, 1982-88; gen. mgr. ICL Devont Computer, Toronto, 1983-88; transplant coord. Toronto Gen. Hosp., 1982-86; dir. P.O.R.T. Program, Vancouver, B.C., Can., 1986-87; owner, exec. v.p. Simple Surg. Solutions, Denver, 1988—. Contbr. articles to profl. jours. Recipient Humanitarian award Can. Kidney Found., Ottawa, Can., 1980, Culver award of merit NATCO, New Orleans, 1986. Mem. Can. Assn. for Transplantation (founder, pres. 1986), N.Am. Transplant Coords. Assn. (founder, rsch. dir. 1980-84), Kidney Found. (asst. 1982-90). Office: Simple Surg Solutions 15428 E Hampden Aurora CO 80013

COHEN, MELVIN JOSEPH, neuroscientist, educator; b. Los Angeles, Sept. 28, 1928; s. Samuel and Bessie (Firman) C.; m. Catherine Black, Dec. 27, 1963; children: Frank M., Renée C., Sarah R., Samuel D. B.A., UCLA, 1949, M.A., 1952, Ph.D., 1954; student, U. Calif., Berkeley, 1950-51. Instr. biology Harvard, 1955-57; asst. prof. to prof. biology U. Oreg., 1957-69; prof. biology Yale U., 1969-95, prof. emeritus, 1995—. Contbr. articles to profl. jours. NSF postdoctoral fellow Stockholm, 1954-55; Guggenheim fellow Oxford, Eng., 1965. Fellow AAAS; mem. Nat. Acad. Scis., Internat. Brain Research Orgn., Soc. Gen. Physiologists (pres. 1976-77), Am. Soc. Zoologists, Soc. Neurosci.

COHEN, MELVIN LEE, pediatrician, child and adolescent psychiatrist; b. San Antonio, Mar. 18, 1950; s. Melvin David and Elizabeth Catherine (Brown) C. BA summa cum laude, Rice U., 1972; MD, U. Va., 1977. Diplomate Am. Bd. Pediatrics, Am. Bd. Psychiatry and Neurology. Chief pediatric clinic 97th Gen. Hosp., U.S. Army, Frankfurt, Fed. Republic of Germany, 1980-83; fellow in developmental pediatrics William Beaumont Army Med. Ctr., El Paso, Tex., 1983-85; regional coord. Army exceptional family mem. program, cons. Brooke Army Med. Ctr., San Antonio, 1985-87; pvt. practice pediatrics San Antonio, 1987-89; chief of staff Bowling Green Hosp., San Antonio, 1988-89; resident in gen. and child psychiatry U. Tex. Health Sci. Ctr., San Antonio, 1989-93; pvt. practice child and adolescent psychiatry, San Antonio, 1993—; med. dir. child and adolescent partial hospitalization Laurel Ridge Hosp., San Antonio, 1992-95; clin. assoc. prof. pediats. U. Tex. Health Sci. Ctr., 1994—, clin. asst. prof. psychiatry, 1994—; mem. exec. com. Laurel Ridge Hosp., San Antonio, 1987-88, 93-94. Bd. dirs. Jewish Family Svc., 1993—, sec. bd. dirs., 1996—; mem. sci. adv. bd. WInston Sch., 1993—. Maj. U.S. Army, 1980-87, lt. col. USAR, 1987-92. Rotary Found. scholar Rice U., 1972; recipient Cert. of Appreciation, Fres. Azcona of Honduras, 1986. Fellow Am. Acad. Pediatrics; mem. Tex. Med. Asn., Tex. Med. Found., Bexar County Med. Soc., Rice U. Alumni Assn., Phi Beta Kappa. Jewish. Office: 14800 San Pedro Ave # 1110 San Antonio TX 78232-3733

COHEN, MICHAEL, psychologist; b. Yonkers, N.Y., Mar. 14, 1950; s. Joseph and Mary (Harris) C.; m. Amy Beth Siskind, Nov. 1, 1987; 1 child, Laura Reneé. BA, SUNY, Binghamton, 1972; MA, PhD, CUNY, N.Y.C., 1992. Pvt. practice psychotherapist N.Y.C., 1973-89; rsch. cons. N.Y.C. Bd. Edn., 1986-87; sr. rsch. analyst Kennan Rsch. and Cons., N.Y.C., 1987-90; dir. qualitive rsch. KRC Rsch. and Cons., N.Y.C., 1990-91, pres., 1992-95; pres., founding ptnr. ARC Cons. LLC, N.Y.C., 1995—; mem. adv. bd. Handprints Prodns., N.Y.C., 1990—. Editor: The Einstein Connection, 1979. Office: ARC Cons LLC 295 Lafayette St New York NY 10012

COHEN, MICHAEL I., pediatrician; b. Bklyn., Feb. 9, 1935; s. Nat L. and Fannie (Wechsler) C.; m. Nancy Ann Wood, Oct. 28, 1963; children—Adam Wood, Amy Melissa, Meg Rebecca. B.A., Columbia U., 1956, M.D., 1960. Intern Mary Imogene Bassett Hosp., 1960-61; resident Babies Hosp., N.Y.C., 1961-63; USPHS postdoctoral fellow in gastroenterology Albert Einstein Coll. Medicine, 1965-67, mem. faculty, 1967—, prof. pediatrics, 1976—, chmn. dept., 1980—; pres., chief exec. officer Montefiore Med. Ctr., 1985-86; dir. div. adolescent medicine Montefiore Hosp., N.Y.C., 1967-80. Author numerous papers in field; contbr. chpts. to books. Served with M.C. USAF, 1963-65. Decorated Air Force Commendation medal. Mem. Inst. Medicine of NAS, Am. Acad. Pediatrics (chmn. com. adolescence 1977-80, award sect. adolescence 1980), Soc. Adolescent Medicine, Am. Fedn. Clin. Research, Ambulatory Pediatrics Assn., Soc. Pediatric Research, Am. Psychosomatic Soc., Am. Pediatrics Soc., Am. Gastrointestinal Assn., Alpha Omega Alpha. Office: Montefiore Med Ctr 111 E 210th St Bronx NY 10467-2490

COHEN, MURRY JOSEPH, psychiatrist; b. Bklyn., Jan. 17, 1941; s. Oscar and Beatrice (Kowalski) C. BA in Psychology, Lehigh U., 1961; MD, U. Chgo., 1965. Intern Montefiore Hosp., Bronx, N.Y., 1965-66; resident Mount Sinai Hosp., N.Y.C., 1970-73; asst. prof. clin. psychiatry, asst. attending psychiatrist Mt. Sinai Hosp., N.Y.C., 1977-85, dir. narcotics rehab. ctr., 1975-85; asst. in psychiatry Beth Israel Hosp., N.Y.C., 1980-85; assoc. psychiatrist, chief psychiatric clinic Lenox Hill Hosp., N.Y.C., 1985-89; pvt. practice N.Y.C., 1973-90, Va., 1990—. Mem. adv. bd. Jews for Animal Rights, 1987—, Concern for Helping Animals in Israel, 1990—, Assn. Vets. for Animal Rights, 1991—, Ctr. for Health Sci. Policy, 1993—; bd. dirs. Friends of Animals, 1985. Mem. Am. Holistic Med. Assn., Med. Rsch. Modernization Commn. (chmn. 1987—), Physicians Com. for Responsible Medicine, Inst. Noetic Scis., Med. Soc. Va., Alpha Omega Alpha. Jewish. Office: No Va Inst Psychiat 5537 Hempstead Way Springfield VA 22151-4010

COHEN, NEIL, oral and maxillofacial surgeon; b. S.I., N.Y., May 8, 1933; s. Sam and Sylvia (Kirschner) C.; student U. Miami, 1950-53; D.D.S., U. Md., 1957; postgrad. NYU, 1958-59; m. Cynthia Jane English, June 26, 1976; 1 son, Jason English; children by previous marriage: Jane Elizabeth, Jennifer Ann. Intern, Beth Israel Hosp., Boston, 1957-58; resident Harlem Hosp., N.Y.C., 1959-60; practice dentistry specializing in oral and maxillofacial surgery, Miami, Fla., 1960, Belmont, Mass., 1961, Burlington, Mass., 1961—; chief oral surgery Winchester (Mass.) Hosp., 1969-79; chief oral and maxillofacial surgery Choate Hosp., Woburn, Mass., 1984-89; mem. staff Boston Regional Med. Ctr., Stoneham, Mass., Winchester Hosp., Mass.; oral surgeon Harvard U. Health Svs., Cambridge, 1962-91; clin. asst. in oral and maxillofacial surgery Harvard U. Sch. Dental Medicine, 1970-93. Fellow Internat. Assn. Oral Surgeons, Royal Soc. Health; mem. New Eng. Soc. Oral Surgeons, ADA, Mass. Dental Soc. Mass. (v.p. 1967-68, pres. 1968-69) dental socs. anesthesiology, Am. Assn. Oral and Maxillofacial Surgeons, Mass. Soc. Oral and Maxillofacial Surgeons, Middlesex Dist. Dental Soc., Harvard Sch. Dental Medicine Sr. Soc., Alpha Omega. Contr. articles to profl. jours. Home: 54 Temple St Arlington MA 02174-6343 Office: 175 Cambridge St Burlington MA 01803-2930

COHEN, NOEL LEE, otolaryngologist, educator; b. N.Y.C., Sept. 20, 1930; s. Victor Max and Esther Lily (Schonfeld) C.; m. Baukje Philippina Boersma, June 1, 1957; 1 child, Mark Bennett. AB, NYU, 1951; MD, U. Utrecht, The Netherlands, 1957. Intern Stads-en Aacademish Ziekenhuis, Utrecht, 1955-57; resident in otolaryngology Bellevue Med. Ctr., NYU, 1959-62; instr. NYU Sch. Medicine, 1962-64, asst. prof., 1964-69, assoc. prof., 1969-73, clin. prof., 1973-80, prof. otolargyngology, 1980—, chmn. dept., 1981—; bd. dirs. League for Hard of Hearing, Am. Auditory Soc.; mem. rsch. adv. bd. EAR Found., Nashville, 1987—; mem. adv. bd. Self Help for Hard of Hearing People, 1995. Mem. editl. bd. Am. Jour. Otology, 1986—, Otolaryngology-Head and Neck Surgery; reviewer articles and books for profl. jours.; contbr. numerous articles to profl. jours.; author chpts. in books. Lt. USNR, 1957-59. Fellow ACS, Am. Acad. Otolaryngology-Head-Neck Surgery (Honor award 1985), Am. Laryngol., Rhinol. and Otol. Soc., Am. Soc. Head and Neck Surgery, Am. Bronchoesophagol. Assn., Am. Otol. Soc., N.Y. Acad. Medicine, N.Y. State Soc. Otolaryngology-Head and Neck Surgery (pres. 1988-89), N.Y. Head and Neck Soc. (charter mem. Pres.' award 1984), Soc. Univ. Otolaryngologists, Soc. Acad. Depts. Otolaryngology, N.Y. Acad. Scis., Acoustic Neuroma Soc., Alexander Graham Bell Assn. (med. adv. bd.). Democrat. Jewish. Office: NYU Med Ctr 530 1st Ave New York NY 10016-6402

COHEN, NORMAN GIRARD, social worker; b. Rochester, N.Y., Nov. 5, 1940; s. Abraham Joseph and Ethel (Weinstein) C.; B.S., Syracuse U., 1962; student Babson Coll., 1958-60; M.S.W., U. Tenn., 1964; postgrad. U. Mich., 1962-63. Diplomate Am. Bd. of Clin. Social Workers; m. Mary Catherine Serafine, Dec. 26,1964; children—Jonathan, Adrian, Jordan. Supervising psychiat. social worker Beeman Clinic, Niagara Falls, N.Y., 1966-73; psychotherapist, assoc. H.W Goldfarb, M.D., Niagara Falls, 1973-76; pres., clin. dir. Quantum Bionomics, Inc., Niagara Falls, 1977-80; project dir., systems analyst Williams Group of Cos., Kenmore, N.Y., 1980-81; project analyst Office Mental Health, Albany, N.Y., 1981-83; pvt. practice psychotherapy, Albany, 1983-86; assoc. and acting exec. sec. N.Y. State Bds. Social Work, Chiropractic, Albany, 1986-91; exec. sec. N.Y. State Bds. for Social Work and Chiropractic, 1991—; part-time faculty SUNY-Albany; part-time columnist The Spotlight, Delmar, N.Y., 1982-86; part time faculty Niagara County Community Coll., Sanborn, N.Y., 1974-75; project cons. sch. systems, govt. agys., profl. agys. Bd. dirs. Golden Agers; v.p. bd. dirs. Metanoia Drug Program, 1972-73; coach Little League, 1976. NIMH fellow, 1962-63. Mem. Acad. Cert. Social Workers, Nat. Assn. Social Workers, Am. Fedn. Musicians, Biofeedback Soc. Am. Home: 18 Hawthorne Ave Delmar NY 12054-3116 Office: NY St Bd Social Work & Chiropractic State Edn Dept Cultural Edn Ctr Rm 3041 Albany NY 12230

COHEN, PETER ARTHUR, educational psychologist, consultant; b. L.A., Apr. 15, 1951; s. David Robert Cohen and Beverlee Merle (Peterson) Brazil; m. Bonnie Lee Cunningham; children: Jennifer Anne, Jillian Lane, Alaina Marie. AB, U. Calif., 1973; MA, San Diego State U., 1976; PhD, U. Mich., 1980. Rsch. assoc. Ctr. for Rsch. on Learning & Teaching, Ann Arbor, Mich., 1977-80; asst. dir. Office Instrnl. Svcs. & Ednl. Rsch. Dartmouth Coll., Hanover, N.H., 1980-83; evaluation specialist U. Tex. Health Scis. Ctr., San Antonio, 1983-88; dir. ednl. devel. Med. Coll. Ga., Augusta, 1988-92; assoc. dean acad. planning and devel. Baylor Coll. of Dentistry, 1992—; cons. Kans. State U., Manhattan, 1989—; mem. editorial rev. bd. Jour. Dental Edn., Washington, 1989-96. Author 11 book chpts., 10 abstracts, 55 conf. papers, 40 jour. articles. Dir. Ga. Dental Edn. Found., Atlanta, 1990-92. recipient rsch. grants Am. Fund for Dental Health, 1990-91, 94—, tng. grant Health Careers Opportunity Program Dept. Health & Human Svcs., 1990-93; U.S. Pub. Health fellow NIMH, 1976-77. Fellow APA; mem. Am. Ednl. Rsch. Assn. (SIG chmn. 1990-92), Am. Assn. Dental Schs. (sect. chair 1993-94), Sigma Xi, Phi Beta Kappa. Office: Baylor Coll Dentistry Acad Planning & Devel 3302 Gaston Ave Dallas TX 75246-2013

COHEN, PETER J., osteopath; b. Boston, July 17, 1952; m. Isabelle Alice Darula, June 7, 1987. BS, Gordon Coll., 1979; DO, U. Osteopathic Medicine, 1990. Diplomate Am. Bd. Internal Medicine. Physician Blue Cross Hawaii, Lihue, 1993-94, Northeast Colo. Family Health Ctr., Brush, 1994—; asst. dir. Eben Ezer Retirement Home, Brush, 1994—. Served in USAR, 1987-95. Mem. Am. Coll. Physicians. Home: 7211 Longview Dr Niwot CO 80503

COHEN, PHILIP LAWRENCE, medical/surgical nurse, educator; b. Bklyn., Mar. 28, 1954; s. Isidore and Laura (Wolf) C.; m. Nidia Altagracia Arias, Jan. 29, 1979; children: Jeffrey, Joshua. BSN, L.I. U., 1981. LPN, Md., N.Y.; RN, N.Y. LPN St. John's Hosp., 1985-91, RN, 1991-95; nurse New Hosp. Delray Cmty. Hosp., 1995—. With U.S. Army, 1979-85. Mem. Nat. League Nursing. Home: 21392 Town Lakes Dr 10-12 Boca Raton FL 33486

COHEN, PINYA, microbiologist; b. Burlington, Vt., Dec. 23, 1935; married; 1 child. B.S., Delaware Valley Coll., 1957; MS, U. Ga., 1959; PhD, Purdue U., 1964. Research microbiologist NIH, Bethesda, Md., 1964-68, chief blood and blood derivatives sect., 1968-72; dir. plasma derivatives br. FDA, Bethesda, Md., 1972-76; dir. quality control and regulatory affairs Merieux Inst., Inc., Miami, Fla., 1976-79, v.p. quality control and regulatory affairs, 1979-90, asst. sec., 1977—, asst. treas., 1978—; v.p. regulatory affairs Connaught Labs., Swiftwater, Pa., 1990-92; v.p. quality assurance and regulatory affairs N.Am. Biologicals, Inc., 1992-95, sr. v.p. quality assurance and regulatory affairs, 1995—; adv. Univ. without Walls Morgan State Coll., Balt., 1972-74; mem. adv. panel to com. on public-pvt. sector relations in vaccine innovation Nat. Acad. Scis., 1983-84, mem. Inst. of Medicine NAS com. blood safety and availability. U. Ga. scholar, 1957; NIH fellow, 1961-64. Mem. AAAS, Am. Soc. Microbiology, Internat. Assn. Biol. Standardization, Internat. Soc. Blood Transfusion, N.Y. Acad. Scis., Sigma. Xi. Contbr. article to profl. jours. Office: No Am Biologicals Inc 5800 Park of Commerce Blvd NW Boca Raton FL 33487

COHEN, RALPH LUNTZ, psychiatrist; b. Pitts., Dec. 1, 1938; s. Robert and Ruth Cohen; m. Susan Chase, Nov. 3, 1968; children: Rachael, David. BA in Sociology, U. Colo., 1960, MD, 1965. Intern Orange County (Calif.) Med. Ctr., 1965-66; resident in psychiatry, fellow in child psychiatry U. So. Calif. Med. Ctr., L.A., 1966-70; ward chief, cons. Dept. Def. Schs. USAF Hosp., Tachikawa, Japan, 1970-72; child psychiatrist, clin. dir. Child Mental Health Svcs., Bangor, Maine, 1973-78; exec. dir. Holyoke-Chicopee (Mass.) Area Mental Health, 1978-80; clin. asst. prof. Smith Coll. Social Work, Northampton, Mass., 1979-80; pvt. practice Amherst, Mass., 1980—; med. dir. Mt. Tom Inst., Holyoke, 1980-92, Osborn Clinic, Agawam, Mass., 1985-92, Cmty. Svcs. Inst., Inc., Springfield, 1989—; cons. psychiatrist Holyoke Hosp. Adolescent Clinic, 1980—, Key Youth Program, 1979-92; cons. psychiatrist Mediplex Psychosocial Neuro Behavioral Rehab. Program, 1986—, psychiat. dir., 1986-96. Maj. USAF, 1970-72. Mem. Internat. Soc. for Study of Dissociation, Physicians for Social Responsibility, Am. Psychiat. Assn., Mass. Psychiat. Assn., Western Mass. Psychiat. Soc. (pres.), Am. Acad. Child Adolescent Psychiatry, New Eng. Coun. Child Adolescent Psychiatry, Pioneer Valley Child Psychiatry Group (chmn.), Am. Soc. Clin. Psychopharmacology. Office: 664 Main St Amherst MA 01002-2428

COHEN, ROBERT, medical device manufacturing-marketing executive; b. Glen Cove, N.Y., Sept. 23, 1957; s. Alan and Selma (Grossman) C.; m. Nancy A. Arey, Jan. 17, 1981. BA, Bates Coll., 1979; JD, U. Maine, 1982. Bar: N.Y. 1983, U.S. Dist. Ct. (so. and ea.) N.Y. 1983. Atty. Pfizer Inc., N.Y.C., 1982-86; asst. corp. counsel, asst. sec. Pfizer Hosp. Products Group, Inc., N.Y.C., 1986-88; v.p. bus. devel., dir. for med. device mfr. and marketer Deknatel Inc., Fall River, Mass., 1988-92; pres., CEO GCI Med., Braintree, Mass., 1992-93; v.p. bus. devel. Sulzermedica USA, Inc., Angleton, Tex., 1993-94, group v.p., 1994—. Author: 19th Century Maine Authors, 1978. Mem. ABA, Am. Corp. Counsel Assn., Am. Mgmt. Assn., Licensing Execs. Soc. Republican. Home: 58 Heathrow Ln Sugar Land TX 77479-2500 Office: Sulzermedica 4000 Technology Dr Angleton TX 77515-2523

COHEN, ROBERT ABRAHAM, retired physician; b. Chgo., Nov. 13, 1909; s. Ezra Harry and Catherine (Kurzon) C.; m. Mabel Jean Blake, Mar. 21, 1933 (dec. Oct. 1972); children—Donald Edward, Margery Jean; m. Alice L. Muth, Mar. 31, 1974. B.S., U. Chgo., 1930, Ph.D., M.D., 1935. Intern Michael Reese Hosp., Chgo., 1936-37; resident Henry Phipps Psychiat. Clinic Johns Hopkins U., 1937-38; resident Sheppard-Pratt Hosp., Towson, Md., 1938-39, 40-41; sr. fellow Inst. Juvenile Research, Chgo, 1939-40; pvt. practice psychiatry Washington, 1946-48; clin. dir. Chestnut Lodge, Rockville, Md., 1948-53, dir. psychotherapy, 1981-91; dir. clin. investigations NIMH, Bethesda, Md., 1953-69; dir. div. clin. and behavioral research NIMH, 1969-81, dep. dir. intramural research program, 1969-81; pres. Washington Sch. Psychiatry, 1973-82; Bd. dirs. Founds. Fund for Research in Psychiatry, 1960-63, chmn. bd., 1962-63; trustee William Alanson White Psychiat. Found. Served from lt. (j.g.) to comdr. M.C. USNR, 1941-46. Recipient Salmon medal N.Y. Acad. Scis., 1978, Fromm-Reichmann award Am. Acad. Psychoanylsis, 1979, HEW Disting. Service award, 1970. Fellow Am. Psychiat. Assn. (life); mem. Am. Psychoanalytical Assn., Am. Psychopathol. Assn., Assn. Research in Nervous and Mental Disease, Washington Psychoanalytic Soc. (pres. 1951-53), Washington Psychiat. Soc. (pres. 1958-59), Washington Psychoanalytic Inst. (chmn. edn. com. 1953-58, dir. 1959-63), Washington Acad. Medicine. Home: 5216 Elsmere Ave Bethesda MD 20814-5734

COHEN, RONALD JAY, neurological surgeon; b. Pitts., Apr. 8, 1947; s. Albert K. and Dorothy (Fisher) C.; m. Margaret Callanan, June 11, 1972; children: Sarah, Jessica, Jacob. BA, U. Pitts., 1968; MD, Johns Hopkins U., Balt., 1972. Am. Bd. Neurological Surgery. Asst. resident gen. surgery Johns Hopkins Hosp., Balt., 1972-74; clin. assoc. Nat. Cancer Inst., Balt., 1974-76; asst. resident, Neurological Surgery Johns Hopkins Hosp., Balt., 1976-81; asst. prof. dept. neurological surgery Johns Hopkins Med. Inst., Balt., 1981—; neurological surgery pvt. practice, 1981—; chmn. Peer Rev. Mgmt. Com. Med. and Chirurgical Faculty of Md. Fellow Am. Coll. Surgeons, Am. Assn. Neurological Surgeons, Cong. Neurological Surgeons, Stroke Soc. of Am. Heart Assn. Office: 1777 Reisterstown Rd Baltimore MD 21208-1313

COHEN, SALLY SOLOMON, health policy nurse, educator; b. New Rochelle, N.Y., Dec. 5, 1953; d. Louis Arnold and Bernice (Fiering) Solomon; m. Arnold Cohen, Jan. 3, 1987; 1 child, Aaron Moss. BA, Cornell U., 1975; MSN, Yale U., 1980; PhD, Columbia U., 1993. Coord. for continuing edn. U. N.Mex., Albuquerque; pediatric nurse practitioner Children's Hosp., Newark; dir. pub. policy and rsch. NLN, N.Y.C.; assoc. dean, asst. prof. Columbia U. Sch. Nursing, N.Y.C.; asst. prof. Yale U. Sch. Nursing; dir. Ctr. for Health Policy; bd. dirs. Global Alliance Women's Health. Contbr. articles to profl. jours. Recipient Disting. Alumnae award Yale U. Sch. Nursing, 1988. Mem. ANA, Am. Acad. Nursing, Am. Polit. Sci. Assn., Am. Pub. Health Assn., Sigma Theta Tau.

COHEN, SANFORD CHARLES, radiation company executive, nuclear engineer; b. Chgo., May 14, 1936; s. George Cohen and Evelyn (Aron) C.; m. Gail Hirsch, July 4, 1966; children: David, Thomas. BS, Northwestern U., 1958; PhD, U. Mich., 1964. Mem. staff Gen. Atomic, San Diego, 1964-70; div. mgr. Sci. Applications Internat. Corp., San Diego, 1971-75; v.p. Teknekron Inc., Berkeley, Calif., 1975-81; pres. SC&A, Inc., McLean, Va., 1981—. Contbr. articles to profl. jours. Fulbright fellow, 1959, AEC fellow, 1960-62, Ford-Phoenix fellow, 1963. Mem. IEEE, Am. Nuclear Soc., Health

Physics Soc. Home: 8200 Riding Ridge Pl Mc Lean VA 22102-1314 Office: SC&A Inc 1355 Beverly Rd Mc Lean VA 22101-3623

COHEN, SANFORD IRWIN, physician, educator; b. N.Y.C., Sept. 5, 1928; s. George A. and Gertrude (Slater) C.; m. Jean Steinbrecker, Nov. 30, 1952; children—Jeffrey, Debra, John, Robert. A.B. magna cum laude, N.Y. U., 1948; M.B., M.D., Chgo. Med. Sch., 1952. Intern Jackson Meml. Hosp., Miami, Fla., 1952-53; resident psychiatry U. Colo. Med. Center, 1953-54; resident Duke Med. Center, 1954-55, 57-58, mem. faculty, 1956-68, prof. psychiatry, 1964-68, head div. psychosomatic medicine and psychophysiol. research, 1964-68, lectr. psychology, 1960-68; instr. Washington Psychoanalytic Inst., 1964-68; cons. VA Hosp., Durham, N.C., 1957-65, NIMH, 1963-66; prof. psychiatry Boston U. Med. Sch., 1970-86, chmn. dept., 1970-86; vis. research scientist health and behavior br., div. basic scis. NIMH, 1986-88; prof. psychiatry U. Miami (Fla.) Sch. Medicine, 1988—, vice chmn. dept., 1990—; Markle scholar med. sci., 1957-62. Contbr. articles to profl. jours., chpts. to books. Recipient Robert Morse award excellence in sci. writing, 1965. Fellow Am. Psychiat. Assn. (life), Am. Coll. Clin. Pharmacology (life); mem. AAAS, Am. Psychosomatic Soc. Home: 6844 Sunrise Ct Miami FL 33133-7018

COHEN, SEYMOUR MARTIN, oncologist, hematologist, educator; b. N.Y.C., Dec. 19, 1936; s. Harry and Rose (Ehrlich) C.; B.A., Bklyn. Coll., 1957; B.Med. Sci., U. Geneva, 1959; M.D., U. Pitts., 1962; m. Carole J. Pomerantz, Aug. 16, 1976; children—Roger, Michael. Intern, Montefiore Hosp., N.Y.C., 1962-63, asst. resident in medicine, 1963-64; resident in medicine Mt. Sinai Hosp., N.Y.C., 1964-65, Am. Cancer Soc. fellow in hematology, 1965-66, mem. staff, 1969—; fellow in hematology L.I. Jewish Hosp., 1968-69; pvt. practice medicine specializing in med. oncology and hematology, N.Y.C., 1969—; clin. assoc. in medicine Mt. Sinai Med. Sch., 1969-73, sr. clin. asst. physician in medicine, 1969-73, asst. clin. prof. medicine, 1973-78, assoc. clin. prof. medicine, 1979—; mem. Cancer and Leukemia B Group. Mem. exec. com. Jewish Am. Polit. Action Com., 1975-79, v.p., 1979-81, pres., 1981-83; bd. govts. State of Israel Bonds, 1979—. Capt. M.C., USAF, 1966-68. Diplomate Am. Bd. Internal Medicine and Subspecialty. in Med. Oncology. Fellow A.C.P.; mem. AMA, AAUP, Am. Soc. Clin. Oncology, Internat., Am. Socs. Hematology, N.Y. Cancer Soc. (sec. 1983-86, v.p. 1987, pres. 1989), N.Y. State Soc. of Med. Oncologists and Hematologists (pres. 1989-92), N.Y. Alliance of Physicians and Surgeons (bd. dirs. 1988-89, co-chmn. 1990—), New York County Med. Soc. Assoc. editor Cancer Investigation, 1993—; contbr. articles to profl. publs.; research on malignant melanoma. Office: 1045 Fifth Ave New York NY 10028-0138

COHEN, SEYMOUR STANLEY, biochemist, educator; b. N.Y.C., Apr. 30, 1917; s. Herman and Lena (Tanz) C.; m. Elaine Pear, July 12, 1940; children: Michael, Sara. B.S., CCNY, 1936; Ph.D. in Biol. Chemistry, Columbia U., 1941; Dr.h.c., U. Louvain, Belgium, 1972, U. Kuopio, Finland, 1982. NRC fellow Rockefeller Inst., 1941-42; mem. faculty U. Pa., 1943-71, prof. biochemistry in pediatrics, 1954-71, Charles Hayden-Am. Cancer Soc. prof. biochemistry, 1957-71, Hartzell prof., chmn. dept. therapeutic research Sch. Medicine, 1963-71; Am. Cancer Soc. prof. microbiology U. Colo. Sch. Medicine, Denver, 1971-76; distinguished prof., Am. Cancer Soc. prof. pharm. scis. State U. N.Y., Stony Brook, 1976-85, prof. emeritus, 1985—; chmn. council analysis and projection Am. Cancer Soc., 1972-74, adviser research, 1974-76; Guggenheim fellow Pasteur Inst., Paris, 1947-48; Jesup lectr. Columbia U., 1967; guest investigator Institut du Radium, Paris, 1967-68; vis. prof. Collège de France, Paris, 1970; vis. fellow Smithsonian Instn., 1973-74, 86; vis. prof. U. Tokyo, 1974, Hadassah Med. Sch., 1974, Zuckerman lectr. tropical disease, 1979; Guggenheim and Lady Davis fellow Faculty Agr., Israel, 1983; fellow Nat. Humanities Ctr., N.C., 1982-83, 85; research assoc. history of sci., Smithsonian Inst., 1986; presdl. scholar U. Calif., San Francisco, 1988; lectr. Academia Sinica, R.O.C., 1989; trustee Marine Biol. Lab., Woods Hole, Mass.; bd. sci. cons. Sloan-Kettering Inst. Author: Virus-Induced Enzymes, 1968, Introduction to the Polyamines, 1971; editorial bd.: Virology, 1954-59, Jour. Biol. Chemistry, 1959-65, Jour. Cell Physiology, 1966-71, Bacteriol. Revs, 1969-73, Hist., Philos. Life Scis., 1985—. Recipient cert. for war research OSRD, 1945, War Manpower Commn., 1945; War Research medal Columbia U., 1943; Eli Lilly award and medal Am. Soc. Bacteriology, Immunology and Pathology, 1951; 1st Mead Johnson award Am. Acad. Pediatrics, 1952; medal Soc. de Chimie Biologique France, 1964; Borden award Am. Assn. Med. Colls., 1967; Passano award, 1974; Townsend Harris medal CCNY Alumni Assn., 1978; Forster award German Acad. Sci. and Letters, Mainz, 1978; Fogarty scholar NIH, 1973-74. Fellow AAAS (Newcomb Cleveland award 1955); mem. NAS, Am. Acad. Arts and Scis., Soc. Gen. Physiologists (councilor, pres. 1967-88), Serbian Acad. Scis. and Art, Inst. Medicine, Am. Assn. Cancer Rsch. (hon., bd. dirs. 1974-77), French Soc. Microbiology, Phi Beta Kappa. Home: 10 Carrot Hill Rd Woods Hole MA 02543-1206

COHEN, SIDNEY MAXIMILIAN, neurologist; b. Morristown, N.J., May 26, 1919; s. Abraham Isaac and Shaina Rachel C.; m. Lea Ostrojinsky, Feb. 26, 1955; children: Ron, Navah, Oren. BS, Columbia U., 1939; MD, L.I. Med. Coll., Bklyn., 1943; DMS, Columbia U., 1952. Diplomate Am. Bd. Psychiatry and Neurology. Rotating intern Cumberland Hosp., Bklyn., 1943; asst. resident medicine Cumberland Hosp., 1944; resident in neurology Mt. Sinai Hosp., N.Y.C., 1947; asst. resident neurology Neurol. Inst., N.Y.C., 1948; fellow dept. neurology Columbia U., N.Y.C., 1949-54; attending neurologist Roosevelt/St. Luke's Hosp., N.Y.C., 1952-91; sr. attending neurologist Roosevelt St. Luke's Hosp., 1991—; assoc. neurologist Neurol. Inst., 1952—. Contbr. articles to profl. jours. Capt. M.C., U.S. Army, 1944-46. Recipient Scroll of Honor United Jewish Appeal, 1971. Fellow Am. Acad. Neurology; mem. Am. Psychiat. Assn., Assn. for Rsch. Nervous & Mental Diseases. Office: 1213 Park Ave New York NY 10128

COHEN, STANLEY, pathologist, educator; b. N.Y.C., June 4, 1937; s. Herman Joseph and Eva (Lapidus) C.; m. Marion Doris Cantor, Aug. 30, 1959; children: Laurie Ellen, Ronald Nelson, Kenneth Stuart. A.B., Columbia U., 1957, M.D., 1961. Diplomate Am. Bd. Pathology (mem. immunopathology com.). Intern Albert Einstein Med. Ctr., Bronx, N.Y., 1961-62; resident Mass. Gen. Hosp., 1962-64; fellow NYU Med. Ctr., 1964-66; prof. pathology SUNY, Buffalo, 1968-74; acting dir. Ctr. for Immunology, Buffalo, 1973-74; prof. pathology U. Conn. Health Ctr., Farmington, 1974-87; assoc. chmn. U. Conn. Health Ctr., 1976-80; prof., chmn. bd. Hahnemann U., Phila., 1987-94; prof., chmn. U. Medicine Dentistry-N.J. Med. Ctr., 1994—; mem. study sect. allergy and immunology, 1981-85; chair study sect. tumor immunology ahd therapy TRORP, 1992-94; co-chmn. 3d, 4th and 5th Internat. Lymphokine Workshops, 1982, 84, Congress on Cytokines, 1987, UCLA colloquism: molecular pathways of cytokines, 1990—, Keystone Symposium, 1992. Author: Mechanisms of Cell-Mediated Immunity, 1974, Mechanisms of Tumor Immunity, 1976, Mechanisms of Immunopathology, 1978, Biology of the Lymphokines, 1979, Interleukins, Lymphokines and Cytokines, 1983, Molecular Basis of Lymphokine Action, 1987, Role of Lymphokines in the Immune Response, 1989; assoc. editor-in-chief Clin. Immunology and Immunopathology; mem. editorial bds. 8 profl. jours.; contbr. more than 185 articles to profl. jours. Served to capt. U.S. Army, 1966-68. Recipient Kinne award, 1954, Borden award, 1961, Parke-Davis award in Exptl. Pathology, 1977, Outstanding Investigator award Nat. Cancer, Inst., 1986; Witobsky Meml. lectr., 1995. Mem. Am. Assn. Pathologists, Am. Assn. Immunologists, Clin. Immunol. Soc. (councilor), Pluto Soc. Home: 611 Bryn Mawr Ave Narberth PA 19072-1612 Office: Hahnemann U Sch Medicine Philadelphia PA 19102

COHEN, STANLEY, biochemistry educator; b. Brooklyn, N.Y., Nov. 17, 1922; s. Louis and Fannie (Feitel) C.; m. Olivia Larson, 1951 (div.); children: Burt Bishop, Kenneth Larson, Cary; m. Jan Elizabeth Jordan, 1981. BA, Bklyn. Coll., 1943; MA, Oberlin Coll., 1945, PhD, 1989; PhD in Biochemistry, U. Mich., 1948; PhD, U. Chgo., 1985, Washington U., 1993. Instr. dept. biochemistry and pediatrics U. Colo., Denver, 1948-52; Am. Cancer Soc. fellow in radiology Washington U., St. Louis, 1952-53, assoc. prof. dept. zoology, 1953-59; asst. prof. biochemistry, sch. medicine Vanderbilt U., Nashville, 1959-62, assoc. prof., 1962-67, prof. biochemistry, 1967-86, disting. prof., 1986—; rsch. prof. biochemistry Am. Cancer Soc., Nashville, 1976—; Charles B. Smith vis. rsch. prof. Sloan Kettering, 1984; Feodor Lynen lectr. U. Miami, 1986, Steenbock lectr. U. Wis., 1986. Mem. editorial bd. Abstracts of Human Developmental Biology, Jour. of Cellular Physiology. Cons. Minority Rsch. Ctr. for Excellence. Recipient Research Career Devel. award NIH, 1959-69, William Thomson Wakeman award Nat. Paraplegia Found., Earl Sutherland Research Prize Vanderbilt U., 1977, Albion O. Bernstein MD award Med. Soc. State N.Y., 1978, H.P. Robertson Meml. award Nat. Acad. Sci., 1981, Lewis S. Rosentiel award Brandeis U., 1982, Alfred P. Sloan award Gen. Motors Cancer Research Found., 1982, Louisa Gross Horwitz prize Columbia U., 1983, Disting. Achievement award UCLA Lab. Biomed. and Environ. Scis., 1983, Lila Gruber Meml. Cancer Research award Am. Acad. Dermatology, 1983, Bertner award MD Anderson Hosp. U. Tex., 1983, Gairdner Found. Internat. award, 1985, Fred Conrad Koch award Endocrine Soc., 1986, Nat. Medal Sci., 1986, 89, Albert and Mary Lasker Found. Basic Med. Research award, 1986, Nobel Prize in physiology or medicine, 1986, Tennessean of Yr. award Tenn. Sports Hall of Fame, 1987, Franklin Medal, 1987, Albert A. Michaelson award Mus. Sci. and Industry, 1987. Fellow Jewish Acad. Arts and Sci.; mem. Nat. Acad. Sci., Am. Soc. Biol. Chemists, Am. Chem. Soc., AAAS, Internat. Inst. Embryology, Internat. Acad. Sci. (hon. internat. coun. for sci. devel.). Office: Vanderbilt U Sch Medicine Dept Biochemistry 607 LH Nashville TN 37232-0146*

COHEN, STANLEY ALLEN, pediatric gastroenterologist; b. Columbus, Ohio, June 3, 1947; s. Norman Saul and Esther (Schlansky) C.; m. Judith Dee Adler, Mar. 22, 1970; children: David, Adam, Lauren. BS, Case Western Res., 1969; MD, Ohio State U., 1972. Diplomate Am. Bd. Pediatrics and Pediatric GI/Nutrition. Intern Johns Hopkins Hosp., Balt., 1972-73, resident, 1973-75, intern, resident, 1972-75; pediatrician USAF, Langley AFB, Va., 1975-77; fellow Mass Gen. Hosp., Boston, 1977-80; pediatrician Roswell (Ga.) Pediatrics, 1980-87; physician, dir. Ctr. Pediatric Gastroenterology/Nutrition, Atlanta, 1987—; med. dir. Hug Ctr., Altanta, 1989—. Author: Healthy Babies, Happy Kids, 1985, poem Two, 1990, Seeping Into/Out of the Well, 1991, Beyond Hell, 1992; editor: Pediatric Emergency Management, 1983; patentee in field. Chmn. 20th Century Art Acquisition Fund, Atlanta, 1985-86; pres. Scottish Rite Childrens Med. Ctr., Atlanta, 1986. Maj. USAF, 1975-79. Recipient Premiere Physicians award Crohn's and Colitis Found. Ga. chpt., 1995. Fellow Am. Acad. Pediatrics (chmn. com. on nutrition Ga. chpt.); mem. Greater Atlanta Pediatric Soc., N.Am. Soc. Pediatric Gastroenterology and Nutrition, Poetry Atlanta. Office: Ctr Pediatric Gastroenterology/Nutrition 5455 Meridian Mark Ste 100 Atlanta GA 30342

COHEN, STEPHEN MICHAEL, physician assistant; b. Washington, Dec. 27, 1957; s. Herbert Jay and Lucille (Walter) C. AA, cert. paramedic, Santa Fe Community Coll., Gainesville, Fla., 1981; BS in Allied Health, U. Ala., 1984; MS in Health Care Adminstrn., LaSalle U., 1995. Paramedic instr. Santa Fe Community Coll., 1981-82; surg. and trauma physician's asst. Halifax Hosp. Med. Ctr., Daytona Beach, Fla., 1985-86; surg. and orthopedics physician's asst. U. Ala., Birmingham, 1986-88; surg. physician's asst. Maui Plastic Surgery, Kahului, Hawaii, 1988-89; paramedic instr. Western Carolina U., Cullowhee, N.C., 1990-91; surg. physician's asst. Carolina Hand Surgery, Ashville, N.C., 1990-91; with Denver (Colo.) Orthopedic Clinic, 1993-95; acad. dir., asst. prof. Nova-Southeastern U., 1995—. Co-chmn. Juvenile Justice Com. Youth Action Group, Asheville. Fellow Am. Acad. Physician's Assts., Fla. Acad. Physician Assts., Phi Kappa Phi. Office: 3200 S Univ Dr Ste #1290 Fort Lauderdale FL 33328

COHEN, STEPHEN MITCHELL, optometrist; b. Bklyn., Sept. 24, 1956; s. Herbert William Cohen and Diana Kalifowitz Flax; m. Stephanie Helene Shapiro, Apr. 6, 1986; children: Joshua, Arielle, Zachary. BA in Sci. Edn., Ariz. State U., 1980; BS in Optical Sci., Pa. Coll. Optometry, Phila., 1983, OD, 1985. Optometrist Family Vision Care, Scottsdale, Ariz., 1985-88, Ariz. Eye and Vision Care, Scottsdale, 1988-93, Scottsdale Vision Ctr., Scottsdale, 1993—; vision cons. Kachna Country Day Sch., Scottsdale, 1987—. Pres. Scottsdale "TIPS" Bus. Group, 1986-91, Desert Foothills Cmty. Theatre, Carefree, Ariz., 1985-94; v.p. Project Prevention, Phoenix Children's Hosp., 1986-92, mem. parent adv. bd., 1993-94; mem. Valley Leadership, Phoenix, 1989-90; treas. Coun. for Jews with Spl. Needs, Phoenix, 1993—. Named Outstanding Actor, Desert Foothills Cmty. Theater, 1988, 91. Mem. Am. Optometric Assn., Ariz. Optometric Assn. (Service award 1988, membership com.), Rotary (pres. 1986-93, Outstanding Svc. award 1991). Republican. Jewish. Office: Scottsdale Vision & Achieve 10505 N 69th St #1000 Scottsdale AZ 85253

COHEN, TERRENCE JAY, cardiologist; b. Bklyn., June 23, 1950; s. Irving I. and Myra J. Cohen; m. Connie Rose Holck Swales, May 29, 1988; children: John Palmer, Holly Beth. BA, Columbia Coll., 1971; MD, SUNY, Bklyn., 1975. Intern, resident in medicine Charity Hosp. New Orleans-Tulane U., 1975-78; fellow in cardiology North Shore Univ. Hosp.-Cornell U., Manhasset, N.Y., 1978-79; with Nassau County Med. Ctr.-SUNY Stony Brook, East Meadow, N.Y., 1979-80; attending cardiologist JF Kennedy Med. Ctr., Atlantas, Fla., 1981—, Palm Beach Regional Hosp., Lake Worth, Fla., 1981-95; cons. cardiologist Wellington Regional Med. Ctr., West Palm Beach, Fla. Fellow Am. Coll. Cardiology; mem. AMA, Am. Soc. Internal Medicine, Am. Coll. Cardiology (Fla. chpt.), Fla. Soc. Internal Medicine. Office: 4801 S Congress Ave #206 Lake Worth FL 33461

COHEN, WILLIAM NATHAN, radiologist; b. Balt., Dec. 10, 1935; s. Herbert and Lillian (Goldberg) C.; m. Sylvia Weinstein, Feb. 9, 1964; children: Elaine, Shirah, Jonathan. Student, Johns Hopkins U., 1952-55; M.D., U. Md., 1959. Intern U. Mich. Hosp., Ann Arbor, 1959-60; resident in radiology Mallinckrodt Inst., Washington U., St. Louis, 1960-63; chief radiology sect. Gallup Indian Hosp., USPHS, 1963-65; asst. prof. radiology U. Iowa, Iowa City, 1965-69; asso. prof. U. Iowa, 1969-73, prof., 1973-76; prof. radiology SUNY Health Sci. Ctr., Syracuse, 1976-83, clin. prof. radiology, 1983—; attending radiologist Crouse-Irving Meml. Hosp., Syracuse; vis. prof. radiology Hebrew U., Jerusalem, 1971-72; examiner Am. Bd. Radiology, 1981-87. Contbr. articles in field to med. jours. Fellow Am. Coll. Radiology; mem. Radiol. Soc. N. Am., Am. Roentgen Ray Soc., Am. Inst. Ultrasound in Medicine (sr.), Alpha Omega Alpha. Office: Crouse Irving Meml Hosp 736 Irving Ave Syracuse NY 13210-1690

COHN, BERTRAM DOUGLAS, pediatric surgeon; b. N.Y.C., May 7, 1926; s. Isaac H. and Anna (Stein) C.; B.S. cum laude, N.Y. U., 1945, M.D., 1948; m. Rita Brettschneider, June 30, 1991; children by previous marriage—Jonathan, Mark, Jeanne, Susan. Intern, Bellevue Hosp., N.Y.C., 1948-49, Maimonides Med. Center, Bklyn., 1949-50; resident Montreal (Que.) Children's Hosp., 1950-51, 53-55, VA Hosp., N.Y.C., 1955-56; practice medicine specializing in pediatric surgery, Bklyn., 1956—; dir. pediatric surgery service Maimonides Med. Ctr., S.I. Hosp.; cons. surgeon to hosps.; prof. clin. surgery State U. N.Y. Downstate Med. Center; teaching fellow in surgery McGill U., Montreal, 1954-55. Served with M.C., USAF, 1951-53. NIH grantee, 1960-62; NIH research fellow, 1960-62. Diplomate Am. Bd. Surgery. Fellow A.C.S., Am. Acad. Pediatrics; mem. Am. Pediatric Surg. Assn. (charter), N.Y. Soc. Pediatric Surgery (founder), Phi Beta Kappa, Alpha Omega Alpha. Contbr. articles to med. jours.; patentee caval filter, inserter; inventor slide-rule calculater, surg. instruments. Home and Office: 8420 Ridge Blvd Brooklyn NY 11209-4328

COHN, DAVID LESLIE, health facility executive; b. Chgo., May 24, 1949; s. Herman and Elsa (Kahn) C.; m. Valerie Kaye Smith, June 11, 1974; children: Joshua Smith, Zachary Smith. BA in Zoology, U. Mich., 1971; MD, U. Ill., Chgo., 1975. Diplomate Am. Bd. Internal Medicine, Am. Bd. Infectious Diseases. Resident in internal medicine U. Wis., Madison, 1975-78; fellow in infectious diseases U. Colo., Denver, 1979-81; contract physician Denver Health & Hosps., 1979-81, asst. dir. disease control svc., 1981-87, dir. disease control svc., 1987—, assoc. dir. Denver Pub. Health, 1989—, dir. AIDS svcs., 1989—; temporary advisor WHO, Geneva, 1992, med. officer, 1994-95; instr. U. Colo. Health Sci. Ctr., Denver, 1981-83, asst. prof., 1983-88, assoc. prof., 1988—. Contbr. chpts. to books, articles and revs. to profl. jours. Hon. bd. dirs. Colo. AIDS Project, Denver, 1987—; Gov.'s AIDS Coun., 1988-94; mem. Leadership Denver, 1987-88. Recipient Outstanding Sr. award Chgo. Tribune, 1967, Citation for AIDS/HIV Rsch. and Prevention, U.S. Dept. Health and Human Svcs., Denver, 1988; named Hero in the AIDS Epidemic, Colo. AIDS Project, Denver, 1992. Fellow Am. Coll. Physicians, Infectious Disease Soc. Am.; mem. Am. Thoracic Soc., Internat. AIDS Soc., Western Soc. Clin. Investigation, Internat. Union Against TB, Phi Eta Sigma. Jewish. Office: Denver Health & Hosps 605 Bannock Denver CO 80204

COHN, ERIC ALAN, ophthalmologist; b. Kansas City, Mo., June 2, 1955; s. Kenneth G. and Rosalie (Reichman) C.; m. Joan Marie Darnell, Feb. 26, 1983; children: Alexandra Lynn, Brandon Mitchell. BA in Chemistry, U. Mo., Kansas City, 1977; DO, U. Health Scis., Kansas City, 1982. Diplomate Nat. Bd. Osteopathic Physicians and Surgeons, Am. Bd. Ophthalmology. Commd. 2d lt. U.S. Army, 1978, advanced through grades to maj., 1988, resigned, 1991; rotating intern Chgo. Osteo. Hosp., 1982-83; resident in ophthalmology Fitzsimons Army Med. Ctr., 1985-88; fellow in glaucoma Houston Eye Assocs., 1991-92; staff physician U.S. Army Family Practice Clinic Patch Health, Stuttgart, Germany, 1983-84; family practice clinic cmmdr. Panzer Troop Clinic, Stuttgart, 1983-84, Nellingan Health Clinic, Stuttgart, 1984-85; staff ophthalmologist Moncrief Army Comty. Hosp., Columbia, S.C., 1988-91; ophthalmologist, glaucoma specialist Seltzer Eye Assocs., Florence, S.C., 1992-94; pres., ophthalmologist, glaucoma specialist Surgical Eye Care of Fla., Orange Park, 1995—. Fellow Am. Acad. Ophthalmology; mem. AMA, Fla. Med. Assn., Inc., Clay County Med. Soc., Duval County Soc. Ophthalmology, Rotary Club of Orange Park. Republican. Jewish. Office: Surgical Eye Care of Fla PA Ste 138 772 Foxridge Center Dr Orange Park FL 32065

COHN, ISIDORE, JR., surgeon, educator; b. New Orleans, Sept. 25, 1921; s. Isidore and Elsie (Waldhorn) C.; m. Jacqueline Heymann, July 4, 1944 (div. Aug. 1971); children: Ian Jeffrey, Lauren Kerry; m. Marianne Winter Miller, Jan. 3, 1976. MD, U. Pa., 1945; M.Med. Sci. in Surgery, 1952, DMS in Surgery, 1955; LHD (hon.), U. S.C., 1995. Diplomate Am. Bd. Surgery (bd. dirs. 1969-75). Intern Grad. Hosp. U. Pa., 1945-46, resident in surgery, 1949-52; fellow dept. surg. rsch. U. Pa., 1947-48; vis. surgeon Charity Hosp., New Orleans, 1952-62, sr. vis. surgeon, 1962—; surgeon in chief La. State U. Svc., Charity Hosp., New Orleans, 1962-89; prof. surgery La. State U. Sch. Medicine, New Orleans, 1959—; cons. surgeon VA Hosp., New Orleans, Touro Infirmary, New Orleans; instr. surgery La. State U. Sch. Medicine, New Orleans, 1952-53, asst. prof., 1953-56, assoc. prof., 1956-59, prof., 1959—, chmn. dept. surgery, 1962-89; mem. surg. rsch. rev. com. VA, Washington, 1967-68; dir. Nat. Pancreatic Cancer Project, 1975-84; mem. Soc. Surg. Chairmen, 1962-89. Mem. editl. bd. Am. Surgeon, 1963-87, Current Surgery, 1964-90, Am. Jour. Surgery, 1968—, Digestive Diseases and Scis., 1978-82, Surg. Gastroenterology, 1982—, Cancer, 1992—, Digestive Surgery, 1995—. Served to capt. M.C., AUS, 1946-47. Isidore Cohn, Jr. Professorship named in his honor at La. State U., 1987. Fellow ACS (exec. com., bd. govs. 1987-91, vice-chmn. 1989-90, chmn. 1990-91, 1st v.p. 1993-94); mem. AMA, Am. Surg. Assn., So. Surg. Assn. (1st v.p. 1979-80, treas.-recorder 1981-82, pres. 1982-83), La. Surg. Assn. (pres. 1968), So. Med. Assn., La., Orleans Parish med. socs., Soc. Univ. Surgeons, Southeastern Surg. Congress (chmn. forum on progress in surgery 1967-69, councillor for La. 1967-73, pres. 1972), Surg. Biology Club II, Assn. Acad. Surgery, James D. Rives Surg. Soc., Internat. Surg. Soc., Am. Gastroenterol. Assn., Bockus Soc. Gastroenterology, Soc. Surgery Alimentary Tract (trustee 1969-80, recorder 1973-76, pres. 1976-77, chmn. bd. 1977-78), Am. Soc. Microbiologists, Soc. Surg. Oncology, N.Y. Acad. Scis., Am. Assn. Cancer Research, Southeastern Cancer Research Assn. (pres. 1975), Collegium Internationale Chirurgiae Digestivae, Am. Cancer Soc. (vice chmn. clin. investigation adv. com. 1969, chmn. clin. investigation adv. com. 1969-73), Sigma Xi, Phi Beta Kappa, Alpha Omega Alpha, Omicron Delta Kappa. Office: La State U Med Sch New Orleans LA 70112

COHN, JESS VICTOR, psychiatrist; b. Cin., Jan. 1, 1908; s. Samuel L. and Hannah (Pritz) C.; m. Norma J. Hana, Sept. 7, 1947; children: Jess Victor Jr., William S., James D. M.D., U. Cin., 1933. Diplomate Am. Bd. Psychiatry and Neurology. Rotating intern Cin. Gen. Hosp., 1933, resident psychiatry, 1934; resident neurology Bellevue Hosp., N.Y.C., 1935; pres. neuro-psychiat. dept. Broward Gen. Hosp., Ft. Lauderdale, Fla., 1961, mem. active staff, 1955-63; cons. psychiatry Meml. Hosp., Hollywood, Fla., 1957-63, Mt. Sinai Hosp., Miami Beach, Fla., 1956-63; mem. active staff North Broward Provident Hosp., Ft. Lauderdale, 1956-63, Holy Cross Hosp., Ft. Lauderdale, 1957-63, Ft. Lauderdale Beach Hosp., 1957-63; mem. active staff Boca Raton (Fla.) Community Hosp., 1969-88, emeritus chief div. psychiatry; cons. psychiatry Social Security Adminstrn., 1963-69, 69—, Sinai Hosp., Balt., 1964-69, Carroll County Gen. Hosp., 1965-69, Jerusalem Mental Health Ctr., 1973; asst. supt. Central State Hosp., Indpls., 1948-50; instr. neuro-psychiatry Ind. U. Med. Sch., 1948-50; dir. clerkship in applied practical psychology Butler U., 1949-50; supt. Embreevill (Pa.) State Hosp., 1950-55; assoc. psychiatry U. Pa. Med. Sch., 1952-55, U. Pa. Med. Sch. (Grad. Sch. Medicine), 1952-55; asst. prof. psychiatry U. Miami, 1957; supt. Springfield State Hosp., Sykesville, Md., 1963-69; asst. prof. psychiatry Johns Hopkins Med. Sch., 1963-69; psychiatrist Johns Hopkins Hosp., 1963-69; mem. faculty U. Md. Med Sch., 1963-69; clin. prof. psychiatry U. Miami (Fla.) Sch. Medicine, 1979—; psychiatrist Univ. Hosp., 1963-69; regional dir. mental health for Western Md. Founding mem., chmn. med. adv. com. Mental Health Assn. S.E. Fla., 1944-48; chmn. Fla. commn. Internat. Congress Mental Health, 1948. Author: Sane, Insane, or Maybe: From the Notebook of the Psychiatrist, 1993; contbr. articles to sci. jours., books and bulls. Fellow ACP, AMA, Am. Psychiat. Assn. (life, examining bd. adminstrv. psychiatry); mem. Assn. Med. Supts. Mental Hosps., Am. Assn. Psychiat. Adminstrs. (editor emeritus newsletter, jour.), So. Psychiat. Assn., Pa. Psychiat. Soc., Phila. Psychiat. Soc. (chmn. program com.), Med. Chirurgical Faculty Md., Broward County Med. Assn. (chmn. med. adv. com. to mental health clinic), Broward County Neuropsychiat. Assn. (founding mem., 1st pres.), Fla. Psychiat. Soc., Delaware Valley Group Psychotherapy Soc. 9founding mem., chmn. program com., mem. exec. com.), Am. Acad. Psychotherapists, Eastern Psychoanalytic Assn., Am. Coll. Psychiatrists, Am. Coll. Physicians. Address: 23371 Blue Water Cir # C323 Boca Raton FL 33433-7048

COHN, JOSEPH DAVID, surgeon; b. N.Y.C., Jan. 26, 1937; s. Samuel Theodor and Gertrude (Emsheimer) C.; m. Barbara Ester Forst, July 27, 1966; children: Michael, Russell. SB, MIT, 1957; MD, NYU, 1961; MBA, Rutgers U., 1993. Diplomate Am. Bd. Surgery, Am. Bd. Thoracic Surgery, Am. Bd. Critical Care Surgery. Intern Duke Hosp., Durham, N.C., 1961-62; surg. resident Bronx Mcpl. Hosp. Ctr., N.Y., 1962-67; thoracic surgery resident U. Calif., San Diego, 1969-71; from asst. dir. surgery to dir. St. Barnabas Med. Ctr., Livingston, N.J., 1971-83; thoracic surgeon Northfield Surg. Assn., Livingston, 1978—; clin. asst. prof. surgery UMDNJ, Newark, 1972-79, assoc. prof., 1979-90, prof., 1990—; bd. dirs. Daltex Corp., N.Y.C., 1983—. Editor: scientific jours.; author: software programs, 1988; contbr. articles to profl. jours. Capt. USAF, 1967-69. Fellow Am. Heart Assn. 1966-67, NIH 1964-66. Fellow Am. Coll. Surgeons, Am. Coll. Critical Care Medicine; mem. Sigma Xi, Phi Lambda Upsilon, Alpha Omega Alpha. Office: Northfield Surg Assocs 299 E Northfield Rd Livingston NJ 07039-4811

COHN, LAWRENCE, podiatrist; b. Bklyn., Mar. 14, 1952; s. Norman and Elsie (Belkin) C.; m. Susan Cohn, June 11, 1982; 1 child, Erica. BS, Bklyn. Coll., 1973; D in Podiatry, Ohio Coll. Podiatric Medicine, 1980. Diplomate AACPPS, AIFM. Pvt. practice podiatrist Miami, Fla., 1981—. Fellow AAFS.

COHN, LAWRENCE H., cardiothoracic surgeon; b. San Francisco, Mar. 11, 1937; s. Harold Edward and Dorothy Harriet (Cohen) C.; m. Roberta Lee Cohn, June 26, 1960; children—Leslie Anne, Jennifer Lynne. B.A., U. Calif., Berkeley, 1958; M.D., Stanford U., 1962. Diplomate Am. Bd. Surgery, Am. Bd. Thoracic Surgery. Sr. cardiothoracic surgeon Brigham & Woman's Hosp., Boston, 1980-87, chief div. cardiac surgery, 1987—; prof. surgery Harvard Med. Sch., Boston, 1980—. Served to lt. comdr. USPHS, 1964-66. Fellow Am. Coll. Cardiologists, Am. Coll. Chest Physicians, Soc. Thoracic Surgeons, Am. Assn. Thoracic Surgery, Am. Surg. Soc. Office: Brigham Womens Hosp 75 Francis St Boston MA 02115-6110

COHN, LAWRENCE STEVEN, physician, educator; b. Chgo., Dec. 21, 1945; s. Jerome M. and Francis C.; BS, U. Ill., 1967, MD, 1971; m. Harriett G. Rubin, Sept. 1, 1968; children: Allyson and Jennifer (twins). Intern, Mt. Zion Hosp., San Francisco, 1971-72, resident, 1972-73; resident U. Chgo., 1973-74; practice medicine specializing in internal medicine, Paramount, Calif.; pres. med. staff Charter Suburban Hosp., 1981-83; mem. staff Long Beach Meml. Hosp., Harbor Gen. Hosp; assoc. clin. prof. medicine UCLA. Maj. USAF, 1974-76. Recipient Disting. Teaching award Harbor-UCLA Med. Ctr., 1980, 90; diplomate Am. Bd. Internal Medicine. Fellow Am. Coll. Physicians; mem. A.C.P., AMA, Calif. Med. Assn., L.A. County Med.

Assn., Am. Heart Assn., Soc. Air Force Physicians, Phi Beta Kappa, Phi Kappa Phi, Phi Lambda Upsilon, Phi Eta Sigma, Alpha Omega Alpha. Home: 6608 Via La Paloma Palos Verdes Peninsula CA 90275-6449 Office: 16415 Colorado Ave Ste 202 Paramount CA 90723-5054

COHN, MICHAEL JAY, psychologist, consultant, educator; b. Chgo., Apr. 22, 1951; s. Myron and Jacqueline P. (Gollob) C.; m. Linda Dock, Mar. 22, 1986. BA, Ariz. State U., 1973, M of Counseling, 1975; EdD, Ball State U., 1979. Lic. psychologist; diplomate Am. Bd. Forensic Examiners. Doctoral fellow Ball State U., Muncie, Ind., 1977-79; prevention cons. Ind. Dept. Edn., Indpls., 1980-83; staff therapist Tri-County Mental Health Ctr., Carmel, Ind., 1983; asst. adminstr. Fairbanks Hosp., Indpls., 1983-86; CEO Treatment Ctrs. of Am., Scottsdale, Ariz., 1986; pres. Michael Jay Cohn, P.C., Scottsdale, Ariz., 1986—; mem. faculty U. Phoenix, 1988—; faculty assoc. Ariz. State U., Tempe, 1988—; lectr. Internat. Conf. on Drugs, Atlanta, 1984-86. Author: Technoshock: Combatting Stress in the 90's and Beyond, Al K. Hall Talks About Alcohol and Your Safety, 1986, (chpt.) Psychological Maltreatment of Children and Youth, 1987. Mem. community adv. com. U. Phoenix Counseling Dept., 1990—; pres. Ind. Juvenile Justice Task Force, Indpls., 1985; prevention com. chair Ind. Mental Health Assn., Indpls., 1985. Recipient Key to City, City of Indpls., 1986, Placque of Appreciation, Fairbanks Hosp., 1986, Placque of Appreciation, Ind. Juvenile Justice Task Force, 1986; named Hon. Lt. Col., Ind. State Police, 1986. Mem. APA, Ariz. Psychol. Assn. (conv. co-chair 1985—), Am. Soc. Clin. Hypnosis, Am. Bd. Forensic Examiners. Office: Michael J Cohn PC 7330 E Earll Dr Scottsdale AZ 85251-7221

COHN, PETER FRANK, cardiologist; b. N.Y.C., Jan. 19, 1939; s. Archie and Clare (Miller) C.; m. Joan Kirschenbaum, Mar. 23, 1968; children: Alan Douglas, Clifford David. BA, Columbia U., 1958, MD, 1962. Diplomate Am. Bd. Internal Medicine and Cardiovascular Diseases. Instr., asst. prof., assoc. prof. Harvard Med. Sch., Boston, 1971-81; attending physician, dir. Cardiac Catheterization Lab. Brigham and Women's Hosp., Boston, 1971-81, dir. Clin. Cardiology Svc.; prof. medicine, chief cardiology divsn. SUNY Health Scis. Ctr., Stony Brook, N.Y., 1981—. Author: Silent Myocardial Ischemia and Infarction, 3 edits., 1986, 89, 94; editor Cardiology Rev., Greenwich, Conn., 1984—; contbr. over 200 articles to profl. jours. Capt. U.S. Army, 1964-66. Fellow Am. Coll. Cardiology, Am. Heart Assn. (Coun. on Clin. Cardiology); mem. Assn. U. Cardiologists, Assn. Profs. Cardiology. Democrat. Jewish. Office: SUNY Health Scis Ctr Cardiology Divsn Stony Brook NY 11794-8171

COHN, STEVEN JAY, cardiologist, internist; b. Queens, N.Y., Aug. 26, 1950; s. Gerald and Estelle (Glasser) C.; m. Randie S. Messinger, Mar. 19, 1977; children: Pamela, Jason. BS in Biomed. Engring., Boston U., 1972; MS in Biomed. Engring., Columbia U., 1974; MD, SUNY, Bklyn., 1977. Diplomate Am. Bd. Internal Medicine and Cardiovasc. Diseases. Intern Maimonides Med. Ctr., Bklyn., resident; pvt. practice Lauderhill, Fla., 1983—. Rsch. grantee Dynamics in Lung Disease, 1975. Fellow Am. Coll. Cardiology; mem. Tau Beta Pi. Office: 4300 N University Dr A103 Lauderhill FL 33351

COHN, THEODORE ELLIOT, optometry educator, vision scientist; b. Highland Park, Ill., Sept. 5, 1941; s. Nathanand Marjorie (Kurtzon) C.; m. Barbara Adler, Nov. 29, 1975; children: Avery Samon, Adrienne Leah, Harris Samuel. SB in Elec. Engring., MIT, 1963; MS in Bioengring., U. Mich., 1965, MA in Math., 1966, PhD in Bioengring., 1969. Asst. prof. U. Calif., Berkeley, 1970-76, assoc. prof., 1976-84, prof., 1985—; vis. fellow John Curton Med. Sch., Australian Nat. U., Canberra, 1977; vis. scholar U. Calif., San Diego, 1981-90. Author, editor: Visual Detection, 1993. Bd. dirs. Berkeley-Richmond Jewish Cmty. Ctr., 1995—. Fellow Optical Soc. Am. (chairvision tech. group 1984-86); mem. IEEE (sr. mem.), Soc. Neurosci., Sigma Xi. Office: U Calif Sch Optometry 360 Minor Hall Berkeley CA 94720-2020

COHN-HAFT, HERA MARIA, psychiatrist; b. N.Y.C., July 5, 1947; d. Louis and Athena Iris (Capraro) Cohn-H.; m. David Brian Cohn-Haft Johnston, May 4, 1969; children: Rebekah, Mariah, Alexander, Isaac. BA, Barnard Coll., N.Y.C., 1971; MD, Med. Coll. Pa., 1979. Resident in psychiatry U. Conn., Farmington, 1984; pvt. practice psychiatry West Hartford, Conn., 1984—; staff psychiatrist Manchester (Conn.) Meml. Hosp. Mental Health Clinic, 1984—; supr. Collaborative Counselling, Manchester, 1985-90. Vol. Nat. Abortion Rights Action League, Hartford, 1983—; lectr. in field. Mem. Am. Med. Women's Assn., Am. Psychiat. Assn., Am. Assn. Women Psychiatrists. Home: 22 Beverly Rd West Hartford CT 06119-1710 Office: 10 N Main St West Hartford CT 06107-1901

COILEY, MARIAN, critical care nurse; b. Bayonne, N.J., Nov. 8, 1959; d. Ernest John and Irene Marie (Kakascik) Hannig; m. Gerard K. Coiley Jr., June 13, 1987; children: Megan Alisse, Erin Elizabeth, Peter John. BSN, Seton Hall U., 1981; MS, Rutgers U., 1987. Staff nurse med./surgical Beth Israel Med. Ctr., Newark, N.J., 1981-84; nurse cardiovascular/surgical Beth Isarel Med. Ctr., Newark, N.J., 1984, staff nurse critical care unit, 1985; cardiac clin. specialist Summit (N.J.) Med. Group, 1986-94; cardiothoracic surgical nurse clinician Cardiac Surgical Assocs., Ltd., Richmond, Va., 1994—. Mem. Am. Assn. Critical Care Nurses, Sigma Theta Tau. Home: 11425 Briarcrest Dr Richmond VA 23236

COKELET, GILES ROY, biomedical engineering educator; b. N.Y.C., Jan. 7, 1932; s. Roy S. and Anna M. (Trippel) C.; m. Sarah Drew, June 15, 1963; children—Becky, Bradford. B.S., Calif. Inst. Tech., 1957, M.S., 1958; Sc.D., MIT, 1963. Research engr. Dow Chem. Co., Williamsburg, Va., 1958-60; asst. prof. Calif. Inst. Tech., Pasadena, 1964-68; assoc. prof. Mont. State U., Bozeman, 1969-76, prof., 1976-78; prof. U. Rochester, N.Y., 1978—. Contbr. articles to profl. jours. Served with U.S. Army, 1954-55, Japan. Recipient Sr. U.S. Scientist award Humboldt-Stiftung, Bonn, Fed. Republic Germany, 1981-82, 88. Fellow AAAS; mem. Biomed. Engring. Soc., Microcirculatory Soc., Am. Inst. Med. and Biol. Engring., Soc. Rheology, No. Am. Soc. Biorheology, Internat. Soc. Biorheology (pres.), European Microcirculation Soc. Office: U Rochester Dept Biophysics 601 Elmwood Ave Rochester NY 14642-0001

COKER, DONALD WILLIAM, economic, healthcare, valuation and banking consultant; b. Mobile, Ala., Nov. 26, 1945; s. William Mack and Gloria Antoinette (Croker) C.; m. Linda Carol Sandlin, July 12, 1969; children: Caroline Tiffany, Brittany Blaire. BA, U. Ala., 1968, postgrad., 1968; MA, Spring Hill Coll., 1996. Approved comml. arbitrator Am. Arbitration Assn. Trust mortgage officer AmSouth Bank, Mobile, 1968-72; sr. loan officer Gibraltar Savs., Houston, 1972-73; mortgage officer, asst. treas. Citicorp Real Estate, Houston, 1973-74; comml. loan officer M Bank-Houston, 1974-77; regional mgr. Comml. Credit Co., Houston, 1977-83, Ford Motor Credit, Houston, 1983-84; sr. v.p., mgr. lending and mortgage banking First Fed. Savs., San Antonio, 1984-85; exec. v.p. Home Savs., Houston, 1985-86; also bd. dirs. Home Savs.; supr. banking Tex. Savs. & Loan Dept., Houston, 1986-88; chmn. Fin. Inst. Mgmt. Svcs., Mobile, Ala., 1988—; mng. dir. Coker Consulting, Mobile, 1995—, Corp. Intelligence and Analysis, Mobile, 1994—; mng. dir. Present Value Econs., 1989—, Capstone Computer, 1990—, Capstone Ednl. Consulting, 1990—; CEO All Am. Asset Mgmt., 1988—, First Internat. Investment Bank, 1994; pres. 1st Nat. Sports Bank, 1989—; cons. Prentice-Hall Pub., IRS, FDIC, Resolution Trust Corp.; CEO All-Am. Mortgage, 1995; cons. to fin. instns., attys., corps. and govt. agys.; legis. and govtl. cons.; nat. healthcare and profl. practice valuation cons.; expert witness on valuation, econ., fin. and banking. Author: Complete Guide to Income Property Financing, 1984, Self-Management, 1985; editor: Complete Real Estate Computer Workbook, 1986, The Complete Loan Officers' Handbook, 1996; contbr. articles to profl. jours. Trustee Katy Ind. Sch. Dist., Houston, 1987; treas. Nottingham Country Civic Club, Houston; precinct leader, del. and dep. voters registrar Rep. party. Mem. Nat. Assn. of State Savs. and Loan Suprs., Mortgage Bankers' Assn., Am. Bankers Assn., U.S. Savs. & Loan League, Houston C. of C. (bus. devel. com.). Republican. Episcopalian. Clubs: Sweetwater Country. Home and Office: PO Box 91182 Mobile AL 36691-1182

COKER, SAMUEL TERRY, pharmacology and toxicology educator; b. Evergreen, Ala., Nov. 29, 1926; s. Zollie Watson and Lillie Mae (Anthony) C.; m. Carolyn Sue Ridnour, Aug. 15, 1954; children: Ann Louise, Susan Teri, Blair Anthony, Cheryl Ruth. BS in Pharmacy, Auburn U., 1951; MS, Purdue U., 1953, PhD, 1955. Registered pharmacist, Ala. Asst. prof. of pharmacology U. Miss., Oxford, 1955-56; assoc. prof. U. Mo., Kansas City, 1956-59; prof. of pharmacology Auburn (Ala.) U., 1959-92, prof. of toxicology, 1973-92, prof. emiritus of Pharmacology, 1992, dean Sch. Pharmacy, 1959-73; sec.-treas. Dist. III Bds. and Colls. of Pharmacy, Auburn, 1979—. Pres. Kiwanis Club of Auburn, 1980. Cpl. USAF, 1945-47. Am. Found. for Pharm. Edn. fellow, 1954. Methodist. Office: Auburn U Sch Pharmacy Dept Pharm Sci Auburn AL 36849

COKINOS, STEPHAN GEORGE, cardiologist; b. Bklyn., Aug. 28, 1949; s. George Stephan and Katina Olga (Papanastasopoulos) C.; m. Paula Panagopoulos, Jan. 10, 1982; children: Giorgios, Katina, James. BA, Adelphi U., 1971; MD, SUNY, Stony Brook, 1974. Diplomate Am. Bd. Internal Medicine. Intern in internal medicine Nassau County Med. Ctr., East Meadow, N.Y., 1974, resident in internal medicine, 1975-77, cardiology fellow, 1977-79, dir. cardiac catherization lab., 1979-81, dir. coronary care unit, 1981-85, attending cardiologist, 1979-85; cardiologist in group practice Ea. Cardiac Group, PC, West Islip, N.Y., 1985-96; attending cardiologist Good Samaritan Hosp., Southside Hosp., West Islip, N.Y., 1985—; cardiologist Southbay Cardiovascular Assocs., West Islip, N.Y., 1994—. Fellow Am. Coll. Cardiology, Am. Coll. Angiology, N Y. Cardiologic Soc.; mem. Am. Soc. Internal Medicine, Am. Heart Assn. Greek Orthodox. Office: Southbay Cardiovascular Assocs Ea Cargiac Group 1111 Montauk Hwy West Islip NY 11795

COKLEY, KAREN F., psychotherapist; b. Chicago Heights, Ill., July 28, 1944; m. Robert L. Cokley, Aug. 31, 1963; children: Kimberli, Kellie. AS, Richland C.C., Decatur, Ill., 1976; BS, Millikin U., 1978; MSW, U. Ill., 1980. Diplomate Clin. Social Work; registered social worker, Ill.; lic. psychotherapist. Counselor, cons. Family Svc. Decatur, 1980-87; psychotherapist, cons. Thomas Radecki & Assocs., Decatur, 1986-91, Cokley, Sunderland & Cokley, Decatur, 1992—. Mem. NASW (cert.). Office: 348 W Prairie Ave Ste 3 Decatur IL 62522

COLAIANNI, RANA A., nurse practitioner; b. Pitts., Aug. 6, 1954; d. Raymond and Alberta (Ricci) C.; m. Michael K. Armbruster, Apr. 16, 1983. Diploma, St. Margeret's Hosp., Pitts., 1976, U. Pitts., 1980. Cert. adult nurse practitioner, cervical cap fitter Am. Nurses Credentialing Ctr. Staff nurse, team leader, charge nurse St. Clair Hosp., Pitts., 1976-80; staff nurse practitioner, Family Practice Group Williamsport (Pa.) Hosp. and Med. Ctr., 1980-88; pvt. practice Loyalsock Family Practice, Williamsport, Pa., 1989—; preceptor nurse practitioner students; nurse colposcopist; mem. colposcopy faculty, family practice residency Williamsport Hosp. and Med. Ctr. Mem. Am. Soc. for Colposcopy and Cervical Pathology, Am. Acad. Nurse Practitioners (Pa. award for Excellence 1996), Pa. Nurses Assn. Home: RR 1 Box 518 Williamsport PA 17701-9754 Office: 901 Westminster Dr Williamsport PA 17701-3909

COLAIZZI, JOHN LOUIS, college dean; b. Pitts., May 10, 1938; s. Peter Richard and Lena M. (Sebastian) C.; m. Maria Rose Santoro, Aug. 12, 1967; children—James J., Patricia R., John Louis. B.S., U. Pitts., 1960; M.S., Purdue U., 1962, Ph.D., 1965. Asst. prof. Sch. Pharmacy, W.Va. U., Morgantown, 1964-65; asst. prof., asso. prof. Sch. Pharmacy, U. Pitts., 1965-76, prof., chmn., asso. dean, 1976-78; prof., dean Coll. Pharmacy, Rutgers U., Piscataway, N.J., 1978—; bd. dirs. Robert Wood Johnson Univ. Hosp., New Brunswick, N.J., 1985—; mem. Medicaid Drug Utilization Rev. Bd. N.J., 1996—. Mem. Am. Pharm. Assn., Am. Assn. Pharm. Scis., Am. Soc. Health-system Pharmacists, Am. Assn. Coll. Pharmacy, Am. Inst. of History Pharmacy, Rho Chi, Alpha Zeta Omega, Sigma Xi. Democrat. Roman Catholic. Home: 21 Jason Dr East Brunswick NJ 08816-3342 Office: Rutgers U Coll Pharmacy Piscataway NJ 08855-0789

COLAN, STEVEN DONALD, pediatrician, cardiologist; b. Omaha, Nebr., June 2, 1950; s. Robert Joseph Colan and Cathy Jean Cathroe Lyon; m. Margaret Ruth Wermer, Sept. 4, 1971; children: Henry Alexander Wermer Colan, Ariana Wermer Colan. BS in Math. and Philosophy, MIT, 1973; MD, Boston U., 1977. Diplomate Am. Bd. Pediatrics with subspecialty in pediatric cardiology; lic. physician, Mass. Intern in pediatrics Mass. Gen. Hosp., Boston, 1977-78, from asst. resident to chief resident in pediatrics, 1978-81; fellow in pediatric Cardiology The Children's Hosp., Boston, 1981-84; pvt. practice Boston, 1984—; instr. pediatrics Harvard Med. Sch., Boston, 1984-85, asst. prof., 1985-90, assoc. prof., 1990—; asst. in pediatrics Mass. Gen. Hosp., Boston, 1980-81; asst. in cardiology The Children's Hosp., Boston, 1984-85, assoc. in cardiology, 1985-90, sr. assoc. in cardiology, 1990—, dir. cardiovascular exercise lab., 1984—, staff echocardiographer noninvasive lab., 1984—, dir. divsn. cardiology info. svcs., 1994—, dir. divsn. noninvasive cardiology, 1994—; lectr. in field. Contbr. numerous articles to profl. jours. Janeway fellow, 1983-84. Fellow Am. Coll. Cardiology, Soc. for Pediatric Rsch.; mem. IEEE, AAAS, Am. Heart Assn., Am. Acad. Pediatrics, Internat. Soc. for Optical Engring., Soc. for Pediatric Rsch., Alpha Omega Alpha. Home: 11 Amelia Rd Needham MA 02194 Office: Childrens Hospital 300 Longwood Ave Boston MA 02115

COLANGELO, JAMES JOSEPH, psychotherapist; b. Jamaica, N.Y., Jan. 8, 1950; s. Joseph and Amalia (Bove) C.; m. Kathy DeGuardi, Nov. 12, 1983; children: Nicole, Steven, Christina. BA, Manhattan Coll., 1971; MSEd, St. John's U., 1974; PD, L.I. U., 1987, cert. in marriage, family therapy, 1987; PhD candidate, Calif. Coast U. Diplomate Am. Bd. Sexology; cert. clin. mental health counselor; nat. cert. counselor; registered profl. hypnotherapist; bd. cert. sex therapist; cert. sex counselor. Ind community mental health counselor Queens, N.Y.; caseworker N.Y.C. Dept. Social Svcs., Queens; clin. cons. Ea. Met. Counseling and Consulting Svcs., Queens; supr. Dept. Health & Human Svcs., Adminstrn. Children & Families, N.Y.C.; specialist Children and Families Program (DHHS/ACF); adj. faculty C.W. Post Ctr., L.I. U.; EEO counselor; mem. Region II AIDS com., DHHS. Recipient C. Eugene Morris award in mental health counseling L.I. U., 1992; named to Nat. Disting. Svc. Registry in Counseling, 1990. Mem. ACA, Am. Assn. Marriage and Family Therapists (clin. mem., approved supr.), Am. Assn. Profl. Hypnotherapists, Am. Assn. Sex Educators, Counselors and Therapists (cert.), Internat. Assn. Marriage and Family Counselors, N.Y. Assn. Marriage and Family Counselors, Am. Bd. Sexology, N.Y. Mental Health Counselors Assn. (v.p. N.Y.C. area), Psi Chi, Chi Sigma Iota.

COLARDYN, FRANCIS ACHILLE, physician; b. Kortrijk, Belgium, Dec. 3, 1944; s. Evariste and Carolina (Tarkanyi) C.; m. Michelle Fauconnier, July 10, 1967 (div. 1989); children: Gregory, Ancuk; m. Marie-Antoinette Van Den Berghe, Sept. 10, 1989 (div. 1993). MD, State U., Ghent, Belgium, 1970, postgrad., 1973-76, specialist in internal medicine degree, 1975. Asst. in internal medicine Univ. Hosp., Ghent, 1970-75, asst. prof. intensive care unit and emergency room, 1976-86, head dept. intensive care, 1981—, prof. intensive care, 1986—; mem. Med. Bd., 1979-80; pres. dept. medicine Internat. Faculty Schelde, 1994—; mem. Nat. Coun. on Blood, 1995—. Mem. med. adv. bd. Internal Medicine Digest, 1983-87. Mem. Commn. to the Ministry of Health for med. urgencies, 1976-85. Mem. Belgium Soc. Ultrasonography, Belgian Soc. Med. Informatics, Belgian Soc. Intensive Care (bur., tchg. commn., pres. 1993-94), N.Y. Acad. Scis., Belgian Soc. Endoscopy, Belgian Assn. Burn Injuries, European Soc. Intensive Care Medicine, Belgian Soc. Oxygen Metabolisms, Toxicological Soc. Belgium and Luxembourg, Belgian Working Group on Cardiac Pacing and Electrophysiology, Am. Soc. for Microbiology, Dutch-Belgian Soc. for A.R.D.S. (bd. dirs. 1990—), Soc. Critical Care Medicine, European Soc. Parenteral and Enteral Nutrition, Reanimation Soc. French Lang., Flemish Soc. Clin. Nutrition Metabolism (founding). Office: Univ Hosp, De Pintelaan 185, B 9000 Ghent Belgium

COLBATH, JOHN DENIS, nursing educator, nursing administrator; b. North Conway, N.H., June 21, 1949; s. George Banfill and Margaret Kenny C.; m. Lynne Marie Cayer, June 4, 1977; children: Courtney Ann, Geoffrey Alan, Benjamin Banfill. ADN, N.H. Tech. Inst., Concord, 1976; BSN, U. N.H., 1982; MBA, Plymouth State Coll., 1986; MSN, Simmons Coll., 1996. RN, N.H., Mass., Maine. Staff nurse The Meml. Hosp., North Conway, 1976-78, insvc. edn. dir., 1978-80, asst. adminstr., 1980-87; critical care nurse Nurse Finders, Boston, 1987-88; prof. nursing N.H. Tech. Coll., Berlin, 1988—; nursing supr. Androscogin Valley Hosp., Berlin, 1990—; adj. prof. nursing Coll. for Lifelong Learning, Conway, N.H., 1989—; adv. bd. N.H. Vocat.-Tech. Coll., Berlin, 1983-88. Chmn. blood drive ARC, Conway, 1984—; chmn. bd. dirs. Am. Cancer Soc., 1985-87; affiliate faculty for ACLS, N.H. Heart Assn., 1987—; chmn. Children's Health Ctr., 1995—; mem. Zoning Bd. of Adjustment, Conway, 1988—. Recipient Outstanding Vol. award ARC, Conway, 1990, 91, Am. Cancer Soc., North Carroll County, 1986, 87, past pres.'s award, 1988. Mem. Nat. League Nursing, N.H. Coun. Nurse Educators, Sigma Theta Tau. Republican. Roman Catholic. Office: NH Tech Coll 2020 Riverside Dr Berlin NH 03570-3717

COLBORN, GENE LOUIS, anatomy educator, researcher; b. Springfield, Ill., Nov. 23, 1935; s. Adin Levi and Grace Downey (Tucker) C.; divorced; children: Robert Mark, Adrian Thomas, Lara Lee Colborn Russell; m. Sarah Ellen Crockett, Aug. 14, 1976; children: Jason Matthew, Nathan Tucker. BA with honors, Ky. Christian Coll., 1957; BS with honors, Milligan Coll., 1962; MS in Anatomy, Wake Forest U., 1964, PhD in Anatomy, 1967. Postdoctoral fellow U. N.Mex. Sch. Medicine, Albuquerque, 1967-68; asst. prof. U. Tex. Health Sci. Ctr., San Antonio, 1968-72, assoc. prof., 1972-75; assoc. prof. anatomy Med. Coll. Ga., Augusta, 1975-88, prof. anatomy, 1988—, prof. surgery, 1993—, dir. Ctr. for Clin. Anatomy, 1987—, dir. med. gross anatomy, 1975—, cons. dept. surgery, 1977—, prof. surgery, 1993—; pres. Ga. State Anatomical Bd., 1983-93; cons. Eisenhower Army Med. Ctr., 1990—. Author: Practical Gross Anatomy, 1982, Surgical Anatomy, 1987, Hernias, 1988, Musculoskeletal Anatomy, 1989, Workbook of Surgical Anatomy, 1990, Clinical Gross Anatomy, 1993, Modern Hernia Repair, The Embryological and Anatomical Basis of Surgery, 1996; mem. editl. bd. Clin. Anatomy Jour.; contbr. numerous articles on cardiac conduction, nervous sys., primate anatomy, cell culture and clin. and surg. anatomy to profl. jours. Active San Antonio Symphony Mastersingers, 1970-75, Augusta Opera, 1975—, Augusta Choral Soc., 1975—; judge Regional Sci. Fairs, Augusta, 1978-90. Recipient Golden Apple award U. Tex. Health Sci. Ctr., 1975; Outstanding Med. Educator award Med. Coll. Ga., 1976, 77, 78, 82, 87, 88, 90, 91, Disting. Faculty award, 1978. Mem. AAUP, Am. Assn. Clin. Anatomists (membership chmn. 1982-86, councillor 1992-95, mem. editl. bd. Jour. Clin. Anatomy 1994—), Am. Assn. Anatomists, N.Y. Acad. Scis., KC (4th degree). Republican. Office: Med Coll Ga 15th At Laney Walker Blvd Augusta GA 30912

COLBURN, ALBERT PRESBY, physician assistant; b. Bklyn., June 15, 1942; s. Arthur Presby and Marjorie Roberta (Wyatt) C.; m. Linda Gale Simmons, May 26, 1962; children: Arthur Presby II, Eric Lee, Jennifer Leigh. BS in healthcare Adminstrn., San Diego State U., 1978; BS in Allied Health Care, George Washington U., 1981. Commd. USN, 1961-85, advanced through grades, physician asst./hosp. corpsman, 1961-85; physician asst. Presbyn. Med. Svcs., Farmington, N.Mex., 1985-90, FHP N.Mex., Albuquerque, 1990-93, Alamo (Nev.) Med. Clinic, 1992-93, Lincoln County Med. Ctr., Ruidoso, N.Mex., 1993-95, San Juan Regional Med. Ctr., Farmington, 1995—. Deacon So. Bapt. Ch. Fellow Am. Acad. Physician Assts. Republican. Home: 5605 E Greenwood Dr Farmington NM 87402 Office: Immediate Care Ctr 4820 E Main St Farmington NM 87402

COLBURN, HAROLD LEWIS, dermatologist, state legislator; m. Jane Harrison, 1949; children: Robert, Suzanne. AB, Princeton U., 1947; MD, Albany Med. Coll., 1949. Diplomate Am. Bd. Dermatology. Intern Hosp. Ctr., Orange, N.J., 1949-50; resident in dermatology U. Pa., 1952-55; dermatologist Moorestown and Mt. Holly, N.J., 1955-95; sec. chief emeritus of dermatology Meml. Hosp. Burlington County, Mt. Holly, 1955-92; sect. chief dermatology Zurbrugg Meml. Hosp., Riverside, N.J., 1955-92; asst. clin. prof. dermatology Thomas Jefferson U., 1971; rep. N.J. Assembly, 1984-95, chmn. health and human svcs. com., 1986-89, 91-95, fin. instns. com., 1993-95, drug and alcohol abuse com., 1987-89; med. dir. N.J. State Bd. Med. Examiners, 1995—. Freeholder Burlington County, 1971-84, freeholder dir., 1976, 80, 84. Mem. Burlington County Med. Soc. (past pres.), Med. Soc. N.J. (past trustee), Nat. Assn. Counties (chmn. subcom. for health resources 1977-80).

COLBY, FRANK GERHARDT, scientific consultant; b. Mulhausen, Germany, Apr. 10, 1915; came to U.S., 1946; s. Fritz and Paula (Oppenheimer) Cohn; m. Renee Hiller, Oct. 15, 1952 (dec. Mar. 1995); children: Audrey B., Leonard F. ChemE, U. Geneva, 1939, DSc, 1941. Consulting chemist various cos., Havana, Cuba, 1941-46; rsch. chemist Indsl. Tape Corp., New Brunswick, N.J., 1946-47; chem. lit. specialist Comml. Solvents Corp., Terre Haute, Ind., 1947-51; dir. rsch. info. R.J. Reynolds Tobacco, Winston-Salem, N.C., 1951-70; mgr. sci. info. R.J. Reynolds Tobacco, Winston-Salem, 1970-79, assoc. dir. sci. issues, 1979-83; sci. cons. rsch. analysis and product liability N.Y.C., 1983—. Fellow AAAS; mem. Am. Chem. Soc. Home: 186 Riverside Dr Apt 6A New York NY 10024 Office: 90 Park Ave 28th Fl New York NY 10016

COLDITZ, PAUL BERNARD, perinatal medicine educator, medical researcher; b. Australia, Dec. 30, 1951; s. Bernard Trevor and Doris (Wright) C.; m. Rhonda Kathleen Jarrett, Dec. 30, 1972; children: Stephen, Michael, Jennifer. MB BS, U. NSW, 1977, M in Biomed. Engring., 1985; PhD, Oxford (Eng.) U., 1988. Registrar The Children's Hosp., Sydney, 1980-83, neonatal fellow, 1984; rsch. scholar Oxford U., 1985-88; dir. Neonatal Care Unit King George V Hosp./, Sydney, 1989-91; prof. perinatal medicine U. Queensland, Brisbane, 1992—. Author: Obstetrics and the Newborn, 1996; contbr. articles to profl. jours. Bd. dirs. Queensland Sudden Infant Death Rsch. Found., Brisbane, 1994-96. Fellow Royal Australian Coll. Physicians; mem. Paediatric Rsch. Soc. Australia (pres. 1994-96), Australian Coll Paediatrics, Australian Perinatal Soc., Neonatal Soc. (Eng.). Office: Royal Womens Hosp, Perinatal Rsch Centre, Brisbane QLD 4029, Australia

COLE, DAVID JEFFERSON, surgeon; b. Albuquerque, May 25, 1960; s. James Kenneth and Joan (Meadow) C.; m. Kathryn Cochran, Aug. 20, 1988; children: Jacquelyn Paige, Andrew Jefferson. BS, N.Mex. State U., 1982; MD, Cornell U., 1986. Diplomate Am. Bd. Surgery. Resident in gen. surgery Emory U. Affil. Hosp., Atlanta, 1986-91; surg. oncological fellowship NCI/NIH, Bethesda, Md., 1991-94; sr. med. staff fellow Surgery Brn. NCI/NIH, Bethesda, 1992-94; asst. prof. surgery Med. U. of S.C., Charleston, 1994—; primary investigator NSABP, Pitts., 1995—; grad. faculty Med. U. S.C., 1995—, charter mem. Hollings Cancer Ctr., 1995. Republican. Presbyterian. Office: Med U SC Dept Surgery Rm 420 CSB 171 Ashley Ave Charleston SC 29425

COLE, EDITH FAE, dietitian, consultant; b. Benchley, Tex., Jan. 8, 1925; d. Horace and Bessie Mae (Seale) Cook; m. Charles Edward Cole, Feb. 12, 1979. BS, Tex. Woman's U., 1945, MA, 1947. Registered dietitian Am. Dietetic Assn. Intern Okla. A & M State U., 1946; asst. dietitian Tex. Woman's U., Denton, 1946-48; dietitian, asst. prof. U. Southwestern La., Lafayette, 1948-52; asst. dir. dietetics Hermann Hosp., Houston, 1952-55, dir. dietetics, 1955-74; pvt. practice cons. Crosby, Tex., 1974—; adj. asst. prof. U. Tex. Sch. Allied Health Sci., Houston, 1977-79. Author: Crosby's Heritage Preserved 1823-1949, 1992. Mem. Am. Dietetic Assn. (treas. 1973-75), Tex. Dietetic Assn. (pres. 1958-59, del. 1959-61, 69-71, Tex. Disting. Dietitian 1984), South Tex. Dietetic Assn. (treas. 1957-58, Disting. Dietitian of Yr. 1984), Crosby Huffman C. of C. Mem. Church of Christ. Home and Office: 1331 Hare Cook Rd Crosby TX 77532-7605

COLE, HAROLD SAMUEL, retired health facility administrator, physician; b. Bklyn., Apr. 20, 1916; s. Morris and Celia (Lilienfeld) C. BS, U. Md., 1937; postgrad., Princeton U., 1938; MD, NYU, 1942; postgrad., N.Y. Med. Coll., 1947-48. Intern New Rochelle (N.Y.) Hosp., 1942-43; resident Willard Parker Hosp., N.Y.C., 1946, Met. Hosp., 1947; pvt. practice in pediatrics Rutherford, N.J., 1948-65; prof. pediatrics N.Y. Med. Coll., N.Y.C., 1965-80, emeritus prof. pediatrics/community and preventive medicine, 1980—; med. dir. Flower-Fifth Ave. Hosp., N.Y.C., 1978-80, Bronx (N.Y.) Devel. Ctr., 1983-95. Co-editor: Early Diabetes, 1972, Early Diabetes in Early Life, 1973, Vascular and Neurological Changes in Early Diabetes, 1973, Prediabetes, 1989. Capt. U.S. Army, 1943-46, PTO. Fellow Am. Acad. Pediatrics; mem. Am. Diabetes, Am. Pediatric Soc., Lawson Wilkins Pediatric Endocrine Soc. Home: 8876 Wine Valley Cir San Jose CA 95135

COLE, JACK ELI, physician; b. Matamoras, Pa., Jan. 7, 1915; s. Eli Martin and Louise (Henneberg) C. m. Evelyn Gaston Darragh, Apr. 26, 1941;

children: Jack Eli, Thomas, Beverly, Martin, Robert, Leslie, Christopher, Candace, Champa. BS, Pa. State U., 1937; MD, U. Pa., 1941. Diplomate Am. Bd. Family Practice. Intern Wilkes-Barre (Pa.) Gen. Hosp., 1941-42; practice medicine, specializing in family practice Matamoras, Pa., 1946-47; staff St. Luke's Hosp., Bethlehem, Pa., 1948—; practice medicine, specializing in family practice Bethlehem, 1952-68, 1973-89; sec. dept. family practice St. Luke's Hosp., Bethlehem, 1973-88; incorporator, mem. med. staff Muhlenberg Hosp., Bethlehem, 1960—, pres. med. staff, 1961-62; student health physician Lehigh U., Bethlehem, 1948-52; physician Peace Corps, Afghanistan, Swaziland, India, 1968-73; leader mission med. team United Ch. Christ, Honduras, 1987; preceptor Temple U. Med. Sch., Phila., 1978-86. Contbr. poetry to anthologies, children's stories and articles to profl. publs. Charter mem. mission partnership com. N.E. Pa. conf. United Ch. of Christ, 1984. With U.S. Army, 1942-45. Decorated Purple Heart, Combat Medic badge; recipient Recognition award Temple U. Med. Sch., 1979; Boss of Yr. award Allentown Bus. Womens Assn., 1975. Fellow Am. Acad. Family Physicians; mem. AMA, Northampton County Med. Soc., Pa. Med. Soc., Lehigh Valley Acad. Family Physicians (v.p. 1979-81, pres. 1981-83), Pa. Acad. Family Physicians, Am. Acad. Family Physicians. Republican. Home: 782 Barrymore Ln Bethlehem PA 18017-2522

COLE, JEANE KAY, pediatric nurse practitioner; b. New Castle, Ind., Sept. 17, 1954; d. Fred Nelson and Shirley Dean (Plunkett) Criswell. Diploma in nursing, Marion County Gen. Hosp., Indpls., 1975; cert. PNP, Mt. St. Joseph Coll., Cin., 1980; BSN, Fla. So. Coll., 1986. Charge nurse Hancock County Meml. Hosp., Greenfield, Ind., 1975; head pediat. nurse Henry County Meml. Hosp., New Castle, 1975-79; PNP New Castle Pediat., 1979-80, New Castle Cmty. Schs., 1980-81; dir. Spina Bifida Ctr., Arnold Palmer Hosp. for Children & Women, 1981-93; cons. Agent Orange Class Assistance project Spina Bifida Assn. Am., 1992-95; pvt. practice PNP, 1994—; pvt. practice PNP, 1994—; owner, mgr. image cons. co. Me! Inside & Out, St. Cloud, Fla., 1984—; mem. adv. bd. Humana Lucerne Spinal Cord Injury Unit, Orlando, 1987—; mem. Interagy. Coun. for Handicapped Children, Orlando, 1987; chmn. coms., state rep. United Cerebral Palsy, Orlando, 1986-89; chmn. Nat. Nursing Coun. for Spina Bifida, 1990-92; sec. Nat. Cert. Bd. for PNPs and Nurses, 1991—. Designer playground for handicapped and able-bodied children. chmn. Friends of Playground, Orlando, 1987—; vol. All Children's Playground, 1988; v.p. Winter Park (Fla.) Ch. Religious Sci., 1989—. Recipient Citation for Vol. Efforts, U.S. Pres. Ronald Reagan, 1988; featured in So. Living Mag., Nov. 1989. Fellow Nat. Assn. PNPs (cert., dir. pub. rels. Fla. chpt. 1988-89, pres.-elect chpt. 1991-92, Outstanding Mem. award 1991), Spina Bifida Assn. Am. (editor newsletter 1986), Spina Bifida Assn. Ctrl. Fla. (v.p., treas. 1981-85), Fla. Nurses Assn. (speaker 1989, Clin. Excellence in Nursing award 1989). Home: 910 Marabon Ave Orlando FL 32806-1806 Office: Orlando Regional Health Aff 2875 S Orange Ave Ste 540 Orlando FL 32806-5454

COLE, JULIA PATRICIA, healthcare facility administrator; b. Altoona, Pa., Apr. 6, 1952; d. Dale Thomas and Norma Rae (Thomas) Shaffer; m. Charles R. Cole, Nov. 28, 1984; children: Victor, Candace. AS in Nursing, Community Coll. Allegheny Co., 1972; BS in Edn. and Pub. Health, California (Pa.) State U., 1976; M in Health Mgmt., St. Thomas U., Miami, Fla., 1989. Dir. nursing Hanover House, Miami; head nurse North Miami (Fla.) Med. Ctr.; adminstrv. dir., med.-psychiat. head nurse Hialeah (Fla.) Hosp.; asst. adminstr. Palace Gardens-ACLF, Homestead, Fla.; instr., leader workshops in field. Recipient Exceptionally Able Youth award Allegheny County. Mem. Psychiat. Nursing Network. Home: 11201 SW 55 St #9 Miramar FL 33025-3103

COLE, KIMBERLY ALICE, critical care and post-anesthesia care nurse; b. Mt. Pleasant, N.Y., Sept. 8, 1962; d. Elhannah and Mrytle (Tedford) C. BSN, Ea. Ky. U., 1985. RN, Ky., N.C.; cert. in ACLS, CCRN. Nurse apprentice U. Ky. Med. Ctr., Lexington; med. surgical staff nurse, post anesthesia care unit and CCU Humana U. Hosp., Louisville; staff nurse open heart unit Duke U. Med. Ctr., 1991-95; SICU/MICU Rex Health Care, Raleigh, 1996—. Mem. AACCN.

COLE, MALVIN, neurologist, educator; b. N.Y.C., Mar. 21, 1933; s. Harry and Sylvia (Firman) C.; A.B. cum laude, Amherst Coll., 1953; M.D. cum laude, Georgetown U. Med. Sch., 1957; m. Susan Kugel, June 20, 1954; children: Andrew James, Douglas Gowers. Intern, Seton Hall Coll. Medicine, Jersey City Med. Ctr., 1957-58; resident Boston City Hosps., 1958-60; practice medicine specializing in neurology, Montclair and Glen Ridge, N.J., Montville, N.J., 1963-72, Casper, Wyo., 1972—; teaching fellow Harvard Med. Sch., 1958-60; Research fellow Nat. Hosp. for Nervous Diseases, St. Thomas Hosp., London, Eng., 1960-61; instr. Georgetown U. Med. Sch., 1961-63; clin. assoc. prof. neurology N.J. Coll. Medicine, Newark, 1963-72, acting dir. neurology, 1965-72; assoc. prof. clin. neurology U. Colo. Med. Sch., 1973-88, clin. prof., 1988—; mem. staff Wyo. Med. Ctr., Casper, U. Hosp., Denver. Served to capt. M.C., AUS, 1961-63. Licensed physician, Mass., N.Y., Calif., N.J., Colo., Wyo.; diplomate Am. Bd. Psychiatry and Neurology, Nat. Bd. Med. Examiners. Fellow ACP, Am. Acad. Neurology, Royal Soc. Medicine; mem. Assn. Research Nervous and Mental Disease, Acad. Aphasia, Am. Soc. Neuroimaging, Internat. Soc. Neuropsychology, Harveian Soc. London, Epilepsy Found. Am., Am. Epilepsy Soc., Am. EEG Soc., N.Y. Acad. Sci., Osler Soc. London, Alpha Omega Alpha. Contbr. articles to profl. jours. Office: 246 S Washington St Casper WY 82601-2921

COLE, MARILYN BUSH, occupational therapy educator; b. N.Y.C., Jan. 29, 1945; d. George Lyman and Theis Odette (Maurer) Bush; m. Carl E. Cole, Aug. 31, 1968 (div. June 1981); children: Charlot E. Cole, Bradley Eric Cole; m. Martin M. Schiraldi Sr., July 3, 1982. BA, U. Conn., 1966; grad. cert., U. Pa., 1969; MS, U. Bridgeport, 1982. Registered occupational therapist, Conn. Staff occupational therapy Ea. Pa. Psychiat. Inst., Phila., 1968-69; dir. occupational therapy Middlesex Meml. Hosp., Middletown, Conn., 1973-76; supervising occupational therapist Lawrence & Meml. Hosps. Day Treatment Ctr., New London, Conn., 1976-79; staff occupational therapist Newington Children's Hosp., Newington, Conn., 1980-82; asst. prof. occupational therapy Quinnipiac Coll., Hamden, Conn., 1982-95, assoc. prof., 1995—; cons. psychiat. svcs. VA Med. Ctr., West Haven, Conn., 1983-91; cons. Fairfield Hills Hosp., Newtown, Conn., 1989-91. Author: (textbook) Group Dynamics in Occupational Theray, 1993; co-author Structured Group Experiences, 1982, chpt. in Group Process and Structure, 1988; contbr. articles to profl. jours. Grantee Quinnipiac Coll, 1986. Mem. Am. Occupational Therapy Assn. (Communications award 1976, cert.), Conn. Occupational Therapy Assn. (sec. 1978, nominations chair 1982-89), World Fedn. Occupational Therapists, AAUW (cultural chair 1972, publicity chair 1973-76, edn. chair 1989-91, nominations 1993-96), Ctr. for Study Sensory Integrative Dysfunction (cert. 1979). Republican. Episcopalian. Office: Quinnipiac Coll Dept Occupl Therapy Mount Carmel Ave Hamden CT 06518

COLE, MICHAEL ALLEN, microbiologist, educator; b. Denver, Dec. 15, 1943; s. William J. and Marcella T. (Soll) C.; m. Iris K. Stovall, Feb. 20, 1978. BS, Cornell U., 1967; M in Microbiology, N.C. State U., 1970, PhD, 1972. Asst. prof. So. Ill. U., Edwardsville, 1972-73; asst. prof. U. Ill., Urbana, 1974-80, assoc. prof., 1980—; cons. 3M Co., St. Paul, 1989—, Green Cycle, Inc., Northfield, Ill., 1992—, Dow-Elanco, Indpls., 1995—; bd. dirs., sr. v.p. Solum Remediation Svcs., Lake Bluff. Contbr. articles to profl. jours. Mem. Am. Chem. Soc., Am. Soc. Microbiology, Am. Soc. Agronomy. Home: 101 W George Huff Dr Urbana IL 61801-5181 Office: U Ill Natural Resources and Environ Scis Dept 1102 S Goodwin Ave Urbana IL 61801-4730

COLE, ROBERT EDWARD, psychologist, consultant; b. July 2, 1946. BS, Cornell U., 1968, MS, 1973, PhD, 1976. Instr. U. Rochester, N.Y., 1974-78, asst. prof., 1978-86, clin. assoc. prof., 1986—; ptnr. Cole-Schwartzman Assocs., Rochester, 1984—; cons. NIMH, 1982—, Nat. Inst. on Alcohol Abuse & Alcoholism, 1990—. Author: Fireproof Children Handbook, 1990, Fireproof Children Education Kit, 1990, (monograph) Parent Psychopathology, Family Interaction and Child Competence, 1982; editor: Families and Chronic Illness, 1991. Grantee N.Y. State, 1983-86, Robert Wood Johnson Found., 1984-88. Mem. Am. Psychol. Assn., Soc. Rsch. in Child Devel. Office: Cole-Schwartzman Assocs 20 N Main St Pittsford NY 14534-1303

COLE, STEPHEN ADAMS, psychiatrist; b. Washington, Dec. 18, 1940; s. Gordon Henry and Malvine Stuart (Gescheidt) C.; m. Dalen Lucia Sciarra; 1 child, Julietta Lorraine. BA with honors, Cornell U., 1961; AM, Harvard U., 1964; MD, Columbia U., 1970. Diplomate Am. Bd. Psychiatry and Neurology. Vol. U.S. Peace Corps, Kathmandu, Nepal, 1964-66; intern Roosevelt Hosp., N.Y.C., 1970-71; resident in psychiatry Albert Einstein Coll. Medicine, Bronx, N.Y., 1971-74, fellowship in social and community psychiatry, 1974-75; Robert Wood Johnson Found clin. scholar Columbia U. Coll. Phsycians and Surgeons, N.Y.C., 1975-77; dir. family treatment program N.Y. VA Med. Ctr., 1977-87; chief partial hospitalization program St. Vincent's Hosp. Med. Ctr., N.Y.C., 1988-92, chief continuing day treatment program, 1992-95; med. dir. Healthcare and Rehab. Svc. Southeastern Vt., Bellows Falls, 1995; lectr. in chemistry Amrit Sci. Coll., Kathmandu, 1964-66; instr. in psychiatry Columbia U. Coll. of Physicians and Surgeons, 1976-78; asst. prof. psychiatry, NYU, 1977-84; clin. assoc. prof. psychiatry, 1984—; assoc. attending physician St. Vincent Hosp. and Med. Ctr., N.Y., 1983—; asst. attending physician U. Hosp., N.Y.C., 1977—; examiner Am. Bd. Psychiatry and Neurology, 1980, 83, 84, 86. Author: (with others) Treatments of Psychiatric Disorders, 1989, 95, Families of the Mentally Ill, 1987, Comprehensive Group Psychotherapy II, 1983, Less Time to Do More, 1993; contbr. articles to profl. jours. Dir. Patient-Family Support Project, N.Y.C., 1981—; mem. Curriculum and Tng. com. N.Y. State Alliance for the Mentally Ill, N.Y.C., 1988—; bd. advisors Friends and Advocates of the Mentally Ill, N.Y.C., 1989—. Lt. comdr. USPHS, 1971-75. Recipient Deans prize for rsch. Columbia Coll. Physicians and Surgeons, 1969, Exemplary Psychiatrist award Nat. Alliance for Mentally Ill, 1993, 96; grad. fellow NSF, 1961-64; internat. fellow Columbia U., 1967-68. Fellow Assn. for Clin. Psychosocial Rsch., N.Y. Acad. of Medicine, Am. Orthopsychiat. Assn., Am. Psychiat. Assn.; mem. Am. Family Therapy Acad., Am. Assn. for Marriage and Family Therapy, Am. Assn. for Behavior Therapy. Democrat. Office: Healthcare and Rehab Svc Southeastern Vt Med Dir 1 Hospital Ct #410 Bellows Falls VT 05101

COLE, THEODORE JOHN, osteopathic physician; b. Covington, Ky., May 30, 1953; s. John N. and Florence R. (Bruener) C.; m. Ellen Cole; children: Joren, Emily, Kevin. BA, Centre Coll., Danville, Ky., 1975; MA, Western Ky. U., 1978; DO, Ohio U., 1986. Diplomate Am. Osteo. Bd. Gen. Practice, Nat. Bd. Osteo. Examiners. Psychologist Comprehensive Mental Health Svcs., St. Petersburg, Fla., 1978-82; intern Detroit Osteo. Hosp., 1986-87; resident Doctors Hosp., Columbus, Ohio, 1987-88; pvt. practice, West Chester, Ohio, 1989—; preceptor Ohio U. Coll. Osteo. Medicine, Athens, 1990—, U. Cin. Med. Sch., 1990—; dir. So. Ohio Coll. Nursing. Coach, Soccer Assn. for Youth, West Chester, 1989, 90, Liberty Sports Orgn., West Chester, 1990. Mem. Am. Osteo. Assn., Am. Assn. Osteopathy, Am. Coll. Gen. Practitioners, Ohio Osteo. Assn., Am. Acad. Environ. Medicine, Cranial Acad., Am. Acad. Advancement of Medicine. Office: West Chester Family Practice 9678 Cincinnati Columbus Rd Cincinnati OH 45241-1071

COLE, WILLIAM FRANK, orthopaedic surgeon; b. Houston, Nov. 23, 1940; s. W. Frank and Lora Elizabeth (Cammack) C.; m. Mayron Ann Ellis, Aug. 24, 1961; children: Ellisa Carol Cole Goldsmith, Colleen Mayron. BA, Baylor U., 1962, MD, 1966. Diplomate Am. Bd. Orthopaedic Surgery. Orthopaedic surgeon pvt. practice, Houston, 1973—. Lt. comdr. USN Med. Corps, 1967-69. Recipient Guy Whitt Meml. award Tex. Neuropsychiat. Assn., 1964. Fellow Am. Coll. Surgeons; mem. Am. Acad. Orthopaedic Surgery, Western ORthopaedic Assn., Tex. Orthopaedic Assn., Houston Orthopaedic Soc. (pres. 1986). Baptist. Office: 1 Meml SW Ste 344 7777 Southwest Fwy Houston TX 77074-1887

COLECCHI, STEPHEN, lawyer, hospital administrator; b. Ravenna, Ohio, July 28, 1954; s. Paul and Josephine (Ventura) C.; m. Diane Balazs, Aug. 5, 1978; children: Matthew, Sarah. BBA, Kent (Ohio) State U., 1976; JD, U. Akron, Ohio, 1979. Bar: Ohio 1979, U.S. Dist. Ct. (no. dist.) Ohio 1979, U.S. Supreme Ct. 1982. Ptnr. Martell, Cimino & Colecchi, Ravenna, 1979-85; gen. counsel Robinson Meml. Hosp., Ravenna, 1985-94, pres., CEO, 1994—; asst. prosecutor Portage County, Ravenna, 1989-94. Asst. law dir. City of Kent, 1979-85; mem. Ravenna Planning Commn., 1988—; treas. Portage County Dems., Ravenna, 1990-91, vice-chmn., 1991-94. Mem. Am. Acad. Healthcare Attys., Ohio Bar Assn., Portage County Bar Assn., Nat. Health Lawyers Assn., Ravenna C. of C. (pres. 1990). Home: 1110 Woodbend Rd Ravenna OH 44266-8750 Office: Robinson Meml Hosp PO Box 1204 Ravenna OH 44266-1204

COLELLA, DONALD FRANCIS, pharmaceutical licensing executive; b. Utica, N.Y.; s. Frank Joseph and Marie Josephine (Barbano) C.; m. Joanne DiNovo; 1 child, Teresa Anne. BS in Biology, Rensselaer Polytech. Inst.; MS in Biology, Coll. of St. Rose, Albany, N.Y.; MBA in Mktg. and Fin., Drexel U. Assoc. biologist Sterling-Winthrop Rsch. Inst., Rensselaer; pharmacologist Smith Kline Beecham, Phila., N.Y.; U.S. and Internat. product mgr. Smith Kline Beecham, Phila., dir. worldwide bus. devel.; dir. bus. devel. and pharms. Alfred Benzon, Inc., Phila.; v.p. pharms. Brit. Tech. Group U.S.A., Gulph Mills, Pa. Contbr. articles to profl. jours. Home: 1508 Wynnemoor Way Fort Washington PA 19034-2829 Office: Brit Tech Group USA Inc 2200 Renaissance Blvd Gulph Mills PA 19406-2755

COLEMAN, ALEX, psychologist, lawyer; b. Champaign, Ill., Aug. 7, 1949; 1 child, Benjamin David. BA in Psychology, SUNY, Buffalo, 1971; JD, Boston U., 1974; MA in Clin. Psychology, Fielding Inst., Santa Barbara, Calif., 1980; PhD in Clin. Psychology, Fielding Inst., 1982. Lic. psychologist provider, Mass.; bar: Mass. 1974, U.S. Dist. Ct. Mass. 1975, U.S. Supreme Ct. 1979. Legal analyst NIMH Rsch.-Child Abuse/Neglect, Boston, 1974-75; atty. child abuse team Children's Hosp., Boston, 1975; hearing officer Bur. Spl. Edn. Appeals, Boston, 1976; atty. State Adv. Commn. Spl. Edn., Boston, 1977; pvt. practice psychotherapy Brookline, Watertown, Mass., 1978-84; pvt. practice psychology Brookline, 1986—, pvt. practice law, 1975—; guardian ad litem, cons., expert witness and presenter concerning child custody, adoption, child abuse, lesbian, gay and transgender issues; adj. faculty Boston U., 1987-94; adj. asst. prof. Simmons Coll. Sch. Social Work, 1990-92. Author: The Psychotherapeutic Potential of the Judge: Child Abuse/Neglect, 1983; newsletter editor Assn. for Women in Psychology, 1984-88; contbr. articles to profl. jours. Bd. dirs. Boston Women's Fund, 1988-94, Brookline Cmty. Mental Health Ctr., 1984-93; mem. adv. com. gifted & talented program Brookline Pub. Schs., 1995—; cooperating atty. GLAD, Boston, 1985—; steering com. Am Tikva, Boston, 1984-88, 93-94, adv. com., 1995—. Recipient Outstanding Svc. award Am Tikva, Boston, 1987, 88; fellow Boston U. Human Relations Lab., 1972-74. Mem. APA, Assn. for Women in Psychology (implementation collective 1984-89), Mass. Lesbian & Gay Bar Assn., Mass. Assn. Guardians Ad Litem, Phi Beta Kappa. Home and Office: 246 Tappan St Brookline MA 02146-4309

COLEMAN, ARLENE FLORENCE, nurse practitioner; b. Braham, Minn., Apr. 8, 1926; d. William and Christine (Judin) C.; m. John Dunkerken, May 30, 1987. Diploma in nursing, U. Minn., 1947, BS, 1953; MPH, Loma Linda U., 1974. RN, Calif. Operating room scrub nurse Calif. Luth. Hosp., L.A., 1947-48; indsl. staff nurse Good Samaritan Hosp., L.A., 1948-49; staff nurse Passavant Hosp., Chgo., 1950-51; student health nurse Moody Bible Inst., Chgo., 1950-51; staff nurse St. Andrews Hosp., Mpls., 1951-53; pub. health nurse Bapt. Gen. Conf. Bd. of World Missions, Ethiopia, Africa, 1954-66; staff pub. health nurse County of San Bernadino, Calif., 1966-68, sr. pub. health nurse, 1968-73, pediatric nurse practitioner, 1973—. Contbr. articles to profl. jours. Mem. bd. dist. missions Bapt. Gen. Conf., Calif., 1978-84; mem. adv. coun. Kaiser Hosp., Fontana, Calif., 1969-85, Bethel Sem. West, San Diego, 1987—; bd. dirs. Casa Verdugo Retirement Home, Hemet, Calif., 1985—; active Calvary Bapt. Ch., Redlands, Calif., 1974—; mem. S.W. Bapt. Conf. Social Ministries, 1993—. With USPHS, 1944-47. Calif. State Dept. Health grantee, 1973. Fellow Nat. Assn. Pediatric Nurse Assocs. and Practitioners; mem. Calif. Nurses Assn. (state nursing coun. 1974-76). Democrat.

COLEMAN, BERNELL, physiologist, educator; b. Jefferson County, Miss., Apr. 26, 1929; s. Percy and Julia (Nailor) C.; m. Annie C. Richardson, Jan. 30, 1962; children—Rochelle, Ronald. BS, Alcorn A&M Coll., 1952; Ph.D. (Univ. fellow), Loyola U. Stritch Sch. Medicine, Chgo., 1964. Research asst. in biochemistry U. Chgo., 1956-57; research in cancer Hines (Ill.) VA Hosp., 1957-59; instr. St. Louis U. Sch. Medicine, 1963-65, asst. prof. physiology, 1965-67; asst. prof. Chgo. Med. Sch., 1967-69, asso. prof., 1969-76, prof., 1976; prof. Howard U. Coll. Medicine, Washington, 1976—; chmn. dept. physiology and biophysics Howard U. Coll. Medicine, 1979—; lectr. Cook County Grad. Sch. Medicine, U. Ill. Med. Sch.; vis. prof. Rush Med. Coll.; external examiner Godfrey Huggins Sch. Medicine, U. Zimbabwe, Salisbury, 1981; mem. cardiovascular and pulmonary study sect. Nat. Heart, Lung and Blood Inst./NIH, 1982-83, rsch. tng. rev. com., 1990-94. Peer rev. com. Am. Heart Assn., 1988-93, 95—, rsch. com., 1993—. With U.S. Army, 1953-56, Korea. Recipient research award Chgo. Med. Sch. Bd. Trustees, 1975; NIH research fellow, 1960-61; NIH grantee, 1966-68, 69-74, 74-76, 79—; USPHS fellow, 1961-63; Dept. Def. grantee, 1965-67. Mem. AAUP, Am. Physiol. Soc. (cardiovascular fellow 1985), Am. Heart Assn. (basic sci. coun.), AAAS, Fedn. Am. Socs. Exptl. Biology (vis. scientist for minority instns. programs 1982-83, 1989-90), N.Y. Acad. Scis., Am. Soc. Hypertension (charter), Sigma Xi, Phi Rho Sigma. Democrat. Home: 14200 Myer Ter Rockville MD 20853-2350 Office: 520 W St NW Washington DC 20001-2337

COLEMAN, C. NORMAN, radiologist, oncologist, researcher, educator; b. N.Y.C., Jan. 24, 1945; s. Samuel A. and Minna (Kramer) C.; m. Karolynn Forsburg, May 25, 1970; children: Gabrielle, Keith. BA, U. Vt., 1966; MD, Yale U., 1970. Diplomate Am. Bd. Internal Medicine, Am. Bd. Radiology, Am. Bd. Med. Oncology. Intern in internal medicine U. Calif., San Francisco, 1970-71, resident in internal medicine, 1971-72; clin. assoc. Nat. Cancer Inst., NIH, Bethesda, Md., 1972-74; clin. fellow therapeutic radiology Stanford (Calif.) U. Med. Sch., 1975-78, asst. prof. dept. radiology and medicine, 1979-84, assoc. prof., 1984-85; prof., chmn. Joint Ctr. for Radiation Therapy, Harvard U. Med. Sch., Boston, 1985—; prin. investigator radiation therapy oncology group, chem. modifiers of cancer treatment NIH, 1983—; chmn. sensitizer protector working group DCT, NIH, Bethesda, 1985—; mem. radiation study sect. NIH, Bethesda, 1988-92; mem. Nat. Cancer adv. bd. subcom. Nat. Cancer Program, 1993-94; mem. Nat. Cancer Inst. Divsn. of Treatment Bd. of Sci. Councilors, 1995—. Author: (monograph) Chemical Modifiers of Radiotherapy and Chemotherapy, 1989; editor: (monograph) Interaction of Radiation and Chemotherapy, 1986. Lt. col. USPHS, 1972-74. Fellow ACP, Am. Coll. Radiology (sec.-treas., soc. chmn. acad. radiology oncology programs), Am. Soc. Therapeutic Radiology and Oncology, Am. Soc. Clin. Oncology (bd. dirs.), Radiation Rsch. Soc. (counselor 1992-94, v.p. elect 1995); mem. Phi Beta Kappa, Alpha Omega Alpha. Democrat. Office: Joint Ctr Radiation Therapy 330 Brookline Ave Boston MA 02115-6013

COLEMAN, D. JACKSON, ophthalmologist, educator; b. Waverly, N.Y., Dec. 1, 1934; s. Max Elliot and Frances Agnes (Henton) C.; m. Jane Marie Holmes, July 6, 1963; children: Jeffrey, Jonathan, Jeremy. B.S., Union Coll., 1956; M.D., U. Buffalo, 1960. Intern Columbia Med. Div., Bellevue Hosp., N.Y.C., 1960-61; lt. comdr. USPHS Bur. State Services Heart Disease Control Program, Washington, 1961-64; resident in ophthalmology Edward S. Harkness Eye Inst., Columbia Presbyn. Med. Center, N.Y.C., 1964-67, mem. faculty, staff, 1967-79; John Milton McLean prof. Cornell U. Med. Coll., N.Y.C., 1979—; chmn. dept. ophthalmology N.Y. Hosp.-Cornell Med. Ctr., 1979—, ophthalmologist-in-chief, 1979—. Sr. author: Ultrasonography of Eye and Orbit, 1977; contbr. articles to med. jours. Recipient Wacker award of Club Jules Gonin Internat. Retina Soc., 1976, Lucien Howe medal, 1988; NIH grantee. Fellow ACS, Am. Acad. Ophthalmology; mem. Am. Inst. Ultrasound Medicine (bd. govs. 1970-73), Am. Ophthamolgy Soc., Am. Retina Soc. (v.p. 1989-91, pres. 1991-93), Assn. Rsch. Ophthamology (Weisenfeld award 1996), Societas Interationalis de Diagnostic Ultrasonica in Ophthalmology (exec. bd. 1971-81), World Fedn. Ultrasound Medicine and Biology (exec. bd. 1973-82, sec.treas. 1973-77, treas. 1977-82), Am. Intraocular Lens Soc. (sci. advisor 1976-79), Am. Soc. Ophthalmic Ultrasound (bd. govs. 1976—), AMA, N.Y. County Med. Soc., Am. Eye Study Club, Jules Gonin Club (exec. com. 1992—, v.p. 1993—). Republican. Methodist. Office: NY Hosp-Cornell Med Ctr 525 E 68th St New York NY 10021-4873

COLEMAN, FRANCIS XAVIER, health systems administrator; b. Carbondale, Pa., Aug. 7, 1956; s. Francis and Rosemary (Mussari) C.; children: Kevin, David, Kellie. BS, U. Scranton, 1978; physician asst. degree, King's Coll., 1981. Cert. physicians asst. Surg. physicians asst. St. Vincent's Med. Ctr., S.I., N.Y., 1982-83; staff physician asst. Fed. Bur. of Prisons, Otisville, N.Y., 1983-88, asst. health svc. adminstr., 1988-90; health svc. adminstr. Fed. Bur. of Prisons, Loretto, Pa., 1990-91, Butner, N.C., 1991-92; regional health systems adminstr. Fed. Bur. of Prisons, Annapolis Junction, Md., 1992-95; asst. nat. health systems adminstr. Fed. Bur. of Prisons, Washington, 1995—. Office: Fed Bur of Prisons 320 First St NW Washington DC 20534

COLEMAN, JAMES EUGENE, national laboratory administrator; b. Bronx, N.Y., Sept. 6, 1945; s. James Michael and Helen Mary (Nathan) C.; m. Therese A. Carrieres, Aug. 8, 1970; 1 child, Jean Marie. BA in English, Coll. Santa Fe, 1969; MA in Pub. Adminstrn., U. N.Mex., 1971. Adminstrv. asst. to city mgr. City of Albuquerque, 1971-73; dean, asst. prof. U. Albuquerque, 1973-76; asst. dir. Tng. Ctr. Dept. Energy, Rsch. and Devel., Oak Ridge, Tenn., 1976-78; assoc. dir. Exec. Seminar Ctr. CSC, Office Pers. Mgmt., Kings Point, N.Y., 1978-80; chief of staff Adminstrn. Divsn. Lawrence Berkeley Lab. U. Calif., Berkeley, 1980-84; v.p. human resources AmeriWest Fin. Corp., Albuquerque, 1984-85; assoc. dir for adminstrn. Thomas Jefferson Nat. Accelerator Facility (formerly CEBAF), Newport News, Va., 1985—; adj. instr. U. N.Mex., Albuquerque, 1975. Mem. charter revision com. City Govt. Albuquerque, 1974. With USMC, 1965-67, Vietnam. Mem. ASPA, Peninsula Track Club (pres. 1995, 96), Peninsula Triathlon Club, Peninsula Bicycling Assn., Phi Delta Kappa. Office: CEBAF 12000 Jefferson Ave Newport News VA 23606-4323

COLEMAN, JEAN BLACK, nurse, physician assistant; b. Sharon, Pa., Jan. 11, 1925; d. Charles B. and Sue E. (Dougherty) Black; m. Donald A. Coleman, July 3, 1946; children: Sue Ann Lopez, Donald Ashley. RN, Spencer Hosp. Sch. Nursing, Meadville, Pa., 1945; student Vanderbilt U., 1952-54. Nurse, dir. nursing Bulloch Meml. Hosp., Statesboro, Ga., 1948-51, nurse supr. surgery, 1954-67, dir. nursing, 1967-71; physicians asst., nurse anesthetist to Robert H. Swint, Statesboro, 1971—; mem. Pa. adv. com. Ga. Med. Bd., 1989—. Recipient Dean Day Smith Svc. to Mankind award, 1995; named Woman of Yr. in Med. Field, Bus. and Profl. Women, 1980. Mem. ANA, Ga. Nurses Assn., Am. Acad. Physicians Assts., Ga. Assn. Physicians Assts. (bd. dirs. 1975-79, v.p. 1979-80, pres. 1980-81), Ga. Bd. Med. Examiners (mem. physician assts. adv. com. 1987—, ex-officio mem. 1994). Democrat. Roman Catholic.

COLEMAN, JOHN WILLIAM, urologist; b. Jersey City, Jan. 26, 1939; s. John William and Marion Cecille (McAuliffe) C.; m. Rosemary Elizabeth Romano, July 13, 1963 (div. 1984). AB, Georgetown U., 1960, MD, 1964. Diplomate Am. Bd. Urology. Intern, resident, chief resident surgery NY Hosp., 1964-72, asst. attending surgeon urology, 1972-75; assoc. attending urologist NY Hosp./Cornell Med. Ctr., 1975—; assoc. prof. urology Cornell Med. Coll., 1975—. Fellow Am. Coll. Surgeons, Am. Acad. Pediatrics; mem. Asian Surg. Soc., Chinese Am. Med. Soc., Soc. Pediat. Urology, Soc. Urologie Internat. Roman Catholic. Office: 53 E 70th St New York NY 10021

COLEMAN, MORTON, oncologist, hematologist; b. Norfolk, Va., Sept. 15, 1939; s. Isadore and Bessie (Levin) C.; m. Joyce Goodman, May 26, 1968; children: Ingrid Alexandra, Benjamin Lee, Abigail Rachael. AA, Coll. William and Mary, 1958; BA, Johns Hopkins U., 1959; MD, Med. Coll. Va., 1963. Diplomate Nat. Bd. Med. Examiners, Am. Bd. Internal Medicine, Am. Bd. Hematology, Am. Bd. Clin. Oncology. Intern Grady Meml. Hosp.-Emory U. Med. Ctr., Atlanta, 1963-64, resident, 1964-65; resident N.Y. Hosp.-Cornell U. Med. Ctr., N.Y.C., 1967-68; NIH fellow in hematology Cornell U. Med. Coll., 1968-70, asst. prof. medicine, 1970-74, assoc. prof., 1974-86, clin. prof., 1986—; asst. attending N.Y. Hosp., N.Y.C., 1970-74, assoc. attending, 1974-85, attending, 1986—, assoc. dir. oncology svc., 1974-86, assoc. program dir. Nat. Cancer Inst. Clin. Chemotherapy Program in Cancer Control, 1974-80; attending staff Manhattan Eye and Ear Hosp., 1972-82, Doctors Hosp., 1973-90, Beth Israel North Med. Ctr., 1990-94. Chmn. new agts. com. Cancer and Leukemia Group B, 1975-82; chmn. bd. dirs. Fund for Blood and Cancer Rsch., 1975—; sci. advisor United Leukemia Fund, 1976-82; cons. New Rochelle Med. Ctr., N.Y., 1986—;

assoc. editor Cancer Investigation, 1987—; program chmn. N.Y. Cancer Soc., 1992-93, sec., 1993-94, treas., 1994-95, v.p., 1995—; chmn. lymphoma/Hodgkin's diseases symposium com. Internat. Union Against Cancer Congress, 1993-94; internat. adv. bd. Indian Jour. Med. and Pediatric Oncology, 1994—; co-chairman clin. rsch. rev. com. Israel Cancer Rsch. Fund., 1988-93, Internat. Adv., Cancer Care Trust and Rsch. Found. India, 1994— V.p. alumni coun. Cornell U. Med. Ctr., 1992-94, pres., 1994-96. Lt. comdr. USN, 1965-67. Disting. Alumni award Old Dominion U., 1994. Fellow ACP; mem. AAAS, AMA, Am. Assn. Cancer Rsch., Am. Fedn. Clin. Rsch., Am. Radium Soc., Am. Soc. Clin. Oncology, Am. Soc. Hematology, Am. Heart Assn., Cornell U. Med. Ctr. Alumni Assn., Harvey Soc., Internat. Soc. Hematology, Internat. Soc. Thrombosis and Hemostasis, N.Y. Acad. Sci., N.Y. State Soc. Med. Oncology and Hematology (mem. exec. com., 1991—), Soc. Study of Blood, N.Y. State Med. Soc., N.Y. County Med. Soc., Indian Soc. Med. and Pediat. Oncology, Alpha Omega Alpha, Sigma Zeta. Research publs. on blood, cancer. Office: 407 E 70th St New York NY 10021-5302 also: NY Hosp-Cornell U Med Ctr Div Hematology-Oncology 525 E 68th St New York NY 10021-4873

COLEMAN, RALPH EDWARD, nuclear medicine physician; b. Otwell, Ind., Jan. 2, 1943; s. Ralph H. and Roxie Ellen (Arnold) C.; children: Kathryn Kinsley, Emily Elizabeth, Matthew Edward. BA, U. Evansville, 1965; MD, Washington U., 1968. Diplomate Am. Bd. Nuclear Medicine, Am. Bd. Internal Medicine. Intern Barnes Hosp., St. Louis, 1968-69; med. resident Royal Victoria Hosp., Montreal, Que., Can., 1969-70; resident Mallinckrodt Inst. Radiology, St. Louis, 1972-74, asst. prof., 1974-76; assoc. prof. U. Utah Med. Ctr., Salt Lake City, 1976-78; prof. Duke U. Med. Ctr., Durham, 1978—. Author: ACR Nuclear Radiology Syllabus, 1983, 2d edit., 1990, Diagnostic Nuclear Medicine, 3d edit., 1995; assoc. editor Jour. Nuclear Medicine, 1989—. Capt. U.S. Army, 1970-72. Fellow Am. Coll. Radiology, Am. Coll. Chest Physicians; mem. Soc. Nuclear Medicine (trustee 1985-88, 89-93, pres. Southeastern chpt. 1987-88), Am. Coll. Nuclear Physicians, Radiol. Soc. N.Am., Inst. for Clin. Positron Emission Tomography (pres. 1990). Office: Duke U Med Ctr PO Box 3949 Rm 1419 Durham NC 27710

COLEMAN, RICHARD WALTER, biology educator; b. San Francisco, Sept 10, 1922; s. John Crisp and Reta (Walter) C.; m. Mildred Bradley, Aug. 10, 1949 (dec.); 1 child, Persis C. BA, U. Calif., Berkeley, 1945, PhD, 1951. Rsch. asst. div. entomology and parasitology U. Calif., Berkeley, 1946-47, 49-50; ind. rsch., 1951-61; prof. biology, chmn. dept. Curry Coll., Milton, Mass., 1961-63; chmn. div. scis. and math. Monticello Coll., Godfrey, Ill., 1963-64; vis. prof. biology Wilberforce U., Ohio; 1964-65; prof. sci. Upper Iowa U., Fayette, 1965-89; prof. emeritus sci., 1989—; collaborator natural history div. Nat. Park Svc., 1952; spl. cons. Arctic Health Rsch. Ctr., USPHS, Alaska, 1954-62; apptd. explorer Commr. N.W. Ty., Yellowknife N.W. Ty., Can., 1966. Contbr. articles to profl. reports. Mem. AAAS, Nat. Health Fedn., Iowa Acad. Sci., Geol. Soc. Iowa (affiliate), Am. Inst. Biol. Scis., Nat. Sci. Tchrs. Assn., Ecol. Soc. Am., Am. Soc. Limnology and Oceanography, Am. Bryological and Lichenological Soc., Arctic Inst. N.Am., N.Am. Benthological Soc., Am. Malacological Union, Assn. Midwestern Coll. Biology Tchrs., The Nature Conservancy, Nat. Assn. Biology Tchrs., Fla. Auctioneers Assn., Nat. Auctioneers Assn., Sigma Xi. Methodist.

COLEMAN, RICKEY JOE, physician; b. San Diego, Mar. 11, 1961; s. Ronnie Joe Coleman and Janie Sue (Crane) Payte; m. Angela Marie Lawler, Mar. 6, 1981; children: Jeremy, Paige, Austin. Odessa Jr. Coll., Tex., 1988, U. Tex. of the Permian Basin, 1989; DO, Tex. Coll. Osteopathic Medicine, 1993. Family practice resident U. Tex. Tech. Health Scis. Ctr., Odessa, 1993-95; Carson City Hosp., Mich., 1995—. Office: Carson City Hosp 406 E Elm St Box 879 Carson City MI 48811-0879

COLEMAN, ROBERT TRENT, social worker, rehabilitation consultant; b. Gary, Ind., Feb. 4, 1936; s. Robert Clinton and Lucille Verna C.; m. Dorothy Agnes, Aug. 1957; children: Sean, Bryce, Daniel; m. 2d, Patricia Lou, June 13, 1976; m. 3d Polly Anderson, Sept. 15, 1984. BA in Speech Therapy, U. Wash., Seattle, 1962; postgrad. in speech U. Redlands, 1963-64; MS in Rehab. Counseling, U. Oreg., 1971. Cert. rehab. counselor, cert. ins. rehab. specialist. Social worker, San Bernardino City Welfare Dept., 1963-64; correctional counselor Calif. Rehab. Center, Norco, 1964-67; sr. counselor Job Corps, Clearfield, Utah, 1967; assoc. dir. Ednl. Systems Corp., Washington, 1968-69; ptnr. Black Fir Jade Mines, Big Sur, Calif., 1971-76; vocat. specialist Internat. Rehab. Assn., San Diego, 1976-77; vocat. rehab. counselor Sharp Hosp., San Diego, 1977-80; clin. coord. San Diego Pain Inst., 1981; cons. in rehab. counseling, career guidance, human rels., Carlsbad, Calif., 1981—; propr. R.T.C. Cons. Svcs., Escondido, 1983—; vocat. rehab. expert Civil Ct., 1983—. Commr., Handicapped Appeals Commn., San Marcos, Calif., 1981-83. Served with U.S. Army, 1955-58. Mem. ACA, San Diego Career Guidance Assn. (pres. 1984), Assn. Indsl. Rehab. Reps. (pres. 1983), Am. Rehab. Counseling Assn., Nat. Assn. Rehab. Profls. in Pvt. Sector (standards and ethics com. 1986—, chmn. 1988-90). Republican. Home: 538 Glenheather Dr San Marcos CA 92069-2005 Office: 538 Glenheather Dr San Marcos CA 92069

COLEMAN, ROGER DIXON, bacteriologist; b. Rockwell, Iowa, Jan. 18, 1915; s. Major C. and Hazel Ruth Coleman; A.B., UCLA, 1937; postgrad. Balliol Coll., Oxford (Eng.) U., 1944; MS, U. So. Calif., 1952, PhD, 1957; m. Lee Aden Skov, Jan. 1, 1978. Sr. laboratorian Napa (Calif.) State Hosp., 1937-42; dir. Long Beach (Calif.) Clin. Lab., 1946-86, pres., 1980-86; mem. Calif. State Clin. Lab. Commn., 1953-57. Served as officer AUS, 1942-46. Diplomate Am. Bd. Bioanalysts. Mem. Am. Assn. Bioanalysts, Am. Assn. Clin. Chemists, Am. Soc. Microbiologists, Am. Chem. Soc., Am. Venereal Disease Assn., AAAS (life), Calif. Assn. Bioanalysts (past officer), Med. Research Assn. Calif., Bacteriology Club So. Calif., Sigma Xi, Phi Sigma (past chpt. pres.). Author papers in field. Home: 7 Laguna Woods Dr Laguna Niguel CA 92677-2829 Office: PO Box 7073 Laguna Niguel CA 92607-7073

COLEMAN, ROGER LEWIS, psychiatrist; b. N.Y.C., Feb. 14, 1945; s. Jerome Byron and Evelyn Rose C.; m. Dalia Gelman; children: Jenifer Suzanne, Claire Elise, Jonathan Charles; stepchildren: Miri Goldman, Avi Laub. BA cum laude, Harvard U., 1967; MD, Tufts U., 1971; MPH, U. Calif., Berkeley, 1976. Intern Mary's Help Hosp., Daly City, Calif., 1971-72; resident in psychiatry San Mateo (Calif.) Mental Health Service, 1971-72; asst. profl. psychology U. Alaska, Fairbanks, 1972-73, lectr. behavioral scis., 1973-74; asst. profl. health scis. Alaska Meth. U., Anchorage, 1974-75; resident, fellow dept. psychiatry Yale U., New Haven, 1976-78; dir. psychiatry inpatient unit Danbury (Conn.) Hosp., 1978-83; dir. psychiatry Meml. Hosp., Meriden, Conn., 1983-92; chief profl. svcs. Cedarcrest Regional Hosp, Newington, Conn., 1992—; assoc. clin. prof. psychiatry U. Conn.; asst. prof. psychiatry N.Y. Med. Coll., 1979-83; asst. clin. prof. psychiatry Yale U., 1983—. Served with USPHS, 1972-75. Fellow Am. Psychiat. Assn.; mem. AMA, Am. Statis. Assn., Soc. for Med. Decision Making, Am. Soc. Quality Control. Office: 525 Russell Rd Newington CT 06111-1538

COLEMAN, ROY MELVIN, psychiatrist; b. N.Y.C., June 10, 1930; s. Samuel C. and Augusta (Singer) C.; children: David, Robert. AB, Harvard U., 1952; MD, U. Rochester, 1959. Diplomate Am. Bd. Psychiatry and Neurology, Am. Psychoanalytic Assn. Intern Michael Reese Hosp., Chgo., 1959-60; resident in psychiatry McLean Hosp., Belmont, Mass., 1960-62, 63-64, Beth Israel Hosp., Boston, 1962-63; clin. practice of psychiatry Boston and Washington, 1960—; clin. practice psychoanalysis Washington, 1967—; teaching fellow in psychiatry Harvard Med. Sch., Boston, 1960-64; instr. psychiatry Harvard Med. Sch., 1964-67; faculty Washington Psychoanalytic Inst., Washington, 1976—; asst. prof. George Washington U. Med. Ctr., Washington, 1967-72; assoc. prof. George Washington U. Med. Ctr., 1972-74, assoc. clin. prof., 1974-78, clin. prof. psychiatry, 1978—; participant psychoanalytical tng. Wash. Psychoanalytic Inst., Washington, 1967-74; cons. St. Elizabeth Hosp., Washington, 1983-88; adj. prof. dept. psychiatry Georgetown U. Sch. Medicine, 1994—. Book reviewer Am. Jour. Psychiatry, 1968-74; corr. editor The Am. Psychoanalyst, 1988—; bd. editors Jour. Clin. Psychoanalysis, 1990—. Bd. trustees Nat. Capital Med. Found., Washington, 1981-84. Fellow Am. Psychiat. Assn. (cons. ethics com. 1994-95); mem. AMA, Am. Psychoanaltic Assn., Washington Psychiat. Soc. (chmn. ethics com. 1977-89), Washington Psychoanalytic Soc. (chmn. ethics com. 1979-80), Ctr. for Advanced Psychoanalytic Studies, Harvard Club Washington, Cosmos Club. Home: 1404 Cola Dr Mc Lean VA 22101-3102 Office: 2201 L St NW Apt 701 Washington DC 20037-1412

COLEMAN, TIMOTHY LOUIS, neurologist; b. Balt., May 31, 1946; s. Wilbur Jerome and Mildred Marie (Pivec) C.; m. Deborah Ann Helfrich, Aug. 22, 1970; 1 child, Sarah Slater. BA in Econs., U. Va., 1968, MD, 1972. Diplomate Am. Bd. Internal Medicine, Am. Bd. Psychiatry and Neurology. Intern Med. U. S.C., Charleston, 1972-73; resident in neurology U. Ky. Med. Ctr., Lexington, 1974-77; resident internal medicine Med. U. S.C., 1973-74; pvt. practice Lexington, Ky., 1979—. Bd. dirs. Single Parent Housing, Lexington, 1986-91, Sena Neighborhood Assn., Lexington, 1989—, Lexington Philharm., 1995—. Lt. comdr. M.C., USNR, 1977-79. Fellow Am. Acad. Neurology; mem. ACP, AMA, Ky. Med. Assn., Fayette County Med. Soc. Home: 1363 Strawberry Ln Lexington KY 40502-2744 Office: 1800 Nicholasville Rd Lexington KY 40503-1433

COLEMAN, WARREN OSWIN, thoracic and cardiovascular surgeon, educator; b. New Orleans, July 5, 1930; s. Warren O. and Thelma (Furey) C.; m. Elizabeth Jean Fortenberry, Jan. 1, 1955; children: Pamela, Mark, Michael, Susan. BS, Tulane U., 1951; MD, La. State U., 1955. Diplomate Am. Bd. Surgery, Am. Bd. Thoracic Surgery Resident in surgery Sch. Medicine La. State U., New Orleans, 1956-57, 59-62, resident in thoracic surgery, 1962-64; pvt. practice New Orleans, 1964-74; capt., dep. chief of surgery USPHS, New Orleans, 1975-81; assoc. prof. surgery Sch. Medicine La. State U., Shreveport, 1981—; dep. chief of surgery Conway Divsn. La. State U., Monroe, La., 1981—. Mem. exec. com. KEDM Pub. Radio, Monroe, 1991-95; v.p., bd. dirs. Monroe Symphony Orch., 1989-90. Capt. Med. Corps, USAF, 1957-59. Fellow ACS, Am. Coll. Chest Physicians, Am. Coll. Angiology; mem. AMA, So. Thoracic Surg. Assn., Southeastern Surg. Congress, Alpha Omega Alpha. Democrat. Roman Catholic. Home: 3505 Deborah Dr Monroe LA 71201 Office: La State U Shreveport-EA Conway Divsn 4864 Jackson St Monroe LA 71201

COLEN, LAWRENCE BRUCE, plastic surgeon; b. N.Y.C., May 14, 1951; s. Leslie Colen and Ruth (Mintz) C.; married, 1982; children: Eva, Henry, David. BA, Colgate U., 1972; MD, Dartmouth U., 1975. Intern in surgery U. Calif. San Francisco, 1975-76, resident in surgery, 1976-81, resident in plastic surgery, 1981-83; fellow in hand and microsurgery Davies Med. Ctr., San Francisco, 1978-79; assoc. prof. surgery Dartmouth Med. Sch., 1983-90, Eastern Va. Med. Sch., Norfolk, 1990—. Recipient Marko Godina award Am. Soc. for Reconstructive Microsurgery. Mem. numerous plastic surgery socs. Office: Eastern Va Med Sch 880 Kempsville Rd Ste 2600 Norfolk VA 23509

COLERIDGE, SAMUEL TIMOTHY, osteopath, family physician, army officer, educator; b. Akron, Ohio, Aug. 18, 1945; m. Maryann Belko, May 16, 1978; children: Elizabeth, Jessica, Megan, Melissa. BS, U. Akron, 1967; DO, Coll. Osteo. Medicine, Kansas City, Mo., 1971. Diplomate Am. Bd. Family Practice, Am. Bd. Emergency Medicine, Am. Osteo. Bd. Family Practice, Am. Osteo. Bd. Emergency Medicine. Commd. 2d lt. U.S. Army, 1971, col., 1985, ret., 1991; chief family practice, emergency svc. U.S. Army 2d Gen. Hosp., Landstuhl, Germany, 1972-75; chief emergency med. svcs. Silas Hays Army Hosp., Monterey, Calif., 1975-76; cmmdr. 913th med. detachment 7th med. command U.S. Army, Kaiserslauter, Germany, 1976-79; chief Ambulatory Care & Emergency Svcs. Army Regional Med. Ctr., Landstuhl, 1979; commdr. 24th med. detachment 7th med. command, Germany, 1979-80; resident emergency medicine Madigan Army Med. Ctr., Tacoma, Wash., 1980-81; chief resident Madigan Army Med. Ctr., Tacoma, 1981; chair emergency svcs., vice chair primary care William Beaumont Army Med. Ctr., El Paso, Tex., 1982-85; chair dept. emergency medicine Brooke Army Med. Ctr., Fort Sam Houston, Tex., 1985-91; prof., chmn. dept. family medicine U. North Tex. Health Sci. Ctr., Fort Worth, 1991—; bd. advisors EMT Tactical Course, Washington, 1990—; chmn. family practice adv. com. Tex. Higher Edn. Coord. Bd, Austin, 1991—; mem. Children's Health Coun., Ft. Worth, 1992—. Author: (with others) Clinical Procedures in Emergency Medicine, 1985, 91, Emergency Medicine: An Approach to Clinical Problem Solving, 1991, Medical Malpractice: Handling Emergency Cases, 1991; reviewer Acad. Emergency Medicine, Jour. Am. Osteo. Assn. Cons. in Emergency Medicine, Surgeon Gen. U.S., Washington, 1986-91, Health Svcs. Command in Emergency Medicine, Fort Sam Houston, Tex., 1985-91; mem. Tarrant County Cancer Consortium, Ft. Worth, 1992—, Tarrant County Med. Edn. Consortium, Primary Care Inst., Ft. Worth, 1994-95. Fellow Am. Coll. Emergency Physicians (bd. dirs. govt. svcs. chap, pres. elect 1986, pres. 1987), Am Coll. Osteo. Emergency Physicians (bd. dirs., sec.-treas. 1992-96); mem. Am. Osteo. Assn. (bd. dirs., v.p. 1987-92), Assn. of Mil. Osteo. Physicians (bd. dirs., v.p., pres. 1984), Nat. Registry Emergency Med. Technicians (treas., vice chmn. 1989—). Roman Catholic. Office: U N Tex. Health Sci Ctr 3500 Camp Bowie Blvd Fort Worth TX 76107

COLES, ANNA LOUISE BAILEY, university official, nurse; b. Kansas City, Kans., Jan. 16, 1925; d. Gordon Alonzo and Lillie Mai (Buchanan) Bailey; children: Margot, Michelle, Gina. Diploma, Freedmen's Hosp. Sch. Nursing, 1948; B.S. in Nursing, Avila Coll., Kansas City, Mo., 1958; M.S. in Nursing, Cath. U. Am., 1960, Ph.D. in Higher Edn., 1967. Instr. VA Hosp., Topeka, 1950-52; supr. VA Hosp., Kansas City, Mo., 1952-58; asst. dir. inservice edn. Freedmen's Hosp., Washington, 1960-61; adminstrv. asst. to dir. nursing Freedmen's Hosp., 1961-66, assoc. dir. nursing services, 1966-67, dir. nursing, 1967-69; dean Howard U. Coll. Nursing, Washington, 1968-86, dean emeritus, 1986—; cons. pvt. practice, Kansas City, Kans.; dir. minority devel. U. Kans., 1991-95; cons. Gen. Research Support Program, NIH, 1972-76, VA health care com. NRC-Nat. Acad. Scis., 1975-76, VA Central Office continuing edn. com., 1976—; pres. Nurses Examining Bd., 1967-68; mem. Inst. Medicine, Nat. Acad. Scis., 1974—; Mem. D.C. Health Planning Adv. Com., 1968-71, Tri-State Regional Planning Com. for Nursing Edn., 1969, Health Adv. Council, Nat. Urban Coalition 1971-73. Contbr. articles to profl. jours. Bd. dirs. Iona Whipper Home for Unwed Mothers, 1970-72; bd. dirs. Nursing Edn. Opportunities, 1970-72; trustee Community Group Health Found., 1976-77, cons., 1977—; bd. regents State Univ. System Fla., 1977; adv. bd. Am. Assn. Med. Vols., 1970-72. Recipient sustained superior performance award HEW, 1962, Meritorious Pub. Svc. award Govt. of D.C., 1968, medal of honor Avila Coll., 1969, Disting. Alumni award Howard U. Nat. Assn. for Equal Opportunity in Higher Edn., 1990, cmty. svc. award Black Profl. Nurses Kansas City, 1991, lifetime achievement award Assn. Black Nursing Faculty in Higher Edn., 1993, svc. award Midwest Regional Conf. on Black Families and Children, 1994. Mem. Nat. League Nursing (dir.), Am. Nurses Assn., Freedmen's Hosp. Nursing Alumni Assn., Am. Congress Rehab. Medicine, Am. Assn. Colls. of Nursing (sec. 1975-76), Societas Docta, Inc. (charter, pres. 1996—), Sigma Theta Tau, Alpha Kappa Alpha. Home: 15107 Interlachen Dr #205 Silver Spring MD 20906

COLES, ROBERT, child psychiatrist, educator, author; b. Boston. Mass., Oct. 12, 1929; s. Philip and Sandra (Young) C.; m. Jane Hallowell; children—Robert, Daniel, Michael. A.B., Harvard U., 1950; M.D., Columbia U., 1954; M.D. (hon.), Temple U., Notre Dame U., Bates Coll., 1972, Wayne State U., 1973, Western Mich. U., Holy Cross Coll., 1974, Hofstra U., 1975, Coll. William and Mary, Bard Coll., U. Lowell, U. Cin., 1976, Stonehill Coll., Lesley Coll., Rutgers U., 1977, Wesleyan U., Columbia Coll., Knox Coll., Cleve. State U., Wooster Coll., 1978, U. N.C., Manhattan Coll., St. Peter's Coll., Coll. New Rochelle, Pratt Inst. and Sch. Design, 1979, Berea Coll., Bklyn. Coll., Emmanuel Coll., 1980, Colby Coll., 1981, Sienna Heights Coll., Salem State Coll., Williams Coll., 1983, Beloit Coll., 1984, Emory U., Fairfield U., Macalaster Coll., Colgate U., 1986, Dartmouth Coll., 1987. Intern U. Chgo. Clinics, 1954-55; resident in psychiatry Mass. Gen. Hosp., Boston, 1955-56, McLean Hosp., Belmont, Mass., 1956-57, Judge Baker Guidance Center-Children's Hosp., 1957-58; mem. staff children's Unit Met. State Hosp., Waltham, Mass., 1957-58; mem. staff alcoholic clinic Mass. Gen. Hosp.; teaching fellow in psychiatry, mem. psychiat. staff and clin. asst. in psychiatry Harvard Med. Sch., 1955-58; research psychiatrist Harvard U. Health Services, 1963—; lectr. gen. edn. Harvard U., 1966—, prof. psychiatry and med. humanities, 1977—; child psychiat. fellow Judge Baker Guidance Center, Children's Hosp., Boston, 1960-61; mem. Nat. Adv. Com. on Farm Labor, 1965—; cons. Appalachian Vols., 1965—, Rockefeller Found., 1969—, Ford Found., 1969—; mem. Inst. of Medicine, Nat. Acad. Scis., 1973-78; vis. prof. public policy Duke U., 1973—; cons. supr. dept. psychiatry Cambridge (Mass.) Hosp., 1976—; cons. Center for Study of So. Culture, U. Miss., 1979—; bd. dirs. Ctr. for Documentary Studies, Duke U.; vis. prof. psychiatry, Dartmouth Coll., 1989. Author: Children of Crisis: A Study of Courage and Fear, 1967, Dead End School, 1968, Still Hungry in America, 1969, The Grass Pipe, 1969, The Image is Yours, 1969; Wages of Neglect, 1969, Uprooted Children: The Early Lives of Migrant Farmers, 1970, Teachers and the Children of Poverty, 1970, Erik H. Erikson: The Growth of His Work, 1970, The Middle Americans, 1970, Migrants, Sharecroppers and Mountaineers, 1972, The South Goes North, 1972, Saving Face, 1972, Farewell to the South, 1972, A Spectacle Unto the World, 1973, Riding Free, 1973, The Darkness and the Light, 1974, The Buses Roll, 1974, Irony in the Mind's Life: Essays on Novels by James Agee, Elizabeth Bowen and George Eliot, 1974, Headsparks, 1975, The Mind's Fate, 1975, Eskimos, Chicanos and Indians, 1978, Privileged Ones, Vol. V of Children in Crisis book series, 1978, (with Jane Hallowell Coles) Women of Crisis Lives of Struggle and Hope, 1978, Walker Percy: An American Search, 1978, Flannery O'Connor's South, 1980, Women of Crisis; Lives of Work and Dreams, 1980, Dorothea Lange: Photographs of a Lifetime, 1982, (with Ross Spears) Agee, 1985, The Political Life of Children, 1986, Dorothy Day: A Radical Devotion, 1987, Simone Weil: A Modern Pilgrimage, 1987, Times of Surrender: Selected Essays, 1988, Harvard Diary, 1988, That Red Wheelbarrow, 1988, The Call of Stories: Teaching and the Moral Imagination, 1989, Rumors of Separate Worlds, 1989, The Spiritual Life of Children, 1990; contbg. editor: The New Republic, 1966—, Am. Poetry Rev, 1972—, Aperture, 1974—, Lit. and Medicine, 1981—, New Oxford Rev, 1981—; mem. editorial bd.: Integrated Edn., 1967—, Child Psychiatry and Human Devel., 1969—, Rev. of Books and Religion, 1976—, Internat. Jour. Family Therapy, 1977—, Grants mag., 1977—, Learning mag., 1978—, Jour. Am. Culture, 1977—, Jour. Edn., 1979—; bd. editors: Parents' Choice, 1978—; editor: Children and Youth Services Rev., 1978—. Bd. dirs. Field Found., 1968—; trustee Robert F. Kennedy Meml., 1968—, Robert F. Kennedy Action Corps, State of Mass., 1968—, Miss. Inst. Early Childhood Edn., 1968—, Twentieth Century Fund, 1971—; bd. dirs. Reading is Fundamental, Smithsonian Inst., 1968—, Am. Freedom from Hunger Found., 1968—, Am. Parents Com., 1971—; mem. corp. Boston Children's Service, 1970; mem. adv. council Inst. for Nonviolent Social Change of Martin Luther King, Jr. Meml. Center, 1971—, Ams. for Children's Relief, 1972—; mem. nat. com. for Edn. of Young Children, 1972—; mem. nat. adv. council Rural Am., 1976—; trustee Austen Riggs Found., Stockbridge, Mass., 1976—; mem. nat. adv. com. Ala. Citizens for Respor ive Public Television, 1976—; mem. adv. com. Nat. Indian Edn. Assn., 1976—; visitor's com. mem. Boston Mus. Fine Arts, 1977; bd. dirs. Boys Club Boston, 1977; vis. com. Boston Coll. Law Sch., 1977; adv. Center for So. Folklore, 1978—; mem. children's com. Edna McConnell Clark Found., 1978—; bd. dirs. Lyndhurst Found., 1978—; mem. nat. adv. bd. Foxfire Fund, Inc., 1979—. Recipient Ralph Waldo Emerson prize Phi Beta Kappa, 1967; Anisfield-Wolf award in race relations Saturday Rev., 1968; Hofheimer award Am. Psychiat. Assn., 1968; Sidney Hillman prize, 1971; Weatherford prize Berea Coll. and Council So. Mountains, 1973; Lilliam Smith Award So. Regional Council, 1973; McAlpin medal Nat. Assn. Mental Health, 1972; Pulitzer prize, 1973 (all received for Children of Crisis, Vols. II, III); disting. scholar medal Hofstra U., 1974; William A. Shonfeld award Am. Soc. Adolescent Psychiatry, 1977; MacArthur Found. award, 1981; Josepha Hale award, 1986; fellow Davenport Coll., Yale U., 1976—. Fellow Am. Acad. Arts and Scis., Inst. Soc., Ethics and the Life Scis.; mem. Am. Psychiat. Assn., Am. Orthopsychiat. Assn. (past dir.), Acad. Psychoanalysis, Nat. Orgn. Migrant Children. Home: 81 Carr Rd Concord MA 01742-1852 Office: Harvard U Univ Health Svcs 75 Mt Auburn St Cambridge MA 02138-4901

COLES, TAMMY LYNNE, obstetrician-gynecologist, military officer; b. Salem, N.J., Feb. 22, 1968; d. William Henry and Betty Jane (Leoni) C. BS in Biology, Fla. Inst. Tech., 1990; DO, U. Medicine & Dentistry N.J., 1994. Diplomate Nat. Bd. Osteopathic Examiners. Intern, divisional chief Stratford divsn. Kennedy Meml. Hosp., Stratford, N.J, 1994-95; ob-gyn. resident Monmouth Med. Ctr., Long Branch, N.J, 1995—. Fellow Am. Coll. Ob-Gyn (jr.); mem. AMA, Am. Osteopathic Assn., N.J. Assn. Osteopathic Physicians & Surgeons. Office: Monmouth Med Ctr Dept Ob-Gyn 300 Second Ave Long Branch NJ 07740

COLES, WILLIAM HENRY, ophthalmologist, educator; b. Rochester, N.Y.. BA, Ohio Wesleyan U., 1958; MD, Emory U., 1962; MS, La. State U., 1970. Diplomate Am. Bd. Ophthalmology. Intern Grady Hosp., Atlanta, 1962-63; resident Charity-La. State U., New Orleans, 1966-70; prof. ophthalmology Emory U., Atlanta, 1980-86, dir. postgrad. edn., 1981-86; prof. ophthalmology SUNY, Buffalo, 1986—, chmn. dept., 1986—; clin. assoc. prof. Med. Univ. S.C., Charleston, 1980-86; chief of svc. Grady Meml. Hosp., Atlanta, 1981-84; chief ophthalmology svc. VA Hosp., Atlanta, 1984-86. Author: Ophthalmology: A Diagnostic Text, 1989; sect. editor: Medicine for the Practicing Physician, 1984 (Med. Textbook of Yr. award). Nat. Eye Inst. grantee, 1975-78. Mem. AMA, ACS, AAUP, Am. Acad. Ophthalmology (Disting. Svc. award 1989), Med. Soc. State of N.Y., Assn. Rsch. and Vision in Ophthalmology, Assn. Univ. Profs. in Ophthalmology (trustee). Home: RR 96 Box 503 E Booth Bay ME 04544 Office: SUNY Dept Ophthalmology 462 Grider St Rm 1168 Buffalo NY 14215-3075

COLESON, SARRAH LYNN, women's health nurse, critical care nurse; b. Quonset Point, R.I., June 11, 1954; d. William Peter and Glenda Sue (Young) C. BA, U. Albuquerque, 1978, ADN, 1986. Staff nurse labor and delivery Presbyn. Hosp., Albuquerque, 1980-88; staff nurse ICU, house coord. St. Hoseph's Heights Hosp., Albuquerque, 1988—.

COLLADO, CAROL BUTLER, international health consultant, nursing educator; b. N.Y.C., Aug. 28, 1940. BS, Nazareth Coll. of Rochester, 1962; MN, U. Wash., 1968. RN, N.Y., Md. Staff nurse various N.Y.C. hosps., 1962-64; asst. clin. instr. Bellevue-Mills Sch. Nursing, N.Y.C., 1964-65; asst. instr., staff nurse II Cornell U. N.Y. Hosp., N.Y.C., 1965-67; nurse educator (Mex. and Dominican Republic) Pan Am. Health Orgn., WHO, Washington, 1969-76; asst. prof. Coll. Human Devel., Pa. State U., University Park, 1977-79, Duke U., Durham, N.C., 1981-83; staff nurse med.-surg. unit Raleigh (N.C.) Community Hosp., 1981-87; project dir. PINCAP, NEWH, Nursing Consortium, Rocky Mount, N.C., 1983-86; mem. adj. faculty Sch. Nursing George Mason U., Fairfax, Va., 1989—; cons. World Bank, 1988—, Pan Am. Health Organ., 1977—, Coll. of Nursing, Madrid, 1989-90, U. Ill., 1989—, NIH, 1991. Contbr. articles to profl. jours. Mem. ANA, Am. Pub. Health Assn., Nat. League for Nursing (N.C. League for Nursing bd. dirs. 1984-87, program com. 1984-85, membership chmn. 1985-87), Sigma Theta Tau. Home: 13211 Collingwood Ter Silver Spring MD 20904-1419

COLLATT, MARGARET M., nurse; b. John Day, Oreg., Aug. 1953; d. Buddie L. and Oradell F. (Miller) Weaver; children: Lester W. Wall, Joann A. Wall, Jennifer F. AAS, ASN, Blue Mountain Community Coll., 1980; Oreg. Health Scis. U., 1995. Cert. corrections health profl. Staff nurse, charge nurse Ea. Oreg. Tng. Ctr., Pendleton; staff nurse Oreg. Dept. Corrections, Salem, health svcs. mgr.; nursing adv. bd. Ea. Oreg. Hosp. and Tng. Ctr.; tng. specialist health svcs. Oreg. Dept. of Corrections. Mem. Correctional Health Svcs. Assn., Oreg. Nurses Assn. Home: 1985 Oxford St SE Salem OR 97302

COLLAZOS GONZALEZ, JULIO, internist, researcher; b. Tordehumos, Valladolid, Spain, Mar. 11, 1955; s. Pablo Collazos and Concepción González. MD with honors, U. Complutense, Madrid, 1978, internal medicine specialist, 1984; PhD cum laude, U. Autonoma, Madrid, 1990. Resident Found. Jimenez Diaz, Madrid, 1980-84; attending physician Hosp. Provincial, Alicante, Spain, 1984-87; assoc. prof. U. Alicante, 1984-87; attending physician Hosp. de Galdácano, Vizcaya, Spain, 1987-93, chief infectious diseases sect., 1993—. Author, editor: The Tumor Markers in Benign Liver Diseases, 1990; also numerous articles. Grantee Fondo de Investigaciones Sanitarias, Madrid, Dept. de Sanidad del Gobierno Vasco, Vitoria. Mem. Am. Soc. for Microbiology, European Soc. Clin. Microbiology and Infectious Diseases, Assn. Infectious Diseases (pres. Vizcaya, Spain). Office: Sect Infectious Diseases, Hosp de Galdácano, Bo Labeaga s/n Vizcaya 48960, Spain

COLLEN, MORRIS FRANK, physician; b. St. Paul, Nov. 12, 1913; s. Frank Morris and Rose (Finkelstein) C.; m. Frances B. Diner, Sept. 24, 1937; children: Arnold Roy, Barry Joel, Roberta Joy, Randal Harry. BEE, U. Minn., 1934, MB with distinction, 1938, MD, 1939. Diplomate Am. Bd. Internal Medicine. Intern Michael Reese Hosp., Chgo., 1939-40; resident Los Angeles County Hosp., 1940-42; chief med. service Kaiser Found. Hosp., Oakland, Calif., 1942-52; chief of staff Kaiser Found. Hosp., Oakland, 1952-53; med. dir. Permanente Med. Group, West Bay Div., 1953-79, dir. med. methods research, 1962-79, dir. tech. assessment, 1979-83, cons. div. research, 1983—; chmn. exec. com. Permanente Med. Group, Oakland, 1953-73; dir. Permanente Services, Inc., Oakland, 1958-73; lectr. Sch. Pub. Health, U. Calif., Berkeley, 1966-78; lectr. info. sci. U. Calif., San Francisco, 1970-85; lectr. U. London, 1972, Stanford U. Med. Ctr., 1973, 75, 84-86, Harvard U., 1974, Johns Hopkins U., 1976, also others; cons. Bur. Health Services, USPHS, 1965-68, chmn. health care systems study sect., 1968-72, mem. adv. com. demonstration grants, 1967; advisor VA, 1968; cons. European region WHO, 1968-72; cons. med. fitness program U.S. Air Force, 1968; cons. Pres.'s Biomed. Research Panel, 1975; mem. adv. com. automated Multiphasic Health Testing, 1971; discussant Nat. Conf. Preventive Medicine, Bethesda, Md., 1975; mem. com. on tech. in health care NAS, 1976; mem. adv. group Nat. Commn. on Digestive Diseases, U.S. Congress, 1978; mem. adv. panel to U.S. Congress Office of Tech. Assessment, 1980-85; mem. peer rev. adv. group TRIMIS program Dept. Def., 1978-90; program chmn. 3d Internat. Conf. Med. Informatics, Tokyo, 1980; chmn. bd. sci. counselors Nat. Library Medicine, 1985-87. Author: Treatment of Pneumococcic Pneumonia, 1948, Hospital Computer Systems, 1974, Multiphasic Health Testing Services, 1978, Medical Informatics: A Historical Review, 1995; editor: Permanente Med. Bull., 1943-53; mem. editl. bd. Preventive Medicine, 1970-80, Jour. Med. Sys., Methods Info. Medicine, 1980-94, Diagnostic Medicine, 1980-84, Computers in Biomed. Rsch., 1987-94; contbr. articles to med. jours., chpts. to books. Recipient Computers in Health Care Pioneer award, 1992; Johns Hopkins Centennial scholar, 1976; fellow Ctr. Advanced Studies in Behavioral Scis., Stanford U., 1985-86; scholar-in-residence Nat. Libr. Medicine, 1987-96. Fellow ACP, Am. Coll. Cardiology, Am. Coll. Chest Physicians, Am. Inst. Med. and Biol. Engring.; mem. AMA, Inst. Medicine of NAS (chmn. tech. subcom. for improving patient records 1990, chmn. workshop on informatics in clin. preventive medicine 1991), Am. Fedn. Clin. Rsch., Am. Coll. Med. Informatics (pres. 1987-88, Morris F. Collen medal named in his honor 1993), Salutis Unitas (v.p. 1972), Soc. Adv. Med. Sys. (pres. 1973), Nat. Acad. Practice in Medicine (chmn. 1982-88, co-chmn. 1989-91), Am. Med. Informatics Assn. (bd. dirs. 1985-95, Lifetime Achievement award 1992), Internat. Health Evaluation Assn. (pres. 1995-96), Sr. Officers Club, Internat. Med. Informatics Assn., Alpha Omega Alpha, Tau Beta Pi. Home: 4155 Walnut Blvd Walnut Creek CA 94596-5834 Office: 3505 Broadway Oakland CA 94611-5714

COLLEY, KAREN J., medical educator, medical researcher; b. Nov. 3, 1958. BS in Chemistry, Duke U., 1981; PhD in Molecular Biology, Washington U., St. Louis, 1987. Postdoctoral fellow dept. biol. chemistry UCLA, 1987-91; asst. prof. dept. biochemistry U. Ill., Chgo., 1991—; mem. med. adv. bd. Leukemia Rsch. Found., reviewer study sect., 1994—; outside reviewer NSF Grants, 1995—, VA Rsch. Grants, 1995—; reviewer Jour. Biol. Chemistry, Jour. Cell Biology, Molecular and Chem. Neuropathology, Jour. Cell Sci., Devel. Biology. Contbr. articles to profl. jours.; patentee in field. Postdoctoral fellow NIH, 1990, grantee, 1992; Sr. fellow Am. Cancer Soc., 1991, grantee, 1992; U. Ill. grantee, 1992, 96, Leukemia Rsch. Found., Inc., 1993; recipient Established Investigator award Am. Heart Assn., 1996. Mem. AAAS, Am. Soc. Cell Biology, Am. Soc. Biochemistry and Molecular Biology, Soc. Glycobiology, Sigma Xi. Office: U Ill Dept Biochemistry M/C 536 1953 W Polk St Chicago IL 60612

COLLIER, ALBERT M., pediatric educator, child development center director; b. Elba, Ala., May 3, 1937; s. Milford William and Ida Ruth C.; m. Mary Gynell Wehler, July 17, 1960; children: Albert Mark, Dennis Murray, Jonathan Lee. BS, U. Miami, 1959, MD, 1963. Pediatric resident U. Miami, Coral Gables, Fla., 1963-66; infectious diseases fellow U. N.C., Chapel Hill, 1968-70, from asst. prof. to assoc. prof., 1971-80, prof., 1980—, divsn. chief infectious disease, 1980—, assoc. dir. ctr. environ. med. lung bio, 1980—, acting dir. Frank Porter Graham Child Devel. Ctr., 1990-92. Contbr. over 100 articles to profl. jours. Recipient Louis Dienes award Internat. Orgn. Mycoplasmology, Vienna, Austria, 1988. Mem. Gideons (zone leader 1990-93). Baptist. Office: U NC Chapel Hill Dept Pediatrics 535 Burnett-Womack CB 7220 Chapel Hill NC 27599

COLLIER, RICHARD EARL, oncologist; b. St. Louis, Mar. 28, 1927; s. Earl Matthew and Wilma (Pilkinston) C.; m. Marilyn Loomis, Oct. 2, 1950; children: Vivian Collier O'Dell, Barbara Collier Sponberg. BA, Hardin-Simmons U., Abilene, Tex., 1945; MD, U. Tex., Dallas, 1948. Diplomate Am. Bd. Radiology. Intern Baylor U. Med. Ctr., Dallas, 1948-49, asst. resident surgery, 1949-50, resident in radiology, 1953-55, radiologist, 1950—, dir. radiation oncology, 1967—; asst. resident pathology Parkland Meml. Hosp., Dallas, 1950; prof. Baylor U. Med. Ctr., Dallas, 1967-92; clin. prof. U. Tex., Dallas, 1967—; bd. dirs. North Tex. Oncology Ctr., Dallas, North Tex. Regional Cancer Ctr., Dallas, 1987—. Contbr. articles to profl. jours. Chmn. community task group Legis. Task Force on Cancer in Tex., 1985-86, community adv. com. Tex. Cancer Coun., 1986—. Lt. jg. USNR, 1950-52. Fellow Am. Coll. Radiology; mem. AMA, Tex. Med. Assn., Am. Soc. Therapeutic Radiologists, Am. Soc. Clin. Oncology, Am. Radium Soc., Dallas County Med. Soc. (del. 1971—), Tex. Radiol. Soc. (radiation oncology com. 1989—), Park Cities Club. Republican. Baptist. Home: 4019 University Blvd Dallas TX 75205-1714 Office: Tex Oncology Physician Asst Dept Radiation Oncology 3500 Gaston Ave Dallas TX 75246-2045

COLLIER, R(OBERT) JOHN, biomedical researcher, academic dean; b. Wichita Falls, Tex., Aug. 6, 1938; s. Eric Knox and Julia (Spearman) C.; m. Joan McCarthy, June 23, 1962; children: Andree, Erin, Brittany. BA in Biology, Rice U., 1959; PhD in Biology, Harvard U., 1964. Postdoctoral fellow Molecular Biology Inst., Geneva, 1964-66; asst. prof. bacteriology UCLA, 1966-70, assoc. prof. bacteriology, 1970-74, prof. microbiology, 1974-84; prof. microbiology and molecular genetics Harvard Med. Sch., Boston, 1984-88, faculty dean for grad. edn., 1988—, Maude and Lillian Presley prof. microbiology and molecular genetics, 1989—; DuPont lectr. Harvard, 1981; chmn. Gordon Conf., Microbial Toxins and Pathogenicity, 1982; cons. Cetus Corp., Berkeley, Calif., 1984-89, Xoma Corp., Berkeley, 1989—, Virus Rsch. Inst., 1992—. Mem. editorial bd. Infection and Immunity, Molecular Microbiology, Microbiological Revs. Guggenheim fellow, 1973-74; recipient Eli Lilly award, 1972, co-recipient Pierce Immunotoxin award, 1988, Paul Ehrlich prize, 1990. Mem. NAS, Am. Field Svcs. (treas. local chpt. 1986-90), Phi Beta Kappa. Office: Harvard Med Sch Dept Microbiology & Molec Generics 220 Longwood Ave Boston MA 02115-5701*

COLLIER, WILLIAM J., II, dentist; b. Oakland, Calif., Aug. 18, 1953; s. William J. and Mary Evelyn (Fisher) C. BS in Agr., Kans. State U., 1976; DDS, U. Mo., Kansas City, 1983. Pvt. practice dentistry Juneau, Alaska, 1983—. Mem. ADA, Juneau Dental Soc., S.E. Alaska Dental Soc., Acad. Gen. Dentistry, Elks, Moose, Eagles. Office: 1600 Glacier Ave Juneau AK 99801-1430

COLLIGAN, JOSEPH FRANCIS, psychiatrist; b. Ft. Wayne, Ind., July 18, 1933; s. Joseph P. and Marie F. (Hoffman) C.; m. Gretchen B. Rauch, Nov. 30, 1963; children: Joseph Jr., Sean, Daniel, Kevin, Terrance. BS in Premedicine, U. Notre Dame, 1954; MD, Loyola U., 1958; MA in Philosophy, De Paul U., 1959. Cert. psychiatrist, Am. Psychiat. Assn. Intern, resident Cook County Hosp., Chgo., 1958-59; pvt. practice family medicine Buchanan, Mich., 1959-64; resident in psychiatry U. Mich., Ann Arbor, 1964-68; fellow lab. comm. psychiatry Harvard Med. Sch., Boston, 1968-69; med. dir. psychiat. unit Duplin Gen. Hosp., Kenansville, N.C., 1991—. Office: Joseph F Colligan MD 825 Gum Branch Rd Ste 121 Jacksonville NC 28540

COLLIN, JACK, vascular surgeon, medical educator; b. Catchgate, Eng., Apr. 23, 1945; s. John and Amy Maud (Burton) C.; m. Christine Frances Proud, July 19, 1971; children: Beth, Neil, Graham, Ivan. MB, BS, U. Newcastle, Eng., 1968, MD, 1976; MA (hon.), Oxford (Eng.) U., 1980. Med. registration 1968. Anatomy demonstrator U. Newcastle, 1969-70; surg. registrar Royal Victoria Infirmary, Newcastle, 1970-80; found. fellow Mayo Clinic, Rochester, Minn., 1977; cons. surgeon John Radcliffe, Oxford, 1980—; reader Oxford U., 1980—, professorial fellow, Trinity Coll., 1980—, chair of faculty, 1991-93; dir. Nuffield Orthopaedic Hosp., Oxford, 1991-94; vascular advisor Nat. Confidential Enquiry into Perioperative Deaths, Eng., 1992—. Contbr. articles to profl. jours. Recipient Jacksonian Prize Royal Coll. Surgeons, Eng., 1976; Moynihan fellow, Assn. Surgeons, Eng., 1980; Hunterian Prof. Royal Coll. Surgeons, 1988. Fellow Royal Coll. Surgeons; mem. European Surg. Assn., Vascular Surg. Soc. (coun. mem. 1992-94). Office: U Oxford Dept Surgery, John Radcliffe Hospital, Oxford OX3 9DU, England

COLLINE, MARGUERITE RICHNAVSKY, maternal, women's health and pediatrics nurse; b. Bayonne, N.J., Nov. 30, 1953; d. John P. and Margaret M. (Conaghan) Richnavsky; m. Richard L. Colline, Oct. 8, 1977; children: Jennifer, Nicole, Danielle, James Michael. Diploma in practical nurse, Union County Tech. Inst., Scotch Plains, N.J., 1973; BSN, Seton Hall U., 1978. RN, N.J., Md. Practical nurse oncology unit John E. Runnell's Hosp., Berkley Heights, N.J.; staff nurse infant unit Johns Hopkins Hosp., Balt.; staff nurse neonatal unit Overlook Hosp., Summit, N.J. Mem. Nat. Assn. Neonatal Nurses, Sigma Theta Tau. Home: 8 Overlook Dr Bridgewater NJ 08807-2105

COLLINS, ALLEN HOWARD, psychiatrist; b. Washington, Sept. 6, 1942; s. Murray and Bertha (Baccalman) C.; m. Stephanie Evelyn Awn, May 22, 1976; children: Sasha Marie, Matthew Allen, Alyssa Beth. AB, Columbia Coll., 1964; MD, Tufts U., 1968; MPH, Columbia U., 1974. Diplomate Am. Bd. of Psychiatry and Neurology; Nat. Bd. of Med. Examiners; cert. psychoanalysis. Mental health career develop. fellow NIMH, Rockville, Md., 1968-74; staff psychiatrist Region II NIMH, N.Y.C., 1972-74, psychiat. cons., 1974-90; chief psychiat. consultation liaison svcs. Lenox Hill Hosp., N.Y.C., 1974-76, chief psychiat. inpatient svc., 1976-78, chief of psychiatry svc., 1978-86, dir. dept. of psychiatry, 1986—; examiner in psychiatry Am. Bd. of Psychiatry and Neurology, Evanston, Ill., 1979—; clin. prof. of psychiatry N.Y. Med. Coll., Valhalla, 1988-90; tng. and supervisory psychoanalyst divsn. of psychoanalytic tng., 1986-90; assoc. clin. prof. psychiatry Cornell U. Med. Coll., 1990-93; clin. prof. psychiatry NYU Med. Ctr., 1993—. Author: (with others) Provider's Guide To Hospital-Based Services, 1986; contbr. articles to profl. jours. With USPHS, 1968-74. Fellow Am. Psychiatr. Assn., Am. Acad. of Psychoanalysis.

COLLINS, CHRISTINE M., occupational health nurse; b. Long Beach, Calif., Apr. 29, 1952; d. Owen Ward and Marion Almy (Maltby) Collins; m. Robert Blair Reynolds, July 1, 1973 (div. 1985); stepchildren: Pamela Jean, Yvonne Kay; 1 child, Edwin Blair (dec.). BSN, Calif. State U., 1980; MSN, U. Pa., 1994. Staff nurse ICU Marshall Hosp., Placerville, Calif., 1980-83; FNP Sierra Family Clinic, Placerville, 1983-84; occupational nurse, nurse practitioner Hewlett Packard, Roseville, Calif., 1984-85; mgr. employee health svc. U. Calif. Davis Med. Ctr., Sacramento, 1985-86; nurse practitioner Children's Hosp. Pitts., 1987-88; dir. employee health Med. Ctr. Del., Wilmington, 1988—. Mem. AAHEP, Assn. Occupational Health Nurses, Sigma Theta Tau. Office: Med Ctr Del 501 W 14th St Wilmington DE 19801-1013

COLLINS, CLARA, pediatric critical care nurse; b. Jersey City, Feb. 10, 1958; d. Lawrence and Mildred (DeRiso) Caputi; m. James J. Collins, 1991. BSN, Boston Coll., 1980; MA, NYU, 1991. RN, N.Y. Nurse neonatal ICU, Presbyn. Hosp., N.Y.C., 1980—. Mem. ANA, N.Y. State Nurses Assn. Home: 154 Eagle St North Arlington NJ 07031-5819

COLLINS, COREY EMMANUEL, organ bank administrator; b. Stamford, Conn., May 15, 1966; s. Cornelius Joseph Collins and Joanna Barbara Bracchi Nowlan; m. Cristina Falcione, June 22, 1996. BS, U. Conn., 1996; postgrad., U. New England, 1996—. Cert. tissue banking specialist; cert. procurement coord. Lab. technician Hartford (Conn.) Hosp., 1991-93; procurement coord. New Eng. Organ Bank, Newton, Mass., 1993-94, donation coord., 1994-96; profl. educator Lahey Hitchcock Med. Ctr., Burlington, Mass., 1994-96; speaker in field. With USNR, 1987-95. Mem. N.Am. Transplant Coords. Orgn. Roman Catholic.

COLLINS, DELWOOD CHARLIE, biomedical researcher, university administrator; b. Cairo, Ga., Oct. 7, 1937; m. Patricia Ann Burg, May 18, 1981; children: Robert, Susan, Christina. BS in Biology, Emory U., 1959; MS in Zoology, U. Ga., 1963, PhD in Physiology, 1966. Postdoctoral researcher Worchester (Mass.) Found., 1966-67; med. rsch. assoc. dept. biochemistry U. Ottawa (Can.), 1967-69; asst. prof. medicine, biochemistry Emory Sch. Medicine, Atlanta, 1969-72, assoc. prof. medicine, biochemistry, 1972-76, prof. medicine, assoc. prof. biochemistry, 1976-91; vice chancellor rsch. and grad. studies U. Ky. Med. Ctr., Lexington, 1991—, prof. ob-gyn. and biochemistry, 1991—; assoc. rsch. scientist Dept. of Vet. Affairs, 1982—. Contbr. over 300 articles to profl. jours. Office: U Ky Med Ctr 204 Health Scis Rsch Bldg Lexington KY 40536-0305

COLLINS, DIANA JOSEPHINE, psychologist; b. Potsdam, N.Y., Apr. 27, 1944; d. Philip Joseph and Janet Dorothy (Lynke) C.; grad. with high honors, SUNY; Psy.D., Mass. Sch. Profl. Psychology, 1981. Psychologist, N.H. Hosp., Concord, 1974-79; asst. dir. forensic unit, 1979-80; founder, dir. Victim/Witness Service County of Hillsborough, Manchester, N.H., 1980-84; pvt. practice, Bedford, N.H.; adj. assoc. prof. U. N.H., 1974; adj. assoc. prof. Antioch Coll. of New Eng. Mem. APA, Assn. Applied Psychophysiology and Biofeedback, Biofeedback Soc. Am. (cert.), N.H. Psychol. Assn. (bd. dirs.), Mass. Psychol. Assn., Eastern Psychol. Assn., Internat. Assn. Psychotherapists and Counselors, Am. Assn. Female Execs., Roman Catholic. Home: 17 Pine Ln Warner NH 03278 Office: 40 S River Rd Unit 63 Bedford NH 03110-6724

COLLINS, EARLINE BROWN, medical and surgical and nephrology nurse; b. Canton, Miss., Apr. 30, 1955; d. Oresa and Thelma Holbert (Nichols) Brown; m. James Byron Collins, Jan. 23, 1982 (div. Dec. 1995). Cert., Holmes Jr. Coll., Goodman, Miss., 1975; AAS, Shelby State C.C., Memphis, 1989. Nurse Canton Nursing Home; charge nurse Canton Manor; nurse St. Dominic, Jackson, Miss.; staff nurse nephrology med./surg. unit, 1979-90; nurse hemodialysis unit Meth. Hosp., Memphis, 1990-91, patient educator continous ambulatory peritoneal dialysis, 1991—; clin. instr. nursing asst. program Rice Coll., 1989-90. Mem. Am. Nephrology Nurses Assn., Phi Theta Kappa. Home: 4132 Arrowhead Rd Memphis TN 38118

COLLINS, ERIK, psychologist, researcher; b. Grand Rapids, Mich., May 17, 1938; s. Kreigh Taylor and Theresa (Van Der Laan) C.; divorced; children: Brett and Brian; m. Janice Louise Lloyd, Dec. 19, 1987; children: Nicole, Ben, Toby. BBA, U. Mich., 1959, MA, 1963, PhD, 1969. Lic. psychologist, Pa., Del. Tchr. Plymouth (Mich.) Community Schs., 1963-67; vis. lectr. edn. Eastern Mich. U., Ypsilanti, 1967-69; asst. prof., rsch. project dir. SUNY, Fredonia, 1969-74; rsch. assoc., project dir. U. Md., Princess Anne, 1974-76; dir. rsch. Geneva Acad., Phila., 1976-77; ptnr. Greely, Collins & Assocs., N.Y.C., 1977-78; psychologist Embreeville Ctr., Coatesville, Pa., 1978-87, Haverford (Pa.) State Hosp., 1987-89, Del. State Hosp., New Castle, 1989—; cons. test devel. SUNY, Brockport, 1971-72, evaluation N.Y. Bd. Edn., 1974-78, rsch. projects and proposal devel. N.Y.C. Community Sch. Dists. Stoney Pointe, N. Y., U. Md., 1976-78; consulting psychologist Pinehill Rehab. Ctr., Phila., 1986-84; pvt. practice West Chester, Pa., Wilmington, Del., 1980—; consulting psychologist, Phila., Elwyn, 1991—. Author poetry and tech. reports on assessment of emotional devel. and screening for learning disabilities; contbr. articles to profl. jours. Evaluation grantee N.Y. State Ctr. for Migrant Studies, Geneseo, 1971-72, Innovative Project grantee ESEA Title I and VII, Appalachian Regional Commn., 1972-78, rsch. grantee Coop. State Rsch. Svcs., 1974-76, Innovative Project grantee Dept. of Spl. Edn., Harrisburg, Pa., 1977. Mem. Am. Psychol. Assn., Lower Shore Assn. for Children Learning Disabilities (pres. Eastern Shore chpt. 1975-76), Dunkirk Yacht Club (fleet capt. 1971-72).. Democrat. Episcopalian.

COLLINS, FRANCIS S., medical research scientist. PhD in Phys. Chemistry, Yale U., 1974; MD, U. N.C., 1977. Former staff mem. Howard Hughes Med. Inst., U. Mich. Med. Ctr., Ann Arbor; now dir. Nat. Ctr. for Human Genome Rsch. NIH, Bethesda, Md. Co-recipient Gairdner Found. Internat. award for work on cystic fibrosis, 1990. Mem. NAS. Office: Nat Ctr Human Genome Rsch Bldg 31 Rm 4B09 31 Center Dr MSC2152 Bethesda MD 20892-2152

COLLINS, FUJI, mental health professional; b. Tokyo, Nov. 3, 1954; s. Boyd Leslie and Kimiko (Terayama) C.; 1 child, Lacey Nichole. BS, Ariz. State U., 1977; MS, Ea. Wash. U., 1989; MA, The Fielding Inst., 1993, PhD, 1994. Commd. 2d lt. U.S. Army, 1978, advanced through grades to maj., 1989, lt. platoon leader, adminstrv. officer, 1978-79; lt. bat. adjutant 509th Airborne Bat. Combat Team, 1977-80; capt., air def. fire coordination officer U.S. Army, 1981-83, capt. battery comdr., 1983-85, capt., 1985-86; clin. therapist Wash. State Patrol, 1985-95; dir. of administrn., Japanese Counseling Program Richmond Area Multi-Svcs., Inc., San Francisco, 1995—; registered clin. therapist, coord. Wash. State Patrol Critical Incident/Peer Support Team, Wash. State Hostage Negotiator; mem. Thurston/Mason County Critical Incident Stress Debriefing Team. Vol. Thurston/Mason County Crisis Clinic; mem. steering com. Thurston/Mason County Critical Incident Team. Mem. ACA, APA, Wash. State Psychol. Assn., Asian Am. Psychol. Assn., Soc. for Psychol. Study of Ethnic Minority Issues, Am. Critical Incident Stress Found., Wash. State Hostage Negotiation Assn., Assn. Police Planning and Rsch. Officers. Home: 3 Bayside Ct Richmond CA 94804 Office: NAAPTC 3626 Balboa St San Francisco CA 94121

COLLINS, GWENDOLYN BETH, health administrator; b. Akron, Ohio; d. Emmert Samuel and Lillice Elizabeth (Matthews) Shaffer; divorced; 1 child, Holly Marie. BA, Case Western Res. U. Exec. dir. Canton Area Regional Health Edn. Network, 1981-88; project dir. Region VII Cancer Registry, Canton, Ohio, 1984-88; program dir. Diabetes Mgmt. Ctr., St. Petersburg, Fla., 1988-89, 92-94, Pasadena Sr. Health Ctr., St. Petersburg, 1995-96; pvt. practice health program mgmt. cons. Largo, Fla., 1995—; health mgmt. cons., 1986-88, 95—; mem. continuing med. edn. com. Aultman Hosp., 1983-88; planner and evaluator Directions for Mental Health, Inc., Clearwater, Fla., 1990-92. Mem. adv. com. Camp Y-Noah, 1985-86. HHS grantee, Canton, 1986-88. Mem. Cancer Control Consortium Ohio (mem. cancer incidence mgmt. com. 1986-87). Republican. Home: 13013 89th Ave N Largo FL 34646-2706

COLLINS, HAROLD THEODORE, urologist; b. N.Y.C., Nov. 30, 1942; s. Harold Reeves and Atanaska (Vitonoff) C. BA in Chemistry, Kent State U., 1964; MD, Ohio State U., 1968. Urologist North Bend Med. Ctr., Coos Bay, Oreg., 1975—. Capt. U.S. Army, 1969-71. Mem. AMA, Am. Urol. Assn. Home: 1040 East Bay Dr North Bend OR 97459 Office: North Bend Med Ctr 1900 Woodland Dr Coos Bay OR 97420

COLLINS, H(ERSCHEL) DOUGLAS, retired physician; b. Caribou, Maine, Jan. 19, 1928; married, 1950, 87; 3 children.; BA, U. Maine, 1949; MD, Harvard U., 1952. Diplomate Am. Bd. Internal Medicine. Intern Mass. Gen. Hosp., 1952-53, asst. resident in medicine, 1953-54, 72-73, resident, 1954-55, staff surgeon, dir. patient care, 1974-87; sr. asst. surgeon USPHS, 1955-57; pvt. practice Caribou, 1957-72, 73-75, 1980-84, group practice, 1984-87; dir. Ctrl. Maine Family Practice Residency, 1975-79, Maine-Dartmouth Family Practice Residency, 1979-80; gov. Am. Bd. Internal Medicine, 1988-91. Mem. Inst. Med.-Nat. Acad. Sci., AMA, ACP. Home: RFD Box 2179 Kingfield ME 04947

COLLINS, JAMES FRANCIS, lawyer, financial consultant; b. Evanston, Ill., July 31, 1943; s. James Francis Jr. and Jeanne (Moss) C.; m. Ann Peake Rogers, Apr. 5, 1983. BSc in Mktg., U. Louisville, 1969, JD, 1977; JD, Xavier U., 1971; MEd in Bus. Adminstrn. Bar: Ky. 1977, Ill. 1977, Fla. 1978, U.S. Dist. Ct. (we. dist.) Ky. 1978, U.S. Mil. Ct. Appeals 1978, U.S. Tax Ct. 1978, U.S. Customs Ct. 1978, U.S. Ct. Appeals (6th cir.) 1980, U.S. Supreme Ct. 1980, U.S. Dist. Ct. (so. dist.) Ind. 1981, U.S. Dist. Ct. (mid. dist.) Fla. 1982, Wis. 1989, Ind. 1989; cert. secondary tchr., Ill., Ky., Ohio. Br. mgr., mcht. rep. Household Fin. Corp., Chgo., 1962-66; tchr. bus. Jefferson County Bd. Edn., Louisville, 1968-77; pvt. practice Louisville, 1977-82; criminal def. trial lawyer Pub. Defender, Sanford, Fla., 1982-83; pvt. practice Schaumburg, Ill., 1984—; arbitrator, chairperson Cir. Ct. Cook. County, Mandatory Ct. Annexed Arbitration, 1990—; part-time instr. in comml. and internat. law Watterson Coll., Louisville, 1974-75. Dist. ct. judge candidate Jefferson County, Ky., 1981; cir. ct. judge candidate Dem. Primary, Chgo., 1986, 88, 92, 96; appellate ct. judge candidate, Chgo., 1990, Dem. Primary, Chgo., 1994; Dem. cir. ct. judge candidate, 1996; mem. S.E. Side Community Orgn.; legal counsel election day Dem. Party of Proviso Twp., 1985-90, 37th Ward of Chgo., 1991-94, 27th Ward of Chgo., 1991-94, election day legal counsel to Sen. Richard Hendon, 1989—; mem. Berkeley (Ill.) Citizens Party, 1987. Recipient ICLE 32 Hour Bankruptcy Course award, 1985, Recognition award Berkeley (Ill.) Citizens party, 1986, Continuing Legal Edn. Recognition award Ky. Bar Assn., 1987, 91, 92, 93, 94, 95, 96, Recognition awards Westside Chgo. Black Polit. Leaders Assn., 1990, 92, Recognition award Cook County Dem. Party Fair Coalition, 1992; named Disting. Citizen of Louisville, Ky. by Mayor Harvey Stone, 1976, Hon. Cpt. Belle Louisville by County Judge Exec. Todd Hollenbach, 1974, Hon. Ky. Col. by Gov. Wenden Ford, Lt. Gov. Thelma Stoval, 1974. Mem. Internat. Platform Assn., Chgo. Bar Assn. (Ill. indsl. comm. worker's compensation com., adminstrv. law com.), U. Louisville Bus. Sch. Alumni Assn., Xavier U. Alumni Assn., United Hellenic Voters of Am. (life), Sigma Delta Kappa. Office: 3 Golf Ctr PO Box 68042 Schaumburg IL 60168-0042

COLLINS, JAMES FRANCIS, toxicologist; b. Balt., Jan. 26, 1942; s. James Murphy and Mary M. (Dolan) C.; m. Barbara Joan Betka, June 21, 1969; children: Chris, Cavan. BS, Loyola Coll., Balt., 1963; PhD, U.N.C., 1968. Diplomate Am. Bd. Toxicology. Fellow NIH, Bethesda, Md., 1968-75; faculty mem., rsch. chemist U. Tex. Health Sci. Ctr. and VA Med. Ctr., San Antonio, 1975-86; staff toxicologist Calif. EPA and Dept. Health Svcs., Berkeley, Calif., 1986—; instr. U. Calif. Berkeley/Extension, 1987-95; instr. U. San Francisco, 1995—. Contbr. numerous articles to profl. jours., publs. Mem. Am. Soc. Biochemistry and Molecular Biology. Democrat. Roman Catholic. Home: 822 Rogers Way Pinole CA 94564-2409 Office: Calif EPA 2151 Berkeley Way Annex 11 Berkeley CA 94704-1011

COLLINS, JEANNE SIMONNE, telemetry nurse; b. Fall River, Mass., July 5, 1968; d. Theodore J. and Simonne Bernier; m. Michael E. Collins, May 26, 1990; children: Christopher M., Elora J. BSN, Southeastern Mass. U., North Dartmouth, 1990. RN St. Anne's Hosp., Fall River, Mass., 1993—.

COLLINS, JERRY CLAYTON, biomedical engineering educator; b. Nashville, Mar. 19, 1941; s. Seldon Clayton and Hilda (Copeland) C.; m. Sandra Lynn Johnson, Aug. 22, 1964; children: Leslie, Reid, Erin. B of Engring., Vanderbilt U., 1962; MSEE, Purdue U., 1965; PhD, Duke U., 1970. Registered profl. engr., Tenn. Asst. prof. U. Ky., Lexington, 1968-74, cons. dept. surgery, 1974, sr. rsch. assoc., 1975-77; rsch. instr. Vanderbilt U., Nashville, 1977-81, rsch. asst. prof., 1981-87, rsch. assoc. prof., 1987—; cons. Clin. Rsch. Ctr. Meharry Med. Coll., Nashville, 1987-90, dir. computers and biostats., 1990-93; cons. Aids Clin. Trials Unit, Meharry Med. Coll., 1993-96. Author 80 articles and 90 abstracts. Deacon Southside Ch. of Christ, Lexington, 1974-77, Otter Creek Ch. of Christ, Nashville, 1980-93; mem. exec. bd. Youth Hobby Shop, Nashville, 1982, 84, pres. exec. bd., 1983; bd.

dirs. Christian Campus Ministries, Inc., Nashville, 1989-90, pres. bd. dirs., 1991—; bd. dirs. Internat. Christian U., Vienna, Austria, 1995—. Mem. IEEE, Engring. in Medicine and Biology Soc. of IEEE, Am. Physiol. Soc., Biomed. Engring. Soc. (sr. mem., bull. editor 1991—), Tau Beta Pi, Eta Kappa Nu, Sigma Xi. Democrat. Office: Vanderbilt Univ AA-3228 Med Ctr N Nashville TN 37232

COLLINS, MARY S., dean; b. Sayre, Pa., Nov. 13, 1945; d. Robert L. and Dorothy Mae (McCormick) Shaffer; m. Christopher M. Collins, June 25, 1966; children: Robert M. Collins, Charles A. Collins. BS, Keuka Coll., 1966; MS, Syracuse U., 1975, PhD, 1981. RN, N.Y. Pub. health nurse City-County Health Dept., Colorado Springs, Colo., 1966-69; instr. Broome C. C., Binghamton, N.Y., 1972-74; lectr. Binghamton (N.Y.) U., 1976-81, asst. prof., 1981-86, dean Decker Sch. Nursing, 1988—; mem. N.Y. State Bd. for Nursing, 1995—. Contbr. articles to profl. jours. Bd. dirs. Fairview Good Shepard Home, Binghamton, N.Y., 1986—. Mem. Am. Nurses Assn., Am. Assn. Colls. Nursing (edn. and credentialing 1986—), Nat. League Nursing (state vis. 1991—), N.Y. State Coun. Deans (pres. 1992-94), Sigma Theta Tau (Zeta Iota chpt. pres., v.p. 1980—). Home: 225 Smith Hill Rd Binghamton NY 13905 Office: Decker Sch Nursing P O Box 6000 Binghamton NY 13902

COLLINS, MICHAEL DAVID, environmental health educator, development toxicologist; b. Yonkers, N.Y., Oct. 4, 1949; s. Gilbert and Millicent (Sorkness) C.; m. Karen Lynn Mitchell, May 21, 1977; children: Brock Damon, Kyna Monique. BS, U. Ill., 1971, MS, 1977; MSPH, U. Mo., 1981, PhD, 1982. Interdisciplinary Programs in Health fellow Harvard Sch. Pub. Health, Boston, 1982-84; rsch. fellow Children's Hosp. Rsch. Found., Cin., 1984-87; rsch. instr. dept. pediatrics U.Cin., 1986-88, rsch. asst. prof., 1988-93; asst. prof. environ. health scis. UCLA Sch. Pub. Health and Ctr. Occup. and Environ. Health, 1993-95, assoc. prof., 1995—; vis. scientist Freie U. Berlin, 1989-90; mem. biology faculty Raymond Walters Coll., U. Cin., 1992-93, Environ. Sci. and Engring. Program, 1994—, Ctr. Environ. Risk Reduction, 1996—. First Ind. Rsch. Support and Transition grantee NIH, 1987. Mem. Teratology Soc., The Oxygen Soc., Am. Inst. Nutrition. Home: 4044 Jim Bowie Rd Agoura Hills CA 91301 Office: UCLA School Public Health 10833 Le Conte Ave Los Angeles CA 90095

COLLINS, NANCY S., medical publisher; b. Long Branch, N.J., July 17, 1958; d. Luke Kenneth and Marilyn (Tarnopolsky) McS.; m. Steven Thomas Collins, May 5, 1984; children: Emily, Grace. BA, Beaver Coll., 1980. Nat. sales mgr. Appleton-Century-Crafts, N.Y.C., 1980-83; med. acquisitions editor Appleton-Century-Crafts, Norwalk, Conn., 1983-85; med. editor Williams & Wilkins, Balt., 1985-87, dir. jour. mktg., 1987-90, v.p., pub., 1990—. Office: Williams and Wilken 351 W Camden St Baltimore MD 21201

COLLINS, PAUL STEVEN, vascular surgeon; b. Portsmouth, Ohio, July 24, 1954; s. Paul Whitney and Geralda Pearl (Hoskins) C.; m. Cathy Ann McWicker, Jan. 17, 1981; children: Lauren Elizabeth, Paul McWicker, Andrew Steven. BS, Davidson Coll., 1976; MD, U. South Fla., 1979. Diplomate Am. Bd. Surgery, spl. qualifications in gen. vascular surgery and surg. critical care; diplomate Nat. Bd. Med. Examiners; lic. surgeon, Fla., Va. Commd. 2d lt. U.S. Army, 1979, advanced through grades to lt. col., 1990; resident in gen. surgery Walter Reed Army Med. Ctr. U.S. Army, Washington, 1979-84; chief gen. surg. svc. U.S. Army, Würzburg, West Germany, 1984-86; fellow peripheral vasc. surgery Walter Reed Army Med. Ctr. U.S. Army, Washington, 1986-87; chief vascular surgery Letterman Army Med. Ctr. U.S. Army, San Francisco; resigned U.S. Army, 1992; pvt. practice St. Petersburg, Fla., 1990—; asst. clin. prof. surgery Uniformed Svcs. U. of Health Scis., Bethesda, Md., 1984—; profl. mem. Keystine, Tampa, Fla., 1993—; pres. Bay Blaza Outpatient Surgery; dir. vascular lab. St. Anthony's Hosp., St. Petersburg, 1994—; bd. dirs, trustee St. Anthony's Found. Contbr. chpts. to books, articles to med. jours. Bd. dirs. St. Anthony's Found. Recipient Physicians Recognition award AMA, 1992, Sigvaris award Camp Internat., 1987. Fellow ACS (Regional Trauma award 1984), Internat. Soc. for Cardiovascular Surgeons; mem. So. Assn. for Vascular Surgery (Pres.'s award 1992), Fla. Vascular Soc., Fla. Med. Assn., Pinellas County Med. Soc. Office: 1201 5th Ave N Ste 200 Saint Petersburg FL 33705-1425

COLLINS, PEGGY ANN, medical writer; b. Denver, Dec. 5, 1948. Student, Rockmont Coll., 1967-69; diploma, Colo. Coll. Med. Assts., 1970; BS, Met. State Coll., 1976. Legisl. liaison Health Med. Services of Colo., Denver, 1977; assoc. dir. Aspen Health Resources, Denver, 1977, 78; state info. officer State and Fed. Assocs. Report Service, Washington, 1978-80; editorial assoc. Am. Jour. of Sports Medicine, Columbus, Ga., 1980-81; freelance med. writer, editor Denver, 1981—; owner Medinform Comms., Arvada, Colo., 1981—; sec. U. Colo. Health Sci. Ctr., Denver, 1986-89. Contbr. articles to profl. jours.; mem. editorial bd. Jour. Operating Room Research Inst., Denver, 1983. Rep. precinct committeewoman, Denver, 1986-88, 93-95. Mem. Am. Med. Writers Assn. (pres. 1986-87), Council of Biology Editors. Republican. Baptist. Home: 11535 W 70th Pl Unit D Arvada CO 80004-1382 Office: Medinform Communications 11535 W 70th Pl Unit D Arvada CO 80004-1382

COLLINS, RICHARD ANDREW, pathologist, biochemist; b. Norristown, Pa., Oct. 27, 1924; s. George W. and Blanche (Latshaw) C.; m. Carmen Portillo, Oct. 29, 1955 (dec.); children: Cynthia, Deborah, Daniel. BS, Pa. State U., 1948; MS, U. Wis., 1950, PhD, 1952; MD, Marquette U., 1962. Diplomate Am. Bd. Clin. and anatomic Pathology. Intern Mary Fletcher Hosp., Burlington, Vt., 1962-63; resident in pathology U. Va., Burlington, 1963-65; pathologist Regional Med. Labs., Battle Creek, Mich., 1972-81, St. Luke's Med. Ctr., Milw., 1981—. 1st lt. USAF, 1943-46, PTO. Republican. Office: Saint Lukes Med Ctr 2900 W Oklahoma Ave Milwaukee WI 53215-4330

COLLINS, RICHARD FRANCIS, microbiologist, educator; b. St. Paul, Minn., Jan. 22, 1938; s. Francis Bernard and Maude Roegene (Night) C.; m. Deanne Margaret Scafati, Dec. 28, 1960 (div. 1970); children: Lisa, Mark, Michael; m. Judy A. Wright, Feb. 15, 1978; children: Kristyn, Todd. AB, Shepherd Coll., 1962; MA, Wake Forest U., 1968; PhD, U. Okla., 1973. Tchr. Alexandria (Va.) Schs., 1962-66; instr. U. Okla., Oklahoma City, 1972-73; lab. dir. Infectious Disease Svc. U. Ill./Rockford Sch. of Medicine, 1974-80; asst. prof. U. Ill., Rockford, 1973-80; assoc. prof. U. Osteo. Medicine and Health Scis., Des Moines, 1980-85, faculty pres., 1990-91, prof., dept. head, 1985-95; cons. U.S. EPA, Washington, 1975-81; mem. Nat. Bd. Podiatry Examiners, Princeton, N.J., 1983—, Nat. Bd. Osteo. Med. Examiners, Des Plaines, Ill., 1994—; participant mission project Christian Med. Soc., Dominican Republic, 1977. Mem. editorial bd. African Jour. Clin. Exptl. Immunology, 1979-83; contbr. articles to profl. jours. Vol. Blank Guild, Iowa Meth. Hosp., Des Moines, 1988-91. Recipient awards NSF, 1962-67, fellowship NIH, 1969-70, Gov.'s Vol. awards State of Iowa, 1988, 89. Mem. Am. Soc. for Microbiology, Am. Soc. Tropical Medicine and Hygiene, Iowa Acad. of Sci., Sigma Xi (pres. 1987-90, 96-97, treas. 1990-91). Home: 1215 S 60th St West Des Moines IA 50266-5740 Office: U Osteo Medicine & Health Scis 3200 Grand Ave Des Moines IA 50312-4104

COLLINS, ROBERT ELLWOOD, surgeon; b. Cottage City, Md., Aug. 4, 1932; s. Edward Clarence and Edith (Blough) C.; m. Barbara Kauffmann Murray, June 28, 1964; children: Garret, Randy, Robin, Bill, Bruce, Brad, Beth. BS, Ea. Mennonite Coll., 1954; MD, Med. Coll. Va., 1958. Diplomate Am. Bd. Orthopaedic Surgeons. Intern Washington Hosp. Ctr., 1958-59, orthopaedic resident, 1961-64; pvt. practice medicine Broadway, Va., 1959-60; resident in gen. surgery Med. Coll. Va., Richmond, 1960-61; pvt. practice medicine specializing in orthopaedic surgery Washington, 1964—; acting orthopaedic chief Children's Hosp., 1970-72; chief orthopaedics Washington Hosp. Ctr., 1973-75, vice-chmn. dept. orthopaedics, 1975-80, bd. dirs., pres. med. and dental staff, 1981, 83-85; assoc. prof. Georgetown U. Hosp., 1975—; courtesy staff Sibley Meml. Hosp.; pres. med. staff Nat. Rehab. Hosp., Washington, 1988; bd. dirs. Medlantic Health Corp., Washington. Bd. dirs. Easter Seal Soc. of Washington and Md., 1986—, chmn. bd. dirs., 1990-92; chmn. bd. dirs. Nat. Orthopedic Hosp., Washington, 1990; bd. dirs. Nat. Easter Seals Soc., 1995—. Recipient Teaching award Georgetown U., Washington, 1985; Children's Orthopaedic's fellow Children's Hosp., 1963, Cerebral Palsy fellow Children's Rehab. Inst. Johns Hopkins U., 1965. Fellow ACS (chmn. D.C. trauma com.), Am. Acad. Cerebral Palsy, Am. Acad. Orthopaedic Surgeons, Am. Acad. Orthopaedic Foot Surgeons; mem. Med. Soc. D.C. (pres. 1985-86), Washington Clin. Club (past pres.), Georgetown Club, Congl. Country Club (Bethesda, Md.). Presbyterian. Office: Drs Collins Gordon Johnson PC 106 Irving St NW Ste 318 Washington DC 20010-2927

COLLINS, ROBERT KEITH, health center administrator, physician; b. Aztec, N.Mex., Oct. 27, 1947; s. Clifford Calvin and Margaret Etta (Flaugh) C.; m. Pamela Cole Capps, May 28, 1972. BS in Biology, BA in Chemistry, Millsaps Coll., 1969; MD, U. Miss., 1974. Diplomate Am. Bd. Family Practice; cert. sports medicine. Resident in family practice U. Miss. Med. Ctr., Jackson, 1974-77; staff physician Miss. State U. Med. Ctr., Starkville, 1977-88; dir. John C. Longest Student Health Ctr. Miss. State U., Starkville, 1988—; mem. staff, sec., vice chief staff Oktibbeha County Hosp., Starkville, 1977-88, chief staff, 1990-92; chmn. edn. com. AIDS task force, Miss. Bd. Health, 1987-95; profl. and tech. adv. com. Ambulatory Healthcare for Joint Commn. for Accreditation Health Orgns., 1993—. Contbr. articles to med. jours. Fellow Am. Acad. Family Practice; mem. AMA, Am. Coll. Health Assn. (chmn. athletic medicine sect. 1989-90, bd. dirs. 1990-92), So. Coll. Health Assn. (pres. 1988-89), Am. Coll. Sports Medicine, Am. Med. Soc. Sports Medicine, Sigma Xi. Home: 507 N Montgomery St Starkville MS 39759-2331 Office: Miss State U John C Longest Student Health Ctr Starkville MS 39759

COLLINS, STEPHEN BARKSDALE, health care executive; b. Houston, Mar. 14, 1932; s. Ray George and Ruth Ella (Davis) C.; m. Katherine Jane Justice, June 6, 1955; children: Nancy Catherine, Rebecca Jane, Ruth Anne, Stephen Barksdale, Cynthia Marye. B.A., Baylor U., 1954; M.H.A., Washington U., 1956. Asst. adminstr., adminstr. Good Samaritan Hosp., Vincennes, Ind., 1959-65; adminstr. Rosewood Gen. Hosp., Houston, 1965-72; chief exec. officer Lake Charles Meml. Hosp., La., 1972-85; v.p. shareholder rels. and membership VHA, Inc., Irving, Tex., 1985—. Bd. dirs. Better Bus. Bur. Served with USAF, 1956-59. Decorated Meritorious Service medal, Commendation medal. Fellow Am. Coll. Hosp. Adminstrs.; mem. C. of C. (dir.), Southeastern Hosp. Conf. (bd. dirs. 1981-82, exec. com. 1983, chmn.-elect 1984), La. Hosp. Assn. (chmn.-elect 1981, chmn. 1982), Am. Hosp. Assn. Baptist. Club: Rotary. Home: 3541 Meadowside Dr Bedford TX 76021-3546 Office: VHA Inc PO Box 160909 Irving TX 75061

COLLINS, SYLVIA DURNELL, nurse, health promotion consultant; b. Phila., Nov. 17, 1934; d. Frank Edward and Catherine Florence (Sanford) Durnell; 1 child, Dawn Catherine. BSN, U. Pa., 1959; MEd, Temple U., 1973. RN, Pa. Cons. Phila. Health Plan, 1976-79; instr. in-svc edn. Luth. Home, Phila., 1977-79; staff nurse ACT Drug Rehab., Phila., 1981-82; cons. for health promotion Phila Corp. for Aging, 1981—; vis. lectr. Community Coll., Phila., 1978-80; guest lectr. Sec., Gratz St. Neighbors, Phila., 1984-86; mem. Phila. Coun. on Neighborhoods, 1985; bd. dirs. Chas. R. Drew Commun. Mental Health/Mental Retardation Ctr.; bd. dirs., chmn. health ministry Zion Bapt. Ch.; bd. dirs. YWCA, Phila.; trustee Phila. YWCA, North Ctrl. Phila. YWCA.; adv. com. N. Ctrl. Phila. Mem. NAACP (life), Am. Cancer Soc. (Keys to Living bd. dirs., profl. edn. com.), Pub. Edn. Commn. Arthritis Assn., Am. Pub. Health Assn., PHiladelphia County Nurses Assn. (corr. sec. 1981-84, 3d v.p.), Ethnic Nurses of Color (vice chmn. 1984-86), Alzheimer's Assns. of Greater Phila., Sigma Theta Tau, Alpha Kappa Alpha, Chi Eta Phi. Democrat. Baptist. Office: Phila Corp Aging 642 N Broad St Philadelphia PA 19130-3409

COLLINS, TUCKER, pathologist, molecular biologist; b. Lorain, Ohio, Nov. 3, 1952; s. Robert James and Catherine (Meisner) C.; m. Mary Judith Whitley, June 15, 1985. BA, Amherst Coll., 1975; MD, PhD, U. Rochester, 1981. Diplomate Am. Bd. Pathology. Clin., rsch. fellow Brigham and Women's Hosp., Boston, 1981-85; instr. pathology Harvard Med. Sch., Boston, 1985-86, asst. prof. pathology, 1986-91, assoc. prof. pathology, 1992—; assoc. pathologist Brigham and Women's Hosp., 1986—; charter mem. pathology study sect. NIH. Assoc. editor Am. Jour. Pathology; contbr. articles to profl. jours. Scholar Pew Scholars Program, 1987-91; grantee NIH, 1985, 90, 93, Am. Heart Assn Established Investigator, 1991-96; recipient Warner-Lambert/Parke-Davis award Am. Society for Investigative Pathology, 1994. Master Francis Weld Peabody Soc. (assoc.); mem. Am. Assn. Pathologists, Am. Assn. Univ. Pathologists, N.Am. Vascular Biology Orgn. Home: 160 Fairoaks Ln Cohasset MA 02025-1314 Office: Brigham and Women's Hosp Boston MA 02115

COLLINS, VINCENT PATRICK, radiologist, physician, educator; b. Toronto, Ont., Can., Nov. 11, 1912; came to U.S., 1940, naturalized, 1945; s. John and Laura (Doyle) C.; m. Lois Cowan, Dec. 26, 1942; children: Cowan, Ross, Christopher. M.D., U. Toronto, 1937; J.D., U. Houston, 1964. Diplomate: Am. Bd. Radiology. Intern Toronto Gen. Hosp., 1937-38; demonstrator anatomy, fellow physiology U. Toronto, 1938-39; research fellow Banting Inst., 1939-40; sr. resident pathology N.E. Deaconess Hosp., Boston, 1940-42; resident surg. pathology, instr. surgery Presbyn. Hosp., Columbia, 1942-43, resident radiology, 1945-47, attending radiologist, 1950-52; instr. radiology Columbia U., 1947-49; cons. radiology USPHS Marine Hosp., S.I., 1948-52; asst. prof. Columbia U., 1949-50, assoc. prof. radiology, 1950-52; chief radiotherapy Francis Delafield Hosp., 1950-52; prof. radiology, chmn. dept. Baylor U., 1952-68; radiologist-in-chief Jefferson Davis Hosp., Houston, 1952-68, Ben Taub Gen. Hosp., Houston, 1963-68; chief cons. radiology VA Hosp., Houston, 1952-68; attending radiologist Meth. Hosp., Houston, 1955-68; cons. radiology Tex. Children's Hosp., Houston, 1956-68; dir. radiotherapy Rosewood Gen. Hosp., 1969-82, cons., 1982—; cons. radiotherapy Ochsner Clinic, New Orleans, 1968-82, U. Tex. Med. Br., Galveston, 1969-84; prin. cons. radiology Nat. Inst. Gen. Med. Scis., Bethesda, Md., 1966, Lawrence Labs. U. Calif. at Berkeley, 1972-77; med. dir. Houston Inst. for Cancer Research, Detection and Treatment, 1974—; mem. med. adv. com. U.S. Nuclear Regulatory Commn., clin. prof. radiology therapy dept., U. Tex. Med. Br., 1984—. Served from 1st lt. to capt., M.C. AUS, 1943-45. Decorated Silver Star. Fellow Am. Coll. Radiology, Am. Coll. Legal Medicine; mem. Am. Roentgen Ray Soc., Radiol. Soc. N.Am., Tex. Radiol. Soc., Soc. Surg. Oncology, Am. Radium Soc., N.Y. Acad. Scis., Arthur Purdy Stout Soc., Am. Soc. Therapeutic Radiologists, A.A.A.S., Internat. Acad. Pathology, Sigma Xi. Home: 105 Shasta Dr Houston TX 77024-6914 Office: 8811 Gaylord #100 Houston TX 77024

COLLINS, VINCENT PETER, pathologist; b. Dublin, Ireland, Dec. 3, 1947; s. James Vincent and Mary Ann (Blanche) C. MB, BCh, BAO, Nat. U. Ireland, 1971; MD, Karolinska Inst., Stockholm, 1978. Registered med. practitioner, Ireland, Eng., Sweden; specialist in pathology, Eng., Ireland, Sweden, specialist in clin cytology, Sweden. Assoc. prof. pathology Karolinska Inst., Stockholm, 1979-93, dir. studies Inst. Pathology, 1983-84; cons. pathologist and cytologist Karolinska Hosp., Stockholm, 1982-86, sr. cons. pathologist, 1986-90; chief for clin. research Ludwig Inst. for Cancer Research, Stockholm, 1986—; prof. pathology U. Gothenburg, Sweden, 1990-93; sr. cons. pathologist Salgrenska Hosp., Gothenburg, 1990-93; prof. tumor pathology Karolinska Inst., Stockholm, 1993—; sr. cons. pathologist Karolinska Hosp., Stockholm, 1993—, chmn. Inst. Oncology and Pathology, 1996—; mem. sci. bd., chmn. subcom. A, Swedish Cancer Assn., Stockholm, 1988-93; mem. sci. rev. bd. Swedish Med. Rsch. Coun., 1991—; William O. Russell lectr. in anatomical pathology U. Tex. M D Anderson Cancer Ctr., Houston, 1990; Lucien J. Rubinsten Neuropathology Rsch. lectr. U. Va., Charlottesville, 1994. Edtl. bd. Cancer Letters, 1985—, Brain Pathology, 1990—, Jour. Neuropathology and Exptl. Neurology, 1995—, Neuropathology & Applied Neurobiology, 1995—; internat. edtl. bd. Excerpta Medica, 1985—; contbr. articles to profl. jours. Recipient Minerva Found. prize, 1987, Joanne Vandenberg Hill award U. Tex. M D Anderson Cancer Ctr., 1990; grantee NIH, 1991-95, Swedish Cancer Soc., 1980-86, 90—, Stockholm Cancer Soc., 1974-86; Karolinska Inst. rsch. fellow, 1982, 86. Fellow Royal Coll. Physicians Ireland, Royal Coll. Pathologists (London); mem. Brit. Neuropath. Soc., Am. Cell Biology Assn., N.Y. Acad. Scis., Swedish Med. Soc., Stockholm Cancer Soc. Home: Skillinganand 9, S-11220 Stockholm Sweden Office: Karolinska Hosp Dept Pathology, Box 100, S-17176 Stockholm Sweden

COLLINS, WILLIAM F., JR., neurosurgery educator; b. New Haven, Conn., Jan. 20, 1924. MD, Yale U., 1947. Diplomate Am. Bd. Neurol. Surgery. Intern Barnes Hosp., St. Louis, 1947-49, asst. resident in neurosurgery, 1951-52, resident, 1952-53; fellow neurophysiology Washington U., 1953-54; instr. neurosurgery Western Res. U., Cleve., 1954-55, sr. instr., 1955-57, asst. prof., 1957-60, assoc. prof., 1960-63; prof., chmn. div. neurosurgery Med. Coll. Va., 1963-67; prof. Yale U., New Haven, 1967—, chmn. sect. neurosurgery, 1967-86, chmn. dept. surgery, 1986-93, prof. neurosurgery, 1993-94, prof. neurosurgery emeritus, 1994—. With M.C., U.S. Army, 1949-51. Office: Yale Sch Medicine Sect Neurosurgery PO Box 208039 New Haven CT 06520-8039

COLLINS-EILAND, KAREN WISLER, psychologist; b. Oklahoma City, Mar. 25, 1949; d. Charles C. and Frances Joan (Higgins) Wisler; BA with honors, Stephen F. Austin State U., Nacogdoches, Tex., 1973; MA, Tex. Christian U., 1978, PhD, 1979; m. David C. Eiland, Jr. Lic. psychologist. Asst. prof. Dickinson (N.D.) State Coll., 1979-80; rsch. asst. prof. psychiatry U. Tex. Med. Br., Galveston, 1980-81, asst. prof. dept. ob-gyn and sr. assoc. Office Ednl. Devel., 1981-85; dir. acad. counseling, 1986-89; asst. prof. dept. psychiatry and behavioral scis., 1986-88; cons. Med. Educators and Galveston Ind. Sch. Dist., 1981-88; asst. prof. dept. psychiatry and behavioral scis., U. Tex.-Southwestern Med. Ctr., Dallas, 1992-93. Contbr. articles to profl. jours. Mem. Am. Psychol. Assn., Am. Ednl. Rsch. Assn., Sigma Xi, Psi Chi, Alpha Kappa Delta, Alpha Chi, Delta Zeta. Methodist.

COLLINSON, JEFFREY JOSEPH, venture capitalist; b. Springfield, Ohio, Nov. 26, 1941; s. Joseph Bruard and Jean Brock (Crayton) C.; m. Sharon Jewils, July 2, 1966; children: Robin, Christy, Andrew. BA, Yale U., 1963; MBA, Harvard Bus. Sch., 1966. Pres. Schroder Venture Mgrs., N.Y.C., 1981-90, Collinson Howe Venture Ptnrs., Stamford, Conn., 1990—; bd. dirs. Incyte Pharms., Palo Alto, Calif., Neurogen Corp., Bramford, Conn., Transitional Care Am., Clayton, Mo., Advanced Rehab. Resources, St. Louis. Office: Collinson Howe Venture Ptnr 1055 Washington Blvd Stamford CT 06901

COLLOTON, JOHN WILLIAM, university health care executive; b. Mason City, Iowa, Feb. 20, 1931; s. Harold and Miriam (Kelly) C.; m. Mary Ann Hagglund, Oct. 8, 1960; children—Steven, Laura, Ann. B.A. with high honors, Loras Coll., 1953; M.A., U. Iowa, 1957. Hosp. relations rep. Hosp. Service Inc. of Iowa, Des Moines, 1957-58; with U. Iowa, Iowa City, 1958—; assoc. dir. U. Iowa Hosps. and Clinics, 1969-71, dir., asst. to univ. pres. for statewide health svcs., 1971-93; v.p. statewide health svcs. U. Iowa, 1993—; bd. dirs. Baxter Internat., Inc., Nat. Med. Waste Inc., Iowa State Bank & Trust Co., MidAm. Energy Co., Premier Anesthesia, Atlanta, 1992, Assn. Health Svcs. Rsch., 1992; cons. HIH; pres. adminstrv. bd. Assn. Am. med. Colls. Coun. of Teaching Hosps., 1979-80; mem. presdl. search com. Assn. Am. Med. Colls., 1984; mem. adv. bd. Duke U. Hosp., 1985; mem. task force on acad. health ctrs. Commonwealth Fund, chmn. selection com. exec. nurse leadership program, 1983; mem. prospective payment commn. Congl. Office Technology Assessment, 1983; chmn. bd. dirs. Iowa-S.D. Health Svcs. Corp. (now Blue Cross and Blue Shield Iowa, Blue Cross S.D.), 1993—. Contbr. articles to profl. publs. Served with Finance Corps U.S. Army, 1953-55. Fellow Am. Coll. Hosp. Adminstrs.; mem. Inst. Medicine NAS, Am. Hosp. Assn. (coun. on financing 1977, med. edn. com. 1984-87), Iowa Hosp. Assn. (chmn. bd. trustees 1977-78, trustee 1978—), Am. Assn. Hosp. Planning, Assn. Am. Med. Colls. (chmn. 1987-88, disting. svc. mem. 1991), Johnson County (Iowa) Med. Soc., U. Iowa Alumni Assn., Rotary. Roman Catholic. Home: 1899 Brown Deer Rd Coralville IA 52241-1160 Office: U Iowa Hosps & Clinics 200 Hawkins Dr Iowa City IA 52242-1009

COLMAN, ROBERT WOLF, physician, medical educator, researcher; b. N.Y.C., June 7, 1935; s. Jack K. and Miriam (Greenblatt) C.; m. Roberta Fishman, June 16, 1957; children: Sharon, David. AB summa cum laude, Harvard U., 1956, MD cum laude, 1960. Intern Boston City Hosp., 1960-61; resident Beth Israel, Brookline, Mass., 1961-62; clin. assoc. USPHS, NIH, 1962-64; resident Barnes Hosp., St. Louis, 1964-65, fellow in hematology, 1965-67; assoc. in medicine Harvard Med. Sch., Cambridge, Mass., 1967-69, asst. prof., 1969-73, assoc. prof., 1973; assoc. prof. U. Pa., Phila., 1973-77, prof. medicine, 1977-78; prof. medicine Temple U. Sch. Medicine, Phila., 1978—, prof. thrombosis rsch., 1981—, prof. physiology, 1992—, dir. Sol Sherry Thrombosis Rsch. Ctr., 1979—, Sol Sherry prof. of medicine, 1989—; mem. hematology study sect. NIH, Bethesda, Md., 1977-81; mem. parent com. to review SCORs in Ischemic Heart Disease; invited lectr. Gordon confs., Internat. Congress Hemostasis and Thrombosis, Fedn. Am. Socs. Exptl. Biology meetings; plenary lectr. Internat. Soc. Kallikreins and Kinins, others. Editor: Hemostasis and Thrombosis, 3d edit., 1994; editor Platelet Jour.; mem. editorial bd. Jour. Clin. Investigation, Blood, Procs. Soc. Exptl. Biology, Thrombosis Rsch. Platelets, Thrombosis Hemostasis; contbr. numerous articles to profl. jours. Surgeon USPHS, 1962-64. Recipient Leon Resnick prize Harvard U., Career Devel. award NIH, Sr. Investigator award S.E. Pa. chpt. Am. Heart Assn., Disting. Career award Internat. Soc. Thrombosis and Hemostasis. Fellow ACP; mem. Assn. Am. Physicians. Am. Soc. Clin. Investigation, Am. Soc. Biochemistry and Molecular Biology, Internat. Soc. Hemostasis and Thrombosis (councillor 1989-95), Peripatetic Club, Interurban Clin. Club, Phi Beta Kappa, Sigma Xi, Alpha Omega Alpha. Office: Temple U Sch Medicine Sol Sherry Thrombosis Rsch Ctr 3400 N Broad St Philadelphia PA 19140-5196

COLOMBO, ANTONIO, cardiologist; b. Busto Arsizio, Varese, Italy, June 17, 1950; s. Luigi and Lidia (Filippini) C.; m. Antonia Busetto, Mar. 30, 1978; children: Andrea, Paola. MD summa cum laude, U. Milan, 1975; degree in cardiology, U. Parma, Italy, 1978. Resident Centro Gasperis, Milan, 1975-78; intern N.Y. Med. Coll., N.Y.C., 1978-79, resident in cardiology, 1979-80, chief resident, 1980-82; fellow in cardiology VA Med. Ctr., Long Beach, Calif., 1982-84, dir. cardiology wards, 1985-86, asst. dir. cath. lab., 1985-86; fellow in cardiology St. Joseph's Hosp., Syracuse, N.Y., 1984-85; asst. prof. medicine U. Calif., Irvine, 1985-89; dir. Catheterization Lab. Columbus Hosp., Milan, 1986-95; chief investigational coronary angioplasty Lenox Hill Hosp., N.Y., 1995—; cons. for interventional cardiology Clinica Villa Bianca, Bari, 1991—; chmn. cardiopulmonary resuscitation VA Med. Ctr., Long Beach, Calif., 1985-86. Recipient Best Teaching award Cabrini Med. Ctr., N.Y., 1981, Ethica award Erasmus U., Rotterdam, 1994, Andreas Gruntzig ETHICA award, 1995. Fellow Am. Coll. Cardiology, Am. Heart Assn. Office: Columbus Hospital, Via M Buonarroti N 48, Milan 20145, Italy

COLOMER, VERONICA, medical educator, researcher; b. Mexico City, Mex., Nov. 9, 1957; married. BS, U. Mexico City, Mex., 1983; PhD, NYU, 1990. Postdoctoral fellow in lab. dept. cell biology NYU Med. Ctr., 1990-94; instr. lab. dept. cell biology Cornell Med. Coll., 1995; instr. in lab. dept. psychiatry Johns Hopkins U. Sch. Medicine, 1996—; guest investigator in lab. dept. cellular physiology and immunology Rockefeller U., 1982-84. Contbr. articles to profl. jours. Recipient Minority Scientist Devel. award Am. Heart Assn., 1996, Career award MSDA Am. Heart Assn., 1996—; Undergrad. Student fellowship Consejo Nacional de Ciencia y Tecnologia, 1981-82, Grad. Student fellowship, 1984-87, Ella Fitzgerald fellow Am. Heart Assn., 1991, Postdoctoral Participating Lab. award fellowship Am. Heart Assn., 1991-94. Mem. Am. Soc. Cell Biology, Royal Soc. Tropical Medicine and Hygiene, N.Y. Acad. Scis., Mex. Soc. Biochemistry, Mex. Soc. Immunology.

COLONNA, JOSEPH GEORGE, urologist; b. Jersey City, Jan. 20, 1949; s. Joseph Anthony and Ednamae (Kuppler) C.; m. Maria Rotundo, Nov. 3, 1979; children: Laura, Kathrine, Christine. BA, Ohio No. U., 1973; MD, U. Autonoma de Guadalajara, Mex., 1977. Diplomate Am. Bd. Urology. Fifth pathway Coll. Medicine and Dentistry N.J., Hackensack (N.J.) Hosp., 1978-79; gen. surgery resident Coll. Medicine and Dentistry N.J., Rutgers div., Piscataway, 1979-80; resident urology Hahneman Med. Coll. and Hosp., Phila., 1980-81, W.Va. U. Med. Ctr., Morgantown, 1981-84; pvt. practice urology Waldorf, Md., 1985—; mem. active staff surgery/urology Physician Meml. Hosp., Laplata, Md., 1987—; mem. active staff surgery/urology St. Mary's Hosp., Lenardtown Md., 1989—, So. Md. Hosp., Clinton, 1985—, Doctors Community Hosp., Lanham, Md., 1987—. Fellow ACS; mem. AMA, Am. Urol. Assn., Am. Fertility Soc., Med. and Chirurgical Faculty Md., Charles County Med. Soc. Roman Catholic. Home: 1017 Suffolk Dr La Plata MD 20646-3507 Office: 11350 Pembrooke Sq Ste 311 Waldorf MD 20603-4809

COLONNIER, MARC LEOPOLD, neuroanatomist, educator; b. Quebec, Que., Can., May 12, 1930; s. Jean and Enilda (Bourguignon) C.; m. Lise De

Gagne, Oct. 24, 1959; 1 son, Jean. B.A., B.Ph., U. Ottawa, 1951, M.D., 1959, M.S., 1960; Ph.D., U. Coll. London, 1963. Asst. prof. anatomy U. Ottawa, 1963-65; asst. prof. dept. physiology U. Montreal, Que., Can., 1965-67; assoc. prof., assoc. fellow neurol. scis. group Med. Research Council Can., 1967-69; prof., head dept. anatomy U. Ottawa, 1969-76; prof. dept. anatomy Laval U., Quebec City, Que., 1976-91; ret., 1991. Recipient Lederle Med. Faculty award, 1966, Charles Judson Herrick award Am. Assn. Anatomists, 1967. Fellow Royal Soc. Can.; mem. Am. Assn. Anatomists; Mem. Soc. Neurosci.; mem. Can. Assn. Anatomists (pres. 1973-75). Club: Cajal.

COLONY-COKELY, PAMELA CAMERON, medical researcher; b. Boston, Apr. 18, 1947; d. Donald Gifford Colony and Priscilla (Adams) Pratley; m. E. Paul Cokely Jr., Apr. 26, 1986; children: Daniel Patrick, John Travis. BA, Wellesley (Mass.) Coll., 1969; PhD, Boston U., 1976. Rsch. asst. sch. medicine Boston U., 1969-71, U. Hosp., 1971-73, Peter Bent Brigham Hosp., Boston, 1973-75; instr. dept. anatomy Harvard Med. Sch., 1975-77; assoc. staff in medicine Peter Bent Brigham Hosp., Boston, 1976-79; sr. fellow, instr. Harvard Med. Sch., Boston, 1979-81; asst. prof. anatomy and medicine Pa. State Coll. Medicine, Hershey, Pa., 1981-88; assoc. prof. rsch., pre-health advisor Franklin and Marshall Coll., Lancaster, 1988-91; adj. assoc. prof. of surgery Pa. State Coll. Medicine, Hershey, 1988-91, sr. rsch. assoc. dept. surgery, 1991-95; program dir. histotechnology SUNY, Cobleskill, 1995—; ind. assessor Nat. Health and Med. Rsch. Coun., Australia, 1985—; ad-hoc reviewer NIH, Nat. Cancer Inst., Bethesda, Md., 1986; lectr., adj. instr. Harrisburg Area Cmty. Coll., 1991—. Contbr. articles to profl. jours. Fellow Nat. Found. Ileitis and Colitis, 1979-81; grantee Fed. Republic Germany, 1978, Cancer Rsch. Ctr., 1982-83, NIH, 1982-91. Mem. AAAS, Am. Soc. Cell Biology, N.Y. Acad. Sci., Am. Gastroent. Assn., Nat. Assn. Advisors Health Profls. Office: SUNY Cobleskill Dept Liberal Arts and Sci Cobleskill NY 12043

COLOSIMO, ANN MARIE, orthopaedic nurse; b. Red Bank, N.J., May 19, 1939; d. Donald and Anna Veronica (Kelly) Hickey; m. Anthony Colosimo, June 28, 1958 (div. 1985); children: Lynn Marie, Susan. AAS, Brookdale Community Coll., 1975; BSN, Trenton State Coll., 1983. Cert. nat. orthopaedic nurse, case mgr. Staff and charge nurse Perth Amboy (N.J.) Gen. Hosp., 1975-77; staff nurse othopaedics Riverview Med. Ctr., Red Bank, N.J., 1977-83, asst. clin. coord. othopaedics, 1983-86, staff nurse orthopaedics, 1986-90, nurse case mgr. orthopaedics, 1990-95, nurse case mgr. occupational health, 1995—. Mem. Nat. Assn. Orthopaedic Nurses (pres. 1984-85, 92-93, pres.-elect 1991-92, sec. 1995—), Collaborative Practice Com., Discharge Planning Nurse Coords. of N.J., Inc., Sigma Theta Tau (Lamgda Delta chpt., cmty. leader award 1992). Home: 53-04 Grassmere Ct Freehold NJ 07728 Office: Riverview Med Ctr 1 Riverview Plz Red Bank NJ 07701-1864

COLOSKI, DENNIS JOHN, critical care nurse; b. New Haven, Jan. 15, 1954; s. Denny J. and Mary V. (Swiatek) C.; children: Cassandra, Barbara. ASN with honors, Norwalk Community Coll., 1985. RN, CCRN. Staff nurse med. ICU Hosp. of St. Raphael, New Haven; staff nurse ICU Pa. Hosp., Phila.; staff nurse Cardiac Cath. Lab. Phila. (Pa.) Heart Inst., 1991-96, U. Pa. Presbyn. Med. Ctr. campus, 1996—. Co-author: Continuous Arteriovenous Hemofiltration Patient: Nursing Care Plan DCCN, vol. III, 1990. With U.S. Army, 1971-73. Mem. AACN, Phi Theta Kappa.

COLOSO, VICTOR FRANCISCO, pediatrician; b. Manila, Nov. 2, 1960; came to U.S., 1986; s. Ernesto Cruz Coloso and Ramona De Guzman Francisco; m. Regina Sanson Sitchon, Jan. 12, 1992; children: Nina Therese, Patrick Angelo. BS in Zoology cum laude, U. of The Philippines, Quezon City, 1982; MD, U. of The Philippines, Manila, 1986. Bd. cert. Am. Bd. Pediats. Resident in pediats. Monmouth Med. Ctr., Long Branch, N.J., 1991-94; neonatal fellow U. Miami-Jackson Meml. Hosp., Miami, Fla., 1994—. Mem. Am. Acad. Pediats. Home: 12364 SW 143 Ln Miami FL 33186 Office: U Miami Jackson Meml Hosp Miami FL 33136

COLP, RALPH, JR., psychiatrist; b. N.Y.C., Oct. 12, 1924; s. Ralph Colp and Miriam (Mirsky) Ittelson; children: Ruth, Judith. BA, Columbia Coll., 1945; MD, Columbia U., 1948. Diplomate Am. Bd. Psychiatry and Neurology. Intern Michael Reese Hosp., Chgo., 1948-49; resident in surgery Mount Sinai Hosp., N.Y.C., 1950-53; instr. in medicine Tulane Med. Sch., New Orleans, 1949-50; instr. in psychiatry Harvard U., Cambridge, 1957-59; resident in psychiatry Mass. Mental Health Ctr., Boston, 1957-59, St. Luke's Hosp., N.Y.C., 1959-60; attending psychiatrist St. Luke's-Roosevelt Hosp. Ctr., N.Y.C., 1960-84, sr. attending psychiatrist, 1984—; asst. prof. clin. psychiatry Columbia U., N.Y.C., 1974—; attending psychiatrist Columbia U. Health Svc., 1960-93; rsch. fellow Psychohistory Forum, N.Y.C., 1984—. Author: To Be an Invalid: The Illness of Charles Darwin, 1977. Capt. USAF, 1953-55. Fellow Am. Assn. Sex Educators, Counselors and Therapists, Am. Psychiat. Assn., N.Y. Acad. Medicine; mem. Ea. Assn. Sex Therapists, Internat. Psychohistory Assn. Jewish. Home and Office: 301 E 79th St Apt 12A New York NY 10021-0938

COLTEN, HARVEY RADIN, pediatrician, educator; b. Houston, Jan. 11, 1939; s. Oscar Aaron and Zina Mae (Radin) C.; m. Susan J. Kaplowitz, July 29, 1959; children: Jennifer J., Lora, Charles Thomas. B.A., Cornell U., 1959; M.D., Western Res. U., 1963; M.A. (hon.), Harvard U., 1978. Diplomate Am. Bd. Allergy and Clin. Immunology, Am. Bd. Pediatrics. Intern Univ. Hosps., Cleve., 1963-64, resident in pediatrics, 1964-65; resident in pediatrics Children's Hosp. of D.C., Washington, 1968-69; rsch. assoc. Nat. Inst. Child and Human Devel., NIH, Bethesda, Md., 1965-67; asst. prof. pediatrics George Washington U., 1969-70; asst. prof. pediatrics Harvard U., 1970-73, assoc. prof., 1973-79, prof., 1979-86; chief div. cell biology, dir. cystic fibrosis program Children's Hosp. Med. Ctr., Boston, 1976-86; Harriet B. Spoehrer prof. pediats. Washington U. Med. Sch., St. Louis, 1986—, chmn. dept. pediats., 1986-95, prof. molecular microbiology, 1986—; pediatrician-in-chief Children's and Barnes Hosps., 1986-95, Jewish Hosp., 1986-90; pediatrician Children's, Barnes and Jewish Hosps., 1995—; past chmn. pediatric allergy Nat. Inst. Allergy and Infectious Disease Task Force on Asthma and Allergy; past mem. Nat. Inst. Child and Human Devel. Task Force on Cystic Fibrosis; past bd. dirs. rsch. rev. com. Nat. Cystic Fibrosis Found.; past mem. pulmonary diseases adv. com. NIH. Assoc. editor Jour. Immunology, 1971-74, Immuno-chemistry, 1972-75, Jour. Allergy and Clin. Immunology, 1977-80, New Eng. Jour. Medicine, 1978-81, Jour. Clin. Investigation, 1982-85, Am. Jour. Respiratory Cell and Molecular Biology, 1988-91, New Insights into CF, 1993; mem. editorial bd. Molecular and Cellular Biochemistry, 1983-87, Jour. Pediatrics, 1981-88, Jour. Clin. Immunology, 1985-89, Ann. Rev. Immunology, 1986-90, Clin. Immunology and Immunopathology, 1987-91, Blood, 1987-92, New England Journal of Medicine, 1990—, Jour. Biomedical Sci., 1992—, Proc. Assn. Am. Physics, 1995—; contbr. articles to profl. jours. Parents As Tchrs. Nat. Ctr.; past mem. pediatric scientist program selection com. AMSPDC; mem. sci. adv. coun. Mar. Dimes; mem. Nat. Heart, Lung, Blood Adv. Coun., NIH. Recipient Spl. faculty rsch. award Western Res. U., 1963, E. Mead Johnson award, 1979. Fellow AAAS, Am. Acad. Allergy and Immunology, Am. Acad. Pediatrics; mem. Fedn. Am. Socs. for Exptl. Biology (mem. fin. com.), Inst. Medicine of NAS (mem. coun.), E. Mead Johnson Award Program Com. (past chmn.), Am. Assn. Immunologists (sec.-treas.), Am. Soc. Clin. Investigation, Assn. Am. Physicians, Soc. Pediatric Rsch., Am. Pediatric Soc., Am. Thoracic Soc., Cen. Inst. for Deaf (bd. mgrs.), Am. Soc. Biochem. & Molecular Biol., St. Louis Pediatric Soc. Office: Washington U Sch Medicine Dept Pediats One Children Place Saint Louis MO 63110

COLTRANE, TAMARA CARLEANE, intravenous therapy nurse; b. Greensboro, N.C., Oct. 18, 1963; d. Charles Floyd and Nancy Jane (Lemons) C. BS in Nursing, U. N.C., Greensboro, 1986. RN, N.C.; cert. in intravenous therapy. Nursing asst. (summer) Mary Field Nursing Home, High Point, N.C., 1984; med.-surgical nurse Wesley Long Cmty. Hosp., Greensboro, 1986-88, IV team nurse, 1988—; mem. nursing policy com. Wesley Long Cmty. Hosp., Greensboro, 1987-88, nursing adv. com., 1987-89, 91-93, mem. nursing edn. coun., 1996—. Mem. coun. on ministries, pianist, coord. comm. Sandy Ridge United Meth. Ch., High Point, N.C., 1990—, mem. adminstrv. bd., 1986-88, 90—; vol. worker Starmount Villa Nursing Home, Greensboro, 1984. Mem. Nat. Intravenous Nurses Soc., N.C. Intravenous Nurses Soc., Sigma Theta Tau. Office: Wesley Long Cmty Hosp 501 N Elam Ave Greensboro NC 27403-1118

COLVARD, MICHAEL DAVID, periodontist, oral medicine and laser surgery specialist; b. Salem, Ore., Oct. 11, 1954; s. William Douglas and Othelene (Lee) C.; m. Kathleen Marie Perkowitz, July 14, 1984; children: Christopher Michael, Jonathon David. BA in Edn., Ariz. State U., 1978; DDS, Loyola U., 1985, cert. periodontist, 1985-87; postgrad., U. Ill., 1993—. Diplomate Am. Acad. Pain Mgmt. Surg. asst. Evanston (Ill.) Hosp., 1978-85; pvt. practice Schaumburg, Ill., 1985—; vis. lectr. Dept. Oral and Maxillofacial Surgery Loyola U., Maywood, Ill., 1990-95; clin. asst. prof. Stritch Sch. Medicine Loyola U., 1995—; adj. prof. dental hygiene William R. Harper Coll., Palatine, Ill., 1987—. Speaker Am. Acad. Gen. Dentistry, 1988—. Named One of Outstanding Young Men Am., U.S. Jaycees, 1975, Outstanding Dental Corp. Officer of Air Nat. Guard, 1991; recipient Outstanding Achievement medal, Air Force, 1994, Air Force Meritorious Medal, 1992, Order of the Med. Minuteman N.G. Bur., Washington, 1991. Fellow Am. Acad. Oral Medicine, Am. Soc. Laser Medicine and Surgery; mem. ADA, Am. Acad. Periodontology (speaker 1988—), Assn. of Mil. Surgeons, Air Force Assn., Aerospace Medicine Assn., Nat. Jr. Coll. Athletic Assn. (all-Am. 1st team gymnastics 1975). Republican. Office: Ste 1 South 650 E Higgins Schaumburg IL 60173

COLVIN, CLIFFORD NORMAN, medical technologist; b. McMinnville, Oreg., Dec. 1, 1941; s. Norman Taylor and Agnes May (Lindsay) C.; m. Phyllis Bertha Hegney, Aug. 30, 1964; children: Larry Lee, Linda Sue DeClue. BS in Biology, Warner Pacific Coll., 1973. Cert. Am. Med. Technologists, Ltd. Permit Diagnostic Radiologic Technology. Med. technologist United Med. Labs., Portland, 1964-66, United Med. Labs./ICN Med. Labs., Portland, 1968-78; production mgr. Intersci. Diagnostics, Portland, 1978-86; chief technologist Rinehart Meml. Hosp., Wheeler, Oreg., 1986-88; lab. mgr. Oakridge Med. Clin., Lake Oswego, Oreg., 1988-96. With U.S. Army, 1966-68. Home: 8041 SE Henry Portland OR 97206 Office: Oakridge Med Clin 4309 Oakridge Rd Lake Oswego OR 97035

COLVIN, GEORGE LESLIE, osteopath; b. Morristown, N.J., Nov. 23, 1934; m. Natalie Colvin, July 11, 1964; children: Gerald, Rachel, Andrew. BS, Davis & Elkins Coll., 1956; DO, Phila. Coll. Osteo. Medicine, 1960, MSc in Radiology, 1964. pres. N.Y. State Osteo. Med. Soc., 1989-91. Contbr. articles to profl. jours. Dist. dep. grand master Masonic, Queens, 1993, 94, 95. Recipient Disting. Svc. citation N.Y. State Chiropractic Assn., 1988, Disting. Practitioner award Nat. Acads. Practice, 1988. Fellow Am. Osteo. Coll. Radiology (bd. cert. radiology, cert. nuclear medicine), Am. Osteo. Coll. Family Practice (bd. cert. family practice, geriat.); mem. N.Y.C. Soc. Osteo. Physicians (pres. 1977, 95, 96). Home: 785 Longview Ave North Woodmere NY 11581 Office: 7819 18th Ave Brooklyn NY 11214

COLVIN, HARRY WALTER, JR., physiology educator; b. Schellsburg, Pa., Dec. 5, 1921; s. Harry Walter and Maude Elizabeth (Girven) C.; m. Marie Catherine McNinch, Apr. 8, 1950; children: Sarah Lee, William McNinch. BS, Pa. State U., 1950; PhD, U. Calif., Davis, 1957. Instr. Okla. State U., Stillwater, 1955-57; assoc. prof. physiology U. Ark., Fayetteville, 1957-65; prof. U. Calif., Davis, 1965—; cons. Pel-Freez Biologicals, Inc., Rogers, Ark., 1960-65. Assoc. editor Hilgardia, 1981-92; contbr. articles to profl. jours. Served with U.S. Army, 1942-45, ETO. Recipient Fulbright award CIES, Washington, 1972, 86. Mem. Am. Dairy Sci. Assn., Am. Soc. Animal Sci., Sigma Xi, Phi Kappa Phi, Alpha Zeta, Gamma Sigma Delta, Phi Sigma , Phi Eta Sigma. Republican. Club: El Macero (Calif.) Country. Home: 3340 Biscayne Bay Pl Davis CA 95616-2602 Office: U Calif Davis Dept Neurobiol & Physiol Behavior Davis CA 95616

COLVIN, ROBERT ALAN, neurobiology educator; b. Buffalo, Apr. 26, 1953; s. John D. and Martha L. (Jaworska) C. BA, SUNY, Buffalo, 1975; PhD, Rutgers U., 1980. Instr. U. Conn. Health Ctr., Farmington, Conn., 1980-85; asst. prof. pharmacology Oral Roberts U., Tulsa, 1985-90; assoc. prof. biology Ohio U., Athens, 1990—. Office: Coll Osteopathic Medicine Ohio Univ Athens OH 45701

COLVIN, ROBERT BARNES, pathologist, researcher; b. Columbus, Ohio, May 7, 1942; s. Robert M. and Ellen M. (Barnes) C.; m. Gatewood Warwick Wise, July 23, 1966; children: Jessica. BS, MIT, 1964; MD, Harvard U., 1968. Lic. anatomic and immunopathologist. Intern-resident/fellow Mass. Gen. Hosp., Boston, 1968-72, from asst. pathologist to pathologist, 1975-91, dir. immunopathology unit, 1980-91; chief Dept. of Pathology Mass. General Hosp., Boston, 1991—; maj. Walter Reed Army Inst. Rsch., Washington, 1972-75; from asst. prof. to prof. pathology Harvard Med. Sch., Boston, 1975-91, Benjamin Castleman prof. pathology, 1991—, master Holmes Soc., 1990-92; chief pathology svcs. Mass. Gen. Hosp., Boston, 1991—; mem. test com. Nat. Bd. Med. Examiners, Phila., 1983-87, 89-90, Am. Bd. Pathology, Tampa, Fla., 1985-91. Editor: Diagnostic Immunopathology, 1996, Organ Transplantation in Children, 1989; contbr. over 200 articles to profl. jours. Maj. U.S. Army, 1972-75. Recipient Merit award NIH, 1987; grantee NIH, 1975—. Mem. Am. Assn. Pathologists, Am. Assn. Immunologists, Am. Soc. Nephrology, Transplantation Soc., Internat. Acad. Pathology. Episcopalian. Office: Mass Gen Hosp Dept Pathology Boston MA 02114

COLVIN, SUSAN PUGLIESE, nurse educator; b. Pitts., Jan. 5, 1943; d. Peter M. and Guida (Ambrosino) Pugliese; m. Gerald C. Colvin, June 27, 1970; children: Michael, David, Anne. BSN, Duquesne U., 1965; M of Nursing, U. Pitts., 1971, postgrad., 1990—. RN, Pa.; cert. trauma nurse ANA, pediatric nurse ANCC. Clin. nurse NIH, Bethesda, Md., 1965-66, VA Hosp., Pitts., 1966-67; instr. nursing Presbyn. U. Hosp. Sch. Nursing, Pitts., 1967-70, Community Coll. Allegheny County, Pitts., 1978-88; asst. prof. Duquesne U. Sch. Nursing, Pitts., 1988—; staff nurse Children's Hosp. Pitts., 1981—. Vol vision screening Pitts. Blind Assn., 1982—. Mem. Duquesne U. Sch. Nursing Alumni Assn. (exec. com.), Sigma Theta Tau Internat. (chmn., faculty advisor, exec. com.). Home: 16 Bryn Mawr Rd Pittsburgh PA 15221-3822 Office: Duquesne U Sch Nursing College Hall Pittsburgh PA 15282

COLWELL, JOHN AMORY, physician; b. Boston, Nov. 4, 1928; s. Arthur Ralph and Jeane (Haskins) C.; m. Jane Kuebler, June 19, 1954; children: John Clayton, Ann Kimbell, Karen Elizabeth, James Lewis. A.B., Princeton U., 1950; M.D., Northwestern U., 1954, M.S. in Medicine, 1957, Ph.D. in Physiology, 1968. Intern Univ. Hosps., Cleve., 1954-55; resident in internal medicine Passavant Meml. Hosp., Chgo., 1955-57, VA Research Hosp., Chgo., 1959-60; from instr. to assoc. prof. medicine Northwestern U. Med. Sch., 1960-71; fellow in neuroendocrinology and diabetes Northwestern U. Med. Ctr., Chgo., 1960-63; clin. investigator, then chief metabolic sect. VA Research Hosp., 1961-71; prof. medicine Med. U. S.C., Charleston, 1971—; dir. endocrinology-metabolism-diabetes div., dept. medicine Med. U. S.C., 1972-94; dir. diabetes ctr. Med. U. S.C., Charleston, 1994—; rsch. coord. Med. U. S.C., 1973-79; assoc. chief staff rsch. and devel. VA Med. Center, Charleston, 1971-93; bd. dirs. Am. Diabetes Assn., 1982-88, v.p. 1985, pres. elect 1986, pres., 1987; bd. dirs. S.C. Diabetes Assn., 1971-80/. Author: Clinical Recognition and Treatment of Diabetic Vascular Disease, 1975; co-author: Diabetes and Metabolic Disorders, 1975, 82, Diabetes, Endocrinology and Metabolic Disorders, 1981; contbr. articles med. jours. Served to capt. M.C. USAF, 1957-59. Grantee: NiH, VA, 1962-94. Fellow ACP; mem. AAAS, Am. Diabetes Assn., Am. Fedn. Clin. Rsch., Am. Physiol. Soc., Ctrl. Soc. Clin. Rsch., Endocrine Soc., So. Soc. Clin. Investigation. Republican. Episcopalian. Clubs: Skokie Country (Glencoe, Ill.), Carolina Yacht (Charleston), Yeamans Hall (Charleston), Cloister Inn (Princeton U.). Home: 182 Broad St Charleston SC 29401-2429

COLWELL, RITA ROSSI, microbiologist, molecular biologist, educator; b. Nov. 23, 1934; m. Jack H. Colwell, May 31, 1956; children: Alison E.L., Stacie A. BS in Bacteriology with distinction, Purdue U., 1956, MS in Genetics, 1958; PhD, U. Wash., 1961; DSc, Heriot-Watt U., Edinburgh, Scotland, 1987; DSc (hon.), Hood Coll., 1991; DSc, Purdue U., 1993; LLD, Notre Dame Coll., 1994; DSc (hon.), U. Surrey, Eng., 1995. Rsch. asst. genetics lab. Purdue U., West Lafayette, Ind., 1956-57; rsch. asst. U. Wash., Seattle, 1957-58, predoctoral assoc., 1959-60, asst. rsch. prof., 1961-64; asst. prof. biology Georgetown U., Washington, 1964-66, assoc. prof. biology, 1966-72; prof. microbiology U. Md., 1972—, v.p. for acad. affairs, 1983-87; dir. Ctr. Marine Biotech., 1987-91; pres. Md. Biotech. Inst. U. Md., 1991—; hon. prof. U. Queensland, Brisbane, Australia, 1988; cons., advisor Washington area comms. media, congressman, legislators, 1978—; external examiner various univs. abroad, 1964—; mem. coastal resources adv. com. dept. natural resources State of Md., 1979; NAS ocean scis. bd., 1977-80, vice-chair polar rsch. bd., 1990-94; mem. Nat. Sci. Bd., 1984-90, sci. adv. bd. Oak Ridge Nat. Labs., 1988-90, 93-96, adv. com. FDA, 1991-92, food adv. com., 1993-96. Author 16 books including (manual numerical taxonomy) Collecting the Data, 1970, (with M. Zambruski) Rodina-Methods in Aquatic Microbiology, 1972, (with L. H. Stevenson) Estuarine Microbial Ecology, 1973, (with R. Y. Morita) Effect of the Ocean Environment on Microbial Activities, 1974, (with A. Sinsky and N. Pariser) Marine Biotechnology, 1983, Vibrios in the Environment, 1985, Nucleic Acid Sequence Data, 1988, (with others) Marine Biotechnology, 1995; mem. editorial bd. Microbial Ecology, 1972-91, Applied and Environ. Microbiology, 1969-81, Oil and Petrochemical Pollution, 1980-91, Jour. Washington Acad. Scis., 1981-87, Johns Hopkins U. Oceanographic Series, 1981-84, Revue de la Fondation Oceanographique Ricard, 1981-92, Estuaries, 1983-89, Zentralblatt fur Bacteriologie, 1985—, Jour. Aquatic Living Resources, 1987—, System. Applied Microbiology, 1985—, World Jour. Microbiology and Biotechnology, 1988—; contbr. articles and revs. to profl. jours. including Can. Jour. Fisheries and Aquatic Scis., Soc. Gen. Microbiology, Jour. Bacteriology, others. Recipient Gold medal Internat. Biotech. Inst., 1990, Purkinje Gold medal Achievement in Scis. Czechoslavakian Acad. Scis., 1991, Civic award Gov. Md., 1990, Cert. Recognition, NASA, 1984, Alice Evans award Am. Soc. Microbiol. Com. on Status of Women, 1988, Andrew White medal Loyola Coll., 1994, medal of distinction Barnard Coll./Columbia U., 1996; named Phi Kappa Phi Scholar of Yr., 1992, Outstanding Women on Campus U. Md., 1979. Fellow AAAS (chmn. sect. biol. scis. 1993-94, pres. 1995, chmn. bd. 1996), Grad. Women Sci., Can. Coll. Microbiologists, Am. Acad. Microbiology (chmn. bd. govs. 1989-94), Washington Acad. Scis. (bd. mgrs. 1976-79), Marine Tech. Soc., (exec. com. 1982-88), Sigma Delta Epsilon; mem. Am. Soc. Microbiology (various sci. coms. 1961—, pres. 1985, chmn. program com. REGEM-1 1988, Fisher award 1985), World Fedn. Culture Collections, Internat. Union Microbiol. Soc. (v.p. 1986-90, pres. 1990-94), Am. Inst. Biol. Scis. (bd. govs. 1976-82), Am. Soc. Limnology and Oceanography, Internat. Coun. Sci. Unions (gen com., exec. bd. 1993—), U.S. Fedn. Culture Collections (governing bd. 1978-88), Soc. Indsl. Microbiology (bd. govs. 1976-79), Classification Rsch. Group Eng. (charter), Soc. Gen. Microbiology, Phi Beta Kappa, Sigma Xi (Ann. Achievement award 1981, Rsch. award 1984, nat. pres. 1991), Omicron Delta Kappa, Delta Gamma. Office: U Md Biotech inst Ste 550 4321 Hartwick Rd College Park MD 20740-3210

COLWILL, JACK MARSHALL, physician, educator; b. Cleve., June 15, 1932; s. Clifford V. and Olive A. (Marshall) C.; m. Winifred Stedman, 1954; children: James F., Elizabeth Ann, Carolyn. B.A., Oberlin Coll., 1953; M.D. (George Whipple scholar), U. Rochester, 1957. Diplomate Am. Bd. Med. Examiners, Am. Bd. Internal Medicine, Am. Bd. Family Practice. Intern Barnes Hosp., Washington U. Sch. Medicine, St. Louis, 1957-58; resident in medicine U. Washington Affiliated Hosps., Seattle, 1958-60; chief resident U. Hosp., 1960-61; instr. medicine, dir. med. outpatient dept. U. Rochester (N.Y.) Sch. Medicine and Dentistry, 1961-62, sr. instr. medicine, dir. med. outpatient dept., 1962-64; asst. dean, asst. prof. medicine, asst. prof. community health and med. practice U. Mo. Sch. Medicine, Columbia, 1964-67; assoc. dean, asst. prof. U. Mo. Sch. Medicine, 1967-69, assoc. dean for acad. affairs, asst. prof., 1969-70, assoc. dean, assoc. prof., 1970-76, interim chmn. dept. family and community medicine, 1976-77, prof., 1976—, chmn. dept., asso. prof. medicine, 1977—; cons. Office Div. Dir., USPHS, 1977—, Bur. Health Manpower, NIH, 1969-75; mem. Coun. on Grad. Med. Edn. Health Resources and Svcs. Adminstrn., 1990—. Contbr. articles to profl. jours. Dir. Robert Wood Johnson Found. Generalist Physician Initiative, 1991—. Mem. AMA, Assn. Med. Am. Colls. (chmn. Midwest-Gt. Plains Group on Student Affairs 1971-73, nat. vice chmn. Group 1973-74, chmn. working group on non-cognitive assessment-adv. to com. on admissions assessment 1974-77), Soc. Tchrs. Family Medicine (bd. dirs. 1978-82, 83-87, pres.-elect 1987-88, pres. 1988-89), Am. Acad. Family Physicians (commn. on govtl. legis. affairs 1984-87, coun. on grad. med. edn., 1990—), Inst. Medicine NAS, Alpha Omega Alpha. Office: U Mo-Columbia Sch Medicine Dept Family and Medicine Columbia MO 65212

COLYER, JAMES DANIEL, surgeon; b. Hays, Kans., Apr. 2, 1950; s. James D. and Lorene M. (McKee) C.; m. Toni K. farha, June 3, 1972; children: James, Kelli, Christopher, Kami. BA in Biology, U. Kans., 1972; DDS, Baylor Coll. of Dentistry, 1976; Cert. Oral and Maxillofacial Surgery, U. Okla., 1980. Diplomate Am. Bd. Oral and Maxillofacial Surgery. Pvt. practice oral and maxillofacial surgery Tempe, Ariz. Contbr. articles to profl. jours. Fellow AAOMS; mem. ADA, Ariz. Soc. Oral Surgerons (sec./treas. 1988-90, v.p., 1990-92, pres. 1992-94), Southside Dental Soc. (pres. 1981-85), ADA, Phoenix Soc. Oral Surgeons, Ariz. Dental Assn., Cen. Ariz. Dental Soc. Republican. Office: 6200 s McClintock # 6 Tempe AZ 85283

COMA-CANELLA, ISABEL, cardiologist; b. Vigo, Pontevedra, Spain, Sept. 12, 1948; d. Fernando and Rosina (Canella) C. License in medicine, Navarra U., Pamplona, Spain, 1971. Resident Cantabria Hosp., Santander, Spain, 1972-73; resident in internal medicine Puerta de Hierro Hosp., Madrid, 1973-74, resident in cardiology, 1974-76; cardiology asst. coronary care unit La Paz Hosp., Madrid, 1977-95; head dept. cardiology U. de Navarra, Pamplona, Spain, 1995—. Author: Ischemic Heart Disease, 1981, 88, Cholesterol and Infarction, 1991; contbr. articles to profl. jours.; editorial bd. Spanish Jour. Cardiology, 1982; reviewer European Jour. Cardiology, 1990. Founder Verin Cultural Orgn., Madrid, 1991. Recipient award Knoll Labs., 1982, Rsch. award, 1992, 95. Fellow European Soc. Cardiology, Am. Coll. Cardiology; mem. Spanish Soc. Cardiology. Roman Catholic. Office: Dept Cardiology Clinica U, U de Navarra Apt 4209, 31080 Pamplona Spain

COMBE, BERNARD MARIE-JOËL, physician; b. Avignon, France, May 24, 1947; s. John and Alberte (Vernède) C.; m. Annie Genevieve Bartoccioni, June 30, 1973; 1 child, Guillaume. Bachelor's degree, Lycee Carnot, Cannes, 1968; MD, Sci. and Med. U. Grenoble, France, 1975. Intern CHU Grenoble, 1971-74, asst. instr., 1972-74, practice med., 1975; staff pvt. gerontological hosp., 1977-81, Civil Soc. Coberome, LeCannet, 1982—; pres. Hosp. staff, 1973-74; med. creative staff S.O.S., Cannes, 1977-78. Served with the French mil., 1974-1975. Mem. Gerontologic Meridional Fedn. Soc. Roman Catholic. Home: Gen de Gaulle Ave 1291, 06250 Mougins France

COMBE, IVAN DEBLOIS, drug company executive; b. Fremont, Iowa, Apr. 21, 1911; s. Louis Abel and Elsie (Mange) C.; m. Mary Elizabeth Deming, Dec. 10, 1938; children—Diana M. Combe Bickford, Juliette M. Combe Larson, Christopher Bryan. BS, Northwestern U., 1933, postgrad. Law Sch., 1933-35. Salesman, sales promotion exec. Nat. Dairy Products, Chgo., 1935-36; div. sales mgr. Wilbert Products Co., N.Y.C., 1936-40; merchandising account exec. Young & Rubicam, Inc., N.Y.C., 1940-43; v.p. sales and advt. Pharmacraft Corp. (subs. Seagram Distillers), N.Y.C., 1944-49; pres., founder Combe Inc., White Plains, N.Y., 1949-70; chmn. , 1970—. Chmn. Council on Family Health, N.Y.C., 1972-79; bd. dirs. White Plains Hosp. Ctr., 1962—; trustee Northwestern U., 1968—, life trustee, 1979—, life regent. Recipient Alumni Service award Northwestern U., 1962, Merit award, 1971. Mem. U.S. Nonprescription Drug Mfrs. Assn. (bd. dirs., exec. com. 1958—, chmn. 1964-66), World Fedn. Proprietary Medicine Mfrs. (bd. dirs., exec. com. 1977—, chmn. 1977-79), Met. Club (N.Y.C.), Blind Brook Club (Purchase, N.Y.), Country Club of Fla. (Delray), Ekwanok Country

Club, (Manchester, Vt.), Svc. Club, Rotary, Alpha Delta Phi. Home: 25 Wilshire Rd Greenwich CT 06831-2723

COMBEMALE, PATRICK ABEL, dermatologist; b. Mende, Lozere, France, July 30, 1953; s. Jean Abel and Colette (Lauraire) C.; m. Isabelle Marie Girardin, Sept. 24, 1977; children: Thomas, Claire. MD, U. Lyon, 1978. Resident in sports medicine U. Paris, 1978-79, resident in leprology, 1986, resident in dermatology, 1987; resident in aero. medicine Cerma, Paris, 1979; asst. physician Hosp. Begin, Paris, 1983-87; dermatologist, asst. Hosp. Desgenette, Lyon, France, 1987-89, head dept., 1989—; cons. Air Force Base 941,Taverny, France, 1979-83. Maj. M.C., French Air Force, 1979-83. Mem. French Soc. Dermatology, Rhone Alie Soc. Dermatology. Home: 32 rue Chaziere, 69004 Lyon France Office: Hosp Desgenette, 108 blvd Pinel, 69004 Lyon France

COMBERG, DIETRICH WILHELM, retired oculist; b. Berlin, Dec. 27, 1928; s. Wilhelm and Käthe (Ruhnke) C.; m. Sabine Baerbel Berg; children: Kai, Ute. Dr. Med., U. Rostock, Fed. Republic Germany, 1955; Dr. med. habilitation, Humboldt U., Berlin, 1965, Free U., West Berlin, 1973. Prof. Free Univ., Berlin, 1975-93; ret. Mem. Deutsche Ophthalmoi Gesellschaft. Home: Treiberpfad 28, D-13469 Berlin Germany

COMBS, GERALD FUSON, SR., nutritionist; b. Olney, Ill., Feb. 23, 1920; s. Lloyd Roscoe and Ina Roe (Fuson) C.; children: Gerald Fuson Jr., Lawrence Luther, John Wallace, Gregory Lloyd. BS, U. Ill., 1940; PhD, Cornell U., 1948. Prof. nutrition U. Md., College Park, 1948-69; dep. chief nutrition program USMHA HEW, Rockville, Md., 1969-71; coord. human nutrition and food safety USDA, Washington, 1971-73; head dept. food and nutrition U. Ga., Athens, 1973-75; dir. nutrition program Nat. Inst. Arthritis, Diabetes and Digestive and Kidney Disease NIH, Bethesda, Md., 1975-83; asst. dep. adminstr. human nutrition Agrl. Rsch. Svc., USDA, Beltsville, Md., 1983-91; adj. prof. U. So. Miss., 1992—; cons. Internat. Com. on Nutrition for Nat. Def. NIH, 1956-69, OMNI, USAID, 1994-95, various indsl. cos., 1953-85; dir. U.S. sponsored nutritional survey Republic of Korea, 1956, Ecuador, 1959. Contbr. 150 articles to profl. jours. Chmn. bd. dirs. Good Shepherd Meth. Ch., Silver Spring, Md., 1981-82. Maj. U.S. Army, 1941-46, ETO. Decorated Bronze Star; recipient Ann. Rsch. award Am. Feed Mfrs., 1953, Meritorious Svc. award Delmarva Poultry Industries, 1969, Disting. Nutritionist award Distillers Rsch. Coun., 1970, Meritorious Svc. award Agrl. Rsch. Svc., USDA, 1988; named Man of the Yr. Md. Agr., 1959. Fellow Am. Inst. Nutrition; mem. FAO, Internat. Union Nutritional Scis. (past chmn. U.S. nat. com.), Fedn. Am. Socs. for Exptl. Biology (pres. 1979-80), Alpha Gamma Rho, Omicron Mu, Gamma Sigma Delta, Sigma Xi, Phi Kappa Phi, Phi Tau Sigma, Alpha Zeta.

COMBS, RONALD DEAN, physicians assistant; b. Washington, Apr. 12, 1955; s. Leslie Clay and Billie Lee (Burkhart) C.; m. Maryann Ferrigno, July 18, 1982; children: Ronald John, Christina Marie, Jaclyn Roseann, Jonathan Dean, Maryann Norma Catherine. AA, Polk C.C., 1975; BS, Alderson Broaddus Coll., 1979. Cert. physicians asst. Physicians asst. N.Y. Hosp. Med. Ctr. of Queens, 1979-82, sr. physicians asst., 1982-87, chief physicians asst., 1987—; clin. prof. Alderson Broaddus Coll. Physician Assts. Program, 1989-95; faculty mem. dept. of surgery N.Y. Hosp. Med. Ctr. of Queens, 1984—, surg. intensive care quality assurance com., 1984—, surg. continous quality assurance, 1994—, N.Y. Hosp. Med. Ctr. transplant com., 1984—; lectr. in field. Mem. Am. Acad. of Physicians Assts., N.Y. Soc. of Physicians Asst., Soc. Critical Care Medicine (specialty sect. treas. 1994-95, chmn. 1996-97), K.C. Roman Catholic. Office: NY Hosp Med Ctr of Queens 56-45 Main St Flushing NY 11577

COMBS, STEVEN PAUL, orthopedic surgeon; b. Ft. Dodge, Iowa, Apr. 9, 1944; s. Eugene Charles and Marie Wilhelmina (Mack) C.; m. Penelope Ann Calvey, July 6, 1974; children: Patrick, Mary Katherine, Meaghan, Bridgett. BS, U. Iowa, 1966, MD, 1970; MBA, Lake Erie Coll., 1991. Diplomate Am. Bd. Orthopedic Surgery. Intern Robert Packer Hosp., Sayre, Pa., 1970-71; resident in orthopedics Cleve. Clinic, 1971-75; orthopedic surgeon Drs. DeMarco & Irwin, Willoughby, Ohio, 1979—. Served to maj. USAF, 1975-79. Fellow Am. Coll. Surgeons; mem. Am. Acad. Orthopedic Surgeons, Orthopedic Rsch. Soc., Lake County Med. Soc. (pres. 1991), Lake Hosp. Found. (chmn. 1993-96). Republican. Roman Catholic. Home: 8685 King Memorial Rd Mentor OH 44060-7960

COMER, J. WILLIAM, physician; b. Louisville, Oct. 2, 1948. BA in Chemistry, U. Louisville, 1970, MD, 1974. Diplomate in internal medicine and cardiovascular medicine Am. Bd. Internal Medicine. Pvt. practice Louisville, 1977-94; assoc. area med. dir. U.S. Postal Svc. Mid-Atlantic Area, Louisville, 1994—. Founding mem. Jewish Hosp. Heart and Lung Insts. Fellow Am. Coll. Cardiology, Am. Heart Assn. Coun. on Clin. Cardiology; mem. AMA, Ky. Med. Assn., Jefferson County Med. Assn., Am. Soc. Nuclear Cardiology (founding), Am. Heart Assn., Am. Soc. Echocardiography, Am. Coll. Occupational & Environ. Medicine. Office: PO Box 6653 Louisville KY 40206-0653

COMER, JAMES PIERPONT, psychiatrist, educator; b. East Chicago, Ind., Sept. 25, 1934; s. Hugh and Maggie (Nichols) C.; m. Shirley Ann Arnold, June 20, 1959 (dec. Apr. 1994); children: Brian Jay, Dawn Renee. AB, Ind. U., 1956; MD, Howard U., 1960; MPH, U. Mich., 1964; DSc (hon.), U. New Haven, 1977; LittD (hon.), Calumet Coll., 1978; LHD (hon.), Bank St. Coll., N.Y.C., 1987, Albertus Magnus Coll., 1989, Quinnipiac Coll., 1990, DePauw U., 1990; DSc (hon.), Ind U., 1991, Wabash Coll., 1991; EdD (hon.), Wheelock Coll., 1991; LLD (hon.), U. Conn., 1991; LHD (hon.), SUNY Buffalo, 1991, New Sch. for Social Rsch., 1991; D Pedagogy (hon.), R.I. Coll., 1991; DSc (hon.), Amherst Coll., 1991; LHD (hon.), John Jay Coll. Criminal Justice, 1991, Wesleyan U., 1991; DH (hon.), Princeton U., 1991; DSc (hon.), Northwestern U., 1991, Worcester Poly. Inst., 1991; LHD (hon.), U. Pa., 1992; DPD (hon.), Niagara U., 1992; LHD (hon.), Hamilton Coll., 1992; DSc (hon.), Brown U., 1992; LHD (hon.), U. Mass. at Lowell, 1992; DSc (hon.), Med. Coll. Ohio, 1992, Howard U., 1993, W.Va. U., 1993; LLD (hon.), Lawrence U., 1993; DSc (hon.), Morehouse Sch. Medicine, 1993; LLD (hon.), Columbia U., 1994, Boston Coll., 1994; LHD (hon.), Briarwood Coll., 1994. Served with USPHS, Washington and Chevy Chase, Md., 1961-68; intern St. Catherine's Hosp., East Chicago, 1960-61; resident Yale Sch. Medicine, 1964-67; asst. prof. psychiatry Yale Child Study Center and dept. psychiatry, 1968-70, assoc. prof., 1970-75, prof., 1975-76, Maurice Falk prof. psychiatry, 1976—; assoc. dean Yale Med. Sch., New Haven, 1969—; dir. pupil svcs. Baldwin-King Sch. Project, New Haven, 1968-73; dir. sch. devel. program Yale Child Study Ctr., 1973—; dir. Conn. Energy Corp., 1976—; co-dir. Black Family Roundtable Greater New Haven, 1986—; cons. Joint Commn. on Mental Health of Children, Nat. Commn. on Causes and Prevention of Violence, NIMH; mem. nat. adv. mental health coun. HEW; Henry J. Kaiser Sr. fellow Center for Advanced Study in the Behavioral Scis., Stanford, 1976-77. Author: Beyond Black and White, 1972, Black Child Care, 1975, 2d edit., 1992, School Power, 1980, 2d. edit., 1993, Maggie's American Dream, 1988; mem. editl. bd. Am. Jour. Orthopsychiatry, 1970-76, Youth and Adolescence, 1971-87, Jour. Negro Edn., 1978-83; guest editor Jour. Am. Acad. Child Psychiatry, 1985; columnist Parents mag.; contbr. articles to profl. jours. Bd. dirs. Dixwell Soul Sta. and Yale Afro-Am. House; truste Carnegie Corp. of N.Y., 1990, Albertus Magnus Coll., 1989—, Conn. State U., 1991-94, Nat. Coun. for Effective Schs., 1985—; bd. dirs., mem. profl. adv. bd. Children's TV Workshop, 1972-88; trustee Wesleyan U., 1978-84, Hazen Found., 1975-79, Field Found., 1981-88, Carnegie Corp., 1990; mem. profl. adv. coun. Nat. Assn. Mental Health; mem. ad. hoc adv. com. Conn. Rsch. Commn.; mem. adv. coun. Nat. Com. for Citizens in Edn.; mem. nat. adv. coun. Hogg Found. for Mental Health, 1983-86; mem. adv. com. adolescent pregnancy prevention Children's Def. Fund. Recipient Child Study Assn.-Wel-Met Family Life book award, 1975, Howard U. Disting. Alumni award, 1976, John and Mary Markle Found. scholar, 1969—, Rockefeller Public Service award, 1980, Media award NCCJ, 1981, Community Leadership award Greater New Haven C. of C., 1983, Disting. Fellow award Conn. chpt. Phi Delta Kappa, 1984, Elm and Ivy award New Haven Found., 1985, Disting. Service award Conn. Assn. Psychologists, 1985, Disting. Educator award Conn. Coalition of 100 Black Women, 1985, Outstanding Leadership award Children's Def. Fund, 1987, Whitney M. Young Jr. Svc. award Boy Scouts Am., 1989, Prudential Leadership award Prudential Found., 1990, Harold W. McGraw Jr. prize in Edn., 1990, James Bryant Conant award Edn. Commn. States, 1991, Charles A. Dana prize in Edn., 1991, Disting. Svc. award Coun. Chief State Sch. Officers, 1991; James Comer NIMH Minority Fellowship established in his honor, 1991. Mem. APA (Disting. Svc. award 1993) Am. Acad. Child Adolescenttry, Nat. Med. Assn., Nat. Mental Health Assn. (Lela Rowland Prevention award 1989), Am. Psychiat. Assn. (Agnes Purcell McGavin award 1990, Solomon Carter Fuller award 1990, Spl. Presdl. Commendation 1990, Disting. Svc. award 1993), Am. Orthopsychiat. Assn. (Vera S. Paster award 1990), Am. Acad. Child Psychiatry, Black Psychiatrists of Am., NAACP, Black Coalition of New Haven, Greater New Haven Black Family Roundtable (co-dir. 1986—), Alpha Omega Alpha, Alpha Phi Alpha. Office: Yale U Child Study Ctr 230 S Frontage Rd PO Box 207900 New Haven CT 06520-7900

COMER, NATHAN LAWRENCE, psychiatrist, educator; b. Phila. Nov. 10, 1923; s. Rubin L. and Fannie (Cassover) C.; m. Rita Ellis, June 19, 1949 (dec. Mar. 1978); children: Robert, Susan Comer Kitei, Debra R., Marc J. BA, U. Pa., 1944; MD, Hahnemann Med. Coll., 1949; postgrad., U. Pa. Diplomate Am. Bd. Psychiatry and Neurology, Am. Bd. Profl. Disability Cons., Sr. Disability Analyst of Am. Bd. Disability Analysts, Am. Bd. Forensic Examiners, Am. Bd. Forensic Medicine. Intern Hahnemann Med. Coll., Phila., 1949-50; resident, NIMH fellow Inst. of Pa. Hosp., Phila., 1951-53, sr. attending psychiatrist, 1968—, resident in psychiatry, 1951-53; chief of psychiatry Ford Rd. campus Thomas Jefferson U. Hosp., Phila., 1978-94; clin. assoc. prof. psychiatry and human behavior Jefferson Med. Coll., Thomas Jefferson U., Phila., 1994—; clin. assoc. prof. psychiatry Med. Coll. Pa. and Hahnemann U., 1978—; pres. med. staff Phila. Psychiat. Ctr., 1975-77, emeritus sr. attending physician, 1988—; pres. med. staff Inst. of Pa. Hosp., 1983-85. Contbr. articles to profl. jours. Bd. dirs. Temple Adath Israel of Main Line, Merion, Pa., 1958-78. Fellow Coll. Physicians Phila., Am. Psychiat. Assn. (life); mem. AMA, Am. Soc. for Adolescent Psychiatry, Hehnemann Med. Coll. Alumni Assn. (pres. 1973-74), B'nai B'rith. Republican. Jewish. Home: 1100 Hillcrest Rd Narberth PA 19072-1224 Office: Inst Pa Hosp 111 N 49th St Philadelphia PA 19139-2718

COMERFORD, CYNTHIA ANN, family nurse practitioner; b. Camden, N.J., June 16, 1961; d. Philip M. and Diana Comerford. BSN, Lynchburg (Va.) Coll., 1983; MSN, U. Va., 1987. RN, Md., Va., D.C.; cert. family nurse practitioner. Staff nurse George Washington U., Washington, 1983-86, U. Va. Hosp., Charlottesville, 1986-88; family nurse practitioner George Washington U. Health Plan, Washington, 1988-91; family nurse practitioner employees' health unit NASA, Washington, 1991-93; pvt. practice ob-gyn nurse practitioner Fairfax, Va., 1994—. Mem. Am. Acad. Nurse Practitioners.

COMEROTA, ANTHONY JAMES, vascular surgeon, biomedical researcher; b. Newark, Aug. 4, 1948; s.Louis Anthony and Eleanor Dorothy (Dombroski) C.; m. Elsa Benavides, Aug. 18, 1973; children: Anthony James, Maya Christine, Mark Anthony. BA, Millikin U., 1970; MD, Temple U., 1974. Diplomate Am. Bd. Surgery. Surg. resident Temple U. Hosp., Phila., 1974-78; vascular surgery fellow Good Samaritan Hosp., Cin., 1979-81; from asst. prof. to prof. surgery Temple U. Hosp, Temple U. Sch. Medicine, Phila., 1981-88, prof. surgery, chief vascular surgery, 1988—; dir. Ctr. for Vascular Diseases Temple U. Hosp., Temple U. Sch. Medicine, Phila., 1995—; dir. ctr. vascular diseases Temple U. Sch. Medicine, Phila., 1995—. Editor: Thrombolytic Therapy for Peripheral Vascular Disease, 1995; co-editor: Prevention of Venous Thromboembolism, 1994. Fellow ACS, Royal Australian Coll. Surgeons; mem. Am. Surg. Assn., Soc. Vascular Surgery, Internat. Soc. Cardiovascular Surgery, Phila. Acad. Surgery (pres. 1996-97), Temple U. Sch. Medicine Alumni Assn. (pres. 1993-95), Alpha Omega Alpha. Office: Temple Univ Dept of Surgery Broad & Ontario St Philadelphia PA 19140

COMIS, ROBERT LEO, oncologist, educator; b. Troy, N.Y., July 16, 1945; s. James Carl and Mary (Casile) C.; m. Virginia Martin; children: Larissa, Robert Leo Jr., Anthony. BS, Fordham U., 1967; MD, SUNY, Syracuse, 1971. Diplomate Am. Bd. Internal Medicine, Am. Bd. Internal Medicine-Med. Oncology. Intern SUNY Upstate Med. Ctr., Syracuse, 1971-72, resident, 1974-75, chief med. oncology, 1978-84; staff assoc. cancer evaluation program Nat. Cancer Inst., NIH, Bethesda, Md., 1972-74; dir. Cen. N.Y. Regional Oncology Ctr., N.Y.C., 1984-88; chmn. med. oncology Fox Chase Cancer Ctr., Phila., 1984-88, med. dir., 1984-93, v.p. med. sci., 1987-93; prof. medicine Temple U. Hosp., Phila., 1987-93; dir. div. neoplastic diseases Thomas Jefferson U., Phila., 1993—; clin. dir. Kimmel Cancer Ctr., Phila., 1993—; asst. prof. medicine, chief solid tumor oncology svc., sect. hematology/oncology SUNY Upstate Med. Ctr., 1976-78, assoc. prof., 1978-83, prof. medicine, 1983-84, chief sect. med. oncology, 1978-84; chmn. respiratory disease com. Cancer and Leukemia Group, 1979-84; assoc. chmn. lab. sci. Ea. Coop. Oncology Group, 1991-95, group chmn., 1995—; mem. cancer award selection com. Bristol Myers-Squibb, 1985-91; asst. in medicine Peter Pent Brigham Hosp., Boston, 1975-76. Contbr. articles to profl. publs. V.p. Am. Cancer Soc., Onodaga County, N.Y., 1981-82, pres., 1982, mem. med. affairs com. N.Y. State div. With USPHS, 1972-74. Grantee, Ea. Coop. Oncology Group, 1985—, Bristol-Myers, 1985-89, Small Instrumentation Program, 1989-90, Biomed. Rsch. Support, 1989-90, Clin. Oncology Rsch. Career DEvel. Program, 1992—. Mem. AAAS, Am. Soc. Clin. Oncology (program chair 1985-86, editorial bd. jour. 1985, chmn. program com. 1985, clin. trial com.), Am. Radium Soc. (resident awards com. 1990—, sci. program com. 1990-91), Am. Assn. Cancer Rsch., Inc., Internat. Assn. for Study of Lung Cancer, N.Y. State Cancer Programs Assn., Pa. Soc. Hematology/Oncology, Pa. Med. Soc., Phila. County Med. Soc., Soc. Biol. Therapy. Office: Kimmel Cancer Ctr Ste 1014 1025 Walnut St Philadelphia PA 19107

COMISKEY, MARY ALICE, nursing supervisor; b. Somerville, N.J., Dec. 29, 1940; d. John V. and Mabel M. (Stryker) Sharp; m. James P. Comiskey, Apr. 12, 1969; 1 child, Kevin R. Diploma, St. Francis Sch. Nursing, Trenton, N.J., 1961; BSN cum laude, Rutgers U., 1970. Cert. nursing adminstrn. Staff nurse St. Francis Med. Ctr., Trenton, 1961-62; staff and charge nurse VA Hosp., Lyons, N.J., 1962-66; instr. med.-surg. nursing Muhlenberg Hosp., Plainfield, N.J., 1968-72; nursing adminstrv. supr. John F. Kennedy Med. Ctr., Edison, N.J., 1972-96; instr. Sch. Nursing, Muhlenberg Regional Med. Ctr., Plainfield, N.J., 1996—. Mem. Fiscataway Twp. Health Commn., 1972—, past chair. Nat. League for Nursing scholar Rutguers U., 1969-70. Mem. ANA (N.J. dist. nominating com. med.-surg. div.), Coun. on Nursing Adminstrn., Sigma Theta Tau (Alpha Tau chpt. del. to biennial conv., 1974, co-chmn. program com.). Office: Muhlenberg Regional Med Ctr Sch Nursing Park Ave and Randolph Rd Plainfield NJ 07060

COMIZIO-ASSANTE, DELVA MARIA, nurse; b. Yonkers, N.Y., Nov. 8, 1964; d. Vito Joseph and Delva Maria (Ciucci) Comizio; m. William J. Assante, Nov. 5, 1988. BSN, Coll. Mt. St. Vincent, Bronx, N.Y., 1986; postgrad., Pace U. RN, N.Y., Va.; cert. med.-surg. nurse. Staff nurse St. Joseph's Med. Ctr., Yonkers, N.Y., 1986-87, sr. nurse, 1987-89, nurse clinician, 1989-90; med.-surg., ambulatory surgery-recovery rm. nurse Community Hosp at Dobbs Ferry, N.Y., 1991—; mem. quality assurance coun. St. Joseph's Med. Ctr., Yonkers, 1989, chmn. nurse practice coun., 1987-90, mem. leadership coun., 1987-90, mem. exec. coun., 1987-90, mem. documentation com., 1989, mem. com. for the system of nursing care delivery, 1989. Mem. All County Head Nurse Assn., Nat. League for Nursing, Am. Soc. Post-Anesthesia Nurses, Sigma Theta Tau (chpt. treas. 1987-92, chpt. v.p. 1992-93). Republican. Roman Catholic. Home: 137 Hosner Mt Rd Hopewell Junction NY 12533 Office: Community Hosp Dobbs Ferry 128 Ashford Ave Dobbs Ferry NY 10522-1924

COMMITO, RICHARD WILLIAM, podiatrist; b. Chgo., May 2, 1951; s. Mario Fiore and Aileen Margaret Commito. BS, U. Ill., Chgo., 1972; DPM, Ill. Coll. Podiatric Medicine, 1976. Diplomate Nat. Bd. Podiatry Examiners, Am. Bd. Podiatric Surgery, Am. Bd. Profl. Disability Cons., Am. Bd. Forensic Examiners, Am. Coun. Cert. Podiatric Physicians and Surgeons, Am. Acad. Pain Mgmt. Podiatrist Chgo., 1976—; dir. podiatry svcs. Community Hosp., Evanston, Ill., 1978-80; cons. staff podiatry Ridgeway Hosp., Chgo., 1981—; owner Conserv Environ. Products, FootDoc Products, NewFoot Pharmical; dir. podiatry svc. Lawndale Pla. Surgicenter, Chgo.; ind. med. examiner of counsel R. S. Connors Assocs., Chgo. Bd. dirs. Little Village unit Boys Clubs, 1981—, mem. One Hundred Club, 1982. 400 Club, Marshall Square unit, 1981-82; mem. Art Inst. Chgo., 1980-96, Lincoln Park Zool. Soc., Chgo., 1980-96. Fellow Acad. Ambulatory Foot Surgery, Am. Inst. Foot Medicine (cert.); mem. Soaring Soc. Am., Ill. Podiatry Edn. Group, Am. Podiatric Med Assn., Ill. Podiatry Soc., Am. Med. Soc. Vienna (life), Nat. Assn. Professions, Am. Coll. Forensic Examiners, Am. Bd. Profl. Disability Consultants, Am. Soc. Podiatric Legal Medicine, Am. Podiatric Circulatory Soc., Am. Acad. Pain Mgmt., Am. Soc. Podiatric Physicians and Surgeons, Am. Coun. Cert. Podiatric Physicians and Surgeons (cert.), Internat. Inst. Reflexology (cert.), Am. Pain Soc., Nat. Assn. of the Self-Employed, Internat. Inst. Continuing Med. Edn. Roman Catholic.

COMOSS, PATRICIA B., cardiac rehabilitation nurse, consultant; b. Shamokin, Pa., Apr. 20, 1947; d. William J. and Lucille M. (Shipulski) McCall; m. Eugene J. Comoss, Nov. 25, 1970. Diploma, St. Joseph's Hosp., Reading, Pa., 1968; BS in Health Care Mgmt., Pa. State U., Harrisburg, 1982. CCU staff nurse Polyclinic Med. Ctr., Harrisburg; head nurse, cardiac rehab. Rehab. Hosp., Mechanicsburg, Pa.; dir. edn. AMSCO/Rehab., Mechanicsburg; founder, pres. Nursing Enrichment Consultants, Harrisburg. Co-author: Cardiac Rehabilitation: A Comprehensive Nursing Approach, 1979; contbr. articles to profl. jours. Fellow Am. Assn. Cardiovascular and Pulmonary Rehab. (bd. dirs. 1986-88, v.p. 1988-90, pres.-elect 1990-91, pres. 1992, chair fed. project on clin. practice guidelines on cardiac rehab. 1992-95); mem. ANA, AACCN, Am. Coll. Sports Medicine, Am. Heart Assn. Home: 4100 Elmerton Ave Harrisburg PA 17109-1327

COMPANS, RICHARD W., microbiology educator; b. Syracuse, N.Y., Sept. 15, 1940; m. Marian Merly Compans. BA magna cum laude, Kalamazoo Coll., 1963; PhD, Rockefeller U., 1968. Asst. prof. The Rockefeller U., 1969-73, assoc. prof., 1973-75; prof. dept. microbiology The U. Ala., Birmingham, 1975-92, prof. dept. biochemistry, 1985-92; prof., chmn. dept. microbiology and immunology Emory U., 1992—; guest investigator Inst. Rsch., Villejuif, France, 1968; vis. investigator Scripps Clinic and Rsch. Found., 1982; vis. prof. U. Geneva, 1988-89; numerous univ. appointments including sr. scientist Cancer Rsch. and Tng. Ctr., U. Ala., 1975-92, dir. Electron Microscope Core Facility, 1975-92, sr. scientist Diabetes Rsch. and Tng. Ctr., 1977-92, Multipurpose Arthritis Ctr., 1977-92, Cystic Fibrosis Rsch. Ctr., 1982-93, dir. Molecular Cell Biology Grad. Program, 1982-92, others; mem. various virology task forces. Editor: Virus Research, 1983—; editorial bd.: Jour. Gen. Virology, 1972-77, Jour. Virology, 1974-82, 91-94, Intervirology, 1974-90, Virology, 1974-76, CRC Handbook Series in Clin. Lab. Sci., Archives of Virology, 1980-83, Jour. Biol. Chemistry, 1983-88, Current Topics Microbiology and Immunology, 1985—, Virology, 1992—; contbr. numerous articles to profl. jours. Recipient Wright A. Gardner award Ala. Acad. Scis., 1988; grantee NIH, 1972—, others. Mem. Am. Acad. Microbiology, Am. Soc. Virology, Am. Soc. Biol. Chemists, Am. Soc. Cell Biology, Am. Assn. Immunologists, Soc. Gen. Microbiology, Am. Soc. Microbiology, Soc. Mucosol Immunology, Phi Beta Kappa. Office: Emory U Sch Medicine Dept Microbiology and Immunology Atlanta GA 30322

COMPTON, RONALD E., insurance and financial services executive; b. 1933; married. B.S., Northwestern U., 1954. With Aetna Life & Casualty Co., 1954—; sr. v.p. Am. Re-Ins. Co., N.Y.C., 1980-81, exec. v.p., 1981-83; pres., dir. Am. Re-Ins. Co. unit Aetna Life and Casualty Co., N.Y.C., from 1983; corp. sr. v.p. Aetna Life and Casualty Co., 1987-88, exec. v.p., 1988—, now pres., chief operating officer; sr. v.p., exec. asst. to chmn. Aetna Life Ins. Co., 1986-87, exec. v.p., 1987-88, pres., 1988—; with Aetna Casualty and Surety Co., 1954-80, 1987—, sr. v.p., 1987-88, exec. v.p., office of chmn., 1987-88, now pres., 1988—; now chmn., pres., CEO, dir. Aetna, 1993—. Office: Aetna Financial Services Corp Hdqrs 151 Farmington Ave Hartford CT 06156-0001

CONANT, EMILY FOX, radiology educator; b. Washington, Mar. 17, 1958; d. Samuel Mickle III and Mary Alice (Vann) Fox; m. Jonathan Brewster Conant, May 27, 1987; children: Hannah Randall, Alice Benson, Samuel Vann. BA, U. Vt., 1980; MD, U. Pa., 1984. Resident Hosp. U. Pa., Phila., 1984-89; asst. prof. radiology Thomas Jefferson U. Hosp., Phila., 1989-96, assoc. prof. radiology, 1996—. Contbr. articles to profl. jours. Mem. Am. Coll. Radiology, Radiologic Soc. N.Am., Soc. Breast Imagery. Office: THomas Jefferson U Hosp Breast Imaging Ctr 1100 Walnut St Philadelphia PA 19107

CONANT, STEVEN GEORGE, psychiatrist; b. Elkhart, Ind., July 8, 1949; s. Hubert Eugene and Ruth (Weaver) C. BA in Zoology with distinction, DePauw U., 1971; MD, Ind. U., 1975. Diplomate Am. Bd. Psychiatry and Neurology. Intern Ind. U. Med. Ctr., Indpls., 1975-76, resident in psychiatry, 1976-78, asst. prof. psychiatry, 1978-80, asst. clin. prof. psychiatry, 1988-93; cons. psychiatry Gallahue Mental Health Ctr., Indpls., 1979-85; staff psychiatrist Metro Health, Indpls., 1983—; staff privileges at Meth. Hosp., Indpls., 1979—; cons. psychiatrist Ind. Prison Sys., 1986, Ctrl. State Hosp., 1992-94, Hamilton Ctr., 1994—. Mem. Conductor's Cir. Indpls. Symphony, 1984—, Indpls. Symphonic Choir Orch., 1976-83; trustee Indpls. Mus. Art, 1988—. Mem. AMA, Am. Acad. Clin. Psychiatrists, Mensa, The Hoosier Group, Wash. DePauw Soc. Republican. Presbyterian. Office: Metro Health 4850 Century Plaza Rd Indianapolis IN 46254-2483

CONAWAY, DOUGLAS CAMDEN, rheumatologist; b. Charlotte, N.C., July 21, 1950; s. Camden Garlow and Patricia Ann (Graham) C.; m. Margaret Ann Willekes MacDonald, Jan. 26, 1995. BA, Rice U., 1972; MD, Baylor U., 1975. Diplomate Am. Bd. Internal Medicine. Intern, resident internal medicine U. Oreg. Health Sci. Ctr., Portland, 1975-78; staff internist Travis AFB, Calif., 1978-80; chief internal medicine & flight medicine Hellenicon AFB, Athens, Greece, 1980-82; chief aerospace medicine McGuire AFB, N.J., 1982-83; fellow rheumatology, then assoc. prof. Temple U., Phila., 1983—; program dir. Temple U., 1986—, chair med. practice com., 1988—; chair Cytotec Adv. Coun., Searle Pharms., Chgo., 1993-95. Author, editor: Geriatrics, 1988, 89; contbr. articles to profl. jours., chpts. to book. Bd. dirs. Phila. Lupus Found., 1995—. Fellow Am. Coll. Rheumatology; mem. Am. Coll. Physicians, Phila. Rheumatism Soc. Democrat. Home: 2318 Green St Philadelphia PA 19130 Office: Temple U Hosp 3401 N Broad St Philadelphia PA 19140

CONAWAY, MARY JO, nurse, epidemiologist; b. Johnstown, Pa., May 3, 1936; d. Victor F. and Frances T. (Longo) Amistadi; m. Charles H. Conaway, July 20, 1957; children: Lynn, Patrick. Diploma, Queen of Angels Sch. Nursing, L.A., 1957; BS, Christian Coll., 1978; MS, Chapman U., 1985. Cert. infection contorl, Calif.; cert. tchr. Nurse, epidemiologist Mission Hosp., Regional Med. Ctr., Mission Viejo, Calif.; owner Conaway & Assocs., Monarch Beach, Calif.; nurse cons. video, tech.cons., video producer, lectr., AIDS educator. Mem. Assn. Practitioners in Infection Control (pres.). Home: 33581 Capstan Dr Monarch Beach CA 92629-4484

CONCA, WALTER, rheumatologist, educator; b. Malles, Bolzano, Italy, Apr. 2, 1952; arrived in Germany, 1983; s. Pietro and Anna (Hafner) C.; m. Mirella Birgit Wurzer, July 14, 1979; children: Anina, Tiziana. MD, Vienna (Austria) U., 1979; Medico Chirurgo, Bologna (Italy) U., 1982. Med. diplomate internal medicine and rheumatology. Rsch. fellow Inst. Pharmacology, Vienna, 1979-81; intern dept. internal medicine U. Vienna, 1981-82, resident in internal medicine, 1982-83; resident in internal medicine Medizinische Poliklinik, U. Munich, 1983-85; resident in rheumatology Medizinische Poliklinik, 1985-87; rsch. fellow Harvard Med. Sch., Boston, 1987-90; asst. prof. Max Planck Inst., Munich, 1990-91; asst. prof. internal medicine U. Freiburg, Germany, 1991-95, dir. lab. molecular rheumatology, 1991—, assoc. prof., 1995—. Co-author: Sonographische Diagnostik, 1987, Klinische Immunologie, 1995. Recipient Promotio sub auspiciis Praesidentis rei publicae Pres. of Austria, Vienna, 1979, Rudolf Schoen Stiftung Deutsche Gesellschaft Rheumatologie, 1991. Mem. Deutsche Gesellschaft Rheumatologie, Am. Coll. Rheumatology, N.Y. Acad. Sci. Office: U Freiburg, Dept Rheumatology, Hugstetter Strasse 55, D-79106 Freiburg Germany

CONDE, CESAR AUGUSTO, cardiologist, educator; b. Lima, Peru, Oct. 31, 1942; s. Aurelio Vicente and Mercedes (Portocarrearo) C.; M.D., San Marcos U. (Lima, Peru), 1967; m. Maria C. Perez-Teran, Sept. 8, 1972; children: Cesar R., Jorge C., Enrique A. Intern, Phila. Gen. Hosp., U. Pa., 1968-69; resident Henry Ford Hosp., Detroit, 1969-71; resident cardiology Mt. Sinai Hosp. and Mt. Sinai Sch. Medicine, 1971-73, asst. prof. medicine and cardiology, 1973-74; asst. clin. prof. medicine and cardiology U. Miami,

1974-78, asso. clin. prof., 1978-84, clin. prof., 1984—, chief div. cardiology Parkway Gen. Hosp., Miami, Fla., 1977-84; chief staff Parkway Regional Med. Ctr., Miami, 1984—, bd. dirs.; chief cardiology Cedars Med. Ctr., 1990-92; dir. internat. cardio-vascular program Mt. Sinai Med. Ctr., Miami Beach, 1991—. Pres. Am. Heart Assn. of Greater Miami, 1986-87. Fellow Am. Coll. Cardiology, A.C.P., Nat. Council Clin. Cardiology; mem. Am. Heart Assn. (pres.-elect Greater Miami), Miami Heart Assn. (dir.). Roman Catholic. Clubs: Big Five (Miami), Fisher Island, Peruano de la Fla. Home: 8100 Los Pinos Blvd Miami FL 33143-6457 Office: 16800 NW 2nd Ave North Miami Beach FL 33169-5549 also: 4302 Afton Rd Ste 100 Miami FL 33140

CONDIE, VICKI COOK, nurse, educator; m. Michael J. Condie; children: Jennifer, Jamie, Stephen. Diploma, Deaconess Hosp. Sch. Nursing, 1969; BSN summa cum laude, SUNY, 1983; MS, Syracuse U., 1986; CAS in Nursing Edn., Widener U., 1991. RN, N.Y. Dir. nursing edn. Cayuga Community Coll., N.Y., 1987—, prof. nursing; SIDS educator Western N.Y. Sids Ctr., 1987—; mem. utilization rev. com. Cayuga County Dept. Health, 1985—, profl. adv. com. for Cert. Home Health Agy., 1987—; adj. prof. SUNY Health Sci. Ctr., Syracuse.; active N.Y. State Coun. ADN Programs. Active Florence Nightengale Mus. Assn., London. Mem. ANA, N.Y. State Nurses Assn. (mem. coun. nursing edn.), SUNY Health Sci. Ctr. Honor Soc., Sigma Theta Tau.

CONDIT, JOHN RUSSELL, cardiologist; b. West Caldwell, N.J., Oct. 6, 1954; s. John Russell Sr. and Catherine (Sharp) C.; m. M. Diane Condit, Dec. 14, 1987; children: Caitlin Susan, Courtney Anne. BS, Fairleigh Dickinson U., 1976; DO, U. Osteo. Medicine/Health Scis, 1986. Rsch. asst. Nat. Heart, Lung and Blood Inst., NIH, Bethesda, Md., 1976-81; rotating internship Chgo. Osteo. Med. Ctr., 1986-87; internal med. resident Henry Ford Hosp., Detroit, 1987-90, chief med. resident, 1990-91; cardiology fellow Georgetown U. Med. Ctr., Washington, 1991-93, transplant fellow, 1993-94, instr. of medicine, 1993-94; cardiologist Chesapeake Cardiology Clinic, Easton, Md., 1994—; bd. dirs. Bd. of Quality Assurance, Easton Meml. Hosp. Contbr. articles to profl. jours. Co-chair AHA Walk-A-Thon, Easton, 1996. Named Jr. Resident of the Yr. Henry Ford Hosp., 1989; recipient Cert. of Merit Dept. of Health, Edn. and Welfare, 1978. Mem. AMA, ACP; mem. Am. Coll. of Cardiology, Am. Osteo. Assn., Am. Soc. of Gen. Internal Medicine, W. Proctor Harvey Soc., Am. Heart Assn. (bd. dirs. 1994—). Home: 8108 Laurel Ln Denton MD 21629 Office: Chesapeake Cardiology Clinic 403 Marvel Ct Easton MD 21601

CONDON, ROBERT EDWARD, surgeon, educator; b. Albany, N.Y., Aug. 13, 1929; s. Edward A. and Catherine (Kilmartin) C.; m. Marcia Jane Pagano, June 16, 1951; children: Sean Edward, Brian Robert. AB, U. Rochester, 1951, MD, 1957; MS, U. Wash., 1965. Diplomate Am. Bd. Surgery, Nat. Bd. Med. Examiners. N.Y. Bd. Regents scholar U. Rochester, 1957; intern King County Hosp., Seattle, 1957-58; resident dept. surgery U. Wash. Sch. Medicine (and affiliated hosps.), 1958-65; postdoctoral rsch. fellow Nat. Heart Inst., 1961-63; asst. prof. surgery Baylor Coll. Medicine, Houston, 1965-67; assoc. prof. surgery U. Ill. Coll. Medicine, Chgo., 1967-69, prof., 1969-70; prof., head dept. surgery U. Iowa Coll. Medicine, Iowa City, 1971-72; prof. surgery Med. Coll. Wis., Milw., 1972—, chmn. dept. surgery, 1979-95; chief surg. svcs. Wood VA Hosp., Milw., 1972-81; attending surgeon Columbia Hosp., 1972—, Froedtert Meml. Luth. Hosp., 1982—; cons. Mt. Sinai, Samaritan, St. Luke's, St. Mary, St. Joseph hosps., Milw. Author: (with others) Abdominal Pain: A Guide to Rapid Diagnosis, 2d edit., 1995, Manual of Surgical Therapeutics, 9th edit., 1996, Hernia, 4th edit., 1995, Surgical Care, 1980; mem. editl. bd. Jour. Clin. Therapeutics, Surgery, Jour. Surg. Oncology. Recipient sr. class award as Outstanding Faculty Member Baylor U. Coll. Medicine, 1966, Excellence in Teaching award Phi Chi, 1967, Cert. Appreciation U. Iowa Coll. Medicine, 1971, Tchr. of Yr. award 1972, Med. Coll. Wis., 1983; rsch. fellow Guggenheim Found., 1963-64. Mem. ACS, Am. Surg. Assn., Surg. Infection Soc. (pres.), Am. Assn. Surgery of Trauma, Internat. Soc. Surgery, Collegium Internationale Chirurgiae Digestivae (pres.), Assn. for Acad. Surgery, Cen. Surg. Assn. (pres.), So. Surg. Assn., Western Surg. Assn., Wis. Surg. Soc. (pres.), Milw. Surg. Soc. (pres.), Chgo. Surg. Soc., Soc. U. Surgeons, Soc. Clin. Surgery, Med. Rsch. Soc. (London), Milw. Acad. Medicine, Royal Soc. Medicine, Soc. Surgery Alimentary Tract, Milw. Acad. Surgery (pres.). Home: 2300 E Kensington Blvd Milwaukee WI 53211-1248 Office: 9200 W Wisconsin Ave Milwaukee WI 53226-3522

CONDON, THOMAS BRIAN (BRIAN CONDON), hospital executive; b. Beverly, Mass., June 1, 1942; s. Thomas William and Marguerite Mary (Welch) C.; m. Carol Therese Sicilliano, Apr. 29, 1969; children: Therese Beth, Tara Bridget, Colleen Marguerite, Caroline Susan. BA in English, Boston Coll., 1964; MPA, U. New Haven, 1973, MA in Community Psychology, 1975, MA in Indsl. and Organizational Psychology, 1977. Dir. unit mgmt. Yale New Haven Hosp., 1971—, asst. adminstr., 1975, v.p., 1980-94, v.p. clin. adminstrn., 1994—; lectr. Quinnipiac Coll., Hamden, 1982—; bd. dirs. Nat. Inst. Cmty. Health Edn., Hamdah, Conn., Hill Devel. Corp., New Haven, Spectronics, Phila.; mem. adv. coun. New Eng. Organ Bank; chmn. bd. dirs. Gateway Tech. and C.C. Found., New Haven, 1988-96. Elected mem. Cheshire (Conn.) Planning and Zoning Commn., 1976-87; chmn., dir. Conn. Student Loan Found., Rocky Hill, 1976—; mem. Gov.'s Task Force on Student Aid, Hartford, Conn., 1986-87; bd. dirs. So. Conn. Jr. Achievement, 1994—; bd. advisors Clelian Ctr. Adult Day Care Ctr., Maden, Conn., 1990. Capt. U.S. Army, 1964-70. Recipient Community Svc. award Bd. Trustees Conn. State Coll., 1991. Mem. Grad. Club Assn. New Haven (bd. dirs. 1993—). Roman Catholic. Home: 150 Hotchkiss Rdg Cheshire CT 06410-3041 Office: Yale New Haven Hosp 20 York St New Haven CT 06510-3220

CONDRY, ROBERT STEWART, retired hospital administrator; b. Charleston, W.Va., Aug. 16, 1941; s. John Charles and Mary Louise (Jester) C.; m. Mary Purcell Heinzer, May 21, 1966; children: Mary-Lynch, John Stewart. BA, U. Charleston, 1963; MBA, George Washington U., 1970. Asst. hosp. dir. Med. Coll. of Va., Richmond, 1970-73, assoc. adminstr., 1973-75; assoc. hosp. dir. McGaw Hosp., Loyola U., Maywood, Ill., 1975-84, hosp. dir., 1984-93, ret., 1993; pres. Inter-Hosp. Planning Assn. of Western Suburbs, Maywood, 1983-93; bd. dirs. PentaMed, Inc., San Antonio. Bd. dirs. Met. Chgo. Healthcare Coun., 1985-93, mem. exec. com., 1989-93; bd. dirs. Cath. Hosp. Alliance, 1992, chmn. bd. dirs., 1992, mem. exec. com. 1988-94; mem. Ill. Gov.'s Adv. Bd. on Infant Mortality Reduction, 1988-93, Rev. Bd. on Emergency Medicine Svcs., 1989-93. With U.S. Army, 1964-66. Recipient preceptorship George Washington U., 1985, U. Chgo., 1984, St. Louis U., 1984, Tulane U., 1984, Yale U., 1991. Fellow Am. Coll. Healthcare Execs., Am. Acad. Med. Adminstrs.; mem. Am. Hosp. Assn., Cath. Hosp. Assn., Am. Mgmt. Assn. Republican. Roman Catholic.

CONE, LAWRENCE ARTHUR, research medicine educator; b. N.Y.C., Mar. 23, 1928; s. Max N. and Ruth (Weber) C.; m. Julia Haldy, June 6, 1947 (dec. 1956); m. Mary Elisabeth Osborne, Aug. 20, 1960; children: Lionel Alfred. AB, NYU, 1948; MD, U. Berne, Switzerland, 1954; DSc (hon.), Rocky Mountain Coll., 1993. Diplomate Am. Bd. Internal Medicine, Am. Bd. Infectious Diseases, Am. Bd. Allergy and Immunology, Am. Bd. Med. Oncology. Intern Dallas Meth. Hosp., 1954-55, resident internal medicine, 1955; resident Flower 5th Hosp., N.Y.C., 1957-59, Met. Hosp., N.Y.C., 1959-60; rsch. fellow infectious diseases and immunology NYU Med. Sch., N.Y.C., 1960-62; from asst. prof. to assoc. prof. N.Y. Med. Coll., N.Y.C., 1962-72, chief sect immunology and infectious diseases, 1962-72; assoc. clin. prof. medicine Harbor UCLA Med. Sch., 1984—; career scientist Health Rsch. Coun. N.Y.C., 1962-68; chief sect. immunology and infectious diseases Eisenhower Med. Ctr., Rancho Mirage, Calif., 1973—, chmn. dept. medicine, 1976-78, pres. elect, pres., past pres. med. staff, 1984-90; cons. infectious disease Desert Hosp., Palm Springs, Calif., 1980-85. Contbr. articles to profl. jours. Bd. dirs. Desert Bighorn Rsch. Inst., Palm Desert, Calif., 1986—, pres., bd. dirs., 1995—; nat. adv. coun., mem., bd. trustees Rocky Mountain Coll., Billings, Mont.; mem. med. adv. staff Coll. of Desert, Palm Desert; active Desert Mus., Palm Springs, Calif., Idaho Conservation League, Gilcrease Mus., Tulsa, Sun Valley Ctr. for Arts and Humanities. Fellow ACP, Royal Soc. Medicine, Am. Coll. Allergy, Am. Acad. Allergy and Immunology, Am. Soc. Infectious Diseases, Am. Geriatric Soc. (founding fellow western divsn.); mem. Internat. AIDS Soc., Am. Soc. Microbiology, Reticulocudothelial Soc., Am. Fedn. for Clin. Rsch., Assn. for the Advancement of Sci., Faculty Soc. UCLA, Woodstock Artists Assn., Harvey Soc., N.Y. Acad. Scis., Lotos Club, Tamarisk Country Club, Coachella Valley Gun and Wildlife Club Faculty Soc. UCLA Harbor Med. Ctr., Sigma Xi. Republican. Home: 765 W Via Vadera Palm Springs CA 92262-4170 Office: Probst Profl Bldg # 308 39000 Bob Hope Dr Rancho Mirage CA 92270-3221

CONERLY, ALBERT WALLACE, dean; b. Tylertown, Miss., Dec. 14, 1935; m. Francis Marie Bryan; children: Albert Wallace Jr., Charles Franklin. BS, Millsaps Coll., 1957; MD, Tulane U., 1960. Diplomate Am. Bd. Internal Medicine, Am. Bd. Pulmonary Disease. Intern The McLeod Infirmary, S.C., 1960-61; fellow in medicine sect. on cardiology Ochsner Found. Hosp., New Orleans, 1971; resident in medicine U. Miss. Sch. of Medicine, Jackson, 1971-72, fellow in pulmonary disease, 1972-74; vis. prof. U. Ky. Sch. of Medicine Dept. of Anesthesiology, 1981; attending staff Miss. Bapt. Hosp., St. Dominic Hosp. and Hinds Gen. Hosp., Jackson, Miss., 1966-70; asst. instr. in medicine U. Miss. Sch. of Medicine, Jackson, 1971-73, instr. in medicine divsn., 1973-74, asst. prof. medicine divsn. of pulmonary diseases, 1974-79, prof. respoiratory care, sch. of health related professions, 1978-93, assoc. prof. medicine, 1990-94; attending physician Univ. Hosp., U. Miss. Med. Ctr., 1973—, med. dir. adult intensive care unit, 1977-79, med. dir. acute care lab., 1978-82, dir. divsn. on continuing health profl. edn., 1979-93, asst. vice chancellor, 1981-94; med. dir. dept. respiratory therapy U. Hosps. and Clinics, U. of Miss., 1973—, med. dir. dept. of respiratory care Sch. of Helath Related Professions, 1975-93; med. advisor Tri-State Respiratory Therapy Conf., Ala., La., Miss., 1975-85, 90—; med. cons. Respiratory Care Svcs., Inc., Jackson, 1976-84; med. cons. Tuberculosis Control Unit, Miss. State Bd. of Health, 1976-82; oral examiner Nat. Bd. for Respiratory Care, 1977-79, others. Editl. rev. bd. Jour. of Respiratory Diseases, 1981-82; contbr. articles to profl. jours. With USAF, 1960-66. Grantee Am. Lung Assn., 1975-78, VA grant U. Miss. Med. Ctr., 1975-83. Mem. AMA, ACP, Aerospace Med. Assn., Am. Acad. of Gen. Practice, Am. Soc. Internal Medicine, Miss. Acad. Scis., Miss. State Med. Assn., Ctrl. Med. Soc. of Miss., Am. Coll. Chest Physicians, Am. Thoracic Soc., Miss. Thoracic Soc., Assn. of Am. Med. Colls., Miss. Soc. of the Am. Assn. for Respiratory Care (med. advisor 1974-85, 91—). Office: U Miss Med Ctr 2500 N State St Jackson MS 39216-4505*

CONFER, ANTHONY WAYNE, veterinary pathologist, educator; b. Hot Springs, Ark., July 29, 1947; s. Edwin M. and Gloria V. (Parker) C.; m. Carolyn Gay Pope, Aug. 15, 1970; children: Andrew W., Aaron J., Michael E., Christina A. DVM, Okla. State U., 1972; MS, Ohio State U., 1974; PhD, U. Mo., 1978. Diplomate Am. Coll. Vet. Pathologists. Assoc. prof. La. State U., Baton Rouge, 1978-81; assoc. prof. Okla. State U., Stillwater, 1981-85, prof., 1985—, dept. head, 1986—, endowed chair food animal rsch., 1995—; vis. prof. U. B.C., Vancouver, 1990-91; cons. Ft. Dodge (Iowa) Lab., 1987-92, Baxter Healthcare Corp., Round Lake, Ill., 1988-89, Vet. Reference Lab., Dallas, 1988-89, Smith Kline Beechan Ltd., Lincoln, Nebr., 1990; mem. Conf. Rsch. Workers-Animal Diseases, 1981—; cons. Diamond Animal Health, Des Moines, 1994—. Mem. editl. bd. Am. Jour. Vet. Rsch., 1993—, Vet. Pathology, 1995—. V.p. Stillwater Soccer Assn., 1987-91, pres., 1992-93; pub. rels. specialist Stillwater H.S. Soccer Club, 1990-96; cub master Cub Scout pack 22, Stillwater, 1987-89. Capt. USAF, 1974-76. Recipient Beecham award for Rsch., Smith Kline Beecham Lab., 1985, Norden Disting. Tchr. award Norden Labs., 1987. Mem. AVMA (Vet. Rsch. award 1992), Am. Coll. Vet. Pathologists (chair standing edn. com. 1994-96, program chair 1995), Morris Animal Found. (sci. advisor 1991-95), Sigma Xi (chpt. lectr. 1993). Mormon. Home: 2817 W 28th Ave Stillwater OK 74074-2212 Office: Dept Anatomy Pathology and Pharmacology Okla State Univ Stillwater OK 74078

CONFUSIONE, MICHAEL JOSEPH, psychologist; b. Bklyn., Oct. 19, 1947; s. John and Francesca Rachael (Sardo) C.; m. Linda Elizabeth Otvas, Sept. 6, 1986 (div. 1992); step-children: James, Virginia, Jennifer, Matthew, Thomas. BA, John Jay Coll., 1969; MA, New Sch. for Social Rsch., 1971; PhD, Calif. Sch. Profl. Psychology, 1979. Diplomate Am. Bd. Med. Psychotherapists; lic. psychologist, N.Y. Drug abuse counselor N.Y. State Drug Abuse Svcs., Bklyn., 1971-72; methadone clinic supr. Suffolk County Drug Abuse Svcs., Bayshore L.I., N.Y., 1972-75; clinics coord. Suffolk County Drug Abuse Svcs., Hauppauge L.I., 1975-76; psychology intern various agys., Calif., 1976-79; rsch. asst. SUNY, Stony Brook, 1979-80; cons. Comprehensive Home Care-Hospice, Smithtown, N.Y., 1979-81; psychologist Suffolk County Correctional Facility, Riverhead, N.Y., 1981-82; cons. Suffolk County Drug Abuse Svcs., Hauppauge, 1979-88; asst. prof. clin. family medicine SUNY Dept. Family Medicine, Stony Brook, 1980—; clin. psychologist pvt. practice Rocky Point, N.Y., 1983—; cons. in field. Contbr. articles to profl. jours. Hon. mem. North Shore Youth Coun., Rocky Point, N.Y., 1981—. Recipient Nat. Innovations in Clin. Teaching award, 1986, Achievement award for Drug Abuse Edn. and Prevention for Primary Care Physicians, 1983. Mem. APA, Am. Assn. Family Counselors/Mediators, Nat. Assn. Alcoholism and Drug Abuse Counselors, Coun. Nat. Register Health Svc. Providers Psychology. Office: Michael J Confusione PO Box 5011 Rocky Point NY 11778-0962

CONGDON, MARY ANN, health facility administrator, consultant; b. Bethesda, Md.. Diploma in nursing, Grace New Haven Sch. Nursing; BA in Health Care Adminstrn., St. Joseph's Coll., Windham, Maine. Med. surg. nurse Yale New Haven Hosp.; pediat. nurse Yale U. Health Svcs., New Haven; vis. nurse UNH, New Haven; supr. HHA UNH, Southbury, Conn.; case mgr. CHCP; dir. provider rels. MD Health Plans; regional dir. med. mgmt. Oxford Health Plans, 1993—. Office: Oxford Health Plans 48 Monroe Turnpike Trumbull CT 06611

CONGEDO, CAROL ZINN, retired otolaryngologist; b. N.Y.C., Aug. 18, 1973; d. Philip and Matilda (Gimberg) Zinn; m. Thomas V. Congedo, Aug. 18, 1973; children: Isaac, Benjamin. BS, Bklyn. Polytech. U., 1972; MD, U. Pitts., 1976. Diplomate Am. Bd. Otolaryngology. Resident surgeon Western Pa. Hosp., Pitts., 1976-78; resident Eye and Ear Hosp. U. Pitts., 1978-81; pvt. practice McKeesport, Pa., 1981-91; mem. cons. staff dept. otolaryngology U. Pitts. Med. Ctr., 1991—; physician advisor KEPRO, Pitts., 1987-90, McKeesport Hosp., 1987-90; clin. instr. U. Pitts., 1981—; exec. com. mem. McKeesport Hosp., 1990-91; bd. dirs. Lupus Found. Am. S.W. Pa. chpt. Fellow ACS; mem. Pitts. Otologic Soc. (v.p. 1990-92, sec.-treas. 1988-90, pres. 1992-94).

CONGER, JOHN D., vascular physiologist, nephrologist; b. Cottonwood, Idaho, Jan. 15, 1939; s. Earnest A. and Helen M. (Hines) C.; m. Carol A. Cherberg, May 13, 1961; children: David, James, Paul, Carolyn, Catherine. BS in Chemistry, Seattle U., 1961; MD, U. Wash., 1965. Diplomate Am. Bd. Internal Medicine. Rsch. fellow U. Calif., San Francisco, 1971-73; asst. prof. U. Colo., Denver, 1973-77, assoc. prof., 1977-87, prof., 1988—; chief of staff for rsch. VA Med. Ctr., Denver, 1995—; cons. Cole Labs., Lakewood, Colo., 1974-80; mem. adv. bd. SmithKline & Beecham, Phila., 1974—; chmn. rsch. com. Am. Heart Assn. Colo., Denver, 1995—. Contbr. chpt. to book, articles to profl. jours. Chmn. minority com. U. Colo., Denver. Lt. comdr. USN, 1965-71. NIDDK/NIH grante, 1989-93. Fellow ACP; mem. Am. Phys. Soc., Am. Soc. Clin. Investigation, Internat. Soc. nephrology. Office: Rsch Svcs (151) VA Med Ctr 1055 Clermont St Denver CO 80220

CONGER, JOHN JANEWAY, psychologist, educator; b. New Brunswick, N.J., Feb. 27, 1921; s. John C. and Katharine (Janeway) C.; m. Mayo Trist Kline, Jan. 1, 1944; children: Steven Janeway, David Trist. BA magna cum laude, Amherst Coll., 1943; MS, Yale U., 1947, PhD, 1949; DSc (hon.), Ohio U., 1981, Amherst Coll., 1983, U. Colo., 1989. Asst. prof. psychology Ind. U., 1949-53; chief staff psychologist U.S. Naval Acad., 1951-52; mem. faculty U. Colo. Sch. Medicine, prof. psychology, 1957-88, assoc. dean, 1961-63, v.p. for med. affairs, 1963-70, dean, 1963-68, acting chmn. dept. psychiatry, 1983-84, acting chancellor, 1985-86, prof. emeritus, 1988—; fellow Ctr. for Advanced Study in Behavioral Scis., Stanford, Cal., 1970-71; vis. scholar Inst. Human Devel., U. Calif., Berkeley, 1978; v.p., dir. health program John D. and Catherine T. MacArthur Found., 1980-83, cons., 1983-85; cons. to NIH, VA, USPHS; vice chmn. Colo. Bd. Psychology Examiners, 1961-64; mem. Gov. Colo. Com. Mental Health, 1957; chmn. mental health adv. council Colo. Dept. Pub. Health, 1957-61; mem. tng. com. Nat. Inst. Mental Health, 1959-62; mem. Western council mental health research and tng. Western Interstate Commn. Higher Edn., 1959-66; chmn. research com. President's Com. Traffic Safety, 1960-63; vice chmn. nat. motor vehicle safety adv. council Dept. Transp., 1967-70; mem. inter-council com. constrn. univ.-affiliated facilities for mentally retarded Dept. Health, Edn. and Welfare, 1967-70, mem. sec.'s adv. com. traffic safety, 1966-69; council research and planning Am. Hosp. Assn., 1965-68; nat. adv. mental health council USPHS, 1965-69; nat. adv. com. John F. Kennedy Center for Research on Edn. and Human Devel., 1965-76, chmn., 1970-74; mem. adv. com. on undergrad med. edn. AMA, 1969-70; adv. com. on casualty ins. Dept. Transp., 1970; mem. Pres.'s Task Force on Hwy. Safety, 1970, President's Commn. on Mental Health, 1977-78; mem. com. study nat. needs for biomed. and behavioral sci. research personnel Nat. Acad. Scis., 1976-80; mem. Inst. Medicine/Nat. Acad. Scis., 1983—, bd. mental health and behavioral medicine, 1986-92. Author: Child Development and Personality, 7th edit., 1990, Readings in Child Development, 1964, 3d edit., 1984, Personality, Social Class and Delinquency, 1965, Adolescence and Youth: Psychological Development in a Changing World, 5th edit., 1996, The Shape of the Tree: Selected Poems, 1993, Basic and Contemporary Issues in Developmental Psychology, 1975, Contemporary Issues in Adolescent Development, 1975, Psychological Development: A Life-Span Approach, 1979, Essentials of Child Development and Personality, 1980, also articles; mem. editl. coun. Applied and Preventive Psychology, 1991—. Served to lt. USNR, 1944-46, 51-52. Recipient Stearns Alumni medal for extraordinary service U Colo., 1970, U. Colo. medal, 1986, disting. profl. achievement award Am. Bd. Profl. Psychology, 1979. Fellow APA (mem. policy and planning bd. 1967-70, rec. sec., dir. 1974-79, pres. 1980-82, award for outstanding contbns. health psychology 1983, award for disting. contbns. psychology in pub. interest 1986), AAAS, Soc. Rsch. in Child Devel. (program chmn. 1975, fin. com. 1989-93, Disting. Contbns. to Pub. Policy for Children award 1995); mem. Am. Psychol. Found. (bd. dirs. 1982-86, pres. 1985-86), Denver Med. Soc. (hon. mem.), Colo. Psychol. Assn. (pres. 1959, Disting. Svc. award 1963, 84), Colo. Med. Soc. (Disting. Svc. award 1970), Phi Beta Kappa, Sigma Xi, Alpha Omega Alpha (hon.). Home: 130 S Birch St Denver CO 80222-1017

CONIBEAR, SHIRLEY ANN, occupational health consultant, physician; b. Amboy, Ill., Aug. 20, 1946; d. Herbert Louis and Margaret (Cenkar) C.; m. Bertram Carnow, Oct. 31, 1975; children: Rebecca, Kalinka, Tina. BA, Shimer Coll., 1968; MD, U. Ill., 1973, MPH, 1976. Diplomate Am. Bd. Preventive Medicine. Intern Conemaugh Valley Meml., Johnstown, Pa., 1973-74; resident family practice McNeal Hosp., Berwyn, Ill., 1974; resident family practice, occupational medicine Cook County Hosp., Chgo., 1975-76, dir. health hazard evaluation, 1977-78; dir. programs in medicine, occupational medicine residency U. Ill. Coll. Medicine, Chgo., 1978-82, assoc. prof. occupational medicine, 1982-88; v.p. Carnow, Conibear & Assocs., Chgo., 1977-88, pres., 1988—; epidemiologist Argonne Nat. Lab., Lemont, Ill., 1979-81; chief med. officer Milw. RR, Chgo., 1982-86; cons. to Dept. Energy, Washington, 1986-93; pres. Athena Analytical Lab., Inc.; apptd. to Nat. Adv. Com. on Occupational Safety and Health, 1994. Author: Medical Surveillance of Hazardous Waste Workers, 1990; editor: First Aid Manual for Chemical Accidents, 1989; contbr. chpts. to books; editorial adviser Occupational Health and Safety Jour. Fellow Am. Coll. Preventive Medicine; mem. Am. Coll. Epidemiology, Am. Coll. Toxicology, Am. Indsl. Hygiene Assn., Am. Coll. Occupation and Environ. Medicine, Am. Pub. Health Assn. Office: Carnow Conibear & Assocs 333 W Wacker Dr Ste 1400 Chicago IL 60606-1226

CONKLIN, FRANCES PHILLIPS, retired radiologist, educator; b. Port Jervis, N.Y., July 8, 1924; d. Robert Conkling and Marion (Rice) Phillips; m. J. Wallace Conklin, July 31, 1949 (div. 1983); children: Jonathan, Jennifer, Elizabeth, Suzanne. BA, U. Wis., 1945; MD cum laude, U. Vt., 1951. Diplomate Am. Bd. Radiology, Nat. Bd. Med. Examiners. Rotating intern Santa Barbara (Calif.) Coll. Hosp., 1951-52; resident in radiology U. Minn. and U. Minn. Hosps., Mpls., 1952-55; staff radiologist Temple U. Hosp., Phila., 1955-56; radiologist in-charge radiation therapy R.I. Hosp., Providence, 1958-72; pvt. practice, Providence, 1972-89; ret., 1989; clin. asst. prof. radiation medicine Brown U., Providence, 1984—; mem. bd. med. discipline and licensure State of R.I., Providence, 1987-93; del. from Am. Med. Women's Assn. to Med. Women's Internat. Assn., The Hague, The Netherlands, 1995—. Author: (with Coleman and Olfelt) Manual of Radiation Therapy, 1957; contbr. articles to med. jours. Med. dir. reach to recovery, past chmn. svc. and rehab. com. R.I. divsn. Am. Cancer Soc.; past trustee Episcopal Housing Found. R.I.; past bd. mgrs. Hallworth House; past mem. med. adv. com. Hospice Care R.I., Inc.; past bd. dirs. R.I. Lung Assn. Recipient Therese Lasser award Am. Cancer Soc., 1988, Woman Physician of Yr. award R.I. Med. Women's Assn., 1989; named to R.I. Heritage Hall of Fame, 1991. Fellow Am. Coll. Radiology (emeritus); mem. R.I. Med. Soc. (treas. 1986-90, Charles L. Hill award 1991), Providence Med. Assn. (pres. 1984-85, exec. com. 1989, Cmty. Svc. award 1995), U. Vt. Med. Alumni Assn. (Svc. to Medicine and Cmty. award 1996), Save the Bay, Am. Assn. Ret. Persons. Republican. Home: 54 Hybrid Dr Cranston RI 02920-5807

CONKLIN, SUSAN JOAN, psychotherapist, corporate staff development; b. Bklyn., Feb. 7, 1950; d. Joseph Thomas Hallek and Stella Joan (Kubis) Kuceluk; m. John Lariviere Conklin, July 25, 1981; children: Genevieve Therese, Michelle Therese. BA, CCNY, 1972; MSW, CUNY, 1975. Lic. ind. clin. social worker; cert. diplomat. Shop counselor Assn. for Help of Retarded Citizens, N.y.C., 1971-75; dir. social svcs., acting exec. dir. North Berkshire Assn. for Retarded Citizens, North Adams, Mass., 1975-77; project dir. Title XX tng. grant State of Mass., North Adams, 1978-79; pvt. practice psychotherapy Williamstown, Mass., 1979—; human resources cons., 1996—; asst. prof. North Adams State Coll., 1977-85, Berkshire C.C., Pittsfield, Mass., 1985-86, 95; therapeutic touch practitioner, 1978—; human resources cons., 1996—. Pres. Williamstown PTO, 1989-91; bd. dirs., edn. com., spl. events coord. Hospice No. Berkshire, Inc., 1989—. Mem. NASW (bd. dirs. 1981-83, regional coun. mem. 1980-83, 93—), LWV, Nurse Healers-Profl. Assn., Inc. (trustee 1981-83, rec. sec., editor-in-chief Coop. Connection newsletter 1983-88). Democrat. Episcopalian. Home and Office: 85 Hawthorne Rd Williamstown MA 01267-2700

CONLAN, IRENE ESTELLE, health care administrator; b. Emmett, Idaho, Sept. 25, 1935; d. Carl O. Danielson and Mona A. Cardwell; m. John B. conlan, Sept. 13, 1968 (div. 1993); children: Christopher, Kevin. BS in Nursing, The Cath. U. Am., 1964, MS in Nursing, 1965; RHT, Nat. Hypnotherapy Tng. Ctr., 1996. Dir. St. Anthony Sch. Nursing, Oklahoma City, 1965-66; mem. faculty Coll. Nursing Ariz. State U., Tempe, 1966-67, Sch. Nursing No. Ariz. U., Flagstaff, 1966; dir. nursing adminstrn. St. Luke's Hosp Med. Ctr., Phoenix, 1967-72; asst. dir. div. emergency med. services and health care facilities Ariz. State Health Dept., Phoenix, 1987-89; founder, CEO Cartridge Care, Inc., Scottsdale, Ariz., 1989-95; founder, pres. The Power Zone, Scottsdale, 1995—; cons. grant rev. office child and family services HHS, Washington, 1985, office adolescent pregnancy, 1986—. Author: Women We Can Do It, 1976; co-author: 1984 and Beyond, 1984. Pres. Scottsdale Rep. Women, 1978; bd. dirs. The Enterprise Network, Ariz. Women's Employment and Edn.; mem. St. Luke's Svc. League, Phoenix, 1970—, Scottsdale Leadership Class IX, 1995. Mem. Nat. Assn. Women Bus. Owners, Nat. Spkrs. Assn., Sigma Theta Tau. Home: 11349 E Poinsettia Dr Scottsdale AZ 85259-3143

CONLAN, MAUREEN GERALDINE, internist, hematologist, oncologist; b. Teaneck, N.J., Sept. 12, 1955; d. Andrew K. and Gloria L. (Serrichio) C. BS, Fairleigh Dickinson U., 1977; MD, U. N.J., 1981. Diplomate Am. Bd. Internal Medicine, Am. Bd. Hematology, Am. Bd. Med. Oncology. Resident internal medicine SUNY-Upstate Med. Ctr., Syracuse, N.Y., 1981-84; fellow hematology U. Wis., Madison, 1984-87; fellow med. oncology Nebr. Med. Ctr., Omaha, 1987-88; asst. prof. U. Tex. Med. Sch., Houston, 1988-93; assoc. dir. clin. rsch. and devel. R.W. Johnson Pharm. Rsch. Inst., Raritan, N.J., 1993—. Fellow Am. Coll. Physicians; mem. Am. Soc. Hematology, Am. Soc. Clin. Oncology, Am. Fedn. Clin. Rsch. Home: 18 William Barnes Rd Flemington NJ 08822 Office: RW Johnson Pharm Rsch Inst 700 Rt 202 Raritan NJ 08869

CONLEY, DANIEL PETER, psychologist, writer; b. Erie, Pa., Jan. 14, 1935; s. Joseph Peter and Theresa (Heible) C.; m. Sally Anderson, July 4, 1960 (div. Nov. 1982); m. L.J. Reynolds, Nov. 18, 1987; children: Arlene Belinda Conley Gaffney, Kolleen. BS, Edinboro (Pa.) U., 1959; MA, Ariz.

State U., Tempe, 1966, PhD, 1973. Lic. Ariz. State Bd. Psychologists Examiners. Speech pathologist Elk County Pub. Schs., Ridgway, Pa., 1964-66; dir. spl. edn. Glendale (Ariz.) Schs., 1966-72; clin. dir. Adaptive Stress Ctr. P.C., Phoenix, 1972—; psychol. cons. Ariz. Dept. Correction, 1980—; bd. dirs. Nova Drug Program, Phoenix, 1994—. Editor East High Alumni Assn., 1993-95. Sgt. USAF, 1952-56, Korea. Recipient Cert. award Tinnnitis, Kreske Inst., 1994. Mem. APA, Ariz. Psychol. Assn., Biofeedback Soc. (pres. 1974-76). Republican. Roman Catholic. Home: PO Box 384 Paulden AZ 86334

CONLEY, KAREN ANN, hematology, oncology and bone marrow transplant nurse; b. Winchester, Mass., July 28, 1966; d. John Joseph and Lynda Ann (Porter) Nugent; m. Brian Michael Conley, Aug. 9, 1986; children: Thomas Patrick, Meghan Kathleen. Student, U. Rochester (N.Y.), 1986-87; BSN, Boston Coll., 1988; MS in Nursing Adminstrn., Northeastern U., 1996. Staff RN Brigham Women's Hosp., Boston, 1988-91, nurse-in-charge, 1991-96, asst. nurse mgr., 1996—. Mem. ANA, Oncology Nursing Soc., Boston Oncology Nursing Soc., Sigma Theta Tau Internat. (Gamma Epsilon chpt.). Roman Catholic. Office: Brigham Women's Hosp Tower 6 75 Francis St Boston MA 02115-6110

CONLEY, SUSAN BERNICE, medical school faculty pediatrician; b. Coldwater, Mich., Feb. 3, 1948; d. Kenneth D. and Mary F. (Spence) C. MD, U. Mich., 1973. Instr. Washington U. Med. Sch., St. Louis, 1977-78; asst. prof. pediatrics U. Tex. Med. Sch., Houston, 1978-84, dir. pediatric nephrology, 1983—, assoc. prof. pediatrics, 1984-91; dir. pediatric renal ctr. Calif. Pacific Med. Ctr., San Francisco, 1991-94; prof. pediatrics sch. medicine Stanford (Calif.) U., 1994—; med. dir. dialysis and renal transplantation, chief clin. nephrology Packard Children's Hosp. at Stanford, Calif., 1994—; chmn. med. adv. bd. No. Calif. chpt. Nat. Kidney Found., pres. region V western states. Mem. kidney/pancreas com. United Network Organ Sharing. Fellow Am. Acad. Pediatrics; mem. Am. Soc. Nephrology, Am. Soc. Pediatric Nephrology, Soc. for Pediatric Rsch. Office: Sch Medicine Dept Pediatrics Stanford U Stanford CA 94305-5119

CONLEY, THOMAS ANTHONY, minister, counselor; b. Oak Hill, Ohio, Aug. 7, 1954; s. David C. and Jean (Wheeler) C.; m. Susan B. Kemp, June 21, 1981; children: Gabriel S., Zachary D., Caleb B. Student, Ohio U., 1972-74; BA, Circleville (Ohio) Bible Coll., 1981; MPC, Olivet Nazarene U., 1991; postgrad., Trinity Evangel. Divinity Sch., Deerfield, Ill., 1991—. Ordained to ministry Ch. of the Nazarene, 1983. Min. Ch. of the Nazarene, Mt. Sterling, Ill., 1984-86, Crothersville, Ind., 1986-90, Salem, Ohio, 1990-94, Bradford, Pa., 1994—; pastoral counselor Nazarene Counseling Svcs., Salem, 1990-94. Home: 31 Interstate Pky Bradford PA 16701-1010 Office: Ch of the Nazarene 55 N Bennett Bradford PA 16701-1010

CONLON, CHRISTOPHER PETER, infectious diseases physician, consultant; b. Sheffield, Eng., July 29, 1955; m. Jennifer Lortan; 1 child, Sophie. BA with honors, Oxford (Eng.) U., 1977; MB BChir, London U., 1980, MD, 1991. Med. registrar St. Thomas' Hosp., London, 1985-86; rsch. fellow St. Mary's Hosp., London, 1986-89; lectr. in medicine U. Zambia, 1986-88; sr. registrar in infectious diseases Oxford, 1989-92, cons. physician, 1992—. Contbr. articles and chpts. to profl. publs. Fellow Royal Coll. Physicians U.K. Office: John Radcliffe Hosp, Nuffield Dept Medicine, Oxford OX3 9D6, England

CONLON, PATRICK C., health facility administrator, nurse educator; b. Sioux City, Iowa, July 24, 1962; s. James Ambrose and Mary Lee Emily (Donahue) Conlon. Diploma in Nursing, St. Joseph Mercy Hosp., Sioux City, 1986; BSN, Briar Cliff Coll., Sioux City, 1988, BA in Psychology. Cert. in gen. nursing practice; cert. diabetes educator; cert. BCLS; cert. case mgr. Staff nurse, charge nurse Marian Health Ctr., Sioux City, 1979-89; staff nurse Western Med. Svcs., Sioux City, 1987-89; asst. nurse mgr., orthopaedic nurse adminstr. Michael Reese Hosp. and Med. Ctr., Chgo., 1989-91; edn. dir. ADA Iowa Diabetes Childrens Camp, 1989-93; health team coord., nurse educator, teaching faculty Triangle D Childrens Diabetes Camp, No. Ill., 1990-93; dir., clin. coord. diabetes edn. Mt. Sinai Hosp., 1991-96. Manuscript reviewer Jour. of Care Mgmt.; contbr. articles to profl. jours. Mem. ANA (chmn. 1992-94), Am. Nurses Credentialing Ctr., Am. Diabetes Assn. (bd. dirs., camp com. No. Ill. affiliate, peer reviewer of recognition program 1994—), Iowa Nurses Assn. (nursing adminstrn. commn. 1993-97), Am. Psychol. Soc. (charter), Nat. Nurses in Bus. Assn. (charter), St. Joseph Mercy Sch. Nursing Alumni Assn., Am. Assembly for Men in Nursing, Am. Assn. Diabetes Educators (manuscript reviewer jour.), Diabetes Educators Chgo. Area (v.p. 1991-92, pres.-elect 1992-93, pres. 1993-94, past pres./symposium chair 1994-95), Sigma Theta Tau, Alpha Tau Delta. Home: 2059 Roundtable Rd Sergeant Bluff IA 51054-9743 Office: Mt Sinai Hosp and Med Ctr Dept Medicine F-908 15th and California Ave Chicago IL 60608

CONN, HADLEY LEWIS, JR., physician, educator; b. Danville, Ind., May 6, 1921; s. Hadley L. and Fyrne (Holtsclaw) C.; m. Betty Jean Aubertin, Sept. 18, 1946; children: Eric Hadley, Jeffrey Wood, Thomas Brian, Andrew Randall, Lisabeth Ann. B.A., U. Ind., 1942, M.D., 1944; M.S. (hon.), U. Pa., 1972. Assoc. scientist Brookhaven Nat. Lab., N.Y., 1953-55; asst. prof. U. Pa. Sch. Medicine, Phila., 1956-59; assoc. prof. U. Pa. Sch. Medicine, 1959-64, prof. medicine, 1964-72; dir. Clin. Research Center Hosp. of U. Pa. Sch. Medicine, 1970-72; chmn. dept. medicine Presbyn.-U. Pa. Med. Center, Phila., 1964-69; vis. prof. medicine Am. U. Beirut, 1969-70; chmn. dept. medicine Univ. Medicine and Dentistry N.J.-Rutgers Med. Sch., Piscataway, 1972-83, dir. Cardiovascular Inst., 1982-91, prof. medicine, chmn. emeritus, 1992. Author: Myocardial Cell, 1966, Cardiac and Vascular Disease, 1971, Platelets, Prostaglandins and Lipids, 1980, Health and Obesity, 1983. Sec. Nat. Bd. Med. Examiners, 1962-65; bd. govs. Am. Heart Assn., 1969-72; pres. Heart Assn. S.E. Pa., 1967, Detweiler Found., 1973-85. Served to capt. M.C., AUS, 1946-48. Mem. ACP, Am. Coll. Cardiology (trustee 1963-69), AMA, Am. Soc. Clin. Investigation, Am. Clin. and Climatological Soc., Assn. Univ. Cardiologists, Am. Phys. Soc., Assn. Profs. Medicine, Phi Beta Kappa, Alpha Omega Alpha. Republican. Clubs: Rittenhouse; Merion Cricket (Phila.). Home: 253 Wendover Dr Princeton NJ 08540-2434

CONN, HAROLD O., physician, educator; b. Newark, Nov. 16, 1925; s. Joseph H. and Dora (Kobrin) C.; m. Marilyn Barr, May 2, 1951; children: Chrysanne, Steven A., Dorianne. BS, U. Mich., 1946, MD, 1950; MS, Yale U., 1972. Diplomate: Am. Bd. Internal Medicine. Intern Johns Hopkins Hosp., 1950-51; asst. resident Grace New Haven Community Hosp., 1951-52, chief resident, 1955-56; James Hudson Browne research fellow, 1952-53; dir. med. edn. Middlesex Meml. Hosp., 1956-57; clin. investigator VA, 1957-61; chief med. svc. VA Hosp., West Haven, Conn., 1959-60; chief hepatic rsch. lab. VA Hosp., 1961-89; instr. Yale Sch. Medicine, 1955-58, asst. prof., 1958-66, assoc. prof., 1966-71, prof., 1971-91, prof. emeritus, 1991—, dir. continuing med. edn. program, 1988-91; clin. prof. surgery divsn. liver/intestinal transplantation U. Miami, 1995—; vis. assoc. prof. Washington U. Sch. Medicine, 1982-83; CEO, Med., Med.-Legal and Led.0Lit. Consultations; dir. Continuing Med. Edn. dept. medicine Yale U. Sch. Medicine, 1990-92; cons. Miami Vascular Inst., 1994-95. Author: (with M.M. Liebenthal) The Hepatic Coma Syndromes and Lactulose, 1979; co-author: (with G. Klatskin) Histopathology of the Liver, 1990; editor: Cyanidanol in Diseases of the Liver, 1981; (with J. Palmaz, J. Rösch, and M. Rössle) Transjugular Intrahepatic Partial Systemic Stent-shunts Tips, 1995; mem. editl. bd.: Viewpoints on Digestive Disease, 1968-73, Jour. Gastroenterology, 1970-80, Jour. Clin. Trials, Italian Jour. Gastroenterology, 1977-87, Jour. Internal Medicine, 1988-96; assoc. editor Hepatology, 1980-90; book editor: Hepatology, 1985-88; editor Hepatology Elsewhere, 1985-91; editor: (with J. Bircher) Hepatic Encephalopathy: Management with Lactulose and Related Carbohydrates, 1988, (with J. Bircher) Hepatic Encephalopathy: Syndromes and Therapies, 1994. Bd. dirs. Am. Liver Found., 1977-80. Ensign USNR, 1943-44; 1st lt. USAR, 1953-54, USAFR, 1954-55. Recipient Rorer award, 1973, William Beaumont award clin. rsch., 1974. Fellow ACP; mem. Assn. Am. Physicians, Am. Soc. Clin. Investigation, Internat. Assn. Study Liver, Sydenham Soc. (sec. 1968-88, mem. med. adv. bd. Seminars and Symposia 1974-80), Hepatic Perfusion Soc. (pres. St. Louis chpt.), Am. Assn. Study Liver Disease (v.p. 1971, pres. 1972), Am. Fedn. Clin. Rsch., Am. Gastroenterol. Assn. (councillor 1974-77, Hugh Butt-Miles and Shirley Fiterman award for clinical rsch. in hepatology 1990), Soc. for Clin. Trials (dir. 1978-83), Nat. Assn. Va. Physicians (bd. dirs. 1986-88, chmn. continuing med. edn. com. 1987-89); hon. mem. Australian Soc. Gastroenterology, Brazilian Assn. for Study of Liver, China Med. Assn. (Shanghai br.; Taiwan), Hungarian Gastroent. Soc. (hon.). Home and Office: 160 Morgan Ave East Haven CT 06512-4519 Summer home: 1620 S Ocean Blvd Apt PHB Pompano Beach FL 33062-7703

CONN, REX BOLAND, JR., physician, educator; b. Marengo, Iowa, Aug. 3, 1927; s. Rex Boland and Helena Dorothea (Schoenfelder) C.; m. Victoria Grace Sellens, Dec. 28, 1950; children: Elizabeth Marian, Victoria Anne, Mary Catherine. BS, Iowa State U., 1949; MD, Yale U., 1953; BSc U. Oxford, Eng., 1955; MS, U. Minn., 1960. Prof. pathology, dir. clin. labs. W.Va. Med. Center, Morgantown, 1960-68; prof. lab. medicine, dir. dept. Johns Hopkins Med. Instns., Balt., 1968-77; prof. pathology and lab. medicine, dir. clin labs. Emory U., Atlanta, 1977-87; prof. and vice chmn. dept. pathology and cell biology, dir. clin. labs. Thomas Jefferson Med. Coll., Phila., 1987—; mem. pathology tng. com. NIH, 1972-73, mem. pathology A study sect., 1968-72; cons. Walter Reed Army Med. Center, 1972-77; cons. Armed Forces Inst. of Pathology, 1984-88. Editor: Current Diagnosis, 1996, Yearbook of Pathology and Clinical Pathology, 1980, Applied Laboratory Medicine, 1992. Served with USNR, 1945-46. Mem. Coll. Am. Pathologists, Am. Soc. Clin. Pathologists (dir. 1975-81, pres. 1993-94), Acad. Clin. Lab. Physicians and Scientists (pres. 1972). Office: Thomas Jefferson Univ Hosp 204 Pavilion Philadelphia PA 19107

CONNAUGHTON, JAMES PATRICK, psychiatrist; b. Dublin, Mar. 13, 1931; came to U.S., 1965; s. Patrick and Julia (Barrett) C.; children: Bernadette, Eileen, James, Paul, John. MB, ChB, Univ. Coll., Dublin., 1956. Diplomate Am. Bd. Psychiatry & Neurology, Am. Bd. Child & Adolescent Psychiatry. Intern Mater Univ. Hosp., Dublin, 1956-57; resident in psychiatry Seton Psychiat. Inst., Balt., 1958-61; sr. staff psychiatrist Milw. Psychiat. Hosp., 1961-65; fellow dept. child psychiatry, dept. pediatrics Johns Hopkins Hosp., Balt., 1965-67; sr. staff div. child psychiatry Johns Hopkins Hosp., 1967—; family practice medicine, Manchester, Eng., 1957-58; psychiat. cons. VA Hosp., Wood, Wis., 1961-65; cons. dept. medicine West Allis Meml. Hosp., Milw., 1962-65; psychiat. cons. Peace Corps Tng. Projects, 1963-64; dir. adolescent program Milw. Psychiat. Hosp., 1961-65; treas. Milw. Psychiat. Clinic Chartered, 1963-64, v.p., 1964-65; asst. prof. psychiatry Marquette U., 1962-65; dir. Dundalk Mental Health Clinic, Baltimore County, Md., 1966-67; assoc. dir. div. child psychiatry Johns Hopkins Hosp., 1971—; assoc. prof. psychiatry and pediatrics Johns Hopkins U. Med. Sch., 1972—; dir. child in-patient neuropsychiatric unit and psychiatric unit, 1969-72, liaison-cons. svcs, children-adolescents, 1972-74, dir. psychiat. and mental health scis., 1972-81, psychiatric svcs. and mental health svcs. Comprehensive Pediatric Child Care Clinic, 1973-81, The Children and Adolescent Mental Health Ctr., 1981-93, psychosomatic clinic divsn. child adolescent psychiatry, 1993—; cons. Assoc. Catholic Charities, 1965-81, Villa Maria-Residential Treatment Ctr., 1981—, Children's Guild, 1969-78, Oldfields Sch., 1968-78, John F. Kennedy Inst. 1971—, Francis Scott Key Community Psychiatry Program, 1994—; dir. child & adolescent neuropsychiat. unit Johns Hopkins Hosp., 1969-73, mem. child care com., 1971-73, bed utilization com., 1971-74, pediatric intern selection com., 1971-74, mental health com. Comprehensive Pediatric Care Clinic, 1974-81, chmn. child abuse and neglect com. dept. pediats., 1975-80, directorate com. community mental health programs, 1981—, dir. child and adolescent community mental health program, 1981-93. Mem. steering com. East Balt. Mental Health Ctr.; goals and objectives com. Villa Maria Children's Inst., med. adv. com.; div. spl. edn. Balt. City Dept. Edn.; directorate com. community mental health programs Balt. City Health Dept., 1981—, mem. children's mental health planning com. Fellow Am. Psychiat. Assn. (life), Am. Acad. Child Psychiatry, Royal Coll. Psychiatrists; mem. AAAS, Balt. County Med. Soc., Md. Psychiat. Soc. Roman Catholic. Home: 45 Thornhill Rd Lutherville MD 21093-5806 Office: Johns Hopkins Hosp 600 N Wolf St Baltimore MD 21287

CONNELL, ALASTAIR MCCRAE, physician; b. Glasgow, Scotland, Dec. 21, 1929; came to U.S., 1970; s. Alex McCrae and Maud (Crawford) C.; m. Joyce Dethlefs, 1983; children: Stewart, Fiona, Alison, Iain, Andrew. BS, U. Glasgow, 1951, MB, ChB, 1954, MD, 1969. Intern Western Infirmary, Glasgow, 1954-55; resident in gastroenterology Cen. Middlesex and St. Mark's Hosp., London, 1957-60; practice medicine specializing in gastroenterology, 1960—; mem. med. staff Med. Rsch. Coun., 1960-64; sr. lectr. clin. sci. Queen's U., Belfast, No. Ireland, 1964-70; Mark Brown prof. medicine Med. Ctr., U. Cin., 1970-79, dir. div. digestive diseases, 1970-79, prof. physiology, 1972-79, assoc. dean, 1975-77; dir. Office Clin. Affairs, 1975-77; dean Coll. Medicine, U. Nebr. Med. Ctr., 1979-84, prof. internal medicine, 1979-84; v.p. health scis. Va. Commonwealth U., Richmond, 1984-88; scholar-in-residence Inst. Medicine, 1988-89; vice chancellor health scis. Ea. Carolina U., 1989-90; dir. Office Healthcare Inspections, Dept. Vets. Affairs, Washington, 1991—; adj. prof. med. George Washington U., 1992—; adj. prof. humanities E. Carolina U; vis. prof. dept. moral philosophy U. St. Andrews, Scotland, 1984-86; mem. sci. adv. bd. Nat. Found. for Ileitis and Colitis, 1974-80, chmn. rsch. devel. com., 1974-78; mem. Personal Health Com. Ohio, 1974-76; trustee Medco Peer Rev., 1974-79. Author: Clinical Tests of Gastric Function, 1973; Assoc. editor: Am. Jour. Digestive Diseases; Contbr. articles to profl. jours. Served with M.C. Royal Army, 1955-57. Fellow Royal Coll. Physicians (Edinburgh), ACP; mem. Am. Gastroent. Assn., Brit. Soc. Gastroenterology, Internat. Group for Study Intestinal Motility (past pres.). Address: 2341 W Island Rd Williamsburg VA 23185

CONNELLY, CYNTHIA DONALDSON, nursing educator; b. Barre, Vt.; d. Dugald Campbell and Jennie Gould (Smith) Donaldson; m. Robert F. Connelly, Dec. 19, 1978. Diploma, Hartford Hosp. Sch. Nursing, 1971; BA, U. Redlands, 1977, MA, 1980; MS in Nursing, U. San Diego, 1984; PhD in Nursing, U. R.I., 1993. Postdoctoral fellow U. Wash. Sch. Nursing, Seattle, 1995—. Mem. ANA, N.H. Nurses Assn., Sigma Theta Tau.

CONNER, KEITH CAMERON, pharmacist, consultant; b. Guntersville, Ala., Apr. 16, 1960; s. Elmer Randolph and Virginia Grace (Cameron) C. BS in pharmacy, Auburn U., 1983. Pharmacist Big B Drugs, Birmingham, Ala., 1983; pharmacist/mgr., cons. Pharmacy Corp. Am., Birmingham, Ala., 1983-89; tech. svcs. mgr. Vital Care, Inc., Livingston, Ala., 1989—; dir. pharmacy Hill Hosp., York, Ala., 1989—; mem. adv. bd. Tombigbee Hospice, Livingston, 1991—; pres. Vital Care West Ala., C and M Vital Care. Fellow Am. Soc. Cons. Pharmacists; mem. Am. Pharm. Assn., Am. Soc. Hosp. Pharmacists, Ala. Soc. Hosp. Pharmacists, Ala. Pharm. Assn. Home: PO Box 38 Livingston AL 35470-0038 Office: Vital Care Inc PO Box 1249 Livingston AL 35470-1249

CONNER, REBECCA ELAINE, molecular biologist, researcher; b. Bowling Green, Ky., Mar. 2, 1960; d. James Ewing and Dorothy Marie (Hogan) C. BS, Western Ky. U., 1983, MS, 1986. Rsch. asst. III dept. pathology Vanderbilt U., Nashville, 1986-87; grad. teaching asst. biology dept. Tex. Woman's U., Denton, 1987—. Contbr. articles to Jour. Photochemistry and Photobiology. Mem. Phi Kappa Phi. Office: Tex Woman's U Biology Dept PO Box 425799 Denton TX 76204-1971

CONNEY, ALLAN HOWARD, pharmacologist; b. Chgo., Mar. 23, 1930; s. Leo Younkers and Celia (Gasway) C.; m. Diana, Sept. 5, 1954; children—Michael Raymond, Steven Herbert. B.S., U. Wis., 1952, M.S., 1954, Ph.D., 1956. Research asst. McArdle Lab., Madison, Wis., 1952-56; guest investigator Nat. Heart Inst., Bethesda, Md., 1957-58, pharmacologist, 1958-60; head dept. biochem. pharmacology Burroughs Wellcome & Co., Tuckahoe, N.Y., 1960-70; dir. dept. biochemistry Hoffmann-La Roche Inc., Nutley, N.J., 1970-71, dir. dept. biochemistry and drug metabolism, 1971-83, assoc. dir. exptl. therapeutics, 1979-83, dir. lab. exptl. carcinogenesis and metabolism, 1983-85; head Lab. of Exptl. Carcinogenesis and Metabolism Roche Inst. Molecular Biology, Nutley, N.J., 1985-87; chmn. dept. chem. biology Rutgers U. Coll. Pharmacy, Piscataway, N.J., 1987—. Mem. NAS, AAAS, Am. Soc. Biol. Chemists, Am. Soc. Pharmacology and Exptl. Therapeutics (ASPET award), Am. Assn. Cancer Rsch. (G.H.A. Clowes award), Soc. Toxicology, Inc. (Arnold J. Lehman award). Office: Rutgers U Coll Pharmacy Piscataway NJ 08855

CONNOLLY, DAVID PAUL, surgeon; b. Pitts., Oct. 1, 1936; s. John Wray and Pauline (Rock) C.; m. Joeanne Clare Perrone, Oct. 2, 1965; children: Colleen A., David J., Meghan G., Cara M., Anne W. BA, John Carroll U., 1957; MD, Loyola U., Chgo., 1961. Diplomate Am. Bd. Surgery. Intern Akron (Ohio) Gen. Hosp., 1962; resident Mercy Hosp., Pitts., 1964-69; dir. surg. edn. St. Margaret Meml. Hosp., Pitts., 1976—, pres. med. staff, 1990-92; mem. exec. com. Am. Cancer Soc., Pitts., 1977-82, chmn. profl. edn. com., 1977-82; lectr. Am. Cancer Soc., Pitts; fellow Am. Cancer Soc., Meml.-Sloan-Kettering Inst., 1967-68. Maj. USAF, 1962-64. Fellow ACS (bd. govs. S.W. Pa. chpt. 1975-79, sec. 1995—; liaison fellow commn. on cancer 1977—), Soc. Surg. Oncology; mem. AMA, Pa. Med. Soc. (coun. edn./sci. 1976-78), Pitts. Surg. Soc. (pres.-elect 1992-94, prse. 1994-95), Allegheny County Med. Soc., Internat. Coll. Surgeons, Am. Soc. Clin. Oncologists, Am. Soc. Gastrointestinal Endoscopy, Soc. Surgery Alimentary Tract, Soc. Laparoscopic Surgeons, Am. Soc. Laser Medicine and Surgery, Soc. Surg. Oncologists, Soc. Am. Gastrointestinal Endoscopic Surgeons. Roman Catholic. Office: 100 Delafield Rd Ste 203 Pittsburgh PA 15215-3247

CONNOLLY, DONNA LEE, nurse; b. Framingham, Mass., Oct. 26, 1955; d. George T. Jr. and Nancy L. (Kemp) Busby; m. Thomas P. Connolly Jr., Aug. 7, 1976; children: Thomas, Jeffrey, Matthew. Diploma, Whidden Meml. Hosp., 1976; BSN, Bowie State U., 1990. CCRN, cert. BLS instr., ACLS. Staff nurse med.-surg. unit Drs. Hosp., Lanham, Md., 1976-77; staff nurse ICU Ami Drs. Hosp., Lanham, Md., 1977-80, asst. clin. dir. intensive care unit, 1980-87; patient care coord Drs. Hosp., Lanham, Md., 1987-89, head nurse IMCU, 1989—. Mem. AACN, GWAC.

CONNOLLY, JAMES LEO, physician, pathologist; b. Lynn, Mass., Apr. 8, 1948; s. Owen James and Marion Louise (Battles) C.; m. Alison Mull Connolly, April 10, 1982; children: Caitlin, Brianna. MA, Merrimack Coll., N. Andover, Mass., 1970; MD, Vanderbilt Med. Sch., Nashville, 1974. Cert. Am. Bd. Anatomic Pathology. Resident, chief resident pathology Beth Israel, Boston, 1974-78; instr. Harvard Med. Sch., Boston, 1979-82, asst. prof., 1982-88, assoc. prof., 1988—; pathologist Beth Israel Hosp., Boston, 1979-91, co-dir. anatomic pathology, 1991-92, dir. anatomic pathology, 1992—; cons. in pathology Dana Farber Cancer Inst., Boston, 1981—; mem. editl. bd. Cancer Manual, Mass., 1989—, Case Studies in Pathology, Washington, 1995—; mem. European Orgn. for Rsch. and Treatment of Cancer, 1989—. Recipient award NIH, 1979, (2) 1993. Mem. Am. Soc. Cell Biology, New England Soc. Pathologists, New England Cancer Soc., Internat. Acad. Pathology (U.S.-Can. divsn.), Assn. Dirs. Anatomic & Surg. Pathology. Office: Beth Israel Hosp Pathology Dept 330 Brookline Ave Boston MA 02215

CONNOLLY, JOHN EARLE, surgeon, educator; b. Omaha, May 21, 1923; s. Earl A. and Gertrude (Eckerman) C.; m. Virginia Hartman, Aug. 12, 1967; children: Peter Hart. John Earle, Sarah. A.B., Harvard U., 1945, M.D., 1948. Diplomate: Am. Bd. Surgery (bd. dirs. 1976-82), Am. Bd. Thoracic and Cardiovascular Surgery, Am. Bd. Vascular Surgery. Intern. in surgery Stanford U. Hosps., San Francisco, 1948-49, surg. research fellow, 1949-50, asst. resident surgeon, 1950-52, chief resident surgeon, 1953-54, surg. pathology fellow, 1954-55, 1957-60, John and Mary Markle Scholar in med. scis., 1957-62; surg. registrar professional unit St. Bartholomew's Hosp., London, 1952-53; resident in thoracic surgery Bellevue Hosp., N.Y.C., 1955; resident in thoracic and cardiovascular surgery Columbia-Presbyn. Med. Ctr., N.Y.C., 1956; from instr. to assoc. prof. surgery Stanford U., 1957-65; prof. U. Calif., Irvine, 1965—, chmn. dept. surgery, 1965-78; attending surgeon Stanford Med. Ctr., Palo Alto, Calif., 1959-65; chmn. cardiovascular and thoracic surgery Irvine Med. Ctr. U. Calif., 1968—; attending surgeon Children's Hosp., Orange, Calif., 1968—, Anaheim (Calif.) Meml. Hosp., 1970—; vis. prof. Beijing Heart, Lung, Blood Vessel Inst., 1990, A.H. Duncan vis. prof. U. Edinburgh, 1984; Hunterian prof. Royal Coll. Surgeons Eng., 1985-86; Kinmonth lectr. Royal Coll. Surgeons, Eng., 1987; mem. adv. coun. Nat. Heart, Lung, and Blood Inst.-NIH, 1981-85; cons. Long Beach VA Hosp., Calif., 1965—. Contbr. articles to profl. jours.; editorial bd.: Jour. Cardiovascular Surgery, 1974—, chief editor, 1985—; editorial bd. Western Jour. Medicine, 1975—, Jour. Stroke, 1979—, Jour. Vascular Surgery, 1983—. Bd. dirs. Audio-Digest Found., 1974—; bd. dirs. Franklin Martin Found., 1975-80; regent Uniformed Svcs. U. of Health Scis., Bethesda, 1992—. Served with AUS, 1943-44. Recipient Cert. of Merit, Japanese Surg. Soc., 1979, 90. Fellow ACS (gov. 1964-70, regent 1973-82, vice chmn. bd. regents 1980-82, v.p. 1984-85), Royal Coll. Surgeons Eng. (hon.), Royal Coll. Surgeons Ireland (hon.), Royal Coll. Surgeons Edinburgh (hon.); mem. Am. Surg. Assn., Soc. Univ. Surgeons, Am. Assn. Thoracic Surgery (coun. 1974-78), Pacific Coast Surg. Assn. (pres. 1985-86), San Francisco Surg. Soc., L.A. Surg. Soc., Soc. Vascular Surgery, Western Surg. Assn., Internat. Cardiovascular Soc. (pres. 1977), Soc. Internat. Chirurgie, Soc. Thoracic Surgeons, Western Thoracic Surg. Soc. (pres. 1978), Orange County Surg. Soc. (pres. 1984-85), James IV Assn. Surgeons (councillor 1983—). Clubs: California (Los Angeles); San Francisco Golf, Pacific Union, Bohemian (San Francisco); Cypress Point (Pebble Beach, Calif.); Harvard (N.Y.C.); Big Canyon (Newport Beach). Home: 7 Deerwood Ln Newport Beach CA 92660-5108 Office: U Calif Dept Surgery Irvine CA 92717

CONNOLLY, JOHN JOSEPH, health care company executive; b. Worcester, Mass., Feb. 4, 1940; s. Nicholas John and Margaret Anne (Flynn) C.; m. Ingrid Schlemminger, Apr. 11, 1964; children: Sean Timothy, Cheryl Lea. BS, Worcester State Coll., 1962; MA., U. Conn., 1963; EdD, Columbia U., 1972; LLD, Mercy Coll., 1980. Tchr., counselor Worcester Pub. Schs., 1963-65; dir. admissions, registrar Sullivan County Community Coll., South Fallsburg, N.Y., 1965-67; asst. dean faculty, dir. community and extension svcs. Mercer County Community Coll., Trenton, N.J., 1967-68; asst. to pres., dir. community and extension svcs. Mercer County Community Coll., Trenton, 1968-70; dean of coll. Harford C.C., Bel Air, Md., 1970-72; pres. Dutchess Community Coll., Poughkeepsie, N.Y., 1972-81; pres., CEO N.Y. Med. Coll., Valhalla, N.Y., 1981-92, Castle Connolly Med. Ltd., N.Y.C., 1991—; bd. dirs. Mortons Rest Group, McCormack & Schmick Mgmt. Co., Alpha Gene Inc., Lynx Worldwide Ltd., Homestead Nat. Ins. Bd. dirs. United Way of Dutchess County, pres., 1978; chmn. bd. trustees St. Francis Hosp., Poughkeepsie, 1976-80; chmn. Dutchess County Indsl. Devel. Agy., 1978-81; trustee N.Y. Med. Coll., chmn. acad. affairs com.; trustee Culinary Inst. Am., 1976—, vice chair, 1995—, Poughkeepsie Area Fund, 1973-78, St. Agnes Hosp., White Plains, 1988-91; bd. dirs. Econ. Devel. Corp. Dutchess County, Westchester County Mental Health Assn.; hon. chmn. Dutchess/Columbia br. Am. Lung Assn., 1979; pres. Westchester Hist. Soc., 1985-88; mem. pres. adv. coun. United Hosp. Fund. Recipient Disting. Svc. award Poughkeepsie Jaycees, 1974, Marie Y. Martin award Assn. Community Coll. Trustees, 1978; named Man of Yr. Dutchess County Legislature, 1980, One of 100 Outstanding Young Leaders in Higher Edn. Change mag., 1979. Fellow N.Y. Acad. Medicine; mem. N.Y. Acad. Scis., Assn. Colls. Mid-Hudson Area (pres. 1976-79), Am. Lyme Disease Found. (chmn.), Friends of the Nat. Libr. Medicine (dir.), Friends of Hudson Valley (chmn. 1990), Westchester County Assn. (bd. dirs. 1991—), S.L.E. (Lupus) Found. (bd. dirs.), Phi Delta Kappa. Roman Catholic. Office: Castle Connolly Med Ltd 150 E 58th St New York NY 10155-0001

CONNOLLY, NEVILLE K., surgical educator; b. London, Nov. 13, 1920; came to U.S., 1954; s. William Frederick and Kathleen Maud (Knott) C.; m. Agnes Haskell Flather, Apr. 5, 1945 (dec. Feb. 1994); m. Jocelyn Irene Rountree, June 3, 1994; children: Catherine Anne West, Angela Haskell Ray. MA, Cambridge (Eng.) U., 1944; MD, Harvard U., 1944; MB BChir, Cambridge (Eng.) U., 1945. Diplomate Am. Bd. Surgery, Am. Bd. Pediat. Surgery. Assoc. prof. surgery Georgetown U., Washington, 1956—; sr. attending surgeon Washington Hosp. Ctr., 1966-96, pres. med. staff, 1982; sr. attending surgeon Children's Nat. Med. Ctr., Washington, 1966-92. Squadron leader Royal Air Force, 1946-47. Fellow ACP, Royal Coll. Surgeons (Eng.), Am. Acad. Pediats.; mem. D.C. Med. Soc., Osler Soc. (pres., mem. emeritus), Clinico Pathol. Soc. (pres., mem. emeritus). Episcopalian. Office: 9 Russell Rd Cabin John MD 20818

CONNOLLY, PAUL MARTIN, industrial and organizational psychologist; b. Natick, Mass., Jan. 20, 1955; s. Joseph M. and Margaret P. Connolly; m. Kathleen Groll. BA, Holy Cross Coll., 1977; MA, Fordham U., 1979, PhD, 1983. Human resource cons. Lopez Assocs., Port Washington, N.Y., 1980-82; dir. cons. svcs. Mgmt. Decision Systems, Darien, Conn., 1982-87; pres. Performance Programs, Inc., Old Saybrook, Conn., 1987—. Author: Career Building in the 80's, 1985, Entrepreneurs in Corporations, 1986, Create Your Own Employee Handbook, 1989, Competing for Employees, 1991. Mem.

APA, Met. N.Y. Assn. Applied Psychology, Soc. Indsl. Orgnl. Psychology, Norwalk Seaport Assn. (trustee 1988). Office: Performance Programs 123 Elm St Ste 1500 Old Saybrook CT 06475

CONNOLLY, RUTH CAROL, critical care nurse; b. Pitts., Oct. 2, 1944; d. Chester John and Mary Elizabeth (Sansbury) Williams; separated; children: Patrick L., Sean M. Diploma in nursing, Allegheny Gen. Hosp., Pitts., 1965; cert. nurse practitioner, Allegheny Gen. Hosp., 1983, La Roche Coll., Pitts., 1983. RN, Pa. Staff nurse critical care Divine Providence Hosp., Pitts.; asst. clin. supr. Allegheny Gen. Hosp., clin. supr. neuroscis. unit; nurse practitioner Triangle Urol. Group, Pitts. Contbr. articles to nursing jours. Mem. AACCN, Am. Assn. Urology Allied Nurses, Am. Urol. Assn. Allied (founding mem. and pres.-elect Pitts. chpt.), Am. Assn. Office Nurses. Home: 5549 Pocusset St Pittsburgh PA 15217-1912

CONNOLLY, WILLIAM S., radiologist; b. Phila., Nov. 17, 1943; s. William J. and Wanda F. (Gortat) C.; m. Judyann Ginn, Sept. 5, 1970 (div. 1988); m. Nada Laguna, Oct. 30, 1993. BS, St. Joseph's U., 1965; DO, Phila. Coll. Osteo. Medicine, 1969. Diplomate Am. Bd. Radiology. Intern J.F. Kennedy Hosp., Stratford, N.J., 1969-70; resident Hahnemann Univ. Hosp., Phila., 1970-74; assoc. radiologist Pottsville (Pa.) Hosp., 1974-88; dir. radiology Pottsville Hosp., Warne Clinic, 1988—; bd. dirs. Pottsville Hosp. Bd. edn. Schuylkill Haven (Pa.) Sch. Dist., 1981-87. Mem. AMA, Am. Coll. Radiology, Radiol. Soc. N.Am., Pa. Radiol. Soc., Pa. Med. Soc., Pa. Osteopathic Med. Soc. Office: Pottsville Hosp 420 S Jackson St Pottsville PA 17901

CONNOR, JOHN DENNIS, pharmacologist, consultant; b. Coatesville, Pa., Jan. 15, 1933; s. Matthew Edward and Mabel Anna (McCollum) C.; m. B. Norine Steele, June 15, 1963; children: Paula, Michael. BS, Phila. Coll. Pharmacy & Sci., 1960, MS, 1962, PhD, 1966. Registered pharmacist, Pa. Pharmacist Campbell & Bro., Phila., 1956-66; grad. rsch. assoc. Eastern Pa. Psychiatric Inst., Phila., 1962-66; staff fellow Nat. Inst. Mental Health, Washington DC, 1966-69; asst. prof. Pa. State U., Coll. of Medicine, Hershey, 1969-72, assoc. prof., 1972-75, prof., 1975--; cons. Pa. Dept. of Health, Harrisburg, 1982-90; assoc. editor Karger Publs., Switzerland, 1980--. Contbr. over 60 articles to profl. jours. With U.S. Coast Guard, 1952-56. NIH rsch. grantee, 1970-90; Fogarty fellow, NIH, Washington DC, 1978-79, Fulbright fellow Coun. for Internat. Exch. of Scholars, Washington DC, 1988-89. Mem. Lions Club (sec. 1970-78, named Lion of the Yr. 1978). Democrat. Roman Catholic. Home: 808 Twin Oaks Dr Hummelstown PA 17036-9740 Office: Penn State Univ PO Box 850 Hershey PA 17033-0850

CONNOR, PAUL EUGENE, social worker; b. Atchison, Kans., Aug. 11, 1921; s. Samuel Walters and Juanita Marie (Fry) C.; m. Louise Dorothy Schiddel, June 28, 1959 (div. 1964). BS in History with honors, Columbia U., 1962, MA, 1963; grad. cert. in social work, Fordham U., 1973; postgrad. summer history program, Cambridge U., 1990-96. Lectr. Am. History Rutgers State U., 1966-67; lectr. S.E. Asian history New Sch. Social Rsch., 1967-68; caseworker Bergen Ctr., South Bronx, N.Y., 1970-73; caseworker Protective Svcs. Bur. of Child Welfare, Bronx, N.Y., 1973-76; caseworker preventive svcs. Spl. Svcs. for Children, N.Y.C., 1976-83; supr. I family program Crisis Intervention Svcs., N.Y.C., 1983-87; tchr. The Internat. Ctr., N.Y.C., 1977-86. Rec. sec. Bronx Coun. for Environ. Quality, 1981-83, bd. dirs., 1983—; docent Mus. of City of N.Y., 1988-91, Abigail Adams Smith Mus., 1993-95, South St. Seaport Mus., 1993-96. Mem. Internat. Coun. Social Welfare, Asia Soc., Am. Hist. Assn., S.C. Hist. Soc., N.c. Lit. and Hist. Assn., Soc. of Boonesborough, Clan Buchanan Soc. in Am., English Speaking Union. Democrat. Home: 2755 Reservoir Ave Apt 5A Bronx NY 10468-2730

CONNOR, WILLIAM ELLIOTT, physician, educator; b. Pitts., Sept. 14, 1921; s. Frank E. and Edna S. (Felt) C.; m. Sonja Lee Newcomer, Sept. 19, 1969; children: Rodney William, Catherine Susan, James Elliott, Christopher French, Peter Malcolm. B.A., U. Iowa, 1942, M.D., 1950. Diplomate Am. Bd. Internal Medicine, Am. Bd. Nutrition. Intern USPHS Hosp., San Francisco, 1950-51; resident in internal medicine San Joaquin Gen. Hosp., Stockton, Calif., 1951-52; practice medicine specializing in internal medicine Chico, Calif., 1952-54; resident in internal medicine VA Hosp., Iowa City, 1954-56; cons., 1967-75; mem. faculty U. Iowa Coll. Medicine, 1956-75, prof. internal medicine, 1967-75; acting dir., then dir. Clin. Research Center, 1967-75, dir. lipid-atherosclerosis sect., cardiovascular div., 1974-75; vis. prof. Basic Sci. Med. Inst., Karachi, Pakistan, Ind. U., 1961-62, Baker Med. Rsch. Inst., Melbourne, Australia, 1982; vis. fellow clin. sci. Australian Nat. U., Canberra, 1970; prof. cardiology and metabolism-nutrition, dept. medicine, 1975-79, head sect. clin. nutrition, 1979-90, acting head, head div. endocrinology, metabolism and nutrition, 1984-90, prof. sect. clin. nutrition, 1990—, dir. lipid-atherosclerosis lab., assoc. dir. Clin. Rsch. Ctr., Oreg. Health Scis. U. Portland, 1975-94; chmn. heart and lung program project com. Contbr. numerous articles to med. jours.; editor Jour. Lab. and Clin. Medicine, 1970-73; mem. editorial bds., reviewer profl. jours. Mem. Johnson County (Iowa) Cen. Dem. Com., 1965-69; mem. nat. council Fellowship Reconciliation; nat., North Central and Pacific Northwest bds. Am. Friends Service Com. Served with AUS, 1943-46. Research fellow Am. Heart Assn., 1956-58; ACP traveling fellow Sir William Dunn Sch. Pathology, Oxford, Eng., 1960; recipient Career Devel. Research award Nat. Heart Inst., 1962-73, Discovery award Med. Research Found. Oreg. Mem. AAAS, ACP, AMA, AAUP (pres. U. Iowa chpt. 1968-69, pres. Oreg. Health Sci. U. chpt. 1978-79), Am. Diabetes Assn. (vice chmn. food and nutrition com. 1972-74), Am. Dietitic Assn. (hon.), Am. Fedn. Clin. Rsch., Am. Heart Assn. (chmn. coun. arteriosclerosis 1975-78, exec. com. coun. epidemiology 1967-70, exec. com. coun. cerebral vascular disease 1966-68, C. Lyman Duff meml. lectrue 1989), Am. Soc. Clin. Nutrition (pres. 1978), Nat. Acad. Sci. (food and nutrition bd. 1986-89), Am. Inst. Nutrition, Am. Oil Chemists Soc., Am. Physiol. Soc., Am. Soc. Clin. Investigation, Am. Soc. Study Arteriosclerosis, Assn. Am. Physicians, Ctrl. Soc. Clin. Rsch., Nutrition Soc., Soc. Exptl. Biology and Medicine (coun. 1971-72, pres. Iowa sect. 1971-72), Western Assn. Physicians, Western Soc. Clin. Rsch., Phi Beta Kappa, Sigma Xi, Alpha Omega Alpha. Home: 2600 SW Sherwood Pl Portland OR 97201-2285 Office: Oreg Health Scis U L465 Portland OR 97201

CONNORS, ROBERT EDWARD, health facility administrator; b. Rochester, N.Y., May 22, 1956; s. Edward William and Esther Josephine (Doyle) C.; m. Jeannie Lee Righini, Dec. 11, 1982 (div. June 1991); 1 child, Andrew Paul; m. Helene Judith Hook, Apr. 1, 1995; 1 child, Patrick Brendan. BA cum laude, SUNY, 1978; MA in Healthcare Adminstrn., George Washington U., 1980. Adminstrv. resident North Miami (Fla.) Gen. Hosp., 1979-80; commd. lt. (j.g.) USN, 1980, advanced through grades to comdr., 1994; asst. adminstr. Naval Hosp., Phila., 1980-84; dir. Office of Med./Dental Affairs, Great Lakes, Ill., 1984-87; staff analyst USN Bur. Medicine and Surgery, Washington, 1987-90; asst. adminstr. Naval Hosp., Rota, Spain, 1990-94; dir. for adminstrn. Naval Hosp., Twenty-nine Palms, Calif., 1994—. V.p. Van Dorn Village Homeowners Assn., Alexandria, Va., 1987-90. Fellow Am. Coll. Healthcare Execs. (membership com. 1995—); mem. Am. Acad. Med. Examiners (assoc., Charles U. Letourneau award 1979). Republican. Roman Catholic. Office: Naval Hosp MCAGCC Twenty-nine Palms CA 92277

CONRAD, EDGAR M., IV, internist; b. Pittsburg, Kans., Nov. 18, 1962; s. Edgar M. Conrad III and Maxine Conrad-Emerson; m. Roberta Conrad (div. Jan. 1996); children: Elizabeth, Edgar V. Resident Iowa Meth. Hosp., Des Moines, 1991-94, chief resident, 1994—. Home: Ste 108 2817 Mc Clelland Blvd Joplin MO 64804-1630

CONRAD, HAROLD THEODORE, psychiatrist; b. Milw., Jan. 25, 1934; s. Theodore Herman and Alyce Barbara C.; A.B., U. Chgo., 1954, B.S., 1955, M.D., 1958; m. Elaine Marie Blaine, Sept. 1, 1962; children—Blaine, Carl, David, Erich, Rachel. Intern USPHS Hosp., San Francisco, 1958-59; commd. sr. asst. surgeon USPHS, 1958, advanced through grades to med. dir., 1967; resident in psychiatry USPHS Hosp., Lexington, Ky., 1959-61, Charity Hosp., New Orleans, 1961-62; chief of psychiatry USPHS Hosp., New Orleans, 1962-67, clin. dir., 1967; dep. dir. div. field investigations NIMH, Chevy Chase, Md., 1968; chief NIMH Clin. Research Center, Lexington, 1969-73; cons. psychiatry, region IX, USPHS, HEW, San Francisco, 1973-79; dir. adolescent unit Alaska Psychiat. Inst., Anchorage, 1979-81, supt., 1981-85 ; clin. assoc. prof. psychiatry U. Wash. Med. Sch., 1981-85; med. dir. Bayou Oaks Hosp., Houma, La., 1985—. Decorated Commendation medal; recipient various community awards for contbns. in field of drug abuse and equal employment opportunity for minorities. Diplomate Am. Bd. Psychiatry. Fellow Royal Soc. Health, Royal Soc. Medicine, Am. Psychiat. Assn.; mem. AMA, Alpha Omega Alpha, Alpha Delta Phi. Contbr. to publs. in field. Office: 855 Belanger St Houma LA 70360-4463

CONRAD, MARCEL EDWARD, hematologist, educator; b. N.Y.C., Aug. 15, 1928; s. Marcel Edward and Lulu Marie (Geraghty) C.; children—Marcel Edward, III, Mark E., Carol J., Erin E., Julia P. B.S., Georgetown U., 1949, M.D., 1953. Diplomate Am. Bd. Internal Medicine, Am. Bd. Hematology. Intern Walter Reed Gen. Hosp., Washington, 1953-54; resident, then chief resident in internal medicine Walter Reed Gen. Hosp., 1955-60; mem. staff Walter Reed Army Inst. Research, 1961-74, chief dept. hematology, 1965-74; chief clin. investigation service Walter Reed Army Med. Center, 1971-74; clin. asst. prof., then clin. assoc. prof. medicine Georgetown U. Med. Sch., 1964-74; prof. medicine U. Ala. Med. Sch., Birmingham, 1974-83; also dir. div. hematology and oncology U. Ala. at Birmingham Med. Sch., 1974-83; prof. medicine, dir. div. hematology and oncology U. South Ala., 1983—, dir. USA Cancer Ctr., 1985—. Contbr. numerous articles to med. publs. Commd. 1st lt. M.C. U.S. Army, 1953; advanced through grades to col. 1968. Decorated Legion of Merit with oak leaf cluster; recipient Skinner medal U.S. Army, 1955, Hoff medal, 1962, John Shaw Billings award, 1967, William Beaumont award, 1972, Walter Reed award, 1974. Fellow Internat. Soc. Hematology, ACP (Laureate award 1989); mem. Assn. Am. Physicians, Internat. Soc. hematology, Am. Soc. Clin. Investigation, Am. Physiol. Soc., Internat. Soc. Blood Transfusion, Am. Soc. Hematology, Am. Soc. Clin. Oncology, Soc. Exptl. Biology and Medicine, AAAS, So. Soc. Clin. Investigation, Am. Fedn. Clin. Rsch. Roman Catholic. Home: 1314 Dauphin St Mobile AL 36604-2122 Office: U South Ala USA Cancer Ctr Mobile AL 36688

CONRAD, NANCY LU, podiatrist, retired; b. Chillicothe, Ohio, June 26, 1927; d. Earl Leroy and Mabel Leona (Ellifritt) C. BSc, Capital U., 1949; D of Podiat. Medicine, Ohio Coll. Podiat. Medicine, 1957. Med. technologist Ohio State U. Hosp., Columbus, 1950-53, Cleve. Foot Clinic, 1955-57; pvt. practice podiatry Circleville, Ohio, 1957-95; judge Amour awards Am. Podiatric Honor Soc., 1974; vis. lectr. Ohio Coll Podiat. Medicine Alumni Assn., 1985-87. Bd. editors: Jour. Am. Podiatric Med. Assn.; contbr. articles to profl. jours. Vis. vol. Clin. Inst., Cleve., 1976-77; bd. dirs., pres. Pickaway County unit Am. Cancer Soc., Cleve.; trustee Pickaway County Hist. Soc., Cleve., 1979; co-instr. defensive driver tng. and babysitting course Bus. and Profl. Women's Club, 1966-68; tutor ops. Boost; instr. sports medicine, bookbinding YMCA, 1982. Recipient Bronze award, Ann. Maxwell Cupshon Sci. Paper award, 1977, Podiatrist of Yr. award State of Ohio, 1988, Editors Recognition award, 1992, Disting. Svc. award Am. Podiatric Med. Assn., 1993; elected to The Ross C. of C. Women's Hall of Fame, 1993. Fellow Royal Soc. Health; mem. Am. Soc. Med. Technologists, Ohio Soc. Med. Technologists, Am. Assn. for Women Podistrists (organizer, 1st pres., editor 1965-82, nomination com. 1983-84, chmn. by-laws com. 1984-85), Am. Coll. Sports Medicine, Can. Podiatric Sports Medicine Acad., Am. Podiatric Med. Writers Assn., Altrusa Internat., NRA, Pi Delta, Delta Phi Alpha (editor alumni mag.). Home: 190 Vine St Chillicothe OH 45601-2414

CONRAD, STEVEN ALLEN, physician, biomedical engineer, educator, researcher; b. St. Martinville, La., Aug. 23, 1953; s. Karl Donovan and Dolores Beatrice (Bienvenu) C.; m. Mona Theresa Hollier, Aug. 9, 1974; children: David, Lesley, Taylor. BS, U. S.W. La., 1974; MD, La. State U., Shreveport, 1978; MS, Case Western Reserve, Cleve., 1980, PhD, 1985; MS in Engring., La. Tech. U., 1981. Diplomate Am. Bd. Internal Medicine, Critical Care Medicine, Am. Bd. Emergency Medicine. Asst. prof. medicine La. State U. Med. Ctr., Shreveport, 1986-91, assoc. prof. medicine, 1991—, dir. crit. care svc., 1986—, dir. med. ICU, 1986—, assoc. prof. emergency medicine, 1996—, chmn. dept. emergency medicine, 1996—; mem. adj. assoc. prof. biomed. engring. La. Tech. U., Ruston, 1989—. Editor: Pulmonary Function Testing: Principles and Practice, 1984; contbr. articles to profl. jours. Fellow ACP, Am. Coll. Crit. Care Med., Am. Coll. Chest Physicians, Am. Coll. emergency Physicians; mem. IEEE, Biomed. Engring. Soc., Shock Soc., Am. Soc. Artificial Internal Organs, Internat. Soc. for Artificial Organs. Office: La State U Med Ctr 1501 Kings Hwy Shreveport LA 71103

CONROY, RICHARD ALAN, ophthalmologist; b. New Haven, Mar. 18, 1944; s. John Thomas and Rita (Byrne) C.; m. Mary Hucksam, June 29, 1968; children: Catherine, Brian, Christopher. BA, Georgetown U., 1966, MD, 1970. Diplomate Am. Bd. Ophthalmology. Resident dept. ophthalmology Georgetown U., Washington, 1973-76; pvt. practice ophthalmology Paolillo & Conroy, P.A., Venice, Fla., 1976-94, Advanced Eye Care (Conroy & Ehrlich), Venice, 1994—; staff physician Venice Hosp., 1976—, chief of surgery, 1984. Lt. USN, 1971-73. Fellow Am. Acad. Ophthalmology; mem. AMA, Fla. Med. Assn., Fla. Soc. Ophthalmology, Castroviejo Corneal Soc., Am. Soc. Cataract and Refractive Surgery, Alpha Omega Alpha. Office: 1299 Jacaranda Blvd Venice FL 34292-4522

CONSIDINE, KEVIN CHARLES, family physician; b. San Diego, Aug. 21, 1963; s. Timothy Malcolm and Sharon Elaine (Culver) C.; m. Sally Anne Grant, July 23, 1988; children: Krystind Lynne, Lisa Marie, Brian Timothy. BS in Biology, San Diego State U., 1987; DO, U. Health Scis./Coll. Osteo., 1991. Diplomate Am. Bd. Family Practice, Am. Bd. Osteopathic Family Physicians. Family practice resident Warren Hosp., Phillipsburg, N.J., 1991-94; family practice physician Scripps Clinic Med. Group, San Diego, 1994—; utilization rev. com. Scripps Clinic Med. Group, San Diego, 1995—, adv. bd. for manual medicine, 1995—. Mem. 717 Club, Coranado, Calif., 1995—. Mem. Am. Acad. Osteopathy, Am. Osteopathic Assn., Am. Acad. of Family Physicians, Osteopathic Physicians and Surgeons of Calif., Am. Coll. Osteopathic Family Physicians, Calif. Acad. of Family Physicians. Republican. Roman Catholic. Office: Scripps Clinic Rancho Bernardo 15025 Innovation Dr San Diego CA 92128

CONSIDINE, WILLIAM HOWARD, health care adminstrator; b. Akron, Ohio, July 7, 1947; s. G. Howard and Gene Marie (Nelson) C.; m. Rebecca Diane Krenrick, Oct. 14, 1972; children: Michael, Cathryn, Matthew. BA, Akron U., 1969; MS, Ohio State U., 1971; LHD U. Arkon, 1996. Program cons. USPHS, Bethesda, Md., 1971-73; with patient care mgmt. N.C. Meml. Hosp., Chapel Hill, 1973-75, with gen. svcs., 1975-76, dir. ambulatory care, 1977-79; pres. Children's Hospital, Akron, Ohio, 1979—; cons. search com. Children's Hosp., Nat. Med. Ctr., Washington, 1982, Robert Wood Johnson Found. on Ambulatory Care Dental Program, 1978-79; bd. dirs. Child Health Corp Am., Children's Hosps. Exec. Coun., Children's Miracle Network Telethon. Chmn. Akron Health Coordinating Coun., 1978-79, EEO com. NIH, 1972-73. Lt. USPHS, 1971-73. Rsch. asst. grantee Kellogg Found., 1971; recipient Appreciation award Ohio State U. Alumni in Health Svcs. Adminstrn., 1975, Outstanding Hoban Alumni award, 1984, Honor award U. Akron, 1986, Outstanding Leader award Mental Health Assn., 1992, Exec. of Yr. award Sales and Mktg. Assn., 1994, Crystal Cross award Am. Lung Assn., 1994. Fellow Am. Coll. of Hosp. Adminstrs.; mem. Am. Hosp. Assn., Assn. of Am. Med. Colls., Nat. Assn. of Children's Hosps. and Related Insts., Children's Hosp. Exec. Coun., Assn. of Univ. Programs in Health Adminstrn., Ohio Hosp. Assn., Ohio State U. Alumni Assn. (Disting. Alumni award 1984), North Hosp. Assn., Chapel Hill C. of C. Roman Catholic. Clubs: City, Fireston Country, Portage Country (Akron). Office: Children's Hosp Med Ctr of Akron One Perkins Sq Akron OH 44308-1062

CONSIGLI, RICHARD ALBERT, virologist; b. Bklyn., Mar. 2, 1931; s. Benjamin Martin and Maria Rose (Corchia) C.; m. Barbara J. Seel, June 2, 1960 (dec. Feb. 1988); children: Linda, Joanne, Maria. BS, Bklyn. Coll., 1954; MA, U. Kans., 1956, PhD, 1960. Rsch. asst. U. Kans., Lawrence, 1954-59, instr., 1959-60; postdoctoral fellow U. Pa., Phila., 1960-63; asst. prof. Kans. State U., Manhattan, 1963-65, assoc. prof., 1965-69, prof., 1969-85, disting. prof., 1985—; panel mem. Nat. Cancer Inst. (Manpower), Bethesda, Md., 1983-86, NSF, Washington, 1974-82. Editorial bd. mem. Applied & Environ. Microbiology, Washington, 1973-82; contbr. articles to profl. jours. Recipient Rsch. Career Devel. award NIH, 1968-73, silver medal Prof. of Yr., Coun. for Advancements & Support of Edn., Washington, 1985, 86, Olin Petefish Basic Sci. award, 1992; named Mid.-Am. U. Assn. Honor Lectr., Big Eight Univs., 1976. Fellow Am. Acad. for Microbiology; mem. Am. Soc. for Microbiology, Am. Soc. for Virology, Am. Assn. for Cancer Rsch., Fogarty Internat. Rsch. Award Panel, Sigma Xi. Office: Kans State U Div Biology Sect of Virology & Oncology Manhattan KS 66506

CONSIGLIO, MICHAEL A., neurologist; b. Bklyn., Aug. 4, 1941; s. Michael A. and Jennie M. (Todaro) C. BA, NYU, 1962; MD, N.J. Coll. Medicine, 1967. Pvt. practice Bklyn., 1972—. Capt. U.S. Army, 1971-75. Mem. Am. Acad. Neurology, Bklyn. Neurologic Soc. Democrat. Roman Catholic. Home: 318 Albemarle Rd Brooklyn NY 11218-2310 Office: 415 Albemarle Rd Brooklyn NY 11218-2310

CONSTANDIS, DECEBAL DAVE, general surgeon; b. Oituz, Tg-Ocha, Romania, Jan. 1, 1938; came to U.S., 1971; s. Constantin and Aurelia (Vleja) C.; m. Michelle Renée Melamede, Jan. 18, 1975; children: Nicole, Danielle, Andrea. MD, Faculty of Medicine, Cluj, Romania, 1960. Diplomate Am. Bd. Surgery. Resident in surgery N.Y.C., 1971-75; fellow in gastrointestinal endoscopy Beth Israel Med. Ctr., N.Y.C., 1977-78; pvt. practice in gen. surgery N.J., 1976; chmn. dept. surgery J.F.K. Med. Ctr., Edison, N.J., 1994—. Fellow Am. Soc. for Laser Medicine and Surgeons, Internat. Coll. Surgeons, Am. Coll. Gastroenterology, Am. Soc. Abdominal Surgeons; mem. Med. Soc. N.J., Union County Med. Soc. (treas. 1995-96). Eastern Orthodox. Office: 415 Avenel St Avenel NJ 07001

CONSTANTINO-BANA, ROSE EVA, nursing educator, researcher; b. Labangan Zamboanga del Sur, Philippines, Dec. 25, 1940; came to U.S., 1964; naturalized, 1982; d. Norberto C. and Rosalia (Torres) Bana; m. Abraham Antonio Constantino, Jr., Dec. 13, 1964; children: Charles Edward, Kenneth Richard, Abraham Anthony III. BS in Nursing, Philippine Union Coll., Manila, 1962; MNursing, U. Pitts., 1971, PhD, 1979; J.D., Duquesne U., Pitts., 1984. Lic. clin. specialist in psychiatric-mental health nursing; registered nurse. Instr. Philippine Union Co., 1963-65, Spring Grove State Hosp., Balt., 1965-67, Montefiore Sch. Nursing, Pitts., 1967-70; instr. U. Pitts., 1971-74, asst. prof., 1974-83, assoc. prof., 1983—, chmn. Senate Athletic Com., 1985-86, 89-90, univ. senate sec., 1991-92, univ. senate v.p., 1993-95; project dir. grant divsn. of nursing HHS, Washington, 1983-85; prin. investigator NIH NINR, 1991-94; bd. dirs. Internat. Coun. on Women's Health Issues, 1986—. Author: (with others) Principles and Practice of Psychiatric Nursing, 1982; contbr. chpts. to books and articles to profl. jours. Mem. Republican Presdl. Task Force, Washington, 1980, Rep. Senatorial Com., Washington, 1980. Fellow Am. Acad. Nursing; mem. ABA, ATLA, Allegheny County Bar Assn. (bd. cert. forensic examiner), Pa. Bar Assn., Women's Bar Assn., Am. Assn. Nurse Attys., Am. Nurses Assn., Pa. Nurses Assn., Nat. League Nursing, Pa. League Nursing (chairperson area 6), Allegheny County Bar Assn., U. Pitts. Sch. Nursing Alumni Assn., U. Duquesne Law Alumni Assn., Sigma Theta Tau, Phi Alpha Delta. Seventh-Day Adventist. Avocations: cooking, playing the piano. Home: 6 Carmel Ct Pittsburgh PA 15221-3618 Office: U Pitts Sch Nursing 415 Victoria St Pittsburgh PA 15261

CONSTINE, LOUIS SANDERS, pediatric oncologist, radiation oncologist; b. San Francisco, Feb. 4, 1948; s. Louis Sanders and Nancy Jane (Meyer) C.; m. Sally Joanne Baxter; children: Alysia, Joshua. BA, Stanford U., 1969; MD, Johns Hopkins U., 1973. Diplomate Am. Bd. Pediatrics, sub.-bds. Pediatric Hematology/Oncology, Therapeutic Radiology. Resident in pediatrics U. Calif., San Francisco, 1973-75; resident in pediatrics Stanford U., 1975-76, resident in radiation oncology, 1978-81; fellow in pediatric hematology/oncology U. Wash., Seattle, 1976-78; asst. prof. pediatrics and radiation oncology U. Rochester (N.Y.) Med. Ctr., 1981-87, assoc. prof., 1987-96, prof., 1996—. Author: Pediatric Radiation Oncology, 1989, 94; editor: Survivors of Childhood Cancer, 1994. Mem. Phi Beta Kappa. Office: U Rochester Cancer Ctr 601 Elmwood Ave Rochester NY 14642

CONTE, JEAN JACQUES, medical educator, nephrologist; b. Tours, France, Nov. 6, 1938; s. Rene G. and Anne J. (Grangier) C.; m. Anne Y. Viatge, June 4, 1970; 1 dau., Stephanie C. MD, Faculte de Medecine, Toulouse, France, 1966. Cert. nephrologist Comité Consultatif des Universités. Prof. medicine Universite P. Sabatier, Toulouse, France, 1971—, cons. Mission de la Recherche, 1983—; chief nephrology dept. Centre Hospitalo-Universitaire Purpan, Toulouse, 1974—; vice doyen Faculte de Medecine Purpan, Toulouse, 1980—; dir. Rsch. Unit in Renal Immunopathology and Immunopharmacology, Inst. Nat. de la Santé et de la Recherche Médicale, 1984—; expert in medicine Toulouse Ct. Appeals, 1984—; pres. U. Paul Sabatier, Toulouse III, 1986-91; v.p. de la Conf. des Pres. Univ., 1987-89, Assn. des Univs. Partiellement ou Entièrement de Langue Française, 1987-91, Conseil Economique et Social de la Région Midi-Pyrénées, 1989—; v.p. de l'Agence de Coopération Midi-Pyrénées; conseiller Mcpl. de Portet Sur Garonne, Tech. de la Found. HARIRI, mem. Chargé de Mission au Ministére de l'Edn. Nationale, 1991; mem. Union Internat. Journalistes & Presse Langue Française, 1991; tech. cons. Chambre de Commerce et d'Industrie de Toulouse, 1992; pres. du Groupement Interprofessionnel Régional pour la Promotion de l'Emploi des Personnes Handicappés, 1992; mem. com. indsl. Action Economique Région Toulouse, 1993; tech. cons. dept. health City of Hanoi, Viet Nam, Ho Chi Minh City, Mil. Acad. Hanoi, Ctr. Internat. Rsch. and Teaching of Thermalism, 1994; bd. govs. Eurosud Assn., 1994; mem. office Transports & Comms. Midi; v.p. Edn./Teaching Commn. C. of C. & Industry, Toulouse; bd. govs. HANDIPRO 31, 1996; pres. Nat. Fedn. Groupement Interprofl. Régional pour Promotion Emploi Travailleurs Handicapés, 1996. Co-author: Glomerulonephritis, 1973; Advanced in Nephrology, 1974, 76; Plasmapheresis, 1983. Mem. European Soc. for Clin. Investigation, Internat. Soc. Nephrology, French Soc. Immunology, French Soc. of Plasma Exchange (founding mem.), Chevalier dans l'Ordre Nat. de Mérite, de l'Ordre du Lion du Sénégal, chevalier des Palmes Académiques, médaille d'Or de la Ville de Toulouse, Compagnie des Mousquetaires d'Armagnac (Auch, France), Confrérie des Vins de Cahors, Golf of Vieille-Toulouse (Toulouse), Golf of Pals (Costa Brava). Roman Catholic. Office: U Purpan Centre Hosp, Dept Néphrologie-Hémodialyse, 31059 Toulouse France

CONTE, SARAH RODWICK, therapeutic recreation specialist, nurse; b. Ridgewood, N.J., Oct. 21, 1965; d. Marvin Joseph and Martha Jane (Scott) Rodwick; m. Michael John Conte III, Oct. 14, 1989. BS, East Carolina U., 1987; postgrad., Watts Sch. Nursing, Durham, N.C., 1994-96. Recreation therapist Bergen Pines County Hosp., Paramus, N.J., 1987-90, Greenery Rehab. Ctr., Durham, N.C., 1990-94; RN cardiovascular intensive care unit Duke U. Med. Ctr., Durham, N.C., 1996—. Christ Epis. Ch. scholar, 1983-87, Coll. Club of Ridgewood scholar, 1983, 85, 86. Mem. Nat. Student Nursing Assn., Santa Filomena (nat. honor soc.), Chi Omega. Republican. Episcopalian. Home: 3105 Synnotts Pl Durham NC 27705-1403

CONTENTO, ANNETTE, optometrist; b. N.Y.C., Jan. 14, 1965; d. Anthony Joseph and Marie (Buonanno) Picchione; m. Albert John Contento, Aug. 20, 1989; children: Michael Anthony, Marissa Nicole. BA magna cum laude, CUNY, Flushing, 1987; OD, SUNY, N.Y.C., 1991. Optometrist, low vision specialist Westchester (N.Y.) Lighthouse, 1992-93; pvt. practice Contento & Kaplan, Optometrists, P.C., Bronx, 1992—; lectr. in field. Mem. Morris Park Cmty. Assn., 1993—, Pelham Bay Cmty. Assn., 1992—, Chester Civic Assn., 1994—. Recipient Columbia Class of 1936 award for acad. and clin. achievement in ocular pathology, 1991, Sola/PBH award for outstanding proficiency in contact lenses, 1991; Optometric Coun. N.Y. scholar, 1988-89, 90-91. Fellow Am. Acad. Optometry; mem. Am. Optometric Assn., N.Y. State Optometric Assn., N.Y. Acad. Optometry, Golden Key, Phi Beta Kappa, Beta Sigma Kappa. Roman Catholic. Home: 2214 Wickham Ave Bronx NY 10469 Office: Eye Care Unlimited 1745 Crosby Ave Bronx NY 10461

CONTI, DAVID J., surgeon; b. Chgo., July 5, 1955; s. Louis Leo and Elaine (Sassetti) C.; m. Laura Lynn Bryant, Dec. 16, 1978; children: Lauren, Sondra, Alexander, Benjamin. BA in Biology, Washington U., St. Louis, 1977; MD, Northwestern U., 1981. Diplomate Am. Bd. Surgery. Sr. rsch. fellow transplant surgery Northwestern U. Med. Ctr., Chgo., 1984-85, resdient in surgery, 1985-87; clin. fellow in transplant surgery Mass. Gen. Hosp., Boston, 1987-88, rsch. fellow in transplant surgery, 1988-89; clin. in rsch. fellow in transplantation Harvard Med. Sch., Boston, 1987-89; asst. prof. surgery Albany (N.Y.) Med. Coll., 1989-92, assoc. prof., 1992—, dir. organ transplantation, 1992—, chief sect. gen. surgery, 1992—; assoc. counselor United Network for Organ Sharing, 1994—, mem. membership and profl. standards com., 1994—. Editor newsletter The Chimera, 1995—. Fellow ACS; mem. Ctrl. Surg. Soc., Cell Transplant Soc., Surg. Infection Soc., Transplant Soc., Am. Soc. Transplant Surgeons (mem. membership com.), Phi Beta Kappa. Office: Albany Med Coll 47 New Scotland Ave Albany NY 12208

CONTI, ISABELLA, psychologist, consultant; b. Torino, Italy, Jan. 1, 1942; came to U.S., 1964; d. Giuseppe and Zaira (Melis) Ferro; m. Ugo Conti, Sept. 5, 1964; 1 child, Maurice. J.D., U. Rome, 1966; Ph.D. in Psychology, U. Calif.-Berkeley, 1975. Lic. psychologist. Sr. analyst Rsch. Inst. for Study of Man, Berkeley, Calif., 1967-68; postgrad. rsch. psychologist Personality Assessment and Rsch. Inst., U. Calif.-Berkeley, 1968-71; intern U. Calif.-Berkeley and VA Hosp., San Francisco, 1969-75; asst. prof. St. Mary's Coll., Moraga, Calif., 1978-84; cons. psychologist Conti Resources, Berkeley, Calif., 1977-85; v.p. Barnes & Conti Assocs., Inc., Berkeley, 1985-90; pres. Lisardco, El Cerrito, Calif., 1989—; bd. dirs. ElectroMagnetic Instruments, Inc., El Cerrito, Calif., 1985—. Trustee Monterey Inst. Internat. Studies, 1996—. Author: (with Alfonso Montuori) From Power to Partnership, 1993; contbr. articles on creativity and mgmt. cons. to profl. jours. Regents fellow U. Calif.-Berkeley, 1972; NIMH predoctoral rsch. fellow, 1972-73. Mem. APA. Office: Lisardco 1318 Brewster Dr El Cerrito CA 94530-2526

CONTI, JOAN NOEL, social worker; b. Rome, N.Y., May 21, 1958; d. Joseph J. and Jean (Norelli) c.; m. Stewart B. Whitney III.; 1 child, Stewart Bowman Whitney Jr. BA in Sociology, Niagara U., 1980; MSW, SUNY, Buffalo, 1987. Cert. sch. social worker, N.Y.; cert. social worker N.Y. Human svc. data base adminstr. Cen. Referral Svc., Inc., Buffalo; editl. asst., rschr. Niagara Rsch. Inst., Niagara Falls, N.Y.; sch. social worker, employee assistance program coord. Cheektowaga (N.Y.) Cen. Sch. Dist.; pvt. practice E. Amherst Counseling Ctr. Editor PeoplePeople Newletter, SUNY, Buffalo. Mem. Nat. Assn. Social Workers, N.Y. State Sch. Social Workers Assn., N.Y. State Coun. Family Rels.

CONTI, JOSEPH JOHN, internist; b. Paterson, N.J., June 21, 1962; s. Joseph James and Rose Marie (Giannella) C.; m. Marie Alice Popjoy, July 16, 1988; children: Joseph William, Alexander Donald. BA, Gettysburg Coll., 1984; DO, Phila. Coll. Osteopathic Med, 1990. Diplomate Am. Bd. Intenal Medicine. Ptnr. Siculerville (N.J.) Internal Medicine Assocs., 1994—. Roman Catholic. Office: Siculerville Internal Med 550 Williamstown Rd Siculerville NJ 08081

CONTI, VINCENT ROY, cardiothoracic surgery educator; b. N.Y.C., Dec. 6, 1943; s. Vincent S. and Rose Helen (Maletta) C.; m. Andrea J. Gruszecki, Mar. 20, 1971. AB, Coll. of Holy Cross, 1965; MD, Tufts U., 1969. Diplomate Am. Bd. Surgery, Am. Thoracic Surgery, Nat. Bd. Med. Examiners. Surg. intern UCLA, 1969-70, resident in surgery, 1970-74; resident in cardiovascular surgery U. Ala. Med. Ctr., Birmingham, 1977-78, instr., 1979; asst. prof. surgery U. Tex. Med. Br., Galveston, 1979-82, assoc. prof., 1982-86, prof., 1986—, chief div. cardiothoracic surgery, 1986—. Contbr. articles and abstracts to med. jours. Maj. M.C., U.S. Army, 1974-76. Mosley scholar, 1968. Mem. AMA, ACS, Am. Coll. Chest Physicians, Am. Heart Assn., Am. Coll. Cardiology (cardiovascular surgery com.), Soc. Univ. Surgeons, Soc. Thoracic Surgeons, Am. Assn. Thoracic Surgeons, Longmire Surg. Soc., Kirklin Surg. Soc., Galveston County Med. Soc., Alpha Omega Alpha, Phi Delta Epsilon. Home: 6 Lakeview Dr Galveston TX 77551-1564 Office: U Tex Med Br Divsn Cardiothoracic S Galveston TX 77555

CONTIGUGLIA, JOSEPH JUSTIN, preventive medicine physician, internist; b. N.Y.C., Jan. 8, 1948; s. Joseph and Doris (Justin) C.; m. Sylvie Blaise, Nov. 23, 1982; children: Dorothy Justine, Joseph Henry, Catherine Emily. AB in Sociology, Columbia Coll., N.Y.C., 1969; MD, U. Siena (Italy), 1975; MPH and Tropical Medicine, Tulane U., 1981; MBA, St. Mary's U., San Antonio, 1990. Diplomate Am. Bd. Preventive Medicine, Am. Bd. Med. Mgmt. Resident internal medicine Cabrini Med. Ctr., N.Y.C., 1975-78; commd. USAF, advanced through grades to col.; chief hyperbaric medicine USAF Clinic, Kadena AFB, Okinawa, Japan, 1978-80; resident aerospace medicine USAF Sch. Aerospace Medicine, Brooks AFB, San Antonio, 1980-82; chief aeromed. svcs. USAF Hosp., Seymour Johnson AFB, Goldsboro, N.C., 1982-85; chief occupational medicine and environ. health Royal Australian Air Force, Canberra, Australia, 1985-87; chief aerospace medicine div. Air Tng. Command, Randolph AFB, San Antonio, 1987-90; hosp. comdr. USAF Hosp., Reese AFB, Lubbock, Tex., 1990-92; dep. comdr. 5th med. group comdr. 5th aerospace medicine squadron, Minot AFB, N.D., 1992-96; comdr. 5th Air Transportable Hosp.; clin. assoc. prof. preventive medicine and rural health U. N.D. Sch. Medicine, 1992—; dir. med. ops. USAF-Europe, 1996—. Editor: Flight Surgeons Check List, 1982. Fellow Royal Soc. Medicine, Am. Coll. Preventive Medicine, Aerospace Med. Assn. (chmn. mil. aviation safety subcom., chmn. AIDS subcom.); mem. ACP, Am. Col. Physician Execs., Am. Soc. Tropical Medicine and Hygiene, Royal Aero. Soc., Aviation Med. Soc. Australia and New Zealand. Republican. Roman Catholic. Office: PSC 2 Box 7945 APO AE 09012

CONTIS, JOHN CHRIS, surgeon; b. Ioannina, Greece, Apr. 1, 1958; came to the U.S., 1991; s. Christos and Chido Contis. MD, Aristotelian U., 1982; PhD, Kapodestrian U., 1989. Intern. gen. surgery Hellenic Airforce Gen. Hosp., 1984-85; resident gen. surgery 2d dept. surgery U. Atehens Aretaeion Hosp., 1985-89; attending surgeon dept. surgery Univ. Hosp. Ioannina, 1990-91; fellow in liver transplantation U. Chgo., 1991-92; fellow in transplant surgery U. Pa., Phila., 1992-94, instr. in surgery, 1992-94; asst. prof. St. Louis U. Med. Sch., 1994—. Recipient Rsch. award A. Onassis Found., 1990-92. Mem. European Liver Transplant Assn. (founding), European Soc. Organ Transplantation, Internat. Liver Transplant Soc., Transplantation Soc., Internat. Pancreas and Islet Transplantation Assn., Assn. for Acad. Surgery. Office: Saint Louis U Health Scis 3635 Vista Ave at Grand Blv Saint Louis MO 63110

CONVERSE, GEORGE MARQUIS, pediatrician, educator; b. N.Y.C., Aug. 18, 1940; s. George M. Jr. and Barbara (Delany) C.; m. Juliet Bodin; children: George M. IV, Christopher G. BA, Lehigh U., 1963; MD, U. Va., 1969. Diplomate Am. Bd. Pediatrics. Attending pediatrician Charity Hosp. La., New Orleans, 1973-74; clin. asst. prof. pediatrics U. Ala. Sch. Medicine, Birmingham, 1980-85, clin. assoc. prof., 1985—, chairperson joint edn. com., 1981—; pediatrician Lloyd Noland Hosp., Fairfield, Ala., 1976—, dir. med. edn., 1980—; dir. nat. continuing med. edn. for physicians. Contbr. articles to profl. jours. Served with USPHS, 1972-74. Fellow Am. Acad. Pediatrics; mem. Med. Assn. Ala. (council on med. edn.), Assn. for Hosp. Med. Edn., Alliance for Continuing Med. Edn., So. Society for Pediatric Research. Office: Lloyd Noland Hosp 701 Lloyd Noland Pky Fairfield AL 35064-2660

CONVERTINO, VICTOR ANTHONY, physiologist, educator, research scientist, civil servant; b. Troy, N.Y., Apr. 26, 1949; s. Roger Orazio and Yolanda Ann (Trunfio) C.; m. Barbara Anne Bow, June 3, 1978; children: Laura, Pamela, Kevin, Brian. BA, San Jose State U., 1971, BS, 1972; MA, U. Calif.-Davis, 1974, PhD, 1981. Research assoc. U. Calif.-Davis, 1977-78, exercise test supr., 1978-79; research assoc. Stanford U., Palo Alto, Calif., 1979-82, lectr., 1982; asst. prof. U. Ariz., Tucson, 1982-85; cons. Stanford U., 1982-85, NASA, Moffett Field, Calif., 1982-85; research physiologist The Bionetics Corp., Kennedy Space Ctr., Fla., 1985-87; sr. research physiologist NASA, Kennedy Space Ctr., Fla., 1987-93; rsch. physiologist USAF, Brooks AFB, Tex., 1993—. Mem. editorial bd. Med. Sci. Sports Exercise, 1986, Jour. Applied Physiology, 1991; contbr. chpts. to profl. publ., also articles. Recipient award Univ. Consortium, NASA, 1984, Performance award, 1990, 92, 94, 95; Chancellor's Patent grantee U. Calif., Davis, 1973. Fellow Am. Coll. Sports Medicine (new investigator award 1982, lectureship award 1984, 90, vis. scholar award 1986, trustee, 1988, v.p., 1991), Aerospace Med. Assn. (Ellingson Literary award 1985); mem. Am. Physiol. Soc. (travel grant 1981, 84). Office: Physiology Rsch Br AL/AOCY 2507 Kennedy Cir Brooks AFB TX 78235-5117

CONVERY, F. RICHARD, surgeon, orthopedist; b. Olympia, Wash., June 12, 1932; m. Martha Ann Minteer; children: Kristine Helen, Linda Lea, Mark Richard. BA, U. Wash., 1954, MD, 1958. Instr. orthopedics U. Wash., Seattle, 1967-68, asst. prof., 1968-71, assoc. prof., 1971-72; assoc. prof. U. Calif., San Diego, 1972-77, surgeon in residence, prof. surgery, 1977—; Diplomate Am. Bd. Orthopaedic Surgery (examiner 1980—). Inventor prosthetic fixation technique. Mem. med. and sci. com. Western Wash. chpt. The Arthritis Found., 1968-72, San Diego chpt., 1973, chmn., 1977-78; mem. Calif. State Arthritis Coun., 1974-76. Grantee Johnson & Johnson, 1994. Fellow Am. Acad. Orthopaedic Surgeons (exam. and evaluation com. 1974-82, Kappa Delta award 1972); mem. Am. Rheumatism Assn. (sect. arthritis, program com. 1973-75), Western Orthopaedic Assn. (Vernon P. Thompson award for Resident Rsch. 1964), Acad. Orthopaedic Soc., Am. Orthopaedic Assn. (resident guest 1966), Orthopaedic Rsch. Soc., Internat. Soc. of the Knee, Assn. for Arthritic Hip and Knee Soc., Wilson-Bost Interurban Club. Office: U Calif San Diego Med Ctr 200 W Arbor Dr San Diego CA 92103

CONVISER, RICHARD, health services researcher; b. N.Y.C., Apr. 21, 1944; s. Harry and Pauline (Diner) C. BA, Reed Coll., Portland, Oreg., 1965; PhD, Johns Hopkins U., 1970. Asst. prof. U. Pitts., 1970-73, U. Ill., Urbana, 1973-76; freelance writer Woodford Creek, Glendale, Oreg., 1976-78; lectr. So. Oreg. State Coll., Ashland, 1978-80; asst. prof. Rensselaer Poly. Inst., Troy, N.Y., 1980-84; health policy specialist Empire Blue Cross/Blue Shield, N.Y.C., 1984-86; health policy analyst N.J. Dept. Health, Trenton, 1986-88; cons. Health Policy Rsch. and Analysis, West Linn, Oreg., 1988-96; policy analyst Oregon Health Plan Admnstr.'s Office, Salem, Oreg., 1995-96; chief evaln. br. Office of Sci. and Epidemiology U.S. Dept. Health and Human Svcs., Rockville, Md., 1996—; chair alumni-student rels. com. Reed Coll. Mem. alumni-student rels. com. Reed Coll., mem. alumni bd., 1991-95; vice chmn. Coalition for AIDS Edn., Portland, 1990-92; mem. Cascade AIDS Project Speakers Bur., Portland, 1991-95. Fellow NSF, 1965-70, 70, NEH, 1979. Mem. APHA, AHSR.

CONWAY, BRIAN PETER, ophthalmologist, educator; b. N.Y.C., Dec. 20, 1942; s. Francis Xavier and Marie Theresa (Bohan) C.; m. Dora Linda Rubin, July 23, 1971; children: Jennifer, Matthew, Michael. AB in Econs., Georgetown U., 1964, MD, 1968. Intern Peter Bent Brigham Hosp., Boston, 1968-69, asst. resident in internal medicine, 1969-70; resident in ophthalmology Johns Hopkins Hosp., Balt., 1972-75, asst. chief of svc., 1976-77; asst. prof. Johns Hopkins U., Balt., 1977-78; prof. ophthalmic surgery, chmn. dept. U. Va. Med. Sch., Charlottesville, 1978—; mem. data monitoring com. Nat. Eye Inst., Bethesda, Md., 1982—. Lt. cmdr. USPHS, 1970-72. Retinal disease fellow Bascom Palmer Eye Inst., Miami, Fla., 1975-76. Episcopalian. Office: Univ of Va Sch Medicine Dept of Ophthalmology Charlottesville VA 22901

CONWAY, JAMES BERNARD, hospital administrator, consultant; b. Boston, Jan. 6, 1947; s. John J. and Nora M. (O'Leary) C.; m. Joanne M. Duffy, Nov. 30, 1969; children: Christopher, Kerry, Peter. BS, Boston State Coll., 1969; MA in Applied Mgmt., Lesley Coll., Cambridge, Mass., 1992. Diplomate Am. Coll. Healthcare Execs. Radiology adminstr. Children's Hosp., Boston, 1972-85, asst. to v.p. fin., 1985-87, dir. ops., 1987-95; COO Dana-Farber Cancer Inst., Boston, 1995—; faculty Sch. of Mgmt. Lesley Coll., Cambridge, Mass., 1995—; bd. dirs. Children's Hosp. Fed. Credit Union, 1973-80; speaker, presenter in field. Mem. editorial bd. Risk Mgmt. Found., Cambridge, 1991-95; author articles. Bd. dirs. Ronald McDonald House, 1992—, Hospitality Program, 1992—, Boy Scouts Am. Recipient Dist. award of Merit boy Scouts Am., 1984, Oliver Morrill award Mass. Soc. Radiologic Technologists, 1980, others. Fellow Am. Healthcare Radiology Adminstrs. (bd. dirs., chair 1978-85, Gold award 1982); mem. Am. Soc. for Quality Control, Healthcare Mgmt. Assn. Roman Catholic. Home: 8 Mt Pleasant St Woburn MA 01801

CONWAY, JAMES DONALD, internist, educator; b. Newark, May 2, 1946; s. James M. and Dorothy (Kelly) C. BA, St. Olaf Coll., 1968; MD, U. Ill., 1972, MS, 1972. Bd. cert. internal medicine and infectious diseases. Intern Cornell Coop. Hosp., N.Y.C., 1972, resident, 1973-74; fellow infectious disease U. Mich., Ann Arbor, 1974-76; sr. resident medicine La. State U., New Orleans, 1978-79; co-dir. critical care medicine So. Md. Hosp., Clinton, 1979; assoc. prof. internal medicine, emergency medicine La. State U., 1980—; practice medicine specializing in internal medicine and infectious diseases, New Orleans, 1980—; dir. ICU Touro Hosp., 1985-86; chmn. dept medicine, dir. infection control Doctor's Hosp., ACP, 1994—; bd. dirs. Doctor's Hosp, Ponchatran IFA. Contbr. articles to profl. jours. Recipient Rsch. award U. Ill., 1973; Mich. Heart Assn. fellow rsch. award, 1974. Mem. Am. Soc. Microbiology, ACP. Home and Office: 4300 Houma Blvd Ste 205 Metairie LA 70006-2924

CONWAY, JAMES JOSEPH, physician; b. Chgo., July 1, 1933; s. Frank and Mary (Tuohy) C.; m. Dolores Mazer, June 30, 1956; children: Laurie, John, Cheryl. BS, DePaul U., 1959; MD, Northwestern U., 1963. Asst. instr. U. Pa., 1964-68; assoc. in radiology McGaw Med. Ctr. Northwestern U., Chgo., 1968-71, asst. prof. to assoc. prof. radiology, 1974-80; attendant radiology, chief nuclear medicine div. Children's Meml. Hosp., Chgo., 1968—, prof. radiology, 1980—. Contbr. 107 articles to profl. jours. Served with U.S. Army, 1953-55. Fellow Am. Coll. Nuclear Physicians, Am. Coll. Radiology; mem. AMA, P.R. Soc. Nuclear Medicine (hon.), Radiol. Soc. N.Am. (Scroll of Appreciation award 1983, pres. 1994-95), Soc. Nuclear Medicine. Office: Children's Meml Hosp # 42 2300 N Childrens Plz Chicago IL 60614-3394

CONWAY, PATRICIA LEIGH, healthcare consultant; b. Richmond, Va., Nov. 9, 1954; d. Mack Howard Jr. and Mae (Powell) C. Diploma, Riverside Hosp. Sch. Nursing, 1978; BSBA, Christopher Newport U., 1984; MA, Lynchburg (Va.) Coll., 1990. Staff nurse labor and delivery Riverside Regional Med. Ctr., Newport News, Va., 1978-83; adminstrv. IV, labor and delivery nurse Sentara Norfolk (Va.) Gen. Hosp., 1984-86; sr. risk mgmt. cons. Va. Profl. Underwriters, Inc., Roanoke, 1987-91; healthcare cons. Carilion Health System, Roanoke, 1991-96, dir. accreditation and lic., 1996—. Mem. Assn. Women's Health, Obstetric and Neonatal Nurses, Va. Orgn. Nurse Execs. (program chmn., bd. dirs., pres. elect), Nat. Assn. Healthcare Quality, Am. Coll. Healthcare Execs.

CONWAY, PAUL GARY, neuropharmacologist; b. Monson, Mass., July 31, 1952; s. Andrew Paul and Joan Sarah (Haley) C.; m. Malana Frances Seniuk, Aug. 21, 1976. BS in Pharmacy, Ohio No. U., 1975; MS in Pharmacology, U. Toledo, 1978; PhD in Pharmacology, Ohio State U., 1982. Postdoctoral fellow U. Pa., Phila., 1982-84; sr. rsch. pharmacologist Hoechst Roussel Pharm. Inc., Somerville, N.J., 1984-86, rsch. assoc., 1986-88, group leader, 1988-92, project mgr., 1992-95, sr. project mgr., 1995-96; dir. project planning Janssen Rsch. Found., Titusville, N.J., 1996—; adj. asst. prof. Fairleigh-Dickinson U., Madison, N.J., 1986; pharmacology instr. Ohio No. U., Ada, 1975-76. Editor Clin. Neuropharmacology, 1991; contbr. more than 40 articles to profl. jours.; patentee in field. Mem. Am. Soc. Pharmacology and Exptl. Therapeutics, Soc. for Neurosci., Internat. Brain Rsch. Orgn., Drug Info. Assn., Sigma Xi. Office: Janssen Rsch Found 1125 Trenton-Harbourton Rd Titusville NJ 08560

CONWAY, SAMUEL ANTHONY, chiropractor; b. Dallastown, Pa., Jan. 19, 1917; s. Clarence C. and Coletta Elizabeth (Smith) C.; student Lebanon Valley Coll., 1947-48; D.C., Nat. Coll. Chiropractic, 1951; m. Irene May Runkle, Feb. 6, 1944; 1 son, Samuel A. Gen. practic chiropractic medicine, Hanover, Pa., 1951-83; chmn. bd., pres. Golden Age Nursing Home, Inc., Hanover, 1961-82; trustee Nat. Coll. Chiropractic, 1960-80, mem. exec. bd. dirs., 1969-80, ret., 1982, chmn. bldg. fund com. 1961-64; participant internat. profl. confs. Served with Signal Corps, U.S. Army, 1942-46. Recipient Disting. Service award Nat. Coll. Chiropractic, 1972; lic. nursing home adminstr., Pa. Mem. VFW, DAV, Nat. Coll. Alumni Assn., Am., Pa. chiropractic assns., Pa. Assn. Drugless Therapists (pres. 1968-69, Disting. Service award 1969, dir.), Health Care Facilities of Pa., Am. Nursing Home Assn., York County (Pa.), Hanover Area hist. socs., Antique Automobile Club, Am. Legion, York-Adams Fish and Game Assn., Hanover Area C. of C. Democrat. Mem. United Ch. of Christ (trustee). Clubs: Masons, Shriners, Elks. Address: 434 Deerfield Dr Hanover PA 17331-5203

CONWAY-WELCH, COLLEEN, dean, nurse midwife; b. Monticello, Iowa, Apr. 26, 1944; d. John Andrew and Lorraine (Digman) Conway; m. Ted Houston Welch, Mar. 31, 1985. BSN, Georgetown U., 1965; CNM, Catholic Maternity Inst., 1969; MSN, Catholic U., Washington, 1969; PhD, NYU, 1973. Staff nurse Georgetown U. Hosp., Washington, 1965; staff nurse labor & delivery Queens Med. Ctr., Honolulu, 1966; nurse cons. U. So. Calif. Med. Ctr., L.A., 1967; staff assoc. Nat. League Nursing, N.Y.C., 1969-70; asst. prof. Downstate Med. Ctr., Bklyn., 1970-74; asst. prof. Georgetown U., 1974-76, assoc. dean, 1975-76; assoc. prof. George Mason U., Fairfax, Va., 1976-78, Calif. State U., Long Beach, 1978-80; prof. nursing U. Colo., Denver, 1980-84; dean Vanderbilt Sch. Nursing, Nashville, 1984—; mem. Presdl. Commn. on HIV Epidemic, Washington, 1988, adv. coun. NIH Nat. Ctr. Nursing Rsch., Washington, 1989-93, bd. trust Healthcare Leadership Coun., Washington, 1990; chair nursing leadership coun. Inst. Healthcare Improvement, 1992; bd. dirs. Diversicare, Franklin, Tenn., Nat. League Nursing Community Health Accreditation, N.Y.C., Commonwealth Fund Nurse Exch. Fellowship Program, N.Y.C. Contbr. articles to profl. jours. Bd. govs. United Way, Middle, Tenn., 1989; active Mayor's Task Force for Substance Abuse, 1990, JFK Adv. Com. on Arts, Washington, 1991, Jr. League, 1973—. Recipient Dempsey Humanitarism award St. Clare's Hosp. AIDS Ctr., 1989; commencement speaker, Columbia Sch. Nursing, 1991. Fellow Am. Acad. Nursing; mem. Soc. Advancement Women's Health Rsch. (bd. dirs. 1991—), Rotary Club, Cosmos Club, Sigma Theta Tau (bd. dirs. 1968—). Home: 109 Lynnwood Ter Nashville TN 37205-2911 Office: Vanderbilt U Sch Nursing 111 Godchaux 21st Ave S Nashville TN 37240*

CONWELL, HALFORD ROGER, physician; b. Cin., Jan. 28, 1924; s. Halford Fredrick and Erma Pearl (Cornelius) C.; BA, U. Wooster, 1948; MA, U. Louisville, 1950; MD, U. Cin., 1955, ATP; diplomate crew coordination tng. Continental Airlines; m. Margaret Ann King, Dec. 15, 1965; children: Mark A., Sherri L. Aviation medicine, Huntsville, Tex., 1959—; mem. staff Huntsville (Tex.) Meml. Hosp., chief of staff, 1974-75, chief medicine, 1976-80, bd. trustees, 1991—; sr. U.S. med. officer Brit. Caledonian Airways, 1977-89; cons. Aeromexico; sr. cons. aviation medicine, flight ops. Continental Airlines, 1996—; mem. Walker County Hosp. Dist., 1975-79, chmn., 1976-79; asst. dean of men, instr. psychology Heidelberg U., Tiffin, Ohio, 1950-51; instr. psychology Cin. Coll.; sr. med. examiner FAA; sr. examiner C.A.A. (U.K.), C.A.A. (Australia); newspaper columnist, 1992—. Trustee Biol. Analysis and Research Found.; capt. (hon.) Tex. Internat. Airline; founder Bomber Command Mus. (R.A.F.). Served to lt. USNR, 1942-46. Recipient safe pilot award Nat. Pilots Assn., Pilot Proficiency award FAA, Profl. Svc. Citation. Assoc. fellow Brit. Assn. Aerospace Medicine, Latin Am. Aviation Med. Assn., Scottish Assn. Aviation Med. Examiners; mem. Airline Med. Dirs. Assn., Civil Aviation Med. Assn. (v.p. 1968-80, dir. 1968—, pres. 1980-81, award of merit 1994), Mitchell Pediatric Soc., Academie Internationale de Medicine Aeronatque et Spatiale, Aircraft Owners and Pilots Assn. (med. adv. panel), Confederate Air Force (founding mem.), Order Ky. Cols., Quiet Birdmen, Masons, Psi Chi, Alpha Psi Omega (hon.). Office: 2800 Lake Rd Huntsville TX 77340-5632

CONWILL, DAVID E., preventive medicine educator; b. Laramie County, Wyo., Jan. 31, 1950; m. Gloria Ann Kennedy, May 26, 1973; children: Amanda Elizabeth, Andrew David. AA, Itawamba Jr. Coll., Fulton, Miss., 1973; BS in Biology, U. Miss., University, 1972; MD, U. Miss., Jackson, 1976; MPH, U. Calif., Berkeley, 1980. Diplomate Am. Bd. Preventive Medicine; lic. physician, Miss. Commd. USNR, 1972; advanced through grades to lt. comdr USN, 1984; intern flexible anesthesiology Naval Regional Med. Ctr., Oakland, Calif., 1976-77; resident infectious disease epidemiology Calif. State Dept. Health Svcs., U. Calif. Sch. Pub. Health, Berkeley, 1978-80; head epidemiology dept. Navy Environ. and Preventive Medicine Unit No. 5, San Diego, 1980-82; head epidemiology and infectious disease control div. Navy Environ. Health Ctr., Norfolk, Va., 1982-84; commanding officer Naval Res. Environ. and Preventive Medicine Unit, West Monroe, La., 1985-88; med. officer Naval Res. Fleet Hosp., Naval Res. Ctr., Jackson, Miss., 1988-89; assoc. prof. preventive medicine U. Miss. Sch. Medicine, Jackson, 1989—; cons. epidemiologist Miss. State Dept. Health, 1984—; vis. prof. gen. preventive medicine and pub. health, occupational medicine dept. U. Cin. Sch. Medicine. Contbr. articles to profl. jours. Mem. 3d Va. Infantry, Civil War Reenactment Group, 32d Miss. Infantry/60th N.Y. Infantry and Cleburne's Brigade; mem. 1st Confederate Brigade, Nat. Civil War Reenactment Group; sustaining mem. Rep. Nat. Com., 1979-89; v.p. bd.dirs. Miss. Seabelt Coalition, 1986-88, pres. bd. dirs., 1989-90. With USN, Persian Gulf, 1991. Recipient award Am. Coalition for Traffic Safety State of Miss., 1989. Fellow Am. Coll. Preventive Medicine; mem. Am. Venereal Disease Assn., Assn. Mil. Surgeons U.S., U.S. Naval Inst., Res. Officers Assn., Northeast Miss. Hist. and Geneal. Soc., Sons Confederate Wars, Itawamba County Hist. Soc., Civil War Roundtable of JAckson (pres. 1990-91), Scottish-Am. Mil. Soc. Office: U Miss Sch Medicine Dept Preventive Medici Jackson MS 39216

CONWILL, WILLIAM LOUIS, psychologist, consultant; b. Louisville, Jan. 5, 1946; s. Adolph Giles and Mary Luella (Herndon) C.; m. Faye Venetia Harrison, May 17, 1980; children: Giles Burgess, Leonart Mondlane, Justin Neal. BA, U. San Diego, 1968; MA, Calif. State U., 1973; PhD, Stanford U., 1980. Lic. psychologist. Trainer, rsch. asst. family crisis intervention tng. Richmond (Calif.) and San Francisco Police Dept, 1972-73; sr. tng. counselor Santa Clara (Calif.) County Juvenile Probation Dept., 1971-73; counseling psychologist II U. Calif., Santa Cruz, 1974-77; chief consultation and edn. San Mateo (Calif.) County Dept. Mental Health, 1980-82; chief outpatient psychologist Psychiatry Clinic U. Louisville, 1983-88; dir. creative pain mgmt. program U. Louisville Sch. Medicine, 1983-87, asst. project dir. AIDS health care profl. tng. contract, 1987-88; community statis. rsch. assoc. City of Louisville HHS, 1988-89; psychologist Lakeshore Mental Health Inst., Knoxville, Tenn., 1990—; pres. Family Stress Inst., Inc., Louisville, 1988—; lectr. in field. Contbr. articles to profl. jours. Cons., lectr. Community Action Agy, Louisville, 1986, Highlands Baptist Hosp. Med.-Surg. Symposium, Louisville, 1986-87, N.E. Ecumenical Devel. Ctr., Louisville, 1986; mem. edn. com. Jefferson County AIDS, Louisville, 1987-89, Minority Community, 1989-90, AIDS Edn. Coalition, 1988-89; mem. planning, presenter Knoxville Coll. Black Family Health Conf., 1989; bd. dirs. Black-aleidoscope Cultural Ctr., Louisville, 1982-84, Suicide Edn. and Prevention Ctr., Louisville, 1985-87, Knoxville County Head Start, Knoxville Alliance for Mentally Ill; lectr. dept. psychiatry U. Tenn. Med. Sch., Memphis; regional trainer APA HIV Office for Psychology Edn. Program. Mem. APA, Am. Pain Soc., Ky. Soc. Psychologists, Tenn. Psychol Assn., Assn. Black Psychologists, Behavioral Medicine Soc., Am. Group Psychotherapy Assn. Roman Catholic. Office: Lakeshore Mental Health Inst Children & Youth Svcs-Child & Family 5908 Lyons View Dr Knoxville TN 37919

COODLEY, EUGENE L., internist; b. L.A., Jan. 14, 1920; s. Oscar and Rae (Karot) C.; m. Gloria B. Coodley, July 11, 1946; children: Lauren, Cheryl, Gregg. BA, UCLA, 1939; MD, U. Calif., San Francisco, 1943. Diplomate Am. Bd. Internal Medicine. Chief medicine Phila. Gen. Hosp., 1967-73; prof. medicine Hahnemann U. Sch. Medicine, Phila., 1973-80, chief internal medicine, 1973-80; chief internal medicine sect. VA Med. Ctr., Long Beach, Calif., 1985—; prof. medicine V U. Calif.-Irvine Sch. Medicine, Orange, 1980—; Chief medicine Kern County Hosp., Bakersfield, Calif., 1965-67; asst. clin. prof. Calif. Coll. Medicine, Orange, 1965-67. Author: Clinical Enzymology, 1978, Geriatric Heart Disease, 1987, Odyssey of a Physician, 1995; contbr. chpts. to books. Chmn. 61st Dist. Dem. Club, L.A., 1979. Capt. M.C., U.S. Army, 1944-46, PTO. Recipient 1st prize for sci. exhibit AMA, Chgo., 1969. Fellow ACP, Am. Coll. Cardiology (3rd prize 1974). Home: 490-102 Medford Ct Long Beach CA 90803 Office: VA Med Ctr 5901 E 7th St Long Beach CA 90822

COOGAN, FRANK NEIL, health and social services administrator; b. Watertown, Wis., June 14, 1929; s. Neil Christopher and Lilian (Nelson) C.; m. Mary Louise Block, Apr. 14, 1951; children: Michael, Thomas, Karen. BS, U. Wis., 1951, MSW, 1955. Psychiatric social worker VA, 1955-62; dist. mental health cons. Wis. State Div. Mental Hygiene, 1962-65; dir. Bur. Alcohol and Other Drug Abuse, Wis. Dept. Health, 1965-77; v.p. DePaul Health Corp., 1977-90; behavioral health cons. Corphealth, West Allis, Wis., 1990-94; psychotherapist Family Social and Psychotherapy Svc., 1994—. With U.S. Army, 1951-53. Fellow Am. Coll. Addiction Treatment Adminstrs.; mem. Alcohol and Drug Problems Assn. N. Am. (chmn. membership com.), Wis. Alcohol and Drug Treatment Providers Assn. (bd. dirs.), Wis. Assn. Alcohol and Other Drug Abuse (bd. dirs., Outstanding Profl. award 1990), Am. Legion. Lutheran. Home: 2127 S 99th St Milwaukee WI 53227-1452

COOGAN, PHILIP SHIELDS, pathologist; b. Peoria, Ill., Feb. 13, 1938; s. Paul Mathew and Elizabeth Ann (Shields) C.; m. Carol Jean Gerlach, June 18, 1960 (div. 1985); children: Mary Brighid, Philip Gerlach, Joseph Baker,

Clare Ann; m. Joan C. Storozynski, Dec. 24, 1987. Student, U. Notre Dame, 1955-58; M.D., St. Louis U., 1962. Diplomate: Am. Bd. Pathology. USPHS summer research trainee pathology St. Louis U. Med. Sch., 1959-61; intern Presbyn.-St. Luke's Hosp., Chgo., 1962-63; resident Presbyn.-St. Luke's Hosp., 1963-67; research pathologist, chief histopathology U.S. Air Force Sch. Aerospace Medicine, 1967-69; asst. prof. pathology Rush Med. Coll., Chgo., 1971-73; assoc. prof. Rush Med. Coll., 1972-75; assoc. prof. pathology Northwestern U., Chgo., 1974-78; dir. anatomic pathology Northwestern Meml. Hosp., Chgo., 1974-78; prof., chmn. dept. pathology James H. Quillen Coll. Medicine, East Tenn. State U., Johnson City, 1978—; cons. FDA, 1972-81, USPHS, 1962-67. Assoc. editor: Year Book Pathology and Clinical Pathology, 1978-80. Served with USAF, 1967-69. Recipient Hektoen award Chgo. Path. Soc., 1969; named Outstanding Tchr. East Tenn. State U. Coll. Medicine, 1980, 81, 83, 84, 85. Mem. AMA, AAAS, U.S. and Can. Acad. Pathology, Am. Soc. Exptl. Pathology, Am. Soc. Clin. Pathology, Coll. Am. Pathology, Am. Soc. Investigative Pathology, Alpha Omega Alpha. Roman Catholic. Home: 3409 Stoneridge Dr Johnson City TN 37604-2182 Office: East Tenn State U Dept Pathology Johnson City TN 37614

COOK, BRIAN F., optometrist; b. Charleston, W. Va., Feb. 10, 1968; s. Frank B. and Marilyn G. (Haas) C. OD, Ill. Coll. of Optometry, 1993. Lic. optometrist, Wis. Optometrist Foresight Optical, Inc., Sheboygan, Wis., 1993-95; partner Alternative Vision Svcs., Wausau, Wis., 1993—; owner Brillion Family Eye Care, Brillion, Wis.; mgr. optometric svcs. Lenscrafters, Green Bay, Wis., 1995—. Assoc. mem. Wis. Healthcare Assn., Wis. Assn. of Homes and Svcs. for the Aging; mem. Am. Optometric Assn., Wis. Optometric Assn., Brillion C. of C., Green Bay Jaycees, Brillion Optimist Club. Home: 2212 Nicolet Dr #8 Green Bay WI 54311 Office: Brillion Family Eye Care 544 Fairway Dr Brillion WI 54110

COOK, CHARLES ANDREW, physician assistant; b. Cin., Oct. 21, 1944; s. Jesse Lee and Mary Esther (Cuttingham) C.; m. D. Darlene Weich, May 16, 1969; children: Andrew Charles, Melissa Dee. X-Ray Technician, Cin. Gen. Hosp., 1964; AS in Physician Asst., Cin. Tech. Coll., 1976; BA in Premed./Psychology, U. Cin., 1979. Registered X-Ray technologist. X-Ray technologist Cin. Gen. Hosp., 1962-64, Cin. Childrens Hosp., 1963-64, Columbus (Ohio) Childrens Hosp., 1964-65, Bethesda Base Hosp., Cin., 1969-71, Bethesda North Hosp., Montgomery, Ohio, 1971-74; physician's asst. Physician Assocs., Cin., 1975—; mem. adv. bd. Am. Cancer Soc., Cin., 1985-89, Navaree (Franciscan Health Sys.), Cin., 1992-94; vice chair bd. dirs. Carewise Home Health, Cin., 1992—. With USN, 1965-69. Mem. Am. Acad. Physician's Assts., Ohio Assn. Physician's Assts. (S.W. region rep. 1975-95). Republican. Methodist. Home: 9560 Millbrook Dr Cincinnati OH 45231 Office: Physician Assocs 5049 Crookshank Rd Cincinnati OH 45238

COOK, CHARLOTTE DASHER, rehabilitation counselor; b. Nashville, Ga., Sept. 11, 1948; d. Johnny Vestus and Alma Lee (Griner) Dasher; m. James Mitchell Cook, Sept. 1, 1984 (div. Aug. 1994); children: Lynne Michele, Tina Marie, Jodie Ann. AA, DeKalb Jr. Coll., 1972; BS, Ga. State U., 1974; MEd, U. Ga., 1977. Encode operator 1st Nat. Bank, Atlanta, 1966-67; stenographer II, State Dept. Edn., Atlanta, 1967-70, stenographer III, 1970-71; rehab. intern State Dept. Human Resources, Augusta, Ga., 1974-76, counselor I, Tifton, Ga., 1976-80, sr. rehab. counselor, 1980—; mem. adv. com. for Handicapped, Fitzgerald, Ga., 1979—, mem. adv. com. Vocat. Edn., Tifton, 1983—; pres.-elect Coun. for Exceptional Children, Tifton, 1983-84; mem. South Ga. Pvt. Industry Coun., 1992—. Projects chmn. Tiftarea Civitan, 1981—; Sunday Sch. tchr. 1st Bapt. Ch., Tifton, 1982—; Spl. Olympics coord. Tift County, 1982—; chmn. Tift County Com. for the Disabled; dir. Lowndes Leadership Devel. Inst., 1994—; chmn.-elect Valdosta Mayor's Coun. for Persons with Disabilities; mem. bus. and profl. com. Valdosta C. of C., pub. rels. com.; Recipient Service awards Tiftarea Civitan, 1982-83, Honor Key, 1983, Cert. Recognition Tifton Jr. Womens Club, 1984, Lewis Hine award Nat. Child Labor Com., 1985; named Outstanding Young Woman of Am., 1981, 82, 84, Handicapped Profl. Woman of Yr., Tifton Pilots Club, 1988, Lt. Col. ADC Gov.'s Staff, 1979. Mem. Ga. Rehab. Counseling Assn. (sec.-treas. 1983-84, pres. SW Dist. chpt. 1980-81, program chmn. 1985, pres. 1989, Currie Counselor of Yr. 1982, Counselor of Yr. 1992), Soc. Human Resource Mgmt., Nat. Rehab. Assn., Ga. Composite Bd. Profl. Counselors, Social Workers, Marriage and Family Therapists (lic. profl. counselor). Democrat. Baptist. Home: Rte 1 Box 541-73 Valdosta GA 31602 Office: Div Rehab Svcs 2517 Bemiss Rd Ste A Valdosta GA 31602-1900

COOK, COLIN BURFORD, psychiatrist; b. London, Jan. 20, 1927; came to U.S., 1952, naturalized, 1975; s. Bertram William and Anna Marie (Forster-Jones) C.; M.D., London U., 1951. Rotating intern Bridgeport (Conn.) Hosp., 1952-53; resident Goodmayes Hosp., Warlingham Park Hosp., London, 1955-57; gen. med. practitioner, London, 1960-66; resident in psychiatry Marquette Sch. Medicine, Wis., 1968-69; resident in psychiatry Cornell U., White Plains, N.Y., 1969-71; fellowship Nat. Neurol. Disease U. London, 1973; practice medicine, specializing in psychiatry, Stamford, Conn., 1975—; prof. psychiatry, Columbia U., N.Y.C., 1992-95; attending physician, psychiatrist Regional Network Programs, Inc., Conn., 1995—. Served with Brit. Navy, 1953-55, 57-59. Diplomate Am. Bd. Psychiatry and Neurology. Mem. AMA. Address: 373 Strawberry Hill Ave Stamford CT 06902-2512

COOK, DAVID ALASTAIR, pharmacology educator; b. Haslemere, Surrey, Eng., May 19, 1942; emigrated to Can., 1967; s. James W. and Monica (Reekes) C. M.A., Oriel Coll., Oxford U., D.Phil. Postdoctoral fellow U. Alta., Edmonton, 1967-70, asst. prof., 1970-74, assoc. prof., 1974-79, prof., 1979—, chmn. dept. pharmacology, 1981-91, dir. div. study med. edn., 1990—. Contbr. articles to profl jours. Named Tchr. of Yr., Med. Students Assn., 1974, 79, 81, 83, 94, Hon. Graduating Class Pres., 1987; recipient Pharm. Soc. Jour. award, 1977, Teaching award 3M, 1996. Mem. Pharm. Soc. Can. (past pres.), Can. Soc. Clin. Pharmacology, Can. Assn. Med. Edn., Western Pharm. Soc., Soc. Toxicology of Can., Brit. Pharm. Soc., Soc. Dirs. Rsch. in Med. Edn. Office: U Alta Divsn Studies Med Edn, Dept Pharmacology, Edmonton, AB Canada T6G 2R7

COOK, DAVID BURFORD, biochemistry educator; b. Sheffield, Yorkshire, Eng., Mar. 11, 1945; s. Edward William and Ada (Wimsey) C.; m. Elizabeth Hepplewhite, Apr. 3, 1971; children: Katherine, Steven. BSc, U. Newcastle on Tyne, Eng., 1966, MSc, 1967, PHD, 1971. Lectr. dept. clin. biochemistry U. Newcastle on Tyne, 1970—. Contbr. articles to profl. publs., chpt. to book. Sch. gov. Walbottle Campus, Newcastle on Tyne, 1992—, Lemington Mid. Sch., 1987—. Mem. Assn. Clin. Biochemists, Inst. Biology, Benwell Sports Club (chmn.). Mem. Brit. Labour Party. Office: U Newcastle on Tyne Med Sch, Framlington Pl, Newcastle on Tyne NE2 4HH, England

COOK, DONALD E., pediatrician; b. Pitts., Mar. 24, 1928; s. Merriam E. and Bertha (Gwin) C.; BS, Colo. Coll., 1951; MD, U. Colo., 1955; m. Elsie Walden, Sept. 2, 1951; children: Catherine, Christopher, Brian, Jeffrey. Intern, Fresno County Gen. Hosp., Calif., 1955-56; resident in gen. practice Tulare (Calif.) County Gen. Hosp., 1956-57; resident in pediatrics U. Colo., 1957-59; practice medicine specializing in pediatrics, Aurora, Colo., 1959-64, Greeley (Colo.) Med. Clin., Greeley Sports Medicine Clin., 1964-93; med. adv. Centennial Develop. Svcs., Inc., clin. faculty U. Colo., clin. prof., 1977—; organizer, dir. Sports Medicine Px Exam Clinic for indigent Weld Co. athletes, 1990-95; mem. adv. bd. Nat. Center Health Edn., San Francisco, 1978-80; mem. adv. com. on maternal and child health programs Colo. State Health Dept., 1981-84, chmn., 1981-84; preceptor Sch. Nurse Practitioner Program U. Colo., 1978-88. Mem. Weld County Dist. 6 Sch. Bd., 1973-83, pres., 1973-74, 76-77, chmn. dist. 6 accountability com., 1972-73; mem. adv. com. dist. 6 teen pregnancy program, 1983-85; mem. Weld County Task Force on teen-aged pregnancy, 1986-89, Dream Team Weld County Task Force on sch. dropouts, 1986-92, Weld County Interagy. Screening Bd., Weld County Cmty. Ctr. Found., 1984-89, Weld County Task Force Speakers Bur. on AIDS, 1987—; mem. Weld County Task Force Adolescent Health Clinic; mem. Task Force Child Abuse, C. of C.; bd. dirs. No. Colo. Med. Ctr., 1993—, No. Colo. Med. Ctr. Found., 1994—; mem. Sch. Dist. 6 Health Coalition, Task Force on access to health care; group leader neonatal group Colo. Action for Healthy People Colo. Dept. Pub. Health, 1985-86; co-founder Colorodoans for seatbelts on sch. buses, 1985-90; co-founder, v.p. Coalition of primary care physicians, Colo., 1986; mem. adv. com. Greeley Cen. Drug and Alcohol Abuse, 1984-86, Rocky Mtn. Ctr. for Health Promotion and Edn., 1984—, bd. dirs., 1984—, v.p., 1992-93, pres. 1994; rep. coun. on med. specialty soc., AAP, 1988-89, mem. coun. pediatric rsch., 1988-89, oversight com. fin., oversight com. communications, rep. to nat. PTA, 1990-94, mem. coun. on govt. affairs, 1989-90, rep. to coun. sects. mgmt. com., mem. search com. for new exec. dir.; med. cons. Sch. Dist. 6, 1989—; adv. com. bd. comm., adv. com. bd. membership comm., adv. com. bd. finance, adv. com. bd. dirs. AAP 1990-95, AAP com. govt. affairs, 1990; bd. dirs. N. Colo. Med. Ctr., 1993—, United Way Weld County, 1993—; founder, med. dir. Greeley Children's Clinic, 1994—. With USN, 1946-48. Recipient Disting. Svc. award Jr. C. of C., 1962, Disting. Citizenship award Elks, 1975-76, Svc. to Mankind award Sertoma Club, 1972, Spark Plug award U. No. Colo., 1981, Eta Sigma Gamma Svc. award, 1996; Mildred Doster award Colo. Sch. Health Coun. for sch. health contbns., 1992, Citizen of Yr. award No. Colo. Med. Ctr. Found., 1996, Humanitarian of Yr. award Weld County United Way, 1996, Alfred Winchester Humanitarian award Greeley/Weld Sr. Found., Inc., 1996. Diplomate Am. Bd. Pediatrics. Mem. Colo. Soc. Sch. Health Com. (chmn. 1967-78), Am. Acad. Pediatrics (alt. dist. chmn. 1987-93, dist. chmn. dist. VIII 1993, chmn. alt. dist. chmn. com. 1991-93, chmn. sch. health com. 1975-80, chmn. Colo. chpt. 1982-87, mem. task force on new age of pediatrics 1982-85, Ross edn. and award com. 1985-86, media spokesperson Speak Up for Children 1983—, mem. coun. sects. mgmt. 1991-92, mem. search com., exec. dir.), AMA (chmn. sch. and coll. health com. 1980-82, James E. Strain Community Svc. award 1987, 94, com. pediatric practice), Adams Aurora Med. Soc. (pres. 1964-65), Weld County Med. Soc. (pres. 1968-69), Colo. Med. Soc. (com. on sports medicine, 1980-90, com. chmn. 1986-90, chmn. com. sch. health 1988-91, A.H. Robbins Community Svc. award 1974), Centennial Pediatric Soc. (pres. 1982-86), Rotary (bd. dirs. Greely chpt. 1988-91, mem. immunization com. 1994—, chmn. immunization campaign Weld county, 1994). Republican. Methodist. Home: 171reeley CO 80631-5143 Office: Greeley Sports Medicine Clinic 1900 16th St Greeley CO 80631-5114

COOK, DONALD EUGENE, orthopedist; b. Cromwell, Ala., Oct. 19, 1935; s. Frances Aubrey and Ethie Francis (Nicholson) C.; m. Myrna Nell Shadow, June 20, 1959; children: Janet Lynn, Donald Scott. Student, U. Miss., 1959, MD, 1963. Extern Miss. State Hosp., Whitfield, 1962-63; intern Mobile (Ala.) Gen. Hosp., 1963-64; resident U. Miss. Med. Ctr., Jackson, 1964-68, chief resident, 1967-68; cons. physician Miss. Crippled Children's Service, Meridian, 1968-72; staff Riley Meml. Hosp., Meridian, 1968-76, Meridian Regional Hosp., 1968-89, Anderson Med. Ctr., Meridian, 1968—; pres. East. Cen. Orthopaedics, Ltd., Meridian, 1982—; CEO Astro Devel. Co., Meridian, 1986-92; pres., chief exec. officer Planetary Products, Inc., Meridian, 1986-93. Patentee. Mem. bd. dirs. ARC, Meridian, 1978-80; team physician Meredian Boxing Club, 1980-95. Served with U.S. Army, 1954-57. Mem. AMA, East Miss. Med. Assn., Miss. Orthopaedic Assn., Nat. Assn. Disability Examiners, So. Med. Assn., Miss. State Med. Assn., So. Orthopaedic Assn., Masons (32 degree), Shriners. Baptist. Home: 6485 Highway 493 Meridian MS 39305-9281 Office: East Cen Orthopaedics Ltd 5002 Highway 39 N Meridian MS 39301-1071

COOK, JAMES FRANCIS, medical technologist; b. Jacksonville, Fla., Oct. 14, 1960; s. Charles Leo and Agnes Cecilia (Kearny) C.; m. Nancy Jean Householder; children: Cameron James, Valerie Ann. BS Medical Technology, George Mason U., 1984; MBA, Marymount U., 1990. Medical technologist Fairfax Hosp., Falls Church, Va., 1984-87, microbiologist, faculty, 1987-89; laboratory manager Va. Med. Assoc., Springfield, Va., 1989-90; legis. analyst Am. Med. Labs., 1990-92; lab. dir. Charleston (S.C.) Meml. Hosp., 1992—; mem. faculty Trident Tech. Coll., 1996—. Mem. editl. bd. Advance for Adminstrs. the Lab., 1992—; contbr. articles to profl. jours. Mem. Am. Soc. Clin. Pathologists (cert. med. tech., diplomate lab. mgmt., chmn. mem. awards 1987-90, sec. AMS, workshop dir. 1989-94, task force on recruitment, retention and image lab. pers. 1992-94, S.E. Region Assoc. of Yr. 1995), Am. Soc. Med. Tech. (cert. clin. lab. scientist), Clin. Lab. Mgmt. Assn. (pres. Carolina Low Country chpt. 1993—, gen. chmn. Carolinas clin. connection 1995), Toastmasters (sec. Fairfax Hosp. Assn. chpt. 1987-89). Roman Catholic. Office: Charleston Meml Hosp 326 Calhoun St 11091 Main St Charleston SC 29401

COOK, JOSEPH E., medical technologist; b. Duncan, Okla., Mar. 23, 1954; s. Joseph Edwin and Mary Jewell (Bell) C.; m. Darlene M. Sparrgrove, Dec. 30, 1974; children: Amy Leigh, Melissa Layne. Student, U. Okla., 1974-75. Staff med. tech. Meml. Hosp. Southern Okla., Ardmore, 1979-87; med. tech. supervisor Med. Ctr. Southeast Okla., Durant, Okla., 1987-88; adminstrv. dir. lab. Arbuckle Meml. Hosp., Sulphur, Okla., 1988—. Home: HCR 70 Box 102A Ardmore OK 73401 Office: Arbuckle Meml Hosp Lab 2011 W Broadway Sulphur OK 73086

COOK, KENNETH RAY, radiologist; b. Sublette, Kans., Sept. 16, 1953; s. Curtis Carl and Carmen Madonna (Countryman) C.; m. Paula Rose Petryzyn, July 22, 1978; children: Erin Michelle, Leah Nicole, Tara Rachelle. AA, Hutchinson Community Coll., Kans., 1976; BA, U. Kans., 1979, MD, 1983. Diplomate Am. Coll. of Radiology. Resident in diagnostic radiology U. Kans. Med. Ctr., 1983-87; diagnostic radiologist Radiology Assocs., Corpus Christi, Tex., 1987—; staff radiologist Meml. Med. Ctr., Columbia Northwest, Corpus Christi, Tex., 1987—; chief radiology Bay Area Med. Ctr., 1993—, vice chmn., trustee, 1993-94, chmn., 1994-96; chief radiology Rehab. Hosp. South Tex., 1989-91; asst. clin. prof. family practice U. Tex., San Antonio; med. dir. Del Mar Coll. Ultrasound Technol. Sch. Recipient Resident Teaching award, Dept. Radiology, U. Kans., Kansas City, 1985-86, Resident Teaching award, Med. Ctr. Kans. U., 1986-87. Mem. AMA, Am. Coll. Radiology, Radiologic Soc. N. Am., Tex. Med. Soc., Tex. Radiologic Soc., Am. Inst. Ultrasound in Medicine, Nueces County Med. Soc. Republican. Roman Catholic. Office: Radiology Assocs PO Box 5608 Corpus Christi TX 78465-5608

COOK, PATRICK JOSEPH, cardiologist; b. Houston, Dec. 15, 1954; s. Joseph Bernard and Mary Margaret (Fail) C. BA in History, U. Tex., 1975; MD, Baylor U., 1979. Bd. cert. in internal medicine, in cardiovascular disease. Intern St. Luke's Episcopal Hosp., Houston, 1979-80; resident Baylor Coll. Affiliated Hosps., Houston, 1980-82; fellow Tex. Heart Inst., Houston, 1983-84; cardiologist Kelsey-Seybold Clinic, Houston, 1985-89, Med. Clinic Houston, 1989—; clin. instr. Baylor Coll. Medicine, Houston, 1985—. Fellow Am. Coll. Cardiology; mem. Tex. Heart Inst. (med. exec. com. 1991-93), Lakeside Country Club, KC. Republican. Roman Catholic. Office: Med Clinic Houston 1707 Sunset Blvd Houston TX 77005-1713

COOK, QUENTIN LAMAR, healthcare executive, lawyer; b. Sept. 8, 1940; s. J. Vernon and Bernice (Kimball) C.; m. Mary Gaddie, Nov. 30, 1962; children: Katheryn Cook Knight, Quentin Laurance, Joseph Vernon III. BS, Utah State U., 1963; JD, Stanford U., 1966. Bar: Calif. 1966. Assoc. Carr, McClellan, Ingersoll, Thompson & Horn, Burlingame, Calif., 1966-69, ptnr., 1969-93; interim pres., CEO Calif. Healthcare Sys., San Francisco, 1993-94, pres., CEO, 1994-95; vice chmn. Sutter Health/Calif. Healthcare Sys., San Francisco, 1996—; bd. dirs. Burlington Bank & Trust Co., Guittard Chocolate Co., Calif. Healthcare Sys., San Francisco; mem. adv. bd. KOIT AM/FM, 1994—. City atty. Town of Hillsborough, Calif., 1982-93; mem. adv. bd. Utah State U., Logan, 1985-95; mem. bd. visitors Brigham Young U. Law Sch., Provo, 1994—; area authority Ch. of Jesus Christ of Latter-day Saints, 1994-1995. Mem. Nat. Health Lawyers Assn., Am. Soc. Hosp. Attys., Pacific Union Club San Francisco. Republican. Home: 595 Pullman Rd Hillsborough CA 94010-6748 Office: Sutter Health Calif Healthcare Sys 1 California St Fl 15 San Francisco CA 94111-5401

COOK, ROY RODNEY, health facility administrator, psychologist; b. Oklahoma City, June 1, 1951; s. Ralph Vern and Rita Lee (Hedge) C.; m. Nancy Lynn Brinkmeyer, Sept. 13, 1986; 1 child, John Streeter. BS, Okla. State U., 1973; PhD, U. Miss., 1980. Diplomate Am. Bd. Med. Psychology. Psychologist VA Med. Ctr., Balt., 1980-81, dir. ADTP, 1981-85, acting chief psychology dept., 1983-84; chief psychology svc. VA Med. Ctr., Tuskegee, Ala., 1985—; coord. R&D, VA Med. Ctr., Tuskegee, 1985—; expert witness in field, 1985—; mem. adj. faculty Auburn U., Montgomery, 1985—. Cons. editor Internat. Jour. of Criminal Justice, 1991-93. Grantee U.S. Dept. VA, 1987-88, 89, 90-94, 95, 96. Mem. APA. Office: VA Med Ctr VA med Ctr Tuskegee AL 36083

COOK, STUART DONALD, physician, educator; b. Boston, Oct. 23, 1936; s. Martius and Nina (Schwartzman) C.; m. Josepha Emdin, June 26, 1960; children—Andrew, Peter, Jonathan. A.B., Brandeis U., 1957; M.S., U. Vt., 1959, M.D., 1962. Diplomate: Am. Bd. Psychiatry and Neurology. Intern Upstate Med. Center, Syracuse, N.Y., 1962-63; resident in neurology Albert Einstein Coll. Medicine, Bronx, N.Y., 1965-67; chief resident Albert Einstein Coll. Medicine, Bronx, 1967-68, instr. dept. neurology, 1968-69; asst. prof. neurology Coll. Physician and Surgeons, Columbia U., N.Y.C., 1969-71; prof. medicine N.J. Med. Sch., Newark, 1971—, chmn. dept. neuroscis., 1972—, acting dean, 1987-89; chief neurology svc. VA Med. Center, East Orange, N.J., 1971-86; vis. scientist div. virology Nat. Inst. Med. Research, London, 1977-78; vis. scientist Swiss Inst. for Cancer Research, 1985. Contbr. articles to profl. jours. Served with USN, 1963-65. Mem. Am. Acad. Neurology (S. Weir Mitchell award 1968), Am. Assn. Neuropathologists, AAUP, Am. Fedn. Clin. Research, Assn. Univ Profs. Neurology, Harvey Soc., Am. Neurol. Assn., Sigma Xi, Alpha Omega Alpha. Home: 26 Dogwood Dr Morristown NJ 07960 Office: U Medicine and Dentistry NJ MS Dept Neuroscis 185 S Orange Ave Newark NJ 07103-2407

COOK, TODD MCCLURE, health care executive; b. Frankfort, Ind., Nov. 3, 1962; s. Robert Eugene and Patricia (McKinney) C. Student Calif. State U., 1981-82; BA in Econs./English George Mason U., 1983; MBA in Health Care Administrn., Columbia Pacific U., 1990. Asst. dir./acting dir. This Way House, Alexandria, 1983-85; pvt. cons., 1985-86; bus. mgr. Falls Church (Va.) Med. Ctr., Va., 1986-88; adminstr., Neurology Svcs., Inc., Fairfax, Alexandria, Woodbridge, Va. and Washington, 1989-92; sr. ptnr. Cook & Miele Assocs., Alexandria and L.A., 1989-93; health care exec. RehabCare Corp., Rio Hondo Hosp., Downey, Calif., Valley Presbyn. Hosp., Van Nuys, Calif., Alhambra (Calif.) Hosp., 1993—; cons. St. Elizabeth's Hosp. Crisis Intervention Tng., Washington, 1985, Alexandria's Child Safety Day, 1984; Bd. dirs. Help in Emotional Trouble, Fresno, 1982, v.p., bd. dirs., 1983; bd. dirs. Mental Health Assn., Alexandria, 1984, v.p. bd., 1985; del. Nat. Network of Runaway and Youth Services Symposium, Bethesda, Md., 1985; v.p. Alexandria Mental Health Assn., 1983-86; active Nat. Head Injury Found., Va. Head Injury Found., Calif. Head Injury; vol. Alexandria Crisis Hot-Line. Grantee Youth Devel. Bur., 1984, 85, Alexandria City grantee, 1985. Mem. SAR, Am. Coll. Health Care Execs. (affiliate), Am. Coll. Med. Quality (affiliate), Am. Bd. Quality Assurance and Utilization Rev. Physicians (diplomate), Am. Acad. Med. Adminstrs., Am. Coll. Neuromusculoskeletal Adminstrs. Democrat. Presbyterian. Club: Entrepreneur Orgn. (Alexandria) (pres. 1985). Lodge: Demolay. Avocation: tennis.

COOKE, GARY SCOTT, health facility administrator; b. Indpls., Nov. 30, 1962; s. Gary Gene and Betty Hager (Meade) C.; m. Kristine Ann Cramer, June 27, 1987; children: Rayann, Emma, Garett. BA, Cedarville Coll., 1985. Adminstr. Ossian (Ind.) Health Care, 1990-92, Evergreen Woods Health & Rehab., Spring Hill, Fla., 1992-95, Eagle Crest Rehab. & Health Ctr., Jacksonville, Fla., 1995—. Recipient Pres.'s award Nat. Health Care Affiliates, Buffalo, 1995. Mem. Am. Coll. Health Care Adminstrs., Ind. Health Care Assn. (legis. com. 1991-92, pub. rels. com. 1991-92). Republican. Office: Eagle Crest Rehab & Health 2802 Pareital Home Rd Jacksonville FL 32216

COOKE, GILBERT MILES, physician assistant; s. Gilbert Orson and Jewel E. (Hollander) C.; m. Nancy Gayle Simonton, June 16, 1969 (div. June 1994); children: Gayle Marie Cooke Truitt, Tracy Leigh; m. E. Jane Allen, July 22, 1994. Physician Asst., USAF Sch. Health Care Scis./, U. Nebr., 1976. Cert. physician asst. Medic, served to master sgt. USAF, 1960-80; physician asst. Franklin (Ga.) Family Medicine Clinic, 1980-81, Jack E. Binge, MD, Carrollton, Ga., 1981-93, Jewett (Tex.) Med. Ctr., 1993-94, Fayette Meml. Hosp., LaGrange, Tex., 1994-95, John G. Bates, Cuthbert, Ga., 1995—. Moderator, founder Lee County Diabetic Group Support, Tex., 1994-95, Randolph Diabetes Group Support, Cuthbert, Ga., 1995—. Msgt. USAF, 1960-80. Fellow Am. Acad. Physician's Assts., Ga. Assn. Physician's Assts. (mem. conf. planning com. 1982-93, chmn. 1988-89), Soc. Air Force Physician's Assts., Am. Acad. Diabetic Educators, Noncommissioned Officer Assn., Retired Enlisted Assn., DAV. Republican. Mem. Christian Ch. Home: PO Box 178 Cuthbert GA 31740-0178 Office: c/o John G Bates MD 208 McDonald Ave Cuthbert GA 31740

COOKE, JOHN P., cardiologist, medical educator, medical researcher. BA in Biology, Cornell U., 1976; MD, Wayne State U., 1980; PhD in Physiology, Mayo Grad. Sch. of Medicine, 1985. Diplomate Am. Bd. Internal Medicine, Am. Bd. Cardiovascular Disease; cert. instr. advanced cardiac life support Am. Heart Assn. Assoc. physician Brigham and Women's Hosp., Boston, 1987-90; asst. prof. medicine Harvard Med. Sch., Boston, 1987-90; asst. prof. medicine Stanford (Calif.) U. Sch. of Medicine, 1990-95, dir. sect. vascular medicine, 1991—, assoc. prof. medicine, 1995—. Mem. editl. bd. Jour. Vascular Medicine and Biology, 1990—; contbr. articles to profl. jours. Rsch. fellow Mayo Grad. Sch. of Medicine, 1980-87; Merck fellow Am. Coll. Cardiology, 1985-86; recipient Henry Christian award Am. Fedn. Clin. Rsch., 1990, Vascular Acad. award NIH, 1991. Mem. Soc. Vascular Medicine and Biology (fouder). Office: Stanford U Sch of Medicine Divsn Cardiovascular Medicine 300 Pasteur Dr Stanford CA 94305-5246*

COOKE, MARY A., hospice director; b. Hoboken, N.J., Sept. 22, 1944; d. John F. and Mary A. (Schmidt) C. RN, St. Joseph Sch. Nursing, Syracuse, N.Y., 1966; BS, Seton Hall U., South Orange, N.J., 1968; MA, NYU, 1972. Staff nurse St. Mary's Hosp., Hoboken, N.J., 1966, Holy Name Hosp., Teaneck, N.J., 1967-68, St. Barnabas Med. Ctr., Livingston, N.J., 1969; instr. Elizabeth (N.J.) Gen. Hosp., 1969-72, clin. nurse specialist, 1972-74; nursing care coordinator Cabrini Med. Ctr., N.Y.C., 1974-82; nursing dir. Cabrini Hospice, N.Y.C., 1982-83; dir. Cabrini Hospice, 1983—; ptnr., prog. dir. Ahmed, Gordon & Mancino, N.Y.C., 1981-83; adj. faculty Sch. Nursing, Columbia U., 1992—. Contbr. articles to profl. jours. Mem. ANA, N.Y. State Nurses Assn. (bd. dirs. 1996—), N.J. Nurses Assn. (v.p. 1971, bd. dirs. 1972-76), Sigma Theta Tau. Democrat. Roman Catholic. Home: 240 E 27th St Apt 26C New York NY 10016-9023 Office: Cabrini Hospice 227 E 19th St New York NY 10003-2600

COOKE, NELSON ROGER, neurologist, educator; b. Webster, S.D., June 27, 1943; s. Chester Nelson Cooke and Helen Charlotte Shively; m. Judith Hill, June 10, 1969; children: Amanda, Daniel, Mark. BA, Pomona Coll., 1965; MD, Yale U., 1969. Diplomate Am. Bd. Psychiatry and Neurology, Am. Bd. Neurodiagnostic Medicine. Intern Alameda County Hosps., Oakland, Calif., 1969-70; resident in internal medicine Mayo Clinic, Rochester, Minn., 1971-72, resident in neurology, 1972-75; asst. prof. U. Wash., Spokane, Wash., 1985-91, assoc. prof., 1992—; cons. Neurology Assocs. of Spokane, 1975—; mem. med. com. Sacred Heart Hosp., 1981—, mem. profl. adv. com. Multiple Sclerosis Soc. Inland N.W. chpt., 1986—, chmn. neuroscience com. Sacred Heart Hosp, 1991—. Vol. physician Am. Mission, Ethiopia, 1971. Mem. AMA, Am. Acad. Neurology, Am. Assn. Electrodiagnostic Medicine. Office: Neurology Assocs of Spokane 711 S Cowley Spokane WA 99202

COOKE, ROBERT EDMOND, physician, educator, former college president; b. Attleboro, Mass., Nov. 13, 1920; s. Ronald Melbourne and Renee Jeanne (Wuillumier) C.; m. Sharon Riley, Nov. 20, 1978; children: Susan R., Anne R.; children from previous marriage: Robyn (dec.), Christopher, Wendy, W. Robert, Kim. BS, Yale U., 1941, MD, 1944, postgrad., 1948-50; DSc (hon.), U. Miami, 1970. Intern, then asst. resident dept. pediat. New Haven Hosp., 1944-46; instr. pediat. Yale U., New Haven, 1950-51, asst. prof. pediat. and physiology, 1951-54, assoc. prof., 1954-56; from resident to assoc. pediatrician Grace-New Haven Cmty. Hosp., 1951-56; pediatrician-in-chief Johns Hopkins Hosp., 1956-73; chmn. dept. Johns Hopkins Sch. Medicine, 1956-73; Grover Powers prof. pediat. Nat. Assn. Retarded Children, 1957-59, Given Found. prof., 1962-73; vis. prof. Harvard U., 1972-73; vice chancellor health scis., prof. pediat. U. Wis., 1973-77; pres. Med. Coll. Pa., 1977-80; A. Conger Goodyear prof., med. dir. SUNY, Buffalo, 1982-88, prof. emeritus, 1988—, chmn. dept. pediat., 1985-88; pediatrician-in-chief Children's Hosp. of Buffalo, 1985-88; chief med. officer Spl. Olympics Internat.; with Mass. Dept. Mental Health, 1980-82; chmn. med. adv. bd. Kennedy Found.; mem. adv. bd. Nat. Ctr. Rehab. Rsch., Nat. Inst. Child Health and Human Devel., 1991—. Editor, contbr. to pediat. textbooks, profl. jours. Trustee Children's Rehab. Inst. Capt. M.C., AUS, 1946-48. NIH postdoctoral fellow Sch. Medicine Yale U., 1948-50, John and Mary Markle scholar, 1951-55; recipient Mead Johnson award in pediat., 1954, Kennedy Internat. award for disting. svc. in field of mental retardation, 1968, Howland medal, 1992, medallion of the Surgeon Gen., 1993. Fellow Am. Acad. Pediat., Am. Psychiat. Assn. (disting.); mem. APHA, Am. Pediat. Soc. (John Howland award 1991), Soc. for Pediat. Rsch. (pres. 1965-66), Am. Soc. for Clin. Investigation, Md. Med. Soc., Am. Fedn. Clin. Rsch., Inst. of Medicine, Aurelian Hon. Soc., Phi Beta Kappa, Sigma Xi, Alpha Omega Alpha. Home: 865 Painted Bunting Ln Vero Beach FL 32963-2026

COOKE, THERESA ROBSON, nurse; b. Phila., Oct. 5, 1942; d. Harry S. and Theresa M. (Mack) Robson; m. Joseph W. Cooke, Apr. 30, 1966 (div. Jan. 1990); children: Mary T., Eileen P., Kevin J. Diploma in nursing, Thomas Jefferson U. Hosp., 1963; BS, Phila. Coll. Textiles & Sci., 1993. RN, Pa.; cert. oper. rm. nurse. Staff nurse Thomas Jefferson U. Hosp., Phila., 1963-65; pvt. scrub nurse, office nurse pvt. practice med. office, Bryn Mawr, Pa., 1965-66; staff nurse oper. rm. Germantown Hosp. and Med. Ctr., Phila., 1977-82, Holy Redeemer Hosp. and Med. Ctr., Meadowbrook, Pa., 1982-86; staff nurse, asst. head nurse, head nurse orthopedics Med. Coll. Pa. Hosp., Phila., 1986-91; mgr. clin. edn. programs Surg. Laser Tech. Inc., Oaks, Pa., 1991-95; mgr. continuing edn. Maxillo-Facial divsn. Synthes, 1995—. Mem. Assn. Oper. Rm. Nurses (v.p. Phila. chpt. 1983-87, pres. 1988-89, nominating com. 1990-92), Am. Soc. Lasers in Medicine and Surgery, Jefferson Hosp. Sch. Nursing Alumnae Assn. Republican. Roman Catholic. Home: 3200 Carriage Ct S North Wales PA 19454

COOKER, PHILIP GEORGE, psychology educator; b. Oswego, N.Y., Jan. 20, 1942; s. George Joseph and Rose Marie (Lille) C.; m. Barbara J. Buongiorne, Aug. 4, 1947; children: Jeremy Philip, Joshua Edward. BS, SUNY, Oswego, 1963; MS, SUNY, 1968; PhD, Fla. State U., 1971. Lic. psychologist, Miss. Elem. sch. counselor Enlarged City Sch. Dist., Oswego, 1966-69; intern Deer Park (Tex.) Hosp., 1978-79; prof. U. Miss., Oxford, 1971—; prof., dir. tng., counselor tng. programs U. Miss. Co-author: Gestalt Therapy, 1976; contbr. articles to profl. jours.; producer (film) Counselor Competencies, 1988. Named Outstanding Young Educator, Jaycees. Mem. APA, Am. Counseling Assn., Miss. Counseling Assn. (pres. 1987-88, Researcher of Yr.), Miss. Assn. Sch. Adminstrs. (bd. dirs. 1987-90). Home: Box 488H RR 1 Box 488H Oxford MS 38655-9729 Office: U Miss Sch Edn University MS 38677

COOKINHAM, LORI-ANN BETH, pediatrics nurse; b. Bklyn., May 4, 1962; d. Thomas Charles Sr. and Mildred Margaret (Hutchinson) Amundsen; m. Robert Lee Cookinham Jr., June 25, 1988. ADN, Gloucester County Coll., Sewell, N.J., 1992; student, Widener U., 1992—. RN, N.J., Pa.; cert. pediatric nurse; cert. PALS. Dental asst., office mgr. Dr. Leonard E. Zbikowski, Runnemede, N.J., 1982-92; nurse St. Christopher's Hosp. for Children, Phila., 1992—. Home: 411 Whitman Dr Turnersville NJ 08012 Office: St Christophers Children Hosp Erie and Front Sts Philadelphia PA 19134

COOLEY, SHEILA LEANNE, psychologist, consultant; b. Oakland, Calif., July 25, 1956; d. Philips Theadore and Helen Ellene (Newbill) C. BA, St. Leo Coll., 1979; MS, U. So. Miss., 1986; PhD, Miss. State U., 1990. Lic. psychologist, Ky. Counselor Charter Counseling Ctr., Jackson, Miss., 1988-89; staff psychologist Rivendell Psychiat. Ctr., Bowling Green, Ky., 1989-90; program dir. MidSouth Hosp., Memphis, 1990-91; resource ctr. dir. Mid-South Resource Ctr., Ridgeland, Miss., 1991-92; partial hosp. dir. Pathways Partial Hospitalization, Ridgeland, 1991-92; edn. specialist, sr. position Miss. Dept. of Edn., Bur. Spl. Svcs., Jackson, 1993-94; psychologist Western State Hosp., Hopkinsville, Ky., 1994—, Caring Connections, Hopkinsville, Ky., 1995; pvt. practice Hopkinsville, Ky., 1996—. Campaign organizer for Dem. mayor, Jackson, 1992. Mem. APA, Ky. Psychol. Assn., Phi Delta Kappa, Psi Chi, Theta Pi Sigma. Baptist. Home: 4081 Singletree Dr Hopkinsville KY 42240 Office: PO Box 2200 Hopkinsville KY 42241-2200

COOLEY, TONYA TRUONG, physician; b. Saigon, Vietnam, Dec. 24, 1957; came to U.S., 1973; d. Bobby Jean and Mia Phuong (Nguyen) C. BS in Pharmacy, U. Mo., 1983; DO., U. Health Scis., 1989. Pharmacist May's Pharmacy, Joplin, Mo., 1983-84; staff pharmacist Harry Truman-VA Hosp., Columbia, Mo., 1984-85; staff physician Blue Springs (Mo.) Primary Care Physicians, 1993-96. Home: 16305 E 26th Independence MO 64055 Office: Blue Springs Physician Pri Care 205 W RD Mize Ste 408 Blue Springs MO 64014

COOLEY, WILLIAM EDWARD, regulatory affairs manager; b. St. Louis, Mar. 7, 1930; s. Charles Frederic and Lillian Marie (Williams) C.; m. Marion Grace Sherman, June 5, 1952; children: Charles, Marilyn, Harold, Noele. AB, Cen. Coll., 1951; PhD, U. Ill., 1954. Rsch. chemist Procter & Gamble Co., Cin., 1954-61, product devel. chemist, 1961-65, product devel. group leader, 1965-75, product devel. regulatory sect. mgr., 1975-90, regulatory affairs sect. mgr., 1990-91; worldwide regulatory coordination sect. mgr., 1991-94; pres. Cooley Cons., Inc., 1994—; bd. dirs. Nonprescription Drug Mfrs. Assn., Washington, 1987-91. Contbr. articles to profl. jours.; inventor, patentee in field. Mem. Am. Assn. Dental Rsch., Internat. Assn. Dental Rsch., Drug Info. Assn., Assn. Food Drug Ofcls., Regulatory Affairs Profl. Soc. (bd. editors 1990). Republican. Home: 531 Chisholm Trl Cincinnati OH 45215-2517 Office: Cooley Cons Inc 531 Chisholm Trail Wyoming OH 45215

COOLEY, WILLIAM EMORY, JR., radiologist; b. Charlottesville, Va., Jan. 28, 1941; s. William Emory Sr. and Madelle Elizabeth (Fullen) C.; m. Janella Mahoney Haney, Dec. 26, 1966; children: Angela Janette, William Emory, James Haney. BA, Emory U., 1963; MD, U. Va., 1967. Diplomate Am. Bd. Radiology. Rotating intern. U.S. Naval Hosp., Phila., 1967-68; resident radiology U.S. Naval Regional Med. Ctr., Phila., 1972-75; radiologist U.S. Naval Regional Med. Ctr., Portsmouth, Va., 1975-76, asst. chief radiology, 1976-77; radiologist Bloomington (Ill.) Radiology S.C., 1977-79, pres., 1979—; chief radiologist Brokaw Hosp., Normal, Ill., 1979-85, St. Joseph Hosp., Bloomington, Ill., pres. med. staff, 1981; med. dir. radiology Bromen Health Care System, Bloomington, 1985—, pres. med. staff, 1990. Mem. citizens adv. coun. Sch. Dist. 87, Bloomington, 1981-84; v.p. McLean County unit Am. Cancer Soc., 1989-90, pres., 1990-94. Comdr. USN, 1966-77. Fellow Am. Coll. Radiology (alt. councillor 1987-92, councillor 1993—); mem. AMA, Radiol. Soc. N.Am., Am. Roentgen Ray Soc., Am. Inst. Ultrasound Medicine, Ill. Radiol. Soc. (exec. com. 1986—, pres. 1994-95), Ctrl. Ill. Radiol. Soc. (pres. 1990-91), Bloomington Country Club, Masons. Republican. Presbyterian. Office: Bloomington Radiology SC 200 S Towanda Ave Normal IL 61761-2132

COOLICAN, PAUL PATRICK, social services administrator, consultant, educator; b. Watkins Glen, N.Y., Jan. 23, 1959; s. John G. and Jean E. (Martine) C.; m. Patricia A. Hurst, Nov. 22, 1986; children: Rachel, Nicole. AS in Science, Mohawk Valley Community Coll., 1979; BA in Psychology, SUNY, Geneseo, 1981; MSW, SUNY, Buffalo, 1983. CSW, ACSW, NYSDOH. Foster care counselor NYS Div. for Youth, Elmira, N.Y., 1980-81; mental health/substance abuse counselor Mid Erie Mental Health, Cheektowaga, N.Y., 1983-84; med. social worker Visiting Nurses Assn., Buffalo, 1984-87; social svcs. dir. Episcopal Ch. Home, Buffalo, 1987-91, adult day health dir., 1988-94; sr. adminstr. Wegman Cos., Inc., 1994-95; adminstr. Episcopal Gen. Homecare, Inc., 1995—; instr. Hilbert Coll., Hamburg, N.Y., Niagara C.C., Sanborn, N.Y., 1988-92, SUNY Sch. Social Work, Buffalo, 1991—; cons. Odd Fellows RHCF, Lockport, N.Y., 1989-91, Blind Assn. Western N.Y., 1990-91, Rosa Coplon RHCF, Buffalo, 1990. Mem. profl. adv. bd Niagara Hospice, 1991-94, Stulzman Alcoholic Treatment Ctr., 1993—. Mem. NASW, Acad. of Cert. Social Workers. Democrat. Roman Catholic. Home: 45 Tanglewood Dr Buffalo NY 14224-4444

COOMARASWAMY, MICHAEL ANANDA, physician, surgeon; b. N.Y.C., Jan. 2, 1959; s. Rama P. and Bernadette (Martocchio) C.; m. Patricia Loi Yeh, Jan. 1, 1993; children: Grace, Teresa, Aoife. BS, We. Wash. U., Bellingham, 1982; MD, Albert Einstein Coll. Medicine, 1986. Diplomate Am. Bd. Surgery, Sub-Bd. Critical Care. Intern Montefiore Med. Ctr., Bronx, N.Y., 1986, resident in gen. surgery, 1987-90, chief resident surgery, 1991, fellow in head and neck surgery, 1994-95; attending surgeon in trauma surgery svc. Bronx Mcpl. Hosp. Ctr., 1991—; asst. prof. surgery Albert Einstein Coll. Medicine, Bronx, 1993—. Contbr. articles to profl. jours.; lit. reviewer Ednl. Revs. Inc., 1994—. Mem. Assn. for Surg. Edn. Roman Catholic. Office: Montefiore Med Park 1575 Blondell Ave Bronx NY 10461

COOMBES, RAOUL CHARLES, medical oncology educator; b. Swindon, Wiltshire, Eng., Apr. 20, 1949; s. Raoul Charles and Doreen Mars (Ellis) C.; m. Caroline Sarah Oakes, July 24, 1984; children: Jack, Sophie, Matilda. MBBS, U. London, 1971; MD, PhD, London U., 1981. Sr. clin. scientist Ludwig Inst. Cancer Rsch., London, 1978-86; cons. physician Royal Marsden Hosp., Sutton, Eng., 1978-86; cons. med. oncologist St. Georges Hosp., London, 1986-90; prof. med. oncology, head dept. Charing Cross Hosp., Westminster Med. Sch., Fulham, London, 1990—; hon. cons. med. oncologist Charing Cross Hosp., London, 1990—; mem. cell bd. MRC. grants com. CRC. Editor 2 books on breast cancer; contbr. 320 articles on breast cancer to profl. jours.; patentee on antistrogen for breast cancer. Recipient awards MRC & CRC, 1986-88. Fellow RCP; mem. Brit. Assn. Cancer Rsch., Am. Assn. Cancer Rsch. Office: Charing Cross Westminster Med Sch, Saint Dunstan Rd, London W6 SW, England

COOMES, DONNA F., medical records administrator; b. Princeton, W.Va., Nov. 2, 1964; d. Dennis and Judith (Shrewsbury) Hatfield; m. Jody S. Coomes, Oct. 7 1983. Cert., AHIMA, Chgo., 1993. Accredited record technician. Clerk, coder, abstractor Princton (W.Va.) Cmty. Hosp., 1986-93; dir. med. records dept. NoraCare So. Hills Rehab. Hosp., Princeton, 1993-94; asst. dir. med. records dept. Floyd Med. Ctr., Rome, Ga., 1994—. Mem. Am. Health Info. Mgmt. Assn., Ga. Health Info. Mgmt. Assn., Northwest Ga. Health Info. Mgmt. Assn., Phi Theta Kappa. Home: 173 Addington Dr Rome GA 30165 Office: Floyd Med Ctr Rome GA 30162

COOMES-HILL, LESLIE ANN, registered nurse; b. Guam, Mich., Mariannas Islands, Dec. 8, 1959. ADN, Eastern Ky. U., 1979; BSN, U. Tex., 1990. RN, Tex., Ky. Nurse U. Ky. Med. Ctr., Lexington, 1980-82, Hermann Hosp., Houston, 1982-86; transplant coord. Meth. Hosp., Houston, 1986—. Mem. Nat. Assn. Transplant Coord. Orgn. Office: Meth Hosp 6565 Fannin SM 447 Houston TX 77030

COON, PENNY K., administrator; b. Penn Yan, N.Y., May 21, 1959; d. Wilfred Orval and Marilyn Estelle (Wells) Knapp; m. Thomas Allen Gray, Aug. 30, 1980 (div. July 1990); m. David Charles Coon, May 23, 1992; 1 child, Rachel Mariah. BSW, Keuka Coll., 1980. Residence counselor Cath. Charities Residential Program, Penn Yan, N.Y., 1981-82, residence mgr., 1982-92, residential supr., 1992—; bd. dirs. Yates County (N.Y.) ARC, Penn Yan, 1993—, mem. human rights com., 1989; co-chmn. Keuka Lake Conf. Com., Rochester, N.Y., 1986—; mem. Yates County Devel. Disabilities Subcom., 1990. Recipient Direct Care award, N.Y. State Assn. Community Residence Adminstrs., 1985. Mem. DAR, Daughters Am. Colonists. Republican. Home: 2599 Knapp Rd Dundee NY 14837-9730 Office: Cath Charities Residential Program 607 W Washington St Geneva NY 14456-1804

COOPER, ALAN ROBERT, optometrist; b. Newark, June 28, 1942; s. Herbert and Freda (Edelman) C. BS, Ill. Coll. Optometry, 1965, OD, 1966. Cert. therapeutic pharm. agts. Pvt. practice optometry specializing in contact lenses, Paterson, N.J., 1969—; clin. investigator soft contact lenses FDA. Served to capt. AUS, 1967-69. Diplomate Nat. Bd. Examiners in Optometry. Mem. Nat. Eye Research Found., Better Vision Inst., Optometric Refractive Surgery Soc., Alumni Assn. Ill. Coll. Optometry, U.S. Power Squadrons. Home: 151 Pine Brook Rd Montville NJ 07045-9693 Office: 136 Market St Paterson NJ 07505-1402

COOPER, ARNOLD MICHAEL, psychiatrist; b. N.Y.C., Mar. 9, 1923; s. Morris and Clara (Aronow) C.; m. Madge Huntington, June 28, 1973; children by previous marriage: Andrew, Melissa, Thomas. AB, Columbia U., 1943, cert. psychoanalytic medicine, 1956; M.D., U. Utah, 1947. Research fellow in medicine Harvard U., 1947-48; asst. in medicine Thorndike Meml. Lab., Boston City Hosp., 1947-48; intern internal medicine Presbyn. Hosp., N.Y.C., 1948-50; psychiat. resident Bellevue Hosp., N.Y.C., 1950-53; mem. faculty Columbia U. Coll. Physicians and Surgeons, 1968—, clin. prof. psychiatry, 1971-74; lectr. Columbia U. Div. Humanities and Contemporary Civilization, 1964-79, adj. prof. comparative lit., 1985—; prof. psychiatry N.Y. Hosp.-Cornell U. Med. Ctr., 1974—, Stephen P. Tobin and Dr. Arnold M. Cooper prof. consultation liaison psychiatry, 1992-94, Stephen P. Tobin and Dr. Arnold M. Cooper prof. emeritus, 1994—; assoc. chmn. edn., dept. psychiatry N.Y. Hosp.-Cornell U. Med. Ctr.-Payne Whitney Clinic, 1974-88; supr., tng. psychoanalyst Columbia U. Psychoanalytic Ctr. Trg. and Research, 1961—; mem. instnl. rev. bd. Rockefeller U., 1990—. Editorial bd. Psychoanalysis and Contemporary Thought, 1987—; editor Psychoanalysis: The Second Century, 1989; editorial bd. Psychiatry Textbook, Am. Jour. Psychiatry, 1987-91, Jour. Am. Psychoanalytic Assn., 1988-91, Jour. Acad. Psychiatry; dep. editor Am. Jour. Psychiatry, 1992—, N.Am editor, Internat. Journal Psychoanalysis, 1993—; consulting editor: Jour. Psychotherapy Practice and Rsch.; contbr. articles on masochism, narcissism, applied psychoanalysis, psychoanalytic concepts, psychoanalytic technique, psychoanalytic and psychiat. edn. to profl. jours. Mem. Am. Psychoanalytic Assn. (pres. 1980-82), Am. Assn. Dirs. Psychiat. Residency Tng., Internat. Psychoanalytic Assn. (v.p. 1985-89, assoc. sec. 1989—), Am. Coll. Psychiatry, Am. Psychiat. Assn. (pres. N.Y. County dist. br. 1988-89), N.Y. Psychiat. Soc., Assn. Dirs. Med. Student Edn., Assn. Psychoanalytic Medicine (pres. 1975-77), Am. Coll. Psychoanalysis, Vidonian Soc., Century Club (N.Y.C.), Alpha Omega Alpha. Office: 50 E 78th St New York NY 10021-1809

COOPER, BARRY, hematologist; b. Louisville, Jan. 22, 1945; s. Rudey and Rosalie (Schwarz) C.; m. Lynn Myra Cantor; children: Stephanie, Andrew, Mallory. AB, Franklin and Marshall Coll., 1967; MD, Johns Hopkins U., 1971. Diplomate Am. Bd. Internal Medicine, Am. Bd. Hematology and Med. Oncology. Intern and resident in medicine Johns Hopkins Hosp., Balt., 1971-73; clin. assoc. NIH, Balt., 1973-75; rsch. fellow hematology Peter Bent Brigham, Harvard Med. Sch., Boston, 1975-77, jr. assoc. medicine, 1977-79; chief of hematology West Roxbury (Mass.) VA Med. Ctr., 1977-79; asst. prof. medicine Harvard Med. Sch., Boston, 1977-79; co-dir. hematology Baylor U. Med. Ctr., Dallas, 1982—; clin. prof. medicine Southwestern Med. Ctr., University and Dallas, Tex., 1995—; ptnr. Tex. Oncology, Dallas, 1979—. Editl. bd. Jour. Clin. Applied Hemostasis and Thrombosis; contbr. articles to profl. jours. Lt. comdr. USPHS, 1973-75. Fellow ACP; mem. Am. Soc. Hematology, Am. Soc. of Clin. Oncology, Tex. Med. Assn., Phi Beta Kappa. Jewish. Office: Texas Oncology PA 3535 Worth St Ste #200 Dallas TX 75246

COOPER, CAROL J., medical technologist; b. Winner, S.D., Nov. 15, 1957; d. George C. and Donna J. (Bailey) Mayes; m. Wayne W. Cooper, Dec. 31, 1988; children: Tisha A., Kyle W. AD, Dakota Wesleyan U., 1978. Lab. technician Hand County Hosp., Miller, S.D., 1978-86, St Joseph Hosp., Polson, Mont., 1986—.

COOPER, DAVID YOUNG, science educator; b. Henderson, N.C., Aug. 14, 1924; s. James Allison and Frances Howe (Cheatham) C.; m. Cynthia Laughlin, Aug. 6, 1955; children: Lucy C., Allison Y. BS in Medicine, U. N.C., 1948; MD, U. Pa., 1948. Asst. prof U. Pa., Phila., 1959-60, assoc. prof., 1965-68, prof., 1968—, prof. pharmacology, 1969—. Editor N.Y. Acad. Sci. Symposia, 1973, (with Marshall Ledger) Innovation and Tradition at the School of Medicine of the University of Pennsylvania, 1990. Lt. USN. Mem. ASPET, Am. Phys. Soc., Am. Soc. Biol. Chemistry and Molecular Biology, Endocrine Soc., Am. Chem. Soc., Alpha Omega Alpha. Episcopalian. Office: U Pa Sch of Medicine 36th and Hamilton Walk Philadelphia PA 19104-1999

COOPER, DEBORA A., dietitian; b. Scranton, Pa., Dec. 3, 1958; d. Frank Thomas and Eleanor Jean (Kulesa) Conrad; m. Donald F. Cooper. BS, Marywood Coll., Scranton, Pa., 1981; student, Pa. State U., 1976-78. Cert. fitness instr. Bookkeeper/teller Third Nat. Bank, Scranton, Pa., 1977; salesperson J.C. Penney Co., Scranton, 1977-81; food svc. employee Marywood Coll., Scranton, 1980-81; clin. dietitian The Wood Co. at Easton Hosp., Easton, Pa., 1981-83; nutrition support dietitian The Wood Co. at Easton Hosp., 1983-85, clin. nutrition mgr., 1984-95, cons. nutritionist, 1988-94, asst. dir. nutritional svc., 1995—; mem. nutrition com., profl. svc. men's and women's health care adv. com., clin. path steering com., infection control, wellness com., patient edn. com. Easton Hosp.; presenter Clin. Congress ASPEN, 1995—; numerous speaking engagements-profl. and cmty. Contbg. author: Handbook of Therapeutic Intervention, 1994. Mem. Two Rivers Health Promotion Coun., Pa. State Coop. Family Living Adv. Coun., Am. Health Assn. Adv. Com. Named Young Dietitian of Yr. in Pa., 1988, Quality Valley USA Team award Am., 1995. Mem. Am. Dietetic Assn., Pa. Dietetic Assn., Lehigh Valley Dietetic Assn., Am. Soc. Parenteral and Enteral Nutrition, Aerobic and Fitness Assn. Am. Roman Catholic. Home: 2664 Washington St Easton PA 18045 Office: Easton Hosp 250 S 21st St Easton PA 18042

COOPER, DONALD LEE, physician; b. Columbus, Kans., Aug. 11, 1928; s. Calvin M. and J. Pearl (Mullen) C.; m. Dona Faye Maddux, June 4, 1950; children—Donald Lee, Catherine Susan, Cheryl Lyn, Tad Houston. A.B., Kans. State Coll., 1949; M.D., U. Kans., 1953. Intern St. Mary's and Childrens Mercy hosps., Kansas City, Mo., 1953-54; pvt. practice medicine Manhattan, Kans., 1956-57; team physician, asst. dir. Health Center Kans. State U., 1957-60; dir. health service, team physician Okla. State U. Hosp. and Clinic, Stillwater, 1960-90, dir. athletic medicine, 1990—; vis. lectr. div. sportsmedicine, dept. orthopedic surgery Coll. Medicine U. Okla. Health Scis. Center, 1974—; liaison officer Am. Coll. Health Assn. to Nat. Athletic Trainers Assn., 1963—; Am. chmn. 1st Am.-Soviet Conf. on Student Health, Moscow, Russia, 1967; team physician U.S. Olympic Team, 1967-68; mem. Pres.'s Coun. Phys. Fitness and Sports, 1981-92, del. to Moscow to rev. phys. culture and olympic tng. sites in Russia, 1989; team physician U.S. Deaf Olympic Team, Los Angeles, 1985; elected chmn. Joint Commn. on Competitive Safegaurds and Med. Aspects of Sports, 1986. Author: (with others) Standard Nomenclature of Athletic Injuries, 1966; Contbr. (with others) articles med. jours. Served to capt. USAF, 1954-56. Recipient Pres.'s Challenge Sportsmedicine award Nat. Athletic Trainers Assn., 1974, Bill Coltrin Meml. award Western Athletic Conf. Sports Writers Assn., 1974, Edward Hitchcock award Am. Coll. Health Assn., 1975; named among 10 healthy American fitness leaders Nat. Jaycees, Pres.'s Coun. on Physical Fitness and Sports, Allstate Ins. Co., 1995. Mem. AMA (chmn. com. med. aspects sports 1971-76, chmn. 1976-77, mem. coun. sci. affairs 1976-79), Nat. Collegiate Athletic Assn. (med. cons. to football rules com. 1969—), Am. Coll. Health Assn. (past pres., exec. com.), Southwestern Coll. Health Assn. (past pres.), Nat. Athletic Trainers Assn., Alpha Omega Alpha, Nu Sigma Nu. Presbyterian (elder 1971—). Club: Lion. Home: 1001 W Liberty Ln Stillwater OK 74075-2113 Office: Okla State U Hosp and Clinic Stillwater OK 74074

COOPER, EDWARD SAWYER, internist, educator; b. Columbia, S.C., Dec. 11, 1926; s. Henry Howard and Ada Crosland (Sawyer) C.; m. Jean Marie Wilder, Dec. 2, 1951; children—Lisa Marie Cooper Hudgins, Edward Sawyer Jr. (dec.), Jan Ada, Charles Wilder. A.B., Lincoln U., Pa., 1946; M.D., Meharry Med. Coll., Nashville, 1949; M.S., U. Pa., 1972. Diplomate Nat. Bd. Med. Examiners, Am. Bd. Internal Medicine. Intern Phila. Gen. Hosp., 1949-51, resident in medicine, 1951-54, NIH fellow in cardiology, 1956-57, pres. med. staff, 1969-71, co-dir. Stroke Research Ctr., 1968-74, chief med. service, 1973-76; prof. medicine U. Pa., Phila., 1973—; dir. Independence Blue Cross; mem. adv. bd. Hypertension Detection and Followup Program, Phila., 1974—. Trustee Am. Found. Negro Affairs, 1969—, Rockerfeller U., 1992—. Served to capt. USAF, 1954-56. Fellow Phila. Coll. Physicians (council), Am. Coll. Chest Physicians; mem. ACP (master), Am. Heart Assn. (chmn., dir., past nat. pres.), Alpha Omega Alpha. Democrat. Methodist. Research on stroke and hypertension. Home: 6710 Lincoln Dr Philadelphia PA 19119-3155 Office: University of Pa Hosp 3400 Spruce St Philadelphia PA 19104

COOPER, ELAINE JANICE, physical therapist; b. Detroit, Apr. 26, 1937; d. Morris and Sally (Mack) Braverman; divorced; children: Jeffrey, Michael, Jonathan. BS, U. Mich., 1959; cert. in massage therapy. Supr. Rehab. Inst., Detroit, 1959-61; cons. Redford (Mich.) Community Hosp., 1963-73; cons. in field Detroit, 1970-78; asst. dir. William Beaumont Hosp., Royal Oak, Mich., 1979-81; pres., cons. Cooper & Assoc. Physical Therapy P.C., Farmington Hills, Mich., 1981—; cons. Drs. Sobel & Castle, Detroit, 1965-66. Mem. Am. Phys. Therapy Assn. (edn. com. 1969), Mich. Phys. Therapy Assn., Biofeedback Soc. Mich., Am. Massage Therapy Assn., Mich. Dance Assn., Mich. State C. of C. (health care com.), Brookfield Highlands Club (chmn. land devel., restrictions coms. 1979-85). Office: Cooper & Assocs Phys Therapy PC 31800 Northwestern Hwy Ste 110 Farmington MI 48334-1663

COOPER, ELIZABETH MARIE, nurse midwife; b. Norman, Okla., Aug. 20, 1946; m. Gerard M. LaRusso,; children: John G., Kathryn E. Student, U. Dallas, 1964-65; BSN, U. Tex., 1969; MS in Maternity Nursing, Midwifery, Columbia U., 1971; EdD, U. Rochester, 1992. RN, N.J., N.Y.; lic. nurse-midwife, N.Y. Staff nurse-midwife, adminstr. midwifery svc. Bklyn.-Cumberland Med. Ctr./Williamsburg Health Ctr., 1971-74; instr. nursing Orange County C.C., Middletown, N.Y., 1974; nurse-midwife Community Health Ctr., Middletown, 1974-75, Planned Parenthood of Orange and Sullivan County, Newburgh, N.Y., 1974-75; cons., acting dir. midwifery svc. North Hudson Hosp., Weehawken, N.J., 1975; coord. nurse-midwifery dept. ob.-gyn. U. Rochester, N.Y., 1975-80, 84—, asst. prof. ob-gyn and clin. nursing, 1992—; bd. dirs. Genesee Region Family Planning Program, 1975-79; chair N.Y. State Med. Record Access Rev. Com., 1987-89; perinatal adv. com. N.Y. State Assembly Health Com., 1989-90; maternal and infant care adv. com. Monroe County Legislature Human Svcs. Com., 1990—; mem. Monroe County Infant Mortality Rev. Com., 1990—; mem. ob. access task force Finger Lakes Health Sys., 1992; mem. perinatal data base adv. com. Hosp. Consortium of Rochester; presenter profl. confs. Contbr. articles to profl. publs. Fellow Am. Coll. Nurse-Midwives (clin. practice com. 1985-88, treas. N.Y. chpt. 1984-88, 91-95); mem. APHA, N.Y. State Perinatal Assn. (bd. dirs. 1986-93, v.p. 1987-88, pres. 1989-90, founding mem. Finger Lakes chpt. 1991—), Midwives' Alliance N.Am., Nat. Perinatal Assn., Internat. Childbirth Edn. Assn., Jacobs Inst. Women's Health, Kappa Delta Pi. Office: U Rochester 601 Elmwood Ave Rochester NY 14642-8668

COOPER, GEORGE DAVID, psychologist; b. Hagerstown, Md., July 7, 1935; s. George Emmanuel and Mary Elva (Longanecker) C. BA, Sheperd Coll., 1958; PhD in Clin. Psychology, Duke U., 1962. Lic. psychologist, Va., W.Va., Md. Chief psychologist Petersburg (Va.) Tng. Sch., 1961-63; clin. psychologist Springfield Youth Ctr., Sykesville, Md., 1963-64, Newton D. Baker Vets. Ctr., Martinsburg, W.Va., 1964-73; assoc. prof. George Mason U., Fairfax, Va., 1973-79; clin. dir. Glaydin Sch., Leesburg, Va., 1979-83; chief psychologist MCTC Div. of Correction, Hagerstown, Md., 1984—; vis. assoc. prof. W.Va. U., Morgantown, 1968-69. Mem. APA, Kiwanis. Republican. Methodist. Office: Md Correctional Tng Ctr 18800 Roxbury Rd Hagerstown MD 21746

COOPER, GEORGE WALLACE, JR., human in vitro fertilization biologist; b. Warrensburg, Mo., June 7, 1936; s. George Wallace and Mildred Jo (Humphreys) C. AB, Brown U., 1958; PhD, Stanford U., 1964. Asst. prof. anatomy Coll. of Physicians & Surgeons Columbia U., N.Y.C., 1967-72; assoc. prof./asst. prof. reproductive biology/ob-gyn. Cornell U. Med. Coll., N.Y.C., 1972-79; rsch. scientist North Shore U. Hosp., Manhasset, N.Y., 1979—. Contbr. articles on sperm ultrastructure, biology, immunology, zona pellucida receptor physiology to profl. jours. Mem. AAAS, Am. Soc. for Reproductive Medicine, N.Y. Acad. Sci. Office: North Shore U Hosp 300 Community Dr Manhasset NY 11030-3801

COOPER, HOWARD, plastic and reconstructive surgeon; b. N.Y.C., Jan. 24, 1934; s. Benjamin and Jean (Harrison) C.; m. Adela Lander; children: Stephanie Anne, Benjamin, Anna Laura. BS in Pharms., L.I. U., 1955; MD, Mcpl. U. Amsterdam, The Netherlands, 1962. Sr. attending surgeon plastic surgery Lenox Hill Hosp., N.Y.C., 1972—, Pennisula Hosp., N.Y.C., 1972—. Capt. U.S. Army, 1962-69. Office: Howard Cooper MD 911 Park Ave New York NY 10021-0337

COOPER, HOWARD NORVIN, psychiatrist, educator, consultant; b. Chgo., July 13, 1922; s. Benjamin and Gertrude Cooper. BS, Northwestern U., 1945; MD, Columbia U., 1949. Diplomate Am. Bd. Psychiatry and

Neurology. Intern in medicine Bellevue Hosp., N.Y.C., 1949-50; residency in psychiatry Payne Whitney Hosp. Cornell U., 1950-53; pvt. practice N.Y.C., 1953—; asst. prof. psychiatry Cornell U. Med. Sch., N.Y.C., 1957—; attending psychiatrist N.Y. Hosp., N.Y.C., 1957—; psychiatrist emeritus, 1991—; dir. N.Y.C. Community Mental Health Bd., 1960-62; med. dir. N.Y. Coun. on Alcoholism, N.Y.C., 1962-65; cons. N.Y.C. Bd. Edn., 1980—. Fellow Am. Psychiat. Assn. (life). Office: 450 E 63rd St New York NY 10021-7928

COOPER, JACK ROSS, pharmacology educator, researcher; b. Ottawa, Ont., Can., July 26, 1924; came to U.S., 1948; s. Harry and Jean (Levine) C.; m. Helen Achbar, Aug. 14, 1951; children: Marilyn, Sheila, Nancy. B.A., Queen's U. Kingston, Ont., 1948; M.A., George Washington U., 1952, Ph.D., 1954; M.A. hon., Yale U., 1971. Asst. prof. pharmacology Yale U., New Haven, 1953-63, assoc. prof., 1963-71, prof., 1971—. Author: The Biochemical Basis of Neuropharmacology, 6th edit., 1991; mem. editorial bd. Biochem. Pharmacology. Served with RCAF, 1944. Smith, Kline and French research fellow, 1950-52; USPHS predoctoral fellow, 1952-54; postdoctoral fellow USPHS, 1954-56; spl. fellow USPHS, London, 1965-66. Mem. Am. Soc. Neurochemistry, Internat. Soc. Neurochemistry, Am. Soc. Pharmacology and Exptl. Therapeutics, Soc. Neurosci. Democrat. Jewish. Home: 11 Jenick Ln Woodbridge CT 06525-1935 Office: Yale U Sch Medicine 333 Cedar St New Haven CT 06510-3206

COOPER, JAMES CLINTON, social services administrator, consultant; b. Brinson, Ga., Feb. 3, 1929; s. James and Hattie Lue (Speights) C.; m. Anne Elizabeth Brown, July 14, 1959. BA, Savannah State U., 1956; MSW, Atlanta U., 1958. Lic. ind. social worker, Ohio. Clin. social worker VA Hosp., Tuskegee, Ala., 1958-61; social work supr. State Hosp., Fulton, Mo., 1961-64; dir. resident ctr. Community Action for Youth, Cleve., 1964-67; exec. dir. Goodrich-Bell Social Settlement, Cleve., 1967-69; dir. social svc. Cleve. State Hosp., 1969-74, Fairhill Mental Health Ctr., Cleve., 1974-84; dir. social svc. Cleve. Psychiat. Inst., 1984-85, cons. on quality assurance, 1985-95; owner Northcoast Vending Co., Cleve., 1992—; pres., chief exec. officer Wayne Morrie, Inc., cons., Cleve., 1983—. Bd. dirs. Hough Area Devel. Corp., Cleve., 1967-77, 1st vice-chmn., 1976-77. Sgt. U.S. Army, 1951-53. Recipient Editors' Choice award Nat. Libr. Poetry, 1993, 96; NASW fellow U. Pitts., 1977-79. Mem. Acad. Cert. Social Workers, Nat. Assn. Quality Assurance Profls. Home: 14420 Onaway Rd Cleveland OH 44120-2841

COOPER, JANELLE LUNETTE, neurologist, educator; b. Ann Arbor, Mich., Dec. 11, 1955; d. Robert Marion and Madelyn (Leonard) C.; children: Lena Christine, Nicholas Dominic. BA in Chemistry, Reed Coll., 1978; MD, Vanderbilt U., 1986. Diplomate Nat. Bd. Med. Examiners; diplomate in neurology Am. Bd. Psychiatry and Neurology; registered med. technologist Am. Soc. Clin. Pathologists. Med. technologist Swedish Hosp. Med. Ctr., Seattle, 1978-80, U. Wash. Clin. Chemistry, Seattle, 1980-82, Vanderbilt U. Hosp., Nashville, 1983-84; intern medicine Vanderbilt U. Med. Ctr., Nashville, 1986-87, resident neurology, 1987-90; instr. neurology Med. Coll. Pa., Phila., 1990-91, asst. prof., clerkship dir., 1991—, mem. curriculum com., 1990-91, vis. asst. prof., 1991-95; neurologist Greater Ann Arbor Neurology Assocs., 1991-93; dir. neurological svcs., med. dir. Industrial Rehab. Program St. Francis Hosp., Escanaba, Mich., 1993—; founder, dir. No. Neuroscis., Escanaba, 1993—; physician MCP Neurology Assocs., Phila., 1990-91; emergency rm. physician Tenn. Christian Med. Ctr., 1989-90. Contbr. articles to Annals of Ophthalmology, Ophthalmic Surgery. Vol. Rape and Sexual Abuse Ctr., Nashville, 1988-90; mem. adminstrv. bd. Edgehill United Meth. Ch., Nashville, 1989-90; mem. editorial bd. Nashville Women's Alliance, 1989-90; bd. dirs. Upper Peninsula Physicians Network; mem. adv. bd. Perspective Adult Daycare Ctr., 1996—. Recipient Svc. award for outstanding contbns. Rape and Sexual Abuse Ctr., 1990; epilepsy minifellow Bowman Gray U., 1995. Mem. AMA (physician's Recognition award 1989-92), NOW, AAAS, NAFE, Am. Med. Women's Assn., Am. Acad. Neurology, Am. Psychol. Soc., Mich. State Med. Soc., N.Y. Acad. Scis., Upper Peninsula Physician Network (bd. dirs. 1995—), Aircraft Owners and Pilots Assn., Women in Aviation Internat. (charter). Democrat (mem. nat. com.). Methodist. Home: 519 S 8th St Escanaba MI 49829-3608 Office: Northern Neurosciences 3415 Ludington St Ste 201 Escanaba MI 49829-1300

COOPER, JEFFREY STUART, orthodontist; b. Hackensack, N.J., Apr. 11, 1947; s. H. Miton and Gladys L. (Levitas) C.; m. Marcia G. Cohen, June 22, 1969; children: Jill, Karen, Greg. BS, U. Md., 1969, DDS, 1972; MS in Dentistry, Farleigh Dickinson U., 1976. Diplomate Am. Bd. Orthodontics. Pvt. practice Ramsey, N.J., 1976—. Lt. USNR, 1972-74. Mem. Coll. of Diplomates of Am. Bd. Orthodontics, Am. Assn. Orthodontists, N.J. Assn. Orthodontists. Independant. Jewish. Home: 282 Pine St Wyckoff NJ 07481-2825 Office: 42 N Franklin Tpke Ramsey NJ 07446-2034

COOPER, JOEL, psychology educator; b. N.Y.C., Dec. 3, 1943; s. Samuel Cooper and Sarah Tobias; m. Barbara Orenstein, Dec. 17, 1966; children: Jason, Aaron, Grant. BS, CCNY, 1965; PhD in Social Psychology, Duke U., 1969. Asst. prof. psychology Princeton (N.J.) U., 1969-73, assoc. prof., 1973-78, prof., 1978—, chmn. psychology dept., 1985-92, dir. grad. studies dept. psychology, 1976-83; chmn. Inst. Rev. Bd. Princeton U., 1974-81, 84-87, com. appointments and advancements, com. on grad. sch.; sr. fellow East-West Population Inst., 1975. Author: Understanding Social Psychology, 1976, 5th edit. 1991; editorial bd. Jour. Personality, Jour. Exptl. Social Sychology, Social Psychology Quar.; contbr. chpts. to books in field, articles to profl. jours. Office: Princeton U Dept Psychology Green Hall Princeton NJ 08544

COOPER, JOHN ALLEN DICKS, medical educator; b. El Paso, Tex., Dec. 22, 1918; s. John Allen Dicks and Cora (Walker) C.; m. Mary Jane Stratton, June 17, 1944; children: Margaret Ann, John Allen Dicks, Patricia Alison, Randolph Arend Stratton. B.S. in Chemistry, N.Mex.State U., 1939, LL.D. (hon.), 1971; Ph.D. in Biochemistry, Northwestern U., 1943, M.D., 1951, D.Sc. (hon.), 1972; D.Honoris Causa, U. Brasil, 1958; D.Sc. (hon.), Duke U., 1973, Med. Coll. Ohio, Toledo, 1974, Med. Coll. Wis., 1978, N.Y. Med. Coll., 1981, Wake Forest U., 1985, Georgetown U., 1986; D.Med. Sci (hon.), Med. Coll. Pa., 1973; DHL (hon.), Thomas Jefferson U., 1984. Intern Passavant Meml. Hosp., Chgo., 1951; mem. attending staff Passavant Meml. Hosp., 1955-69; mem. faculty Northwestern U., 1943-69, prof. biochemistry, 1957-69; assoc. dean Northwestern U. (Med. Sch.), 1959-63, dean scis., 1963-69; mem. faculty Georgetown U., Washington, 1970-90; prof. practice of health policy Duke U., Durham, N.C., 1973-78; faculty Baylor Coll. Medicine, Houston, 1987—; Disting. physician VA, 1987-92; vis. prof. U. Brasil, 1956, U. Buenos Aires, 1958, Harvard Med. Sch., 1985; mem. policy adv. bd. Argonne Nat. Lab., 1957-63, mem. review com. divs. biol. and med. research and radiol. physics, 1958-63, chmn. review com., 1958-62; mem. com. on licensure AEC, 1956-69, cons. div. edn. and tng., 1963; mem. adv. council on health research facilities NIH, 1965-69; organizing com. Pan Am. Fedn. of Assn. Med. Colls., 1962-64, treas., 1963-76; adv. com. personnel for research Am. Cancer Soc., 1962-66; cons. commr. food and drugs FDA, 1965-70; spl. cons. to dir. NIH, 1968-70; cons. to div. physician and health professions edn. Bur. Health Manpower Edn. NIH, 1970-73; mem. Inst. Medicine, Nat. Acad. Scis., 1972—; mem. bd. higher edn., Ill., 1964-69; chmn. Gov.'s Sci. Adv. Council, State Ill., 1967-69; mem. council Assn. Midwest Univs., 1963-68, v.p., bd. dirs., 1964-65, pres., bd. dirs., 1965-66; v.p., bd. trustees Argonne Univs. Assn., 1965-68; bd. dirs. Nat. Fund Med. Edn., 1970-79. Editor: Jour. Med. Edn, 1962-71. Trustee Georgetown U., 1986-89. Served to 1st lt., San. Corps AUS, 1945-47. Recipient Outstanding Alumnus award N.Mex. State U., 1960; Alumni medal Northwestern U., 1976; Abraham Flexner award Assn. Am. Med. Colls., 1985; John and Mary R. Markle scholar in acad. medicine, 1951-56. Mem. AMA, AAAS, Am. Hosp. Assn. (hon.), Inst. Medicine of NAS, Am. Soc. Biol. Chemists, Assn. Am. Med. Colls. (del. numerous confs., mem. various coms., pres. 1969-86, pres. emeritus 1986), Asociación Venezolana Para el Avance de la Ciencia (hon.), Tavern Club, Sigma Xi, Alpha Omega Alpha. Home: 4118 N River St Mc Lean VA 22101-5815

COOPER, JOHN EDWARD, psychiatrist; b. Sheffield, Yorkshire, Eng., July 27, 1929; s. Cyril Martin and Enid Alexandra (Greaves) C.; m. Chloë W. Simpson, July 1959 (div. Nov. 1990); children: Elizabeth, Polly, Martin. BA in Physiology, Oxford (Eng.) U., 1951, B.M., B.Ch., 1953. D.P.M. (London). Sci. officer Med. Rsch. Coun., U.K., 1962-65; dep. dir. in U.K. U.S.-U.K. Diagnostic Project, 1965-69; vice-dean Inst. of Psychiatry, London, 1969-71; cons. psychiatrist Royal Bethlem and Maudsley Hosps., London, 1969-71; found. prof. psychiatry U. Nottingham (Eng.) Med. Sch., 1971-90; emeritus prof. psychiatry U. Nottingham, 1990—; psychiat. cons.; mem. WHO Expert Panel on Mental Health, Geneva, 1970—. Co-author: Psychiatric Diagnosis in New York and London, 1971, Measurement of Psychiatric Symptoms, 1974; cons. to WHO for ICD-10, 1991; contbr. articles to profl. jours. Fellow Royal Soc. Medicine (U.K.), Royal Coll. Psychiatry. Home: 25 Ireton Grove, Attenborough, Nottingham NG9 6BJ, England

COOPER, JOHN THOMAS, psychologist, consultant; b. Thomasville, Ga., Mar. 31, 1945; s. Arnold Ervin and Era (Stewart) C.; m. Sandra Jean Page, June 9, 1972 (div. Aug. 1975). BA, Fla. State U., 1967, MS, 1973; PhD, Atlanta U., 1989. Cert. counselor; diplomate Am. Acad. Pain Mgmt.; cert. Eye Movement Desensitization and Reprocessing Network. Tchr. Pinetta Jr. High Sch., Madison, Fla., 1968-70; asst. to v.p. RexAir, Inc., Troy, Mich., 1975-76; asst. mgr. AMC Orange Park (Fla.) Five Theatres, Atlanta, 1976-78; gen. mgr. AMC Tower Pl. Six Theatres, Atlanta, 1979-81; sr. caseworker Gwinnett County Dept. Family & Children Svcs., Lawrenceville, Ga., 1981-82; sr. disability adjudicator Disability Adjudication Sect., Decatur, Ga., 1982-88; intern in psychology N.W. Ga. Mental Health Ctr., Ft. Oglethorpe, Ga., 1988-89, Ga. Regional Hosp., Decatur, 1988-89; psychotherapist Bayles & Assocs., Atlanta, 1986-91; pvt. clinic psychotherapist and counselor Atlanta, 1989-91, clinic dir., 1989-91; psychologist, pres. Cooper Psychol. Svcs., P.C., Atlanta, 1991—; cons. Bayles & Assocs., Atlanta, 1987-91. Mem. Ga. Coun. on Child Abuse, Atlanta, 189-95, Georgians for Victim Justice, Atlanta, 1987. Mem. ACA, APA, Ga. Psychol. Assn., Soc. for Personality Assessment, Am. Soc. Clin. Hypnosis (cert. in clin. hypnosis), Am. Inst. Forensic Examiners (diplomate). Democrat. Baptist. Home: 145 Copeland Rd NE Apt 1H Atlanta GA 30342-1067

COOPER, KAREN RENÉ, health facility administrator, nurse; b. Pleasanton, Calif., Oct. 15, 1957; d. Homer L. and Rosa B. (Upton) C.; m. Tommy Joe McCarty, Nov. 1, 1981. BSN, U. Ala., Birmingham, 1980. Cert. Profl. in Healthcare Quality, Healthcare Cert. Bd. Nat. Commn. Certifying Agencies, cert. profl. Utilization Rev., Interqual Nat. Registry; cert. chemotherapy, rehab. nurse, tissue therapy. Internship in SICU/MICU Cedars of Lebanon Hosp., Miami, Fla., 1980; mem. head injury/CVA and chronic pain team Spain Rehab. Ctr. U. Ala. Hosps., Birmingham, 1980-82, rheumatology charge nurse Spain Rehab. Ctr., 1982-88, staff nurse, 1988-90, coord. utilization rev./quality assurance med. care rev., 1990-91, coord. quality improvement med. care rev., 1991-93, sr. nurse coord. med. care rev., 1993, interim dir. med. care rev., 1993-94, sr. coord. dept. quality resources, 1994—; Mem. Com. for Quality Improvement U. Ala. Birmingham Hosps., mem. Discharge Planning Com., Emergency Svcs. Quality Improvement, 1991-93, Key 100 Com., Med./Dental Staff Task Force, Mobile ICU Quality Com. APACHE Study, 1990-92, Neurology Quality Com., 1990-92, Nursing Stds. Com., 1982-85, Nursing Task Force Com., 1984-88, Resuscitation Com., 1990-94, Skin Care/Tissue Therapy Com., 1986-89, Surg. Quality Improvement Com., 1991-93; mem. Arthritis Newsletter Com. U. Ala. Birmingham Multi-Purpose Arthritis Ctr., 1983-89; active Value Improvement Project of Birmingham Hosp. Network; participant, presenter numerous confs. and workshops in field. Contbr. articles to Arthritis Today and Arthritis Newsletter of U. Ala. Birmingham Multi-Purpose Arthritis Ctr. Pres. Coalnugget Ala. Mining Mus., 1987-89, chair literacy daycamp, 1990-92; participant Ala. State Fair Family Craft Divsn., 1975—; co-chair AHPA Nat. Nursing Coun., 1986-88; vol. Children's Hosp., Dixie Wheelchair Assn. Regional Wheelchair Games, Goodwill Industries Doll Sale, Caring and Sharing Drive; troop leader Cahaba Coun. Girl Scouts Am., 1982—, POGO advisor, 1985-93, advisor outdoor interest group, 1995—, mem. program operating unit, 1984-93, coun. trainer, 1984-93, 94—, cons. svc. area events/programs, 1984-92, svc. area mgr. Upper 78 West, 1995—, assn. chair, 1991-92, mem. nominating com., 1993-95, facilities com., 1992-94, chair long-range property planning com., 1993, del. to nat. conv., 1993, life mem., 1993; mem. Ala. Assn. Healthcare Quality, Am. Juvenile Arthritis Orgn., 1982-88, Arthritis Found., 1982-90, liaison ACT Club support group, 1984-86; mem. UHC: Quality and Risk Mgmt. Coun., United Way/Benevolent Fund com. U. Ala. Birmingham Hosps., 1990. Recipient Thanks award Girl Scouts Am. Cahaba Coun., 1989; fellow Girl Scouts U.S.A., 1976. Mem. NAFE, Nat. Assn. Healthcare Quality, U. Ala. Birmingham Alumni Assn. Home: 30 Scurlock Rd Dora AL 35062 Office: Dept Quality Resources U Ala Birmingham Hosp Birmingham AL 35223-6507

COOPER, KUM, pathologist, educator; b. Durban, Natal, South Africa, May 14, 1955; s. Ap and Ar Cooper; m. Dhana Suku, June 1977 (div. 1983); 1 child, Mahesh; m. Nimmie Naidoo, Dec. 9, 1984; 1 child, Suven. BSc with honors, U. Durban, 1975; M.B.Ch.B., U. Natal, 1980; DPhil, U. Oxford, U.K., 1992. Intern King Edward VIII Hosp., Durban, 1981; resident in anatomical pathology U. Natal, Durban, 1982-86, pathologist, 1987-89; Oxford Nuffield fellow U. Oxford, 1990-92; prof. anatomical pathology U. Witwatersrand, Johannesburg, South Africa, 1992—, prof. and head dept., 1993—. Recipient Phyllis-Knocker award Coll. Medicine, South Africa, 1990, Daubenton award Witwatersrand U., 1995. Fellow Coll. Pathologists; mem. Royal Coll. Pathologists London, Internat. Assn. Pathologists (sec. South Afican divsn., pres.-elect 1995—). Office: Witwatersrand Univ, Anatomical Pathology, PO Box 1038, Johannesburg 2000, Republic of South Africa

COOPER, LINDA TATKO, emergency services clinical nurse specialist; b. Buffalo, Oct. 12, 1955; d. Joseph and Caroline (Krol) Tatko; m. Steven Louis Cooper, Oct. 14, 1984; children: Jacqueline, Benjamin. BS in Nursing summa cum laude, Niagara U., 1977; MS in Med.-Surg. Nursing, Boston Coll., 1980. RN, Mass.; critical care RN AACN, cert. emergency nurse Emergency Nurses Assn., advanced cardiac life support Am. Heart Assn., pediatric advanced life support instr. Staff nurse surg. trauma floor U. Miami/Jackson Meml. Hosp. Med. Ctr., Miami, Fla., 1977, staff nurse surg. intensive care unit, 1979-80, assoc. head nurse intensive care unit, 1980-82, clin. adminstr., 1982-83, asst. dir. nursing Surg. Svcs. Hosp. Ctr., 1983-84; trauma nurse specialist coord. Baystate Med. Ctr., Springfield, Mass., 1984-87, clin. nurse specialist emergency svcs., 1987—; lectr. in field. Contbr. articles to profl. jours. Mem. Emergency Nurses Assn. (Pioneer Valley chpt., chairperson nurse practice com. 1989-90, chairperson edn. com. 1990-91, pres.-elect 1991-92, mem. state faculty emergency nursing pediatric course, trauma nursing core course), Sigma Theta Tau.

COOPER, LISA DAWN, health services administrator; b. Charleston, W.Va., Oct. 20, 1974; d. Arthur Ernest and Veronica Lareme (Cooper) Priddy. BA in Health Svcs. Adminstrn., W.Va. Inst. Tech., Montgomery, 1996. Adminstrv. asst., vol. Marmet (W.Va.) Health Care, 1995—. Mem. Am. Coll. Health Care Adminstrs. Home: PO Box 37 Dawes WV 25054

COOPER, MARK EMMANUEL, medical educator, researcher; b. Sydney, NSW, Australia, Sept. 8, 1956; s. Hercz Kupferminc and Rochelle Melman; m. Frances Helen Irving, Dec. 6, 1988; children: Samara, Zachary. MB, BS, Melbourne (Australia) U., 1979, PhD, 1989. Resident Austin Hosp., Heidelberg, 1980-82, registrar, 1983-84; sr. rsch. officer Melbourne U., 1988-90, sr. lectr., 1991-95; assoc. prof., 1996—. Contbr. more than 100 articles to profl. jours. Mem. Australia Diabetes Soc. (Young Investigator award 1987), Endocrine Soc. Australia, European Assn. Study Diabetes, Coun. High Blood Pressure Rsch., Australian Atherosclerosis Soc. (com. 1992-94), Australia Soc. Med. Rsch.

COOPER, MAX DALE, physician, medical educator, researcher; b. Hazelhurst, Miss., Aug. 31, 1933; s. Ottis Noah and Lily (Carpenter) C.; m. Rosalie Lazzara, Feb. 6, 1960; children: Owen Bernard, Melinda Lee Cooper Holladay, Michael Kane, Christopher Byron. Student, Holmes Jr. Coll., 1951-52, U. Miss., 1952-54; postgrad., U. Miss. Med. Sch., 1954-55; MD, Tulane U., 1957. Diplomate Am. Bd. Pediatrics. Intern Saginaw (Mich.) Gen. Hosp., 1957-58; resident dept. pediatrics Tulane Med. Sch., New Orleans, 1958-60; house officer Hosp. for Sick Children, London, 1960, rsch. asst. dept. neurophysiology, 1961; allergy fellow dept. pediatrics U. Calif. Med. Ctr., San Francisco, 1961-62; instr. Tulane Med. Sch., New Orleans, 1962-63; med. fellow specialist U. Minn., Mpls., 1963-64, instr., 1964-66; asst. prof. dept. pediats. U. Ala., Birmingham, 1967-71, assoc. prof. dept. microbiology, 1967-71, dir. rsch. Rehab. Rsch. and Tng. Ctr., 1968-70, prof. dept. microbiology, 1971—, dir. Cell. Identification Lab., 1987-90, dir. Ctr. Interdisciplinary Rsch. in Immunological Diseases, 1987-95, dir. Div. Devel./Clin. Immunology, 1987—, prof. dept. medicine, 1987—, investigator Howard Hughes Med. Inst., 1988—; sr. scientist Comprehensive Cancer Ctr. U. Ala., Birmingham, 1971—, Multipurpose Arthritis Ctr., 1979—, Cystic Fibrosis Rsch. Ctr., 1981—; dir. Cellular Immunobiology Unit of Tumor Inst. U. Ala., Birmingham, 1976-87; vis. scientist tumor immunology unit dept. zoology, U. Coll. London, 1973-74, Inst. D'Embryologie, Nogent-Sur-Marne and Inst. Pasteur, Paris, 1984-85. Co-author: Acute Hemiplegia in Childhood, 1962, Ontogeny of Immunity, 1967, Immunologic Incompetence, 1971, Immunodeficiency in Man and Animals, 1975, numerous others; mem. editl. bds. Immunology Today, 1986, Immunodeficiency Revs., 1987-94, Clin. Immunology and Immunopathology, 1987-90, Internat. Immunology, 1988—; assoc. editor Jour. Immunology, 1972-76, 77-79, Arthritis and Rheumatism, 1985-90, Jour. Clin. Immunology, 1979—; co-editor Seminars in Immunopathology, 1988-91; editor Current Topics in Microbiology and Immunology, 1981—; contbr. numerous 450 articles to profl. jours. Faculty rsch. assoc. Am. Cancer Soc., 1966-71; mem. bd. sci. advisors St. Jude Hosp., Memphis, 1981-84, 91—, Becton-Dickinson Monoclonal Antibody Ctr., 1980-90; mem. med. adv. com. Immune Deficiency Found., 1981-99; mem. bd. sci. counselors Nat. Cancer Inst., Bethesda, Md., 1982-86, Nat. Inst. Allergy and Infectious Diseases, 1978-82, 91—, Inst. Merieux, Lyons, France, 1985-90, Med. Biology Inst., La Jolla, Calif., 1986; mem. internat. sci. adv. bd. Basel (Switzerland) Inst. Immunology, 1987-91; NIH Immunobiology Study Sect., 1974-78; trustee Leukemia Soc. Am., 1983-88. Special Postdoctoral Rsch. fellow USPHS, 1964-66; recipient Teaching Traineeship award Nat. TB Assn., 1962-63, Samuel J. Meltzer Founder's award Soc Exptl. Biology and Medicine, 1966, Life Scis. award 3M, 1990, Sandoz Prize for Immunology, 1990. Mem. NAS, AAAS, AAUP, Am. Assn. Immunologists (pres. 1988-89, councilor 1983-86, chmn. mem. com. 1974-77), Am. Soc. Exptl. Pathology, Am. Soc. Clin. Investigation, Am. Assn. Cancer Rsch., Am. Acad. Pediatrics, Am. Pediatric Soc., Fedn. Am. Scientists, Med. Assn. State Ala., Internat. Soc. Devel. and Comparative Immunology, Soc. Francaise d'Immunologie (life Membre d'Honneur), Soc. Pediatric Rsch. (v.p. 1978), So. Soc. Pediatric Rsch. (pres. 1975), Cen. Soc. Clin. Rsch., Jefferson County Med. Assn., Clin. Immunology Soc., Am. Acad. Scis., Inst. Medicine, Am. Acad. Arts and Scis., Soc. Mucosal Immunology, Alpha Omega Alpha, Sigma Xi. Office: Howard Hughes Med Inst U Ala 1824 Sixth Ave S #378 Birmingham AL 35294-3300

COOPER, NORMAN STREICH, pathologist, medical educator; b. N.Y.C., Dec. 23, 1920; s. Samuel and Edith (Streich) C.; m. Evelyn Fickler, Apr. 13, 1945; 1 child, Jonathan Samuel. B.A., Columbia Coll., 1940; M.D., U. Rochester, 1943. Diplomate Am. Bd. Pathology. Intern, resident pathology N.Y. Hosp., N.Y.C., 1944-46, intern in medicine, 1948-49; scientist Oak Ridge Nat. Lab., Tenn., 1947-48; instr. microbiology NYU Sch. Medicine, N.Y.C., 1949-51, instr. pathology, 1951-54, asst. prof., 1954-56; assoc. prof NYU Sch. Medicine, 1956-67, prof. pathology, 1967—; chief pathology and lab. medicine svc. DVA Med. Ctr., N.Y.C., 1967—; founding pres. Assn. VA Lab. Service Chiefs, 1974-76. Mem. editorial bd. Clin. Immunology and Immunopathology, 1979-82. Vice pres., treas. Arthritis Found., N.Y. chpt., 1978-84. Served to capt. U.S. Army, 1946-48. Mem. Am. Assn. Immunologists, Am. Soc. for Investigative Pathology, U.S. and Can. Acad. Pathology, Transplantation Soc., Assn. VA Pathologists (pres. 1987-89), Soc. for In Vitro Biology, Am. Soc. for Cell Biology, Army and Navy Club (Washington), Dunes Racquet Club. Home: PO Box 1887 228 Cove Hollow Rd East Hampton NY 11937-0902 Office: NYU DVA Med Ctrs 423 E 23rd St New York NY 10010-5050

COOPER, REGINALD RUDYARD, orthopedic surgeon, educator; b. Elkins, W.Va., Jan. 6, 1932; s. Eston H. and Kathryn (Wyatt) C.; m. Jacqueline Smith, Aug. 22, 1954; children—Pamela Ann, Douglas Mark, Christopher Scott, Jeffrey Michael. B.A. with honors, W.Va. U., 1952, B.S., 1953; M.D., Med. Coll. Va., 1955; M.S., U. Iowa, 1960. Diplomate Am. Bd. Orthopedic Surgeons (examiner 1968-70). Orthopedic surgeon U.S. Naval Hosp., Pensacola, Fla., 1960-62; assoc. in orthopedics U. Iowa Coll. Medicine, Iowa City, 1962-65; asst. prof. orthopaedics U. Iowa Coll. Medicine, 1965-68, assoc. prof. orthopedics, 1968-71, prof. orthopedics, 1971—, chmn. orthopedics, 1973—; research fellow orthopedic surgery Johns Hopkins Hosp., Balt., 1964-65; exchange fellow to Britain for Am. Orthopedic Assn., 1969. Trustee Jour. Bone and Joint Surgeons, 1989—, chmn. 1993—. Trustee Nat. Easter Seals Research Found., 1977-81, chmn., 1979-81. Served to lt. comdr. USNR, 1960-62. Mem. Iowa, Johnson County Med. Socs., Orthopedic Rsch. Soc. (sec.-treas. 1970-73, pres. 1974-75), Am. Acad. Orthopedic Surgeons (Kappa Delta award for outstanding rsch. in orthopedics 1971), Canadian, Am. Orthopedic Assns., N.Y. Acad. Sci., Assn. Bone and Joint Surgeons, AMA, Am. Rheumatism Assn., Am. Acad. Cerebral Palsy, Am. Acad. Orthopedic Surgeons (chmn. exams. com. 1978-82, sec. 1982, 2d v.p. 1985-86, 1st v.p. 1986-87, pres. 1987-88, ortho residency rev. com. 1989-95, chmn. 1993-95). Home: 201 Ridgeview Ave Iowa City IA 52246-1625 Office: U Iowa Hosps & Clinics 450 Newton Rd Iowa City IA 52242

COOPER, RUBIN SEYMOUR, pediatric cardiologist; b. Bklyn., Mar. 22, 1946; s. Isaac Samuel Cooper and Frances Lillian Podzieba; m. Toby Ann Kaufman, Dec. 28, 1969; children: Shulie, Keli, Daniel, Michael. BA, N.Y. Med. Coll., ., 1967; MD, NYU, 1971. Diplomate Am. Bd. Pediatrics, Pediatric Cardiology. Instr. Health Sci. Ctr. SUNY, Bklyn., 1977-78; asst. prof. pediatrics SUNY Health Sci. Ctr., Bklyn., 1978-86, assoc. prof. pediatrics, 1986—, co-dir. div. pediatric cardiology; chief div. pediatric cardiology Brookdale Hosp. Med. Ctr., Bklyn., 1985-91; chief pediatric cardiology N. Shore U. Hosp., Manhasset, N.Y., 1991—; prof. clin. pediatrics Cornell Med. Coll.; cons. pediatric cardiology Meth. Hosp., Bklyn., 1981—, Coney Island Hosp., Maimonedes Hops., Bklyn., 1985—, Luth. Hosp., Bklyn., 1988—, Hungtington, Glencove, South Nassau Cmty. Jamaica, Good Samaritan Southside Hosp., 1994—. Pres. Holliswood (N.Y.) Jewish Ctr., 1988-91. Named Lieberman Memorial Fellow, Yeshiva U., 1967, Samuel Claussen Memorial Fellow, U. Rochester, N.Y., 1973-75. Fellow Am. Acad. Pediatrics, Am. Coll. Cardiology, N.Y. Acad. Sci., N.Y. Cardiology Soc.; mem. Pediatric Cardiology Soc. N.Y. (pres. 1989-90). Office: North Shore Univ Hosp 300 Community Dr Manhasset NY 11030-3801

COOPER, RUTH, nurse; b. Boston, Dec. 17, 1958; d. Saul and Sylvia (Singer) C.; children: Justin Nestor, Brittany Nestor, Abby Nestor. BS in Health Edn., Northeastern U., Boston, 1982; BSN, Simmons Coll., 1995. Health educator Neponset Health Ctr., Dorchester, Mass., 1982-84, family planner, 1984-87, health educator, 1987-90, HIV case mgr., 1990-95, HIV nurse, clin. coord., 1995—. Mem. Mass. Nurses Assn., Assn. of Nurses in AIDS Care. Home: 16 Nutty Hill Rd Hingham MA 02043

COOPER, SANFORD, nephrologist; b. Bklyn., Oct. 29, 1954; s. Charles Louis and Beverly (Insel) C.; m. Carol Beth Anekstein, July 30, 1978; 2 children. BS magna cum laude, Tufts U., 1976; MD, N.Y. Med. Coll., 1980. Intern in medicine L.I. Jewish Med. Ctr., New Hyde Park, N.Y., 1980-81, resident in internal medicine, 1981-83; fellow in nephrology Mt. Sinai Med. Ctr., N.Y.C., 1983-85; pvt. practice The Nephrology Group, West Orange, N.J., 1985—; attending nephrologist Newark Beth Israel Med. Ctr., 1985—; chief hemodialysis Christ Hosp., Jersey city, 1990—, dir. nutrition support group, 1991—; lectr. Lupus Support Group, Jersey City, 1990, 95, Christ Hosp. Grand Rounds, 1995. Mem. AMA (Physician Recognition award 1994), N.J. Med. Soc., Tau Beta Pi. Office: The Nephrology Group 111 Northfield Ave West Orange NJ 07052

COOPER, SIGNE SKOTT, retired nurse educator; b. Clinton County, Iowa, Jan. 29, 1921; d. Hans Edward and Clara Belle (Steen) Skott. BS, U. Wis., 1948; MEd, U. Minn., 1955. Head nurse U. Wis. Hosp., Madison, 1946-48; instr. U. Wis. Sch. Nursing, Madison, 1948-51, asst. prof., 1952-57, assoc. prof., 1957-62; prof., assoc. dean U. Wis. Sch. Nursing, 1948-83, prof. emeritus, 1983—; prof. U. Wis. Extension, 1955-83. Contbg. author: American Nursing: A Biographical Dictionary, Vol. 1, 1988, Vol. 2, 1992; contbr. articles to profl. jours. 1st Lt. U.S. Army Nurse Corps, 1943-46. Recipient NLN Linda Richards award, ANA Honorary Recognition award, Adult Edn. Assn. Pioneer award; named Fellow Am. Acad. Nursing. Mem. ANA, Am. Assn. for History Nursing, Wis. Nurses Assn. (pres.).

COOPER, SUZANE, physician; b. Phila., Oct. 12, 1954; d. Entriken E. Ruth. BS in medical tech., BA in biology, U. Pa., 1976; MD, Temple Univ., 1980. Diplomate Am. Bd. Anesthesiology. Asst. prof. anesthesia Temple Univ. Hosp., Phila., 1986-91, assoc. prof. anesthesia, 1991-93; dir. of anesthesia Citizens Bapt. Medical Ctr., Talladega, Ala., 1993—; v.p. med. staff Citizens Bapt. Medical, 1995, chief staff, 1996. Named Outstanding New Med. Dir. Premier Anesthesiology, 1994, Woodbridge Teaching award Temple U., 1988. Mem. Talladega County Medical Soc. (pres. 1996). Office: Citizens Bapt Medical Ctr Anesthesiology dept 604 Stone Ave Talladega AL 35160

COOPER, TODD YOUNG, medical technologist; b. San Antonio, Dec. 9, 1961; s. Edward Young and Georgette Dwanelle (Lackey) C.; m. Debra Flynt, July 13, 1990; children: Alexander Young, Aaron William. BS in Med. Technology, U. Tex. San Antonio, 1984. Med. technologist Northeast Bapt. Hosp., San Antonio, 1984-86; asst. supr. lab. Southwest Immunodiagnostics, San Antonio, 1986-92; asst. dir. Histocompatibility Lab. Stewart Regional Blood Ctr., Tyler, Tex., 1992-96; supr. tissue antigen lab. U. Tex. Med. Br., Galveston, 1996—; med. technologist Immuno-D, Inc., San Antonio, 1988-92; adj. faculty U. Tex. Tyler, 1995-96. Contbr. articles to profl. jours. Coach Tyler Soccer Assn., 1995-96. Mem. Am. Soc. Clin. Pathologists (cert.), Am. Soc. Histocompatibility and Immunogenetics (by-laws com. 1994—), Am. Soc. Clin. Lab. Sci. (Tex. treas. dist XI 1995-96), East Tex. Organ Donation Awareness Group (sec. 1995). Home: 17702 Heritage Cove Dr Webster TX 77598 Office: U Tex Med Br Tissue Antigen Lab 301 University Blvd # 9140 Galveston TX 77550

COOPER, TOM SMYTHE, ophthalmologist; b. Memphis, Mar. 31, 1944; s. Tom Smythe and Maggie Sherman (Taylor) C.; m. Marjorie Allyne Nix, Sept. 20, 1970; children: Tom, John, Jean. BS, U. Miss., Oxford, 1966; MD, U. Miss., Jackson, 1969. Diplomate Am. Bd. Ophthalmology. Intern Bapt. Hosp., Memphis, 1969-70; resident in ophthalmology U. Tenn., Memphis, 1974-76; pvt. practice Cooper-Pang Eye Clinic, Clarksdale, Miss., 1976—. Capt. USAF, 1970-72. Mem. Rotary Club (bd. dirs.). Episcopalian. Office: Cooper-Pang Eye Clinic 561 Medical Dr Clarksdale MS 38614

COOPER, WILLIAM ALLEN, JR., audiologist; b. Detroit, Aug. 16, 1932; s. William Allen and Ida Louise (Ford) C.; m. Auguste Ingrid Schneider, Oct. 5, 1957; children: Ingrid Louise, Robert William, James Allen. Student, Adrian Coll., 1950-52; BS, Wayne State U., 1957; PhD, Okla. U., 1964. Chief audiology VA Hosp., Oklahoma City, 1963-71; asst. prof. U. Okla., Oklahoma City, 1964-71; assoc. prof. Purdue U., West Lafayette, Ind., 1971-81; prof. U. S.C., Columbia, 1981—, chair dept. speech pathology and audiology, 1981-83, 96—; vis. fellow Inst. Sound & Vibration Rsch., Southampton, U.K., 1979. Contbr. articles to profl. jours. Chmn. bd. dirs. Unitarian Fellowship, Lafayette, Ind., 1975; bd. dirs. Unitarian Ch., Oklahoma City, 1969-70, Columbia, S.C., 1990-91. With U.S. Army, 1954-56, Germany. Am. Speech and Hearing Assn. fellow, 1978; recipient Honors of Assn. award S.C. Speech and Hearing Assn., 1989. Fellow Am. Acad. Audiology; mem. AAAS, Internat. Soc. Audiology, Am. Auditory Soc. Unitarian. Home: 6503 Christie Rd Columbia SC 29209-2049

COOPER, WILLIAM CLARK, physician; b. Manila, P.I., June 22, 1912 (father Am. citizen); s. Wibb Earl and Pearl (Herron) C.; MD, U. Va., 1934; MPH magna cum laude, Harvard U., 1958; m. Ethel Katherine Sicha, May 1, 1937; children: Jane Willoughby, William Clark, David Jeremy, Robert Lawrence. Intern, asst. resident U. Hosps., Cleve., 1934-37; commd. asst. surgeon USPHS, 1940, advanced through grades to med. dir., 1952; chief occupational health Field Hqrs., Cin., 1952-57; mem. staff div. occupational health USPHS, Washington, 1957-62, chief div. occupational health, 1962-63; ret., 1963; rsch. physician, prof. occupational health in residence Sch. Pub. Health, U. Calif.-Berkeley, 1963-72; med. cons. AEC, 1964-73; sec.-treas. Tabershaw-Cooper Asso., Inc., 1972-73, v.p., sci. dir., 1973-74; v.p. Equitable Environ. Health Inc., 1974-77; cons. occupational medicine, 1977-94. Served to 1st lt. M.C., U.S. Army, 1937-40. Diplomate Am. Bd. Internal Medicine, Am. Bd. Preventive Medicine, Am. Bd. Indsl. Hygiene. Fellow AAAS, Am. Pub. Health Assn., Am. Coll. Chest Physicians, Am. Coll. Occupational Medicine, Royal Soc. Medicine (London); mem. Internat. Commn. on Occupational Health, Western Occupational Med. Assn., Am. Indsl. Hygiene Assn., Cosmos Club. Contbr. articles to profl. jours. Home: 8315 Terrace Dr El Cerrito CA 94530-3060

COOPER-LEWTER, NICHOLAS CHARLES, psychotherapist, educator, minister; b. Washington, June 25, 1948; s. Ernest Charles and Constance (Hoage) Cooper; m. Marcia Jean Wyatt; children: Michelle, Sonia, Sean, Nicholas. BA, Ashland U., 1970; MSW, U. Minn., 1976; PhD, Calif. Coast U., 1988; LHD, Treamer Sch. Religion, 1976. Lic. marriage family therapist, Minn., marriage family child counselor, Calif. Rsch. specialist Ctr. Youth Devel. and Rsch. U. Minn., St. Paul, 1972-73; group worker Hallie Q Brown MLK Ctr., St. Paul, 1973-74; teaching asst. Sch. Social Work, U. Minn., St. Paul, 1974-75; field investigator, rep. City of St. Paul Human Right Dept., 1974; owner, dir. Cooper-Lewter Cons., Minn., Calif., 1978—, C.R.A.V.E. Christ Counseling Ctrs., Minn., Calif., 1984—; sr. pastor New Garden of Gethsemane B.C., L.A., 1985-90; founder, chief exec. officer C.R.A.V.E. Christ Ministries, St. Paul, 1987—; assoc. minister New Hope Bapt. Ch., St. Paul, 1990-93; assoc. prof. Bethel Coll. and Sem., St. Paul, 1990-95, coord. McKnight Found. cultural diversity grant, 1991-95; founder, CEO Cooper-Lewter Rites of Passage, Inc., St. Paul, 1995—; founder, pastor, CEO Committed by Choice Ministries, Inc., Mpls., 1995—; consulting agt. Met. Protection Bur., St. Paul, 1993—. Co-author: Soul Theology: Heart of American Black Culture, 1986. Mem. NAACP, Nat. Assn. of Social Workers, Acad. Cert. Social Workers, Am. Acad. Med. Hypnoanalysts (cert.), Rotary Internat., Omega Psi Phi (founder Xi Theta chpt.).

COOPERSMITH, BERNARD IRA, obstetrician, gynecologist, educator; b. Chgo., Oct. 19, 1914; s. Morris and Anna (Shulder) C.; m. Beatrice Klass, May 26, 1940; children: Carol, Cathie. BS cum laude, U. Ill., 1936, MD cum laude, 1938. Diplomate Am. Bd. Ob-Gyn. Intern Michael Reese Hosp., Chgo., 1938-39, resident in ob-gyn., 1939-42; pvt. practice medicine specializing in ob-gyn. Chgo., 1942—; mem. staff Prentice Women's Hosp. of Northwestern Meml. Hosp., Michael Reese Hosp., Mt. Sinai Hosp., Chgo. Maternity Ctr.; asst. prof. ob-gyn Northwestern U. Med. Sch., Chgo., 1948—. Contbr. articles to profl jours. Pres. Barren Found. Chgo., 1971-73. Fellow ACS; mem. AMA, Ill. Med. Soc., Chgo. Med. Soc., Chgo. Gynecol. Soc., Cen. Assn. Ob-Gyn, Am. Coll. Ob-Gyn, Alpha Omega Alpha. Jewish. Clubs: Bryn Mawr Country, Carleton. Home: 1110 N Lake Shore Dr Chicago IL 60611-1054 Office: 680 N Lake Shore Dr Ste 1030 Chicago IL 60611-4402

COOPERSMITH, SEYMOUR EDWARD, psychoanalyst; b. Boston, June 19, 1931; s. Leon and Bella (Winokur) C.; m. Valerie Lynn Pinhas, June 5, 1988; 1 child, Andria Bari. BA, Bates Coll., 1953; MA, New Sch. for Social Rsch., 1965; EdD, Columbia U., 1984. Cert. psychoanalyst. Pvt. practice N.Y.C. Pres. cooperative 257 Central Park West, N.Y.C., 1994—; bd. dirs. Univ. Gardens, Great Neck, N.Y., 1995—. With U.S. Army, 1956-58. Mem. Nat. Psychol. Assn. for Psychoanalysts (bd. dirs. 1974—, pres. 1980-84, 90-94, bd. dirs. tng. inst. 1974—, pres. tng. inst. 1980-84, Past Pres. award 1988), Coun. Psychoanalytic Psychotherapists (pres. 1985-87, Past Pres. award 1987). Home: 10 Sussex Rd Great Neck NY 11020 Office: 257 Central Park West Apt 11-C New York NY 10024

COOPERSTEIN, SHERWIN JEROME, medical educator; b. N.Y.C., Sept. 14, 1923; s. Joseph and Bessie (Berger) C.; m. Alice Ruth Peskin, June 1, 1947; children—Rhonda Ann, Lawrence Alan. B.S., Coll. City N.Y., 1943; D.D.S., N.Y. U., 1948; Ph.D. in Anatomy, Western Res. U., 1951. Instr. biology Coll. City N.Y., 1943, 46-48; research asso. physiology N.Y. U., 1946-48; instr. anatomy Western Res. U., 1948-49, fellow anatomy, 1949-51, sr. instr., 1951-52, asst. prof. anatomy, 1952-55, assoc. prof., 1955-64, asst. dean, 1957-64; prof., head dept. anatomy U. Conn. Schs. Medicine and Dental Medicine, Farmington, 1964-92, prof. emeritus, acting head dept., 1992-94; prof. emeritus, 1994—; Mem. adv. panel on med. student research NSF, 1960-61; mem. anatomical scis. tng. com. Nat. Inst. Gen. Med. Scis., 1966-70; mem. spl. study sect. on diabetes centers NIH, 1973-75, mem. ad hoc study sect. on research tng. grants in systems and integrative biology, 1977; mem. adv. panel on research personnel needs in basic biomed. sci. Nat. Acad. Scis./NRC, 1976-83. Contbr. articles profl. jours.; editorial adviser: Diabetes Lit. Index, 1966-79. Served with AUS, 1943-44. Mem. AAAS, Am. Chem. Soc., Marine Biol. Lab., Am. Assn. Anatomists, Am. Soc Biol. Chemists, Am. Diabetes Assn., Sigma Xi. Home: 10 Hillsboro Dr West Hartford CT 06107-1011 Office: U Conn Health Ctr Farmington Ave Farmington CT 06030

COOVERT, DALE LEE, psychologist; b. Dayton, Ohio, Aug. 20, 1948; s. Harold E. and Rita (Baeder) C.; m. Lynn D. Coovert, June 30, 1989; children: Brigitte, Nicole. BA with hons., Eckerd Coll., St. Petersburg, Fla., 1984; MA, U. S. Fla., Tampa, 1987; PhD, U. S. Fla., 1989. Lic. psychologist, Fla., 1991. Psychologist Fla. Mental Health Inst., Tampa, 1989—, chief of profl. staff, 1994—; program dir. clin. psychology Sch. Profl. Psychology U. Sarasota, Fla., 1995—; adj. prof. psychology Eckerd Coll., 1987—. Contbr. articles to profl. jours. U. S. Fla. grad. fellow, 1984. Mem. APA, Fla. Psychol. Assn., Mensa, Sigma Xi (Disting. PhD Rschr. 1988). Office: U Sarasota Sch Profl Psychology 410 Ware Blvd Ste 300 Tampa FL 33619

COPANS, STUART ALAN, psychiatrist, cartoonist; b. Springfield, Mass., Feb. 16, 1943; s. Lawrence William and Rosaline (Davidoff) C.; m. Mary Omer Webb, Dec. 9, 1972; children: Laurie, Roy, Jonathan, Benjamin. AB magna cum laude, Harvard U., 1964; MD, Stanford U., 1969. Diplomate Am. Bd. Psychiatry and Neurology; bd. cert in gen. psychiatry and child and adolescent psychiatry. Intern U. Vt. Med. Ctr. Hosps., 1969-70, resident in neurology, 1970-71; resident in psychiatry George Wash. U. Hosp., 1973-74; resident in psychiatry Mary Hitchcock Hosp., Darmouth, Vt., 1976-77, fellow in child psychiatry, 1974-76; asst. prof. psychiatry Dartmouth Med. Sch., Hanover, N.H., 1976-85, assoc. prof., 1985—; med. dir. adolescent alcohol and drug abuse treatment divsn. Brattleboro (Vt.) Retreat, 1985-92, interim med. dir., 1988-90, divsn. dir. adolescent divsn., 1992-94; chmn. New Eng. Children's Mental Health Task Force, 1982-83. Co-author: Who's the Patient Here, 1978, Baseball Fever, 1991, Twelve Jewish Steps to Recovery, 1991, Smart Moves: Your Guide Through the Emotional Maze of Relocation, 1996; editor: Home Health Handbook, 1970; illustrator: How to Avoid the Evil Eye, 1985, Loosening the Grip, 1978, 83, 87, 91, 95, Understanding Alcohol, 1992. Mem. Brattleboro Town Meeting, 1982—; bd. dirs. Brooks Meml. Libr., Brattleboro, 1984-95, Brattleboro Mus. and Art Ctr., 1996—; Surgeon USPHS, 1974-76. Recipient Henry Kempe award Nat. Conf. on Child Abuse and Neglect, 1978, award for brochure Nat. Assn. Pvt. Psychiat. Hosps., 1980. Fellow Am. Psychiat. Assn. (mem. task force on rural psychiatry 1995—), Am. Acad. Child and Adolescent Psychiatry (com. chmn. 1983-86); mem. New Eng. Coun. Child Psychiatry (bd. dirs. 1987-90), Vt. Assn. Child and Adolescent Psychiatry (founding mem., 1st pres.), Vt. Pataphys. Assn., Harvard Club Vt., Stanford Club Vt., Graphic Artist's Guild, Nat. Cartoonist's Soc., Nat. Writer's Union, Guild Am. Papercutters. Home: 44 Putney Rd Brattleboro VT 05301-2944 Office: Brattleboro Retreat 75 Linden St Brattleboro VT 05301-4807

COPE, WINSTON THOMAS, ophthalmologist; b. St. Petersburg, Fla., Feb. 21, 1947; s. Paul Thomas and Ruth (Winston) C.; m. Margaret MacArthur Clark, Mar. 18, 1978; children: David, Christine. BA in Chemistry, Oberlin Coll., 1968; MD, U. Fla., 1972. Intern U. Miami (Fla.), 1972-73; resident Duke U., Durham, N.C., 1975-78; ophthalmologist pvt. practice, St. Petersburg, Fla., 1979—; clin. asst. prof. U. South Fla., 1992—; adv. coun. Tampa Bay Rsch. Inst., St. Petersburg, 1992—; med. adv. com. Morton Plant East Lake, Palm Harbor, Fla., 1995—; presenter in field. Contbr. articles to profl. jours. Lt. USN, 1973-75. Fellow Am. Acad. Ophthalmology, Am. Coll. Surgeons. Office: Advanced Refractive Surgery 5666 Seminole Blvd Seminole FL 34642

COPELAND, ADRIAN DENNIS, psychiatrist; b. N.Y.C., Aug. 30, 1928; s. Leslie and Belle (Tockerman) C.; m. Elise Lilienthal (div. 1983; dec.); children: Loren, Ron, Graham, Daniel. BA, NYU, 1949; MD, Med. U. Geneva, Switzerland, 1956; MS, Temple U., 1960. Intern Jersey City Med. Ctr., 1956-57; resident dept. psychiatry Temple U. Med. Sch., Phila., 1957-60, assoc. prof., 1969-72; clin. prof. Thomas Jefferson Med. Sch., Phila., 1972—; pvt. practice Phila., 1960—; med. dir. St. Francis Hosp. for Boys, Phila., 1986—; med. dir. St. Gabriel's System Outpatient Svcs., 1993. Author: Textbook of Adolescent Psychopathology and Treatment, 1974, Childhood Symptoms of Maladjustment: 1993, Adolescent Psychiatry, 1993. Fellow Am. Psychiat. Assn., Am. Soc. Adolescent Psychiatry (mem. editorial bd.), Phila. Coll. Physicians; mem. Union League Phila., Rotary, Psi Chi, Sigma Xi. Office: Warwick Hotel 1200 Locust St Ste 1922 Philadelphia PA 19107-5605

COPELAND, BRADLEY ELLSWORTH, physician; b. Pitts., Sept. 8, 1921; s. Warren Ellsworth and Josephine May (Bradley) C.; m. Jacqueline Jamieson, Feb. 11, 1982; children: Margaret Ann, Priscilla Jean. BS, Dartmouth Coll., 1943; MD, U. Pa., 1945. Diplomate Am. Bd. Pathology. Pathologist to dir. pathology New Eng. Deaconess Hosp., Boston, 1950-79; pathologist to dir. pathology New Eng. Bapt. Hosp., Boston, 1950-79, chief of staff, 1975-78; inst. to assoc. prof. Harvard Med. Sch., Boston, 1951-79; prof. pathology U. Cin., 1979-91, prof. pathology emeritus, 1991—; chmn. stds. com. Coll. of Am. Pathologists, Chgo., 1960-68; chmn. coun. on chemistry, Am. Soc. Clin. Pathologists, 1956-62; chmn. commn. on world stds, World Assn. of Pathology Socs., Chgo., 1959-74. Author: (book) Quality Control in Clinical Chemistry, 1956. Lt. (j.g.) USN, 1945-48. Office: U Cin Hosp 256 Eden Ave Cincinnati OH 45267

COPELAND, EDWARD MEADORS, III, surgery educator; b. Augusta, Ga., Oct. 6, 1937; s. Edward Meadors Jr. and Louise (Leggitt) C.; m. Martha Patterson, Ar. 24, 1964; children: Edward Meadors IV, Catherine Leggit. BA, Duke U., 1959; MD, Cornell U., 1963. Diplomate Am. Bd. Surgery (bd. dirs. 1983-91, chmn. 1990-91). Intern in surgery U. Pa. Hosp., Phila., 1963-64, resident in gen. surgery, 1964-69; resident surg. oncology Anderson Hosp., Houston, 1971-72; asst. prof. to prof. U. Tex. Med. Sch., Houston, 1972-82, U. Tex. M.D. Anderson Hosp. and Tumor Inst., Houston, 1972-82; prof., chmn. dept. U. Fla. Coll. Medicine, Gainesville, 1982—; project dir. Nat. Large Bowel Cancer Project, Nat. Cancer Inst., Houston, 1981-82. Bd. dirs. Sun Bank, Gainesville, 1987—. Maj. U.S. Army, 1969-71, Vietnam. Decorated Bronze Star Rep. Vietnam; recipient Seale Harris award So. Med. Assn., 1984. Disting. Alumnus award M.D. Anderson Hosp. and Tumor Inst., 1987. Fellow Am. Surg. Assn., So. Surg. Assn.; mem. ACS, Assn. for Acad. Surgery (pres. 1978-79), Soc. Univ. Surgeons, Gainesville Golf and Country Club. Home: 2605 NW 7th Rd Gainesville FL 32607-2600 Office: Univ Fla Coll Medicine Dept of Surgery PO Box 100286 Gainesville FL 32610-0286*

COPELAND, LOIS JACQUELINE (MRS. RICHARD A. SPERLING), physician; b. Malden, Mass., Sept. 16, 1943; d. Arnold Alan and Ann (Goldfarb) C.; BA magna cum laude with distinction in all subjects, Cornell U., 1964, MD, 1968; m. Richard A. Sperling, June 7, 1970; children: Mark Edward, Larissa Lynn, Lauren Anne, Lorraine Elizabeth. Intern N.Y. Hosp., N.Y.C., 1968-69, resident, 1969-70; resident Bellevue Hosp., NYU Med. Ctr., 1970-72; teaching asst. internal medicine NYU Med. Ctr., 1971—; attending physician Pascack Valley Hosp., Westwood, N.J., 1974—; courtesy staff Valley Hosp., Ridgewood, N.J., 1980—. Mem. secondary schs. com. Cornell U., 1978—; bd. dirs. Found. For Free Enterprise; steering com. physicians coun. Heritage Found., 1993—; pres. coun. Cornell Women, 1993-95. Mem. Bd. Assn. Am. Physicians and Surgeons, Assn. Am. Physicians and Surgeons (bd. dirs. 1991—, pres. 1995), Phi Beta Kappa, Phi Kappa Phi, Alpha Lambda Delta. Home: 25 Sparrowbush Rd Saddle River NJ 07458-1411 Office: 47 Central Ave Hillsdale NJ 07642-2118

COPELAND, ROBERT BODINE, internist, cardiologist; b. Arab, Ala., Jan. 24, 1938; s. Haden Paul and Jimmie Alice (Bodine) C.; m. Jenny Trammell, June 26, 1960; children: Robert Theodore, Haden McTieyre. BS, Auburn U., 1960; MD, U. Ala., Birmingham, 1963. Diplomate Am. Bd. Internal Medicine; cert. cardiovascular diseases and geriatrics. Intern then resident, clin. rsch. fellow in cardiology Mass. Gen. Hosp., Boston, 1963-67; physician Clark Holder Clinic, LaGrange, Ga., 1967-77; founder, dir. Ga. Heart Clinic, LaGrange, 1972—; founder, pres. So. Cardiopulmonary Assocs., LaGrange, 1977—; clin. prof. med. U. Ala., Birmingham, 1980—, Emory U., Atlanta, 1980—; bd. dirs. Nations Bank, La Grange; bd. govs. Am. Bd. Internal Med., Phila., 1980-86, Joint Commn. on Accreditation of Healthcare Orgns., Chgo., 1991—. Contbr. articles to profl. jours. Recipient Disting. Alumni award U. Ala., Birmingham, 1985. Fellow ACP (gov. Ga. chpt. 1987-91, master 1993, regent 1993), Am. Coll. Cardiology; mem. Am. Heart Assn. (pres. Ga. affiliate 1985-86), Nat. Acad. Sci., Inst. of Medicine. Office: 1551 Doctors Dr Lagrange GA 30240

COPEMAN, HERBERT ARTHUR, endocrinologist; b. Brisbane, Queensland, Australia, Sept. 24, 1923; s. Arthur Bradby and Ellen (Briggs) C.; m. Margaret Jean Hill, Nov. 29, 1947; children: Richard, Ann, Peter, Andrew. M.B., B.S., U. Queensland, 1951. Resident Royal Brisbane Hosp., 1952-53, registrar, 1954-56, endocrinologist, 1957-74; coord. postgrad. studies U. Western Australia, Royal Perth Hosp., 1975-88; hon. rsch. fellow U. Western Australia, Perth, 1989—; cons. physician and endocrinologist Albany Regional Hosp., 1989-92; ret., 1992; rschr., writer on endocrine aspects of arterial disease. Author: Let Us Not Forget to Remember: Reminiscences of an Australian World War, 1995. Australian postgrad. fedn. in medicine fellow and patron, 1994. Fellow Royal Australasian Coll. Physicians. Home: 36 Mermaid Ave, Emu Point 6330, Australia Office: 102 Aberdeen St, Albany 6330, Australia

COPLEY, WILLIAM MCKINLEY, III, mental health counselor, human relations consulting company executive; b. Orlando, Fla., July 10, 1943; s. William McKinley Jr. and Dorothy (Rathbun) C.; m. Suzanne Howard Montgomery, June 14, 1985. BA, East Carolina U., 1966; MA, Ball State U., 1971; AS, Fla. Community Coll., 1976. Nat. cert. counselor. Dir. aftercare Univ. Hosp., Jacksonville, Fla., 1972-80; exec. dir. Orange County Crisis Unit, Orlando, 1980-81, Hillcrest House, Inc., Orlando, 1981-83; dir. CSP Mental Health Svcs. Orange County, Orlando, 1983-85; mng. ptnr. Montgomery, Copley & Assocs. Inc., Jacksonville, 1985—. Mem. Jacksonville Cmty. Coun., 1986—, Leadership Jacksonville, 1987-88; bd. dirs. Vol. Jacksonville, 1988-90; mem. citizens adv. com. Long-Range Corridor/Park and Ride study Jacksonville Transp. Authority, 1990; mem. Youth Leadership Jacksonville selection com., 1991, 93. With U.S. Army, 1967-70. Mem. ACA, Mental Health Assn. (bd. dirs. 1989, chmn. adv. com., treas. 1991), Fla. Counseling Assn. Republican. Episcopalian. Office: Montgomery Copley & Assocs Inc 1812 Atlantic Blvd Jacksonville FL 32207-3404

COPMAN, LOUIS, radiologist; b. Phila., Jan. 17, 1934; s. Jacob and Eve (Snyder) C.; m. Avera Schuster, June 8, 1958; children: Mark, Linda. BA, U. Pa., 1955, MD, 1959. Diplomate Am. Bd. Radiology; Nat. Bd. Med. Examiners. Commd. ensign Med. Corps USN, 1958; advanced through grades to capt. M.C. USN, 1975; ret.; asst. chief radiology dept. Naval Hosp., Pensacola, Fla., 1966-69; chief radiology dept. Doctors Hosp., Phila., 1969-73; radiologist Mercer Hosp. Ctr., Trenton, N.J., 1973-75; chmn. radiology dept. Naval Hosp., Phila., 1975-84; chief. radiology dept. Naval Med. Clinic, Pearl Harbor, Hawaii, 1984-89; pvt. practice radiologist Honolulu, 1989-92; cons. Radiology Services, Wilmington, Del., 1978-84, Yardley (Pa.) Radiology, 1979-84. Author: The Cuckold, 1974. Recipient Albert Einstein award in Medicine, U. Pa., 1959. Mem. AMA, Assn. Mil. Surgeons of the U.S., Royal Soc. Medicine, Radiol. Soc. N.Am., Am. Coll. Radiology, Photographic Soc. Am., Sherlock Holmes Soc., Phi Beta Kappa, Alpha Omega Alpha. Home: PO Box 384767 Waikoloa HI 96738-4767 Office: 68-1771 Makanahele Pl Waikoloa HI 96738-4767

COPP, DOUGLAS HAROLD, physiologist, educator; b. Toronto, Jan. 16, 1915; s. Charles Joseph and Edith Mabel (O'Hara) C.; m. Winnifred A. Thompson, July 15, 1939; children: Mary Louise Copp Macdonald, Carolyn Ann Copp Malchy, Patricia Jane Copp Montpellier. B.A., U. Toronto, 1936, M.D., 1939, LL.D., 1970; Ph.D., U. Calif., Berkeley, 1943; LL.D., Queen's U., 1970; D.Sc., U. Ottawa, 1973, Acadia U., 1975, U. B.C., 1980. Instr., asst. prof. physiology U. Calif., Berkeley, 1943-50; prof., head dept. physiology U. B.C., Vancouver, 1950-80; pres. Nat. Cancer Inst. Can., 1968-70. Research and publs. in bone metabolism, phosphate depletion, calcium regulation in vertebrates. Decorated officer Order of Can., 1971, companion, 1980; recipient Gairdner Found. ann. award, 1967, Nicolas Andry award, 1968, Steindler award, 1974, Gold medal in sci. and engring. B.C. Sci. Coun., 1980, William F. Neuman award Am. Soc. Bone and Mineral Rsch., 1983, Disting. Svc. award Can. Soc. Endocrin. Metab., 1988. Fellow Royal Soc. Can. (Flavelle gold medal 1972, coun. 1973-75, 77-84, pres. acad. sci. 1978-81), Royal Soc. (London), Royal Coll. Physicians (Can.); mem. Can. Physiol. Soc. (pres. 1963-64), Faculty Assn. U. B.C. (pres. 1965-66), Sci. Coun. B.C., Can. Orthopedic Assn. (hon.), Deutsche Gesellschaft of Osteologie (hon.), Canadian Med. Hall of Fame (founding laureate 1994). Home: 4755 Belmont Ave, Vancouver, BC Canada V6T 1A8

COPPENS, THOMAS ADRIAAN, retired pharmaceutical manufacturing executive; b. Rotterdam, Netherlands, Feb. 2, 1923; came to U.S., 1927; s. Philip Adriaan and Evelyn (van Capelle) C.; m. Sylvia Helen Scofield, Feb. 26, 1944; children: Laura Kathryn, Carole Elizabeth, John Philip, Barbara Helen. Student, McGill U., 1941-43, Lafayette Coll., 1944; D LL (hon.), Inst. Applied Rsch., London, 1973. Internat. rep. Sharp & Dohme, Inc., Mediterranean area, 1946-52; mng. dir. Merck, Sharp & Dohme, Manila, 1952-57; v.p. Merck & Co., Inc., Rahway, N.J., 1957-77; pres. Merck, Sharp & Dohme, BV, Haarlem, Netherlands, 1977-82; cons. Merck & Co., Inc., Rahway, 1982-84; prin. Camelot Antiques, Cooperstown, N.Y., 1984-90. Contbr. articles to profl. publs. Sr. warden St. Andrews Episcopal Ch., Harrington Park, N.J., 1958-67; bd. dirs. Hubbard Farms, Walpole, N.H., 1975-77, Walden U., Naples, Fla., 1984—; trustee Naples Cmty. Hosp., 1988-94; mem. Collier County (Fla.) Emergency Med. Svcs. Adv. Coun., 1993-95. Decorated Purple Heart. Mem. Rotary (Paul Harris fellow), Am. C. of C. of Hague, Netherlands (bd. dirs. 1977-83). Home and Office: 6075 Pelican Bay Blvd Naples FL 34108

COPPERMAN, STUART MORTON, pediatrician; b. Bklyn., June 5, 1935; s. Irving and Anne (Reisfield) C.; m. Renee Stein, Aug. 17, 1958; children: Beth, Alan, Cara. B.A. cum laude, Bklyn. Coll., 1956; M.D., SUNY-Bklyn., 1960. Diplomate Am. Bd. Pediatrics. Rotating intern. L.I. Jewish Hosp., New Hyde Park, N.Y., 1960-61, resident in pediatrics, 1961-63; practice medicine specializing in pediatrics Merrick, N.Y., 1965—; mem. staff L.I. Jewish Hillside Med. Ctr., Schneider Children's Hosp., New Hyde Park, Nassau County Med. Ctr., East Meadow, Winthrop U. Hosp., Mineola, North Shore Univ. Hosp., Manhasset, Hempstead (N.Y.) Gen. Hosp.; clin. assoc. prof. pediatrics SUNY Med. Sch.-Stony Brook, 1972—; assoc. prof. clin. health studies Sch. Allied Health, 1977—; clin. instr. physicians asst. program Stony Brook Med. Ctr., 1972—; prof. pediatrics St. George's Med. Coll., St. Vincent, W.I., acting chmn. pediatrics, 1979-80; med. advisor Assn. Children with Downs Syndrome, 1971—; mem. com. for handicapped Bellmore Sch. Dist., 1976-86; mem. ad hoc com. on cmty. as sch. Merrick-Bellmore Schs., 1976-90; bd. dirs. L.I. Sch. Health Edn. Coalition; mem. Nassau County Sch. Health Edn. Commn., 1990-93; mem. ad hoc com. on prevention of birth defects March of Dimes; preceptor in pediat. Physicians Asst. Program; mem. doctor's adv. com. Shaare Zedek Hosp., Jerusalem, 1974—; med. cons. Matchbox Toys, 1985-88, Proctor & Gamble, 1988, Carnation Co., 1989-90, Disney Ednl. Svcs., 1990-95; cons., mem. spkrs. bur. N.Y. State Senate Com. Mental Hygiene, 1988—; mem. spkrs. bur. Lederle Labs., 1989—. Appearance TV shows on Downs Syndrome, learning disabilities, CPR, first aid, infant exercise programs, TV's effects on children, infectious disease, parent-infant bonding, prevention of cigarette smoking among children, 1972—, also on HealthLinks (Life Time TV), 1990-93; mem. editl. adv. bd. Jour. Assn. for Physician Assts., 1987—; editl. cons. Jour. Pediat. Mgmt., 1991—; contbr. articles to profl. jours.; contbr. chpt. to Textbook Pediat. Sports Medicine; developer Babycise (infant parent interactive program in video tape and book form), 1985; rschr. on hetacillin, 1966, pyridoxine effect on serotonin level and performance in children with Down's Syndrome, 1970-75, Alice in Wonderland syndrome as presenting sympton of infectious mononucleosis, 1966-77, on transmission of group A Beta hemolytic strep infection from pet reservoirs to children, 1963-81; med. editor Air Fair Mag., 1991-93, L.I. Parent Mag., 1985-93, L.I. Family Magazine, 1994-95. Mem. sch. bd. Temple Beth Am., Merrick, 1972-78, mem. exec. com., 1973-74, chmn. com. Israel and World Affairs, 1976-78, mem. sch. com., 1976-78, mem. ritual com., 1976-93; mem. N.Y. State Senate com. on mental hygiene, 1990—; mem. profl. adv. bd. So. Shore divsn. YM-YWHA; benefactor Merrick Libr., 1992—. With U.S. Army, 1963-65. Recipient Physician Recognition award AMA, 1966-96, testimonial dinner and plaque Assn. Children with Down Syndrome, 1972, Best Clin. Tchrs. of Pediat. award Nassau County Med. Ctr., 1981-82; named Merrick Profl. of Yr., 1994. Fellow Am. Acad. Pediatrics (chmn. com. TV effects on children1976—, nat. com. comm. and pub. info. 1984-85, media spokesperson 1988—, tobacco, alcohol & drug-free generation coord. 1988—, chmn. substance abuse com. 1992—, N.Y. state chmn. substance abuse com. 1992-94, managed care com. chpt. 2 1993-95), Internat. Coll. Pediatrics; mem. AMA, N.Y. State Med. Soc., Nassau County Med. Soc. (com. on mental health 1980—, project assist 1992—, Nassau Acad. Medicine Pub. Health com. 1991—, libr. com. 1993—, chmn. pediatric section 1995—), Nassau Pediatric Soc. (mem. exec. bd. 1972—, chmn. com. on mental health 1972-88, v.p. 1994-95, pres. 1995-96). A Non-Smoking Generation Internat. (organizer, med. dir. Am. divsn.), Am. Lung Assn., Nassau-Suffolk Lung Assn. (life mem., dir. 1982-84), Am. Physicians Fellowship for Israel Med. Assn., Assn. Children with Learning Disabilities (mem. profa Leche League, Latin Am. Parents Assn., L.I. Sch. Health Edn. Coun. (bd. dirs. 1989-92), Alpha Epsilon Pi (chancellor Phi Theta chpt. 1955-56), Phi Delta Epsilon (counsul Zeta chpt. 1960), B'nai Brith. Office: 3137 Hewlett Ave S Merrick NY 11566-5328

COPPOLECCHIA, ROSA, internist; b. Hoboken, N.J., Mar. 28, 1964; d. Sergio and Maria Corrada (Annese) C. BS in Biology, St. Peter's Coll., 1986; DO, UMDNJ-SOM, 1992. Diplomate Nat. Bd. Osteopathic Med. Examiners. Intern Union Hosp., U. Medicine and Dentistry of N.J., 1992-93; resident in internal medicine Overlook Hosp., Summit, N.J., 1993-96; resident in environ. and occupl. medicine UMDNJ-Robert Wood Johnson Med. Sch., Piscataway, N.J., 1996—. Mem. AMA, ACP (assoc.), Am. Coll. Occupl. and Environ. Medicine, Am. Osteo. Assn., N.J. Med. Soc. Home: 213 Clinston St Hoboken NJ 07030

COPPOLILLO, HENRY PETER, psychiatrist; b. Cervicati, Cosenza, Italy, July 27, 1926; s. Vincent Louis and Maria Giovanna (Chidichimo) C.; m. Ruthann Butler, June 6, 1962 (dec. Apr. 1993); children: Catherine, Peter, Robert. Student, U. Ill., 1943-44; MD, U. Rome, 1955. Lic. physician, Ill., Mich., Tenn., Colo.; diplomate Am. Bd. Psychiatry and Neurology. Intern Cook County Hosp., Chgo., 1955-56; resident U. Chgo. Clinics, Chgo., 1956-59; assoc. attending physician Michael Reese Hosp., Chgo., 1959-66; asst. prof. to prof. U. Mich., Ann Arbor, 1966-70; prof. psychiatry Vanderbilt U., Nashville, 1970-76, U. Colo. Med. Sch., Denver, 1976-85; pvt. practice specializing in psychiatry Englewood, Colo., 1985—; clin. instr. dept. psychology U. Colo., Boulder, 1985—, Denver U., 1985—. Author: Psychodynamic Psychotherapy of Children, 1987; contbr. articles to profl. jours. Mem. Nat. Assn. Christians & Jews. Named Tchr. of the Yr., Residents & Fellows Psychiatry U. Mich., 1971, Disting. Tchr., Child. Psychiatriy Fellows, U. Colo., 1985. Fellow Am. Psychiatric Assn., Am. Acad. Child and Adolescent Psychiatry.

COPPRIDGE, ALTON JAMES, urological surgeon; b. Roanoke, Va., Dec. 8, 1926; s. William Maurice Coppridge and Ferrie (Patterson) Coppridge Choate; m. Helen Allen Burnett, June 24, 1950; children: William Allen, Virginia Choate. BA, U. N.C., 1949; MD, U. Va., 1953. Diplomate Am. Bd. Urology. Intern N.C. Meml. Hosp., Chapel Hill, 1953-54; surg. resident State U. of Iowa Hosp., Iowa City, 1954-56; urology resident U. Mich., Ann Arbor, 1956-59; mem. Coppridge Urologic Group, P.A., Durham, N.C., 1959-89; dept. chmn. Durham County Gen. Hosp., 1978-84; asst. clin. prof. Duke Med. Ctr., Durham, 1970-89; clin. instr. U. N.C. Med. Sch., Chapel Hill, 1960-75. Contbr. articles to urologic lit. Served with U.S. Army, 1944-46; Japan. Mem. Am. Urol. Assn. (exec. com. Southeast sect. 1983-86), Durham-Orange Med. Soc. (pres. 1978), N.C. Med. Soc. (pres. sect. urology 1978), Carolina Urol. Soc. (pres. 1985), ACS. Democrat. Presbyterian. Clubs: Hope Valley Country (Durham); Safari Internat. (Tucson) (pres. N.C. chpt. 1979-80); Kiwanis of Tobaccoland (Durham). Avocations: hunting, shooting, farm work. Home: 3605 Rugby Rd Durham NC 27707-5456

COPULSKY, JOSEPH V., urologist; b. Bklyn., June 26, 1943; s. Nathaniel and Edith (Goldstein) C.; m. Maxine Schneier, Aug. 19, 1967; children: Erica, Dena, Nicole. AB, U. Vt., 1965, MD, 1970. Diplomate Am. Bd. Urology. Intern Beth Israel Med. Ctr., N.Y.C., 1970-71, resident in gen. surgery, 1971-72, resident in urology, 1972-76; pvt. practice, Boca Raton, Fla., 1976—; chief surgery Delray Cmty. Hosp., Delray Beach, Fla., 1981-83, pres. med. staff, 1983-85. Capt. USAR, 1970-76. Fellow ACS. Home: 7027 Ayrshire Ln Boca Raton FL 33496 Office: 899 Meadows Rd Ste 202 Boca Raton FL 33486

CORAN, ARNOLD GERALD, pediatrician, surgeon; b. Boston, Apr. 16, 1938; s. Charles and Ann (Cohen) C.; m. Susan Myra Williams, Nov. 17, 1960; children: Michael, David, Randi Beth. AB, Harvard U., 1959, MD, 1963. Diplomate Am. Bd. Surgery, Am. Bd. Thoracic Surgery, Am. Bd. Pediat. Surgery. Intern in surgery Peter Bent Brigham Hosp., Boston, 1963-64, resident in general and thoracic surgery, 1964-69; resident in pediatric surgery Children's Hosp., Boston, 1966-68; chief pediat. surgery, assoc. prof. surgery U. South Calif. Med. Sch., L.A., 1972-74; chief pediat. surgery, prof. surgery U. Mich., Ann Arbor, 1974—; surgeon in chief C.S. Mott Childrens Hosp., Ann Arbor, 1981—. Contbr. articles to profl. jours. Lt. comdr. USN, 1970-72. Home: 505 E Huron St # 802 Ann Arbor MI 48104 Office: CS Mott Childrens Hosp Rm F3970 Ann Arbor MI 48109-0245

CORAZZINI, JOHN GERALD, psychologist, counseling center executive, consultant; b. Boston, Dec. 15, 1938; s. Pasquale and Eileen Cecelia (Burke) C.; m. Agnes Elizabeth Kilduff, Mar. 20, 1971; children: Seth Aaron, Jeremy Luke. AB, St. Johns Sem., 1961; S.T.B., Gregorian U., 1963; PhD, U. Notre Dame, 1974. Lic. clin. psychologist, Va.; lic. psychologist, Va. Sr. staff psychologist Colo. State U., Ft. Collins, 1974-78; asst. dir. Univ. Counseling Ctr., Colo. State U., Fort Collins, 1978-80; dir. Univ. Counseling Svcs., Va. Commonwealth U., Richmond, 1980—, assoc. prof. dept. psychology, 1980-88, prof., 1988—; cons. Midlothian, Va., 1981—; mem. Va. Bd. Psychology, vice-chmn., 1994-95, chmn., 1995-96. Contbr. articles to profl. jours. 2d v.p. PTA, Midlothian, 1984-86. Fellow Am. Psychol. Assn.; mem. Va. Psychol. Assn. Home: 13430 Glendower Rd Midlothian VA 23113-3807 Office: Va Commonwealth U Univ Counseling Svcs 907 Floyd Ave Rm 225 Richmond VA 23284-9026

CORBEN, ROBERTA JOY, physical therapist; b. Rockaway, N.Y.; d. Henry Aaron and Jeanne (London) C. BS, NYU, 1963; MS, L.I. U., 1974. Cert. phys. therapist. Staff phys. therapist Hosp. for Joint Diseases, N.Y.C., 1963-67, Nacka (Sweden) Sjukhuset, 1967-68; coord. rehab. medicine Booth Meml. Med. Ctr., Flushing, N.Y., 1968-78; dir. phys. therapy Long Beach (N.Y.) Meml. Hosp. and Nursing Home, 1979-82; cons., supr. Vis. Nurse Svc., Flushing, 1982—; pvt. practice phys. therapist Queens, N.Y., 1982—; lectr. various orgns., N.Y., 1968—; developer, therapist Multiple Sclerosis Patients, Flushing, 1979-81; examiner, mem. N.Y. State Bd. Examiners, N.Y., 1985-91. Mem. Am. Arbitration Assn. (comml. panel mem. 1980—), Am. Congress Rehab. Assn., Am. Phys. Therapy Assn. (sect. on geriatrics, del. N.Y. chpt., ho. of dels. 1973-76, rec. sec. Greater N.Y. dist. 1974-77, chmn. nominating com. 1977, chmn. prgram com. N.Y. chpt. 1985). Home and Office: 270-14L Grand Central Pkwy Floral Park NY 11005

CORBET, LORRAINE, hospital administration consultant; b. June 23; d. Gil and Karen Chassie; m. Michael Corbet; children: Karen, Michael. BS, Harvard, MBA. Admin. Kings County Hosp., Labrador, Pa., dir. admin.; dir. admin. Mercy Pvt. Hosp. and Nursing Home, Reading, Pa.; cons. Blue Cross, Blue Shield Pa., Phila.; chief admin. officer Phila. Meml. Hosp., 1986—. Office: Meml Hosp Admin Offices 2322 Werik Plaza Ste 22 Phila PA 19104

CORBETT, JAMES JOHN, neurologist, neuroophthalmologist; b. Chgo., July 2, 1940; s. Maxwell Melville and Rose Marie (Evanchak) C.; m. Joyce Roberta Zymali, Dec. 29, 1962; children: John Christopher, Jill Stephanie, Jennifer Sarah. BA in Biology, Brown U., 1962; MD, Chgo. Med. Sch., 1966. Diplomate Am. Bd. Neurology and Psychiatry. Intern. and resident R.I. Hosp., Providence, 1966-68; resident in neurology Univ. Hosps Cleve., 1968-71; instr., clin. asst. prof. Jefferson Med. Coll., Phila., 1973-77; pvt. practice Phila., 1973-77; asst. prof. neurology U. Iowa, Iowa City, 1977-80, assoc. prof., 1980-85, prof. neurology and ophthalmology, 1985-90; prof. and chmn. dept. neurology, prof. ophthamology U. Miss., Jackson, 1991—. Lt. comdr. M.C., USNR, 1971-73. Fellow Am. Neurol. Assn., Am. Acad. Neurology; mem. N.Am. Neuroophthalmology Soc. (v.p 1990-93), Alpha Omega Alpha. Democrat. Episcopalian. Home: 1402 Bay Vista Brandon MS 39042-8654 Office: UMC 2500 N State St Jackson MS 39216-4505

CORBETT, RICHARD EDWARD, psychotherapist; b. Newton, Mass., Jan. 6, 1949; s. Edward J. and Ardrith A. (Cossaboom) C. BA in Psychology, Northeastern U., 1974; MA in Counseling Psychology, Assumption Coll., Worcester, Mass., 1977. Lic. mental health counselor; nat. cert. addictions counselor; masters addiction counselor; cert. alcohol and drug abuse counselor. Mental health worker Framingham (Mass.) Union Hosp., 1974-78; prin. psychologist Wrentham (Mass.) State Sch., 1978-81; psychotherapist Marsalin Inst., Holliston, Mass., 1981-84; coord. dual diagnosis program Arbor Hosp., Boston, 1984-87; coord. outpatient addictions svcs. New Eng. Meml. Hosp., Stoneham, Mass., 1987-92; clinician Boston ASAP, 1992-93; addiction svcs. program coord. Emerson Hosp., Concord, Mass., 1993—; mem. adv. coun. Middlesex County Driving Under the Influence of Liquor Program, Waltham, Mass., 1990-92. Mem. Nat. Assn. Alcoholism and Drug Abuse Counselors, Mass. Assn. Alcoholism Counselors, Mass. Mental Health Counselors Assn. Office: Emerson Hosp PO Box 9120 Concord MA 01742-9120

CORBETT, SIOBHAN AIDEN, surgeon; b. Aug. 11, 1959. Diplomate Am. Bd. Surgery. Postdoctoral fellow Princeton (N.J.) U. Recipient Clin. Sci. award Am. Heart Assn., 1995-96.

CORBIN, KENDALL BROOKS, physician, scientist; b. Oak Park, Ill., Dec. 31, 1907; s. William Sherman and Emma (Heacock) C.; m. Eryl Portia Wallace, Jan. 2, 1932; children: Kendall Wallace, Edwin Malcolm. Student, UCLA, 1926-29; AB cum laude, Stanford, 1931, MD, 1935. Diplomate: Am. Bd. Psychiatry and Neurology. Instr. anatomy Stanford, 1934-38; NRC fellow in medicine Neurology Inst., Northwestern U., 1937-38; assoc. prof. anatomy Tenn. U., then prof. and chief div. anatomy, 1938-46, in charge neurology, 1943-46; prof. neurology Mayo Found., Minn. U., and; cons. in neurology Mayo Clinic, 1946-72, head sect. neurology, 1956-63, sr. cons. neurology, 1963-72, pres. staff, 1968; asso. dir. Mayo Found. for Med. Edn. and Research, Grad. Sch. of U. Minn., 1950-54; chmn. bd. devel. Mayo Found., 1969-73, emeritus, 1973—; mem. residency rev. com., neurology and psychiatry, 1952-56. Contbr. articles on nervous system to med. jours., chpts. to med. books. Chmn. Rochester Com. Higher Edn., 1955-60; bd. dirs. United Fund Rochester, 1962-68. Mem. Am. Neurol. Assn., Am. Acad. Neurology, A.M.A., Am. Assn. Anatomists, Am. Physiol. Soc., Soc. Exptl. Biology and Medicine, Minn. Med. Assn., Central Neuropsychiat. Assn., Minn. Soc. Neurology and Psychiatry, Phi Beta Kappa, Sigma Xi, Alpha Omega Alpha. Home: 211 2nd St NW Apt 1817 Rochester MN 55901-2899 Office: Mayo Clinic Rochester MN 55901

CORCIONE, GIUSEPPE, physician, vice minister of health; b. Panama, Panama, Nov. 19, 1939; s. Nicolas and Maria (Lavena) C.; m. Margarita Maria Perez-Balladares, Mar. 19, 1966; 3 children. MD, Sch. Medicine, Panama, 1964. Cert. Bd. Urology. Attending Social Security, Panama, 1970—, chief OR, 1976, med. dir., 1982-83, chief urology svc., 1986—; vice min. of health Panama, 1994—; del. Assn. Medica Nacional, 1987, 88, 89. Mem. Urology Soc. Panama (pres. 1986, 90), Rotaly Club. Home: PO Box 55, 2729 Paitilla Panama City Panama Office: Cons Medicos, Paitilla, Panama Panama

CORCORAN, PAUL JOHN, physician; b. Washburn, Wis., June 8, 1934; s. Thomas F. and Mary Rose (McCauley) C., m. Patricia Ann Bounds, Nov. 10, 1956; children: Mary Colbourne, Ann Campbell, Clare Bounds, Thomas Bounds, Peter Campbell, David Pusey. B.S., Georgetown U., 1955; M.D., 1959; M.S. in Phys. Medicine and Rehab., U. Wash., 1968. Diplomate Am. Bd. Phys. Medicine and Rehab. Intern U. Oreg. Hosps., 1959-60; resident in rehab. medicine NYU, 1963-66; postdoctoral fellow dept. rehab. medicine HEW-Social and Rehab. Services; Acad. Career trainee dept. rehab. medicine U. Wash. Med. Center, 1966-68; asst. attending physiatrist Presbyn. Hosp. City N.Y.; asst. prof. rehab. medicine Columbia U., 1968-72; dir. residency tng. in rehab. medicine Columbia-Presbyn. Med. Center, N.Y.C., 1969-72; assoc. prof. rehab. medicine Boston U., 1972-76; chief rehab. medicine Boston City Hosp., 1975-77; asso. prof. Tufts U., 1976-78, prof., 1978-85, clin. prof., 1985-95, acting chmn. dept. rehab. medicine, 1976-77, 89-90, chmn. dept., 1977-81; physiatrist-in-chief Rehab. Inst., New Eng. Med. Center Hosp., Boston, 1976-81, 89-90; chief rehab. medicine service Boston VA Med. Center, 1980-85; med. dir. Easter Seal Soc./N.H., Manchester, 1985-91; chief phys. medicine and rehab. New Eng. Sinai Hosp. and Rehab. Ctr., Stoughton, Mass., 1989-90, Newton-Wellesley (Mass.) Hosp., 1991-93; dir. rehab. medicine Spaulding Rehab. Hosp., Boston, 1992-96; vis. prof. Harvard Med. Sch., Boston, 1993-95, interim dir. divsn. phys. medicine and rehab., 1993-96; assoc. in neurology Mass. Gen. Hosp., Boston, 1993—; instr. NYU Grad. Sch. Prostheticws and Orthotics, 1970-77; vis. physician rehab. medicine Univ. Hosp., Boston, 1972-76; project dir. New Eng. Regional Rehab. Rsch. and Tng. Ctr., 1977-81; chief med. cons. Mass. Rehab. Commn., 1991-96. Contbr. chpts. to books, articles to profl. publs.; editorial bd. Archives Phys. Med. and Rehab., 1971-77. Trustee Easter Seal Rsch. Found., 1975-78, 88-90, Carroll Rehab. Ctr. for Blind, 1975-78; mem. rehab. svcs. nat. adv. com. HEW, 1976-77; chmn. Mass. Interagy. Coun. on Ind. Living, 1977-79. Lt. M.C., USN, 1960-63. Recipient Licht award Am. Congress Rehab. Medicine, 1985, Physician of Yr. award Pres.'s Com. on Employment of Handicapped, 1986, Disting. Clinician award Am. Acad. Phys. Medicine and Rehab., 1995. Mem. Am. Assn. Acad. Physiatrists (pres. 1981-83, Outstanding Svc. award 1996). Home: 37 Main St Hancock NH 03449 Office: Spaulding Rehab Hosp 125 Nashua St Boston MA 02114-1101

CORDASCO, FRANK ANTHONY, orthopaedic surgeon, educator; b. Jersey City, Oct. 22, 1957; s. Frank Peter and Ruth Ann (Monico) C.; m. Monique Andre Swierbutowicz, Dec. 6, 1991; 1 child, Luke Edward. BS in Biology, U. Ariz., 1979; MS in Physiology, Rutgers U., 1981; MD, UMDNJ, 1985. Diplomate Am. Bd. Orthopaedic Surgery. Asst. clin. prof. dept. orthopaedic surgery U. Calif., San Diego, 1990-92, Columbia Coll. Physicians and Surgeons, N.Y.C., 1992—; cons. San Diego Track Club, 1990-92; tournament physician Virginia Slims Tennis Tournament, N.Y.C., 1992-96. Author: Upper Extremity in Sports Medicine, 1995; contbr. articles to profl. jours. Recipient Neer award Am. Shoulder and Elbow Surgeons, 1990. Fellow Am. Acad. Orthopaedic Surgeons; mem. AMA, N.Y. County Med. Soc., Alpha Omega Alpha. Office: Orthopaedic Assocs NY 343-345 W 58th St New York NY 10019

CORDELL, RONALD EUGENE, radiologist; b. Nashville, Oct. 31, 1949; s. Ernest H. and Sadie D. (Williams) C.; m. Joann Meredith, Sept. 24, 1976; children: Chad, Andrea. BA, Vanderbilt U., 1971; postgrad., U. Ky. Coll. Dentistry, 1971-72; MD, U. Tenn., 1975. Diplomate Am. Bd. Diagnostic Radiology. Resident in pediatrics U. Tenn., LeBonheur Hosp., Memphis, 1976-78; resident in diagnostic radiology U. Tenn., Memphis, 1978-81; diagnostic radiologist Associated Radiologists, Inc., Charleston, W.Va., 1981—; v.p. Associated Radiologists, Inc., 1989; vice chief dept. med. imaging Charleston Area Med. Ctr., 1984, chief, 1985-87; clin. prof. dept. radiology Charleston divsn., W.Va. U. Asst. scoutmaster Boy Scouts Am., Charleston, 1982-84, 90-92; mem. pastor-parish com. Christ Ch. United Meth., Charleston, 1987-89, mem. adminstrv. bd., 1984-86, 93-95. Fellow Am. Coll. Radiology (cert. added qualifications interventional radiology 1995—); mem. Radiol. Soc. N.Am., Am. Roentgen Ray Soc., Soc. Cardiovasc. and Interventional Radiology, W.Va. Radiol. Soc. (sec.-treas. 1991-95), W.Va. Med. Assn. (state legis. com. 1990—, constn. and bylaws com. 1993-96, v.p. 1994, pres.-elect 1995, pres. 1996), Kanawha Med. Soc. (chmn. legis. com. 1990—, exec. coun. 1991—, v.p. 1993, pres. 1994, 95, chmn. exec. coun. 1996). Office: Associated Radiologists Inc PO Box 11137 Charleston WV 25339-1137

CORDER, MICHAEL PAUL, physician, educator; b. Zanesville, Ohio, Jan. 20, 1940; s. Thurman E. and Dorothy S. C.; children: Anita, Jennifer, Wendy. BS, Capital U., 1963; MD, Ohio State U., 1965. Diplomate Am. Bd. Internal Medicine, Am. Bd. Med. Oncology, Am. Bd. Quality Assurance and Utilization Review Physicians, Am. Acad. Pain Mgmt., Am. Bd. Med. Mgmt. Asst. chief hematology and oncology service Letterman Med. Ctr., San Francisco, 1971-75, chief oncology sect., 1972-75; from asst. prof. to assoc. prof. medicine U. Iowa, Iowa City, 1975-83; chief div. oncology and hematology Kern Med. Ctr., Bakersfield, Calif., 1983-93; adj. prof. medicine UCLA, 1984-94, clin. prof., 1994—; dir. UR/QA/RM Bakersfield Med. Ctr., 1990-93, chief of staff, 1990-93; dir. clin. resources Heritage Med. Sys., 1993—; cons. Nat. Cancer Inst., Bethesda, Md., 1978—, Am. Joint Com. on Cancer, 1980-88; med. dir. Cancer Registry Ctrl. Calif., 1988-91;pres. Kern Unit Am. Cancer Soc., 1988. Contbr. articles to profl. jours. Col. USAR, 1964-91. Fellow ACP (A. Blaine Brower Traveling scholar 1981), Internat. Soc. Hematology, Am. Coll. Med. Quality, Am. Coll. Physician Execs.; mem. Am. Soc. Clin. Oncology (membership com. 1984), Western Soc. Clin. Investigation, Calif. Acad. Medicine, Res. Officers Assn. (nat. surgeon 1987-88), Soc. Med. Cons. to Armed Forces, Sr. Army Res. Comdrs. Assn., Calif. Yacht Club. Unitarian. Home: 12430 Cattle King Dr Bakersfield CA 93306-9767 Office: 4570 California Ave Bakersfield CA 93309-1143

CORDERO, JOSE FERNANDO, pediatrician; b. Camuy, P.R., July 25, 1948; s. Fernando and Ana T. Cordero; m. Milagros J. Garcia, June 18, 1970; children: Jose F., Ana M., Joann M., Maria M. BS in Biology, U. P.R., Rio Piedras, 1969; MD, U. P.R., San Juan, 1973; MPH, Harvard U., 1979. Diplomate Nat. Bd. Med. Examienrs, Am. Bd. Med. Genetics, Am. Bd. Pediatrics; lic. physician, Ga. Intern Boston City Hosp., 1973-74, jr. asst. resident dept. pediatrics, 1974-75; clin. and rsch. fellow pediatrics Mass. Gen. Hosp., 1975-77; pediatrican South End Cmty. Health Ctr., Boston, 1977-79; epidemiology intelligence svc. officer Bur. Epidemiology Ctrs. for Disease Control & Prevention, Atlanta, 1979-81, dep. chief birth defects and genetic diseases br., 1985-88, acting chief birth defects and genetic diseases bd., 1988-89, asst. dir. sci. divsn. birth defects and devel. disabilities, 1989-94, dep. dir. nat. immunization program, 1994—; dir. genetics clinic, clin. asst. prof. pediatrics Boston U., 1978-79; clin. instr. pediatrics Children's Hosp., Boston, 1978-79; clin. asst. prof. pediatrics Emory U., 1982—. Co-editor jour. Teratology, 1983-86; mem. editoril bd. Birth Defects Ency., 1988; reviewer jours.; contbr. numerous articles and abstracts to pubs. Mem. working group cancer chemotherapy Internat. Agy. Cancer Rsch., 1980; mem. task force on child health and related issues FDA, 1980-83; mem. rev. coms. NIH; coord. U.S. Govt. Task Force Premature Thelarche in P.R., 1982-85; trustee Calif. Birth Defects Monitoring Program, 1983-89; mem. adv. bd. TERIS, Seattle, 1986—, Fla. Teratogen Info. System, 1986-90; cons. WHO, Guatemala, 1990, 91, 92, Copenhagen, 1991; founding mem. Emmaus Community, 1992—; mem. troop 547 com. Boy Scouts Am., 1983-94. Recipient Arthur S. Flemming award, 1988, Physician's Recognition award AMA, 1980, 84, 88. Mem. APHA, Am. Soc. Human Genetics, Am. Bd. Med. Genetics, Am. Acad. Pediatrics (nutrition com. 1980, com. on drugs 1988-93, genetic com. 1985), Am. Epidemiology Soc., Mass. Med. Soc., Genetics Soc. Ga., Coalition of Spanish Speaking Mental Health and Human Svcs. Orgn., Teratology Soc., Soc. Pediatric Rsch. Roman Catholic. Office: Ctrs for Disease Control & Prevention Nat Immunization Program 1600 Clifton Rd E05 Atlanta GA 30333*

CORDOVA, MARIA ASUNCION, dentist; b. Punta Arenas, Magallanes, Chile, May 14, 1941; came to U.S., 1972; d. Miguel Cordova and Maria Asucion Requena; m. Carlos F. Salinas, July 27, 1963; children: Carlos M., Claudio A., Lola. DDS, U. Chile, Santiago, 1965; DMD, Med. U. S.C., 1986. From instr. to assoc. prof. medicine U. Chile Dept. Physiology, Valparaiso, 1965-72; postdoctoral fellow Johns Hopkins U., Balt., 1972-75; from instr. to asst. prof. M.U. S.C. Dept. Physiology, Charleston, 1975-86; pvt. practice Charleston, 1987—; vis. scientist N.Y. Med. Coll., 1975. Contbr. articles to profl. jours. Program coord. Circulo Hispanic Charleston; coord. Amnesty Internat. U.S.A., Spoleto, Neighborday, Charleston, S.C.; bd. dirs. YWCA; active NOW. Mem. Charleston Women's Network (pres. 1989-90). Roman Catholic. Office: 159 Wentworth St Charleston SC 29401-1731

CORDTS, PAUL ROGER, surgeon; b. Cumberland, Md., Sept. 27, 1958; s. Harold J. and Jeanne (Moore) C. BA, Johns Hopkins U., 1980; MD, USUHS, 1984. Diplomate Am. Bd. Surgery, Am. Bd. Surg. Critical Care, Am. Bd. Gen. Vascular Surgery. Commd. med. officer U.S. Army, 1980; intern, resident in surgery William Beaumont Army Med. Ctr., El Paso, Tex., 1984-89; staff surgeon Munson Army Community Hosp., Ft. Leavenworth, Kans., 1989-90; fellow in vascular surgery Boston U. Med. Ctr., Boston, 1990-92; chief vascular surgery sect. Tripler Army Med. Ctr., Honolulu, 1992-93, chief gen. surgery svc., tng. dir. surg. residency program, 1993—. Fellow ACS; mem. Uniformed Svcs. U. Health Scis. Surg. Assocs., Am. Venous Forum, Peripheral Vascular Surgery Soc., 38th Parallel Med. Soc., Soc. of Critical Care Medicine, Soc. for Clin. Vascular Surgery, Assn. of Mil. Surgeons of U.S., Am. Legion (Farrady Post 24), Omicron Delta Kappa Nat. Leadership Soc., Assn. for Acad. Surgery. Home: 98-1323 Kaonohi St Aiea HI 96701-2836 Office: Tripler Army Med Ctr Gen Surgery Svc Honolulu HI 96859-5000

CORE, GRADY B., plastic and reconstructive surgeon; b. DeQueen, Ark., Feb. 27, 1955; s. Orval Ben and Pollyanna (Williams) C.; m. Heidi Karen Holloway, July 28, 1990; children: Taylor Ben, Jared James. BS in Zoology with honors., U. Ark., 1977, MD, 1981. Diplomate Am. Bd. Surgery, Am. Bd. Plastic Surgery. Surgical resident U. Ark. for Med. Sci., Little Rock, 1981-84, Oral Roberts U., Tulsa, 1984-86, Flushing (N.Y.) Hosp. Affiliat Einstein U., 1986-88; staff gen. surgeon Oral Roberts City of Faith Hosp., Tulsa, 1988-89; plastic surgery resident Mayo Clinic, Rochester, Minn., 1989-91; clin. instr. in plastic surgery U. Ala., Birmingham, 1991-92; staff plastic surgeon Ochsner Clinic, New Orleans, 1992-93, chief sect. plastic surgery, 1993-95; pvt. practice in plastic surgery McCullough-Grotting Clinic, Birmingham, Ala., 1995—; asst. prof. surgery Oral Roberts U., Tulsa, 1988-89; asst. clin. prof. plastic surgery Tulane U., New Orleans, 1992-95; cons. endoscopic plastic surgery Smith-Nephew-Richards, Inc., Memphis, 1992—; mem. endoscopic adv. panel Am. Soc. Aesthetic Plastic Surgery; instr. endoscopic plastic surgery continuing edn. courses, U. Ala., 1994, Am. Soc. Aesthetic Plastic Surgery, 1995, 96, Australia and New Zealand U., 1995, U. Utah, 1996, St. Louis U., 1996. Editor: (book) Minimally Invasive Plastic Surgery; Clinics in Plastic Surgery, 1995; contbr. articles to profl. jours., chpts. to books. Named for Best Paper in Microvascular Surgery Nat. Sr. Resident Conf. in Plastic Surgery, Madison, Wis., 1991. Fellow Am. Coll. Surgeons, Am. Soc. Reconstructive Surgery; mem. AMA, Am. Soc. Plastic and Reconstructive Surgery, Ala. Soc. Plastic and Reconstructive Surgery, Priestly Soc. Mayo Alumni., Phi Eta Sigma. Republican. Baptist. Office: McCullough-Grotting Assocs 1600 20th St S Birmingham AL 35205

CORE, HARRY MICHAEL, psychiatric social worker, mental health therapist/administrator; b. Core, W.Va., Oct. 7, 1933; s. Earl Lemley and Freda Bess (Garrison) C.; m. Jane Ann Boggs, Oct., 1976; children: Kevin M., Brian D. BS, W.Va. U., 1955; MSW, U. N.C., 1957. Psychiat. social worker Lake County Mental Health Ctr., Mentor, Ohio, 1960-67, asst. dir., 1967-72, exec. dir., 1972-87; psychiat. social worker Simon & Bertschinger MDs, Inc., Eastlake, Ohio, 1966-92; trustee Tri-Care, Inc., Westlake, Ohio, 1986-87. Trustee Western Res. Counseling, Inc., 1988—. 1st lt., U.S. Army, 1957-60. Fellow Am. Orthopsychiat. Assn. (life); mem. Acad. Cert. Social Workers, Nat. Assn. Social Workers Ohio Council of Community Mental Health Agencies (trustee 1981-84, v.p. 1984). Democrat. Mem. Disciples of Christ Ch. Home: 6707 Stratford Rd Painesville OH 44077-1533 Office: Lake Ambulatory Care Ctr 9500 Mentor Ave Ste 320 Mentor OH 44060

CORE, MARY CAROLYN W. PARSONS, radiologic technologist; b. Valparaiso, Fla., Dec. 8, 1949; d. Levi and Mary Etta (Elliott) Willey; m. Joel Kent Core, Aug. 3, 1979; 1 child, Candace W. Parsons. Student, Peninsula Gen. Hosp. Sch. Radiologic Tech., Salisbury, Md., 1969; student, U. Del., 1969-73, Del. Tech. Community Coll., 1973-79, St. Joseph's Coll., 1983-86; BSBA, St. Joseph's Coll., 1987; MGA, U. Md., 1995. Technologist Peninsula Gen. Hosp., Salisbury, 1967-72; tech. dir. edn. Sch. Radiologic Tech., Salisbury, 1973-75; technologist Johns Hopkins Hosp., Salisbury, 1972-73, Nanticoke Meml. Hosp., Seaford, Del., 1975-79; adminstrv. chief technologist, imaging depts. Shady Grove Adventist Hosp., Rockville, Md., 1979-81; dir. dept. radiol. scis. Anne Arundel Diagnostics, Inc., Annapolis, Md., 1981-92; COO Anne Arundel MRI (Magnetic Resonance Imaging, Annapolis, Md., 1981-92; CEO Anne Arundel Diagnostics, Inc. and Anne Arundel MRI, Annapolis, Md., 1981-92; v.p. corp. svcs. Anne Arundel Healthcare Systems, Inc., 1992—. Mem. Ctrl. Md. Coun. Girl Scouts Am., Pres.'s award svc. team, 1989; bd. mem. Anne Arundel Trade Coun., 1996—; adv. bd. YWCA Careers, 1994—. Recipient twin awards YWCA, 1988. Mem. NAFE, Md. Soc. Radiologic Technologists (pres. 1980-81, sr. bd. mem. 1982-83, various awards including 1st Pl. Essay awards 1974, 76, 84, 87), Am. Hosp. Radiology Adminstrs. (v.p. 1984-85, chmn. by-laws com. 1984-85, statis. resources com. 1985-86), Am. Mgmt. Assn., Radiology Bus. Mgrs. Assn., Ea. Shore Dist. Radiologic Technologists (pres. 1976-78), Md.

Assn. Healthcare Execs., Project Mgrs. Inst., Phi Kappa Phi. Republican. Methodist. Home: 1907 Harcourt Ave Crofton MD 21114-2103 Office: 135 E 55th St New York NY 10022-4049

COREA, LUIGI, cardiologist, educator; b. Taverna, Italy, Apr. 6, 1939; s. Ulisse and Antonia (Garcea) C.; M.D., U. Perugia, 1964; postgrad. U. Pisa, 1969-71; m. Maria Federica Tei, Oct. 7, 1972; children—Francesco, Pierluigi. Intern, resident U. Pisa, 1964-71; house physician Patologie Medica, U. Perugia, Italy, 1964-69, asst. at semeiotica medica, 1969—, registrar, 1972—, sr. registrar, 1974—, assoc. prof. semeiotica medica and cardiology, 1981-83, prof. cardiology Sch. Medicine, 1983—; faculty cardiology Nat. Heart Hosp. and St. Mary's Hosp., London, 1967. Decorated commendatore of St. Gregorio Magno of Vaticano (Rome). Fellow Internat. Coll. Angiology, European Soc. Cardiology, Am. Coll. Cardiology; mem. Italian Soc. Cardiology (council 1970-80, 86—), Italian Soc. Hypertension, Italian Soc. Vascular Pathology, Italian Fedn. Medicine of Sport, Internat. Soc. Hypertension, Italian Soc. Internal Medicine, European Soc. Clin. Investigation. Democrat. Roman Catholic. Author: The Pheocromocytoma, 1980; L'ipertrofia cardiaca; contbg. author: Trattato di Patologia Medica, Trattato Italiano di Cardiologia; contbr. articles on cardiovascular pathology to profl. jours. Home: 8 Degli Olivetani, 06100 Perugia Italy Office: Policlinico Universitario, Cattedra di Cardiologia, 06100 Perugia Italy

CORIASSO, RONALD JOSEPH, osteopathic physician, educator; b. Flint, Mich., Jan. 29, 1957; s. Louis Bartholomew and Margaret Ann (O'Leary) C.; m. Kathryn Elaine Coriasso, Aug. 9, 1980; children: Sheila Ann, Ronald Joseph Jr., Michael Louis. BS, Mich. State U., 1979; DO, U. Osteo. Medicine-Health Sci., Des Moines, 1984. Intern Flint Osteo. Hosp., 1984-85; resident in family practice Genesys St. Joseph Hosp.-Mich. State U., Flint, 1985-87, assoc. prof., 1987—; emergency room physician Genesee St. Joseph Hosp.-Mich. State U., Flint, 1987—; pvt. practice, Flint, 1987—; sch. physician Mich. Sch. Deaf, Flint, 1989—; bd. dirs., mem. fin. com. Health Plus Mich., 1993—; bd. dirs. Genesys P.H.O. Integrated Group, Flint, 1993—; incorporator Genesys P.H.O., Flint, 1994—. Mem. AMA, Am. Acad. Family Practice, Mich. Med. Soc., Genesee Med. Soc., Mich. Ind. Physicians Assn. (bd. dirs. 1993—). Republican. Roman Catholic. Home: 603 Boutell Dr Grand Blanc MI 48439-1535

CORK, LINDA KATHERINE, veterinary pathologist, educator; b. Texarkana, Tex., Dec. 14, 1936; d. Albert James and Martine Sessions (Buntyn) Collins; m. P.S. Cork Jr., Mar. 1955 (div. 1965); children: Robin E., Jerald W. BS, Tex. A&M U., 1969, DVM, 1970; PhD, Wash. State U., 1974. Diplomate Am. Coll. Vet. Pathologists. Fellow Wash. State U., Pullman, 1970-74; asst. prof. U. Ga., Athens, 1974-76; asst. prof. Johns Hopkins U., Balt., 1976-82, assoc. prof., 1982-88, assoc. dir. rsch. Alzheimer's Disease Rsch. Ctr., 1985-93, prof., 1988-93; prof., chmn. Dept. Comparative Medicine Stanford U., 1994—; coun. mem. NIH div. Rsch. Resources, Bethesda, Md., 1985-89; adv. bd. Registry Comparative Pathology, Bethesda. Grantee Nat. Inst. on Aging, 1985-89, Nat. Inst. Health, 1986-91, 86-93, 87-92. Mem. Inst. Medicine, Am. Assn. Neuropathologists (chmn. June 1988), Am. Assn. Pathology, U.S.-Can. Acad. Pathology. Methodist. Office: Stanford Univ Dept Comparative Medicine MSOB Bldg Stanford CA 94305-5415*

CORKER, FRANK THOMAS, physician, retired military officer; b. Atlanta, Dec. 12, 1935; s. Newman and Thayer Davenport (Hopper) C.; m. Diane Blankenship, Sept. 22, 1955; children: Thayer Diane Corker, Frank Thomas Jr., Thomas Angel. BA, Emory U., 1957, MD, 1961; MPH, Johns Hopkins U., 1969. Diplomate Am. Bd. Preventive Medicine. Commd. 1st lt. USAF, 1960, advanced through ranks to col., 1976, ret., 1981; intern USAF Hosp. Lackand AFB, San Antonio, Tex., 1961-62; jr. asst. resident ob-gyn Grady Meml. Hosp., Atlanta, 1964-65; resident in aerospace medicine Sch. Aerospace Medicine, Brooks AFB, San Antonio, 1969-70; flight surgeon 832 TAC Hosp., Cannon AFB, N.M., 1962-64; asst. chief aerospace med. div. USAFE Hdqrs., Wiesbaden, Fed. Republic Germany, 1965-68; dispensary cmmdr., dir. med. svcs. 56th USAF Dispensary, Thailand, 1970-71; cons. preventive medicine USAF Hdqrs., Washington, 1971-76, chief of preventive medicine, 1976-77; hosp. commdr., dir. med. svcs. USAF Hosp., Moody AFB, Ga., 1977-81; pvt. practice in occupational and aerospace medicine Valdosta, Ga., 1981—; cons. in aerospace medicine USAF Surgeon Gen., 1977-81. Contbr. articles to profl. jours. Active Cub Scouts, Potomac, Md., 1973-75 (past chmn.); team leader United Way of Valdosta and Lowndes County, 1982-86. Decorated Legion of Merit, D.F.C., Air medal with silver oak leaf cluster, Meritorious Svc. medal. Fellow Aerospace Med. Assn., Am. Coll. Preventive Medicine; mem. AMA, Am. Coll. Occupational and Environ. Medicine, Med. Assn. Ga., South Ga. Med. Soc. (sec., treas. 1982-84), Norfolk So. Assn. Physicians, Valdosta C. of C. (past dir.), Rotary (past dir.), Alpha Tau Omega (chpt. sec. 1954-55, v.p. 1955-56). Episcopalian. Office: 2704 N Oak St Bldg N Valdosta GA 31602-1738

CORLESS, DOROTHY ALICE, nurse educator; b. Reno, Nev., May 28, 1943; d. John Ludwig and Vera Leach (Wilson) Adams; children: James Lawrence Jr., Dorothy Adele Carroll. RN, St. Luke's Sch. Nursing, 1964. Clinician, cons., educator, author, adminstr. Fresno County Mental Health Dept., 1970-94; pvt. practice mental health nurse Fresno, 1991-94; instr. police sci. State Ctr. Tng. Facility, 1991-94; pvt. practice, mental health con., educator Florence, Oreg., 1994—. Vol. ARC, Disaster Mental Health Svcs., 1993—. Maj. USAFR, 1972-94. Mem. NAFE, Forensic Mental Health Assn. Calif., Calif. Peace Officer's Assn., Critical Incident Stress Found. Home: 1580 Kalla Kalla Ct Florence OR 97439-8963

CORLEW, DANIEL SCOTT, plastic surgeon; b. Murfreesboro, Tenn., Apr. 8, 1955; s. Robert Ewing and Mary Saille (Scott) C.; m. Katherine Weidhaas, Sept. 18, 1982; children: Christopher James, David Andrew. BA, Vanderbilt U., 1977; MD, Emory U., 1981. Diplomat Am. Bd. Plastic Surgery, Am. Bd. Surgery. Resident, gen. surgery Emory U., Atlanta, 1981-82, 84-86; physician Nat. Health Svcs. Corps, Atlanta, 1982-84; resident, gen. surgery U. Md., Balt., 1986-88; gen. surgeon Murfreesboro Med. Clinic, 1988-89; plastic and reconstructive surgeon Murfreesboro Med. Clinic, 1991—; fellow, plastic and reconstructive surgery U. Fla., Gainesville, 1989-91. With USPHS, 1982-84. Fellow Am. Coll. Surgeons; mem. Am. Soc. Plastic and Reconstructive Surgeons, Southeastern Soc. of Plastic and Reconstructive Surgeons, Tenn. Soc. Plastic and Reconstructive Surgeons.

CORLEY, CAROL L., school nurse; b. Waco, Tex., Feb. 2, 1943; d. Henry Lee (dec.) and Irma Geraldine (King) Cranfill; m. Thomas Lane Corley, May 22, 1965; 1 child, Christopher Lyn. ADN, McLennan C.C., 1974; BSN, U. Tex.-Arlington, 1983. Staff nurse ICU Providence Health Ctr., Waco, Tex.; sch. nurse Crawford (Tex.) Ind. Sch. Dist.; coord. sch. nurse Midway Ind. Sch. Dist., Waco. Mem. ANA, Tex. Nurses Assn. (dist. 10 pres. 1992-94, past v.p.), Tex. Assn. Sch. Nurses (dist. 12 pres. 1990), Tex. Sch. Nurses Adminstrs. Assn., Sigma Theta Tau. Home: 8930 Raven Dr Waco TX 76712-3453

CORLEY, THOMAS EDWARD, urologist; b. Prentiss, Miss., Feb. 28, 1938; s. Suber Singleton Corley and Willie Rite (Boure) Corley Morie; m. Lea Reynolds, June 7, 1985; children: Tim, Cherry, Traci, Cerae, Megan. BS, Millsaps Coll., 1959; MD, U. Miss., 1963. Diplomate Am. Bd. Urology. Rotating intern U. Miss. Med. Sch. Hosp., Jackson, 1964; resident in urology Naval Hosp., Oakland, Calif., 1967-71; chief urology U.S. Naval Hosp., Camp Pendelton, Calif., 1971-72; staff urologist North Broward Med. Ctr., Pompano Beach, Fla., 1972—, vice chief surgery, 1980-82, chief of surgery, 1982-84, vice-chief of staff, 1987-89, chief of staff, 1989-91. Comdr. USN, 1964-71. Mem. Broward County Med. Soc. (treas. 1990-91, v.p. 1991-92, pres.-elect 1992-93, pres. 1993-94, trustee 1994—). Methodist. Office: 1 W Sample Rd Pompano Beach FL 33064

CORLEY, WILLIAM EDWARD, hospital administrator; b. Pittsburgh, Sept. 2, 1942; s. Robert Ray and Helen (Wise) C.; m. Angela Irvine Blose, Mar. 22, 1969; children: Laura, Matt. BA in Bus. and Econs., Coll. of William and Mary, 1964; MHA in Hosp. Adminstrn., Duke U., Durham, 1966. Adminstrv. asst. Duke U., Durham, N.C., 1965-66; mgmt. cons. Booz, Allen & Hamilton, Chicago, 1968-71; assoc. hosp. dir. U. Ky., Lexington, 1971-75; hosp. dir. Milton S. Hersey Med. Ctr. of Pa. State U., Hershey, 1975-78; pres. Akron Gen. Med. Ctr., Ohio, 1978-84, Community Hosps. of Ind., Inc., 1984—; Bd. dirs. Vol. Hosps. Am. Tri-State, Irving, Tex., 1982—, tri-state chmn.; chmn. United Hosp. Svcs., Indpls., 1986-88; lectr. Ind. U.-Purdue U. at Indpls., 1984—. Author: Ray E. Brown-A Manager's Manager: Lectures, Messages, Memoirs, 1990; contbr. articles to profl. jours. Chmn. United Hosp. Svc., 1986-88, Vol. Hosp. Am. Tri-State, 1989-91; active Indpls. Children's Mus. Bd., United Way Bd., 500 Festival Bd., 400 Festival Bd. 1st lt. U.S. Army, 1966-68. Presbyterian. Home: 13570 N Gray Rd Carmel IN 46033-9708 Office: Community Hosps 1500 N Ritter Ave Indianapolis IN 46219-3027

CORMACK, ALLAN MACLEOD, physicist, educator; b. Johannesburg, South Africa, Feb. 23, 1924; came to U.S., 1957, naturalized, 1966; s. George and Amelia (MacLeod) C.; m. Barbara Jeanne Seavey, Jan. 6, 1950; children: Margaret, Jean, Robert. BS, U. Cape Town, South Africa, 1944, M.Sc., 1945; research student, Cambridge (Eng.) U., 1947-50. Lectr. U. Cape Town, 1946-47, 1950-56; research fellow Harvard U., 1956-57; asst. prof. physics Tufts U., Medford, Mass., 1957-60, assoc. prof., 1960-64, prof., 1964-80, University prof., 1980-94, emeritus prof., 1994—; researcher nuclear and particle physics, computed tomography and related math. topics. Named hon. fellow St. John's Coll., Cambridge, Eng., 1993, Korean Acad. Sci. and Tech., 1995; recipient Ballou medal Tufts U., 1978, Nobel prize in medicine and physiology, 1979. medal of merit U. Cape Town, 1980, Nat. medal sci. NSF, 1990. Fellow AAAS, Am. Phys. Soc., Am. Acad. Arts and Scis., Royal Soc. South Africa (fgn.); mem. NAS, South African Phys. Soc., Am. Assn. Physicists in Medicine (hon.), Inst. Medicine, Korean Acad. Sci. and Tech. (hon.), Sigma Xi. Office: Tufts U Dept Physics Medford MA 02155

CORMAN, MARVIN LEONARD, surgeon; b. Phila., Dec. 17, 1939; s. Joseph Mayer and Dorothy Frances (Stern) C. m. Bonnie Ruth Podrat, June 14, 1964; children: John Mayer, Alexander Stern. BA, U. Pa., 1961, MD, 1965. Diplomate Nat. Bd. Med. Examiners, Am. Bd. Surgery, Am. Bd. Colon and Rectal Surgery; lic. surgeon, Mass., N.J., Fla., Calif. Sr. registrar, vis. lectr. gen. infirmary, profl. surg. unit U. Leeds, Eng., 1968-69; surg. intern Boston City Hosp.-Fifth (Harvard) Surg. Svc., 1965, surg. resident, 1966-68, surg. resident, chief surg. resident, 1969-71; staff surgeon divsn. colon and rectal surgery, dept. surgery Lahey Clinic Med. Ctr., Boston, 1971-81, Sansum Med. Clinic, Santa Barbara, Calif., 1981-95; surgeon divsn. colon and rectal surgery UCLA, 1996—; instr. surgery Sch. Medicine Harvard U., Boston, 1972-77, clin. asst. prof surgery, 1977-82; co-dir. tng. program colon and rectal surgery Sansum Med. clinic, 1981-95, chmn. divsn. edn., 1983-90; credentials com. Santa Barbara Cottage Hosp., 1984-95, mem. libr. com., 1985-95, mem. com. on grad. med. edn., 1989-94, vice-chmn. dept. surgery, 1994-95; pres. alumni assn. Harvard Surg. Svc., Boston City Hosp., 1983-84; vis. prof. U. Tex. Health Sci. Ctr., San Antonio, 1982, Throckmorton Surg. Soc., Des Moines, 1985, Ogden (Utah) Surg. Soc., 1985, 20th ann. Surg. Congress Orange County Surg. Soc., Newport Beach, Calif., 1988, Royal Australasian Coll. Surgeons, Adelaide, Australia, 1989, Northwest Permanente Dept. Surgery, Portland, Oreg., 1990, Hahnemann U., Phila., 1991, El Colegio de Cirujanos Gererales de Mexicali, Mexico, 1991, Cleve. Clinic Fla., Ft. Lauderdale, Fla., 1992, Univ. Hosp. de Clinicas do Parana, Curitiba, Brazil, 1993; Ralph Coffey vis. prof. Sch. Medicine, U. Mo., Kansas City, 1988; Ralph B. Samson Meml. lectr. Grant Med. Ctr., Columbus, Ohio, 1991; Louis A. Buie vis. lectr. Mayo Med. Sch., Rochester, Minn., 1992; ann. vis. surgeon Queen Elizabeth Hosp. Ctr. of Montreal, Que., 1993; vis. prof. U. So. Calif. Sch. Medicine, L.A., 1995; del. leader Citizen Amb. Program Colon and Rectal Surgery Del. to Russia, Hungary and Czechoslovakia, 1992. Author: (textbook) Colon and Rectal Surgery, 1984, 89, 93; assoc. editor: Diseases of the Colon and Rectum, 1977-92, Lahey Clinic Bull., 1972-81; contbr. numerous articles to profl. jours. Recipient Hoffman-LaRoche award, 1965, Piedmont Proctologic Soc award, 1973, 1st prize of Med. Book award, 1985. Fellow ACP; mem. ACS (So. Calif. chpt.), AMA (chmn. residency rev. com. for colon and rectal surgery 1985-86), Internat. Soc. Univ. Colon and Rectal Surgeons, Am. Soc. Colon and Rectal Surgeons (v.p. 1995-96), Am. Surg. Assn., Am. Med. Writers Assn. (hon.), Am. Coll. Gastroenterology, Assn. for Program Dirs. in Colon and Rectal Surgery, We. Surg. Assn., Pan Am. Med. Assn. (coun. sect. on colon and rectal surgery 1989—), Royal Australasian Coll. Surgeons (hon., sect. colon and rectal surgery 1989), New Eng. Surg. Soc., Calif. Med. Soc., New Eng. Soc. Colon and Rectal Surgeons (sec.-treas. 1977-81), Boston Surg. Soc., Northeastern Soc. Colon and Rectal Surgeons, Soc. Surgery Alimentary Tract, Santa Barbara County Med. Soc., So. Calif. Soc. Colon and Rectal Surgeons, Piedmont Proctologic Soc. (hon.). Office: Dept Surgery UCLA School Medicine Box 957060 Rm 3360H PVUB Los Angeles CA 90095-7060

CORMICAN, MARTIN GERARD, pathologist; b. Galway, Ireland, Nov. 7, 1962; came to the U.S., 1994; s. David and Bridget (Murphy) C.; m. Fiona M. Nicholson, Apr. 25, 1992; children: David, Sarah, Ruth. MB, BChir, Nat. U. Ireland, Galway, 1986, MD, 1992. Registered med. practitioner, Ireland. Intern Western Health Bd., Galway, 1986-87; sr. house officer medicine South Lincolnshire (U.K.) Area Health Authority, 1987-89; sr. house officer microbiology Western Health Bd., Galway, 1989-90, registrar microbiology, 1990-94; fellow pathology U. Iowa Hosps. and Clinics, Iowa City, 1994-96; cons. immunologist U. C.H., Galway, 1996—. Editl. bd. mem. Diagnostic Microbiology Infectious Disease, 1996; contbr. chpt. to book and articles to profl. jours. Recipient Rsch. award Royal Acad. Medicine in Ireland, 1992. Mem. Royal Coll. Physicians, Royal Coll. Pathologists, Am. Soc. for Microbiology, Assn. Clin. Pathologists (U.K.), Royal Acad. Medicine in Ireland. Office: U Iowa Hosps & Clinics 200 Hawkins Dr Iowa City IA 52242

CORNBLATH, MARVIN, pediatrician, educator; b. St. Louis, June 18, 1925; s. David and Sophia (Kornblett) C.; m. Joan Senturia, Aug. 29, 1948; children—Nancy Moshe, Polly Cornblath Manin, Ben S. Student, Washington U., St. Louis, 1944, M.D. cum laude, 1947. Diplomate: Am. Bd. Pediatrics. Rotating intern St. Louis Jewish Hosp., 1947-48; resident pediatrics St. Louis Children's Hosp., 1948-50; asst. pediatrics Washington U. Sch. Medicine, 1948-50; instr., then asst. prof. pediatrics Johns Hopkins Sch. Medicine, 1953-59; lectr. John Hopkins Sch. Medicine, 1975—; research asso., adj. attending pediatrician Sinai Hosp., Balt., 1953-59; pediatrician out-patient dept. Johns Hopkins Hosp., 1956-59; asst. prof., then asso. prof. Northwestern U. Med. Sch., 1959-61; asst. chmn. div. pediatrics Michael Reese Hosp., Chgo., 1959-61; asso. prof., then prof. pediatrics U. Ill. Coll. Medicine, 1961-68; attending physician, physician-in-charge neonatal service Research and Ednl. Hosps., Chgo., 1961-68; attending physician Cook County Hosp., Chgo., 1963-68; prof. pediatrics U. Md. Sch. Medicine, 1968—, chmn. dept., 1968-78; spl. asst. to sci. dir. Nat. Inst. Child Health and Human Devel., NIH, 1978-82; med. cons. Nordisk-U.S.A., 1982-87. Author numerous articles in field. Served to 1st lt. M.C. AUS, 1951-53. Mem. Soc. Pediatric Research, Am. Acad. Pediatrics, AAAS, Am. Pediatric Soc., Brit. Biochem. Soc., Am. Soc. Biol. Chemists, Endocrine Soc., Am. Physiol. Soc., Am. Diabetes Assn., Sigma Xi, Alpha Omega Alpha. Home: 3809 St Paul St Baltimore MD 21218-1821

CORNEJO SAN MILLÁAN, MARGARITA, pediatrician, infectious diseases consultant; b. Salta, Argentina, Mar. 31, 1940; d. Nolasco Cornejo Costas and Carmen San Millán Bane. MD, U. Salboa, Argentina, 1966. Bd. cert. pediats., pediat. infectious disease. Pediats. resident Univ. Hosp., Jacksonville, Fla., 1971-73; asst. Children's Hosp. Salta, 1974-80, chief infectious diseases, 1980-90, chief pediats. dept., 1990—. Roman Catholic. Home: Belgran 1040 6A, 4400 Salta Argentina Office: J M Leguizamon 232, 4400 Salta Argentina

CORNELIS, PIETER ARSÈNE, psychology educator, consultant; b. Yzendyke, Zeeland, The Netherlands, Mar. 13, 1927; s. Jerôme Charles and Caecilia Maria (Aspeslagh) C.; m. Elisabeth Elvira van Grootel, Oct. 2. BA, U. Nijmegen, The Netherlands, 1955, MBA, 1957, PhD in Social Scis., 1970; student, U. Calif., Berkeley, 1955. Cert. psychologist. Indsl. psychologist DeWit's Textiel N.V., Helmond, The Netherlands, 1958-62; mgr. ednl. dept. P de Gruyter & Zn N.V., 's Hertogenbosch, 1962-66; owner, operator Rsch. Inst. P.A. Cornelis, Helmond, 1966-72; assoc. prof. Free U., Amsterdam, The Netherlands, 1972-80, prof. indsl. psychology, 1980—; bd. dirs., mgr. promotion retng. acads. for informatics Free U., Amsterdam, The Netherlands.; part-time prof. indsl. psychology Royal Mil. Acad. Breda, 1981-84; cons. European Combined Terminals, Rotterdam, The Netherlands, 1980-96, CAP Gemini/Pandata Holland, The Hague, 1992-94, China Europe Mgmt. Program, Beijing, 1988-92; IBM Holland, Amsterdam, 1988-90; bd. dirs. Found. Work Amsterdam, 1986-94, Bus. Adminstrn. and Informatics Rsch. Group, 1985-92. Author, editor: Europeans About Europe, 1970, Work With Sense, 1974, Shared Control in Orgns., 1978, Community Problems, 1982, Automation With A Human Face, 1986, Innovation and Management, 1992. With Royal Dutch Army, 1948-52. Decorated officer Royal Order Orange-Nassau (The Netherlands); recipient van Meeteren prize for informatics Combined Employers Orgns. in The Netherlands, 1990; pure sci. rsch. grantee, 1986, grantee NATO, 1969, European Commn., 1970. Mem. Netherlands Profl. Inst. Psychologists, Soc. for Applied Psychology (bd. dirs. 1973-88), Nat. Soc. for Informatics. Democrat. Roman Catholic. Home: Jacob van Lenneplaan 20, 3743 AR Baarn Utrecht, The Netherlands Office: Pion, Faculty of Econs, De Boelelaan 7, 1083 HT Amsterdam The Netherlands

CORNELL, ANNIE AIKO, nurse, administrator, retired army officer; b. L.A., Sept. 23, 1954; d. George and Fumiko (Iwai) Okubo; m. Max A. Cornell, Dec. 10, 1990. BSN, U. Md., 1976. RN, Calif. Enlisted U.S. Army, 1972, advanced through grades to maj.; clin. staff nurse surg. ICU U.S. Army, Presidio of San Francisco; clin. head nurse ICU U.S. Army, Seoul, Korea; clin. head nurse gen. medicine ward U.S. Army, Ft. Ord, Calif., chief nursing adminstrn.; ret. U.S. Army, 1992; nursing supr. Home Health Plus; dir. patient svcs. Hollister Vis. Nurs Assn., Calif. Recipient Walter Reed Army Inst. nursing scholarship. Mem. Sigma Theta Tau. Home: 199 Linde Cir Marina CA 93933-2206

CORNELL, DEWEY GENE, psychologist; b. Louisville, June 22, 1956; s. Dewey Cornell Jr. and Patricia L. (Gehring) Dotson; m. Nancy Emily Trinka, Aug. 19, 1978; children: Cristina, Allison, Erin. AB, Transylvania U., 1977; MA, U. Mich., 1979, PhD, 1981. Lic. clinical psychologist. Intern U. Mich. Psychol. Clinic, Ann Arbor, 1979-81; postdoctoral scholar U. Mich, Psychiatry Dept., Ann Arbor, 1981-83; clin. psychologist Ctr. Forensic Psychiatry, Ann Arbor, 1983-86; asst. prof. Sch. Edn., U. Va., Charlottesville, 1986-91, assoc. prof., 1991—; asst. dir. Ctr. Clin. Psychology Svcs., U. Va., Charlottesville, 1989—; faculty assoc. Inst. Law, Psychiatry and Pub. Policy U. Va., Charlottesville, 1986—; asst. prof. psychology Mich. State U., East Lansing, 1985-86; pvt. practice, Charlottesville, 1986—. Author: Families of Gifted Children, 1984; co-editor Juvenile Homicide, 1989; co-author: Recommended Practices in Gifted Education, 1991; contbr. articles to profl. jours. Sponsor Charlottesville Go Club, 1987—. Fellow Am. Orthopsychiat. Assn., Internat. Soc. Rsch. Aggression; mem. APA, Am. Psychology Law Soc., Am. Ednl. Rsch. Assn., Nat. Assn. Gifted Children, Va. Psychol. Assn. Office: U Va Sch Edn 405 Emmet St Charlottesville VA 22903-2495

CORNELL, EUGENIA ANN, psychiatrist; b. Erie, Pa., May 29, 1943; d. Carl. John and Regina Theresa (Weiner) C. BA in Chemistry, Villa Maria Coll., 1965; MA in Biochemistry, Boston U., 1970; MD, U. Mass., 1980. Diplomate Am. Bd. Psychiatry. Intern U. Rochester (N.Y.) Med. Ctr., 1980-81, resident in psychiatry, 1981-84; pvt. practice Rochester, 1984—; psychiatrist Rochester Psych. Ctr., 1984-86; cons. psychiat. health svcs. Western Monroe Mental Health Svcs., Rochester, 1985-86; cons. Rochester Rehab. Ctr., 1986-87, DePaul Mental Health Svcs., 1986-88, 90—. Mem. APA (rep. 1989-91, 93-94, dep. rep. 1993-95, editor newsletter Genesee Valley Dist. br. 1988-92, pres.-elect 1991-93, pres. 1993-95). Office: 300 White Spruce Blvd Rochester NY 14623-1606

CORNELY, PAUL BERTAU, physician, educator; b. Guadeloupe, French W.I., Mar. 9, 1906; came to U.S., 1921, naturalized, 1934; s. Eleodore and Adrienne (Mellon) C.; m. Mae Stewart, June 23, 1934; 1 child, Paul Bertau. A.B., U. Mich., 1928, M.D., 1931, Dr. P.H., 1934, D.Sc. (hon.), 1968; D. Pub. Service (hon.), U. of Pacific, 1972; ScD (hon.), Howard U., 1992. Diplomate: Bd. Preventive Medicine and Pub. Health. Intern Lincoln Hosp., Durham, N.C., 1931-32; mem. faculty Howard U. Coll. Medicine, Washington, 1934—; chief div. phys. medicine and rehab. Howard U. Coll. Medicine, 1959-64, prof., chmn. dept. preventive medicine and pub. health, 1955-73, prof. emeritus, 1973—; pres. Tech. Assos., Inc., 1977-84; med. dir. Freedmen's Hosp., Washington, 1947-58; chmn. bd. dirs. Profl. Exam. Service, 1978-81; cons. AID, 1960-74; asst. to exec. med. officer United Mine Workers Welfare and Retirement Fund, Inc., 1971-74; sr. med. cons. System Scis. Inc., Bethesda, Md., 1973-81; mem. Pres.'s Commn. on Population and Am.'s Future, 1970-72; mem. com. of cons. on cancer Senate Com. on Labor and Pub. Welfare, 1970-72; mem. exec. com. Pres.'s Com. on Employment of Handicapped, 1971-85; bd. dirs. Physicians Forum, 1947-67, pres., 1960-61; pres. Community-Group Health Found., 1968-73. Bd. dirs. Pub. Citizen Found., 1992. Recipient Sesquicentennial award U. Mich., 1967; Nat. Merit award Delta Omega Soc., 1979; Disting. U.S. Immigrant award Citizens Com. Immigration Reform, 1982. Fellow Am. Coll. Preventive Medicine, Am. Coll. Hosp. Adminstrs. (hon.); mem. Med. Soc. D.C. (Community Service award 1964), Am. Cancer Soc. (v.p. 1962- 63), Am. Pub. Health Assn. (exec. com. 1964-71, pres. 1969-70, chmn. exec. bd. 1970-71, Sedgwick Meml. award 1972), D.C. Pub. Health Assn. (pres. 1963-65, Disting. Service award 1971). Home: 1220 E West Hwy Apt 622 Silver Spring MD 20910-3271 Office: Howard U Sch Med 520 W St NW Washington DC 20001-2337

CORNETT, WALTER GOZA, III, medical products executive; b. Jacksonville, Ill., Dec. 6, 1940; s. Walter G. Cornett II and Mary Helen (Norris) Miller; m. Rosanne T. Shilskey, Dec. 7, 1985; children: Cynthia, Cristin, Meredith, Megan. BSChemE, Ga. Inst. Tech., 1963; MBA, Harvard U., 1966. Asst. to pres. Baxter, Deerfield, Ill., 1966-68; pres., co-founder Convacare, Arlington Heights, Ill., 1968-70, Respiratory Care, Inc., Arlington Heights, 1970-80; founder Viridian/Corpak, Wheeling, Ill., 1980-87; pres., founder WGC Enterprises/Cerulean Fund, Glenview, Ill., 1987—; bd.dirs. Success Mag.; founder Ashley/Norris, Glenview, 1987—; mng. dir. Monona Ptnrs., 1994—; dir. Econometrics, 1993—; adv. bd. The Harbour, Des Plaines. Recipient High Tech Entrepreneur award Peat Marwick, 1987, Supporter of Entrepreneurship award Arthur Young, 1989. Mem. Westmoreland Country Club (bd. dirs. 1979-82), Harvard Bus. Sch. Club (Chgo., bd. dirs. 1990—), Econ. Club (Chgo.). Republican. Mem. Ch. of Christ. Home: 12 Old Hunt Rd Northfield IL 60093 Office: WGC Enterprises 1701 E Lake Ave Ste 170 Glenview IL 60025-2088

CORNETTE DE SAINT-CYR, BERNARD, plastic surgeon; b. Meknes, Morocco, May 27, 1944; s. Cornette de Saint-Cyr; children: Guillaume, Faustine. MD, U. Paris, 1976. Intern, Hopitaux de Paris-Ambroise Paré-Necker-St. Louis-Pitie, 1975-76; resident Hopital Jean Rostand, Paris-Iury, 1977-80; practice medicine specialising in plastic surgery, Paris, 1980—. Mem. ISAPS, Assn. de la Noblesse Franç aise, Société Française de Chirurgie Plastique, Reconstructice et Ethetique, Internat. Soc. Aesthetic Plastic Surgery, Golf Racing Club, Maxim Bus. Club, St. James Club (Paris). Address: 15 Rue Spontini, 75116 Paris France

CORNFIELD, JOEL Z., urologist; b. Milw., Aug. 25, 1957; s. Jerome Roy and Rachel Pearl (Katz) C.; m. Anne Michele Kaufmann, Mar. 25, 1984; 3 children. BA, U. Wis., 1979, MD, 1983. Intern U. Ill./Cook County Hosp., 1983-84, resident, 1984-88; sr. attending physician LaGrange (Ill.) Meml. Hosp., 1988—; attending physician Hinsdale (Ill.) Hosp., 1988—; asst. clin. prof. urology West Side VA Hosp./U. Ill., Chgo., 1991—; med. dir., founder Elm Kidney Stone Ctr., Hinsdale, 1994—. Asst. den leader Boy Scouts Am., 1995—. Office: York Urologic Assocs 950 N York Rd # 208 Hinsdale IL 60521

CORNWALL, CLAUDE CYRIL, JR., pathologist; b. Salt Lake City, Mar. 31, 1934; s. Claude Cyril Sr. and Evelyn (Thurston) C. BA, Cornell U., 1955, MD, 1959. Intern, resident St. Vincents Hosp., Manhattan, N.Y., 1959-62; resident pathology N.Y. Hosp. Cornell Med. Ctr., Manhattan, 1965-67, NYU Bellevue Med. Ctr., Manhattan, 1967-70; trainee immunopath Manhattan VA Hosp., Manhattan, 1970-71; asst. prof. pathology SUNY Upstate Med. Ctr., Syracuse VA Hosp., Syracuse, N.Y., 1971-77; assoc. pathologist Wilson Hosp., Johnson City, N.Y., 1977-80; dir. lab. Corning (N.Y.) Hosp., 1980-87; assoc. pathologist United Health Svc. Hosps., Johnson City, 1987—; clin. asst. prof. SUNY Health Sci. Ctr., Syracuse, 1988—. Capt. US Army Med. Corps., 1962-65. Fellow Coll. Am. Pathologists, Am. Soc. Clin. Pathologists; mem. U.S./Can. Acad. Pathology, N.Y. Acad. Scis. Mem. LDS Ch. Home: 512 Reynolds Rd # J-22 Johnson City

NY 13790 Office: United Health Svcs Hosps 33-57 Harrison St Johnson City NY 13790-2143

CORNWELL, ERIC LERAY, surgeon; b. L.A., Nov. 2, 1957; s. Raymond and Maple Cornwell; m. Valerie K. Mortensen, Dec. 4, 1993; 1 child, Taylor Leray. BS, Dartmouth Coll., 1979; MD, Dartmouth Med. Sch., 1982. Intern U. Calif., Davis, Calif., 1982-83, resident, 1983-87; chief of surgery and asst. physician in chief Kaiser Permanente, Stockton, Calif., 1988—. Office: 7373 Westlane Stockton CA 95209

CORNWELL, KATRINA SUE, ultrasound and x-ray technician; b. Paducah, Ky., Aug. 22, 1954; d. Albert Richard and Jo Nell (Davis) C. Grad. in Radiologic Tech., Vanderbilt U., 1974; AS, Murray State U., 1989. Registered diagnostic med. sonographer, vascular and cardiac sonographer, Ky. X-ray technician Vanderbilt U., Nashville, 1974; radiologic technologist Harlan (Ky.) Appalachian Regional Hosp., 1974-76, St. Thomas Hosp., Wichita, Kans., 1977-94, Lourdes Hosp., Paducah, Ky., 1977-94; CT technologist Ohio Cmty. Hosp., Hartford, Ky., 1990-91; ultrasound/CT technologist Crittenden Health Sys., Marion, Ky., 1992—. Mem. Right to Life, Western Ky., 1983. Mem. Soc. Diagnostic Med. Sonograph, Soc. Vascular Tech., Purchase Area Ultrasound Soc. (sec. 1995), Am. Soc. Echocardiography (watch mem. for legislation 1994—), Am. Registry Radiologic Tecnologists. Office: Crittenden Health Sys PO Box 386 Marion GA 42064-0386

CORNWELL, PAMELA LOU, nurse; b. Pittsfield, Mass., Dec. 21, 1955; d. Frank John and Doris May (Jordan) Soldo; m. Anthony Bruce Cornwell, Apr. 8, 1972; children: Chad Anthony, Rebecca Lynn, Lindsay Lee. LPN, McCaan Tech., North Adams, Mass., 1982; AS with honors, Berkshire Community Coll., Pittsfield, 1987; BSN, U. Mass., 1996. RN Mass., 1987. LPN Mapleview Nursing Home, Washington, Mass., 1982-83; LPN Berkshire Med. Ctr., Pittsfield, 1983-87, RN, 1987—. Mem. Mass. Nurses Assn. Home: 369 Old Windsor Rd Dalton MA 01226-1342

CORRAO, RICHARD GAETANO, pharmacist, scientist; b. Bklyn., Sept. 9, 1946; s. Antonio Salvatore and Salvatrice Caroline (Intoci) C.; m. Kathleen Anne Knapp, June 5, 1977; children: Carol Susan, Brandalyn Alyce, Jessica Katherine, Sarah Anne. BS in Pharmacy, St. John's U., 1969. Registered pharmacist, N.Y. Rsch. scientist Bristol Labs., Syracuse, N.Y., 1970-74; pharmacist Plaza 81 Pharmacy, Syracuse, 1974-80, Cazenovia (N.Y.) Pharmacy, 1980, Church Drugs, East Syracuse, 1980-90; sr. rsch. scientist Bristol-Myers Squibb Co., Syracuse, 1980—; pharmacist Fay's Pharmacy, Syracuse, 1990—. Mem. Am. Assn. Pharm. Scientists, Delta Sigma Theta (rec. sec. 1966-67, historian 1967-68). Roman Catholic. Home: 1 E Dickens Ct Jackson NJ 08527 Office: Bristol-Myers Squibb Co 1 Squibb Dr New Brunswick NJ 08903

CORREA, ROY JAY, JR., urologist, educator; b. Seattle, Feb. 24, 1932; s. Roy J. Correa and Flora Marie (Horst) Benaroya; m. Mabelan Nesbit, Oct. 27, 1962; children: Jay, Annemarie. BS, U. Wash., 1953; MD, U. Mich., 1956. Diplomate Am. Bd. Urology. Intern U. Colo., Denver, 1956-57; resident in urology U. Mich., Ann Arbor, 1960-65; staff urologist Virginia Mason Clinic, Seattle, 1965—, bd. dirs., 1971-73, 79-82; bd. dirs. Virginia Mason Hosp., 1985-93; clin. prof. urology U. Wash., Seattle, 1980—. Contbr. articles to med. jours. Lt. comdr. M.C., USNR, 1956-60. Fellow ACS; mem. Am. Urol. Assn. (pres.-elect 1996), Western Sect. Am. Urol. Assn. (pres. 1987), N.W. Urology Soc. (pres. 1981), Columbia Tower Club. Office: Virginia Mason Clinic 1100 9th Ave Seattle WA 98101

CORREA-PEREZ, MARGARITA, rehabilitation physician; b. Ponce, P.R., Nov. 10, 1954; d. Raul and Luisa M. (Perez) Correa; m. Julian E. Maeso-Hernandez; 1 child, Julian A. BS magna cum laude, U. Puerto Rico, Rio Pedras, P.R., 1976, MD, 1980; physical medicine and rehabilitation, U. Puerto Rico, U. Hosp., 1984. Diplomate Am. Bd. Phys. Medicine and Rehab. Dir. physical fitness program Med. Scis. Campus U. Puerto Rico, Rio Pedras, 1984—; assoc. prof. phys. medicine and rehab. U. Puerto Rico, Rio Pedras, 1984—; dir. cardiac rehab. program U. Puerto Rico Hosp., Rio Pedras, 1990—. Fellow Am. Acad. Phys. Medicine and Rehab; mem. Am. Coll. Sports Medicine, Am. Assn. Cardiovascular and Pulmonary Rehab., Am. Assn. Electrodiagnostic Medicine. Roman Catholic. Office: Ctr Fisiatrico Am Miranda # 1261 Americo Miranda Ave Rio Piedras PR 00921

CORREA-VILLASEÑOR, ADOLFO, epidemiologist, physician; b. Mazatlán, Sinaloa, Mex., Mar. 2, 1946; came to U.S., 1961; s. Adolfo and Estela (Villaseñor) Correa; m. Ana Isabel Alfaro, June 2, 1978. MS, U. Calif., San Diego, 1970, MD, 1974; MPH, Johns Hopkins U., 1981, PhD, 1987. Diplomate Am. Bd. Pediatrics, Am. Bd. Preventive Medicine. Intern San Francisco Gen. Hosp., 1974-75; resident in pediatrics U. Calif., San Francisco, 1975-77, chief resident in pediatrics, 1977-78; epidemic intelligence service officer Ctr. for Disease Control, Atlanta, 1978-80; resident in preventive medicine Johns Hopkins Sch. Hygiene and Pub. Health, Balt., 1980-83, asst. prof. epidemiology, 1987-95, assoc. prof. epidemiology, 1995—, asst. prof. pediatrics, 1988-92, assoc. prof. population dynamics, 1990—, assoc. prof. epidemiology, 1995—; vis. rsch. prof. Sch. of Pub. Health of Mex., 1993. Mem. Soc. for Epidemiologic Rsch., Teratology Soc., Am. Statis. Assn., Ambulatory Pediat. Assn., Internat. Soc. Environ. Epidemiology. Home: 419 Kensington Rd Baltimore MD 21229-2436 Office: Johns Hopkins U Dept Epidemiology 615 N Wolfe St Baltimore MD 21205-2103

CORRIERE, JOSEPH N., JR., urologist, educator; b. Easton, Pa., Apr. 3, 1937; s. Joseph N. and Rosa Ada (Poinsetta) C.; m. Evelyn Pavia Mossey, June 25, 1960 (div. July 1984); children—Joseph N., Christopher John, Gregory James, Evelyn Anne; m. Eileen Doyle Brewer, Oct. 17, 1987. B.A., U. Pa., 1959; M.D., Seton Hall Coll. Medicine, 1963. Diplomate Am. Bd. Urology (trustee). Intern Pa. Hosp., Phila., 1963-64; asst. instr. surgery, fellow in Harrison Dept. Surg. Research, Hosp. U. Pa., Phila., 1964-65, asst. instr. urology, 1965-68, USPHS urol. research trainee, 1967-68, instr. urology, 1968-69, assoc. in urology, 1969-71, asst. prof. urology, 1971-74; venereal disease trainee Phila. Dept. Pub. Health, 1965; radioisotope trainee William H. Donner Ctr. for Radiology, Phila., 1965-66; prof., dir. div. urology, dept. surgery U. Tex. Med. Sch., Houston, 1974-93, interim chmn. dept. surgery, 1980-82, assoc. chmn. dept. surgery, 1984-86; chief urology service Hermann Hosp., 1974-93, Tex. Med. Ctr., Houston; cons. Lyndon Baines Johnson Hosp., residency review com. urology, NASA. Contbr. numerous articles to profl. jours. Trustee Am. Bd. Urology. Served to maj. USAF, 1969-71. Mem. Am. Urol. Assn. (dir. edn. 1993—), Soc. Univ. Surgeons, ACS, Soc. Univ. Urologists (pres. 1987-88, sec.-treas. 1984-86, pres. 1987-88), Am. Assn. Genitourol. Surgery, Am. Assn. for Surgery of Trauma. Roman Catholic. Home: 7511 Morningside Dr Houston TX 77030-3619 Office: U Tex Med Sch Dept Urology 6431 Fannin St Ste 6018 Houston TX 77030-1501

CORRIGAN, CHRISTOPHER JOHN, medical educator; b. Grays, Essex, U.K., Apr. 16, 1958; s. George and Glenda (Tyler) C.; m. Anne Rhiannon Richards; children: Jonathan Ariel, Philip Corin. MSc, U. Oxford, Eng., 1980, MA, 1985; PhD, U. London, 1990. Gen. med. intern Queen Mary's Hosp., Sidcup, U.K., 1984-86; registrar Royal Brampton Hosp., London, 1986-91; sr. registrar in medicine Royal Brampton Hosp./Nat. Heart & Lung Inst., London, 1991-93, hon. cons. physician, sr. lectr. in medicine, 1993-96; hon. cons. physician, sr. lectr. in medicine Charing Cross and Westminster Med. Sch., London, 1996—. Contbr. articles to profl. publs., chpts. to books. Recipient Charlton Briscoe Meml. prize for med. rsch. King's Coll. Hosp. Med. Sch./U. London, 1992; Allergy 200 Internat. Young Investigator award EAACI/Schering-Plough, 1993. Mem. Brit. Soc. for Allergy and Clin. Immunology (coun. mem. 1995—), Royal Coll. Physicians (com. on immunology and allergy 1993-95). Roman Catholic. Home: Chrannies Messons Ln, Grays Essex RM17 5EE, England Office: Charing Cross/Westminster, Fulham Palace Rd, London W6 8RF, England

CORRIGAN, JAMES JOHN, JR., pediatrician, dean; b. Pitts., Aug. 28, 1935; s. James John and Rita Mary (Grimes) C.; m. Carolyn Virginia Long, July 2, 1960; children: Jeffrey James, Nancy Carolyn. B.S., Juniata Coll., Huntingdon, Pa., 1957; M.D. with honors, U. Pitts., 1961. Diplomate: Am. Bd. Pediatrics (hematology-oncology). Intern, then resident in pediatrics U. Colo. Med. Center, 1961-64; trainee in pediatric hematology-oncology U. Ill. Med. Center, 1964-66; asso. in pediatrics Emory U. Med. Sch., 1966-67; asst. prof. Emory U. Med. Sch., Atlanta, 1967-71; mem. faculty U. Ariz. Coll. Medicine, Tucson, 1971-90; prof. pediatrics U. Ariz. Coll. Medicine, 1974-90; chief sect. pediatric hematology-ongology, also dir. Mountain States Regional Hemophilia Center, U. Ariz., Tucson, 1978-90; chief of staff U. Med. Ctr. U. Ariz., Tucson, 1984-86; prof. pediatrics, vice dean for acad. affairs Tulane U. Sch. Medicine, New Orleans, 1990-93, interim dean, 1993-94, dean, 1994—. Assoc. editor Am. Jour. Diseases of Children, 1981-89, 90-93, interim editor, 1993; contbr. numerous papers to med. jours. Grantee NIH, Mountain States Regional Hemophilia Ctr., Ga. Heart Assn., GE, Am. Cancer Soc. Mem. Am. Acad. Pediatrics, Am. Soc. Hematology, Soc. Pediatric Rsch., Western Soc. Pediatric Rsch., Am. Heart Assn. (coun. thrombosis), Internat. Soc. Thrombosis and Haemostasis, Am. Pediatric Soc., World Fedn. Hemophilia, Pima County Med. Assn. (v.p., 1986—, pres. 1988—), Alpha Omega Alpha. Republican. Roman Catholic. Office: Tulane U Sch Medicine Office of Dean 1430 Tulane Ave New Orleans LA 70112-2699

CORRIGAN, MICHELLE ANN, critical care nurse; b. Carbondale, Pa., Nov. 20, 1963; d. James E. and Rosemary (Frisbie) C. Diploma, Community Med. Ctr. Sch. Nursing, Scranton, Pa., 1986; student, Marywood Coll. RN, Pa. Staff nurse ICU Marion Community Hosp., Carbondale. Home: 142 8th Ave Carbondale PA 18407-2474

CORRIGAN, PATRICK WILLIAM, psychologist, educator; b. Evanston, Ill., Apr. 19, 1956; s. Lloyd and Eileen (Hardt) C.; m. Georgeen Marie Carson, Aug. 8, 1981; children: Abraham, Elizabeth. BS, Creighton U., 1978; MA, Roosevelt U., 1981; D in Psychology, Ill. Sch. Profl. Psychology, 1989. Lic. psychologist, Ill. Assoc. prof. psychiatry and dir. U. Chgo., Ctr. for Psychiat. Rehab., 1990—; dir. Ill. Staff Tng. Inst., Chgo., 1993—. Author: Rehab Teams that Work, 1996; editor: Cognitive Rehabilitation of Neuropsychiatry, 1996; editor-in-chief Psychiat. Rehab. Skills, 1996; contbr. articles to profl. jours. Leadership in the Rehab. Team grantee U.S. Dept. Edn., 1995—. Office: Univ Chgo Ctr Psychiat Rehab 7230 Arbor Dr Tinley Park IL 60477

CORRY, DALILA BOUDJELLAL, internist; b. El-Arrouch, Algeria, July 7, 1943; came to U.S., 1981; MD, U. Algiers, 1974. Intern Hosp. Mustapha Algiers, 1972-73; resident Hosp. Tenon, Paris, 1975-79; fellow in nephrology UCLA, 1981-83; chief renal divsn. Olive View-UCLA Med. Ctr., Sylmar, Calif.; assoc. prof. clin. medicine UCLA. Recipient Clinician-Scientist award Am. Heart Assn., 1995-96. Mem. Am. Hosp. Assn., Am. Soc. Nephrology. Office: Olive View-UCLA Med Ctr 14445 Olive View Dr Sylmar CA 91342-1495

CORSON, RICHARD HOWELL, gynecologist; b. Woodbury, N.J., Nov. 2, 1931; s. James Clark and Elizabeth (Ayars) C.; m. Estelle Marie McCann, Sept. 15, 1959 (dec.); children: Elizabeth Ayars, George Westmoreland; m. Kathy S. Bridges, May 5, 1995. BS, Haverford Coll., 1953; MD, Temple U., 1957. Diplomate, Am. Bd. Ob-Gyn. Intern Jackson (Fla.) Meml. Hosp., 1957-58, resident in ob-gyn., 1963-67; pvt. practice Miami, Fla., 1967—; asst. chief dept. ob-gyn Bapt. Hosp., 1976-77, dept. chief, 1978-79; clin. assoc. prof. Sch. Medicine U. Miami, 1976-85. Fellow Am. Coll. Ob-Gyn (regional rep. 1988—); mem. AMA, Fla. Med. Assn., Dade County Med. Assn., Fla. Ob-Gyn Soc., Miami Ob-Gyn Soc. (sec. 1980-83, v.p. 1983-84, pres. 1984-85), South Atlantic Assn. Ob-Gyn, Am. Fertility Soc., Soc. Desc. Signers of Declaration of Independence (past pres.), John Bartram Assn. Office: 568 E Oaks Shopping Ctr Hwy 6 E Batesville MS 38606

CORTA, NANCY RUTH, nurse; b. Gorman, Tex., Feb. 15, 1957; d. Dale Newton and Perelene Ruth (Wright) Johnson; 1 child, Joseph Henry Johnson. BSN, Tex. Woman's U., Denton, 1980. Staff nurse Baylor U. Med. Ctr., Dallas, 1980-81; charge nurse ICU/CCU DeLeon Hosp., Tex., 1981-82; staff nurse MICU/CCU VA Med. Ctr., Phoenix, 1982-83; staff nurse Harris Hosp. Meth., Ft. Worth, 1983-84, Tex. Dept. Health, Stephenville, 1984-95; nurse Dublin Ind. Sch. Dist., 1995—. Mem. Tex. Women's U. Alumni Assn., Epsilon Sigma Alpha. Lodge: Order Eastern Star. Home: Rt 2 Box 192 De Leon TX 76444 Office: 701 Thomas Dublin TX 76446

CORTRIGHT, LOUISE VERA, retired medical technologist, small business owner; b. Buffalo, Apr. 22, 1938; d. Asa Lawrence and Mary Lois (Ward) C. BS with honors, Fairleigh Dickson U., 1960; postgrad., Rutgers U., 1965-67. Nationally registered med. technologist. Bacteriology supr. Middlesex Gen. Hosp., New Brunswick, N.J., 1963-64; hematology supr. Princeton Hosp., Princeton, N.J., 1964-65; teaching supr. Somerset Med. Ctr., Somerset, N.J., 1965-67; chief technologist Somerset Med. Ctr., 1966-79; owner, operator Aurora Kennel, Bridgewater, N.J., 1973-92; cons. N.J. State Dept. of Health, Trenton, 1979-80. Treas., v.p. Bridgewater Twp. Bd. of Health, 1974, 1975; chmn. Regional Animal Shelter, 1978-81. Mem. Morris Hills Dog Training Club (founding mem. 1961), North Jersey Shetland Sheepdog Club (founding mem. 1965).

CORWIN, BERT CLARK, optometrist; b. Rapid City, S.D., Oct. 4, 1930; s. Meade and Adeline (Clark) C.; m. Lydia M. Forehand; children: B. Clark II, Kelley Linette Fromm. AS, S.D. State U., 1952; BS, Ill. Coll. Optometry, Chgo., 1956, OD, 1957. Pvt. practice optometry Rapid City, 1957—; projects chmn. S.D. Lions Sight and Svc. Found., 1964; chmn. med. adv. com. to S.D. Dept. Pub. Welfare, 1968-76; mem. S.D. Adv. Coun. for Regional Med. and Health Planning, 1971; cons. S.D. Dept. Human Svcs., 1989—; mem. adv. bd. S.D. Dept. of Svc. to Visual Impaired. Contbr. articles to profl. jours. Pres. Cleghorn PTA, Rapid City, 1968-70; bd. dirs. Am. Optometric Found., 1989-90, v.p., 1990-94, pres., 1994—. Fellow Am. Acad. Optometry (diplomate contact lens sect., sec.-treas. 1985-86, pres.-elect 1987-88, pres. 1988-90, chmn. 1st internat. meeting 1992); mem. Am. Optometric Assn. (exec. com. 1974-76, Am. Optometrist of the Yr. 1993), S.D. Optometric Soc. (pres. 1970-71), North Ctrl. State Optometric Conf. (bd. dirs. 1970-71), Black Hills Optometric Soc. (sec.-treas. 1958-69), S.D. State Bd. Examiners (pres. 1982-85), Nat. Acad. Practice Optometry (sec.-treas. 1990-94, Disting. Practitioners award, co-chair 1994—). Republican. Methodist. Club: Black Hills Water Ski (pres. 1963). Lodges: Masons, Elks, Lions (pres. Rushmore chpt. 1961-62). Home: 5436 Timberline Trl Rapid City SD 57702-1806 Office: 810 Mountain View Rd Rapid City SD 57702-2520

CORWIN, WILLIAM, psychiatrist; b. Boston, Oct. 28, 1908; M.D., Tufts Coll., 1932; m. Frances M. Wetherell (dec.) m. Joyce S. Newman, 1965. Intern Wesson Meml. Hosp., Springfield, Mass., 1932-33; physician Met. State Hosp., Waltham, Mass., 1933-37, asst. supt., 1937-42; rsrch. fellow Harvard, 1937-46; practice medicine, specializing in psychiatry, Springfield, Mass., 1946-54, Miami, Fla., 1954-88, Ocala, Fla., 1988—; mem. staff Charter Springs Hosp., Ocala., Marion Community Hosp., Ocala; instr. psychiatry Boston U., 1937-46, Tufts Coll., 1941-46; clin. assoc. prof. psychiatry U. Miami, 1955-70, clin. prof., 1970-88. Past mem. State Fla. Adv. Com. on Mental Health; agy. ops. com. United Fund. Bd. dirs. Family and Childrens Svcs. Miami. Served to lt. col. M.C., USAAF, 1942-46. Diplomate Am. Bd. Psychiatry and Neurology, Am. Bd. Forensic Psychiatry. Fellow Am. Psychiat. Assn. (life), Am. Coll. Psychiatrists; mem. AMA, S. Fla. Psychiat. Soc. (councillor), Fla. Psychiat. Soc. Contbr. articles on physiology of schizophrenia to profl. publs. Office: 1111 NE 25th Ave Ocala FL 34470-5675

COSCAS, GABRIEL JOSUE, ophthalmologist, educator; b. Tunis, Mar. 1, 1931; s. Jules Joseph and Gilda (Guez) C.; M.D., U. Paris, 1963; m. Gisele Nataf, Mar. 23, 1957; children—Florence, Brigitte. Chief ophthalmology clinic Hotel Dieu, Paris, 1963-70; maitre conf. agrege Univ. Paris-Val de Marne, 1970-79, prof. ophthalmology, chmn. dept. Univ. Eye Clinic de Creteil, 1979—; founder Conf. Angiographie de Creteil, 1972—. Served as med. lt. French Army, 1958-60. Decorated chevalier de l'Ordre de Palmes Academiques, 1984, chevalier de l'Ordre Nat. de la Legion d'Honneur, 1985. Mem. Internat. Orgn. Against Trachoma (pres. 1977), French Soc. Photocoagulation (pres. 1988), Acad. Internat. Ophthalmology, Assn. U. Profs. of Ophthalmology of France (gen. sec. 1994, pres.), Joint Eurpean Soc. Rsch. Opthalmology and Vision (pres.). Author books, articles in field. Home: 203 Vaugirard, 75015 Paris France Office: 40 Ave Verdun, 94010 Creteil France

COSCIA, ROBERT L., physician; b. Memphis, Feb. 16, 1937; s. Louis and Anne (Lingua) C.; m. Joan K. Kingsbury, Dec. 27, 1964 (div. Jan. 1981); children: Paul, Matthew, Lori; m. Karen Kaye Kennedy, June 1, 1989. BS, Tex. A&M U., 1959; MD, U. Tenn., 1962. With Surg. Assocs. of Ozarks, Springfield, Mo.; asst. clin. prof. U. Mo., Kansas City, 1986—; bd. dirs. Mo. Chpt. Am. Cancer Soc., Springfield, 1975-83; instr. ATLS, 1982—; chmn. Mo. Dist. 3 com. on applicants ACOS, Sprinfield, 1987-94, mem., 1978-94, chmn. com. on trauma, Chgo., 1989—, site visature, 1993—; del. Mo. State Med. Assn., Jefferson City, 1984; chmn. sub-com. adv. coun. Pediatric EMS, Jefferson City, 1991-94; mem. state adv. coun. EMS, Jefferson City, 1991-94; cons. Mo. Patient Rev. Found., Jefferson City, 1986—. Maj. USAF, 1969-71. Recipient EMS Leadership award Mo. Dept. Health, Jefferson City, 1994, Trauma Achievement award ACOS, Chgo., 1994. Mem. N.Am. Limousin Found. (bd. dirs. 1986-92, pres. 1990), Internat. Limousin Coun. (pres. 1990-92). Baptist. Home: 5724 E Farm Rd 132 Springfield MO 65802 Office: Surg Assocs of Ozarks 1900 S National Springfield MO 65802

COSCO, JOHN ANTHONY, health care executive, educator; b. Cin., July 13, 1947; s. Adolph John and Pasqualina Marie (Saluppo) C.; m. Anne Patricia Ward, Aug. 5, 1978; children: Stephen Ward, Justin Thomas. BS, Xavier U., Cin., 1969, MEd, 1972, MBA, 1975; postgrad. U. Cin., 1972, PhD in Health Svcs. and Mgmt., Columbia-Pacific U., 1986; dir. edn. and staff devel. Jewish Hosp., Cin., 1972-77; exec. dir. Region IX Peer Rev. Systems, Inc., Portsmouth, Ohio, 1977-78; exec. dir. Region II Med. Rev. Corp., Dayton, Ohio, 1978-81; asst. adminstr., sr. v.p. Mercy Hosp., Tiffin, Ohio, 1981-87; adminstr. Grafton (W.Va.) City Hosp., 1987-89; sr. v.p., COO The St. Francis Acad., Inc., Salina, Kans., 1989—; ptnr. Hos-Con & Assocs., 1974-79; pres. & CEO hale foster & stunning, 1993—; bd. dirs. Sunflower Health Network, Inc.; bus. instr. Kans. State U., Salina, 1996—; adj. asst. prof. in bus. mgmt. and health svcs. adminstrn. Benedictine Coll. at Marymount, 1990-96; past adj. faculty mem., Southern Ohio Coll, 1975-76, Xavier U., 1976-81, Sinclair Community Coll., 1979-80, Tiffin U., 1982-87, Columbia-Pacific U., 1986-89, Wichita State U., 1990. Lt. AUS, 1969-71. Decorated Bronze Star. Fellow Am. Coll. Health Care Execs.; mem. Kans. Intergenerational Network. Roman Catholic. Home: 1224 Fredrich Dr Salina KS 67401-5276 Office: St Francis Academy Inc 509 E Elm St Salina KS 67401-2353

COSENZA, MARIO ANTHONY, emergency medicine physician; b. Bklyn., Oct. 19, 1962; s. Anthony and Teresa (Torchiano) C. BA, NYU, 1984; DO, UOMHS, Des Moines, 1990. Diplomate Am. Bd. Osteo. Emergency Medicine Physicians. Osteo. rotating intern Delaware Valley Med. Ctr., Langhorne, Pa., 1990-91; osteo. emergency medicine resident St. Barnabas Hosp./NYCOM, Bronx, 1991-94; allopathic pediatric emergency medicine fellow Jacobi Hosp., Bronx, 1994-96; emergency medicine attending Morristown (N.J.) Meml. Hosp., 1996—. Home: 70 Wildflower Ln Morristown NJ 07960 Office: Morristown Meml Hosp 100 Madison Ave Morristown NJ 07962

COSERIU, GEORGE V., physician and surgeon; b. Youngstown, Ohio, Mar. 28, 1949; s. Vasile G. and Sylvia (Corujan) C.; m. Penny Louise Billo, Dec. 28, 1973 (div. 1996); children: Gregg, Allison, Marc and Stephanie (twins). AB in Biol. Chemistry, Washington U., St. Louis, 1971; postgrad., Cleve. State U., 1971-72, Autonomous U. Guadalajara, Mex.; MD, Case Western Res. U., 1977. Diplomate Am. Bd. Urology. Resident in gen. surgery Cleve. Clinic, 1977-79, resident in urology, 1979-82, spl. fellow in renal transplant, 1982-83; pvt. practice Urology Assocs. West, Inc., Lakewood, Ohio, 1983-94, S.W. Urology Inc., Parma, Ohio, 1994—; chmn. dept. urology Parma Hosp., 1991—; mem. med. adv. bd. Kidney Found. N.E. Ohio, 1992—; mem. physician adv. bd. Coram Inc., 1991—; organ recovery surgeon Life Bone Transplant Program N.E. Ohio, 1980—. Contbr. articles to profl. jours. Fellow ACS; mem. AMA, Am. Assn. Clin. Urologists, Urol. Soc. Transplantation and Vascular Surgery, Ohio State Med. Assn., Cleve. Acad. Medicine, Ohio Urol. Soc. Republican. Roman Catholic. Home: 8173 Dalebrook Blvd Independence OH 44131 Office: SW Urology Inc 6707 Powers Blvd Parma OH 44129

COSGRIFF, JAMES ARTHUR, physician; b. Lamberton, Minn., Mar. 18, 1924; s. James Arthur and Elsie Ann (Forster) C. BS summa cum laude, Coll. St. Thomas, 1944; MD, U. Minn., 1946. Diplomate Am. Bd. Family Practice. Intern St. Mary's Hosp., Duluth, Minn.; pvt. practice Olivia, Minn., 1949—. With USN, 1947-49. Fellow Am. Acad. Family Physicians; mem. Minn. Acad. Family Physicians (pres. 1963, Merit award 1964). Roman Catholic. Home: 802 E Park Ave Olivia MN 56277 Office: Olivia Clinic 619 E Lincoln Ave Olivia MN 56277

COSGRIFF, STUART WORCESTER, internist, consultant; b. Pittsfield, Mass., May 8, 1917; s. Thomas F. and Frances Deford (Worcester) C.; m. Mary Shaw, Jan. 23, 1943; children: Mary, Thomas, Stuart, Richard, Robert. B.A. cum laude, Holy Cross Coll., 1938; M.D., Columbia U., 1942, D.Med. Sci., 1948. Diplomate: Am. Bd. Internal Medicine. Intern Presbyterian Hosp., N.Y.C., 1942-43; asst. resident in medicine, 1943, 46-47, chief resident, 1947-48; instr. in medicine Columbia U., N.Y.C., 1948-50, clin. asst. prof. medicine, 1951-63, clin. assoc. prof., 1963-73, clin. prof. medicine, 1973-83, clin. prof. emeritus, 1983—; attending physician Presbyn. Hosp., N.Y.C., 1948-83; cons. emeritus Presbyn. Hosp., 1984—; individual practice medicine, specializing in internal medicine and vascular diseases, 1948—; cons. in medicine to dir. Selective Svc., N.Y.C., 1957-73, N.Y. Giants Baseball Club, 1951-57, San Francisco Baseball Club, 1958-61; dir. thrombo-embolic clinic Vanderbilt Clinic, N.Y.C., 1948-83. Contbr. articles to med. jours. Served to capt. M.C., U.S. Army, 1943-45, ETO. Fellow ACP, Pan Am. Med. Assn.; mem. Am. Heart Assn., N.Y. Heart Assn., Alpha Omega Alpha. Roman Catholic. Club: Knickerbocker Country (Tenafly, N.J.). Home and Office: 11 Park St Tenafly NJ 07670-2217 Office: 161 Ft Washington Ave New York NY 10032-3713

COSKEY, RALPH JOSEPH, dermatologist, dermapathologist; b. Detroit, July 29, 1929; s. Leo Alexander and Hedwig Coskey; married; children: Laura, Larry. BS, U. Mich., 1951; MD, Wayne State U., 1955. Diplomate Am. Bd. Dermatology. Intern Sinai Hosp., Detroit, 1955-56; dermatology resident Henry Ford Hosp., Detroit, 1958-61; pvt. practice specializing in dermatology Farmington, Mich., 1962—; clin. prof. dept. dermatology Wayne State U. Sch. Medicine, Detroit, 1982-96; chmn. sect. dermatology Sinai Hosp., Detroit, 1975-96. Contbr. numerous articles on dermatology to profl. jours. Pres., treas., sec. graphic arts coun. Detroit Inst. Arts, 1973-80, 77, 81, 82-84. Capt. USAF, 1956-58. Mem. AMA, Am. Acad. Dermatology (adv. coun. 1986-92), Noah Worcester Dermatol. Soc. (bd. dirs. 1981-84), Mich. Dermatol. Soc. (past pres., sec.-treas.), Oakland County Med. Soc. (bd. dirs. 1988-91, treas. 1991-92), Alpha Omega Alpha. Office: Farmington Dermatologists 23133 Orchard Lake Rd Farmington MI 48336

COSMAN, BARD CLIFFORD, surgeon, educator; b. N.Y.C., Mar. 1, 1963; s. Bard and Madeleine (Pelner) C.; m. Pamela Caren Feldman, mar. 26, 1989; children: Benjamin, Rafael. AB magna cum laude, Harvard U., 1983; MPH, MD, Columbia U., 1987. Diplomate Nat. Bd. Med. Examiners, Am. Bd. Surgery. Resident in surgery Stanford (Calif.) U., 1987-89, postdoctoral fellow, 1989-91; fellow spinal cord injury svc. Palo Alto (Calif.) VA Med. Ctr., 1989-91; resident in surgery Stanford U. Hosp., 1991-94; resident in colon and rectal surgery U. Minn., 1994-95; asst. clin. prof. surgery U. Calif., San Diego, 1995—. Contbr. articles to profl. jours. NRSA Tng. grantee Nat. Cancer Inst., Bethesda, 1990; Giannini Found. Postdoctoral Rsch. fellow Bank of Am., San Francisco, 1990. Home: 3303 Caminito Gandara LaJolla CA 92037-2906 Office: VA Med Ctr Surgical Svc 112E 3350 LaJolla Village Dr San Diego CA 92161-5017

COSMAN, FELICIA, endocrinologist, educator; b. N.Y.C., June 12, 1958. BA with distinction, Cornell U., 1979; MD, Stony Brook Med. Sch., 1983. Diplomate Am. Bd. Internal Medicine, Am. Bd. Internal Medicine, Endocrinology and Metabolism, Nat. Bd. Med. Examiners. Intern dept. medicine Columbia Presbyn. Med. Ctr., N.Y.C., 1983-84, resident, 1984-86; NIH fellow divsn. endocrinology Columbia Coll. Phys. and Surg., N.Y.C., 1986-88, instr. clin. medicine, 1988-90, asst. prof. medicine, 1990-96; endocrinologist, metabolic bone specialist Helen Hayes Hosp., West Haverstraw, N.Y., 1988—; cons. St. Luke's Roosevelt Hosp., N.Y.C., 1993; clin. dir. Nat. Osteoporosis Found., 1996—. Assoc. editor Osteoporosis: Index and Reviews, 1995—; contbr. articles to profl. jours., chpts. in books. NIH grantee, 1993—. Mem. ACP (assoc.), Am. Soc. Bone and Mineral Rsch. Office: Helen Hayes Hosp West Haverstraw NY 10993

COSMIDES, GEORGE JAMES, medical scientist, consultant; b. Pitts., July 23, 1926; s. James George and Katina Nikola (Palogari) C.; m. Nasia Murlas, Sept. 12, 1948; 1 child, Leda. BS, U. Pitts., 1952; MS, Purdue U., 1954, PhD, 1956. Registered pharmacist, Pa. Pharmacist Ind. and Pa., 1952-56; psychopharmacologist Smith Kline & French Labs., Phila., 1956-57; asst. prof. pharmacology U. R.I., Kingston, 1957-59; pharmacologist NIMH, Bethesda, Md., 1959-63; dir. pharmacology and toxicology Nat. Inst. Gen. Med. Scis., Bethesda, Md., 1963-74, dep. dir. divsn. specialized info. svcs., 1974-94; assoc. dir. Nat. Libr. Medicine, Bethesda, Md., 1994—; pres. P-T Info. Svcs., Rockville, Md., 1995—; mem. NIH Prevention Coord. Com., Bethesda, 1989-95; dir. pharmacology rsch. assoc. tng. NIH, Bethesda, 1963-74; disting. lectr. award AAAS, Washington, 1971. Editor: Microsomes and Drug Oxidations, 1969, The Handling of Toxicological Information, 1978, Information Transfer in Toxicology-Proceedings, 1981 (Excellence award 1982); editor Toxicology Info. Series, Fundamental & Applied Toxicology, 1990. Mem. parish coun. St. George's Ch., Bethesda, 1970-80; organizer, coach Rockville City Girls Softball League, 1965-68; pres. PTA Montgomery County Schs., Rockville, 1963-74; mem. Citizens for Good Govt., Rockville, 1962-72. Staff sgt. U.S. Army, 1944-46, PTO. Decorated Bronze Star, Purple Heart; recipient Disting. Alumnus award U. Pitts., 1966. Mem. Soc. Toxicology (chmn. info. handling com. 1983-87), Am. Soc. for Pharmacology & Exptl. Therapeutics, Internat. Union of Pharmacology, Internat. Coun. Sci. Unions (com. on data for sci. and tech. 1977—), Internat. Soc. Regulatory Toxicology and Pharmacology (coun. 1995—), Toastmasters Internat. (pres. NIH chpt. 1973). Home: 639 Crocus Dr Rockville MD 20850-2046

COSTA, ERMINIO, pharmacologist, cell biology educator; b. Cagliari, Italy, Mar. 9, 1924; s. Oreste and Gigina (Murgia) C.; divorced; children: Max, Robert Henry, Michael John; m. Ingeborg Hanbauer, July 13, 1973. MD, U. Cagliari, 1947, PhD in Pharmacology, 1953; PhD in Biol. Sci. (hon.), U. Cagliari, Italy, 1986; DSc (hon.), Georgetown U., 1992; MD (hon.), U. Tampere, Finland, 1992. Asst. prof., assoc. prof. U. Cagliari, 1948-54, prof. pharmacology, 1954-56; physician II, med. rsch. assn. Thudichum Psychology Rsch., Galesburg, Ill., 1956-60; vis. scientist NIH, Bethesda, Md., 1960-61; dep. chief lab. chem. pharmacology Nat. Heart Inst., Bethesda, 1961-63, head sect. clin. pharmacology, 1963-65; assoc. prof. pharmacology Columbia U., N.Y.C., 1965-68; chief lab. preclin pharmacology St. Elizabeth's Hosp., Washington, 1968-85; dir. Fidia-Georgetown Inst. for the Neurosci. Georgetown U., Washington, 1985-94; McDonnel vis. prof. neurology Washington U. Sch. Medicine, St. Louis, 1994—; now sci. dir. U. Ill. at Chgo. Psychiat. Inst. Editor Neuropharmacology, 1967, Advance Biochem Psychopharmacology, 1968; contbr. 915 articles to profl. jours. Recipient Bennet award and Gold medal Soc. Biol. Psychiatry, Gold medal Fed. II Univ., Naples, 1990, Premio Fiuggi award Fiuggi Rsch. Found., 1988. Mem. NAS, Academia Nazionale Lincei, Am. Soc. Pharmacology and Exptl. Theareutics., Am. Soc. Physiology., Am. Soc. Biol. Chemistry and Molecular Biology, Cosmos Club, Pepipathetic Club. Office: Psychiatric Ins. Univ of Illinois at Chicago 1601 West Taylor St Chicago IL 60612*

COSTA, MAX, health facility administrator, pharmacology educator, environmental medicine educator; b. Jan. 10, 1952. BS in Biology, Georgetown U., 1974; PhD in Pharmacology, U. Ariz., 1976. Rsch. asst. NIMH, Bethesda, Md., 1970-72, Lab. Tumor Cell Biology, Nat. Cancer Inst., Bethesda, Md., 1972-74; rsch. assoc., divsn. radiation oncology U. Ariz. Sch. of Medicine, Tucson, 1976; asst. prof. lab. medicine U. Conn. Sch. Medicine, Farmington, Conn., 1977-79; asst. prof. dept pharmacology and toxicology Coll. Medicine, Tex. A & M Univ., Coll. Sta., Tex., 1979-80; asst. prof. dept. pharmacology U. Tex. Medical Sch., Houston, 1980-81, assoc. prof. dept pharmacology, 1981-85, prof. dept. pharmacology, 1985-86; prof. environ. medicineand pharmacology NYU Med. Ctr., N.Y.C., 1986-92; dep. dir. Inst. Environ. Medicine, NYU Med. Ctr., N.Y.C., 1986-92, prof., chmn. dept. environ. medicine, 1993—; dir. The Nelson Inst. Environ. Medicine, Tuxedo, N.Y., 1993—; Burroughs Wellcome prof. U. South Ala. Coll. Medicine, 1996; expert witness testified U.S. Congressional Hearing, 1979, Dept. Labor, OSHA, 1990; cons. Amax Inc., 1977-80, NiPera, 1981, 82; vis. prof. Kurume U., Japan, 1989; invited lectr., speaker Nat. Cancer Ctr. Rsch. Inst., Tokyo, Kitasato U., Tokyo, Shizuoka Coll., Japan, Kurume U., Japan, Robert Wood Johnson Med. Sch., N.J., Temple U., Pa., U. Milan, Italy, U. Tenn., U. Calif., Rutgers U., Cornell U., Brown U., and numerous others. Author: Metal Carcinogenesis Testing: Principles and In Vitro Methods, 1980; Editor: Environmental Carcinogenesis Chemosphere, 1981-83, Biology of Metals, 1988-90, Journal of Pharmacology and Experimental Therapeutics, 1992—; editorial bd. Cell Biology and Toxicology, 1987—, Biological Trace Element Research, 1988—, BioMetals, 1992—; editor in chief Molecular Toxicology, 1989-91; contbr. to numerous profl. jours. including Journal Biological Chemistry, Biochemistry Journal, Science, Cancer Research and numerous others;. Recipient Young Environ. Scientist award NIH, 1978-81, Kenneth Morgareidge award Internat. Life Scis. Inst., 1984; Hoffmann-La Roche Inc. grantee, 1974-76, Conn. Rsch. Found, 1977-78, NIH-NIEHS, 1978-81, 78-79, 79-80, 80-81, 89—, 88—, 91—, 90—, NIH-NCI CA, 1982-85, 85-90, Amax. Inc., 1978, 79, U.S. EPA, 1980-84, 1985-88, 90-93, U.S. Dept. Energy, 1981-86, Chem. Mfr. Assn., 1987-88, Rutgers U., 1994—. Mem. AAAS, Am. Soc. Cell Biology, Am. Soc. Biochemistry and Molecular Biology, Am. Soc. Pharmacology and Experimental Therapeutics, Soc. Toxicology, Am. Assn. Cancer Rsch., Internat. Assn. Bioinorganic Scientists, Internat. Assn. Environ. Analytical Chemistry. Office: NYU Med Ctr Inst of Environ Medicine 550 1st Ave New York NY 10016-6481*

COSTA, ROBIN LEUEEN, psychologist, counselor; b. Hackensack, N.J., Dec. 9, 1948; d. Frank G. and Hazel L. (Brown) C. BA, Colby Coll., 1970; MA in Clin. Psychology, Fairleigh Dickinson U., 1973; MBA, Fla. Atlantic U., 1984. Lic. mental health counselor, sch. psychologist, Fla.; nat. cert. sch. psychologist. Sch. psychologist Broward County Sch. Bd., Ft. Lauderdale, Fla., 1973-91; pres., chief exec. officer Silver Linings Fin. Care, Ft. Lauderdale, 1986—; pvt. practice Ft. Lauderdale, 1991—. Mem. Jung Generations Soc. (founder). Home: 3750 Galt Ocean Dr Fort Lauderdale FL 33308-7656

COSTABEL, ULRICH, pneumologist; b. Schramberg, Germany, Jan. 31, 1949; s. Armin and Ingeborg (Rasche) C.; m. Josune Guzman y Rotaeche, Sept. 2, 1982. MD, U. Freiburg, Germany, 1975, Dr. med. habil., 1986. Diplomate in internal medicine, pulmonary and allergy. Intern, resident, clin. and rsch. fellow dept. medicine U. Freiburg, 1978-85, staff mem. sect. of pulmonary diseases, 1985-87; chief pulmonary and allergy sect. Ruhrlandklinik, Essen, Germany, 1988—; assoc. prof. medicine U. Essen, 1988-94, prof. medicine, 1994—; vis. scientist Chest Disease Rsch. Inst., Kyoto (Japan) U., 1992-93. Chief editor European Respiratory Jour., 1994—; author: Atlas der Bronchoalveolären Lavage, 1994; contbr. about 250 articles to sci. jours. and about 50 chpts. to books. Recipient Karl-Hansen prize German Soc. Allergy, 1987, Sarcoidosis Rsch. prize German Sarcoidosis Assn., 1994; Japan Soc. for Promotion of Sci. rsch. fellow, 1992. Fellow Am. Coll. Chest Physicians; mem. German Soc. Pneumology, German Soc. Cytology, European Respiratory Soc. (sci. group chmn. 1991-93), Am. Thoracic Soc. (internat. advisor sci. program com. 1990—), World Assn. Sarcoidosis (exec. com. 1991—, v.p. 1995—). Office: Ruhrlandklinik, Tüschener Weg 40, D-45239 Essen Germany

COSTALL, BRENDA, university official, research neuropharmacologist; b. York, Eng., Sept. 12, 1947; d. John and Eileen Stella (Austin) C.; m. Robert John Naylor, Dec. 13, 1969. BPharm with honors, U. Bradford, Eng., 1969, PhD in Neuropharmacology, 1972, DSc, 1984. Rsch. fellow U. Bradford, 1972-73, from lectr. to sr. lectr. pharmacology, 1973-83, reader neuropharmacology, 1983-85, prof., 1985—, pro vice-chancellor planning and resources, 1990-92, sr. pro vice chancellor, 1992-94, dep. vice chancellor, 1994—; presenter in field. Patentee use of novel anxiolytics, antipsychotics and memory enhancing compounds; contbr. articles to profl. jours. Grantee Med. Rsch. Coun., Sci. and Engring. Rsch.Coun., Wellcome Trust, Parkinson's Disease Soc., Assn. To Combat Huntington's Chorea, Brit. Tech. Group, pharm. cos. in Europe, U.S. and Japan, 1975-94. Mem. British Pharmacol. Soc. (com. mem.), Brain Rsch. Assn., Collegium Internat. Neuro-Psychopharmacologicum, European Neuroscis. Assn., British Assn. Psychopharmacology, European Coll. Neuropsychopharmacology, N.Y. Acad. Scis.

COSTANZO, RICHARD MICHAEL, physiologist, educator; b. Bklyn., July 18, 1947; s. William H. and Agatha (Maraventano) C.; m. Linda Schupper, July 3, 1971; children: Daniel, Rebecca. BS in Biology, SUNY, Stony Brook, 1969; PhD in Physiology, SUNY, Syracuse, 1975. From asst. rsch. scientist to instr. Med. Sch. NYU, 1977-79; asst. prof. Va. Commonwealth U.-MCV, Richmond, 1979-85; assoc. prof. Med. Coll. Va., Richmond, 1985-93; prof., 1993—; adj. rsch. assoc. Rockefeller U., N.Y.C., 1977-79. Developer: Sense of Smell Kit; contbr. chpts. in books and articles to profl. jours. With USAFR, 1970-76. NIH fellow, 1975-77; NINCDS and NIDCD grantee, 1975—; recipient Rsch. Career Devel. award NIH, 1984-89. Mem. Assn. Chemoreception Scis., Soc. for Neuroscis., Am. Physiol. Soc., Sigma Xi. Home: 1908 Tunbridge Dr Richmond VA 23233-3517 Office: Va Commonwealth U Med Coll Va PO Box 980551 Richmond VA 23298-0551

COSTARELLA, ANTHONY RICHARD, emergency physician; b. Youngstown, Ohio, Feb. 3, 1946; s. Adam Earle and Lucy (Wooley) C.; m. Mildred Elizabeth Buoscio, Oct. 6, 1973; 1 child, Elizabeth Angelina. BS in Biology cum laude, Youngstown State U., 1968; MD, Loyola U., 1972. Emergency physician Mercer County Twp. Hosp., Coldwater, Ohio, 1979-80, Mease Hosp., Dunedin, Fla., 1980-81, DeSoto Meml. Hosp., Arcadia, Fla., 1981-86, Citrus Meml. Hosp., Inverness, Fla., 1986-88, Bartow (Fla.) Meml. Hosp., 1988-91, Walker Meml. Hosp., Avon Park, Fla., 1988-91, North Bay Med. Ctr., New Port Richey, Fla., 1991-95, Lakeland (Fla.) Regional Med. Ctr., 1995—; dir. emergency rm. DeSoto Meml. Hosp., 1983-85. Lt. comdr. USN, 1968-79. Fellow Am. Coll. Emergency Physicians. Democrat. Mem. Ch. of Jesus Christ. Home: 5729 W Shore Dr New Port Richey FL 34652

COSTOFF, ALLEN, physiology and endocrinology educator; b. Milw., Sept. 26, 1935; s. Steve and Katherine (Kutzaroff) C. BS, Marquette U., 1957, MS, 1959; PhD, U. Wis., 1969. Organic chemist Aldrich Chem. Co., Milw., 1959-61; teaching asst. U. Wis., Madison, 1961-63, rsch. asst., 1963-65, predoctoral trainee, 1965-69, postdoctoral trainee, 1969-70; asst prof. Med. Coll. Ga., Augusta, 1970-76, assoc. prof., 1976—. Author: Ultrastructure of Rat Adenohypophysis, 1973; co-author: Essentials of Medical Physiology, 1996; contbr. articles to profl. jours. Bd. dirs. Cen. Savannah Area Sci. Fair, Augusta, 1980—, chmn., 1970-89; v.p. AAUP, Augusta, 1976-77, pres., 1977-78, chair rsch. com. Sigma Xi, Augusta, 1982-83. Grantee NIH, 1977, 78, 81, 82, 88. Fellow Am. Fertility Soc. (reviewer); mem. Endocrine Soc. (reviewer), Am. Soc. Cell Biology (reviewer), Am. Assn. Anatomist (reviewer), Am. Physiol. Soc. (reviewer), Internat. Soc. Neuroendocrinology (reviewer), Electron Microscopic Assn. Program Com. Am., N.Y. Acad. Sci., Gerontol. Soc. Democrat. Greek Orthodox. Home: 224 Gardners Mill Rd Augusta GA 30907-3720 Office: Med Coll Ga Dept Physiology and Endocrinology Augusta GA 30912

COTÉ, KATHRYN MARIE, psychotherapist, stress management educator; b. Oceanside, Calif., May 31, 1953; d. Richard Alfred Kauth and Carole Maxine Brue Potter; m. Dennis Malcolm Coté, Dec. 23, 1983; children: Claire Marie, Simone Gloria, Jesse Patrick. BA, St. Norbert Coll., DePere, Wis., 1975; MSSW, U. Wis., 1977. Lic. clin. social worker; cert. clin. social worker. Psychiat. social worker Napa (Calif.) State Hosp., 1977-79, team leader, 1979-80; supr. adolescent clin. svcs. Solano County Mental Health, Vallejo, Calif., 1980-83; sect. head of residential svcs. for children and adolescents London Borough of Camden, 1983-84; mental health program mgr. Solano County Mental Health, Fairfield, Calif., 1985-87; clin social worker, county liaison West Ctrl. Cmty. Svc. Ctr., Montevideo, Minn., 1987-90; pvt. practice as psychotherapist and stress mgmt. educator Berlin, N.H., 1990—; profl. cons. North Bay Suicide Prevention and Stressline, Napa, 1985-87. Bd. dirs. Coos County Family Health, Berlin, 1990—. Recipient Cert. of Appreciation, Solano County Mental Health Adv. Bd., 1987. Democrat. Roman Catholic.

COTE, LUCIEN J., neurologist, educator; b. Angers, Quebec, Can., Jan. 4, 1928; came to U.S., 1940; s. Gaston and Yvonne (Scantland) C.; m. Joanne Waseleski, Apr. 23, 1960; children: Gabrielle, Paul Andrew. BS, U. Vt., Burlington, 1951, MD, 1954. Lic. neurologist, N.Y. Assoc. prof. neurology Columbia U., N.Y.C., 1978—; assoc. attending in neurology Columbia Presbyn. Med. Ctr., N.Y.C., 1978—. Capt. USAF, 1956-58. Home: 223 Cross Ridge Rd Tuxedo Park NY 10987

CÔTÉ-ARSENAULT, DENISE Y., maternal and women's health nurse; b. Syracuse, N.Y., Sept. 30, 1954; d. Wilfred A. Jr. and Irene M. (Campbell) Côté; m. Peter J. Arsenault, June 26, 1976; children: Yvonne, Jean-Pierre, Elise, Renee. BS, Syracuse U., 1976, MS, 1985; PhD, U. Rochester, 1995. Cert. Nurses Assn. of Am. Coll. Obstetricians and Gynecologists, Internat. Bd. Lactations Cons. Prin. Family Nursing Assocs., Manlius, N.Y.; faculty Syracuse U. Author: (pamphlets) Early Pregnancy Loss, 2d Trimester Loss, Late Pregnancy Loss; contbr. articles to profl. jours. Mem. N.Y. State Nurses Assn., Sigma Theta Tau (past treas. Omicron chpt.).

COTLER, JEROME MARVIN, orthopaedic surgeon; b. Bridgeton, N.J., July 26, 1928; s. Mitchell George and Elizabeth (Shapiro) C.; m. Florence, Aug. 19, 1951; children: Howard Bruce, Michelle Gail. BS, Ursinus Coll., 1948; MD, Jefferson Med. Coll., 1952. Intern Jefferson Med. Coll. Hosp., Phila., 1952-53, resident, 1953-57; orthopaedic surgeon pvt. practice, Bridgeton, N.J., 1957-73; instr. orthopaedic surgery Jefferson Med. Coll., Phila., 1957-70, clin. asst. prof., 1970-73; orthopaedic surgeon Jefferson Orthopaedic Assocs., Phila., 1973—; clin. prof. orthopaedic surgery Jefferson Med. Coll., 1973-81, prof. orthopaedic surgery, 1981—, Dr. Everett J. and Marian Gordon prof., 1991—. Co-editor: Spinal Fusion: Science and Techniques, 1990, Spinal Instrumentation, 1992; contbr. articles to profl. jours. Mem. Union League Phila., 1974—. Fellow Am. Acad. Orthopaedic Surgeons (bd. dirs. 1972-76), Am. Coll. Surgeons (bd. govs. 1962—, adv. coun. 1985-90, 93-96); mem. Am. Orthopaedic Assn. (v.p. 1993-94), Masons. Home: 4 E Kings Hwy Haddon Heights NJ 08035 Office: 130 S 9th St Ste 106 Philadelphia PA 19107

COTNER, DAN BARRETT, dentist; b. Cape Girardeau, Mo., Apr. 11, 1923; s. Barrett and Bertha Alma (Kassel) C.; m. Thelma Paulette Sturgeon, Dec. 25, 1948; children: Danna Cotner-Blackwell, Danice C. Dean, Daniel C. Burch, Paul B. DDS, St. Louis U., 1949; BSS, Southeast Mo. State U., 1977. Gen. practice dentistry Cape Girardeau, 1949—. Organist Westminster Presbyn. Ch., Cape Girardeau, 1964—. 1st lt. USAF, 1951-54. Recipient Dingeldein award S.E. Mo. Arts Council, Cape Girardeau, 1982, Golden Deeds award Exchange Club, 1989. Mem. ADA, Mo. Dental Assn., S.E. Mo. Dental Soc. (pres. 1961-62), Am. Guild Organists, Rotary (pres. Cape Girardeau 1961-62, Outstanding Rotarian 1989, 95). Home: 1222 Hillcrest Dr Cape Girardeau MO 63701-4729 Office: 937 Broadway Ste 100 Cape Girardeau MO 63701

COTRUVO, JOSEPH ALFRED, federal agency administrator; b Toledo, Aug. 3, 1942; s. Nicholas and Angela (Campanale) C.; m. Marcia J. Ramm, Dec. 28, 1968 (div. 1970); m. Karen Shrum, June 18, 1983; 1 child, Joseph Alfred Jr. BS in Chemistry, U. Toledo, 1963; PhD, Ohio State U., 1968; postdoctoral, U. Bologna, Italy, 1969. Mgr. R & D Chem. Samples Co., Columbus, Ohio, 1970-72; programs analyst EPA, Washington, 1973-76, dir. drinking water criteria and stds. divsn., 1976-90, dir. health and environ. rev. divsn., 1990-92; dir. risk assessment divsn., 1992—; mem. Coun. Pub. Health Cons., Nat. Sanitation Found., Ann Arbor, Mich. Co-editor: Ozone/Chlorine Dioxide, 1978, Water Chlorination, 1983; chmn., editor book series NATO/CCMS Drinking Water Pilot, 1980; contbr. articles to jours. in field. Recipient Environ. Leadership award Nat. Sanitation Found., Ann Arbor, 1988, Donald R. Boyd award Assn. Met. Water Agys., 1990; named Meritorious Exec., Pres. U.S., 1983. Mem. Am. Chem Soc., Am. Water Works Assn. (life, mem. editorial adv. bd. Jour., 1987-90). Roman Catholic. Office: EPA Risk Assessment Divsn 401 M St NW Washington DC 20460-0002

COTTEN, CATHERYN DEON, medical center international advisor; b. Erwin, N.C., Apr. 13, 1952; d. Ben Hur and Minnie Lee (Smith) C. BS in Anthropology, Duke U., 1975. Asst. internat. advisor Med. Ctr. Duke U., Durham, N.C., 1975-76; internat. advisor Med. Ctr. Duke U., Durham, 1976—. Editor and contbr. chpt. to Advisors Manual of Federal Regulations Affecting Foreign Students and Scholars. Key vol. City of Durham, 1990-91; pres. Durham County Lit. Coun., 1992-94. Recipient Cert. Recognition So. Regional Coun. Black Am. Affairs, Atlanta, 1985. Mem. Nat. Assn. Fgn. Student Affairs/Assn. Internat. Educators (gov. regulations adv. com. 1985-96, nat. chair 1991-94, chair Southeastern region 1989-90), Altrusa Club (pres. Durham chpt. 1987-89). Office: Duke U Med Ctr PO Box 3882 Durham NC 27710

COTTEN-HUSTON, ANNIE LAURA, psychologist, educator; b. Oxford, N.C., Nov. 18, 1923; d. Leonard F. and Laura Estelle (Spencer) Cotten; diploma Hardbarger Bus. Coll., 1944; AB, Duke U., 1945; MEd, U. Hartford, 1965; PhD, The Union Inst., 1979; children: Hollis W., Rebecca Ann, Laura Cotten. Diplomate Am. Bd. Sexology. Asst. to pres. So. Meth. U., 1953; rsch. asst. Duke U., 1947-49; exec. sec. Ohio Wesleyan U., 1955-56, Conn. Coun. Chs., 1958-60; adj. prof. U. Hartford, 1976-78; clin. pastoral counselor Hartford Hosp., 1962-65; asst., then asso. dir. social svcs. Hartford Conf. Chs., 1965-67; teaching fellow U. N.C., 1970-71; adj. prof. U. Hartford, 1976-78; assoc. prof. Cen. Conn. State U., New Britain, 1967-93, adj. prof. 1994—; adj. prof. St. Joseph Coll., 1986-96; clinical internship, Montefiore Med. Ctr., 1995; dir. elderhostel programs, Cen. Conn. State U., 1989—; organizer ctr. adult learners Cen. Conn. State U., 1991—; cons. Somers Correctional Ctr. (Conn.), 1980-81, instr./researcher, 1980-81; cons. Life Ins. Mktg. Rsch., 1981—; amb. to China, spring, 1986; presenter 3d Internat. Interdisciplinary Cong. on Women, 1987; vis. prof., scholar Duke U., 1989; vis. prof. Conn. Coll. New London, Conn., 1990; dir. Ctr. Adult Learners Cen. Conn. State U., 1991—, Sex Info. and Edn. Conn., 1995— (named Human Sexuality Educator of the Yr., 1996); clin. faculty, supr. Am. Bd. Sexology, 1991, 94. Elder hostel dir. Cen. Conn. State U., 1987-93, organizer Elder Hostel Affiliate Network, 1991. Mem. AAUW, Am. Assn. Marriage and Family Therapists (cert.), Am. Psychol. Assn. (chair divsn. 1987), Nat. Coun. Family Rels., Am. Assn. Sex Educators, Counselors and Therapists (cert., presenter conf. 1993), Conn. Psychol. Assn., Conn. Council Chs. (dir.), Hartford Women's Network. Contbr. articles to profl. jours. Home: 193 Westland Ave West Hartford CT 06107-3057 Office: Ctrl Conn State U Dept Psychology New Britain CT 06050

COTTER, DOUGLAS ADRIAN, healthcare executive; b. Brockport, N.Y., Aug. 15, 1943; s. Adrian Edwards and Rita Elizabeth (Marshall) C.; m. Rosalyn DeVaughn, June 12, 1965 (div.); children: Elizabeth D., Anne R.; m. Anne Holmes Thompson, Oct. 4, 1986. BS, Duke U., 1965; MS, N.C. State U., 1967, PhD, 1970. Rsch. engr. Corning Glass Works, Raleigh, N.C., 1966-69, mgr. rsch. & devel., 1970-78; bus. devel. mgr. Corning Med. Europe, Halstead, Essex, England, 1978-80; portfolio mgr. Corning (N.Y.) Glass Works, 1980-83; dir. info. systems Corning Med., Medfield, Mass., 1984-85; pres. Healthcare Decisions Inc., Norwood, Mass., 1986-96; v.p. Decision Resources Inc., Waltham, Mass., 1996—; adj. prof. Boston U., 1985—, N.C. State U., 1973-76; dir. Respironics Inc., Murrysville, Pa., 1989—; dir. Applied Microbiology, Tarrytown, N.Y., 1995-96. Inventor/patentee in field. Mem. Inst. Elec. Engrs. (sr. mem.), Assn. Corp. Growth, Licensing Exec. Soc. Office: Decision Resources Inc 1100 Winter St Waltham MA 02154

COTTER, JANIS M., optometrist; b. Boston, May 24, 1957; d. Philip Michael and M. Patricia Cotter. BS in Edn., Northeastern U., Boston, 1979; OD, New Eng. Coll. Optometry, Boston, 1985. Resident in hosp.-based optometry VA Med. Ctr., West Roxbury, Mass., 1985-86; pvt. practice Revere, Mass., 1986—; mgr. contact lens svc. Mass. Eye and Ear Infirmary, Boston, 1986-92; instr. New. Eng. Coll. Optometry, Boston, 1986-94. Contbr. chpt. to book, articles to profl. jours. Bd. dirs., exec. v.p. Boston Found. for Sight, Chestnut Hill, 1992—; vol. optometrist Vision U.S.A., VOSH, 1994-95. Named woman of Excellence, Mt. St. Joseph Acad., 1996. Mem. APHA, Am. Optometric Assn., Mass. Soc. Optometrists. Roman Catholic. Home: 19 Andrew Rd Swampscott MA 01907 Office: Boston Foundation for Sight 1244 Boylston St #202 Chestnut Hill MA 02967

COTTER, LEO PATRICK, mental health counselor; b. Detroit, Sept. 28, 1951; s. Leo Anthony and Marie Deloris (Bell) C.; m. Gretchen Centers, Sept. 27, 1994; children: Rita-Marie, Seth Patrick. BS, No. Mich. U., 1973; MA, Mich. State U., 1974; PhD, Fla. State U., 1982. Lic. mental health counselor, marriage and family therapist. Counseling intern Ingham County Jail-Drug Program, Mason, Mich., 1973-74; therapist intern Eaton County Community Mental Health Ctr., Charlotte, Mich., 1974; psychologist II Avon Park (Fla.) Correctional Inst., 1975-77; staff psychologist Hillsborough Correctional Inst., Riverview, Fla., 1977-78; planner, evaluator D.O.C. cen. office Dept. Corrections Bur. Planning, Rsch. and Statistics, Tallahassee, 1978-80; planner, evaluator H.R.S. cen. office Dept. Health and Rehab. Svcs., Tallahassee, 1980-82; assoc. Profl. Counseling Assocs., Inc., Tallahassee, 1982; staff psychologist Zephyrhills (Fla.) Correctional Inst., 1982-83; systems adminstr. Pinellas-Pasco Dist. Mental Health Bd. V, 1983-84; asst. prof. Fla. Mental Health Inst., U. South Fla., Tampa, 1985-89; dir. SHARE Program I, Tampa, 1982—, SHARE Jr. Program, Tampa, 1989—; adj. prof. dept. law and mental health Fla. Mental Health Inst., U. South Fla., 1989—. Chairperson Coalition for the Effective Supervision of Sex Offenders, 1987; family protection team com. Coordination of Svcs. for Sexually Abused Children; chair Human Rights Advocacy Com., Tampa, 1990. Mem. ACA, APA, Pub. Offender Counselors Assn., Am. Psychology-Law Soc., Assn. for Treatment of Sex Offenders, Am. Assn. Sex Educators, Counselors and Therapists. Office: 7819 N Dale Mabry Hwy Ste 212 Tampa FL 33614-3221

COTTON, WILLIAM ROBERT, dentist; b. Miami, Fla., Nov. 29, 1931; s. Robert Lee and Mamie Bell (Daniel) C.; m. Marye Ruth Hartz; children: Caroline Ruth, William Robert Jr., David Michael, Lynn Cathryn. DDS, U. Md., 1955; MS, Northwestern U., Chgo., 1963; MA, Roosevelt U., 1973; EdS, George Washington U., Washington, 1980. With USN, 1955-81, commd. capt., 1973, ret., 1981; asst. dental officer Marine Corps Schs. and USS F.D. Roosevelt CVA 42, Quantico, Va. and Mayport, Fla., 1957-61; head exptl. pathology div. Naval Med. Rsch. Inst., Bethesda, Md., 1963-67; dental officer USS Fulton AS-11, New London, Conn., 1967-69; chief histopathology div. Naval Dental Rsch. Inst., Great Lakes, Ill., 1969-72, exec. officer, 1972-73; dep. commanding officer Naval Dental Rsch. Inst., Great Lakes, 1973-76; chmn. dental scis. dept. Naval Med. Rsch. Inst., Bethesda, Md., 1976-79; dir. Casualty Care Rsch. Program Ctr., Naval Med. Rsch. Inst., Bethesda, Md., 1979-81; assoc. prof dept. operative dentistry Temple U., Phila., 1981-83; prof., chmn. dept. operative dentistry Georgetown U., Washington, 1983-90; pvt. practice Bethesda, Md.; mem. spl. study sect. NIH, Washington, 1984, 87; mem. adv. com. Dental Tech. Program, So. Ill. U., Carbondale, 1976-85; cons. Naval Dental Rsch. Inst., Great Lakes, 1981-85, Dentsply Internat., York, Pa., 1984-88. Contbg. author: Biology Dental Cares, 1968, Dental Clinics of North America, 1986; editorial bd. Jour. Dental Rsch., 1976-86, 88, Jour. Operative Dentistry, 1986-92. Fellow Am. Coll. Dentists, Internat. Coll. Dentists; mem. ADA, D.C. Dental Soc. (bd. dirs. 1986-89). Democrat. Presbyterian. Home: 11816 Winterset Ter Potomac MD 20854-2846

COTTONE, FRANCIS JOHN, physician; b. Trenton, N.J., Apr. 24, 1929; s. Rosario John and Martha (Brood) C.; m. Irene Mae Yuhas, May 18, 1963; children: Peter, Mary, Elizabeth, Thomas, Ellen. BS, Georgetown U., 1950, MD, 1954. Diplomate Am. Bd. Surgery. Intern D.C. Gen. Hosp., 1954-55; resident in gen. surgery Mayo Found., Rochester, Minn., 1955-57, 59-61; pvt. practice surgery Trenton, 1961-65; ptnr. Fares Surg. Assocs., Trenton, 1965-91; dir. surgery St. Francis Med. Ctr., Trenton, 1991—; assoc. prof. Hahneman U., Phila., 1972—; clin. asst. prof. surgery Robert Wood Johnson U., 1991—. Lt. USNR, 1957-59. Fellow Am. Coll. Surgeons; mem. AMA, Alpha Omega Alpha. Roman Catholic. Office: Saint Francis Med Ctr 601 Hamilton Ave Trenton NJ 08629-1915

COTTONE, JUDITH, healthcare administrator, nurse; b. Greenville, S.C., Oct. 12, 1943; d. Arthur L. Anderson and Doris Virginia (Brison) Nathan; divorced; children: Elizabeth, Amy, Ruth. BSN, Loyola U., Chgo., 1985; MBA, U. Ill., Chgo., 1990, MS, 1990. RN, Ill., Fla.; cert. nurse adminstr. Staff nurse Rush Presbyn. St. Luke's Med. Ctr., Chgo., 1976-78, 82-85, supr., 1978-82; head nurse Rush Presbyn. St. Luke's Med. Ctr., 1985, rsch. asst., 1987-89, asst. to chair, 1989-90; DON Lakeland (Fla.) Regional Med. Ctr., 1990-92, ops. dir., 1992-93, dir. profl. nursing devel., 1994—; mem. health occupations adv. bd. Traviss Tech. Ctr., Lakeland, Fla., 1995—. Capt. Paint Your Heart Out Lakeland, 1990-96. Mem. Fla. Orgn. Nurse Execs. (mem. edn. com.), Fla. Nurses Assn. (pres.-elect 1993-95, pres. 1995—). Home: 1645 Sir Henrys Trl Lakeland FL 33809 Office: Lakeland Regional Med Ctr Box 95448 Lakeland FL 33804

COTTRELL, ALFRED CHARLES, medical educator; b. Takoma Park, Md., May 15, 1956. BS, Muhlenberg Coll., 1978; MD, Hahne Mann U., 1982. Asst. prof. medicine Loma Linda (Calif.) U., 1993—. OFfice: Loma Linda U Med Ctr Rm 1405 11234 Anderson St Loma Linda CA 92354

COTTRELL, DAVID C., II, orthopedic surgeon; b. Phila., Sept. 19, 1933; s. James Ewing and Mary Elizabeth (Murray) C.; m. Sandra Lee Beaver, May 27, 1967; children: David Chadwell III, Catherine Ann. BA, U. Tenn., 1955; MD, U. Pa., 1959. Diplomate Am. Bd. Orthop. Surgery. Rotating intern U. Pa. Hosp., Phila., 1959-60, resident in gen. surgery, 1962-63, resident in orthop. surgery, 1963-66, attending staff orthopedist, 1966-72; pvt. practice in orthopedics Del. County Meml. Hosp., Bryn Mawr Hosp., Drexel Hill, Bryn Mawr, Pa., 1972-86, Sunbury (Pa.) Cmty. Hosp., Evangelical Cmty. Hosp., Lewisburg, Pa., 1986—. Capt. U.S. Army, 1960-62, Okinawa. Fellow Am. Acad. Orthop. Surgeons, Am. Coll. Surgeons; mem. Eastern Orthop. Assn. Republican. Lutheran. Office: 113 N Market St Selingrove PA 17870

COTTRELL, THOMAS SYLVESTER, pathology educator, university dean; b. Chgo., Feb. 2, 1934; s. Sylvester Vincent and Cleo (Medley) C.; m. Jane Chichester, July 3, 1959; children: Matthew Thomas, Anne Medley, Sarah Jane. AB, Brown U., 1955; MD, Columbia U., 1965. Diplomate Am. Bd. Pathology. Asst. prof. N.Y. Med. Coll., Valhalla, 1968-79; assoc. prof. pathology SUNY Sch. Medicine, Stony Brook, 1979—, assoc. dean clin. affairs, 1979-88, exec. assoc. dean, 1988—; interim exec. dir. U. Hosp. SUNY, Stony Brook, 1983-84, interim chmn. dept. ob-gyn. Sch. Medicine, 1991-92, interim chmn. dept. surgery Sch. Medicine, 1996—. Lt. USNR, 1957-60. Scholar John and Mary R. Markle Found., 1969-73. Fellow Coll. Am. Pathologists, N.Y. Acad. Medicine; mem. AAAS. Home: PO Box 1292 3775 Skunk Ln Cutchogue NY 11935-1541 Office: SUNY Sch Medicine Office Of Dean Stony Brook NY 11794

COUCH, JAMES RUSSELL, JR., neurology educator; b. Bryan, Tex., Oct. 25, 1939; married; 2 children. BS, Texas A&M U., 1961; MD, Baylor U., 1965, PhD in Physiology, 1966; postgrad. fellow, Lab of Neuropharmacology, NIMH, 1966-68; postgrad., Nat. Inst. Neurol. Diseases and Stroke, 1969-72. Diplomate Am. Bd. Psychiatry and Neurology; lic. physician, Tex., Md., Kans., Mo., Ill. Intern Barnes Hosp., St. Louis, 1966-67; resident in neurology Washington U. Sch. Medicine, St. Louis, 1969-72; mem. staff Kans. U. Med. Ctr., Kansas City, asst. prof. div. neurology, 1972-76, assoc. prof., 1976-79; prof., chief div. neurology So. Ill. U. Sch. Medicine, Springfield, 1979-92; mem. staff VA Hosp., Kansas City, Mo., Marion, Ill., VA Hosp., Oklahoma City, St. Joseph (Mo.) Hosp., Kansas U. Med. Ctr., Atchison (Kans.) Hosp., Kansas City Gen. Hosp.; mem. staff Meml. Med. Ctr., Springfield, dir. EEG lab., muscular dystrophy clinic, cons. speech and hearing lab., 1979-92; mem. staff St. John's Hosp., Springfield; prof., chmn. dept. neurology Okla. U. Coll. Med. and Health Sci. Ctr., Oklahoma City, 1992—; mem. staff Presbyn. Hosp., Oklahoma City, Univ. Hosp., Oklahoma City; investigator Mental Retardation Rsch. Ctr. Kans. U. Med. Ctr., Kansas City, 1972-79; bd. dir. postgrad. neurology course Continuing Med. Edn.; examiner Am. Bd. Psychiatry and Neurology, 1975-77, 79, 84-85, 89-95, Am. Bd. Neurosurgery, 1977; cons. Richland Meml. Hosp., Olney, Ill., 1981-85, Abraham Lincoln Meml. Hosp., Lincoln, Ill., 1981—; staff cons. Lincoln Devel. Ctr., Outpatient Clinics, Lincoln, 1981—; vis. prof. Northwestern U., Chgo., 1982, 93, U. Nebr., 1992, Wayne State U. Med. Sch., 1992, Ind. Univ. Med. Sch., 1992, U. Rochester, 1992, U. Ala., Birmingham, 1994, U. W.Va., Morgantown, U. Mo., Columbia, Med. Sch. Kans. U., 1996, Med. Coll. S.C., 1996, U. South Fla., 1996, Med. Sch. Brown U., 1996; presenter at profl. confs.; mem. various coms. med. sch. Kans. U., 1972-79, So. Ill. U., 1980-92. Mem. editorial bd. Headache, 1979-92; contbr. numerous articles to profl. jours. Mem. med. adv. bd. Lincoln Land Epilepsy Assn., 1980—; mem. exec. bd., chmn. edn. com. Am. Soc. Neurorehab. Fellow Nat. Heart Inst., 1965-66, NIH, NIMH, 1967-69; recipient numerous grants for neurology rsch., 1969—. Fellow Am. Acad. Neurology (bd. dirs. asst. sec.-treas. 1984-86, sec.-treas. 1986-88, chmn. sect. neurorehab. 1996—), Stroke Coun. of Am. Heart Assn.; mem. AMA, Am. Neurological Assn. (elected), Am. Assn. for Study of Headache (exec. com. ad hoc 1983-85, winter headache course, membership com. 1983-85, chmn., 1994—, faculty Continuing Med. Edn. courses 1983-84, edn. com. 1983-85, 86—, achievement recognition com., publs. com. 1986—, bd. dirs. 1983-85, 86-92, treas. 1992-94, sec. 1994-96, pres.-elect 1996—), Am. Geriatric Soc., Am. Assn. Univ. Profs. Neurology (chmn. undergrad. edn. com, sec.-treas. 1992—) Am. Soc. Neurorehab. (bd. dirs., chmn. edn. com. 1989—), Neurosci. Soc. (sec. Kansas City chpt. 1976-77, pres. 1977-78, pres. Sangamon County chptr. of Neurosci. 1986-87), Ill. Med. Soc., Sangamon County Med. Soc., Okla. State Med. Soc., Okla. County Med. Soc., Baylor U. Med. Alumni Assn., Washington U. Med. Alumni Assn., Sigma Xi, Alpha Omega Alpha, Phi Eta Sigma, Phi Kappi Phi. Home: 1616 Queenstown Rd Oklahoma City OK 73116-5523 Office: U Okla Health Sci Ctr Dept of Neurology 3SP203 PO Box 26901 Oklahoma City OK 73190-3048

COUCH, RICHARD ALAN, research chemist; b. Mason, W.Va., Jan. 23, 1957; s. Walter Roberts and Isabelle Virginia (Stobart) C. BSc in Pharmacy, Ohio State U., 1980, PhD, 1986. Registered pharmacist, Del. Rsch. chemist ICI Pharms., Wilmington, Del., 1986-88; sr. analytical chemist ICI Pharms., Macclesfield, Eng., 1989; group leader analytical devel. ICI Pharms., Wilmington, 1990-92; sr. dir. analytical R & D, Pharmavene Inc., Gaithersburg, Md., 1992—. Contbg. author: Pharmaceutical Analysis: Modern Methods, 1984; contbr. articles to sci. jours. Grad. fellow Ohio State U., 1980-81, Am. Found. for Pharm. Edn., 1981-84. Mem. Am. Assn. Pharm. Scientists, Am. Chem. Soc. Office: Pharmavene Inc 1550 E Gude Dr Rockville MD 20850

COUCH, ROBERT BARNARD, physician, educator; b. Guntersville, Ala., Sept. 25, 1930; s. Ezekiel Harvey and Frances Jane (Barnard) C.; m. Katherine Frances Klein, Apr. 23, 1955; children—Robert Steven, Leslie Ann, Colleen Frances, Elizabeth Lee. BA, Vanderbilt U., 1952, MD, 1956. Diplomate: Am. Bd. Internal Medicine. Intern Vanderbilt U. Hosp., Nashville, 1956-57; resident in medicine Vanderbilt U. Hosp., 1959-60, chief resident in medicine, 1960-61; clin. asso. NIH, Washington, 1957-59; sr. investigator NIH, 1961-65, head clin. virology sect., 1965-66; asso. prof. Baylor Coll. Medicine, Houston, 1966-71; dir. influenza research center Baylor Coll. Medicine, 1974—, prof. microbiology and immunology and medicine, 1971—, head infectious diseases sect. medicine, 1987-92, chmn. dept. microbiology and immunology, 1989—; mem. rsch. rev. panels infectious diseases; cons. NIH, Dept. Def., FDA. Contbr. articles to med. jours. Served to sr. surgeon USPHS, 1957-66. Mem. ACP, AAAS, Soc. Exptl. Biology and Medicine, Am. Soc. Microbiology, Infectious Diseases Soc. Am., Am. Assn. Immunologists, Am. Fedn. Clin. Rsch., Am. Soc. Clin. Investigation, So. Soc. Clin. Investigation, Am. Assn. Physicians, Am. Soc. Epidemiology, Am. Soc. Virology. Office: Baylor Coll Medicine 1 Baylor Plz Houston TX 77030-3411

COUCH, ROBERT CHESLEY, hospital administrator; b. Troy, Ala., Sept. 23, 1930; s. James Joshua and Margaret (White) C.; m. Barbara Allen Joyce, Sept. 3, 1952; children: Joyce, Gayle, Leslie, Karen. B.S., Auburn U., 1953; M.Hosp. Administrn., Ga. State U., 1957. Cons., Ga. State Health Dept., Atlanta, 1955-56; administr. Cherokee County Hosp., Centre, Ala., 1957-59; pres. Cumberland Med. Ctr., Crossville, Tenn., 1959-92; cons. to surgeon gen. U.S. Air Force, 1973-83. Past pres. Cumberland County ARC, Tenn., 1960—, United Fund of Cumberland County, 1966—. Served to col. USAFR, 1953-83. Recipient Outstanding Service award USAF Hosp. and 97th Bomb Wing, Blytheville AFB, 1973-83; Meritorious Service award Tenn. Hosp. Assn., Nashville, 1983; Bus. Assoc. Yr., Am. Bus. Womens Assn., Crossville, 1984. Mem. Am. Coll. Hosp. Administrs., Healthcare Fin. Mgmt. Assn., Am. Hosp. Assn., Tenn. Hosp. Assn. (Disting. Svc. award 1989), Crossville C. of C. Club: Exchange (pres. 1963). Lodge: Rotary. Avocations: tennis, boating, fishing. Home: 76 Short Sawmill Rd Crossville TN 38555

COUGHLIN, FRANCIS RAYMOND, JR., surgeon, educator, lawyer; b. N.Y.C., Feb. 22, 1927; s. Francis Raymond and Isabel (Archibald) C.; B.S., Fordham U., 1948; M.D., Yale, 1952; M.S. (Hosmer Teaching fellow), McGill U., Montreal, Que., Can., 1955, diploma in surgery, 1959, J.D., U. Bridgeport, 1988; m. Barbara Ann Blunt, June 9, 1951; children—Hilary, Mary, Patricia, Christopher Francis, Geoffrey Blunt, Daniel Taylor, Isabel, David Carleton. Intern, N.Y. Hosp., N.Y.C., 1952-53; resident in surgery McGill U. Teaching Hosp., Montreal, 1953-57; resident in thoracic surgery Overholt Thoracic Clinic, Boston, 1958-60; practice medicine, specializing in thoracic surgery, Stamford, Conn., 1960-88; medico-legal cons., 1988—; teaching fellow Harvard U., 1958; dir. div. thoracic and vascular surgery Stamford Hosp., 1970-73; dir. thoracic and vascular surgery St. Josephs Hosp., Stamford, 1970-73, 80-85, assoc. chief surgery, 1971-73, chief surgery, 1973-77; assoc. prof. clin. surgery N.Y. Med. Coll., 1981—; mem. staff Norwalk Hosp.; vice chair Conn. State Commn. on medicolegal investigations, 1990—. With U.S. Maritime Svc., 1945-46. Recipient Encaenia award Fordham U., N.Y.C., 1958. Diplomate Am. Bd. Surgery, Am. Bd. Thoracic Surgery. Fellow ACS (sec.-treas. Conn. chpt. 1966-70), Royal Coll. Surgeons (Can.), Am. Coll. Cardiology, Am. Coll. Chest Physicians, Royal Soc. Health, Royal Soc. Medicine, Am. Coll. Legal Medicine; mem. Soc. Thoracic Surgeons (founding mem.), N.Y. Acad. Medicine, Conn. Heart Assn. (dir. 1961-64), Conn. Lung Assn. (dir. and exec. com. 1963-69, v.p. 1967-69), Lung Assn. So. Fairfield County (pres. 1963-68, dir. 1960-70), Soc. Med. Jurisprudence (v.p. 1992-93, pres. 1996—), English-Speaking Union, Scottish-Am. Found., Canadian Soc., Yale Club N.Y. Republican. Roman Catholic. Office: 20 Mead St New Canaan CT 06840-5701

COUGHLIN, RICHARD JOHN, colon and rectal surgeon; b. Newark, Ohio, Aug. 21, 1953. BS in Nutrition Sci., U. Calif., Davis, 1976; MD, U. So. Calif., L.A., 1982. Diplomate ACS, Am. Coll. Colon and Rectal Surgeons. Intern Swedish Hosp. Med. Ctr., Seattle, 1982-83, resident, 1985-89; pvt. practice Los Gatos, Calif., 1991—; assoc. clin. prof. Stanford (Calif.) Med. Sch., 1995—. With USPHS, 1983-85. Fellow ACS, Am. Coll. Colon and Rectal Surgeons. Office: 14850 Los Gatos Blvd Los Gatos CA 95032

COUK, DAVID EDGAR, orthopaedic surgeon; b. Jonesville, Va., Oct. 1, 1935; s. Morgan Donnelly and Thelma Elizabeth (Smiley) C.; m. Phyllis Dennison James, Dec. 20, 1959 (dec. Oct. 1982); children: David Jr., Suzanne Blair, James Donnelly. BS, Emory (Va.) and Henry Coll., 1957; MD, Med. Coll. Va., 1963. Lic. physician and surgeon, Va. Intern Med. Coll. Va., 1963-64, resident, 1964, 67-71, fellow in hand surgery, 1971; pvt. practice Blue Ridge Orthopaedics, Warrenton, Va., 1971—; chief of staff Fauquier Hosp., Warrenton, 1971—. Contbr. articles to profl. jours. Capt. USAF, 1964-67. Decrorated Air Force Commendation medal. Mem. AMA (featured in jour. 1982), Am. Coll. Orthopaedic Surger, Va. orthopaedic Soc., Va. Med. Soc. (mal practice rev. bd.), Fauquier County med. Soc. (pres.), chmn. ethics com. 1975—). Republican. Home: 7510 Stonelea Ln Warrenton VA 22186 Office: Blue Ridge Orthopaedics Inc 550 Hospital Dr Warrenton VA 22186

COULDWELL, WILLIAM TUPPER, neurosurgeon; b. Vancouver, B.C., Can., Dec. 15, 1955; s. William John and Janet Mary (Tupper) C.; m. Marie Francoise Simard; children: Sandrine, Mitchell, Genevieve. MD, McGill U., 1984, PhD, 1991. Resident in neurosurgery U. So. Calif., L.A., 1984-89; fellow neuroimmunology Montreal Neurol. Inst., 1989-91, fellow epilepsy surgery, 1990; fellow neurosurgery CHUV, Lausanne, Switzerland, 1990-91; asst. prof. dept. neurol. surgery U. So. Calif., L.A., 1991-95, assoc. clin. prof., 1995—; ICU dirs. com. U. So. Calif. Med. Ctr., L.A., 1991-95; assoc. clin. prof. U. N.D., Minot, 1995—. Contbr. articles to profl. jours. Recipient Preuss award Am. Assn. Neurol. Surgeons, 1991, Clinician Investigator award, 1993; Med. Rsch. Coun. Can. Centennial fellow, 1990; McGill U. scholar, 1984, Wood Gold medal. Fellow ACS; mem. Am. Assn. Neurol. Surgeons (joint sect. on tumors 1991—), Congress of Neurol. Surgeons. Office: Trinity Med Ctr 1 Burdick Expressway W Minot ND 58701

COULTER, JOHN BREITLING, III, biochemist, educator; b. Stamford, Tex., Nov. 28, 1941; s. John Breitling and Sue Madeline (Morrow) C.; m. Brenda Kay Norman, May 27, 1966; children: Grace Kathleen, John Paul, Peter Stephen. BS, U. Tex., Arlington, 1966; PhD, Baylor U., 1970. Dir. rsch. and diagnostic labs. Scott and White Meml. Hosp. and Clinic, Temple, Tex., 1971—; assoc. prof. pathology and biochemistry Coll. Medicine Tex. A&M U., Temple, 1978—; adj. asst. prof. chemistry Baylor U., Waco, Tex., 1975-81; cons. chemist Lab. Svc., VA Ctr., Temple, 1973-90. Founder, pres. Christian Info. Coun., Inc., 1981—. With U.S. Army, 1960-63. HEW rsch. grantee, 1971-81; NDEA Title IV fellow Baylor U., 1970. Mem. AAAS, Am. Chem. Soc., Assn. for Rsch. in Vision and Ophthalmology, Am. Assn. Clin. Chemists, Sigma Xi (pres. Temple chpt. 1975). Baptist. Office: Scott & White Hosp and Clinic 2401 S 31st St Temple TX 76508-0001

COULTER, MURRAY WHITFIELD, biology educator; b. El Dorado, Ark., May 2, 1932; s. Edward Herbert and Estella (Pruthru) C.; m. Ingrid Glaesser, Dec. 26, 1959; children: Keith Edward, Kenneth Carr. AA, U. Ark., 1951; BA, Emory U., 1954; MS, U. Ariz., 1956; PhD, UCLA, 1963. Rsch. fellow U. Ariz., Tucson, 1954-55; asst. prof. Calif. State U., Northridge, 1959-61; rsch. botanists U. Calif., L.A., 1962-63; asst. prof. Tex. Tech. U., 1964-67, assoc. prof., 1967—, faculty senate pres., 1995-96, pres. faculty senate, 1995-96; cons. N.Am. Aviation, Inc., Burbank, Calif., 1961-62, UN/Food and Agrl. Orgn., New Deli, India, 1985. Contbr. articles to profl. jours. Election judge County of Lubbock, 1986—; bd. pres. Unitarian-Universalist Ch., Lubbock, 1970-71, 80-81. Fellow AAAS; mem. USTA (sport sci. com. 1990—), Am. Soc. Plant Physiologists, Indian Soc. Plant Physiologists, Genetics Soc. Am., Tex. Assn. Coll. Tchrs. (chpt. pres., state v.p. 1970-74, 96—), Sigma Xi (chpt. pres. 1969-70). Home: 3805 62nd Dr Lubbock TX 79413-5211 Office: Tex Tech U Dept Biol Scis PO Box 4149 Lubbock TX 79409-0006

COULTER, NORMAN ARTHUR, JR., biomedical engineering educator emeritus; b. Atlanta, Jan. 9, 1920; s. Norman Arthur and Carabelle (Clark) C.; m. Elizabeth Harwell Jackson, June 23, 1951; 1 child, Robert Jackson. B.S., Va. Poly. Inst., 1941; M.D., Harvard U., 1950; postdoctoral fellow, Johns Hopkins U., 1950-52. Instr. math. dept. Va. Poly. Inst., 1946; asst. to assoc. prof. physiology dept. Ohio State U., 1952-65; dir. biophysics div., physiology dept., 1962-65; assoc. prof. depts. surgery and physiology U. N.C., Chapel Hill, 1965-67; prof. U. N.C., 1967-90, prof. emeritus, 1990—, chmn. bioengring.-biomath. program, 1969-82, dir. grad. studies, 1982-90. Author: Synergetics: An Adventure in Human Development, 1976; also articles in profl. jours. Served to maj. A.A. AUS, 1941-46. Mem. AMA, IEEE, Biophys. Soc., Am. Physiol. Soc., Biomed. Engring. Soc., Soc. Gen. Sys. Rsch., Physicians for Social Responsibililty, Sigma Xi. Home: 1825 N Lakeshore Dr Chapel Hill NC 27514-6734

COULTON, ROBERT WILLIAM, JR., medical administrator; b. Cleve., June 7, 1950; s. Robert William and Lavern Lois (Tice) C.; m. Mary Ruth Simpson, June 8, 1974; children: Elizabeth, Robert, Kathleen. BS, Rio Grande Coll., 1972; MBA, Baldwin Wallace Coll., 1981. Asst. adminstr. Euclid (Ohio) Park Nursing Ctr., 1972-73; svcs. coord. adminstrv. svcs. Cleve. Clinic Found., 1973-75, asst. dept. head, adminstrv. svcs., 1975-80, adminstr., neurology, 1981-87, adminstr. profl. staff affairs, 1987—. Mem. Ohi State Med. Assn. Office: Cleveland Clinic Found 9500 Euclid Ave Cleveland OH 44195

COUNSELL, LEE ALBERT, dentist, educator, Hispanist; b. Neillsville, Wis., July 5, 1923; s. Clarion and Henrietta (Clemens) C. D.D.S., Northwestern U., 1948; B.A., U. Wis.-Madison, 1949; diploma grad. pedodontics Forsyth Dental Center, Boston, 1949; M.P.H., U. Mich., 1967; M.A. Spanish, So. Ill. U., 1984. Commd. lt. Dental Corps, U.S. Navy, 1950, advanced through grades to comdr., ret., 1972; intern staff Naval Hosp., Gt. Lakes, Ill., 1950; asst. dir. dept. pediatric dentistry Marquette U., 1952-54; practice pediatric dentistry, Milw. and Washington, 1954-55; house staff Naval Hosp., Boston, 1959-62; dir. dental dept. Naval Constrn. Bn. Center, Davisville, R.I., 1964-66; head preventive dentistry program Naval Base, Gt. Lakes, Ill., 1968-70; asst. chief clin. investigations div. Naval Dental Research Inst., 1971, chief, 1972; asst. dir. Bur. Dental Health, Div. Health, State of Fla., 1972-73; fellow U. Dundee (Scotland), 1973; research assoc. Am. Dental Assn., Chgo., 1973-74; assoc. prof. So. Ill. U., Carbondale, 1974-77, adj. assoc. prof., 1979-86; apptd. adj. prof. Northwestern U., 1990; cons. dental health edn., 1977-86, dental pub. health, 1977-86. Decorated Navy Commendation medal, 1972. Fellow Am. Assn. Endodontists, Am. Coll. Dentists; mem. ADA (life), G.V. Black Soc. (life), Organ Hist. Soc., Xi Psi Phi (life), Phi Kappa Phi, Omicron Kappa Upsilon (hon. mem.). Episcopalian. Contbr. numerous articles to profl. publs. Home: 140 E Franklin Pl #107 Lake Forest IL 60045

COUNTRYMAN, DAVID MARK, general, vascular and throacic surgeon; b. Honolulu, July 18, 1953; s. Ralph Lyon and Dorothy Jean (Doherty) C.; m. Vickie Ann Johnson, Dec. 17, 1979; children: Andy, Scott, John, Becky. BS in Applied Biology highest honors, U. Ga. Tech., 1975; MD, Med. Coll. Ga., 1979. Diplomate Am. Bd. Surgery, Nat. Bd. Med. Examiners. Commd. 2d lt. USAF, advanced through ranks to maj.; intern USAF Med. Ctr., Keesler, Miss., 1979-80; resident USAF Med. Ctr., Keesler, fellow in non-cardiac thoracic surgery, 1984-85; chief thoracic surgery USAF Med. Ctr., Scott AFB, Ill., 1985-89; chief gen. surgery USAF Med. Ctr., Scott AFB, 1987-89; attending thoracic surgeon John Cochran VA Hosp., St. Louis, 1987-89; asst. clin. prof. surgery Uniformed Svcs. U. Health Scis., Bethesda, Md., 1988-89; dir. surgical edn. family practice residency USAF Med. Ctr., Scott AFB, 1986-89; resigned USAF, 1989; surgeon Piedmont Surg. Assocs., Rock Hill, S.C., 1989—; asst. dir. rotating internship program USAF Med. Ctr., Scott AFB, 1986-89; privileges at Mercy Hosps., Charlotte, N.C., chief of surgery Piedmont Med. Ctr., 1992.; dir. surgical sect. Air Force Emergency Physician Tng. Program. Contbr. articles to profl. jours.; presenter at many Air Force med. clinics and confs. Mem. sch. bd. Westminster Catawba Christian Sch., team physician for athletes; deacon Westminster Prebyn. Ch.; bd. dirs. Winthrop U. Eagles Club; coach of various youth sports. Recipient Achievement medal USAF, for handling of civilian crash at Scott AFB, commendation medal for svcs. as head of surgery. Mem. AMA, Am. Coll. Surgeons, So. Med. Assn., Soc. Am. Gastrointestinal Endoscopic Surgeons, York County Med. Assn., S.C. Med. Assn., Southeastern Surgical Assn., Soc. Critical Care Medicine. Office: Piedmont Surg Assocs 200 S Herlong Ave Ste G Rock Hill SC 29732

COUNTRYMAN, ELLEN WITT, hospital administrator; b. Pineville, Ky., Dec. 18, 1951; d. Cecil and Sylvia (Tolliver) Witt; m. Daniel Lee Countryman, Jan. 2, 1972; children: Sarah Ellen, Kathryn Elizabeth. Student, Ball State U., 1986-88; grad., Ind. U., 1993. Sec., dispatcher Franklin (Ohio) Police Dept., 1971; legal sec. De Armond & De Armond Law Office, Anderson, Ind., 1972; exec. sec. J.C. Penney Distbrn. Ctr., Anderson, 1972-74; reading tutor, aide Jay Sch. Corp., Portland, Ind., 1974-79; billing clk. Jay County Hosp., Portland, 1979-80, med. records clk., 1980-86, interim dir. med. records, 1986-87, dir. health info. mgmt. and med. staff svcs., 1988—. Mem. Headwaters Heritage, Portland, 1983-88, pres., 1983-86; deacon Presbyn. Ch., Portland, 1984-86, pres., 1986, trustee; mem. solicitation com. Jay Arts Coun.; mem. cmty. rels. com. Jay County Hosp.; mem. Jay County Friends of the Libr.; mem. Dem. Women's Com., pres., 1994; bd. dirs. Literacy Coalition, 1992—. Mem. Nat. Assn. Med. Staff Svcs., Am. Health Info. Mgmt. Assn., Ind. Health Info. Mgmt. Assn., Ctrl. Ea. Ind. Health Info. Mgmt. Assn. (pres. 1996), Altrusa Internat., Cincinnatus League, Phi Theta Kappa. Democrat. Office: Jay County Hosp 500 W Votaw St Portland IN 47371-1322

COUPEY, SUSAN MCGUIRE, pediatrician, educator; b. Montreal, Que., Can., June 29, 1942; came to U.S., 1978; d. Clarence Herbert and Paulette (Lefevre) McGuire; m. Pierre M.L. Coupey, July 1964 (div. 1981); children: Marc M.R., Ariane S.; m. James R. English III, Nov. 23, 1988. BA, Queen's U., Kingston, Ont., Can., 1962; postgrad., McGill U., Montreal, 1962-63; MD, U. B.C., Vancouver, Can., 1975. Diplomate Am. Bd. Pediatrics, subboard in adolescent medicine. Devel. chemist Merck, Sharp & Dohme, Ltd., Montreal, 1963-64; rotating intern Montreal Gen. Hosp., 1975-76; resident in pediatrics Montreal Children's Hosp., 1976-78; fellow in adolescent medicine Montefiore Med. Ctr., Bronx, N.Y., 1978-79, attending pediatrician, 1980—; rsch. asst. Cancer Rsch. Ctr., U. B.C., 1967-72; instr., asst. prof. pediatrics Albert Einstein Coll. Medicine, Bronx, 1979-85, assoc. prof., 1985-93, prof., 1993—, assoc. dir. div. adolescent medicine, 1984—, course dir. introduction to clin. medicine, 1989—, mem. faculty senate, 1983-84, 88-90; attending pediatrician North Ctrl. Bronx Hosp., 1979—; cons. in adolescent medicine Flushing (N.Y.) Hosp. and Med. Ctr., 1982—; Maricopa-Pima vis. prof. U. Ariz., 1989; vis. prof. Children's Hosp. Ea. Ont., U. Ottawa and Ea. Can. chpt. Soc. for Adolescent Medicine, 1990; chmn. health svcs. adv. com. Children's Aid Soc., 1985—, bd. trustees, 1993—; mem. adv. bd. Office Substance Abuse Ministry, Archdiocese of N.Y., 1983-85. Assoc. editor Adolescent Medicine: State of the Art Revs., 1990—, Jour. Devel. & Behavioral Pediatrics, 1992-96, Jour. Pediat. & Adolescent Gynecology, 1992—; contbr. articles to med. jours., also chpts. to books and monographs. Fellow Am. Acad. Pediatrics; mem. Soc. for Adolescent Medicine (nominations com. 1984-85, chmn. jour. adv. com. 1987—, program com. 1991-93, awards com. 1992-95), Ambulatory Pediatric Assn., Soc. for Behavioral Pediatrics, N.Am. Soc. Pediat. and Adolescent Gynecology (bd. dirs.), Ea. Soc. Pediat. Rsch., Soc. Rsch. in Adolescence, Sex Info. and Edn. Coun. U.S., Am. Acad. Physicians & Patients, Albert Einstein Coll. Medicine Alumni Assn. (v.p. pediatrics 1983-84, pres. 1984-85). Office: Albert Einstein Coll Medicine Montefiore Med Ctr 111 E 210th St Bronx NY 10467-2490

COUREY, NORMAN LEON, anesthesiologist; b. Montreal, Que., Can., July 4, 1942; came to U.S., 1982; s. Leon and Laurice Courey; m. Susan Silverman, Nov. 27, 1971. BSc, McGill U., Montreal, 1963, MD, 1966, diploma in anesthesia, 1971. Diplomate Am. Bd. Anesthesiology. Intern Jewish Gen. Hosp., Montreal, 1966-67; resident Royal Victoria Hosp., Montreal Children's Hosp., 1967-71, Montreal Chest Hosp., Montreal Neurol. Inst., 1967-71; anesthesiologist Grace Hosp., Ottawa, Ont., Can., 1971-73, St. Mary's Hosp., Montreal, 1973-82, Royal Victoria Hosp., Montreal, 1980-81, Newton-Wellesley Hosp., Boston, 1982-90, St. Margaret's Hosp., Boston, 1991-93, Norwood Hosp., 1993—. Fellow Royal Coll. of Physicians; mem. Mass. Med. Soc. Eastern Orthodox.

COURNOYER, PAUL A., podiatrist; b. Southbridge, Mass., Aug. 22, 1961; s. Russell Wilfrid and Anita Mary Cournoyer; m. Kathleen A. Cournoyer, May 28, 1988; children: Ryan, Kaley. BS, Mass. Coll. Pharmacy, 1982; DPM, Scholl Coll. Podiatristy, Chgo., 1986. Diplomate Am. Bd. Podiatric Surgery; lic. Fla., Mass. Resident in surgery Bapt. Med. Ctr., Bklyn., 1986-88; attending physician Wyckoff Heights Hosp., Bklyn., 1988-91, Fallon Clinic, Inc., Worcester, Mass., 1991—; attending physician Bklyn. Caledonia Hosp., 1988-91, St. Vincent Hosp., Worcester, 1991—. Fellow Am. Coll. Foot and Ankle Surgeons; mem. Am. Podiatric Med. Assn., Mass. Podiatric Med. Assn. Office: Fallon Clinic Inc 135 Gold Star Blvd Worcester MA 01606

COURSEY, JOY HAMMOND, critical care nurse; b. Oxford, Ala., July 14, 1963; d. Franklin D. Hammond and Gloria Hammond Myers; m. Michael T. Coursey, July 31, 1988. BSN, Med. Coll. Ga., 1985; M in Biomed. Scis., U. S.C., 1996. CCRN, Ga. Staff nurse trauma ICU Med. Coll. Ga., Augusta, Ga., 1985-92; asst. nurse mgr. cardiovascular ICU Richland Meml., Columbia, S.C., 1990-94, staff nurse, 1994—, nurse anesthetist, 1996—; staff nurse float pool Humana Hosp., Augusta, 1991-92. Mem. AACN, Am. Assn. Nurse Anesthetists. Home: 19 Wheatstone Columbia SC 29223-9029

COURT-BROWN, CHARLES MICHAEL, orthopaedic surgeon; b. Edinburgh, Scotland, Feb. 3, 1948; s. William Michael and Caroline (Gordon) C.-B.; m. Jacqueline Yek Quen Mok, July 6, 1974; children: Johanna, Michael. BS in Zoology, U. Aberdeen, 1970; MBChB, U. Edinburgh, 1975, MD, 1984. Lectr. Edinburgh U., 1982-84, sr. lectr., 1985-90; fellow Sunnybrook Hosp., Toronto, 1984-85; cons. surgeon Edinburgh, 1990—; chmn. Scottish Orthopaedic Rsch. Trust into Trauma, 1992—. Author: Closed Nailing of the Tibia and Femur, 1991; editor: Management of Open Fractures, 1996; contbr. articles to profl. jours.; mem. Brit. Trauma Soc. (founder 1989). Mem. British Orthopaedic Assn., Orthopaedic Trauma Assn., Secot. Office: Royal Infirmary Edinburgh, Orthopedic Surgery Edinburg, Lauriston Pl EM3 9YW, Scotland

COURTEMANCHE, JUDY BELLISARIO, hospital administrator; b. Putnam, Conn., Feb. 13, 1950; d. Henry J. and Isabelle A. (Bartholic) Bellisario; m. Gary E. Courtemanche, June 19, 1971; children: John E., Jeffrey A. BSN, Worcester State Coll., 1983; MS in Adminstrn. and

Nursing, Boston U., 1985. RN, Conn., Mass., R.I.; CEN. Adminstrv. supr. Day-Kimball Hosp., Putnam, 1979-84; adminstrv. mentor U. Mass. Med. Ctr., Worcester, 1984-85; emergency/outpatient service coordinator St. Joseph Hosp., Providence, R.I., 1985-91; dir. St. Joseph Ctr. Health and Human Svcs., Providence, 1991-93, chief nurse coord., 1993-94; field rep. Joint Commn. for Accreditation Healthcare Orgns., Oakbrook Terrace, Ill., 1994—; coord. trauma nursing State of R.I., 1987-91. Mem. ANA, Emergency Nurses Assn. (R.I. coun. 1986-90), Providence Regional Emergency Med. Svcs. Coun. (vice chair 1990), Zonta, Sigma Theta Tau. Home: 7 Wakefield Pond Rd Thompson CT 06277-2325 Office: Joint Commn Accreditation Healthcare Orgns 1 Renaissance Blvd Oakbrook Terrace IL 60181 also: Courtemanche & Assocs, Inc. Thompson CT 06277

COURTEMANCHE, LINDA AILEEN, emergency nurse, poison control nurse, administrator; b. Lebanon, N.H.. Diploma, Jeanne Mance Sch. of Nursing, Burlington, Vt., 1970. RN, N.H., Vt.; cert. poison info. specialist. Emergency flight nurse Kalispell (Mont.) Regional Hosp., 1978-81; staff nurse emergency and pediatric dept. Dartmouth Hitchcock Med. Ctr., Lebanon, N.H., 1973-76, asst. head nurse emergency dept., 1976-78, 81-85, supr. N.H. poison control, 1985—. Contbr. articles to profl. jours. Capt. Nurse Corps, U.S. Army, 1970-72. Mem. Am. Assn. Poison Control Ctrs., Emergency Nurses Assn.

COURTIEU, ANDRE-LOUIS, retired microbiology educator; b. Lyons, France, Sept. 2, 1925; s. Paul Marie and Aimee (Robellet) C.; m. Suzanne-Paule Kempf, July 10, 1950 (dec. Mar. 1979); children: Claude, Francoise; m. Marie-Anne Deschamps, Sept. 7, 1985. MD, U. Lyons, 1952. Asst. Inst. Pasteur Lyon, 1952-59, chief, 1959-61; chief microbiologist Hopital Centre Hospitalier, St. Etienne, France, 1960-66, Hopital Centre Hospitalier Regional, Nantes, France, 1966-93; prof. microbiology Faculty Medicine, Unite De Formation et de Recherche, Nantes, 1966-93, prof. emeritus, 1993. With French Air Force, 1945-46. Recipient Merite Nat., 1965. Mem. Soc. Francaise Biologie Clinique (pres. 1982-83), AAAS, Am. Soc. Microbiology, Mutuelle Nat. des Sports (Paris, pres. 1994), Rotary. Home: Rue des Onchères, 44230 Saint Sebastien sur Loire France

COURTNAY, WILIAM GERARD, osteopathic physician; b. Guthrie, Okla., Aug. 22, 1962; s. Clarence Clive and Patricia Ann (Pike) C.; m. Sandra Louise Ferrell, June 4, 1994. BS, U. Ctrl. Okla., Edmond, 1986; DO, Okla. State U., Tulsa, 1994. Emergency dept. technician Midwest City (Okla.) Meml. Hosp., 1979-88; med. examiner investigator Office of Chief Med. Examiner, Oklahome City, 1988-90; intern Hillcrest Health Ctr., Oklahome City, 1994-95; physician in pvt. practice Moore, Okla., 1995—. Vol. med. examiner Office of Chief Med. Examiner, Oklahoma City, 1995. Mem. Am. Osteo. Assn., Okla. Osteo. Assn. Republican. Roman Catholic.

COURTNEY, ANN, nursing educator. AS in Nursing magna cum laude, Nassau Community Coll., 1984; BSN magna cum laude, SUNY, Stony Brook, 1993. RN, N.Y.; cert. advanced neonatal life support Am. Heart Assn. Staff nurse surg. ICU Booth Meml. Med. Ctr., Flushing, N.Y., 1984-86; staff nurse ICU St. Charles Hosp., Port Jefferson, N.Y., 1986; nursing instr. mem. breastfeeding support team Rssch. Ctr. II, Univ. Hosp., Stony Brook, 1986—. Mem. NAACOG (cert.), Nat. Assn. Neonatal Nurses, L.I. Assn. Neonatal Nurses, Internat. Lactation Cons. Assn. (cert., coord. bd. examiners 1990), L.I. Lactation Cons. Assn. (corr. sec. 1989-92, chmn. pub. rels. com. 1992-94), Golden Key, Sigma Theta Tau. Office: Univ Hosp Suny Stony Brk Stony Brook NY 11794

COURTNEY, JAMES WHITFIELD, optometrist; b. Paducah, Ky., Jan. 8, 1951; s. James Elvis and Mary Ruth (Carlin) C.; m. Lana Jill Hatcher, Aug. 2, 1986; children: Jacob, Carlin, Addie, Jamie, Anne. BS in Optometry, U. Houston, 1974, OD, 1976. Pvt. practice Murray, Ky., 1976—. Mem. Am. Optometric Assn. (contact lens sect.), Ky. Optometric Assn., Murray Rotary (pres. 1994-95). Republican. Baptist. Office: Courtney Vision Ctr 1208 Johnson Blvd Murray KY 42071-2961

COUTINHO, ROELAND ARNOLD, microbiologist, epidemiologist; b. Laren, The Netherlands, Apr. 4, 1946; s. Maurice Sigismund and Lore (Frensdorf) C.; m. Johanna Wiggelendam, Mar. 21, 1970; children: Hannah, Marye, Jonathan. MD, U. Amsterdam, The Netherlands, 1972, PhD, 1984. Head rural hosp. Provisional Govt. Guinee-Bissao, Ziguinchor, Senegal, 1973-74; gen. practitioner The Netherlands, 1974; head dept. pub. health Mcpl. Health Svc., Amsterdam, 1977—; rsch. fellow dept. virology U. Amsterdam, 1974-77, prof. epidemiology and control of infectious diseases, 1989—; cons. smallpox eradication WHO, Geneva, 1975; cons. infectious diseases Nat. Inst. Pub. Health, Bilthoven, 1988-90; vis. scientist CDC, Atlanta, 1990-91; mem. several pub. health adv. bds. Contbr. over 280 articles to profl. jours. Mem. Am. Pub. Health Assn., Internat. Epidemiol. Assn., Internat. AIDS Soc., Am. Soc. for Epidemiologic Rsch., Med. Soc. for the Study of Venereal Diseases, Dutch Soc. for Microbiology, Dutch Soc. for the Study of Venereal Diseases, Dutch Soc. for Infectious Diseases. Home: Dorpsstraat 164, 1393 NL Nigtevecht The Netherlands Office: Mcpl Health Svc Pub Health, Nieuwe Achtergracht 100, 1018 WT Amsterdam The Netherlands

COUTURE, JOSIE BALABAN, foundation director, insurance executive; b. Chgo., Dec. 10, 1922; m. Louis Couture, May 20, 1945 (div. 1948); 1 child, Dan B. Student, Tobias Matthay Sch. Pianoforte, London, Eng., 1938-39; studied with, Tobias Matthay; student, Yale U., 1939-40, Manhattan Sch. Music, 1940-42. Debut concert pianist Civic Theatre Chgo. Opera House, 1941; concert pianist live performances, radio, TV, 1941-50; entertainer USO tours; stockbroker N.Y. Stock Exch., 1955-60; ins. agt., broker, cons. N.Y.C., 1956—; internat. pub. info. coord. Al-Anon Hdqs., N.Y.C., 1970-76; founder, pres. TOVA (The Other Victims of Alcoholism, Inc.), N.Y.C., 1976—; lectr., speaker in field. Editor: Domino Quar., 1977—; past mem. editorial adv. bd. Alcoholism Digest, Labour-Mgmt. Alcoholism Jour.; contbr. articles to profl. jours. Liaison rep. nat. adv. coun. Nat. Inst. on Alcohol Abuse and Alcoholism U.S. Dept. Health and Human Svcs., Washington, 1977—; testified at senate hearings Women and Alcoholism, 1976, Impact Alcohol and Drug Abuse on Family Life, 1977, Comprehensive Alcohol Abuse and Alcoholism Prevention, Treatment, and Rehab. Act Amendments, 1979. Recipient New Pioneer award Office Women and Alcoholism Nat. Coun. Alcoholism Inc. and Women's Inst. Am. Univ., 1977; recognized in Congl. Record for New Nat. Orgn. TOVA, 1976. Home: 100 W 57th St New York NY 10019-3327 Office: TOVA PO Box 1528 Radio City Sta New York NY 10101

COUTURE, NORMA W., nursing educator; b. Stoneham, Mass., July 9, 1930; children: Jeanne, Steven, John. RN, Lawrence Gen. Hosp., Mass., 1950; BSN, U. Lowell (Mass.), 1977; MSN, Boston U., 1980. Instr. No. Essex Community Coll., Haverhill, Mass.; clin. nurse specialist N.E. Rehab. Hosp., Salem, N.H.; asst. dir. nursing First healthcare Corp., Methuen, Mass.; nurse clincian Gillette A.M.C., Andover, Mass.; now instr. nursing North Essex C.C. Co-author: A Guide to Chemotherapy, 1980. Mem. Lawrence Gen. Hosp. Sch. Nursing Alumnae Assn., U. Lowell Alumnae Assn., Boston U. Alumnae Assn., NLN, Sigma Theta Tau. Home: 165 Haverhill St Methuen MA 01844-3445

COUTURIER, LANCE CORNELIUS, psychologist; b. Humboldt, Nebr., May 17, 1948; s. Gerard Morency and Jean (Cornelius) C.; m. Katherine Jean Devlin, Dec. 26, 1976; children: Graham, Gregory, Anna. BA cum laude, U. Md., 1970; MA, Temple U., 1974, PhD, 1980. Teaching assoc. Temple U., Phila., 1972-76; tng. inst. dir. Juvenile Justice Ctr. Pa., Phila., 1976-80; clin. dir. Southeast Secure Treatment Unit, West Chester, Pa., 1980-85; chief psychologist State Correctional Institution at Graterford, Graterford, Pa., 1985-92; chief psychol. svcs. div. Dept. of Corrections, Camp Hill, 1992—; cons. United Cerebral Palsy Assn., Pottstown Drug and Alcohol Rehab. Program, Collegeville, Pa., 1985-88, Pub. Mgmt. Info. Systems, Washington; vis. lectr. Neumann Coll., Aston, Pa., 1983. Contbr. articles to profl. jours. Bd. dirs. Crime Prevention Assn., Phila., 1980-86; mem. adv. bd. South Phila. Unemployment Project, 1977-80, Family Resource Ctr., Greaterford, 1989—. Sgt. USNG, 1976-80. Mem. APA, Am. Correctional Psychologists Assn., Nat. Alliance for Mentally Ill, Family and Corrections Network, ACLU, Amnesty Internat., Phi Kappa Phi. Home: 110 W End Ave Lititz PA 17543-2620 Office: PO Box 598 Camp Hill PA 17001-0598

COVAS, AMELIA M., critical care and rehabilitation nurse, intravenous therapy nurse; b. Bunheiro, Portugal, Jan. 29, 1960; d. Jose Santos and Beatriz Oliveira (Amador) Matos; m. Albert A. Covas, Sept. 19, 1981; children: Lauren, Amanda. ADN, Felician Coll., Lodi, N.J., 1982; BSN, Seton Hall U., 1986. Cert. critical care nurse, intravenous therapy nurse, ALS. Head nurse in same day surgery St. James Hosp., Newark, emergency rm. staff nurse; nurse, v.p. Health Network, Inc., Kenilworth, N.J. Mem. Women in Ins. Assn. (pre-admission testing coord.). Home: 10 Nolan Ct Atlantic Highlands NJ 07716-2104

COVELL, LINDA M., pathologist; b. Winchester, Mass., June 26, 1947; m. Jonathan H. Davis, 1977; 4 children. BA, Wellesley Coll., 1969; MD, Harvard U., 1973. Diplomate Am. Bd. Pathology; lic. MD, Mass. Resident, fellow pathology Beth Israel Hosp., Boston, 1973-78; pathologist Brigham & Women's Hosp., Boston, 1980, 82-84, Mount Auburn Hosp., Cambridge, Mass., 1986-93. Author: A Purim Story, 1988; author, composer (audiocassette) Carpools and Kippahs, 1991, More Carpools and Kippahs, 1995; illustrator Gribbenes, 1984—. Mem. Acad. Pathology (Am.-Can. divsn.), New Eng. Soc. Pathologists.

COVELL, RUTH MARIE, medical educator, medical school administrator; b. San Francisco, Aug. 12, 1936; d. John Joseph and Mary Carolyn (Coles) Collins; m. James Wachob Covell, 1963 (div. 1972); 1 child, Stephen. m. Harold Joachim Simon, Jan. 4, 1973; 1 child, David. Student, U. Vienna, Austria, 1955-56; BA, Stanford U., 1958; MD, U. Chgo., 1962. Clin. prof. and assoc. dean sch. medicine U. Calif. San Diego, La Jolla, 1969—; dir. Acad. Geriatric Resource Ctr.; bd. dirs. Calif. Coun. Geriatrics and Gerontology, Beverly Found., Pasadena, Alzheimer's Family Ctr., San Diego, San Diego Epilepsy Soc., Devel. Svcs. Inc., San y Sidro Health Ctr., NIH SBIR Stude Sect. Geriatrics; cons. Agy. Health Care Policy and Rsch. Contbr. articles on health planning and quality of med. care to profl. jours. Mem. AMA, Am. Health Svcs. Rsch., Assn. Tchrs. Preventive Medicine, Am. Pub. Health Assn., Assn. Am. Med. Colls. Group on Instl. Planning (chair 1973-74, sec. 1983-84), Phi Beta Kappa, Alpha Omega Alpha. Home: 1604 El Camino Del Teatro La Jolla CA 92037-6338 Office: U Calif San Diego Sch Medicine M-002 La Jolla CA 92093

COVERT, MICHAEL HENRI, healthcare facility administrator; b. Chgo., Apr. 7, 1949; s. Leonard and Shirley Gladys (Jeffe) C.; children: Jason, Tiffany, Briennm; m. Janie Covert; 1 child, Madison. BS in Bus., Washington U., St. Louis, 1970, M in Health Adminstrn., 1972. Adminstrv. asst. St. Agnes Hosp., White Plains, N.Y., 1969; adminstrv. resident Hillcrest Med. Ctr., Tulsa, 1971-72, asst. adminstr., 1972-73, adminstr., 1973-80; exec. v.p., chief operating officer St. Francis Regional Med. Ctr., Wichita, Kans., 1980-85; CEO Ohio State Univ. Hosps., Columbus, 1985-88; sr. v.p. Physician Corp. of Am., Wichita, Kans., 1988-89; ind. mgmt. cons. Wichita, 1989-91; acting dir. community health Wichita/Sedgwick County, Wichita, Kans., 1991-92; pres., CEO Sarasota (Fla.) Meml. Hosp., 1992—; pres.-elect Franklin County Hosp. Coun., Columbus, 1987-88; adj. faculty Ohio State U., 1985—, Washington U., St. Louis, 1992—. Bd. dirs. United Way Sarasota, 1993—, campaign chair, 1995-96; del. Am. Hosp. Assn., State of Fla. Fellow Am. Coll. Healthcare Execs. (mem. accreditation commn. grad. edn. in health care adminstrn. 1988-94, chair commn. 1991-94); mem. Fla. Hosp. Assn. (bd. dirs. 1995—), U. South Fla. Leadership Coun., Healthcare Alumni Assn. (chair Washington U., St. Louis 1994-95, past chair 1996—), Sarasota C. of C. (chair 1995-96), Univ. Club (v.p. 1996). Home: 1598 Peregrine Point Dr Sarasota FL 34231 Office: Sarasota Meml Hosp 1700 S Tamiami Trail Sarasota FL 34239

COVI, LINO, psychiatrist; b. Trento, Italy, Mar. 19, 1926; came to U.S., 1956, naturalized, 1965; s. Giuseppe and Giuseppina (Mariotti) C.; m. Beverly A. Yeutsy, Dec. 30, 1958 (dec.); children: Lisa Martina, Michelle Peppina, Gina Albina, Tina Maria. Student in philosophy, U. Florence, Italy, 1945-47, Sch. Social Work, Trento and Rome, 1949-51; MD, U. Rome, 1955. Asst. U. Rome Neuropsychiat. Clinic, 1955-56; intern Albert Einstein Med. Ctr., Phila., 1956-57; resident fellow psychiatry Johns Hopkins Hosp., Balt., 1957-60, dir. outpatient clin. rsch. unit, 1968-83, dir. Cognitive Therapy Clinic, 1982—, dir. treatment assessment rsch. unit, 1983—; assoc. clin. prof. U. Md. Med. Sch., Balt., 1986—; instr. psychiatry Johns Hopkins U., 1960-67, asst. prof., 1967-72, assoc. prof., 1972—; vis. psychiatrist Balt. City Hosp., 1960-80; vis. scientist Nat. Inst. Drug Abuse-Addiction Rsch. Ctr., Balt., 1988—; psychiatrist Francis Scott Key Med. Ctr.-Hopkins Bayview Med. Ctr., Balt., 1988—; med. dir. Friends Health Svcs., 1994—; staff psychiatrist Patuxent Instn., Jessup, Md., 1960-62; chief out-patient dept. Gundry Hosp., Balt., 1962-86, pres. bd. dirs., 1972-84, rsch. dir., 1973-86; mem. bd. govs. Cen. Md. Health Systems Agy., 1978-83; rsch. psychiatrist NIMH Collaborative Studies, 1962-64, co-prin. investigator, 1964-65, prin. investigator, 1965-83, prin. investigator clin. trials of new drugs for depression and anxiety, 1970—6, studies of group cognitive therapy in depression, 1980—; tchg. assoc. Sheppard and E. Pratt Hosp., 1973-79; cons. Pharm. Rsch. Labs., 1971—, Centro Psicologia Clinica, Milan, 1981—. Editor: The Md. Psychiatrist, 1974-80, Today's Psychiatry, Md. Med. Jour., 1985—; contbr. articles to profl. jours. Mem. human rights com. Coop. Studies Program, VA, 1981-84. Mem. AMA (prof. staff drug evaluation con. on drugs 1968-71), Am. Coll. Neuropsychopharmacology (coms.), Md. Psychiat. Soc. (coms.), Am. Psychiat. Assn. (nat. coms., dep. rep. Md., Newsletter award 1977), Am. Soc. Clin. Psychopharmacology, World Fedn. Mental Health, Johns Hopkins Med. Soc., Assn. Advancement Behavior Therapy, Md. Med. Soc., Balt. Med. Soc. (chmn. coms.), Collegium Internat. Neuropsychopharmacologicum, Italian-Am. Hist. Assn. Democrat. Roman Catholic. Office: PO Box 10676 505 Baltimore Ave Baltimore MD 21285 Office: PO Box 10676 505 Baltimore Ave Towson MD 21285

COVINGTON, PAUL STEVEN, internist; b. Birmingham, Ala., Feb. 20, 1956; s. Joseph Frances and Ruth Mary (Schileci) C.; m. Anita Gail Vines, Dec. 21, 1979; children: Steven, Andrew, Philip. BS, U. Ala., 1978, MD, 1982. Intern Carroway Meth. Med. Ctr., Birmingham, Ala., 1982-83; resident Carroway Meth. Med. Ctr., Birmingham, 1983-85; pvt. practice Clanton, Ala., 1985-90; med. dir. Future Healthcare Rsch. Ctrs., Birmingham, 1990-91; med. dir. Pharm. Product Devel., Wilmington N.C., 1991-93, exec. med. dir., 1993-94, v.p. med. affairs, 1994—. Republican. Roman Catholic. Home: 3116 Braemar Ln Wilmington NC 28409 Office: Pharm Product Devel 115 N 3d St Wilmington NC 28401

COVINGTON, STEPHANIE STEWART, psychotherapist, writer, educator; b. Whittier, Calif., Nov. 5, 1942; d. William and Bette (Robertson) Stewart; children: Richard, Kim. BA cum laude, U. So. Calif., 1963; MSW, Columbia U., 1970; PhD, Union Inst., 1982. Pvt. practice psychotherapy, co-dir. Inst. for Relational Devel., La Jolla, Calif., 1981—; instr. U. Calif., San Diego, 1981—, Calif. Sch. Profl. Psychology, San Diego, 1982-88, San Diego State U., 1982-84, Southwestern Sch. Behavioral Health Studies, 1982-84, Profl. Sch. Humanistic Psychology, San Diego, 1983-84, U.S. Internat. U., San Diego, 1983-84, UCLA, 1983-84, U So. Calif., L.A., 1983-84, U. Utah, Salt Lake City, 1983-84; co-dir. Inst. Relational Devel.; cons. L.A. County Sch. Dist., N.C. Dept. Mental Health, Nat. Ctrs. Substance Abuse Treatment and Prevention, Nat. Inst. Corrections, others; designer women's treatment, cons. Betty Ford Ctr.; presenter at profl. meetings; lectr. in field; addiction cons. criminal justice sys. Author: Leaving the Enchanted Forest: The Path from Relationship Addiction to Intimacy, 1988, Awakening Your Sexuality: A Guide for Recovering Women and Their Partners, 1991, A Woman's Way Through the Twelve Steps, 1994; contbr. articles to profl. jours. Mem. NASW (diplomate), Am. Assn. Sex Educators, Counselors and Therapists, Am. Bd. Med. Psychotherapists (diplomate), Am. Bd. Sexology (diplomate), Am. Pub. Health Assn., Am. Assn. Marriage and Family Therapy, Assn. Women in Psychology, Calif. Women's Commn. on Alcoholism (Achievement award), Ctr. for Study of the Person, Friends of Jung, Internat. Coun. on Alcoholism and Addictions (past chair women's com.), Kettil Brun Soc. (Finland), San Diego Soc. Sex Therapy and Edn., Soc. for Study of Addiction (Eng.). Office: 7946 Ivanhoe Ave Ste 201B La Jolla CA 92037-4517

COVITZ, WESLEY, medical educator, physician; b. Winthrop, Mass., Oct. 12, 1944. BA in Biochem. Scis., Harvard U., 1966; MD, U. Cin. 1970. Diplomate Am. Bd. Pediatrics, Sub bd. Pediat. Cardiology. Asst. prof. pediats. Med. Coll. Ga., Augusta, 1976-81, assoc. prof. pediats., 1981-86, prof. pediats., 1986-89; prof. pediats., chief divsn. pediat. cardiology Bowman Gray Sch. Medicine, Winston-Salem, N.C., 1989—. Office: Bowman Gray Sch Medicine Medical Center Blvd Winston Salem NC 27157-1081

COWAN, DALE HARVEY, internist, lawyer; b. Cleve., Jan. 25, 1938; s. Milton Jerome and Clara (Umans) C.; m. Deborah Wolowitz, Jan. 28, 1967; children: Rachel, Morris Benjamin, William Ezra. AB, Harvard U., 1959, MD, 1963; JD, Case We. Res. U., 1981 Diplomate Am. Bd. Internal Medicine. Bar: Ohio 1981. Intern Cleve. Met. Gen. Hosp., 1963-64, resident, 1964-65, 67-70; practice medicine specializing in internal medicine, hematology and oncology; dir. hematology and oncology Marymount Hosp., Cleve., 1982—; asst. prof. medicine Case We. Res. U., Cleve., 1970-75, assoc. prof., 1975-84, clin. prof. environ. health scis.) 1985—, assoc. Health Systems Mgmt. Ctr., 1982-90; of counsel firm Burke, Haber & Berick, 1984-86; spl. cons. President's Commn. on Bioethics, Washington, 1981-82; mem. nat. adv. coun. Nat. Heart Lung and Blood Inst., Bethesda, Md., 1982-85. Author: Preferred Provider Organizations, 1984; co-editor Human Organ Transplantation, 1987; contbr. articles to profl. jours. Bd. dirs. Bur. Jewish Edn., 1977-87, Northeast Ohio affiliate Am. Heart Assn., 1982-86; pres. Ohio/W.Va. Oncology Soc., 1990-94. Served to lt. comdr. USPHS, 1965-67. Fellow ACP, Am. Coll. Legal Medicine; mem. AMA, ABA, Am. Soc. Hematology, Am. Soc. Clin. Oncology, Am. Assn. for Cancer Research, Nat. Health Lawyers Assn. (bd. dirs. 1988-94), Am. Acad. Hosp. Attys., Am. Soc. Law and Medicine, Acad. Medicine Cleve. (pres.-elect). Home: 19600 Shaker Blvd Cleveland OH 44122-1830 Office: 6100 W Creek Rd #15 Cleveland OH 44131-2133

COWAN, GARY MILTON, ophthalmologist, consultant; b. Honolulu, Nov. 30, 1955; s. Claud Milton and Evah Lee (Arrington) C.; m. Marilyn Suzanne Smith, Nov. 15, 1980; children: Lara, Melissa. MD, U. Tex. Southwestern, 1980. Diplomate Am. Bd. Ophthalmology. Intern in internal medicine Baylor U. Med. Ctr., Dallas, 1980-81; resident in ophthalmology Yale U., 1981-84; fellow in vitreoretinal UCLA Jules Stein Eye Inst., L.A., 1984-86; asst. prof. ophthalmology U. Tex. Med. Sch., San Antonio, 1986-88; pvt. practice Trinity Valley Retina Cons., Ft. Worth, Tex., 1988—; assoc. clin. prof. ophthalmology U. Tex. Southwestern Med. Sch., 1988—; assoc. adj. prof. anatomy and cell biology U. North Tex. Health Sci. Ctr., 1995—; cons. Tex. State Bd. Med. Examiners, Austin, 1991—, assoc. examiner Am. Bd. Ophthalmology, 1992—; v.p. bd. Plaza Med. Group, Ft. Worth, 1994—; mem. Healthcare adv. com. U.S. congressman Joe Barton, Ft. Worth, 1993—; mem. health care task force state senator Jane Nelson, Ft. Worth, 1993—. Contbr. articles to profl. jours. including Glaucoma, Am. Jour. Ophthalmology. Tex. Merit scholar U. Tex. Southwestern Med. Sch., 1978, 79. Fellow Am. Acad. Ophthalmology; mem. The Vitreous Soc., Tex. Ophthalmological Soc., Tex. Med. Assn., Tarrant County Med. Soc., Tarrant County Ophthalmological Soc., Alpha Omega Alpha. Republican. Office: Trinity Valley Retina Cons 800 5th Ave Ste 214 Fort Worth TX 76104

COWAN, ROBERT JENKINS, radiologist, educator; b. Greensboro, N.C., Apr. 22, 1937; s. John Columbus and Edith (Jenkins) C.; m. Leila Caroline Sikes, June 18, 1960; children: Caroline Cowan Morris, Barbara Haynes. AB, U. N.C., 1959, MD, 1963. Diplomate: Am. Bd. Radiology (guest examiner), Am. Bd. Nuclear Medicine. Intern in medicine Presbyn. Hosp., Columbia-Presbyn. Med. Center, N.Y.C., 1963-64; resident Presbyn. Hosp., Columbia-Presbyn. Med. Center, 1966-67; resident in radiology N.C. Bapt. Hosp., Winston-Salem, 1967-70; instr. radiology Bowman Gray Sch. Medicine, Wake Forest U., Winston-Salem, 1970-71; asst. prof. Bowman Gray Sch. Medicine, Wake Forest U., 1971-74, asso. prof., 1974-79, prof., 1979—; dir. nuclear medicine N.C. Bapt. Hosp., Winston-Salem, 1977—; med. dir. nuclear med. tech. tng. program Forsyth Tech. Inst., Winston-Salem, 1977—. Contbr. articles to profl. jours. Adv. bd. Stone Mountain State Park, 1994—. Served to capt., M.C. U.S. Army, 1964-66. Decorated Bronze Star medal; Am. Cancer Soc. fellow, 1969-70; James Picker scholar, 1970-73; recipient James Quinn M.D. Teaching Excellence award, 1983. Fellow Am. Coll. Radiology; mem. AMA, Soc. Nuclear Medicine (coun. Southeastern chpt. 1972-84, pres. 1978, trustee 1983-84), Radiol. Soc. N.Am., Am. Coll. Nulear Physicians, N.C. Radiol. Soc., Med. Soc. N.C., Alpha Omega Alpha. Methodist. Office: Bowman Gray Sch Medicine Winston Salem NC 27103

COWDERY, JOHN STEWART, physician; b. Phila., Oct. 22, 1949; s. John Stewart and Patricia (Collins) C.; m. Suzanne Brittingham, June 22, 1974; children: Karen, Andrew. BA, Duke U.; MS, MD, Emory U. Diplomate Am. Bd. Internal Medicine, Rheumatology. Med. resident Emory U., Atlanta, 1978-79; med. staff fellow NIH, Bethesda, Md., 1979-82; sr. med. resident U. Iowa, Iowa City, 1982-83; asst. prof. U. Iowa Coll. Medicine, Iowa City, 1983-88, assoc. prof., 1988-94, prof., 1994—; mem. immunology, virology, and pathology study sect., NIH, 1994—. Contbg. author: Am. Coll. Physicians publs., 1993-94; contbr. articles to profl. jours. Comdr. USPHS, 1978-82. Rsch. grantee NIH, 1984-95, Am. Heart Assn., Dallas, 1985-88, Dept. Vets. Affairs, Washington, 1991-96, Am. Cancer Soc., Atlanta, 1987-93. Mem. Am. Soc. Clin. Investigation, Am. Assn. Immunologists, Am. Fedn. for Clin. Rsch., Am. Coll. Rheumatology (sec./treas. 1988-90), Cen. Soc. for Clin. Rsch. Office: Univ of Iowa College of Medicine 200 Hawkins Dr Iowa City IA 52242

COWELL, KAREN W., nursing educator; b. Perth Amboy, N.J., Sept. 25, 1952. AA, Frederick Community Coll., 1984; BSN, W.Va. U., 1987; MSN, Marymount U., 1989; PhD, U. Md., 1996. RN, Md. Nursing supr. Frederick (Md.) Meml. Hosp., 1989-90; instr. Frederick County Sch. Practical Nursing, 1987-88; asst. prof. Frederick C.C., 1988-93, assoc. prof., 1993—. Mem. ANA (cert. med.-surg. nursing), Md. Nurses Assn. (dist. 8 pres.), Sigma Theta Tau, Delta Epsilon Sigma. Office: Frederick C C 7932 Opossumtown Pike Frederick MD 21702-2964

COWEN, BARRETT STICKNEY, microbiology educator; b. Lebanon, N.H., May 23, 1939; s. Frank Young and Elsie (Stickney) C.; m. Ruth Maria Consuegra, Sept. 3, 1966; children: Marcella Lucia, Matthew Alfredo. BS, U. Vt., 1963; MS, U. N.H., 1968; PhD, Cornell U., 1973. Lab. asst. Hubbard Farms, Inc., Walpole, N.H., 1963-65; grad. asst. U. N.H., Durham, 1965-67; rsch. specialist Cornell U., Ithaca, N.Y., 1967-73, rsch. assoc., 1973-78; lab. dir. Cobb, Inc., Concord, Mass., 1978-82; assoc. prof. vet. sci. Pa. State U., University Park, 1982—, cons. microbiology dept., 1983; cons. Cobb, Inc., 1983, Pilch, Inc., Troutmen, N.C., 1984, Croton Egg Farms, Ohio, 1985; tech. advisor Pa. Egg Producers, Lancaster, 1984, Biomune, Inc., Lenexa, Kans., 1989—, Super Pollo, Rancaqua, Chile, 1993—, Incubator Anhalzer, Quito, Ecuador, 1994, Grandparents Poultry (PVT) Ltd., Lahore, Pakistan, 1995. Contbr. articles to profl. jours. Served with U.S. Army, 1960. Pa. Dept. Agr. grantee, 1984—; J. William Fulbright Fgn. scholar, 1994. Mem. Am. Assn. Avian Pathologists, Am. Soc. Microbiology, Conf. Rsch. Workers in Animal Diseases, Am. Assn. Vet. Lab. Diagnosticians, World Vet. Poultry Assn., Sigma Xi, Phi Kappa Phi. Republican. Methodist. Lodges: St. John's, Masons. Avocations: hunting and fishing, tennis, skiing, stamp collecting. Home: 724 Cornwall Rd State College PA 16803-1427 Office: Wiley Lab University Pa State U University Park PA 16802

COWEN, DONALD EUGENE, retired physician; b. Ft. Morgan, Colo., Oct. 8, 1918; adopted s. Franklin and Mary Edith (Dalton) C.; BA, U. Denver, 1940; MD, U. Colo., 1943; m. Hulda Marie Helling, Dec. 24, 1942; children: David L., Marilyn Marie Cowen Dean, Theresa Kathleen Cowen Cunningham Byrd, Margaret Ann Cowen Koenigs. Intern, U.S. Naval Hosp., Oakland, Calif., 1944; gen. practice medicine, Ft. Morgan, 1947-52; resident internal medicine U. Colo. Med. Ctr., Denver, 1952-54; practice medicine specializing in allergy, Denver, 1954-90, ret., 1990; mem. staff Presbyn. Med. Ctr., Denver, Porter, Swedish hosps., Englewood, Colo.; clin. asst. prof. medicine U. Colo. Med. Center, 1964-91, ret., 1991; postgrad. faculty U. Tenn. Coll. Medicine, Memphis, 1962-82; cons. Queen of Thailand, 1973, 75, 77. Pres. Community Arts Symphony Found., 1980-82. Served to lt. M.C., USN, 1943-47. Fellow ACP, Am. Coll. Chest Physicians (vice chmn. com. on allergy 1968-72, 75-87, sec.-treas. Colo. chpt. 1971-77, pres. 1978-80), Am. Coll. Allergy and Immunology, Acad. Internat. Medicine, West Coast Allergy Soc., Southwest Allergy Forum, Am. Acad. Otolaryngic Allergy, Colo. socs. internal medicine, Colo. Allergy Soc. (past pres.), Ill. Soc. Opthalmology and Otolaryngology (hon.), Denver Med. Soc. (chmn. library and bldg. com. 1963-73), Arapahoe Med. Soc. (life emeritus mem.). Presbyterian (ruling elder 1956—). Club: Lions. Contbr. numerous articles to profl. jours. Home: 18560 Polvera Dr San Diego CA 92128-1120

COWEN, JOSEPH ROBERT, psychiatrist; b. Washington, Mar. 1, 1923; s. Samuel and Sarah Lillian (Davis) C.; m. Beatrice Mosner, Sept. 21, 1951 (dec.); 1 child, James S. Student, U. Chgo., 1942-44, Johns Hopkins U., 1944-46; MD, U. Md., Balt., 1950. Diplomate Am. Bd. Psychiatry and Neurology, Nat. Bd. Med. Examiners. Intern Wayne County (Mich.) Hosp., 1950-51; resident in psychiatry Spring Grove (Md.) Hosp., 1951-54, chief of svc., 1954-56; sr. psychiatrist Sheppard Enoch Pratt Hosp., Md., 1956-58; pvt. practice Balt., 1958—. Contbr. poems to profl. jours., newspapers and mags. Fellow Am. Psyciat. Assn. (life); mem. AMA. Home and Office: 7307 Rockridge Rd Baltimore MD 21207-4642

COWLEY, LUIS M., psychiatrist, educator; b. Havana, Cuba, June 22, 1921; came to U.S., 1960, naturalized, 1967; s. Luis M. and Guillermina (Morales) C.; m. Yolanda M. Perez, Aug. 29, 1948; children: Ana, Margarita, Luis, Maria, Yolanda, Felipe. M.D., Havana U., 1944. Student house officer Havana (Cuba) U. Hosp., 1940-44, intern, 1944-45; resident psychiatry San Juan de Dios Psychiat. Sanatorium, Havana, 1945-47; psychiatrist, vice dir. San Juan de Dios Psychiat. Sanatorium, 1947-49, psychiatrist, 1949-60; psychiatrist, clin. dir. Perez Vento Psychiat. Sanatorium, Havana, 1957-60; asso. psychiatry Havana U. Hosp., 1946-50; instr., adjoined prof. clin. therapeutic Havana U. Sch. Medicine, 1946-50; asso. in psychiatry Elizabeths Hosp., Washington, 1947; staff, physician charge intensive treatment Terrell (Tex.) State Hosp., 1961, staff physician, supr. psychiat. residency tng. and white female acute treatment program, 1961-62, clin. dir., 1963-64, supt., 1967-81; psychiat. resident Parkland Meml. Hosp., Dallas, 1962-63; clin. prof. psychiatry U. Tex. Southwestern Med. Sch., 1965-81. Recipient ann. award Tex. Assn. Mental Health, 1967; hon. mem. Psychology Club, East Tex. State U., 1969. Fellow Am. Psychiat. Assn. (life); mem. AMA, Pan Am., Tex., Dallas County med. assns., Tex., Dallas neuropsychiat. assns., Guild Catholic Psychiatrists, N.Y. Acad. Scis. Address: 1800 Hanover Dr Richardson TX 75081-3134

COWX, IAN GRAHAM, biology educator, researcher, consultant; b. Rhyl, Wales, Apr. 7, 1952; s. William Marriot and Francis Jesse (Hunt) C.; m. Julia Caroline Hardick, Apr. 5, 1986; children: Dafydd Owain, Hans Joost. BSc with honors, Liverpool (Eng.) U., 1975; PhD, Exeter (Eng.) U., 1980. Fisheries biologist Severn Trent Water Authority, Eng., 1980-81, fisheries scientist, 1981-85; lectr. Humberside Coll. Higher Edn., Eng., 1985-89, U. Hull, Eng., 1989—. Editor: Fishing with Electricity, 1990, Developments in Electric Fishing, 1990, Catch Effort Sampling Strategies, 1991, Rehabilitation of Freshwater Fisheries, 1994, Jour. Fisheries Mgmt. and Ecology. Mem. Am. Fisheries Soc., Fisheries Soc. the British Isles, Inst. Fisheries Mgmt., Freshwater Biol. Assn., Network Tropical Fisheries Scientists, Network Tropical Aquaculture Specialists. Office: U Hull, Hull Internat Fisheries Inst, Hull HU6 7RX, UK

COX, ANN BRUGER, biological scientist, editor, researcher; b. Salinas, Calif.; d. Albert Matthews and Adrienne (Bruger) C. SB, U. Chgo.; MA in Biology, Boston U., PhD, 1976. Rsch. technician U. Chgo. Clinics, 1965-69, Mass. Gen. Hosp., Boston, 1970; rsch. asst. Harvard Sch. Pub. Health, Boston, 1975; rsch. assoc. Colo. State U., Ft. Collins, 1979-86; rsch. physiologist Sch. Aerospace Medicine USAF, San Antonio, 1987-91; rsch. physiologist USAF Armstrong Lab., Brooks AFB, 1991—; adj. asst. prof. Health Sci. Ctr. U. Tex., San Antonio, 1990—. Assoc. editor Advances in Radiation Biology, Academic Press, 1982-94. Singer Brooks (AFB) Chorus Unlimited, Tex., 1987-92; bd. dirs. High Plains Arts Ctr., Ft. Collins, Colo, 1980-84. Recipient pre-doctoral fellowship NIH, post doctoral fellowship, summer fellowships NASA-Am. Soc. for Engring. Edn., 1983, 84. Mem. Am. Soc. Cell Biology, Aerospace Med. Assn., Radiation Rsch. Soc., Com. on Space Rsch. (exec. com. 1988-92), Am. Soc. for Gravitational and Space Biology, Sigma Xi. Home: PO Box 35506 San Antonio TX 78235-0506 Office: USAF Armstrong Lab AL/OERT Brooks AFB TX 78235-5102

COX, DAVID RICHARD, neuropsychologist; b. Chgo., Mar. 2, 1958; s. Richard H. and Betty (Ervin) C. BA, U. Calif., San Diego, 1978; MA, U.S. Internat. U., San Diego, 1981, PhD, 1982. Clin. psychologist Univ. Calif. San Diego Med. Ctr., 1983-86, Duke Univ. Med. Ctr., Durham, N.C., 1986-87; dir., neuropsychology Learning Svcs.-Carolina, Durham, 1987-90, Fla. Hosp. Med. Ctr., Orlando, Fla., 1990-94; pres. Neuropsychology & Behavioral Health Cons., Inc., Winter Park, Fla., 1994—; cons. IBM, Boca Raton, Fla., 1988—. Contbr. articles to profl. jours. Mem. Am. Psychol. Assn., Internat. Neuropsychol. Soc., Nat. Acad. Neuropsychologists, Am. Congress of Rehab. Medicine, Am. Assn. for Marriage and Family Therapy, Internat. Assn. for Study of Traumatic Brain Injury. Office: Ste C-210 1555 Howell Branch Rd Winter Park FL 32789

COX, DIANE DEBORAH, nurse, educator; b. Pitts., Sept. 23, 1953; m. Dan R. Cox, Feb. 12, 1977; children: Christopher, Brittany. AS, Allegheny Community Coll., Pitts., 1973; BSN magna cum laude, La Roche Coll., Pitts., 1983, MSN, 1987; PhD, U. Pitts., 1995. RN, Pa. Critical care staff nurse Suburban Gen. Hosp., Pitts., 1973-80, nursing supr., 1980-84, cmty. educator, 1984-88; asst. prof. La Roche Coll., Pitts., 1988-94, assoc. prof., 1994—; researcher in field. Recipient Nursing Leadership Grad. Aluman award LaRoche Coll., 1989. Mem. Sigma Theta Tau (past pres. chpt., faculty counselor 1992—). Home: 206 Ridgeview Dr Wexford PA 15090-9434 Office: 9000 Babcock Blvd Pittsburgh PA 15237

COX, JAMES LEWIS, surgeon; b. Fair Oaks, Ark., 1942. MD, U. Tenn. Ctr. Health Scis., Memphis, 1967. Diplomate Am. Bd. Surgery, Am. Bd. Thoracic Surgery. Intern Duke U. Med. Ctr., Durham, N.C., 1967-68; resident gen. surgery Duke U. Med. Ctr., Durham, 1963-76, resident thoracic surgery, 1976-78; surgeon in charge cardio-thoracic surgery Barnes Hosp., St. Louis, 1983—; prof. surgery, chief cardio-thoracis surgery divsn., 1983—. Mem. editorial bd. Cardiac Chronicle, 1985—, Clin. Cardiology, 1988—, Heart and Vessels, 1989—, Trends in Cardiovascular Medicine, 1991&, Med. Intelligence Unit, 1993—, others; contbr. more than 250 articles to profl. jours.; patentee in field. Mem. AMA, AAAS, AAUP, Am. Assn. Thoracic Surgeons, Assn. Hosp. Adminstrs., Soc. Thoracic Surgeons, Soc. Univ. Surgeons, Am. Coll. Chest Physicians, Am. Heart Assn., others. Office: One Barnes Hosp Pla 3108 Queeny Twr Saint Louis MO 63110-1013*

COX, JAMES SIDNEY, physician; b. Homer, La., Nov. 17, 1950; s. Sidney and Rita (Haynes) C.; m. Judy Katherine Vickers, Oct. 21, 1984; children: Shannon Ruth, Sarah Anne, Megan Elizabeth. Student, La. State U., 1968-71; MD, Tulane U., 1971-75. Diplomate Am. Bd. Family Practice, Am. Bd. of Emergency Medicine. Intern, resident in family practice John Peter Smith Hosp., Ft. Worth, 1975-78; city health officer family practice City of Athens, Tex., 1978-84; pvt. practice Athens, 1978-84, Ft. Worth, 1984—; mem. staff Henderson County Meml. Hosp., Athens, vice chief med. staff, 1981-82; mem. staff Lakeland Med. Ctr., Athens, chief med. staff, dir., 1983-84; vice chief emergency medicine dept. Harris Meth. Hosp., Ft. Worth, 1988-91; dir. occupational medicine Harris Meth. Hosp., 1989—; chief emergency dept. Harris Meth. Hosp., Ft. Worth, 1992-93, sec. med. staff, 1994-95, sec. emergency medicine divsn., 1996—; pres., chmn. bd. dirs. Occuhealth Physicians Group, P.A., Ft. Worth; mem. faculty U. Tex. Health Sci. Ctr.-Dallas Community Medicine Dept., John Peter Smith Hosp., Ft. Worth, 1978—, course dir. ACLS, 1989—, mem. affiliate faculty ACLS, 1991—, med. rev. officer for urine drug testing; med. bd. Harris Meth. Hosp., 1992-95. Author: Intestinal Obstruction: A Programmed Text, 1975. Fellow Am. Acad. Family Physicians, Am. Coll. Emergency Physicians; mem. AMA (Physician's Recognition award), Am. Coll. Occupl. and Environ. Medicine, Tex. Med. Assn. (alt. del. 1994-96), Tarrant County Med. Soc. (bd. dirs. 1994-96), Rotary (bd. dirs. Athens chpt. 1983-84), Alpha Epsilon Delta. Presbyterian. Home: 3458 Lantern Holw Fort Worth TX 76109-2411 Office: Harris Meth Hosp Ft Worth Emergency Dept 1301 Pennsylvania Ave Fort Worth TX 76104-2122 also: Occuhealth Physicians Group 1525 Merrimac Cir Ste 107 Fort Worth TX 76107-6536

COX, JEROME ROCKHOLD, JR., electrical engineer; b. Washington, May 24, 1925; s. Jerome R. and Jane (Mills) C.; m. Barbara Jane Lueders, Sept. 2,1951; children—Nancy Jane Cox Battersby, Jerome Mills, Randall Allen. S.B., Mass. Inst. Tech., 1947, S.M., 1949, Sc.D., 1954. Mem. faculty Washington U., St. Louis, 1955—, prof. elec. engring., 1961—, prof. biomed. engring. in physiology and biophysics, Sch. Medicine, 1965—, dir. Biomed. Computer Lab., 1964-75, chmn. computer labs., 1967-83, program dir. tng. program tech. in health care, 1970-78; chmn. dept. Computer Sci., 1975-91; prof. biomedicine, Inst. for Biomed. Computing Washington U., St. Louis, 1983—; Harold and Adelaide Welge prof. computer sci., 1989—; dir. Applied Rsch. Lab, 1991-95; co-chmn. computers in cardiology conf., 1974-88; cardiology adv. com. Nat. Heart and Lung Inst., 1975-78; mem. epidemiology biostatistics and bioengring. cluster Pres.'s Biomed. Rsch. Panel, 1975-76; chmn. Divsn. computer Rsch. and Tech. rev. com. NIH, 1983—; mem. PROPHET adv. com. NIH, 1983-88; mem. adv. com. Harvard-MIT Health Scis. and Tech., Boston, 1988-92; mem. Nat. Neural Circuitry Database com. Inst. of Medicine, NAS, 1989-91; mem. Nat. Adv. Coun. Human Genome Rsch., 1990-95. Mem. editorial bd. Computers and Biomed. Research, 1967—, Applied Mathematics Letters, 1987—; assoc. editor, IEEE, trans. biomed. engring., 1969-71. Mem. bd. mgrs. Ctrl. Inst. Deaf, 1993—. Served with U.S. Army, 1943-44. Fellow IEEE, Acoustical Soc. Am., Am. Coll. Med. Informatics; sr. mem. Inst. Medicine; mem. Assn. Computing Machinery, Sigma Xi, Eta Kappa Nu, Tau Beta Pi. Office: Washington U Dept Computer Sci Campus Box 1045 One Brookings Dr Saint Louis MO 63130-4899

COX, JOHN MICHAEL, cardiologist; b. Toledo, June 21, 1952; s. William E. and Laura M. (Carroll) C.; m. Sandra Helen Kemner, Aug. 19, 1972 (div. Mar. 1978); 1 child, Justin Michael; m. Vickie Diane Humphreys, May 27, 1978; children: Sarah Elizabeth, Aaron Alexander, Gabriel John. BA magna cum laude, Westminster Coll., 1974; DO, Kirksville Coll. Osteo. Medicine, 1978. Cert. Am. Bd. Osteo. Cardiology, Internal Medicine. Rotating intern Riverside Hosp., Trenton, Mich., 1978-79, resident in internal medicine, 1979-81, fellow in cardiology, 1981-83; practice medicine specializing in cardiology Sedalia and Columbia, Mo., 1983-88, Joplin, Mo., 1988—; chmn. dept. internal medicine Oak Hill Hosp., 1991, 95; chmn. dept. internatl medicine Freeman Hosp., 1992; chmn. dept. internal medicine Bothwell Regional Health Ctr., 1985—. Grantee Detroit Osteo. Hosp. Corp., Burroughs Wellcome Fellowship, Meade Johnson Fellowship. Fellow Am. Coll. Osteo. Internistis, Am. Coll. Cardiology; mem. Am. Heart Assn., Am. Osteo. Assn., Mo. Assn. Osteo. Physicians and Surgeons (v.p. west cen. dist. 1985-87, pres. 1987), Am. Soc. Echocardiography, N.Am. Soc. Pacing and Electrophysiology, Psi Sigma Alpha, Sigma Sigma Phi. Methodist.

COX, KATHRYN CULLEN, laboratory executive; b. Sedalia, Mo., June 29, 1943; d. Bernard Joseph and Ann (Matthews) Cullen; m. Paul John Cox, Oct. 3, 1964 (div. Sept. 1980); children: Donna, Eric. Diploma, St. John's Mercy Med. Ctr., 1964; BS, Coll. St. Francis, 1986. Staff RN Bapt. Med. Ctr., Kansas City, Mo., 1969-80, staff RN surgery, 1980-84; oper. rm. supr. Ctr. Eye Surgery, Kansas City, 1984-86; dir. nursing Hunkeler Eye Clinic, Kansas City, 1986-93; staff nurse Glendale (Calif.) Eye Med. Group, 1993-94; consumer affairs supr. Alcon Labs., Irvine, Calif., 1994—; cons. ophthalmology, 1988—. Mem. Am. Soc. Ophthalmic Registered Nurses (pres. local chpt. 1984-86), Assn. Oper. Rm. Nurses, Am. Soc. Cataract & Refractive Surgery. Home: 23592 Windsong Apt 10H Aliso Viejo CA 92656-1324 Office: Alcon Labs 15800 Alton Pky Irvine CA 92718-3818

COX, NEIL HARRISON, dermatologist; b. Leeds, England, July 21, 1956; s. George Harrison and Yvonne Pamela (Sheriff) C.; m. Fiona Helen Dawson, July 12, 1980; children: David Harrison, Katherine Joyce. BSc in Med. Cell Biology with honors, Liverpool U., 1978, MBChB, 1980. Registrar in dermatology Western Infirmary, Glasgow, Scotland, 1984-87; sr. registrar Royal Victoria Infirmary, Newcastle, England, 1987-89; cons. dermatologist Cumberland Infirmary, Carlisle, England, 1990—; chmn. East Cumbria Med. Rsch. Ethics Com., Carlisle, 1991—. Mem. editl. bd. Dermatology in Practice, 1993—; author: Physical Signs in Dermatology, 1994 (Atlas prize 1994), Diagnostic Picture Tests in Clinical Dermatology, 1995; contbr. articles to profl. jours. Recipient Wycombe prize Brit. Assn. Dermatologists, 1995-97. Fellow Royal Coll. Physicians (London and Edinburgh). Office: Cumberland Infirmary, Dermatology Dept, CA2 7HY Cumbria England

COX, PAUL ALAN, biologist, educator; b. Salt Lake City, Oct. 10, 1953; s. Leo A. and Rae (Gabbitas) C.; m. Barbara Ann Wilson, May 21, 1975; children: Emily Ann, Paul Matthew, Mary Elisabeth, Hillary Christine, Jane Margaret. BS, Brigham Young U., 1976; MSc, U. Wales, 1978; AM, Harvard U., 1978, PhD, 1981. Teaching fellow Harvard U., Cambridge, Mass., 1977-81; Miller research fellow Miller Inst. Basic Research in Sci., Berkeley, Calif., 1981-83; asst. prof. Brigham Young U., Provo, Utah, 1983-86, assoc. prof., 1986-91, prof., 1991-93, dean gen. edn. and honors, 1993—; ecologist Utah Environ. Coun., Salt Lake City, 1976; project ecologist Utah MX Coordination Office, Salt Lake City, 1981. Mem. editorial bd. Pacific Studies. Recipient Bowdoin prize; Danforth Found. fellow, 1976-81, Fulbright fellow, 1976-77, NSF fellow, 1977-81, Melbourne Univ. fellow, 1985-86, named NSF Presdl. Young Investigator, 1985-90. Mem. AAAS, Brit. Ecol. Soc., Internat. Soc. Ethnopharmacology (pres.), Am. Soc. Naturalists, Assn. Tropical Biology, Soc. Econ. Botany (pres.), New Eng. Bot. Club. Mormon. Office: Brigham Young U General Edn and Honors 302 Maeser Bldg PO Bx 22600 Provo UT 84602

COX, ROBERT SAYRE, JR., pathologist, researcher, educator; b. Jan. 30, 1925; s. Robert Sayre and Helen Covington (Barnard) C.; m. Brenda Kay Walker, Apr. 14, 1974 (dec. Nov. 1989); children: Charles Thomas, Leslee Ann Cox Stout, Robert S. VI, Nancy E. Cox Jones, Kristina S.; stepchildren: Kevin W. Walker, David B. Walker. Student, MIT, U. Idaho, St. Louis U.; BS with distinction, Stanford U., 1946, BA, MS, 1948, PhD, 1952; MD, U. Chgo., 1952. Diplomate in anat. and clin. pathology Am. Bd. Pathology. Intern Letterman Army Hosp., San Francisco, 1952-53, 54, resident in pathology, 1954-57; chief clin. pathology, dir. R&D, 1957-59; chief lab. svc. Rodriguez Army Hosp., 1959-62; rsch. dir., pres. Inst. for Med. Rsch. Santa Clara County, 1962-80; chief clin. pathology Santa Clara Valley Med. Ctr., 1962-66, dir. labs., 1966-80; prof. Creighton U., Omaha, 1980-95, emeritus prof., 1995—, chmn. dept. pathology, 1980-91; assoc. clin. coord. Sunderbruch Corp.-NE (PRO), 1994—. Pres. Indian Hills Homeowners, Omaha, 1984-87; mem. blood tech. adv. com. ARC, San Jose, Calif. and Omaha, 1966—, chmn., 1968-80; bd. dirs. midwest blood svc. ARC, Omaha, 1992-96. Col. U.S. Army, 1943-46, 52-62, ret.; with USAR, 1946-52, 62-85. Mem. Phi Beta Kappa, Sigma Xi, Phi Lambda Upsilon, Alpha Omega Alpha, Delta Psi. Republican. Congregationalist. Home: 102 S 89th St Omaha NE 68114-4026 Office: Creighton Univ Saint Joseph Hosp 6843 B 601 N 30th St Omaha NE 68131

COX, RODY P(OWELL), medical educator, internist; b. New Brighton, Pa., June 24, 1926; s. Raymond James and Hazel (Powell) C.; m. Jane Beverly Birks, Sept. 5, 1953; children: Shelley Lea, Rody Powell, Sue Ellen. Student Franklin and Marshall Coll., 1946-48; MD, U. Pa., 1952. Diplomate Am. Bd. Internal Medicine. Intern U. Mich., 1952-53, resident in medicine, 1953-54; resident in medicine U. Pa., Phila., 1953-57, asst. prof. medicine, 1957-60; rsch. assoc. U. Glasgow, Scotland, 1960-61; prof. medicine NYU, N.Y.C., 1961-79, prof. pharmacology, 1972-79, chief div. human genetics, 1972-79; prof., vice chmn. dept. medicine Case-Western Res. U., Cleve., 1979-88; chief med. svc. VA Med. Ctr., Cleve., 1979-88; dean Med. Sch. U. Tex. Southwestern Med. Ctr., Dallas, 1988-89, prof. internal medicine, 1988—; mem. metabolism study sect. NIH, 1970-74, chmn. genetics study sect., 1978-79, chmn. mammalian genetics study sect., 1979-81; mem. panel on clin. scis. NRC, 1976-86. Editor: Cell Communication, 1974; co-editor: Epithelial Cell Culture, 1981. Contbr. articles to profl. publs. Sgt. U.S. Army, 1944-46, NATOUSA. Fellow ACP; mem. Am. Soc. Clin. Investigation (emeritus), Assn. Am. Physicians, Cen. Soc. Clin. Research, John Morgan Soc. of U. Pa., Harvey Soc., Am. Clin. Climatol. Assn., Am. Soc. Human Genetics, Interurban Clin. Club, Alpha Omega Alpha (councillor NYU chpt. 1970-76). Home: 3701 Turtle Creek Blvd Dallas TX 75219-5541 Office: U Tex Southwestern Med Ctr 5323 Harry Hines Blvd Dallas TX 75235-8889

COX, RUSSELL SCOTT, toxicologist; b. Memphis, Nov. 7, 1966; s. John Payne Cox and Betty Joyce Woods; m. Cathy Jo Pasco, July 8, 1990 (div. July 1992); 1 child, Joseph Orren. BS in Biol. Scis., U. Miss., 1988. Cert. med. technologist Am. Med. Technologists; cert. lab. scientist in chemistry Nat. Certification Agy. Radio immuno assay technologist Roche Biomed. (Lab. Corp.), Southaven, Miss., 1991-92; technologist toxicology confirmation Roche Biomed. (Lab. Corp.), Southaven, 1992-93, technologist toxicology screening, 1993-94, technologist group leader screening, 1994-95, certifying scientist, 1995—. mem. Am. Assn. Med. Pers., Alpha Epsilon Delta, Beta Beta Beta, Golden Key. Methodist. Home: 69 Quinn Rd Byhalia MS 38611 Office: Lab Corp Am 1120 Stateline Rd Southaven MS 38671

COX, SHARON KARLIN, health facility administrator; b. Denver, Dec. 1, 1950; d. Robert and Wanda Karlin; m. Donald W. Cox. BA in Edn., U. No. Colo., Greeley, 1972; MS in Mgmt., Regis U., Denver, 1992. Dir. outreach amb. svcs. Swedish Med. Ctr., Denver, 1985-93; v.p. mktg. and support svcs. Ea. N.Mex. Med. Ctr., Roswell, 1993—; apptd. by gov. Rural Devel. Response Coun. N.Mex., 1993—; cons. staff devel. Ea. N.Mex. U., 1996—. Mem. N.Mex. Soc. for Healthcare Mktg. and Pub. Rels., Soc. for Healthcare Planning and Mktg. of Am. Hosp. Assn. Home: 1209 San Juan Dr Roswell NM 88201 Office: Ea NMex Med Ctr 405 W Country Club Rd Roswell NM 88201

COX, WILLIAM ANDREW, cardiovascular thoracic surgeon; b. Columbus, Ga., Aug. 3, 1925; s. Virgil Augustus and Dale Jackson C.; m. Nina Recelle Hobby, Jan. 1, 1948; children: Constance Lynn Cox Rogers, Patricia Ann Cox Brown, William Robert, Janet Elaine. Student Presbyn. Coll., 1942, Harvard U., 1944-45, Cornell U., 1945, BS, Emory U., 1950, MD, 1954, MS in Surgery, Baylor U., 1961. Active duty USN, 1943-46; lt. (sr.g.) USNR, 1946-54; commd. 1st lt. M.C., U.S. Army, 1954, advanced through grades to col., 1969; intern Brooke Army Med. Ctr., San Antonio, 1954-55, resident in gen. surgery, 1956-60; resident in cardiovasc. thoracic surgery Walter Reed Army Med. Ctr., Washington, 1960-62, staff cardiothoracic surgeon, 1962; asst. chief cardiothoracic surgery Letterman Gen. Hosp., 1962-65; chief dept. surgery and cardiothoracic surgery 121 Evacuation Hosp., Seoul, Korea, cons. cardiothoracic surgery Korean Theatre, 1965-66; asst. chief cardiothoracic surgery Brooke Army Med. Ctr., 1966-69, chief, 1969-73, bd. dirs. thoracic surgery residency programs, 1966-73, ret., 1973; clin. prof. cardiothoracic surgery U. Tex. Sch. Medicine, San Antonio, 1971—; practice medicine specializing in cardiovasc. thoracic surgery, Corpus Christi, Tex., 1973-93; cons. cardio-thoracic surgery Brooke Army Med. Ctr., San Antonio, 1977—; chief staff Meml. Med. Ctr., 1980; dir. disaster med. care region 3A Tex. State Dept. Health, 1973-88; mem. Coastal Bend Coun. Gov.'s Emergency Med. Svc. Commn., 1979-88; mem. adv. bd. on congenital heart disease Tex. Dept. Health, 1980-88; participant joint confs. on cardiovasc. surgery and thoracic surgery Am. People Ambassador Program, Leningrad, Moscow, Bucharest, Romania, Belgrade, Yugoslavia, Prague, Czechoslovakia, 1987; del. Vanderbilt U. joint conf. vascular surgery Dublin, Ireland, Edinburgh, Scotland, London, 1986; participant joint confs. cardiovasc. surgery and thoracic surgery Am. Amb. People to People Program Singapore, Kuala Lumpur, Malayasia, Hanoi, Vietnam, DaNang, Vietnam, Hue, Vietnam, Saigon, Vietnam, Hong Kong, Feb.-Mar., 1993, People to People Am. Ambassador Program, Eng., Scotland, Wales, 1996. Ruling elder Presbyn. Ch., 1960—. Decorated Legion of Merit, Army Commendation medal; recipient A Prefix award Surgeon Gen. U.S. Army, commendation Surgeon Gen. South Korea; named hon. citizen Phila. by Mayor Edward G. Rendell, 1995; diplomate Am. Bd. Surgery, Am. Bd. Thoracic Surgery. Fellow Am. Coll. Chest Physicians; mem. AMA, Soc. Thoracic Surgeons, Denton A. Cooley Cardiovasc. Surgery Soc., Tex. Med. Assn. (del. conf. infectious diseases Bankgkok, Hong Kong, Beijing, Shanghai, 1983), So. Thoracic Surgery Assn., Nueces County Med. Soc., Corpus Christi Surg. Soc., 38th Parallel Med. Soc., U.S. Power Squadron, People to People Internat., Internat. Platform., USN League (life), Retired Officers Assn. (life), Navy Meml., Yacht Club (past commodore presidio San Francisco), T-Bar-M Racquet Club, Corpus Christi Country Club, Corpus Christi Athletic Club, Corpus Christi Town, Club, Ft. Sam Houston Officers Club. Republican. Contbr. numerous articles in field to profl. jours. Home: 5214 Wooldridge Rd Corpus Christi TX 78413-3833

COYE, MOLLY JOEL, state agency administrator; b. Bennington, Vt., May 11, 1947; d. Robert Dudley Coye and Janet (Loper) Coye Nelson; m. Daniel Noah Lindheim, Sept. 22, 1974 (div. 1980); m. Mark Douglas Smith, Feb. 22, 1980; 1 child, Langston Matthew Coye. BA, U. Calif., Berkeley, 1968; MA, Stanford U., 1972; MPH, Johns Hopkins U., 1977, MD, 1977. Chief of occupational health clinic U. San Francisco, 1979-84; med. officer Nat. Inst. for Occupational Safety & Health, 1980-85; advisor health and environment Gov.'s Office of Policy & Planning, Trenton, N.J., 1985-86; dep. commr. N.J. Dept. Health, Trenton, 1986—; chair adv. com. graduate program in pub. health U. Medicine and Dentistry of N.J., Newark, 1986—; mem. tech. bd. Milbank Meml. Fund, N.Y.C., 1986-88; mem. com. role of primary care physician in occupational/environ. medicine Nat. Acad. Scis, Inst. Medicine, Washington, 1986-88; mem. adv. com. AIDS U.S. Pub. Health Svc., Washington, 1989; mem. adv. coun. Nat. Inst. for Environ. Health Scis., Betheseda, Md., 1989. Co-author, editor: China: Inside the People's Republic, 1972, co-editor: China Yesterday and Today. Contbr. peer review articles to profl. jours. Recipient Virginia Apgar award March of Dimes, Plainsboro, N.J., 1988, Woman of the Yr. award Jersey Woman mag., 1989. Mem. AMA, Am. Coll. Preventive Medicine, Am. Pub. Health Assn. (chair exec. bd. 1988), Assn. for Health Svcs. Rsch., Assn. State and Territorial Health Officers (chair exec. bd. 1988—, mem. AIDS com. 1988—), Soc. for Occupational and Environ. Health (mem. governing coun. 1988—). Office: NJ Health Dept Cn #360 John Firch Pla Trenton NJ 08625*

COYLE, JOSEPH THOMAS, psychiatrist; b. Chgo., Oct. 9, 1943; s. Joseph Thomas and Mercedes (Sartor) C.; m. Genevieve Sansoucy, Aug. 19, 1968; children: Andrew, Peter, David. AB, Coll. of the Holy Cross, 1965; MD, Johns Hopkins Sch. of Medicine, 1969; MA (hon), Harvard U., 1991. Diplomate Am. Bd. Psychiatry and Neurology. Asst. prof. pharmacology Johns Hopkins Sch. of Medicine, Balt., 1974-76, asst. prof pharmacology and psychiatry, 1976-78, assoc. prof pharmacology and psychiatry, 1978-80, prof of neurosci., psychiatry and pharmacology, 1980-91, dir. div. of child psychiatry, 1982-91, Disting. Svc. prof. of child psychiatry, 1985-91; Eben S. Draper prof. of psychiatry and neurosci. Harvard U., Boston, 1991—; chair consol. dept. psychiatry Harvard Med. Sch., Boston, 1991—; co-dir outpatient pharmacotherapy clinic Johns Hopkins Hosp., Balt., 1977-82; mem. sci. adv. bd. Pfizer Scholars Program, N.Y.C., 1989-94 John F. Merck Found., Boston, 1990—. Abbott Pharms., North Chgo. Ill., 1990—, Trophix Pharms., Piscataway, N.J., 1993—. Contbr. articles to profl. jours. Mem. adv. bd. NIMH, Washington, 1990-94. Recipient Gold Medal award Soc. Biol. Psychiatry, Washington, 1991, McAlpin award, Mental Health Assn., Washington, 1992. Fellow Am. Psychiat. Assn. (Found. prize 1985), Am. Acad. of Arts and Scis.; mem. Soc. Neurosci. (pres. 1991-92), Am. Coll. Neuropsychopharmacology (Efron award 1982), Am. Acad. Child and Adolescent Psychiatry, Am. Soc. Pharmacology and Exptl. Therapeutics (John Jacob Abel award 1979), Inst. of Medicine of the Nat. Acad. Sci. Office: Harvard Med Sch Dept Psychiatry 115 Mill St Belmont MA 02178-1041

COYLE, MARIE BRIDGET, microbiology educator, laboratory director; b. Chgo., May 13, 1935; d. John and Bridget Veronica (Fitzpatrick) C.; m. Zheng Chen, 1995. BA, Mundelein Coll., 1957; MS, St. Louis U., 1963; PhD, Kans. State U., 1965. Diplomate Am. Bd. Med. Microbiology. Sci. instr. Sch. Nursing Columbus Hosp., Chgo., 1957-59; research assoc. U. Chgo., 1967-70; instr. U. Ill., Chgo., 1970-71; asst. prof. microbiology U. Wash., Seattle, 1973-80, assoc. prof., 1980-94, prof., 1994—; assoc. dir. microbiology labs Univ. Hosp., Seattle, 1973-76; dir. microbiology labs Harborview Med. Ctr., Univ. Wash., 1976—; co-dir. Postdoc Training Clinic Microbiology, Univ. Wash., 1978—. Contbr. articles to profl. jours. Fellow Am. Acad. Microbiology; mem. Acd. Clin. Lab. Physicians and Scientists (sec.-treas. 1980-83, exec. com. 1985-90), Am. Soc. Microbiology (chmn. clin. microbiology divsn. 1984-85, recipient bioMerieux Vitek Sonnenwirth Meml. award 1994), Kappa Gamma Pi. Office: Harborview Box 359743 325 9th Ave Seattle WA 98104-2499

COZ, MARY KATHLEEN, respiratory therapist; b. Ravenna, Ohio, Aug. 1, 1952; d. John and Kathleen (Bronson) C. A in Secretarial Sci., U. Akron, 1972, A in Respiratory therapy, 1979, BS, 1986, MS in Tech. Edn., 1990. Registered and lic. respiratory therapist. Sec. Kent (Ohio) Bd. Edn., 1970; exec. sec. Ernst & Ernst, Akron, Ohio, 1972-75; respiratory therapist, tech. support assoc. Akron City Hosp. Summa Health Syss., 1977—. Mem. Am. Assn. Respiratory Care, Ohio Soc. Respiratory Care, Nat. Bd. Respiratory Care. Roman Catholic. Home: 1236 Chelton Dr Kent OH 44240-3240 Office: Akron City Hosp 525 E Market St Akron OH 44304-1619

COZAN, LEE, clinical research psychologist; married, 1947. B.A., Am. U., 1948; M.A., George Washington U., 1951, Ph.D., 1964. Research psychologist U.S. Govt., Washington, 1954-64; pvt. practice psychology N.J., 1964-74; regional dir. Fla. Div. Mental Health, Ft. Lauderdale, 1974-76; mental hosp. adminstr. So. Fla. State Hosp., Hollywood, 1976-79; pres. Inst. Mental Health, Hollywood, 1979-81; dir. mental health program Fla. Dept. Health and Rehab. Services, Ft. Lauderdale, 1979-82; clin. psychologist Assocs. in Psychiatry, 1983-85; pres. Applied Psychology Corp., 1983-86, Children Residential and Day Treatment Ctr., Inc., 1987-96; health care cons. Fort Lauderdale, Fla., 1996—; adj. prof. Fla. Atlantic U., 1974-79, Nova U., 1979-80. Editor: Jour. Indsl. Psychology, 1961-65, Jour. Engring. Psychology, 1963-68; cons. editor: Jour. Schizophrenia, 1970-71. Mem. Broward County (Fla.) Republican Exec. Com., 1976-80. Served with U.S. Army, 1941-46. Mem. APA, AAAS, Nat. Geog. Soc., Human Factors Soc., Fla. Psychol. Assn., Children's Hosp. Internat. Greek Orthodox.

COZEN, LEWIS, orthopedic surgeon; b. Montreal, Aug. 14, 1911; came to U.S. 1922; AB, U. Calif., San Francisco, 1929, MD, 1934. Diplomate Am. Bd. Orthopedic Surgery. Intern San Francisco Hosp., 1933-34; resident orthopedic surgeron U. Iowa, 1934-35; resident and fellow orthopedic surgery San Francisco County Hosp., 1935-36, Children's Hosp. and Mass. Gen. Hosp., Boston, 1936-39; pvt. practice orthopedic surgery L.A., 1939-40, 45—; clin. prof. orthopedic surgery UCLA, 1965-93; assoc. clin. prof. emeritus Loma Linda Med. Sch., 1963—; attending orthopedic surgeon, emeritus Cedars Sinai Med. Ctr., 1939—, Orthopaedic Hosp., 1939—; chief orthopedic surgery City of Hope, 1948-67; sr. attending orthopedic surgeons, emeritus Unit One L.A. County Hosp., 1950-63; vis. lectr. U. Santo Tomas, Manila, U. Madrid, Spain; Far East Sch. of Medicine, Manila, 1994, Hadassah Med. Ctr., Jerusalem, 1994; lectr. in field. Author: Office Orthopedics, 1955, 4th edit. 1973, Operative Orthopedic Clinics (with Dr. Avia Brockway), 1960, Atlas of Orthopedic Surgery, 1966, Difficult Orthopedic Diagnosis, 1972, Plannings and Pitfalls in Orthopedic Surgery, Natural History of Orthopedic Disease, 1993, Supplement Book, 1996; mem. editl. bd. Resident & Staff Physician; contbr. numerous articles to profl. jours. Vol. physician Internat. Children's Program, Orthopedic Hosp., Mexicali, Mexico. Lt. col. U.S. Army, 1940-45. Fellow ACS, Internat. Coll. Surgeons; mem. Am. Rheumatism Assn., Am. Coll. Rheumatism, Am. Orthopaedic Assn. (sr.), Am. Acad. Orthopaedic Surgeons, So. Calif. Rheumatism Assn. (pres. 1979), Western Orthopaedic Assn., Phi Beta Kappa, Alpha Omega Alpha.

COZORT, AMBER LYNNE, nurse; b. West Plains, Mo., Jan. 4, 1963; d. Norris Bert and Chlora Ivene (Brickey) C. BSN, Rockhurst Coll. and Rsch. Coll. of Nursing, Kans. City, Mo., 1985. Psychiat. staff nurse Cox Med. Ctr. North, Springfield, Mo., 1985; psychiat. technician Park Cen. Hosp., Springfield, 1985-86; orthopedic staff nurse St. John's Regional Health Ctr., Springfield, 1986—. Mem. com. St. John's Med. Explorer Post 339, 1989-90, pres., 1990-91; mem. Greene County Rep. Party-TARGET; mem. Rep. Nat. Com., 1995; mem. com. S.W. Mo. Nurses Recognition Dinner, 1992-94, chair, 1994—. Mem. Mo. Nurse Assn. (corr. sec., past bd. dirs., 4th dist. nominating com., mem. med.-surg. spl. interest group 1993-95, sec. 1996—, region F regional dir. 1994—, mem. MONA-PAC com. 1996—), Nat. Assn. Orthopedic Nurses, Rsch. Nursing Alumni Assn., Rsch. Coll. Nursing Alumni Assn., Rsch. Coll. Nursing Honor Soc.

CRABB, KENNETH WAYNE, obstetrician, gynecologist; b. Glendive, Mont., June 17, 1950; s. Kenneth Willard and Marjorie Jane (Martin) C.; m. Gwen Aldean Wendelschafer, June 8, 1974; children: Kenneth Wendel, Richard David. BS with honors in Biochemistry, U. Iowa, 1971, MD, 1975. Diplomate Am. Bd. Ob-Gyn. Intern, then resident in ob-gyn St. Paul Ramsey Med. Ctr., 1975-79; practice medicine specializing in ob-gyn St. Paul, 1979—; clin. asst. prof. ob.-gyn. U. Minn., Mpls., 1981-82, clin. assoc. prof., 1989—; vice chmn. dept. ob.-gyn. United Hosp., St. Paul, 1984-86, 91-93, pharm. and therapeutics com., 1980-84, cance com., 1995—; preceptor family practice resident St. John's Hosp., St. Paul, 1979—, maternal health com., 1979-88, cancer com., 1984-85; quality assurance com. St. Joseph's Hosp., St. Paul, 1981-83; mem. Med. Affairs Coun. for Health One, 1989-93; chmn. bd. dirs. ParaNatal Svcs., Inc., 1990-94; bd. dirs. Preferred One Physicians Assn., 1987—, pres. 1994-96, Preferred One PPO, Preferred One Mgmt. Co.; physician advisor Medtrac, Health Mark, Found. for Health Care Evaluation. Trustee Actors Theatre of St. Paul, 1980-90, bd. dirs, 2d v.p., 1984-85; mem. council Grace Luth. Ch., 1984-87; bd. dirs. Indianhead Council Boy Scouts Am., 1986—. Recipient Eagle Scout award Boy Scouts Am., 1966, Appreciation award Am. Acad. Family Physicians, 1979-90. Fellow Am. Coll. Ob-Gyn. (jr. fellow dist. chmn. 1978-79, jr. fellow adv. coun. 1978-80, chmn. 1989 Dist. VI meeting, appreciation award 1978-79, chmn. higher edn. loan program com. 1989-91, adv. coun. Minn. sect. 1996—), Am. Fertility Soc.; mem. AMA (Physicians Recognition award 1985, 88, 90, 93, 96), Ctrl. Assn. Obstetricians & Gynecologists, Am. Soc. Coloscopy & Cervical Pathology, Am. Assn. Gynecologic Laparoscopists, Minn. Med. Assn. (nominating com. 1986-87, legis. com. 1988-94, vice chmn. 1989-94, med. practice and planning com. 1995—, vice chmn. 1995—), Minn. Obstetric and Gynecologic Soc. (program com. 1984), Ramsey Med. Soc. (bd. trustees 1993-94, med. practice com. 1982-87, del. 1983, 85-87, fin. com. 1984-89, med. svc. com. 1986-88, nom. com. 1992-93, polit. action com. 1988—, pres.-elect 1995, pres. 1996), Assn. Profs. Ob-gyn., Found. Health Care Evaluation, Rotary (chmn. various coms. 1983-84, 87-88, bd. dirs. 1984-86, 89-91, v.p. 1991-92, pres. 1992-93, sgt. at arms 1986-87), Phi Beta Sigma, Omicron Delta Kappa, Phi Beta Phi (sec. U. Iowa chpt. 1972-73, 2d vice archon 1982-83, supreme sec. treas. 1984-89, supreme archon 1989-92). Office: Advanced Specialty Care for Women 310 Smith Ave N Ste 390 Saint Paul MN 55102-2378

CRABBÉ, JEAN, physiology and medicine educator; b. Brussels, Aug. 12, 1927; s. François and Simone (Doutreligne) C.; m. Marie De Guchteneere, Aug. 10, 1954; children: Isabelle and François (twins), Christine, Bruno, Nicolas. MD magna cum laude, Cath. U. Louvain, Belgium, 1951, DSc, 1962. Guest asst. dept. medicine U. Hosp. Zurich, Switzerland, 1951-52; rsch. asst. dept. medicine U. Hosp. Louvain, 1952-54; clin. and rsch. fellow U. Hosp., Geneva, 1954-55; asst. in medicine Peter Bent Brigham Hosp., Boston, 1955-58, intern in medicine, 1958-59; clin. and rsch. fellow Mass. Gen. Hosp., Boston, 1959-60; asst. dept. medicine Univ. Clinics, Louvain, 1961-62; cons. physician in endocrinology Univ. Clinics, Louvain and Brussels, 1964-94; mem. faculty dept. physiology Cath. U. Louvain, 1966-67, assoc. prof. medicine and physiology, 1967-72, prof., 1972-92, prof. emeritus, 1992—; vis. prof. Facultés Notre Dame de la Paix, Namur, Belgium, 1968, Dartmouth Med. Sch., Hanover, N.H., 1974, Pahlavi Med. Sch., Shiraz, Iran, 1978, Cath. U. Córdoba, Argentina, 1980; Am. Heart Assn. vis. scientist U. Kans. Med. Ctr., 1968; hon. prof. Nat. U. Tucamán, Argentina, 1980; ofcl. guest Venezuelan Inst. Sci. Investigation, Caracas, 1970, Acad. Scis. USSR, 1981, Technion, Haifa, Israel, 1986, 89; bd. dirs. Cercle Alumni Fond. U., Belgium, 1974-78. Editorial bd. Jour. Steroid Biochemistry, 1971-92, Archives Internat. de Physiologie et Biochimie, 1971-94, Physiol. Revs., 1971-78, Molecular and Cellular Endocrinology, 1974-79, Pflügers Archiv, 1978-83; contbr. numerous articles and abstracts to sci. jours., chpts. to books. With Belgian Army, 1952-54. Recipient René Beckers award, 1955, John J. Larkin award St. Luke's Guild Boston, 1958, Med. Scis. Alumni prize Fond. U., 1963, award Spa Found., 1988; fellow Belgian Am. Ednl. Found., 1955-56, 72, WHO, 1956, Jane Coffin Childs Meml. Fund, 1956-58, Helen Hay Whitney Found., 1959-62. Mem. AAAS (life), N.Y. Acad. Scis. (life), Belgian Endocrine Soc. (gen. sec. 1977-88, pres. 1991-93), Belgian Acad. Medicine (hon.), Belgian Soc. Internal Medicine, Belgian Soc. Physiology, Belgian Soc. Gastroenterology (hon.), European Fedn. Endocrine Socs. (mem. exec. com. 1985-90), Assn. Physiologistes, French Soc. Endocrinology. Office: Cath U Louvain Med Sch, 55 Ave Hippocrate, B-1200 Brussels Belgium

CRABLE, JOHN V., chemist; b. New Castle, Pa., Sept. 14, 1923; s. Charles McDonough and Margaret Cecilia (O'Connor) C. Student, Geneva Coll., 1942-43, Va. Poly. Inst., 1943-44; BS in Chemistry, Duquesne U., 1949; postgrad., U. Wis., 1949-50. Jr. fellow Mellon Inst. Indsl. Rsch., Pitts., 1950-57; rsch. chemist Gulf R&D, Pitts., 1957-62; rsch. chemist phys. & chem. analysis br. BOSH, Cin., 1962-69; chief phys. & chem. analysis br. Nat. Inst. Occupl. Health & Safety, Cin., 1970-76; chief measurments/methods rsch. br. NIOSH, Cin., 1976-90; cons., Cin., 1990—; mem. intersoc. com. ambient air sampling & analysis Am. Conf. Govt. Indsl. Hygiene, N.Y.C., 1969-80; mem. analytical chemistry com. Am. Indsl. Hygiene Assn., Akron, Ohio, lab. accreditation com., 1971-78; mem. Am. del. Internat. Orgn. Standardizaton, Geneva, 1972-86; project officer U. Alexandria, Egypt; temporary cons. Inst. Occupl. Health WHO, Beijing, 1984; chmn. subcom. biol. monitoring com. lab stds. and practices APHA, 1981-83. Coeditor Biol. Monitoring, 1983-88; editl. bd. Applied Indsl. Hygiene, 1985-90; contbr. articles to profl. jours. Mem. Am. Chem. Soc. (emeritus), Am. Conf. Govtl. Indsl. Hygienists (emeritus), Am. Indsl. Hygiene Assn. (emeritus).

CRABTREE, MARK ANDERSON, dentist; b. Welch, W.Va., Sept. 21, 1959; s. Estel and Frances Ann (Collins) Crabtree Armstrong; m. Rebecca Alice Alice Williams, June 7, 1986. BA, Wake Forest U., 1981; DDS, Med. Coll. Va., 1986-90. Pvt. practice Martinsville, Va., 1985—; mem. dental staff Meml. Hosp., Martinsville, 1985—; mem. Va. State Bd. Dentistry, 1994—. Chmn. Martinsville Rep. Com., 1986-90; pres. United Meth. Men, 1st United Meth. Ch., Martinsville, 198—; founding bd. dirs. Gateway Streetscape Found., 1991—; bd dirs. Martinville Ptnrs. for Progress; mem. Martinsville City Coun., 1994—; bd. visitors Wake Forest U., 1994—. Chmn. Martinsville Rep. Com., 1986-90; pres. United Meth. Men, 1st United Meth. Ch., Martinsville, 1988—; founding bd. dirs. Gateway Streetscape Found., 1991—; bd. dirs. Martinville Ptnrs. for Progress. Named Outstanding Young Virginian, Va. Jaycees, 1988. Fellow Internat. Coll. Dentists, Va. Dental Assn.; mem. ADA, Am. Assn. Hosp. Dentists, Am. Acad. Implant Dentistry, Acad. Gen. Dentistry, Patrick Henry Dental Soc. (sec.-treas. 1988-89), Martinsville C. of C. (pres. 1991-92), Martinsville Jaycees, Kiwanis (pres. 1990-91), Piedmont Arts Assn. (bd. dirs.). Home: 1100 Mulberry Rd Martinsville VA 24112-5220 Office: 407 Starling Ave Martinsville VA 24112-3700

CRABTREE, TANIA OYLAN, home health nurse, administrator, consultant; b. Panama City, Panama, Sept. 8, 1942; d. German and Rosa America (Tason) Tortosa; m. Robert Crusoe, Feb. 27, 1969 (div. 1982); children: Greta, Bryan; m. Ben C. Crabtree II, May 5, 1992. Student, Radcliffe Coll., 1960; BSN, Ctrl. U., Quito, Ecuador, 1964. RN, Fla., Tex. Oper. rm. nurse Peter Bent Brigham Hosp., Boston, 1965-66; oper. rm. staff nurse Lakeland (Fla.) Gen. Hosp., 1966-69; surg. head nurse Miami (Fla.) Heart Inst., 1970-71; oper. rm. head nurse Mercy Hosp., Miami, 1971-74; staff nurse Gorgas Army Cmty. Hosp., Panama City, 1974-75, oper. rm. nurse, 1975-82, home health nurse practitioner, 1982-93; DON Ace Personal Health Care, Inc., San Antonio, 1993-95; cons. edn. coord. Precision Consulting, Inc., San Antonio, 1994—; dir. profl. and clin. svcs. River City Fin. Health Group, San Antonio, 1995-96; adminstr., dir. nurses A&E Quality Home Health Care, Inc., San Antonio, 1996—; geriatrics nursing cons. Hurley, Galvan and Assocs., Panama City, 1989-93. Mem. Tex. Nurses Assn. Roman Catholic. Office: A&E Quality Home Health Care Inc 10221 Desert Sands Ste 107 San Antonio TX 78216

CRACCO, ROGER QUINLAN, medical educator, neurologist; b. Union City, N.J., June 1, 1934; s. Frederick A. and Ruby Ann (Quinlan) C.; m. Joan Marie Bender, June 9, 1962. A.B., Cornell U., 1956; M.D., N.J. Med. Sch., 1960. Diplomate Am. Bd. Psychiatry and Neurology, Am. Bd. Electrodiagnostic Medicine, Am. Bd. Clin. Neurophysiology (bd. dirs. 1984-88). Intern Phila. Gen. Hosp., 1960-61; resident in neurology Jersey City Med. Ctr., 1961-64; fellow in neurophysiology Mayo Grad. Sch., Mayo Clinic, 1964-66; asst. prof. neurology Jefferson Med. Coll., Phila., 1968-71, assoc. prof., 1971-73; prof. neurology SUNY Health Sci. Ctr. at Bklyn., 1973-80, prof., chmn. neurology, 1980—; head neurology service State U. Hosp.-Kings County Hosp. Ctr., Bklyn., 1980—; mem. program project rev. com. Nat. Inst. Neurology, Communicative Disease and Stroke, NIH, USPHS, 1984-88, chmn. 1987-88. Editor: (with I. Bodis-Wollner) Evoked Potentials, 1986; mem. editorial bd. Ann. Neurology, Electroencephalography Clinical Neurophysiology, Muscle and Nerve jour., others.; contbr. articles to profl. jours. Served to capt. M.C., U.S. Army, 1966-68. NIH grantee, 1970-86. Fellow Am. Acad. Neurology; mem. Am. Neurol. Assn., Am. Electroencephalographic Soc. (pres. 1981-82), Eastern Assn. Electroencephalography (pres. 1979-80), Am. Assn. Electromyography and Electrodiagnosis, Am. Epilepsy Soc., Soc. for Neurosci., Assn. U. Profs. of Neurology, Am. Acad. Clin. Neurophysiology (pres. 1987-89), Alpha Omega Alpha. Office: SUNY Health Sci Ctr Bklyn Dept Neurology 450 Clarkson Ave Brooklyn NY 11203-2012

CRADDOCK, NICHOLAS JOHN, psychiatrist, consultant; b. Birmingham, Eng., Mar. 13, 1959; s. Maxwell Hammersley and Marie Rose (Urquhart) C.; m. Bridget Cottingham, July 13, 1985; children: Alexander Nicholas, Joseph Duncan, Rosie Anne. MA with honors, Cambridge (Eng.) U., 1984; MB BChir with honors, Birmingham (Eng.) U., 1985, M of Med. Sci., 1991; PhD, U. Wales, 1995. Sr. house officer in neurology Dudley Rd. Hosp., Birmingham, 1986; registrar in psychiatry Birmingham Hosp., 1986-90; rsch. fellow Birmingham U., 1990-92; rsch. fellow U. Wales Coll. Medicine, Cardiff, 1992-95, rsch. fellow, cons., 1995—; vis. lectr. Washington U., St. Louis, 1993-94; hon. cons. psychiatrist U. Hosp. Wales, Cardiff, 1995—, hon. sr. registrar, 1992-95. Contbr. sci. articles to profl. jours. Grantee Wellcome Trust, 1992, 95. Mem. Royal Coll. Psychiatrists, Am. Soc. Human Genetics, Internat. Soc. Psychiat. Genetics. Office: U Wales Coll Medicine, Dept Psychol Medicine, Cardiff CF4 4XN, Wales

CRAFT, CHERYL MAE, neurobiologist, anatomist, researcher; b. Lynch, Ky., Apr. 15, 1947; d. Cecil Berton and Lillian Lovelle (Ellington) C.; m. Laney K. Cormney, Oct. 14, 1967 (div. Sept. 1980); children: Tyler Craft Cormney, Ryan Berton Cormney. BS in Biology/Chemistry/Math., Valdosta State Coll., 1969; Cert. in Tchg. Biol./Math., Ea. Ky. U., 1971; PhD in Human Anatomy/Neurosci., U. Tex., San Antonio, 1984. Undergrad. rsch. asst. Ea. Ky. U., Richmond, 1965-67; tchg. asst. dept. cell-structural biology U. Tex. Health Sci. Ctr., San Antonio, 1979-84; postdoctoral fellowship lab. devel. neurobiology NICHD and LMDB/NEI, Bethesda, Md., 1984-86; instr. dept. psychiatry U. Tex. Southwestern Med. Ctr., Dallas, 1986-87, asst. prof. dept. psychiatry, 1987-91; dir. lab. molecular neurogenetics Schizophrenia Rsch Ctr. VA Med. Ctr., Dallas, 1988-94, Mental Health Clinic Rsch. Ctr., U. Tex. Southwestern Med. Ctr., Dallas, 1990-94; assoc. prof. dept. psychiatry U. Tex. Southwestern Med. Ctr., Dallas, 1991-94; Mary D. Allen prof. Doheney Eye Inst. U. So. Calif. Sch. Medicine, L.A., 1994—, chair dept. cell and neurobiology, 1994—; ad hoc reviewer NEI/NIH, Bethesda, 1993—; reviewer Molecular Biology, NSPB Fight for Sight Grants, 1991-94; STAR-sci. adv. bd. U. So. Calif./Bravo Magnet H.S., L.A., 1995—. Author: (chpt.) Melatonin: Biosyn., Physio. Effects, 1993; exec. editor Exptl. Eye Rsch. jour., 1993—. Recipient Merit award for rsch. VA Med. Ctr., 1992, 93, 94, nomination for Women in Sci. and Engring. award Dallas VA, 1992, 93; NEI fellow, 1986, NICHD/NIH fellow, 1986. Mem. AAAS, AAUW, Assn. for Rsch. in Vision and Ophthalmology (chair program planning com. 1991-94), Am. Soc. for Neurochemistry (Jordi Folch Pi Outstanding Young Investigator 1992), Sigma Xi (sec./treas. 1986-93, pres. 1993-94). Home: 1191 Brookmere Rd Pasadena CA 91105 Office: Univ So Calif Sch of Medicine 1333 San Pablo St BMT 401 Los Angeles CA 90033

CRAFT, JAMES H., radiologist; b. Gaffney, S.C., May 2, 1945; s. William M. and Ruth (Hord) C.; m. Mary Theresa Timko, May 3, 1969; children: Elena, Christina, Lauren. BS, U. S.C.; MD, Med. U. S.C. Diplomate Am. Bd. Radiology. Radiologist Wilson (N.C.) Meml. Hosp., 1980-82, Shallowford Hosp., Atlanta, 1982-86, HCA Aiken Reg. Med. Ctr., Aiken, S.C., 1986—; asst. clin. prof. radiology Med. Coll. Ga., Augusta, 1989— 1st lt. U.S. Army, 1966-69. Mem. S.C. Med. Soc., S.C. Radiol. Soc., Am. Coll. Radiology, Radiol. Soc. N.Am., Soc. of 1324 of Med. U. S.C., U. S.C. Alumni Assn. Home: 1764 Ponder Ct Aiken SC 29803-5248

CRAFT, JEROME WALTER, cosmetic plastic and reconstructive surgeon; b. Erie, Pa., Oct. 20, 1932; s. Walter Sion and Elizabeth Mabel (Bowen) c.; divorced; children: Jerome Robert, Christine Anne, David William. MD, Case Western Res. U., 1948. Cert. Am. Bd. Plastic and Reconstructive Surgeons. Intern gen. surgery St. Vincent's Hosp., Erie, 1949, gen. surgery preceptee, 1949-52; flight surgeon USAF, 1952-54; resident gen. surgery, 1954-56; resident, clin. instr. plastic/reconstructive/hand surgery U. Rochester, N.Y., 1956-58; fellow in head and neck surgery Roswell Pk. Cancer Inst., U. Buffalo, 1957-58; clin. practice in plastic and reconstructive surgery, head and neck surgery, surgery of hand Erie, 1958-66; chief Craft Surg. Ctr., W. Palm Beach, 1966—; pres. Craft Cosmetic Surgery Ctr., W. Palm Beach, Fla., 1974—; mem. Senator Paula Hawkins Med. Adv. Com. to U.S. Congress, Fla., 1986-87; bd. dirs. Octagon Large Wild Animal Treatment Ctr., Ft. Myers, Fla. Author: Reconstruction Hypophanynx, 1959, Burn Cardiac Arrest, 1958, Cosmetic Surgery Book, 1987; rschr. Arterial Grafts, 1957. Med. advisor Congress, Washington, 1986. Capt. USAF, 1952-54. Mem. Palm Beach County Med. Soc., Fla. Med. Soc., AMA, Am. Soc. Plastic & Reconstructive Surgeons, Am. Bd. Plastic & Reconstructive Surgeons. Republican. Office: Craft Cosmetic Surgery Ctr 535 S Flagler Dr West Palm Beach FL 33401-5903

CRAIG, CAROL MILLS, marriage, family and child counselor; b. Berkeley, Calif.. BA in Psychology with honors, U. Calif., Santa Cruz, 1974; MA in Counseling Psychology, John F. Kennedy U., 1980; doctoral student, Calif. Sch. Profl. Psychology, Berkeley, 1980-87, Columbia Pacific U., San Rafael, Calif., 1987—. Psychology intern Fed. Correction Inst., Pleasanton, Calif., 1979-81, Letterman Army Med. Ctr., San Francisco, 1980-82; psychology intern VA Mental Hygiene Clinic, Oakland, Calif., 1981-82, Martinez, Calif., 1982-83; instr. Martinez Adult Sch., 1983, Piedmont Adult Edn., Oakland, 1986; biofeedback and stress mgmt. cons. Oakland, 1986—; child counselor Buddies-A Nonprofit, Counseling Svc. for Persons in the Arts, Lafayette, Calif., 1993—; founder Chesley Sch., 1994; rsch. asst. Irvington Pubs., N.Y.C., 1979, Little, Brown and Co., Boston, 1983. Mem. Calif. Assn. Marriage and Family Therapists (clin.), Musicians Union Local 424, Calif. Scholarship Fedn. (life).

CRAIG, CLIFFORD LINDLEY, orthopaedic pediatric surgery educator; b. Detroit, Mar. 25, 1944; s. Paul Forrest and Dorothy Madeline (Denhart) C.; m. Laura Ann Hackley, June 20, 1976; children: Paul Edward, Julia Marie. BS, Tufts U., 1965; MD, U. Mich., 1969. Diplomat Am. Bd. Orthopaedic Surgery. Asst. prof. orthopaedic surgery Tufts U. Sch. Medicine, Boston, 1979-94, assoc. prof. orthopaedic surgery, 1994—. Fellow Am. Coll. Surgery; mem. AMA, Am. Acad. Orthopaedic Surgery, Am. Acad. Pediatrics, Am. Acad. Cerebral Palsy, Am. Assn. Clin. Anatomy, Pediatric Orthopaedic Surgery. Office: New England Med Ctr 750 Washington St Boston MA 02111

CRAIG, JAMES LYNN, physician, consumer products company executive; b. Columbia, Tenn., Aug. 7, 1933; s. Clifford Paul and Maple (Harris) C.; m. Suzanne Anderson, July 20, 1957; children: James Lynn, Margaret; m. Roberta Anne, May 17, 1980. Ed., Mid. Tenn. State U., 1953; MD, U. Tenn., 1956; MPH, U. Pitts., 1963. Diplomate Am. Bd. Preventive Medicine, Am. Bd. Family Practice. Intern U. Tenn. Meml. Hosp., Knoxville, 1957; resident in occupl. medicine U. Pitts., 1962-64; resident in occupl. medicine TVA, Chattanooga, 1964-65, physician, 1966-69, chief med. officer, 1969-74; corp. med. dir. Gen. Mills Corp., Mpls., 1974-76, v.p. corp. med. dir., 1976-80, v.p., dir. health and human svcs., 1980—; clin. prof. U. Minn., Mpls., 1979—, chmn. cmty. adv. com. Ctr. for Environ. and Health Policy, 1994—, mem. adv. coun. health in scis., 1992-95, chmn. adv. bd. Ctr. for Environ. and Health Policy, 1994—; clin. instr. U. Tenn., Memphis, 1970-74, Meharry Med. Sch., Nashville, 1972-74; bd. dirs. Inst. Rsch. and Edn. Health Sys. Minn. Contbr. articles to profl. jours. Bd. dirs. Mpls. Blood Bank, 1976-88, Minn. Bible Coll., Rochester, 1978-83, Minn. Safety Coun., 1981-90, Minn. Heart Assn., Mpls., 1976-87, Children's Heart Fund, 1976-88, Meth. Hosp. Found., 1979-87, Park Nicolett Med. Found., 1987-93, Altcare, 1983-95, Meth. Hosp. Health Assn., 1987-93, Minn. Wellness Coun., 1986-91, Health Sys. Minn. Assocs., 1993-94; bd. dirs. Health Systems Minn. Inst. for Rsch. and Edn., 1996—. Recipient Physician Recognition award AMA, 1975, 78,81, 85, 89, 93, Cmty. Svc. award Park Nicolett Med. Ctr., 1995. Fellow Am. Occupl. Medicine Assn. (bd. dirs. 1974-78), Am. Acad. Occupl. Medicine (treas. 1982-83, sec. 1983-84, v.p. 1984-85, prs. 1986-87), Health Achievement in Occupl. Medicine, Am. Acad. Family Practice; mem. AMA (alt. del. Ho. Dels. 1990-92, del. 1992—), Occupl. Health Inst. (chmn. 1983-84), North Ctrl. Occupl. Medicine Assn. (pres. 1977), Mpls. Acad. Medicine (sec. 1983-85, pres. 1985-86), Emergency Physicians Assn. (bd. dirs. 1984-92). Home: 10008 S Shore Dr Minneapolis MN 55441-5011 Office: Gen Mills Corp General Mills Blvd Minneapolis MN 55426

CRAIG, JAMES WILLIAM, physician, educator, university dean; b. West Liberty, Ohio, Jan. 23, 1921; s. J. Frank and Clara Helen (Scarborough) C.; m. Helen Catherine Lang, Sept. 18, 1948 (dec.); children: Maribeth, Jon, William, Barbara; m. Wendy Burnip Johnson, June 23, 1972; stepchildren: Steven, Barbara, Philip, Laura Johnson. BS, Western Res. U., 1943, MD, 1945. Intern, asst. resident in medicine Presbyn. Hosp., N.Y.C., 1945-46, 48-50; fellow in medicine Western Res. U. Sch. Medicine, Cleve., 1950-52; from instr. to assoc. prof. medicine Western Res. U. Sch. Medicine, 1952-72; assoc. dean Sch. Medicine U. Va., Charlottesville, 1972-89, prof. medicine, 1972-90, prof. emeritus, 1991—. Condr. research; contbr. articles on diabetes mellitus and intermediary metabolism to publs. Served with AUS, 1946-48. Recipient Lederle med. faculty award, 1962-64. Mem. Am. Diabetes Assn., Am. Inst. Nutrition, Soc. for Exptl. Biology and Medicine, Cen. Soc. for Clin. Rsch., Med. Soc. Va., Phi Beta Kappa, Sigma Xi, Alpha Omega Alpha. Home: 101 Indian Spring Rd Charlottesville VA 22901-1019 Office: Univ Va Sch Medicine Charlottesville VA 22908

CRAIG, JOHN MERRILL, psychiatrist; b. Pasadena, Calif., Oct. 14, 1913; s. Volney Howard and Elinor (Merrill) C.; m. Elsa Fay Hartshorne, May 30, 1949 (dec. Dec. 1970); m. Margery Merrill, July 21, 1973; stepchildren: Robin Hartshorne, Caroline Hartshorne, Mariana Hartsong. AB, U. Calif., Berkeley, 1936, MA, 1938; MD, Havard U., 1941. Asst. to pathologist Boston Children's Med. Ctr., 1950-58; dir. labs. Magee Women's Hosp., Pitts., 1958-59; from pathologist to chief pathologist Boston Hosp. for Women, 1960-79; resident in psychiatry Wes Ros Park Mental Health Ctr., Roslindale, Mass., 1979-82, psychiatrist, 1982-90; assoc. in psychiatry Brigham Women's Hosp., Boston, 1983-91, ret., 1991. Contbr. numerous articles to profl. jours.; assoc. editor: Am. Jour. Pathology, 1962-79. Mem. Greater Boston Health Planning Coun., 1972-76. Lt. comdr. USN, 1942-46. Mem. Mass. Med. Soc., New Eng. Pathology Soc. (pres. 1966-67), Pediatric Pathology Soc. (pres. 1976), Country Club. Home: 41 Sargent Beechwood Brookline MA 02146-7519

CRAIG, KENNETH DENTON, psychologist, educator, researcher; b. Calgary, Alta., Can., Nov. 21, 1937; s. William Denton and Wilhelmina Wylie (MacIntyre) C.; m. Sydney Grace Smith, Apr. 10, 1971; children: Kenneth Deane, Alexandra Grace, Christopher James, Daniel Smith (dec.). BA, Sir George Williams U., Montreal, Que., Can., 1958; MA, U. B.C., Vancouver, Can., 1960; PhD, Purdue U., 1964. Cert. clin. psychologist. Prof. psychology, assoc. dean faculty of grad. studies U. B.C., 1963—; assoc. prof. U. Calgary, 1969-71; dir. Banff Internat. Confs., 1981—, pres., 1994—. Editor Can. Jour. Behavioural Sci., 1986-89; assoc. editor Pain, 1994—; contbr. articles to profl. jours. Nat. advisor first aid svc. Can. Red Cross Soc., 1987-90. Can. coun. Killam rsch. fellow 1992-93. Fellow APA, Can. Psychol. Assn. (pres. 1986-87); mem. Internat. Assn. for Study Pain (founding), B.C. Psychol. Assn. (pres. 1977), Social Sci. Fedn. Can. (treas. 1988-92), Can. Pain Soc. (pres. 1994—). Office: U BC, Dept Psychology, Vancouver, BC Canada V6T 1Z4

CRAIG, MARY ELIZABETH, nurse. RN, Jefferson Hosp. RN, Pa. Staff devel. coord. oper. rm. Thomas Jefferson U. Hosp., Phila. Mem. Am. Soc. for Laser Medicine and Surgery, Assn. Oper. Rm. Nurses (cert.).

CRAIG, NADINE KARAMARKOVICH, pharmaceutical executive; b. Sewickley, Pa., Aug. 18, 1951; d. Nicholas and Mildred (Torbica) Karamarkovich; m. Jeffrey Lynn Craig, Oct. 10, 1977; 1 child, Jacquelyn Leslie. Nursing diploma, U. Pitts., 1972. RN, Fla. Staff nurse St. Francis Hosp., Pitts., 1972-74, Orlando (Fla.) Regional Med. Ctr., 1974-75; dir. aftercare Seminole Community Mental Health Ctr., Altamonte Springs, Fla., 1975-76; sales rep. Searle Pharm., Orlando, 1976-85; sales tng. supr. Searle Pharm., Skokie, Ill., 1985-86; dist. sales mgr. Searle Pharm., New Orleans, 1986-91; prod. mgr. Searle Pharm., Skokie, Ill., 1991-92; assoc. dir. Sci. Mktg. Comm., 1992—; regional sales dir Searle Pharm., Irving, Tex., 1992-96, exec. dir. S.W.-Ctrl. Geog. Customer unit, 1996—. Office: Ste 1170 909 E Las Colinas Blvd Irving TX 75039

CRAIG, ROBERT GEORGE, dental science educator; b. Charlevoix, Mich., Sept. 8, 1923; s. Harry Allen and Marion Ione (Swinton) C.; m. Luella Georgine Dean, Sept. 29, 1945; children: Susan Georgine, Barbara Dean,

Katherine Ann. BS, U. Mich., 1944, MS, 1951, PhD (E.I. du Pont research fellow 1952-53), 1955; MD (hon.), U. Geneva, Switzerland, 1989. Rsch. chemist Linde Air Products Co., 1944-50, Texaco, Inc., Beacon, N.Y., 1954-55; rsch. assoc. U. Mich. Engring. Rsch. Inst., 1955-57; faculty dept. dental materials Sch. Dentistry, U. Mich., Ann Arbor, 1957-87, asst. prof., 1957-60, assoc. prof., 1960-64, prof., 1964-87, chmn. dept., 1969-87, prof. biologic and material sci., 1987-93, Marcus Ward prof. dentistry, 1990-93, prof. emeritus, 1993—; dir. Specialized Materials Sci. Ctr. Nat. Inst. Dental Rsch., Ann Arbor, 1989-93; mem. exec. com. Sch. Dentistry, U. Mich., Ann Arbor, 1972-75; mem. budget priorities com. U. Mich., Ann Arbor, 1978-81; chmn. U. Mich. Budget Priorities Com., 1979-81; mem. sci. adv. com. Dental Research Inst., 1980-89, chmn., 1984-89; cons. Walter Reed Army Hosp., 1969-75; assessor for Nat. Health and Med. Rsch. Coun., Commonwealth Australia. Author: Restorative Dental Materials, 9th edit., 1993, (with K.A. Easlick, S.I. Seger and A.L. Russell) Communicating in Dentistry, 1973, (with W.J. O'Brien, J.M. Powers) Dental Materials-Properties and Manipulation, 6th edit., 1996, (with J.M. Powers) Workbook for Dental Materials, 1979; editor, contbr. Dental Materials Rev., 1977, Dental Materials-A Problem Oriented Approach, 1978; asst. editor Jour. Biomed. Materials Rsch., 1983-93; editl. assoc. Jour. Oral Rehab., 1995—; cons. editor Jour. Dental Rsch., 1971-73, 77-80, Jour. Dental Edn., 1971-76, Jour. Oral Rehab., 1974-94, Mich. State Dental Jour., 1973-77, Jour. Oral Implantology, 1988—; mem. adv. bd. Saudi Dental Jour., 1989—; contbr. articles to profl. jours. Prin. investigator specialized material Scis. Rsch. Ctr. (funded by NIDR 1989-94). Rsch. grantee Nat. Inst. Dental Rsch., 1965-76, 84-94; Nat. Scis. Res. Svc. Tng. grantee, 1976-93. Mem. ADA (cons. coun. on dental materials and devices 1983-95), Am. Nat. Stds. Inst. (chmn. spl. com. 1968-77, subcom. with ADA on mouth protectors and materials 1996—), Internat. Assn. Dental Rsch. (pres.-elect dental materials group 1972-73, pres. 1973-74, Wilmer Souder award 1975), Am. Assn. Dental Schs. (chmn. biomaterials sect. 1977-79), Am. Chem. Soc., Soc. Biomaterials (Clemson award for basic rsch. in biomaterials 1978, program chmn. 1983), Acad. Operative Dentistry (George Hollenbach Meml. prize 1991), Sigma Xi (sec. U. Mich chpt. 1978-81), Phi Kappa Phi, Phi Lambda Upsilon, Omicron Kappa Upsilon. Home: 1503 Wells St Ann Arbor MI 48104-3914 Office: U Mich Sch Dentistry Sch Dentistry 1011 N University Ave Ann Arbor MI 48109-1078

CRAIG, ROBERT JAMES, healthcare executive; b. Newport, R.I., Oct. 27, 1958; s. James E. and Shirley A. (Terry) C.; m. Rebecca T. Thurmond, May 26, 1985; children: Sean Michael, Shelby Jane. BS cum laude, Indiana U. Pa., 1981; M in Health Adminstrn., Duke U., 1983. Adminstrv. resident Meth. Hosps., Memphis, 1983-84, spl. projects coord., 1984; adminstrv. asst. Meth. Health Systems, Memphis, 1984-85; v.p. mktg. Lancaster (Ohio)-Fairfield Community Hosp., 1985-91; v.p. profl. svcs. Union Hosp., Dover, Ohio, 1991—; sec. Home Health Resources, Inc., Lancaster, 1986-87, Zane Properties, Inc., Lancaster, 1987-91. Bd. dirs. Info. and Crisis Fairfield County, Lancaster, 1987-91; mem. com. Forward Lancaster, 1987; div. chmn. United Way of Tuscarawas County, Ohio, 1992; bd. dirs. Forum of Health Svcs. Execs., Valley Healthcare Inc., Tuscacarawas County Coun. for Ch. and Cmty. Named Outstanding Young Man of Am., 1984. Mem. Am. Coll. Healthcare Execs. (diplomate), Ohio Soc. of Healthcare Planning and Mktg. Republican. Roman Catholic. Office: Union Hosp 659 Boulevard St Dover OH 44622-2026

CRAIG, RUSSELL WAYNE, osteopath; b. Detroit, Nov. 17, 1964; s. Kenneth Edward and Lorraine Antonette (Fitchena) C. BA cum laude, Wayne State U., 1987; DO, Mich. State U., 1991. Diplomate Nat. Bd. Osteo. Med. Examiners. Pathology lab. asst. William Beaumont Hosp., Troy, Mich., 1985-87; intern, resident Mt. Clemens (Mich.) Gen. Hosp., 1991-96; clinician Schoenherr Med. Assocs., Warren, Mich., 1993—; instr. oncology dept. Wayne State U., Detroit, 1984-87. Contbr. articles to profl. jours. Mem. AMA (Physicians Recognition award 1994-97), Am. Osteo. Assn., Am. Acad. Facial Plastic and Reconstructive Surgery, Am. Acad. Otolaryngic Allergy, Am. Acad. Otolaryngology, Head and Neck Surgery (Achievement award 1995-96), Am. Osteo. Colls. Ophthalmology and Otolaryngology, Head and Neck Surgery, Pi Kappa Alpha. Office: Mount Clemens Gen Hosp 1000 Harrington Blvd Mount Clemens MI 48043

CRAIG, STACEY ANN, medical and surgical nurse; b. Balt., Sept. 4, 1967; d. Thomas Edward and Barbara Mae (Fauver) G. Student, Loyola Coll., Balt., 1985-87; BS in Nursing, Towson (Md.) State U., 1990. Med./surg. staff nurse St. Agnes Hosp., Balt., 1990-93; neurosci. staff nurse Fairfax Hosp., Falls Church, Va., 1993—. Mem. Sigma Theta Tau (Iota Epsilon chpt.). Home: 10929 Decatur Dr Fairfax VA 22030-5385

CRAIG, WILLIAM DAVID, rheumatologist; b. Bristol, Tenn., May 3, 1962; s. Orlyn Winfred and Betty Josephine (Wright) C.; m. Julia Marie Mullins, Aug. 10, 1985; children: Elizabeth, Spencer, Andrew. BS, East Tenn. State U., Johnson City, 1985; DO, W.Va. Sch. Osteo. Medicine, Lewisburg, 1989. Diplomate Am. Bd. Internal Medicine. Resident internal medicine U. Tenn. Chattanooga unit Erlanger Med. Ctr., 1990-93; fellow rheumatology Med. Coll. Ga., Augusta, 1993-95; physician in rheumatology Arthritis Assocs., Chattanooga, 1995—. Mem. ACP, Am. Coll. Rheumatology. Baptist. Home: 8503 Creek Stone Dr Chattanooga TN 37421 Office: Arthritis Assocs 605 Glenwood Ave Ste 100 Chattanooga TN 37404

CRAIG, ZANE GRANT, obstetrician, gynecologist; b. Wilmington, Ohio, Feb. 11, 1952; s. Hollis Summers and Marjorie Ellen (Clevenger) C.; m. Cheryl Lee Ross, Sept. 26, 1981; 1 child, John Taylor. BA in Zoology magna cum laude, Miami U., Oxford, Ohio, 1975; DO, U. Osteo. Medicine/Health Sci., 1978. Intern William Beaumont Army Med. Ctr., El Paso, Tex., 1978-79; commd. 2d lt. U.S. Army, 1979, advanced through grades to maj.; med. officer Army Med. Corps U.S. Army, various locations, 1979-90; resigned U.S. Army, 1990; resident in ob-gyn. Grandview Hosp., Dayton, Ohio, 1990-91; resident in ob-gyn. Carson City Hosp., 1991-94, attending physician dept. ob-gyn., 1994—, chmn. dept. ob-gyn., 1994-95. Mem. Am. Osteo. Assn., Am. Coll. Osteo. Obstetricians and Gynecologists, Am. Assn. Gynecologic Laparoscopists, Soc. Laparendoscopic Surgeons, Mich. Assn. Osteo. Physicians and Surgeons, Phi Kappa Phi. Home: 10406 West Camper's Trail Perrinton MI 48871-9631 Office: Ctr for Ob-Gyn 121 N Pine River St Ithaca MI 48847

CRAIGE, DANNY DWAINE, dentist; b. Okla., Mar. 25, 1946; s. William and Ruby G. (Sinor) C.; m. Mary Ann Thompson, Dec. 22, 1970. BS in Math., Southeastern Okla. State U., 1967; MS, Okla. U., 1968, DDS, 1980. Tchr. Yuba (Okla.) Pub. Schs., 1968-69, Sherman (Tex.) Pub. Schs., 1971-73; asst. mgr. Thompson Book and Supply Co., Durant, Okla., 1973-76; pvt. practice Durant, 1980—; cons. Med. Ctr. of S.E. Okla., Durant, 1980—, Bryan County (Okla.) Nursing Homes, 1980—. Bd. dirs. Texoma chpt. Boy Scouts Am., Durant and Denison, Tex., 1983-90, chmn. sustaining membership drive, Durant, 1989, 90; bd. dirs. Durant Western Days Talent Contest, 1989, 90, 91. Capt. USNR. Okla. U. fellow, 1968. Mem. ADA, Okla. Dental Assn., Naval Res. Assn. (life), Naval Order U.S., Texoma Dental Study Club (chmn. 1980—), Lions (past chpt. pres. and bd. dirs.). Home: 601 W Pine St Durant OK 74701-3735 Office: 203 N 16th Ave Durant OK 74701-3607

CRAIGE, ERNEST, physician, educator; b. El Paso, Tex., June 3, 1918; s. Branch and Else (Kohlberg) C. B.A., U. N.C., 1939; M.D., Harvard U., 1943. Intern in medicine Mass. Gen. Hosp., Boston, 1943; asst. resident Mass. Gen. Hosp., 1946-47, resident, 1947-48, clin. and research fellow in medicine and resident in cardiology, 1949-50, asst. in medicine, 1950-52; teaching fellow in medicine Harvard U. Med. Sch., Boston, 1949-50; asst. prof. medicine U. N.C., Chapel Hill, 1952-55; asso. prof. U. N.C., 1955-62, prof., 1962-85, Henry A. Foscue disting. prof., 1971-78; chief cardiology N.C. Meml. Hosp., Chapel Hill, 1952-78. Served with U.S. Army, 1944-46, ETO. Rhodes scholar Oxford U., 1939. Fellow Am. Coll. Cardiology, Philippine Coll. Cardiology; mem. Am. Heart Assn., Am. Clin. and Climatological Assn., Am. Soc. Echocardiography, Assn. Univ. Cardiologists, Argentina Soc. Cardiology, Alpha Omega Alpha. Home: 235 Mt Bolus Rd Chapel Hill NC 27514-2749

CRAIGHEAD, JOHN EDWARD, pathology educator; b. Pitts., Aug. 14, 1930; s. Samuel Judson and Madeleine Rose (Schmalz) C.; m. Dorothy Ellen Ford, July 29, 1957 (div. June 1992); 2 children; m. Christina Ann Canon, Aug. 29, 2992; 7 children. BS, U. Utah, 1952, MD, 1956. Diplomate Am. Bd. Pathology, Nat. Bd. Med. Examiners (pathology com. 1978-81). Intern ward med. svc. Barnes Hosp., St. Louis, 1956-57; jr. asst. resident in pathology Peter Bent Brigham Hosp., Boston, 1960-61, sr. asst. resident, 1961-62, chief resident, 1962-63, assoc. in pathology, 1963-68; assoc. in pathology Harvard U. Med. Sch., Boston, 1963-66, assoc. prof., 1966-68; assoc. prof. U. Vt. Coll. Medicine, Burlington, 1968-69, prof., 1969—, chmn. dept. pathology, 1974-90; attending physician Med. Ctr. Hosp. Vt., Burlington, 1970-94, Fletcher Allen Health Care, Burlington, 1995—; Harry B. Harding meml. lectr. Evanston (Ill.) Hosp., 1981; 4th ann. Karl Sohlberg lectr. U. Ill., 1981; Finlayson seminar lectr. McGill U., Montreal, Que., Can., 1987; George Hoyt Whipple lectr. U. Rochester, N.Y., 1989; assoc. mem. Commn. Viral Infections, Armed Forces Epidemiol. Bd., 1966-68; mem. adv. com. on infectious diseases Nat. Inst. Allergy and Infectious Diseases, 1971-75; mem. pathology A study sect. NIH, 1984-86, mem. nat. adv. environ. health scis. coun., 1985-89; mem. adv. com. Registry Comparative Pathology, Armed Forces Inst. Pathology, 1993—; mem. Vt. Regional Cancer Ctr., 1988-91; mem. med. sci. adv. bd. Juvenile Diabetes Found., 1978-80; mem. residency rev. com. for pathology Accreditation Coun. for Grad. Med. Edn., 1979-83, vice chmn., 1982-84; dir. sci. program, chmn. environ. pathology task force Univs. Assoc. for Rsch. and Edn. in Pathology, 1991—; mem. pulmonary panel Am. Registry Pathology, 1992—. Editor: The Pathology of Environmental and Occupational Disease, 1995; mem. editl. bd. Lab. Investigation, Archives Pathology and Lab. Medicine, Human Pathology, Am. Jour. Pathology, 1980-92; contbr. numerous articles and abstracts to med. jours., chpts. to books. Surgeon USPHS, 1957-60. Recipient David Rumbough sci. award, 1976, Moses Barron award, 1977; spl. fellow NIH, 1963; travel fellow Royal Soc. Medicine, 1971. Mem. AAAS, AMA (coun. sci. affairs, adv. panel on asbestos related diseases, chmn. 1982-83), Am. Acad. Pathology, Am. Assn. for Cancer Rsch., Am. Assn. Pathologists, Am. Soc. Clin. Pathologists (basic sci. rsch. symposium com. 1978-82, H.P. Smith Meml. award 1987), Am. Thoracic Soc., Assn. Pathology Chairmen (past sec.-treas., v.p., pres. 1981-82), Internat. Acad. Pathology (councillor 1980-84), Coll. Am. Pathologists (environ. resource com. coun. on pathology practice 1980-81), Am. Soc. for Virology, New Eng. Soc. Pathologists (pres. 1980-81), Mass. Soc. Pathologists (exec. com. 1967), Vt. Med. Soc., Chittenden County Med. Soc. Office: U Vt Dept Pathology 55A S Park Dr Colchester VT 05446

CRAIGO, JOYCE KAREL, long term care administrator; b. South Charleston, W.Va., Aug. 8, 1960; d. Everett Luster Carroll and Phyllis Ann (Withrow) Hill; m. Robert Samuel Craigo, Apr. 2, 1983; children: Jennifer Marie, Jason Mark, Samuel Parker. BBA, Marshall U., 1982. Cert. nursing home administr., W.Va. Credit mgr. Charleston (W.Va.) Marriott, 1982-86; credit adjuster E-Z Go/Textran, Augusta, Ga., 1987; account receivable rep. Manpower, Charleston, 1987-88; credit rep. GMAC, Charleston, 1988-89, acct. II, 1989-90; contr. Arthur B. Hodges Ctr., Charleston, 1990-94, asst. adminstr., 1994—. Mem. Am. Coll. of Healthcare Adminstrs. Office: Arthur B Hodges Ctr Inc 500 Morris St Charleston WV 25301

CRAIS, THOMAS FLOYD, JR., plastic and reconstructive surgeon; b. New Orleans, Nov. 22, 1943; s. Thomas F. and Myrtle (Laresche) C.; divorced; children: Vanessa, Hilary, Thomas III. Student Tex. A&M U., 1961-63; MD, La. State U., 1968. Diplomate Am. Bd. Plastic Surgery, Am. Coll. Surgeons. Rotating intern William Beaumont Hosp., El Paso, Tex., 1968-69; aerospace medicine fellow Naval Aerospace Med. Inst., Pensacola, Fla., 1969-70; chief outpatient clinic U.S. Army Hosp., Berlin, 1970-73; resident gen. surgery Boston U., 1973-77; resident plastic surgery NYU, N.Y.C., 1977-79, microsurgery fellow, 1979; practice medicine specializing in plastic and reconstructive surgery, New Orleans, 1980—; clin. instr. plastic surgery La. State U. Med. Ctr., New Orleans, 1980—; med. dir. microsurg. research and tng. lab. So. Bapt. Hosp., New Orleans, 1981—, course dir. ann. microsurgery symposium, 1981-87. Contbr. articles to med. publs. Patentee microarterial bridge. Bd. dirs. Holy Cross Sch., New Orleans, 1983-89, headmaster's coun., 1990-95, Big Bros./Sisters, 1989-96; mem. Operation Smile Internat. missions to Manizales and Duitama, Colombia, Hanoi, Haiphong, Vietnam, Bucharest, Romania; founder La. chpt. Operation Smile (pres. bd. dirs.); exec com. So. Baptist Hosp. New Orleans; past mem. first sci. cultural mission People's Republic China, 1984. Served to maj. M.C., U.S. Army, 1968-73, Fed. Republic Germany. Mem. AMA, Am. Soc. Reconstructive Microsurgery, Am. Soc. Plastic and Reconstructive Surgery, La. Soc. Plastic and Reconstructive Surgeons (past pres.), La. State Med. Soc., Orleans Parish Med. Soc., Southeastern Soc. Plastic and Reconstructive Surgeons, So. Med. Assn., Surg. Assn. La., Internat. Soc. Reconstructive Microsurgery, Am. Soc. for Aesthetic Plastic Surgery Inc., New Orleans Surg. Soc., Lipoplasty Soc. N.Am., Pan Am. Med. Assn., Soc. Peripheral Nerve Surgery. Roman Catholic. Avocations: equestrian activities, jogging, languages, gardening, private pilot. Office: 804 Heavens Dr Ste 205 Mandeville LA 70471-2890

CRAKE, ROGER F., general surgeon; b. Wilkes Barre, Pa., Dec. 24, 1952; s. Fred Alfred and Margaret Rose (Yuknavich) C.; m. Michele Robin Andreyko, June 3, 1978; children: Michael, Stephen. BS, U. Scranton, 1974; MD, Jefferson Med. Coll., 1978. Diplomate Am. Bd. Surgery, Nat. Bd. Med. Examiners. Staff Berwick (Pa.) Hosp., 1983—; chmn. div. surgery Berwick Hosp., 1987-89, sec.-treas. staff, 1991-93, v.p. staff, 1993, pres. staff, 1993-95, chmn. credentials, 1995—. Fellow Am. Coll. Surgeons; mem. AMA, Soc. Am. Gastrointestinal Endoscopic Surgeons, Soc. Laparoscopic Surgeons, Pa. Med. Soc., Columbia County Med. Soc. Home: 737 E Front St Berwick PA 18603 Office: 695 E 16th St Berwick PA 18603

CRAMER, EVA BROWN, anatomy and cell biology educator; b. N.Y.C., June 6, 1944; d. Saul and Sylvia (Casler) Edward; m. Marvin Edward Cramer, May 30, 1968; children: Jocelyn, Jeff. BS, Cornell U., 1965; PhD, Jefferson Med. Sch., 1969. Instr. Coll. Physicians and Surgeons Columbia U., N.Y.C., 1970-71; instr. Med. Sch. Harvard U., Boston, 1971-73; instr. Downstate Med. Sch. SUNY, N.Y.C., 1973-76, asst. prof. Downstate Med. Sch., 1976-80, assoc. prof. Downstate Med. Sch., 1980-88; prof. Health Sci. Ctr. SUNY, Bklyn., 1988—, acting assoc. provost for sci. affairs Health Sci. Ctr., 1988-94, assoc. v.p. for sci. affairs, 1994—; adj. assoc. prof. The Rockefeller U., N.Y.C., 1982-86. Contbr. articles to profl. jours. NIH predoctoral fellow Jefferson Med. Sch., 1965-69; NIH postdoctoral fellow Coll. Physicians and Surgeons, Columbia U., 1969-70. Mem. Am. Assn. Anatomists, Am. Soc. for Cell Biology, N.Y. Soc. Electron Microscopists, Harvey Soc. Office: SUNY Health Sci Ctr at Bklyn 450 Clarkson Ave Brooklyn NY 11203-2012

CRAMER, JOHN SANDERSON, health care executive; b. Butte, Mont., Feb. 22, 1942; s. John Dale and Angela Rita (Sanderson) C.; m. Ellen E. McGrath, Apr. 15, 1968; children: Jennifer, Jon. BBA in Small Bus. Adminstrn., Adelphi U., 1964; MBA in Hosp. Adminstrn., George Washington U., 1969. Asst. to assocs. John G. Steinle and Assocs., Garden City, N.Y., 1960-64, jr. assoc., 1964-67, assoc., 1969-70; adminstrv. resident Harrisburg (Pa.) Hosp., 1968-69, asst. dir., 1970-73, dir. planning, 1973-78; v.p. corp. planning Capital Health System, Harrisburg, 1978-84, sr. v.p. corp. planning, 1984-88, pres., chief exec. officer, 1988—. Author: (with others) Organizational Theory, Cases and Applications, 1990. Mem. Coun. for Pub. Edn., Harrisburg, 1991—; bd. dirs. Harrisburg Symphony Assn., 1992-95, mem. long range planning com., 1992-93; mem. adv. com. Harrisburg Acad., 1992—, Greater Harrisburg YWCA, 1994—; mem. Pa. Health Care Cost Containment Coun., 1993—. Recipient Businessman of Yr. award City of Harrisburg, 1992. Fellow Am. Coll. Healthcare Execs.; mem. Am. Hosp. Assn. (charter mem., soc. for healthcare planning and mktg., bd. dirs. 1990-93, nat. recognition award 1985, Pa. del., mem. regional policy bd. 2 1995—), Hosp. Assn. Pa. (blue ribbon vision 2000 panel 1990, bd. dirs. 1991—, mem. exec. com., chmn. strategic planning com. 1993—, ann. creative energy award 1981, chmn. bd. dirs. 1996), Vol. Hosps. Pa. (sec. 1991—, bd. dirs. 1988—, officer, mem. exec. com. 1992—), Capital Area C. of C. (bd. dirs. 1993-95), Capital Region Econ. Devel. Corp. (ambassador 1994—), Colonial Country Club, Tuesday Club, Country Club of Harrisburg.

CRAMER, JOYCE JACOBS, medical researcher; b. Worcester, Mass., Feb. 18, 1943; m. Marvin B. Cramer, Aug. 30, 1964. BS, Simmons Coll., 1964. Rschr. Yale U. Sch. Medicine, VA Med. Ctr., West Haven, Conn., 1964-79; project dir. VA-Yale Epilepsy Ctr., West Haven, 1975-91; project coord. Health Svcs. Rsch., VA Med. Ctr., West Haven, 1991—; cons. various pharm. cos. Author 4 books; contbr. more than 70 articles to profl. jours. Chmn. bd. trustees Lennox Trust Fund, 1993—. Recipient Clin. Trial prize Internat. League Against Epilepsy, 1985; named Amb. for Epilepsy, Internat. League Against Epilepsy, 1995. Mem. Am. Epilepsy Soc. (treas. 1990-93), Soc. Clin. Trials (bd. dirs.). Office: Health Svcs Rsch 116A 950 Campbell Ave West Haven CT 06516

CRAMER, STANLEY HOWARD, psychology educator, author; b. N.Y.C., Oct. 1, 1933; s. Louis and Sophie (Zimmerman) C.; m. Rosalind Faber, Nov. 26, 1959; children: Elizabeth, Lauren, Matthew. BA, U. Mass., 1955; MA, SUNY, Albany, 1957; EdD, Columbia U., 1963. Prof. counseling psychology SUNY at Buffalo, Amherst, 1965—. Author: (with E.L. Herr) Critical Issues in the Helping Professions, 1987, Career Guidance and Counseling Through the Lifespan, 1972, 5th edit., 1996, (with J.C. Hansen and R.H. Rossberg) Counseling: Theory and Process, 1994. Mem. Am. Counseling Assn., Am. Psychol. Assn. Home: 21 Foxboro Ln East Amherst NY 14051-1828 Office: SUNY Buffalo 423 Christopher Baldy Hall Amherst NY 14260

CRAMPTON, GEORGE HARRIS, science educator, retired army officer; b. Spokane, Wash., Nov. 20, 1926. BS, Wash. State U., 1949, MS, 1950; PhD, U. Rochester, 1954. Enlisted U.S. Army Res., 1944; advanced through grades to col. U.S. Army M.S.C., 1969; ret. U.S. Army, 1971; prof. Wright State U., Dayton, Ohio, 1971-86, prof. emeritus, 1987—. Home: 790 SW Dawnview Ter Oak Harbor WA 98277-8116

CRAMPTON, RICHARD SAVINGTON, cardiologist, educator; b. Norwalk, Conn., Sept. 29, 1931; s. Savington Warren Crampton and Louise (Michel) Welch; m. Julia Mary Synolda Butler, June 6, 1959; children: Anne Cordelia, Suzanna Louise, Thomas William Butler. Student, Princeton U., 1949-52; MD, U. Va., 1956. Intern in internal medicine St. Luke's Hosp., N.Y.C., 1956-57; resident in internal medicine St. Luke's Hosp., N.Y.C., 1957-58, 59-60, resident in cardiovascular surgery, 1960-61, physician, 1963-69; resident St. Bartholomew's Hosp., London, 1958-59; assoc. prof. U. Va., University, 1969-75, prof., 1975—; head cardiovascular br. U.S. Naval Hosp., Phila., 1961-63; jr. registrar St. Bartholomew's Hosp., London, 1958-59; instr. Columbia U., N.Y.C., 1963-69, U. Pa., Phila., 1961-63; mem. scientific adv. bd. Sudden Arrhythmia Death Syndrome Found., Salt Lake City, 1992—. Contbr. articles to profl. jours. and chpts. to books. Lt. comdr. USNR, 1961-63. Fellow Coun. on Clin. Cardiology Am. Heart Assn., Am. Coll. Cardiology (gov. for Va. 1976-79), ACP (life); mem. N.Y. Acad. Sci. (life). Episcopalian. Office: Health Scis Ctr Cardiovascular Divsn Box 158 University VA 22908

CRANDALL, DAVID LEROY, research scientist; b. Creston, Iowa, Sept. 1, 1952; s. Robert Miles and Margaret (Duncan) C.; m. Sarah Jane Scholl, June 12, 1982. B.S., Tulane U., 1974; M.S., Iowa State U., 1977, Ph.D., 1979. Research fellow Emory U., 1979-81; sr. research scientist Am. Cyanamid Co., Pearl River, N.Y., 1981-95, prin. scientist Wyeth Res., Princeton, N.J., 1995—; adj. asst. prof. dept medicine, SUNY; vis. lectr. N.Y. Med. Coll., Vahalla, 1985—; adj. asst. prof. SUNY Downstste Med. Ctr., 1987-88. Contbr. articles on biochem. and physiol. adaptations to obesity to profl. jours.; mem. editorial bd. Am. Jour. Physiology. Bd. dirs. Union County Baseball League, Afton, Iowa, 1970-73. Mem. Am. Physiol. Soc., Eastern Hypertension Soc., Sigma Xi. Roman Catholic. Avocations: jogging, golfing. Home: 181 Sunset View Dr Doylestown PA 18901 Office: Wyeth Rsch CN 8000 Princeton NJ 08543

CRANDALL, EARLE ELLSWORTH, neurosurgeon, educator; b. Chgo., Feb. 17, 1933; s. Theodore Anton and Jeanette Crandall; m. Arlette Louise Passy, Oct. 6, 1963; children: Phillip Reddington, Carolyn Janet, Marc Stephen. BS, U. Ill., Chgo., 1955, MS, 1956, MD, 1956; PhD, U. Minn., 1967. Diplomate Am. Bd. Neurol. Surgery. Intern U. Ill. Hosps., 1956-57; neurosurgery fellow Mayo Found., 1957-62; chief of neurosurgery St. Vincent Med. Ctr., L.A., 1990—; mem. staff Cedars Sinai Med. Ctr., L.A., 1965—, Hosp. of the Good Samaritan, L.A., 1965—, Queen of Angels/Hollywood Prsbyn. Med. Ctr., L.A., 1965—; assoc. clin. prof. depts. neurosurgery and neurobiology UCLA Med. Sch. Bd. dirs. South Calif. Regional Organ Procurement Agy., U. So. Calif. Friends of Sch. Fin. Arts. Lt. comdr. USN, 1963-65, Vietnam. Spl. NIH Brain Rsch. fellow Coll. of France, Paris, 1962-63; recipient Nat. Rsch. award Am. Acad. Neurosurgery, 1964. Office: 8920 Wilshire Blvd Ste 618 Beverly Hills CA 90211-2006

CRANDALL, SONIA JANE, medical educator; b. Quincy, Ill., Sept. 2, 1952; d. Gerald Madison and Roselma Louise (Zeiger) Syrcle; m. Edward Young Crandall, June 28, 1975. Diploma, Michael Reese Med. Ctr., Chgo., 1974; BS, Western Ill. U., 1974; MED, U. Ill., 1980; PhD, U. Okla., 1989. Med. tech. U. Mo. Med. Ctr., Columbia, 1974-75; med. tech., clin. instr. St. Johns Hosp., Springfield, Ill., 1976-81; med. tech., supr. Okla. Teaching Hosp., 1982-85, tng. officer, 1985-87; Kellog fellow U. Okla., Norman, Okla., 1987-89; asst. prof., dir. faculty devel. and edn. resources, dept. family medicine U. Okla. Health Scis. Ctr., Oklahoma City, 1989-94; asst. prof., dept. family and community medicine Bowman Gray Sch. of Medicine, Wake Forest U., 1994—. Contbr. articles to prof jours. Named one of Outstanding Young Women in Am.; elected to Women's Inner Circle of Achievement, 1995, 500 Leaders of Influence, 1993, 2,000 Notable Am. Women, 1992. Mem. Am. Edn. Rsch. Assn., Am. Assn. for Adult and Continuing Edn., Am. Soc. Clin. Pathology, Soc. Tchrs. Family Medicine, Alliance for Continuing Med. Edn., World Found. of Successful Women (charter), Phi Kappa Phi. Home: 3969-E Valley Ct Winston Salem NC 27106-4379 Office: Dept Family & Cmty Medicine Bowman Gray Sch Medicine Wake Forest U Medical Center Blvd Winston Salem NC 27157

CRANE, DAVID MARK, physician; b. Minot, N.D., Feb. 9, 1948; s. Curtis Wilbur and Betty Anne (Mertins) C.; m. Mary Margaret Disbrow, June 17, 1971; children: Meghan Kathleen, Jennifer Erin. BS cum laude, Georgetown U., 1970; MD, Tufts U., 1974. Diplomate Am. Bd. Emergency Medicine, Am. Bd. Internal Medicine, Am. Bd. Quality Assurance and Utilization Rev. Physicians. Resident in internal medicine Bapt. Meml. Hosp., Memphis, 1974-76; resident in emergency medicine U. Cin. Gen. Hosp., 1976-78; dir. emergency med. svcs. Deaconess Hosp., Evansville, Ind., 1981-83; asst. dir. emergency med. svcs. Reston (Va.) Hosp., 1985-86; corp. dir. quality assurance Emergency Medicine Assocs., Rockville, Md., 1984-86; dir. emergency med. svcs. Capitol Hill Hosp., Washington, 1987-91; v.p. pers. Emergency Medicine Assocs., Rockville, 1992—; dir. emergency med. svcs. Carroll County Gen. Hosp., Westminster, Md., 1996—; clin. faculty Georgetown U. Sch. Medicine, Washington, 1985—. Fellow Am. Coll. Emergency Physicians; mem. AMA, Am. Coll. Physician Execs., Am. Coll. Med. Quality. Roman Catholic. Home: 7709 Ivymount Ter Rockville MD 20854-3216 Office: Emergency Medicine Assocs 9210 Corporate Blvd #210 Rockville MD 20850-4697

CRANE, DEBORAH L., clinical research nurse; b. Wilmington, Del., Dec. 6, 1962; d. James A. and Patricia (Drake) Peel; m. Dennis L. Crane, May 18, 1985; 1 child, Alexandra. Student, U. Del., 1980-81; ADN, Del. Tech. and Community Coll., 1983. Cert. orthopaedic nurse; cert. BCLS; cert. in vascular access. Nurse's aide Emily Bissell Hosp., Wilmington, 1983; staff nurse Med. Ctr. Del., Newark, 1984-92; clin. rsch. nurse Med. Rsch. Inst. Del., 1992—. Mem. Nat. Assn. Orthopaedic Nurses, Phi Theta Kappa. Home: 572 Capitol Trl Newark DE 19711-3874

CRANE, FRANCINE T., physician; b. Darby, Pa., Oct. 3, 1958; d. Francis R. and Elizabeth T. (Giberson) C. Nursing diploma, Thomas Jefferson U., 1981, BSN, 1985; MD, Jefferson Med. Coll., 1995. Resident in internal medicine. Mem. AMA. Home: 49 Orchard Park Greenville SC 29615

CRANE, JOSEPH STROTHER, human services manager; b. Parkersburg, W.Va., Sept. 6, 1934; s. James Cloud and Hazel Elizabeth (Meadows) C.; m. Ruth Naomi Dobbins, Nov. 2, 1957. BA, Johns Hopkins U., 1955; MA, George Washington U., 1963; postgrad., Am. U., 1964-69. Sr. analyst IRS, Washington, 1962-67; sr. analyst U.S. Dept. Housing and Urban Devel., Washington, 1967-68, mgmt. officer model cities program, 1968-70, dir. mgmt., community planning & devel., 1970-81; govt. affairs adminstr. AIA, Washington, 1981-84; pvt. practice mgmt. cons. Washington, 1984-86; ind. realty contractor Bethesda, Md., 1986-88; regional adminstr. Va. Div. Child

Support Enforcement, Williamsburg, 1988-91, asst. dir. program devel. and adminstrn., 1991-95, interim divsn. dir., 1995—. Capt. U.S. Army, 1955-63. Presbyterian. Office: Child Support Enforcement 730 E Broad St Richmond VA 23219-1836

CRANE, MARK ALAN, physician assistant, orthopedic surgery; b. Santa Monica, Calif., May 11, 1958; s. Stanley Albert and Eva Christine (Sjursen) C.; m. Randi Christine Campagnam Jan. 11, 1994. BS in Biology, U. Calif., Irvine, 1982; BBA in Healthcare Adminstrn., Chapman Coll., 1986; PA-C, George Washington U., Washington, DC, 1991; MBA in Mktg., U. So. Calif., L.A., 1993. Lic. and cert. for orthopedic surgery, Boston Coll., Boston. Ski patrol mem. Vail (Colo.) Assocs., 1976-79; operating rm. tech. Hoag Meml. Hosp., Newport Beach, Calif., 1979-81; surgical tech. II U.S. Navy/Sharp Healthcare, San Diego, 1981-89; PA-C, Lt. Jr. Grade U.S. Navy, Coronado, Calif., 1989-91; v.p. sales and mktg. Coast Med., Inc., Orange, Calif., 1994—; PA-C orthopedic surgery Orthopedic Med. Group, San Diego, Calif., 1991—; team health care provider Navy Seals, Coronado, Calif., 1982-85; total joint specialist Orthopedic Med. Group, San Diego, 1991—; med. device cons. Coast Med., Inc., Orange, 1994—. Inventor: Endostachial Tube Stylett, 1994 (patent 1994). Regional ACLS instr. ARC, San Diego, 1993; mem. Dennis Conner crew in Am.,s Cup races, San Diego, 1995. Decorated numerous mil. medals; recipient Orthopedic Rsch. scholarship, Boston Coll., 1991. Fellow Nat. Bd. Orthopedic Surgery; mem. Assn. Physician Assts., U. So. Calif. Alumni, San Diego Yacht Club (pres. 1989—). Republican. Roman Catholic.

CRANE, PATRICIA SUE, probation services administrator, social worker; b. Rockway, N.Y., Jan. 17, 1948; d. Herbert Milton and Miriam (Rosenblum) Brager; m. Marvin J. Crane, May 2, 1971; 1 child, Elizabeth A. BA, U. Wis., 1969; MS in Criminal Justice with honors, Wayne State U., 1984. Cert. social worker. Dir. probation svcs. 52d dist. ct. 1st div. State of Mich., Novi, 1979—. Jewish. Home: 5042 Meadowbrook Dr West Bloomfield MI 48322-1570 Office: 52nd Dist Ct 1st Divsn 48150 Grand River Ave Novi MI 48374-1222

CRANE, REA BABCOCK, nurse; b. Oakland, Calif., June 2, 1942; d. William Joy and Adeline Hazel (Gunnufson) Babcock; m. Charles Truman Crane, Apr. 2, 1966 (div. 1977); children: Audra Joy, Elise Deborah. Diploma, Calif. Hosp. Sch. Nursing, Los Angeles, 1963. RN, Calif.; cert. ins. rehab. specialist; cert. case mgr. Emergency room nurse Kaiser Found., San Francisco, 1963-64, Santa Monica (Calif.) Hosp., 1964-65; med.-surg. floor nurse West L.A. VA Hosp., 1964-65; rehab. nurse Internat. Rehab. Assocs., L.A., 1970-76; rehab. nurse Fremont Compensation Ins. Co., L.A., 1976-79, rehab. supr., 1979-84, asst. dir. rehab., 1984-86, dir. rehab., 1986-91; rehab. mgr. T.I.G. Ins. (formerly TransAmerica), Woodland Hills, Calif., 1991-95; med./dir. coord. Calif. Worker's Compensation Inst., San Francisco, 1995—; mem. Cert. Ins. Rehab. Specialist Commn. Mem. Rehab. Nurses Soc. (pres. 1978-82, T. Gucker award 1992), Nat. Assn. Rehab. Profls. in Pvt. Sector (founding pres. Calif. chpt. 1984-86, regional rep., chmn. constn. by-laws 1986—, Bd. Mem. of Yr. 1985, Lifetime Contbn. to Pvt. Sector Rehab. award 1989), Rehab. Pres.' Coun. (founder), Calif. Workers Compensation Inst. (chair rehab. com. 1995), Ins. Rehab. Study Group (sec. 1995). Democrat. Episcopalian. Office: Calif Workers' CompensationInst 120 Montgomery St Ste 1300 San Francisco CA 94104

CRANEFIELD, PAUL FREDERIC, physiology educator, physician, scientist; b. Madison, Wis., Apr. 28, 1925; s. Paul Frederic and Edna (Rothnick) C. Ph.B., U. Wis., 1946, Ph.D., 1951; M.D., Albert Einstein Coll. Medicine, 1964. Fellow biophysics Johns Hopkins U., 1951-53; from instr. to assoc. prof. physiology State U. N.Y. Downstate Med. Center, N.Y.C., 1953-62; research fellow psychiatry Albert Einstein Coll. Medicine, 1960-64; exec. sec. com. publs. and med. information, editor bull. N.Y. Acad. Medicine, 1963-66; adj. assoc. prof. pharmacology Columbia Coll. Physicians and Surgeons, 1964-75, adj. prof., 1975—; assoc. prof. Rockefeller U., 1966-75, prof., 1975—. Author: (with Hoffman) The Electrophysiology of the Heart, 1960, Paired Pulse Stimulation of the Heart, 1968, (with C. McC. Brooks) The Historical Development of Physiological Thought, 1959, The Way In and the Way Out, 1974, The Conduction of the Cardiac Impulse, 1975, Claude Bernard's Revised Edition of his Introduction à L'Étude de la Médicine Expérimentale, 1976, (with Aronson) Cardiac Arrhythmias, The Role of Triggered Activity and Other Mechanisms, 1988, Science and Empire: East Coast Fever in Rhodesia and the Transvaal, 1991, Born Wanderer: The Life of Stanley Portal Hyatt, 1995; also numerous articles; editor: Two Great Scientists of the Nineteenth Century, 1982, Jour. Gen. Physiology, 1966-96; mem. editorial bd.: Circulation Research, Spl. Collections, Jour. of Electrocardiology; cons. editor: Internat. Microform Jour. Legal Medicine, 1969-77. Chmn. bd. dirs. LaMama Exptl. Theatre Club, 1965-69; chmn. bd. dirs. Circle Repertory Co., 1970-76, The Working Theatre; trustee Milton Helpern Library Legal Medicine. Recipient Einthoven medal U. Leiden, 1983, Disting. Scientist award N.Am. Soc. Pacing and Electrophysiology, 1994. Fellow N.Y. Acad. Medicine (medal 1988), Internat. Acad. History of Medicine; mem. Am. Physiol. Soc., Biophys. Soc., Am. Assn. History Medicine, Bibliog. Soc., Episcopal Actors Guild (mem. coun. 1990-92), Century Club, Players Club, Nat. Arts Club, Grolier Club, Coffee House Club, Cosmos Club (Washington), Savile Club (London). Home: 310 E 9th St New York NY 10003-7901 Office: Rockefeller U 1230 York Ave New York NY 10021-6307

CRANE-TREISTER, PAMELA HEIDI, nurse; b. Bklyn., May 6, 1963; d. Barry and Saundra (Schwartz) C. BSN cum laude, Hunter Coll., 1985, MSN, 1989. RN; cert. in med./surg. nursing. Nurse Roosevelt Hosp., N.Y.C., 1985; nurse neurosurgery ICU, emergency trauma ctr. Bellevue Hosp., N.Y.C., 1986-89; clin. nurse specialist Beth Israel Med. Ctr., N.Y.C., 1989; instr. med., surg. nursing, bone marrow transplant Cabrini Med. Ctr., N.Y.C., 1989-93; adj. clin. instr. CUNY, 1994—; adj. lectr. Hunter Coll. CUNY, 1989-92, EMT, 1984-94. N.Y. Nurses Regents scholar, Jeanettte L. Arons scholar. Mem. ANA, N.Y. State Nurses Assn., Am. Assn. for Spinal Cord Injury Nurses, Sigma Theta Tau.

CRANFORD, CLIFFORD A., surgeon. MD, Emory U., 1979; postgrad. in endoscopy GI, U. Dundee, Scotland, 1985. Diplomate Am. Bd. Surgery. Mem. Am. Bd. Surgery, ASGE, SAGES.

CRANIN, ABRAHAM NORMAN, oral and maxillofacial surgeon, researcher; b. Bklyn., June 17, 1927; s. Samuel Leonard and Henrietta C.; m. Marilyn Sunners, June 14, 1953; children: Jonathan, Andrew, Elizabeth. A.B., Swarthmore Coll., 1947; D.D.S., NYU, 1951; cert., Mt. Sinai Hosp., 1952, 53; DEng. (hon.) Rose-Hulman Inst. Tech., 1987. Assoc. attending oral surgeon Mt. Sinai Hosp., N.Y.C., 1961—; practice dentistry specializing in oral and maxillofacial surgery and implantology; chief oral surgery Greenpoint Hosp., Bklyn., 1961-63; attending oral surgeon Cmty. Hosp., Bklyn., 1962-72; assoc. clin. prof. Mt. Sinai Sch. Medicine, N.Y.C., 1974—; adj. prof. oral & maxillofacial surgery & hosp. dentistry Sch. Dental Medicine U. Pa., 1993—; clin. prof. oral and maxillofacial surgery NYU, 1975—, mem. carr com., 1994—; dir., chmn. dental and oral surgery Brookdale U. Hosp. & Med. Ctr., Bklyn., 1965—, mem. med. exec. bd.; chmn. oral surgery Linroc S.N.F., Bklyn, 1995; cons. Nat. Patent Devel. Corp., N.Y.C., 1964-70, N.J. State Bd. Dental Examiners, 1989; pres. Internat. Congress Implantology and Biomaterials in Stomatology, 1988—; chmn. study sect. NIH Oral Biology and Medicine, 1982—, mem. study sect. Clin. Scis. Rev. Group Div. Research Group; clin. prof. oral and maxillofacial surgery N.J. Dental Sch., 1987—, dir. dental implant ctr., 1987-91; cons. oral surgeon Bklyn. Devel. Ctr., 1973—, U.S. Surg. Corp., 1987-90, USPHS Gen Practice Residencies, 1995—. Author 5 books, including Atlas of Oral Implantology, 1992; editor-in-chief: Jour. Oral Implantology Quar, 1973 (Gold Key 1974), 1987—. Jour. Biomed. Materials Research, 1978-88 (cert. 1981, award Am. Assn. Pubs.); editor Brookdale Prof. Newsletter, 1992—; contbr. 121 articles to profl. jours., chpts. to textbooks. Pres. Informed Citizens Com. Hewlett Bay Park, N.Y., 1976. Ensign USN, 1950-51. Recipient medal/plaque Univ. Mojes das Cruzes, Brazil, 1980, award of honor Met. Conf. Hosp. Dentists, 1982, cert. of honor Brit. Dental Implant Soc., 1989, Medal of Paris Mayor Jacques Chirac, 1989, medal Alpha Implant Group, 1989, Pierre Fauchard Acad., 1990, Pierre Fauchard medal, 1993; named Man of Yr. Fedn. of Jewish Philanthropies, Bklyn., 1973, Adm. Gt. Navy of Nebr., 1978, Tchr. of Yr. Internat. Coll. Oral Implantology, 1986, NYU, 1984, Outstanding Implantologist of Yr. Internat. Assn. Dental Rsch., 1990; AAID award Comm. 1st formal Implant Tng. Program, Pioneer's medal Implant Hall of Fame AAIP; honoree United Jewish Appeal, Brookdale Hosp., 1980; grantee USPHS, 1993-95; v.p. Am. Assn. Hosp. Dentists. Am. Assn. Dental Schs.; founder, dir. Brookdale Implant Maxicourse, 1988. Fellow Internat. Coll. Oral Implantology, Am. Acad. Implant Dentistry (founder, pres. 1972), Internat. Coll. Dentists, Am. Dental Soc. Anesthesiology, Royal Soc. Health, Internat. Coll. Dentistry, Brazilian Soc. Oral and Maxillofacial Surgery (hon., Rene Lefort medal 1980), Acad. Dental Materials, Soc. for Biomaterials (bd. dirs. San Antonio chpt. 1973—, pres. 1988-89, Clemson award 1976), Japanese Soc. for Biomaterials, Am. Coll. Dentists; mem. Am. Bd. Oral Implantology (founder, diplomate), Japanese Soc. Implant Dentistry (hon.; medal and plaque 1980), Argentina Soc. Implantology (hon.), Israeli Soc. Implantology Soc., Woodmere Bay Club (Bay Park, N.Y.), Woodmere (N.Y.) Club. Office: Brookdale Hosp Med Ctr One Brookdale Plz Brooklyn NY 11212

CRANNY, ANNE, nurse; b. Darby, Pa., July 29, 1953; d. James P. and Gertrude (Gill) Gallagher; m. May 13, 1978; children: Julia Anne, Colleen. AD, Del. County Community Coll., 1973. RN; cert. emergency nurse, basic life support, advanced cardiac life support. Supr., staff nurse emergency room South Chester County Med. Ctr., West Grove, Pa.; staff nurse emergency room Paoli (Pa.) Meml. Hosp., staff nurse oper. rm. Home: 2509 Mansfield Ave Drexel Hill PA 19026-1016

CRANSTON, ROBERT EARL, neurologist; b. West Palm Beach, Fla., June 21, 1955; s. Robert Jerrell and Carolyn Lucille (Shaw) C.; m. Barbara Jean Finger, June 11, 1977; children: Daniel, Sarah, Joanna. BA, Greenville Coll., 1977; MD, U. Ill., 1982. Diplomate Am. Bd. Psychiatry & Neurology. Intern Valley Med. Ctr., Fresno, Calif., 1982-83; staff physician L.B.J. Tropical Med. Ctr., Pago Pago, American Samoa, 1983-85, Jay (Okla.) Meml. Hosp., 1985-87; resident U. Ariz., Tucson, 1987-90; staff neurologist Carle Clinic, Urbana, Ill., 1991—. Active layman Mattis Ave. Free Meth. Ch., Champaign, 1991-96. Epilepsy fellow U. Minn., Mpls., 1990-91. Mem. AMA, Am. Epilepsy Soc. (recognition award 1993), Am. Acad. Neurology, Ill. State Med. Soc., Champaign County Med. Soc. (exec. com. 1991-96). Republican. Office: Carle Clinic Divsn Neurosci 602 W University Ave Urbana IL 61801

CRANTZ, FRANK RICHARD, endocrinologist; b. Detroit, June 25, 1948; s. Theodore and Jewel (Usiak) C.; m. Joanne Gittleson, May 23, 1982; children: Julia, Emily. BA, U. Mich., 1969; MA, Cambridge U., England, 1971; MD, Johns Hopkins U., 1975. Diplomate Am. Bd. Internal Medicine, sub-bd. Endocrinology and Metabolism. Intern The N.Y. Hosp., 1975-76, asst. physician, 1976-78; fellow in medicine Harvard Med. Sch., Boston, 1978-81; clin. asst. prof. Medicine Georgetown U., Washington, 1983-87, clin. assoc. prof. Medicine, 1987—; assoc. dir. Diabetic Treatment Ctr. Georgetown U. Hosp., Washington, 1985-90; dir. Diabetic Treatment Ctr., Reston (Va.) Hosp., 1990-91. Pres. Washington Affiliate Am. Diabetes Assn., 1988-89. Named Power Scholar, Cambridge U., 1969-71, Goldberger Fellow, AMA, 1973. Fellow Am. Coll. Endocrinology, ACP; mem. AMA, The Endocrine Soc., Am. Thyroid Assn., Am. Assn. Clin. Endocrinologists. Office: Endocrine Assocs 6888 Elm St Mc Lean VA 22101-3829

CRAPO, LAWRENCE MARTIN, physician; b. Portland, Oreg., Sept. 12, 1938; s. Philip Madison and Audrey Vivienne (Petterson) C.; children: Larisa, Bryan, Kevin, Alexandra. BS, U. Calif., Berkeley, 1960; PhD, Harvard U., 1964; MD, Stanford U., 1973. Cert. Bd. Internal Medicine, Bd. Endocrinology and Metabolism. Asst. prof. medicine Stanford (Calif.) U., 1978-84, assoc. prof., 1984—. Author: Vitality and Aging, 1981, Hormones: The Messengers of Life, 1985. Mem. ACP, Am. Fedn. Clin. Research, Endocrine Soc. Home: 528 Kendall Ave #11 Palo Alto CA 94306 Office: Santa Clara Valley Med Ctr 751 S Bascom Ave San Jose CA 95128-2604

CRAPOTTA, JOSEPH ANTHONY, ophthalmologist; b. Queens, N.Y., May 20, 1959. BSChE, Columbia U., 1981; MD, N.Y. Med. Coll., 1985. Intern Winthrop U. Hosp., Mineola, N.Y., 1985-86; resident in ophthalmology Cath. Med. Ctr., Queens, 1986-89; fellow in vitreoretinal surgery U. Calif., San Diego, 1989-91; asst. prof. ophthalmology St. Louis U., 1991-93; pvt. practice Howard Beach, N.Y., 1993—. Author: Ophthalmology Clinics of North America, 1992; contbr. articles to profl. jours. Mem. AMA, Am. Acad. Ophthalmology.

CRATE, STEPHEN CHURCH, vocational rehabilitation specialist, consultant, author, politician; b. Doylestown, Pa., Aug. 2, 1952; s. Douglas Willits and Sally (Alexander-Church) C.; m. Allison Catherine Ferris, Aug. 23, 1975; children: Matthew Stephen, Daniel Church. Assoc., U. Me., Augusta, 1977; BA, U. Me., Farmington, 1980; postgrad., Northeastern U., 1981, Thomas Coll., 1991. Fellow Am. Bd. Vocat. Experts; cert. rehab. counselor, vocat. evaluation specialist, case mgr. Counselor Halcyon House Emergency Shelter, Hinckley, Me., 1978-80; activities dir. Hinckley Home Sch. Farm, 1980-82; employment, tng. specialist Me. Dept. Labor, Skowhegan, 1982-83; vocat. evaluator Waterville (Me.) Sch. Dept., 1983-85; chief exec. officer Employee Devel. Corp. of New England, Waterville, 1986—; rehab. cons. N.E. Occupational Cons., Waterville, 1984-86. Co-author: I Lost My Job, Now What Do I Do?, 1990; syndicated columnist The Changing Workplace, Allied Feature Syndicate. Elected Waterville City Counselor, 1994-95, elect4ed chair of coun., 1995—; past v.p. Opera House Assn. Mem. Nat. Rehab. Assn. (pres. pvt. sector div. 1994—), Rehab. Profls. Maine, Better Bus. Bur. (consumer div.), Rotary Internat. Office: Employee Devel Corp New Eng PO Box 256 Waterville ME 04903-0256

CRAVEN, DONALD EDWARD, epidemiologist researcher; b. Omaha, Jan. 13, 1944; s. Orvin William and Florence (Waite) C.; m. Margaret McClave, July 21, 1966 (div. 1971); m. Dianne Munson, Sept. 10, 1983 (div. 1994); children: Natalie, Hillary; m. Kathleen Walsh Steger, Apr. 1, 1995; children: David, Jenny, Kristina. BA, Wesleyan U., 1966; MD, Union Coll., 1970. Rsch. assoc. NIH Bur. Biologics, Bethesda, Md., 1976-79; hosp. epidemiologist Boston City Hosp., 1979-87, dir., AIDS Pub. Health, 1987-89, dir., AIDS program, 1989—; asst. prof. Boston U. Sch. Medicine and Pub. Health, 1979-84; assoc. prof. Boston U. Sch. Medicine, 1984-89, prof. medicine, microbiology, epidemiology and biostatics, 1989—; mem. adv. bd. AIDS Action Com., 1988—, mem. hosp. infection control practices adv. com., 1991-95, Ctrs. for Disease Control, 1991, Best Drs. Am., 1992, 94. Contbr. 110 articles on hosp. epidemiology and AIDS to med. jours. Sr. surgeon USPHS, 1976-79. Recipient Gov. Recognition award for AIDS Rsch., 1987. Fellow ACP, Royal Coll. Physicians, Infectious Disease Soc.; mem. Soc. Health Care Epidemiologists (pres. 1993), Mass. Hosp. Assn. (mem. adv. bd. for AIDs 1988-93). Home: 20 Clifford St Wellesley MA 02181-6041 Office: Boston City Hosp 818 Harrison Ave Boston MA 02118-2905

CRAVEN, LINDA NELL COOK, psychotherapist; b. Shamrock, Tex., Nov. 16, 1943; d. Worthy R. and Virgie N. (Gaither) Cook; m. Jerry A. Craven, Oct. 3, 1974; children: Chris Cain, Schelle Stewart, Lauri Watanabe, David. BA, West Tex. State U., 1974, MA, 1979, MEd, 1986. Lic. prof. counselor, marriage and family therapist, Tex. Counselor Amarillo (Tex.) Drug Abuse Program, 1974-75; instr. Tex. State Tech. Inst., Amarillo, 1975-76; teaching asst. West Tex. State Univ., Canyon, Tex., 1977-78; freelance writer Canyon, 1980-82; pubs. specialist West Tex. State Univ., Canyon, 1983-85; counselor/psychotherapist Profl. Social Work Assn., Amarillo, 1986-87; instr. Inst. Tech. MARA, Shah Alam, Malaysia, 1987-88, Tex. Tech. Med. Sch., Amarillo, 1988-89; adminstr., clin. mgr., dept. behavioral scis. Bivins Ctr. for Phys. Medicine and Rehab., Amarillo, 1989-92; psychotherapist, Amarillo, 1992—. Author: (book) Stepfamilies, 1982 (award non-fiction book Tex. Press Women 1983), Jaguar: King of Cats, 1991, Rolls Royce: Leader in Luxury, 1991; contbr. numerous articles to profl. jours. Mediator, bd. dirs. Dispute Resolution Ctr., Amarillo, 1989-92; bd. dirs. Amarillo Womens Network, 1987-89; bd. dirs., newsletter editor Stepfamily Assn. Am., Palo Alto, Calif., 1983-86. Mem. Am. Counseling Assn., Tex. Counseling Assn., Internat. Assn. Marriage and Family Therapists. Democrat. Unitarian Universalist. Office: The Atrium 6900 W Interstate 40 Ste 100 Amarillo TX 79106-2525

CRAWFORD, E. MAC, health facilities executive; b. 1949. Grad., Auburn U., 1971. With Salem Nat. Corp., 1977-78, Arthur Young & Co., 1971-77, 78-81, GTI Ltd., 1981-85, 86, Oxylance Corp., 1985-86, Mulberry St. Investment Co., 1986-90; exec. v.p. hosp. ops. Charter Med. Corp., Atlanta, 1990-92, pres., COO, 1992—. Office: Charter Med Corp 3414 Peachtree Rd Ste 1400 Atlanta GA 30326

CRAWFORD, FRED ALLEN, JR., cardiothoracic surgeon, educator; b. Columbia, S.C., Oct. 17, 1942; s. Fred Allen and Susan Valery Floyd C.; m. Mary Jane Dantzler, June 11, 1966; children: Fred Allen, III, Mary Elizabeth. MD, Duke U., 1967. Diplomate Am. Bd. Surgery, Am. Bd. Thoracic Surgery (bd. dirs.). Intern, Duke U. Med. Ctr., Durham, N.C., 1967-68, resident in surgery, 1971-76, instr. surgery, 1975-76; asst. prof. surgery, chief div. cardiac surgery U. Miss., Med. Ctr., Jackson, 1976-79; prof. surgery pediatrics, chief div. cardiothoracic surgery Med. U. of S.C., Charleston, 1979—, chmn. dept. surgery, 1988—. Maj. U.S. Army, 1969-71. Decorated Bronze Star. Mem. ACS, Am. Surg. Assn., Charleston County Med. Soc., S.C. State Med. Assn., Soc. Thoracic Surgeons, So. Surg. Assn., So. Thoracic Surg. Assn., Am. Heart Assn., Am. Assn. Thoracic Surgery, Am. Coll. Cardiology, Phi Beta Kappa, Alpha Omega Alpha. Presbyterian. Club: Ducks Unltd. Contbr. numerous articles to profl. jours. Office: 171 Ashley Ave Charleston SC 29403

CRAWFORD, GEORGE EVERETT, internist, geriatrician, military officer; b. Tucson, Nov. 14, 1946; s. Charles Edward and Elizabeth (Winkler) C.; m. Sharon Rajala, May 12, 1972; children: Laurel, Jennifer. BS, U. Notre Dame, 1968; MD, Northwestern U., 1972. Diplomate Am. Bd. Internal Medicine, Am. Bd. Infectious Diseases, Am. Bd. Geriatric Medicine. Resident internal medicine Mass. Gen. Hosp., Boston, 1972-74; commd. capt. USAF, 1972, advanced through grades to col., 1986; flight surgeon USAF, Patrick AFB, Fla., 1974-76; fellow infectious diseases U. Wash., Seattle, 1976-78; staff infectious disease Wilford Hall Med. Ctr., Lackland AFB, Tex., 1978-80; cons. AF Surgeon Gen., Bolling AFB Washington, DC, 1980-83; chmn. dept. medicine Malcolm Grew Med. Ctr., Andrews AFB, Md., 1983-85, David Grant Med. Ctr., Travis AFB, Calif., 1988-93; chief divsn. medicine, internal medicine program dir. Wilford Hall Med. Ctr., Lackland AFB, 1993—. Contbr. articles to profl. and mil. jours. Fellow ACP; mem. Soc. Air Force Physicians (bd. govs., pres. 1991-93), Infectious Disease Soc. N.Am., Armed Forces Infectious Disease Soc. (pres. 1995-96). Home: 311 Bluffcrest San Antonio TX 78216 Office: Wilford Hall Med Ctr Divsn Medicine Lackland A F B TX 78236

CRAWFORD, JEAN ANDRE, clinical therapist; b. Chgo., Apr. 12, 1941; d. William Moses and Geneva Mae (Lacy) Jones; student Shimer Coll., 1959-60; BA, Carthage Coll., 1966; MEd, Loyola U., Chgo., 1971; postgrad. Nat. Coll. Edn., Evanston, Ill., 1971-77, Northwestern U., 1976-83; m. John N. Crawford, Jr., June 28, 1969; lic. profl. counselor; cert. sch. counselor Nat. Bd. Cert. Counselors, elem. edn., spl. edn. and pupil personnel services, Ill. Med. technologist, Chgo., 1960-62; primary and spl. edn. tchr. Chgo. Pub. Schs., 1966-71, counselor maladjusted children and their families, 1971-88; counselor juvenile first-offenders, 1968-88, post-secondary vocat. counselor, 1988-93; tchr., transition coord. Cook County Dept. Corrections Alternative High Sch., Chgo., 1993-94; clin. therapist St. Mary of Nazareth Hosp. Ctr., Chgo., 1994—. Vol. Sta. WTTW-TV; vol. counselor deaf children and their families; counselor post-secondary students; vol., mem. community devel. bd. New City YMCA, 1987-92. Mem. scholarship com. Chgo. Urban League. Mem. AACD, Ill. Assn. Counseling and Devel., Am. Sch. Counselors Assn., Ill. Sch. Counselors Assn., Ill. Vocat. Counselors Assn., Am. Mental Health Counselor Assn., Ill. Mental Health Counselor Assn., IIll. Assn. Advancement Black Ams. in Vocat. Edn., Coun. Exceptional Children, Coordinating Coun. Handicapped Children, Shimer Coll. Alumni Assn. (sec. 1982-84), Phi Delta Kappa. Home: # 1200 601 E 32nd St Chicago IL 60616-4054 Office: 2233 W Division St Chicago IL 60622-3043

CRAWFORD, JOHN LITTLEFIELD, III, ophthalmologist; b. McAllen, Tex., Nov. 18, 1943; s. John Littlefield and Dorothy (Rose) Crawford; m. Donna Taylor, June 12, 1971; children: Caroline Taylor, Robert Littlefield. BS, Davidson Coll., 1966; MD, Bowman Gray Sch. Medicine, 1974. Diplomate Am. Bd. Ophthalmology, Am. Bd. Eye Surgery. Intern Brooke Army Med. Ctr., Fort Sam Houston, Tex., 1974-75; resident N.C. Bapt. Hosp., Bowman Gray Sch. of Medicine, Winston-Salem, 1975-78, chief resident, 1977-78; pvt. practice, Hendersonville, N.C., 1978—. Capt. U.S. Army, 1966-69, 74-75. Fellow Am. Acad. Ophthalmology, Am. Coll. Surgeons; mem. Lions. Presbyterian. Office: Carolina Ophthalmology PA 1701 Old Village Rd Hendersonville NC 28791

CRAWFORD, MALLORY, counselor; b. Sweetwater, Tex., Jan. 4, 1942; d. Leslie Charles and Marjorie Eliose (Crawford) Edie; children: Alma Willow Whitten, Amedeo Michael Cacciutto. BA, Barnard Coll., 1964; MA, Beacon Coll., 1981. Co-dir. Crisis Ctr. Touch, alcohol counselor Tri-County Alcohol Coun., Middletown, Conn.; dir. social svcs. Town of Portland, Conn.; counselor, group leader YWCA, Hartford, Conn.; pvt. practice psychotherapy Hartford; speaker at profl. confs.; ambassador to China Citizen Ambassador Program. Mem. Out Town/Our Planet; adv. bd. Hartford area Birthright, La Leche League; past pres. Hartford Gay and Lesbian Health Collective. Grantee Conn. Humanities Coun. Mem. ASGPP, Gestalt Therapists Assn., Capitol Region Conf. Chs. (chair sexual minorities com.), Hartford Women's Ctr., Mensa.

CRAWFORD, SALLY SUE, nursing educator; b. LaGrange, Ga., Nov. 17, 1944; children from previous marriage: Patricia Anne, Elizabeth Sue, James Burton Jr. AA, DeKalb Coll. Nursing, 1973; BA, Ga. State U., Atlanta, 1971, MEd, 1978; EDS, U. Ga., 1987; BSN, Clayton State Coll., 1994. RN. Sr. health educator Ga. Dept. Human Resources, Lawrenceville, 1975-88; asst. dir. staff devel. ARC, Atlanta, 1988; with Atlanta Eye Screening, 1988-89; outreach coord. Cataract Inst., Atlanta, 1989-90; tng. coord. S.E. Regional Ctr. For Drug-Free Schs. & Communities, 1990; tng. planner Atlanta Community Prevention Coalition, 1991-92; sole propr. Health Lifestyles, 1992-95; nursing instr. Griffin Tech. Sch., 1992-93; sr. nurse Clayton Ctr., Jonesboro, Ga., 1993-95; adminstrv. supr. Peachtree Regional Hosp., 1994—; clin. nursing instr. Gordon Coll. Nursing Students, 1995—; supr. Healthways, Morrow, Ga., 1995; health svcs. adminstr. Correctional Healthcare Solutions, 1996—; chmn. bd. dirs. Canine Vision, Inc. Author: 6 manuals; contbr. articles to profl. jours. Mem. NAFE, ASTD, AAPHERD, UDC (state chmn. 1988-90, nat. chmn. of pages 1989), Ga. Fedn. Profl. Health Educators, Internat. Platform Assn., Daus. of 1812 (local officer 1989—, state officer 1992-94), Continental Soc., Daus. of Indian Wars (nat. officer, state officer 1990-94), DAR (organizing regent chpt. 1982-84, nat. spkrs. staff 1986-89), Daus. Am. Colonists (chpt. regent 1988-91, state officer 1991—), Colonial Dames of XVII Century (local registrar), Ga. Soc. Magna Charta Dames (state officer 1986—), First Families of Ga., Lions (1st female mem. Atlanta club, chmn. sight and vision 1989-90, officer 1990-91), Sigma Theta Tau. Episcopalian. Home: 2305 Luther Bailey Rd Senoia GA 30276-9218 Office: Griffin RYDC 105 Justice Blvd Griffin GA 30223

CRAWFORD, SUSAN, library director, educator; b. Vancouver, B.C., Can.; d. James Y. and S. Young; m. James Weldon Crawford, July 5, 1955; 1 son, Robert James. B.A., U. B.C., 1948; M.A., U. Toronto, 1950, U. Chgo., 1954; Ph.D., U. Chgo., 1970. With bur. library and indexing service ADA, 1954-56; with office exec. v.p. AMA, Chgo., 1956-60; dir. div. library and archival services AMA, 1960-81; asso. prof. Sch. Library Sci., Columbia U., N.Y.C., 1972-75; prof., dir. Sch. Medicine Library and Biomed. Communications Ctr. Washington U., 1981-92; adj. prof. U. Ill., Chgo., 1994—. Author over 160 books and sci. papers; mem. editl. bd. Med. Socioecon. Rsch. Sources, Index to Sci. Revs., Jour. Am. Soc. Info. Sci., Med. Libr. Assn. News, Health Libr. Rev. (London), Health and Info. Librs. (Budapest); assoc. editor Jour. Am. Soc. Info. Sci., 1979-82; editor Med. Info. Systems, 1988-90; editor-in-chief Bull. of Med. Libr. Assn., 1982-88, 91-92. Bd. regents Nat. Library Medicine, NIH, 1971-75; mem. bd. overseers for univ. libraries Tufts U., 1988-89. Janet Doe hon. lectr., 1983; recipient Disting. Alumni award U. Toronto, 1987, Grad. medal U. Toronto, 1989. Fellow AAAS, Med. Libr. Assn. (life, Eliot award 1976, chmn. com. on surveys and stats. 1966-75, publs. panel 1977-80, chmn. consulting editors panel 1981-88, 91-92, spl. award to editor of bull. 1988, Noyes award 1992, pres.'s award 1992); mem. ALA, Soc. Social Studies of Sci., Assn., Acad. Health Scis. Libr. Dirs., Am. Soc. Info. Sci. (chmn. med. info. sys. 1987-88, outstanding specialty group award 1988, 89, bd. and program chair Chgo. chpt. 1984-95), Am. Med. Informatics Assn., Acad. Health Info. Profls.

(disting. mem.), Sigma Xi (chmn. coms.).. Home: 2418 Lincoln St Evanston IL 60201-2151

CRAWLEY, JOHN CROMANTIE, physician assistant; b. Fayetteville, N.C., Dec. 10, 1953; s. Lewis Marvin Sr. and Urbanna (Cromantie) C.; m. Martha Irene Burns, July 22, 1978; children: Laura Elizabeth, Jonathan Burns. BA in Biology, U. N.C., Wilmington, 1976; MS in Pub. Health, U. N.C., 1977; Cert. Physician Asst., MUSC, 1981. Physician asst. Chadbourn (N.C.) Med., 1981-84, FCF Butner (N.C.), 1984-85, Carolina Neurosci., Fayetteville, 1985-90, VAMC, Fayetteville, 1990-92, Raeford (N.C.) Hoke Family Care, 1992-95, St. Pauls (N.C.) Med. Ctr., 1995—. Deacon Cedar Falls Bapt. Ch., Fayetteville, 1994—. Mem. Am. Assn. Physician Assts., N.C. Assn. Physician Assts., N.C. Med. Soc. Republican. Home: 1803 Kelly St Fayetteville NC 28305 Office: St Pauls Med Ctr 128 E Broad St Saint Pauls NC 28384

CRAWSHAW, RALPH, psychiatrist; b. N.Y.C., July 3, 1921. A.B., Middlebury (Vt.) Coll., 1943; M.D., N.Y. U., 1947. Diplomate: Nat. Bd. Med. Examiners, Am. Bd. Psychiatry and Neurology. Intern Lenox Hill Hosp., N.Y.C., 1947-48; resident Menninger Sch. Psychiatry, Topeka, 1948-50, Oreg. State Hosp., Salem, 1950-51; practice medicine specializing in psychiatry Washington, 1954; staff psychiatrist C.F. Menninger Meml. Hosp., Topeka, 1954-57; asst. chief VA Mental Hygiene Clinic, Topeka, 1957-60; staff psychiatrist Community Child Guidance Clinic, Portland, Oreg., 1960-63; founder, clinic dir. Tualatin Valley Guidance Clinic, Beaverton, Oreg., 1961-67; pvt. practice medicine, specializing in psychiatry Portland, 1960—; mem. staff Holladay Park Hosp., 1961—; lectr. dept. child psychiatry Med. Sch. U. Oreg., 1961-63, clin. prof. dept. psychiatry, 1976; lectr. Sch. Social Work, Portland State U., 1964-67; founder Benjamin Rush Found., 1968, pres., 1968—; founder Friends of Medicine, 1969, Ct. of Man, 1970, Club of Kos, 1974, Oreg. Health Decisions, 1983, Am. Health Decisions, 1989, Health Vol. Overseas, 1984; Sonian Machanic vis. prof. South African Coll. Medicine, 1993. Contbr. editor: AMA Jour. of Socio-Econs, 1972-75; Columnist: Prism mag, 1972-76, The Pharos, 1972—, Portland Physician, 1975, Western Jour. Medicine, 1980—; Contbr. articles to med. jours. Cons. Bur. Hearings and Appeals, HEW, 1964-90; cons. Albina Child Devel. Center, Portland, 1965-75, HEW Region 8 Health Planning, 1979; mem. Inst. Medicine, Nat. Acad. Sci., 1978, Oreg. Health Coordinating Council, 1979; Mem. Gov.'s Adv. Com. on Mental Health, 1966-72; ad hoc com. Nat. Leadership Conf. on Am. Health Policy, 1976, Gov.'s Adv. Com. on Med. Care to Indigent, 1976—; trustee Millicent Found., 1964-67, Multnomah Found. for Med. Care, 1977; vis. scholar Center for Study Democratic Instns., 1969, Jack Murdock Charitable Trust, 1977, U.S.-USSR exchange scholar, 1973. Served with AUS, 1943-46; to lt., M.C. USN, 1951-54. Named Oreg. Dr./Citizen of Yr., 1978; U.S.-USSR rsch. scholar, 1973, 79; recipient I.N. Piragou medal for humanitarian Svcs., Russian Govt., 1992; Ralph Crawshaw Ann. Lectr. in Civic Medicine named in honor by Oreg. Found. for Med. Excellence, 1987. Fellow Am. Psychiat. Assn.; mem. AMA, APA, AAAS, Nat. Med. Assn., Oreg. Med. Assn. (trustee 1972—), Multnomah County Med. Soc. (pres. 1975), Royal Soc. Medicine, Inst. of Medicine of NAS, North Pacific Soc. Neurology and Psychiatry, Soc. for Psychol. Study Social Issues, Western European Assn. Aviation Psychology, Am. Med. Writers Assn., Portland Psychiatrists in Pvt. Practice (pres. 1971), Russian Acad. Natural Scis. (fgn. mem.), Alpha Omega. Address: 2525 NW Lovejoy St Ste 404 Portland OR 97210-2865

CRAYTON, BILLY GENE, physician; b. Holden, Mo., May 15, 1931; s. John Reuben and Carrie Zona (Head) C.; student Central Mo. State Coll., 1948-49; BS, Stetson U., 1958; postgrad. U. Kansas City, summer 1955; MD, U. Mo., 1962. Intern, Mound Park Hosp., St. Petersburg, Fla., 1962-63; practice gen. medicine Latham Hosp., California, Mo., 1963-64, Kelling Clinic and Hosp., Waverly, Mo., 1964-88, vice chief of staff, 1980-88; preceptor in community health and med. practice U. Mo. Sch. Medicine, Waverly, 1968-88; sec., dir. Kelling Hosp., Inc., 1969-80; pres. Kelling Clinic, 1971-88; med. dir. Waverly Ambulance Co., 1985-86; pres. Riverview Heights, 1972-88. Adviser, Mo. chpt. Am. Assn. Med. Assts., 1973-79. Adviser, Explorer Post Boy Scouts Am., 1968-70. Served with AUS, 1952-54. Fellow Am. Acad. Family Physicians. Baptist. Home: 1231 W 69th Ter Kansas City MO 64113-2054

CREANZA, NICHOLAS ERNEST, pharmacist; b. Springfield, Mass., Apr. 24, 1948; s. Peter and Pauline Marie Creanza; m. Paula V. D'Angelo, June 11, 1976; children: Peter J., Angela M. BS, Hampden Coll. Pharmacy, 1974; MBA, Western New Eng. Coll., 1979. Mem. staff Springfield Mcpl. Hosp., 1972-85, aide to hosp. dir. with pharm. duties, 1974-79, asst. hosp. dir. adminstrv. services, 1979-83, dir. tech. edn. and employment program, 1983-85; supr. spl. projects City of Springfield, 1985-87; pres., owner Campus Pharmacy & Med. Equipment, Springfield, 1987—; instr. Springfield adult edn. program, 1979-89; adj. asst. prof. pharmacy practice Mass. Coll. Pharmacy & Allied Health Sci., 1995—, trustee. Recipient award Springfield YWCA, 1980, Joseph Gagne award Mass. Coll. of Pharmacy, 1993. Mem. Mass. Pharm. Assn., Western Mass. Pharm. Assn. (pres. 1989-91), Nat. Assn. Retail Druggists, Western New Eng. Coll. Alumni Assn. (mem. exec. bd., pres. 1991), UNICO. Democrat. Lodges: Masons, Shriners, Elks. Home: 3 Wilbraview Dr Wilbraham MA 01095-2021

CREASEY, DAVID EDWARD, physician, psychiatrist, educator; b. Santa Barbara, Calif., Aug. 26, 1944; s. Edward Louis Aja and Ruth (Bryan) Creasey; m. Beverly Dewolfe, Apr. 8, 1972. BA cum laude, Tufts U., 1966, MD, 1970. Surgical intern, then OB/GYN resident Tufts-New England Med. Ctr., Boston, 1970-72; gen. med. officer Newport (R.I.) Naval Hosp., 1972-74; resident in psychiatry Boston VA Hosp., Boston, 1974-77; fellow in psychiatry Mt. Auburn Hosp., Cambridge, Mass., 1977-78; staff psychiatrist Westwood (Mass.) Lodge Hosp., 1978-79, Mass. Mental Health Ctr., Boston, 1979—; psychiat. dir. New Eng. Psychiat. Rehab. Tng. program, Cambridge, Mass., 1978—; cons. Mass. Rehab. Com. and Com. for the Blind, Boston, 1984—; adj. assoc. prof. Boston U., 1986—; assoc., pre-med. adv. North House Harvard U., 1982—; ind. med. reviewer, Metupe, 1994—. Contbr. articles to profl. jours.; reviewer Am. Jour. Psychiatry, Hosp. and Cmty. Psychiatry, Jour. Clin. Neuropsychiatry; author interactive videodisc tchg. program, 1985; med. editor Ency. Disability and Rehab. Mem. various community orgns. Lt. cmdr. USN, 1972-74. Recipient Excellence in Media award Nat. Rehab. Assn., 1996. Mem. Am. Psychiat. Assn. (physician's recognition award 1978, 82, 85, 88, 91, 94), Mass. Psychiat. Soc. Office: 8th Fl 1101 Beacon St Fl 8 Brookline MA 02146-5502

CREASIA, DONALD ANTHONY, toxicologist, researcher; b. Milford, Mass., Mar. 28, 1937; s. Dominic and Minnie (Bufalo) C.; m. Joan Labelle, June 29, 1963; children: Karen Joan, Tracey Dawn. BS in Biology, U. Vt., 1961; DSc, Harvard U., 1967; PhD, U. Tenn., 1981. Rsch. assoc. Sch. Pub. Health, Harvard U., Cambridge, Mass., 1963-69; toxicologist Oak Ridge (Tenn.) Nat. Lab., 1970-77; program dir. Frederick (Md.) Cancer Rsch. Ctr., 1977-83; rsch. chemist U.S. Army R&D, Frederick, 1983—; cons. toxicology, 1963—. Author: (chpts. in books with others) Internat. Symposium on the Biological Effects of Ozone and Related Photochemical Oxidents, 1983, Trycothecine Mycotoxicosis: Pathophysiological Effects, 1989; contbr. over 120 articles to profl. jours. NSF scholar, 1965-67; NRC fellow, 1981-83. Mem. AAAS, Soc. Toxicology, Am. Coll. Toxicology, Soc. Govt. Toxicologists, Internat. Soc. Toxicology, Sigma Xi. Home: 6187 Viewsite Dr Frederick MD 21701-6750 Office: US Army R&D Ft Detrick Frederick MD 21702

CREASIA, JOAN CATHERINE, nurse educator; b. Burlington, Vt., Aug. 14, 1941; d. Ramon J. and Marjorie E. (Rising) LaBelle; m. Donald A. Creasia, June 29, 1963; children: Karen, Tracey. BSN, U. Vt., 1964; MS in Nursing, U. Tenn., 1978; PhD, U. Md., 1987. Staff nurse psychiat. unit Mass. Mental Health Ctr., Boston, 1964-65; instr. D'Youville Sch. Nursing, Cambridge, Mass., 1965-66; staff nurse Boston Lying-In Hosp., 1966-67; staff nurse med. surg. units Norwood (Mass.) Hosp., 1967-70; staff nurse, nursing supr. Oak Ridge (Tenn.) Hosp., 1971-74; staff nurse, supr. Frederick (Md.) Meml. Hosp., 1977-78, 86-92; instr. in nursing U. Tenn., Knoxville, 1974-77; rsch. asst. U. Md., Balt., 1980-83; instr., coord., asst. prof. med. surg. nursing Frederick (Md.) C.C., 1978-80, 81-83; asst. prof., coord. RN-BSN program U. Md. Sch. Nursing, Balt., 1983-90, assoc. prof., chair RN-BSN/MS programs, 1990-94; dir. statewide programs U. Md. Sch. Nursing, 1991-94; assoc. dean for acad. programs and interim dean Med. U. of S.C. Coll. of Nursing, Charleston, 1994-95; dean, Coll. of Nursing U. Tenn., Knoxville, 1995—; cons. in field. Author: Conceptual Foundations of Professional Nursing Practice, 1991, 96 (Book of Yr. award Am. Jour. Nursing 1992); contbr. articles to profl. jours. and books. Recipient Outstanding Achievement in Indirect Nursing Rsch. award, 1987, Nat. Rsch. Svc. award, 1982, 83, Profl. Nurse Traineeship award, 1981, Outstanding Leadership award Md. Nurses Assn., 1990. Mem. ANA, NLN, Sigma Theta Tau, Phi Kappa Phi. Home: 605 Scotswood Cir Knoxville TN 37919

CREAVEN, PATRICK JOSEPH, physician, research oncologist; b. Eng., Jan. 31, 1933. MB, BS, St. Mary's Hosp. Med. Sch., U. London, 1956, PhD, 1964. House surgeon Bedford Gen. Hosp.; also house physician Barnet Gen. Hosp., Eng., 1956-57; asst. lectr. biochemistry U. London, St. Mary's Hosp. Med. Sch., 1963-64, lectr., 1964-66; chief biochemistry Tex. Rsch. Inst. Mental Sci., 1966-69; chief, oncological pharmacology Nat. Cancer Inst., VA Med. Oncology Br., 1969-75; assoc. chief, cancer rsch. clinician Roswell Park Meml. Inst., Buffalo, 1975-79, chief cancer rsch. clinician, 1979—, chief dept. clin. pharmacology and therapeutics, 1979-89, chief div. clin. pharmacology and therapeutics, Dept. Medicine, 1989-91, sr. investigator dept. investigational therapeutics, 1991—; rsch. prof. medicine Dept. Medicine, SUNY, Buffalo, 1994—. Contbr. articles to profl. jours. Fellow Am. Coll. Clin. Pharmacology, Royal Soc. Health; mem. Am. Assn. Cancer Rsch., Am. Soc. Clin. Oncology, Am. Soc. Pharmacology and Exptl. Therapeutics, Am. Soc. Clin. Pharmacology and Therapeutics. Office: Roswell Park Cancer Inst Elm And Carlton St Buffalo NY 14263-0001

CREECH, RICHARD HEARNE, oncologist; b. Boston, Apr. 6, 1940; s. Hugh J. and E. Marie (Hearne) C.; m. Charlotte E. Goetz, Dec. 28, 1963; children—Susan Marie, Nancy Elizabeth. A.B., Johns Hopkins U., 1961; M.D., U. Pa., 1965. Diplomate: Am. Bd. Internal Medicine (subspecialty in med. oncology, hematology, geriatrics). Intern, resident in medicine Hosp. of U. Pa., 1965-67; clin. assoc. lab. molecular pharmacology Nat. Cancer Inst., Bethesda, Md., 1967-70; fellow in hematology and immunology U. of Pa., 1970-71; chief med. oncology service Phila. Gen. Hosp., U. Pa. Service, 1971-72; assoc. attending physician Am. Oncologic Hosp., Fox Chase Cancer Ctr., Phila., 1972-84, Jeanes Hosp, 1984—, chmn. dept. medicine, 1992—; assoc. attending physician Holy Redeemer Hosp., 1987—; med. dir. Holy Redeemer-Nazareth-St. Mary Hospice, 1996—. Contbr. articles to profl. jours. Served with USPHS, 1967-70. Fellow ACP; mem. Am. Soc. Clin. Oncology, Am. Assn. Cancer Research, AMA, Coll. Physicians Phila. Republican. Episcopalian. Office: 7500 Central Ave Suite 203 Philadelphia PA 19111

CREELMAN, WAYNE LEWIS, psychiatrist, research director; b. Hartford, Conn., Aug. 11, 1951; s. Henry Lewis and Agnes Catherine (Zurowski) C.; m. Margaret Ann Higbie, June 11, 1977; children: Chad Lewis, Evan Randall. AB, Boston Coll., 1974; MD, Georgetown U., 1978. Diplomate Am. Bd. Psychiatry and Neurology. Intern Hartford Hosp., 1978-79; resident Inst. of Living, Hartford, 1979-82; Asst. sect. chief Inst. of Living, Harford, 1984-86; dir. research and psychopharmacology dept. psychiatry Maine Med. Ctr., Portland, 1986-91; assoc. med. dir. Jackson Brook Inst., South Portland, Maine, 1991-93; med. dir. Brylin Hosps., Buffalo, N.Y., 1993—; assoc. prof. psychiatry Sch. Medicine, U. Vt., 1986-93; clin. assoc. prof. psychiatry SUNY, Buffalo, 1996—. Contbr. psychiat. and psychopharmacology articles to profl. jours. Town councilor Cape Elizabeth, Maine, 1988-93. Mem. AMA, Am. Psychiat. Assn., Western N.Y. Psychiat. Soc., N.Y. State Med. Soc., Erie County Med. Soc. Republican. Roman Catholic. Office: Brylin Hosps 1263 Delaware Ave Buffalo NY 14216

CREGLER, LOUIS LEONARD, medical educator. MD, SUNY, Bklyn., 1975. Diplomate Am. Bd. Internal Medicine. Intern Bklyn. Jewish Med. Ctr., 1975-76; resident Mt. Sinai Med. Ctr., Bronx, N.Y., 1976-79; fellow in cardiology Mt. Sinai Med. Ctr., N.Y.C., 1979-81; asst. chief cardiology Bronx (N.Y.) VA Med. Ctr., 1981-85, asst chief medicine, 1985-91, chief med. svc., 1991-92; assoc. prof., assoc. dean Med. Coll. Ga. Sch. Medicine, Augusta, 1992-94; prof., dep. dean CUNY Med. Sch., N.Y.C., 1994—; resident Bronx VA Med. Ctr., 1976-79; asst. prof. med. Mt. Sinai Sch. Medicine, N.Y.C., 1986-89, assoc. prof. medicine, 1989-92. Bd. trustees SUNY Alumni Fund, Bklyn., 1995—. Recipient Outstanding Svc. award Internat. Soc. Hpertension, Balt., 1988. Fellow ACP, Am. Coll. Cardiology, Am. Coll. Angiology, Assn. Black Cardiologists (bd. dirs. 1991—, editor newsletter 1990—), N.Y. Acad. Medicine; mem. Am. Heart Assn. N.Y. (bd. dirs. 1989—, nat. bd. dirs. 1996—, Louis B. Russel award 1995, Louis H. Stark award N.Y. State 1987, Outstanding Svc. award N.Y. State 1991), Assn. Am. Med. Colls., SUNY Alumni Assn. (bd. mgrs. 1994—). Office: CUNY Med Sch 138th St & Convent Ave New York NY 10031

CREGO, CLYDE ALLAN, psychology educator; b. Missoula, Mo., June 6, 1936; s. Clyde Allan Crego and June (Gaskins) Soderholm; m. Carol Maxwell, Sept. 6, 1958 (div. 1978); children: Terri Jo, Allan Mason; m. Marilyn Wendland, Oct. 7, 1978. BA, U. Mont., 1958; PhD, Mich. State U., 1966. Lic. psychologist, Calif., Ariz., Va., Mo. Instr. Mich. State U., East Lansing, 1964-66; asst. prof. psychology U. N.C., Chapel Hill, 1966-67, Wash. State U., Pullman, 1967-69; cons. to mgmt. U.S. Intelligence Community, Washington, 1969-71; chief of counseling svc. U. Mo., Columbia, 1971-83; prof., dept. head Calif. State U., Long Beach, 1983—; adj. prof. U. So. Calif., L.A., 1988—; cons. numerous univs. and med. ctrs., 1971—. Author: Crisis Intervention, 1982; cons. editor Profl. Psychology, 1980—; contbr. articles to profl. jours. Recipient 2 awards City Coun., 1977, 83. Mem. Fellow Am. Psychol. Assn. (pres. div. cons. psychology 1988-89). Lutheran.

CRENSHAW, DAVID ALLEN, clinical psychologist; b. Hannibal, Mo., May 9, 1944; s. Joel Vetrece and Genevieve (Elizabeth) C.; m. Mary Kerfoot Lupton, Dec. 27, 1970; children: Stefanie Lee, Gillian Elizabeth. BA, William Jewell Coll., Liberty, Mo., 1965; PhD, Washington U., St. Louis, 1969. Staff psychologist St. Louis VA Hosps., 1969-71; clin. dir. Rhinebeck (N.Y.) Country Sch., 1972-78; pvt. practice Rhinebeck, 1977—; clin. dir. Astor Home for Children, Rhinebeck, 1978—; bd. dirs. Dutchess County Mental Hygiene Dept., Poughkeepsie, N.Y., 1979-83; cons. in field; mem. adv. bd. Hospice in Dutchess and Ulster Counties, 1995—. Author: Bereavement: Counseling the Grieving Throughout the Life Cycle, 1990; contbr. articles to profl. jours. Fellow Am. Assn. Grief Counselors; mem. Am. Psychol. Assn., N.Y. State Psychol. Assn., Hudson Valley Psychol. Assn., Assn. for Death Edn. and Counseling, N.Y. State Assn. for Play Therapy (chmn. legis. com.). Republican. Lodge: Rotary (pres. Rhinebeck chpt. 1978). Home: 181 Academy St Unit 205 Poughkeepsie NY 12601 Office: 91-93 Montgomery St Rhinebeck NY 12572

CRENSHAW, JERE WALTON, orthodontist; b. Union City, Tenn., Oct. 10, 1950; s. Walton B. and Farra Mae (Carter) C.; m. Linda Diane Pollard, Dec. 19, 1970; children: Brian Walton, Benjamin Hardy, Jeremy Carter. BS, U. Tenn., Martin, 1972; DDS, U. Tenn., Memphis, 1974, MS in Orthodontics, 1976. Pvt. practice orthodontics Union City, 1976—; instr. U. Tenn., dept orthodontics, Memphis, 1993—. Cubmaster Boy Scout Am., Union City, 1985-90, dist. leader tng. chmn. Three Rivers Dist., 1988-89. Recipient Dist. award of merit Boy Scouts Am., 1989. Mem. ADA, Tenn. Dental Assn., Am. Assn. Orthodontists, So. Assn. Orthodontists, Tenn. Assn. Orthodontists (bd. dirs. 1987-90, v.p. 1990-91, pres.-elect 1991-92, pres. 1992-93), Charles H. Tweed Internat. Found. for Orthodontic Rsch., So. Tweed Edgewise Study Club. Methodist. Home: 1319 Oaklawn St Union City TN 38261-8836 Office: 1623 E Reelfoot Ave Union City TN 38261-6031

CREPAGE, RICHARD ANTHONY, school system administrator; b. Youngstown, Ohio, May 1, 1948; s. Edward Joseph and Mary Lucille (Maskulka) C.; m. Ruth Anne Schneider Fife-Crepage, June 15, 1991; children: Lori, Teri. BA, Youngstown State U., 1970, MS in Edn., 1978. Math. tchr. East Jr. High-Warren (Ohio) City Schs., 1972-78; math. tchr. Warren G. Harding High, Warren, 1978-81, asst. prin., 1981-88; prin. Harry B. Turner Middle Sch., Warren, 1988-94; supr. pers./grants Ashtabula County Bd. Edn., Jefferson, Ohio, 1994—. treas., bd. mem. Trumbull Art Gallery, Warren, 1985—. Scholar Martha Holden Jennings Found., Cleve., 1978. Mem. ASCD, Ohio ASCD, Nat. Mid. Sch. Assn., Ohio Mid. Sch. Assn., Buckeye Assn. Sch. Admisntrs., Phi Delta Kappa. Roman Catholic. Office: Ashtabula County Bd Edn PO Box 186 Jefferson OH 44047-0186

CRESCI, MARY K., critical care nurse, educator; b. Detroit, Aug. 15, 1946; d. William B. and Mary F. (Schneider) Krug; m. Peter P. Cresci, Aug. 28, 1971; 1 child, Jonathan B. BSN, Mercy Coll., Detroit, 1968; MS, U. Md., Balt., 1975; postgrad., Wayne State U., 1988—. Cert. critical care nurse. Clin. nurse specialist St. Agnes Hosp., Balt.; instr. St. Joseph Sch. Nursing, Towson, Md.; staff devel. instr. Johns Hopkins Hosp., Balt., instr. Sch. Nursing. Mem. AACN, Soc. Applied Learning Tech., Am. Heart Assn., Sigma Theta Tau.

CRESPI, TONY D., psychologist; b. Plattsburgh, N.Y., Oct. 19, 1955; s. David Emanuel Crespi and Hope Gloria (Leeger) Pinkerton; m. Cheryl Susan Raudis, June 22, 1984. BA, U. Hartford, 1975; MA, Western State Coll., 1976; EdD, U. Mass., 1985. Lic. psychologist, Conn. Sch. counselor Wallingford (Conn.) Bd. of Edn., 1977-79; sch. psychologist Altobello Psychiat. Hosp., Conn., 1979-91; adj. asst. prof. counseling psychology program U. Conn., 1992-94; assoc. prof. psychology U. Hartford, 1995—; vis. faculty U. Mass., Amherst, summers 1985-86. Consulting editor Profl. Psychology: Rsch. and Practice, 1992, 93. Mem. APA, Nat. Assn. Sch. Psychologists (contbg. editor NASP Communique 1988—), Am. Assn. Marriage and Family Therapy (clin.). Home: 420 Swain Ave Meriden CT 06450-7220

CRESPO, LUIS DANIEL, plastic and reconstructive surgery; b. Panama, Panama, Sept. 24, 1958; s. Luis and Elsa (Perez) C.; m. Mercedes Carmen Arias, June 21, 1984; children: Luis D., Tatiana, Lucas. MD, U. Guadalajara, 1981. Bd. cert. gen. surgery, plastic surgery. Intern Harvard U., Boston, 1983-84, resident in plastic surgery, 1989-91, fellow in microsurgery, 1991; resident in gen. surgery Tufts U., Springfield, Mass., 1984-89; fellow in aesthetic surgery U. Miami, Fla., 1991; plastic surgeon Social Security Hosp., Panama, 1992, Centro Medico Paitilla, Panama, 1992, Gorgas Hosp., Balboa, Panama, 1993, Plastic Surgery Inst., Panama, 1994—; asst. prof. surgery Med. Sch. of Panama, 1992. Contbr. articles to profl. jours. Mem. Am. Soc. Plastic and Reconstructive Surgery, Am. Soc. Aesthetic Plastic Surgery, Internat. Fedn. Plastic Surgery, Panamanian Plastic Surgery Soc. Home: Limajo St, Panama City Panama Office: PO Box 55-2306, Panama City Panama

CRESS, RONALD DANEWOOD, orthopedic surgeon; b. Mexia, Tex., Dec. 29, 1927; s. Samuel Oliver and Roxie Lee (Wright) C.; m. Mary Gwendolyn Whitfield, June 4, 1950; children: Ronda Kay, Donna Berna, Samuel Edward. AS, Tarlton State U., 1950; DVM, Tex. A&M U., 1954; MD, U. Tex., 1961. Intern John Sealy Hosp., Galveston, Tex., 1961-62, orthopedic resident, 1962-66; orthopedic surgeon Orthopedic clinic of Galveston County Assn., Tex. City, 1966—. Sergeant USMC, 1947, China. Methodist. Office: Orthopedic clinic of Galv 6501 Memorial Dr Texas City TX 77591

CRESSMAN, MICHAEL DAVID, internist, researcher; b. Quakertown, Pa., July 30, 1952; s. Richard S. and Ruth L. (Swartz) C. BS, Muhlenberg Coll., Allentown, Pa., 1974; DO, Phil. Coll. Osteo. Medicine, 1978. Diplomate Am. Bd. Internal Medicine with subspeciality in nephrology. Asst. prof. medicine Thomas Jefferson U., Phila., 1985-86; asst. staff, then staff Cleve. clinic, 1986-94; assoc. prof. medicine U. Pitts. Med. Ctr., 1994—; lipid edn. faculty Bristol-Mayers Squibb, Princeton, N.J., 1990—. Contbr. articles to profl. jours. Cleve. Clin. Internat. Traveling fellow, Australia, 1983. Mem. Am. Soc. Nephrology, Am. Soc. Clin. trials, Internat. Soc. for Clin. Trials. Office: Univ of Pitts Med Ctr 623 Scaife Hall Pittsburgh PA 15213

CRESSMAN, RALPH DWIGHT, surgeon, educator; b. Oglesby, Ill., Jan. 17, 1909; s. Ralph Gates and Emily (Blackmore) C.; m. Bernice Moore Klein, Aug. 16, 1935; children—Russell R., Ann Cressman Anderson. A.B., U. Calif. at Berkeley, 1929, M.A., 1931, M.D., 1934. Intern Alameda County Hosp., Oakland, Calif., 1935; postgrad. surg. tng. U. Calif., Vanderbilt U. and San Francisco Gen. hosps., 1935-41; practice surgery Palo Alto (Calif.) Med. Clinic, 1946-78, head sect. gen. surgery, 1960-74; clin. prof. surgery Stanford Med. Sch., 1970-74, emeritus, 1974—. Author articles in field. Served with M.C. AUS, 1942-45. Mem. A.C.S. (gov. 1962- 68, sec. bd. govs. 1967-68), San Francisco Surg. Soc., Pacific Coast Surg. Assn. (sec.-treas. 1964-68, pres. 1975). Home: 360 Everett Ave Palo Alto CA 94301-1422

CRETEKOS, CONSTANTINE J. G., psychiatrist. BA in Gen. Sci., U. Rochester, 1955; MD, U. Buffalo, 1959. Diplomate Am. Bd. Psychiatry and Neurology. Intern, then resident Robert Packer Hosp., Sayre, Pa., 1959-61; resident in adult and child psychiatry N.Y. Med. Coll., N.Y.C., 1961-66; chief of psychiatry dept. Ireland Army Hosp., Ft. Knox, Ky., 1967-69; med. dir. Parent & Child Guidance Ctr., Pitts., 1969-77, staff psychiatrist, 1978--; pvt. practice specializing in adolescence psychiatry Pitts., 1969--; cons. in field; clin. asst. prof. child psychiatry U. Pitts. Med. Sch., 1970-90. Contbr. articles to profl. jours. Bd. dirs. Wesley Inst., 1976-82. Fellow Am. Psychiat. Assn., Am. Acad. of Psychoanalysis; mem. Pa. Med. Soc., Allegheny Med. Soc., Pitts. Psychiat. Soc. Office: 2644 Banksville Rd Pittsburgh PA 15216-2812

CREVELING, CYRUS ROBBINS, chemist, neuroscientist; b. Washington, May 30, 1930; s. Cyrus Robbins and Edith Lois (Hill) C.; m. Cornelia Mills Rector, Sept. 3, 1954; children: Victoria Anne Mariano, Diana Rector Mears. BS, George Washington U., 1954, MS, 1955, PhD, 1962. Chemist Naval Ordinance Lab., Washington, 1953-54; med. tech. Sibley Meml. Hosp., Washington, 1955-57; chemist Nat. Heart Inst., Bethesda, Md., 1957-62; rsch. assoc. Harvard U., Boston, 1963-64; chemist NIH, Bethesda, 1964—; prof. of pharmacology Howard U. Sch. Medicine, Washington, 1967-86; coord. technology dept. NIH, Bethesda, 1989-95; dir. office tech. devel. Nat. Inst. Diabetes and Digestive and Kidney Diseases, 1995—; prof. pharmacology and toxicology Med. Coll. Va., Richmond, 1985—; mem. divsn. rsch. grants NIH, 1966-70; lectr. in field; mem. task force on environ. cancer and heart and lung diseases, Project Group on standardization, measurements and tests, EPA, 1979-82; project adv. bd. screening food additives, FDA, 1979-83; organizer 8th Internat. Catecholamine Symposium, 1995—. Contbr. numerous articles to profl. jours., chpts. to books; editor: Transmethylation Series I, 1979, II, 1982, III, 1986; reviewer Analytical Biochemistry, Archives of Biochemistry and Biophysics, Biochem. Jour., Biochem. Pharmacology, Brain Rsch., Drug Metabolism and Disposition, Endocrinology, European Jour. Pharmacology, Life Scis., Jour.Neurosci., Jour. Neurochemistry, Jour. Molecular Pharmacology, Jour. Medicinal Chemistry, Jour. Biol. Chemistry, Jour. Am. Chem. Soc., others. Chmn. adv. bd. Montgomery Libr., Kensington, 1984-86; mem. Bethesda HELP, 1987—; mem. BB Telecasts, Channel 7, Washington, 1982-91. Fellow Am. Diabetes Found., 1955, Mass. Gen. Hosp., 1963-64; recipient Disting. Sci. award Soc. Exptl. Biology and Medicine, 1979, Pub. Health Svc. award NIH, 1991; rsch. grantee Eli Lilly, 1984, E.I. duPont de Nemours & Co., 1985. Mem. Am. Fedn. Scientists, Am. Chem. Soc., Am. Soc. Pharmacol. Exptl. Therapeutics, Soc. Exptl. Biology and Medicine (pres. 1977-78, councilor 1975—), Washington Acad. Scis. (fellow, bd. mgrs. 1979-80, chmn. biol. scis. panel 1980—, v.p. membership affairs 1991—), Fdn. Advanced Edn. in Scis. (chair scholarship com. 1989—), Catecholamine Club (pres. 1980-81), Soc. Neurosci., Gordon Conf. on Cyclic Nucleotides, Chem. Soc. Washington, Internat. Soc. Study Xenobiotics, Internat. Union Physiol. Scis., Internat. Union Pure and Applied Chemistry (affiliate), Internat. Narcotics Rsch. Conf. 1989—, Internat. Union Physiol. Sci., many others. Republican. Methodist. Home: 4516 Amherst Ln Bethesda MD 20814-4008 Office: NIH 31/9A-35 9500 Rockville Pike Bethesda MD 20814-3915

CREWS, JOHN ERIC, rehabilitation administrator; b. Marion, Ind., Aug. 4, 1946; s. Odis Earl and Beatrice True (Wright) C.; m. Nancy J. Murphy, Aug. 9, 1975; 1 child, Katherine. BA in English, Franklin Coll., 1969; MA in English, Ind. U., 1971; MA in Blind Rehab. with honors, Western Mich. U., 1977, D in Pub. Adminstrn., 1990. Mem. English faculty Ball State U., Muncie, Ind., 1971-73, S.W. Mo. State U., Springfield, 1973-76, Western Mich. U., Kalamazoo, 1976-77; rehab. tchr. Mich. Commn. for the Blind, Saginaw, 1977-80; program mgr. Sr. Blind Program, Saginaw, Southeastern Mich. Ctr. for Ind. Living, Detroit, 1980-92, Ind. Living Rehab. Program, 1986-92; rsch. health scientist Rehab. R&D Ctr. Va. Med. Ctr., Decatur, Ga., 1992, chief behavioral sect. Rehab. R&D Ctr., 1992-93; acting dir.

Rehab. Rsch. and Devel. Ctr. VA Med. Ctr., Decatur, Ga., 1993-95; adj. sr. assoc. rehab. medicine Emory U. Sch. Medicine, Atlanta, 1992—; clin. prof. dept. mental health and human svcs. Ga. State Univ., Atlanta, 1993—; exec. dir. Gov.'s Coun. Devel. Disabilities, Atlanta, 1995—; v.p. bd. Midland County Coun. on Aging, 1982-84; bd. dirs. Saginaw Valley Spl. Needs Vision Clinic, 1981-88; mem. adv. bd. rehab. continuing edn. program So. Ill. U., Carbondale, 1985-90, Lighthouse Nat. Ctr. on Vision and Aging, 1992—; sec. Statewide Ind. Living Coun., 1987-92; mem. editl. bd. Jour. Visual Impairment and Blindness, 1984-90; regional bd. mem. Am. Found. for the Blind-S.E., Atlanta, 1995—; exec. dir. gov.'s coun. on devel. disabilities, Atlanta, 1995—. Contbr. to books and profl. publs. Exec. dir. Gov.'s Coun. on Devel. Disabilities, 1995—. Recipient Grant award Ind. Living Svcs. for Older Blind Rehab. Svcs. Adminstrn., 1986, Community Svc. award Saginaw Valley Rehab. Ctr., 1992; grantee Ctr. Ind. Living U.S. Dept. Edn., 1980, 82, Ind. Living for Elderly Blind, 1986; All-Univ. grad. rsch. and creative scholar Western Mich. U., 1988. Mem. Nat. Coun. Aging, Assn. Retarded Citizens (pres. Midland 1981-87, Ann. award 1981). Methodist. Home: 5287 Candleberry Dr SW Lilburn GA 30247-6769 Office: Govs Coun on Devel Disabili Suite 210 Third Floor 2 Peachtree Street NE Atlanta GA 30303

CRIARES, NICHOLAS JAMES, obstetrician and gynecologist; b. Bronx, N.Y., Apr. 2, 1934; s. James George and Christina (Brim) C.; M.D., St. Louis U., 1960; D.Sc., U. Pa., 1963; m. Helen Athos, July 3, 1966; 1 son, Peter. Diplomate Am. Bd. Ob-Gyn. Commd. 2d lt. U.S. Air Force and U.S. Army, 1960-88, advanced through grades to brig. gen., 1960-88, ret.; intern Meadowbrook Hosp., 1960-61; resident in ob-gyn Met. Hosp., N.Y.C., 1961-62, Misericordia Hosp., Phila., 1962-65, Johns Hopkins U., 1965-66; asst. attending staff Montefiore-Morrisania Affiliation, Bronx, N.Y., 1968-69; asst. prof. ob-gyn Upstate Med. Ctr., Syracuse, N.Y., 1969-72; surgeon N.Y. State Troopers Med. Evacuation, 1983-85, surgeon gen., 1985-96, ret., 1996; pres. Nicholas J. Criares, M.D., P.C., Hartsdale, N.Y., 1972-88, ret.; asst. attending staff Hosp. of Albert Einstein Coll. Medicine, Bronx Mcpl. Hosp. Ctr., Keller Army Hosp. of U.S. Mil. Acad.; clin. asst. prof. ob-gyn and psychiatry Albert Einstein Coll. Medicine. Mem. Soc. Urban Physicians, 1968-69, Doctors Council, 1978-80. Fellow Am. Coll. Obstetricians and Gynecologists, Internat. Coll. Obstetricians and Gynecologists, Am. Coll. Quality Assurance and Utilization Rev. Physicians (cert.); mem. Bronx Ob-Gyn Soc., Assn. Mil. Surgeons U.S., AMA (Physicians Recognition award), Med. Soc. State N.Y., Westchester County Med. Soc., Am. Coll. Legal Medicine. Greek Orthodox. Club: West Point Officers. Contbr. articles profl. jours. Research on alkaline phosphatase during pregnancy, teratology, the Feto-Placental Unit, anomalies in gynecology. Office: 34 Andover Rd Hartsdale NY 10530-2003

CRICK, FRANCIS HARRY COMPTON, science educator, researcher; b. June 8, 1916; s. Harry and Annie Elizabeth (Wilkins) C.; m. Ruth Doreen Dodd, 1940 (div. 1947); 1 son; m. Odile Speed, 1949; 2 daus. B.Sc., Univ. Coll., London; PhD, Cambridge U., Eng. Scientist Brit. Admiralty, 1940-47, Strangeways Lab., Cambridge, Eng., 1947-49; with Med. Rsch. Coun. Lab. of Molecular Biology, Cambridge, 1949-77; Kieckhefer Disting. prof. Salk Inst. Biol. Studies, San Diego, 1977—, pres., 1994-95, non-resident fellow, 1962-73; adj. prof. psychology U. Calif., San Diego; vis. lectr. Rockefeller Inst., N.Y.C., 1959; vis. prof. chemistry dept. Harvard U., 1959, vis. prof. biophysics, 1962; fellow Churchill Coll., Cambridge, 1960-61; Korkes Meml. lectr. Duke U., 1960; Henry Sidgewick Meml. lectr. Cambridge U., 1963; Graham Young lectr., Glasgow, 1963; Robert Boyle lectr. Oxford U., 1963; Vanuxem lectr. Princeton U., 1964; William T. Sedgwick Meml. lectr. MIT, 1965; Cherwell-Simon Meml. lectr. Oxford U., 1966; Shell lectr. Stanford U., 1969; Paul Lund lectr. Northwestern U., 1977; Dupont lectr. Harvard U., 1979, numerous other invited meml. lectrs. Author: Of Molecules and Men, 1966, Life Itself, 1981, What Mad Pursuit, 1988, The Astonishing Hypothesis: The Scientific Search for the Soul, 1994; contbr. papers and articles on molecular, cell biology and neurobiology to sci. jours. Recipient Prix Charles Leopold Mayer French Academies des Scis., 1961; (with J.D. Watson) Rsch. Corp. award, 1961, Warren Triennial prize, 1959, (with J.D. Watson & Maurice Wilkins) Lasker award, 1960, Nobel Prize for medicine, 1962; Gairdner Found. award, 1962, Royal Medal Royal Soc., 1972, Copley medal, 1975, Michelson-Morley award, 1981, Benjamin P. Cheney medal, 1986, Golden Plate award, 1987, Albert medal Royal Soc. Arts, London, 1987, Wright Prize VIII Harvey Mudd Coll., 1988, Joseph Priestly award Dickinson Coll., 1988, Order of Merit, 1991, Disting. Achievement award Oreg State U. Friends of Libr., 1995. Fellow AAAS, Univ. Coll. London, Royal Soc., Indian Nat. Sci. Acad., Rochester Mus., Indian Acad. Scis. (hon.), Churchill Coll. Cambridge (hon.), Royal Soc. Edinburgh (hon.), Caius Coll. Cambridge (hon.), John Muir Coll. U. Calif., San Diego (hon.); mem. Acad. Arts Scis. (fgn. hon.), Am. Soc. Biol. Chemists (hon.), U.S. Nat. Acad. Scis. (fgn. assoc.), German Acad. Sci., Am. Philos. Soc. (fgn. mem.), French Acad. Scis. (assoc. fgn. mem.), Royal Irish Acad. (hon.), Hellenic Biochemical and Biophysical Soc. (hon.). Office: Salk Inst Biol Studies PO Box 85800 San Diego CA 92186-5800

CRIDER, ANDREW BLAKE, psychologist; b. Cleve., June 11, 1936; s. Blake and Doris (Towne) C.; m. Anne Horrocks, Apr. 25, 1964; children: Juliet Gage, Jonathan Andrew. BA, Colgate U., 1958; MS, U. Wis., 1960; PhD, Harvard U., 1964. Lic. psychologist, Mass. Research assoc. Harvard Med. Sch., Boston, 1964-68; asst., then assoc. prof. psychology Williams Coll., Williamstown, Mass., 1968-77, prof., 1977-84, Warren prof. psychology, 1984-94, chmn. dept., 1986-91, dir. Oxford program, 1991-93, prof. emeritus, 1994—; cons. Berkshire Med. Ctr. Psychiatry Dept., Pittsfield, Mass., 1979-85. Author: Schizophrenia, 1979; (with others) Psychology, 1983; contbr. articles to profl. jours. Bd. dirs. No. Berkshire Mental Health Assn., 1982-91. Fulbright scholar U. Brussels, 1958-59; NIH research grantee, 1964-74. Mem. Am. Psychol. Assn., Soc. Psychophysiol. Research, Assn. for Applied Psychophysiol. and Biofeedback. Home: PO Box 234 Williamstown MA 01267-0234 Office: Williams Coll Dept Psychology Williamstown MA 01267

CRIDER, RUDYARD LEE, psychotherapist; b. Abilene, Kans., Oct. 16, 1942; s. Clarence A. and Myrtle (Cox) C.; m. Doris Elaine Heisey, Aug. 3, 1962; 1 child, Michele Renee. BA, Messiah Coll., 1971; MS, Shippensburg U., 1978. Cert. clin. mental health counselor; nat. cert. counselor. Mental health worker King's View Hosp., Reedley, Calif., 1966-68; crisis intervention counselor Holy Spirit Hosp. Mental Health, Camp Hill, Pa., 1974-78; sr. psychotherapist Holy Spirit Hosp. Mental Health, Camp Hill, 1978—, asst. coord. outpatient svcs., 1989—; pvt. practice psychotherapy, 1992—; sr. peer reviewer Holy Spirit Hosp. Mental Health, Camp Hill, 1990—, quality assurance com., 1990—, clin. site supr., 1983—, mem. extended mgmt. team, 1994. Recipient Recognition for Outstanding Svc. award Cumberland Perry County Mental Health-Mental Retardation Program, 1993. Mem. Acad. Clin. Mental Health Counselors, Am. Counseling Assn., Am. Mental Health Counselors Assn., Pa. Counselors Assn., Pa. Psychol. Assn. Lutheran. Home: 438 Parkside Rd Camp Hill PA 17011-2127 Office: Holy Spirit Hosp 21st St Camp Hill PA 17011

CRIM, GARY ALLEN, dental educator; b. Louisville, Ky., July 13, 1949; s. John W. Crim and Ruby M. Willis. DMD, U. Ky., 1974; MS in Dentistry, Ind. U., 1981. Asst. prof. U. Louisville Sch. Dentistry, 1981, assoc. prof., 1987-93, prof., chmn., 1993—. Contbr. articles to profl. jours. Mem. ADA, Internat. Assn. Dental Rsch., Am. Assn. Dental Schs., Acad. Operative Dentistry. Office: U Louisville Sch Dentistry 501 S Preston St Louisville KY 40292

CRIMLISK, JANET THERESE, pulmonary clinical nurse specialist; b. Newton, Mass., June 25, 1945; d. Frank J. and Helen R. (Roman) C. BS, Boston Coll., 1967; MS, Boston U., 1971, geriatric nurse practitioner, 1978; adult nurse practitioner, Mass. Gen. Hosp. Inst. Health, Professions, 1995. RN, Mass.; cert. med.-surg. nurse, ANCC. Staff nurse Boston City Hosp., 1967-69, med. clin. nurse specialist, 1974-77, pulmonary clin. nurse specialist, 1977—; mem. faculty St. Elizabeth's Hosp. Sch. Nursing, Boston, 1971-73, Boston City Hosp. Sch. of Nursing, 1973-74, Boston State Coll., 1975. Contbr. numerous articles to profl. jours. H.E.W. fellow, Boston U., 1971; named Outstanding Nurse of Yr., City of Boston, 1985. Mem. ANA, AACN, Am. Acad. Nurse Practitioners (cert. nurse practitioner), Am. Heart Assn., Am. Thoracic Soc., Respiratory Nurses Assn., Sigma Theta Tau.

CRINO, MARJANNE HELEN, anesthesiologist; b. Rochester, N.Y., Aug. 18, 1933; d. Michael Jay and Helen Barbara (Kennedy) C.; m. Michael Anthony La Iuppa, Nov. 12, 1960; children: James Michael, Barbara Anne, John Christopher. BS, Coll. St. Teresa, 1955; MD, Med. Coll. Wis., 1959; MA in Theology, St. Bernard's Inst., 1991. Diplomate Nat. Bd. Med. Examiners. House staff Genesee Hosp., Rochester, 1959-61; perinatal mortality rsch., resident in anesthesiology Jackson Meml Hosp.-U. Miami, 1962-65; attending staff in anesthesiology Genesee Hosp., Rochester, N.Y., 1969—; mem. exec. com., med. staff sec., 1980, 82; acting chmn. dept. anesthesiology Genesee Hosp., Rochester, N.Y., 1989, 91, chmn. pain control com., 1989—; clin. instr. anesthesiology U. Rochester Sch. Medicine, 1983—; cons. anesthesiology Rochester Psychiat. Ctr., 1975-85; instr. anesthesiology U. Miami Sch. medicine, 1966, 67; attending staff anesthesiology Jackson Meml. Hosp., Miami, 1966, 67. Mem. adv. bd. Isaiah House Hosp., 1994—, com. Pittsford (N.Y.) Republican Party, 1970's-80's; vol. chaplain Genesee Hosp. Mem. N.Y. State Soc. Anesthesiologists (bd. dirs., vice spkr. 1983-86, del. 1971-82, 87—), Am. Soc. Anesthesiologists (del. 1979-86), AMA, N.Y. State Med. Soc., Med. Soc. County of Monroe, Rochester Acad. Medicine, Cath. Physicians Guild Rochester (pres. 1988-89), Margaret Roper Guild (pres. 1975-76). Roman Catholic. Office: Genesee Hosp Dept Anesthesiology 224 Alexander St Rochester NY 14607-4002

CRISAFULLI, JOSEPH ANTHONY, podiatrist; b. Mar. 3, 1960. BS in Biology, Niagara U., 1982; D in Podiatric Medicine, Ohio Coll. Podiatric Medicine, Cleve., 1986. Diplomate Am. Bd. Podiatric Surgery; lic. podiatrist, N.Y., Mass. Intern West Roxbury (Mass.) VA, 1986, Balt. VA, 1986; resident West Roxbury (Mass.) VA Med. Ctr., 1987, St. Vincent Hosp., Worcester, Mass., 1989; assoc. Dr. Raymond P. Esper, Westboro, Mass., 1989-90; pvt. practice Albany, N.Y., 1990—; mem. staff Capital Dist. Psychiatric Ctr., Albany, N.Y., Albany County Nursing Home, Ann Lee Home, Albany; cons. in field. Contbr. articles to profl. jours. Trustee Westland Hills, Albany. Fellow Am. Coll. Foot and Ankle Surgeons; mem. Am Podiatric Med. Assn., West Albany Italian Benevolent Soc., KC, Kiwanis (bd. dirs.). Office: 120 Russell Rd Albany NY 12205

CRISCI, PAT DEVITA, retired psychology educator; b. N.Y.C., Oct. 29, 1931; d. Victor Anthony and Christine Marie (Capobianco) De V.; m. S. George Crisci, Jan. 10, 1954; children: Debra Leah, George Sabato, Wayne Lawrence, Lorraine I. BA, CUNY, 1952; MA, John Carroll U., 1968; PhD, Kent State U, 1974. Lic. psychologist, Ohio; cert. sch. supt., counselor, sch. psychologist, Ohio. Psychology intern Cleveland Heights-University Heights (Ohio) City Sch. System, 1968-69, sch. psychologist, counselor, 1969-70, supr. intern sch. psychologists, 1970-71, supr. spl. edn., 1971-72, dir. edn., 1972-74; supt. schs. Tallmadge (Ohio) City Sch System, 1974-78; asst. supr. pub. instrn. Dept. Edn. State Ohio, Columbus, 1978-79; assoc. prof. then prof. ednl. psychology and leadership Kent (Ohio) State U., 1979-93, dir. Ctr. for Sch. Pers. Rels., 1981-93, dir. KEDS Desegregation Assistance Ctr., 1986-88; prof. emeritus, 1993—; cons. numerous orgns. including Greater Cleve. Rouondtable, The Cleve. Found., Shaker Heights Bd. Edn., Lakewood Bd. Edn., Cleve. Bd. Edn., Youngstown City Sch. Dist., others. Contbr. numerous articles to profl. jours. Mem. Am. Ednl. Rsch. Assn., Am. Assn. Sch. Adminstrs. (chmn. governance subcom. platform and resolutions com. 1987-88, mem. Blue Ribbon task force on evaluation 1988, exec. com. Women's Caucus), Am. Edn. Finance Assn., Am. Psychol. Assn., Nat. Assn. Mediation in Edn., Assn. Negotiators and Contract Adminstrs. (adv. bd.), Nat. Coun. Profs. of Edn. Adminstrn., Nat. Assn. Sch. Psychologists, Ohio Assn. Gifted Children, Ohio Assn. Children with Learning Disabilities, Phi Delta Kappa. Home: 4501 S Atlantic Ave New Smyrna Beach FL 32169-4005 also: 3068 Kent Rd Stow OH 44224

CRISMON, MILES LYNN, clinical psychopharmacologist; b. Tulsa, Feb. 13, 1951; s. Isaac Edward and Geneva Angeline (Pate) C.; m. Camille Hemlock; children: Teresa Lynne, Anthony Edward. BS in Pharmacy, U. Okla., 1974; D in Pharmacy, U. Tex., 1979. Registered pharmacist, Tex., N.Mex. Resident in hosp. pharmacy USPHS Gallup Indian Med. Ctr., 1974-75; resident in psychopharmacology U. Tex., San Antonio, 1979; asst. prof. Coll. Pharmacy U. Tex., Austin, 1979-85, assoc. prof., 1984-91; prof. U. Tex., 1991—; asst. dean U. Tex., Austin, 1984-85, head clin. div., 1985—; clin. pharmacologist Austin State Hosp., 1973—, Healthcare Rehab. Ctr., Austin, 1985—; dir. neuropsychiatry rsch. Ctr Clin. Rsch., Austin, 1991—; vis. prof. Coll. Arts and Sci. and Tech., Kingston, Jamaica, 1989, 91; cons. Tex. Dept. Mental Helath, 1983-91, Healthcare Financing Adminstrn., Balt., 1986—, Okla. Dept. Mental Health, 1988; chmn. splty. coun. on psychiat. pharmacy practice, ex-officio mem. bd. Bd. Pharm. Spltys.; preceptor ASHP Found. Psychiat. Drug Therapy Fellowship, 1989-90, 93-95, TSHPR&E Found., treas., 1989-91, pres., 1992-93, v.p., 1994-95, bd. dirs., 1989-91, 92-93, 94—. Contbr. articles to profl. jours., chpts. to books. Lt. sgt. USPHS, 1974-76. Grantee NEH, 1981, Am. Coll. Clin. Pharm., 1989; Regents fellow Psychiat. Pharmacy U. Tex., Austin, 1985-86, S.W. Drug Corp. fellow, 1986—. Fellow Am. Coll. Clin. Pharmacy (CNS Rsch. award 1989); mem. Am. Soc. Health-System Pharmacists (chmn. psychopharmacy splty. practice group 1991), Tex. Soc. Health-Sys. Pharmacists (treas. 1987-89, bd. dirs. 1981-84, 86-89, 92—, pres. 1993-94), Acad. Pharm. Rsch. and Sci. (mem.-at-large clin. sci. sect. 1989-90), Nat. Head Injury Found. (Outstanding Rsch. Presentation 1994). Democrat. Roman Catholic. Office: U Tex Coll Pharmacy Austin TX 78712

CRISOSTOMO, EDGARDO ABAD, neurologist; b. Philippines, Feb. 8, 1952; came to U.S., 1979; m. Arminda Espenilla, Jan. 19, 1980; children: Abigail, Ashley, Allison. BS, U. Santo Tomas, 1972, MD, 1976. Resident Albany Med. Coll., 1980-84; rsch. fellow Duke U., Durham, N.C., 1984-86; rsch. assoc. U. N.Mex., Albuquerque, 1986-88; neurologist Duluth (Minn.) Clinic, 1988—. Contbr. articles to profl. jours. Med. adv. regional stroke program St. Luke's. Fellow Am. HEart Assn. (stroke coun.); mem. Am. Soc. Neurorehab., Am. Soc. Neuroimaging, Am. Acad. Neurology, Minn. Stroke Assn. (dir. 1993—), Soc. Neurosci. Office: Stroke Office St Lukes Hosp 915 E First St Duluth MN 55805

CRISP, BRAULIA-NELIDA SORIANO, surgeon; b. Barceloneta, P.R., July 8, 1933; d. Rafael Soriano-Pintor and Virginia Soriano-Vega; m. George B. Crisp, Jr., June 13, 1959; 1 son, George Rafael. Pre-med, U. P.R., 1949-51; M.D., U. Madrid, 1955. Intern, Lebanon Hosp., N.Y.C., 1956; resident in surgery VA Hosp., Bklyn., 1957-59, 64-65. practice medicine specializing in gen. surgery, Bklyn., 1965-67, Atlanta, 1970-72, Fort Worth, 1974—; attending surgeon VA Adminstrn. Clinics, Bklyn., 1966-67, Atlanta, 1970-71; cons. Mem. AMA. Club: Petroleum (Ft. Worth).

CRISPIN, KATHLEEN MARGARET, nursing educator; b. Chico, Calif., Feb. 28, 1945; d. James V. and Hazel Kathleen (Coppage) O'Brien; m. William David Crispin, Jan. 15, 1972 (dec.). BS in Nursing, U. Va., 1969; MSN, U. N.C., 1971; EdD, Bob Jones U., 1994. Staff nurse VA Hosp., Gulfport, Miss., 1971-79; nursing faculty Bob Jones U., Greenville, S.C., 1981-83, chmn. div. nursing, 1983—; mem. State. Bd. Nursing for S.C. Mem. S.C. Coun. Deans and Dirs. of Nursing Edn., Sigma Theta Tau.

CRISSMAN, JOHN D., physician; b. Detroit, Feb. 3, 1939; m. Lynn B. Crissman, Sept. 12, 1964; children: John, Allison. SBME, MIT, 1961; MD, Western Res. U., 1966. Physician U. Cin., 1974-81, Wayne State U., Detroit, 1981-87, 90—, Henry Ford Hosp., Detroit, 1987-90. Capt. USAF, 1968-70.

CRISWELL, ELEANOR CAMP, psychologist; b. Norfolk, Va., May 12, 1938; d. Norman Harold Camp and Eleanor (Talman) David; m. Thomas L. Hanna. BA, U. Ky., 1961, MA, 1962; EdD, U. Fla., 1969. Asst. prof. edn. Calif. State Coll., Hayward, 1969; prof. psychology, chair Calif. State U., Sonoma, 1969—; faculty adviser Humanistic Psychology Inst., San Francisco, 1970-77; dir. Novato Inst. Somatic Research and Tng; editor Somatics jour.; cons. Venturi, Inc., Autogenic Systems, Inc.; clin. dir. Biotherapeutics, Kentfield Med. Hosp., 1985-90. Founder Humanistic Psychology Inst., 1970. Co-editor: Biofeedback and Family Practice Medicine, 1983, How Yoga Works, 1987, Biofeedback and Somatics, 1993. Mem. APA, Biofeedback Soc. Calif. (dir.), Aerospace Med. Assn., Assn. for Transpersonal Psychology. Patentee optokinetic perceptual learning device. Office: Sonoma State U Psychology Dept 1801 E Cotati Ave Rohnert Park CA 94928-3613

CRITCHLOW, HOWARD ARTHUR, oral and maxillofacial surgeon, educator; b. Littleborough, Lancashire, Eng., Apr. 22, 1943; s. Arthur and Edith Ellen (Evans) C.; m. Avril Pyne, Dec. 4, 1970; children: Edward, Bridget. BDS, Sheffield U., 1965. Pvt. practice gen. dentistry Sheffield, 1965-68; sr. house officer/registrar Charles Clifford Dental Hosp., Sheffield, 1968-71; registrar Royal South Hants. Hosp./Odstock Hosp., Eng., 1971-73; first asst. U. Newcastle-upon-Tyne, Eng., 1973-76; cons. Glasgow (Scotland) Dental Hosp. and Sch., 1976—, chmn. ethical com., 1980—; chmn. area dental com. Greater Glasgow Health Bd., 1979-92; chmn. ethical com. Stobhill Hosp., Glasgow, 1986-95. Contbr. articles to profl. jours. Recipient Bronze medal U. Sheffield, 1962. Fellow Brit. Assn. Oral and Maxillofacial Surgeons. Office: Glasgow Dental Hosp/Sch, Sauchiehall St, Glasgow G2 3JZ, Scotland

CRITCHLOW, JONATHAN FRANCIS, surgeon; b. L.A., Jan. 31, 1953; s. Francis B. and Marion C.; m. Wenda Junge Gantz, Sept. 7, 1973; children: Ashley, Taylor, Blair; m. Barbara DuBos, May 2, 1992. BS, Stanford U., 1974; MD, U. Calif. San Diego, 1978. Diplomate Am. Bd. Surgery. Resident in surgery Beth Israel Hosp., Boston, 1978-84, assoc. surgeon, 1984—; co-dir. RSICU Beth Israel Hosp., 1984-95, chief, surg. crit. care, 1995—; instr. in surgery Harvard Med. Sch., Boston, 1984-92, asst. prof. of surgery, 1992—. Fellow Am. Coll. Surgeons, Coll. Crit. Care Medicine; mem. New Eng. Ctr. Care Soc. (exec. bd. 1992), Soc. for Surgery of Alimentary Tract, Boston Surg. Soc. Office: Beth Israel Hosp 330 Brookline Ave Boston MA 02215

CROCI, HENRY GEORGE, ophthalmologist; b. Toledo, Ohio, July 11, 1939; s. Leander and Rosemary (Goshia) C.; m. Suzanne Croci, Aug. 31, 1963; children: Michael A., Michele A. BS in Chemistry, U. Detroit, 1961; MD, Ohio State U., 1965. Diplomate Am. Bd. Ophthalmology. Resident in ophthalmology Ohio State U. Dept. of Ophthalmology, 1968-71; pvt. practice in ophthalmology Atheus Ohio, 1971-81; ptnr. Eye Physicians and Surgeons of Athens Inc., 1981—. Capt. USAF, 1966-68. Mem. Am. Acad. of Ophthalmology, Am. Cataract and Refractive Soc., Ohio Ophthalmology, Ohio State Med. Assn., Athens County Med. Soc. (pres. 1986). Roman Catholic. Office: Eye Physician and Surgeons Athens Inc 444 W Union St Athens OH 45701

CROCK, HENRY VERNON, surgeon, writer; b. Perth, Australia, Sept. 14, 1929; arrived in Eng. 1986; s. Vernon John and Annie (Doyle) C.; m. Mary Carmel Shorten, Mar. 15, 1958; children: Catherine, Elizabeth, Carmel, Vernon, Damian. Student in Dental Sci., U. Western Australia, 1947-48; MB, BS with honors in Anatomy, Physiology, Bateriology, Medicine and Surgery, U. Melbourne, Victoria, Australia, 1953, MD, 1967, MS, 1977. Jr. resident med. officer with med. and surgical rotations St. Vincent's Hosp., U. Melbourne, 1954, sr. resident med. officer gen. urological and orthopaedic surgery, 1955; sr. demonstrator anatomy dept. U. Melbourne, 1956; resident tutor in anatomy Newman Coll, U. Melbourne, 1956; sr. surgical regisrar St. Vincent's Hosp., U. Melbourne, 1957; Nuffield Dominions clin. asst. orthopaedic surgery Nuffield Orthopaedic Ctr., U. Oxford, 1957-60; lectr. in orthopaedic Surgery Oxford U., 1959-60; sr. honorary orthopaedic surgeon St. Vincent's Hosp., U. Melbourne, 1961-86; assoc. prof. dept. surgery U. Melbourne, 1978-85; honorary cons. orthopaedic surgery Royal postgrad. Med. Sch., Hammersmith, 1986—; honorary rsch. fellow anatomy dept. Royal Coll. Surgeons, Eng., 1986—; spl. lectr. orthopaedic surgery U. Melbourne, 1961-86, Naughton Dunn lectr Birmingham Royal Infirmary, 1988; guest lectr. U. Dusseldorf, Japanese Orthopaedic Assn., U. Nottingham, Norfolk and Norwich Hosps, U. Oporto, U. Bologna, U. Manchester, Internat. Soc. Study of Lumbar Spine, Japan, Switzerland, Saudi Arabia. Author: The Blood Supply of the Lower Limb Bones in Man, 1967, Practice of Spinal Surgery, 1984, A Short Practice of Spinal Surgery, 1992; co-author: (with Yoshizawa) The Blood Supply of the Vertebral Column and Spinal Cord in Man, 1977, (with Yamagishi and M C Crock) The Conus Medullaris and Cauda Equina in Man, 1986, An Atlas of the Vascular Anatomy of the Skeleton and Spinal Cord, 1996; contbr. numerous chpts. in books (with others) including Spinal Stenosis, 1991, The Lumbar Spine and Back Pain, 1991, The Adult Spine: Principles and Practice, 1991; contbr. to numerous profl. jours. Recipient Prosector and Gold medallist (with G W Crock) U. Melbourne, 1949, Gold medals in Medicine and Surgery St. Vincent's Hosp. Clin. Sch., 1953, L O Betts Meml. Gold medal Australian Orthopaedic Assn., 1976; Michael and Margaret Ryan scholar, 1949-53; named officer Order of Australia, 1984. Fellow Royal Coll. Surgeons (Wood Jones medal 1981, Arnott Demonstrator, 1988), Royal Australasian Coll. Surgeons (Sir Allan Newton prize 1977), British Orthopaedic Assn. Office: Cromwell Hosp, Crock Spinal Disorders Unit, London SW5 0TU, England

CRODELLE, MARY E., nurse; b. Poughkeepsie, N.Y., Sept. 21, 1954; d. Vincent A. and Yolande M. (Gaetano) C. BSN, Regents Coll., Albany, N.Y., 1993. RN, N.Y.; cert. ACLS. Nurse St. Francis Hosp., Poughkeepsie; nurse Albany Med. Ctr., asst. nurse mgr.

CROFT, BARBARA YODER, medical educator; b. Port Chester, N.Y., Aug. 11, 1940; d. Paul Henry Yoder and Harriet French (Postle) McBride; m. Joseph Edward Croft, Dec. 15, 1977 (dec. 1988); m. Jerry Porter, Oct. 15, 1989. BS, Swarthmore Coll., 1962; MS, Johns Hopkins U., 1964, PhD, 1967. Sr. scientist Johnston Labs., Inc., Balt., 1967-68; programmer U. Va., Charlottesville, 1968, instr. dept. radiology, 1969-72, asst. prof. dept. radiology, 1972-87, assoc. prof. dept. radiology, 1987—; rsch. assoc. Oak Ridge (Tenn.) Associated Univs., 1972; vis. scholar U. N.Mex., Albuquerque, 1975. Co-author: Basics of Radiopharmacy, 1974; author: Single Photon Emission Computed Tomography, 1986. Fellow Am. Coll. Nuclear Physicians; mem. AAAS, AAUP, Am. Chem. Soc., Am. Coll. Radiology, Soc. Nuclear Medicine (pres. 1988-89). Democrat. Episcopalian. Office: U Va Dept Radiology PO Box 170 Charlottesville VA 22908

CROFT, DESMOND NICHOLAS, physician; b. Devonport, Eng., June 14, 1931; s. Charles Richard and Phyllis Mary (Lee) C.; m. Hilary Diana Rendle, Feb. 6, 1960; children: Charles Desmond, Nicholas Michael, Hilary Mary. MA, Oxford (Eng.) U., 1957, DM, 1966. Cert. cons. physician. Resident St. Thomas Hosp., London, 1957-59; med. registrar, sr. med. registrar St. Thomas & West Middlesex Hosps., London, 1961-64; med. fellow to Prof. F.J. Ingelfinger, Boston, 1964-65; sr. med. registrar St. Thomas Hosp., London, 1965-69, cons. physician, clin. dir. nuclear medicine, 1961—. Contbr. articles to profl. jours. Capt. Brit. Army, 1959-61. Rsch. grantee St. Thomas' Hosp., London, 1962, USPHS Rsch. & Tng. grantee Nat. Inst. Arthritis & Metabolic Diseases; Nuffield Found. Med. fellow, U.K., 1964-65. Fellow Royal Coll. Physicians, Royal Coll. Radiologists, Royal Soc. Medicine; mem. Brit. Nuclear Med. Soc. (pres. 1976), Brit. Soc. Gastroenterology, Clin. Rsch. Soc., European Nuclear Medicine Soc. (founder), European Union of Med. Specialists (pres. nuclear medicine sect. 1990—). Conservative. Anglican. Home: Bourne House, Hurstbourne Priors, Priors Whitechurch RG28 7SB, England England Office: St Thomas Hosp, Lambeth Palace Rd, London SE1 7EH, England

CROFT, ROXANNE GAYLE FRALLEY, clinical psychologist; b. Honolulu, Jan. 24, 1947; d. George Harry and Jacqueline Arkin (Snedeker) Fralley; m. Mark Clyde Croft (div. Feb. 1992). BA in Biol. Scis. cum laude, Goncher Coll., 1970; MA in Clin. Psychology, U. Rochester, 1976, PhD in Clin. Psychology, 1977. Lic. clin. psychologist, N.J. Asst. prof., rsch. assoc. U. Rochester, N.Y., 1976-77; staff psychologist counseling ctr. Rutgers U., New Brunswick, N.J., 1977-78, field supr. Grad. Sch. for Applied and Profl. Psychology, 1977—; pvt. practice, specializing in posttraumatic stress disorder Highland Park, N.J., 1977—. Mem. APA, N.J. Psychol. Assn., N.J. Acad. Psychology. Office: 114 S 1st Ave # B Highland Park NJ 08904-2164

CROFTCHECK, STEVEN RAY, nurse; b. Muskogee, Okla., Nov. 7, 1972; s. Thomas Joseph and Judy Ann (Hutson) C. ADN, Bacone Coll., Muskogee, 1993; BSN, Northeastern State U., Tahlequah, Okla., 1996. RN, Okla. Nurse Muskogee Regional Med. Ctr., 1993—. Bur. Indian Affairs scholar, 1994-95; Regents scholar, 1994-95. Mem. Emergency Nurses Assn. Democrat. Baptist. Home: 11020 S 25th St E Muskogee OK 74401

CROLEY, GRANVILLE GILTZ, II, surgeon; b. Johnson City, Tenn., Dec. 15, 1959; s. Giltz Wymer and Dorothy Rae (Moss) C.; m. Jill Reneé Peters, June 22, 1985; children: Granville Mason, Mallory Reneé. BS, East Tenn.

State U., 1982, MD, 1987. Diplomate Am. Bd. Surgery. Intern U. Miss. Med. Ctr., Jackson, 1987-88, resident in gen. surgery, 1988-92; gen./vascular surgeon Piedmont Surg. Clinic, PA, Concord, N.C., 1992—. Contbr. articles to med. jours. Fellow ACS (assoc.), James D. Hardy Soc.; mem. AMA, N.C. Med. Soc. Office: Piedmont Surg Clinic PA 56 Lake Concord Rd NE Concord NC 28025

CROMARTIE, WILLIAM JAMES, medical educator, researcher; b. Garland, N.C., May 19, 1913; s. Robert Samuel and Mary Blanche (Jester) C.; m. Josephine Colter Rule, Nov. 19, 1945; children: William James, Robert Colter, Mary Blanche, John Benjamin, Martha Anne. Student, Presbyn. Jr. Coll., 1929-30, U. N.C., 1931, U. Ala., 1931-33; MD, Emory U., 1937. Diplomate Am. Bd. Internal Medicine. Intern Emory U. divsn. Grady Hosp., Atlanta, 1937-38; resident Vanderbilt U. Hosp., Nashville, 1938-40; instr. pathology Vanderbilt U., 1939-41; asst, prof. bacteriology and medicine U. Minn., Mpls., 1949-50, assoc. prof., 1950-51; assoc. prof. bacteriology and medicine U. N.C., Chapel Hill, 1951-59; chief div. infectious diseases, dept. medicine N.C. Meml. Hosp., Chapel Hill, 1952-65, chief of staff, 1967-72; prof. microbiology-immunology-medicine U. N.C., Chapel Hill, 1959-85, prof. emeritus, 1985—; mem. adv. panel microbiology Office Naval Rsch., Washington, 1950-55; mem. Nat. Bd. Med. Examiners, Phila., 1966-68; mem. infectious disease adv. com. NIH, Bethesda, Md., 1971-75. Mem. bd. govs. Capital Health Planning Agy., Durham, N.C.; mem. exec. com. Regional Med. Program N.C., 1972-76. Maj. U.S. Army, 1942-46, ETO. Decorated Legion of Merit; named Alumni Disting. Prof. U. N.C., 1980. Fellow ACP, Am. Acad. Microbiology (chmn. bd. govs. 1974-75); mem. Soc. Am. Microbiologists (mem. coun. 1974-75), Am. Assn. Pathologists, Infectious Disease Soc. Am., U. N.C. Med. Alumni Assn. (Disting. Faculty award 1983, Disting. Svc. award 1989). Democrat. Home: Glendale 204 Weaver Rd Chapel Hill NC 27514-5947 Office: U NC Sch Medicine Dept Microbiology and Immunology 804 FLOB 23L-H Chapel Hill NC 27514

CROMEANS, LINDA MCCARLEY, sales executive; b. Booneville, Miss., Apr. 7, 1949; d. Norwood Sherrod and Katie Lou (Yarber) McCarley; m. Larry David Cromeans, Dec. 26, 1973. AS, North Miss. Jr. Coll., 1974; BS, U. North Ala., 1987. Lab. asst., phlebotomist Northeast Miss. Hosp., Booneville, 1968-72; tech. asst. lab. Meth. Hosp. Lab., Memphis, 1973-74; staff technologist Union County Gen. Hosp., New Albany, Miss., 1974-75, Colonial Manor Hosp., Florence, Ala., 1975-80; supr. Humana Hosp., Florence, Ala., 1980-88; sales rep. Infolab, Inc., LaGrange, Ky., 1988—; mem. presdl. adv. com. Infolab, Inc., Clarksdale, Miss., 1990-92; area sales mgr., tech. cons. Lab. Supply Co., 1996. Contbr. tech. articles to profl. publs. Vol. Free Clinic Owensboro, Ky., 1995; mem. Rep. Nat. Com., 1994—. Mem. Am. Soc. Clin. Pathologists, Am. Med. Technologists (bd. dirs., treas. 1992-93, v.p. 1993-95, pres. 1995-96, 96—), Clin. Lab. Mgmt. Assn. Baptist. Home: 3216 New Moody Ln LaGrange KY 40031 Office: Am Med Technologists 710 Higgins Rd Park Ridge IL 60068

CROMWELL, FLORENCE STEVENS, occupational therapist; b. Lewistown, Pa., May 14, 1922; d. William Andrew and Florence (Stevens) C. BS in Edn., Miami U., Oxford, Ohio, 1943; BS in Occupational Therapy, Washington U., St. Louis, 1949; MA, U. So. Calif., 1952; cert. in health facility adminstrn., UCLA, 1978. Mem. staff, then supervising therapist Los Angeles County Gen. Hosp., 1949-53; occupational therapist Goodwill Industries, L.A., 1954-55; staff therapist Vis. Nurse Assn., Phila., 1955-56; rsch. therapist United Cerebral Palsy Assn., L.A., 1956-60; dir. occupational therapy Orthopaedic Hosp., L.A., 1961-67; coordinator occupational therapy Rsch. and Tng. Ctr. U. So. Calif., L.A., 1967-70, assoc. prof., 1970-76, acting chmn. dept. occupational therapy, 1973-76, mem. adv. bd. project SEARCH, Sch. Medicine, 1969-72; founding editor Occupational Therapy in Health Care jour., 1984-88, editor emerita, 1988—; assoc. dir. L.A. Job Corps Ctr., 1977-78, cons. in edn. and program devel., 1976-95; free-lance editor, 1986—. Author: Manual for Basic Skills Assessment, 1960; also articles. Mem. scholarship com. Los Angeles March of Dimes, 1963-70; bd. dirs. Am. Occupational Therapy Found., 1965-69, v.p., 1966-69; bd. dirs. Nat. Health Council, 1975-78; mentor U. Tex. Class 1990 Occupational Therapy. Served to lt. (j.g.) WAVES, 1943-46. Recipient Disting. Alumni award Washington U., 1978, Disting. Lectr. Calif. Occupational Therapy Found., 1986. Fellow Am. Occupational Therapy Assn. (pres. 1967-73); mem. Inst. Medicine NAS (sr. 1989), So. Calif. Occupational Therapy Assn. (pres. 1950-51, 75-76), Coalition Ind. Health Professions (chmn. 1973-74), Assn. Schs. Allied Health Professions (dir. 1973-74), Cwen, Mortar Bd., Kappa Delta Pi, Kappa Kappa Gamma.

CROMWELL, TERRY ALAN, plastic and reconstructive surgeon; b. Danville, Ill., Aug. 20, 1938; s. Howard Tex and Catherine (Osborn) C.; m. Janice Graziadei, Oct. 18, 1976; children: Tyson, Timothy, Kaitlin; m. Jenna V., Aug. 6, 1960 (div. 1974); children: Janelle, Casey. BA, DePauw U., 1960; MD, U. Cin., 1964. Diplomat Am. Bd. Plastic and Reconstructive Surgery. Intern gen. surgery resident Henry Ford Hosp., Detorit, 1964-65, 69-71; asst. residency St. Joseph Mercy Hosp., Ann Arbor, Mich., 1967-69; plastic surgery resident U. Mich. Med. Ctr., Ann Arbor, Mich., 1971-73; practicine MD Plastic Surgery Assoc., Lafayette, La., 1973—; chmn. Dept. of Surgery Lafayette Gen. Med. Ctr., Lafayette, 1991; clinical asst. prof. Tulane Med. Sch., New Orleans, 1980—. Contbr articles to profl. jours. Vestry mem. St. Barnabus Espiscopal Ch., Lafayette, 1990-91; pres. Lafayette Parish Med. Soc., 1991-92. Lt. USN, 1965-67. Recipient Charles G. Johnson award Detroit Surgical Soc., 1971. Fellow ACS; mem. Am. Soc. Plastic and Reconstructive Surgeons, Southeastern Soc. Plastic and Reconstructive Surgeons, La. Soc. Plastic and Reconstructive Surgeons (sec., treas., v.p. 1989-90, pres. 1992-93), Lafayette Parish Med. Soc. (pres. 1991), Am. Assn. Hand Surgery. Republican, Episcopalian. Office: Plastic Surgery Assoc 1101 S College Rd Ste 400 Lafayette LA 70503-3038

CRONBERG, STIG, infectious diseases educator; b. Malmö, Sweden, Jan. 20, 1935; s. Nils Ebbe and Gerd (Carlander) C.; m. Gertrud Hellsten, May 28,1960; children: Nils, Hans, Olof, Per, Truls, Barbro, Cecilia. MD, Lund (Sweden) U., 1960. Intern Dept. of Medicine, Malmö, 1960-68; scientist Hôpital Saint-Louis, Paris, 1969-70; cons. Dept. of Infectious Diseases, Malmö, 1970-76; asst. prof. dept. infectious diseases Malmö Gen. Hosp., 1976—. Author: Infektioner, 5 edits., 1976-91, Maladies Infectieuses, 1988; co-author: Platelets: Physiology and Pathology, 1977. Home: Tygelsjövägen 127, S 23042 Tygelsjö Sweden Office: Malmö Gen Hosp, Dept Infectious Diseases, S 21401 Malmö Sweden

CRONCE, PAUL CALVIN, physician; b. Trenton, N.J., Dec. 25, 1931; s. Paul Ross and Rachie Cathryn (Allen) C.; m. Nancy Elizabeth Dorrien, Aug. 27, 1960 (div. Aug. 1979); children: Paul Allen, Charles Scott, Thomas Taylor. BA summa cum laude, Duke U., Durham, N.C., 1954; attended, Duke U. Grad. Sch. Arts & Scis., Durham, N.C., 1954-55; MD, Duke U. Sch. Medicine, Durham, N.C., 1960. Diplomate Am. Bd. Dermatology, 1965. Rotating med. intern USPHS Hosp., Boston, 1960-61; acting dermatology resident USPHS Hosp., Staten Island, N.Y., 1961-62, dermatology resident, 1962-65, asst. chief dermatology, 1965-66; vis. fellow in dermatology Columbia-Presbyn. Med. Ctr., N.Y.C., 1964-65; ptnr. Alden & Cronce Dermatology, Atlanta, 1966-73; pres. and treas. Alden Dermatology Assocs., P.A., Atlanta, 1973—; instr. medicine, dermatology Emory U. Sch. Medicine, 1967-71, asst. clin. prof. dermatology, 1971-78, assoc. clin. prof. dermatology, 1978-89, clin. prof. dermatology, 1989—. Contbr. articles to profl. jours. Fellow Am. Acad. Dermatology; mem. Southeastern Dermatological Assn., Ga. Soc. Dermatologists (vice chmn. 1971), Med. Assn. Ga., Internat. Soc. Dermatologic Surgery, Atlanta Dermetological Assn. (sec.-treas. 1967, pres. 1968), Med. Assn. Atlanta, Phi Beta Kappa, Alpha Omega Alpha. Republican. Presbyterian. Office: Alden Dermatological Assocs PA 3312 Piedmont Rd NE Ste 400 Atlanta GA 30305

CRONE, JOHN ROSSMAN, pharmacist; b. Franklin, Pa., Apr. 11, 1933; s. Wilmer Jennings and Lydia Juanita (Rossman) C.; m. Shirley Mae Parker, July 27, 1955; children: Michael John, David Jennings, Alan Parker. BS in Pharmacy, U. Pitts., 1955. Pharmacist King's Drug Store, Clarion, Pa., 1955-56; pharmacist, mgr. Cowdrick's Drug Stores, Inc., Philipsburg, Pa., 1956-57; pharmacist Warren, Pa., 1959-80, pharmacist, mgr., 1980-88; prin., pharmacist Crone's Drug Store, Warren, 1988—. Mem. adv. bd. Salvation Army, Warren, 1984—; bd. dirs. Warren County United Way, 1983—, pres. bd. dirs., 1993-95; chmn. Warren Bus. Group, 1990-92; bd. dirs. Pa. Lions Eye Rsch. Found., 1970-79; bd. dirs. Pa. Lions Hearing Rsch. Found., 1980—, chmn. bd., 1994—. Recipient Warren Lions Club Melvin Jones Fellow award, 1990, C. of C. Community Svcs. award, 1990. Mem. Am. Pharm. Assn., Pa. Pharm. Assn., Warren County Pharm. Assn., Nat. Assn. Retail Druggists, Warren County C. of C. (bd. dirs. 1988-95, pres.-elect 1992-93, pres. 1993-94). Republican. Methodist. Home: 605 Madison Ave Warren PA 16365-2940 Office: Crones Drug Store 212-214 Liberty St Warren PA 16365-2347

CRONE, RICHARD ALLAN, cardiologist, educator; b. Tacoma, Nov. 26, 1947; s. Richard Irving and Alla Marguerite (Ernst) C.; m. Becky Jo Zimmerlund, Dec. 11, 1993. BA in Chemistry, U. Wash., 1969, MD, 1973. Intern Madigan Army Med. Ctr., Tacoma, 1973-74, resident in medicine, 1974-76, fellow in cardiology, 1977-79; commd. med. officer U.S. Army, Tacoma, Denver, San Francisco, 1972; advanced through grades to lt. col. U.S. Army, 1981; dir. coronary care unit Fitzsimons Army Med. Ctr., Denver, 1979-81; practice medicine specializing in cardiology Stevens Cardiology Group, Edmonds, Wash., 1981—, also dir. coronary care unit, cardiac catheter lab, 1982—; clin. assoc. prof. medicine U. Wash., Seattle, 1983—. Fellow Am. Coll. Angiology; mem. AMA, Am. Coll. Cardiology, Am. Heart Assn., Seattle Acad. Internal Medicine, Wash. State Soc. Internal Medicine, Wash. State Med. Assn. Republican. Roman Catholic. Home: 10325 66th Pl W Mukilteo WA 98275-4559 Office: 21701 76th Ave W Ste 100 Edmonds WA 98026-7536

CRONEN, ARTHUR CLARK, psychiatrist; b. Bklyn., June 4, 1946; s. Herbert and Cecily Pearl (Sapadin) C.; m. Julie Carhart, May 24, 1970; children: Rachel, Deborah, Herbert Joseph. AB, Columbia U., 1967; MD, SUNY, Buffalo, 1971. Diplomate Am. Bd. Psychiatry and Neurology. Intern USPHS Hosp., S.I., 1971-72; resident in psychiatry Mt. Sinai Hosp., N.Y.C., 1974-76, chief resident, 1976-77; asst. attending psychiatrist Elmhurst (N.Y.) Hosp., 1977-87, assoc. attending psychiatrist, 1987-92; pvt. practice N.Y.C., 1977-92; attending psychiatrist Tompkins Cmty. Hosp., Ithaca, N.Y., 1992—, chmn. dept. psychiatry, 1993—; clin. instr. Mt. Sinai Sch. Medicine, N.Y.C., 1977-89, asst. clin. prof. psychiatry, 1989. With USPHS, 1971-77. Mem. Am. Psychiatric Assn. Office: Tompkins Community Hosp Ithaca NY 14850

CRONEN, PAUL WILLIAM, surgeon; b. Louisville, Ky., June 6, 1951; s. Paul William Sr. and Martha Victoria (Marsiglio) C.; m. Cherri Ann Bright, May 26, 1979; children; Paul Drew, Kellen Bright. Student, Tulane U.; MD, U. Louisville, 1976. Ptnr. Madison (Ind.) Clinic, 1991—. Fellow ACS; mem. SSAT, ASGE, Shock Soc. Office: 703 Green Rd Madison IN 47250

CRONIN, ERNEST DATTNER, plastic surgeon; b. Houston, Nov. 12, 1945; s. Edward and Elaine (Dattner) C.; m. Kathleen Kane, June 14, 1969; children: Erin, Christopher, Tracy, Mary Lynn, Brendan, Carol, Sean, Sheila. MD, U. Tex., Galveston, 1971. Intern Kansas City (Mo.) Gen. Hosp.; gen. surgery resident St. Joseph Hosp., 1972-73, plstic surgery resident, 1976-78; otolaryngology resident Med. Br. U. Tex., Galveston; pvt. practice plastic surgery Houston, 1978—. Office: Cohen & Cronin Clin Assocs 1315 Calhoun Ste 920 Houston TX 77002

CRONIN, MICHAEL THOMAS IGNATIUS, pathologist; b. Glasgow, Scotland, Feb. 1, 1924; came to U.S., 1952, naturalized, 1958; s. Thomas Mary and Susan Dorothea (O'Keeffe) C.; M.R.C.V.S., U. Dublin, 1945, M.Sc. in Bacteriology, 1946, Ph.D. in Pathology and Bacteriology (Med. Research Council Ireland fellow), 1948; cert. in mgmt., N.Y. U., 1959; M.D., Georgetown U., 1965; postgrad. Yale U., 1965-68; m. Carmel Sheridan, Nov. 21, 1950; children—Susan Mary Ingrid, Thomas Michael Sheridan, Agnes Wilhelmina Carmel, Geraldine Teresa Ruth, Charles Patrick Desmond, Arthur John Christopher, Carmel Marie Louise, Brenda Juliana Patricia, Michael Terence Richard. Research fellow Irish Racing Bd., 1947-50; research officer Equine Research Sta., Eng., 1950-52; dir. Regional Lab., Warrenton, Va., 1952-53; bacteriologist dept. animal pathology U. Ky., 1953-55; assoc. pathologist Penrose Lab., Phila. Zoo, also asst. prof. vet. pathology U. Pa., 1955-57; head dept. pathology and toxicology Schering Corp., N.J., 1957-61; pathologist Woodard Research Corp., Herndon, Va., 1961-65, Vets. Meml. Med. Ctr., Meriden, 1990-93. dir. labs. east campus, 1990-93; intern, asst. resident, postdoctoral research fellow Yale-New Haven Hosp. and Yale U., 1965-67; resident VA Hosp., West Haven, Conn., 1967-68; pathologist, dir. labs. Meml. Hosp., Meriden, Conn., 1968-72, 74-90, chief of staff, 1981-83; cons. pathologist Meml. Hosp., Meriden, 1972-74; pathologist, dir. labs. Masonic Hosp., Wallingford, Conn., 1968-70, 72-76; cons. pathologist Bradley Hosp., Southington, Conn., 1970-91; attending physician, assoc. pathologist Hosp. of St. Raphael, New Haven, 1972-76; asst. clin. prof. Yale U., 1972—. Diplomate Am. Bd. Pathology. Mem. Am. Soc. Investigative Pathology, Am. Coll. Vet. Pathologists (cert.), Conn. Med. Soc., U.S. and Can. Acad. Pathology, Meriden Med. Soc., New Haven County Med. Assn., Sigma Xi, Alpha Omega Alpha. Roman Catholic. Cons. editor Am. Scientist, 1971-89. Home: 71 Turtle Bay Dr Branford CT 06405-4977 Office: Vets Meml Med Ctr East Campus PO Box 1009 1 King Pl Meriden CT 06450-1099

CRONIN, RANDALL COURTNEY, JR., family practice physician; b. Balt., June 23, 1951; s. Randall Courtney and Adeline Rosalie (Mosberg) C.; m. Laura Catherine van Valzan, June 29, 1974; children: Katherine Grace, Marian Virginia, Randall Van Valzan. BS in Zoology with honors, Mich. State U., 1973; MD, Hahnemann U., 1977. Diplomate Am. Bd. Family Physicians. Family practice resident Franklin Sq. Hosp., Balt., 1977-80; pvt. practice, owner Enfield Family Health Ctr., Whiteford, Md., 1980-86; part-time staff Fallston (Md.) Gen. Hosp. Ambulatory Clinic, 1981-86; med. dir., chief physician Prime Care Med. Ctrs. Newton (N.J.) Meml. Hosp., 1986-90; chief physician Geisinger Mountaintop (Geisinger Med. Group), Mountaintop, Pa., 1990—. Mem. AMA, Am. Acad. Family Physicians, Pa. Acad. Family Physicians (pres. Luzerne County chpt. 1994—), Pa. Med. Soc., Luzerne County Med. Soc. Methodist. Office: Geisinger Mountaintop 12 Kirby Ave Mountain Top PA 18707

CRONIN-GOLOMB, ALICE MARY, neuropsychologist; b. New Haven, Mar. 27, 1957. BA, Wesleyan U., 1979; PhD, Calif. Inst. Technology, 1984. Lic. psychologist, Mass. Assoc. prof. psychology Boston U., 1989—; cons. in field. Author: (book chpts.) Handbook of Neuropsychology, 1990, Dementia, 1993. Recipient Individual Rsch. Svc. award NIH, 1985-88, Del E. Webb fellowship Calif. Inst. Tech., 1985; grantee Alzheimer's Assn., 1988-89, , 95—, Sandoz Found. for Gerontol. Rsch., 1993-94. Mem. APA, AAAS, Soc. for Neuroscience, Am. Psychol. Soc., Ea. Psychol. Assn., Gerontol. Soc. Am., Phi Beta Kappa. Office: Dept Psychology Boston U 64 Cummington St Boston MA 02215-2407

CRONKHITE, LEONARD WOLSEY, JR., physician, consultant, research foundation executive; b. Newton, Mass., May 4, 1919; s. Leonard Wolsey and Orpah Glencor (Brewster) C.; m. Linda M. Marchky, Aug. 14, 1976; children: Judith, Marcia, Janice, Wendy. B.S., Bowdoin Coll., 1941, LL.D., 1979; M.D., Harvard U., 1950; LL.D., Northeastern U., 1970; L.H.D. (hon.), Curry Coll., 1977. Intern Mass. Gen. Hosp., Boston, 1950-51, resident, 1951-54; practice medicine Boston; mem. staff Children's Hosp. Med. Center, 1962-77, exec. v.p., 1971-73, pres., 1973-77; cons. staff Mass. Gen. Hosp., 1955-77, Boston Hosp. for Women, 1967-77; lectr. Harvard U. Med. Sch., 1953-77; pres. Med. Coll. Wis., Milw., 1977-84, MCW Research Found., Milw., 1984-86; trustee Northwestern Mut. Life Ins. Co., 1979-89; dir. Universal Health Services, Inc. Contbr. articles to profl. publs. Trustee Bowdoin Coll., chmn., 1995; trustee Maine Maritime Mus., chmn., 1995; trustee Nancy Sayles Day Found., Bigelow Lab. for Ocean Sci., 1995—, chmn., 1991—. With U.S. Army, 1940-45, 61-62. Decorated Legion of Merit with oak leaf cluster, Army Commendation medal, D.S.M.; recipient Bowdoin prize, 1973. Mem. Soc. Med. Adminstrs. (pres.), Assn. Am. Med. Colls. (chmn. 1975-76), Council Teaching Hosps. (chmn. 1972-73), Children's Hosps. Execs. Council, Nat. Acad. Scis. (Inst. Medicine). Clubs: Harvard (Boston), Army and Navy (Washington).

CRONKITE, EUGENE PITCHER, physician; b. Los Angeles, Dec. 11, 1914; s. Clarence Edgar and Anita (Pitcher) C.; m. Elizabeth Erna Kaitschuk, Aug. 17, 1940; 1 dau., Christina Elizabeth. AB, Stanford U., 1936, MD, 1940; DSc (hon.), L.I. U., 1962; MD (hon.), U. Ulm, Fed. Republic of Germany, 1987, U. Parma, Italy, 1991. Intern Stanford U. Hosps., San Francisco, 1939-40; resident in medicine Stanford U. Hosps., 1941-42; commd. lt. (s.g.) U.S. Navy, 1942, advanced through grades to rear adm., 1969, ret., 1954; head hematology Naval Med. Research Inst., Bethesda, Md., 1945-54; sr. scientist med. dept. Brookhaven Nat. Lab., 1954—, chmn., 1967-79; prof. medicine Health Sci. Center, SUNY, Stony Brook, 1979—; doctor of medicine Health Ctr. U. Ulm, Fed. Republic Germany, 1987—. Contbr. articles to med. jours. Recipient Alfred Benzon award Denmark, 1969; Ludwig Heilmeyer medal Fed. Republic Germany, 1974; Semmelwiess award Hungary, 1975; Alexander von Humboldt sr. scientist award Fed. Republic Germany, 1977; deVilliers prize and medal Leukemia Soc. Am., 1989. Mem. Am. Soc. Hematology (pres. 1970), Internat. Soc. Exptl. Hematology (pres. 1976), U.S. Nat. Acad. Scis., Am. Soc. Clin. Investigation, Assn. Am. Physicians, Am. Soc. Hematology, Am. Assn. Physiologists. Office: Brookhaven Nat Lab Med Dept Upton NY 11973

CRONKLETON, THOMAS EUGENE, physician; b. Donahue, Iowa, July 22, 1928; s. Harry L. and Ursula Alice (Halligan) C.; BA in Biology, St. Ambrose Coll., 1954; MD, Iowa Coll. Medicine, 1958; m. Wilma Agnes Potter, June 6, 1953; children: Thomas Eugene, Kevin P., Margaret A., Catherine A., Richard A., Robert A., Susan A., Phillip A. Diplomate Am. Bd. Family Practice. Rotating intern St. Benedict's Hosp., Ogden, Utah, 1958-59; Donahue, Iowa, 1959-61, practice family medicine, Davenport, Iowa, 1961-66, Laramie, Wyo., 1966-95; asso. The Davenport Clinic, 1961-63, partner, 1963-66; active staff St. Luke's Hosp., Mercy Hosp., Davenport; staff physician U. Wyo. Student Health Service, 1966-69, 70-71, 74-75, 76-95, acting dir., 1988-89, ret., 1995; staff physician outpatient dept. VA Hosp., Iowa City, 1969-70: staff physician outpatient dept. VA Hosp., Cheyenne, Wyo., 1971-74, chief outpatient dept., 1973-74; dir. Student Health Service Utah State U., Logan, 1975-76; physician (part-time) dept. medicine VA Hosp., Cheyenne, 1976-81. Active Long's Peak council Boy Scouts Am., 1970-95, scout chaplain Diocese of Cheyenne, 1980-95, mem. Diocesan Pastoral Council, 1982-85. Served with USMC, World War II, Korea. Recipient Dist. Scouter award Boy Scouts Am., 1974, St. George Emblem, Nat. Cath. Scouter award, 1981, Silver Beaver award Longs Peak Coun. Boy Scouts, 1995, Bronze Pelican award Diocese of Cheyenne Adult Scouts, 1995; also 5, 10, 15, 20 and 25-yr. service pins Boy Scouts Am. Fellow Am. Acad. Family Practice; mem. Wyo. State Med. Soc., Albany County (Wyo.) Med. Soc., Iowa Med. Soc., Johnson County (Iowa) Med. Soc. Democrat. Roman Catholic. Club: K.C. (4 deg.). Home: 6414 N Mokane Ct Kansas City MO 64151

CRONSHAW, JAMES, biology educator; b. Lancashire, Eng., Mar. 11, 1933; came to U.S., 1962; s. William and Edith (Wilkinson) C.; m. Patricia Birtwhistle, Sept. 1, 1956; 1 child, Caroline Anne. BS in Botany, U. Leeds, Eng., 1954, PhD, 1957, DSc, 1973. Demonstrator dept. botany U. Leeds, 1955-57; research officer, div. forest products Commonwealth Sci. and Indsl. Research Orgn., Melbourne, Australia, 1957-62; demonstrator dept. botany U. Melbourne, 1957-62; asst. prof. biology Yale U., New Haven, 1962-65; assoc. prof. biol. scis. U. Calif., Santa Barbara, 1965-71, prof., 1971-93; prof. emeritus, 1993—. Contbr. articles to profl. jours. Grantee NSF, 1962-64, 65-66, 67-69, 69-72, 75-78, 80-86, 88-91, 91-93, NIH, 1962-67, Santa Barbara Med. Found. Clinic, 1974-76, Dickson Blanchard Pathology Group, 1978, U.S. Dept. Interior, 1976-80, USDA, 1985, U.S. Dept. Energy, 1985. Fellow AAAS, Royal Microscopical Soc.; mem. Am. Soc. Cell Biology, Bot. Soc. Am., Electron Microscopy Soc. Am., So. Calif. Soc. for Electron Microscopy, Sigma Xi. Office: U Calif Dept Biol Scis Santa Barbara CA 93106

CRONSTEIN, BRUCE NEIL, rheumatologist, educator; b. Cin., May 24, 1951; s. Ralph and Carolyn (Spiwak) C.; m. Susan Marion Goodman, June 28, 1975; children: Jessica, Alexander. BA, Lake Forest (Ill.) Coll., 1972; MD, U. Cin., 1976. Intern in internal medicine U. Cin. Med. Ctr., 1976-77; resident in internal medicine Lenox Hill Hosp., N.Y.C., 1978-80; resident in pathology NYU Med. Ctr., 1977-78, fellow in rheumatology, 1980-81, chief fellow in rheumatology, 1981-82, instr. medicine, 1983-86, asst. prof., 1986-92, assoc. prof., 1992-96, prof. medicine and pathology, 1996—; clin. investigator, NIH, 1985-90; arthritis investigator, Arthritis Found., 1988-91, med. & sci. com. N.Y.C. chpt., 1990. Contbr. articles to profl. jours. Fellow Arthritis Found., 1985-87. Fellow Am. Coll. Rheumatology; mem. ACP, Am. Fedn. Clin. Rsch., N.Y. Rheumatism Assn. (bd. dirs. 1988, pres. 1994-95), Am. Soc. Clin. Investigation. Office: NYU Med Ctr 550 1st Ave New York NY 10016-6481

CROOKE, ROSANNE M., pharmacologist; b. Pittsfield, Mass., Oct. 30, 1955; d. Myron Michael and Marian Geneva (Russell) Muzyka; m. Stanley T. Crooke, Sept. 5, 1986. BA, Williams Coll., 1978; PhD, U. Pa., 1986. Rsch. asst. endocrine sec. dept. medicine U. Pa., Phila., 1978-81; fellow Wistar Inst. Anatomy and Biology, Phila., 1986-89; sr. scientist ISIS Pharms., Carlsbad, Calif., 1989—. Contbr. articles to profl. jours. Mem. AAAS, Soc. for In Vitro Biology. Home: 3211 Piragua St Carlsbad CA 92009-7840 Office: ISIS Pharms 2280 Faraday Ave Carlsbad CA 92008-7208

CROOKE, STANLEY THOMAS, pharmaceutical company executive; b. Indpls., Mar. 28, 1945; m. Nancy Alder (dec.); 1 child, Evan; m. Rosanne M. Snyder. BS in Pharmacy, Butler U., 1966; PhD, Baylor Coll., 1971, MD, 1974. Asst. dir. med. rsch. Bristol Labs., N.Y.C., 1975-76, assoc. dir. med. rsch., 1976-77, assoc. dir. R&D, 1977-79, v.p. R&D, 1979-80; v.p. R&D Smith Kline & French Labs., Phila., 1980-82; pres. R&D Smith Kline Beckman, Phila., 1982-88; chmn. bd., chief exec. officer ISIS Pharms., Inc., Carlsbad, Calif., 1989; cons. Enzytech, Cambridge, Mass., 1988, Bachem Biosci., Phila., 1988, Centocor, Malvern, Pa., 1988, BCM Techs., Houston, 1988; chmn. bd. dirs. GES Pharms., Inc., Houston, 1989-91; adj. prof. Baylor Coll. Medicine, Houston, 1982, U. Pa., Phila., 1982-89; bd. dirs. GeneMedicine, Houston, Calif. Healthcare Inst., Indsl. Biotech. Assn., Washington, 1993; mem. sci. adv. bd. SIBIA, La Jolla, Calif.; adj. prof. pharmacology UCLA, 1991, U. Calif. San Diego, 1994. Editor: Anti Cancer Drug Design, 1984; mem. editl. adv. bd. Molecular Pharmacology, 1986-91, Jour. Drug Targeting, 1992; editl. bd. Antisense Rsch. and Devel., 1994; sect. editl. bd. for biologicals and immunologicals Expert Opinion on Investigational Drugs, 1995. Trustee Franklin Inst., Phila., 1987-89; bd. dirs. Mann Music Ctr., Phila., 1987-89; children's com. Children's Svcs., Inc., Phila., 1983-84; adv. com. World Affairs Coun., Phila. Recipient Disting. Prof. award U. Ky., 1986, Julius Stermer award Phila. Coll. Pharmacy and Sci., 1981, Outstanding Lectr. award Baylor Coll. Medicine, 1984. Mem. AAAS, Am. Assn. for Cancer Rsch. (state legis. com.), Am. Soc. for Microbiology, Am. Soc. Pharmacology and Exptl. Therapeutics, Am. Soc. Clin. Pharmacology and Therapeutics, Am. Soc. Clin. Oncology, Indsl. Biotech. Assn. (bd. dirs. 1992-93). Office: ISIS Pharms Inc 2280 Faraday Ave Carlsbad CA 92008-7208

CROOKS, G(ARY) WALTER, physician, educator; b. Warrington, England, Sept. 22, 1955; s. Walter Broadhurst and Barbara Lillian (Johnson) C.; m. Bridget Anne King, Sept. 6, 1986. AB, Stanford U., 1977; MD, Harvard U., 1981. Diplomate Am. Bd. Internal Medicine. Intern, resident U. Pa., Phila., asst. prof., 1994-96, assoc. prof., 1996—. Mem. ACP, Phila. Coll. Physicians. Home: 429 W Moreland Ave Philadelphia PA 19118-4223 Office: Hosp of U Pa 3400 Spruce St Philadelphia PA 19104

CROOKS, PETER ANTHONY, pharmacy educator; b. Maltby, Eng., Oct. 17, 1942; came to U.S., 1981; s. Francis Benjamin and Daisy (Roberts) C.; m. Denise Gail Lord, Sept. 16, 1972; children: Stephen Edward, Sara Jane, David Michael, Elizabeth Anne. BS with honors, Manchester U., 1966, MS, 1967, PhD, 1970. Asst. lectr. Manchester (Eng.) U., 1968-70, lectr., 1970-80, sr. lectr., 1980-81; rsch. assoc. Yale U. Med. Sch., New Haven, Conn., 1976-78; assoc. prof. pharmacy U. Ky., Lexington, 1981-91, dir. grad. study, 1989—, prof., 1991—; cons. pharm. industry, 1991; mem. adv. com. NIH, Washington, 1992—. Regional (U.S.A.) editor Jour. Enzyme Inhibition, 1987—; mem. editorial bd. Jour. Biopharm. Scis., London, 1989—, Drug Metabolism Drug Interactions, Tel Aviv, 1987; patentee in field; contbr. over 200 articles to profl. publs. Recipient Geigy prize U. Manchester, 1966; grantee Wellcome Found., 1976, 78, ICI Pharms., Eng., 1972-75, Sci. Rsch. Coun., Eng., The Royal Pharm. Soc., The Brit. Coun., NIH, The Tobacco and Health Rsch. Inst., R.J. Reynolds Tobacco Co. Fellow Royal Soc. Chemistry, Royal Pharm. Soc.; mem. AAAS, Internat. Assn. for Study of Xenobiotics, Am. Chem. Soc., Pharm. Soc. Am., Assn. Pharm. Scientists (founder), Royal Pharm. Soc. Gt. Britain (conf. sci. com. 1980-82), Sigma Xi,

Rho Chi. Home: 3233 Raven Cir Lexington KY 40502-3305 Office: U Ky Coll of Pharmacy Lexington KY 40536

CROOKS, RICHARD HUGHEY, dermatologist; b. Greenville, S.C., Dec. 17, 1937; s. Job Hughey and Edith Mary (Wilde) C. BS, Furman U., Greenville, 1959; MD, Med. U. S.C., Charleston, 1962. Diplomate Am. Bd. Dermatology. Inern Piedmont Hosp., Atlanta, 1962-63; resident in dermatology Baylor Coll. Medicine, houston, 1965-68; pvt. practice Greenville, 1969—; alumni advisor Sigma Alpha Epsilon, 1982-96. Capt. USAF, 1963-65. Recipient Merit Key award Sigma Alpha Epsilon, 1995. Fellow Am. acad. Dermatology; mem. Piedmont Dermatol. Soc. S.C., Greenville Country Club, Pouisett Club (Greenville). Republican. Methodist. Office: 7-A Cleveland Ct Greenville SC 29607

CROSBY, GORDON EUGENE, JR., insurance company executive; b. Remsen, Iowa, Nov. 14, 1920; s. Gordon E. and Florence (Plummer) C.; m. Serena Chesnut Fitz Randolph Mac Rae, Apr. 23, 1992; children: Gordon Eugene III, Douglas H. Grad., Kemper Mil. Sch., 1938; student, U. Mo., 1938-40. Agt. New Eng. Mut. Life Ins. Co., Knoxville, Tenn., 1945; supr. New Eng. Mut. Life Ins. Co., Oakland, Calif., 1946; agy. mgr. New Eng. Mut. Life Ins. Co., Seattle, 1947, gen. agt., 1948-59; v.p., dir. agys. U.S. Life Ins. Co., N.Y.C., 1959-62, sr. v.p., dir. agys., 1962-64, exec. v.p., 1964-66, pres., CEO, 1966; pres., dir., mem. exec. com. USLIFE Corp., N.Y.C., 1966, chmn., pres., CEO, 1967-94, chmn. bd. dirs., chmn. exec. com., 1995—; chmn. U.S. Life Ins. Co., N.Y.C., All Am. Life Ins., Chgo., USLIFE Credit Ins. Co., Schaumburg, Ill., USLIFE Equity Sales Corp., N.Y.C., USLIFE Advisers, Inc., N.Y., USLIFE Sys. Corp., N.Y., USLIFE Income Fund, Inc., USLIFE Real Estate Svcs. Corp., USLIFE Ins. Svcs. Corp., USLIFE Fin. Instn. Mktg. Group, Inc., The Old Line Life Ins. Co. Am., Milw.; mem. nat. adv. bd. Chase Bank Corp. Mem. steering com. on fed. taxation Am. Coun. Life Ins.; past trustee Pace U.; past pres., bd. trustees Fifth Ave. Presbyn. Ch.; past bd. dirs. The Anglers Club of N.Y. Lt. USNR, WWII, PTO. Decorated Bronze Star medal. Mem. Manhattan's India House, Royal Palm Yacht Club, Anglers Club, Linville (N.C.) Golf Club, Univ Club (Ft. Myers, Fla.), Beta Gamma Sigma, Sigma Chi (Significant Sig award 1977). Episcopalian. Home: 429 E 52d St New York NY 10022 Office: USLIFE Corp 125 Maiden Ln New York NY 10038-4992*

CROSBY, LLOYD L., medical technologist; b. Parker, Kans., Nov. 13, 1934; s. Marion Lee and Bertha Gertrude (Gilderhause) C.; m. Mary Ann Hickerson, Jan. 3, 1959; children: Stephen, Paul Michael. BS, Kansas State Jr. Coll., 1956. Supt. Osawatomie (Kans.) State Hosp., 1953-55; chief of staff Osteopathic Hosp., Kansas City, 1955-73; lab. officer, pathologist Munson Amry Cmty. Hosp., Ft. Leavenworth, Kans., 1973-93.

CROSBY, LON OWEN, scientist, researcher; b. Webster City, Iowa, Aug. 6, 1945; s. Owen S. and Viola (Short) C.; m. Ann E. Sonerholm, Aug. 5, 1967; children: Brian, Teresa. BS, Iowa State U., 1967; PhD, Purdue U., 1971. Rsch. asst. Purdue U., Lafayette, Ind., 1967-71; rsch. assoc. Cornell U., Ithaca, N.Y., 1971-73; group leader Syntex Corp., Palo Alto, Calif., 1973-75; sr. scientist Enviro Control, Rockville, Md., 1975-79; rsch. assoc., rsch. asst. prof. U. Pa., Phila., 1979-85, exec. dir. clin. nutrition ctr., 1979-84; dir. cen. lab. VA Med. Ctr., Phila., 1983-86; pres. Numedloc, Inc., Bryn Mawr, Pa., 1979—; cons. Brookhaven Nat. Lab., Upton, N.Y., 1988-91. Author rsch. papers, abstracts and book chpts.; editor 1 book. Fellow Am. Coll. Nutrition. Office: 1687 301st St Webster City IA 50595-7450

CROSIGNANI, PIER GIORGIO, obstetrics and gynecology educator; b. Ziano, Piacenza, Italy, Oct. 14, 1933; s. Luigi and Agata (Casella) C.; m. Giuliana Nava (div. 1991); children: Andrea, Cristina, Laura, Marco; m. Maria Teresa Giavazzi, Mar. 5, 1952; 1 child, Matteo. MD, U. Pavia, Italy, 1958; PhD in Ob-Gyn., Sch. Medicine, Milan, Italy, 1964. Intern ob-gyn. U. Milan, 1958-62, asst. prof. dept. ob-gyn., 1962-69, assoc. prof., 1969-75, prof., 1975-79, prof., chief dept. ob-gyn. III, 1979-89, prof., chief dept. II, 1990-92, prof., chief dept. I, 1992—, dir. II Sch. Medicine, 1987—, dir I Inst. Ob-Gyn., 1993—; NIH Internat. fellow Dept. Ob-gyn. UCLA at Torrence, Calif., 1968-69; vis. prof. dept. ob-gyn. U. So. Calif., 1970; mem. WHO steering com. Task Force on Prevention and Mgmt. of Infertility, 1994—; mem. sci. program com. Internat. Fedn. Fertility Socs., 1989—; coord. human reprodn. area for U.S/Italy Coop. Rsch. Program, 1985—. Editor: Endocrinology of Human Infertility: New Aspects, 1981, In Vitro Fertilization and Embryo Transfer, 1983, Clinical Obstetrics and Gynecology: Induction of Ovulation, 1990, Endometriosis and Pelvic Pain: Time of Review, 1994. Mem. European Soc. Human Reprodn. and Embryology (past chmn.), Am. Fertility Soc., Chgo. Soc. Ob-Gyn. (hon.), Finnish Soc. Ob-Gyn. (hon.).

CROSS, CHARLOTTE LORD, social worker; b. Andalusia, Ala., Dec. 1, 1941; d. Roy Olice and Laura Emily (Smith) Lord; m. Jack Allen Cross, May 5, 1960; children: Jack Allen III, James Duane, Jeffrey Miles. BA in English, Auburn U., Montgomery, Ala., 1979, MS in Psychology, 1980, MS in Secondary Edn./English, 1993. Social worker dept. human resources State of Ala., Andalusia, 1980—; tchr. in English conversation to Nat. Cancer Inst. research scientists, Tokyo, 1965-66; adj. instr. psychology Lurleen B. Wallace State Jr. Coll, 1988-89, Troy State U., Fort Rucker, 1991. Recipient Dept. of Human Resources Commr.'s Merit award, 1989. Mem. United Coun. on Welfare Fraud (cert. welfare fraud investigator), Ala. Coun. on Welfare Fraud. Baptist.

CROSS, K.C., health facility administrator; b. Charleston, W.Va., Nov. 28, 1967; s. Robert Lee and Cynthia May (Kolb) C.; m. Melissa Combest, June 22, 1991; children: Savannah Jane, Hayley Elizabeth. AA in Bus. Mgmt., Potomac State Coll., 1988; BA in Bus. Adminstrn., Maryville Coll., 1990; MA in Health Adminstrn., Lynn U., 1993. Adminstr. in tng. Healthcare & Retirement, Boynton Beach, Fla., 1993; asst. adminstr. Healthcare & Retirement, Tamarac, Fla., 1993-94; adminstr. Unicare Health Facilities, Winter Haven, Fla., 1994-95, Integrated Health Svcs., Ft. Myers, Fla., 1996—. Fellow Am. Coll. and Health Care Adminstrs.; mem. Fla. Health Care Assn. Home: 1281 Bittmore Dr Fort Myers FL 33901 Office: Integrated Health Svcs 13755 Golf Club Pkwy Fort Myers FL 33919

CROSS, LYNDA LEE, health facility administrator, nurse; b. L.A., June 18, 1943; d. Fredrick Lewis Heyle and Bonnie Verda (Fridell) Covey; m. Jim Carl Eckler, June 7, 1963 (div. Sept. 1972); children: Barry, Dennis, Shantel, Candace; m. Douglas William Cross, Apr. 10, 1981. Diploma, Paradise Valley Sch. Nursing, 1964; BSN, Sonoma State U., 1981. RN; cert. infusion therapist, 1987. Clin. coord. urology San Diego Urological Med. Group, 1965-71; relief head nurse nursery Grossmont Hosp., La Mesa, Calif., 1971-75; relief head nurse neonatal ICU Balboa Naval Hosp., San Diego, 1976-77; coord. IV therapy St. Helena Hosp. and Health Ctr., Deer Park, Calif., 1977-79; staff nurse, IV therapist Mass. Eye and Ear Infirmary, Boston, 1982-84; pres., owner, IV clinician I.V. Lifeline, Inc., Berkley, Mass., 1984—. Developer IV homecare module, 1984 (1st Nurse award), coop. extended IV therapy in physicians setting, 1993. Fellow New Eng. Intravenous Nurses Soc. (scholarship chmn. 1985-86); mem. Intravenous Nurses Soc. Home and Office: 15861 Hwy 101 South Brookings OR 97415

CROSSEN, JOHN JACOB, radiologist, educator; b. Chgo., Mar. 28, 1932; s. John Shelly and Viola Catherine (Geis) C.; divorced; children: John, Pamela, Gregory, Terrence; m. Esther Aileen Cowie, Aug. 4, 1972. BS, U. Ill., 1953; MD, Loyola U., Chgo., 1957. Diplomate Am. Bd. Radiology, Nat. Bd. Med. Examiners. Intern Mercy Hosp., Buffalo, 1957-58; resident in radiology Cook County Hosp., Chgo., 1960-63; radiologist San Pedro and Long Beach, Calif., 1963-79; attending radiologist Harbor Hosp. of UCLA, Torrance, 1964-69; radiologist Tacoma, 1979-82; radiologist United Hosp. Ctr., Clarksburg, W.Va., 1982-93, dir. diagnostic radiology, 1992-93; asst. clin. prof. W.Va. U. Med. Sch., Morgantown, 1982-93; pres. Clarksburg Radiology Group Inc., 1992-94; with Columbia E Hosp. and Diagnostic Ctr., El Paso, Tex., 1993—. Capt. M.C., USAF, 1958-60. Recipient tchr. recognition Am. Acad. Family Practice, 1983-91. Fellow Am. Coll. Radiology, Internat. Coll. Surgeons, Am. Coll. Angiology; mem. AMA, Radiol. Soc. N.Am., Am. Inst. Ultrasound in Medicine, Tex. Radiology Soc., El Paso County Med. Soc., Coronado Country Club. Democrat. Roman Catholic. Home: 804 Pintada Pl El Paso TX 79912-1805

CROSSEN, ROBERT J., retired ophthalmologist, medical educator; b. Indpls., Apr. 13, 1923; s. Edward C. and Gladys (Gray) C.; m. Bettejane Mott, Apr. 23, 1945; children: Kathleen, Janet, Phyllis. BS in Medcine, Ind. U., 1944; MD, Ind. U., Indpls., 1946. Bd. cert. Am. Bd. Ophthalmology. Pvt. practice ophthalmologist Detroit, Grosse Pointe, Mich., 1952-82; prof. Wayne State Sch. Medicine, Detroit, 1953-88, U. Mich. Sch. Medicine, Ann Arbor, 1975-88; cons. Bausch & Lomb, Dow-Corning, 1970-77; sec., v.p. Am. Assn. Ophthalmology, 1970-80; pres. Mich. Ophthalmol. Soc., 1972-73, Med. Eye Svcs. Am., 1975-76; couselor Am. Acad. Ophthalmology, 1979-82. Contbr. chpt. to book and articles to profl. jours. Mem. Cable Com., James City County, Va., 1995—. Capt. U.S. Army, 1947-49. Fellow Am. Bd. Ophthalmology. Presbyterian. Home: 155 Fords Colony Dr Williamsburg VA 23188

CROSSLAND, ANN ELIZABETH, psychotherapist; b. Cambridge, Ohio, Apr. 24, 1940; d. H. Stewart and Laura Geraldine (Geese) Hastings; m. Eugene Joseph Szmuc, Nov. 30, 1963 (dec. Oct. 1976); m. Richard Ray Crossland, July 16, 1988; children: Rae Ann, Nancy, Carol. BS in Edn., Kent State U., 1965; MSEd in Counseling, U. Akron, 1981. Third grade tchr. Bertha Bradshaw Elem. Sch., Rootstown, Ohio, 1963-64; substitute tchr. Kent (Ohio) City Schs., 1967-84, Portage County Schs., Ravenna, Ohio, 1979-84; assoc. tchr. severely behaviorally handicapped Portage County Schs., Ravenna, 1984-88, H.S. tchr. severe behavior handicap, 1988-92; therapist Child & Adolescent Svc. Ctr., Canton, Ohio, 1992—. Bd. dirs., facilitator Oncology Support Group, Akron, 1977-81; bd. dirs., vol. trainer, counselor WomanShelter, Ravenna, 1980-87, organizer, group facilitator Portage County Cancer Group, Ravenna, 1982-83; mem. steering com. Portage County Adolescent Network, Ravenna, 1987-92. Mem. ACA, Am. Mental Health Counselors Assn., Delta Kappa Gamma (Theta chpt.). Democrat. Unitarian Universalist. Office: Child & Adolescent Svc Ctr 1226 Market Ave N Canton OH 44714-2604

CROSSON, CLAY FREDERICK, healthcare administrator; b. Jackson, Tenn., May 7, 1957; s. Fred Julius and Paula Irene (Turner) C.; m. Julie Marie Jacques, Aug. 15, 1981; children: Matthew Clayton, Caroline Anne. BSBA, U. Tenn., 1980; MBA, Mid. Tenn. State U., 1993. Adminstr. Nat. Health Corp., Tenn., Mo. and Ky., 1980-89; regional v.p. Nat. Health Corp., Greenwood, S.C., 1989-91; regional v.p Care More, Inc., Dalton, Ga., 1991-93, v.p., COO, 1994—; adj. faculty mem. So. Coll., Collegedale, Tenn., 1992—. Bd. dirs. Rotary Club, Dalton, 1991, United Way, 1984, 86, 90; pres. Boy Scouts Am., McMinnville, Tenn. 1988. Named Man of Yr. McMinnville C. of C., 1990. Mem. Am. Heart Assn. (pres. 1993), Am. Coll. Health Care Adminstrs. (pres. Tenn. chpt. 1989-90, Ga. gov. 1992-94, regional gov. 1995—, Adminstr. of Yr. 1989), Ga. Nursing Home Assn. (sec. 1995-96, vice chmn. 1996-97). Baptist. Home: 1905 Coventry Dalton GA 30720 Office: Care More Inc 1219 Memorial Dr Dalton GA 30720

CROUCH, FRED MICHAEL, physician, surgeon; b. Montgomery, Ala., Feb. 25, 1956; s. Robert Perry Crouch and Betty Ann Dover Featherstone; m. Karen Lynn Quesenberry, June 10, 1978; children: Caroline Elizabeth, Melissa Lynn, Katherine Marsha. BA in Chemistry, U. N.C., 1978; MD, Bowman Gray Sch. Medicine, 1982. Resident in surgery Hennepin County Med. Ctr., Mpls., 1982-88; fellow in vascular surgery Carolinas Med. Ctr., Charlotte, N.C., 1989; fellow in cardiothoracic surgery Carolinas Med. Ctr., Charlotte, 1990-91; pvt. practice Hickory Cardiovascular and Thoracic Surg. Assocs., Hickory, N.C., 1992—. John Motley Morehead scholar, 1978. Fellow So. Thoracic Surg. Assn., Am. Med. Soc., N.C. Med. Soc. Baptist. Home: 356 44th Ave Dr NW Hickory NC 28601 Office: Hickory Cardiovascular and Thoracic Surg Assocs 419 2d St NW Hickory NC 28601

CROUSHORE, THERESA MARIE, health facility administrator; b. Oct. 25, 1950. Diploma with honors, St. Barnabas Sch. Nursing, Mpls., 1972; BSN and BA in Psychology cum laude, Gwynedd Mercy Coll., 1982, BBA summa cum laude, 1983; M in Health Adminstrn., Wilkes Coll., 1987. RN, Pa., Minn., Fla., Calif.; cert. psychiat. nurse, advanced nurse adminstr., infection control. Staff and charge nurse surg. ICU, emergency dept. Winter Park (Fla.) Meml. Hosp., 1972-78; clin. editor Intermed Communications, Inc., Horsham, Pa., 1979; adminstrv. supr. Warminster (Pa.) Gen. Hosp., 1979-81, dir. mental health nursing svcs., 1981-85; dir. nursing svcs. First Hosp. Wyoming Valley, Wilkes-Barre, Pa., 1985-89, asst. adminstr., 1989-95; nursing dir. behavioral health divsn. Wyoming Valley Healthcare Sys., Wilkes Barre, 1995—; practitioner infection control; mem. adv. bd. Wilkes U., Coll. Misericordia; mem. adv. bd. and faculty Luzerne C.C.; cons. on survey preparation Joint Commn. Accreditation of Health Orgns. Contbr. articles to profl. jours. and books. Mem. Psi Theta Tau. Home: 14 Woodcrest Dr Wilkes Barre PA 18702-6957 Office: First Hosp Wyoming Valley 149 Dana St Wilkes Barre PA 18702-4825

CROUT, J(OHN) RICHARD, physician, pharmaceutical researcher; b. Portland, Oreg., Dec. 30, 1929; s. John Shaw and Georgia (Jacobs) C.; m. Carol Jean Keith, June 19, 1954; children: Linda Jane, Keith Richard, Andrew Richard. AB, Oberlin Coll., 1951; MD, Northwestern U., 1955, MS, 1956; DMed (hon.), U. Uppsala, Sweden, 1977. Intern Passavant Meml. Hosp., Chgo., 1955-56; asst. resident in internal medicine VA Rsch. Hosp., Chgo., 1956-57; clin. assoc. Nat. Heart Inst., Bethesda, Md., 1957-60; asst. resident in Medicine NYU-Bellevue Med. Ctr., N.Y.C., 1960-61; USPHS fellow, instr. pharmacology Harvard U., 1961-63; asst. prof. pharmacology and internal medicine U. Tex. Southwestern Med. Sch., Dallas, 1963-65; assoc. prof. U. Tex. Southwestern Med. Sch., 1965-70; prof. pharmacology and medicine Mich. State U., 1970-71; dep. dir. Bur. Drugs FDA, Rockville, Md., 1971-72; dir. office sci. evaluation Bur Drugs FDA, 1972-73, dir. Bur. Drugs, 1973-82; dir. Office of Med. Applications of Rsch. NIH, 1982-84; v.p. med. and sci. affairs Boehringer Mannheim Pharms., 1984-94; scholar in residence Inst. Medicine, 1994-95; pres. Crout Cons., Bethesda, 1994—; mem. drug rsch. bd. NAS-NRC; cons. WHO, 1974-84; trustee U.S. Pharmacopeia, 1985-95; mem. coms. Inst. Medicine, 1990, 92, 93; mem. bd. Genetics Inst., Inc., Cambridge, Mass., 1994—. Contbr. articles to profl. jours. Served to sr. asst. surgeon USPHS, 1957-60; asst. surgeon gen. 1976-84. Recipient Dist. Svc. award USPHS, 1977, Spl. Citation Commr. of FDA, 1981, 82, Disting. Career award Drug Info. Assn., 1994; Burroughs Wellcome scholar in clin. pharmacology, 1965-70. Fellow ACP; mem. Am. Fedn. Clin. Rsch., Am. Soc. Pharmacology and Exptl. Therapeutics, Am. Soc. Clin. Investigation, Am. Soc. Clin. Pharmacology and Therapeutics, Heart Assn., Soc. Clin. Trials, Phi Beta Kappa, Alpha Omega Alpha. Home and Office: 5300 Alta Vista Rd Bethesda MD 20814-1629

CROUTHAMEL, DAVID WAYNE, oral and maxillofacial surgeon; b. Augsburg, Germany, May 1, 1953; (parents Am. citizens); s. George N. and Vera E. (Gildersleve) C.; m. Janice Nolan, Aug. 28, 1976; 1 child, Joshua David. BS, Monmouth Coll., 1976; DDS, Temple U., 1982; cert. in oral and maxillofacial surgery, U. Pa., 1990. Diplomate Am. Bd. Oral and Maxillofacial Surgery. Med. technologist J.C. Blair Meml. Hosp., Huntingdon, Pa., 1976-78; gen. dentist Indian Health Svc., Sacaton, Ariz., 1982-87; oral and maxillofacial surg. resident U. Pa., 1987-90; pvt. practice, Chandler, Ariz., 1991—. Mem. ADA, Am. Assn. Oral and Maxillofacial Surgeons, Ariz. Soc. Oral and Maxillofacial Surgeons, Ariz. Dental Assn., Ctrl. Ariz. Dental Soc., Phoenix Soc. Oral and Maxillofacial Surgeons, Rotary (bd. dirs. Chandler Horizon 1995-96). Office: Ste 3 800 W Chandler Blvd Chandler AZ 85224

CROUTHAMEL, WILLIAM GUY, pharmaceutical research scientist, administrator, pharmacokineticist; b. Sellersville, Pa., Feb. 11, 1942; s. G. William and Susan (Walters) C.; m. Joanne Marie Kiszka, Jan. 29, 1966; children: Brian, Lori, David, Matthew. BS, Phila. Coll. Pharmacy, 1965, MS, 1967; PhD, U. Ky., 1970. From asst. to assoc. prof. W.Va. U., Morgantown, 1970-75; assoc. prof. U. Md., Balt., 1975-78; group leader Hoffmann-La Roche Inc., Nutley, N.J., 1978-79, rsch. sect. head, 1979-83, asst. dir., 1983-84, dir., 1984-90, sr. dir., 1990—; on spl. assignment Roche Basel (Switzerland) Rsch. Ctr., 1990-91; internat. mgr. Drug Metabolism & Pharmacokinetics, 1992-95, internat. adv., 1995—, v.p., 1993—; asst. v.p. Hoffmann-La Roche Inc., Nutley, N.J., 1991-93. Author: (with others) Disease States on Drug Pharmacokinetics, 1976, Methodology in Analytical Toxicology, 1982, G.I. Physiology and Dosage Form Design, 1989; editor: Animal Models for Oral Drug Delivery, 1983. Scoutmaster Boy Scouts Am., West Milford, N.J., 1984-88, com. chmn., 1988—. Named Disting. Kentuckian U. Ky., 1989; recipient FDA Commn.'s Spl. citation, 1993. Fellow Am. Assn. Pharm. Assn. (sect. chmn. 1986), Pharm. Rsch. Mfrs. Assn. (steering com. 1982-86, 93—). Home: 332 High Crest Dr West Milford NJ 07480-3712 Office: Hoffmann-La Roche Inc Dept Drug Metabolism Nutley NJ 07110

CROVITZ, ELAINE SANDRA, clinical psychologist; b. N.Y.C., Oct. 18, 1936; d. Sydney and Jennie (Papier) Kobrin; children—Gordon, Deborah, Sara Pi. B.A., Bklyn. Coll., 1956; M.A., Duke U., 1960, Ph.D., 1964. Instr. med. psychology, staff psychologist Duke U. Med. Center, Durham, N.C., 1963-64, assoc. med. psychology, supervising psychologist, 1964-67, asst. prof. med. psychology, 1967-75, assoc. prof., 1975—; bd. dirs. Maferr Found., Va.; vis. assoc. prof. N.C. Cen. U., Durham, 1976-79. Mem. Am. Psychol. Assn., Southeastern Psychol. Assn., N.C. Psychol. Assn., Assn. for Advancement Psychology, Internat. Council Psychologists, Internat. Assn. Applied Psychology, Nat. Register Health Service Providers Psychology, AAUW. Author: (with Elizabeth Buford) Courage Knows No Sex, 1978; author research papers; contbr. articles to profl. jours. Home: 419 Gentry Ln Hillsborough NC 27278-8811 Office: Duke U Med Ctr PO Box 3895 Durham NC 27710

CROW, CHARLES BRANDON, III, internist; b. Balt., Nov. 20, 1944; s. Charles Brandon Jr. and Catherine (Carey) C.; m. Carol Catherine Connor, Dec. 20, 1969; children: Patricia, Charles IV, Amy, Ellen. BA, U. Va., 1966; MD, U. Ala., 1974. Diplomate Am. Bd. Internal Medicine. Intern and resident Carraway Meth. Med. Ctr., Birmingham, Ala., 1975-78; pvt. practice internal medicine Birmingham, 1978—. Office: 516 Brookwood Blvd Birmingham AL 35209

CROW, HAROLD EUGENE, physician, family medicine educator; b. Farber, Mo., Jan. 17, 1933; s. Leslie J. and Laura L. (Sparks) C.; m. Mary Kay Krenke, July 5, 1974; children—Janet L., Jason P. MD, U. Mo., 1963. Diplomate Am. Bd. Family Practice, Am. Bd. Med. Examiners. Intern E.W. Sparrow Hosp., Lansing, Mich., 1963-64; pvt. practice medicine specializing in family practice Lansing, 1964-70; dir. family practice residency E.W. Sparrow Hosp., Lansing, Mich., 1970-82; chmn. dept. family and community medicine Sch. Medicine U. Nev., Reno, 1982-87, dir. office Rural Health Sch. Medicine, 1984-87; med. dir. S.W. Med. Assocs., Reno, 1987-88; dir. Lynchburg (Va.) Family Practice Resident Program, 1988-96; dir. Outer Banks Project East Carolina U. Sch. of Medicine, Nags Head, N.C., 1996—; dir. Outer Banks Edn. and Program Devel. Project. Developer non-rotational residency model for family practice tng., tng. model for rural med. practice; innovator computerized health info. systems for family physicians. Numerous civic activities. With U.S. Army, 1955-57. Mem. Am. Coll. Phys. Exec., numerous profl. assns. Presbyterian. Home: 2604 Bridge Ln Nags Head NC 27959-9693

CROW, SAMUEL ALFRED, II, physician, army officer; b. Topeka, Dec. 10, 1950; s. Samuel Alfred and Ruth Marie (Rush) C.; m. Cheryl Venita Browne, June 13, 1973; children: Andrew Marcus, Melissa Jean. BA in Psychology, Washburn U., 1973; MA in Counseling Psychology, Chapman Coll., 1975; DO, U Health Scis., 1985. Commd. capt. U.S. Army, 1981, advanced through grades to lt. col., 1994; missile launch officer USAF, Wichita, Kans., 1985-86; brigade surgeon Berlin Brigade, 1986-88; resident Womack Army Hosp., Ft. Bragg, N.C., 1988-90; brigade surgeon Saudi Arabia, 1990-91; family practice physician Reynolds Army Hosp. Ft. Sill, Lawton, Okla., 1991-92; family practice physician, chmn. Dept. Family Practice Springfield (Mo.) Clinic, 1992—. Mem. AMA, AOA, Am. Acad. Family Physicians (bd. cert.). Home: 4926 S Wellington Dr Springfield MO 65810-1638 Office: 1660 E Kearney St Springfield MO 65803-4106

CROWDER, MILES KEENEY, psychiatry educator; b. Chattanooga, Jan. 25, 1943; s. Miles Samuel and Leone (Biggers) C. AB, Emory U., 1963, MD, 1967. Intern W.Va. U., Morgantown, 1968; resident in psychiatry U. Wis., Madison, 1971; from asst. to assoc. prof. Vanderbilt U. Med. Ctr., Nashville, 1973-88; assoc. prof. Emory U. Sch. Medicine, Atlanta, 1988—; sr. examiner Am. Bd. Psychiatry and Neurology, Deerfield, Ill., 1983—. Reviewer Am. Jour. Psychiatry, 1981—; contbr. articles to profl. jours. With USN, 1971-73. Fellow Am. Psychiat. Assn.; mem. Am. Coll Psychiatrists, Am. Assn. of Dirs. Psychiat. Residency Tng. (chmn. membership com. 1979-88), Assn. for Acad. Psychiatry, Soc. for Psychotherapy Rsch., Chi Phi. Office: Emory U 1701 Uppergate Dr NE Atlanta GA 30322

CROWE, HAL SCOTT, chiropractor; b. Atlanta, Apr. 19, 1953; s. Hugh Lee and Dorothy Elizabeth (Cooke) C.; m. PiHsiou Hsu, Mar. 29, 1980; children: Hal Scott Jr., Colleen Jao. Student, Johns Hopkins U., 1971-72, Ga. State U., 1973-76, 78-80; D of Chiropractic, Life Chiropractic Coll., 1983; post D. in Chiropractic Neurology, Logan Chiropractic Coll., 1992. Diplomate Nat. Bd. Chiropractic Examiners; cert. chiropractic orthopinologist, cert. chiropractic neurologist Logan Chiropractic Coll.; cert. advance open water scuba diver, cavern diver. Radiol. technician Crowe Chiropractic Offices, College Park, Ga., 1979-83; chiropractic practitioner Crowe Chiropractic Offices, College Park and Brunswick, Ga., 1983—; clin. rschr. Sweat Found., Atlanta, 1984—; resident in neurology Am. Coll. of Chiropractic Neurology, 1989-92; mem. postgrad. faculty Life Chiropractic Coll.; interim chmn. Acad. Upper Cervical Chiropractic Orgn., 1994; preceptor faculty mem. Palmer Chiropractic Coll.; participant 4th through 12th Ann. Upper Cervical Confs., 1987-95; mem. Dolphin Project Rsch. Program. Contbr. articles to profl. jours.; 2d chair trombonist Jekyll Island Big Dance Band, 1985-94, condr., 1993-95. Host Columbus Ship Replica exhibit, 1992; missionary United Meth. Ch., Petite Goave, Haiti, 1986; mem. coun. on ministries McKendree United Meth. Ch., Brunswick, 1986-87. Recipient Appreciation award Grostic Study Club, Life Chiropractic Coll., 1985. Mem. Internat. Chiropractors Assn., Ga. Coun. Chiropractic, Soc. Chiropractic Orthospinologists (cert. doctor, instr.), Chiropractic Atlas Orthogonists, Nat. Upper Cervical Chiropractic Assn., Acad. Upper Cervical Chiropractic Orgns. Inc., Reef Environ. Edn. Found., Nat. Speleological Soc. (cave diving sect.), Lions (bd. dirs. 1986-88, Lion Tamer 1986-87, presdl. appreciation award 1986, pres. 1988-89, Tail Twister 1991), Diver's Alert Network, Ian Fleming Found. Home: 792 S Beachview Dr Jekyll Island GA 31527-0638 Office: Crowe Chiropractic Offices 2321 Parkwood Dr Brunswick GA 31520-4720

CROWE, RAE LORD, nurse educator researcher, nurse practitioner; b. Binghamton, N.Y., Aug. 19, 1933; d. Roy F. and Valerie W. (Kreski) Lord; m. Kenneth Crowe, Sept. 8, 1956; children: Kenneth, Roy, Daniel, Carol. BSN, Cornell U., 1956; MA, NYU, 1977, PhD, 1989; gerontol. nurse practitioner, Adelphi U., 1995. Cert. nurse practitioner Am. Nurses Credentialing Ctr. Pub. health nurse Vis. Nurse Svc., N.Y.C., 1956-57; evening charge nurse various orgns., 1957-74; instr. Bd. Cooperative Ednl. Svcs., Syosset, N.Y., 1974-77; asst. prof. CCNY, N.Y.C., 1977-86; asst. prof. SUNY, Bklyn., 1989-94, assoc. prof., 1994—; cons. N.Y. State Health Dept., N.Y.C., 1975-76, discharge planning nurse, 1977; workshop leader in therapeutic touch and meditation. Contbr. artivles to profl. jours.; appeared on Let's Talk Arthritis (cablevision), 1993. Asst. coord. Nurse Healers Profl. Assn., 1983-85. Am. Heart Assn. grantee, 1991-92, 94-95. Mem. ANA, N.Y. State Nurses Assn. (functional unit nurse educator liaison 1992), Cornell N.Y. Hosp. Alumni (bd. dirs. 1980-84, class sec. 1992—), Sigma Theta Tau. Home: 37 E Lyons St Melville NY 11747-1121

CROWELL, KENNETH LELAND, biology educator; b. Glen Ridge, N.J., July 19, 1933; s. Thomas Irving Jr. and Pauline (Whittlesey) C.; m. Marilyn Nancy Reed, Jan. 12, 1939; children: David, Thomas. BS, Yale U., 1955; PhD, U. Pa., 1961. Instr. Duke U., Durham, N.C., 1961-62; faculty Marlboro Coll., Marlboro, Vt., 1962-66; rsch. assoc. U. Alberta, Calgary, Alberta, Can., 1966-67; prof. biology St. Lawrence U., Canton, N.Y., 1967—; stewardship com. Nature Conservancy, Deer Isle, Maine, 1970—. Contbr. sci. papers to profl. jours.; regional editor Federated Bird Clubs N.Y., 1984—. Rsch. grantee NSF, 1962-73. Fellow Linnean Soc. London, AAAS; mem. Am. Ornithologists Union (elective). Universalist-Unitarian. Office: St Lawrence U Canton NY 13617

CROWELL, SHERRY DIEGEL, clinical psychologist; b. Colorado City, Tex., Oct. 19, 1951; d. Charles Ambrose and Jo Ellen (Elliot) Diegel; 1 child, Charles Michael. BA, Tex. Tech U., 1983, MA, 1985, PhD, 1992. Lic. psychologist, Tex. Sr. dir. Psychol. Clinic, Lubbock, Tex., 1987-89; psychometrist Med.-Surg. Neurology Clinic, Lubbock, 1987-89; assoc. clin.

psychologist Big Spring (Tex.) State Hosp., 1987-89; psychology intern Austin (Tex.) State Hosp., 1989-90; pvt. practice psychotherapy Abilene, Tex., 1990-93; clin. psychologist Abilene Regional Mental Health Mental Retardation Ctr., 1991-93; pvt. practice psychology Abilene; cons. and chief psychologist Young County Family Resource & Advocacy Ctr., Child Advocacy of Tex., 1996—; adj. prof. psychology McMurry U., 1994—; chair symposium Tex. Assn. on Mental Retardation, 1992; presenter in field. Contbr. rsch. articles to profl. publs. Mem. adv. bd. Big Country AIDS Support Group, Abilene, 1992—; mem. Lubbock AIDS Health Care Planning Group, Lubbock, 1987-89; founding mem., trustee West Tex. AIDS Found., Lubbock, 1986-89, mentoring program, 1995—. Mem. APA, Tex. Psychol. Assn. (chair symposium 1987, 88, 92-93, Alexander award for Rsch. Excellence in Psychobiologic Field 1992), Abilene Philharmonic. Home: 1217 Ross Ave Abilene TX 79605-4230 Office: 3301 N 3rd St Ste 113 Abilene TX 79603-7033

CROWLEY, ANGELA ANTOINETTE, nurse, educator; b. Washington, Dec. 29, 1949; d. Constantino F. and Doreen A. (Rasmussen) Cinquegrana; m. John D. Crowley, Nov. 24, 1973; children: Matthew, Elizabeth. BSN, Cath. U. Am., 1971; MA in Nursing, NYU, 1975; PNP, U. Conn., Farmington, 1975; PhD, U. Conn., 1995. Staff nurse Nat. Naval Med. Ctr., Bethesda, Md., 1973; pediatric nurse practitioner Bridgeport (Conn.) Hosp., 1975-76, Norwalk (Conn.) Hosp., 1977-80; mem. collaborative pediatric practice Brookfield, Conn., 1981-84, New Haven, Conn., 1994—; pediatric nurse practitioner Washington-Warren (Conn.) Vis. Nurses Agy., 1982-84, Guilford (Conn.) Pediatrics, 1985-94, 94—; assoc. prof. nurse practitioner program Yale U. Sch. Nursing, New Haven, 1984—; collaborative practice PNP, New Haven, Conn. Contbr. articles to profl. publs. Mem. adv. group Child Care Coalition South Ctrl. Ct., 1986—. Mem. ANA, Am. Acad. Nurse Practitioners (State Excellence award 1991), Conn. Nurses Assn., Nat. Assn. Pediatric Nurse Assocs. and Practitioners (co-chair child care spl. interest group, liaison to Am. Acad. Pediatrics), Sigma Theta Tau.

CROWLEY, DANIEL D., health insurance executive. BBA, MBA. Exec. v.p. Blue Cross and Blue Shield of Ohio; chmn., pres. CEO Found. Health Corp., Cordova, Calif., 1989—. Office: Found Health Corp 3400 Data Dr Rancho Cordova CA 95670-7956*

CROWLEY, DAVID JEREMIAH, psychiatrist, neurologist; b. Lynn, Mass., Jan. 6, 1941; s. John J. and Mary T. (McGillicuddy) C.; m. Martha Cotter, Apr. 15, 1967; children: Maureen, David Jr., Kevin. AB, Holy Cross Coll., 1962; MD, Tufts U., 1966. Diplomate Am Bd. Neurology and Psychiatry. Intern St. Elizabeth's Hosp., Brighton, Mass., 1966-67, resident in internal medicine, 1967-69; resident in neurology New England Med. Ctr., Boston, 1969-72; pvt. practice Essex Neurol. Assn., Salem and Lynn, Mass., 1972—. Mem. AMA, Am. Acad. of Neurology, Mass. Med. Soc. Roman Catholic. Home: 4 Wilson Rd Gloucester MA 01930 Office: Essex Neurol Assocs 225 Boston St Lynn MA 01904

CROWLEY, MARILYN, critical care nurse, educator; b. Geuda Springs, Kans., Sept. 29, 1935; d. Wyatt Julian and Mary Alice Swaim; m. Dale Crowley, June 7, 1958; 1 child, Debra Crowley Schrag. Diploma, William Newton Meml. Hosp., Winfield, Kans., 1956. Cert. critical care nurse, emergency nurse, emergency med. svcs. instr., ACLS, BLS, others. Dir. emergency med. tech. program Southwestern Coll. of Kans., Winfield, 1975-90; coord. fire med. rescue svcs. Wichita Fire Dept., 1981-86; mobile intensive care nurse Winfield Ambulance Svc. William Newton Meml. Hosp., 1970-76, charge ICU and emergency dept., house supr., 1990-93, travel nurse emergency dept., trama ctr., critical care, 1993—, supr., head nurse, 1970-77; surg. and emergency nurse Snyder Clin. Assn., Winfield, 1957-70; per diem nurse emergency dept. Trauma Ctr. St. Francis Regional Med. Ctr., Wichita, Kans., 1993—; travel nurse Robert Wood Johnson Univ. Hosp., New Brunswick, N.J.; travel nurse emergency dept. Trauma Ctr. Hendrick Med. Ctr., Abilene, Tex.; night nursing and ER supr. Mt. Desert Island Hosp., Bar Harbor, Maine, 1994; staff nurse ICU N.W. Miss. Med. Ctr., Clarksdale, Miss., 1994—; house mgr. Penobscot Valley Hosp., Lincoln, Maine, 1995; interim DON Perry (Okla.) Meml. Hosp., 1995-96; adj. staff edn., tng. and exam. Kans. Bd. Emergency Med. Svcs., Topeka; instr. nursing continuing edn. St. Francis Regional Med. Ctr. Outreach Edn. Active Am. Heart Assn., Am. Cancer Soc. Recipient Spl. award Kans. Emergency Med. Technicians Assn., 1980, Wichita Fire Dept., 1985, 86, Winfield Area Emergency Med. Svcs., 1978, numerous others. Home: 1002 E 13th Ave Winfield KS 67156-4513

CROWN, BARRY MICHAEL, psychologist; b. Waukegan, Ill., June 23, 1943; s. Frank Edward and Sara (Babel) C.; m. Sheryl Joyce Lowenthal, Oct. 31, 1982. B.A., U. Miami, 1965; M.Ed., Fla. Atlantic U., 1966; Ph.D., Fla. State U., 1969; JD Thomas Jefferson Coll. Law, 1983. Diplomate Am. Acad. Behavioral Medicine, Am. Bd. Profl. Neuropsychology, Am. Bd. Adminstrv. Psychology; cert. addictions specialist. Research coordinator Gov. Office State Fla., 1967-69; postdoctoral fellow in psychology Mass. Gen. Hosp., Boston, 1969-70; asst. prof. psychiatry U. Ill. Med. Sch., Chgo., 1970-71, U. Miami Med. Sch., 1971-74; assoc. prof. psychology Fla. Internat. U., Miami, 1974-78, Courtesy Prof. psychology, 1980—; pvt. practice psychology, Miami, 1978—. NIMH postdoctoral fellow, 1969, fellow Am. Coll. Forensic Psychology, 1986; recipient Disting. Sci. Contbn. award Nat. Council on Drug Abuse, 1975. Fellow Royal Soc. Medicine; mem. Am. Psychol. Assn., Am. Coll. Psychology, Am. Psychology-Law Soc., Soc. Behavioral Medicine, Soc. Nuclear Medicine, Nat. Acad. Neurpsychology. Democrat. Jewish. Club: Tiger Bay (Miami).

CROWN, EMILIE BALDWIN KNAPP, critical care nurse; b. Washington, Feb. 28, 1952; d. Harold A. and Barbara I. (Baldwin) Knapp; m. Dale Montgomery, Apr 21, 1981; children: Matthew, Kelly. Christopher. AA, Montgomery Coll., Takoma Park, Md., 1979; BA, Goucher Coll., 1974. RN, Md.; CEN; cert. TNCC instr., ACLS, PALS, PALS instr., ENPC instr. Recovery room nurse Suburban Hosp. Assn., Bethesda, Md., 1979-83; charge nurse Montgomery Gen. Hosp., Olney, Md., 1984-85; head nurse emergency dept. Montgomery Gen. Hosp., Olney, 1985-89; clin. dir. emergency dept. Montgomery Gen. Hosp., 1989-90; staff nurse emergency dept. Shady Grove Adventist Hosp., Rockville, Md., 1990—. Mem. Emergency Nurses Assn. (pres. Md. coun. 1993, Mid-Md. chpt. 1993, treas. Md. state coun. 1994-95, treas. mid Md. chpt. 1996), Sigma Theta Tau. Home: 17113 Berclair Ter Rockville MD 20855-2520

CROYLE, BARBARA ANN, health care management executive; b. Knoxville, Tenn., Oct. 22, 1949; d. Charles Evans and Myrtle Elizabeth (Kellam) C. BA cum laude in Sociology, Coll. William and Mary, 1971; cert. corp. tax and securities law Inst. Paralegal Tng., 1971; JD, U. Colo., 1975; cert. program mgmt. devel. Colo. Women's Coll., 1980; MBA, U. Denver, 1983. Bar: Colo. 1976. Paralegal Holland & Hart, Denver, 1972-73; law clk. Colo. Ct. Appeals, Denver, summer 1976; assoc. firm Shaw Spangler & Roth, Denver, 1976-77; mgr. acquisitions/lands Petro-Lewis Corp., Denver, 1977-85; mgr. strategic planning Westinghouse, Transp. Div., 1985-87; mng. dir. Benefit Resource Mgmt. Group (subs. Blue Cross We. Pa.), 1987-92; COO and v.p. D.T. Watson Rehab. Hosp., 1992-93; regional dir. Franciscan Med. Ctr., Dayton campus, Ohio, 1994—; tchr. oil and gas law Colo. Paralegal Inst., 1978, 79; arbitrator Am. Arbitration Assn.; mediator Dayton Mediation Ctr. Mem. NAFE, ABA, Pa. Bar Assn., Inst. Noetic Scis., Am. Coll. Healthcare Execs. (ethics com., assoc.). Home: 330 Jones St Dayton OH 45410-1104 Office: Franciscan Med Ctr Dayton Campus 601 S Edwin C Moses Blvd Dayton OH 45408-1424

CRUES, JOHN VERNON, III, radiologist, educator; b. Lubbock, Tex., Nov. 21, 1949; s. John Vernon Jr. and Dorothy Katherine (Sievers) C.; m. Jayne Ausanka, Aug. 7, 1976; children: Drew, Ry, Melissa. AB, Harvard U., 1972; postgrad., U. Salzburg, Austria, 1972; MS, U. Ill., 1975; MD, Harvard U., 1979. Diplomate Am. Bd. Internal Medicine, Am. Bd. Radiology, Nat. Bd. Med. Examiners; lic. physician, Calif.; cert. drug enforcement adminstrn., basic life support in cardiopulmonary resuscitation; lic. amateur radio operator, sr. parachute rigger, single engine pvt. pilot. Intern. L.A. County-U. So. Calif. Med. Ctr., L.A., 1979-80; resident in internal medicine Cedars-Sinai Med. Ctr., L.A., 1980-82, resident in diagnostic radiology, 1982-85; rsch. engr. dept. elec. and computer engring. U. Calif., Santa Barbara; asst. clin. prof. radiology UCLA, 1987—; dir. magnetic resonance, musculoskeletal and emergency radiology Cedars-Sinai Med. Ctr., L.A., 1993—; med. cons. Future Diagnostics Inc., L.A.; bd. dirs. Future Diagnostics Inc.; mem. rsch. bd. F. I. Internat.; mem. adv. bd. Teleradiology Svcs. Inc., Boston. Assoc. editor: Jour. Magnetic Resonance Imaging, 1993-96; column editor: Applied Radiology; mem. editl. bd.: Magnetic Resonance Quar., 1990-95; manuscript reviewer; contbr. articles to med. jours.; editor book chpts. Recipient Crues and Kressel award for outstanding contbns. to edn. of magnetic resonance technologists Sect. for Magnetic Resonance Technologists, 1991; Schlumberger scholar Harvard U., 1968-72. Mem. Soc. Magnetic Resonance (pres.), Radiol. Soc. N.Am., Am. Coll. Radiology (commn. on neurology and magnetic resonance; com. stds. and accreditation 1991—, com. mktg. and pub. rels. 1991—, com. human resources 1991—, com. magnetic resonance biol. effects 1993—, com. rsch. and tech. assessment 1993—), Internat. Soc. for Magnetic Resonance in Medicine (pres. 1994-95), Am. Soc. Emergency Radiology (charter), Internat. Skeletal Soc.

CRUESS, RICHARD LEIGH, surgeon, university dean; b. London, Ont., Can., Dec. 17, 1929; s. Leigh S. and Martha A. (Peever) C.; m. Sylvia Crane Robinson, May 30, 1953; children: Leigh S., Andrew C. B.A., Princeton U., 1951; M.D., Columbia U., 1955. Diplomate Am. Bd. Orthopedic Surgery. Intern Royal Victoria Hosp., Montreal, Que., 1955-56; resident surgery Royal Victoria Hosp., 1956-57; resident surgery N.Y. Orthopedic Hosp., 1959-60, asst. resident orthopedic surgery, 1960-61, resident orthopedic surgery, 1961-62, Annie C. Kane fellow orthopedic surgery, 1961-62; research asso. depts. orthopedic surgery and biochemistry Columbia U., N.Y.C., 1962-63; John Armour Travelling fellow, 1962-63, Am.-Brit.-Can. Travelling fellow, 1967; practice medicine specializing in orthopedic surgery Montreal, 1963—; orthopedic surgeon Royal Victoria Hosp., orthopedic surgeon-in-charge, 1968-81, asst. surgeon-in-chief, 1970-81; chief surgeon Shriner's Hosp. for Crippled Children, Montreal, 1970-82; prof. surgery McGill U., Montreal, 1970—, chmn. div. orthopedic surgery, 1976-81, dean faculty medicine, 1981-95, prof. Ctr. for Med. Edn., 1995—; bd. dirs. Carter-Wallace, Inc., N.Y.C.; hon. cons. orthopedic surgery Queen Elizabeth Hosp., 1972—; mem. clin. grants com. Med. Rsch. Coun., 1972-75, mem. coun., 1980-86, mem. exec., 1983-86. Contbr. articles on surgery to profl. jours.; mem. editl. bd. Jour. Internat. Orthopedics, 1976-85, Jour. Bone and Joint Surgery, 1977-83, Current Problems in Orthopedics, 1977-83, Jour. Orthopaedic Rsch., 1986-88. Served to lt. M.C., USN, 1957-59. Fellow Royal Coll. Physicians and Surgeons Can. (chief examiner orthopedic surgery 1970-72), ACS, Am. Acad. Orthopedic Surgeons, Royal Soc. Can.; mem. Order of Can., Can. Orthopedic Assn. (sec. 1971-76, pres. 1977-78), Can. Orthopedic Rsch. Soc. (pres. 1971-72), Am. Orthopedic Rsch. Soc. (pres. 1975-76), Am. Orthopedic Assn., Ann. Orthopedic Surgeons Province Que. (treas. 1971-72), Société Française de Chirurgie Orthopedique (hon.), McGill Osler Reporting Soc., Assn. can. Med. colls. (pres. 1987-89). Home: 526 Mount Pleasant Ave, Montreal, PQ Canada H3Y 3H5 Office: McGill U, 3655 Drummond St, Montreal, PQ Canada H3G 1Y6

CRUFT, GEORGE EDWARD, surgeon; b. Keokuk, Iowa, 1924. MD, U. Ill. Coll. Medicine, 1947. Diplomate Am. Bd. Surgeons. Intern Indpls. Gen. Hosp., 1947-48; resident surgery Phila. Naval Hosp., 1958-62; adminstr. Am. Bd. Surgery, Phila. Fellow ACS; mem. AMA. Office: Am Bd Surgery 1617 John F Kennedy Blvd Philadelphia PA 19103-1847*

CRUM, ALBERT BYRD, psychiatrist, consultant; b. Omaha, Nov. 17, 1931; s. J. Rufus and Alberta (McCreary) C.; m. Rosa Maria Hennessy y Sinclair; children: Rosa Maria Crum O'Brien, Elsie Crum Coy, Alberta Crum Fousek. BS, U. Redlands, Calif., 1953; MD, Harvard U., 1957; MS, NYU, 1987; DS (hon.), U. Redlands, 1974. Med. intern Columbia U. div. Bellevue Med. Ctr., N.Y.C., 1957-58; rsch. fellow, psychiat. resident Creedmoor Inst. for Psychol. Studies, Queens Village, N.Y., 1958-59; chief, neuropsychiatric svcs., Continental Air Command USAF Hosp., 1959-61; psychiat. resident Columbia U. Psychiat. Inst. of Columbia-Presbyn. Hosp., N.Y.C., 1961-63; pvt. practice Brooklyn Heights, N.Y., 1963—; active attending staff Gracie Sq. Hosp., N.Y.C., 1963—; med. dirs. Psychiatric Svcs. Internat. P.C., Brooklyn Heights, 1980—; ednl. dir. med. and health seminars Internat. Inst. for Human Behavior, Inc., Brooklyn Heights, 1983—; advisor Office of Tibet, N.Y.C., 1984—; clin. prof. behavioral scis. NYU, N.Y.C., 1987—; pres., dir. behavioral scis. Way of Life/N.Y., Ltd., Brooklyn Heights, 1989—; pres. Y.F. One/N.Y., Ltd., Brooklyn Heights, 1991—, Y.F. Nationwide, Inc., Brooklyn Heights, 1991—; co-chmn. U.S. Coordinating Commn. for Nomination of His Holiness the Dalai Lama of Tibet for the Nobel Peace Prize, Brooklyn Heights, 1986—; adj. prof. anatomy and neuroanatomy, NYU, 1987—; ptnr. Burdick Assocs. Investment Firm, Brooklyn Heights, 1976—; pres. Burdick Assocs. Owners Corp., Brooklyn Heights, 1983—; chmn. Human Behavior Found., Brooklyn Heights, 1968—; chmn. selection com. Human Behavior Found.'s Albert Schweitzer Humanitarian Award, Brooklyn Heights, 1986—. Author (chpt.) The Triumphant Person, 1989. Bd. dirs. Albert Schweitzer Fellowship, N.Y.C., 1982—; chmn. William James Found., Brooklyn Heights, 1989—; bd. dirs. Burdick Internat. Ancestry Library, Sarasota, Fla., 1985—; mem., chn., bd. advisors NYU's Coll. of Dentistry, N.Y.C., 1988—; mem. Brooklyn Heights Assn., 1970—. Capt. USAF, 1959-61. Recipient Disting. Svc. award Bklyn. Jr. C. of C., 1966, Bicentennial award Nat. Jogging Assn., 1976. Fellow Royal Coll. Physicians and Surgeons in Psychiatry; mem. Pan Am. Med. Assn., Nat. Bd. Med. Examiners, Med. Coun. of Can., Am. Acad. Clin. Psychiatrists, Am. Orthopsychiatric Assn., Am. Psychiat. Assn., AMA, Med. Soc. State of N.Y., Kings County (N.Y.) Med. Soc., World Med. Assn., World Fedn. Mental Health, Am. Physicians Art Assn., Harvard Med. Soc., English Speaking Union, Harvard Club of N.Y., Bklyn. Club, Heights Casino and Racquet Club, MENSA (life, nat. coord. 1980-84), Phi Beta Kappa (councillor 1981-84). Home and Office: Psychiat Svcs Internat PC 77 Remsen St Brooklyn NY 11201-3401

CRUM, DEBRA LYNN, geriatrics nurse, consultant; b. Flint, Mich., Jan. 28, 1960; m. Dale Crum, Nov. 30, 1991. BSN summa cum laude, No. Mich. U., 1981; MA in Gerontology summa cum laude, U. South Fla., 1991. RN, Fla.; cert. geriatric care mgr. Nurse St. Joseph Hosp., Flint, 1982; nurse on open heart unit Borgess Hosp., Kalamazoo, 1982-83; nurse, med.-surg. and orthopedic McLaren Hosp., Flint, 1983-87; oncology and home health nurse St. Joseph Hosp., Tampa, Fla., 1987-89; lab. facilitator St. Petersburg (Fla.) Jr. Coll., 1989-90; nurse, rev. coord. PRO, Tampa, 1990-91; nurse, edn. coord. Mease Home Health, Safety Harbor, Fla., 1991-92; clin. supr. Care One Home Health, Tarpon Springs, Fla., 1992-93; adminstr. home health First Am. Home Health, Tarpon Springs, 1993-95; pres., CEO, owner Forerunner Med. Health Cons. Inc., Clearwater, Fla., 1995—; mem. adv. bd. House-Calls, Clearwater, 1996—. Fellow Nat. Assn. Geriatric Care Mgrs., Nat. Assn. Geriatric Care Mgrs. of Fla.;mem. Palm Harbor C. of C., Rotary of Palm Harbor. Office: Forerunner Med Cons Inc 2765 Brattle Ln Clearwater FL 34621

CRUM, JOHN EVAN, physician, executive; b. Mpls., Dec. 5, 1953; s. Gerald Pollert and Vivian Dorothy (Wonning) Crum; m. Kimberly Anne Garts, Sep. 10, 1983; children: Susanna, Elizabeth. BS in Biol. Scis., Ind. U., 1973; MD, Ind. U., Indpls., 1978. Diplomate Am. Bds. Family Practice, Med. Mgmt.; lic. Ind., Ky. Family practice resident U. Iowa, Iowa City, 1978-81; pvt. practice family medicine Williamsburg, Iowa, 1981-86; med. dir. Maxicare Ky. HMO, Louisville, 1987-88, Humana Helath Plan HMO, Louisville, 1988; physician dir. Humana Inc., Louisville, 1988—. Bd. mem. Chance Sch., Louisville, 1989-90. Fellow Am. Acad. Family Physicians; mem. Am. Coll. Physician Execs., Health Ins. Assn. Am. (health care tech. com.), Jefferson County Med. Soc., Ky. Med. Assn. Presbyterian. Home: 7006 Shallow Lake Rd Prospect KY 40059-9361 Office: Humana Inc 101 E Main St Louisville KY 40202-1349

CRUMBAUGH, JAMES CHARLES, psychologist; b. Terrell, Tex., Dec. 11, 1912; s. Charles Miller and Hallie Virginia (Dansby) C.; m. Edna Mae Bailey, 1938 (dec. 1946); 1 child, Charles; m. Teresa Amanda Croteau, June 14, 1975 (dec. Feb. 1989); m. Lois Dickson Hicks, Nov. 10, 1992. AB, Baylor U., 1935; AM, So. Meth. U., 1938; PhD, U. Tex., 1953. Lic. psychologist, Miss.; cert. logotherapist. Psychologist, tchr. Memphis State U., 1947-56; chmn. Dept. Psychology MacMurray Coll., Jacksonville, Ill., 1957-59; rsch. dir. Bradley Ctr., Inc., Columbus, Ga., 1959-64; staff psychologist VA Med. Ctr., Augusta, Ga., 1964-65, Gulfport, Miss., 1965-80; so. regional dir. Inst. Logotherapy, Berkeley, Calif., 1980—; rsch. cons. Internat. Graphoanalysis Soc., Chgo., 1968—. Author: Counseling for Graphoanalysts, 1970, Everything to Gain, 1973; co-author: Logotherapy, 1980; co-editor: Primer of Projective Techniques, 1990. With U.S. Army air Corps, 1941-45. Rsch. fellow Duke U., 1954-55. Mem. APA, Miss. Psychol. Assn. (Kinlock Gill award 1989), Southeastern Psychol. Assn., So. Soc. Philosophy and Psychology, Psi Chi. Roman Catholic. Home: 140 Balmoral Ave Biloxi MS 39531-4701

CRUMLEY, ROGER LEE, surgeon, educator; b. Perry, Iowa, Oct. 8, 1941; s. Dwight Moody and Helen Ethelwyn (Anderson) C.; m. Janet Lynn Conant, Nov. 13, 1987; children: Erin Kelly Helen, Danielle Nicole. BA, Simpson Coll., 1964; MS, U. Iowa, 1975, MD, 1967. Diplomate Am. Bd. Otolaryngology. Intern L.A. County Gen. Hosp., 1967-68; resident in surgery Highland-Alameda Hosp., Oakland, Calif., 1968-69; battalion surgeon 1st Marine Div., Vietnam, 1968-69; resident in otolaryngology U. Iowa, Iowa City, 1971-75; chief otolaryngology San Francisco Gen. Hosp., 1975-81; assoc. prof., then prof. U. Calif., San Francisco, 1981-87; prof., chief otolaryngology-head and neck surgery U. Calif., Irvine, 1987—; guest prof. Humboldt U., East Berlin, 1982, M.S. McLeod vis. prof. S. Australian Postgrad. Edn. Ctr., Adelaide, 1988; treas., pres. 1994-95 Am. Acad. Facial Plastic Surgeons. Contbr. articles and book chpts. to profl. publs. With USN, 1969-71, Vietnam. Recipient Alumni Achievement award Simpson Coll., 1984. Fellow ACS, Am. Acad. Otolaryngology (treas., bd. dirs. 1988—, award 1989); mem. Soc. Univ. Otolaryngologists, Bohemian Club (San Francisco), Center Club (Costa Mesa, Calif.). Republican. Methodist. Office: U Calif-Irvine Med Ctr Dept Otolaryngology/Head/Neck 101 City Blvd W Orange CA 92868-3298

CRUMMY, ANDREW BERNARD, JR., radiologist, medical educator; b. Newark, Jan. 30, 1930; s. Andrew Bernard and Kathleen (Higgins) C.; m. Elsa Ann Esser, 1958; children: Colleen, Kevin, Timothy. AB, Bowdoin Coll., 1951; MD, Boston U., 1955. Diplomate Am. Bd. Radiology. Intern U. Wis., Madison, 1955-56, resident in radiology, 1958-61, from asst. prof. to prof. radiology, 1964—; med. officer USN, Atsuji, Japan, 1956-58; fellow in radiology Mt. Auburn Hosp., Cambridge, Mass., 1961-62; USPHS fellow in radiology Yale U., New Haven, Conn., 1962-63; asst. prof. radiology U. Colo., Denver, 1963-64. Contbr. over 200 articles to profl. jours.; editor: Paul and Juhl's Essentials of Radiologic Imaging, 1993, Digital Subtraction Arteriography, 1972. Lt. USNR, 1956-68. Mem. Am. Coll. Radiology (counselor 1981-83), Radiol. Soc. N.Am. (counselor 1983-87), Soc. Cardiovascular and Interventional Radiology (pres., v.p., sec. 1978-82), Am. Roentgen Ray Soc., Assn. Univ. Radiologists, State Med. Soc. Wis. (bd. dirs. 1992-95). Home: 3535 Lake Mendota Dr Madison WI 53705 Office: U Wis Hosp and Clinics 600 Highland Ave Madison WI 53792-3252

CRUMP, KENNY SHERMAN, biostatistician; b. Haynesville, La., Oct. 13, 1939; s. Sherman and Travis Elsie (Hardaway) C.; m. Shirley Rae Edmondson, June 2, 1961; children: Frankie Faith Crump Alexander, Tanya Travis Crump Bernard, Kenny Sherman, Jr. BSEE, La. Tech., 1961; MS math., U. Denver, 1963; PhD Math., Mont. State U., 1968. Prof. math. La. Tech. U., Ruston, 1966-80; pres. K.S. Crump & Co., Ruston, 1980-87; v.p. IEF-Kaiser, Ruston, 1987—.

CRUMPLIN, MICHAEL KENNETH HUGH, surgeon; b. Glasgow, Scotland, Aug. 12, 1942; s. William Cahrles Digby and Muriel Elizabeth Kerr (Barley) C.; m. Elizabeth Anne Bunting, May 20, 1965; children: Ian, Patrick, Fiona. M.B.B.S., Middlesex Hosp. London, 1965. House surgeon Middlesex Hosp., London, 1965-66, registrar in surgery, 1971-73; house physician Ctrl. Middlesex Hosp., London, 1966, casualty officer, sr. house officer, 1966-67; sr. house officer surgery Colchester Hosp., 1967-68; registrar surgery Swindon Hosp., 1968-71; hon. rsch. fellow/hon. sr. registrar United Birmingham (Eng.) Hosps., 1973-74, sr. registrar surgery, 1973-77; cons. gen. surgeon Wrexham Clwyd, U.K., 1977—; mem. ct. of examiners Royal Coll. Surgeons of Eng., chmn. ct. examiners; higher specialist tng. examiner; examiner United Examining Bd. U.K. Contbr. articles to profl. jours., chpts. to books; editl. bd. Brit. Jour. surgery, 1990-95. Welsh Office Rsch. grantee. Fellow Royal Coll. Surgeons (Eng.); mem. Royal Coll. Physicians (Eng., licentiate), Assn. Surgeons of Gt. Britain (past coun. mem.), Brit. Assn. Surg. Oncology, Welsh Surg. Soc. Mem. Ch. of Eng. Home: 57 Wynnstay Ln, Marford Wrexham LL12 8LH, Wales Office: Wrexham Maelor Hosp, Croesnewydd Rd, Wrexham Clwyd LL13 7TD, Wales

CRUSE, JULIUS MAJOR, JR., pathologist, educator; b. New Albany, Miss., Feb. 15, 1937; s. Julius Major and Effie (Davis) C. BA, BS with honors, U. Miss., 1958; D.Microbiology with honors (Fulbright fellow), U. Graz, Austria, 1960; MD, U. Tenn., 1964, Ph.D. in Pathology (USPHS fellow), 1966, USPHS postdoctoral fellow, 1964-67. Mem. faculty U. Miss. Med. Sch., 1967—; prof. immunology, biology Grad. Sch., 1967-74, prof. pathology, 1974—, asso. prof. microbiology, 1974—, dir. grad. studies program in pathology, 1974—, dir. clin. immunopathology, 1978—, dir. immunopathology sect., 1978—, dir. tissue typing lab., 1980—, assoc. prof. medicine, 1989—; lectr. pathology U. Tenn. Coll. Medicine, 1967-74; aj. prof. immunology Miss. Coll., 1977—; mem. sci. adv. bd. Immuno Tech. Corp., L.A.; active FDA Expert Panel on Alternatives to Silicone Breast Implants, 1994—. Author: Immunology Examination Review Book, 1971, rev. edit., 1975, Introduction to Immunology, 1977, Principles of Immunopathology, 1979; editor-in-chief Immunologic Research, 1981—, Pathology and Immunopathology Research, 1982-90, Concepts in Immunopathology, 1985—, The Year in Immunology, 1984—, Pathobiology: Jour. Immunopathology, 1990—, Molecular and Cellular Biology, 1990, Transgenics: Biological Analysis Through DNA Transfer; contbns. to Microbiology and Immunology; editor Immunomodulation of Neoplasia, Antigenic Variation: Molecular and Genetic Mechanisms of Relapsing Disease, 1987, Autoimmunoregulation and Autoimmune Disease, 1987; The Year in Immunology, vol. 1, 1984-85, vol. 2, 1985-86, The Year in Immunology, vol. 3, 1987, The Year in Immunology, vols. 4, 5, 1988, vol. 6, 1989-90, Genetic Basis of Autoimmune Disease, 1988, Cellular Aspects of Autoimmunity, 1988, Therapy of Autoimmune Diseases, 1989, B Lymphocytes: Function and Regulation, Conjugate Vaccines, 1989, Molecules and Cells of Immunity, 1990, Immunoregulation and Autoimmunity, 1986, Organ-Based Autoimmune Diseases, 1985, Autoimmunity: Basic Concepts, Systematic and Selected Organ-Specific Diseases, 1985, Clinical and Molecular Aspects of Autoimmune Diseases, 1990, Immunoregulatory Cyrokines and Cell Growth, 1989, Complement Profiles, 1992; author chpts. to books on immunology; co-editor: Self-Nonself Discrimination in the Immune System, 1992, Complement Profiles, vol. 1, 1992, Illustrated Dictionary of Immunology, 1995; contbr. articles to profl. jours. Recipient Pathologists award in continuing edn. Coll. Am. Pathologists-Am. Soc. Clin. Pathologists, 1976; Julius M. Cruse collection in immunology established in his honor Middleton Med. Libr., U. Wis., Madison, 1979; Wilson Found. grantee, 1990-95, 93-94. Fellow AAAS, Royal Soc. Promotion Health, Am. Acad. Microbiology, Am. Soc. for Histocompatibility and Immunogenetics (chmn. publs. com. 1987-95), Intercontinental Biog. Assn.; mem. AMA (Physicians Recognition award 196-75), Clin. Immunology Soc., Am. Inst. Biol. Scis., Am. Soc. Clin. Pathologists, Can. Soc. Microbiologists, N.Y. Acad. Scis. Exptl. Biology and Medicine, Soc. Francaise d'Immunologie, Reticuloendothelial Soc., Transplantation Soc., Electron Microscopy Soc. Am., Am. Assn. History Medicine, The Paul Ehrlich Soc., Am. Assn. Pathologists, Am. Chem. Soc., Brit. Soc. Immunology, Can. Soc. Immunology, Am. Soc. Microbiology, Internat. Acad. Pathology, Am. Assn. Immunologists (historian 1990—), Sigma Xi, Phi Kappa Phi, Phi Eta Sigma, Alpha Epsilon Delta, Gamma Sigma Epsilon, Beta Beta Beta. Episcopalian. Office: U Miss Med Ctr Dept Pathology 2500 N State St Jackson MS 39216-4500

CRUVANT, ETHAN MILTON, physician; b. St. Louis, July 31, 1958. BA, Harvard U., 1980; MD, Washington U., St. Louis, 1984. Internist in pvt. practice St. Louis, 1987-89, Las Vegas, 1989—. Mem. ACP. Office: 3006 S Maryland Pkwy # 750 Las Vegas NV 89109

CRUZ, IVAN J., medical technologist; b. Havana, Cuba, Mar. 3, 1959; came to U.S., 1967; s. Ivan R. and Mureya (Docampo) C.; m. Nilda R. Muguercia, May 2, 1981; children: Ivan J., Alexander. BS, CUNY, 1985. Radiographic technologist St. Michaels Med. Ctr., Newark, 1990-95; MRI specialist, cons. Health Imaging Svcs., Middletown, N.Y., 1993-94; MRI technologist Med. Resources, Inc., West Orange, N.J., 1994—; MRI imaging chief technologist Beth Israel Med. Ctr., Newark, 1991—. CUNY scholar, 1985. Republican. Roman Catholic. Home: 828 Sherman Ave Plainfield NJ 07063

CRUZ, JUDITH A., nursing administrator; b. Utica, N.Y., Feb. 27, 1938; d. Leon G. and Anne Marie (McGillis) Beekman; 1 child, Sharon Ann. Diploma, Eilizabeth (N.J.) Gen. Hosp., 1961; BS in Nursing, Salve Regina U., 1986; MS, Salve Regina Coll., 1991. Asst. head nurse R.I. Nursing Hosp., Providence, 1964-70, nurse leader, 1970-78, asst. dir. emergency svcs., 1978-86, dir. emergency nursing hosp., 1986-90, med. legal cons., 1991-92, clin. reviewer, 1992-94, case mgr., 1995—.

CRUZ, NELSON XAVIER, healthcare executive; b. N.Y.C., June 30, 1950; s. Jaime and Angela (Vega) C.; m. Asuncion Rosado, July 10, 1971 (div. 1976); children: Celena, Jasmin; m. Lydia Cordero, 1987; 1 child, Lauren A. BA, Hunter Coll., 1974; MS, Herbert H. Lehman Coll., 1978; MBA, Manhattan Coll., 1985. CLU, ChFC. Recreation therapist Bronx (N.Y.) Children's Psychiat. Hosp., 1974-78; dir. rehab. svc. Rockland Children's Psychiat. Hosp., Orangeburg, N.Y., 1978-79; dir. mkgt. Fordham-Tremont Community Mental Health Ctr., Bronx, 1979-83; adminstr. dept. emergency Woodhull Hosp., Bklyn., 1983-85, assoc. dir. quality assurance, 1985-86; mgr./cons. patient accounts Promesa, Inc., Bronx, 1986-87; adminstr. ambulatory care network Bronx-Lebanon Hosp. Ctr., 1987-92; project dir. United Cmty. Health Plan/United Hosps. Med. Ctr., Newark, 1992-95; dir. network devel. PruCare HMO, Prudential Life Ins. Co. of Am., Iselin, N.J., 1995—; project coord., cons. Inst. Puerto Rican Hispanic Elderly, N.Y.C., 1983; med. computer account exec. Medi-Scan, Inc., Worcester, Mass., 1983. Adv. bd. Bronx Legal Aid Soc.; bd. dirs. Community Planning Bd. 6, 1981-82; mem. Bronx-Boro-Wide Mental Health Svcs. Com., 1979-81. Leadership Mgmt. Urban Execs. Inst. fellow, Rutgers U., 1996; Leadership N.J. fellow, 1994—; Hispanic Leadership Opportunity Program fellow, 1993-94. Fellow Am. Managed Care and Rev. Assn. (cert.); mem. Am. Coll. Healthcare Execs. (diplomate, cert. health care exec.), Assn. Healthcare Execs. of N.J., Med. Group Mgmt. Assn., Am. Coll. Med. Practice Execs., Group Health Assn. Am., Am. Coll. CLUs and ChFCs, N.J. Med. Group Mgmt. Assn., Am. Coll. Healthcare Mktg., Hispanic Assn. Health Svcs. Execs. (mktg. cons. 1986-87), N.Y. Assn. Ambulatory Care, Health Adminstrs. Assn. N.Y., Acad. Health Svcs. Mktg., Nat. Assn. Health Svcs. Execs. Democrat. Roman Catholic. Office: Prudential Life Ins Co Am 200 Wood Ave S Iselin NJ 08830

CRUZ, OSCAR ALFREDO, ophthalmologist; b. Baton Rouge, June 7, 1961; s. Oscar Jose and Maria Teresa (Portela) C.; m. Mary Harris, Aug. 10, 1985; children: Lauryn Marie, Oscar Adam, Dana Kathryn. BS, La. State U., 1982, MD, 1987. Intern St. Joseph Hosp., Houston, 1987-88; resident Baylor Coll. Medicine, Houston, 1988-91; fellow Bascom Palmer Eye Inst., Miami, Fla., 1991-92; cons., attending physician Cardinal Glennon Children's Hosp., St. Louis, 1992—, dir. pediatric ophthalmology, 1993—; cons., attending physician Anheuser-Busch Eye Inst., St. Louis, 1992—; cons. St. Louis U. Sch. Medicine, 1992, sst. prof., 1992; mem. adv. bd. Delta Gamma Ctr. for Visually Impairedchildren, Mo., 1995—. Office: Cardinal Glennon Childrens Hosp 1465 S Grand Blvd Saint Louis MO 63104

CRUZ, SYLVIA SANTOS, obstetric gynecologist; b. Tamuning, Guam, Nov. 7, 1966; d. Antonio G. and Isabel (Santos) C.; m. John Alexander Burgess IV, Jan. 13, 1993; children: John Alexander Burgess V, Isabella Antoinette Burgess. BS in Biology, Ea. Oreg. State Coll., 1987; DO, Kirksville Coll. Osteo., 1993. Med. asst. Family Med. Clinic, Tamuning, Guam, 1983-84; sec. infection control Guam Meml. Hosp., Tamuning, 1987-89; resident ob-gyn. Riverside Osteo. Hosp., Trenton, Mich., 1993-96. Mem. Am. Osteo. Assn., Am. Acad. Osteopathy, Cranial Acad. Home: 29956 Ostreich Rd Rockwood MI 48173 Office: Riverside Osteo Medicine 150 Truax St Trenton MI 48184

CRUZE, KENNETH, retired surgeon; b. Takoma Park, Md., Oct. 10, 1927; s. Conrad Ellis and Claudia Eleanore (Carpenter) C.; B.A., Columbia Union Coll., 1949; M.D., Loma Linda U., 1955; m. Jean Anna Hansen, June 13, 1948; children: Wendy Jean, Lori Ann, Barbara Lee. Diplomate Am. Bd. Gen. Surgery, Am. Bd. Thoracic Surgery. Intern L.A. County Gen. Hosp., 1955-56; resident in surgery Wadsworth Gen. Med. and Surg. Hosp., West Los Angeles, 1956-60; resident in pediatric surgery Children's Hosp. Los Angeles, 1958-59; fellow in thoracic and cardiovascular surgery U. Fla., Gainesville, 1960-62; practice medicine specializing in thoracic and cardiovascular surgery, Takoma Park, Md., 1962-89; mem. staff Washington Adventist Hosp., Takoma Park, 1962-89, dir. open heart surgery program, 1970-89; ret. Mem. exec. com., bd. trustees D.C. Blue Shield, Columbia Union Coll., Takoma Park. Served to capt. M.C., U.S. Army, 1956-63. Fellow ACS, Am. Coll. Chest Physicians, Am. Coll. Angiology; mem. Am. Thoracic Soc., Am. Trauma Soc., Med. and Chirurg. Faculty Md., Md. Heart Assn., Soc. Thoracic Surgeons. Republican. Club: Civitan. Mem. editorial bd. Md. State Med. Jour., 1972-77; contbr. articles to med. jours. Home: 12804 Gaffney Rd Silver Spring MD 20904-3517

CRYAN, STEPHEN EDWARD, pediatric cardiologist; b. Elizabeth, N.J., Apr. 28, 1955; s. Edward Joseph and Doris (Mazur) C.; m. Margaret Rose Hannagan, Dec. 29, 1979; children: Edward John, Stephanie Rose, Megan Alexandra. BS in Chemistry, U. Del., 1977; MD, George Washington u., 1981. Resident in pediatrics Hershey (Pa.) Med. Ctr., 1981-84; fellow in pediatric cardiology Children's Hosp., Cin., 1984-87; assoc. prof. pediatrics Pa. State U., Hershey, 1987-94; chief divsn. pediatric cardiology Hershey Med. Ctr., 1994—. Contbr. numerous articles to profl. jours. Bd. dirs. Dauphin County dist. Am. Heart Assn., Harrisburg, Pa., 1995—; bd. dirs. Cub Scouts, Hershey, 1992-94; cantor local ch., Hershey, 1989-95. Am. Heart Assn. grantee, 1988-90, 91-93. Fellow Am. Coll. Cardiology, Am. Acad. Pediatrics (subsect. pediatric cardiology); mem. Am. Heart Assn., Am. Coll. Sports Medicine. Roman Catholic. Home: 1670 Brookline Dr Hummelstown PA 17036 Office: Pa State U Hershey Med Ctr PO Box 850 Hershey PA 17033

CRYER, DENNIS ROBERT, pharmaceutical company executive, researcher; b. Dearborn, Mich., Mar. 30, 1944; s. Earl Wilton and Marguerite Gladys (Root) C.; m. Leilani Chen, 1974 (div.); 1 child, Jonathan Eric; m. Sharon Therese Kniezewski, July 26, 1986; children: Catherine Grace, Laura Rose. BA in Biology, Johns Hopkins U., 1968; MD, Albert Einstein Coll. Medicine, 1977. Intern Children's Hosp. Phila., 1977-78, resident, 1978-79, 80-81; fellow in pathology and molecular biology U. Pa. Sch. Medicine, Phila., 1979-80; fellow in human genetics Sch. Medicine U. Pa., Phila., 1981-84, clin. asst. prof. pediatrics Sch. Medicine, 1983-84, asst. prof. pediatrics Sch. Medicine, 1984-87; assoc. clin. rsch. dir. E.R. Squibb and Sons, Princeton, N.J., 1987-89; assoc. med. devel. dir. Squibb U.S. Pharm. Group, Princeton, 1989-90, med. ops. dir., 1990-91, med. dir., 1991-94; v.p. cardiovascular metabolism Women's Healthcare, 94-96; sr. med. dir. Bristol-Myers Squibb U.S. Pharm., Princeton, 1996—; v.p. cardiovascular and metabolic products E.R. Squibb and Sons, Princeton, N.J., 1996—; corp. rep., corp. affairs com. Am. Soc. Hypertension, 1991—; mem. internat. adv. bd. XII Internat. Symposium on Drugs Affecting Lipid Metabolism, 1993-95. Author: with others Cold Spring Harbor Symposium on Quantitative Biology, 1974, Methods in Cell Biology, 1975; contbr. articles Jour. of Molecular Biology, Jour. Lipid Rsch., Jour. Clin. Investigation. Grantee Nat. Heart, Lung, and Blood Inst. , NIH, 1986, Am. Heart Assn., 1987; recipient Merck Faculty Devel. award Merck, Sharp, and Dohme, 1984. Fellow Am. Heart Assn. (arteriosclerosis coun.); mem. AAAS, Am. Diabetes Assn., Am. Fedn. Clin. Rsch., Am. Soc. Human Genetics, Am. Soc. Hypertension (corp. rep., corp. affairs com.), Endocrine Soc. N.Y. Acad. Scis., Alpha Epsilon Delta. Home: 7 North Cir Yardley PA 19067-3212 Office: Bristol-Myers Squibb Co PO Box 5400 Princeton NJ 08543-4500

CRYER, PHILIP EUGENE, medical educator, scientist, endocrinologist; b. El Paso, Ill., Jan. 5, 1940; s. Clifford Eugene and Carol Ruth (Cherry) C.; m. Susan Odette Shipman, Dec. 23, 1963 (div. May 1990); children: Philip Clifford, Justine Laurel; m. Carolyn Elizabeth Havlin, Sept. 16, 1994. BA, Northwestern U., 1962, MD, 1965. Diplomate Am. Bd. Internal Medicine, diplomate Am. Bd. Endocrinology and Metabolism. Intern Barnes Hosp., St. Louis, 1965-67; fellow in endocrinology Barnes Hosp./Washington U., 1967-68, resident in medicine, 1968-69, 71-72; investigator Naval Med. Rsch. Inst., Bethesda, Md., 1969-71; from instr. to assoc. prof. Washington U. Sch. Medicine, St. Louis, 1971-80, prof., 1981—, Irene E. and Michael M. Karl prof. endocrinology/metabolism, 1995—, dir. gen. clin. rsch. ctr., 1978—, dir. div. endocrinology, diabetes and metabolism, 1985—; Connaught-Novo lectr. Can. Diabetes Assn., 1987; Pimstone lectr. Soc. Endocrinology, Metabolism and Diabetes, South Africa, 1989; Kellion lectr. Australian Diabetes Soc., 1992; Plenary lectr. Japan Diabetes Soc., 1994. Author: Diagnostic Endocrinology, 1976, 2d edit., 1979, 61 book chpts.; editor: Diabetes; mem. editl. bd. Jour. Clin. Investigation, Am. Jour. Physiology, Jour. Clin. Endocrinology and Metabolism; contbr. over 260 articles to profl. jours. Recipient Rorer Clin. Investigator award Endocrine Soc., 1988, Rumbough Sci. award Juvenile Diabetes Found., 1989, Banting medal Am. Diabetes Assn., 1994, Excellence in Clin. Rsch. award NIH, 1994, Am. Diabetes Clin. Rsch. grantee, 1996. Fellow ACP; mem. Am. Fedn. Clin. Rsch. (councilor 1979-80), Am. Soc. Clin. Investigation (v.p. 1985-86), Assn. Am. Physicians, Am. Diabetes Assn. (pres. 1996—), Phi Beta Kappa, Alpha Omega Alpha. Office: Washington U Sch Medicine 660 South Euclid Ave Box 8127 Saint Louis MO 63110

CRYER, THEODORE HUDSON, ophthalmologist, educator; b. Chgo., May 8, 1946; s. Arthur William and Maxine Ritter C.; AB in Chemistry, Taylor U., 1968; MD, U. Md., 1972; children: Timothy Hudson, Jordan Tinley, Megan Elizabeth, Rebecca Jeanne. Straight med. intern South Balt. Gen. Hosp., 1972-73; jr. asst. resident, 1973-74; asst. resident U. Md. Hosp., Balt., 1974-76, resident, 1976-77; practice medicine specializing in ophthalmology, Waynesboro, Pa., 1977—, Westminster, Md., 1977-85; instr. U. Md. Sch. Medicine, 1979-91, clin. asst. prof. medicine, 1991—; chmn. com. on ethics Waynesboro Hosp., 1984, chmn. com. quality assurance, 1987—, v.p. med. staff, 1987-89, 96—, pres. med. staff, 1989-91, trustee, 1991—. Clk. session Westminster Reformed Presbyn. Ch., 1980-83. Fellow ACS; mem. AMA, AAAS, Am. Acad. Ophthalmology, Pa. Med. Soc., Franklin County Med. Soc., Md. Eye Physicians and Surgeons, Pa. Acad. Otolaryngology and Ophthalmology, Nat. Soc. to Prevent Blindness (charter mem.), Ophthal. Assn. Rsch. to Prevent Blindness, Ind., 1978. Republican. Methodist. Office: 45 Roadside Ave Waynesboro PA 17268-2537

CSÁNGÓ, PÉTER ANDRÁS, microbiologist; b. Budapest, Hungary, May 14, 1942; s. Ferenc and Magda (Herczeg) C.; m. Gerda Patricia Dub, Oct. 25, 1969; children: Monica, Miriam, Michelle. MD, U. Medicine, Pécs, Hungary, 1967; postgrad., U. Birmingham, Eng., 1972-73. Registrar County Lung Hosp., Szombathely, Hungary, 1967-68 Semmelweis Hosp., Budapest, 1968-69, State Lung Hosp., Tromsø, Norway, 1969-70; registrar Nat. Inst. Pub. Health, Oslo, 1970-73, sr. registrar, 1973-78, virologist, 1978; dir. Dept. Clin. Microbiology Ctr. Hosp., Kristiansand, 1978—. Contbr. articles to profl. jours. Grantee Royal Ministry Social Affairs, Norway, 1972, Royal Ministry Fgn. Affairs, Norway, 1986, Mid. East Eye Rsch. Inst., Israel, 1987. Mem. Norwegian Med. Assn., Norwegian Soc. Infectious Diseases, Norwegian Soc. Med. Microbiology (chmn. 1989-91), Swedish Soc. Med. Microbiology, Scandinavian Soc. of Vaginal Bacteriosis, N.Y. Acad. Scis., Scandinavian Soc. Genitourinary Medicine (bd. dirs. 1986—), European Soc. Chlamydia Rsch. (bd. dirs. 1987—), Am. Soc. Microbiology, European Group Rapid Viral Diagnosis, Internat. AIDS Soc. Home: PO Box 2126, Kristiansand N-4602, Norway Office: Vest-Agder Ctrl Hosp, Dept Clin Microbiology, N-4604 Kristiansand Norway

CSERR, ROBERT, psychiatrist, physician, hospital administrator; b. Perth Amboy, N.J., May 29, 1936; s. Frank Joseph and Helen (Bodzany) C.; m. Helen Fitzgerald, May 28, 1962; 1 dau., Ruth. A.B. magna cum laude, Harvard, 1958, M.D., 1962. Med. intern U. Va. Hosp., 1962-63; resident, fellow in psychiatry Mass. Gen. Hosp., Harvard Med. Sch., 1963-66; alcohol coordinator Mass. Gen. Hosp., 1967-68, clin. assoc. psychiatry, 1968—; asst. supt. Medfield State Hosp., Harding, Mass., 1968-70, supt., 1970-74, area program dir., 1970-74; dir. Outlook Psychiat. Facility, Hampstead, N.H., 1974-76; med. dir. Charles River Hosp., Wellesley, Mass., 1976-80; psychiatrist-in-chief Charles River Hosp., 1980-87, Hahnemann Hosp., Boston, 1982—; med. dir. Taunton Hosp. and Regional Svc. Ctr., 1990-92; assoc. med. dir. psychiatry PHCS, Lexington, Mass., 1991-93; v.p., med. dir. mental health svcs. PHCS, Waltham, Mass., 1993—; v.p. clin. affairs Community Care Systems Inc., 1979-86, sr. cons., 1986—; asst. clin. prof. psychiatry Boston U. Sch. Medicine, 1968-74, assoc. clin. prof., 1975—; asst. psychiatrist Beth Israel Hosp., 1970—; lectr. in psychiatry Harvard Med. Sch., 1972-89. Pres. Medfield Found.; bd. overseers Mt. Desert Island Biol. Lab. Served with AUS, 1966-68. Mem. Am. Psychiat. Assn., Am. Coll. Mental Health Adminstrn., Mass. Med. Soc., Mass. Psychiat. Soc. Home: Green Acres North Dighton MA 02764 Office: Chase St North Dighton MA 02764

CUATRECASAS, PEDRO MARTIN, research pharmacologist; b. Madrid, Sept. 27, 1936; came to U.S., 1947; s. Jose and Martha C.; m. Carol Zies, Aug. 15, 1959; children: Paul, Lisa, Diane, Julia. AB, Washington U., St. Louis, 1958, MD, 1962; DSc honoris causa, U. Barcelona, 1984, Mt. Sinai Sch. Medicine, 1985. Intern, then resident in internal medicine Osler Svc. Johns Hopkins Hosp., 1962-64, asst. physician, 1972-75; clin. asso., clin. endocrinology br. Nat. Inst. Arthritis and Metabolic Diseases, NIH, 1964-66; spl. USPHS postdoctoral fellow Lab. Chem. Biology, 1966-67, med. officer, 1967-70; professorial lectr. biochemistry George Washington U. Med. Sch., 1967-70; assoc. prof. pharmacology and exptl. therapeutics, assoc. prof. medicine, dir. div. clin. pharmacology, Burroughs Wellcome prof. clin. pharmacology Johns Hopkins U. Med. Sch., 1970-72, prof. pharmacology and exptl. therapeutics, assoc. prof. medicine, 1972-75; v.p. rsch., devel. and med. Wellcome Rsch. Labs.; dir. Burroughs Wellcome Co., Research Triangle Park, N.C., 1975-86; sr. v.p. R&D Glaxo Rsch. Labs., Glaxo Inc., 1986-89; also bd. dirs. Glaxo Rsch. Labs., Glaxo Inc., Glaxo Internat. Rsch., Ltd., London, 1986-89; v.p., pres. pharm. rsch. div. Warner-Lambert Co., Ann Arbor, Mich., 1990—, pres.; adj. prof. Duke U. Med. Sch., 1975-89; adj. prof., mem. adv. com. cancer rsch. program U. N.C. Med. Sch., 1975—; adj. prof. dept. pharm. and medicinal chemistry, U. Md., 1990; bd. dirs. Burroughs Wellcome Fund, 1975-86. Editor: Receptors and Recognition Series, 1975, Jour. Solid-Phase Biochemistry, 1975-80; editorial bd.: Jour. Membrane Biology, 1973, Internat. Jour. Biochemistry, 1973, Molecular and Cellular Endocrinology, 1973-77, Biochimica Biophysica Acta, 1973-79, Life Scis., 1978—, Neuropeptides, 1979—, Jour. Applied Biochemistry, 1978-91, Cancer Research, 1980-81, Jour. Applied Biochemistry and Biotech., 1980—, Toxin Revs., 1981—, Biochem. Biophys. Research Communications, 1981—; contbr. articles to profl. jours. Active Am. Diabetes Assn., 1972—, PMA Commn. on Drugs and Rare Diseases, 1982-89. Recipient John Jacob Abel prize, 1972, Laude prize Pharm. World, 1975, Beerman award Soc. Investigative Dermatology, 1981, Isco award U. Nebr., 1985, Dupont Splty. Diagnostics award Clin. Ligand Assay Soc., 1986, Alumni Achievement award Washington U. Sch. Medicine, 1987, Wolf Found. prize, 1987; inducted into Johns Hopkins Soc. Scholar, 1990. Fellow Am. Acad. Arts. and Scis.; mem. Am. Soc. Biol. Chemists, Nat. Acad. Scis., Inst. Medicine of Nat. Acad. Scis. (governing council 1988—), Am. Soc. Pharmacology and Exptl. Therapeutics (Goodman and Gilman award 1982), Am. Soc. Clin. Investigation, Am. Soc. Clin. Research, Spanish Biochem. Soc., Md Acad. Scis. (Outstanding Young Scientist of Year 1970), Am. Cancer Soc., Endocrine Soc., Am. Chem. Soc., Am. Diabetes Assn. (Eli Lilly award 1975), Am. Diabetes Assn., Sigma Xi. *

CUCCI, CESARE ELEUTERIO, pediatric cardiologist; b. Spoleto, Italy, Dec. 22, 1925; came to U.S., 1954, naturalized, 1958; s. Otto and Anna (Morelli) C.; m. Gilda Morillo, Oct. 22, 1966; children: Susanna, Gardenia, Otto. Diploma in Classics, Coll. St. Maria, Rome, 1943; MD, State U. Perugia (Italy), 1949. Diplomate: Am. Bd. Pediatrics, Am. Bd. Pediatric Cardiology. Chief, pediatric cardiology service Lenox Hill Hosp., N.Y.C., 1963-81; cons. pediatric cardiologist, 1981-89; cons. pediatric cardiology Flushing Hosp., Queens, N.Y., 1970-89, Methodist Hosp., Bklyn., 1966-89, Booth Meml Hosp., Queens, 1964-89; prof. clin. pediatrics N.Y.U. Hosp., 1976-83. Contbr. articles to med. jours. Fellow ACP, Am. Acad. Pediatrics, Am. Coll. Cardiology, Am. Coll. Chest Physicians. Roman Catholic. Club: 7th Regt. Rifle (N.Y.C.).

CUCIN, ROBERT LOUIS, plastic surgeon, lawyer; b. N.Y.C., Apr. 17, 1946; s. Robert and Julia C.; BA magna cum laude, Cornell U., 1967, MD, 1971; JD, Fordham U., 1985. Bar: N.Y. 1988, N.J. State Supreme Ct., Washington Ct. of Appeals; bd. cert. legal medicine. Intern, Cornell-N.Y. Hosp., N.Y.C., 1971-72, resident in gen. surgery, 1972-76, resident in plastic surgery, 1977-79; fellow in surgery Meml.-Sloan Kettering Found., 1972-76, 77-79; practice medicine specializing in plastic surgery, N.Y.C., 1979—; instr. surgery Cornell U. Med. Coll., 1980—; asst. attending plastic surgeon Beth Israel North, N.Y. Downtown Hosp., 1979—, N.Y. Hosp., 1980—, Drs. Hosp., 1987—; pres. Esquire Cadillac Limousine Svc. Inc., 1977-93, Beaux Arts Holdings, 1979—, Rocin Labs., Inc., 1981—. Mem. N.Y. County Health Svc. Rev. Orgn., 1976—; founder, dir. Rocin Found. for Plastic Surg. Rsch., 1979—; Maj. M.C., USAF, 1976-77; Japan. Diplomate Am. Bd. Surgery, Am. Bd. Plastic Surgery; licensed physician, N.J., N.Y. State, Calif., Va. Fellow ACS, Internat. Coll. Surgeons, Am. Soc. Abdominal Surgeons, Am. Coll. Legal Medicine; mem. Am. Soc. Plastic and Reconstructive Surgery, Royal Soc. Medicine, AMA (physicians recognition award 1978, 81), N.Y. State Med. Soc., N.Y. County Med. Soc. (health systems, pub. rels., peer rev. coms.), N.Y. Acad. Scis., Am. Trial Lawyers Assn., ABA, Le Club, N.Y. Athletic Club, Cornell Club, Phi Beta Kappa. Republican. Author: The Kindest Cut; Keeping Face, Medical Malpractice: Handling Plastic Surgical Cases; contbr. articles to profl. publs. Office: 120 Central Park S New York NY 10019-1560

CUDDIHY, JUNE TUCK, pediatrics nurse; b. Buffalo, June 15, 1936; d. John R. Sr. and Monica A. (Donahue) Tuck; m. Robert V. Cuddihy, Aug. 24, 1957; children: Robert V., Timothy, Kathleen. BSN, D'Youville Coll., Buffalo, 1957; MA, Seton Hall U., 1972, MSN, 1979. Cert. primary care nurse practitioner. Pub. health nurse Monroe County, Rochester, N.Y.; health coord. Early Childhood Learning Ctrs. N.J., Morristown; asst. prof. Seton Hall U., South Orange, N.J., 1977-81, William Paterson Coll., Wayne, N.J., 1981-94; clin. assoc. Coll. Nursing Ohio State U., 1994—; cons. Berkeley BioMedical Group, Inc., 1991—. Contbr. articles to profl. jours. Named Outstanding Grad. Student, Seton Hall U., 1979. Mem. ANA (vice chmn. bd. examiners for cmty. health nursing practice, chmn. sch. nurse practice subcom.), N.J. State Nurses Assn., Nat. Child Abuse Assn., Nat. Burn Victim Found., Pub. Health Assn., Sigma Theta Tau. Home: 8798 Killie Ct Dublin OH 43017-8333 Office: Ohio State U Coll Nursing Dept Cmty Parent Child Psyc 1585 Neil Ave Columbus OH 43210-1289

CUDDY, BRIAN GERARD, neurosurgeon; b. Syracuse, N.Y., July 13, 1959; s. Edward Michael and Mary Elizabeth (O'Brien) C. BS in Biology, SUNY, Albany, 1981; MS in Physiology, Albany Med. Coll., 1983, MD, 1987. Asst. prof. neurosurgery Med. U. S.C., 1994—, Med. Coll. Wis., 1993-94. Contbr. articles to profl. jours. Mem. Am. Assn. Neurol. Surgeons, Sigma Xi. Roman Catholic. Office: Med U of SC Dept Neurosurgery 171 Ashley Ave Charleston SC 29425-0001

CUELLAR, TERRENCE MICHAEL, pediatrics nurse; b. Des Moines, Jan. 10, 1964; s. John and Peggy Cuellar. BSN, U. Mo., 1988; MN Pediatric Nurse Practitioner, U. Fla., 1994. RN, Fla., Mo.; cert. BLS, pediatric advanced life support, BLS instr. Pediatrics staff nurse Univ. Hosp. and Clinics, Columbia, Mo., 1988-90; nurse Camp Winadu, Pittsfield, Mass., 1989; adolescent unit nurse Univ. Hosp. and Clinics, Columbia, 1990-91; pediatrics staff nurse Shands Hosp. U. Fla., Gainesville, 1991—; nurse Alachua Regional Juvenile Detention Ctr., Gainesbille, Fla. (student asst.), 1992; instr. Nursing Simulated Lab., Santa Fe C.C. Nursing Programs, Gainesville, 1993-95, pediat. clin. instr. ADN program, 1994-95. Vol. nurse Camp Quality, Columbia, 1991, Big Bros./Big Sisters, Columbia, 1983-86; vol. height/weight screener for children Health Fair, Columbia Mall, 1991. Staff scholar Univ. Hosp. and Clinics, 1987, scholar Fla. chpt. Nat. Assn. Pediatric Nurse Assocs. and Practitioners, 1991, W.K. Kellogg Found., 1992; grantee HHS, 1991, 92; recipient U.S. Achievement Acad. Nat. award. Mem. ANA, Fla. Nurses Assn., NAPNAP, Sigma Theta Tau. Home: 2370 SW Archer Rd Apt 49 Gainesville FL 32608-1056

CUELLO, AUGUSTO CLAUDIO GUILLERMO, medical research scientist, author; b. Buenos Aires, Argentina, Apr. 7, 1939; came to Can., 1985; s. Juan Andres and Rita Maria (Sagarra) Cuello-Freyre; m. Martha Maria J. Kaes, Mar. 10, 1967; children: Paula Marcela, Karina Rosa. MD, U. Buenos Aires, 1965; MA (hon.), Oxford (Eng.) U., 1978, DSc, 1986; hon. degree, U. Fed. do Ceará, 1991. Asst. prof. Sch. Biochemistry, U. Buenos Aires, 1974-75; scientist MRC Neurochem. Pharmacology, Cambridge, Eng., 1975-78; lectr. depts. pharmacology and human anatomy U. Oxford, 1978-85; med. tutor, E.P. Abraham sr. research fellow Lincoln Coll., Oxford, 1978-85; chmn., prof. pharmacology and therapeutics McGill Univ., Montreal, Que., Can., 1985—; cons. Seralab Ltd., Sussex, Eng., 1981-85, Sandoz Ltd., Basel, Switzerland, 1982-84, Medicorp-Immunocorp, Montreal, 1985—, Synthelabo, Paris, 1977-78, Fidia Rsch. Labs., 1991-93, UN Inst. Biotech. and Genetic Engring., Italy, 1993; internat. advisor Cajal Inst., Madrid, 1983-88. Editor: Co-Transmission 1, 1982, Immunohistochemistry, 1983, Brain Microdissection Techniques, 1983, Substance P and Neurokinins, 1987, Pain and Mobility, 1987, Neuronal Cell Death and Repair, 1993, Cholinergic Function and Dysfunction, 1993, Immunohistochemistry II, 1993, Pharmacological Sciences: Perspectives For Research and Therapy in the Late 1990's, 1995, NeuroReport, 1990—, Jour. Chem. Neuroanatomy, 1987-93; mem. editl. bd. profl. jours. Recipient Estela A. de Goytia prize Argentinian Assn. Advancement Sci., 1968, Prof. A. Rosenblueth award Grass Found., 1979, Robert Feulgen prize Gesellschaft für Histochemie, 1981; NIH Postdoctoral fellow, 1970-72; named Hon. Prof. faculty of Pharmacy and Biochemistry, Buenos Aires U., 1992, Norman Bethune U. Med. Scis., China., Hon. Citizen of New Orleans, 1992, Heinz Lehman award Can. Coll. Neuropsychopharmacology, 1995. Mem. Brit. Pharm. Soc., Brain Rsch. Assn., Can. Coll. Neuropsychopharmacology, Am. Soc. Neurochemistry, European Neurosci. Assn., Internat. Soc. Neuroendocrinology, Soc. for Neurosci., Assn. Med. Sch. Pharmacology, Can. Assn. Neurosci., Internat. Soc. Neurochemistry, Can. Assn. Acad. Pharm., Internat. Brain Rsch. Orgn., Internat. Neuropeptide Soc., World Health Orgn., Am. Soc. Pharmacology and Exptl. Therapeutics, Oxford Soc., Physiol. Soc. Gt. Britain, Pharm. Soc. of Can., Gesellschaft fur histochemie, Corr. Pharma. Soc. of Argentina, Can. Fed. of Bio. Sci., Oxford and Cambridge United Club, Univ. Club Montreal. Avocations: tennis, reading, theatre, history, Spanish and Latin American literature. Office: McGill U Dept Pharmacology, 3655 Drummond St, Montreal, PQ Canada H3G 1Y6

CUEVAS, DAVID, psychologist; b. Mt. Vernon, Ohio, Sept. 28, 1947; s. Robert Myron Ryan and Wanda Mae Carter; m. Belia Cuevas, Apr. 1, 1980; 1 child, Angela Marie. AA in Gen. Edn., Lassen Coll., 1975; BS in Psychology, U. Md., 1984; MA in Psychology, Webster U., 1986; PhD in Psychology, Columbia Pacific U., 1989. Drafted USN, 1964-67; enlisted U.S. Army, 1971, advanced through ranks to sgt., specialist behavioral sci., 1966-86, ret., 1986; faculty El Paso (Tex.) Community Coll., 1986—; cons. Cuevas Cons. Svcs., El Paso, 1986—; sch. dir. Computer Career Ctr., El Paso, 1987-89; speaker conf. Fed. Women's Assn., Ft. Bliss, Tex., 1990. Advisor, vol. Paralyzed Vets. Am., El Paso, 1991—. 2d jr. vice-comdr. DAV. Mem. APA, ASCD, VFW (life), Spl. Forces Assn. Home: 11640 Lake Erie Dr El Paso TX 79936 Office: El Paso Community Coll PO Box 20500 El Paso TX 79998-0500

CUEVAS, RITA ESTHER, internist, reheumatologist; b. N.Y.C., Dec. 14, 1958; d. Vicente and Maria (Santana) C.; m. Raul Yordan, Mar. 16, 1985; children: Raul V., Ileana V. BS, U. P.R., 1981, MD, 1985. Diplomate Am. Bd. Internal Medicine, Am. Bd. Rheumatology. Resident in internal medicine Tulane U. Med. Sch., New Orleans, 1985-89; fellow in rheumatology U. Tex. Health Sci. Ctr., San Antonio, 1989-91; pvt. practice, San Antonio, 1994—. Maj. M.C., USAF, 1991-94. Roman Catholic. Office: 215 E Quincy St Ste 417 San Antonio TX 78215

CUFFE, ROBIN JEAN, nursing educator; b. Frankfurt, Sept. 8, 1951; d. Russell Bates and Jean May (Clark) Preuit; m. Ronald Frederick Cuffe, Mar. 9, 1974; 1 child, Matthew David. Diploma, Richmond Meml. Hosp., 1973; BSN, Marymount U., 1982; MS in Edn., Va. Technol. and State U., 1990. RNC; cert. in cardiac rehab. nursing AACN; cert. health edn. specialist. Staff nurse Fairfax Hosp., Falls Church, Va., 1973-75; asst. head nurse, staff nurse, supr. ICU Arlington (Va.) Hosp., 1975-78, asst. coord. cardiac rehab., 1978-81, coord. cardiopulmonary rehab., 1981—. Bd. dirs. Am. Heart Assn., Northern, Va., 1982-91; jr. high youth group leader Ch. of the Holy Comforter, Vienna, Va., 1988-90, mem. adult edn. comm., 1990—. Fellow Am. Assn. Cardiovascular and Pulmonary Rehab. (chair stds. and reimbursement com. 1991—, pres.-elect 1994-95, pres. 1995-96, treas. 1996—), Sigma Theta Tau (pres. chpt. 1984-86). Episcopalian. Home: 2607 Midway St Falls Church VA 22046-1928

CUI, KE-HUI, embryologist, obstetrician, gynecologist; b. Guangzhou, Guangdong, China, May 15, 1948; arrived in Australia, 1989; s. Shen-Zhi and Zi-Jian (Chen) C.; m. Ling-Jia Wang, Dec. 31, 1982; children: Jing,

Yong-Yan. MD, Sun Yat-sen U. Med. Scis., Guangzhou, 1982; PhD, U. Adelaide, Australia, 1993. Tech. officer 1st Affiliated Hosp. Sun Yat-sen U. Med. Scis., 1976-78, resident in ob-gyn., 1982-86; postdoctoral fellow U. Fla., Gainesville, 1986-89; scientist in charge preimplantation diagnosis U. Adelaide, 1993-96; dir. molecular and preimplantation genetics The Ctr. For Human Reproduction, Chgo., 1996—; honorable assoc. prof. Sun Yat-sen U. Med. Scis., Guangzhou, China, 1995—. Referee Human Fertilisation and Embryology Authority, London, 1995; mem. panel assessors Nat. Health and Med. Rsch. Coun., Australia, 1995—. Mem. Fertility Soc. Australia (Marion Merrell Dow prize 1991, 94). Office: Ctr Human Reprodn 750 North Orleans St Chicago IL 60610

CULBERSON, JAMES LEE, anatomist, educator; b. Pana, Ill., Sept. 18, 1941; s. Rex Melvin and Norma Elaine (Mills) C.; m. Judith Francis DeMoulin, Apr. 8, 1962; children: Carole Lynne, Laura Joan, Sarah Jane. BA in Biology, Ill. Wesleyan U., 1963; PhD in Anatomy, Tulane U., 1968. Instr. anatomy Tulane U., New Orleans, 1967-68; instr. anatomy W.Va. U., Morgantown, 1968-69, asst. prof., 1969-72, assoc. prof., 1972-84, prof., 1984—, acting chair dept., 1986-88; assoc. chair dept., 1994—; vis. sr. lectr. U. Otago, Dunedin, New Zealand, 1978; rsch. assoc. U. Tasmania, Hobart, Australia, 1978—; cons. Nat. Bd. Examiners in Optometry, 1989-90; reviewer, cons. neurosci. textbooks various pubs., 1985—. Contbr. articles to profl. jours. Fogarty Sr. Rsch. fellow Fogarty Ctr. NIH, Cambridge, Eng., 1990; grantee NIH, 1974—; P.I. Rsch. grantee NSF W.Va. U., 1988—. Mem. Am. Assn. Anatomist, Soc. Neurosci., Clare Hall (life), Phi Kappa Phi. Democrat. Methodist. Home: RR 7 Box 618 Morgantown WV 26505-9116 Office: WVa U Health Sci Ctr Dept Anatomy Morgantown WV 26506

CULBERT, GRETCHEN ANN, women's health care nurse; b. Cleve., Feb. 23, 1943; d. Henry Timothy and Edith Pauline (Zwilling) Fenderbosch; m. Charles Culbert, Nov. 23, 1963; children: Patricia Ann, Charles Timothy. ADN, Ctrl. Tex. Coll., Killeen, 1985; student, U. Tex. Southwestern Med. Sch., Dallas, 1987. RN, Tex.; cert. women's health care nurse practitioner. Women's health nurse practitioner Family Planning Program, Copperas Cove, Tex., 1977-91, Scott and White Clinic, Temple, Tex., 1991—; speaker and presenter in field. Mam. Nat. Assn. Nurse Practitioners in Reproductive Health, Tex. Nurse Practitioners, Am. Acad. Nurse Practitioners, Ctrl. Tex. Nurse Practitioners. Home: 604 End O Trail Harker Heights TX 76543 Office: Scott and White Clinic 2401 S 31st St Temple TX 76503

CULBERTSON, MARVIN CRIDDLE, JR., physician; b. Vernon, Tex., Aug. 30, 1927; s. Marvin Criddle and Henrietta May (Beal) C.; m. Elizabeth Abshier, Dec. 9, 1950; children: Marvin C. III, Kathryn Lynn, Donald G., Diane Seward. MD, U. Tex., 1950. Diplomate Am. Bd. Pediat., Am. Bd. Otolaryngology. Ruling elder P.C.A., 1948—; moderator North Tex. Presbyn. Ch. in Am., 1986-87, mission to world com., 1989—; gen. assembly rep. Presbyn. Ch. Am., Dallas, 1991—; pvt. practice, Dallas, 1956-93; clin. prof. U. Tex. S.W. Med. Ctr., 1956—; med. tchr. India, Korea and others. Lt. USN, 1950-53. Mem. ACS, Am. Acad. Otolargyn. Home: 3405 Colgate Ave Dallas TX 75225-4830 Office: U Tex Southwestern Med Ctr 5323 Harry Hines Blvd Dallas TX 75235

CULLARI, SALVATORE SANTINO, clinical psychologist, educator; b. Caroniti, Calabria, Italy, Apr. 1, 1952; came to U.S., 1955; s. Carmelo and Carmela (Cullari) C.; m. Kathryn Plesce, Apr. 26, 1985; children: Catherine, Dante. BA, Kean Coll., 1974; MA, Western Mich. U., 1976, PhD, 1981. Lic. psychologist, Pa., W.Va. Dir. psychology White Haven (Pa.) Ctr., 1982-83; psychologist Danville (Pa.) State Hosp., 1983-84; coord. of psychology Harrisburg (Pa.) State Hosp., 1984-86; prof., dept. chair Lebanon Valley Coll., Annville, Pa., 1986—; cons. Harrisburg State Hosp., 1986—, Bur. Disability Determination, Harrisburg, 1987—. Author acad. questionaire acad. social evaluation scales, 1990, Treatment Resistance, 1996; contbr. numerous articles to profl. jours. Mem. APA, Assn. Advancement of Behavior Therapy, Pa. Psychol. Assn. Office: Lebanon Valley Coll Psychology Dept Annville PA 17003

CULLEN, BRUCE F., anesthesiologist; b. Iowa City, May 6, 1940. MD, UCLA, 1966. Intern Blodgett Meml. Hosp., Grand Rapids, Mich., 1966-67; resident in anesthesiology U. Calif., San Francisco, 1967-70; attending anesthesiologist Harborview Med. Ctr., Seattle; prof. U. Wash. Office: U Wash HMC Anesthesiology 325 9th Ave Seattle WA 98104-2420*

CULLEN, LUNDA AHERN, nurse; b. Presque Isle, Maine, Feb. 9, 1943; d. John Joseph and Sarah Ann (McCrossin) A.; m. Gerald John Cullen, June 20, 1964; children: Kimberly Ann, Michael Sean. Diploma in nursing, R.I. Hosp. Sch. Nursing, 1964; BA, St. Joseph Coll., 1975; postgrad., N.H. Coll. Operating room nurse R.I. Hosp., Providence, 1964; infirmary nurse Dartmouth Coll., Hanover, N.H., 1965-70; instr. med.-surg. nursing Mary Hitchcock Meml. Hosp., Hanover, 1970-78; cmty. health nurse Town of Hanover, 1978-79, acting dir. cmty. health, 1979-80; supr. home health Dartmouth Hitchcock Med. Ctr., Hanover, 1980-92; dir. clin. svcs. Visiting Nurse Alliance Vt. and N.H., White River Junction, Vt., 1992—; cons. Vt. Assembly Home Health, Montpelier, 1995; speaker in field. Contbr. articles to profl. jours. Mem. com. Steering Com. for Sr. Residents, Hanover, 1985—. Recipient Citizen award Hanover High Sch., 1982. Mem. Homecare Assn. N.H. (bd. dirs. 1989-91), Vt./N.H. Continuing Care Assn. Democrat. Roman Catholic. Home: Haystack Rd Grantham NH 03753 Office: Visiting Nurse Alliance Vermont and New Hampshire 20 S Main St White River Junction VT 05001

CULLEY, JUNE ELIZABETH, clinical reviewer, quality improvement specialist; b. Valley Station, Ky., July 22, 1933; d. Wilbur W. and Elizabeth Piper (Dodge) C. Diploma, Ky. Bapt. Hosp., Louisville, 1954; BSN, Case Western Res. U., 1963; MPH, Johns Hopkins U., 1970, ScD, 1981. Dir. nursing State Tb Commn., Louisville; dir. nursing svcs. Louisville/Jefferson County Dept. Pub. Health; dir. nursing, long-term care svcs. City Health Dept., Balt.; quality mgmt. analyst VA Med. Ctr., Ft. Howard, Md.; coord. Palliative Care ProgramFt. Howard divsn. Va./Md. Health Care Sys. Mem. AAUW, VA Nat. Nurses Rsch. Coun., VA Regional Nurses Rsch. Com., Sigma Theta Tau, Delta Omega (nat. award).

CULLIS, PAUL ANTHONY, neurologist; b. London, May 15, 1952; came to U.S., 1960; s. Frank and Angela Maria (Hammond) C.; m. Anne Hilary Greaves, May 31, 1980; children: Jonathan James, Emma Louise. MB, ChB with distinction, U. Birmingham, 1979. Diplomate Am. Bd. Neurology, reg. Gen. Med. Coun. Gt. Britain. Resident in neurology Wayne State U. Sch. Medicine, Detroit, 1980-82, chief resident in neurology, 1982-83, fellow dept. neurology, 1983-84, from clin. instr. to clin. assoc. prof. dept. neurology, 1983—; staff Harper Hosp., Detroit, 1984—, Macomb Hosp. Ctr., Warren, Mich., 1984—, dir. Parkinson's Disease clinic, 1990—, dir. neuro care, 1993—; courtesy staff Bon Secours Hosp., Grosse Pointe, Mich., 1991—; staff, dir. movement disorder clinic Detroit Receiving Hosp. U. Health Ctr., Detroit, 1984-87, co-dir., 1989—, dir. headache clin., 1984-87, med. ctr. affiliate staff, 1987—; year III student coord. dept. neurology Wayne State U. Sch. Med., Detroit, 1983-86, year IV student coord., 1986-87, continuing med. edn. coord., 1983-87; cons. Huron Valley Hosp., Milford, Mich., 1986-91, Rehab. Inst., Detroit, 1985-91; med. adv. Project ST, Warren, 1980—, Am. Spasmodic Torticollis Assn, Hendon, Va., 1990-91; mem. scientific adv. bd. NeuroMed Corp., 1985-87, Allergan Pharmaceuticals, 1990-92; local media contact person Dystonia Med. Rsch. Found., 1988—; mem. profl. adv. bd. Mich. Parkinson's Found., 1991—; TV guest various programs; spkr., lectr. in field. Contbr. articles to profl. pubs., chpts. to books. Vol. Heroin Addiction Clin., Harper Hosp., Detroit, 1970; leg. asst. to Rep. Jackie Vaughn III, Lansing, Mich., 1970; pres. Citizens United for the Vote at 18, Inc., 1969-71. Recipient Sandoz award, 1983; grantee A.H. Robins Co., 1983, Roche Labs., 1984, 87, 90, Wayne State U. Sch. Med. dept. neurology, 1984, Athena Neuroscience, 1993; Wayne State U. Sch. Med. dept. neurology fellow, 1983-84. Fellow Am. Acad. Neurology (neurol. rehab. sect. 1988—); mem. AMA, Mich. State Med. Soc., Macomb County Med. Soc., Assn. Rsch. Nervous and Mental Disease, Am. Assn. Electrodiagnostic Medicine, Movement Disorder Soc., Am. Soc. Neurorehab., Mich. Neurol. Assn., Nat. Spasmodic Torticollis Assn. (chmn. med. adv. bd., bd. dirs. 1982—, rep. to NIH consensus devel conf. on clin. use botulinum toxin 1990), Nat. Spasmodic Dysphonia Assn. (med. adv. bd. 1990—), Mensa. Republican. Roman Catholic. Office: Neurol Rehab Assocs 11900 E 12 Mile Rd # 209 Warren MI 48093

CULLISON, SAMUEL WILKINSON, III, physician; b. Chgo., Jan. 14, 1948; s. Samul Wilkinson Jr. and Eleanor (Wilkins) C.; m. Beth Roberta Trussell, Dec. 21, 1971; children: Samuel Wilkinson IV, Robert John. BA, Ind. U., 1970; MD, U. Mo., 1975. Diplomate Am. Bd. Family Practice, subspecialty in geriatrics; cert. in addiction medicine. Resident in family practice U. Wash., Seattle, 1975-78; pvt. practice specializing in family practice, Monroe, Wash., 1978-94; residency dir. in family practice Providence Hosp., Seattle, 1994—; med. dir. Evergreen Treatment Ctr., Seattle, 1978—; pres. med. staff Valley Gen. Hosp., Monroe, 1982-84; med. dir. Midvale Treatment Ctr., Seattle, 1986-94, Alcohol Drug Treatment Ctr., Monroe, 1986-94; assoc. clin. prof. U. Wash. Sch. Medicine, 1980—; bd. dirs. Snohomish County Physicians Corp., Everett, Wash, 1985-94, pres. bd., 1987-88; bd. dirs. Wash. Physician Health Program, 1995—. Contbr. articles to med. jours. Mem. AMA, Wash. State Med. Assn. (trustee 1985—, del. nat. convs. 1987—), Am. Acad. Family Physicians, Wash. Acad. Family Physicians (pres. 1987-88), Am. Med. Soc. for Alcoholism and Other Drug Dependencies. Democrat. Methodist. Office: Providence Family Practice Residency 550 16th Ave Ste 100 Seattle WA 98122

CULLUM, ELAINE WARDEN, medical and surgical nurse, health facility manager; b. Orange, N.J., Jan. 9, 1931; d. Arthur G. and Lilyan A. (Kunz) Warden; m. Paul F. Cullum, Jr., Feb. 13, 1954; children: Paul, Stephen, Noreen, Caren, Margo, Diana. AA in Speech and Drama, Bradford Coll., Haverhill, Mass., 1950; LPN, St. Barnabas Nursing Sch., Livingston, N.J., 1975; AA in Nursing, SUNY, Albany, 1981, BSN, 1990. RN, N.Y.; cert. med.-surg., critical care nephrology. Staff nurse-renal div. St. Barnabas Med. Ctr., Livingston, 1975-81, lic. practical nurse, 1981-82, nursing supr., 1982-89, asst. dir. nursing, 1989—; nursing supr. Union (N.J.) Hosp., 1992—. Mem. ANA, N.J. State Nurses Assn. Home: 26 Franklin St Cedar Grove NJ 07009-2208

CULPEPPER, MICHAEL IRVING, researcher, educator; b. Mobile, Ala., Sept. 28, 1951; s. Milton Irving and Betty Jean (Wimpee) C.; m. Cynthia Ann Langner, Mar. 11, 1972; children: Amber Joy, Amy Celeste, Amanda Kaye. Student Auburn U., 1969-71; BS, U. Ala.-Birmingham, 1973, MS, 1975, CASE, 1978; EdD, U. Ala., 1981. Cert. tchr., Ala. Asst. lab. technician div. orthopaedic surgery U. Ala.-Birmingham, 1971-72, lab. asst., 1972-73, research technician, 1973-74, research asst., 1974-75, research assoc., 1975-81, instr. stats., biomechanics/kinesiology, 1981-87, asst. prof., 1987; dir. research Kerner-Quarterback Sports Medicine Inst., Children's Hosp., Birmingham, 1982—; lectr. to orgns. on sports medicine and health care. Tchr., coach Chelsea High Sch. (Ala.), 1987; bd. dirs. Dixie Softball Inc., Central Shelby League; chmn. long-range planning com. Chelsea Youth Club. Recipient M. Ray Loree research award U. Ala., Tuscaloosa, 1981. Fellow Am. Coll. Sports Medicine; mem. Ala. Acad. Sci., Am. Alliance Health Phys. Edn., Recreation and Dance, Am. Coll. Sports Medicine (chpt. membership com.), Nat. Athletic Trainers Assn., Soc. for Biomaterials, U.S. Sports Acad. (nat. faculty)Sigma Xi, Kappa Delta Pi. Baptist. Contbr. articles to profl. jours.; developer U. Ala.-Birmingham sports injury/illness data storage and retrieval system. Home: 165 Rich Dr Chelsea AL 35043-9575 Office: Chelsea High Sch Chelsea AL 35043

CULPEPPER, WALTER SHELLEY, III, pediatric cardiology; b. New Orleans, Jan. 28, 1947; s. Walter Shelley and Mary Louise (McLean) C.; m. Martha Trautman, Feb. 15, 1974; 1 child, Jennifer Elizabeth. BA in English Lit., U. Va., 1968; MD, La. State U., 1972. Diplomate pediatrics and pediat. cardiology Am. Bd. Pediat. Staff pediat. cardiologist Ochsner Clinic, New Orleans, 1978—, sect. chief pediat. cardiology, 1987—, assoc. med. dir., 1993—; staff cons. Children's Spl. Health Svcs., La., 1978—. Contbr. articles to profl. jours. Fellow Am. Coll. Cardiology, Am. Acad. Pediat.; mem. Southeastern Pediat. Cardiology Soc. (pres. 1989-90). Republican. Episcopalian. Office: Pediat Cardiology Ochsner Clinic 1514 Jefferson Hwy New Orleans CA 70121

CULROSS, RITA ROMAINE, psychology educator; b. Monmouth, Ill., Jan. 31, 1950; d. Lee Acheson and Dorothy Julia (Baltz) Rodgers; m. Claude Culross, June 17, 1972. B.A. with highest distinction, Purdue U., 1972, M.S. in Edn., 1973, Ph.D., 1976. Asst. prof. psychology Marycrest Coll., Davenport, Iowa, 1976-78; instr. psychology N Harris County Coll., Houston, 1978-79; asst. prof. U. Houston-Clear Lake City, 1979-83, assoc. prof., 1983-91; pvt. practice psychology, Houston, 1980-85; cons. psychologist Clear Creek Schs. Gifted Program, 1980-86; fellow Am. Coun. on Edn., 1990-91; prof. La. State U., 1991—. David Ross fellow, 1974-76; Purdue Research Found. grantee, 1974-76; U. Houston Organized Research grantee, 1982. Mem. Mental Health Assn. (edn. com. 1979-81, liaison to children's com. 1979-81, speaker's bur. 1979—), Am. Psychol. Assn., Am. Ednl. Research Assn., Am. Assn. for Higher Edn., La. Psychol. Assn., Soc. for Pediatric Psychology, Presbyterian. Author: Counseling the Gifted: Developing the Whole Child, 1981. Home: 16027 Chantilly Ave Baton Rouge LA 70817-2410 Office: 388 Pleasant Hall Baton Rouge LA 70803

CULTON, PAUL MELVIN, counselor, educator, interpreter; b. Council Bluffs, Iowa, Feb. 12, 1932; s. Paul Roland and Hallie Ethel Emma (Paschal) C. BA, Minn. Bible Coll., 1955; BS, U. Nebr., 1965; MA, Calif. State U., Northridge, 1970; EdD, Brigham Young U., 1981. Cert. tchr., Iowa. Tchr. Iowa Sch. for Deaf, Council Bluffs, 1956-70; ednl. specialist Golden West Coll., Huntington Beach, Calif., 1970-71, dir. disabled students, 1971-82, instr., 1982-88; counselor El Camino Coll., Via Torrance, Calif., 1990-93, acting assoc. dean, 1993-94; counselor El Camino Coll., Via Torrance, Caif., 1994—; interpreter various state and fed. cts., Iowa, Calif., 1960-90; asst. prof. Calif. State U., Northridge, Fresno & Dominguez Hills, 1973, 76, 80, 87-90; vis. prof. U. Guam, Agana, 1977; mem. allocations task force, task force on deafness, trainer handicapped students Calif. C.C.s, 1971-81. Editor: Region IX Conf. for Coordinating Rehab. and Edn. Svcs. for Deaf proceedings, 1970, Toward Rehab. Involvement by Parents of Deaf conf. proceedings, 1971; composer Carry the Light, 1986. Bd. dirs. Iowa NAACP, 1966-68, Gay and Lesbian Cmty. Svcs. Ctr., Orange County, Calif., 1975-77; founding sec. Dayle McIntosh Ctr. for Disabled, Anaheim and Garden Grove, Calif., 1974-80; active Dem. Cent. Com. Pottawattamie County, Council Bluffs, 1960-70; del. People to People N.Am. Educators Deaf Vis. Russian Schs. & Programs for Deaf, 1993. League for Innovation in Community Coll. fellow, 1974. Mem. Registry of Interpreters for Deaf, Congress Am. Instrs. Deaf, Am. Deafness and Rehab. Assn., Calif. Assn. Postsecondary Educators Disabled, Am. Fedn. Tchrs., Nat. Assn. Deaf. Mem. Am. Humanist Assn. Home: 2567 Plaza Del Amo Apt 203 Torrance CA 90503-8962 Office: El Camino Coll Spl Resource Ctr 16007 Crenshaw Blvd Torrance CA 90506-0001

CULTON, SARAH ALEXANDER, psychologist, writer; b. Burwell, Nebr., Nov. 12, 1927; d. James Claude and Frances Ann (Evans) Alexander;m. Verlen Ross Culton, June 19, 1949; children: James Verlen, Sarah Ann. BA in Edn., Ea. Wash. U., 1953, MA in Edn., 1956; EdD in Psychology, U. Idaho, 1966. Tchr. pub. schs. Kennewick, Northport, Wash., Potlatch, Idaho, 1946-56; prof. Lewis-Clark U. of Idaho, Lewiston, 1956-59, North Idaho Jr. Coll., Coeur d'Alene, 1961-66; sch. psychologist Sch. Dist. 81, Spokane, Wash., 1966-67; prof. psychology Spokane Falls Community Coll., 1967-88; author Colville, Wash., 1988—; sch. psychologist Adna (Wash.) Spl. Edn. Coop., 1994; mid. sch. counselor Soda Springs (Idaho) Sch. Dist., 1994—; sch. psychologist, sch. counselor vol. Northport Schs., 1989-92; presenter convs. in field. Author: Psychology of Stress and Nutrition, 1991. Doctoral fellow Wash. State U., 1959, U. Idaho, 1964; recipient Faculty Achievement award Burlington No. Found., 1988. Fellow Am. Inst. Stress; mem. NEA, APA, Internat. Coun. Psychologists, Internat. Stress Mgmt. Assn. (newsletter editor), Nat. Stroke Assn., Western Psychol. Assn., Am. Counseling Assn. (writer invitation 1992), Nat. Assn. Sch. Psychologists, Alpha Delta Kappa. Home and Office: 50 E Second S #5 Soda Springs ID 83276

CULVER, ROBERT ELROY, osteopathic physician; b. Toledo, Oct. 1, 1926; s. Elroy and Helen Mary C.; m. Sallie Jane Corder, June 10, 1972; children: Diana L., Galen R., Ronald A., Richard A., Patricia A., Robert B. B.S., U. Toledo, 1951; D.O., Chgo. Osteo. Medicine, 1959. Cert. med. boxing profl. Intern Sandusky Meml. Hosp., Ohio, 1960; practice medicine specializing in family practice and sports medicine Oregon, Ohio, 1960—; health commr. Village of Harbor View, 1990—; dir. osteo. svcs. Riverside Hosp., 1996—; mem. City of Oregon Bd. Health, staff Parkview, Riverside, Toledo, Mercy Hosps.; physician Oregon Sch. Sys.; police surgeon City of Oregon; chief dep. coroner, 1978-80; chmn. wrestling divsn. physicians Nat. AAU; U.S. med. rep. Fedn. Internat. Lute Amateur; physician U.S. Wrestling Team; med. dir. World Cup of Wrestling; pres. Northwestern Ohio AAU; 3rd v.p. Ohio AAU; med. cons. Ohio Profl. Boxing Commn. Mem. Air Force Mus., Toledo Mus. Art; dir. Toledo Zoo; mem. Smithsonian Instn.; apptd. to sr. coun. of Ohio Acad. of Sci., 1993. With C.E., U.S. Army, 1944-46; col. Ohio Def. Svc. Recipient commendation Ohio Ho. of Reps., 1983, 93, honor award Oreg. Sch. Sys., 1983; named Outstanding Team Physician State of Ohio, 1984, World Sports Medicine Hall of Fame, 1993. Mem. Am. Osteo. Assn., Ohio Osteo. Assn., 1st Dist. Acad. Osteo. Medicine (state trustee, past pres.), Am. Coll. Gen. Practitioners in Osteo. Medicine and Surgery, Ohio Osteo. Assn. Physicians and Surgeons, Chgo. Coll. Osteo. Med. Alumni Assn., Ohio Acad. Sci. (mem. sr. coun.), NRA (life), U. Toledo Alumni Assn. (life), Air Force Assn., Aircraft Owners and Pilots Assn., Nat. Hist. Soc., Ohio Hist. Soc., Am. Legion, Atlas Club, Masons, Elks, Shriners. Methodist. Office: 5517 Corduroy Rd Oregon OH 43616-1511

CULYBA, MICHAEL JOHN, physician, medical administrator; b. Charleroi, Pa., Oct. 9, 1946; s. Michael and Lillian Helen (Gaydos) C.; m. Joyce Carol Grochocinski, Aug. 15, 1970; children: Michael Christian, Rebecca Janine, Matthew Justin. BA in Chemistry, Washington and Jefferson Coll., 1968; MD, Loyola U., 1972. Diplomate Am. Bd. Internal Medicine. Resident in internal medicine Northwestern U., Evanston, Ill., 1976-78; physician Marshall/Culyba Partnership, Beaver, Pa., 1979-84, Beaver Internal Medicine Assocs., 1984-93; assoc. med. dir. Health America, Pitts., 1993-94, physician-in-charge network, 1994-96, ops. v.p., med. dir., 1996—; chmn. bd. Riverside Health Plan, Beaver, 1986-93; v.p. med. staff The Med. Ctr., Beaver, 1991-92, pres.-elect, 1992-93, pres., 1993. Bd. dirs. Beaver County Heart Assn., 1984-90, pres., 1989-90; bd. dirs. The Med. Ctr., Beaver, 1992-93. Lt. comdr. USNR, 1973-76. Mem. ACP, AMA, Pa. Med. Soc., Beaver County Med. Soc., Am. Coll. Physician Execs. Home: 460 2d St Beaver PA 15009 Office: Health America 5 Gateway Ctr Pittsburgh PA 15222

CUMES, DAVID M., urologist; b. Johannesburg, South Africa, Aug. 12, 1944; came to U.S., 1975; s. Jack and Lillian (Beare) C.; children: Lila, Terence, Paul, Roni. M.B.B.Ch., U. Witwatersrand, Johannesburg, 1967. Diplomate Am. Bd. Urology. Intern, resident in gen. surgery Johannesburg, 1968-75; resident in urology Stanford (Calif.) Med. Sch., 1975-79, staff urologist, 1979-80; staff urologist Mason Clinic, Seattle, 1980-81; pvt. practice Santa Barbara, Calif., 1981—. Mem. Am. Urol. Assn. (western sect.), Santa Barbara Med. Soc. Office: 601 E Arrellaga Santa Barbara CA 93109

CUMMING, JANICE DOROTHY, clinical psychologist; b. Berkeley, Calif., Nov. 20, 1953; d. Gordon Robertson and Helen (Stanford) Cumming; 1 child, Shauna Cumming Keddy. BA, U. Calif., Davis, 1975; MA, Calif. State U., Sacramento, 1980; PhD, Calif. Sch. Profl. Psychology, Berkeley, 1985. Lic. psychologist, Calif. Counselor and instr. Serendipity Diagnostic/Treatment, Citrus Hts., Calif., 1978-79; reg. psychologist asst. John Gibbins, PhD, Castro Valley, Calif., 1984-87, Enrico Jones, PhD, Berkeley, Calif., 1985-86; asst. rsch. specialist U. Calif., Berkeley, 1985-90; clin. cons. Family Guidance, Children's Hosp., Oakland, Calif., 1987-90; clin. supr. psychiat. svcs. Children's Hosp., San Francisco, 1987-90; pvt. practice psychology Castro Valley, 1987-90, San Francisco, 1987-90, Oakland, Calif., 1990—; mem. rschr. San Francisco Psychotherapy Rsch. Group, 1987—, instr., 1991, conf. chair, 1992-93; conv. chair Calif. State Psychol. Assn., Sacramento, 1985, 86; asst. clin. prof. U. Calif., San Francisco, 1992—. Mem. APA, Calif. Psychol. Assn. (continuing edn. com. chair 1986, co-chair 1987), Psychologists for Social Responsibility (bd. dirs. 1984-87, chair 1987-89), No. Calif. Soc. Psychoanalytic Psychology, Alameda County Psychol. Assn., Phi Beta Kappa. Office: 5835 College Ave Ste C Oakland CA 94618-1653

CUMMINGS, CHARLES WILLIAM, physician, educator; b. Boston, Nov. 16, 1935; s. Harry Blanchard and Madge (Frey) C.; m. Jane Drake Cummings, July 1, 1983; children—Charles William, Lee Blanchard, Evelyn Howard. A.B., Dartmouth Coll., 1957; M.D., U. Va., 1961. Intern Mary Hitchcock Meml. Hosp., Hanover, N.H., 1961-62; resident otolaryngology Harvard U. Med. Sch., 1965-68; practice medicine specializing in otolaryngology Seattle, 1978—; assoc. prof. otolaryngology Upstate Med. Sch., SUNY, Syracuse, 1976-78; prof., chmn. dept. otolaryngology-head and neck surgery U. Wash. Med. Sch., Seattle, 1978-91, Johns Hopkins Hosp. and Med. Ctr., Balt., 1991—; Bd. dirs. Am. Bd. Otolaryngology. Author: Atlas of Laryngeal Surgery; co-author: Comprehensive Text of Otolaryngology-Head and Neck Surgery; contbr. sci. articles to profl. jours. Served to capt., M.C. USAF, 1963-65. Mem. ACS (chmn. adv. coun.), Soc. Head and Neck Surgeons, Am. Soc. for Head and Neck Surgery (sec., pres.), Soc. Univ. Otolaryngologists, Assn. Acad. Depts., Otolaryngology (past pres.), Triological Soc., Laryngological Soc., Bronchoesophagological Soc. (past pres.), Am. Acad. Otolaryngology-Head and Neck Surgery (bd. dirs., past pres.). Episcopalian. Office: Johns Hopkins U Dept Otolaryngology/Head/Neck/Surgery 601 North Carolina St Baltimore MD 21287

CUMMINGS, FRANK JOSEPH, oncologist; b. New Haven, Sept. 6, 1940; s. Thomas E. and Mary A.C. Cummings. BS, Trinity Coll., Hartford, Conn., 1962; MD, U. Va., 1966. Intern, Presbyn.-U. Pa. Hosp., Phila., 1966-67, resident in medicine, 1967-68; instr. Brown U., Providence, 1970-73, asst. prof., 1973-80, assoc. prof. medicine, 1980—; mem. div. oncology-hematology Roger Williams Gen Hosp., Providence, 1970-73, head div., 1974-85, univ. dir. div. med. oncology, 1974-88. Mem. Am. Assn. Cancer Rsch., ACP, Am. Fedn. Clin. Research, Am. Soc. Clin. Oncology. Office: Roger Williams Med Ctr Divsn Hematology/Oncology 825 Chalkstone Ave Providence RI 02908

CUMMINGS, LARRY LEE, psychologist, educator; b. Indpls., Oct. 28, 1937; s. Garland R. and Lillian P. (Smith) C.; children—Lee Anne, Glenn Nelson. A.B. summa cum laude, Wabash (Ind.) Coll., 1959; postgrad. in psychology (Woodrow Wilson fellow), U. Calif., Berkeley; M.B.A., Ind. U., 1961, D.B.A., 1964. Asst. prof., then assoc. prof. Grad. Sch. Bus., Ind. U., Bloomington, 1964-67; vis. assoc. prof. Grad. Sch. Bus., Columbia U., 1967-68; mem. faculty U. Wis., Madison, 1968-81; prof. Grad. Sch. Bus. and Indsl. Relations Research Inst., lectr. univ. dept. psychology, 1970-81; dir. Center Study Organizational Performance, 1973-81, H.I. Romnes faculty fellow, 1975-81, Slichter research prof., 1980-81; assoc. dean social scis. Center Study Organizational Performance (Grad. Sch.), 1975-78; Kellogg disting. research prof. orgnl. behavior Kellogg Grad. Sch. Mgmt., Northwestern U., Evanston, Ill., 1981-88; Carlson prof. Carlson Sch. Mgmt. U. Minn., Mpls., 1988—; Ford. Found. sr. research fellow, Brussels, Belgium, 1969-70; vis. prof. Faculty Commerce and Bus. Adminstrn., U. B.C., Vancouver, 1971-72. Co-author: Organizational Decision Making, 1970, Performance in Organizations, 1973, Introduction to Organizational Behavior, 1980; co-editor: Readings in Organizational Behavior and Human Performance, rev. edit., 1973, Research in Organizational Behavior, vol. 2, 1980, vol. 3, 1981, vol. 4, 1982, vol. 5, 1983, vol. 6, 1984, vol. 7, 1985, vol. 8, 1986, vol. 9, 1987, vol. 10, 1988, vol. 11, 1989, vol. 12, 1990, vol. 13, 1991, vol. 14, 1992, vol. 15, 1993, vol. 16, 1994, vol. 17, 1995, vol. 18, 1996, Publishing in the Organizational Sciences, 1985; cons. editor Irwin series in mgmt. and behavioral scis.; contbr. profl. publs. Bd. trustees Wabash Coll., 1992—. Woodrow Wilson fellow, 1959-60; fellow Ford Found., 1961-62, summer 1965, grantee; Richard D. Irwin Dissertation fellow, 1963-64; co-recipient McKinsey Found. Mgmt. Research Design award, 1968-69; grantee Richardson Found., 1968-71; grantee Am. Soc. Personnel Adminstrn., 1974-75. Fellow Am. Psychol. Soc. (charter), Acad. Mgmt. (editor jours., bd. govs., v.p., nat. programs chmn., pres., dean of fellow of acad., Disting. Educator award 1995), APA, Am. Inst. Decision Scis. (v.p., exec. bd.); mem. Midwestern Psychol. Assn., Indsl. Rels. Rsch. Assn., Am. Sociol. Assn., Soc. Pers. Adminstrn., Phi Beta Kappa, Sigma Xi, Beta Gamma Sigma, Tau Kappa Alpha, Delta Phi Alpha, Sigma Chi. Office: U Minn Carlson Sch Mgmt 271 19th Ave S Minneapolis MN 55455-0430

CUMMINGS, LUIS EMILIO, anesthesiologist, consultant; b. Mayagüez, P.R., Nov. 2, 1954; s. Luis and Gladys (Carrero) C.; m. Hazel Ruiz, 1993; 1

child, Luisito. MD, U. P.R., 1979; postgrad., U. Miami, 1983. Diplomate Am. Bd. Anesthesia. Intern U. P.R., 1979-80; resident in anesthesiology Jackson Meml. Hosp., Miami, Fla., 1980-83. Mem. P.R. Soc. Anesthesia (pres. 1995—), Caribbean Anesthesia Soc. (bd. dirs. 1992—). Roman Catholic. Home: Cond Alhambra Plz # 403 Ponce PR 00733 Office: Caribbean Anesthesia Soc PO Box 1790 Ponce PR 00733

CUMMINGS, MARTIN MARC, medical educator, physician, scientific administrator; b. Camden, N.J., Sept. 7, 1920; s. Samuel and Cecelia (Silverman) C.; m. Arlene Sally Avrutine, Sept. 27, 1942; children: Marc Steven, Lee Bernard, Stuart Lewis. B.S., Bucknell U., 1941, D.Sc., 1969; M.D., Duke U., 1944; DHL (hon.), Georgetown U., 1971; D.Sc. (hon.), Duke U., 1985; D.Sc., U. Nebr., Emory U.; MD (hon.), Karolinska Inst., 1972, U. Lvov, 1975; DHL, Georgetown U., 1976. Diplomate Am. Bd. Microbiology. Intern, resident Boston Marine Hosp., 1944-46; resident Tb Grasslands Hosp., Valhalla, N.Y., 1946-47; dir. Tb evaluation lab. Communicable Disease Ctr., USPHS, Atlanta, 1947-49; instr. medicine Emory U. Sch. Medicine, 1948-50, assoc. medicine, 1950-52, asst. prof., 1953; chief Tb sect., also dir. Tb research lab. VA Hosp., Atlanta, 1949-53; dir. research services VA Cen. Office, Washington, 1953-59; MD (hon.) U. Lwow, 1975; prof. microbiology, chmn. dept. Okla. U. Sch. Medicine, 1959-61; chief Office Internat. Research, NIH, USPHS, 1961-63; dir. Nat. Library of Medicine, 1964-84, dir. emeritus, 1984—; cons. Council on Library Resources, 1984—; chmn., bd. dirs. Coun. on Libr. Resources, 1994-96; assoc. dir. for research grants NIH, 1963-64; chmn. com. med. research Nat. Tb Assn., 1958-59; chmn. panel Sarcoidosis NRC-Nat. Acad. Scis., 1958-60; dist. prof. community medicine Georgetown U. Sch. Medicine, 1986-90. Author: (with Dr. H.S. Willis) Diagnostic and Experimental Methods in Tuberculosis, 1952, The Economics of Research Libraries, 1986; contbr. chpt. on Tubercle Bacilli, Diagnostic Procedures and Reagents, 1950; editor: Influencing Change in Research Libraries, 1989. Served with AUS, 1943-44. Recipient Exceptional Service award VA, 1959; Distinguished Service award HEW, 1968; Rockefeller Pub. Service award, 1973; Disting. Achievement award Modern Medicine, 1976; Disting. Service award Am. Coll. Cardiology, 1978; John C. Leonard award Assn. Hosp. Med. Edn., 1979. Fellow AAAS (dir.), Royal Soc. Medicine, Med. Libr. Assn., N.Y. Acad. Medicine (hon.), Phila. Coll. Physicians; mem. Am. Soc. Clin. Investigation (sr. mem.), Am. Fedn. Clin. Rsch., Inst. Medicine, Coun. Libr. Resources (bd. dirs.). Home: 605 Sutton Pl A-402 Longboat Key FL 34228 Office: Coun Libr Resources 1400 16th St NW Washington DC 20036-2217

CUMMINGS, NANCY BOUCOT, nephrologist, biomedical ethicist; b. Phila., Feb. 21, 1927; d. Arthur B. Guest and Katharine (Rosenbaum) Sturgis; m. Milton Curtis Cummings Jr., July 1959 (div. 1985); children: Christopher Ronald, Jonathan Benton, Susan Sturgis. BA, Oberlin Coll., 1947; postgrad., Radcliffe Coll., 1947; MD, U. Pa., 1951. Rotating intern Pa. Hosp., Phila., 1951-52; resident in internal medicine Hosp. of the U. Pa., Phila., 1952-54; rsch. and clin. asst. Royal Hosp. St. Bartholomew, London, 1954-55, Manchester (Eng.) Royal Infirmary, 1955; rsch. fellow in internal medicine, nephrology Harvard Med. Sch., Boston, 1955-58; asst. medicine Peter Bent-Brigham Hosp., Boston, 1955-58; rsch. fellow in biochemistry Harvard Med. Sch., Boston, 1958-59; guest worker Lab. Intermediary Metabolism Nat. Inst. Arthritis and Metabolic Diseases, Bethesda, 1959-62; rsch. med. officer Walter Reed Army Inst., Washington, 1962-66; exptl. medicine researcher USN Med. Rsch. Inst., Bethesda, Md., 1966-72; clin. instr. medicine Georgetown U., Washington, 1960-70, clin. asst. prof. medicine, 1970-81, clin. assoc. prof. medicine, 1981-88, clin. prof. medicine, 1988—; clin. scholar ctr. for clin. ethics Georgetown U., 1995—; officer Kidney Disease Collaborative Program Nat. Inst. for Arthritis, Metabolism and Digestive Diseases (now Nat. Inst. of Diabetes and Digestive and Kidney Diseases)/NIH, Bethesda, 1972-73, spl. asst. to dir., 1973-74, acting assoc. dir. for kidney, urologic and blood diseases, 1974-76, assoc. dir. for kidney, urologic, and blood diseases, 1976-84, assoc. dir. for research and assessment, 1984-96; mem. core faculty coll. medicine, assoc. prof. cmty. medicine and family practice Howard U.; nephrological cons. NIH, 1972—, USN Hosp., Bethesda, 1966-72; vis. scholar Ctr. for Clin. Med. Ethics, U. Chgo., 1992-93; assoc. prof. dept. cmty. & family medicine Howard U. Coll. Medicine, 1994-96; rsch. fellow Kennedy Inst. Ethics, Georgetown U., 1994—. Editor: Prevention of Kidney and Urinary Tract Diseases, 1978, Immune Mechanisms in Renal Disease, 1982, Chronic Renal Failure, 1985. Lay reader (now called lay liturgical eucharistic minister) Cathedral of St.Peter and Paul (Washington Nat. Cathedral), Washington, 1976—; vestry St. Albans Ch., Washington, 1975-79, 89-92; chmn. St. Albans Sunday Forum, 1986-89, chmn. com. med. ethics Diocese (Episcopal) of Washington, 1990-94, standing com., 1996—; diocesan del. St. Albans Ch., 1992-95; mem. Standing Commn. on Health of Gen. Conv. Episcopal Ch., 1992—, vice chair, 1993—; bd. dirs. Collington Episcopal Life Care Cmty., 1991-93; bd. govs., bd. mgrs. quality care Strategic Planning Commn. Wash. Home, 1992—, chair credentialing com. 1996—. Recipient Jacob Ehrenzeller award Pa. Hosp., 1986, Hall of Fame award Cheltenham High Sch. Alumni Assn., 1984. Mem. Am. Soc. Nephrology, Internat. Soc Nephrology, Am. Fedn. Clin. Rsch., Nat. Kidney Found. (sci. adv. bd. 1973-79, Disting. Svc. award 1981), Washington Acad. Medicine (bd. dirs. 1989-92, v.p. 1991-94, pres. 1994-96), European Dialysis and Transplant Assn., Exec. Women in Govt. (treas. 1978-79), Women in Nephrology (program chmn. 1987—, sec. 1990-92, mem. women's health seminar com., 1992—, NIH chair 1993-94, pres.'s vis. com. Mt. Vernon Coll.), Cosmos Club (program com. 1992-95). Home: 3900 Connecticut Ave NW Washington DC 20008-2412 Office: NIH Nat Inst Diabetes Digestv Kidney Diseases Bethesda MD 20892

CUMMINGS, NICHOLAS ANDREW, psychologist; b. Salinas, Calif., July 25, 1924; s. Andrew and Urania (Sims) C.; m. Dorothy Mills, Feb. 5, 1948; children—Janet Lynn, Andrew Mark. AB, U. Calif., Berkeley, 1948; MA, Claremont Grad. Sch., 1954; PhD, Adelphi U., 1958. Chief psychologist Kaiser Permanente No. Calif., San Francisco, 1959-76; pres. Found Behavioral Health, San Francisco, 1976—; chmn., chief exec. officer Am. Biodyne, Inc., San Francisco, 1985-93; chmn., CEO Kendron Internat., Ltd., Reno, Nev., 1992—; chmn. Nicholas & Dorothy Cummings Found., Reno, 1994—; co-dir. South San Francisco Health Ctr., 1959-75; pres. Calif. Sch. Profl. Psychology, Los Angeles, San Francisco, San Diego, Fresno campuses, 1969-76; chmn. bd. Calif. Community Mental Health Ctrs., Inc., Los Angeles, San Diego, San Francisco, 1975-77; pres. Blue Psi, Inc., San Francisco, 1972-80, Inst. for Psychosocial Interaction, 1980-84; mem. mental health adv. bd. City and County San Francisco, 1968-75; bd. dirs. San Francisco Assn. Mental Health, 1965-75; pres., chmn. bd. Psycho-Social Inst., 1972-80; dir. Mental Rsch. Inst., Palo Alto, Calif., 1979-80; pres. Nat. Acads. of Practice, 1981-93. Served with U.S. Army, 1944-46. Fellow Am. Psychol. Assn. (dir. 1975-81, pres. 1979); mem. Calif. Psychol. Assn. (pres. 1968). Office: Nicholas & Dorothy Cummings Found 561 Keystone Ave Ste 212 Reno NV 89503-4304

CUMMINGS, RICHARD J., otologist; b. Topeka, Nov. 18, 1932; s. John Edward and Mary J. (Harrington) C.; m. Laura Roberta Herring, Dec. 21, 1956; children: Thomas, Anne, William, John. BA, U. Kans., 1954, MD, 1957. Intern St. Benedict Hosp., Ogden, Utah, 1957-58; resident U. Okla. Med. Ctr., Oklahoma City, 1959-62; practice medicine specializing in ear, nose, throat Colorado Springs Med. Clinic, Colo., 1961-62; practice medicine specializing in otology Wichita (Kans.) Ear Clinic, 1962—; clin. asst. prof. U. Kans. Sch. Medicine; pres. med. staff St. Francis Hosp., Wichita, 1974-75; mem. med. staff St. Joseph Hosp., Wichita, pres., 1990-91; host M.D. Radio program, Wichita, 1978-79. Contbr. articles to med. jours. Bd. dirs. Kans. State Bd. of Healing Arts, 1981-83, Kans. Commn. for Deaf and Hearing Impaired, 1988-91; mem. Kans. tissue transplantation com. ARC, 1990-94; chmn. St. Joseph Charity Classic Tournament, 1981; physician's group chmn. United Way Campaign, 1968, 69, 77, 84; mem. U. Kans. Athletic Bd., 1991-95. With USPHS, 1958-59. Fellow ACP, ACS, Am. Acad. Otolaryngology; mem. AMA, Am. Audiol. Soc., Kans. Med. Soc., Kans. Ear Nose Throat Soc. (pres. 1975), Wichita Surg. Soc. (pres. 1989), Sedgwick County Med. Soc. (pres. 1978), Otosclerosis Study Group, Hearing Conservation Assn., Pan Am. Soc. Otolaryngology, Wichita Cochlear Implant Program (bd. dirs.), Rotary (bd. dirs. Wichita chpt. 1978-79), U. Kans. Nat. Alumni Assn. (bd. dirs. 1979-84, vice chmn. 1994-95, chmn. 1995-96). Home: 1258 Burning Tree Dr Wichita KS 67230-1410 Office: 427 N Hillside St Wichita KS 67214-4917

CUMMINGS, ROBERT EUGENE, retired counseling psychologist; b. Honolulu, Aug. 15, 1930; s. Bernard Joseph and Mary (Moran) C.; m. Margit Castle, May 16, 1973; children: Michael Robert, Caroline Marie. BA, U. Calif., 1953; MA, San Diego State U., 1962; EdD, U. Mo., 1969. Lic. Psychologist, Tenn. Psychology intern Jefferson Barracks Vets. Hosp., Columbia, Mo., 1965-66; staff psychologist Agnew State Hosp., San Jose, Calif., 1967-72; counseling psychologist Mt. Home VA Med. Ctr., Johnson City, Tenn., 1971-95; ret., 1995; with Office Vocat. Rehab., 1962-66. Author: (poem) Now and Then, (book) Poems & Sculpture, 1977; contbr. articles to profl. jours. Lt. (j.g.) USN, 1953-57, Korea. Mem. Psi Chi (hon.).

CUMMINS, CECIL STRATFORD, former microbiology educator; b. Monkstown, Co. Cork, Ireland, Nov. 20, 1913; came to U.S., 1967; s. James and Fanny (Exham) C.; m. Morag Fraser Cameron, Oct. 3, 1959 (dec. 1992); children: Patricia (dec. 1990), James. BA with honors, Trinity Coll., Dublin, Ireland, 1941, M.B.,B.Ch., 1943, ScD, 1964. Asst. to prof. dept. microbiology Trinity Coll., Dublin, 1944; pathologist Royal Army Med. Corps, 1944-47; sr. lectr. Med. Coll. London Hosp., 1948-64, reader, 1964-67; prof. microbiology Va. Poly. Inst. and State U., 1967-89, prof. emeritus, 1989—.

CUMMINS, KARL PATRICK, chemical engineer; b. Bitburg, Germany, Mar. 17, 1965; s. Charles Gayle and Gabriele Karia (Huhndorf) C.; m. Kimberly Vern Hart, Oct. 20, 1990; 1 child, Geoffrey Charles. AAS Chem. Technology, Alfred State Coll., 1986, AS Engring. Sci., 1986; BS Chem. Engring., U. Buffalo, 1989; MBA, Rochester Inst. of Tech., 1993. Intern engr., N.Y. Assoc. process engr. Varflex Corp., Rome, N.Y., 1989-91; scientist Bausch & Lomb, Rochester, N.Y., 1993—. Mem. Internat. Soc. for Pharm. Engring. Republican. Home: 11 Green Ln Hilton NY 14468 Office: Bausch & Lomb Personal Products Divsn 1400 N Goodman St Rochester NY 14692

CUMMINS, THOMAS DEMAREE, physician; b. Louisville, Aug. 15, 1952; s. Demaree Thomas and Mildred Susan (Harrelson) C. BA in Biology with honors, U. Louisville, 1974, MS, 1980, MD, 1983. Diplomate Am. Bd. Plastic Surgery. Intern in gen. surgery Quillen-Dishner Coll. Medicine East Tenn. State U., Johnson City, 1983-84, resident in gen. surgery, 1984-86; resident in plastic and reconstructive surgery Med. Coll. Ohio, Toledo, 1987-89; fellow in surgery of the hand Wayne State U., Detroit, 1986-87; mem. staff Alliant Health Sys., Audubon Regional Med. Ctr., Bapt. Hosp. East, Suburban Med. Ctr., Jewish Hosp., Caritas Med. Ctr., Tri-County Cmty. Hosp., S.W. Med. Ctr., Clark Meml. Hosp., Floyd County Hosp.; presenter Ohio Valley soc. for Plastic and Reconstructive Surgery, 1989, St. Anthony Med. Ctr., 1990, Bapt. Hosp. East, 1996, Jewish Hosp. Contbr. articles to profl. jours. Recipient Alumni Fellow award U. Louisville, 1992. Fellow ACS; mem. AMA, Am. Soc. Plastic and Reconstructive Surgeons, Louisville Soc. Plastic and Reconstructive Surgeons (sec.-treas. 1995), Ky. Med. Assn., Jefferson County Med. Soc. Republican. Roman Catholic. Home: 516 Blankenbaker Ln Louisville KY 40207 Office: Ste G 6002 Brownsboro Park Blvd Louisville KY 40207

CUMPSTON, GRAHAM NEIL, cardiologist; b. Perth, Australia, Mar. 21, 1935; s. Lancelot Graham and Rosalie Jean (Gollan) Bowser Cumpston; m. Beverley Anne Greig, Aug. 15, 1959. MB, BS, U. Adelaide, South Australia, 1958. Registrar, med. officer Royal Perth Hosp., Princess Margaret Hosp., 1959-61; registrar Brompton Hosp., London, 1962-64, Royal Perth Hosp., Sir Charles Gairdner Hosp., 1965-67; cons. cardiologist Princess Margaret Hosp. for Children, Perth, 1968-72, Royal Perth Hosp., 1968—. Editl. bd. Catheterisation and Cardio-Vascular Diagnosis, 1994. V.p. Fremantle (West Australia) divsn. Liberal Party; councillor Shire Peppermint Grove, West Australia, 1973—, pres., 1995—; pres. Royal Western Australian Hist. Soc., 1979. Travelling fellow Nat. Heart Found., 1970. Fellow Royal Australasian Coll. Physicians (chmn. West Australia divsn. 1978-80), Soc. Cardiac Angiography and Interventions (U.S., gov.); mem. Cardiac Soc. Australia and New Zealand (chmn. West Australia divsn. 1988—, councillor 1991—), Weld Club, Lake Karrinyup Country Club. Democrat. Mem. Ch. of Eng. Office: 2/11 Colin Grove, West Perth, West Australia 6005, Australia

CUNEO, JOHN ANDREW, JR., health facility administrator; b. N.Y.C., May 5, 1929; s. John A. Sr. and Adele (Neive) C.; m. Gloria Britting, June 28, 1952; children: Susan, Richard. BS, Fordham U., 1951; MS, Columbia U., 1955. Asst. adminstr. Mid Island Hosp., Beth Page, N.Y., 1955-59; adminstr. Pelham Bay Gen. Hosp., Bronx, N.Y., 1959-74; exec. dir. Parkway Hosp., Forest Hills, N.Y., 1974-87; sr. v.p. LaGuardia Hosp., Forest Hills, 1987-92; adminstrv. officer surg. svcs. VA Med. Ctr., Bklyn., 1993-95, adminstrv. officer radiation oncology svcs., 1995—. Capt. USAF, 1951-53. Fellow Royal Soc. Health; mem. APHA, Am. Coll. Healthcare Execs., Am. Hosp. Assn., Assn. Pvt. Hosps. Inc. (sec., v.p., past pres.), Pub. Health Assn. N.Y.C., Healthcare Execs. Club.

CUNHA, DENISE ANNE, clinical psychologist; b. Brockton, Mass., May 2, 1956; d. James Denis and Josephine Anne (Gonsalves) C. BS, Rensselaer Poly. Inst., 1978; MA, U. Del., 1982, PhD, 1985. Lic. psychologist, Maine, Md., Del. Clin. psychologist Wilmington, Del., 1990—. Mem. APA, Del. Psychol. Assn. (sec. 1994—). Office: 1504 N Broom St Apt 2 Wilmington DE 19806-3056

CUNHA-VAZ, JOSE GUILHERME FERNANDES, ophthalmologist; b. Coimbra, Portugal, Nov. 5, 1938; s. Antonio Manso and Maria Izilda (Calado) Cunha-Vaz; m. Teresa Maria Deniz Coutinho, Dec. 6, 1962; children: Ricardo Jose, Maria Cecilia, Eduardo Henrique. MD, U. Coimbra, 1962, D Med Scis., 1967; PhD, U. London, 1966. Rsch. and clin. asst. Inst. Ophthalmology, Morfields Eye Hosp., London, 1963-66; asst. prof. ophthalmology U. Coimbra, 1966-74, assoc. prof., chmn. dept., 1974-79, dean faculty medicine, 1976; prin. investigator L.F.E.N. Biology, Lisbon, Portugal, 1968-69; prof. ophthalmology U. Ill., U. Ill. Hosp., Chgo., 1979-81, 84-86; prof. ophthalmology, chmn. dept. ophthalmology U. Coimbra and Hosp., 1981—; dir. Ctr. for Ophthalmology Rsch., Coimbra, 1975—; pres. Assoc. Biomed. Inst. Rsch. in Light and Image, Coimbra, 1989—; adj. prof. U. Ill., Chgo., 1986—. Editor Experientia Ophthalmologica, Jour. Francais D'Ophthalmologie, Internat. Ophthalmology, others; editor 4 books; co-inventor Vitreous Fluorophotometry, 1975; contbr. articles to sci. jours., chpts. to books. Mem. Coordinating Commn. Health Rsch., Jnict, Portugal, 1990-95, Nat Coun. Sci. and Tech., Portugal, 1990-95; Portuguese del. to European Community Biomed. Rsch. Program, 1991—. Lt. Portugal mil., 1969-71. Recipient medicine prize U. Coimbra, 1962, prize Inst. Alta Cultura, 1965, prize Soc. Med. Scis. Lisbon, 1975, Order Pub. Instrn., Portugal, 1993, Diaz-Caneja medal U. Valladolid, 1993; Internat. rsch. scholar Prevention of Blindness; NIH rsch. grantee, 1979, 81, 84, 89, Junta Nacional Investigacao Cientif, Portugal. Fellow Am. Acad. Ophthalmology, Coll. of Ophthamologists (U.K.); mem. Portuguese Soc. Ophthalmology (pres. 1981-83, 90-92), Internat. Soc. Ocular Fluorometry (pres. 1992-94), European Soc. Engring. and Medicine (bd. dirs. 1991—), European Soc. Cataract Refractive Surgery (bd. dirs. 1991—), Easd-Diabetic Eye Complications (v.p. 1989), Internat. Ocular Microsurgery Study Group, Club Jules Gonin (bd. dirs. 1994—). Roman Catholic. Home: R Penedo da Saudade 30, 3000 Coimbra Portugal Office: Hosp U Coimbra, Dept Ophthalmology, Coimbra Portugal

CUNNANE, PATRICIA S., medical facility administrator; b. Clinton, Iowa, Sept. 7, 1946; d. Cyril J. and Corinne Spain; m. Edward J. Cunnane, June 19, 1971. AA, Mt. St. Clare Coll., Clinton, Iowa, 1966. Mgr. Eye Med. Clinic of Santa Clara Valley, San Jose, Calif. Mem. Med. Adminstrs. Calif. Polit. Action Com., San Francisco, 1987. Mem. Med. Group Mgmt. Assn., Am. Coll. Med. Group Adminstrs. (nominee). Nat. Notary Assn., NAFE, Exec. Women Internat. (v.p. 1986-87, pres. 1987—), Profl. Secs. Internat. (sec. 1979-80), Am. Soc. Ophthalmic Adminstrs., Women Health Care Execs., Healthcare Human Resource Mgmt. Assn. Calif. Roman Catholic. Home: 232 Tolin Ct San Jose CA 95139-1445 Office: Eye Med Clinic of Santa Clara Valley 220 Meridian Ave San Jose CA 95126-2903

CUNNINGHAM, DENNIS DEAN, microbiology, molecular genetics educator; b. Des Moines, Iowa, Aug. 16, 1939; s. Melvin B. and Laura (Jones) C. BA, U. Iowa, 1961; PhD, U. Chgo., 1967. Postdoctoral fellow Princeton (N.J.) U., 1968-70; asst. prof. U. Calif., Irvine, 1970-74, assoc. prof., 1974-78, prof. microbiology and molecular genetics, 1978—, chmn. microbiology and molecular genetics, 1987—; mem. study sect. NIH, Bethesda, Md., 1975-80, Am. Cancer Soc., 1982-86. Editor: Control of Cellular Division and Development, 1980, Proteases in Biological Control and Biotechnology, 1986; assoc. editor Jour. Cellular Physiology, 1978—; mem. editorial bd. Jour. Cellular Biochemistry, 1979—, Jour. Biol. Chemistry, 1990—; contbr. articles to sci. jours. Recipient Research Career Devel. award NIH, 1975-80; research grantee NIH, 19706. Fellow AAAS; mem. Am. Soc. Biol. Chemists, Am. Soc. Cell Biology. Home: 1215 Brangwyn Way Laguna Beach CA 92651-2924 Office: U Calif Irvine Dept Microbiology & Molecular Genetics Irvine CA 92717*

CUNNINGHAM, GLENN D., orthopaedic surgeon; b. Davenport, Iowa, Jan. 25, 1945; s. Glenn D. and Grace Cunningham. BA, Yale U., 1967; MD, U. Iowa, 1976. Diplomate in orthopaedic surgery and hand surgery Am. Bd. Orthopaedic Surgery. Commd. ensign USN, 1968, advanced through grades to comdr.; surg. intern Naval Hosp., San Diego, 1976-77, resident in orthopaedic surgery, 1977-81; orthopedic surgeon U.S. Naval Hosp., San Diego, 1981-84; orthopedic surgeon U.S. Naval Hosp., San Francisco, 1984-86, chief orthopedic surgery, 1984-86; chief orthopedic surgery U.S. Naval Hosp., Camp Pendleton, Calif., 1986-89; ret. USN, 1989; pvt. practice orthopaedic surgery Palm Springs, Calif., 1989—; chief of surgery Desert Hosp., Palm Springs, 1995—. Fellow ACS, Am. Acad. Orthopaecid Surgery. Republican. Roman Catholic. Office: Palm Springs Orthopaedics 1100 N Palm Canyon # 212 Palm Springs CA 92262

CUNNINGHAM, JACQUELINE LEMMÉ, psychologist, educator; b. Biddeford, Maine, Apr. 22, 1941; d. S. James and Alice (Fréchette) Lemmé; m. Seymour Cunningham II, Dec. 16, 1960 (dec. 1987); children: Macklin Todd, Danielle, Alyssa. BA in Psychology cum laude, U. Maine, Orono, 1963; MS in Psychology, U. South Ala., 1983; PhD, U. Tex., 1994. Tchr. Mobile (Ala.) Pub. Schs., 1976-81; intern Devereux Found., Devon, Pa., 1988-89; fellow in developmental disabilities Med. Sch. Harvard U., Cambridge, Mass., 1990; prof. U. S.D., Vermillion, 1994-95; fellow in pediat. neuropsychology Children's Nat. Med. Ctr., Washington, 1995—; cons. in field. Contbr. articles to profl. jours. Mem. APA (outstanding dissertation of yr. award divsn. 16 1994), Internat. Neuropsychol. Soc., Nat. Acad. Neuropsychology, Soc. History Behavioral Scis., Phi Kappa Phi.

CUNNINGHAM, KATRINA SUE, nurse; b. Dayton, Ohio, May 15, 1943; d. Bertram Susdorf and Helen Cook Palm; m. Bruce A. Cunningham, Feb. 27, 1965; children: Jennifer Ruth, Douglas James. Diploma in nursing, Rockford Meml. Hosp., 1964. Cert. peri-operative nurse. Nurse Yale New Haven (Conn.) Hosp., 1964-66, N.Y. Hosp., 1966-71; office nurse Dr. M. Buckman, N.Y., 1971-72; nurse United Hosp. Med. Ctr., Port Chester, N.Y., 1980-89, asst. nursing care coord. oper. rm., 1989-92; unit coord. Scripps Surgery Ctr., La Jolla, Calif., 1993—. Mem. Assn. Oper. Room Nurses. Home: 13455 Roxton Cir San Diego CA 92130-1843

CUNNINGHAM, MADELEINE WHITE, microbiologist, immunologist; b. Greenville, Miss., Feb. 24, 1946; d. L.C. and Josephine (Kersh) White; m. Curtis Phillip Cunningham, Dec. 19, 1969 (div. 1986); children: Catherine, Nicole, Luke. BS, Miss. U. for Women, 1968; MS, U. Tenn., 1971, PhD, 1973. Postdoctoral fellow Okla. Med. Rsch. Found., Oklahoma City, 1973-76; rsch. assoc. U. Okla. Health Sci. Ctr., Oklahoma City, 1980-81, asst. prof., 1981-86, assoc. prof. microbiology, 1986-93, prof., 1993—, dir. Flow Cytometry Core Ctr., 1990-92; mem. bacteriology-mycology study sect. NIH, Washington, 1989-93, myocarditis working group, 1985; mem. grant-in-aid rev. com. Am. Heart Assn., 1993—, co-chmn., 1996, chair, 1996-97; bd. dirs. Presbyn. Health Fedn., Oklahoma City, 1996—. Contbr. articles to sci. jours. Bd. dirs. Canterbury Choral Soc., Oklahoma City, 1988; bd. dirs. Presbyn. Health Found., 1995—. Grantee Am. Heart Assn., 1984-86, Nat. Heart, Lung and Blood Inst., 1986-89, 89-94, 95—, others; recipient NIH Rsch. Career Devel. award, 1986-91, Provost's Rsch. award U. Okla., 1986, Regent's award for outstanding rsch. and creative activity, 1994. Mem. AAAS, Am. Soc. Microbiology, Am. Assn. Immunologists, Internat. Cardiovascular Immunology Soc. (sci. bd. dirs.), Lancefield Soc. for Streptococci and Strep Diseases (pres., v.p. 1991-93). Presbyterian. Office: U Okla Health Sci Ctr Dept Microbiology PO Box 26901 Oklahoma City OK 73126-0901

CUNNINGHAM, MARK DOUGLAS, clinical and forensic psychologist; b. Dallas, Sept. 3, 1951. BA in Psychology magna cum laude, Abilene Christian U., 1973; MS, Okla. State U., 1976, PhD, 1977; postgrad., Yale U., 1979-81. Diplomate Am. Bd. Profl. Psychology (forensic); lic. psychologist, Tex. Clin. psychology intern Nat. Naval Med. Ctr., Bethesda, Md., 1977-78; asst. prof. psychology Hardin-Simmons U., Abilene, Tex., 1981-83; pvt. practice Abilene, 1981—; cons. Hendrick Med. Ctr, Abilene, Abilene Regional Med. Ctr. Columnist Abilene Reporter News, 1986—. Lt. USNR, 1977-81. Decorated Navy Commendation medal; recipient Al Brown Meml. award Yale U., 1981. Fellow Am. Acad. Forensic Psychology; mem. Am. Psychol. Assn., Tex. Psychol. Assn., Abilene Psychol. Assn., Nat. Register Health Svc. Providers in Psychology. Office: 2501 S Willis St Ste B Abilene TX 79605-6249

CUNNINGHAM, MILAMARI ANTOINELLA, anesthesiologist; b. Cody, Wyo., Oct. 4, 1949; d. Milo Leo and Mary Madeline (Haley) Olds; m. Michael Otis Webb, June 4, 1970 (div. Feb. 1971); m. James Kenneth Cunningham, June 14, 1975. BA with honors, U. Mo., 1971, MD, 1975. Diplomate Am. Bd. Anesthesiologists. Intern and resident U. Mo., Columbia, 1975-78; jr. ptnr. Anesthesiologist, Inc., 1979-82, ptnr., 1982-86; owner Cunningham Anesthesia, 1986—; dir. anesthesia dept. Ellis Fischel Cancer Ctr., 1991-92; acting chief anesthesia Harry S. Truman Meml. Vets. Hosp., 1994-95; mem. med. staff Columbia Regional Hosp., Boone Hosp. Ctr., Columbia U. Mo. Hosp. and Clinics, Columbia; cons. staff Audrain Med. Ctr., Mexico, Mo., Harry S Truman Meml. Vets. Hosp., Columbia. Active Mo. Med. Polit. Action Com., 1991—, Friends of Music, Friends of Libr., Boone County Fair, 1978-94, with ham breakfast divsn., 1978-85, with draft horse and mule show, 1986-88; bd. dirs. A Call to Serve Mo., 1996—. Fellowship Am. Coll. Anesthesiologists, 1977. Mem. AMA (physicians recognition award 1978, 85, 87, 91, 95), Am. Soc. Regional Anesthesia, Am. Med. Women's Assn., Internat. Anesthesia Rsch. Soc., Mo. Soc. Anesthesiologists (v.p. 1986-87, pres. elect 1987-88, pres. 1988-89, Am. Soc. Anesthesiologists del. 1989—), Boone County Med. Soc. (alt. del. 1986, del. 1987-89, membership chair 1982-84, sec.-treas. 1996—), Mo. State Med. Assn. (commn. econs. third party payors 1986—, chair 1989), Vis. Nurses Assn. (bd. dirs. 1982-89, chair 1984-86, adv. bd. 1989-93), Phi Beta Kappa. Home: 8202 S Bennett Dr Columbia MO 65201-9804 Office: PO Box 1301 Columbia MO 65205-1301

CUNNINGHAM, PAUL JOHNSTON, surgeon; b. Princeton, Ky., Oct. 10, 1928; s. Paul Clemens and Marie (Johnston) C.; children: Suzanne Davis, Cynthia Duffy, P. Ray; m. Patricia Tate, July 22, 1989. BS in BA, U. Ky., 1950; MD, U. Louisville, 1955. Intern/resident U. Tex. Med. Br., Dept. Surgery, Galveston, 1955-62; clin. instr. U. Tex. Med. Br., Dept. Surgery, 1962-68; ptnr. Galveston Surg. Group, 1962-84; clin. asst. prof. surgery U. Tex., Galveston, 1968—; pres. The Gulf Coast Med. Group, 1994—; cons. in field. Contbr. articles to profl. jours. Bd. regents Galveston Coll., 1978—, chmn. bd., 1984-86; mem. Tex. State Rep. Exec. Com., 1990-92; pres. Gulf Health Network, 1991-92; mem. Tex. State Bd. Med. Examiners, 1978-84. Capt. M.C., USAF, 1957-59; lt. col. USAFR, 1978-89. Recipient S. Graham medal, Ga. Mil. Acad., 1946; Am. Cancer Soc. fellow, 1960. Fellow ACS; mem. Tex. Surg. Soc., S.W. Surg. Soc., Singleton Surg. Soc. (pres. 1981-82). Republican. Baptist. Office: Galveston Surgical Group 200 University Blvd Ste 922 Galveston TX 77550-2726

CUNNINGHAM, PAUL RAYMOND GOLDWYN, surgery educator; b. Jamaica, July 28, 1949; came to U.S., 1974; s. Winston Pommells and Sylvia Fenella (Marsh) C.; m. Bridget Ann Mulvany, 1974 (div. 1985); children: Rachel Louise, Lucinda Jane; m. Sydney Louise Keniston, Feb. 14, 1987. MB, BS, Univ. West Indies, Jamaica, 1972. Diplomate Am. Bd. Surgery. Commd. maj. U.S. Army Res. Med. Corp., 1990; resident surgeon Mt. Sinai Hosp., N.Y.C., 1974-78, chief resident surgery, 1978-79, clin. instr., 1978-81; asst. dir. surgery and joint diseases North Gen. Hosp., N.Y.C., 1979-81, instr., 1981-84; attending surgeon Bertie County Meml. Hosp., Windsor, N.C., 1981-84, vice chief of staff, 1981-84; clin. instr. surgery East Carolina U. Sch. Medicine, Greenville, N.C., 1981-84, asst. prof. surgery Dept. Surgery, 1984-89, assoc. prof. and tenure, 1989-93, prof., 1993—; med. dir. Pitt County Meml. Hosp. Trauma Svc., Greenville, 1986—, chief of staff, 1991, various coms.; mem. N.C. Com. on Trauma, 1985—; cons., mem. Bertie County Dept. Health, Windsor, 1982-84. Contbr. articles to profl.

jours. Mem. AMA, Am. Coun. on Transplantation, N.C. Med. Soc., Pitt County Med. Soc. A. Trauma Soc. (pres. N.C. chpt. 1989-91). Office: Pitt County Meml Hosp PO Box 6028 Greenville NC 27835-6028

CUNNINGHAM, SAM ROLAND, state government official; b. Greenwood, S.C., Oct. 11, 1951; s. Claude R. and Emily J. (Nahil) C.; m. Mary Frances Fortson, Nov. 15, 1975; children: Jason Ryan, Kristin Leigh. BA, U. Ga., 1973. Cert. paramedic. Dir. emergency med. svcs., adminstrv. asst. Elbert Meml Hosp., Elberton, Ga., 1971-90; coord. regional emergency med. svcs. Ga. Dept. Human Resources/Northeast Health Dist. EMS Prog., Athens, 1990—; dist. chmn. CPR Com., N.E. Ga. Dist. 5, 1989-92; sec. Ga. Trauma Sys. Adv. Coun., 1994—; mem. EMS for children adv. coun. State of Ga., 1994—, pres. BLS subcom., 1992-94, nat. faculty, 1994—, emergency cardiac care com., 1992—, ambulance zoning task force, 1995, acting dir. state emergency med. svcs. dir., 1996—. Editor (newsletters) Ga. EMS News, 1990—, N.E. Ga. EMS News, 1988—; writer: The EMS Messenger, 1989-91, Emergency, 1988—. Bd. dirs., chmn. Arts Coun. Elberton, Inc., 1990-94; gen. chmn. Elbert County Bicentennial Celebration, 1989-90; pub. rels. Literacy Vols. Am., Elbert County, 1989-90; active Ga. Pub. Health Disaster Plan Revision Team, 1995—; mem. pub. health coord. com. Olympic Games, 1994—, Athens '96 med. resource team, 1994—, EMS and transp. com., 1996—. Recipient coll. scholarship Elberton Granite Assn., 1969, state advt. award Distributive Edn. Club, Ga., 1969, numerous awards Am. Heart Assn., 1979-91, and civic/profl. orgns.; named NE GA EMT of the Yr., 1989, USA EMS of the Yr., Nat. Assn. EMS, Nashville, 1980. Mem. EMS Dirs. Assn. Ga., Ga. EMT Assn., Ga. Assn. EMTs, Inc. (pres. 1994—), Elbert County C. of C. (bd. dirs.). Home: 1623 Melody Ln Elberton GA 30635-4708 Office: Northeast Georgia EMS 468 N Milledge Ave Athens GA 30601-3808 also: Ga Office EMS Legis Office Bldg 47 Trinity Ave Ste 104 Atlanta GA 30334-5600

CUNNINGHAM, TERENCE THOMAS, III, hospital administrator; b. Bell, Calif., Feb. 13, 1943; s. Terence Thomas and Leone (Scheuerell), C.; m. Mary Katherine Kasarda, Apr. 22, 1967; children: Wendy Victoria C., Terence Thomas IV. BS in Microbiology, Calif. State U., Long Beach, 1967; MA in Hosp. Adminstrn., George Washington U., Washington, 1974. Commd. 2d lt. USAF, 1967, advanced through grades to col., 1989; adminstrv. resident USAF Hosp., MacDill AFB, Fla., 1973-74; adminstr. Rhein-Main Clinic, Frankfurt, Germany, 1974-79; med. inspector Air Force Inspection Ctr., San Bernardino, Calif., 1979-81; dir. med. resource mgmt. David Grant Med. Ctr., Fairfield, Calif., 1981-82; adminstr. Torrejon Hosp., Madrid, 1982-85; chief resources mgmt. div. Office Command Surgeon, Hdqrs. Mil. Airlift Command, Bellville, Ill., 1985-87; adminstr. Wright Patterson Med. Ctr., Dayton, Ohio, 1987-92, Wilford Hall Med. Ctr., San Antonio, 1992-94; v.p. adminstrn. Johns Hopkins Hosp., Balt., 1994—; instr. grad. program health care adminstrn. Chapman Coll., Calif., 1981-82; preceptor grad. students in hosp. and health care adminstrn. Xavier U., Cin., 1987—, Baylor U., San Antonio, 1988—, George Washington U., Washington, 1995—, Johns Hopkins U., Balt., 1995—; asst. clin. prof. Wright State U. Sch. Medicine, Dayton, Ohio, 1990—; cons. Surgeon Gen. USAF, 1986, 89, Air Force Logistics Command surgeon, 1987. Book reviewer Hosps. and Health Svcs. Adminstrn., Jour. Quality Assurance, Mil. Medicine; editorial bd. Frontiers of Health Svcs. Mgmt. Fellow Am. Coll. Healthcare Execs. (various coms., regent to U.S. Air Force); mem. Ohio Hosp. Assn. (chmn. accreditation com.), Greater Dayton Area Hosp. Assn. (bd. dirs.), Tex. Hosp. Assn. (edn. com.), Assn. Mil. Surgeons U.S. (Young Fed. Healthcare Adminstr. of Yr. 1983, Fed. Healthcare Adminstr. of Yr. 1989), Interagy. Inst. Fed. Health Care Alumni Assn.

CUOMO, FRANCES, orthopaedic surgeon; b. Rockville Center, N.Y., May 19, 1956. BS in Biology, Cortland State U., 1978; MD, NYU, 1983. Diplomate Am. Bd. Orthopaedic Surgery. Intern gen. surgery Beth Israel Med. Ctr., N.Y.C., 1983-84; resident orthop. surgery Lenox Hill Hosp., N.Y.C., 1984-88; fellow Columbia Presbyn. Med. Ctr., N.Y. Orthop. Hosp., N.Y.C., 1988-89; assoc. chief shoulder svc., assoc. dir. shoulder rsch. group Hosp. for Joint Diseases Orthop. Inst., N.Y.C., 1989—; attending physician Cath. Med. Ctr., Jamaica, N.Y., 1989—; dir. Occupl. and Indsl. Orthop. Ctr., N.Y.C., 1991—; clin. instr. dept. orthop. Cornell U. Med. Ctr., N.Y.C., 1989—; asst. prof. orthop. surgery NYU, N.Y.C.; lectr. in field. Presenter in field; contbr. chpts. in books and articles to profl. jours. Grantee N.Y. Acad. Medicine 1990, Reicher Found., 1990-91. Fellow Am. Acad. Orthop. Surgeons; mem. AMA, Med. Soc. State N.Y., N.Y. County Med. Soc., Queens County Med. Soc., Am. Shoulder and Elbow Surgeons. Office: Hosp Joint Diseases Inst Dept Orthop Surgery 301 E 17th St New York NY 10003

CUONO, CHARLES BOSETTI, plastic burn surgeon; b. N.Y.C., Nov. 21, 1943; s. Joseph and Dorothy (Bosetti) C.; m. Ada Cheung, May 21, 1994. BS cum laude, Wheeling Jesuit Coll., 1965; MD summa cum laude, PhD, W.Va. U., 1971; MA (hon.), Yale U., 1990. Diplomate Nat. Bd. Med. Examiners, Am. Bd. Surgery, Am. Bd. Plastic Surgery; cert. advanced burn life support instr., ACLS. Clin. assoc. surgery br. Nat. Cancer Inst., NIH, Bethesda, Md., 1973-75; clin. fellow W.Va. U., Morgantown, 1975-76; fellow in hand surgery U. Conn./Yale U., Hartford, 1977-78; asst. prof. Yale U., New Haven, Conn., 1978-83, assoc. prof., 1983-90, prof., 1990—, dir. Yale Burn Ctr., 1990—; consulting physician West Haven (Conn.) VA Hosp., 1978—; attending physician Yale-New Haven Hosp., 1978—, Hosp. of St. Raphael, New Haven, 1980—; founder, med. dir. Yale Skin Bank Yale Sch. Medicine, New Haven, 1984—; dir. Yale Burn Ctr., Yale-New Haven Hosp., 1989—; dir. hand surgery sect. plastic surgery Yale U. Sch. Medicine, 1990—, dir. ad interim sect. plastic surgery, 1991-92; med. dir. multi-state Burn Camp, High Rock, Mass., 1991—; co-dir. Conn. Burn Consortium, 1992—. Author book chpts.; assoc. editor Plastic and Reconstructive Surgery, 1990—; reviewer Annals of Plastic Surgery, 1990—, Jour. Investigative Dermatology, 1989—, and others; mem. editl. bd. Computerized Med. Imaging and Graphics, 1992—, Skin Rsch. and Tech., 1995—, Jour. Burn Care and Rehab., 1990—; contbr. articles to profl. jours. Lt. comdr. USPHS, 1973-76. NSF Chemistry fellow, 1965-66, NASA Pre-doctoral fellow, 1966-68, Am. Cancer Soc. Pre-doctoral fellow, 1969-71; recipient Sci. award Wheeling Coll., 1963, Hoffman LaRoche award, 1969, Lange Med. award, 1970, 71, Disting. Alumnus award Wheeling Jesuit Coll., 1982; named one of Outstanding Young Men Am., 1974. Mem. AAAS, Am. Acad. Physician Assts., Am. Assn. Hand Surgery, Am. Assn. Plastic Surgeons, Am. Soc. Plastic and Reconstructive Surgeons (Ednl. Found., Cert. of Merit 1978, 88), Am. Assn. Tissue Banks (Cert. of Merit 1988), Assn. for Acad. Surgery, Am. Soc. Reconstructive Microsurgery, Am. Soc. Surgery of Hand, Am. Burn Assn., Am. Chem. Soc., Am. Coll. Surgeons, Conn. Soc. Am. Bd. Surgeons, Conn. Soc. Plastic and Reconstructive Surgeons, Electrophoresis Soc., Internat. Soc. Reconstructive Microsurgery, Internat. Soc. for Digital Imaging of Skin (bd. dirs. 1992—), NIH Alumni Assn., New Eng. Hand Soc., Northeastern Soc. Plastic Surgeons, Plastic Surgery Rsch. Coun., Soc. for In Vitro Biology, Soc. Head and Neck Surgeons, Soc. Magnetic Resonance in Medicine, Soc. Univ. Surgeons, Soc. Investigative Dermatology, Wound Healing Soc., Alpha Sigma Nu, Alpha Omega Alpha, Phi Lambda Upsilon, Sigma Xi. Office: Yale Univ Sch Medicine 333 Cedar St New Haven CT 06510

CUPIDO, MARILYN MCCOLLUM, medical/surgical nurse; b. Niagara Falls, N.Y., Feb. 13, 1935; d. Melville McCollum and Marion G. (Robinson) Giordano; m. John Cupido, Oct. 22, 1976; children: Debra, Pamela, Mark, Marcia. Student, Millard Fillmore Hosp.; AS, Mercer County Community Coll., 1972; BSN, Trenton State Coll., 1983. RN, N.J., N.Y.; cert. med.-surg. nurse. Staff nurse Helene Fuld Med. Ctr., Trenton, N.J., 1972, asst. head nurse, head nurse, 1977—. Mem. Oncology Nursing Soc., Acad. Med.-Surg. Nurses. Home: 2320 Liberty St Trenton NJ 08629-2005

CURATI-ALASONATTI, WALTER, radiology educator; b. Geneva, Nov. 8, 1943; arrived in U.K., 1984; s. Mario A. and Clotilde N. (Alasonatti) C.-A. MD, U. Geneva, 1970, P.D., 1980. Cert. F.M.H. in radiology and nuclear medicine. Resident dept. radiology Univ. Hosp., Geneva, 1971-73, resident dept. medicine, 1973-74; clin. fellow dept. radiology McGill u., Montreal, Can., 1974-76; jr. rsch. fellow Hammersmith Hosp., London, 1976; chief resident dept. radiology Univ. Hosp., Geneva, 1977, cons. dept. radiology, 1978-83; sr. rsch. fellow Hammersmith Hosp., London, 1984-86, cons., 1987—; sr. lectr. Royal Postgrad. Med. Sch., London, 1987—; cons. U. Mainz (Germany), 1987-89, Swiss Paraplegic Ctr., Notswil, Switzerland, 1989-90, MRI Unit Project Coord., London, 1990—. Contbr. more than 100 med. articles to profl. jours. Fellow Royal Coll. Radiologists, Swiss Soc. Radiology, Royal Soc. Medicine; mem. Radiol. Soc. N.Am. Office: Royal Postgrad Med Sch, Du Cane Rd 150, London W12 OHS, England

CURE, DEANN KAY, medical facility executive; b. Colorado Springs, Jan. 18, 1955; d. Glenn F. and Leona Marie (Pickard) Edmunds; m. Robert G. Cure, May 1, 1976; children: R. Wesley, Stephen, Anthony. Student, Blair Bus. Coll., Colorado Springs, 1974, U. Minn., 1994. Ins. clk. Kit Carson County Meml. Hosp., Burlington, 1985—, bus. office mgr., 1986—, chief fin. officer, 1988—, asst. adminstr., 1990-93, CEO, 1993—; chmn., bd. dirs. High Plains Rural Health Network; mem. State Trauma Adv. Coun., 1996—; dist. chair Colo. Farm Bur., 1988-92; sec. bd. dirs. Kit Carson County Farm Bur., 1982-94; precinct chair Kit Carson County Reps., 1982-94, chair, 1990-94; bd. dirs. CHA Trust for Workers' Compensation. Dist. chair Colo. Farm Bur., 1984—; sec. bd. dirs. Kit Carson County Farm Bur., 1982-94; precinct chair Kit Carson County Reps., 1982-94, chair, 190-94. Rep. Leadership Program scholar, 1989. Roman Catholic. Office: Kit Carson County Meml Hosp 286 16th St Burlington CO 80807-1651

CURFMAN, DAVID RALPH, neurological surgeon, musician; b. Bucyrus, Ohio, Jan. 2, 1942; s. Ralph Oliver and Agnes Mozelle (Schreck) C.; m. Blanche Lee Anderson, June 6, 1970. Student, Capital U., 1960-62; AB, Columbia Union Coll., 1965; MS, George Washington U., 1967, MD, 1973. Diplomate Nat. Bd. Med. Examiners. Asst. organist, choirmaster Peace Luth. Ch., Galion, Ohio, 1956-62; bus. mgr. Mansfield/Galion Ambulance Svc., Galion, Ohio, 1962-66; with news div. Sta. WTOP-TV (CBS), Washington, 1965; choirmaster, assoc. organist Grace Luth. Ch., Washington, 1966-73, historian, curator, 1969—; teaching fellow in anatomy George Washington U., Washington, 1966-67, gen. surgery intern, 1973-74, resident in neurol. surgery, 1974-78; resident in neuropathology Armed Forces Inst. Pathology, Washington, 1975; resident in pediatric neurol. surgery Children's Hosp. Nat. Med. Ctr., Washington, 1976; teaching fellow in anatomy Georgetown U., Washington, 1967-69, clin. instr. neurol. surgery, 1978—, practice medicine specializing in neurol. surgery, 1978—; chief divsn. neurol. surgery Jefferson Hosp., Alexandria, Va., 1989-93, Wash. Hosp. Ctr. Soc., 1992—; vice-chmn. bylaws com. Providence Hosp., 1987-95; panelist ann. meeting ethical issues in neurol. surgery Am. Assn. Neurol. Surgery. Chmn., chief author: Physician's Reference Guide for Medicolegal Matters, 1982. Elected mem. D.C. Rep. Com., 1988—; bd. dirs., historian The Christmas Pageant of Peace, Inc., Washington, The Leo Sowerby Found.; pres., bd. govs. Washington Columbus Celebration Assn. Hon. mem. Quiz Kid Show, 1953. Mem. AMA (Phys. Recognition award 1983—), Assn. Am. Med. Colls. (nat. student chmn. rules and regulations com. 1971-73), Am. Soc. Law, Medicine and Ethics, Med. Soc. D.C. (chmn. medicine and religion com. 1981-83, chmn. medico-legal com. 1986-88), Pan Am. Med. Soc. (mem. exec. bd. 1993—, sec. 1994-95, pres.-elect 1996), Congress Neurol. Surgeons (joint section on neuro-trauma and critical care), Am. Coll. Legal Medicine, Washington Acad. Neurosurgery, Assn. Mil. Surgeons U.S. (Continuing Edn. Neurosurgery award 1993—), Galion Hist. Soc. (charter), Children Am. Revolution (pres. Ohio 1963-64, hon. pres.), SR, N.Y./D.C. Socs., U.S. Capitol Hist. Soc. (founding supporting mem., trust mem.), Nat. Cathedral Assn., Cathedral Choral Soc. (v.p. bd. trustees 1981-83, pres. 1984-86, repertoire chmn. 1981-92), Am. Guild Organists (dean D.C. chpt. 1974-76, publicity chmn. nat. conv. 1982, state chmn. 1984-91, nat. com. long-range devel. 1990—), Internat. Congress Organists (Washington program chmn. 1977), Royal Sch. Ch. Music (Eng.), English-Speaking Union, Luth. Laymen's Fellowship, Soc. War 1812 (D.C./Md. chpts.), Pilgrim Soc. (Plymouth chpt.), Hymn Soc. Am., Mil. Hospitaller Order Saint Lazarus Jerusalem, Sovereign Mil. Order Temple of Jerusalem (grand chirurgeon), Sons & Daughters of Colonial & Antebellum Bench & Bar, Mil. Order Loyal Legion U.S., Sons of Union Vets. Civil War (chmn. historic Memorial Day observances), Hospitaller Order of St. John (companion), St. Andrew's Soc. Washington, Crawford County Coin Club (charter mem.), Am. Polit. Items Collectors Assn., George Washington U. Club, Elks (Galion Lodge No. 1191, hon. founder Elks Nat. Found.), Ordo Sancti Constantini Magni, Sons/Daus. of the Pilgrims, Soc. Colonial Wars, Sons Am. Colonists, Vet. Corps Artillery State N.Y., Am. Revolution Soc., Soc. of 1812, Hereditary Order Descendants of the Loyalists and Patriots of the Am. Revolution, Sigma Xi (pres. chpt. 1981-82), Soc. Colonial Wars in D.C., Phi Delta Epsilon. Home: 4201 Massachusetts Ave NW Washington DC 20016-4701 Office: 3301 New Mexico Ave NW Ste 210 Washington DC 20016-3622

CURFMAN, WAYNE CORBET, psychiatrist; b. Center, Tex., July 29, 1949; s. Hugh Wendell and Jayne Elizabeth (Locke) C.; m. Bashie Garmon (div. 1980); children: Corbet Clarke, Colin Locke; m. Cindi Landrum, Mar. 8, 1984; children: Mary-Catherine E., Clarke Andrew. BA, So. Meth. U., 1971; MD, U. Tex. Southwestern, Dallas, 1975. Diplomate Am. Bd. Psychiatry and Neurology. Resident in psychiatry U. Utah, Salt Lake City, 1978; staff psychiatrist Helen McNabb Ctr., Knoxville, 1978-81; asst. med. dir. Helen Ross McNabb Ctr., Knoxville, 1981-86; chief psychiatry U. Tenn. Med. Ctr., Knoxville, 1986—, asst. prof., 1986-94, assoc. prof., 1994—; dir. psychiat. svcs. U. Tenn. Med. Ctr., Knoxville, 1986—. Mem. Am. Psychiat. Assn., Tenn. Psychiat. Assn. (pres. Smoky Mountain br. 1986-88), Am. Assn. of Geriatric Psychiatrists, Tenn. Geriatric Soc., Acad. of Psychosomatic Medicine. Republican. Mem. LDS Ch. Home: 9508 Middleground Ln Knoxville TN 37923-2027 Office: U Psychiatric Assocs 1928 Alcoa Hwy Ste 214 Knoxville TN 37920-1504

CURLEY, JOHN F., pediatrician; b. Phila., Sept. 12, 1958; s. John B. and Mary Joan (Birchill) C.; m. Kathleen Joan Smith, May 23, 1981; children: Kara Lynne, Kevin John. BS in Biology, Ursinus Coll., 1980; DO, Phila. Coll. Osteo. Medicine, 1984. Mem. med. staff Bucks County Hosp., Warminster, Pa., 1987—, Northeastern Hosp. Phila., 1989—, Doylestown (Pa.) Hosp., 1993—, St. Christopher's Hosp. for Children, Phila., 1994—. Fellow Am. Coll. Osteo. Pediatricians. Office: Kantor-Curley Pediat Assocs 205 Newtown Rd Warminster PA 18974

CURLEY, MARTHA ANNIE QUATRANO, critical care clinical specialist; b. Springfield, Mass., Nov. 14, 1952; d. Angelo and Annette (Watson) Quatrano; m. John G. Curley, June 23, 1973; children: Joseph, Paul. Grad. RN, Springfield (Mass.) Hosp., 1973; BS, U. Mass., 1985; MSN, Yale U., 1987; PhD, Boston Coll., 1996. Cert. critical care RN. Pediatric critical care instr., staff RN PICU Baystate Med. Ctr., Springfield, 1981-85; critical care clin. specialist The Children's Hosp., Boston, 1987—; lectr. in field. Author, editor Critical Care Nursing of Infants and Children, 1996; contbr. articles to profl. jours. Louise Mellen fellow in critical care. Mem. ANA, AACN, Soc. Crit. Care Medicine, Sigma Theta Tau. Office: Childrens Hosp Multidisciplinary ICU 300 Longwood Ave Boston MA 02115-5724

CURLIN, JOHN PASCHAL, obstetrician, gynecologist; b. Memphis, Aug. 28, 1939; s. James Howard and Johnny Valentine (Paschal) C.; m. Elizabeth Andrews, May 7, 1966; children: David, Majorie, Micah, Farr, Howard, John Reid, Caleb. MD, U. Ark., Little Rock, 1965. Diplomate Am. Bd. Ob-Gyn. Straight ob-gyn intern Univ. Hosp., Little Rock, 1965-66, resident in ob-gyn, 1966-69; pvt. practice, Carbondale, Ill., 1972-73, Jackson, Tenn., 1973—. Lt. comdr. USN, 1969-72. Fellow Am. Coll. Obstetricians and Gynecologists, Ams. for Health Soc. Evangelical. Home: 8 Deepwood Dr Jackson TN 38305-9679 Office: Jackson Clinic 616 W Forest Ave Jackson TN 38301-3902

CURNS, EILEEN BOHAN, counselor, author, speaker; b. Chgo., May 22, 1927; d. Alvin Joseph and Lorraine Bohan; m. John R. Curns, July 1, 1950 (div. 1975); children: James Richard, Barbara Obrokta. BA in Sociology, DePaul U., Chgo.; MEd in Psychology and Edn., Loyola U., Chgo.; postgrad. in health edn., U. Wis. Cert. Gestalt therapist. Prin. ACCORD, Vernon Hills, Ill.; cons. in health care cost containment, stress researcher, inner healing; lectr. on the five stress signals leading to disease and how to reverse them. Recipient Golden Deeds award Exchange Club, 1965, commendation Queen Mary Vets. Hosp., Montreal, 1975. Mem. Am. Bd. Med. Psychotherapists (cert.), Nat. Wellness Assn., Midwest Satir Inst. Home: 825 Waterview Cir Vernon Hills IL 60061-2550

CURRAN, ANDREW ROGER, orthopedic surgeon; b. Phila., Apr. 12, 1966; s. John Roger and Anne (Robinson) C. BA, U. San Diego, 1988; DO, Midwestern U., Chgo., 1994. Orthopedic surgery resident Rush Presbyn.-St. Luke's Med. Ctr., Chgo., 1994—. Vol. med. student assisting orthopedic surgery in Lithuania, Lithuanian Children's Hope Orgn., 1993. Mem. Sigma Sigma Pi. Republican. Presbyn. Home: Coach House 1414 W Henderson Chicago IL 60657

CURRAN, EILEEN ELIZABETH, geriatrics nurse; b. Tyrone, Pa., July 18, 1938; d. Karl and Mary Frances (Gleeson) Engerud; m. J. THomas Curran, Jr., Jan. 9, 1960; children: Maureen, Kevin, Timothy, Kellie. RN, N.J. Nurse Hunterdon Med. Ctr., Flemington, N.J., 1959-61, Carrier Found., Belle Mead, N.J., 1965-69, Physician's Offices, Flemington, Bridgewater, 1972-83; dir. social svcs. Hillsborough Twp., Somerville, N.J., 1983-86; coord. health promotion Somerset County Office Aging, Somerville, 1986-95, Somersety County Divsn. Health, Somerville, 1995—; Mem. breast task force Somerset Med. Ctr., Somerville, 1993—. Mem. planning com. Somerset County, somerville, 1995—. Recipient Exemplary Contributions to Aging award AARP, 1992. Republican. Roman Catholic. Home: 875 River Rd Somerville NJ 08876 Office: Somerset County Divsn Health PO Box 3000 20 Grove St Somerville NJ 08876

CURRAN, JAMES W., epidemiologist, educator; b. Monroe, Mich., Sept. 16, 1944; married; two children.; BS, U. Notre Dame, 1966; MD, U. Mich., 1970; MPH, Harvard U., 1974. Rsch. instr. dept. preventive and cmty. medicine U. Tenn. Med. Sch., 1971-73; career devel. tng. Ctr. Disease Control, USPHS, 1973-75; asst. commr. health med. svc. Columbus (Ohio) City Health Dept., 1975-78; chief oper. rsch. br. Venereal Disease Control Ctr. Disease Control and Prevention, 1978-82; dir. Acquired Immune Deficiency Syndrome Activ, 1982-84; chief AIDS br. Divsn. Viral Diseases, Ctr. Infectious Diseases, 1984-85; dir. WHO Referal Ctr. AIDS & Retroviruses, 1985-92; assoc. dir. human immunodeficiency virus/AIDS Ctr. Disease Control and Prevention, 1992—; L. Vernon Scott lectr. U. Okla. Health Sci. Ctr., 1985, Verna & Mars lectr. Baylor Coll. Medicine, 1988, Oliver Cope lectr. Mass. Gen. Hosp., 1988; clin. rsch. investigator Venereal Disease Br., Ctr. Disease Control, 1971-73; med. dir. Influenza Immunication Program, Franklin County, 1976-77; clin. rsch. investigator, coord. Oper. Rsch. Br., Venereal Disease Control Divsn., Ctr. Disease Control, 1975-78; clin. asst. prof. dept. preventive and cmty. medicine, Coll. Medicine, Ohio State U., 1976-79; John Forbes fellow infectious disease Fairfield Hosp., Melbourne, Australia, 1985; vis. prof. Coll. Medicine, U. Ill., 1988; asst. surgeon gen. USPHS, 1991. Recipient William C. Watson Jr. award, 1987. Fellow Infectious Disease Soc. Am., Am. Coll. Preventive Medicine, Am. Epidemiol. Soc.; mem. AAAS, Inst. Medicine-NAS, Am. Venereal Disease Assn., Sigma Xi. *

CURRAN, SISTER MARY ANDREA, gerontology nurse; b. Phila., Aug. 16, 1943; d. Vincent S. and Marian M. (Ford) C. BS in Edn., Marillac Coll., 1968; AD, Felician Coll., 1977. RN, Pa. House supr. Divine Providence Hosp., Williamsport, Pa., preceptor in critical care, staff nurse CCU; dir. nursing Holy Family Convent Hosp., Danville, Pa.; nursing info. systems coord. Divine Providence Hosp., Williamsport, Pa.; local superior, computer trainer Holy Spirit Hosp., Camp Hill, Pa.

CURRAN, THOMAS, molecular biologist, educator; b. Broxburn, West Lothian, Scotland, Feb. 14, 1956; came to U.S., 1982; s. Thomas and Jane Holden (McGovern) C.; m. Frances Ko-Fang Yao, Dec. 27, 1979; 1 child, Sean Philip. BS, U. Edinburgh, Scotland, 1978; PhD, U. Coll. London, 1982. Postdoctoral fellow Salk Inst., San Diego, 1982-84; sr. scientist Hoffman-La Roche Inc., Nutley, N.J., 1984-85; asst. mem. Roche Inst. Molecular Biology, Nutley, 1985-86, assoc. mem., 1986-88, full mem., 1988-95, head dept., 1989-92, assoc. dir., 1991-95; adj. prof. Columbia U., N.Y.C., 1989—; mem. and chmn. dept. devel. neurobiology St. Jude Children's Rsch. Hosp., Memphis, 1995—; mem. adv. bd. study sect. NIH, Washington, 1991-94, Damon Runyan/Walter Winchell Cancer Rsch. Fund, N.Y.C., 1992—; Merton F. Utter Meml. lectr. Case Western Res. U., 1992. Editor: The Oncogene Handbook, 1988, Origins of Human Cancer, 1991; contbr. over 150 articles to sci. jours. and books. Recipient Young Scientist award Passano Found., 1992, Rita Levi Montalcino Lecture award Fidia Rsch. Found., 1992, Glasgow U.-Tenovus-Scotland medal, 1992, Litchfield Lecture award Oxford U., 1994, Golgi award Italian Acad. Neurosci. and Camillo Golgi Found., 1994.; Imperial Cancer Rsch. Fund grantee. Fellow AAAS, Am. Acad. Microbiology; mem. Am. Assn. for Cancer Rsch. (Rhoads award 1993), Am. Soc. for Cell Biology, Am. Soc. Biochemistry and Molecular Biology, Soc. for Neurosci., Harvey Soc. Roman Catholic. Office: St Jude Childrens Rsch Hosp 332 N Lauderdale Memphis TN 38105-2794

CURRERI, JOSEPH PETER, pulmonary physician; b. Cherry Hill, N.J., Mar. 6, 1964; s. John Francis and Kathleen Patricia (Doyle) C.; m. Kathleen Jo Sweeney, Oct. 23, 1993. BSE with highest honors, Rutgers Coll. Engrng., Piscataway, N.J., 1986; DO, Pa. Coll. Osteopathic Medicine, Phila., 1990. Intern U. Med. and Dentistry N.J.-Sch. Osteo. Medicine, Stratford, 1990-91, resident in internal medicine, 1991-93, chief resident medicine, 1993-94, pulmonary fellow, 1993-95, chief pulmonary fellow, 1995. Recipient Tourigian Surg. award Pa. Coll. Osteopathic Medicine, 1989, Lindback Scholarship award, 1987. Mem. Am. Osteo. Assn., Am. Coll. Osteo. Internists (Manuscript award 1995), Am. Thoracic Soc., Am. Coll. Chest Physicians, Tau Beta Pi, Eta Kappa Nu. Office: 124 Lexington Ave Merchantville NJ 08109

CURRERI, P. WILLIAM, health policy consultant; b. Milw., Sept. 2, 1936; s. Anthony Rudolph and Dorothea Christiana (Heubsch) C.; m. Patricia Ann Egry, Aug. 14, 1958 (div. 1975); children: Charles Anthony, James Bradley, Regina Dawn. BA, Swarthmore Coll., 1958; MD, U. Pa., 1962. Asst. prof. surgery U. Tex., Southwestern MEd. Ctr., Dallas, 1971-74; assoc. prof. surgery U. Wash. Med. Sch., Seattle, 1974-77; prof. surgery Cornell U. Med. Ctr., N.Y.C., 1977-81; prof., chmn. surgery U. South Ala. Med. Sch., Mobile, 1981-88; pres. Strategem of Ala., Inc., Mobile, 1988—; dir. LifeCell Corp., The Woodlands, Tex., 1992—, Colonial Banl, Mobile, 1985-89, Strategem, Inc., 1988-92; commr. Physician Payment Rev. Commn., Washington, 1988—. Contbr. articles to profl. jours. Chmn. sirgery anesthesiology & trauma study sect. NIH, Washington, 1986-88, mem., 1980-84. Lt. col. U.S. Army, 1968-71. Decorated Meritorious Svc. medal; recipient Rsch. Career Devel. award NIH, 1972, Curtis P. Artz award Am. Trauma Soc., 1989. Mem. Am. Assn. for Surgery og Trauma (pres. 1989-90), Am. Burn Assn. (pres. 1983-84), Am. Coll. Surgeons (sec. bd. govs. 1987-89), Halstead Surg. Soc. (pres. 1988-89), Soc. Univ. Surgeons (pres. 1980-81), Assn. Acad. Surgery (recorder 1972-74). Baptist. Office: Strategem Inc 3103 Airport Blvd Ste 630 Mobile AL 36606

CURREY, THOMAS ARTHUR, ophthalmologist; b. Itawamba County, Miss., July 9, 1933; s. Charles Edward and Anna L. (Williams) C; m. Carol Ann Clabough, Nov. 7, 1959; children: Thomas A. Jr., C. Russell. Degree, U. Miss., 1955; MD, U. Tenn., 1958. Diplomate Am. Bd. Ophthalmology. Intern City of Memphis Hosps., 1958-59; resident in ophthalmology U. Tenn., Memphis, 1962-65; pvt. practice Memphis, 1965—; mem. staff St. Francis Hosp., 1965—, pres. med. staff, 1985; assoc. instr. ophthalmology dept. family practice, 1990—, asst. clin. instr. ophthalmology U. Tenn., 1965—. Fellow ACS; mem. Tenn. Med. Assn. (v.p. 1987), Tenn. Acad. Ophthalmology (pres. 1975), Memphis & Shelley County Med. Soc. (treas. 1983-86). Office: Eye Specialists Assoc PC 1900 Kirby Pky Memphis TN 38138-3690

CURRIER, ROBERT DAVID, neurologist; b. Grand Rapids, Mich., Feb. 19, 1925; s. Frederick Plummer and Margaret (Hoedemaker) C.; m. Marilyn Jane Johnson, Sept. 1, 1951; children: Mary Margaret, Angela Maria. AB, U. Mich., 1948, MD, 1952, MS in Neurology, 1956; postgrad., Nat. Hosp., U. London, 1955; postgrad. Medico-Social Research Bd, Dublin, Ireland, 1972. Intern, then resident in neurology Univ. Hosp., Ann Arbor, 1952-56; from instr. to asso. prof. U. Mich. Med. Sch., 1956-61; mem. faculty U. Miss. Med. Ctr., Jackson, 1961—, prof. neurology, 1971—, chief div., 1961-77, chmn. dept., 1977-90, H.F. McCarty prof., 1987-94, prof. emeritus, 1994—; mem. adv. bd. Nat. Ataxia Found., rsch. dir., 1985-93; mem. clin. adv. coun. Amyotrophic Lateral Sclerosis Soc. Am., 1979-85; mem. Ataxia com. World Fedn. Neurology, 1981-95, sec., 1985-93. Co-editor; Yearbook of Neurology and Neurosurgery, 1981-88, editor, 1989-92; co-editor (jour.) Key Quar. Neurology and Neurosurgery, 1986-92; asst. editor for history Archives of Neurology, 1983—; assoc. editor Jour. Neuroscis., 1990-95; contbr. articles to med. jours. Served with USAAF, 1943-45, ETO. Decorated Air medal with 2 oak leaf clusters; NIH grantee, 1961-74. Fellow Am. Acad.

Neurology (chmn. history com. 1980-82, treas. 1991-95); mem. Am. Neurol. Assn., Ctrl. Soc. Neurol. Rsch. (pres. 1971), Sigma Xi, Alpha Omega Alpha. Home: 5529 Marblehead Dr Jackson MS 39211-4249 Office: 2500 N State St Jackson MS 39216-4500

CURRY, CYNTHIA J.R., geneticist; b. Cleve., July 20, 1941. MD, Yale U., 1957. Diplomate Am. Bd. Med. Genetics; Am. Bd. Pediatrics. Intern U. Wash., Seattle, 1967-68, resident, 1968-69; resident U. Minn., Mpls., 1969-70; fellow med. genetics U. Calif., San Francisco, 1975-76; med. faculty UCSF, Fresno, Calif.; med. dir. genetics Valley Children's Hosp., Fresno, Calif., 1976-96. Contbr. 15 chpt. to books, numerous articles to profl. jours. Office: Valley Children's Hosp 3151 N Millbrook Fresno CA 93703-1425

CURRY, JUDITH CAROLYN, nurse; b. West Columbia, S.C., Dec. 6, 1939; d. Charlie Haskell and Carolyn Eunice (Boland) Bickley; m. John Edward Curry, Jan. 31, 1970. BSN, U. S.C., 1962; cert. U. Calif.-San Francisco, 1964; MSN, Boston U., 1967, cert. advanced grad. study, 1968. Staff nurse Columbia (S.C.) Hosp., 1962-63; pub. health nurse Richland County Health Dept., Columbia, 1963-64; clin. nurse Child Evaluation Clinic, S.C. Dept. Health, 1964-66; instr., cons. Shriver Ctr., Waltham, Mass., 1968-70; asst. prof., chief of nursing Ohio State U. Nisonger Center, Columbus, 1970-74; health liaison specialist Am. Acad. Pediatrics Head Start Consultation Project, Evanston, Ill., 1974-76, Westinghouse Health Systems Head Start Project, Chgo., 1976-82; Concord unit dir. Met. State Hosp., Waltham, Mass., 1982-84; dir. mental retardation svcs. Lowell Area Office, Mass. Dept. Mental Health, 1984-88; dir. support svcs. Dept. Mental Retardation, 1988—. Registered nurse, S.C., Ill., Ohio, Mass. Fellow Am. Assn. Mental Retardation (life, regional nursing chmn. 1972-75, nat. nursing v.p. 1984-85). Lutheran. Editor: (Kathryn K. Peppe) Mental Retardation: Nursing Approaches to Care, 1978. Home: 44 Brassie Way North Reading MA 01864-3411 Office: PO Box A Hathorne MA 01937

CURRY, ROBERT WHITNEY, JR., physician, medical educator; b. Bradenton, Fla., July 3, 1945; s. Robert W. and Jessie Beth (Longino) C.; m. Ruthanne Lamason, June 14, 1969; children: Mary K., Robert L. BS, U. Fla., 1967; MD, Duke U., 1971. Diplomate Am. Bd. Family Practice, Am. Bd. Internal Medicine. Intern, resident Stanford (Calif.) U. Med. Ctr., 1971-74; clin. fellow Cmty. Health Family Medicine, Gainesville, Fla., 1976-77; dir. Inpatient Svcs., Gainesville, 1977-82; program dir. family practice residency program U. Fla., Gainesville, 1982-91, acting chmn., prof. dept. cmty. health and family medicine, 1991-92, chmn., prof. dept. cmty. health and family medicine, 1992—; rsch. asst. dept. surgery Shands Tchg. Hosp., Gainesville, 1967-68; physician Kaiser Emergency Svc. and Clinics, Redwood City, Calif., 1974; med. dir. Family Practice Med. Group, Inc., Gainesville, 1978-82; asst. prof. divsn. family practice U. Fla., Gainesville, 1978-82, assoc. prof., 1982-91. Author: Clinical Electrocardiography, 1992; contbr. articles to profl. jours. Disting. mem. scholarship adv. com. Picacano Scholars Program, 1993-96. Fellow ACP, Am. Acad. Family Physicians; mem. Soc. Tchrs. Family Medicine, Fla. Med. Assn., Alachua County Med. Assn., Fla. Acad. Family Physicians, Phi Beta Kappa. Democrat. Methodist. Office: U Fla Coll Medicine PO Box 103588 Gainesville FL 32610

CURRY, THOMAS EDWARD, JR., research scientist; b. Honolulu, Dec. 6, 1953; s. Thomas Edward and Ramona Sophia (Fotos) C.; children: Joshua Thomas, Jordan Michael. BS, U. South Fla., 1976, MS, 1979; PhD, East Carolina U., 1983. Research assoc. East Carolina U., Greenville, N.C., 1983; postdoctoral fellow U. Miami, 1983-84, rsch. assoc., 1984-86; asst. prof. U. Ky., Lexington, 1986-91, assoc. prof., 1991—; bd. dirs. Sci. and Tech. Camp, Lexington, RIA Lab. Dept. Ob-Gyn., Lexington; reviewer March of Dimes Found., NSF, NIH, Lexington, 1988, seven sci. jours., Lexington, 1987—. Contbr. book chpts. and articles to profl. publs. Scientific grantee NIH, 1986—, U. Ky., 1986—. Mem. AAAS, Am. Assn. Anatomists, Soc. for the Study of Reprodn., Am. Fertility Soc., Endocrine Soc., Sigma Xi, Phi Kappa Phi. Democrat. Methodist. Office: Dept Ob-Gyn U Kentucky 800 Rose St Lexington KY 40536-0084

CURTIN, BRIAN JOSEPH, ophthalmologist; b. N.Y.C., July 25, 1921; s. James Joseph and Julia Margaret (Smith) C.; m. Claire Margaret Flood, June 18, 1955; children: Edward Brian, James Martin, Thomas Hayes, Deirdre Claire. BS, Fordham U., 1942; MD, NYU, 1945. Intern St. Vincent's Hosp., N.Y.C., 1945-46; resident surgeon Manhattan Eye, Ear and Throat Hosp., 1950-53, asst. attending surgeon, asso. attending surgeon, 1953-74, surgeon dir., 1974-89, surgeon dir. emertus, 1990—, pres. med. bd., 1977-79, vice chmn. dept. ophthalmology, 1983-89, med. dir., 1989-91; attending ophthalmologist, chief svc. Misericordia-Lincoln Affiliated Hosps., 1958-79; attending ophthalmologist N.Y. Hosp., 1969-84; assoc. attending ophthalmologist Columbia Presbyn. Med. Ctr., 1985-92; asst. prof. clin. ophthalmology NYU, 1954-70; assoc. prof. clin. ophthalmology Cornell Med. Coll., 1970-84, Columbia U. Coll. Physicians and Surgeons, 1985—; med. adv. bd. Eye Bank for Sight Restoration, N.Y.C., 1978-90, chmn., 1988-90; attending ophthalmologist, chmn. dept. St. Clare's Hosp. and Health Ctr., 1978-81. Author: The Myopias: Basic Science and Clinical Management, 1985; mem. editorial bd. Cornea, 1981-85; contbr. chpts. to textbooks, articles to med. jours. With U.S. Navy, 1946-48. Recipient Achievement award Fordham U., 1976. Mem. ACS, AMA, AAAS, Am. Ophthalmol. Soc., N.Y. State Med. Soc., N.Y. County Med. Soc., N.Y. Acad. Medicine, N.Y. Acad. Scis., Am. Acad. Ophthalmology, N.Y. Ophthal. Soc. (v.p. 1981-82, pres. 1982-83), Am. Eye Study Club, Siwanoy Country Club, Knights of Malta. Home: 2 Stoneleigh Bronxville NY 10708-2652 Office: 1001 Park Ave New York NY 10028-0935

CURTIN, LINDA JEANNE, critical care nurse, educator; b. Quincy, Mass., Dec. 7, 1958; d. Lawrence M. and Dorothy A. (Gallo) C. Diploma, St. Elizabeth's Hosp., Brighton, Mass., 1980; BSN, Boston Coll., 1982, MSN, 1984. CCRN, ACLS, BLS instr. Staff nurse in surgery Quincy City Hosp., 1980-82, staff nurse ICU, 1982-84, critical care instr., 1984-86, critical care clin. nurse specialist, 1986-92; critical care clin. nurse specialist Brockton Hosp., 1994—. Trustee Braintree (Mass.) Future Med. Club. Recipient Dr. Frist Humanitarian award. Mem. ANA, AACN, Mass. Nurses Assn., Sigma Theta Tau.

CURTIN, THOMAS LEE, ophthalmologist; b. Columbus, Ohio, Sept. 9, 1932; s. Leo Anthony and Mary Elizabeth (Burns) C.; m. Constance L. Sallman; children: Michael, Gregory, Thomas, Christopher. BS, Loyola U., L.A., 1954; MD, U. So. Calif., 1957; cert. navy flight surgeon U.S. Naval Sch. Aviation Medicine, 1959. Intern, Ohio State U. Hosp., 1957-58; resident in ophthalmology U.S. Naval Hosp., San Diego, 1961-64; practice medicine specializing in ophthalmology, Oceanside, Calif., 1967—; mem. staff Tri City, Scripps Meml. Mercy hosps.; sci. adv. bd. So. Calif. Soc. Prevention Blindness, 1973-76; bd. dirs. North Coast Surgery Ctr., Oceanside, 1987-96; cons. in field. Trustee, Carlsbad (Calif.) Unified Sch. Dist., 1975-83, pres., 1979, 82, 83; trustee Carlsbad Libr., 1990—, pres, 1993. Served as officer M.C., USN, 1958-67. Diplomate Am. Bd. Ophthalmology. Mem. Am., Calif. med. assns., San Diego County Med. Soc., Am. Acad. Ophthalmology, Aerospace Med. Assn., San Diego Acad. Ophthalmology (pres. 1979), Calif. Assn. Ophthalmology (dir.), Carlsbad Rotary, El Camino Country Club. Republican. Roman Catholic. Office: 3231 Waring Ct Ste S Oceanside CA 92056-4510

CURTIN, VIRGINIA MARIE, nurse; b. Needham, Mass., June 26, 1958; d. David John and Eileen Mary (Foley) C. BS, Simmons Coll., 1980; MS, U. Calif., San Francisco, 1986. Cert. RN, Pediatric Nurse Practitioner. Student nursing asst. Children's Hosp. Med. Ctr., Boston, 1978-80, patient activities dept., 1979-80; staff nurse surgical unit Children's Hosp. Nat. Med. Ctr., Washington, 1980-81, staff nurse pediatric med. unit, 1981-84; staff nurse med. respiratory unit Children's Hosp., Oakland, Calif., 1985-86; coord. cord blood screening program hemoglobinopathies Children's Hosp., Oakland, 1986-87, craniofacial clin. nurse specialist, 1986—; research asst. Pediatric Pain Study Univ. Calif., San Francisco, 1985-86. Recipient Commendation for Outstanding Primary Nursing Children's Hosp. Nat. Med. Ctr., 1984, Donna Pruzansky Meml. Fund Scholarship Am. Cleft Palate Conf., 1988. Mem. Assn. for the Care of Children's Health, Calif. Nurse's Assn., Am. Cleft Palate Craniofacial Assn., Clin. Nurse Specialists No. Calif., Sigma Theta Tau. Democrat. Roman Catholic. Office: Craniofacial Clinic Children's Hosp 747 52nd St Oakland CA 94609-1809

CURTIS, ADAM SEBASTIAN GENEVIEVE, biologist, educator; b. London, Jan. 3, 1934; s. Herbert Lewis and Nora Patricia (Stevens) C.; m. Ann Park, May 3, 1958; children: Penelope Jane, Susanna Clare. BA, Cambridge (Eng.) U., 1955; PhD, Edinburgh U., 1957; MA, Cambridge U., 1958. Chartered biologist. Rsch. asst. Univ. Coll. London, 1957-62, lectr. in zoology, 1962-67; prof. cell biology U. Glasgow, Scotland, 1967—, head molecular and celluar biology, 1991-94; bd. dirs. Co. Biologists Ltd., Cambridge; gov. Westbourne Sch., Glasgow, 1984-90; pres. Soc. for Exptl. Biology, Lond, 1991-93; dir. Ctr. for Clin. Engring., 1996—. Author: The Cell Surface, 1967; editor several books on cell biology; contbr. articles to profl. jours.; editor-in-chief Exptl. Biology on Line, 1996—. Pres. Scottish Sub-Aqua Club, Glasgow, 1970-76. Recipient Zool. medal Soc. Zool. de France, 1976. Fellow Inst. Biology, Royal Soc. Edinburgh; mem. numerous sci. socs., Lansdowne Club. Home: 2 Kirklee Circus, Glasgow G12 OTW, Scotland Office: U Glasgow, Dept Biomed & Life Scis, Glasgow G12 8QQ, Scotland

CURTIS, ALEXIS CASSANDRA, clinical nurse specialist; b. N.Y.C., Sept. 5, 1957; d. Alexander John and Theresa Rose (Svetics) Borris; m. Joseph Gerard Patrick Curtis, Aug. 9, 1980; children: Gordon William, Douglas Alexander, Courtney Ann, Emily Theresa. BSN, Adelphi U., 1979, MSN, 1988. RN, N.Y., Mass., Conn.; cert. childbirth educator NACES. Perinatal student nurse intern maternal/child health John Hopkins Hosp., Balt., 1979; nurse costep nursing adminstrn. sudden infant death program HEW Office Maternal/Child Health, Rockville, Md., 1979; staff nurse stepdown cardiac unit labor and delivery suite South Nassau Communities Hosp., Oceanside, N.Y., 1979-81; staff nurse neonatal intensive care unit North Shore Univ. Hosp., Manhasset, N.Y., 1981-82; staff nurse, alternating charge nurse labor/delivery suite Winthrop Univ. Hosp., Mineola, N.Y., 1982-87; ob-gyn. nurse educator Long Island Jewish Med. Ctr. New Hyde Park, N.Y., 1987-90; acting asst. dir. nursing ob./gyn. L.I. Jewish Med. Ctr., 1990, perinatal clin. nurse specialist, 1990—; childbirth educator in pvt. practice, 1982—; maternal/child home care nurse Nursing Home Care, Wilton, Conn., 1995—; Lamaze instr. Westport (Conn.)/Weston Health Dist., 1995-96; presenter in field; hon. faculty mem. Adelphi U. Preceptor Program, N.Y.C., 1982-92; clin. instr. obstetrics Nassau C.C., Garden City, N.Y., 1991-92. Author: (annotated bibliography) Sudden Infant Death Syndrome, 1979. Winthrop U. Hosp. Acad. scholar, 1986; recipient Nurse Traineeship award Adelphi U., 1981, 85. Mem. AWHONN, Coun. Childbirth Edn. Specialists of N.Y., Internat. Childbirth Edn. Assn., Sigma Theta Tau.

CURTIS, BRIAN ALBERT, physiologist, neuroscientist, educator; b. N.Y.C., Nov. 25, 1936; s. Howard James and Dorothy Ruth (Albert) C.; m. Dade Tull, Apr. 9, 1960; 1 child, Elliot Warfield. BA, U. Rochester, 1958; PhD, Rockefeller U., 1963. From asst. to assoc. prof. Tufts U. Med. Sch., Boston, 1965-74, asst. dean, 1970-73; asst. dean coll. medicine U. Ill., Peoria, 1974-79, assoc. prof., 1974—; mem. rsch. com. Am. Heart Assn., Dallas, 1980—. Author: An Introduction to the Neurosciences, 1972, Neurosciences: the basics, 1990; Computer Basic Instruction: PLATO System; contbr. articles to profl. jours. Mem. adv. com. Town of Hingham, Mass., 1970-73; bd. dirs. Am. Cancer Soc., Peoria, 1977-79, Lake of the Woods Homeowners, Dunlap, Ill., 1981-85; bd. dirs. Ill. affiliate Am. Heart Assn., 1982-87, 92—. Rsch. grantee NIH, Am. Heart Assn., 1965—. Mem. Am. Physiol. Soc. (edn. com. 1969-75, chmn. pub. affairs com. 1975-81), Soc. Gen. Physiologists (sec. 1967-69), Biophys. Soc., Cosmos Club. Office: U Ill Coll Medicine-Peoria Box 1649 One Illini Dr Peoria IL 61656

CURTIS, JOHN J., medical educator; b. Rochester, N.Y., Jan. 16, 1944; s. John Joseph and Mabel (Leatherman) C.; m. Vicky Burleson, Oct. 2, 1987. BS, U. Scranton, 1966; MD, Georgetown U., 1970. Diplomate Am. Bd. Internal Medicine, Am. Bd. Nephrology. Asst. prof. medicine U. Ky. Med. Ctr., Lexington, Ky., 1974-79; assoc. prof. medicine U. Ala., Birmingham, 1979-85, prof. medicine, 1985—, prof. surgery, 1991—; program dir. Gen. Clin. Rsch. Ctr., Birmingham, 1988—; mem. med. adv. bd. Ala. Kidney Found., Birmingham, 1989—. Asst. editor Am. Jour. Kidney Diseases, 1987-92; transplantation editor (book) Yearbook of Nephrology, 1992—. 1st lt. USAR, 1970-72. Mem. Am. Soc. Nephrology, Internat. Soc. Nephrology, The Transplantation Soc., Am. Soc. Transplant Physicians, Am. Fed. Clin. Rsch., European Dialysis & Transplant Assoc. Office: U Ala Divsn Nephrology 1900 University Blvd Birmingham AL 35294-0007

CURTIS, ROSANNE JEANNE, nursing educator, educational administrator; b. N.J., Mar. 7, 1952; d. George F. and Helen (Novick) Sigler; m. Ralph S. Curtis, Mar. 27, 1982; children: Victoria Ashley, Justine Elyse. BSN magna cum laude, Mount St. Mary's Coll., 1979; M in Nursing, UCLA, 1983; postgrad., Pepperdine U., 1995—. RN, Calif.; cert. pub. health nurse. Nurse oncology St. John's Hosp. and Health Ctr., Santa Monica, Calif., 1979-80, charge nurse med./surg., 1980-81; nurse oncology Encino (Calif.) Hosp., 1981-82; clin. nurse specialist oncology, med./surg. educator Holy Cross Hosp., Mission Hills, Calif., 1982-84; clin. care specialist oncology Johnson and Johnson Home Health Care, Inc., Long Beach, Calif., 1984; nurse editor Williams and Wilkins/Nurseco, Pacific Palisades, Calif., 1984-85; instr. Mount St. Mary's Coll., L.A., 1985-36; nurse per diem St. John's Hosp. and Health Ctr., Santa Monica, Calif., 1985-86; clin. educator Kaiser Permanente, Panorama City, Calif., 1986-87; asst. dir. edn. Kaiser Found. Hosp., Panorama City, Calif., 1987-89; dir. edn. Kaiser Found. Hosp., Panorama City, 1989—, leader/mem. nursing exec. team, 1994—; asst. clin. prof. UCLA, 1987—; mem. adj. clin. faculty Mount St. Mary's Coll., 1989—. Past bd. dirs. Calif. divsn. Am. Cancer Soc. Recipient Career award March of Dimes, 1978. Mem. Orgn. Nurse Execs. Calif., Valley Nursing Edn. Coun., Sigma Theta Tau. Office: Kaiser Permanente 13652 Cantara St Panorama City CA 91402-5423

CURTIS, WILLIAM HENRY, III, psychology educator; b. Phila. June 25, 1939; s. William Henry and Kathryn Helen (McCorkle) C.; B.A., Mt. St. Mary's Coll., 1961; M.Ed., Loyola Coll., Balt., 1964; S.T.B., St. Mary's U., 1963; Ph.D. equivalent, Cath. U., 1966; Ph.D., Walden U., 1975; clin. behavior therapy trainee Eastern Pa. Psychiat. Inst., 1975-76. Clin. intern Marriage Counseling Center, Cath. U., Washington, 1964-66; sch. psychology extern Pennsauken (N.J.) Sch Dist., 1979-80; charter faculty mem., prof. psychology, sociology Camden County Coll., Blackwood, N.J., 1967—, chmn. div. behavioral scis., 1970-71, chmn. psychology discipline, 1991—; pvt. practice as clin. psychologist, Phila., 1966—; staff psychologist N.E. Phila. Community Mental Health Center, 1974-82; staff neuropsychologist Assocs. for Health and Guidance, Phila., 1978—; staff psychologist Phila. Protestant Home, 1992-93. Cert. Am. Bd. Family Psychology, Cert. Addictions Specialist, Am. Bd. Profl. Neuropsychology. Lic. clin. psychologist, Pa.; cert. sch. psychologist, Pa., N.J.; cert. Hypnotist. Active mem. Brigantine Alliance to Prevent Alcoholism and Drug Abuse Commn.; faculty moderator Psi Beta Honor Soc. Camden County Coll., 1993—; recreation bd. dirs. Upper Providence Twp., Delaware County, Pa. Mem. APA, Am. Soc. Clin. Hypnosis, Ea. Psychol. Assn., Phila. Clin. Neuropsychology Group, Soc. Personality Assessment, Am. Arbitration Assn. (family disputes panel), Nat. Acad. Neuropsychologists, Greater Phila. Soc. Clin. Hypnosis, Soc. Friendly Sons St. Patrick, Assn. Sociology of Religion, Brigantine Residents Assn. Lodge: KC (4 deg.). Address: 1101 Ocean Ave Brigantine NJ 08203-2239 also: 454 Kirk Ln Media PA 19063

CURTISS, CAROL PERRY, nursing consultant; b. Worcester, Mass., Dec. 9, 1946; d. Joseph Anthony and Marjorie Ruth (Riedle) Perry; m. Jack Daniel Curtiss, Feb. 8, 1970; children: Paul Daniel, Jennifer Perry. Diploma in nursing, Mass. Gen. Hosp. Sch. Nursing, Boston, 1967; BS, Am. Internat. Coll., Springfield, Mass., 1978; MSN, Yale U., 1981. RN, Mass.; cert. Oncology Nursing Cert. Corp. Staff nurse Franklin Med. Ctr., Greenfield, Mass., 1970, Greenfield Ob-Gyn. Assocs., 1972-74, Greenfield V.s. Nurses, 1974-75; instr. Slim Living Program YMCA, Greenfield, 1977-78; instr. nursing Greenfield C.C., 1978; asst. prof. nursing Elms Coll., Chicopee, Mass., 1981-84; oncology program mgr. Franklin Med. Ctr, Greenfield, 1986-93; cancer care cons. Greenfield, 198—; mem. faculty Greenfield C.C., 1985-87; vis. lectr., clin. instr. Fitchburg (Mass.) State Coll., 1985-86; vis. lectr. Elms Coll., Chicopee, Mass., 1984-85; mem. adj. faculty SUNY, 1987-90, U. Mass., Amherst, 1989—; mem. U.S. com. Internat. Union Against Cancer, NRC, 1992—, mem. nursing project, 1992-95; peer reviewer Agy. for Health Care Policy and Rsch., Cancer Pain Guidelines, Health & Human Svcs., 1993; presenter numerous instns., U.S. and fgn. countries, 1981—. Co-author: Cancer Doesn't Have to Hurt, 1996; guest editor Oncology Nursing Forum, 1993; contbr. articles to profl. jours. Bd. dirs. Franklin County, Am. Cancer Soc., Greenfield, 1979-95, mem. nurse and social work scholarship com., 1988—, nursing com. liaison, 1990—; mem. steering com. Mass. Cancer Pain Initiative, 1988-90, liaison, 1990—; trustee Oncology Nursing Found., 1995—. Mem. Oncology Nursing Soc. (mem. numerous sub coms. 1987—, bd. dirs. 1991—, pres. elect 1991-92, pres. 1992-93, corp. adv. bd. 1991-93, Oncology Nursing Press pres. 1992-94, co-chair conf. on pain 1994, pres. 1993-94), Internat. Union Against Cancer (U.S. com. 1992—, nursing project 1992-94), Sigma Theta Tau. Home: 73 James St Greenfield MA 01301-3607

CURTISS, ROY, III, biology educator; b. May 27, 1934; m. Josephine Clark, Dec. 28, 1976; children: Brian, Wayne, Roy IV, Lynn, Gregory Clark, Eric Garth, Megan Kimberly. B.S. in Agr., Cornell U., 1956; Ph.D. in Microbiology, U. Chgo., 1962. Instr., research asst. Cornell U., 1955-56; jr. tech. specialist Brookhaven Nat. Lab., 1956-58; fellow microbiology U. Chgo., 1958-60, USPHS fellow, 1960-62; biologist Oak Ridge Nat. Lab., 1963-72; lectr. microbiology U. Tenn., 1965-72; lectr. Grad. Sch. Biomed. Scis. U. Tenn., Oak Ridge, 1967-69; prof. U. Tenn. (Grad. Sch. Biomed. Scis.), 1969-72, assoc. dir., 1970-71, interim dir., 1971-72; Charles H. McCauley prof. microbiology U. Ala., Birmingham, 1972-83; sr. scientist Inst. Dental Research, 1972-83, Comprehensive Cancer Center, 1972-83; dir. molecular cell biology grad. program, 1973-82; dir. Cystic Fibrosis Research Center, 1981-83; prof. cellular and molecular biology Sch. Dental Medicine Washington U., St. Louis, 1983-91, George William and Irene Koechig Freiberg prof. biology, 1984—, chmn. dept. biology, 1983-93, dir. Ctr. Plant Sci. and Biotech., 1991-94; vis. prof. Instituto Venezolana de Investigaciones Científicas, 1969, U. P.R., 1972, U. Católica de Chile, 1973, U. Okla., 1982; Mem. NIH Recombinant DNA Molecule Program Adv. Com., 1974-77, NSF Genetic Biology Com., 1975-78; mem. NIH Genetic Basis of Disease Rev. Com., 1979-83, chmn., 1981-83. Editor: Jour. Bacteriology, 1970-76, Infection and Immunity, 1985-92, Escherichia coli and Salmonella: Cellular and Molecular Biology, 1993-96. Mem. Oak Ridge City Coun., 1969-72, Cystic Fibrosis Found. (rsch. devel. program rev. com. 1984-89), Conf. Rsch. Workers on Animal Diseases; bd. dirs. Am. Type Culture Collection, 1989—; founder, dir. and sci. adv. MEGAN Health, Inc., 1992—. Fellow AAAS, Am. Acad. Microbiology; mem. Genetics Soc. Am. (chmn. genetics stock ctrs. com. 1987-89), Am. Assn. Avian Pathologists, Internat. Soc. Mucosal Immunology, Soc. Gen. Microbiology, Am. Soc. Microbiology (Parliamentarian 1970-75, dir. 1977-80, 89-94, editorial bd. ASM News 1987—), N.Y. Acad. Scis., Coun. Advancement Sci. Writing (dir. 1976-82, v.p. 1978-82), World Health Orgn. (steering com. immunology of Tb 1982-85), Sigma Xi. Home: 6065 Lindell Blvd Saint Louis MO 63112-1009 Office: Washington U Dept Biology Saint Louis MO 63130

CURZON, MARTIN EDWARD JOHN, pediatric dentistry educator, consultant; b. Greenwich, Kent, Eng., May 11, 1940; s. Stanley Arthur and Antoinette Carmela (Davies) C.; m. Jennifer Anne Hall, Aug. 29, 1964 (div.); children: Richard Martin, Thomas Paul, Neil Simon; m. Anne Pinfield, Apr. 30, 1994. BDS, U. London, 1964; MS, U. Rochester, 1968; PhD, U. London, 1977. House surgeon Univ. Coll. Hosp., London, 1964; dental extern Govt. British Columbia, Can., 1964-65; lectr. children's dentistry U. Bristol, 1968-70; sr. dental officer Govt. Can., Frobisher Bay, NWT, 1970-73; asst. prof. dental rsch. U. Rochester (N.Y.), 1973-77, assoc. prof. dental rsch., 1977-83; prof. pediatric dentistry U. Leeds, Eng., 1983—. Author, editor: Trace Elements and Dental Disease, 1983; contbr. over 145 articles to profl. jours. Chmn. Ilkley Conservative Party, 1981-83. Fellow Royal Coll. Surgeons, Royal Coll. Dentists (Can.); mem. European Acad. Pediatric Dentistry (pres. 1990-94), European Orgn. Caries Rsch. (treas. 1989-93). Home: 488 Otley Rd, Leeds LS6 8AE, England Office: U Leeds, Clarendon Way, LS1 9LU Leeds England

CUSACK, GRETCHEN ANNE, nurse case manager, career officer; b. Chateauroux, France, May 1, 1962; came to U.S., 1980; d. Gerard and Patricia Ermentrout (Evans) Akerhuis; m. John Patrick Cusack, III, May 28, 1988; children: John Patrick III, Aindrea Erin. BSN, U. Pa., 1985; MSN, Boston Coll., 1992. RN, Pa., Mass.; cert. BLS, ACLS; cert. gerentol. clin. nurse specialist, AACN. Resident counselor Pathways, Inc., Greenwich, Conn., 1985; nurse intern Wilford Hall Med. Ctr. USAF, San Antonio, Tex., 1986; asst. charge nurse USAF Hosp. Laughlin, Del Rio, Tex., 1986-89; staff nurse 509th Strategic Hosp., Portsmouth, N.H., 1989-91; oncology clin. nurse specialist USAF Med. Ctr. Scott, Scott AFB, Ill., 1992-94; nurse case mgr. USAF Med. Ctr. Scott, Scott AFB, 1994-96; med. case mgr. 3rd Med. Group SGOMI, Elmendorf AFB, Alaska, 1996—; quality improvement coord., cardiac care coord. USAF Hosp. Laughlin, Del. Rio, 1986-89; edn. and procedures stds. com. USAF Med. Ctr. Scott, Scott AFB, 1992-94; region V utilization mgmt. group USAF, Scott AFB, 1994-96. Bd. dirs. Am. Cancer Soc., chair staff devel. com., nominating com., income devel. com.; vol. staff fitness ctr., Scott AFB, 1994. Capt. USAF, 1986—. Recipient Air Force Benchmark, Case Mgmt. awards USAF, 1994. Mem. ANA, Oncology Nurses Soc. (oncology cert. nurse), Gerentology Nursing Assn., Officers Club. Office: 3rd Med Group SGOMI Elmendorf AFB AK 99506

CUSCHIERI, ALFRED, surgeon; b. Sliema, Malta, Sept. 30, 1938; s. Saviour and Angela (Galea) C.; m. Margeurite Holley, Mar. 31, 1966; children: Rosalind, Elizabeth, Katie. MD, U. Malta, 1961; ChM, U. Liverpool, 1968. Lectr. in surgery U. Liverpool, Eng., 1967-69, sr. lectr. in surgery, 1969-74, reader in surgery, 1974-76; prof. surgery, head dept. U. Dundee, Scotland, 1976—; dir. Minimal Access Therapy Tng. Unit, Scotland, 1992—. Author: Operative Manual of Endoscopic Surgery, 1992, Tissue Approximation in Endoscopic Surgery, 1995; editor: Essential Surgical Practice, 1988, 2d edit., 1991, 3d edit., 1995; editor jours. Surg. Endoscopy, 1991—, Seminar in Laproscopic Surgery, 1992—. Recipient Moynihan prize Assn. Surgeons Gt. Britain, 1972, prize Internat. Soc. Surgeons. Fellow Royal Coll. Physicians and Surgeons (mem. coun. Edinburgh 1985—). Office: U Dundee Dept Surgery, Ninewells Hosp & Med Sch, Dundee DD1 9SY, Scotland

CUSHING, MATTHEW, internist; b. Salem, Mass., Apr. 29, 1932; s. Matthew and Marita Jane (Teague) C.; m. Mary Genevieve Connors, June 22, 1957; children: Hugh Austin, Evan Albert. A.B., Harvard U., 1953; M.D., Tufts U., 1957. Diplomate Am. Bd. Internal Medicine. Intern, Colorado General Hosp. Denver, 1957-58; resident Univ. of Calif., San Francisco 1958-59; San Francisco General 1959-61; practice medicine specializing in internal medicine, Andover, Mass., 1963-94; pres. Andover Internal Medicine P.C., 1963—; mem. staffs Lawrence General, Bon Secours; 1963-94, chief internal medicine, 1982-84; med. dir. Suburban Healthcare Ctr., Andover, 1986-94. Contbg. editor MD Computing, 1983—. Served to lt. comdr. USNR, 1960-62. Mem. Mass. Soc. Internal Medicine (councillor 1978-84, pres. 1986-87), Mass. Med. Soc. (exec. councillor 1977-80), Essex N. Dist. Med. Soc. (pres. 1980-82), Alpha Omega Alpha. Democrat. Unitarian. Home: 7 Elizabeth Cir Greenbrae CA 94904-3033 Office: Mill Valley Med Group 591 Redwood Hwy Ste 2310 Mill Valley CA 94941-6004

CUSHMAN, INA SUE, physician assistant; b. Malden, Mass., May 11, 1954; d. Frank Melvin and Julia (Krasnow) C. BA in Zoology, Conn. Coll., New London, 1976; student, Yale U., 1986. Nat. cert. physician asst. Physician asst. pvt. office, Plymouth, Mass., 1987-88; sr. physician asst. Harvard Cmty. Health Plan, Braintree, Mass., 1988—. Recipient Profl. Achievement award Am. Acad. Physician Assts./Pfizer Pharms, 1995. Fellow Am. Acad. Physician Assts. (chair pub. edn. com. 1995-96), Mass. Assn. Physician Assts. (chief del. 1995, 96, sec. 1989-92, pres. 1994). Office: HCHP 111 Grossman Dr Braintree MA 02184

CUSHMAN, LAURA ANN, physical medicine and rehabilitation professor; b. Rochester, N.Y., May 11, 1958; d. Eugene S. Cushman and Rita Norene (Ames) Nordquist; m. Alan K. Stetler, Sept. 19, 1987. BA, Wheaton (Ill.) Coll., 1979; PhD, Wayne State U., 1984. Lic. psychologist N.Y. Assoc. prof. U. Rochester (N.Y.), Sch. of Medicine and Dentistry, 1984—. Contbr. articles to profl. jours. Bd. dirs. Mental Health Assn., Rochester Ctr. for Ind. Living, 1985—. Recipient Thomas G. Rumble fellowship Wayne State U., Detroit, 1979. Mem. Internat. Neuropsychological Soc., Am. Psychol. Assn., Nat. Acad. Neuropsychologists, Am. Assn. Spinal Cord Injury Psychologists and Social Workers. Democrat. Episcopalian. Office: U Rochester Med Ctr 601 Elmwood Ave # 664 Rochester NY 14642-0001

CUSHMAN, ORIS MILDRED, retired nurse, hospital education administrator; b. Springfield, Mass., Nov. 22, 1931; d. Wesley Austin and Alice Mildred (Vaile) Stockwell; m. Laurence Arnold Cushman, Apr. 16, 1955; children: Lynn Ann Cushman Wronker, Laurence Arnold III. Diploma in nursing Hartford Hosp. Sch. Nursing (Conn.), 1953; BS, Western Mich. U., 1978, MA, 1980. Staff nurse Wesson Maternal Hosp., Springfield, 1953-54, acting supr., 1954-55; staff nurse Hartford Hosp., 1955-56, head nurse, 1956, staff nurse, 1957-59; staff nurse, charge nurse Reed City Hosp. (Mich.), 1961-67; supr. Meml. Hosp., St. Joseph, Mich., 1967-75, clin. supr. maternal/child health, 1975-77, dir. maternal/child health 1977-80; dir. edn. Pawating Hosp., Niles, Mich., 1980-87; ret., 1987. Sec. Women's aux. Reed City Hosp., 1964-65, v.p., 1965-66, pres., 1966-67; mem. adv. bd. on family life edn. St. Joseph Sch. Bd. (Mich.), 1979-80, Krasl Art Ctr., St. Joseph, 1987-94. Republican.

CUSHMAN, PAUL, physician, educator; b. N.Y.C., Feb. 4, 1930; m. Paulette Bessire; children: Paul, III, Clare Hepburn. BA, Yale U., 1951; MD, Columbia U., 1955. Intern Barnes Hosp. St. Louis, 1955-56; asst. resident Strong Meml. Hosp., Rochester, N.Y., 1956-57, 1959-61; asst. resident attending physician St. Lukes Hosp., N.Y.C., 1961-77; instr. Columbia U, N.Y.C., 1961-65, asst. prof. medicine, 1965-77; assoc. prof. medicine, pharmacology, psychiatry Med. Coll., Wis., Milw., 1977-81; from assoc. prof. to prof. medicine, pharmacology and psychiatry Med. Coll. Va., Richmond, 1982-87; prof. psychiatry, prof. clin. medicine NYU, 1987-90; prof. psychiatry SUNY, Stony Brook, 1990—. Bd. dirs. Cathedral Ch. St. John the Divine, Episcopal Mission Soc., Sheltering Arms Children's Svc., Milw. Found. Capt. USAF, 1957-59. Recipient Caleb Fiske prize, 1967; Henry E. Sigerist prize Yale U., 1973. Fellow ACP, Am. Coll. Clin. Pharmacology; mem. AAAS, Endocrine Soc., Am. Physiol. Soc., Am. Fedn. Clin. Rsch., Union Club, St. NIcholas Soc., Ch. Club, Century Assn. Episcopalian.

CUSHMAN, PHILLIP WAYNE, psychiatrist, educator; b. Evansville, Ind., June 19, 1941; s. William Robert and Cora (Smith) C. BS, Purdue U., 1962; MD, Ind. U., 1966. Diplomate Am. Bd. Psychiatry and Neurology. Intern Meml. Hosp. South Bend, Ind., 1966-67; resident in psychiatry U. Fla. Hosp. and Clinics, Gainesville, 1993—; pvt. practice, Gainesville, 1972—; staff psychiatrist Apalachee Ctr. for Human Svcs., Tallahassee, 1978—; clin. asst. prof. psychiatry U. Coll. Medicine, 1993—. Bd. dirs. North Ctrl. Fla. AIDS Network, Gainesville, 1987, newsletter editor, 1985-88. Maj. Med. Corps, U.S. Army, 1970-72, Vietnam. Named Vol. of Yr. North Ctrl. Fla. AIDS Network, 1987. Fellow Am. Psychiat. Assn., Fla. Psychiat. Soc. (counselor 1993-94, treas. 1994-95, v.p. 1995-96, pres.-elect 1996-97, assoc. editor newsletter 1994—); mem. Assn. Gay and Lesbian Psychiatrists (sec. 1985-90). Home: 5801 NW 83rd Ter Gainesville FL 32653 Office: 2830 NW 41st St Ste B Gainesville FL 32606

CUSHMAN, WILLIAM CHANDLER, physician researcher; b. Lakehurst, N.J., Oct. 6, 1948; s. Townsend Hamilton Jr. and Virginia Marie (Benoit) C.; m. Susan Dell Johnson, June 13, 1970; children: Jonathan David, Jason Chandler, Elizabeth Ann. BA, U. Miss., 1970, MD, 1974. Diplomate Am. Bd. Internal Medicine; ordained to priesthood, Antiochian Orthodox Christian Ch., 1987. Resident U. Miss. Sch. Medicine, Jackson, 1974-77, instr., medicine, 1977-78, asst. prof., medicine, 1978-86; chief hypertension sect. VA Med. Ctr., Jackson, 1978-88; assoc. prof., medicine U. Miss. Sch. Medicine, Jackson, 1986-88; chief hypertension sect. VA Med. Ctr., Memphis, 1988—; assoc. prof., medicine, preventive medicine U. Tenn. Coll. Medicine, Memphis, 1988-94, prof. medicine and preventive medicine, 1994—; speaker in field. Contbr. articles to profl. jours. Asst. pastor St. John Orthodox Ch., Memphis, 1988—, St. Peter Orthodox Ch., Jackson, 1976-88. Fellow ACP, Am. Heart Assn. (fellow coun. high blood pressure rsch., mem. coun. epidemiology); mem. Internat. Soc. & Fedn. Cardiology (coun. epidemiology and prevention), Am. Fedn. Clin. Rsch., Am. Soc. Hypertension, Inter-Am. Soc. Hypertension, So. Soc. Clin. Investigation, Alpha Omega Alpha, Phi Kappa Phi. Office: VA Med Ctr 1030 Jefferson Ave Memphis TN 38104-2127

CUSICK, JOANNE, speech and language therapist; b. Pitts., Dec. 2, 1952; d. Joseph F. and Anne A. (Fiorillo) C. BS in Edn. Speech Correction, Indiana U. of Pa., 1974, MS in Speech Pathology, 1979; postgrad., Slippery Rock U. of Pa., 1985-87, Duquesne U., 1990-92. Cert. clin. competence speech-lang. pathology, Pa., cert. spl. edn. supr., sch. psychologist, lic. speech-lang. pathologist, Pa. Speech and language therapist Seneca Valley Sch. Dist., Zelienople, Pa., 1974—; 1990-92; mem. Students-at-Risk Rowan Elem. Sch., Cranberry Twp., Pa., 1990-92. Legislative contact Pa. State Edn. Assn., 1987—, PSEA Task Force Disparity in Edn., 1989-91. Mem. NEA, ASCD, AHSA (cert. clin. competency-speech pathology), Am. Speech and Hearing Assn., Pa. Speech and Hearing Assn., State Edn. Assn., Seneca Valley Edn. Assn. (pres. 1986-90, v.p. 1990-92, negotiations com. 1983-95, instrnl.-devel. com. 1985—, co-chief negotiator 1989, 92, co-chief negotiator 1995, instrnl. support team mem., long-range planning com. 1991—, mem. Seneca Valley S.D. Strategic Planning Adv. and Dist. Com., 1994—, SVEA Health Care Com., Seneca Valley S.D. Joint Health Care Com. 1992—), Phi Delta Kappa. Democrat. Office: Connoquenessing Valley Elem Sch 300 S Pittsburgh St Zelienople PA 16063

CUSICK, JOSEPH F., neurosurgeon; b. Binghamton, N.Y., May 10, 1939; m. Darby; children: Joseph, Darby, John, Matthew, Patrick. BS, Fordham U., 1961; MD, Georgetown U., 1965. Intern Rush Presbyn.-St. Luke's, Chgo., 1966-72; resident U. Ill., Chgo., 1972; neurosurgeon Richmond (Va.) Neurosurgery Ctr., 1972-74; prof. Med. Coll. Wis., Milw., 1974—; co-dir. Neurosci. Rsch. Labs., 1991—. Assoc. editor Spine, 1989—; reviewer Archives Neurology, 1980-82, Jour. Spinal Disorders, 1991—, Surg. Neurology, 1994—; contbr. articles to profl. jours. Mem. Cervical Spine Rsch. Soc. (exec. com. 1990-96). Office: Med Coll Wis 9200 W Wisconsin Ave Milwaukee WI 53226

CUSMANO, KAREN ANN, critical care nurse; b. Union, N.J., Aug. 27, 1963; d. John Cornell and Nancy Alice (Wallace) C.; m. Thomas Joseph Cusmano; children: Thomas Carmine, Robert Cornell. BSN, Seton Hall U., 1986. RN, N.J.; CCRN. EKG technician John F. Kennedy Med. Ctr., Edison, N.J., 1984, nursing unit asst., 1984-86, nurse CCU, 1986-89, asst. nursing care coord., 1989-90, staff nurse CCU, 1990—. Mem. AACN. Office: John F Kennedy Med Ctr James St Edison NJ 08820

CUSSEL, GEORGE HAROLD, physician assistant; b. Hannover, Germany, May 29, 1932; s. John Jacob and Margarete (Pincus) C.; m. Wilma Jackson Cussel, Aug. 11, 1951 (wid. Jan. 1979); children: Margaret, Deborah, Kris, Kim, Hannah; m. Patricia Marlene Kuhn, May 23, 1980. Cert. physicians asst., Ga. Enlisted USAF, 1951, advanced through grades to master sgt., ret., 1971; v.p. The Med. Ctr., Columbus, Ga., 1971-87; exec. dir. Columbus Hospice, Columbus, 1987-91; v.p. St. Francis Hosp., Columbus, 1991-94; physician's asst. Dr. Marvyn Cohen, Columbus, 1995—; pres. Columbus Hospice, 1973-75, bd. dirs. Health care advisor Columbus Hospice, 1979—; bd. dirs. TB and RD Assocs. Columbus, 1972-76; v.p. GSRT, Atlanta, 1975. Mem. Ga. Assn. Physician Assts., Am. Assn. Physician Assts., Respirator Care Assn. (pres. 1975-79). Jewish. Office: Marvyn Cohen Doctors Bldg Columbus GA 31902

CUSUMANO, CHARLES, physician assistant; b. Newark, Oct. 23, 1943; s. Carl Vanmiller and Edith Marie (Johnson) C.; children: Carl Alexander, Andrea Meryl; m. Sandra Jeanene VanWye, June 14, 1980. BS, Cornell U. Med. Sch., 1975. Physician asst. N.E. Colo. Surg. Assoc., Sterling, 1976-80, Kaiser Permanente, Denver, 1981-92, Family Medicine Clinic, Campbellsville, Ky., 1993—; pediat. trauma instr. child health assoc. program Colo. U. Med. Ctr., Denver, 1990. Author: Isshin Shorinji Justsu Ryu: a Manual of Practice, 1979, Ischemic Necrosis in Sibling Athletes, 1991. Hon. Ky. Col., 1994. Fellow Am. Acad. Physican Asst. Home: 804 Lebanon Ave Campbellsville KY 42718 Office: Family Medicine Clinic 307 Broadway Campbellsville KY 42718

CUSUMANO, PHILIP A., physician; b. Bedford, Ohio, Sept. 9, 1950; s. Philip A. and Mary A. (Famiano) C.; m. Barbara Stockdale Cusumane, May 6, 1978; children: Laura, Christy, Katy, Chelcie. BS in Pharmacy, Ohio No. U., 1973; MD, Wright State U., 1983. Diplomate Am. Bd. Internal Medicine. Intern, resident Cleve. Met. Gen. Hosp., 1983-86; assoc. clin. prof. Case Western Res. U. Med. Sch., 1986—; pvt. practice in internal medicine Beachwood, Ohio, 1986-95; staff St. Luke's Med. Ctr., 1986—; physician Outreach Profl. Svcs. Inc., Beachwood, 1990—; med. review officer Centerior Elec. Co., Cleve., 1987-92; staff Meridia Hillcrest Hosp., 1994—; quality assurance com. St. Luke's Med. Ctr., resident tng. com., bus. adv. com. 1993, primary care task force, 1993, profl. rels. appellate review com., 1995; bd. dirs. Outreach Profl. Svcs., Inc., 1992—; mem. Med. Leadership Coun., Washington, 1995—. Mem. Valley Christian Acad. Sch. Bd., 1991-93; candidate bd. elders Parkside Ch., Solon, Ohio; mem. N.E. Ohio Roundtable; Sunday sch. tchr. Parkside Ch., Bainbridge, Ohio, 1994—. Recipient Achievement award Upjohn, 1973. Mem. AMA, Am. Coll. Physicians, Christian Med. Soc., Phi Eta Sigma, Phi Kappa Phi, Omicron Delta Kappa, Rho Chi, Sigma Phi Epsilon. Office: 24755 Chagrin Blvd Beachwood OH 44122

CUTILLO-SCHMITTER, TERRI ANN, psychiatric and mental health nurse, consultant; b. Pheonixville, Pa., Aug. 22, 1942; d. Louis J. Cutillo and Anne C. Korbel-Cutillo; children: Maureen, Michelle, Robert, Julie Ann. BSN, Villanova U., 1965; MSN, U. Pa., 1982. RN, Pa.; cert. child and adolescent psychiat. mental health clin. nurse specialist. Program dir. geriatric psychiatry program Wills Eye Hosp., Phila.; pvt. practice, cons., family therapy. Contbg. author: Family Psychiatric Nursing, 1993; contbr. articles to profl. jours. Mem. ANA, Nurses in Advanced Practice, Pa. Nurses Assn., Am. Assn. Marriage and Family Therapy (clin.). Home: 212 Old Trinity Pl Lancaster PA 17602-3514

CUTLER, JOHN CHARLES, physician, educator; b. Cleve., June 29, 1915; s. Glenn Allen and Grace Amanda (Allen) C.; m. Eliese Helene Strahl, Nov. 21, 1942. B.A., Western Res. U., 1937, M.D., 1941; M.P.H., Sch. Hygiene and Pub. Health, Johns Hopkins U., 1951. Diplomate: Am. Bd. Preventive Medicine and Pub. Health. Commd. asst. surgeon (lt. j.g.) USPHS, 1941, advanced through grades to asst. surgeon gen. (rear adm.), 1958; intern USPHS Hosp., Staten Island, N.Y., 1941; venereal disease investigations Pub. Health Service Venereal Disease Research Lab., Stapleton, N.Y., 1943-46; venereal disease rsch. and demonstration Guatemala, 1946-48; assigned WHO, 1949-50; with venereal disease div. USPHS, 1951-54; program office Bur. State Svcs., 1954-57; asst. dir. Nat. Inst. Allergy and Infectious Diseases, 1958; asst. surgeon gen. for program, 1958-59; health officer Central dist. Allegheny County Health Dept., 1959-61; dep. dir. Pan Am. San. Bur., regional office for Americas WHO, 1961-68; prof. internat. health, dir. population program Grad. Sch. Public Health, U. Pitts., 1968-79, chmn. dept. health svcs. adminstrn., 1979-80, assoc. dept. chmn., prof. internat. health, 1980-85, prof. emeritus, 1985—; pres. Family Planning Council Southwestern Pa., 1971-72; sec. Am. Social Health Assn., 1972-76; pres. Internat. Health Soc., 1972-73, Am. Assn. World Health, 1973-75, Assn. Voluntary Sterilization, 1977-83; sec.-treas. World Fedn. Health Agys. for Advancement Vol. Surg. Contraception, 1975-81, pres.-elect., 1981-85, pres. 1985-87. Contbr. articles to med. publs. Pres. UN Assn., Pitts., 1988-90. Fellow Am. Pub. Health Assn.; mem. Phi Beta Kappa. Home: 210 S Dallas Ave Pittsburgh PA 15208-2626 Office: U Pitts Grad Sch Pub Health Pittsburgh PA 15261

CUTLER, LINDA M., nursing administrator; b. Exeter, N.H., Apr. 25, 1947; d. William O. and Eleanor W. Cutler. BSN, U. N.H., 1970; MS, Boston U., 1979. Staff, sr. staff, per diem Children's Hosp., Boston, 1970-74; head nurse Marth Elliot Health Ctr., Jamaica Plain, Mass., 1974-75; asst. prof. nursing U. N.H., Durham, 1979-85; dir. med.-surg. nursing and nursing edn. Lowell (Mass.) Gen. Hosp., 1985-88; assoc. v.p. nursing, then v.p. nursing Frisbie Meml. Hosp., Rochester, N.H., 1988-94; quality improvement/risk mgmt. coord. Tri-Area Vis. Nurses Assn., Somersworth, N.H., 1994-96; health occupations instr. Seacoast Sch. Tech., Exeter, 1996—; presenter in death and dying, advance directives, health assessment of the adult and primary nursing; cons. home health care, safety, documentation, quality improvement; asst. prof. nursing cmty. health U. N.H., Durham, 1995—. Coord. med. svcs. N.H. Spl. Olympics Summer Games, 1989—. Mem. N.H. Hosp. Assn. (mem. steering com. worker's compensation trust 1995—), Sigma Theta Tau.

CUTLER, MARK OWEN, psychiatrist; b. Boston, Nov. 29, 1947; m. Saul J. and Anne Shirley (Lazrus) C.; m. Sandrea Joan Gashin, Sept. 5, 1971; children: Adam Michael, Alex Jay, Michelle Amanda. MD, Boston U., 1971. Diplomate Am. Bd. Psychiatry and Neurology. Dir. cons. liaison psychiatry Worcester Meml. Hosp., Worcester, Mass., 1977-79; pvt. practice psychiatry Worcester, 1979—; cons. post tramatic stress disorder unit Rutland (Mass.) Heights Hosp., 1979-90. Contbr. articles to Internat. Jour. Group Psychotherapy, 1978, Psychosomatics, 1980. Sec. Temple Emanuel Worcester, 1988-91; v.p. Worcester Jewish Fedn., 1987-89, 91-92, pres., 1992-94, campaign chmn., 1989-91. Maj. U.S. Army, 1975-77. Decorated Army Commendation medal. Mem. Shriners, Masons (master Level lodge 1985). Republican. Home: 14 Leyton Rd Worcester MA 01609-1100 Office: Psychotherapy Assocs 55 Cedar St Worcester MA 01609-2132

CUTLER, TODD LOHMAN, health facility executive; b. Akron, Ohio, July 2, 1966; s. Harloe P. and Hariet I. (Yount) C.; m. Beth Ann Bouy, Oct. 28, 1989; 1 child, Timothy. BS in Pharm. Sales and Mktg., U. Toledo, 1989. Bidding and instnl. mktg. coord. Harris Wholesale Co., Solon, Ohio, 1989-90; Rx mktg. coord., contract adminstr. Harris Wholesale/Fox Meyer Corp., Solon, 1990-93; Rx cons. Fox Meyer Corp., Carrollton, Tex., 1993-94; owner ElectroMed Claims, Sandusky, Ohio, 1993-94; mktg. and planning exec. Mercy Hosp., Willard, Ohio, 1994—; bd. dirs. Willard Area Provider Hosp. Orgn.; mem. planning coun. mission svcs. com. Mercy Health Sys., Cin., 1994—; mem. Health Care Adv. Bd., Washington, 1994—. Mem. Italian Am. Beneficial, U. Toledo Alumni Assn. (bd. dirs. Sandusky Bay chpt. 1994—), Kiwanis. Roman Catholic. Office: Mercy Hosp Willard 110 E Howard St Willard OH 44890

CUTLIP, RANDALL BROWER, retired psychologist, college president emeritus; b. Clarksburg, W.Va., Oct. 1, 1916; s. M.N. and Mildred (Brower) C.; m. Virginia White, Apr. 21, 1951; children: Raymond Bennett, Catherine Baumgarten. AB, Bethany Coll., 1940; cert. indsl. personnel mgmt., So. Meth. U., 1944; M.A., East Tex. U., 1949; Ed.D., U. Houston, 1953; LL.D., Bethany Coll., 1965, Columbia Coll., 1980; L.H.D., Drury Coll., 1975; Sc.D., S.W. Bapt. U., 1978; Litt.D., William Woods U., 1981. Tchr. adminstr. Tex. pub. schs., 1947-50; dir. tchr. placement U. Houston, 1950-51, supr. counselling, 1951-53; dean students Atlantic Christian Coll., Wilson, N.C., 1953-56, dean, 1956-58; dean personnel, dir. grad. div. Chapman U., Orange, Calif., 1958-60; pres. William Woods Coll., Fulton, Mo., 1960-81, pres. emeritus, 1981—; trustee William Woods U., Fulton, Mo., 1981-85, 92—; chmn. bd. dirs. Mo. Colls. Fund, 1973-75; chmn. Mid-Mo. Assn. Colls., 1972-76; bd. dirs. Marina del Sol, bd. pres., 1985-90, 92—. chmn. bd. dirs. Mo. Colls. Fund, 1973-75; chmn. Mid-Mo. Assn. Colls., 1972-76; bd. dirs. Marina del Sol, bd. pres., 1985-90, 92-95. Mem. visitors' bd. Mo. Mil. Acad., 1966-90, chmn., 1968-72; trustee Shreiner Coll., Kerrville, Tex., 1983-92, Amy Shelton McNutt Charitable Trust, 1983—, Permanent Endowment Fund, Scholarship Found. and Res. Fund of Christian Ch.; bd. dirs. Univ. of the Americas, 1984—, exec. v.p., 1985—; bd. dirs. Tex. State Aquarium, 1994; elder Life Christian Ch. Recipient McCubbin award, 1968, Delta Beta Xi award, 1959. Mem. Am. Personnel and Guidance Assn., Alpha Sigma Phi, Phi Delta Kappa, Kappa Delta Pi, Alpha Chi. Address: 1400 Ocean Dr Corpus Christi TX 78404-2109

CUTTER, JOHN MICHAEL, dentist; b. Columbus, Ohio, May 28, 1952; s. John Raymond and Betty Mae (Paripovich) C.; m. Alice May Mcquitty, Aug. 6, 1977 (div. May 1984); 1 child, John David Benjamin; m. Linda Ann Hovis-Smith, Oct. 20, 1990. BA, Ohio State U., 1974, DDS, 1976. Pvt. practice family dentistry and laser-assisted care Fairfield, Ohio, 1976—, Loveland, Ohio, 1993—; assoc. staff dental outpatient dept. Jewish Hosp. Cin., 1977-80, courtesy staff mem. 1980-84; also dental outpatient rep. to med. records and ambulatory care com.; instr. radiology div. dental hygiene U. Cin., 1977, supervising dentist clin. affairs; clin. dentist Rockdale Elem. & Condon Schs. for Handicapped, 1977-79; founding mem., trustee DenCare, 1986-89. Contbr. articles to profl. jour. Sr. clin. dentist Cin. Bd. Edn.; mem. programming com. Southwestern Ohio chpt. Am. Heart Assn., 1983; co-chmn. fin. com., ch. bd. Lindenwald United Meth. Ch., 1982;. Mem. ADA, Ohio Dental Assn., Acad. Gen. Dentistry (nat. spokesdentist in laser-assisted dentistry), Am. Endodontic Soc., Internat. Acad. Laser Dentistry, Cin. Dental Soc. (assoc.), Keely Dental Soc. (co-chmn. programming com. 1980, chmn. continuing edn. 1979-82, editor Keely Bull. 1982-85, mem.-at-large coun. 1982), Psi Omega. Republican. Office: 1251 Nilles Rd Fairfield OH 45014-7205

CUTTIC, CHARLES EDWARD, physician assistant; b. Newark, June 14, 1955; s. Charles and Luba (Hall) C.; m. Nancy Jean Odegard, May 30, 1982; children: Evan Ford, Alexander Hall. BA, Lafayette Coll., 1977; B Health Scis. magna cum laude, Duke U., 1984. Cert. physician asst., Pa. and Nat. Commn. on Cert. Physician Assts. Physician asst. in cardiac surgery Temple U. Hosp., Phila., 1984-86; physician asst. in gen./orthopaedic surgery Paoli Meml. Hosp., Pa., 1986-88; dir. surg. svcs. Hosp. Phila. Coll. Osteopathic Medicine, 1988-89; physician asst. in cardiac surgery Hahnemann U. Hosp., Phila., 1989-95, Crozer Chester Med. Ctr., Upland, Pa., 1995—. Recipient spl. recognition in surgery Nat. Commn. on Cert. Physician Assts., 1991. Fellow Am. Acad. Physician Assts., Assn. Physician Assts. in Cardiovasc. Surgery. Russian Orthodox. Home: 1707 Marsha Ln Downingtown PA 19335

CUTTINO, CHARLES LYNUM, III, oral and maxillofacial surgeon; b. Sumter, S.C., Nov. 19, 1940; s. Charles Lynum Jr. and Anne Elizabeth (Marsh) C.; m. Peggy J. Jepsen, Aug. 8, 1964 (div. Sept. 1984); children: Charles Marsh, David Scott; m. Anne C. Adams, Apr. 26, 1986. BS, Clemson U., 1962; DDS, Med. Coll. Va., 1966. Diplomate Am. Bd. Oral and Maxillofacial Surgery. Oral surgery intern Med. Coll. Va., Richmond, 1969-70, resident, 1970-72; oral and maxillofacial surgeon Peters, Green, Cuttino, Nelson, Miller, Eschenroeder et al, Richmond, 1972—; assoc. clin. prof. dept. oral maxillofacial surgery Med. Coll. Va., 1983—; chief oral surgery St. Mary's Hosp., Richmond, 1978—. Contbr. articles to profl. jours. Pres. Dorset Wood Civic Assn., Richmond, 1990-91. Capt. USAF, 1969-72. Recipient awards Am. Cancer Soc. Fellow Am. Coll. Dentists, Internat. Coll. Dentists, Va. Dental Assn. (exec. coun. 1986-92, sec.-treas. 1993—); mem. ADA, Am. Assn. Oral and Maxillofacial Surgeons, Southeastern Soc. Oral and Maxillofacial Surgeons (bd. dirs. 1994—, sec./treas. 1996-97), Va. Soc. Oral and Maxillofacial Surgeons (pres.-elect 1991-93, pres. 1993-95), Richmond Dental Soc. (bd. dirs., pres. 1983-84), Chalmers J. Lyons Oral Surgery Soc., Pierre Fauchard Acad. (vice-chmn. 1992-94), Commonwealth Dental Acad. (pres. 1975), Sigma Xi, Sigma Zeta, Omicron Kappa Upsilon, Psi Omega. Methodist. Home: 512 Welwyn Rd Richmond VA 23229-8106 Office: Peters Green Cuttino et al 3217 Grove Ave Richmond VA 23221-2815

CUVIELLO, PATRICK VICTOR, medical technologist; b. West New York, N.J., Mar. 30, 1926; s. Daniel and Mildred (Candelmo) C.; m. Norma Jean Nitzschke; children: Patrick, Linda, Kimberly, Elice. BS, Seton Hall U., 1949; MS, East Tex. U., 1971. Med. technologist VA Hosp., MArlin, Tex., 1953-55; clin. lab. dir. Navarro Regional Hosp., Corsicana, Tex., 1955-95, retired, 1995; instr part-time Navarro Coll., Corsicana, Tex., 1968—, Hill Jr. Coll., Hillsboro, Tex., 1975-78; cons. in field. Author: Cuviello Reference Manual vol. I and vol. II, 1982, revised edit., 1996, A Reference Manual of Medical Technology, 1970. Scoutmaster Boy Scouts Am., Corsicana, 1962-72, sea explorer advisor, 1962-65. With USN, 1944-46. Mem. Am. Med. Technologist (v.p., treas., pres., bd. dirs.). Methodist. Home: 1911 Fairfax Corsicana TX 75110

CUZICK, JACK MARTIN, epidemiologist, statistician; b. Hawthorne, Calif., Aug. 11, 1948; s. Martin J. and Margaret M. (Gaughran) C.; m. Jane V. Beanland, May 11, 1971; children: Alayne, John. BSc, Harvey Mudd Coll., 1970; MSc, U. London, 1971; PhD, Claremont (Calif.) Grad. Sch., 1974. Sr. systems analyst Carson Systems Inc., Newport Beach, Calif., 1970-74; asst. prof. Columbia U., N.Y.C., 1975-78; IARC rsch. fellow Oxford (Eng.) U., 1978-79; rsch. fellow Imperial Cancer Rsch. Fund, London, 1979-82, head dept. math. statistics and epidemiology, 1982—. Editor: Geographical and Environmental Epidemiology, 1992; contbr. articles to profl. jours. Recipient Biomedicine Prize, 1988. Fellow Inst. of Math. Stats., Royal Statis. Soc. Office: Imperial Cancer Rsch Fund, Lincoln's Inn Fields PO Box 123, London WC2A 3PX, England

CYBULSKI, JOANNE KAREN, nutritionist, diabetes educator; b. N.Y.C., May 8, 1950; d. Willard Schmelz and Else (Mikifer) Brown; m. Lee Andrew Cybulski, Dec. 28, 1974; children: David Mark, Michael Ryan. BS in Food and Nutrition, SUNY, Plattsburgh, 1972; MS in Nutrition, Case Western Res. U., 1975. Cert. diabetes educator. Dietitian White Plains (N.Y.) Hosp., 1972-73; instr. W.Va. State Coll., Institute, 1977; dietitian W.VA. Dept. Health, Charleston, 1975-77; adminstrv. dietitian Drake Meml. Hosp., Cin., 1978; clin. dietitian U. Hosp., Louisville, 1978-82; nutritionist I Louisville-Jefferson County Bd. Health, 1982, coordinator nutrition services, 1982-89; dietitian Caritas Med. Ctr., Louisville, 1989—; adj. instr. Ind. U. S.E., New Albany, 1985-90. Contbr. articles to profl. jours. Ruling elder Bardstown Rd. Presbyn. Ch., 1984-86; mem. fin. dept. Presbytery of Louisville, 1986-89. Mem. Am. Dietetic Assn. (registered), Ky. Dietetic Assn. (treas. 1989-91), Diabetes Care and Edn. Practice Group, Am. Diabetes Assn., Am. Assn. Diabetes Educators, Greater Louisville Assn. Diabetes Educators (v.p. 1984-86, pres. 1989-91, treas. 1996—). Office: Diabetes & Caritas Med Ctr 1850 Bluegrass Ave Louisville KY 40215-1161

CYGAN, MARIA DOROTA, ultrasound physician; b. Warsaw, Poland, Feb. 7, 1955; d. Henryk and Jolanta Antonina (Walicka) Rutkowska; m. Bohdan Leszek Cygan, Mar. 4, 1978; children: Szymon, Olga, Hanna-Bronka. MD, Med. Acad. Warsaw, 1982. Specialist in radiology. Chief ultrasound dept. Oncology Ctr., Warsaw, 1990—. Contbr. book chpt.: Colonic Cancer, 1995. Mem. Polish Ultrasonic Soc. Home: ul Lachmana 2 m 72, 02-786 Warsaw Poland Office: Inst Oncology, ul Wawelska 15, 02-034 Warsaw Poland

CYNADER, MAX SIGMUND, psychology, physiology, brain research educator, researcher; b. Berlin, Feb. 24, 1947; arrived in Can., 1951; s. Samuel and Maria (Kraushar) C.; m. Moira Elizabeth Langton, May 30, 1985; children: Madeleine Maria, Rebecca Kay, Alexandra Josephine. BSc, Mc Gill U., Montreal, Que., Can., 1967; PhD, MIT, 1972. Fellow neuroanatomy Max-Planck Inst. Psychiatry, Munich, 1972-73; asst. prof. psychology Dalhousie U., 1973-77, assoc. prof., 1977-81, assoc. prof. physiology, 1979-84, prof. psychology, 1981-84, Killam rsch. prof., 1984-88, prof. physiology, 1984-88; prof. psychology U. B.C., 1988—, prof. physiology, 1988—, prof., dir. rsch. dept. ophthalmology, 1988—; mem. pres.'s workshop on five yr. plan strengthening sci. support in Can. Natural Scis. and Engring. Rsch. Coun. Can., 1984, workshop for Steacie fellows, 1988; mem. task force on curricular devel. in Can. neurosci., 1984; mem. spl. adv. panel on rsch. preparedness USAF, 1985; rep. Internat. Human Frontiers Sci. program Med. Rsch. Coun. Can., 1988; mem. grants com. behavioural scis. Med. Rsch. Coun. Can., program grants com. 1989—; referee senate rev. grad. program in neurosci. U. Western Ont., 1989; mem. math., computational and theoretical spl. rev. com. NIMH, 1989—; external reviewer Med. Rsch. Coun. Can., Alta. Heritage Fund Med. Rsch., NIH, NSF, USAF Office Sci. Rsch., Multiple Sclerosis Soc. Can., Vancouver Found., March of Dimes, Fight for Sight. Mem. editorial bd. jours. Behavioral Brain Rsch., Clin. Vision Scis., Concepts in Neurosci., Devel. Brain Rsch., Exptl. Brain Rsch., Neural Networks, Visual Neurosci.; mem. adv. bd. series Rsch. Notes in Neural Computing; contbr. articles to profl. jours. Recipient Killam Rsch. prize U. B.C., 1989—; E.W.R. Steacie fellow Natural Sci. and Engring. Rsch. Coun. Can., 1979; Can. Inst. Advanced Rsch. fellow, 1986—; grantee Med. Rsch. Coun. Can., 1973—, Natural Sci. and Engring. Rsch. Coun. Can., 1975—, NIH, 1978-81. Fellow Can. Inst. Advanced Rsch., Royal Soc. Can.; mem. Soc. Neurosci. (Halifax chpt., pres. 1985, edn. com. 1986-89), Can. Assn. Neurosci. (pres. 1986), Assn. Rsch. Otolaryngology, Assn. Rsch. in Vision and Opthalmology, Can. Physiol. Soc., Internat. Brain Rsch. Orgn., Internat. Soc. Devel. Neurosci., Internat. Strabismol. Assn., World Fedn. Neuroscientists. Office: U of BC Dept Opthalmology, 2550 Willow St, Vancouver, BC Canada V5Z 3N9

CYR, KENNETH A., psychiatric and mental health nurse; b. Portland, Maine, Aug. 23, 1946; s. Merle Richmond and Eunice Priscilla (Ramsey) C.; m. Maria Centenera, Aug. 20, 1967; children: Bryan L, Steven J., Michael A. ASN, U. of State N.Y., Albany, 1977; BS cum laude, U. Nebr., Omaha, 1975; MA in Hosp. Mgmt., Webster U., 1978; MA in Mental Health, St. Mary's U., 1980; PhD in Clin. Psychology, Union Inst., 1994. Lic. profl. counselor, marriage and family therapist, Tex.; lic. psychologist. Professional lectr. psychology U. of Philippines, Manila, 1983-84; instr. psychology Cen. Tex. Coll., Killeen, Tex., 1984-88; clin. dir. Assoc. Counseling Svcs., Harker Heights, Tex., 1990-91; dir. Advanced Counseling Ctr., Harker Heights, 1991—. Contbr. articles to profl. jours. Major USAF, 1964-88. Home: 1704 Beaver Trl Harker Heights TX 76548-7010

CYTOWIC, RICHARD EDMUND, neurologist; b. Trenton, N.J., Dec. 16, 1952; s. Edmund R. and Margaret A. (Ganyo) C. BA, Duke U., 1973; MD, Bowman Gray Sch. Medicine, 1977; postgrad. Nat. Hosp. for Nervous Diseases, London, 1976. Diplomate Nat. Bd. Med. Examiners. Intern, N.C. Bapt. Hosp./Bowman Gray Sch., Winston-Salem, N.C., 1977-78, resident in neurology, 1978-79, fellow in neurology, neuropsychology, cerebral blood flow, 1979-80; resident in neurology George Washington U., Washington, 1980-81; attending physician dept. neurology Washington Hosp. Ctr., 1981—; pres. Capitol Neurology, Washington, 1981—; med. advisor Med-Scene Teleconfs., Alexandria, Va., 1984—; resident fellow Hambridge Ctr. for Creative Arts and Scis., Rabum Gap, Ga., 1988, 89, 90, Va. Ctr. for Creative Arts, 1992. Author: Studies in Nonfocal Brain Injury, 1987, Synesthesia: A Union of the Senses, 1988, Nerve Block for Common Pains, 1989, The Neurological Side of Neuropsychology, 1996, The Man Who Tasted Shapes, 1993; contbr. articles to profl. jours., various newspapers. Pulitzer prize nominee, 1982; mem. editorial bd. Brain and Language, Brain and Cognition, 1987—. Fellow Royal Soc. Medicine; mem. AAAS, AMA, Internat. Neuropsychol. Soc., Med. Soc. D.C. (publs. com. 1984—, pub. info. and edn. bd. 1987—), Am. Acad. Neurology, Am. Assn. for History of Medicine, N.Y. Acad. Scis., Sigma Xi. Republican. Roman Catholic. Home: 2737 Devonshire Pl NW Washington DC 20008-3479 Office: Capitol Neurology 1611 Connecticut Ave NW Ste 2B Washington DC 20009-1033

CZAJKA, GREGORY ALLAN, physician assistant; b. Buffalo, N.Y., June 1, 1956; s. Ronald J. and Lois B. Czajka; m. Camilla S. Czajka, Jan. 1, 1982; children: Sarah, Kathryn, Kimberly, Meghan, Brittany, Matthew. BS in Health Sci., Canisius Coll., 1977; cert. physician asst., Hahnemann U., 1979. Cert. physician asst., Nat. Comm. Cert. Physician Assts. Physician asst. Cleveland Hill Med. Group, Buffalo, 1979-82, Buffalo Gen. Hosp., 1982-83, Health Care Plan Med. Ctr., West Seneca, N.Y., 1983-84, Lakeshore Family Medicine, Hamburg, N.Y., 1984-86; dir. physician asst. Sisters of Charity Hosp., Buffalo, 1986-91; physician asst. Cosgriff, Heyden, Wiles & Gage Surg. Assocs., Buffalo, 1991—; mem. adv. bd. D'Youville Coll., Buffalo, 1993—, adj. faculty, 1993—, mem. admissions com., 1993—; mem. admissions com. Daemen Coll., Buffalo, 1995—. Vol. fireman Alden (N.Y.) Fire Dept., 1974—, past rescue squad capt.; surg. house coord. Sister's of Charity Hosp., Buffalo, 1993—. Fellow Am. Acad. Physician Assts., N.Y. State Soc. Physician Assts., Am. Acad. Surgeon Assts.; mem. Western N.Y. Physician Asst. Assn. (sec. 1990—). Home: 1596 Homecourt Alden NY 14004 Office: Cosgriff Heyden Wiles & Gage Surg Assoc 2121 Main St Ste 301 Buffalo NY 14214

CZARNECKI, CASIMIR, ophthalmologist; b. Phila., Dec. 29, 1936; s. Jacob and Anastasia (Konopka) C.; m. Dorothy Julia Geremsky; children: Mark, Christine, Karen, Janine, Barbara, Julie, David. AB, U. Pa., 1958; MD, Hahnemann U., 1962. Diplomate Am. Bd. Ophthalmology. Resident Phila. Gen. Hosp., 1963-66; pvt. practice ophthalmology Phila., 1966—. Served to capt. USAF, 1963-69. Fellow Am Acad. Ophthalmology; mem. AMA, Nat. Med. & Dental Assn., Pa. Med. Soc. Phila. County Med. Soc. Roman Catholic. Home: 9412 Academy Rd Philadelphia PA 19114-2693

CZARNIONKA, SUSAN STARKEY, clinical nurse; b. Wausau, Wis., Jan. 10, 1948; d. Fred Jefferson and Lita Irene (Nelson) Starkey; m. Paul A. Czarnionka, Sept. 5, 1981; children: Mary J., Paul J. Diploma, Mass. Gen. Hosp. Sch. Nursing, Boston, 1974; BSN, Northeastern U., 1980; MBA, Keller Grad. Sch. Mgmt., Milw., 1990. Supr. nursing Mass. Gen. Hosp., Boston; nurse mgr. St. Francis Hosp., Milw.; nursing dir. St. Mary's Hosp., Milw., clin. nurse; adminstrv. dir. Heart Inst., York, Maine; cardiovascular health specialist So. Maine Med. Ctr., Biddeford. Mem. Sigma Theta Tau. Home: 122 Raydon Road Ext York ME 03909-1626

CZEISLER, JEFFREY LANCE, pharmaceutical scientist; b. N.Y.C., July 20, 1942; s. Nicholas and Bessie (Naidich) C.; m. Miriam Ingrid Straus, May 20, 1973; children: Paula Stephanie, Barry Michael. BA, SUNY, Binghamton, 1964, MA, 1966; PhD, Case Western Res. U., 1970. Postdoctoral fellow Johns Hopkins U., Balt., 1970-75; rsch. investigator G.D. Searle & Co., Skokie, Ill., 1975-78, lab. head, 1978-80, mgr., 1980-83, sect. head, 1984-85; dir. project mgmt. G.D. Searle & Co., Skokie, 1985-86; dir. Pharmacy R & D, Wayne, N.J., 1986-94; head pharm. products dept. Berlex Labs., Inc., Wayne, N.J., 1994-96. Editorial adv. bd. Drug Devel. & Indsl. Pharmacy, 1989—; contbr. articles to profl. jours. Named N.Y. State Regents scholar, 1960-64, NIH postdoctoral fellow, 1972, 74, Fulbright fellow, 1973. Mem. Am. Chem. Soc., Am. Assn. Pharm. Scientists. Office: Berlex Labs 300 Fairfield Rd Wayne NJ 07470-7300

CZERNER, THOMAS B., physician, educator; b. Prague, Sept. 27, 1938; s. Max and Irma (Frölich) C.; m. Cynthia Silvert Wax, Nov. 21, 1967; children: Suzanne, Elizabeth. BA, U. Ill., Urbana, 1959; MD, U. Ill., Chgo., 1962. Diplomate Am. Bd. Ophthalmology. Pvt. practice San Francisco; clin. prof. U. Calif., San Francisco, 1971—. Lt. Comdr. USN, 1962-64. Office: 3838 California St San Francisco CA 94118

DACRE, JACK CRAVEN, toxicologist, consultant; b. Auckland, New Zealand; came to U.S., 1970; s. George Craven and Grace (Piper) D.; m. Jean Rosina Olney, Dec. 10, 1950; children: Kenneth J.C., Terrence M., Paul C. BS, U. New Zealand, 1943, MS with honors, 1946; PhD, U. London, 1950, DS, 1982. Sr. rsch. biochemist Toxicology Rsch. Unit/NZ Med. Rsch. Coun., Dunedin, New Zealand, 1954-61, head of unit, 1968-70; chief toxicologist pathol. rsch. dept. U. Otago Med. Sch., Dunedin, 1961-67; assoc. prof. Lab. Environ. Medicine Tulane U. Med. Sch., New Orleans, 1970-74; rsch. toxicologist U.S. Army Med. Bioengring. R & D Lab/Ft. Detrick, Frederick, Md., 1974-84, mgr. chem. weapons rsch., 1985-90; chief toxicologist U.S. Army Biomedical R & D Lab./Ft. Detrick, Frederick, 1990-92; cons. toxicologist Geo-Ctrs. Inc. at Ft. Detrick, Frederick, 1993-95; pvt. practice Frederick, Md., 1996—; toxicology cons., 1996—; expert mem. Joint WHO/FAO Expert Com. on Food Additives, Geneva, Rome, 1968-84. Contbg. author: Metabolic Aspects of Food Safety, 1969, Environmental Risk Analysis of Chemicals, 1981, Cholinesterases--Fundamental and Applied Aspects, 1983, Lewisite: Its Chemistry, Toxicology and Biological Effects, 1989, Toxicology and Pharmacology of the Chemical Warfare Agent Sulfur Mustard (A Review), 1996. Recipient Chem. Essay prize New Zealand Inst. Chemistry, 1959, 68, ICI (Imperial Chem. Industries) Silver medal and prize, New Zealand, 1974, Commr.'s Spl. Citation award and Harvey W. Wiley medal Nat. Ctr. for Toxicological Rsch., FDA, 1990. Fellow Acad. Toxicological Scis., New Zealand Inst. Chemistry. Home and Office: 7209 E Sundown Ct Frederick MD 21702-2950

DADO, CLAUDIA M., dentist; b. Evergreen Park, Ill., Mar. 12, 1957; d. Ralph Natale Sr. and Violet Mary (Mlejnek) D.; m. Brodie Glenroy Secrest, III. BS in Biology, St. Xavier Coll., 1979; DDS, Loyola U., Maywood, Ill., 1983. Gen. practice dentistry Chgo., 1983—; instr. histology Loyola U., Maywood, 1983-84. Mem. ADA, Hispanic Dental Assn., Ill. Dental Soc., Chgo. Dental Soc.

DAESCHNER, CHARLES WILLIAM, JR., retired physician, educator; b. Houston, Dec. 24, 1920; s. Charles William and Maxie Virginia (Hulsey) D.; m. Norma Sederholm, Nov. 14, 1948 (dec. Aug. 1991); children: Charles William III, Mary Lynn, Martha Ann; m. Martha Murray Brown, May 2, 1992. BA, Rice Inst., 1942; MD, U. Tex., 1945. Diplomate Am. Bd. Pediatrics (bd. dirs., past pres.). Rotating intern Hermann Hosp., Houston, 1945-46; resident St. Louis Children's Hosp., 1948-50, Children's Med. Center, Boston, 1950-51; instr., then asso. prof. Baylor U. Med. Coll., 1951-60; prof. pediatrics, chmn. dept. U. Tex. Med. Br., Galveston, 1960-89, Ashbel Smith prof. emeritus, 1989-91; mem.-at-large bd. Nat. Bd. Med. Examiners, 1978—, vice-chmn. exec. bd., 1981-83, chmn. exec. bd., 1983-87, past mem. adv. com. undergrad. med. edn. Mem. sci. publs. com.: Tex. Medicine, 1973-81, mem. editorial bd., 1975-81, chmn., 1977-81 ; editorial bd.: Am. Jour. Diseases of Children, 1973-81. Trustee Moody Retirement Home; bd. dirs. Galveston Hist. Dist., 1963-75; mem. Galveston Planning Commn., 1963-75. Served to capt., M.C. USAF, 1946-48. Recipient Disting. Svc. award Nat. Bd. Med. Examiners, 1991; named Disting. Alumnus Rice Inst., 1989. Mem. Am. Acad. Pediatrics (chmn. com. med. edn. 1965-70, Abraham Jacobi award 1982, Lifetime Achievement in Med. Edn. award 1991), Am. Pediatric Soc., So. Soc. Clin. Research, So. Soc. Pediatric Research, AMA, Tex. Pediatric Soc. (Kaliski award 1981), Galveston County Med. Soc., Assn. Med. Sch. Pediatric Dept. Chmn. (pres. 1970—), Assn. Pediatric Program Dirs., Sigma Xi. Home: 7518 Beluche Galveston TX 77551-1518

DAFFORN, GEOFFREY ALAN, biochemist; b. Cunningham, Kans., Feb. 4, 1944; s. Francis Elston and Anna Elizabeth Dafforn; m. Gail McLaughlin, July 14, 1973; 1 child, Christine Elizabeth. BA cum laude, Harvard U., 1966; PhD, U. Calif., Berkeley, 1970. Postdoctoral fellow U. Calif., Berkeley, 1973; asst. prof. U. Tex., Austin, 1974; from asst. prof. to assoc. prof. Bowling Green (Ohio) State U., 1974-81; sr. chemist Syva Co., Palo Alto, Calif., 1982-87, rsch. fellow, 1987—. Author articles and abstracts; patentee in field. Grantee Army Rsch. Office, 1979-82, Am. Chem. Soc., 1975-80. Mem. AAAS, Am. Chem. Soc., Sierra Club. Office: Behring Diagnostics Inc 3403 Yerba Buena Rd San Jose CA 95135

DAFOE, DONALD CAMERON, surgeon, educator; b. Appleton, Wis., Nov. 22, 1949. BS in Zoology, U. Wis., 1971, MD, 1975. Diplomate Am. Bd. Surgery. Intern Hosp. of U. of Pa., Phila., 1975-76, resident, 1976-80, Measey rsch. fellow, 1978-80, chief resident, 1980-81, clin. fellow, Culpeper Found. fellow, 1981-82; asst. prof. surgery U. Mich., Ann Arbor, 1982-87; dir. clin. pancreas transplantation program u. Mich., Ann Arbor, 1984-87; assoc. prof. surgery U. Mich., Ann Arbor, 1987; assoc. prof. surgery, chief divsn. transplantation Hosp. of U. of Pa., Phila., 1987-91, Stanford (Calif.) U. Med. Ctr., 1991—; cons., physician advisor Keystone Peer Rev. Orgn., Inc., 1990-91. Reviewer various publs.; mem. editorial bd. Transplantation Sci., 1992, The Chimera, 1993; contbr. over 100 articles to profl. jours; also numerous book chpts. Mem. ACS, Am. Diabetes Assn., Am. Soc. Transplant Surgeons (membership com. 1989-90, sci. studies com. 1991—, newsletter com. 1991—, program & publs. com. 1994—), Assn. for Acad. Surgery, Soc. Internat. de Chirurgie, The Transplantation Soc., Ctrl. Surg. Assn., Frederick A. Coller Surg. Soc., Soc. Univ. Surgeons, Surg. Biology Club II, Ravdin-Rhoads Surg. Soc., United Network for Organ Sharing, Calif. Transplant Donor Network, Western Assn. Transplant Surgeons. Office: Dept Surgery MSOB X-300 Stanford Univ Med Ctr Stanford CA 94305

DAFOE, WILLIAM ALFRED, surgeon; b. Wautoma, Wis., July 21, 1917; s. George Eber And Gertrude (Collins) D.; m. Muriel Isabel Sprissler, July 13, 1942; children: Barbara, Nancy, Diane, Donald, Richard, Jane, Willem, Sarah. BA, U. Wis., 1937; MD, Harvard U., 1940; MS in Surgery, U. Minn., 1947. Diplomate Am. Bd. Surgery. Intern Faulkner Hosp., Boston, 1941; resident Boston City Hosp., 1942-44; surg. fellow Mayo Clinic, Rochester, Minn., 1944-47; pvt. practice Appleton, Wis., 1947-85, Orlando, Fla., 1985—. Fellow Am. Coll. Surgeons; mem. AMA, Wis. Surg. Soc., Southeastern Surg. Congress. Home and Office: 1915 N Forest Ave Orlando FL 32803-1520

DA FONSECA, AUGUSTO J., social worker; b. Elizabeth, N.J., May 18, 1952; s. Abilio and Emilia (Rodrigues) da F.; m. Maryann Tokasz, Aug. 7, 1976; children: Amanda Marie, Andrea Augusta. BA, U. Miami (Fla.), 1975; MSW, Barry U., Miami Shores, Fla., 1977. Diplomate Am. Bd. Examiners in Clin. Soc. Work; lic. clin. social worker, N.J.; notary public, N.J. Clin. social worker Mt. Carmel Guild Community Mental Health Ctr., Newark, 1977-78; psychiat. clinician dept. psychiatry Elizabeth Gen. Med. Ctr., 1978-81; psychiat. social worker U. Medicine and Dentistry of N.J.-N.J. Med. Sch., Newark, 1982-86; social svc. adminstr. Ironbound Ednl. and Cultural Ctr., Newark, 1986-87; renal social worker Alexian Bros. Hosp., 1988-90, Elizabeth Gen. Med. Ctr., 1990—. Active coun. of nephrology social workers Nat. Kidney Found., legis. chairperson, 1993-94; Dem. committeeman, Elizabeth, 1977-82. Mem. Nat. Assn. Social Workers, Acad. Cert. Social Workers, Soc. for Clin. and Experimental Hypnosis (assoc.), The Internat. Soc. Hynosis, KC, Elizabeth Portuguese Lions (sec. 1983-84, pres. 1984-85, 88-89, dist. 16E region chmn. 1988-89, zone chmn. 1986-87, treas. 1996—), Portuguese Instructive Social Club (Elizabeth), Portuguese Am. Congress N.J. (bd. dir. 1986—), Soc. Clin. and Exptl. Hypnosis, Internat. Soc. Hypnosis, Internat. Assn. Lions, Inc. (dist. 16 E regional chmn., treas.), Elizabeth Portuguese Lions (pres. 1984-85, 88-89). Office: 973 Grove St Elizabeth NJ 07202-3223

D'AGOSTINO, RALPH BENEDICT, mathematician, statistician, educator, consultant; b. Somerville, Mass., Aug. 16, 1940; s. Bennedetto and Carmela (Piemonte) D'A.; m. Lei Lanie Carta, Aug. 28, 1965; children: Ralph Benedict, Lei Lanie Maria. AB, Boston U., 1962, MA, 1964; PhD, Harvard U., 1968. Lectr. math. Boston U., 1964-68, asst. prof., 1968-71, assoc. prof., 1971-76, lectr. law, 1975-91, assoc. dean Grad. Sch., 1976-78, prof. math. and stats., 1976—, prof. pub. health, 1982—, dir. stats. unit Framingham Heart Study, 1985—, chmn. dept. math., 1986-91, dir. stats. cons. unit, 1986—, dir. Biostats MA/PhD Program, 1988—, prof. law, 1991—; vis. lectr. Am. Statis. Assn., 1975-86, 88—; vis. prof. biostats. clin. epidiology unit Univ. Hosp., Geneva, 1993; Rankin vis. prof. U. Wis., 1995; spl. lectr. clin. trials symposium U. Fla., 1995; vis. scientist Nat. Heart, Lung and Blood Inst., 1993; spl. scientist Boston City Hosp., 1981—, New Eng. Med. Ctr., 1990—; mem. Health Inst. New Eng. Med. Ctr., 1990—; cons. stats. United Brands, 1968-76, Diabetes and Arthritis Control Unit, Boston, 1971-75, City of Somerville, Mass., 1972, ednl. Harvard U. Dental Sch., 1969, Lahey Clinic Found., 1973-85, Walden Rsch., 1974-79, FDA Biometrics Divsn. and Over-the-Counter Divsn., 1975—, Cardio and Renal Divsn. FDA, 1987—, Gastrointestinal Drug Divsn., FDA, 1994—, Arnold & Porter, 1980, Bedford Rsch. Assn., 1976-81, Corneal Scis., 1976, Biotek, 1979-88, GCA, 1979-87, Lever Bros., 1982-87, Conrail, 1981, FBI, 1984, Ctr. Psychiat. Rehab., Boston U., 1985—, NIMH, 1985, Dade Clin. Assays, 1986-90, Millipore, 1983—, VLI Corp., 1985-90, New England Coll. Optometry, 1985—, Dupont Corp., 1985, Bristol Myers, 1986, Cheeseborough Ponds, 1987—, med. decision making divsn. and health svcs. rsch. unit Tufts New England Med. Ctr., 1986—, Am. Inst. Rsch. in Social Scis., 1983-88, New England Rsch. Insts., 1987—, Thompson Med. 1987—, Merck, Sharpe and Dohme, 1988—, Carter Ctr., Emory U., 1969—, Unilever, 1991—, Miles, 1991—, Ultra Fem., 1991-93, Health Effects Inst., 1992—, Forsyth Dental Clinic, 1992-93, 95—, Bard Vascular, 1990—, Ultra Slim Fast, 1990—, Block Med., 1993—, Bayer Pharmaceutical, 1993—, Astra Pharmaceutical, 1993—, Cytyc, 1993—, Regua, 1994—, SmithKline Beechman, 1994—, Proctor and Gamble, 1994—, Sandoz, 1994—; mem. various FDA coms. including fertility and maternal health drugs adv.com, 1978-81, life support subcom., 1979-81, drug abuse adv. com., 1987-90, gastrointestinal drugs adv. com., 1990-94, nonprescriptive drug adv. com., 1995—, chair, 1996—; mem. task force on design and analysis of dental and oral rsch., Harvard U., 1979—, health tech. com., 1986-90; mem. Honolulu Heart Study Adv. Com., NIH, 1989-96, Balt. Longitudinal Study of Aging Adv. Com., 1990, Consensus Panel on Liver Transplantation, 1983, Consensus Panel on Fresh Frozen Plasma, 1984, Consensus Panel on Geriatric Assessment Methods for Clin. Decision Making, 1987; mem. task force Office Tech. Assessment, 1980; mem. consensus panel on intraoral techniques ADA, 1990; mem. study sect. Agy. for Health Care Policy and Rsch., 1990-94; mem. Bethesda Conf. on Matching Intensity of Risk Factor Mgmt. With the Hazard for Coronary Disease Events; prin., co-prin. investigator or sr. statistician on grants Nat. Ctr. Health Svcs. Rsch., 1976-82, Nat. Heart Lung and Blood Inst., 1982—, USAF, 1980-85, Nat. Cancer Inst., 1985—, Nat. Inst. Criminal Justice, 1982-85, Nat. Ctr. Child Abuse and Neglect, 1982-85, Robert Wood Johnson Found., 1981-85, Social Security Adminstrn., 1982-86, 90-93, Motor Vehicles Mem. Assn., 1987, NIOSH, 1985, Nat. Insts. Aging, 1986—, Agency for Health Care Policy and Rsch., 1989—; grant and contract reviewer NAS, 1979—, Nat. Ctr. Health Svcs. Rsch., 1976, 89, NIH, 1983, NSF, 1987—, AHCPR, 1990—. Author: (with E.E. Cureton) Factor Analysis, An Applied Approach, 1983, (with Shuman and Wolf) Mathematical Modeling, Applications in Emergency Health Services, 1984,986, (with D. Schiff) Practical Engineering Statistics, 1996; assoc. editor Am. Statistician, 1972-76, Jour. Am. Statis. Assn., 1993—; editor Emergency Health Svc. Rev., 1981-88, Stats. in Medicine (biostat. tutorials), 1993—; mem. editl. bd. Biostatistica, 1990—; book reviewer Houghton-Mifflin, Holden, Day, Duxbury Press, Prentice Hall, 1969; contbr. articles to profl. jours.; co-developer instrument for predicting acute ischemic health disease and stroke health risk appraisal function. Recipient Spl. citation FDA Commr., 1981, 95, Metcalf awrd for excellence in teaching Boston U., 1985; Am. Heart Assn. fellow, 1991; pre-doctoral fellow NIH, 1962-68. Fellow Am. Statis. Assn. (pres. Boston chpt. 1972, v.p. 1971, mem. nat. coun. 1973-75, vis. lectr. 1976-78, 80—, Statistician of Yr. Boston chpt. 1993, chmn. sect. Health Policy Stats. 1996); mem. Am. Heart Assn. (cardiovascular epidemiology coun.), Inst. Math. Stats., Am. Soc. Quality Control, Biometrics Soc. (regional adv. com. 1989-94), Am. Pub. Health Assn. (chmn. sect. emergency health svcs. 1982-83, governing coun. 1983-85), Phi Beta Kappa, Sigma Xi. Home: 5 Everett Ave Winchester MA 01890-3523 Office: Boston U Dept Math 111 Cummington St Boston MA 02215-2411

DAHL, ANDREW WILBUR, health services executive; b. N.Y.C., Feb. 19, 1943; s. Wilbur A. and Margret L. Dahl; BS, Clark U., 1968; MPA, Cornell U., 1970; ScD, Johns Hopkins U., 1974; m. Janice White, Sept. 4, 1965; children: Kristina, Jennifer, Meredith. Staff asst. Md. Comprehensive Health Planning Agy., Balt., 1970-72; dir. planning St. John Hosp., Detroit, 1972-79; exec. v.p., COO St. John Health Corp., Detroit, 1979-85; pres., CEO United Health System, Detroit, 1983-88; v.p. devel. Hosp. Corp. Am. Mgmt. Co., 1988-90; pres., CEO IVF America Inc., Greenwich, Conn., 1990-94; pres., CEO HealthNet, Kansas City, 1994—; instr. U. Mich. Bur. Hosp. Adminstrn., 1981-88. Bd. dirs. Detroit Sci. Ctr., 1984-91; mem. Nat. Com. for Quality Health Care, Washington, 1984-89; bd. dirs. Forum Health Care Planning, Kansas City Sci. Ctr., Kansas City (Mo.) Mus., 1995—. Served with USN, 1965-67. Recipient Disting. Service award Mich. Jaycees, 1977, Outstanding Contbns. to Profl. Mgmt. award, Cornell U., 1980. Mem. AAAS, APHA, Am. Coll. Hosp. Adminstrs., Am. Hosp. Assn. (rehab. sect. bd.), Am. Assn. Health Plans, Internat. Health Econs. and Mgmt. Inst., Hallbrook Country Club, Cornell Club N.Y. Methodist. Office: 2300 Main St Ste 700 Kansas City MO 64108-2415

DAHL, DAVID S., physician, medical educator; b. Albert Lea, Minn., Mar. 17, 1936; s. Selmer J. and Dorothy L. (Lee) D.; m. Janet M. Orr, June 15, 1963; children: Sarah, Elizabeth, Christopher. AA magna cum laude, Waldorf Coll., 1956; BAin Chemistry with honors, St. Olaf Coll., 1958; MS in Anatomy, U. Iowa, 1961, MD, 1963. Diplomate Am. Bd. Psychiatry and Neurology. Straight med. intern 3rd, 4th divsns. Bellevue Med. Ctr. NYU, 1963-64; resident neurology U. Hosps., Iowa City, 1964-66; asst. prof. neurology Med. Sch. U. Wis., Madison, 1968-74; assoc. prof. neurology Med. Sch. U. Wis., Milw., 1974-79, prof. neurology, dept. chmn., 1979-91, clin. prof. neurology, 1991—; attending physician Wis. Gen. Hosp., 1968-74; head sect. neurology dept. medicine Sinai Samaritan Med. Ctr., Milw., 1974-95, attending physician, 1974—, med. dir. Variety Club Epilepsy Ctr., 1974-95; cons. neurologist Madison (Wis.) Gen. Hosp., St. Mary's Hosp., Methodist Hosp., Madison, 1968-74, Family Hosp., Milw., 1979-83; dir. chronic pain mgmt. program Mt. Sinai Med. Ctr., Milw., 1980-87, mem. exec. com. behavioral medicine program, 1981—, med. dir. dept. physical therapy, 1984-88; chmn. ethical issues in med. practice com. Sinai Samaritan Med. Ctr., Milw., 1986-94, med. dir. Headache Clinic, Mt. Sinai campus, Milw., 1987-88; mem. med. adv. coun., 1974—, affiliation computer com. , 1979-87, pharmacy and dietetic com., 1980, behavioral medicine sttering com., 1980—, ambulatory svcs. com., 1982—, ethics in med. practice com., 1982—. Contbr. numerous articles to profl. jours., chpts. to books. Grantee Muscular Dystrophy Assn. Am., 1968-74; recipient Vol. of Yr. award Epilepsy Assn. S.E. Wis., 1984, Outstanding Med. Svcs. award, 1991. Fellow Am. Acad. Neurology; mem. Am. Pain Soc., Am. Acad. Pain Medicine, Internat. Pain Soc., Alpha Omega Alpha, Sigma Xi (full mem.-at-large). Home: 2428 E Beverly Rd Milwaukee WI 53211 Office: Aurora Med Group Ste 120 1575 N River Ctr Dr Milwaukee WI 53212

DAHL, GERALD LUVERN, psychotherapist, educator, consultant, writer; b. Osage, Iowa, Nov. 10, 1938; s. Lloyd F. and Leola J. (Painter) D.; m. Judith Lee Brown, June 24, 1960; children: Peter, Stephen, Leah. BA, Wheaton Coll., 1960; MSW, U. Nebr., 1962; PhD in psychotherapy (Hon.), Internat. U. Found., 1987. Juvenile probation officer Hennepin County Ct. Svcs., 1962-65; cons. Citizens Coun. on Delinquency and Crime, Mpls., 1965-67; dir. patient svcs. Mt. Sinai Hosp., Mpls., 1967-69; clin. social worker Mpls. Clinic of Psychiatry, 1969-82, G.L. Dahl & Assocs., Inc., Mpls., 1983—; assoc. prof. social work Bethel Coll., St. Paul, 1964-83; spl. instr. sociology Golden Valley Luth. Coll., 1974-83; pres. Strategic Team-Makers, Inc., 1985—; adj. prof. U. Wis., River Falls, 1988-90. Founder Family Counseling Svc., Minn. Baptist Conf., bd. stewards, 1994—; bd. dirs. Edgewater Baptist Ch., 1972-75, chmn., 1974-75; vice-chmn. bd. stewards Minnetonka Bapt. Ch., 1995. Mem. AAUP, Am. Assn. Behavioral Therapists, Pi Gamma Mu. Author: Why Christian Marriages Are Breaking Up, 1979; Everybody Needs Somebody Sometime, 1980, How Can We Keep Christian Marriages from Falling Apart, 1988, The Sandwich Family, 1995; contbr. articles to profl. jours. Office: 4825 Highway 55 Ste 140 Minneapolis MN 55422-5155

DAHL, LAUREL JEAN, human services administrator; b. Chgo.; d. James Edward and Gladys Uarda (Boquist) Findlay; m. Philip Nels Dahl, Aug. 29, 1970; children: Eric Nels, John Philip. BA, Trinity Coll., 1970; MS in Human Svcs., Nat. Louis U., 1992. Cert. sr. alcohol and other drug preventionist. Tchr. Grove Sch., Lake Forest, Ill., 1971, Little Bear Child Care Ctr., Waukegan, Ill., 1975-77; sec. to dir. Strang Funeral Home, Antioch, Ill., 1981-87; comptroller, office mgr. Village of Antioch, 1987-92; prevention specialist Lake County Dept. of Health: Mental Health Div., 1992; community coord. Fighting Back Project of Lake County, Round Lake, Ill., 1992-94; prevention adminstr. No. Ill.Coun. on Alcoholism and Substance Abuse, Lake, 1994—; adj. faculty Nat. Louis U., 1994—. Mem. Antioch Comty. H.S. Bd. Edn., 1987-95, pres., 1991-95, sec., 1989-91; mem. Antioch Comty. H.S. Drug Task Force, MADD; past pres. PTO; mem. adv. bd. WAY; bd. dirs. COURAGE; vice chair Human Svc. Coun., 1994-96, chmn., 1996—; mem. peer rev. com. Ill. Alcohol and Other Drug Abuse Profl. Cert. Assn., 1996—; mem. women's bd. No. Ill. Coun. on Alcoholism and Substance Abuse, 1996—; pres. Human Svc. Coun., 1996—. Recipient commendation for Gt. Lakes Naval Tng. Ctr. for Drug Edn. for Youth, 1994-95, Disting. Svc. award Ill. chpt. Nat. Sch. Pub. Rels. Assn., Enrique Camarena "One Person Can" award, 1995. Mem. Alliance Against Intoxicated Motorists, Ill. Student Assistance Profls., Ill. Assn. for Prevention. Home: PO Box 613 Antioch IL 60002-0613

DAHL, SANDRA TRIMBLE, nursing administrator; b. Birmingham, Ala., Nov. 4, 1952; d. Robert M. Jr. and Margaret Ann (Smith) Trimble Sessons; m. W. Alan Dahl, Aug. 25, 1973; children: Matthew Alan, David Stuart, Robert Drayton. BSN, Alderson-Broaddus Coll., Philippi, W.Va., 1974; MA in Mgmt./Healthcare Adminstrn., Coll. of Notre Dame, Balt. RN, Pa., Md.; cert. CPR instr., childbirth edn. specialist, cmty. health nurse ANA. Project coord. Tel-A-Teen, Health Edn. Ctr., Pitts., 1983-86; staff nurse Balt. Med. System, Inc., 1986-87, dir. patient edn. and staff devel., 1987-88, dir. support svcs., 1988-89, dir. contract and grants devel., 1989-90; dir. Helix Tele Health Ctr./Ask-A-Nurse, Balt., 1990—; dir. ask-a-nurse program Helix Health System. Recipient M. Frances Etchberger Nursing award Md. Pub. Health Assn. Mem. Am. Assn. Ambulatory Care Nursing (co-chair telephone nursing practice spl. interest grop), Am. Acad. Ambulatory Care Nursing (program chmn. Mid-Atlantic networking group). Home: 7924 34th St Baltimore MD 21237-1408 Office: 4979 N Mercantile Rd Baltimore MD 21236

DAHLBEN, SALIN ABRAHAM, neuropsychiatrist; b. Rio de Janeiro, Brazil, Nov. 2, 1945; s. Abraham and Emilia D.; m. Sonia Sapolnik, July 8, 1971 (div. 1975); m. Jean Annette Leupold, Nov. 7, 1982 (div. 1996); children: Deborah, Rachael Emily, Lindsay Johanna, Joshua Robert, Brian Andre. BS, Hebrew Coll., Rio de Janeiro, 1963; MD, Fed. U. Rio de Janeiro, 1969. Cert. Bd. Med. Quality Assurance, Calif., Diplomate Am. Bd. Psychiatry and Neurology, Mem. med. staff Naval Hosp., Rio de Janeiro, 1970-71; intern, Mt. Sinai Hosp. Services, N.Y.C., 1973-74; resident Boston City Hosp., 1974-75; fellow in neurosurgery Lahey Clinic, Boston, 1975-76; resident in neurosurgery, U. Iowa Hosps., Iowa City, 1976-78, resident in psychiatry, 1979-80; chief resident Mt. Sinai Hosp. Med. Ctr., Chgo., 1981; med. unit dir. Bridgewater State Hosp., 1983-85; med. dir. Dorchester Mental Health Ctr., Mass., 1985-87; asst. psychiatrist McLean Hosp., Belmont, Mass., 1983—; clin. instr. psychiatry Harvard Med. Sch., Boston, 1983—; clin. assoc. Mass. Gen. Hosp., 1988—; assoc. Cambridge Hosp., 1990—. Served to 1st lt. M.C. Brazilian Navy, 1970-71. Recipient prize, Assn. Med. Students, Rio de Janeiro, 1968, 1969; Nat. Council for Research scholar, 1969-70; recipient Abbey Norman Prince award, Mt. Sinai Hosp.

Med. Ctr., Chgo., 1981. Mem. Am. Psychiat. Assn., Mass. Psychiatric Soc., Mass. Med. Soc., N.Y. Acad. Scis., Sigma Xi. Club: Harvard Faculty. Office: 10 Hammond Pond Pkwy Ste 606 Chestnut Hill MA 02167-2125

DAHLE, CHARLENE G., administrator; b. Balt., May 3, 1951; d. John Aaron Dettmer and Alice May (Holdorf) Wells; m. Elkins William Dahle III, Jan. 9, 1971; children: Elkins W. IV, Reneé T. ADN, Essex C.C., 1980; BS in Health Care Adminstrn., St. Joseph's Coll., 1991; postgrad. Utilization/quality assurance retrospective reviewer Delmarva Found. for Med. Care, Inc., 1987-88; lead quality assurance/risk mgmt. coord. Johns Hopkins Med. Svcs. Corp., 1988-92; dir. quality improvement/risk mgmt. patient advocacy Desert Springs Hosp., 1992-93; total quality mgmt. cons. Mission Hosp., 1994; dir. health svcs. Delmarva Rural Ministries, 1995, managed care rev. mgr., 1995—. Mem. NAFE, Am. Coll. Health Care Execs., Nat. Assn. for Healthcare Quality, Am. Hosp. Assn. Risk Mgmt. Soc., Soroptimist Internat. Democrat. Roman Catholic. Home: 21385 Island Club Rd Tilghman MD 21671 Office: Delmarva Found for Med Care Inc 9240 Centreville Rd Easton MD 21601

DAHLEN, ROGER WAYNE, health science administrator; b. Iola, Wis., Sept. 7, 1935; s. Orin E. and Marian (Tobie) D.; m. Karen Hackleman, may 3, 1986; children: Peggy A., Garth M., Todd S., Tara L. BA, Luther Coll., 1956; MS, U. Iowa, 1958, PhD in Physiology, 1960. Instr. Boston U. Sch. Medicine, Boston, 1960-62; asst. prof. N.J. Coll. Medicine, Jersey City, 1962-68; program officer Nat. Heart Lung & Blood Inst., Bethesda, Md., 1968-71; chief biomed. info. Nat. Libr. Medicine, NIH, Bethesda, 1971—; bd. regents Upsala Coll., East Orange, N.J., 1964-68. Contbr. 15 sci. articles to profl. jours. Grantee NIH, Am. Heart Assn., N.J. Heart Assn. Home: 10958 Trotting Ridge Way Columbia MD 21044-2834 Office: Nat Libr Medicine 8600 Rockville Pike Bethesda MD 20894-0001

DAHLQUIST, KAREN, emergency services nurse, educator; b. Phila., Mar. 14, 1957; d. Robert Henry and Merle Louise (Hollingsworth) Oetting; m. Paul Joseph Dahlquist, June 1, 1984; children: Kathleen, Amanda, Paul, Jr. ADN, Gloucester County Coll., 1978; BSN, Thomas Jefferson U., 1986. Flight nurse Nat. Air Ambulance, Phila.; charge nurse emergency dept. Meth. Hosp., Phila., evening adminstr.; supr. emergency dept. Sacred Heart Med. Ctr., Chester, Pa.; instr. Presbyn. Med. Ctr. Sch. of Practical Nursing; mem. faculty Meth. Hosp. Sch. Nursing; mem. Delaware County Emergency Health Svcs. Coun., 1988, 89; mem. adj. faculty Gloucester County Coll., 1991-93. Mem. Delaware County Emergency Nurses Assn. (treas. 1989, pres.-elect 1990), Sigma Theta Tau. Home: 214 Colonial Ave Woodbury NJ 08096-1008

DAHLSTRÖM, HANS ALBERT, physician; b. Stockholm, May 14, 1920; s. Albert Fabian and Olga Maria (Aberg) D.; m. Kerstin Cecilia Amelin, June 7, 1947; children: Göran D., Birgitta Holmberg, Louise D., Olov Amelin. MD, Karolinska Inst., Stockholm, 1950. With Clin. Physiol. Labs., Stockholm and Umeå, Sweden, 1950-51, 55-60; rsch. asst. Washington U., St. Louis, 1952-54; rsch. dir. Ab Kabi, Stockholm, 1960-71; gen. mgr. Serono, Stockholm, 1981-85, chmn. bd., 1986-90. Editor Contenta Serono, 1982-92; contbr. articles on clin. physiology and pharmacology, 1948-93. Home: Nockebybacke 8B/485, 16840 Bromma Sweden

DAHM, LIDA INGE SWAFFORD, pediatric anesthesiologist; b. Norfolk, Va., Aug. 18, 1937; d. Chester Arthur and Lida Tunstall (Inge) Swafford; m. Karl Heinz Dahm, Dec. 21, 1968; children: Elizabeth, Karl, Paul, AnneMarie. BA, Tulane U., 1959, MD, 1962. Cert. Am. Bd. Anesthesiology. Resident in anesthesiology Columbia-Presbyn. Med. Ctr., N.Y.C., 1963-66; vis. physician, chief resident Columbia Presbyn. Med. Ctr., N.Y.C., 1965-66; attending physician, asst. prof. Children's Meml. Hosp. Northwestern U., Chgo., 1966-68; asst. prof. anesthesiology and pediatrics Baylor Coll., Houston, 1969-85, clin. asst. prof. anesthesiology and pediatrics, 1985-90; dir. of anesthesiology Angleton (Tex.)-Danbury Gen. Hosp., 1990-94; dir. anesthesiology Yale Hosp., Houston, 1992—; vis. prof. numerous colls. Contbg. author: Management of Spasticity, 1985, Principle and Practice Nurse, 1987; contbr. articles to profl. jours. Layreader St. John the Divine Episcopal Ch., Houston, 1984—. Fellow Am. Acad. Pediatrics (sect. sec. 1972, vice-chmn. 1978), Am. Coll. Anethesiology, Kappa Alpha Theta. Club: Briar (Houston). Home: 4634 Banning Dr Houston TX 77027-4706 Office: Yale Hosp 510 W Tidwell St Houston TX 77091

DAHMS, KATHY GREENE, maternal women's health nurse, educator; b. Stamford, Conn., June 6, 1952; d. Clark Harper and Mabel (Foster) Greene; m. Russell W. Dahms, Sept. 11, 1982; children: Caitlin, Russell W. Jr., Evan. BA, U. So. Maine, 1974; cert., Paralegal Inst., N.Y.C., 1976; ADN, Westbrook Coll., Portland, Maine, 1981. RN, Maine. Exec. paralegal Moskowitz & Passman, N.Y.C., 1975-79; paralegal Ainsworth & Ainsworth, Portland, Maine, 1979-80; nursing supr. Osteo. Hosp. Maine, Portland, 1986-87, staff nurse maternal-women's health unit, 1980-96; staff nurse Mercy Hosp. "Birthplace", 1995—; expert med./legal cons. Author: (coloring book) Big Brother/Big Sister to Be. Co-founder Childbirth Discovery Edn. Mem. AWOHNN (cert.).

DAI, JING CHU LING, medical writer, researcher, consultant; b. Tacoma, Wash.; d. Yunan and Yet Sze Ling; m. Shenyu Dai (div.); children: Alexander M., Benjamin M. Student Temple U., 1960-63; BA in Journalism, Calif. State U., Long Beach, 1968; MPH, UCLA, 1977; CME, U. So. Calif., 1984. Mgr. med. order dept. J.B. Lippincott Co., Phila., 1956-62; copy editor Annals Internal Medicine, 1962; pub. rels. asst., editor Linton's Inc., Phila., 1962-64; exec. editor Bearing & Transmission Specialist, 1971-72; dir. publs. City of Hope Nat. Med. Ctr., Duarte, Calif., 1972-74; sr. proposal engr., writer, subcontractor for aerospace cos., 1965-66, 79-82, 86—; med. affairs rsch. cons., Gravity Guidance, Inc., Pasadena, Calif., 1982-84; freelance writer, cons.; rsch. cons. Musculo-Skeletal Clinic, Pasadena, 1982-84. Condr. study on Calif. marriage laws as preventative for congenital syphilis and congenital rubella, 1977; contbr. articles to profl. jours. Bd. dirs., v.p. Bougless-White Scholarship Found., Long Beach, 1967-71, mem., 1965—; publicity adviser Am. Cancer Soc., L.A., 1975; adv. Metric Cert. Specialist Bd., U.S. Metric Assn., 1981—. USPHS grantee, UCLA, 1975-77. Mem. Women in Comm. (chmn. careers conf., L.A., 1975, award 1975), Am. Med. Writers Assn., Am. Pub. Health Assn., Nat. Assn. Female Execs., Assn. Health Svc. Rsch., Soc. Tech. Comm. (chmn. ways/means, internat. tech. com. conf. 1978), Women's Internat. Friendship League (co-founder 1943), Coun. Biology Editors, U.S. Metric Assn. (planning com. ann. conf. 1987). Home: 320 S Gramercy Pl Los Angeles CA 90020-4543

DAICOFF, BARBARA BLUE, nursing education, researcher; b. Chgo., May 7, 1947; d. Thurman Edward and Sara Elizabeth (McCarthy) Blue; m. George Ronald Daicoff, June 24, 1972 (div. May 14, 1982); 1 child, Nicholas George Daicoff. BSN, Ind. U., Indpls., 1970; MSN, U. Fla., 1976, PhD, 1993. RN, Mass.; cert. pediat. advanced life support. Staff nurse, asst. burn unit James Whitcomb Riley Hosp., Indpls., 1968-70; staff nurse pediat. ICU James Whitcomb Riley Hosp. for Children, Indpls., 1970; head nurse NICU Univ. Hosp., Jacksonville, Fla., 1971-72; head nurse ICU No. Fla. Regional Hosp., Gainesville, Fla.; office mgr., nurse cons. private MD practice, St. Petersburg, Fla., 1977-80; staff nurse ICU, nurse mgr. All Children's Hosp., St. Petersburg, 1985-90; per diem ICU nurse Shands Hosp., Gainesville, 1990-91; asst. prof. rsch. asst. U. Fla., Gainesville, 1991-94; asst. prof. Boston Coll. Sch. Nursing, Chestnut Hill, Mass., 1994—; per diem Cardiovascular ICU, Children's Hosp., Boston. Grantee Gatorade, 1991-92, Boston Coll., 1995. Mem. ANA, AACN, Nat. Assn. Neonatal Nurses, Soc. Pediat. Cardiovascular Nurses Soc., N.E. Pediat. Cardiology Nurses Assn., Coun. on Cardiovascular Nursing, Sigma Theta Tau. Home: 93 Arrowhead Circle Ashland MA 01721 Office: Boston Coll. Sch. Nursing Cushing Hall 334E Chestnut Hill MA 02167-3812

DAIGLE, DARLENE, psychotherapist; b. White Castle, La., Sept. 10, 1951; d. Floyd Joseph and Marian Ann (Labarthe) D. BSW, U. Tex., Arlington, 1981, MSW, 1983. Lic. social worker, Tex., marriage and family therapist, Tex., chem. dependecncy counselor, Tex. Edn. cons. psychotherapist Parenting Guidance Svc., Ft. Worth; psychotherapist, cons. Family Svcs., Ft. Worth, 1983-85, Porfl. Svc. assn., Hurst, Tex., 1984-85; psychotherapist Daigle Counseling Svcs., Summer Sky, Tex., 1985—; mem. Tarrant Coun. on Alcoholism and Drug Abuse.; participant workshops on eating disorders, sexual abuse, co-dependency, dissociation, alcohol and drug abuse, marriage, families, child abuse, HIV/AIDS, ethics. Mem. Nat. Assn. social Workers, Mental Health Assn., Tex. Alcohol and Drug Abuse Assn., Alpha Delta Mu, Alpha Chi, Alpha Kappa Delta. Office: 2201 Midway Ste 304 Carrollton TX 75006

DAILEY, HARRY ALVA, microbiology educator, biomedical researcher; b. Santa Cruz, Calif., Feb. 21, 1950; s. Harry Alva and Eleanor Florence (Bradbury) D.; m. Tamara Lynn Andrew, Nov. 25, 1989. BA, U. Calif., Los Angeles, 1972, PhD in Microbiology, 1976. Teaching asst. dept. microbiology U. Calif., Los Angeles, 1972-73, rsch. asst., 1973-76; postdoctoral fellow dept. biochem. U. Conn. Health Ctr., Farmington, 1976-80; asst. prof. microbiology U. Ga., Athens, 1980-85, assoc. prof. and actind head, 1985-90, prof. and head, 1990—. Editor and author: Biosynthesis of Heme and Chlorophyll, 1990; contbr. articles to profl. jours. Recipient summer undergrad. fellowship NSF, Los Angeles, 1971; postdoctoral fellow Am. Heart Assn., Conn., 1977-78; recipient Rsch. Career Devel. award NIH, 1982-87; rsch. grantee NIH, 1981—. Mem. Am. Soc. Biochem. and Molecular Biology, Am. Soc. Microbiology, Protein Soc(tetrapyrrole group). Office: Univ Ga Dept Microbiology Athens GA 30602-2605

DAILEY, THOMAS HAMMOND, surgeon; b. Orange, N.J.; s. Louis Bird and Evelyn (Hammond) D.; m. Denise Benzacar Dailey, Aug. 22, 1959; children: Andrea, Erika, Seth. AB, Princeton U., 1957; MD, Cornell U. Med. Coll., 1961. Assoc. prof. clin. surgery Coll. Physicians and Surgeons, N.Y.C., 1991; sr. attending dept. surgery St. Luke's-Roosevelt Hosp. Ctr., N.Y.C., 1982, dir. div. colon and rectal surgery, 1990-96, chief med. officer, 1996—; pres. med. bd. St. Luke's-Roosevelt Hosp., N.Y.C., 1989-91; v.p. Rsch. Found. of Am. Soc. Colon and Rectal Surgeons, pres., 1995. Capt. M.C., U.S. Army, 1966-68, Vietnam. Capt. U.S. Army Med. Corps., 1966-68, Vietnam. Mem. Med. Strollers, Physician's Sci. Soc., N.Y. Soc. of Colon and Rectal Surgeons (pres. 1979-81). Office: St Lukes Roosevelt Hosp Ctr 1111 Amsterdam Ave New York NY 10025

DAILY, LOUIS, ophthalmologist; b. Houston, Apr. 23, 1919; s. Louis and Ray (Karchmer) D.; B.S., Harvard U., 1940; M.D., U. Tex. at Galveston, 1943; Ph.D., U. Minn., 1950; m. LaVerl Daily, Apr. 5, 1958; children: Evan Ray, Collin Derek (dec.). Intern, Jefferson Davis Hosp., Houston, 1943-44; resident in ophthalmology Jefferson Davis Hosp., 1944-45, Mayo Found., Rochester, Minn., 1947-50; individual practice medicine, specializing in ophthalmology, Houston, 1950—; clin. assoc. prof. ophthalmology U. Tex-Houston, 1972-86, Baylor Med. Sch., Houston, 1950—. Vice pres. bd. dirs. Mus. Med. Sci., 1973-85, pres., 1980-82. Served as lt. (j.g.) USNR, 1945-46. Diplomate Am. Bd. Ophthalmology. Fellow A.C.S., Internat. Coll. Surgeons; mem. Soc. Prevention of Blindness (med. chmn. Tex. 1968-70), Contact Lens Assn. Ophthalmologists (exec. bd. 1976-78), Tex. Ophthal. Assn. (pres. 1963-64), Houston Ophthal. Soc. (pres. 1970-71), numerous other med. socs., Sigma Xi, Alpha Omega Alpha. Jewish. Clubs: Doctors, Harvard (dir. 1965-66) (Houston). Editorial bd. Jour. Pediatric Ophthalmology, 1964-68; asso. editor Eye, Ear, Nose and Throat Monthly, 1962-65, Jour. Ophthalmic Surgery, 1970; contbr. numerous articles to profl. publs., also contbr. to books. Home: 2523 Maroneal St Houston TX 77030-3117 Office: 1517 Med Towers 1709 Dryden Rd Houston TX 77030-2400

DAILY, WILLIAM ALLEN, retired microbiologist; b. Indpls., Nov. 10, 1912; s. Thomas Alvin Daily and Mary Bernice Swengel; m. Eva Fay Kenoyer, June 24, 1937. BS, Butler U., 1936; MS, Northwestern U., 1938. Asst. sr. microbiologist Eli Lilly Co., Indpls., 1941-77. Co-author: Coccoid Myxophceae, 1956, History of Indiana Academy of Science 1885-1984, 1984. Curator cryptogamic bot. herbarium biology dept. Butler U., Indpls. 1941—. Mem. Ind. Acad. Sci. (pres. 1958), Phycological Soc. Am. (pres. 1958), Bot. Soc. Am., Sigma Xi. Republican. Home: 5884 Compton St Indianapolis IN 46220-2653

DAJANI, ESAM ZAPHER, pharmacologist; b. Jaffa, Palestine, May 30, 1940; came to U.S., 1958; s. Zapher Rageb and Mamdouha (Dajani) D.; m. Najwa Said Beidas, July 16, 1964; children: Mona, Zapher, Nora. BS in Pharmacy, U. Mo., 1963; MS in Pharmacology and Med. Chemistry, Auburn U., 1966; PhD in Pharmacology, Purdue U., 1969. Sr. pharmacologist Rohm and Hass Co., 1968-72; sr. rsch. investigator G.D. Searle and Co., Chgo., 1972-74, group leader, 1974-80, chmn. G.I. diseases, 1974-80, sect. head, 1980, asst. dir., 1980-82, assoc. dir., 1982-85, dir. Cytotec sci. and med. affairs, 1985-87, dir. clin. rsch., 1987-93; pres. Internat. Drug Devel. Cons. Corp., Long Grove, Ill., 1993—; mem. editl. adv. bd. Drug Devel. Rsch., Dallas, 1983-93, Jour. Assn. Acad. Minority Physicians, Bklyn., 1992—, Jour. Physiology and Pharmacology, Krakow, Poland, 1993—; adj. prof. medicine UCLA, 1984-95; adj. prof. medicine Loyola U., Chgo., 1995—. Editor: Gastrointestinal Cytoprotection, 1987; author: (with others) Prostaglandins and GI Mucosa, 1987, Pharmacology of Misoprostol, 1989, Prostaglandins and Esophagus, 1991, Pharmaceutical Industry Perspective, 1991, Prevention and Treatment of Ulcers induced by NSAIDS, 1995; contbr. numerous rsch. papers, book chpts., and presentations in field; patentee in field. Mem. Arab-Am. Anti-discrimination Com., Washington, 1972, Arab-Am. U. Grads., Washington, 1991. Recipient Edward M. Queeny award, Monsanto Corp., 1991; named Disting. Alumnus Purdue U., 1991. Fellow Am. Coll. Gastroenterology; mem. Am. Soc. Pharmacology and Exptl. Therapeutics, Am. Gastroent. Assn., Am. Pharm. Assn., European Soc. Gastroenterology and Endoscopy, Assn. Acad. Minority Physicians, N.Y. Acad. Sci., Rho Chi, Phi Kappa Phi. Office: Inter Drug Devel Cons Corp Divsn Mid Gulf USA Inc 1549 RFD Long Grove IL 60047-9532

DAKAS, JEFFREY LEE, cardiologist; b. Belle Vernon, Pa., Oct. 23, 1955; s. Jack Edward and Elaine Victoria (Wood) D.; m. Sherri Ann Harnsberger, Mar. 21, 1986; children: Erin, Nora. BS in Biology, St. Vincent Coll., 1977; MS in Physiology, Georgetown U., 1979, MD, 1993. Intern Mercy Hosp. of Pitts., 1983-84; resident Letterman Army Med. Ctr., San Francisco, 1986-88; commd. U.S. Army, 1984-94; ret.; staff internist U.S. Army, Ft. Monmouth, N.J., 1988-90; chief dept. of medicine, 1989-90; staff internist U.S. Army, Ft. Belvoir, Va., 1990-94; asst. prof. med. U.S. Univ. Health Scis., Bethesda, Md., 1992-94; chief emergency rm. U.S. Univ. Health Scis., Soto Cano Air Base, Honduras, 1993; staff physician VA Med. Ctr., Huntington, W.Va., 1994-95; cardiology fellow Marshall U., Huntington, 1995—. Mem. ACP, Am. Coll. Cardiology (affiliate-in-tng.). Office: Univ Physicians Surgeons 2828 1st Ave Ste 300 Huntington WV 25702

DAKOFSKY, LADONNA JUNG, radiation oncologist, educator; b. N.Y.C., Oct. 30, 1960; d. George S. and Kay (Han) Chung. BA magna cum laude, Columbia U., N.Y.C., 1982; MD, NYU, 1987. Bd. cert. radiation oncologist. Rsch. asst. dept. neurology UCLA, 1980-81, Harvard U., Boston, 1982; tchr. chemistry St. Ann's Sch., Brooklyn Heights, N.Y., 1982-83; resident in internal medicine Lenox Hill Hosp., N.Y.C., 1987-88; resident in radiation oncology Hosp. of U. Pa., Phila., 1988-91; instr. in radiation oncology New Eng. Med. Ctr., Boston, 1991-92; attending physician Norwalk (Conn.) Hosp., 1992—; clin. asst. prof. radiation oncology Yale U., 1994—; prin. investigator RTOG cancer rsch. Norwalk Hosp. Mem. jr. com. Boys Club N.Y.; sponsor Mus. City of N.Y.; mem. com. Vocat. Found., N.Y.c.; mem. Jr. League of Stamford-Norwalk. Marine Biol. Lab. scholar, 1981. Mem. AMA, Assn. Therapeutic Radiology and Oncology, Fairfield County Med. Assn., New Eng. Cancer Soc., Met. Breast Cancer Group. Presbyterian. Office: Norwalk Hosp Radiation Oncology Box 5050 Norwalk CT 06856

DALBY, ALAN JAMES, pharmaceutical company executive; b. Glasgow, Scotland, Jan. 15, 1937; s. William J. P. and Elizabeth Jean (MacKenzie) D.; children: A. Royce, Mark. B.S., Paisley Coll., 1958. Analytical chemist Smith Kline & French Labs., Can., 1958; mgmt. trainee SK&F, Phila., 1960-61; gen. mgr. consumer products div. Menley & James Labs., Can., 1963-65; dir. mktg. SK&F, Can., 1966-71; v.p. comml. devel. Worldwide Pharms., Phila., 1971-72, v.p. Europe, Africa, India, Brussels, 1972-75, v.p. internat., 1975-80, pres., from 1980; exec. v.p. therapeutics products group Smith Kline Corp. (now SmithKline Beecham), Phila., 1980-87; pres. SmithKline and French Labs., Phila., 1980-87, also mem. corp. bd. dirs., 1987-94; bd. dirs. Reckitt & Colman, PLC, 1995—; chmn. Reckitt & Colman, PLC, Immulogic Pharm. Corp., Alteon, Inc., Mass. Eye & Ear Infirmary. Mem. Hyannisport Golf Club, Somerset Club (Boston). Republican. Episcopalian. Office: Reckitt & Colman, 1 Burlington Ln, London W4 2RW, England

DALDAL, M. FEVZI, molecular biologist, geneticist; b. Istanbul, Turkey, Mar. 3, 1950; came to U.S., 1978; s. Mustafa Rebi and Ayse Kadriye (Abaci) D.; m. Nur Selamoglu, May 7, 1988. BS and MS, INSA, 1974; PhD, U. Strasbourg, 1977. Rsch. assoc. Harvard Med. Sch., Boston, 1981-82; staff scientist Cold Spring Harbor (N.Y.) Lab., 1983-87, sr. staff scientist, 1987-88; assoc. prof. U. Pa., Phila., 1988-95, prof., 1995—; reviewer in field. Contbr. over 70 articles to profl. jours. NIH, DOE grantee. Mem. AAAS, Am. Soc. for Microbiology, Biophys. Soc. Home: 409 S Taney St Philadelphia PA 19146-1042 Office: U Pa Dept Biology Philadelphia PA 19104

DALDERUP, LOUISE MARIA, medical and chemical toxicologist, nutritionist; b. Rotterdam, Netherlands, Oct. 22, 1925; d. Clemens Bernardus Franciscus Maria and Jacoba Diedericka Louise (Wever) D. PhD in Physiol. Chemistry, U. Amsterdam, 1949, MD, 1957. Cert. social medicine, pub. health, Amsterdam, 1966, occupational health, Leiden, 1974. From jr.rsch. asst. to mgr. lab. and animal dept. Netherlands Inst. Nutrition, Amsterdam, 1948-70; sr. med. inspector to factory inspectorate Ministry of Social Affairs and Employment, Amsterdam, 1971-90; ret.; mem. Netherlands Nutrition Coun. and its expert coms. on dental caries (fluoride), cardiovascular diseases, 1958-85; mem. expert com. pesticide first aid measures for gen. practitioner Netherlands Pub. Health Coun., 1980-90; mem. expert com. prevention of radioactive contamination of food and feed Ministry of Agr. and Fishery, 1966-90; cons. Netherlands Office Nutritional Edn., 1970-79, Netherlands Heart Assn., 1972-80; expert com. Treshold Limit Values for Chem. in working environ., 1976-91. Author: Nutrition and Dental Caries, 1959, Myocardial Infarction and Risk Factors and Prevention, 1974; contbr. over 150 articles to profl. jours. Mem. med. com. drafting safety cards, 1980—, com. safety and hygiene in hosps., 1988-93. Decorated Officer of Order of Oranje-Nassau, 1990. Mem. Netherlands Med. Assn., Netherlands Chem. Assn.

DALE, DAVID C., physician, medical educator; b. Knoxville, Tenn., Sept. 19, 1940; s. John Irvin and Cecil (Chandler) D.; m. Rose Marie Wilson, June 22, 1963. BS magna cum laude, Carson-Newman Coll., 1962; MD cum laude, Harvard U., 1966. Intern and resident Mass. Gen. Hosp., 1966-68; resident U. Wash. Hosp., Seattle, 1971-72; clin. assoc. NIH, 1968-71; prof., assoc. chmn. dept. medicine U. Wash., Seattle, 1976-82, dean Sch. of Medicine, 1982-86. Contbr. numerous articles to profl. jours. Served to comdr. USPHS, 1968-70, 72-74. Mem. Am. Soc. Hematology, Assn. Am. Physicians, Am. Soc. for Clin. Investigation, ACP. Office: U Wash Sch of Medicine RG-22 Seattle WA 98195

DALE, KATHY GAIL, rehabilitation rheumatology nurse; b. Evansville, Ind., Sept. 28, 1954; d. Albert Joseph and Doris Maxine (Dunning) D. ADN, U. Evansville, 1975, BSN, 1986; MS in Health Svcs. Adminstrn., Coll. of St. Francis, Joliet, Ill., 1992. RN, Tenn., Ind.; cert. rehab. registered nurse. Staff nurse St. Mary's Med. Ctr., Evansville, Ind., 1975-86, Vanderbilt Med. Ctr., Nashville, 1986-87; head nurse St. Thomas Hosp., Nashville, 1987-89; referral coord. Edgefield Rehab. Ctr., Nashville, 1989-90; nurse educator Arthritis and Osteoporosis Care Ctr. at Bapt. Hosp., Nashville, 1990—. Contbr. articles to profl. jours. Mem. Assn. Rehab. Nurses, Tenn. Assn. Rehab. Nurses (pres.-elect 1990, 94, pres. 1991, 95, bd. dirs. 1992, 96), Am. Assn. Neurosci. Nurses. Home: 865 Bellevue Rd Apt D-18 Nashville TN 37221-2759 Office: Arthritis and Osteoporosis Care Ctr at Bapt Hosp Bapt Hosp-Med Office Bldg 300 20th Ave N Ste G-1 Nashville TN 37203-2115

DALEN, JAMES EUGENE, physician, educator; b. Seattle, Apr. 1, 1932; s. Charles A. and Muriel E. (Joanise) Robinson. BS, Wash. State U., 1955; MA, U. Mich., 1956; MD, U. Wash., 1961; MS, Harvard U., 1972. Intern and asst. med. resident Boston City Hosp., 1961-63; sr. resident New Eng. Med. Ctr., Boston, 1963-64; research fellow in cardiology Peter Bent Brigham Hosp., Boston, 1964-67, asso. dir. cardiovascular lab., 1967-75; instr., asst. prof., asso. prof. medicine Harvard Med. Sch., 1967-75; chmn. dept. cardiovascular medicine U. Mass. Med. Sch., 1975-77, prof., chmn. dept. medicine, 1977-88; physician-in-chief U. Mass. Hosp., 1977-88; acting chancellor U. Mass. at Worcester, 1986-87; dean, vice provost med. affairs U. Ariz. Coll. of Medicine, Tucson, 1988-92; v.p., dean coll. medicine Health Scis., Tucson, 1995; v.p. health scis. U. Ariz. Coll. Medicine, Tucson, 1995—. Contbr. articles to med. jours.; editor: Archives of Internal Medicine, 1987—. Served with USN, 1951-53. Mem. A.C.P., Am. Clin. and Climatol. Soc., Assn. Univ. Cardiologists, Am. Coll. Cardiology, Am. Coll. Chest Physicians (pres. 1985-86), Am. Fedn. Clin. Research. Home: 5305 N Via Velazquez Tucson AZ 85715-5989 Office: U Ariz Coll Medicine Tucson AZ 85724-5018

DALE RIIKONEN, CHARLENE BOOTHE, international health administrator; b. Washington, June 10, 1942; d. John Edward and Frances Elizabeth (Jett) Boothe; m. Esko Riikonen, 1989; children: Cynthia Lee, Anthony John, Jennifer Elizabeth. AA with high honors, Howard Community Coll., 1977; BA magna cum laude, U. Md., 1979. Asst. dir. univ. rels., alumni dir. U. Md., Catonsville, 1977-81; assoc. dir. univ. rels. and devel. U. Md., College Park, 1982-83; sr. devel. officer Internat. Ctr. Diarrhoeal Disease Rsch., Dhaka, Bangladesh, 1984-86; exec. v.p. Child Health Found. (formerly Internat. Child Health Found.), Columbia, Md., 1985—; cons. to organize symposium oral rehydration therapy Nat. Coun. Internat. Health, Washington, 1987; organizer internat. symposium on food-based oral rehydration therapy Aga Khan U., Pakistan, 1989; organizer consensus conf. cereal-based oral rehydration therapy, Columbia, Md., 1993. Author: (tng. manual) Prevention and Treatment of Childhood Diarrhea with Oral Rehydration Therapy, Nutrition and Breastfeeding, 1992; editor procs. Oral Rehydration Therapy Symposia, 1987, 89, 93, 94; editor Child Health News, 1993—; contbr. articles to profl. jours. Pub. affairs chmn. United Way, Washington Capital Area, Prince Georges County, 1981-83; v.p. Waterfowl Assn.; pres. Windstream Assn., 1988-89; v.p. Waterfowl Terrace Assn., 1994—; mem. pub. rels. com. Md., Del. Cable TV Assn., Balt., 1981-83. Mem. APHA (internat. maternal-child health com.), AAUW, Nat. Coun. Internat. Health Assn., U. Md. Balt. County Alumni Assn. (bd. dirs. 1979-83), Women's Internat. Pub. Health Network. Democrat. Club: Columbia Assn. Athletic (Md.) (capt. women's traveling racquetball team 1979-83).

DALES, ELSA REUTERWALL, nurse; b. Ossining, N.Y., Apr. 7, 1937; d. Owen and Helda (Nelson) Reuterwall; m. Lawrence Graham Dales, Sept. 14, 1958; children: Victoria, Barbara, Kenneth, Janet. Diploma, St. Luke's Sch. Nursing, N.Y.C., 1958. Cert. RN in intravenous therapy. IV therapy and critical care nurse St. Agnes Hosp., White Plains, N.Y., 1980-88; coord. IV therapy, coord. outpatient infusion svcs. Greenwich (Conn.) Hosp., 1988-96; nurse supr. ARC-Conn. Blood Svcs., White Plains, 1996—. Patentee in field. Mem. Intravenous Nurses Soc. (CRNI cert.).

D'ALESANDRO, PHILIP ANTHONY, parasitologist, immunologist, retired educator; b. Bound Brook, N.J., Apr. 2, 1927; s. Philip and Antoinette Ann (Vaccaro) D'A.; m. Rosemary Natale Falzarine, Nov. 25, 1961. BSc, Rutgers U., 1952, MSc, 1954; PhD, U. Chgo., 1958. Rsch. assoc. U. Chgo., 1958-59; assoc. prof. Rockefeller U., N.Y.C., 1959-75; assoc. prof., acting head divsn. tropical medicine Columbia U., N.Y.C., 1975-92, emeritus prof., 1992—; chmn. tropical medicine and parasitology study sect. NIH, Bethesda, Md., 1976-80. Author: (with others) Immunity to Parasitic Animals, 1970, Pathogenicity of Trypanosomes, 1979, Parasitic Protoza, Vol. 1, 1991; editor Jour. Protozoology, 1980-88; contbr. articles to profl. jours. Sgt. U.S. Army Air Corps, 1945-46. Grantee NIH, 1972-90, 79-82. Fellow AAAS; mem. Phi Beta Kappa.

DALESSANDRI, KATHIE MARIE, surgeon; b. Stambaugh, Mich., May 4, 1947; d. Paris Henry and Kathryn Mary (Macuga) D. BS in Biology, Mich. Tech. U., 1969; MS in Biophysics, Purdue U., 1971; MD, U. Mich., 1976. Intern, resident Martinez (Calif.) VA Hosp., 1976-79; resident U. Calif., Davis, 1979-81; staff surgeon Martinez (Calif.) VA Med. Ctr., 1982-92, Palo Alto (Calif.) VA Med. Ctr., 1992—; asst. prof. surgery U. Calif., Davis, 1982-88, assoc. clin. prof. surgery, 1989-95; clin. assoc. prof. surgery Stanford (Calif.) U., 1993—; Diplomate Am. Bd. Surgery; chairperson mammography action com. Reviewer jours.; contbr. articles to profl. jours. Recipient 1st prize in rsch. nat. VA Surgeons, 1981. Fellow ACS; mem. East Bay Surg. Soc. (1st prize in rsch. 1981), Assn. Acad. Surgery, Internat. Coll. Surgeons, Soc. Internat. de Chirurgie, Assn. Surg. Edn. Home: PO Box 1173

Point Reyes Station CA 94956 Office: Palo Alto VA Med Ctr Surgery Dept 3801 Miranda Ave Palo Alto CA 94303

D'ALESSANDRI, ROBERT M., dean; b. N.Y.C., June 26, 1945. BA, Fordham U., 1967; MD, N.Y. Med. Coll., 1971. Diplomate Am. Bd. Internal Medicine, Am. Bd. Infectious Diseases. Intern Dept. Medicine, Met. Hosp., N.Y.C., 1971-72; fellowship Divsn. Infectious Diseases, U. Fla., Gainesville, 1974-76; resident Dept. Medicine, U. Fla., Gainesville, 1976-77; instr., chief resident Dept. Medicine, W.Va. U. Sch. Medicine, 1977-78, asst. prof., 1978-81, assoc. prof., 1981-84, prof., 1985—, chief sect. of comprehensive medicine, 1979-87, assoc. dean ambulatory svcs., 1987-90, dean Sch. of Medicine, 1989—; v.p. for health scis. W.Va. U., 1992—; bd. dirs. Nat. Bank of W.Va., Morgantown, MountainView Regional Rehab. Hosp., W.Va. U. Rsch. Corp., Chestnut Ridge Psychiat. Hosp., W.Va. U. Hosps., W.Va. U. Med. Corp., Morgantown HealthRight Clinic, Morgantown Hospice; commentator Sta. WNPB, W.Va. Pub. Radio; host weekly Doctors on Call; weekly med. corr. Sta. WCHS-TV, Charleston, Sta. WDTV, Clarksbur, Sta. WTRF, Wheeling; elected shc. medicine rep. Univ. Faculty Senate, 1980-84; chair credentials com. W.Va. Hosps., 1984-85, med. exec. bd. chair 1985-86, chair infection control com., 1985-86, exec. com. chair 1986-87, mem. 1983-87, chair hosp. med. records com., 1986-87, chair hosps. patient care rev. com., 1986-87, chair ambulatory care bldg. com., 1987-89, chair dean's com. VA Med. Ctr., Martinsburg, 1991—, Clarksburg, 1989—; chair sch. of medicine ednl. adv. coun. W.Va. U. Health Scis. Ctr., 1989—, chair sch. of medicine exec. faculty, 1989—, chair health scis. ctr. exec. com., 1992—; coord. intro. clin. medicine dental studies, 1979-84, coord. intro. to clin. medicine, phys. diagnosis course, 1979-84; spl. lectr. Guiyang (China) Med. Coll., 1988, Hangzhou (China) Red Cross Hosp., 1988. Contbr. numerous articles to profl. jours. Bd. dirs. Monongalia Arts Ctr., Morgantown, 1989—. Mem. AMA, Am. Coll. of Physicians, Infectious Diseases Soc., Soc. for Gen. Internal Medicine, Nat. Rural Health Assn., W.Va. State Med. Assn., Monongalia County Med. Soc. Office: 1150 Health Sciences North Robert C Byrd Health Scis Po Box 9000 Morgantown WV 26506-9000

DALESSIO, DONALD JOHN, physician, neurologist, educator; b. Jersey City, Mar. 2, 1931; s. John Andrea and Susan Dorothy (Minotta) D.; m. Jane Catherine Schneider, Sept. 4, 1954; children: Catherine Leah, James John, Susan Jane. BA, Wesleyan U., 1952; MD, Yale U., 1956. Diplomate Am. Bd. Internal Medicine. Intern in medicine N.Y.C. Hosp., 1956-57, asst. resident in medicine and neurology, 1959-61; resident in medicine Yale Med. Ctr., 1961-62; pres. med. staff Scripps Clinic, La Jolla, Calif., 1974-78; chmn. dept. medicine Scripps Clin., La Jolla, Calif., 1974-89, chmn. emeritus, 1989—, cons., 1982—, pres. med. group, 1980-81; clin. prof. neurology U. Calif., San Diego, 1973—; physician in chief Green Hosp., La Jolla, 1974-89; Musser-Burch lectr. Tulane U., 1979, Kash lectr. U. Ky., 1979; pres. Am. Assn. Study Headache, Chgo., 1974-76, Nat. Migraine Found., Chgo., 1977-79; chmn. Fedn. Western Soc. Neurology, Santa Barbara, Calif., 1976-77. Author: Wolff's Headache, 6th edit., 1993, Approach to Headache, 1973, 5th edit., 1992; editor: Headache jour., 1965-75, 79-84, Scripps Clinic Personal Health Letter; mem. editorial bd.: Jour. AMA, 1977-87; columnist San Diego Tribune. Capt. U.S. Army, 1957-59. Recipient Disting. Alumnus award Wesleyan U., Middletown, Conn., 1982. Fellow ACP; mem. Am. Acad. Neurology (assoc.), World Fedn. Neurology (Am. sec. 1980-90, rsch. group on migraine), La Jolla Country Club, La Jolla Beach/Tennis Club. Republican. Roman Catholic. Home: 8891 Nottingham Pl La Jolla CA 92037-2131 Office: Scripps Clinic & Rsch Found 10666 N Torrey Pines Rd La Jolla CA 92037-1027

DALINKA, MURRAY KENNETH, radiologist, educator; b. Bklyn., May 13, 1938; s. Joseph and Gertrude (Cohen) D.; m. Janice L. Kolber, Feb. 28, 1982; 1 son, Bradford Gordon; children by previous marriage: Ilene, Ian Scott. B.S., U. Mich., 1960, M.D., 1964. Am. Bd. Radiology. Intern Pa. Hosp., Phila., 1964-65; resident in radiology Montefiore Hosp., N.Y.C., 1965-68; instr. radiology Harvard Med. Sch., 1970-71; asst. prof. radiology Thomas Jefferson U. Hosp., Phila., 1971-73, assoc. prof., 1973-76, chief diagnostic radiology, 1974-76, prof., 1976—; chief orthopaedic radiology Hosp. U. Pa., 1976—; cons. Phila. Naval Hosp., 1974-79, Walson Hosp., Ft. Dix Army Base, 1972-77. Author: Arthography, 1980, Symposium on Orthopedic Radiology, 1983; mem. editorial bd. Bone Syllabus IV, 1982—, Skeletal Radiology, 1982—, Conversations in Radiology, 1977-79; guest editor Emergency Medicine Clinics of North America, Vol. 3, 1985; editor: (with J.J. Kaye) Radiology in Emergency Medicine Clinics in Emergency, Vol. 3, 1984, (with J. Edeiken and D. Karasick) Edeiken's Roentgen Diagnosis of Diseases of Bone, 4th edit. Served to capt. USAF, 1968-70. James Picker research fellow, 1972-73. Mem. Internat. Skeletal Soc. (pres.), Radiol. Soc. N.Am., Assn. Univ. Radiologists, Am. Coll. Radiology, Phila. Roentgen Ray Soc. (pres.-elect). Home: 318 S 21st St Philadelphia PA 19103-6531 Office: U Pa Hosp Dept Radiology 3400 Spruce St Philadelphia PA 19104

DALLACHIE, NORMA LORINE, nurse; b. Alex, Okla., Mar. 9, 1936; d. Joyce Erington McClellan and Zelma Florine (Naylor) Cato; m. Robert Allan Dallachie, Sept. 4, 1957; children: Isabel, Suzanne, Matthew. ADN, Santa Rosa Jr. Coll., 1957; postgrad., Calif. State U., Rohnert Park, 1974-75; family nurse practitioner cert., U. Calif., Davis, 1977. RN, Calif. Staff nurse med.-pediatric wards Sonoma County Hosp., Santa Rosa, Calif., 1957-64; staff nurse Sonoma County Juvenile Hall and Dependent Unit, Santa Rosa, 1966-78; family nurse practitioner Cmty. Hosp., Santa Rosa, 1976-90, Meml. Hosp., Santa Rosa, 1992—; cons., clin. supr. Family Practice Ctr., Santa Rosa, 1988-90, Sonoma State U., 1982-90; mem. Sonoma County Hypertension Task Force, 1987-89; cons. occupational medicine Hewlett-Packard Corp., Santa Rosa, 1978-83; mem. occurrence com. Cmty. Hosp., 1980-83. Leader Girl Scouts Am., Santa Rosa, 1969-73; mem. precinct com. Costa for Sheriff, Santa Rosa, 1982. Republican. Methodist. Home: 2021 E Haven Dr Santa Rosa CA 95404

DALLAS, DANIEL GEORGE, social worker; b. Chgo., June 8, 1932; s. George C. and Azimena P. (Marines) D.; B.A., Anderson (Ind.) Coll., 1955; B.D., No. Bapt. Theol. Sem., 1958; M.S.W., Mich. State U., 1963; M.Div., No. Bapt. Theol. Sem., 1972, D.Min., 1981; m. G. Aleta Leppien, May 26, 1956; children—Paul, Rhonda. Mem. faculty Mich. Dept. Corrections, Mich. State U., 1963-66; med. social adminstr. Med. Services div. Mich. Dept. Social Services, 1966-68; cons. Outreach Center of DuPage County, 1976—, also dir. social service Meml. Hosp. of DuPage County, Elmhurst, Ill., 1968—; therapist, lectr. Traffic Sch., Elmhurst Coll.; pvt. practice; indsl. cons. Mem. Elmhurst Sr. Citizen Commn., 1976—. Recipient Outstanding Service award Mental Health Assn. Ill., 1978. Mem. Nat. Assn. Social Workers, Soc. Hosp. Social Work Dirs., Am. Hosp. Assn., Nat. Registry of Health Care Providers, Mental Health Assn. Chgo. Club: Rotary. Contbr. articles to profl. jours. Office: 242 N York St Ste 203 Elmhurst IL 60126-2747

DALLAS, ROBERT VALINE, radiologist; b. Methuen, Mass., Dec. 17, 1942; s. Matthew and Hilda Anne Marie (Valine) D.; B.S., Rensselaer Poly. Inst., 1964; M.D., Albany Med. Coll., 1969; children—Heather Anne Lee, Robert Matthew. Intern, Albany (N.Y.) Med. Center Hosp., 1969-70, resident in radiology, fellow, 1970-74, attending radiologist, 1977-80, head div. diagnostic radiology, 1977-80, acting radiologist-in-chief, 1977-78; attending radiologist Geneva (N.Y.) Gen. Hosp., 1974-76; attending radiologist, chmn. dept. radiology Altoona (Pa.) Hosp., 1980-85; radiologist Centre Community Hosp., State College, Pa., 1986-92; asst. prof. Dartmouth Coll. Med. Sch., Hanover, N.H., 1992—; acting chmn. dept. radiology Albany Med. Coll., 1977-78, asst. prof. radiology, 1977-80, exec. faculty, 1977-78; adv. Health Systems Agy. of Northeastern N.Y., 1977-80; med. bd. Albany Med. Center Hosp., 1977-78; cons. Albany VA Hosp., 1979-80; radiologist Dartmouth-Hitchcock Med. Ctr., Hanover, 1992—. Served to capt. USAR, 1970-76. Diplomate Am. Bd. Radiology (examiner 1979—). Mem. Am. Coll. Radiology, Radiol. Soc. N.H., N.H. Radiol. Soc. Home: 39 College Hl Hanover NH 03755-3208 Office: Dartmouth-Hitchcock Med Ctr Dept Diagnostic Radiology Hanover NH 03755

DALLMAN, MARY F., physiology educator. BA in Chemistry, Smith Coll., 1956; PhD in Physiology, Stanford U., 1967; postgrad., Swedish Royal Vet. Sch., 1968, U. Calif., San Francisco, 1969-70. Lectr. U. Calif. Dept. Physiology, San Francisco, 1970-72, aast., 1972-76, assoc. prof., 1976-81, prof., 1981—, vice-chair, 1987—. Assoc. editor: Am. Jour. Physiol.: Endocrinology and Metabolism, 1979-85, Steroids, 1985-87, Am. Jour. Physiol.: Regulatory, Integrative and Comparative Physiology, 1990-92; contbr. articles to profl. jours. Recipient Am. Diabetes Rsch. award, 1996. Mem. NIH (mem. endocrine study sect. 1977-81, mem. diabetes, digestive, kidney grants rev. subcom. 1988-92, chair 1992-93), Women in Endocrinology (pres. 1993-95), Internat. Soc. Neuroendocrinology (pres. 1996). Office: U Calif Dept Physiology Box 0444 513 Parnassus Ave Rm S-762 San Francisco CA 94143*

DALLOCA, LUCA LORENZO, dental prosthodontist, educator; b. Bellinzago Novarese, Italy, Dec. 30, 1962; s. Lorenzo Guido Adolfo and Paola (Storti) D.; m. Paola Giovanna Donati; children: David, Lorenza. Cert. dental technician, Dental Tech. Inst., Orange, Calif., 1980; D of Dental Medicine, Tufts U., 1991; advanced edn. in prosthodontics tng., UCLA, 1991-92; degree in dentistry & dental prosthesis, U. Pavia, Italy, 1993. Co-owner Factory Dental House, 1983-87; owner dental lab. Arcodent, 1983-87; specialist in prosthetics Studio di Odont. Special., Oral Design Ctr., Arcore and Milan, Italy, 1992—; clin. assoc. Tufts U. Sch. Dental Medicine, Boston, 1995—; prof. dental anatomy Istituto di Anat. Umana Normale, U. Milan, 1995—; vis. prof. postgrad. program restorative dentistry dept. oral sci. U. Siena, 1994—. Extern USCG, Boston, 1990. With Alpin, 1981-82. Mem. ADA, Am. Prosthodontic Soc., Am. Coll. Prosthodontists. Office: via Gilera 12, 20043 Arcore Italy

DALLURA, SAL ANTHONY, physician; b. Flushing, N.Y., Nov. 7, 1960; s. Russ and Mayann (Taranto) D.; m. Donna Ann Baldassare, Aug. 6, 1983 (div. Mar. 1993); children: Christopher Anthony, Corinne Elizabeth; m. Stacy Elizabeth Carberry, July 1, 1995; 1 child, Matthew Anthony. BS, U. Notre Dame, 1982; DO, N.Y. Coll. Osteo. Medicine, 1986. Diplomate Am. Acad. Family Physicians. Mng. ptnr. Flashner Med. Ptnrship., Babylon, N.Y., 1989-91; assoc. physician Moriches Med. Care, Center Moriches, N.Y., 1989-91, Digiovanna, Massepequa Park, N.Y., 1991-92; physician Tippecanoe Family Physicians, Tipp City, Ohio, 1992—; physician mng. ptnr. After Hours Family Care, Tipp City, 1994—. Mem. Am. Osteo. Assn., Am. Coll. Family Practice, Am. Coll. Legal Medicine. Republican. Roman Catholic. Office: 450 N Hyatt St Tipp City OH 45371-1433

D'ALMEIDA, MICHAEL JUDE, osteopath, surgeon; b. Hong Kong, Hong Kong, July 29, 1957; came to U.S., 1958; s. Julio Arturo and Gwendolyn Rita (Dragon) D'A.; m. Diana Lee Baglietto, Dec. 24, 1983 (dec. June 1990); m. Colleen Marie O'Connor, July 4, 1992; children: Carolyn Marie, Christina Ann, Carly Lynn. BA, Calif. State U., Fullerton, 1980; DO, U. Health Scis., 1985. Intern Pontiac (Mich.) Osteo. Hosp.; resident in osteopathy Mt. Clemens (Mich.) Gen. Hosp.; gen. surgeon N.E. Surg. Group, P.C., Mt. Clemens, 1994—; assoc. clin. prof. medicine Mich. State U., Lansing, 1995—. Lt. comdr. USN, 1990-94. Mem. Am. Osteo. Assn., Am. Coll. Osteo. Surgeons, Am. Soc. Parenteraly Enteral Nutritionist, Macomb County Osteo. Assn. Republican. Roman Catholic.

DALRYMPLE, DEBORAH LEE, nursing educator; b. Attleboro, Mass., Apr. 18, 1950; d. Joseph W. and Lorraine (Glines) Belcher; m. Robert Dalrymple, Jan. 23, 1972; children: Thomas, Jessie Ann. BSN, U. R.I., Kingston, 1972; MS in Nursing, Villanova (Pa.) U., 1984. RN, Pa., R.I. Staff nurse Kent County Meml. Hosp., West Warwick, R.I., 1973-78, Doylestown (Pa.) Hosp., 1978—; assoc. prof. nursing Montgomery County Community Coll., Blue Bell, Pa., 1979—; clin. practitioner IV therapy and oncology; ednl. cons. Ctr. for Nursing Excellence. Mem. Intravenous Nurses Soc. (pres. Pennsylvania Valley chpt. 1994, 95), CRNI, Nat. League for Nursing, Pa. League Nursing, Sigma Theta Tau.

DALTON, CLAUDETTE ELLIS HARLOE, anesthesiologist, educator, university official; b. Roanoke, Va., Jan. 18, 1947; d. John Pinckney and Dorothy Anne (Ellis) Harloe; m. Henry Tucker Dalton, May 17, 1973 (div. 1979); 1 child, Gordon Tucker. BA, Sweet Briar Coll., 1969; MD, U. Va., 1974. Resident in anesthesiology U. N.C., Chapel Hill, 1974-77; med. edn. Lenoir County Meml Hosp./East Carolina U., Kinston, N.C., 1978-80; med. edn. in intensive care Presbyn Hosp., Charlotte, N.C., 1981-82; practice anesthesiology Charlotte Eye, Ear, Nose and Throat Hosp., 1982-85, Medivision of Charlotte and Orthopedic Hosp. of Charlotte, 1985-89; asst. dean alumni affairs, 1989-92; asst. dean med. edn. U. Va. Health Scis. Ctr., Charlottesville, 1992—, cmty. preceptor coord., 1992-94; dir. Office of Cmty. Based Med. Edn., 1994—; bd. dirs. Kinston Bd. Health, 1979-81. Author developer patient edn. materials for illiterate patients, 1979—, emergency med. svc. tng. program, 1981. Bd. dirs. Charlottesville Family Svcs., Family Svcs. Albemarle County, 1992-93, Coun. on Aging, Lenoir County C.C., Am. Cancer Soc.; exec. dir. Cmty. Involvement Coun. Lenoir County, Kinston, 1979; county coord. Internat. Yr. of Child, Kinston, 1979; mem. women's task force U. Va. Med. Sch.; also others. Recipient Gov.'s award State of N.C., 1980, cert. of merit for svc. to children N.C. Dept. Human Resources, Outstanding Teaching award U. Va. Sch. Medicine, 1993; named Commencement speaker U. Va. Sch. Medicine Graduation, 1993. Mem. Va. Med. Soc. (editor med. news. Va. Med. Quar., mem. legis. com., mem. health acess com., bd. dirs. Va. Health Quality Coun. 1995—, chair ad hoc com. on telemedicine 1996—, del. to ann. meeting, reference com.), Albemarle County Med. Soc. (sec.-treas. 1995—), Va. Soc. Anesthesiology, U. Va. Med. Alumni Assn. (assoc. bd. dirs. 1989-92), Alpha Omega Alpha. Office: U Va Med Sch PO Box 325 Charlottesville VA 22902-0325

DALTON, DAVID LANDRESS, urologist, educator; b. Chattanooga, Feb. 17, 1944; s. Sethur White and Elizabeth (Landress) D.; m. Suzanne Burns, Mar. 15, 1980; children: Nathalie, David, Clare, William, Stewart. BA, Vanderbilt U., 1966; MD, U. Tenn., 1969. Diplomate Am. Bd. Urology, Inc. Resident in urology Duke U., Durham, N.C., 1969-73, instr. dept. surgery, 1973-74; assoc. dept. surgery Duke U., Durham, 1975; pvt. practice urologist Jacksonville, Fla., 1976—; asst. clin. prof. surgery Jacksonville (Fla.) Hosp., 1976—; chair dept. urology St. Lukes Hosp. Assn., Jacksonville, 1982—, bd. dirs., 1994—; v.p. Ctr. Jacksonville Urol. Soc., 1988; exec. com. Fla. Urol. Soc., 1989-90. Contbr. articles to profl. jours. Maj. USAR, 1970-79. Recipient Mosby Scholar Book award U. Tenn., 1969. Fellow ACS, Am. Soc. for Laser Medicine and Surgery; mem. Am. Urol. Soc. (southeastern sect.), Am. Fertility Soc., Soc. Urol. Cryosurgeons, Fla. Med. Assn., Duval County Med. Soc., Alpha Omega Alpha. Office: 4203 Belfort Rd #365 Jacksonville FL 32116

DALTON, RORY RALPH, surgeon, researcher; b. Huntsville, Ala. Jan. 29, 1960; s. Ralph Ables and Louise (Nance) D.; m. Jane Louise Cooper, Nov. 10, 1992. BS, Birmingham Southern Coll., 1982; MD, U. Ala., 1986. Diplomate Am. Bd. Surgery. Resident physician Mayo Clinic, Rochester, Minn., 1986-92; fellow in surgical oncology Fox Chase Cancer Ctr., Phila., 1992-94; staff surgeon Washington Cancer Inst., Washington Hosp. Ctr., 1994—. Contbr. articles to profl. jours. and chpt. to book; editl. advisor Silver Platter Edn. Inc., Norwood, Mass., 1995—. Mem. Met. Opera Guild, 1994—. Recipient Med. Rsch. grant Midlantic Rsch. Inst., Washington, 1995. Fellow Am. Coll. Surgeons (assoc.); mem. AAAS, Priestly Soc., Alpha Omega Alpha, Phi Beta Kappa. Episcopalian. Home: PO Box 72 11610 Rokeby Ave Garrett Park MD 20896 Office: Washington Cancer Inst 110 Irving St NW Washington DC 20010

DALTON, RUTH MARGARET, retired pathologist; b. Chgo., Apr. 30, 1926; d. Maurice Jewett and Madeline Irene (Murphy) D. Student, DePaul U., 1946-48; BS, U. Ill., Chgo., 1950, MD, 1953. Diplomate Am. Bd. Pathology. Intern Madison (Wis.) Gen. Hosp., 1953-54, resident in pathology, 1954-57; resident in pathology Phila. (Pa.) Gen. Hosp., 1957-58; pathologist St. Francis Med. Ctr. Assocs. in Lab. Medicine, La Crosse, Wis., 1958-86; instr. St. Francis Hosp. Sch. Med. Tech., La Crosse, 1953-86; ret., 1986; instr. Madison (Wis.) Gen. Hosp. Sch. Med. Tech., 1954-57; lectr. in field; past inspector Am. Assn. Blood Banks; pres. bd. advisors Viterbo Coll., La Crosse, 1978-81; past med. adv. com. Badger Regional Red Cross Blood Ctr., Madison; past adv. bd. Community-Med. Dietetics Program Viterbo Coll.; bd. dirs. Viterbo Coll. Mem. Girl Scout Am. (life, pers. com., bd. dirs. Riverland chpt.); past bd. mem.La Crosse (Wis.) Symphony Orch.; bd. dirs. La Crosse (Wis.) Community Found., Riverfront Found. Fellow Am. Soc. Clin. Pathologists; mem. Am. Assn. Blood Banks, Internat. Soc. Pathologists, AAAS, Univ. Ill. Alumni Assn. (life), Nat. Wildlife Fedn. (life), Rotary. Roman Catholic. Home: N1946 Forest Ridge Dr La Crosse WI 54601-2467

DALTON, STEVEN PAUL, physician assistant; b. New Milford, Conn., Aug. 3, 1955; s. John Edgar and Callie Nettie (Wheeler) D.; m. Claudia Tinnin, Aug. 15, 1981; children: Rebecca, Matthew. Diploma in Nursing, Harlem Valley Sch. Nursing, Wingdale, N.Y., 1976; BS, Western Conn. State Coll., 1980; Physician Asst., Pa. State U., 1983. Cert. physician asst. Physician asst. Commerce St. Med. Ctr., Clinton, Conn., 1983-85, Rural Internists of Maine, P.A., Skowhegan, 1985-93, Cmty. Health Plan, North Adams, Mass., 1993-94, Shaftsbury (Vt.) Med. Assocs., Inc., 1994—, Vt. Vets. Home, Bennington, 1994—; lectr. health occupations Southwestern Vt. Sch. Union, Bennington, 1995. Bd. trustees Old First Ch. of Bennington, 1995—. Fellow Am. Acad. Physician Assts. Office: Shaftsbury Med Assocs Inc Box 379 Shaftsbury VT 05262

DALTON, SUZANNE LATACZ, health facility administrator; b. Bayonne, N.J., Jan. 7, 1948; d. Anthony John and Dorothy Ann (Miller) Latacz; m. Thomas Francis Dalton Jr., Oct. 7, 1991. Diploma in nursing, Bayonne Hosp. Sch. Nursing, 1968; BS, Monmouth Coll., 1974; EdM, Rutgers U., 1978. RN, N.J. Head nurse Bayonne (N.J.) Hosp., 1971-75; nursing supr. Middlesex Hosp., New Brunswick, N.J., 1975-78; assoc. dir. nursing Middlesex Gen. U. Hosp., New Brunswick, 1978-86; v.p. nursing Barnert Hosp., Paterson, N.J., 1986—; adj. prof. William Paterson Coll., Wayne, N.J., 1988—. Johnson and Johnson-Wharton fellow, 1983. Mem. Nat. League Nursing, N.J. League Nursing, Am. Orgn. Nurse Execs., Orgn. Nurse Execs. N.J.

DALVI, RAMESH R., toxicologist, educator, consultant; b. Bombay, India, Nov. 8, 1938; s. Rajaram S. and Sundar R. (Sawant) D.; m. Rekha B. Jadhav, Jan. 22, 1969; children: Rajan, Samir. BSc with honors, U. Bombay, 1962, BSc in Tech., 1964, MSc in Tech., 1967; PhD, Utah State U., Logan, 1972. Diplomate Am. Bd. Toxicology. Research fellow Univ. Grants Commn., New Delhi, 1964-67; biochemist Hindustan Lever, Ltd., Bombay, 1967; sci. research officer Bhabha Atomic Research Ctr., Bombay, 1967-69; grad-research fellow Utah State U., 1969-72; postdoctoral fellow Vanderbilt U., Nashville, 1972-74; asst. prof. to prof. toxicology Tuskegee (Ala.) U., 1974—; cons. Nat. Acad. Scis., Boston U. Editorial bd., internat. adv. bd.: Tropical Veterinarian, 1982—, mem. bd. reviewers Am. Jour. Vet. Research, 1987-89; contbr. over 100 articles to profl. jours., chpts. in book. Recipient award So. Regional Edn. Bd., 1975; Tuskegee U. Faculty Achievement award, 1985-86; SmithKline Beecham award for rsch. excellenc, 1991; numerous research grants, 1975—. Mem. Soc. Toxicology, Am. Coll. Vet. Toxicologist, Am. Chem. Soc., Am. Soc. Vet Physiol. Pharmacology, AAAS, Inst. Food Tech., Internat. Soc. Study of Xenobiotics, Am. Assn. Vet. Med. Colls., Pharm. Soc. Japan, Sigma Xi. Home: 375 Oakridge Dr Auburn AL 36830-6796 Office: School Vet Medicine Tuskegee U Tuskegee AL 36088

DALY, BENEDICT DUDLEY THOMAS, JR., cardiothoracic surgeon; b. Boston, Nov. 28, 1939; s. Benedict Dudley Thomas and Alice Margaret (Groden) D.; m. Joan Marie Behenna, Sept. 25, 1971; children: Jennifer, Benedict, Matthew. AB, Georgetown U., 1961; MD, Boston U., 1965. Intern, Boston City Hosp., 1965-66, resident, 1966-72; assoc. surgeon Tex. Heart Inst., Houston, 1972-75; dir. cardiothoracic surgery St. Elizabeth Hosp., Brighton, Mass., 1976-78; surgeon New Eng. Med. Ctr., Boston, 1978-87, sr. surgeon, 1987—; chief cardiothoracic surgery VA Med. Ctr., Boston, 1978-92, Newton Wellesley Hosp., 1986-93; assoc. prof. Tufts U., Boston, 1976-84, prof. cardiothoracic surgery, 1984—; Contbr. articles to profl. jours. NIH-NHLBI grantee, 1978-84; Am. Heart Assn. grantee, 1973-74. Fellow ACS, Coll. Chest Physicians, Am. Coll. Cardiology; mem. Soc. Thoracic Surgeons, Am. Assn. Thoracic Surgery. Home: 12 Wildwood Cir Wellesley MA 02181-6465 Office: 171 Harrison Ave Boston MA 02111-1854

DALY, MARGARET REDDY, rehabilitation nurse; b. Phila., Sept. 19, 1940; d. Patrick and Ellen (Cavanagh) Reddy; m. D. Michael Daly, Nov. 24, 1989. ADN, Gwynedd Mercy Coll., 1967, BSN, 1972; MA in Nursing, NYU, 1980. RN, Pa. With Fitzgerald Mercy Hosp., Darby, Pa., head nurse, supr.; asst. nursing dir. Thomas Jefferson U. Hosp., Phila.; cons. Nursing Cons. Svcs., Norristown, Pa. Mem. ANA, Assn. Rehab. Nurses (dir.-at-large 1996, program chair nat. conf. 1986), Nat. Assn. Orthop. Nurses, Assn. Legal Nurse Consultants (bd. dirs. 1993-96). Home: 243 Yale Rd Wayne PA 19087-2649

DALY, ROBERT W., psychiatrist, medical educator; b. Watertown, N.Y., Oct. 1, 1932; s. Robert Joseph and Margaret Florence (Ward) D.; m. Elizabeth Mary McCarthy, July 4, 1958; children: Kendra, Lauren, Robert, John, Erik. BS, St. Lawrence U., 1957; MD, SUNY, Syracuse, 1957. Diplomate Am. Bd. Psychiatry and Neurology, Nat. Bd. Med. Examiners. Resident in psychiatry SUNY, Syracuse, 1958-60, chief resident in psychiatry, 1960-61; chief Dept. Psychiatry & Neurology, Barksdale AFB, Bossier City, La., 1961-63; asst. prof. psychiatry SUNY Upstate Med. Ctr., Syracuse, 1963-69, assoc. prof. psychiatry, 1969-75; visiting scholar U. Cambridge, England, 1969-70; sr. fellow Nat. Endowment for the Humanities, 1974-75; prof. psychiatry SUNY Upstate Med. Ctr., Syracuse, 1975—; adj. prof. philosophy Syracuse U., 1980—; prof. med. humanities, dir. program in med. humanities SUNY Health Sci. Ctr., Syracuse, 1984—; exec. dir. Syracuse Consortium for the Cultural Found. of Medicine, 1978—; chmn. bd., pres. Inst. for Ethics in Health Care, Inc., 1995—; examiner Am. Bd. Psychiatry and Neurology, 1980-90; pvt. practice psychiatry, Syracuse, 1963—; cons. to hosps., govt. agencies, religious orgns., law firms, 1964—. Contbr. articles to profl. jours.; co-editor: The Cultures of Medicine, Vol. 8 of Literature and Medicine. Mem. mental health adv. bd., County Onondaga, N.Y., 1976-77. Capt. USAF, 1961-63. Rsch. fellow N.Y. State Dept. Mental Hygiene, 1969-70; recipient award in recognition of svcs. Ctrl. N.Y. Eye Bank & Rsch. Corp., 1985. Fellow Am. Psychiat. Assn. (life; pres. Onondaga dist. bd. 1968-69); mem. N.Y. State Med. Soc., Internat. Soc. for Comparative Study Civilization (coun. 1977-80), Soc. Health and Human Values, Assn. Faculty in Med. Humanities (program chmn. 1986-87, pres., program dir. sect. 1995-96), Assn. for Advancement of Philosophy and Psychiatry, Soc. for Bioethics Cons. Democrat. Roman Catholic. Home: 101 Revere Rd Syracuse NY 13214-1938 Office: SUNY Health Sci Ctr 750 E Adams St Syracuse NY 13210-2306

DALY, WALTER JOSEPH, physician, educator; b. Michigan City, Ind., Jan. 12, 1930; s. Walter Hayes and Nellie Martha (Stipp) D.; m. Joan Brown, June 12, 1953; children: Lois Kay, Alice Louise. AB, Ind. U., 1951, MD, 1955. Diplomate Am. Bd. Internal Medicine. Intern Ind. U., 1955-56, resident, 1956-57, 59-62, instr. medicine, 1962-63, asst. prof., 1963-65, assoc. prof., 1965-68, prof., 1968-77, John B. Hickam prof., 1977-80, J.O. Ritchey prof., 1980-95, J.O. Ritchey prof. emeritus, 1995—; chmn. dept. medicine, 1970-83, dean Sch. Medicine, 1983-95; dean emeritus Ind. U., 1995—; dir. Regenstrief Inst. Health Rsch., 1976-83. Capt. M.C., U.S. Army, 1957-59. Mem. ACP (master, gov. 1980-84), Am. Physiol. Soc., Cen. Soc. Clin. Rsch. (pres. 1980-81), Am. Soc. Clin. Investigation, Am. Clin. and Climatol. Assn., Assn. Am. Physicians. Home: 2048 Oldfields Indianapolis IN 46228 Office: Ind U Sch Medicine 1120 South Dr Indianapolis IN 46202-5135

DALY, WILLIAM JAMES, retired health industry distributing company executive; b. Lawrence, Mass., Aug. 29, 1917; s. James W. and Alice Gertrude D.; m. Cornelia Mahony, July 18, 1942; children: Jane, Cornelius, James, William James, Christopher. B.S. in Elec. Engring, U.S. Naval Acad., 1941. With James W. Daly, Inc. (health care distbn.), Lynnfield, Mass., 1946-87; pres. James W. Daly, Inc. (health care distbn.), 1967-87. Served to comdr. U.S. Navy, 1941-46, 50-52. Mem. Nat. Wholesale Druggists Assn., Health Industry Distbrs. Assn. (past chmn.), Nat. Assn. Wholesalers, Am. Mgmt. Assn. Clubs: Salem Country, Lanam.

DAMAN, HARLAN RICHARD, allergist; b. N.Y.C., Nov. 1, 1941; s. D. Leon and Frances (Weissler) D.; AB cum laude, Harvard U., 1963; MD, Albert Einstein Coll. Medicine, 1967. Diplomate Am. Bd. Pediatrics, Am. Bd. Allergy and Immunology. Intern, then resident Yale-New Haven Hosp./Med. Ctr., 1967-69; fellow in allergy and clin. immunology Nat. Jewish Hosp. Research Ctr./U. Colo. Med. Ctr., Denver, 1971-73, instr., 1974-81; clin. asst. prof. pediatrics Albert Einstein Coll. Medicine, N.Y.C., 1981—; dir. pediatric allergy clinic Bronx Mcpl. Hosp. Ctr., 1982-92; mem. Med. Ctr./Sch. Medicine, 1976-90. Co-editor: Psychobiologic Aspects of Allergic Disorders, 1986; contbr. chpt. to Outpatient Medicine, 1980; contbr. articles on pulmonary function testing in asthmatic disorders. Served to maj. M.C., USAF, 1969-71. Fellow Am. Acad. Pediatrics, Am. Coll. Allergists,

Am. Coll. Chest Physicians, Am. Acad. Allergy; mem. N.Y. Allergy Soc., Westchester Allergy Soc. (ednl. program dir. 1978-89, treas. 1980-81, pres. 1982-83), Westchester Acad. Medicine. Office: 769 Kimball Ave Yonkers NY 10704-1534

DAMASIO, ANTONIO R., physician, neurologist; b. Lisbon, Portugal, Feb. 25, 1944; came to U.S., 1975; m. Hanna Damasio. MD, U. Lisbon, 1969, DMS, 1974. Intern U. Hosp., Lisbon, 1969-72; prof. auxiliar in neurology Med. Sch., U. Lisbon, 1971; assoc. prof. dept. neurology U. Iowa, Iowa City, 1976-80, prof. neurology, 1980-86, prof. neurology, head dept., 1986—, Van Allen Disting. prof., 1989, chief div. behavioral neurology and cognitive neurosci., 1977—; adj. prof. Salk Inst., San Diego, 1989—. Author: Lesion Analysis in Neuropsychgology, 1989 (award Assn. Am. Pubs. 1990); mem. editorial bd. Trends in Neurosci., 1986-91, Behavioral Brain Rsch., 1988—, Cerebral Cortex, 1990—, Jour. Neurosci., 1990, spl. brain issue Sci. Am, 1992; contbr. articles to profl. jours. Recipient Disting. prof. award U. So. Calif., 1985, Nelson Urban Rsch. award Mental Health Assn. Iowa, 1990, Dr. William Beaumont award AMA, 1990, Pessoa prize Portuguese govt., 1992. Fellow Am. Acad. Neurology, Am .Neurol. Assns.; mem. Soc. for Neurosci., Acad. Aphasia (pres. 1983), Behavioral Neurology Soc., (pres. 1985), Royal Soc. Medicine Belgium (elected) European Acad. Arts and Scis. (elected). Office: U Iowa Hosp & Clinic Dept Neurology 200 Hawkins Dr Iowa City IA 52242-0009*

D'AMATO, KEITH ROCKY, clinical psychologist; b. Paterson, N.J., July 28, 1952; b. Henry Joseph and Lillian Marie D'Amato. BA, Newark State Coll., 1973; MEd, William Paterson Coll., 1978; MA, Calif. Sch. Profl. Psychology, 1980, PhD, 1981. Diplomate Am. Bd. Forensic Examiners. Tchr., counselor Paterson Pub. Schs., 1973-78; sch. psychologist Fresno (Calif.) Pub. Schs., 1979-80; intern Merced (Calif.) Dept. Mental Health, 1978-79, Madera (Calif.) Dept. Mental Health, 1981; chief psychologist Agy. for Children and Youth, Wellsboro, Pa., 1981-83; exec. dir. Mental Health Care Ctr. Monroe County, Key West, Fla., 1983-85, dir. Ctr. Psychol. Services, Orange Park, Fla., 1986—, dir. Sexual Abuse Treatment Programs, 1986—, cons. child protection team, 1987—, Sch. Blind & Deaf, 1988; with dept. of Health & Rehab., 1986—, psychology William Paterson Coll., Fla. Keys Community Coll., 1983-85. Pres. N.E. Fla. Coalition Against Sex Abuse. Contbr. articles to profl. jours. Named Outstanding Young Floridian, Fla. Jaycees, 1984; Clinician of Yr., Fla. Council for Community Mental Health, 1984. Mem. Am. Psychol. Assn., Am. Assn. Marriage and Family Therapy (clin.), N.E. Fla. Psychological Assn. (chairperson ethics, 1991). Home: PO Box 175 Orange Park FL 32067-0175 Office: 1665 Kingsley Ave Orange Park FL 32073-4435

DAMBERG, DAVID VERN, health facility consultant; b. Duluth, Minn., May 24, 1933; s. Alvern Carl and Ruth Viola (Peterson) D.; m. Ellen Pauline Olsen, July 12, 1958; children: Kristen, Tague, Berik. BS, Macalester Coll., 1954; MHA, U. Minn., 1958. Adminstrv. resident R.I. Hosp., Providence, 1957, asst. adminstr., 1958-60; hosp. cons. James A. Hamilton Assocs., Mpls., 1960—, ptnr., 1966-75, sr. v.p., 1975-84, mng. ptnr. Mpls. office, 1984-87, also bd. dirs.; of counsel James A. Hamilton Assocs. (name now Hamilton/KSA), Mpls., 1987-91; pres. DamBerg, Ltd., St. Paul, 1991; lectr. Program in Health Services Adminstrn., U. Minn.; bd. dirs. EMPI, Inc., Mpls. Contbr. articles to profl. jours. Named to Hamilton Soc., U. Minn. Alumni Found., 1984. Fellow Am. Assn. Healthcare Cons.; mem. Am. Coll. Health Care Execs., Am. Hosp. Assn., Internat. Hosp. Fedn., AIA Architecture for Health Com. Republican. Presbyterian. Home: 433 Otis Ave Saint Paul MN 55104-4929 Office: DamBerg Ltd 433 Otis Ave Ste Mg Saint Paul MN 55104-4929

D'AMBROSIO, JOSEPH ANTHONY, dentist; b. Bklyn., May 20, 1954; s. Joseph and Rose (Ambrosio) D'A. BA, Columbia U., 1976; DDS, SUNY, Buffalo, 1980, MS, 1986. Diplomate Am. Bd. Oral Medicine. Coord. dental residency Erie County Med. Ctr., Buffalo, 1981-87; asst. prof. dentistry SUNY, Buffalo, 1983-87; vice chmn. dentistry Michael Reese Hosp./Med. Ctr., Chgo., 1987-89; asst. prof. dental medicine U. Conn., Farmington, 1989—, dir. grad. oral medicine, 1991—; attending staff John Dempsey Hosp.; cons. ADA, Chgo., 1988—. Editorial rev. bd. Oral Surgery, Oral Pathology, Oral Medicine Jour., St. Louis, 1988—; contbr. articles to sci. publs. Mem. ADA, Am. Acad. Oral Medicine, Am. Assn. Hosp. Dentists (newsletter editor), Orgn. Tchrs. Oral Diagnosis (pres. 1992), Am. Assn. Dental Schs., Omicron Kappa Upsilon. Office: Univ Conn Health Ctr 263 Farmington Ave Farmington CT 06030-0001

DAMESHEK, H(AROLD) LEE, physician; b. Balt., Mar. 16, 1937; s. Samuel and Rose (Rudick) D.; m. Michelle Zubasic, Sept. 12, 1965; children: Lynne R. Shine, Amy D. Brumbaugh, David, Deborah. BS in Chemistry, Franklin and Marshall Coll., 1959; MD, Tufts U., 1963. Diplomate Am. Bd. Internal Medicine. Intern Presbyn.-Univ. Hosp., Pitts., 1963-64, resident in internal medicine, 1966-68; hematology fellow Ohio State U. Hosp., Columbus, 1968-69; practice medicine specializing in hematology and oncology Pitts., 1969—; clin. instr. medicine U. Pitts., 1969-74, clin. asst. prof., 1974-81, clin. assoc. prof., 1981—; instr. West Penn Hosp., Pitts., 1969-77; chmn. cancer com. Presbyn.-Univ. Hosp., 1980—; cons. various hosps.; bd. dirs. Physicians' Healthg Plan Pa., 1986—. Contbr. articles to med. jours. Bd. dirs. Leukemia Soc. West Pa., 1971—, v.p., 1977-79, Am. Cancer Soc.; treas. Presbyn.-Univ. Hosp., 1984-86, v.p., 1986-88, pres. med. staff, 1988-90, mem. med. quality improvement com., 1991—; mem. med. adv. com. Cancer Support Ctr., 1987—; vol. faculty promotions com. U. Pitts. Med. Ctr., 1994—. Capt. U.S. Army, 1964-66. Fellow ACP; mem. AMA, Am. Soc. Hematology, Allegheny County Med. Soc. (treas. 1980-81, v.p. 1982, pres. 1984, bd. dirs., peer rev. bd. 1991-94, Frederick Jacob award 1988), Pa. Med. Soc., Pitts. Acad. Medicine (treas. 1981—), Westmoreland Country Club (sec., bd. dirs.), Univ. Club Pitts. Home: 421 Radcliff Dr Pittsburgh PA 15235-5326 Office: 580 S Aiken Ave Pittsburgh PA 15232-1531

DAMIAN, GUILLERMO RUSTIA, physiatrist, educator; b. Manila, Aug. 24, 1925; s. Luis Aristorenas and Marciana Javier (Rustia) D.; m. Rita Reyes Abriol, Sept. 2, 1958; children: Judith, Teresita. MD, U. Philippines, 1952. Diplomate, Philippine Bd. Phys. Medicine and Rehab. Resident in phys. medicine and rehab. D.C. Gen. Hosp., Washington, 1955-56, NYU-Bellevue Med. Ctr., N.Y.C., 1956-58; coll. sec. Sch. Allied Med. Professions, U. Philippines, Manila, 1962-72; dir., then dean Sch. Allied Med. Professions, U. Philippines, 1972-87, mem. faculty in phys. medicine and rehab., 1962-90; chmn. dept. phys. medicine and rehab. Coll. Medicine, U. Philippines, Manila, 1972-74; mem. faculty phys. medicine and rehab. Coll. Medicine, U. Philippines, 1959-90; chmn. dept. phys. medicine and rehab. Manila Doctors Hosp., St. Lukes Med. Ctr., 1965-87, Med. City Gen. Hosp.; chmn. med. commn. Philippine Found. of Rehab. of Disabled, 1975-77. Chmn. Coll. Allied Med. Prof. Found., chmn., 1991—. Grantee, WHO, 1965. Fellow Philippine Soc. Phys. Medicine and Rehab. (pres. 1965-67), Sports Medicine Assn. of Philippines (pres. 1985-87), Philippine Rheumatism Assn. (ppres. 1988-92, immediate past pres. 1992-95); mem. Am. Congress Rehab. Medicine, Asian Pacific League Against Rheumatism (coopted mem. 1992—), Quezon City Sports Club. Roman Catholic. Home: 29 Scout de Guia, Quezon City Luzon, The Philippines Office: Manila Drs Hosp, 667 United Nations Ave, Manila The Philippines

D'AMICO, CHRISTINE J., nursing administrator; b. Canonsburg, Pa., Aug. 29, 1961; d. Domenick and Laberta (DiFlauro) D'Amico. BSN, Duquesne U., Pitts., 1983; MSN, Duquesne U., 1993. Nurse labor and delivery room Magee Women's Hosp., Pitts., 1983-86, nurse clinician, 1986-87, asst. nurse mgr., 1987-89; instr. Louise Suydam McClintic Sch. Nursing, St. Margaret Hosp., Pitts., 1989-92; head nurse labor and delivery room St. Clair Hosp., Pitts., 1992-93, dir. maternal child health svcs., 1993-94; nurse clinician emergency rm. Magee Women's Hosp., Pitts., 1994—. Mem. Assn. Women's Health Obstetrics and Neonatal Nursing (Pa. mem. coord. Pitts. chpt. 1992-93, Pa. state chair 1993-96).

D'AMICO, LEON, pharmacist; b. Phila., Mar. 2; s. Louis and Elizabeth (Pappa) D'A.; m. Amanda D'Amico (div. 1982); 1 child, Denise; m. Angela Santucci, Mar. 22, 1992. B Pharmacy, Phila. Coll. Pharmacy and Sci., 1970. Owner, mgr. Penn Towers Pharmacy, Phila., 1971-88, Med. & Safety Group, Phila., 1988—. Office: Med & Safety Group 525 Spring Garden St Philadelphia PA 19123

DAMJANOV, IVAN, pathologist, educator; b. Subotica, Yugoslavia, Mar. 31, 1941; came to U.S., 1967; s. Milenko and Ana (Pavkovic) D.; m. Andrea Zivanovic, Jan. 18, 1964; children: Nevena, Ivana, Milena. MD, U. Zagreb (Yugoslavia), 1964, PhD, 1971. Lic. physician, Yugoslavia; diplomate Am. Bd. Pathology. Intern Gen. Hosp., Zagreb, Yugoslavia, 1964-65; resident in pathology U. Zagreb, 1966-67; intern in pathology Cleve. Met. Gen. Hosp., Cleve., Phila., 1967-68; resident in pathology Mt. Sinai Hosp., N.Y.C., 1968-69; asst. in pathology U. Zagreb, 1969-71; postdoctoral fellow Fels Rsch. Inst., Temple U., Phila., 1971-72; asst. prof. pathology U. Zagreb, 1972-73; from asst. prof. to assoc. prof. U. Conn., Farmington, 1973-77; from assoc. prof. to prof. Hahnemann Med. Coll. and Hosp., Phila., 1977-86; prof. pathology Jefferson Med. Coll. of Thomas Jefferson U., Phila., 1986-94; prof. pathology, chmn. U. Kans. Sch. Med., Kansas City, 1994—; cons. pathologist VA Hosp., Newington, Conn., 1975-77, Cancer Info. Dissemination and Analysis Ctr. for Virology, Immunology and Cancer-Related Biology, Franklin Inst., Phila., 1977-82; mem. group for rsch. in pathology edn. U. Iowa, 1977-82; ad hoc reviewer, mem. site vis. teams and study sects. NIH, Bethesda, Md., 1978—; mem. basic sci. merit award bd. VA, 1989-92. Mem. editl. bd. Ultrastructural Pathology, 1985-96, Virchows Archiv A, 1986—, In Vivo, 1988—, Hosp. Physician, 1990-96, Human Pathology, 1991—; assoc. editor Lab. Investigation, 1982-94; regional editor N.Am. Differentiation, 1985-96. Recipient Christian R. and Mary F. Lindback award for disting. teaching Jefferson Med. Coll., Phila., 1988. Mem. Am. Assn. Pathologists, Am. Assn. for Cancer Rsch., Internat. Acad. Pathology, Internat. Soc. Differentiation, Developmental Biology Soc., Am. Soc. for Cell Biology. Office: U Kansas Sch of Med Dept Pathol & Lab Med 3901 Rainbow Blvd Kansas City KS 66160-0001

DAMM, SALLY ANN, health facility administrator; b. Lemmon, S.D., May 21, 1955; d. Saliah and Irene (Holmes) Pazie; m. Philip H. Damm, Sept. 9, 1979. BA, Huron Coll., 1977. Lic. nursing home adminstr., social work assoc., S.D. Social worker S.D. Dept. Social Svcs., Huron, 1976-77; dir. cmty. ctr. for devel. disabled Parkview, Redfield, S.D., 1977-79; case mgr. for devel. disabled Redfield State Hosp. and Sch., 1980-87; adminstr. Sun Dial Manor Inc., Bristol, S.D., 1987—; bd. dirs. Dacotah Bank Webster; preceptor for new nursing home adminstrs. State Bd. Examiners Nursing Home Adminstrs., 1991. Pres. Am. Cancer Soc.; bd. dirs. St. John's Luth. Ch., Webster, 1990-93; bd. dirs., mem. ednl. com. S.D. Assn. Homes and Svcs. for Aged, 1990-95. Mem. Am. Coll. Health Care Adminstrs., S.D. Assn. Healthcare Orgns. (ednl. com. 1996). Office: Sun Dial Manor Inc 410 2d St Box 337 Bristol SD 57219

DAMMON, JAMES WARREN, JR., cardiovascular and thoracic surgeon; b. Waco, Tex., Jan. 22, 1956; s. James Warren Sr. and Patsy Jean (Walker) D.; m. Cynthia Gail Bowling, Aug. 5, 1978; 1 child, Lauren Grace. BS in Chemistry cum laude, Baylor U., 1978; MD, U. Tex., Dallas, 1982. Diplomate Am. Bd. Surgery, Am. Bd. Thoracic Surgery with added qualifications in surg. critical care. Resident in gen. surgery N.C. Bapt. Hosp., Winston-Salem, 1982-87; resident in thoracic surgery U. Tenn., Memphis, 1987-89; cardiovascular and thoracic surgeon Kans. Heart Inst., Topeka, 1989—. Fellow ACS, Am. Coll. Chest Physicians, S.W. Surg. Congress, Internat. Coll. Surgeons; mem. Soc. Critical Care Medicine, Soc. Thoracic Surgeons, Nat. Eagle Scout Assn. Baptist. Office: Kans Heart Inst 830 SW Mulvane Topeka KS 66606

DAMON, MICHAEL CRAIG, nursing administrator; b. Watertown, N.Y., Apr. 14, 1951; s. Ronald David and Helen I. (O'Hara) D.; m. Carmella Chiumento, Feb. 23, 1970 (div. May 1981); children: Carrie Lynn, Michael C.; m. Gerrilynn A. Sprague, Oct. 21, 1982; children: Elliott R., Jeremy S. AAS in Nursing, Jefferson Coll., 1974; BS in Health Svcs. Adminstrn., Fla. Internat. U., 1987. RN, advanced nurse practitioner, Fla. Staff nurse Mercy Hosp., Watertown, 1974-76; pub. health nurse Jefferson County Pub. Health Dept., Watertown, 1976-77; nursing supr. ICU, CCU, pediatric ICU, emergency rm., chief supr. nurses North Dade Hosp., Opalacka, Fla., 1977-79; advanced nurse practitioner geriatrics Miami (Fla.) Jewish Home for Aged, 1979-84; advanced nurse practitioner Public Health Trust - Human Resources Health Ctr., Miami, 1984—, dir. nursing; mem. South Fla. AIDS Network, Miami, 1984—; cons./ expert on long term sub-acute and AIDS care, 1984—; co-dir. Prism Med. Svcs., Dade Corrections Inst., Miami, 1989-90; v.p. J&M Med. Legal Cons., Mirimar and Sunrise, Fla., 1992—; developer spl. care unit for long term AIDS care, 1989-91. Grantee Ryan White Funds, 1990. Mem. ANA, Assn. Nurses in AIDS Care (founder, treas. 1988-91, Miami chpt. 1992—, bd. dirs.), Am. Acad. Nurse Practitioners, Fla. Nurses Assn., Fla. Assn. Dirs. Long Term Care. Home: 13250 NW 11th Dr Sunrise FL 33323

DAMROSCH, SHIRLEY PATCHEL, social psychologist, educator; b. Wilkes-Barre, Pa.; d. Charles and Sophie (Ruch) Petchel; m. William Ludlow Damrosch, June 4, 1970; 1 child, Guy Donahoo. BA, Ohio State U.; PhD, U. Minn., 1975. Assoc. prof. social psychology and rsch. cons. Ctr. for Methodological Rsch., Sch. Nursing, U. Md., Balt., 1977—. Contbr. articles to profl. jours., chpts. to books. Mem. AIDS Prevention Edn. Adv. Com. of the Howard County Pub. Sch. System, Columbia, Md., 1990—. Mem. APA, Phi Beta Kappa. Office: Univ of Md 655 W Lombard St Baltimore MD 21201-1512

DAMSBO, ANN MARIE, psychologist; b. Cortland, N.Y., July 7, 1931; d. Jorgen Einer and Agatha Irene (Schenck) D. B.S., San Diego State Coll., 1952; M.A., U.S. Internat. U., 1974, Ph.D., 1975. Diplomate Am. Acad. Pain Mgmt. Commd. 2d lt. U.S. Army, 1952, advanced through grades to capt., 1957; staff therapist Letterman Army Hosp., San Francisco, 1953-54, 56-58, 61-62, Ft. Devers, Ft. Devens, Mass., 1955-56, Walter Reed Army Hosp., Washington, 1958-59, Tripler Army Hosp., Hawaii, 1959-61, Ft. Benning, Ga., 1962-64; chief therapist U.S. Army Hosp., Ft. McPherson, Ga., 1964-67; ret. U.S. Army, 1967; med. missionary So. Presbyterian Ch., Taiwan, 1968-70; psychology intern So. Naval Hosp., San Diego, 1975; predoctoral intern Naval Regional Med. Ctr., San Diego, 1975-76, postdoctoral intern, 1975-76, chief, founder pain clinic, 1977-86; chief pain clinic, 1977-86; adj. tchr. U. Calif. Med. Sch., San Diego; lectr., U.S., Can., Eng., France, Australia; cons. forensic hypnosis to law enforcement agys.; approved cons. in hypnosis. Contbr. articles to profl. publs., chpt. to book. Tchr. Sunday sch. United Meth. Ch., 1945—; Rep. Nat. Candidate Trust Presdl. adv. com., platform planning commn. at-large-del. Fellow Am. Soc. Clin. Hypnosis (psychology mem.-at-large, exec. bd. 1989-90), San Diego Soc. Clin. Hypnosis (pres. 1980); mem. AAUW, Am. Phys. Therapy Assn., Calif. Soc. Clin. and Hypnosis (bd. govs.), Am. Soc. Clin. Hypnosis Edn. Rsch. Found. (trustee 1992-94), Internat. Platform Assn., Am. Soc. Clin. Hypnosis (exec. bd.), Ret. Officers Am., Ret. Officers Assn. (rep. presdl. task force, pres. adv. com.), Toastmasters (local pres.), Job's Daus. Republican. Home and Office: 1062 W Fifth Ave Escondido CA 92025-3802

DAN, BRUCE B., internist; b. Memphis, Dec. 20, 1946; s. Merrill D. and Hope B. Dan. BS, MIT, 1968; MD, Vanderbilt U., 1974, postgrad., 1979-81. Diplomate Nat. Med. Examiners, Am. Bd. Internal Medicine. Sr. engr., computer scientist Mass. Gen. Hosp., Boston, 1969-70; instrument systems analyst NASA, Cambridge, Mass., 1970; postdoctoral computerized medicine U. Tex. Health Sci. Ctr., Dallas, 1975-76; intern in internal medicine Vanderbilt U. Hosp., Nashville, 1975-76, resident in internal medicine, 1976-78; epidemic intelligence officer Ctrs. for Disease Control, Atlanta, 1979-81; dir. sci. affairs AMA, Chgo., 1984-92; sr. editor Jour. of AMA, 1984-92; William Benton fellow U. Chgo., 1990-91; exec. v.p., exec. editor Med. News Network, N.Y.C., 1993-94; sr. fellow Nat. AIDS Fund, Washington, 1995—; dir. med. affairs Ctr. for Biomed. Comm., 1994—; mem. steering com. Internat. Congress on Peer Rev., Chgo., 1986-89; mem. adv. com. Am. Heart Assn., Chgo., 1987-91; pres. MedNet Comm., 1996—. Editor: A Piece of My Mind, 1988, AMA Manual of Style, 8th edit., 1988, Roundsmanship Series, 1989-94. Hon. chmn. Muscular Dystrophy Assn., Chgo., 1989-91. Lt. comdr. USPHS, 1979-81. Rsch. project grantee So. Med. Assn., 1976; recipient Alexandr Langmuir Prize, Ctrs. for Disease Control, Atlanta, 1981, Commendation medal USPHS, 1982, Emmy award NATAS, 1989, John McGovern award Am. Med. Writers Assn., 1991; Morris Fischbein Med. Journalism fellow AMA, 1983. Mem. Coun. Biology Editors, Epidemic Intelligence Svc. Alumni Assn. (pres. 1990-92), Soc. Scholarly Pub., Nat. Assn. Sci. Writers.

DANA, EDWARD RUNKLE, physician, educator; b. Columbus, Ohio, May 20, 1919; s. Lowell Brockway and Helen (Runkle) D.; m. Lorraine Kirschner, Aug. 2, 1945; children—Edward R., H. Richard. A.B., Wesleyan U., 1941; M.D., Johns Hopkins U., 1944. Diplomate: Am. Bd. Radiology. Intern Univ. Hosps., Cleve., 1944-45; resident radiology Johns Hopkins Hosp., 1947-50; dir. radiology Mercy Hosp., Balt., 1950-64; asst. prof. radiology Johns Hopkins Med. Sch., 1960-68, asso. prof., 1968-69; chief diagnostic radiology Orange County Med. Center, Orange, Calif., 1969—; asso. prof. radiology U. Calif. Med. Sch., Irvine, 1969-79; prof. U. Calif. Med. Sch., 1979—, joint prof. gastroenterology, 1969—, chief gastrointestinal radiology, 1976-77, co-chief, 1977—; co-dir. swallowing ctr. U. Calif. Med. Ctr., Coll. Medicine, Irvine; cons. gastroent. radiology Long Beach (Calif.) VA Hosp., 1974—. Contbr. articles to profl. jours. Served to capt. M.C. U.S. Army, 1945-47. Named Tchr. of Yr. U. Calif. Irvine Coll. Med., 1996. Mem. Soc. Gastrointestinal Radiologists, Mensa, Sigma Chi, Phi Chi. Club: Md. Home: 2523 Altamar Dr Irvine Cove Laguna Beach CA 92651 Office: U Calif Irvine Med Ctr Orange CA 92668

DANCER, RICHARD EDWIN, chemical dependency psychotherapist, nursing educator; b. Toledo, July 4, 1930; s. Lloyd Russell and Margaret Loretta (Lafountain) D.; m. Mary Jane Watkins, Sept. 1, 1950 (div. Sept. 1978); children: John, Mark; m. Cynthia Ayres Fox, Jan. 9, 1979. BA, U. Toledo, 1955; MS, U. North Fla., 1980. Cert. addictions profl. Program dir. Flint Gen. Hosp. (Mich.), St. Joseph Hosp., Flint, Flint Osteo. Hosp., 1975-77; program dir. 4 county area St. Joseph Hosp., Tawas City, Mich., 1977-79; pres. Dancer & Assocs., Inc., 1978—; chief, aftercare svcs., alcoholism therapist Palm Beach Inst., Jupiter, Fla., 1982-84; program dir. Awareness Ctr. for chem. and other dependencies, Jupiter, Fla., 1984—; chem. dependency/co-dependency educator. Served with U.S. Army, 1952-54. Mem. Nat. Assn. Alcoholism and Drug Abuse Counselors, Fla. Assn. Alcoholism and Drug Abuse Counselors, Rotary (Tawas City), Masons, Phi Kappa Phi. Home and Office: 1008 Stillwater Dr Jupiter FL 33458-6821

DANCIS, JOSEPH, pediatrics educator, researcher; b. N.Y.C., Mar. 19, 1916; s. Abraham Goldberg and Sarah Dancis; m. Bernice Schrier, July 4, 1948; children: Andrew, Dale. AB, Columbia U., 1934; MD, St. Louis U., 1938. Intern Queens Gen. Hosp., N.Y., 1938-40; resident NYU-Bellevue Hosp., 1945-46; prof. pediatrics Sch. Medicine NYU, 1960—, chmn. dept. pediatrics, 1974-89; cons. Nat. Inst. Child Health and Human Devel. NIH, 1971-78. Mem. edit. bds. sci. jours. Served to capt. Med. Service Corp. U.S. Army, 1941-45. John and Mary Markle scholar, 1956-61; NIH grantee, 1962-74; recipient nutrition studies award, Borden Co., 1966. Mem. Am. Pediatrics Soc. (council 1973-80, pres. 1983-84), Soc. Gynecol. Investigation (hon.), Alpha Omega Alpha. Office: NYU Sch of Medicine Dept of Pediatrics 550 1st Ave New York NY 10016-6481

D'ANCONA, SILVIA, medical educator; b. Rome, June 25, 1927; d. Umberto and Luisa (Volterra) D'A. MD, U. Padova, Italy, 1952; Specialization in Oncology, U. Pavia, 1955. Internal physician U. Padovs, 1952-53, vol. asst., 1954-55, prelist asst., 1960-66, asst., 1966-83, assoc. prof., 1983—; prelist asst. U. Pavia, 1955-56; internal physician U. Milan, 1956-58; scholarship oncology Heidelberg, Germany, 1959-60; visitor Chester Beatty, London, 1968. Overseas fellow Royal Soc. Medicine, London, 1992. Home: Via Scalcerle 9, 35123 Padova Italy

DANDO, THERESA MARIE, medical and surgical nurse; b. Phoenix, Feb. 4, 1964; d. Walter Mathias Jr. and Helen Louise (Glennie) Kelting; m. Michael Edward Dando June 6, 1987; children: Stephanie Marie, Eric Michael. BSN, U. Ariz., 1988. RN Tex., Ariz., BLS Tex., Ariz., ACLS, CNIII, Ariz. Med./surg. nurse St. Luke's Episcopal Hosp., Houston, 1988-89; cardiovascular telemetry nurse Good Samaritan Regional Med. Ctr., Phoenix, 1989-91; resource team nurse Thunderbird Samaritan Med. Ctr., Glendale, Ariz., 1991-95; asst. dir. HSDRC, 1995—; chair med./surg. LTC divsn. Scope practice com. Ariz. State Bd. Nursing, Phoenix, 1994—; orientation speaker the Cerner Project Samaritan Health Svc., Phoenix, 1995-96; co-founder specialized orientation for resource team nurses project Thunderbird Samaritan Med. Ctr., Glendale, Ariz., 1994—. Contbr. articles to profl. jours. Alumni recruitment vol. U. Ariz., Phoenix, 1994—; founder Parish Nurse Ministry Comty Ch. of Joy, Glendale, Ariz., 1996—.

DANDOY, SUZANNE EGGLESTON, physician, state agency executive; b. Los Angeles, Jan. 2, 1935; d. Leonard Lester and Catherine (Wheelwright) Eggleston; m. Jeremiah Richard Dandoy, June 14, 1958; children: Kevin, Bret, Jolyn. BA, UCLA, 1956, MD, 1960, MPH, 1963. Diplomate: Am. Bd. Preventive Medicine. Intern, Los Angeles Harbor Gen. Hosp., Torrance, Calif., 1960-61; resident Los Angeles Health Dept., 1961-62, 63-64; epidemiologist San Diego Dept. Pub. Health, 1967-68; bur. chief Ariz. Dept. Health Service, Phoenix, 1970-72; asst. commr. Ariz. Dept. Health Service, 1973-74, asst. dir., 1974-75, dir., 1975-80; prof. health adminstrn. Ariz. State U., Tempe, 1981-85; exec. dir. Utah Dept. Health, Salt Lake City, 1985-92; dep. commr. Va. Dept. Health, Richmond, 1992-94; dir. Va. Beach Health Dept., 1994—; clin. prof. Eastern Va. Med. Sch., 1995—; adj. prof. U. Utah; bd. dirs. Pub. Health Found. Chair editl. bd. Am. Jour. Pub. Health; contbr. articles to profl. jours.; assoc. editor: Am. Jour. Preventive Medicine, 1996—. Chair Nat. Vaccine Adv. Com., HHS; adv. com. on immunization practices HEW; pres. Utah Women's Forum. Recipient award Ariz. Dietetic Assn., 1976; award Maricopa County Med. Soc., 1980. Fellow APHA, Am. Coll. Preventive Medicine (pres. 1991-93, Disting. Svc. award 1995); mem. AMA, Nat. Assn. County and City Health Ofcls., Assn. State Health Officers (pres. 1990-91), Phi Beta Kappa, Delta Omega. Democrat. Mormon. Home: 1321 Botetourt Gardens Norfolk VA 23517 Office: Va Beach Health Dept 3432 Virginia Beach Blvd # 103 Virginia Beach VA 23452

D'ANDRADE, HUGH A(LFRED), pharmaceutical company executive, lawyer; b. Metuchen, N.J., Nov. 7, 1938; s. Herman and Lucille D'A.; m. Nancy K. Koyen (div.); 1 dau., Janine; m. Mary T. Bohner. BA in Econs., Rutgers U., 1961; LLB cum laude, Columbia U., 1964. Bar: N.J. 1964. Law sec. to assoc. justice N.J. Supreme Ct., 1964-65; assoc. Toner, Crowley, Woelper & Vanderbilt, Newark, 1965-68; gen. atty. CIBA Corp., Summit, N.J., 1968-70; counsel to pharms. div. CIBA-GEIGY Corp., Summit, 1970-75, v.p. and counsel pharms. div., 1975-77; sr. v.p. and counsel for planning and adminstrn. dept. CIBA-GEIGY, Summit, 1980-81; sr. v.p. adminstrn. Schering-Plough Corp., Kenilworth, N.J., 1981-84; exec. v.p. adminstrn. Schering-Plough Corp., Madison, N.J., 1984-95, vice chmn., chief adminstrv. officer, 1996—; mem. bd. dirs. AutoImmune Inc. Trustee Drew U.; mem. bd. visitors Columbia U. Law Sch. Mem. ABA, N.J. Bar Assn., Biotech. Industry Orgn. (bd. dirs.). Office: Schering-Plough Corp 1 Giralda Farms Madison NJ 07940-1027

D'ANDREA, MARK, radiation oncologist; b. Palos Park, Ill., May 24, 1960; s. Anthony E. and Adriene (Boka) D'A. BA in Chemistry, Religion, and Biology, Luther Coll., 1981; MD, Ponce (P.R.) Sch. Medicine, 1985. Diplomate Am. Acad. Pain Mgmt., Am. Bd. Radiology in Radiation Oncology. Resident in internal medicine Cabrini Med. Ctr., N.Y.C., 1985-86; resident in radiation oncology Meth. Hosp., Bklyn., 1986-89; radiation oncologist East Tex. Cancer Ctr., Tyler, 1989-94, Mother Frances Hosp., Tyler, Med. Ctr. Hosp., Tyler, U. Tex. Health Ctr., Tyler, St. Josephs Hosp., Paris, Tex., McCuistion Hosp., Paris, Tex., Longview (Tex.) Radiation Oncology Ctr.; resident U. Tex. Med. Branch, Galveston, 1991-92; dir. radiation oncology Bayshore Hosp., Pasadena, Tex., 1994—; prof. radiation biology Tyler Jr. Coll., 1990-91; chief resident in radiation oncology Meth. Hosp., Bklyn., 1988-89; cons. Longview Regional, Good Shepherd Hosp., 1989-94, pres., chmn. bd. Danhul Corp., 1992. Patentee diagnostic marking catheter system for use in radiation diagnosis procedures. Chmn. Com. Pub. health Kings and Bklyn. County, N.Y., 1988-89. Named One of Outstanding Young Men Am., 1987; recipient Outstanding award Ill. Jr. Acad. Sci., 1978. Fellow Am. and Internat. Coll. Angiology, InterAm. Coll. Physicians and Surgeons; mem. Am. Inst. Chemists (ethics com.), Am. Chem. Soc., Am. Soc. Clin. Oncology, Am. Soc. Therapeutic Radiology and Oncology, AMA, Radiol. Soc. N.Am., Med. Soc. N.Y. State, Kings County Med. Soc., Acad. Medicine Bklyn., Smith County Med. Soc., Tex. Med. Assn., Circilo de Radioterapeutas ibero Latino Americanos. Office: Bayshore Hosp Ctr Dept Radiation Oncology 4000 Spencer Hwy Pasadena TX 77504-1221

D'ANDREA-SMITH, VIVIEN, internist; b. Detroit, Nov. 1, 1958; m. Stephen D'Andrea; 1 child, Lauren. BA, U. Calif., San Diego, 1982; MD, U. Calif., San Francisco, 1986. Diplomate Am. Bd. Internal Medicine. Intern, then resident in internal medicine Santa Clara County Med. Ctr., San Jose, Calif., 1986-89, chief resident, 1989-90; pvt. practice, Los Altos, Calif., 1990—; site med. dir. Camino Med. Group, Los Altos, 1994—. Med. Explorer's advisor Boy Scouts Am., Mountain View, Calif., 1990—. Mem. AMA, ACP, Am. Med. Women's Assn. Office: Camino Med Group 4906 El Camino Real Los Altos CA 94022

DANDRIDGE, WALTER CURTIS, JR., surgeon; b. San Angelo, Tex., Oct. 31, 1943; s. Walter Curtis Sr. and Inez (Colwell) D.; m. Cheryl Ann Bennett, Oct. 23, 1973 (div. May 1992); children: Michael, Andrea, Alisha. BA, U. Okla., 1965, MD, 1969. Diplomate Am. Bd. Surgery. Intern U. Hosp., Oklahoma City, 1969-70; resident in surgery Okla. Health Scis. Ctr., Oklahoma City, 1970-74; ptnr. Joplin Surgical Assocs., Joplin, Mo., 1976—; med. staff St. John's Regional Med. Ctr., Joplin, Mo., 1976—, also dir. metabolic support svcs., 1978—, trauma dir., 1991—, chmn. dept. surgery, 1993—; med. dir. clin. nutrition svcs. Freeman Hosp., Joplin, Mo., 1976—; med. staff McCune Brooks Hosp., Carthage, Mo., 1978—; chmn. trauma com. State of Mo. Southern Regional Bureau Emergency Med. Svcs., Jefferson City, 1993—; bd. dirs. McCune Brooks Hosp., 1993—. Pres. Jasper County chpt. Am. Cancer Soc., Joplin, Mo., 1981-86, 91-94; v. p., bd. dirs. Mo. Div. Am. Cancer Soc., Jefferson City, Mo., 1987. Lt. comdr. USN, 1974-76. Recipient recognition award AMA, 1979. Fellow Am. Coll. Surgeons; mem. Am. Trauma Soc., Southwestern Surgical Cong., Am. Soc. Parainternal Internal Nutrition (pres.), Soc. Am. Gastrointestinal Endoscopic Surgery. Republican. Presbyterian. Office: Joplin Surgical Assocs Inc PO Box 3058 Joplin MO 64803

DANDRIDGE, WILLIAM SHELTON, orthopedic surgeon; b. Atoka, Okla., May 21, 1914; s. Theodore Oscar and Estelle (Shelton) D.; m. Pearl Sessions, Feb. 3, 1941; children: Diana Dawn, James Rutledge. B.A., U. Okla., 1935; M.D., U. Ark., 1939; M.S., Baylor U., 1950. Intern, St. Paul's Hosp., Dallas, 1939-40; surg. residence Med. Arts Hosp., Dallas, 1940; commd. 1st lt. USAF, advanced through grades to lt. col., 1950; chief reconditioning svc. and reconstructive surgery Ashburn Gen. Hosp., McKinney, Tex., 1945-46; neurosurg. resident Brooke Army Med. Center, San Antonio, 1946-47; orthopedic surg. resident, 1947-50; chief orthopedic svc. and gen. surgery Francis E. Warren AFB, Cheyenne, Wyo., Travis AFB, Susan, Calif., 1950-51; chief orthopedic svc. and gen. surgery Shepherd AFB, 1951-52; comdg. officer, chief orthopedic svc., chief gen. surgery Craig AFB Hosp., Selma, Ala., 1952-53; pvt. practice medicine specializing in orthopedic surgery, Muskogee, Okla., 1954-69, 72-94; courtesy staff Muskegon Gen. Hosp.; orthopedic cons. McAlester (Okla.) Gen. Hosp., VA Hosp., Muskogee. Exec. mem. Eastern Okla. council Boy Scouts Am. Fellow ACS, Internat. Coll. Surgeons; mem. Am. Fracture Assn., Nat. Found. (adviser 1958-61), N.Y. Acad. Scis., Okla. State, Pan-Am., So., Aerospace Med. Assns., AMA, So. Orthopaedic Assn., Garfield County Med. Soc., S.W. Surg. Congress, Am. Rheumatology Soc., Air Force Assn. (life). Republican. Methodist. Masons, K.T. Shriners, Jesters, Lions, Club of Enid. Contbr. articles to profl. jours.; research and evaluation of various uses of refrigerated homogenous bone. Home: 802 S Hayes St Apt 13 Enid OK 73703-6655

DANDRIFOSSE, GUY AUBIN, biochemist, physiologist; b. Stavelot, Walloony, Belgium, June 15, 1940; s. Theodore Martin Dandrifosse and Julia Ferdinande Blockman; m. Jeannine Marie Lamborelle, Aug. 1, 1964; children: Jean-François, Anne-Catherine. B Biology, U. Liege, Belgium, 1960, M in Zoology, 1962, PhD in Zoology, 1968, Agrege Enseignement Superieur, 1977. Asst. U. Liege, 1962-68, 1st asst., 1968-72, chef de travaux, 1972-77, agrege de l'enseignement superieur, 1977-79, charge de cours associe, 1979-87, prof. biochemistry, 1987—. Contbr. over 200 articles to sci. jours., chpts. to books. Decorated officier Ordre de Leopold II, comdr. Ordre de la Couronne (Belgium). Mem. Kiwanis (officer). Office: U Liege Faculty Medicine, Sart Tilman, 4000 Liege Belgium

DANE, FRANCIS CHARLES, psychology educator; b. Milw., July 21, 1952; s. Joseph Henry Oorszynski and Jacquelyn Alfreda (Klotz) Fussell; m. Pamela Jean Metzelfeld, Aug. 4, 1973 (div. Mar. 1986); m. Linda Ruth Kirchofer, Sept. 9, 1988. Student, U. Wis., Waukesha, 1971-73; BS in Psychology, U. Wis., Milw., 1974; MA in Psychology, U. Kans., 1977, PhD in Psychology, 1979. Teaching asst. U. Wis., Milw., 1974-75; rsch. asst. U. Kans., Lawrence, 1975-77, asst. instr., 1977-79; asst. prof. SUNY, Oswego, 1979-83; asst. prof. Clemson (S.C.) U., 1983-86, assoc. prof., 1986-88; asst. prof. Mercer U., Macon, Ga., 1988-91, assoc. prof., chair psychology dept., 1991—; pres. Pairadane Enterprises, Macon, 1988—. Author: Common and Uncommon Sense of Social Psychology, 1988; Research Methods, 1990; coauthor: Social Psychology in the Nineties, 1992; editor Contemporary Social Psychology, 1990—. Mem. APA, Am. Psychol. Soc., Soc. for Advancement Social Psychology (sec.-treas. 1983—), Soc. Psychol. Study Social Issues, Soc. Personality and Social Psychology, Am. Statis. Assn. Office: Mercer U Psychology Dept Macon GA 31207

DANEHOLT, PER BERTIL EDVARD, molecular geneticist; b. Borås, Sweden, Nov. 25, 1940; s. Alva Frisk, Nov. 25, 1967. B Medicine, U. Gothenburg (Sweden), 1962; MD, Karolinska Inst., Stockholm, 1970. Asst. prof. Karolinska Inst., Stockholm, 1970-77, prof. molecular genetics, 1981—, chmn. dept. molecular genetics, 1987-92, chmn. dept. cell and molecular biology, 1993—; researcher Swedish Natural Sci. Rsch. Coun., Stockholm, 1978-80; mem. faculty bd. Karolinska Inst., Stockholm, 1984-90, mem. Nobel Com., 1990—; bd. mem. Swedish Natural Sci. Rsch. Coun., Stockholm, 1983-89; mem. Coun. of European Molecular Biology Lab., Heidelberg, 1983-89. Contbr. articles to profl. jours. Mem. Swedish Hybrid DNA Delegation, Stockholm, 1983-91; chmn. ethical com. Royal Swedish Acad. Scis., Stockholm, 1990—; bd. mem. Göran Gustafsson Found., Stockholm, 1989—. Recipient Eric K. Fernström prize Karolinska Inst., Stockholm, 1984; E. Roosevelt Internat. Cancer fellow Internat. Union Against Cancer, Geneva, 1987-88. Mem. Royal Swedish Acad. Scis. (mem. bd.), Royal Physiographic Soc., Academia Europaea, European Molecular Biology Orgn. Home: Vallstigen 13, S-17246 Sundbyberg Sweden Office: Karolinska Inst, S-17177 Stockholm Sweden

DANEV, STOYAN, clinical laboratory medicine educator; b. Sofia, Bulgaria, Jan. 10, 1932; s. Ivailo and Olga (Oertel) D.; m. Maria Assenova, Aug. 11, 1963; 1 child, Tatiana. Grad. in English philology, State U. Bulgaria, Sofia, 1953; MD, Med. Acad. Bulgaria, Sofia, 1964, PhD, 1977, D Med. Sci., 1991. Asst. Postgrad. Med. Sch., Sofia, 1965-73; asst. Med. Acad. Bulgaria, 1974-78, assoc. prof., 1978-91, chmn. clin. lab. chair, prof., 1991—; tchr. WHO, Sofia, 1982, 85, Lisbon, Portugal, 1985, WHO advisor, Geneva, 1984; mem. Med. Faculty Bd., Sofia, 1990—; v.p. Denis de Rougemont Culture Ctr., Sofia, 1991—; coord. TEMPUS Teaching Project, Sofia, Plovdiv, Namur, Liege, Bonn, Hamburg med. schs., 1995—; exec. bd. Euroclub, Sofia, 1995—. Author: (monograph) Diagnostic Enzymology, 1974, Antibody Deficiency in Children, 1975, Acid State Balance, 1981; editor Lab. Abstract Bull., 1991; also articles on clin. chemistry and enzymology and 15 tech. innovations. Recipient 100 Yrs. Bulgarian Pub. Health medal Bulgarian Ministry of Health, 1980, medal for outstanding profl. achievements State Coun., 1987. Mem. Internat. Soc. Clin. Enzymology (founding), Internat. Fedn. Clin. Chemistry (nat. rep.), Balkan Clin. Lab. Found. (pres. 1993—), N.Y. Acad. Scis., Bulgarian Clin. Lab. Soc. (pres. 1991—, sec. 1981), Assn. Clin. Biochemists (U.K.). Greek Orthodox. Home: Z Zerkovski 3, 1421 Sofia Bulgaria Office: Med Acad Clin Lab, Georgui Sofiisky 1, 1431 Sofia Bulgaria

DANFORTH, DAVID NEWTON, JR., physician, scientist; b. N.Y.C., June 25, 1942; s. David Newton and Gladys Margaret (Blaine) D.; m. Anne Walker Nickson, Apr. 13, 1985. BA, Northwestern U., Evanston, Ill., 1965; MD, Northwestern U., Chgo., 1971; MS, U. N.Mex., Albuquerque, 1967. Diplomate Am. Bd. Surgery. Intern, then resident Cornell Med. Ctr., N.Y.C., 1971-74, 77-79; clin. assoc. NIH, Bethesda, Md., 1974-77; surg. fellow M.D. Anderson Hosp., Houston, 1979-80; sr. staff fellow NIH, Bethesda, 1980-82; sr. investigator Nat. Cancer Inst., NIH, Bethesda, 1982—. Editor: Diagnosis and Management of Breast Cancer, 1988; contbr. articles to profl. jours. Served to lt. comdr. USPHS, 1974-76. Fellow Am. Cancer Soc., 1979-80. Fellow ACS, Soc. Surg. Oncology, Am. Soc. Clin. Oncology, Am. Assn. Cancer Research, Endocrine Soc. Republican. Episcopalian. Home: 7301 Meadow Ln Chevy Chase MD 20815 Office: Nat Cancer Inst Surgery Br Bldg 10 Rm 2B38 Bethesda MD 20892

DANFORTH, WILLIAM HENRY, retired academic administrator, physician; b. St. Louis, Apr. 10, 1926; s. Donald and Dorothy (Claggett) D.; m. Elizabeth Anne Gray, Sept. 1, 1950; children: Cynthia Danforth Prather, David Gray, Maebelle Danforth Reed, Elizabeth D. Sanhey. A.B., Princeton U., 1947; M.D., Harvard U., 1951. Intern Barnes Hosp., St. Louis, 1951-52; resident Barnes Hosp., 1954-57; now mem. staff; asst. prof. medicine Washington U., St. Louis, 1960-65, asso. prof., 1965-67, prof., 1967-95; vice chancellor for med. affairs Washington U., 1965-71, chancellor, 1971-95; chmn., bd. trustees Washington U., St. Louis, 1995—; pres. Washington U. Med. Sch. and Assoc. Hosps., 1965-71; program coord. Bi-State Regional Med. Program, 1967-68; dir. Ralston Purina Co., McDonnell Douglas Corp., Ralcorp Holdings. Trustee, chmn. bd. Danforth Found.; trustee Am. Youth Found., 1963—, Princeton U., 1970-74; pres. St. Louis Christmas Carols Assn., 1958-74, chmn., 1975—; co-chair Barnes/Jewish Hosp., 1996—; bd. dirs. BJC Health Systems, 1996—. Named Man of Yr. St. Louis Globe-Democrat, 1978. Fellow AAAS, Am. Acad. Arts and Scis.; mem. Inst. Medicine. Home: 10 Glenview Rd Saint Louis MO 63124-1308 Office: Washington U West Campus Campus Box 1044 7425 Forsyth Blvd Ste 262 Saint Louis MO 63105-2198

DANG, CHI VAN, hematology and oncology educator; b. Saigon, Vietnam, Nov. 2, 1954; came to U.S., 1967; s. Chieu Van and Nga Ngoc (Nguyen) D.; m. Mary Doreen Seeley, May 18, 1985; children: Eric Van, Vanessa Marie. BS in Chemistry, U. Mich., 1975; PhD in Chemistry, Georgetown U., 1978; MD, Johns Hopkins U., 1982. Diplomate Am. Bd. Internal Medicine. Resident in internal medicine Johns Hopkins Hosp., Balt., 1982-85; fellow in hematology and oncology U. Calif., San Francisco, 1985-87; asst. prof. medicine Johns Hopkins U., 1987-91, assoc. prof., 1991—, assoc. prof. oncol., pathology, molecular biology & genetics, 1995—, dir. hematology, 1993—; mem. oncological scis. path B NIH, Bethesda, Md., 1993—; cons. Sandoz, East Hanover, N.J., 1993—, Genentech, South San Francisco, Calif., 1995—. Contbr. articles to Nature, Molecular and Cellular Biology, Genes and Devel. Scholar Leukemia Soc. Am., 1992-97. Mem. Am. Soc. for Clin. Investigation, Phi Beta Kappa, Alpha Omega Alpha. Home: 217 Upnor Rd Baltimore MD 21212-3425 Office: Johns Hopkins U Sch Med Ross 1025 720 Rutland Ave Baltimore MD 21205-2109

DANG, MICHAEL H., cardiologist; b. Honolulu, May 19, 1943; s. Arthur C. and Helen L. Dang; m. Joan T. Dang, Dec. 10, 1967; children: Lindsey, Marshall, Travis. BA, U. Hawaii, 1964; MD, U. Colo., 1968. Intern Santa Clara Valley Med. Ctr., San Jose, Calif., 1968-69; resident cardiothoracic Baylor Coll. Medicine, Houston, 1972-78; pvt. practice Honolulu Med. Corp., 1979—. Capt. U.S. Army, 1969-71. Fellow ACS; mem. Hawaii Med. Assn., Hawaiian Surg. Assn., DeBakey Surg. Soc. (bd. dirs.). Office: 550 S Beretania St Honolulu HI 96813

D'ANGELO, ALFRED RICHARD, family practice physician; b. Phila., Aug. 14, 1951; s. Alfred Joseph and Rosemarie M. (Haughney) D.; m. Denise Anne Boyd, Oct. 22, 1977; children: Andrew J., Matthew R., Stephanie M., Alexis M. BA in Chemistry cum laude, Cheyney U., 1975; DO, Phila. Coll. Osteo. Medicine, 1979. Rotating internship Meml. Hosp., York, Pa., 1979-80, emergency physician, 1980-85; family physician, ptnr. Dairyland Med. Ctr., Red Lion, Pa., 1980-91, Keller Med. Ctr., York Haven, Pa., 1980-91; family practice residency dir. Michiana Cmty. Hosp., South Bend, Ind., 1991—, med. dir., 1991—; founder., chmn. bd. dirs. Physicians Diagnostic Ctr., York, 1985-91; mem. Pa. State Bd. Osteopathic Medicine, 1990-91, Pa. Atty. Gen. Task Force for Drug Abuse, 1989-91, Pa. Occupl. Medicine Task Force, 1990-91. Team physician East End Boys Club, York, 1980-91; camp physician Camp Setabaid, Berwyk, Pa., 1987-91. Mem. Ind. Assn. Osteo. Physicians and Surgeons (conv. chmn. 1991—), Am. Osteo. Assn., Am. Coll. Family Practice, Am. Coll. Physician Execs., Alpha Kappa Mu, Phi Sigma Gamma (pres. 1976-77). Democrat. Roman Catholic. Office: Michiana Cmty Hosp 2515 E Jefferson Blvd South Bend IN 46615

D'ANGELO, MARC SCOTT, neurologist; b. Phila., May 21, 1952; s. George Anthony and Antonia Scott (Billett) D'A. BA in Chemistry, U. Pa., 1973; MD, Univ. Autonoma de Guadalajara, Jalisco, Mex., 1980 Diplomate Am. Bd. Psychiatry and Neurology. Intern Meml. U. of Newfoundland, St. John's, Can., 1980-81; with social svc. dept. Angel Leaño Hosp., Zapopan, Jalisco, Mex., 1981-82; fellow in neuropathology Thomas Jefferson U., Phila., 1982-83; resident in neurology U. Cin., 1984-85; resident in neurology Vanderbilt U., Nashville, 1986-87, muscular dystrophy assn. neurology fellow, 1987-88; neurologist South Ga. Neurol. Inst., Thomasville, 1988-92, Hattiesburg (Miss.) Clinic, 1993—. Mem. AMA, Am. Acad. Neurology, Am. Assn. Electrodiagnostic Medicine. Office: Hattiesburg Clinic 415 S 28th Ave Hattiesburg MS 39401

D'ANGIO, GIULIO JOHN, radiologist, educator; b. N.Y.C., May 2, 1922; s. Carlo and Rosa (Calderazzo) D'A.; m. Jean Chittenden Terhune, Aug. 27, 1955; children: Carl, Peter. AB, Columbia U., 1943; MD, Harvard U., 1945; D. Medicine and Surgery (hon.), U. Bologna, 1983. Diplomate: Am. Bd. Radiology, Am. Bd. Therapeutic Radiology. Surg. intern Children's Hosp., Boston, 1945-46, tng. in pathology, 1948-49; resident in radiology Boston City Hosp., 1949-53; also mem. staff; radiation therapist Children's Hosp., Boston, 1956-62; researcher Donner Lab., also Lawrence Radiation Lab., U. Calif., Berkeley, 1962-63; dir. div. radiation therapy U. Minn. Med. Sch., 1964-68; chmn. dept. radiation therapy Meml. Hosp., N.Y.C., 1968-76; dir. children's cancer rsch. ctr. Children's Hosp., Phila., 1976-89; prof. radiation oncology Hosp. of U. Pa., Phila., 1976-92, vice chmn., clin. dir. dept. radiation oncology, 1989-92, prof. emeritus, 1992—; prof. pediatric oncology U. Pa. Med. Sch., Phila., 1976-92; chmn. Nat. Wilms Tumor Study Com., 1968-91; past chmn. cancer clin. investigation rev. com. Nat. Cancer Inst. Editor-in-chief Med. and Pediat. Oncology, 1996—; contbr. numerous articles to med. jours. Capt. M.C. AUS, 1946-48. Decorated Commendation medal; recipient ann. award Am. Cancer Soc., 1978, Heath Meml. award M.D. Anderson Tumor and Cancer Inst., 1979. Fellow Royal Coll. Radiology, Am. Acad. Pediatrics; mem. Am. Acad. Pediatrics (past chmn. sect. oncology-hematology), AAAS, Am. Assn Cancer Rsch., Am. Coll. Radiology, Am. Soc. Therapeutic Radiologists, Mass. Med. Soc., Pa. Med. Soc., Royal Soc. Medicine, Internat. Soc. Pediatric Oncology (pres. 1987), Radiol. Soc. N.Am., Am. Radium Soc., Soc. Pediatric Radiology, Phi Beta Kappa. Episcopalian. Home: 518 Cedar Ln Swarthmore PA 19081-1105 Office: U Pa Hosp Dept Radiation Oncology 3400 Spruce St Philadelphia PA 19104

DANGLER, DAVID WALLER, health center executive, former banker; b. Chgo., Nov. 14, 1915; s. David and Lucy Alexander (Knott) D.; BA, Yale U., 1937; postgrad. Northwestern U., 1939-40. With No. Trust Co., Chgo., 1938-79, v.p. trust dept., until 1979, ret., 1979. Pres. Johnston R. Bowman Health Ctr. for the Elderly, Chgo., 1979-89, hon. pres., 1989—; former pres. bd. trustees Allendale Assn.; life trustee Rush Presbyn., Newberry Libr.; life trustee St. Luke's Med. Ctr.; bd. dirs. Erie Neighborhood House; former elder 1st Presbyn. Ch., Lake Forest, Ill. Club: Univ. (Chgo.).

DANIEL, CARLTON RALPH, III, dermatologist; b. Columbus, Ohio, Mar. 22, 1952; s. Carlton Ralph Jr. and Beverly (Gordon) D.; m. Melissa Paisios, June 15, 1974; children: Carlton Maxwell, Jonathan Gordon. Student, Vanderbilt U., 1970-73; MD, U. Miss., 1973-77. Diplomate Am. Bd. Dermatology. Intern U. Miss. Med. Ctr., Jackson, 1977-78; resident in dermatology U. Ala., Birmingham, 1978-81; pvt. practice Jackson, Miss., 1981—; chief dermatology VA Med. Ctr., Jackson, 1982-94; clin. prof. dermatology U. Miss. Med. Ctr., Jackson, 1985—. Author: Differential Diagnosis of Onychomycosis, 1995; author, editor: The Nail, 1990; contbr. more than 60 articles to profl. jours. Mem. fin. com. Hinds County, Miss.; advisor Lupus Found. Named to Outstanding Young Am., 1984. Fellow Am. Acad. Dermatology (mem. editl. bd.), Am. Soc. Dermatol. Surgery; mem. Jackson Acad. Medicine (pres. 1988-89), Miss. Dermatol. Soc. (pres. 1988-89), Noah Worcester Soc., Jackson Dermatol. Soc. (pres. 1995-96). Office: 971 Lakeland Dr Ste 659 Jackson MS 39216-4608

DANIEL, FRANCES KAY, dental investigator; b. Cin., Oct. 2, 1944; d. William Cassius and Frances (Irving) Eversole; m. Phillip Richard Daniel, 1963; children: Diana K., Stephen R. AS, Angelina Jr. Coll., Lufkin, Tex., 1986; BFA summa cum laude, Stephen F. Austin State U., 1988. Intern Mus. East Tex., 1988; claims examiner Tex. Employment Commn., Lufkin, 1988-89; facilitator Tex. Employment Commn., Houston, 1989-90; investigator Dental Info. Resource Ctr., Houston, 1991-95; motor vehicle divsn. investigator Tex. Dept. Transp., Austin, 1995—; Mem. Rep. Women-Magic Circle, Houston, 1992. Mem. AAUW (sec. Lufkin 1989), Bus. and Profl. Women's Club Houston, Alpha Chi. Office: Tex Dept Transp 410 East Fifth St Austin TX 78768

DANIEL, KENNETH VICTOR, geriatrics services professional; b. Allentown, Pa., Apr. 22, 1955; s. Victor Asher and LaRue Elizabeth (Laubach) D.; m. Barbara Kershner, Apr. 26, 1986; children: Mark Andrew, Christopher S. BA, Kutztown U., 1977; MDiv, United Theol. Sem., 1981; MA, Moravian Theol. Sem., 1989. Ordained to ministry United Ch. of Christ, 1981. Pastor St. Andrew's United Ch. of Christ, Reading, Pa., 1981-89; mgr. Phoebe Terr., Allentown, Pa., 1989-91; asst. adminstr. Phoebe Home, Allentown, 1991-94; adminstr. Phoebe Berks Health Care Ctr., Wernersville, Pa., 1994—; pastoral counselor Wylie House Pastoral Counseling Svc., Bethlehem, Pa., 1988. V.p. Berks Women in Crisis, Reading, 1988; pres. coun. United Ch. Ministry, Reading, 1988; mem. coun. United Ch. Health and Human Svc. Ministries. Mem. Assn. for Clin. Pastoral Edn., Am. Assn. Pastoral Counselors (profl. affiliate), Pa. Non Profit Homes for the Aging, Am. Assn. Homes for the Aging, Am. Coll. Health Care Adminstrs. Office: Phoebe Berks Hlth Care Ctr 1 Heidelberg Dr Wernersville PA 19565

DANIEL, RAMON, JR., psychologist, consultant, bilingual educator; b. Phoenix, Oct. 30, 1936; s. Ramon Sr. and Rosario (Lopez) D.; m. Lydia Cadriel, June 4, 1960; children: Lynda Ruth, Michael Ray, Patricia Lynn. BA in Edn., Ariz. State U., 1964, MA in Edn., 1966; PhD, U.S. Internat. U., 1990. Lic. psychologist, Calif.; cert. bilingual and math. tchr., Calif. Tchr. Phoenix Sch. Dist., 1964, Garden Grove (Calif.) Unified Sch. Dist., 1964-75, Cypress (Calif.) Coll., 1975-77; psychologist Santa Ana (Calif.) Unified Sch. Dist., 1978—; dropout prevention program specialist, student success teams coord. Santa Ana Unified Sch. Dist.; mem. adj. faculty Nat. U., Irvine, Calif., 1991—; with Mexican Consulate, Orange County (Calif.) Office Ednl. Affairs, 1991. Columnist (newspapers) La Conexion Humana, 1988. Mem. Least Restrictive Edn. Task Force, Santa Ana, 1990, Task Force on Linguistic and Cultural Differences, Santa Ana, 1990-91, Community Svc. Bd., Anaheim, Calif., 1990—. Mem. Calif. Assn. Sch. Psychologists, Coun. for Exceptional Children, Assn. Mex.-Am. Educators, Phi Delta Kappa (pres. Calif. chpt. 1988-89, Svc. Key 1989). Office: Santa Ana Unified Sch Dist 1601 E Chestnut Ave Santa Ana CA 92701-6322

DANIEL, SAMUEL MICHAEL, social worker, psychotherapist; b. Badarpur, Assam, India, Mar. 9, 1929; came to U.S., 1955; s. Michael and Yerushabai (Penkar) D.; m. Gussie Silberstein, Dec. 5, 1959 (div. Apr. 1963); m. Erna Weber, Jan. 15, 1975. BSc, Bombay U., 1951; MSW, Howard U., 1957. Social worker N.Y.C. Bd. of Edn., 1965—; pvt. practice psychotherapist N.Y.C., 1965—; psychotherapist N.Y. Cons. & Referral Svc., N.Y.C., 1970—. Hon. pres. Congregation Bina, N.Y.C., 1981—. Mem. NASW, Coun. Psychoanalytical Psychotherapists. Home: 600 W End Ave Apt 1C New York NY 10024-1643 Office: NY Cons and Referral Svc for Psychotherapy 211 W 56th St Ste 6-h New York NY 10019-4312

DANIELL, HERMAN BURCH, pharmacologist; b. Cadwell, Ga., May 25, 1929; s. Walter and Ruby Florence (Burch) D.; m. Lorraine Smith, June 30, 1957; children: Kimberley Ann, Anthony Burch, Walter Herman. B.S. in Pharmacy, U. Ga., 1951, M.S. in Pharmacology, 1964; Ph.D. in Pharmacology; USPHS trainee 1964-66, Med. Coll. S.C., Charleston, 1966. Owner-operator retail pharmacies Savannah, Ga., 1953-62; instr. U. Ga., 1962-64; mem. faculty Med. U. S.C., 1966-92, prof. pharmacology, 1978-92; prof. emeritus, 1992—. Author papers in field. Served to capt. Med. Service Corps, AUS, 1951-53. Grantee USPHS, 1966-85, S.C. Heart Assn., 1966-73. Mem. Am. Soc. Pharmacology and Exptl. Therapeutics, Sigma Xi, Rho Chi, Kappa Sigma. Episcopalian. Home: 1549 Burningtree Rd Charleston SC 29412-2630 Office: 171 Ashley Ave Charleston SC 29425-0001

DANIEL-LEMOINE, JO-ANN C., nurse; b. Woonsocket, R.I., Aug. 8, 1953; d. John and Simonne (Tancrede) Daniel; m. Raymond Paul Lemoine, Mar. 16, 1991; children: Jody, Joshua, Hillary. AA, ASN, Greater Hartford Community Col, 1982; BSN, U. S. Fla., 1989; MBA, Chadwick U., 1994; postgrad., Lasalle U., 1995—. RN, Fla., R.I., Mass., Conn.; cert. basic cardiac life support tchr., advanced cardiac life support, critical care nurse, hospice nurse, IV therapy homecare, PICC/Landmark Cath., cert. cmty. health. Staff nurse ICU, critical care unit New Britain (Conn.) Gen. Hosp.; IV team leader Nat. Med. Home Care, Newington, Conn.; staff nurse Bristol (Conn.) Hosp.; staff nurse surg. ICU St. Anthony's Hosp., St. Petersburg, Fla.; staff nurse trauma unit R.I. Hosp., 1990-91; hospice nurse, case mgr., clin. nurse coord., nurse mgr. Woonsocket VNS, 1991—, quality improvement mgr., 1995—; owner, founder, educator New Eng. Rsch. and Edn., 1991—; N.E., IV cons. Menlo Care, Menlo Park, Calif., 1990—. Mem. ANA, AACN, NAFE, USF-Bayboro Nurses Assn. (pres.), Nat. Platform Soc., Internat. Nursing Soc., Am. Running and Fitness Assn., Golden Key Nat. Honor Soc., Phi Theta Kappa, Sigma Theta Tau, Omicron Delta Kappa. Home: 111 Pine Grove Ave Bellingham MA 02019-2139

DANIELS, JOHN SCOTT, emergency room nurse; b. Burlington, Vt., July 20, 1952; s. Horace J. and Gladys M. (Milligan) D.; m. Cynthia Kuliniewicz, Sept. 2, 1985; children: Jason E., Leah A. BS in Biology, Va. Poly. Inst. and State U., 1974; BSN, Va. Commonwealth U., 1976. Cert. CEN, TNCC, ACLS, ABLS. Rehab. attendant, orderly/patient aide Woodrow Wilson Rehab. Ctr., Fishersville, Va., summers 1972-74; nursing asst. Med. Coll. Va./Va. Commonwealth U., Richmond, summer 1975; gen. duty nurse MCV Hosps., Richmond, 1976-77; staff nurse emergency dept., charge nurse St. Vincent Hosp., Santa Fe, 1977-81; staff nurse emergency dept., charge nurse, med.-surg. team leader Barnes Hosp., St. Louis, 1981—; crisis intervention counselor The Raft, Blacksburg, Va., 1973-74; dep. med. investigator State of N.M., 1978-80. Life mem. Va. Poly. Inst. and State U. Rescue Squad, 1975—; mem. Mayoral Bd. Disaster Svcs., Santa Fe, 1980. Mem. ENA, ARC (life). Office: Barnes Hosp Emergency Dept 1 Barnes Plz Saint Louis MO 63110

DANIELS, JOSEPH, neuropsychiatrist; b. Linden, N.J., Mar. 18, 1931; s. Bennie and Dora (Chese) D.; m. June 28, 1958 (div. Dec. 1988); children: Joan Marie, Jean Dorene. BA cum laude, Lincoln U., Oxford, Pa., 1953; MD, Howard U., 1957. Rotating enter Med. Ctr. Jersey City, 1957-58; resident in internal medicine Worcester (Mass.) City Hosp., 1958-59; resident in psychiatry Ancora (N.J.) Hisp., 1962-65; dir. outpatient clinic Christian Health Care Ctr., Wyckoff, N.J., 1966-70; dir. outpatient dept. Community Mental Health Ctr., N.J. Coll. Medicine, Newark, 1970-79; med. dir., pres. Ctr. for Growth and Reconciliation, East Orange, N.J., 1979-87; sr. staff psychiatrist Pine Rest Christian Hosp., Grand Rapids, Mich., 1987—; mem. Healthy Kent 2000 Health Com., 1993-94; cons. psychiatrist Newark Bd. Edn., 1976-84, East Orange Bd. Edn., Victory House, Newark, 1976-82, Project Rehab, Grand Rapids, 1990-91. Author: The Urban Mission, 1974. Founder, pres., chmn. bd. Ministry Reconciliation Fellowship, 1980-87; bd. dirs. Grand Rapids Reach Inc., pres., 1991-93; selected mem. Leadership Grand Rapids, 1993-94. Capt. M.C., U.S. Army, 1959-62. Mem. Beta Kappa Chi. Baptist. Office: Pine Rest Christian Hosp PO Box 165 300 68th St SE Grand Rapids MI 49501-0165

DANIELS, KURT R., speech and language pathologist; b. Chgo., Oct. 22, 1954; s. Donald R. and Phyllis D. (Lenz) D.; m. Renee Perry, July 5, 1980. BS, Ea. Ill. U., 1976, MS, 1977. Cert. clin. competence speech/lang. pathology; lic. speech/lang. pathologist, nursing home adminstr; tchr's. cert. spl. K-12th grades. Hearing and speech specialist Shapiro Devel. Ctr., Kankakee, Ill.; dysphagia specialist W.A. Howe Devel. Ctr., Tinley Pk., Ill.; cons. in field; presenter in field of dysphagia and developmental disabilities. Recipient Editor's Choice award Nat. Libr. Poetry, 1994, 95. Mem. Am. Speech, Lang. and Hearing Assn., Ill. Network for Augmentative and Alternative Comm., Internat. Soc. Poets.

DANIELS, LYDIA M., health care administrator; b. Louisville, Dec. 21, 1932; d. Effort and Gladys T. (Turner) Williams; student Calif. State U., Hayward, 1967, 69-72; BA, Golden Gate U., 1992, MS, 1993; cert. Samuel Merritt Hosp. Sch. Med. Record Adminstrs., 1959; student Cen. State Coll.,

Ohio, 1950-52; children by previous marriage: Danny Winston, Jeffrey Bruce, Anthony Wayne. Sec. chemistry dept. Cen. State Coll., Wilberforce, Ohio, 1950-52; co-dir. Indian Workcamp, Pala Indian Reservation, Pala, Calif., 1956-58; clk.-typist Camarillo (Calif.) State Hosp., 1956-58; student med. record adminstr. Samuel Merritt Hosp., Oakland, Calif., 1958-59, asst. med. record adminstr., 1962-63, asst. chief med. record adminstr., 1965, chief med. record adminstr., 1965-72; med. record adminstr. Albany (Calif.) Hosp., 1964-65; asst. med. record adminstr. Children's Hosp., San Francisco, 1960; co-dir. interns in community svc. Am. Friends Svc. Com., San Francisco, 1960-61; med. record adminstr. Pacific Hosp., Oakland, Calif., 1963-64; med. record cons. Tahoe Forest Hosp., Truckee, Calif., 1969-73; chief med. record adminstr. Highland Gen. Hosp., Oakland, 1972-74; dir. med. record svcs. U. Calif. San Francisco Hosps. and Clinics, 1975-82; mgr. patient appointments, reception and registration Kaiser-Permanente Med. Ctr., 1982-88; dir. ambulatory adminstrv. svcs., 1988-94, asst. dir. human resources, 1994-96, dir. human resources Brookside Hosp., San Pablo, Calif., 1996—; adj. prof. mgmt., labor mgmt. rels. Golden Gate U., 1978—; pres. Daniels Consultation Svcs., 1988—. Leader Girl Scouts Am. Oakland area council, 1960-62; sunday sch. tchr. Soc. of Friends, Berkeley, Calif., 1961-63, mem. edn. com., 1965-68; mem. policy and adv. bd. Far West Lab. Demonstration Sch., Oakland, 1973-75; bd. dirs. The Californians, Oakland, 1993—, Patrons of the Arts and Humanities, Oakland, 1994—, YWCA, Berkeley, 1995—. Recipient Mgmt. Fellowship award U. Calif., San Francisco, 1979-80. Mem. Am. Med. Record Assn., Calif. Med. Record Assn. (editorial bd. 1976-77, pres. 1974-75), East Bay Med. Record Assn. (chmn. edn. com. 1971-72, pres. 1969-70), Assn. Systems Mgmt., Am. Mgmt. Assn., San Francisco Med. Records Assn. (pres.-elect 1982-83, pres. 1983-84), Am. Assn. Tng. and Devel. (Golden Gate chpt., v.p. prof. devel. 1994—). Author: Health Record Documentation: A Look at Cost, 1981; Inservice Training as a Tool in Managing the Changing Environment in the Medical Record Department, 1983; the Budget as a Management Tool, 1983. Issues editor Topics in Health Record Management, Parts I and II, 1983. Home: 545 Pierce St Apt 1105 Albany CA 94706-1048 Office: Brookside Hosp 2000 Vale Rd San Pablo CA 94806

DANIELS, MADELINE MARIE, psychotherapist, author; b. Newark, Oct. 14, 1948; d. William and Dorothy Barlow; BA cum laude, CCNY, 1971; PhD, Union Grad. Sch., Yellow Springs, Ohio, 1975, PhD, Union Grad. Sch., Cin., 1988; m. Peter W. Daniels, Oct. 18, 1976; children: Jonathan, Jedediah, Jeremiah. Lectr., Westchester C.C., also Bronx C.C., 1973-74; mem. adj. faculty SUNY, Purchase, 1974-76; data processing coordinator GTE Internat., 1976-78; lectr. div. continuing edn. U. N.H., 1979-87; exec. dir. Crossroads Center Human Integration, East Kingston, N.H., 1979-88; administrator Spectrum Cross-Cultural Inst. Youth Inc., East Kingston, 1988-93; rsch./comm. cons. North Bay, Calif., 1994—; rsch./comm. cons. Metis Assocs., Eureka, Calif., 1994—. psychotherapist, lectr., cons. in field. Cert. ind. biofeedback practitioner, clin. mental health counselor. Mem. APA, Internat. council Psychologists (area chair 1988), Biofeedback Soc. Am., Soc. Psychol. Athropology, N.H. Psychol. Orgn., Phi Beta Kappa. Author: Realistic Leadership, 1983, Living Your Religion in the Real World, 1985, A Culturally Different Perspective on Psychology, 1989, (video) The Rainbow Classroom, 1991.

DANIELS, RICHARD ALAN, internist, educator; b. Newark, May 8, 1930; s. Helen Frances (Cooper) D.; m. Norma M. Kasoff, Nov. 16, 1956; children: Steven, Jeffrey, Cathy, Barrie. BA in Chemistry magna cum laude, Syracuse U., 1951; MD summa cum laude, SUNY, Bklyn., 1955. Diplomate Am. Bd. Internal Medicine, Am. Bd. Geriatric Medicine, 1992. Rotating intern Mt. Sinai Hosp., N.Y.C., 1955-56, resident in internal medicine, 1957-59, chief resident in medicine, 1958-59; resident in internal medicine VA Hosp., Bronx, N.Y., 1956-57; practice internal medicine Oakhurst, N.J., 1961—; assoc. clin. prof. medicine Hahnemann Med. Coll., Phila., 1977—; attending physician Monmouth Med. Ctr., Long Branch, 1977—, chief internal medicine sect., 1981-88; instr. phys. diagnosis U. Medicine and Dentistry of N.J. Contbr. articles to profl. jours. Trustee, pres. Monmouth County (N.J.) Heart Assn., 1968-69. Served to maj. USAF, 1959-61. Fellow ACP, N.J. Acad. Medicine; mem. Am. Coll. Cardiology (assoc.), Am. Soc. Internal Medicine, Soc. Tchrs. of Family Practice, N.J. State Med. Soc., Monmouth County Med. Soc., Phi Beta Kappa, Alpha Omega Alpha. Republican. Jewish. Office: 200 Norwood Ave Oakhurst NJ 07755-1713

DANIELS, ROBERT SANFORD, psychiatrist, administrator; b. Indpls., Aug. 12, 1927; s. Harry H. and Mary (Bassett) D.; m. Vikki Ashley; children: Stephen, Allen, Lynn, Judith. BS, U. Cin., 1948, MD, 1951. Intern Cin. Gen. Hosp., 1951; resident U. Cin. Hosp., 1954-57; mem. faculty U. Chgo., 1957-71, dir. psychiat. cons. service, 1961-63, asso. prof. psychiatry, acting chmn. dept., 1963-66, clin. dir., 1966-68, asso. dean community and social medicine, 1968-71, prof. psychiatry and social medicine, 1970-71; dir. Center Health Adminstrn. Studies, Grad. Sch. Bus., 1970-71; dir. dept. psychiatry U. Cin., 1971-75; interim dean U. Cin. (Coll. Medicine), 1972-75; dean Coll. Medicine, U. Cin., 1975-86, also sr. v.p., 1982-86; dean La. State U. Sch. Medicine, New Orleans, 1986-95, exec. asst. to chancellor, 1995—; chief staff Cin. Gen. Hosp., 1972-86, Holmes Hosp., 1972-86; vis. prof. social medicine and clin. epidemiology St. Thomas' Hosp. Med. Coll., London, Eng.; sci. exchange visitor Ministry Health, Moscow, USSR; vis. scholar King Edward VII Hosp. Fund, London, 1977; cons. Cook County Hosp., Ill. State Psychiat. Inst.; spl. research community and group psychiatry, health planning, community health, 1967-69; Chmn. Ill. Mental Health Planning Bd.; mem., chmn. rev. com., psychiatry edn. br. Health Services and Mental Health Adminstrn., 1971-75; mem. nat. mental health adv. bd. NIMH, 1975-79; bd. dirs. Hamilton County Bd. Mental Health and Retardation, 1974-78. Asso. editor: Social Psychiatry. Bd. dirs. Central Ohio River Valley Planning Authority, 1979—. Served with AUS, 1946-47; Served with USAF, 1952-54. Recipient Stella Feis Hoffheimer award U. Cin., 1951. Mem. AMA, Am. Psychiat. Assn., Am. Group Psychotherapy Assn., Assn. Am. Med. Colls. (exec. coun. 1982-87, psychiatry residency rev. coun. 1990—, Daniel Drake medal 1988), Ill. Group Psychotherapy Soc. (pres. 1965-66), Ill. Psychiat. Soc. (pres. 1967), Phi Beta Kappa, Alpha Omega Alpha. Office: La State U Sch Medicine Office of the Chancellor 433 Bolivar St Rm 820 New Orleans LA 70112

DANIELS, SUZANNE MADELEINE, medical technologist; b. Worcester, Mass., July 23, 1941; d. George Edward and Ruth Bernadette (St. Martin) Brodeur; student Central New Eng. Coll. Tech., 1959-62; M.T., Worcester City Hosp. Sch. Med. Tech., 1962; B in Profl. Studies Mgmt. cum laude U. N.H., 1993; children—Edward, Jennifer. Flight exam technician Pratt & Whitney, E. Hartford, Conn., 1962-63; sect. head chemistry/radioisotopes Mt. Sinai Hosp., Hartford, Conn., 1963-65; gen. technician Meml. Hosp., Worcester, 1965-69; blood bank supr. Milford-Whitinsville Regional Hosp., Milford, Mass., 1969-70; asst. clin. supr., sect. head chemistry Worcester Hahnemann Hosp., 1970-75; lab. supr. Weeks Meml. Hosp., Lancaster, N.H., 1975-87; clin. teaching staff Vt. Coll. Sch. Med. Lab. Technicians, 1975-87; office supr. Gulf Coast Pathology and Med. Lab. Services, Inc., Bradenton, Fla., 1987-88; mgr. lab. Littleton (N.H.) Regional Hosp., 1988-93; lab. mgr., asst. office mgr. Family Dr., Bradenton, Fla., 1993—. Mem. Am. Soc. Clin. Pathologists, Clin. Lab. Mgmt. Assn. Roman Catholic. Home: 2220 Holyoke Ave Bradenton FL 34207-5141

DANIELS, WORTH B., JR., retired internist; b. N.Y.C., Jan. 3, 1925. MD, Johns Hopkins U., 1948. From asst. med. rschr. to rschr. Balt. City Hosp., 1954-57; physician, assoc. prof. Johns Hopkins U., 1958—; ret.; med. dir. Union Meml. Hospice. Mem. AMA, ACP, Inst. Medicine-NAS, Am. Soc. Internal Medicine. Address: 11 E Chase St Baltimore MD 21202-2516*

DANIELSEN, RANDY DEE, physician assistant; b. Preston, Idaho, June 14, 1949; s. Henry Grant Danielsen and Lola Deanne (Wilson) Parker; m. Alisa Jean Bridges, Oct. 22, 1971; children: Kathleen, Robert, John, Sarah, Stan, Lynda. BS cum laude, U. Utah, 1979; Physician Asst., U. Utah Medex, 1974. Cert. physician asst. Physician asst. Kearns (Utah) Med. Ctr., 1974-79, ABC HMO, Phoenix, 1979-80, Ariz. Heart Inst., Phoenix, 1980-81, Rainbow Health Svcs., Show Low, Ariz., 1981-82, Maricopa Med. Assocs., Phoenix, 1982-84, Samaritan Health Svcs., Phoenix, 1984-89, USAF, Luke AFB, Ariz., 1989-92, Healthcare Assocs., Inc., Phoenix, 1992-94, Wichita (Kans.) State U., 1994-95, KCOM Southwest Ctr. for Osteo. Med., Phoenix, 1995—; v.p. Healthcare Assocs., Inc., Phoenix, 1981—; bd. dirs. Ariz. Joint Bd. on Regulation of Physician Assts., Phoenix, 1988-92. Contbr. revs. to med. mags. Med. Corpsman USAF, 1970-73, Utah Air Nat. Guard, 1973-74; sgt. 1st class Utah Army Nat. Guard, 1974-80; res. capt. USAFR, 1989, maj. 1989-92; maj. ARiz. Army Nat. Guard, 1992-94, 94—, Kans. Army Nat. Guard, 1994-95. Recipient Nat. Def. Svc. medal bronze Svc. Star, Southwest Asia Svc. medal, 1 bronze Svc. Stars, Army Res. Componenets Achievement Ribbon, Bronze Oak Leaf Cluster, Army NCO Profl. Devel. ribbon, 2 attachments. Fellow Am. Acad. Physician Assts. (pub. edn. chmn. 1977-79, bd. dirs. 1979-81, chmn. nominating com. 1981-83, ho. of dels. 1977—, sec. ho. of dels. 1985-86, 2d vice speaker ho. of dels. 1986-87, 1st spkr. ho. of dels. 1987-88, chmn. nominating com. 1988-89, AAPA Outstanding Physician Asst. of Yr. 1993), Ariz. Assn. Physician Assts. (bd. dirs. 1979-80, chmn. ethics & grievances 1980-81, pres. 1982-83, 85-86, newsletter editor 1984-85, 88-89, chmn. legis. and legal affairs 1989, chmn. CME com. 1990-91, pres. 1993-94), Assn. Physician Asst. Program, Vets. Caucus of Am. Acad. Physician Assts. (pres. 1989, dir. external rels. 1993—, newsletter editor 1994—). Democrat. LDS. Office: KCOM Southwest Ctr PO Box 11037 3210 W Camelback Phoenix AZ 85061

DANIELSON, CHARLES ERIC, public health officer; b. Greenwich, Conn., July 19, 1947; m. Judy Danielson; children: Eric, Andrea. MD, U. Conn., 1974; MPH, U. N.C., 1987. Med. cons. divsn. maternal and child health Maine Dept. Human Svcs., 1990-91; med. dir. family and cmty. health Iowa Dept. Pub. Health, 1991-94; dir. N.H. Divsn. Pub. Health Svcs., 1994-96; med. dir. N.H. Divsn. Pub. Health Svcs., Concord, 1996—. Office: NH Dept Health & Human Services 6 Hazen Dr Concord NH 03301

DANIELSON, DAVID GORDON, health science facility administrator, general legal counsel; b. Minot, N.D., Dec. 18, 1954; s. Gordon Everett and Myla Eunice (Torgerson) D.; m. Lisbeth Annette Roehrich, June 9, 1979; children: Michael, Katherine, Laura, Anna, Emily. BSBA, U. N.D., 1977, JD, 1980; postdoctoral, U. Minn., 1980-82. Bar: N.D. 1980, U.S. Dist. Ct. N.D. 1983; CPA, Minn., N.D. Tax specialist Deloitte, Haskins & Sells, Mpls., 1980-82, Eide Helmeke and Co., Fargo, N.D., 1982-84; exec. adminstr. Med. Arts Clinic, Minot, 1984—; exec. v.p. Teamcare, Inc., Minot, 1990—, also bd. dirs.; gen. legal counsel Med. Arts Out Patient Svcs., Inc., Magic City Fin. Group, Inc., South Park Fin. Group, Inc.; gen. legal counsel Key Care Investment Co., also bd. dirs.; bd. dirs. Credit Bur. Minot; mem. electronic data interchange planning commn. State of N.D.; mem. dean's coun. Coll. Bus., Minot State U., mem. bd. regents, 1994—. Bd. dirs. Domestic Violence Crisis Ctr., 1984-87, Minot Area C. of C., 1995; mem. planning commn. City Minot, 1995—. Mem. AICPA (area IV planning com. 1994—), N.D. Soc. CPAs (chmn. legis. com. 1986-88, 94—), N.D. Bar Assn. (CLE com. 1982—), Nat. Health Lawyers Assn., Med. Group Mgmt. Assn. (legis. com.), Lambda Chi Alpha, Rotary, Elks. Home: 2412 11th Ave NW Minot ND 58703-1770 Office: Med Arts Clinic PC PO Box 1489 Minot ND 58702-1489

DANIELSON, GORDON DOUGLAS, dentist; b. Everett, Wash., Nov. 11, 1942; s. Marvin and Elanor (Weers) D.; m. Jamie Lynn Waters, Jan. 9, 1977. BS with honors, U. Oreg., 1968; postgrad., MIT, 1968-69; MA in Molecular Biology, U. Calif., 1974, BS in Med. Sci., DDS, 1975. DDS. Pvt. practice Larkspur, Calif., 1975—; exec. v.p. Atmospheric Rsch. Tech., Sacramento, Calif., 1984-85; cons. Freeport Fin. Svcs., Denver, 1985-87; pres. Lynmar Enterprises Inc., Rno, 1987—; bd. dirs. Freeport Venture Fund. MIT fellow, 1968-69; U. Calif., Berkeley fellow, 1969-71; U. Calif., San Francisco fellow, 1973-75, pres. fellow, 1973-75. Mem. U. Calif. Dental Alumni Assn., U. Oreg. Alumni Assn., Marin County Dental Soc. (chmn. emergency care 1975-81), St. Francis Yacht Club (mem. com. 1973—), Aircraft Owners and Pilots Assn., Omicron Kappa Upsilon. Republican. Office: 5 Bon Air Rd Ste 114 Larkspur CA 94939-1127

DANIELSON, GORDON KENNETH, JR., cardiovascular surgeon, educator; b. Burlington, Iowa, Dec. 5, 1931; s. Gordon Kenneth and Helen H. (Hill) D.; m. Sondra Jean Bolich, Jan. 21, 1961; children: Gordon Kenneth III, Laura, Karen, Keith, Bruce, Susan, Jennifer. B.A. in Chemistry, U. Pa., 1953, M.D. (Pfizer, Senatorial, Clark scholar, Albert Einstein award 1956, Roche award 1956, Spencer Morris prize 1956), 1956; postgrad., Oak Ridge Inst. Nuclear Studies, 1960. Diplomate Am. Bd. Surgery, Am. Bd. Thoracic Surgery. Intern U. Mich. Hosp., Ann Arbor, 1956-57; asst. resident in surgery Hosp. of U. Pa., 1957-61, chief resident in surgery, 1961-62, gen. and thoracic surgeon, 1962-65, asst. chief surg. div. I, 1962-65; vis. fellow in thoracic surgery Thorax Kliniken, Stockholm, 1963-64; practice medicine specializing in thoracic and cardiovascular surgery Phila., 1963-65, Lexington, Ky., 1965-67, Rochester, Minn., 1967—; assoc. prof. surgery U. Ky. Med. Sch.; also chief cardiac surgery Univ. Hosp., 1965-67; mem. faculty Mayo Grad. Sch. Medicine, Rochester, Minn., 1967—, prof. surgery, 1975—, Joe M. and Ruth Roberts prof. surgery, 1987—; past chmn. divsn. thoracic and cardiovascular surgery, cons. cardiovascular and thoracic surgery Mayo Clinic/Mayo Found., 1967—, St. Mary's Hosp., Meth. Hosp., Rochester, 1967—; Am. Heart Assn. vis. tchr., Singapore, 1975, Amman, Jordan, 1981. Editor Cardiovascular Surgery, 1972-78; contbr. numerous articles to med. jours. Markle scholar in acad. medicine, 1962-67. Fellow ACS, Am. Coll. Cardiology; mem. Am. Assn. Thoracic Surgery, Am. Surg. Assn., Am. Heart Assn. (fellow coun. cardiovascular surgery), Soc. Thoracic Surgeons (a founder), Soc. Univ. Surgeons, Soc. Vascular Surgery, Mexican Soc. Cardiology (hon.), Assn. Thoracic and Cardiovascular Surgeons of Asia (hon.), India (hon.), Chile Soc. Cardiology and Cardiovascular Surgery (hon.), Colombian Soc. of Cardiology (hon.), Congenital Heart Surgeons Soc., Phi Beta Kappa, Alpha Omega Alpha. Home: 6000 16th Ave NW Rochester MN 55901-2107 Office: Mayo Clinic 200 1st St SW Rochester MN 55905-0001

DANIELSON, MARK VERNON, surgeon; b. Chgo., Feb. 24, 1954; s. Vernon Simon and Dorothy Evelyn (Oyer) D.; m. Carol Jean Ritzena; children: Eric, Jenna, Brian. BA, Vanderbilt U., 1976; MD, Northwestern U., 1981. Intern, resident Med. Coll. Wis., Milw., 1981-86; staff surgeon St. Joseph's Hosp., Joliet, Ill., 1986—. Fellow ACS. Office: 1301 Copperfield Joliet IL 60432

DANIELSON, PAUL ALBERT, oral and maxillofacial surgeon, educator; b. S.I., N.Y., Dec. 20, 1945; s. Rolf E. and Lillian (Fry) D.; m. Carol Bisby, June 14, 1969; children: Gregory P., Emily J. BS, St. Lawrence U., Canton, N.Y., 1967; DMD, Tufts U., 1971. Diplomate Am. Bd. Oral and Maxillofacial Surgery (bd. dirs. 1993—). Dental intern Med. Ctr. Hosp. Vt., Burlington, 1971-72, attending oral and maxillofacial surgeon, 1978—; resident in oral surgery Hartford (Conn.) Hosp., 1972-75, attending surgeon, 1975-78; pvt. practice, South Burlington, Vt., 1978—; assoc. clin. prof. U. Vt. Coll. Medicine, Burlington, 1978. Contbg. editor: The 5 Minute Clinical Consult for Dental Professionals, 1996. Capt. USAR, 1975-79. Fellow Am. Coll. Dentists, Am. Assn. Oral and Maxillofacial Surgeons; mem. ADA. Office: Oral Surgery Assocs 44 Timber Ln South Burlington VT 05403

DANILOWICZ, DELORES ANN, pediatric cardiologist, pediatrics educator; b. Bradford, N.Y., Feb. 3, 1935; s. Kajetan Joseph and Bronislawa Anna (Luta) D.; m. Hugh Paul Gabriel, June 3, 1960. A.B., NYU, 1956, M.D., 1960. Diplomate: diplomate am. bd. pediatrics, diplomate am. bd. pediatrics, diplomate am. bd. pediatrics; am. bd. pediatric cardiology am. bd. neonatology. Inter, resident pediatrics Jacobi Hosp., Bronx, 1960-63, cardiac fellow, 1963-65; postdoctoral fellow Johns Hopkins, Balt., 1965-66, Nat. Heart Inst., Bethesda, Md., 1966-68; asst. prof. NYU Med. Ctr., N.Y.C., 1968-72; assoc. prof. NYU Med. Ctr., N.Y.C., 1972-80; prof. pediatrics NYU Med. Ctr., N.Y.C., 1980—; dir. pediatric cardiac catheterization lab. U. Hosp., 1968—; admitting physician Univ. Hosp., Bellevue Hosp., Lenox Hill Hosp.; mem. am. sub-bd. Pediatric Cardiology, 1985-89. Contbr. articles to profl. jours. NYU scholar, 1952-56; NYU Scholar, 1957-60; named Disting. Tchr. NYU Med. Sch., 1971, Disting. Tchr., 1976; NYU Pediatric House Staff, 1975. Fellow Am. Acad. Pediat, Am. Coll. Cardiology; mem. Am. Heart Assn.

DANKLE, MARK DEWITT, family practice physician; b. Cristobol, Panama Canal Zone, Jan. 7, 1957; parents Am. citizens; s. W.K. and Marilyn J. (DeWitt) D.; m. Zoe T. Dankle; children: Katherine A., Geoffrey M. BS, U. Iowa, 1979; DO, Coll. Osteo. Med. Scis., Des Moines, 1983. Diplomate Am. Bd. Family Practice. Resident U. Iowa Hosp. and Clinics, Mason City, Iowa, 1983-86; staff/pvt. physician Mercy Hosp., Mason City and Clear Lake, Iowa, 1989—; aviations med. examiner FAA, Clear Lake, 1992—. Maj. USAF, 1986-89. Mem. AMA, Am. Acad. Family Practice. Office: Clear Lake Med Group 15 Plaza Dr PO Box 248 Clear Lake IA 50428

DANN, FRANCIS JOSEPH, dermatologist, educator; b. N.Y.C., Aug. 26, 1946; s. Richard William and Helen (Brennan) D. BA, Columbia U., 1968, MD, 1972. Bd. cert. dermatologist Am. Bd. Dermatology. Pvt. practice specializing in dermatology, 1976-90; asst. clin. prof. dermatology UCLA, 1993—; recognized expert med. reviewer State of Calif., 1995; specialized tng. in leprosy USPHS Hosp., Carville, La., 1972, 95. Contbr. articles to profl. and med. jours. Recipient Cert. of Appreciation for charitable med. missions to The Philippines, 1986, 88, 92. Mem. AMA, Am. Acad. Dermatology, Philippine Med. Assn. Hawaii, L.A.-Metro Dermatology Soc., Pacific Dermatology Soc., L.A. Acad. Medicine (bd. dirs. 1995-97), Aloha Med. Mission. Roman Catholic. Office: 100 UCLA Medical Plz # 545 Los Angeles CA 90024

DANNENBERG, ANDREW LOEB, epidemiologist, educator; b. Phila., Sept. 4, 1952; s. Arthur M. Jr. and Aileen (Hart) D.; m. Katherine Singley, May 30, 1983; children: Edward, Alice. BA, Swarthmore Coll., 1974; MD, Stanford U., 1979; MPH, Johns Hopkins U., 1983. Diplomate Am. Bd. Preventive Medicine. Resident in family practice Med. U. (Charleston) S.C., 1979-82; med. epidemiologist Nat. Heart Lung and Blood Inst., Bethesda, Md., 1982-89; epidemiologist injury prevention ctr. Johns Hopkins Sch. Hygiene and Pub. Health, Balt., 1989—, asst. prof. dept. health policy mgmt. and dept. epidemiology, 1989—, dir. preventive medicine residency program, 1989—. Contbr. over 40 articles to jours. in cardiovascular and injury epidemiology. Recipient USPHS citation, 1989. Fellow Am. Coll. Preventive Medicine; mem. AAAS, APHA, Soc. Epidemiol. Rsch. Office: Johns Hopkins Sch Pub Health 624 N Broadway Rm 545 Baltimore MD 21205-1901

DANNER, DEAN JAY, geneticist; b. Milw., Sept. 26, 1941; s. Julius Alexis and Evalyn Anna (Pautz) D.; m. Susan Melissa Reddin, Aug. 25, 1968; children: Mark Jay, Kirstin Melissa. BS in Chemistry/Biology, Lakeland Coll., 1963; PhD in Biochemistry, U. N.D., 1968. Postdoctoral fellow St. Jude Children's Rsch. Hosp., Memphis, 1968-70; asst. prof. Northwestern State U., Natchitoches, La., 1970-73; asst. prof. Emory U., Atlanta, 1973-78, assoc. prof., 1978-89, prof., 1989—; mem. NIH Study Sect. Med. Biochemistry, Bethesda, Md., 1989-93. Presbyterian. Home: 266 Winnona Dr Decatur GA 30030-3854 Office: Emory U Dept Genetics Molecular Medicine 1462 Clifton Rd NE Atlanta GA 30322-1063

DANOFF, DUDLEY SETH, surgeon, urologist; b. N.Y.C., June 10, 1937; s. Alfred and Ruth (Kauffman) D.; m. Hevda Amrani, July 1, 1971; children: Aurele Alfie, Doran. BA summa cum laude, Princeton U., 1959; MD, Yale U., 1963. Diplomate Am. Bd. Urology. Surg. intern Columbia-Presbyn. Med. Ctr., N.Y.C., 1963-64; resident in surgery Yale New Haven Med. Ctr., 1964-65; resident in urologic surgery Squier Urologic Clinic, Columbia-Presbyn. Med. Ctr., 1965-69; NIH trainee Francis Delafield Hosp., N.Y.C., 1969; asst. in urology Columbia U..Columbia-Presbyn. Hosp., N.Y.C., 1969; cons., surgeon New Orleans VA Hosp., 1970; asst. surgeon Tulane U., New Orleans, 1970; pvt. practice urologic surgery L.A., 1971—; attending urologic surgeon Cedars-Sinai Med. Ctr., L.A., Midway Hosp., L.A., Century City Hosp., L.A. VA Hosp., L.A.; attending urologic surgeon, clin. faculty UCLA. Author: Superpotency, 1993, Research: Laparoscopic Urologic Procedures; contbr. articles to profl. jours. Bd. dirs. Tel-Hashomer Hosp., Israel, Christian Children's Fund, Beverly Hills Edn. Found.; trustee Anti-Defamation League; mem. prof. adv. bd. The Wellness Comty.; mem. nat. exec. bd. Gesher Found.; mem. adv. com., past pres. Med. divsn. L.A. Jewish Fedn. Coun.; mem. nat. leadership cabinet United Jewish Appeal; chmn. Am. Friends of Assaf Harofeh Med. Ctr., Israel; pres. western states region and internat. bd. govs. Am. Friends Hebrew U. Jerusalem; pres. western region Am. Commn. for Shaare Zedek Med. Ctr. Jerusalem. Fellow ACS; mem. AMA, Internat. Coll. Surgeons, Israeli Med. Assn., Am. Fertility Soc., Soc. Air Force Clin. Surgeons, Am. Urologic Assn., Societe International d'Urologie, Transplant Soc. So. Calif., Los Angeles County Med. Assn., Soc. for Minimally Invasive Surgery, Am. Technion Soc., Profl. Men's Club of L.A. (past pres.), Princeton Club So. Calif., Yale Club So. Calif., Hillcrest Country Club, Phi Beta Kappa, Sigma Xi, Alpha Omega Alpha, Phi Delta Epsilon (past pres., mem. exec. com.). Jewish. Office: Cedars-Sinai Med Ctr Towers 8631 W 3rd St Ste 915E Los Angeles CA 90048-5912

DANS, PETER EMANUEL, medical educator; b. N.Y.C., June 17, 1937; s. Emanuel and Filomena (Lisanti) D.; m. Colette Lumina Lizotte, May 28, 1966; children: Maria Cristina, Paul Edouard, Thomas Emanuel, Suzanne Elise. BS in Chemistry, Manhattan Coll., 1957; MD, Columbia U., 1961. Intern, resident medicine Johns Hopkins Hosp., Balt., 1961-63; resident medicine Presbyn. Hosp., N.Y.C., 1963-64; fellow rsch. NIH, Bethesda, Md., 1964-67; infectious diseases fellow Harvard U., Boston, 1967-69; asst. prof. medicine U. Colo., Denver, 1969-74, assoc. prof., 1974-78; Robert Wood Johnson health policy fellow Inst. Medicine, Washington, 1976-77, sr. prof. assoc., 1977-78; assoc. prof. medicine Johns Hopkins U. Sch. Medicine, Balt., 1978—; mem. Md. Physician Bd. Quality Assurance, sec. 1988-92. Co-author: New Medical Market Place A Physician's Guide to the Health Care Revolution, 1988; dep. editor Annals of Internal Medicine, 1991-94; assoc. med. dir. GMIS, Inc., 1994-95; mem. editl. bd. Pharos, 1988—; contbr. articles to profl. jours., chpts. to books; film reviewer Physician at the Movies, Pharos. Pres. Falls Rd. Cmty. Assn., Cockeysville, Md., 1980-84, 87-90; mem. adv. com. on gifted talented program Baltimore County, 1981-90, mem. zoning adv. com., 1985-86, mem. commn. on aging, 1996—; pres. parish coun. Shrine of Sacred Heart, Balt., 1981-83. Fellow ACP; mem. AAAS, AMA, Epsilon Sigma Pi, Alpha Omega Alpha. Roman Catholic. Home and Office: 11 Hickory Hill Rd Cockeysville MD 21030-1624

DANTO, ELIZABETH ANN, social worker, administrator; b. Detroit, May 31, 1952; m. Paul Werner. BA, Sarah Lawrence Coll., 1973; MS, Columbia U., 1984; PhD, NYU, 1996. ACSW, CSW, N.Y. Coord. social svcs. United Storeworkers Union, N.Y.C., 1983-86; EAP dir. N.Y.C. Office of Mayor, 1986-91; ind. cons. N.Y.C., 1992—; founding dir. Stillpoint, N.Y.C., 1996. Contbr. articles to profl. jours. Mem. NASW (commr. 1989-92).

D'ANTONIO-KRUMM, THERESA, nursing administrator, educator, nursing consultant; b. Bklyn., May 27, 1947; d. Julian and Josephine Dorothy (Noyes) D'A; m. Ronald C. Krumm. AA, Rockland C.C., 1972; BS in Behavior Sci. & Criminal Justice, Mercy Coll.; MA in Psychology, L.I. U., 1982; PhD in Counseling, S.W. U., 1992. RN, N.Y., N.J.; cert. nurse adminstr. Adj. prof. psychology Mercy Coll., Dobbs Ferry, N.Y.; bus. and nursing instr. BOCES Rockland County; secretarial asst., legal & safety cons. Town of Orangetown, N.Y. Maj. N.Y. ARNG. Home: 470 Washington St Tappan NY 10983-2701

DANTZKER, DAVID ROY, internist. MD, SUNY, Buffalo, 1967. Diplomate Am. Bd. Internal Medicine, Am. Bd. Pulmonary Medicine, Am. Bd. CCM. Intern Buffalo Gen. Hosp., 1967-68; resident in medicine SUNY Affiliated Hosp., Buffalo, 1968-70; fellow in pulmonary medicine U. Calif., San Diego Med. Ctr., 1972-74; medicial staff Long Island (N.Y.) Jewish Med. Ctr., 1974—; prof. medicine Albert Einstein Coll. Medicine, Long Island, N.Y., 1974—. Fellow Am. Coll. Physicians, Am. Coll. Cardiac Physicians. Office: LI Jewish Med Ctr Med Adminstrn 270-05 76th Ave New Hyde Park NY 11040*

DANTZLER, KELLEY DIANE, nurse; b. San Diego, Nov. 1, 1959; d. Wilbert Dantzler and Phyllis Eloise Estridge. BA in Biology, Whittier Coll., 1981; diploma, Los Angeles County Med. Ctr. Sch. Nursing, 1984. RN. Nurse Los Angeles/U. So. Calif. Med. Ctr., 1986—. Democrat. Mem. AME. Home: 12360 Riverside Dr Apt 303 North Hollywood CA 91607-3659 Office: Los Angeles County U So Calif Med Ctr 1200 N State St Los Angeles CA 90033-4525

DANZANSKY, JOAN COX, child and family advocate and consultant, riding therapist; b. Phila., Mar. 1, 1941; d. Joseph Winston Cox Jr. and Edna Lee Gilchrist; m. Stephen Ira Danzansky, Apr. 29, 1967; children: Michael Winston, Katharine Cox. BA in Sociology and Psychology, Mt. Holyoke Coll., 1963. Founder, exec. dir. Family Stress Svcs. D.C. and D.C. chp. Nat.

Com. Prevention Child Abuse, Washington, 1975-88; cons. on child abuse and neglect to pvt. agys. Washington, 1986—; instr. Nat. Ctr. for Therapeutic Riding, Washington, 1990—; instr. and program adminstr. Nat. Ctr. for Therapeutic Riding, Washington, 1994—; mem. faculty family crisis intervention program Met. Police Dept., 1979-88; mem. Task Force Exploited Children Met. Washington Coun. Govts., 1984-85; mem. Fed. Region III Task Force Child Abuse and Neglect, HHS, Phila., 1985-86; chmn. Washington Mayor's Adv. Com. Child Abuse and Neglect, 1986-93. Chmn. alumnae honors rsch. com. Mt. Holyoke Coll., South Hadley, Mass., 1988-91, 93—; bd. dirs. Child Health Ctr., Children's Hosp., Washington, 1977; mem. sustainer adv. rsch. group Internat. Assn. Jr. Leagues, N.Y.C., 1988-91; elephant interpreter Nat. Zoo, Washington, 1989—; mem. cmty. adv. com. Friends Nat. Zoo, 1989-91; mem. parents activities com. Nat. Cathedral Sch., Washington, 1989-91. Mem. alumnae honors rsch. com. Mt. Holyoke Coll., South Hadley, Mass., 1989-91, chmn., 1993—; bd. dirs. child Health Ctr., Children's Hosp., Washington, 1977—; mem. sustainer adv. rsch. group Internat. Assn. Jr. Leagues, N.Y.C., 1988-91; elephant interpreter Nat. Zoo, Washington, 1989—; mem. cmty. adv. com. Friends Nat. Zoo, 1989-91; mem. parents activities com. Nat. Cathedral Sch., Washington, 1989-91. Recipient Marian Chace award D.C. Mental Health Assn., 1978, Regional Dir.'s Disting. Vol. award HHS, 1982, Outstanding Community Svc. award Psychiat. Inst. Found., 1983, Washingtonian of Yr. award Washingtonian mag., 1985, Sesquicentennial award Mt. Holyoke Coll., 1987, Outstanding Svc. Recognition Resolution, Coun. of D.C., 1989. Mem. Am. Assn. for Protecting Children, Am. Profl. Soc. on Abuse Children, N.Am. Riding for Handicapped Assn., Am. Assn. Suicidology (vice chmn. local arrangements com. 1987-88), Elephant Mgrs. Assn. Episcopalian. Home: 3609 Edmunds St NW Washington DC 20007-1434 Office: Nat Ctr Therapeutic Riding 5110 Glover Rd NW Washington DC 20015-1006

DANZL, DANIEL FRANK, emergency physician; b. Cin., Apr. 2, 1950; s. Frank Bernard and Mary Ellen (Doerger) D.; m. Joanna Colosimo Danzl, Nov. 25, 1978; children: Maggie, Julia. BS magna cum laude, U. Cin., 1972; MD, Ohio State U., 1976. Diplomate Am. Bd. Emergency Medicine. Intern St. Francis Med. Ctr., Peoria, Ill., 1976-77; resident in emergency medicine U. Louisville, 1977-79, asst. prof. emergency medicine, 1979-83, assoc. prof. emergency medicine, 1983-89, prof. emergency medicine, 1989-91, prof., chair, 1991—; bd. dirs., councilman-at-large Univ. Assn. for Emergency Medicine, 1988-89, indsl./govtl. rels. com., 1984-85, nominating com., 1987-88; bd. dirs. Soc. for Acad. Emergency Medicine, 1989, mem. annals of emergency meidcine task force, 1989; bd. dirs. Am. Bd. Emergency Medicine, sec.-treas., 1995-96, mem. ad hoc com., oral examiner, 1982—; mem. Com. to Advise the Nat. ARC, 1984-87; reviewer for various med. jours. Author book chpts., monographs and textbooks including Airway Management in the Trauma Patient in the Clinical Practice of Emergency Medicine, 1991; editorial bd. Jour. Emergency Medicine, 1983—, Poisindex-Emergindex, 1982—, Jour. Wilderness Medicine, 1991—; contbr. more than 70 articles to Jour. Wilderness Medicine, Jpur. Emergency Medicine, Annals of Emergency Medicine, Am. Jour. Emergency Medicine, others. Mem. Water Safety Com. Nat. Safety Coun.-Pub. Safety Div., 1981-84; alternate med. dir. Jefferson Vocat. Edn.-Louisville EMS Paramedic Training Program, 1989-90, 90-91. Recipient Silver Tongue Orator award Soc. Tchrs. of Emergency Medicine, 1986, 88; grantee Office of Naval Resources, 1983-85, Key Pharmaceuticals, 1985, Hoffman-LaRoche, Inc., 1988, 89. Fellow Am. Coll. Emergency Physicians (nat. coun. mem. 1981-93, reference com. mem. 1981, 85, 89, rsch. com. mem. 1982-83, 83-84); mem. AMA (Physician's Recognition awards), NAS, Am. Soc. Circumpolar Health, Soc. for Academic Emergency Medicine (bd. dirs. 1989, task force 1989), Nat. Rsch. Coun., Undersea and Hyperbaric Oxygen Med. Soc., Ky. Chpt. Am. Coll. Emergency Physicians (councillor 1981-93, sec.-treas. 1983-84, pres.-elect 1984-85, pres. 1985-86), Wilderness Med. Soc., Phi Beta Kappa, Beta Theta Pi. Roman Catholic. Home: 4804 Smith Rd Floyds Knobs IN 47119-9214 Office: U Louisville Dept Emergency Med 530 S Jackson St Louisville KY 40202-1675

DANZON, PATRICIA M., medical educator. BA, U. Oxford, 1968; MA, U. Chgo., 1969, PhD of Econs., 1973. Lectr. U. Chgo., 1972; rsch. economist, instr. Rand Corp., 1974-80; sr. rsch. fellow Hoover Inst. Stanford U., 1980-84; assoc. prof., adj. prof., lectr. Duke U., Durham, N.C., 1984-85; Celia Moh prof. Health Care Sys. Ins. & Risk Mgmt. U. Pa., Phila., 1985—; vis. asst. prof. Econ. Dept. U. Calif., 1978; vis. prof. Ctr. Study Economy and State U. Chgo., 1988-89. Office: U Pa Wharton Sch Health Care Sys Dept 3641 Locustwalk Philadelphia PA 19104*

DAOUD, GEORGES ISSA, physician; b. Lattakiat, Syria, Mar. 27, 1927; came to U.S., 1954; s. Issa and Rose (Jawish) D.; m. Sonia Boustany, June 3, 1954; children: Rosine, Micheline, Emile. Diploma, French Med. Sch., 1952. Diplomate Am. Bd. Internal Medicine, Am. Bd. Cardiovascular. Intern Sibley Meml. Hosp., Washington, 1954-55; resident Providence Hosp., Washington, 1955-57; cardiology fellow NYU, Bellevue, N.Y., 1957-95; pediat. cardiology fellow Children's Hosp., 1959-60; dir. cardiac catheterization lab. Children's Hosp., Cin., 1960-65, Good Samaritan Hosp., Cin., 1965-95; chmn., dir. cardiology dept. Good Samaritan Hosp., Cin., 1972-94; clin. prof. medicine U. Cin., 1968, assoc. clin. prof. pediat. cardiology. Fellow Am. Coll. Cardiology, Am. Coll. Physicians, Am. Heart Assn. (Visionary award 1995). Roman Catholic. Home: 1030 Grandin Ridge Cincinnati OH 45208

DAOUST, DONALD ROGER, pharmaceutical and toiletries company executive, microbiologist; b. Worcester, Mass., Aug. 13, 1935; s. G. Arthur and Alice Anne (Lavalee) D.; m. Johanna K. Kalinoski, May 30, 1959; children: Donna Jean, Stephen Michael, Sandra Marie. BA, U. Conn., 1957; MS, U. Mass., 1959, PhD, 1962. Sr. research microbiologist Merck Sharp & Dohme, Rahway, N.J., 1962-70, research fellow, 1970-72; mgr. biol. quality control Merck Sharp & Dohme, West Point, Pa., 1972-75; dir. quality control Armour Pharm. Co., Kankakee, Ill., 1975-76; v.p. quality assurance and regulatory compliance Armour Pharm. Co., Phoenix, 1976-78; v.p., quality control Carter-Wallace, Inc., Cranbury, N.J., 1978—. Contbr. articles to profl. jours., chpts. to books; patentee in field. Mem. Borough Council, South Plainfield, N.J., 1970-72; treas. George Washington council Boy Scouts Am., 1981-84, pres., 1984-87, area v.p., bd.dirs. NE region U.S., 1987—. Recipient Disting. Svc. award South Plainfield Jaycees, 1969, silver Beaver award Boy Scouts Am., 1988, Silver Antelope award N.E. region, 1992; named Outstanding Young Man, N.J. Jaycees, 1970. Mem. AAAS, Am. Soc. Microbiology, Am. Soc. for Quality Control, Pharm. Mfrs. Assn. (quality control adminstrn. 1979-82, adv. bd. 1982-94, rec. sec. 1986-88, vice chmn. 1988-90, chmn. 1990-92), Bedens Brook Club (Skillman, N.J.). Home: 8 Fairway Dr Cranbury NJ 08512-1726 Office: Carter-Wallace Inc PO Box 1001 Cranbury NJ 08512-0181

DARBY, BONNIE MAE HANSON, anesthetist; b. Wheeling, W.Va., Dec. 26, 1945; d. Andrew Jackson and Betty Mae (McKitrick) Hanson; 1 child, Brian Alan Darby. RN, Wheeling Hosp. Sch. Nursing, 1966; cert., Wheeling Hosp. Sch. Anesthesia, 1971; BSA, Wheeling Coll., 1979; MA, W.Va. U., 1984. RN; cert. BLS, ACLS. Nurse Wheeling Hosp., 1966-69; anesthetist Ohio Valley Med. Ctr., Wheeling, 1971-73; clin. instr. and anesthetist Ohio Valley Hosp., Steubenville, Ohio, 1973-79; dir. of anesthesia East Ohio Regional Hosp., Martins Ferry, 1979-88; anesthetist and quality assurance coord. Palm Lakes Anesthesia Cons., Loxahatchee, Fla., 1988-95; pvt. practice West Palm Beach, Fla., 1995—. Mem. Am. Assn. Nurse Anesthetists, Anesthesia Patient Safety Found., Fla. Assn. Nurse Anesthetists. Home and Office: 5593 Berry Blossom Way W West Palm Beach FL 33415

DARBY, WILLIAM JEFFERSON, JR., physician, biochemistry and nutrition educator; b. Galloway, Ark., Nov. 6, 1913; s. William J. and Ruth (Douglass) D.; m. Elva Louise Mayo, June 12, 1935; children—William J., James Richard, Thomas Douglass. B.S., U. Ark., 1936, M.D., 1937; M.S. (Univ. Sigma Xi fellow 1939-40, Horace H. Rackham fellow 1940-41), U. Mich., 1941, Ph.D., 1942, D.Sc. (hon.), 1966; D.Sc. (hon.), Utah State U., 1973; DSc (hon.), U. Ark., 1984. Instr. phys. chemistry U. Ark. Sch. Medicine, 1937-39; asst. prof. nutrition U. N.C. Sch. of Pub. Health, 1942-43; instr. preventive medicine Duke U. Sch. Medicine, 1942-43; asst. prof. biochemistry, also asst. prof. medicine Vanderbilt U. Sch. Medicine, 1944-46, assoc. prof. biochemistry, 1946-48, prof. biochemistry, chmn. dept., dir. div. nutrition, 1949-71, prof. nutrition, 1964-79, prof. medicine in nutrition, 1965-79, prof. biochem. in nutrition, 1972-79, prof. emeritus, 1979—, hon. curator spl. collections-nutrition Med. Ctr. Library, 1977—; pres. Nutrition Found., Inc., 1972-82; mem. study sect. biochemistry and nutrition, div. rsch. grants and fellowships USPHS, 1948-53, chmn. study sect. on metabolism and nutrition, 1948-53, chmn. study sect. on gen. medicine, 1956-59, mem. com. on selection sr. research fellowships, 1956-59, chmn. study sect. nutrition, 1959-61; mem. food and nutrition bd. NRC, 1949-71, mem. food protection com., 1950-71, chmn., 1954-71; mem. adv. bd. Inst. Nutrition Central Am. and Panama, 1950-64; mem. WHO Expert Adv. Panel on nutrition, 1950-82, FAO and WHO Joint Expert Com. on Nutrition, 1954, 57, 61, 66; sci. adv. com. Samuel R. Noble Found., 1953-63, 78, chmn., 1955, 58, 61, 78; chmn. Joint FAO-WHO Expert Com. on Food Additives, 1956; cons. Interdeptl. Com. on Nutrition for Nat. Def., 1955-66; co-ordinator WHO Protein adv. group, 1956-60; mem. bd. sci. counselors Nat. Inst. Arthritis and Metabolic Diseases NIH, 1957-59, mem. adv. com. diet, nutrition and cancer program Nat. Cancer Inst., 1975-77; mem. FAO/WHO/UNICEF Protein Adv. Group, 1960-62; mem. sci. adv. com. Nutrition Found., 1958-65, 67-71, Sci. Adv. Com. Nat. Vitamin Found., 1950-64; Kempner lectr. U. Tex. Med. Bd., Galveston, 1961; Negus lectr. Med. Coll. Va., 1972, Va. Acad. Sci., 1975; W.O. Atwater lectr. U.S. Dept. Agr., 1975, Underwood-Prescott Meml. lectr., MIT, 1979; chmn. adv. com. United Health Found., 1962-70; chmn. food sci. mission to Europe USDA, 1963; tech. adv. com. Inst. Nutrition Scis., Columbia U., 1966-70; vis. com. dept. nutrition and food sci. Mass. Inst. Tech., 1963-68, 74-76; nat. cons. USAF Surgeon Gen., 1967-72; mem. council on foods and nutrition AMA, 1948-62, 65-73, chmn., 1967-70; mem. commn. on pesticides sec. HEW, 1969-71; mem. long range planning com. FASEB, 1969-70; mem. Tenn. Gov.'s Adv. Commn. on Consumer Protection, 1969-70; mem. adv. com. on nutrition AID, 1968-72; vis. prof. U. Calif. at Davis, 1967; adv. com. on personnel for research Am. Cancer Soc., 1962-65; pub. trustee Food Law Inst., 1962—; mem. bd. basic sci. examiners State of Tenn., 1961-72, pres., 1962-72; mem. bd. commrs. Navajo Health Authority, 1972-77; adv. task force world hunger Presbyn. Ch. U.S., 1972-76; mem. Tenn. Gov.'s Commn. Aging, 1972-76; co-chmn. hazardous materials adv. com. EPA, 1971-74, environ. health adv. com., 1974-79; trustee Internat. Life Scis. Inst. 1978-82, Oley Found., Albany, N.Y., 1983-87, Food Safety Coun., 1977-82, Food Processors Inst., 1973-76; trustee, mem. med. advi. coun. Alcoholic Beverage Med. Rsch. Found., 1981-89, chmn. 1986-87, emeritus trustee, 1989—; mem. rev. bd. biomed. div. Samuel Roberts Noble Found., 1977-79; mem. environ. health adv. com. EPA, 1974-79; bd. dirs., trustee Swanson Ctr. for Nutrition, 1973-89; pub. trustee Nutrition Found., 1972-82; advisor on nutrition program Howard Heinz Endowment, 1981—. Co-author: Fermented Food Beverages in Nutrition; Food, the Gift of Osiris; assoc. editor: Nutrition Revs., 1944-50, Jour. Clin. Investigation, 1950-54. Pres. Williamson County (Tenn.) Hist. Soc., 1984-85, v.p., 1985-86. Decorated Order Rodolf Robles Guatemala; Star of Jordan, 1963; Order Cedars of Lebanon, 1972; recipient Mead-Johnson B-Complex award, 1947; Joseph Goldberger Award AMA, 1964; Thomas Jefferson award Vanderbilt U., 1969; Charles Franklin Craig lectr. Am. Soc. Tropical Med., 1950; Roberts Meml. lectr. U. P.R., 1966; Phi Beta Kappa scholar, 1966-67; Forty-Niner award, 1975. Fellow A.C.P. (master 1973); mem. Nat. Acad. Scis., Am. Chem. Soc. (Spencer award 1972), Am. Inst. Nutrition (pres. 1958, Elvehjem award 1972, Osborne-Mendel award 1962), Am. Public Health Assn., AMA (chmn. council foods and nutrition 1960-62, 67-70), Am. Soc. Biol. Chemists, Soc. Exptl. Biology and Medicine, Nutrition Soc. (Gt. Britain), So. Soc. Clin. Research (v.p. 1948), Am. Fedn. Clin. Research, Am. Soc. Clin. Investigation, Assn. Am. Physicians, Austrian Pub. Health Assn. (hon.), Nat. Med. Assn. Panama, Am. Acad. Scis., Serbian Acad. Scis. (hon. mem.), Philippine Dietetic Assn. (hon.), L'Institute d'Egypte (asso.). Office: Vanderbilt U Med Ctr Libr Nashville TN 37235*

DARDANO, ANTHONY NICHOLAS, obstetrician and gynecologist; b. Utica, N.Y., May 27, 1942; s. Nicholas Salvatore and Catherine (Matt) D.; m. Marjorie Gamello, Aug. 8, 1963; children: Anthony, Kathryn. BS, Niagara U., 1963; MD, Bologna (Italy) U., 1968. Diplomate Am. Bd. Obstetrics and Gynecology. Intern Ellis Hosp., Schenectady, 1969-70; resident St. Mary's Hosp., Rochester, N.Y., 1970-73; pvt. practice Utica, 1973—; med. staff pres. St. Elizabeth Hosp., Utica, 1980-81, chief dept. ob-gyn., 1980-90, chmn. laser com., 1986—. Fellow ACS, ACOG, Internat. Coll. Surgeons; mem. AMA, N.Y. Med. Soc. Republican. Roman Catholic. Office: 2405 Genesee St Utica NY 13501

DARDICK, KENNETH REGEN, physician, educator; b. Bklyn., Oct. 16, 1946; s. Bruce S. and Leila Mae (Regen) D.; children from previous marriage: Lauren E., Jeremy S.; m. Judith Stein, 1996. AB cum laude, Dartmouth Coll., 1968, BMS, 1969; MD, Harvard U., 1971; D in Tropical Medicine and Hygiene, London Sch. of Hygiene and Tropical Medicine, 1989. Intern, Cambridge (Mass.) Hosp., 1971-72, resident in internal medicine, 1973-74; resident in pediatrics Children's Med. Ctr., Boston, 1972-73; with USPHS, Rochester, N.Y., 1974-76, pres., med. dir. med. dental staff Westside Health Svcs., Rochester, N.Y., 1975-76,; practice medicine specializing in internal medicine and family practice, Storrs, Conn., 1976—; mem. staff, chmn. dept. medicine Windham (Conn.) Cmty. Meml. Hosp., 1993-95, asst. chief med. staff, 1994-95; asst. clin. prof. U. Conn. Med. Sch., dir. health, Windham, 1993-94; dir. of health, Mansfield, Conn., 1936—, sch. physician, Mansfield, 1990—; chmn. Hypertension Task Force, Am. Heart Assn., 1981-84; dir. Capital area IPA, 1987—, HealthOne Conn., 1995—; mem. adv. bd. Comm. Datalink, 1994—. Author: Foreign Travel and Immunization Guide, 13th edit. Founder, pres. Conn. Safety Belt Coalition, 1984—; pres., med. dir. Immunization Alert, 1983—; censor Windham County Med. Assn, 1992-94. Jeffrey Richardson fellow Harvard U., 1988; recipient Patient Care award for excellence in patient edn., 1983, 1988. Fellow ACP (George C. Griffith Traveling scholar 1988), Royal Soc. Tropical Medicine, Am. Acad. Family Practice; mem. Am. Soc. Tropical Medicine and Hygiene. Office: Mansfield Profl Park Storrs CT 06268

DARDIK, HERBERT, vascular surgeon, general surgeon; b. Long Branch, N.J., May 17, 1935; s. Morris and Sarah D.; m. Janet E. Goldstein, June 23, 1958; children: Alan, Michael, Sharon. BA magna cum laude, NYU, 1956, MD, 1960. Diplomate Am. Bd. Med. Examiners, Am. Bd. Surgery, cert. spl. competency in vascular surgery; lic. M.D. N.J., N.Y., Calif. Intern Montefiore Hosp. and Med. Ctr., N.Y.C., 1960-61, asst. surg. resident to chief surg. resident, 1961-64; instr. surgery Albert Einstein Coll. Medicine, N.Y.C., 1964-65, asst. prof. surgery, 1967-77; clin. assoc. prof. surgery N.J. Coll. Medicine, Newark, 1981-91; clin. assoc. in surgery U. Pa. Sch. Medicine, Phila., 1991—; clin. prof. surgery Mt. Sinai Sch. Medicine, N.Y.C., 1991—; staff surgeon USAF Hosp. Andrews AFB, Washington, 1965-67; assoc. dir. surgery to dir. surgery Montefiore-Morrisania Affiliate, N.Y.C., 1967-71, cons. in surgery, 1971-76; assoc. attending surgeon Montefiore Hosp. and Med. Ctr., N.Y.C., 1970-77; cons. surgery North Ctrl. Bronx Hosp., N.Y., 1976; assoc. attending surgeon Englewood (N.J.) Hosp., 1973-79, active attending surgeon and chief vascular surg. svc., 1979—, chief dept. surgery, 1984—; sr. rsch. scientist Lab. for Exptl. Medicine and Surgery in Primates, NYU Med. Ctr., 1973-78; numerous visiting professorships, 1976-95, at Good Samaritan Hosp., Cin., U. Munich, U. Laval, Que., Can., Rigshospitalet, Copenhagen, Karolinska Inst., Stockholm, Semmelweis Med. U., Budapest, First Internat. Course on Vascular Traumatology, Mexico City, Inst. of Vascular Surgery of U. Milan, Groote Schuur Hosp., Cape Town, South Africa, U. Orange Free State, Bloemfontein, South Africa, Johannesburg Hosp. of U. of Witwatersrand, South Africa, Allegheny Gen. Hosp., Pitts., Wilmington (Del.) Med. Ctr., Mercy Hosp., Pitts., U. Cologne, Germany, Jewish Gen. Hosp., Montreal (Harry C. Vallon Vis. Prof.), U. Md., Balt., Maritime Vascular Soc., North Sydney Hosp., N.S., Can., Pa. Hosp., Phila., U. Colo. Health Sci. Ctr. and Affiliated Hosps., Denver, Mary Imogene Basset Hosp., Cooperstown, N.Y., Cooper Hosp./Univ. Med. Ctr., Camden, N.J., Gulf Coast Vascular Soc., Tulane U., La. State U. Ochsner Med. Clinic, New Orleans, St. Vincent's Med. Ctr., N.Y.C., U. Trondheim, Norway, Broadgreen Hosp., Liverpool, Eng., U. Colo. Rose Med. Ctr. (guest lectr.), Queen Elizabeth Hosp., Montreal, Wright State U., Dayton, Ohio, Cleve. Vascular Soc., N.Y. Meth. Hosp., Bklyn.; surgeon by invitation Mass. Gen. Hosp., Bosotn, 1979, Milan, 1981, Sydney, N.S., 1985, Colo. Health Sci. Ctr., 1985, U. Trondheim, 1992, Paul Brousse Hosp., Paris, 1995; internat. adv. com. Internat. Vascular Symposium, London, 1981, Internat. Coll. Angiology, Athens, 1985, 14th World Congress Internat. Union Angiology, Munich, 1986. Contbr. over 300 articles and abstracts to profl. jours., chpts. to books; presenter in field; creator exhibits in field; dir. numerous symposia in field; patentee in field; editor SCVS Newsletter, 1987—; editl. bd. Jour. Englewood Hosp., 1989—, Fitness Swimmer, 1992—, Vascular Forum, 1993-95, guest editor 1994, Vascular Surgery, 1995—; creativity editor Jour. Am. Coll. Physician Inventors, 1992—; invited reviewer Jour. Vascular Surgery, European Jour. Vascular Surgery, Am. Jour. Surgery. Capt. USAF Med. Corps, 1965-67. Recipient George Schwartz prize in biology, 1954, Wortis Biol. prize, 1956; honoree 10th Ann. Vascular Fellows Abstract Presentation (Herbert Dardik awards). Mem. ACS (bd. govs. 1991-94), ACP, AMA (Hektoen Gold medal 1976), Assn. Acad. Surgery, Soc. Vascular Surgery, Internat. Soc. Cardiovasc. Surgery, Soc. Internat. de Chirurgia, Soc. Clin. Vascular Surgery (hon., various offices and coms., pres. 1984-85, exec. com. 1982—), Soc. Surgery of the Alimentary Tract, Am. Coll. Gastroenterology, Collegium Internat. Chirurgia Digestive, Am. Coll. Physician Inventors (founding mem., sec. 1992—), Eastern Vascular Soc. (adv. coun. 1991—, exec. com. 1986—, pres. 1990-91), N.J. Vascular Soct 1983-84, pres. 1984-85, dir. exec. com. 1982-83, postgrad. surg. edn. award 1983), N.Y. Soc. Cardiovasc. Surgery, N.Y. Surg. Soc., Bergen County Med. Soc., Maine Vascular Soc. (hon.), Mex. Soc. Angiology (hon.), Israel Soc. Vascular Surgery (hon.), Rocky Mountain Vascular Soc. (hon.), Cleve. Vascular Soc., Phi Beta Kappa. Office: Englewood Surg Assocs 375 Engle St Englewood NJ 07631

DARGA, RICHARD JEROME, health facility administrator; b. Alpena, Mich., Mar. 20, 1955; s. Harry Martin and Alice Bernice (Krawczak) D.; m. Anne Florence Davis, Aug. 8, 1981; children: Jessica, Sara. BA in Edn. and Geography, Ctrl. Mich. U., 1977; diploma in Polish lang., Jagellonian U., Krakow, Poland, 1980; MA in Spl. Edn., Ea. Mich. U., 1984; EdD in Edn. Adminstrn., U. Mich., 1994. Tchr. Child Psychol. Hosp./U. Mich., Ann Arbor, 1981-85, Manchester (Mich.) Pub. Schs., 1985-86, Romulus (Mich.) Pub. Schs., 1986-87, 88-89, Dexter (Mich.) Pub. Schs., 1987-88, Wayne (Mich.) County Ind. Sch. Dist., 1989-90; cons. No. Mich. Hosp., Petoskey, 1990-92, dir. behavioral svcs., 1992-95, dir. mgmt. info. sys., 1995—; mem. ad hoc com. for CON, Mich. Dept. Pub. Health, Lansing, 1995. Mem. Mich. Hosp. Assn. (mem. coun. for psychiat. and substance abuse 1992-95). Roman Catholic. Home: 8530 Page Hill Harbor Springs MI 49740 Office: No Mich Hosp 416 Connable Petoskey MI 49770

DARIEN, STEVEN MARTIN, pharmaceutical executive; b. N.Y.C., Oct. 29, 1942; s. Leo and Laura (Kalish) D.; m. Susan Ruth Kinsley, Nov. 29, 1942; children: Jodi Ellen, Andrew Todd. AB, Rutgers Coll., 1963; MBA, Columbia U., 1966. Claims settler Equitable Life, N.Y.C., 1963-64; mgmt. trainee Merck & Co., Inc., Rahway, N.J., 1966-69, mgr. coll. rels., 1969-74, exec. dir. pers. resources, 1974-79, exec. dir. U.S. Pers., 1979-85, v.p. employee rels., 1985-89, v.p. worldwide pres., 1989-90, v.p. human resources, 1990—; bd. dirs. Somerset Hosp. Mem. Labor Policy Assn. (exec. com. 1994—), Columbia U. Bus. Sch. Alumni Assn. (v.p.). Office: Merck & Co Inc PO Box 100 Whitehouse Station NJ 08889

DARITY, EVANGELINE ROYALL, dean, educator; b. Wilson, N.C., June 16, 1927; B.Sc. in Religious Edn., Barber-Scotia Coll., Concord, N.C., 1949; M.Ed., Smith Coll., 1969; Ed.D., U. Mass., Amherst, 1978; m. William A. Darity; children: William, Janki Evangelia. Various YWCA positions 1949-53; tchr., Egypt, N.C. and Mass., 1953-67; asst. to class deans Smith Coll., Northampton, Mass., 1968-75; v.p. student affairs Barber-Scotia Coll., 1978-79; exec. dir. YWCA, Holyoke, Mass., 1979-81; assoc. dean studies, assoc. dean third world affairs Mt. Holyoke Coll., South Hadley, Mass., 1981—; corp. mem. Community Savs. Bank, Holyoke. Mem. Amherst Town Meeting, 1971-80; mem. adv. bd. Community Adolescent Resource and Edn. Ctr.; trustee Barber-Scotia Coll., Concord, N.C. Mem. AAUW (br. pres. 1971-74, 86-88), Am. Assn. Counseling and Devel., Nat. Assn. Women Deans, Counselors and Adminstrs., LWV, Alpha Kappa Alpha, Phi Delta Kappa. Home: 105 Heatherstone Rd Amherst MA 01002-1698

DARKOVICH, SHARON MARIE, nurse administrator; b. Ft. Wayne, Ind., Dec. 10, 1949; d. Gerald Antone LaCanne and Ida Eileen (Bowman) LaCanne Cutler; m. Robert Eliot Ness, July 17, 1971 (dec. Aug. 1976); m. Paul Darkovich, Jan. 23, 1981 (div. May 1994); 1 child, Amy Elizabeth. BS in Nursing, Case Western Res. U., 1973, BA in Psychology, 1978; cert. in advanced bioethics, Cleve. State U., 1990, MA in Philosophy & Bioethics, 1994. RN, Ohio. Staff nurse Univ. Hosps., Cleve., 1973, asst. head nurse, 1973-76; quality improvement coord. St. Luke's Med. Ctr., Cleve., 1976-83, 84—, dir. nursing, 1983-84. cons. to long-term care facilities, 1986-92, pressure ulcer dressing devel. B.F. Goodrich Co., 1988-92; JCAHO coord., 1993—; cons. to long term care facilities, 1989-93, cons. to ambulatory faculty for JCAHO Accreditation, 1994; cons. to cmty. hosp. med. staff, bylaws and JCAHO, 1996; adj. instr. U. Akron, Northeast Ohio U. Coll. Medicine. Mem. ANA, Greater Cleve. Nurses Assn. (mem. dist. coun. on practice, 1982-84), Sigma Theta Tau. Avocations: reading, needlework, sewing, camping.

DARLEY, JOHN MCCONNON, psychologist; b. Mpls., Apr. 3, 1938; s. John Gordon and Kathleen (McConnon) D.; m. Susan Ellen Ancell, July 2, 1966 (div.); children: Lea Shannon, Piper Eve; m. Genevieve Pére, Aug. 16, 1990. BA, Swarthmore Coll., 1960; MA, Harvard U., 1962, PhD, 1965. Asst. prof. psychology NYU, 1964-68; assoc. prof. Princeton (N.J.) U., 1968-72, prof., 1972—, Dorman T. Warren prof. psychology, 1989—; mem. adv. com. for behavioral and neural scis. NSF, 1977-79, mem. exec. com. of adv. com., 1978-79; mem. com. on behavioral and social aspects of energy consumption NAS, 1980—. Author: (with B. Latané) The Unresponsive Bystander: Why Doesn't He Help, 1970 (Appleton-Century Crofts Book award), (with P. Robinson) Justice, Liability and Blame: Community Voices and the Criminal Law, 1995; mem. edit. com. Ann. Rev. Psychology, 1994—. Co-recipient Media award Am. Psychol. Found., 1979; Guggenheim Found. fellow, 1990-91. Fellow Am. Psychol. Assn. (bd. sci. affairs 1969-72, policy and planning bd. 1975-77); mem. AAAS (co-recipient Socio-Psychol. Essay prize 1968), Soc. Exptl. Social Psychologists (exec. com. 1980-83), Soc. for Psychol. Study Social Issues, Soc. Personality and Social Psychology (pres. 1989-90). Episcopalian. Home: 20 Gordon Way Princeton NJ 08540-3957 Office: Princeton U Dept Psychology Washington Rd Princeton NJ 08544-1010

DARLINGTON, RICHARD BENJAMIN, psychology educator; b. Woodbury, N.J., Nov. 16, 1937; s. Charles Joseph and Eleanor (Collins) D.; m. Elizabeth Day, June 13, 1959; children: Jean Susan, Lois Heather. BA, Swarthmore Coll., 1959; PhD, U. Minn., 1963. Asst. prof. psychology Cornell U., Ithaca, N.Y., 1963-68, assoc. prof., 1968-80, prof., 1980—. Author: Radicals and Squares, 1975, (with others) Lasting Effects of Early Education, 1982, (with Patricia M. Carlson) Behavioral Statistics: Logic and Methods, 1987, Regression and Linear Models, 1990; contbr. articles to profl. jours.; contbr. chpts. to books. Project dir. Am. Friends Service Com., 1960, 61. Fellow NSF, 1959-60; fellow Woodrow Wilson Found., 1959-60; grantee HEW, 1977-81, Office of Edn., 1966-67, 70-71, Dept. of Labor, 1980-81. Fellow AAAS; mem. Phi Beta Kappa. Quaker. Home: 204 Fairmount Ave Ithaca NY 14850-4804 Office: Cornell Univ Dept Psychology Uris H Ithaca NY 14853

DARMANI, NISSAR AHMAD, pharmacologist, educator; b. Kabull, Afghanistan, Dec. 29, 1955; came to U.S., 1988; s. Aziz Ahmad and Zainab (Kurban) D.; m. Faridah Shahbaz, Sept. 30, 1988; children: Mariam, Nielofar. BS with honors, Leeds U., U.K., 1979; MS, U. Wales, 1984, PhD, 1988. Sci. officer Bllod Transfusion and Immunohaematology Ctr., Cambridge, U.K., 1979-83; postdoctoral fellow Richmond (Va.) MCV, 1988-90, asst. prof. dept. pharmacology, 1990-91; asst. prof. dept. pharmacology Kirksville (Mo.) Coll. Osteo. Medicine, 1991-95, assoc. prof., 1995—; editl. cons. CRC Book Co., 1993—. Contbr. articles to profl. jours. Grantee Warner Fund, 1993, NIDA, 1993, EPA, 1993, INVEST NIH, 1995. Mem. Soc. for Neurosci., APAIA. Office: Kirksville Coll Osteo Med Dept Pharmacology 800 W Jefferson St Kirksville MO 63501-1443

D'ARMIENTO, THERESA, nurse; b. New Brunswick, N.J., Sept. 9, 1963; d. Rocco William and Judith Anne (Ettinger) D'A. LPN, Princeton (N.J.) Nursing Sch., 1985; ASN, SUNY, Albany, 1991; postgrad., 1992—. RN, N.Y.; cert. plastic surgery nurse, BCLS, ACLS, operating rm. nurse. Staff nurse ICU Princeton Med. Ctr., 1985-86, staff nurse pediatric unit, 1986, staff nurse, med./surgical, 1989-90; pvt. scrub nurse, oper. rm. asst., plastic surgery Nurse Dr. M. Drimmer, Princeton, 1986-87, 90-94, Dr. Steven Zax, Beverly Hills, Calif., 1987-89; oper. rm. charge nurse/staff nurse Middlesex Surg. Ctr., East Brunswick, N.J., 1994—; nurse mgr. oper. rm. N.J. Vein & Cosmetic Surgery Ctr., Livingston, 1996—. Mem. Am. Soc. Plastic and

Reconstructive Surg. Nurses, Assn. Oper. Rm. Nurses, Princeton Breast Inst. Home: 278 Andover Pl Robbinsville NJ 08691 Office: NJ Vein & Cosmetic Surgery Ctr Livingston NJ 07052

DAROS, ANTONY JAMES, osteopath; b. Big Rapids, Mich., Feb. 10, 1970; s. Evtishios James and Connie (Contos) D.; m. Amy Jo Locke, June 15, 1996. BS in Physiology, Mich. State U., 1992; OD, Kirksville Coll. Osteo. Lifeguard, swim instr. Springfield Oaks, Davisburg, Mich., 1987-90; computer tech. Dar-Ware Inc., Grand Blanc, Mich., 1990; profl. waterskier Marine World-Africa USA, Vallejo, Calif., 1991; intern Genesys Regional Med. Ctr., 1996—; owner Dream Quest, Linden, Mich., 1995—. Scholar Kirksville Coll. Osteo. Medicine, 1992-96. Greek Orthodox. Office: Genesys Regional Med Ctr 3921 Beecher Rd Flint MI 48532-3679

DARROW, WILLIAM RICHARD, pharmaceutical company executive; b. Middletown, Ohio, Sept. 7, 1939; s. Richard William and Nelda Virginia (Darling) D.; BA, Ohio Wesleyan U., 1960; MD, Western Res. U., 1964; PhD in Pharmacology, Case-Western Res. U., 1969; m. Janet Elizabeth Swan, June 20, 1964; children: James William, Susan Elizabeth, Margaret Ellen. Intern, Univ. Hosps., Cleve., 1964; sr. clin. rsch. assoc. CIBA Pharm. Co., 1969, asst. dir. clin. pharmacology, 1969-70; dir. clin. pharmacology CIBA-GEIGY Corp., 1970-75, exec. dir. clin. rsch., 1975-76; sr. v.p. rsch., med. dir. Wallace Labs. div. Carter Wallace, Inc., Cranbury, N.J., 1976-80; med. dir. Schering Labs. div. Schering-Plough Corp., Kenilworth, N.J., 1980, v.p. med. and regulatory affairs, 1981-82, sr. v.p. med. ops., 1982-94, sr. med. advisor, 1994—. Chmn. rsch. com. N.J. Health Scis. Group, 1973-76, mem. exec. com., 1973-74, 76-86, treas. 1977-80, v.p., 1980-86, Bernards Twp. Bd. Health, 1979-93, v.p., 1980, pres., 1981-85, 86-93; bd. dirs. N.J. Arthritis Found., 1990—, exec. com., 1991—, vice chmn., 1995—, Pharm. Rsch. Mfrs. Am. Ednl. and Rsch. Inst., 1993—, chmn. curriculum com., 1993-95; bd. dirs. Junior Achievement No. N.J., 1996—; mem. sci. adv. bd. Clin. Rsch. Ctr. Robert Wood Johnson Med. Ctr., 1990—; mem. U.S. del. Internat. Conf. on Harmonization, 1991—. Recipient Roche award, 1962, Humanitarian of Yr. award Arthritis Found. N.J., 1994; USPHS postdoctoral fellow, 1965-69. Fellow Royal Soc. Medicine, Am. Acad. Pharm. Physicians; mem. AMA, Am. Acad. Pharm. Physicians (life), Drug Info. Assn., N.J. Acad. Scis., Pharm. Rsch. Mfrs. Am. (mem. steering com. med. section 1984—, program chmn. 1988-89, vice-chmn. 1989-90, chmn. 1990-92, past chmn. 1992—), Pharm. Rsch. Mfrs. Am. Found. (sci. adv. bd. 1990—, chmn. 1994—), Phi Gamma Delta, Phi Rho Sigma, Omicron Delta Kappa, Pi Delta Epsilon. Republican. Presbyterian. Home: 42 Palmerston Pl Basking Ridge NJ 07920-2524 Also: 521 E Lake Rd Penn Yan NY 14527-9422 Office: Galloping Hill Rd Kenilworth NJ 07033

DAS, MOHAN POTTETH, psychiatrist; b. Kerala, India, July 15, 1947; s. V. K. Krishnan Unni and Nanikutty Amma; m. Suma Das, 1979; 1 child, Priya. MD, Med. Coll., Trivandrum, India, 1972. Diplomate Am. Bd. Psychiatry and Neurology. Mem. faculty U. London, Cambridge (Eng.) U., 1976-83, U. Ottawa (Ont., Can.) Health Scis. Ctr., 1984-87; med. dir. Behavioral Health Ctr. Texoma Med. Ctr., Sherman, Tex., 1989—. Contbr. articles to med. jours. Fellow Royal Coll. Physicians; mem. Tex. Med. Assn., Tex. Soc. Psychiatric Physicians, Grayson County Med. Soc., Royal Coll. Psychiatrists. Office: 2601 Cornerstone Dr Sherman TX 75092

DAS, SANKAR KUMAR, cardiopulmonologist; b. Calcutta, India, Dec. 1, 1933; s. D.N. and Nilima (Roy-Chowdaury) D.; m. Enakshi Roy; children; Shumit, Priya. MB, BS, Calcutta U., 1956. Intern Mil. Hosps. India, 1956-59; med. registrar, sr. house officer Victoria Hosp., Blackpool, 1964-66; fellow VA Hosp., Milw., 1966-69; sr. med. registrar, lectr. King's Coll. Hosp., London, 1970-74; cons. physician St. Helier Gen. Hosp., Sutton, England, 1974—; sr. med. registrar St. Francis Hosp., London, 1970-74; cons. phys. Derby City Hosp., U.K., 1974-77; sr. lectr. U. London, 1977—. Author medical books; contbr. articles to med. jours.; inventor physiotherapy machines. Recipient Nat. Health Svc. Meritorious award, 1993, Man of Yr. award A.B.A. Cambridge, 1994, Mother India Internat. Svcs. to Elderly & Cmty. Svcs. award, 1995. Fellow Royal Soc. Health, Royal Coll. Physicians, Am. Coll. Chest Physicians; mem. N.Y. Acad. Scis., Br. Geriatric Soc., Royal Inst. Great Britain. Home: 62 Rose Hill, SM1 3EX Sutton England Office: St Helier NHS Trust Hosp, Wrythd Ln, SM5 1AA Carshalton England

DAS, SUMAN KUMAR, plastic surgeon, researcher; b. Calcutta, India, May 6, 1944; came to U.S., 1980; s. Bisweswar and Devi Rani (Ghosh) D.; m. Carole Ellen Simmons, July 10, 1976 (div. Apr. 1984); children: Louise Angelique, Natalie Krishna; m. Rosyln Tanner, Mar. 22, 1991. B of Medicine and Surgery, Calcutta (India) U., 1967; MD, Ednl. Commn. Fgn. Med. Grad., 1981. Diplomate Am. Bd. Plastic Surgery. Intern R.G. Kar Med. Coll. and Hosp., Calcatta, 1966-67, resident in gen. surgery, house officer, 1967-68; sr. house officer in accident and emergency, orthopaedics Royal Infirmary, Bolton, Lancs, Eng., 1968-69, house surgeon in gen. surgery, 1969-70; sr. house officer in gen. surgery Royal United Hosp., St. Martins's Hosp., Bath, Eng., 1970-72; house officer in medicine Whiston Hosp., Prescot, Liverpool, Eng., 1970; registrar in gen. surgery Frenchay Hosp., Bristol, Eng., 1972-73, sr. house officer in plastic surgery, 1973-74; registrar in plastic surgery Frenchay Hosp., Bristol, Eng., 1974, Royal Victoria Infirmary, Fleming Meml. Children's Hosp., Newcastle-Upon-Tyne, Eng., 1974-77; fellow in plastic and reconstructive surgery Hosp. for Sick Children, Toronto, Ont., Can., 1978; fellow in micro and hand surgery St. Vincent's Hosp., Melbourne, Australia, 1979-80, asst. plastic surgeon, 1979-80; rsch. assoc. in plastic surgery UCLA Med. Ctr., 1980-82; co-dir. microsurgery tng. program Harbor/UCLA Med. Ctr., 1980-82; dir. plastic surgery rsch. VA Wadsworth Med. Ctr., L.A., 1980-82; resident in plastic surgery U. Miss. Med. Ctr., Jackson, 1982-83, sr. and chief resident in plastic surgery, 1983-84; pvt. practice Jackson, 1984-86; chief and asst. prof. div. plastic surgery U. Miss. Med. Ctr., Jackson, 1986-87, chief and assoc. prof. div. plastic surgery, 1987-90, prof. plastic surgery, chief div. plastic surgery, chief, 1990-95, clin. prof. plastic surgery, 1995—; cons. plastic surgery Meth. Hosp., Miss. Bapt. Med. Ctr., River Oaks Hosp.; attending Meth. Rehab. Ctr., U. Miss. Med. Ctr., River Oaks East Hosp., Parkview Hosp., Vicksburg, Miss.; vis. prof. dept. surgery divsn. plastic surgery U. Calif., San Francisco, 1981, U. Ala., 1992; mem. patient care com. U. Miss., Jackson, 1990—; presenter and exhibitor in field at numerous profl. meetings. Author: (with others) Manual of Operative Plastic and Reconstructive Surgery, 1980, Textbook of Surgery, 2nd edit., 1988, Ency. of Flaps, 1990; mem. editorial bd. So. Med. Jour., 1993—; contbr. articles to Brit. Jour. Surgery, Brit. Jour. Plastic Surgery, Indian Jour. Dermatology, Hand, Plastic Surgery Forum, Jour. Singapore Acad. Sci., Jour. Oral Surgery, Plastic Reconstrn. Surgery, Acta Anatomica, Jour. Clin. Pathology, others; inventor turmeric on wound healing. Donor Miss. Symphony Orch., Jackson, 1991, Indian Assn., 1991; archangel New Stage Theatre, 1991. Recipient prize North Eng. Surg. Soc., 1977, Plastic Surgery Ednl. Found. Rsch. grant 1983-84, other grants Eli Lilly 1989, Tyra, 1989, Collagen Corp. 1989, 90-91, NIH, 1989, Am. Soc. Aesthetic Plastic Surgery, 1990, 91. Fellow ACS, Royal Coll. Surgeons London, Royal Coll. Surgeons Edinburgh (traveling scholarship 1976); mem. AMA, AAAS, Am. Fedn. for Clin. Rsch., Am. Assn. Hand Surgery (rsch. grant com. 1990-91, chmn. rsch. grant com. 1992), Am. Assn. Acad. Plastic Surgeons (fellowship com. 1990), Am. Soc. Plastic and Reconstructive Surgeons, Am. Assn. Plastic Surgeons, Internat. Soc. Burn Injuries, Internat. Soc. Reconstructive Microsurgery, Internat. Soc. Surgery, Internat. Soc. Emergency Medicine and Critical Care (charter), Brit. Assn. Plastic Surgeons (best prize and cert. 1967), Brit. Soc. Surgery of Hands (European traveling scholarship 1977), Soc. N.Am. Skull Base Surgery (founding), Miss. State Med. Assn., Plastic Surgery Rsch. Coun., N.Y. Acad. Sci., S.E. Soc. Plastic and Reconstructive Surgeons (program com. 1990—), Miss. Acad. Scis. (chmn. 1992), Acad. Surgical Rsch., Assn. for Acad. Surgery, Southeastern Surgical Congress, Internatdn. Surgical Colls., Southern Med. Assn. (chmn. elect 1991, chmn. 1992), Sigma Xi. Home: 242 Highland Hills Ln Flora MS 39071 Office: 764 Lakeland Dr Ste 306 Jackson MS 39216-4500

DASGUPTA, AMITAVA, chemist, educator; b. Calcutta, India, May 6, 1958; came to U.S., 1980; s. Anil Kumar and Hasi Dasgupta. BS with honors, U. Calcutta, India, 1978; MS in Chemistry, U. Ga., 1981; PhD in Chemistry, Stanford U., 1986. Diplomate Am. Bd. Clin. Chemistry. Fellow in clin. chemistry U. Wash., Seattle, 1986-88; asst. dir. clin. chemistry U. Chgo., 1988-93; dir. clin. chemistry lab. U. N.Mex. Hosp., Albuquerque, 1993—; assoc. prof. pathology and biochemistry U. N.Mex., Albuquerque, 1993—; lectr in field. Reviewer jours. Clin. Chemistry, Nephron, Jour. Liquid Chromatography; contbr. articles to Clin. Chemistry, Am. Jour. Clin. Pathology, Jour. Am. Soc. Nephrology.. SYVA, 1990-91, Home Health Care, 1992-93. Fellow Nat. Acad. Clin. Biochemistry (Grannis award 1993); mem. Am. Assn. Clin. Chemistry, Acad. Clin. Labs. Physicians and Scientists. Hindu. Home: 801 Locust Pl NE # 2257 Albuquerque NM 87102 Office: U NMex Hosp Pathology Svcs Albuquerque NM 87106

DASH, BARRY HAROLD, pharmaceutical company executive; b. N.Y.C., June 9, 1931; s. Joseph and Anna (Levine) D.; m. Selma Magid, Dec. 19, 1953; children: Faith, Neil, Jeffrey. BS, Columbia U., 1952, MS, 1954; PhD, U. Fla., 1956. Asst. prof. Columbia U., N.Y.C., 1956-60; dir. rsch. and devel. Whitehall Labs., N.Y.C., 1960-70, v.p. sci. affairs, 1970-76; v.p., dir. labs. Am. Can Co., Greenwich, Conn., 1976-78; v.p. rsch. and devel. J.B. Williams Co., Div. Nabisco, N.Y.C., 1978-82; v.p. sci. affairs Whitehall div. Am. Home Products, N.Y.C., 1983-91, sr. v.p. sci. affairs, 1991-94, v.p. adv. tech., 1994-95; pres. Dash Assocs. LLC, N.J., 1995—; indsl. cons., 1956-60; vis. staff Pfizer & Co., Bklyn., 1958; clin. prof. Coll. Podiatry, L.I. U., 1958-60; nat. seminar chmn. Soc. Cosmetic Chemists, N.Y.C., 1962. Contbg. editor: Remington's Practice of Pharmacy, 12th edit. 1960. Patentee in field. Mem. N.J. Fed. Bds. of Edn., Englewood Cliffs, 1965-68, v.p., 1965-68. Fellow Am. Found. Pharm. Edn., 1954-56; recipient Lascoff award, Columbia U., 1950, Merck award, 1952. Mem. AAAS, Am. Pharm. Assn., N.Y. Acad. Sci., Soc. Cosmetic Chemists, Phi Kappa Phi, Rho Chi. Avocations: boating, tennis. Home: 168 Wood Rd Englewood Cliffs NJ 07632 Office: Dash Assoc LLC 168 Wood Rd Englewood Cliffs NJ 07632

DASHEF, STEPHEN SEWELL, psychiatrist; b. Boston, Nov. 1, 1941; s. Oscar Z. and Selma Flashner D.; m. Carolyn Nast, Mar. 18, 1979; children: Alysia Ahavah, Jennifer Kerry, Lauren Elizabeth. AB in Am. Lit. with highest honors, Brown U., 1963; MD, U. Rochester, 1968. Diplomate Am. Bd. of Psychiatry and Neurology. Intern in medicine U. Fla., Gainesville, Fla., 1968-69; resident in psychiatry U. Colo., Denver, 1969-72, chief resident in psychiatry, 1971-72; dir. mental health svc. U. Md., College Park, Md., 1974-76; staff Holyoke Area Mental Health Ctr., Holyoke, Mass., 1976-77; pvt. practice psychiatry Northampton, Mass., 1976—; cons. Franklin Hampshire Cmty. Mental Health Ctr./Svc. Net, 1989—, VA Hosp., Northampton, 1977—, Northampton Area Mental Health Svcs., 1977-84; founder Northampton Conf. on Psychotherapy, 1982. Contbr. articles and book revs. to profl. publs. Lt. comdr. USN, 1972-74. Fellow Am. Psychiat. Assn.; mem. Western Mass. Psychiat. Soc. (pres. 1980-81), Mass. Psychiat. Soc. (coun. mem. 1979-81, fellowship com. 1989—), Phi Beta Kappa. Democrat. Jewish. Home: 78 Harrison Ave Northampton MA 01060-2911 Office: 57 Gothic St Northampton MA 01060-3047

DASKAL, PAUL L., psychiatric and mental health professional; b. Chgo., Jan. 19, 1955; s. Jordan and Jewel D.; m. Jenny E. Velarde, Aug. 3, 1986; children: Janelle M., Michelle N., Matthew J. Diploma, Luth. Gen. Hosp. Sch. Nursing, 1985; AA, Oakton Jr. Coll., 1986; BSN, No. Ill. U., 1991. Cert. psychiat. and mental health nurse. Staff nurse Hines (Ill.) VA Hosp., 1985-89; unit mgr. Macneal Hosp., Berwyn, Ill., 1989-90; staff nurse North Chgo. VA Hosp., North Chgo., Ill., 1990; psychiatric staff nurse Luth. Gen. Hosp., Park Ridge, Ill., 1990—. With USN, 1976-80. Home: 498 Buckingham Dr Grayslake IL 60030-3474

DASMAHAPATRA, BIMALENDU, molecular virologist, researcher; b. Negua, W. Bengal, India, Oct. 12, 1948; came to U.S., 1979; s. Basanta and Bisweswari (Das) D.; m. Jaya Sengupta, Mar. 7, 1976; 1 child, Sanchita. BSc in Chemistry with honors, U. Calcutta, W. Bengal, India, 1969, MSc in Biochemistry, 1971, PhD in Biochemistry, 1977. Sr. sci. asst. Indian Inst. of Chem. Biology, Calcutta, India, 1978-79; rsch. assoc. dept. biochemistry, Med Coll. Wis., Milw., 1979-81; project assoc. Biophysics Lab., Madison, Wis., 1981-85; sr. scientist Schering-Plough Rsch. Inst., Kenilworth, N.J., 1985-87, prin. scientist, 1987-91, sr. prin. scientist, 1991-95, rsch. fellow, 1995—. Gen. sec. Indian Student Orgn., U. Wis., Madison, 1984. Rsch. fellow Coun. for Sci. and Indsl. Rsch., Govt. of India, Indian Inst. Chem. Biology, Calcutta, 1973-77. Mem. Am. Soc. Virology. Office: Schering-Plough Rsch Inst 2015 Galloping Hill Rd Kenilworth NJ 07033-1310

DASTGEER, GHULAM MOHAMMAD, surgeon; b. Kabul, Afghanistan, Apr. 27, 1939; came to U.S., 1979; s. Sofi Ghulam and Zubaida Majida (Tarin) D.; m. Nassrin Sadiqua Saidy, Sept. 1, 1960; children: Nazifa, Walid A., Afifa, Khalid A. MD, Kabul U., 1963. Cert. ACLS; lic. physician, Mass., N.Y. Intern medicine/surgery Kabul U. Med. Sch., 1963-64; gen. surgeon Jalalabad, Afghanistan, 1965-68; resident sr. house officer orthopedics Singleton/Morriston Hosps., Swansea, Wales, 1970-73, resident (sr. house officer) oncology, 1973-74; chief resident, registrar gen. and thoracic surgery Wales and London, 1974-77; sr. resident surgery Leicester, Eng., 1973-74; chief resident gen. surgery Neath Gen. Hosp., Wales, 1974-77; chief resident thoracic surgery St. Helier/St. Thomas Hosps., Surrey and London, 1977-78; assoc. prof. gen. surgery, sr. registrar North Middlesex Hosp., London, 1978; staff physician ambulatory care/surgery VA Med. Ctr., Springfield/Northampton, Mass., 1987—; instr. gen. surgery Nangerhar (Afghanistan) Med. Sch., 1965-68; rsch. fellow U. Coll. Hosp. Med. Sch. Surg. Unit, London, 1969-70; hon. clin. instr. gen. surgery Neath. Gen. Hosp./Cardiff Med. Sch., Wales, 1975-79; lectr. gen. surgery Kabul U. Med. Sch., Afghanistan, 1978-79; instr. somatic medicine dept. psychiatry U. Mass. Med. Ctr., Northampton, 1980-83; asst. physician, asst. prof., chief somatic svcs. Harvard/McLean/Northampton Program, 1983-86; attending surgeon Mil. Hosp., Kabul, 1978-79; lectr. EMT pre-med program U. Mass., Amherst, 1985-90. Contbr. articles to profl. jours.; patentee in field. Recipient Honor award and letter VA, 1989, Spl. Contbn. award VA Med. Ctr., Northampton, 1988, Medallion Acad. Psychosomatics, 1985. Fellow Royal Coll. Surgeons (Scotland), Internat. Coll. Surgeons, Acad. Psychosomatic Medicine; mem. AMA (Physician's Recognition award 1983, 86, 89, 92, 95), Royal Coll. Physicians (London, licensiate), Islamic Med. Assn., Afghan Physicians Assn. Am. (pres.). Republican. Islam. Office: Dept Vets Affairs Springfield Ambulatory Care 1550 Main St Ste 304 Springfield MA 01103-1422

DATE, ELAINE SATOMI, physician; b. San Jose, Calif., Feb. 19, 1957. BS, Stanford U., 1978; MD, Med. Coll. Pa., 1982. Diplomate of Nat. Bd. Med. Examiners. Diplomate Am. Bd. Phys. Medicine and Rehab. Dir. phys. medicine and rehab. Stanford (Calif.) U. Sch. Medicine, 1985—, rehab. medicine sect. chief, 1988-90, head phys. medicine and rehab. div., 1990—, assoc. prof. dept. functional rehab., 1995—; rehab. medicine chief Palo Alto (Calif.) VA Med. Ctr., 1988—. Fellow Am. Acad. Phys. Medicine and Rehab., Am. Assn. Electromyography & Electrodiagnosis. Office: Stanford U Sch of Medicine 300 Pasteur Dr Palo Alto CA 94305

DATO, ROBERT ANTHONY, psychoanalyst, stress consultant; b. Reading, Pa., Dec. 11, 1942. s. Anthony and Millie (DeLuco) D.; m. Joyce Jewell Sinagoga, Jan. 26, 1974. BS, Pa State U., 1964; MHW cert., NIMH, 1965; cert., Family Inst. Phila., 1969; PhD, Heed U., 1975; cert. Phila. Sch. Psychoanalysis, 1976. Program dir. Phila. State Hosp., 1966-67; rsch. dir. Harrisburg State Hosp., Harrisburg, Pa., 1967-71; coord. family therapy Haverford State Hosp., Pa., 1971-72; clin. dir. Phila. Psychiat. Ctr., Phila., 1972-74; pres. Stress Management Sys., 1974—. Author: The Dato Stress Inventory, 1974, The Law of Stress, 1978, Strategic Stress Management, 1990. Fellow Am. Inst. Stress, Internat. Stress Mgmt. Assn.; mem. Nat. Assn. Advancement of Psychoanalysis, Am. Counseling Assn., Assn. for Assessment in Counseling, Employee Assistance Profls. Assn. Home and Office: 900 Clover Hill Rd Wynnewood PA 19096-1631

DATTA, PRADIP, clinical chemist. MS, Yale U., MPhil, PhD. Diplomate Am. Bd. Clin. Chemistry. Asst. dir. Clin. Chem. Lab., U. Tex. Med. Br., Galveston, 1983-84; sr. scientist Photest Diagnostics, N.J., 1984-89, Cirrus/DPC, N.J., 1989-92; staff scientist CIBA Corning Diagnostics, East Walpole, Mass., 1992—; mem. adj. faculty William Paterson Coll., N.J., 1984-89, County Coll. of Morris, N.J., 1989-92; speaker various clin. chemistry rsch. meetings. Contbr. articles to sci. jours.; patentee in field. Office: CIBA Corning Diagnostics 333 Coney St East Walpole MA 02032

DATTA, SYAMAL KUMAR, medical educator, researcher; b. Cuttack, Orissa, India, Sept. 21, 1943; came to U.S., 1967; s. Jitendra Nath and Kalyani (Hazra) D.; m. Tapati Chaudhury, 1976; 1 child, Ronjon. BS, U. Calcutta, India, 1960, MB, BS, 1966. Diplomate Am. Bd. Internal Medicine. Resident in medicine Cook County Hosp., Chgo., 1969-71, fellow in hematology, 1971-72; rsch. assoc. Tufts U./New Eng. Med. Ctr., Boston, 1972-74, instr. in medicine, 1974-76, asst. prof. medicine, 1976-79, assoc. prof. medicine, 1979-85, prof. medicine, 1985-93; Solovy Arthritis-Rsch. Soc. prof., prof. medicine Northwestern U. Med. Sch., Chgo., 1993—; sr. faculty mem. grad. program immunology Sackler Sch., Boston, 1975-93; mem. study sects. NIH, Bethesda, 1987—. Assoc. editor Jour. Immunology, 1984—. Leukemia Soc. Am. fellow, 1972-74; Am. Cancer Soc. scholar, 1975-78. Mem. AAAS, Am. Assn. Immunologists, N.Y. Acad. Scis., Am. Coll. Rheumatology. Office: Northwestern Univ Med Sch Arthritis Div Ward 3-315 303 E Chicago Ave Chicago IL 60611-3008

DATYE, SHREEKRISHNA SHANTARAM, surgeon, consultant; b. Pune, Maharashtra, India, June 8, 1950; arrived in Iceland, 1978; s. Shantaram Narayan and Vimal Shantaram (Joshi) D.; m. Surekha Shreekrishna Tikekar, Dec. 5, 1980; children: Shlok, Som. MBBS, G.S. Med., Mumbai, India, 1972, M Surgery, 1976. House surgeon K.E.M. Hosp., Mumbai, 1973-74; surg. registrar Cooper Hosp., Mumbai, 1974-76, sr. registrar, 1976-78; sr. registrar F.S.A., Akureyri, Iceland, 1978-84, specialist, 1984-90, chief surgery, 1991—. Hindu.

DAUBE, PATRICIA BARRETT, health facility administrator; b. Pitts., July 12, 1943; d. James Patrick and Lena Gottlieba (Eyering) Barrett; m. Donald Gerard Daube, Apr. 17, 1971; children: Christa Ann, Donald Gerard, Jason Barrett, Jeremy Patrick. BA, LaRoche Coll., 1966; BSN, Carlow Coll., 1986. Cert. psychiat./mental health nurse. RN, psychiat. home health care Personal Touch, Pitts., 1987-89; RN, hosp. home health/mental health care Hosp. Home Health, Pitts., 1989-90; psychiat. nurse Nurses Inc., Monroeville, Pa., 1990—; staff RN Mayview State Hosp., Bridgeville, Pa., 1986-89; asst. mgr. clin. nursing Western Psychiat. Inst. and Clinic, U. Pitts. Med. Ctr., Pitts., 1989-93; nursing informatics coord. Office of Nursing Adminstrn. Western Psychiat. Inst. and Clinic, U. Pitts. Med. Ctr., 1993—; computer liaison nurse WPIC Info. Systems, 1992-93. Mem. Tri-State Computer Network. Home: 931 Lebanon Ave Pittsburgh PA 15234-2157

DAUBERT, ELIZABETH ANNE, health facility administrator; b. Danbury, Conn.; d. Robert Sr. and Bridget (Keating) D. Diploma, Danbury Hosp. Sch. Nursing, 1954; BSN, U. Bridgeport, 1966; MPH, U. Mich., 1971. RN, Conn. Staff nurse, supr., asst. dir., assoc. dir. VNA of New Haven, 1966-83; exec. dir. Conn. Assn. for Home Care, Inc., Wallingford, Conn., 1983-88; commr. Commn. on Hosps. and Health Care, State of Conn., Hartford, 1988-91; v.p. Vis. Nurse Svcs. of Conn., 1991—; guset lectr. Yale U. Sch. Nursing, U. Hartford, Conn., Quinnipiac Coll., Tex. Woman's U., U. Minn., U. Md. Contbr. articles to profl. publs. Recipient Emile Sargeant award for excellence in pub. health nursing. Mem. ANA, APHA, Am. Acad. Nursing, Conn. Pub. Health Assn., Sigma Theta Tau. Home: 96 Jones Hill Rd # 4 West Haven CT 06516-7000

DAUGAVIETIS, ANDREW, rheumatologist; b. Riga, Latvia, Mar. 22, 1943; came to U.S., 1949; s. Peter and Mirdza Daugavietis; m. Pamela Harman, June 25, 1989; children: Peter, Elizabeth. MD, U. Mich., 1969. Diplomate Am. Bd. Internal Medicine, Am. Bd. Rheumatology. Staff physician Burns Clinic, Petoskey, Mich., 1975-89; sr. cons. in rheumatology King Fahad N.G. Hosp., Riyadh, Saudi Arabia, 1989-91; staff physician Arthritis Clinic, Grand Rapids, Mich., 1991—. Home: 6255 Heathmore Ct SE Grand Rapidss MI 49546 Office: Arthritis Clinic 1000 E Paris Ave SE Grand Rapids MI 49546

DAUGHERTY, J(AMES) PATRICK, oncologist; b. Athens, Tenn., May 17, 1948; s. James Larson and Dorothy Mae D.; m. Rebecca Poteet, Sept. 6, 1969; children: Lori, Andrea, Amy. BS in Natural Sci. cum laude, Lee Coll., 1969; postgrad., U. Chattanooga, 1967, Cleve. State C.C., 1968, E. Tenn. State U., 1969-70; PhD, U. Tenn., 1975; MD, U. Ala., 1981. Diplomate Am. Bd. Internal Medicine. Intern, resident Carraway Meth. Med. Ctr., Birmingham, Ala., 1982-84; fellow med. oncology Fox Chase Cancer Ctr., Phila., 1985-87; staff physican Med. Ctr. Shoals, Muscle Shoals, Ala., 1987—; founder, dir., physician N.W. Ala. Cancer Ctr., Muscle Shoals, Florence, 1987—; staff physician Helen Keller Meml. Hosp., Sheffield, Ala., 1988—; staff physician Eliza Coffee Meml. Hosp., Florence, 1987—, Florence Hosp., 1987—; adj. prof. biomed. sci., co-dir. Lab. Applied Tech., U. North Ala.; grad. tech. asst. East Tenn. State U., Johnson City, 1969-70, U. Tenn., Knoxville, 1973-74; postdoctoral investigator Oak Ridge Grad. Sch. med. Sci. and Biology divsn. Oak Ridge Nat. Lab., 1974-76; vis. lectr. Lee Coll., Cleveland, Tenn., 1976-77; rsch. assoc. Lab. Molecular Biology, U. Ala., Birmingham, 1976-80, assoc. scientist Comprehensive Cancer Ctr., 1980-84; mem. dir. Chandler Hall Hospice, Newton, Pa., 1986-87; mem., chmn. several coms. Florence Hosp., ECM Hosp., Med. Ctr. Shoals, Helen Keller Meml. Hosp. Contbr. numerous articles to profl. jours. Bd. dirs. Lauderdale County chpt. Am. Cancer Soc., 1987—, pres., 1992—; bd. dirs. R&D coun. Riverbend Mental Health Ctr., Florence, 1992—, United Way of the Shoals, 1990—, Shoals Area C. of C., exec. com., vice chair pub. policy; chmn. bd. trustees Woodmont Christian Sch., Florence, 1994—; deacon Woodmont Bapt. Ch., 1994—; pres. cabinet U. No. Ala.; bd. dirs., investment com. U. No. Ala. Found.; steering com. Conf. Spiritual Renewal. Named Disting. Alumnus Lee Coll., Cleveland Tenn., 1992, Small Bus. of Yr. Shoals Area C. of C., 1994; NDEA fellow, 1971-73. Mem. ACP,AMA, Am. Soc. Internal Medicine, Am. Assn. Cancer Rsch., Am. Soc. Clin. Oncology, So. Assn. Oncology, Med. Assn. Ala. (alt. del 1989, del 1992), Lauderdale County Med. Soc., Colbert County Med. Soc., So. Med. Assn., Ala. Cattleman's Assn., Shoals Area C. of C. (bd. dirs., exec. com., vice chmn. pub. policy), Christian Booksellers Assn., Rotary, Sigma Xi. Home: 1914 N Beechwood Dr Florence AL 35630-1007 also: NW Ala Cancer Ctr 302 W Dr Hicks Blvd Florence AL 35630 also: 101 WH Blake Jr Dr Muscle Shoals AL 35661

DAUGHERTY, ROBERT MELVIN, JR., university dean, medical educator; b. Kansas City, Mo., May 2, 1934; s. Robert Melvin and Mildred Josephine (Johnson) D.; m. Sandra Allison Keller, Aug. 10, 1957; children—Robert Melvin III, Allison, Christopher. BS, Kans. U., 1956; MD, U. Kans., 1960; MS, U. Okla. Med. Ctr., 1964; PhD, U. Okla., 1965. Intern Jefferson Davis Hosp., Houston, 1960-61; resident U. Okla. Med. Ctr., Oklahoma City, 1961-63, asst. prof. physiology and medicine, 1965-66; assoc. prof. physiology and medicine Mich. State U. Coll. Human Medicine, East Lansing, 1969-71; prof., dir. Office Curriculum Implementation, 1969-76; prof. physiology and medicine U. Wyo. Coll. Human Medicine, Laramie, 1976-78; dean U. Wyo. Coll. Human Medicine, 1976-78; prof. physiology and medicine Ind. U. Sch. Medicine, Indpls., 1978-81; assoc. dean Ind. U. Sch. Medicine, 1978-81, dir. continuing med. edn., 1978-81; dean Sch. Medicine, U. Nev., 1981—; teaching scholar Am. Heart Assn., 1970-75. Mem. AMA (coun. med. edn. 1991—), LCME, Am. Physiol. Soc., Am. Heart Assn., Ctrl. Soc. for Clin. Investigation. Presbyterian. Home: 820 Marsh Ave Reno NV 89509-1945 Office: U Nev Sch Medicine Reno NV 89557

DAUGHTRY, DEWITT CORNELL, surgeon, physician; b. Clinton, N.C., Feb. 1, 1914; s. James Guilford and Lorena (Grantham) D.; m. Lucille Carr, June 3, 1939; children: Janet (Mrs. Lester E. Moody), James DeWitt. A.B., Atlantic Christian Coll., 1935; M.D., Med. Coll. Va., 1939, postgrad., 1945-46; postgrad., Wayne U. Coll. Medicine, 1939-42, George Washington U., 1948, Cook County Grad. Sch., 1951. Intern Detroit Receiving Hosp., 1939-40, sr. intern surgery, 1940-41; asst. resident surgery Alexander Blain Hosp., Detroit, 1941-42; resident surgery Med. Coll. Va. Hosp., 1945-46; resident thoracic surgery McGuire Gen. Hosp.; mem. dean's com. VA Hosp. Med. Coll. Va., 1946-48; pvt. practice medicine, specializing in thoracic and cardiovascular surgery Miami, Fla., 1948—; instr. surgery Wayne U. Coll. Medicine, 1940-42, Med. Coll. Va., 1945-48, Am. Coll. Surgeons, 1952; clin. prof. surgery U. Miami Sch. Medicine, 1969—, founder, endower dept. thoracic surgery, endower sect. gen. surgery chief dept., prof., 1978-92, ret.; cons. thoracic surgery VA Hosp. and Regional Office, Southeast Fla. Tb Hosp.; Asst. sec.-treas. Papanicolaou Cancer Research Inst., Miami; chmn. asso. hosp. com. Jackson Meml. Hosp., U. Miami Sch. Medicine, 1967-68;

mem. adv. bd. com. Internat. Congress on Smoking and Health, 1965-67; pres. med. staff Miami Heart Inst., 1970-72, chief of surgery, 1962-68, mem. med. exec. com., 1962-78, chmn. surg. audit com., 1965-70, 1972-74; chief thoracic surgery Mt. Sinai Med. Center of Greater Miami, 1949-63, also Baptist Hosp., and; Mercy Hosp.; chief surgery Nat. Children's Cardiac Hosp., 1950-60; chief thoracic surgery Dade County Hosp., 1950-65, McGuire Gen. Hosp., Richmond, Va., 1946-48; mem. staff Jackson Meml., Miami Heart Inst. (also mem. Endowment Fund and Benefactors Guild), Mt. Sinai, Cedars of Lebanon, Baptist, South Miami, Doctors, Variety Children's Mercy, St. Francis, North Shore, North Miami Gen., Palm (Springs, Hialeah hosps.); ret. Pres. Anatomical Models, Inc.; Physician mem. Met. Pollution Control Bd., 1964-69; mem. exec. com. South Fla. Inter-Profl. Council, 1964, pres., 1976, 79; mem. med. adv. bd. Vocational Rehab. Service, 1955-56; mem. Gov.'s Com. Employment Handicapped, 1962-64; v.p., bd. govs. Com. of 100, 1970—, mem. exec. com., 1980—. Sr. author: Pulmonary Tumors for Tice's Practice of Medicine, 1967, Thoracic Trauma, 1980; author, editor: Thoracic Trauma, 1980; 55 med. publs.; contbr. numerous articles to med., sci. jours. Trustee Miami Shores Presbyn. Ch., 1992—, elder, 1993—, trustee endowments, 1992—, trustee 1995; trustee Pulitzer Found., 1993. Recipient merit award Miami Med. Forum, 1968, 69; silver medal Miami Heart Inst., 1972, Builder's award, 1985; Benefactors Guild, 1978; epidemiology bldg. at Daughtry bldg. dedicated in his name U. Miami Sch. Medicine, 1989, endowed dept. gen. surgery, 1988, thoracic surgery sect., 1980. Fellow A.C.S., Am. Coll. Chest Physicians (gov. 1964-70, bd. regents 1971-77), Am. Coll. Cardiology; mem. Am. Assn. Thoracic Surgery, Soc. Thoracic Surgeons, So. Thoracic Surg. Assn. (pres. 1964), Nat. Tb Assn. (dir. 1956-73), Am. Thoracic Soc. (council 1971-74), Am. Heart Assn., Am. Med. Assn., So. Med. Assn., Pan-Am. Med. Assn., Fla. Med. Assn., Dade County Med. Assn. (pres. 1964), Am. Med. Writers Assn., So. Tb Conf., So. Thoracic Soc., Fla. Thoracic Soc. (pres. 1956-57) thoracic socs), Fla. Tb and Health Assn. (pres. 1956-57), Dade County Tb Assn. (dir. 1950-81, v.p. 1960-61, exec. com. 1962-63), Heart Assn. Greater Miami (pres. 1967), Miami Med. Forum (pres. 1970), Hesperian Lit. Soc. (pres. 1934-35), So. Thoracic Surg. Assn. (v.p. 1957, pres. 1961, chmn. council 1962), So. Coll. Chest Physicians (sec. treas. 1959, v.p. 1960, pres. 1961), Fla. Tb and Respiratory Disease Assn. (v.p. 1955-56, dir. 1950—, mem. exec. com., pres. 1958, chmn. research com. 1956), Soc. Univ. Founders, Alpha Kappa Kappa. Clubs: Miami Shores Country, Ponte Vedra (Fla.). Home: 4201 Lake Rd Miami FL 33137-3334

DAUM, CONRAD HENRY, psychiatrist; b. N.Y.C., Mar. 23, 1943; s. Conrad Ferdinand and Clara Francesca D.; m. Beverly Jean Burwell; children: Denise, Jennifer, Daniel. BA, Grinnell Coll., 1965; MS, U. Wash., 1970; MD, U. Ky., 1971. Diplomate Am. Bd. Psychiatry and Neurology with qualification in geriatric, addiction and forensic psychology. Intern, then resident in psychiatry Bowman Gray Sch. Medicine, Winston-Salem, N.C., 1971-74; pvt. practice Salem, Va., 1978—. Contbr. articles to profl. jours. Maj. U.S. Army, 1974-76. Mem. S.W. Va. Psychiat. Soc. (pres. 1990-91). Lutheran. Office: 1906 Braeburn Dr Salem VA 24153-7304

DAUM, ROBERT STEVEN, pediatrics educator; b. Boston, Dec. 5, 1946; s. Arnold Edward and Phyllis (Simblist) D.; m. Diane Susan Vinikoor, Aug. 23, 1970 (div. Aug. 1984); children: Michael, Jeremy; m. Karen Paula Goldstein, Apr. 5, 1992; 1 child, Abigail. BSc with honours in Genetics, McGill U., Montreal, Que., Can., 1968, MD, CM, 1972, MSc in Genetics, 1973. Diplomate Am. Bd. Pediatrics. Straight intern in pediatric medicine Montreal Children's Hosp., 1972-73, resident, 1972-75, chief resident, 1974-75, fellow in infectious diseases, 1975-78; asst. prof. pediat., head sect. infectious diseases Tulane U. Sch. Medicine, New Orleans, 1978-82, assoc. prof., head sect. infectious diseases, 1982-88, adj. asst. prof. microbiology and immunology, 1979-82, adj. assoc. prof., 1982-88; prof. pediat., chief sect. pediatric infectious diseases U. Chgo., 1988—, dir. antibiotic monitoring svc. dept. pediat., 1988—; mem. Chgo. Communicable Disease Tech. Adv. Group, 1993—; chmn. spl. rev. com. on vaccine evaluation units Nat. Inst. Arthritis and Infectious Diseases, 1994, mem. spl. rev. com. on multi-component vaccine devel., 1994; invited reviewer Nat. Vaccine Compensation Act, 1993—; mem. nat. vaccine adv. com. ad hoc subcom. on childhood vaccinations HHS, Washington, 1994; also others. Mem. editl. bd. Pediatric Infectious Diseases Jour., 1984-88; contbr. numerous articles, revs., abstracts, and book revs. to med. jours. Recipient honor roll for tchg. excellence Owl Club of Tulane U. Sch. Medicine, 1979-81, 85, 87, Best Faculty award, 1982, 84; rsch. grantee Lederle Labs., 1985-92, Merck Sharp & Dohme Rsch. Labs., 1988-92, Inst. Merienx/Connaught, 1990—, Praxis-Lederle Labs., 1991-93, Children's Rsch. Found., 1992-93, Blowitz-Ridgeway Found., 1993-94, Joyce Found., Cubs Care, U. Chgo. Hosps., 1993; fellow Pediatric Infectious Diseases Soc., 1988-92. Fellow Am. Acad. Pediat. (com. on infectious diseases 1983-89, sec. 1983-86, cons. to com. 1989-91); mem. Am. Soc. Microbiology, Infectious Diseases Soc. Am., Soc. for Pediatric Rsch. Office: Wyler Childrens Hosp Dept Pediatrics 5841 S Maryland Ave MC 6054 Chicago IL 60637-1463*

D'AURORA, JAMES JOSEPH, psychologist, consultant; b. Canton, Ohio, Feb. 10, 1949; s. James Joseph Sr. and Arsilia (Lombardi) D'A.; m. Denise Marie Linkenhoker, Dec. 28, 1974; children: Andrew David, Elizabeth Clare. BA, U. Notre Dame, 1971; MEd, Kent State U., 1974; PhD, U. Minn., 1984. Lic. psychologist, Minn., marriage and family therapist, Minn. Pre-major adv. Coll. of Liberal Arts U. Minn., Mpls., 1974-75; intern Bach Inst., Mpls., 1975-77, staff psychologist, 1977-79; psychologist Loring Family Clinic, Mpls., 1979-81; pvt. practice Mpls., 1981-86; cons. psychologist Solstice: A Ctr. for Psychotherapy and Learning, St. Paul, 1986-89; pvt. practice St. Paul, 1989—; cons. in field, 1975—; researcher Family Renewal Ctr., Mpls., 1982-85, Golden Valley Health Ctr. Psychology Subsect., 1988-92. Lectr., lay homilist preacher Christ the King Ch., mem. parish pastoral coun., 1991-96; interim sch. bd. Christ the King-St. Thomas the Apostle Sch., 1992, bd. rs., 1992—, mem. governance com., 1992. Mem. APA, Minn. Psychol. Assn. (chairperson ins. com. 1988-94), Notre Dame Club Minn. (bd. dirs. 1986-91, sec. 1987-88, v.p. 1988-89, pres. 1989-90). Mem. Democratic Farm Labor Party. Roman Catholic. Home: 5536 Merritt Cir Edina MN 55436-2026 Office: 91 Snelling Ave N Ste 200 Saint Paul MN 55104-6753

DAUS, ARTHUR STEVEN, neurological surgeon; b. Louisville, Feb. 6, 1957; s. Arthur Theodore Daus Jr. and Marilyn Ann (McCord) Hanish; m. Victoria Lynn Schilla, July 10, 1982; children: Arthur S. Jr., Haley N. BS in Physics magna cum laude, Vanderbilt U., 1977; MD, St. Louis U., 1981. Diplomate Nat. Bd. Med. Examiners, Am. Bd. Neurol. Surgery; lic. physician, Ky., N.Mex., Ariz., Mo., Calif. Rotating intern in surgery U. Ky. Med. Ctr., Lexington, 1981-82, resident neurosurgeon, 1982-88; pvt. practice Midwest Neurosurgery Ctr., Joplin, Mo., 1988—; instr. cervical spine instrumentation A.M.E. Med. Co., Kansas City, Mo., 1992. Mem. Nat. Coalition of Physicians Against Family Violence, Chgo., 1994—. Named Ky. Col. State of Ky., 1985—. Mem. AMA (Physician's Recognition award 1990-94, Physician's Recognition award with spl. commendation 1993—), So. Med. Assn., Jasper-Newton County Med. Soc., So. Neurosurg. Soc., Congress of Neurol. Surgeons, Am. Assn. Neurol. Surgeons (continuing edn. award 1990-92), Nat. Audubon Soc., Phi Beta Kappa. Republican. Roman Catholic. Home: 5 Teal Dr Joplin MO 64804 Office: Midwest Neurosurgery Ctr Ste 101 1020 McIntosh Circle Dr Joplin MO 64804

DAUSER, KIMBERLY ANN, physician assistant; b. Detroit, Nov. 20, 1947; d. George Leonard and Jeanne (Austin) Wilkie; m. Steven Kent Dauser, Nov. 10, 1983; 1 child, Aaron Thomas. AA, Pensacola Jr. Coll., 1971; BS in medicine, physician's asst. cert. in medicine, U. Ala., Birmingham, 1976; cert. in mgmt., Am. Mgmt. Assn., 1989; postgrad., U. West Fla., 1995—. Cert. physician's asst. Asst. mgr. Christo's, Gulf Breeze, Fla., 1966-67; teller, bookkeeper loan dept. Bank Gulf Breeze, 1967-72; med. tech. aide USN Hosp., Pensacola, 1972, physician's asst., 1972-73; physician's asst. John Kingsley, MD, Pensacola, 1976, Mountain Comprehensive Health Corp., Whitesburg, Ky., 1976-78; physician's asst. N.W. Fla. Nephrology, Pensacola, 1978-87, med. adminstr., 1987-95; med. adminstr. Nephrology Ctr. of Pensacola, Fla., 1987-95; COO Nephrology Ctr. Inc., Crestview, Pensacola, 1995—, Nephrology Ctr., Inc., Crestview, Pensacola, 1995—, Nephrology Ctr. Assocs., Pensacola, 1995—. Fellow Am. Acad. Physician's Assts. (del. nat. mtg. 1978-95), Nat. Commn. on Cert. Physician's Assts., Fla. Acad. Physician's Assts. (mem. jud. com. 1979-80), Natural Wildlife Assn. Republican. Roman Catholic. Office: Nephrology Ctr Inc 1717 N E St Ste 501 Pensacola FL 32501-6334

DAUSSET, JEAN, immunologist; b. Toulouse, France, Oct. 19, 1916; s. Henri and Elizabeth D.; m. Rose Mayoral, Mar. 17, 1962. AB, Lycee Michelet, 1939; MD, U. Paris, 1945. Intern, then resident in internal medicine and hematology Paris Mcpl. Hosps., 1946-50; dir. lab. Nat. Transfusion Ctr., 1950-63; prof. immunohematology U. Paris, 1963-77; prof. exptl. medicine Coll. de France, Paris, 1977-87; dir. research unit on immunogenetics Hopital Saint-Louis, Paris, 1969-84; dir. Human Polymorphism Study Ctr., 1984—; researcher in field of man's histocompatibility system anbd human genome. Served to capt., World War II. Recipient Nobel prize in physiology and medicine, 1980, Honda prize Honda Found. Japan, 1987. Mem. Academie des Sciences de l'Institut de France, Am. Acad. Arts and Sci., NAS (Washington). Home: 9 rue Villersexel, 75007 Paris France Office: 27 Rue Juliette Dodu, 75010 Paris France

DAVALLI, MARY, women's health nurse; b. Cumberland, Md.; d. Leonard A. and Harriet (Carolan) McKenzie; m. Paul A. Davalli, Feb. 20, 1971; children: Jacob, Joshua. AA in Nursing, Essex C.C., Balt., 1981; AA, Allegany C.C., Cumberland. Gen. staff nurse St. Joseph's Hosp., Balt.

DAVANT, CHARLES, III, physician; b. Charleston, S.C., Jan. 16, 1946; s. Charles and Harriet (Browning) D.; m. Teena Brewer, June 14, 1969; 1 child, Charles Davant IV. BS in Psychology, Duke U., 1968; MD, U. N.C., Chapel Hill, 1972. Diplomate Am. Bd. Family Practice; cert. Added Qualifications in Geriatric Medicine. Residency Riverside Hosp., Newport News, Va., 1972-75; physician Blowing Rock (N.C.) Med. Clinic P.A., 1975—; asst. prof. community and family medicine Duke U., 1980—. U. N.C., 1980—; dir. Med. Rev. N.C. Contbg. editor Med. Econs. Mag., 1989—. Chmn. Blowing Rock Planning and Zoning Bd., 1980—. Fellow Am. Acad. Family Physicians; mem. Watauga County Med. Soc. (past pres.), N.C. Med. Soc., AMA, Am. Med. Athletic Assn., Man Will Never Fly Meml. Soc. Internat., Yonohlossee Racket Club, Blowing Rock Country Club, Flat Earth Soc., Procrastinators Club. Episcopalian. Home: Rt 2 Box 5 378 1 Chestnut Cir Blowing Rock NC 28605 Office: Blowing Rock Med Clinic PO Box 8 Blowing Rock NC 28605-0008

DAVENPORT, ANTHONY PETER, clinical pharmacology educator; b. Edinburgh, Scotland, Nov. 27, 1955; s. Peter Thomas and Kathleen Cynthia (Buckley) D.; m. Ann Judith Payne, July 17, 1982; children: Emma Elisabeth, Rebecca Ann, James Anthony. BS, Nottingham (Eng.) U., 1978; PhD, London U., 1983; MA, Cambridge U., 1995. Postdoctoral fellow U. Cambridge, Eng., 1981-86, rsch. assoc. Parke-Davis Rsch. Unit, 1988; sr. lectr. U. Cambridge, 1988—; ofcl. fellow St. Catherine's Coll., Cambridge, 1995—; sr. mem. Hughes Hall, Cambridge, 1995—. Author sci. papers and book chpts. Rsch. grantee Brit. Heart Found., 1989, 90, 93, 94, 95, Nuffield Trust, 1990, Royal Soc., 1991, 92, Royal Soll. Ob-Gyn., 1991, Sci. and Engring. Rsch. Coun., 1992; rsch. fellow Hughes Hall, Cambridge, 1992-95. Fellow Cambridge Philos. Soc.; mem. Brain Rsch. Assn., European Neurscis. Assn., Brit. Pharmacology Soc., Soc. Exptl. Biology. Mem. Ch. of England. Office: U Cambridge, Clin Pharmacology Dept. F&G Block Addenbrookes Hosp, Cambridge CB2 2QQ, England

DAVENPORT, HORACE WILLARD, physiologist; b. Phila., Oct. 20, 1912; s. Horace Willard and Elizabeth (Langendorf) D.; m. Virginia Dickerson, Feb. 1, 1945 (dec. Mar. 1968); 2 sons; m. Ingeborg L. Epstein, Aug. 15, 1969. B.S., Calif. Inst. Tech., 1935, Ph.D., 1939; B.A., U. Oxford, Eng.; B.A. (Rhodes scholar 1935-38), 1937, B.Sc., 1938, D.Sc., 1961. Instr. physiology U. Pa. Med. Sch., Phila., 1941-1943; instr. physiology Harvard Med. Sch., 1943-45; prof., head dept. physiology U. Utah Med. Sch., 1945-56; prof. dept. physiology U. Mich., Ann Arbor, 1956—; chmn. dept. U. Mich., 1956-78, William Beaumont prof., 1978-83, prof. emeritus, 1983—; vis. prof. Mayo Found., 1962-63. Contbr. to articles on med. history to profl. jours. Recipient Friedenwald medal Am. Gastroent. Assn., 1980. Mem. NAS, Am. Physiol. Soc. (pres. 1961-62), Brit. Soc. Gastroenterology (hon.). Home: 3850 Galleria Woods Dr Birmingham AL 35244

DAVENPORT, JUDITH ANN, social work educator; b. Gulfport, Miss., Sept. 21, 1944; d. Tom and Jessie (Roberts) Reaves; m. Joseph Davenport, Sept. 11, 1966; 1 child, Jennifer Ann. AA, Meridian (Miss.) Community Coll., 1964; BA, Miss. State U., Starkville, 1966; MSW, U. Tenn., 1970; PhD, U. Wyo., 1985. Lic. clin. social worker, Mo. Social worker Clover Bottom Hosp., Nashville, 1966-68; dir. outpatient svcs. Weems Mental Health Ctr., Meridian, 1973-75; asst. prof., dir. health counseling agy. Miss. State U., 1975-78; assoc. prof., dir. Wyo. human svcs. U. Wyo., Laramie, 1978-80, assoc. prof., dir. BSW proram, 1980-82; assoc. prof., dir. BSW program U. Ga., Athens, 1985-89; prof., dir. Sch. Social Work, U. Mo., Columbia, 1989—; cons. HEW, Washington, 1979, U.S. Bur. Land Mgmt., Reno, 1981, Territorial Govt. N.W. Territory, Can., 1982, The Bush Found., St. Paul, 1990-92, The Durrant Group, 1993. Editor: Social Work in Rural Areas, 1979, Boom Towns and Human Services, 1979, Human Side of Energy, 1981; contbr. over 100 articles to profl. jours. Adv. bd. mem. CARE, Columbia, 1989—; pres. bd. dirs. Laramie Child Devel. Corp. 1984-85. Named Social Worker of Yr., NASW, Wyo. chpt. 1991, Athens Unit 1988, Cen. Mo. Unit 1993; recipient Martha Davis Lectureship Ky. Conf. on Social Welfare 1981, Victor I. Howery award Nat. Assn. Rural Mental Health 1982. Mem. NASW (nat. comm. com. 1990-92, Columbia chpt. unit com. 1989—), Nat. Assn. Deans and Dirs. (nominating com. 1991-93), Internat. Assn. Schs. of Social Work (U.S. liaison children project 1990-92), Mo. Assn. Social Welfare (bd. dirs. Columbia chpt. 1991), Coun. Social work Edn. (nominating com. 1990-93, editorial bd. Jour. 1993, Columbia Svcs. for Ind. Living (bd. dirs. 1993—), Phi Kappa Phi. Democrat. Episcopalian. Office: U Mo Sch Social Work Clark Hall Columbia MO 65211

DAVEY, LYCURGUS MICHAEL, neurosurgeon; b. N.Y.C., Feb. 20, 1918; s. Michael Marco and Elizabeth (Delaveris) D.; m. Artemis Diana Pappas, June 7, 1942; children: Michael Dean, Elaine Anne, Elizabeth. BA, Yale U., 1939, MD, 1943. Diplomate Am. Bd. Neurol. Surgery, 1954. Surg. intern New Haven Hosp., 1943-44, asst. resident in surgery, 1946-50, William Harvey Cushing fellow, 1947-48, resident neurosurgeon, 1951-52; asst. resident in neurosurgery Hartford Hosp., 1950-51; clin. clk. Nat. Hosp., London, summer 1954; clin. instr. neurosurgery Yale U., 1952-60, asst. clin. prof., 1960-68, asso. clin. prof., 1968-77, clin. prof., 1977—; assoc fellow Trumbull Coll. Yale U., 1959—; cons. practice in neurosurgery New Haven, 1952—; attending neurosurgeon Vets. Meml. Med. Ctr. (formerly Meriden-Wallingford Hosp.), Hosp. St. Raphael; assoc. sect. chief emeritus Yale-New Haven Med. Ctr.; bd. dirs. MD Health Plan, Tex. Citrus Found. Served to comdr. USNR, 1942-46, 52-54; capt. Res. ret. 1973. Fellow ACS, Internat. Coll. Surgeons; mem. AMA, Conn. Med. Soc. (chmn. sect. on neurosurgery 1971-72), Conn. Soc. Neurol. Surgeons, New Haven County Med. Soc. (pres. 1987), New Haven Med. Assn. (pres. 1972), Am. Assn. Neurol. Surgeons, New Eng. Neurosurg. Soc., Congress Neurol. Surgeons (Disting. Svc. award 1966), Assn. Rsch. in Nervous and Mental Diseases, Soc. Med. Cons. to Armed Forces, Internat. Platform Assn., Assn. Yale Alumni in Medicine (pres. 1995-97). Home: 1010 Hartford Tpke North Haven CT 06473-3038 Office: 60 Temple St New Haven CT 06510-2716 also: 2 Church St S New Haven CT 06519-1717

DAVID, BARBARA MARIE, medical, surgical nurse; b. Wisconsin Rapids, Wis., Mar. 3, 1935; d. Stanley Spencer and Olga Agatha (Bissig) Stark; m. Russell Paul David, Jan. 19, 1957; children: Dennis James, John Paul. Diploma, St. Joseph's Hosp. Sch. Nursing, Marshfield, Wis., 1956. Cert. med./surg. nurse, clin. nurse 3. Asst. to dir. nursing rsch. St. Joseph's Hosp., 1968-70, head nurse, ICU, 1964-67, 70-71, staff nurse, 1983—. Mem. ANA, Wis. Nurses Assn. (treas. dist. 18), Acad. Med.-Surg. Nurses, Nat. League Nurses. Home: 2007 S Maple Ave Marshfield WI 54449-4957 Office: St Josephs Hosp 611 St Joseph Ave Marshfield WI 54449

DAVID, GEORGE, psychiatrist, economic theory lecturer; b. N.Y.C., Feb. 19, 1940; s. Norman and Jennie (Danziger) D. BA, Yale U., 1961; MD, NYU, 1965. Intern Children's Hosp., San Francisco, 1965; resident in psychiatry Colo. Psychiat. Hosp., Denver, 1965-66; practice medicine specializing in psychiatry San Francisco; staff Calif. Pacific Med. Ctr., San Francisco, 1966-67, San Mateo County (Calif.) Mental Health Svcs., 1968-71; lectr. on application of econ. theory to personal decision making. Mem. San Francisco Clin. Hypnosis (v.p. 1973-74). Libertarian. Office: 399 Laurel St San Francisco CA 94118-1846

DAVID, HENRY PHILIP, psychologist; b. Hagen, Germany, May 28, 1923; came to U.S., 1937; s. Ferdinand and Ilse (Gerson) D.; m. Tema Seidman, Mar. 28, 1953; children: Jonathan (dec.), Gail. BA, U. Cin., 1948, MA, 1949; PhD, Columbia U., 1951. Diplomate Am. Bd. Profl. Psychology. Sr. clin. psychologist Topeka State Hosp., 1951-52; instr. Western Psychiat. Inst. U. Pitts. Med. Sch., 1952-55; asst. prof. and head dept. psychology, Lafayette Clinic Wayne State U. Med. Sch., Detroit, 1955-56; chief psychologist N.J. State Dept. Instns. and Agys., Trenton, 1956-63; assoc. dir. World Fedn. for Mental Health, Geneva, 1963-65; assoc. dir., Internat. Rsch. Inst. Am. Insts. for Rsch., Washington, 1965-71; dir. Transnat. Family Rsch. Inst., Bethesda, Md., 1971—; assoc. clin. prof. psychology U. Md. Med. Sch., Balt., 1975-91; lectr. Rutgers U., 1960-63, Princeton U., 1962; cons. Nat. Inst. Medicine, 1975, WHO, Geneva, Copenhagen and Washington, 1975—, Nat. Acad. Scis., 1984, UN Population Div., 1983-84, UN Fund for Population Activities, 1984-85. Author: International Resources in Clinical Psychology, 1964, (with H. von Bracken) Perspectives in Personality Theory, 1956, (with J.C. Brengelmann) Perspectives in Personality Research, 1960, (with others) Reproductive Behavior: Central and Eastern European Experience, 1981, Born Unwanted: Developmental Effects of Denied Abortion, 1988, Child Mental Health in International Perspective, 1972, Family Planning and Abortion in the Socialist Countries of Central and Eastern Europe, 1970; editor: Population and Mental Health, 1964, Migration, Mental Health, and Community Services, 1968, others; editorial cons. various jours. Recipient Harold M. Hildreth Meml. award for Disting. Pub. Svc. in Psychology, 1974, medal Charles U., Prague, 1991. Fellow APA (chmn. task force on psychology and family planning 1969-72, pres. div. population and environ. psychology 1977-78, chmn. com. on internat. rels. in psychology 1989-92, Award Disting. Contbns. to Internat. Advancement Psychology, 1992); mem. AAAS, APHA, Am. Orthopsychiat. Assn., Population ssn. Am., Internat. Coun. Psychologists (pres. 1967-69), Population and Devel. Internat. (sec., treas. 1983—), D.C. Psychol. Assn., World Fedn. for Mental Health, Interam. Soc. Psychology, Internat. Assn. Applied Psychology. Home and Office: 8307 Whitman Dr Bethesda MD 20817-6820

DAVID, JOHN R., internist, educator; b. Eng., Feb. 15, 1930; married; 2 children. BA, U. Chgo., 1951, BS, 1955, MD, 1955; D (hon.), U. F. Ceara, 1991. Diplomate Am. Bd. Internal Medicine. From intern to asst. resident Mass. Gen. Hosp., 1955-57; clin. assoc. Nat. Inst. Arthritis and Metab Dis., 1957-59; trainee Rheumatism Rsch. Unit, Eng., 1959-60; resident med. Mass. Gen. Hosp., 1960-61; fellow NYU, 1961-64, asst. prof. medicine, 1964-66; asst. physician-in-chief Robert B. Brigham Hosp., 1966-82; prof., chair dept. tropical pub. health Harvard Sch. Pub. Health, Boston, 1981—; prof. medicine NYU, 1973—; sr. assoc. med. Brigham & Women's Hosp., 1980-82, asst. chief Dept. Rheumatol-immunol., 1982—, sr. physician Dept. Medicine, 1982—, sci. adv. bd. Internal Lab. Rsch. Animal Disease, 1980—, Burroughs Wellcome vis. prof. Johns Hopkins U., Balt., 1983, Royal Soc. Medicine, Eng., 1984; cons. sci. working group Dir. Cmty. Disease, 1981—. Mem. steering com. Cmty. Immunology Tuberclosis, 1984—; mem. sci. adv. com. New Eng. Biolabs, 1982—; ad hoc cons. Bd. Sci. Coun. Rev. Lab. Parasitic Diseases, NIH, 1984—. Mem. Inst. Medicine Nat. Acad. sci., Am. Soc. Tropical Medicine and Hygiene (pres. 1989), Am. Soc. Clin. Investigation, Am. Assn. Immunologists, Am. Fedn. Clin. Rsch., Am. Rheumatism Assn., Infectious Disease Soc. Am., Soc. Exptl. Biology and Medicine, Am. Assn. Physicians, Am. Acad. Arts and Sci. Rsch. Office: Harvard Sch Pub Health Dept Tropical Medicine 665 Huntington Ave Boston MA 02115*

DAVID, RONALD BRIAN, child neurologist; b. Richmond, Va., Aug. 3, 1937; m. Candace M. Heiderich; children: Ronald Bryan, Susan D. Soueidan, Elizabeth D. Kurtz, Thomas Edwin, Whitney Pund, Jennifer Pund. BS, Eastern Mennonite Coll., 1960; MD, Med. Coll. Va. Sch. Medicine, 1964. Diplomate Am. Bd. Psychiatry & Neurology, Am. Bd. Pediatrics, Nat. Bd. Med. Examiners, Am. Bd. Child Neurology. Fellow in pediatrics Mayo Grad. Sch. Medicine, Rochester, Minn., 1965-67, fellow in child neurology, 1967-70; from asst. prof. to assoc. prof. Med. Coll. Va., Richmond, 1970—; vis. prof. Coll. William & Mary. Editor: Pediatric Neurology for the Clinician, 1992; series editor: Mosby Neurology-Psychiatry Access Series, 1996; editor: Child and Adolescent Neurology, 1996; contbr. articles to profl. jours., chpts. to books. Fellow Am. Acad. Neurology, Am. Acad. Cerebral Palsy & Child Devel., Am. Acad. Pediatrics; mem. Am. Neurol. Assn., Child Neurology Soc., Internat. Neuropsychol. Soc., Learning Disabilities Coun., Am. Epilepsy Found., Va. Neurol. Soc., Va. Pediat. Soc., Orton Soc. Office: Children's Neurol Svcs 1825 Monument Ave Richmond VA 23220

DAVIDGE, ROBERT CUNNINGHAME, JR., hospital administrator; b. Schenectady, Jan. 1, 1942; s. Robert Cunninghame and Jean (Humphrey) D.; m. Margie Ann Green, May 20, 1961; children: Robert Cunninghame, III, Donna Marie, Christopher Hayne, Michael Rayburn. B.S., Fla. State U., 1965; M.B.A., U. Fla., 1967. Asst. adminstr. Tallahassee Meml. Hosp., 1967-69; adminstr. Cathedral Health and Rehab. Center, Jacksonville, Fla., 1969-73; exec. v.p. Tallahassee Meml. Regional Med. Center, 1973-79; pres., chief exec. officer Our Lady of Lake Regional Med. Center, Baton Rouge, 1979—; mem. Fla. Bd. Examiners Nursing Home Adminstrs., 1970-75; bd. dirs. Big Bend Med. Edn. Found., 1974-79, Neighborhood Health Center, Inc., Tallahassee, 1974-79, Big Bend Health Plan, 1974-79, Easter Seals N. Fla., 1971-73; mem. White House Health and Mental Health Task Force, 1971, Fla. Conf. Aging, 1971; mem. devel. bd. Fla. State Bank, 1973-79; Bd. dirs. Jacksonville Art Mus., 1972-73, Safety Council Greater Baton Rouge, 1981. Chmn. Southeast Hosp. Conf., 1985-86; vol. bd. dirs. Baton Rouge, Inc., 1987—; bd. dirs. Sta. WRKF pub. radio, 1987—, adv. bd. La. State U. Grad. Sch. Social Work; bd. dirs. La. Sr. Olympics, 1990—, chmn. Greater Baton Rouge United Way, 1992, bd. dirs. La. Assn. of bus. and industry, 1992, Greater Baton Rouge Healthcare Alliance, 1992, La. Pan Am. Commn., 1990—, chmn. medical com. With USAF, 1959-63. Grantee HEW, 1974. Fellow Am. Coll. Healthcare Execs. (regent for La. 1984-90); mem. Am. Hosp. Assn. (sect. on aging and long-term care services 1987-90), La. Hosp. Assn. (sec.-treas. 1982-83, chmn. 1983-84), Southeastern Hosp. Conf. (chmn. 1985-86), Res. Officers Assn., Soc. Air Force Res. Med. Svc. Corps Officers (pres. 1989-90), Beta Gamma Sigma. Republican. Roman Catholic. Clubs: Rotary (past dir. Tallahassee, bd. dirs. Baton Rouge club 1988-91), KC. Home: 12115 Oakshire Ave Baton Rouge LA 70810-7106 Office: Our Lady Lake Regional Med Ctr 5000 Hennessy Blvd Baton Rouge LA 70808-4350

DAVIDMAN, LEONARD, psychologist, educator; b. N.Y.C., Sept. 19, 1947; s. Irving and Matilde (Melmid-Vargas) D.; m. Naomi Olkon, Sept. 8, 1969; m. 2d Beverly Yvonne Dyer, Dec. 13, 1981. B.A. in Psychology, Yeshiva U., 1969; M.S., Bklyn. Coll., 1971; Ph.D., Fordham U., 1982; student Hebrew U. Jerusalem, 1967-68. Lic. psychologist, N.Y.; cert. sch. psychologist, N.Y. Intern sch. psychology Coney Island Hosp., Bklyn., 1971; part-time sch. psychologist The Archway Sch., Bklyn., 1971-72; staff psychologist Kings County Hosp., Bklyn., 1971-73, sr. psychologist, 1973-77; chief psychologist Met. Hosp., N.Y.C., 1977—; asst. prof. psychiatry N.Y. Med. Coll., 1984—; clin. instr. psychiatry Downstate Med. Ctr., Bklyn., 1971-77; instr. psychiatry N.Y. Med. Coll., 1978-84, 94—, acting co-dir. psychology Met. Hosp., 1983-85, 94—; pres. local 1189 dist. coun. 37 AFSCME, AFL-CIO, 1994—; field supr. psychology Yeshiva U., Pace U., Fordham U., 1976—. Bd. dirs. The Family Youth Ctr., Bklyn., 1975-77; chmn. community adv. bd. Playing to Win Community Computer Ctr., 1986-95; elected to bd. trustees Lincoln Sq. Synagogue; chmn. Jewish Chapel Adv. Com. Met. Hosp. Mem. Am. Psychol. Assn., N.Y. State Psychol. Assn., Nat. Assn. Sch. Psychologists, Manhattan Psychol. Assn. Democrat. Jewish Orthodox. Office: NY Med Coll Met Hosp 1900 2nd Ave New York NY 10029-7406 also: 19 E 83rd St Apt B New York NY 10028-0429

DAVIDOFF, ANN L., psychologist; b. Cin., Oct. 13, 1942; d. Samuel Bert and Edith (Litwack) Lee; m. Merrill Edward Milham, Apr. 27, 1996. BA, Barnard Coll., 1964; MA, Syracuse U., 1968, PhD, 1971. Cert. psychologist, Md. Psychologist St. Joseph's Outpatient Psychiat. Svcs., Syracuse, N.Y., 1969-70; intern VA Mental Hygiene Clinic and Day Treatment Ctr., Syracuse, 1970-71; dir. Weight Control Clinic Essex Community Coll., Balt., 1972-73; assoc. prof. dept. psychology Essex Community Clinic, Balt., 1972-88; post doctoral fellow div. occupational health Johns Hopkins U. Sch. Hygiene and Pub. Health, Balt., 1989-91, rsch. assoc., 1991-92; postdoctoral fellow divsn. geriatric medicine Johns Hopkins U., 1992-95, asst. prof. geriatric medicine, 1995—; staff psychologist Sheppard and Enoch Pratt Hosp., Balt., 1995—; presenter in field. Pre-doctoral fellow NIMH, 1965-66, postdoctoral fellow Nat. Inst. Environ. Health Scis., 1989-91, Nat. Inst.

Aging, 1992-95; tuition remission scholar U. Wis., 1964-65; recipient N.Y. State Scholar Incentive award, 1966-69. Mem. APHA, APA. Home: 13803 Manor Glen Rd Baldwin MD 21013-9714 Office: Sheppard and Enoch Pratt Hospital Beacham Clinic 6501 N Charles St A405 Baltimore MD 21285

DAVIDSON, AARON HERSHEL, physician; b. Macon, Ga., July 17, 1960; s. Abraham Nathan and Ida (Radetsky) D. BS magna cum laude, U. Ga., 1982; MD, Med. Coll. Ga., 1986. Diplomate Am. Bd. Ophthalmology. Transitional intern Med. Coll. Ga., 1986-87, ophthalmology resident, 1987-90; pvt. practice Aaron H. Davidson, MD, Statesboro, Ga., 1990—; adj. faculty Ga. So. U., Statesboro, 1994—; sec.-treas. Physicians' Group of Southeast Ga., Statesboro, 1994—; sec. med. staff Bulloch Meml. Hosp., Statesboro, 1996. Mem. bd. dirs., past v.p. planned giving chair, tobacco project chair Am. Cancer Soc., Statesboro, 1992—. Fellow Am. Acad. Ophthalmology; mem. AMA, Med. Assn. Ga., Ogeechee River Med. Soc. (pres. 1994, sec. 1995-96), Phi Beta Kappa, Phi Kappa Phi, Alpha Omega Alpha. Office: Aaron H Davidson MD 108 Northside Dr E Statesboro GA 30458

DAVIDSON, ALICE WARE, nurse, educator; b. Warren, Ohio, Feb. 24, 1945; d. Harold V. and Ruby Arlene (Brunson) Ware; widowed; children: Anne Claire, William John. Diploma, St. Luke's Hosp., Cleve., 1966; BSN, Case Western Res. U., 1969, MSN, 1971; PhD, U. Colo., 1988. Rsch. asst. Coll. Environ. Design U. Colo., Boulder; coord. ambulatory care Mercy Med. Ctr., Springfield, Ohio; asst. prof. Wright State U., Dayton, Ohio; rsch. educator Boulder Community Hosp., 1989-93; asst. prof. U. Colo., Denver, 1989-95; rsch. fellow Harvard Med. Sch., McLean Hosp., Boston, 1994-95; with Ware Davidson Environ. Consulting, Boulder, 1995—; cons. on environ. design, Denver. Contbr. articles to profl. publs. Mem. ANA, Colo. Nurses Assn., Sigma Theta Tau. Home: 1045 Pine St Boulder CO 80302

DAVIDSON, BERNARD, psychiatry educator; b. Newark, Aug. 11, 1950; s. Mildred Davidson. BA, Seton Hall U., 1973; MA, Fairleigh Dickinson U., 1976; PhD, U. Ga., 1980, MSW, 1989. Lic. psychologist, Ga. Asst. prof. Tex. Tech U., Lubbock, 1980-86, assoc. prof., 1986-88, assoc. chairperson dept. human devel., 1985-88; assoc. prof. dept. psychiatry Med. Coll. Ga., Augusta, 1989—, assoc. prof. Sch. of Nursing, 1992—; part-time assoc. prof. Coll. Edn. Augusta Coll., 1990—; cons. Humana Hosp., Augusta, 1990-92; adj. fellow Inst. for Behavioral Rsch., U. Ga., Athens, 1989—. Author: (with others) The Inexpressive Male, 1988; contbr. articles to profl. jours. Mem. APA, Am. Assn. for Marriage and Family Therapy (clin. mem.), Ga. Psychol. Assn. Office: Dept Psychiatry and Health Behavior MCG 1515 Pope Ave Augusta GA 30912

DAVIDSON, CHARLES SPRECHER, physician; b. Berkeley, Calif., Dec. 7, 1910; s. Charles Sprecher and Mary (Blossom) D. A.B., U. Calif. at Berkeley, 1934; M.D., C.M., McGill U., 1939; M.A. (hon.), Harvard, 1953. Intern, house officer medicine San Francisco Hosp., 1939-41; research fellow medicine Harvard Med. Sch. and asst. resident physician Thorndike Meml. Lab., Boston City Hosp., 1941-42; various appointments, 1942-44; asso. dir. of II and IV Harvard Med. Services, Boston City Hosp. and asso. physician (Thorndike Meml. Lab.), 1948-63, asso. dir., 1964-70, acting dir., 1970-74; vis. physician (Boston City Hosp.), 1965, acting head dept. medicine, 1970-74; asso. prof. medicine Harvard Med. Sch., 1953-68, prof., 1969-73, William Bosworth Castle prof. medicine, 1974-77, prof. emeritus, 1977—; vis. prof. medicine MIT, 1974-77, sr. lectr. health scis. and tech., 1977—, program dir. Clin. Rsch. Ctr., 1974-77; assoc. dir. Harvard U. med. unit, Boston City Hosp., 1972-73; cons. Mt. Auburn Hosp., Cambridge, Cambridge Hosp.; hon. dir. Med. Found., Inc.; scholar-in-residence Fogarty Internat. Ctr., NIH, 1972-73; bd. dirs. Theobald Smith Rsch. Inst., 1984—; chair Truro (Mass.) Conservation Commn., 1976-93; trustee Truro Conservation Trust. Contbr. to profl. jours. Recipient Alexander D. Stewart Meml. prize, 1939, E.V. McCollum award Am. Soc. Clin. Nutrition, 1966, Joseph Goldberger award AMA, 1991, Environ. Excellence award Ctr. for Coastal Studies, 1993. Master ACP; mem. Am. Gastroent. Soc., Am. Acad. Arts and Scis., Assn. Am. Physicians. Home: Union Field Rd Truro MA 02666 Office: 100 Memorial Dr Cambridge MA 02142-1314

DAVIDSON, DEBRA ANN, medical and surgical, diabetes, critical care nurse; b. Dayton, Ohio, June 18, 1956; d. Charles E. and Daisy I. (Waterhouse) Badders. BSN magna cum laude, Wright State U., Dayton, 1978, MS in Nursing summa cum laude, 1987. RN, Ohio, Fla.; cert. diabetes educator. Primary nurse I and II Miami Valley Hosp., Dayton, 1979-84, clin. nurse specialist in endocrinology, 1984-93, primary nurse II, ICU, diabetes cons., 1993; diabetes clin. nurse specialist, diabetes program coord. Florida Hosp., Orlando, Fla., 1993—; cons. in insulin pump therapy Fla. Hosp., Miami Valley Hosp.; cons. diabetes program devel.; developer, coord. profl. diabetes workshop; presenter, nat. known spkr. on diabetes and other endocrine disorder to various orgns.; coord. various inpatient and outpatient diabetes programs; charter mem. Miami Valley Hosp. nursing coun., com. mem. clin. ladder and case mgmt.; mem. diabetes collaborative practice and diabetes med. adv. com. Fla. Hosp.; adj. faculty mem. Valencia C.C., Orlando, Fla. Author: Diabetes: Making It Part of Your Lifestyle; rsch. in field. Recipient award Recognition, Ohio Dept. Health; scholar Advanced Studies Inst. Diabetes Edn. Mem. Am. Assn. Diabetes Educators (past pres. Western Ohio chpt.), Ctrl. Fla. Assn. Diabetes Educators, Am. Diabetes Assn. (Nat. Recognition for Miami Valley Hosp. Diabetes Patient Edn. Program 1992), Diabetes Assn. Dayton Area (past bd. dirs.). Office: Fla Hosp Diabetes Program 601 E Rollins St Orlando FL 32803-1248

DAVIDSON, EUGENE ABRAHAM, biochemist, university administrator; b. N.Y.C., May 27, 1930; s. Jack and Sophie Miriam (Deutsch) D. B.S., UCLA, 1950; Ph.D., Columbia U., 1955. Postdoctoral fellow, instr. U. Mich., 1955-58; asst. prof. biochemistry Duke U., 1958-62, assoc. prof., 1962-65, prof., 1965-67; prof., chmn. dept. biol. chemistry M.S. Hershey Med. Center, Pa. State U., 1967-87, assoc. dean for edn., 1975-87; prof., chmn. dept. biochemistry and molecular biology Georgetown U., Washington, 1988—; mem. Nat. Bd. Med. Examiners, Part I; cons. in field. Author: Carbohydrate Chemistry, 1967; contbr. numerous articles to profl. publs.; Editorial reviewer for numerous jours. Guggenheim fellow, 1965-66; NIH grantee, 1958—. Mem. AAAS, Am. Soc. Biol. Chemists, Assn. Med. Sch. Depts. Biochemistry, Biochem. Soc., Am. Assn. Cancer Research, Soc. Complex Carbohydrates, Glycoconjugate Soc. (pres. 1985-87), Sigma Xi. Home: 5506 Nebraska Ave NW Washington DC 20015-1256 Office: Georgetown U Dept Biochem/Molecular Biology Washington DC 20007

DAVIDSON, EVELYNE MONIQUE, internist; b. Knoxville, Tenn., Apr. 5, 1961; d. Elvyn Verone and Esther M. (Johnson) D. BS, Vanderbilt U., 1983; MD, Ea. Tenn. State U., 1987. Intern New Hanover Meml. Hosp., Wilmington, N.C., 1987-88, resident in internal medicine, 1988-90; pvt. practice, Knoxville, 1990-94; physician Bapt. Primary Care System, 1994—; med. dir. east office Housecall Home Health, Knoxville, 1990—. Mem. AMA, Nat. Med. Assn., Am. Soc. Internal Medicine. Office: 710 N Cherry St Knoxville TN 37914

DAVIDSON, EZRA C., JR., physician, educator; b. Water Valley, Miss., Oct. 21, 1933; s. Ezra Cap and Theresa Hattie (Woods) D.; children: Pamela, Gwendolyn, Marc, Ezra K. B.S. cum laude, Morehouse Coll., 1954; M.D., Meharry Med. Coll., 1958. Diplomate: Am. Bd. Ob-Gyn. (examiner 1973—). Intern San Diego County Gen. Hosp., 1958-59; resident in ob-gyn. Harlem Hosp., N.Y.C., 1963-66, asst. attending ob-gyn, obstet. coordinator maternal and infant care clinics, 1967-68; dir. departmental research, assoc. attending, acting chmn. ob-gyn, co-dir. coagulation research lab. Roosevelt Hosp., N.Y.C., 1968-70; fellow blood coagulation, asst. ob-gyn Columbia U. Coll. Physicians and Surgeons, N.Y.C., 1966-67, instr. dept. ob-gyn, 1967-69, asst. clin. prof., 1970; cons. ob-gyn Office Health Affairs, OEO, Washington, 1970-72; prof., chmn. dept. ob-gyn. Charles R. Drew U. of Medicine and Sci., L.A., 1971—, acad. v.p., 1982-87; prof. U. So. Calif., Los Angeles, 1971-80, UCLA, 1980—; chief svc. dept. ob-gyn. King/Drew Med. Ctr., L.A., 1971—; attending physician dept. ob-gyn. L.A. County-U. So. Calif. Med. Ctr., 1971-80; mem. nat. med. adv. com. Nat. Found. March of Dimes, 1972-76; bd. cons. Internat. Childbirth Edn. Assn., 1973-81; mem. sec.'s adv. com. population affairs HEW, 1974-77, chmn. svcs. task force, 1975-77; chmn. bd. dirs. L.A. Regional Family Planning Coun., 1975-77; bd. dirs. Nat. Alliance Sch. Age parents, 1975-79; mem. corp. bd. Blue Shield, Calif., 1989—; chmn. fertility and maternal health drugs adv. com. FDA, 1992—, active, 1990—, reproductive health drugs adv. com., 1996; chmn. sec.'s adv. com. on infant mortality Dept. of Health and Human Svcs., 1991-95; mem. adv. com. to the dir. NIH, 1995—, mem. dirs. adv. panel on clin. rsch., 1995; mem. roundtable on health care quality Inst. of Medicine, 1995—. Bd. dirs. The Calif. Wellness Found., 1995—, Children's Bur. So. Calif., v.p., 1995—. Served with USAF, 1959-63. Johnson Found. Health Policy fellow Inst. Medicine, Nat. Acad. Scis., 1979-80. Fellow ACS, Am. Coll. Ob-Gyns. (nat. sec. 1983-89, pres.-elect 1989—, pres. 1990-91), Royal Coll. Ob-Gyn., L.A. Ob-Gyn. soc. (pres. 1982-83); mem. Inst. Medicine of NAS, Am. Ob-Gyn. Soc., N.Am. Soc. Pediatric and Adolescent Gynecology (pres.-elect 1993-94, pres. 1994-95), Pacific Coast Ob-Gyn. Soc., L.A. Regional Family Planning Coun., Inc., Ob-Gryn. Assembly So. Calif. (chmn. 1989-90), Nat. Med. Assn. (chmn. nat. sect. ob-gyn. 1975-77, mem. sci. coun. 1979-88, trustee 1989-95, chmn. bd. trustee 1992-95), Golden State Med. Assn. (pres. 1989-90), Assn. Profs. Ob-Gyn. (pres. 1989-90). Office: 12021 Wilmington Ave Los Angeles CA 90059-3019

DAVIDSON, GRACE EVELYN, nursing educator, retired administrator; b. Wabash, Ind., Aug. 2, 1920; d. William Alexander and Jennie Lavinia (Baker) Davidson. Diploma, Columbia Presbyn. Sch. Nursing, 1942; BS, U. Minn., 1948; MA in Teaching, Columbia U., 1954, postgrad. 1961, 63-64. Instr. Sch. Nursing, Columbia U., N.Y.C., 1948-51; assoc. prof. Skidmore Coll., Saratoga Springs, N.Y., 1954-66; asst. adminstr., dir. nursing Univ. Hosp., NYU Med. Ctr., 1966-79, assoc. prof., 1977-79, prof. 1979—; cons. nursing svc. adminstrn., N.Y.C., 1980-88. Contbr. articles to profl. jours. Served to Maj. Army Nurse Corps, 1943-46, World War II, 51-53, Korea, Res., 53-60, Ret. Recipient Alumni Fedn. medal Columbia U., 1981, Plaque for leadership in nursing NYU Med. Ctr., 1983; Grace Davidson award established in her honor NYU, 1991. Mem. AAUW, Nursing Edn. Alumnae Assn. Tchrs. Coll. Columbia U. (achievement award 1977), Am. Nurses Assn., Nat. League Nursing, Columbia U.-Presbyn. Hosp. Sch. Nursing Alumnae Assn. (pres. 1970-76, edn. bd. 1985-93, bd. dirs. 1993—, Disting. Alumnae award 1981), Fedn. Alumni Assn. Columbia U., Ret. Officers Assn., Ret. Army Nurse Corps., The Woman's Club of Dumont, Republican Club of Dumont. Presbyterian. Home: 67 Chestnut St Dumont NJ 07628-3214

DAVIDSON, JAMES ARTHUR, physician assistant; b. Anaconda, Mont., Aug. 21, 1946; s. Norman B. and Emily Alice (Pechar) D.; m. Nancy Elaine Sackmann, June 27, 1970; children: Jon Eric, Jeanette Marie. AA, Big Bend Community Coll., 1966; student, Wash. State U., 1966-67, U. Wash., 1973, Cen. Wash. U., 1980. Health technician Job Corps, Moses Lake, Wash., 1971-72; physician asst. Grandview (Wash.) Med. Ctr., 1972-89, Hanford Environ. Health Found., Richland, Wash., 1989—; instr. emergency med. svc. program Yakima County, Wash., 1974-83; sports medicine adviser Grandview (Wash.) Schs., 1979—, guest lectr., 1984—; preceptor, health adv. program Yakima Valley Coll., 1986-89. Assoc. editor Physician Asst. jour., 1985—; moderator PA Forum e-mail list, 1995—. Chmn. local bd. Selective Svc. Sys., 1981—; active local Boy Scouts Am., Grandview, 1982—, chmn. Chief Kamlakin Dist., 1987-90, coun. exec. bd., 1987—; trustee Bleyhl Cmty. Libr., Grandview, 1982-93. Recipient Wood Badge award Boy Scouts Am., 1986, Award of Merit, 1986, Silver Beaver award, 1989, Vigil Honor, 1992, Grandview Youth Svc. award, 1992, HEHF Cmty. Svc. award, 1993. Fellow Am. Acad. Physician Assts. (quality and risk mgmt. com. 1995—), Wash. Aca. Physician Assts. (bd. dirs. 1975-76, v.p. 1985-86, newsletter editor 1975-86); mem. Am. Legion (local comdr. 1985-96, boy scouting chmn.), Phi Kappa Phi. Republican. Presbyterian. Home: 606 Cherry Lane PO Box 56 Grandview WA 98930-0056 Office: Hanford Environ Health Found PO Box 100 Richland WA 99352-0100

DAVIDSON, JAMES WILSON, clinical psychologist; b. Muncie, Ind., Apr. 22, 1950; s. James Wayne and Mary Marguerite (Sanford) D.; m. Nancy Lee Hendershott, Aug. 30, 1969; children: Melissa Ann, Amanda Corynne, Kevin Patrick. BS, Mich. State U., 1972; PhD, Kent State U., 1975; postgrad., Ashland (Ohio) Theol. Sem., 1980-82. Ordained to ministry Assemblies of God, 1988. Coord. Ctr. on Rsch. and Evaluation, Ashtabula, Ohio, 1974-77; pres. The Children's Ctr., Ashtabula, 1978-80, Computech Data Systems, Ashtabula, 1978-82; v.p. Davidson Assocs., Ashtabula, 1977-86; assoc. pastor First Assembly of God, Ashtabula, 1986-88; sr. pastor Metro Ch., Cleve., 1988-94; CEO Heart and Hand Found., Cleve., 1988—, LifeLine Counseling Ctr., 1994—; dir. Ohio Dist. Coun. Urban Missions Ministries, Columbus, 1990—. Recipient 414th Point of Light award White House, 1991, Health award UNICEF, 1992, 93, Ptnr. Agy. Excellence award CMHA, 1992, 93; Kent State U. fellow, 1973-74. Mem. APA, Am. Assn. Christian Counselors. Republican. Home: 2627 Courtland Blvd Cleveland OH 44118 Office: Heart and Hand Found PO Box 93813 2570 Woodhill Rd Cleveland OH 44104-5813

DAVIDSON, JOAN GATHER, psychologist; b. Long Branch, N.J., Jan. 26, 1934; d. Ralph Paul and Hilde (Bresser) Gather; m. Harry Gene Davidson, Sept. 14, 1957; children; Guy, Marc, Kelly. BA, Shorter Coll., 1956; BA cum laude, U. South Fla., 1982; MS, Fla. Inst. Tech., 1986, PsyD, 1987. Lic. psychologist, Fla., RN, Ga. Clin. instr. Ga. Bapt. Sch. Nursing, Atlanta, 1956-59; dir. nurses Aidmore Hosp., Atlanta, 1959-60; dir. insvc. edn., asst. dir. nurses Bayfront Med. Ctr., St. Petersburg, Fla., 1960; instr. St. Petersburg Jr. Coll., 1971-76; pvt. practice St. Petersburg-Clearwater, 1987—. Mem. Am. Psychol. Assn., Fla. Psychol. Assn., Nat. Register Health Svc. Providers in Psychology, Assn. for Advancement Psychology, Am. Assn. Christian Counselors, Psi Chi, Phi Kappa Phi. Republican. Baptist. Home: 11600 87th Ave Largo FL 34642-3613 Office: 25400 US Highway 19 N Ste 105 Clearwater FL 34623-2143

DAVIDSON, JOHN KNIGHT, radiologist; b. Edinburgh, Scotland, Aug. 17, 1925; s. John Rose and Edith Jane (Good) D.; m. Edith Elizabeth McKelvie, June 25, 1950; children: Fiona, Alastair, Neil. MBCHB, Edinburgh U., 1948, MD, 1963. Registrar Edinburgh U. Hosp., 1953-56, St. Bartholomews Hosp., London, 1956-60; radiologist Southern Gen. Hosp., Glasgow, Scotland, 1960-67, Western Infirmary & Gartnavel Gen. Hosp., Glasgow, 1967-90; dir. Yorkhill NHS Trust, Glasgow, 1993-95; council Med. and Dental Def. Union, Scotland, 1971-95; radiology advisor Bone Disease in Divers, 1965-92, USN, 1976-78. Editor Aseptic Necrosis of Bone; contbr. numerous articles to profl. jours. Fellow Royal Coll. Physicians Edinburgh, Royal Australian Coll. Radiology (hon.), Am. Coll. Radiology (hon.), Internat. Skeletal Soc. (hon.), Royal Coll. Radiologists; mem. Scottish Radiol. Soc. (hon.), Royal and Ancient Golf Club, U.S. Golf Assn., Glasgow Art Club. Home: 15 Beechlands Ave, Glasgow G44 3YT, Scotland

DAVIDSON, JOHN ROBERT, dentist; b. Peru, Ind., Apr. 28, 1947; s. John Howard and Kathryn (Loughran) D.; m. Jean-Marie Dobler, Jan. 23, 1965 (div. Oct. 1972); children: James Michael, Jennifer Renee; m. Linda Mary Seasock, Oct. 22, 1977; children: Kathryn Cherise, John Richard. BS, Purdue U., 1969; DDS, UCLA, 1972. Gen. practice dentistry Granada Hills, Calif., 1972-74; prof. clin. and community dentistry, dir. of clinics Ferris State Coll., Big Rapids, Mich., 1974-75; pvt. practice dentistry specializing in oral implantology Peru, Ind., 1975—; dental staff mem. Dukes Meml. Hosp., Peru, 1975—; dep. coroner Miami County, 1987—. Drive chmn. United Way of Miami County, Peru, 1977, 78, bd. dirs., 1977-84; mem. Utility Service Bd., Peru, 1984-86, chmn., 1986; trustee 1st Bapt. Ch., Peru, 1979-82, 84-86, chmn. bd. trustees, 1986. Recipient Citizen of Yr. award, Peru, 1978, Pride award, Grissom AFB Community Council, Peru, 1980. Fellow Internat. Congress of Oral Implantologists, Am. Coll. Oral Implantologists (assoc.); mem. Am. Dental Assn., Ind. Dental Assn., Wabash Valley Dental Soc., Peru Area C. of C. (bd. dirs. 1976-83, Outstanding Service award 1979), Mensa, Masons, Elks, Rotary (chmn. scholarship com. Peru, 1975—). Home and Office: 27 N Park Ave Peru IN 46970-1718

DAVIDSON, JONATHAN ROBERT TOLME, psychiatrist; b. West Kirby, Eng., Sept. 29, 1943; came to U.S., 1972; s. Joseph Robert and mary Kathleen (Overman) D.; m. Meg. G. Hodge, June 24, 1969; children: Benjamin, Rebecca. MBBS, London U., 1967. Diplomate in psychiatry Am. Bd. Psychiatry and Neurology. Resident Royal Edinburgh Hosp., 1969-72; prof. psychiatry Duke U. Med. Ctr., Durham, N.C., 1994—. Co-author: Post Traumatic Stress, 1994; contbr. over 200 articles to profl. jours. Fellow Am. Psychiat. Assn., Royal Coll. Psychiatry (U.K.). Office: Duke University Box 3812 DUMC Durham NC 27710

DAVIDSON, KENNETH HARVEY, cardiologist; b. Portland, Maine, Dec. 16, 1941; s. Herman I. and Violet E. (Forman) D.; m. Arlene Rosenstein, June 16, 1944; children: Lauri Sue, Eric Scot. AB magna cum laude, Boston U., 1964; MD, Columbia U., 1968. Cert. Nat. Bd. Med. Examiners; diplomate Am. Bd. Internal Medicine. Intern Roosevelt Hosp., N.Y.C., 1968-69; med. resident Roosevelt Hosp., 1969-70, Boston City Hosp., 1970-71; cardiology fellow Tufts New Eng. Med. Ctr., Boston, 1971-72; chief internal medicien Ft. McPherson Army Hosp., Atlanta, 1973-74; cardiology fellow West Roxbury VA Hosp., Harvard Med. Sch., Boston, 1974-76; clin. instr. in medicine Harvard Med. Sch., Boston, 1975-76, U. Rochester Med. Sch., Rochester, N.Y., 1978—. Contbr. articles to Rev. of the Lit. Annals Internal Medicine, 1977, Am. Jour. Med. Scis., 1985. Major U.S., 1972-74. Fellow Am. Coll. Cardiology; mem. Am. Heart Assn., ACP, Phi Beta Kappa. Home: 3 Brookwood Rd Pittsford NY 14534-1807 Office: 1445 Portland Ave Rochester NY 14621-3008

DAVIDSON, LARRY, psychologist; b. Bklyn., Dec. 31, 1960; s. Bernard and Faye (Bernstein) D.; m. Maryanne Loetterle, Oct. 28, 1990. BA, Emory U., Atlanta, 1982, MA, 1982; MA in Psychology, Duquesne U., Pitts., 1983, PhD, 1989. Counseling coord. Duquesne U. Health Svc., Pitts., 1985-86; predoctoral fellow Duquesne U. Psychology Dept., Pitts., 1986-87; predoctoral intern Danbury (Conn.) Hosp., 1987-88; predoctoral fellow Yale U. Med. Sch., New Haven, 1988-89; lectr. Yale U. Nursing Sch., New Haven, 1989; adv. resident Danbury Hosp., 1989-90, clin. cons., 1990; postdoctoral fellow Yale U. Med. Sch., 1990-92, asst. prof. psychiatry, 1992—. Cons. editor Jour. Phenomenological Psychology, Pitts., 1986—. Contbr. articles to profl. jours. Named Disting. Young Investigator, Soc. for Life History Rsch., 1990, Karl Jaspers prize, Assn. for Advancement of Philosophy and Psychiatry, 1991. Mem. APA, Conn. Psychol. Assn., Human Sci. Rsch. Conf., Internat. Soc. for Theoretical Psychology, Am. Assn. Applied and Preventive Psychology, Soc. for Phenomenology and Psychiatry (sec. 1990-94). Democrat. Jewish. Office: Yale Univ Med Sch 34 Park St New Haven CT 06519-1109

DAVIDSON, LESLIE LODGE, epidemiologist; b. N.Y.C., Apr. 3, 1948; d. Richard Ralph and Elizabeth (Kellermann) D.; m. Marcus Richards; children: Alexis, Elizabeth. BA cum laude, Harvard U., 1970, MD, Columbia U., 1978; MSc, London Sch. Hygiene, 1982. Lectr. Columbia U., N.Y.C., 1983-84, asst. prof. pub. health and pediatrics, 1984-91, assoc. prof. pub. health and pediatrics, 1992; regional pediatric epidemiologist S.E. Thames Region, 1992-95; hon. sr. lectr. Kings Coll. Sch. Medicine, 1992—; cons. pub. health medicine Lambeth, Southwark and Lewisham Health Authority, London, 1995—; mem. profl. com. Child Accident Prevention Trust, London, 1992—; mem. expert com. on single parent families European Coun. Strassbery, France, 1993-96; mem. Working Party on Alcohol and the Young, Royal Coll. Physicians, 1993-96; mem. faculty publ. health medicine, 1994. Contbr. articles to profl. jours. Grantee Ctrs. for Disease Control, Atlanta, 1987. Mem. APHA, Royal Coll. Physicians, Brit. Pediatric Assn., British Assn. Cmty. Child Health (exec. com. 1996), Alpha Omega Alpha. Office: Lambeth Southwark and, Lewisham Health Authority, 1 Lower Marsh, London SE1 7NT, England

DAVIDSON, MAUREEN KATHRYN, microbiology educator, biomedical researcher; b. Portsmouth, Va., July 14, 1951; d. Robert Allen and Norma Rosamond (Calhoun) D.; m. Jerry Kendall Davis, July 30, 1981; 1 child, Kendra Rosamond. BS, U. Ala., Birmingham, 1972, U. Ala., Birmingham, 1973; MS, U. Ala., Birmingham, 1981, PhD, 1988. Cert. med. technologist. Lab. instr. in anatomy and biology U. Ala., Birmingham, 1970-72; staff med. technologist Univ. Hosps., Birmingham, 1973-77; clin. instr. clin. pathology U. Ala., Birmingham, 1972-77; tech. supr. microbiologo Univ. Hosp., Birmingham, 1976-77; rsch. asst. in comparative medicine U. Ala., Birmingham, 1977-81, asst. prof., then assoc. prof. comparative medicine, 1988-93; microbiologist VA Med. Ctr., Birmingham, 1978-92; assoc. prof. of Div. of Comparative Medicine, pathobiology U. Fla., Gainesville, Fla., 1993—, head Clin. Vet. Lab. Div. Comparative Medicine, 1993—; mem. Internat. Rsch. Program on Comparative Mycoplasmology, 1986. Contbr. chpts. to books, articles to profl. jours. Mem. AAAS, Am. Soc. for Microbiology, Internat. Orgn. for Mycoplasmology, Am. Assn. for Lab. Animal Sci., Soc. for Mucosal Immunology. Office: U Fla Divsn Comp Medicine Rm CB 159 Box 100006 1600 SW Archer Blvd Gainesville FL 32610

DAVIDSON, MAYER B., medical educator, researcher; b. Balt., Apr. 11, 1935; s. David and Esther (Crockin) D.; m. Naomi Berger, Nov. 25, 1961 (div. 1977); children: Elke W., Seth J.; m. Roseann Herman, Aug. 31, 1980. AB, Swarthmore Coll., 1957; MD, Harvard U., 1961. Diplomate Am. Bd. Internal Medicine, Am. Bd. Endocrinology and Metabolism. Intern Bellevue Hosp., N.Y.C., 1961-62, jr. asst. resident, 1962-63; sr. asst. resident U. Wash. Affiliated Hosps., Seattle, 1963-64; rsch. fellow dept. endocrinology and metabolism King County Hosp., U. Wash., Seattle, 1964-66; asst. prof. medicine UCLA Sch. Medicine, 1969-74, from assoc. prof. to prof., 1974-95, clin. prof., 1996—, acting chief div. endocrinology and metabolism, 1973-74; dir. diabetes program Cedars-Sinai Med. Ctr., L.A., 1979-95; assoc. dir. clin. diabetes City of Hope Nat. Med. Ctr., 1995—; nat. advisor Diabetes Ctr. Humana Hosp., Phoenix, 1985-91; attending physician diabetic clinic Boston City Hosp., 1966-68; clin. asst. Harvard Med. Sch., 1968-69; cons. AMA Dept. Drugs. Author: Diabetus Mellitus: Diagnosis and Treatment, 1991, 3d rev. edit., 1991; contbr. 23 chpts. to books, numerous revs., editls., articles and abstracts; presenter 126 sci. papers; mem. editl. bd. Jour. Clin. Endocrinology and Metabolism, 1981-84, 93-95, Jour. Diabetes Care, 1984-87, Geriatrics, 1986—, Diabetes Reports, 1987-89, Today in Medicine,1987-88, Clin. Diabetes, 1989-92, Diabetes Spectrum, 1989-92, Diabetes Rsch. & Clin. Practice, 1992-95. Co-founder, bd. dirs. free med. facility Venice (Calif.) Family Clinic, 1970. Maj. Med. Svc. Corps U.S . Army, 1966-69. USPHS rsch. fellow Nat. Inst. Arthritis and Metabolic Diseases, 1965-66; recipient Upjohn award for Outstanding Diabetes Educator, 1990, Robert H. Williams/Rachmiel Levine award for sci. contbns. and humanism in tng. young rschrs., 1995; named to Best Doctors in Am., 1992-93. Fellow ACP; mem. AAAS, Am. Diabetes Assn. (rsch. prizes 1965, 66, R&D award 1974-75, rsch. 1978-81, bd. dirs. 1986-89, 93—, v.p. 1995-96, pres.-elect 1996-97), Am. Fedn. Clin. Rsch., Western Soc. Clin. Rsch., Endocrine Soc., Am. Soc. Clin. Investigation, Western Assn. Physicians, Am. Assn. Diabetes Educators (editl. bd. jour. 1980-83), Boylston Med. Soc., Sigma Xi. Democrat. Jewish.

DAVIDSON, NEIL, physiology educator; b. Aberdeen, Scotland, Sept. 17, 1941; s. Charles and Isobel (Wood) D.; m. Susan Lemon, June 16, 1980; children: Sarah Jane Fisher, Rachel Lynne Wood. BSc with honors, U. Aberdeen, 1963; PhD, SUNY, Bklyn., 1967. Lectr. dept. physiology U. Aberdeen, 1967-74, sr. lectr., 1974-83; prof., chmn. dept. physiology Aga Khan Med. Coll., Karachi, Pakistan, 1983-90; prof., acting chmn. United Arab Emirates U. Med. Coll., Al-Ain, 1990—; vis. prof. Florence (Italy) Med. Coll., 1980. Contbr. chpts. to books in field. Fellow Rsch. Found., SUNY, 1964-66, Grass Found., 1965; Welcome Found. travel grantee, 1972-73. Mem. Physiol. Soc. U.K., Pharmacol. Soc. U.K., Inst. Biology U.K., Pakistan Physiol. Soc. (founding mem.). Episcopalian. Home and Office: PO Box 17666, Al-Ain, Abu Dhabi United Arab Emirates

DAVIDSON, RICHARD LAURENCE, geneticist, educator; b. Cleve., Feb. 22, 1941. B.A., Case Western Res. U., 1963, Ph.D., 1967. Asst. prof. Harvard Med. Sch., Boston, 1970-73, assoc. prof. microbiology and molecular genetics, 1973-81; research assoc. human genetics Children's Hosp. Med. Ctr., Boston, 1970-81; head dept. genetics U. Ill. Med. Ctr., Chgo., 1981—, Benjamin Goldberg prof. genetics, 1981—; co-dir. Cell Cult Ctr., MIT, Boston, 1975-81; mem. mammalian genetics study sect. NIH, 1975-81; mem. human cell biology adv. panel NSF, 1973-75. Editor-in-chief: Somatic Cell Genetics. U.S. Air Force Office Research-NRC fellow, 1967-68, Ctr. Molecular Genetics, Paris, 1967-70. Mem. AAAS, Tissue Culture Assn., Cell Biology Assn. Office: U Ill Med Ctr Ctr Genetics Chicago IL 60612

DAVIDSON, ROBERT C., JR., manufacturing executive; b. Memphis, Oct. 3, 1945; s. Robert C. Sr. and Thelma (Culp) D.; m. Alice Faye Berkley, Jan. 5, 1978; children: Robert III, John Roderick, Julian. BA, Morehouse Coll., 1967; MBA, U. Chgo., 1969. V.p. Urban Nat. Corp., Boston, 1972-74, Avant Garde Enterprises, Los Angeles, 1974-76; pres. Surface Protection, Industries, Los Angeles, 1976—. Bd. dirs. Pasadena Art Workshop, 1986—;

planning commr. City of Pasadena, 1986—. Mem. Young Pres. Orgn. Club: 100 Black Men (Los Angeles). Office: Surface Protection Industries Inc 3411 E 14th St Los Angeles CA 90023-3804*

DAVIDSON, SALLY HOPE, anesthesiologist; b. Ft. Worth, Tex., June 17, 1938; arrived in Sweden, 1978; d. John Francis and Elizabeth Catherine (Hope) D.; m. Bengt Erik Alfred Lindgren, Apr. 26, 1980; 1 child, Birgitta Lindgren. BS, Oreg. State U., 1960, MD, 1964. Intern Milwaukee County, Milw., 1964-65; resident Portland, Oreg., 1965-67; instr. Portland, 1967-68; staff mem. Physicians & Surgeons, Portland, 1968; instr. Ulleual Hosp., Oslo, 1969-76; asst. prof. Drammen (Norway) Hosp., 1976-77; instr. St. Eriks Hosp., Stockholm, 1978-79, Norrtälje (Sweden) Hosp., 1979-81; instr. Danderyd Hosp., Sweden, 1981-85, head of gen. surgery anesthesia, 1985-87, head of orthopedic anesthesia, 1987—; asst. prof. Built Up Anesthesia Block Svc. Ortho. Surgery, Svensk. Contbr. studies to profl. publs. Mem. Swedish Föening Anestesi Intensivvård, Swedish Med. Assn.

DAVIDSON, SHELDON JEROME, hematologist; b. N.Y.C., Oct. 21, 1939; s. Leo and Lee (Levy) D.; m. Golda Feldman, Sept. 16, 1962; children: Larry, Debra, Sara. BA summa cum laude, NYU, 1960; MD, Albert Einstein U., 1964. Diplomate Am. Bd. Internal Medicine, Am. Bd. Hematology. Intern Maimonides Med. Ctr., Bklyn., 1964-65; fellow in hematology Mt. Sinai Med. Ctr., N.Y.C., 1967-68, resident internal medicine, 1965-67; fellow in hematology, oncology U. So. Calif. Med. Ctr., Los Angeles, 1971-72; with So. Calif. Hematol-Oncology Med. Group, Los Angeles, 1972-77, Valley Hematol-Oncology Med. Group, Los Angeles, 1977-88, Hematology-Oncology Cons., 1988-91, North Valley Hematology-Oncology Med. Group, 1991—; bd. dirs. oncology Holy Cross Hosp., Mission Hills, Calif., 1978—; assoc. clin. prof. dept. medicine UCLA Sch. Medicine, 1976—; chief dept. medicine Holy Cross Hosp., 1985-87, Valley Presbyn. Hosp., Van Nuys, Calif., 1986-88; dir. cancer rsch. Northridge Hosp. Med. Ctr., 1992—. Served to maj. U.S. Army, 1968-71. Cert. of Appreciation dept. medicine UCLA, 1984, 87. Fellow ACP; mem. Am. Legion, Am. Soc. Hematology, Am. Soc. Clin. Oncology, Med. Oncology Assn. So. Calif. (bd. dirs.), Alpha Omega Alpha. Democrat. Jewish. Home: 15232 Greenleaf St Sherman Oaks CA 91403-4009 Office: N Valley Hematology Onoclogy Med Group 18533 Roscoe Blvd # 233 Northridge CA 91324-4632

DAVIDSON, STEVEN J., emergency physician; b. Phila., Mar. 9, 1950; s. Jay Howard and Claire Beverly (Silverman) D.; m. Simone F. Mogul, June 21, 1987; children: Zoey Samuel, Masha Kalinkina. AB in Chemistry, Temple U., 1971, MD, 1975; MBA, U. Pa., 1989. Diplomate Am. Bd. Emergency Medicine. Intern in acute care Med. Coll. Pa., 1975-76, resident in emergency medicine, 1976-78; instr., asst. prof., assoc. prof. surgery Med. Coll. Pa., Phila., 1978-84, assoc. prof. emergency medicine, 1984-89, prof. emergency medicine, 1989—, head divsn. emergency med. svc., 1988—; chmn. emergency medicine Maimonides Med. Ctr., Bklyn., 1996—; med. dir. Phila. Emergency Med. Svc., 1983-94; oral examiner Am. Bd. Emergency Medicine, 1980—, bd. dirs., 1986-95. Assoc. editor Yearbook of Emergency Medicine, 1981—; guest reviewer Annals of Emergency Medicine, 1983—, Prehosp. and Disaster Medicine, 1992—, Acad. Emergency Medicine, 1993—. Fellow Am. Coll. Emergency Physicians (bd. dirs. Pa. chpt. 1979-85, Emergency Svc. award 1992), Soc. Acad. Emergency Medicine (pres. 1985-86), Nat. Assn. Emergency Med. Svc. Physicians. Office: Maimonides Med Ctr Dept Emergency Medicine 4802 Tenth Ave Brooklyn NY 11219

DAVIDSON, THOMAS SCOTT, physician; b. Wawautosa, Wis., Jan. 3, 1949; s. Thomas H. and A. Elaine (Carroll) D.; m. Toni W. Davidson, June 15, 1975; children: Scott J., Chad L. BA, Emory U., 1971; MD, Southwestern Med., 1975. Intern and resident U. Miami, 1976-78; cardiology fellowship Southwestern Med., 1978-81; pvt. practice Dallas, 1981—. Office: PO Box 800187 Balch Springs TX 75180-0187

DAVIE, JOSEPH MYRTEN, physician, pathology and immunology educator, science administrator; b. La Porte, Ind., Oct. 14, 1939; s. John James and Dorothy Elizabeth (Hash) D.; m. Janet Sue Whorwell, Dec. 17, 1960; children: Shelley, Jennifer, Melissa. A.B., Ind. U., 1962, M.A., 1964, Ph.D., 1966; M.D., Washington U., St. Louis, 1968. Intern Washington U., 1968-69; staff assoc. NIH, 1969-71; resident Nat. Cancer Inst., 1971-72; assoc. prof. pathology Washington U. Sch. Medicine, 1972-75, asst. prof. microbiology, 1972-73, assoc. prof. microbiology, 1973-75, prof., head microbiology and immunology, prof. pathology, 1975-87; sr. v.p. research G.D. Searle and Co., Skokie, Ill., 1987, pres. research and devel., 1987-92, corp. sr. v.p. sci. and tech., 1993; v.p. rsch. Biogen, Inc., Cambridge, Mass., 1993—. Asso. editor: Jour. of Immunology, 1975-78; sect. editor, 1978-82. Served with USPHS, 1969-71. Mem. Am. Soc. Microbiology, Am. Assn. Immunologists, Am. Assn. Pathologists, Inst. Medicine, Royal Soc. Medicine. Office: Biogen Inc 14 Cambridge Ctr Cambridge MA 02142-1401

DAVIES, ALUN HUW, surgeon, educator; b. Swansea, Wales, U.K., Jan. 16, 1960; s. Stanley Charles and Vera (Thomas) D.; m. Anne Elizabeth Mary Richards, Sept. 23, 1988; children: Emma Bronwen, Bethan Mary. BA, Cambridge (U.K.) U., 1981, MA, 1985; BMBCh, Oxford (U.K.) U., 1984, MA, MD, 1993. House officer John Radcliffe Hosp., Oxford, 1984-85, sr. house officer, 1986-87, registrar, 1988-90; demonstrator anatomy Cambridge (U.K.) U., 1985-86; sr. house officer Bristol (U.K.) Royal Infirmary, 1987-88, fellow, 1990-92, sr. registrar, 1992—; lectr. U. Bristol, U.K., 1992-95; sr. lecturer, cons. Charing Cross Westminster Med. Sch., London, 1995—. Contbr. articles to profl. jours. Moynihan Traveling fellow Assn. Surgeons Gt. Britain and Ireland, 1994. Fellow Royal Coll. Surgeons England (Arris & Gale lectr. 1987, Hunterian prof. 1993-94); mem. Vascular Soc. Gt. Britain and Ireland, European Soc. Vascular Surgeons, European Assn. Vascular Surgeons in Tng. (founding com. mem. 1994), Surg. Rsch. Soc. Home: 4 York Ave East Sheen, London SW14 7LG, England Office: Charing Cross Hosp, Dept Surgery, London W6 8RF, England

DAVIES, BARBARA L., physician, plastic surgeon; b. Lock Haven, Pa., Oct. 23, 1954. BA, Pa State U., University Park, 1976; MD, Jefferson Med. Coll., Phila., 1983. Diplomate Am. Bd. Plastic Surgery. Pvt. group practice Brunswick, Ga., 1991-92, pvt. solo practice, 1992-93; pvt. group practice Savannah Plastic Surgery Assocs., Savannah, Ga., 1993—. Fellow Am. Coll. Surgeons (assoc.); mem. Am. Soc. Plastic & Reconstructive Surgeons, Assn. Women Surgeons, Alpha Omega Alpha. Office: Savannah Plastic Surgery Assocs 4750 Waters Ave Ste 500 Savannah GA 31404

DAVIES, BRIAN W., plastic surgeon; b. Muncie, Ind., Nov. 9, 1953; s. Carroll Frederick and Helen Ann (Curran) D.; m. Deanna; children: Eric, Ian, Allison. BA, Ind. U., 1975, MD, 1978. Diplomate Am. Bd. Plastic and Reconstructive Surgery. Intern in surgery Ind. U. Hosps., Indpls., 1979-80, resident in surgery, 1980-83; resident in surgical subspecialties Akron Gen. Med. Ctr., 1983-84; resident in plastic surgery Akron City Hosp., 1984-85, chief resident, 1986-87; fellow in aesthetic plastic surgery Manhattan Eye, Ear and Throat Hosp., N.Y.C., 1986-87; fellow in craniofacial surgery Mt. Sinai Hosp., Cleve., 1987; fellow in microsurgery Royal Melbourne Hosp., Australia, 1987-88; pvt. practice plastic surgery Akron, 1988—. Mem. AMA, Am. Soc. Plastic and Reconstructive Surgeons, Northeast Ohio Soc. Plastic and Reconstructive Surgeons, Am. Assn. Hand Surgery, Am. Soc. Maxillofacial Surgery, Lipoplasty Soc. N.Am., Am. Soc. Aesthetic Plastic Surgery, Am. Soc. Reconstructive Microsurgery. Office: 2569 Romig Rd Ste 101 Akron OH 44320

DAVIES, CHRIS THOMAS, plastic and reconstructive surgeon; b. Rantoul, Ill., 1954; s. Robert C. and Jan Davies. BS in Biology cum laude, U. Calif., Irvine, 1976, BA in Psychology cum laude, 1977; MD, Tulane U., 1982. Diplomate Am. Bd. Plastic Surgery; qualified med. examiner in plastic surgery, Calif. Resident gen. surgery U. Calif.-Irvine Med. Ctr., Orange, 1982-85; resident plastic surgery St. Francis Meml. Hosp., San Francisco, 1985-88; resident/fellow in microvascular surgery Davies Med. Ctr., San Francisco, 1988; pvt. practice Encinitas, Calif., 1988-95; plastic surgeon, mem. active staff Scripps Hosps., La Jolla, Calif., 1992-95, Encinitas, Calif., 1988-95; plastic surgeon, mem. active staff Tri-City Med. Ctr., 1988-95; assoc. plastic and reconstructive surgery Gutire Clinic, Ltd., Sayre, Pa., 1995—; chief divsn. subspecialty surgery Tri City Med. Ctr., Oceanside, Calif., 1991-92. Recipient Physicians Recognition award AMA, 1989-96. Mem. Am. Soc. Plastic and Reconstructive Surgeons, Inc., Calif. Soc. Plastic Surgeons, Inc., Alpha Omega Alpha. Office: Guthrie Clinic Dept Plastic Surgery Guthrie Sq Sayre PA 18840

DAVIES, GEORGE JAMES, physical therapist, educator; b. La Crosse, Wis., June 9, 1947; m. Carol J. Riley, June 7, 1969; children—Scott, Steven. B.A. in Health and Phys. Edn., Trenton (N.J.) State Coll., 1969, M.Ed. with high honors, 1972; postgrad. Rutgers U., 1973, Columbia U., 1973-75, Fairleigh-Dickinson U., 1974, U. Wis., 1977, U. Wis.-La Crosse, 1978. Cert. phys. therapist Columbia U., 1975; lic. phys. therapist Wis.; cert. athletic trainer Nat. Athletic Trainers Assn.; cert. exercise technician Am. Coll. Sports Medicine; cert. emergency med. technician Nat. Registry of Emergency Med. Technicians, Wis.; cert. cardiopulmonary resuscitation instr., trainer Am. Heart Assn.; cert. cardiopulmonary resuscitation instr., standard first aid and personal safety instr., advanced first aid and emergency care instr., ARC. Student athletic trainer Trenton (N.J.) State Coll., 1967-79, grad. asst. in health and phys. edn., 1971-72; instr. health and phys. edn. Bergen Community Coll., Paramus, N.J., 1972-74, athletic training cons., 1974-75; mem. faculty, asst. prof. phys. therapy U. Wis.-La Crosse, 1975-80, assoc. prof., 1980—, dept. chmn., 1978-79, clin. supr., 1979—, vis. asst. prof. grad. program Inst. Grad Health Scis., 1980—, prof. phys. therapy; nat. faculty mem. U.S. Sports Acad., Mobile, Ala., 1977—; mem. staff La Crosse (Wis.) Exercise Program, 1976—; assoc. dir., bus. mgr. sole practice Orthopaedic and Sports Phys. Therapy, La Crosse, 1979—; cons. in field; exec. dir. Western Wis. Sports Med. Served with USMC, 1969-70. Recipient Cramer Products Athletic Tng. award, 1981; grantee numerous profl. orgns. and govt. agys. Mem. Am. Phys. Therapy Assn. (pres. sports phys. therapy sect. 1992, editor jour., chmn. publs. com.), Am. Coll. Sports Medicine, Nat. Athletic Trainers Assn., Great Lakes Athletic Trainers Assn., Wis. Athletic Trainers Assn., Nat. Registry Emergency Med. Technicians, Wis. Registry Emergency Med. Technicians, Nat Jogger's Assn., Phi Epsilon Kappa (nat. merit scholar, key award 1972), Sigma Xi. Am. Baptist. Author: (with J. Tesch, et al) Laboratory and Field Tests for Cross Country Skiers, 1980; co-editor: Textbook of Physical Therapy: Orthopaedics and Sports, 1984; contbr. chpts. to books, over 50 articles to profl. jours.; editor Sports Medicine column Cardio-Gram, La Crosse, 1976—, Isokinetics and Exercise Science; co-editor Jour. Orthopaedic and Sports Phys. Therapy, 1979—. Home: 1707 Jennifer Ct Onalaska WI 54650-3135 Office: U Wis 2036 Cowley Hall La Crosse WI 54601-3791

DAVIES, HUW TALFRYN OAKLEY, health services researcher; b. Holyhead, Anglesey, Wales, June 1, 1962; s. Derek Graham Oakley and Margaret Mary (Walsh) D.; m. Catherine Mary Grant; children: Thomas Cybi Grant, Bryn Rhodri Grant, Padrig Llew Grant. BA with honors, Cambridge (Eng.) U., 1983; MS, Sussex (Eng.) U., 1985; PhD, Dundee (Scotland) U., 1996; MA (hon.), Cambridge U., 1990. Rsch. fellow Polytechnic of South Bank, London, 1985-88, Dundee U., 1989-96; lectr. in health care mgmt. U. St. Andrews, Scotland, 1996—. Author: The Audit Handbook, 1993, Research into Healthcare, 1996. Mem. Faculty Pub. Health Medicine (hon.). Office: Dept Mgmt, U Saint Andrews, Saint Andrews Fife, Scotland

DAVIES, KEITH G., neurosurgeon; b. Merthyr Tydfil, Wales, June 10, 1953; came to U.S. 1994; s. Evan Thomas and Freda D.; m. Sandra Lobo, Sept. 17, 1981; children: Owen, Leela. MB, BCh, U. Wales, 1976. Sr. registrar neurosurgery U. Hosp. Wales, Cardiff 1985-89, 91-93; rsch. fellow in neurosurgery Baylor Coll. Medicine, Houston, 1989-90; clin. fellow specialist neurosurgery U. Minn., Mpls., 1990-91; surg. dir., asst. prof Epi-Care Ctr. Semmes-Murphey Clinic U. Tenn., Memphis, 1994—. Contbr. articles to profl. jours. Fellow Royal Coll. Surgeons. Office: Semmes-Murphey Clinic 930 Madison Ave Ste 700 Memphis TN 38103

DAVIES, PATRICIA JEAN, nursing educator; b. Oil City, Pa.. Diploma in nursing, Sewickley (Pa.) Valley Hosp., 1971; BSN, Slippery Rock U., 1980; MS in Nursing, U. Pitts., 1985. RN, Pitts.; cert. BCLS, ACLS, CCRN. Staff nurse ICU and CCU, Sewickley Valley Hosp., 1971-72, evening supr., 1975-77, charge nurse CCU, 1977-82; staff nurse surg. ICU, Allegheny Gen. Hosp., Pitts., 1972-74, team leader CCU, 1982-83; nurse educator critical care nursing Mercy Hosp., Pitts., 1983-85; rsch. asst. U. Pitts., 1985, mem. adj. faculty, 1986-93; coord. patient care CCU, Butler (Pa.) Meml. Hosp., 1986; critical care clin. specialist VA, Pitts., 1986-93; instr. Sch. of Nursing U. Pitts., 1993—; cons. to outlying VA med. ctrs., Pitts., 1986—. Nursing fellow Am. Lung Assn., 1984. Mem. AHA (chmn. western branch edn. com.), AACN (cert.), Assn. Pulmonary Nurses (chmn. edn. com. 1987-88), Sigma Theta Tau. Home: 308 Mcintosh Dr Coraopolis PA 15108-2708 Office: Univ of Pitts Sch Nursing Acute/Tertiary Care Pittsburgh PA 15260

DAVIES, PETER DAVID OWEN, cardiologist; b. Trieste, Italy, Apr. 30, 1949; arrived in U.K., 1952; s. Herbert Lewis and Mary Ann (Currie) D.; m. Eleanor Mary Mynors, Mar. 29, 1975; children: Richard, Edward, Mary, Michael. MA DM, U. Coll., Oxford, Eng., 1971; BM BCh, St. Thomas Hosp., London, 1973. Sr. house officer West Middlesex Hosp., London, 1975-76; registrar Mt. Vernon Hosp., London, 1976-78; clin. sci. officer Med. Rsch. Coun., Brompton Hosp., London, 1978-80; registrar Llandough, Cardiff, U.K., 1980-82, sr. registrar, 1982-88; cons. physician Cardiothoracic Ctr. and Aintree Hosps. Trust, Liverpool, Eng., 1988—; cons. physician H.M. Prison, Liverpool, 1988—. Editor: Clinical Tuberculosis, 1994. Reader Diocese of Chester, U.K. Fellow Royal Coll. Physicians; mem. Am. Thoracic Soc., Brit. Thoracic Soc. Mem. Anglican Ch. Office: Cardiathoracic Ctr, Thomas Dr, Liverpool L14 3PE, England

DAVIES, ROBERT BRUCE, osteopath; b. New Cumberland, Pa., Oct. 13, 1925; s. Cecil Douglas and Mary Evelyn (Wieder) D.; m. Martha Alice Snyder, Dec. 29, 1951; children: Robin L., Robert B., Steven T., Cynthia L. Student, Dickinson Coll., 1946-48, Albright Coll., 1948-49; DO, Phila. Coll. Osteo. Medicine, 1954. Intern Allentown (Pa.) Osteo. Hosp., 1954-55; pvt. practice, Kutztown, Pa., 1955-74; dir Student Health Ctr., team physician Indiana U. Pa., 1974-83; physician specialist II, safety advisor Pa. Disability Determination Svc., Greensburg, 1983-93. With USN, 1943-46, PTO. Mem. Masons, Shriners. Democrat. Home: 16 Unity Square Dr Greensburg PA 15601

DAVIES-HATHEN, NANCY DANELLA, critical care nurse; b. Phila., Dec. 12, 1953; d. G. Douglas and Margaret Howells (Llewellyn) Davies; m. Ronald Hathen, June 29, 1985. AB, Lafayette Coll., 1976; MEd, Lehigh U., 1977; diploma, Einstein Med. Ctr., 1982; BSN, Thomas Jefferson U., 1984; MSN, U. Pa., 1991. RN, Pa., N.J.; CCRN. Staff nurse Thomas Jefferson U. Med. Ctr., Phila., 1982-85, WCHS at Pa. Hosp., Phila., 1985-86, Cooper Hosp./U. Med. Ctr., Camden, N.J.; asst. nurse mgr. Cooper Hosp./U. Med. Ctr., Camden, 1986-93; dir. heart failure/transplant program Hahnemann U., Phila., 1993—. Mem. AACN, Nat. League for Nursing, Soc. Critical Care Medicine. Home: 720 Marietta Dr Ambler PA 19002-1523

DAVILA, C. EDGAR, dentist, maxillofacial prosthodontist, dental oncologist, educator; b. Lima, Peru, June 28, 1965; came to U.S., 1993; s. Julian Alfonso and Alicia Bertha (Castillo) D.; m. Martha Patricia Gamarra, Dec. 29, 1989; children: Christian Daniel, Alexandra Alicia. BS, Cayetano Heredia Peruvian U., Lima, 1986, DDS, 1987; cert. advanced gen. dentistry, Eastman Dental Ctr., U. Rochester, Rochester, N.Y., 1990; MS, cert. combined prosthodontics, U. Louisville, Sch. of Dentistry, 1992; cert. maxillofacial prosthetics and dental oncology, U. Tex., M.D. Anderson Cancer Ctr., Houston, 1993. Intern Rimac Hosp., Lima, 1986; asst. prof. Cayetano Heredia Peruvian U., 1987-89; pvt. practice, Lima, 1987-89; resident in advanced gen. dentistry Eastman Dental Ctr., 1989-90; resident in combined prosthetics U. Louisville, 1990-92, VA Med. Ctr., Louisville, 1991-92; resident in maxillofacial prosthetics James Graham Brown Cancer Ctr., Louisville, 1991-92; fellow in maxillofacial prosthetics M.D. Anderson Cancer Ctr., Houston, 1992-93; maxillofacial prosthodontist H. Lee Moffitt Cancer Ctr. and Rsch. Inst., Tampa, Fla., 1993—; asst. prof. U. South Fla., Tampa, 1993—. Contbr. articles and astracts to dental jours. Mem. ADA, Am. Acad. Maxillofacial Prosthodontists, Am. Coll. Prosthodontists, Internat. Assn. for Dental Rsch., Acad. Osseointegration, Fla. Dental Assn. Roman Catholic. Home: 17707 Parkway Green Ln Tampa FL 33647 Office: Med Arts Ctr. Ste 5 4600 N Habana Tampa FL 33614

DAVILA, NORMA, developmental psychologist and program evaluator; b. Rio Piedras, P.R., Dec. 17, 1962; d. Fernando and Ana (Maldonado) D. BA in Psychology, Yale U., 1985; MA in Behavioral Sci., U. Chgo., 1988, PhD in Psychology, 1991. Asst. edn. coord. Head Start, New Haven, 1984-85; rsch. asst. Disengagement of Talent Project, Chgo., 1985-86; rsch. asst. Chgo. Stress Project, 1986-87, project coord., 1987; sr. pro-analyst Rsch. Pros, Chgo., 1988-89; instr. dept. psychology St. Xavier Coll., Chgo., 1988-89, 90, Roosevelt U., Chgo., 1990-91; asst. prof. dept. psychology U. P.R., Rio Piedras, 1991-96; dir. evaln. PR-SSI Project, Rio Piedras, 1993-95, dir. evaln. and assessment, 1996—; career counselor and career devel. instr. Women Employed, Chgo., 1991. Recipient Trustee's Fellowship U. Chgo., 1985-86, Minority Grad. Incentive Program Fellowship, State of Ill., 1986-89, Dissertation of Yr. Fellowship, Dorothy Danforth Compton Found., 1990-91. Mem. APA, Psychol. Assn. of P.R., Am. Ednl. Rsch. Assn., Am. Evaluators Assn. Office: Dept Psychology U Puerto Rico Rio Piedras PR

DAVIS, ADA ROMAINE, nursing educator; b. Cumberland, Md., June 7, 1929; d. Louis Berge and Ethel Lucy (Johnson) Romaine; m. John Francis Davis, Aug. 1, 1953; children: Kevin Murray, Karen Evans-Romaine, William Romaine. Diploma in nursing, Kings County Hosp., Bklyn., 1949; BSN, U. Md., Balt., 1973, MS, 1974; PhD, U. Md., College Park, 1979, postdoctoral student, 1985-89. Cert. editor in life scis. Asst. prof. grad. program U. Md., Balt., 1974-79; chmn. dept. nursing Coll. of Notre Dame, Balt., 1979-82; assoc. dean grad. program Georgetown U. Sch. Nursing, Washington, 1982-87; nurse cons. Health Resources and Svcs. Adminstrn., Rockville, Md., 1987-93, HHS, USPHS, Bur. Health Profls., Rockville, 1987-93; assoc. prof. and dir. undergrad. program Johns Hopkins U. Sch. of Nursing, Balt., 1993—; reviewer Choice, ALA; evaluator methodology and findings for rsch. studies; hist./med. biographer. Editor: Ency. of Home Care for the Elderly, 1995; contbr. articles to nursing jours. Recipient excellent performance award HRSA; rsch. grantee U. Md. Grad. Sch. Mem. ANA (cert. adult nurse practitioner), Soc. for Neoplatonic Studies, Nat. Orgn. Nurse Practitioner Faculties, Am. Acad. Nurse Practitioners, Md. History of Medicine Soc., Soc, for the Social History of Medicine (Oxford U.), N.Y. Acad. Scis., Sigma Theta Tau. Office: 1830 E Monument St Baltimore MD 21205-2114

DAVIS, ANN LOUISE, health services administrator, educator; b. Dubuque, Iowa, Nov. 5, 1942; d. John Dubuque and Louise Mae D. AAN, Chgo City Coll., Chgo., 1967; BSN, U. Ill., 1972, MSNA, 1976. Staff nurse, asst. dir. Michael Reese Rehab. Inst., Chgo., 1967-70, dir. staff devel., 1970-71, dir. edn., 1972-73; assoc. dir. nursing U. Wisc. Med. Ctr., Madison, 1978-82; assoc. dir. nursing Drake Hosp., Cin., 1982-84, dir. nursing, 1984-86; divsn. dir. patient care Findley Hosp., Dubuque, Iowa, 1986-91, v.p. patient care and quality mgmt., 1991—; mem. Clarke Coll. Sch. Nursing, Dubuque, 1986—, U. of Dubuque Sch. Nursing, 1986—. Contbr. articles to profl. jours. Bd. dirs. Salvation Army Dubuque chpt., 1990; active Rotary (Key City sgt.-at-arms, environment com., edn. com.) Dubuque chpt., 1987-94. Named Iowa Nurse Executive of Yr. IHA, 1992. Mem. Iowa Orgn. Nurse Execs. (chair edn. com., 1992-93, dist. pres.-elect, 1994-95, pres. 1994-96).

DAVIS, ANNE SHERVINGTON, social services administrator; b. Balt., Aug. 23, 1935; d. E. Walter and Charlotte (Watson) Shervington; m. Gerald Davis, Dec. 28, 1957 (div. Sept. 1979); children: Lynnette Morris, Alison Hiller, Melanie. BA, Morgan State U., 1957; MEd, Coppin State Coll., 1973. Supr. juvenile probation Dept. Juvenile Svcs., Balt., 1964-73, tng. specialist, 1973-76; tng. officer Sch. Bus. Howard U., Washington, 1976-77; exec. dir. Florence Crittendon Svcs. Balt., Inc., 1977—; owner Etcetera Boutique, 1983—. Vice chair Woman's Commn., 1988-89; bd. dirs. Juvenile Justice Adv. Coun., Balt., 1990—; sec. bd. dirs. Morgan State U. Found., 1986—; bd. dirs. Md. Commn. for Children, 1979-82; mem. Leadership Balt., 1991. Recipient Bus. Achievement award Bus. and Profl. Women's Club, Balt., 1990; named Woman on the Move, Sigma Gamma Rho, Balt., 1987, Disting. Black Marylander, Towson State U., 1989. Mem. Child Welfare League Am. (chair Mid. Atlantic region 1991-93), Alpha Kappa Alpha. Democrat. Roman Catholic. Home: 2225 Deerfern Cres Baltimore MD 21209-4605 Office: Florence Crittenton Svcs 3110 Crittenton Pl Baltimore MD 21211-2723

DAVIS, ARCHIE G., cardiologist, internist; b. Charlotte, N.C., Aug. 5, 1947; s. John W. and Lucy Friend (Hassell) D.; m. Donna Jew, Apr. 27, 1974; 1 child, Ginger Blair. BS, Davidson (N.C.) Coll., 1968; MD, U. N.C., 1972. Diplomate Am. Bd. Internal Medicine, Am. Bd. Cardiology. Resident in internal medicine U. Ala., Birmingham, 1975-77; internal medicine specialist Selma (Ala.) Internal Medicine Assocs., 1977-86; fellow in cardiology Med. Corps U.S. Army, Mobile, 1986-89, U. South Ala., Mobile, 1989; pvt. practice Heart Group, Mobile, 1989—; cons. Coastal Clin. Rsch., Mobile, 1989—. Maj. U.S. Army, 1975-77. Fellow ACP, Am. Coll. Cardiology; mem. Mobile County Med. Soc. Republican. Presbyterian. Office: Heart Group 1 Mobile Infirmary Cir Mobile AL 36607

DAVIS, BRIAN ADAM, physician; b. Chgo., Jan. 21, 1966; s. Paul Michael and Arlene Carol (Feinman) D.; m. Edith Carpio Bautista, May 23, 1992. BS, No. Ill. U., 1986; MD, Meharry Med. Coll., 1992. Intern Hosp. of U. Pa./Presbyn. Med. Ctr., Phila., 1992-93; resident U. Medicine and Dentistry N.J., Newark, 1993-96; assoc. attending Runnells Specialized Hosp., Berkeley Heights, N.J., 1994—; fellow Kessler Sports Inst., West Orange, N.J., 1996—. Contbr. articles to profl. jours. Student asst. I Have a Future, Nashville, 1991. Mem. AMA, Am. Coll. Sports Medicine, Am. Acad. Physicians Med. & Rehab., N.J. Assn. Electrodiagnostic Medicine, N.J. Soc. Physicians Med. & Rehab., Assn. Acad. Psychiatrists, KC (participant, fundraiser 1985-86), Phi Kappa Delta (participant health screening 1990-92), Sigma Alpha Mu (participant, fundraiser 1985-86), Alpha Omega Alpha. Independent. Home: 308 Williams Ct Edgewater NJ 07020 Office: Kessler Inst Rehab 1199 Pleasant Valley Way West Orange NJ 07052

DAVIS, BRUCE ALLEN, psychologist; b. Monett, Mo., Aug. 13, 1948; s. William Lester and Mable Caroline (Frederickson) D.; m. Jill Suzanne Keene, Aug. 1, 1992. AB in Psychology, Drury Coll., 1970, MBA, 1980; MS in Guidance and Counseling, S.W. Mo. State U., 1974. Diplomate Disability Cons.; lic. psychologist, sch. psychol. examiner; cert. marriage and family therapist. Prison psychologist U.S. Bur. Prisons, Springfield, Mo., 1976; staff psychologist Greene County Guidance Clinic, Springfield, 1975-80; clin. psychologist Davis Psychol. Testing Svc., Springfield, 1975—; child clin. psychologist Springfield Park Cen. Hosp., 1985-87; divorce psychologist Springfield Divorce Ctr., 1987—; psychol. cons. Social Security Adminstn., Springfield, 1981-89, Mo. Div. Family Svcs., Springfield, 1985-89, Syntex Corp., Springfield, 1984, Springfield Pub. Sch., 1984-86. Contbr. articles to profl. jour. Cons. Greene County Mental Health Soc., Springfield, 1985-91. Mem. Am. Psychol. Assn., Mo. Psychol. Assn., Ozark Area Psychol. Assn., Am. Assn. Marriage and Family Therapists, Mo. Assn. Marriage and Family Therapists, Ozark Area Marriage and Family Therapists, Nat. Assn. Disability Examiners, Mo. Assn. Disability Examiners, Mensa (test adminstr. 1984—), Kappa Alpha. Republican. Mem. Christian Ch. Home: 1240 S Saratoga Ave Springfield MO 65804-0562

DAVIS, CAROLE JOAN, psychologist; b. Norristown, Pa., Aug. 15, 1942; d. John Morgan and Eva (Pierson) D.; children: Kevin Jae, Kara Megan. AB in English Lit., U. Pa., 1964; MA in Psychology, Temple U., 1967; PhD in Child Devel. and Clin. Evaluation, Bryn Mawr (Pa.) Coll., 1973. Lic. psychologist Pa. Sr. clin. psychologist Camden County Psychiat. Hosp., Lakeland, N.J., 1967-76; psychologist counselling ctr. staff Chestnut Hill Coll., Phila., 1976-89; psychologist hearing impaired programs Phila. (Pa.) Sch. Dist., 1984-85; pvt. practice Phila., 1974-89, New Britain, Pa., 1989—; cons. psychologist Pa. Sch. for Deaf, Phila., 1970-84, Luth. Children & Family Svc., Phila., 1974-80, Willis & Elizabeth Martin Sch., Phila., 1975-84, Overbrook Sch. for Blind, 1978-94; psychologist Colonial Sch. Dist. 1994-95; lectr. in psychology Chestnut Hill Coll. Grad. Divsn., Phila., 1980—; psychologist APOGEE, 1995—. Mem. Am. Psychol. Assn., Pa. Psychol. Assn., Phila. Soc. Clin. Psychologists (exec. bd. 1981-83), Nat. Register of Health Svc. Providers in Psychology, Psychologists for the Ethical Treatment Animals. Home: 62 Shady Grove Cir Doylestown PA 18901-2132

DAVIS, CAROLYNE KAHLE, health care consultant; b. Penn Yan, N.Y., Jan. 31, 1932; d. Paul Frederick Kahle and Alice Edgerton (Kahle) Cargill; m. Ott Howard Davis, June 28, 1953; 1 son, Richard Ott. BS in Nursing, Johns Hopkins U., 1954; MS in Nursing, Syracuse U., 1965, PhD in Higher Edn. Adminstrn., 1972; LittD (hon.), Georgetown U., 1982; DSc (hon.), U. Evansville, 1982, U. Medicine & Dentistry N.J., 1984; LLD (hon.), Adelphi U., 1985; LHD (hon.), Med. U. S.C., 1986; DSc (hon.), Eastern Mich. U., 1989; DHL (hon.), Med. Coll. of N.Y., 1992. Chmn. baccalaureate nursing program Syracuse U., 1969-73; dean sch. nursing U. Mich., Ann Arbor, 1973-75, prof. nursing and edn., 1973-81, assoc. v.p. acad. affairs, 1975-81; adminstr. Health Care Fin. Adminstrn. HHS, Washington, 1981-85; cons. Ernst & Whinney, Washington, 1985-89, Ernst & Young, Washington, 1989—; bd. dirs. Pharm. Mktg. Svcs., Inc., Scottsdale, Ariz., Beckman Inst., Irvine, Calif., Prudential Ins. Co. of Am., Newark, Merck, Rahway, N.J., Sci. Applications Internat. Corp., San Diego. Mem. editorial bd. Nursing Economics, Pitman, N.J.; contbr. more than 100 articles to profl. jours. Bd. dirs. ARC, 1988-94; trustee U. Pa. Med. Ctr., Phila., 1987—; vice chmn. bd. trustees Nat. Rehab. Hosp., 1993-96; mem. health adv. com. GAO, 1990—. Recipient Disting. Alumnus award Johns Hopkins U., 1981, Alumni award Syracuse U. Sch. Edn., 1983, Alumni award U. Mich., 1984, Spl. Recognition award Assn. Am. Med. Colls., 1986; named one of the Top Young Leaders in Am. Acad. Mag., 1978. Mem. NAS Inst. Medicine, Nat. League for Nursing (bd. dirs. 1979-81, chmn. Cmty. Health Accreditation Program 1987-92, Presdl. award 1993). Sigma Theta Tau, Phi Delta Kappa. Republican. Office: Ernst & Young 1225 Connecticut Ave NW Washington DC 20036-2604

DAVIS, CYNTHIA GAIL, otolaryngologist, naval officer; b. Cleve., Jan. 13, 1956; d. Donald B. and Joyce Robertson; m. Martin Alex Davis, Apr. 10, 1980. B.A., UCLA, 1978; M.D., Uniformed Services U., 1982. Diplomate Am. Bd. of Otolaryngology. Commd. ensign U.S. Navy, 1978, advanced through grades to cmdr., 1993; staff physician Br. Hosp., U.S. Marine Corps, Twenty Nine Palms, Calif., 1983-84; med./surg. intern U.S. Naval Hosp., San Diego, 1982-83, postdoctoral tng. in head and neck surgery, 1984-88; dir. otolaryngology head and neck surgery Naval Hosp., Phila., 1988-91; head otolaryngolgy dept. Naval Hosp., Camp Pendleton, Calif., 1991-94; pvt. practice, Solana Beach, Calif., 1994——; organizer, com. mem. biology of cancer program UCLA, 1978; vol. Cystic Fibrosis Clinic, UCLA, 1977-78. Latter Day Saints Hosp. research fellow, 1977. Fellow ACS; mem. AMA, Calif. Med. Soc., San Diego Med. Soc., Assn. Mil. Surgeons U.S., Am. Acad. Otolaryngology, Am. Acad. Facial Plastic and Reconstructive Surgery, Alpha Phi. Republican. Presbyterian. Home: 9954 Rocky Ridge Rd Escondido CA 92026-6620 Office: 100 Pacific Ave Solana Beach CA 92075

DAVIS, DAVE MCALISTER, psychiatrist; b. Chattanooga, May 22, 1937; s. Thomas Lee and Maurice (Jernigan) D.; m. Joan Winfield Barber, Dec. 29, 1960; children: Scott Winfield, Breton Kingsland. Student, Goettingen U., Fed. Republic Germany, 1957-58; AB in German, U. N.C., 1960, MD, 1963. Diplomate Am. Bd. Clin. Psychiatry, Am. Bd. Forensic Psychiatry, Am. Bd. Adminstrv. Psychiatry. Intern in medicine U. Fla., Gainesville, 1963-64; fellow in psychiatry Mass. Gen. Hosp., Boston, 1964-65; resident in psychiatry Emory U. Hosp., Atlanta, 1967-69; dir. psychiatry Peachtree-Parkwood Mental Health Ctr. and Hosp., Atlanta, 1969-80; med. dir. Piedmont Psychiat. Clinic, Atlanta, 1980—; pres. Ga. Adminstrv. Psychiatrists, Atlanta, 1987; chmn. Am. Psychiat. Assn. Consultation Svc., Washington, 1986-90, ethics com. Med. Assn. Atlanta, 1974-75; adj. asst. prof. psychology Ga. State U., examiner clin. psychiatry Am. Bd. Psychiatry and Neurology. Editorial Bd. Adolescent Psychiatry, 1983-94; contbr. numerous articles profl. jours. Founder Fist Adolescent Psychiat. Unit in South, 1971, First Child's Psychiatry Unit in South, 1972, Fist Psychiat. Halfway House in South, 1974; activist Handgun Control Inc., Washington, 1979—, Action Against Smoking, Washington, 1975—; mem. Govs. Commn., Atlanta; treas. Mental Health Assn. Ga., Atlanta, 1984-89; chmn. psychiat. panel Atlanta Found. Med. Care. John Motley Morehead scholar U. N.C., 1955-60, Goettingen U. scholar, 1957-58. Fellow Ga. Psychiat. Assn. (pres. 1976-77), Am. Assn. Psychiat. Adminstrs. (pres. 1986-87), Am. Psychiat. Assn. (chmn. cons. svcs. bd.); mem. AMA, Am. Coll. Forensic Psychiatry, Am. Coll. Psychiat. Adminstrs., Am. Coll. Mental Health Adminstrn., Am. Soc. Adolescent Psychiatry, Nat. Forensic Ctr., Nat. Mental Health Assn., So. Med. Assn., So. Psychiat. Assn., Med. Assn. Ga., Ga. Acad. Psychiatry and Law (pres. 1986-87), Ga. Soc. Adolescent Psychiatry, Med. Assn. Atlanta (chmn. mental health com., judicial coun.), Capital City Club, Peachtree Racquet Club (pres. 1995-96). Unitarian. Office: 1938 Peachtree Rd NW Atlanta GA 30309-1254

DAVIS, DAVID OLIVER, radiologist, educator; b. Danville, Ill., June 25, 1933; s. Oliver and Anna Marie (Collignon) D.; m. Agnes Layden, Dec. 26, 1955; children: Karen, Kathy, Diane, Janet, Nancy. BS, U. Ill., 1954; MD, St. Louis U., 1958. Diplomate Am. Bd. Radiology. Intern Starkloff Meml. Hosp., St. Louis, 1958-59; resident USPHS Hosp., S.I., N.Y., 1959-61, Columbia Presbyn. Med. Center, N.Y.C., 1962-63; asst. prof. radiology Washington U., St. Louis, 1966-68; assoc. prof. Washington U., 1968-70; prof. U. Utah, 1970-72; prof. George Washington U., 1972—, prof. neurology, 1977—, chmn. dept. radiology, 1978-82, 1991—, prof. neurosurgery, 1985—; vis. prof. U. Calif., San Francisco, 1985; cons. UCLA, 1995-96, UNS; sec.-gen. 12th Internat. Symposium on Neuroradiology. Editor: Principles of Diagnostic Radiology, 1971, Reconstruction Tomography in Diagnostic Radiology and Nuclear Medicine, 1977; mem. editl. bd. Jour. Computer Assisted Tomography, 1977—, Am. Jour. Neuroradiology, 1979—, Neuroradiology, 1971-80; mem. editl. exec com. Jour. Investigative Radiology, 1971-80. Served with USPHS, 1959-64. NIH spl. fellow, 1964-66. Fellow Am. Coll. Radiology (mem. coun. steering com. 1992-94, mem. bd. chancellors 1994—), Am. Heart Assn. (stroke coun.); mem. AMA, Am. Soc. Neuroradiology (sec. 1971-74, pres. 1979-80, chmn. publs. com. 1988-92, alt. counselor 1991-92, counsellor 1992-94), D.C. Med. Soc., D.C. Radiol. Soc. (pres. 1983-84, alt. counselor 1982-85, counsellor 1985-91), Assn. Univ. Radiologists, Soc. Chmn. Acad. Radiology Depts. (sec.-treas. 1981-83), Internat. Microcirculation Soc., Blue Grass Radiology Soc. (hon.), Radiol. Soc. N.Am., Am. Roentgen Ray Soc. (mem. exec. coun. 1992-95, alt. del. to AMA 1995—), North Pacific Soc. Neurology and Psychiatry (hon.), Am. Head and Neck Radiology, Phila. Roentgen Soc. (hon.), Western Neuroradiology Soc., Am. Assn. Neuro. Surgeons. Office: George Washington U Med Ctr Dept Radiology 901 23rd St NW Washington DC 20037-2377

DAVIS, DEBORAH ANN, health science facility administrator; b. Largo, Fla., June 13, 1959; d. John James and Carolyn Ann (Clark) D. BS, Grace Coll., Winona Lake, Ind., 1981; MA, Webster U. Staff acct. St. Anthony Hosp. Systems, Denver, 1981-86; bus. systems mgr. Alina Health Systems, Denver, 1986-90; v.p. Superior Cons. Co., Plano, Tex., 1990—; chmn. St. Anthony Hosp. Credit Com., 1983-90; treas. North Fork Fire Dept., Pine County, 1983-84. Mem. Assn. Hosp. Fin. Mgmt. Assn., Healthcare Info. Sys. Soc. Home: 2617 Brookside Ct McKinney TX 75070 Office: Superior Cons Co 101 E Park Blvd Ste 413 Plano TX 70574

DAVIS, DONALD IRVIN, psychiatrist, family therapist; b. Portland, Oreg., Oct. 18, 1942; s. Aubrey Milton and Clara Ethel (Dickson) D.; BA magna cum laude (NSF grantee), Harvard Coll., 1964; MD, U. Pa., 1968; m. Susan Lynn Rabinowitz, Aug. 16, 1964; children: Kenneth Bernard, Joshua Ian. Intern, Case-Western Res. U. Hosps. Cleve., 1968-69; resident in psychiatry U. Chgo.-Billings Hosp., 1969-72; clin. asso. Alcoholism Clin. Rsch. Lab., Nat. Inst. on Alcohol Abuse and Alcoholism, NIMH, Washington, 1972-74; clinic instr. Georgetown U., 1973-74; asst. prof. psychiatry and behavioral scis. George Washington U., 1974-79, attending psychiatrist, dir. family therapy program, psychiat. inpatient unit, 1977-79, clin. assoc. prof. psychiatry, 1979-87, clin. prof. psychiatry, 1987—; adj. prof., Dept of Child and Family Devel., Va. Polytechnic Inst., 1985—; trainee in family therapy Family Therapy Inst. D.C., 1975-76, med. cons., 1976-77; co-founder, dir. Family Therapy Inst. Alexandria (Va.), 1978—, NLP Resource Ctr., 1987—; clin. cons., Employee Assistance Svcs. Inc., 1994—; condr. profl. workshops, panels, U.S. and abroad. Served to lt. comdr. USPHS, 1972-74. Nat. Inst. Drug Abuse grantee, 1974-77; Nat. Inst. Alcohol Abuse and Alcoholism grantee, 1974-77, Diplomate Am. Bd. Psychiatry and Neurology; cert. master practitioner, trainer Neuro-Linguistic Programming. Fellow Am. Psychiat. Assn., Am. Orthopsychiat. Assn., Am. Assn. Marriage and Family Therapy (approved supr.), N.Am. Assn. Neuro-Linguistic Programming (charter); mem. Am. Family Therapy Acad. (charter), Washington Psychiat. Soc., No. Va. Psychiat. Soc. (exec. com. 1981-82), Alexandria Med. Soc., Va. Med. Soc., Phi Rho Sigma. Democrat. Jewish. Author: Alcoholism Treatment: An Integrative Family and Individual Approach, Allyn and Bacon, 1987. Research, publs. on alcoholism, the family, family therapy, neurolinguistic programming. Office: Family Therapy Inst Alexandria 220 S Washington St Alexandria VA 22314-3626

DAVIS, DONALD ROBERT, nutritionist, researcher, consultant; b. La Jara, Colo., Mar. 19, 1941; s. Robert Cristopher and Ida Mary (Blissard) D.; m. Vera Elaine Wilson, June 27, 1980 (div. Aug. 15, 1989). Grad., Calif. Inst. Tech., 1962; PhD, UCLA, 1965; post-doctoral fellow, Calif. Inst. Tech., 1965-67. Instr. Calif. Inst. Tech., Pasadena, 1965-67; asst. prof. U. Calif., Irvine, 1967-74; rsch. scientist assoc. U. Tex., Austin, 1974-86, rsch. assoc., 1986—; mem. bd. trustees Internat. Acad. Nutrition and Preventive Medicine, 1983-85, The Wacker Found., 1987—; dir. Roger J. Williams Nutrition Inst., 1987-90; sr. rsch. cons. Ctr. for Improvement of Human Functioning, Wichita, Kans., 1989—. Editor-in-chief Jour. Applied Nutrition, 1986-91; mem. edtl. bds. Jour. Applied Nutrition, 1978—, Jour. Internat. Acad. Preventive Medicine, 1983-85; contbr. over 40 articles to profl. jours; co-developer nutrient content software, Nutricircles, 1985. Instr. Lifetime Learning, Austin, 1978—. Recipient Rsch. fellowship NSF, Washington, 1965-67; grantee Found. for Nutritional Advancement, Washington, 1986. Mem. AAAS, Am. Coll. Nutrition, Internat. Acad. Nutrition and Preventive Medicine, Acad. Orthomolecular Medicine, Coun. Biology Editors. Office: Biochem Inst Univ Tex Austin TX 78712

DAVIS, DORINNE SUE TAYLOR LOVAS, audiologist; b. East Orange, N.J., Mar. 29, 1949; d. William Henry and Evelyn Doris (Thorp) Taylor; BA, Montclair State Coll., 1971, MA, 1973; children: Larissa Louise, Peter Alexander. Ednl. audiologist Kinnelon (N.J.) Bd. Edn., 1972-94, Inst. for Career Advancement, Inc., 1980-82, Dover Gen. Hosp., 1984-86; pres. Hear You Are, Inc., 1987—; kindergarten tchr. Kinnelon (N.J.) Bd. Edn., 1994—; adj. prof. Kean Coll., Union, N.J., 1993-95. Cert. tchr. of hearing impaired, speech correctionist, tchr. speech and drama, supr. nursery sch. endorsement N.J. Dept. Edn. Mem. NEA, Internat. Orgn. Educators Hearing Impaired, Am. Speech and Hearing Assn. (cert. of clin. competence in audiology), Am. Acad. Audiology, Alexander Graham Bell Assn., N.J. Speech and Hearing Assn., Morris County Speech and Hearing Assn., N.J. Edn. Assn., Morris County Edn. Assn., Kinnelon Edn. Assn., Self Help for the Hard of Hearing, Ednl. Audiology Assn. (past pres.). Methodist. Home: 4 Musconetcong Ave Stanhope NJ 07874-2936 Office: Kiel Sch Kiel Ave Kinnelon NJ 07405 also: Hear You Are Inc 125 Main St Netcong NJ 07857

DAVIS, DORIS MAURINE, nurse manager, researcher, consultant; b. Bryan, Tex., Jan. 30, 1946; d. D.B. and Lera M. (Barnett) Pilgreen. AD summa cum laude, Tyler (Tex.) Jr. Coll., 1974; diploma with honors, Tex. Eastern Sch. Nursing, Tyler, 1975; BSN cum laude, U. Tex., Tyler, 1989; postgrad., Stephen F. Austin State U., 1993-94. RN, Tex.; lic. interior design Tex. Bd. Archtl. Examiners. Staff nurse, emergency room Mother Frances Hosp., Tyler, 1974-81; staff nurse, asst. supr. surgery U. Tex. Health Ctr., Tyler, 1975-76; clin. coord. O.E. McClusky, M.D., Tyler, 1977-84; staff nurse, emergency room Panola Gen. Hosp., Carthage, Tex., 1984-85; charge nurse, staff nurse III U. Tex. Health Ctr., 1985-86, nurse clinician, protocol coord., dept. biochemistry, 1986-89, dir. gen. medicine clinic, ambulatory svcs., 1989-91; protocol coord. TexCAPS Clinic, Ft. Worth, 1992; house supr. Univ. Pk. Hosp., Tyler, 1992-93; staff nurse part-time U. Tex. Med. Branch, Nacogdoches, 1993-94; exec. dir. nursing Briarcliff Village Health Ctr., Inc., Tyler, 1994; facility nurse assessor, quality assurance coord. Colonial Manor-Summit Care Corp., Tyler, 1996—; nurse cons. Strength Devel. Corp., Tyler, 1989-91; design cons. health care facilities and residential. Contbr. articles to profl. jours.; presenter in field. Vol. Am. Lung Assn., March of Dimes, People Attempting to Help Tyler. Named Office Nurse of the Year, Tex. Nurses Assn., 1981. Mem. ANA, Am. Soc. Interior Designers, Tex. Nurses Assn. (dist. 19 sec. 1988-91), East Tex. Fine Arts Assn., Tyler Art League, U. Tex. at Tyler Alumni Assn., Tex. Alpha Chi, Sigma Theta Tau, Inc.

DAVIS, DWIGHT, cardiologist, educator; b. Winston-Salem, N.C., Apr. 11, 1948; s. James C. Davis; m. Lorna Jean Enck, July 30, 1988; 1 child, Nathan James. BS, N.C. A&T State U., 1970; MD, U. Rochester, 1975. Rsch. asst. U. Rochester, N.Y., 1970-71; intern in medicine Boston U. Hosp., 1975-76, resident in medicine, 1976-78; cardiology fellow Duke U. Med. Ctr., Durham, N.C., 1978-81; asst. prof. medicine, cardiology divsn. Pa. State U., Hershey, 1981-87, assoc. prof., 1987-92, disting. lectr., 1986, prof. medicine, 1992—, cardiology dir. heart transplantation, artificial organs and preclinical tchg. program, dir. cardiology preclinical tng. program, 1984—, dir., cardiology fellow tng. program, 1984-87, dir. cardiac catheterization lab., 1987—, med. dir. cardiac rehab. program, 1988—, dir. clin. cardiology program, 1991—, asst. dean for admissions, 1994—; vice chmn. faculty affairs faculty senate Pa. State U., University Park, 1988—; mem. med. alumni coun. U. Rochester Sch. Medicine and Dentistry, 1992—; various disting. lectureships. Contbr. numerous articles to profl. jours.; editorial reviewer Annals Internal Medicine, 1983—; editorial adv. bd. Primary Cardiology, 1985—. Mem. Pa. Coun. on Aging, Harrisburg, 1989—. Recipient Outstanding Physician award Pa. State U. Sch. Medicine, 1984, Disting. Tchg. awards, 1988-89, Tchr. of Yr. award, 1991, Disting. Prof. award for tchg., 1991, Outstanding Tchr. of Yr. award med. sch. class of 1995, 93, Outstanding Tchr. of Yr. award med. sch. class of 1997, 1995, Alumni Excellence award N.C. A&T State U., 1986, Disting. Alumni award Nat. Assn. Equal Opportunity in Higher Edn., 1987. Fellow Am. Coll. Cardiology, Am. Coll. Angiology; mem. AAAS, Am. Heart Assn. (fellow coun. on clin. cardiology, rsch. com. Pa. affiliate 1992—), Am. Fedn. Clin. Rsch., Am. Assn. Cardiovasc. and Pulmonary Rehab. (expert panel cardiac rehab. guidelines project 1992—, chair cardiac rehab. criteria devel. panel 1995—), N.Y. Acad. Scis., Alpha Omega Alpha. Mem. United Ch. of Christ. Office: Pa State U Coll Medicine Divsn Cardiology PO Box 850 Hershey PA 17033-0850

DAVIS, EDGAR GLENN, science and health policy executive; b. Indpls., May 12, 1931; s. Thomas Carroll and Florence Isabelle (Watson) D. m. Margaret Louise Alandt, June 20, 1953; children: Anne-Elizabeth Davis Polestra, Amy Alandt, Edgar Glenn Jr. AB, Kenyon Coll., 1953; MBA, Harvard U., 1955. With Eli Lilly & Co., Indpls., 1958-91, mgr. budgeting and profit planning, 1963-66, mgr. econ. studies, 1966-67, mgr. Atlanta sales dist., 1967-68, dir. market research and sales manpower planning, 1968-69, dir. mktg. plans, 1969-74, exec. dir. pharm. mktg. planning, 1974-75, exec. dir. corp. affairs, 1975-76, v.p. corp. affairs, 1976-90, v.p. health care policy, 1990; pres., chmn. bd. dirs. Centre for Health Sci. Info., Boston, 1990—; fellow Ctr. for Bus. and Govt. Kennedy Sch. of Govt. Harvard U., 1991—; exec.-in-residence Butler U. Coll. of Bus., Indpls.; exec. in residence Coll. of Bus., Butler U.; pres. Eli Lilly and Co. Found., 1976-88; mem. Inst. Ednl. Mgmt., Harvard U. Grad. Sch. Edn., 1987; mem. Inst. Medicine NAS, 1981—; chmn. staff Bus. Roundtable Task Force on Health, 1981-85; U.S. rep. UN Indsl. Devel. Orgn. Conf., Lisbon, 1980; participant UNIDO meeting of experts on pharms., 1981; rep. to UN Commn. on Narcotic Drugs, Vienna, 1981, UN Econ. and Social Coun., N.Y.C., 1981, UN Indsl. Devel. Orgn. Conf. Casablanca, 1981, Budapest, 1983, Madrid, 1987; trustee Boston Biomed. Rsch. Inst., 1991—; fellow Ctr. for Bus. and Govt., Kennedy Sch. Govt., Harvard U.; co-chmn. Harvard Conf. on Govt. Role in Civilian Tech., 1992, Harvard Conf. Pharmaceutical Rsch., Innovation and Pub. Policy, 1993; co-chmn. Harvard Biotech. Roundtable, 1991—; vis. scholar and advisor Health and Welfare Unit, Inst. for Econ. Affairs, London, vis. scholar Green Coll. Oxford (Eng.) U., 1994—; chmn. Nat. Fund for Med. Edn., San Francisco; lectr. in field. Contbr. articles to profl. jours. Pres., chmn. bd. Indpls. Health Inst., 1988-91; trustee Kenyon Coll., Gambier, Ohio, Eiteljorg Mus. Am. Indian and Western Art; pres. bd. trustees Boston Biomed. Rsch. Inst.; chmn. Nat. Fund for Med. Edn., 1996—; bd. dirs. Carnegie Coun. on Ethics and Internat. Affairs and accredited nongovtl. observer rep. to UN, Goodwill Found. Ind. Inc., 1987-95, Sta. WFYI Pub. TV, Indpls., 1983-91, Indpls. Mus. Art, Am. Symphony Orch. League, 1987-92, Nat. Health Coun., 1984-91, Pub. Affairs Coun., Washington, Nat. Fund for Med. Edn.; bd. advisors Christian Theol. Sem., N.C. Schl Arts, Bishops Sch., LaJolla, Calif.; chmn. bd. dirs. Ind. Repertory Theatre, 1979-85; vice chmn., exec. com., bd. dirs. Indpls. Symphony Orch. and Ind. State Symphony Soc., 1977-91; chmn. task force on fine arts Commn. for Future of Butler U.; chmn. exec. com. Pan Am. Econ. Leadership Conf., 10th Pan Am. Games, Indpls.; mem. Chgo. Coun. on Fgn. Rels. Fellow The Hudson Inst. (sr. adj. Indpls.); mem. NAM (bd. dirs., vice-chmn. health policy com. 1987-91), Met. Club (Washington), Overseas Press Club, Edgartown Yacht Club, Naples (Fla.) Yacht Club, Woodstock Club, Royal Poinciana Golf Club (Fla.), Contemporary Club, Lambs Club, Crooked Stick Golf Club, Chappaquiddick Beach Club, N.Y. Yacht Club, Traders Point Hunt Club, Reform Club London. Office: Harvard U Ctr for Bus and Govt Kennedy Sch of Govt Weil Hall 79 JFK St Cambridge MA 02138

DAVIS, EILEEN PEARL, emergency room nurse; b. Hartland, Maine, Apr. 27, 1957; d. Arthur A. and Roslyn Bernice (Sklar) Firestone; m. William Joseph Davis, June 29, 1980; 1 child, Ashley Mary. BSN, San Jose State U., 1979. RN II, Calif., Md.; cert. in ACLS and PALS; CPR instr. Nurse neurosurg. floor O'Connors Hosp., Santa Clara, Calif.; nurse emergency dept. St. Mary's Hosp., Leonardtown, Md. Home: 45265 Elm Brook Dr California MD 20619-3215

DAVIS, ELIZABETH ANN, nursing administrator; b. West Chester, Pa., Oct. 4, 1955; d. George Thomas and Elizabeth Jean (Lockard) D. Diploma in nursing, Gowanda Psychiatric Sch., Helmuth, N.Y., 1976; BSN, So. Oreg. State Coll., 1982; MSN, Tex. Woman's U., 1992. RN, N.Y., Oreg.; cert. clin. specialist psychiat. and mental health nursing, nursing adminstrn., advanced. Head nurse Ea. Oreg. Hosp. & Tng. Ctr., Pendleton, 1977-80; community health staff nurse Lane County Mental Health, Eugene, Oreg., 1982-83; mental health coord. Mercy Med. Ctr., Roseburg, Oreg., 1984-87; dir. quality assurance/utilization rev./risk mgmt. Community Psychiat. Ctrs., Cypress Pt. Hosp., Houston, 1988-91; psychiat. clin. nurse specialist Starbranch Psychiatry Assocs., P.A., Houston, 1991; dir. nursing svc. Carondelet Psychiat. Care Ctr., Richland, Wash., 1992; nurse mgr. inpatient psychiatry Med. Ctr., Roseburg, Va., 1992—; cons. Community Psychiat. Ctrs., Houston, 1988-91. Chairperson, bd. dirs. Springville (N.Y.) Youth Ctr., 1975-77. Mem. ANA, Nat. Assn. Psychiat. Nurses. Home: 755 NE Nash St Roseburg OR 97470-3534

DAVIS, FLOREA JEAN, social worker; b. Crossett, Ark., Jan. 10, 1953; d. Richard Davis and Geneva (Bedford) Williams. BA in Psychology and Social Work cum laude, Park Coll., Parksville, Mo., 1975; MSW, Kans. U., 1982. Cert. secondary tchr. social studies; lic. social worker, Kans.; lic. specialist clin. social work. Asst dir. Northeast Coordination and Devel. Ctr., Kansas City, Kans., 1975; asst. dir., clin. supr. DRAG Alcohol Ctr., Kansas City, 1975-83; substance abuse counselor Johnson County Substance Abuse Ctr., Shawnee, Kans., 1983-85; clin. social worker Family & Children Services, Inc., Kansas City, 1975-88; area svc. mgr. Agy. Heart of Am. Family Svcs., Kansas City, 1988-90; sr. practitioner Crittenton, Kansas City, Mo., 1990—; dir. Wyandotte Christian Counseling Ctr., Kansas City, Kans., 1995—; instr. U. Kans., Lawrence, 1976: substance abuse specialist, cons. Kansas City area, 1985—; part-time instr. Avila Coll., Kansas City, Mo., 1987—; sr. practitioner Kansas City Outpatient Clinic, Crittenton, Kans., 1990—. Vol. United Way Speakers Bur., 1986—; sec. Women to Women Ministry. Mem. NASW (clin. diplomat), Acad. Cert. Social Workers, Next Step Counseling & Consulting Assn. (pres., founder). Home: 1216 N 77th St Kansas City KS 66112-2408 Office: Crittenton S Kans City 10920 Elm Ave Kansas City MO 64134-4108

DAVIS, GARY JACK, cardiologist, educator; b. Chgo., Feb. 16, 1949; s. Jack and Ellen (Bergman) D.; m. Janet Marie Hubbard, May 10, 1987; children: Chris, Molly, Blake, Quinn. AB, Harvard Coll., 1974; MD, U. Va., Charlottesville. Diplomate Am. Bd. Med. Examiners, Am. Bd. Cardiovascular. Intern and resident in medicine Northwestern Meml. Hosps., Chgo.; attending cardiologist Evanston (Ill.) Hosp., 1980—; clin. assoc. Northwestern U. Med. Sch., Evanston, Ill., 1980—. Fellow Am. Coll. Cardiology. Home: 1861 Hilltop Ln Bannockburn IL 60015

DAVIS, GAY RUTH, psychotherapist, social welfare educator, author, researcher, consultant; b. Bellingham, Wash., Sept. 19, 1935; d. Lee Laverne Wickersham and Altha (Lund) Wickersham Knight; m. Paul Cushing Davis, Dec. 20, 1956; children: Jeffrey Richards, Jennifer Lynn. Student, Brigham Young U., 1953-55; BA summa cum laude, Western Wash. U., 1976; MSW, U. Wash., 1978, PhD, 1985. Diplomate in clin. social work. Dir. Social Svcs. Sound Health Assn., Tacoma, 1977-78; social work profl. Harborview Med. Ctr., Seattle, 1979-81; instr. Sch. Social Work U. Wash., Seattle, 1984-85; pvt. practice cons. social work and psychotherapy Seattle, 1985—; prin. investigator NINCDS Rsch., 1980-81; coord. Adult Svcs. Tng. Project, U. Wash., 1983-84. Contbr. articles to profl. jours. Mem. adv. bd. LDS Social Svcs., 1990-91. Grantee Wash. Dept. Health and Human Services, 1981-82. Mem. NASW (qualified clin. social worker), Nat. Registry Clin. Social Work, Am. Profl. Soc. on Abuse of Children, Gerontol. Soc. Am., Wash. Assn. Social Workers, Wash. Profl. Soc. on Abuse of Children, Assn. Mormon Counselors and Psychotherapists. Democrat. Mormon.

DAVIS, GENEVIEVE ANNA, clinical counselor, marriage and family therapist; b. Detroit, Oct. 31, 1953; m. Thomas William Laga, May 18, 1976 (div. Jan. 1987). Student, Calif. State U., Fullerton, 1971-73; BA in Theater Edn., Prescott Coll., 1975; MA in Psychology and Counseling, Antioch U., 1986. Dir. clin. counselor, marriage and family therapist Biofeedback Clinic of Santa Fe, 1984—; clin. counselor, marriage and family therapist Women's Health Svcs., Santa Fe, 1990—; mem. clin. stds. com. N.Mex. Counseling and Therapy Practice Bd., Santa Fe, 1994—; grief intervention counselor Office of the Med. Investigator, State of N.Mex.; small group coord., advisor N.Mex. Dept. Health, Women's Wellness Project, Santa Fe, 1985—. Mem. smoking cessation group Smoke Free Santa Fe-Nat. Cancer Inst.; mem. adv. bd. N.Mex. Respiratory Therapy, 1988—; mem. N.Mex. Acupuncture Bd., Santa Fe, 1994. Mem. Assn. for Applied Psychophysiology and Biofeedback, N.Mex. Soc. Biofeedback and Behavioral Medicine (pres. 1993-94, treas. 1995-96), N.Am. Soc. Psychol. Assn., Biofeedback Cert. Inst. Am. (cert.). Office: 546 Harkle Rd Ste C Santa Fe NM 87505

DAVIS, GEORGE A., pharmacologist, medical researcher. Pharmacy intern Kroger Pharmacy, Little Rock, 1990-93; pharmaceutics lab asst. Clin. Pharmacokinetics Lab. U. Ark., 1991-93; clin. staff pharmacist Med. Ctr. U. Ky., Lexington, 1993—, lectr., 1995—; mem. resident recruitment com., resident survey com. U. Ky. Med. Ctr., 1993-95; presenter in field. Jour. referee Pharmacotherapy, Annals of Pharmacotherapy, Am. Jour. Health Sys. Pharmacy; contbr. articles to profl. jours. Psychiat. Drug Therapy fellow Am. Soc. Hosp. Pharmacists, 1995, Geriatric Drug Therapy fellow, 1996. Mem. Am. Soc. Health Sys. Pharmacists, Am. Coll. Clin. Pharmacy, Kappa Psi. Office: U Ky Coll Pharmacy 800 Rose St Rm 117 Lexington KY 40536-6973*

DAVIS, JAMES ANTHONY, psychiatrist; b. Orange, Calif., Dec. 10, 1941; s. Robert Perry and Ethel (Sturbaum) D.; m. Margaret Moloney Davis, 1978; children: Meghan, Ryan. BA with honors, Stanford U., 1966, MD, 1968. Cert. Am. Bd. Psychiatry and Neurology. Rotating intern and resident internal medicine USPHS Hops., Staten Island, N.Y., 1968-71; resident psychiatry Montefiore Hosp., Bronx, N.Y., 1972-75; fellow in adult psychotherapy L.I. Jewish Hillside Med. Ctr., N.Y., 1975-77; Med. dir. Project Outreach L.I. Jewish Hillside Med. Ctr., Glen Oaks, N.Y., 1975-80; med. dir. young adult program Four Winds Hosp., Katonah, N.Y., 1980-89; med. dir. Southgate Four Winds Hosp., 1989-93; program dir. Lodge Four Winds Hosp., 1993—. Sr. asst. surgeon USPHS, 1968-71. Mem. Am. Psychiat. Assn., Phi Beta Kappa. Democrat. Home: PO Box 371 Cross River NY 10518-0371 Office: Four Winds Hosp 800 Cross River Rd Katonah NY 10536-9640

DAVIS, JAMES EVANS, general and thoracic surgeon, parliamentarian, author; b. Goldsboro, N.C., Mar. 2, 1918; s. Daniel Wilborn and Annie Maude (Evans) D.; m. Margaret Royall, June 14, 1943; children James Evans Jr. (dec.), Kenneth Royall, George Harrison. AB in Chemistry, U. N.C., 1940; MD, U. Pa., 1943; DSc (hon.), U. N.C., 1988. Diplomate Am. Bd. Surgery. Intern N.Y. Hosp. Cornell U. Med. Ctr., 1944-45, resident in surgery, 1946-50, chief surg. resident, 1950-51; instr. surgery Med. Sch., Cornell U., N.Y.C., 1945-51; prof. clin. surgery Sch. Medicine, U. N.C., Chapel Hill, 1954—; assoc. prof. clin. surgery Med. Sch., Duke U., Durham, N.C., 1954—; chmn. dept. surgery Watts and Durham Regional Hosp., 1954-80; founding chmn. bd. dirs. N.C. Inst. Medicine, Durham, 1983—; founding pres. Med. Mut. Ins. Co. N.C., Raleigh, 1975-88. Author: Major Ambulatory Surgery, 1987, Rules of Order, 1992; mem. editorial bd. Jour. Ambulatory Care Mgmt., 1980—; contbr. articles to profl. jours. Chmn.

City of Medicine Program, Durham, 1981—; mem. Bipartisan Commn. on Comprehensive Health Care, 1989-90; trustee Durham Gen. Hosp., 1991—, N.C. Sch. Sci. and Math., 1995—. Lt. (j.g.) USNR, 1945-46, lt. comdr. res. ret., Korea. Recipient Disting. Svc. award U. N.C. Sch. Med., Chapel Hill, 1960, Disting. Svc. award Gen. Alumni Assn. U. N.C., 1975, Man of Yr. civic award, Durham, 1988. Mem. AMA (pres. 1988-89, speaker ho. dels. 1983-87), ACS (gov. 1980-86, pres. N.C. chpt. 1978-79, Disting. Surgeon award 1991), N.C. Med. Soc. (pres. 1975-76), N.C. Surg. Soc. (pres. 1980-81), Am. Soc. Gen. Surgeons (founding pres. 1992—), Med. Speakers Assn. (founding pres. 1992—), Greater Durham C. of C. (pres. 1983-84), N.C. Sch. Sci. and Math. (trustee), Hope Valley Country Club, Country Club N.C., Coral Bay Beach Club. Democrat. Episcopalian. Home: 7 Beverly Dr Durham NC 27707-2223

DAVIS, JAMES ROYCE, microbiologist, educator; b. Rison, Ark., Apr. 6, 1938; s. Robert Hugh and Juanita (Pierson) D.; m. Barbara Ann Martin, May 29, 1959; children—Lezlie Dyan, Kimberly Nicole, Amy Suzanne. Student Miss. Delta Jr. Coll., 1956-57; B.S., Tex. A&I U., 1960; M.S. in Microbiology, U. Houston, 1962, Ph.D., 1965. Research asst. U. Houston, 1960-65, lab. teaching asst., 1960-62, teaching fellow in gen. biology, 1962-63, lectr. med. microbiology for nurses, 1963-64, instr. in microbiology, 1965; asst. prof. in microbiology Dental Br. U. Tex., Houston, 1965-68; dir. microbiology sect. clin. lab. Methodist Hosp., Houston, 1968—, assoc. dir. labs., 1983—; asst. prof. microbiology Baylor Coll. Medicine, Houston, 1968-84, asst. prof. pathology, 1973-84, assoc. prof. pathology, microbiology and immunology, 1984—; cons. clin. pathology service Harris County Hosp. Dist. Adv. bd. Bac/Talk newsletter; contbr. papers to sci. publs. and confs. Mem. Am. Soc. Microbiology (nat. and Tex. br.), Tex. Med. Ctr. Research Soc. (treas. 1967-68), Houston Soc. Clin. Pathologists, Southwestern Assn. Clin. Microbiologists, Sigma Xi, Beta Beta Beta. Office: Methodist Hosp 6565 Fannin St # 205 Houston TX 77030-2704

DAVIS, JESSICA G., clinical geneticist, pediatrician; b. Bklyn., Apr. 3, 1934; d. Nathan S. and Sylvia (Teplitz) Grosof; m. Andrew C. Davis, June 17, 1956; children: Jennifer Davis Hall, David. BA, Wellesley Coll., 1955; MD, Columbia U., 1959. Diplomate Am. Bd. Med. Genetics. Intern pediatrics St. Luke's Hosp.-Columbia U.; fellow Albert Einstein Coll. Medicine Yeshiva U., N.Y.C., 1961-68, instr. Albert Einstein Coll. Medicine, 1962, asst. prof. Albert Einstein Coll. Medicine, 1968-74; assoc. prof. clin. pediatric Coll. Medicine Cornell U., N.Y.C., 1974—; cons. March of Dimes, N.Y.C., 1974—, Hastings Inst., Briarcliff, N.Y., 1979—. Contbr. articles to profl. jours. Recipient numerous grants. Founding fellow Am. Coll. Med. Genetics; mem. Am. Soc. Human Genetics (past chmn.), Coun. Regional Genetics Network (pres. 1991-94). Office: Cornell U/NY Hosp 525 E 68th St Rm HT 150 New York NY 10021-4873

DAVIS, JOAN, medical laboratory administrator; b. Clayton, Ga., July 9, 1952; d. Lawrence and Elzie Shook; m. John C. Davis; children: Jonathan Chad, Jamie Elaina. AAS, Truett-McConnell Coll., 1996. Med. lab. mgr. Rabun G. Meml. Hosp., Clayton, 1982—; med. tech. adv. bd. Southwest C.C., Sylva, N.C., 1988. Mem. Phi Theta Kappa. Home: PO Box 762 Clayton GA 30525

DAVIS, JOHN CRISPEN, family physician; b. Beaumont, Tex., Jan. 22, 1928; s. Earle Davis and Merle (Blackwell) D.; m. Bettye Pickens, June 20, 1953 (dec. Aug. 1990); children: Susan, Steven, Charles, Nancy; m. Emily Davis, July 27, 1991. BA, U. Tex., 1950; MD, U. Tex. Med. Br., Galveston, 1954. Intern Robert B. Green Hosp., San Antonio, 1954-55; pvt. practice Trott Clinic, Yoakum, Tex., 1955-58, High-Davis Clinic, Cuero, Tex., 1958—. Cpl. U.S. Army, 1946-48. Fellow Am. Acad. Family Practice. Republican. Methodist. Home: 1210 E Morgan Cuero TX 77954 Office: Cuero Rural Health Clinic 2500 N Esplanade #102 Cuero TX 77954

DAVIS, JOHN MIHRAN, surgeon, educator; b. N.Y.C., Aug. 13, 1946; s. Drought Delaney and Ruth Radcliff (Kalaidjian) D.; m. Marlene Morgan, Oct. 13, 1973; children—Nicholas Mihran, Elisabeth Whitfield. B.A., Columbia Coll., 1968; M.D., Wayne State U., 1972. Diplomate Am. Bd. Surgery. Intern, then resident N.Y. Hosp., N.Y.C., 1972-77; asst. attending surgeon N.Y. Hosp.-Cornell U. Med. Ctr., N.Y.C., 1977—, Jamaica Hosp., N.Y., 1980—; asst. prof. surgery Cornell U. Med. Coll., 1977-84, assoc. prof., 1984—, also assoc. dir. trauma, 1984—. Author: Andrew W. Mellon, Teacher-Scientist, 1983. Fellow ACS; mem. Am. Burn Assn., Surg. Infection Soc. (charter), N.Y. County-State Med. Soc., N.Y. Surg. Soc., Soc. Univ. Surgeons. Home: 450 E 63rd St New York NY 10021-7928

DAVIS, JOHN T., optometrist; b. Leavenworth, Kans., June 14, 1965; s. Gerald Lynn and Karen Sue (Doebelle) D. AS, Dodge City (Kans.) C.C., 1985; BS, Kans. State U., 1987; OD, U. Houston, 1992. Registered optometrist, Kans. Pvt. practice, Overland Park, Kans., 1992—. Mem. Am. Optometric Assn., Kans. Optometric Assn. Roman Catholic. Office: Eye Assocs Overland Park 10120 W 119th St Overland Park KS 66213

DAVIS, JOHN WANDELL, JR., medical laboratory technology educator, researcher; b. Far Rockaway, N.Y., Jan. 12, 1946; s. John Wandell Sr. and Mary Ann (Schust) D.; m. Maria Antonia Milan, Aug. 2, 1975; children: Matthew, Peter. BS in Biology, U. Notre Dame, Ind., 1967; MS, PhD in Biology, St. John's U., Jamaica, N.Y., 1975. Tchr. Long Beach (N.Y.) Jr. High Sch., 1967-68; lectr. Bronx Community Coll. CUNY, 1970-74, asst. prof., 1974-78, assoc. prof., 1978-82, prof., 1982—; adj. assoc. prof. CUNY Med. Sch., N.Y.C., 1980-88 Pace U. Grad. Sch. Nursing, Pleasantville, N.Y., 1980-82; project counselor space life scis. tng. program NASA, Cape Canaveral, Fla., summer 1989. Contbr. articles to profl. jours. Coach White Plains (N.Y.) Youth Soccer Assn., 1987—, pres. 1991-92; elected parent White Plains Post Rd. Sch. Leadership Coun., 1989-91; faculty adv. coun. Rsch. Found. CUNY, 1992—, bd. dirs., 1994—. CUNY fellow, 1978-79, 88; grantee NIH, 1982-85, 85-88, 89-91, 91-94, 94—. Mem. Am. Soc. for Microbiology (chair G. divsn. 1990-91), Internat. Orgn. for Mycoplasmology, N.Y. Acad. Scis. (spkr. Scientists in the Schs. program 1981—). Home: 100 Concord Ave White Plains NY 10606-2232 Office: CUNY/Bronx Community Coll University Avenue St Bronx NY 10453

DAVIS, JOSEPH E., JR., urologist; b. Sumter, S.C., July 1, 1949; s. Joseph E. and Elizabeth (Hobbie) D.; m. Ruth Roper Hutchinson, July 25, 1981; children: Joseph E. III, Ann Hughston. BS in Chemistry, Clemson U., 1971; MD, Med. U. S.C., 1975. Pvt. practice Montgomery, Ala. Maj. USAF, 1980-84. Recipient Commendation medal, 1984. Episcopalian. Office: 2015 Normandie Dr Montgomery AL 36111

DAVIS, JUDI RATLIFF, dietitian; b. San Antonio, Nov. 5, 1944; d. Wortham Wayne and Margaret (Bales) Ratliff; m. Frank Eugene Davis, Feb. 11, 1967 (dec. 1994); children: Darrell Wayne, Douglas Alexander, Deborah Michelle. BS, U. Tex., 1966; MS, Tex. Women's U., 1978. Clin. dietitian Rex Hosp., Raleigh, N.C., 1967-69; nutrition cons. nursing homes S.W. Va., 1969-70; clin. dietitian Bapt. Meml. Hosp., San Antonio, 1970-71, Park North Gen. Hosp., San Antonio, 1972-73; food and nutrition cons. The Sugar Assn., Washington, 1975-78; instr. Tarrant County Jr. Coll., Ft. Worth, 1976-78; dietitian Greenhouse Health Spa, Arlington, Tex., 1979-81; pvt. practice cons. dietitian Arlington, 1981-87; chief dietitian Fort Worth State Sch., 1987-90; dept. head nutrition therapy Rehab. Hosp. North Tex., Arlington, 1990-91; cons. Headstart Program, Ft. Worth, 1992—; chief dietitian home and cmty. based svcs. Tarrant County Mental Health Mental Retardation, Fort Worth, 1994—. Author: Diabetic Meal Plan Handbook, 1987, (with others) Applied Nutrition and Diet Therapy, 1988, 2d edit., 1994, Nurturing Young Minds and Bodies, 1995; created several slide presentations, 1978-79. Dir. Nutrition Task Force Am. Heart Assn. Tarrant County, 1978-80. Mem. Am. Dietetic Assn., Tex. Dietetic Assn., Ft. Worth Dietetic Assn. Home: 3103 Westador Dr Arlington TX 76015-2353

DAVIS, JUDITH EVELYN, retired nurse, consultant; b. Denison, Ohio, Dec. 19, 1939; d. Willard Albert and Lilyan E. (Thomas) O'Neil; m. Michael Kinney O'Heeron, July 24, 1960 (div. 1966); children: Michael Rollie, Patrick Todd, Peter Timothy; m. Maurice Eugene Davis, Aug. 19, 1966; 1 dau., Dawn Denise. Student Sam Houston U., 1957-60, Baylor Coll. Medicine, 1957-59, U. Houston, 1971; grad. Meth. Hosp. Sch. Nursing, 1960; B.S. in Nursing, U. Tex., 1979. Office nurse pediatrics, Bryan, Tex., 1960-62; charge nurse A&M Coll. Hosp., College Station, Tex., 1962-63; inservice instr. Meth. Hosp., Houston, 1963-64; dir. nursing Moody House, Galveston, Tex., 1964-65; sch. nurse Brazosport Ind. Sch. Dist., Freeport, Tex., 1966-78, supr. nurses, 1978-81; nurse cons. Infant Devel. Ctr., Brazoria County Activity Ctr. for Retarded, Lake Jackson, Tex., 1982-83; ednl. coord. Intermedics Inc., Angleton, Tex., 1983-85; health educator Tex. Sch. for Deaf, Austin, 1985-88, supr. health svcs., 1987-88, coord., 1988-90; sch. nurse Dahlstrom Mid. Sch. Hays Consol. Sch. Dist., Buda, Tex., 1990-95; ret., 1995; part-time surg. and med. ICU nurse Community Hosp., Freeport, 1966-71, part-time med. intensive care nurse and recruitment nurse, 1981-83; part-time instr. St. Philips Sch. Nursing, New Braunfels, Tex., 1996—; tchr. constrn. miniature dolls and plaques, owner The Calico Owl. Brazoria County Med. Aux. scholar, 1957-60; Good Samaritan scholar, 1957-60; Brazoria County Nurses Assn. scholar, 1978. Mem. Brazoria County Assn. for Prevention of Teenage Pregnancies. Baptist. Club: Miniature of Brazosport. Author nurse's manual for Tex. Pub. Law sch. dists. 94-142; co-author physicians manual for pub. law. dists. 94-142.

DAVIS, JUNE LEAH, retired psychologist; b. Craigsville, W.Va., Nov. 10, 1922; d. Ernest Layton and Bessie May (Bostic) Taylor; m. Charles William Heasley, Jan. 16, 1943 (div. 1961); children: Denasse Ann Heasley Dugan, Wanda Lori Heasley Schwartz. BA, Glenville (W.Va.) State Coll., 1962; MA, Ohio State U., 1967. Cert. psychologist, Ohio. Tchr. Nicholas County Bd. Edn., Summersville, W.Va., 1943-46, 1958-60; tchr. Columbus (Ohio) Bd. Edn., 1962-70, sch. psychologist, 1970-96; ret., 1996. Active First Baptist Ch., Columbus, 1975—. Mem. Sch. Psychologists Ctrl. Ohio (pres.; Best Practice award 1987), Ohio Sch. Psychologists Assn., Ctrl. Ohio Psychologists Assn. (Hueslman award for outstanding svc. 1989). Democrat. Home: 5392 Ponderosa Dr Columbus OH 43231

DAVIS, KAREN PADGETT, fund executive; b. Blackwell, Okla., Nov. 14, 1942; d. Walter Dwight and Thelma Louise (Kohler) Padgett; 1 child, Kelly Denise Collins. BA, Rice U., 1965, PhD, 1969. Asst. prof. econs. Rice U., 1969-70; econ. policy fellow Social Security Adminstrn. Brookings Instn., Washington, 1970-71, rsch. assoc., 1971-74, sr. fellow, 1974-77; dep. asst. sec. for planning and evaluation, health HEW, Washington, 1977-80; adminstr. health resources adminstrn. USPHS, Washington, 1980-81; prof. Johns Hopkins U., Balt., 1981-92; chmn., 1983-92; exec. v.p. Commonwealth Fund, N.Y.C., 1992-94, pres., 1995—; bd. dirs. Somatix Therapy Corp.; bd. dirs. Mt. Sinai MEd. Ctr., 1995—; mem. Physician Payment Rev. Commn., 1986-94; dir. Commonwealth Health Fund Commn. on Elderly People Living Alone, 1985-91; vis. lectr. Harvard U., 1974-75. Author: National Health Insurance: Benefits, Costs and Consequences, 1975, Health and the War on Poverty, 1978, Medicare Policy: New Directions for Health and Long-Term Care, 1986, Health Care Cost Containment, 1990. Bd. dirs. Mt. Sinai Med. Ctr., 1995—. Mem. Inst. Medicine, Am. Econs. Assn., Phi Beta Kappa. Democrat. Methodist. Home: 176 E 77th St New York NY 10021-1908 Office: The Commonwealth Fund The Harkness House 1 E 75th St New York NY 10021-2601

DAVIS, KEITH EUGENE, psychologist, educator, consultant; b. Clifton, N.C., May 15, 1936; s. Ted Eugene and Mary Flossie (Rol) D.; m. Dorothy Ann Reeves, Feb. 23, 1968; 1 child, Kristin Lee; children from previous marriage: Rachel, Rebecca, Jessica. BA, Duke U., 1958, PhD, 1963. Instr. psychology Princeton U., 1961-62; asst. prof. U. Colo., Boulder, 1962-67, assoc. prof., 1967-70; prof., chmn. dept. psychology Livingston Coll., Rutgers U., New Brunswick, N.J., 1970-73; prof. U.S.C., Columbia, 1973—; adj. prof. health adminstrn., health promotion/edn. U. S.C., Columbia, 1991—, univ. provost, 1974-78; chair dept. psychology U.S.C., Columbia, 1994—; founder The Paradigm Group, mgmt. cons.; mgmt. cons., mem. population study sect. Nat. Inst. Child Health and Human Devel., 1973-76; mem. mental health rsch. edn. rev. com. NIMH, 1979—, chmn., 1980-83; chmn. State Plan Adv. Com., S.C. State Dept. Mental Health, 1976-78; pres. past participants Greater Columbia Forum, 1975-76. Author: Advances in Experimental Social Psychology, 1963; author, editor: Advanced in Descriptive Psychology, 1981; editor: The Social Construction of the Person, 1985; contbr. to Thoretical Perspectives on Personal Relationships, 1993; assoc. editor: Personal Relationships; contbr. 85 articles to profl. jours. Bd. dirs. Columbia Area Mental Health Ctr., 1976-82, chmn. bd. dirs., 1981. Woodrow Wilson fellow, 1958-59, So. Fellowships Fund fellow, 1958-61. Mem. APA, Am. Sociol. Assn., Internat. Soc. for Study of Personal Relationships (program chair 1992), Mind Assn., Nat. Coun. Family Rels., Soc. Descriptive Psychology (1st pres. 1979-81), Phi Beta Kappa, Omicron Delta Kappa. Home: 1808 Catawba St Columbia SC 29205-3010 Office: U SC Dept Psychology Columbia SC 29208

DAVIS, KENNETH, physician; b. Cin., Dec. 22, 1950; s. Kenneth Sr. and Flora Margaret (Smothers) D.; m. Johnie Mae Brocks, Oct. 14, 1978; children: Rhiannon, Naima, Olivia. BS in Biology, U. Cin., 1972; MD, St. Louis U., 1976. Instr. surgery N.Y. Med. Coll., N.Y.C., 1982-84; asst. prof. surgery U. Cin., 1984-91, assoc. prof. surgery & anesthesia, 1991—. Office: U Cin 231 Bethesda Ave Cincinnati OH 45267-0558

DAVIS, LANAY FLINT, psychologist; b. Pocatello, Idaho, Apr. 25, 1933; d. Franklin Hyde and Adelia (Smith) Flint; m. Gordon B. Davis, Aug. 19, 1954; children: Alison, Jennifer, Clark, Flint. BA, Idaho State U., 1954; MSW, U. Minn., 1981, PhD, 1987. Lic. marriage and family therapist, lic. psychologist. Psychologist, therapist Loring Family Svc., Mpls., 1987-89; psychologist Mpls. and St. Paul, 1989—. Mem. LDS Ch. Office: 2301 Como Ave Saint Paul MN 55108-1718

DAVIS, LAWRENCE WILLIAM, radiation oncologist; b. N. Braddock, Pa., Sept. 5, 1935; s. William Paul Davis and Julia Helen Zukas; children: James G., Karen E. BS, Juniata Coll., Huntington, Pa., 1957; MA, U. Pa., 1969; MBA, Temple U., 1984; MD, Georgetown U., 1961. Diplomate Am. Bd. Radiology (trustee 1981-95, asst. exec. dir. radiation oncology 1994—); lic. physician Pa., Md., N.Y., Ga. Asst. instr. radiology U. Pa., Phila., 1962-66, instr. radiology, 1966, 68-69, asst. prof. radiology, 1969-72, assoc. prof. radiology, 1972-75; prof. radiation therapy Thomas Jefferson Sch. Medicine, 1975-84; prof. and chmn. radiation oncology Albert Einstein Coll. Medicine, Bronx, 1984-91, Emory U., Atlanta, 1991—; cons. Armed Forces Radiobiology Rsch. Inst., Bethesda, 1968-70; exec. com. of med. staff Montefiore Med. Ctr., 1984-87, 1990-91, div. coun., 1988-89; prof. svc. com. Phila. div. Am. Cancer Soc., 1970-75. Contbr. numerous articles to profl. jours.; assoc. editor Internat. Jour. Radiation Oncology, 1986—; editorial bd. Neuro Oncology, 1989—, assoc. editor, 1991—; editorial bd Am. Jour. Clin. Oncology, 1991—. Capt. USAF, 1966-68. Fellow Am. Cancer Soc., Phila., 1963-64, NIH, 1964-66, Am. Cancer Soc. traineeship, 1968-71. Fellow Am. Coll. Radiology; mem. AMA, AAAS, Am. Assn. Cancer Rsch., Am. Coll. Radiology (commn. on radiation oncology 1981-90, bd. chancellors 1993—), Am. Soc. Therapeutic Radiology and Oncology (chmn. bd. 1988-89, pres. 1987-88), Am. Coll. Hosp. Adminstrs., Am. Mgmt. Assn., Am. Radium Soc. (pres. 1992-93), Am. Soc. Clin. Oncology, Med. Assn. Atlanta, N.Y. Acad. Scis., Ga. State Med. Soc., Ga. State Radiol. Soc., Radiation Rsch. Soc., Radiol. Soc. N.Am., Alpha Omega Alpha Office: Emory Clinic 1365 Clifton Rd NE Atlanta GA 30307-1013

DAVIS, LILA ROSS, public health officer; b. Balt., June 16, 1941; d. Robert P. and Lila (Norfleet) D. BA in Psychology, Mary Washington Coll., 1963; cert. in med. record adminstrn., USPHS Sch. for Med. Record Adminstrs., 1964. Chief med. record dept DePaul Hosp., Norfolk, Va., 1964-66, Kings Daughters Children's Hosp., Norfolk, 1966-69; research analyst Norfolk Gen. Hosp., 1969-73; commd. officer USPHS, 1973, advanced through grades to capt., 1983; dep. chief med. record dept. USPHS Hosp., Norfolk, 1973-74; chief USPHS Hosp., 1974-79; chief med. record dept. USPHS Hosp., San Francisco, 1979-81; dep. dir. USPHS Health Data Ctr., Lanham, Md., 1981-83, dir., 1983-86; dir. USPHS Health Data Ctr., GWL Hansen's Disease Ctr., Carville, La., 1986—; cons. Fed. Bur. Prisons; participant, cons. disaster med. assistance program Bur. Health Care and Delivery, Rockville, Md., 1983-86. Mem. Am. Med. Record Assn., La. Med. Record Assn., Commd. Officer Assn. USPHS, Assn. Mil. Surgeons U.S. Presbyterian. Lodge: Zonta. Office: GWL Hansens Disease Ctr Carville LA 70721

DAVIS, LINDA ANN, anesthesiologist, physician; b. Riverside, Calif., Aug. 2, 1957. DO, Kirksville (Mo.) Coll. Osteo., 1985. Diplomate Am. Bd. Pain Mgmt., Am. Bd. Anesthesiology. Intern Phoenix Gen. Hosp., 1985-86; resident in anesthesiology and pain mgmt. Cleve. Clinic, 1987-88, U. Ariz., 1988-90; anesthesiologist Marcus Lawrence Med. Ctr., Cottonwood, Ariz., 1990—; pain mgmt. specialist Ctr. for Back Pain and Headache, Cottonwood, Ariz., 1992—; med. dir. Cottonwood Day Surgery Ctr., 1994—. Recipient Achievement award Janet Glasgow Found., 1985. Mem. Am. Soc. Anesthesiologists, Am. Acad. Pain Mgmt., Am. Soc. Pain Practitioners, Ariz. Soc. Anesthesiologists, Ariz. Osteo. Med. Assn., Phi Beta Kappa. Office: Ctr for Back Pain and Headache 55 S 6th St Cottonwood AZ 86326

DAVIS, LUCY TOLBERT, psychologist, educator; b. Greenville, S.C.; d. Joseph Augustus and Margaret (Shirley) Tolbert; m. Ron Willson Davis, Aug. 28, 1948; children: Ronald Redd, Margaret Willson, Elisabeth Southard. BA, Erskine Coll, 1946; MA, Columbia U., 1948, EdD, 1955. Lic. psychologist, N.C. Guidance testing New Trier High Sch., Winnetka, Ill., 1948-50; exec. dir. Student Life Office Columbia U., N.Y.C., 1950-54; dir. counseling and guidance Centennial Schs., Southampton, Pa., 1954-57; dir. pupil services Bucks County Schs., Doylestown, Pa., 1957-64; research assoc. Greater Cleve. Research Council, 1964-67; edn. dir. therapeutic edn. program program Duke Med. Ctr., Durham, N.C., 1967-70; prof. dept. edn. Duke U., Durham, 1970—; chmn. of dept., 1982-94; clin. assoc. dept. of child psychiatry Duke U. Med. Ctr., Durham, 1970—; cons. Pa. and N.C. Sch. Systems and State Depts., research assoc. Gov.'s and State's Commns., N.C. Author, editor four books; contbr. articles to profl. jours. Div. head Am. Heart Assoc. and Cancer Drives. President's scholar Columbia U., 1955. Fellow N.C. Psychol. Assn. (program chmn. 1978); mem. N.C. Sch. Psychologist Assn.(Most Outstanding Woman 1985), Am. Psychol. Assn., Nat. Coun. Health Care Psychology Providers. Episcopalian. Home: 705 Gimghoul Rd Chapel Hill NC 27514-3814 Office: Duke U W Duke Bldg Durham NC 27708

DAVIS, MARGARET THACKER, critical care, medical and surgical nurse; b. Greensboro, N.C., June 7, 1925; d. Tiller Foltz and Lucy Wright (Spencer) Thacker; m. Joe Southard Davis, Feb. 4, 1961; 1 child, Dana Lee. Diploma in nursing, Baylor U., Dallas, 1947; student, Ea. N.Mex. U., Roswell, 1978. RN, N.Mex., Tex., Fla. Office nurse Drs. Britt & Cafaro, St. Augustine, Fla., 1947-50, Dr. Robert J. Rowe, Dallas, 1950-61, Dr. F.A. English, Roswell, 1964-74; charge nurse post anesthesia care unit Ea. N.Mex. Med. Ctr., Roswell, 1990-91, ret., 1991. Named Employee of Month, Ea. N.Mex. Med. Ctr., 1985. Mem. ANA, Am. Soc. Post Anesthesia Nurses (charter), Post Anesthesia Nurses Assn. N.Mex. (bd. dirs. 1980-86, sec. 1986-87, legis. com. 1989-90), N.Mex. Nurses Assn. (dist. 5 sec. 1983-85, 91-93, pres. 1986-88, bd. dirs. 1988-90, 92-94, 96—, membership chmn. 1988-90, chmn. nominating com. 1990, Nurse of Yr. award 1989, search for excellence award 1990, dist. 5 honored nurse 1995), Baylor U. Sch. Nursing Alumni Assn.

DAVIS, MARK M., microbiologist, educator; b. Paris, Nov. 27, 1952. BA in Molecular Biology, Johns Hopkins U., 1974; PhD in Molecular Biology, Calif. Inst. Tech., 1981. Fellow lab. of immunology NIH, Bethesda, Md., 1980-82, staff fellow lab. of immunology, 1982-83; asst. prof. med. microbiology Stanford (Calif.) U. Sch. Medicine, 1983-86, assoc. prof. microbiology and immunology, 1986-91, prof. microbiology and immunology, 1991—, dir. predoctoral program in immunology, 1994—; assoc. investigator Howard Hughes Med. Inst., Stanford U., 1987-91, faculty coord., 1989—, investigator, 1991—; instr. Cold Spring Harbor (N.Y.) Lab., 1983; mem. sci. adv. bd. Damon Runyon-Walter Cancer Found., 1985-88; co-organizer UCLA Symposium, 1987; mem. allergy and immunology study sect. divsn. rsch. grants NIH, 1988-92. Recipient Intra-Sci. Rsch. Found. award 1980, Youth Scientist award Passano Found., 1985, Eli Lilly award 1986, Kayden award N.Y. Acad. Scis., 1986, Howard Taylor Ricketts award U. Chgo., 1988, Gairdner Found. award, 1989, King Faisal Internat. prize 1995, Sloan prize Gen. Motors Rsch. Found., 1996; scholar PEW Found. 1985-89. Mem. Nat. Acad. Scis. Office: Stanford U Sch Medicine Howard Hughes Med Inst Beckman Bldg Stanford CA 94305-9991

DAVIS, MARK S., podiatric surgeon; b. Bklyn., May 23, 1965; s. Howard and Ellen (Seeman) D.; m. Tammy Friedman, Sept. 16, 1989; children: Courtney Leigh, Jordan Taylor. Student, Boston U., 1982-85; D in Podiatric Medicine, N.Y. Coll. Podiatric Medicine, 1989. Diplomate Am. Bd. Podiatric Surgery. Podiatric surgeon Footcare Svcs. of S.I. Fellow Am. Coll. Foot and Ankle Surgeons. Office: Footcare Svcs Staten Island 2795 Richmond Ave Staten Island NY 10314

DAVIS, MARTIS JAMES, government official; b. Atlanta, Jan. 25, 1944; s. Martis and Juanita (Turner) D. BA in Liberal Arts, So. Ill. U., 1966, MA in History and Pub. Policy, 1975. Program dir. Nat. Parks Svc., Washington; tchr. govt. and journalism Washington; dir. comm. program Am. U., Washington; v.p. pub. affairs Joint Ctr. for Polit. Studies, Washington, 1970-72; dir. pub. rels. Washington Post, 1972-76; sr. v.p., dir. pub. rels. The Uniworld Group, N.Y.C., 1976-79, 88-89; nat. media rels. mgr. AT&T, N.Y.C., 1979-86; v.p. pub. affairs, dep. commr. N.Y.C. Health & Hosp. Corp., 1986-88; dir., prin. Duke Ellington Sch. of the Arts, Washington, 1989-93; dep. asst. sect. health comm. HHS, Washington, 1993—.

DAVIS, MARY HELEN, psychiatrist, psychoanalyst, educator; b. Kingsville, Tex., Dec. 2, 1949; d. Garnett Stant and Emogene (Campbell) D.; m. Timothy Krenke, Oct. 3, 1992. BA, U. Tex., 1970; MD, U. Tex., Galveston, 1975. Cert. Nat. Bd. Med. Examiners, Am. Bd. Psychiatry and Neurology, Child and Adolescent Psychiatry. Intern, then resident in psychiatry SUNY, Buffalo, 1975-78; fellow in child psychiatry U. Cin., 1978-80; tng. in adult and child psychoanalysis Inst. for Psychoanalysis, Chgo., 1982-92; asst. prof. Med. Coll. Wis., Milw., 1980-89, clin. assoc. prof., 1989-93; med. dir. adolescent treatment unit Milw. Psychiat. Hosp., 1981-86, Schroeder Child Ctr., 1986-89; pvt. practice, 1989-93; med. dir. Devereux-Victoria (Tex.) Psych. Residential Treatment Ctr., 1993-94; pvt. practice Lancaster, Pa., 1995—; cons. Milw. Mental Health Cons., 1980-93, Children's Svc. Soc., Milw., 1982-93. Bd. dirs. Next Generation Theatre, Milw., 1988-90, Next Act Theatre, Milw., 1990-92. Mem. Am. Psychiat. Assn., Am. Soc. Adolescent Psychiatry, Am. Med. Women's Assn., Assn. for Child Psychoanalysis. Baptist.

DAVIS, MARY VIRGINIA, medical and surgical nurse; b. Sumter County, Ala., Nov. 17, 1956; d. Coleman and Eliza Mae (Chambers) Danner; m. Iris Davis, Dec. 25, 1986. Cert. in geriatric nursing, U. Ala., Tuscaloosa, 1979, BSN, 1981; MS in Nursing, Miss. U. for Women, 1990. RN, Ala.; cert. adult nurse practitioner, ANA. Staff nurse Druid City Hosp. Regional Med. Ctr., Tuscaloosa, 1981-85, asst. head nurse, 1985-1990, head nurse, 1990-92; adult nurse practitioner Tuscaloosa County Health Dept., 1992, Bibb Med. Ctr., Centreville, Ala., 1992—. Home: 5607 34th Pl Tuscaloosa AL 35401-6273

DAVIS, MICHAEL, medical educator; b. Bronxville, N.Y., Nov. 14, 1942; s. Pearce and Lucia (Bates) D.; children: Nathaniel, Alexander. BA, Northwestern U., 1965; PhD, Yale U., 1969. Rsch. assoc. Yale U. Sch. Medicine, New Haven, 1969-70, asst. prof., 1970-75, assoc. prof., 1975-84, prof., 1984—. Contbr. over 150 articles to profl. jours.; author 25 book chpts. USPHS Rsch. Scientist award NIMH, 1975-79, 80-85, 85-90, 90-95, 95—; Sterling fellow Yale U., 1969. Fellow Am. Psychol. Assn., Am. Psychol. Soc., AAAS; mem. Soc. for Neurosci., Am. Coll. Neuropsychopharmacology, Soc. for Psychophysiology, Phi Beta Kappa. Office: Yale U 34 Park St New Haven CT 06508

DAVIS, MICHAEL AUSTIN, physician assistant; b. L.A., Mar. 6, 1947; s. John Austin and Clara Ellen (Iiams) D.; m. Linda Ann Morenz, Nov. 23, 1969; children: Michelle Lynn, John Austin. BS in Medicine, Western Mich. U., Kalamazoo, 1974; postgrad., Alderson Broaddus Coll., 1995—. Cert. physician asst. Physician asst. Vicksburg (Mich.) Profl. Svcs., 1974-80; commd. USN, 1980, advanced through grades to lt. comdr., 1994; physician asst. Naval Clinic, Quantico, Va., 1980-83, 87-90, Rota, Spain, 1983-87; physician asst. Med. Dept. USS J.F. Kennedy, Norfolk, Va., 1990-92; White House physician asst. OEOB, WHMU, Washington, 1993-95. Fellow Am. Acad. Physician Assts., Navy Acad. Physician Assts. (bd. dirs. 1995—), Va. Acad. Physician Assts. Lutheran. Home: 14 Sarasota Dr Stafford VA 22554 Office: White House Med Unit Rm 105 OEOB Washington DC 20500

DAVIS, MICHAEL JOHN EARLS, cardiologist; b. Launceston, Tasmania, Australia, July 26, 1952; s. Russell Earls and Irene Merle (Michel) D.; m. Wendy Paterson Manuel, Feb. 10, 1996; children from previous marriage: Rebecca, Timothy, Stephanie. MB, BS, U. Western Australia, Perth, 1976. Rsch. fellow in medicine Harvard U., Cambridge, Mass., 1984-86; clin. rsch. fellow Mass. Gen. Hosp., Boston, 1984-86; specialist lectr. Curtin U., Perth, 1986-89; sr. lectr. U. Western Australia, Perth, 1991—; cardiologist Royal Perth Hosp., 1985—, head dept. cardiology, 1996—; vis. med. officer Repatriation Gen. Hosp., Perth, 1986-94, Hollywood Hosp., Perth, 1994—, head dept. cardiology, 1994—, mem. med. adv. com., 1994—, deputy chmn., 1995; vis. specialist Mount Hosp., Perth, 1988—; cons. cardiologist Princess Margaret Hosp., Perth, 1989—. Rsch. grantee Commonwealth Australia, 1989-93; clin. fellow Nat. Heart Found., 1984-85. Fellow Royal Australian Coll. Physicians; mem. Cardiac Soc. of Australia and New Zealand (sec. electrophysiology working group 1990-91), N.Am. Soc. Pacing and Electrophysiology, Am. Coll. Cardiology (assoc.). Office: Royal Perth Hosp, Wellington St, GPO Box K823, Perth 6001, Australia

DAVIS, MICHAEL RAYNER, physician; b. Tifton, Ga., Dec. 20, 1953; s. Woodrow Alvin and Sadie (Bohorfoush) D.; m. Barbara Ficarino. BS, U. Ala., 1976; MD, U. Ala., Birmingham, 1981. Diplomate Am. Bd. Internal Medicine, Am. Bd. Endocrinology and Metabolism. Resident U. Ala., Mobile, 1984; fellow U. Va., Charlottesville, 1986; physician Internal Medicine, Mobile, 1986-94, Providence Endocrinology and Metabolism, Mobile, 1994-96. Fellow Am. Coll. Physician, Am. Coll. Endocrinology. Office: Providence Endocrinology Metabolism 6701 Airport Blvd Mobile AL 36608

DAVIS, MICHAEL WILLIAM, orthopedic surgeon; b. L.A., Aug. 20, 1934. BS, U. Minn., 1956, BA magna cum laude, 1957, MD, 1959. Pvt. practice orthopedic surgeon Mpls., 1964-66, 69—; chief orthopedic surgery U.S. Army Hosp., Neubrucke, Germany, 1966-69. Contbr. articles to profl. publs. Maj. U.S. Army, 1966-69. Fellow Am. Acad. Orthopedic Surgery, Am. Bd. Orthopedic Surgery, Phi Beta Kappa, Alpha Omega Alpha. Office: Western Orthopedic Surgery 5100 Gamble Dr Ste 310 Saint Louis Park MN 55416

DAVIS, MITCHELL, JR., healthcare planning administrator; b. Neptune, N.J., Jan. 21, 1955; s. Mitchell Sr. and Elizabeth (Ellington) D.; m. Cheryl A. Henderson, Nov. 30, 1980; children: Chanel A., Mitchell III. BSBA, Oakwood Coll., Huntsville, Ala., 1980; postgrad., U. Minn., 1989—. Cert. healthcare strategic planning. Fin. analyst RCA Co., West Palm Beach, Fla., 1978-79; contract specialist Dept. Def., Ozark, Ala., 1979-80; acct. Cargill, Inc., Chgo., 1980-82, Mpls., 1982-83; tax cons. Community Svcs. Agy., Mpls., 1982-83; fin. analyst Minn. Hosp. Assn., Mpls., 1983-85; mgr. Minn. Hosp. Assn., 1983-96; planning assoc. North Meml. Med. Ctr., Mpls., 1996—. Contbr. article to mag. Mem. United Way Health Coun., 1993—; active Met. Health Planning Bd., Mpls., 1990-92. Mem. Am. Mktg. Assn. (v.p. comms. 1987-89, Achievement award), Nat. Assn. Health Data Orgns., Minn. Assn. Parliamentarians, Healthcare Fin. Mgmt. Assn. (program chmn. 1989-91, treas. 1991-92, sec. 1992-93, pres.-elect 1993-94, pres. 1994-95), Met. Vis. Nurses Assn. (bd. dirs. 1995—), Inst. of Diversity for Health Mgmt. (bd. dirs. 1995—), Nat. Matrix. Home: 2310 18th Ave N Minneapolis MN 55411-2804

DAVIS, PAMELA ANN, women and childrens health education manager; b. Salem, Mass., Feb. 11, 1960; d. Donald Lee Gorrell and JoAnn Patricia (Hanna) Butcher; m. Joseph Patrick Davis, Aug. 3, 1964; children: Ryan, Cory. BSN, U. Calif., Chico, 1984; MPA, U. San Francisco, 1988. RN, Calif.; RN cert., cert. BLS instr.; Am. Heart Assn./Am. Acad. Pediats. neonatal resuscitation; cert. hosp. based instr. Staff nurse Sutter Meml. Hosp., Sacramento, 1984-92, exracoporeal membrane oxgenator coord., 1989-92, asst. nurse mgr. spl. care nursery, 1990-91, acting nurse mgr. spl. care nursery, 1991-92, womens and childrens health edn. mgr., 1992—; instr. grandparenting class Sutter Meml. Hosp., Sacramento, 1992—, neonatal resuscitation instr., 1992—, BLS instr., 1995—. Assoc. bd. mem. Women Escaping a Violent Environment, Sacramento, 1994—. Mem. Intern. Child Edn. Assn.

DAVIS, PAUL JOSEPH, endocrinologist; b. Chgo., Oct. 28, 1937; s. Paul Albert and Maxine Lydia (Mason) D.; m. Faith Ainsworth Baker, Dec. 8, 1962; children: Matthew, John, Sarah. B.A. magna cum laude, Westminster Coll., 1959; M.D. cum laude, Harvard U., 1963. Intern Bronx Municipal Hosp. Center, 1963-64, resident in medicine, 1964-67; clin. assoc. NIH, Bethesda, Md., 1967-69; sr. staff assoc. NIH, 1969-70; head endocrinology div. Balt. City Hosps., 1970-75; prof. medicine, head endocrinology div. SUNY, Buffalo Med. Sch., 1975-90, also vice chmn. dept. medicine; prof., chmn. dept. medicine Albany Med. Coll., Albany Med. Ctr., N.Y., 1990—; chief med. svc. VA Med. Ctr., Buffalo, 1980-90; mem. merit rev. bd. endocrinology VA; bd. dirs. Am. Bd. Internal Medicine. Fellow ACP (gov.-elect Upstate N.Y. region), Gerontol. Soc.; mem. Am. Fedn. Clin. Rsch., Am. Soc. Biochemistry and Molecular Biology, Am. Thyroid Assn. (bd. dirs.), Endocrine Soc., Bd. Sci. Counselors, Nat. Inst. Aging. Home: 35 Old South Rd West Sand Lake NY 12196 Office: Albany Med Coll Dept Medicine # A-57 Albany NY 12208

DAVIS, RICHARD ALLEN, neurosurgeon; b. Chgo., June 15, 1925; s. Loyal and Pearl (McElroy) D.; m. Shirley Hull Hegeler, Aug. 25, 1950 (div. July 1957); 1 child, Barton; m. Patricia Marie Herzing, Nov. 22, 1960; children: Geoffrey, Anne. AB, Princeton U., 1949; MD, Northwestern U., 1951, MS, 1956. Diplomate Am. Bd. Neurol. Surgery. Dennis fellow anatomy Northwestern U. Med. Sch., Chgo., 1951-56, Kanavel fellow neurosurgery, 1952-58; attending surgeon U.S. Vet. Rsch. Hosp., Chgo., 1958, Hosp. U. Pa., Phila., 1958-91; prof. neurosurgery U. Pa. Sch. Medicine, Phila., 1967-91, prof. emeritus, 1991; council Coll. Physicians, Phila., 1987-96. Author: Principle of Neurosurgery, 1963, Collected Papers of Loyal Davis, 1973; contbr. 60 articles on neurosurgery to profl. jours. Sr. lt. USN, 1952-54. U.S. Pub. Health Rsch. grantee Chgo., Phila., 1955-70. Mem. Phila. Acad. Surgery, Halsted Soc., James IV Assn. Republican. Office: Dept Neurosurgery 8 Penn Towers 3400 Spruce St Philadelphia PA 19104

DAVIS, RICHARD C., JR., cardiologist; b. Sept. 15, 1942. BA, Tex. A&M U., 1963, PhD, 1968; MD, Columbia U., 1974. Diplomate in internal medicine and cardiology Am. Bd. Internal Medicine. Chief of cardiology Fitzsimons Army Med. Ctr., Aurora, Colo., 1986—.

DAVIS, RICHARD CALHOUN, dentist; b. Manhattan, Kans., Jan. 4, 1945; s. William Calhoun and Alison Rae (Wyland) D.; Danna Ruth Ritchel, June 13, 1968; 1 child, Darin Calhoun. Student, Ariz. State U., 1963-65, BA, 1978; BA, U. Ariz., 1966; DDS, U. of Pacific, 1981. Retail dept. head Walgreens, Tucson, 1965-66; mgmt. trainee Walgreens, Tucson, San Antonio, 1967-70; asst. store mgr. Walgreens, Baton Rouge, 1970-72; field rep. Am. Cancer Soc., Phoenix, 1972-74; dept. head Lucky Stores Inc., Tempe, Ariz., 1976-78; practice dentistry specializing in gen. dentistry Tucson, 1981—; bd. dirs. Home Again, Inc. Chmn. bd. Capilla Del Sol Christian Ch., Tucson, 1984. Mem. ADA, Acad. Gen. Dentists, Am. Straight Wire Orthodontic Assn., Am. Assn. Functional Orthodontics, Sleep Disorders Dental Soc., So. Ariz. Bus. Assn., N.W. Dental Study Club, Optimists (past pres. N.W. club), Elks. Republican. Mem. Disciples of Christ Ch. Office: 2777 N Campbell Ave Tucson AZ 85719-3101

DAVIS, ROBERT A., psychiatrist; b. N.Y.C., Dec. 15, 1948; s. Arthur W. and Dorothea (Dietrich) D.; m. Marianne Couglin, May 17, 1987. BA in Chemistry, Hofstra U., 1970; MD, N.Y. Med. Coll., 1974. Resident psychiatry Albert Einstein Coll. Medicine, N.Y.C., 1974-75; resident SUNY, Stony Brook, 1975-76, Albert Einstein Coll. Medicine, N.Y.C., 1976-77; research fellow Albert Einstein Coll. Medicine, 1977-78; staff psychiatrist L.I. Jewish Hillside Med. Ctr., Glen Oaks, N.Y., 1978-84, N.Y. Med. Coll., Coler Meml. Hosp., N.Y.C., 1984—; inst. clin. psychiatry SUNY, Stony Brook, 1978-80, asst. prof. clin. psychiatry, 1980-84; asst. prof. clin. psychiatry N.Y. Med. Coll., N.Y.C., 1984—. Contbr. articles to profl. jours. Full acad. scholar Hofstra U., 1966-70; psychiat. research fellow Albert Einstein Coll. Medicine, 1977. Mem. Am. Psychiat. Assn. (com. on aging N.Y. dist. br. 1985—), N.Y. Geriatric Soc., Manhattan Geriatric Com. Office: 65 E 96th St New York NY 10128-0792

DAVIS, ROBERT PAUL, physician, educator; b. Malden, Mass., July 3, 1926; s. Samuel and Sarah (Lemberg) D.; m. Ruby Black, Sept. 5, 1953; children—Edward L., John R., Elizabeth A. A.B. cum laude, Harvard U., 1947, M.D. magna cum laude, 1951, A.M., 1955; A.M. (ad eundem), Brown U., 1967. Diplomate: Am. Bd. Internal Medicine, subsplty. bd. nephrology. Intern Peter Bent Brigham Hosp., Boston, 1951-52; asst. medicine Peter Bent Brigham Hosp., 1952-55, sr. asst. resident physician, 1955-56, chief resident physician, 1956-57; jr. fellow Soc. of Fellows Harvard, 1952-55; asst. medicine Harvard Med. Sch., 1956-57; asst. prof. medicine U. N.C., 1957-59; asst. prof. medicine Albert Einstein Coll. Medicine, 1959-66, assoc. prof., 1967; career scientist Health Research Council, N.Y.C., 1962-67; asst. vis. physician Bronx Mcpl. Hosp. Center, 1959-65, assoc. vis. physician, 1966-67; physician in chief Miriam Hosp., Providence, 1967-74; dir. renal and metabolic diseases Miriam Hosp., 1974-79; prof. med. sci. Brown U., 1967-84, prof. emeritus, 1984—, chmn. sect. in medicine div. biol. and med. scis., 1971-74; vis. scientist Ins. Biol. Chemistry of U. Copenhagen, 1965-66; past mem. corp. Butler Hosp., Jewish Family and Children's Service; mem. sci. adv. council N.E. Regional Kidney Program; vice chmn. R.I. Advisory Commn. Med. Care and Edn. Found.; chmn. med. adv. bd. R.I. Kidney Found.; past bd. dirs. Associated Alumni Brown U.; mem. med. adv. bd. New Eng. sect. Am. Liver Found., 1986—; trustee New Eng. Organ Bank, Boston, 1969—, treas., 1970—; pres. End-Stage Renal Disease Coordinating Council Network 28, New Eng., 1978-79. Assoc. editor: R.I. Med. Jour, 1971-80; contbr. articles to profl. jours. Served as ensign USNR, 1944-46; as lt. (j.g.) M.C. 1951. Traveling fellow Commonwealth Fund, 1965-66; Willard O. Thompson Meml. traveling scholar A.C.P., 1965. Fellow AAAS, ACP; mem. Am. Fedn. Clin. Research, Am. Soc. Transplant Physicians, Harvey Soc., Biophys. Soc., N.Y. Acad. Medicine, Am. Heart Assn., N.Y. Acad. Sci., Am. Soc. Cell Biology, Soc. Gen. Physiologists, Am. Physiol. Soc., Am. Soc. Artificial Internal Organs, Internat. Soc. Nephrology, Clin. Diabetes Assn. R.I. (pres. 1970-71), Providence, R.I. med. socs., Am. Soc. Nephrology, Am. Soc. Pediatric Nephrology, Soc. for Health and Human Values, Am. Philos. Assn., Phi Beta Kappa, Sigma Xi. Home: 75 Prospect St Providence RI 02906-1330 Office: Brown U 245 Waterman St Ste 105 Providence RI 02906-5215

DAVIS, RONALD STEPHEN, dermatologist; b. Dallas, July 29, 1946; s. Quilman B. and Margaret (Dunlevy) D.; m. Suzanne Hunt; children: Laura, Sarah. BS, So. Meth. U., 1968; MS, Mich. State U., 1971; MD, Tulane U., 1975. Diplomate Am. Bd. Dermatology. Intern U. Utah, S.L.C., 1975; resident in dermatology Tulane U., Charity Hosp., New Orleans, 1976-79; assoc. Wayne L. Simmonds, M.D., Pasadena, Calif., 1979-81; pvt. practice Tyler, Tex., 1981—; clin. assoc. prof. dept. dermatology U. Tex., Dallas, 1982—. Editor: (with others) Outpatient Surgery of the Skin, 1983; contbr. articles to profl. jours. Fellow Am. Soc. for Dermatologic Surgery, Am. Acad. Dermatology; mem. AMA. Methodist. Office: 700 Olympic Plz Cir Ste 404 Tyler TX 75701-1952

DAVIS, RUSSELL HADEN, association executive, pastoral psychotherapist; b. Washington, Nov. 26, 1940; s. Walter Haden Davis and Virginia (Russell) Edge; m. Iva Lee Crocker, 1964; children: Brandon Denise, Haden Arnold. BA, U. Va., 1962; MDiv, Union Theol. Sem., N.Y.C., 1965; ThM, So. Bapt. Theol. Sem., Louisville, 1966; STM, Union Theol. Sem., N.Y.C., 1978, PhD, 1986. Ordained to ministry So. Bapt. Ch., 1961. Clin. chaplain Ky. State Reformatory, LaGrange, 1966-71, Ctrl. State Hosp., Milledgeville, Ga., 1971-77; assoc. minister The Riverside Ch., N.Y.C., 1977-86; asst. prof. psychiatry and religion Union Theol. Sem., N.Y.C., 1986-91; mem. faculty Blanton-Peale Grad. Inst. Pastoral Psychotherapy, N.Y.C., 1989-91; dir. Psy-Law, N.Y.C., 1989-91; asst. prof. U. Va., 1994, assoc. prof., 1994-95; pvt. practice pastoral psychotherapy, 1974—; asst. prof. Union Theol. Sem., 1981-83; exec. dir. Assn. for Clin. Pastoral Edn., Inc., Decatur, Ga., 1995—. Author: Freud's Concept of Passivity, 1993; also articles. Bd. dirs. Inst. for Relationship Therapy, N.Y., 1981-88, Counseling Ctr., Riverside Ch., 1978-82. Named Ky. Col., State of Ky., 1970; fellow Union Theol. Sem., 1979-81, rsch. grantee, 1987-90; fellow Oaklawn Found., 1980. Fellow Coll. Chaplains (bd. cert.), Commonwealth Ctr. Lit. and Cultural Change (assoc.); mem. Assn. Clin. Pastoral Edn. (cert. supr.), Am. Assn. Pastoral Counselors.

DAVIS, RUTH C., pharmacy educator; b. Wilkes-Barre, Pa., Oct. 27, 1943; d. Morris David Davis and Helen Jane Gillis. BS, Phila. Coll. Pharmacy and Sci., 1967. Cert. pharmacist, Pa., Md. Mgr. pharmacist Fairview Pharmacy, Etters, Pa.; mgr., pharmacist Neighborcare Pharmacy, Balt.; dir. ambulatory svcs. Rombro Health Svcs., Balt.; tchr., pharmacist Boothwyn Pharmacy, Phila.; pharm. cons. Nat. Rx Svcs. of Pa.; Eagle Managed Care, 1996. Republican. Baptist. Home and Office: 75 Lion Dr Hanover PA 17331-3849

DAVIS, SAMUEL, hospital administrator, educator, consultant; b. N.Y.C., Sept. 30, 1931; s. Morris and Ethel (Levowitz) D.; m. Ellen Darce Kalker, June 16, 1957; children: Joseph Evan, Thomas Adam, Jonathan Edward, Jessica Ann. B.A., CCNY, 1952; M.S., Columbia U., 1957. Acct. Roosevelt Hosp., N.Y.C., 1954-55; relief adminstr. Meml. Center Cancer and Allied Diseases, N.Y.C., 1955-56; adminstrv. resident, then adminstrv. asst. to dir. and dir. ambulatory care services Roosevelt Hosp., 1956-59; mem. adminstrv. staff Hillside Hosp., Glen Oaks, N.Y.C., 1959-72, exec. v.p., 1970-72; exec. cons. L.I. Jewish-Hillside Med. Center, New Hyde Park, N.Y., 1972; exec. pres. Mt. Sinai Hosp., Mpls., 1972-75; dir. Mt. Sinai Hosp., N.Y.C., 1975-81, pres., 1981-85; sr. v.p. Mt. Sinai Med. Center, N.Y.C., 1975-77, exec. v.p., 1978-84; pres. EcuMed, N.Y.C., 1984-85; prin. Sam Davis & Assocs., White Plains, N.Y., 1986—; sr. dir. Delta Cons. Group, N.Y.C., 1990—; assoc. prof. adminstrv. medicine Mt. Sinai Med. Sch., 1975-79, acting chmn., 1977-79, Edmond A. Guggenheim prof. health care mgmt., chmn. health care mgmt., 1979-84, disting. service prof. health care mgmt., 1984—; adj. prof. health care adminstrn. Baruch Coll., CUNY, 1978-87; prof. mgmt., clin. prof. Sch. Pub. Health Columbia U., 1988—; cons. health care strategy and orgnl. change, 1976—; dir. health care research, The Ctr. for Mgmt., CUNY; vice chmn. bd. dirs. Hennepin County (Minn.) Health Coalition, 1973-75; mem. health adv. com. Minn. Met. Health Bd., 1974-75; mem. Hennepin County Health and Social Services Adv. Bd., 1974-75. Author: Decision Analysis in Hospital Administration, 1974; contbr. articles to profl. jours. Trustee Mpls. Fedn. Jewish Service, 1973-75; chmn. health and welfare div. N.Y.C. Fedn. Jewish Philanthropies, 1975-76; trustee, mem. exec. com. Montefiore Med. Ctr., Bronx, N.Y., 1985—. Served with AUS, 1952-54. Recipient Humanitarian award NCCJ, 1984; fellow social studies and humanities CCNY, 1952; WHO fellow, 1970; sr. fellow Wharton Sch. U. Pa., 1986—. Fellow Am. Coll. Hosp. Adminstrs., Am. Pub. Health Assn.; mem. Am. Assn. Hosp. Planning, Am., N.Y. State hosp. assns., Am. Mgmt. Assn., Herman Biggs Soc. Office: Delta Cons Group 1177 Avenue Of The Americas New York NY 10036-2714

DAVIS, SARA LEA, pharmacist; b. Knoxville, Tenn., Aug. 1, 1951; d. Horace William and Margaret Jewel (Hill) D. BS in Liberal Arts, U. Tenn., 1973; BS in Pharmacy, U. Tenn., Memphis, 1976, PharmD, 1977. Asst. mgr. Pharmaco Nuclear, Inc., Chgo., 1977-79; nuclear pharmacist Kansas City, Mo., 1979, Bapt. Meml. Hosp., Memphis, 1979-83; asst. mgr. Syncor, Inc., Washington, 1983-84; staff pharmacist Rite Aid Corp., Knoxville, 1984-87, pharmacist-in-charge, 1987—; rep. 3d High Country Nuclear Medicine Conf., Vail, Colo., 1983; mem. adv. bd. V.I.P. Home Nursing & Rehab., Knoxville, 1985-86. Active Leconte Exec. Women's Coun. Mem. Am. Pharm. Assn., Acad. Pharm. Sci. (sect. nuclear pharmacy), Soc. Nuclear Medicine, Memphis Bus. and Profl. Women's Assn. (bd. dirs. 1982-83), Club Leconte, U. Tenn. Century Club, Mortar Bd., Phi Beta Kappa, Phi Kappa Phi, Rho Chi, Alpha Lambda Delta. Baptist. Office: Rite Aid Pharmacy 508-B E Tri-County Blvd Oliver Springs TN 37840-1436

DAVIS, SARAH JANE, health care professional; b. Cheyenne, Wyo., Feb. 8, 1949; d. Frederick Eugene and Bernice (Deaver) Fowler; m. David Allen Davis, Dec. 21, 1968 (div. 1973); 1 child, Jacoby. Key punch operator San Antonio Coll., 1967-70; with personnel dept. Bapt. Meml. Hosp., San Antonio, 1970-71; key punch operator Frost Bank, San Antonio, 1971-72; mgr. Stop and Go, Inc., San Antonio, 1971-72; engring. coord. constrn., dir. facilities mgmt. S.W. Tex. Meth. Hosp., San Antonio, 1973—. Mem. Nat. Fire Protection Assn. Office: SW Tex Meth Hosp 7700 Floyd Curl Dr San Antonio TX 78229-3902

DAVIS, SHIRLEY CAROL SPENCE, nurse; b. Drexel Hill, Pa., Sept. 8, 1938; d. William Lloyd and Hilda Irene (Marshall) Spence; m. Davis Louis Davis, Feb. 6, 1960 (dec. May 1979); 1 son, David Louis. Diploma in nursing Orange Meml. Hosp., 1959; student in nursing Lake Superior State Coll., 1977-78; BS in Nursing, U. South Fla., 1981, MS in Nursing, 1985. Cert. critical care RN. Operating room nurse Eastern Maine Gen. Hosp., Bangor, 1960-62, S. Community Hosp., Oklahoma City, 1972-75; staff nurse recovery room float team Doctors Hosp., Shreveport, La., 1969-70; infectious care unit nurse Bayfront Med. Ctr., St. Petersburg, Fla., 1970-71, staff nurse float team to med./surg./neurol. units, 1978-85, James A. Haley VA Hosp., Tampa, Fla., 1985-89, nurse med./surg. unit, 1989-91, med. intensive care, 1991—, Fla. Surg. Intensive Care, 1985. Vol., Family Services, Scott AFB, Ill., 1975-77, ARC, Scott AFB, Ill., 1975-77. Mem. Am. Nurses Assn., Fla. Nurses Assn., Am. Heart Assn., Sigma Theta Tau. Republican. Methodist. Clubs: Squadron Wives (Barksdale AFB) (treas. 1965-66), Officers' Wives. Home: 30 Sycamore Ct Palm Harbor FL 34683-3020 Office: James A Haley VA Hosp 13000 Bruce B Downs Blvd Tampa FL 33612-4745

DAVIS, SHIRLEY HARRIET, social worker, editor; b. Brookline, Mass., June 27, 1922; d. Jacob and Matilda (Goldberg) Freedman; m. Edward H. Davis, Nov. 11, 1943; children: Anita Maureen Davis Winn, Lawrence Paul. AB, Calvin Coolidge Coll., 1944; postgrad., Simmons Sch. of Social Work, 1944-45. Social worker Travelers Aid of N.Y., N.Y.C., 1944-48; dir. Community Svc. Workshop of Woodmere (N.Y.) Acad., 1966-70; v.p. for program and membership West End Aux. Peninsula Hosp. Ctr., Edgemere, N.Y., 1973-80; dir. Family Practice Playroom Coll. Medicine, Downstate Med. Ctr., Bklyn., 1977-83; officer mgr. Edward H. Davis, M.D., Loxahatchee, Fla., 1983-93; dir. publicity and pub. rels. Fla. Atlantic Region of Hadassah, 1994—; med. office mgr.; chair Fla. Atlantic Region of Hadassah Women's Health Symposium, 1996. Editor: Hadassah of Wellington Fla., 1990-93. V.p. membership Hadassah of Wellington, 1992-94, bulletin bus. mgr.; dir. publicity and pub. rels., bd. dirs., staff worker thrift shop Fla. Atlantic Region of Hadassah, 1994—; chair Fla. Atlantic Region of Hadassah Women's Health Symposium, 1996. Wellingtn chpt. honoree Fla. Atlantic Region of Hadassah ann. Woman of Valor awards, 1996; recipient Nat. Hadassah Love of a Lifetime award, 1996. Republican. Jewish. Home: 13604 Firewood Ct West Palm Beach FL 33414-8522

DAVIS, STEPHEN ALVIN, internist; b. Guntersville, Ala., May 24, 1946; s. Woodrow Alvin and Sadie Celestine (Bohorfoush) D.; m. Beverly Crawford, Aug. 2, 1969; children: Christopher, Colin. BS, U. Ala., Tuscaloosa, 1968; MD, U. Ala., Birmingham, 1972. Diplomate Am. Bd. Internal Medicine. Pvt. practice Providence Endocrinology & Metabolism, Mobile, Ala., 1978-96; pres. Providence Hosp. staff, Mobile, 1992-93; pres. Ala. Soc. Internal Medicine, 1991-92. Major AUS, 1972-75. Fellow ACP. Episcopalian. Office: Providence Endocrinology C-137 6701 Airport Blvd Mobile AL 36608

DAVIS, STEVEN ANDREW, dermatologist; b. San Antonio, May 28, 1947; s. Herbert and Phyllis D.; m. Jolene Bryant; children: Bryant, Suzanne. BA in Econs., Yale U., 1969; MD, U. Tex., 1973. Diplomate Am. Bd. Dermatologists. Pvt. practice in dermatology San Antonio, Tex., 1977—. Author: (book) How to Stay Healthy in an Unhealthy World, 1983; columnist Syndicated King Features, Speaking of Your Health, 1984-86; CBS Radio Show, Speaking of Health, 1976— (Am. Heart Assn., Am. Acad. Family Physicians and Am. Assn. Blood Banks awards). Fellow Am. Acad. Dermatology; mem. AMA, Tex. Med. Assn., Bexar County Med. Assn. Office: Steven A Davis MD PA 8038 Wurzbach Rd Ste 450 San Antonio TX 78229

DAVIS, STEVEN GABE, physician; b. Indpls., June 22, 1960; s. Gale and Jean Alice (Kucuz) D. BS, BA, Purdue U., 1982; MD, Ind. U., 1986. Diplomate Nat. Bd. Med. Examiners, Am. Bd. Internal Medicine, Am. Bd. Infectious Diseases. Intern in internal medicine Meth. Hosp., Ind.; staff physician Winona Hosp., Indpls., 1988-89; med. staff asst. physician HIV divsn. Harris County Hosp., Houston, 1990-91; physician Dallas Infectious Disease Assn., 1991—; med. dir. infection control Irving (Tex.) Healthcare Sys., 1994—. Mem. AMA, Am. Coll. Physicians, Infectious Disease Soc. Am. (assoc.), Am. Soc. Microbiology, Tex. Med. Soc., Dallas County Med. Soc. Office: Dallas ID Assocs 5939 Harry Hines Blvd 545 Dallas TX 75235

DAVIS, SUSAN LYNN RABINOWITZ, psychiatric social worker, family therapist, trainer; b. Bklyn., Feb. 27, 1944; d. Murray and Jeanette (Baumgarten) Rabinowitz; B.A., Conn. Coll. for Women, 1964; M.S.S. (NIMH grantee), Bryn Mawr Coll., 1968; m. Donald Irvin Davis, Aug. 16, 1964; children—Kenneth Bernard, Joshua Ian. Caseworker, Phila. State Reception Center, Phila. Gen. Hosp., 1965-66; field work Eastern Pa. Psychiat. Inst., Phila., 1966-67, Child Devel. Center, Bryn Mawr Coll., 1967-68; social worker Mental Devel. Center, Case Western Res. U., 1968-69; clin. instr. Northwestern U. Med. Sch., 1969-70; co-leader parent-student group U. Chgo. Lab. Schs., 1972; adj. fac. dept. of child and family devel. Va. Polytech. Inst., 1985—; trainee in family therapy Family Therapy Inst. Washington, 1975-76; pvt. practice family mential and individual therapy, Alexandria, Va., 1972—; co-founder, co-dir. Family Therapy Inst. Alexandria 1978—, NLP Resource Ctr., 1987—; developer, co-dir. Habit Mgmt. Workshops, Alexandria, 1981-90; cons. local schs.; workshop presenter and panelist, local, nat., internat. mental health meetings on family therapy, couples therapy, attention deficit, goals and values elicitation, communication skills and Neurolinguistic Programming; faculty Vir. Poly. Inst. Active in campaigning for polit. candidates. Lic. social worker, Md., Va.; cert. trainer neurolinguistic programming; diplomate in clin. social work. Fellow Am. Orthopsychiat. Assn.; mem. Nat. Assn. Social Workers, Acad. Cert. Social Workers, Am. Family Therapy Acad. Contbr. articles to profl. jours. Home: 7805 Elba Rd Alexandria VA 22306-2559 Office: 220 S Washington St Alexandria VA 22314

DAVIS, T. BOB, dentist, pianist; b. Luverne, Ala., Apr. 10, 1941; s. John Wilson and Vera Elizabeth (Willis) D.; m. Janis Margaret Murphy, Nov. 29, 1969; children: Shawn Timothy, Angie Beth, Creth Andrew. AA, Mars Hill Jr. Coll., 1961; BA, Samford U., 1963; DMD, U. Ala., 1967. Gen. practice dentistry, Dallas, 1969—; clin. asst. prof. dept. gen. dentistry Baylor Coll. Dentistry, 1991; with Baylor Med. Ctr. at Garland, Garland Cmty. Hosp.; accompanist 1st Bapt. Ch., Dallas, 1967—; staff pianist Prestonwood Bapt. Ch., Dallas, 1983—; pianist So. Bapt. Conv., Tex. Bapt. Evangelism Conf., Tex. Bapt. Conv. Super Summer Conf. Record albums include Gratefully T Bob, 1981, T. Bob-Piano, 1983, T. Bob-Late Nite, 1986, T. Bob & Bill-Sunday Sounds, 1986. Vol. Buckner Childrens Home, Dallas, 1970—, Dallas County Juvenile Shelter, 1983—; deacon 1st Bapt. Ch., Dallas, 1976—, Prestonwood Bapt. Ch., 1987; vol. dentist Matamoris Mex. Bapt. Orphanage, 1977—; guest artist Sta. KCBI Radio Sharathon, Dallas, 1976—, Dino's 7 piano Pianorama Concerts, 1983—. Capt. USAF, 1967-69. Fellow Acad. Gen. Dentistry (del. 1981-92, mem. pub. info. coun. 1984-90, chmn. pub. info. coun. 1986-90, chmn. reference com. 1984, sec. region XII 1983-84, pres. Dallas chpt. 1982-83, editor Dallas chpt. 1987-89, dir. Dallas chpt. 1980-90, advisor Dallas chpt. 1990—), Internat. Coll. Dentists, Am. Coll. Dentists; mem. ADA (mem. ann. session com. 1979, del. to Tex. Dental Assn., 1989-91, alternate del. 1993), Tex. Dental Assn., Tex. Acad. Gen. Dentistry (sec. 1982-83, pres. 1984-85, dir. 1986-90, v.p. dental care 1991-92, chmn. interprofl. rels. com., chmn. budget-fin. and nominating coms.), Dallas Acad. Gen. Dentistry (pres. 1982-83, dentist of yr. award 1987), Dallas County Dental Soc. (bd. dirs. 1982-84, 88-91, sec.-treas. 1983-84, mem. fin. com. 1984-85, parliamentarian 1986-87, mem. strategic planning com. 1990-91, chmn. cmty. health com.), Christian Med. Dental Soc., Baylor Coll. Dentistry Alumni Assn. (hon.). Republican. Avocation: concert pianist. Home: 11925 Loch Ness Dr Dallas TX 75218-1325 Office: 8499 Greenville Ave Dallas TX 75231-2412

DAVIS, THOMAS JOEL, cardiologist; b. Duluth, Minn., Sept. 14, 1951; s. Benjamin and Blanche (Greenberg) D.; m. Gail A. Bernstein, June 8, 1978; children: Aaron, Andrew. BS, U. Minn., 1973, MD, 1976. Intern in internal medicine U. Wis., Madison, 1976-79, cardiology fellow, 1980-82; dir. coronary care Fairview Downtown Hosp., 1984-87; heart catheterization dir. Ramsey Hosp., St. Paul; asst. clin. prof. U. Minn. Med. Sch., Mpls., 1986-94, assoc. clin. prof., 1995—. Fellow Am. Coll. Cardiology (bd. mem. 1988-92);

mem. Am. Heart Assn. Home: 3516 Green Ridge Rd Minnetonka MN 55305 Office: Healthpartners 2220 Riverside Ave S Minneapolis MN 55454

DAVIS, VICKIE BEENE, pharmacist, engineer, educator; b. Atlanta, Tex., Apr. 6, 1951; d. Leonard D. and Grace Evelyn (Dial) B.; m. Paul Gaylon Davis, Nov. 27, 1971. Student, Texarkana (Tex.) Jr. Coll., 1969-70, Northwestern State U., Natchitoches, La., 1970-71; BS in Pharmacy magna cum laude, U. Houston, 1974, BSEE summa cum laude, 1992, postgrad., 1992—. Registered pharmacist, Tex. Pharmacist intern Hillcroft Pharmacy, Houston, 1974-75; staff pharmacist K-Mart, Inc., Houston, 1975-76, Bissonnet Pharmacy, Houston, 1976-79; staff pharmacist HCA Woman's Hosp. Tex., Houston, 1979-85, 90-93, asst. dir. pharmacy, 1985-90. Recipient Appreciation award HCA Info. Svcs., Inc., Nashville, 1987; named Hosp. Pharmacy Preceptor of Yr., U. Houston Coll. Pharmacy, 1989; Stella Ehrhardt fellow for grad. studies, 1992-93, Texaco fellow, 1992-93, Motorola fellow, 1993-95. Mem. IEEE, Aircraft Owners and Pilots Assn., Exptl. Aircraft Assn., Phi Kappa Phi, Rho Chi, Kappa Epsilon, Eta Kappa Nu (pres. 1992), Tau Beta Pi (pres. 1992-93). Home: 2708 Maple Ln Pearland TX 77584-1074 Office: Dept Elec Engring Electromagnetics Lab U Houston Houston TX 77402

DAVISON, FREDERICK CORBET, foundation executive; b. Atlanta, Sept. 3, 1929; s. Frederick Collins and Gladys (Carsley) D.; m. Dianne Castle, Sept. 3, 1952; children—Frederick Corbet, William Castle, Anne Harper. D.V.M., U. Ga., 1952; Ph.D., Iowa State U., 1963; H.H.D. (hon.), Presbyn. Coll., 1977; LL.D. (hon.), Mercer U., 1979; hon. degree, U. N.B., Can., 1985. Pvt. practice veterinary medicine Marietta, Ga., 1952-58; rsch. assoc. Iowa State U., Ames, 1958-60, asst. prof., 1960-63; assoc. Inst. Atomic Research, Ames, 1960-63; asst. dir. dept. sci. activities AVMA, Chgo., 1963-64; dean sch. vet. medicine U. Ga., Athens, 1964-66; vice chancellor Univ. System Ga., 1966-67, pres., 1967-86; pres. U. Ga., Athens, 1967-86, prof. vet. medicine, Fred C. Davison chair Sch. Vet. Medicine, 1986-88; pres., chief exec. officer Nat. Sci. Ctr. Found., Inc., Augusta, Ga., 1988—; bd. dirs. 1st Union Nat. Bank Ga., So. Ctr. for Internat. Studies; bd. trustees Presbyn. Coll. Contbr. articles to profl. jours. Mem. NE Ga. commn. Boy Scouts Am., past pres. Area 5; hon. mem. bd. counselors Oxford Coll. Recipient Disting. Achievement award Iowa State U., 1979, Disting. Svc. award Univ. Ga., 1975, Appreciation award, 1976; named Georgian of Yr. Ga. Assn. Broadcasters, 1980. Mem. Am., Ga. vet. med. assns., Sigma Xi, Phi Kappa Phi, Sigma Alpha Epsilon, Omega Tau Sigma, Alpha Zeta, Phi Zeta, Gamma Sigma Delta. Office: Nat Sci Ctr Found Inc PO Box 15577 Augusta GA 30919-1577

DAVISON, RICHARD, physician, educator; b. Buenos Aires, Nov. 7, 1937; came to U.S., 1966; s. Charles Edward and Matilde (Muller) D.; m. Lisette Glusberg, July 1, 1965; 1 child, Sebastian. MD, U. Buenos Aires, 1963. Diplomate Am. Bd. Internal Medicine, Am. Bd. Cardiovascular Diseases, Am. Bd. Critical Care Medicine. Intern Inst. Med. Rsch., Buenos Aires, 1964; resident Passavant Meml. Hosp., Chgo., 1966-68, chief resident, 1968-69; cardiology fellowship VA Hosp., Chgo., 1969-71; asst. prof. Northwestern U. Sch. Medicine, Chgo., 1973-81, assoc. prof., 1981—, chief sect. critical care medicine, 1982—, chief sect. cardiology, 1988-92; dir. med. intensive care area Northwestern Meml. Hosp., Chgo., 1973—. Contbr. articles to profl. jours. Recipient Thrombolysis in Myocardial Infarction award NIH. Fellow Am. Coll. Cardiology, Am. Coll. Physicians, Council of Clin. Cardiology (Am. Heart. Assn.), Soc. Critical Care Medicine; mem. Am. Heart Assn., Alpha Omega Alpha. Office: Northwestern Meml Hosp Sect Critical Care 251 E Chicago Ave Ste 726 Chicago IL 60611-2614

DAWES, ROBYN MASON, psychology educator; b. Pitts., July 23, 1936; s. Norman H. and Zita (Hill) D.; children by previous marriage: Jennifer, Molly. B.A. in Philosophy, Harvard U., 1958; M.A. in Clin. Psychology, U. Mich., 1960, Ph.D. in Math. Psychology, 1963. Researcher Ann Arbor (Mich.) VA Hosp., 1962-67; lectr. U. Mich., Ann Arbor, 1963-66, asst. prof., 1966-67; assoc. prof. psychology U. Oreg., Eugene, 1967-71, prof., 1971-85, co-head dept. psychology, 1972-73, acting head, 1979-80, head, 1981-85; prof. psychology, Carnegie Mellon U., 1985—, univ. prof., 1992—, head dept. social and decision scis., 1985-90, 95—; rsch. scientist Oreg. Rsch. Inst., 1995—, Eugene, 1967-76, v.p., 1973-74; NATO lectr., The Hague, The Netherlands, 1968; vis. prof. U. Calif.-Santa Barbara, 1975-76; pres. Oreg. Psychol. Assn., 1984-85; cons. numerous insts. and orgns. Rackham Summer fellow, 1961; James McKean Cattell Sabbatical fellow, 1978-79; del. NAS, USA-USSR Acad. Scis. Seminar Decision Making, Moscow/Tblisi, USSR, 1979; Ctr. Advanced Study in Behavioral Scis. fellow, 1980-81; fellow Ctr. for Rationality and Interactive Decision Making The Hebrew U. of Jerusalem, 1994. Fellow AAAS, Am. Psychol. Soc., Am. Assn. Applied and Preventative Psychology (mem. exec. bd. 1991—); mem. Oreg. Psychol. Assn. (pres. 1984-85), Am. Statis. Assn., Pub. Choice Soc., Psychometric Soc., West Coast Small Group Research Soc. (pres. 1977-78), Judgement and Decision Making Resch. Soc. (chmn. exec. bd. 1988, exec. bd. 1994—), Soc. for Advancement of Socio-Econs. (exec. bd. 1991—), Sigma Xi. Author: Fundamentals of Attitude Measurement, 1972, Rational Choice in an Uncertain World, 1988 (William James book award div. gen. psychology Am. Psychol. Assn.), House of Cards: Psychology and Psychotherapy Built on Myth, 1994; co-author: (with C.H. Coombs and A. Tversky) Mathematical Psychology: An Elementary Introduction, 1970; contbr. articles to profl. jours.; mem. editorial bds., cons. numerous profl. jours. and publs. Office: Carnegie Mellon U Dept Social & Decision Scis Pittsburgh PA 15213

DAWKINS, CERIDWEN ELIZABETH, chemical pathologist; b. Harwell, England, June 22, 1952; d. Herbert Charles and Elsie May (Williams) Cole; m. Richard William Spence, July 16, 1977 (div. 1988); children: Dawn, Michaela (twins), Eleanor; m. Martin Scott Dawkins, Sept. 29, 1990. BSc, Bristol U., 1973, MB ChB, 1976. Cons. chemical pathologist Frenchay Hosp., Bristol, England, 1986—; inspector CPA U.K., Ltd., 1992—; mem. panel for chem. pathology Nat. Quality Assurance Advisory, 1993—. Mem. Royal Coll. Pathology, Assn. Clin. Pathologists (sec. Wessex branch 1993—). Office: Frenchay Hosp, Frenchay Park Rd, Bristol BS16 1LE, England

DAWKINS, MARVA PHYLLIS, psychologist; b. Jacksonville, Fla., Apr. 12, 1948; d. Ralph and Altamese (Padgett) D.; student U. Freiburg, Germany, 1969-70; BS, Stetson U., 1971; MS, Fla. State U., 1972, PhD, 1975. Rsch. asst. Fla. State U., Tallahassee, 1970-72; clin. intern, psychology dept. Presbyn.-St. Luke's Med. Ctr. and mental health dept. Mile Square Health Ctr., Chgo., 1973-74; staff psychologist, dir. aftercare treatment program, mental health dept. Mile Square Health Ctr., Chgo., 1974-75, staff psychologist, coordinator devel. disabilities program, 1976-79; asst. prof. psychology U. North Fla., Jacksonville, 1975-76, Rush U.-Presbyn. St. Luke's Med. Ctr., Chgo., 1976—; pvt. practice clin. psychology, 1977—; exec. dir. Inst. for Community Mental Health, 1979—; cons. safety evaluation program Isaac Ray Ctr., 1986-91; dir. Ctr. for Applied Psychology and Forensic Studies, 1991—; psychology cons. Disability Policy Br. Social Security Adminstrn., Chgo, 1980—. Registered psychologist, Ill. Mem. Am. Psychol. Assn., Assn. Black Psychologists.

DAWKINS, MAX REID, physicians assistant; b. Dayton, Ohio, Feb. 26, 1948; s. Philip Marion and Doris Maxine (Krall) D.; m. Rebecca Jane Brown, Aug. 25, 1972; children: Emily, Nathan, Aaron. Student, Miami U., Oxford, Ohio, 1966-68; BS, NYU, Albany, 1989; cert. physician asst., Ind. U., Fort Wayne, 1975. Diplomate Nat. Comm. on Cert. of Physician Assts. Physicians asst. Office of Robert Acher, MD, Greensburg, Ind., 1975-80; joined USN, advanced through grades to lt.; physicians asst. family practice/pediatrics MCDEC, Va., 1980-83; officer in charge Camp Upshur Clinic, Quantico, summer 1981, 82; physicians asst. outpatient clinic USNAS, Glenview, Ill., 1983-86; ships physician asst. USS Coral Sea, Norfolk, Va., 1986-88; ADSC U.S. Naval Clinic Kings Bay, St. Marys, Ga., 1988-91; emergency dept. refugee work Fleet Hosp. 5, Zagreb, Croatia, 1994-95; physicians asst. internal medicine Naval Hosp., Pensacola, Fla., 1991-96. Mem. Am. Acad. Physicians Assts. (ho. of dels. 1977, 78, 79), Ind. Assn. Physicians Assts. (sec.-treas. 1976-77, 79-80). Office: US Naval Hosp 98 West Pensacola FL 32508

DAWOOD, MOHAMED YUSOFF, obstetrician, gynecologist; b. Singapore, Singapore, Sept. 13, 1943; came to U.S., 1974; s. Sheikh and Fatimah (Hussein) D.; m. Firyal Sultana Khan, July 14, 1978; children: Fatimah Sultana, Fauzia Sultana, Firdaus Sultana, Hassan Yusoff. MB, ChB, U. Sheffield, Yorkshire, Eng., 1968, MD with gold medal, 1974; M of Medicine, U. Singapore, 1972. Diplomate Am. Bd. Obstetrics and Gynecology, Am. Bd. Reproductive Endocrinology. First asst. in ob-gyn. U. Melbourne, 1974; from instr. to assoc. prof. ob-gyn. Cornell U. Med. Coll., N.Y.C., 1974-79; prof. ob-gyn. U. Ill., Chgo., 1979-90; Bere Held prof. ob-gyn. and reproductive scis. U. Tex. Med. Sch., Houston, 1990—; lectr. U. Singapore, 1973-74; cons., editorial cons., reviewer in field. Author: Green's Gynecology, 1990, Dysmenorrhea, 1981, Premenstrual Syndrome and Dysmenorrhea, 1985, Oxytocin, vol. 2, 1984, Prostaglandin Inhibition in Obstetrics and Gynecology, 1983; contbr. articles to profl. jours. Recipient Gold medal Jaycee Jr. C. of C. Singapore, 1973. Fellow ACS, ACOG, Am. Gynecol. & Obstet. Soc., Royal Coll. Ob-Gyn. (Edgar Gentilli prize 1974, Gold medal 1973); mem. Endocrine Soc. Office: Univ Texas Medical School 6431 Fannin Ste 3204 Houston TX 77030

DAWSON, EARL BLISS, obstetrics and gynecology educator; b. Perry, Fla., Feb. 1, 1930; s. Bliss and Linnie (Calliham) D.; BA, U. Kans., 1955; student Bowman Gray Sch. Medicine, 1955-57; MA, U. Mo., 1960; PhD, Tex. A&M U., 1964; m. Winnie Ruth Isbell, Apr. 10, 1951; children: Barbara Gail, Patricia Ann, Robert Earl, Diana Lynn. Rsch. instr. dept. ob-gyn. U. Tex. Med. br., Galveston, 1963-65, rsch. asst. prof., 1965-68, rsch. assoc. prof., 1968-89, assoc. prof. dept. ob-gyn., 1989—; cons. Interdeptl. Com. on Nutrition for Nat. Def., 1965-68; cons. Nat. Nutrition Survey, 1968-69. Scoutmaster Boy Scouts Am., 1969—. With USNR, 1951-52. Nutrition Rsch. fellow, 1960-61; NSF scholar, 1961-62; NIH Rsch. fellow, 1962-63. Mem. Tex., N.Y. Acads. Scis., Am. Fert. Soc. Am. Inst. Nutrition, Am. Soc. Clin. Nutrition, Am. Coll. Nutrition, Am. Fertility Soc., Soc. Exptl. Biology and Medicine, Soc. Environ. Geochemistry and Health, Sigma Xi, Phi Rho Sigma. Baptist. Mason. Club: Mic-O-Say (Kansas City, Mo.). Author: Effect of Water Borne Nitrites on the Environment of Man; contbr. numerous articles to profl. jours., chpts. to books. Achievements include research on prenatal nutrition, male fertility, epidemiology of lithium in Tex., biochemical changes associated with pre-menstrual syndrome. Home: 15 Chimney Corners Dr La Marque TX 77568-5274 Office: U Tex Med Br Dept Ob-Gyn Galveston TX 77550

DAWSON, HARRY EUGENE, JR., plastic surgeon; b. Augusta, Ga., Apr. 29, 1942; s. Harry Eugene and Ethlyn Winn (Moseley) D.; m. Frances Patricia Devlin, July 13, 1968; children: Angela, Bebhinn, Ceara, Frances Elizabeth. BA, Emory U., 1964; MD, Med. Coll. Ga., 1969. Diplomate Am. Bd. Plastic Surgery. Intern in surgery Meml. Med. Ctr., Savannah, Ga., 1969-70; resident in gen. surgery Meml. Med. Ctr., Savannah, 1970-73; resident in plastic surgery Baylor Coll. Medicine, Houston, 1973-76, instr. plastic surgery, 1973-76; pvt. practice, Rome, Ga., 1976—. Capt. USAFR, 1971-76. Fellow ACS; mem. Am. Soc. Plastic Surgeons, Am. Soc. for Asthetic Plastic Surgery, Southeastern Soc. Plastic Surgeons, Med. Assn. Ga., Ga. Soc. Plastic Surgeons (pres. 1985-86), Ga. Surg. Soc. Roman Catholic. Office: Harbin Clinic Plastic Surg Assocs 1825 Martha Berry Blvd Rome GA 30165-1625

DAWSON, MARCIA ANN, nurse administrator; b. Annapolis, Md., Aug. 17, 1956; children: John, Jason, Michael. Nursing diploma, Union Meml. Hosp., 1977; BSN, U. Md., Catonsville, 1985. Cert. med.-surg. nursing and nursing adminstrn. ANCC. Med.-surg. charge nurse Union Meml. Hosp., Balt., 1977; ICU and psychiat. charge nurse Univ. Hosp. and Clinic, Pensacola, Fla., 1977-78; acute care unit staff nurse Eskaton Am. River Health Care Ctr., Carmichael, Calif., 1978-79; ICU relief charge nurse Riverside Hosp., Jacksonville, Fla., 1979; ICU charge nurse Regional Meml. Hosp., Brunswick, Maine, 1979-82; ICU relief charge nurse Anne Arundel Med. Ctr., Annapolis, 1982-85; lead nursing office supr. Anne Arundel Med Ctr., Annapolis, Md., 1990-91; relief staff nurse PRN Med. Pers. Pool, Norfolk, Va., 1986-87; night shift nursing supr. Kaiser Permanente Med. Ctr., Santa Clara, Calif., 1988-90; nurse mgr. orthopaedic and neuro surgery, admitting nurse, IV therapy North Arundel Hosp., Glen Burnie, Md., 1992—. Mem. Md. Orgn. Nurse Mgrs., Sigma Theta Tau. Democrat. Home: 3 Tyler Pl Annapolis MD 21403 Office: North Arundel Hosp 301 Hospital Dr Glen Burnie MD 21061-5803

DAWSON, NANCY ANN, hematologist, oncologist; b. San Francisco, Nov. 21, 1953; d. Malcolm Bryon and Helen Dorothy (Jones) D.; m. Neal Thomas Baron, Aug. 22, 1981; children: Blake Bryon Baron, Drew Randall Baron. AB, U. Calif., Berkeley, 1975; MD, Georgetown U., 1979. Diplomate Am. Bd. Internal Medicine, Am. Bd. Internal Medicine-Hematology, Am. Bd. Internal Medicine-Oncology, Nat. Bd. Med. Examiners; lic MD, Md., Va. Commd. 2nd lt. U.S. Army, 1976, advanced through grades to lt. col., 1991; intern in internal medicine Walter Reed Army Med. Ctr., Washington, 1979-80, residency internal medicine, 1980-82, fellowship hematology-oncology, 1982-85; teaching fellow, instr. dept. medicine Uniformed Svcs. U. of Health Scis., Bethesda, Md., 1980-82, 83-85, asst. prof. dept. medicine, 1985-92, assoc. prof. dept. medicine, 1992—; staff physician hematology-oncology svcs., asst. chief Walter Reed Army Med. Ctr., Washington, 1985—, 88-90, asst. dir. intern tng. and transitional year program, 1990-91, dir. intern tng. and transitional year program, 1991-94, transitional program advsor to chief grad. med. edn., 1992-94, chief hematology-oncology clinic, 1994-95, dir. clin. rsch., 1995—. Editor: Prostate Cancer, 1994; contbr. chpts. to books and articles to profl. jours. Recipient Am. Med. Women's Assn. Disting. Student citation, 1979. Fellow Am. Coll. Physicians; mem. AMA, Am. Soc. Clin. Oncology, Assn. Mil. Surgeons of U.S., Am. Soc. Hematology, Women in Cancer Rsch., Am. Urol. Assn. Democrat. Roman Catholic. Home: 7721 Curtis St Chevy Chase MD 20815-4913 Office: Walter Reed Army Med Ctr Hematology Oncology Cl Washington DC 20307

DAWSON, PATRICIA BOGAN, medical and surgical nurse, administrator; b. Milford, Del., Sept. 15, 1958; d. Raymond J. and Louise (Burlingame) Bogan; m. Brian K. Dawson, Sept. 7, 1985. BSN, U. Del., 1980. Project coord. Critical Pathways Johns Hopkins Hosp., Balt. Mem. Nat. Assn. Orthopedic Nurses.

DAWSON, PETER JOHN, pathologist, educator; b. Wolverhampton, Eng., Feb. 17, 1928; came to U.S., 1960; s. Sydney and Bertha (Richards) D.; m. Nancy Sexton Taylor, Apr. 10, 1953 (div. 1969); m. Elizabeth Ann Coombs, Mar. 1, 1982. BA, Cambridge U., 1949, MA, 1953, MB, BCh, 1952, MD, 1960. Diplomate Am. Bd. Pathology. Intern, Royal Berkshire Hosp., Reading, Eng., 1952-53, Victoria Hosp. for Children, London, 1953; resident St. George's Hosp., London, 1953-54, Royal Postgrad. Med. Sch., 1954-55, 58-59; vis. asst. prof. U. Calif., San Francisco, 1960-62; lectr. U. Newcastle, Eng., 1962-64; assoc. prof. U. Oreg., Portland, 1964-67, prof. pathology, 1967-76; prof. pathology, dir. lab. surg. pathology U. Chgo., 1977-89, prof. pathology and lab. medicine U. of South Fla., Tampa, 1989—; chief pathology and lab. svcs. James Haley VA Hosp., Tampa, 1994—. Contbr. articles to profl. jours. Fellow Royal Coll. Pathologists; mem. Chgo. Pathology Soc (v.p. 1984-86, pres. 1986-88), Internat. Acad. Pathology, Am. Assn. Cancer Rsch., Am. Assn. Pathologists Episcopalian. Avocation: sailing.

DAWSON, ROBERT EDWARD, SR., ophthalmologist; b. Rocky Mount, N.C., Feb. 23, 1918; s. William and Daisy (Wright) D.; m. Julia Belle Davis, Mar. 10, 1950; children: Dianne Elizabeth, Janice Elaine, Robert Edward, Melanie Lorraine. BS, Clark Coll., 1939; MD, Meharry Med. Coll., 1943. Diplomate Am. Bd. Ophthalmology (examiner 1979-82). Intern Homer G. Phillips Hosp., St. Louis, 1943-44, resident, 1944-46; preceptor Duke Hosp., Durham, N.C., 1946-50, clin. instr. ophthalmology, 1968-70; pvt. practice Durham, 1946-55, 57-88; mem. attending staff ophthalmology Lincoln Hosp., Durham, 1946-55; cons. ophthalmology N.C. Cen. U. Health Svc., Durham, 1950-64; chief ophthalmology and otolaryngology Lincoln Hosp., Durham, 1959-76; mem. attending staff ophthalmology Watts Hosp., Durham, 1966-76; mem. attending staff ophthalmology, v.p. med. staff Durham County Gen. Hosp., 1976-88; med. dir. Lincoln Hosp., Durham, 1968-70; lectr. ophthalmology Lincoln Hosp. Sch. Nursing, Durham, 1948-56; clin. assoc. Duke U., Durham, 1969-75; clin. asst. prof. ophthalmology Duke U. Eye Ctr., Durham, 1975-87, cons. in ophthalmology, 1987-89, ophthalmology scholar in residence, 1991—; chair dept. ophthalmology 3310th Hosp., Scott AFB, Belleville, Ill., 1956-57; mem. N.C. Adv. Com. on Med. Assistance, 1972-85; mem. adv. bd. N.C. State Commn. for Blind, 1965-75; mem. Gov.'s Adv. Com. Med. Assistance; regional surg. dir. Eye Bank Assn. Am., Inc., 1968-79. Mem. Durham Coun. Human Rels., 1967-69; mem. Pres. Com. on Employment of Handicapped, 1971-79; bd. dirs. Durham County Tb Assn., 1950-54, Better Health Found., 1960-66, Durham Community House, 1966-68, Lincoln Community Health Ctr., Am. Cancer Soc., Durham United Fund, Durham County Mental Health Ctr., 1976-79, Found. for Better Health of Durham County Gen. Hosp., 1975-79; bd. dirs., v.p. Nat. Soc. Prevention of Blindness; trustee Durham Acad., 1969-72, Durham County Gen. Hosp.; life trustee Meharry Med. Coll.; trustee emeritus N.C. Cen. U., Mut. Savs. & Loan; mem. bd. mgmt. Meharry Med. Coll. Alumni Assn.; bd. assocs. Greensboro Coll., N.C.; chmn. bd. dirs. Lincoln Pvt. Diagnostic Clinic; bd. visitors Clark Coll., Atlanta. Served as maj., M.C., USAF, 1955-57. Recipient Disting. Svc. award Clark Coll., 1984, Nat. Assn. Equal Opportunity in Higher Edn., 1985, Physician of Yr. award Old North State Med. Soc., 1981, Meritorious Svc. Highest award, 1991. Fellow ACS, Acad. Ophthalmology; mem. AMA, Nat. Soc. to Prevent Blindness (v.p.), Am. Assn. Ophthalmology, Soc. Eye Surgeons, Nat. Med. Assn. (trustee 1971-80, pres. 1979-80, Disting. Service award 1983), Pan Am. Med. Assn. (diplomate), Old North State Med. Soc. (pres. 1966-67), Durham Acad. Medicine (pres. 1967-68), NAACP (life), Durham Bus. and Profl. Chain, C. of C., Meharry Nat. Alumni Assn. (past pres.), Alpha Omega Alpha, Alpha Phi Alpha (past pres.), Sigma Pi Phi (pres.), Chi Delta Mu (pres.). Democrat. Mem. A.M.E. Ch. (stewards bd. 1968—). Mason (33d degree, Shriner). Club: Toastmasters (pres. 1969-70). Home: 817 E Lawson St Durham NC 27701-4534 Office: 512 Simmons St Durham NC 27701-4334

DAWSON, TED MURRAY, neurologist, educator; b. Idaho Falls, Idaho, Apr. 19, 1959; s. Oliver Murray and Goldy (Mehas) D.; m. Valina Lynn Camilli, June 14, 1986. BS, Mont. State U., 1981; MD, U. Utah, 1986, PhD, 1986. Diplomate Am. Bd. Med. Examiners, Am. Bd. Psychiatry and Neurology. Intern in medicine U. Utah Affiliated Hosps., Salt Lake City, 1986-87; resident in neurology Hosp. of U. Pa., Phila., 1987-90; tchg. and rsch. asst. dept. pharmacology U. Utah, Salt Lake City, 1984-86; asst. instr. dept. neurology U. Pa., Phila., 1989, instr., 1989-90; postdoctoral fellow, sr. clin. fellow dept. neurosci. Johns Hopkins U., Balt., 1990-92, instr. dept. neurosci. and neurology, 1992-93, asst. prof. dept. neurology and neurosci., 1993-96, assoc. prof., 1996—. Contbr. articles to profl. jours. Mem. AMA, AAAS, Am. Acad. Neurology, Am. Fedn. Clin. Rsch., Soc. Neurosci., Molecular Medicine Soc. Office: Johns Hopkins U 600 N Wolfe St Path 2-210 Baltimore MD 21287-9999

DAWSON, THOMAS WAYNE, dentist; b. Marshall, Tex., May 30, 1947; s. Weldon C. and Mary Jane (Preston) D.; m. Karen Ann Surley, Aug. 21, 1971. BS in Biology, Lammar U., 1969; DDS, U. Tex., 1974. Pvt. practice Arlington, Tex., 1974—; bd. dirs., assoc. faculty L.D. Pankey Inst., Miami, Fla. Chm. com. Leadership Arlington, 1982-83. Fellow Acad. Gen. Dentistry; mem. ADA, Tex. Dental Assn., Arlington Dental Study Club (treas. 1974-87, pres. 1987—), Tex. Acad. Dental Practice Adminstrn. (pres. bd. dirs., chmn. program), S.W. Acad. Restorative Dentistry, Am. Acad. Fixed Prosthodontics, Class One Triple Plus Club L.D. Pankey Inst. Republican. Mem. Ch. of Christ. Office: 903 W Mitchell St Arlington TX 76013-2507

DAY, ANGELA RIDDLE, occupational health nurse, educator; b. Greenville, S.C., Oct. 23, 1963; d. Earl C. and Sandra (Grooms) Riddle; m. Herbert Day, May 26, 1984; 2 children. BSN, Clemson U., 1985. RN, S.C.; cert. occupational health nurse; cert. occupational hearing conservationist, pulmonary function technician, CPR, first aid instr. Staff nurse St. Francis Hosp., Greenville, 1985-86; dir. occupational health nursing, ednl. coord. North Hills Med. Ctr., Greenville, 1986-94; occupational health nrse BMW Mfg. Corp., Greer, S.C., 1994—. Mem. Am. Assn. Occupational Health Nurses, S.C. State Assn. Occupational Health Nurses (com. chmn.). Office: BMW Mfg Corp PO Box 11000 Spartanburg SC 29304-4100

DAY, ANNE WHITE, retired registered nurse; b. Cin., July 9, 1926; d. Pinkney McGill and Anna Pearl (Glendenning) White; m. Raymond Eric Parker, Mar. 6, 1948 (div. 1969); children: Douglas McGill, Stephanie Morse. Diploma, Christ Hosp. Sch. Nursing, Cin., 1947. RN, Ohio; cert. chem. dependency nurse Consol. Assn. Nurses in Substance Abuse. Staff nurse to asst. head nurse Holmes div. U. Cin., 1948-84; nursing supr. Villa Hope Extended Care Facility, Cin., 1970-72; staff nurse Hillenbrand Nursing Home, Cin., 1980-82, Emerson A. North Hosp., Cin., 1982-94. Vol. Group Against Smoke Pollution, Cin., 1989—; donor Zoo, Cin., 1989—, Voters for Choice, Ohio, 1989—, Ams. for Non-Smokers Rights, Calif., 1989—, Action on Smoking or Health, 1989—, Stop Teenage Addiction to Tobacco; tutor for adult literacy. Mem. DAR (life). Episcopalian.

DAY, LUCILLE LANG, health facility administrator, educator, author; b. Oakland, Calif., Dec. 5, 1947; d. Richard Allen and Evelyn Marietta (Hazard) Lang; m. Frank Lawrence Day, Nov. 6, 1965 (div. 1985); 1 child, Liana Sherrine; m. 2nd, Theodore Herman Fleischman, June 23, 1974; 1 child, Tamarind Channah. AB, U. Calif., Berkeley, 1971, MA, 1973, PhD, 1979. Teaching asst. U. Calif., Berkeley, 1971-72, 75-76, research asst., 1975, 77-78; tchr. sci. Magic Mountain Sch., Berkeley, 1977; specialist math. and sci. Novato (Calif.) Unified Sch. Dist., 1979-81; instr. sci. Project Bridge, Laney Coll., Oakland, Calif., 1984-86; sci. writer and mgr. precollege edn. programs, Lawrence Berkeley (Calif.) Nat. Lab., 1986-90, life scis. staff coord., 1990-92; mgr. Hall of Health, Berkeley, Calif., 1992—. Author numerous poems, articles and book reviews; author: (with Joan Skolnick and Carol Langbort) How to Encourage Girls in Math and Science: Strategies for Parents and Educators, 1982; Self-Portrait with Hand Microscope (poetry collection), 1982. NSF Grad. fellow, 1972-75; recipient Joseph Henry Jackson award in lit. San Francisco Found., 1982. Mem. No. Calif. Sci. Writers Assn., Nat. Assn. Sci. Writers, Math/Sci. Network, Phi Beta Kappa, Iota Sigma Pi. Home: 1057 Walker Ave Oakland CA 94610-1511 Office: Hall of Health 2230 Shattuck Ave Berkeley CA 94704-1424

DAY, ROBERT WINSOR, cancer research administrator; b. Framingham, Mass., Oct. 22, 1930; s. Raymond Albert and Mildred (Doty) D.; m. Jane Alice Boynton, Sept. 6, 1957 (div. Sept. 1977); m. Cynthia Taylor, Dec. 16, 1977; children: Christopher, Natalia, Julia. Student, Harvard U., 1949-51; MD, U. Chgo., 1956; MPH, U. Calif., Berkeley, 1958, PhD, 1962. Intern USPHS, Balt., 1956-57; resident U. Calif., Berkeley, 1958-60; research specialist Calif. Dept. Mental Hygiene, 1960-64; asst. prof. sch. medicine UCLA, 1962-64; dep. dir. Calif. Dept. Pub. Health, Berkeley, 1965-67; prof., chmn. dept. health services Sch. Pub. Health and Community Medicine, U. Wash., Seattle, 1968-72, dean, 1972-82, prof., 1982—; dir. Fred Hutchinson Cancer Rsch. Ctr., Seattle, 1981-91, pres., 1991—; mem. Nat. Cancer Adv. Bd., 1992—; cons. in field. Served with USPHS, 1956-57. Fellow AAAS, Am. Pub. Health Assn., Am. Coll. Preventive Medicine; mem. Am. Soc. Clin. Oncology, Soc. Preventive Oncology, Am. Assn. Cancer Rsch., Assn. Schs. Pub. Health (pres. 1981-82), Am. Assn. Cancer Insts. (bd. dirs. 1983-88, v.p. 1984-85, pres. 1985-86, chmn. bd. dirs., 1986-87). Office: Fred Hutchinson Cancer Rsch Ctr 1124 Columbia St #LY-301 Seattle WA 98104-2015

DAY, STACEY BISWAS, physician, educator; b. London, Dec. 31, 1927; came to U.S. 1955, naturalized 1977.; s. Satis B. and Emma L. (Camp) D.; m. Ivana Podvalova, Oct. 18, 1973; 2 children. M.D., Royal Coll. Surgeons, Dublin, Ireland, 1955; Ph.D., McGill U., 1964; D.Sc., Cin. U., 1971. Intern King's County Hosp., SUNY Downstate Ctr., 1955-56; resident fellow in surgery U. Minn. Hosp., 1956-60; hon. registrar St. George's Hosp., London, Eng., 1960-61; lectr. exptl. surgery McGill U., Montreal, Que., Can., 1964; asst. prof. exptl. surgery U. Cin. Med. Sch., 1968-70; assoc. dir. basic med. research Shriner's Burn Inst., Cin., 1969-71; from asst. to assoc. prof. pathology, head Bell Mus. Pathobiology U. Minn., Mpls., 1970-74; dir. biomed. communications and med. edn. Sloan-Kettering Inst., N.Y.C., 1974-80; mem. Sloan-Kettering Inst. for Cancer Research, 1974-80; mem. adminstrv. council, field coordinator, 1974-75; prof. biology Sloan Kettering div. Grad. Sch. Med. Sci. Cornell U., 1974-80, ret., 1980; clin. prof. medicine div. behavioral medicine N.Y. Med. Coll., 1980-92; prof. biopsychosocial medicine, chmn. dept. community health U. Calabar (Nigeria) Sch. Medicine, 1982-85; prof. internat. health, dir. Internat. Ctr. for Health Scis. Meharry Med. Coll., Nashville, 1985-89, dir. WHO Collaborating Ctr. ICHS, 1987-89; founding dir. WHO Collaborating Ctr., Nashville, 1987-89, emeritus dir., 1989; adj. prof. family and community medicine U. Ariz. Coll. Med. Scis., Tucson, 1985-89; univ. prof. internat. health U. Calabar, Nigeria, 1989—;

permanent vis. prof. med. edn. Oita Med. Univ., Japan, 1992—; Arris and Gale lectr. Royal Coll. Surgeons, Eng., 1972, vis. lectr., Ireland, 1972; vis. prof. U. Bologna, 1977, Kyushu, Japan, 1990, U. Mauritius, 1991, Bratislava U., 1991, Japan, 1992, 1993, Beijing, China, 1993; vis. prof. health comm. U. Santiago, Chile, 1979-80, Kuala Lumpur, Malaysia, 1996, Colombo, Sri Lanka, 1996, South India, 1996, U. S.F. De Quito, Ecuador, 1996; vis. prof. Oncologic Rsch. Inst., Tallinn, Estonia, 1976, All India Insts. Health, 1976, U. Maiduguri, 1982, Kyushu, Japan, 1990; vis. acad. Oxford (Eng.) U. 1993-95; moderator med. cartography and computer health Harvard U., 1978, Acad. Scis., Czechoslovakia, 1987, Australia, 1988; Fulbright prof. Charles U., Czechoslovakia, 1989; cons. Pan Am. Health Assn., 1974-90, U.S.-USSR Agreement for Health Cooperation, 1976, WHO Collaborating Centre Meharry Med. Coll., Nashville, 1985, NAFEO/AID, 1986-89; mem. expert com. for health, manpower devel., WHO, 1986-90; cons. Div. Strengthening Health Care Resources WHO, Geneva, 1987-90, UN-FSSTD, 1987, AID/Joint Memorandum of Understanding, W. Africa, Kenya, Sudan, So. Africa, 1985-89, to dean med. coll., faculty Med. and Health Scis., ABHA, Province of Asir, Saudi Arabia, 1981, to dir. High Tatras symposia Post Grad. Med. Inst., Bratislavia, 1990—, to rector Universidad Autonama Agraria Antonio Narro, Saltillo, Mexico, 1987-89; pres., chmn., Pub. Cultural and Ednl. Prodns., Montreal, U.S., 1966-85; bd. dirs. Internat. Health, African Health Consultancy Svc., Nigeria, Ekológia & Život, Slovakia; bd. dirs., v.p. Am. Sci. Activities Mario Negri Rsch. Found. 1975-80; hon. founding chmn., bd. dirs. Lambo Found. U.S.; v.p., trustee Cancer Relief Found., Calabar; pres., exec. dir. Internat. Found. for Biosocial Devel. and Human Health, 1978-86, chmn., 1986—; mem. Medzinárodny Poradny Vybor Nadácie Ekológia Život, Rep. Slovakia, 1995—; cons. Inst. Health, Lyfford Cay, Bahamas, 1981, Govt. Cross River State, Nigeria, Itreto State and H.H. Obong of Calabar, Nat. Bd. Advs., Am. Biog. Inst., 1982—; cons. cmty. health and health comms. Navaho Nation, Sage Meml. Hosp., Ganado, Ariz., 1984; founder, cons. Primary Self-Health Clinics, Oban, Ikot Oku Okono, and Ikot Imo, Nigeria, 1982-84; cons. High Tatras Internat. Health Symposia, Slovakia, 1990—; apptd. ambassador Gov. State of Tenn., 1986—; adj. clin. prof. medicine N.Y. Med. Coll.; researcher in field. Writer, 1965—; author: (verse) Collected Lines, 1966, (play) By the Waters of Babylon, 1966, (verse) American Lines, 1967, (play) The Music Box, 1967, Three Folk Songs Set to Music, 1967, Poems and Etudes, 1968, (novel) Rosalita, 1968, The Idle Thoughts of a Surgical Fellow, 1968, Edward Stevens-Gastric Physiologist, Physician and American Statesman, 1969, (novella) Bellechasse, 1970, A Leaf of the Chaatim, 1970, Ten Poems and a Letter from America for Mr. Sinha, 1971, Curling's Ulcer: An Experiment of Nature, 1972, Tuluak and Amaulik: Dialogues on Death and Mourning with the Innuit Eskimo of Point Barrow and Wainwright, Alaska, 1974, East of the Navel and Afterbirth: Reflections from Rapa Nui, 1976, Health Communications, 1979, The Biopsychosocial Imperative, 1981, What Is Survival: The Physician's Way and the Biologos, 1981, Developing Health in the West African Bush, 1995; editor: Death and Attitudes Toward Death, 1972, Membranes, Viruses and Immune Mechanisms in Experimental and Clinical Disease, 1972, Ethics in Medicine in a Changing Society, 1973, Communication of Scientific Information, 1975, Trauma: Clinical and Biological Aspects, 1975, Molecular Pathology, 1975, (with Robert A. Good) series Comprehensive Immunology, 9 vols., 1976-80, Cancer Invasion and Metastasis-Biologic Mechanisms and Therapy, 1977, Some Systems of Biological Communication, 1977, Image of Science and Society, 1977, What Is a Scientist, 1978, Sloan Kettering Inst. Cancer Series, 1974-80, (with K. Inokouchi) Selections From the Chronicle of The Hagakure as Wisdom Literature: The Way of The Samurai of Saga Domain, 1993; editor-in-chief, mem. editl. bd.: Health Communications and Informatics, 1974-80; editor in chief: The American Biomedical Network: Health Care System in America Present and Past, 1978, A Companion to the Life Sciences, Vol. 1, 1979, A Companion to the Life Sciences, Vol. 2, Integrated Medicine, 1980, A Companion to the Life Sciences, Vol. 3: Life Stress, 1981, Advance to Biopsychosocial Health, 1984; editor in chief, mem. editorial bd. Health Communications and Biopsychosocial Health; editor: (with others) Cancer, Stress and Death, 1979, 2d edit., 1986, Computers for Medical Office and Patient Management, 1981, Readings in Oncology, 1980, Biopsychosocial Health, 1981; editor: Primary Health Care Guidelines: A Training Manual for Community Health, 2d edit., 1986, (with T.A. Lambo) Contemporary Issues in International Health, 1989; sr. editor (with Salat and others): Health and Quality of Life in Changing Europe in the Year 2000, 1992, Hagakure-Spirit of Bushido, (with H. Koga), 1993, (with K. Inokuchi) Selections from the Chronicles of the Hagakure as Wisdom Literature: The Way of the Samurai of Saga Domain, 1993, (with Salát) Health Management, Organization, and Planning in Changing Eastern Europe, 1993, The Medical Student and the Mission of Medicine in the Twenty First Century, (in Japanese, with M. Kobayashi and K. Inokuchi), 1995, The Wisdom of Hagakure, 1996, Developing Health in the West African Bush (2 parts), 1995, Letters of Owen Wagensteen to a surgicl fellow: with a memoir, 1996; mem. editl. bd.: Annual Reviews on Stress, Jour. Stress; also co-editor various publs.; contbr. articles to profl. lit.; producer TV and radio health edn. programs, Nigeria, TV film River Blindness (Onchocerciasis) in Africa, 1988. Served with Brit. Army, 1946-49. Recipient Moynihan medal Assn. Surgeons Gt. Britain and Ireland, 1960, Reuben Harvey triennial prize Royal Coll. Physicians, Ireland, 1957, disting. scholar award Internat. Communication Assn., 1980, Sama Found. medal, 1982, disting. citation Hagakure Soc., 1992, Nat. Svc. medal Royal Brit. Legion, 1993; named to Hon. Order Ky. Cols., 1968; named Chieftan Ntufam Ajan of Oban Ejagham People, Cross River State, Nigeria, 1983; recipient Chieftan Obong Nsong Idem Ibibio Nigeria, 1983, Mgbe (Ekpe) honor Nigeria, commendation WHO address Fed. Govt. Nigeria, Calabar, 1983, Leadership in Internat. Med. Health citation Pres. U.S., 1987, WHO medal, 1987, Agromedicine citation Commr. of Agr., State of Tenn., 1987, Assembly citation State of N.Y., 1987, Citation Congl. Record., 1987; Maestro Honorifo, U. Autonoma Agraria, Coahuila, Mex., 1987; presented Key to the City of Nashville, 1987; recipient Vice-Chancellor's Citation and Presentation for Primary Health Care Teaching in Nigeria, U. Calabar, 1988; Pamétni medal Postgrad. Med. Coll., Prague, 1991, Gold medal U. of Bratislava, 1991, Disting. Citation Hagakure Rsch. Soc., Japan, 1992, Nat. Svc. medal Royal Brit. Legion, 1993; addresses presented by people of Ikot Imo, Nsit Anyang, Oban, 1982-84, Commendation from King of Calabar, 1984; Ciba fellow Can., 1965; Stacey Day Ward named in his honor by Fed. Min. and Gov. of Cross River State, Calabar Med. Ctr., Nigeria, 1986; charter mem. U.S. Normandy Com., 1988; 1st fgn. hon. mem. Hagakure Res. Soc. (Samurai), Kyushu, Japan, 1991. Fellow Zool. Soc. London Royal Micros. Soc., Royal Soc. Health, World Acad. Arts and Scis., Japanese Found. for Biopsychosocial Health (internat. hon. fellow and most disting. mem.), African Acad. Sci., African Acad. Med. Scis. (founder); mem. AAS, AMA, Am. Burn Assn., Internat. Burn Assn., Can. Authors Assn., N.Y. Acad. Scis., Am. Assn. History Medicine, Am. Inst. Stress (bd. dirs.), Am. Anthrop. Assn., Am. Rural Health Assn. (v.p. internat. sci. affairs, bd. dirs.), Soc. Med. Geographers USSR. Home: 6 Lomond Ave Chestnut Ridge NY 10977-6901

DAY, THOMAS KEVIN, consultant surgeon; b. Cranford, Middlesex, Eng., Aug. 20, 1946; s. Thomas Duncan and Joan Elsa (Lowenthal) D.; m. Christine Elizabeth Harpham, May 5, 1973; children: Catherine Sarah, Elizabeth Anne. MChir, U. Cambridge (Eng.), 1969. Intern Guy's Hosp., London, 1972-73, resident, 1976-77; jr. lectr. Kings Coll., London, 1974; lectr. dept. surgery Guy's Hosp., London, 1978; cons. surgeon Altnagelvin Hosp., Londonderry, No. Ireland, 1983—. Fellow Royal Soc. Medicine, Internat. Coll. Surgeons. Anglican. Home: 46 Lower Ballyartan Rd, Killaloo BT47 3SY, Northern Ireland Office: NW Independent Hosp, Glen Shane Rd, Bally Kelly Ct, Londonberry BT49 9HS, Northern Ireland

DAY, WILLIAM VANCE, health care executive; b. Rochester, Pa.; s. George Etzwiler and Willa Emma (Vance) D.; m. Loraine Charlotte Day, July 19, 1958; children: Valerie Day Wilden, Douglas William Day. BS, Geneva Coll., 1956; EdD, Ohio U., 1969. Asst. dir. of pub. rels. Geneva Coll., Beaver Falls, Pa., 1956-60; dir. coll. rels. Robert Morris Coll., Pitts., 1960-65; v.p. Mgmt. Adv. and Rsch., Pitts., 1965-67; mng. ptnr. Day and Mowry, Pitts., 1967-74; pres. St. Barnabas Health System, Gibsonia, Pa., 1974—; cons. Pitts. Steelers, 1960-85; bd. dirs. Allied Ins. Brokers, Inc., Pitts.; bd. govs. ACHCA, Alexandria, Va.; bd. regents LaRoche Coll., Pitts.; cons. to numerous orgns. including Allegheny Acad., Pitts., 1970-71, Don Parker Sales, Inc., Pitts., 1981-84, Exhibitor's Svc. Co., McKeesRocks, Pa., 1967-77, Thiel Coll., Greenville, Pa., 1973-74, The Congregational Homes, Pitss., 1972-76, Meth. Home and Hosp., Pitts., 1968-69, others. Founder Presents for Patients, 1983, St. Barnabas Leadership Conf., 1987; pres. Lighthouse Cove Owners Assn., Conneaut Lake, Pa., 1990-93; adv. bd. Port Authority of Allegheny, Pitts., 1990—; trustee Nat. Retiree Vol. Co., Mpls., 1989—; task force Nat. Chamber Found., Washington, 1986-93; bd. dirs. Long-Term Care Coalition, Washington, 1992—; trustee Nat. Retiree Vol. Coalition Adv. Bd., Mpls., 1989—; elder Highland Presbyn. Ch., Pitts., 1979-81; numerous others civic activities. Named Community Leader of Yr., North Hills News Record, Pitts., 1993, Nat. Disting. Adminstr., ACHCA, Nashville, 1993, ARCADIA award N. Allegheny C. of C., Pitts., 1994. Fellow Am. Coll. Healthcare Adminstrn. (regional gov. 1993), Continuing Care Accreditation Com. (evaluator 1984), Am. Mgmt. Assn., Med. Group Mgmt. Assn., Internat. Platform Assn., others. Republican. Presbyterian. Office: St Barnabas Health System 5850 Meridian Rd Gibsonia PA 15044-9605

DAYAL, VIJAY SHANKER, medical educator, physician; b. Ranchi, Bihar, India, Sept. 20, 1936; came to U.S., 1986; s. Ram Shanker Dayal and Vindhyachal (Devi) Devi; m. Susheela Sadhu, Oct. 10, 1961; children: Aneeta, Anjali, Amit. MBBS, Patna (India) Med. Coll., 1959; MSc, McGill U., Montreal, Can., 1966. Resident in otolaryngology McGill U., Montreal, 1960-61, 62-64, resident in surgery, 1961-62; clin. tchr. U. Toronto (Can.), 1967-68, asst. prof., 1968-75, assoc. prof., 1975-81, prof., 1981-86; prof. U. Chgo., 1986—. Mem. editorial rev. bd. Am. Jour. Otolaryngology, 1989—, Otolaryngology Head and Neck Injury, 1990—; author: Clinical Otolaryngology, 1981; contbr. over 70 articles to profl. jours. V.p. Am. Neurotology Soc., 1983-84. Fellow Am. Acad. Otolaryngology, Am. Otological Soc., Am. Trilogical Soc., Barany Soc. Office: U Chgo Dept Surgery 5841 S Maryland Ave # 412 Chicago IL 60637-1463

DAYHOFF, RUTH ELIZABETH, research physician, medical computer system developer; b. N.Y.C., May 16, 1952; d. Edward Samuel and Margaret Belle (Oakley) Dayhoff; m. Vincent Michael Brannigan, May 26, 1975; children: Margaret Elaine Dayhoff-Brannigan, Eleanor Maurine Dayhoff-Brannigan. BS, U. Md., 1973; MD, Georgetown U., 1977. Computer programmer Nat. Bur. Standards, Gaithersburg, Md., 1974-75; pathology resident George Washington U. Sch. Medicine, Washington, 1977-79, Johns Hopkins U. Sch. Medicine, Balt., 1979-80; rsch. physician Dept. Vets. Affairs, Washington, 1980-82; rsch. asst. prof. Georgetown U. Sch. Medicine, Washington, 1982-87; pres. Ruth Dayhoff Rsch. Assoc., Bethesda, Md., 1988-89; imaging project dir. Dept. Vets. Affairs, Silver Spring, Md., 1989—; bd. dirs. Internat. Fed. MUMPS Users Group, College Park, Md.; assoc. prof. George Washington U. Sch. Medicine, Washington, 1989—; lectr. Johns Hopkins U. Sch. Medicine, Balt., 1980—. Editor MUMPS Users Group jour., 1980—; developer DHCP Imaging System; contbr. articles to profl. jours. Recipient Fed. 100 award Fed. Computer Week, 1991, Sci. grant NIH, 1986-88; named Fed. Office Profl. of Yr., Info. Resources Adv. Coun., 1990. Fellow Am. Coll. Med. Informatics; mem. IEEE, Assn. Computing Machinery, MUMPS Users Group (exec. dir. 1980-83, chmn. 1983-85). Office: Vets Affairs Info Systems 8403 Colesville Rd Ste 200 Silver Spring MD 20910-3365

DAYTON, MARTIN, health care company administrator; b. N.Y.C., Aug. 7, 1944; s. Jack Dayton and Ruth Buchbiner; m. Barbara Prats, Apr. 16, 1985; children: Heather, Robert Jason, Matthew Dalton. BS, Rutgers U., 1966; DO, Kirksville (Mo.) Coll., 1970; MD, Ross U., Dominica, 1983. Diplomate Am. Bd. Chelation Therapy, Am. Acad. Family Physicians, Am. Coll. Osteo. Physicians in Gen. Practice; ACLS. Emergency room dir. Daytona Beach (Fla.) Hosp., 1971-72; med. dir. Med. Ctr. Sunny Isles, Miami Beach, Fla., 1973—, Dayton Preventative Med. Ctr., Miami Beach, 1980—; clin. asst. prof. family medicine, Coll. Osto. Medicine of the Pacific, N.Y. Coll. Osteo. Medicine; bd. dirs. Moneyworks Bank. Contbr. articles to Health & Medicine mag. Fellow Am. Coll. Applied Nutrition; mem. AMA, Am. Osteo. Assn., Am. Acad. Med. Preventics, Soc. Tchrs. in Family Medicine, Am. Coll. for Advancement in Medicine, Dade County Osteo. Med. Assn., Fla. Soc. Am. Coll. Gen. Practitioner ins Osteo. Medicine, Am. Holistic Med. Assn., Am. Acad. Acupuncture Medicine, Soc. Ultramolecular Medicine, others. Office: Med Ctr Sunny Isles 18600 Collins Ave Miami FL 33160-2426

DEAL, WILLIAM THOMAS, school psychologist; b. Canton, Ohio, Dec. 18, 1949; s. Richard Lee and Rheta Lucille (Gerber) D.; m. Paula Nespeca, Aug. 5, 1972. BS, Bowling Green State U., 1972; MA, John Carroll U., 1977; postgrad. Kent State U., 1979—. Sci. tchr. Westlake Schs., 1972-76, head bldg. sci. dept., 1974-76; intern sch. psychologist Garfield Heights Schs., 1976-77, sch. psychologist, 1977—; pvt. practice psychology, Parma Heights, Ohio, 1982-84. Alternate mem. adv. council Cuyahoga County Spl. Edn. Service Ctr., 1977—. Recipient Cert. of Recognition, Garfield Heights Bd. Edn., 1980; Outstanding Achievement award Cleve. Assn. for Children with Learning Disabilities, Inc., 1980; named Psychologist of Yr. Cleveland Sch., 1990. Mem. Nat. Assn. Sch. Psychologists, United Teaching Profession, Ohio Sch. Psychology Assn., Cleve. Assn. Sch. Psychologists, Phi Delta Kappa. Republican. Mem. Reformed Ch. Home: 5290 Kings Hwy Cleveland OH 44126-3059 Office: 4900 Turney Rd Cleveland OH 44125-2501

DEAN, ANDREW GRISWOLD, epidemiologist; b. Rochester, N.Y., Apr. 4, 1938; m. Consuelo Beck-Sagué; 1 child, Jeffrey A. Student, Wesleyan U., Middletown, Conn., 1956-58; AB summa cum laude, Oberlin Coll., 1960; MD cum laude, Harvard U., 1964, MPH, 1972. Diplomate Am. Bd. Preventive Medicine; lic. Ga. Intern King County Hosp., Seattle, 1964-65; SA surgeon and surgeon USPHS (Peace Corps), Hargeisa, Somali Republic, 1965-67; staff Pacific Rsch. Sect. Nat. Inst. Allergy and Infectious Diseases, Honolulu, Hawaii, 1967-71; resident in preventive medicine U. Hawaii, Honolulu, 1968-70; epidemologist WHO, Arua, Uganda, 1972-73; asst. prof. tropical pub. health Harvard Sch. Pub. Health, Cambridge, Mass., 1973-74; epidemic intelligence svc. officer Ark. State Dept. Health Bur. Disease Control, Atlanta, Ga., 1974-76; project dir. Pacific Ctr. for Geographic Disease Rsch., Honolulu, 1976-78; state epidemologist and dir. communicable disease control Minn. Dept. Health, Mpls., 1978-79, dir. divsn. disease prevention and control, 1979-84; med. epidemiologist Ctr. for Disease Control, Atlanta, 1984-90; chief systems devel. and support br. divsn. surveillance and epidemiology Ctrs. for Disease Control and Prevention, Atlanta, 1991—; asst. clin. prof. tropical medicine and microbiology, U. Hawaii Sch. Medicine, 168-72, clin. assoc. prof., 1977-78; assoc. prof. biometry U. Ark., 1974-76; adj. assoc. prof. epidemiology U. Minn. Sch. Pub. Health, 1978-84; human subjects coord. Epidemiology Program Office, 1986—; mem. med. adv. com. Ctrs. for Disease Control, 1986—; adj. assoc prof. Internat. Health, Rollins Sch. of Pub. Health, Emory U., 1994—. Contbr. numerous articles to profl. jours; author users manuals for med. computer use; contbr. chpts. to books in pub. health field. Vol. Waikiki Drug Clinic, Honolulu, Cambridge (Mass.) Med. Clinic, 1971-72; bd. mem. Internat. Health Vols., Minn., 1979-83. Served in USPHS, 1965-71, 74-76, 1984— Dir. (0-6). Recipient Philip S. Brachman award Ctrs. for Disease Control and Prevention, 1987, Nat. Applied Eipdemilogy award Coun. State and Territorial Epidemiologists, 1996. Fellow Am. Coll. Epidemiology; mem. Am. Pub. Health Assn., Phi Beta Kappa, Sigma Xi, Alpha Omega Alpha. Home: 2877 McClave Dr Doraville GA 30340-1941 Office: Ctrs for Disease Control Bldg 6 Rm 276 Mailstop G34 1600 Clifton Rd NE Atlanta GA 30333

DEAN, ELIZABETH M., rehabilitation medicine educator, physical therapist; b. Birmingham, Eng., Dec. 2, 1948; came to Can., 1965; d. Cyril Lemuel and Marian Emma (Rogers) Isitt. BA, U. Man., 1972, Diploma in phys. therapy, 1975, PhD, 1987; MS, U. So. Calif., 1978. Rsch. asst. Can. Agr., Winnipeg, Man., Can., 1966-71; phys. therapist St. Boniface Gen. Hosp., Winnipeg, 1975-78, rsch. assoc., 1978-79; part-time tchr. U. Man., Winnipeg, 1978-81; assoc. prof., rsch. fellow U. B.C., Vancouver, 1983-87, rsch. fellow, 1985-87; phys. therapist, dir. Ergometric Performance Lab., Sch. Rehab. Med. U. of B.C., Vancouver, 1985—, asst. prof. Sch. Rehab. Med., 1987-92; assoc. prof. Sch. Rehab. Med., 1992—. Contbr. articles to profl. jours. and chpts. to books on cardiorespiratory phys. therapy. Mem. Can. Physiotherapy Assn., Am. Phys. Therapy Assn., Am. Phys. Soc. Home: 203-3784 W 16th Ave, Vancouver, BC Canada V6R 3C4 Office: U BC Sch Rehab Med, 2211 Westbrook Mall, Vancouver, BC Canada V6T 1W5

DEAN, GARY EDWARD, molecular biologist, educator; b. L.A., Aug. 26, 1950; s. Francis Hill and Myrtle Oda (Enoltt) D.; m. Adele Mazzari, Sept. 7, 1978; children: Benjamin Adam, Lily Susanna. BA, U. Calif., Santa Cruz, 1975; PhD, Yale U., 1983. Postdoctoral assoc. dept. pharmacology Yale U. Sch. Medicine, New Haven, 1983-85; assoc. prof. dept. molecular genetics U. Cin. Coll. Medicine, 1985—, dir. molecular biology div.-Alzheimer's Rsch. Ctr., 1988—; exec. com. Alzheimer Ctr., Cin., 1990—; reviewer Am. Heart Assn., Columbus, Ohio, 1990—. Contbr. chpt. to Methods in Enzymology, 1988; contbr. articles to Proceedings of the Nat. Acad. Sci., Jour. Biol. Chemistry, Jour. Neurochemistry. Recipient grants, Am. Heart Assn., 1987, Am. Cancer Soc., 1988, NIH, 1988, 89. Mem. Am. Soc. for Microbiology, Am. Soc. for Cell Biology, Am. Soc. for Biochemistry and Molecular Biology, Soc. for Neuroscience. Democrat. Office: U Cin Coll Medicine 231 Bethesda Ave Cincinnati OH 45229-2827

DEAN, JAMES FRANKLIN, psychologist; b. Berea, Ky., Aug. 20, 1951; s. Carl Lincoln Dean and Barbara Louise (Lockmiller) Woody. BA, U. Ky., 1976; MA, U. Ark., 1983, PhD, 1986. Staff psychologist Astor Home for Children, Bronx, N.Y., 1987-88, Met. Hosp. Ctr., N.Y.C., 1988-90; sr. psychologist Woodhull Med. & Mental Health Ctr., Bklyn., 1990—; pvt. practice Bklyn., Manhattan, N.Y.C., N.Y., 1990—. Mem. APA, N.Y. State Psychol. Assn., Am. Orthopsychiat. Assn., Westchester County Psychol. Assn., Bklyn. County Psychol. Assn. Home: 527 6th Ave St Brooklyn NY 11215-4908

DEAN, JAMES WENDELL, military officer, nurse; b. Hamtramck, Mich., Apr. 29, 1948; s. Albert Jack and Kathleen Elizabeth (Freeman) D.; m. Iris Viola Rankine, Sept. 10, 1971; children: James W. Jr., Christopher N., Veronica V. AS in nursing, Wayne County Community Coll., Detroit, 1975; BSN, Madonna Coll., Livonia, Mich., 1980, B in Natural Sci., 1980. RN, Pulmonary Function tech., audiometric tech. Charge nurse Lakeside Gen. Hosp., Detroit, 1975-76, Detroit Gen. Hosp., 1976-77; nursing instr. Automated Acad., Detroit, 1976-77; occupl. health nurse GM-Cadillac Motor Co., Detroit, 1977-83, Walt Disney World, Orlando, 1983-84; supr. occupl. health nurse Dept. of Def., USN, Orlando, 1984-87; occupl. health nurse VA, Orlando, 1987—; commd. capt. USAF, 1990, advanced through grades to maj., 1992. Crime watch patrolman Buena Ventura Lakes Crimewatch, Kissimmee, Fla., 1986. Maj. USAF, 1989—. Recipient sustained superior performance award Dept. Def., Orlando, 1985, 86, presdl. unit citation USAF, Wurtsmith AFB, Mich., 1968. Mem. ANA, Fla. Nurses Assn., Nurses Orgn. Va. (chpt. rep. 1988—), Cen. Fla. Occupational Health Nurses Assn. (v.p. 1985-86), Res. Officers Assn., AMVETS Post #30, Am. Legion, VFW. Democrat. Baptist. Home: 612 Redwood Ct Kissimmee FL 34743-9028

DEAN, KAREN ABBEY, psychologist; b. Columbus, Ohio, Jan. 28, 1962; d. Wallace Dare and Gerda (Rauch) Abbey; m. William Blair Dean, Nov. 11, 1989; children: Michael William, Jessica Abbey. BA in Psychology cum laude, Furman U., 1984; MS in Psychology, Fla. State U., Tallahassee, 1986, PhD in Clin. Psychology, 1989. Lic. psychologist Ga. Therapist Arthur G. Dozier Sch. for Boys, Marianna, Fla., 1986-87; psychometrician Psychology Assocs., Tallahassee, 1985-88; therapist Psychol. & Family Cons., Tallahassee, 1984-88; extern Tallahassee Meml. Psychiat. Ctr., 1987-88; intern in psychology Med. Coll. of Ga., Augusta, 1988-89; pvt. practice Lawrenceville, Ga., 1989—; workshop leader State Ofcl. Secondary Prins., Tallahassee, 1985; speaker Fla. State Nursing Coun., Tallahassee, 1986, State of Ga. Sch. Tchrs., Augusta, 1989; cons. task force on adolescent suicide State of Fla. Interagy., Tallahassee, 1985-86. Mem. Am. Psychol. Assn. (assoc.), Southeastern Psychol. Assn., Soc. Pediatric Psychology, Ga. Psychol. Assn. Office: 1655 Lebanon Rd Ste B Lawrenceville GA 30243

DEAN, LYDIA MARGARET CARTER (MRS. HALSEY ALBERT DEAN), nutrition coordinator, author, consultant; b. Bedford, Va., July 11, 1919; d. Christopher C. and Hettie (Gross) Carter; m. Halsey Albert Dean; children: Halsey Albert Jr., John Carter, Lydia Margerae. Grad., Averett Coll.; BS, Madison Coll., 1941; MS, Va. Poly. Inst. and State U., 1951; postgrad., U. Va., Mich. State U.; PhD, D Nutrition Sci., UCLA, 1985. Cert. nutrition specialist Am. Coll. Bd. Nutrition, 1994. Dietetic intern, clin. dietitian St. Vincent de Paul Hosp., Norfolk, Va., 1942; jr. physicist U.S. Naval Op. Base, Norfolk, 1943-45; clin. dietitian Roanoke Meml. Hosps., 1946-51; assoc. prof. Va. Poly. Inst. and State U., 1946-53; community nutritionist Roanoke, Va., 1953-60; dir. dept. nutrition and dietetics Southwestern Va. Med. Ctr., Roanoke, 1960-67; food and nutrition cons. Nat. Hdqs. ARC, Washington, 1967—; staff and vol. Nat. Hdqs. ARC, 1973—; nutrition scientist, cons. Dept. Army, Washington, 1973—, Dept. Agr., 1973—; pres. Dean Assocs.; cons., assoc. dir. Am. Dietetic Assn., 1975—; coord. new degree program U. Hawaii, 1974-75; dir., nutrition coord. pub. health HHS, Washington, 1973-95, vol., 1996; mem. task force White House Conf. Food and Nutrition, 1969—; chmn. fed. com. Interagy. Com. on Nutrition Edn., 1970-71; tech. rep. to AID and State Dept.; chmn. Crusade for Nutrition Edn., Washington, 1970—; participant, cons. Nat. Nutrition Policy Conf., 1974. Author: (with Virginia McMasters) Community Emergency Feeding, 1972, Help My Child How to Eat Right, 1963, rev. edit., 1978, The Complete Gourmet Nutrition Cookbook: The Joy of Eating Well and Right, 1978, rev. edit., 1982, The Stress Foodbook, 1980; contbr. articles to profl. jours. Trustee World U., 1987—; apptd. rsch. bd. advisors Am. Biog. Inst., 1990. Named Women's Inner Cir. of Achievement N.Am., 1990. Fellow APHA, Internat. Inst. Cmty. Svc.; mem. AAUW (Hall of Fame 1992), Am. Dietetic Assn., Bus. and Profl. Women's Club (cons. 1970—, pres. 1981-82), Am. Home Econs. Assn. (rep. and treas. joint congl. com.), Inst. Food Technologists (blue ribbon spkr. 1972). Home: 7816 Birnam Wood Dr Mc Lean VA 22102-2709

DEAN, ODELL JOSEPH, JR., urologist, educator; b. Nashville, Mar. 9, 1958; s. Odell Joseph and Barbara Jean (Crowther) D. BS, Howard U., 1979; MD, La. State U., New Orleans, 1983. Diplomate Am. Bd. Urology. Resident in surgery and urology Howard U. Hosp., Washington, 1984-86; resident in urology Tulane U. Med. Ctr., New Orleans, 1986-89, fellow in renal transplantation, 1989-91; asst. prof. surgery and urology U. Mo., Columbia, 1991-93; asst. prof. urology Tulane U., 1993-95; attending urologist Meml. Hosp. Sys., Houston, 1996—; cons. Ellis Fischel Cancer Ctr., Columbia, 1991-93, Tulane Cancer Ctr., 1993-95; med. edn. adv. com. Tulane Med. Sch., 1994-95; residency program dir. Tulane dept. urology, 1994-95; assoc. rsch. fellow NIH, Bethesda, 1979-80. Contbr. articles to profl. jours. Advisor Neighborhood Youth Corps, New Orleans, 1980-91; sr. cons. Total Cmty. Action, New Orleans, 1993-95. Grantee Atrium Med., 1989, Medtronic, 1989, Searle Pharms., Chgo., 1992, Pfizer Pharms., 1994. Fellow ACS; mem. Am. Urological Assn., Soc. Univ. Urologists, S.W. Oncology Group, Harris County Med. Soc., Assn. Acad. Minority Physicians. Roman Catholic. Office: Urology Assocs 11914 Astoria Ste 300 Houston TX 77089

DEAN, RICHARD HENRY, surgeon, educator; b. Radford, Va., June 16, 1942; s. Howard Lee and Minnie Yates (Crowder) D.; children: Richard Lancaster, Harrison Blaylock, Howard Lee Alexander; m. Stephanie Williams Frey, Feb. 14, 1987; 1 child, Williams Cabler. BA, Va. Mil. Inst., 1964; MD, Med. Coll. Va., 1968. Diplomate Am. Bd. Surgery (bd. dirs. 1993—), Am. Bd. Gen. Vascular Surgery. Surg. intern Vanderbilt U. Hosp., 1968-69, surg. asst. resident, 1969-73, chief. surg. resident, 1973-74, asst. prof. surgery sch. medicine, 1975-77, assoc. prof. surgery, 1977-81, prof. surgery, 1981-86, head divsn. vascular surgery sch. medicine, 1978-86; vascular rsch. fellow, instr. surgery Northwestern U. Hosp, 1974-75; Richard T. Meyers prof. and chmn. surgery Bowman Gray Sch. Medicine Wake Forest U., Winston-Salem, N.C., 1987-89, dir. divsn. surg. scis., chmn. dept. gen. surgery Bowman Gray Sch. Medicine, 1989—; vis. prof. U. Vienna, Austria, 1980, U. NSW, Sydney, Australia, 1982, U. Queensland, Brisbane, Australia, 1984, U. Rochester (N.Y.) Med. Ctr., 1986, 2nd Internat. Symposium on Ischemia, Madrid, 1986, U. Health Scis., Bethesda, Md., 1987, East Carolina U., Greenville, N.C., 1987, Ga. Bapt. Med. Ctr., Atlanta, 1988, Roanoke (Va.) Meml. Hosp., 1988, Ea. Va. Med. Sch., Norfolk, 1988 (two lectures), Mayo Clinic, Rochester, Minn., 1989, Med. Coll. Va., Richmond, 1990, W.Va. U. Health Sci. Ctr., Charleston, 1990, Va. Vascular Soc., Hot Spring, 1990, First All-Union Congress Cardiovascular Surgery, Moscow, 1990, Carolinas Heart Inst., Charlotte, 1991, U. Miami Sch. Medicine, 1991, Allegheny Gen. Hosp., Pitts., 1992, Northwestern U. Med. Sch., Chgo., 1992, U. Minn., Mpls., 1992, Nat. Naval Med. Ctr., Bethesda, 1992, Emory U. Sch. Medicine/Emory Hosp., Atlanta, 1992, Internat. Symposium Hosp. Universitario, Madrid, 1993, Ruprect-Karls-Universitat Heidelberg, Germany, 1993, La. State U. Med. Ctr., Shreveport, 1993, U. N.C., Chapel Hill, 1993, U. Man., Winnipeg, Can., 1993, U. Cin. Med. Ctr., 1993; Paul Dudley White vis. prof. U. Sao Paulo and Campinas, Brazil, 1982; Deryl Hart lectr. Duke U. Med. Sch., 1991; mem. Coun. on Cardio-Thoracic and Vascular Surgery, 1990-91; dir. Am. Bd. Plastic Surgery, 1995—; guest lectr.

in field. Editor: (with J.A. O'Neill Jr.) Vascular Disorders of Childhood, 1983, (with W.P. Ritchie and G. Strele Sr.) General Surgery, 1994, (with J.S.T. Jao and D.C. Brewster) Current Diagnosis and Treatment in Vascular Surgery, 1995; mem. editl. bd. Jour. Vascular Surgery, Annals of Vascular Surgery; contbr. 104 chpts. to books, 125 articles to sci. and profl. jours. Fellow ACS (N.C. chpt., cardiovascular com. 1987), Am. Heart Assn. (stroke coun., coun. high blood pressure rsch.); mem. AMA, Am. Bd. Surgery (cons. com. on vascular surgery 1986-92, dir. 1993—), Am. Surg. Assn. (adv. membership com. 1991—), Internat. Soc. Cardiovascular Surgery (vis. prof. First Sci. Congress 1992), Internat. Soc. for Surgery, Pan-Pacific Surg. Assn., Soc. Univ. Surgeons, Soc. for Vascular Surgery (recorder, publs. com. 1992—), Assn. for Acad. Surgery (exec. coun. 1978-80, nominating com. 1980), So. Assn. Vascular Surgery (program com. 1982-85, exec. coun. 1985-88, pres.-elect 1988-89, pres. 1990-91), Forsyth-Stokes-Davie County Med. Assn., So. Calif. Vascular Surgery Soc. (hon.), So. Med. Assn., So. Surg. Assn., S.E. Surg. COngress, Va. Surg. Assn. (hon.), H. William Scott, Jr. Soc. (sec. 1982-87, pres. 1988-89). Home: 268 S Pine Valley Rd Winston Salem NC 27104-1810 Office: Wake Forest U Bowman Gray Sch Med Divsn Surg Scis Medical Center Blvd Winston Salem NC 27157-1095

DEANE, LELAND MARC, plastic surgeon; b. N.Y.C., June 18, 1952; s. Maurice Allen and Barbara Elaine (Ushkow) D.; m. Danielle Anne Sheft, Nov. 21, 1993. BS, Union Coll., 1974; MD, SUNY, Bklyn., 1978. Intern, then resident in surgery New Eng. Med. Ctr., 1978-83; resident in plastic surgery Ea. Va. Grad. Sch. Medicine, 1983-85; fellow in hand surgery Jefferson Med. Coll., 1986; pvt. practice L.I. Plastic Surg. Group P.C., Garden City, N.Y., 1986—; mem. surg. rev. com. Winthrop U. Hosp., Mineola, N.Y., 1986—, mem. resident edn. com., 1992—. Contbr. articles to profl. jours. Advisor Mothers of Super Twins, L.I., 1995—. Grantee So. Med. Assn., 1984. Fellow ACS, Am. Acad. Pediatrics; mem. Am. Soc. Plastic and Reconstructive Surgeons, Northeastern Soc. Plastic Surgeons, N.Y. Regional Soc. Plastic and Reconstructive Surgery. Office: LI Plastic Surg Group PC 999 Franklin Ave Garden City NY 11530

DEANE, SALLY JAN, health services administrator, consultant; b. Downey, Calif., Sept. 24, 1948; d. Virgil Eldred and Pearl Jan (Kettell) D. BA, Whittier Coll., 1970; MEd, Boston U., 1971, MPH, 1988. Mgr. community health Peter Bent Brigham Hosp., Boston, 1974-76; coord. WIC program Martha Eliot Health Ctr., 1976-78; dir. S.W. Boston WIC program Shattuck Hosp. Corp., 1978-80; exec. dir. Fenway Community Health Ctr., 1980-84; exec. asst. commr. Boston Dept. Health & Hosps., 1984-86; assoc. dir. spl. projects Health Policy Inst. Boston U., 1986-87; dir. ambulatory reimbursement Mass. Medicaid, 1987-88; assoc. Cambridge (Mass.) Mgmt. Group, 1989; ptnr. Integrated Health Strategies Inc., Cambridge, Mass., 1990-96; asst. prof. Pub. Health Boston U., 1994—; v.p. Chadwick Martin Bailey, Boston, 1996—; cons. Mass. Dept. Pub. Health, Boston, 1978-80, Citicorp Corp. Hdqrs., N.Y.C., 1986. Mem. Mayor's Task Force on AIDS, Boston, 1983-86; v.p. Trustees Charitable Donations, Boston, 1984-88. Mem. Mass. Pub. Health Assn., Am. Pub. Health Assn., Women in Health Care Mgmt. Presbyterian. Home: 115 University Rd Brookline MA 02146-4545 Office: Chadwick Martin Bailey 179 South St Boston MA 02111

DEANGELIS, CATHERINE D., pediatrics educator; b. Scranton, Pa., Jan. 2, 1940; m. James C. Harris. BA, Wilkes Coll., 1965; MD, U. Pitts., 1969; MPH, Harvard U., 1973. RN, Pa., N.Y.; diplomate Nat. Bd. Med. Examiners, Am. Bd. Pediatrics. Intern in pediatrics Children's Hosp., Pitts., 1969-70; resident in pediatrics Johns Hopkins Hosp., Balt., 1970-72, teaching fellow pediatrics dept. internat. health Sch. Pub. Health, 1972; pediatrician Roxbury Comprehensive Health Clinic, Boston, 1972-73; asst. prof. pediatrics Coll. Physicians and Surgeons, asst. prof. health svc. adminstrn. Sch. Pub. Health Columbia U., 1973-75; mem. staff divsn. pediatric ambulatory care, dir. med. edn. Child Care Project Columbia Presbyn. Med. Ctr., 1973-75; asst. prof. pediatrics Sch. Medicine U. Wis., 1975-77, assoc. prof. pediatrics Sch. Medicine, 1977-78; dir. ambulatory pediatric svcs. U. Wis. Hosps., 1975-78; assoc. prof. pediatrics Johns Hopkins Sch. Medicine, 1978-85; dir. pediatric primary care and adolescent medicine Johns Hopkins Hosp., 1978-84, co-dir. adolescent pregnancy program, 1979-82; with dept. health svcs. adminstrn. and dept. internat. health Johns Hopkins Sch. Hygiene and Pub. Health, 1980-90; dir. residency tng. dept. pediatrics Johns Hopkins Hosp., 1983-90, dir. divsn. gen. pediatrics and adolescent medicine, 1984-90; deputy chmn. dept. pediatrics Johns Hopkins Sch. Medicine, 1983-90, prof. pediatrics, 1986—, assoc. dean acad. affairs, 1990-93, sr. assoc. dean acad. affairs and faculty, 1993-94; vice dean acad. affairs and faculty, 1994—; mem. Gov.'s Task Force to Evaluate Health Care in Wis. State Prisons, 1975-78; chmn. ambulatory care com. U. Wis. Hosp., 1976-78; mem. med. sch. admissions com. U. Wis. Sch. Medicine, 1976-78, chmn., 1977-78; mem. exec. coun. dept. pediatrics and Children's Ctr., Johns Hopkins U. Sch. Medicine, 1982-90, chmn. fin. com. dept. pediatrics, 1984-85, chmn. assoc. prof.'s promotion com., 1985-88; chmn. com. developing Women's Health Ctr. at Johns Hopkins Med. Instns., 1993—; mem. Gov.'s Task Force on Women's Health, Md., 1993—, chair 1994—; mem. search com. U. Wis., 1976, Johns Hopkins Sch. Medicine, 1984, 88, 92, 93; mem. nat. review com. for accreditation of nurse practitioners Am. Nurses' Assn., 1975-79, co-chmn., 1977; mem. peer review com. nurse practitioner programs divsn. nursing Health Resources Agy., Dept. Health, Edn. and Welfare, 1979-81; mem. Nat. Commn. on Nursing, 1985-86, Physician Consortium on Substance Abuse Edn., 1989—; mem. clin. scholar's adv. com. Robert Wood Johnson Found., 1992-94, Assn. Acad. Health Ctrs., 1993—; mem. Assn. Health Svcs. Rsch., 1993—; with immunization team, Nicaragua, 1969; subintern Harbel Hosp., Liberia, West Africa, 1969; organizer immunization program Peru, 1972, West Indies Sch. Nursing, 1977; mem. editorial bd. The Hosp. Med. Staff, 1982—, Pediatrician, 1984—, Jour. of Pediatrics, 1986—, Pediatric Annals, 1990—, Pediatrics in Review, 1990—, Archives of Pediatrics and Adolescent Medicine, 1993—; reviewer Acad. Medicine, Am. Jour. Diseases of Children, Am. Jour. Medicine, Clin. Pediatrics, Jour. Pediatrics, Med. Care, Pediatrics; writer weekly column Balt. Sun, 1987-90. Author: Basic Pediatrics for the Primary Care, 1984; editor: An Introduction to Clinical Research, 1990; editor: (with others) Principles and Practice of PEdiatrics, 1990, 2d edit., 1994; assoc. editor Pediatric Annals, 1990—; editor Archives of Pediatrics and Adolscent Medicine, 1993—. Mem. steering com. Rural Health Planning, Wis.; cons. Robert Wood Johnson Found., 1973—; mem. adv. group on improving outcomes for children Pew Charitable Trusts, 1991-92; mem. adv. panel medicine Pew Health Profession's Commn.; mem. nat. adv. com. Robert Wood Johnson Clin. Scholars Program, 1992—. NIH fellow, 1973; recipient George Armstrong award Ambulatory Pediactric Assn., Acad. Adminstrn. and Health Policy scholarship Assn. Acad. Health Ctrs., 1993. Fellow APHA, Am. Acad. Pediatrics (govt. affairs com. 19that com. N.Y. chpt. 1974-75, chmn. adolscent com. Md. chpt. 1981-84); mem. Am. Pediatr. Soc. (sec., treas. 1989—), Am. Bd. Pediatrics (examiner 1986—, long range planning com. 1990-91, chmn. ling range planning com. 1992—, bd. dirs. 1990—, fin. com. 1991—, sec., treas. 1993-95, chair-elect 1995-96, chair 1996, search com. 1990), Soc. Adolscent Medicine, Alpha Omega Alpha. Office: Johns Hopkins Sch Medicine 720 Rutland Ave Ste 106 Baltimore MD 21205-2109

DEANGELIS, ROBERT NEAL, dermatologist; b. Connellsville, Pa., Dec. 5, 1942; s. Fulvio Garibaldi and Ruth margaret (Nordlund) DeA.; m. Nance Lee Barbour, June 20, 1940 (div.); children: Diana Lee, Robert Neal Jr., Nancy Carol, Julie Ann, David Andrew. MD, Med. Coll. of Va., 1968. Diplomate Am. Bd. Dermatology, Am. Bd. Dermatopathology. Intern MCV Hosps., Richmond, Va., 1968-69; resident dermatology MCV Hosps., 1969-72; pvt. practice dermatology Springfield, Va., 1973—. Major USAF, 1972-74. Fellow Am. Acad. Dermatology, Am. Soc. Dermatopathology. Baptist. Home and Office: 8346 Traford Ln Springfield VA 22152-1645

DEANGELIS, ROGER THOMAS, surgeon; b. Yonkers, N.Y., Sept. 9, 1941; s. Anthony Marion and Carolyn Chambers (Hutchison) DeA.; m. Lynn Ann Beloin, Dec. 19, 1964 (div. Jan. 1975); children: Lara Elizabeth, Christian Roger; m. Mary Frances Therese Nelson, June 21, 1975; children: Mary Frances, Roger Thomas III, Rebecca Marie. BA, Columbia U., 1963, MD, 1967. Diplomate Nat. Bd. Med. Examiners, Am. Bd. Surgery. Intern surgery St. Luke's Med. Ctr., N.Y.C., 1968, resident surgery, 1968-72; sec. med. staff St. John's Hosp., Yonkers, 1979-85, vice chief med. staff, 1985-87, 89-91, dir. surgery, chief gen. surgery sect., 1991—; chmn. quality assurance com. St. John's Hosp., Yonkers, 1985-87, 89-91, chmn. operating rm. com., 1991—, chmn. intensive care com., 1991—, trustee, 1994; sci. chmn., bd. dirs. Yonkers Acad. Medicine, 1975-80; pres. Yonkers Practioners Club, 1977-79. Lt. comdr. USN, 1972-74, Vietnam. Fellow ACS; mem. AMA, Am. Soc. Gen. Surgeons, Am. Soc. Abdominal Surgery, N.Y. Surg. Soc., Westchester Surg. Soc. (sec.-treas. 1995), Soc. Laparoendoscopic Surgeons. Republican. Episcopalian. Office: 17 Greenvale Ave Yonkers NY 10703-1803

DEAN-ZUBRITSKY, CYNTHIA MARIAN, psychologist, reseacher; b. Urbana, Ill., Oct. 27, 1950; d. William Bonaparte and Lois (Doran) Dean; m. John Jay Zubritsky , Sept. 15, 1979; 1 child, Grant Doran. BA, Ind. U., 1972; M in Psychology, Pa. State U., 1978; PhD, Temple U., 1989. Counselor New Castle (Pa.) Youth Devel. Ctr., 1972-76; dir. Ill. Family Edn. Ctr., Danville, 1976-77; researcher Pa. State U., University Park, 1977-78, 89—; film cons. Ill. Devel. Disabilities Council, Springfield, 1978; psychologist Atkins House, York, Pa., 1978-82; quality assurance specialist Pa. Office Mental Retardation, Harrisburg, 1982-84; dir. tng. and staff devel. Pa. Office Mental Health, Harrisburg, 1984-89; pvt. practice psychology Harrisburg, 1989—; bd. dirs. children and youth svcs. Vermilion County Mental Health Program, Danville, 1975-77; psychologist Loysville (Pa.) Youth Devel. Ctr., 1981-82; tchr. Danville Community Coll., 1975; cons. U. Ill., Urbana, 1976, Danville Sch. System, 1975-76; faculty dept. psychiatry U. Pa., 1989—; rsch. alliance for mentally ill Pa., 1989-92. Vol. ARC, 1967-87, YWCA, 1970-89; mem. Pa. Task Force on Mental Health: Women, Harrisburg, 1986-87. Fed. rsch. grantee NIMH, CSAD, AOA; Human Resource Devel. grantee NIMH, 1985—, Office of Substance Abuse Prevention grantee, 1992—. Mem. Internat. Psychogeriatric Assn., Nat. Assn. State Mental Health Program Dirs., Am. Horticulture Soc., Phi Delta Kappa, Phi Mu. Republican. Presbyterian. Office: U Pa Dept Psychiatry Philadelphia PA 19104

DEAR, RONALD BRUCE, social work educator; b. Phila., Sept. 23, 1933; s. John David and Margaret (McDade) D.; 1 child, Bruce. BA, Bucknell U., 1955; honors cert., U. Aberdeen, Scotland, 1955; MSW, U. Pitts., 1957; PhD in Social Work, Columbia U., 1972. Cert. social worker, N.Y., Wash. Chief social worker Mental Hygiene Cons. Svc., Aberdeen Proving Ground, Md., 1958-60; chief Neuropsychiat. Clinic, 7th Inf. Divsn., Korea, 1960-61; residence dir. Horizon House, Inc., Phila., 1961-64; prof. U. Wash., Seattle, 1970—; vis. prof. U. Bergen, Norway, 1984, U. Trondheim, Norway, 1996; faculty lobbyist U. Wash., 1985-88, 88-91, faculty pres., 1993-95; master tchr. Coun. on Social Work Edn., 1991, 93, 94; mem. adv. bd. Internat. Population and Family Assocs., 1994—; bd. dirs. Wash. Future, 1994—. Editor: Poverty in Perspective, 1973; contbr. articles to profl. jours. and encys. Mem. income assistance adv. com., 1987-93, to adv. com. for Dept. Social and Health Svcs., 1980-83. 1st lt. U.S. Army, 1957-61. Mem. NASW (Social Worker of Yr. Wash. chpt. 1981), Acad. Cert. Social Workers, Coun. on Social Work Edn. Home: 7328 16th Ave NE Seattle WA 98115-5737 Office: U Wash Sch Social Work 4101 15th Ave NE Seattle WA 98195-6299

DEARBORN, MAUREEN MARKT, speech and language clinician; b. Brockton, Mass., Jan. 19, 1948; d. Francis Joseph and Marjorie Agnes (White) M.; m. James Clement Bovin, Nov. 6, 1970 (div. June 1973); m. David C. Dearborn, Jan. 14, 1989. BA in Speech Pathology and Audiology, U. Mass., 1970; MA in Ednl. Psychology, Am. Internat. Coll., Springfield, Mass. Speech and lang. clinician Holyoke (Mass.) Pub. Schs., 1970—. Chmn. Holyoke Cancer Crusade, 1985; voter registration chmn. Holyoke Dem. Com., 1987; chmn. deaconesses 2d Congl. Ch. Holyoke. Mem. Hampden County Tchrs. Assn. (pres. 1981, 87, sec. 1982, v.p. 1984-86, treas. 1988—), Holyoke Tchrs. Assn. (treas. 1989, DAR historian), Am. Speech, Hearing and Langs. Assn. (continuing edn. adv. bd. 1988-91, congl. action contact continuing edn. adv. bd. 1988-90), Mass. Tchrs. Assn., Mass. Speech, Hearing and Langs. Assn., New England Hist. and Geneal. Soc., Friends of the Lib. Coun. (treas. 1992—), Mass. Genealogical Soc., Assn. for Gravestone Studies, DAR (historian Eunice Day 1984), Wrentham Hist Soc., Dorchester Hist. Soc. Home: 257 W Franklin St Holyoke MA 01040-2210 Office: Holyoke Pub Schs 57 Suffolk St Holyoke MA 01040-5015

DEARDEN, ROBERT JAMES, retired pharmacist; b. Phila., Sept. 25, 1932; s. Raymond Francis and Genevieve (Hendershot) D.; m. Marie Elizabeth Harrell, Aug. 21, 1954; children Cherylanne, James, Jeanette, Denise. BS in Pharmacy, Temple U., 1955. Registered community pharmacist, Fla., N.J., Pa. Pharmacist, mgr. Merck Sharp and Dohme, Phila., 1955-57, Roman Pharmacy, Phila., 1957-63; pharmacist Phila. Polio Immunization Drive, 1963; pharmacist, pres. Barclay Pharm. Surg. Corp., Cherry Hill, N.J., 1964-83; pharmacist, mgr. Eckerd Drug Corp., Clearwater, Fla., 1983-95; ret., 1995; preceptor Fla. State Bd. Intern Program, Sarasota, 1986-95. V.p., treas. Wedgewood Lakes Condo. Assn. Mem. Am. Pharm. Assn., Fla. Pharm. Assn., Nat. Audubon Soc., Kappa Psi. Republican. Roman Catholic. Home: 5202 Wedgewood Ln Sarasota FL 34235-7020

DEARDORFF, JOHN ANDREW, health care company administrator; b. Dallastown, Pa., Oct. 10, 1970; s. Richard Paul and Jean Marie (McKernan) D. BS with honors, Towson (Md.) State U., 1993; M Health Svcs. Adminstrn., George Washington U., 1996. Activities asst. Inova Health Sys., Fairfax, Va., 1993-94, coord. accounts receivable, 1994-95; adminstrv. resident Manor Healthcare Corp., Silver Spring, Md., 1995-96, asst. adminstr., 1996—. Mem. Am. Coll. Healthcare Execs., Am. Coll. Healthcare Adminstrs. Republican. Baptist. Home: 20511 Via Marisa Boca Raton FL 33498 Office: Manor Care Nursing & Rehab Ctr 375 NW 51st St Boca Raton FL 33431

DEARDORFF, WILLIAM ALVA, radiologist, educator; b. Charleston, W. Va., Mar. 27, 1928; s. William Henry and Rose Eldora (McCallister) D.; m. Anita Page Gentry, June 1, 1957; children: Michael Barry, Jennifer Page McClung, David Alva. BS, W. Va. U., 1952, MS, 1954, MD, 1956. Diplomate Am. Bd. Radiology, Am. Bd. Nuclear Medicine. Resident in radiology Henry Ford Hosp., Detroit, 1957-60; pvt. practice radiology Elkin, Kugel & Deardorff, Charleston, W. Va., 1960-78, W Alva Deardorff Ltd., S. Charleston, 1978—; radiologist Thomas Meml. Hosp., S. Charleston, 1960—, St. Francis Hosp., Charleston, 1973—; asst. prof. Nuclear Medicine, W. Va. State Coll., 1975-80. Mem. Bd. Radiologic Tech. State of W. Va., 1996. Fellow Am. Coll. Radiology; mem. Am. Coll. Nuclear Medicine, W. Va. Med. Assn. (treas. polit. action com. 1985—). Home: 1417 Robin Hood Rd Charleston WV 25314 Office: W Alva Deardorff Ltd 4620 MacCorkle Ave SW South Charleston WV 25309

DEATON, FAE ADAMS, clinical social worker, counselor; b. Phila., Feb. 19, 1932; d. Charles Sizemore and Dorothea Lucia (Adams) Deaton; children: Dorothea Fae Stein Scott Krause, Caroline Louise Stein, Erich Charles Stein. Mus.B., Salem Coll., 1953; postgrad. Oxford U., Eng., 1961-63, U. Alaska, 1968-69, Alaska Methodist U., 1969, Wright State U., 1971-73; M.S. in Edn., Old Dominion U., 1975; M.S.W., Norfolk State U., 1980; postgrad. Santa Clara U., 1980. Diplomate Am. Bd. Social Workers, Am. Bd. Clin. Social Workers. Tchr. music, Mifflin, Ohio, 1953-54; supr. high sch. USN Dependents Sch., Argentia, Nfld., 1956-57; tchr. USAF Dependents Sch., Croughton, Eng., 1960-63, Upper Heyford, Eng., 1963-64; mag. editor Scott AFB, Ill., 1966-67; mem. staff Hist. and Fine Arts Mus., Anchorage, 1968-70; music and arts reviewer Anchorage Evening Times, 1968-70; publicity chmn., mem. publicity staff Alaska Council on Arts, 1969-70; counselor Youth Services Bur., Dayton, Ohio, 1973; engring. research aide Wright Patterson AFB Biophysics Lab., Dayton, 1973; writer Dayton Daily News, 1973; field research aide Am. Inst. Research, Palo Alto, Calif., 1974-75; counselor, patient advocate Norfolk (Va.) Free Clinic, 1975-76; adminstrv. asst. econs. dept. Old Dominion U., Norfolk, 1975-76; tchr., counselor Blessed Sacrament Sch., Norfolk, 1976-77; mem. mental health team, young adolescent unit, milieu therapist Portsmouth (Va.) Psychiat. Center, 1977-79, children's unit, 1979-80, child, adult, family and marital therapist sexual trauma treatment center Psychiatrists/Portsmouth Psychiat. Center, 1980-82; therapist, social worker children's services, sexual trauma treatment unit, Community Mental Health Ctr. and Psychiat. Inst. Dept. Psychiatry, Eastern Va. Med. Sch., Norfolk, Va., 1983-88; dir., psychotherapist Hampton Roads Psychotherapy Assocs. and Childhood Trauma Treatment Ctr., Norfolk, 1988-95; mem. lt. gov.'s subcom. on sexual victimization prevention in Va., 1992-95. Mem. Tidewater Profl. Assn. on Child Abuse, 1978-82, pres., 1981-82; mem. Tidewater Rape Info. Services, Norfolk, 1978-88; adminstr./author, bd. dirs. Sexual Abuse Helpline of Tidewater, 1979-95; mem. VBDSS Sexual Abuse Treatment Team, 1979-82; mem. ad hoc com. Nat. Coalition on Sexual Abuse, 1980-81; bd. dirs. Tidewater Alliance on Sexual Abuse, 1981-88, pres., 1984-87; mem. admissions/release bd. Norfolk Lakehouse Girls Detention Home, 1978-79; program chmn. Conf. Internat. Yr. of the Child, Norfolk, 1979; mem. Middle Atlantic Coalition on Sexual Victimization of Children, 1980-83, sec., 1981-82; bd. dirs. Tidewater Assembly on Family Life, 1981-82, Va. chpt. Nat. Com. on Prevention of Child Abuse, 1981-82, Parents Anonymous of Va., 1984-86; mem. Virginia Beach Dept. Social Services Multi Discipline Team, 1983-86; mem. Norfolk Com. for Prevention of Child Abuse, 1983—. Chmn. task force spl. children Children's Art Center, Norfolk, 1979-81; co-chmn. Gov.'s Child Abuse sub-com.; bd. dirs. Norfolk Little Theater, 1977-78; chmn. FamiliesUnited Va., Inc., 1980-95; sponsor/coor. Virginia Beach chpt. Parents United, 1979-92; bd. dirs. Parents United Internat., chmn. quality assurance com., regional chairperson mid.-Atlantic chpts., 1987-92, chmn. 20th Anniversary Conf., Norfolk, 1991; historian Alaska Arts Club, 1969-70; mem. Elmendorf AFB Sch. Bd., 1967-68; state dir. Parents United Inc., Va., 1979-92, Families United-Human Potentials Inc., Va., 1992; clin. supr. Families United, Tidewater, 1992-95; bd. mem. Parents United Internat. San Jose, Calif., 1987-92. Recipient Gov.'s award for work in child abuse treatment, 1986. Mem. Nat. Assn. Social Workers, Am. Assn. Counseling and Devel., Va. Assn. Counseling and Devel., Va. Assns. Specialists in Group Work, Internat. Soc. for Traumatic Stress Studies, Nat. Soc. for Traumatic Stress Studies, Am. Profl. Soc. on the Abuse of Children, Calif. Profl. Soc. on the Abuse of Children. Contbr. papers and lectures various confs. and tng. programs in U.S., 1967—. Ofce: Albemarle Mental Health Ctr 202 1/2 Hicks St PO Box 791 Edenton NC 27932

DEAVER, DAVID C., III, general surgeon; b. Cheyenne, Wyo., May 18, 1953; s. David C. and Lois H. (Hofmann) D.; m. Mary M. Stengel, Sept. 10, 1988; children: Sean, Colin, Margaret. BS, U. Denver, 1975; MD, Creighton U., 1979. Diplomate Am. Bd. Surgery. Staff physician Mercy Med. Ctr., Durango, Colo., 1984—. Fellow ACS, Soc. Am. Gastrointestinal and Endoscopic Surgeons, Southwestern Surg. Soc. Office: 1810 E Third Ave Ste 102 Durango CO 81301-5046

DEB, SANJAY KUMAR, surgeon; b. Calcutta, India, Apr. 23, 1938; came to U.S., 1968; s. Soroj Ranjan and Uma (Burdhan) D.; m. Mary Szylinski, June 23, 1972 (dec. Feb. 1978); 1 child, Ravi; m. Mary Ann Fiordaliso, Jan. 3, 1981; 1 child, Anita. MD, Caclutta U., 1961; M Surgery, Delhi U., 1965. Diplomate Am. Bd. Gen. Surgery. Intern Med. Coll. Hosp., Calcutta, 1961-62; resident Maulana Azala Med. Coll. Group Hosps., Delhi, India, 1963-67, South Buffalo (N.Y.) Mercy Hosp., 1968-69; resident Sisters Hosp., Buffalo, 1969-72, attending surgeon, 1972—; attending surgeon St. Joseph Hosp., Buffalo, 1972—. Fellow ACS, Royal Coll. Surgeons Can. Office: 3527 Harlem Rd Buffalo NY 14225-1552

DEBAKEY, MICHAEL ELLIS, cardiovascular surgeon, educator, scientist; b. Lake Charles, La., Sept. 7, 1908; s. Shaker Morris and Raheeja (Zorba) DeB.; m. Diana Cooper, Oct. 15, 1936; children: Michael Maurice, Ernest Ochsner, Barry Edward, Denis Alton, Olga Katerina; m. Katrin Fehlhaber, July 1975. BS, Tulane U., 1930, MD, 1932, MS, 1935, LLD (hon.), 1965; Docteur Honoris Causa, U. Lyon, France, 1961, U. Brussels, 1962, U. Ghent, Belgium, 1964, U. Athens, 1964; DHC, U. Turin, Italy, 1965, U. Belgrade, Yugoslavia, 1967; LLD, Lafayette Coll., 1965; MD (hon.), Aristotelean U. of Thessaloniki, Greece, 1972; DSc, Hahnemann Med. Coll., 1973; Docteur honoris causa, U. Louis Pasteur, Paris, 1991. Diplomate Nat. Bd. Med. Examiners, Am. Bd. Surgery, Am. Bd. Thoracic Surgery. Intern Charity Hosp., New Orleans, 1932-33, asst. surgery, 1933-35; asst. surgery U. Strasbourg, France, 1935-36, U. Heidelberg, Fed. Republic of Germany, 1936; instr. surgery Tulane U., New Orleans, 1937-40, asst. prof., 1940-46, assoc. prof., 1946-48; prof., chmn. dept. surgery Baylor Coll. Medicine, 1948-93, Disting. svc. prof., 1968—, v.p. med. affairs, 1968-69, CEO, 1968-69, pres., 1969-79, Olga Keith Weiss prof. of surgery, 1981—, Olga Keith Weiss prof. of surgery, chancellor, 1978-96; chancellor emeritus, 1996—; pres. The DeBakey Med. Found., 1961—; dir. Nat. Heart Blood Vessel Rsch. Demonstration Ctr. Baylor Coll. Medicine, Tex., 1975-85; dir. DeBakey Heart Ctr., Baylor Coll. Medicine, 1985—; chancellor emeritus Baylor Coll. Medicine, 1996—; surgeon-in-chief Ben Taub Gen. Hosp., 1963-93; sr. attending surgeon Meth. Hosp.; clin. prof. surgery U. Tex. Dental Br., Houston; cons. surgery VA Hosp., St. Elizabeth's Hosp., U. Tex., M.D. Anderson Hosp., St. Luke's Hosp., Tex. Children's Hosp., Tex. Inst. Rehab. and Rsch. Brooke Gen. Hosp., Brooke Army Med. Ctr., Ft. Sam Houston, Tex., Walter Reed Army Hosp., Washington, D.C.; mem. med. adv. com. Office Sec. Def., 1984-50, Ams. for Substance Abuse Prevention, 1984; mem. adv. bd. Internat. Brotherhood Teamsters, 1985—; chmn. com. surgery NRC, 1953, mem. exec. com. 1953; mem. com. med. svcs. Hoover Commn.; founding bd. dirs.Friends of Nat. Libr. of Medicine, 1985—, mem. bd. regents Nat. Libr. Medicine, 1994—, chmn., 1959; past mem. nat. adv. heart coun. NIH; mem. Nat. Adv. Health Coun., 1961-65, Nat. Adv. Coun. Regional Med. Programs, 1965—, Nat. Adv. Gen. Med. Scis. Coun., 1965, Program Planning Com., Com. Tng., Nat. Heart Inst., 1961—; mem. civilian health and med. adv. coun. Office Asst. Sec. Def.; chmn. Pres.'s Commn. Heart Disease, Cancer and Stroke, 1964; mem. adv. coun. Nat. Heart Lung and Blood Inst., 1982-87; mem. Tex. Sci. and Tech. Coun., 1984-86; chmn. Found. Biomed. Rsch., 1988—, Physicians for Health in the Middle East, 1991—; trustee, v.p. Baylor Med. Found.; chmn., med. adv. bd. The DeBakey Heart Ctr. Health Letter; adv. bd. Family Cir.; internat. sci. coun. Fondation Cardiologique Princesse Liliane; adv. Dag Hammarskjöld Med. Sci. Prize Com.; mem. bd. visitors Uniformed Svcs. U. Health Scis., U. Calif.-Davis Sch. Medicine. Author: (with Robert A. Kilduffe) Blood Transfusion, 1942; (with Gilbert W. Beebe) Battle Casualties, 1952; (with Alton Ochsner) Textbook of Minor Surgery, 1955; (with T. Whayne) Cold Injury, Ground Type, 1958, A Surgeon's Visit to China, 1974, The Living Heart, 1977, The Living Heart Diet, 1985, The Living Heart Brand Name Shopper's Guide, 1992, The Living Heart Guide to Eating Out, 1993, The New Living Heart Diet, 1996; editor: Yearbook of Surgery, 1958-70; chmn. adv. editl. bd. Medical History of World War II; editor Jour. Vascular Surgery, 1984-88; contbr. over 1500 articles to med. jours. Mem. Tex. Constl. Revision Commn., 1973. Col. Office Surgeon Gen., AUS, 1942-46; now Col. Res.; cons. to Surgeon Gen., 1946—; disting. mem. U.S. Army Med. Dept. Rgt., 1989. Decorated Legion of Merit, 1946, Independence of Jordan medal 1st Class, Merit order of Republic 1st Class Egypt, comdr. Cit Pro Utiliate Hominum Sovereign Order Knights of Hosp. of St. John of Jerusalem in Denmark; recipient Rudolph Matas award, 1954, Internat. Soc. Surgery Disting. Svc. award, 1958, Modern Medicine award, 1957, Leriche award Internat. Soc. Surgery, 1959, Great medallion U. Ghent, 1961, Grand Cross, Order Leopold Belgium, 1962, Albert Lasker award for clin. research, 1963, Order of Merit Chile, 1964, St. Vincent prize med. scis. U. Turin, 1965, Orden del Libertador Gen. San Martin Argentina, 1965, Centennial medal Albert Einstein Med. Ctr., 1966, Gold Scalpel award Internat. Cardiology Found., 1966, Baylor Alumni Disting. Faculty award, 1973, Eleanor Roosevelt Humanities award, 1969, Meritorious Civilian Service medal Office Sec. Def., 1970, USSR Acad. Sci. 50th Anniversary Jubilee medal, 1973, Phi Delta Epsilon Disting. Service award, 1974, La Madonnina award, 1974, 30 Yr. Service award Harris County Hosp. Dist., 1978, Knights Humanity award honoris causa Internat. Register Chivalry, Milan, 1978, diploma de Merito Caja Costarricense de Seguro Social, San Jose, Costa Rica, 1979, Disting. Service plaque Tex. Bd. Edn., 1979, Britannica Achievement in Life award, 1979, Medal of Freedom with Distinction Presdl. award, 1969, Disting. Service award Internat. Soc. Atherosclerosis, 1979, Centennial award ASME, 1980, Marian Health Care award St. Mary's U., 1981, Inst. Med. Nat. Acad. Sci., 1981, Soc. Biomaterials award for clin. rsch. in biomaterials Clemson U. and Soc. Biomaterials, 1983, Humana Heart Inst. award, 1985, Theodore E. Cummings award, 1987, Nat. Med. of Sci. award 1987, Markowitz award Acad. Surg. Rsch., 1988, Assn. Am. Med. Colls. award 1988, George Crile award Internat. Platform Assn., 1988, Thomas Alva Edison Found. award, 1988, first issue Michael DeBakey medal ASME, 1989, Inaugural award Scripps Clinic and Rsch. Found., 1989, DeBakey-Bard Chair in Surgery, Baylor Coll. of Medicine, 1990, Disting. Svc. award Am. Legion, 1990, Lifetime Achievement award Found. for Biomed. Rsch., 1991, Jacobs award Am. Task Force for Lebanon, 1991, Maxwell Finland award Nat. Found. for Infectious Diseases, 1992, Lifetime Achievement award Acad. Med. Films, 1992, Order of Independence First Class medal United Arab Emirates, 1992, Academy of Athens award, 1992, Cmdrs. Cross Order of Merit (Fed. Germany), 1992, Pres. Disting. Svc. award Baylor Coll. Medicine, 1992, Gibbon award Am. Soc. Extracorporeal Tech., 1993, named in his honor Michael E. DeBakey Libr., Svc. Outreach award Friends of the Nat. Libr. Medicine, 1993, Alton Ochsner award relating smoking to health, 1993, Thomas Jefferson award AIA, 1993, Ellis Island Medal of Honor, 1993,

Lifetime Achievement award Am. Heart Assn., 1994, Caring Spirit award Inst. Religion Tex. Med. Ctr., 1994, Samaritan Living Legend award Women's Internat. Ctr., 1994, Giovanni Lorenzini Med. Fedn. prize for basic biomed. rsch., 1994, Disting. Svc. award Tex. Soc. Biomedical Rsch., 1994, Heart Saver award Save A Heart Found., Cedars-Sinai Med. Ctr., 1994, Honor award United Meth. Assn. Health & Welfare Ministries, 1995, Michael E. DeBakey chair in Pharm. Baylor Coll. Med., 1995, Nat. Order of Vasco Nunez de Balboa (Panama), 1995, Health Care Hall of Fame Modern Healthcare, 1996, Sci. Rschr. of XX Century award govt. of Argentine Republic, 1996, others; named Dr. of Yr., Med. World News, 1965, Med. Man of Yr., 1966, Disting. Service Prof., Baylor U., 1968, Humanitarian Father of Yr., 1974, Tulane U. Alumnus of Yr., 1974, Tex. Scientist of Yr., Tex. Acad. Sci., 1979; Michael E. DeBakey Heart Inst. Wis. named in his honor Kenosha Hosp. and Med. Ctr., 1992; Michael E. DeBakey, M.D. award for Excellence in Visual Edn. named in his honor, 1993; DeBakey Scholar in Cardiovasc. Scis. MD-PhD Program named in his honor Baylor Coll. Medicine, 1994; Michael E. DeBakey, MD Excellence in Rsch. award named in his honor Baylor Coll. Medicine, 1994, dedication of Northwestern U. Med. Sch. book, 1995. Fellow ACS (Ann. award Southwestern Pa. chpt. 1973), Inst. of Medicine Chgo. (hon.), Royal Coll. Physicians and Surgeons of U.S. (hon., disting. fellow 1992), Am. Inst. Med. and Biol. Engring. (founding fellow 1993), Biomaterials Sci. and Engr., Soc. Biomaterials, Am. Coll. Cardiology (hon.), Am. Coll. Health Care Execs. (hon.); mem. AAAS, Royal Soc. Medicine, Halsted Soc., Am. Heart Assn., So. Soc. Clin. Rsch., Southwestern Surg. Congress (pres. 1952), Soc. Vascular Surgery (pres. 1954), Soc. Vascular Surg. Lifeline Found. (pres. 1989), AMA (Disting. Svc. award 1959, Hektoen Gold medal 1954, 70), Am. Surg. Assn. (Disting. Svc. award 1981, pres. 1989), So. Surg. Assn. (pres. 1989-90, chmn. coun. 1995—), Western Surg. Assn., Am. Assn. Thoracic Surgery (pres. 1959), Internat. Cardiovascular Soc. (pres. 1958, pres. N.Am. chpt. 1964), Assn. Internat. Vascular Surgeons (pres. 1983), Mex. Acad. Surgery (hon.), Soc. Clin. Surgery, Nat. Acads. Practice Medicine, Soc. Univ. Surgeons, Internat. Soc. Surgery, Soc. Exptl. Biology and Medicine, Hellenic Surg. Soc. (hon.), Bio-med. Engring. Soc. (bd. dirs. 1968), Houston Heart Assn. (mem. adv. coun. 1968-69), Soc. Nacional de Cirugia (hon., Cuba), Japanese Assn. Thoracic Surgery (first fgn. hon. mem. 1989), Assn. Française de Chirurgie (hon.), University Club (Washington), Acad. of Athens, Sigma Xi (William Procter prize for scientific achievement 1995), Alpha Omega Alpha. Episcopalian. Office: Baylor Coll Medicine 1 Baylor Plz Houston TX 77030-3498 also: Tex Med Ctr 6535 Fannin St Houston TX 77030-3498

DEBARDELEBEN, MARTHA GRAVES, counselor; b. Atlanta, Dec. 26, 1925; d. Charles Wilbur and Edith Helen (Klooz) Graves; m. John Thomas DeBardeleben Jr., 1946 (div. 1989); children: John Thomas III, Charles Graves, Eve Lamar Roebu ck. BA, Vanderbilt U., 1947; MA, Rider U., 1986. Pvt. practice Christian Counseling, Princeton, N.J. Author: Fear's Answer, 1980, Belief Systems Inventory, 1989. Home: 219 Mercer St Princeton NJ 08540-6818

DEBAS, HAILE T., gastrointestinal surgeon, physiologist, educator; b. Asmara, Eritrea, Feb. 25, 1937; came to U.S., 1980; s. Tesfaye and Keddes (Gabre) D.; m. Ignacia Kim Assing, May 23, 1969. BS in Biology, U. Coll., Addis Ababa, Ethiopia, 1958; MD,CM, McGill U., Montreal, Que., Can., 1963. Intern Ottawa (Ont.) Civic Hosp., Can., 1963-64; resident in surgery U. B.C., Vancouver, Can., 1964-69, asst. prof. surgery, 1970-76, assoc. prof., 1976-79; fellow in gastrointestinal physiology UCLA, 1972-74, assoc. prof. surgery, 1979-81, prof. of surgery, 1981-85; chief gastrointestinal surgery U. Wash., Seattle, 1985-87; prof., chmn. dept. surgery U. Calif., San Francisco, 1987-93; dean U. Calif.-San Francisco Sch. Medicine, 1993—; key investigator Ctr. for Ulcer Rsch. and Edn., UCLA, 1980-87; cons. NIH, Bethesda, Md., 1983-87, Bd. Med. Quality Assurance, Calif., 1983-85; bd. dirs. Am. Bd. Surgery. Mem. editorial bd. Am. Jour. Physiology, Am. Jour. Surgery, Jour. Surg. Rsch., Western Jour. Medicine, Gastroenterology; contbr. over 250 articles and abstracts to jours. and chpts. to books. Recipient Merit awards, Va., 1981-87; fellow Med. Rsch. Coun. of Can., 1972-74; rsch. grantee NIH, 1976—. Fellow AAAS, ACS, Royal Coll. Physicians and Surgeons Can.; mem. Am. Surg. Assn., Am. Gastroent. Assn. (bd. govs. 1995—), Am. Assn. Endocrine Surgeons, Collequium Internat. and Chirugiae Digestivae, Soc. Univ. Surgeons, Soc. Surgeons Alimentary Tract (trustee 1985-89), Inst. Medicine NAS, Inst. Medicine, Am. Acad. Arts and Scis., Internat. Hepato-Biliary Pancreatic Assn. (pres. 1991-92), Assn. Minority Acad. Physicians (pres. 1992-93). Office: U Calif Office of the Dean 505 Parnassus Ave # S-224 San Francisco CA 94122-2722*

DE BENEDICTIS, ANTHONY, dentist; b. Mount Vernon, N.Y., Nov. 26, 1964; s. Flavio and Emanuela (Frongillo) De B.; m. Patricia Alexandra Cepeda, Mar. 4, 1995; 1 child, Jonathan. BS, Fordham U., 1986; DDS, NYU, 1990. Gen. resident in dentistry Montefiore Hosp., Bronx, 1990-91, prosthodontics resident, 1991-93, gen. dentist, 1993-94; pvt. practice Mt. Vernon, N.Y., 1994—. Mem. ADA, Am. Coll. Prosthodontists, Omicron Kappa Upsilon. Office: 562 Gramatan Ave Mount Vernon NY 10552

DE BETHUNE, GUY JACQUES, pediatrician; b. Marke, Belgium, Apr. 17, 1934; s. Jean Marie and Louise-Marie (de Vinck) de B.; m. Josephine-Marie van der Kelen, Sept. 5, 1959; children: Bernadette, Veronique, Elizabeth, Francis. MD, Cath. U. Louvain, Leuven, 1960; degree in paediatrics, Cath. U. Louvain, Leuven, Belgium, 1965. Chief dept. paediatrics Kliniek Maria's Voorzienigheid, Kortrijk, Belgium, 1965—. Contbr. articles to profl. jours. Home: Patersmotestraat 40, B 8500 Kortrijk Belgium Office: Kliniek Maria's Voorzienigheid, Loofstraat 43, B 8500 Kortrijk Belgium

DEBEYSSEY, MARK SAMMER, molecular and cellular biologist; b. Putnam, Conn., Mar. 24, 1966; s. Ghaleb and Widad Debeyssey. BS cum laude, U. Conn., 1988, MS in Moledular and Cell Biology, 1992. Sr. toxicologist Ciba-Geigy, Farmington, Conn., 1988-89; rsch. scientist U. Conn. Health Ctr., Farmington, 1989-90; molecular and cellular biologist VA Med. Ctr., West Haven, Conn., 1990-94, Albert Einstein Sch. Medicine, Bronx, N.Y., 1994—. Contbr. articles to profl. jours. Chmn. Am. Druze Soc., Conn., 1990-91. Recipient Superior Performance award Dept Vets. Affairs, 1991. Mem. AAAS, Am. Chem. Soc., Planetary Soc. (assoc.), Am. Mus. Natural History, Archaeol. Inst. Am. (assoc.), Smithsonian Nat. Assocs. Office: St Francis Hosp and Med Ctr 114 Woodland St Hartford CT 06105

DE BLEECKER, JAN LEON EMIEL, neurologist; b. Oudenaarde, Flanders, Belgium, Feb. 7, 1961; s. Georges and Paula De B.; m. Katrien De Keukelaere, Sept. 6, 1986; children: Emiel, Leonie, Henri. MD in Neuropsychiatry, Ghent (Belgium) State U., 1986, PhD in Neurology, 1992. Clin. fellow dept. neurology Ghent U. Hosp., 1986-91; postdoctoral rsch. fellow Mayo Clinic Neuromuscular Rsch. Lab., Rochester, Minn., 1991-93; with Univ. Hosp., Ghent, Belgium, 1993—; lectr. in field. Rsch. grantee NATO, Brussels, 1991-93; rsch. fellow MDA, 1993. Roman Catholic. Home: F Ferrerlaan 88, B-9000 Gent Flanders, Belgium

DEBOLT, MERLAN EDWARD, retired psychiatrist, psychoanalyst; b. Newton, Iowa, Aug. 19, 1922; s. Daniel Clarke and Grace Irene (Langmaid) DeB.; m. Idola Ruth Hubbard, Dec. 12, 1942; children: Margo, Michael, Laura, Mary. MD, State U. Iowa, 1948. Intern USPHS Hosp., S.I., N.Y., 1948-49; resident psychiatry USPHS Hosp., Ft. Worth, 1949-51, Lexington, Ky., 1951-52; asst. chief dept. USPHS Hosp., New Orleans, 1952-54; chief Mental Hygiene Clinic VA, New Orleans, 1954-55; pvt. practice psychiatry New Orleans, 1955-59; pvt. practice psychoanalysis Dallas, 1959-90; clin. prof. psychiatry Southwestern Med. Sch., Dallas, 1960-90; tng. and supervising analyst New Orleans Psychiat. Inst., 1975-94, Dallas Psychoanalytic Inst., 1983-90. Fellow Am. Psychiat. Assn.; mem. AMA, Am. Psychoanalytic Assn. Home: 101 Rainbow Dr # 4707 Livingston TX 77351-9330

DEBONS, ANTHONY, psychologist, information scientist; b. Msida, Malta, Apr. 6, 1916; came to U.S., 1923; s. Philip and Carmela (Guiffrida) DeB.; m. Aug. 15, 1948; children: Janet Marie, Eugene A. BA, Bklyn. Coll., 1948; MS, Columbia U., 1952, PhD, 1954. Commd. 2d lt. USAF, 1942, advanced through grades to col., 1964, retired, 1964; chmn. dept. psychology U. Dayton, Ohio, 1964-67, chmn. dept. infor. sci., 1967-69; vice chmn. dept. info. sci. U. Pitts., 1969-86, prof. emeritus, 1986; visiting prof. Robert Morris Coll., Coropolis, Pa., 1986-90. Author: Information Science: Integrated View, 1986. Consul, Republic of Malta; Jilin. of Tech., Chung Chu, People's Republic of China, 1987. Fellow APA, AAAS; mem. Human Factros Soc., Soc. Info. Display (pres.), Sigma Xi. Home: 115 Edgecliff Rd Carnegie PA 15106-1045 Office: U Pitts 135 N Bellefield Ave Pittsburgh PA 15213-2609

DEBOW, DWIGHT ARLES, orthodontist; b. Hot Springs, Ark., Sept. 8, 1943; s. Arles O. and Floy Mae (Wisener) DeB.; m. Carol J. Modin; children: Elizabeth, Laure, Julie. DDS, U. Tenn., Memphis, 1967; MS in Orthodontics, U. Mich., 1973. Dentist USPHS, Atlanta, 1967-71; dental instr. Emory U., Atlanta, 1970-71; orthodonic instr. U. Mich., Ann Arbor, 1972-73; pvt. practice Kingsport, Tenn., 1973—. Pres. Kingsport Dental Soc., 1980-81, Southeastern Med. Dental Soc., Arlington, Va., 1985-87; bd. dirs. Beech Mt. (N.C.) Club, 1984-89, Beech Mt. Ski Edn. Found., 1991-96. Recipient Merit cert. Am. Soc. Dentistry Children, 1968. Mem. ADA, Am. Orthodontic Assn., Omicron Kappa Upsilon. Home: 1417 Linville St Kingsport TN 37664 Office: 1203 N Wilcox Dr Kingsport TN 37660-4922

DEBOY, JOHN MICHAEL, II, public health microbiologist, laboratory director; b. Balt., June 14, 1946; s. John Michael and Margaret Ruth (Christian) DeB. BS, U. Md., 1969, U. Md., Balt., 1977; MPH, U. N.C., 1978, DrPH, 1980. Rsch. asst. Schs. Medicine and Pub. Health, Johns Hopkins U., Balt., 1972-77; vis. fellow Ctrs. Disease Control, Atlanta, 1979-80; lab. scientist Labs. Adminstrn. State Health Dept., Balt., 1969, 74-77, chief div. lab. licensure, cert., tng., 1984-94, asst. dir., 1988—; dir. lab. ops. diagnostic lab. N.Y. State Coll. Vet. Medicine, Ithaca, 1980-83; postdoctoral fellow in med. and pub. health microbiology Washington U. Med. Ctr., St. Louis, 1983-84; chmn. Nat. Registry of Microbiologists, 1987-93; advisor Ctr. for Disease Control, 1991—; cons. in field. Contbr. articles to profl. jours. and author state regulations. Served with U.S. Army, 1970-72. USPHS grantee, 1977-79. Mem. Am. Soc. Microbiology, Md. Pub. Health Assn. (bd. dirs.), Nat. Registry Microbiologists, Conf. Pub. Health Laboratorians, Sigma Xi, Delta Omega. Avocations: racquetball, genealogy. Office: Labs Adminstrn 201 W Preston St Baltimore MD 21203-2355

DE BRAUD, FILIPPO GUGLIELORO, oncologist, researcher; b. Firenze, Italy, Sept. 19, 1956; s. Mario Tenrico de Braud and Maria Luisa Buy; m. Titiana Sparolazzi; children: Laurenzia, Jacofo. Lic., Liceo G. Pacini, Milan, Italy, 1976; degree in medicine, U. Milan, 1984. Cert. Italian Bd. Oncology, European Bd. Oncology. Rsch. fellow Nat. Cancer Inst., Milan, 1980-84, fellow in med. oncology, 1984-87; rsch. fellow Wayne State U., Detroit, 1987-88, rsch. asst., 1988-89; rschr. Inst. Gustav, Paris, 1989-90; asst. prof. med. oncology Nat. Cancer Inst., Milan, 1990-94; vice dir. med. concology European Inst. Oncology, Milan, 1994—. With Italian Air Force, 1977-78. Home: Via Dello Moscova 27, 20121 Milan Italy Office: Inst Oncologia Eurofeo, Via Ripamonti 435, 20141 Milan Italy

DE BREMAECKER, SUSAN, osteopath; b. Englewood, N.J., Jan. 23, 1956; d. Jean-Claude and Arlene Anne (Parker) DeB.; m. Larry Lee Dove, July 5, 1991. BA, Rice U., 1977; MDiv, Pacific Sch. Religion, 1982; DO, W.Va. Sch. Osteopathic Med., 1992. Diplomate Am. Bd. Family Practice. Resident family practice East Tenn. State U., Johnson City, 1992-95; family practitioner St. Claire Med. Ctr., Frenchburg, Ky., 1995—. Episcopalian. Office: Menifee County Med Ctr MCR 71 Box 220 Frenchburg KY 40322

DE BRUIJN, CHRIS HENRY, health care science and biotechnology consultant, biomedical and health care technology educato; b. Geleen, Limburg, The Netherlands, Oct. 9, 1946; s. Johannes Wilhelmus and Anne-Marie (van de Wall) De B.; 1 child, Chérine. Grad. in biochemistry, U. Nijmegen, The Netherlands, 1970; PhD in Medical Scis., U. Nijmegen, 1974; postgrad., Nyenrode Bus. U., The Netherlands, 1991-92. Rsch. fellow U. Nijmegen Med. Sch., 1971-74, sr. researcher, 1974-79, assoc. prof., 1979-83; sr. researcher Pasteur Inst., Paris, 1974-79; R&D dir. Haarlem (The Netherlands) Allergy Labs., 1983-85; prof. physiol. chemistry U. Eindhoven, The Netherlands, 1983—; pres., chief exec. officer Euro-Diagnostics B.V., Apeldoorn, The Netherlands, 1985-92; vis. prof. several univs., U.S. and Austria, 1979-83; referent several sci. jours., U.S. and Europe, 1978—; cons. biosci. and healthcare industry, The Netherlands and Germany, 1985—; bd. dirs. Innovation Ctr., Zutphen, The Netherlands, 1988—; mem. govt. adv. com. on Food Safety, Ministry of Agr., Fisheries and Environ. Mgmt., The Netherlands, 1990—. Author: Purine Metabolism in Man III: Clinical and Therapeutic Aspects, 1980, Purine Metabolism in Man III: Biochemical, Immunological and Cancer Research, 1980, Purine Metabolism in Man IV: Clinical and Therapeutic Aspects, Regulatory Mechanisms, 1984, Purine Metabolism in Man IV: Biochemical, Immunological and Cancer Research, 1984, Leadership in a Creative Organisation, 1991; author TV and radio courses on biotech., 1983—; contbr. over 120 articles to sci. jours. Bd. dirs. Sch. for Higher Edn., Deventer, The Netherlands, 1989-93. Mem. European Orgn. for Cancer Rsch., Dutch Orgn. Biotech. (com. 1989-93), N.Y. Acad. Scis., Rotary. Office: Ctr Biomed and Healthcare Tech, PO Box 513, 5600 MB Eindhoven The Netherlands

DEBUONO, BARBARA ANN, physician, state official; b. N.Y.C., Apr. 13, 1955; d. Richard Francis and Catherine (Brutto) DeB.; m. David Lavington Farren, June 1, 1980; children: Adam, Douglas. BS, U. Rochester, 1976, MD, 1980; MPH, Harvard U., 1984. Diplomate Am. Bd. Internal Medicine, Nat. Bd. Med. Examiners. Intern in internal medicine New Eng. Deaconess Hosp., Boston, 1980-81, jr. med. resident, 1981-82, sr. med. resident, 1982-83; clin. fellow Brown U., Providence, 1984-86, clin. instr. dept. medicine, 1987-90, clin. asst. prof. medicine, 1990—; med. epidemiologist R.I. Dept. Health, Providence, 1986, state epidemiologist, med. dir. Office Disease Control, 1986-91; dir. dept. health State of R.I., 1991-94; commr. NY State Dept. Health, Albany, 1994—; lectr. in field. Contbr. articles to profl. jours. Robert Wood Johnson Found. Ednl. scholar U. Rochester Sch. Med., 1976-80; recipient James L. Tulis Disting. Study Lectureship award New Eng. Deaconess Hosp., 1992; named Women of Yr. by Bus. and Profl. Women's Club Providence, 1989, Person of Yr. by The Women's Youth League R.I., 1990, Woman of Yr. by R.I. Fedn. Bus. and Profl. Women's Clubs, 1991. Fellow Am. Coll. Physicians (mem. CDC cancer project adv. panel 1992—); mem. AMA, APHA, Am. Soc. Microbiology, Assn. State and Territorial Health Officials (mem. HIV com. 1989—, mem. breast and cervical cancer com. 1991—, mem. immunizations task force 1991—), Coun. State and Territorial Epidemiologists (mem. HIV com. 1989-91, mem. exec. com. 1991), Infectious Disease Soc. Am., Providence Med. Assn., R.I. Med. Soc. (mem. AIDS exec. com. 1988—), R.I. Med. Women's Assn. (R.I. Women Physician of Yr. 1988), R.I. Environ. Health Assn., Hosp. Assn. R.I. (mem. AIDS task force 1988—), Am. Coll. Physicians (mem. R.I. chpt., mem. exec. coun.), Women Execs. in Govt. Office: NY State Dept of Health Corning Tower Empire State Plaza Albany NY 12237*

DECANIO, SALVATORE MICHAEL, JR., optometrist; b. Miami, Fla., Sept. 9, 1953; s. Salvatore Michael Sr. and Leticia (Miranda) DeC.; m. Carol Ann Murante, Aug. 28, 1982; children: Margaret Anne, Michael Rocco. BA cum laude, Wake Forest U., 1975; OD, U. Houston, 1980; residency cert., VA Med. Ctr., Albuquerque, 1981. Pvt. practice Boynton Beach, Boca Raton, Fla., 1981—; co-chmn. Palm Beach Winter Seminar, 1985—; lectr. in field; optometric clin. affiliate Summit Tech. Excimer Laser, PRF, 1994—; clin. coord. 20/20 Laser Svc. S. Fla., 1996—. Contbr. articles profl. jours. Trustee Boynton Beach Area Commerce Polit. Action Com., 1990-91; mem. Downtown Re-Devel. Com., 1984-85; nat. chmn. legis. affairs com. Am. Optometric Student Assn., 1977-79; pres. Boynton Beach Blvd. Assn., 1995—. Named one of Outstanding Young Men of Am., Jaycees, 1979. Fellow Am. Acad. Optometry; mem. Am. Optometric Assn., Fla. Optometric Assn., Palm Beach County Optometric Soc. (treas. 1986-89), Greater Boynton Beach C. of C., Gold Key Internat., Omicron Delta Kappa. Republican. Roman Catholic. Office: Palm Beach Eyes 211 E Boynton Beach Blvd Boynton Beach FL 33435-3839 also: Palm Beach Eyes 4400 N Federal Hwy Ste 134 Boca Raton FL 33431-5181

DE CASTRO, ANDREW ARREOLA, physician; b. Bulan, Sorsogon, The Philippines, Sept. 15, 1956; s. Elmer Gerona De Castro and Esmeralda Pascua Arreola; m. Maria Theresa Rectra Ong, Apr. 11, 1987; children: Aya Aisa, André Austin Ahmer, Elmer Jhon Arlowe. BS in Zoology, Far Eastern U., Manila, 1978; MD, Perpetual Help Coll. Medicine, Binan, The Philippines, 1983. Diplomate. Physician Mary Immaculate Hosp., Manila, 1985-86, Bulan (The Philippines) Gen. Hosp., 1986-87, Sorsogon Provincial Hosp., 1987—. Mem. Sorsogon Amateur Radio Assn., Sorsagon Med. Assn. Roman Catholic. Home: Brgy Sta Remedios, Bulan 4706, The Philippines Office: Sorsogon Provincial Hosp, Macabog, Sorsogon 4700, The Philippines

DECASTRO, FERNANDO JOSE, pediatrics educator; b. Havana, Cuba, Nov. 11, 1937; s. Fernando R. and Maria A. (Freyre) deC.; m. Catalina, June 9, 1962; children: Maria, Ana, Fernando, Ramon, Teresa, Pablo, Jose Manuel. MD, Tulane U., 1962; MPH, U. Mich., 1966. Clin. prof. pediatrics St. Louis U., 1976—; dir. toxicology Arcadia Valley Hosp., Pilot Kove, Mo., 1992—. Contbr. articles to profl. jours. Fellow APHA, Am. Acad. Pediatrics, Am. Coll. Emergency Physicians, Am. Coll. Med. Toxicology, Am. Acad. Clin. Toxicology, Am. Fedn. Clin. Rsch.

DECATO, CLIFFORD MILES, psychology educator; b. Lebanon, N.H., Feb. 1, 1940; s. Harold H. and Yvonne R. (Beaudry) DeCato; m. Kathleen M. Orlando, Sept. 10, 1966; children: Leah A., Todd D. BA cum laude, U. N.H., 1963, MA, 1965; PhD, Temple U., 1971. Diplomate Internat. Acad. Behavioral Medicine, Am. Bd. Med. Psychotherapists, Am. Coll. Forensic Examiners. Postdoctoral fellow Irving Schwartz Inst., Phila., 1970-71; sr. instr. grad. edn. in psychology Hahnemann Med. Coll. and Hosp., Phila., 1971-72, asst. dir. grad. edn. in psychology, 1972-75, asst. prof., 1972-76, acting dir. div. of psychology, 1975-77; assoc. prof., assoc. dir. div. psychology Hahnemann U., Phila., 1977-85, prof., 1985-89; prof., assoc. dir. Inst. for Grad. Clin. Psychology Widener U., Chester, Pa., 1989—; chief psychologist Div. Mental Health Svcs., Phila. Prisons, 1977-84. Contbr. numerous articles to profl. jours. Recipient award for Outstanding Svc. to Pa. Psychol. Assn., 1984, award for Valuable Contributions to the Assn., 1977. Fellow Soc. for Personality Assessment, Am. Bd. Med. Psychotherapists; mem. APA, Assn. for Advancement Psychology, Internat. Assn. Behavioral Medicine (coun. psychotherapies), Internat. Rorschach Soc., Pa. Psychol. Assn., Phila. Soc. Clin. Psychologists, Sigma Xi. Roman Catholic. Office: Widener U Inst Grad Clin Psychology One University Pl Chester PA 19013

DE CERTAINES, JACQUES DONALD, biophysicist; b. Lyon, France, Apr. 10, 1946; s. Edme and Brigitte (Dillon) de C.; m. Madeleine Neunier, June 29, 1974; children: Gwenola, Olivier, Anne-Gael. MS, U. Sorbonne, 1973; PhD, U. Rennes, 1977. Fellow Nat. Ctr. Sci. Rsch. (CNRS), Dakar, 1968-71, Ecole des Hautes Etudes en Sci. Sociales, Paris, 1971-74; asst. Med. Sch., Rennes, 1974-81; dir. NMR lab. U. Rennes, 1981—; dir. dept. clin. biology Rennes Cancer Inst., 1995—; rsch. asst. U. Copenhagen, 1989-90; adminstr. Rennes-Atalante Sci. Park, France, 1984-89; project mgmt. group European Projects in MRI and MRS, 1985-94. Author: Resonance Magnetique Nucleaire, 1987, La Fievre des Technopoles, 1988, Magnetic Resonance Spectroscopy of Biofluids, 1989, Magnetic Resonance Spectroscopy in Biology and Medicine, 1992; editl. bd. Jour. MRI; chief editor Jour. Magnetic Resonance Analysis, 1995. Vice-mayor Rennes, 1983-89. Mem. Soc. Magnetic Resonance, European Soc. Magnetic Resonance in Biology and Medicine (bd. dirs. 1989-92). Home: 93 rue Ange Blaise, 35000 Rennes France Office: U Rennes, Lab NMR, 35043 Rennes France

DECHAINE-DHALIWAL, LINDA MICHELLE, medical technologist; b. Halifax County, Va., May 24, 1965; d. Joseph Vincent and Barbara Ann (Overstreet) Dechaine; m. Seraj Singh Dhaliwal, Apr. 30, 1994; 1 child, Wyatt Singh. Diploma med. lab. technician, Sentara Sch. Allied Health, 1988; BS in Biology, Averett Coll., 1990. Cert. med. technologist Am. Med. Technology, hematologist Am. Soc. Clin. Pathologists, med. lab. technician Am. Soc. Clin. Pathologists. Med. technologist Bon Secours St. Francis Xavier Hosp., Charleston, S.C., 1989-91, Patient First Urgent Care, Virginia Beach, Va., 1992, Sentara Leigh Hosp., Norfolk, Va., 1992-94, Maryview Med. Ctr., Portsmouth, Va., 1993-94; microbiology technician Baxter-Cardiovascular Group, Irvine, Calif., 1994—. Mem. Am. Soc. Clin. Pathologists (assoc.). Home: 3149 B Tamayo Ct Irvine CA 92714 Office: Baxter Cardiovascular Group Microbiology 14410 Redhill Ave Irvine CA 92714

DE CHAMPLAIN, RICHARD WILLIAM, dentist, educator; b. Berlin, N.H., Jan. 12, 1934; s. William John and Virginia (Boulay) De C.; m. Edwina Pope, Apr. 4, 1959; children: Jennifer, Suzanne, Richard. BS, U. N.H., 1954; DMD, Tufts U., 1958. Diplmate Am. Bd. Oral & Maxillofacial Surgery. Intern, resident Walter Reed Army Hosp., 1958-65; oral and maxillofacial surgeon Walter Reed Army Hosp., Washington, 1967-70, Tripler Army Med. Ctr., Honolulu, 1970-73, Letterman Med. Ctr., San Francisco, 1973-77, William Beaumont Army Med. Ctr., El Paso, Tex., 1977-79; from chair oral surgery to dean coll. dental medicine Med. U. S.C., Charleston, 1979—. Col. U.S. Army, 1958-79. Decorated commendation medal U.S. Army, 1970, meritorious svc. medal, 1978, legion of merit, 1973, 79; recipient meritorious svc. medal S.C. Dental Assn., 1995. Fellow Am. Coll. Dentists, Internat. Coll. Dentists, Am. Soc. Oral Surgeons, Internat. Ass. Oral Surgeons, Hawaiian Soc. Oral Surgeons (pres.), S.C. Soc. Oral Surgeons (pres.); mem. Am. Assn. Dental Schs. (v.p.). Roman Catholic. Office: Med U SC 171 Ashley Ave Charleston SC 29425

DECHANT, JOSEPH MICHAEL, audiologist; b. Lorain, Ohio, Feb. 11, 1958; s. Leonard Francis and Arlene Catherine (Thome) D.; m. Donna Anne Campbell, Dec. 29, 1984. BS, Kent State U., 1980, MA, 1982; postgrad. studies in psychology, U. Cen. Fla., 1988. Audiologist Orange County Pub. Schs., Orlando, Fla., 1981-82, Ear, Nose and Throat Surgical Assn., Winter Park, Fla., 1982-84; dir. of audiology and hearing conservation U.S. Naval Hosp., Orlando, 1984-89; audiologist Naval Med. Command Mid Atlantic Region, Norfolk, Va., 1989, U.S. Naval Hosp., Portsmouth, Va., 1989—; audiology cons. Orlando (Fla.) Regional Med. Ctr., 1981-82, Health South Rehab. Ctr., Winter Park, Fla., 1986-87. Bd. dirs. Ctr. for Ind. Living, Orlando, 1982-84. Fellow Am. Acad. of Audiology; mem. Am. Speech, Lang., Hearing Assn. (cert. mem., continuing edn. award 1987, 91), Speech and Hearing Assn. of Va. Democrat. Roman Catholic. Office: US Naval Hosp Audiology Div Portsmouth VA 23708-5100

DE CHERNEY, ALAN HERSH, obstetrics and gynecology educator; b. Phila., Feb. 13, 1942; s. William Aaron and Ruth (Hersh) DeC.; m. Deanna Faith Saver, June 26, 1966; children: Peter, Alexander, Nicholas. BS in Natural Scis., Muhlenberg Coll., 1963; MD, Temple U., 1967; MA (hon.), Yale U., 1985. Diplomate Am. Bd. Ob.-Gyn. (examiner 1984—, bd. mem. 1993—), Am.Bd. Reproductive Endocrinology (bd. dirs. 1988-94), Nat. Bd. Med. Examiners (examiner 1987-90). Intern in gen. medicine U. Pitts., 1967-68; resident in ob-gyn. U. Pa., Phila., 1968-72, instr. dept. ob-gyn, 1970-72; asst. prof. ob-gyn. Yale U. Sch. Medicine, New Haven, 1974-78, assoc. prof., 1979-84, prof., 1984-91, John Slade Ely prof. ob-gyn, 1987-92, dir. div. reproductive endocrinology, dept. ob-gyn, 1982-92, lectr. dept. biology, 1985-92; Louis E. Phaneur prof., chmn. dept. ob-gyn. Tufts U. Sch. Medicine, 1992-96; chmn. dept. ob-gyn. UCLA, 1996—. Maj. U.S. Army, 1972-74. Recipient Disting. Alumni award Temple U., 1989, Muhlenberg Coll., 1994. Fellow ACOG, Am. Fertility Soc. (pres. 1994-95), Am. Assn. History of Medicine, Soc. for Assisted Reproductive Tech. (pres. 1987-88), Soc. Reproductive Endocrinologists (pres. 1988), Soc. Reproductive Surgeons (charter, pres. 1991), Endocrine Soc., European Soc. Human Reproductions and Embryology, Soc. Gynecologic Surgeons, Soc. for Study of Reproduction, Soc. Gynecologic Investigation (pres. 1994-95). Office: Tufts U Dept Ob-Gyn 750 Washington St Boston MA 02111-1533

DECICCO, BENEDICT THOMAS, microbiologist, educator; b. Rahway, N.J., Feb. 7, 1938; s. Ralph and Anna (Mancuso) DeC.; BA, Rutgers U., 1960, MS, 1962, Ph.D., 1964; m. Doris P. Scholl, June 11, 1960; children: Richard, Lauren, Michael, Daniel, Anthony, Kathleen. Lab. technician Rutgers U., 1962-63; asst. prof. Cath. U. Am., Washington, 1964-68, asso. prof., 1968-77, prof., 1978—, chmn. dept. biology, 1973-77, 86-92; cons. environ. microbiology, 1978—. Contbr. articles to profl. jours. Mem. troop com. Boy Scouts Am., 1980-82; coach Boys Club, 1972-78. Named D.C. Prof. of Yr., 1989; NSF fellow, 1962; USPHS fellow, 1963-64; grantee NASA, 1965-73, NSF, 1974, Dept. Interior, 1975-79, Dept. Army, 1980-81. Mem. Am. Soc. Microbiology (v.p. D.C. br. 1982-83, pres. 1983-84), Coun. for Advancement and Support of Edn. (recipient Silver medal 1989), AAAS, Sigma Xi. Roman Catholic. Club: KC. Home: 12505 Caswell Ln Bowie MD 20715-1522 Office: Michigan Ave Washington DC 20064

DECK, JAMES DAVID, SR., anatomy educator; b. Atlanta, Nov. 6, 1930; s. Lucius Linton Sr. and Rosalie Elizabeth (Wootten) D.; m. Pauline Curtis

Phelps, Aug. 6, 1955; children: Sarah Deck Stevens, James David Jr., Stewart Linton, Emily Deck Harrill. BS cum laude, Davidson Coll., 1951; MA, Princeton U., 1953, PhD in Biology, 1954. Grad. teaching asst. Princeton (N.J.) U., 1952-54; instr., anatomy U. Va., Charlottesville, 1954-56, asst. prof., anatomy, 1956-62, assoc. prof., 1962-65, 66—; cons., rsch. contractor in field. Bd. dirs. , pres. Oratorio Soc., 1970-78, Youth Orch., Charlottesville, 1981-85; bd. dirs. City Polit. Party, Charlottesville, 1972-82; ann. solicitor United Way, Charlottesville, 1976-95; bd. dirs. Westminster Organ Concert Series, Charlottesville, 1992-96; officer Presbyn. Ch., Charlottesville, 1956-83. Capt. U.S. Army Res., 1954-64. Postdoctoral fellow Harvard Med. Sch., 1965-66; Rsch. grantee NSF, 1956-64, NIH, 1974-82; Rockefeller Foundation graduate scholar, 1951-52. Mem. AAAS, AAUP (chpt. pres. 1986-96), Am. Soc. Cell Biology, Am. Assn. Anatomists, Faculty Club U. Va. Democrat. Office: U Va Med Sch Dept Cell Biology PO Box 439 Health Sci Ctr Charlottesville VA 22908-0439

DECKER, CHRISTINE MARIE, healthcare administrator; b. Morristown, N.J., Feb. 4, 1947; d. George and Jenneke (Van Dyken) Laufenberg; m. James J. Decker, Oct. 5, 1968; children: James, Johanna. BSN, Villanova U., 1968; postgrad., Rider Coll., 1984—. RN, N.J., Pa. Supr. residential and profl. svcs. State of N.J., Skillman, 1981-82; mgr. quality assurance Managed Care System, Mt. Holly, N.J., 1987-88; program dir. health care accreditation programs N.J. Hosp. Assn., Princeton, 1982-87; asst. v.p. corp. quality assessment U.S. Healthcare, Blue Bell, Pa., 1988-95; quality mgmt. cons., northeast health svcs. team AETNA, Wayne, Pa., 1995-96; sr. cons. Coopers & Lybrand LLP, Phila., 1996—. Mem. Nat. Assn. Healthcare Quality, N.J. Assn. Quality Assurance Profls. (sec. bd. dirs.). Home: 6 Charred Oak Ln Hightstown NJ 08520-1804

DECKER, JAMES THOMAS, psychotherapist; b. Dayton, Ky., Jan. 16, 1944; s. Frank and Edith (Mountain) D.; m. Jane Campbell Fisher, May 6, 1972; children: Peter Campbell, James Mountain, Christina Campbell. AA, Los Angeles Pierce Coll., 1970; BA, Calif. State U., Northridge, 1972; MSW, SUNY, Stony Brook, 1974; PhD, U. Minn., 1976, Pacifica Grad. Inst. Research asst. U. Minn., Mpls., 1974-76; asst. prof. San Diego State U., 1976-78; dir., assoc. prof. U. Tex., El Paso, 1978-80; dir. cons. Kern View Hosp., Bakersfield, Calif., 1980-82; exec. dir. J.T. Decker Profl. Group, Bakersfield, Calif., 1982—; adj. prof. Calif. State Coll., Bakersfield, 1981—; sch. psychotherapist Friends Sch., Bakersfield, 1983—; nursing mgmt. cons. Meml. Hosp., Bakersfield, 1983—; out placement cons. Tosco Inc., Bakersfield, 1983—; employee asst. coordinator various orgns., Bakersfield, 1982—. Contbr. articles to profl. jours. Bd. dirs. Consumer Credit Counselors, Bakersfield, 1982—; chmn. Human Resources Com., Bakersfield, 1980-85; bd. dirs. Health Care Mgmt. Adv. Council, Bakersfield, 1982—; bd. dirs. United Way., San Diego and El Paso, Tex., 1977-80. Served with U.S. Army, 1960-64. Recipient Outstanding Alumni award Sch. Social Work, SUNY. Mem. Assn. Labor Mgmt. Adminstrs. and Cons. on Alcoholism, Nat. Assn. Social Workers (cert.). Home: 231 Oleander Ave Bakersfield CA 93304-2751

DECKER, JOSEPHINE I., clinic administrator; b. Barling, Ark., May 24, 1933; d. Ralph and Ada A. (Claborn) Snider; BS in Health Mgmt., Kennedy Western U., 1986, MS in Bus. Adminstrn., 1987; m. William Arlen Decker, Feb. 4, 1952; 1 son, Peter A. With Southwestern Bell Telephone Co., Ft. Smith, Ark., 1951-52; with Holt Krock Clinic, Ft. Smith, 1952—, bus. adminstr., 1970—. Bd. dirs. Sparks Credit Union, Adv. Council Northside and Southside high schs., Ft. Smith, Ft. Smith Girls Shelter, Ft. Smith Credit Bur. Mem. Credit Women Internat., Soc. Cert. Consumer Credit Execs. Office: Holt Krock Clinic 1500 Dodson Ave Fort Smith AR 72901-5128

DECKER, RICHARD HENRY, science consultant; b. Grand Rapids, Mich., Aug. 12, 1934; s. Dennis H. and Helen (Lucille) D.; m. Mary Elizabeth Burris, Aug. 5, 1960; children: Stephen, Richard, Stephanie. AB, Hope Coll., 1956; MS, U. Ill., 1958; PhD, Okla. State U., 1960. NIH postdoctorial fellow U. Wis., 1960-62; rsch. assoc., instr. Mayo Clinic, Rochester, Minn., 1962-71; rsch. scientist Abbott Labs, North Chgo., 1971-95, ret., 1996, dir. rsch. and devel., 1981—; sr. Volwiler fellow, Abbott Labs.; worldwide cons. on hepatitis, Wiesbaden, Gemany, 1990-91. Contbr. over 100 articles on AIDS, Hepatitis rsch. to books. Church elder, Reformed Ch., Rochester, 1962-70; symposium faculty Internat. Hepatitis Symposium, 1984, 87, 90; chmn. USSR Hepatitis Symposium, Moscow, 1984, Berlin HCV Symposium, 1990, Internat. AIDS Symposium, 1993, Hepatitis C and Beyond, 1996; mem. adv. com. W.H.O., 1996; mem. subcom. rev. panels NIH, 1994-96. Served with USNR, 1952-60. Fellow NIH, 1960-62, grantee, 1965, 68; recipient Chemistry award, Hope Coll., 1956. Mem. Fed. Socs. Expl. Biology, Nat. Com. Lab Standards (chmn. hepatitis subcom. 1988-90, Outstanding Scientist award 1989), Eurohep. Presbyterian. Avocations: Jogging; traveling; photography; music. Home: 924 Castlewood Ln Deerfield IL 60015-2608

DECKER, SUSAN DEE, nursing educator; b. Dayton, Ohio, Mar. 4, 1947; d. Sylvan Earl and Marcia Elnor (Lodge) Decker; children: Brennan William, Jonathan William. Diploma, Christ Hosp. Sch. of Nursing, Cin., 1968; BA, Miami U., Oxford, Ohio, 1970; MSN, U. Cin., 1973; PhD, Portland State U., Oreg., 1982. RN, Ohio, Oreg. Assoc. prof. Nursing U. Portland, Oreg. Contbr. articles to profl. jours., also rsch. Home: 2315 N Willamette Blvd Portland OR 97217-4410

DECKER, SUSAN JANET, electron microscopy educator; b. Chgo., Feb. 29, 1944; d. Edwin Henry and Mildred Lucille (Bowman) D. BA in Biology, Ind. U., 1968. Cert. technologist electron microscopy, open water scuba instr., water safety instr. Transmission electron microscopy supr. Northwestern U. Med. Sch., Chgo., 1966-73; transmission electron microscopy supr./instr. biology dept. U. Ill., Chgo., 1973-79; transmission and scanning electron microscopy supr./instr. U. Miami (Fla.) Sch. Medicine, 1979—; manuscript reader Twayne Pub. Co., Chgo., 1974-77; owner, operator Marine Specialty, Hollywood, Fla., 1984—. Med. writer Ency. Britannica, 1971-72; assoc. editor Underseas Jour., 1972-74; contbr. articles to profl. jours. Mem. Wildlife Care Ctr., Ft. Lauderdals, Fla., 1986—; founder Pet Trust Inc., Hollywood, Fla., 1990—. Recipient Good Citizen award DAR, Bensenville, Ill., 1962. Mem. Fla. Assn. Electron Microscopy, Midwest Soc. Microscopy, So. Calif. Soc. Electron Microscopy, Humane Soc. Am., Microscopy Soc. Am. Office: U Miami Med Sch Dept Anatomy 1600 NW 10th Ave Miami FL 33136-1015

DECKER, WALTER JOHNS, toxicologist; b. Tannersville, N.Y., June 13, 1933; s. H. Russell and Leola May (Coons) D.; m. Barbara Allen Hart, Aug. 19, 1961; children: Karl Hart, Reid Johns, Sam Travis. BA, SUNY, Albany, 1954, MA, 1955; PhD, George Washington U., 1966. Commd. 2d lt. U.S. Army, 1955, advanced through grades to lt. col., 1970, ret., 1975; assoc. prof. U. Tex. Med. Br., Galveston, 1976-83; pres. Toxicology Cons. Svcs., El Paso, Tex., 1984—; adj. clin. prof. Tex. Tech. U., El Paso, 1992—. Contbr. articles to jours. Clin. Toxicology, Vet. and Human Toxicology, Toxicology and Applied Pharmacology, others. Mem. sci. rev. panel Nat. Libr. Medicine's Hazardous Substance Data Bank, Bethesda, Md., 1985—; chair steering com. West Tex. Poison Ctr., El Paso, 1994—. Recipient Aesculapius award Tex. Med. Assn., 1977. Fellow Am. Acad. Clin. Toxicology; mem. Soc. Toxicology. Episcopalian.

DECKERS, PETER JOHN, dean; b. Boston, Feb. 13, 1941; married, 1964; 7 children. BA cum laude, Coll. of the Holy Cross, 1962; MD cum laude, Boston U., 1966. Diplomate Nat. Bd. Med. Examiners, Am. Bd. Surgery. Med. intern Boston City Hosp., 1966-67; jr. asst. resident gen. surgery Boston U. Med. Ctr., Univ. Hosp., 1967-68; clin. assoc. surgery br. Nat. Cancer Inst., NIH, Bethesda, 1968-70; resident gen. surgery Boston U. Med. Ctr., U. Hosp., 1971, UPSHS trainee in acad. surgyer, 1971-72, resident in gen. surgery, 1972-73, chief resident in gen. surgery, 1973-74; staff surgeon Boston City Hosp., 1974-84; asst. prof. surgery Boston U. Sch. Medicine, 1974-78; dean U. Conn. Sch. of Medicine, 1995—; cons., attending staff gen. surgery John Dempsey Hosp./U. Conn. Health Ctr., 1984—, VA Med. Ctr., 1984-89; sr. staff dept. surgery Hartford Hosp., 1984—; program dir. Hartford Hosp.-U. Conn. Integrated Surg. Residency Program, 1984-94; dir. divsn. of gen. surgery Hartford Hosp., 1984-87; adj. prof. surgery Dartmouth Coll., Hanover, N.H., 1984-95; interim chief divsn. of gen. surgery U. Conn. Sch. of Medicine, 1985-86, interim chmn., 1985-86; sr. staff dept. surgery New Britain Gen. Hosp., 1989—, Dept. Surgery, Mt. Sinai Hosp., 1989—, St. Francis Hosp. and Med. Ctr., 1988—; chmn. dept. surgery Hartford Hosp., 1987-94, chmn. dept. surgery, 1987-94; Murray-Heilig prof., chmn. dept. surgery U. Conn. Sch. of Medicine, 1987—; surgeon-in-chief John Dempsey Hosp., 1990-94; program dir. U. of Conn. Integrated Gen. Surg. Residency Tng. Program, 1990-94; interim divsn. chief, divsn. of gen. surgery U. Conn. Sch. Medicine, 1991-92, interim dean, 1992-94; exec. v.p. for clin. affairs U. Conn. Health System, 1994-95; exec. v.p. for physician practice orgn. U. Conn. Health System, 1995—. Editl. bd. Breast Surgery: Index and Reviews, 1993—, Surg. Oncology, 1991—; contbr. numerous articles to profl. jours. Recipient First Prize James Ewing Resident Rsch. award, 1971; recipient numerous grants. Mem. Transplantation Soc., Am. Assn. for Cancer Rsch., Eastern Coop. Oncology Group, Assn. for Acad. Surgery, Am. Assn. for Cancer Edn., Am. Fedn. for Clin. Rsch., Mass. Med. Soc., Am. Radium Soc. (exec. com. 1989-91), Am. Soc. of Clin. Oncology, Soc. of Surg. Oncology (mem. coms.), Soc. of Univ. Surgeons, New England Cancer Soc. (pres. 1993, pres.-elect, 1992, exec. coun. 1991-94), Boston Surg. Soc., N.H. Med. Soc., Societe Internationale de Chirurgie, Bay State Health Care, Soc. for the Surgery of the Alimentary Tract, New England Surg. Soc. (treas. 199—), Pilgrim Ind. Practice Assn., Internat. Acad. of Oncology, Assn. for Surg. Edn. (bd. dirs. Assn. for Surg. Edn. Found. 1993), Assn. of Program Dirs. in Surgeons (pres.-elect 1990-91, pres. 1991-92), Conn. State Med. Soc. (mem. cancer coordinating com. 1990-91), Capital Area Individual Practice Assn., Am. Cancer Soc. (Hartford chpt.), Connecticare, Hartford County Med. Assn., Soc. of Surg. Chmn. Home: 29 Valley View Dr Avon CT 06001 Office: Univ of Conn Health Ctr 263 Farmington Ave Farmington CT 06030-1920

DECKERT, PATRICIA KAY, family practice osteopath, medical director; b. Detroit, Apr. 17, 1947; d. Myrton W. and Kathleen I. (Fitzpatrick) Woehrle; m. George E. Preston, Jan. 6, 1967 (div. 1982); children: Kathleen, Karen; m. Vern R. Deckert, July 1, 1984. BS with honors, Mich. State U., 1969; DO, Coll. Osteo. Med. Pacific, Pomona, Calif., 1991. Intern Michiana Cmty. Hosp., South Bend, Ind., 1992; pvt. practice Alpine Creek Family Medicine, Alpine, Calif., 1992—; chief, family practice Scripps Hosp East County, El Cajon, Calif., 1993—; med. dir. Scripps Med. Assn. East County, El Cajon, Calif., 1995—. Mem. Am. Osteo. Assn., Calif. Osteo. Assn., San Diego Osteo. Assn. Home: 17312 Kumeyai Trail Alpine CA 91901 Office: Alpine Creek Family Med 1349 Tavern Rd Ste 9 Alpine CA 91901

DE CLAIRE, JEFFREY H., orthopaedic surgeon; b. Harper Woods, Mich., Apr. 26, 1955; s. Alton George and Theresa Marie (Zorillo) De C.; m. Penny Sue Shields; children: Maria Louise, Lauren Michelle, Jeffery Hilliard. BS, U. Mich., 1977, MD, 1981. Diplomate Am. Bd. Orthopaedic Surgery. Surg. intern Wayne State Univ. Hosps., Detroit, 1982-83; resident orthopaedic surgery U. Mich. Hosps., Ann Arbor, 1983-86; sports medicine fellow Pa. State U., Hershey Med. Ctr., 1986-87; chief orthopaedics Crittenton Hosp., 1991, 92; mem. outpatient surgery com. Crittenton Hosp., 1987—, outpatient surgery subcom.-planning, 1989—, surgery rev. com., 1989—, chmn. rehab. com., 1989—, sec. dept. surgery, 1991, 92, 93; adv. bd. Crittenton Fitness Inst., 1987—. Contbr. articles to profl. jours. Vol. emergency rm. St. John Hosp., Detroit, 1974; Little League Baseball coach, Grosse Point Woods, Mich., 1975-76; preceptorship Cottage Hosp., Grosse Pointe Farms, 1976; team physician Wayne (Mich.) Meml. H.S., 1983, Hershey (Pa.) Bears Hockey Team, 1986, 87, Andover H.S., Lahser H.S., Troy H.S., Oakland County, Mich., 1987-89, Cranbrook H.S., Bloomfield Hills, Mich., 1987-92, Bloomfield Jets Hockey Team, 1987, Detroit Jr. Red Wings, 1989-92; asst. team physician Pa. U. State Coll., Hershey, 1986, 87; team physician, orthopaedic cons. Oakland U. Athletic Program, Rochester Hills, Mich., 1988—. Mem. AMA, Am. Orthopaedic Soc. for Sports Medicine, Arthroscopy Assn. N.Am., Am. Acad. Orthopaedic Surgeons, Mich. State Med. Soc., Mich. Orthopaedic Alumni Assn., Oakland County Med. Soc., U. Mich. Alumni Soc., Sigma Alpha Epsilon (pledge trainer U. Mich. 1975, pres. 1976). Office: Ste 330 1135 W University Rochester MI 48307

DE CORTE, ERIK WILLY ALBERIC, educational psychology researcher; b. Blankenberge, Belgium, June 15, 1941; m Rita Vanderheyde, Sept. 23, 1964; children: Emmanuel, Karolien. Degree in edn., U. Leuven, Belgium, 1964; D in Pedagogical Sci., 1970. Asst. FNRS U. Leuven, 1964-71, lectr. in ednl. psychology, 1971-72, prof. in ednl. psychology, 1976—; dir. Leuven Lang. Ctr., 1987-93. Co-author: Foundations of School Learning and Teaching, 1972, (transl. German and French) Educational Objectives, 1973, 2d edit., 1976, Research on Teaching-Learning Processes: Present Trends and Issues, 1982, Growing in Teaching, 1988; editor-in-chief jour. Learning and Instrn., 1990-93; editor Internat. Jour. Ednl. Rsch., 1986—; mem. editl com. for various jours in field. First laureate of Concours U. Belgium, 1965; recipient award for best publ. in edn. Ministry of Nat. Edn., 1973, award for outstanding rsch. articles U.S. Nat. Coun. Tchrs. Math., 1987. Mem. APA, European Assn. Rsch. on Learning and Instrn. (pres. 1985-89), Belgian Psychol. Assn., Dutch Edn. Rsch. Assn., Am. Ednl. Rsch. Assn., Internat. Assn. Applied Psychology (pres. divsn. edn. instruction and sch. psychology 1994—), Internat. Soc. for Study of Behavioral Devel., Royal Norwegian Soc. Scis. and Letters, Sect. Humanities (fgn.), Academie Europaea. Home: Panoramalaan 5, B 3360 Bierbeek Belgium Office: U Leuven Dept Sci Pedag, Vesaliusstraat 2, B 3000 Leuven Belgium

DE COURTEN-MYERS, GABRIELLE MARGUERITE, education educator, researcher; b. Fribourg, Switzerland, Aug. 8, 1947; came to U.S., 1979; d. Maurice Edmond and Margrit (Wettstein) De Courten; m. Ronald Elwood Myers, Apr. 18, 1981; 1 child, Maximilian. BSBA, Akademikergemeinschaft, Zurich, Switzerland, 1967; MD, U. Zurich, 1974. Resident in psychiatry Hopital Psycho-Geriatrique, Gimel, Switzerland, 1974-75; resident in pediatrics U. Hosp. Zurich, 1977; resident in neuropathology U. Hosp. of Lausanne, Switzerland, 1976-78; rsch. assoc. NIH, Bethesda, Md., 1979-80; fellow in neuropathology Coll. of Medicine U. Cin., 1980-83, asst. prof. neuropathology Coll. of Medicine, 1983-88, assoc. prof. neuropathology Coll. of Medicine, 1988-89, tenured assoc. prof. Coll. of Medicine, 1989—; cons. Vets. Affairs Med. Ctr., Cin., 1983—, Children's Hosp. Med. Ctr., Cin., 1984—, Good Samaritan Hosp., Cin., 1990—. Grantee VA, 1985—, NIH, 1986-90, 93—, Am. Heart Assn., 1991-94, Am. Diabetes Assn., 1995. Mem. AAAS, Am. Assn. Neuropathologists, Am. Acad. Neurology, AAUP, Soc. Acad. Emergency Medicine, Soc. Exptl. Neuropathology. Office: U Cin Coll of Medicine 231 Bethesda Ave Cincinnati OH 45229-2827

DEDEAUX, PAUL J., orthodontist; b. Pass Christian, Miss., Feb. 22, 1937; s. Mack and Harriet D.; m. Janet Louise Harter, June 29, 1971; children: Michele, Kristen, Kelly. BA, Dillard U., 1959; DDS, Howard U., 1963; MS, Fairleigh Dickinson U., 1975. Pvt. practice, Washington, 1976-93, Santa Ana, Calif., 1976-93; instr. Howard U., Washington, 1967-69; dental dir. Dr. Martin Luther King Health Ctr., Bronx, N.Y., 1969-70, dentist, 1970-76; chief dentist Calipatria State Prison, Calif., 1993-96, Calif. Med. Facility, Vacaville, 1996—; instr. Howard U., Washington, 1967-69; cons. Hostos C.C., Bronx, 1971-76; mem. adv. panel Dental Econs. mag., 1976; adj. assoc. prof. Columbia U., N.Y.C., 1970-72. Contbr. articles to profl. jours. Capt. U.S. Army, 1963-67, comdr. USAR, 1975—. Mem. Am. Assn. Orthodontists, Pacific Coast Soc. Orthodontists, ADA, Calif. Dental Assn., Assn. Mil. Surgeons of U.S. Democrat. Methodist. Home: 12181 Anzio St Garden Grove CA 92840 Office: Calif Med Facility PO Box 2000 1600 California Dr Vacaville CA 95696

DEDERICK, DONALD HENRY, medical librarian; b. N.Y.C., July 10, 1935; s. Peter James and Clara (Hesse) D.; m. Arline Theresa Montgomery, Aug. 24, 1958; children: Donald Henry Jr., Diana Elizabeth, Desiree Clare, Deborah Tereza, Douglas Richard, Dawn Alexandra. BA in History, CCNY, 1966; MA in History, Queens Coll., 1975; MLS, Pratt Inst., 1976, postgrad., 1988—. Social caseworker N.Y.C. Dept. Social Svcs., 1965-76; head reader svcs. div. Bloomfield (N.J.) Pub. Library, 1976-78; pub. svcs. librarian Rio Grande (Ohio) Coll. and Community Coll., 1978-80; head circulation dept. Seton Hall U., South Orange, N.J., 1980-82; library dir. Mt. Holly (N.J.) Library, 1982-84; head inter-library loan dept. SUNY Health Sci. Ctr., Bklyn., 1984-92, serials libr., 1992-95, reference libr., 1995—; trustee Burlington County Lyceum History and Natural Scis., Mt. Holly, 1988-91. contbr. columns, revs. to profl. publs. Vice-chmn. Preservation Commn. Historic Mt. Holly, 1980-95; mem. del. assembly United Univ. Professions, 1986—. Mem. ALA, Med. Libr. Assn. (chmn. archives com. N.Y.-N.J. regional group 1987-92), Bklyn. Queens S.I. Health Sci. Librs. Group (membership chmn. 1988-92), N.J. Libr. Assn., N.Y. State Hist. Assn., Bklyn. Hist. Soc., N.Y. Hist. Soc., N.Y. Libr. Club. Democrat. Episcopalian. Home: 37 Union St Mount Holly NJ 08060-1824 Office: SUNY Health Scis Ctr Med Rsch Libr 450 Clarkson Ave Brooklyn NY 11203-2098

DEDERT, STEVEN RAY, marketing professional, consultant; b. Franklin, Ind., Feb. 17, 1953; s. Ralph Edward and Martha Elizabeth (Weisman) D.; children: Eric Allen, Tammi Michelle. AA, St. John's Coll., Winfield, Kans., 1973; BSBA, U. Denver, 1975. CPA, Ind. Audit sr. Coopers & Lybrand, Indpls., 1975-78; controller Am. Med. Mgmt., Inc., Indpls., 1978-82, Moorfeed Corp., Indpls., 1982-84; chief fin. officer, controller Midwest Energy Mgmt., Indpls., 1984-86; pres. Cleaning Solution, Inc., Indpls., 1986-89; chief fin. officer, dir. ops. Corinthian Pharm. Systems, Inc., Indpls., 1990-93; ptnr. Hometown Living Ctrs., Inc., Indpls., 1991—; cons. acct., 1980—. Treas. bd. dirs. Greater Indpls. Assn. for Luth. Secondary Edn., 1978-82; mgr. Franklin Twp. Little League, 1985-87. Mem. Ind. CPA Soc., AICPA. Home: PO Box 39251 Indianapolis IN 46239-0251 Office: 115 N Pennsylvania Ste 856 Indianapolis IN 46204

DEDONATO, DONALD MICHAEL, obstetrician/gynecologist; b. Bridgeport, Conn., Apr. 25, 1952; s. Michael Anthony and Mary Jane (Zawadski) DeD.; m. Susan Mary Naulty, June 15, 1974; children: Mark Dominic, David Nicholas. BA in Chemistry cum laude, Coll. Holy Cross, 1974; MD, Loyola U., Maywood, Ill., 1977. Intern Loyola Foster McGaw Hosp., Maywood, Ill., 1977-78; resident Ohio State U. Hosp., Columbus, Ohio, 1978-81; ob-gyn. Ob-Gyn. Assocs., Arlington Heights, Ill., 1981-87, DeDonato, Goodnough and Geittmann, Ob-Gyn, Arlington Heights, 1987-92; pres. N.W. Women's Cons., Arlington Heights, 1993—; Clin. instr. Northwestern U. Med. Ctr., Chgo., 1981—. Recipient CIBA award. Mem. AMA, Am. Assn. Med. Colls. (Loyola rep.), Chgo. Med. Soc., Ill. State Med. Soc., Am. Bd. Ob-Gyn., Am. Assn. Gyn. Laparoscopists, Garden Camera (pres. 1985-86, 92-93), Phi Beta Kappa, Alpha Sigma Nu. Office: NW Womens Cons 1614 W Central Rd Arlington Heights IL 60005-2490

DE DUVE, CHRISTIAN RENÉ, chemist, educator; b. Thames-Ditton, Eng., Oct. 2, 1917; s. Alphonse and Madeleine (Pungs) de D.; m. Janine Herman, Sept. 30, 1943; children: Thierry, Anne, Françoise, Alain. M.D., U. Louvain, Belgium, 1941, Ph.D., 1945, M.Sc., 1946; D honoris causa, U. Turin, 1969, U. Leiden, 1970, U. Sherbrooke, 1970, U. Lille, 1973, Cath. U. Santiago, Chile, 1974, U. René Descartes, Paris, 1974, State U. Liege, 1975, State U. Ghent, 1975, Gustavus Adolphus Coll., St. Peter, Minn., 1975, U. Rosario, Argentina, 1975, U. Aix-Marseille II, 1979, U. Keele, 1982, Katholieke U. Leuven, 1984, Karolinska Inst., Stockholm, 1986, U. Montreal, 1992. Lectr. physiol. chemistry faculty medicine Cath. U. Louvain, 1947-51, prof., head dept. physiol. chemistry, 1951-85, emeritus prof., 1985—; prof. biochem. cytology Rockefeller U., N.Y.C., 1962-74, Andrew W. Mellon prof., 1974-88, prof. emeritus, 1988—; vis. prof. Albert Einstein Coll. Medicine, Bronx, N.Y., 1961-62, Chaire Francqui State U. Ghent, 1962-63, Free U. Brussels, 1963-64, State U. Liège, 1972-73, Facultés Universitaires Notre-Dame de la Paix, Namur, 1990-91; Mayne guest prof. U. Queensland, Brisbane, Australia, 1972; pres. Internat. Inst. Cellular and Molecular Pathology, Brussels, 1974-91. Mem. editorial bd. Subcellular Biochemistry, 1971-87, Preparative Biochemistry, 1971-80, Molecular and Cellular Biochemistry, 1973-80. Mem. Conseil d'Adminstrn. du Fonds Nat. de la Recherche Scientifique, 1958-61; mem. Conseil de Gestion du Fonds de la Recherche Scientifique Medicale, 1959-61; mem. Commn. Scientifique du Fonds de la Recherche Scientifique Medicale, 1958-61; mem. Comite des Experts du Conseil Nat. de la Politique Scientifique, 1958-61; mem. adv. bd. Ciba Found., 1960-85; mem. adult devel. and aging research and tng. rev. com. Nat. Inst. Child Health and Devel., NIH, 1970-73; mem. adv. com. for med. research WHO, 1974-79; mem. sci. adv. com. Max Planck-Inst. für Immunbiologie, 1975-78, Ludwig Inst. Cancer Research, 1985-91 , Mary Imogene Bassett Research Inst., 1986-90, Clin. Research Inst. Montreal, 1986—; mem. biology adv. com. N.Y. Hall of Sci., 1986—; adv. sci. com. Basel Inst. for Immunology, 1989-93. Recipient Prix des Alumni, 1949, Prix Pfizer, 1957, Prix Francqui, 1960, Prix Quinquennal Belge des Sciences Médicales, 1967 (Belgium); Gairdner Found. Internat. award merit (Can.), 1967; Dr. H.P. Heineken prize (The Netherlands), 1973; Nobel prize for physiology or medicine, 1974; Harden award Biochem. Soc. (Gt. Britain), 1978; Theobald Smith award Albany Med. Coll., 1981; Jimenez Diaz award, 1985. Fellow AAAS; mem. NAS, Royal Acad. Medicine, Royal Acad. Belgium, Am. Chem. Soc., Biochem. Soc., Am. Philos. Soc., Am. Soc. Biol. Chemists, Pontifical Acad. Sci., Am. Soc. Cell Biology (coun. 1966-69, E.B. Wilson award 1989), Soc. Chimie Biologique, Soc. Belge Biochim. (pres. 1962-64), Deutsche Akademie der Naturforscher Leopoldina, Koninklyke Akademie voor Geneeskunde (Belgium), European Assn. Study Diabetes, European Molecular Biology Orgn., European Cell Biology Orgn., Internat. Soc. Cell Biology, N.Y. Acad. Scis., Soc. Belge de Physiologie, Sigma Xi; fgn. assoc. Am. Acad. Arts and Scis., Royal Soc. London, Royal Soc. Can., Académie des Sciences de Paris, Académie des Sciences d'Athènes, Academia Europaea, Deutsche Gesellschaft für Zellbiologie; numerous hon. memberships. Office: Rockefeller U 1230 York Ave New York NY 10021-6307 also: ICP, 75 Ave Hippocrate, B-1200 Brussels Belgium

DEE, ROBERT FORREST, retired pharmaceutical company executive; b. Cin., July 8, 1924; s. Raymond H. and Mary (Owen) D.; m. Virginia Winston Verner, Sept. 10, 1948 (div. 1979); children: Jacqueline, Robert R., John, Catherine, Thomas; m. 2d Jean T. Tanney, Jan. 2, 1980; 1 child, Patrick. A.B., Harvard U., 1946; LL.D. (hon.), Phila. Coll. Pharmacy and Sci., 1978; L.H.D. (hon.), Med. Coll. Pa., 1979. With SmithKline Corp., Phila., 1948-87; successively market research analyst, asst. to adminstrv. v.p., dir. Animal Health div., dir. consumer, animal and instrument products, v.p., dir. consumer, animal and instrument products, exec. v.p., pres., chief exec. officer, chmn.; bd. dirs. United Techs. Corp., Air Products and Chems. Inc.; mem. adv. bd. Volvo Internat. Bd. dirs. U.S. Council for Internat. Bus., Com. Econ. Devel.; trustee Heritage Found. Served with AUS. Mem. Nat. Assn. Mfrs. (chmn. exec. com.), Bus. Council, Conf. Bd., Council Fgn. Relations, Mgmt. Execs. Soc. Episcopalian. Office: PO Box 1539 709 Swedeland Rd King Of Prussia PA 19406

DEE, VIVIEN, nursing administrator; b. Manila, Nov. 12, 1944; came to U.S., 1962; d. David Hawkins and Ivy Marie (Woo) D.; m. John Robert Smith, Sept. 30, 1984. BSN, Loma Linda U., 1966; MN, UCLA, 1974; D of Nursing Sci., U. Calif., San Francisco, 1986. Cert. advanced nursing adminstrn. Staff nurse White Meml. Med. Ctr., L.A., 1966; pub. health nurse Los Angeles County Health Dept., L.A., 1966-69; program nurse specialist Child Devel. and Mental Retardation ctr. U. Wash., Seattle, 1969-72; asst. prof. nursing Calif. State U., L.A., 1974-75; nursing cons. Western Regional Ctr. for the Developmentally Disabled, Santa Monica, Calif., 1974-75; clin. nurse coordinator child ambulatory svcs. UCLA, 1975-76; asst. dir. nursing Neuropsychiat. Inst. and Hosp. UCLA, L.A., 1977-87, assoc. hosp. adminstr., dir. nursing, 1987—; asst. dean clin. affairs Sch. Nursing UCLA, 1987—; pres. Psychiatric Healthcare Cons., Rolling Hills Estates, 1989—; vis. prof. Nat. Def. Med. Ctr., China, 1991; trustee Loma Linda U., 1996. Contbr. articles to profl. jours. and chpts. to books. Fellow Am. Acad. Nursing, Am. Psychiatric Nurses Assn. (Excellence in Psychiatric Nursing award 1992); mem. ANA, Am. Orgn. Nurse Execs., Sigma Theta Tau (Leadership award 1994). Home: 1509 Via Fernandez Palos Verdes Estates CA 90274

DEEB, G. MICHAEL, surgery educator; b. Franklin, Pa., June 25, 1949; m. Nancy Dryer; children: Jayme, Andrea. BS, U. Pitts., 1971, MD, 1975. Diplomate Am. Bd. Surgery, Am. Bd. Thoracic Surgery. Intern in surgery U. Pitts., 1975-76, resident in gen. surgery, 1976-80, resident in cardiothoracic surgery, 1980-82; asst. prof. surgery Temple U. Hosp., Phila., 1982-86; asst. prof. surgery U. Mich. Hosps., Ann Arbor, 1986-91, assoc. prof., 1991—, dir. heart-lung transplant and artificial devices program, 1986-95, dir. adult cardiac surgery, 1990—; cons. heart transplantation program Newark Beth Israel Med. Ctr.; attending cardiothoracic surgery St. Christopher's Hosp. for Children, Phila., 1982-86, Germantown Hosp., Phila., 1982-86, Brandywine Hosp., Phila., 1982-86, Abington Hosp., Phila., 1982-86, VA Hosp., Ann Arbor, 1986—; numerous presentations in field, 1979—. Contbr. over 75 articles and absracts to med. jours., chpts. to books. Recipient best resident rsch. award Pitts. Acad. Medicine, 1980; grantee Am. Heart Assn. Mich., 1989-91, NIH, 1988-89, 93-98, Miles Inc.,1992-94, also others. Mem. ACS (award for best resident rsch. presentation Southeastern Pa. chpt. 1979), AMA, Am. Soc. Transplant Surgeons, Internat. Soc. for Heart and Lung Transplantation, Assn. for Acad. Surgery, Soc. Thoracic Surgeons, Assn. Am. Med. Colls., Soc. Univ. Surgeons, Am. Assn. for Thoracic Surgeons, Transplantation Soc. Mich. (trustee), Mich. Soc. Thoracic and Cardiovasc. Surgeons, Phi Beta Kappa, Alpha Omega Alpha, Alpha Epsilon Delta, Beta Beta Beta. Office: U Mich Med Ctr 1500 E Medical Center Dr Ann Arbor MI 48109

DEED, MARTHA LOUISE, psychologist; b. Nyack, N.Y., May 1, 1941; d. Robert Frederick and Louise Eleanor (Salls) D.; 1 child, Mildred Elizabeth; m. David H. Suckow. Student, Carleton Coll., 1959-62; BA, New Sch. for Social Research, 1964; PhD, Boston U., 1969. Lic. psychologist, N.Y. Staff psychologist Rockland County Mental Health Ctr., Pomona, N.Y., 1969-73, Western N.Y. Inst. for Psychotherapies, Niagara Falls, 1981-82; psychologist, researcher Paris, 1973-75; pvt. practice psychology N.Y.C., 1976-81, Snyder, East Amherst, N.Y., 1982—; mem. adj. faculty SUNY Sch. Law, 1994-96; seminar leader and trainer for counselors of adults abused as children: speaker in field, 1984—; vis. lectr. SUNY, 1994. Contbg. editor Am. Jour. of Orthopsychiatry, 1989—; contbr. articles to various publs. Hester Ann Beebe fellow Boston U., 1965-68, Am. Friends Svc. Com. Campbell fellow; Friends World Com. for Consultation research grantee, 1968-69. Mem. APA, N.Y. State Psychol. Assn. (pres.-elect clin. divsn. 1993-94, pres. 1994-95, Disting. Svc. award 1996), Am. Orthopsychiat. Assn., Psychol. Assn. Western N.Y., Authors Guild, Nat. League Am. Penwomen. Mem. Religious Soc. Friends. Home and Office: 6 Coriander Ct East Amherst NY 14051-1265

DEEMER, ALBERT EARL, social worker; b. USSR, Nov. 10, 1912; came to U.S., 1921; s. Barney and Rose Deemer; m. Estelle Soffen, June 28, 1940; 1 child, Lee Bruce. AB, U. Pitts., 1934, MSW, 1937. Caseworker Juvenile Ct., Pitts., 1936-38; caseworker, supr., asst. dir. Jewish Children's Bur., Chgo., 1938-48; regional dir. Joint Distbn. Com. Midwest, N.Y.C., 1948-50; case cons. Jewish Family Svc., Kansas City, Mo., 1950-53; exec. dir. Jewish Family Svc. Assn., Buffalo, 1953-87, exec. dir. emeritus, 1987-90, ret., 1990; cons. Erie County Dept. Mental Health, Buffalo, 1962-64; peer reviewer Coun. Accreditation, Family & Children's Assn., N.Y.C., 1983-86. Mem. Mayors Com. Alcoholism, Buffalo, 1965; arbitrator Dispute Settlement Ctr., Better Bus. Bur., Buffalo, 1987—; bd. dirs. Rsch. and Planning Coun., 1972-80, Family Svc. N.Am.; pres. Meals on Wheels Buffalo and Erie Counties, 1979-81, bd. dirs., 1989; bd. dirs., pres. Found. for Crisis Svc., 1988; treas. Crisis Svcs., Buffalo, 1986-88, bd. dirs., 1988. 2d lt. U.S. Army, 1943-45. Recipient Outstanding Vol. Svc. award Meals on Wheels Buffalo, 1981, statuette Found. for Crisis SVcs., 1988. Mem. NASW (cert., editor newsletter N.Y. chpt., western div. 1991—, chair N.Y. State chpt. western div., western N.Y. div. Lifetime Achievement award 1993, N.Y. state chpt., 1993), Nat. Assn. Vocat. Svcs. (bd. dirs. 1970-80).

DEER, PHILIP JAMES, JR., ophthalmologist; b. El Dorado, Ark., Sept. 27, 1933; s. Philip James and Polly Pearl (Dial) D.; m. Florence Elizabeth Ross, June 2, 1955; children: Philip James III, Ashley Ross, Sloan Deer Powell. Student, Hendrix Coll., 1951-53; MD, U. Tenn., Memphis, 1957; postgrad., Harvard U., Boston, 1961. Diplomate Am. Bd. Ophthalmology. Resident in ophthalmology U. Tenn., 1961-64; pvt. practice, Little Rock, 1964—; med. cons. Ark. Rehab. for Blind, Little Rock, 1967—. Bd. dirs. Hendrix Coll., Conway, Ark., 1972-89. Lt. M.C., USN, 1958-60. Mem. Ark. Med. Soc., Pulaski County Med. Soc., Little Rock Country Club. Democrat. Methodist. Home: 16 Longfellow Ln Little Rock AR 72207 Office: 8500 Markham St Ste 133 Little Rock AR 72205

DEERING, GEORGE EDWIN, psychiatrist; b. Worcester, Pa., May 27, 1917; s. George Edwin and Agatha Louise (Small) D.; m. Ruby E. Sternlof, Aug. 7, 1925; children: George Edwin, Martha Pearl, Rebecca Jane. BA, Clark U., Worcester, Mass., 1939; MD, Harvard U., 1943. Psychiatrist Worcester Hahnemann Hosp., Worcester, Mass., 1945-84; chief neuropsychiat. svc. and mental hygiene clinic U.S. Army Hosp., 1951-53; sr. psychiatrist emeritus St. Vincent Hosp., Worcester, Mass., 1954—, co-founder alcoholism clinic, 1954; psychiat. dir. Belmont Rehab. Program, Worcester, Mass., 1955-69; courtesy staff qualified physician Worcester State Hosp., Worcester, Mass., 1972-83; asst. prof. psychiatry U. Mass. Med. Sch., Worcester, 1973-90. co-author with others: Alcohol Dehydrogenase and Etiological Factor in Alcoholism, 1968, Effect of Ethanol on Serotonin Metabolism in Alcoholic and Normal Subject; producer, dir. Theatre Six. Lay leader Fairlawn United Meth. Ch., Shrewsbury, Mass., 1980-96, cert. lay speaker, 1989—. Mem. AMA, Am. Psychiat. Assn., Am. Group Psychotherapy Assn., Mass. Med. Soc., Acad. Religion and Mental Health, Assn. Gen. Hosp. Psychiatrists, Nat. Council on Alcoholism. Republican. Office: 85 Crescent St Shrewsbury MA 01545-2827

DEES, TOM MOORE, internist; b. Dallas, Mar. 4, 1931; s. Tom Hawkins and Maida Elizabeth (Board) D.; m. Suzanne Settle, Feb. 20, 1971; children: Tom Moore III, David Walsh. BA, Johns Hopkins U., 1952; MD, Southwestern Med. Sch., 1956. Intern Bellevue Hosp., N.Y.C., 1957, resident, 1958-59; rsch. fellow in cardiology Southwestern Med. Sch., Dallas, 1961; internist, ptnr. pvt. practice med. office Dallas, 1962—; dir. and mng. ptnr. Swiss Ave. Med. Bldg., Dallas, 1984—; clin. asst. prof. medicine Southwestern Med. Sch., Dallas, 1962—; assoc. attending physician Baylor Med. Ctr., Dallas, 1962—. Mem. dist. commn. Boy Scouts Am., Dallas, 1963-72; mem. ofcl. bd. Highland Park Meth. Ch., Dallas, 1963-72. Capt. USAF, 1959-61. Mem. ACP (life), AMA, Am. Soc. Internal Medicine, Johns Hopkins U. Alumni Assn. (pres. North Tex. chpt 1964-68), Tex. Club of Internists (pres. 1992-93). Republican. Home: 3649 Stratford Ave Dallas TX 75205-2810 Office: 3434 Swiss Ave Ste 420 Dallas TX 75204-6239

DEESE, JAMES EARLE, psychologist, educator; b. Salt Lake City, Dec. 14, 1921; s. Thomas D. and Serena Jane (Johnson) D.; m. Ellin Ruth Krauss, Dec. 24, 1948; children: Elizabeth Ellin, James Lawrence. A.B., Chapman Coll., 1944; A.M., Ind. U., 1946, Ph.D., 1948; D.Litt., Chapman Coll., 1982. From asst. prof. to prof. psychology Johns Hopkins U., Balt., 1948-72; Commonwealth prof. U. Va., 1972-80, Hugh Scott Hamilton prof., 1980-90, prof. emeritus, 1990—; vis. prof. U. Calif., Berkeley, 1958-59, Georgetown U., 1990. Author: Psychology of Learning, 5th edit., (with S.H. Hulse and H. Egeth), 1980, (with W. Lado and R. Goodale) Principles of Psychology, 2d edit., 1975, The Structure of Associations in Language and Thought, 1965, General Psychology, 1967, Psycholinguistics, 1969, Psychology as Science and Art, 1972, (with L.B. Szalay) Subjective Meaning and Culture, 1978, Thought into Speech, 1984, (with E.K. Deese) How to Study, 1978, rev. edit., 1992, American Freedom and the Social Sciences, 1985; contbg. author: Introduction to Psychology (C.T. Morgan), 1955; assoc. editor Jour. Exptl. Psychology, 1963-68; editor Psychol. Bull., 1968-74; cons. editor Psychology Rev. Recipient Raven award U. Va., 1990. Fellow Soc. Exptl. Psychologists, Am. Psychol. Assn. (dir.); mem. AAAS (v.p. 1971-72), Ea. Psychol. Assn. (pres. 1966-67), Linguistic Soc. Am. Clubs: 14 West Hamilton Street (Balt.); Greencroft (Charlottesville), Colonnade (Charlottesville); Cosmos (Washington). Home: 1829 Westview Rd Charlottesville VA 22903-1632

DE FABO, EDWARD CHARLES, photobiology and photoimmunology, research scientist, educator; b. Wilkes-Barre, Pa., June 10, 1937; s. Giovanni and Anna (Marconi) De F.; m. Athena Macris, Aug. 17, 1967 (dec. June 1985); m. Frances Patricia Noonan. BS, Kings Coll., 1958; PhD, George Washington U., 1974. Rsch. scientist USDA, Beltsville, Md., 1974-75, NCI-Frederick (Md.) Cancer Rsch. Ctr., 1978-81; scientist, adminstr. U.S. EPA, Washington, 1975-78; asst. rsch. prof. dept. dermatology George Washington U., Washington, 1981-86, assoc. rsch. prof. dept. dermatology, 1986-92, rsch. prof. dept. dermatology, 1992—; chmn. project Sci. Com. on Problems of Environ. SCOPE ozone depletion and UV radiation, Paris, 1989-92; cons. U.S. EPA, 1984-85; chmn. project Internat. Arctig Sci. Com., Oslo, 1993—. Editor, organizer publ. Sci. Com. on Problems of Environment, 1992; contbr. articles to rsch. jours.; author: Immunology Today, 1992. Dir. congl. sci. fellowship program Am. Soc. Photobiology, Bethesda, 1981-85. Grantee Internat. Union Against Cancer, 1983, Am. Cancer Soc., 1987-89, U.S. EPA, 1987—, NIH, 1989—; fellow Smithsonian Inst., 1970-74, NSF, 1963-64. Mem. AAAS, Am. Soc. Photobiology (councilor 1980-83). Office: George Washington U Med Ctr Ross Hall Rm 101-B 2300 I St NW Washington DC 20037-2337

DEFELICE, EUGENE ANTHONY, physician, medical educator, consultant, magician; b. Beacon, N.Y., Dec. 24, 1927; s. Domenick and Louise (Grippo) DeF. B.S., Columbia U., 1951; M.D., Boston U., 1956. Ciba fellow, lectr. pharmacology Boston U. Sch. Medicine, 1954-57; intern Newton (Mass.) Wellesley Hosp., 1957; practice medicine specializing in internal medicine North Miami, Fla., 1958-61; asst. dir. clin. research Warner Lambert Research Inst., Morris Plains, N.J., 1961-64; dir. clin. pharmacology Bristol Labs., Syracuse, N.Y., 1965-66, Sandoz Inc. (formerly Sandoz-Wander, Inc.), East Hanover, N.J., 1967-68; exec. dir. clin. research Sandoz Inc., 1969-70; dir. sci. affairs and comml. devel. Sandoz Inc. (formerly Sandoz-Wander, Inc.), 1970-74, dir. corp. sci. devel., 1974, v.p. corp. sci. devel., 1974-77, v.p. internat. med. liaison, 1977-81; v.p., med. adviser Sandoz Inc., 1982-83; prof. biol. scis. New Eng. Coll. Pharmacy, 1956-58; pvt. practice, cons. in medicine, Morristown, N.J., 1961-87, East Schodack, N.Y., 1988-94, Albany, N.Y., 1995—; clin. assoc. prof. medicine Coll. Medicine and Dentistry N.J.-Rutgers Med. Sch., 1975-85; clin. prof. medicine UMD-Robert Wood Johnson Med. Sch., 1985—; clin. prof. anesthesiology UCLA, 1978-83. Contbr. numerous articles to profl. jours. cons. to editor; mem. internat. editorial com.: Triangle, Sandorama, 1979-81. Served with U.S. Army, World War II. Named hon. citizen of Italy; named to Notable Italian-Am. Hall of Fame. Fellow Am. Geriatrics Soc., Acad. Psychosomatic Medicine; mem. N.Y. Acad. Scis., Soc. Am. Magicians, Internat. Brotherhood Magicians. Home and Office: PO Box 9160 Albany NY 12209-0160

DEFENDI, VITTORIO, medical research administrator, pathologist; b. Treviglio, Italy, Nov. 16, 1928; married, 1955; 3 children. MD, U. Pavia, 1951. Instr. pathology dept. U. Pavia, 1951-52; pathologist virus sect. Lederle Labs., N.Y.C., 1956-58; assoc. pathologist Med. Sch., U. Pa., 1958-64, assoc. prof., 1964-68, Wistar prof., 1968-74; prof. pathology, chmn. dept. Sch. Med. NYU, N.Y.C., 1974—; Brit. Coun. scholar Postgrad. Med. Sch., U. London, 1952-53; Fulbright fellow Med. Sch., U. Vt., 1953-54; rsch. fellow Detroit Inst. Cancer Rsch., 1954-56; assoc. mem. Wistar Inst., 1958-64, mem. staff, 1964-74; rsch. prof. Am. Cancer soc., 1973—. Leukemia Soc. scholar, 1962-66. Mem. Am. Soc. Cell Biology, Am. Soc. Exptl. Pathology, Histochem. Soc., Am. Assn. Immunology, Am. Assn. Cancer Rsch. Office: NYU Sch Medicine Dept Pathology 550 First Ave New York NY 10016-6402

DE FEO, LUCIO, medical company executive; b. Avellino, Campania, Italy, Nov. 12, 1934; s. Giuseppe and Adriana (Alvino) De F.; m. Giovanna Colarusso, Dec. 10, 1960; children: Giuliana, Marina. A.Pharm. Chemistry, U. Naples, Italy, 1958. Salesman Dow Chem.-Lepetit, Naples, 1960-63; supr. Dow Chem.-Lepetit, Turin, 1964-68; North Italy area mgr. Dow Chem.-Lepetit, Milan, 1968-69, product mgr., 1970-72, sales/promotion mgr., 1972-74; mktg. mgr. Farmitalia C. Erba, Milan, 1974-78; exec. v.p. Apsia Med. S.p.A., Rome, 1979-85; pres. Med I Trade, Rome, 1986-89, Gen. Med. Supply, Rome, 1989-95; cons. L. De Feo & Ptnrs., Rome, 1996—. Co-author: (movie) Physiology and Pathology of Gut: Influence of Metoclopramide, 1971, Pharmacokinetic of Antibiotics, 1972; editor: (monograph) Biological Aspects of Atherosclerosis, 1976, Inflammation, 1977, others. Nat. Rsch. Coun. scholar, 1958-59. Mem. Italian Microbiologists Assn. Home: Via dei Laghi KM 8.600, 00047 Marino Rome Italy

DE FERREIRE, MARY ELIZABETH, psychologist, consultant; b. Rio Grande City, Tex., Sept. 13, 1949; d. Manuel Jr. and Tomasa (Garza) DeF.; 1 child, Leigh DeFerreire Rowen. Student, U. Md., 1967-68; BA, U. Tex., 1970, PhD, 1984; MS, Wright State U., 1973. Tchr. English San Felipe Ind. Sch. Dist., Del Rio, Tex., 1970; tchrs. aide Livingston (Calif.) Day Care Ctr., 1971; dir. head start program Migrant Ministry Program, Tipp City, Ohio, 1974; fellow population research ctr., dept. sociology U. Tex., Austin, 1977-78, asst. instr. dept. ednl. psychology and home econs., 1978-80; intern psychology VA Hosp., San Antonio, 1980-81; psychotherapist Robert E. Buxbaum & Assocs., San Antonio, 1981-82; supr., budget analyst Tex. Gen. Land Office, Austin, 1983-86; psychologist Tex. dept. mental health and mental retardation Austin State Hosp., 1986—; presenter psychol. rsch. and scholarly work Tex. Assn. marriage and Family Ann. Conf., 1987, Tex. Psychol. Assn., 1988, 89, 90, 91, 94, 95, Hosp. de Santo Dimongo, Ecuador, 1990, APA, 1990, Exec. Women in Tex. Govt., 1990. Contbr. articles to profl. jours. Nat. del. Tex. Dems., 1984, mem. nominations com., 1986; sec. capitol chpt. Mex. Am. Dems. Tex., 1983-84, vice-chmn., 1984-85, vice chairperson fin. com., 1985-87, state treas., 1985-87; founder Wenceslao R. "Benny" Matias, Jr. Mex. Am. Dems., 1995; charter mem., chair pub. rels. com. Hispanic Women's Polit. Caucus, Austin, 1987; mem. Hispanic Coalition for Quality Edn. Austin, 1985-87, Austin Ind. Sch. Dist. Affirmative Action Com., 1986-92; pres., co-founder Tex. Hispanic Commn., Austin, 1986-89; vol. Am. Cancer soc., Am. Heart Assn.; bd. dirs. Univ. YWCA, Austin, 1986; pres., bd. dirs. Internat. Hospitality Coun. of Austin. Nat. Inst. Child Health Dept. fellow, 1977-78. Fellow Nat. Assn. Ptnrs. Am. (Kellogg Internat. Leadership 1988-90); mem. Nat. Ptnrs. of Ams., Tex. Ptnrs. of the Ams. (bd. dirs. 1987—), Capital Area Psychol. Assn. (Austin chpt.), Mex.-Am. Bus. and Profl. Women's Assn. (v.p. community issues and concerns com. 1987-88), Phi Kappa, Kappa Delta Pi, Psi Chi. Democrat. Home: 1507 Lupine Ln Austin TX 78741-1147 Office: Austin State Hosp Mental Health Mental Retardation 4110 Guadalupe St Austin TX 78751-4223

DEFIORE, JOSEPH C., JR., orthopedic surgeon; b. N.Y.C., Jan. 14, 1938; m. Jayne Crumpler; children: Missy, Caroline. AB, Fordham Coll., 1959; MD, Stritch Sch. Medicine, 1963. Me. Diplomate Am. Bd. Orthopedic Surgery; cert. of added qualification in Havel surgery. Intern St. Vincent's Hosp., N.Y.C., 1963-64; capt. U.S. Army 8th Special Forces, Canal Zone, 1964-66; surgical resident U. Calif., San Francisco, 1966-67; research fellow The Hosp. for Special Surgery, N.Y.C., 1967-68, resident, 1968-71, hand/rheumatoid fellow, 1971-72; hand fellow U. Louisville, 1972; surgeon Knoxville (Tenn.) Orthopedic Clinic, 1972—; orthopedic cons. Rheumatoid Arthritic Clinic, Knoxville, 1985—; clin. dir. Hand Clinic Ea. Tenn. Children's, Knoxville, 1979—, U. Tenn., 1972—. Contbr. articles to profl. jours. Bd. dirs. Knoxville Symphony Soc., 1976-89; chmn. Arthritis Found., Tennessee, 1976-79; med. advisor Am. Med. Asst. Assn., Tennessee, 1977-79. Fellow ACS; mem. Knoxville Orthopedic Soc. (pres. 1985-87), Tenn. Orthpaedic Assn. (sec., treas. 19876), Southeastern Hand Club (pres. 1989—), Tenn. Hand Soc. (pres. 1987), Am. Acad. Orthopedic Surgeons, Soc. Internat. de Chiurgie Orthopedique et de Traumatologie, Rotary. Republican. Roman Catholic. Home: 4 Hillvale Cir Knoxville TN 37919-6620 Office: Knoxville Orthopedic Clinic 1128 E Weisgarber Rd Knoxville TN 37909-2674

DEFLORIO, MARY LUCY, physician, psychiatrist; b. Chgo.; d. Anthony Ralph adn Bernice B. (Bounell) DeF.; m. Robert Y. Shapiro, Dec. 27, 1986. BA with distinction, U. Wis.; MD, MPH, U. Ill., Chgo., 1984; cert. writing program, Columbia U., 1988-91. Cert. emergency med. technician. Adjudicator Fed. Disability Program, Ill. and Mass.; vocat. counselor U. Ill., Chgo.; resident internal medicine Mercy Hosp., Chgo., 1984-85; med. examiner Dept. Pub. Aid State of Ill., Chgo., 1985-87; resident psychiatrist St. Vincent's Hosp., N.Y.C., 1987-90; fellow cons. liaison psychiatry Meml. Sloan Kettering/Cornell Med. Ctr., N.Y.C., 1991-93; chief fellow Meml. Sloan Kettering, N.Y.C., 1992-93; attending physician Div. Psychiatry/Dept. Neurology Meml. Sloan Kettering and Cornell Med. Coll., N.Y.C., 1993-95; pvt. practice N.Y., 1996—. Recipient Med. Econs. Writing award, 1987; James scholar U. Ill., Gen. Assembly scholar. Mem. AMA (Nutritional scholar 1983-84), Am. Women's Assn., Nat. Rehab. Assn., Assn. Acad. Psychiatrists (Mead-Johnson fellow 1990), Am. Psychiat. Assn. (Br. Rsch. award 1990), Am. Psychiat. Arts Assn. (black and white photography award 1993, 96, poetry award 1993). Roman Catholic. Home: 605 W 113th St Apt 21 New York NY 10025-7951

DEFORT, DALE K., nursing educator, psychiatric and mental health nurse; b. Gloucester, Mass.; d. Edward E. and Gunvor L. (Carlson) Oakes; m. Mark G. DeFort, Aug. 1, 1969; children: Brian, Tracie. BSN, U. Mass.s, 1971; MS, Boston U., 1985; MEd, Antioch U., Yellow Springs, Ohio, 1980. RN, Mass. Staff nurse Beverly (Mass.) Hosp.; nurse, therapist Danvers State Hosp., Hathorne, Mass.; nurse, social worker Rockport (Mass.) Sch. System; asst. prof. psychiat.-mental health nursing Salem (Mass.) State Coll., counselor; psychotherapist, Salem, 1985—. Boston U. scholar, 1983-85. Mem. ANA (cert. clin. specialist in adult psychiat.-mental health nursing), NEA, Nurses United for Responsible Svcs., Sigma Theta Tau.

DEGENER, JOHN EDWARD, medical microbiologist; b. The Hague, S. Holland, The Netherlands, July 19, 1950; s. Edward Henry Degener and Clementine Louise Petronella Maria Paijens; m. Wilhelmina Louisa Ruiter, Mar. 4, 1977; children: Loes, Clementine. MD, State U. Leiden, The Netherlands, 1976; registered med. microbiologist, U. Hosp. Rotterdam, The Netherlands, 1979, PhD, 1983. Mem. staff U. Hosp./Childrens Hosp. Sophia, Rotterdam, 1979-81, U. Hosp./Dijkzigt Hosp., Rotterdam, 1981-88; head dept. lab. med. microbiology Pub. Health Lab., Leeuwarden, Friesland, The Netherlands, 1988-96; head dept., prof. med. microbiology U. Hosp., Groningen, The Netherlands, 1996—. Contbr. articles to profl. jours. Mem. European Soc. Med. Microbiology and Infectious Diseases, Am. Soc. Microbiology, Netherlands Soc. Med. Microbiology (sec.), Rotary Internat. Office: Dept Med Microbiology U Hosp Groningen, Hanzeplein 1, 9713 GZ Groningen The Netherlands

DE GENNARO, MADELINE H., oncology nurse; b. Montclair, N.J., Feb. 28, 1947; d. Vincent and Lena (Ferrante) De G. B.S.N., Seton Hall U., South Orange, N.J., 1970; M.A., Columbia U., 1979. Staff nurse Cornell Med. Ctr., N.Y.C., 1970-71, staff nurse Meml. Sloan-Kettering Cancer Ctr., N.Y.C., 1971-73; asst. head nurse, 1973-75, head nurse, 1975-81, supr. cancer info. service Office Cancer Communications, 1981-85; dist. dir. Phila. div. Am. Cancer Soc., 1985—. Home: 802 Stonycreek Ct Lansdale PA 19446-4336

DEGEORGE, PAMELA J., nurse; b. McKeesport, Pa., Oct. 25, 1960; d. Bernard J. and Jean (Claar) Riggs; m. Vincent DeGeorge, May 4, 1985. BSN, Pa. State U., 1982, MEd, 1990. Staff nurse Forbes Regional Health Ctr., Monroeville, Pa., 1986; office nurse Three Rivers Orthopedics, Pitts., 1986-89; clin. instr. Community Coll. Allegheny County, West Mifflin, Pa., 1989-90; staff nurse U. Pitts. Med. Ctr. (formerly Presbyn. U. Hosp.), 1982-86, 89—. Mem. Nat. Assn. Orthopedic Nurses (treas. 1990-92). Home: 11161 Hunters Woods Ln Irwin PA 15642-1940

DEGIORGIO, CHRISTOPHER MICHAEL, neurology and neurosurgery physician; b. Encino, Calif., Oct. 7, 1956; s. Eugene R. and Rose Marie DeGiorgio; m. Judy Marie Apodola, Jan. 16, 1986; children: Andrew Charles, Anne Elizabeth. BS, Loyola Marymount U., L.A., 1978; MD, Loyola U., Chgo., 1981. Intern L.A. County-U. So. Calif. Med. Ctr.; resident UCLA-Wadsworth; William Gowers fellow Epilepsy Soc. Am., Md., 1985-87; asst. prof. neurology U. So. Calif., L.A., 1987-94, assoc. prof. neurology and neurosurgery, 1994—, dir. Epilepsy Ctr., 1987—; dir. divsn. epilepsy and critical care neurology Epilepsy Soc. Am., 1996—; reviewer Jour. Neurosurgery, 1995-96. Mem. Am. Acad. Neurology, Alpha Sigma Nu. Office: U So Calif Sch Medicine HCC Rm 620 1510 San Pablo St Los Angeles CA 90033-4586

DEGIOVANNI-DONNELLY, ROSALIE FRANCES, biology researcher, educator; b. Bklyn., Nov. 22, 1926; d. Frank and Rose (Quartuccio) DeGiovanni; m. Edward Francis Donnelly, Sept. 23, 1961; children: Edward F. Jr., Francis M. BA, Bklyn. Coll., 1947, MA, 1953; PhD, Columbia U., 1961. Adj. prof. microbiology and genetics George Washington U., Washington, 1968—; research biologist FDA, Washington, 1968-88. Contbr. articles to profl. jours. Recipient Merit award FDA, 1970. Mem. AAAS, AAUW, Italian Cultural Soc., Environ. Mutagen Soc., N.Y. Acad. Scis., Am. Soc. Microbiology, Sigma Xi, Sigma Delta Epsilon. Democrat. Roman Catholic. Clubs: Hylands, McLean Indoor. Avocations: theater, swimming, tennis, travel, photography. Home: 1712 Strine Dr Mc Lean VA 22101-4744 Office: George Washington U Microbiology Dept Washington DC 20052

DEGNAN, ELIZABETH JOSEPHINE, psychologist, educator; b. East Newark, N.J., June 19, 1927; d. James A. and Elizabeth J. (Berkise) D. BA, Montclair State Coll., 1949; MA, Cath. U., 1961; EdD, Rutgers U., 1971. Lic. psychologist; diplomate Sch. Psychology. Tchr. Sparta, Wayne, Oceanport, N.J., 1949-56, USAF Dependent Schs., Morocco, Eng., Rep. Germany, 1956-59; student activities coord. Cath. U., Washington, 1959-60, asst. dean of women, dir. women's residences, 1960-61; math. tchr. Farmingdale (N.Y.) High Sch., 1961-62; guidance counselor Shore Regional High Sch., West Long Branch, N.J., 1962-68; psychologist Middletown (N.J.) Twp. Bd. Edn., 1970-89; pvt. practice psychologist Holmdel, N.J., 1976—; supr. psychologist Family and Cmty. Svcs., Red Bank, N.J., 1987-91, Family Life Bur.-Diocese, Trenton, West Long Branch, 1989—; ednl. and psychol. cons., spkr. at confs. in field. Mem. Monmouth County (N.J.) Right-to-Life, 1987—; advocate Children and Adults with Learning Disabilities, Oceanport, 1970-90; task force substance abuse, Borough of Oceanport, 1988-89; ministry bd. Cath. Women of Zion, Middletown, 1989—. Recipient Psychol. Recognition award N.J. Acad. Psychologists, 1980-83, 84-86. Mem. APA, N.J. Psychol. Assn. (exec. bd. 1976-79), Monmouth-Ocean County Psychol. Assn. (Outstanding Contbrn. award 1977-78, 74-89), Monmouth County Ret. Edn. Assn.

DEGRAFF, ARTHUR CHRISTIAN, JR., internist; b. N.Y.C., June 18, 1929; s. Arthur Christian and Dorothy (Dodd) D.; m. Sandra Ketelhut, June 30, 1956; children: Arthur C. III, Betsy Dodd Sands. BA, Wesleyan U., Middletown, Conn., 1951; MD, NYU, 1955. Intern Bellevue Hosp., N.Y.C., 1955-56, resident, 1956-57; resident Bronx V.A. Hosp., N.Y.C., 1957-58; fellow Tulane U., New Orleans, 1958-59; fellow cardio-pulmonary lab. U. Tex. Southwestern Med. Sch., Dallas, 1961-62, instr. in medicine, 1961-63, asst. prof., 1963-65; med. dir. pulmonary lab. Hartford (Conn.) Hosp., 1965—; pvt. practice Hartford, 1967—; clin. asst. prof. medicine Yale U., New Haven, Conn., 1965—; asst. clin. prof. U. Conn. Health Ctr. Sch. Medicine, Farmington, 1976-78, assoc. clin. prof., 1979-89, clin. prof., 1990—; bd. dirs. Com. for Promotion Med. Rsch., pres., 1986—. Contbr. articles to profl. jours. With USAF, 1959-61. Fellow Am. Coll. Chest Physicians, ACP; mem. Am. Physiol. Soc., Am. Thoracic Soc., Am. Heart Assn., Am. Fedn. for Clin. Rsch., Conn. State Med. Soc., Conn. Thoracic Soc. (program com. 1985-89, exec. com. 1987-89), Hartford County Med. Soc., John C. Leonard Soc. (sec.-treas. 1971-72, pres. 1972-73), Alpha Omega Alpha, Sigma Xi. Home: 160 Hunter Dr West Hartford CT 06107-1017 Office: Hartford Lung Physicians 85 Seymour St Hartford CT 06106-5501

DE GRAFFENRIED, VELDA MAE CAMP (MRS. THOMAS P. DE GRAFFENRIED), retired clinical laboratory executive; b. Kirwin, Kans.; d. George Robert and Laura (Woodward) Camp; student No. Ill. U., 1959-60; m. Thomas P. deGraffenried, May 23, 1942; children: Donna Rae McCaffrey, Albert Lawrence II, Nicholas Thomas. Office mgr. deGraffenried & Fisher Clin. Labs., DeKalb, Ill., 1957-64, exec. sec., 1964-85, dir. pub. affairs until 1985; dir. public affairs deGraffenried Med. Cons. Service, Inc., 1985-86; ret. 1987. Vice pres. Haish Sch. PTA, DeKalb, 1958-59; den mother cub scouts Chief Shabbona council Boy Scouts Am., 1957-60; supr. Teen Age Club, Louisville, 1949-50; county crusade chmn. Am. Cancer Soc. (recipient commendation, 1987), 1965, mem. exec. bd. DeKalb County, 1964—, dir. public affairs, 1970—, chmn. bd., 1978-80, chmn. Radiothon, 1972-82, 83-87, sec. DeKalb County Soc., 1969—, mem. state bd. Ill. div., 1985—. Recipient commendations Am. Cancer Soc., 1965, 74, Boy Scouts Am., 1955. Mem. DeKalb County Med. Soc. Aux. (sec. 1959-60, 76—, pres. 1973-74), DeKalb Hosp. Aux. Methodist. Home: 1208 Sunnymeade Trl De Kalb IL 60115-2358

DEGRANDE, GARY CHRISTOPHER, physician; b. West Long Branch, N.J., Aug. 14, 1949; s. Natale and Diana (Fingo) DeG.; m. Elaine Frances Smorra, Aug. 21, 1971; children: Laura, Michael. BS, Monmouth Coll., 1971; MD, U. Guadalajara, 1977. Diplomate Am. Bd. Obstetrics and Gynecology. Intern, resident SUNY, Syracuse, 1979-83; pvt. practice Montclair, N.J., 1983—; chmn. dept. ob-gyn. Mountainside Hosp., Montclair. Fellow Am. Coll. Obstetrics and Gynecology; mem. AMA. Office: 33 N Fullerton Ave Montclair NJ 07042-3412

DEGRASSI, DAVID JOHN, physical therapist; b. Bronx, July 5, 1961; s. Lucio and Emilia (Maraspin) D.; divorced. BS, SUNY, Stony Brook, 1984. Lic. phys. therapist, N.Y., Fla. Staff phys. therapist Nassau County Med. Ctr., E. Meadow, N.Y., 1984-87; phys. therapist John Papalia's Sports Medicine Practice, Merrick, N.Y., 1984-86; chief therapist Hofstra Health

Dome, Hempstead, N.Y., 1984-85; home care therapist Top of the Line Nursing Agy., Deer Park, N.Y., 1985-86; self-employed home care therapist Bellmore, N.Y., 1986-89; dir. phys. therapy dept. Island Phys. Therapy, Levittown, N.Y., 1987-89; home care therapist Olsten Temporary Svcs., Westbury, N.Y., 1988-89; owner/therapist Seaford Phys. Therapy, Seaford, N.Y., 1989—. Mem. Am. Running & Fitness Assn., Am. Phys. Therapy Assn., Nat. Strength & Conditioning Assn. Republican. Roman Catholic. Office: Seaford Physical Therapy 4007 Merrick Rd Seaford NY 11703

DE GREEFF, LOUIS E., obstetrician, gynecologist; b. St. Louis, May 9, 1946; s. Vincent Alois and Walburgine (Wiess) De G.; m. Marilyn Ann Burns, Dec. 23, 1979; 1 child, Lauran Elaine. AB, St. Louis U., 1969; MD, U. Mo., 1080. Diplomate Am. Bd. Ob-Gyn. Pvt. practice, Quincy, Ill., 1983—. With U.S. Army, 1980-81. Mem. ACOG. Office: Quincy Med Group 1025 Maine St Quincy IL 62301

DEGROATE, LINDA S., correctional nurse; b. Waterbury, Conn., Dec. 20, 1958; d. Harvey W. and Rita M. (Popke) Richardson; children: William, Ashley. LPN, W.F. Kaynor Tech. Sch., Waterbury, 1988. EMT. WSI/camp first-aid person Easter Seals Day Camp, Wolcott, Conn.; EMT-A Capitol County Ambulance, Bristol, Conn.; mental retardation worker I Southbury (Conn.) Tng. Sch., LPN; correctional nurse New Haven Correctional Ctr. Recipient Nat. Citizenship award.

DE GROOTE, ROBERT DAVID, general and vascular surgeon; b. Hackensack, N.J., Aug. 30, 1951; s. Emiel and Filomena Lillian (Candio) De G. BS in Biology, Fordham U., 1973; MD, Autonomous U. Guadalajara, Jalisco, Mex., 1978. Diplomate Am. Bd. of Surgeons. Resident gen. surgery U. Medicine and Dentistry N.J. Med. Sch., Newark, 1979-84, fellow critical care medicine, 1981-82, fellow vascular surgery, 1984-86; fifth pathway St. Joseph's Hosp., Paterson, N.J., 1978-79; attending surgeon Hackensack (N.J.) Med. Ctr., 1986—. Contbr. articles to Surgery, Stroke, Archives of Surgery, Annals of Vascular Surgery. Named Man of Yr., Lyndhurst, N.J. chpt. Italian-Am. Nat. Svc. Orgn., 1993. Fellow ACS; mem. AMA, Internat. Soc. for Cardiovascular Surgery, Soc. for Critical Care Medicine, Ea. Vascular Soc. Roman Catholic. Office: 83 Summit Ave Hackensack NJ 07601

DEGUIRE, MARGARET ANN, nurse; b. Detroit, June 7, 1950; d. Gerard John and Althea Wenona (Orrill) DeG. AA, Riverside City Coll., 1973; AS, SUNY, Albany, 1981; postgrad., 1991—. RN, Calif.; CCRN; lic. vocat. nurse; cert. ACLS. Nurse Dr. Stamper, Riverside, Calif., 1973-75; team leader Knollwood Community Hosp., Riverside, Calif., 1975-77; nurse, critical care Riverside Community Hosp., 1977-78; staff nurse Kaiser Hosp., Fontana, Calif., 1978-81, 81-82, nurse, critical care, relief unit leader, 1982-86, treadmill nurse, 1986—. Mem. AACN, Am. Coll. Sport Medicine(exercise technologist), Internat. Dance Excercise Assn. (cert. fitness instr.), Am. Coun. Exercise (cert. aerobics instr.), Loma Linda Lopers. Home: 8809 Bennett Ave Fontana CA 92335-8648 Office: SCPMG 9961 Sierra Ave Fontana CA 92335-6720

DEHAAN, CLAYTON RICHARD, surgery educator; b. Plano, Ill., Jan. 11, 1924; s. Richard Thomas and Florence Helen (Ruschulte) DeH.; children: Lise, Richard, Dorian, Christopher. BS, U. Fla., 1949; MD, Columbia U., 1953. Diplomate Am. Bd. Plastic Surgery. Intern St. Luke's Hosp., N.Y.C., 1953-54, resident in gen. surgery, 1954-58, resident in plastic surgery, 1968-60; pvt. practice, Middletown, N.Y., 1960—; program dir. plastic surgery St. Luke's-Roosevelt Hosp., 1981-83; chief staff Horton Meml. Hosp., Middletown, 1992-95; adj. prof. Adelphi U., L.I., N.Y. Contbr. articles to profl. jours. Mem. polit. action com. Orange County Citizens Found. With USN, 1943-45. Mem. Am. Soc. Plastic Surgery (ombudsman N.E. U.S.), Am. Assn. Plastic Surgeons, Internat. Soc. Plastic Surgery, Northeastern Soc. Plastic Surgery, Pan Am. Men Assn., N.Y. Regional Soc. Plastic Surgery (chmn. pub. info. com.), N.Y. State Med. Soc. (polit. action com.), Phi Beta Kappa. Office: 10 Benton Ave Middletown NY 10940

DEHAAN, EDDIE DALE, physician, family practitioner; b. Helena, Mont., Nov. 3, 1944; s. Henry and Mae (DeBoer) DeH.; m. Joyce I. Okken, June 17, 1967; children: Shane, Luke. BA, U. Minn., 1966, MD, 1969. Diplomate Am. Bd. Family Practitioners. Intern Marion County Gen. Hosp., Indpls.; clinic physician Elliot Park Clinic, Mpls., 1972-76, Owatonna (Minn.) Clinic, 1976-79, Ft. Dodge (Iowa) Med. Ctr., 1980—. Bd. dirs. Iowa Found. for Med. Care, Des Moines, 1988-91, Iowa Bd. Med. Examiners, Des Moines, 1993—. Capt. USAF, 1970-71. Mem. Am. Acad. Family Practitioners, Iowa Med. Assn. Democrat. Baptist. Office: Ft Dodge Med Ctr 800 Kenyon Rd Fort Dodge IA 50501-5713

DE HAAN, HENRY JOHN, research psychologist; b. St. Clair County, Ill., Nov. 23, 1920; s. Henry J. and Fanny (Haislip) de H.; m. Mary J. Farrell, Oct. 22, 1943. AB, Washington U., St. Louis, 1942, AM, 1949; PhD, U. Pitts., 1960. Postdoctoral Coatesville (Pa.) VA Hosp., 1960-62; rsch. scientist George Washington U., Washington, 1962-64; rsch. pscyhologist Armed Forces Radiobiol. Rsch. Inst., Bethesda, Md., 1965-69, U.S. Army Rsch. Inst., Alexandria, Va., 1969-86; mem. faculty U.S. Dept. Agr. Grad. Sch., Washington, 1967-77. Author 10 U.S. govt. sci. and tech. reports, 1954-82; contbr. articles to Perception and Psychophysics, Jour. Comparative and Physiol. Psychology and other jours. With USN, 1944-46, PTO. Mem. AAAS (emeritus), APA (life), Am. Psychol. Soc., N.Y. Acad. Scis. (emeritus), Ea. Psychol. Assn. (life), Internat. Neuropsychol. Soc. (emeritus), Soc. Neurosci. (emeritus), U.S. Tennis Assn. (life), Internat. Primatological Soc. (life), Psychonomic Soc., Sigma Xi (emeritus). Home: 5403 Yorkshire St Springfield VA 22151-1203

DE HAAS, DAVID DANA, emergency physician; b. Hollywood, Calif., May 31, 1956; S. Martin and Norma (Deutsch) De H.; m. Mary Danuta Przybylowski, June 27, 1982; children: Lindsay Alexandra, Heather Brittany, Lance Austin. BS in Biochemistry, UCLA, Westwood, Calif., 1979; MD, Chgo. Med. Sch., 1983. Diplomate Am. Bd. Internal Medicine, Am. Bd. Emergency Medicine, Nat. Bd. Med. Examiners; cert. provider advanced trauma life support, ACLS, Pediatric Advanced Life Support, BCLS, Med. Disaster Response, instr. ACLS, Pediatric Advanced Life Support, Med. Disaster Response. Resident emergency medicine/internal medicine Kern Med. Ctr., Bakersfield, Calif., 1983-87; assoc. med. dir. Family Care Med. Assocs., Huntington Beach, Calif., 1987—; emergency physician Anaheim (Calif.) Meml. Hosp., 1988—; asst. clin. prof. medicine dept. internal medicine U. Calif.-Irvine Med. Ctr., Orange, 1989—; emergency physician St. Bernardine Med. Ctr., San Bernardino, Calif., 1991—; ptnr. Calif. Emergency Physicians Med. Group, San Bernardino, 1991—; expert reviewer Med. Bd. Calif.; affiliate faculty ACLS, Pediatric Advanced Life Support, Am. Heart Assn.; vice chmn. dept. emergency medicine St. Bernardine Med. Ctr., ACLS dir., quality assurance/continuins quality improvement dept. emergency medicine; mem. edn. com. Med. Disaster Response; ptnr.Calif. Emergency Physician Med. Group. Fellow ACP, Am. Coll. Emergency Physicians; mem. AMA, Calif. Med. Assn., Orange County Med. Soc., Soc. Orange County Emergency Physicians (bd. dirs.), Assn. Clin. Faculty U. Calif., Irvine Coll. Medicine. Home: 26882 Via La Mirada San Juan Capistrano CA 92675 Office: St Bernardine Med Ctr 2101 N Waterman Ave San Bernardino CA 92404

DE HAËN, CHRISTOPH, pharmaceutical company executive; b. St. Gallen, Switzerland, Sept. 6, 1940; s. Heinz Hans and Frieda Elsa (Frei) de H.; m. Ilse Nagel, Sept. 5, 1967; children: Katrin, Stephanie, Sandra Joyce. Diploma Chem. Engring., Swiss Fed. Inst. Tech., Zurich, 1966, DSc, 1970. Rsch. asst. prof. dept. medicine and biochemistry U. Wash., Seattle, 1974-79, rsch. assoc. prof, 1979-87, rsch. prof., 1987-88; head dept. biochemistry Bracco SpA, Milan, 1988-90, vice-dir. preclin. rsch., 1989-90, dir. preclin. rsch., 1990-94; dir. Milano Rsch. Ctr., 1994—; cons. Imré Corp., Seattle, 1984-88, Tech. Dynamics, Inc., Woodinville, Wash., 1985-86. Acting assoc. editor: Biochemistry, Seattle, 1986; mem. editorial bd.: Jour. Biol. Chemistry, 1986-87, Minerva Biotech., 1989—; contbr. articles to profl. jours. Grant reviewer Drug and Alcohol Abuse Inst., State Wash., Seattle, 1980-84, Am. Diabetes Assn., Wash. Affiliate, Seattle, 1984-89; bd. dirs., treas., pres. Pottery Northwest, Seattle, 1986-88; dir. com. Italian Assn. Devel. Biotechnology, Milan, 1990-92. 1st lt. Swiss Army, 1959-70. Fellow Stiftung Stipendien a.d. Geb. d. Chemic, Basel, Switzerland, 1970, Battelle Meml. Inst., Sealle Ctr., Columbus, Ohio, 1971; recipient Pub. Health Svc. Career Devel. award NIH, Bethesda, 1979-84. Mem. Am. Soc. Biochem. Molecular Biology, Soc. Mag. Resonance Medicine, Am. Chem. Soc. Home: Viale 1 Maggio 2/13, I-20068 Peschiera-Borromeo Italy Office: Bracco SpA, Via Folli 50, I-20134 Milano Italy

DEHAVEN, KENNETH LE MOYNE, retired physician; b. The Dalles, Oreg., Mar. 28, 1913; s. Luther John and Dora (Beeks) DeH.; m. Ledith Mary Ewing, Jan. 11, 1937; children: Marya LeMoyne DeHaven Keeth, Lisa Marguerite DeHaven Jordan, Camille Suzanne DeHaven. BS, North Pacific Coll. Oreg., 1935; MD, U. Mich., 1946. Intern USPHS Hosp., St. Louis, 1947; intern Franklin Hosp., San Francisco, 1947-48, resident, 1949; clinician Dept. Pub. Health, City San Francisco, Dept. V.D., 1949-51; practice family medicine, Sunnyvale, Calif., 1955-87; mem. staff El Camino Hosp., Mt. View, Calif., San Jose (Calif.) Hosp. Pres. Los Altos Hills Assn. Served to capt., USAF, 1952-55. Fellow Am. Acad. Family Practice; mem. AMA, Ariz. Med. Assn., Calif. Med. Assn., N.Y. Acad. Scis., Santa Clara County Med. Soc., Astron. Soc. Pacific, Sunnyvale C. of C. (bd. dirs. 1955-56), Book Club (San Francisco), Masons, Alpha Kappa Kappa. Republican. Home: 9348 E Casitas Del Rio Dr Scottsdale AZ 85255-4313

DEHMER, GREGORY JOSEPH, cardiologist; b. Milw., Sept. 26, 1949; s. Joseph Anton and Bernadine Elizabeth (Bloom) D.; m. Sue Jane Vencil, Jan. 21, 1977; children: Jeffrey, Laura. BS, Carroll Coll., 1971; MD, U. Wis., 1975. Diplomate Am. Bd. Internal Medicine, Am. Bd. Cardiology. Dir. cardiac catheterization lab. VA Med. Ctr., Dallas, 1984-88; from assoc. prof. to prof. medicine U. N.C., Chapel Hill, 1988—; asst. prof. medicine U. Tex. Health Sci. Ctr., Dallas, 1984-88; dir. cardiac catheterization lab. U. N.C. Hosps., 1988-96. Editl. bd. Circulation, 1993—, Am. Jour. Cardiology, 1990—. Maj. USAF, 1981-83. Fellow Am. Coll. Cardiology, Am. Heart Assn., Soc. Cardiac Angiography and Interventions, Am. Coll. Physicians; mem. AMA (panelist DATTA program 1991—). Mem. Ch. of Christ. Office: U NC Hosps 101 Manning Dr Chapel Hill NC 27514

DEHN, PAULA FAYE, biology educator; b. Richmond, Ind., Feb. 15, 1951; d. Leonard Franklin and Joyce Alyadean (Murphy) D. AB in Zoology, DePauw U., 1973, MA in Zoology, 1974; PhD in Biology, U. South Fla., 1980. Vis. fellow Nat. Sci.-Engring. Rsch. Coun. Can., 1980-82; asst. prof. U. Tex., San Antonio, 1982-89; assoc. prof. biology Canisius Coll., Buffalo, 1989-95, prof. biology, 1995—, chmn. dept., 1989—; rsch. asst. EPA and U. South Fla., Tampa, 1974-76; cons. minority access to rsch. careers program Nat. Inst. Gen. Med. Sci.-NIH, 1984-88, finfish mariculture program U. Tex. Marine Sci. Inst., Port Arkansas, 1987-88; collaborator Agrl. Rsch. Svc., USDA, 1985-87; faculty advisor Alpha Phi Omega, 1983; chmn. organizer Expanding Your Horizons in Sci. and Math. Consortium, San Antonio, 1985-88, Buffalo, 1990—; participant San Antonio Target 90 Scientist-Sci. Tchrs. Coop., 1987-88. Contbr. articles to profl. jours. Pres. bd. dirs. Unity Ch. San Antonio, 1987-89. Named Sunday's Woman, San Antonio Light, 1988; Ind. State scholar, 1969; grantee NIH, 1985—, NSF, 1991—. Fellow Tex. Acad. Sci. (pres. 1990); mem. AAAS, Coun. Undergrad. Rsch., Soc. in Vitro Biol., Am. Soc. Zoologists, Sigma Xi. Democrat. Office: Canisius Coll Biology Dept 2001 Main St Buffalo NY 14208-1035

DE HOFF, JOHN BURLING, physician, consultant; b. Balt., May 28, 1913; s. George William and Pearle Ann (Burling) De H.; m. Mabelle Audrey Dunn, July 9, 1938; children: Susan De Hoff Montgomery, John Howard. MD, Johns Hopkin's U., 1939, MPH, 1967. Diplomate Am. Bd. Preventive Medicine, Am. Bd. Pub. Health. Med. intern Mt. Sinai Hosp., N.Y.C., 1939-41; asst. resident in psychiatry N.Y. Hosp., 1946; pvt. practice internal medicine Balt., 1947-65; asst. commr. Balt. City Health Dept., 1965-69, resident in pub. health, 1966-68, dep. commr., 1969-75, commr., 1975-84; advisor to mayor City of Balt., 1984-87; med. cons. Bd. Phys. Quality Assurance, State of Md., Balt., 1987—; med. cons. Social Security Adminstrn., 1986-89. Contbr. articles to profl. jours. and community health publs. Col. USAR, 1935-65, ETO. Commonwealth fellow N.Y. Hosp., 1946; Jacobi medalist Mt. Sinai Med. Ctr., N.Y.C., 1983. Fellow APHA (mem. governing coun.); mem. Am. Assn. Pub. Health Physicians (pres. 1977), U.S. Conf. Local Health Officers (pres. 1979), Md. Med. Soc. (councillor, del.), Balt. City Med. Soc. (pres. 1974). Democrat. Presbyterian. Home: 13801 York Rd Unit N-7 Cockeysville MD 21030-1825

DEHOVITZ, JACK ALAN, physician, educator, health facility administrator; b. Oceanside, Calif., Aug. 12, 1952; s. Bernard and Ruth (Senturia) DeH. BS, U. Calif., Davis, 1974; MPH, U. Tex., Houston, 1975; MD, U. Tex., Galveston, 1980. Diplomate Am. Bd. Internal Medicine, Am. Bd. Preventive Medicine, Am. Bd. Infectious Disease. Intern medicine St. Vincent's Hosp. and Med. Ctr., N.Y.C., 1980-81; asst. resident medicine N.Y. Hosp.-Cornell Med. Ctr., N.Y.C., 1981-82; Strang fellow in pub. health Cornell U. Med. Coll., N.Y.C., 1983-85; fellow in internat. medicine, infectious diseases N.Y. Hosp., N.Y.C., 1983-85; asst. med. dir. Spellman Ctr. of HIV Disease, N.Y.C., 1985-88; asst. prof. Cornell U. Med. Coll., N.Y.C., 1985—; asst. prof. SUNY, Bklyn., 1985-91, assoc. prof., 1991—, dir. AIDS Prevention Ctr., 1988-93, dir. HIV Ctr., 1993—; cons. infectious diseases N.Y. State Dept. Health, Albany, 1989-91; cons. Czech Min. Health, Prague, 1990-92. Editor AIDS Manual, 1988, HIV Infection in Women, 1995; contbr. articles to profl. jours. Mem. organizing com. Czech-Am. Med. Com., Prague, 1990. Fellow ACP, N.Y. Acad. Medicine, Infectious Diseases Soc. Am.; mem. APHA, N.Y. Soc. Tropical Medicine, Internat. AIDS Soc. Jewish. Office: SUNY Health Sci Ctr Bklyn 450 Clarkson Ave # 43 Box 1240 Brooklyn NY 11203-2012

DEIDAN, CECILIA THERESA, neuropsychologist; b. N.Y.C., Oct. 24, 1964. BA Biology, Spanish, Psychology, St. Louis U., 1985; MEd in Counseling Psychology, U. Mo., 1987, PhD in Counseling Psychology, 1992. Lic. psychologist, Fla., sch. psychol. examiner, Mo. Counselor, detoxification asst. McCambridge Ctr. for Women, Columbia, Mo., 1986-88; shc. psychol. examiner Columbia Pub. Schs., 1988-90; geriatric neuropsychology postdoctoral fellow U. Miami Sch. Med., 1992-93; pvt. practice Pembroke Pines, Fla., 1993—; adj. prof. Fla. Internat. U., Miami, 1993—. Mem. ACA, NAN, APA, Kappa Delta Pi, Psi Chi, Sigma Delta Pi, Alpha Sigma Nu, Beta Beta Beta.

DEINES, JOHN THOMAS, psychologist; b. Kansas City, Mo., Aug. 19, 1937; s. Joseph Ernest and Gladys Bernadette (Farrell) D.; m. Beverly Jane Brown, Jan. 29, 1965; children: Sara Jane, George Thomas. BA, U. Dayton, 1961; MEd, Miami U., Oxford, Ohio, 1967; PhD, Mich. State U., 1974. Lic. psychologist, Tex., Mich. Tchr. St. Henry (Ohio) Local Sch. Dist., 1962-66; counselor, asst. prof. Ctrl. Mich. U., Mt. Pleasant, 1968-74; dir. counseling ctr. Tex. Women's U., Denton, 1974-81; dir. counseling Mich. Tech. U., Houghton, 1981-82; pvt. practice psychologist Denton, 1982—; asst. prof. psychology Tex. Christian U., Ft. Worth, 1989-91; adj. prof. psychology U. North Tex., Denton, 1992; cons. psychologist Brookwood Adolescent Ctr., Denton, 1984-86, Parkside Med. Svcs. (formerly Brookwood Recovery Ctr.), Denton, 1985-92; med. adviser Social Security Adminstrn., Washington, 1986—. Contbr. chpts. Handbook for University Counseling Centers, 1978, Bereavement Counseling, 1980; contbr. articles to profl. publs. Cons. Family Guidance Ctr., Dallas, 1989. Mem. APA, Tex. Psychol. Assn., Dallas Psychol. Assn., Soc. Psychoanalytic Psychotherapy, Assn. Advancement of Psychology, Denton C. of C., Kiwanis, K.C. Roman Catholic. Home: 1822 Nevada St Denton TX 76201-3414 Office: 1810 Teasley Ln Suite A Denton TX 76205

DEISS, WILLIAM PAUL, JR., physician, educator; b. Shelbyville, Ky., Feb. 1, 1923; s. William Paul and Florence (Schilling) D.; m. Bettye Jane Baker, May 5, 1948 (div. 1979); children: Diana Elizabeth Deiss Mysliwiec, William David, Paula Jane Deiss Roberts.; m. Elizabeth Matson Benham, June 27, 1981. B.S., U. Notre Dame, 1943; M.D., U. Ill., 1945. Diplomate: Am. Bd. Internal Medicine (mem.). Intern U. Wis., 1945-46, resident, fellow in medicine, 1948-54; asst. prof., asso. prof. medicine Duke, 1954-58, asst. prof. biochemistry, 1954-58; assoc. prof., prof. medicine and biochemistry Ind. U., 1958-68; prof. U. Tex., Galveston, 1968-84, 90—, chmn. dept. medicine, 1968-84; prof. medicine Med. Coll. Va., 1984-90; mem. adv. com. NIH. Contbr. articles to profl. jours. Served from 1st lt. to capt. M.C., U.S. Army, 1946-48. Fellow ACP; mem. Am. Fedn. Clin. Rsch. (past sec.-treas.), Am. Soc. Clin. Investigation, Assn. Am. Physicians, Endocrine Soc. Home: 2878 Dominique Dr Galveston TX 77551-1569

DEITER, NEWTON ELLIOTT, clinical psychologist; b. N.Y.C., Dec. 12, 1931; s. Benjamin and Anna (Leibowitz) D. BS, UCLA, 1957; MS, Leland Stanford, 1960; PhD in Clin. Psychology, U. Chgo., 1965. Cert. in clin. psychology. Pvt. practice clin. psychology L.A., 1965-90; exec. dir. Nat. Family Planning Coun., L.A., 1965-76, Gay Media Task Force, L.A., 1976—; staff cons. Aaron Spelling Prodns., L.A., 1980-90, spl. cons. NBC, L.A., 1970-79, cons. broadcast standards dept. CBS, L.A., 1968-82, cons. City Coun., City of L.A., 1975-85. Columnist Bottomline Mag., 1992—. Mem. Dem. Ctrl. Com., L.A., 1972-76; bd. dirs. Gay Cmty. Svcs. Ctr., L.A., 1970-75, Am. Cancer Soc., L.A., 1972-77, Palm Springs Gay Tourism Coun., 1993-95; commr. L.A. Probation Commn., 1977-85; bd. advisors San Francisco Sheriffs Dept., 1969-79. Lt. col. USAFR, 1950-75. Inductee Internat. Gay Travel Assn. Hall of Fame, 1994. Mem. Acad. TV and Scis., Press Club L.A., Internat. Gay Travel Assn. (bd. dirs. 1986-93, pres. 1991-92), Desert Bus. Assn. (v.p. 1993, bd. dirs. 1992), Internat. Food, Wine and Travel Writers Assn. (bd. dirs., v.p./treas. 1995—), Air Force Assn., Am. Mensa, Masons. Home: 71426 Estellita Dr Rancho Mirage CA 92270-4215 Office: Rancho Mirage Travel 71-428 Us Highway 111 Rancho Mirage CA 92270-4130

DEITRICK, GEORGE ALBERT, III, biopharmaceutical executive; b. Ashland, Pa., Apr. 17, 1946; s. George Albert and Sabina Mary (Cortellini) D.; m. Tara Lynne Gleason, Nov. 28, 1981; 1 child, Taryn Christine. Student, U. Pa., 1964-66; AB, Gettysburg Coll., 1970; MD, Temple U., 1976. Cert. Am. Bd. Surgery, Nat. Bd. Med. Examiners. Intern The Pa. Hosp., Phila., 1976-77, resident in surgery, 1977-81; gen. surgeon, asst. clin. prof. surgery U. Pa. Sch. Medicine, Phila., 1981-91; v.p. med. affairs and med. dir. Curative Health Svcs, Inc. (was Curative Technologies Inc.), East Setauket, N.Y., 1991—; cons. W.L. Gore and Assocs., Flagstaff, Ariz., 1983-91. Mem. Union League of Phila., 1985—. Fellow ACS, Am. Coll. Physician Execs.; mem. Sigma Alpha Epsilon. Office: Curative Health Services Inc 14 Research Way East Setauket NY 11733-3469

DEITZ, IRA JEFFREY, psychiatrist, author, educator; b. Balt., Feb. 3, 1949; s. William and Minnie (Lapin) D.; m. JoAnn Smith, Nov. 1, 1981; children: William, Andrew. BA, U. Pa., 1970; MD, U. Md., 1974. Diplomate Am. Bd. Psychiatry and Neurology. Pvt. practice psychiatry Phila. and Trumbull, Conn., 1977—; attending psychiatrist St. Vincents Med. Ctr., Bridgeport, Conn., 1982—; instr. Albert Einstein Coll. of Medicine, Bronx, 1988—; cons. psychiatrist D.C. Police and Fire Clinic, Washington, 1981-82; dir. Fairfield Behavioral Medicine, Trumbull; mem. Faculty Tng. and Rsch. Inst. for Self Psychology, N.Y.C., 1992—. Contbg. author: Using Self Psychology in Psychotherapy, 1991; book reviewer Am. Jour. of Psychiatry, 1986—; contbr. articles to profl. jours. Mem. Am. Psychiat. Assn., Assn. Advancement of Psychotherapy, Am. Acad. Psychoanalysts, Am. Soc. Clin. Psychopharmacology. Office: 160 Hawley Ln Ste 1 Trumbull CT 06611-5379

DE JESÚS, NYDIA ROSA, anesthesiologist; b. Humacao, P.R., Sept. 8, 1930; d. Manuel Aurelio De Jesus and Luz María González. BS, U. P.R., 1949, MD, 1955; cert. med. tech., Sch. Tropical Medicine, San Juan, P.R., 1950; cert. anesthesiology, Columbia Presbyn. Med. Ctr., 1958. Diplomate Am. Bd. Anesthesiology. Intern St. Mary's Coll., Rochester, NY, 1955-56; resident in anesthesiology Columbus Presbyn. Med. Ctr., N.Y.C., 1956-58; dir. dept. anesthesiology U. Hosp. & Sch. Medicine, San Juan, 1960-65; dir. div. anesthesiology P.R. Med. Ctr., San Juan, 1965-76; vis. prof., fellow in anesthesiology Harvard Med. Sch., Boston, Mass., 1973-74; dean acad. affairs Med. Scis. Campus, U. P.R., San Juan, 1976-78; dir. cardiovascular surg. ctr. P.R. Med. Ctr., San Juan, 1980-85; prof. anesthesiology U. P.R. Sch. Medicine, San Juan, 1965-90, dean, 1986-90; ret., 1990; staff mem. anesthesiology Las Americas Amb. Surg. Ctr., San Juan, 1990—; dir. intensive care unit Univ. Hosp., San Juan, 1974-75; chief sect. anesthesiology VA Hosp., San Juan, 1963-76; mem. cardiovascular commn. Sec. of Health, Commonwealth of P.R., 1985; cons. div. medicine, health resources adminstrn. Bur Health Manpower, USPHS, 1977-79; pres. cons. bd. Pediatric U. Hosp., San Juan, mem. bd. dirs., 1986. Fellow Am. Coll. Anesthesiology; mem. ACP, N.Y. Acad. Scis., AAAS, Am. Soc. Anesthesiology. Home: #8 Jardines de Vedruna San Juan PR 00927 Office: U PR Med Sci Campus San Juan PR 00936

DE JESUS-MCCARTHY, FE TERESA, physician; b. Samar, Philippines, Dec. 31, 1942; came to U.S., naturalized, 1978; d. Felicisimo V. and Baslia E. de J.; M.D., U. Philippines, 1966; m. Thomas J. McCarthy, Mar. 3, 1973 (dec.); children—Amour Fe, Vida Linda; m. D. Vincent Cerrito, July 18, 1992. Practice medicine specializing in ob-gyn, Schenectady; mem. staff Bellevue Maternity Hosp., Ellis Hosp., St. Clare's Hosp. Mem. AMA, Am. Med. Women's Assn., Am. Fertility Soc., Am. Coll. Ob-Gyn, Am. Assn. Gynecol. Laparoscopists, N.Y. State Med. Soc., Med. Soc. of Schenectady County. Home: 21 Covington Ct Schenectady NY 12309-1323 Office: PO Box 1030 2210 Troy Rd Schenectady NY 12309-4725

DE JONG, JAN WILLEM, cardiochemist; b. The Hague, The Netherlands, Aug. 13, 1942; s. Willem and Johanna (Kuiper) De J.; m. Meiskelina Elizabeth van Lier, Oct. 9, 1968; stepchildren: Martha H., Harmanna M. BS, Leiden U., The Netherlands, 1964; MS, Leyden U., The Netherlands, 1966; PhD, Erasmus U., Rotterdam, The Netherlands, 1971. Instr., asst. prof. Med. Faculty, Rotterdam/Biochem., Rotterdam, 1966-74; tchr. Adv. Analysis Sch./Biochem., Rotterdam, 1968-69; assoc. prof., dir. Cardiochem. Lab., Erasmus U., 1974—; established investigator Netherlands Heart Found., The Hague, 1975-80; vis. prof. U. Brescia, Italy, 1992-93; cons. Igen Inc., rockport, Md., 1994-95; cons. U. Tex. Med. Ctr., Houston, 1982-83; mem. exec. com. Med. Faculty, Rotterdam, 1979-81; vice chmn. presidium Erasmus U., Rotterdam, 1991—; evaluator European Commn. Biomed 2, 1995; mem. sci. adv. bd. Netherlands Heart Found., 1992-93. Editor: Myocardial Energy Metabolism, 1988, The Carmitine System, 1995; mem. editorial bd. Internat. Jour. Purine/Pyrim. Res., Lugano, Switzerland, 1989-93, Thoraxctr. Jour., Leiden, 1990—, Cardiovascular Drug Therapy, Norwell, Mass., 1994—; guest editor 10 sci. jours., Europe and U.S. Inspector Birds Protection Act, The Hague, 1971-85. Fulbright fellow, 1973; recipient award Chris Barnard Fund, Cape Town, Republic of South Africa, 1986, 88, 92, German Acad. Exch. Svc., Berlin, 1981. Fellow European Soc. Cardiology (chmn. work group 1990-92); mem. Am. Heart Assn., Am. Physiol. Soc. (corr.), Internat. Soc. Heart Rsch. (coun. 1984-93, chmn. Euopean sector 1989-90), Internat. Union Biochemistry and Molecular Biology. Home: Stad en Landschap 51, 2923 BL Krimpen a/d IJssel The Netherlands Office: Erasmus U Thorax Ctr, PO Box 1738, 3000 DR Rotterdam The Netherlands

DE JONG, RUSSELL NELSON, JR., obstetrician, gynecologist, educator; b. Ann Arbor, Mich., Sept. 19, 1945; s. Russell Nelson and Madge Anna (Brook) De J.; m. Janetha Ann Benson, Mar. 15, 1972; children: Sarah Benson, Mark Benson. AB, U. Mich., 1967; MD, Columbia U., 1971. Diplomate Am. Bd. Ob-Gyn. Intern L.A. County Med. Ctr.-U. So. Calif., L.A., 1971-72; resident in ob-gyn U. Wash., Seattle, 1972-75, acting instr. dept. Ob-Gyn, 1975-76, instr., 1976-80; pvt. practice Belgrade, Maine, 1980—; chief ob-gyn. Harborview Med. Ctr., Seattle, 1975-80; asst. prof. cmty. and family medicine Dartmouth Med. Ctr., Hanover, N.H. Fellow Am. Coll. Obstetricians and Gynecologists. Home: RR 2 Box 1011 Belgrade ME 04917-9734 Office: Maine-Dartmouth Family Practice Residency 4 Sheridan Dr Fairfield ME 04937

DEJTER, STEPHEN WILLIAM, JR., urologist; b. Phila., Apr. 12, 1957; s. Stephen William and Patricia (McKenzie) D.; m. Theresa Todd Lee, Jan. 4, 1981; children: Stephen William III, Chase, John. BS, U. Md., College Park, 1979; MD, U. Md., Balt., 1983. Diplomate Am. Bd. Urology. Resident in surgery Georgetown U. Hosp., Washington, 1983-84, resident in urology, 1985-89; pvt. practice, Washington, 1989—. Contbr. articles to sci. jours., chpts. to books; patentee for biopsy needle. Recipient 1st prize Washington Urol. Assn., 2d place award Washington Acad. Surgery, 1989, William Maxted award divsn. urology Georgetown Hosp., 1995. Fellow ACS, Osler Soc. (sec.); mem. Am. Urol. Soc., Washington Urol. Soc. Republican. Lutheran. Office: Spence Constantinople Et Al Ste 311 3301 New Mexico Ave NW Washington DC 20016

DEKOSKY, STEVEN TRENT, neurologist; b. Camden, N.J., Mar. 23, 1947; s. Aaron and Evelyn (Gorlen) DeK.; m. Sheila, June 20, 1971; children: Allison. Lauren. AB in Psychology, Bucknell U., 1968; MD, U. Fla., 1974. Post-doctoral fellow, instr. neurology U. Va. Sch. Medicine, Charlottesville, 1978-79; asst. prof. neurology, anatomy U. Ky. Coll. Medicine, Lexington, 1979-85; grad. faculty U. Ky. Grad. Sch., Lexington, 1981-90; assoc. prof. anatomy and neurology U. Ky. Coll. Medicine, Lexington, 1985-90, interim chmn. dept. neurology, 1985-87; prof. psychiatry U. Pitts. Sch. Medicine, 1990—, prof. neurology, neurobiology, 1990—, grad. faculty, 1991—; vis. prof. psychology U. Calif., Irvine, 1983; co-dir. Alzheimer's disease rsch. ctr. U. Pitts. Med. Ctr., 1990-94, dir., 1994—, U. Ky. Med. Ctr., 1985-90; task force on Alzheimer's disease State of Ohio, Columbus, 1986-92; med. sci. adv. bd. Alzheimer's Assn., 1992—; dir. behavioral neurology of aging tng. program U. Pitts., 1990—. Mem. Am. Neurol. Assn. (Presd. award 1988), Am. Acad. Neurology, Am. Soc. Neurochemistry, Am. Heart Assn. (stroke coun.), N.Y. Acad. Scis., Soc. Neurosci., Soc. Exptl. Neuropathology (councillor 1990-92), Behavioral Neurology Soc. Office: U Pitts 3811 Ohara St Pittsburgh PA 15213-2593

DEKREY, JEANNE MARIE, physical therapist; b. St. Paul, Sept. 5, 1960; d. Frank A. and Margaret Mary (Collins) Likar; m. Bruce Douglas DeKrey, Feb. 23, 1985. BS in Phys. Therapy, U. N.D., 1983, M of Phys. Therapy, 1993. Staff phys. therapist St. Alexius Med. Ctr., Bismarck, N.D., 1983-84; out patient phys. therapist, group leader Medcenter One, Bismarck, N.D., 1984-92; phys. therapist, ptnr. PT-OT Assocs., Bismarck, N.D., 1992-93; phys. therapist, owner The Phys. Therapy Ctr., Bismarck, N.D., 1993—. Mem. Am. Phys. Therapy Assn., N.D. Phys. Therapy Assn. (Outstanding Svc. award 1989), Federation State Bd. Phys. Therapists (chmn. ethics stds. of practice com. 1989—). Independent. Office: The Phys Therapy Ctr 811 E Interstate Ave Ste A Bismarck ND 58501

DE LA CANCELA, VICTOR, psychologist; b. Bronx, N.Y., Dec. 18, 1952; s. Luis Fernandez and Guillermina (Ortiz) De La C. BA cum laude, CCNY, 1974, MPhil, 1979, MPH, 1995, PhD, 1981. Lic. marriage, family and child counselor, Calif.; lic. psychologist, Calif., Mass., N.Y.; cert. health svcs. provider, Mass.; cert. HIV counselor, N.Y. Intern, clin. fellow Med. Sch. Harvard U., 1977-79; supervising psychologist Boston City Hosp., 1979-81; dir. outpatient svcs. San Fernando Valley Cmty. Mental Health Ctr., Van Nuys, Calif., 1982-83; dir. Latino mental health Cambridge (Mass.) Hosp., 1983-85; dir. family svcs. Brookside Cmty. Health Ctr., Boston, 1985-88; dir. cmty. programs Dr. S.C. Fuller Cmty. Mental Health, Boston, 1988-89; sr. v.p. N.Y.C. Health and Hosps. Corp., 1990-95; prof. Coll. Physicians and Surgeons Columbia U., N.Y.C., 1990-92, 93—; pres., CEO Salud Mgmt. Assocs., Riverdale, N.Y., 1995—; asst. in psychology Beth Israel Hosp., Boston, 1979-81; network supr. Boston City Hosp., 1983-89; assoc. psychologist Brigham and Women's Hosp., Boston, 1985-88; asst. prof., psychologist Columbia-Presbyn. Med. Ctr., N.Y.C., 1990-96; instr. Harvard Med. Sch., Boston, 1979-81, lectr., 1983-88; lectr. U. Mass., Boston, 1985-89; cons. Puerto Rican Youth Devel. Leadership, Boston, 1983-86, Concilio Hispano Cambridge, Inc., 1988-90, Martha Eliot Health Ctr., Boston, 1989-90, Boriken Health Ctr., N.Y., 1995, Bronx Ctr. Cmty Svcs., 1995, Comprehensive Habilitation Svcs., 1995, Gateways Counseling Ctr., N.Y., 1995—, Ctr. for Substance Abuse Prevention, SAMHSA, 1995—, Ctr. for Substance Abuse Treatment, 1996. Contbr. numerous articles to profl. jours. Recipient Pres. Svc. award N.Y. Assn. Black Psychologists, 1990, Outstanding Contbn. award, 1991, U.S. Surgeon Gen.'s cert. of appreciation, 1993. Fellow APA (commr. 1994-96, 5th ann. achievement award, cert. HIV/AIDS trainer), Am. Orthopsychiat. Assn., Soc. Pub. Health Edn., Prescribing Psychologists Register; mem. Nat. Hispanic Psychol. Assn. (pres. 1986-90, Outstanding Contbn. award 1989, Exemplary Leadership and Svc. 1990), Nat. Congress Puerto Rican Rights, NAACP, Nat. Puerto Rican Coalition, Nat. Puerto Rican Policy Network. Home: 2727 Palisade Ave Apt 4H Riverdale NY 10463-1020 Office: Salud Management Assocs Highpoint-on-the-Hudson Riverdale NY 10463-1020

DE LACHARRIÈRE, OLIVIER ROGER, dermatologist; b. Rabat, Morocco, Mar. 19, 1953; s. Bertrand Marie and Roselyne (Castaing) L.; m. Patricia Christine Le Huu, July 10, 1987; children: Robinson, Colombe. MD, Necker Enfants Malades U., Paris, 1982; PhD in Pharm. Sci., U. Paris, 1992. Resident Hosp. of Paris, 1979-84; asst. prof. Necker Enfants Malades U., 1984-88; researcher advanced rsch. labs. L'Oréal, Aulnay Sous Bois, France, 1988-91, head rsch. unit advanced rsch. labs., 1991-94, head of clin. rsch. dept., 1995—; dermatology cons. dept. of medicine Inst. Pasteur, Paris, 1987—; dermatology cons. Hopitaux Paris, 1988—; sci. cons. European Space Agy., Noordwijk, Nederlands, 1989-91. Silver Laureate U. Necker Enfants Malades, 1982. Mem. Assn. for Prevention of AIDS, Soc. for Investigative Dermatology, French Soc. Dermatology, Soc. French Dermatology and Venerology, European Soc. for Dermatol. Rsch., French Soc. Psychosomatic Dermatology, Soc. Francaise de Gerontologie. Office: L'Oréal Advanced Rsch, 90 rue general Rogvet, 92100 Clichy France

DE LA CRUZ, MARIANO VILLAROMAN, JR., physician, anatomy educator; b. Manila, Philippines, Aug. 23, 1928; s. Mariano Gonzales Sr. and Valeriana L. Villaroman. AA, U. Philipines, 1949, MD, 1954. Diplomate Am. Bd. Colon and Rectal Surgery, Philippine Bd. Colon and Rectal Surgery, Philippine Soc. Anatomists. Rsch. asst. U. Philippines, Quezon City, 1962-63; instr. anatomy Coll. Medicine U. Philippines, Manila, 1963-66, asst. prof., 1966-71, assoc. prof., 1971-74, prof., 1974-93, chmn. dept. anatomy, 1972-85, clin. assoc. prof. surgery, 1981-88, clin. prof. surgery, 1988-93, sec. Coll. of Medicine, 1985-88, assoc. dean, 1988-91; prof. anatomy De La Salle U., Dasmarinas, Cavite, 1994-97. Professorial chair Philippine Medicare Commn., Quezon City, 1981-84, United Labs., Mandaluyong, Philippines, 1984-88, E.S. Garcia Found., Manila. Recipient Disting. Leadership award Am. Biographical Inst., 1986. Fellow Philippine Soc. Colon and Rectal Surgeons (bd. dirs.), Philippine Coll. Surgeons, Internat. Biographical Ctr.; mem. Philippine Soc. Anatomists (councilor/auditor 1983-84, v.p. 1985, pres. 1986, bd. dirs. 1989-91, Pres. Plaque 1986, Most Outstanding Anatomist award 1992), Sports Medicine Assn. Philippines (treas., bd. dirs. 1985-90), Cath. Physician Guild (life). Home: 36 Marilag UP Village, Quezon City 1101, The Philippines Office: U Philippines Coll Medicine, 547 Pedro Gil Ermita, Manila 1000, The Philippines

DELANEY, JOHN FRANCIS, neurologist, psychiatrist; b. Pitts., June 23, 1938; s. John Francis and Annette R. (Caress) D.; B.S., U. Pitts., 1960, M.D., 1964, MPH, 1992. Intern, Health Center Hosp. U. Pitts., 1964-65, teaching fellow in neurosurgery, 1965-66; teaching fellow Western Psychiat. Inst., Pitts., 1966-69; teaching fellow in neurology Health Center Hosps. U. Pitts., 1970-72; instr. psychiatry Sch. Medicine U. Pitts., 1969-70, asso. prof. neurology and psychiatry, 1972—, asst. dean, 1977-82, chief neurology Oakland VA Hosp., Pitts., 1972-77, chief staff, 1977-82; practice medicine specializing in neurology, psychiatry and geriatric psychiatry Pitts., 1982—. Mem. profl. bd. Transitional Living Services, 1969-72. Served to USAR, 1964-91 . Fellow ACP, Am. Acad. Neurology, Am. Coll. Angiology, Acad. Psychosomatic Medicine; mem. Acad. Pain Medicine, Am. Neuro-Rehab. Soc., Am. Psychiat. Assn., Assn. for Research in Nervous and Mental Disease, Pitts. Acad. Medicine, N.Y. Acad. Sci. Home: 404 Fox Chapel Rd Pittsburgh PA 15238-2226 Office: 4815 Liberty Ave Ste 123 Pittsburgh PA 15224-2156

DELANEY, SYLVIA ANNE MARIE, nurse, consultant; b. Berlin, N.H., Nov. 17, 1945; d. Laurier M. and Marie Anne E. (Morneault) Berube; m. James K. Delaney, Aug. 10, 1968; 1 child, Kevin J. BS, St. Anselm Coll., 1967; MS, Adelphi U., 1992. RN, N.Y.; internat. bd. cert. lactation cons. Staff nurse, supr. Columbia Presbyn. Med. Ctr., N.Y.C., 1967-72; staff nurse, clin. nurse specialist L.I. Jewish Med. Ctr., New Hyde Park, N.Y., 1974—; co-chair Provider Network Steering Com. to Promote Breastfeeding in N.Y.C., 1989—; lectr. in maternal-child health. Assoc. producer ednl. video, book: Breastfeeding, the Art of Mothering, 1987. Block capt. Bellerose (N.Y.) Commonwealth Civic Assn., 1973—. Mem. AWHONN, Internat. Lactation Cons. Assn., N.Y. Lactation cons. Assn. (v.p. 1993), N.Y. State Breastfeeding Adv. Coun. Roman Catholic. Home: 84-20 252nd St Bellerose NY 11426-2119 Office: LI Jewish Med Ctr 270-01 76th Ave New Hyde Park NY 11040-1433

DE LA PIEDRA, JORGE, orthopedic surgeon; b. Peru, Feb. 11, 1923; came to U.S., 1960; naturalized, 1963; s. Luis G. and Rosa M. (Quinones) de la P.; m. June M. Daugherty, May 1, 1955; children: Ana Maria, Jorge Antonio, James Michael. grad. Facultad de Ciencias, Universidad de San Marcos, Lima, Peru, 1942, Facultad de Medicina, MD, 1950. Diplomate Am. Bd. Orthopedic Surgery, Am. Bd. Profl. Disability Cons. Intern, Army Hosp., Lima, 1951-52; rotating intern Augustana Hosp., Chgo., 1952-53; resident in orthopedic surgery St. Francis Hosp., Peoria, Ill., 1953-54, Charlotte (N.C.) Meml. Hosp., 1954-57; fellow in orthop. divsn. Duke U. Hosp., 1956-57; acting chief orthopedic dept. Social Security Adminstrn. Hosp. #1, Lima, 1958-59; orthopedic Surgeon Mullens (W.Va.) Hosp., 1960-66; practice medicine specializing in orthopedic surgery, Princeton, W.Va., 1966—; mem. staff Princeton Community Hosp., 1966—, dir., 1974—. Served with Peruvian Army, 1951-52. Recipient award Disting. Physicians of Am. Fellow Internat. Coll. Surgeons, Am. Acad. Disability Evaluating Physicians; mem. AMA (physician's award 1969, 72-74, 77, 80, 84), W.Va. State Med. Assn., Mercer County Med. Soc., Am. Fracture Assn., So. Med. Soc., Latin Am. Soc. Orthopedic Surgeons, Orthopedic Rsch. and Edn. Found. (life), Peruvian Acad. of Surgery. So. Orthopedic Soc., W.Va. Orthopedic Soc., Peruvian Am. Med. Soc., Nat. Assn. Disability Evaluating Physicians (charter). Roman Catholic. Lodge: K.C. Office: Morrison Dr Princeton WV 24740-2322

DELAPLAIN, LAURA ZULEME, psychologist; b. Berkeley, Calif., Oct. 2, 1955; d. James Lisle Jr. and Mary Kathryn (Hickman) D.; m. Donald Richard Zook; children: Nathan Walker Delaplain-Zook, Joshua David Delaplain-Zook. BA, U. Wis., 1977; MDiv., Garrett-Evang., 1981; PhD, Boston U., 1989. Lic. psychologist, Mass.; ordained minister United Meth. Ch., 1980. Clin. fellow Danielsen Inst. for Psychotherapy, Boston, 1984-86; pastor United Meth. Ch., Swampscott, Mass., 1984-88, Hingham, Mass., 1988-90; interim pastor United Ch. of Christ in Abington, Mass., 1990-91; clin. psychologist Beechwood Counseling Svcs. Inc., Quincy, Mass., 1988—; exec. dir. Norma Kent Pastoral Counseling Ctr., Abington, 1986—. Named Danielsen fellow Boston U., 1984-86, Johnson Teaching fellow Boston U., 1986-87. Fellow Am. Assn. Pastoral Counselors. Home: 16 Copeland Tannery Dr Norwell MA 02061-2837 Office: Norma Kent Ctr 10 Bedford St Abington MA 02351-2441

DE LA ROCHA, CARLOS A., physician; b. Santo Domingo, Dominican Republican, Aug. 12, 1934; s. Carlos A. and Germania (Contin) de la R.; m. Penelope Lynn Lansing, May 20, 1961; children: C. Andrew, Maria L., Michael J., David L., Alicia M., Juan A. MD, Univ. de Santo Domingo, 1958. Diplomate Am. Bd. Surgery. Rotating intern City Hosp. at Elmhurst, Queens, N.Y., 1958-59; asst. resident surgery Albert Einstein Med. Ctr., Phila., 1959-60; asst. resident surgery Ellis Hosp., Schenectady, N.Y., 1960-62, chief resident surgery, 1962-63; tchg. fellow surgery St. Clares Hosp., Schenectady, 1963-65; asst. attending surgeon St. Clares and Ellis Hosp., 1965-69, attending surgeon, 1969—; chmn. tissue unit Ellis Hosp., 1985-90; mem. Ellis Hosp. Found. Bd., 1988-94. Fellow Am. Coll. Surgeons; mem. Am. Soc. Gen. Surgeons, N.Y. State Surgery, N.Y. State and County Med. Soc. Republican. Roman Catholic.

DÉ LA ROCHA, JOSÉ JULIÁN, physician assistant; b. Danto Domingo, Dominican Republic, Nov. 14, 1952; came to U.S., 1965; s. Julio Cesar Dé La Rocha and Maria Altagracia (Cambero) Dé La Rocha Guillandeaux; m. Jane Ann Grzanowski, Dec. 15, 1975 (div.); children: Tania Anayansi, Aliccia Francesca; m. Seviap Lewis, Feb. 14, 1996. AA, Anne Atundel C.C., Arnold, Md., 1983; BA, SUNY, Albany, 1985; BS with honors, U. Okla., 1992. ACLS; PALS. Enlisted USAF, 1979, advanced through grades to 1st lt., 1992; clin. specialsit U.S. Army 10th mash, Ft. Meade, Md., 1979-85; EMT U.S. Army Kimbrough Hosp., Ft. Meade, Md., 1985-87; combat medicine specialist Md. Army Nat. Guard, Balt., 1987-91; rsch. physician asst. Facilitator of Applied Clin. Trials, San Antonio, 1992-96; physician asst. emergency med./family practice 6th Med. Group USAF, McDill AFB, Fla., 1992—; physician asst. Am. Health Choice/Rural Health Clinic, Von Ormy, Tex., 1996—. Decorated Expert Field Med. badge. FEllow Am. Acad. Physician Assts., Soc. Mil. Surgeons, Soc. Air Force Physician Assts. Home: 1114 Oak Path San Antonio TX 78258 Office: Am Health Choice/ Rural Clinic Hwy 16 S Von Ormy TX 78073

DELATEUR, BARBARA L., medical educator; b. Hoquiam, Wash., Nov. 17, 1936. Student, Marylhurst (Oreg.) Coll., 1954-56; BS in Philosophy, St. Louis U., 1959; MD, U. Wash., 1963, MSc, 1968. Cert. Am. Bd. Phys. Medicine and Rehab.; lic. physiatrist, Wash., Md. Rotating intern U. Hosp., U. Wash., 1963-64; resident dept. phys. medicine and rehab. U. Hosp., 1964-67; instr. dept. phys. medicine and rehab. U. Wash. Sch. Medicine, 1967-68, asst. prof., 1968-71, assoc. prof., 1971-76, prof. dept. rehab. medicine, 1976-93; prof., dir. dept. phys. medicine and rehab. Johns Hopkins U. Sch. Medicine, Balt., 1993—, Lawrence Cardinal Shehan chair phys. medicine and rehab., 1993—, joint prof. health policy & mgmt. Sch. Hygiene & Pub. Health, 1994—; acting physiatrist-in-chief Rehab. Medicine Svc. Harborview Med. Ctr., Seattle, 1970-72, physiatrist-in-chief, 1972-93; dir. Muscular Dystrophy Clinic Meml. Hosp., Yakima, Wash., 1979-88; dir. dept. phys. medicine and rehab. Johns Hopkins Hosp., Balt., 1993—; med. dir. dept. rehab. medicine Good Samaritan Hosp., Balt., 1993—; vis. prof. dept. rehab. medicine and dept. internal medicine SUNY, Syracuse, 1988; cons. physiatrist Johns Hopkins Geriatrics Ctr., Johns Hopkins Bayview Med. Ctr., Balt., 1994—; vis. lectr. dept. phys. medicine Coll. Medicine, Ohio State U., 1985; Arthur Grant lectr. U. Tex., San Antonio, 1992; Marquette lectr. Jefferson Med. Coll., Phila., 1993; spkr. various univs. and orgns.; pres. Phys.Medicine and Rehab./Edn. and Rsch. Found., 1990-94; mem. governing coun. sect. rehab. hosps. and programs Am. Hosp. Assn., 1993—; mem. adv. bd. Wash. State Divsn. Vocat. Rehab., 1979-84. Contbr. articles to profl. jours.; mem. editl. bd. Archives Phys. Medicine and Rehab., 1978-84, Health After 50, Johns Hopkins Hosp., 1994—; reviewer Jour. Am. Geriatrics Soc., 1994—. Recipient Elizabeth and Sidney Licht award for sci. writing, 1990, Excellence in Tchg. award N.J. Med. Sch., 1992, Excellence in Rsch. Writing award Assn. Acad. Physiatrists and Am. Jour. Phys. Medicine and Rehab., 1992, Golden Goniometer award Phys. Medicine and Rehab. Residents, 1995, Labe Scheinberg award, Meeting of Consortium of MS Ctrs., Portland, Oreg., 1995. Fellow Am. Acad. Phys. Medicine; mem. AMA, Am. Acad. Phys. Medicine and Rehab. (bd. govs. 1983-90, v.p. 1986-887, pres-elect 1987-88, pres. 1988-89, past-pres. 1989-90), Am. Burn Assn., Am. Congress Rehab. Medicine, Assn. Acad. Physiatrists, Interntnt. Assn. for Study of Pain, King County Med. Assn., Northwest Assn. Phys. Medicine and Rehab. (pres. 1974-76), Gerontol. Soc. Am. (clin. medicine sect.), Wash. State Med. Assn. Office: Good Samaritan Profl Bldg Rm 403/ 406 5601 Loch Raven Blvd Baltimore MD 21239*

DELAUTER, DAVID EUGENE, respiratory therapist; b. Frederick, Md., Dec. 5, 1959; s. Eugene Elwood and Janice Louise (Cashour) D.; m. Kimberly Sue Cramer; children: Joshua David, Rebekah Elizabeth. BS magna cum laude, Valley Forge Christian Coll., 1989; cert. in respiratory care, Biosystems Inst., 1983. Registered Nat. Bd. Respiratory Care, Pa. Laborer CAM Constrn. Co., Frederick, Md., 1978; asst. mgr. Kenny Shoe's, Frederick, 1977; security guard Boone Investigating Agy., Frederick, 1978; nursing asst. Frederick (Md.) Meml. Hosp., 1977-78, respiratory technician, 1978-85; respiratory technician Chester County Hosp., West Chester, Pa., 1987-88, Phoenixville (Pa.) Hosp., 1987-89; respiratory therapist Homedco, Hagerstown, Md., 1990; respiratory care practitioner Chambersburg (Pa.) Hosp., 1991—; instr. BLS Am. Heart Assn., Chambersburg, 1994—, instr. ACLS and PALS, 1995—. Mem. Delta Epsilon Chi. Republican. Home: 43 W Dahlgren St Greencastle PA 17225-1503 Office: Chambersburg Hosp 112 N 7th St Chambersburg PA 17201

DELAWDER, ROBERT EUGENE, consultant to healthcare porviders, entrepreneur; b. Ironton, Ohio, June 10, 1951; s. Delbert Eugene and Norma June (Riley) D.; m. Glenda Kay Beckett, July 28, 1972; children: Robert Christopher, William Britton. AA, Ohio U., 1972, BBA cum laude, 1974. CPA, Ohio, West Va. Various acctg. positions Hayflich & Steinberg CPAs, Huntington, W. Va., 1974-80; v.p. healthcare Hayflich & Steinberg CPAs, Huntington, 1980—; mem. adv. bd. Huntington Rehab., 1990—; instr., guest lectr. Marshall U., Huntington, W. Va.; speaker, recognized expert in Healthcare Financial Field. Mem. editorial rev. bd. Healthcare Fin. Mgmt. Rev., 1992—. Ground Crew Mem. Marshall U. Soc. Yeager Scholars, Huntington, 1985—; pacesetter United Way of River Cities,, Huntington, 1985—; chmn. of bd. Jr. Achievement of Ohio Valley, Tri-State Area, 1987-90. Fellow Healthcare Fin. Mgmt. Assn. (cert. fin. mgr., Follmer award 1992); mem. AICPA, Ohio Soc. CPAs, W. Va. Soc. CPAs (numerous coms., offices), Am. Coll. Healthcare Execs. (cert. health exec.). Republican. Home: 150 Scherer Rd Ironton OH 45638 Office: Hayflich & Steinberg CPAs 517 Ninth St Huntington WV 25701

DELBANCO, THOMAS LEWIS, medical educator, researcher; b. London, Dec. 7, 1939; came to U.S., 1948; s. Kurt and Barbara Gabriele (Bernstein) D.; m. Jill Martin Behrens, Dec. 13, 1964; children: Steven, Suzanne, Jennifer. BA, Harvard U., 1961; MD, Columbia U., 1965. Diplomate Am. Bd. Internal Medicine. Intern in medicine Bellevue Hosp., N.Y.C., 1965-66, resident, 1967-68; resident Presbyn. Hosp., N.Y.C., 1966-67; chief resident Harlem Hosp. Ctr., N.Y.C., 1968-69; prof. medicine Harvard Med. Sch., Boston, 1971—; mem. staff, dir. div. gen. medicine and primary care Beth Israel Hosp., Boston, 1971—; dir. Picker/Commonwealth Program Patient-Centered Care, 1987—; chmn. Picker Inst., 1994—; mem. coun. APHA, 1983-85; mem. program com. Inst. Medicine, NAS, 1991—. Editor: 4 books; contbr. numerous articles to profl. jours. Vice chmn. United Way Mass. Bay, Boston, 1987-91; co-dir. Learning Through Drama Program, Lexington, Mass., 1982-90; bd. dirs. Health Commons Inst., 1994—. Maj. U.S. Army, 1969-71. Robert Wood Johnson Health Policy fellow Inst. Medicine, 1977-78. Fellow ACP; mem. Am. Fedn. Clin. Rsch., Soc. Gen. Internal Medicine (pres. 1986-87, councillor), Nat. Pub. Health and Hosps. Inst. (bd. dris.), Inst. of Medicine (program com), Nat. Acad. Scis. Jewish. Office: Beth Israel Hosp 330 Brookline Ave Boston MA 02215-5400

DEL CASTILLO, JULIO CESAR, retired neurosurgeon; b. Havana, Cuba, Jan. 21, 1930; came to U.S., 1961, naturalized, 1968; s. Julio Cesar and Violeta (Diaz de Villegas) Del C.; m. Rosario Freire, Sept. 18, 1955; children: Julio Cesar, Juan Claudio, Rosemarie. BS, Columbus Sch., Havana, 1948; MD, U. Havana, 1955; Diploma Am. Coll. of Surgeons, 1971. Intern, Michael Reese Hosp., Chgo., 1955-56; resident Cook County Hosp., Chgo., 1957, Lahey Clinic, Boston, 1957-58, U. Pa. Grad. Hosp., 1958-60; rsch. asst. dept. gen. surgery Jackson Meml. Hosp., Miami, Fla., 1962-64; practice medicine, specializing in neurosurgery, Havana, 1960-61, Quincy, Ill., 1965—; mem. staff Blessing Hosp., Quincy, pres. staff, 1972-74; mem. staff Blessing at 14th, Quincy, trustee, 1987; owner Top Hat Hobbies, Inc., Quincy. Bd. dirs. Western Ill. Found. for Med. Care, 1970-73; trustee Blessing Hosp., 1972-74, St. Mary's Hosp., 1988-90. Mem. Am. Acad. Model Aeros., Congress Neurol. Surgeons, AMA, A.C.S., Adams County Med. Soc. (sec., treas. 1966-75, pres.), Ill. Med. Soc., Exptl. Aircraft Assn. Rotarian (dir. 1970-72, pres. 1976-77). Home: 14 Curved Creek Rd Quincy IL 62301-6580 Office: 126 N 5th St Quincy IL 62301-2916

DELCOMYN, FRED, physiology and neurobiology educator; b. Copenhagen, June 4, 1939; came to U.S., 1947, naturalized, 1960; s. Niels Theodor and Erna A. Delcomyn; m. Nancy Ann Nigg, Dec. 14, 1969; children—Julia C. M., Michael T.W., Erik A.W. B.S., Wayne State U., 1962; M.S., Northwestern U., 1964; Ph.D., U. Oreg., 1969. Research assoc. dept. zoology U. Glasgow (Scotland), 1969-71, lectr. inst. physiology, 1971-72; asst. prof. dept. entomology U. Ill.-Urbana, 1972-77, assoc. prof., 1977-95, prof., 1995—. Contbr. articles to profl. jours., chpts. to books. Fellow U. Ill., 1973; Sr. Fulbright scholar U. Kaiserslauten, Germany, 1987-88; grantee NIH, NSF, Whitehall Found. Fellow AAAS; mem. Soc. Exptl. Biology, Soc. Neurosci. Office: U Ill Dept Entomology 505 S Goodwin Ave Urbana IL 61801-3707

DELCROS, MICHEL JACQUES, neuropsychiatrist, geriatrician; b. France, May 20, 1942. Cert. neuropsychiatrist, 1972. Intern Hosp. Paris, 1967-72; chef de clinique Paris, 1972-79; head geriatric svc. Hosp. Corentin Celton, Issy, France, 1979—. With French Nat. Navy, 1967-68. Mem. Internat. Psychogeriatric Assn. (bd. dirs. 1985-89). Office: Hosp Corentin Celton, 37 Bd Gambelta, 32130 Issy France

DELEDICQUE, ALAIN-GEORGES, rehabilitation physician; b. Roubaix, Nord, France, Jan. 17, 1944; s. Georges-Paul and Yvonne (Destailleur) D.; m. Brigitte Poillion (div. 1980); 1 child, Robin; m. Danielle Gedon, Sept. 29, 1981; children: Roland, Carole. Grad. in medecine, U. Lille, France, 1969; grad. in rehab. phys. medecine, U. Paris, 1971. Medecin dir. Thalassotherapy, Oleron, France, 1973-77; medecin chief Thalassotherapy, Carnac, France, 1978-83, Quiberon, France, 1983-90, Dinard, France, 1990-94; chief medicine Thalasso-Deauville, France, 1994, Thalassotherapie, Siouville, France, 1995—; sr. spine cons.; expert Cour d'Appel, Poitiers, France, 1974-78. Author: The Thalassoth, 1978, The Fitness, 1986; editor: Thalassotherapy, 1991, T.T.J., Tokyo. Mcpl. conseiller, St. Trojan, France, 1976. Mem. Societe Francaise de Thalassotherapie (treas.), French Ctr. of Young Mgrs. Republican. Roman Catholic. Lodge: Rotary. Office: Thalassa Siouville Ctr Edn, 17 Rue Marcel Grillard, F-50340 Siouville Normandy Brittany, France

DE LEENHEER, INGEBORG ALMA, biologist, researcher; b. Aalst, Belgium, May 4, 1965; d. Frieda De Pril; m. Peter Gaston Van Damme, June 18, 1994; 1 child, Laurens. MS in Biology with distinction, State U., Ghent, 1989; grad. with greatest distinction, Econ. Sch., 1992. Scientist Sugar Refinery, Tienen, Belgium, 1988-90; rschr. Innogenetics & State U., Ghent, Belgium, 1990-91, Inst. Hygiene and Epidemiology, Brussels, 1991; clin. rsch. assoc. Bristol-Myers Squibb, Brussels, 1991-94; sr. clin. rsch. assoc. Pharmaco-LSR, Brussels, 1994—.

D'ELETTO, MARIA JOSEPHINE, pediatric and occupational health nurse; b. Bronx, N.Y., Oct. 7, 1960; d. Adolph T. and Frances M. (Palermo) D'E. BS in Biology, Va. Poly. Inst. and State U., 1982; BSN magna cum laude, Seton Hall U., 1987. Internal medicine and family practice office nurse Michael Ambrosio, M.D., Aberdeen, N.J., 1982—; pediatrics staff nurse Newark Beth Israel Med. Ctr., 1987; disability adminstrn. nurse, cons.. supr. Pathmark Stores, Inc., Woodbridge, N.J., 1991—. Mem. Sigma Theta Tau. Home: 226 Claire Ct Aberdeen NJ 07747-2219

DEL GIUDICE, AMORE, hospital administrator; b. Waterbury, Vt., Oct. 31, 1913; s. Alfonso and Sebastiana (Imbruglia) Del G.; m. Helen E. Chubb, Oct. 1940; children: Richard, Joan; m. Marie Maschino Berning, Dec. 5, 1953. B.S., U. Vt., 1936, M.D., 1939. Diplomate: Am. Bd. Psychiatry and Neurology. Intern Vassar Bros. Hosp., Poughkeepsie, N.Y., 1939-40; resident psychiatrist Binghamton (N.Y.) State Hosp., 1946-51; asst. dir. St. Lawrence State Hosp., Ogdensburg, N.Y., 1961-66; dir. Middletown (N.Y.) Psychiat. Center, 1966-79. Served with M.C., AUS, 1940-46. Fellow Am. Psychiat. Assn. (life). Home: 3866 County Rt 6 Hammond NY 13646-9707

DEL GUERCIO, LOUIS RICHARD MAURICE, surgeon, educator, company executive; b. N.Y.C., Jan. 15, 1929; s. Louis and Hortense (Ardengo) Del G.; m. Paula Marie Helene de Vautibault, May 18, 1957; children: Louis, Francsca, Paul, Catherine, Maria, Michelle, Christopher, Anthony. BS, Fordham U., 1949; MD, Yale U., 1953. Diplomate: Am. Bd. Surgery, Am. Bd. Thoracic Surgery. Intern Columbia-Presbyn. Med. Center, N.Y.C., 1953-54; resident St Vincent's Hosp., N.Y.C., 1954-58, Cleve. City Hosp., 1958-60; practice medicine specializing in thoracic surgery, 1960—; mem. faculty Albert Einstein Coll. Medicine, N.Y.C., 1960-71; assoc. prof. Albert Einstein Coll. Medicine, 1966-70, prof. surgery, 1970-71, dir. Clin. Research Center-Acute, 1967-71; dir.; clin. prof. surgery N.J. Coll. Medicine, Newark, 1971-76; prof. surgery N.Y. Med. Coll., N.Y.C., 1976—; chmn. dept. N.Y. Med. Coll., 1976—; chief surgery Westchester County Med. Center, 1976—; cons. surgeon other hosps.; mem. surg. study sect. NIH, 1970-74; mem. com. on shock NRC-Nat. Acad. Scis., 1969-71; mem. merit rev. bd. VA, 1971-74; mem. health care tech. study sect. Dept. HHS, 1980-84; cons. Nat. Ctr. Health Services Research, 1980-84; chmn. bd. dirs. Daltex Med. Scis., Inc. Author: (with B.G. Clarke) Urology, 1956, The Multilingual Manual for Medical History Taking, 1972, (with S.G. Hershey, R. McConn) Septic Shock in Man, 1971; editor-in-chief Critical Care Monitor, 1980-85, Complications in Surgery, 1990—; contbr. articles to med. jours.; patentee in field. With Mcht. Marine, 1946-47; with AUS, 1949-51; col. med. dept. USAR, 1990—. Recipient award in medicine Fordham U. Alumni Assn., 1974, Gold award Am. Acad. Pediats., 1973, Humanitarian award Boys' Towns of Italy, 1994; Am. Thoracic Soc. fellow, 1959-60; grantee Health Rsch. Coun. N.Y., 1965-71, NIH, 1962-71. Fellow ACS, Coll. of Critical Care Medicine; mem. Am. Trauma Soc. (founding mem.), Soc. Critical Care Medicine (founding mem., pres. 1976), Am. Surg. Assn., Am. Physiol. Soc., Soc. Univ. Surgeons, Equestrian Order of HOly Sepulchre of Jerusalem. Home: 14 Pryor Ln Larchmont NY 10538-4021 Office: NY Med Coll Munger Pavilion Valhalla NY 10595

DELIGNÉ, PIERRE, physician, anesthesiologist, researcher; b. Fontaines, Vendée, France, June 24, 1926; s. Auguste and Madeleine (Bonnaud) D.; m. Germaine Harscöet, Aug. 25, 1954 (dec. Feb. 1974); children: Pascal, Francois, Daniel. Cert. Phys. Chem. Biol., Faculty of Sci., Paris, 1945; MD, Faculty of Medicine of Paris, 1953; Cert. in Anesthesiology, 1953. Anesthesiologist Neurosurg. Ctr. St. Anne's Hosp., Paris, 1953-66; asst. anesthesiologist Pitié Hosp., Paris, 1959-66; anesthesiologist St. Antoine's Hosp., Paris, 1966-70; aggregate prof. Faculty of Medicine, Paris, 1966-81; anesthesiologist Tenon Hosp., Paris, 1970-92; prof. anesthesiology St. Antoine Faculty of Medicine Paris VI U., 1981-92; hon. prof. of French Univs., 1992; hon. anesthesiologist Paris Hosps., 1992; chief dept. anesthesiology Tenon Hosp., Trousseau Hosp., Paris, 1971-92; clin expert in anesthesiology for Ministerial Agreement of New Drugs, 1966-74; jud. expert in anesthesiology Appeal Ct. of Paris, 1972-81; sci. advisor Nat. Ctr. of Sci. Rsch., Informasci., 1977-86. Editor: Anesthésie-Analgésie-Réanimation, 1954-60, Essor Médico Social dans l'Union Française, 1955-56, Agressologie, 1960-62, Annales de l'Anesthésiologie Française, 1963-81, Convergences Médicales, 1982-88, Urgences Médicales, 1989-96; contbr. over 300 articles to profl. jours. and chpts. to book. Named comdr. of Order of Sci. Merit, Paris, 1968; recipient cert. of merit for disting. svc. to the advancement of anaesthetics, London, 1967. Mem. Soc. Neuro-Surgery in French-Speaking Countries (assoc. mem.), French Soc. Anesthésie-Analgésie-Réanimation (exec. mem. 1954-60), Assn. French Anesthesiologists (co-founder, exec. mem., pres. 1978), French Soc. Clin. Pharmacology (co-founder, exec. mem. 1968-76), French Soc. Parenteral Nutrition, Assn. Convergences Médicales (co-founder, v.p. 1981-95), Soc. for Free Radical Rsch. Home: 72 Avenue du Général Leclerc, 72 Ave Généal Leclerc, 75014 Paris France

DE LISA, JOEL ALAN, rehabilitation physician, rehabilitation facility executive; b. Seattle, Mar. 18, 1942; s. Joseph Phillip and Alice Georgia (Jensen) DeL.; m. Janet Hopper, July 25, 1971. BS in Zoology, Wash. State U., 1964; MD, U. Wash., 1968, MS, 1976. Diplomate Am. Bd. Phys. Medicine and Rehab. (chmn. 1993—). Intern St. Josephs Hosp., Phoenix, 1968-69; resident in phys. medicine and rehab. U. Wash., Seattle, 1972-75; med. dir., chief med. officer Kessler Inst. Rehab., West Orange, N.J., 1987-93; sr. v.p., chief med. officer Kessler Rehab. Corp., West Orange, 1994—; prof., chmn. dept. phys. medicine and rehab. Univ. Medicine and Dentistry N.J., Newark, 1987—; chmn. dept. phys. medicine and rehab. St. Barnabas Med. Ctr., Livingston, N.J., 1990—; spkr. Taiwan Nat. U. Hosp., 1995, 23d ann. meeting Korea Acad. Rehab. Medicine, 1995. Author: Manual of Nerve Conduction Velocity and Clinical Neurophysiology, 1994, Principles and Practice of Rehabilitation Medicine, 1993. Mem. AMA, Assn. Acad. Physiatrists, Am. Acad. Phys. Medicine and Rehab., Am. Congress Rehab. Medicine, Am. Paraplegic Soc. (hon., pres. Jackson Heights chpt. 1989-91, Excellence award 1995). Office: Kessler Inst Rehab 1199 Pleasant Valley Way West Orange NJ 07052-1419

DELL, STEPHEN OWEN, neurosurgeon; b. N.Y.C., June 13, 1944; s. Joseph Bernard and Laura Rachel (Lubowitz) D.; m. Julia Anne Walsh, Jan. 17, 1972; children: Elizabeth, Emily, Rebecca, Joseph. AB, Harvard U., 1964; postgrad., Oxford (Eng.) U., 1965-66; MA, Princeton U., 1967; MD, NYU, 1972. Intern, resident U. Calif., San Francisco, 1972-74; chief Friends' Hosp., Kaimosi, Kenya, 1974-75; resident N.Y. Neurol. Inst., N.Y.C., 1975-79; instr. Tufts U., Boston, 1979-82; neurosurgeon Spine Clinic New Eng. Neuromuscular Cons., Epsom, N.H., 1992—, Brookdale Hosp., Bklyn., 1990-91; founder Med. Diagnostics, Burlington, Mass., 1984-95; dir. Lifesource, Hooksett, N.H., 1992—; vis. sr. lectr. U. Zimbabwe, 1992, U. Ghana, 1994. Contbr. articles to sci. jours. Fellow Rockefeller Found., 1982. Mem. AMA, Am. Assn. Neurol. Surgeons, Congress Neurol. Surgeons, Soc. Pediatric Neurosurgery. Unitarian Universalist. Home: 230 Wildwood Ave Piedmont CA 94610-1102 Office: Neuromuscular Cons 56 Standish Rd Bellingham MA 02019 also: 411 30th St Ste 508 Oakland CA 94609

DELLANDE, WILLIAM DREW, optometrist; b. Dyersburg, Tenn., Jan. 20, 1926; s. Armand Joseph and Georgianna (Collins) D.; m. Alice Hassebrock, Oct. 1, 1947; children—Brian William, Elaine Alison. O.D. Ill. Coll. Optometry, 1949; M.A. U. Mo., 1966. Diplomate Am. Acad. Optometry. Pvt. practice St. Louis, 1950-54, Columbia, Mo., 1955—; instr. reading improvement progam U. Mo., Columbia, 1963-68; mem. adv. com. Sch. Optometry U. Mo.-St. Louis, 1982-84. Contbr. articles profl. jours. Named Optometrist of Yr. Mo. Optometric Assn., 1990. Fellow Am. Acad. Optometry; mem. Am. Optometric Assn. (mem. contact lens com. 1972-73, assoc. editor Contact Lens sect. 1983-84), St. Louis Optometric Soc. (pres. 1952), Heart of Am. Contact Lens Soc. (pres. 1970-71, man of the year 1975), Mo. Chapt. Am. Acad. Optometry (pres. 1983-84), Cen. Mo. Optometric Soc. (pres. 1986). Club: Webster Groves Toastmaster (Toastmaster of Yr. 1953). Home: 2409 Cimarron Dr Columbia MO 65203-2997 Office: 111 E Broadway Suite 310 Columbia MO 65201

DELLA SELVA, PATRICIA COUGHLIN, psychology educator, psychologist; b. Paterson, N.J., Sept. 19, 1954; d. James Dominic and Patricia (Sanglyn) Coughlin; children: Megan, Katherine, Anthony. BS, Ohio U., 1976; MS, Syracuse U., 1978; PhD, Syracuse (N.Y.) U., 1981. Lic. psychologist, N.Y. Asst. prof. Med. Sch. Northwestern U., Chgo., 1981-88; prin. psychologist Albany (N.Y.) Psychol. Assocs., 1989-90; asst. prof. Albany Med. Coll., 1989—; pvt. practice psychologist Albany, 1989—; mem. vis. faculty Inst. for Short-Term Dynamic Psychotherapy, St. Clare's-Riverside Med. Ctr., Denville, N.J., 1992—. Author: Intensive Short-Term Dynamic Psychotherapy: Theory and Technique, 1996, (book chpt.) Sleep Disorder, 1986; contbr. articles to profl. jours. Mem. APA, Assn. Psychologists in Ind. Practice, N.Y. Psychol. Assn. Home: 2632 Troy Rd Niskayuna NY 12309-1410 Office: 435 New Karner Rd # 204 Albany NY 12205-3809

DELLAVECCHIA, MICHAEL ANTHONY, ophthalmologist. BA in Physics, LaSalle Coll., Phila., 1970; MS in Biomedical Sci. and Engring., Drexel U., 1972, PhD in Biomedical Sci. and Engring., 1984; MD, Temple U., 1976. Diplomate Am. Bd. Med. Examiners; lic. physician, Pa., N.J. Resident in anatomical and clin. pathology Temple U. Hosp., Phila., 1977-80, chief resident, 1979-80, fellow in surg. pathology, 1980-81, resident in ophthalmology, 1981-84; fellow in ophthalmology Project Orbis, Inc., N.Y.C., 1985; v.p., med. dir., co-founder Mega Med. Electronics, Hatfield, Pa., 1984-86; assoc. John Reichel MD, Ltd., Bryn Mawr, Pa., 1984-95; assoc. staff, clin. instr. Temple U. Hosp., Phila., 1986—; instr. Wills Eye Hosp., Phila., 1986—, Scheie Eye Inst., Phila., 1986—; prof. dept. biomed. engring. Drexel U., Phila., 1991—; attending staff ophthalmology Grad. Health Sys. Phila. Coll. Osteo. Medicine, 1995—; med. dir. Interstate Blood Bank, Inc., 1977-80, Info. Mgmt. Corp., 1984-87, Sonic Technologies, Inc., 1984-86; med. dir., adv. bd. Lehigh Ultrasonics Group, 1985-87; pres., founder Dell Med. Inc., 1985—; pres., treas., co-founder Med. Design Assoc., 1985-86; co-founder, med. dir. Omega Nutrients, Inc., 1987-89; tech. adv. Project Orbis, Inc., 1986—; clin. instr. ophthalmology svc. Wills Eye Hosp., 1986—, U. Pa., 1986—, Temple U., 1984—; dir. labs. Am. Clin. Labs., 1985-94, Phila. Union Health Ctr., 1988—; radiological officer Emergency Mgmt. Assn., State of Pa., 1993—, co-founder Med. Surveillance Group, 1993-95; cons. Keystone Clin. Labs., 1994-95, NASA, Nat. Aero. and Space Adminstrn., 1992—. Contbr. articles to profl. jours. including Clin. Rsch., Jour. of the AMA, Procs. of SPIE. Recipient numerous Fed. Emergency Mgmt. Assn. certificates; rsch. fellow Drexel U., 1976-77, Surg. Pathology fellow Temple U. Hosp., 1980-81; Pa. State Senatorial scholar; recipient numerous grants for rsch. Mem. IEEE, AMA (Physician Recognition award 1990-93, 93, 96—), Am. Soc. Laser Medicine and Surgery, Internat. Bioelectrochem. Soc., Internat. Soc. Photoinstrumentation Engrs., Internat. Biomedical Optics Soc. (inaugural), Laser and Electr-Optics Soc., Engring. in Medicine and Biology, Am. Soc. Clin. Pathology, Am. Acad. Ophthalmology (Lifetime Edn. in Ophthalmology award), N.Y. Acad. Scis., Del. Valley Ophthal. Soc., Intercounty Ophthal. Soc., Phila. County Med. Soc., Pa. Med. Soc., Montgomery County Med. Soc., Newtonian Soc., Chymian Soc., Sigma Xi, Kappa Mu Epsilon, Alpha Epsilon Delta. Home: 6131 Grays Ave Philadelphia PA 19142-3207

DELLINGER, EVAN PATCHEN, surgery educator; b. Newark, Jan. 2, 1944; s. David and Elizabeth (Peterson) D.; m. Lissa D'Orlando, July 1, 1967; children: Kira Lauren, Seth Berton. BA in Math., Swarthmore Coll., 1966; MD, Harvard U., 1970. Diplomate Am. Bd. Surgery; Cert. Crit. Care. Resident in surgery Beth Israel Hosp., Boston 1970-73, 1975-77; research fellow Tufts U.-New Eng. Med. Ctr., Boston, 1973-75; asst. prof. surgery U. Wash., Seattle, 1977-82, assoc. prof., 1982-90, prof., 1990—. Contbr. articles to profl. jours., chpts. to books. Fellow ACS, Infectious Diseases Soc. Am.; mem. Soc. Univ. Surgeons, Surg. Infection Soc. (sci. studies com. 1983-86, treas. 1986-90), Am. Soc. Microbiology, Am. Assn. for Surgery Trauma, Assn. Acad. Surgery, Soc. for Surgery Alimentary Tract, Soc. for Health Care Epidemiology Am. Office: Univ Wash Dept Surgery Box 356410 Seattle WA 98195-6410

DELLOJOIO, PENNY CAROL, medical and surgical nurse; b. San Francisco, Mar. 6, 1947; d. Herbert P. and Katherine I. (Ruger) Ferrara; m. Frank John DelloJoio, June 20, 1987; children: Cynthia Silverman, Jerry Wilson. AAS in Nursing, Orange County C.C., Middletown, N.Y., 1976. RN, N.Y. Head nurse Sylcox Nursing Home. Newburgh, N.Y., 1977-84; staff nurse oper. rm. St. Francis Hosp., Beacon, N.Y., 1984-89; mgr. oper. rm. St. Anthony Hosp., Warwick, N.Y., 1990-91; staff nurse III CNOR St. Francis Hosp., Poughkeepsie, N.Y., 1991—. Mem. Assn. Oper. Rm. Nurses (pres. mid-Hudson chpt.).

DELLON, A. LEE, plastic surgeon; b. Bronx, N.Y., Apr. 18, 1944; s. Alfred and Irene (Samuels) D.; divorced; children: Evan, Glenn, Brian. BA, Johns Hopkins U., 1966, MD, 1970. Prof. plastic surgery and neurosurgery Johns Hopkins U. Sch. Medicine, Balt. Author 3 books in field; contbr. over 250 articles to profl. publs. Office: 2328 W Joppa Rd Ste 325 Lutherville Timonium MD 21093

DELLSPERGER, KEVIN CHARLES, internist, medical educator, researcher. BS in Biomed. Engring. summa cum laude, Tulane U., 1978; MD, La. State U., 1983, PhD in Physiology, 1983. Resident in internal medicine U. Iowa, 1983-85, fellow in cardiovasc. diseases, 1985-87, chief resident in internal medicine, 1987-88, assoc. in cardiovasc. diseases, 1988-89, asst. prof. medicine, 1989-94, assoc. prof. medicine, 1994—. Mem. editl. bd. Am. Jour. Physiol., Heart Circ. Physiology; contbr. articles to profl. jours., chpts. to books. Recipient Nat. Rsch. Svc. award NIH, 1986, Cardiovasc. Health Sci. Assoc. Young Investigator award Merck, Sharp and Dohme, 1988, Clin. Investigator award NIH, 1989; La. Undergrad. Student Rsch. fellow Am. Heart Assn., 1977. Mem. Am. Heart Assn. (mem. peer group C rev. com. 1995, established investigator award 1995), Am. Coll. Cardiology-European Soc. Cardiology (internat. acad. exch. participant). Office: U Iowa Dept Medicine E329-1GH Iowa City IA 52242*

DELMAN, MICHAEL ROBERT, physician; b. N.Y.C., Oct. 29, 1942; s. Alex and Dorothy (Scher) D.; m. Joan Ellen Dubin, July 9, 1967; children: Keith Andrew, Danna Lee. BA, Alfred U., 1963; MD, N.Y. Med. Coll., 1968. Diplomate Am. Bd. Internal Medicine. Intern N.Y. Med. Coll.-Met. Hosp. Ctr., 1968-69, resident in internal medicine, 1969-70, chief resident in internal medicine, 1971-72, fellow gastroenterology, 1972-73; asst. clin. prof. medicine SUNY, Stony Brook, 1974—; chief chmn. dependency svcs. Southside Hosp., Bay Shore, N.Y., 1989—, chmn. med. staff quality assurance, 1992—, v.p. med. staff, 1995—. Surgeon and vol. fireman East Islip (N.Y.) Fire Dept., 1978—. Recipient McAulay award East Islip Soccer Club, 1984, citation Town of Islip, 1992. Fellow ACP, Am. Coll. Gastroenterology; mem. Am. Gastroenterology Assn., Am. Soc. Addiction Medicine (cert.), Am. Soc. Gastrointestinal Endoscopy, N.Y. Acad. Gastroenterology, N.Y. State Med. Soc. Office: East Islip Med Assocs 45 E Main St East Islip NY 11730

DE LOACH, ERVIN DANIEL, physician; b. Valdosta, Ga., May 12, 1948; s. Bruce Daniel and Ann Louise (Sellars) De L.; m. Cameron Carpenter; children: E. Daniel, W. Alexander, J. Graham. BS in Chemistry, Valdosta State Coll., 1970; MD, Med. Coll. Ga., 1973. Diplomate Am. Bd. Surgery, Am. Bd. Plastic Surgery. Intern in surgery Meml. Med. Ctr., Savannah, Ga., 1974, resident in surgery, 1975-78, chief resident in surgery, 1977-78; resident in plastic surgery U. Tenn. Clin. Edn. Ctr., Chattanooga, 1978-80, chief resident in plastic surgery, 1979-80; asst. clin. prof. dept. surgery Med. Coll. Ga., Augusta, 1983—; assoc. clin. prof. dept. surgery Mercer U. Sch. of Medicine, Macon, 1989—; chief of staff Meml. Med. Ctr., 1988-89, med. affairs officer, 1996—; presenter in field. Contbr. articles to profl. jours. Bd. dirs. First Liberty Bank, Savannah, Meml. Med. Ctr. Found. Recipient Prin. Investigator award SSI Corp., 1985-87, Squibb Corp., 1989, 91, Howmedica Corp., 1989-90, 91, Abbott Labs., 1992. Fellow Am. Coll. Surgeons, Internat. Coll. Surgeons; mem. AMA, Am. Soc. Plastic and Reoncstructive Surgeons, Internat. Soc. Clin. Plastic Surgeons, Southeastern Soc. Plastic and Reconstructive Surgeons, Ga. Soc. Plastic Surgeons, Savannah Soc. Plastic Surgeons, Plastic Surgery Edn. Found., Lipoplastic Soc. N.Am., Am. Cleft Palate Assn., Am. Burn Assn., Wound Healing Soc., Med. Assn. Ga., Ga. Med. Soc. Republican. Baptist. Office: Savannah Plastic Surgery 4750 Waters Ave Ste 500 Savannah GA 30458

DELOACHE, WILLIAM REDDING, pediatrician; b. Camden, S.C., Mar. 27, 1920; s. William Redding and Louise Blakeney (Zemp) DeL.; m. Bond Davis, Sept. 7, 1943; children: Frances D., William Redding Jr. Student, Furman U., Greenville, S.C., 1937-38; BA, Vanderbilt U., 1941, MD, 1943. Diplomate Am. Bd. Pediatrics; lic. Tenn. Healing Arts.; cert. med. examiner, S.C. Intern pediatrics Vanderbilt Hosp., Nashville, 1944, resident pediatrics, 1947-48; resident pediatrics N.C. Bapt. Hosp., Bowman Gray, Winston-Salem, 1948-49; pvt. practice Greenville, S.C., 1949-53; ptnr. Christie Pediatric Group, Greenville, 1953-72; dir. nurseries Greenville Hosp. Sys., 1972-77, dir. med. edn., 1977-82; assoc. exec. dir. Am. Bd. Pediatrics, Chapel Hill, N.C., 1982-87; ofcl. examiner Am. Bd. Pediatrics, Chapel Hill, 1976-90; assoc.,sr. assoc. Greenville Meml. Hosp., Greenville Hosp. Sys., 1994-92; mem. pediatric staff St. Francis Hosp., Greenville, 1949-92; assoc. prof. pediatrics Med. U. S.C., 1973-87; mem. bd. Vanderbilt U. Med. Ctr., Nashville, 1985-91, mem. adv. bd., 1991—. Contbr. articles to profl. jours. Elder Fourth Presbyn. Ch., Greenville. Capt. U.S. Army, 1944-46. Mem. AMA, Am. Acad. Pediatrics (career achievement award S.C. chpt. 1987), Greenville County Med. Soc. (pres. 1971), S.C. Med. Assn., So. Soc. Pediatric Rsch., So. Perinatal Assn., Greenville C. of C. (bd. mem.), Rotary Club (mem. bd. 1976—), Greenville Country Club, Poinsett Club. Home: 72 Round Pond Rd Greenville SC 29607

DELORENZO, DAVID W. J., health facility administrator, human resources consultant; b. Auburn, N.Y., Jan. 15, 1957; s. David J. and Margaret M. (Pinckney) DeL.; m. Lori DeLorenzo, June 5, 1981 (div. Mar. 1996); 1 child, David C. AAS, Cayuga County C.C., Auburn, 1978; student, Niagara U.; diploma in environ. health/battlefield, flight nurse, Brooks AFB Sch. Aerospace Med., San Antonio. Cert. occupl. hearing conservationist, EMT, ACLS, BLS and first aid instr.; cert. hazardous material tech., spirometry NIOSH; bd. cert. occupl. health nurse specialist Am. Bd. Occupl. Health Nurses; FAA lic. pvt. pilot. RN, trauma ICU S.U.H. Upstate Med. Ctr., Syracuse, N.Y.; RN ICU Niagara Falls (N.Y.) Meml. Med. Ctr.; RN, surgical ICU VA Med. Ctr., Buffalo, N.Y.; mgr. employee health svcs., human resources cons. Cummins Engine Co., Inc., Lakewood, N.Y. Active Jamestown Area Safety Coun., Chautauqua County Health Coalition. Maj. USAFR. Decorated Meritorious Svc. medal, Air Force Commendation medal for nursing mgmt., Nat. Def. medal, Armed Forces Res. medal, USAF Suggestion award, Armed Forces Volunteerism medal; Andrew Murphy Meml. scholar, Flight Nurse Honor Grad. scholar. Mem. Am. Occupl. Health Nurses, N.Y. State Assn. Occupl. Health Nurses, Northeastern Assn. Occupl. Health Nurses, Res. Officers Assn. (life mem.). Home: 136 Frederick Blvd Jamestown NY 14701-4270

DE LORIMIER, ALFRED ALEXANDRE, physician, pediatric surgeon, medical educator; b. Washington, May 30, 1931; s. Alfred Alexandre and Emilie Blanche (Kidder) de L.; m. Sandra Marie Veano, Nov. 21, 1953; children: Robert Maurice, Sally Renee, Nancy Denise. BS, U. Calif., Berkeley, 1953; MD, U. Calif., San Francisco, 1956. Diplomate Am. Bd. Surgery. Intern San Joaquin Gen. Hosp., Stockton, Calif., 1956-57; resident in gen. surgery U. Calif., San Francisco, 1957-62; fellow in pediat. surgery Ohio State U., Columbus, 1962-64; asst. prof. surgery U. Calif., San Francisco, 1964-71, assoc. prof. surgery, 1971-80, prof. surgery, 1980—, chief pediat. surg. divsn., 1965-88; chief pediat. surg. divsn. Calif. Pacific Med. Ctr., San Francisco, 1994—. Maj. USAFR, 1966-71. Office: U Calif 533 Parnassus Ave San Francisco CA 94143

DE LOS ANGELES, REYNALDO ADRILLANA, psychiatrist, consultant; b. Manila, July 2, 1945; came to U.S., 1976.; s. Amancio Nicdao and Consolacion (Adrillana) D.; m. Olivia Paula Olmedo, Jan. 25, 1947 (dec.); children: Karlo, Reynaldo Amancio II, Olivia Renee, Oliver Rinaldi. BS, U. of the East, Quezon City, Philippines, 1964, MD, 1969. Diplomate Am. Bd. Addiction Medicine, Am. Bd. Forensic Medicine, Am. Bd. Forensic Examiners. Med. dir. New Horizons Community Mental Health, Clinton, Okla., 1982-83; clinical dir. Western State Hosp., Ft. Supply, Okla., 1983-86, Muskogee Regional Med. Ctr., Psychiatric Intervention Ctr., Muskogee, Okla., 1986-88; med. dir. Muskogee Psychiatric Clinic, Muskogee, Okla., 1986-89; active staff Shawnee Mission Med. Ctr., Overland Park, Kans., 1989-91; med. dir. Chem. Dependency Unit Richard H. Young Hosp., Kearney, Nebr., 1991—, chief med. officer, 1993-95; chmn. dept. psych. Good Samaritan Hosp., Kearney, Nebr., 1993-95; bd. dirs. Good Samaritan Health Sys., Kearney, 1993-95. Recipient physician's recognition award AMA., 1982—. Mem. Am. Psychiat. Assn., Acad. Clin. Psychiatrists, Acad. Psychomatic Medicine. Home: 2014 W 36th St Kearney NE 68847-2211

DELP, LARRY BRUCE, psychologist, educator; b. Caretta, W.Va., May 11, 1942; s. Omer James and Dorothy Ruth Delp; m. Carol Jean Elswick, June 5, 1971; 1 child, Bruce Allen. AA, Hiwassee Coll., Madisonville, Tenn., 1965; BS, East Tenn. State U., 1968, MA, 1969, postgrad. Asst. prof. psychology Lincoln Meml. U., Harrogate, Tenn., 1969-70; field engr. Neely and Gibson Coal Co., Spartanburg, S.C., 1971-85; psychologist County of Dickenson, Clintwood, Va., 1988-89, Va. Dept. Corrections, 1991—. With U.S. Army, 1961-63. Mem. APA. Baptist.

DELPH, EMMA JEAN, nurse administrator; b. Norton, Va., Nov. 14, 1934; d. John and Stella Jane (Justice) Trusley; m. Hobert Ray Delph, Nov. 15, 1952; children: Louis Wayne, Regina Lynn. BSN, East Tenn. State U., 1990. Cert. nursing administrator, ANA. Staff nurse Lonsome Pine Hosp., Big Stone Gap, Va., 1974-76, shift supr. and chmn. nurse practice com., 1976-92, dir. home health svcs., 1992—. Bd. dirs. Lendwised Hospice, Duffield, Va., 1994-95. Mem. Sigma Theta Tau (Epsilon Sigma chpt.). Democrat. Pentecostal Ch. Home: PO Box 167 East Stone Gap VA 24246 Office: Lonesome Pine Hosp Home Health Cloverleaf Sq Big Stone Gap VA 24219

DEL PRIORE, ANASTASIA, health organization administrator; b. Ft. Wayne, Ind., Jan. 5, 1967; d. John E. and Eilleen Schaab; m. Don Del Priore, Jr., Nov. 25, 1989; 1 child, Mona. BA in Comm. and Nursing, Purdue U., 1989. Lic. nursing home adminstr., Ind.; lic. ins. agt.; qualified mentally retarded profl. Announcer WLKI Radio, Angola, Ind., 1989; admission/social svcs. staff Three Rivers Convalescent Ctr., Fort Wayne, Ind., 1989-90; instr. bus. comm. St. Francis Coll., Fort Wayne, Ind., 1990-92; admissions/social svcs. staff Anthony Wayne Living Ctr., Fort Wayne, Ind., 1990-92; instr. speech and med. transcription Internat. Bus. Coll., Fort Wayne, Ind., 1990-95; asst. adminstr., dir. mktg. Life Care Ctr. Ft. Wayne, Fort Wayne, Ind., 1992—. Mem. aging com. Ind.-Purdue U.; bd. dirs. Tri-State Ethics Consortium; pres. N.E. Ind. Continuity of Care; past pres. Allen County Coord. Coun. on Aging; pub. rels. chair Am. Diabetes Assn.; mem. Sr. Health Care Coord. Com., Minority Health Coalition of Allen County; co-dir. Admission Coord. Group; mem. Coun. on Sr. Svcs.; mem. Profl. Adv. Com. for Vis. Nurse Svc. and Hospice. Mem. Case Mgrs. Soc. Am. Home: 8608 Winchester Fort Wayne IN 46819 Office: Life Care Ctr of Fort Wayne 1649 Spy Run Fort Wayne IN 46805

DEL PRIORE, LUCIEN V., medical researcher; b. Italy, Dec. 13, 1953; m. Susan Panzarine, Oct. 16, 1981; children: Lia, Eric. BS in Physics summa cum laude, Cooper Union for Advancement of Sci. and Art, N.Y.C., 1975; MS in Physics, Cornell U., 1977, PhD in Physics, 1984; MD with distinction in rsch., U. Rochester, 1982. Diplomate Am. Bd. Ophthalmology, Nat. Bd. Med. Examiners. Intern in internal medicine Greater Balt. Med. Ctr., 1983-84; resident in ophthalmology Wilmer Ophthalmol. Inst., 1984-87, fellow in glaucoma, 1987-88; fellow in vitreoretinal surgery, asst. surgeon Wilmer Ophthalmol. Inst.-Johns Hopkins Hosp., Balt., 1988-89; attending ophthalmologist Washington Eye Physicians and Surgeons, Chevy Chase, Md., 1989-91; attending surgeon Washington Hosp. Ctr., 1989-91, Wilmer Opthalmol. Inst.-Johns Hopkins Hosp., Balt., 1988-91; attending surgeon in ophthalmology Ctr. for Sight Georgetown U. Hosp., Washington, 1990-91, clin. asst. prof. ophthalmology Ctr. for Sight, 1990-91; asst. surgeon in ophthalmology Jewish Hosp., St. Louis, 1991—, St. Louis Children's Hosp., 1991—; asst. ophthalmologist Barnes West County Hosp., St. Louis, 1991—, Barnes Hosp. at Washington U. Med. Ctr., St. Louis, 1991—; asst. prof. ophthalmology and visual scis., asst. prof. biochemistry and molecular biophysics Washington U. Sch. Medicine, St. Louis, 1991—; ophthalomology surgery cons. Loch Raven VA Hosp., Balt., 1987-91; physician cons. in ophthalmology VA Hosp., St. Louis, 1991—. Contbr. articles to profl. jours.; presenter in field. Heed Found. fellow, 1987-88, Heed/Knapp Found. fellow, 1988-89. Mem. AAAS, AMA, Am. Acad. Ophthalmology, Assn. for Rsch. in Vision and Ophthalomology, Am. Diabetes Assn. (rsch. award 1995), Internat. Soc. for Eye Rsch., Retina Soc., Vitreous Soc., Rsch. to Prevent Blindness. Office: Washington U Sch Medicine Barnes Hosp Plz Barnes Retina Inst Ste 17413 E Pavillion Saint Louis MO 63110*

DEL REGATO, JUAN ANGEL, radiotherapeutist, oncologist, educator; b. Camagüey, Cuba, Mar. 1, 1909; came to U.S., 1937, naturalized, 1941; s. Juan and Damiana (Manzano) del R.; m. Inez Johnson, May 1, 1939; children: Ann Cynthia del Regato Jaeger, Juanita Inez del Regato Peters, John Carl. Student, U. Havana, Cuba, 1930; M.D., U. Paris, France, 1937, Laureat, 1937; D.Sc. (hon.), Colo. Coll., 1969, Hahnemann Med. Coll., 1977, Med. Coll. Wis., 1981. Diplomate Am. Bd. Radiology. Asst. radiotherapist Radium Inst., U. Paris, 1934-37; assoc. radiotherapist Chgo. Tumor Inst., 1938; radiotherapeutist Warwick Cancer Clinic, Washington, 1939-40; researcher Nat. Cancer Inst., Balt., 1941-43; chief dept. radiotherapy Ellis Fischel State Cancer Hosp., Columbia, Mo., 1943-48; dir. Penrose Cancer Hosp., Colorado Springs, Colo., 1949-73; prof. clin. radiology U. Colo. Med. Sch., 1950-74; prof. radiology U. South Fla., Tampa, 1974-83, prof. emeritus, 1983—; mem. Nat. Adv. Cancer Coun., Bethesda, Md., 1967-71; mem. med. adv. com. Milheim Found., Denver; David Gould lectr. Johns Hopkins U., 1983. Author: (with L.V. Ackerman, M.D.) Cancer: Diagnosis Treatment and Prognosis, 1947, 54, 62, 70, (with H.J. Spjut and J.D. Cox), 1985, Radiological Physicists, 1985, Radiological Oncologists, 1993; editor Cancer Seminar, 1950-82; adv. editor Internat. Jour. Radiation Oncology, 1975—; contbr. articles to profl. jours. Active Colo. Springs Round Table, 1950-74. Honored by dedication of Juan A. del Regato Radiation Therapy Ctr., James Haley VA Hosp., Tampa; decorated Order of Carlos Finlay of Cuba, Order Francisco de Miranda Republic of Venezuela, Béclère medal à titre exceptionnel, 1980; recipient Gold medal Radiol. Soc. N.Am., 1967, Gold medal Inter-Am. Coll. Radiology, 1968, Gold plaque, 1975, Laureat Nat. Acad. Medicine of France, 1948, Grubbe Gold medal Ill. Radiol. Soc., 1973, Prix Bruninghaus French Acad. Medicine, 1979, Disting. Scientist award U. South Fla. Coll. Medicine, 1980, Disting. Svc. award Am. Cancer Soc., 1983, Ellis Fischel Disting. Achievement Oncology award Cancer Commn. State of Mo. and Fischel State Cancer Ctr., 1990; named Disting. Physician VA, 1974. Fellow Am. Coll. Radiology (bd. chancellors, chmn. commn. radiation therapy, com. awards and honors), AMA (coord. radiology jour. 1979—, Sci. Achievement award 1993, Gold Medallion award 1993); mem. Radiol. Soc. N.Am. (v.p. 1959-60, Arthur Erskine lectr. 1978, Roentgen Centennial medal 1995, X-Ray Discovery Centennial medal 1995), Am. Roentgen Ray Soc., Am. Radium Soc. (v.p. 1963-64, treas. 1966-68, pres. 1968-69, chmn. exec. com. 1971-72, historian 1969—, Janeway gold medal 1973), Assn. Am. Med. colls., Internat. Club Radiotherapists (pres. 1962-65), Inter-Am. Coll. Radiology (pres. 1967-71, U.S. counselor 1971-79), Am. Soc. Therapeutic Radiology (founder, sec. 1956-68, historian 1968—, pres. 1974-75, chmn. bd. dirs. 1975-76, gold medal 1977), Fedn. Clin. Oncologic Socs. (pres. bd. dirs. 1976-77); hon. mem. Rocky Mountain, Pacific N.W., Tex., Oreg., Minn. radiol. socs., radiol. socs. Cuba, Mex., Panama, Ecuador, Peru, Paraguay, Can., Argentina, Buenos Aires (Argentina), Am. Inst. Radiology (historian 1978-91, hon. mem. 17th Internat. Congress Radiology, Paris 1989), Arthur Purdy Stout Soc. Pathologists, Am. Soc. Physicists in Medicine. Home: University Village E-107 12401 N 22nd St Tampa FL

33612-4623 Office: U South Fla Coll Medicine VA Med Ctr Dept Radiation Oncology 124 Tampa FL 33618 also: VA Med Ctr 13000 Bruce B Downs Blvd Tampa FL 33612-4745

DE LUCA, ANTHONY JAMES, psychoanalyst, theologian; b. N.Y.C.; s. James Carl and Antoinette (Scarano) DeL. BA, St. John's U., 1957; STB, Catholic U. Am., 1961; BS, Queens Coll., 1963; MA, Fordham U., 1965; PhD, 1971; MA, St. John's U., 1973; DD Lafayette U. cert. in psychoanalysis and psychotherapy Postgrad. Center Mental Health, 1975. Installed as Monsignor Orthodox Cath. Ch., 1991; lic. clin. psychologist, Pa., marriage counselor, N.J., sch. psychologist, N.Y., N.J. Asst. prof. philosophy and psychology Notre Dame Coll., N.Y.C., 1967-71, Fordham U., N.Y.C., 1972-73; exec. dir Am. Inst. for Creative Living Inc., Bklyn., S.I., N.Y., Morrisville, Pa., and East Brunswick, N.J., 1972—; assoc. pastor Bklyn Diocese, Roman Catholic Ch., 1961-67, cons. Marriage Tribunal, 1967—; archbishop Syrian Orthodox Ch. Am. Western Rite; UN rep. for Ch.; chaplain to students, dean Internat. Sch. for Mental Health Practitioners, S.I. and Pa.; cons. N.Y.C. Police Dept., 1980—; dean Internat. Sch. Mental Health Practitioners, Morrisville, Pa.; dir., producer S.I. Cmty. TV. Author: Freud and Future Religious Experience, 1976. Mem. S.I. Mental Health Council, 1975—. Fellow Am. Orthopsychiat. Assn.; mem. APA, Am. Philos. Assn., Am. Sociol Assn., Am. Group Psychotherapy Assn., Am. Assn. Marriage and Family Therapists (supr.), Am. Found Religion and Psychiatry, Alzheimer's Assn. (bd. dirs.), N.Y. Soc. Clin. Psychologists, Am. Assn. Psychoednl. Therapists (adv. bd.), Council Register Health Providers in Psychology. Home: 2295 Victory Blvd Staten Island NY 10314-6625 also: 78 N Pennsylvania Ave Morrisville PA 19067

DE LUCA, CARLO JOHN, biomedical engineer; b. Bagnoli del Trigno, Italy, Oct. 12, 1943; came to U.S., 1973; s. John and Josephine (De Blasio) De L.; B in Applied Sci. U. B.C., Can., 1966; MS, U. N.B., Can., 1968; PhD, Queen's U., 1972; m. Christine M. Rafferty. Lectr. U. N.B. Computing Ctr., Fredericton, 1968; lectr. biomed. engring. unit Queen's U., Kingston, Ont., Can., 1969-70, lab. instr. dept. anatomy, 1970-71, lectr. dept. anatomy, 1971-72, asst. prof. dept. anatomy, 1972-73; lectr. M.I.T., Cambridge, 1973—; rsch. assoc. in orthopaedic surgery Children's Hosp. Med. Ctr., Harvard U. Med. Sch., Boston, 1973-79, prin. rsch. assoc. in orthopaedic surgery, 1979-84, dir. Neuromuscular Rsch. Lab., 1980-84; adj. assoc. prof. biomed. engring. Boston U., 1977-84, prof. biomed. engring., 1984—, rsch. prof. neurology, 1985—, dir. NeuroMuscular Rsch. Ctr., 1984—, chmn. dept. of biomed. engring., 1986; dean Coll. of Engring., Boston U., 1986-89; founder, pres. DelSys, Inc., 1993—; cons. Liberty Mut. Rsch. Ctr., Hopkinton, Mass., 1973—; rsch. mem. Harvard-M.I.T. div. of health sci. and tech., 1978-84; affiliated scientist New Eng. Regional Primate Ctr., 1977-87; mem. nat. and internat. coms. Ont. Govt. fellow, 1969-70. Founding editor-in-chief Jour. Electromyography and Kinesiology, 1990; mem. editorial bds. sci. jours.; co-author: Muscles Alive; contbr. articles on biomed. engring. and neurophysiolgy to sci. publs. Founder, pres. Neuromuscular Rsch. Found., 1985—. RSA grantee, VA grantee, NIH grantee, NASA grantee; recipient Volvo award Internat. Soc. for Study of Lumbar Spine, 1989, Wartenweiler Lecture award Internat. Soc. Biomechanics, 1993, Stuart Reiner Meml. Lectr. award Am. Assn. Electrodiagnostic Medicine, 1994; named to Italian Cultural Ctr. Hall of Fame, Vancouver, Can., 1991. Fellow Am. Inst. Med. and Biol. Engring. (founding fellow 1993), IEEE; mem. AAAS, Biomed. Engring. Soc., Internat. Soc. of Electrophysiol. Kinesiology (sec. gen. 1976-80, sec. 1980-84, v.p. 1985-88, pres. 1988-92), Can. Med. and Biol. Engring. Soc., Soc. Neurosci., Orthopaedics Rsch. Soc., Dante Alighieri Soc. (bd. govs. 1986-88), Mass. Tech. Park Corp. (bd. govs. 1987-90), Sigma Xi. Club: Harvard of Boston. Home: 107 Livingston Rd Wellesley MA 02181 Office: Boston U NeuroMuscular Rsch Ctr 44 Cummington St Boston MA 02215-2407

DELUCA, DOMINICK, medical educator, researcher. BA in Bacteriology, UCLA, 1969, PhD in Microbiology, 1974. Predoctoral fellow NIH dept. bacteriology UCLA, 1970-74, rsch. asst. dept. bacteriology, 1974; postdoctoral fellow Leukemia Soc. Am., Walter and Eliza Hall Inst., Parkville, Australia, 1974-77; scientist cancer biology program Frederick (Md.) Cancer Rsch. Ctr., 1977-80; asst. prof. biochemistry Med. U. S.C., Charleston, 1980-85, assoc. prof. biochemistry, 1985-90; assoc. prof. microbilogy and immunology U. Ariz., 1990—. Mem. editl. adv. bd. Devel. and Comparative Immunology, 1995—; contbr. articles to profl. jours., chpt. to books. Recipient Developing Scholar award Health Scis. Found. Med. U. S.C., 1987, Rsch. award Am. Diabetes Assn., 1995. Mem. Am. Assn. Immunologists, Southeastern Immunology Conf. (pres. elect 1982-83, pres. 1983-84, bd. dirs. 1985), Ariz. Cancer Ctr. Office: U Ariz Dept Micro Immuno Lifescis N Rm 644 PO Box 245049 Tucson AZ 85724-5049

DELUCA, PATRICK PHILLIP, pharmaceutical scientist, educator, administrator; b. Scranton, Pa., Sept. 7, 1935; m. Judy Beitzel, June 16, 1956; children: Paul, Thomas, Patrick, Donald, Michelle, Michael. BS in Pharmacy, Temple U., 1957, MS in Pharmacy, 1960, PhD in Pharmacy (SKF W.G. Karr fellow), 1963. Analytical chemist SKF Co., 1957-59; instr., research asso. Temple U., 1959-62; sr. research pharmacist CIBA Co., Summit, N.J., 1963-66; plant mgr. CIBA Co., 1966-69, dir., 1969-70; dir. Cormedics Corp., Somerville, N.J.; mem. faculty U. Ky., 1970—; prof., asso. dean U. Ky. (Coll. Pharmacy), 1972-87, dir. ctr. for pharmaceutical sci. and tech., 1987-88; cons. to pharm. industry and FDA. Editor-in-chief Jour. Pharm. Devel. and Tech., 1995; contbr. numerous articles and sci. papers to profl. jours. Recipient Leo G. Penn award Temple U., 1957, Lunsford-Richardson Pharmacy Rsch. award Richardson Merrell Co., 1960, 62, Best Paper Toward Advancement Indsl. Pharmacy award N.J. Pharmacy Discussion Group, 1965, Disting. Alumni award Temple U., 1989, Outstanding Educator award in U.S., 1974, Sturgill Rsch. award U. Ky., 1995; also numerous grants. Fellow Am. Assn. Pharm. Scientists (bd. dirs. 1986-88, Rsch. Achievement award 1988), Acad. Pharm. Sci. (pres. 1979-80), Inst. for Advanced Biotech. (sr.); mem. Am. Pharm. Assn., Parenteral Drug Assn. (Rsch. Achievement award 1975), Am. Soc. Hosp. Pharmacists (Rsch. award 1975), N.Y. Acad. Sci., Am. Soc. Enteral and Parental Nutrition, Sigma Xi, Rho Chi. Home: 3292 Nantucket Rd Lexington KY 40502-3269 Office: U Ky Coll Pharmacy Rose St Lexington KY 40536-0082

DELUCA-KRANZ, EILEEN THERESA, cardiovascular telemetry, long term and subacute care nurse; b. Elizabeth, N.J., Apr. 11, 1956; d. Lawrence Joseph and Virginia Clair (Mahoney) DeLuca; m. Andrew Joseph Kranz; 1 child, Mackenzie Martin. BSN, Villa Maria Coll., Erie, Pa., 1978; MSN, Edinboro U., 1990. RN, Pa., N.J. Staff nurse/team leader/charge nurse Hamot Med. Ctr., Erie, assoc. unit nursing dir., 1983-96. Recipient award for Excellence in Nursing Practice, Dist. 9 Pa. Nurses Assn., 1991. Mem. ANA (cert. med./surg. nurse), Affiliated Orgn. Nurse Mgrs. of Pa., Soc. Peripheral Vascular Disease, Sigma Theta Tau. Home: 4639 Idyllbrook Village Ln Erie PA 16506

DELUCCA, LEOPOLDO ELOY, otolaryngologist, head and neck surgeon; b. Santurce, P.R., Nov. 1, 1952; s. Leopoldo Claudio and Laura Iris (Juncos) DeL.; m. Judith Lynn McClellan, June 11, 1977; children: Lauren Denise, Gina Fay. Pre-med. degree, U. P.R., 1973; MD, Jefferson Med. Coll., Phila., 1977. Diplomate Am. Bd. Otolaryngology. Otolaryngologist Ft. Dodge (Iowa) Med. Ctr., 1981-86; practice medicine specializing in otolaryngology Ft. Dodge, 1986—; active med. staff Trinity Regional Hosp., Ft. Dodge, 1981—, chief of surgery, 1985—, pres. med. staff, 1991—; vol. faculty Coll. Osteo. Medicine and Surgery, Des Moines, 1981-82. Bd. dirs. Trinity Regional Hosp., 1993—. Fellow ACS, Am. Acad. Otolaryngology-Head and Neck Surgery, Am. Acad. Facial Plastic and Reconstructive Surgery. Republican. Roman Catholic. Home: 2626 Woodland Dr Fort Dodge IA 50501-7130 Office: Physicians Office Bldg 200 Kenyon Rd Ste 200 Fort Dodge IA 50501-5762

DELUZE, JAMES ROBERT, physician; b. L.A., Sept. 14, 1948; s. James Vierea and Jean Ruth (Hanna) DeL. BA, U. Hawaii, 1974; student, Andrews U., 1980-82; DO, U. Health Scis., Kansas City, 1987. Product specialist Hanna Enterprise, Kailua, Hawaii, 1972-74; pres. Ecol. Engring., Honolulu, 1976-79; intern Kirksville (Mo.) Osteo. Med. Ctr., 1987-88; pvt. practice medicine Kailua, 1988-89; physician Mental Health Systems, San Diego, 1989-90; pvt. practice Waialua, Hawaii, 1991-95. Rep. candidate U.S. Ho. of Reps., 1992, U.S. Senate, 1994; pres. Waialua Rep. Precinct, 1992; del. Rep. State Conv., Honolulu, 1992. Mem. Am. Assn. Clin. Anatomists, Am. Coll. Occupational and Environ. Medicine, Am. Osteo. Assn. (del. 1992), Hawaii Assn. Osteo. Physicians and Surgeons (v.p. 1991-92, pres. 1992-93), Nat. Space Soc., U.S. C. of C. Republican. Seventh Day Adventist. Home and Office: PO Box 541 Waialua HI 96791-0541

DELZER, DAMIEN RANEY, optometrist, optometric physician; b. Bismarck, N.D.. BS, Oral Roberts U., Tulsa; OD, Ohio State U. Bd. cert. internat., nat., Alaska, Minn. Chief optometry svc. Bassett Cmty. Hosp., Fairbanks, Alaska, 1993—; adj. asst. prof. optometry Pacific U., Forest Grove, Oreg.; asst. prof. clin. optometry Ferris State U., Big Rapids, Mich.; owner Interior Alaska Eyecare, Fairbanks; staff doctor West Valley Vision Ctr. Capt. U.S. Army, 1993—. Mem. Am. Optometric Assn. (contact lens sect.), Armed Forces Optometric Soc., So. Coun. Optometrists. Office: USA MEDDAC AK MCUC-OPT 1060 Gaffney Rd # 7480 Fort Wainwright AK 99703-7480

DEMAIN, ARNOLD LESTER, microbiologist, educator; b. N.Y.C., Apr. 26, 1927; s. Henry and Gussie (Katz) D.; m. Joanna Kaye, Aug. 2, 1952; children: Pamela Robin Demain McCloskey, Jeffrey Brian. BS, Mich. State U., 1949, MS, 1950; PhD, U. Calif., Berkeley, 1954. Rsch. asst. U. Calif., Davis, 1952-54; rsch. microbiologist Merck & Co., Inc., Danville, Pa., 1954-56, Rahway, N.J., 1956-65; founder, head of dept. ferm. microbiology Merck & Co., Inc., Rahway, 1965-69; prof. of ind. microbiology MIT, Cambridge, 1969—. Editor 7 books; contbr. over 395 articles to profl. jours. With U.S. Navy, 1945-47. Recipient hotpack award Can. Soc. Microbiology, 1978, Rubro award Australian Soc. Microbiology, 1978, indsl. microbiology award Italian Pharm. Assn., 1989, Hans Knoll meml. award, Germany, 1990. Mem. NAS, Soc. Indsl. Microbiology (pres. 1990, Charles Thom award 1978, Waksman Tchg. award 1995), Am. Soc. Microbiology (Waksman award N.J. br. 1975, Biotech. award 1990, Disting. Svc. award 1994), French Soc. Microbiology (hon.). Office: MIT 77 Massachusetts Ave Cambridge MA 02139-4301

DEMAIO, DOROTHY J., dean, nurse, educator; b. Jersey City, Jan. 12, 1927; d. John Joseph and Agnes (McEnroe) Jengo; m. Laurence R. DeMaio, Oct. 15, 1950; children: Maureen, Michele, Laurence J., Diane, James. BS, Jersey City State Coll., 1948; MA, NYU, 1970; postgrad., Rutgers U., 1970—. Supr. pediatrics svc. and edn. Jersey City Med. Ctr., 1964-65; instr. nursing Charles E. Gregory Sch. Nursing, Perth Amboy, N.J., 1965-68; instr. Rutgers U., Newark, 1970-75, dir. pediatric nurse practitioner program, from 1972, coord. nurse practitioner programs, from 1974, assoc. prof. nursing, 1975-76, assoc. prof. grad. program parent-child nursing, from 1976, now dean Coll. of Nursing, prof. Coll. of Nursing; sec., treas. N.J. Bd. Nursing, from 1975; chmn. Ad Hoc Com. to Redefine Nursing, 1973-74. Bd. dirs. Crossroads Girl Scouts U.S., 1963-69; active Colonia Sch. 17 PTO, 1959-72. Recipient Outstanding Alumnae award Jersey State Coll., 1956, Thanks badge Girl Scouts U.S., 1969. Office: Rutgers-State U Coll Nursing Ackerson Hall 180 University Ave Newark NJ 07102-1803*

DEMANN, MICHAEL MARCUS, psychologist; b. Mpls., June 1, 1932; s. George S. and Mary Hazel (Short) DeM.; B.A., U. Minn., 1955, M.A., 1958, Ph.D., 1960; m. Carol L. Knutson, Feb. 10, 1961; children—James G., Susan M., John P. Staff mem. VA Hosp., Mpls., 1960-61; cons. psychologist Rohrer, Hibler and Replogle, Mpls., 1961-65; cons. psychologist in pvt. practice, Mpls., 1965—; dir. Internat. Graphics Corp., Mpls., 1967—; cons. Social Security Adminstrn., Mpls., 1966-67. Bd. dirs. Opportunity Workshop, Mpls., 1962-69; bd. govs. St. Mary's Jr. Coll., Mpls., 1973. Served with M.C., U.S. Army, 1950-52. Mem. Am. Psychol. Assn., Minn. Psychol. Assn. (exec. council 1971-73), Am. Legion. Episcopalian. Home: 10248 Colorado Rd S Bloomington MN 55438-1842 Office: 8200 Humboldt S Minneapolis MN 55431

DEMAR, ANDREW RICHARD, JR., surgeon; b. Kittery, Maine, Apr. 1, 1959; s. Andrew Richard and Geraldine (Potter) DeM.; m. Catherine Norberth Grinstead, June 11, 1982 (div.). BA, Carleton Coll., 1981; MD, Ohio State U., 1985. Resident gen. surgery UCLA, 1985-92; assoc. Capitol Surg. Assocs., Sacramento, 1992—; trauma surgeon Sutter Roseville (Calif.) Med. Ctr., 1994—. Office: 2800 L St Ste 200 Sacramento CA 95816

DEMARCO, GAIL K., nursing association administrator; b. N.Y., Oct. 20, 1940. BS, SUNY, Plattsburgh, 1961; MS, Russell Sage Coll., 1979. Dir. satellite clinics St. Mary's Hosp., Amsterdam, N.Y., faculty Sch. of Nursing, dir. Sch. of Nursing; assoc. dir. nursing practice and svcs. N.Y. State Nurses Assn., Latham, N.Y. Mem. ANA, N.Y. State Nurses Assn., N.Y. State Assn. Sch. Nurses, Sigma Theta Tau. Home: 18 Empire Cir Rensselaer NY 12144-9314

DEMARCO, MARYELLEN, rehabilitation and critical care nurse; b. Coatesville, Pa.; d. Michael David and Helen Mary (Rovka) Baylog; m. Ronald Anthony DeMarco, June 24, 1972; children: Daniel Lawrence, Debra Lynn, Donna Lenore. Diploma, St. Francis Med. Ctr., Trenton, N.J., 1964; BSN, Trenton State Coll., 1984. RN, N.J.; ACLS, BLS, CRRN. Staff RN med.-surg. St. Francis Med. Ctr., 1964-66, head nurse, 1966-74, evening charge nurse, 1974-76, float nurse, 1976-93; ICU staff nurse St. Francis Med. Ctr., Trenton, N.J., 1993—; adminstrv. supr. St. Lawrence Rehab. Ctr., 1985—, chairperson recruitment and retention com., 1992, 95, 96. Mem. AACN, Assn. Rehab. Nurses. Roman Catholic. Home: 229 Lambertville Hopewell NJ 08525 Office: Saint Lawrence Rehab Ctr 2381 Lawrenceville Rd Lawrenceville NJ 08648-2024 also: St Francis Med Ctr ICU Dept 601 Hamilton Ave Trenton NJ 08629-1915

DEMAREE, ROBERT GLENN, psychologist, educator; b. Rockford, Ill., Sept. 20, 1920; s. Glenn and Ethel Mae (Champion) D.; BS, U. Ill., 1941, MA, 1948, PhD (univ. fellow 1949-50), 1950; m. Alyce Anisia Jones, Sept. 4, 1948; children— Dee Anne, Marta, James, David. Chief performance br. Pers. and Tng. Rsch. Ctr., Lowry AFB, Denver, 1951-57; dir. human factors Martin Space Flight div. Bell Aircraft Corp., Balt., 1958-60; dir. programs Matrix Corp., Arlington, Va., 1960-61; dir. office instructional rsch. U. Ill., 1961-63; projects dir. Life Scis., Inc., Hurst, Tex., 1963-66; mem. faculty Tex. Christian U., Ft. Worth, 1966-85, prof. psychology, prof. Inst. Behavioral Rsch., 1970-85, emeritus, 1985—; cons., 1985—. Served with AUS, 1941-46. Mem. APA, Am. Statis. Assn., Psychometric Soc., Soc. Multivariate Exptl. Psychology, Sigma Xi. Home: 4813 Eldorado Dr Fort Worth TX 76180-7227

DE MARGERIE, JEAN-M., ophthalmology educator; b. Prud'homme, Sask., Can., Dec. 11, 1927; s. Antonio (Agnes) and Lavergne de M.; m. Therese-E. Brochu, Aug. 31, 1955; children: Claudine, Michele, Andre, Monique, Jean-Pierre. B.A., U. Ottawa, 1947; M.D., U. Laval, Que., 1952; D.Phil., Oxford U., Eng., 1955. Intern Quebec City Univ. Hosps., 1951-52; resident in ophthalmology Oxford, Eng., 1955-57, Edinburgh, Scotland, 1957-59; asst. prof. ophthalmology Queen's U., Kingston, Ont., 1960-66; prof. ophthalmology U. Sherbrooke, Que., 1966—, head dept., 1966-76, vice dean for research Faculty of Medicine, 1973-79, dean Faculty of Medicine, 1979-83; exec. mem. Que. Health Research Council, 1974-78; v.p., then. pres. Med. Research Council Can., 1976-79. Assoc. editor: Can. Jour. Ophthalmology, 1965-79. Trustee Kingston Separate Sch. Bd., 1962-66; pres. Nat. Fedn. Can. Univ. Students, 1951-52; v.p. Mus. of Fine Arts of Sherbrooke, 1986-87. Fellow Royal Coll. Physicians and Surgeons Can., ACS; mem. Que. Assn. Opthalmologists (pres. 1976-77); mem. Can. Ophthal. Soc. (pres. 1975-76). Office: University of Sherbrooke CHUS, Faculty of Medicine, Sherbrooke, PQ Canada J1J 5N4

DE MARIA, ALFRED ANTHONY, neurologist; b. Sewickley, Pa., Mar. 27, 1952; s. Alfred Anthony and Helen Josephine (Goray) De M.; m. Katherine Grace Bridge, June 25, 1977; children: Genevieve Camille, Gabrielle Christine. BA, Johns Hopkins U., 1973; MD, Ohio State U., 1976. Diplomate Am. Bd. Psychiatry & Neurology. Intern N.C. Baptist Hosp., Winston-Salem, 1976-77; resident in neurology N.C. Meml. Hosp., Chapel Hill, 1977-80; fellow in EEG Mayo Clinic, Rochester, Minn., 1980-81; attending physician Neurol. Assocs., Columbus, Ohio, 1981-92, Wilmington (N.C.) Health Assocs., 1993—; med. dir. EEG lab. Riverside Meth. Hosp., Columbus, Ohio, 1981-92; med. dir. sleep lab. Cape Fear Meml. Hosp., Wilmington, 1993—. Host (TV show) Sound Opinion, 1996—. Mem. Am. Acad. Neurology, Am. Sleep Disorders Assn., Am. EEG Soc., Am. Epilepsy Soc., Nat. Stroke Assn., Nat. Headache Found., Nat. Assn. Physician Broadcasters. Office: Wilmington Health Assocs 1202 Medical Ctr Dr Wilmington NC 28401

DEMARIA, MICHAEL BRANT, psychologist; b. Norwalk, Conn., Apr. 23, 1962; s. Francesco and Jacqueline (Campbell) DeM.; m. Kathleen Jean Kies, July 4, 1982; 1 child, Danielle. BA in Psychology magna cum laude, U. West Fla., 1982, BA in Philosophy magna cum laude, 1982; MA in Psychology, Duquesne U., Pitts., 1983, PhD in Clin. Psychology, 1987. Lic. clin. psychologist, Fla.; registered play therapist; diplomate in expressive therapy. Doctoral intern Bapt. Hosp. and Lakeview Ctr., Pensacola, Fla., 1985-86; resident Clin. Psychology Assn., Pensacola, 1986-88, clin. psychologist, 1988-89; clin. psychologist, pres., clin. dir. DeMaria and Assoc., Pensacola, 1989—; therapist Counseling Ctr. Point Park Coll., Pitts., 1983-84, Ctr. Tng. and Rsch. in Psychology Duquesne U., 1983-86, instr. Psychology Dept., 1983-85, rsch. asst., 1983-85; faculty assoc. U. West Fla., 1985—; cons. Adolescent Stress Ctr. Bapt. Hosp., Pensacola, 1985-89, IMPACT Program, 1986-88, Child Protection Team, 1986-89; cons./expert witness State Atty. Office, Pensacola, Renascence Recovery Ctr., Anchorage Counseling Svcs., Community Drug & Alcohol Commn., Rivendale Hosp.; speaker in field. Author: Horns and Halos: Towards the Blessing of Darkness, 1992; contbr. articles to The Humanistic Psychologist, Internat. Journey of Play Therapy, The Arts in Psychotherapy: An International Jour. Mem. Fla. Legis. Task Force on Child Abuse and Neglect Reports, 1988—. Recipient Merit scholarship Dept. Psychology, Dept. Philosophy U. West Fla., Alumni Found. scholarship. Mem. APA, Soc. for Personality Assessment, Assn. for Play Therapy, Southeastern Psychol. Assn., Fla. Psychol. Assn. (treas. 1989—), Psi Chi, Phi Kappa Phi. Office: 512 E Zarragossa St Pensacola FL 32501-6155

DEMARIA, THOMAS PATRICK, psychologist; b. Long Beach, N.Y., Feb. 20, 1960; s. William and Margaret (Roche) D.; m. Mary Kate Magee, Sept. 8, 1990. BA, St. John's U., 1982; MA, Hofstra U., 1983, PhD, 1986. Lic. psychologist, N.Y. Staff therapist Inst. for Behavior Therapy, Manhattan, N.Y., 1984-87; sch. psychologist Rockville Centre (N.Y.) Sch. Dist., 1983-87; chief psychologist South Nassau Community Hosp. Mental Health Clinic, Oceanside, N.Y., 1987-92, dir., 1992—; trainer, cons. psychology, N.Y., 1985—. Contbr. articles to profl. jours. Chair svc. area coun. Nassau County Dept. Mental Health, 1990-92, 95— ; mem. Community Disaster Task Force, 1991—. Mem. Am. Psychol. Assn., Assn. Advancement Behavior Therapy, Nassau County Psychol. Assn. Roman Catholic. Office: South Nassau Community Hosp 2277 Grand Ave Baldwin NY 11510

DE MARNEFFE, FRANCIS, psychiatrist, hospital administrator; b. Brussels, May 7, 1924; arrived in England, 1940; came to U.S., 1950; s. Armand Gustave and Esther Magdalen (Loveday) de M.; m. Nancy Marie Edmonds, Aug. 5, 1955 (div. Sept. 1967); children: Peter Loveday, Daphne Elizabeth, Colette; m. Barbara Cassard Rowe, Dec. 5, 1969. MB, BS, U. London, 1950. Diplomate Am. Bd. Psychiatry and Neurology. Intern Muhlenberg Hosp., Plainfield, N.J., 1950-51; asst. resident in psychiatry Mass. Gen. Hosp., Boston, 1952; teaching fellow in psychiatry Med. Sch. Harvard U., Boston, 1955-56, rsch. fellow, 1955-56; resident in psychiatry McLean Hosp., Belmont, Mass., 1953-54, staff psychiatrist, 1955-90, cons. psychiatrist, 1990—; gen. dir. McLean Hosp., Belmont, 1962-87, gen. dir. emeritus, 1987—, pres., CEO McLean Health Svcs., Inc., 1986-89; med. dir. Holly Hill Mental Health Svcs., Raleigh, N.C., 1990-93; instr. psychiatry Med. Sch. Harvard U., 1961-66, lectr. 1966—; mem. accreditation coun. psychiat. faciltities Joint Commn. on Accreditation of Hosps., Chgo, 1979-84, mem. tech. adv. com., 1979-84, chmn. accreditation, 1970-72, mem. coun., 1970-79; adminstr. McLean divsn. Hall-Mercer Hosp., Phila., 1969-87; v.p. Hall-Mercer Hosp., 1980-87; exec. v.p. Belmont programs Mass. Gen. Hosp., Boston, 1986-87; clin. prof. psychiatry U. N.C., Chapel Hill, 1991-93; assoc. cons. prof. psychiatry Duke U. Med. Sch., 1991-93, v.p. Wake County Mental Health Assn., 1992-93, med. staff Rex Hosp., Raleigh, N.C., 1993; mem. Corp. Ptnrs. Health Care Inc., Boston, 1994—; trustee working group McLean Hosp., 1996; cons. Exec. Svcs. Corps., Boston, 1996. Author: Introduction to Adolescent Patients in Transition, 1974, contbg. author: The Changing Mental Health Scene, 1976; mem. editorial bd. McLean (Hosp.) Jour., 1976—. Trustee Guidance Camps, Inc., Boston, 1968-90, Preschool, Inc., Cambridge, Mass., 1961-62, Concord Acad. Mass., 1975-78, Nat. Assn. Pvt. Psychiat. Hosps., Washington, 1982-85, 93-94, McLean Hosp. Corp., Belmont, 1985-87; mem. Corp. of Family Svc. Assn. Greater Boston, 1978-81; hon. trustee Concord Acad., 1978—; bd. dirs. Mass. chpt. Nat. Com. for Prevention of Child Abuse, Boston, 1979-81, Health Planning Coun. Greater Boston, 1972-76; chmn. med. divsn. United Way, 1986; mem. Mass. Gen. Hosp. Corp., 1988-94, coll. Des Conseillers of French Libr. & Cultural Ctr., Boston, 1995—; bd. dirs. Friends of McLean, 1995—. Served as flying officer RAF, 1943-46. Recipient Presdl. award Nat. Assn. Pvt. Psychiat. Hosps., 1991. Licentiate Royal Coll. Physicians; fellow Am. Psychiat. Assn., Am. Coll. Psychiatrists (hon. fellowship com.), Royal Coll. Psychiatrists (hon. fellowship com.), Royal Coll. Psychiatrists, Mass. Med. Soc., Am. Coll. Mental Helth Adminstrn.; mem. Roayl coll. Surgeons, Eng. Ctrl. Neuropsychiat. Hosp. Assn. (pres. 1986-87), The Country Club (Brookline), Somerset (Boston) Club, Harvard of Boston, Leander (Henley-on-Thames, England), Cambridge Boat, Thames Rowing (London), Lake (Dublin, N.H.) Club. Home: 126 Coolidge Hl Cambridge MA 02138-5522 Office: McLean Hosp 115 Mill St Belmont MA 02178-1041

DEMARTINO, ANTHONY GABRIEL, cardiologist, internist; b. Bronx, Oct. 7, 1931; s. Agostino and Vincenzina (Clarizia) DeM.; BS cum laude, Iona Coll., 1953; MD, SUNY, 1957; m. Marlene Mignone, Aug. 8, 1964; children: Anthony Augustin, Laura Jean. Intern, Univ. div. Kings County Med. Center, Bklyn., 1957-58, med. resident, 1960-62; fellow cardiopulmonary Cornell U., N.Y. Hosp., 1962-64; acting chief medicine Fordham div. Misericordia Fordham Affiliation, Bronx, 1964-65; physician in charge cardiac lab. Misericordia-Fordham Affiliation, 1965-69; attending physician dept. medicine and cardiology Our Lady of Mercy Med. Ctr., Bronx, 1967—, sr. physician, 1995—, mem. med. bd., 1985-93; attending physician dept. medicine and cardiology Lawrence Hosp., Bronxville, N.Y., 1977—, mem. med. bd., 1989-94, sec., treas. Med. Bd. Lawrence Hosp., 1996—, assoc. dir. Dept. Medicine, Lawrence Hosp., Bronxville, N.Y., 1993—; practice medicine, specializing in cardiology and internal medicine, Bronx and Bronxville, 1964—; v.p. med. bd. Misericordia Hosp. Med. Center, Bronx, 1973-75, pres., 1975-77; clin. asst. prof. medicine N.Y. Med. Coll., 1971—; hon. police surgeon N.Y.C. Trustee, Misericordia Hosp., 1977-83; sec., treas. med. bd. Lawrence Hosp., 1996—. Served to capt., M.C., U.S. Army, 1958-60. Nat. Heart Inst. fellow, 1962-64. Diplomate Nat. Bd. Med. Examiners, Am. Bd. Internal Medicine (cardiovascular disease). Fellow ACP, Am. Coll. Cardiology, Council Clin. Cardiology of Am. Heart Assn., Am. Coll. Chest Physicians, N.Y. Cardiol. Assn.; mem. Am. Soc. Internal Medicine, AMA, Westchester County, N.Y. County Med. Soc. Roman Catholic. Contbr. articles to profl. jours; editorial bd. N.Y. Med. Quar., 1980-84. Office: 4350 Van Cortlandt Park E Bronx NY 10470-1867 also: 77 Pondfield Rd Bronxville NY 10708-3809

DEMARZO, JEANNE PATRICIA, neonatal critical care nurse; b. N.Y.C., Apr. 4, 1961; d. Thomas Michael and Barbara Ann (Ostrander) Whelan; m. Joseph Andrew DeMarzo, June 15, 1990; 1 child, Sarah Elizabeth. BSN, Coll. New Rochelle, 1983, MSN in Adminstrn., 1990. RN, N.Y.; cert. in neonatal intensive care. Staff nurse pediatrics Weiler Hosp., Albert Einstein Coll. Medicine, Bronx, N.Y., 1983-86, 1986-89, assoc. adminstrv. supr., 1989-90; adminstrv. nursing supr. neonatal ICU Einstein Hosp.-Montefiore Med. Ctr., Bronx, N.Y., 1990—. Mem. AWHOON, NANN, AONE, NAACOG, Sigma Theta Tau. Home: 11 Bloomer Rd Mahopac NY 10541-3708 Office: Einstein Hosp-Montefiore Med Ctr 1825 Eastchester Rd Bronx NY 10461-2373

DEMAY, HELEN LOUISE, nursing services administrator; b. Pitts., July 9, 1927; d. Patrick J. and Ellen (Kennedy) Duffy; m. John A. DeMay, Sept. 2, 1950; children: John A. III, Patrick J., Ann L., Mary Ellen, Theresa, Michael, Elizabeth, Stephen, Paul, David, Maureen. Nursing diploma, Braddock Gen. Hosp., 1948; postgrad., Cook County Hosp., 1949. Staff nurse Homestead (Pa.) Hosp., 1948; asst. head nurse Children Hosp., U. Pitts., 1949-52; staff nurse Kane Hosp., Pitts., 1978; activity dir. Jefferson Hills Nursing Home, Pitts., 1979-82; founder, officer Concerned Care Inc., Pitts., 1983-92; ret., 1992. Bd. dirs. St. Germaine Roman Cath. 1st Parish Coun., Bethel Park, Pa.; founding mem. Sch. House Arts Ctr., Bethel Park;

bd. dirs., sec. Germaine Harbor, Bethel Park, 1990—; mem. Allegheny County Bd. Assistance, 1981-87; bd. advisor Allegheny County Single Parent Program, Pitts., 1984-94. Mem. S.W. Pa. RN Club. Republican. Home: 7166 Keith Rd Bethel Park PA 15102-3741

DEMB, HOWARD BERTRAM, psychiatry educator, pediatrics educator; b. N.Y.C., Oct. 30, 1931. BS, CCNY, 1953, MA, 1957; MD, SUNY, Syracuse, 1962. Asst. clin. prof. psychiatry and pediatrics Albert Einstein Coll. Medicine, N.Y.C., 1972-86, asst. prof. psychiatry, 1986—, asst. prof. pediatrics, 1986-90, assoc. prof. pediatrics, 1990—. Office: Albert Einstein Coll Medicine 1410 Pelham Pky S Bronx NY 10461-1101

DEMBO, DONALD HOWARD, cardiologist, medical administrator, educator; b. Balt., Jan. 27, 1931; s. Sydney Harry and Yetta (Bank) D.; m. Leatrice Cohen, Aug. 10, 1952; children: Steven Jay, Michael Brian, Susan Ann Weinstein Dembo. BA, Johns Hopkins Univ., 1951; MD, Univ. Md, 1955. Diplomate Am. Bd. Internal Medicine, Am. Bd. Cardiovascular Disease. Internship Sinai Hosp., Balt., 1955-56; residency in medicine Univ. Hosp., Balt., 1956-58; asst. cardiologist in chief U.S. Army Hosp., Frankfurt, Germany, 1958-60; fellow in cardiology Univ. Hosp., 1960-61; chief of cardiology Md. Gen. Hosp., Balt., 1961-91, Good Samaritan Hosp., Balt., 1975-95; assoc. physician in chief, vice chair of medicine Sinai Hosp., 1995—; asst. prof. medicine Univ. Md., 1970-91, Johns Hopkins Univ., 1991—; pres. Cen. Md. Cardiology, Balt., 1976-95. Contbr. articles to profl. jours. Bd. trustees Cardiopulmonary Resuscitation, Inc., 1975-77.; chmn. adv. bd. Easton Waterfowl Festival, Easton, Md., 1990-93. Capt. U.S. Army, 1958-60. Recipient Bronze, Silver & Gold award Am. Heart Assn. (Md. affiliate), Svc. award Md. Gen. Hosp., Svc. award Good Samaritan Hosp., Disting. Physician award Sinai Hosp.; Cardiology tchg. scholar Hopkins/Sinai Internal Med. Program. Fellow Am. Coll. Physicians, Am. Coll. Cardiology; mem. Am. Coll. Cardiology (Md. chpt., trustee 1990—), Am. Heart Assn. (Md. affiliate pres. 1971-72), Md. Soc. Cardiology (pres. 1976-78), Balt. City Medical Soc. (pres.-elect 1993-94, 96), Medical & Chirurgical Faculty (pres. 1994-95). Democrat. Jewish. Home: 6103 Ivydene Terrace Baltimore MD 21209 Office: Sinai Hosp Balt Ste 205 Weinberg Bldg 2411 W Belvedere Ave Baltimore MD 21215

DEMBOSKE, RICHARD MICHAEL, trauma nurse; b. Saddle Brook, N.J., Sept. 19, 1962; s. Richard Thomas and Patricia Ann (Mathyas) D.; children: Richard Michael Jr., Victoria Lynn. AAS, County Coll. of Morris, Randolph, N.J., 1992. RN, N.J. Staff nurse U. Medicine and Dentistry, Newark, 1993-95; Tb control nurse Essex County Corrections, Newark, 1995; nurse on cardiac telemetry unit Meadowlands Hosp., Secaucus, N.J., 1995—. With USN, 1980-85. Mem. Am. Legion, N.J. Coun. for Children's Rights, Theta Chi Alumni Assn. Roman Catholic. Home: 268 President St Saddle Brook NJ 07663 Office: Univ Medicine and Dentistry 150 Bergen St Newark NJ 07107-3000

DE MENESES, MARY ROADES, assistant dean; b. Alton, Ill., Apr. 16, 1939; d. Charles Franklin and Eunice Lorea (Nolan) Roades; m. William C. Meneses, July 31, 1973; children: Luis Alberto, Daniel William. BS in Nursing, DePaul U., 1970, MA in Edn., 1973, MS in Nursing, 1975; EdD, Northern Ill. U., 1982. RN, MO. Emergency room nurse St. Luke's Hosp., St. Louis, 1960-61; ICU nurse Our Lady of Lourdes Hosp., Binghampton, N.Y., 1961-64; evening nursing supr. St. Joseph's Hosp., Alton, 1964-65, head nurse, 1965-66; med. surg. nurse St. Joseph's Hosp., Chgo., 1966-67, head nurse, 1967-69; instr. med. surg. nursing Michael Reese Med. Ctr., Chgo., 1969-74; from instr. to assoc. prof. sch. nursing DePaul U., Chgo., 1974-81, assoc. prof. sch. nursing, 1981-82; assoc. prof. sch. nursing So. Ill. U., Edwardsville, Ill., 1982-89; prof. sch. nursing So. Ill. U., Edwardsville, 1989—; coord. grad. programs sch. nursing So. Ill. U., Edwardsville, 1985-92, asst. project dir. Project GAIN, 1989-92, asst. project dir. nurse anesthesia, 1992-95, acting assoc. dean academic affairs, 1994-95, assoc. dean ednl. svcs., 1996—; cons. local and regional law firms, 1983—, VA Hosps., St. Louis, 1985—, Alzheimer's Disease Rsch. Ctr. Wash. U. Sch. Medicine, 1990; tutor Illinois League Nursing, 1978-79; lectr. Ill. Trauma Nurses Assn., 1977-79; mem. obstetrical task force So. Ill. Med. Assn., 1990-91; presenter, rschr. in field. Co-author: (with N. Pinnell) Nursing process: Theory, application and related processes, 1986; guest reviewer (textbooks) Prentice-Hall, 1984, Brady Book Co., 1985, (books) F.A. Davis Co., 1988, W.B. Saunders Co., 1991, 92, 93, (market rsch. project) Oncology Nursing Soc., 1990; reviewer Midwest Nursing Rsch. Soc., 1987, 88, 92, 96, Sigma Theta Tau Internat., 1995; mem. rev. panel Am. Jour. Nursing, 1988, Focus on Critical Care, 1988-90, editl. bd., 1990-94; item writer C.V. Mosby Company, 1986—, N.Y. Regent's Coll. Examination in Adult Nursing, 1987; contbr. 20 chpts. to books, articles to profl. pubs. Mem. adv. bd. NBC-TV Health Fair '80, 1979-81; mem. East St. Louis, Ill. Housing Authority Consortium, 1993—, Cmty. Edn., 1993—, task force, 1993—; mem. Hosp. Sys. Agency DuPage County, Ill., 1977-82. Danforth scholar Danforth Found., 1957-60; grantee HHS, 1983-86, 89-91, HECA, 1991, 92. Mem. ANA (coun. nurse rschrs, coun. nurse educators), AACN (So. Ill. Chpt. treas. 1983-85, bd. dirs., pub. com., bylaws com., chair ways and means com. 1983-86), Ill. Nurses Assn. (delegate, 1982-85, coun. nurse educators sec., exec. com. 1994-95), MidAmerica Regional Nursing Diagnosis Special Interest Group, (chair rsch. com. 1983-85), Midwest Nursing Rsch. Soc., Oncology Nursing Soc., Am. Heart Assn. (Ill. Affiliate cmty. edn. com. 1993-96, chair programs com. 1994-96, So. Madison County bd. dirs. 1984-90, sec. 1988-90, chair program com. 1988-90), Am. Cancer Soc., Ill. Alliance for Aging, 10th Dist. Nurses' Assn. (bd. dirs. 1983-87, 93—, bylaws com., alternate senator 1983-87, v.p. 1985-87, student advisor 1993-94, nominating com. 1993-94), DePaul U. Nursing Alumni (pres.-elect 1979-80, pres. 1980-81), DePaul U. Alumni Assn., No. Ill. U. Alumni Assn., So. Ill. U. Med. Assn. (obstetrical task force so. Ill. 1990-91), So. Ill. U. Student Nurses Assn. (faculty advisor 1994-95), Sigma Theta Tau Internat. (Epsilon Eta Chpt. exec. bd. 1983-87, chair eligibility com. 1988-88, chair rsch. day 1989, faculty advisor 1994-96), Kappa Delta Pi, Phi Kappa Phi (nominating com. 1992, chair nominating com. 1994, sec.-treas. 1995—), Sigma Phi Omega, Phi Delta Kappa. Republican. Roman Catholic. Home: 4710 Fantasy Ln Alton IL 62002 Office: So Ill Univ Sch Nursing Box 1066 Edwardsville IL 62026

DEMENT, WILLIAM CHARLES, sleep researcher, medical educator; b. Wenatchee, Wash., July 29, 1928; s. Charles Frederick and Kathryn (Severyns) D.; m. Eleanor Weber, Mar. 23, 1956; children: Catherine Lynn, Elizabeth Anne, John Nicholas. B.S., U. Wash., 1951; M.D., U. Chgo., 1955, Ph.D., 1957. Bd. cert. in clin. polysomography. Intern Mt. Sinai Hosp., N.Y.C., 1957-58, research fellow dept. psychiatry, 1958-63; assoc. prof. dept. psychiatry and behavioral scis. Stanford U., 1963-67, prof., 1967—; dir. Stanford Sleep Disorders Clinic and Lab., 1970—, Sleep Research Lab., Stanford, Calif., 1963—; chmn. U.S. Surgeon Gen.'s Joint Coord. Coun., Project Sleep, 1979—, Nat. Commn. on Sleep Disorders Rsch., 1990-92. Author: Some Must Watch While Some Must Sleep, 1972, The Sleep Watchers, 1992; editor-in-chief: Sleep, 1977—; mem. editorial bd. Neurobiology of Aging, 1982—. Recipient medal Intra-Sci. Research Found., 1981; recipient Disting. Service award U. Chgo. Med. Alumni Assn., 1978. Mem. Sleep Research Soc. (founder), Assn. Sleep Disorders Ctrs. (pres. 1982 Nathaniel Kleitman prize), Inst. Medicine of Nat. Acad. Scis., Psychiat. Research Found., Soc. Neurosci., Western EEG Soc., Am. EEG Soc., Am. Physiol. Soc. Office: Stanford Sleep Disorders Ctr 701 Welch Rd Ste 2226 Palo Alto CA 94304-1709

DEMENTI, BRIAN ARMSTEAD, toxicologist; b. Richmond, Va., Mar. 3, 1938; s. Frank Armstead and Connie Mae (Sims) D.; m. Patricia Ann Long, Jan. 21, 1967; children: Briana Carol, Frank Dorset. BS in Chemistry, Hampden-Sydney Coll., 1960; MS in Chemistry, U. Richmond, 1964; PhD in Biochemistry, Med. Coll. Va., 1977. Diplomate Am. Bd. Toxicology. Sci. tchr. Henrico County Pub. Sch. System, Richmond, Va., 1967-68; polymer chemist Allied Chem. Corp., Colonia Heights, Va., 1968-73; regulatory toxicologist Va. State Health Dept., Richmond, 1977-80; biochemist A.H. Robins Pharm. Co., Richmond, 1980-82; biochemist/toxicologist cons. Richmond, 1982-84; regulatory toxicologist U.S. EPA, Washington, 1984—; pres. Toxicol. and Environ. Cons. Svc., Richmond, 1982—. Contbr. articles to profl. jours.; patentee in field. Chmn. bd. deacons Lakeside Presbyn. Ch., Richmond, 1973, elder, 1974—, adult tchr. Sun. sch., 1978—. Med. Coll. Va. grantee, 1976. Mem. Am. Chem. Soc., Soc. for Occupational and Environ. Health, Soc. for Risk Analysis, Sigma Xi. Republican. Presbyterian. Home: 7519 Oakmont Dr Richmond VA 23228-3726 Office: US EPA 401 M St SW Washington DC 20460-0001

DEMEO, WILLIAM JOSEPH, social worker, educator; b. Waltham, Mass., Jan. 11, 1950; s. Joseph Anthony and Nora Jane (Carresi) D.; m. Mary Elizabeth Martel; children: Alexander, Sarah, Katherine. BA, U. Mass., 1971; MSW, U. Md., 1973; D Social Work, Cath U. Am., 1990. Lic. social worker, Md., D.C. Clin. social worker Family Svcs. of Montgomery County, Gaithersburg, Md., 1973-78; supr. social work Family Svcs. of Prince Georges County, Lanham, Md., 1974-79; pvt. practice clin. social work Washington, 1978—; psychiat. social worker George Washington U. Hosp., Washington, 1982-86; E.A.P. counselor Brownlee Dolan & Stein Assoc., Washington, 1986-89; mem. adj. faculty Nat. Cath. Sch. Social Svc., Washington, 1987-89, Va. Commonwealth U. Sch. Social Work, 1991-92; cons. Cope, Inc., Washington, 1986-90. Mem. Nat. Assn. Social Workers (chmn. com. on inquiry and grievances Washington Met. chpt. 1981-84), Acad. Cert. Social Workers. Office: 5255 Connecticut Ave NW # 311 Washington DC 20015-1813

DEMERS, MARLENE A., health facility inspector; b. Lowell, Mass., Sept. 30, 1951; d. Edward A. and Bernice G. (Anderson) Perry; m. Andrew M. Demers Jr., Oct. 10, 1968; children: Edward P., Jennifer E. ADN, N.H. Tech. Inst., 1978; BS in Human Svc. Administrn., N.H. Coll., 1983; MS in Psychology, Springfield Coll., 1990. RN, Mass. PSRO coord. N.H. Found. for Med. Care, Dover, 1981-83; utilization rev. coord. Nashua (N.H.) Meml. Hosp., 1983-84; dir. nursing Casa Grande LTCF, Tewksbury, Mass., 1984-85; nurse mgr. DUI unit Tewksbury Hosp., 1985-86; clin. dir. Habit Mgmt., Lowell, Mass., 1987-88; psychiat. nurse Solomon Mental Health Ctr., Lowell, 1988-89; dir. quality assurance Erich Lindemann Mental Health Ctr., Boston, 1989—; health care facility insp. Dept. Pub. Health, Boston, 1993—. Mem. ANA, NAFE, Mass. Nurses Assn., Nat. Soc. DAR. Home: 3 Castle Hill Rd Pelham NH 03076-2102

DEMETS, DAVID L., medical educator, biomedical researcher; b. Austin, Minn., Nov. 27, 1944; married; 2 children. BA in Math., Gustavus Adolphus Coll., St. Peter, Minn., 1966; MS in Biostats., U. Minn., 1968, PhD in Biostats., 1970. Statistician, divsn. computer rsch. and tech. NIH, Bethesda, Md., 1970-72, math. statistician, Nat. Heart, Lung and Blood Inst., 1973-79, chief, mathematical and applied statistics br., 1979-82; dir. biostats. Ctr., prof. stats. and biostats. U. Wis., Madison, 1982-91, assoc. dir. Clin. Cancer Ctr., 1982-91, chair dept. biostats., prof. stats. and biostats., 1991—, assoc. dir. Comprehensive Cancer Ctr., 1991—; lectr., cons. in field; bd. scientific counselors Nat. Cancer Inst., 1993—. Co-author: Fundamentals of Clinical Trials, 1981, 2d edit. 1985, 3d edit. 1995; contbr. numerous articles to profl. jours., chpts. to books; presenter in field; mem. adv. bd. jour. Controlled Clin. Trials, 1993—, editl. bd. 1994—; assoc. editor Jour. Clin. Rsch. and Drug Devel., 1987-90. Recipient Disting. Alumni award Gustavus Adolphus Coll., 1990, Gaylord Anderson Leadership award U. Minn. Sch. Pub. Health Alumni Soc., 1993. Fellow Am. Statis. Assn. (bd. dirs. 1987-89), Internat. Statis. Inst.; mem. Biometrics Soc. (regional adv. bd. 1975-77, 80-82, exec. com. Ea. N.Am. region 1992-94, pres. 1993), Soc. for Controlled Clin. Trials (bd. dirs. 1983-87, program com. 1984, 85, program chmn. 1988, v.p. 1988-89, pres. 1989-90, joint program com. with Internat. Soc. Clin. Biostats., Brussels, 1991, policy com. 1993—), Internat. Soc. Clin. Biostats. Office: U Wis Clin Science Ctr Dept Biostatistics 600 Highland Ave Madison WI 53792*

DE MEYER, JOSEPH ALEXANDRE AUGUST, clinical psychologist; b. Amsterdam, Netherlands, June 13, 1950; came to U.S., 1977; s. Joseph François and Constance Maria (van Delft) de M.; m. Elizabeth Maria Meijers, Feb. 17, 1978 (div. 1993); children—Robert Joseph, Melanie Constance; m. Sophie Bramoullé, Jan. 14, 1995; 1 child, Ilka Marine Bramoullé-Phillips. Doctoral degree State U. Leyden (Netherlands), 1977. Clin. psychologist Retreat Hosp., Decatur, Ala., 1977-80; clin. dir. North Central Ala. Mental Health Center, Decatur, 1980-83; dir adult outpatient psychiatry, 1985-86; dir. child and adolescent psychiatry Jersey City Med. Ctr. (N.J.), 1984-88 ; pvt. practice, 1984—; attending psychologist Chilton Meml. Hosp.; supr. Washington Square Inst., N.Y.C.; adj. prof. Am. Inst. Psychotherapy, Huntsville, Ala., 1981-83; candidate William Alanson White Inst., N.Y.C., 1983-87 . Cert. psychoanalyst N.Y.C., N.J.; Lic. psychologist, N.J. Mem. Am. Psychol. Assn., N.J. Psychol. Assn., William Alanson White Psychoanalytic Soc., Netherlands Inst. Psychologists, N.J. Psychologists in Pvt. Practice. Home: 15 W 73d St New York NY 10023 Office: 1330 Hamburg Tpk Wayne NJ 07470

DEMICK, JACK, psychologist; b. Hartford, Conn., May 18, 1952; s. Joel Yale and Jayne Katherine (Distefano) D.; m. Joan Kellerman, Aug. 30, 1981; children: Kate Kellerman-Demick, Daniel Kellerman-Demick. AB, Yale U., 1974; MA, Clark U., Worcester, Mass., 1977, PhD, 1981. Lic. psychologist, Mass. Chief psychology Fuller Meml. Hosp., South Attleboro, Mass., 1982-84; lectr. psychology Harvard U., Cambridge, Mass., 1985-89; rsch. assoc. Clark U., Worcester, 1984—, assoc. prof., 1986-89; assoc. prof. and chair Suffolk U., Boston, 1989-94, prof. and chair dept. psychology, 1994—; cons. Clark U., 1987-90; pvt. practice clin. psychology, Sharon, Mass., 1982—; co-organizer 4th Japan-U.S. Seminar on Environment-Behavior Relations, Worcester, 1995. Editor Jour. of Adult Devel., 1992—; editor: Parental Development, 1993, Development in Workplace, 1993; contbr. articles to profl. jours. AARP Rsch. grantee, 1995—, NSF grantee, 1995. Mem. APA, Soc. for Rsch. in Child Devel., Am. Psychol. Soc., Psychonomic Soc., Soc. for Psychol. Study of Social Issues, Ea. Psychol. Assn. (local arrangements chair 1991—). Democrat. Jewish. Office: Suffolk Univ Dept Psychology 41 Temple St Boston MA 02114

DEMIDOWICH, GEORGE, cardiologist; b. Buenos Aires, Oct. 18, 1949; came to U.S., 1960; s. Paul and Nadia Demydowycz; m. Christine R. Romaniw, June 3, 1978; children: Andrew, Lisa. BS, CCNY, 1971; MD, N.Y. Med. Coll., 1975. Diplomate Am. Bd. Internal Medicine, Cardiovascular Diseases. Intern Northshore Hosp./Sloan Kettering Cancer Ctr., Manhasset, N.Y., 1975-76; resident Northshore Hosp./Sloan Kettering Cancer Ctr., 1976-78; fellow in cardiology Beth Israel Med. Ctr., Newark, 1978-80; cardiologist Cardiovascular Cons. N.J., Livingston, 1980—; dir. Cardiac Rehab. St. Barnabas Med. Ctr., Livingston, 1992—. Fellow Am. Coll. Cardiology; mem. AMA, N.J. Med. Soc., Essex County Med. Soc. Office: Cardiovascular Cons N J 340 E Northfield Rd Livingston NJ 07039

DEMLING, ROBERT HUGH, surgeon, researcher; b. Grand Rapids, Mich., July 17, 1943; s. Gerry James and Margaret Helen (Boucher) D.; m. Patricia Ann Huber, Nov. 6, 1971; children: Jill, Kate. BS, Notre Dame U., 1965; MD, Med. Coll. Wis., 1969. Diplomate Am. Bd. Surgeons (cons. 1986—). Intern U. Calif., San Francisco, 1969, resident, 1970-76; dir. Burn Ctr. U. Wis., Madison, 1976-79, U. Calif., Davis, 1979-82; prof. surgery Harvard Med. Sch., Boston, 1982—; dir. Burn-Trauma Ctr. Brigham and Women's Hosp., Boston, 1982; dir. Longwood Area Trauma Ctr., Boston, 1982—; cons. NIH, 1984—. Author: 2 books; contbr. numerous articles to profl. publs. Mem. ACS (chmn. pre and post operation care com. 1987—), Univ. Surgeons (treas. 1986-89), Am. Burn Assn. (program chair 1990-94, pres. 1994-95). Republican. Roman Catholic. Home: 15 Bakers Hill Rd Weston MA 02193-1708 Office: Longwood Area Trauma Ctr 75 Francis St Boston MA 02115-6110

DEMONTIGNEY, JAMES MORGAN, health services administrator; b. Wilkes-Barre, Pa., Aug. 2, 1947; s. James DeMontigney and Elizabeth Morgan-DeMontigney; m. Sharon Ann Frake-DeMontigney, Dec. 11, 1971; children: Rachelle Ann, Marc James. BA in Polit. Sci., U. Tenn., 1969, MSW, 1975. Caseworker Burlington County Welfare, Mt. Holly, N.J., 1969-71; parole officer N.J. Bur. Parole, Trenton, 1971; social worker N.J. Divsn. Pub. Welfare, Hamilton Township, 1971-73. N.J. Divsn. Youth and Family Svcs., Trenton, 1973, 75-78; casework supr. N.J. Divsn. Youth and Family Svcs., Camden, 1981-83; rsch. assoc. Bur. Rsch. N.J. Divsn. Youth and Family Svcs., Trenton, 1983-85, standards and procedures technician, 1986-87; social worker N.J. Divsn. Med. Assistance and Health Svcs., Trenton, 1978-79, social work supr., 1979-81; field svc. supr. N.J. Divsn. Med. Assistance and Health Svcs., Woodbury, 1987; program devel. specialist office of home care programs N.J. Divsn. Med. Assistance and Health Svcs., Trenton, N.J., 1987—; with Mathematica Policy Rsch. Inc., Princeton, N.J., 1996. Mem. Mt. Holly (N.J.) Twp. Rep. Com., 1983—, chmn., 1985—; mcpl. coord. Reagan for Pres. Campaign, Mt. Holly, 1984, Bush for Pres. Campaign, Mt. Holly, 1988, 92, Saxton for Congress Campaign, Mt. Holly, 1988, 90, 92, 94, Smith, Sosa, Anderson Campaign, Mt. Holly, 1991; phonebank coord. Kean for Gov. Campaign, Burlington County, N.J., 1985; mcpl. coord. Whitman for Gov. Campaign, 1993; mem. Mt. Holly Twpl. Planning Bd., 1986-93, chmn. 1990-96; mem. Mt. Holly Bd. Ethics, 1986-92; bd. dirs. Strength to Love, Inc., Mt. Holly, 1992-96. Mem. Comm. Workers Am., Mt. Holly Twp. Rep. Club (charter mem. 1983—, pres. 1984, 89, 90, 91). Home: 305 Ridgway St Mount Holly NJ 08060-1443 Office: NJ Divsn Med Assistance Cn # 712 Trenton NJ 08060

DEMOREST, ALLAN FREDERICK, retired psychologist; b. Omaha, Dec. 20, 1931; s. Byron Peter and Minerva Gladys (Heine) D.; 1 child, Steven M. BA, U. Omaha, 1957; MA, U. Mich., 1959, postgrad., 1960. Lic. psychologist, Iowa, Nat. Register Health Svc. Providers. Counselor Mayor's Com. on Skid Row Problems, Detroit, 1959-61; psychologist Macomb County Schs., Mt. Clemens, Mich., 1961-64; chief psychologist Jasper County Mental Health Ctr., Newton, Iowa, 1964-68; exec. dir. North Cen. Iowa Mental Health Ctr., Ft. Dodge, 1968-75; pvt. practice Ft. Dodge, 1968-85; psychologist Iowa Luth. Hosp., Des Moines, 1985-87; clin. dir. United Behavioral Systems, Des Moines, 1987-94, sr. psychologist, 1994-96; cons. pvt. practice, Des Moines, 1996—; cons. psychologist Des Moines, 1996—; adj. prof. psychology Buena Vista Coll., Ft. Dodge, 1974-85. Contbr. articles on rational therapy to profl. jours. Founding bd. dirs. Rape and Sexual Assault Victim Program, Ft. Dodge, 1976-85, Family Violence Ctr., Ft. Dodge, 1976-85, Youth Shelter Svcs., Ft. Dodge, 1979. With U.S. Army, 1952-54, Korea. Recipient appreciation award Community Mental Health Ctrs. Assn., 1968, community svc. award Iowa Dept. Human Svcs., 1985. Fellow Inst. Rational Psychotherapy; mem. Am. Psychol. Assn., Midwestern Psychol. Assn., Iowa Psychol. Assn., Adminstrv. Mgmt. Soc. (pres. Ft. Dodge 1979-80, 84-85), Iowa Assn. for Advancement Psychology (pres. 1984, Appreciation award 1988), Elks (Exalted Ruler 1979). Home and Office: 4225 Hickman Rd Des Moines IA 50310-3334

DEMPSEY, BARBARA MATTHEA, medical, surgical and critical care nurse; b. The Netherlands, July 27, 1943; d. Petrus Antonius and Hendrika Petronella (Kemp) Petersen; m. James D. Dempsey, June 13, 1981; children: Jennifer, Daniel. AA, Santa Monica (Calif.) Coll., 1970; cert. lactation educator, UCLA, 1982. Staff nurse med./surg. Santa Monica Hosp., 1967-72; surg. intensive care nurse VA Wadsworth Hosp., L.A., 1973-77; staff nurse med./surg. Community Hosp., Santa Rosa, Calif., 1988-90; staff nurse Redwood Nurses Registry, Santa Rosa, 1990-93, Norrell Healthcare, Santa Rosa, Calif., 1990-93; charge nurse Creekside Convalescent Hosp., 1994; ret., 1994.

DEMPSEY, CAROLE L., pharmaceuticals company executive; b. Phila., June 10, 1940; d. Herbert and Dorothy (McCoy) Lomax; children: Alexander P. Martinez, Christopher S. Martinez. BA, Vassar Coll., 1961; MA, Columbia U., 1965. From med. interviewer to exec. dir. health care policy Sandoz Pharms., East Hanover, N.J., 1965-95; cons. Medipharmix, San Louis Opisbo, 1995—; alt. delivery sys. subcom. Nat. Pharm. Coun. Bd. dirs. Laguna Lakes Homeowners Assn., San Luis Obispo, Calif., 1995. Mem. Pharm. Mfrs. Assn., Health Care Bus. Women's Assn. Office: Medipharmix 1817 Gathe Dr San Luis Obispo CA 93405

DEMPSEY, DANIEL THOMAS, surgeon, educator; b. Cambridge, N.Y., Mar. 30, 1953; s. Harry Francis and Jennie (Vairo) D.; m. Barbara Ann Seneca, Oct. 19, 1975; 1 child, Patrick. AB, Princeton U., 1975; MD, U. Rochester, 1979. Resident surgery U. Pa., Phila., 1979-86, lectr. surgery, 1987-88; assoc. prof. surgery Temple U., Phila., 1986-87, 88—. Office: Temple U Hosp Broad And Ontario St Philadelphia PA 19104

DEMPSEY, RAYMOND LEO, JR., radio and television producer, moderator, writer; b. Providence, June 18, 1949; s. Raymond Leo Sr. and Louise Veronica (Gambuto) D.; m. Patricia Batchelder (div. 1984); children: Joab, Jahdeam, Deezsha, Nathaniel, Talitha. BA in Liberal Arts, R.I. Coll., 1973; Cert. in Bus., U. R.I., 1979; cert., Blake Computer Programming Inst., 1977, Billy Graham Sch. Evangelism, 1989. Lic. real estate agt., R.I.; lic. radio sta. operator FCC; cert. secondary tchr., videographer, contractor, R.I. Writer local and nat. publs., 1980—; producer, moderator Chapter & Verse TV, RICA-TV, Providence, 1983—; tchr. R.I. Pub. High Schs., Providence and Cranston, 1988—; producer, moderator radio programs Ch. Focus and People, WRIB AM Radio, East Providence, R.I., 1989—; bd. dirs. Blessing, Inc., Providence; spl. corr. Songtime U.S.A. Radio Network, 1988—, spl. reporter, spl. contbr., 1991; host Straight Talk, Sta. WKRI, 1989, dir. World Exch., 1991-93; co-host The Bible Answer Program, Sta. WARV, 1986; judge The Ace Awards, 1992, Cable Ace Awards, 1992; interviewer Gallup Poll, 1987; trainee N.E. Law Enforcement Officers Assn., 1991; elector Radio Hall of Fame, 1993, Stellar Awards, 1993; nursing asst. nursing homes, R.I., 1979; pvt. nurse's asst. R.I. Hosp., 1979; patient attendant R.I. Mental Hosp.; papers placed in permanent reference res. Brit. Libr., London, N.Y.C. Pub. Libr., Libr. Congress, Washington; donated reference libr. U. Steubenville, Ohio, 1995. Bd. dirs. R.I. Right to Life, Cranston, 1973—; witness R.I. Gen. Assembly, 1973—, R.I. Bd. Health, 1973—; vol. ARC, R.I. Hosp.; registrar voters State of R.I., 1980, 91, 92; del. Rep. Nat. Conv. 1980; sponsor World Vision, Pasadena, Calif., 1981—, Compassion Internat., Colo. Springs, Colo., 1989—; chief boys instr. karate Mattson Acad., Providence, 1968-71; mem. Providence Sci. Outreach of Brown U.; del. Gov.'s Conf. on Libr. and Info. Svcs., 1991; elector White House Conf. on Libr. and Info. Svcs.; Justice of Peace, 1991; regional rep. Students Against Vietnam War, 1971, Taxpayers Action Network, 1991; ptnr. Food for the Hungry, 1984—; del. Ellen McCormack for Pres., 1976; vol. U.S. Fish and Wildlife Svc.; elected Rep. City Com. and Rep. State Ctrl. Com.; chmn. Issues and Rsch. Com. Rep. party Providence. Named One of Top 4 Local Cable TV Prodrs. in Nation, Nat. Assn. Local Cable Programming, 1987, ofcl. Jerusalem Pilgrim, State of Israel, 1990, Ptnr. in Philanthropy, 1995; recipient 2 Internat. Angel awards for excellence in Cable TV presentations, 1991, cert. U.S. SBA, 1990, Diamond award, 1992, 1st prize for excellence in pub. affairs in R.I. and Mass., 1992, Achievement award Dale Carnegie Orgn., 1992, 1st pl. award Mastermedia: The Spotlight award, 1993; nominated for J.C. Penney Golden Rule award. Mem. AAAS, ASCD, NRA, Am. Math. Soc., Coll. Sci. Tchrs., Sons Union Vets., Nat. Assn. H.S. Tchrs. English, Evangel. Theol. Soc., Soc. for Coll. Tchrs., Nat. Assn. Edn. of Young Children, Nat. Assn. Tchg. Sci., Am. Soc. Oriental Rsch., Archaeol. Inst. Am., R.I. Assn. for Edn. Young Children, R.I. Assn. for Supervision and Curriculum Devel., Mental Health Assn. R.I., N.Y. Acad. Scis., Internat. Press Assn. (founding mem.), Nat. Geog. Soc., Nat. Assn. Broadcasters, Nat. Assn. Radio Talk Show Hosts, Nat. Acad. Cable Programming, Near East Archaeol. Soc., Internat. Platform Assn., Nat. Assn. Tchrs. Sci., Jewish TV Inst. (charter), Smithsonian Air and Space Mus., Smithsonian Instn. (assoc.), Royal Inst. Pub. Health and Hygiene London (affiliate), Bread for the World, Evangs. for Social Action, Mus. Heritage Soc., Interscholastic Inst., Libr. Co. Phila., John Russell Bartlett Soc. (Brown U.), Intertel, Mensa, USCG Aux., Golden Key, Abraham Lincoln Soc., Internet Soc., Rel. Heritage Am., Providence Athenaeum, Toastmasters Internat., R.I. Pilots Assn., Phi Theta Kappa. Home and Office: PO Box 41000 Providence RI 02940-1000

DEMPSEY, SAMUEL JOHNS, plastic surgeon; b. Chgo., Jan. 20, 1966; s. Bertholde and Ernestine D.; m. Donna Loveland, Aug. 24, 1996. BS, U. Calif., Berkeley; MD, U. Calif., San Francisco. Diplomate Am. Bd. Plastic Surgery. Intern Kings County Hosp., Seattle, 1989-90, resident surgery, 1990-91; resident in plastic surgery U Wash. Hosps., Seattle, 1991-92; staff Valley Ridge Hosp., Seattle, 1992—; with Werik Surgical and Assoc., Seattle, 1993-; prof. surgery Seattle U. Author: Cuts Like A Knife, 1992; cntbr. numerous articles to profl. jours. AMA, Surgeons Assn. Am. Office: Werik Surgical and Assoc 992 Perry Hwy Seattle WA 98101

DEMUTH, BARBARA R., health facility administrator; b. Waynesburg, Pa., Apr. 6, 1949; d. Oliver S. and Irene P. (Phillips) Robson; m. Jack B. Demuth, June 27, 1971; 1 child, Jennifer. BSN, W.Va. Wesleyan Coll., 1971; MSN, Pa. State U., 1976. Instr. health-related svcs. Hiram Andrews Ctr., Johnstown, Pa.; pub. health nurse II Pa. Dept. Health, Somerset; nurse instr. II Pa. Dept. Health/Mercy Hosp., Johnstown; dir. of nursing Am. Red Cross, Johnstown; mem. adv. bd. to Gov. Pa. Cardiovascular Risk Reduction; instr. Profl. Edn. of RNs.; nursing subject matter expert on mfg. and computer standardization project ARC, Washington; cons. Critical Care Assocs.; speaker in field. Cons. Am. Lung Assn.'s Black Lung Clinics tng. program. Mem. Am. Assn. Blood Banks, Sigma Theta Tau. Home: 194 Orlando St Johnstown PA 15905-4723

DENAMUR, THOMAS JOSEPH, dentist; b. Green Bay, Wis., Aug. 20, 1950; s. Lloyd Francis and Muriel Janet (Delfosse) DeN.; m. Lynn Marie Vetter, Aug. 26, 1972; children: Christopher Thomas, Nicole Lynn. BS in Chemistry, St. Norbet Coll., 1972; DDS, Marquette U., 1976. Lic. dentist, Wis. Gen. practice dentistry Algoma, Wis., 1976—; cons. dentist Algoma Meml. Hosp., 1985-86. Contbr. articles to profl. jours. Mem. Concerned Citizens Com. St. Mary's Ch., 1982, Algoma Citizens Together, 1984. Fellow Acad. Gen. Dentistry; mem. Am. Equilibration Soc., Soc. Occlusal Studies, Wis. Dental Assn. (alternate del. 1986), Bay Lakes Dental Soc., Chgo., Brown Door Kewanee Dental Soc. (bd. dirs. 1983-86, peer rev. com. 1984-86), Chgo Dental Soc. (assoc.), Am. Assn. Functional Orthodontists (Hon. Mention Case Solvers 1986), Omicron Kappa Soc. Lodges: Algoma Optimists (v.p. 1979-80, pres. 1980-81, Honor Club mem. 1981, Disting. Pres. 1981). Home: 520 Ohio St Algoma WI 54201-1451 Office: 800 Jefferson St Algoma WI 54201-1734

DENARO, ANTHONY THOMAS, psychiatrist; b. N.Y.C., Aug. 9, 1929; s. Joseph and Maria (DeGennaro) Denaro; m. Mitsuru Suzuki, Nov. 23, 1963. BS, CCNY, 1960; MD, U. Okla., 1969; MPA, U. Hartford, 1981. Diplomate Nat. Bd. Med. Examiners, Am. Bd. Psychiatry, Am. Bd. Gen. Psychiatry and Child Psychiatry, Adminstrv. Psychiatry. Intern Nassau County Med. Ctr., East Meadow, N.Y., 1969-70; resident in child psychiatry U. Pa., Phila., 1970-72, resident in gen. psychiatry, 1972-74; dir. child psychiatry U. Conn. Health Ctr., Farmington, 1974-78; dir. adolescent unit Natchaug Psychiat. Hosp., Willamantic, Conn., 1978-80; assoc. dir. child and adolescent service Mt. Sinai Hosp., Hartford, Conn., 1980-82; assoc. dir. child and adolescent psychiatry Elmcrest Psychiat. Inst., Portland, Conn., 1982-84; dir. outpatient psychiatry Woodhull Med. and Mental Health Ctr., N.Y.C., 1984-85; dir. child and adolescent psychiatry First Hosp. Wyoming Valley, Wilkes-Barre, Pa., 1985—; asst. prof. dept. psychiatry U. Conn. Sch. Medicine, Farmington, 1974-83. With U.S. Army, 1947-49. Fellow Am. Acad. Child and Adolescent Psychiatry; mem. AMA, Am. Psychiat. Assn., Am. Assn. Psychiat. Adminstrs., Northeastern Pa. Psychiat. Soc. (pres. 1990-91), Phi Beta Kappa. Republican. Office: First Hosp Wyoming Valley 149 Dana St Wilkes Barre PA 18702-4825

DENEGRI, GUILLERMO MARIA, parasitologist, educator; b. Puan, Buenos Air, Argentina, Dec. 8, 1956; s. Guillermo Ambrosio Felipe and Raquel Antonia (Rosell) D.; m. Maria Luisa Romero, Nov. 11, 1985; 1 child, Laura Beatriz. Lic. of Zoology, Natural Scis., La Plata, Buenos Aires, 1982, D of Natural Scis., 1987, Lic. of Philosophy, 1991. Fellow Coun. Sci. Rsch. Argentina, La Plata/Buenos Aires, 1983-89, researcher, 1989-90; fellow Internat. Soc. Hydatidology, Madrid, 1991—; asst. prof. dept. parasitology/vet. sci., La Plata, 1987; prin. prof. Method of Sci. Univ. of Belgrano, Buenos Aires, 1990; vis. prof. U. Alcala, Spain, 1992-95. Recipient Cordero del Campillo prize Pamplona, Spain, 1993. Mem. Platense Epistemology Assn. (pres. 1986-90), Argentina Soc. Parasitology (v.p. 1989-92, titular mem. 1994), Internat. Soc. Hidatidology (titular mem. 1991). Home: Calle 45 N 491, P3 Dept E, 1900 Buenos Aires Argentina Office: 60 y 118, Sch of Veterinary Scis, 1900 Buenos Aires Argentina

DENENBERG, HERBERT SIDNEY, health association administrator, journalist, lawyer, former state official; b. Omaha, Nov. 20, 1929; s. David Aaron and Fannie (Rothenberg) D.; m. Naomi N. Glushakow, June 22, 1958. BS, Johns Hopkins U., 1958; JD, Creighton U., 1954; LLM, Harvard U., 1959; PhD, U. Pa., 1962; LLD, Allentown Coll. St. Francis de Sales, 1989; LHD, Spring Garden Coll., 1992. CLU; CPCU. Mem. firm Denenberg & Denenberg, Omaha, 1954-55; asst. prof. ins. U. Iowa, Iowa City, 1962; asst. prof. ins. Wharton Sch. Fin. and Commerce, U. Pa., 1962-65, assoc. prof., 1965-68, Harry J. Loman prof. ins., 1968-73; commr. ins. State of Pa., 1971-74; commr. Pa. Pub. Utility Commn., 1975; columnist Phila. Bull., 1975-79; consumer columnist Phila. Daily News, 1979-81, Phila. Jour., 1981-82, Del. County Daily and Sunday Times, 1987-90, Bucks County Courier Times, 1987-90, Pottstown Mercury, 1988-94, Burlington County Daily Times, 1987-90, Reading Eagle, 1989—, Doylestown Patriot, 1991—, Citizen's Choice of Wilkes-Barre, Pa., 1992—, Mainliner, 1992-94, Auto Insider, 1992-93, Collector's Guide, 1992-93, New Chester Jour., 1992—, Del. County Bus. Monthly, 1993—, Hellenic News, 1993—, 1994; consumer columnist Phoenixville, Phoenix, 1994—; consumer and investigative reporter Sta. WCAU-TV (NBC), Phila., 1975—; talk show host Sta. WCAU-AM CBS, Phila., 1976-80; columnist Sales and Mktg. Mag., 1976-80; regular on Real People, NBC-TV, 1979-80; consumer reporter Nat. Public Radio, 1979; Spl. counsel, rsch. dir. Pres.'s Nat. Adv. Panel on Ins. in Riot-Affected Areas., 1967-68; spl. adviser to Gov. Pa. on consumer affairs, 1974-75; assoc. dir. Wis. Ins. Laws Rev. Project, 1966-71; cons. Dept. Labor, 1965-68, Coop. Devel. Adminstrn. P.R., 1967-68, John F. Kennedy Ctr., Washington, 1966-71, Small Bus. Adminstrn., 1968-71, Dept. Justice, 1969, FTC, 1968, Dept. Transp., 1969-70, State of Nev., 1969-71; cons. Alaska Legislature, 1976; spl. cons. to Mayor Washington, 1968-69; mem. Bd. of Health Promotion and Disease Prevention of Inst. Medicine, Nat. Acad. Scis., 1973—. Author: (with others) Risk and Insurance, 2d edit, 1973, (with Spencer L. Kimball) Insurance Government and Social Policy, 1969, (with J.R. Ferrari) Life Insurance and/or Mutual Funds, 1967, (with S.L. Kimball) Mass. Marketing of Property and Liability Insurance, 1970, The Insurance Trap, 1972, Shopper's Guide to Surgery, 1972, Shopper's Guide to Dentistry, 1973, Shopper's Guide to Insurance on Mobile Homes, 1973, A Citizens Bill of Hospital Rights, 1973, Shopper's Guide to Bankruptcy, 1974, Shopper's Guide Book, 1974, Herb Denenberg's Smart Shopper's Guide, 1980, Shoppers Guide to Medical Equipment, 1990; columnist, mem. editorial bd. Caveat Emptor, 1971-79; mem. adv. bd. medicine and health newsletter The Dr.'s People, 1989-93. Dem. candidate for U.S. Senate, 1974; mem. adminstrv. bd. S.S. Huebner Found., 1968-71; bd. dirs. Consumers Union, 1973-76; mem. bd. trustees Ctr. for Proper Medication Use, 1994—. 1st lt. JAGC, AUS, 1955-58. Recipient awards for articles Jour. Risk and Ins., Lambert award, 1972, Nat. Press Club award, 1276, 77, 80, 84, 88, Journalism award Am. Osteol. Assn., 1976, Journalism award Am. Chiropractors Assn., 1977-80, 88, citation Columbia U., Media award Am. Trial Lawyers Assn., 1986, Enterprise Reporting award Phila. Press Club, 1986, 87, Grand Pub. Svc. award, 1987, 89, Enterprise Reporting award Pa. Associated Press, 1988, Nat. Headliner award, 1987-88, 90, 92, 28 Emmy awards, Best TV Pub. Svc. award Sigma Delta Chi, 1987, 88, 90, 92, 93, 94, TV Feature award, 1989, 94, 95, TV Mag. Feature award, 1989, 92, Best Media Criticism, 1990, 93, Best Investigation, 1990, 92, 93, 94, 95, Best Health and Sci. Report, 1995, Outstanding Media Consumer Svc. award Consumer Fedn. of Am., 1990, Sam Beber Disting. AZA Alumnus award B'nai B'rith, 1990, Outstanding Citizen award Firemen's Assn. Pa., 1991, Consumer of Yr. award Pa. Assn. Weights and Measures, 1991, Phila. award integrity in journ988; inducted Phila. Press Club Hall of Fame, 1995. Mem. Am. Risk and Ins. Assn. (2nd v.p. 1967-68, bd. dirs. 1967-71, pres. 1969-70), Internat. Assn. Ins. Law (v.p. sci. sect. Am. chpt. 1967-71), Old Clunker Club (founder, pres. 1982—). Home: PO Box 7301 Saint Davids PA 19087-7301 Office: Sta WCAU-TV Philadelphia PA 19131

DENENBERG, VICTOR HUGO, psychology educator; b. Chgo., Apr. 3, 1925; s. Jacob Herman and Gussie (Denenberg) D.; m. Ruth Adele Orner, Aug. 27, 1950 (div. Sept. 1975); children: Carol Faith, Susan Vicki, Nancy Gay, Julie Orner; m. Evelyn B. Thoman, Nov. 1975. B.A., Bucknell U., 1949; M.S., Purdue U., 1951, Ph.D., 1953. Research asso. Human Resources Research Office, Ft. Knox, Ky., 1952-54; from asst. prof. to prof. Purdue U., 1954-69; prof. biobehavioral scis. U. Conn., Storrs, 1969—; cons., writer in field.; Mem. study sect. NIH, 1967-71; mem. com. brain scis. NRC-Nat. Acad. Scis., 1967-73. Served with AUS, 1943-45. Decorated Purple Heart, Combat Inf. badge; NIH spl. fellow Cambridge (Eng.) U., 1963-64. Fellow Am. Psychol. Assn. (exec. com. div. exptl. psychology 1971-74, exec. com. div. comparative and physiol. psychology 1980-83, mem. bd. sci. affairs 1989-92, AAAS (council 1971-75), Animal Behavior Soc.; mem. Internat. Soc. Devel. Psychobiology (pres. 1970). Home: 796 Stafford Rd Storrs Mansfield CT 06268-2023

DÉNES, JÓZSEF, dentist, dental educator; b. Szolnok, Hungary, Jan. 10, 1939; s. József D. and Anna Gajda; m Marianne Gratzer, Sept. 15, 1962; 1 child, Zsolt. DMD, Semmelweis U. Medicine, Hungary, 1963; PhD, Hungarian Acad. Sci., 1973. Prof.'s asst. U. Med. Budapest, 1963-69, asst. lectr., 1969-74, assoc. prof., 1974-80, prof., head dept. pedodontics and orthodontics, 1980—; assoc. dean Semmelweis U. Medicine, Budapest, 1983-86, dean, 1986-92. Author: Gyermekfogászat-fogszabályozás, 1978, 95. Fellow Hungarian Dental Assn. (asst. sec., gen. sec. 1982-86, pres. pedodontics and orthodontics sect., 1992—). Office: Dept Pedondontics and Orthodontics, Mária u 39, 1085 Budapest Hungary

DENES, MICHEL JANET, physical therapist, consultant in rehabilitation; b. Detroit, Apr. 29, 1950; d. Seymore Bernard and Clarine (Stierer) Swartz; m. George Denes, Jan. 22, 1984; 1 child, Zachary Todd. BS in Phys. Therapy, U. Mich., 1972. cert. in phys. therapy; cert. in neuro-devel. treatment in adult hemiplegia. Staff phys. therapist Sinai Hosp. of Detroit, 1972-77, supr., phys. therapist, 1977-78, chief phys. therapy supr., 1979-88; phys. therapist Rehab. Physicians, P.C., Birmingham, Mich., 1989; phys. therapy cons. closed head injury program Spl. Tree Rehab. Sys., Birmingham, 1989—; adj. instr. Wayne State U. Coll. Allied Health Professions, Detroit, 1982-90; lectr. in field. Mem. Neurodevel. Treatment Assn., Am. Acad. Oral Medicine. Office: Spl Tree Rehab Sys Ste 300 2100 E Maple Rd Birmingham MI 48009-6516

DENEV, STEFAN ANGELOV, microbiologist; b. Russe, Bulgaria, Sept. 25, 1954; s. Angel Denev and Katina Nikolovna Atanasova; m. Evangelina Geleva Manafova-Deneva, Mar. 13, 1954; 1 child, Desislava. Grad., U. Zootechnics/Vet. Medicine, Stara Zagora, Bulgaria, 1979, PhD, 1987. Cert. mgr. in animal husbandry. Asst. prof. U. Zootechnics and Vet. Medicine, 1979-90, assoc. prof., 1991—; dept. microbiology, head sect. Thracian U., 1992. Author 75 articles, books, textbooks and guide books; patentee chem. preservative for green fodder, USSR, 1986. Mem. Union of Scientists, N.Y. Acad. of Sci., Am. Soc. Microbiology, Am. Dairy Sci. Assn., Internat. Soc. for Human and Animal Mycology, Am. Biograph. Inst. (rsch. bd. advisors), Bulgarian Soc. Microbiology, European Fedn. Food Sci. and Tech. Home: Bratya Jekovi 38A ap 35, 6000 Stara Zagora Bulgaria Office: Thracian Univ, Dept Microbiology, PO Box 208, 6000 Stara Zagora Bulgaria

DENG, ROSALINE ZHUANG, biologist; b. Beijing, Hebei, People's Republic of China, July 28, 1933; came to U.S., 1980; d. Shu-Qun Deng (S.C. Teng) and Gui-Ling Lou; m. Yaguan Li, Aug. 10, 1963. BS, Shenyang Agrl. Coll., 1954; PhD equivalent, Microbiology Inst. Acad. Sinica, 1961. Rsch. assoc. Microbiology Inst. Acad. Sinica, Beijing, 1961-64, Lab. Mycology, Canton, People's Republic of China, 1964-66, U. Wis. Dept. Botany, Genetics, Madison, 1980-83; rsch. biologist The Upjohn Co., Kalamazoo, 1984—. Author: Entomogenous Fungi and Their Application to Pests Control, 1964, co-author: Edible and Poisonous Mushrooms in China, 1966; contbr. articles to profl. jours. the on cultivating of edible mushrooms. Sr. Rsch. fellow, Guangdong Microbiology Inst., Canton, 1973-79. Office: The Upjohn Co Kalamazoo MI 49001

DENHART, CHARLES FORD, physician; b. Zanesville, Ohio; s. Paul Raymond and Ruth Ann (Ford) D. BA, Hope Coll., 1972; MD, Ohio State U., 1975. Diplomate Am. Bd. Phys. Medicine and Rehab., Am. Bd. Electrodiagnosis. Asst. prof. Ohio State U., Columbus, 1978-79; pvt. practice Des Moines, 1980—; med. dir. Younker Rehab. Ctr., Des Moines, 1992—. Bd. dirs. On With Life, Ankeny, Iowa, 1989-95. Mem. AMA, Am. Acad. Electrodiagnosis, Am. Acad. PM&R. Episcopalian. Office: Younker Rehab Ctr 1200 Pleasant St Des Moines IA 50409

DENIĆ, SRDJAN, oncologist, hematologist; b. Belgrade, Serbia, Yugoslavia, Oct. 28, 1952; came to U.S., 1981; s. Mioljub and Jelena (Simić) D.;m. Danica Nikola Došlov, Dec. 6, 1989; children: Vladimir, Nikolas, Klara. MD, U. Belgrade, 1978. Diplomate Am. Bd. Internal Medicine, Am. Bd. Hematology, Am. Bd. Med. Oncology, Yugoslav Bd. Internal Medicine. Intern U. Hosps. Belgrade, 1979; clin. physician Children's Hosp., U. Belgrade, 1979-81; gen. physician Tjesno, Yugoslavia, 1978; resident, fellow hematology The Bklyn. Jewish Hosp., 1981-85; fellow oncology Mt. Sinai Hosp., N.Y.C., 1985-87; physician Inst. Oncology and Radiology, Belgrade, 1987-88; cons. oncology-hematology Ibn Al-Bitar Hosp., Baghdad, Iraq, 1988-90; pvt. practice oncology-hematology Lewistown (Pa.) Hosp., 1991—. Mem. ACP, ASCO, Internat. Soc. for Study of Comparative Oncology. Mem. Orthodox Ch. Home: 809 Middle Rd Lewistown PA 17044

DENKO, JOANNE D., psychiatrist, writer; b. Kalamazoo, Mich., Mar. 29, 1927; d. John S. and Marian Mildred (Boers) Decker; m. Charles Wasil Denko, June 17, 1950; children: Christopher Charles, Nicholas Charles, Timothey Charles. BA summa cum laude, Hope Coll., 1947; MD, Johns Hopkins U., 1951; MS in Psychiatry, U. Mich., 1963. Lic. psychiatrist Md., Ill, Mich., Ohio. Pvt. practice Columbus, Ohio, 1961-68; staff psychiatrist Fairview Gen. Hosp., Cleve., 1968—; pvt. practice Rocky River, Ohio, 1968—; cons. Juvenile Diagnostic Ctr., Columbus, 1967-68, VA Hosp., Cleve., 1968-72, Cmty. Mental Health Ctrs., Greater Cleve., 1974-80; clin. instr. Case Western Res. U., Cleve., 1981-83. Author: Through the Keyhole at Gifted Men and Women, 1977, (monograph) The Psychiatric Aspects of Hypoparathyroidism, 1962; contbr. articles to profl. jours.; author poetry, 1960—. Mem. AAAS (reviewer children's books), Cleve. Astron. Soc. (bd. dirs. 1984-86), Mensa (Cleve. area br. pres. 1986-87), Great Books Discussion Group (Rocky River, chmn. 1985-92, 94—), Kiwanis Internat. Russian Orthodox. Home and Office: 21160 Avalon Dr Cleveland OH 44116-1120

DENMARK, STANLEY JAY, orthodontist; b. Queens, N.Y., May 26, 1927; s. Jack and Frieda (Kirschenbaum) D.; m. Florence Levin, June 7, 1953 (div. June 1973); children—Valerie, Pamela and Richard (twins); m. Anita Goodman, Jan. 2, 1983. B.S., Queen's Coll., 1950; M.Sc., NYU, 1955; D.D.S., U. Pa., 1955, orthodontics cert., 1957. Diplomate Am. Bd. Orthodontics. Asst. prof. orthodontics Fairleigh Dickinson U., Hackensack, N.J., 1974-79; practice dentistry specializing in orthodontics, Westbury, N.Y., 1955-91; clin. asst. prof. growth and devel. scis. (orthodontics) Sch. Dentistry N.Y.U., 1991—. Served with USN, 1945-47. Mem. Am. Assn. Orthodontists, Northeastern Soc. Orthodontists, Coll. Diplomates of Am. Bd. Orthodontists, ADA, Sigma Xi. Jewish. Avocations: painting; woodcuts; tennis; cross-country skiing. Home: 330 E 80th St New York NY 10021-0915 Office: NYU Coll Dentistry 345 E 24th St New York NY 10010-4020

DENNEHY, JOHN JOSEPH, internist; b. Phila., Jan. 30, 1930; s. John and Winifred (Byrne) D.; children: Michael, John, Patrick, Kathleen, Mary, Thomas. BA, La Salle Coll., Phila., 1952; MD, Hahnemann U., 1956. Diplomate Am. Bd. Internal Medicine, Am. Bd. Infectious Disease. Intern St. Agnes Hosp., Phila., 1956-57, resident in family practice, 1957-58; resident in internal medicine Hahnemann Hosp., Phila., 1958-61; dir. dept. infectious disease Geisinger Med. Ctr., Danville, Pa., 1964-88, sr. cons., 1988—; drug reviewer U.S. Pharmacopeial Conv., Washington, 1980-96. Contbr. articles to med. jours. Mem. exec. bd. Columbia-Montour coun. Boy Scouts Am., 1970—, pres., 1984-85, scoutmaster troop 33, Riverside, Pa., 1972-74; pres. St. Joseph Parish coun., Danville, 1987-89. Capt. Med. Corp., U.S. Army, 1961-64. Recipient Silver Beaver award Boy Scouts Am., 1980. Fellow ACP; mem. AMA, Infectious Disease Soc. Am., Am. Soc. Tropical Medicine and Hygiene, Am. Venereal Disease Assn., Am. Fedn. for Clin. Rsch., Am. Soc. for Microbiology, Pa. Med. Soc. (mem. DUR com., mem. coun. on edn. and sci.), Montour County Med. Soc. (pres. 1976), Kiwanis, Elks. Republican. Roman Catholic. Office: Geisinger Med Ctr Danville PA 17822

DENNER, ALAN MATTHEW, internist; b. N.Y.C., Feb. 14, 1951; s. David and Ida (Anselowitz) D.; m. Valerie Louise Vaino, May 29, 1976; children: Tami Danielle, Robert Albert. BS, Bklyn. Coll., 1972; MD, Albany Med. Coll., 1976. Diplomate Am. Bd. Internal Medicine. Resident in internal medicine St. Raphael's Hosp., New Haven, 1979; pvt. practice internal medicine Sharon, Mass., 1979-80, Orlando, 1981—; med. dir. Nurse World, Orlando, 1983-89, Abbey Home Health Care, Orlando, 1994—. Mem. AMA. Jewish. Office: Arden Hill Internists 6388 Silver Star Rd Ste 1L Orlando FL 32818

DENNER, MELVIN WALTER, retired life sciences educator; b. North Washington, Iowa, Aug. 27, 1933; s. Norbert William and Petronella Nettie (Eischeid) D.; m. N. Anne Greer, June 19, 1965; children: Mark Andrew, Michael Alan (twins). BS, Upper Iowa U., 1961; MS (NSF fellow), U. Ky., 1963; PhD, Iowa State U., 1968. Asst. prof. life scis. U. So. Ind., Evansville, 1968-71, assoc. prof., 1971-76, prof., 1976-95, Disting. prof., 1989-90, premed. advisor, chmn. dept., 1969-95, assoc. chmn. div. scis. and math., 1975-77, acting chmn. div. scis. and math., 1976-77, chmn., 1979-87; dean Sch. of Sci. and Engring. Tech., 1994; coord. univ. self-study U. So. Ind., Evansville, 1976, 86, 96; Eucharistic minister Corpus Christi Ch., 1981—; panelist Ind. Com. Higher Edn., 1993. Contbr. articles to profl. jours. Vice chmn. Iowa Young Dems., 1958-60; bd. dirs. Deaconess Hosp. Allied Health Programs, chmn. radiation tech. adv. com., 1987-95; bd. dirs. Evansville Mus. Arts and Scis.; mem. alumni adv. bd. U. So. Ind., 1982—; spl. minister Corpus Christi Ch., 1981—. With USN, 1953-57. Named Ind. Prof. of Yr., 1989, Sagamore of the Wabash, 1989; NSF fellow 1962, 64, NIH fellow, 1966-67, Alumni Achievement fellow, 1967-68. Fellow AAAS (film critic); mem. Internat. Soc. Invertebrate Pathology (founding), Am. Soc. Parasitologists, Am. Micros. Soc. (nat. treas.), North Ctrl. Assn. Colls. and Secondary Schs. (visitation team 1976-94), Am. Inst. Biol. Scis., Sigma Xi (pres. So. Ind. chpt.), Sigma Zeta. Home: 100 S Peerless Rd Evansville IN 47712-3043 Office: U So Ind Sch Sci & Engring Tech Evansville IN 47712

DENNING, DAVID WEMYSS, research physician; b. Gosport, U.K., May 18, 1957; s. Basil Wemyss and Antoinette (Gossett) D.; m. Merian Llewelyn, June 16, 1985; children: Thomas, Robert. MB BS, Guy's Hosp., London, 1980. Sr. registrar Northwick Park Hosp., Harrow, Middlesex, Eng., 1985-87; fellow Stanford (Calif.) U., 1987-90; sr. lectr. U. Manchester, Eng., 1990—; cons. Zeneca Pharms., Macclesfield, U.K., 1991—, Hoffmann La Roche, Kamakura, Japan, 1992—, Pfizer Inc., Sandwich, Eng., 1992—. Author: Opportunistic Fungal Diseases, 1994; contbr. articles to profl. jours. Office: U Manchester, Hope Hosp Eccles Old Rd, Salford M6 8HD, England

DENNIS, CLARENCE, surgeon, educator; b. St. Paul, June 16, 1909; s. Warren Arthur and Clara May (Van Orman) D.; m. Eleanor Mary Smith, June 17, 1939; children: Jane E. Dennis Wigertz, Richard, James, David; m. Mary Elise Mott, Mar. 12, 1977; stepdaughter, Mrs. Katherine Elise Franda. B.S., Harvard U., 1931; M.D., Johns Hopkins U., 1935; M.S., U. Minn., 1938, Ph.D., 1940; DSc (hon.) ., SUNYHealth Sci. Ctr., Bklyn., 1988. Diplomate: Am. Bd. Surgery. Trained in surgery under Dr. O. H. Wangensteen, U. Minn., 1935-40; in physiology with Dr. M. B. Visscher, 1937-38, instr. in physiology, 1938-39, in surgery, 1940-41, asst. prof., 1941-44, asso. prof., 1944-47, prof. surgery, 1947-51; prof. SUNY Downstate Med. Ctr., 1951-72, chmn. dept. surgery, 1952-72; dir. div. tech. applications Nat. Heart and Lung Inst., NIH, Bethesda, Md., 1972-73; spl. asst. for tech. Office of Dir., Nat. Heart, Lung and Blood Inst., 1973-74; prof. surgery SUNY at Stony Brook, 1974-88; clin. prof. surgery U. Minn., Mpls., 1989—; assoc. chief staff for R & D VA Med. Ctr., Northport, N.Y., 1975-88; surg. cons. VA Med. Ctr., Minn., 1989—; dir. Cancer Detection Ctr., U. Minn., 1991-96; former surgeon-in-chief Kings County Hosp. Contbr. articles to profl. publs. and textbooks. Recipient Modern Medicine award for disting. achievement, 1973, John H. Gibbon award Am. Soc. Extracorporeal Technicians, 1974, dedication Forum on Fundamental Surg. Problems, ACS, 1987. Fellow ACS (past gov., dedication The Forum Vol. 1987); mem. Assn. Advancement Med. Instrumentation (pres. 1980-82, chmn. bd. 1982-84, Laufman-Greatbatch award for contbns. to instrumentation 1984), Am. Heart Assn., Am. Soc. for Artificial Internal Organs (past pres.), Internat. Surg. Soc. (past pres. U.S. chpt.), Soc. Vascular Surgery (past pres.), N.Y. Surg. Soc. (past pres.), Bklyn. Surg. Soc. (past pres.), Am. Assn. Surgery Trauma, Am. Assn. Thoracic Surgery, Soc. U. Surgeons, Am. Surg. Assn. (past v.p.), Soc. Clin. Surgery, Soc. Exptl.. Biology and Medicine, N.Y. Cancer Soc. (past pres.), Internat. Cardiovascular Soc., Soc. Surgery Alimentary Tract, Nat. Soc. Med. Research (pres. 1977-79), N.Y. Soc. Thoracic Surgery, Soc. U. Surg. Chmn. (past pres.), Found. Biomed. Rsch. (bd. dirs. 1989—). Home: 2332 Field Stone Dr Mendota Heights MN 55120

DENNIS, DONALD PATRICK, otolaryngologist; b. Macon, Ga., May 8, 1947. BS in Chemistry, U. Ga., 1969; MD, Med. Coll. Ga., 1974; Diploma otolaryngology, Johns Hopkins Hosp., Balt., 1979. Intern in straight medicine Emory U., Atlanta, 1974; resident gen. surgery Union Meml. Hosp., Balt.; faculty Dept. Otolaryngology, Head and Neck Surgery, Johns Hopkins, Balt., 1979-80; fellow Facial Plastic Surgery, Dr. Eugene Tandy, Chgo., 1979, Otology -Ugo Fisch, Zurich, Switzerland, 1980; chief ear, nose and throat dept. West Paces Ferry Hosp., Atlanta, 1986-88; laser surgeon Piedmont Hosp., West Paces Hosp., Atlanta, 1980—; Inventor in field. Fellow Am. Acad. Otolaryngology (cert. Head and Neck Surgery 1981), Am. Acad. Facial Plastic and Reconstructive Surgery, Am. Coll. Surgeons. Office: 3193 Howell Mill Rd NW Ste 215 Atlanta GA 30327-2100

DENNIS, JOHN MURRAY, health facility administrator, radiologist; b. Willards, Md., Jan. 31, 1923; s. John Murray and Bettie Lee (Hearne) D.; m. Mary Helen France, Oct. 8, 1947; children: Lori Dennis Raneri, John M., Patrick F., Terry Dennis Passano. BS, U. Md., 1943; MD, U. Md., Balt., 1945. Cert. radiologist. Resident in radiology U. Md., Balt., 1948-50, instr., assoc. sch. medicine, 1951-53, prof., chmn. sch. medicine, 1953-74, dean sch. medicine, 1974-90, dean emeritus sch. medicine, 1990—; fellow in radiology U. Pa., Phila., 1950-51; chmn. of coun. Am. Coll. Radiology, N.Y., 1969-71, chmn. bd. chancellors, 1975-76, pres., 1976-77 (Gold medal 1980). Contbr. articles to profl. jours. Bd. dirs. Am. Cancer Soc., N.Y., 1963-69. Capt. USAF, 1946-48. Recipient Andrew White award Loyola Coll., 1982, Gold medal Am. Roentgen Ray Soc., 1990; named Outstanding Alumnus of Yr. U. Md., 1984, U. Md. Sch. Medicine, 1990. Mem. Md. Club, Balt. Country Club. Roman Catholic. Home: 803 Huntsman Rd Baltimore MD 21286-1456

DENNIS, RICHARD CLARENCE, surgery and anesthesia educator; b. Mpls., Nov. 29, 1944; s. Clarence and Eleanor (Smith) D.; children: Elissa, Sara, Johanna. BA, Dartmouth Coll., 1967; MD, Union U., Albany, N.Y., 1971. Diplomate Am. Bd. Surgery. Intern Univ. Hosp., Boston; resident Boston Univ. and Affiliated Hosp., 1972-77; acad. fellow Boston U., 1973-75; fellow Harvard U. and PBBH, 1978-79; assoc. dir. surg. ICU, Boston U. Med. Ctr. Hosp., 1981-87, dir. surg. ICU, 1987—; assoc. dir. surg. ICU, Boston VA Hosp., 1981-87, dir. surg. edn., 1984-87; assoc. dir. critical care medicine Boston U. Med. Ctr. Hosp., 1981-87, chief critical care medicine, 1987—; asst. prof. anesthesia Boston U. Sch. Medicine, 1983-88, assoc. prof. surgery and anesthesia, 1988—. Contbg. author: Critical Care, 1995. Lt. comdr. M.C., USN, 1977-79. Fellow ACS, Am. Coll. Critical Care Medicine; mem. Soc. Critical Care Medicine, New Eng. Soc. Critical Care Medicine, Alpha Omega Alpha. Office: Boston U Med Ctr Hosp 88 E Newton St Ste A2707 Boston MA 02118

DENNISON, ALLEN MANSFIELD, internist; b. N.Y.C., Sept. 28, 1952; s. Ethan Allen Jr. and Frances (Ferry) D.; m. Jane Atkinson Mackenzie, May 26, 1979; children: Eric, Ethan Allen, Malcolm Thayer, John Francis. BA magna cum laude in Biology, Harvard U., 1975; MD, Columbia U., 1980. Diplomate Am. Bd. Internal Medicine. Intern in internal medicine R.I. Hosp., Providence, 1980-81, resident, 1981-83, asst. attending physician, 1983—; practice medicine specializing in internal medicine Providence, 1983—; asst. prof. medicine Brown U., Providence, 1984—. Cubmaster pack 88 Boy Scouts Am., Providence. Named one of Five Top Internists in R.I., R.I. Monthly, 1994. Mem. ACP, Am. Soc. Internal Medicine, West Chop Club (Vineyard Haven, Mass.). Episcopalian. Office: Medical Assocs R I 286 Maple Ave Barrington RI 02806-3430

DENNY, FLOYD WOLFE, JR., pediatrician; b. Hartsville, S.C., Oct. 22, 1923; s. Floyd Wolfe and Marion Elizabeth (Porter) D.; m. Barbara H. Denny, Apr. 27, 1946; children: R. Zoe, Mark W., Timothy P. BS, Wofford Coll., 1944; MD, Vanderbilt U., 1946. Diplomate Am. Bd. Pediatrics. Intern Vanderbilt Hosp., Nashville, 1946-47; resident in pediatrics Vanderbilt Hosp., 1947-48; instr. pediatrics U. Minn., 1951-52, asst. prof., 1952-53; asst. prof. pediatrics Vanderbilt U. Sch. Medicine, 1953-55; asst. prof. preventive medicine and pediatrics Western Res. U. Sch. Medicine, 1955-60, asso. prof. preventive medicine, 1960; prof. Sch. Medicine, U. N.C., Chapel Hill, 1960—, chmn. dept. pediatrics, 1960-81, alumni disting. prof., 1974—; vis. scholar dept. epidemiology Sch. Pub. Health and Child Devel. Inst., 1977-78; vis. worker Med. Research Council Clin. Research Centre, London, 1970-71; mem. Commn. on Streptococcal and Staphylococcal Diseases Armed Forces

Epidemiol. Bd., 1954-72, dep. dir., 1959-63; mem. Commn. on Acute Respiratory Diseases Armed Forces Epidemiol. Bd., 1960-73, dep. dir., 1963-67, dir., 1967-73; mem. Inst. Medicine, Nat. Acad. Scis., 1981—. Mem. editorial bd.: Am. Rev. Respiratory Diseases, 1971-74; mem. publs. com.: Jour. Infectious Diseases, 1973-78; contbr. articles to med. jours. Served to maj. M.C. U.S. Army, 1948-51. Mem. Am. Acad. Pediatrics, Am. Assn. Immunologists, Am. Epidemiology Soc., Am. Fedn. Clin. Rsch., Am. Pediatric Soc. (pres. 1980-81, Howland award 1995), Am. Soc. Clin. Investigation, Am. Soc. Microbiology, Am. Thoracic Soc., Assn. Am. Physicians, Infectious Diseases Soc. Am. (pres. 1979-80), Soc. Exptl. Biology and Medicine, Soc. Pediatric Rsch. (pres. 1968-69), So. Soc. Clin. Rsch., So. Soc. Pediatric Rsch., Phi Beta Kappa, Alpha Omega Alpha. Home: 9210 Dodsons Crossroads Chapel Hill NC 27516-7681 Office: U NC Sch of Medicine Dept Pediatrics 356 B Wing C CB # 7225 Chapel Hill NC 27599

DENSEN, PAUL MAXIMILLIAN, former health administrator, educator; b. N.Y.C., Aug. 1, 1913; s. Charles Edwin and Carrie (Weinberg) D.; m. Elizabeth A. Reed, Dec. 19, 1939; children—Rebecca E. (Mrs. John Rothfuss), Peter. A.B., Bklyn.Coll., 1934; D.Sc., Johns Hopkins U., 1939; M.A. (hon.), Harvard U., 1968. From instr. to assoc. prof. preventive medicine Vanderbilt U. Med. Sch., 1939-46; chief div. med. research statistics VA, Washington, 1946-49; assoc. prof., then prof. biometry Grad. Sch. Pub. Health, U. Pitts., 1949-54; dir. div. research and statistics Health Ins. Plan Greater N.Y., 1954-59; dept. commr. N.Y.C. Dept. Health, 1959-66; dept. adminstr. N.Y.C. Health Services Adminstrn., 1966-68; dir. Harvard Center Community Health and Med. Care, 1968-85; prof. community health Harvard Sch. Pub. Health, 1968-85, prof. emeritus, 1985—. Fellow Am. Statis. Assn., Am. Pub. Health Assn., AAAS; mem. Am. Epidemiol. Soc., Inst. Medicine. Home: PO Box 405 165 Fremont Rd Sandown NH 03873-2204

DENSEN-GERBER, JUDIANNE, psychiatrist, lawyer, educator; b. N.Y.C., Nov. 13, 1934; d. Gustave A. and Beatrice D.; m. Michael M. Baden, June 14, 1958; children: Trissa Austin, Judson Michael, Lindsey Robert, Sarah Densen. A.B. cum laude, Bryn Mawr Coll., 1956; JD, Columbia U., 1959; MD, NYU, 1963. Bar: N.Y. 1961. Rotating intern French Hosp., N.Y.C., 1963-64; resident psychiatry Bellevue Hosp., N.Y.C., 1964-65, Met. Hosp., N.Y.C., 1965-67; mem. core staff Addiction Services Agy., N.Y.C., 1966-67; founder Odyssey House (psychiat. residence for rehab. narcotics addicts), N.Y.C., Mich., Maine, N.H., Utah, La., Australia, N.Z., 1967, clin. dir., 1967-69, exec. dir., 1967-74, pres. bd., 1974-82; pres., founder, chief exec. officer Odyssey Inst. Am., 1974-82; pres. Odyssey Inst. Australia, 1977-86, Odyssey Inst. Internat., Inc., 1978—; chairwoman Odyssey Inst. Corp. Conn., 1974—; attending physician Gracie Sq. Hosp., N.Y.C., 1982-93; attending physician Park City Hosp., Bridgeport, Conn., 1985—, mem. ethics com., 1988-93; mem. ethics com. Bridgeport Hosp., attending physician, 1985—; attending physician Northwest Gen. Hosp., Detroit, 1985-86; active staff St. Vincent's Hosp., Bridgeport, 1987—; courtesy staff Norwalk Hosp., 1993—; assoc. vis. prof. law U. Utah Law Sch., 1973-75; adj. prof. law N.Y. Law Sch., 1973-76; chairperson plenary session drug abuse Am. Acad. Forensic Scis., 1972, sec. psychiatry sect., 1973, chmn. sect., 1974—; founder, 1973, since pres. Inst. Women's Wrongs; founder, since pres. Odyssey Inst. (health care for socially disadvantaged), 1974—; bd. dirs. Simpson St. Devel. Assn., An Extraordinary Event (One to One for Mental Retardation), Bridge House; mem. Nat. Adv. Commn. Criminal Justice Standards and Goals, 1971-74, Pres.'s Commn. on White House Fellows, 1972-76; mem. drug experience adv. com. HEW, 1973-76; v.p. psychiat. sect. Internat. Forensic Medicine Conf., Budapest, 1967; pres. N.Y. Council Alcoholism, 1978—; co-chair com. on reproductive rights vs. best interest of the child Mich. State Senate, 1984-86; trustee Nat. Forensic Ctr., Princeton, N.J., 1985—, keynote speaker nat. conf., 1988, lectr., 1988; speaker Conf. for Multiple Personality Disorder, Chgo., 1985—; cons. to Mich. State Legislature to draft legislation on The Best Interests of the Child vs. the New Reproductive Techs., 1986; amicus curiae brief in Mary Beth Whitehead appeal Surrogate Mothering, 1987; sr. non-govt. psychiatrist L'Ambiance Plaza disaster, Bridgeport, 1987; guest lectr. narcotics addiction NYU Sch. Medicine, also Sch. Law.; in field dir. Daitch Shopwell, Inc.; cons. substance abuse device Insight Inc., Flint, Mich., 1987-88; guest speaker Cornell U., 1989, Internat. Hypnosis Soc. of Yale, 1989, Cumberland Law Sch., 1989, Sacred Heart U., 1994; founder, CEO, pres. The Family Maintenance Health Orgn., LLC; guest speaker Nat. Ctr. Forensic Scis. Author: (with Trissa Austin Baden) Drugs, Sex, Parents and You, 1972, We Mainline Dreams, The Odyssey House Story, 1973, Walk in My Shoes, 1976; (with David Sandberg) The Role of Child Abuse in Delinquency and Juvenile Court Decision-Making, 1984, Chronic Acting-Out Students and Child Abuse: A Handbook for Intervention, 1986, Shortened Forms: A Manual for Teachers On; (with John Dugan) Issues in Law and Psychiatry, 1988; contbr. articles to profl. jours.; editor: Jour. Corrective and Social Psychiatry, 1975; co-developer, co-inventor virocidal surface cleaner against AIDS, 1988. Mem. N.Y.C. Crime Control Commn., 1975-79, Gov.'s Task Force on Crime Control, Albany, N.Y., 1977-79, N.Y. State Crime Control Planning Bd., 1975-79; del. White House Conf. on Youth, 1971; bd. dirs. Nat. Coalition for Children's Justice, 1975—, Am. Soc. for Prevention of Cruelty to Children, 1979—, Mary E. Walker Found., 1978; psychiat. cons. Good Shepherd Home for Girls, 1989-90. Recipient Woman of Achievement award AAUW, 1970; Myrtle Wreath award Hadassah, 1970; B'nai B'rith Woman of Greatness award, 1971; Otty awarce to N.Y.C. Our Town Newspaper, 1977; named Dame of White Cross Australia, #1 Dame of Malta, Ky. Col., N.Y. State Hon. Fire Chief. Fellow Am. Coll. Legal Medicine (Congl. cert. merit 1990); mem. AMA, N.Y. State, N.Y. County Med. Socs., Soc. Med. Jurisprudence, Therapeutic Communities of Am. (founding mem., 1st v.p. 1975—), Am. Acad. Psychiatry and Law (mem. AIDS ad hoc com 1988—), Am. Psychiat. Assn., Women's Forum N.Y. (founding mem.), Nat. Women's Forum, Internat. Women's Forum, Internat. Soc. Multiple Personality and Dissociative States, Conn. Med. Assn., Am. Orthopsychiat. Assn., ABA, N.Y. State Bar Assn., N.Y. County Women's Bar Assn., N.Y. Assn. Vol. Agys. Narcotics Addiction and Substance Abuse (dir. 1968—), Am. Psychiat. Assn., N.Y. Med. Assn., Post Traumatic Stress Syndrome Soc., Fairfield County Med. Soc. (physicians health subcom. 1986-92). Republican. Unitarian. Club: Women's City (N.Y.C.). Office: Odyssey Inst Internat 5 Hedley Farms Rd Westport CT 06880-6335

DENSON, DONALD D., pharmacologist, educator; b. Beverly, Mass., July 11, 1945; s. Derby A. and Ruth (Smith) D.; m. F. Jeanine Overholser, Sept. 5, 1980; children: Chad Edward, Todd Christopher, Zachary David. BS, U. Ga., 1967, PhD, 1970. B.E. clin. pharmacologist. Assoc. prof. anethesiology pharmacokinetics, dir. rsch. U. Cin., 1978-90; asst. prof. anesthesiology pharmacokinetics, dir. labs. Emory U., Atlanta, 1990-92; assoc. prof., 1992—. Author 20 chpts. in books; contbr. 160 articles to profl. jours. Capt. USAF, 1970-72. Fellow Am. Coll. Clin. Pharmacology (McKeen Cattell Disting. Achievement award 1991); mem. Internat. Assn. for Study of Pain, Am. Soc. Anesthesiologists, Assn. Univ. Anesthesiologists, Am. Soc. Regional Anesthesia (editorial bd. 1988—). Office: Emory U Sch Medicine Dept Anesthesiology 1364 Clifton Rd NE Atlanta GA 30322-1059

DENT, ERNEST DUBOSE, JR., pathologist; b. Columbia, S.C., May 3, 1927; s. E. Dubose and Grace (Lee) D.; m. Dorothy McCalman, June 16, 1949; children: Christopher, Pamela; m. 2d, Karin Frehse, Sept. 6, 1970. Student, Presbyn. Coll., 1944-45; M.D., Med. Coll. S.C., 1949. Diplomate clin. pathology and pathology anatomy Am. Bd. Pathology. Intern U.S. Naval Hosp., Phila., 1949-50; resident pathology USPHS Hosp., Balt., 1950-54; chief pathology USPHS Hosp., Norfolk, Va., 1954-56; assoc. pathology Columbia (S.C.) Hosp., 1956-59; pathologist, dir. labs. Columbia Hosp., S.C. Baptist Hosp., 1958-69; with Straus Clin. Labs., L.A., 1969-72; staff pathologist Hollywood (Calif.) Community Hosp, St. Joseph Hosp., Burbank, Calif., 1969-72; dir. labs. Glendale Meml. Hosp. and Health Ctr., 1972-94; ret.; bd. dirs. Glendale Meml. Hosp. and Health Ctr. Author papers nat. med. jours. Mem. Am. Cancer Soc., AMA, L.A. County Med. Assn. (pres. Glendale dist. 1980-81), Calif. Med. Assn. (councillor 1984-90), Am. Soc. Clin. Pathology, Coll. Am. Pathologists (assemblyman S.C. 1965-67; mem. publs. com. bull. 1968-70), L.A. Soc. Pathologists (trustee 1984-87), L.A. Acad. Medicine, S.C. Soc. Pathologists (pres. 1967-69). Lutheran. Home: 1605 La Plaza Dr San Marcos CA 92069 Office: S Central and Los Feliz Aves Glendale CA 91225-7036

DENTE, GINO ALDO, anesthesiologist, educator; b. Barre, Vt., Apr. 12, 1917; s. Basilio Dente and Mary Elizabeth Pianfetti; m. Carmen Amanda Lavin. MD, U. Vt., 1941. Diplomate Am. Bd. Anesthesiology. Intern Greenpoint Hosp., Bkyln., 1941-42; resident, fellow in anesthesiology Mary Fletcher Hosp., Degoesbriand Hosp., Burlington, Vt., 1948-50; practice medicine specializing in anesthesiology Burlington, 1950—; prof. surgery, anesthesia Coll. Medicine U. Vt., Burlington, 1972-86, prof. emeritus, 1987; attending anesthesiologist Med. Ctr. Hosp. Vt., Burlington, 1954-86 bd. dirs. Merlin Inc., Burlington. Served to capt. USMC, 1942-46, PTO. Roman Catholic. Club: Ethan Allen (Burlington). Home: 41 Elsom Pky South Burlington VT 05403

DENTINGER, MARK PETER, neurologist; b. Rochester, N.Y., June 22, 1945; s. John Cyril and Mary Louise (Peters) D.; m. Nancy Tufano, Aug. 28, 1965; children: Adam, Aaron, Kelleen. BA in Chemistry, St. John Fisher Coll., Rochester, 1967; MD, Albany (N.Y.) Med. Coll., 1971. Neurology resident Albany Med. Coll., 1971-74; staff neurologist VA Med. Ctr., Albany, 1974-87; prof. neurology Albany Med Coll., 1987—, asst. dean, 1987—, acting chair neurology, 1993-95. Fellow Am. Acad. Neurology; mem. Am. Nuerol. Assn., Neurosci. Soc., Am. Soc. Exptl. Neuropathology, Hudson-Mohawk Neurosci. Soc. Democrat. Roman Catholic. Office: Albany Med Coll 47 New Scotland Ave Albany NY 12208

DENTON, KEITH G., psychologist; b. Mansfield, Eng., Sept. 23, 1945; came to U.S., 1947; s. Peter Robert and Gertrude (Rosenstrauch) D.; m. Elaine Karten, Aug. 3, 1969; children: Michael, Amy. BA, Adelphi U., 1967; MA, New Sch. for Social Rsch., 1970; PhD, Hofstra U., 1977, postdoctoral cert. in clin. psychology, 1979. Nat. cert. sch. psychologist, 1989. Spl. edn. tchr. Queens (N.Y.) Public Schs., 1968-72; sch. psychologist Island Trees, N.Y., 1973-75, East Rockaway, N.Y., 1978-80, East Meadow, N.Y., 1981—; prof. spl. edn. C.W. Post Center, 1977—; pvt. practice clin. psychology, 1979—; psychologist L.I. Council Chs. Clinic, Albertson, N.Y., 1979-94. Trustee Nassau Psychol. Svcs. Inst. Mem. APA, Nat. Assn. Sch. Psychologists, N.Y. State Psychol. Assn., Nassau County Psychol. Assn. (dir.), Round Robin Model R.R. Club. Jewish. Home and Office: 43 Melanie Ln Syosset NY 11791-5118

DENUZZO, RINALDO VINCENT, pharmacy educator; b. Cleve., Oct. 21, 1922; s. Luigi and Domenica Mary (Razzano) DiNuzzo; m. Lucy Bernadine Sneed, June 29, 1946; 1 child, Lisa Ann. BS, Albany Coll. Pharmacy, 1952; MS in Edn., SUNY-Albany, 1956. Registered pharmacist, N.Y., Fla., Vt. Prof. pharmacy N.Y. Coll. Pharmacy, Albany, 1952—, adminstrv. asst., 1963-80; pharmacist, N.Y., Fla., Vt., 1968-95; sr. pharmacist inspector N.Y. State Dept. Health, 1966-95; field dir. Market Measures, Inc.; chmn. tech. pharmacy adv. com.; lectr. drug product substitution and generic drugs. Author: Ann. Albany Coll. Pharmacy Prescription Survey, 1956-84, Substitution, The New York State Experience, 1980, RX Servcies, XIII Winter Games, 1980, Annual DeNuzzo Prescription Survey, 1985—, Impact of One-Line Prescription Form on Generic Drug Use, 1987, Cipro, Vasotec, Voltaren Post Biggest Gains, 1987, Using the Right Tools to Achieve Personal Success, 1990, Personal Selling, 1991, Annual Survey Tracks Drug Prescribing Trends, 1990, Consumer Prescription Prices Increase, 1991, Changes in Dental Prescribing, 1991, How to Reduce Prescription Medical Costs, 1992, Are Dental Prescriptions a Viable Target for RPhs?, 1992, Financial Success: A Challenge for the Future, 1996; editor: Albany Coll. Pharmacy Alumni News, 1961-81; mem. editl. bd. MMM, 1977-80. Instr. first aid, responding to emergencies, CPR ARC; mem. East Greenbush Ctrl. Sch. Dist. Bd. Edn., 1974-92, v.p., 1975-76, pres., 1976-78, 91-92, East Greenbush Edn. Found.; mem. adv. bd. Merrell-Dow Hosp., 1987; sec.-treas. Union U. Pharmacy Coll. Coun., 1970-80; cons. pharmacist, coord. pharm. svcs. XIII Olympic Winter Games, Lake Placid, N.Y., 1980; chmn. Albany Coll. Pharmacy Faculty, 1987-89, com. on cons., 1984-87, promotions com. 1989-92, exec. com., grievance com., chair strategic planning steering com., 1995-96, faculty affairs chmn. and rev., 1990-94, mission statement com., 1995, faculty ombudsman, 1991—; mem. profl. adv. com. Albany Vis. Nurses Assn.; mem. rev. panel on prescription payment rev. commn. of Office Tech. Assessment U.S. Congress, 1988; mem. ethics panel Siena Coll., 1992; mem., dir. So. Rensselaer County Taxpayers Assn.; liaison Health Sys. Mgmt. degree, Joint MS with Union Coll. With U.S. Army, 1941-46, USAF, 1946-47, capt. M.C. USAFR, 1948-63, ret., 1982. Named Francis J. O'Brien Pharmacy Man of Yr., 1979; recipient 25 Yr. Svc. citation ARC, 30 Yr. Svc. citation, Svc. plaque East Greenbush Ctrl. Sch. Dist., Svc. plaque East Greenbush Edn. Found., 25 Yr. Svc. award N.Y. State Dept. Health. Fellow Am. Coll. Apothecaries; mem. Am. Assn. Colls. Pharmacy (sec.-treas., coun. faculties 1979-80, coun., chmn. elect 1982-83, chmn. 1984-87, dir. 1984-89, Am. Pharm. Assn., N.Y. State Pharm. Soc., N.Y. Sch. Bd. Assn., AARP, N.Y. State Pub. Employees Fedn., Albany Coll. Pharmacy Alumni Assn. (exec. dir. 1965-86, disting. svc. medal 1975), AAUP (pres. 1978—), Kappa Psi (2 Disting. Svc. Plaques 1988, Cert. of Commendation 1989, 96), Beta Delta (ann. Rinaldo V. DeNuzzo luncheon 1988—), Nat. Italian-Am. Found. (coun.), 46th and 72nd Recon Assn., Albany Coll. Pharmacy Pres.'s Club (chmn. bd. 1962-87), Army Five Star, Kappa Psi (dep. grand coun. Beta Delta chpt., Albany grad., sec.-treas., regent protemp), Officers Club (West Point, N.Y.). Republican. Roman Catholic. Home: 19 Alva St East Greenbush NY 12061-2027 Office: 106 New Scotland Ave Albany NY 12208-3425

DEORIO, ANTHONY JOSEPH, surgeon b. Chgo., June 27, 1945; s. Joseph John and Catherine Marie Deorio; m. Janet Ann Balskus, Jan. 10, 1970; children: Joseph, Catherine. BS, Loyola U., Chgo., 1967; MD, Loyola U., Maywood, Ill., 1971. Diplomate Am. Bd. Surgery. Intern St. Joseph Hosp., Chgo., 1971-72; resident in surgery Loyola Med. Ctr., Maywood, 1972-76, clin. instr. surgery, 1976-77, asst. prof. surgery, 1977—; pvt. practice Resurrection Hosp., Chgo., 1977—, dir. surg. edn., 1977—, chmn. dept. surgery, 1984-88, sec. med. staff, 1986-88; assoc. examiner Am. Bd. Surgery, 1993, 96. Contbr. articles to profl. jours. Fellow ACS; mem. AMA, Ill. Med. Soc., Chgo. Med. Soc., Chgo. Surg. Soc., Ill. Surg. Soc., Alumni Assn. Stritch Sch. Medicine (bd. govs.), Columbian Club, KC, Blue Key, Alpha Omega Alpha. Roman Catholic. Office: 7447 W Talcott Ave Chicago IL 60631-3745

DE ORIO, LINDA LEE, gerontology nurse practitioner; b. Cranston, R.I., Nov. 21, 1959; d. Edmond and Lena (Sylvester) Boulanger; m. Carl A. De Orio Jr., June 14, 1986; children: Carl A. III, Lindsay A., Rachael E. BSN, Northeastern U., Boston, 1982; MS, U. Lowell (Mass.), 1989. Staff nurse Mass. Gen. Hosp., Boston, 1982-84, 87-90, clin. tchr., 1984-87; nurse practitioner Dept. Vets. Affairs Med. Ctr., Manchester, N.H., 1990—. Mem. ANA, N.H. Nurses Assn., Sigma Theta Tau. Home: RR 1 Box 190A Deering NH 03244-9330 Office: Dept Vets Affairs Med Ctr Intermediate Medicine 718 Smyth Rd Manchester NH 03104-7004

DEPACE, NICHOLAS LOUIS, physician; b. Nutley, N.J., Oct. 18, 1953; s. Nicholas Frank and Rose (Piro) DeP.; m. Marilyn Tomaro, Jan. 17, 1981. BS, Seton Hall U.; MD, N.J. Sch. Medicine, Mt. Sinai, N.Y.C.; internal medicine cardiology, Hahnemann U., Phila. Diplomate Am. Bd. Internal Medicine and Cardiology. Intern in internal medicine Overlook Hosp., Summit, N.J., Columbia U., N.Y.C., 1978-79; resident internal medicine Hahnemann Med. Coll. and Hosp., Phila., 1979-81; practice medicine specializing in internal and cardiology medicine Phila., 1982—; with Sta. WPEN, Phila., 1990; clin. prof. medicine Med. Coll. Pa., 1987-89; chief divsn. preventive cardiology Grad. Hosp. Med. Coll. Pa., Center City, 1991-93; dir. heart repair program Phila. Heart Inst., Presbyn. Med. Ctr., Phila., 1993-95; chief divsn. of preventive cardiology Grad. Hosp., 1995—. Co-author: The Heart Repair Manual. Fellow Am. Coll. Cardiology, Am. Coll. Chest Physicians; mem. AMA, N.Y. Acad. Scis., Pa. Med. Soc. Republican. Roman Catholic. Home: 109 Jefferson Ave Haddonfield NJ 08033-3411 Office: Ste N-2 188 Fries Mill Rd Turnersville NJ 08012

DEPALMA, RALPH GEORGE, surgeon, educator; b. N.Y.C., Oct. 29, 1931; s. Frank and Maria (Sibilio) deP.; m. Maleva Tankard, Sept. 17, 1955; children: Ralph L., Edward F., Maleva B. Malinda G. AB, Columbia U, 1953; MD, NYU, 1956. Diplomate Am. Bd. Surgery, Am. Bd. Vascular Surgery. Resident in surgery Univ. Hosps., Cleve., 1962-64; instr. to assoc. prof. surgery Case Western Res. U., Cleve., 1964-80, prof. surgery, 1973-80; prof., chmn. surgery U. Nev., Reno, 1980-82, George Washington U. Sch. Medicine, Washington, 1982-92; Lewis B Saltz prof. of surgery George Washington U. Med. Ctr., Washington, 1992-94; prof. surgery, vice chair dept. surgery, assoc. dean U. Nev., Reno, 1994—. Editor: (with J.M. Giordano) Reoperative Vascular Surgery, 1987, Basic Science of Vascular Surgery, 1988; assoc. editor: Haimovici Vascular Surgery: Principles and Techniques, 1989; co-editor: Basic Science in Vascular Disease, 1996; mem. editl. bd. Internat. Vascular Surgery, Internat. Jour. Impotence Rsch.; contbr. articles to profl. jours. Stroke liaison nat. chpt. Am. Heart Assn., 1992-94. Capt. USAF, 1958-61. Grantee USPHS, 1974-82. Fellow ACS; mem. Cleve. Vascular Soc. (pres. 1977-78), Rocky Mt. Vascular Soc. (pres. 1981-82), Am. Surg. Assn., Soc. Vascular Surgery, Washington Acad. Surgery (sec. 1991-92, v.p. 1992-93, pres. 1993-94), Am. Venous Forum (sec. 1991-94, bd. dirs. found. 1992-95), Western Vascular Soc., Cosmos Club (Washington) (admissions com. 1992-94).

DEPAOLA, DOMINICK PHILIP, academic administrator, dean; b. Bklyn., Dec. 29, 1942; s. Dominick and Marie (DeStefano) DeP.; m. Rosemary Elizabeth Femiano, Aug. 2, 1969; 1 child, Alexis Jane. BS, St. Francis Coll., 1964; DDS, NYU, 1969; PhD, MIT, 1974; ScD (hon.), Baylor U., 1995. Assoc. prof. Va. Commonwealth U., Med. Coll. Va., Richmond, 1974-78; dean Dental Sch. U. Tex. Health Sci. Ctr., San Antonio, 1983-87, interim dean Grad. Sch. Biomed. Scis., 1986-87; dean Dental Sch. U. Medicine and Dentistry N.J., Newark, 1988-90; pres., dean Baylor Coll. Dentistry, Dallas, 1990—; mem. dental adv. com. Pew Commn. for Health Professions, 1991; bd. dirs. Am. Fund for Dental Health, Baylor Rsch. Inst.; mem. Commn. on Dental Accreditation, 1992—. Editor: Preventive Dentistry, 1979. Mem. exec. com. Cancer Ctr., Baylor U. Med. Ctr. Recipient Presdl. award San Antonio Dist. Dental Soc., 1987, Alumni Achievement award NYU Coll. Dentistry, 1993. Fellow Am. Acad. Oral Medicine (hon.); mem. ADA (cons. commn. 1990—, coun. on dental edn.), Am. Inst. Nutrition, Am. Assn. Dental Schs. (past pres. 1989-91), Am. Soc. for Clin. Nutrition, Am. Assn. Dental Rsch., Internat. Assn. Dental Rsch., Hispanic Dental Assn. (hon.), Lakewood Country Club, Crescent Club. Office: Baylor Coll Dentistry 3302 Gaston Ave Dallas TX 75246-2013

DE PAULO, J(OSEPH) RAYMOND, JR., psychiatrist; b. Charleston, W.Va., May 21, 1946; s. J. Raymond Sr. and Mary Catherine (Wilson) DeP.; m. Elizabeth Anne Ratterman, June 8, 1970 (dec. Dec. 1993); children: Marianne, Margaret. BS in Arts and Scis., Xavier U., 1968; MD, John's Hopkins U., 1972. Asst. prof. psychiatry Johns Hopkins U., Balt., 1977-83, assoc. prof. psychiatry, 1983-92, prof. psychiatry, 1993—; dir. affective disorders clinic Johns Hopkins U., Balt., 1977—. NIMH grantee, 1988-89, 91, 94-96. Fellow Am. Psychiat. Assn., Am. Psychopathol. Assn. Roman Catholic. Office: Johns Hopkins U Dept Psychiatry Meyer 3-181 Baltimore MD 21287-7381

DEPERSIO, RICHARD JOHN, otolaryngologist, plastic surgeon; b. Oak Ridge, Tenn., July 10, 1949; s. John Dominick DePersio and Genevieve (Kellerman) Weinberg; m. Melissa Eddleman, Nov. 23, 1994; children: Lauren Elizabeth, Katherine Genevieve, Gerard Edward. BS with honors, U. Tenn., Knoxville, 1971; MD, U. Tenn., Memphis, 1974. Diplomate Am. Bd. Facial, Plastic and Reconstructive Surgery, Am. Bd. Otolaryngology. Intern City of Memphis Hosps., 1975; surgery resident Meth. Hosp., Memphis, 1976-77; otolaryngology resident U. Tenn., Memphis, 1977-80; pvt. practice Knoxville Otolaryngology Facial Surgery Clinic, 1980—; clin. asst. prof., U. Tenn. Dept. Surgery, Knoxville, 1980—. Fellow ACS, Am. Acad. Cosmetic Surgery, Am. Acad. Facial, Plastic and Reconstructive Surgery, Am. Acad. Otolarygology/Head and Neck Surgery, Am. Rhinologic Soc., Am. Acad. Aesthetic & Restorative Surgery, Am. Soc. TMJ Surgeons. Roman Catholic. Home: 7841 Embercrest Trl Knoxville TN 37938-3404 Office: Knoxville Otolaryngology 930 E Emerald Ave Knoxville TN 37917-4539

DEPNER, THOMAS ARNOLD, nephrology educator; b. Medford, Oreg., Apr. 8, 1943; s. Arnold Martin and Helen Lois (Swan) D.; m. Celeste Marie White, June 29, 1968; children: Charles, Kristine, Ivy. BS, U. Portland, 1965; MD, Johns Hopkins U., 1969. Intern Case Western Res. U. Hosps., Cleve., 1969-70, resident in medicine, 1970-72, fellow in nephrology, 1972-74; asst. prof. nephrology U. Calif., Davis, 1974-81, assoc. prof., 1981-89, prof., 1989—; dir. renal dialysis unit U. Calif.-Davis Med. Ctr., 1980—. Mem. Internat. Soc. Nephrology, Am. Soc. Nephrology, Internat. Soc. Artifical Organs, Am. Kidney Found. Democrat. Roman Catholic. Office: U Calif 4301 X St Sacramento CA 95817-2214

DEPP, DAVID ALAN, thoracic and cardiovascular surgeon; b. New Orleans, Oct. 26, 1942; s. Oren Richard and Alma (Cates) D.; m. Karen Lee Deener, June 13, 1967; children—Kristin Elizabeth, Natalie Andrea. B.A., Tulane U., 1966, M.D., 1967. Diplomate Am. Bd. Surgery, Am. Bd. Thoracic Surgery. Intern U. Utah affiliated Hosps., Salt Lake City, 1967-68; resident in surgery and cardiovascular surgery, 1968-76; surgeon, ptnr. Thoracic and Cardiovascular Clinic, Baton Rouge, 1976—; clin. asst. prof. dept. surgery La. State U. Sch. Medicine. Pres. Baton Rouge chpt. Am. Cancer Soc., 1976-77; pres. Baton Rouge unit Am. Heart Assn., 1981-82. Served to lt. comdr. USN, 1973-75. Mem. ACS, Am. Coll. Cardiology, Am. Coll. Chest Physicians, Soc. Thoracic Surgeons, So. Thoracic Surg. Assn., Baton Rouge Oncology Group (pres. 1996). Republican. Episcopalian. Lodge: Rotary. Office: Thoracic and Cardiovascular Clinic 4750 North Blvd Baton Rouge LA 70806-4016

DEPPOLITI, DENISE BRAMLEY, mental health nurse; b. Oneida, N.Y., Nov. 2, 1948; d. Amos and Bernice (Hemming) Bramley; children: Bruce, Brian. BS in Nursing, Syracuse U., 1971, MS, 1977. Staff nurse VA Hosp., Syracuse, 1971-73; coord. mental health psychiat. nursing Crouse Irving Meml. Hosp. Sch. Nursing, Syracuse, 1977-89; clin. nurse specialist psychiatry St. Joseph's Hosp. Health Ctr., Syracuse, 1987-91, dir. clin. resource and devel., 1991—; cons. James Sq. Residential Health Care, Syracuse, 1986-93; pvt. practice, Liverpool, N.Y. Mem. Syracuse Area Psychiat. Nurses (pres. 1986-88), Ctrl. N.Y. Hosp. Assn. (conf. chairperson staff educators, 1993-95), Sigma Theta Tau. Office: Ste 2Z 7209 Buckley Rd Liverpool NY 13088

DE PRIEST, IONE ELIZABETH, occupational health nurse; b. Lewistown, Pa., Aug. 2, 1945; d. Jacob T. and Ione (Carmichael) Stayrook; m. John Vernon De Priest; children: Michelle Reneé, William Byron. Diploma, Bapt. Hosp. Sch. Nursing, Nashville, 1966; BS, St. Francis Coll., Joliet, Ill., 1990. RN, Tenn.; cert. occupational health nurse; cert. case mgr. Oper. rm. nurse Bapt. Hosp., Nashville, 1966-67; charge nurse Gen. Hosp., Macon, Ga., 1967-68, Nautilus Hosp., Waverly, Tenn., 1968-69; vol. ARC, Baumholder, Germany, 1969-72; indsl. nurse II Oscar Mayer Foods, Goodlettsville, Tenn., 1972, indsl. nurse I, 1973-92, benefits coord., 1993-95; worker's compensation adminstr. Oscar Mayer, Madison, Wis., 1995—. Office: PO Box 7188 Madison WI 53707-7188

DEPUMPO, LESTER JOHN, JR., nursing educator; b. Elmira, N.Y., June 22, 1942; s. Lester and Louise (Dieffenbauch) DeP.; m. Elaine Blaisure, Oct. 30, 1965; children: Denise, John. Diploma, Binghamton (N.Y.) State Hosp., 1965; BS in Nursing Edn., Wilkes (Pa.) U., 1971; MED, Elmira (N.Y.) Coll., 1976; MSN, Syracuse U., 1986. RN, N.Y., Pa. Instr. St. Joseph's Hosp. Sch. Nursing, Elmira; coord. practical nursing program Bradford County Area Vocat. Tech. Sch., Towanda, Pa.; with psychiat. clin. nursing dept. St. Joseph's Hosp. Sch. Nursing, Elmira; instr. Arnot Ogden Meml. Hosp. Sch. Nursing, Elmira; asst. prof. Robert Parker Dept. Nursing Mansfield (Pa.) U. Capt. U.S. Army, 1966-69. Mem. N.Y. State Nurses Assn., Sigma Theta Tau. Home: 1227 Weaver Rd Waverly NY 14892

DERISE, NELLIE LOUISE, nutritionist, educator, researcher; b. Jeanerette, La., Aug. 9, 1937; d. O'Niell Paul and Anita (Savoy) D. BS, U. Southwestern La., 1962; MS, U. Ala., 1964; PhD, Va. Poly. Inst., 1973. Grad. asst. U. Ala., Tuscaloosa, 1962-64; asst. prof. Iowa State U., Ames, 1968-70; asst. prof. U. Southwestern La., Lafayette, 1964-68, assoc. prof., 1973-81, prof. home econs., 1981-94; ret., 1994; Chmn La. State Nutrition Council, 1977-78. Contbr. articles to profl. jours. Mem. Am. Home Econs. Assn., Am. Dietetic Assn., U.S. Metric Assn., Soc. Nutrition Edn., La. Home Econs. Assn. (bd. dirs. 1973-75), La. Dietetic Assn. (bd. dirs. 1982-86), Inst. Food Tech., Sigma Xi. Democrat. Roman Catholic. Home: 1108 Highway 668 Jeanerette LA 70544-8611

DERIVAN, ALBERT THOMAS, psychiatrist; b. Yonkers, N.Y., Nov. 2, 1939; s. Albert Joseph and Beatrice (Lister) D.; m. Mary Collins, July 4,

1961; children: Janice, Nancy, Linda, Donna. BChE, Manhattan Coll., 1961; MD, N.J. Coll. of Medicine, 1966. Diplomate Am. Bd. Psychiatry and Neurology, Nat. Bd. Med. Examiners, Child Psychiatry. Intern/resident Johns Hopkins Hosp., Balt., 1966-68; resident/fellow J.F. Kennedy/Johns Hopkins Hosp., Balt., 1971-72; resident Sheppard Pratt Hosp., Towson, Md., 1972-75, dir. tng. outpatient, 1975-79; asst. prof. psychiatry Johns Hopkins Hosp., Balt., 1974-80; pvt. practice Balt., 1972-80; asst. prof. Thomas Jefferson U. Sch. Medicine, Phila., 1980—; asst. v.p. clin. rsch. Wyeth Ayerst Rsch., Radnor, Pa., 1980—; corp. rep. Am. Coll. Neuropsychopharmacology, Nashville, 1987—. Author: (chpt.) Disorders of Bonding in Failure to Thrive, 1981. Deacon Cath. Archdiocese Phila. Fellow Am. Acad. Child Psychiatry, Soc. for Devel. Disabilities; mem. Pa. Regional Coun. for Child and Adolescent Psychiatry, Am. Psychiatric Assn., AMA, Collegium Internationale Neuropsychopharmacolgium (Milan, Italy). Roman Catholic. Home: 226 Hardwicke Ln Villanova PA 19085-1405 Office: Wyeth Ayerst Rsch PO Box 8299 Philadelphia PA 19101-0082

DERIVAN, MARY COLLINS, oncology, medical and surgical nurse; b. N.Y.C., Apr. 2, 1939; d. John Francis and Anne Frances (Connare) Collins; m. Albert T. Derivan, July 4, 1961; children: Janice, Nancy, Linda, Donna. BSN, Hunter/Bellevue, 1960; MSN, Villanova U., 1987. Cert. oncology nurse. Staff nurse Vis. Nurse Svc. N.Y., N.Y.C., 1960-61, Vis. Nurse Assn. Plainfield, N.J., 1961-62; head nurse St. Francis Hosp., Jersey City, N.J., 1962-63; instr. St. Francis Hosp. Sch. Nursing, Jersey City, N.J., 1963-64; dir. insvc. edn. Yonkers (N.Y.) Gen. Hosp., 1964-65; staff nurse Stella Maris Hospice, Towson, Md., 1979-80; asst. dir. nursing Wayne (Pa.) Nursing Ctr., 1981-82; staff nurse Fitzgerald Mercy Hosp., Darby, Pa., 1982-83, nurse mgr., 1983-89, nurse educator, 1989—; bd.dirs., profl. edn. csubcom. Delaware County unit Am. Cancer Soc., 1988—, mem. Acad. of Med. Surg. Nursing. Presenter in field. Vol. Am. Home Missions Owingsville Ky., 1991. Mem. Oncology Nursing Soc. (founding mem., co-chair program com. Penns Wood chpt.). Roman Catholic. Home: 226 Hardwicke Ln Villanova PA 19085-1405 Office: Fitzgerald Mercy Hosp 1500 Lansdowne Ave Darby PA 19023-1225

DE RIVAS, CARMELA FODERARO, psychiatrist, hospital administrator; b. Cortale, Italy, Nov. 25, 1920; came to U.S., 1935, naturalized, 1942; d. Salvatore and Mary (Vaiti) Foderaro; m. Aureliano Rivas, Oct. 30, 1948; children: Carmen, Norma, Sandra, David. Student, U. Pa., 1940-42; M.D., Women's Med. Coll. Pa., 1946. Diplomate: Am. Bd. Psychiatry and Neurology. Intern women's Med. Coll. Pa. Hosp., 1946; gen. practice Phila., 1947-49, Tex., 1947-49; mem. staff Norristown (Pa.) State Hosp., 1949-63, supt., 1963-70, dir. family planning, 1979-87, clin. dir. spl. assignments, 1979-82; assoc. psychiatry U. Pa., 1963-75; psychiatrist Penn Found. Mental Health, Sellersville, Pa., 1970-72; dir. intake coping svcs. Ctrl. Montgomery Mental Health/Mental Retardation Ctr., Norristown, Pa., 1972-77, med. dir., 1977-82, psychiatrist, 1980-82; cons. surveyor HEalth Care Fin. Adminstrn., 1987—; dir. program evaluation Norristown State Hosp., 1979-82, med. dir., 1982-87. Named to Hall of Fame S. Phila. H.S., 1968; recipient citation Women's Med. Coll. Pa., 1968, Amita achievement award, 1976, achievement award Grad. Club Phila., 1976; named Woman of Yr. Pa. Fedn. Bus. and Profl. Women, 1979. Fellow Am. Psychiat. Assn., Pa. Psychiat. Soc. (rep. assembly of dist. brs. 1979-88); mem. AMA, Phila. Psychiat. Soc. (councilor), Montgomery County Med. Soc. (bd. dirs., past pres.), Pa. Med. Soc. (chmn. adv. com. to aux. 1981-88, mem. ho. of dels., mem. commn. on med. edn. 1991-94, mem. com. on continuing med. edn. 1994—). Home: 700 Joseph Dr Wayne PA 19087-1021

DE ROSA, GUY PAUL, orthopedic surgery educator; b. Napoleon, Ohio, Oct. 25, 1939; married. BS, Notre Dame U., 1961; MD, Ind. U., 1965. Diplomate Am. Bd. Orthopedic Surgery (oral examiner 1983—, site investigator residency rev. com. 1983—, bd. dirs. 1990—, mem. credentials com. 1990-93, mem. oral examinations com. 1990—, mem. grad. edn. com. 1990—, chmn. 1995-97, mem. oral recertification examination com. 1992-93, mem. practice audit com. 1992-93, ABMS rep. alt. 1992-93, ACS adv. coun. 1992-94, sec. 1993-94, mem. exec. com. 1993-94, mem. cert. renewal com. 1993-94, mem. fin. com. 1993-94, vice chmn. residency rev. com. 1994—). Resident in gen. surgery Sch. Medicine, Ind. U., Indpls., 1965-66, resident in orthopedic surgery, 1966-70; fellow in pediat. orthopedics Hosp. for Sick Children, London, 1969-70; asst. prof. orthopedic surgery Sch. Medicine, Ind. U., Indpls., 1970-76, assoc. prof., 1976-82, dir. undergrad. edn. dept. orthopedic surgery, 1972—, chief neuromuscular disease, 1972—, coord. Garceau-Wayu Lectureships dept. orthopedic surgery, 1975—, dir. Cerebral Palsy Clinic, 1978-88, orthopedic cons. Hemophilia Clinic, 1978-91, prof. orthopedic surgery, 1981—, orthopedic cons. Rheumato-Orthopedic Clinic, 1984—, chmn. dept. orthopedic surgery, 1986-95; attending physician Wishard Meml. Hosp., Indpls., 1970-95, Ind. U. Med. Ctr., Indpls., 1970-95, James Whitcomb Riley Hosp. for Children, Indpls., 1970-95; coord. Ctrl. Ind. and So. Ind. State Bd. Health Programs, Scoliosis and Sch. Screening, 1977; mem. orthopedic surgery steering com. Children's Cancer Study Group, 1990; mem. residency rev. com. for orthopedic surgery Accreditation Coun. for Grad. Med. Edn., 1990—; vis. prof. Children's Hosp., Columbus, Ohio, 1977, St. Joseph Hosp., Ft. Wayne, Ind., 1977, Miami Valley Hosp., Dayton, Ohio, 1978, 82, 85, 86, Deaconess Hosp., Evansville, Ind., 1980, Bloomington (Ind.) Hosp., 1982, U. Tex., Galveston, 1982, U. Mo. Med. Ctr., Columbia, 1983, Southwestern Mich. Area Health Edn. Ctr., Kalamazoo, 1985, Newington (Conn.) Children's Hosp., 1988, Children's Hosp. Med. Ctr., Akron, Ohio, 1992, and numerous others; active Hemophilia Med. Adv. Coun., 1978—; presenter in field. Contbr. numerous articles to profl. jours. Bd. dirs. United Cerebral Palsy, 1973-85, Hemophilia Found., 1978—, New Hope of Ind., 1984-86, also mem. long range planning com. 1984-85, mem. task force on serving brain injured 1988, Ind. Found. Hand Surg. Rsch. and Edn., 1989-95; mem. adv. bd. Head Injury Found., 1983-95, Children's Limb Found., 1992—; mem. pub. rels. and promotion com. Ind. Gov. Coun. on Phys. Fitness and Sports Medicine, 1986-92, mem. promotion com. 1988-92; dir. State of Ind. Orthop. Rsch. and Edn. Found., 1993, bd. trustees, 1994. Maj. USAF, 1970-72. Grantee in field; recipient Ensminger award for rsch. in trauma, 1967, Willis Gatch award, 1968. Mem. AMA, Am. Orthop. Assn. (mem. nominating com. 1988-89, del.-at-large exec. com. 1988-89, mem. com. on N.Am. travelling fellowship 1989-93, mem. com. planning and devel. 1991—, 2nd pres.-elect 1994—), Am. Fracture Assn. (Wellmerling award 1982), Am. Acad. Pediats., Am. Acad. Orthop. Surgeons (mem. com. undergrad. edn. 1976-83, chmn. 1979-83, mem. com. pediat. orthopedics 1988-94, mem. subcom. on spine 1990, mem. subcom. on pediats program com. 1992, mem. coun. clin. resources 1993-94), Am. Acad. Cerebral Palsy and Devel. Medicine, Am. Orthop. Foot and Ankle Soc. (mem. com. biomechanics 1982-84, mem. program com. 1985—), Ind. Orthop. Soc. (mem. exec. com. 1986-95), Ind. State Med. Soc., Assn. Orthop. Chmn., Clin. Orthop. Soc., Acad. Orthop. Soc. (mem. undergrad. edn. com. 1983-87), Little Orthop. Club, Marion County Med. Soc., Mid-Am. Orthop. Assn. (chmn. program com. 1986-87, bd. dirs. 1986—, sec. 1990-93, 2nd v.p. 1993-94, 1st v.p. 1994—), Orthop. Letters Club, Pediat. Orthop. Soc. N.Am. (mem. com. on fellowships 1986-92, bd. dirs. 1990-92, 2nd v.p. 1994, 1st v.p. 1995, pres. 1996), Russell Hibbs . Soc. (mem. edn. com. 1985—), Internat. Soc. Orthop. Surgery and Traumatology, Spectators Orthop. Letters Club, 20th Century Orthop. Assn., Alpha Omega Alpha, Alpha Epsilon Delta. Office: ABOS 400 Silver Cedar Ct Chapel Hill NC 27514

DE ROSE, SANDRA MICHELE, psychotherapist, educator, supervisor, administrator; b. Beacon, N.Y.; d. Michael Joseph Borrell and Mabel Adelaide Edic Sloane; m. James Joseph De Rose, June 28, 1964 (div. 1977); 1 child, Stacey Marie. Diploma in nursing, St. Luke's Hosp., 1964; BA in Child and Community Psychology, Albertus Magnus Coll., 1983; MS in Counseling Psychology with honors, Century U., 1986, PhD in Counseling Psychology with honors, 1987. Gen. duty float nurse St. Luke's Hosp., Newburgh, N.Y., 1964-65; supr. nurses Craig House Hosp., Beacon, N.Y., 1986-94; dir. staff devel., team dir. divsn. outpatient treatment svc. Conn. Mental Health Ctr., New Haven, 1986-94; dir. edn., 1994-95; clin. instr. Sch. Nursing Yale U., New Haven, 1979-84, clin. instr. dept. psychiatry, 1989-95; dir. edn. outpatient divsn. Conn. Mental Health Ctr., New Haven and Norwich, Conn., 1994-95; pvt. practice Comprehensive Psychiat. Care, New Haven, 1975—; clin. dir. Comprehensive Psychiat. Care, Norwich, Colchester and Willimantic, Conn., 1994—. Mem. AAUW, ANA (cert.), Conn. Nurses Assn., Conn. Soc. Psychoanalytic Psychologists, Conn. Soc. Nurse Psychotherapists, Assn. for Advancement Philosophy and Psychiatry, Ea. Conn. Psychiat. Assn. (exec. dir.), Sigma Theta Tau, Delta Mu, Alpha Sigma Lambda. Office: 203 Starro Rd Willimatic CT 06415 Office: 210 Prospect St New Haven CT 06511-2186 Office: 200 W Town St Norwich CT 06360-2112 also: 188 Norwich Ave Colchester CT 06415

DERRY, CONNIE SUSIE, psychogeriatrics nurse; b. Elmira, N.Y., Oct. 24, 1958; d. Robert G. and Phyllis B. (Duggan) Wilber; m. James Derry; children: Melissa, Elizabeth. AAS, Corning (N.Y.) Community Coll., 1983; BSN, Alfred (N.Y.) U., 1990; MSN, Syracuse U., 1994. Cert. clin. nurse specialist. Charge nurse Tioga Gen. Hosp., Waverly, N.Y., 1983-84; head nurse rehab. unit Elmira Psychiat. Ctr., 1984-89; charge nurse Arnot Ogden Meml. Hosp., Elmira, 1989-91; asst. unit mgr. Founder's Pavilion, Corning (N.Y.) Hosp., 1991-93; dir. nursing Three Rivers Health Care Ctr., Painted Post, N.Y., 1993—, acting adminstr., 1994-95. Mem. ANA (cert. gerontological nursing), Am. Psychiat. Nurses' Assn., N.Y. League of Nursing. Home: 405 Wisteria Way Horseheads NY 14845-1818

DERSH, JEROME, physician, ophthalmologist; b. N.Y.C., Mar. 27, 1928; s. Philip and Selma (Gallanty) D.; m. Rhoda E. Eisman, Dec. 23, 1956; children: Debra Lori, Jeffrey Jonathan. BS, Albright Coll., 1949, DH (hon.), 1989; postgrad. in Bacteriology, U. Pa., 1949-50; MD, Thomas Jefferson U., 1954; DH (hon.), Albright Coll., 1989. Diplomate Am. Bd. Ophthalmology, Am. Bd. Med. Examiners. Intern St. Joseph Hosp., Reading, Pa., 1954-55; resident in surgery Wills Eye Hosp., Phila., 1955-58; capt., chief ophthalmology Westover USAF, Springfield, Mass., 1958-60; pres. Eye Physicians Assocs. Ltd., Reading, Pa., 1960—; pres. med. staff St. Joseph's Hosp., Reading, 1977-79, chief ophthalmology dept., 1979-92; cons. Reading Area C.C., 1976-79. Contbr. articles to profl. jours. Trustee Albright Coll., Reading, 1974—, chmn. fine arts commn., 1972—; fine arts bd. Reading Redevel. Authority, 1977-85, Reading Mus., 1977-82; collection mgmt. com. Reading Pub. Mus., 1993—, bd. dirs., 1994—. Recipient Dist. Alumnus award Albright Coll., 1979. Fellow ACS (diplomate); mem. AMA (Physicians Recognition award 1977, 80, 83, 86, 89, 92, 95), Am. Acad. Ophthalmology, Pa. Med. Soc., Pa. Acad. Ophthalmology and Otoloaryngology (editor-in-chief Transaction 1968-78, coun. mem. 1964-81, pres. 1980-81), Reading Ear, Nose, Throat Soc. (pres. 1969-70), Berks County Med. Soc. Home: RR 1 Box 1488 Mohnton PA 19540-9609 Office: Eye Physicians Assoc Ltd 606 Court St Ste 200 Reading PA 19601-3542

DERTIEN, DONALD CHARLES, prosthodontist, air force officer; b. Ravenna, Neb., Sept. 9, 1936; s. Charles John and Florence Hilda (Voetberg) D.; m. Helen Dolores Henson, Apr. 5, 1963; children: Craig Charles, Evan Carleton, Sarah Angela, Cheyenne Anita. D.D.S., U. Nebr., 1960; MS U. Tex.-Houston, 1969. Diplomate Am. Bd. Prosthodontics. Commd. 1st lt. U.S. Air Force, 1960, advanced through grades to lt. col., 1978; dental intern U.S. Army, Ft. Benning, Ga., 1960-61; gen. dentist, RAF Croughton, Eng. and Myrtle Beach AFB, S.C., 1961-66; prosthodontist, Wright-Patterson AFB, Ohio, USAF Acad., Colo., Yokota Air Base, Japan, 1969-79; chief prosthodontist, Edwards AFB, Calif., 1979-85; pvt. practice prosthodontics and gen. dentistry Colorado Springs, Colo., 1985—. Active Boy Scouts Am., 1975-85. Fellow Am. Coll. Prosthodontists; mem. ADA, Am. Bd. Prosthodontists, Internat. Acad. Gnathology. Republican. Home: 1314 Shrider Rd Colorado Springs CO 80920-3122 Office: Chapel Hills Dental Bldg 7970 N Academy Blvd Colorado Springs CO 80920-3902

DERVAN, JOHN PATRICK, cardiologist; b. Boston, Aug. 3, 1950; s. Peter Brendan and Ellen (Comer) D. BS, Boston Coll., 1972; MD, St. Louis U., 1976. Diplomate Am. Bd. Internal Medicine, also Sub-bds. Cardiovascular Disease, Critical Care Medicine. Intern Faulkner Hosp., Boston, 1976-77, jr. and sr. resident, 1977-79, chief resident in internal medicine, 1979-80; fellow cardiology Beth Israel Hosp., Boston, 1980-83; instr. medicine Harvard Med. Sch., Boston, 1982-83; clin. asst. prof. medicine Jefferson Med. Coll., Phila., 1983-85, asst. prof. medicine, 1985-86; asst. prof. medicine SUNY, Stony Brook, 1986-93, assoc. prof. medicine, 1993—; dir. cardiac catheterization lab. Univ. Hosp., SUNY, Stony Brook, 1986—, dir. interventional cardiology, 1986—. Fellow Am. Coll. Cardiology, Soc. Cardiac Angiography and Intervention; mem. ACP, Soc. Critical Care Medicine, Am. Heart Assn. Office: SUNY at Stony Brook Divsn Cardiology Health Scis Ctr T17 # 020 Stony Brook NY 11794

DERWINSKI, DENNIS ANTHONY, dentist; b. Chgo., Oct. 18, 1941; s. Anthony Joseph and Julie Donata (Pochron) D.; m. Mary Pamela Butler, Feb. 11, 1964 (div. Dec. 1975); children: Julie, Nancy, John, Amy, Mollie, Camy; m. Gayle Marie Sondelski, Oct. 8, 1977; 1 child, Anthony. DDS, Marquette U., 1965. Resident Cook County Hosp., Chgo., 1967-68; dentist Riverview Dental Assocs., Wausau, Wis., 1968-81; also pres. Riverview Dental Assocs., Wausau, 1971-81; dentist, pres. Hosp. Dental Assocs., Wausau, 1981-92; with Westhill Profl. Ctr., Wausau, 1989—; vice chmn. Wausau Hosp. Dental Staff, Wasau, 1983-87, chmn., 1987-90. Contbr. articles to profl. jours. Dental chmn. United Way, Wausau, 1983; pres. Montessori Sch. Wausau, 1984; bd. dirs. St. Francis Cabrini Sch., 1978-85. Served to capt. USAF, 1965-67. Fellow Acad. Gen. Dentistry (cert.); mem. Soc. Occlusal Studies, ADA, Wis. Dental Assn. (Continuing Edn. award), Am. Equilibration Soc. Republican. Roman Catholic. Club: Wausau. Home: 1209 E Crocker St Wausau WI 54403-2378 Office: Westhill Profl Ctr 2800 Westhill Dr Ste 104 Wausau WI 54401-3769

DESAI, BARIN G., psychiatrist; b. Bombay, India, Apr. 3, 1933; came to U.S., 1959; s. Darbar Gopaldas and Bhaktiben (Amin) D.; m. Heide S. Golitz; children: Monika, Mark, Mira. MD, Grant Med. Coll., Bombay, 1958; MA, U. Iowa, 1963. Diplomate Am. Bd. of Psychiatry and Neurology. Intern St. Francis Hosp., Honolulu, 1959-60; resident Gowanda Psychiat. Ctr., Helmuth, N.Y., 1960-61; rsch. assoc. U. Iowa, Iowa City, 1961-63; sr. psychiatrist Gowanda Psychiat. Ctr., Helmuth, 1963-67; supr. psychiatrist Rockland Psychiat. Ctr., Orangeburg, N.Y., 1968-74; unit chief Rockland Psychiat. Ctr., N.Y., N.J., 1974-80; clin. dir. Rockland Psychiat. Ctr., N.Y., 1980-83; staff psychiatrist Mental Hygiene Clinic, VA Med. Ctr., Lyons, N.J., 1986—; clin. asst. prof. NYU Med. Sch., Rutgers U. Med. Sch. Dir. United Way of Gujarat-affiliate of United Way Internat., Alexandria, Va. Lt. col. USAR, 1983—. Fellow Am. Psychiat. Assn. (del. to assembly, 1982-88, pres. West Hudson dist. branch, 1981-82). Democrat. Unitarian. Home and Office: 495 King George Rd Basking Ridge NJ 07920

DESAI, KARVIN HIRENDRA, pediatrician; b. Bombay, Oct. 8, 1963. MD, Wayne State U., 1988. Resident in pediatrics Stanford U., Palo Alto, Calif., 1989-91, fellow in pediatric cardiology, 1991—; staff pediatrician Lucille Salter Packard Children's Hosp., Palo Alto, 1994—. Recipient Clinician-Scientist award Am. Heart Assn., 1995-96. Office: Lucille Salter Packard Childrens Hosp 751 University Ave Palo Alto CA 94022*

DESAI, MANUBHAI HARIBHAI, surgeon; b. Kosamba, Bulsar, India, Aug. 21, 1933; came to U.S., 1976; m. Sudha. Nathubhai; 3 children. MBBS, U. Bombay, 1957, M in Surgery, 1962. Lic. surgeon, Tex., Mass., N.Y., N.J.; cert. Edn. Coun. for Fgn. Med. Students, Fed. Licensing Exam. Bd. Intern Grant Med. Coll., Allied J.J. Group Teaching Hosps., Bombay, 1958; resident house surgeon in gen. surgery Allied J.J. Group Teaching Hosps., Bombay, 1959, resident house surgeon in ENT, 1959-60, resident surg. registrar in gen. surgery, 1960-62; locum thoracic registrar in exptl. thoracic surgery J.J. Group Teaching Hosps., Bombay, 1962; resident surg. registrar Bombay Hosp., 1962-63; govt. med. officer Ministry of Health, Zambia, 1963-64; surg. specialist Kitwe Cen. Hosp., Zambia, 1965-72; chief surgeon Comml. and Indsl. Med. Aid Hosps., Kitwe, Ndola, Zambia, 1972-75; clin. fellow Cornell Med. Ctr., 1977-78; assoc. dir. critical care svcs. Baystate Med. Ctr., Springfield, Mass., 1978-83; assoc. prof. surgery divsn. gen. surgery U. Tex. Med. Br., Galveston, 1983-91, prof., 1992—, dir. Blocker Burn Ctr., 1992—; asst. chief of staff Shriners Burns Inst., Galveston, 1983—; cons. surgeon to Nchanga Consolidated Group of Copper Mind Hosps., Rokana divsn., Zambia, 1972-75; guest speaker in field; prin. investigator rsch. U. Tex. Med. Br., 1989—, Baystate Med. Ctr., Springfield, Mass., 1982-84. Author: (with others) Art and Science of Burn Care, 1987; contbr. articles to Med. Jour. Zambia, Maharashtra Med. Jour., Current Med Practice (Bombay), Arch. Surg., Nutritional Support Svcs., Cancer Treatment Reports, Am. Surgeon, Jour. Burn Care Rehab., Critical Care Quar., Jour. Trauma, Pediatric Clinics in N.Am., Emergency Care Quar., Surg. Forum, Annals of Surgery, Metabolism, Emergency Medicine, Jour. Pediatric Surgery, Postgrad. Medicine, Burns, Surg. Gynecology and Obstetrics. Recipient Appreciation placque Critical Care Founders Circle, 1989; grantee Shriners Hosps. for Crippled Children, 1986-89; HHS grantee Baystate Med. Ctr., 1982-84. Fellow ACS, Am. Coll. Critical Care Medicine, Internat. Coll. Surgeons, East African Assn. Surgeons, Royal Coll. Surgeons of Edinburgh; mem. AMA (Physician Recognition award 1980-82, 84-90), Surg. Infection Soc., Galveston County Med. Soc., Tex. Med. Assn., Singleton Surg. Soc., Pan Am. Med. Assn., Am. Trauma Soc., Soc. Critical Care Medicine, Mass. Med. Soc., Internat. Soc. for Burn Injuries, Hampden Dist. Med. Soc., Assn. for Acad. Surgery, Am. Burn Assn., Zambia Med. Assn., East African Assn. Surgeons, Rotary. Office: Shriners Burns Inst 815 Market St Galveston TX 77550-2725

DE SALVA, SALVATORE JOSEPH, pharmacologist, toxicologist; b. N.Y.C., Jan. 14, 1924; s. Nicola Carlo and Frances Agnes (Caldarella) De S.; m. Elaine Mae Radloff, June 14, 1948; children: Salaine Claire De Salva Bonanne, Christopher Joseph, Stephanie De Salva Farrelly, Steven William, Gregory Vincent, Peter Nicholas, Philip Anthony, Deidre De Salva Berry. BS, Marquette U., 1947, MS, 1949; postgrad., U. Ill., Chgo., 1951-53; PhD, Stritch Sch. Medicine, Loyola U., Chgo., 1958. Research and teaching asst. Marquette U., Milw., 1947-49; research biochemist Milw. County Gen. Hosp., 1954; instr. U. Ill., Chgo., 1951-52; asst. prof. Chgo. Coll. Optometry, 1951-53; pharmacologist Armour Pharm. Lab., Chgo, 1953-59, sect. head Colgate Palmolive Co., Piscataway, N.J., 1959-66, sr. research assoc., 1966-72, mgr., 1972-76, assoc. dir. research for pharmacology and toxicology, 1976-83, dir. research pharmacology and toxicology, 1983-88, worldwide ops. dir., 1988-90, corp. dir. human and environ. safety worldwide, 1990-92; pres. Salva Cons. Svcs., Somerset, N.J., 1992—; lectr. Loyola U., 1957-59; mem. technician tng. N.J. Council for Research and Devel., Rutgers U., 1969-72. Editor: Symposium for Biomedical Electronic Instrumentation, 1965; contbr. articles to profl. jours.; patentee in field; current work in pharmaco-toxicology of flourides, sequestering agts. and surfactants, nitrosamine risk assessment, alternative safety testing method devel. Mem. Park Forest (Ill.) Mosquito Abatement Program, 1952-55, Franklin Twp. (N.J.) Sch. Bd., 1969-70, Somerset (N.J.) Bd. Health, 1965-67, Cath. Youth Orgn., Somerset; v.p. Cedar Hill Swim Club, Somerset; active Boy Scouts Am., Somerset, 1965-67; trustee Franklin Twp. Day Care Ctr., 1969. Served with USN, 1942-46. Mem. AAAS, Soc. Exptl. Biology and Medicine, Am. Soc. Pharmacology and Exptl. Therapeutics, Soc. Toxicology, Internat. Union Pharmacology (toxicology sect.), N.Y. Acad. Scis., Internat. Soc. Regulatory Pharmacology and Toxicology, Internat. Soc. Study of Xenobiotics, Sigma Xi. Roman Catholic. Home: 83 Demott Ln Somerset NJ 08873-1604

DESANCTIS, ROMAN WILLIAM, cardiologist; b. Cambridge Springs, Pa., Oct. 30, 1930; s. Vincent and Margherita (Marini) DeS.; m. Ruth Ann Foley, May 7, 1955; children: Ellen Ruth, Lydia Marie, Andrea Jean, Marcia Louise. B.S. summa cum laude, U. Ariz., 1951; M.D. magna cum laude, Harvard U., 1955; D.Sc. (hon.), Wilkes Coll., 1984. Diplomate: Am. Bd. Internal Medicine, Sub Bd. Cardiovascular Diseases. Successively intern, asst. resident, sr. resident in medicine Mass. Gen. Hosp., Boston, 1955-56, 58-60; fellow in cardiology Mass. Gen. Hosp., 1960-62; dir. CCU, 1967-80, dir. clin. cardiology, 1980—, physician, 1970—; mem. faculty Harvard U. Med. Sch., 1964—, prof. medicine, 1973—. Co-author: Cardiac Clinico-Pathological Conferences of the Mass. Gen. Hosp, 1972, The Practice of Cardiology, 1989; contbr. articles to med. jours. Served as officer M.C. USNR, 1956-58. Decorated Order of Dynasty of Alouite (Morocco); recipient Excellence in Clin. Teaching award Harvard U. Med. Sch., 1990, Centennial Achievement award U. Ariz., 1989. Fellow ACP (master of the coll. 1994), Am. Coll. Cardiology (Gifted Tchr. award 1991); mem. Am. Heart Assn. (David Littmann award 1996), Assn. Am. Physicians, Inst. of Medicine, Assn. Univ. Cardiologists, New Eng. Cardiovasc. Soc. (pres. 1979-80), Am. Clin. and Climatol. Soc. Roman Catholic. Clubs: Winchester Country; York Golf and Country; Harvard (Boston); Aesculapian. Lodge: Knights of Malta. Home: 5 Thoreau Cir Winchester MA 01890-3340 Office: Mass Gen Hosp 15 Parkman St # 467 Boston MA 02114-3117

DE SAN LAZARO, CAMILLE MARIA, pediatrician. MBBS, Bangalore U., 1969. Sr. registrar Royal Victoria Infirmary, Newcastle, England, 1981; sr. lectr. Newcastle U., 1989; dir. Lindisfarne Forensic Ctr., Newcastle, 1990—; Contbr. articles to profl. jours. and chpts. to textbooks. Ch. organist; bd. dirs. Foster Care Assn.; accompanist regional choir. Office: Lindisfarne Ctr, Royal Victoria Infirmary, Newcastle NE1 4LP, England

DESANTIS, JOSEPH ANTHONY, orthopaedic surgeon; b. Bklyn., Jan. 25, 1933; s. Joseph Anthony and Angela (Saponaro) DeS.; m. Mary Margaret Rizzo, Sept. 5, 1954; children: Joseph G., Lisa M., Kristin M. BS, CCNY, 1954; MD, U. Bologna, Italy, 1960. Diplomate Am. Bd. Orthopaedic Surgery. Rotating intern Flushing (N.Y.) Hosp., 1960-61, resident in gen. surgery, 1961-62; resident in orthopedic surgery Monmouth Med. Ctr., Long Beach, N.J., 1964-67; pvt. practice, Trenton, N.J., 1967—. Capt. M.C., U.S. Army, 1962-64. Fellow ACS, Am. Acad. Orthopaedic Surgeons, Ea. Orthopaedic Assn.; mem. AMA, N.J. Orthopaedic Soc., Acad. Medicine N.J. Office: 3240 E State St Ext Mercerville NJ 08619

DESANTIS, JOSEPH GERARD, plastic surgeon; b. Bologna, Italy, Feb. 2, 1958; came to the U.S., 1960; s. Joseph Anthony and Mary (Rizzo) DeS.; m. Jeanne Abruzzo; children: Joseph Anthony, Elaina Maria, Jennifer Angela. BA, Franklin & Marshall Coll., 1980; MD, Yale U., 1984. Diplomate Am. Bd. Plastic Surgery, Am. Bd. Surgery. Resident in gen. surgery Thomas Jefferson U. Hosp., Phila., 1984-89; resident in plastic surgery George Washington U. Hosp., Washington, 1989-91, clin. instr. plastic surgery, 1991-94; assoc. in plastic surgery Geisinger Med. Ctr., Danville, Pa., 1994—; clin. asst. prof. surgery Thomas Jefferson Med. Coll., Phila., 1996—; presenter in field. Contbr. chpt. to book. Fellow ACS; mem. Am. Soc. Plastic and Reconstructive Surgery, D.C. Med. Soc. (sec. 1992, mem.-at-large 1993), Nat. Capital Soc. Plastic Surgeons. Office: Geisinger Med Ctr 100 N Academy Ave Danville PA 17822

DE SANTIS, MARK, osteopathic physician; b. Amityville, N.Y., Jan. 2, 1954; s. Vera De S.; m. Elizabeth Anne King, July 15, 1989; children: Mark Anthony, Matthew Robert. AS in Phys. Sci., Nassau C.C., 1975; BS in Nuclear Medicine, C.W. Post Coll., 1982; MS in Med. Biology, L.I. U., 1991; DO, Kirksville Coll. Osteo. Med., 1993. Registered nuclear medicine technologist. Asst. Brookhaven Nat. Lab., Upton, N.Y., 1978-87; staff nuclear medicine technologist Sloan-Kettering Meml. Med. Ctr., N.Y.C., 1977-78; asst. radiophysicist, nuc. cardiology tech. L.I. Jewish Med. Ctr., New Hyde Park, N.Y., 1978-88; med. intern Massapequa Gen. Hosp., Seaford, N.Y., 1993-94; radiology resident St. Barnabas Hosp., Bronx, N.Y., 1994-95; nuclear medicine resident VA Med. Ctr., Northport, N.Y., 1995—; clin. instr. Sch. Allied Health Profls., Stony Brook U. Health Sci. Ctr., SUNY, 1986-87; medicine clerkship aerospace flight surgeon tng. course NASA, 1993. Contbr. articles to profl. publs. With USN, 1982. Recipient Still Kickin' Editor award KCOM. Mem. Am. Osteo. Assn., Soc. Nuclear Medicine, Am. Roentgen Ray Soc., Am. Osteo. Coll. Radiology. Home: 55 Lincoln Blvd Bethpage NY 11714-5517

DE SANTO, DONALD JAMES, psychologist, educational administrator; b. Bklyn., July 5, 1942; s. Vincent James and Rose Ann (Dowd) DeS. BA cum laude, St. Francis Coll., N.Y., 1964; MA in Clin./Child Psychology, St. John's U., 1966, profl. diploma, 1976; m. Loretta DePippo, Aug. 25, 1962; children: Dolores, Jennifer, Marisa. Asst. law libr. rsch. asst. Dewey, Ballantine, Bushby, Palmer & Wood, N.Y.C., 1960-64; rsch. asst. St. John's U., N.Y., 1964-65, teaching fellow, 1965-66, project dir. 2 federally funded grants, 1975-76; dir. The Rugby Sch., Freehold, N.J., 1977—. Mem. Youth Guidance Com., Freehold, 1983—, chmn. econ. devel. com., 1984-86; mem. Econ. Devel. Com., Freehold, 1983-87; mem. Zoning Bd. Adjustment, Freehold, 1985-86; commr. Lake Topanemus Commn., 1990-94; Rep. campaign chmn., Freehold, 1990, 91; bd. dirs. Monmouth County Transp. Assn., 1990, 91-92; mem. U.S. Selective Svc. Bd., 1991—; apptd. Selective Svc. Commn, 1992; v.p. Freehold Rep. Club, 1991-92; mem. adv. bd. Congl. Awards Com., 1994—; mcpl. chmn. Freehold Borough Rep. Party, 1995—; appt. Rep. Nat. Com., 1995; participant, amb. People to People, Beijing, 1995. Contbg. editor Channels jour. special educators, 1986-90, 96—. Recipient Fire Prevention medal, N.Y.C., 1954; citation for outstanding contbn. to arts in edn. N.J. Commr. Edn., 1981, Pres. award Assn. Schs. and Agys. for the Handicapped, 1995-96, N.J. Very Spl. Arts award, 1996, N.J. Gov's. Arts in Edn. award, 1996; Title VIb Fed. grantee, 1972-78. Mem. NRA (life), APA (pub. relations com. div. 16), Nat. Assn. Pvt. Schs. Exceptional Children, Council for Exceptional Children, N.J. Assn. Schs. and Agys. for Handicapped (sec., conf. chmn. 1983-84, pub. relations chmn. 1984-86, Pres. award 1995-96), Nat. Soc. Psychologists in Mgmt., Assn. for Help Retarded Children, Monmouth County Hist. Assn., Internat. Platform Assn., N.J. Assn. Children With Learning Disabilities, Nat. Assn. Pvt. Schs. for Exceptional Children (Coll. bd. 1992—), Nat. Trust for Historic Preservation, Optimists, Elks, Psi Chi, Phi Delta Kappa. Roman Catholic. Home: 222 Park Ave Freehold NJ 07728-2006 Office: PO Box 1403 Belmar NJ 07719-1403

DESAULNIERS, RENE GERARD LESIEUR, optometrist; b. Danielson, Conn., Oct 21, 1922; s. Egide A. and Rose (Regis) D.; student Georgetown U., 1943, Boston U., 1944, Pa. Coll. Optometry, 1948, grad. J. Brinkman Profl. Umpire Sch., Fla.; children: Suzanne Rose (Mrs. R. Bauzys), Maureen Frances (Mrs. R. Russe), Michelle Elizabeth (Mrs. Van Haagen), Thomas Benedict, John Christopher. Individual practice optometry, Putnam, Conn., 1948—; externship Gessel Inst. Child Devel. Yale U., 1964-92; past pres. Conn. Bd. Examiners in Optometry, 1957-91; past pres. Internat. Assn. Bd. Examiners in Optometry; past pres. Nat. Bd. Examiners in Optometry, 1975-85. Past pres. Putnam Little League, Quinebaug Valley Assn. for Retarded; past mem. Putnam Sch. Bd.; life mem., former nat. dir. Am. Optometric Found.; chmn. DK Hosp. Devel. Fund., 1984-85. Served from pvt. to lt., inf. AUS, 1943-46; maj. Res. Recipient Sam Levitt Meml. award, 1948; named Conn. Optometrist of Yr., 1989. Fellow Am. Acad. Optometry, Nat. Acad. Practices (Disting. Practitioner); mem. New Eng. Council Optometrists (chmn. 42d Congress), Am. Optometric Assn., Conn. Assn. Optometrists, VFW, Am Legion (baseball com.), Am. League Umpires Baseball (vision cons.), Conn. Approved Baseball Umpires (eastern bd., past pres. 1981-82), Omega Delta. Clubs: KC (4 deg.), Elk, Rotary (P. Harris fellow). Home: 41 Grove St Putnam CT 06260-2107

DESCHNER, ELEANOR ELIZABETH, retired biologist, cancer researcher; b. Jersey City, Oct. 18, 1928. BA, Notre Dame Coll., Staten Island, N.Y., 1949; MS, Fordham U., 1951, PhD, 1954. Assoc. prof. medicine & radiology Cornell U. Med. Sch., 1976—; assoc. radiobiologist Dept. Medicine Meml. Hosp., N.Y.C., 1978—; head lab of digestive tract carcinogenesis Sloan Kettering Inst. for Cancer Rsch., N.Y.C., 1980—. Contbr. numerous articles to profl. jours. Recipient grants from Nat. Cancer Inst., Am. Cancer Soc., Nat. Inst. Health, Am. Coll. of Gastroenterology. Mem. AAAS, Am. Assn. Cancer Rsch., Am. Gastroent. Assn., Royal Soc. Medicine, Am. Soc. Cell Biologists, Cell Kinetics Soc., Genetics Soc., Am. Inst. Biol. Scis., Radiation Rsch. Soc., Am. Soc. Preventive Oncology, Bus. and Profl. Women's Club, Women's Club, Sigma Xi. Republican. Roman Catholic. Office: Meml Sloan Kettering Cancer Ctr 1275 York Ave New York NY 10021-6007

DESCHNER, WILLIAM P., cardiothoracic and vascular surgeon; b. Brownsville, Tex., Feb. 17, 1953; m. Luretta Susan Schoby, Aug. 6, 1977; children: Kate Elizabeth, Benjamin William, Matthew Nicholas, Daniel Jacob. MD, Ind. U., 1978. Diplomate Am. Bd. Surgery, Am. Bd. Thoracic Surgery. Resident in gen. surgery Ind. U. Sch. Medicine, Indpls., 1974-78, chief resident in gen. surgery, 1982-83, resident in thoracic and cardiovascular surgery, 1983-85; staff surgeon dept. cardiovascular and thoracic surgery St. Joseph Mercy Hosp., Ypsilanti, Mich., 1985-91; pvt. practice Ind./Ohio Heart, Ft. Wayne, Ind., 1991—; staff surgeon Luth. Hosp., Parkview Meml. Hosp., St. Joseph Med. Ctr., Ft. Wayne, Ind., 1991—; clin. asst. prof. Ind. U. Medicine, 1993—; FDA co-investigator TCI HeartMate VAD Program, No. Ind. Heart Inst., Luth. Hops. Ind., Ft. Wayne, 1991—; presenter in field. Contbr. articles to profl. jours. Fellow Am. Coll. Cardiology, Am. Coll. Surgeons; mem. AMA, Soc. Thoracic Surgeons, Am. Coll. Chest Physicians, Chest Club of Midwest, Ind. State Med. Assn., Mich. Soc. Thoracic Surgeons, Mich. State Med. Soc., Southeastern Mich. Surg. Soc., Washtenaw County Med. Soc., Ind. Thoracic Soc., Midwestern Vascular Surg. Soc., Internat. Soc. Cardiovascular Surgery (N.Am. chpt.), Alpha Omega Alpha. Office: Ind/Ohio Heart Ste 102 7910 W Jefferson Blvd Fort Wayne IN 46804

DE SÉGUIN DES HONS, LUC DONALD, physician, medical biologist; b. Paris, Nov. 4, 1919; s. Gabriel and Florence Louisa (Payne) de S. des H.; m. Macha Plaoutine, Dec. 12, 1952; children: Michel, Andre, Cyril. MD, U. Algiers (Algeria), 1943; biologist, Ordre Nat. Medecins, Paris, 1952. Master rsch. C.S.F. and Pasteur Inst., Paris, 1946-53; pres. Labs. Seguin, Drancy, France, 1948—; researcher biol. properties of microwaves French Acad. Scis., 1945-52. Patentee automatic analyzers. Served with Free French Forces, 1943-45. Mem. Union Syndicats Medicaux Region Parisienne (founder, pres. 1966-70), Union 93 (founder, pres. 1967-92).

DE SETTON, LEA SOFER, psychotherapist, educator; b. Panama, Republic of Panama, Jan. 25, 1949; d. Jacobo and Reina Sofer; m. Salomon Setton; children: Joseph, Gabriel, Ilain. Licenciature, U. Santa Maria, Panama, 1973; MEd, U. Okla., Albrook, Panama, 1981; M in Clin. Psychology, Inst. Clin. Psychology, Panama, 1982; PhD, U. Miami, Fla., 1988; postgrad., Washington Sch. Psychiatry, 1993-95, Internat. Inst. Object Rels., 1995-96. Sch. psychologist Albert Einstein Inst., Panama, 1972-78, prin., 1979-83; psychotherapist Clinica Psicologica Alameda, Panama, 1984—; mem. faculty Sch. Psychology, U. Santa Maria, Panama, 1988—. Mem. APA, Panamanian Psychol. Assn. (v.p. 1986-91), World Orgn. for Edn. Preschoolers, ASCD, Nat. Assn. for Edn. Young Children. Jewish. Office: Clinica Psicologica Alameda, Box 318 Zone 1, Panama Republic of Panama

DESFORGES, JANE FAY, medical educator, physician; b. Melrose, Mass., Dec. 18, 1921; d. Joseph Henry and Alice (Maher) Fay; m. Gerard Desforges, Sept. 11, 1948; children—Gerard Joseph, Jane Alice. BA cum laude (Durant scholar), Wellesley Coll., 1942; MD cum laude, Tufts U., 1945; ScD (hon.), Holy Cross Coll., 1990. Diplomate: Am. Bd. Internal Medicine, Am. Bd. Hematology. Intern in pathology Mt. Auburn Hosp., Cambridge, Mass., 1945-46; intern in medicine Boston City Hosp., 1946-47, resident in medicine, then chief resident, 1948-50; USPHS research fellow in hematology Salt Lake Gen. Hosp., Salt Lake City, 1946-47; research fellow in hematology hosp. Thorndike Lab., 1950-52; physician-in-charge RH lab., 1952-53; mem. faculty Tufts U. Med. Sch., 1952—, prof. medicine, from 1972, disting. prof., from 1992, prof. emerita, 1994; asst. dir. Tufts Med. Svc., Boston City Hosp., 1952-67; assoc. dir. Tufts Med. Svc., 1967-68; acting dir., physician in charge, 1968-73; dir. Tufts Med. Svc., 1968-69; assoc. dir. Tufts hematology lab., 1954-67, asst. dir. hosp. labs., 1958-67, acting dir. labs., 1967-68; sr. physician in hematology, rsch. assoc. blood rsch. lab. New Eng. Med. Ctr. Hosp., Boston, 1973—; attending physician VA Hosp., Jamaica Plain; cons. in hematology to various area hosps., 1955-72. Assoc. editor New Eng. Jour. Medicine, 1960-93; mem. editl. bd. Blood, 1976-79; contbr. numerous articles to med. jours. Bd. dirs. Med. Found., Inc., 1976-82; trustee Boston Med. Libr., 1977-81; chmn. automation in med. lab. scis. rev. com. Nat. Inst. Gen. Med. Scis., 1974-76; chmn. consensus com. of infectious disease testing for blood transfusions NIH, 1995—; mem. subcom. on hematology Am. Bd. Internal Medicine, 1976-82, bd. dirs., 1980-88, exec. com., 1984-88; chmn. blood diseases and resources adv. com. Nat. Heart, Lung and Blood Inst., 1978-81. Recipient Disting. Alumna award Wellesley Coll., 1981; NIH fellow, grantee, 1955-88. Fellow AAAS; mem. ACP (Master 1983, Disting. Tchr. award 1987, chmn. med. knowledge self assessment program IX 1989-92), Am. Fedn. Clin. Rsch., Am. Soc. Clin. Pathology, Am. Soc. Hematology (exec. com. 1975-78, adv. bd. 1980-82, v.p. 1982-83, pres. 1984-85), Internat. Soc. Hematology, Mass. Med. Assn., N.Y. Acad. Scis., Am. Assn. Physicians, Inst. Medicine, Phi Beta Kappa, Alpha Omega Alpha (Outstanding Tchr. award 1994). Home: 49 Lake Ave Melrose MA 02176-2701 Office: New England Med Ctr 750 Washington St Boston MA 02111-1533

DESHIELDS BROOKS, DELORA, medical technologist, medical writer; m. Eugene L. Brooks; children: DeLora D. Brooks II, Eugenia L. Brooks. Student, various colls., 1949-61, Vassar Coll., 1968; BS, SUNY, New Paltz, 1981. Medical technician, technologist Westchester County Dept. of Labs. and Rsch., Valhalla, N.Y., 1953, Grassland Hosp., County of Westchester Dept. Pub. Welfare, 1953-55, Scarsdale (N.Y.) Med. Group, 1958, Pvt. Med. Group of New Rochelle, N.Y., 1958, Greenwich (Conn.) Hosp., 1962, Ossining Med. Lab., 1960-61; rsch. asst. Columbia Presbyn., N.Y.C., 1962-63; med. technician, technologist Demir Lab., Mt. Vernon, N.Y., 1960-61; owner, dir. DeShields Med. Lab., New Rochelle, 1961-63; med. technician, technologist Harlem Valley State Hosp., Wingdale, N.Y., 1967; rsch. technologist Wassaic Devel. Ctr., 1982. Contbr. articles to profl. jours. Chmn. ARC Blood Bank, New Rochelle, 1965, procurement disaster unit, 1965; mem. Civil Air Patrol; cons., leader Town of North East Dutchess County Girl Scout Troop; v.p. Millerton Day Care Ctr.; co-capt. Heart Fund; chmn. Am. Cancer Crusade; pres. Friends of the Millerton Free Libr., 1982, St. Patrick's Rosary Altar Soc., 1991; lectr. New Rochelle Girl Scout Coun., 1963; mem., lectr. New Rochelle Girl Scout Coun., 1963; mem., fund raiser North East Heart Assn., 1964. Scholarship Urban League of Westchester County, 1952. Mem. Am. Coll. of Med. Technology. Roman Catholic. Home: Dutchess Ave Box 67 Millerton NY 12546

DESHOTELS, JAMES MICHAEL, nurse practitioner, priest; b. Euclid, Ohio, Nov. 5, 1956; s. Warren J. and Patricia Mary (Cronin) D. BA in Philosophy, Marquette U., 1978, MA in Philosophy, 1982; BSN, St. Louis U., 1986; MDiv, Weston Sch. Theology, 1991, ThM, 1992; MPH, Emory U., 1995, MSN, 1995. Joined Soc. of Jesus, 1982; ordained priest Roman Cath. Ch., 1993. Staff nurse Charity Hosp., New Orleans, 1986-88, 90, Pine St. Inn Clinic, Boston, 1989-91, Stillman Infirmary-Harvard U., Cambridge, Mass., 1990-91; retreat dir. Jesuit Spirituality Ctr., Grand Coteau, La., 1991-93; staff nurse Emory Student Health Ctr., Atlanta, 1994-95; family nurse practitioner Excelth, Inc., New Orleans, 1995—; part-time nurse practitioner Mercy Mobile Health Care, Atlanta, 1995. Mem. Bread for the World, Pax Christi USA; vol. ARC, 1989-91, Ephphany Cmty. Relief Ctr. Clinic, New Iberia, La., 1992, Bridge Over Troubled Waters Med. Outreach Van, Boston, 1988-91, Mercy Mobile Health Care, 1995, Ga. Nurses Found. Clinics, 1994-95; mentor in students' clinic Inst. Latin Am. Concern, Dominican Republic, 1988; chaplain St. Louis U. Med. Ctr., 1985-86. Mem. ANA, APHA, NAACP, Nat. League for Nursing, Nat. Resource Persons Network, Am. Coll. Nurse Practitioners, Amnesty Internat., Knights of Peter Claver, Sigma Theta Tau. Home: Immaculate Conception Ch 130 Baronne St New Orleans LA 70112-2377 Office: St Bernard Cmty Health Ctr 3639 St Bernard Ave New Orleans LA 70122 also: Algiers-Fischer Health Clinic 2030 Whitney Ave New Orleans LA 70114

DESILETS, LYNORE DUTTON, nursing educator; b. Ohio, Feb. 23, 1941; d. Leland S. and Ruth Genevive (Clitty) Dutton; children: Robert L., Michelle Lyn. BSN, Case Western Res. U., Cleve., 1964; MSN, U. Pa., 1978; EdD, Temple U., Phila., 1990. Cert. continuing edn. and staff devel. Clin. instr. Lankenau Hosp. Sch. Nursing, Phila., 1966-68, 74, Delaware County C.C., Media, Pa., 1976-77; clin. instr. Villanova (Pa.) U. Coll. Nursing, 1979, dir. continuing edn. in nursing and healthcare, 1978—. Contbr. articles to profl. jours. Recipient Cert. of Appreciation for outstanding svc. Pa. Nurses Assn. Mem. Pa. Nurses Assn. (Nursing Edn. award 1990), Am. Nurses Assn. (site visitor), Am. Nurses Credentialing Ctr., (commn. on accreditation), Mid-Atlantic Regional Nurses Assn. (v.p 1987), Nat. League for Nursing, Sigma Theta Tau. Office: Villanova U Coll Nursing 800 Lancaster Ave Villanova PA 19085-1690

DE SILVA, HEMA NIHAL, neonatologist; b. Colombo, Sri Lanka, Nov. 3, 1940; came to U.S., 1972, naturalized, 1974; s. Davi Hamilton and Beatrice N. (Sugathapala) De S.; MBBS with honors U. Ceylon, 1965; diploma in child health U. Sri Lanka, 1972; divorced; children Thanushpa Manjula, Nimalie Indhira; m. Paula Ballantyne. Med. officer Dept. Health Svcs., Colombo, Sri Lanka, 1965-72; rotating intern St. Peters Hosp., Albany, N.Y., 1972-73, pediatric resident, 1973-74; pediatric resident and fellow in neonatal-perinatal medicine U. Conn. Health Ctr./Sch. Medicine, Farmington, 1974-77; dir. Sect. Neonatology, St. Francis Hosp. and Med. Ctr., Hartford, Conn., 1977—, dir. pediatric ICU, 1982-85; asst. prof. pediatrics U. Conn. Health Ctr., Farmington, 1978-92, asst. prof. family medicine, 1986-92, assoc. prof. pediatrics and family medicine, 1993—; mem. adv. bd. family devel. resource ctr. St. Joseph Coll., West Hartford, Pediatric Rsch. and Tng. Ctr., Newington, Conn.; mem. profl. health adv. subcom. Conn. chpt. March of Dimes, bd. dirs., 1992—, chmn. Hartford chpt. Diplomate Am. Bd. Pediatrics (subcert. in neonatal/perinatal medicine). Recipient Community Svc. award Hartford County Med. Assn., 1993; named Vol. of Yr., Conn. chpt. March of Dimes, 1992. Fellow Am. Acad. Pediatrics; mem. Sri Lanka Med. Assn., New Eng. Perinatology Soc., Conn. Perinatal Assn., Hartford Med. Soc. (asst. sec. 1986-87, v.p. 1988-89, trustee 1987-90, v.p. 1992, pres. 1993), Nat. Perinatal Assn. (mem. program com. 1992-94, state forum 1994, mem. nominating com. 1995). Contbr. articles to profl. jours. Office: 114 Woodland St Hartford CT 06105-1200

DE SILVA, MERL, radiologist; b. Colombo, Sri Lanka, Aug. 2, 1935; arrived in Australia, 1970; s. Wilson and Soma (Cooray) De S.; m. Nilangani De Silva, Apr. 15, 1960; 1 child, Ruwani. MBBS, U. Ceylon, Colombo, 1960. Radiology registrar Cen. Middlesex Hosp., London, 1966-68; cons. radiologist Jaffna Hosp., Sri Lanka, 1969-70; staff radiologist Children's Hosp., Sydney, N.S.W., Australia, 1970-74 dir. radiology, 1975—; cons. radiologist Westmead Hosp., Sydney, 1985—, Balmain Hosp., Sydney, 1970—. Fellow Royal Coll. Physicians and Surgeons, Royal Australasian Coll. Radiologists; mem. Soc. Paediatric Radiology, Australian Paediatric Radiology, Assn. Neurologists, Coll. Paediatrics Australia. Home: 14 Tryon Ave, Wollstonecraft New South Wales 2065, Australia Office: Children's Hosp, Hawxesbury Rd Westmead, Sydney NSW 2145, Australia

DE SIMONE, ALBA, psychotherapist, counselor, psychologist; b. Mirabella Eclano, Avellino, Italy, June 7, 1948; came to U.S., 1965; d. Gennaro and Anna Recupero; m. Vittorio De Simone, May 25, 1966; children: Anthony, Rosana, Victor, Jr. AS in Community Svcs., Bunker Hill C.C., Boston, 1981; BS in Psychology, Northeastern U., 1984; MEd in Community Counseling with honors, Salem State Coll., 1987; PhD in Human Svcs., Walden U., 1993. Lic. mental health counselor, Mass.; cert. hypnotherapist Internat. Assn. Counselors and Therapists. Spl. edn. tchr. Whelan Sch., Revere, Mass., 1979-80; counselor, social worker Prospect Hill Manor, Somerville, Mass., 1983-84; grad. sch. Italian tchr. Salem (Mass.) State Coll., 1986-90, counselor, examiner, cons., 1987-88; psychotherapist, counselor, community counseling Town of Chelsea, Mass., 1986-93; psychotherapist, prin. Alba & Assocs., Chelsea, 1986—; received advanced certificates for postgrad. study in counseling couples, addiction, families, 1989-90. Congrl. campaign worker, Malden, Mass., 1984, nat. senate campaign supporter, Revere, Mass. 1976, Chelsea, Mass., 1988, Boston, 1993. Salem State Coll. Found. Recipient award Doctorate Assn. N.Y., 1994, Community Svc. award Commonwealth Mass., 1994. Mem. ACA, APA, MPA, Am. Assn. Counseling and Devel., Mass. Mental Health Coun., Doctoral Assn. N.Y. Educators, Mass. Psychol. Assn., Salem State Coll. Alumni Assn., Dante Aligheri Soc. Democrat. Home: 225 Sargent St Revere MA 02151-2164 Office: Alba & Assocs 80 Everett Ave Ste 10 Chelsea MA 02150-2333

DESISTO, ELIZABETH AGNES, medical records specialist; b. Medford, Mass., May 15, 1954; d. John Anthony and Josephine Loretta (Passero) DeS. AS cum laude, Mass. Bay Community Coll., 1974; BS magna cum laude, Northeastern U., 1979. Sr. med. record technician Children's Hosp. Med. Ctr., Boston, 1974-76; asst. dir. med. records dept. Glover Meml. Hosp., Needham, Mass., 1980-82; asst. dir. med. records dept. McLean Hosp., Belmont, Mass., 1982-83, acting dir. med. records dept., 1983-84, dir. med. records dept., 1984-91; dir. med. records dept. New Eng. Meml. Hosp., Stoneham, Mass., 1991-95; project mgr. home health Vis. Nurse Assn., Inc., Haverhill and Andover, Mass., 1995-96; med. record coord. Harvard Pilgrim Health Care, Boston, 1996—. Vol. Big Sister Assn. Greater Boston, 1985-87, Greater Boston Walk for Hunger, 1983-94, nat. and local congl. campaigns; bd. dirs. New Eng. Meml. Hosp. Aux., 1992-95. Mem. Am. Health Info. Mgmt. Assn. (registered records adminstr., mental health record sect., bd. dirs. 1987-90, chmn. 1988-90), Mass. Health Info. Mgmt. Assn. (bd. dirs. 1985-96, sec. 1989-90, pres.-elect 1996—, del. 1994-96). Democrat. Roman Catholic. Home: 235 Winthrop St # 7701 Medford MA 02155 Office: Harvard Pilgrim Health Care 1 Fenway Plz Boston MA 02215

DESJARDINS, BARBARA ANN, psychiatric, mental health nurse; b. Melrose, Mass., Mar. 2, 1946; d. Roy Samuel and Bernadette (Hurley) Fletcher; children: Michael, Danielle, Christa. RN, St. Joseph Hosp. Sch. Nursing, Lowell, Mass., 1966; BS in Psychology/Sociology, New Eng. Coll., Henniker, N.H., 1987, MS in Human Svcs. and Edn., 1996. RN, N.H., Mass.; cert. prof. in health care quality; cert. psychiat./mental health nurse, legal nurse cons. Psychiat. liaison nurse, nurse mgr. Portsmouth (N.H.) Hosp., 1979-84; day supr. HCA Portsmouth Pavilion, 1984, dir. utilization and quality mgmt., 1984-94. Mem. ANA, N.H. Nurses Assn., Nat. Assn. Quality Healthcare Profls., Am. Assn. Legal Nurse Cons.

DESJARDINS, CLAUDE, physiologist, dean, administrator; b. Fall River, Mass., June 13, 1938; s. Armand Louis and Marguerite Jean (Mercier) D.; m. Jane Elizabeth Campbell, June 30, 1962; children: Douglas, Mark, Anne. BS, U. R.I., 1960; MS, Mich. State U., 1964, PhD, 1967. Staff fellow The Jackson Lab., Bar Harbor, Maine, 1967; asst. prof. dept. physiology Okla. State U., Stillwater, 1968-69, assoc. prof., 1969-72; assoc. prof. physiology U. Tex., Austin, 1970-75, prof. Inst. Reproductive Biology, Patterson Labs., 1975-86; NIH sr. fellow U. Va. Med. Sch., Charlottesville, 1983-84, prof. physiology, 1987-96, dir. Ctr. for Rsch. in Reproduction, 1990-96; prof. physiology & biophysics, sr. assoc. dean coll. of medicine, dir. office of rsch. U. Ill., Chgo., 1996—; mem. Ctr. for Advanced Studies, 1986; cons. NIH, ASA, VA, FDA, U.S. Dept. Agr. Danforth Found. fellow, 1960; C.F. Wilcox Found. scholar, 1958. Mem. Am. Physiol. Soc., Soc. Neurosci., Soc. Study Reprodn. (pres. 1982-83), Endocrine Soc., Am. Soc. for Cell Biology, The Microcirculatory Soc. Author: Cell and Molecular Biology of the Testis, 1993, Molecular Physiology of Testicular Cells, 1996; editor: Am. Jour. Physiology: Endocrinology and Metabolism, 1991-95; editor in chief Jour. Andrology, 1989-91, Encyclopedia of Reproduction, 1996; mem. editorial bd. Biology of Reproduction, Endocrinology; contbr. articles to profl. jours.; patentee techs. for male contraception, mechanisms of peptide hormone transport in the microcirculation and liquid-dependent and liquid ind. actions of steroid hormones in peripheral vasculature. Office: U Ill at Chgo Office of Dean M/C 784 1853 Polk St Chicago IL 60612-7332

DESJARDINS, RAOUL, medical association administrator, financial consultant; b. Montreal, Quebec, Can., Oct. 8, 1933; came to U.S., 1962; s. Elso and Blanche (Lemieux) D.; m. Regina Turgeon, Oct. 10, 1961; children: Bryan-Claude, John Andrew. BA, U. Montreal, 1953, MD, 1958; MS, Baylor U., 1964, PhD, 1966; MBA, Rutgers U., 1990. Diplomate Am. Bd. Medicine. Chief intern, resident St. Joan of Arc Hosp., Montreal, 1958-59; med. dir. Candiac (Can.) Med. Clinic, 1953-62, Ortho Research Found., Raritan, N.J., 1966-72; pres. Raoul Desjardins Assocs. Inc., Mendham, N.J., 1972-83, Research Cons. Inc., Mendham, 1983—, APG Internat., Inc., 1991—; med. dirs. Iroquois Class Co., Candiac, 1959-62; asst. prof. Hahnemann Hosp. and U., Phila., 1976-80; bd. govs. Internat. Medicines Exch. and Devel., Georgetown, Ga., 1986—; chmn. bd. advisors Fed. Inst. Health, 1991—; chmn. bd. govs. Grand Masters Found., 1989—. Prodr. video: The Apgram: A New Tool to Measure Cardiovascular Performance, 1995. Recipient physician's recognition award AMA, 1969. Fellow Am. Coll. Angiology, The Royal Soc. Health, Am. Coll. Clin. Pharmacology, N.Y. Acad. Medicine; mem. Doctors Club, Met. Club (membership com. 1991—), Med. Execs. Club, Sigma Xi, Beta Gamma Omega. Roman Catholic. Home: 135 Talmage Rd Mendham NJ 07945-1508 Office: Rsch Cons Inc 135 Talmage Rd Mendham NJ 07945

DESMOND, PATRICIA L., psychotherapist, writer, publisher; b. Boston, June 25, 1946; d. Francis X. and Mary L. (Donohue) D.; children: June, Timothy. AB, Stonehill Coll., 1968; MEd, U. Mass., Boston, 1994. Reporter The Patriot Ledger, Quincy, Mass., 1968-81; publisher Hingham (Mass.) Mariner, 1981-83, The Women's Jour., Hingham, 1985, Milton (Mass.) Times, 1995—; assoc. editor The Hingham Jour., 1985-86; copy editor Boston Herald, 1987-89; columnist Hull (Mass.) Times, 1988-94; editor Mariner Newspapers, Marshfield, Mass., 1989-91; pvt. practice Milton, Mass., 1993-95; pub. Milton (Mass.) Times, 1995—; outpatient therapist High Point, Plymouth, Mass., 1994—; case mgr. Harbor Light Ctr., Boston, 1995; columnist Tiny Town Gazette, Cohasset, Mass., 1993-96; publicist Share New Eng., Canton, Mass., 1993-95; therapist S. Mental Health Ctr., Weymouth, 1995; relapse prevention counselor Nazareth Residence, Roxbury, 1995-96. Author: Cinnamon, 1988; co-author: How to Heal Your Heart, 1988; editor On the Edge, 1992-93; counselor/case mgr. St. Elizabeth's Comprehensive Alcoholism and Addictions Program, 1994-95. Recipient Honorary Mention Mass. Womens Press Assn., 1971, New England Press Assn., 1983. Mem. NOW (state coord. 1973-74), Am. Counseling Assn., Nat. Writers Union, Mass. Assn. Alcoholism and Drug Abuse Counselors, The Women's Poetry Collective. Home: 39 Willoughby Rd Milton MA 02186

DESNICK, ROBERT JOHN, human geneticist; b. Mpls., July 12, 1943; s. Theodore David and Celia Janice (Marcus) D.; m. Julie E. Herzig, Oct. 23, 1988; 1 child, Jonathan Phillips. B.A., U. Minn., 1965, Ph.D., 1970, M.D., 1971. Diplomate Am. Bd. Med. Examiners, Am. Acad. Pediatrics, Am. Bd. Med. Genetics (bd. dirs. 1990—, treas. 1991-93). Rsch. assoc. U. Minn., Mpls., 1970-72, intern and resident dept. pediatrics, 1971-73, asst. prof. lab. medicine and pathology, 1973-75; assoc. prof. genetics and cell biology U. Minn. (Coll. Biol. Sci.), 1975-77; asst. prof. pediatrics U. Minn. (Dight Inst. Human Genetics), 1973-75, assoc. prof. pediatrics, 1975-77, prof. pediatrics, 1977; Arthur J. and Nellie Z. Cohen prof. pediatrics and genetics, 1977—, chief divsn. med. and molecular genetics Mt. Sinai Sch. Medicine, N.Y.C., 1977-93, chair dept. Human Genetics, 1993—; dir. Mt. Sinai Ctr. Jewish Genetic Diseases, 1981—; program dir. Mt. Sinai Gen. Clin. Rsch. Ctr., 1990—; attending physician pediatrics Mt. Sinai Hosp.; cons. physician pediatrics Beth Israel Med. Ctr., N.Y.C., City Ctr. Hosp. Elmhurst, N.Y.; med. adv. bd. Nat. Tay-Sachs and Allied Diseases Assn., 1975—, chmn. med. adv. bd., 1989-93; med. adv. bd. Nat. Neurofibromatosis Found., 1978-81; med. adv. bd. Nat. Found. Jewish Genetic Diseases, 1981—, Am. Porphyria Assn., 1984—, Mucolipidosis IV Found., 1984—, Nat. MPS Soc., 1987—; sci. adv. bd. Dysautonomia Found., 1990—; med. adv. bd. Internat. Incontinenta Pigmenti Found.; bd. dirs. Soc. Inherited Metabolic Diseases, 1983-92; mem. N.Y. Gov.'s Adv. Com. on Genetics, 1982—; sci. adv. bd. Ara Parseghian Med. Rsch. Found., 1994—. Editor: Enzyme Therapy in Genetic Diseases, 1972, 79, Molecular Genetic Modification of Eucaryotes, 1978, Gaucher Disease: A Century of Delineation and Research, 1982, Animal Models of Inherited Metabolic Disorders, 1982, Recent Advances in Inborn Errors of Metabolism, 1987, Treatment of Genetic Diseases, 1991; mem. editl. bd. Enzyme, 1979—, Am. Jour. Human Genetics, 1980-84, Clinica Chemica Acta, 1984—, Pediatrics, 1991—, Human Mutation, 1991—, Biochem. Medicine and Metabolic Biology, 1991—, Jour. Clin. Investigation, 1992—, Jour. Inherited Metabolic Disease, 1996—; contbr. articles to profl. jours. Pres. 5th Internat. Congress of Inborn Errors of Metabolism, 1990. USPHS fellow, 1968-70; recipient Ross award Soc. Pediatric Rsch., 1972, C.J. Watson award U. Minn. Med. Sch., 1973, NIH Rsch. Career Devel. award, 1975-80, E. Mead Johnson award Am. Acad. Pediatrics, 1981, Outstanding Faculty award Mt. Sinai Sch. Medicine, 1991, NIH Merit award, 1992. Mem. AAAS, Am. Soc. Human Genetics, Genetics Soc. Am., Am. Acad. Pediatrics, Minn. Human Genetics League (dir. 1970-77), Soc. Complex Carbohydrates, Behavior Genetics Assn., Am. Fedn. Clin. Rsch., Am. Coll. Med. Genetics (founding fellow), Am. Soc. Biochemistry and Molecular Biology, Assn. Profs. Human/Med. Genetics (pres-elect 1994, pres. 1996-98), Midwest Soc. Pediatric Rsch., Ea. Soc. Pediatric Rsch., Soc. Pediatric Rsch., Soc. Exptl. Biology and Medicine, Am. Soc. Exptl. Pathology, Cen. Soc. Clin. Rsch., Soc. Study Social Biology, Soc. Study Inborn Errors of Metabolism, N.Y. Acad. Sci., European Soc. Human Genetics, Harvey Soc. (sec. 1984-89), Soc. Inherited Metabolic Diseases (pres. 1989-90), Am. Pediatric Soc., Am. Soc. Microbiology, Am. Assn. Physicians, Am. Soc. Clin. Investigation, Japanese Soc. Inherited Diseases (hon.), Societá Italiana di Pediatrica (hon.), Peripatetic Club, Sigma Xi. Office: Mt Sinai Sch Med Dept Human Genetics Fifth Ave & 100th St New York NY 10029

DESOTO, B. MELVIN, orthodontist; b. El Dorado, Ark., July 14, 1941; s. Raymond Melvin DeSoto and Torry Florence (Waller) Rountree; m. Laura Katherine Roddie, June 15, 1962; children: Robert J., David J., Kathleen Ann. DDS, U. Tex. Dental Br., 1965, MS, 1967. Diplomate Am. Bd. Orthodontics. Pvt. practice Shreveport, La., 1967—; asst. clin. prof. La. State U. Med. Ctr., Shreveport, 1980—. Mem. offices thru pres. Rotary Club of SN Shreveport, 1980—; bd. dirs. YMCA Shreveport Southside, 1974-81. Mem. Southwestern Soc. of Orthodontists (sec.-treas. 1967—, 2d v.p. 1967—, trustee to Am. Assn. of Orthodontists 1996—), La. Assn. of Orthodontists (pres., all offices 1967—). Republican. Baptist. Home: 9335 Midvale Shreveport LA 71118 Office: Mel DeSoto Corp 2525 Southside Shreveport LA 71118

DESOTO, CLINTON BURGEL, psychologist, educator; b. Hartford, Conn., Jan. 13, 1931; s. Clinton Burgel and Ruth Esther (Higbie) D.; m. Jane Louise Everhardt, Feb. 4, 1956; children: Brian, William, Stewart; m. Janet Louise Tolbert, Feb. 7, 1975. Student Eau Claire State Coll., Wis., 1948-50; B.A., U. Wis., 1952, M.A., 1953, Ph.D., 1956. Instr. Johns Hopkins U., 1956-57, asst. prof., 1957-61, assoc. prof., 1961-69, prof. psychology, 1969—. Contbr. chpts. to books, articles to profl. jours. Mem. Am. Psychol. Assn., Psychonomic Soc., Soc. Exptl. Social Psychology, Eastern Psychol. Assn., AAAS, Sigma Xi. Home: 923 Beaverbank Cir Baltimore MD 21286-3314 Office: Johns Hopkins U Dept Psychology Baltimore MD 21218

DE SOTO, HERNANDO, pediatric anesthesiologist; b. San Juan, P.R., Mar. 17, 1956; s. Moises and Rosario (Carreno) De S.; m. Hortensia Zeno, July 14, 1979; children: Lara, Pedro Urena. BS, U. P.R., 1977; MD, U. Pedro Humena, 1982. Diplomate Am. Bd. Anesthesia. Intern, resident Mt. Sinai Hosp., N.Y.C., 1985; fellow Children's Hosp., Washington, 1986; asst. prof. anesthesia Med. Coll. Ga., Augusta, 1986-88; chief anesthesia Riverside Hosp., Jacksonville, Fla., 1988-92; dir. pediat. anesthesia U. Fla., Jacksonville, 1992—. Fellow Am. Acad. Pediatrics; mem. Am. Soc. Anesthesiologists, Interam. Soc. Physicians, Soc. Pediat. Anesthesia, Soc. Ambulatory Anesthesia (pubs. com. 1990—), Fla. Soc. Anesthesiology. Office: Univ Med Ctr 655 W 8th St Jacksonville FL 32209

DE SOUSA, BYRON NAGIB, physician, anesthesiologist, clinical pharmacologist, educator; b. Goiania, Goias, Brazil, Jan. 15, 1949; came to the U.S., 1972; s. Lazaro Jose and Zarife (Chaul) de.; m. Ana Maria Soares, Nov. 15, 1991; stepchildren: Thiago M., Thais Martins; children: Daniela N., Elisabeth L. BS in Biology, U. Brasilia, Brazil, 1970, BS in Biology Edn., 1971, MD, 1973; PhD in Physiol. Chemistry, Ohio State U., 1976. Prin. CASEB & CSL biology tchr. Adult Sr. H.S., Brazil, 1969-71; instr. biochemistry U. Goias, Brazil, 1972; rsch. asst. prof. neurology UCLA-Wadsworth V.A. Med. Ctr., L.A., 1978-79; cons. physician Brentwood V.A. Med. Ctr., L.A., 1979-80; intern Wadsorth-Brentwood V.A. Med. Ctr., L.A., 1980-81; resident in Anesthesiology U. So. Calif. Med. Ctr., L.A., 1981-83; anesthesiologist Simi Valley Presbyn. Hosp., Calif., 1983-85, Simi Valley Community Hosp., Calif., 1983-85, Rio Hondo Meml. Hosp., L.A., 1983-85, Kaiser Permanente Med. Ctr., Orange County, Calif., 1983-84, Hollywood Presbyn. Med. Ctr., L.A., 1983-84, Pacoima Community Hosp., L.A., 1984; assoc. prof. biochemistry, pharmacology Fed. U. Goias, 1986-89; adj. prof. pharmacology U. North Tex. Health Sci. Ctr., Ft. Worth, 1993; anesthesiologist UTSMC affiliated hosps., Dallas, 1993; vis. prof. pharmacology, med. microbiology and immunology U. North Tex. Health Sci. Ctr., Ft. Worth. Author, editor (book) Arts of Politics: Thoughts and Quotations, 1988; reviewer sci./clin. jours.; contbr. over 60 articles to sci. jours.; inventor in field. NIA postdoctoral fellow Med. Coll. Pa., 1976-77, postdoctoral fellow U. Wis., 1977-78, Internal Medicine fellow UCLA Med. Ctr., 1979-80. Fellow Am. Coll. Internat. Physicians (trustee, pres. Dallas-Ft. Worth chpt.); mem. AAAS, AMA, Am. Soc. Anesthesiologists, Am. Soc. Neurochemistry, Western U.S.A. Pain Soc., Calif. Med. Assn., Calif. Soc. Anesthesiologists, Tex. Med. Assn., Tarrant County Med. Soc. Orange County Anesthesiology Soc., L.A. County Soc. Anesthesiologists, L.A. County Med. Soc., Internat. Anesthesia Rsch. Soc., Internat. Soc. Neurochemistry, European Brain and Behavior Soc., European Soc. Regional Anesthesia, Brazilian Coun. Ophthalmology, British Brain Rsch. Assn., Gerontological Soc., Soc. Neurosci. Office: U North Tex Health Sci Ctr Dept Pharmacology 3500 Camp Bowie Blvd Fort Worth TX 76107-2699

DESPAIN, BECKY ANN, dental educator; b. Oklahoma City, July 14, 1948; children: Brian Thomas, Meredith Lynn. BS in Dental Hygiene, Baylor U., 1970; MEd, Cen. State U., Okla., 1982. Registered dental hygienist. Pvt. practice clin. dental hygienist Oklahoma City, 1970-73; instr. Coll. Dentistry, Okla. U. Health Scis. Ctr., Oklahoma City, 1973-82, asst. prof., 1982-85, acting chair dept. dental hygiene, 1984-85, clin. dental hygienist faculty practice, 1977-85; assoc. prof., dir. Caruth Sch. Dental Hygiene Baylor Coll. Dentistry, Dallas, 1985-93, assoc. prof. dept. pub. health scis., 1993—; clin. dental hygienist Drs. Israelson, Plemons & Jaynes, Richardson, Tex., 1995—; clin. instr. Rose Jr. Coll., Midwest City, Okla., 1972; mem. affil. staff Okla. Children's Meml. Hosp., Oklahoma City, 1977-85; clin. dental hygienist North Tex. Periodontal and Implant Assn., Richardson, 1988-91; clin. dental hygienist Drs. Hilton Israelson and Jacqueline Plemons, Richardson, Tex., 1995—; mem. text constrn. com. Nat. Bd. Dental Hygiene, ADA, Chgo., 1987-91, dental hygiene cons. Commn. on Dental Accreditation, 1989-96; investigator grants and contracts HHS, NIH. Editorial rev. bd.: Jour. Dental Hygiene, Chgo., 1982—; contbr. abstracts and articles to profl. jours. Spkr. Sch. Vols. Program, Oklahoma City Pub. Schs., 1976-85; project dir. Oral Healthlink: Dallas/Ft. Worth Coalition for Oral Health 2000; bd. dirs. Dallas chpt. ACLU of North Tex., pres., 1996; Tex. coord. Nat. Spit Tobacco Edn. Program, Oral Health Am., 1996. Recipient small grant award Rsch. Coun., OUHSC, Oklahoma City, 1985, Dental Hygiene Rsch. grant Oral-B Labs., Redwood City, Calif., 1985. Mem. ACLU (pres. Dallas chpt.), Am. Assn. Dental Schs., Am. Assn. Dental Rsch., Am. Dental Hygienists Assn. (del. 1980-84), Tex. Dental Hygienists Assn., Tex. Dental Hygiene Dirs. Assn. (sec. 1990-92), Dallas Dental Hygienists Soc. (v.p. 1994, pres.-elect 1995, pres. 1996), The Woman's Ctr. of Dallas (chair health care task force, bd. dirs. 1994-96, health com. Women's Coun. of Dallas County 1995—), Sigma Phi Alpha, Kappa Delta Pi. Office: Baylor Coll Dentistry PO Box 660677 Dallas TX 75266-0677

D'ESPOSITO, MARK THOMAS, neurologist, researcher; b. N.Y.C., May 12, 1961; s. Raymond and Janet (Volpe) D'E.; m. Judith M. Sonnenblick, May 27, 1987; 1 child, Zoe. BS, BA, U. Rochester, 1983; MD, SUNY, Syracuse, 1987. Diplomate Am. Bd. Psychiatry and Neurology. Intern Nassau County Med. Ctr., East Meadow, N.Y., 1987-88; resident in neurology Boston U. Med. Ctr., 1988-91, fellow in behavioral neurology, 1991-93; asst. prof. in neurology U. Pa., Phila., 1993—. Contbr. articles to profl. jours. Recipient McDonnell-Pew award in cognitive neurosci., 1992, Clin. Investigative Devel. award NIH, 1993. Mem. Internat. Neuropsychol. Soc., Behavioral Neurology Soc., Acad. Neurology, Soc. for Neurosci. Office: U Pa Hosp Dept Neurology 3400 Spruce St Philadelphia PA 19104

DESROSIERS, RONALD CHARLES, microbiology and molecular genetics educator; b. Manchester, N.H., June 16, 1948; s. Armand Joseph and Stella Anne (Rogala) D.; m. Marguerite Ann Arel, Aug. 15, 1970; children: Aimee, Jesse. BA, Boston U., 1970; PhD, Mich. State U., 1975. Instr. microbiology, molecular genetics Harvard Med. Sch., Southborough, Mass., 1977-79, asst prof. microbiology, molecular genetics, 1979-85; acting chmn. div. microbiology New Eng. Regional Primate Rsch. Ctr., Southborough, 1983-84, chmn. div. microbiology, 1984—; assoc. prof. microbiology, molecular genetics Harvard Med. Sch., Southborough, 1985-91, prof. microbiology, molecular genetics, 1991—; coord. AIDS unit New Eng. Regional Primate Rsch. Ctr., Southborough, 1988—; rsch. assoc. Yale U., 1977; lectr. in field. Editor Intervirology, 1988-90, AIDS Rsch. and Human Retroviruses, 1990—, Jour. of Virology, 1991—, Current Biology, 1993—; contbr. numerous articles and revs. to profl. jours. NIH Postdoctoral fellow, 1975-77, Med. Found. of Boston Inc. fellow, 1979-81, Leukemia Soc. Am. Spl. fellow, 1982-84. Office: New Eng Regional Primate Rsch Ctr 1 Pine Hill Rd # 9102 Southborough MA 01772-1312

DESSER, KENNETH BARRY, cardiologist, educator; b. N.Y.C., Mar. 24, 1940; s. George and Sarah Ruth (Kaplan) D.; m. Carmen Yvonne Fletcher; children: Brett Karen, Lori Helene. BA, NYU, 1961; MD, N.Y. Med. Coll., 1965. Diplomate Am. Bd. Internal and Cardiovascular Disease. Intern Beth Israel Med. Ctr., N.Y.C., 1965-66, resident in medicine, 1968-70; cardiology fellow Inst. Cardiovascular Diseases, Phoenix, 1970-72. asst. dir., 1977-83; fellowship dir. cardiology Good Samaritan Med. Ctr., Phoenix, 1995—; prof. medicine U. Ariz., Tucson, 1985—; editorial cons. to med. jours. Mem. emeritus Am. Jour. Cardiology, 1980-82; contbr. articles to profl. jours., chpts. to books. Capt. U.S. Army, 1966-68, Vietnam. Decorated Bronze Star with oak leaf, Purple Heart, Air medal, Cross of Gallantry; recipient Best Rsch. award Beth Israel Med. Ctr., 1966. Fellow ACP, Am. Coll. Cardiology (mem. editl. bd. 1983-85), Am. Coll. Chest Physicians, Am. Heart Assn.; mem. Am. Fedn. Clin. Rsch. Office: Cardiology and Internal Medicine 1144 E Mcdowell Rd Phoenix AZ 85006-2664

DEST, VANNA M., clinical nurse specialist; b. New Haven, Dec. 13, 1962; d. Joseph F. and Blanche H. (Denegris) D. BSN, So. Conn. State U., 1984; MSN, Yale U., 1992. Radiation oncology clin. nurse specialist Hosp. St. Raphael, New Haven. Vol. Am. Cancer Soc. Recipient Lane Adams award Am. Cancer Soc., 1995. Mem. Oncology Nursing Soc., Conn. Oncology Assn., Southwestern Conn. Oncology Nursing Soc. (pres.), Sigma Theta Tau. Home: 768 Pine Rock Ave Hamden CT 06514-3815

D'ESTE, MARY ERNESTINE, health administration executive; b. Chgo., Apr. 1, 1941; d. Ernest Gregory and Mary (Turcich) D'E. Student, Mundelein Coll., 1958-61. Sec. MMM, Bedford Park, Ill., 1961-69, Michael Reese Med. Ctr., Chgo., 1969-73; adminstrv. asst. Thomas Jefferson U., Phila., 1973-85, divisional adminstr., 1985-86; adminstr. dept. cardiothoracic surgery Hahnemann U., Phila., 1986-94, Med. Coll. Pa.-Hahnemann U. Hosps., Phila., 1994-96, Allegheny U. Hosps.-Center City, 1996—; v.p. CTS Cardiac & Thoracic Surgeons PC, Phila., 1986—. V.p. archtl. review com. GTV Homeowners Assn., Marlton, N.J., 1979-85. Mem. Med. Group Mgmt. Assn., Am. Assn. Notaries, NAFE. Roman Catholic. Office: Allegheny U Hosp/Ctr City MS 111 Broad & Vine Sts Philadelphia PA 19102-1192

DESTEFANO, JOSEPH LOUIS, physician; b. Bklyn., June 6, 1943; s. Louis and Frances DeStefano; m. Rita Calouri, Sept. 28, 1968; children: Danielle, Lila, Joseph Jr. MD, Georgetown Med. Coll., 1969. Diplomate Am. Bd. Ob/Gyn. Intern Thomas Jefferson U. Hosp., Phila., 1969-70; resident Georgetown U., Washington, 1970-73; mem. interview com. Georgetown Coll., Washington, 1974—; prin. Drs. DeStefano, Feldman & Kaufman, PA, Atlantic City, N.J., 1973—; dir. dept. ob/gyn. Atlantic City Med. Ctr., 1987—. Mem. exec. com. Atlantic City Tomorrow, 1990-92; mem. Holocaust com. Ann Frank exhibit Stockton State Coll., Pomona, N.J., 1991. Fellow Am. Coll. Ob/Gyn., Am. Coll. Surgeons; mem. AMA, Am. Coll. Ob/Gyn., (dist. II adv. coun.), Am. Fertility Soc., N.J. Med. Soc. (com. on child health and maternal care, subcom. maternal mortality), Atlantic County Med. Soc. (exec. com. 1980-84, pres. 1982). Office: 4401 Ventnor Ave Atlantic City NJ 08401-5736

DESTEFANO, MARIE STEENBERG, oncological nurse; b. Darby, Pa., May 8, 1955; d. Kenneth Orvil and Agnes (McCullough) Steenberg; m. Stephen V. DeStefano, Sept. 25, 1982; children: Kathleen, Kimberly, Kaitlyn, Kenneth. BSN, Our Lady of Angels, 1977; MSN, U. Pa., 1986. Cert. in oncology. Adminstrv. dir. oncology svcs. Crozer Keystone Health Sys., Del. County, Pa. Bd. dirs. Delaware County unit Am. Cancer Soc. Mem. Oncology Nursing Soc. (Ednl. Exhibit award 1987), SGNO, Am. Orgn. Nurse Execs., ACS, Nurse to Nurse Cons., Am. Coll. of Oncology Adminstrs., Sigma Theta Tau (UpJohn Quality of Life award 1988).

DE SZALAY, HELGA KERSTEN, laboratory safety officer; b. Stolp, Germany, Oct. 9, 1936; came to U.S., 1961; d. Gottfried A. and Erna A. (Renius) K.; m. Csaba J. de Szalay, July 1, 1962; children: Péter J., Ferenc A., Krisztina K. Cert. med. technologist, U. Frankfurt/Main, Fed. Republic Germany, 1957; BS in Biology, SUNY, Saratoga Springs, 1982; MS in Medical Biology, L.I. U., 1988, MPA in Health Administrn., 1993. Lic. lab. supr.; C/ASCP; CLS/S. Research technician NYU Med. Ctr., N.Y.C., 1961-63; technician North Shore Univ. Hosp., Manhasset, N.Y., 1971-75; sr. technician North Shore Univ. Hosp., Manhasset, 1975-78, technologist, 1978-86, sr. technologist, 1986-88; asst. supr. Columbia Presby. Med. Ctr., N.Y.C., 1988-89; lab. safety officer dept. Math. and Nat. Scis. CUNY, Flushing, 1993—; tchr. of med. technology North Shore Univ. Hosp., Manhasset, 1982-86. Contbr. articles to profl. jours. Mem. N.Y. Acad. Scis., Am. Soc. Clin. Pathologists, Am. Soc. for Med. Tech., Internat. Assn. Med. Lab. Technologists, Clin. Lab. Mgt. Assn. Lutheran.

DE THIBAULT DE BOESINGHE, LÉOPOLD BARON, physician; b. Gent, Belgium, Sept. 4, 1943; married; children: Isabel, Fernando. MD. Dir. dept. occupl. health U. Ghent, Belgium, prof. radiotherapy and nuclear medicine Univ. Clinic; chief dept. Aalsters Stedelijk Ziekenhuis ASZ. Contbr. articles to profl. jours. Mem. Assoc. Europ. de Thermologie (past pres.), Provincial Chamber of the Bd. of Physicians of Oost-Vlaanderen (past pres.), Internat. Coll. of Thermology (past pres.), Oost Vlaanderen Belgisch Werk Tegen Kanker, Provincial Med. Commn. Oost Vlaanderen (pres.), Belgian Assn. of Radiationprotection (past pres.), Gand Club, Sté des redoutés Club, Univ Found. Club, Flemisch Ligue against Cancer O.VL. BWK. (pres.). Home: Sint-Martensstraat 10, B9000 Ghent Belgium Office: Univ Ziekenhuis, De Pintelaan 185, B9000 Ghent Belgium

DETMER, DON EUGENE, medical educator, health policy researcher, surgeon; b. Winfield, Kans., Feb. 3, 1939; s. Lawrence Oscar and Esther Beulah (McCormick) D.; m. Mary Helen McFerson, Aug. 26, 1961; children: Mary Catherine, Emily Anne. Student, U. Kans., 1957-59, 60-61, U. Durham, 1959-60; MD, U. Kans., Kansas City, 1965. Intern, then resident in surgery Johns Hopkins U., Balt., 1965-67; clin. assoc. surg. br. Nat. Heart Inst. NIH, Bethesda, Md., 1967-69; resident in surgery Duke U., Durham, N.C., 1969-72; Global Cmty. Health fellow Dept. HEW, Inst. Medicine/NAS, Washington, 1972-73; prof. preventive medicine and surgery U. Wis., Madison, 1973-84; v.p. health scis., prof. surgery and med. info. U. Utah, Salt Lake City, 1984-88; univ. prof. surgery and health policy U. Va., Charlottesville, 1988-93, v.p., provost for health scis., 1993-95, sr. v.p., Louise Nurancy prof. health scis. policy, 1996—; cons. China, Australasian Coll. Surgeons, U. Algeria, Robert Wood Johnson Found., Princeton, N.J.; bd. dirs. China Med. Bd. N.Y., Inc., 1991—, Am. Med. Informatics Assn., Assn. Acad. Health Ctrs., Assn. Health Svcs. Rsch., NAS Inst. Medicine, Washington, chmn. bd. healthcare svcs., 1994—; bd. dirs. Vet. Affairs Spl. Med. Adv. Group; chmn. nat. com. vital health stats. HHS, Washington, 1996—; regent Nat. Libr. Medicine, NIH, Bethesda, 1987-91; bd. dirs., developer adminstrv. medicine U. Wis. Contbr. articles on compartment syndromes, shin splints, health svcs. rsch. and policy to profl. jours. Chmn. pub. svc. com. bd. dirs. United Way, Salt Lake City, 1986-88, Charlottesville, Va., 1992—; pres. Peace Luth. Ch., 1996—. With USPHS, 1967-69, 72-73. Global Community Health fellow HEW, 1972-73. Fellow ACS (vice chmn. com. allied health pers. 1989-90, chmn. 1990-94, internat. health com. 1996—), Am. Coll. Sports Medicine; mem. Inst. of Medicine of NAS, Soc. Med. Adminstrs., Am. Surg. Assn., So. Surg. Assn., Am. Acad. Physician Assts. (hon.), Am. Hosp. Assn. (chmn. coun. hosp. med. staffs 1984-87), Am. Coll. Med. Info., Assn. Health Svcs. Rsch., Cosmos Club Washington, Alpha Omega Alpha. Lutheran. Home: Pavilion I West Lawn Charlottesville VA 22903 Office: Univ Va The Rotunda Box 9016 Charlottesville VA 22906

DE TOMASI, DENNIS CARL, oral and maxillofacial surgeon; b. Vallejo, Calif., Dec. 5, 1954; s. Donald Henry and Dorlene (Wanlass) De T.; m. Dawn Marie Theis, Apr. 17, 1982; children: Dustin Louis, Drake Edward. DDS, U. of Pacific, San Francisco, 1979. Diplomate Am. Bd. Oral and Maxillofacial Surgery. Oral and maxillofacial surgeon Med. U. S.C., Charleston, S.C., 1981-84; pvt. practice Yuba city, Calif. Bd. dirs. Butte-Sierra Dental Found., Yuba City, 1995—. Fellow Am. Assn. Oral and Maxillofacial surgeons; mem. ADA, Calif. Dental Assn., Buttel-Sierra Dental Soc. (pres. 1995—), Calif. Assn. Oral and Maxillofacial surgeons. Home: 555 Estates Dr Yuba City CA 95993 Office: 1215 Plumas St Ste 300 Yuba City CA 95991-3453

DE TOMBE, PIETER PHILIPPUS, physiologist; b. Voorburg, The Netherlands, Mar. 25, 1957; s. Pieter Philippus and Gerbedina (Ver Gouwe) de T.; married, July 8, 1987. MS in Analytical Chemistry, U. Leiden HBO, Leiden, The Netherlands, 1978; PhD, U. Calgary, Alta., Can., 1989. Rsch. asst. dept. cardiology U. Rotterdam, The Netherlands, 1979-84; systems programmer dept. physiology U. Leiden, 1984; postdoctoral fellow dept. biomed. engring. Med. Sch., Johns Hopkins U., Balt., 1989-91; asst. prof. Dept. Medicine Wake Forest U., Winston-Salem, N.C., 1992—. Contbr. articles to profl. jours. including Circulation Rsch. Mem. basic sci. coun. Am. Heart Assn., 1988—. Am. Heart Assn. fellow, Md., 1990-91. Mem. Am. Physiol. Soc., Biophys. Soc., Cardiovascular Systems Dynamics Soc. Office: Wake Forest UDept Medicine Bowman Gray Sch Medicine 300 S Hawthorne Rd Winston Salem NC 27157-0002

DETRE, THOMAS, psychiatrist, educator; b. Budapest, Hungary, May 17, 1924; came to U.S., 1953, naturalized, 1958; m. Katherine Maria Drechsler, Sept. 15, 1956; children: John Allan, Antony James. BA, Gymnasium of Piarist Fathers, Kecskemet, Hungary, 1942; postgrad., Horthy Miklos U. and Pazmany Peter U., Hungary, 1945-47; MD, Rome U., 1952. Diplomate: Am. Bd. Psychiatry and Neurology (assoc. examiner). Intern Morrisania City Hosp., N.Y.C., 1953-54; resident in psychiatry Mt. Sinai Hosp., N.Y.C., 1954-55; resident in psychiatry Yale U., 1955-57, chief resident, instr., 1957-58, instr., 1958-59, asst. prof., 1959-62; dir. psychiat. inpatient service Yale-New Haven Hosp., 1960-68, assoc. prof., 1962-70, asst. chief psychiatry div., 1965-68, psychiatrist in chief, 1968-73, prof., 1970-73; prof., chmn. dept. psychiatry U. Pitts., 1973-82, assoc. sr. vice chancellor, 1982-84, disting. svc. prof. health scis., 1982—, disting. prof. psychiatry and neurosci., 1993—, sr. v.p. health scis., 1984-92, sr. vice chancellor for health scis., 1992—, pres. med. and health care div., 1986-90, pres. med. ctr., 1990-92; dir. Western Psychiat. Inst. and Clin. Western Psychiat. Inst. and Clin., 1973-94; mem. Nat. Adv. Mental Health Coun., NIH, 1994—. Author: (with H.G. Jarecki) Modern Psychiatric Treatment, 1971; contbr. chpts. to books. Fellow Am. Coll. Psychiatrists, Am. Coll. Neuropsychopharmacology (pres. 1994), Acad. Behavioral Medicine Rsch., Am. Psychiat. Assn. (life fellow); mem. AAAS, Collegium Internat. Neuropsychopharmacologicum, Pan Am. Med. Assn., Am. Soc. Clin. Pharmacology and Therapeutics, Phi Beta Kappa. Office: U Pitts Western Psychiat Inst & Clinic 3811 Ohara St Pittsburgh PA 15213-2593

DETTINGER, GARTH BRYANT, surgeon, physician, retired air force officer, county health officer; b. Syracuse, N.Y., Dec. 23, 1921; s. Maurice and Maxine Bryant (Giddings) D.; m. Gladys Ruth Hickingbotham, Aug. 5, 1939; children—Holly Maxine Dettinger Dixon-Keane, Ronald Mark, Michael James. A.B., Harvard U., 1948; M.D., Columbia U., 1952; M.S. in Surgery, Baylor U., 1956. Diplomate: Am. Bd. Surgery. Commd. officer U.S. Air Force, 1952, advanced through grades to maj. gen., 1977; intern Valley Forge Army Hosp., Phoenixville, Pa., 1952-53; resident in surgery Brooke Army Hosp., San Antonio, 1953-57; chief surgery MacDill Hosp., Tampa, Fla., 1957-59, Elmendorf Hosp., Alaska, 1959-62, Davis-Monthan Hosp., Tucson, 1962-64; hosp comdr. Roswell, N.Mex., 1964-67; chief profl. services Air Forces Europe, 1967-70; hosp. comdr. Vandenberg, Calif., 1970-72; surgeon Air Force Mil. Personnel Center, San Antonio, 1972-74; command surgeon Air Tng. Command, 1974-75; dir. plans and resources U.S. Air Force, Washington, 1975-77; dep. surgeon gen. U.S. Air Force, 1977-80; asst. health dir. Fairfax County, Va., 1980—; surg. cons. Surgeon Gen. U.S.; clin. assoc. prof. Georgetown U. Med. Sch., 1983—;. Editor-in-chief: Surgeons Comments, 1967-70. Fellow A.C.S. (bd. govs.); mem. Soc. Med. Cons. to Armed Services, Alpha Omega Alpha. Republican. Episcopalian. Home: M-305 9120 Belvoir Woods Pky Fort Belvoir VA 22060-2721 Office: Fairfax County Health Dept 10777 Main St Ste 203 Fairfax VA 22030-6903

DEUEL, KENNETH HARRINGTON, optometrist, miltary officer; b. Oxford, N.Y., June 7, 1929; s. Walter C. and Mildred (Harrington) D.; m. Jane F. Popek, May 12, 1973. OD, Pa. Coll. Optometry, 1952, post grad. cert. Ocular Therapeutics, 1987. Commd. 2d lt. USAF, 1953, advanced through grades to col., 1974, ret., 1979; pvt. practice optometry Gulf Breeze, Fla., 1979—; optometry cons. to Surgeon Gen. USAFE, Germany, 1975-78. Part-time mem. Pensacola Ch. Symphony Choral. Decorated Bronze Star USAF, Vietnam, 1970. Fellow Am. Acad. Optometry; mem. Armed Forces Optometric Assn. (life, pres. 1972-73), Am. Optometric Assn. (contact lens sect.), Fla. Optometric Assn., W. Fla. Optometric Assn. (trustee, bd. dirs. 1990-94), Ret. Officers Assn., Gulf Breeze C. of C. (v.p. 1981-82), Rotary (bd. dirs. local chpt. 1980-82, Paul Harris fellow). Methodist. Office: Dr Kenneth Deuel 97 Bay Bridge Dr Gulf Breeze FL 32561-4468

DEUPREE, ROBERT MARSHALL, physician, minister, author; b. Elizabeth, Colo., Dec. 26, 1912; s. Elmer Burton and Mary Ayer (Griffin) DeuP.; m. Harriett Ann Janetos, Oct. 11, 1963; children: Carol J., R. Scott. Student, Santa Ana Coll., 1930-33, L.A. City Coll., 1937-38; DO, Coll. Osteo. Physicians and Surgeons, 1942; MD, Met. U., 1948; postgrad., UCLA, 1952-53; AB, Calif. State U., Fullerton, 1962; MA, Calif. State U., Long Beach, 1963; PhD, Purdue U., 1963-64; DD, Am. Fellowship Ch., 1988. Diplomate in aerospace medicine and occupational medicine. Editor-pub. San Juan Capistrano Coastline Dispatch, 1930-33; intern Wilshire Hosp., L.A., 1942-43, resident in neurology, 1943-44; pvt. practice medicine L.A., 1944-57, El Monte, Calif., 1957-58, Newport Beach, Calif., 1958-59; dir. Rush-Merced Clinic, 1957-58; assoc. med. dir. Aerojet Gen. Corp., Azusa, Calif., 1967-69, Am. Airlines, L.A., 1969; ships surgeon U. Calif. Scripps Inst. Oceanography, 1969; assoc. prof. U. Calif., San Diego, 1969; area med. officer Divsn. Fed. Employee Health USPHS, L.A., 1970-85; head dept. internal medicine and radiology Hiss Orthopedic Clinic, L.A., 1953-57; instr. differential diagnosis Coll. Osteo. Physicians and Surgeons, L.A., 1945-49; instr. med. terminology N. Orange Community Coll. Dist., 1966-78; pres., Deustar Internat. Corp.; rsch. fellow VA Hosp., Long Beach State Coll., UCLA Inst. Laryngol. Rsch., 1962-6; guest lectr. abnormal psychology Fuller Theol. Seminar, 1978-81. Author: The Cross and the Caduseus Deustar, 1996; author, editor: DeuPree International Emergency Medical Translations, 1972; co-author: Travis' Handbook of Speech Pathology and Audiology, 1972; editor Jour. Pro-Re-Nata, 1947-50; author, prodr. med. motion pictures, USN, 1950-51; cons. med. TV, films, 1952—. Nat. Inst. Dental Health fellow Purdue U., 1963-64. Fellow Royal Soc. Health, N.Y. Acad. Scis., Am. Aerospace Med. Assn. (assoc.), Am. Coll. Occupational Medicine, Royal Soc. Medicine, Internat. Clergy Soc.; mem. Aviation Hall of Fame (charter), Asclepiad. Home: 2625 Huckleberry Rd Santa Ana CA 92706-2106

DEUSCHLE, KURT WALTER, physician, educator; b. Kongen, Germany, Mar. 14, 1923; came to U.S., 1924, naturalized, 1949; s. John and Marie (Schaefer) D.; m. Jeanne Magagna, 1975; children by previous marriage—Kurt J., Sally, James. B.S. cum laude, Kent State U., 1944; M.D., U. Mich., 1948. Intern Colo. Gen. Hosp., Denver, 1948-49; resident medicine, fellow oncology Upstate Med. Ctr. SUNY, Syracuse, 1950-52, instr. medicine, 1954-55; asst. prof. pub. health and preventive medicine Cornell Med. Coll., 1955-60; prof., chmn. dept. community medicine U. Ky., 1960-68; Ethel H. Wise prof., chmn. and dir. dept. community medicine Mt. Sinai Sch. of Medicine, CUNY, 1968-90, prof. emeritus, 1990—; prof. emeritus, disting. svc. prof. Mt. Sinai Hosp.; Ethel H. Wise chmn. emeritus Mt Sinai Sch. of Medicine, CUNY, 1993—, Disting. Svc. prof. dept. community medicine, 1993—; Merrimon lectr. U. N.C., Chapel Hill, 1975; mem. N.Y.C. Bd. Health, 1982-89; vis. prof. U. Lagos, Nigeria, 1977, Chinese Med. Assn., People's Republic China, 1986; mem. tech. bd. Milbank Meml. Fund; mem. Tb control adv. com. Center Disease Control Dept. HEW; cons. manpower intelligence NIH; mem. Inst. Medicine of Nat. Acad. Scis., Washington; mem. rural health systems del. to China, 1978; mem. Nat. Adv. Environ. Health Scis. Coun. NIH, 1982-86; sr. advisor Report of U.S. Preventive Services Task Force, The Guide to Clinical Preventive Servcies, HHS, 1989; mem. com. pub. health N.Y. Acad. Medicine, 1983—, N.Y. State Council on Grad. Med. Edn., 1987—, adv. com. Am. Ba. Family Practice, 1986—. Author: (with J. Adair) The People's Health: Anthropology and Medicine in a Navajo Community, 1970, rev. and expanded edit., 1988; Contbr. to: (ed. John Norman) Medicine in the Ghetto, 1969, Community Medicine: Teaching, Research and Health Care, (ed. Lathem and Newberry), 1970. Served with AUS, 1943-46. Recipient Award of Honor, Mayor of N.Y.C., 1989, Jacobi award Associated Alumni Mt. Sinai Med. Ctr., 1989, Alexander Richman Commemorative award Mt. Sinai Med. Ctr., 1991; Duncan Clark award Assn. Tchrs. Preventive Medicine, 1990; Commonwealth Fund sr. health fellow, 1966-67. Fellow AAAS, Am. Coll. Preventive Medicine (past pres., Disting. Svc. award 1975); mem. Am. Pub. Health Assn. (award for excellence in domestic health 1975), Am. Thoracic Soc., Internat. Epidemiol. Assn., Alpha Omega Alpha. Home: 1212 Fifth Ave New York NY 10029-5210 Office: Fifth Ave New York NY 10029*

DEUS FOMBELLIDA, JAVIER, surgeon, educator; b. Renteria, Guipuzcoa, Spain, Dec. 27, 1950; s. Alfonso Prieto and M. Dolores Diego (Fombellida; m. M. Angeles Ortiz Alonso, Mar. 31, 1987; children: Javier, Natalia, Borja. BS, St. Ignatius Loyola, San Sebastian, Spain, 1967; MD, U. Zaragoza, Spain, 1973, Dr. Medicine and Surgery, 1981. Specialist in gen. and digestive surgery Faculty Medicine U. Zaragoza, specialist in thoracic surgery; asst. Hosp. Med. Sch., Lausanne, Switzerland, Med. Sch. Paris; titular prof. surgery U. Zaragoza, dir. dept. surgery, 1990-93; clin. chief svc. surgery U. Hosp. Zaragoza. Editor: Pathology of the Adrenal Glands, 1982; contbr. articles to profl. jorus. Mem. Spanish Assn. Surgeons, Francophone Thoracic and Cardiovascular surgery Soc., French Assn. Surgery, Am. Coll.

Chest Physicians, Internat. Soc. Surgeons, European Soc. for Surg. Rsch. Roman Catholic. Home: Plaza de Salamero 14-12A, 50004 Zaragoza Spain Office: Plaza del Carmen 1-3 5A, 50004 Zaragoza Spain

DEUSINGER, SUSAN SCHAEFER, physical therapist; b. St. Louis, June 21, 1946; d. Kenneth Miller and Miriam (Glaze) Schaefer; m. Thomas Hunter McCrackin III, June 15, 1968 (div. Dec. 1979); m. Robert Henry Deusinger, Mar. 15, 1980; children: Christopher James, Marcus Jay, Leigh Elizabeth. BS, U. Kans., 1969; MA, Washington U., St. Louis, 1980, PhD, 1987. Phys. therapist Rehab. Inst., Kansas City, Mo., 1969, George Washington U. Hosp., Washington, 1969-70, Santa Clara Valley Med. Ctr., San Jose, Calif., 1971; chief phys. therapist Southeast Mo. Hosp., Cape Girardeau, Mo., 1972-73; phys. therapist St. John's Mercy Med. Ctr., St. Louis, 1975-76, St. Louis County Spl. Sch. Dist., St. Louis, 1976-78; faculty Washington U., St. Louis, 1978-90, dir., 1990—; instr. riding dir. therapeutic programming Therapeutic Horsemanship, St. Louis, 1975-88, mem. adv. bd., 1988—; Jesse Ball lectr. U. Kans., 1988. Contbr. articles to profl. jours. Mem. Am. Phys. Therapy Assn. (bd. dirs. 1991-94, accreditation program 1984—, Lucy Blair Svc. award 1995), Am. Ednl. Rsch. Assn. (co-chair program com. 1991-92), Mo. Phys. Therapy Assn. (pres. 1986-90, Outstanding Svc. award 1994). Office: Washington U Sch Medicine 4444 Forest Park Blvd Saint Louis MO 63108

DEUTCH, JULIA FLUGER, dietitian; b. N.Y.C., Feb. 26, 1919; d. Max Lowenthal and Clara (Hoffman) Fluger; m. Samuel Deutch, Mar. 6, 1943; 1 child, Reesa Joan. BA, Hunter Coll., 1939; postgrad., 1944-45; postgrad. Columbia U., 1945-46. Dietetic intern City Home & Cancer Hosp., N.Y.C., 1939-41; dietitian Triboro Hosp., N.Y.C., 1941-43; with VA Hosp., Bronx, N.Y., 1943-62, asst. chief dietitian, to 1962; chief dietitian VA Hosp., Coral Gables, Fla., 1962-68, Miami, Fla., 1968-75; coord. dietetic work experience Barry Coll., Miami, 1967-68; lectr. diet therapy U. Miami, 1968-69; mem. task force VA Personnel Utilization, Washington, 1969; chmn. curriculum planning adv. bd. Fla. Internat. U., Miami, 1969—, assoc. community prof., 1972-74; dir. Orientation in Hosp. Dietetics, Marymount Coll., Tarrytown, N.Y., 1970-72; chmn. ad hoc adv. com. VA, 1972-73; chmn. spl. edn. com. Dade County Vocat. Schs., 1968-74; dir. dietetic mgmt. job tng. Miami-Dade Community Coll., 1969-74. Author: Doctors Information Guide, 1970, (monthly pamphlets) Diet-Grams, 1970-74. Recipient Commendation U.S. VA, 1953, Outstanding Performance award, 1966, Superior Performance award, 1969, 71, 72, commendation, 1974, citation Fla. Rehab. Assn., 1968, Cert. of Merit, Jewish War Vets., 1970, Cert. of Appreciation, Lindsay Hopkins Vocat. Sch., Miami, 1974, Fla. Internat. U., 1974. Mem. Am. Dietetic Assn., Fla. Dietetic Assn., Miami Dietetic Assn. (dir. career guidance com. 1970-72, chmn. nominating com. 1971). Republican. Jewish.

DEUTSCH, FLORENCE ELAYNE GOODILL, nursing and health care consultant; b. San Diego, Aug. 1, 1923; d. George Ehrlich and Beatrice Marie (Urick) Goodill; m. Edward Thomas Deutsch, June 27, 1953 (dec.); 1 son, George Edward. Student, San Diego State Coll., 1942-43; B.S.N., Villa Maria Coll., 1948; diploma in nursing Evanston Hosp., Northwestern U., 1947; M.Ed., Edinboro U., 1961. Staff nurse St. Vincent Hosp., Erie, Pa., 1947; clin. instr.-supr. Hamot Med. Ctr., Erie, 1948-58, dir. edn., 1958-62, dir. Sch. Nursing, 1962-66, asst. adminstr., dir. Sch. Nursing, 1969-73; exec. dir. Florence Crittenton Home, Erie, 1966-69; asst. adminstr., dir. nursing Capitol Hill Hosp., Washington, 1974-79; assoc. adminstr. profl. services Millcreek Community Hosp., 1980-82; v.p. nursing East Liverpool City Hosp. (Ohio), 1982-87; lectr., cons. on nursing and nursing law, 1988-89; lectr. Gannon U., Erie, Pa. Editor newsletter U.S. Brig Niagara, 1991-93. Past bd. dirs. Columbiana County Cancer Soc.; bd. dirs. Sarah A. Reed Retirement Ctr., Erie, 1991—, treas. 1992-95; treas. Spl. Purpose Fund, 1995—. Served with USNR, 1948-53. Recipient Vol. of the Year award U.S. Brig Niagara, 1993, Named Most Outstanding Nurse Erie County, 1969, Disting. Nursing Alumna Villa Maria Coll. Gannon U., 1989, Disting. Alumnus Gannon U., 1991. Mem. Nat. League Nursing, Am. Orgn. Nurse Execs., Svc. Corps Of Ret. Execs. (vice-chmn. Erie chpt. 193 1988-90, chmn. 1995—), Sigma Theta Tau, Delta Kappa Gamma. Republican. Presbyterian. Editor: Penn League News, 1968-70; contbr. articles to profl. jours. Address: 3207 Georgian Ct Erie PA 16506-1109

DEUTSCH, GARY MICHAEL, internist; b. Chgo., Sept. 26, 1951; s. Sidney Deutsch and Olivia Sellinger; m. Debra Melshenker, May 2, 1976; children: Gordon, Adam, Ryan, Tyler. AB in Biology, Washington U., 1973; MD, Rush U., 1977. Diplomate Am. Bd. Internal Medicine. Resident in internal medicine U. Calif., San Francisco, 1980; pvt. practice Santa Paula, Calif., 1980—; asst. clin. prof. Ventura (Calif.) County Med. Ctr. UCLA Sch. Medicine, 1980—; qualified med. evaluator Calif. Indsl. Bd., Sacramento, 1994—. Bd. dirs., safety dir. Am. Youth Soccer Orgn., Ventura, 1994—. Mem. Calif. Med. Soc., Ventura County Med. Soc., Phi Beta Kappa, Alpha Omega Alpha. Office: 243 March St Santa Paula CA 93060

DEUTSCH, JULES S., physician; b. N.Y.C., Mar. 28, 1940; m. Carol F.; 1 child. MD, Tulane U., 1965. Diplomate Am. Bd. Urology. Intern Charity Hosp., New Orleans, 1965-66, resident in urology, 1966-70; resident in urology Charity Hosp., Touro, 1967-69; physician The Urologic Inst. of New Orleans, 1970—; clin. instr. of urology La. State U. Sch. of Medicine, 1983—; clin. asst. prof. urology Tulane U. Sch. of Medicine, 1990—; bd. govs. Jo Ellen Smith Hosp./F. Edward Herbert; chmn. NME Physician Adv. Bd., chmn. gov. bd. Meadowcrest Hosp.; affil. numerous hosps., including Children's Hosp., New Orleans, 1982—, F. Edward Hebert Rehab. Hosp., 1985—, West Jefferson Med. Ctr., 1981—, Univ. Rehab. Hosp., 1995, others. Contbr. articles to profl. jours. Mem. Am. Assn. Clin. Urologists, Am. Coll. Surgeons, Am. Fertility Soc., Am. Inst. Ultrasound in Medicine, Am. Urolog. Assn., Internat. Continence Soc., Jefferson Parish Med. Soc., Soc. of Urologic Cryosurgeons, So. Med. Assn., others. Office: Urologic Inst New Orleans 2600 Belle Chasse Hwy Gretna LA 70056

DEUTSCH, MARSHALL E(MANUEL), medical products company executive, inventor; b. N.Y.C., Aug. 17, 1921; s. David and Madeline Lea (Roth) D.; m. Judith Greene, June 27, 1947; children: Pamina Margret, Ethan Amadeus, Freeman Sarastro. BS, CCNY, 1941; PhD, NYU, 1951. Tech. dir. NEN-Picker Radiopharms., Boston, 1966-68, Picker-Hoechst Inc., Bedford, Mass., 1968-70, Mead Diagnostics, Inc., Bedford, 1970-72, CIS Radiopharms., Bedford, 1972-74, Thyroid Diagnostics Inc., Bedford, 1972-85; chmn. Marshall Diagnostics Inc., Bedford, 1985-87; tech. adv. J&S Med. Assocs., Natick, Mass., 1988—; bd. dirs., corp. sec., v.p. Health Svcs. Internat., Washington, 1983—; contractor Joint Publs. Rsch. Svc., Arlington, Va., 1984-92. Inventor self-contained technetium generator, 1971, various radiopharm. products, 1973, various clin. chem. test kits, devices, 1953-93; contbr. articles to mags. cons. AID, Zaire, 1979, UN Capital Devel. Fund, Benin, 1977. 1st lt. A.C., U.S. Army, 1942-45, ETO. Fellow AAAS; mem. Am. Assn. Clin. Chemistry (chmn. pub. rels. com. 1962), Am. Chem. Soc. (sr., emeritus), N.Y. Acad. Scis., Sci. Rsch. Soc. Am. Unitarian Universalist. Home: 41 Concord Rd Sudbury MA 01776-2328 Office: J&S Med Assocs 19 Strathmore Rd Natick MA 01760-2418

DEUTSCH, MORTON, psychologist, educator; b. N.Y.C., Feb. 4, 1920; s. Charles and Ida (Prager) D.; m. Lydia S. Shapiro, June 1, 1947; children—Anthony Charles, Nicholas Andrew. BS, CCNY, 1939; MA, U. Pa., 1940; PhD, MIT, 1948; LHD, CUNY, 1989. From asst. to assoc. prof. psychology NYU, 1948-56; dir. research interpersonel processes Bell Telephone Labs., Murray Hill, N.J., 1956-63; prof. psychology, edn. Tchrs. Coll. Columbia, N.Y.C., 1963—; Edward Lee Thorndike prof. Tchrs. Coll. Columbia, 1981—; dir. Internat. Ctr. Cooperation and Conflict Resolution Tchrs. Coll. Columbia U., 1986—; vis. scholar Russell Sage Found., 1976-77; vis. disting. fellow La Trobe U., 1993; cons. NIMH, Va. Author: Inter-racial Housing, 1951, Research Methods in Social Relations, 1951, Preventing World War III; Some Proposals, 1962, Theories in Social Psychology, 1965, The Resolution of Conflict: Constructive and Destructive Processes, 1973, Applying Social Psychology, 1975; Distributive Justice, 1985. Trustee Marshall Fund. Served to 1st lt. USAAF, 1942-45. Decorated D.F.C. with cluster, Air medal with three clusters; recipient Helsinki medal U. Helsinki, 1990, Carl Hovland Meml. award Yale U., 1967, Tchrs. Coll. medal, 1992. Mem. AAAS (Socio Psychology prize 1961), Soc. Psychol. Study Social Issues (pres. 1960-61, Kurt Lewin Meml. award 1968, G.W. Allport prize 1972), APA (Disting. Sci. Contbn. award 1987), APS (William James fellow 1988), N.Y. State Psychol. Assn. (pres. 1965-66, Samuel Flowerman Meml. award 1963), Eastern Psychol. Assn. (pres. 1968-69), Internat. Soc. Polit. Psychology (pres. 1981-82, Nevitt Sanford award 1983), Internat. Assn. Conflict Mgmt. (Lifetime Contribution award 1993), Psychol. Soc. Response (Disting. Contribution award 1991), Soc. Exptl. Social Psychology (disting. scientist award 1985). Home: 161 W 86th St New York NY 10024-3411 Office: Columbia U Teachers Coll 525 W 120th St New York NY 10027-6625

DEUTSCH, SID, bioengineer, educator; b. N.Y.C., Sept. 19, 1918; s. Elias and Gussie (Hazen) D.; m. Ruth Appleman, Nov. 15, 1941 (div. June 1969), remarried, 1984; children: Alice, Phyllis, Naomi; m. Jane Arieti, Aug., 1969 (dec. Mar., 1978); m. Annette Page, Apr., 1979 (div. Dec., 1984). BEE, Cooper Union, 1941; MEE, Bklyn. Poly. Inst., 1947, DEE, 1955. Designer Fairchild Camera & Instrument Co., N.Y.C., 1943-44; instr. Madison Inst., Newark, 1946-50; engr. Poly. R & D Co., Bklyn., 1950-54; mem. faculty Bklyn. Poly. Inst., 1954-72, prof. elec. engring., 1962-72; prof. bioengring. Rutgers U. Med. Sch., Piscataway, N.J., 1972-79; vis. prof. U. S.Fla., Tampa, 1983—; vis. prof. Tel Aviv U., Israel, 1977, prof. bioengring, 1979-84; cons. Lewyt Mfg. Corp., 1958-60; affiliate Rockefeller Inst., 1961-64. Author: Theory and Design of TV Receivers, 1951, Models of the Nervous System, 1967; co-author: Biomedical Instruments: Theory and Design, 1976, 2d edit., 1992, Neuroelectric Systems, 1987, Understanding the Nervous System: An Engineering Perspective, 1993; assoc. editor: IEEE Transactions on Biomedical Engring., 1991—; patentee pseudorandom dot scan for TV. Mem. adult edn. com. Roslyn (N.Y.) Pub. Schs., 1955-58. With USNR, 1944-46. Fellow IEEE, Soc. for Info. Display; mem. Sigma Xi, Tau Beta Pi, Eta Kappa Nu. Home: 3967 Oakhurst Blvd Sarasota FL 34233-1447 Office: Univ S Fla Elec Engring Dept Tampa FL 33620

DEUTSCH, STANLEY, anesthesiologist, educator; b. N.Y.C., Apr. 4, 1930; s. Elias and Estelle (Press) D.; m. Margaret R. Zuanic, July 11, 1971; children: Susan, Ellen, Nina, Eva. BA, NYU, 1950; MA, Boston U., 1951, PhD, 1955, MD, 1957. Diplomate Am. Bd. Anesthesiology. Rsch. and teaching fellow in physiology Sch. Medicine Boston U., 1951-55; intern Grad. Hosp. U. Pa., 1957-58; resident in anesthesiology Hosp. U. Pa., 1958-61; asst. prof. anesthesiology U. Pa., 1963-65; asst. prof. Harvard U., 1965-69; prof. U. Chgo., 1969-71; prof., head. dept. anesthesiology U. Okla. Health Scis. Center, 1971-82; prof. anesthesiology U. Tex. Med. Sch., Houston, 1982-89, George Washington Sch. Medicine, Washington, 1989—; cons. VA Med. Center, Oklahoma City. Contbr. articles to profl. publs. Capt., M.C. USAR, 1961-63. Mem. AMA, Am. Soc. Anesthesiologists, D.C. Med. Assn., Sigma Xi, Alpha Omega Alpha. Home: 1508 Colonial Ct Arlington VA 22209-1439 Office: George Washington U Hosp 901 23rd St NW Washington DC 20037-2377

DEUTSCHMAN, CLIFFORD SCOTT, anesthesiologist, internist, researcher, educator; b. N.Y.C., June 27, 1954; s. Arnold Jerome and Blossom Edith (Goldfeder) D.; m. Christine Barbara Hilke, Nov. 30, 1985; children: Catherine Anne, Nicole Charlotte, Elizabeth Diane. BS, Trinity Coll., 1975; MS, Northwestern U., 1976; MD, N.Y. Med. Coll., 1980. Resident in surgery U. Fla. Teaching Hosps., Gainesville, 1980-81; resident in neurosurgery U. Minn. Teaching Hosps., Mpls., 1981-83; fellow in critical care medicine dept. surgery U. Minn., 1983-85; resident in anesthesiology Johns Hopkins U., Balt., 1985-87, instr., 1988, asst. prof., 1988-93; attending anesthesiologist Nat. Naval Med. Ctr., Bethesda, Md., 1990-91; assoc. prof. dept. anesthesia U. Pa., Phila., 1993—. Contbr. articles to profl. jours. Comdr. USNR, 1990—. Rsch. grantee Nat. Inst. Diabetes, Digestive and Kidney Diseases, 1993—. Fellow Am. Coll. Critical Care Medicine; mem. Soc. Critical Care Medicine (mem. adv. bd. anesthesia sect. 1995—, co-chair pub. policy com. 1996—), Am. Soc. Critical Care Anesthesiologists (bd. dirs. 1995—), Am. Soc. Anesthesiologists, Internat. Anesthesia Rsch. Soc., Shock Soc. Office: U Pa Dept Anesthesia Dulles 7/HUP 3400 Spruce St Philadelphia PA 19104-4283

DEVANAND, DAVANGERE PRAHALAD, psychiatrist, researcher; b. Bangalore, India, June 13, 1955; came to U.S., 1980; s. Davangere Krishna and Jaya P. (Rao) D. MBBS, Christian Med. Coll., Vellore, Tamil Nadu, India, 1978; MD, N.Y. State U., 1989. Diplomate Am. Bd. Psychiatry and Neurology, 1985. Resident in psychiatry SUNY Upstate Med. Ctr., Syracuse, 1980-82, Yale U. Sch. of Med., New Haven, 1982-84; rsch. fellow N.Y. State Psychiatric Inst. and Columbia U., N.Y.C., 1985-93; asst. prof. Columbia U., N.Y.C., 1987-93; assoc. prof., 1993—; dir. Electroconvulsive Therapy Svc., N.Y. State Psychiat. Inst., N.Y.C., 1987—, asst. dir. Memory Disorders Clinic, 1988—. Contbr. articles to profl. jours. Rsch. grantee. Office: NY State Psychiat Inst 722 W 168th St New York NY 10032-2603

DEVARIS, JEANNETTE MARY, psychologist; b. Burbank, Calif., Jan. 7, 1947; d. Nicholas Propper Klein and Elizabeth (Von Lichtenberg) Schaeffer; m. Robert Lee Blake, May 20, 1967 (div. 1979); 1 child: Brendon; m. Panayotis Eric DeVaris, Dec. 5, 1988. BA, Adelphi U., 1968; MA, Fairleigh Dickinson U., 1977; PhD, Seton Hall U., 1987. Lic. psychologist, N.J. Caseworker N.Y.C. Welfare Dept., 1968-72; alcohol and drug rehab. counselor U.S. Army, Ft. Monmouth, N.J., 1972-76; psychol. intern N.J. State Intern Program, Trenton, 1977-78; psychologist Greystone Psychiat. Hosp., Greystone Park, N.J., 1979; sr. psychologist R. Hall Community Mental Health Ctr., Bridgewater, N.J., 1979-90; pvt. practice South Orange and Somerset, N.J., 1988—; tng. supr. Grad. Sch. Applied and Profl. Psychology; adj. prof. Seton Hall U.; sponsor and participant in Cable TV program. Contbr. articles to profl. jours. Mem. APA, Nat. Register Health Svc. Providers, N.J. Psychol. Assn. (bd. dirs., interprofl. rels. com.), Soc. Psychologists in Pvt. Practice (bd. dirs., spkrs. bur. com.). Office: 2 Worlds Fair Dr Somerset NJ 08873-1377

DEVARO, JOHN MICHAEL, ophthalmologist; b. Rochester, N.Y., Feb. 23, 1962; s. John Nicholas and Joanne (DiGiacomo) DeV.; m. Josepha Bueno, Oct. 7, 1990; 1 child, Sarah Nicole. AB, Dartmouth Coll., 1984; MD, U. Pa., 1988. Diplomate Am. Bd. Ophthalmology, Nat. Bd. Med. Examiners. Intern Pa. Hosp., Phila., 1988-89; resident in ophthalmology U. Pitts., 1989-92; chief res. U. Pitts., 1991; gen. ophthalmologist Danville (Va.) Eye Ctr., 1992-94; fellow in pediatrics and neuro-ophthalmology Duke U. Eye Ctr., Durham, N.C., 1994-95; assoc. in pediatrics and neuro-ophthalmology Nevyas Eye Assocs., Bala Cynwyd, Pa., 1995—; instr. Wills Eye Hosp., Phila., 1995—. Contbr. chpt. to book Ophthalmology: A Comprehensive Text, 1995; contbr. articles to profl. jours. including Archives of Ophthalmology, Jour. of Pediat. Ophthalmology. Rufus Choate scholar Dartmouth Coll., 1984; short-term experimental rsch. fellow NIH, 1987. Fellow Am. Acad. Ophthalmology; mem. Am. Assn. Pediatric Ophthalmology and Strabismus, Delaware Valley Pediatric Ophthalmology Soc., Phila. Neuro-Ophthalmology Soc. Office: Nevyas Eye Assocs. 2 Bala Plaza 333 City Line Ave Bala Cynwyd PA 19004

DEVENDORF, JOHN RICHARD, psychologist; b. Norwalk, Conn., Jan. 31, 1942; s. George Harvey and Viola Evelyn (Butler) D.; m. Carol Lewis, Sept. 9, 1972; children: Brian Lewis, Sean Lewis. BS, Bates Coll., 1964; MA, NYU, 1974, PhD, 1989. Tchr. secondary sch. U.S. Peace Corps Malawi, 1964-66; tchr. math. Ctr. for Vocat. Arts, Norwalk, 1966-68; tng. chief N.J. Tng. Inst., Trenton, 1969-71; pvt. practice tng. cons. Princeton, N.J., 1971-76; edn. dir. Hudson County Mental Health Bd., Secaucus, N.J., 1977-80, exec. dir., 1980-81; dir. children's partial hospitalization program Jersey City Med. Ctr., 1981-84; psychologist Correctional Med. Systems, Smyrna, Del., 1986-87; rsch. psychologist/therapist Lighthouse Sch., Chelmsford, Mass., 1987-89; clin. dir. Boston Secure Treatment Ctr. Justice Resource Inst., Boston, 1989—. Mem. APA, Am. Psychology-Law Soc. Unitarian. Home: 16 Windsor Rd Milford MA 01757-3830 Office: Boston Secure Treatment Justice Resource Inst 450 Canterbury St Roslindale MA 02131-3216

DEVEREUX, RICHARD BLYTON, internal medicine educator; b. Phila., Oct. 23, 1945; s. Robert T. and Dorothea A. (Kern) D.; m. Corinne Keating, Oct. 3, 1970; children: Jane Helena, Robert Jed. BA, Yale U., 1967; MD, U. Pa., 1971. Diplomate Am. Bd. Internal Medicine, Sub-bd. Cardiovascular Diseases. Intern, resident in internal medicine N.Y. Hosp., N.Y.C., 1971-74; fellow in cardiology Hosp. of U. Pa., Phila., 1974-76; dir. echocardiography lab. N.Y. Hosp., N.Y.C., 1978—; asst. prof. medicine Cornell U. Med. Coll., N.Y.C., 1978-83, assoc. prof. medicine, 1983-92, prof. medicine, 1992—; mem. epidemiology study sect. NIH, Bethesda, Md., 1991-95; chmn. professional adv. bd. Nat. Marfan Found., 1993—. Mem. editorial bd. Am. Jour. Cardiology, Jour. Hypertension, Am. Jour. Hypertension, Circulation; contbr. articles to profl. jours. Recipient Physician-Scientist award Andrew Mellon Found., 1980-82, rsch. award Nat. Marfan Found., 1987. Fellow ACP, Am. Coll. Cardiology, Coun. on High Blood Pressure Rsch. Am. Heart Assn., Am. Soc. Hypertension (chair publs. com. 1994—), Assn. Univ. Cardiologists. Episcopalian.

DEVIERE, JACQUES M. E., gastroenterologist, researcher; b. Charleroi, Belgium, Apr. 2, 1958; s. Jean Deviere and Suzanne Housiaux; m. Michele Palvasie, Oct. 30, 1982; children: Renaud, Florent. MD, Brussels Free U., 1983, degree in gastroenterology, 1988, PhD, 1991. Resident Ulb Erasme Hosp., Brussels, 1988-92, assoc. clin. prof., 1992—. Contbr. articles to med. jours. Lt. Med. Corps, 1990. Recipient Lilly prize, 1989, French Belgian Comty. prize, 1988. Mem. Royal Belgian Soc. Gastroenterology (assoc. sec. 1991-96, gen. sec. 1996-2001). Office: Ulb Hosp Erasme, Rte de Lennif 808, 1070 Brussels Belgium

DEVIN, JERRY PRESTON, orthodontist; b. Dubuque, Iowa, Nov. 9, 1939; s. James Howard ad Edna May (Waltemeyer) D.; m. Irene Kathryn Duvall, June 7, 1964; children: Lance, Shelley, Clint. DDS, U. Iowa, 1963; MS in Dentistry, U. Minn., 1969. Pvt. practice, Laramie, Wyo., 1969—; chmn. bd. Delta Dental Wyo., Cheyenne, 1990-92. Lt. USN, 1964-66. Mem. Pierre Fauchard Acad., Rocky Mountain Soc. Orthodontists (pres. 1992-93), Rotary (pres. Laramie 1989-90). Republican. Lutheran. Home: 3601 Grays Gable Rd Laramie WY 82070 Office: 502 S 4th St Laramie WY 82070

DEVINE, CHARLES JOSEPH, JR., urologist, educator; b. Norfolk, Va., Feb. 23, 1923; s. Charles Joseph and Julia Vera (Campbell) D.; m. Rae Lou Ellis, Sept. 30, 1950; children—Charles Joseph III, Paul E., Jane C., David C., Rachel A. B.A., Washington and Lee U., 1943; M.D., George Washington U., 1947; DSc (hon.), Ea. Va. Med. Sch., 1994. Diplomate: Am. Bd. Urology, Nat. Bd. Med. Examiners. Intern Brady Inst., Johns Hopkins Hosp., 1947-48; fellow in urology Cleve. Clinic, 1948-50; resident in urology U.S. Naval Hosp., Phila., 1951; with Devine Fiveash Urology, Ltd., Norfolk, Va., 1952-91; pres. Devine Fiveash Urology, Ltd., 1975-84; chief urology Med. Center Hosps., 1979-80; pres. med. staff Norfolk Gen. Hosp., 1970; chmn. surgery dept. DePaul Hosp., 1965-66; chief of urology Children's Hosp. of King's Daus., 1977-85; clin. coord. for urology Eastern Va. Med. Sch., 1973-75, prof. urology, 1975-94, chmn. dept., 1975-89, emeritus prof., 1994—; dir. Devine Ctr. for Genito-urinary Reconstruction, Sentara Norfolk Gen. Hosp., 1991—; mem. Project Hope, Alexandria, Egypt, 1977; Royal Australasian Coll., Surgeons Found. lectr., 1982, condr. symposia; vis. prof. univs. Co-editor: Urology in Practice, 1978; mem. editorial bd. Jour. Urology, 1978-89, Weekly Updates in Urology, 1978—; contbr. numerous articles to profl. jours., chpts. in books. Served to lt. M.C. USNR, 1950-52. Fellow ACS (pres. Va. chpt. 1967), Am. Acad. Pediatrics, Am. Soc. Plastic and Reconstructive Surgeons (assoc.); mem. AMA, Med. Soc. Va., Norfolk Acad. Medicine, Am. Urol. Assn. (Disting. Contribution award 1993, others), Va. Urol. Soc. (pres. 1968), Tidewater Urol. Assn., Societe Internationale d'Urologie, Am. Assn. Genitourinary Surgeons, Soc. Pediatric Urology, Soc. Univ. Urologists, Genitourinary Reconstructive Surgeons (founding pres. 1987-88), Seaboard Med. Soc., AAAS, N.Y. Acad. Scis., Alpha Tau Omega, Nu Sigma Nu. Roman Catholic. Clubs: Norfolk Yacht and Country (Norfolk), U.S. Sailing. Home: 2034 Hunters Trl Norfolk VA 23518-4921 Office: 400 W Brambleton Ave Ste 100 Norfolk VA 23510

DEVINE, JAMES VINCENT, psychologist, educational administrator; b. Mason City, Wash., Feb. 28, 1936; s. Vincent James and Mae Ann (Young) D.; m. Shirley Jean Montague, July 16, 1955; children: Vincent James, Gregory Bernard. BS, U. N.Mex., 1960, MS, 1962; PhD, Kans. State U., 1969. Asst. prof. psychology U. Tex., El Paso, 1967-71, assoc. prof., 1971-79, chmn. dept. psychology, 1978-83, prof., 1979—, interim dean Coll. Liberal Arts, 1984-85, dean, 1985-89; supr. programming Teaching Machines, Inc., Albuquerque, 1962-64; health trainee in exptl. psychology Kans. State U., Manhattan, 1964-67. Contbr. articles to profl. jours. Served with U.S. Army, 1954-56. Research grantee Nat. Inst. Mental Health div. NIH, 1980-83, 95-98, Aero. Systems divsn. USAF, 1977-79, Aero. Med. div. AFSC, 1972-77. Mem. Am. Psychol. Soc., Psychonomic Soc., Sigma Xi. Home: 5046 Ocotillo St El Paso TX 79932-2222 Office: U Tex Dept Psychology El Paso TX 79968

DEVITA, VINCENT THEODORE, JR., oncologist; b. Bronx, N.Y., Mar. 7, 1935; s. Vincent Theodore and Isabel DeV.; m. Mary Kay Bush, Aug. 3, 1957; children: Teddy (dec.), Elizabeth. BS, Coll. William and Mary, 1957; MD, George Washington U., 1961; DSc (hon.), N.Y. Med. Coll., 1987, Georgetown U., 1989. Diplomate: Nat. Bd. Med. Examiners, Am. Bd. Internal Medicine (subspecialty hematology, med. oncology). Intern U. Mich. Med. Center, Ann Arbor, 1961-62; resident in medicine George Washington U. Med. Service D.C. Gen. Hosp., 1962-63; clin. assoc. Lab. Chem. Pharmacology, Nat. Cancer Inst. NIH, Bethesda, Md., 1963-65; sr. resident in medicine Yale New Haven Med. Center, 1965-66; sr. investigator solid tumor service, medicine br. Nat. Cancer Inst. NIH, 1966-68, head solid tumor service, medicine br., 1968-71, chief med. br., 1971-74, dir. div. cancer treatment, 1974-80, clin. dir. inst., 1975-80; dir. Nat. Cancer Inst., Nat. Cancer Program, NIH, 1980-88; physician-in-chief Meml. Sloan-Kettering Cancer Ctr., N.Y.C., 1988-91, attending physician, mem., 1988-93, Benno C. Schmidt chair clin. oncology, 1988-93; prof. medicine Cornell U. Med. Coll., 1989-93; dir. Yale Cancer Ctr., New Haven, 1993—; prof. medicine Yale U. Sch. Medicine, New Haven, 1993—; attending physician Yale-New Haven Hosp., 1993—; prof. epidemiology and pub. health, dir. of Yale Cancer Ctr. Yale U. Sch. Medicine, New Haven, 1994—; assoc. prof. medicine George Washington U. Med. Sch., 1971-75, prof. medicine, 1975-89; vis. physician Rockefeller U. Hosp., 1989-93; mem. expert advisory panel WHO, 1976-93; mem. Lasker Award Jury, 1974—; chmn. Com. French-Am. Agreement on Cancer Treatment Research, 1976; vis. prof. Stanford U. Med. Sch., 1972; 1st ann. Clowes lectr. Roswell Park Meml. Inst. Buffalo, 1973; mem. sci. com. 4th Internat. Congress on Anti-Cancer Chemotherapy, 1991-92, 5th Internat. Congress on Anti-Cancer Chemotherapy, also mem. internat. adv. bd., 1993—; mem. sci. adv. bd. Tobacco-Related Disease Rsch. Program State of Calif., 1991—, Hollings Cancer Ctr., 1991—; mem. adv. bd. Stop Cancer, 1991—; mem. sci. com. Italian-Am. Found. For Cancer Rsch., 1991—; mem. clin. adv. bd. Hybridon, Inc., 1993—; bd. dirs. Imclone Systems Inc., Oncotech Inc., Oncos Inc. Mem. editl. bd. Cancer Rsch., 1981-91, Gynecologic Oncology, 1981-91, Hematol. Oncology, 1981-87, Physicians' Drug Alert, 1982—, Jour. Clin. Oncology, 1983—; assoc. editor Online Jour. Current Clin. Trials, 1991—, Cancer Investigation, 1983-87, Am. Jour. Medicine, 1983-88; mem. extramural bd. assoc. editors Physicians Desk Query (PDQ), Nat. Cancer Inst., 1989—; mem. editl. bd. or adv. editor numerous other med. jours.; contbr. numerous articles to med. jours. Mem. awards assembly Gen. Motors Cancer Research Found., 1981-85, adv. council, 1984—; mem. Armand Hammer Cancer Award Com., 1983—. Served with USMCR, 1955-61. Tobacco Rsch. Industry fellow, 1959; decorated Oren del Sol en el Grando de Official, Govt. of Peru, 1970; recipient Albert and Mary Lasker Med. Rsch. award, 1972; Superior Svc. award HEW, 1975; Esther Langer Found. award, 1976; Alumni medallion Coll. William and Mary, 1976; Jeffrey Gottlieb award, 1976; Bronze medal Am. Soc. Therapeutic Radiology, 1978, Karnofsky prize and lecture, 1979, Griffuel prize Assn. for Devel. Rsch. on Cancer, 1980, James Ewing award Soc. Surg. Oncology, 1982; Meml. Sloan-Kettering Cancer Ctr. award, 1972; Disting. Svc. medal USPHS, 1983; Meyer and Anna Prentiss award, 1984; Second Emmanuel Cancer Found. award, 1984; Pierluigi Nervi award, Rome, 1985; Medal of Honor, Am. Cancer Soc., 1985; Barbara Bohen Pfeifer award Am.-Italian Found. Cancer Rsch., 1985; Stratton lectr. Am. Soc. Hematology, 1985, Leukemia Rsch. Fund lectr., London, 1985; Tenth Richard and Hilda Rosenthal Found. award, Am. Assn. Cancer Rsch., Inc., 1986; Stanley G. Kay Meml. award, D.C. Am. Cancer Soc., 1986, Sci. award Brady Cancer Rsch. Inst., 1987, Prix Cino del Duca, Paris, 1988, Pezcoller award Eur. Sch. Oncolog 1988, Surgeon Gen.'s Exemplary Svc. medal, 1988, Armand Hammer Cancer prize, 1990, Outstanding Achievement in Clin. Rsch. award Assn. Cmty. Cancer Ctrs., 1992; elected Conn. Acad. Sci. and Engring., 1994; recipient City of Medicine award, 1995. Fellow ACP, N.Y. Acad. Medicine; mem. AMA, Am. Soc. Clin. Oncology (chmn. program com. 1972, dir. 1973-76, pres. 1977-78), Am. Cancer Soc., Am. Soc. Hematology, Am. Assn. Cancer Rsch. (dir. 1976-79), Am. Fedn. Clin. Rsch., Am. Soc. Clin. Investigation, Assn. Am. Physicians, Soc. Surg. Oncology,

Smith-Reed-Russel Med. Soc., Internat. Coun. for Coordinating Cancer Rsch. (pres. Am. bd. 1989-92), Alpha Omega Alpha.

DEVITO, PAUL LEONARD, psychology educator; b. Pitts., Nov. 19, 1953; s. Albert and Bertha (Aragonese) DeV.; m. Rebecca Sue Lipner, Aug. 24, 1980; 1 child, Zachary Lipner. BS, U. Pitts., 1975, MS, 1978, PhD, 1980. Asst. prof. St. Joseph's U., Phila., 1980-86, assoc. prof., 1986—, chair dept. psychology, 1987—; presenter at profl. confs. Contbr. articles to profl. publs. Mem. Am. Psychol. Assn., Am. Psychol. Soc. (charter), Ea. Psychol. Assn., Midwestern Psychol. Assn., Psychonomic Soc., Sigma Xi. Office: Dept Psychology Saint Josephs Univ 5600 City Ave Philadelphia PA 19131-1308

DE VITO, ROBERT, psychiatrist, educator; b. Portsmouth, N.H., July 19, 1935; s. Alexander and Ethel (Barnett) deV.; m. Joan Jenette Pratte, May 23, 1964; 1 child, Stefani. AB, Harvard U., 1957; MD, Loyola U., Chgo., 1961. Diplomate Am. Bd. Psychiatry and Neurology. Intern St. Elizabeth Hosp., Boston, 1961-62; resident Ill. State Psychiat. Inst., Chgo., 1962-65; pvt. practice psychiatry Maywood, Ill., 1967—; dir. jr. clerkship in psychiatry Stritch Sch. Medicine, Loyola U., Chgo., 1967-69, clin. prof. psychiatry, 1977-80, prof., chmn. dept., 1980—; lectr. speakers burs. Pfizer Labs., 1972—, Squibb Pharms., 1975, Lederle Labs., 1976—, Merrill Pharms., 1979—; cons. inpatient alcoholism treatment programs Chgo. Alcoholic Treatment Ctr., 1967-69, Hines Hosp., 1967-72; organizer Internat. Symposium on Schizophrenia, Chgo., 1977. Sr. editor, contbr.: A View Into a Modern State-Operated Mental Health Facility, 1975; contbr. articles to profl. pubs. With USAF, 1965-67. Decorated Air Force Commendation medal; named Clin. Tchr. of Yr., 1969, Outstanding Clin. Tchr. of Yr., 1981, Dept. Psychiatry Faculty Mem. of Yr., 1981-82 Stritch Sch. Medicine, Loyola U. Fellow Am. Psychiat. Assn. (cert. adminstrv. psychiatrist); mem. Ill. Psychiat. Assn. (editor newspaper 1970-72, chmn. constn. revision com. 1972-74, treas. 1974-78, chmn. edn. com. 1976-77, pres.-elect 1980-81, pres. 1981-82), AMA., Ill. Med. Soc., Chgo. Med. Soc., Nat. Assn. Mental Health Program Dirs. (bd. dirs. 1978-79, v.p. 1979-80, Am. Assn. chmn. depts. psychiatry 1980—), Alpha Omega Alpha (Faculty Initiate award Epsilon chpt. 1973). Home: 95416 Helen Ct Downers Grove IL 60516 Office: 2160 S 1st Ave Maywood IL 60153-3304

DEVITT, NEAL FRANCIS, family practice physician; b. Milw., Nov. 18, 1952; s. John Robert and Elizabeth Margaret (Maier) D.; m. Paula Lewis, May 7, 1983; children: Sheila, Gabriel, Jessica, Nicholas. AB, Harvard U., 1977; MD, Rush Presbyn. St. Lukes Hosp., 1981. Resident Luth. Gen. Hosp., Park Ridge, Ill., 1981-84; physician La Familia Med. Ctr., Santa Fe, N.Mex., 1984—; assoc. clin. prof. U. N.Mex. Sch. Medicine, Albuquerque, 1988—; mem. affiliate faculty N.Mex. chpt. Am. Heart Assn., Albuquerque, 1988—. Reviewer: Am. Family Physician, 1992—. Recipient Cmty. Svc. award Am. Heart Assn., 1987, Disting. Svc. award USPHS, 1986. Mem. Am. Acad. Family Practice (sec. N.Mex. chpt. 1995-96). Office: La Familia Med Ctr 1035 Alto St Santa Fe NM 87505-8395

DEVITT-GRASSO, PAULINE VIRGINIA, civic volunteer, nurse; b. Salem, Mass., May 13, 1930; d. John M. and Mary Elizabeth (Cologey) Devitt; m. Frank Anthony Grasso, Oct. 26, 1968; 1 stepson, Christopher Anthony. BSN, Boston Coll., 1952; student, Boston U., 1954-55, Boston State Tchrs. Coll., 1953-54. RN. Staff nurse J.P. Kennedy Jr. Meml. Hosp., Brighton, Mass., 1952-53; head nurse, day supr. J.P. Kennedy Jr. Meml. Hosp., Brighton, 1953-54, day supr., 1955, clin. instr., 1955-58, adminstrv. asst., 1968, dir. nursing edn., 1958-68; vis. instr. Boston Coll., Mass. State Coll., Meml. Hosp. Sch. Nursing, Newton, Mass. Meml. Hosp. Sch. Nursing, 1955-68, CUA S of N, 1990; bd. dirs. Behavioral Health Svcs. Inc. Pres. Project H.O.P.E., Manhattan Beach, Calif., 1982; pres. adv. coun. Meals on Wheels, Salvation Army, 1989, 90, 91, bd. dirs. Redondo Beach, 1992—, sec. bd. dirs., 1994; cons. Manhattan Beach Housing Found., 1986—, Manhattan Beach Case Mgr., 1982—; mem. adv. coun. South Bay Sr. Svcs., Torrance, Calif., 1986—, pres., 1994; sr. advocate City of Manhattan Beach, 1982; bd. dirs. Ret. Sr. Vol. Program, Torrance, 1986-90, Behavioral Health Svcs., 1992—, treas. 1993, hosp. com., fin. com., exec. com.; neighborhood chair Girl Scouts U.S.; mem. Beach City Coun. on Aging, 1983-91; mem. Salvation Army Ladies Aux.; mem. adv. bd. Salvation Army Corps, Redondo Beach. Recipient Cert. of Appreciation, County of L.A., 1988, Vol. of the Yr. award City of Manhattan Beach, 1988, Award of Honor County of L.A., 1989, State of Calif. Senate Rules Com. Resolution Commendation, 1988; named Outstanding Vol. Cath. Daus. of Am., 1986, Vol. of Yr. City Manhattan Beach, 1986-87; Rose and Scroll award Manhattan Beach C. of C., 1989, Art Michel Meml. Community Svc. award Manhattan Beach Rotary Club, 1989, Cert. of Appreciation KC's Queen of Martyrs Coun., 1989, Redondo Beach Lila Bell award Salvation Army, 1989, others, Manhattan Beach Vol. Appreciation award, 1982, 83, 84, 85, 86, 88, 90, 91, 92, 93, cert. South Bay Centinela Credit Union, 1990; nominated for Pres's. Vol. Action award Project H.O.P.E., 1987. Mem. AARP, South Bay Geneal. Soc., New Eng. Hist. and Geneal. Soc., Polish Genal. Soc. So. Calif., Am. Martyrs Altar Soc. (pres. 1983, coun. mem.-at-large 1992), Cath. U. Am. Nat. Alumni Assn. (hon.), Cath. U. Am. Sch. Nursing Alumni Assn. (hon.), Boston Coll. Alumni Assn., Manhattan Beach Sr. Citizens Club (pres. 1985-86, 88-89), Lions (Citizen of Yr. award Manhattan Beach club 1986), DAV (comdr.'s club 1990, 91, 92), Lady in Equestrian Order of Holy Sepulchre of Jerusalem. Democrat. Roman Catholic. Home: 329 3rd St Manhattan Beach CA 90266-6410

DE VIVO, DARRYL CLAUDE, pediatric neurologist; b. Everett, Mass., Aug. 28, 1937; m. Ruth Marie Crock, Feb. 6, 1965; children: Cynthia, Jessica, Kristin. BA, Amherst Coll., 1959; MD, U. Va., 1964. Diplomate Am. Bd. Psychiatry and Neurology (dir. for neurology 1991—). Intern Univ. Hosp., Boston, 1964-65; resident in pediatrics and neurology Mass. Gen. Hosp., Boston, 1965-67; clin. assoc. NIH, 1967-69; fellow in pediatric neurology St. Louis Children's Hosp., 1969-70; mem. faculty Wash. U. Sch. Medicine, St. Louis, 1970-78, prof. pediatrics and neurology, 1977-78; Sidney Carter prof. neurology and prof. pediatrics Coll. Physicians and Surgeons, Columbia U., N.Y.C., 1979—; dir. pediatric neurology Columbia-Presbyn. Med. Ctr., N.Y.C., 1979—. Assoc. editor: Rudolph's Textbook of Pediatrics, 17th edit., 1982, 18th edit., 1987, 19th edit., 1990, 20th edit., 1996; assoc. editor Annals of Neurology, 1979-83, Advances in Pediatrics, 1989—; contbr. articles to profl. jours. With USPHS, 1967-69. NIH grantee. Mem. Am. Neurol. Assn., Am. Acad. Neurology, Child Neurology Soc. (pres. 1989-91), Am. Pediatric Soc., Soc. Pediatric Rsch., Am. Soc. Neurochemistry, Internat. Child Neurology Assn., Soc. Neurosci., Alpha Omega Alpha. Office: Presbyn Hosp Columbia-Presbyn Med Ctr 710 W 168th St New York NY 10032-2603

DEVIZIA, JOSEPH FRANCIS, healthcare executive; b. Wilkes-Barre, Pa., Nov. 6, 1942; s. Joseph and Ruth (Miller) DeV.;m . Maura Klemek, July 26, 1969; children: Tania, Joseph, Christa. AB in Sociology, King's Coll., 1969; MS in Edn., Wilkes Coll., 1975. Caseworker White Haven (Pa.) Ctr., 1969, 70, Luzerne County Child Welfare, Wilkes-Barre, 1970-72; community living arrangements coord. Luzerne Wyoming Mental Health and Mental Retardation, Wilkes-Barre, 1970-74, mental retardation coord., 1974-76, county adminstr., 1976-79; assoc. dir. Children's Svc. Ctr., Wilkes-Barre, 1979-84, exec. dir., 1984—. Contbr. articles to profl. jours. Bd. dirs. Children and Adolescent Svc. System Project, Vols. of Am., Project Remain for Elderly Disadvantaged, Reach, Vision, St. Pius X Seminary; chmn. Campaign for Human Devel. Mem. Pa. Assn. Mental Health and Mental Retardation Providers (bd. dirs. 1987-93). Democrat. Roman Catholic. Office: Children's Svc Ctr 335 S Franklin St Wilkes Barre PA 18702-3808

DEVLIN, ROBERT MARTIN, physiologist educator; b. Albany, N.Y., Oct. 13, 1931; s. Patrick C. and Katherine (Martin) D.; m. Wanda Theresa Karandy, July 10, 1960; children: Kristin, Theresa, Michael. BS, SUNY, Albany, 1959; MA, Dartmouth Coll., 1961; PhD, U. Md., 1963; D Honoris Causa (hon.), Szczecin U., Poland, 1990. Asst. prof. N.D. State U., Fargo, 1963-65; asst. prof. U. Mass., Amherst, 1965-68, assoc. prof., 1968-74, prof., 1974—. Author: Plant Physiology, 1966; co-author: Photosynthesis, 1970, Biology of Human Concern, 1972, Exercises in Plant Physiology, 1986. Commr. Town of Barnstable, Mass., 1973-75; bd. dirs. Assn. for Preservation of Cape Cod, Mass., 1971; judge U.S. Figure Skating Assn., 1972-76. Pfc. U.S. Army, 1952-54. Recipient Disting. Mem. award Northeastern Weed Sci. Soc., 1990. Fellow Weed Sci. Soc. Am. (chmn. outstanding rsch. award com., Fellow award 1991); mem. Plant Growth Regulator Soc. Am. (v.p. 1973-74, pres. 1974-76, 80-82), Internat. Weed Sci. Soc., Coun. Agriculture Sci. and Tech. (bd. dirs. 1980—), Am. Coun. Sci. & Health (bd. sci. advisors 1978—). Roman Catholic. Home: 10 Lost Meadows Rd East Sandwich MA 02537-1254 Office: U of Mass Glen Charlie Rd PO Box 569 East Wareham MA 02538-0569

DEVON, BRUCE, urologist; b. N.Y.C., Apr. 25, 1948. AB cum laude, Brandeis U., Waltham, Mass., 1969; MD, Tufts U., 1973. Diplomate Am. Bd. Urology. Fellow ACS; mem. Am. Assn. Clin. Urologists, Am. Urol. Assn. Office: 103 Garland St Everett MA 02149

DEVORE, JON EUGENE, clinical psychologist; b. Chattanooga, June 9, 1945; s. Mark Edwin and Helen (Derengoski) DeV.; m. Nancy Jean Agee, Dec. 10, 1971; children: Jon E. II, William E., Catherine A. BS, U. Chattanooga, 1969; MA, Mid. Tenn. State U., 1973, Memphis State U., 1979; EdS, Memphis State U., 1980, PhD, 1985. Lic. clin. psychologist, Tenn.; cert. sch. psychologist, Tenn. Couselor-instr. Chattanooga Pub. Schs., 1970-72; psychol. examiner Moccasin Bend Mental Health Inst., Chattanooga, 1974-77; sch. psychology intern Memphis City Schs. and Memphis State U., 1979-80; student clinician Memphis State U., 1981-83; clin. psychology intern Vets. Med. Ctr., Memphis, 1984-85; clin. psychologist, coord. psychol. svcs. Regional Rehab. Ctr., Memphis, 1985-88; clin. psychologist Vets. Med. Ctr., Memphis, 1988—, Psychol. Emergency Rm., The Med, Memphis, 1991—; adj. faculty Memphis State U., 1985-90; mem. theses and dissertation coms. Memphis State U.; supr. interns, Regional Rehab. Ctr., Vets. Hosp., chmn. psychology Clinical Privileges Com., mem. training com., mem. tumor bd., cancer com., Vets. Med. Ctr. Illustrator Historical Geology lab. manual, Physical Geology course textbook; contbr. articles to profl. jours. Mem. AAUP, Tenn. Psychol. Assn., Tenn. Acad. Sci., Beta, Beta, Beta, Delta Tau Omega, Pi Gamma Mu, Psi Chi, Kappa Delta Pi, Phi Delta Kappa, Gamma Beta Phi, Phi Kappa Phi, Sigma Xi. Presbyterian. Office: VA Med Ctr 1030 Jefferson Ave Memphis TN 38104-2127

DEVOTI, ANDREA L., hospital administrator; b. St. Louis, Mar. 2, 1955; d. Ernest L. and Wanda I. (Downs) Devoti. BSN, U. Pa., 1972, MSN, 1982; MBA, Widener U., 1991. Nursing instr. Bryn Mawr (Pa.) Hosp., 1985-87, surp. med.-surg., epidemiologist; asst. dir. St. Mary Hosp., Phila., 1987-90; dir. employee health svcs. Bryn Mawr Hosp., 1991-93; dir. compensation, benefits, Human Resource Info. Sys. and employee health The Children's Hosp. Phila., 1994—. Contbr. articles to profl. jours. Bd. dirs. Family and Community Health Svcs. of Delaware County. Home: 507 Covington Rd Havertown PA 19083-5715

DEVRIES, DONALD CHARLES, health care administrator; b. Bklyn., Oct. 19, 1944; s. Charles Francis and Irene Elizabeth (Hoffman) DeV.; children from previous marriage: Peter Ross, Christopher Scott. BS, U. Vt., 1967; MA, Montclair State U., 1986. Lic. nursing home adminstr., N.J. Asst. adminstr. Dunrovon Nursing Home, Cresskill, N.J., 1968-74; adminstr. Dunroven Health Care Ctr., Cresskill, N.J., 1974-90; exec. v.p. GEM Holding Co., Paramus, N.J., 1990—. Comdr. USNR. Mem. Am. Coll. Health Care Adminstrs., N.J. Soc. Nursing Home Adminstrs., N.J. Assn. Care Facility (mem. exec. com. 1986—), Coalition of Concerned Health Care Adminstrs. (mem. exec. bd. 1986—). Office: Dunroven 221 County Rd Cresskill NJ 07626

DEWALD, ERNEST JAMES, retired dental educator, military career officer; b. Springfield Gardens, N.Y., Apr. 30, 1946; s. William Lee and Josephine Lena (Furey) DeW.; m. Joan Eileen Murray, May 5, 1973. BS, St. John's U., N.Y.C., 1967; DDS, Georgetown U., 1972. Commd. 2d lt. U.S. Army, 1972, advanced through grades to col., 1986; dir. dental svcs. Nuernberg Dental, Bamberg, Fed. Republic of Germany, 1980-83; chief restorative dentistry Walter Reed Dental The Pentagon, Washington, 1985; clinic chief U.S. Army Dental, Ft. Meyer, Va., 1985-86; dir. advanced edn. of gen. dentistry U.S. Army Dental, Ft. Campbell, Ky., 1986-87, 1986-91; dir. advanced edn. of gen. dentistry U.S. Army Dental, Ft. Bragg, N.C., 1991-93, retired, 1993; project officer new clinic constrn. West Point Dental, U.S. Mil. Acad., N.Y., 1978-80; forensic odontologist U.S. Army, Ft. Campbell, 1986-91. Contbr. articles to profl. jours. Member fundraising com. Meml. Hospice, Clarksville, Tenn., 1988-91; Sunday sch. instr. Cumberland Presbyn. Ch., Sango, Tenn., 1988-91; instr. in children's bowling DYA, Bamberg, 1980-83; sec. Ft. Campbell Bowling League, 1987-90; mem. Octoberfest planning com. Edelweis German Club, Clarksville, 1987-96. Fellow Am. Coll. Dentists, Internat. Coll. Dentists; mem. ADA, Acad. Gen. Dentistry (sec. Army chpt. 1986-91, self assessment com. 1991-96), Acad. Forensic Sci., Soc. Forensic Odontology, Acad. Oral Medicine, Acad. Operative Dentistry, Fed. Svcs. Bd. Gen. Dentistry, Certifying Bd. Gen. Dentistry (bd. dirs.), United Way (bd. dirs.), Rotary (bd. dirs.). Home: 2074 Roxbury Ln Clarksville TN 37043-2112 Office: 1301 Peachers Mill Rd Clarksville TN 37042-4610

DEWAN, MANTOSH JAIMANI, psychiatrist, educator; b. Bombay, July 22, 1951; came to U.S., 1975; s. Jaimani and Sheel (Krishen) D.; m. Anita Lall, June 21, 1975; children: Amant, Radhika. MB, BS, Bombay U., 1975. Diplomate Am. Bd. Psychiatry and Neurology. Intern SUNY Health Sci. Ctr., Syracuse, 1975-76, resident in psychiatry, 1976-79, asst. to assoc. prof., 1979-92, prof., 1992—, asst. dir. undergrad. edn., 1982-85, co-dir. undergrad. edn., 1985-88, dir. undergrad. edn., 1988-92, dir. residency tng. in psychiatry, 1992—, vice chair dept. psychiatry, 1995—; staff psychiatrist VA Med. Ctr., Syracuse, 1979-85, acting chief, 1985-89; research cons. Hutchings Psychiat. Ctr., Syracuse, 1984—. Contbr. articles to profl. jours. and author chpts. in books, 1982—. Named exemplary psychiatrist Nat. Alliance for Mentally Ill, 1994. Fellow Am. Psychiat. Assn. (counselor-at-large dist. chpt. 1984-85, sec., treas. 1990-91, pres. 1992-93); mem. AAAS, Assn. Am. Psychiatrists from India (life), Soc. for Biol. Psychiatry, Assn. of Dirs. of Med. Student Edn. in Psychiatry, Am. Assn. Dirs. of Psychiat. Residency Tng. Democrat. Home: 5310 Aquarius Dr Syracuse NY 13224-2146 Office: SUNY Health Sci Ctr Dept Psychiatry 750 E Adams St Syracuse NY 13210-2306

DEWART, DOROTHY BOARDMAN, clinical psychologist, consultant, researcher; b. Boston, Aug. 19, 1948; d. Thomas Dennie and Dorothy (Potter) Boardman. BA in Psychology and Sociology, Salem Coll., 1972; MA in Clin. Psychology, Xavier U., 1976; postgrad., U. Cin., 1975-77; PhD in Clin. Psychology, Temple U., 1981. Rsch. asst. Cin. Ctr. Devel. Disorders, 1974-75, psychology trainee, 1975, U. Cin., 1975-76, Rollman' Psychiat. Inst., Cin., 1975-76; psychologist Ctrl. Psychiat. Clinic, Cin., 1976-77; asst. dir. Pyschol. Svcs., Clermont Gen. and Tech. Coll., U. Cin., 1976-77; supr. Psychol. Svcs. Ctr., Temple U., 1978, clin. asst., 1980, psychology intern, 1980-81, staff psychologist, dept. psychiat. and chronic pain clinic, 1981-82; cons. maxillo-facial pain clinic, 1981-83 , clin. instr. dept. psychiatry, 1981-92, clin. asst. prof., dept. psychiatry, Temple U. Hosp., 1992—. Rsch. Incentive Fund grantee Temple U. Hosp., 1981-82; recipient NIMH assistantship, 1977-78. Mem. Am. Psychol. Assn., Phila. Soc. Clin. Psychologists, Nat. Register Health Svcs. Providers, Am. Pain Soc. Research in psychotherapy with patients who present significant physical illness; research in effects of tryptophan on chronic pain; clin. assoc. Am. Bd. Med. Psychotherapists, 1987. Office: 748 Saint Georges Rd Philadelphia PA 19119-3342

DEWEESE, JAMES ARVILLE, surgeon, educator; b. Apr. 5, 1925; s. Arville Ottis and Vergie (Jenkins) DeW.; m. Margaret Brown, June 20, 1950 (dec. 1960); children: James Arville Jr., Margaret Ann, Elizabeth Lynn, Joanne Spencer; m. Patricia Bidwell, May 5, 1962; children; Robert Bidwell, Jamie Susan. Student, Harvard U., 1942-43, Kent State U., 1943-44; MD, U. Rochester, 1949. Diplomate Am. Bd. Surgery (bd. dirs. 1986-91), Am. Bd. Thoracic and Cardiovascular Surgery (bd. dirs. 1987-91); cert. spl. qualifications gen. vascular surgery. Intern Strong Meml. Hosp., Rochester, N.Y., 1949-50, resident, 1950-52, 54-56; instr. surgery U. Rochester (N.Y.) Sch. Medicine and Dentistry, 1955-58, asst. prof. surgery, 1958-63, assoc. prof. surgery, 1963-69, prof. surgery, 1969-74, prof. cardiothoracic surgery, 1975—, chmn. div. cardiothoracic surgery, 1977-91, assoc. chmn. dept. surgery, 1986-90, chief sect. vascular surgery, 1987-91. Bd. dirs. Jour. Vascular Surgery, 1983—; editor: Vascular Surgery, 1985; contbr. over 200 articles to sci. jours. and over 60 chpts. to books. Mem. bd. trustees Clifton Springs (N.Y.) Hosp., 1980—. Mem. Am. Heart Assn. (bd. dirs. 1982-86, chmn. coun. cardiovascular surgery 1982-84), Ea. Vascular Soc. (pres. 1988), Internat. Soc. Cardiovascular Surgery (pres. N.Am. chpt. 1984-85, sec.-gen. 1987-95, pres. 1995—), Pan Pacific Surg. Assn. (pres. 1989-91), Soc. Vascular Surgery (pres. 1977-78), Am. Venous Forum (pres. 1993-94), Sr. Cardiovascular Surg. Soc. (pres. 1996), Oak Hill Country Club (bd. govs. 1978-81). Home: 78 Winding Creek Ln Rochester NY 14625-2175 Office: U Rochester Dept Surgery M&D Cardiothoracic Div 601 Elmwood Ave Rochester NY 14642-0001

DEWERD, LARRY ALBERT, medical physicist, educator; b. Milw., July 18, 1941; s. Anthony Lawrence and Dorothy M. (Heling) DeW.; m. Vada Mary Anderson, Sept. 14, 1963; children: Scott, Mark, Eric. BS, U. Wis., Milw., 1963; MS, U. Wis., 1965, PhD, 1970. Rsch. assoc. U. Wash., Seattle, 1970-72, rsch. asst. prof., 1973-75; vis. asst. prof. U. Wis., Madison, 1975-76, clin. asst. prof., 1976-79, clin. assoc. prof., 1979-86, prof., 1990—; mgr. product devel. Radiation Measurements, Middleton, Wis., 1986-90; dir. Radiation Calibration Lab., Madison, 1990—; cons. Instrumentarium, Milw., 1990; v.p. Standard Imaging, Madison, 1990—; presenter in field to sci. confs., seminars and workshops. Contbg. author: Brachytherapy, Thermoluminescence and Mammography; also numerous articles. Science chmn. Am. Cancer Soc. State of Wis., 1986-90. Grantee Nat. Cancer Inst., 1979-86, 94—. Mem. Am. Assn. Physicists in Medicine (pres. 1990-92), Health Physics Soc., Am. Phys. Soc., Coun. Ionizing Radiation Measurements and Standards (pres. 1995—), Sigma Xi (bd. dirs. 1984-86). Home: 13 Pilgrim Cir Madison WI 53711-4033 Office: U Wis 1530 Med Sci Ctr 1300 University Ave Madison WI 53706-1510

DEWITT, PAUL LESLIE, surgeon; b. Billings, Mont., Apr. 15, 1941; s. Lloyd L. and Lillian Eleanor (Beeler) DeW.; m. Jennifer Jean Jerome; 1 child, Catherine Abigail. MD, George Washington U., 1968. Diplomate Am. Bd. Thoracic Surgery. Cardiac/thoracic/vascular surgeon Fla. Cardiovascular Surgeons, Inc., Miami, 1978-91, Fla. Cardiovascular Surgeons, Clearwater, 1991—. Maj. USAR, 1971-73. Decorated Bronze Star. Home: 1540 Gulf Blvd # 1001 Clearwater FL 34630 Office: Fla Cardiovascular Surgeons 1000 Lakeview Rd # 3 Clearwater FL 34616

DE WOLFF, FREDERIK ALBERT, toxicology educator; b. Schiedam, The Netherlands, Sept. 19, 1944; s. Frederik A. and Andrea J. (Vogely) de W.; m. Deena Rouendaal, June 26, 1971; children: Jacob Frederik, Abraham Ruben. BSc in Biochemistry, U. Leiden, The Netherlands, 1966, MSc in Biochemistry, 1968, BA in Semitic Langs., 1971, PhD in Pharmacology, 1973, MA in Semitic Langs., 1984. Diplomate in clin. chemistry and toxicology. Resident U. Leiden, 1969-73, lectr. dept. Hebrew studies, 1981-87; resident in clin. biochemistry Univ. Hosp., Leiden, 1973-76, assoc. prof., head dept. human toxicology, 1976-91; vis. prof. U. Amsterdam (The Netherlands) Med. Ctr., 1979-91, prof., 1991—; Lady Davis vis. prof. Hebrew U., Jerusalem, 1995; cons. various pharm. cos. and law firms; pres. Eurotox 91 Congress, Maastricht, Netherlands, 1991. Editor: Therapeutic Relevance of Drug Assays, 1979, Medical Toxicology, 1992, Intoxications of the Nervous System I, 1994, and II, 1995, Basic Analytical Toxicology, 1995; contbr. over 250 articles to sci. jours. Mem. Netherlands Soc. Clin. Chemistry (bd. mem. 1991—), Netherlands Soc. Toxicology (pres. 1988-90), Am. Assn. for Clin. Chemistry, Brit. Toxicology Soc., N.Y. Acad. Scis., Internat. Assn. Forensic Toxicologists, Health Coun. of the Netherlands. Jewish.

DEWS, PEOLA BUTLER, government consultant therapist; b. Alexandria, Va., July 16, 1936; d. Edward Godfrey and Mazie Lula (Poindexter) Butler; m. Alphonso Lee Holt, Aug. 8, 1953 (div. 1967); children: Direk, Lisa, Clevin, Cheronne, Lynnette, Deirdre, Janis, Kenyetta; m. Kenneth Stuart Spurlock, Jan. 29, 1972 (div. 1981); m. Robert William Dews, Apr. 5, 1984; stepchildren: Angela, Robert, Jr., Charles, David, Denise. BS, Howard U., 1974, MEd, 1976; postgrad. American U., 1975, Catholic U., 1978, Duke U., 1980, George Washington U., 1982—. Community affairs coordinator WHUR-FM, Washington, 1971-74; univ. rels. info. officer, dep. dir. Howard U., Washington, 1974-76, alumni rels. officer, 1976-78; pres. PJ Cons., Inc., Washington, 1978—; minority rels. coord. Peace Corps, Washington, 1980-85, chmn. minority concerns com., 1982-85; counseling cons. Notre Dame Acad., Washington, 1982—; profl. in residence Wheaton Coll., Norton, Mass., 1983-84; vis. lectr. Population Concern, Eng., Ireland, 1983, Schiller U., Paris, 1985. Author: (book) Mad Nigger Woman, 1971; (play) Black Justice, 1971; (booklet) Prescription for Changing your Life, 1979. Editor Alumni News, 1976. Founder Southwest Community coop. Youth Club, Washington, 1965-67; vol. counselor to runaway youths, battered women, refugees, 1966—; fund-raising chmn. Howard U. Miss. Project, Washington, 1969-71; mem. Coun. of 100 Black Republicans, Washington, 1980—, Rep. Nat. Com., 1980—. Named Woman of Yr., Big Sisters Met. Washington, 1982, One of Outstanding Black Ams. in Met. Washington, 1983; recipient Outstanding Community Service award Mayor's Office, Washington, 1983, Thomas Jefferson award WTTG-TV, 1984; Peola Spurlock Day named in her honor Capitol Hill Homemaker/Health Aid, 1979. Mem. Am. Assn. Counseling and Devel., Assn. for Non-white Concerns, Assn. for Humanistic Edn. and Devel., Assn. for Specialists in Group Work, Am. Mental Health Counselors Assn., Nat. Assn. Personnel Workers, Nat. Council Negro Women, Nat. Urban League, NAACP, Women in Devel. Task Force. Lutheran. Office: PO Box 56595 Washington DC 20040-6595

DEXTER, FREDERICK JAY, dentist; b. Bklyn., Apr. 12, 1947; s. Michael M. and Muriel Dexter; m. Deborah Rosenzweig, Aug. 12, 1972 (div. 1978); 1 child, Michael J. BS in Aerospace Engring., U. Md., 1970, DDS, 1979; BSME, Johns Hopkins U., 1974. Registered profl. engr.; cert. dentist. Mech. engr. U.S. Army, Aberdeen Proving Ground, Md., 1970-75; pvt. practice dentistry Thurmont, Md., 1980—, Reisterstown, Md., 1981—; dental cons. Ivy Hall Nursing Home, Balt., 1979-89, Bent Nursing Home, Reisterstown, 1985-88. Author articles various newspapers, 1981—. Mem. Gen. Practice Orthodontics (adv. to bd. 1987-94, bd. dirs. 1994—), Lions (v.p. Thurmont club 1986-93), Optimists (v.p. Reisterstown club 1984), Tau Beta Pi. Home: 620 Main St Reisterstown MD 21136-1910 Office: 100 S Center St Thurmont MD 21788-1910

DEY, RADHESHYAM CHANDRA, cytologist; b. Calcutta, India, Jan. 30, 1950; came to U.S., 1978; s. Bhairab and Satyabala D.; m. Indrani Roy Chowdhury, July 5, 1981; children: Smita, Anita. BSc, Bangabasi Coll., Calcutta, 1970; MSc, U. Calcutta, 1972, cert. in life sci., 1974; CT, Brooke Army Med. Ctr., San Antonio, 1983; cert. leadership mgmt., ednl. devel., quality improvement and equal opportunity, Walter Reed Army Med. Ctr., 1989; postgrad., Laval U., Quebec City, Can., 1995. Registered cytotechnologist, Am. Soc. Clin. Pathologists, Internat. Acad. Cytology, Calif., Md. Rsch. fellow U. Calcutta, 1975-77; with Anthropol. Survey of India, Indian Mus. Calcutta, 1977-78; biol. science asst. Army Inst. Rsch., Washington, 1980-83; cytology specialist U.S. Army Hosp., Ft. Campbell, Ky., 1983-85, SHAPE Med. Ctr., SHAPE/Mons, Belgium, 1985-87; cytotechnologist Nat. Health Lab., Vienna, Va., 1988; cytologist, supr. and chief Walter Reed Army Med. Ctr., Washington, 1988-94; attended Indian Sci. Congress, U. New Delhi, Calcutta, Waltair, Gujarat, 1972-77, Internat. Congress of Cytology, Brussels, Belgium, 1987, Internat. Cytology Tutorials, Vienna, Austria, 1986, Tokyo, Japan, 1991, Harvard Med. Sch. Advances in Cytology, Boston, 1990, Coll. Am. Pathologists, Las Vegas, 1992, World Congress on Anthropol. & Ethnol. Scis., Mexico City, 1993, Am. Soc. Clin. Pathologists and Cytopathology, Seattle, Advanced Techniques in Human Identification-Armed Forces Inst. Pathology, Washington, 1994; participant New Directions for Leaders Focus 2000, Ft. Belvoir, Va., 1994, Immunol. Markers in Histopathology and Cytology, Inst. of Pathology, Ghent U. Hosp., Belgium, 1987, numerous seminars; mem. symposium for suprs. and team bldg. dynamics for mgrs. U.S. Army Walter Reed Med. Ctr., Washngton, 1995, 96. Contbr. articles to profl. jours. Decorated U.S. Army Commendation medal, 1985, Achievement medal, 1984, Good Conduct medals, 1982, 85; recipient Decree of Merit for outstanding contbn. to medicine and health care, 1995. Mem. AAAS, Internat. Acad. Cytology, Am. Anthropol. Assn., Am. Soc. Cytopathology, Am. Soc. Clin. Pathologists, N.Y. Acad. Scis., Soc. of Armed Forces Med. Lab. Scientists, Belge de Cytologie Clinique (del. visit to People's Repubblic China 1987, 91, internat. team cytologists exch. sci. knowledge with USSR 1990), Ind. Sci. Congress, Indian Anthropol. Soc., Washington Met. Assn. of Cytology. Home: 2313 Snowflake Dr Odenton MD 21113-2237 Office: Walter Reed Army Med Ctr Dept Pathology Cytology Lab Washington DC 20307

DE YCAZA, MANUEL MARIA, physician; b. Panama City, Panama, July 10, 1938; came to U.S., 1956; s. Rogelio E. and Ines E. (Vallarino) De Y.; m. Shirley Ann Murphy, Dec. 7, 1963; children: Manuel, Maria Elena, Roberto, Melissa. BS, Marquette U., 1960; MD, Med. Coll. Wis., 1964. Diplomate Am. Bd. Internal Medicine; recertified 1980. Intern Phila. Gen. Hosp., 1964-65; resident Milw. County Hosp., 1965-68; attending staff St. Thomas Hosp., Panama City, Panama, 1969-96, chief internal medicine, 1989-96; clin. prof. medicine U. Panama, Panama City, 1975-96; attending staff Saitilla Med. Ctr., Panama City, 1975-96; physician Panama Express, Miami, Fla., 1996—. Fellow Am. Coll. Physicians. Roman Catholic. Home: PO Box 4547, Panama Panama Office: Panama Express 8619 NW 68 St Miami FL 33166

DEYO, RICHARD ALDEN, medical educator; b. New Orleans, May 26, 1949; s. Henry Alden and Jane Morse (Cushman) D.; m. Christina D. Chavez, Oct. 28, 1978 (div. Apr. 1995); children: Andrew, Elizabeth. BA, Grinnell Coll., 1971; MD, Pa. State U., 1975; MPH, U. Wash., 1981. Resident U. Tex. Health Sci. Ctr., San Antonio, 1975-79, asst. prof. medicine, 1982-86; assoc. prof. medicine & health scis. U. Wash., Seattle, 1986-92, prof. medicine & health sci., 1992—; dir. health svcs. rsch. & devel. program Seattle VA Med. Ctr., 1986-92; chair adv. com. on rsch. Que. Workers Compensation Agy., Montreal, Can., 1991-93. Data modeling task force Wash. State Dept. Health, Olympia, 1994-95. Treatment Effectiveness grantee Agy. Health Care Policy & Rsch., 1994—; Robert Wood Johnson Clinical scholar U. Wash., 1979-81. Fellow Am. Coll. Physicians; mem. Am. Soc. Clin. Investigation, Am. Pub. Health Assn., Western Assn. Physicians, Soc. Gen. Internal Medicine (coun. mem.), Assn. Health Svcs. Rsch.

DEZELL, NANCY ANN, clinical nurse specialist, nursing administrator; b. Detroit, Mar. 15, 1962; d. Leonard Joseph and Clementine Sabina (Kowalski) Sulkoski; m. Craig Bryan Dezell, Oct. 24, 1987. BSN, Mercy Coll. Detroit, 1985; MSN, U. Cin., 1994. NCC, inpatient obstetric nursing, RNC. Staff nurse med.-surg. Sinai Hosp., Detroit, 1985—; clin. nurse USAF Wurtsmith AFB, Oscoda, Mich., 1986-88, Fairchild AFB, Spokane, Wash., 1988-92; nurse mgr. ob. unit Cannon AFB, N. Mex., 1994-96; maternal child care coord. (flight chief) Cannon AFB, 1995-96; nurse mgr. Elmendorf AFB, Fairbanks, Alaska, 1996—; health promotion coord. Wurtsmith AFB, Oscoda, Mich., 1986-88, ACLS instr., 1989—, neonatal resustication instr., 1992—. Mem. Assn. Women's Health Obstet. and Neonatal Nurses, Sigma Theta Tau. Roman Catholic. Home: 2412 Fairway Terr Clovis NM 88103 Office: 27th Med Group-SGOBN 208 Casablanca Ave Clovis NM 88101

DEZIEL, PAUL JEFFREY, physician assistant, educator; b. Windsor, Ont., Can., Sept. 16, 1961; came to U.S., 1975; s. David and Beatrice (Fraser) D.; m. Ann Christine Jorgensen, Sept. 30, 1988; children: Stephanie Anne, Daniel David. AS, Broward C.C., Ft. Lauderdale, Fla., 1981; BSc in Physician Asst. Studies, U. Detroit-Mercy Hosp., 1984; MSc in Health Adminstrn., Ctrl. Mich. U., 1996. Cert. Nat. Commn. on Cert. Phys. Assts.; cert. bd. primary care. Physician asst. in gen. medicine United Cerebral Palsy, Miami, Fla., 1984-87; physician asst. AIDS svc. U. Miami-Jackson Meml. Med. Ctr., 1987-90; physician asst. infectious diseases consultation svc. Grace Hosp.-Detroit Med. Ctr., 1990—; clin. preceptor physician asst. program U. Detroit-Mercy, 1992—, adj. clin. prof., 1993—; clin. lectr. Oakland U., Rochester, Mich., 1994—; presenter in field. Guest editor Jour. Am. Acad. Physician Assts. Fellow Am. Acad. Physician Assts. (peer reviewer Jour. 1994—), Mich. Acad. Physician Assts. Republican. Roman Catholic. Home: 856 S Brady Rd Dearborn MI 48124

D'HAEM, CHRISTOPHER MICHAEL, physician, cardiologist; b. Albion, Mich., Nov. 15, 1961; s. Michael Eldon D'Haem and Elizabeth Carolyn (Young) Keyes; m. Dana Lynn Drumheller, Dec. 27, 1986; children: Alicia, Cailyn. BS, Mich. State U., 1984; DO, Kirksville Coll. Osteo. Med., 1989. Diplomate in internal medicine and cardiology Am. Coll. Osteo. Internists. Intern Ingham Med. Ctr., Lansing, Mich., 1989-90; resident in internal medicine Lansing Gen. Hosp., 1990-92; fellow in cardiology Mich. Capital Med. Ctr., Lansing, 1992-95; cardiologist Thoracic and Cardiovascular Inst., Lansing, 1995—; asst. clin. prof. Mich. State U. Coll. Osteo. Medicine, East Lansing, 1995—. Mem. Am. Coll. Cardiology, Am. Coll. Osteo. Internists, Am. Osteo. Assn. Office: Thoracic/Cardiovasc Inst 405 W Greenlawn Ste 220 Lansing MI 48910

DHALIWAL, AMRIK SINGH, biology educator; b. Punjab, India, Nov. 17, 1934; came to U.S. 1957; s. Kapur Singh and Kishan Kaur (Bajwa) D.; m. Gurmeet Gill, Nov. 18, 1962; children: Roopinder Kaur, Deepinder Kaur. MA, Utah State U., 1959, PhD, 1962. Postdoctoral fellow Utah State U., Logan, 1962-64, rsch. assoc., 1965-66; asst. prof. biology Loyola U., Chgo., 1966-71, assoc. prof. biology, 1971-75, prof. biology, 1975—. Home: 1415 Woodhill Dr Northbrook IL 60062-4660 Office: Loyola U 6525 N Sheridan Rd Chicago IL 60626-5311

DHOOPER, SURJIT SINGH, social work educator; b. Kartarpur, Punjab, India, May 8, 1934; s. Bachint Singh and Kartar Kaur (Wasson) D.; m. Harpal Kaur Dhooper; children: Amrit Kaur, Devinder Singh, Manjot Kaur, Nimrat Kaur. MA in Polit. Sci., Agra U., India, 1961; MSW, Delhi U., India, 1963; PhD, Case Western Res. U., 1982. Social work supr. Cleve. Metro Gen. Hosp., Cleve.; sr. lectr. Visva Bharati U., Shantiniketan, India; edn. officer Delhi Maternity Hosp., New Delhi; prof. social work U. Ky., Lexington. Author: (books) Social Work and Transplantation of Human Organs, 1994, Social Work in Health Care in the 21st Century, 1996; editor Asian Am. Social Work Educators Newsletter; mem. editl. bd. Jour. Social Work Edn., Health and Social Work, Jour. Gerontol. Social Work, Aratê, Adult Residential Care Jour.; book reviewer. Mem. NASW, Ky. Assn. Social Work Educators, Coun. Social Work Edn. Home: 660 Halifax Dr Lexington KY 40503-4227

DHOPLE, ARVIND MADHAV, microbiologist; b. Ankola, Canara, India, June 13, 1937; came to U.S., 1969; s. Madhav Keshav and Kamala Madhav (Savitri) D.;m. Padmini Arvind, Dec. 26, 1966; children: Anita, Anil. BSc, U. Bombay, 1957, MSc, 1959, PhD, 1963. Rsch. asst. Acworth Leprosy Hosp., Bombay, 1962-63; post-doctoral fellow Johns Hopkins U., Balt., 1963-66; rsch. officer Cen. Leprosy Rsch. Inst., Chinglepu, India, 1966-69; rsch. assoc. Johns Hopkins U., Balt., 1970-75, asst. prof., 1975-80; rsch. prof. Fla. Inst. Tech., Melbourne, 1980—; vis. prof. Japan Soc. for Promotion of Rsch., Kurume, Japan, 1977, Chinese Acad. Med. Scis., Nanjing, People's Republic China, 1985. Contbr. articles to sci. jours. Mem. City of Satellite Beach (Fla.) Comprehensive Planning, 1988—; sec. troop 301 Boy Scouts Am., Satellite Beach, 1986—; mem. Brevard County Sch. Adv. Com., Satellite Beach, 1983—. Mem. Internat. Leprosy Assn., Am. Soc. for Microbiology, Indian Leprosy Assn., Chinese Acad. Med. Scis. (hon.), Fla. Acad. Scis., Sigma Xi. Home: PO Box 372274 Melbourne FL 32937-0274 Office: Fla Inst Tech 150 W University Blvd Melbourne FL 32901-6982

DIAL, JACK GRADY, neuropsychologist; b. Crockett, Tex., Jan. 21, 1947; s. Miller David and Ruth (Sayers) D.; 1 child, Kimberly Ruth Dial Brath. BA, Stephen F. Austin U., 1970, MEd, 1974; PhD, U. North Tex., 1982. Lic. cert. psychologist, Tex. Exec. dir. Baytown (Tex.) Opportunity Ctr., 1970-71; program dir. Dept. Mental Health and Mental Retardation, Beaumont, Tex., 1972-74; asst. prof. rehab. sci. U. Tex. Southwestern Med. Ctr., Dallas, 1975-83, clin. asst. prof., 1985—; clin. and cons. neuropsychologist Dallas, 1983—; clin. asst. prof. U. W.Va., Morgantown, 1986—; vis. lectr. U. Hawaii, Honolulu, 1984-85; clin. asst. prof. dept. psychology Ill. Inst. Tech., Chgo., 1989—; cons. Tex. Commn. for the Blind, Austin, 1981—; dir. McCarron-Dial Systems, Inc., Dallas, 1975-85; dir. rsch., instr. Sch. Allied Health Scis., Dallas Rehab. Inst., U. Tex. Southwestern Med. Ctr., Dallas, 1974-77. Contbr. articles to profl. jours. and chpts. in books. Rsch. grantee U. Tex., 1975, 79, Social Security Adminstrn., 1989. Mem. APA, Nat. Acad. Neuropsychologists, Nat. Rehab. Assn., Vocat. Evaluation and Work Adjustment Assn., Tex. Psychol. Assn., Phi Kappa Phi, Psy Chi, Alpha Kappa Delta, Alpha Mu Gamma. Home: 4507 N O Connor Rd Irving TX 75062-3705

DIAMANT, GREGORY ERIC, medical company executive, consultant; b. N.Y.C., Mar. 7, 1949; s. Fred Jack and Gini Regina (Weiss) D.; m. Irene Althea Williams, Nov. 9, 1979. BA, Boston U., 1973, MA, 1975. Freelance editor Boston, 1976-77; sales exec. Internat. Weekends, Boston, 1977-78; chief operating officer Revelations Shoe Corp., N.Y.C., 1978-88; cons. N.Y.C., 1988-90; ptnr., pres. Automated Med. Products Corp., N.Y.C., 1990—; founding ptnr. Ferris Wheel Prodns., 1989-90. Prodr. (documentary film) At the Crossroads, 1989-90. Mem. Amnesty Internat. USA, N.Y.C., 1980; adv. bd. mem. First Step program Coalition for the Homeless, 1993—. Mem. Footwear Industries Am. (chmn. mktg. steering com. 1985-87), Two-Ten Orgn. (life, endowed scholarship). Jewish.

DIAMOND, BETTY ANN, internist, educator; b. 1948. MD, Harvard U. Diplomate Am. Bd. Internal Medicine. Prof. Albert Einstein Coll. Medicine, N.Y.C. Rsch. fellow Am. Heart Assn., 1995-96. *

DIAMOND, DANIEL LLOYD, surgeon. MD, Tulane U., 1970. Diplomate Am. Bd. Surgery. Intern U. Pitts. Health Ctr. Hosps., 1970-71, resident in surgery, 1971-76; dir. gen. surgery, divsn. surgery Allegheny Genl. Hosp., Pitts., 1976—; assoc. prof. surgery Med. Coll. Pa., Pitts., 1976-95; chmn., prof. dept. surgery U. Tenn. Med. Ctr., Knoxville, 1995—. Mem. ACS. Office: U Tenn Med Ctr 1924 Alwa Hwy U-11 Knoxville TN 37920

DIAMOND, EDWARD, gynecologist, infertility specialist, clinician; b. Newark, N.J., Nov. 25, 1928; s. William D. and Ruth (Stier) Brief; m. Joan Marilyn Chase, June 16, 1951 (div. Apr. 1969); children: Gary Warren, Steven Michael, Stuart Eric; m. Linda Ruth Johnson, Sept. 4, 1969; 1 child, Mira Frieda. BS, Franklin and Marshall Coll. 1949; MB, MD, Chgo. Med. Sch., 1953. Diplomate Am. Bd. Obstetrics and Gynecology. Intern Beth Israel Med. Ctr., Newark, 1953-54, ob.-gyn. resident, 1954-56, attenting physician, 1956—; attenting physician Clara Maass Med. Ctr., Belleville, N.J., 1959—; bd. dirs. Diamond Inst. for Infertility, Irvington, N.J., 1968—; microsurgery cons. Am. Coll. Ob.-Gyn., Washington, 1979-82; design cons.Codman Med. Instruments, Johnson & Johnson, Waltham, Mass., 1973-91, Edward Weck Co. Med. Div., Chapel Hill, N.C., 1973-85; preceptorship in infertility Fertility Inst. of N.Y., N.Y.C., 1967. Author: Microsurgery in Gynecology I and II, 1977, 81, Endoscopy in Gynecology, 1978, Operative Perinatology, 1984; contbr. articles to profl. jours.; speaker in field. Trustee, assoc. Franklin and Marshall Coll., Lancaster, Pa., 1982—; assoc. Nat. Coun. on Arts and Scis., Washington, 1982—, Aspen (Colo.) Ctr. for Environ. Studies, 1985—. Capt. U.S. Army, 1956-58. Recipient Leading Pioneer in Tubal Microsurgery citation Prince George Med. Ctr., Cheverly, Md., 1976, Contbn. to Arts citation Rutgers U., Newark, 1984. Fellow Am. Coll. Ob.-Gyn.; mem. Am. Fertility Soc., Internat. Soc. Advancement of Humanistic Studies in Gynecology, N.Y. Soc. Reproductive Medicine. Hebrew.

DIAMOND, EUGENE CHRISTOPHER, lawyer, hospital administrator; b. Oceanside, Calif., Oct. 19, 1952; s. Eugene Francis and Rosemary (Wright) D.; m. Mary Theresa O'Donnell, Jan. 20, 1984; children: Eugene John, Kevin Seamus, Hannah Rosemary, Seamus Michael. BA, U. Notre Dame, 1974; MHA, St. Louis U., 1978, JD, 1979. Bar: Ill. 1979. Staff atty. AUL Legal Def. Fund, Chgo., 1979-80; adminstrv. asst. Holy Cross Hosp., Chgo., 1980-81, asst. adminstr., 1981-82, v.p., 1982-83, counsel to adminstr., 1980—, exec. v.p., 1983-91; exec. v.p., COO St. Margaret Mercy Healthcare Ctrs., Hammond, Ind., 1991-93, pres. CEO, 1993; cons. Birthright of Chgo., 1979—, mem. benefit com., 1981—; bd. dirs. Hammond C. of C., 1993, North West Ind. Forum. Mem. Ill. State Bar Assn., Chgo. Bar Assn. Mgmt. Roman Catholic. Office: St Margaret Mercy HealthcareCtrs 5454 Hohman Ave Hammond IN 46320-1931

DIAMOND, HERBERT S., physician; b. N.Y.C., Mar. 21, 1938; m. Carol G.; children: Stewart, Elyse. BA, NYU, 1958; MD, SUNY, N.Y.C., 1962. Intern Kings County Hosp., Bklyn., 1962-63, resident, 1963-65; asst. chief gen. med. svc. Fitzsimmons Gen. Hosp., Denver, 1966-68; instr. medicine SUNY Downstate Med. Ctr., N.Y.C., 1968-70; attending physician Kings County Hosp., N.Y.C., 1968-88, SUNY Hosp., N.Y.C., 1968-88; asst. prof. SUNY-Downstate Med. Ctr., N.Y.C., 1970-73, assoc. prof., 1973-77, chief rheumatology, 1977-82; prof. medicine SUNY, Stony Brook, 1985-88; chmn. medicine L.I. Jewish Med. Ctr., New Hyde Park, N.Y., 1982-88, West Penn Hosp., Pitts., 1989—; clin. prof. medicine U. Pitts., 1989—; cons. med./rheumatism St. John's Hosp., Bklyn., 1970-81; dir. Gen. Clin. Rsch. Ctr., SUNY-Downstate Med. Ctr., 1978-82. Contbr. numerous articles and abstracts to profl. jours. Exec. com., bd. trustees Arthritis Found., 1982, v.p. rsch. and edn., 1982-85, mem. med. and sci. com., 1975-85, chmn. med. and sci. com., 1981-85. Recipient Mitchell prize, 1962, Master Tchr. award SUNY Bklyn. Alumni Assn., 1987; Ivan T. Hirschl Trust Career Scientists, 1976-81. Fellow ACP; mem. AMA, Am. Coll. Rheumatology, Assn. of Program Dirs. in Internal Medicine (com. on internat. edn. 1989—, fin. com. 1987-92, 96—, long range planning com. 1991—, mem. coun. 1994—), N.Y. Rheumatism Assn. (pres. 1982-83). Jewish. Office: West Penn Hosp 4800 Friendship Ave Pittsburgh PA 15224-1722

DIAMOND, JEFFREY ALAN, gastroenterologist; b. Bklyn., Nov. 29, 1939; s. Solomon and Martha Edith (Epstein) D.; m. Maria Aparecida Vieira, May 26, 1966; children: Marc, Melize, Glenn. BA, Colgate U., 1961; MD, NYU, 1965. Diplomate Am. Bd. Internal Medicine and Gastroenterology. Intern U. Miami Med. Ctr., Hollywood, Fla., 1965-66; resident in internal medicine Downstate Med. Ctr., Bklyn., 1966-68; fellowship in gastroenterology U. Miami, 1968-69; pres. Gastroenterology Cons., Hollywood, Fla., 1971—; clin. prof. medicine U. Miami, Fla., 1984—; chief dept. internal medicine Meml. Hops., Hollywood, 1982-84. Fellow Am. Coll. Gastroenterology; mem. Fla. Gastroenterology Soc. (pres. 1987-88), Am. Gastroenterology Assn., Am. Soc. Gastrointestinal Endoscopy. Office: Gastroenterology Cons 4700 M Sheridan St Hollywood FL 33021

DIAMOND, MARY ELIZABETH, psychiatrist; b. Phila., Sept. 22 1950; d. William Charles and Elizabeth Theresa (Hinchey) D.; m. O. John Ohanian, Jr., Nov. 20, 1976 (div. Dec. 1984); children: O. John III, Mary Catherine. BA in Psychology, West Chester (Pa.) U., 1971, MA in Psychology, 1976; MPA, Pa. State U., 1979; DO, Phila. Coll. Osteo. Medicine, 1994. Dir. vocat. adjustment svcs. Haverford (Pa.) State Hosp., 1978-84, mgmt. devel. instr., 1983-87; dir. vocat. adjustment svcs. Embreeville (Pa.) Ctr., 1989-92, acting residential svcs. mgr., 1992-93; resident I in family practice Wyoming Valley Family Practice, Kingston, Pa., 1994-95; psychiatry resident II Norristown (Pa.) State Hosp., 1995; resident in psychiatry Albert Einstein Med. Ctr., Bronx, N.Y., 1995—. Cubmaster pack 65 Lenni-Lenape Boy Scouts Am., West Chester, 1987-88; 4th grade Sun. sch. tchr. Westminster Presbyn. Ch., West Chester, 1979-80. Pa. Bus. and Profl. Women's Club scholar, 1987, Downingtown (Pa.) Bus. and Profl. Women's Club scholar,m 1991, Angus Cathie scholar, 1992. Mem. West Chester Bus. and Profl. Women's Club (pres. 1989-90, v.p. 1988-89, treas. 1987-88). Home: 192 Stirling Ct West Chester PA 19380

DIAMOND, MICHAEL RICHARD, chiropractor; b. N.Y.C., Aug. 27, 1961; s. Martin and Charlotte (Hayden) D.; m. Cheryl Gail Nagler, June 28, 1987. BS, Bklyn. Coll., 1984; MS, Western Ill. U., 1985; D Chiropractic, NY Chiropractic Coll., 1990. Intern sports medicine BioFitness Inst., N.Y.C., 1983; dir. fitness Paerdegat Athletic Club, N.Y.C., 1985-87; pvt. practice chiropractic Suffolk Family Chiropractic Ctr., Patchogue, N.Y., 1991—. Mem. Am. Chiropractic Assn., Internat. Chiropractic Assn., Am. Jiu Jitsu Practitioners Assn., N.Y. State Chiropractic Assn., Patchogue C. of C. Office: Suffolk Family Chiropractic 285 Sills Rd Bldg 9 Patchogue NY 11772

DIAMONDS, BLANCA MARIA, mental health counselor; b. Havana, Cuba, Apr. 1, 1944; came to U.S., 1962; d. Mario Vicente and Josefa Basilisa (Suardiaz) Peres; 1 child, Neil Armstrong. BSN, U. Mo., 1968. Lic. realtor. Student nurse asst. med. surgical U. Mo., Columbia, 1963-67; student nurse, psychiat. nursing, head nurse Mid Mo. Mental Health Ctr., Columbia, 1966-68; med. surgical nurse Kuakini Hosp., St. Francis Hosp., Honolulu, 1969—; front office nurse Clay Barton & Thomas Smith, Gardena, Calif, 1971-72; nursing dir. Del Amo Hosp., Torrance, Calif., 1972-74; v.p., sec. Dewhurst Med. Corp., Torrance, 1975-91; mental health counselor Los Angeles County, L.A., 1991; realtor Amber Realty, 1995-96, Bankers Realty, Redondo Beach, Calif., 1996—; founder Cassiopeia Enterprises, Rollings Hills Estates, Calif.; nurse cons. to various profls., 1975—. Mental Health Student Nurse award U. Mo., 1966. Mem. L.A. World Affairs Coun., Wilson Ctr. Assocs., Nat. Trust for Historic Preservation, Nat. History Mus., Smithsonian Inst., Humane Soc. U.S. Democrat. Home: 2018 Farrell Ave # B Redondo Beach CA 90278-1817

DIAMONDSTEIN, NELSON LEE, dentist; b. Bklyn., Sept. 26, 1950; s. Aaron and Matilda (Sorkin) D.; m. Nancy Ilene Swiss, June 30, 1974; children: Amanda, Megan. BA, CUNY, 1971; MS, NYU, 1973, DDS, 1977. Tchr. biology and gen. sci. Midwood High Sch., Bklyn., 1973-74, Franklin D. Roosevelt High Sch., Bklyn., 1974; resident in gen. practice dentistry Luth. Med. Ctr., Bklyn., 1978; pvt. practice Bklyn., 1980—, Woodmere, 1990-95; Lynbrook, 1995—. Mem. ADA, Dental Soc. State of N.Y., 2d dist. Dental Soc., various local dental study groups, K.C. Office: 9229 Flatlands Ave Brooklyn NY 11236-3721 also: 483 Scranton Ave Lynbrook NY 11563

DIANA, JOHN NICHOLAS, physiologist; b. Lake Placid, N.Y., Dec. 19, 1930; s. Alphonse Walton and Dolores (Mirto) D.; m. Anita Louise Harris, May 8, 1966; children: Gina Sue, Lisa Ann, John Nicholas. B.A., Norwich U., 1952; Ph.D., U. Louisville, 1965. Asst. prof. physiology Mich. State U. Med. Sch., 1966-68; assoc. prof., then prof. U. Iowa Med. Sch., 1969-78; prof. physiology, chmn. dept. La. State U. Med. Center, Shreveport, 1978-85; dir. cardiovascular research ctr. U. Ky., 1985-87, assoc. dean research and basic sci., 1987-88; dir. T&H Rsch. Inst., 1988—; cons. Nat. Inst. Neurol. Diseases and Stroke, 1973-75, Nat. Heart, Lung and Blood Inst., 1974—, mem. cardiovascular and renal study sect., 1980-85, mem. clin. scis. study sect., 1986-91, chmn. 1989-91; rsch. com. Iowa Heart Assn., 1974-77, bd. dirs., 1977-79; mem. cardiovascular study sect. Am. Heart Assn., 1981-84. Author papers, abstracts in field. Served with AUS, 1952-54; Served with USAR, 1961-62. NIH postdoctoral fellow, 1965-67. Mem. Am. Fedn. Clin. Research, Am. Physiol. Soc. (editorial bd. jour. 1974-78), Microcirculation Soc. (pres. 1977-78, editorial bd. jour. 1979-85), Am. Heart Assn. (fellow council circulation), N.Y. Acad. Scis., La. Heart Assn. (dir. 1979-81, research com. 1978-82), Sigma Xi. Democrat. Home: 3656 Eleuthera Ct Lexington KY 40509-9525 Office: U Ky Coll Medicine Dean's Office 900 Rose St Rm MN140D Lexington KY 40546

DIANTO, LINDA CHRISTINE, therapeutic activities coordinator, administrator; b. Bklyn., Dec. 11, 1949; d. Salvatore and Josephine (Battaglia) Lore; m. Nicholas L. Dianto, June 26, 1971. AA in Psychology, Staten Island C.C., 1969; BA, Richmond Coll., Staten Island, 1971, MS in Edn., 1974; 6th yr. cert. NYU, 1988. Cert. tchr., N.Y., cert. therapeutic recreation specialist, cert. recreation mgr.; lic. recreation adminstr., N.J. Tchr. St. Mary's Sch., Staten Island, 1971-74; staff Vacation Day Camp, N.Y.C. Bd. Edn., 1973-75; dir. activities and vols. Golden Gate Health Care Ctr., Staten Island, 1974-86; recreation cons. Princeton Nursing Home, N.J., 1980-81, Sheepshead Nursing Home, Bklyn., 1984-86; dir. Coler Goldwater Meml. Hosp., Roosevelt Island, N.Y., 1988—; lectr., seminar presenter. Treas. Deborah Heart Found., Staten Island, 1985-86, v.p. membership com., 1986-88; scholarship chairwoman Chiropractic Edn. Found., Inc., Albany, N.Y., 1985—; pres. Chiropractic Edn. Found. N.Y., 1989-93; treas. Met. N.Y. Rec. and Parks Soc., 1995—. Recipient Worker's Pin, Deborah Hosp. Found., Browns Mills, N.J., 1984; Disting. Svc. award N.Y. State Chiropractic Assn. Dist. 5, 1985; Tom & Ruth Rivers scholar, 1986. Mem. AAUW, N.Y. State Parks and Recreation Soc. (Presdl. citation 1994), Nat. Recreation and Parks Assn., Nat. Therapeutic Recreation Soc., N.Y. State Therapeutic Recreation Assn. (founder), Women's Aux. N.Y. State Chiropractic Assn. (dist. pres. 1981-84, state treas. 1984-85, v.p. 1988-89), World Health and Leisure Assn., Chiropractic Edn. Found., Met. Recreation & Parks Soc. (treas.). Roman Catholic. Lodge: Soroptimist (bd. dirs.). Avocations: travel; interior decorating; playing piano; sewing; antiquing.

DIANZANI, MARIO UMBERTO, pathology educator; b. Grosseto, Italy, June 13, 1925; s. Edgardo and Irma (Bocelli) D.; m. Maria Assunta Mor, Aug. 18, 1956; children: Irma, Chiara, Umberto, Paola. Degree in medicine, U. Siena, Italy, 1948, degree in pharmacy, 1950; hon. doctorate, Brunel U., London, 1978; hon. doctorate in chemistry, U. Genoa, Italy, 1995; hon. doctorate, U. Buenos Aires, 1996. Asst. in gen. pathology U. Siena, 1948-50, prof. gen. pathology, 1964-65; asst. in gen. pathology U. Genoa, Italy, 1950-58; prof. gen. pathology U. Cagliari, Italy, 1958-64, U. Turin, Italy, 1965—; rector magnificus U. Turin, 1984—. Author textbook of gen. pathology, 1970. Recipient Premio Feltrinelli, Accademia del Lincei, Rome, 1979, Trevor Slater award Internat. Free Radical Soc., 1994, In Verizzi prize, 1996. Roman Catholic. Home: Corso D'Azeglio 118, 10126 Turin Italy Office: U Torino, Via PO 17, 10100 Turin Italy

DIAS-KELLEHER, SONIA, critical care nurse; b. Rio de Janeiro, Apr. 11, 1964; came to U.S., 1970; d. Antonio and Isaura (Reis) Dias; m. Denis Gerard Kelleher, Aug. 27, 1989. BSN, Rutgers U., Newark, 1993. RN, N.J.; cert. BLS-C, ACLS, critical care course. Staff nurse Rahway (N.J.) Hosp., 1993-95; staff nurse neurosurg. ICU St. Barnabas Med. Ctr., Livingston, N.J., 1995—; critical care nurse Phoenix Healthcare Corp., Tenafly, N.J., 1994—. Mem. Everett Hatcher Mcpl. Alliance, Roselle, N.J., 1993. Democrat. Roman Catholic. Home: 1245 Grandview Ave Union NJ 07083

DIAZ, CARLOS RICARDO, physician, military officer; b. San Juan, P.R., July 23, 1946; s. Alberto and Beverly Diaz; m. Judy Lynn Kealey, Mar. 14, 1992; children: Carlos A., David R. BA, Johns Hopkins U., 1968; MD, George Washington U., 1972. Bd. cert. Am. Bd. Internal Medicine. Asst. dir., flight surgeon ED-S.E. Cmty. Hosp., Washington, 1977-80; commd. officer USN, 1980, advanced through grades to comdr., sr. med. officer USS Forrestal, 1980-81; head dept. internal medicine NAMI USN, Pensacola, Fla., 1981-83; pvt. practice ED physician West Fla. Hosp., Pensacola, 1983—; ACLS instr. Am. Heart Assn., Pensacola, 1983—; med. dir. Lifeguard Air Ambulance, Pensacola, 1985—. Contbr. articles to profl. jours. Decorated Navy Achievement medal USN, 1982. Mem. ACP, Am. Soc. Microbiology. Home: 11590 Dueling Oaks Dr Pensacola FL 32514 Office: West Fla Regional Med Ctr 8383 N Davis Hwy Pensacola FL 32514

DIAZ, LUIS A., dermatologist educator; b. Cascas, Peru, Sept. 16, 1942; came to U.S. 1970.; m. Dora I. Bielli-Bianchi, Dec. 13, 1969; children: Luis A., Jr., Fernando D., Carlos A. Student, U. Nacional de Trujillo, Trujillo, Peru, 1960-61; MD, U. Nacional de Trujillo, 1962-68. Diplomate Am. Bd. Dermatology, Am. Bd. of Dermatology Immunology. Clinical asst. inst. dermatology Buffalo (N.Y.) Affiliate Hosp., 1971-74; postdoctoral fellow in clinical immunology Mayo Sch. of Med., Rochester, Minn., 1974-76; asst. prof. dermatology U. Mich., Ann Harbor, Mich., 1976-80; assoc. prof. dermatology U. Mich., Johns Hoskins U., Balt., 1982-86; professor dermatology Johns Hoskins U., 1986-88; prof. and chmn. dermotology Med. Coll. Wis., Milw., 1988—; Bd. dirs. Soc. Invest. Dermotology, 1989-92; mem. NIAMS Adv. Counc., 1992—. Recipient Wm. Montagna lecturer award, Mtg. Soc. for Invest. Dermotology, 1991, Sulzberger lecturer award, Mtg. Am. Acad. Dermotology, 1996. Fellow Am. Acad. Dermotology; mem. Soc. Investigative Dermatology, Dermatology Found. (bd. dirs. 1994—), Am. Soc. Clinical Investigation, Am. Dermatol. Assn., Assn. Am. Physicians. Home: 1490 Barrington Woods Dr Brookfield WI 53045 Office: Med Coll of Wis 8701 Watertown Plank Rd Milwaukee WI 53226

DÍAZ DE GONZALEZ, ANA MARÍA, psychologist, educator; b. San Juan, P.R., July 26, 1945; d. Esteban Díaz-González and Petra (Guadalupe) De Díaz; m. Jorge Gonzalez Monclova, Jan. 7, 1968; children: Ana Teresa, Jorge, Julio Esteban. BS, U. P.R., Río Piedras, 1965, MEd, 1973; MS, Caribbean Ctr. Advanced Study, San Juan, 1982, PhD, 1983. Lic. psychologist, P.R. Home economist U. P.R., Fajardo and San Juan, 1965-82; specialist in human devel. and gerontology U. P.R., San Juan, 1983—. Mem. APA, Assn. Economists Hogar (pres. 1965-92, Disting. Svc. award 1973), Assn. Specialists SEA (pres. 1982-93), Assn. Psychology P.R., Epsilon Sigma Phi (sec. 1970—), Gamma Sigma Delta. Roman Catholic. Home: 1325 Calle 23 San Juan PR 00924-5249 Office: U PR Svc Extension Agr Terrenos Estacion Exptl Río Piedras San Juan PR 00928

DIAZ-FRANCO, CARLOS, surgeon, anatomist, anesthesiologist; b. Valparaiso, Chile, Nov. 9, 1956; came to U.S., 1985; s. Ismael Segundo and Aida Rosa (Franco-Huerta) Diaz-Labarca; m. Jennifer Ann Leepard, Mar. 31, 1989 (div. May 1993). MD, U. Valparaiso, Chile, 1981. Instr. anatomy Sch. of Medicine Univ. Valparaiso, Chile, 1982; surgery resident U. Valparaiso, Chile, 1982-85; asst. prof. anatomy, surgery Univ. Valparaiso, Chile, 1983-89; vis. prof. anatomy Med. Coll. of Ohio, Toledo, 1985-86, 88-89; surgeon, pvt. practice Valparaiso U. Hosp., Chile, 1986-89; surgery resident Sinai Hosp., Detroit, 1990-91, anesthesiology resident, 1991-94; with dept. anesthesia Cook County Hosp., Chgo., 1994—. Contbr. articles to profl. jours. Grantee WHO, 1985-86, Ednl. Commn. for Foreign Med.

Grads., 1988-89. Fellow AMA, Am. Soc. Anesthesiologists, Latin Am. Soc. Regional Anesthesia. Roman Catholic.

DIBBELL, DAVID GILMORE, SR., plastic surgeon; b. Evanston, Ill., Mar. 2, 1934; s. David Dibbell; children: David G. Jr., Cherie. BA, Yale U., 1955; MD, U. Pa., 1959. Resident gen. surgery Yale-New Haven Hosp., 1959-64, Palo Alto-Stanford, Lackland AFB, Tex., 1964-66; resident, gen. and thoracic surgery Palo Alto-Stanford, Lackland AFB, 1966-67; resident plastic surgery Palo Alto-Stanford, Madison, 1967-68; resident head and neck Palo Alto-Stanford, Roswell Park, 1968; cons. to surgeon gen. MACV, RVN Med. Corp., 1968-69; chief plastic surgery dept. Wilford Hall, Lackland AFB, 1974-75; prof., chmn. divsn. plastic and reconstructive surgery U. Wis., Madison, 1975—. Mem. ACS, AMA, Am. Soc. Plastic Surgeons, Assn. Plastic Surgeons, Am. Soc. Maxillofacial Surgeons, State Med. Soc. Wis., Alpha Omega Alpha. Office: U Wis Plastic Surgery Dept 600 Highland Ave G5/355 Madison WI 53792

DI BENEDETTO, ROBERT JAMES, physician, educator; b. Bklyn., May 28, 1937; s. Saverio and Margaret (Derbyshire) Di B.; m. Margherita A. Munari, June 24, 1961; children: Robert, Christian, Stephen, David. BS summa cum laude, St. John's Coll. Med., Hillcrest, N.J., 1958; MD magna cum laude, SUNY, Bklyn., 1962. Diplomate Am. Bd. Internal Medicine, Am. Bd. Pulmonary Diseases, Am. Bd. Critical Care. Intern St. Vincent's Hosp., N.Y.C., 1963, chief resident internal medicine, 1965-66; resident in internal medicine Kings County Hosp., Bklyn., 1963-65; fellow pulmonary medicine SUNY, Bklyn., 1968-69; physician Med. Assn. Savannah, Ga., 1969-90; program dir. internal medicine Meml. Med. Ctr., Savannah, 1990-95, chief med. officer, 1995—; med. dir. Armstrong Coll. Sch. Respiratory Therapy, Savannah, 1979—; assoc. dean Mercer Univ. Coll. Med., Savannah, 1995—. Contbr. articles to profl. jours. Bd. dirs. Savannah YMCA, 1974-78; bd. dirs. Ga. Chpt. Am. Lung Assn., 1973-85, chmn. bd., 1985-87, Vol. of Yr., 1987. Lt. comdr. USNR, 1966-68. Fellow ACP (J. Willis Hurst Outstanding Bedside Tchr. award 1992), Am. Coll. Chest Physicians (pres. Ga. chpt. 1984-86); mem. Am. Thoracic Soc. (pres. Ga. chpt. 1977-78), Ga. Thoracic Soc., Italian Heritage Soc. Office: Meml Med Ctr 4700 Waters Ave Savannah GA 31441

DIBIANCO, ROBERT, cardiologist; b. Bklyn., Dec. 20, 1946; m. Joan Marie Bowen, Oct. 29, 1977; children: David Anthony, John-Michael, Regina Marie. BS, CCNY, 1968; MD, SUNY, 1972. Diplomate Am. Bd. Internal Medicine. Intern, resident, chief resident SUNY/Buffalo Affiliated Hosps., 1972-75; fellow in cardiology Georgetown U., Washington, 1975-77, from instr. to assoc. clin. prof. medicine, 1977—. Fellow Am. Coll. Physicians, Am. Coll. Cardiology (gov.'s adv. com. 1985-87), CLin. Coun. Cardiology Am. Heart Assn. (profl. edn. com. 1978-84, allied health profl. subcom. 1978-84, rsch. com. 1980-84, pub. affairs com. 1992—). Home: 4914 30th Pl Washington DC 20008

DI CAPRIO, ROBERT CARL, podiatrist; b. Mount Holly, N.J., Apr. 1, 1963; s. Robert and Elizabeth Anne (Gargiulo) D.C.; m. Patricia Han Kewley, July 30, 1994; children: Kyle, Nicholas. BS in Biology, Fordham U., 1986; DPM, N.Y. Coll. Podiatric Medicine, 1990. Pvt. practice Kosinski & Di Caprio, Schenectady, Albany, N.Y., 1991—. Mem. N.Y. State Podiatric Medicine Assn. (treas. N.E. divsn. 1996—). Roman Catholic. Office: 504 Madison Ave Albany NY 12208-3602

DI CARLO, FREDERICK JOSEPH, toxicologist, editor; b. N.Y.C., Nov. 24, 1918; s. Amilcare and Anna (Manieri) Di C.; m. Nancy Cucco, Oct. 16, 1943; children: Frederick, Nancy Ann, Paul. BS, Fordham U., 1939, MS, 1941; PhD, NYU, 1944. Instr. chemistry dept. NYU, N.Y.C., 1943-44; rsch. assoc. Squibb Inst. for Med. Rsch., New Brunswick, N.J., 1944-46; head biochemistry divsn. Fleischmann Labs., Stamford, Conn., 1946-60; dir. dept. drug metabolism Warner Lambert Rsch. Inst., Morris Plains, N.J., 1960-77; sr. sci. advisor U.S. EPA, Washington, 1977—; adj. prof. Coll. St. Elizabeth, Convent Sta., N.J., 1968-77; editor Drug Metabolism Rev., Marcel Dekker, Inc., N.Y.C., 1971—; dir. toxicology courses Am. Chem. Soc., Washington, 1981—. Fellow AAAS; mem. Soc. for Leucocyte Biology (hon.). Home: 341 Boulevard Mountain Lakes NJ 07046 Office: 401 M St SW Washington DC 20460

DICHTER, MARC A., physician; b. N.Y.C., Dec. 1, 1943; m. Carole Dichter; children: Harold, Eric. BS, CUNY, 1964; MD, NYU, 1969, PhD, 1969. Asst. prof., assoc. prof. neurology Harvard Med. Sch., Boston, 1975-86; prof. neurology U. Pa., Phila., 1986—. Lt. comdr. USPHS, 1970-72. Office: Hosp U Pa Dept Neurology 3400 Spruce St Philadelphia PA 19104

DICK, CAROL LYNNE, psychology educator; b. Ann Arbor, Mich., Oct. 26, 1942; d. C. H. and Lois M. (Wubbena) D. Student, Albion Coll., 1960-62; BA, U. Mich., 1965, MA in Edn., 1970. Rsch. asst. dept. psychology U. Mich., 1966-70; rsch. asst. High/Scope Ednl. Rsch. Found., Ypsilanti, Mich., 1971-72; counselor Cath. Social Svc., Ann Arbor, Mich., 1972-75; communications specialist Ann Arbor (Mich.) Schs., 1975-76; religious coord. U. Mich., Ann Arbor, 1976-77; office asst. U. Mich. Continuing Edn., Ann Arbor, 1977-78; bookkeeper Money Mgrs., Inc. (Debt Aid, Inc.), Ann Arbor, 1978-82; instr. psychology Holyoke (Mass.) Community Coll., 1985—; interviewer psychology dept. U. Mass., Amherst, 1992; mem. support staff Nat. Evaluation Systems, Amherst, 1992-94. Author: (poetry book) Transcendent Ways of God, 1976, (short book) Henry's Mother, 1990. Vol. Project Progress, Friends of the Earth and Ecology Ctr., Ann Arbor, 1976-82; forum coord. Unitarian Ch., Ann Arbor, 1978-79; vol. bd. dirs. LWV, Ann Arbor, 1978-82; active Action for Children's TV, Telecomm. Rsch. and Action Ctr., Coalition for Responsible Genetic Rsch., 1978-82; v.p. Lay Acad. Ecumenical Studies, Amherst, 1990-91, others.

DICK, ELLIOT COLTER, virologist, epidemiologist, educator; b. Miami, Fla., June 30, 1926; s. Elliot C. Dick and Helen Jean Cribb; m. Claire Rebecca Blumer, Sept. 23, 1967; children: Emily diane, Elliot Mayhew, Frederic Krichton, Catherine Virginia. BA in Bacteriology, U. Minn., 1950, MS in Bacteriology, 1953, PhD in Bacteriology, 1955. Asst. prof. Bacteriology U. Kans., Lawrence, 1955-59; asst. prof. medicine Tulane U., New Orleans, 1959-61; asst. prof. Preventive Medicine U. Wis., Madison, 1961-64, assoc. prof., 1964-72, prof., 1972—; cons. Kans. State Bd. Health, Topeka, 1955-59; mem. collaborative com. rhinoviruses WHO, 1966—; vis. scientist Delta Regional Primate Ctr., Tulane U., Covington, La., 1967-72; Sigrid Juselius Found. lectr., Turku, Finland, 1991. Contbr. articles, abstracts to profl. jours. including Jour. Infectious Diseases, Jour. Allergy and Clinical Immunology, Jour. Clinical Investigation, chpts. to books; patentee in field. With U.S. Army, 1944-46, ETO. Recipient Antarctic medal U.S., 1979; grantee U. Kans., 1956-59, Kans. State Bd. Health, 1957-58, USPHS, 1959-70, 71-73, 76, 79, 82, 85, 88, S.C. Johnson, 1966-67, 70-79, Smith, Kline & French, 1966-71, 74, 75, NASA, 1967-82, NSF, 1976-88, Kimberly-Clark, 1981—, Hoffmann-LaRoche, 1986—, Sterling Drug, 1989—. Fellow Am. Acad. Microbiology (diplomat clin. microbiology), Infectious Disease Soc., Explorers Club; mem. AAAS, Am. Soc. Virology (founder), Am. Soc. Microbiology (Wis. legis. rep. 1970—), Soc. Experimental Biology and Medicine, N.Y. Acad. Scis., Phi Sigma, Sigma Xi. Mem. Unitarian Ch. Home: 11 Robin Cir Madison WI 53705-4929 Office: U Wis Respiratory Virus Rsch Lab 465 Henry Mall Madison WI 53706-1501

DICK, HAROLD MICHAEL, orthopedic surgeon; b. Buffalo, Dec. 22, 1933; s. Norman James and Helen (Ryan) D.; m. Schmidt, Apr. 12, 1977 (div. Jan. 1978); m. Joyce Ann Geller, Apr. 28, 1978; 1 child, Victoria Leigh. BA, Princeton U., 1956; MD, NYU, 1960. Diplomate Am. Bd. Orthopaedic Surgery; lic. dr. Hawaii, N.Y., Calif., N.J. Intern Queens Hosp., Honolulu, 1960-61; resident Roosevelt Hosp., N.Y.C., 1961-62; resident orthopaedic surgery Columbia-Presbyn. Med. Ctr., N.Y.C., 1962-66, hand fellow, 1966-67; tumor fellow NYU, 1967-68; prof. orthopaedic surgery Columbia-Presbyn. Med. Ctr., N.Y.C., 1965—; cons. Harlem Hosp. Ctr., N.Y.C., 1967—, Helen Hayes Hosp., West Haverstraw, N.Y., 1967—, Nyack (N.Y.) Hosp., 1974—, Valley Hosp., Ridgewood, N.J., 1976—, Hyannis (Mass.) Hosp., 1976—, Greenwich (Conn.) Hosp. Assn., 1983—, Englewood (N.J.) Hosp., 1985—. Fellow ACS, Am. Acad. Orthopaedic Surgeons, N.Y. Acad. Medicine (Orthopaedic sect. sec. 1982-83, chmn. 1983-84, Hoar com. for rsch. fellowship 1993); mem. AMA, Am. Soc. for Surgery of the Hand, Am. Soc. for Surgery of Trauma, Musculoskeletal Oncology Soc., Am. Orthopaedic Assn. (pres.-elect 1994-95, pres. 1995-96), Orthopaedic Rsch. Soc., Orthopaedic Rsch. and Edn. Found. (bd. dirs., v.p. 1990-94), Pediatric Orthopaedic Soc. N.Am., Am. Bd. Orthopaedic Surgery Inc. (bd. dirs., bd. examiner for certifying exams, 1983—, pres.-elect 1995-96), Acad. Orthopaedic Soc. (pres.-elect 1992-93, pres. 1993-94), Century Assn., Twentieth Century Orthopaedic Assn., Internat. Soc. Orthopaedic Surgery and Traumatology, Internat. Skeletal Soc., Internat. Soc. Orthopaedic Rsch. and Traumatology, Royal Soc. Med. (affiliate), Colombian Soc. Orthopaedic Surgery and Traumatology (hon.), Columbian Soc. Surgery of Hand (corr.), N.Y. Soc. for Surgery of Hand (charter, sec. 1975-77, v.p. 1977-79, pres. 1979-80), N.Y. Med. and Surg. Soc., N.J. Orthopaedic Soc., N.Y. State Soc. Orthopaedic Surgeons, N.Y. County Med. Soc., Pediatric Orthopaedic Club N.Y. (pres.-elect 1979-80, pres. 1980-81), Robert E. Carroll Hand Club, Frank E. Stinchfield Club. Office: Presbyn Hosp Columbia-Presbyn Med Ctr 622 W 168th St New York NY 10032-3702

DICK, PATRICIA A., counselor; b. Indpls., Mar. 31, 1929; d. Harold D. and Mary R. (Crockett) Barton; m. Richard D. Dick, Sr., June 21, 1947; children: G. Daniel, Richard D. Jr., Lynda S., Kevin D., Deborah D. AA, Wm. Rainey Harper Coll., Palatine, Ill., 1976; BA, Mundelein Coll., Chgo., 1978; MA, Northeastern Ill. U., Chgo., 1984; postgrad., Alfred Adler Inst., Chgo. Cert. sr. addiction counselor, clin. hypnotherapist; nat. cert. counselor. Counselor in pvt. practice Barrington, Ill., 1979—. Contbr. articles on alcoholism to local papers. Mem. Am. Mental Health Counselor Assn., Nat. Assn. Alcoholism and Drug Counseling, Nat. Assn. for Adult Children of Alcoholics, Am. Assn. for Counseling and Devel., Nat. Guild of Hypnotists, Internat. Assn. Marriage and Family Counseling. Roman Catholic. Office: 28662 W Northwest Hwy Barrington IL 60010-5928

DICKENS, DORIS LEE, psychiatrist; b. Roxboro, N.C., Oct. 12; d. Lee Edward and Delma Ernestine (Hester) D.; BS magna cum laude, Va. Union U., 1960; MD, Howard U., 1966; m. Austin LeCount Fickling, Oct. 15, 1975. Diplomate Nat. Bd. Med. Examiners. Intern, St. Elizabeth's Hosp., Washington, 1966-67, resident, 1967-70; staff psychiatrist, dir. Mental Health Program for Deaf, St. Elizabeth's Hosp., Washington, 1970-87; clin. prof. Howard U. Coll. Medicine, 1982—. Co-founder Nat. Health Care Found. for Deaf (named now Deaf Reach); med. officer Region 4 Cmty. Mental Health Ctr., Washington, Commn. on Mental Health, 1987—, now acting med. dir. Recipient Dorothea Lynde Dix award, 1980. Mem. Am. Psychiat. Assn. (achievement awards bd. 1988-89), Washington Psychiat. Soc., St. Elizabeth's Med. Soc. (mem. exec. com. 1993—), Alpha Kappa Mu, Beta Kappa Chi. Author: How and When Psychiatry Can Help You, 1972; You and Your Doctor; contbg. author: Hearing and Hearing Impairment, 1979, Counseling Deaf People, Research and Practice. Home: 12308 Surrey Circle Dr Fort Washington MD 20744-6244

DICKER, MARC TODD, psychiatric physician assistant; b. St. Louis, June 3, 1948; s. Jack and Bertha Mae (Barg) D.; m. RoxAnn Banks, Sept. 4, 1976; children: Analee Joy, Sarabeth. AA, Meramec Jr. Coll., 1968; BA in Psychology, Mo. U., 1970; BHS, MA in Clin. Psychology, Wichita State U., 1976; PhD in Counselor Edn., Kans. State U., 1989. Cert. physician asst.; registered profl. counselor, Kans. Clin. coord. Wichita State U., 1975-82, mem. physician asst. faculty, 1982-92; psychiat. physician asst. Charter Clinic Hosp., Wichita, 1989-92, Profl. Affiliates, P.A., Wichita, 1992—, Wichita VA Med. Ctr., 1995—; cons. Rehab. Hosp. Wichita, 1992-93; bd. dirs. Charter Behavioral, Wichita; site reviewer for physician asst. programs Allied Health Edn. and Accreditation, Wichita, 1980-91; mem. faculty Assn. Physician Asst. Programs, Arlington, Va., 1975-92. Author: The Problem Oriented Physical Examination, 1986; contbr. articles to profl. jours. Active Coleman Found. Coleman Jr. High Sch., Wichita. Grantee Stanford U. Sch. Medicine, 1985, Wesley Found., 1990. Fellow Am. Acad. Physician Assts. (chmn., mem. publs. com. 1975—, peer reviewer jour.), Kans. Acad. Physician Assts. (legis. com. 1975—); mem. Kans. Psychol. Assn., Am. Soc. for Psychiat. Physician Assts., Kans. Counseling Assn., Wichita Area Psychol. Assn., Alpha Eta. Home: # 8 Hillcrest Wichita KS 67208-4423

DICKERSON, MARIE HARVISON, nurse anesthetist; b. Leaf, Miss., Oct. 14, 1946; d. Thurman C. and Mary C. (Jarrell) Harvison; m. George T. Dickerson, Sept. 2, 1978; children: George H., Kathryn Marie. AA, Jones County Jr. Coll., 1967; BS, U. Ottawa, Kansas City, Kans., 1976; MEd, U. S. Ala., 1978. RN; cert. registered nurse anesthetist. Oper. rm. supr. George County Hosp., Lucedale, Miss., 1967-70; dir. Sch. Anesthesia, Mobile, Ala., 1972-79; chief anesthesia Wayne Gen. Hosp., Waynesboro, Miss., 1979-84; pres. Wayne Anesthesia, P.A., Waynesboro, 1984—. Maj. USAR. Mem. ANA, Miss. Nurses Assn. (dist. pres. 1983), Am. Assn. for Counseling and Devel., Miss. Assn. Nurse Anesthetists (bd. dirs.), Miss Counseling Assn. Baptist. Club: Waynesboro Home and Garden. Avocations: piano; voice; computers; antiques. Home: 824 Pou Dr Waynesboro MS 39367-2532

DICKES, RICHARD ALEXANDER, psychiatrist; b. Bklyn., Nov. 14, 1942; s. Robert and Bernice (Livingston) D.; m. Ruth Jane Gollance, June 13, 1965; children: Roger M., Carolyn J. AB, Columbia U., 1963; MD, Albert Einstein Coll. Medicine, 1967. Intern Beth Israel Hosp., N.Y.C., 1967-68; resident Albert Einstein Coll. Medicine Jacobi Hosp., Bronx, N.Y., 1968-71, fellow in child psychiatry, 1973-75; pvt. practice Morristown, N.J., 1975—; dir. psychiat. edn. Morristown Meml. Hosp., 1980—, asst. clin. prof. Coll. Physicians and Surgeons, vice chmn., 1980—. Mem. Roebling Soc. Bklyn. Mus., 1984—, Oriental Arts Coun. Bklyn. Mus., 1986—. Lt. comdr. USN, 1971-73. Fellow Am. Psychiat. Assn.; mem. Am. Acad. Child Psychology, Tri County chpt. N.J. Psychiat. Assn. (pres. 1984-85), N.J. Coun. Child and Adolescent Psychiatry (pres. 1984-86). Office: 52 Maple Ave Morristown NJ 07960-5218

DICKES, ROBERT, psychiatrist; b. N.Y.C., Apr. 15, 1912; s. Benjamin and Anna (Adler) D.; m. Bernice Livingston, June 12, 1938; children: Richard A., Susan R. Dickes Hubbard. B.S., CCNY, 1933; M.S., Emory U., 1934, M.D., 1938. Diplomate: Am. Bd. Internal Medicine, Am. Bd. Psychiatry and Neurology. Intern L.I. Coll. Hosp., Bklyn., 1938-39; asst. resident in internal medicine L.I. Coll. Hosp., 1938-39, resident in medicine, 1939-41, dir. med. clinics, 1946-50; asso. in medicine L.I. Coll. Medicine, 1946, asst. prof. psychiatry, 1949; fellow in medicine Western Res. U.-Lakeside Hosp., 1941-42; fellow in psychiatry Kings County Hosp. Center-SUNY Bklyn., 1950-52, mem. staff, 1952—, pres. med. br., 1977-78; clin. assoc. prof. psychiatry Downstate Med. Center SUNY, Bklyn., 1950-54, assoc. prof., 1954-56, clin. assoc. prof., 1956-61, assoc. prof., 1961-63, prof., 1963, 78-82, prof. emeritus, 1982—, tng. and supervising analyst, 1965—, acting chmn. dept. psychiatry, 1965-66, 71-72, dir. infant behavior study lab., 1973, dir. center human sexuality, 1973—, chmn. dept. psychiatry, 1975-78; clin. prof. psychiatry NYU Coll. Medicine, 1982—; cons. VA hosps., Bklyn., Northport, N.Y.; v.p. Am. Bd. Sexology, 1989—. Contbr. articles to profl. publs. Bd. govs., mem. acquisitions com. Bklyn. Museum. Maj. M.C. U.S. Army, 1942-46. Commonwealth fellow, 1941-42, 48-49. Fellow A.C.P., Am. Psychiat. Assn., Am. Coll. Psychiatry; mem. Am. Psychoanalytic Assn., Psychoanalytic Assn. N.Y. (treas. 1962-64), Bklyn. Psychiat. Soc. (pres. 1967), Kings County Med. Soc., Kings County Psychiat. Soc. (pres. 1967-68), Soc. Sex Therapy and Research (pres. 1979-81), Am. Bd. Sexology (v.p. 1989—).

DICKEY, JAMES BURL, ophthalmologist, educator; b. San Antonio, July 1, 1962; s. James C. and Blanche L. (Willbanks) D.; m. Marcella L. Conte, July 21, 1984; children: Connor, Ian. BS in Biology, Oral Roberts U., 1983, MD, 1987. Diplomate Am. Bd. Ophthalmology, Nat. Bd. Med. Examiners. Intern Tucson Hosps., 1987-88; resident ophthalmology Loyola U. Chgo., Maywood, Ill., 1989-92; clin. lectr. U. Ariz. Med. Sch., Tucson, 1992-95; ophthmalogist South Hills Eye Assocs., Ltd., Pitts., 1995—. Contbr. articles to profl. jours. Maj. USAF, 1988-89, 92-95. Office: South Hills Eye Assocs Ltd 713 Washington Rd Pittsburgh PA 15228

DICKEY, SUSAN B., nursing educator; b. Hamilton, Ohio, Dec. 31, 1952; d. Joseph M., Jr. and Mary (Mauntel) D. BSN cum laude, U. Pa., 1975; MSN, U. Pa., Phila., 1980, PhD, 1992. RN, Pa. Staff nurse Children's Hosp. Phila., 1979-91; instr. nursing Temple U., 1981-84, asst. prof., 1984-91, assoc. prof., 1992—; relief clin. coord. obstetrical-neonatal nursing Hosp. U. Pa., 1986-88. Author: A Guide to the Nursing of Children, 1987, Guide to Patient Evaluation, 5th edit., 1988. Nurses' Ednl. Fund scholar, 1985, Am. Nurses' Found. scholar, 1989, grantee, 1989. Mem. ANA (cert.), Pa. Nurses' Assn. (congl. dist. coord., del., Mem. award 1981, 82), Sigma Theta Tau (Kappa Chi chpt. grantee 1989). Home: 1186 Neshaminy Valley Dr Bensalem PA 19020-1222

DICKINSON, CATHERINE SCHATZ, retired microbiologist; b. Cin., Jan. 6, 1927; d. Ralph Marvin and Mabel (Dare) Schatz; student U. Cin., 1944-46, postgrad. 1952; A.B., Miami U., Oxford, Ohio, 1948; m. Willard C. Dickinson, Jr., June 23, 1956; children—Kellie Dare, Bradley Clark. Supr., Bacteriology Lab., Children's Hosp., Cin., 1948-53; supr., sect. head Microbiology Lab., Ochsner Found. Hosp., New Orleans, 1953-95, ret., 1995; lectr. in field. Mem. New Orleans Area Soc. for Microbiology (pres. 1979), Am. Soc. Microbiology, Am. Soc. Clin. Pathologists (specialist in microbiology), New Orleans Soc. Microbiology, Nat. Registry for Microbiologists, Delta Zeta. Episcopalian. Club: Order Eastern Star. Home: 10001 Hyde Pl New Orleans LA 70123-1521

DICKINSON, JOHN INGRAM, surgeon; b. Atlanta, July 5, 1931; s. Ingram and Sylvia (Blair) D.; m. Sarah Richardson Longino, July 10, 1954 (dec. 1978); children: Jerome Brooks, Mary Ann, Blair Hinton, Roy Stokes, Sylvia Blair; m. Paula Copeland, Apr. 18, 1979. BA, Amherst Coll., 1952; MD, Emory U., 1956. Intern, resident in surgery Grady Meml. Hosp., Atlanta, 1956-61; pvt. practice Surg. Assocs. Rome, Ga., 1963—; 1st pres. med. staff Redmond Regional Med. Ctr., Rome, 1972-73, trustee 1987-93; pres. med. staff Floyd Med. Ctr., Rome, 1982-83, mem. hosp. authority, 1976-81. Chmn. county and 7th dist. Rep. Ctrl. Com., Rome, mem. Ga. state com.; active Rome Boys Club; mem. Airport Commn. Floyd County, Rome, 1982-88. Lt. comdr. USN, 1961-63. Fellow ACS (pres. Ga. chpt. 1980-81); mem. Ga. Surg. Soc., Chi Phi, Sigma Xi. Episcopalian. Home: 1396 Stringer Rd Rockmart GA 30153 Office: Surg Assocs Rome PC 310 W 6th St Rome GA 30165

DICKINSON, KATHY LEE, ophthalmic technician; b. Hopkinsville, Ky., July 6, 1954; d. Alex H. and Earlene (Barrow) Lee; m. Jerry Michael Bailey, Nov. 17, 1973 (dec. Sept. 1984); 1 child, Elaina Beth; m. Paul Richard Dickinson, Aug. 7, 1992. Student, U. Louisville, 1985-88, Vanderbilt U., 1988-89, Hopkinsville (Ky.) C.C., 1995—. Cert. ophthalmic technician. Bus. adminstr. Bailey Plumbing & Elec. Co., Elkton, Ky., 1973-85, 91—; cert. ophthalmic technician Dr. J.N. Terhune M.D., Hopkinsville, 1985-92, cert. ophthalmic asst., 1987-89, cert. ophthalmic technician, 1989—. Contbr. articles to publs. Youth dir. Christian Ch. of Elkton, 1982-85; mem. youth membership coun. Trenton Bapt. Ch., 1994—; mem. ARC of todd County, mem. disaster team, 1990-93, CPR ihsntr., 1990-94, 1st aid instr., 1980-94, bd. dirs., 1995—; mem. Todd County Assn. for Retarded Children; pres. Todd County 4-H Coun., 1991-94; mem. Ky. State Area 4-H Coun., 1993-94; pres. Todd County PTSO, 1995-96; bd. dirs. ARC, 1995—. Ky. col., 1990. Mem. Tenn. Ophthalmic Soc. (membership v.p. 1989-91, pres. 1992-93), Joint Commn. of Allied Health Care Pers., Todd County Jaycees (bd. dirs. 1991-92, pres. 1986, 89, 92), Ky. Jaycees (muscular dystrophy program mgr. 1987, dist. mgr. 1988, one of Top 10 Presidents in Ky. Jaycees 1986, Thoroughbred award 1990), Todd County Tennis League (v.p. 1986-88). Democrat. Home: 208 Streets Ave PO Box 144 Elkton KY 42220

DICKINSON, RONALD BRUCE, physician assistant; b. Dallas, Dec. 7, 1950; s. Albert Stanley and Marjorie Nell (Reese) D.; m. Debra Kay Simon, Mar. 26, 1982; children: Sean Wesley, Russell Brandon, Ryan Bradley. AA in Math. and Sci., Mountain View Coll., 1975; BS in Health Care, U. Tex. Southwestern Med. Sch., 1977; MA, U. Tex., Dallas, 1986. Lic. physician asst., Tex. Instr. physician asst. program U. Tex. Southwestern Med. Sch., Dallas, 1977-78, 80-81, asst. prof., 1981-82, assoc. dir., 1982-86, dir., 1986-91; staff physician asst. Cook Surg. Clinic, Dallas, 1978-80; sr. staff physician asst. VA Med. Ctr., Dallas, 1992-93; staff physician asst. Glenn-Garrett Clinic, Linden, Tex., 1993-95, East Tex. Med. Ctr. Rural Clinic, Daingerfield, 1995—; advisor allied health edn. Tex. Med. Assn., Austin, 1980-84; cons. com. on accreditation of family planning clinics Tex. Dept. Human Resources, Austin, 1983-85. Author: Physician Assistant: How to Be One, 1978. Coord. Los Barrios Cmty. Clinic Health Fair, Dallas, 1983-85; soccer and baseball coach YMCA Youth League, Irving, Tex., 1987-95; leader Boy Scouts Am., Linden, 1995—. With USN, 1969-73, Vietnam. Named one of Outstanding Young Men Am., 1983; grantee U.S. Dept. HHS, 1991-92, 1985-89. Fellow Am. Acad. Physician Assts. (speaker of the house 1984-85), Tex. Acad. Physician Assts. (pres. 1983-84), Tex. Soc. Allied Health Professions, VA Physician Asst. Assn., Vets. Caucus Am. Acad. (comptroller 1988-96), Res. Officer Assn. Office: East Tex Med Ctr 1402 Linda Dr Daingerfield TX 75638

DICKINSON, WILLIAM ANDREW, JR., hospital administrator; b. Atlanta, Aug. 25, 1945; s. William Andrew and Nancy McQuown (Ring) D.; m. Barbara Helen Griffin, June 13, 1970; children: William Andrew, III, Laura Craven. B.A. in Econs., U. Va., 1967; M.H.A., Ga. State U., 1973. Adminstrv. resident Ind. U. Hosps., Indpls., 1972-73; asst. adminstr. Med. Coll. VA Hosp., Richmond, Va., 1973-75; v.p. Baptist Hosp., Nashville, 1975-78; v.p. Roanoke Meml. Hosps., Va., 1978-84, sr. v.p., 1984-92, Carilion Health Sys., Roanoke, 1992—; dir. Roanoke Meml. Rehab. Ctr. Bd. dirs. Mental Health Assn. of Roanoke Valley, Va., 1979—, Soc. for the Crippled, Southwest Va., 1978—, Roanoke Neighborhood Partnership, Roanoke, 1983—, Burrell Home for Adults, Roanoke, 1983—, Va. Mus. Transp., 1991—. Served to lt. USNR, 1967-71. Mem. Va. Hosp. Assn., Am. Hosp. Assn., Am. Coll. Hosp. Adminstrs., Menatl Health Assn. Roanoke Valley. Republican. Episcopalian. Lodge: Rotary. Office: Carilion Health System PO Box 13727 Roanoke VA 24036-3727

DICKMAN, ROBERT MOYER, retired pharmacist; b. Kankakee, Ill., July 2, 1927; s. Arthur August and Esther M. (Kilgos) D. BS in Pharmacy, U. Ill., 1951. Registered pharmacist, Ill., Wis., Ariz. Pharmacy apprentice Presbyn. Hosp., Chgo., 1950-51; dir. pharmacy Swedish-Am. Hosp., Rockford, Ill., 1954-60; pharmacy in-patient supr. U. Wis. Hosps., Madison, 1961-62; pharmacy supr Nihan & Martin Clinic Pharmacy, Rockford, 1964-66, Mauk Clin. Pharmacies, Rockford, 1966; dir. pharmacy and med. svcs. H. Douglas Singer Mental Health Ctr. State of Ill. Dept. Mental Health, Rockford, 1966-77; continued edn. specialist H. Douglas Singer Mental Health Ctr. State of Ill., Rockford, 1966-77. Mem. Kiwanis, North Rockford, Ill., 1970-77, Court St. United Meth. Ch., Rockford, 1969-77, Willowbrook United Meth. Ch., Sun City, Ariz., 1977—, staff/parish, trustee; Stephen Ministry coord. Willowbrook United Meth. Ch., 1992—. With USN, 1945-46, mil. intelligence U.S. Army, 1952-54. Mem. Am. Pharm. Assn., Am. Soc. Health Sys. Pharmacists, Ariz. Pharm. Assn., Ariz. Soc. Health Sys. Pharmacists, Maricopa County Pharm. Assn. Home: 9423 W Manzanita Dr Sun City AZ 85373-1735

DICKSON, ANGELA DENISE, critical care nurse; b. Longview, Wash., May 11, 1970; d. Phillip Cecil and Nancy Joy (Adams) Corbin; m. Timothy Glenn Dickson, Nov. 5, 1994. AD, Lower Columbia Coll., Longview, 1991. RN, Wash.; cert. critical care nurse; cert. ACLS, TNCC. Med. nurse Columbia View Nursing Home, Cathlamet, Wash., 1990; nurse, float pool St. John's Med. Ctr., Longview, 1990-91, cardiology nurse, 1991-93, ICU/CCU nurse, 1993—. EMT-paramedic vol. Cathlamet Fire Dept., 1989-96; mem., sec. Cathlamet Law and Justice Coun., 1994—. Pentecostal-Ch. of God.

DICKSON, BETSY G., social worker; b. Columbia, S.C., Apr. 18, 1944; d. Henry C. and Betty (Kabler) Garrett; m. Andrew L. Dickson, June 8, 1965; children: James, Marian. BA, U. S.C., 1965; MSW, U. So. Miss., 1977; MPH, U. Ala., 1987. Lic. cert. social worker Acad. Cert. Social Workers. Libr. Ark. River Valley Regional Libr., Russellville, Ark., 1965-67; art instr. Ark. Valley Cultural Enrichment Project, Russellville, 1967-68; br. libr. Okla. County Librs., Oklahoma City, 1968-70; advt. dir. Woolworth Store #253, Milledgeville, Ga., 1972-73; freelance comml. artist Hattiesburg, Miss., 1973-76; dist. social work supr. Miss. State Dept. Health, Hattiesburg, 1977-94; adj. prof. social work U. So. Miss., Hattiesburg, 1979—; cons. social work children's med. program Miss. State Dept. Health, Jackson, 1994—. Bd. dirs. United Way Emergency Welfare Fund, 1982-92; mem. Common Cause Miss., Hattiesburg, 1988—; mem. Outreach com. Trinity Episcopal Ch., Hattiesburg, 1988-90; mem. Miss. Human Svcs. Agenda, Jackson, 1989—, Miss. Episcopal AIDS commn., Jackson, 1994—; mem. faculty Delta Regional AIDS Edn. Tng. Ctr., Jackson, 1994—; mem. adv. bd. Children's Trust Fund Miss., 1995—. Mem. NASW (local chair 1982-84, various coms.), Miss. Pub. Health Workers Assn., State Employees Assn. Miss., Miss. Coalition Mothers and Babies, Miss. Conf. Social Welfare, Miss.

Assn. State Employees, Assn. State & Territorial Pub. Health Social Workers. Office: Miss State Dept Health Children's Med Program care PO Box 5163 Hattiesburg MS 39406-5163

DICKSON, GARY WAYNE, toxicologist, agricultural products executive; b. Pitts., May 17, 1949; s. Alexander Charles and Mary Eleanor (Toy) D.; m. Barbara Jeanne Norton, July 8, 1972; children: Ryan Alexander, Christopher Jon. BS in Biol. Scis., U. Pitts., 1971; MS in Biol. Scis., Old Dominion U., 1976; PhD in Zoology, U. Ga., 1980. Ecologist EPA, Washington, 1980-81; environ. specialist agrl. div. CIBA-GEIGY Corp., Greensboro, N.C., 1981-85, mgr. R & D planning, 1985-88; dir. corp. planning and analysis CIBA-GEIGY Corp., Ardsley, N.C., 1988-90; mgr. ecol. toxicology CIBA-GEIGY Corp., Greensboro, 1990-91; dir. environ. and pub. affairs CIBA-GEIGY Corp., Greensboro, N.C., 1991-93, dir. environ. fate and effects, 1993—; bd. visitors Duke U. Sch. of the Environment, Durham, N.C., 1989—. Contbr. over 20 articles to profl. jours. Capt. USNR, 1972—. Mem. Soc. Environ. Toxicology and Chemistry (bd. dirs. 1986-89), Ecol. Soc. Am. (cert. sr. ecologist). Office: CIBA-GEIGY Corp 401 S Swing Rd Greensboro NC 27409-2011

DICKSON, JAMES EDWIN, II, obstetrician, gynecologist; b. Pontiac, Mich., Feb. 18, 1943; s. James Edwin and Virginia (Farrar) D.; m. Joan Gayle Coonley, July 21, 1967; children: Alison, Andrew. BS, U. Mich., 1965; MD, Wayne State U., 1969. Diplomate Am. Bd. Ob-Gyn. Intern Harborview Med. Ctr., Seattle, 1969-70; resident U. Mich. Med. Ctr., 1972-75; pvt. practice Geneva, N.Y., 1975—; pres. Geneva Med. Assocs.; chmn. dept. ob-gyn. Geneva Gen. Hosp. Capt. M.C., USAF, 1970-72. Fellow Am. Coll. Obstetricians and Gynecologists; mem. Soc. Am. Laparoscopists, Miller Ob-Gyn Soc., N.Y. State Med. Soc., Buffalo Ob-Gyn Soc., Rotary (pres. Geneva 1988). Home: 16 Maplewood Dr Geneva NY 14456-1420 Office: Geneva Med Assocs 324 W North St Geneva NY 14456-1559

DICKSON, JAMES FRANCIS, III, surgeon; b. Boston, May 4, 1924; s. James Francis Jr. and Mary Elizabeth (Rich) D.; m. Vivian Joan Franco, Dec. 23, 1977. A.B., Dartmouth Coll., 1944; M.D., Harvard Med. Sch., 1947. Diplomate Am. Bd. Surgery. Intern and resident Boston City Hosp., 1947-51; practice medicine specializing in thoracic surgery Boston, 1951-61; rsch. assoc. MIT, Cambridge, 1961-65; dir. engring. in biology and medicine NIH, Bethesda, Md., 1965-75; dep. asst. sec. for health HEW, Washington, 1975-78; asst. surgeon gen. HHS, Washington, 1978-89; sr. advisor to dean Harvard Med. Sch., 1992—, vis. com., 1992—; bd. overseers Dartmouth Med. Sch., C. Everett Koop Inst.; bd. dirs. Tane/Life Med. Fellow ACS, IEEE; mem. Inst. Medicine of NAS.

DICKSON, JESSE H., orthopedic surgeon; b. Houston, Aug. 26, 1933; s. James Charles and Ruth Phelps Dickson; children from previous marriage, Dianne Dickson Rushea, A. Chidsey, Josh D. Jones, Jason Jones, Pual H., K. Kendall Berry; m. Cissy Lowe, Feb. 14, 1982. BA in Biology, So. Meth. U., 1955; MD, U. Tex., Dallas, 1959. Diplomate Am. Bd. Orthopedic Surgery. Intern U. Hosps. U. Okla., Oklahoma City, 1956-60; resident Baylor Coll. Medicine, Houston, 1959-64, prof. orthopedic surgery, 1988—; fellow Cornell Med. Coll., N.Y.C., 1966-67; pvt. practice Houston, 1967-88. Contbr. nuemrous articles to profl. jours. Capt. USAF, 1964-66. Mem. Scolrosis Rsch. Soc. (pres. 1989-90). Methodist. Office: Baylor Coll Medicine Dept Orthopedic Surgery 6560 Fannin St Ste 2501 Houston TX 77030-2709

DICKSON, ROBERT FRANK, nursing home executive; b. Carbondale, Ill., Oct. 23, 1933; s. Jason Milburn and Elizabeth (Krysher) D.; m. Roberta Joan Mellican, May 16, 1964; children: Kevin, Craig, Angela, Rebecca. BS, So. Ill. U., 1960. With Farm Credit System, Ill., 1960-67; credit. rep. Fed. Intermediate Credit Bank, St. Louis, 1967-70; adminstr. Union County Hosp., Anna, Ill., 1970-72; v.p. Heritage Enterprises, Inc., Bloomington, Ill., 1972-85, exec. v.p., 1985—. Contbr. articles to mag. Served with USN, 1952-56. Mem. Ill. Health Care Assn. (bd. dirs. 1975-82, 85-86, pres. 1979, 85), Am. Health Care Assn. (bd. dirs. 1979-82, 86). Republican. Presbyterian. Lodge: Kiwanis. Home: 705 Bradley Dr Bloomington IL 61701-2203 Office: Heritage Enterprises Inc 115 W Jefferson St Bloomington IL 61702-3188

DICKSTEIN, LEAH JOAN, psychiatry educator; b. N.Y.C., Aug. 17, 1934. BA in Edn., Bklyn. Coll., 1955, MS in Edn., 1961; MD, U. Louisville, 1970. Intern U. Louisville, 1970-71, resident, 1972-74, dir., founder MHS student health, 1975-81, psychiatrist counseling ctr., 1981-82, psychiat. cons. counseling ctr., 1982—, asst. prof. psychiatry, 1975-83, assoc. prof. psychiatry, 1985-87, prof. psychiatry, 1987—, assoc. dean for faculty and student advocacy, 1989—, assoc. dept. chairperson, 1993—, chief divsn. attitudinal and behavioral medicine, 1995—. Editor, author: (with others) Women in Leadership roles, 1986, Family Violence, 1988; Career Planning for Psychiatrists, 2d edit.; co-editor: Careers in Psychiatry, 1995; inventor, patentee in field. Bd. dirs. Adath Jeshurun Congregation, Louisville, 1990-92, Jewish Family and Vocat. Svcs., Louisville, 1984-87, Planned Parenthood, Louisville, 1977-80; pres. Wellness Forum, Louisville, 1988-90. Recipient Golden Apple award for teaching, 1982, Grawemeyer award Kentuckiana Metroversity, 1987, Sch. Medicine U. Louisville Alumni award, 1995, U. Louisville Trustees award, 1994; Health Awareness Workshop grantee McLean Found., 1981—. Fellow Am. Psychiat. Assn. (v.p. 1992-94, chair sci. program com. 1995-96), Am. Coll. Health Assn., Am. Coll. Psychiatrists; mem. Am. Assn. for Social Psychiatry (pres. 1996—), Assn. Am. Med. Colls. (women's liaison officer 1982—, Women in Leadership Devel. award 1993), Assn. for Acad. Psychiatry (Educators award 1993), Am. Bd. Adolescent Psychiatry, Assn. Women Psychiatrists (nat. pres. 1987-91), Am. Med. Women's Assn. (nat. pres. 1993). Office: U Louisville Sch of Medicine 500 S Preston St Louisville KY 40202-1702

DICLAUDIO, JANET ALBERTA, health information administrator; b. Monroeville, Pa., June 17, 1940; d. Frank and Pearl Alberta (Wolfgang) DiC. Cert. in Med. Rsch. Libr. Sci., Luth Med. Ctr., 1962; BA, Thiel Coll., 1975; MS, SUNY, Buffalo, 1978. Registered record adminstr. Dir. med. records Bashline Hosp., Grove City, Pa., 1962, St. Clair Meml. Hosp., Pitts., 1963-73; asst. prof. Ill. State U., Normal, 1976-81; corp. dir. med. records Buffalo Gen. Hosp., 1981-85; dir. med. records Candler Hosp., Savannah, Ga., 1985-94, med. records analyst, 1994—; med. record cons. White Cliff Nursing Home, Greenville, Pa., 1973-75; mgmt. cons. Gifford W. Lorenz MD, Savannah, 1992-94. Contbr. articles to periodicals. Bd. dirs. Mid-Ill. Areawide Health Planning Corp., Normal, 1979-81. Mem. Am. Health Info. Mgmt. Assn., Ga. Health Info. Mgmt. Assn. Office: Candler Hosp 5353 Reynolds St Savannah GA 31405-6005

DI DONNA, GEORGE JEROME, cardiologist; b. Amsterdam, N.Y., Mar. 23, 1941; s. George Nicholas and Catherine Albina (Holmes) Di D.; m. Brigid Frances Weiss, Aug. 27, 1966; children: Susan, Michael, Gregory. BS in Preprofl. Studies, U. Notre Dame, 1963; MD cum laude, Union U., Albany, N.Y., 1967. Diplomate Am. Bd. Internal Medicine, Am. Bd. Cardiovasc. Diseases. Cardiologist Rees-Stealy Med. Clinic, San Diego, 1974-76; pvt. practice, El Paso, Tex., 1976—; chief med. staff Suntowers (Columbia West) Hosp., El Paso, 1986-88, Providence Meml. Hosp., El Paso, 1995-96. Bd. dirs. El Paso County Emergency Med. Svcs. Adv. Bd., 1984-87, Paso Del Norte Health Found., El Paso, 1995—. Maj. M.C., U.S. Army, 1969-71. Named Man of Yr., Notre Dame Club, El Paso, 1992. Fellow Am. Coll. Cardiology; mem. AMA, Tex. Med. Assn., Am. Heart Assn. (pres. El Paso divsn. 1988), El Paso County Med. Soc. (pres. 1992—). Republican. Roman Catholic. Office: 1700 Curie Dr Ste 5100 El Paso TX 79902-2905

DIEDRICH, RICHARD CURTIS, consulting psychologist; b. Berlin, Wis., July 8, 1934; s. Frederick William Jr. and Marian Frances (Curtis) D.; m. Ada Brown, Feb. 15, 1958; children: Curtis R., Frederick J. AB, Ripon Coll., 1956; AM, U. Chgo., 1959, PhD, 1966. Lic. psychologist, Mass. Staff assoc. edn. dept. U. Chgo., 1961-63; sch. psychology intern Thornton Twp. High Sch., Harvey, Ill., 1961-62, sch. psychologist, 1962-63; sch. psychologist Niles Twp. Dept. Spl. Edn., Lincolnwood, Ill., 1963-64, South Suburban Sch. Coop., Homewood, Ill., 1964-65; lectr.-instr. edn. dept. U. Chgo., 1965-66; dir. rsch. Thornton Twp. High Schs., Thornton Twp. Jr. Coll., Harvey, 1965-66; asst. prof. dept. edn. Purdue U., West Lafayette, 1966-70; corp. psychologist Rohrer, Hibler & Replogle, Inc., Montreal, Can., Boston, 1970-89; ptnr. McSherry, Diedrich & Stevens, Inc., Framingham, Mass., 1989-92; sr. cons. Hay Group, Boston, 1992—. Author: Guidance Personnel, 1968; co-editor: Group Procedures, 1972; co-editor Spl. Issue: Group Processes, 1969; contbr. articles to profl. jours. 1st lt. U.S. Army, 1956-58. Full Tuition scholar U. Chgo., 1959-62; Internat. Travel grantee Purdue U., 1968. Fellow APA. Home: 35 Blacksmith Dr Sudbury MA 01776-1037 Office: 116 Huntington Ave Boston MA 02116-5749

DIEFENBACH, WILLIAM PAUL, neurosurgeon; b. N.Y.C., Dec. 11, 1949; s. William Carl Ludwig and Martha (Kahle) D.; m. Geraldine Musche, Apr. 10, 1977 (div. Oct. 1992); children: William Alexander, Katherine Murchdon; m. Tracey Jean Sandberg, Apr. 30, 1994. BA, Columbia U., 1972, MD, 1979. Resident in neurosurgery Neurol. Inst., N.Y.C., 1980-85; neurosurgeon Neurol. Assocs., Tucson, 1985-93, St. Vincent Health Ctr., Erie, Pa., 1993—. Capt. U.S. Army, 1973. Fellow ACS; mem. AMA, Congress Neurol. Surgeons, Am. Assn. Neurol. surgeons, Erie County Med. Soc. (pres.-elect 1995-96), Pa. Med. Soc. Republican. Presbyterian. Office: St Vincent Neurol Surgery 311 W 24th St Erie PA 16502

DIEHL, MARK EMORY, dentist, consultant; b. Upland, Calif., Feb. 7, 1951; s. John Earl and Patricia Eileen (Stell) D.; m. Lee Ann Collins, July 17, 1976; children: Erin Lee, Brynn Elyse, Megan Eileen. BS, U. So. Calif., 1973; DMD, Washington U., St. Louis, 1978 Resident gen. dentistry VA Hosp., Palo Alto, Calif., 1978-79, staff dentist, 1979-87, asst. chief dental service, 1987—; dir. Palo Alto Dental Clinic, 1990—; cons. Dental Ins Cons. Inc., Saratoga, Calif., 1985—. Fellow Acad. Gen. Dentists; mem. ADA, Omicron Kappa Upsilon. Republican. Mem. Christian Ch. Home: 6880 Chiala Ln San Jose CA 95129-2853 Office: Dental Svc 3801 Miranda Ave Palo Alto CA 94304-1207

DIELMAN, RAY WALTER, radiologic scientist; b. Napoleon, Ohio, Dec. 25, 1938; s. Walter Carl and Gail Ann (Fenstermaker) D.; m. Diane Tahy, June 1961 (div. 1968); children: Joseph Scott, David Jon; m. Beverly Beavers, Oct. 16, 1994. Student, Defiance Coll., 1956-59; radiologic technologist diploma, St. Joseph Hosp. Sch., Ft. Wayne, Ind., 1962; nuclear medicine technologist cert., U. Mich., 1962; OPM, Harvard U., 1975. Cert mgmt. cons., radiologic, nuclear medicine technologist. Supr. nuclear medicine U. Mich. Hosp., Ann Arbor, 1962-63; dir. nuclear medicine Mercy Hosp & Med. Ctr., Chgo., 1963-64; cons., nuclear medicine Picker Corp., White Plains, N.Y., 1964-67; pres. Dielman Cons., Inc., Chgo., 1967-88; dir. dept. of radiology Loyola U. Med. Ctr., Chgo., 1980-83; co-owner Island Cinema & Theatre, Sanibel Isle, Fla., 1983-87; supr. Fla. Health and Rehabilitative Svcs. Office of Radiation Control, Tampa, 1988—; assoc. mem., com. Conf. Radiation Control Program Dirs., Frankfort, Ky., 1989—; vice chmn. Radiation Control Rsch. and Edn. Found.; del. Internat. Com. of Radionuclide Metrology, London, 1976-85. Co-editor/author: Essentials Nuclear Medicine Technology, 1970; contbr. articles to profl. jours. Recipient scholarship Am. Cancer Soc., 1962. Home: PO Box 778 Anna Maria FL 34216-0778

DIEMER, GERALDINE, women's health nursing educator; b. Milw., Jan. 6, 1936; d. Gerhard Henry and Viola Marie (Webber) Junghans; m. Joel Adolf Diemer, Aug. 19, 1962; children: Stephen, Karen, Kristen, Michael. Diploma, Luth. Hosp., 1961; BSN, U. Wis., 1979, MSN, 1981, PhD, 1988. RN, Wis. Clin. assoc. prof. U Wis., Madison; pres. directing bd. Dane County Advs. for Battered Women. Mem. NAACOG, Wis. Perinatal Assn. (bd. dirs.), Madison Dist. Nurses Assn. (bd. dirs., pres.), Sigma Theta Tau. Home: 1422 Pleasure Dr Madison WI 53704-3824

DIENER, ROYCE, corporate director, retired health care services company executive; b. Balt., Mar. 27, 1918; s. Louis and Lillian (Goodman) D.; m. Jennifer S. Flinton; children: Robert, Joan, Michael. BA, Harvard U.; LLD, Pepperdine U. Comml. lending officer, investment banker various locations to 1972; pres. Am. Med. Internat., Inc., Beverly Hills, Calif., 1972-75, pres., chief exec. officer, 1975-78, chmn., chief exec. officer, 1978-85, chmn. bd., 1986-88, chmn. exec. com., 1986-89; bd. dirs. Calif. Econ. Devel. Corp., Acuson, Inc., Advanced Tech. Venture Funds, Am. Health Properties, AMI Health Svcs., plc., Consortium 2000. Author: Financing a Growing Business, 1966, 4th edit., 1995. Bd. visitors Grad. Sch. Mgmt., UCLA; mem. governing bd., UCLA Med. Ctr.; mem. vis. com. Med. Sch. and Sch. Dental Medicine, Harvard U.; bd. dirs. L.A. Philharm. Assn., L.A. chpt. ARC, Heritage Sq. Mus., Santa Monica. Served to capt. USAF, 1942-45, PTO. Decorated D.F.C. with oak leaf cluster. Mem. L.A. C. of C. (bd. dirs.), Calif. C. of C. (bd. dirs.), Calif. Bus. Round Table (bd. dirs.), Harvard Club, Regency Club, Calif. Yacht Club, Riviera Country Club (L.A.), Marks Club (London).

DIENST, STANLEY G., transplant surgeon, researcher; b. Boise, Idaho, Sept. 1, 1927; s. Charles Franklin and Lillian (Hawk) D.; m. Patricia Anne Perkins; children: Bradford Charles, Krista Lee. BA, Denver U., 1949; MD, U. Colo., 1952. Surg. rsch. dir. Maine Med. Ctr., Portland, 1961-68; surg. rsch. dir. Henry Ford Hosp., Detroit, 1968-84, dir. transplant svc., 1974-88; dir. transplant svc. N.D. Transplant Ctr. (MedCenter One-St. Alexius), Bismarck, N.D., 1988—; mem. bd., pres. Organ Procurement Agy. of Mich., 1972-88; mem. bd., officer Lilfe Source Organ Procurement Agencies of Minn., N.D. and S.D., 1989—; founder, owner One World Coffee House, Bismarck., 1989—. Contbr. articles to profl. jours. Pres. Physicians for Social Responsibility, Detroit, 1983-86. To 2d lt. USAFR, 1952—. Recipient NIH grant, 1964-67. Presbyterian. Office: North Dakota Transplant Ctr c/o MedCenter One 300 N 7th St Bismarck ND 58501

DIENSTAG, JULES LEONARD, physician, medical researcher; b. N.Y.C., Dec. 10, 1946; m. Judy Iris Gordon, Feb. 3, 1974; children: Josh, Jonathan. AB magna cum laude, Columbia Coll., 1968; MD, Columbia U., 1972. Diplomate Am. Bd Internal Medicine. Intern in medicine Billings Hosp., Chgo., 1972-73, resident in medicine, 1973-74; postdoctoral fellow, rsch. assoc. NIH, Bethesda, Md., 1974-76; clin. and rsch. fellow Mass. Gen. Hosp., Boston, 1976-78, clin. asst. medicine, 1978-79, asst. in medicine, 1979-82, asst. physician, 1983-87, assoc. physician, 1988-93, physician, 1993—; asst. prof. of medicine Harvard Med. Sch., Boston, 1978-82, assoc. prof., 1982—; vis. scientist Lab. of Epidemiology, The Lindsley F. Kimball Rsch. Inst. of the N.Y. Blood Ctr., 1980-82; expert panelist on viral hepatitis Lister Hill Nat. Ctr. for Biomed. Comm., Nat. Libr. Medicine, 1980-82, advisor, 1982-86; numerous tchg. appointments; lectr. in field. Mem. editl. bd. Jour. Clin. Microbiology, 1977-86, Hepatology, 1980-86, Infectious Disease Series, Marcel Dekker Med. divsn., 1981-85, Gastroenterology, 1981-86, Jour. Viral Hepatitis, 1993—; editor: Gastroenterology Series, Marcel Dekker, 1983-86, Mass. Gen. Hosp. Liver-Biliary-Pancreas Ctr. Newsletter, 1990—; assoc. editor: Gastroenterology, 1986-91, 96—, Viral Hepatitis Knowledge-Base, New Eng. Jour. Medicine, 1986-89. With USPHS res., 1976-83, surgeon, 1983—. Recipient Clin. Investigator award USPHS, 1978-79. Fellow ACP; mem. AAAS, Internat. Assn. Study of the Liver, European Assn. Study of the Liver (corr.), Am. Soc. Microbiology, Am. Fedn. Clin. Rsch. Am. Assn. Immunologists, Am. Assn. Study Liver Diseases (abstract selection com. hepatitis, immunology 1979-85, 89—, tng. and edn. com. 1980-83, mem. nominations com. 1989-90, mem. publs. com. 1993-96), Am. Gastroent. Assn. (abstract selection com., liver-biliary-bile 1983-84, 89—), Mass. Med. Soc., Phi Beta Kappa. Office: Mass Gen Hosp Gastrointestinal Unit Boston MA 02114

DIERINGER, CINDY SUE, physician; b. Canton, Ohio, Mar. 2, 1949; d. Frank Melvin and Mary Ruth (Van Orman) D. BS in Chemistry, Grove City Coll., 1971; MS in Pharmacology, W.Va. U., 1973, PhD in Pharmacology, 1976; MD, U. N.C., 1982. NIH predoctoral fellow W.Va. U. Dept. Pharmacology, Morgantown, 1972-76; staff fellow, research scientist Nat. Inst. Environ. Health Scis., Research Triangle Park, N.C., 1976-78; internal medicine resident Richland Meml. Hosp., Columbia, S.C., 1982-85; physician, chief emergency dept. Providence Hosp., Columbia, 1985-88; med. dir. Doctor's Care Forest Acres, Columbia, 1989-91; staff physician Lexington Med. Ctr. Emergency Dept. and Urgent Care Ctr., Columbia, S.C., 1991-92; staff physician emergency dept. Kershaw County Med. Ctr., Camden, S.C., 1992—, interim dir., 1996. Contbr. articles to profl. jours. Mem. Eastminster Presbyn. Ch. Choir, Columbia, 1983-95, Ch. Handbell Choir, 1983-95; instr. and course dir. ACLS, 1988—. Mem. AMA, Am. Assn. Physician Specialists, Am. Med. Women's Assn., S.C. Med. Assn., So. Med. Assn., Columbia Med. Soc., Kershaw County Med. Soc., Sierra Club, Planned Parenthood (assoc.), Sigma Xi. Republican. Office: Kershaw County Med Ctr Emergency Dept 1315 Roberts St Camden SC 29020-3737

DIERS, DONNA KAYE, nurse educator; b. Sheridan, Wyo., May 11, 1938; d. Don Carlos and Ilene Helen (Poffenberger) D. BSN, U. Denver, 1960; MSN, Yale U., 1964. Staff nurse Yale Psychiat. Inst., New Haven, 1960-62; mem. faculty Yale U. Sch. Nursing, New Haven, 1964—, prof., 1979—, dean, 1972-75; dir. Yale Health Services, Community Health Care Plan, New Haven, 1972—. Author: Research in Nursing Practice, 1979. Mem. adv. com. Robert Wood Johnson Found., Princeton, N.J., 1980-86; mem. research rev. com. Nat. Ctr. Health Services Research, Washington, 1981-86. Recipient Henderson award Conn. Nurses Assn., 1980, Disting. Alumna award Yale U. Sch. Nursing, 1983. Fellow Am. Acad. Nursing; mem. Am. Nurses Assn. (J.M. Scott award 1986), Inst. Medicine of Nat. Acad. Scis. Home: 220 Osborn Ave New Haven CT 06511-2848 Office: Yale U Sch Nursing 100 Church St S PO Box 9740 New Haven CT 06536-0740*

DIETERICH, DOUGLAS THOMAS, gastroenterologist, researcher; b. Queens, N.Y., Mar. 1, 1951; s. Albert Frederick and Florence Anna (Kilroy) D. BS, Yale U., 1973; M in Health Adminstrn., C.W. Post, 1974; MD, NYU, 1978. Diplomate Am. Bd. Internal Medicine and Gastroenterology. Intern, then resident Bellevue Hosp., N.Y.C., 1978-81, fellow gastroenterology, 1981-83; attending physician NYU Hosp., 1983—; cons. Rockefeller Ctr. Mgmt. Corp., N.Y.C., 1983-87, ITT World Hdqs., N.Y.C., 1983-86; asst. dir. medicine Gouverneur Hosp., N.Y.C., 1983-85; acting med. dir. ITT World Communications, Secaucus, N.J., 1985-86; attending physician Gouverneur Hosp. Walk In Clinic, 1981-83; teaching asst. NYU, 1979-83, clin. instr. medicine, 1983-88, clin. asst. prof., 1988-93, clin. assoc. prof., 1993—; mem. AIDS Clin. Trials Group NIH, 1986-94. Contbr. articles to profl. jours. Mem. Am. Liver Found., N.J. Fellow ACP, Am. Coll. Gastroenterology; mem. AMA, Am. Gastroent. Assn., Am. Soc. Gastrointestinal Endoscopy, Am. Soc. Internal Medicine, N.Y. County Med. Soc., N.Y. State Med. Soc., N.Y. Acad. Gastroenterology, Yale Club, Cherry Valley Club. Republican. Lutheran. Home: 62 Saint James St S Garden City NY 11530-6344 Office: 345 E 37th St New York NY 10016-3217

DIETERICH, HANS ARMIN, pharmaceutical company executive; b. Bad Dürkheim, Germany, Sept. 24, 1950; s. Hermann and Elsbeth Dieterich; m. Christine Elisabeth, Mar. 10, 1978; 1 child, Alexandra. MSc, Johannes-Gutenberg U., Mainz, Germany, 1975; PhD, U. Mainz, 1977; postgrad., Georgetown U., 1989; MD, U. Zurich, Switzerland, 1992. Asst. clin. dir. Marion Merrell Dow, Germany, 1979-82; med. dir. Marion Merrell Dow, Switzerland, Austria, Ea. Europe, 1984-85; head clin.rsch. Marion Merrell Dow, Germany, 1985-89; clin. rsch. dir. Germany and other European countries Marion Merrell Dow, Russelsheim, 1989-95; external asst. Pharm. Inst. Med. Clinic U. Mainz, 1989—; med. dir. cardiovascular rsch. worldwide Parexel Internat., Berlin, 1995—; prof. pharmacology Georgetown U.; lectr. nat. and internat. congresses and symposia. Editor: Therapy in Heart Failures, 1991, Coronary Heart Disease, 1993, Interventions of the Heart, 1995, others; contbr. articles to profl. jours. Fellow Am. Coll. Cardiology, European Soc. Cardiology, Internat. Coll. Angiology, Am. Coll. Angiology; mem. German Soc. Pharmacology and Toxicology, German Soc. Heart and Circulation Rsch., Swiss Soc. Cardiology, German Soc. Med. Documentation, European Acad. Allergology and Clin. Immunology, German Heart Found., Fedn. European Soc. Toxicology, Internat. Soc. Cardiovascular Pharmacotherapy, Internat. League Against Epilepsy, World Med. Assn., German Assn. Cardiothoracic Anaesthesiologists. Home: Am Huhlchen 5, 55130 Mainz Germany Office: Parexel Klinikum Westend Univ, Spandauer Damm 130, D-14050 Berlin Germany

DIETERICH, MICHAEL KARL, psychology educator, psychotherapist; b. Stuttgart, Germany, Jan. 13, 1942; s. Karl and Margarete (Krebser) D.; m. Hilde Luise Schweikert, May 21, 1966; children: Eva Maria, Joerg Michael, Rebekka Magdalena. Diploma in engring., Fachhochschule, Esslingen, Germany, 1965; MSc, U. Hohenheim, Germany, 1972; MA, U. Stuttgart, Germany, 1977, DrPhil, 1980. Lab. engr. Ingenieurschule, Esslingen, 1966; fachschulrat Berufsbildungswerk, Waiblingen, Germany, 1967-72; oberstudienrat Wirtschaftsgymnasium, Waiblingen, 1972-77; asst. U. Stuttgart, 1977-80; study dir. Studienseminar, Stuttgart, 1980-82; prof. psychology and rehab. U. Hamburg, Germany, 1982-95; prof. psychotherapy Theol. Hochschule Friedensau, 1995—; chmn. Deutsche Gesellschaft Biblisch Therapeutische Seelsorge, Kernen, Germany, 1987—; lectr. sci. Inst. for Practical Psychology, Zurich, Switzrland, 1987—, Institut for Psychologie and Counseling Frendenstadt. Author: Hamet, 1980, Foerderdiagnostik, 1986, Handbuch Psychologie und Seelsorge, 1989, Auf dem Wegzum Beruf, 1991, Persoenlichkeitsdiagnostik, 1996. Recipient prize Friends of U. Stuttgart, 1979, Bundesanstalt für Arbeit, 1983. Mem. Rotary. Home: Gartenstrasse 25, 78359 Nenzingen Germany Office: DGBTS, Hackstr 60, 70190 Stuttgart Germany

DIETERICH, RUSSELL BURKS, obstetrician, gynecologist; b. Springfield, Ill., May 9, 1943; s. Charles Russell and Irma Rebecca (Burks) D.; m. Lynn Ellen Heidinger (div. July 1976); 1 child, Kristen; m. Barbara Ann Browning (div. May 1990); children: Paula, Pamela, Patrick; m. Irene Lorraine Carroll, June 27, 1992; children: Kathleen Carroll, Jonathon Carroll. BA, Knox Coll., 1965; MD, U. Ill., 1970. Diplomate Am. Bd. Ob-Gyn., Nat. Bd. Med. Examiners. Intern Blodgett Meml. Hosp., Grand Rapids, Mich., 1970-71, residet, 1971-74; chief of staff ob-gyn. USAF Hosp., Whiteman AFB, 1975-76; chief ob-gyn. Barnes St. Peters (Mo.) Hosp., 1986-87; chief ob-gyn. St. Joseph Hosp., St. Charles, Mo., 1987-89, chief of staff, 1989-90; pres. Dieterich Ob/Gyn Assn., Inc., St. Charles, 1981-95; clin. instr. Sch. Medicine Mich. State U., 1973-74, Sch. Medicine Wash. U., St. Louis, 1988—; speakers bur. Syntex Labs.; adv. bd. Life Seekers, St. Charles. Prodr., condr. (mus. rec.) Sentimental Journey by Request, 1985. Bd. mgrs. St. Charles County YMCA, 1985—; internat. mem. Community YMCA, St. Charles, 1985—; bd. dirs. United Svcs. for the Handicapped, Inc., St. Charles, 1994—. Maj. USAF, 1974-76. Recipient Harvard Book prize Associated Harvard Clubs, 1960, Disting. Alumni award Sigma Nu. Fellow Am. Coll. Ob-Gyn. (presenter, Ephraim McDowell award 1974); mem. AMA, Internat. Soc. for Advancement of Humanistic Studies of Gynecology, Am. Assn. Gynecol. Laproscopists, Am. Fertility Soc., St. Louis Gynecol. Soc. Republican. Free Evangelical. Home: 6 Vicksburg Sta Saint Charles MO 63303-6143 Office: Heritage Ob-Gyn Assocs 2730 S Highway 94 Ste 202 Saint Charles MO 63303-5677

DIETERLE, STEFAN, obstetrician, gynecologist; b. Stuttgart, Germany, May 7, 1961; s. Klaus Hermann Karl and Elisabeth (Seufert) D.; m. Susanne Schmidt, July 1, 1988; children: Franziska, Anne-Sophie. Candidate in geneeskunde, U. Louvain, Belgium, 1982; MD, U. Bonn, Germany, 1988. Resident in ob/gyn. Med. Sch. Hannover, Germany, 1989-93; resident in ob/gyn. U. Bochum, Herne, Germany, 1993-94, specialist in reproductive endocrinology and infertility, 1995—. Author: Klinische Diagnose, 1994; contbr. articles to profl. jours. including Jour. Human Reproedn., Geburtshilfe Frauenheilk, Acta Obstet. Found. of German People scholar, 1982. Mem. Am. Soc. Reproductive Medicine, German Soc. Ob/Gyn., German Soc. Ultrasound in Medicine. Office: U Bochum Dept Ob/Gyn, Hoelkeskampring 40, D 44625 Herne Germany

DIETERT, RODNEY REYNOLDS, immunology and toxicology educator; b. Ft. Lee, Va., Dec. 6, 1951; s. Ralph O. and Beverly (Reynolds) D.; m. Margaret Flowers, May 24, 1975; children: Grant C., Matthew W. BS, Duke U., 1974; PhD, U. Tex., 1977. Asst. prof. immunogenetics Cornell U., Ithaca, N.Y., 1977-83, assoc. prof., 1983-89, prof., 1989—; adj. prof. N.C. State U., 1992—; head grad. program in immunology Cornell U., Ithaca, N.Y., 1989-92, dir. Inst. for Comparative and Environ. Toxicology, 1992—; sr. fellow Ctr. for the Environment, 1993—; cons. pesticide program EPA, Washington, 1984-86, Embrex, Inc., Research Triangle Park, N.C., 1991-95; panelist Nat. Inst. Environ. Health Scis. (AIDS Therapeutics), Research Triangle Park, 1988; USDA grant panel mgr., Washington, 1993-94; mem. Am. Inst. Biol. Scis.-Gulf War Illnesses panel Dept. Def., 1995; invited testimony U.S. Congress Clean Water Act, 1995; spkr. at profl. confs. Jour. editor CRC Press, Inc., Boca Raton, Fla., 1986-90, editor book series, 1990—; editor jour. Elsevier Sci. Publs., Ltd., Oxford, U.K., 1990-95; contbr. to profl. publs. Bd. dirs. Wesley Found., Ithaca, 1979-84; chmn. Minority Edn. Com., Ithaca, 1980; chmn. Environ. Com. on Native Americans, Ithaca, 1994-95. Mem. Am. Assn. Immunologists, Soc. Leukocyte Biology,

Soc. Toxicology. Office: Cornell U Inst Comparative Environ Toxicology 215 Rice Hall Ithaca NY 14853-5601

DIETHELM, ARNOLD GILLESPIE, surgeon; b. Balt., Jan. 13, 1932; s. Oskar Arnold and Grace (Gillespie) D.; m. Nancy Lee Lane, June 21, 1951; children: Nancy Elizabeth, Linda Lane, Eugene Arnold (dec.), Ellen Jeanette, Richard Gillespie. A.B., Wash. State U., 1953; M.D., Cornell U., 1958. Intern, then resident in surgery N.Y. Hosp., 1958-65; asst. in surgery, research fellow Peter Bent Brigham Hosp., Boston, 1965-66; research fellow surgery Harvard U. Med. Sch., 1966-67; instr. Cornell U. Med. Sch., 1964-65; mem. faculty U. Ala. Med. Center, Birmingham, 1967—; prof. surgery U. Ala. Med. Center, 1973—, vice chmn. dept., 1973-82, chmn. dept. surgery, 1982—. Contbr. articles med. jours. Mem. AAAS, ACS., AMA, Am. Soc. Nephrology, Am. Soc. Transplant Surgeons, Am. Surg. Assn., Am. Bd. Surgery (dir. 1987-93), Assn. Acad. Surgery, Transplantation Soc., So. Surg. Assn. Home: 3248 Sterling Rd Birmingham AL 35213-3508 Office: U Ala Hosp Dept Surgery 619 19th St S Birmingham AL 35233-1924

DIETRICH, ROSALIND, radiology educator; b. Burnley, Lancashire, Eng., July 28, 1953; came to U.S., 1979; d. John Robert and Thelma (Pownall) Brown; m. Anthony Paul Dietrich, Mar. 30, 1979 (div. 1988); m. William Guerin Bradley, Jr., Oct. 20, 1988; children: India Jane, Felicity Eliza. MD, U. Manchester (Eng.) Sch. Medicine, 1976. Diplomate Am. Bd. Radiology. Surg. house officer U. South Manchester, Eng., 1976-77, med. house officer, 1977; intern in radiology, medicine Cedars-Sinai Med. Ctr., L.A., 1979-80, resident in diagnostic radiology, 1980-84, fellow CT/Ultrasound, 1984; fellow in pediatric radiology UCLA, 1984-85, asst. prof. Radiology in residence, 1986-90, co-dir. residency tng. program, dept. Radiological Scis., 1986-88; assoc. prof. Radiology in residence, dir. MRI, fellowships, dept. Radiological Scis. U. Calif., Irvine, 1990—; lectr. in Anatomy, U. Manchester, England, 1977-78; vis. prof. Radiology UCLA, 1985-86; presenter numerous meetings, seminars, confs. Author: Magnetic Resonance Teaching File: Pediatric Radiology, 1991; contbr. articles to profl. jours., chpts. to books. Grantee Berlex Labs., Inc., 1987, Nat. Inst. Aging, 1989—, Squibb Labs., Inc., 1990, Calif. State Health Svcs., 1992-93; recipient cum laude award Am. Soc. Neuroradiology, 1986. Mem. Am. Coll. Radiology (com. edn. and tng. standards commn. magnetic resonance 1987-88, com. standards and accreditation commn. neuroradiology and magnetic resonance 1991—), Am. Roentgen Ray Soc. (cert. merit 1986, bronze medal award 1987), Assn. Am. Women Radiologists (com. corp. funding 1990-91, awards com. 1992—), Soc. Magnetic Resonance Imaging (core curriculum com. 1990—, summa cum laude award 1991), Soc. Magnetic Resonance in Medicine (core curriculum com. 1990—), Soc. Pediatric Radiology (com. computed tomography and magnetic resonance imaging. 1992—), Radiological Soc. N.Am. (cert. merit 1986), Calif. Radiological Soc. Home: 950 Laguna Rd Pasadena CA 91105-2250 Office: U Calif Irvine Med Ctr 101 The City Dr S Orange CA 92668-3201*

DIETRICH, TINA R., critical care nurse; b. Lansdale, Pa., Nov. 12, 1962; d. Francis M. and Anita C. (Moore) Russo; m. Gary J. Dietrich, May 2, 1987; 1 child, Jason Patrick. Diploma, St. Luke's Hosp. Sch. Nursing, Bethlehem, Pa., 1982; BSN, Duquesne U., 1990. RN, cert. critical care nurse. Staff nurse stepdown unit and ICU Suburban Gen. Hosp., Norristown, Pa.; staff nurse ICU, CCU, stepdown unit St. Luke's Hosp., Bethlehem; staff nurse in ICU Forbes Met. Health Ctr., Pitts.; nurse cons. Springhouse (Pa.) Book Co.; clin. instr. Lehigh County C.C., Schecksville, Pa.; nursing instr. Ivy Tech. State Coll., South Bend, Ind. Mem. Am. Assn. Critical Care Nurses. Home: 820 Patterson Dr Lansdale PA 19446

DIETSCHY, JOHN MAURICE, gastroenterologist; b. Alton, Ill., Sept. 23, 1932; s. John C. and Clara A. (Sahner) D.; m. Beverly A. Robertson, Apr. 18, 1959; children: John, Daniel, Michael, Karen. AB, Washington U., St. Louis, 1954; MD, Washington U. Sch. Medicine, St. Louis, 1958. Resident VA Hosp., Denver, 1959-61; asst. prof. internal medicine U. Tex. Southwestern Med. Ctr., Dallas, 1965-69; assoc. prof. internal medicine U. Tex. Southwestern Med. Ctr., 1969-71, prof. internal medicine, 1971—; mem. adv. bd. Okla. Med. Rsch. Found., Oklahoma City, 1988-92, Children's Hosp. Rsch. Found., Cin., 1990-95; chmn. adv. com. arteriosclerosis hypertension lipid metabolism NIH, 1989-90. Editor: Clinical Gastoenterology Monograph Series, 1976-85, The Science and Practice of Clinical Medicine, 1977-81, Disorders of the Liver, Nutritional Disorders, 1976; contbr. over 190 articles to profl. jours. NIH rsch. grantee, 1964—; Rsch. fellow Boston U., 1961-63, U. Tex. Southwestern Med. Ctr., 1963-65; Markle scholar Acad. Medicine, 1966-71; recipient Heinrich-Wieland prize Lipid Biochemistry, 1983, McKenna medal Can. Assn. Gastroenterology, 1985. Fellow AAAS (elected); mem. Am. Gastroen. Assn. (pres. 1987-88, Disting. Achievement award 1978), Am. Fedn. Clin. Rsch. (pres. So. sect. 1974-75), So. Soc. Clin. Investigation (pres. 1982). Roman Catholic. Office: U Tex SW Med Ctr 5323 Harry Hines Blvd Dallas TX 75235-8887

DIETZ, WILLIAM HARRY, pediatrician; b. Phila., Oct. 6, 1944; s. William H. and Margaret (Shoemaker) D.; m. Nancy Fenn, May 6, 1966; children: Jonathan, Sarah. BA, Wesleyan U., 1966; MD, U. Pa., 1970; PhD, MIT, 1981. Diplomate Am. bd. Pediatrics. Intern Children's Hosp. Phila., 1970-71; resident Upstate Med. Ctr., Syracuse, N.Y., 1974-76; rsch. assoc. NIH, 1971-74, MIT, Cambridge, 1976-81; assoc. prof. Tufts U. Sch. Medicine, Boston, 1986-96, prof., 1996—; dir. clin. nutrition New England Med. Ctr., Boston, 1983—. Fellow Am. Acad. Pediatrics (chmn. task force on children and TV, Elk Grove Village, Ill. 1984-87); mem. Am. Soc. Clin. Nutrition (counselor), N.Am. Assn. for Study of Obesity (pres.-elect 1992-93, pres. 1993-94). Office: New England Med Ctr Box 213 750 Washington St Boston MA 02111-1526

DIGGS, ORVILLE SYLVESTER, III, dentist; b. L.A., May 14, 1956; s. Orville Sylvester Jr. and Charlene (Smith) D.; m. Wilette C. Diggs, June 30, 1985. BS in Biol., U. Redlands, 1978; D in Dental Surgery, U. Calif., San Francisco, 1983. Extern dentist U. Calif. Dental Clinic, San Francisco, 1983-84; dental staff Kno Community Hosp., Tucson, 1985—; pvt. practice Tucson, 1986—; cons. Kno Med. Rec. Group, Tucson, 1988-89. Mem. NAACP, Am. Dental Assn., Am. Soc. Dentistry for Children, So. Ariz. Dental Soc., Humane Soc. Tucson, Tucson Urban League, Afro-Am. Male State Conf. (com. chmn.), Delta Sigma Delta, Kappa Alpha Psi. Democrat. Episcopalian. Office: Coronado Heights Med Dental Ctr 368 E Grant Rd Tucson AZ 85705-5725

DIGGS, WALTER WHITLEY, health science facilty administrator; b. Memphis, Tenn., June 8, 1932; s. Lemuel Whitley and Beatrice (Moshier) D.; m. Ann T. Thobae, Nov. 29, 1958; children: Jennie, Thomas, Andrew. BS, Washington and Lee U., 1954; MHA, U. Minn., 1956. Adminstrv. resident Stormont-Vail Hosp., Topeka, 1955-56; asst. dir. The Johns Hopkins Hosp., Balt., 1959-66; adminstr. Med. Coll. Ga. Hosp., Augusta, 1966-70; asst. prof. Med. Coll. Ga., Augusta, 1970-71, U. Tenn. and Memphis State U., 1971—; field rep. Joint Commn. Hosps., Chgo., 1981-88, 93—; supt. Memphis Mental Health Inst., 1987-93; cons. Tenn. Dept. Mental Health, 1993-95. Pres. Delta Found., Miss., 1987—, Ballet South, Memphis Ballet, Augusta Civic Ballet. Lt. USNR, 1956-59. Recipient Peter Cooper award, Unitarian Ch., Memphis, 1975, Forrest Fletcher, Washington and Lee, Lexington, Va., 1954. Fellow Am. Coll. Healthcare Execs. Home: 5282 Shady Grove Rd Memphis TN 38120-2404

DI GIACOMO, WILLIAM ARTHUR, internist; b. Newark, Aug. 28, 1948; s. William Henry and Eleanore Grey (Lowney) Di G.; B.S. in Biology, Fairfield U., 1970; M.D., Universidad Autonoma De Guadelajara (Mexico), 1974; m. Celine Pagano, Dec. 20, 1970; children—Scott, Brian, Kristen, Taylor. Intern in medicine St. Michael's Med. Center, Newark, 1975-76, resident in medicine, 1976-77, chief resident in medicine, 1977-78, clin. prof. medicine, 1980—, treas. med. staff, 1985-87, sec. med. staff, 1987—; practice medicine specializing in internal medicine, Newark, 1978—; assoc. prof. of medicine Seton Hall U., 1989—; mem. staff Vailsburg Med. Assos., 1978—, pres., 1980—; mem. staff St. Mary's Hosp., Orange, N.J., St. Michael's Med. Center, Columbus Hosp., Newark, Overlook Hosp., Summit, N.J. Named Resident of Yr., St. Michael's Med. Center, 1977; diplomate Am. Bd. Internal Medicine. Fellow Acad. Medicine N.J.; mem. ACP, N.J. Med. Soc., Essex County Med. Soc. Roman Catholic. Home: 25 Coniston Rd Short Hills NJ 07078-2201 Office: 1072 S Orange Ave Newark NJ 07106 also: 2801 Morris Ave Union NJ 07083

DIGIOVANNA, EILEEN LANDENBERGER, osteopathic physician, educator; b. Columbus, Ohio, Nov. 24, 1933; d. Bernard Holman and Della Belle (Crabtree) Landenberger; m. Joseph Anthony DiGiovanna, Apr. 4, 1959; children: Michael, Mark, Gina, Geri, Vicki, Matthew, Kimberly. Student, Ohio State U., 1952-55; DO, Chgo. Coll. Osteopathy, 1959. Pvt. practice Massapequa Park, N.Y., 1960-81; asst. prof., assoc. prof. N.Y. Coll. Osteo. Medicine, Old Westbury, 1977-91, prof., asst. dean student affairs, 1991—. Author, editor: (textbook) Osteopathic Approach to Diagnosis and Treatment, 1991; contbr. articles to profl. jours. Lay speaker Meth. Ch., N.Y., 1988—, chmn. adminstrn. bd. 1993—. Fellow Am. Acad. Osteopathy (trustee 1992-94, pres. 1994-95); mem. Am. Osteo. Assn. (Educator of Yr. 1995), Am. Coll. Family Practice. Republican. Office: NY Coll Osteo Medicine Old Westbury NY 11568

DIGIOVANNI, ANTHONY MICHAEL, physician, gastroenterologist; b. Detroit, Sept. 26, 1942; s. Michael Anthony and Agatha (Ciaramitaro) DiG.; m. Sharon Anne Sakuta, Aug. 22, 1964; children: Michael, Anthony, Joseph, James. BS in Chemistry, U. Detroit, 1964; DO, Chgo. Coll. Osteopathy, 1968. Mem. staff Bi-County Hosp., Warren, Mich., 1973—, vice chmn. internal medicine dept., 1975-78; sect. chief gastroenterology dept. William Beaumont Hosp., Troy, Mich., 1983—, chmn. endoscopy dept., 1983—; asst. clin. prof. Mich. State U., 1973—. Contbr. articles to profl. jours. U. Mich. fellow 1972-73. Fellow Am. Coll. Osteo. Internists; mem. Am. Osteo. Physicians, Mich. Assn. Osteo. Physicians and Surgeons, Am. Soc. Gastrointestinal Endoscopy, Mich. Soc. Gastroenterology (pres. 1978-79), Am. Gastroent. Assn. Roman Catholic. Office: 44199 Dequindre Rochester MI 48306-4504

DIGIOVANNI, JOAN FIMBEL, psychology educator; b. Jersey City, N.J., June 18, 1935; d. Albert Charles and Selma Caroline (Kugler) Fimbel; m. Philip DiGiovanni, June 23, 1956; children: Juliet Paula, Portia Jonquil. Student abroad, U. Miss., Europe, 1954; BA in Edn., Fla. So. Coll., 1954; MA in Psychology, Columbia U., 1955; PhD in Psychology, Baylor U., 1961. Lic. psychologist, elem. and sch. psychologist, Mass. Counselor women's residence halls, dean of women's office U. Ill., Champaign, 1955-57; teaching asst. psychology dept. Baylor U., Waco, Tex., 1958-61; asst. prof. psychology Old Dominion U. (formerly Norfolk Coll. of William and Mary), Norfolk, Va., 1961-63; rsch. asst. U. Mass., Amherst, 1963; asst. prof. psychology, coord. field work svcs. and rehab. Springfield (Mass.) Coll., 1963-65; dir. counseling svc., asst. prof. psychology Western New Eng. Coll., Springfield, 1966-73, prof. psychology, 1973—, chmn. dept. human studies, 1990-92; adj. prof. psychology Westfield State Coll., 1980—; rsch. assoc. U. Mass., Amherst, 1963; instr. Am. Internat. Coll., Springfield, 1963 vis. scholar Inst. Fine Arts, NYU, 1985, N.Y.U., 1988, U. N. Mex., Albuquerque, 1989; NEH scholar Mex. Colonial Act, U. N. Mex., summer, 1992. Presenter in field. Mem. APA (mem.-at-large div. Psychology of Art 1990—), Am. Soc. Psychopathology of Expression, Am. Assn. Women in Psychology, Mass. Psychol. Assn., New Eng. Psychol. Assn. (steering com. 1993—), Ea. Psychol. Assn., Internat. Coun. Psychologists, N.Mex. Psychoanalytic Assn., Psi Chi, Alpha Kappa Delta, Phi Theta Kappa. Unitarian Universalist. Office: Western New Eng Coll 1215 Wilbraham Rd Springfield MA 01119-2654

DIGMAN, STACIE WRIGHT, physician assistant; b. Charleston, W.Va., Mar. 20, 1962; d. Carl Homer and Carlita Jeane (Newcomer) Wright; m. Olivia Claire Digman, Nov. 29, 1986. BS in Med. Sci., Alderson-Broaddus Coll., Philippi, W.Va., 1984. Cert. physician asst. Physician asst. Dr. Richard H. Sibley Orthopaedic Assocs., Charleston, W.Va., 1984-94; physician asst. Surgery dept. St. Francis Hosp., Charleston, 1994—, CME coord. physician asst. dept., 1995—; instr. Coll. of W.Va., Berkley, W.Va., 1995. Fellow Am. Acad. Physician Assts., W.Va. Assn. Physician Assts. (treas. 1984—). Home: 1432 Wilkie Dr Charleston WV 25314 Office: St Francis Hospital Laidley St Charleston WV 25301

DI LEO, FRANCESCO BIAGIO, psychiatrist; b. Lecce, Puglie, Italy, Feb. 3, 1940; came to U.S., 1958; s. Salvatore and Anna (Bortone) Di L.; m. Cynthia Shobe, Oct. 2, 1979 (div. 1987); m. Theodora McFadden, May 13, 1988. BA, UCLA, 1963; D of Medicine, U. So. Calif., 1967. Diplomate Am. Bd. Psychiatry. Rotating internship Herrick Meml. Hosp., Berkeley, Calif., 1967-68; staff physician Kaiser Permanent Hosp., Vallejo, Calif., 1968-72; rsch. physician Md. Psychiat. Rsch. Ctr., Balt., 1972-75; psychiat. residence Sch. of Medicine U. Md., 1975-78; pvt. practice, researcher Balt., 1978-87; staff psychiatrist Springfield Hosp. Ctr., Sykesville, Md., 1987—. Contbr., co-contbr. articles on drug therapy rsch. to profl. publs. Mem. Phi Beta Kappa. Home: 421 Westgate Rd Baltimore MD 21229-2342

DILEO, KIMBERLY LOUISE, medical records supervisor; b. Feb. 23, 1968; d. Urban Anthony and Sandra Lee (Hubener) Kreppein; m. Eric michael DiLeo, Sept. 20, 1992; 1 child, Dominick Ernest. BS, Ithaca Coll., 1990. Registered record adminstr. Supr. med. records Women's Med. Care, Newburgh, N.Y., 1990—. Mem. Am. Health Info. Mgmt. Assn., N.Y. Health Info. Mgmt. Assn., Southeastern N.Y. Health Info. Mgmt. Assn., Ambulatory Care Section Am. Health Info. Mgmt. Assn.

DILEO, MARY ANGELA, psychiatric nurse; b. S.I., N.Y.; children: Joseph George, Jennifer. AAS in Nursing, SUNY, Delhi, 1988. Staff St. Joseph's By The Sea, 1965, Doctor's Hosp. of S.I., 1965-67; nurse, lab. technician for women, infants, children Del. Opportunities, Delhi, N.Y., 1990; staff nurse A.O. Fox Meml. Hosp., Oneonta, N.Y., 1991—. Tchr. Sun. Sch.; active in past in polit. campaigns. Mem. Phi Theta Kappa.

DILEONE, CARMEL MONTANO, dental hygienist; b. New Haven, Aug. 24, 1926; d. Nicholas and Martha (Ercolano) M.; m. Eugene Francis Dileone, Jan. 28, 1948; children: Gina, Richard. Dental Hygienist, Temple U., 1945; AA, Albertus Magnus Coll., 1980; BS, U. Bridgeport, 1983; MS, So. Conn. State U., 1985. Registered dental hygienist. Dental hygiene practitioner George M. Montano, DDS, New Haven, 1946-50; George V. Montano, DDS, 1959—; dental hygiene practitioner Francis R. Mullen, DDS, West Haven, 1950-55; dental hygiene practioner Herbert Saunders, DDS, Orange, Conn., 1958-63; instr. Huntington Inst., North Haven, Conn., 1983; adj. assoc. prof. U. Bridgeport, Conn., Fones Sch. Dental Hygiene, 1985-96; adj. lectr. U. New Haven, 1994—. Mem. APHA, Am. Soc. Dentistry for Children, Am. Dental Hygienist Assn., Conn. Dental Hygienists Assn. (treas. 1986-88, v.p. 1988-89, pres.-elect 1989-90, pres. 1991, Mabel C. McCarthy award 1983, Pres. award 1994). Roman Catholic. Home: 348 Racebrook Rd Orange CT 06477-3109 Office: George V Montano DDS 436 Whalley Ave New Haven CT 06511-3012

DI LISSIO, GLENYS JEAN, substance abuse counselor, prevention specialist; b. Mt. Holly, N.J., Aug. 3, 1948; d. Earl Ellis and Gwennyth (Wilford) Lippincott; m. Louis E. DiLissio, June 7, 1969; children: Jason, Joni. BA in Liberal Arts and Secondary Edn., Fairleigh Dickinson U., 1970. Lic. counselor, Pa.; cert. addictions counselor, prevention specialist. Substitute tchr. local sch. dists. Perry County, Pa., 1974-85; drug and alcohol prevention specialist, counselor Perry Human Svcs., New Bloomfield, Pa., 1984—. Mem. Tri-County chpt. MADD, Camp Hill, Pa., 1982—; mem. Pa. Student Assistance Program. Mem. Commonwealth Prevention Alliance, Am. Assn. Christian Counselors. Office: Perry Human Svcs PO Box 436 New Bloomfield PA 17068-0436

DILLE, JOHN ROBERT, physician; b. Waynesburg, Pa., Sept. 2, 1931; s. Charles Emanuel and Ruth Emma (South) D.; m. Joan Marie Sirtosky, Dec. 17, 1955; children: Paul Andrew, John Alan. BS, Waynesburg Coll., 1952; MD, U. Pitts., 1956; M in Indsl. Health, Harvard U., 1960. Diplomate Am. Bd. Preventive Medicine. Intern Akron City Hosp., 1956-57; resident in aerospace medicine USAF Sch. Aerospace Medicine, San Antonio, 1960-62; program adv. officer FAA Civil Aeromed. Rsch. Inst., Oklahoma City, 1961-64; western region flight surgeon FAA, L.A., 1965; chief FAA Civil Aeromed. Inst., U.S. Dept. Transp., Oklahoma City, 1966-87, ret., 1987; med. dir. Okla. Dept. Corrections, Oklahoma City, 1990-93; assoc. prof. U. Okla., 1961—, dir. tng. residency in aerospace medicine, 1967-72; state surgeon Okla. Army N.G., 1990-91. Assoc. editor: Ag Pilot Internat. mag., 1980—, Conservation Aeronautics mag., 1989-92, Above All mag., 1992; mem. editorial bd. Aviation, Space and Environ. Medicine; contbr. articles to profl. jours. With USAF, 1957-59; col. M.C., U.S. Army N.G., 1976-91. Recipient Meritorious award William A. Jump Found., 1968; named Army N.G. Flight Surgeon of Yr. 1987, Master Flight Surgeon, 1987. Fellow Aerospace Med. Assn. (mem. exec. coun. 1978-81, 93—, chmn. history and archives com. 1982-90, chmn. sci. program com. 1985, 1st v.p., 1990-91, pres. 1992-93, Theodore C. Lyster award 1978, Harry G. Moseley award 1987), Am. Coll. Preventive Medicine (regent 1974-77); mem. Internat. Acad. Aviation and Space Medicine, Soc. U.S. Army Flight Surgeons (mem. bd. govs. 1990-92, Order Aeromed. Merit), Am. Air Mail Soc. (bd. dirs. 1990-92), Sigma Xi, Nu Sigma Nu. Presbyterian. Home and Office: 335 Merkle Dr Norman OK 73069-6429

DILLENBACK, SCOTT J., health services company executive; b. Cooperstown, N.Y., Nov. 26, 1957; s. Seward John and Marian L. (Ehle) D.; m. Lynne S. Dillenback, Feb. 11, 1984. BA, Hamilton Coll., 1980. Mktg. mgr. YSI Inc., Yellow Springs, Ohio, 1988-89, product focus group mgr., 1989-90, gen. mgr. temperature products group, 1990-92; sales rep. CONMED Corp., Utica, N.Y., 1980-81, product mgr., 1981-85, group product mgr., 1985-88, mktg. mgr., 1992-93, mktg. dir., 1993-95, v.p. mktg., surg. sys., 1995—. Mem. Am. Mgmt. Assn., Med. Mktg. Assn., Delta Upsilon Alumni Corp. (treas. 1981, pres. 1982-84, v.p.). Office: CONMED Corp. 310 Broad St Utica NY 13501

DILLER, EMMELINE ANN, psychiatrist; b. N.Y.C., Dec. 11, 1955; d. Edmund Steven and Eugenia (Brand) D.; m. Michael Bradley Bader, Oct. 20, 1985; children: Caroline Sage, Jeremy Brandon, Jonah Lev. BA, Harvard, Radcliffe, Cambridge, 1977; MD, Harvard Med. Sch., 1982. Diplomate Am. Bd. Psychiatry and Neurology. Residency in psychiatry Cambridge Hosp., Harvard Med. Sch., Cambridge, Mass., 1982-86; pvt. practice Cambridge, 1986—; cons. psychiatrist Acton (Mass.) Mental Health Assn., 1986-88; clin. instr. in psychiatry Harvard Med. Sch., Boston, 1987—. Mem. Am. Psychiat. Assn., Mass. Psychiat. Assn. Office: 1105 Massachusetts Ave # 2D Cambridge MA 02138-4314

DILLIHAY, OTHA ROOSEVELT, hospital administrator; b. Montgomery, Ala., June 26, 1957; s. Charles Elliot Dillihay and Thelma R. (Wooden) Milton; m. Tanya Clarkson, Aug. 8, 1958; children: Kip, Elliot, Adam. BS, Morehouse Coll., Atlanta, 1979; BBA, S.C. State U., Orangeburg, 1988; MBA, Webster U., 1990. Bus. mgr. Crafts Farrow Hosp., Columbia, S.C., 1990-92, asst. adminstr., 1992-93; exec. asst. to state commr. S.C. Dept. Mental Health, Columbia, 1992; dir. hosp. mortgage ins. U.S. Dept. HUD, Washington, 1993-94; hosp. adminstr. Bryan Hosp., Columbia, 1994—. Mem. Pres.'s Cancer Panel, NIH, 1994; bd. dirs. Sickle Cell Found., Friendship Ctr. United Way. Exec. Leadership Inst. fellow, 1992; Project Blueprint fellow United Way Am., 1991. Fellow Am. Coll. Health Care Execs.; mem. Nat. Forum for Black Pub. Adminstrs. Office: Bryan Psychiat Hosp 220 Faison Dr Columbia SC 29209

DILLIN, JAKE THOMAS, JR., healthcare facility executive; b. Jonesboro, Ark., Aug. 19, 1945; s. Jake Thomas and Beatrice B. (Ervin) D.; m. Dec. 26, 1965 (div. Feb. 20, 1992); 1 child, Traci. BS in Chemistry and Biology, Fla. So. Coll.; MBA, Cen. Mich. U., 1982. Cert. Health Care Risk Mgr., Fla. Dir. dept. paramed. tng. Busi U. of Tampa, 1968-73; toxicologist, lab. mgr., v.p., bd. dirs. Drs. Lab. Svcs., Inc., Tampa, Fla., 1972-74; pres. Cen. Fla. Biols., Inc., Tampa and Orlando, Fla., 1974-76; dir. lab., pharmacies and mgmt. engring. Orlando Regional Med. Ctr., Inc., 1976-82; sr. v.p., chmn. governing bd. AMI Single Day Surgery, Ameri Med., Internat., 1982-86; pres., chmn. bd. dirs. Ambulatory Health Care Cons., Inc., 1986—; COO The Ophthalmic Group, 1990-95; exec. dir. Eye Surgery Facility Inc., 1993-95; credentialled cons. field surveyor Joint Commn. Accreditation Healthcare Orgns.; owner Tom Dillin Photography, 1969-72; adj. clin. faculty U. Ctrl. Fla. One-man photographic shows at Tampa Photo, Holiday Hosp., Tampa and Orlando. Mem. Orlando Choral Soc. Messiah Chorus, 1977-90, Bach Music Festival, Rollins Coll.; pres., bd. dirs., coach gymnastics team Lakemont YMCA, 1975-76. Mem. Med. Electronics and Data Soc., Soc. Biomed. Equipment Technicians, Hosp. Mgmt. Sys. Soc., Nat. Health Lawyers Assn., Am. Assn. Clin. Chemists (Recognition award 1978), Am. Soc. Law and Medicine, Am. Soc. Quality Control, Internat. Soc. Blood Transfusion (Paris), Clin. Lab. Mgmt. Assn., Assn. Drug Detection Labs., Soc. Human Resource Mgmt., Am. Soc. Ophthalmic Adminstrs., Fla. Soc. Ophthalmic Adminstrs. (founding mem.), U. South Fla. Men's Glee Club, Masons, Jaguar Club Fla. (founder). Home: 3104 N Kinyon Ave Tampa FL 33603-5336

DILLON, JOHN B., medical educator; b. San Benito, Tex., Oct. 11, 1911; s. John Harper and Lillian (Mitchell) D. M.D., St. Louis U., 1943. Intern Wis. Gen. Hosp., Madison, 1943; cons. anesthesiology Huntington Meml. Hosp., Pasadena, Calif., 1943-46; chief anesthesia service Los Angeles County Hosp., 1946-51, cons., 1951—; asso. clin. prof. surg. anesthesiology U. So. Calif. Med. Sch., 1946-51; mem. faculty U. Calif. at Los Angeles Med. Sch., 1950—, prof., chief anesthesiology, 1953-71, prof., chmn. dept., 1971-73; asst. dean U. Calif. at Los Angeles Med. Sch. (Med. Sch.), 1966-73; field rep. Joint Commn. on Accreditation Hosps., 1979-82, cons., 1980—; cons. anesthesiology Harbor Gen. Hosp., Torrance, Calif., Olive View Sanitarium, San Fernando, Calif., VA Hosp., San Fernando, Cedars of Lebanon Hosp., Los Angeles, St. John's Hosp., Santa Monica, Calif.; cons. Am. Arbitration Assn., 1979—. Bd. dirs. Kauai Found. for Continuing Edn., 1989—. John B. Dillon, M.D. Professorship established in his honor Dept. Anesthesiology, UCLA Sch. Medicine, 1992. Fellow ACP; mem. AMA (mem. coun. on assemblies 1970—, chmn. com. emerging health manpower 1971-72, past ho. of dels.), Am. Soc. Anesthesiology, Rotary (pres. elect Poipu Beach, Hawaii 1991). Home: PO Box 759 Koloa HI 96756-0759

DILLON, SALLY PIERSON, nursing educator; b. St. Joseph, Mich., Oct. 4, 1959; d. Donald Richard and Elizabeth Louise (Collins) Pierson; m. Bruce Arthur Dillon, Nov. 28, 1979; children: Donald Bruce, Michael Charles. AS, So. Missionary Coll., 1979; BS in Health Care Adminstrn., Columbia Union Coll., 1990. RN, Ill.; CCRN. Float nurse Mercy Med. Ctr., Chgo.; staff nurse critical care unit Meth. Med. Ctr., Peoria, Ill.; staff nurse-open heart Washington Adventist Hosp., Takoma Park, Md., asst. head nurse coronary care, critical care instr., 1992; asst. v.p. nursing Shenandoah County Meml. Hosp., Woodstock, Va., 1994; pres. BSJ Assocs., Timberville, Va.; freelance writer; instr., instr. trainer ARC; field supr. Pvt. Nurses Registry, Wilmette, Ill. Mem. AACN, Nat. Nurses Staff Devel. Orgn. (pres. Blue Ridge chpt.).

DILLWORTH, JUDY LYNNE, critical care nurse; b. N.Y.C., Nov. 1, 1959; d. Robert S. and Irene (Kropf) D. BSN, Adelphi U., Garden City, N.Y., 1980; MA in Nursing Adminstrn. Exec., Columbia U., 1989. CCRN, CNA certs., BCLS instr., ACLS, PALS. Staff nurse cardiothoracic and surg. ICU/trauma ctr. N.Y. Hosp. Cornell Med. Ctr., N.Y.C., 1980-82, sr. staff nurse, 1982-84; nurse clinician N.Y. Hosp. Cornell Med. Ctr., 1984-85; nurse mgr. surg. ICU/Trauma Ctr., 1985—, nurse mgr. surg. ICU/Trauma Ctr. and emergency dept., 1994-95. Mem. AACN, Am. Orgn. Nurse Execs., Soc. Critical Care Medicine, Sigma Theta Tau. Home: 19808 Mclaughlin Ave Holliswood NY 11423-1308

DILTZ, EMILY ANN, cardiologist; b. Indpls., June 2, 1951; d. James A. and Betty (Field) D.; m. Thomas W.D. Baird, Aug. 23, 1986; 1 child, Lindsay A. Baird. BS, Purdue U., 1973; MD, Tufts U., Boston, 1981. Intern in internal medicine U. Mich., Ann Arbor, 1981-82, resident in internal medicine, 1982-84, fellow in cardiology, 1984-87; cardiologist W.A. Foote Hosp., Jackson, Mich., 1987-89; clin. instr. U. Mich., Ann Arbor, 1987-89; cardiologist St. Francis Hosp., Beech Grove, Ind., 1990-94, Trinity Med. Ctr., Carrollton, Tex., 1994-96, Lewisville (Tex.) Med. Ctr., 1994-96, Ft. Sanders Hosp., Knoxville, Tenn., 1996—. Fellow Am. Coll. Cardiology; mem. AMA, Am. Soc. Nuclear Medicine, Am. Soc. Echocardiography. Home: 1436 Springpointe Way Knoxville TN 37931 Office: Cardiology Assocs East Tenn Medical Center Knoxville TN 37931

DILUOFFO, SANTINA, chiropractor; b. Yonkers, N.Y., Aug. 29, 1958; d. Leone and Anna (Lanzara) DiL. BS in Biology, Mercy Coll., Dobbs Ferry, N.Y., 1980; D Chiropractic, N.Y. Chiropractic Coll., 1986. Pvt. practice Hempstead, N.Y., 1986—, Glen Cove, N.Y., 1988—; lectr. on chiropractic to pub. schs. and chs. Hempstead Police Dept., 1988—; promoter growing up drug free U.S. Dept. Edn., Washington, 1992—; apptd. to perform scoliosis screenings to Hempstead Pub. Schs.; Amway distbr. Active contbr. Father

Flanagan's Boys' Home. Mem. MADD. Office: 33 Front St Hempstead NY 11550-3601

DILWORTH, EDWIN EARLE, retired obstetrician, gynecologist; b. Jasper, Ala., June 28, 1914; s. Tranny and Bertie (Caldwell) D.; m. Neida May Humphrey, June 17, 1939; children: John Edwin, Robert Earle, Nancy. AB, U. Ala., 1936; MD, Tulane U., 1940. Diplomate Am. Bd. Ob-Gyn. Intern, then resident in ob-gyn. Shreveport (La.) Charity Hosp., 1940-44; pvt. practice Shreveport, 1959-60; chief ob-gyn. Schumpert Meml. Med. Ctr., 1951, pres. staff, 1954; chief ob-gyn. Confederate Meml. Med. Ctr. (now La. State U. Med. Ctr.), Shreveport, 1954-76, pres. staff, 1959; clin. prof. ob-gyn. La. State U., Shreveport, 1967-90, prof. emeritus, 1990—. Contbr. articles to profl. jours. Head med. divsn. Shreveport United Way, 1972. Capt. M.C., AUS, 1944-46. Recipient Disting. Svc. award Shreveport Med. Soc., 1980. Fellow ACOG (founding), ACS; mem. Cen. Assn. Ob-Gyn., Southeastern Assn. Ob-Gyn., So. Gynecol. and Obstet. Soc., Shreveport Photog. Soc. Home: 660 Thora Blvd Shreveport LA 71106-1822

DIMANT, JACOB, internist; b. Rehovot, Israel, Apr. 27, 1947; came to U.S., 1972, naturalized, 1977; s. Simcha and Ita D.; m. Rose Bea Jearolmen, Sept. 11, 1974. MD, Hebrew U., Jerusalem, 1972. Diplomate Am. Bd. Internal Medicine and Rheumatology and Geriatric Medicine, Am. Bd. Quality Assurance and Utilization Rev. Physicians. Intern Maimonides Med. Ctr., Bklyn., 1972-73; resident in medicine Maimonides Med. Ctr., 1973-75; chief resident in medicine Maimonides Med. Ctr., Bklyn., 1975-76; fellow in rheumatology Downstate Med. Ctr., Bklyn., 1976-78; practice medicine specializing in internal medicine and rheumatology Bklyn., 1975—; dir. rheumatology Maimonides Med. Ctr., Bklyn., 1978-89, assoc. dir. med. edn., 1978-80; med. dir. Clove Lakes Nursing Home, Staten Island, N.Y., 1985—; med. dir. Prospect Park Nursing Home, Bklyn., 1977-87, Crown Nursing Home, Bklyn., 1983—, Hillside Manor Nursing Ctr., Queens, N.Y., 1993—; pres. Crown Nursing Home Assocs., Inc., Bklyn., 1989—; asst. prof. medicine SUNY, Bklyn., 1978—. Contbr. articles to profl. jours. Named hon. police surgeon N.Y.C. Police Dept., 1982; fellow Arthritis Found. of N.Y., 1977-78. Fellow ACP; mem. Am. Geriatric Soc., Am. Med. Dirs. Assn. (bd. dirs. 1995-97), N.Y. Med. Dirs. assn. (pres. 1994-96). Office: Crown Nursing Home 3457 Nostrand Ave Brooklyn NY 11229-5131

DIMARIA, ROSE ANN, nursing educator; b. Bronx, N.Y., Nov. 14, 1964; d. Angelo and Julia (Ingenito) DiM. BSN cum laude, Hunter Coll., 1986, MS in Nursing, 1990; postgrad., NYU, 1991—. RN, N.Y.; cert. nutrition support nurse. Staff nurse gen. surgery unit Bronx Mcpl. Hosp. Ctr., 1986-87, staff nurse SICU/burn unit, 1987-89, nutrition nurse clinician, 1989-93, asst. DON surg. critical care, 1993-95; lectr. Sch. Nursing W.Va. U., 1995—. Mem. AACN, Am. Soc. Parenteral and Enteral Nutrition, N.Y. State Nurses Assn., W.Va. State Nurse Assn., W.Va. Soc. for Parenteral and Enteral Nutrition, N.Y. Acad. Sci., N.Y.C. Soc. Parenteral and Enteral Nutrition (pres. 1992-93),.

DIMASI, LINDA GRACE, epidemiologist; b. Trenton, N.J., Feb. 7, 1949; d. Nick and Pearl LaVerne (White) D. BS in Biology, Alderson-Broaddus Coll., 1970; MPA, Rutgers U., 1992. Cert. pub. mgr. Field rep. N.J. State Dept. of Health, Trenton, 1971-85, epidemiologist, 1985—. Contbr. articles to profl. jours. Mem. ASPA, APHA, Phi Alpha Alpha. Home: 35 Jennifer Ln Burlington NJ 08016-1144 Office: NJ State Dept of Health Div AIDS Prevention/Control CN 363 Trenton NJ 08625-0363

DIMATTEO, MARYANNE ROBIN, psychology educator; b. Boston, Mar. 26, 1952; d. Joseph P. and Angeline DiM.; m. Michael J. Esnard; 1 child. BS, Tufts U., 1972; MA, Harvard U., 1974, PhD, 1976. Lic. psychologist, Calif. Asst. prof. psychology U. Calif., Riverside, 1976-81, assoc. prof., 1981-86, prof., 1986—, chair dept. psychology, 1994—; resident cons. RAND Corp., Santa Monica, Calif., 1988—. Author: Achieving Patient Compliance, 1982, The Psychology of Health, Illness & Medical Care, 1991. W.K. Kellogg fellow, 1976. Fellow Am. Psychol. Assn., Am. Psychol. Soc. Office: U Calif Dept Psychology Riverside CA 92521

DIMEN, MURIEL VERA, psychoanalyst; b. N.Y.C., Sept. 24, 1942; d. Alfred and Dora (Zauzmer) D.; m. Seth L. Schein, Sept. 16, 1965 (div. Aug. 25, 1980). BA, Barnard Coll., 1964; MA, Columbia U., 1966, PhD, 1970; cert., NYU, 1983. Asst. prof. Lehman Coll., Bronx, N.Y., 1970-75, assoc. prof., 1975-81; prof. Lehman Coll., Bronx, 1981-88; pvt. practice N.Y.C., 1979—; mem. faculty Nat. Inst. for Psychotherapies, 1989-90; clin. prof. psychology postdoctoral program NYU, 1991—; mem. faculty Derner Inst. Adelphi U., 1993—; co-dir. seminar in sexual difference and psychoanalysis, N.Y. Inst. for Humanities, 1986. Author: The Anthropological Imagination, 1977, Surviving Sexual Contradictions, 1986; co-editor: Regional Variation in Modern Greece, 1976; book rev. editor: Psychoanalytic Dialogues: A Journal of Relational Perspectives; assoc. editor: Gender and Psychoanalysis: An Interdisciplinary Journal. Fellow Am. Anthrop. Assn., N.Y. Inst. for Humanities; mem. APA, Psychoanalytic Soc. Office: 3 E 10th St New York NY 10003-5916

DI MENZA, SALVATORE, psychologist; b. Chgo., May 2, 1938; s. Salvatore and Bartalomea (Gallina) diM. A.B., DePaul U., 1960, M.A., 1964; postgrad. Loyola U., 1961-64, Ill. Inst. Tech., 1964, 68-72. Dir. research Ill. Drug Abuse Program, Chgo., 1972-73; dir. mgmt. systems Ill. Drug Abuse Program, 1973; dir. drug abuse div. Joint Commn. Accreditation of Hosps., Chgo., 1973-76, assoc. program dir. for planning and devel., 1976-78; mng. partner Health Resources Mgmt. Systems, Chgo., 1978-80; pres. AGI, Rolling Meadows, Ill., 1981-84; v.p. J.W. Crawford Assos., Inc., Chgo., 1979-80; research and eval. cons. Cook County Research and Eval. Project, Inc., Chgo., 1985-86; spl. asst. to dir., Nat. Inst. on Drug Abuse, Rockville, Md., 1986-89; acting dep. dir. Office of Treatment Improvement, Rockville, 1990-91; dir. spl. projects group Substance Abuse and Mental Health Svcs. Adminstrn., 1991-92; policy analyst Office of Nat. Drug Control, 1992-93; pres. Rehabilitation Systems, Inc., 1993-95; instrnl. asst. Wayne State U., Detroit, 1995—; cons. bus. formation and mgmt.; developer nat. standards for providing drug abuse treatment svcs., also large scale employee assistance programs and mental health svcs. for industry, drug abuse policies, clin. mgmt. systems. Recipient Superior Achievement award State of Ill., 1972, Spl. Recognition award Office Asst. Sec. Health, 1992, Recognition award Dept. Alcoholism and Substance Abuse, 1995. Contbr. articles to profl. jours. Home: 2837 S Princeton Ave Chicago IL 60616-2609

DIMICK, ALAN ROBERT, surgeon, educator; b. Birmingham, Ala., Sept. 30, 1932; s. Daniel Baker and Jennie Rose (Coplon) D.; m. Eleanor Hamilton, July 17, 1954 (div. May, 1987); children—Susan Elaine, Robert Marshall, Richard Neil; m. Ida Martha Reed, Jan. 27, 1988. B.S., Birmingham So. Coll., 1953; M.D., Med. Coll. Ala., 1958. Diplomate Am. Bd. Surgery. Intern, U. Ala. Hosps., Birmingham, 1958-59, resident, 1959-63; assoc. prof. surgery U. Ala.-Birmingham, 1963-90, prof., 1970—; dir. Burn Ctr., U. Ala. Hosps., 1986-89; chmn. adv. com. Emergency Med. Services City of Birmingham, 1967—; asst. chief staff U. Ala. Hosp., 1993—. chmn. adv. bd. Emergency Med. Services, State of Ala., 1972-87. Recipient Service to Mankind award Birmingham Sertoma Club, 1981. Mem. Med. Assn. State of Ala. (Samuel Buford Word award 1978), AMA (com. on emergency med. services 1974-89, chmn. 1977-78), Am. Burn Assn. (pres. 1978), Am. Coll. Surgeons, Southeastern Surg. Congress, Am. Assn. for Surgery of Trauma, Surg. Infection Soc., N.Am. Burn Soc. (pres. 1984-85), Wound Healing Soc., So. Surgical Assn., Alpha Omega Alpha. Contbr. publs. to profl. lit. Home: 2717 Lockerbie Cir Birmingham AL 35223-2911 Office: Dept Surgery University Station Birmingham AL 35294

DIMINO, WILLIAM JOSEPH, optometrist; b. Norristown, Pa., Apr. 5, 1955; s. Barney and Lena Frances (Indelicato) DiM.; m. Deborah Jean Yoder, Feb. 4, 1978; 1 child, Adrienne. OD, Pa. Coll. Optometry, 1990. Lab. asst. Wyeth Pharm. Co., Radnor, Pa., 1979-85; rsch. asst. Smith Kline Beecham, Paoli, Pa., 1985-86; with Pa. Coll. Optometry, 1986-90; pvt. practice Norristown, Pa., 1992—. Mem. Am. Optometric Assn., Pa. Optometric Assn., Bux-Mont. Optometric Soc. Roman Catholic.

DIMITRI, ELIA CHARLES, medical educator; b. Jenkins, Ky., Aug. 29, 1936; s. Charles Z. and Sofia (Kosova) D.; m. Candace Love, Feb. 14, 1963; children: George E., Sara C., C. Robert. BA, East Tenn. State Coll., 1958; MD, U. Tenn., 1960; MPH, U. N.C., 1978. Diplomate Am. Bd. Pediatrics. Intern Nashville Gen. Hosp., Nashville, 1961; U.S. Army Tripler Gen. Hosp. U.S. Army, Honolulu, 1961-62; pediatric resident Vanderbilt U. Hosp., Nashville, 1964-66; fellow in child psychiatry Children's Hosp. Med. Ctr., Boston, 1966-67; asst. prof. Pediatrics U. Va. Sch. Medicine, Charlottesville, 1967-70; pediatrician Reynolds Meml. Hosp., Winston-Salem, N.C., 1970-72; pediatric cons. N.C. Div. Health Svcs., Winston-Salem, 1972-81; assoc. prof. Family Practice and Community Medicine U. Tex. Southwestern Med. Sch., Dallas, Wichita Falls, Tex., 1981—; dir. pediat. edn. Family Practice Residency Program, Wichita Falls, 1981—; assoc. med. dir. Wichita Falls City/County Health Dept., 1987—; assoc. program dir. Wichita Falls Family Practice Residency, 1992—; children with spl. health care needs adv. com. Tex. Dept. Health, 1995—. Bd. dirs. 1st Step Inc. Battered Women's Shelter, Wichita Falls, 1987-90; mem. Sexual Abuse Team, 1987—; mem. Child Death Rev. Team, Wichita County, 1995—. Capt. U.S. Army, 1961-64. Fellow Am. Acad. Pediat.; mem. AMA, APHA, Tex. Pediat. Soc. (chmn. membership com. 1987-94), Tex. Med. Assn., Ambulatory Pediat. Assn., Wichita County Med. Soc. Home: 4506 Barbados St Wichita Falls TX 76308-4931

DIMMITT, CORNELIA, psychologist, educator; b. Boston, Mar. 16, 1938; d. Harrison and Martha Fredericka (Read) D.; m. (div.); children: Colin Barclay Church, Jeffrey Harrison Church. BA, Harvard U., 1958; MA, Columbia U., 1966; PhD, Syracuse U., 1970; diplomate, C. G. Jung Inst., Zurich, Switzerland, 1985. Asst. prof. Am. U., Washington, 1970-71; from asst. to assoc. prof. (with tenure) Georgetown U., Washington, 1971-82; pvt. practice Boston, 1985—; Mem. admissions com. Coll. Arts and Scis., Georgetown U., Washington, 1974-76, mem. rank and tenure com., 1977-78; dir. admissions com. C. G. Jung Inst., Boston, 1986-89, pres. tng. bd., 1989-91; pres. NESJA, 1993—. Author: Classical Hindu Mythology, 1978. NEH fellow, 1979-80. Mem. Am. Oriental Soc., New England Soc. Jungian Analysts, Assn. Grads. in Analytical Psychology (Switzerland), Internat. Assn. for Analytical Psychology. Home and Office: 4 Otis Pl Boston MA 02108-1036

DINERMAN, MIRIAM, social work educator; b. N.Y.C., Apr. 13, 1925; d. Abraham J. and Frances (Shostac) Goldforb; m. Harold Dinerman, June 12, 1951 (dec. June 1976); children: David, Ellen, Ruth. BA with honors, Swarthmore Coll., 1945; MSW, Columbia U., 1949, D Social Work, 1972. Youth dir. Jewish Assn. for Neighborhood Ctrs., N.Y.C., 1949-50, program dir., 1951-54; various social work partime positions, 1955-60; asst. prof. Rutgers U. Grad. Sch. Social Work, New Brunswick, N.J., 1961-72, assoc. prof., 1972-76, prof., 1976—, asst. dean for acad. planning, 1973-75, assoc. dean, 1975-81, acting dean, 1978, chmn. health care sequence, mem. New Brunswick faculty coun., 1989-93, chair, 1991-92; dir. PhD program Rutgers U. Sch. Social Work, New Brunswick, N.J., 1992—; mem. grants rev. panel Office Human Devel. Svcs., HHS, 1986-90; cons. on health and social svcs. N.J. Legis. Task Force on 21st Century; mem. task force on standard of need N.J. Divsn. Econ. Assistance, 1989-91; manuscript rev. editor Longman's Press, Methuen Press; dir. Ctr. for Internat. and Comparative Social Work, 1977—. Editor: Social Work Futures, 1983; mem. editl. bd. Affilia: Jour. Women and Social Work, 1985-94, 95—, book rev. editor., 1995—; contbr. articles to profl. jours., chpts. to books. Bd. dirs. Def. for Children Internat., 1980-88. Grantee NIMH, 1966-67, Rutgers U. Rsch. Coun. and Samuel Silberman Fund, 1979-80. Mem. NASW (chpt. pres. 1984-86, nat. com. on nominations and leadership identification 1988—, mem. editl. com. 1991-95), AAUP (N.J. task force on health care policy), Acad. Cert. Social Workers, Internat. Assn. Schs. Social Work (bd. dirs., agt. 1988-95), Coun. on Social Work Edn. (program planning com. 1984-89, edn. policy and planning commn. 1989-94), Group for Advancement of Doctoral Edn. (sec. steering com. 1990—). Home: 353 W 29th St New York NY 10001-4784 Office: Rutgers U Sch Social Work 536 George St New Brunswick NJ 08901-1167

DINGFELDER, STEVEN PETER, clinical psychologist, mental health service administrator; b. Mpls., May 9, 1944; s. Sigbert and Elizabeth (Neu) D.; B.A., U. Minn., 1966; M.A., Ind. State U., 1968, Ph.D., 1971; cert. mental health adminstrn. U. Minn., 1981; m. Claire Elaine Shechter, Dec. 19, 1965; children—Jennifer Ann, Scott Allen, Heidi Lynn. Psychologist, Moore-Porter Evaluation Clinic, Terre Haute, Ind., 1968; sch. psychologist Vigo County (Ind.) Sch. Corp., Terre Haute, 1969-70; clin. psychologist Katherine Hamilton Mental Health Ctr., Terre Haute, 1970-72, program dir., 1972-74; chem. dependency coordinator No. Pines Unified Services Ctr., Cumberland, Wis., 1973-77; exec. dir. Sandhills Mental Health Devel. Found., 1980-83; adj. prof. psychology Ind. State U., Terre Haute, 1972, adj. prof. U. Minn., 1981—; cons. psychologist Gibault Sch. for Boys, Terre Haute, 1974; area dir. Sandhills Mental Health Ctr., Pinehurst, N.C., 1977-83; pres., practitioner Growth Inst., Inc., Pinehurst, 1982-83; dir. Matanzas Bay Pavilion for Health Resources, St. Augustine, Fla., 1983-84. pvt. practice, St. Augustine, 1984—; pres. Enrichment Tng. Assocs., 1985—, Prestige Counseling, 1986—, Apogee/Prestige Counseling, 1995—. Mem. Ind. Gov.'s Adv. Council on Alcohol and Drug Abuse, 1974; treas. St. John's Interagy. Council, 1983-85. Recipient Becker award Ind. State U., 1968. Mem. Am. Psychol. Assn., Ind. Psychol. Assn. (chmn. div. sch. psychology 1973-74), Fla. Psychol. Assn. (pres. elect northeast chpt. 1987-88, pres. 1988—), Ind. Assn. Counselors Alcohol and Drug Abuse (v.p. 1973-74), Wis. Assn. Community Human Services Program, Wis. Assn. Chem. Abuse Coordinators (chmn. 1976), Area Dirs. Assn. N.C. (sec.-treas. 1979, v.p. 1982), Lambda Psi Sigma, Phi Delta Kappa. Office: Prestige Counseling Ste A 9 Saint Johns Medical Pk Dr Saint Augustine FL 32086-5343

DINH, ANTHONY TUNG, internist; b. Jan. 1, 1938; s. Hoan B. and Phieu T. (Nguyen) D.; m. Lisa L. Tran, Jan. 8, 1971; children: Andrew A., Thomas A. BS, U. Saigon, Vietnam, 1959, MD, 1967. Diplomate Am. Bd. Internal Medicine, Am. Bd. Infectious Disease, Am. Bd. Med. Microbiology. Intern in internal medicine Phila. Gen. Hosp., 1976-77; resident in internal medicine Wayne State U., 1977-79; fellow in infectious diseases U. Pa., 1979-81; asst. prof. U. Saigon, 1970-75; chief infectious disease VA Med. Ctr., Beckley, W.Va., 1981-82, chief med. svc., 1982-85, chief staff, 1985—; adj. clin. prof. medicine W.Va. Sch. Osteopathic Medicine, Lewisburg, 1987—; cons. in infectious disease. Contbr. articles to profl. jours. Mem. ACP, N.Y. Acad. Scis., Am. Soc. Microbiology, Raleigh County Med. Soc. (chmn. continuing med. edn. 1987—), W.Va. State Med. Assn. Office: Beckley Med Arts 2401 S Kanawha St Beckley WV 25801-6900

DINMAN, BERTRAM DAVID, consultant, retired aluminum company executive; b. Phila., Aug. 9, 1925; s. Meyer and Minnie (Kaufman) D.; m. Gabrielle Stamm, June 11, 1950; children: Stefanie, Jonathan David, Emily, Joshua. Student, Temple U., 1944, 46-51, MD, 1951; ScD, U. Cin., 1957. Asst. prof. to prof. Ohio State U. Coll. Medicine, 1957-65; prof., dir. Inst. Indsl. Health, U. Mich. Sch. Pub. Health, 1965-73; corp. med. dir. Aluminum Co. Am., Pitts., 1973-78, v.p. health and safety, 1978-87; clin. prof. dept. environ. and occupational health U. Pitts., 1987—; trustee Am. Bd. Preventive Medicine, vice chmn., 1976-85; cons. U.S. Army, USN, WHO; mem. U.S. del. ILO, 1980-81, 84-85; vis. fellow Green Coll. U. Oxford, 1986-92. Served with C.E. U.S. Army, 1944-46. Fellow Am. Coll. Occupl. and Environ. Medicine (A.G. Kammer Merit in authorship award 1972, S. Knudsen award 1988, Health Achievement in Occupl. Medicine award 1992); mem. Permanent Commn. and Internat. Assn. Occupational Health (dir., emeritus), Am. Acad. Occupational Medicine (pres. 1973-74, Kehoe award, G. H. Gehrmann Lectr. 1982). Club: Faculty U. Pitts. Home: 4710 Bayard St Pittsburgh PA 15213-1708 Office: Dept Occuaptional and Environ Health U Pitts Pittsburgh PA 15261

DINNEBECK, JAMES DOUGLAS, optometrist; b. Boulder, Colo., Dec. 2, 1960; s. James Edward and Edith Jean Dinnebeck; m. Mildred Ivonne Lopez, June 18, 1994. BS, Colo. State U., 1984; OD, U. Houston, 1992. Diplomate Nat. Bd. Optometric Examiners; lic. optometrist, Colo., Tex. Pvt. practice Ft. Collins, Colo., 1992-94, Longmont, Colo., 1995—. Author: (with others) Efferent Tidings, 1993. Mem. Am. Optometric Assn., Colo. Optometric Assn., Tex. Optometric Assn., Fellowship Christian Optometrists, Sigma Lambda Chi. Baptist. Home: 333 23d Ave # C3 Longmont CO 80501

DINNER, MELVYN IVAN, plastic surgeon; b. Johannesburg, South Africa, Nov. 28, 1942; naturalized 1982; s. Michael and Anne (Levenstein) D.; m. Wendy Green, Dec. 16, 1964; children: Nicole, Grant. MB, BCh, Med. Sch. U. Witwatersrand, 1965. Diplomate Am. Bd. Plastic Surgery. Intern in surgery Johannesburg Group Tchg. Hosps., South Africa, 1966; intern in medicine Gen. Hosp. Johannesburg, 1966; sr. intern in surgery/orthopedics South African Base Mil. Hosp., Pretoria, 1967; sr. intern casualty/trauma Gen. Hosp. Johannesburg, 1967; registrar plastic surgery Gen. Hosp. and Transvaal Meml. Hosp. Children, Johannesburg, 1969; registrar gen. surgery Johannesburg Tchg. Hosps., 1970-71; fellow head & neck surgery Rosewell Park Meml. Inst., 1973; sr. cons. plastic surgery Johannesburg Gen. Hosp., 1974; pvt. practice plastic surgery Johannesburg, 1975-83, Cleve., 1983—; clin. asst. prof. Johannesburg Gen. Hosp., 1975-76; staff Cleve. Clinic Found., 1976-77, chmn. dept. plastic surgery, 1977-83; dir. Breast Care Ctr., Cleve.; asst. prof. Case Western Res. U., Cleve. Fellow Royal Coll. Surgeons (Edinburgh), Royal Coll. Surgeons (London), Royal Coll. Surgeons (Can.), Am. Coll. Surgeons; mem. AMA, Am. Assn. Plastic Surgeons, Am. Soc. Plastic and Reconstructive Surgeons, Am. Soc. Aesthetic Plastic Surgery, Br. Soc. Surgery of Hand, Br. Soc. Plastic Surgeons, Lipolysis Soc. N.Am., South African Soc. Pediatric Surgeons, South African Soc. Surgery of the Hand, Soc. Plastic and Reconstructive Surgeons of South Africa, Ohio Valley Soc. Plastic and Reconstructive Surgeons, Ohio State Med. Assn., Northeast Ohio Soc. Plastic and Reconstructive Surgeons, Cleve. Soc. Plastic Surgeons, Cleve. Surg. Soc., Northest Ohio Soc. Plastic Surgeons, Cleve. Acad. Med., Beechmont Country Club. Office: Mt Sinai Ctr Cosmetic Surg 26900 Cedar Rd Ste 120 Beachwood OH 44122

DINOSO, VICENTE PESCADOR, JR., physician, educator; b. San Marcelino, Philippines, Oct. 17, 1936; came to U.S., 1961, naturalized, 1973; s. Vicente Dinoso and Eugenia Corpus (Pescador) D.; m. Alice M. Dinoso, June 19, 1965; children—Vincent, David. B.S., U. Philippines, 1955, M.D., 1960. Intern Mt. Sinai Hosp., Hartford, Conn., 1961-62; resident St. Mary's Hosp., Waterbury, Conn., 1962-64, Lahey Clinic Found., Boston, 1964-65; research fellow Temple U. Sch. Medicine, Phila., 1965-66, 68-69; instr. medicine Temple U. Sch. Medicine, 1969-72, asst. prof., 1972-74; assoc. prof. medicine Hahnemann U. Sch. Medicine, Phila., 1974-78, prof. medicine, assoc. prof. physiology, 1978—; practice medicine specializing in gastroenterology, 1969—. Co-editor: Gastrointestinal Emergencies, 1976; contbr. articles to med. jours. Mem. Am. Gastroenterol. Assn., Am. Physiol. Soc., Am. Fedn. for Clin. Research, AAAS, Sigma Xi. Republican. Office: Hahnemann U Hosp Broad And Pine St Philadelphia PA 19102-5087

DINSMORE, CHARLES EARLE, developmental biologist, educator; b. Lisbon Falls, Maine, Oct. 10, 1947; s. William J. Jr. and Marion (Earle) D. AB, Bowdoin Coll., 1970; PhD, Brown U., 1974. Asst. prof. biology Emmanuel Coll., Boston, 1974-76; asst. prof. anatomy Rush Med. Coll., Chgo., 1976-83, assoc. prof., 1983—; vis. scholar U. Chgo., 1990-91. Editor: A History of Regeneration Research, 1991; contbr. articles to profl. jours. Am. Coun. Learned Socs. grantee, 1989; NSF fellow, 1990-91. Mem. Am. Soc. Zoologists (div. chmn. 1991-93), Soc. for Devel. Biology, History of Sci. Soc., Sigma Xi. Office: Rush Med Coll Dept Anatomy 600 S Paulina St Chicago IL 60612-3832

DINTER, HARALD JOSEF, molecular biologist; b. Hannover, Germany, Apr. 30, 1956; s. Erich Josef and Hildegard C. (Bultjer) D.; m. Ursula Adele Otte, Feb. 15, 1991. Diploma, U. Braunschweig, Fed. Republic of Germany, 1982, PhD in Natural Sci., 1986. Rsch. asst. German Inst. Biotechnol. Rsch., Braunschweig, 1982-85, postdoctoral fellow, 1986; postdoctoral fellow The Salk Inst., La Jolla, Calif., 1986-89; staff scientist Schering, A.G., Berlin, 1990—. Contbr. articles to profl. jours. With German mil., 1975-76. Mem. AAAS, N.Y. Acad. Scis. Office: Berlex Biosciences 15049 San Pablo Ave Richmond CA 94806-1834

DIODENÉ, ALONZO NELSON, orthopedic surgeon; b. New Orleans, July 10, 1941; s. Alonzo Nelson and Gladys Marie (Knoll) D.; m. Jeanelle Jude Bourgeois, June 15, 1963; children: Paula Jeanelle McCaskell, Alonzo Nelson III. BS, La. State U., 1963, MD, 1967. Diplomate Am. Bd. Orthopaedic Surgery. Intern Charity Hosp. La., New Orleans, 1967-68; prespltу. tng., resident gen. surgery Ochsner Found. Hosp., New Orleans, 1968-69; resident in orthopaedic surgery Walter Reed Army Med. Ctr., Washington, 1969-72, hand surgery fellow, 1976-77; asst. chief orthopaedic surgery Martin Army Hosp., Fort Benning, Ga., 1972-75, chief orthopaedic surgery, 1975-76; asst. chmn. orthopaedics, chief hand surgery D.D. Eisenhower Army Med. Ctr., Ft. Gordon, Ga., 1977-80; pvt. practice New Orleans, 1980-94, Plaquemine, 1994—; commd. 1st lt. U.S. Army, 1969, advanced through grades to col., 1985; comdr. 114th EVAC Hosp. USAR, 1984-88; comdr. 4010th USAR Hosp., 1991—; with Operation Desert Storm, 1990-91; chmn. dept. orthopaedic surgery Touro Infirmary, New Orleans, 1993-94; chief orthopaedic surgery svc. River West Med. Ctr., Plaquemine, La., 1994—; assoc. prof. orthopaedics Tulane Med. Ctr., New Orleans, 1989—, asst. prof., 1982-89. Contbr. articles to profl. jours. Recipient Mayor's award City New Orleans, 1959. Mem. AMA, Am. Acad. Orthopaedic Surgeons, Am. Fracture Assn., Soc. Mil. Orthopaedic Surgeons, Orleans Parish Med. Soc. (chmn. Emergency Med. Svcs. Com.), Greater New Orleans Orthopaedic Soc., La. State Med. Soc. (chmn. Liaison Com. with Health Care Providers), So. Med. Assn., La. Orthopaedic Assn., So. Orthopaedic Assn., Mid-Am. Orthopaedic Assn., Am. Acad. Neurolog. and Orthopaedic Medicine and Surgery, North Am. Spine Soc., AAAS, Alpha Epsilon Delta. Democrat. Roman Catholic. Office: 59335 River West Dr Ste A Plaquemine LA 70764-6553

DION, ISABELLE, clinical reseacher; b. Agen, France, June 13, 1960. M in Chemistry, U. P. Sabatier, Toulouse, France, 1987; DEA in Materials Sci., Ecole Nat. Supérieure de Chimie de Toulouse, 1988; PhD in Biology, U. Bordeaux, France, 1992; MBA in Mktg. Strategy, Inst. Supérieure des Affairs, Hautes Études Commerciales, Jouy-en-Josas, France, 1994. Engr. R&D Teracor, France, 1988-92; clin. specialist Baxter, Maurepas, France, 1994; project mgr. Europe Baxter, Maurepas, 1995—. Contbr. chpt. in book and articles to profl. jours. Mem. ASAIO, CNISF, SFC, HEC Santé, ESB. Home: 53 Ave St Cloud, 78000 Versailles France

DIORIO, JOHN DANIEL, internist; b. Schenectady, N.Y., Mar. 28, 1950; s. John Daniel and Maria (Soler) D.; m. Deborah Sarah Young; children: Amanda, James, Joshua. BA in Natural Scis., Johns Hopkins U., 1972; MD, NYU, 1976. Diplomate Am. Bd. Internal Medicine. Intern in internal medicine St. Elizabeth's Hosp., Brighton, Mass., 1976-79; physician emergency room Symmes Hosp., 1979-80, Brockton (Mass.) Hosp., 1980-83; pvt. practice, Brockton, 1983—. Mem. Mass. Med. Soc., Physicians for Social Responsibility. Office: 1351 Main St Brockton MA 02401

DIPALMA, JOSEPH RUPERT, pharmacology educator; b. N.Y.C., Mar. 21, 1916; s. Frank and Anna (Attanasio) DiP.; m. Mary Solowey, June 26, 1948; children: Maria, Dorothea, Joan, Yvonne, Mary-Jo. BS, Columbia U., 1936; MD, SUNY, Downstate Med. Center, 1941; DSc (hon.), Hahnemann U., 1980. Intern, resident in internal medicine Kings County Hosp., Bklyn., 1942-44; asst. prof. medicine and pharmacology State U. N.Y. Downstate Med. Sch., 1946; prof. pharmacology, chmn. dept. Hahnemann Med. Coll. and Hosp., Phila., 1951-67; dean Hahnemann Med. Coll. and Hosp., 1967-82, v.p., 1971-82, sr. v.p., 1972-82, prof. pharmacology and medicine, 1982-86, emeritus prof. pharmacology and medicine, 1986—, emeritus dean, 1986—; mem. bd. Regional Med. Program Southeastern Pa., 1967-75, Health Systems Agy., 1977—. Editor: Pharmacology in Medicine, 1971, Basic Pharmacology in Medicine, 1976, 4th edit., 1994; contbr. med. jours. Recipient Alumni medallion SUNY, Downstate Med. Sch., 1966, Corp. medal Hahnemann U., 1990. Mem. Coll. Physicians Phila. (council 1969-78), AMA, Pa., Phila. County med. socs., Am. Physiol. Soc., Am. Soc. Pharmacology and Exptl. Therapeutics, Am. Soc. Clin. Pharmacology, Alpha Omega Alpha. Home: 100 Pembroke Ave Wayne PA 19087-4819 Office: 235 N 15th St Philadelphia PA 19102-1122

DIPILLO, FRANK WILLIAM, hematologist, oncologist; b. N.Y.C., Apr. 20, 1929; s. Vincent and Gladys (Newman) DiP.; m. Lenore Boni (div. 1969); children: Mark, Steven, Michael; m. Roberta Ann Schultheis; children: Danielle, Frank Vincent. BS summa cum laude, St. John's U., Bklyn., 1952; MD, SUNY, Bklyn., 1956. Diplomate Am. Bd. Internal Medicine, Am. Bd. Hematology, Am. Bd. Oncology. Intern L.I. Coll. Hosp., Bklyn., 1956-57, asst. resident, 1957-59, chief resident, 1959-60, asst. attending physician, 1960-66, assoc. attending physician, 1966-69, chief hemotology and oncology, 1967—, attending physician, 1969—; hematology fellow

Montefiore Hosp., Bronx, N.Y., 1963-64; clin. instr. medicine SUNY, Bklyn., 1962-69, clin. asst. prof., 1969-76, clin. assoc. prof., 1976—; cons. hematology and oncology. Contbr. articles to profl. jours., also abstracts and chpts. to books. Fellow ACP; mem. AMA, Am. Soc. Hematology, N.Y. State Med. Soc., Kings County Med. Soc., Med. Club Bklyn. (sec. 1986-87), Am. Cancer Soc. (exec. bd. dirs., exec. com., prin. investigator 1980-89, pres. Bklyn. chpt. 1982-88), Soc. for Study of Blood. Home: 12 Roberts Rd Warren NJ 07059-5205 Office: LI Coll Hosp 340 Henry St Brooklyn NY 11201-5525

DIPLOCK, ANTHONY TYTHERLEIGH, biochemistry educator, academic administrator; b. Croydon, Surrey, Eng., July 24, 1935; s. Bernard and Elsie (Besley) D.; m. 1957 (div. 1978); children: Carolann Gillian, Jerome Nigel; m. Lynn Christine Richards, Apr. 1, 1980; 1 child, Charles Bernard. BSc, U. Bristol, Eng., 1956; PhD, U. London, 1965, DSc, 1975. Head dept. biochemistry Vitamins Ltd., Tadworth, 1957-66; from sr. lectr. to reader Royal Free Hosp. Sch. of Medicine U. London, 1966-77; prof., head div. biochemistry United Med. & Dental Schs. Guy's Hosp., U. London, 1977—; elected vice dean faculty medicine U. London, 1982, 85, elected dean, 1986-91; elected senator U. London, 1979—, mem. ct. 1989-94; chmn. com. on selenium in human health WHO, 1985-90; mem. Commonwealth scholarships commn., mem. coun. Brit Postgrad. Med. Fedn., Royal Free Hosp. Sch. Medicine Huntarian Inst., Roedean Sch., 1991—; rsch. programme mgr. (cons.) Minister Agr., Fisheries and Food, 1994—; chmn. EL/ILSI Functional Foods Group on Reactive Oxygen Species, 1996—. Contbr. numerous articles to profl. jours. Recipient Evian Health award, 1986, Caroline Walker award, 1993; numerous rsch. grants. Office: U London United Med Dental, Schs Guys Hosp, Div Biochemistry, London SE1 9RT, England

DIPPO, JEANETTE FAYE, school health educator, nurse; b. Miami, Fla., Sept. 15, 1943; d. Llewellyn and Marie Elizabeth (Wanser) Potter; m. Walter Allen Dippo, June 27, 1964; children: Julie Lynn, Kimberly Michelle. RN, St. Luke's Hosp., Newburgh, N.Y., 1964; BS in Health Edn., SUNY, Cortland, 1967, MS in Health Edn., 1969. Cert. tchr., N.Y. RN Cortland Meml. Hosp., 1964-66; health educator Cortland City Schs., 1966-73; health and drug edn. coord. Cortland-Madison Bd. Coop. Ednl. Svcs., 1973-75; health edn. and wellness coord. Cortland City Schs., 1975—; workshop conf. presenter various drug and health edn. confs., 1974—; cons., turnkey trainer N.Y. State Dept. Edn., Albany, 1968—; coop. master tchr. SUNY, Cortland, 1968—, Ithaca (N.Y.) Coll., 1968—; mentor tchr. Corland Jr./Sr. H.S., 1989-94; freedom from smoking clinic coord. Am. Lung Assn., Cortland, 1990-94; cons. feature TV segment on family dynamics course CBS 30 Minutes, 1978-79; grant co-dir. Healthy Me Project Met. Life Found., SUNY, Cortland, 1988-89. Editor: (newsletter) Health Instrnl. Resource Ctr., 1973-75; mem. editl. bd. Catalyst, 1979-81. Sun. sch. and confirmation tchr. First United Meth. Ch., Cortland, 1986—; original founder's com., mem. Seven Valleys Coun. on Alcohol and Substance Abuse, Cortland, 1987—; mem. Tri-County Tobacco Prevention Coalition, Tompkins, Cortland and Cayuga Counties, 1993—. Recipient commendation award Cortland County Legislature, 1989, Head Start Vol. award, 1995; Project Empathy grantee Zero Adolescent Pregnancy (ZAP), 1992; grantee Project Think It Over, 1995. Mem. NEA, Am. Sch. Health Assn., Cortland United Tchrs., N.Y. State United Tchrs., N.Y. State Fedn. Profl. Health Educators (life, regional chmn. 1974-75, pres. 1976, outstanding sch. health educator 1979, past pres. award 1990), Delta Kappa Gamma (internat. Beta chpt. 1991—). Republican. Methodist. Home: RR 1 2444 Ridge Rd Mc Graw NY 13101-9801 Office: Cortland City Schs 8 Valley View Dr Cortland NY 13045-3296

DIPRIMA, JOSEPH GARY, podiatrist, foot surgeon; b. Rochester, N.Y., Jan. 13, 1957. BS in Chemistry, St. John Fisher Coll., 1979; DPM, Pa. Coll. Podiatric Medicine, Phila., 1983. Cert. Am. Bd. Podiatric Surgery. Chief of podiatry Anthony Jordan Health Ctr., Rochester, N.Y., 1986%—. Bd. dirs. Arthritis Found., Rochester, 1988-92, Diabetes Assn., 1993—. Office: Fairport Podiatry 800 Ayrault Rd Ste 210 Fairport NY 14450-8941

DIRKES, MELISSA, health facility administrator; b. Orlando, Fla., Sept. 3, 1963; d. A. Michael and Karen E. (fogarty) Ogram; m. Carl D. Dirkes, May 27, 1989. BS, U. Fla., 1986. Staff coord. Same-day Surgicenter, Orlando, 1986-89; office coord., surgery scheduler Ctr. for Infertility and Reproductive Medicine, Orlando, 1989-93, adminstr., 1993—. Republican. Roman Catholic. Office: Infertility Reproductive Medicine 3435 Pinehurst Ave Orlando FL 32804

DIRKS, KENNETH RAY, pathologist, medical educator, army officer; b. Newton, Kans., Feb. 11, 1925; s. Jacob Kenneth and Ruth Viola (Penner) D.; m. Betty Jean Worsham, June 9, 1946; children: Susan Jan, Jeffrey Mark, Deborah Anne, Timothy David, Melissa Jane. M.D., Washington U., St. Louis, 1947. Diplomate: Am. Bd. Pathology. Rotating intern St. Louis City Hosp., 1948, asst. resident in gen. surgery, 1948-49; resident in pathology VA Hosp., Jefferson Barracks, Mo., 1951-53; resident in pathology, asst. chief lab. service VA Hosp., Indpls., 1953-54; resident in pathology Letterman Army Hosp., San Francisco, 1956-57; fellow in tropical medicine and parasitology La. State U., Central Am., 1958; asst. in pathology Washington U. Sch. Medicine, 1952-53; asst. chief lab. service VA Hosp., Jefferson Barracks, 1953; instr. pathology U. Ind. Med. Center, Indpls., 1953-54; commd. capt. M.C. U.S. Army, 1954, advanced through grades to maj. gen., 1976; dir. research Med. Research and Devel. Command, Washington, 1968-69; dep. comdr. Med. Research and Devel. Command, 1969-71, comdr., 1973-76; asst. surgeon gen., research and devel. U.S. Army, 1973-76; dep. comdr., comdr. Med. Research Inst. Infectious Diseases, Ft. Detrick, Frederick, Md., 1972-73; comdr. Fitzsimons Army Med. Center, Denver, 1976-77; supt. Acad. Health Scis., Ft. Sam Houston, Tex., 1977-80; assoc. prof. to prof. pathology and lab. medicine Coll. Med. Tex. A&M U., College Station, 1980-95; interim head dept. Coll. Medicine, Tex. A&M U., College Station, 1990-91; prof. emeritus pathology, 1995; prof. emeritus Tex. A&M U., College Station, 1995—; asst. dean coll. Coll. Medicine, Tex. A&M U., College Station, 1985-88; dir. dept. student health svcs. and A.P. Beutel Health Ctr. Tex. A&M U., College Station, 1989-95; dir. student health svcs. emeritus, 1995—; dir. emeritus Tex. A&M U., College Station, 1995—. Contbr. articles to med. jours. Decorated D.S.M., Legion of Merit with oak leaf cluster, Meritorious Service medal, Army Commendation medal with oak leaf cluster. Fellow Coll. Am. Pathologists, Internat. Acad. Pathology. Address: 2513 Oak Cir Bryan TX 77802-2009

DISAIA, PHILIP JOHN, gynecologist, obstetrician, radiology educator; b. Providence, Aug. 14, 1937; s. George and Antoinette (Vastano) DiS.; divorced; children: John P., Steven D.; m. Patricia June; children: Dominic J., Vincent J. BS cum laude, Brown U., 1959; MD cum laude, Tufts U., 1963. Diplomate Am. Bd. Ob-Gyn. (examiner 1975—, bd. dirs. 1994), Am. Bd. Gynecologic Oncology (bd. dirs. 1987—). Intern Yale U. Sch. Medicine, New Haven Hosp., 1963-64, resident in ob-gyn., 1964-67, instr. ob-gyn., 1966-67; fellow in gynecologic oncology U. Tex. M.D. Anderson Hosp. and Tumor Inst., Houston, 1969-70, NIH sr. fellow, 1969-70, instr. ob-gyn., 1969-71; asst. prof. ob-gyn. and radiology U. So. Calif. Sch. Medicine, L.A., 1971-74, assoc. prof., 1974-77; prof., chmn. dept. ob-gyn. U. Calif., Irvine Med. Ctr. Calif. Coll. Medicine, 1977-88, prof., 1977—, prof. radiology, radiation therapy div., 1978—, assoc. vice chancellor for health scis. Irvine Coll. Medicine, 1987-89, Dorothy Marsh chair of reproductive biology, 1989—, dep. dir. cancer ctr., 1989—, pres. med. staff, 1993—; pres. UCI Clin. Practice Group, 1994—; dir. div. gynecol. oncology Am. Bd. Obstetrics & Gynecology, 1995—, bd. dirs., 1994—; bd. dirs. U. Calif. Irvine Med. Ctr., 1995; clin. enterprise adv. coun. to pres. U. Calif., 1995; academic planning task force U. Calif. Irvine, 1994, continuing med. edn. com., 1991-94; cancer liaison commn. on cancer Am. Coll. Surgeons, 1981-94; bd. dirs., dir. at large Am. Cancer Soc., 1985—; clin. prof. dept. ob-gyn. U. Nev. Sch. Medicine, Reno, 1985—; chmn. site visit team for surgery br. Nat. Cancer Inst. NIH, 1983, subcom. surg. oncology rsch. devel., 1982-83, mem. sci. counselors div. cancer treatment, 1979-83; mem. gov.'s adv. coun. on cancer State of Calif., 1980-85; vis. prof., lectr., speaker various sci. meetings, confs., courses. Author: (with E.J. Quilligan) Ovarian Tumors, Current Diagnosis, 1974, (with others) Synopsis of Gynecologic Oncology, 1975, (with W.T. Creasman) Clinical Gynecologic Oncology, 1980, 4th Edit. 1993; contbr. numerous articles to profl. jours., book chpts.; assoc. editor Gynecologic Oncology, Endocurietherapy/Hyperthermia Oncology, Danforth's Textbook of Obstetrics & Gynecology; mem. editorial adv. bd. Am. Jour. Reproductive Immunology, Cancer Clinical Trials, The Female Patient, New Trends in Gynecology and Obstetrics (Italian publ.); reviewer Am. Jour. Ob-Gyn., Med. and Pediatric Oncology, New Eng. Jour. Medicine, Ob-Gyn. jour., Cancer; physician cons. Patient Care Standards jour.; sci. adv. bd. The Clin. Cancer Letter. Recipient Disting. Alumnus award M.D. Anderson Hosp. and Tumor Inst. U. Tex., 1980, Silver Apple award U. Calif. Med. Students, 1983, Lauds and Laurels Profl. Achievement award U. Calif. Alumni Assn., 1983, Hubert Haussel's award Long Beach Meml. Hosp., 1983, Dist. Faculty Lectureship award for Teaching, U. Calif. Irvine Acad. Senate, 1993-94, also various rsch. awards. Fellow Am. Coll. Obstetricians and Gynecologists (com. on human rsch. for cancer 1979—, chmn. 1984—, chmn. subcom. on gynecologic oncology 1984-85, prolog editorial and adv. com. 1986—, various others), ACS, Commn. on Cancer Liaison, Western Assn. Gynecologic Oncologists (founder 1971, pres. 1978-79), Am. Gynecol. and Obstet. Soc. (exec. coun. 1986—), Am. Gynecologic Soc., Pacific Coast Ob/Gyn Soc., South Atlantic Assn. Obstetricians and Gynecologists (hon.); mem. AMA, Am. Cancer Soc. (bd. dirs. L.A. County unit 1975-77, Orange County 1979, unit pres. 1993—; bd. dirs. Calif. div. 1985—, chmn. med. scientific com. 1993-94), Nat. Am. Cancer Soc. (dir.-at-large, bd. dirs. 1985—, chmn. program com. for nat. conf. 1986, vice-chmn. detection and treatment adv. group gynecol. cancer 1993-94, active in others), Am. Coll. Radiology (commn. on cancer 1984-85), Am. Soc. Clin. Oncologists, Soc. Gynecologic Oncologists (exec. coun. 1975-80, pres. 1982-83), Internat. Gynecologic Oncology Cancer Soc., Italian Soc. Ob-Gyn. (Camillo Gia 1991), Calif. Med. Assn., other profl. orgns., Alpha Omega Alpha. Home: 12132 Skyline Dr Santa Ana CA 92705-3150 Office: U Calif Irvine Med Ctr 101 City Blvd W Bldg 23 Rm 313 Orange CA 92668-2901

DI SALVO, ARTHUR FRANCIS, physician, public health official; b. N.Y.C., May 16, 1932; m. Shirley Sayre, 1958; 1 child. AAS, SUNY, Cobbleskill, 1951; BS, U. Ariz., 1954, MS, 1958; MD, Med. Coll. of Ga., 1965. Diplomate Am. Bd. Med. Microbiology. Rsch. asst. dept. med. microbiology Med. Coll. of Ga., 1959-63; bacteriologist Milledgeville (Ga.) State Hosp., 1958-59; intern Eugene Talmadge Meml. Hosp., Augusta, Ga., 1965-66; fellow med. microbiology Nat. Communicable Disease Ctr., Atlanta, 1966-68; practice medicine specializing in med. microbiology, 1968—; chief Bur. of Labs. S.C. Dept. Health and Environ. Control, Columbia, 1968-90; dir. Nev. State Health Lab., Reno, 1990—; clin. asst. prof. lab. medicine Med. U. of S.C., Charleston, 1971-78, clin. assoc. prof., 1978-86, clin. prof. pathology and lab. medicine, 1986—; clin. assoc. prof. med. microbiology U. S.C. Sch. Medicine, Columbia, 1976-80, adj. prof. med. microbiology, 1980—; prof. pathology and lab. medicine U. Nev. Sch. Medicine, Reno, 1991-93; cons. microbiology device classification panel FDA, 1977-81; bd. dirs. Water Co. of Edisto Beach (S.C.), 1974-78. Editor-in-chief Mycopathologia, 1989—; mem. editl. bd. JSC Med. Assn., 1981-90, Diagnostic Microbiology and Infectious Disease, 1982-95; contbr. articles on med. microbiology to profl. jours. With USAF, 1954. Fellow Am. Acad. Microbiology; mem. Am. Soc. Microbiology (sec., treas. S.C. bd. 1969-78), Am. Pub. Health Assn. (mem. governing coun. 1975-78, 81-85), Assn. State and Territorial Pub. Health Lab. Dirs. (pres. 1978-79), S.C. Pub. Health Assn., Med. Mycological Soc. Ams. (coun. 1975-76, sec.-treas. 1979-82, pres. 1984), Nev. Pub. Health Assn., John Henry Newman Soc., Columbia Med. Soc., Internat. Soc. for Human and Animal Mycology, AMA (Physicians Recognition award), S.C. Med. Assn., Nev. State Med. Assn.

DISERIO, FRANK JOSEPH, pharmaceutical company executive; b. N.Y.C., Oct. 3, 1931; s. Anthony and Catherine (Solimando) DiS.; m. Lauretta Christine Brunck, Dec., 14, 1954 (div. May 1984); children: Anthony Mark, Francis Joseph, Paul James; m. Marjatta Niemioja, Oct. 19, 1985). BS, NYU, 1963; MBA, Fairleigh Dickinson U., 1970; PhD, Union Inst., 1979. Ptnr. Foam Age Lounge, Inc. and Dawn W.W. Co., N.Y.C., 1956-59; sales rep. Sandoz Pharmaceuticals, Inc., East Hanover, N.J., 1959-63, tech. rep., 1964-66, research assoc., 1966-68, sr. research assoc., 1969-73, clin. research fellow, 1973-76, asst. dir. clin. research, 1976-80, assoc. dir. clin. research, 1980-85, dir. CNS med. rsch., 1985-90; exec. dir. clin. rsch., head OTC/analgesia clin. rsch. dept. Sandoz Rsch. Inst., East Hanover, 1988-95; pharm. devel. cons. Morristown, N.J., 1995—. Contbr. articles to profl. jours. Capt. USAF, 1952-56. Mem. Internat. Headache Soc., Am. Assn. for Study Headache, Am. Acad. Neurology (non-clin. assoc.), Am. Soc. Clin. Pharmacology and Therapeutics, Am. Coun. for Headache Edn. (bd. dirs.), N.Y. Acad. Scis., Rock Spring Club. Republican. Roman Catholic. Home: 24 Pippins Way Morristown NJ 07960-6971

DISHMAN, REX, health facility administrator; b. New Castle, Ind., Apr. 19, 1948; s. Staley Odel and Pearl (Davis) D.; m. Pamela Hunter, May 28, 1973 (div. Jan. 1992); 1 child, Neil Dishman; m. Karen Ann Bennett, Mar 4, 1995. BS in Psychology, Purdue U., 1970, MS in Edn., 1974. Dir. pers. LaPorte (Ind.) Hosp., 1977-79; mgr. tng. Health Quest Corp., South Bend, Ind., 1980-82; dir. corp. human resources Holy Cross Health Sys., South Bend, 1982-90; sr. dir. human resources St. Catherine's Hosp., Kenosha, Wis., 1991-93; v.p. ops. Meml. Hosp., Logansport, Inc., 1993—. Bd. dirs. YMCA, Cass County, Ind., 1995. Mem. Rotary. Home: 207 Princeton Ln Logansport IN 46947 Office: Meml Hosp of Logansport 1101 Michigan Ave Logansport IN 46947-7013

DI SIMONE, ROBERT NICHOLAS, radiologist, educator; b. Canton, Ohio, Nov. 15, 1937; s. Nicholas Joseph and Margaret Elizabeth (Karas) DiS.; m. Patricia Anne Zwigard, June 22, 1963; children: Christopher, Angela, Elizabeth. BSc summa cum laude, Ohio State U., 1959, MSc, 1963, MD cum laude, 1963. Diplomate Am. Bd. Radiology, Am. Bd. Nuclear Medicine. Intern, fellow Johns Hopkins U. Hosp., Balt., 1963-64, asst. resident, fellow in internal medicine, 1964-65, asst. resident, fellow in radiology, 1967-70, instr., radiologist, 1970-71; dir. nuclear medicine Aultman Hosp., Canton, 1971-95, pres., med. staff, 1986-87, vice chmn. dept. radiology, 1988-96, sec.-treas. med. staff, 1977-79; chmn. nuclear medicine sect. Northeastern Ohio Univs. Coll. of Medicine (NEOUCOM), Rootstown, 1979—; chmn. dept. radiology Northeastern Ohio Univs. Coll. of Medicine (NEOUCOM),, Rootstown, 1992-93. Author: Imaging of the Endocrine System in Organ System Radiology, 1984; contbr. articles to profl. jours. Fellow Am. Coll. Radiology; mem. AMA, Soc. Nuclear Medicine, Ohio State Med. Soc. (del. 1983-95), Radiol. Soc. N.Am., Stark County Med. Soc. (trustee 1979-95, chmn. bd. censors 1980-82, pres. 1993), Unique Club Stark County, Phi Beta Kappa, Sigma Xi, Alpha Omega Alpha, Phi Lambda Upsilon. Home: 2465 Oakway St NW Canton OH 44720-5886 Office: Aultman Hosp 2600 6th St SW Canton OH 44710-1702

DISKIND, FAIGA, speech and language pathologist, administrator. BA, CUNY, 1973, MA, 1975. Cert. elem. and secondary tchr., prin., supr., adminstr., N.J.; lic. speech-lang. pathologist, N.J. Elem. tchr. Yeshiva of Spring Valley, Monsey, N.Y., 1970-71, 72-73, Moriah Acad., Edison, N.J., 1973-74, Jewish Ednl. Ctr., Elizabeth, N.J., 1974-75; speech-lang. pathologist Bd. Edn., Lakewood, N.J., 1975-82; dir. Cen. Jersey Occupational and Speech Therapy Ctr., Lakewood, Jackson, Bricktown, Howell, N.J., 1983—; speech-lang. pathologist nursing homes, geriatric ctrs., Ocean County, N.J., 1975-82. Authhor: Coma and Head Trauma--Handbook for Speech Rehabilitation and Management, 1985. Mem. Am. Speech-Lang.-Hearing Assn. (cert. clin. competence). Home: 1004 Lexington Ave Lakewood NJ 08701-1863 Office: Cen Jersey Occupational & Speech Therapy Ctr 301 Madison Ave Lakewood NJ 08701-3266

DISPENZA, JOAN MARIE, ambulatory care nurse, administrator; b. Buffalo, May 10, 1955; d. Frank J. and Madeline (Miano) D. BSN, D'Youville Coll., Buffalo, 1976, MSN in Cmty. Health, 1989. Staff nurse, CCU Millard Fillmore Hosp., Buffalo, 1976-85, head nurse CCU, 1985-89, DON, 1989-96; mgr. ambulatory care Millard Fillmore Health Sys., Buffalo, 1996—. Mem. AACN, Nat. League Nursing, Am. Coll. Healthcare Execs. (assoc.), Am. Orgn. Nurse Execs., N.Y. State Nurses Assn., Sigma Theta Tau. Office: 901 Washington St Buffalo NY 14203

DISSAIT, FRANCOIS LOUIS, physician; b. Issoire, France, May 11, 1950; s. Suzanne D.; m. Veronique Benonie, Aug. 26, 1985; children: Marie, Juliette. MD, U. Clermont, France, 1977, degree in anesthesiology, 1979; degree in catastrophe medicine, U. Lyon, France, 1986. Med. officer Cen. Hosp. Regional, Clermont, 1977-96, chief med. officer, 1979-96; chief med. officer Clermont Fire Dept., 1981-96; educator emergency med. course Ctr. Enseignement Soc. Urgent, Clermont, 1980-96. Contbr. articles to profl. jours. Mem. Assn. France Transplant, Assn. of Medicine of Catastrophe, French Assn. Earthquake Engring. Home: Chemin de Coronet, 63500 Parentignat France Office: Ctrl Hosp Emergency Med Dept, 30 Place Henry Dunant, 63003 Clermont France

DISTLER, ARMIN GEORG, physician, educator; b. Nürnberg, Germany, Jan. 8, 1935; s. Fritz and Martha (Hesse) D.; m. Heide Hagen, Aug. 12, 1961; 2 children. MD, U. Erlangen, 1962. Bd. cert. diplomate. Prof. medicine U. Mainz, Germany, 1971, Free U. Berlin, 1981—; pres. Soc. Nephrology, 1995-96. Contbr. articles to profl. jours. Office: Klinikum Benjamin Franklin, Hindenburgdamm 45, 12200 Berlin Germany

DITCHIK, JAMES MICHAEL, anesthesiologist; b. New Rochelle, Calif., Feb. 28, 1955; s. Philip Marshall and Harriet Ann (Sarined) D. BS, Stanford U., 1976; MD, U. So. Calif., L.A., 1980. Sr. physician Cigna, Pasadena, Calif., 1981-82; resident in anesthesia UCLA, Westwood, 1982-84; anesthesiologist Med. Ctr. Tarzana, Calif., 1984-91, St. John's Med. Ctr., Santa Monica, Calif., 1984-90, Northridge (Calif.) Hosp., 1984-90, West Hills (Calif.) Hosp., 1987-90, Palmdale, Calif. Home: 4022 Falling Leaf Dr Encino CA 91316-4419

DITO, WILLIAM ROBERT, pathology educator; b. Alameda, Calif., Aug. 8, 1929; s. Salvatore Mario and Mary Josephine (Silvestri) D.; m. Bridget Claire O'Rourke, Sept. 25, 1954; children: Robert W., David M., Matthew T., Mark A., William K. BS, U. San Francisco, 1950; MD, Loyola U., Chgo., 1954. Diplomate Am. Bd. Pathology; Clin. and Anatomical Pathology Radioisotopic Pathology. Commd. capt. U.S. Army, 1955, advanced through grades to major, 1961; chief lab. service U.S. Army Hosp., Nuremberg, Fed. Republic Germany, 1961-64; resigned U.S. Army, 1965; chief clin. lab. Letterman Gen. Hosp., San Francisco, 1964-65; dir. labs., dir. Sch. Med. Tech. Pontiac (Mich.) Gen. Hosp., 1965-73; assoc. prof. pathology U. Ariz., Tucson, 1973-76; med. dir. Sch. Med. Tech. Ariz. Med. Ctr., Tucson, 1974-76; head div. lab. medicine Scripps Clinic and Research Found., La Jolla, Calif., 1978-94; regional commr. lab. accreditation program Coll. Am. Pathologists, San Diego, 1994—; adj. instr. Wayne State U., Detroit, 1970-73; adj. assoc. prof. pathology, U. Calif.-San Diego, La Jolla, 1977-86, assoc. clin. prof., 1986—; chief of labs. VA Hosp., Tucson, 1973-74. Co-editor: (with Nakamura and Tucker) Immunologic Analysis—Recent Progress in Diagnostic Laboratory Immunology, 1982; editor: (jour.) Informatics in Pathology, 1985-88; mem. editorial bd. Lab. Medicine, 1978-85; also numerous articles and monographs in field. Fellow. Coll. Am. Pathologists, Am. Soc. Clin. Pathologists (mem. editorial bd. 1979-82, Disting. Service award 1980), Internat. Acad. Pathology. Republican. Roman Catholic. Club: La Jolla Profl. Mens. Office: 9265 Dowdy Dr Ste 212 San Diego CA 92126

DITZLER, THOMAS FREDERICK, psychologist, educator; b. Flint, Mich., Aug. 28, 1946; s. Thomas Edward and Mary Margaret (McLinden) D.; m. Ann Marie Herrick; children: Benjamin Thomas Edward, Nathan James Herrick. AB, Hilldale Coll., 1968; cert. Edn., U. Mich., 1975, MA, 1976; PhD, Clayton U., 1980. Diplomate Am. Bd. Examiners in Psychotheraphy; lic. psychologist, Ky.; registered Nat. Acad. Cert. Clin. Mental Health Counselors. Counseling supr. Women's Alcoholism Treatment Ctr. St. Francis Hosp., Honolulu, 1980-82; program dir. counseling assistance ctr. Marine Corps Air Station, Kaneohe, Hawaii, 1982-84; dir. edn. tng. rsch. dept. psychiatry Tripler Army Med. Ctr., Honolulu, 1984—; sr. fellow ops. rsch. group, Honolulu; asst. clin. prof. U. Hawaii Coll. Health Scis., Honolulu, 1985-86; assoc. prof. clin. faculty Hawaii Loa Coll., Kaneohe, 1989; adj. asst. prof. psychiatry Uniformed Svcs. U. Health Scis., Bethesda, Md., 1989—. Ad Hoc reviewer Jour. Counseling and Devel.; editor Hawaii Jour. Counseling and Devel., 1986-88. Chmn. adv. bd. Diamond Head Community Mental Health Ctr., Hawaii Dept. Health, 1981. Recipient Profl. Svc. award Hawaii Assn. Counseling and Devel., Honolulu, 1987. Fellow Royal Inst. Pub. Health and Hygiene, Hawaii Psychol. Assn. (bd. dirs. 1986-89); mem. Phi Delta Kappa. Home: 1124 Puwa Pl Kailua HI 96734 Office: Dept Psychiatry Tripler Army Med Ctr Dept Psychiatry # 4D Honolulu HI 96859

DIX, DOUGLAS EDWARD, chemistry educator; b. New Britain, Conn., Mar. 12, 1944; s. Edward Frank and Doris Marie D.; m. Patricia Ann Cohen, July 7, 1970; children: Samuel, Joseph, Benjamin, Aaron, Naomi, Joel. BS, Fairfield (Conn.) U., 1962; PhD, SUNY, 1971. Diplomate Am. Bd. Clin. Chemistry. Dir. Haynes Med. Lab., Manchester, Conn., 1976-80; asst. prof. chemistry U. Hartford, W. Hartford, Conn., 1981-86, assoc. prof., 1986-93, prof., 1993—; co-dir. Community Sci. Program, Hartford, 1990-93. Contbr. articles to profl. jours. Grantee NSF, 1990, Conn. Dept. Higher Edn., 1991, U.S. Dept. Energy, 1991. Mem. Am. Assn. Clin. Chemistry (Clin. Chemist Recognition award, 1982). Home: 6 Cobblestone Rd Bloomfield CT 06002-3004 Office: U Hartford 200 Bloomfield Ave West Hartford CT 06117-1545

DIXIT, BALWANT NARAYAN, pharmacology and toxicology educator; b. Kerawade, India, Jan. 7, 1933; came to U.S., 1962; s. Narayan V. and Janakibai N. (Gokhale) D.; m. Vidya B. Ghanekar, Dec. 26, 1969; children: Sunil, Sanjay. B.S. in Chemistry and Biology, Fergusson Coll., Poona, India, 1954; B.S. in Chemistry with honors, U. Poona, 1955; M.S. in Biochemistry with honors, U.Poona, 1956; M.S. in Pharmacology with honors, U. Baroda, India, 1962; Ph.D., U. Pitts., 1965. Sr. research fellow Baroda U., 1960-61; asst. prof. pharmacology U. Pitts., 1965-68; assoc. prof., 1968-74, prof., 1974—, asst. chmn., 1969-74, acting dean, 1976-78, chmn., 1974-87, assoc. dean, 1974-84; dir. Ctr. for the Performing Arts of India, 1992—. Recipient Disting. Alumnus award U. Pitts. Sch. Pharmacy, 1982; fellow Internat. Union Physiological Scis., 1962. Mem. Am. Soc. Pharmacology and Explt. Therapeutics, Soc. Neurosci., N.Y. Acad. Sci., Internat. Soc. Xenobiotic Metabolism. Home: 608 Ravencrest Rd Pittsburgh PA 15215-1120 Office: U Pitts 541 Salk Hall Pittsburgh PA 15261-1905

DIXIT, VISHVA M., pathology educator. MD, U. Nairobi, Kenya, 1980; postgrad., Washington U., St. Louis, 1982-86. Intern dept. medicine Kenyatta Nat. Hosp., 1980-81; resident pathology and medicine Barnes Hosp., St. Louis, 1981-86; asst. prof. pathology Med. Sch. U. Mich., Ann Arbor, 1986-91, assoc. prof., 1991—, prof. pathology, 1995—. Contbr. articles to profl. jours. Recipient Best Pathology Student award Kenya Med. Assn., 1980, Best Overall Med. Student Kamala Meml. award, 1980, Warner-Lambert/Parke-Davis Exptl. Pathology award, 1996; Josiah Macy Found. fellow, 1989. Office: U Mich Med Sch Dept Pathology 1301 Catherine St Box 0602 Ann Arbor MI 48109*

DIXON, ANDREW DERART, retired academic administrator; b. Belfast, No. Ireland, Oct. 27, 1925; came to U.S., 1963, naturalized, 1972; s. Andrew and Martha (Stewart) D.; m. Mary Elizabeth Henderson, Oct. 14, 1948; children: Penelope Jane, Melinda Sara, Alison Mary. Licentiate in Dental Surgery, Queens U., Belfast, 1948, B in Dental Surgery, 1949, M.Dental Surgery, 1953, B.S. (Nuffield Found. dental fellow), 1954, D.Sc., 1965; Ph.D., U. Manchester, 1958. Asst. lectr. anatomy U. Manchester, 1954-56, lectr., 1956-62, sr. lectr., 1962-63; vis. assoc. prof. anatomy U. Iowa, 1959-61; prof. dental sci. U. N.C., Chapel Hill, 1963-65, prof. dental sci., anatomy, 1965-69, prof. oral biology and anatomy, 1969-73, asst. dean, coordinator research Sch. Dentistry, 1966-69, dir. Dental Research Ctr., 1967-73, assoc. dean research, 1969-73; prof., dean UCLA, 1973-80, assoc. dean for faculty affairs, 1985-92, assoc. dean adminstrn., 1989-92; prof. emeritus, 1993—; chmn. dental tng. com. Nat. Inst. Dental Rsch., 1972-73; mem. No. Ireland Partnership. Author, editor sci. texts; contbr. numerous articles to profl. jours. Studies on early devel. and growth of the jaws, sex chromatin in oral smears as a diagnostic tool, nerve supply to oral mucous membrane, facial tissues and temporomandibular joint, facial skeletal growth, trigeminal pathway, including trigeminal ganglion, using histological histochem. and electron microscopy methods. Fulbright Sr. Fellow award, 1959-61, Commonwealth Fund Travel fellow, 1961. Fellow Am. Coll. Dentists, Internat. Coll. Dentists, AAAS; mem. ADA, Inst. of Medicine (sr.), Pacific Coast Soc. Orthodontists (hon.), Western Conf. Dental Examiners and Dental Deans (pres. 1979-80), Anat. Soc. Gt. Britain and Ireland (sr.), Am. Assn. Anatomists, Internat. Assn. Dental Rsch., AAAS, Am. Soc. Cell Biology, N.Y. Acad. Sci., Internat. Soc. Craniofacial Biology, Pierre Fauchard Acad.,

Sigma Xi, Omicron Kappa Upsilon, Psi Omega. Home: 3136 W Orchard Ct Visalia CA 93277-7116

DIXON, FRANK JAMES, medical scientist, educator; b. St. Paul, Mar. 9, 1920; s. Frank James and Rose Augusta (Kuhfeld) D.; m. Marion Edwards, Mar. 14, 1946; children: Janet Wynne, Frank, Michael. BS, U. Minn., 1941, MB, 1943, MD, 1944; DS (hon.), Med. Coll. Ohio, 1983; DSc (hon.), Washington U., 1992. Diplomate: Am. Bd. Pathology. Intern U.S. Naval Hosp., Great Lakes, Ill., 1943-44; research asst. dept. pathology Harvard, 1946-48; instr. dept. pathology Washington U., 1948-50, asst. prof., 1950-51; prof., chmn. dept. pathology U. Pitts. Med. Sch., 1951-60; chmn. dept. exptl. pathology Scripps Clinic and Research Found., La Jolla, Calif., 1961-74; chmn. biomed. research depts. Scripps Clinic and Research Found., 1970-74, dir. research inst., 1974-86, dir. emeritus, 1987—; rsch. assoc. dept. biology U. Calif., San Diego, 1961-64, prof. in residence dept. biology, 1965-68, adj. prof. dept. pathology, 1968-96; sci. advisor NIH, Nat. Found., Helen Hay Whitney Found., St. Jude's Med. Ctr., Christ Hosp. Inst., Cin.; mem. expert adv. panel on immunology WHO; sci. adv. bd. Nat. Kidney Found.; Pahlavi lectr. Ministry of Sci. and Higher Tech., Iran, 1976: mem. adv. com. Lupus Rsch. Inst., Nat. Multiple Sclerosis Soc., Harold C. Simmons Arthritis Rsch. Ctr., Irvington House Inst., Mass. Gen. Hosp. Editor: Advances in Immunology; mem. editorial bd. Excerpta Medica, Jour. Exptl. Medicine, Am. Jour. Pathology, Cellular Immunology, Kidney Hosp. Practice, Perspectives in Biology and Medicine, Jour. Exptl. Clin. Cancer Rsch., Springer Seminars in Immunopathology, Immunological Revs.; contbr. articles to profl. jours. Served with M.C. USNR, 1943-46. Recipient Theobald Smith award, 1952, Parke-Davis award in exptl. pathology, 1957, Disting. Achievement award Modern Medicine, 1961, Martin E. Rehfuss award in internal medicine, 1966, Von Pirquet medal Ann. Forum on Allergy, 1967, Bunim medal Am. Rheumatism Assn., 1968, Internat. award Gairdner Found., 1969, Mayo Soley award Western Soc. Clin. Research, 1969, Albert Lasker Basic Med. Research award, 1975, Dickson prize U. Pitts., 1975, Homer Smith award N.Y. Heart Assn., 1976, Rous-Whipple award Am. Assn. Pathologists, 1979, So. Calif. Permanente Med. Group Immunology award, 1979, Regents award U. Minn., 1985, H.P. Smith award Am. Soc. Clin. Pathologists, 1985, Gold-Headed Cane award, 1987, Distinguished Service award Lupus Found. Am., 1987, 88; Flame of Hope award Terri Gotthelf Rsch. Inst., 1987, Paul Klemperer award N.Y. Acad. Medicine, 1989, Jean Hamburger award Internat. Soc. Nephrology, 1990. Fellow Am. Coll. Allergists, Am. Acad. Allergy, Royal Coll. Pathologists (hon.); mem. NAS, N.Y. Acad. Scis. Western Assn. Physicians, Western Soc. Clin. Research, Soc. Exptl. Biology and Medicine, Transplantation Soc., AAAS, Am. Soc. Clin. Investigation, Am. Acad. Allergists, Interurban Path. Soc., Harvey Soc. (lectr. 1962), Am. Soc. Exptl. Pathology (pres. 1966), Am. Assn. Immunologists (pres. 1972), Am. Assn. for Cancer Research, Assn. Am. Physicians, Am. Acad. Arts and Scis., Am. Heart Assn., Coun. on the Kidney in Cardiovascular Disease, Fedn. Am. Scientists, Internat. Acad. Pathology, U.S. Acad. Pathologists, Can. Acad. Pathologists, Scandinavian Soc. for Immunology (hon.), Japanese Nephrology Soc. (hon.), Sigma Xi, Nu Sigma Nu, Alpha Omega Alpha. Office: Scripps Clinic & Rsch Found 10666 N Torrey Pines Rd La Jolla CA 92037-1027

DIXON, GEORGE DAVID, radiologist; b. Valley City, N.D., Mar. 27, 1936; s. George Sherman and Isabel Ruth (Eaton) D.; m. Carol Marie Vennerstrom, Feb. 28, 1958; children: Barbara Sarah, George David Jr. Student, Willamette U., 1954-55; BA, U. N.D., 1959; MD, Tulane U., 1961. Diplomate Am. Bd. Radiology. Intern St. Luke's Hosp., Duluth, Minn., 1961-62; gen. practice Lenont-Peterson Clinic, Cook, Minn., 1962-64; resident in radiology Mayo Clinic, Rochester, Minn., 1964-66, 68-70; radiologist St. Luke's Hosp. Radiol. Group, Inc., Kansas City, Mo., 1970—, sec., 1971—; clin. prof. radiology U. Mo. Sch. Medicine, Kansas City, 1985—; sec.-treas. med. staff St. Lukes Hosp., 1992, v.p. med. staff, 1993, pres. med. staff, 1995. Mem. edit. adv. bd. Miller-Freeman Pubs., Inc., 1979—; contbr. articles to med. jours. Pres. Interdenominational Christian Youth Council, Fargo, N.D., 1953-54; lay leader Indian Heights United Meth. Ch., Overland Park, Kans., 1977-79. Served to capt. U.S. Army, 1966-68, Vietnam. Fellow Am. Coll. Radiology (alt. councilor Mo.), Am. Heart Assn., Soc. Cardiovasc. and Interventional Radiology; mem. AMA, Mo. State Med. Soc., Mo. Radiol. Soc. (bd. dirs.), Met. Med. Soc., Greater Kansas City Radiol. Soc. (sec. 1978-79, treas. 1977-78, pres.), Radiol. Soc. N.Am. (counselor Western Mo. dist. 1988-92), Am. Roentgen Ray Soc., New Eng. Hist. Geneal. Soc., Wally Byan Caravan Club (Kansas City), Masons, Phi Beta Kappa, Beta Theta Pi, Phi Beta Pi. Republican. Home: 10416 Mohawk Ln Shawnee Mission KS 66206-2551 Office: St Lukes Hosp Dept Radiology P O Box 119000 Kansas City MO 64171-9000

DIXON, JACK E., biological chemistry educator, consultant. BA, UCLA, 1966; PhD, U. Calif., Santa Barbara, 1971. NSF Found. postdoctoral rsch. fellow U. Calif., San Diego, 1971-73; from asst. prof. to assoc. prof. biochemistry Purdue U., West Lafayette, Ind., 1973-82, prof. biochemistry, 1982-86, Harvey W. Wiley disting. prof. biochemistry, 1986-91; Minor J. Coon prof. biol. chemistry, chmn. dept. U. Mich., Ann Arbor, 1991—; adj. asst. prof. biochemistry, Ind. U. Sch. Medicine, 1976-78, assoc. prof. biochemistry, 1978-91, adj. prof. biochemistry, 1983-91; part-time prof. medicine Ind. U. Sch. Medicine, 1985-91; vis. lectr. Wash. State U., 1985; cons. Wyeth-Ayurst Co., Phila., 1985—, Monsanto Chem. Co., St. Louis, 1985—, Amylin Pharms., Inc., San Diego, 1992—, Mitotix Inc., Cambridge, Mass., 1993—; P.T. Varandani Meml. lectr. Wright State U., Dayton, Ohio, 1987; chmn. rsch. rev. com. Ind. affiliate Am. Heart Assn., 1983; spl. reviewer alcohol study NIH, 1983, 84, endocrine study sect., 1985-90; Nathan O. Kaplan lectr. U. Calif., San Diego, 1991; Vestling lectr. U. Iowa, 1991; Edmund Fischer lectr. U. Wash., Seattle, 1993; Arets Novo Nordisk lectr. U. Copenhagen, 1994; presenter in field. Mem. editl. bd.: Archives Biochem. Biophysics, 1981-84, Am. Jour. Physiology, 1985—, Jour. Biol. Chemistry, 1989—, Endocrinology, 1993—, Biochemistry, 1994—, Analytical Biochemistry, 1985—, exec. editor. Recipient Rsch. award Ind. affiliate Am. Diabetes Assn., 1985-86, MERIT award NIH, 1987, Lions award for cancer rsch., 1990. Fellow Mich. Soc. Fellows, U. Mich. (sr.); mem. AAAS, NAS (elected mem. Inst. Medicine 1993), Am. Chem. Soc., Am. Physiol. Soc., Am. Soc. Biochemistry and Molecular Biology (program chmn. 1994—), Am. Soc. Cell Biology, Am. Soc. Neurosci., Soc. Sigma XI, Phi Kappa Phi. Office: U Mich Dept Biomed Box 0606 5416 Med Sci I Ann Arbor MI 48109*

DIXON, JEROME ANTHONY, osteopathic family physician; b. Dayton, Ohio, June 26, 1959. BS in Dietetics, U. Ky., 1982, M in Nutritional Sci., 1984; DO, Ohio U., 1989. Diplomate Am. Bd. Osteopathic Family Physicians, Nat. Bd. Osteopathic Med. Examiners; PALS instr., ACLS instr., ATLS provider. Intern Richmond Heights Gen. Hosp., 1989-90; resident Doctors Hosp., Columbus, 1990-92; physician Family Med. Clinic, Campbellsville, 1992—; emergency rm. physician Doctors Hosp. of Nelsonville, 1990-92, Immediate Health Assocs., Inc., Westerville, Ohio, 1991, Coastal Emergency Svcs. of Ohio Inc., 1991; night house officer VA Med. Ctr. Dept. Psychiatry, 1991-92; ringside physician State of Ohio Boxing Commn., 1991; instr. Ohio U. Coll. Osteo. Medicine, 1987-89, Doctors Hosp. of Stark County, 1988; med. dir. Taylor County Hosp., patients care procedures com., infection control com., pharmacy and therapeutics com. Contbr. articles to profl. jours. Mem. Ky. Osteo. Med. Assn. (v.p. 1995-96, bd. trustees 1994—, chmn. com. on third party reimbursement 1994—), Am. Coll. Osteo. Family Physicians (sec.-treas. Ky. soc. 1995-96, pres. 1994-95, v.p. 1993-94), Am. Osteo. Assn. (ho. of dels., Ky. state alternate del. 1995), Cranial Acad., Nat. Osteo. Found., Ohio Osteo. Assn., Taylor County Med. Soc., Ky. Med. Assn., Am. Acad. Osteopathy, Am. Soc. Colposcopy and Cervical Pathology, Am. Osteo. Acad. Sports Medicine, Am. Osteo. Coll. Occupl. and Preventative Medicine, Am. Coll. Osto. Family Physicians, Phi Upsilon Omicron (Outstanding Mem. 1981-82). Home: 929 Stray Winds Rd Campbellsville KY 42718 Office: Family Med Clinic PO Box 1097 307 E Broadway Campbellsville KY 42719

DIXON, JOHN HOLLAND, JR., cardiologist; b. Nashville, Dec. 6, 1946; m. Janith Johnston; children: John David, Adam Daniel. BS magna cum laude, Duke U., 1969; MD, Vanderbilt U., 1973. Diplomate in internal medicine and cardiovascular disease Am. Bd. Internal Medicine; lic. physician, Tenn., N.C. Med. intern Vanderbilt U., Nashville, 1973-74, resident in medicine, 1974-75, chief resident in medicine, 1977-78; cardiovascular fellow Duke U. Durham, N.C., 1975-77; cardiologist in pvt. practice Nashville, 1977—. Recipient Albert Weinstein award Vanderbilt U.; Justin Potter scholar. Fellow Am. Coll. Cardiology, Coun. Clin. Cardiology/Am. Heart Assn., Soc. for Cardiac Angiography; mem. AMA, Am. Soc. Internal Medicine, Nashville Cardiovascular Soc., Phi Beta Kappa, Alpha Omega Alpha. Office: St Thomas Med Plaza East 4230 Harding Rd Ste 900 Nashville TN 37205-2013

DIXON, JOHN MATTHEWS, physician; b. Roanoke, Va., Oct. 3, 1942; s. Joseph Moore and Virginia (Matthews) D.; m. Patricia Hoblitzell, June 12, 1965; children: John Scott, Allison Blair. BS, Washington and Lee U., 1964; MD, Med. Coll. Ala., 1968. Diplomate Am. Bd. Ophthalmology. Intern Baylor U. Med. Ctr., Dallas, 1968-69; resident in surgery Emory U. Affiliated Hosps., Atlanta, 1971-74; pvt. practice Albany, Ga., 1974—; chmn. bd. Hosp. Corp. of Am. Palymyra Hosp., Albany, 1984—; asst. clin. prof. of ophthalmology Emory U.; chief of surgery HCA Palmyra Park Hosp., Albany, 1991—. Mem. Sertoma. Home: 2536 W Doublegate Dr Albany GA 31707-9232 Office: 1909 Aberdeen Rd Albany GA 31701-1300

DIXON, JOHN MICHAEL, surgeon, educator; b. Sheffield, Eng., Aug. 27, 1954; s. John Michael and Beatrice (Davies) D.; m. Pamela Machen, May 26, 1984; children: Oliver, Jonathan. BSc with honors, Edinburgh U., Scotland, 1975, MBChB, 1978, MD, 1985. Rsch. fellow Edinburgh U., 1982-84, lectr., hon. sr. surg. registrar, 1987-89, sr. lectr., hon. cons. surgeon, 1989-94, cons. surgeon, sr. lectr., 1994—; surg. registrar Edinburgh/Fife Hosps., 1984-85, Oxford Surg. Rotation Scheme, Eng., 1985-87; house officer Lothian Health Bd., Scotland, 1978-79; sr. house officer Edinburgh U./Lothian Health Bd., 1979-82. Author: Handbook of Diseases of the Breast, 1993; author, editor: ABC of Breast Diseases, 1994/95; editor: Electropotentials in the Clinical Assessment of Breast Cancer, 1995; editor The Breats, 1992—. Rsch. grantee Scottish Hosp. Endowments Rsch. Trust, Scotland, 1991, Chief Scientist's Office, Scotland, 1994, Ciba Geigy Pharms., Eng., 1995. Fellow Royal Coll. Surgeons. Home: 29 Dreghorn Loan Colinton, Edinburgh EH13 0DF, Scotland

DIXON, JOSEPH MOORE, ophthalmologist, consultant; b. Roanoke, Va., Sept. 22, 1910; s. Paul A. and Anna (Kinsey) D.; m. Virginia Matthews, June 27, 1941; children: John, Joseph, Mary Sale. MD, Med. Coll. Va., 1935. Diplomate Am. Bd. Ophthalmology. Ophthalmologist Birmingham; trustee Samford Univ., Birmingham. Contbr. articles to profl. jours. Mem. AMA (chmn. sect. on ophthalmology 1974-76), Am. Assn. Ophthalmology (pres. 1968-69), Contact Lens Assn. of Ophthalmology (pres. 1967-68). Republican. Baptist.

DIXON, LINDA, child, adolescent and adult therapist; b. Bronx, June 2, 1962; d. Joseph and Francine Marilyn (Rega) Incoronato; m. Charles Richard Dixon, Aug. 17, 1987 (div.); children: Joseph Anthony, Danielle Marie. AA, Dutchess C.C., Poughkeepsie, N.Y., 1979; BS, BA magna cum laude, Brockport Coll./SUNY, 1982; MA, Marist Coll., Poughkeepsie, 1986; postgrad., Fordham U., 1985. Behavioral edn. counselor Nutri-System Weight Loss Ctr., Fishkill, N.Y., 1983-85; nutrition/fitness cons. IBM/Mariott Corp., Poughkeepsie, 1985-86; psychol. specialist Eckerd Youth Developmental Found., Okeechobee, Fla., 1986-87; counseling cons. Child Protection Team/Children's Spl. Edn. Needs Team, Okeechobee, Fla., 1987-89; day treatment dir. West County Mental Health Ctr., Belle Glade, Fla., 1988-90; counseling cons. Counseling and Behavioral Assocs., Port St. Lucie, Fla., 1990-93; staff trainer/counseling cons. Calvary Assembly of God, Port St. Lucie, Fla., 1990-91; exec. dir. Network for Christian Counselors, Port St. Lucie, Fla., 1992-95; clin. dir. Renewed Hope Counseling Ctr., Fishkill, N.Y., 1995; mental health case mgr. Wellcare, Kingston, N.Y., 1996; mental health counselor, dir. Renewed Hope Counseling Ctr., Fishkill, N.Y., 1996—; EMT, Alamo Ambulance, Poughkeepsie, 1983-85; grad. asst. Office of Health Svcs., Psychology, Marist Coll., Poughkeepsie, 1984-86; cmty. rep. Sandypines Hosp., Tequesta, Fla., 1989-91; cons. Samaritan House for Boys, Stuart, Fla., 1993-94. Contbr. articles to profl. jours. Bd. dirs. Crisis Pregnancy Svcs., Port St. Lucie, 1992-93; vol. worker Heart Assn. Dutchess County, Poughkeepsie, 1980-81, March of Dimes, 1978-79, Muscular Dystrophy, 1978-79; mem. Congl. Campaign Com./Dutchess County Youth Adv. Com. to Legis, 1980-82. Day Treatment for adolescents Children's Svcs. Coun. grantee, 1988. Mem. Fla. Soc. Psychotherapists, Am. Assn. Christian Counselors, Am. Counseling Assn., Am. Mental Health Counselor Assn., Fla. Sheriff's Assn. Democrat. Home: 14 Rosne Dr #W Wappingers Falls NY 12590-5312 Office: Renewed Hope Counseling 132 Main St Fishkill NY 12590

DIXON, N(ORMAN) REX, speech and hearing scientist, educator; b. Ecorse, Mich., Feb. 24, 1932; s. Theodore Roosevelt and Mary Ann (Barnes) D.; m. Barbara Allen Rose, Sept. 19, 1968; 1 child, Lara Britton. B.A., Western Mich. U., 1958; M.A., Ind. U., 1960; Ph.D., Stanford U., 1966. Instr. Cornell U., Ithaca, N.Y., 1960-61; research staff mem. IBM Corp., San Jose, Calif., 1963-67; adv. scientist IBM Corp., Raleigh, N.C., 1967-72; research staff mem. IBM Corp., Yorktown Heights, N.Y., 1972-83; assoc. editor Jour. Research and Devel. IBM Corp., White Plains, N.Y., 1983-84; editor IBM Corp., 1984-89, cons., 1989—; asst. prof. San Jose State U., Calif., 1964-65; adj. prof. N.C. Central U., Durham, 1967, N.C. State U., 1969-70; vis. prof. Brown U., Providence, 1980—; mem. com. computerized speech recognition NRC, 1983-84. Editor: (with others) Automatic Speech and Speaker Recognition, 1979; contbr. articles to profl. jours. Fellow IEEE (chmn. tech. program Internat. Conf. Acoustics, Speech and Signal Processing 1977, assoc. editor, mem. editorial bd. Jour. Transactions on Acoustics Speech and Signal Processing 1977-81, gen. chmn. Workshop on Automatic Speech Recognition, gen. chmn. Internat. Conf. Acoustics, Speech and Signal Processing 1985, co-chmn. IEEE-Academia Sinica Workshop on Acoustics, Speech and Signal Processing 1986, bd. dirs. 1986-87, Meritorious Service award 1979, 86, vice chmn. pubs. bd. 1987, v.p. tech. activities 1988, chmn. tech. activites bd. 1988); mem. Acoustics Speech and Signal Processing Soc. of IEEE (mem. adminstrv. com. 1976-79, chmn. tech. com. on speech processing 1977-80, chmn. standing com. on conf. standards 1977-81, v.p. 1979-81, pres. 1982-83, Meritorious Service award 1979), Internat. Platform Assn., 1991. Home and Office: 1325 Pembroke Jones Dr Wilmington NC 28405-5205

DIXON, ROBERT W., JR., family physician; b. Traverse City, Mich.; s. Robert W. and Madelon (Hawes) D.; m. Lee Anne Norlyn Van Havep, Oct. 2, 1976; children: Kathryn, Anne, Robert W. III. Undergrad. degree, U. Mich., 1970, MD, 1974. Diplomate Am. Bd. Family Practice. Family practice resident Grand Rapids (Mich.) Area Med. Edn. Ctr., 1974-77; owner, pvt. practice family physician Grand Haven, Mich., 1977—. Fellow Am. Acad. Family Physicians; mem. Am Acad. Family Practice, West Mich. Acad. Family Practice, Mich. State Med. Soc., Ottawa County Med. Soc., Phi Beta Kappa, Alpha Omega Alpha. Episcopalian. Office: 1310 Wisconsin Ste 102 Grand Haven MI 49417

DIXON, ROSINA BERRY, physician, pharmaceutical development consultant; b. Columbus, Ohio, Dec. 3, 1942; d. Loren C. and Florence H. (Bateson) Berry; m. Richard W. Dixon, July 4, 1970; children: Erica H., Douglas R., Andrew D. BA in Chemistry, Radcliffe Coll., 1964; MD, Columbia U., 1968. Diplomate Am. Bd. Internal Medicine. From sr. assoc. to exec. dir. Ciba-Geigy, Summit, N.J., 1972-81; med. dir. Schering Labs., Kenilworth, N.J., 1981-84; v.p. Med. Market Spltys., Boonton, N.J., 1985-86; cons. pharm. devel. Bernardsville, N.J., 1986—; bd. dirs. Cambrex Corp., East Rutherford, N.J., Enzon, Inc., Piscataway, N.J., Church & Dwight Co., Inc., Princeton, N.J.; instr. medicine Coll. Phys. and Surg., Columbia U., 1972—; preceptor in family practice Overlook Hosp., Summit, 1979—; mem. adv. bd. Daytop at Mendham, N.J., 1991—; trustee Bonnie Brae, N.J., 1992. Mem. Am. Coll. Clin. Pharmacology, Am. Soc. Clin. Pharmacology and Therapeutics, Nat. Assn. Corp. Dirs. Episcopalian. Home and Office: 43 Old Wood Rd Bernardsville NJ 07924-1416

DIXON, SHARON DENISE, charge nurse; b. Monroe, La., Mar. 29, 1970; d. Dennis R. and Cecile S. (Dixon) Washington. BSN, Dillard U., 1993. RN, La. Staff/charge nurse North Monroe (La.) Hosp., 1993—. Aliene C. Ewell scholar, Chi Eta Phi, New Orleans, 1991, 1992. Mem. Chi Eta Phi. Democrat. Baptist. Home: 1410 S 9th St Monroe LA 71202

DIXON, SUSAN RENÉE, pediatrics nurse; b. Altoona, Pa., Aug. 11, 1970; d. Gilmore Joseph and Donna Marie (Alamprese) Capouillez; m. Fredrick Allen Dixon, Oct. 12, 1991; 1 child, Eve Nicole. Diploma, Altoona Hosp. Sch. Nursing, 1991. RN, Pa. Med.-surg. nurse Altoona Hosp., 1991; med.-surg. pediatric charge nurse Metro Health Ctr., Erie, Pa., 1991-93.

DJERASSI, ISAAC, physician, medical researcher; b. Sofia, Bulgaria, July 27, 1925; came to U.S., 1954, naturalized, 1962; s. Rahamim and Adela (Tadjer) D.; m. Nira Eskenazy, Jan. 31, 1954; children—Ram Isaac, Ady Lynn. Student, Sofia U. Med. Sch., 1944-49; M.D., Hebrew U., Jerusalem, 1952; D.H. (hon.), Villanova U., 1977. Intern Hadassah Hosp., Tel Aviv, 1951-52; resident Hadassah Hosp., 1953-54; research asso. Harvard U. Med. Sch., Boston, 1955-60; asst. prof. pediatrics U. Pa., Phila., 1960-69; dir. research Mercy Cath. Med. Center, Phila., 1969—; also dir. hematology Mercy Cath. Med. Center; prof. oncology U. Tel Aviv Med. Sch., 1986, dir. Djerassi-Elias Oncology Inst., 1987. Contbr. articles to profl. jours. Mem. med. advisory bd. Nat. Hemophilia Found., Phila., 1964—; mem. med. advisory bd. Leukemia Soc., 1970—. Recipient Albert Lasker award Albert and Mary Lasker Found, 1972, E. Cohn-De Laval award, 1990. Mem. Am. Soc. Cancer Research, Soc. Pediatric Research, Am. Soc. Exptl. Pathology, Am. Assn. Blood Banks. Home: 2034 Delancey Pl Philadelphia PA 19103-6510 Office: Mercy Cath Med Ctr PO Box 19709 Philadelphia PA 19143-0709

DLABAL, PAUL WILLIAM, cardiologist, educator; b. Ellsworth, Kans., Dec. 18, 1949. BA summa cum laude, Kans. State U., 1971; MD, Johns Hopkins U., 1975. Diplomate Am. Bd. Internal Medicine, subsplty. in cardiovasc. disease; lic. Calif., Miss., Tex., Md. Intern in internal medicine Wilford Hall USAF Med. Ctr., Lackland AFB, Tex., 1975-76, resident in internal medicine, 1976-78, fellow in cardiology, 1978-80; staff cardiologist USAF Med. Ctr., Keesler AFB, Miss., 1980-82, chmn. pro tempore cardiology dept., 1981, dir. cardiac catheterization lab., 1981-82; staff cardiologist David Grant Med. Ctr., Travis AFB, Calif., 1982-83, chief of cardiology, 1983-84; pres., CEO Interventional Cardiovasc. Cons., PA, Austin, Tex., 1984—; staff mem. Seton Med. Ctr., Austin, St. David's Comty. Hosp., Austin, Brackenridge Hosp., Austin, South Austin Med. Ctr., Austin, Highland Lakes Med. Ctr., Burnet, Tex.; mem. cons. staff Student Health Ctr., U. Tex., Austin; mem. housestaff coun. Wilford Hall USAF Med. Ctr., 1976; clin. instr. medicine Health Sci. Ctr. U. Tex., San Antonio, 1979-80; clin. asst. prof. medicine and cardiology Tulane U., New Orleans, 1980-82, U. Calif., San Francisco, 1982-84; mem. quality assurance com. South Austin Med. Ctr., 1986, trustee, 1988-92; mem. adv. com. St. David's Health and Fitness Ctr., 1985-86; mem. critical care com. St. David's Hosp., 1985-86; mem. coronary care unit com. Brackenridge Hosp., 1985-88, spl. procedures com., 1987-90, med. staff sec., 1991; mem. critical care com. South Austin Med. Ctr., 1988-90, chmn. 1990—. Reviewer: Jour. AMA, 1979; contbr. articles to med. jours. Maj. USAF, 1982-84. Recipient Best Paper award ACP/Soc. Air Force Physicians, 1982, Physician's Recognition award AMA, 1979, 81, Best Paper award Am. Coll. Chest Physicians, 1980; Kans. Rhodes scholar, 1970. Fellow ACP, Am. Soc. Coronary Angiography and Intervention, Am. Coll. Cardiology, Am. Fedn. Clin. Rsch., Am. Heart Assn. (fellow coun. on clin. cardiology 1992, bd. dirs. Travis County chpt. 1986-90, pres. Travis County chpt. 1991-92), Am. Soc. Coronary Angiography and Intervention, Am. Coll. Cardiology; mem. Soc. Air Force Physicians, Phi Beta Kappa, Phi Kappa Phi. Office: Interventional Cardiovasc 4007 James Casey St Ste A130 Austin TX 78745-1181

DLUGOKINSKI, ERIC L., psychologist, educator; b. Detroit, June 25, 1943; s. Leonard and Rita (Duhr) D.; m. Alfreda Grygiel, May 13, 1965 (div. June 1977); m. Lesley Josephine Boardman, May 13, 1965 (div. June 1977); children: Mark, Damien. BA, U. Detroit, 1965, MA, 1967; PhD, Wayne State U., 1971. Lic. psychologist, Okla. Project dir. summer program Total Action Against Poverty, Detroit, 1966; officer pub. health svc. Nat. Inst. Mental Health, Chgo., 1969-71; asst. prof. U. Okla. Health Scis. Ctr., Oklahoma City, 1971-75, assoc. prof., 1975-91, prof., 1991—; cons. on prevention issues NIMH, Washington, 1979-82; chair high risk children grant rev. Alcohol Drug and Mental Health Assn., Washington, 1990. Author: Emotional Competence I-Dealing with Feelings, 1989, Caring Connections, 1991, Emotional Competence II-I Am. Special, 1982, Living in Self-Esteem, 1994; co-editor (newsletter) Connections, 1993-95; author, primary investigator Listening to the Children Interview, 1995. Co-dir. Emotional Health Ctr., Okla. U. Health Scis. Ctr., Oklahoma City, 1995. Recipient Mayor's award for disting. svc. to the City of Detroit, 1966, Recognition of Outstanding Achievement of facilitating harmony between generations Nat. Coun. on Aging, 1981. Mem. APA (divsn. 37), Southwestern Psychol. Assn., Okla. Psychol. Assn. (chair social issues com. 1989), Nat. Ctr. for Health Edn. (Psychologist of Yr. in Pub. Interest 1995). Home: 5956 N W 71st Oklahoma City OK 73132 Office: Oklahoma U Health Scis Ctr Dept Psychiatry PO Box 26901 Oklahoma City OK 73126

D'LUZANSKY, JAMES JOSEPH, urologist, nephrologist; b. Patton, Pa., Aug. 22, 1929; s. George S. and Mary (Simko) D'L.. BA in Chemistry, St. Vincent Coll., 1950; MD, Hahnemann U., 1954. Diplomate Am. Bd. Urology. Intern Altoona (Pa.) Hosp., 1954; resident in urology Ind. U., Indpls., 1957-61; chief urology U.S. VA Hosp., Altoona Hosp., 1961-80. Lt. comdr. USNR, 1957-77. Fellow Am. Coll. Surgeons; mem. Soc. for Pediat. Urology, Ariz. Urologic Soc. Home and Office: Southwest Ctrl Urology 7617 E Minnezona Ave Scottsdale AZ 85251

DOANE, DAVID GREEN, academic dean, family medicine educator; b. Lynn, Mass., Aug. 6, 1921; s. Mortimer Holden and Elizabeth Mary (Green) D.; m. Joan Larson, June 6, 1946 (div. May 1961); children: Stephen Holden, Geoffrey Hammond, Michael Mortimer, Eric Larsen, Leslie Elizabeth; m. Marjorie Ellen Trelease. BA, Norwich U., 1942; MD, Tufts U., 1946. Diplomate Am. Bd. Family Practice. Intern US Naval Hosp., Annapolis, Md., 1946-47; resident ob-gyn. US Naval Hosp., Chelsea, Mass., 1949-50; chief ob-gyn USMC Air Sta., Cherry Point, N.C., 1950-51; sr. med. officer Naval Ops. Base, Midway Island, 1951-52; practice medicine specializing in ob-gyn Walton, N.Y., 1952-71; commd. US Army M.C., 1971, served to col., 1971-81; chief profl. svcs., dep. commr. Patterson Army Hosp., Fort Monmouth, N.J., 1971-72; cons. family practice, ambulatory care Office of the Surgeon Gen., Washington, 1972-77; commr. DeWitt Army Community Hosp., Ft. Belvoir, Va., 1977-81; retired, 1981; prof., chmn. dept. family medicine, James H. Quillen Coll. Medicine East Tenn. State U., Johnson City, Tenn., 1981-90; assoc. dean for clin. affairs and comty health East Tenn. State U., Johnson City, 1990—; med. dir. Four Oaks Health Care Ctr., Jonesborough, Tenn., 1984—; del. Tenn. Acad. Family Physicians, 1986—. Author: (book chpt.) Textbook of Family Practice, 1984. Deacon Congregational Ch., Walton, 1961-71; elder Presbyn. Ch. Decorated D.S.M.; recipient Legion of Merit, Office of Surgeon Gen., 1977, Disting. Svc. award Tenn. Acad. Family Physicians. Fellow Am. Acad. Family Practice (mem. uniformed services acad., del. 1978-81); mem. AMA (physician recognition award 1976—), U.S. Acad. Family Practice (pres. 1971-73), Soc. Med. Cons. to the Armed Forces, Soc. Tchrs. Family Medicine, Tenn. Med. Assn., Tenn. Aca. Family Physicians. Republican. Presbyterian. Club: Am. Kennel (lic. dog judge, del.). Office: East Tenn State Univ Dept Family Medicine 130A PO Box 21 Johnson City TN 37614

DOANE, HELEN MITZI, psychologist, educator; b. Portsmouth, N.H., Apr. 5, 1952; d. Donald Dexter and Martha Lina (Kurch) D.; m. Stephen Paul Arkulary, Feb. 11, 1984; children: Franklin C. Doane-Arkulary, Reilee M. Doane-Arkulary. BS, St. Bonaventure, 1974; MS, Vanderbilt U., 1976, PhD, 1978. Lic. psychologist, Minn. Rsch. asst. Kennedy Ctr. at Peabody Coll., Nashville, Tenn., 1974-78; asst. prof. U. Minn., Duluth, 1978-81, assoc. prof., 1981—, chair dept. psychology, 1988-92, dean Coll. of Edn. and Human Svc. Professions, 1992—; cons. psychologist St. Luke's Hosp., Duluth, 1986—. Author: Famine at the Feast, 1984; contbr. chpt. to book and articles to profl. jours. Pres. bd. dirs. Human Devel. Ctr., Duluth, 1987-90. Named Outstanding Young Women in Am., 1982. Mem. APA, ACA, Delta Epsilon Sigma, Psi Chi. Episcopalian. Home: 4455 Forest Rd Duluth MN 55803-1957 Office: U Minn CEHSP 125 Bohannon H Duluth MN 55812

DOANE, WOOLSON WHITNEY, internist; b. Worcester, Mass., Mar. 21, 1939; s. Whitney Randall and Mary Helen (Woolson) D.; m. Patricia Louise Morse, June 21, 1962; children: Melinda L., Morse W., Seth J. BA, U. Vt., 1962, MD, 1965. Diplomate Am. Bd. Internal Medicine. Lt. USNR, 1966-68; gen. med. officer Force Troops Fleet, Camp Lejeune, N.C., 1966-68; pvt. practice Franklin Meml. Hosp., Greenfield, Mass., 1971-82; assoc. med. dir.

respiratory therapy Maine Med. Ctr., Waterville, 1982-84; med. dir. Knolls Atomic Power Lab., Schenectady, N.Y., 1984-87; area med. dir. GE Plastics-GE Aerospace, Pittsfield, Mass., 1987-90; med. dir. GE Plastics, Pittsfield, 1991-93; corp. med. dir. Reynolds Metal Co., Richmond, Va., 1993—; bd. dirs. Ctr. and Mass. Am. Lung Assn., Worcester, 1973-82; trustee, bd. dirs. Franklin Meml. Hosp., Greenfield, 1975-79. Bd. dirs. Franklin County Community Action Coun., Greenfield, 1978-81; corporator Berkshire Med. Ctr., Pittsfield, 1987-93; mem. GE Elfan Soc., Pittsfield, Schenectady, 1984-93. Recipient Woodbury Alumni prize U. Vt., 1965. mem. Am. Coll. Occupational and Environ. Medicine, Am. Pub. Health Assn., Am. Coll. Physician Ececs., Va. Thoracic Soc., Med. Soc. Va., Richmond Acad. Medicine. Republican. Episcopalian.

DOBBIE, ROBERT PAUL, surgeon; b. Buffalo, N.Y., June 2, 1924; s. Robert Paul and Adeline Dobbie; m. Barbara Louise Smith, July 2, 1949; cildren: David Scott, Sarah Leigh Burroughs. BA, U. Mich., 1944, MD, 1946. Diplomate Am. Bd. Surgery, Am. Bd. Cardio Thoracic Surgery. Capt. med. corps. USN, 1942-69; intern U. Hosp., Ann Arbor, Mich., 1947-48; resident in gen. surgery U. Hosp., Ann Arbor, 1948-53; resident in cardio-thoracic surgery The Glover Clin. Pres. Hosp., Phila., 1958-60; surg. staff U.S. Naval Hosp., Phila., 1953-54; sr. med. officer U.S. Naval Sta. Hosp., Athens, Greece, 1954-56; cardio-thoracic surgeon U.S. Naval Hosp., Bethesda, Md., 1960-64; chief surgery U.S. Naval Hosp., Memphis, 1964-66, Oakland, Calif., 1966-69; assoc. prof. surgery U. Tenn. Coll. Medicine, 1969-78; prof. surgery U. Tenn. Ctr. Health Scis., 1978-79, clin. prof. surgery, 1980—; jr. clin. instr. surgery Univ. Mich. Med. Sch., 1951-52, sr. clin. instr. in surgery, 1952-53; sr. med. officer surg. team #8, 1950-51, surg. team #4, 1960-64; exec. officer U.S. Naval Hosp., Memphis, 1965-66, Oakland,, 1968-69; mem. cancer com. Regional Med. Program, 1972-79; clin. prof. surgery U. Health Scis. Chgo. Med. Sch., North Chicago, Ill.; med. dir. various divsns. Baxter Healthcare, Inc., Deerfield, Ill., 1979-87 cons. nutrition/flow controller divsn., 1982-85; cons. med. dir. various divsns. Baxter Healthcare Corp., 1985—; med. dir. Clintec Internat., 1989—; clin. prof. surgery U. Health Scis. Chgo. Med. Sch., North Chicago, Ill., 1983—; staff City Memphis Hosps., 1969-79, Baptist Hosp., Memphis, 1969-79, West Tenn. Chest Disease Hosp., Memphis, 1973; cons. in thoracic and gen surgery VA Hosp., Memphis, Naval Hosp., Millington, Tenn., St. Joseph Hosp., Memphis, 1969-79, Meth. Hosp., Memphis, 1969-74, courtesy staff, 1974-79; cons. LeBonheur Children's Hosp., Memphis, 1974-79, courtesy staff, 1969-74; cons. new product devel. program Buckeye Cellulose Corp., Memphis, 1975-79; cons., med. liaison Mead Johnson Rsch. Labs., Evansville, Ind., IVAC Corp., La Jolla, Calif., Ross Labs., Columbus, Ohio, 1975-79, Biosearch Med. Products Inc., Raritan, N.J., 1975-80; dir. Cancer Ctr. Program U. Tenn. Ctr. Health Scis., Memphis, 1971-74; ad hoc mem. inst. grant rev. com. Nat. Cancer Inst., 1976-79, mem. isnt. grant rev. and manpower com., 1977-79; presenter in field. Contbr. articles to profl. pubs. Bd. dirs., mem. closed chest resuscitation com. Memphis Heart Assn., 1970; bd. dirs., mem. profl. edn. com. Am. Cancer Soc., 1971-79; bd. dirs. Memphis Regional Cancer Ctr., 1974-79. Recipient Navy Personal Commendation, Navy Unit Commendation, Nat. Alumni Assn. Pub. Svc. award U. Tenn., 1975. Fellow ACP, ACS; mem. AMA (physician's panel home health care 1988—), Soc. Med. Cons. Armed Gorces, Assn. Mil. Surgeons, S.E. Surg. Congress, Am. Soc. Parenteral Enteral Nutrition, Harwell Wilson Surg. Soc., Assn. Advancement Med. Instrumentation, Am. Soc. Artificial Internal Organs Inc., Am. Acad. Med. Dirs., Am. Coll. Physician Execs, Am. Assn. Home Care Physicians, Frederick A. Coller Surg. Soc., Sigma Xi, Phi Kappa Phi, Galen's Hon. Med. Soc., Alpha Omega Alpha. Home: 128 Rivershire Ln Lincolnshire IL 60069-3803

DOBERENZ, ALEXANDER R., nutrition educator, chemist; b. Newark, Aug. 17, 1936; s. Alexander J. and Marie (Zink) D.; m. Angela Rajoppi, June 7, 1958; children: Annamarie, Judith Lynn, Hoke Jr. B.S. in Chemistry, Tusculum Coll., 1958; M.S., U. Ariz., 1960, Ph.D. in Biochemistry and Nutrition, 1963. Research assoc. dept. physics U. Ariz., Tucson, 1963-69; vis. assoc. prof. nutrition U. Hawaii, 1969; assoc. prof. nutritional scis. U. Wis., Green Bay, 1969-71; prof. U. Wis., 1971-76, assoc. dean Coll. and Sch. Profl. Studies, 1969-76, prof. growth and devel., 1975-76; prof. food sci. and human nutrition U. Del., Newark, 1976—; dean Coll. Human Resources U. Del., 1976-93, coord. home econs. rsch., 1978-93, spl. asst. to the pres., 1993, interim v.p. for student life, 1994-95; cons. food industry, 1976-93; mem. nat. steering com. new initiatives for home econs. U.S. Dept. Agr., 1979-81, USDA Planning com. Workshops on Improving Health Maintenance, 1984-87. Contbr. numerous articles on food chemistry and nutrition to profl. publs. Head underwater recovery unit Pima County Sheriff's Dept., 1966-68; warrant officer CAP, 1965-69; mem. Brown County Comprehensive Health Planning Council, 1973-76; bd. dirs. Pima County Sheriff's Search and Rescue, 1968. Recipient Research Career Devel. award NIH, 1966-69, Outstanding Educator Am., 1971, 72. Fellow Am. Inst. Chemists; mem. Am. Chem. Soc., Am. Home Econs. Soc., Am. Inst. Nutrition (Mead Johnson award nominating com. 1973-76), Nutrition Soc. Today, Soc. for Nutrition Edn., Nutrition Soc. London Soc. Exptl. Biology and Medicine, Am. Soc. Clin. Nutrition, AAAS, Assn. Adminstrs. of Home Econs., Del. Gerontol. Soc. (exec. com. 1978), Nat. Council Adminstrs. Home Econs. (exec. bd. 1982-83), Am. Pub. Health Assn., Del.-Panama Ptnrs. of Ams., Assn. for Devel. Computer Based Instruction, Del. Acad. Sci., Sigma Xi, Phi Lambda Upsilon., Phi Kappa Phi. Roman Catholic. Clubs: University and Whist. Office: U Del 222 Alison Hall Newark DE 19716

DOBES, WILLIAM LAMAR, JR., dermatologist; b. Atlanta, Apr. 16, 1943; s. William Lamar and Sara (Wilson) D.; BA, Emory U., 1965, MD, 1969; m. Martha Husmann, June 16, 1966; children: Margaret Alison, William Shane. Intern Grady Meml. Hosp., Atlanta, 1969-70; fellow dermatology Mayo Clinic, 1970-71; fellow U. Miami, 1971-73; clin. instr. Emory U. Sch. Medicine, Atlanta, 1973-77, asst. prof. dermatology, 1977-83, assoc. prof., 1983—, dir. immunofluorescense lab., 1978-85; mem. staff Crawford Long, Grady Meml., Piedmont hosps. (all Atlanta); dir. Skin Cancer Project, Emory Univ., 1981-89; chmn. profl. edn. unit Atlanta chpt. Am. Cancer Soc., 1980-86, also bd. dirs., pres., 1986-87, chmn. bd. dirs., 1987-88; pres. Carter's Atlanta, project chmn. Physicians Com., 1992-95. Grantee Dermatology Found. Rsch. award, 1979; chmn. Ga. med. bd. Lupus Found., 1988. Diplomate Am. Bd. Dermatology. Fellow Am. Dermatol. Assn.; mem. AMA, ACP, Soc. Investigative Dermatology, Am. Acad. Dermatology (chmn. com. quality assurance 1982-84; adv. council 1985-95, ad coun. exec. com. 1991-95, com. on standards of care 1987-91, chmn. clin. task force, 1993—); So. Med. Assn. (vice chmn. 1983), Pan Am. Med. Assn., Am. Soc. Dermatologic Surgery, Ga. Dermatol. Assn. (pres. 1986-87), Atlanta Dermatol. Assn. (pres. 1979), N.Am. Clin. Dermatologic Soc., Soc. Tropical Dermatology, Med. Assn. Atlanta (bd. dirs. 1985-92, chmn. communications com. 1985-90, sec. 1988-89, pres.-elect, 1989-90, pres. 1990-91), Med. Assn. of Ga. (Intersplty. Council 1984—, com. on cancer, 1988-93, pub. rels. com. 1988-94, del. to Ga. Med. Assn. 1985—, Outstsnding Svc. award 1993), Atlanta Clin. Soc., Atlanta Olympic Med. Com. (chmn. dermatology sect. 1996), Emory U. Med. Alumni Assn. (pres. 1980, 86, exec. com. 1992—), Phi Delta Theta (past pres.), Phi Chi (past pres.). Club: Cherokee Town & Country (Atlanta). Contbr. articles to profl. jours. and texts. Home: 2898 Rivermeade Dr NW Atlanta GA 30327-2010 Office: 478 Peachtree St NE Atlanta GA 30308-3103 also: Emory U Sch Medicine Dept Dermatology Atlanta GA 30308

DOBRO, JEFFREY STEVEN, physician; b. Indpls., Sept. 13, 1955; s. Murray Saul and Barbara (Edinger) D.; m. Candace Lyn Desouza, June 13, 1981; children: Sarah, Gwendolyn. BS, Muhlenberg Coll., 1977; MD, Med. Coll. of Pa., 1981. Med. diplomate. Physician, pres. Dobro and Leslie, Mahwah, N.J., 1987—; pres. Creative Med. Mgmt., Boonton, N.J., 1988—, Ambulatory Care Coop, Inc., Mahwah, 1991; asst. clin. prof. NYU Med. Sch., N.Y.C., 1988—; med. dir. NYCCare Health Plans of N.J., 1995—. Fellow Am. Coll. Rheumotology; mem. Am. Coll. Physicians, AMA. Office: NYCCare Atlantic Region Ste 200 2 Brighton Rd Clifton NJ 07012

DOBROW, HARVEY ROBERT, ophthalmologist; b. N.Y.C., Sept. 19, 1942; s. Benjamin and Eleanor (Rubin) D.; m. Diane Beth Stein, Aug. 24, 1967; children: Lawrence, Julie, Ilyse. Student, Tufts U., 1960-63; MD, SUNY, Bklyn., 1967. Diplomate Am. Bd. Ophthalmology. Intern Montefiore Hosp. Med. Ctr., Bronx, N.Y., 1967-68; resident Manhattan Eye, Ear, Nose, Throat Hosp., N.Y.C., 1968-71; pvt. practice ophthalmology Fair Lawn, N.J., 1973—; sec. Bergen/Passiac Cataract Laser Ctr., Fair Lawn, 1992—; chmn. dept. ophthalmology Barnert Meml. Hosp., Paterson, N.J., 1984-88; sr. staff Valley Hosp., Ridgewood, N.J., 1974—. Maj., U.S. Army, 1971-73. Fellow ACS, Am. Acad. Ophthalmology; mem. AMA, Med. Soc. Stte N.J., N.J. Soc. Ophthalmology and Otolaryngology. Office: Elmwood Profl Bldg 12-15 Broadway Fair Lawn NJ 07410-2031

DOBSON, JAMES CLAYTON, psychologist, author; b. Shreveport, La., Apr. 21, 1936; s. James Clayton Sr. and Myrtle Georgia (Dillingham) D.; m. Shirley Mae Deere, Aug. 27, 1960; children: Danae A., J. Ryan. BA in Psychology, Pasadena (Calif.) Coll., 1958; MS, U. So. Calif., 1962, PhD in Child Devel., 1967; LLD, Pepperdine U., 1983; DHum (hon.), Franciscan U., 1988; DHL, Seattle Pacific U., 1988, Liberty U., 1993, Biola U., 1995; others. Psychometrist, tchr. Hudson Sch. Dist., Hacienda Heights, Calif., 1962-63; psychometrist, counselor Charter Oak H.S., Covina, Calif., 1963-64; sch. psychologist, coord. pers. svcs. Charter Oak Unified Dist., Covina, 1964-66; asst. prof. pediatrics U. So. Calif. Sch. Medicine, L.A., 1969-77, assoc. clin. prof., 1978-83; attending staff div. med. genetics Childrens Hosp. of L.A., 1969-83; pres. Focus on the Family, Colorado Springs, Colo., 1977—; author, speaker, radio and TV host shows relating to successful family living, 1965—; bd. dirs. Focus on the Family/Can., Vancouver, B.C., 1982—; bd. dirs. Family Rsch. Coun., 1992—. Author: Dare to Discipline, 1970, Hide or Seek, 1974, The Strong Willed Child, 1978, Preparing for Adolescence, 1978, Emotions: Can You Trust Them?, 1980, Straight Talk, 1991, When God Doesn't Make Sense, 1994, Life of the Edge, 1995, others; contbr. chpts. to books, articles to profl. jours. Del. White House Conf. on Families, 1980; mem. U.S. Army Task Force on Families, 1986-87, chmn., 1988; mem. Atty. Gen.'s Adv. Bd. on Missing and Exploited Children, 1987-88; mem. Sen. Dole Commn. on Child and Family Welfare, 1994. Served with U.S. Army, 1958-59. Recipient Marian Pfister Anschutz award Family Rsch. Coun., 1987, Humanitarian award Calif. State Psychol. Assn., 1988, Alumni Merit award U. So. Calif. Gen. Alumni Assn., 1989, Paraklesis award Internat. Congress on Christian Counseling, 1992; HHS grantee; NIH grantee, 1975-80.

DOBSON, LEONARD FRANCIS, physician assistant; b. Danville, Pa., Dec. 6, 1957; s. Roman A. and Miranda E. (Gatto) D.; m. Debra Marie Bushick, May 8, 1982; children: Amy E., Melissa N., Michael L. AS, Hahnemann U., 1984, BS, 1990; MS, St. Francis Coll., 1995. With dept. nuclear medicine Geisinger Med. Ctr., Danville, Pa., 1980-82; physician asst. family medicine Geisinger Med. Ctr., Danville, 1984-92, physician asst. neurosurgery, 1992—; physician asst. internal medicine, pediatrics GMG, Lewisburg, Pa., 1991-95. Mem. Am. Acad. Physician Assts. (cert.). Republican. Roman Catholic. Home: 5 Pineview Rd Elysburg PA 17824 Office: Geisinger Med Ctr Dept Neurosurgery N Academy Ave Danville PA 17822

DOBYNS, BROWN MCILVAINE, surgeon, educator; b. Jacksonville, Ill., May 14, 1913; s. Henry D. and Leah (McIlvaine) D.; married; children—Mary Meredith, Courtney Sara, Brown McIlvaine. B.A., Ill. Coll., 1935; M.D., Johns Hopkins, 1939; M.S., U. Minn., 1944, Ph.D., 1946. Diplomate: Am. Bd. Surgery. Intern surgery Johns Hopkins Hosp., 1939-40; fellow surgery Mayo Found., 1940-43; resident surgery Kahler Hosp., Mayo Clinic, 1943-45, 1st asst. surgery, 1945-46, asst. surg. staff, 1946; research fellow surgery, med. sch. Harvard, 1946-48, asst. prof. surgery, 1948-51; grad. asst. surgery Mass. Gen. Hosp., 1946-48, asst. surgery, 1946-51; asso. prof. surgery Western Res. U. Med. Sch., 1951-58, prof. surgery, 1958-84, prof. emeritus, 1984—; asst. chief surg. service Cleve. Met. Gen. Hosp., 1951-66, assoc. chief surg. service, 1967-88; asst. surgeon Univ. Hosp., Cleve., 1951-88; Fulbright lectr., Australia, 1966. Mem. fellowship subcom. Com. on Growth NRC, 1950-54; mem. fellowship com. NSF, 1954-61, chmn., 1955-61; adv. screening com. med. scis. Fulbright, 1955-58; adv. com. research on etiology cancer Am. Cancer Soc., 1956-59, chmn. adv. com. on instnl. grants, 1963-65; mem. Dernham Scholarship com. Calif. Cancer Soc., 1964-74. Recipient Van Meter prize, 1946, award of merit, 1954, Disting. Service award, 1978; all Am. Thyroid Assn.; citation for disting. public service Ill. Coll. Fellow ACS; mem. Soc. Univ. Surgeons, Am. Soc. Clin. Investigation, Am., Central surg. assns., Am. Thyroid Assn. (pres. 1956-57), Cleve. Surg. Soc. (pres. 1966-67), Halstead Soc., Société Internationale de Chirurgie, AAAS, Endocrine Soc., Sigma Xi. Home: 9930 Kirtland Rd Chardon OH 44024-9746

DOBYNS, RICHARD C., general practice physician, medical administrator; b. Swindon, Eng., Jan. 25, 1956; s. James H. and Elizabeth G. (Owens) D.; m. Jean Talzmann. BA, St. Olaf Coll., 1978; MD, U. Minn., 1983; MS, U. Iowa, 1993. Cert. in geriat., 1992. Pvt. practice Family Practice of Willmar (Minn.), P.C., 1980-88; asst. prof. family medicine U. Iowa, Iowa City, 1988-95, assoc. prof. family medicine, 1995—; dir. clin. svcs., dept. family medicine U. Iowa, 1994—. Office: Univ Iowa Dept Family Medicine Iowa City IA 52242

DOCHERTY, JOHN JOSEPH, microbiologist; b. Youngstown, Ohio, Dec. 5, 1941; s. John Henry and Viola Jean (Sovak) D.; m. Pamela Ann Kaminsky, Aug. 21, 1965; children: Patricia, Susan. BA, Youngstown U., 1964; MS, Miami U., Oxford, Ohio, 1966; PhD, U. Ariz., 1970; postgrad., Pa. State U. Coll. Medicine, 1972. Asst. prof. microbiology Pa. State U., University Park, 1972-76, assoc. prof., 1976-86; prof. microbiology, immunology Coll. Medicine Northeastern Ohio U., Rootstown, Ohio, 1987—, chair dept., 1987—; cons. in field. Grantee NIH, Dept. Agriculture. Mem. Am. Soc. Microbiology, Am. Soc. Virology, Assn. Med. Sch. Microbiology & Immunology Chairs, Phi Sigma, Alpha Omega Alpha. Home: 7531 Diagonal Rd Kent OH 44240-5954 Office: Northeastern Ohio U Dept Microbiology/Immunology Coll Medicine Rte 44 Rootstown OH 44272

DOCKHORN, ROBERT JOHN, physician, educator; b. Goodland, Kans., Oct. 9, 1934; s. Charles George and Dorotha Mae (Horton) D.; m. Beverly Ann Wilke, June 15, 1957; children: David, Douglas, Deborah. AB, U. Kans., 1956, MD, 1960. Diplomate Am. Bd. Pediat. Intern Naval Hosp., San Diego, 1960-61; resident in pediat. Naval Hosp., Oakland, Calif., 1963-65; resident in pediat. allergy and immunology U. Kans. Med. Ctr., 1967-69, adj. asst. prof. pediat., 1969—; resident in pediat. allergy and immunology Children's Mercy Hosp., Kansas City, Mo., 1967-69, chief divsn., 1969-83; practice medicine specializing in allergy and immunology Children's Mercy Hosp., Prairie Village, Kans., 1969-94, U. Mo. Med. Sch., Prairie Village, Kans., 1969-94; pres. Internat. Med. Tech. Cons., Inc., Kansas City, 1979—; pres. I.M.T.C.I. (Internat. Med. Tech. Cons., Inc.), Kansas City, 1979—; founder, CEO Internat. Med. Tech. Cons., Inc., Prairie Village, Kans., subs. Immuno-Allergy Tech. Cons., Inc., Clin. Rsch. Cons., Inc. Contbr. articles to med. jours.; co-editor: Allergy and Immunology in Children, 1973. Fellow Am. Acad. Pediatrics, Am. Coll. Allergists (bd. regents 1976—, v.p. 1978-79, pres. 1981-82), Am. Assn. Cert. Allegists (pres. 1991—), Am. Acad. Allergy; mem. AMA, Kans. Med. Soc., Johnson County Med. Soc., Kans. Allergy Soc. (pres. 1976-77), Mo. Allergy Soc. (sec. 1975-76), Joint Coun. Socio-Econs. of Allergy (bd. dirs. 1976—, pres. 1978-79). Home: 8510 Delmar Ln Shawnee Mission KS 66207-1926

DOCKRAY, GRAHAM JOHN, physiologist; b. Leeds, England, July 19, 1946; s. Ben Norman and Elsie (Watson) D.; m. Andrea Varro, Dec. 28, 1985; children: Judith, Mark. BS, Nottingham U., England, 1967, PhD, 1971. Lectr. U. Liverpool (England), 1970-78, sr. lectr., 1978-80, reader, 1980-82. Editor: Cholecystokinin, 1986, The Neuropeptide Cholecystokinin, 1989, Gut Peptides, 1994; contbr. articles to profl. jours. Fogerty fellow VA Hosp., L.A., 1973-76; Program grantee Med. Rsch. Coun., 1988. Mem. Physiol. Soc. (com. mem. 1988—, chmn. 1991—), Med. Rsch. Coun. Physiol. Medicine and Infectious Bd. (chmn. grant com. A 1993—), Bayliss and Starling Soc. (sec. 1989-92). Office: U Liverpool Dept Physiology, Brownlow Hall, Liverpool L69 3BX, England

DODD, DARLENE MAE, nurse, air force officer; b. Dowagiac, Mich., Oct. 11, 1935; d. Charles B. and Lila H. D.; diploma in nursing Borgess Hosp. Sch. Nursing, Kalamazoo, 1957; grad. U.S. Air Force Flight Nurse Course, 1959, U.S. Air Force Squadron Officers Sch., 1963, Air Command and Staff Coll., 1973; BS in Psychology and Gen. Studies, So. Oreg. State Coll., 1987, postgrad., 1987; Commd. 2d lt. U.S. Air Force, 1959, advanced through grades to lt. col., 1975; staff nurse, Randolph AFB, Tex., 1959-60, Ladd AFB, Alaska, 1960-62, Selfridge AFB, Mich., 1962-63; Cam Rahn Bay Air Base, Vietnam, 1966-67, Seymour Johnson AFB, N.C., 1967-69, Air Force Acad., 1971-72; flight nurse 22d Aeromed. Evacuation, Tex., 1963-66; chief nurse Danang AFB, Vietnam, 1967; flight nurse Yokotu AFB, Japan, 1969-71; clin. coordinator ob/gyn and flight nurse, Elmendorf AFB, Alaska, 1973-76; clin. nurse coordinator obstetrics-gynecology and pediatric services USAF Med. Center, Keesler AFB, Miss., 1976-79, ret., 1979. Decorated Bronze Star, Meritorious Service medal, Air Force Commendation medal (3). Mem. Soc. of Ret. Air Force Nurses, DAV, Ret. Officers Assn., Vietnam Vets. Am., VFW, Uniformed Services Disabled Retirees, Air Force Assn., Psy Chi, Phi Kappa Phi. Club: Women of Moose. Home: 712 1st St Phoenix OR 97535-9787

DODD, EMMELINE IRWIN, biology educator; b. Nacogdoches, Tex., Aug. 30, 1939; d. Grady Scott and Addie Mae (Chambers) Irwin; m. Gene Dodd, Jan. 28, 1961 (div. 1967); 1 child, Cathy Denise. BA, Stephen F. Austin State U., Nacogdoches, 1961, MA, 1965; postgrad., Tex. A&M U., 1967-74; MS, U. Houston, 1982. CPA, lic. real estate broker, Tex. Biology tchr. Pasadena (Tex.) Ind. Sch. Dist., 1961-65; prof. of biology San Jacinto Coll., Pasadena, 1965-69; rsch. biologist NASA, Clear Lake, Tex., 1969-71; biology tchr. Houston Community Coll., 1971-72; prof. of biology Coll. of Mainland, Texas City, Tex., 1973—. Chmn. Houston Livestock Show and Rodeo, Clear Lake, 1991-94; staff advisor Lunar Rendezvous, Clear Lake, 1991; mem. com. Tex. Higher Edn. Coord. Bd., Austin, 1989—. Mem. Nat. Assn. Biology Tchrs. (planning com. 1990 conv.), Tex. Jr. Coll. Tchrs. Assn. (pres. 1989-90, state social chmn. 1991-92), Tex. Assn. Real Estate Brokers, Clear Lake Panhellenic Soc., Internat. Platform Speakers Assn., Stephen F. Austin Alumni Assn. (life), Chi Omega. Democrat. Baptist. Office: Coll of Mainland 1200 N Amburn Rd Texas City TX 77591-2435

DODD, GERALD DEWEY, JR., radiologist, educator; b. Oaklyn, N.J., Nov. 18, 1922; s. Gerald Dewey and Anne Aloysius (Keveney) D.; m. Helen Carolyn Glenzing, Apr. 5, 1946; children: Patricia, Michael, Barbara, Gerald Dewey III, Anne, Susan, Thomas. A.B., Lafayette Coll., 1945; M.D., Jefferson Med. Coll., 1947. Diplomate Am. Bd. Radiology. Intern Fitzgerald Mercy Hosp., Darby, Pa., 1947; resident Jefferson Med. Coll., Phila., 1948-50; asst. radiologist, instr. radiology Jefferson Med. Coll. and Hosp., Phila., 1952-55; asst. radiologist, clin. prof. radiology Jefferson Med. Coll. and Hosp., 1961-66; assoc. prof. radiology, assoc. radiologist U. Tex. M.D. Anderson Hosp. and Tumor Inst., Houston, 1955-61; prof. U. Tex. M.D. Anderson Hosp. and Tumor Inst., 1966—, chmn. dept. diagnostic radiology Cancer Ctr., 1966-89, prof., head div. diagnostic imaging, 1984-92, Robert D. Moreton Chair Diagnostic Radiology, 1988-93; prof. radiology U. Tex. Med. Sch., Houston, 1971—; chmn. dept. radiology U. Tex. Med. Sch., 1971-74, prof. radiology Sch. Allied Health Scis., 1971—; cons. radiologist St. Luke's Hosp., Tex. Children's Hosp., Houston, 1966—, Singleton Prof. Radiology, 1995—; vis. mem. grad. faculty Tex. A&M U., College Station, 1969—; adj. prof. radiology Baylor Coll. Medicine, 1983—. Cons. to editor Radiology, 1977-86; cons. editor The Cancer Bull., 1979-89; assoc. editor Cancer, 1991—; referee CRC Critical Revs. in Radiol. Scis., 1969—; contbr. articles to profl. jours. Dir.-at-large Am. Cancer Soc., 1977-90, pres., 1990-91, past officer dir.; mem. coun. Nat. Coun. Radiation Protection and Measurement, 1979-91, bd. dirs., 1981-91. Fellow Am. Coll. Radiology (chmn. bd. chancellors 1982-84, pres. 1984-85, chmn. breast task force 1986, mem. standards task force 1988-92, Gold medal 1989); mem. Radiol. Soc. N.Am. (Gold medal 1986), Am. Roentgen Ray Soc. (Gold medal 1992), Soc. Gastrointestinal Radiologists (Cannon medal 1995), Assn. Univ. Radiologists, Tex. Med. Assn., Tex. Radiol. Soc. (Gold medal 1988), Soc. Breast Imaging (Gold medal 1995), Harris County Med. Soc., Houston Radiol. Soc., Phila. Roentgen Ray Soc. (hon.), Alpha Omega Alpha, Phi Delta Theta, Phi Chi. Republican. Roman Catholic. Office: M D Anderson Hosp 1515 Holcombe Blvd Houston TX 77030-4009

DODD, LORRAINE, medical company executive; b. Dewsbury, Yorkshire, Eng., Oct. 8, 1955; d. Trevor and Audrey (Hughes) Thorpe; m. Nigel Andrew Dodd, Apr. 7, 1984; children: Clare Sophie, Helen Rowena. BSc in Pure Math., U. Warwick, Eng., 1977, MSc in Operational Rsch., 1978. Sr. analyst Rolls-Royce, Derby, Eng., 1978-82; sr. lectr. Royal Military Coll. Science, Shrivenham, Eng., 1982-87; sr. rschr. Royal Signals and Radar Establishment, Malvern, Eng., 1987-91; dir. Neural Solutions Ltd., Cheltenham, Eng., 1991—; rsch. cons. Siemens Med., Mass., 1994-96. Patentee in field; contbr. articles to profl. publs. Recipient Small Firms Rsch. and Technology Merit award Dept. Trade and Industry, 1990-91. Office: Neural Solutions Ltd, 15 Celandine Bank, Gloucester GL52 4HZ, England

DODD, RICHARD, family practice physician; b. Syracuse, N.Y., Mar. 18, 1934; s. Donald Cameron and Irene (Winne) D.; m. Jean Susan Petrock, Nov. 12, 1961; children: Richard Paul, Helen J. Dodd Rodgers. BS, St. Lawrence U., 1956; MD, SUNY, Syracuse, 1960. Diplomate Am. Bd. Family Practice. Rotating intern U. Va., Charlottesville, 1961; resident in orthopedics U. Fla., Gainesville, 1962; pvt. practice family physician Daytona Beach, Fla., 1963-73, Memphis, 1990—; dir family practice residency program Halifax Hosp., Daytona Beach, 1973-83, U. Tenn., Memphis, 1983-90; mem. med. staff Bapt. Meml. Hosp., mem. credentials com., 1987-89, chmn. dept. family practice, 1985-88; asst. prof. dept. family medicine U. South Fla., Tampa, 1976-83, U. Tenn., 1983-90; cons. Am. Acad. Family Physicians, Kansas City, Mo., 1986; spkr. in field. Contbr. articles to profl. jours. Chmn., sec. Fla. Coun. on Grad. En., Jacksonville, 1975-78; bd. dirs., sec., v.p. Fla. Acad. Family Physicians, jacksonville, 1974-83; chmn. com., sec., pres. Volusia County Med. Soc., Daytona Beach, 1967-70; mem. ch. coun. Seabreeze United Ch., Daytona Beach, 1974-76; mem. Daytona Beach Mental Health Bd., 1973; bd. dirs. Daytona Beach C. of C., 1975-78; commr. Daytona Beach City Commn., 1977-83. Maj. USNG, 1962-68. Mem. AMA, Ten. Med. Assn., Memphis Acad. Family Physicians (pres. Shelby chpt. 1990-91). Republican. Methodist. Home: 4203 Poplar Ave Memphis TN 38117 Office: Primary Care Specialists 3445 Poplar Ave Memphis TN 38111

DODDS, BRENDA KAY, nurse; b. Wheeling, W.Va., July 14, 1961; d. Ray Charles and Kathryn June (Ries) D. BS, Graceland Coll., 1983; A in Child Devel., 1990. RN. Staff nurse Resthaven Retirement Home, Independence, Mo., 1983-84; staff nurse telemetry unit Columbia Independence Regional Health Ctr., 1983—; camp nurse Mo-Kan Salvation Army Camp, Kansas City, Mo., 1984; dental asst. Ronald E. Jennings, DDS P.C., Independence, 1985-87; sch. nurse Noland Child Devel. Ctr., Independence Pub. Sch. Dist., 1988—, head tchr., 1990—, morning supr., 1993—. Vol. ARC, Independence, 1983—, Voluntary Action Ctr., 1987—; vocalist Independence Messiah/Festival Choir, 1983—; musician Independence Symphony Band, 1988—. Mem. Nat. Assn. for Edn. Young Children, Mo. Nurses Assn., Profl. Nurses Assn., Mensa.

DODGE, R(ALPH) EDWARD, family physician; b. Salamanca, N.Y., Jan. 14, 1936; s. Ralph Edward and Eunice Elvira (Davis) D.; m. Nancy Lou De Lay, Aug. 14, 1957; children: Randall, Jeffrey, Amy. BA, Taylor U., 1958; MD, Ind. U., 1962; MPH, Johns Hopkins U., 1967. Diplomate Am. Bd. Preventive Medicine, Am. Bd. Family Practice. Rotating intern L.A. County Gen. Hosp., 1962-63; resident gen. preventive medicine sch. hygiene & pub. health Johns Hopkins U., 1966-69; asst. prof. pub. health Haile Sellassie U., Gondar, Ethiopia, 1967-69; staff physician Frontier Nursing Svc., Hyden, Ky., 1970-71; med. dir. Citrus-Levy County Health Dept., Inverness, Fla., 1971-74; physician emergency dept. Waterman Meml. Hosp., Eustis, Fla., 1974-75; pvt. practice Inverness, 1975—; med. dir. Citrus Primary Care Network, 1994-96; clin. asst. prof. U. Fla., 1994—. Contbr. articles to med. jours.; editor Fla. Family Physician, 1991-95; newspaper columnist: Health Simplicity, 1988-90, Life and Health, 1990—. Bd. dirs. Marion-Citrus Mental Health Ctrs., Ocala, Fla., 1972-74, North Cen. Fla. Health Planning Commn., Gainesville, 1979-80, Fla. div. Am. Cancer Soc., 1988-90, Citrus Meml. Health Found., Inverness, 1988-94. Lt. comdr. USPHS, 1964-66. Recipient Disting. Svc. award Fla. Assn. Emergency Med. Technicians, 1976, Community Svc. award Seventh Day Adventist Ch., Inverness, 1978, Citizen of Yr. award Citrus County Chronicle, 1987. Mem. AMA, Am. Coll. Preventive Medicine, Am. Acad. Family Physicians, Fla. Acad. Family Physicians (bd. dirs. 1994—), Fla. Med. Assn., Citrus County Med. Soc. (pres. 1977, sec.-treas. 1981-86), Citrus County C. of C. (Outstanding Comty. Svc. award 1972). Democrat. Office: Citrus Primary Care 511 W Highland Blvd Inverness FL 34452-4719

DODSON, JAMES CARLISLE, internist; b. Louisville, Ky., June 28, 1951; s. Carlisle Victor and Elaine (Burkhead) D.; children: George Victor, Julia Elizabet. Student, U. Ky., 1972; MD, Tulane U., 1976. Diplomate Am. Bd. Internal Medicine. Intern in internal medicine Tulane U. Sch. Medicine, New Orleans, 1976-77; resident in internal medicine U. Louisville, 1977-79; pvt. practice internal medicine Russellville, Ky., 1979—. Mem. AMA, ACP, So. Med. Assn. Office: 147 E 5th St Russellville KY 42276

DODSON, VERNON NATHAN, physician, educator; b. Benton Harbor, Mich., Feb. 19, 1923; m. Shirley Jane Wheelihan: children: Martha Ione, Kathryn Anne, Christine Louise, John Nathan, Elizabeth Marie. Student, Mich. State Coll., 1941-43, 46, Northwestern U., summer 1942, Compton (Calif.) Coll., 1943, U. Oreg., 1943-44, Corpus Christi Coll., U. Oxford, Eng., 1945, U. Mich., 1946-47, 48, 51-52; BS, U. Mich., 1952; MD, Marquette U., 1951. Intern in surgery Henry Ford Hosp., Detroit, 1952-53; asst. in pathology Johns Hopkins U. Hosp., Balt., 1953-54, asst. pathologist, 1953-54; resident in internal medicine Univ. Hosp., Ann Arbor, Mich., 1954-57; rsch. assoc. U. Mich. Med. Sch., Ann Arbor, 1957-60, 60-71, lectr., 1959, from jr. clin. instr. to assoc. prof., 1956-64, assoc. prof. Dept. Indsl. Health, Sch. Pub. Health, 1965-71; attending physician U.S. VA Hosp., Ann Arbor, 1961-70; mem. med. staff Milw. County Gen. Hosp., 1971-72; rsch. assoc. U.S. VA Ctr., Wood, Wis., 1971-72; prof. medicine and environ. medicine Med. Coll. Wis., Milw., 1971-72; vis. prof. dept. preventive medicine U. Wis. Med. Sch., Madison, 1973-74, prof. medicine, sect. internal medicine, and preventive medicine, 1977-94, prof. emeritus medicine and preventive medicine, 1994—; lectr. Sch. Dentistry, U. Mich., Ann Arbor, 1957-58, Sch. Nursing, U. Mich., 1958-60, Coll. Lit., Sci. and Arts, Inst. Social Work, U. Mich., 1957-58; cons. staff physician Rochester, Minn. Meth. Hosp., 1974-77; dir. Univ. Employee Health Svc., U. Wis., Madison, 1977-80, mem. staff Ctr. Health Sci., 1978-95, hon. staff, 1995—; physician cons. VA Hosp., Madison, 1978-95; mem. interdepartmental program in toxicology, U. Mich., 1965-71, vice chair, 1969-71; mem. Environ. Toxicology Ctr., Divsn. Health Scis., U. Wis., Madison, 1972-74, 77-94, acting dir., 1974-76, 78-79, assoc. dir. Sch. Biotron., 1979-84; vis. prof. U. Tex. Health Sci. Ctr., Sch. Pub. Health, Houston, 1986, So. Occupational Health Ctr., U. Calif., Irvine, 1986; mem. com. on edn. and libr., Trinity Meml. Hosp., Cudahy, Wis., 1971-71, assoc. med. staff, 1972-73; mem. assoc. med. staff St. Lukes Hosp., Milw., 1972-73; cons. Joint Commn. on Hosp. Accreditation, Chgo., 1974-76; cons. in preventive medicine and internal medicine, Mayo Clinic, Mayo Found., Rochester, 1974-77; cons. GM, Warren, Mich., 1963-65, 72-84, med. dir. GM, Oak Creek, Wis., 1971-72; cons. Oscar Mayer Co., 1973-74; cons. plant physician, IBM, Rochester, 1976-77; cons. med. dir. George A. Hormel co., Austin, Minn., 1977; mem. occupational health adv. bd. GM, UAW, 1982-85; cons. Owens-Corning Fiberglas, Toledo, 1968—, Gen. Mills, Mpls., 1980—; bd. dirs. Nat. Biogerontology Inst., 1984—; cons. USPHS, Dept. Natural Resources, Wis., Dept. Health and Social Svcs., Wis., U.S. Dept. Agr., OSHA, Wis., Nat. Inst. Occupational Safety and Health, Ctr. for Disease Control, Dept. Industry, Labor and Human Rels., Wis.; mem. Gov.'s Task Force on Occupational Health and Safety, State of Wis., Extramural Ctr. Adv. Rev. Panel, Nat. Inst. for Occupational Health and Safety, Sentinel Event Notification System for Occupational Risks, Divsn. Health, State Dept. Health and Social Svc., Madison, Wis.; vice chair Residency Rev. Com. for Preventive Medicine, Accreditation Coun. for Gen. Med. Edn. Edn. cons. editor Am. Jour. Occupational Medicine, 1979-89; assoc. editor Am. Jour. Indsl. Medicine, 1986-80; author 2 books, 17 book chpts., 44 sci. rsch. papers, 119 abstracts and presentations, 4 TV programs; co-editor 1 book. Mem. spl. citizen's adv. com. on safety Ann Arbor Bd. Edn., 1969, gov.'s com. on crime detection and law enforcement, ad hoc com. on lab. svcs., State of Mich., 1969; chmn., mem. com. on sch. safety, King Sch., Ann Arbor, 1969-70; mem. Kettle Moraine High Sch. Band Parents, Wales, Wis., 1972-74, v.p., 1973-74, citizen's com. on drug abuse, Waukesha County, Wis., 1973-74. With U.S. Army, 1942-45, ETO. Recipient Disting. Svc. award, Occupational Health award UAW, GM, 1988. Fellow ACP, Aml. Occupl. Medicine (bd. dirs. 1987—, award 1988), Am. Coll. Medicine, Am. Occupl. Medicine Assn. (bd. govs. 1985, award 1988), Am. Coll. Occupl. and Environ. Medicine, Am. Coll. Preventive Medicine, Soc. Occupl. and Environ. Health; mem. AAAS, AMA (rep. residency rev. com., vice chair accreditation coun. for gen. med. edn., Physician's Recognition award 1981—), Am. Fedn. for Clin. Rsch., The Biochem. Soc. (London), Wis. State Med. Soc. (environ./occupl. health commn., legis. affairs commn., continuing med. edn. commn., Meritorious Svc. award 1991, 96), Ctrl. States Occupl. Medicine Assn. (bd. govs.), Dane County Med. Soc., Am. Pub. Health Assn., Wis. Pub. Health Assn., Am. Cancer Soc. (award 1987), Internat. Commn. for Occupl. Health (Geneva), alumnae orgns. Mich. State U., U. Mich., Marquette U., Johns Hopkins U., Mayo Clinic, Med. Coll. Wis., U. Wis., Henry Ford Hosp., VFW, 11th Armored Divsn. Assn., Friends of WHA-TV, Smithsonian Instn., Nat. Geog. Soc., World Wildlife Fund, Sierra Club, Natural Resource Def. Coun., Sigma Xi. Office: U Wis Dept Medicine 504 Walnut St Madison WI 53705-2335

DOEPKER, J(OHN) FREDERICK, JR., plastic surgeon; b. Lima, Ohio, Mar. 22, 1949; s. John Frederick and Elizabeth (Merritt) D.; children: John, Justin, Ashley, Derek. BA in Math., Ind. U., 1971; MD, Ind. U., Indpls., 1976. Diplomate Am. Bd. Plastic Surgery. Resident in gen. and plastic surgery Butterworth Hosp., Grand Rapids, Mich., 1976-81; fellow in plastic surgery Vanderbilt U., Nashville, 1981-82; practice medicine specializing in plastic surgery Evansville, Ind., 1982—. Past v.p. Vanderburgh County Am. Cancer Soc., Evansville, 1984-88; bd. dirs. Leadership Evansville, 1989—. Fellow ACS; mem. Am. Soc. Plastic and Reconstructive Surgeons, Vanderburgh County Med. Soc., Am. Med. Assn., John B. Lynch Soc., Lipolysis Soc. N.Am., Ferris Smith Soc., So. Med. Assn., Phi Rho Sigma Med. Soc. Office: 2701 Lincoln Ave Evansville IN 47714-1627

DOERFLER, LEO G., audiology educator; b. N.Y.C., June 25, 1919; s. Gustav S. and Anna (Steiner) D.; m. Alice Laura Turechek, Dec. 19, 1943; children—Dennis Lee, Donald Lee, David Lee, Ann Laura. A.B., N.Y.U., 1939; M.S., Washington U., St. Louis, 1941; Ph.D., Northwestern U., 1948. Tchr.- psychologist Iowa Sch. Deaf, Council Bluffs, 1941-43; instr. audiology Northwestern U., 1946-48; chief dept. audiology-speech pathology Latrobe Area Hosp., 1976—; prof. audiology emeritus (Sch. Medicine); dir. doctoral program bioacoustics U. Pitts., 1948-76; dir. dept. audiology Eye and Ear Hosp., Pitts., 1948-76; pres. Westmoreland Hearing Assocs.; chmn. bd. Audiology Coop.; Cons. in field, 1946—, Nat. Inst. Neurol. and Communicative Diseases and Stroke. Contbr. articles to profl. jours. Bd. dirs. Cerebral Palsy Assn. Pitts., 1958—. Served with AUS, World War II. C.C. Bunch fellow Northwestern U., 1946-47. Fellow AAAS, Am. Speech and Hearing Assn. (pres. 1967); mem. Am. Indsl. Hygiene Assn. (com. on noise), Indsl. Med. Assn. (com. on noise), Am. Acad. Ophthalmology and Otolaryngology (com. on hearing and equilibrium), Am. Bd. Examiners in Speech Pathology and Audiology (pres. 1960), Acad. Dispensing Audiologists (pres. 1978-79), Sigma Xi. Home: 4533 W Barlind Dr Pittsburgh PA 15227-1131

DOERING, CHARLES HENRY, research scientist, educator, editor, publisher; b. Munich, Germany, Jan. 7, 1935; came to U.S., 1950; s. Heinrich and Marianne (Fleischmann) D.; m. Panayiota Maria Thliveris, June 17, 1961; children: Andreanna, Erika, Stefan, Anselm. BS in Chemistry, U. San Francisco, 1956; MS in Organic Chemistry, U. Munich, 1959; PhD in Biochemistry, U. Calif., San Francisco, 1964. Postdoctoral fellow Harvard Med. Sch., Boston, 1964-67; rsch. scientist Stanford (Calif.) U. Sch. Medicine, 1967-76; rsch. assoc. prof. SUNY, Stony Brook, 1976-86; editor Springer Verlag Publs., N.Y.C., 1986-90, Oxford Univ. Press, N.Y.C., 1990-91; exec. editor VCH Publs., Inc., N.Y.C., 1991-94; sr. editor Am. Inst. Physics Press, Woodbury, N.Y., 1994—. Contbr. over 30 articles to profl. jours. Mem. AAAS, Am. Chem. Soc., N.Y. Acad. Scis., Soc. Scholarly Pub. Home: 21 Dyke Rd Setauket NY 11733-3014 Office: AIP Press 500 Sunnyside Blvd Woodbury NY 11797-2999

DOERING, DONALD PAUL, nursing administrator; b. Monroe, Wis., Jan. 28, 1948; s. Paul Henry and Shiela Ann (Ross) D.; m. Jennifer Jane Radmer, April 17, 1971; 1 child, Brian Paul. BSN, U. Wis., 1978; MSN, Vanderbilt U., 1980. med./surg. nursing, nursing administration. Staff nurse med./surg. VA Med. Ctr., Nashville, 1978-80, Hendersonville (Tex.) Cmty. Hosp., 1980-82; staff nurse ICU VA Med. Ctr., Nashville, 1982, head nurse med./surg., 1982-88; assoc. chief nurse trainee VA Med. Ctr., Mpls., 1988-89; assoc. chief nurse med./surg. VA Med. Ctr., Pitts., 1989-90, assoc. chief nurse ambulatory care, 1991, assoc. chief nurse long term care and intermediate medicine, 1991—; lectr. multiple adminstrv. topics, 1989-95, multiple med. surg. topics, 1985-88. Vol. Am. Cancer Soc., Nashville, 1984-88. Sgt. USAF, 1970-73. Mem. Pa. Nurses Assn., Sigma Theta Tau. Office: VA Med Ctr University Dr Pittsburgh PA 15240

DOERKSEN, RUSSELL L., optometrist; b. Newton, Kans., June 22, 1962; s. George and Beverly R. (Vanamberg) D.; m. Veronica L. Kraichely; 1 child, Abigail. BA in Natural Sci. and Chemistry, Tabor Coll., Hillsboro, Kans., 1984; OD, U. Mo., St. Louis, 1989. Pvt. practice, St. Louis, 1989-94, Wichita, Kans., 1994—; examining optometrist Benton Elem. Sch., Unified Sch. Dist. 259, Wichita, 1996. Mem. Am. Optometric Assn., Mo. Optometric Assn., Kans. Optometric Assn., Wichita Optometric Soc., Delta Sigma Kappa. Republican. Menonite. Office: Bldg 1042 Ste A 7570 W 21st St Wichita KS 67205

DOERR, BARBARA ANN, health facility director; b. Poteet, Tex., Apr. 2, 1951; d. William Ira and Margaret Sophia (Lozano) Potts; m. Michael F. Doerr, Aug. 19, 1984; 1 child, Jennifer. BSN, U. Tex., 1975. RN, Tex.; cert. nursing adminstr. Nursing house supr. Brackenridge Hosp., Austin, Tex., 1980-84, clin. coord., 1984-87, dir. med./surg. nursing, 1987-93, acting asst. adminstr., 1989-90, dir. nursing adminstrn., 1993—. Mem. ANA, Tex. Nurses Assn. (dist. V, Nurse of Yr. 1990-91), U. Tex.-Austin Sch. Nursing Alumni Assn. (pres.), Tex. Orgn. of Nurse Execs., Sigma Theta Tau (Epsilon chpt.). Home: 4139 Bee Creek Rd Spicewood TX 78669

DOERR, ROBERT DOUGLAS, psychologist, educator, poet, artist; b. Burlington, Vt., Apr. 9, 1944; s. Robert Joseph and Betty Jane Catlin (Whitney) D.; m. Lorinda Ferland. BA, Rollins Coll., 1966; MA, San Francisco State U., 1969; PhD, Saybrook Inst., San Francisco, 1978 Cert. tchr., Calif. From instr. to prof. Columbia Coll., San Francisco, 1970—; lectr. Golden Gate U., San Francisco; dir. Alameda Biofeedback and Peak Performance Ctr., 1980—; ednl. cons., 1981—. Peace Corps vol., Nepal, 1966-68. Recipient Order of Oseola award Rollins Coll., 1966, Academic Excellence award Columbia Coll., 1987. Fellow Am. Psychol. Assn.; mem. Biofeedback Soc. Am., Am. Fedn. Tchrs. Taoist. Author 9 books poetry; contbr. articles to profl. jours.; editor Saybrook Rev., 1979—. Office: 1810 Eagle Ave Alameda CA 94501-1320

DOERSHUK, CARL FREDERICK, physician, professor of pediatrics; b. Warren, Ohio, Dec. 24, 1930; s. Carl Frederick and Eula Blanche (Mahan) D.; m. Emma Lou Plummer, Aug. 21, 1954; children: Rebecca Lee, John Frederick, David Plummer. BA, Oberlin Coll., 1952; MD, Case Western Res. U., 1956. Pediatric intern U.S. Naval Hosp., Camp Pendleton Ohio, 1956-57; pediatric resident Cleve. Met. Gen. Hosp. and Babies and Children's Hosp., Cleve., 1959-61; postdoctoral pulmonary fellow Babies and Children's Hosp. USPHS, Cleve., 1961-63; sr. instr. to prof. pediatrics specializing in academic pediatric pulmonary medicine Case Western Res. U., Cleve., 1963—. Co-editor Pediatric Respiratory Therapy, 1974, 3d edit., 1986; contbr. numerous articles to profl. jours. Chmn. med. adv. coun. Cystic Fibrosis Found., Washington, 1966-72, bd. trustees, 1969-81, exec. com., 1969-74, v.p. med. affairs Cleve. chpt., 1965-90. Lt. M.C., USN, 1957-59. Named Young Man Yr. Cystic Fibrosis Found., 1970. Mem. Am. Pediatric Soc., Soc. Pediatric Research, Am. Acad. Pediatrics (exec. com. chest sect.), Am. Thoracic Soc. (chmn. pediatric pulmonary sect. 1971), No. Ohio Pediatric Soc., Acad. Medicine. Office: Rainbow Babies and Childrens Hosp 2101 Adelbert Rd Cleveland OH 44106-2624

DOFT, BERNARD HARVEY, ophthalmologist; b. N.Y.C., Aug. 13, 1946; m. Sandra Ferguson, 1969; 3 children. Student, Cornell U., 1964-67; MD, NYU, 1971. Diplomate Am. Bd. Internal Medicine, Am. Bd. Ophthalmology. Intern, asst. resident in internal medicine Barnes Hosp., Washington U. Sch. of Medicine, St. Louis, 1971-73; rsch. assoc. NIH, Nat. Heart & Lung Inst. and Bur. of Biologics, Bethesda, Md., 1973-75; resident in ophthalmology Bascom Palmer Eye Inst., U. Miami Sch. Medicine, 1975-78, fellowship in diseases and surgery of retina and vitreous, 1978-79; asst. prof. ophthalmology U. Pitts. Sch. of Medicine, 1979-84, clin. assoc. prof. ophthalmology, 1984—, clin. assoc. prof. of epidemiology, 1989—; cons. Nat. Eye Inst. Vision Rsch. Rev. Com. NIH, 1985; apptd. ophthalmic steering com., diabetic control and complications trial NIH, 1983; quality assurance com. Bascom Palmer Eye Inst., Ann Bates Leach Eye Hosp., U. Miami Sch. Medicine, 1977-78; co-dir., retina svc. Eye and Ear Hosp., U. Pitts., 1979-84, operating rm. com., 1982-87, chmn. com. on lasers, 1982-85; transplant com. Presbyn.-U. Hosp., U. Pitts., 1982-85; clinic coordinating com. Eye and Ear Hosp., Pitts., 1982-85, ad hoc com. for adminstrn./staff rels., 1983-85, chmn. oversight com. outpatient testing and laser ctr., 1983-85, med. staff nursing oversight com., 1983-84; study chair the endophthalmitis vitrectomy study Nat. Eye Inst., Bethesda, 1989—; SurgiCenter task force U. Pitts. Med. Ctr., 1995, ophthalmology search com. dept. of ophthalmology chmn., 1995. Editl. bd. Vitreoretinal Surgery and Technology, 1989—; contbr. numerous articles to profl. jours. With USPHS, 1973-75. Recipient numerous grants. Fellow ACS, Am. Acad. of Ophthalmology (Honor award 1993); mem. Bascom Palmer Eye Inst. Alumni Assn., Pitts. Ophthalmology Soc. (pres. 1989-91, exec. com. 1980-91, program co-chmn. 1982-83, program chmn. 1983-87, v.p., pres.-elect 1987-88, pres. 1989-91, chmn. nominating com. 1991-93), Pa. Med. Soc., Allegheny County Med. Soc., Atlantic Coast Fluorescein Club, Aspen Retinal Detachment Soc., The Macula Soc., Assn. for Rsch. in Vision and Ophthalmology, British Am. Retinal Group, Vitreous Soc., The Retina Soc., Am. Assn. for Ophthalmic Standardized Echography, Alpha Omega Alpha. Home: 123 South Dr Pittsburgh PA 15238 Office: Retina-Vitreous Cons Ste 500 3501 Forbes Ave Pittsburgh PA 15213

DOGAN, AHMET SEMIH, radiologist; b. Bafra, Turkey, Jan. 24, 1959; s. Durmus and Melahat Dogan; m. Sukran Dogan, Apr. 21, 1995. MD, U. Istanbul, 1983. Diplomate Am. Bd. Nuclear Medicine. Gen. practice medicine Etibank Boron Mines, Bursa, Turkey, 1984-86; resident dept. nuclear medicine U. Istanbul, 1986-90, U. Iowa Hosps., Iowa City, 1990-92; clin. fellow dept. nuclear medicine Children's Meml. Hosp., Chgo., 1992-93; fellow assoc. dept. radiology U. Iowa Hosps., 1993-94; assoc. prof. Dokuz Eylul U., Izmir, Turkey, 1994-96; post-doctoral fellow dept. radiology Johns Hopkins Med. Instns., Balt., 1996—. Mem. Soc. Nuclear Medicine, European Assn. Nuclear Medicine, Turkish Soc. Nuclear Medicine. Home: 3700 N Charles St #209 Baltimore MD 21218 Office: Johns Hopkins Med Instns JHOC Radiology Rm 3245 601 N Caroline St Baltimore MD 21287

DOGOLOFF, LEE ISRAEL, clinical social worker, psychotherapist, consultant; b. Balt., Oct. 19, 1939; s. Mark and Minnie Lottie (Gresser) D.; m. Jane Roberta Greenberg, June 17, 1962 (div. 1973); children: Jody, Ilene; m. Mary Louise Gumpper, Feb. 3, 1974; 1 child, Kathryn Ann. BA in Sociology, U. Md., 1961; MSW, Howard U., 1964. Lic. social worker, Md.; bd. cert. Diplomate in Clin. Social Work, 1990—. Dep. adminstr. Narcotics Treatment Adminstrn., Washington, 1970-72; dir., govt. asst. Spl. Action Office on Drug Abuse Prevention, Washington, 1972-73; dir. div. community assistance Nat. Inst. Drug Abuse, Rockville, Md., 1974-75; dep. fed. drug mgmt. program Office Mgmt. and Budget, Washington, 1975-76; assoc. dir. White House Domestic Policy, Washington, 1977-80; exec. dir. Am. Coun. Drug Edn., Rockville, 1981-92; pres. Employee Health Programs, Inc., Bethesda, Md., 1992-93; ind. counselor drug abuse treatment; field instr. Sch. Social Work, U. Md., 1986-92; moderator edn. sect. White House Conf. for Drug Free Am., 1987-88; Presdl. appointee Pres.'s Drug Adv. Coun., 1989-94. Contbr. numerous articles to profl. publs. Mem. Nat. Assn. Social Workers. Office: 7315 Wisconsin Ave Ste 510E Bethesda MD 20814-3209

DOHENY, JUSTIN EDWARD, hospital president; b. Bklyn., Dec. 29, 1951; s. Justin Edward and Kathryn Marie (Golan) D.; m. Dana O. Ovestrud, July 31, 1976; children: Justin Edward III, Christopher Erik, Timothy Sean. AB, Coll. of the Holy Cross, 1973; M in Healthcare Adminstrn., U. Minn., 1975. Diplomate Am. Coll. Healthcare Execs. Asst. to dir. U. Mich. Hosp., Ann Arbor, 1975-77, sr. hosp. planner, 1977-79; asst. hosp. dir., instr. U. Hosp. & Clinic U. Nebr., Omaha, 1979-82; v.p. Monmouth Med. Ctr., Long Branch, N.J., 1982-85; pres. Wayne (N.J.) Gen. Hosp., 1985—; trustee Bergen Regional Blood Ctr., Paramus, N.J., 1990—, N.J. Hosp. Assn., 1991-95, Qualcare, Piscataway, N.J., 1993—. Contbr. chpts. to books. Trustee N.J. Cystic Fibrosis Found., Parsippany, 1985—; vice chmn. Med. Practitioner Rev. Panel, Trenton, N.J., 1991—. Recipient Chmn.'s award United Way, Passaic Valley, 1991. Mem. Bergen-Passaic Hosp. Coun. (chmn. 1992-94). Office: Wayne Gen Hops 224 Hamburg Turnpike Wayne NJ 07470

DOHERTY, HENRY JOSEPH, anesthesiologist, medical hypnotist; b. Trenton, N.J., Apr. 11, 1933; s. Margaret (McCann) D.; m. Mary Anne Hollman, Dec. 29, 1956; children: Margaret Jo, Henry III, James, Paul, Steven, Marla. AB, Johns Hopkins U., 1954; MD, St. Louis U., 1958. Diplomate Am. Bd. Anesthesiology. Intern Phila. Gen. Hosp., 1958-59, resident in anesthesiology, 1959-61, staff anesthesiologist, 1961-73; attending anesthesiologist Lankenau Hosp., Phila., 1962—, chmn. dept. anesthesiologya, 1987—; assoc. prof. clin. anesthesia Jefferson Med. U., Phila., 1987—. Fellow Am. Coll. Anesthesiologists; mem. Am. Soc. Anesthesiologists, Am. Soc. Clin. Hypnosis, Pa. Soc. Anesthesiologists, Phila. Soc. Anesthesiologists. Republican. Roman Catholic. Home: 601 Ballytore Rd Wynnewood PA 19096-2209 Office: Lankenau Hosp 100 E Lancaster Ave Wynnewood PA 19096-3411

DOHERTY, JAMES EDWARD, III, physician, educator; b. Newport, Ark., Nov. 22, 1923; s. James Edward D.; children: Richard Edward, Margaret Elise. B.S. Medicine, U. Ark., 1944, M.D., 1946. Diplomate: Am. Bd. Internal Medicine (cardiovascular disease). Intern Columbus (Ga.) City Hosp., 1946-47; resident internal medicine U. Ark. Sch. Medicine, 1949-52, instr. medicine, 1952-53, asst. prof., 1953-61, assoc. prof., 1962-68, prof., 1968—, dir. cardiology div., 1969-77, dir. cardiovascular research, 1977—, dir. continuing med. edn., 1977—; chief cardiology sect. VA Hosp., Little Rock, 1956-68; del. U.S. Pharmacopeial Conv., 1970, 85; mem. so. regional research and adv. com. Am. Heart Assn., 1969-70. Contbr. articles to profl. publs. Bd. dirs. Ark. Heart Assn., 1960-70, sec., 1955-56, pres., 1959-60. Served with AUS, 1943-46; with USAF, 1947-49. Recipient Casimir Funk award, 1975, Abernathy award, 1985, Disting. Faculty award U. Ark. Coll. Medicine, 1986. Fellow Am. Coll. Chest Physicians (com. on cardiology 1992—, treas. Coun. on Geriatric Cardiology 1991-92); mem. Am. Coll. Cardilogy (gov. Ark. 1962-65, 68-71), ACP (Ark. gov. 1979-82), Soc. Nuclear Medicine, N.Y. Acad. Scis., So. Soc. Clin. Investigation, Assn. Univ. Cardiologists (sec. 1984-86, v.p. 1987-88, pres. 1988-89), Med. Ctr. Camera Club, Raquet Club, Med. Ctr. Scuba Club (v.p. 1983-84, pres. 1984-85), Masons, Sigma Xi, Alpha Omega Alpha, Alpha Epsilon Delta, Sigma Chi. Office: 4300 W 7th St Little Rock AR 72205-5411

DOHERTY, PETER CHARLES, immunologist; b. Brisbane, Australia, Oct. 15, 1940; came to U.S., 1988; s, Eric C. and Linda Doherty; m. Penelope Stephens, 1965; children: James, Michael. B.V.Sc (hons), U. Queensland, Australia, 1962, MVSc, 1966; PhD, U. Edinburgh, Scotland, 1970; DVs (hon.), U. Queensland; DSc (hon), Australian Nat. U. Vet. officer Animal Rsch. Inst., Brisbane, Australia, 1963-67; sci. officer Moredun Rsch. Inst., Edinburgh, 1967-71; postdoctoral fellow John Curtin Sch. Med. Rsch., Canberra, Australia, 1972-75, prof., head dept. exptl. pathology, 1982-88; from assoc. prof. to prof. The Wistar Inst., Phila., 1975-82; mem., chmn. dept. immunology St. Jude Children's Rsch. Hosp., Memphis, 1988—; Bd. dirs. Internat. Lab. Animal Diseases, Nairobi, 1986-92; mem. NIH exptl. virology study sect., 1982-83, 1990—. Contbr. chpts. to books, articles to profl. jours. Recipient Paul Ehrlich prize Fed. Republic Germany, 1983, Gairdner Internat. award for med. sci. Can., 1986, Lasker award for Basic Med. Rsch., 1995; Royal Soc. London fellow, 1987. Fellow Australian Acad. Sci. Office: St Jude Children's Rsch Hosp PO Box 318 332 N Lauderdale St Memphis TN 38105-2729

DOHMEN, FREDERICK HOEGER, retired wholesale drug company executive; b. Milw., May 12, 1917; s. Fred William and Viola (Gutsch) D.; BA in Commerce, U. Wis., 1939; m. Gladys Elizabeth Dite, Dec. 23, 1939 (dec. 1963); children: William Francis, Robert Charles; m. Mary Alexander Holgate, June 27, 1964. With F. Dohmen Co., Milw., 1939-82, successively warehouse employee, sec., v.p., 1944-52, pres., 1952-82, dir., 1947—, chmn. bd., 1952-82. Bd. dirs. St. Luke's Hosp. Ednl. Found., Milw., 1965-83, pres., 1969-72, chmn. bd., 1972-73; bd. dirs. U. Wis., Milw. Found., 1976-79, bd. visitors, 1978-88, emeritus mem. 1988—; assoc. chmn. Nat. Bible Week, Laymen's Nat. Bible Com., N.Y.C., 1968-82, council of adv., 1983—; elder Presbyn. Ch.; bd. dirs. Riveredge Nature Ctr., Newburg, Wis., 1993-94. Mem. Nat. Wholesale Druggists Assn. (chmn. mfr. relations com. 1962, resolutions com. 1963, mem. of bd. control 1963-66), Nat. Assn. Wholesalers (trustee 1966-75), Druggists Service Council (dir. 1967-71), Wis. Pharm. Assn., Miss. Valley Drug Club, Beta Gamma Sigma, Phi Eta Sigma, Delta Kappa Epsilon, University Club, Town Club (Milw.). Home: 3903 W Mequon Rd Mequon WI 53092-2727

DOHN, HENRY HARRIS, psychiatrist; b. Macon, Ga., Nov. 26, 1951; s. Carl Weiss Sr. and Mary Frances (Harris) D.; m. Paula Anne Grahl, June 15, 1974; children: Robyn, Chuck. BA, Presbyn. Coll., 1973; MD, Med. Coll. of Ga., 1977. Diplomate Am. Bd. Psychiatry and Neurology. Resident, fellow dept. psychiatry Sch. of Medicine U. Ala., Birmingham, 1977-81; pvt. practice Pensacola, Fla., 1985—. Contbr. articles to profl. jours. Maj. USAF, 1981-85. Mem. Am. Psychiat. Assn., Acad. Psychosomatic Medicine, Am. Psychosomatic Soc., AMA, Fla. Psychiat. Soc., Escambia County Med. Soc. Republican. Methodist. Home: 2695 Tambridge Cir Pensacola FL 32503-4256 Office: Creekside Psychiat Ctr 5190 Bayou Blvd Ste 6 Pensacola FL 32503-2162

DOHNER, ROBERT PAUL, osteopathic medical student; b. Stroudsburg, Pa., Aug. 20, 1968; s. Dale Harding and Barbara Joyce (Frantz) D. BA in Psychology, Villanova U., 1991; postgrad., U. New Eng., 1995. Lab. technician Villanova (Pa.) U., 1990-92; orthodontist's asst. Dr. Williams, Malvern, Pa., 1990-92; mental health technician Mapleton Psychiat. Inst., Malvern, 1992-94; tchg. asst. U. New Eng. Coll. Osteo. Medicine, Biddeford, Maine, 1995—. Instr. CPR, ARC, Sanford, Maine, 1994-96. Mem. AMA, Am. Osteo. Assn., Am. Coll. Osteo. Family Practitioners (sec. 1995-96). Home: 5 Depot St Kennebunk ME 04043

DOHRENWEND, BRUCE PHILIP, psychiatric epidemiologist, social psychologist, educator; b. N.Y.C., July 26, 1927; s. Gustav John and Gertrude Elise (Funke) D.; m. Barbara Anne Snell, Sept. 21, 1951 (dec. June 1982); m. Catherine J. Douglass, June 1, 1985. B.A., Columbia U., 1950, M.A., 1952; Ph.D., Cornell U., 1955. Cert. psychologist, N.Y. Research assoc. Cornell U., Ithaca, N.Y., 1954-58; research assoc. Columbia U., N.Y.C., 1958-63, asst. prof., 1963-67, assoc. prof., 1967-70, prof., 1970—; chief social psychiatry N.Y. State Psychiat. Inst., N.Y.C., 1979—; mem. task panel on problems, scope and boundaries Presl. Commn. on Mental Health, Washington, 1977-78; head task group on behavioral effects Presl. Commn. on Accident at Three Mile Island, Washington, 1979; mem. tech. evaluation bd. Vietnam Era Veterans study, VA, Washington, 1983-89. Author: (with others) Social Status and Psychological Disorder, 1969, Mental Illness in the United States, 1980, (with others) Socioeconomic Status and Psychiatric Disorders, 1992; editor: (with others) Stressful Life Events, 1974, Stressful Life Events and Their Contexts, 1981. Served with USNR, 1945-46. Recipient Research Scientist award NIMH, 1971, 76, 81, 86, 91, Emily Mumford award Columbia U., 1992; NIMH grantee, 1964-82, 77—. Fellow Am. Psychol. Assn. (co-recipient disting. contbns. div. community psychology award 1980), AAAS (co-recipient prize for behavioral rsch. 1990), Am. Psychopathol. Assn. (Hamilton award 1994); mem. Am. Pub. Health Assn. (co-recipient Rema Lapouse Mental Health Epidemiology award 1981), Am. Sociol. Assn., Soc. for Study of Social Problems (Disting. Contbrs. award divsn. psychiat. sociology 1994). Home: 1056 Fifth Ave New York NY 10028-0112 Office: NY State Psychiat Inst Box 8 722 W 168th St New York NY 10032-2603

DOLAMORE, MOCHAEL JOHN, physician; b. London, July 27, 1958; came to U.S., 1986; s. John David and Myra Rosemary (Lisson) D.; m. JEanne Marie Procino, Sept. 2, 1984; children: Matthew, Christina, Sophie. MS, London U., 1982. Resident Colchester, England, 1983-86; attending physician Mid Hudson Family Health Svcs. Inst., Livingston, N.Y., 1988—; assoc. clin. prof. N.Y. Med. Coll., Valhalla, N.Y., 1991—; med. dir. Tesbrodeck Coll., Lake Katrine, N.Y., 1995—. Geriatric Medicine fellow Mt. Sinai Sch. Medicine, N.Y.C., 1986-87. Fellow Am. Acad. Family Physicians; mem. Am. Med. Dirs. Assn., Am. Geriatric Soc., N.Y. State Med. Soc., Med. Soc. Ulster County, Royal Coll. Gen. Practitioners. Office: Mid-Hudson Family Health 20 Ricks Rd Woodstock NY 12498

DOLAN, JOHN LEO, III, physician; b. Chicopee Falls, Mass., Jan. 1, 1970; s. John Leo and Teresa Mary (Markley) D.; m. Patricia Havunen, Aug. 24, 1989; 1 child, Jordan Randall. AS, C.C. of the Air Force, Maxwell AFB, Ala., 1991; B in Gen. Studies, La. State U., 1992; DO, U. New Eng. Coll. Osteo. Med., 1996. tchg. asst. gross anatomy UNECOM-Dept. Anatomy, Biddeford, Maine, 1993, tchg. asst. neuroanatomy, 1994. Sr. airman USAF, 1989-92. Mem. Am. Osteo. Assn., Am. Med. Student Assn. Republican. Roman Catholic. Home: 24 State St #5 Biddeford ME 04005

DOLAN, JOHN PATRICK, psychiatrist; b. Bklyn., Jan. 23, 1935; s. James Francis and Agnes Barrett (Lane) D.; m. Mary McLaughlin, Dec. 21, 1964 (div. June 1972); children: Deborah Jean, John McLaughlin; m. Margaret Abel, Sept. 6, 1974. AB in History, Bklyn. Coll., 1958; MD, N.J. Coll. Medicine, 1962. Cert. Am. Bd. Psychiatry and Neurology. Resident Washington U., 1966-69, St. Louis U., 1970-72; intern medicine Kings County Hosp., Bklyn., 1963; resident neurology Washington U., St. Louis, 1969; resident psychiatry St. Louis U. Sch. Medicine, 1972, asst. prof. dept. psychiatry, 1972-78; chmn. dept. psychiatry Conemaugh Valley Meml. Hosp., Johnstown, Pa., 1979-83; clin. asst. prof. dept. psychiatry U. Pitts. Sch. Medicine, 1979-83; chmn. dept. psychiatry St. Vincent's Med. Ctr., Bridgeport, Conn., 1983—; clin. assoc. prof. psychiatry N.Y. Med. Coll., Valhalla, N.Y., 1987—; psychiat. cons. Pru-Care N.Y. and Conn., 1988—; past pres. Fairfield/Litchfield chpt. Conn. Psychiat. Soc., 1988-89; v.p. Alliance for Health IPA, Bridgeport, 1987—; counsellor Conn. Psychiat. Soc., 1985-89. Mem. Catchment Area Coun., Bridgeport, 1983-87, Southwest Regional Mental Health Bd., Fairfield County, Conn., 1983-87, legis. com. (Conn.) State Bd. Mental Health, 1985-86. Mem. Bridgeport Psychiat. Soc. (pres. 1987—), Am. Psychiat. Assn., Am. Acad. Med. Dirs., Am. Acad. Psychiatrists in Alcoholism and Addiction, N.Y. Acad. Scis., South Shore Music Club, Fairfield County Hunt Club. Office: St Vincents Med Ctr 2800 Main St Bridgeport CT 06606-4201

DOLAN, THOMAS CHRISTOPHER, professional society administrator; b. Chgo., Dec. 31, 1947; s. Thomas Christopher and Bernice Mary (Doyle) D.; m. Georgia Ann Siebke, Feb. 14, 1983; children: William, Barbara, Lauren. BBA, Loyola U., Chgo., 1969; PhD, U. Iowa, 1977. Instr. U. Iowa, Iowa City, 1971-72; vis. fellow U. Wash., Seattle, 1973-74; asst. prof. U. Mo., Columbia, 1974-79; assoc. prof., dir. St. Louis U., 1979-86; v.p. Am. Coll. Healthcare Execs., Chgo., 1986-87, exec. v.p., 1987-91, pres., 1991—; mem. Accrediting Commn. on Edn. for Health Svcs. Adminstrn., Washington, 1985-86; chmn. Assn. Univ. Programs in Health Adminstrn., Washington, 1983-84; cons. HEW, Kansas City, Mo., 1974-79, State of Mo., Jefferson City, 1974-79. Author: Systems for Health Care Administration: A Model for the Education of Health Manpower, 1975; contbr. articles to profl. jours. Pres. Mental Health Assn. Boone County, Columbia, Mo., 1977-78, Mental Health Assn. Mo., Jefferson City, 1980-82; bd. mem. Nat. Mental Health Assn., Washington, 1982-83, Alexian Bros. Hosp., St. Louis, 1980-86, Chgo. Soc. Assn. Execs., 1995—, Am. Soc. Assn. Execs. Fedn., Washington, 1995—. Fellow Am. Coll. Healthcare Execs., Am. Soc. Assn. Execs. (cert. assn. exec.); mem. APHA, Chgo. Soc. Assn. Execs., Acad. Mgmt. Roman Catholic. Office: Am Coll Healthcare Execs 1 N Franklin St Ste 1700 Chicago IL 60606-3421

DOLAN, WILLIAM DAVID, JR., physician; b. Westerly, R.I., Apr. 30, 1913; s. William David and Mary E. (Dunn) D.; m. Christine Shea, Nov. 25, 1942; children—William David, III, Mary Anne, John Patrick. B.S., U. R.I., 1935; M.D., Georgetown U., 1942; D.Sc. (hon.), Marymount U., 1975, Georgetown U., 1983. Intern Georgetown U. Hosp., 1942-43, resident, 1943-45; practice medicine specializing in pathology Arlington, Va., 1947-95; dir. pathology Arlington Hosp., 1947-95; pres. med. staff Arlington Hosp., 1982-87, trustee; asst. dean sch. medicine affairs at Arlington Hosp. Georgetown U., clin. prof. dept. pathology. Council to dean Georgetown U., 1977—. Served to maj., M.C. AUS, 1942-47. Recipient Distinguished Service to Pathology award Am. Soc. Clin. Pathologists and Coll. Am. Pathologists, 1976, The Brent award Diocese of Arlington, 1989. Mem. AMA (council on sci. affairs, chmn. 1985), So. Med. Assn., Med. Soc. Va. and D.C., Arlington County Med. Soc. (past pres.), Am. Cancer Soc. (bd. dirs.), Am. Soc. Clin. Pathologists (past pres., disting. svc. award honoring Israel Davidsohn 1991), Am. Blood Commn. (past pres.), Coll. Am. Pathologists, Internat. Acad. Pathology, Va. Soc. for Pathology, Arlington County C. of C. (past dir.), Am. Registry of Pathology (pres. 1991-93), Alpha Omega Alpha. Roman Catholic. Club: Washington Golf and Country. Office: 1701 N George Mason Dr Arlington VA 22205-3671

DOLCOURT, JOHN (JACK) LAWRENCE, pediatrician; b. Denver, May 13, 1949; s. Benjamin and Nessie (Badion) D.; m. Joyce Linda Papper, Sept. 3, 1972; children: Bram, Cameron. BA, U. Colo., 1971, MD, 1975. Diplomate Am. Bd. Pediatrics, Am. Bd. Neonatal, Perinatal Medicine. Asst. prof. pediatrics U. Utah Sch. of Medicine, Salt Lake City, 1990-86, assoc. prof., 1986—; med. dir. Ctr. for Pediatric Continuing Edn., Primary Childen's Med. Ctr., Salt Lake City, Utah, 1986—. Contbr. articles to profl. jours.; inventor percutaneously placed catheter. Bd. dirs. Jewish Reconstructionist Fedn., Phila., 1990-93, v.p., 1993—. Fellow Am. Acad. Pediatrics. Home: 509 E Northmont Way Salt Lake City UT 84103-3324 Office: Primary Children's Med Ctr 100 N Medical Dr Ste 4060 Salt Lake City UT 84113-1100

DOLE, ARTHUR ALEXANDER, psychology educator; b. San Francisco, Oct. 25, 1917; s. Arthur Alexander and Ella Elizabeth (Duncan) D.; m. Marjorie Elizabeth Welsh, Mar. 19, 1949; children: Peter, Steven, Barbara. BA, Antioch Coll., 1946; MA, Ohio State U., 1949, PhD, 1951; MA (hon.), U. Pa., 1973. Diplomate Am. Bd. Examiners in Profl. Psychology. Asst. psychology and edn. Antioch Coll., 1946-48; counselor Ohio State U., 1948-51; dir. Bur. Testing and Guidance, U. Hawaii, 1951-60, from asst. prof. to prof. psychology, 1951-67; prof. psychology in edn. U. Pa., 1967-88, chmn. dept., 1967-88, prof. emeritus, 1988—; mem. internat. adv. bd. Univ MSG, Romero and Cedro, El Salvador. Author articles in field.; cons. editor profl. jours. Bd. dirs. Am. Family Found.; pres. PEACE, Internat. Fellow APA; mem. AAAS, AAUP, ACA, Am. Ednl. Rsch. Assn., Internat. Coun. Psychologists, Internat. Assn. Applied Psychology, Nat. Rehab. Assn., Sigma Xi.

DOLE, VINCENT PAUL, medical research executive, educator; b. Chgo., May 8, 1913; s. Vincent Paul and Anne (Dowling) D.; m. Elizabeth Ann Strange, May 23, 1942 (div. 1965); children: Vincent Paul III, Susan, Bruce; m. Marie Nyswander, 1965 (dec. 1986); m. Margaret E. Cool, 1992. AB, Stanford U., 1934; MD, Harvard U., 1939. Intern Mass. Gen. Hosp., Boston, 1940-41; mem. staff Rockefeller U., N.Y.C., 1941—, mem. staff, prof., 1951—. Developer methadone maintenance treatment program for heroin addiction. Office: Rockefeller U Dept of Medicine 1230 York Ave New York NY 10021-6307

DOLENZ, BERNARD JOSEPH, neurologist, health care law consultant; b. West Bend, Wis., July 10, 1933; s. Joseph and Martha (Kircher) D.; m. Dalila Reyna, Oct. 11, 1959 (div. July 1980); children: Kimble, Bruce, Brenda, Brigid, Brian, Beverly. BS, U. Okla., 1954, MD, 1957; JD, South Tex. U., 1983. Bar: Tex. 1983; diplomate Am. Bd. of Neurology and Psychiatry. Intern Boston City Hosp., 1957, Harris Hosp., Ft. Worth, 1957-58; resident in neurology and psychiatry U. Tex., Galveston, 1958-60, Dallas, 1960-61; clin. instr. med. sch. Tulane U., 1961; pvt. practice Ft. Worth Neuropsychiatric Hosp., 1962-71, med. dir. and chief of staff; dir. Comprehensive Care Corp., Newport Beach, Calif., 1971; cons. Fort Worth Gen. Dynamics, FAA, Bur. of Hearings and Appeals, Cosmetics Internat. Author: Nothing Will Stop Me, Not Even Death, Bariloche Connection, Your Thoughts May Kill You; contbr. articles to profl. jours. Mem. Am. Psychiat. Assn., North Tex. Pscychiat. Soc., Titus Harris Soc., Tarrant County Med. Soc., AMA, Tex. Med. Assn., Ft. Worth Internist Club, Tarrant County Psychiat. Assn., South Ft. Worth Rotary, Serra Internat., MENSA, Internat. Brotherhood of Magicians (past pres. Ring 15), Dallas Bar Assn., U.S. Supreme Ct. Bar, Phi Beta Pi, Pi Alpha Delta. Home: 6102 Swiss Ave Dallas TX 75214-4324

DOLGIN, MARTIN, cardiologist; b. N.Y.C., Apr. 12, 1919; s. Samuel and Bertha (Brodsky) D.; m. Jeanne Rydell, Feb. 12, 1950; children: Barbara, Deborah, Stuart. A.B., NYU, 1939, M.D., 1943. Diplomate: Am. Bd. Internal Medicine; cert. cardivascular disease. Intern, resident in medicine Lincoln Hosp., N.Y.C., 1943, 44; fellow in internal medicine Lahey Clinic, Boston, 1945, 46; fellow in cardiovasc. disease rsch. Michael Reese Hosp., Chgo., 1947; instr. to assoc. prof. medicine NYU, N.Y.C., 1948-73, prof. clin. medicine, 1973—; attending physician Bellevue Hosp. and Tisch Univ. Hosp., N.Y.C., 1973—; adj. attending physician Montefiore Hosp., N.Y.C., 1948-68; cons. in cardiology Will Rogers Hosp., Saranac Lake, N.Y., Columbus Hosp., N.Y.C., 1960-70; chief cardiology sect. N.Y. VA Hosp., 1955-89, cons. cardiology, 1989—. Editorial bd.: Jour. Electrocardiology; contbr. articles in electrocardiography to publs. Served with M.D. U.S. Army, 1952-54. Fellow ACP, Am. Coll. Cardiology, N.Y. Acad. Sci.; mem. Am. Fedn. Clin. Research, Am. Heart Assn., AAAS, Alpha Omega Alpha. Home: 32 Mountainview Ave Ardsley NY 10502-2010 Office: NY VA Hospital 423 E 23rd St New York NY 10010-5050

DOLGIN, STEPHEN ELLIOT, pediatric surgeon; b. S.I., N.Y., July 30, 1949; s. Joseph and Barbara (Lake) D.; m. Ellen Sharon Rosen, Nov. 4, 1979; children: Joanna, David. BA, Yale U., 1971; MD, NYU, 1977. Bd. cert. in surgery, pediat. surgery and surg. critical care. Intern in surgery Peter Bent Brigham Hosp. (Harvard Med. Sch.), Boston, 1977-78, resident in surgery, 1978-82; fellow in pediat. surgery Children's Meml. Hosp., Northwestern U. Sch. Medicine, Chgo., 1982-84; chief pediatric surgery Mt. Sinai Med. Ctr., N.Y.C., 1984—, assoc. prof. surgery, pediatrics and anatomy, cell biology, 1993—; course dir. embryology Mt. Sinai Sch. Medicine, N.Y.C., 1992—. Contbr. numerous articles to profl. jours. Mem. sci. adv. bd. Modell Found., N.Y., Crohns Colitis Found., N.Y. Named Attending Tchr. of Yr., Mt. Sinai Surg. Residents, 1990. Mem. ACS, Am. Acad. Pediatrics, Am. Pediatric Surg. Assn., N.Y. Surg. Soc., Pediatric Oncology Group, Am. Coll. Gastroenterology, Alpha Omega Alpha. Jewish. Home: 53 Paine Ave New Rochelle NY 10804 Office: Mount Sinai Med Ctr PO Box 1259 1 Gustave Levy Pl New York NY 10029

DOLIN, SCOTT LLOYD, physician; b. Hartford, Conn., June 13, 1954; s. Saul and Inez (Heller) D.; m. Diane Ellen Etscovitz; children: Rachel Bethany, Adam Michael. BS, Union Coll., Schenectady, N.Y., 1976; MD, U. Conn., 1980. Diplomate Am. Bd. Ophthalmology. Intern Hartford Hosp., 1980-81; resident Boston U. Med. Ctr., 1981-84; fellow Boston Eye Rsch. Inst., 1984-85; ptnr. Hartford Eye Physicians, 1985—. Contbr. articles to profl. jours. Co-chmn. membership com. Beth EL Temple, West Hartford, 1993—, trustee, 1995—; coach Youth Baseball League, West Hartford, 1990—. Fellow Am. Acad. Ophthalmologists; mem. Soc. Eye Physicians, New Eng. Ophthal. Soc., Hartford County Med. Assn., Conn Seers Med. Soc., Conn. Soc. Prevent Blindness. Office: Hartford Eye Physicians 100 Retreat Ave Hartford CT 06106

DOLLENS, RONALD W., pharmaceuticals company executive; b. Ind., Dec. 17, 1946; s. William Franklin and Louise Anna (Davis) D.; m. Susan Stanley, Aug. 30, 1969; children: Stephanie, Grant. BS, Purdue U., 1970; MBA, Ind. U., 1972. From sales rep. to dir. bus. devel. Eli Lilly & Co., Indpls., 1972-85; from sr. v.p. to ceo Advanced Cardiovasc. Sys., Santa Clara, 1985-91; pres. med. devices divsn. Eli Lilly & Co., 1991-94; pres., ceo Guidant Corp., Indpls., 1994—. Office: Guidant Corp PO Box 44906 Indianapolis IN 46244

DOLNEY, JAMES KENNETH, osteopath; b. Homestead, Pa., Mar. 11, 1950; s. Julius Stephen and Lois Jean Dolney; m. Christine Ann Luptak, Aug. 18, 1973; children: Jason Michael, Matthew James. BS, St. Vincent Coll., 1972; DO, U. Health Scis., Des Moines, 1977. Diplomate Am. Bd. Family Practice, Am. Osteo. Bd. Gen. Practitioners. Commd. ensign USN, 1977, advanced through grades to capt., 1993; intern Naval Hosp., Portsmouth, Va., 1977-78; battalion surgeon First Marine Brigade, Kaneohe Bay, Hawaii, 1978-81; residen in family practice Naval Hosp., Camp Pendleton, Calif., 1981-84; family practice staff Naval Hosp., Orlando, Fla., 1984-88; family practice faculty Naval Hosp., Charleston, S.C., 1988-89, asst. dept. chmn. family practice dept., 1989-90, dept. chmn., residency dir., 1990-94; dept. head family practice Naval Med. Ctr., Portsmouth, Va., 1994—; clin. asst. prof. family practice Uniformed Svcs., U. Health Scis., Bethesda, Md., 1990-94. Fellow Am. Acad. Family Physicians; mem. Assn. Mil. Osteo. Physicians and Surgeons (pres. 1993-94). Roman Catholic. Office: Naval Hosp Family Practice Clinic Naval Med Ctr Portsmouth VA 23708-2197

DOLPH, CAROL JOCH, nursing administrator; b. Hinsdale, Ill., Mar. 13, 1946; d. John and Eleanor Marie (Gannam) Joch; m. Paul Barrett Dolph, Nov. 9, 1968; 1 child, Christina. BSN, U. San Francisco, 1968; MBA, Portland State U., 1993. RN, Oreg.; cert. profl. healthcare quality. Staff nurse oper. rm. Shriner's Crippled Children's Hosp., San Francisco, 1971-75, Edward White Hosp., St. Petersburg, Fla., 1975-76, Middlesex Meml. Hosp., Middletown, Conn., 1976-78; dir. quality improvement and risk mgmt. Mercy Healthcare, Inc., Roseburg, Oreg., 1978—. Mem. Nat. Assn. Healthcare Quality, Oreg. Assn. Healthcare Quality, Am. Bus. Women's Assn. (edn. chair 1996, scholar 1992, 93). Office: Mercy Healthcare Inc 2700 Stewart Pkwy Roseburg OR 97470

DOLSKY, RICHARD LAURENCE, plastic surgeon; b. Newark, Feb. 10, 1946; s. Irving and Frieda (Resnick) D.; m. Lauren Kozinn, June 6, 1971; children: Daniel, Trisha, Gregory Ian. AB, Dartmouth Coll., 1968; MD, Tufts U., 1972. Cert. Am. Bd. Otolaryngology, Am. Bd. Cosmetic Surgery, Am. Bd. Plastic Surgery. Intern Mt. Auburn Hosp., Mass., 1972-73; gen. surg. resident Harvard Surg. Svc., Boston, 1973-74; resident in otolaryngology and maxillofacial surgery Northwestern U., Chgo., 1974-77; fellow in plastic and reconstructive surgery Cleve. Clinic, 1977-79; chmn. dept. plastic and reconstructive surgery Haverford Hosp., Havertown, Pa., 1979—. Mem. Am. Acad. Cosmetic Surgery (pres. 1995—), Am. Soc. Liposuction Surgery (pres. 1995—). Office: 191 Presidential Blvd #105 Bala Cynwyd PA 19004

DOLUISIO, JAMES THOMAS, pharmacy educator; b. Bethlehem, Pa., Sept. 28, 1935; s. Dominic and Sue (Powell) D.; m. Phyllis M. Sabolski, June 20, 1959; children—Thomas, James, Rebecca. B.S. in Pharmacy, Temple U., 1957, M.S., 1959; Ph.D., Purdue U., 1962; DSc, Phila. Coll. Pharmacy and Sci., 1983; DSc (hon.), Purdue U., 1995. From asst. prof. to assoc. prof. pharmacy Phila. Coll. Pharmacy and Sci., 1961-67, also assoc. dir. dept., 1965-67; prof., chmn. dept. pharmacy U. Ky., Lexington, 1967-73; prof., dean U. Tex., Austin, 1973—; bd. dirs. Eckerd Corp., COR Therapeutics; cons. Smith Kline & French Labs., Phila., 1962-67, McNeil Labs., Ft. Washington, Pa., 1967-72, Hoechst Labs., Somerville, N.J., 1973-93, Nat. Inst. Drug Abuse, 1976-78, HEW, U.S. Surgeon Gen., 1975-83. Contbr. to profl. and sci. jours. Active Pharmacists Against Drug Abuse Found, 1984; chmn. U.S. Pharmacopeial Conv., Inc., 1990. NSF fellow, 1959-61; Am. Found. Pharm. Edn. fellow, 1957-59. Mem. Am. Pharm. Assn. (Remington Honor medal 1995), Am. Assn. Colls. Pharmacy, Am. Soc. Hosp. Pharmacy, Am. Assn. Pharm. Scientists, Rho Chi. Office: U Texas Office of Dean Coll Pharmacy Austin TX 78712

DOMBROWSKI, ANNE WESSELING, microbiologist, researcher; b. Cin., Jan. 26, 1948; d. Robert John and Margaret Mary (Bell) Wesseling; m. Allan Wayne Dombrowski, Apr. 17, 1982; children: Amy, Alicia. BA summa cum laude, Xavier U., 1970; MS, U. Cin., 1972, PhD, 1974. Fellow Scripps Clinic & Rsch. Found., La Jolla, Calif., 1974-76; sr. rsch. microbiologist Merck & Co., Inc., Rahway, N.J., 1976-87, rsch. fellow, 1987-96, sr. rsch. fellow, 1996—. Patentee in field; contbt. articles to profl. jours. Mem. AAAS, Soc. Indsl. Microbiology (sec. 1982-85), Am. Soc. Microbiology, Mycol. Soc. Home: 51 Landsdowne Rd East Brunswick NJ 08816-4156 Office: Merck & Co Inc PO Box 2000 Rahway NJ 07065-0900

DOMBROWSKI, FRANK PAUL, JR., pharmacist; b. Nashua, N.H., May 10, 1943; s. Frank Paul and Yvonne Joan (Paris) D.; B.S., Mass. Coll. Pharmacy, 1965, M.S., 1967; m. Eleanor Cassady, June 15, 1968; children—Michael, Peter, Laura, Cheryl, Douglas. Pharmacist, Androscoggin Valley Hosp., Berlin, N.H., 1974-75, Eastern Maine Med. Center, 1975-77; dir. pharm. services and central supply Concord Hosp., N.H., 1977-82; founder, pres. Hosp. Home Health Care of N.H., 1982-91, Hosp. Home Health Care of Maine, 1986-92; founder, pres. Weare Family Pharmacy, 1992-96; commr. N.H. Bd. of Registration of Pharmacy; cons. nurse anesthetist sch. Concord Hosp. Served with U.S. Army, 1968-74. Decorated Combat Inf. badge, Bronze Star medal, Army Commendation medal. Fellow Am. Acad. Med. Adminstrs., Am. Coll. Apothecaries; mem. Am. Pharm. Assn., Am. Soc. Hosp. Pharmacists, N.H. Pharm. Assn., N.H. Soc. Hosp. Pharmacists, Nat. Assoc. Retail Druggists. Club: Lions (chpt. pres.). Home: 164 Dolly Rd Contoocook NH 03229-2712

DOMEN, RONALD EUGENE, pathologist; b. Dennison, Ohio, Apr. 22, 1950; s. George and F. Jean (Berkshire) D.; m. Kathryn Heske, Aug. 30, 1991; children: Michael E., Erika M., Laura K. AB, Youngstown (Ohio) State U., 1972; MD, U. Autonoma de Guadalajara, 1975. Bd. cert. internal medicine, clin. pathology, blood banking, transfusion medicine. Intern, resident internal medicine St. Luke's Hosp., Cleve., 1976-79; fellow in hematology-med. oncology Ohio State U., Columbus, 1979-80, resident clin. pathology, 1980-82; asst. prof. pathology Ohio State U., Columbus, Pa., 1982-84, U. South Fla., Tampa, 1984-88; med. dir. Miller Meml. Blood Ctr., Bethlehem, Pa., 1988-93; staff physician Cleve. Clinic, 1993—. Contbr. articles to profl. jours. Bd. dirs. Pa. Assn. Blood Banks, 1990-93, Ohio Assn. Blood Banks, 1995—. Fellow ACP, Coll. Am. Pathologists; mem. Am. Soc. Hematology, Am. Assn. Blood Banks, Internat. Soc. Blood Transfusion. Office: Cleve Clinic L-20 9500 Euclid Ave Cleveland OH 44195

DOMER, JUDITH ELAINE, microbiologist, educator; b. Millersville, Pa., Apr. 9, 1939; d. Richard Harvey and Dorothy Alice (Peters) Kofroth; m. Floyd Ray Domer, Apr. 15, 1965. BA, Tusculum Coll., Greeneville, Tenn., 1961; PhD, Tulane U., 1966. Diplomate Am. Bd. Med. Microbiology. Asst. prof. St. Mary's Dominican Coll., New Orleans, 1966-68; rsch. assoc. Tulane U. Sch. Medicine, New Orleans, 1968-71, asst. prof., 1972-77, assoc. prof., 1977-88, prof., 1988—; assoc. dean grad. sch. Tulane U., New Orleans, 1994—; rsch. fellow Kennedy Inst. Rheumatology, London, 1971-72; guest rschr. NIH, Bethesda, Md., 1984-85; diagnostic mycologist Tulane Hosp., New Orleans, 1980-83; mem. Bacteriology and Mycology Study Sects., Bethesda, 1975-79, Biomed. Sci. Study Sect., 1988-90, AIDS and Related Diseases Study Sect., 1990-93; vis. scientist Clin. Rsch. Ctr., Northwick Park Hosp., Harrow, Eng., 1991-92. Contbr. numerous articles to profl. jours. Charles Oliver Gray scholar Tusculum Coll., 1958-61; named one of Outstanding Young Women Am., 1967. Fellow Am. Acad. Microbiology, Infectious Disease Soc. Am.; mem. Am. Soc. for Microbiology (divsn. chmn. 1984-85, group rep. 1987-89, vice chmn. gen. meeting 1988-92, chmn. 1992-95), Med. Mycological Soc. Ams. (pres. 1987-89), Am. Assn. Immunologists, Internat. Soc. for Human and Animal Mycology, British Soc. for Mycopathology (Ian Murray Meml. lectr. 1990). Democrat. Methodist. Home: 4420 Copernicus St New Orleans LA 70131-3616 Office: Tulane Med Sch 1430 Tulane Ave New Orleans LA 70112-2699

DOMINGUE, GERALD JAMES, medical scientist, microbiology, immunology and urology educator, researcher, clinical bacteriologist; b. Lafayette, La., Mar. 2, 1937; s. Edgar Paul and Sarah Ann (Prejean) D.; m. Marie H. Dugas, Aug. 30, 1958 (div. 1980); children: Andrea, Yvonne, Michelle, Gerald Jr., Marcel; m. Kathryn H. Colbert, June 20, 1981 (div. 1985). BS in Bacteriology, U. Southwestern La., 1959; PhD in Med. Microbiol. and Immunology, Tulane U., 1964. Post-doctoral research fellow Children's Hosp., asst. research instr. pediatrics SUNY, Buffalo, 1965-66; dir. microbiol. Snodgras Lab. of Pathology and Bacteriology, St. Louis, 1966-67; instr. microbiology St. Louis U., 1966-67; asst. prof. microbiology, immunology and urology Tulane U., New Orleans, 1967-70, assoc. prof. microbiology, immunology and urology, 1970-74, prof. microbiology, immunology and urology, 1974—; lectr. microbiology sch. dentistry Washington U., St. Louis, 1966-67; vis. prof., lectr. Peruvian Urol. Assn., Lima, 1973, First Internat. Congress Bacteriology, Jerusalem, 1973, Internat. Convocation Immunology, Buffalo, 1974, World Health Orgn. Conf. on Sperm Immunology, Aarhus, Denmark, 1974, European Soc. Exptl. Urol. Research, Wurzburg, Fed. Republic Germany, 1976, Internat. Seminar L-Forms, Montpellier, France, 1976, U. Melbourne, Royal Melbourne Hosp., Australia, 1978, XII Internat. Congress Microbiology, Munich, 1978, Internat. Symposium Vaccines and Vaccinations, Institut Pasteur, Paris, 1985; speaker U. Montpellier Sch. Medicine, 1985, 4th Internat. Congress on Pyelonephritis, Goteborg, Sweden, 1986, Orion Diagnostica, Helsinki, Finland, 1986, Nat. Inst. Hygiene, Warsaw, Poland, 1986, Symposium on Molecular Biology and Infectious Diseases, Institut Pasteur, 1987; mem. com. for infection control So. Bapt. Hosp., 1971-75, Charity Hosp. La., 1971-77, Tulane U. Hosp., 1977—; mem. infectious disease com. St. Louis City Hosp., 1966-67; mem., reviewer, visitor project sites NIH Grant Review Study Sects., 1967—, NSF, Kaiser Rsch. Found., Kidney Found. of Can.; cons. bacteriology So. Bapt. Hosp., New Orleans, 1968-84, Tulane U. Hosp., 1978-83, Med. Tech. Corp., Somerset, N.J., 1983—; research cons. VA Hosp., New Orleans, 1970-78; cons., mem. tech. adv. bd. Analytab Products, Inc., N.Y.C., 1972-77, cons. Chiron Corp., Emeryville, Calif.; expert witness to subcom. on dept. investigation oversight and research for Animal Cancer Research Act, U.S. Ho. of Reps., 1980. Author, editor: Cell Wall-Deficient Bacteria, 1962; editorial bd. cons. numerous jours.; contbr. over 100 articles to profl. jours. and chpts. to books. Pres. France-Louisiane de la Nouvelle Orleans, 1985—, pres. fondateur, 1988; apptd. mem. Gov.'s Council for Devel. of French Lang. in La., 1985, 88; mem. Met. Area Com., New Orleans, 1987, Bur. Govtl. Research, New Orleans, 1987; mem. Mayor's Com. New Orleans-Paris Cultural Exchange, 1988; chmn. scholar's com. La. COm. on French Revolution, 1988; mem. Alliance for Good Govt., 1980-84; mem. Greater New Orleans French Bd., 1987—; rep. Coun. for Devel. French and France Louisiane for celebration of French Bicentennial, 1989. Served with La. N.G., USAR, 1955-63. Guaranty scholar U. Southwestern La., 1958; grantee NIH, 1970—, Schlieder Found., Armour Pharm. House, VA, Cadwallader Family Sonation, Med. Tech. Corp., Orion Diagnostica; named to Chevalier in the Order of Palmes Academiques, French Prime Minister; recipient French Medal, 1995. Fellow Am. Acad. Microbiology, Infectious Disease Soc. Am.; mem. Am. Soc. Microbiology (divisional lectr. 1978, found. lectr. 1979-80, symposium lectr. 1994), Soc. Basic Urologic Rsch. (state of art lectr. 1994), Soc. for Exptl. Biology and Medicine, AAAS, Am. Assn. Univ. Profs., Fedn. Am. Scientists, Southwestern Assn. Clin. Microbiology (editor newsletter 1983-85, pres. 1985-86), N.Y. Acad. Scis., Am. Assn. Lab. Animal Sci., Soc. Basic Urological Research (nominating com. 1988), Am. Urological Assn. (affiliate mem.), French-Am. Bus. A88, Sigma Xi. Republican. Roman Catholic. Home: 3540 Rue Michelle New Orleans LA 70131-7220 Office: Tulane U Sch Medicine 1430 Tulane Ave New Orleans LA 70112-2699

DOMINGUEZ, JOHN ANTHONY, health consultant; b. Orange, Calif., Sept. 13, 1961; s. Ralph Jose and Kazilla (Murphy) D.; m. Shair Ilene Brand, June 10, 1995. Student, Ariz. State U., 1990; BS in Cmty. Health, U. Ariz., 1993, MPH, 1996. Paramedic, fire fighter Yuma (Ariz.) Fire Dept., 1985-89; paramedic, lt. Rural Metro Fire Dept., Yuma, 1989-90; paramedic Ariz. Med. Transport, Phoenix, 1990, Rural Metro Fire Dept., Tucson, 1991-95; rsch. asst. U. Ariz., Tucson, 1994-95; health cons. Ariz. Dept. Health Svcs., Phoenix, 1995—; intern Ariz. Gov.'s Office of Drug Policy, Phoenix, 1996—, Ariz. Program for Nicotine and Tobacco Rsch., Tucson, 1995; guest lectr. U. Ariz., Tucson, 1993—. Grad. Student Minority fellow U. Ariz., 1995-96.

DOMINGUEZ-MAYORAL, RODRIGO, pediatrics and radiology educator; b. Malaga, Spain, July 14, 1947; came to U.S., 1974; s. Rodrigo Dominguez-Estevez and Maria Luisa (Mayoral) Dominguez. BA, U. Seville, Spain, 1966; MD, Seville U., 1970. Intern U. Barcelona, Spain, 1971; resident in radiology Madrid U., 1973, U. Ariz., 1976; asst. prof. U. Pitts., 1978-84; assoc. prof. depts. radiology and pediatrics U. Tex. Health Sci. Ctr., Houston, 1984-92; prof. dept. radiology Children's Med. Ctr. Dallas, 1992-94; chief sect. pediatric radiology Brooke Army Med. Ctr., Fort Sam Houston, Tex., 1994—; cons. radiologist Shriner's Hosp. Crippled Children, Houston, 1984-92, Cleft Palate Ctr., Pitts., 1978-84. Author (book) Diagnostic Imaging of the Premature Infant, 1991; contbg. author (books) Atlas of Pediatric, 1987, Monographs in Diagnostic Imaging, 1989; contbr. articles to profl. jours. Spkr., counselor Houston AIDS Found., 1986-92; v.p. Hispanic Assn. Health Edn., Houston, 1987-92, Houston Soc. Flamenco Arts, 1984-92. Mem. Spanish Soc. Radiology, Am. Coll. Radiology, Tex. Med. Assn., Hispanic Profls. USA, U. Tex. Minority Faculty Assn. (pub. 1988-92). Avocations: Flemenco dancing, bird breeder. Office: Brooke Army Med Ctr Radiology Dept 3851 Roger Brooke Dr Fort Sam Houston TX 78234-6200

DOMINGUEZ ORTEGA, LUIS, medical educator, health facility administrator; b. Barcelona, Spain, Oct. 4, 1941; s. Jose Dominguez and Dolores Ortega (Araujo) Dominguez; m. Mercedes Sanchez Tamayo, Jan. 2, 1969; children: Elena, Jose Luis. Cert., Ramiro Maeztu Inst., Madrid, Spain,

1962; MD, Complutense U., Madrid, 1969, diploma in internal medicine, 1975. Postgrad. Clinico Hosp., Madrid, 1969-73; asst. physician emergency svc. Dept. of Internal Medicine, 12 de Octubre Hosp., Madrid, 1974-77, asst. physician, 1977—, asst. prof., 1977-86, assoc. prof., 1986—; dir., coord. sleep disorders unit 12 de Octubre Hosp., Madrid, 1990—; dir., founder sleep unit Ruber Clinic, Madrid, 1988-89, 91—; mem. faculty bd. 12 de Octubre Hosp., 1984-88; mem. hosp. bd. Med. Coll., Madrid, 1984-88, candidate to pres. hosp. bd., 1986; organizer, chmn. internat. meeting Advances in Sleep Disorders, Madrid, 1992; mem. project evaluation com. of Nat. Agy. for Evaluation and Prospective in Interministerial Bd. of Sci. and tech., others coms. in field. Member Club Liberal, Madrid, 1980-89; founder, v.p. Asociacion Nacional Medicos Empresarios, Spain, 1991—. FISS grantee, 1980-90, 92. Mem. Am. Sleep Disorders Assn., Nat. Assn. Internal Medicine, N.Y. Acad. Scis., Internat. Assn. Internal Medicine, European Sleep Rsch. Soc., European Assn. Internal Medicine, Spanish Assn. of Hypnosis, Ibecian Assn. of Sleep Pathology. Roman Catholic. Office: Clinica Ruber, Juan Bravo no 49, 28006 Madrid Spain

DOMINO, EDWARD FELIX, clinical pharmacologist, educator; b. Chgo., Nov. 20, 1924; s. James I. and Mary (Dolerzek) D.; m. Antoinette Kaczorowski, Nov. 20, 1948; children: Karen Barbara, Laurence Edward, Debra Ann, Kenneth Edward, Steven Edward. BS, U. Ill., 1948, U. Ill., Chgo., 1949; MS in Pharmacology, MD with honors, U. Ill., Chgo., 1951. Dilpomate Am. Bd. Med. Examiners, Am. Bd. Clin. Pharmacology. Rotating intern Presbyn. Hosp., Chgo., 1951-52; mem. faculty U. Ill., 1951-53; mem. faculty U. Mich. Med. Sch., 1953—, prof. pharmacology, 1962—; pharmacology cons. Lafayette Clinic, Detroit, 1958-67, dir. pharmacology div., 1967-83; vis. prof. neuropsychopharmacology Wayne State U., 1959-73, clin. prof. psychiatry, 1973-80, clin. prof. pharmacology in psychiatry, 1981-86; vis. prof. pharmacology Dept. Neurosurgery U. Occupational and Environ. Health, Kitakyshu, Japan, 1988-89; vis. scientist Japan Marine Sci. and Tech. Ctr., Yokosuka, 1988; mem. study sect. pharmacology and chemistry Nat. Inst. Mental Health, 1965-69; vis. pharmacologist U.S.-USSR Cultural Exchange Program, 1971; mem. com. on nicotine and smoking antagonist drugs Nat. Cancer Inst., 1972-76; rep. U.S. Pharmacopeia, 1976-79, 95—; spl. fellow Nat. Inst. Gen. Med. Scis., 1972-73; mem. ad hoc com. sci. adv. bd. USAF, 1977-78; mem. med. rsch. and devel. adv. panel to surgeon gen. U.S. Army, 1979-82, nat. sci. adv. bd. Brain Info. Svc., UCLA, 1975-81; mem. ad hoc com. on marijuana and health Nat. Acad. Scis., 1981; cons. Policy Analysis Ctr., The Franklin Inst., Chevy Chase, Md., 1983-87, cons. clin. pharmacology VA Med. Ctr. Dept. Psychiatry, Ann Arbor, Mich., 1980—; cons. clin. pharmacology U. Ill. Inst. Aviation, Savoy, 1981-88; Burroughs Wellcome William N. Creasy vis. prof. clin. pharmacology U. Miss. Med. Ctr., Jackson, 1987. Author and editor books in field; mem. editorial bd. Jour. Clin. Pharmacology and Therapeutics, 1973—, Jour. Pharmacology and Exptl. Therapeutics, 1958-65, Drug Metabolism Disposition, 1991-93, Pharmacology, Biochemistry and Behavior, 1973-88, Rsch. Communications on Substance Abuse, 1980—, Neurobiol. Aging, 1980-82; mem. adv. bd., supporting editor Psychopharmacology, 1966-78, Archives Inter. de Pharmacodynam. et Ther, 1976-90; assoc. editor Exptl. Neurology, 1977-80; contbr. articles to med. jours. With USNR, 1943-46. Recipient Sigma Xi prize medicine, 1951; Research award Mich. Soc. Neurology and Psychiatry, 1955; Sci. Exhibit 1st prize Am. Soc. Anesthesiologists, 1963; Sci. Exhibit cert. of merit AMA, 1964; Kravkov Meml. medal acad. bd. Inst. Pharmacology and Chemotherapy of Acad. Med. Sci., USSR, 1968; Cert. of Merit in Teaching and Research Mich. Psychiat. Assn., 1981; Alumnus award in research and edn. U. Ill., 1981; Cert. for Service with High Distinction U.S. Med. Research and Service Command, 1979-82. Fellow Am. Coll. Neuropsychopharm. (life); mem. Am. Soc. Pharmacology and Exptl. Therapeutics (emeritus), N.Y. Acad. Sci. (emeritus), Internat. Soc. Cerebral Blood Flow and Metabolism (emeritus), Washtenaw County Med. Soc. (emeritus), Soc. Exptl. Biology and Medicine (emeritus), Internat. Soc. Neurochemistry (emeritus), Mich. Psychiat. Assn. (assoc. emeritus), Am. Psychiat. Assn. (emeritus), Soc. Toxicology (emeritus), Sigma Xi (emeritus, councilor 1961-63), Alpha Omega Alpha. Home: 3071 Exmoor Rd Ann Arbor MI 48104-4122

DOMINO, GEORGE, psychology educator; b. Turin, Italy, June 13, 1938; came to U.S., 1949; s. Tommaso and Maria (Oglietti) D.; m. Valerie Gerencser, Aug. 14, 1965; children: Brian, Marisa, Marla. BS, Loyola U., Los Angeles, 1960; PhD, U. Calif., Berkeley, 1967. Registered psychologist. Instr. U. San Francisco, 1962-65; asst. prof. psychology Calif. State U., Fresno, 1965-66; prof., dir. counseling Fordham U., N.Y.C., 1966-75; prof. U. Ariz., Tucson, 1975—. Contbr. articles to profl. jours. Mem. Am. Psychol. Assn., Western Psychol. Assn., Rocky Mountain Psychol. Assn. Roman Catholic. Office: U Ariz Dept Psychology Tucson AZ 85721

DOMIZIO, DAN, physician assistant, consultant; b. N.Y.C., Nov. 5, 1944; s. Joseph and Harriet (Zarmon) DiDomizio; m. Honorah Christina Phillips, Sept. 13, 1973; children: Jude, Zoë. BS, CCNY, 1966; B of Health Sci., Duke U., 1975; MPH, U. N.C., 1982. Cert. physician asst., Hawaii; cert. ACLS, pediat. advanced life support. Health generalist Peace Corps, Satawal, Micronesia, 1966-69; cross cultural trainer Ctr. for Peace Corps, Saipan, Micronesia, 1970; med. officer Peace Corps/Ministry of Health, Barbuda, West Indies, 1976-78; clin. coord./clin. assoc. Duke U. Med. Ctr. Pa. Program, Durham, N.C., 1978-82; field program dir. Project Concern Internat., Belize, Ctrl. Am., 1982-85; physician asst./cmty. health coord. Project Concern Internat., Chilchinbeto, Ariz., 1985-86; physician asst./clinic mgr. Indian Health Svc. Clinic, Supai, Ariz., 1986; cmty. health educator U. N.C. Family Medicine Residency Program, Chapel Hill, 1986-87; program dir./physician asst. Chilchinbeto Health Program, 1988-91; physician asst./ emergency rm. staff Waianae (Hawaii) Coast Comprehensive Health Ctr., 1991-95; dir./cons. Calumet Devel. Svcs. Inc., Pahoa, Hawaii, 1987—; dir. physician asst. program devel. U. Hawaii, Hilo, 1995—; physician asst./med. staff Pahoa (Hawaii) Family Health Ctr., 1995—; cons. Essex C.C., Balt., 1987, Peace Corps, Papua New Guinea, 1987, Chilchinbeto Health and Devel. Corp., 1988-91, physician asst. tng. program U. Hawaii, 1994—; clin. preceptor N.C. Student Rural Health Coalition, summers 1979, 80, 81; chmn. Gov.'s Subcom. Studying Safety and Efficiency of Out of Hosp. Childbirth and Midwifery Practice in N.C., 1981-83; co-organizer Hawaii Health Team's ann. visits to Yap State, Micronesia, Aug. 91, 92, 93, 94; participant Sugarloaf Inst. for New Physicians Assts. Program Dirs., 1994; chmn. Hawaii State Primary Care Roundtable, 1994—. Author: (chpt.) The Unfinished Health Agenda, 1994. Recipient grant Robert Wood Johnson Found., 1989, grant The Queen's Health Sys., 1994. Mem. APHA, Am. Acad. Physician Assts., Hawaii Acad. Physician Assts., Hawaii Pub. Health Assn., Nat. Coun. for Internat. Health. Home: 12-4592 Kalapana Rd Pahoa HI 96778

DOMONDON, OSCAR, dentist; b. Cebu City, Philippines, July 4, 1924; Came to U.S., 1954, naturalized, 1956.; s. Antero B. and Ursula (Maglasang) D. ; m. Vicky Domondon. children—Reinelda, Carolyn, Catherine, Oscar. DMD, Philippine Dental Coll., 1951; DDS, Loma Linda U., 1964. Dentist Manila Sanitarium and Hosp., 1952, U.S. Embassy, Manila, 1952-54; pvt. practice dentistry Long Beach, Calif., 1964—; Dentist, Children's Dental Health Center, Long Beach, part-time, 1964-68; past mem. Calif. State Bd. Dental Examiners. Past pres., Filipino Community Action Services, Inc. With AUS, 1946-49, U.S. Army, 1954-60. Fellow Acad. Dentistry Internat., Acad. Gen. Dentistry, Internat. Inst. Community Svc., Acad. Internat. Dental Studies, Internat. Coll. Dentists, Am. Coll. Dentists (life), Acad. Continuing Edn.; mem. ADA (life), Am. Soc. Dentistry Children, Am. Acad. Oral Radiology (award 1964), Internat. Acad. Orthodontists, Am. Soc. Clin. Hypnosis, Am. Endodontic Soc., Western Conf. Dental Examiners and Dental Sch. Deans, Fedn. of Assns. of Health Regulatory Bds., Calif. Assn. Fgn. Dental Grads. (past pres.), Filipino Dental Soc. (past pres.), Philippine Tech. and Profl. Soc. (v.p.), Am. Acad. Dentistry for Handicapped, Am. Assn. Dental Examiners (life), Nat. Assn. Filipino Dentists in Am. (past pres.), Pierre Fauchard Acad., Knights of Rizal (comdr.), Lions (past pres.), Elks (past chmn. rangers), Masons, Shrine Noble, Am. Legion (comdr. Post 688), Disabled Am. Vets. (vice-comdr. dist. 17), VFW (comdr. post 875). Republican. Home: 3570 Aster St Seal Beach CA 90740-2801 Office: 3714 Atlantic Ave Long Beach CA 90807-3409

DOMONKOS, PATRICIA MAHONEY, nurse; b. Hackensack, N.J., Mar. 13, 1949; d. Harold Joseph and Mary Ann (Skrezec) Mahoney; m. John Wyne Dean, May 1, 1971 (div. 1987); children: Kimberly, Jenette; m. Lawrence L. Domonkos, June 9, 1990. AAS in Nursing, Rockland C.C., Suffern, N.Y., 1970; BS in Nursing, George Mason U., 1985; MA in Human Resource Devel., Marymount U., Arlington, Va. 1995. RN, N.Y., Va. Staff nurse Columbia Presbyn. Hosp., N.Y.C., 1970-71, No. Va. Doctors' Hosp., Arlington, 1971-73; office nurse to pvt. physicians Burke, Va., 1974-78; instr. Loudoun County Schs., Leesburg, Va., 1980-84; asst. dir. nursing Hunt Country Home Health, Reston, Va., 1985-86; pres. TLC Health Care, Inc., Leesburg, 1986-90; instr. ARC, Washington, 1990-93; pvt. practice hypnotherapy Windstone, Va., 1992—; cons. for state guidelines for nursing assts., LPNs, 1984-89; head adult edn. health programs, instr. nursing asst. program No. Va. C.C., Alexandria, 1994. Bd. dirs. ARC. Mem. LWV (past officer, named Entrepreneur of Yr. 1988), Nat. Nurses in Bus., Am. Heart Assn., Am. Red. Cross (bd dirs.). Roman Catholic. Home: 35629 Williams Gap Rd Round Hill VA 20141

DOMURAT, FRANCIS MARIAN, medical oncologist, infectious diseases physician; b. Holyoke, Mass., Apr. 19, 1950; m. Meredith Lynn Dickie, June 30, 1972. AB magna cum laude, Brown U., 1972, MD, 1976. Diplomate Am. Bd. Internal Medicine, Am. Bd. Med. Oncology; lic. N.Y. Resident SUNY, Buffalo, 1979; dir. med. oncology, chief internal medicine svc. Yukon Regional Health Ctr., 1979-82; fellow infectious diseases unit U. Rochester (N.Y.) Sch. Medicine, 1982; physician med. oncology, infectious diseases Anchorage, Alaska, 1987—; attending physician Providence Hosp., Anchorage, Columbia Alaska Regional Hosp., Anchorage. Contbr. articles to profl. jours. Grantee Pub. Health Svc., 1973-76, 79-84, State of Alaska, 1981-82, Am. Cancer Soc., 1984-85, United Cancer Coun., 1984-85, Nat. Cancer Cytology Ctr., 1985-87, Wilmot Cancer Rsch. Found., 1984-87, NIH, NIAID, 1986-92; Wilmot Cancer fellow, 1984. Mem. ACP, Infectious Diseases Soc. Am., Am. Soc. Internal Medicine, Sigma Xi. Office: 1200 Airport Heights Dr 300 Anchorage AK 99508

DONABEDIAN, AVEDIS, physician; b. Beirut, Lebanon, Jan. 7, 1919; came to U.S., 1955, naturalized, 1960; s. Samuel and Maritza (Der Hagopian) D.; m. Dorothy Salibian, Sept. 15, 1945; children: Haig, Bairj, Armen. BA, Am. U., Beirut, 1940, MD, 1944; MPH, Harvard U., 1955. Physician, acting supt. English Mission Hosp., Jerusalem, 1945-47; instr. physiology, clin. asst. dermatology and venereology Am. U. Med. Sch., 1948-51, univ. physician, dir. univ. health service, 1949-54; med. assoc. United Community Services Met. Boston, 1955-57; asst. prof., then assoc. prof. preventive medicine N.Y. Med. Coll., 1957-61; mem. faculty U. Mich. Sch. Pub. Health, Ann Arbor, 1961—, prof. med. care orgn., 1964-79, Nathan Sinai disting. prof. public health, 1979-89, emeritus. Author: A Guide to Medical Care Administration: Medical Care Appraisal--Quality and Utilization, 1969, Aspects of Medical Care Administration, 1973, Benefits in medical Care Programs, 1976, The Definition of Quality and Approaches to Its Assessment, 1980, Medical Care Chartbook, 1986, The Criteria and Standards of Quality, 1982, The Methods and Findings of Quality Assessment and Monitoring, 1985; co-author: Striving for Quality in Health Care: An Inquiry into Policy and Practice, 1991. Recipient Dean Conley award Am. Coll. Hosp. Adminstrs., 1969; Norman A. Welch award Nat. Assn. Blue Shield Plans, 1976; Elizur Wright award Am. Risk and Ins. Assn., 1978; Nat. Merit award Delta Omega, 1978; Richard B. Tobias award Am. Coll. Utilization Rev. Physicians, 1984; Outstanding Contbns. in Health Services Research award Assn. Health Services Research, 1985, Baxter Am. Found. Health Services Research prize, 1986, Gold Medal award Med. Alumni Assn., Am. U. of Beirut, 1986. Fellow Am. Coll. Utilization Rev. Physicians (hon.), Am. Pub. Health Assn., Am. Coll. Healthcare Execs. (hon.); mem. Inst. Medicine of NAS, Nat. Acad. Medicine of Mex. (hon.), Internat. Soc. Quality Assurance in Health Care (hon.), Avedis Donabedian Found. (Barcelona, hon. pres. 1990—, Buenos Aires, hon. pres. 1994—). Home: 1739 Ivywood Dr Ann Arbor MI 48103-4523 Office: HMP-SPH II 109 Observatory St Ann Arbor MI 48109

DONAGHY, MICHAEL JOHN, neurology educator; b. London, Oct. 18, 1950; s. James Donaghy and Jean Low Allardyce; m. Mary Ann Gibbon, Dec. 13, 1975; children: Louise, Josephine, Alexander. BS, Univ. Coll., London, 1972; PhD, U. Cambridge, Eng., 1975; MB BChir, Univ. Coll. Hosp., London, 1978; MA, PhD, U. Oxford, Eng., 1987. Med. registrar Hammersmith Hosp., London, 1981-82; neurology registrar Middlesex and Nat. Hosps., London, 1982-86; neurology sr. registrar Nat. Hosp. and St. Bartholomew's Hosp., London, 1986-87; reader in clin. neurology U. Oxford, 1987—; fellow Green Coll. Oxford, 1987—, sr. tutor, 1991-94. Co-author: Brain's Diseases of the Nervous System, 10th edit., 1993; contbg. author: The Oxford Textbook of Medicine, 3d edit., 1995; contbr. rsch. papers and book chpts. to profl. pubs. Fellow Royal Coll. Physicians London. (examiner 1995—); mem. Assn. Brit. Neurologists (hon. asst. sec. 1992-95, hon. sec. 1995—), Royal Soc. Medicine (coun. mem. 1995—), Assn. Physicians of Gt. Britain. Office: Radcliffe Infirmary, Dept Clin Neurology, Oxford OX2 6HE, England

DONAHOO, JAMES SAUNDERS, cardiothoracic surgeon; b. Jackson, Tenn., Sept. 30, 1937; s. Henry Amos and Ruby Burt (Welch) D.; m. Rose Carol Manasco, June 24, 1961; children: Paige, James. AB, Birmingham So. Coll., 1959; MD, Med. Coll. Ala., 1963. Chief resident surgeon Vanderbilt U. Hosp., Nashville, 1969; chief resident cardiac surgery Johns Hopkins U., Balt., 1971, asst. prof. surgery, 1971-75, assoc. prof. surgery, 1975-82; assoc. prof. surgery Jefferson Med. Coll., Phila., 1983-89; prof. cardiothoracic surgery Univ. Medicine Dentistry N.J., Newark, 1989—; chief thoracic surgery East Orange (N.J.) VA Hosp., 1989-94. Editor: Practical Reviews in Surgery, 1975-82; contbr. articles to profl. jours. Col. USAR, 1964-92, Op. Desert Storm, 1991. Recipient Gold Medal Paper award S.E. Surg. Conv., 1967. Fellow ACS; mem. Am. Assn. Thoracic Surgery, So. Surg. Assn., So. Thoracic Surg. Assn. (coun. mem., Osler Abbott award 1982), N.Y. Soc. Thoracic Surgery, N.J. Soc. Thoracic Surgeons (pres. 1994), Elkridge Harford Hunt Club (exec. com. 1980), Alpha Omega Alpha. Episcopalian. Home: 71 Hillcrest Ave Summit NJ 07901-2012 Office: Univ Medicine and Dentistry NJ 185 Bergen St # G-595 Newark NJ 07103-2406

DONAHUE, CHARLES LEE, JR., health network executive; b. Norwood, Mass., Mar. 31, 1943; s. Charles and Katherine (Gallagher) D.; m. Nancy Turner, Aug. 15, 1971; children: Jessica, Charles, Morgan, Caroline, Matthew. AB, Brown U., 1965; MA, Cornell U., 1973. Vol. U.S. Peace Corps, Trengganu, Malaysia, 1967-68; project co-dir. Mass. Health Rsch. Inst., Boston, 1973-75; health planning analyst Boston U., Boston, 1976-80; regional program analyst U.S. Pub. Health Svc., Boston, 1980-81; exec. dir. Health Planning Coun., Boston, 1981-89; pres. Healthcare VALUE Mgmt., Norwood, Mass., 1990—; pres. Mass. Health Coun., 1990-91; adj. asst. prof. Pub. Health Boston U., 1990—; bd. dirs. Ctr. for Cmty. Responsive Care, Mass. Health Data Consortium, Boston. Contbr. articles to profl. jours. Recipient Schlesinger award Am. Pub. Health Assn. and Am. Health Plan Assn., 1987. Home: 390 High St Westwood MA 02090-1106

DONAHUE, DAVID J., pediatric neurosurgeon; b. Chgo., Mar. 6, 1951; s. Robert James and Mary Charlotte (Tighe) D.; m. Angela Jo Berry, Dec. 29, 1979; children: Benjamin Walton, Kenn Clifton, David Wyatt. BA in History and French, Georgetown U., 1973; student, Université d'Aix-Marseille, Aix-en-Provence, France, 1971-72; postgraduate, Memphis State U., 1975. Intern in pediat. Children's Meml. Hosp., Chgo., 1978-79; resident in gen. surgery Bapt. Meml. Hosp., Memphis, 1979-80; resident in neurosurgery U. Tenn., Memphis, 1980-85; staff neurosurgeon Neurosurgical Group, Memphis, 1985-92; pediatric neurosurgery fellow St. Jude's Hosp., U. Tenn., Memphis, 1992-94; staff neurosurgeon Children's Nat. Med. Ctr., Washington, 1994—. Class agent U. Tenn. devel., 1987—; mil. liaison officer USNR, Memphis, 1993-94. Capt. USNR 1985—. Recipient Think First award, 1993. Fellow Am. Acad. Pediat.; mem. Am. Assn. Neurol. Surgeons and Congress of Neurol. Surgeons (chmn. joint com. mil. neurosurgery), Nat. Assn. Med. Veterans, AMSUS. Office: Children's Nat Medical Ctr 111 Michigan Ave NW Washington DC 20010

DONAHUE, HAYDEN HACKNEY, mental health institute administrator, medical educator, psychiatric consultant; b. El Reno, Okla., Dec. 4, 1912; s. Henry Hilton and Mame (Hackney) D.; m. Patricia Toothaker; children—Erin Kathleen, Kerry Shannon, Patricia Marie. B.S., U. Kans., 1939, M.D., 1941. Cert. mental hosp. adminstr.; cert. mental health adminstr. Draftsman, topographer Wilson Constrn. Co., Salina, Kans., 1934; constrn. engr. Pub. Works Adminstrn., State of Kans., 1935-37, efficiency engr. Dept. Inspections and registration, 1937; intern U. Ga. Sch. Medicine Hosp., 1941-42, resident in psychiatry, 1942; resident in aviation medicine Army Air Force Sch. Aviation Medicine, 1943; resident in psychiatry Ark. State Hosp., Little Rock, 1959-61; asst. chief hosp. ops. VA, Washington, 1946; exec. officer, acting mgr. VA Hosp., North Little Rock, Ark., 1946-49; dir. edn. and research Ark. State Hosp., Little Rock, 1949-51; asst. med. dir. Tex. Bd. for Hosps. and Spl. Schs., 1951-52; dir. mental health State of Okla., 1952-59; supt. Cen. State Hosp., Norman, Okla., 1961-79; asst. dir. dept. mental health State of Okla., 1966-70, dir. dept. mental health, 1970-78; dir. Okla. Inst. for Mental Health Edn. and Tng., Norman, 1979-91; cons. psychiatry Ark. Health Dept., 1949-51, Okla. Crime Bur., 1964-85, Base Hosp., Tinker Field, 1964-70; cons. Okla. State Penitentiary, 1963-67; cons. to NIMH, 1968-70, USMC, Vietnam, 1970, gov. State of Nebr., 1978, mem. legislature, 1980; instr. medicine and psychiatry U. Ga. Sch. Medicine, 1942; lectr. in psychiatry AAF Redistbn. Ctr., Atlantic City, 1944; lectr. legal medicine U. Tex. Sch. Law, 1952; lectr. Homicide Inst., U. Okla, U. Tex., 1953-67; lectr. scholarly lecture series U. Okla. 1965-70, mem. faculty and adv. com. U. Okla. Health Sci. Ctr., 1975-78, 85-86; clin. prof. psychiatry U. Okla. Sch. Medicine, 1967-87, emeritus clin. prof. psychiatry and behavioral scis., 1988—; assoc. prof. psychiatry U. Ark. Sch. Medicine, 1949-51, 1960-61, U. Okla. Sch. Medicine, 1958-67, also numerous others; bd. dirs., treas. Pan Am. Tng. Exch. in Psychiatry, 1961-63; mem. exec. com. ABA Commn. on Mentally Disabled, 1973-80; pres. L.F. Am. Coll. Psychiatrists, 1975-76. Contbr. numerous articles to profl. jours. Advisor Okla. com. President's Com. on Employment of Handicapped, 1957-59, 61-91; mem. Okla. Health Planning Commn.; mem. exec. com. Okla Crime Com. 1967-75; chmn com. Juvenile delinquent, 1969-75, Okla. Mental Health Authority, 1970-78, Okla Drug and Alcohol Authority, 1970-78; mem. Okla Coun. Juvenile delinquent Planning Com., 1969—, Com to Regoranize Exec. Dept. Okla., 1971-73, Okla Med. Rsch. Com. 1963-66, 70-78. Served with M.C., USAAF, 1942-46. Recipient Health Planning award Okla. Health Planning Coun., 1978, Bowis award, 1978, Outstanding Svc. award Okla. Health Welfare Assn., 1967, Donahue Appreciation Day declared State of Okla., 1959, Honor plaque Okla. Assn. on Alcohol and Drug Abuse, 1989, Lifetime Achievement award Alliance Mentally Ill., 1991; elected to Okla. Hall of Fame, 1968; Hayden H. Donahue Mental Health Inst. named in his honor, 1979; hon. chief Choctaw Nation, 1968. Fellow AAAS, Am. Assn. for Mental Deficiency, ACP, Am. Psychiat. Assn. (life, pres. Okla. dist. br. 1963, del. Okla. 1953-59, 66-81, chmn. budget com. 1961-68, treas., exec. com. 1969-73, Disting. Svc. award 1984, Warren Williams award 1992), Am. Geriatrics Soc., Am. Assn. Psychiat. Adminstrs. (pres. 1974-75, dir. 1967-75, com. on continuing edn. 1979-89); mem. AMA, Nat. Assn. for Mental Health (profl. adv. com. 1970-78), Nat. Alliance for Mentally Ill (Exemplary Psychiatrist award 1993), Assn. Mental Health Adminstrs. (Piepenbrink award 1988), Okla. Med. Assn. (chmn. coun. pub. and mental health 1962-70, ho. of dels. 1964-89, A.H. Robins Community Svc. award 1979, Leaders in Medicine award 1988), Cleveland-McClain County Med. Soc., Okla. Health Planning Commn., Okla. Geriatric Edn. Resource Orgn. (sr. advisor 1992), Okla. Geriatric Edn. Ctr. (adv. com. 1991), Psychiat. Assn., Am. Med. Correctional Assn. Nat. Acad. Religion and Mental Health, Nat. Rehab. Assn., Am. Rehab. Assn., Okla. Rehab. Assn. (pres. 1969), Norman C. of C., Okla. Psychiat. Soc. (pres. 1962-66), (Psychiat. award NAMI, 1993), Brookings Inst. Mental Health in Gov., Nat. Adv. Coun. The White House Conf. Aging, Assn. Community Mental Health Ctr. Dirs. Methodist. Lodge: Rotary. Home and Office: 1109 Westbrooke Ter Norman OK 73072-6308

DONAHUE, MARY ROSENBERG, psychologist; b. N.Y.C., Dec. 20, 1932; d. Lester and Ethel (Hyman) Rosenberg; children: Laurie, Rachel. BA, Adelphi U., 1954; MA, N.Y. U., 1958; PhD, St. John U., 1968. Tchr. Elmont, N.Y., 1954-57, sch. psychologist, 1957-63; cons. psychologist NIMH, 1964-65; sch. psychologist Mamaroneck, N.Y., 1966-67; pvt. practice psychology Bethesda, Md., 1971—; expert witness local jurisdictions regarding domestic issues, womens issues, abuse, 1974—; speaker on custody evaluations and expert witness considerations. Co-author: On Your Own, 1993. NIMH grantee, 1962-63, 64-65. Mem. Am. Psychol. Assn., Md. Psychol. Assn., D.C. Psychol. Assn., Am. Orthopsychiat. Assn., Assn. Pvt. Practitioners, Nat. Assn. Women Bus. Owners. Home: 12017 Edgepark Ct Potomac MD 20854-2138 Office: 5902 Hubbard Dr Rockville MD 20852-4823

DONAHUE, MICHAEL J., dermatologist; b. Cornwall, N.Y., Dec. 8, 1941; s. Michael Joseph and Loraine (Swin) D.; m. Theresa MArie Stehno, Dec. 8, 1941; children: Kristine, Stephanie, Michelle. BS, Manhattan Coll., 1963; MD, Creighton U., 1967. Intern Jefferson U., Phila., 1967-70; resident U. Pa., Phila., 1970-71; dermatologist pvt. practice, Wilmington, N.C., 1973—; clin. assoc. prof. dermatology U. N.C. Sch. Medicine, 1973—. Maj. U.S. Army, 1971-73. Fellow Am. Acad. Dermatology; mem. AMA, N.C. MEd. Soc., New Hanover-Pender County Med. Soc. Democrat. Roman Catholic. Home and Office: 1421 Landfill Dr Wilmington NC 28405

DONAHUE, THOMAS JOSEPH, orthodontist; b. Scranton, Pa., Aug. 5, 1965; s. Thomas Joseph and Mary Therese (Pamelia) D.; m. Margie M. Kelley, July 24, 1987; children: Cara, Christopher. BA in Philosophy and Biology, U. Scranton, 1987; DMD, U. Pitts., 1991; Orthodontic Cert., SUNY, Stony Brook, 1993. Pvt. practice Patchogue, N.Y., 1991-93, Wilkes-Barre, Pa., 1993—. Mem. ADA (children's dental health mo. chmn. 1995-96), Am. Assn. Orthodontists, Luzurne County Dental Assn. (bd. dirs. 1995-96), N.E. Soc. Orthodontists (rsch. award 1992), Omicron Kappa Upsilon. Home: 392 Elmcrest Dr Dallas PA 18612 Office: 34 S Main St Wilkes Barre PA 18701

DONALD, ALEXANDER GRANT, psychiatrist, educator; b. Darlington, S.C., Jan. 24, 1928; s. Raymond George and Chesnut Evans (McIntosh) D.; m. Emma Louise Coggeshall, Oct. 25, 1958; children: Sandy, Mary Chesnut, Marion Lide. BS, Davidson Coll., 1948; MD, Med. U. S.C., 1952. Diplomate: Am. Bd. Psychiatry and Neurology. Intern Jefferson Med. Coll., 1952-53; resident in psychiatry Walter Reed Hosp., 1956-59; dir. Mental Health Clinic, Florence, S.C., 1962-66; dept. commr. S.C. Dept. Mental Health, 1966-67; dir. William S Hall Psychiat. Inst., Columbia, 1967-90; prof., chmn. dept. neuropsychiatry and behavioral scis. Sch. Medicine, U. S.C., Columbia, 1975-90, Disting. prof. neuropsychiatry, assoc. dean ednl. planning, 1990-91; Disting. prof. emeritus Sch. Medicine, U. S.C., 1991—; bd. dirs. Health Resource Found. Bd. trustees Richland Meml. Hosp., 1993—; bd. dirs. S.C. Inst. for Med. Edn. and Rsch., pres., 1992—. Fellow Am. Coll. Psychiatrists, Am. Psychiat. Assn. (pres. S.C. chpt. 1967), So. Psychiat. Assn. (v.p.); mem. AMA, Columbia Med. Soc. (v.p. 1981, del. 1981, pres. 1989-90), Evening Music Club (pres. 1989-90), Alpha Omega Alpha. Presbyterian. Office: U SC Sch Medicine 3555 Harden Street Ext # 104 La Columbia SC 29203-6815

DONALDSON, DOUGLAS RAMAGE, surgeon, consultant; b. Hessle, E. Yorks., Eng., Mar. 25, 1951; s. Thomas Eric and Kathleen Mary (Ramage) D.; m. Judith Anne Hudson, July 19, 1980; children: Fiona Helen, James Fergus. BSc, St. Andrews U., Scotland, 1971; M.B.,Ch.B., Dundee U., Scotland, 1974, MD, 1984. House physician/surgeon Ninewells Hosp., Dundee, 1974-75; lectr. anatomy St. Andrews U., Scotland, 1975-76; registrar Leeds Rotation, 1977-82; sr. registrar Wrexham-Cardiff Rotation, 1982-86; resident surg. officer St. Mark's Hosp., London, 1986-87; cons. surgeon St. Peter's Hosp., Chertsey, 1987—; mem. Axis Trial Steering Group, London, 1992—. Contbr. articles to profl. jours., chpts. in books. Recipient R.C. Alexander Meml. Prize in surgery Dundee U., 1974, Leeds Regional Surg. medal, 1980. Fellow Royal Coll. Surgeons Eng., Royal Coll. Surgeons Edinburgh, Brit. Soc. Gastroenterology, Assn. Surgeons of Gt. Britain and Ireland. Office: Saint Peters Hosp, Guildford Rd, Chertsey KT16 0PZ, England

DONALDSON, JAMES ADRIAN, otolaryngology educator; b. St. Cloud, Minn., Jan. 22, 1930; s. Charles Scott and Catharine Agnes (Ritchie) D.; m. Merrilyn Dorothy Ward, June 17, 1950; children: Deborah, Susan, James, Scott, Anne. BA, U. Minn., 1950, BS, 1952, MD, 1954; MS in Otolaryngology, 1961. Diplomate Am. Bd. Otolaryngology. Intern Mpls. Gen. Hosp., 1954-55; sr. asst. surgeon USPHS, 1955-57; resident U. Minn., 1957-60; fellow Otologic Med. Group, L.A., 1960-61; clin. instr. otolaryngology U. So. Calif., L.A., 1960-61; asst. prof. otolaryngology U. Iowa, Iowa City, 1961-63, assoc. prof., 1963-65; prof. otolaryngology U. Wash., Seattle, 1965-92, prof. emeritus, 1992—, dept. chmn., 1965-75. Author (with Barry Anson) Surgical Anatomy of the Temporal Bone, 1967, 4th edit.1992. Recipient

Award of Merit Am. Otological Soc., 1993. Fellow: ACS, Am. Otol. Soc., Am. Neurotology Soc., Triological Soc. Office: Seattle Ear Clinic 600 Broadway # 340 Seattle WA 98122-5371

DONALDSON, JAMES OSWELL, III, neurology educator; b. Butler, Pa., July 19, 1942; s. James Oswell Jr. and Estelle Mathilda (Unverzagt) D.; m. Mary Hoopingarner, Aug. 23, 1969 (div. Dec. 1983); 1 child, Andrew Robert; m. Susan McKernin, Nov. 3, 1984; stepchildren: Brendan McDonald, Ian McDonald. BS, Haverford Coll., 1964; MD, U. Pa., 1968. Diplomate Am. Bd. Psychiatry and Neurology, Am. Bd. Internal Medicine. Intern in medicine Hosp. of U. Pa., Phila., 1968-69, resident, 1969-70, resident in neurology, 1974-76; hon. house physician Nat. Hosp. for Nervous Diseases, London, 1973-74, sr. vis. fellow, 1991; asst. prof. neurology U. Conn. Sch. Medicine, Farmington, 1977-82, assoc. prof., 1982-88, prof., 1988—. Author: Neurology of Pregnancy, 1978, 2d edit., 1989. Maj. M.C., U.S. Army, 1970-73. Fellow ACP, Am. Acad. Neurology; mem. Am. Neurol. Assn. Office: U Conn Health Ctr 263 Farmington Ave Farmington CT 06030-1845

DONALDSON, MARY KENDRICK, nurse; b. Tifton, Ga., June 25, 1937; d. Howard Story and Trudy (Donalson) Marlin; m. Harvey Kendrick Sr., Apr. 13, 1953 (dec. 1965); children: Jerome, Micheal, Harvey Jr., Merry, Sheila, Larry; m. Isaac Hargett, Feb. 16, 1985. AA, Compton (Calif.) Coll., 1969; BS, Pepperdine U., 1972, MA, 1976; diploma in nursing, SW Coll., Los Angeles, 1984. Staff nurse St. Francis Hosp., Lynwood, Calif., 1965-67; pvt. duty nurse Profl. Nurse's Registry, L.A., 1967-82; elem. tchr. Compton Sch. Dist., Calif., 1975-80; caseworker, clk. L.A. County Probation Dept., 1980-90, dep. probation officer, 1990—; pediatric nurse companion Personal Care Health Service, Torrance, Calif., 1984—; home economist Dept. Welfare, Compton, 1970-72; asst. dir. Century Plaza Hotel, Century City, Calif., 1971-72. Chairperson Com. To Elect Garland Hardeman For Councilman, Inglewood, Calif., 1987. Exec. Housekeeping scholarship Century Plaza Hotel, Los Angeles, 1971. Mem. Fellow Am. Home Econs. Assn., Pepperdine Alumni Assn., Pepperdine's Kappa-Kappa Sorority, Am. Nurse's Assn. Democrat. Home: 4730 Falcon Ave Long Beach CA 90807-2377 Office: L A County Probation Dept 1601 Eastlake Ave Los Angeles CA 90033-1009

DONALDSON, SARAH SUSAN, radiologist; b. Portland, Oreg., 1939. BS, RN, U. Oreg., 1961; MD, Harvard U., 1968. Intern U. Wash., 1968-69; resident in radiol. therapy Stanford (Calif.) Med. Ctr., 1969-72; fellow in pediatric oncology Inst. Gustave-Roussy, 1972-73; prof. radiol. oncology Stanford U. Sch. Medicine., 1973—. Office: Stanford U Med Ctr Sch Medicine Stanford CA 94305

DONALDSON, SUE KAREN, dean, nursing educator; b. Detroit, Sept. 16, 1943. BSN, Wayne State U., 1965, MSN, 1966; PhD, U. Wash., 1973. Asst. assoc. prof. physiology and nursing U. Wash., Seattle, 1973-78; assoc. prof. physiology and nursing Rush U., Ill., 1978-84, dir. clin. nursing rsch. program, 1980-84; former assoc. dean rsch. Sch. Nursing, U. Minn., Mpls.; now dean Sch. Nursing, Johns Hopkins U., Balt. Grantee Wash. State Heart Assn., 1973-74, NIH, 1973—, USPHS, 1980—, Muscular Distrophy Assn., 1981—. Mem. ANA, NAS, Am. Heart Assn., Coun. Nurse Rschrs. Office: Johns Hopkins U Sch Nursing 266 Adminstrn Bldg 600 N Wolfe Baltimore MD 21205-2104*

DONATELLI, DANIEL DOMINIC, JR., medical/surgical and oncological nurse; b. Youngstown, Ohio, May 29, 1958; s. Daniel D. Sr. and Nerina J. (Santangelo) D.; m. Deborah I. Pihonsky, May 17, 1986; children: Danamarie, Danielle, Deborah. BS in Zoology and Biology, Ohio U., 1981; BSN, Kent (Ohio) State U., 1986. RN, Ohio; cert. med./surg. nurse, clin. nurse II, oncology nurse. Resident dir. Bromly Corp., Athens, Ohio; asst. mgr. Tel Star Restaurant, Youngstown, 1991—; asst. clin. nurse mgr. oncology unit Western Res. Care System, Youngstown, Ohio. Vol. Athens Mental Health Ctr., 1977-81. Named Nurse of Hope for Mahoning County, Am. Cancer Soc., 1992-94. Mem. ANA, Ohio Nurses Assn. (dist. 3, retention and recruitment com., continuing med. edn. com., chair quality assurance/quality improvement com., chair unit edn. com., products com., nurse practice coun.), Ohio Nursing Soc., Sigma Theta Tau. Home: 7483 Salinas Trl Boardman OH 44512-5513

DONCASTER, HILARY LOUISE, nurse; b. Fitchburg, Mass., Dec. 9, 1960; d. Donald Dempsey and Janet Maryann (McKay) D. BS in Nursing, Fitchburg State Coll., 1982; postgrad computer programming, Cen. N.E. Coll., 1988-89; postgrad. in Mgmt. Info. Systems, Nichols Coll., 1990-96. RN, Mass. Staff nurse neurosurgery USAF Med. Ctr., Lackland AFB, Tex., 1983-86; ambulatory surg. specialist Katy (Tex.) Community Hosp., 1986; community nurse Worcester (Mass.) VNA, 1986; nurse reviewer Mass. Peer Rev. Orgn., Waltham, 1986-89; fin. analyst Paul Revere Ins. Co., Worcester, Mass., 1989—. Capt. USAF, 1983-86. Decorate Air Force Commendation medal. Mem. NAFE, Air Force Assn., Health Ins. Assocs., Loma Level I, Fitchburg State Coll. Alumni Assn., Alpha Sigma Lambda, Delta Mu Delta. Democrat. Roman Catholic. Home: 15 Duncannon Ave Apt 4 Worcester MA 01604-5107

DONDERSHINE, HARVEY EDWARD, psychiatrist, educator; b. Newark, Mar. 9, 1942; s. Nathan Frank and Rose (Haskin) D.; m. Susan Lois Steiger, June 14, 1964; 1 child, Stephen Dedalus. MD, U. Mich., 1966; JD, Santa Clara U., 1981. Diplomate Am. Bd. Psychiatry and Neurology. Intern Mt. Sinai Med. Ctr., N.Y.C., 1966-67; resident in psychiatrist Mt. Sinai Med. Ctr., 1967-70; chief psychiatrist San Mateo (Calif.) County Hosp., 1972-73; child and adolescent psychiatrist San Francisco Community Mental Health, 1973-75; sr. psychiatrist and edn. specialist Nat. Ctr. for PTSD, Menlo Park, Calif., 1975—; clin. faculty Stanford (Calif.) Med. Sch., 1978—. Contbr. articles to profl. jours. Maj. U.S. Army, 1970-72. Fellow Am. Psychiatric Assn.; mem. Calif. Psychiatric Assn. (jud. action com.), Northern Calif. Psychiatric Soc. (constn. and bylaws com.). Office: Nat Ctr for PTSD 3801 Miranda Ave Palo Alto CA 94304-1207

DONDES, ROBERT JONATHAN, healthcare executive, consultant; b. Albany, N.Y., Feb. 14, 1960; s. Seymour and Gloria Hannah (From) D. BS, U. Mich., 1981, postgrad. med. sch., 1979-81; postgrad., SUNY, Albany, 1981-84. Account exec. George Washington U. Health Plan, Washington, 1984-85, dir. mem. svcs., 1985-86; assoc. mktg. dir. WellCare of N.Y., Inc., Newburgh, 1986-87; coord. mktg. ops. The WellCare Mgmt. Group, Kingston, N.Y., 1987-88, dir. planning and devel., 1988-89, dir. ops., 1989-93; exec. dir. Toledo Health Plan, Toledo, 1993-95; COO Chesapeake Health Plan, Balt., 1995—; pres. Potomac Med. Svcs. Corp., Balt., 1994—; v.p. mgmt. svcs. Health Wise of Am., Nashville, 1994—. Author: The WellCare Perspective, 1988. Bd. dirs. Maternal Infant Svcs. Network, 1991-93; asst. to co-chmn. Rep. Nat. Com., Washington, 1984. A.H. Robbins Pharm. Corp. scholar, 1979, U. Mich. scholar, 1978, Am. Heart Assn. scholar, 1978; NSF fellow, 1977. Mem. Group Health Assn. Am., U. Mich. Alumni Assn., Sigma Chi. Jewish. Office: Chesapeake Health Plan 814 Light St Baltimore MD 21230

DONEHOWER, LAWRENCE ALLEN, virologist, molecular biologist; b. Pitts., Jan. 25, 1951; s. Wilford John and Helen Martha (Spahn) D.; m. Michelle Enid Smith, Sept. 1, 1985; children: Michael Jacob, Benjamin Isaac. BS, U. Md., 1974; PhD, George Washington U., 1981. Postdoctoral fellow U. Calif., San Francisco, 1981-85; asst. prof. Baylor Coll. Medicine, Houston, 1985-92, rsch. assoc. prof., 1993-94, assoc. prof., 1995—. Contbr. articles to profl. jours. NIH fellow U. Calif., 1981. Mem. AAAS, Am. Soc. for Microbiology. Democrat. Jewish. Office: Baylor Coll of Medicine Div Molecular Virology Houston TX 77030

DONELAN, PETER ANDREW, dermatologist; b. Memphis, Nov. 13, 1953; s. Richard T. and Irene M. (Jacobson) D.; m. Ivette E. Boler, Apr. 25, 1987. BA in Chemistry, Wake Forest U., 1975; MD, U. South Fla., 1978. Diplomate, Am. Bd. Dermatology. Intern U. South Fla., Tampa, Fla., 1978-79; resident in internal medicine U. South Fla., Tampa, 1979-80, resident in dermatology, 1980-83, assoc. clin. prof. medicine, 1984—; instr. dermatologic surgery VA Hosp., 1993—; pvt. practice, Tampa, 1983—; chief dermatology Tampa Gen. Hosp., 1987-88, U. Conn. Hosp., 1993—. Mem. editorial bd. Bull. Hillsboro County Med. Soc., 1987—. Fellow Am. Acad. Dermatology, Am. Soc. Dermatol. Surgery; mem. Fla. Dermatol. Soc., Leaders Soc. of Dermatology Found., Fla. Med. Soc., Green Jacket Club, Pres.'s Coun. Office: 3000 E Fletcher Ave Ste 390 Tampa FL 33613-4645

DONER, JOHN ROLAND, hospital administrator; b. Ontario, Oreg., May 6, 1949; s. L. L. and Majorie R. (Robinson) D.; m. Kathleen M. Lang, Mar. 6, 1970; children: J. R., Erica C. BA in Bus. Adminstrn., Boise (Idaho) State U., 1971. Lic. nursing home adminstr., Idaho. Disability claims adjucator Idaho Disability Determinators Unit, Boise, 1972-74, quality assurance specialist, 1974-76, unit mgr., 1976-78; mgmt. and fin. cons. Idaho Dept. Health & Welfare, Boise, 1978-81; asst. adminstr. Idaho State Sch. & Hosp., Nampa, 1981-92, adminstrv. dir., 1993—. Sec., treas. bd. dirs. Idaho Spl. Olympics, Boise, 1985-92; vice chmn. Nampa Cmty. Work Release Ctr. Bd., 1987—; mem. adv. bd. Bogus Basin Recreation Assn. Inc., Boise, 1987—; mem., v.p., bd. dirs. Archie B. Teater Fund for Hanidcapped, Inc., 1991—. Mem. Profl. Ski Instrs. Am. (cert.). Home: 10341 Shiloh Dr Boise ID 83704-2736 Office: Idaho State Sch & Hosp 3100 11th Ave N Ext Nampa ID 83687-3188

DONESA, ANTONIO BRAGANZA, neurosurgeon; b. Manila, July 27, 1935; came to U.S., 1959, naturalized, 1969; s. Alfonso Pinson and Flora (Braganza) D.; m. Barbara Louise Quinn, Nov. 30, 1962; children: Carmen, Christopher. BS, U. Philippines, 1955, MD, 1959. Intern St. Mary's Hosp., Waterbury, Conn., 1959-60; resident Huron Road Hosp., 1960-61, U. Ala. Med. Ctr., Birmingham, 1961-65; pvt. practice neurosurgery Ft. Wayne, Ind., 1966—; pres., dir. Neurosurgery, Inc., Ft. Wayne, 1971—; mem. staff Parkview Hosp., Ft. Wayne, St. Joseph's Hosp., Ft. Wayne, Luth. Hosp., Ft. Wayne; cons. Marion (Ind.) Gen. Hosp.; founder, past pres. Liberty for Am. Minority Physicians, LAMP Legal Fund. Recipient Leadership award March of Dimes, 1972, Cert. of Appreciation, Heart Fund, 1971, others. Mem. AMA, Assn. Philippine Physicians in Am. (Community Svc. award 1983), Ft. Wayne Acad. Medicine and Surgery, Ind. Philippine Med. Assn. (past pres.), Am. Coll. Internat. Physicians (founder, exec. dir. 1978-90, chmn. 1985, Leadership award 1975, Disting. Fellow award 1982), Ind. State Med. Assn., Allen (Ft. Wayne, pres. 12th dist. 1985-86) County Med. Soc. (pres. 1990-91), Congress Neurol. Surgeons, Soc. Philippine Neurol. Surgeons in Am. (past pres.), Neurosurg. Soc. Ind., Soc. Philippine Surgeons Am., U. Philippines Med. Alumni Soc. in Am. (nat. pres. 1985-87, Disting. Alumnus Overseas 1985), Masons, Shriners, Summit Club. Office: 3030 Lake Ave Fort Wayne IN 46805-5428

DONKER, RICHARD BRUCE, health care administrator; b. Modesto, Calif., Sept. 29, 1950; s. Luverne Peter and Ruth Bernice (Hoskenga) D.; m. Elizabeth Gail Content, May 3, 1986; children: Elizabeth Anne, Danica Ruth. AA, Modesto Jr. Coll., 1970; BS, Calvin Coll., Grand Rapids, Mich., 1972; MA, Calif. State Coll., Turlock, 1978; EdD, U. Pacific, 1980. Grant dir. Yosemite Community Coll. Dist., Modesto, 1975-77; dir. flight ops. Meml. Hosps. Assn., Modesto, 1980-85, adminstrv. coord., 1985-87, v.p. bus. systems, 1987-89; v.p. clin. svcs. Meml. Hosp. Assn., Modesto, 1989-92; prin. Global Bus. Network, Emeryville, Calif., 1992—; divisional pres. Coastal Health Care Group, Inc., Durham, N.C., 1993—; exec. dir. MediPLUS Health Plans, Inc., Modesto, 1986-92; pres. Calif. Aeromed. Rescue and Evacuation, Inc., Modesto, 1985—; lectr. Am. Hosp. Assn., Chgo., 1984—; bd. dirs. Synergistic Sys., Inc.; cons. in field, 1984—. Author: Emergency Medical Technician Outreach Training, 1977, (with others) The Hospital Emergency Department: Returning to Financial Viability, 1987, Restructuring Ambulatory Care, A Guide to Reorganization, 1990, The Hospital Emergency Department, 1992. Bd. dirs. Stanislaus Paramedic Assn., Modesto, 1978-82, Head Rest, Inc., Modesto, 1980; bd. dirs. regional occupational program Stanislau County Dept. Edn., 1980; del. People-to-People Citizen Amb. Program, People's Republic of China, 1988. Mem. Am. Acad. Med. Adminstrs., Nat. Acad. Scis. Inst. Medicine (com. pediatric emergency med. svcs. 1991-92), Phi Delta Kappa, Commonwealth Club. Presbyterian. Home: 1322 Edgebrook Dr Modesto CA 95354-1537 Office: 1 Kaiser Plz Ste 1700 Oakland CA 94612-3612

DONKIN, SCOTT WILLIAM, chiropractor; b. Rapid City, S.D., June 8, 1955; s. Wilmar and Jeanne Elaine (Sherwood) D.; m. Mary Pat Brugh, Oct. 7, 1977; children: Elizabeth, Peter. Student, Midland Luth. Coll., 1973-76; D Chiropractic, Tex. Chiropractic Coll., 1980. Diplomate Am. Chiropractic Bd. Occupational Health. Pvt. practice Donkin Chiropractic Clinic, Lincoln, Nebr., 1980—; lectr. to chiropractic colls.; cons. Sitting on the Job, Lincoln, 1987—. Author: Sitting on the Job, 1988, Stress Free At Your Computer, 1996; inventor Sidewalk Shuffleboard, 1988; contbr. articles to profl. jours., mags. Mem. Am. Chiropractic Assn. (pres. coun. on occupl. health), Nebr. Chiropractic Physicians Assn., Am. Chiropractic Bd. Occupl. Health (treas.). Office: Chiropractic Assocs PC 5540 South St Ste 200 Lincoln NE 68506-2117

DONLON, JOSEPHINE A., diagnostic and evalution counseling therapist, educator; b. N.Y.C., Apr. 3, 1921; d. Henry R. and Josephine V. (Klarer) Janssen; R.N., Englewood (N.J.) Hosp., 1941; B.A. in Psychology, Colo. Coll., Colorado Springs, 1945; M.Ed., Nat. Coll. Edn., Evanston, Ill., 1975; m. William James Donlon; children—William James, Gregory A., Michele L., DruAnn. Pediatric psychiat. nurse N.Y. State Psychiat. Inst., N.Y.C., 1941-42; supr. psychiat. nursing Colo. U. Psychiat. Inst., 1945-47; pub. health nurse Denver Sch., 1947-48; diagnostic educator Schaumburg (Ill.) Sch. Dist. 54, 1969-78; pvt. practice diagnostic evaluation and counseling, Brookeville, Md., 1979-87, Pineland, Fla., 1987—. Leader, Girl Scouts U.S.A., 1958-62; previously active PTA's in Colo. and Ill. Mem. Council Exceptional Children, Council for Children with Behavioral Disorders, Council for Ednl. Diagnostic Services. Research in genetic endocrine diseases of pancreas and thyroid and relation to learning and behavior. Certified in nursing, spl. edn., Ill., Colo.; specialist in social maladjusted, learning disabled, educable mentally handicapped. Home: PO Box 2212 Pineland FL 33945-2212

DONNELLY, BARBARA SCHETTLER, medical technologist; b. Sweetwater, Tenn., Dec. 2, 1933; d. Clarence G. and Irene Elizabeth (Brown) Schettler; A.A., Tenn. Wesleyan Coll., 1952; B.S., U. Tenn., 1954; cert. med. tech., Erlanger Hosp. Sch. Med. Tech., 1954; postgrad. So. Meth. U., 1980-81; children—Linda Ann, Richard Michael. Med. technologist Erlanger Hosp., Chattanooga, 1953-57, St. Luke's Episcopal Hosp., Tex. Med. Ctr., Houston, 1957-58, 1962; engring. R &D SCI Systems Inc., Huntsville, Ala., 1974-76; cons. hematology systems Abbott Labs., Dallas, 1976-77, hematology specialist, Dallas, Irving, Tex., 1977-81, tech. specialist microbiology systems, Irving, 1981-83, coord. tech. svc. clin. chemistry systems, 1983-84, coord. customer tng. clin. chemistry systems, 1984-87, supr. clin. chemistry tech. svcs., 1987-88, supr. clin. chemistry customer support ctr., 1988-93, supr. clin. chemistry and x-systems customer support ctr., 1993—. Mem. Am. Soc. Clin. Pathologists (cert. med. technologist), Am. Soc. Microbiology, Nat. Assn. Female Execs., U. Tenn. Alumni Assn., Chi Omega. Contbr. articles on cytology to profl. jours. Republican. Methodist. Home: 204 Greenbriar Ln Bedford TX 76021-2006 Office: 1921 Hurd Dr Irving TX 75038-4313

DONNELLY, EDWARD JAMES, JR., medical services company executive; b. Windsor, Ont., Can., May 16, 1946; s. Edward James and Hilda Rae (Cornwall) D.; m. JoDell Tamborello, Dec. 20, 1972 (div. 1982); children: Edward James III, Anna Mistelle. BS, U. Houston, 1973. Pres. Perfusion Assocs., Houston, 1970-85; pres., chief exec. officer Allied Cardiac Svcs., Houston, 1985-95; dir. ops. Tex. SETA/Baxter, Houston, 1995-96, Baxter/New Bus. Initiatives, 1996—. Contbr. articles to profl. publs. Mem. Am. Soc. Extracorporeal Technologists (pres. so. region 1978-80, 84-86), Houston Bd. Realtors, Houston Jaycees. Republican. Episcopalian. Home: 2331 Dorrington St Houston TX 77030-3211 Office: Baxter Perfusion Svcs 10620 Stebbins Cir #E Houston TX 77043

DONNELLY, EDWIN HAROLD, ophthalmologist, surgeon; b. Detroit, Aug. 9, 1947; s. Harold George and Dorothy Ruth (Flemming) D.; m. Andrea Lynn Donnelly, June 14, 1974; children: Erin Kelly, Christopher Patrick. BS, U. Mich., 1970, MD, 1974. Diplomate Am. Bd. Ophthalmology. Intern Baylor U., Houston, 1974-75; resident Duke U. Eye Ctr., Durham, N.C., 1975-78; fellow Emory U., Atlanta, 1978-79; assoc. Hagler and Jarrett Group, Atlanta, 1979-81; pvt. practice Atlanta, 1981—; chief of staff Met. Hosp., Atlanta, 1987-88, chief surgery, 1985-87, chmn. ophthalmology, 1983-85. Contbr. articles to profl. jours. Mem. Ga. Soc. Ophthalmology, Atlanta Ophthal. Soc. (pres. 1987), Am. Acad. Ophthalmology, AMA, Med. Assn. Ga., Med. Assn. Atlanta, Tau Beta Pi. Office: 3193 Howell Mill Rd NW Ste 115 Atlanta GA 30327-2100

DONNELLY, JOHN PATRICK, physician assistant, health services administrator; b. Akron, Ohio, Sept. 30, 1949; s. John Patrick and Rosemary Donnelly; children: Anne Marie, John Patrick. Assoc. in Medicine, Emory U., 1973, BS, 1975. Cert. physician asst. Physician asst. Bechtel Inc., San Francisco, 1974-79, WHO, Zurich, Amsterdam, 1979-83, Ministry of Health, Saudi Arabian Govt., 1983-86, Dept. VA, Johnson City, Tenn., 1986—. Bd. dirs. March of Dimes, Johnson City, 1995; co-chmn. Non-Physician Provider Orgn. of VA, Johnson City, 1995—. Fellow Am. Acad. Physician Assts. (com. chair 1995-96), VA Physician Assn. (pres. 1995-96), Soc. Army Physician Assts.; mem. Nurse Practitioner-Physician Asst. Assn. Tenn. (pres. 1994-95). Republican. Roman Catholic. Office: VA Med Ctr 11 E Mountain Home TN 37684

DONNELLY, LISA MARIE, pediatrics nurse, school nurse; b. Manhasset, N.Y., July 19, 1967; d. Chester and Florence (Kessler) Surowiec; m. Thomas Patrick Donnelly, Aug. 9, 1992; 1 child, Amanda Paige. BSN, Molloy Coll., 1993. RN, N.Y.; cert. CPR. Pediatrics nurse Dr. Susan Gunduz, Northport, N.Y., 1993—. Mem. Deer Pk. Fire Dept. Ladies Aux. Republican. Roman Catholic.

DONNER, WILLIAM TROUTMAN, psychiatrist; b. Sharon Pa., Jan. 8, 1921; s. Raymond H. and Edna (Troutman) D.; student U. Pa., 1939-42, MD, 1946; m. Alice Easby Wilkinson, Apr. 12, 1946; children: William W., Marda Elisa, Mary Alice, Margot Ramona. Intern, Allegheny Gen. Hosp., Pitts., 1945-46; resident Friends Hosp., Phila., 1948-50, Hosp. of U. Pa., 1950-51; practice medicine specializing in psychiatry, Abington, Pa., 1951—; psychiatrist Neuropsychiat. Assocs. of Old York Rd., Abington, 1962-64; dir. mental health clinic Abington Meml. Hosp., 1958-64, interim chmn. dept. psychiatry, 1983-85; instr. U. Pa., 1951-58, assoc. psychiatry, 1958-78; clin. asst. prof. Hahnemann Med. Coll., 1978—; acting chmn. Dept. Psychiatry, Abington (Pa.) Meml. Hosp., 1988-95, chmn. dept. Psychiatry Abington (Pa.) Meml. Hosp., 1994-95. Pres. bd. dirs. Family Svc. Montgomery County, 1966-67. Served with AUS, 1946-48. Mem. Am., Pa. Psychiat. Assns., AMA, Pa. State, Montgomery County Med. Socs., Am. Group Psychotherapy Assn. Contbr. articles to tech. jours. Home: 314 Wellington Ter Jenkintown PA 19046-3832

DONOFRIO, PETER DANIEL, neurology educator; b. Syracuse, N.Y., June 5, 1950; s. Carmin Peter and Donna Marie (Powers) D.; m. Kathleen Ann Fitzgerald, May 29, 1976; children: Molly, Emily, Julie. BS, U. Notre Dame, 1972; MD, Ohio State U., 1975. Diplomate Am. Bd. Internal Medicine, Am. Bd. Neurology, Am. Bd. Emergency Medicine. Resident internal medicine Good Samaritan Hosp., Cin., 1978; resident neurology U. Mich. Med. Ctr., Ann Arbor, 1981, instr., 1982-84; instr. V.A. Hosp., Ann Arbor, 1982-84, asst. prof., 1984-85; asst. prof. U. Mich. Med. Ctr., Ann Arbor, 1984-85, Bowman Gray Sch. of Medicine, Winston Salem, N.C., 1986-89; assoc. prof. Bowman Gray Sch. of Medicine, Winston Salem, 1989—; vice-chmn. dept. neurology, 1993—; cons. in neurology, Winston Salem, N.C., 1984—. Contr. articles to profl. jours. Dept. rep. United Way, Winston-Salem, N.C., 1989—. Recipient Notre Dame U. scholarship, 1968. Fellow Am. Acad. Neurology; mem. Am. Assn. Electrodiagnostic Medicine. Roman Catholic. Home: 3509 Donegal Dr Clemmons NC 27012-8678 Office: Bowman Gray Sch of Medicine Medical Center Blvd Winston Salem NC 27157

DONOGHUE, PAUL JOSEPH, psychologist; b. Easington, Eng., Nov. 23, 1937; came to U.S., 1947, naturalized, 1953; s. Michael Patrick and Mary Elizabeth (Ansboury) D.; B.A. magna cum laude, St. Mary's U., 1959; M.Ed., St. Louis U., 1965, Ph.D., 1969. Tchr., Don Bosco High Sch., Milw., 1959-64; staff psychologist Community Psychol. Cons., St. Louis, 1969-71; dir. Touchstone Communications, Stamford, Conn., 1970—, Community Psychol. Cons., 1971—. Co-author: Sick and Tired of Feeling Sick and Tired: Living With Invisible Chronic Illness, 1992. Mem. Am. Psychol. Assn. Democrat. Roman Catholic. Home and Office: 10 Ocean Dr W Stamford CT 06902-8026

DONOHUE, JOHN PATRICK, urologist; b. Pelham, N.Y., Dec. 25, 1930; s. Gerald and Agnes Donohue; m. Rosemary T. O'Brian, 1960; children: Eileen, Agnes, Margaret Mary, John. AB, Coll. Holy Cross, 1954; MD, Cornell U., 1958. Diplomate Am. Bd. Urology. Intern Cornell U.-N.Y. Hosp., 1958-59, asst. resident in surgery, 1959-60; asst. resident in urology Mass. Gen. Hosp., Boston, 1965; asst. prof. urology Ind. U., 1965-67, assoc. prof., 1967-70, prof., 1970—, chmn. dept. urology, 1971—. With USN, 1960-61. Mem. AAUP, ACS, Am. Soc. Nephrology, Am. Soc. Artificial Internal Organs, Assn. Acad. Surgery, Am. Urol. Assn., Soc. Univ. Urologist, Am. Assn. Genito-Urinary Surgeons, Clin. Soc. Genito-Urinary Surgeons, Am. Fertility Soc., Transplantation Soc., Pan-Pacific Surg. Assn., Woodstock Country Club, Indpls. Athletic Club. Office: Ind U Med Ctr Ste 1725 550 N University Blvd Indianapolis IN 46202

DONOHUE, JOYCE MORRISSEY, biochemist, toxicologist, nutritionist, educator; b. Holyoke, Mass., Jan. 27, 1940; d. Richard Charles and Anna Elizabeth (Joyce) Morrissey; m. John Thomas Donohue, Jan. 27, 1973; children: Maura Joyce, John Thomas, Sean Richard, Eric Patrick. BS, Framingham (Mass.) State Coll., 1961; MS, U. Mass., 1964; PhD, U. N.H., 1972. Cert. secondary sch. tchr.; registered dietitian. Tchr. West Springfield (Mass.) H.S., 1962-66; instr. Framingham State Coll., 1966-68, asst. prof. biochemistry and nutrition, 1971-72, assoc. prof., 1972-73; adj. prof. No. Va. C.C., Annandale, 1974—, Va. Poly. Inst. and State U., Falls Church, 1979—; health scientist VJ Cicconi & Assocs., Woodbridge, Va., 1981-89; toxicology svc. mgr. Law Environ. Washington Svc. Ctr., Woodbridge, Va., 1989-90; program mgr., prin. scientist ICAIR/Life Sys. Inc., Arlington, Va., 1990-94; mgr. toxicology NSF Internat., Washington, 1994—; mem. adv. com. Prince William County Sch. Food Svc., 1983-85. Vice chmn. citizens adv. com. for debris landfill and solid waste mgmt., Prince William County, 1987—; mem. Prince William County Wetlands Bd., 1989—. Recipient Alumni Achievement award Framingham State Coll., 1986. Mem. AAAS, Am. Dietetic Assn., No. Va. Dietetic Assn., Sigma Xi. Home: 11979 William And Mary Cir Woodbridge VA 22192-1314 Office: NSF Internat 1301 K St NW # 225 Washington DC 20005

DONOHUGH, DONALD LEE, physician; b. Los Angeles, Apr. 12, 1924; s. William Noble and Florence Virginia (Shelton) D.; m. Virginia Eskew McGregor, Sept. 12, 1950 (div. 1971); children: Ruth, Laurel, Marilee, Carol, Greg; m. Beatrice Ivany Redick, Dec. 3, 1976; stepchildren: Leslie Ann, Andrea Jean. BS, U.S. Naval Acad., 1946; MD, U. Calif., San Francisco, 1956; MPH and Tropical Medicine, Tulane U., 1961. Diplomate AM. Bd. Internal Medicine. Intern U. Hosp., San Diego, 1956-57; resident Monterey County Hosp., 1957-58; dir. of med. svcs. U.S. Depart. Interior, Am. Samoa, 1958-60; instr. Tulane U. Med. Sch., New Orleans, 1960-63; resident Tulane Svcs. V.A. and Charity Hosp., New Orleans, 1961-63; cons. Internat. Ctr. for Rsch and Tng., Costa Rica, 1961-63; assoc. prof. medicine & preventive medicine La. State U. Sch. Medicine, 1962-63; assoc. prof., 1963-65; vis. prof. U. Costa Rica, 1963-65; faculty advisor, head of Agy. Internat. Devel. program U. Costa Rica Med. Sch., 1965-67; dir. med. svcs. Med. Ctr. U. Calif. (formerly Orange County Hosp.), Irvine, 1967-69; assoc. clin. prof. U. Calif., Irvine, 1967-79, clin. prof., 1980-85; pvt. practice Tustin, Calif., 1970-80; with Joint Commn. on Accreditation of Hosps., 1981; cons. Kauai, Hawaii, 1981—. Author: The Middle Years, 1981, Practice Management, 1986, Kauai, 1988, 3d edit., 1990; co-translator; Rashomon (Ryonosuke Akutagawa), 1950; also numerous articles. Lt. USN, 1946-52, capt. USNR, 1966-84. Fellow Am. Coll. Physicians (life); mem. Delta Omega. Republican. Episcopalian. Home: 4890 Lawai Beach Rd Koloa HI 96756-9675

DONOVAN, ARTHUR JOSEPH, surgeon, educator; b. Concord, N.H., Jan. 10, 1925; s. Joseph Casey and Mary Elizabeth (Callahan) D.; m. Jane Wooddell, Jan. 8, 1955; children: John Arthur, Rachel Jane. Three-yr. cert., Harvard U., 1944; M.D., Tufts U., 1948. Diplomate: Am. Bd. Surgery. Intern Grace-New Haven Community Hosp., 1948-49, resident, 1949-52, 54-55; instr. surgery Tufts U., 1955-57, assoc. prof., 1959-61; asst. clin. prof. U. So. Calif., 1961-64, asst. prof., 1964-67, assoc. prof., 1967-69, prof., 1969-73,

79-90, chmn. dept. surgery, 1979-90, prof. emeritus, 1990—; prof., chmn. dept. surgery U. South Ala., 1973-79, acting dean, 1974-76, v.p. health affairs, 1976-77. Served to lt. USNR, 1952-54, Korea. Mem. L.A. Athletic Club, Alpha Omega Alpha.

DONOVAN, DENIS MILLER, psychiatrist, author, lecturer; b. Chgo., June 5, 1946. BA in Edn., Psychology, Social Sci. and French, Antioch Coll., 1969, MEd in Psychology and Social Sci., 1969; MD, McMaster U., Hamilton, Ont., Can., 1975. Diplomate Am. Bd. Med. Psychotherapists; lic. psychiatrist Fla., Va., N.C.; cert. tchr. Gt. Britain, Calif. Tchr. French Corvallis (Oreg.) Sch. Dist., 1969-70; rsch. psychologist dept. clin. psychology VA O.P. Clinic, L.A., 1970; psychotherapist children's svcs. Camarillo (Calif.) State Hosp., 1970-71; resident in psychiatry Inst. for Social Psychiatry, London, 1971-72, U. N.C., Chapel Hill, 1977-79; psychiat. cons., trainer office edn. and staff devel. S.C. State Dept. Social Svcs., 1975-81; med. dir. child and family svcs. Area Mental Health Program of Vance, Granville, Franklin and Warren Counties, 1979-83; psychiat. cons. region IV adoption resource ctr. U. N.C., Chapel Hill, 1979-80; pvt. practice child, adolescent and gen. psychiatry Chapel Hill, 1979-83; dir. Rsch. Triangle Ctr. for Psychotherapy, Research Triangle Park, N.C., 1981-83; dir. adult impatient svc. Community Mental Health Ctr. and Psychiat. Inst., Norfolk, Va., 1983; med. dir. The Children's Ctr. for Devel. Psychiatry, St. Petersburg, Fla., 1983—; mem. med. staff Dept. Neuropsychiatry All Children's Hosp., St. Petersburg; cons. Nat. Coun. for Adoption, Guardian ad Litem Program Juvenile Ct. 6th Jud. Dist., Fla., Child Protection Team All Children's Hosp., St. Petersburg, Pinellas County Sch. System, Fla. Diagnostic and Learning Recources System, Early Childhood Coun. Pinellas County, Pinellas County Assn. for Learning Disabilities; trainer Fla. Inst. Law Enforcement, Fla. Dept. Law Enforcement Crime Against Children Div.; adj. prof. Union Grad. Sch., 1973; adj. faculty St. Petersburg Jr. Coll., 1987; founder co-founder Kairos Ventures, Ltd.; chair New Traumatology Conf. Co-author: Healing the Hurt Child; mem. editorial bd. Behavior Today, Psychotherapy Today, Children and Teens Today, Jour. of Traumatic Stress, Brunner/Hazel Psychosocial Stress Series; co-editor Jour. Childhood Trauma; mem. adv. editorial bd. to sci. jours. W.S. Hall Psychiatric Inst. fellow, 1975-77. Fellow Am. Assn. Social Psychiatry, Am. Psychol. Soc., Am. Assn. Applied Preventive Psychology, Brit. Assn. Social Psychiatry; mem. AAAS, Am. Acad. Child and Adolescent Psychiatry (book reviewer), Met. Washington Soc. Adolescent Psychiatry, Am. Soc. Adolescent Psychiatry, Am. Acad. Psychiatry and the Law (book reviewer), Fla. Acad. Forensic Psychiatry, N.Y. Acad. Scis., Childhood Trauma Soc. (founder), Soc. for Rsch. in Child Devel., Soc. for Social Studies of Sci., Soc. for Rsch. on Adolescence, Cognitive Sci. Soc., Internat. Soc. for Traumatic Stress Studies. Office: Children's Ctr Devel Psychiatry 6675 13th Ave N Ste 2-A Saint Petersburg FL 33710-5483

DONOVAN, JOAN E., ophthalmologist; b. Canton, Ohio, Jan. 17, 1958; d. Earl Charles and Nancy Allyn (Newton) Sheehan; m. Mark L. Donovan, Dec. 27, 1980; children: Brianna, Alonna, Shauna, Catriana. BS in Biology, Wheaton Coll., 1980; MD, Med. Coll. Ohio, 1984. Part-time ophthalmologist John Wilson Eye Clinic, Johnson City, Tenn., 1988—. Mem. Area Homeschooler Assn., Johnson City, 1994—. Evangelical. Office: Wilson Eye Clinic 118 E Watauga Ave Johnson City TN 37601

DONOVAN, JOHN STEPHEN, otolaryngologist; b. Kansas City, Mo., May 6, 1960; s. Robert Charles and Mary Therese D.; m. Linda, Sept. 2, 1989; children: Lauren, Kathryn. BS in Chemistry and Biology, Stanford U., 1982; MD, Washington U., 1987. Diplomate Am. Bd. Otolaryngology. Intern, resident in otolaryngology U. Okla., Norman, 1987-92; pvt. practice Salem, Oreg., 1992—. Avon scholar, 1978-82, Hallmark scholar, 1981. Mem. Am. Acad. Otolaryngology. Office: 939 Oak St SE Salem OR 97301

DONOVAN, KATHLEEN OWEN, physician; b. Sydney, New South Wales, Australia, Jan. 20, 1931; d. Charles Owen and Dorothy Franklin (Fletcher) D. BSc in Agriculture with honors, Sydney U., 1953, MB, BS with honors, 1962, DTM & H, 1966; PhD, Edinburgh (Scotland) U., 1956; fellow Australian Faculty, of Pub. Health Medicine, 1991. Rsch. fellow Edinburgh U., 1953-56; jr. resident med. officer St. George Hosp., Kogarah, Australia, 1963, sr. resident med. officer, 1964; resident med. officer Crown Street Women's Hosp., 1965, Fairfield Hosp., Sydney, 1965-66; missionary Asia Pacific Christian Mission, med. supt. Balimo Health Ctr., Papua New Guinea, 1966-83; dir. Christian Synergy Ctr., Newcastle, NSW, 1983—; mission rsch. officer, med. coord. Asia Pacific Christian Mission, 1984-85; med. coord. Missions Interlink Australian Evang. Alliance Missions Commn, 1990—; part-time rsch. fellow Sch. Agr. Sydney U., 1957; vis. lectr. El Kanah Christian Comty., Marysville, Victoria, Australia, 1987-91, Pastoral Care Sydney Missionary Bible Coll., 1992—; med. registrar Asia Pacific Christian Mission, 1983-96, Assemblies of God World Missions, 1990-96, Worldwide Evangelization Crusade, 1991—; mem. nat. coun. Sudan Interior Mission Internat. Author: Growing Through Stress, 1991. Mem. NSW coun. Asia Pacific Christian Mission. Recipient Independence medal Papua New Guinea, 1976; Thomas Lawrance Pawlett Travelling scholar U. Edinburgh, 1953-54; Walter and Eliza Hall Travelling fellow U. Edinburgh, 1954-55. Mem. Australasian Coll. Tropical Medicine. Presbyterian. Home and Office: Christian Synergy Ctr, 204 Wommara Ave, Belmont NSW 2280, Australia

DONOVAN-BATSON, COLEEN MOIRA, nurse midwife, researcher, educator; b. Hollywood, Calif., Dec. 12, 1959; d. Patrick Joseph Donovan and Lorraine Dorothy (Robatin) Stratton; m. Michael Wayne Batson, March 14, 1981; children: Sean, Andrew, Caitlin. BSN, Calif. State U., Sacramento, 1991; ob-gyn nurse practitioner, Edn. Programs Assocs., Campbell, Calif., 1992; cert. nurse midwife, 1993. RN, nurse practitioner, nurse midwife, Calif.; RN cert., Nat. Cert. Corp. Staff nurse I Sutter Meml. Hosp., Sacramento, 1987-88; staff nurse II Antelope Valley Hosp., Lancaster, Calif., 1988-89; staff nurse III Kern Med. Ctr., Bakersfield, Calif., 1989-91; ob-gyn nurse practitioner Kern Med. Ctr., Bakersfield, 1991-93, cert. nurse midwife, 1993; cert. nurse midwife L.A. County and Univ. So. Calif. Womens and Childrens Hosp., L.A., 1994-95, Frazier Mt. Cmty. Health Ctr., Frazier Park, 1994-95, North Bay Healthcare Systems, Fairfield, Calif., 1995—; clin. faculty nurse midwifery program U. So. Calif., L.A., 1995. Mem. spkrs. bureau March of Dimes, Burbank, Calif., 1995. Recipient nurse midwifery traineeship State of Calif. Maternal Child Health, 1992. Mem. Am. Coll. Nurse Midwives (cert. nurse midwife), Midwives Alliance of N.Am., Calif. Assn. Midwives, Calif. Nurse Midwife Assn. (legis. com.). Home: 1752 Nantucket Ct Fairfield CA 94533

DONOVAN-KACHAVOS, KATHRYN AGNES, psychiatrist; b. Milw., Apr. 11, 1937; d. Laurence Vincent and Anne Marie (Kremsreiter) Donovan; m. Louis John Kachavos, Feb. 8, 1970; 1 child, David Joseph Kachavos. BS, Mt. St. Vincent, N.Y.C., 1961; MD cum laude, St. Louis U., 1965. Diplomate Am. Bd. Psychiatry and Neurology. Intern, then resident First Columbia Medical Sch., N.Y.C., 1965-67; resident Newton Wellesley Hosp., Newton, Mass., 1967-68; resident in psychiatry Mass. Mental Health Ctr., Boston, 1969-72; pvt. practice New Boston, Nashua and Milford, N.H., 1972—; psychiatrist Matthew Thornton Health Plan, Nashua, N.H., 1972-87, Lake Shore Hosp., Manchester, N.H., 1987-88; cons. N.H. Divsn. Children and Youth, 1972—, Conval Spl. Edn. Team, Peterboro, N.H., 1982-91; pres. Beacon Mental Health Assocs., Milford, N.H., 1987—. Bd. dirs. Odyssey House of N.H., Hampton, 1984-91; mem. advocacy com. Child and Family Svcs. of N.H., Manchester, 1983—, N.H. Alliance for Children and Youth Mental Health Task Force, 1988-90, N.H. Children's Lobby, 1988—; bd. dirs. Philbrook Found., Portsmouth, N.H. Fellow gastroenterology Tufts New England Medical Ctr. Hosp., Boston, 1968-69. Fellow Am. Psychiat. Assn.; mem. N.H. Psychiat. Soc. (pres. 1988-90, chmn. com. on children/youth 1984-90), Alpha Omega Alpha. Office: Beacon Mental Health Assocs 15 Union St Milford NH 03055-4875

DONSON, VICTORIA ANN, health facility administrator; b. Harrisburg, Pa., Mar. 29, 1954; d. Eugen L. and Frances A. (Cooveu) Funk; m. Charles R. Donson, Aug. 14, 1976; children: Amanda E., Eric R. RN, York (Pa.) Hosp. Sch. Nursing. RN, Pa.; lic. nursing home adminstr. Nurse Carlisle (Pa.) Hosp., 1976-78; home health nurse Messiah Village, Menchanicsburg, Pa., 1982-84; companion coord. Presbyn. Homes, Inc., Carlise, Pa., 1984-85; staff devel. coord. Meadows Nursing Ctr., Dallas, Pa., 1987-89; dir. nursing Green Ridge Village, Newville, Pa., 1989-94, health care adminstr., 1994—; cons. in field. Mem. adv. coun. ARC, Carlisle, Pa., 1990—. Mem. Pa. Nurses Assn. (steering com. 1990—), Pa. Assn. Non-Profit Homes for Aging (steering com. 1990—). Democrat. Mem. Assemby of God Ch. Office: Green Ridge Village 210 Big Spring Rd Newville PA 17241

DOOB, LEONARD WILLIAM, psychology educator, academic administrator; b. N.Y.C., Mar. 3, 1909; s. William and Florence (Lewis) D.; m. Eveline Bates, Mar. 21, 1936; children: Christopher Bates, Anthony Newcomb, Nicholas Ellsworth. AB, Dartmouth Coll., 1929; AM, Duke U., 1930; postgrad., U. Frankfurt, Germany, 1930-32; PhD, Harvard U., 1934. Asst. instr. psychology Duke U., Durham, N.C., 1929-30; instr. sociology Dartmouth Coll., 1932-33; mem. faculty Yale U., New Haven, 1934-78, prof. psychology, 1950-77, also div. social scis., chmn. African studies, Sterling prof. emeritus psychology, rsch. scholar, assoc. dir. South African Rsch. program, 1977-94; various positions, to policy coord. overseas br. Office of War Info., 1941-45. Editor Jour. of Social Psychology, 1965—; author 15 books, co-author 3 books on comm., pub. opinion, acculturation, ethics, conflict resolution and sustainability; contbr. articles to profl. jours. Home: 6 Clark Rd Woodbridge CT 06525-1609 Office: PO Box 208205 New Haven CT 06520-8205

DOOLEY, PATRICIA KELLY, physician assistant; b. Balt., Sept. 19, 1944; m. John W. Dooley, Dec. 13, 1980. AA in Physician Asst., Essex C.C., Balt., 1976; student, Coll. Notre Dame, Balt. NCCPA and Md. state lic. Receptionist x-ray dept. North Arundel Hosp., Glen Burnie, Md., 1965-76; physician asst. N.W. Cmty. Med., Balt., 1976-78, Constant Care Med., Balt., 1978-79, Omni-Med. Corp., Balt., 1979-81, Koppers Corp., Balt., 1982-91, Childrens Hosp., Balt., 1991-93, Md. Gen. Hosp., Balt., 1993—; physician asst. Baltimore County Health Dept., 1991—. Fellow Am. Acad. Physician Asst., Md. Physician Asst. Orgn.

DOOLEY, SHARON L., obstetrician-gynecologist; b. 1947. MD, U. Va. Mem. faculty Prentice Womens Hosp. Northwestern U. Med. Sch., Chgo. Office: Northwestern U Med Sch Prentice Womens Hosp 333 E Superior St Rm 410 Chicago IL 60611*

DOOLITTLE, THOMAS MORGAN, clinical psychologist; b. N.Y.C., July 7, 1957; s. George Swift and Nancy Irene (Shanahan) D.; m. Lynne Fraser, June 26, 1982. BA in Psychology, Hamilton Coll., 1979; MA in Theology, Fuller Theol. Sem., 1984, PhD in Psychology, 1987. Lic. clin. psychologist, Conn. Behavior technician Jay Nolan Ctr. for Autism, Newhall, Calif., 1979-80; psychiatric aide Woodview-Calabasas (Calif.) Hosp., 1980; psychol. asst. Robert O. Pasnau, MD and Warren Walker, PhD, L.A., 1983-87; behavioral counselor, Risk Factor Obesity Program UCLA, 1983-87; project dir. Be Free Substance Abuse Program, L.A., 1986-87; case mgr. Klingberg Family Ctrs., New Britain, Conn., 1987-88; dir. Linwood at Klingberg Family Ctrs., New Britain, Conn., 1988-90; v.p. Path, PC, West Hartford, Conn., 1990; clin. dir. Parkview Treatment Ctr., New Britain, 1990-94; pvt. practice New Britain, 1987-95; v.p. clin. ops. The Lexington Group, New Britain, 1991-95; mgr. employee assistance program Caterpillar Inc., Peoria, Ill., 1995—; speaker on numerous issues in psychology, 1987—. Mem. APA, Conn. Psychol. Assn. Office: Caterpillar Inc 100 NE Adams St Peoria IL 61629-1410

DOONE, MICHELE MARIE, chiropractor; b. Oak Park, Ill., Oct. 3, 1942; d. Robert Emmett and Tana Josephine (Alioto) D. Cert., Valley Coll. of Med. and Dental Careers, 1962; student, L.A. Valley Coll., 1960-63, Dallas County Community Coll., 1983-84; D in Chiropractic summa cum laude, Parker Coll. of Chiropractic, 1986. Lic. chiropractic, Calif., Tex.; cert Nat. Bd. Chiropractic Examiners, impairment rater diplomate Am. Acad. Pain Mgmt.; bd. eligible chiropractic orthopedist. Med. asst. William Orlando M.D., Edwin Crost, M.D., 1962-65; nursing supr., chief radiologic technologist Vanowen Med. Group, North Hollywood, Calif., 1965-76; radiologic technologist/purchasing agt. Lanier-Brown Clinic, Dallas, 1976-83; faculty mem./ chief radiologic technologist Parker Coll. of Chiropractic, Irving, Tex., 1983-85; exam and X-Ray doctor Margolies Chiropractic Ctr., Richardson, Tex., 1986; clinic staff doctor, assoc. prof. Parker Coll. of Chiropractic, Irving, Tex., 1986-87; doctor/ mgr. contractor Accident Ctrs. of Am., Garland, Tex., 1987; clinic dir. Back Pain Chiropractic, Carrollton, Tex., 1988-91; assoc. in group practice Mullican Chiropractic Ctr., Addison, Tex., 1991—; adviser health-related matters Inner Devel. Inst., Dallas, 1977—; seminar com. Back Pain Chiropractic, Inc., Metairie, La., 1989-91, clinic dir., 1988-91. Mem. Tex. Chiropractic Assn. (radiology com. chmn. 1990-94, practice protocols and parameters com. 1992-94), Metroplex Neurospinal Diagnostic Med. and Surg. Group (med. adv. com. 1989-95), Parker Chiropractic Rsch. Found., Parker Coll. Alumni Assn. (bd. dirs. 1988-90, 93-94, 95—, Dr. of Yr. 1990), Pi Tau Delta. Home: 4837 Cedar Springs Rd Apt 216 Dallas TX 75219-1280 Office: Mullican Chiropractic Ctr 4021 Belt Line Rd Ste 201 Dallas TX 75244-2330

DOOREY, ANDREW, cardiologist; b. Darby, Pa., Feb. 18, 1952; s. Michael J. and Katherine (Thomas) D.; m. Nancy Ann Small, Feb. 14, 1981; children: Kelsey, Jennifer, Alicia. AB, Princeton U., 1974; MD, Harvard U., Boston, 1978. Diplomate Am. Bd. Internal Medicine, Am. Bd. Cardiovascular Diseases. Intern/resident U. Mich. Hosp., Ann Arbor, 1978-80; fellow in cardiology Brigham & Women's Hosp. and Harvard Med. Sch., Boston, 198-83, staff cardiologist, 1984-85; fellow in invasive cardiology and angioplasty U. Heidelberg, Ger., 1983-84; cardiologist The Lankenau Hosp., Phila., 1985-87; dir. cardiac angioplasty Med. Ctr. of Del., Wilmington, 1987—; instr. medicine Harvard Med. Sch., Boston, 1980-85; asst. clin. prof. medicine Jefferson Med. Coll., Phila., 1985-91, assoc. clin. prof. medicine, 1991—. Contbr. articles to profl. jours. Cons. cardiovascular adv. com. FAA, Oklahoma City, 1986—. Rose Seegal prize, Harvard Med. Sch., 1978; Alexander Vol Humbolt fellow, 1983. Fellow ACP, Am. Coll. Cardiology (bd. govs. 1995—), Am. Coll. Chest Physicians, Soc. for Cardiac Angiography and Interventions; mem. Am. Heart Assn. (fellow coun. on clin. cardiology, chmn. rsch. com. 1995—), Aerospace Med. Assn. Office: Cardiology Cons PA 4745 Ogletown Stanton Rd Ste 2 Newark DE 19713-2070

DOOTSON, LESLIE GAIL, school nurse; b. San Francisco, Aug. 13, 1959; d. Alfred Frank and Gladys Irene (Cardwell) Gordon; m. William Craig Dootson, Aug. 29, 1981; children: Crystal Lynn, Kimberly Anne. BSN, Calif. State U., Long Beach, 1992. Birth attendant Nurse Midwifery Care of Orange County, Anaheim, Calif., 1991; staff nurse neuro ICU Hoag Hosp., Newport Beach, Calif., 1992-94; sch. nurse Newport Mesa Sch. Dist., 1994—. Camp nurse Camp Scherman Girl Scouts of Orange County. Recipient Spirit of Nursing award, 1991. Mem. Calif. Student Nurses Assn. (regional rep. 1990-91), Sigma Theta Tau (Iota Eta chpt. 1991), Golden Key Nat. Honor Soc. Democrat. Home: 318 Esther St Costa Mesa CA 92627-2340

DORAN, DENNIS JAMES, health facility administrator; b. Crookston, Minn., July 2, 1947; s. Elmer James and Grace M. (LaCombe) D.; m. Kathleen Voshart, July 3, 1971; children: Christopher, Benjamin, Michael. BS, St. Mary's Coll., 1969; MS, Moorhead State U., 1982. With credit and collections dept. St. Ansgar, Moorhead, Minn., 1969-71, dir. bus. office, 1971-73, CFO, 1973-78, v.p., 1978-83, pres., CEO St. Francis Med. Ctr., Breckenridge, Minn., 1983-84, St. Ansgar/St. Francis, 1984-85, St. John/St. Ansgar, Fargo, Moorhead, N.D., 1985-86; sr. v.p. St. Joseph's Hosp., Tucson, Ariz., 1986-88; pres., CEO United Samaritans Med. Ctr., Danville, Ill., 1988—; bd. dirs. Palmer Bank, Danville. Chair Econ Devel. Corp., Danville, 1995; vice chair United Way, Danville, 1995. Mem. Am. Coll. Health Care Execs., Acad. for Cath. Health Care Leaders, Ill. Hosp. Assn., Danville C. of C. (past chair), Danville Country Club (v.p. 1995), Rotary. Roman Catholic. Home: 1110 Lake Ridge Rd Danville IL 61832 Office: United Samaritans Med Ctr 812 N Logan Ave Danville IL 61832

DORAZIO, RICHARD ARNOLD, surgeon; b. Washington County, Pa., Oct. 29, 1938; s. Michael Sr. and Helen Hazel (Gregor) D.; m. Sharon Dorazio. AB, Columbia U., 1960; MD, U. Pitts., 1964. Rotating intern and resident in gen. surgery Tripler Army Med. Ctr., Honolulu; chief of surgery 67th Evacuation Hosp., Vietnam, 1969-70; asst. chief gen. surgery Fitzsimons Army Med. Ctr., Denver, 1970-72; staff surgeon, asst. chief, gen. surg. resident, program dir Kaiser Found. Hosp., L.A., 1972-80, chief of surgery, 1980—; clin. prof. surgery U. So. Calif., L.A., 1989—. Contbr. articles to profl. jours. Lt. col. U.S. Army, 1964-72, 91. Fellow ACS; mem. Soc. for Clin. Vascular Surgery, Soc. for Gastrointestinal and Endoscopic Surgeons, So. Calif. Vascular Surg. Soc., L.A. Surg. Soc. (pres. 1994). Office: Kaiser-Permanente 4747 Sunset Blvd Los Angeles CA 90059

DOREY, C(HERYL) KATHLEEN, biomedical researcher, educator; b. Wellsville, N.Y., Sept. 7, 1944; d. Clair E. and Inez Marie (Crandall) Roberts; m. Frederick J. Dorey, Sept. 2, 1967 (div. 1981); m. Roman A. Rustia III, Nov. 24, 1984. BA cum laude, SUNY, Buffalo, 1966; MA, U. Mass., 1969; PhD, Georgetown U., 1975. Fellow U. So. Calif., L.A., 1975-78; asst. prof. anatomy So. Ill. U. Sch. Dental Medicine, Edwardsville, 1978-80; asst. prof. anatomy and cell biology U. So. Calif., L.A., 1980-85; asst. prof. ophthalmology Doheny Eye Found., L.A., 1980-85; asst. scientist Schepens Eye Rsch. Inst., Boston, 1985-91; assoc. scientist Eye Rsch. Inst., Boston, 1991—; inst. Harvard Med. Sch., Boston, 1985-92, asst. prof. ophthalmology, 1992—; rsch. on age-related macular degeneration and neovascularization. Contbr. articles to profl. jours. Rsch. grantee Nat. Eye Inst., 1983-87, 90—, Am. Diabetes Assn., 1980, 92, Am. Cancer Soc., 1978. Mem. Am. Soc. Cell Biology, Assn. Rsch. in Vision and Ophthalmology. Episcopalian. Office: Schepens Eye Rsch Inst 20 Staniford St Boston MA 02114-2508

DORFMAN, DAVID MICHAEL, physician; b. N.Y.C., Mar. 6, 1959; w. Samuel and Florence (Matfus) D.; m. Eve LaPlante, Sept. 8, 1990; children: Rose, Clara, Charlotte. AB, Princeton U., 1980; MD, U. Iowa., 1986, PhD in Genetics, 1986. Diplomate Am. Bd. Pathology. Assoc. pathologist Brigham and Women's Hosp., Boston, 1993—, assoc. med. dir., hematol. lab., 1993—; asst. prof. of pathology Harvard Med. Sch., Boston, 1993—. Contbr. articles to profl. jours., chpts. to med. books. Fellow Coll. of Am. Pathologists; mem. U.S. and Canadian Acad. of Pathology, Am. Soc. for Investigative Pathology, Soc. for Hematopathology. Office: Dept of Pathology 75 Francis St Boston MA 02115

DORFMAN, HOWARD DAVID, pathologist; b. N.Y., July 20, 1928; s. Louis and Helen (Weingarten) D.; m. Esther Novick, June 21, 1952; children: Richard H., Peter W., Leslie Jane. BA, NYU, 1947; MD, SUNY, Bklyn., 1951. Resident in pathology Mt. Sinai Hosp., N.Y., 1952-54, Columbia Presby. Medical Ctr., N.Y., 1954-58; dir. pathology Sharon (Conn.) Hosp., 1958-60; assoc. pathologist Sinai Hosp. Balt., Baltimore, Md., 1960-64; dir. pathology Hosp. Joint Diseases, N.Y., 1964-74; pathologist-in-chief Sinai Hosp. Balt., 1974-85; prof. orthopedic pathology Johns Hopkins Sch. of Medicine, Balt., 1985; prof. pathology, radiology and orthopaedic surgery Albert Einstein Coll. Medicine, Bronx, N.Y., 1985—; Walter Putschar lectr. Mass. Gen. Hosp. Harvard Med. Sch., 1983. Author: Bone Tumors, 1995; co-author: Tumors of Bone and Cartilage, 1971. Recipient Henry Jaffe award Hosp. Joint Diseases, 1984. Mem. N.Y. Pathological Soc. (pres. 1989-91), Internat. Skeletal Soc. (pres. 1986-88). Home: 530 E 72nd St Apt 5G New York NY 10021-4844

DORFMAN, LESLIE J., medical educator, physician; b. Montreal, Que., Can., Sept. 11, 1943; came to U.S., 1973; BSc, McGill U., Montreal, 1964; MD, Albert Einstein Coll. Medicine, 1968. Diplomate Am. Bd. Psychiatry and Neurology, Am. Bd. Electrodiagnostic Medicine. Resident in medicine Greenwich (Conn.) Hosp., 1968-70; resident in neurology Stanford (Calif.) Med. Ctr., 1970-73, asst. prof., 1974-80, assoc. prof., 1980-90, prof., 1990—, acting chmn. neurology, 1989—; fellow in neurophysiology Nat. Hosp., London, 1973, Mayo Clinic, Rochester, Minn., 1973-74. Mem. AAAS, Am. Assn. Electrodiagnostic Medicine (sec.-treas. 1993-96), Am. Acad. Neurology, Am. Neurol. Assn., Am. EEG Soc. Office: Stanford U Med Ctr Neurology H3160 Stanford CA 94305

DORFMAN, LORRAINE MARIE, clinical psychologist, consultant; b. Bethlehem, Pa., Nov. 9, 1952; d. Richard J. Dorfman and Phyllis L. (Wimmer) Schmidt. BA cum laude, Hunter Coll., 1980; MS, U. Wis., Milw., 1983, PhD, 1986. Lic. psychologist, Pa., N.J. Counselor Stanley M. Isaacs Neighborhood Ctr., Inc., N.Y.C., 1979, YWCA, N.Y.C., 1979-80, U. Wis. Milw. Psychology Clinic, Milw., 1983-84; asst. psychologist De Paul Rehab. Hosp., Milw., 1984; therapist Family Ctr., Columbia Hosp., Milw., 1985, The Counseling Ctr. Milw., Wis., 1985-86; psychologist Bristol-Bensalem Human Svcs. Ctr., 1986-87, Phila. (Pa.) State Hosp., 1986-87, Lehigh U. Counseling Svc., Bethlehem, 1987-88; pvt. practice psychology Phila., Bucks County, Pa., Mercer Co., N.J., 1988—; instr. U. Wis., Milw., 1980-86; cons. Human Svcs. Ctr., Wyncote, Pa., 1988—, MBCS Achievement and Guidance Ctrs. Am., Inc., Lawrenceville, N.J., 1988-92, assoc. dir., 1992-93, clin. dir., 1993-94; cons. Hoffmann-LaRoche, Inc., Nutley, N.J., 1990—, CORA Svcs., Inc., Phila., 1991, Plymouth Healthcare Assocs., Plymouth Meeting, Pa., 1990, Operation Par, Inc., St. Petersburg, Fla., 1990—, Bustleton Health Sys., Inc., Huntingdon Valley, Pa., 1991-92, Helpfinders, Fort Washington, Pa., 1989—; pub. edn. workshops and seminars. Contbr. articles to profl. jours. Vol. con. Human Svc. Ctr., Phila., 1988—. Mem. APA, Nat. Register Health Svc. Providers in Psychology, Phila. Soc. Clin. Psychologists (pub. rels. com. 1990-91). Office: One Oxford Valley Ste 815 Langhorne PA 19047

DORFMAN, MARK STEVEN, ophthalmologist; b. Bklyn., Sept. 11, 1965; m. Marcy Fern, Jan. 15, 1989; children: Cory Michael, Avery Ryan. BS magna cum laude, Rensselaer Poly. Inst., 1987; MD cum laude, Albany (N.Y.) Med. Coll., 1989. Diplomate Am. Bd. Ophthalmology. Intern Mt. Sinai Med. Ctr., Miami Beach, Fla., 1989-90; resident in opthalmology Med. Coll. Va., Richmond, 1990-93; fellow in pediatric opthalmology Children's Meml. Hosp./Northwestern U., Chgo., 1993-94. Contbr. articles to profl. jours. Fellow Am. Acad. Ophthalmology; mem. AMA, Am. Assn. Pediatric Ophthalmology and Strabismus, Fla. Soc. Ophthalmology, Broward County Med. Assn. (child and health care com. 1994—), Alpha Omega Alpha. Office: Eye Surgery Assocs 2740 Hollywood Blvd Hollywood FL 33020

DORIAN, NANCY MARILYN, psychologist; b. Shaker Heights, Ohio, May 27, 1933; d. Alex and Elsa (Guttman) Frank; m. Alex Dorian, Aug. 6, 1960 (div. Sept. 1961); 1 child, Andrea McIlwaine. AB, U. Chgo., 1954; MA, Case Western Res. U., 1966. Lic. psychologist, Ohio. Psychologist Euclid (Ohio) Pub. Schs., 1965-74; office mgr. Realtek Industries, Cleve., 1974-77; psychologist Vocat. Guidance and Rehab. Services, Cleve., 1977-79; coordinator psychol. services Townhall II-Drug Edn. and Crisis Intervention Ctr., Kent, Ohio, 1979-81; chief psychologist Trumbull County (Ohio) Children's Services Bd., Warren, 1982—. Bd. dirs. Forensic Psychiat. Ctr. N.E. Ohio, Youngstown, 1985—, v.p., 1991-93, pres., 1993—. Recipient Commendation Ohio Bd. Edn., 1972. Mem. APA (assoc.), Sugarbush Kennel Club of Chardon, ohio (sec. 1980-82, 95-96), Samoyed Club Am., Otterhound Club Am. Home: 15481 Riddle Ln Chagrin Falls OH 44022-3943 Office: Trumbull County Children Svcs Bd 2282 Reeves Rd NE Warren OH 44483-4300

DORIO, MARC ANTHONY, industrial psychologist, consultant; b. Woodbury, N.J., Oct. 8, 1944; s. Marcus Anthony and Marie Antionette (Tortella) D.; m. Patricia Mary King, Mar. 5, 1988; stepchildren: Ian, Christina. BA in Philosophy, St. Bernards Coll., 1966, ThM, 1969, MDiv, 1970; MS in Applied Psychology, Stevens Inst. Tech., 1979. Roman Cath. priest, asst. supt. schs. Diocese of Camden, N.J., 1970-77; adminstr. Stevens Inst. Tech., Hoboken, N.J., 1977-78; v.p. McCooe and Assocs., Ridgewood, N.J., 1978-90; pres. Trine Co. div. Trax Systems Inc., Princeton, N.J., 1990-93, Dorio Assocs., Inc., Titusville, N.J., 1993—; adj. prof. Bloomfield (N.J.) Coll., 1983-88. Author: Personnel Managers Desk Book, 1989, Staffing Problem Solvers for Human Resource Professionals and Managers, 1994, The Complete Idiot's Guide to Getting the Job You Want, 1995; contbr. articles to profl. jours. Mem. Am. Psychological Assn. (assoc.), N.J. Psychological Assn. (assoc.), Soc. Indsl. Organizational Psychology. Home: 6 Maddock Rd Titusville NJ 08560-1309 Office: Dorio Assocs 6 Maddock Rd Titusville NJ 08560-1309

DORN, ROBERT MURRAY, physician, psychiatrist, educator, psychoanalyst; b. Cleve., May 1, 1921; s. Karl and Frieda (Cohan) D.; m. Natalie Ivanovna Borokhovich Reid, Nov. 28, 1964; children: Nancy Dorn-Stuart, Robert Murray Jr., Mary Beth, Anthony J., Michael Reid, Linda Donley-Reid, Douglas Reid. BS, Western Res. U., 1941, MS, 1944, MD, 1945. Intern Strong Meml. Hosp., U. Rochester (N.Y.), 1945-46; tng. U. London, 1948-51; clin. clk. Nat. Hosp. Queens Sq. Inst. Neurology, 1948-49,

Inst. Psychiatry The Maudsley Hosp., 1949-51; psychoanalytic trainee Brit. Inst. Psychoanalysis, 1948-51; pvt. practice psychiatry and psychoanalysis Beverly Hills, Calif., 1953-75; pvt. practice psychiatry Davis, Calif., 1986—, Sacramento, 1986—; prof. psychiatry U. Calif., Davis, 1981-86, clin. prof., 1986—; attending psychiatrist L.A. Psychiat. Svc., 1955-59, instr. Reiss-Davis Clinic Child Guidance, L.A., 1955-59; lectr. L.A. Inst. Psychoanalysis, 1958-65, mem. sr. faculty, 1965-68, tng. analyst, 1968-75, analyst supr., 1969—; cons. Whittier (Calif.) Family Svc. Agy., 1960-68, Reiss Davis Child Study Ctr., 1960—; asst. clin. prof. Sch. Medicine, UCLA, 1962-69, assoc. clin. prof., 1969-75; prof. Med. Sch., Ea. Va. U., Norfolk, 1975-81, interim chair psychiatry, 1979-81. Contbr. articles to profl. jours. Chmn. psychiat. div. Community Chest, L.A., 1959-60; tchr. Beverly Hills YMCA, 1964—; mem. Town Hall, L.A., 1964—; founding patron Huntington Hartford Theatre Wing, Greek Theatre; sustaining mem. Community TV, Los Angeles County Mus. Art;mem. Tidewater Assembly on Family Life, 1977-81, Task Force on Sch. Age Parents, 1977-81; mem. profl. adv. bd. Parents with Heart, 1982-86; mem. Yolo County Mental Health Adv. Bd., 1986-88, Crocker Art Mus.; patron, mem. Sacramento Opera; concertmaster, mem. Sacramento Symphony, 1986—; donor Internat. House Davis. Capt. USAF, 1946-47, U.S. Army, 1953-55. Recipient Disting. Svc. award YMCA, 1966. Fellow Am. Psychiat. Assn., Am. Geriatric Soc., Am. Orthopsychiat. Assn., Royal Soc. Health, Am. Coll. Psychiatrists, Am. Coll. Psychoanalysts, Am. Acad. Child and Adolescent Psychology; mem. AMA, CMA, Calif. Med. Assn. (del. 1960-63, 68-75), So. Calif. Med. Assn. (coun. 1964-68), Yolo County Med. Soc. (exec. com. 1986-88), Brit. Psychoanalytical Soc., Internat. Psychoanalytical Soc., Am. Psychoanalytical Soc., Am. Psychoanalytical Assn., Crocker Soc., El Macero Country Club, Sigma Xi. Office: 79 Scripps Dr Ste 212 Sacramento CA 95825

DORN, SAMUEL O., endodontist; b. N.Y.C., Jan. 1, 1946; s. Benjamin and Mae (Baylin) D.; m. Linda Frances Neuger, Dec. 23, 1984; children: Lanelle, Brian, Adam, Dawn. BA, Queens Coll., 1966; DDS, Fairleigh Dickinson U., 1970; cert., Nassau County Med. Ctr., 1976. Diplomate Am. Bd. Endodontics (bd. dirs.). Capt. USAF, Washington, 1970-72; assoc. Dr. Moodnik, Greenfield & Atkinson, Forest Hills, N.Y., 1972-76; pvt. practice Ft. Lauderdale, Fla., 1976—; clin. instr. Fairleigh Dickinson U. Dental Sch., Hackensack, N.J., 1973-74; cons. in field; chmn. advanced endodontics Dade County Dental Rsch. Clinic, Miami, 1977-93; clin. assoc. prof. U. Fla. Sch. Dentistry; clin. asst. prof. U. Miami Sch. Medicine, 1977-93; dir., treas. Am. bd. Endodontics; dir. Post-Grad. Endodontics Nova Southeastern U. Sch. Dental Medicine; lectr. in field. Trustee Endowment & Meml. Found., Chgo., 1987-88. Named Dentist of the Year East Coast Dental Soc., 1987. Fellow Am. Coll. Dentists, Internat. Coll. Dentists; mem. Am. Assn. Endodontists (bd. dirs. 1988-91), Fla. Assn. Endodontists (pres. 1990-92), Greater Hollywood Dental Soc. (pres. 1988-89), South Fla. Endodontic Soc. (pres. 1982-83), East Coast Dist. Dental Soc. (pres.), Am. Assn. Dental Rsch. Jewish. Home: 1031 SW 91st Ave Fort Lauderdale FL 33324-3817 Office: 8200 W Sunrise Blvd Fort Lauderdale FL 33322 also: 2213 N University Dr Pembroke Pines FL 33024

DORNBURG, RALPH CHRISTOPH, biology educator; b. Nuernberg, Fed. Republic Germany, Aug. 12, 1952; came to U.S., 1986; s. Robert and Freia (Puchtler) D.; m. Ute Pietrass, Aug. 12, 1980; children: Alex, Rebecca. Diploma, Ludwig-Maximilians U., Munich, 1982; postgrad., Max-Planck Inst. Biochemistry, Martinsried, Fed. Republic Germany, 1982-86; PhD, U. Munich, 1986. Deutsche Forschungs-Gemeinschaft postdoctoral fellow McArdle Lab. for Cancer Rsch., Madison, Wis., 1986-89; asst. prof. U. Medicine and Dentistry of N.J., Piscataway, 1989-96; assoc. prof. Thomas Jefferson U., Phila., 1996—. Author: Encyclopedia of Human Biology, 1991; contbr. articles to Molecular and Cellular Biology, Jour. Virology, others. Office: Thomas Jefferson Univ Divsn Infectious Diseases 1010 Locust St Philadelphia PA 19107

DORNER, DOUGLAS BLOOM, vascular surgeon, educator; b. Iowa City, Iowa, Aug. 4, 1941; s. Ralph A. and Gene (Bloom) D.; married, 1970; children: Gillian Austin, Hillary Howell. BA magna cum laude, Amherst Coll., 1963; MD cum laude, Harvard U., 1967. Diplomate Am. Bd. Surgery, Am. Bd. Gen. Vascular Surgery, Nat. Bd. Med. Examiners. Physician intern in surgery U. Calif., San Francisco, 1967-68, asst. resident in surgery, 1968-70, sr. resident, 1971-72, chief resident, 1972-73; surg. registrar St. James' Hosp., London, 1970-71; pvt. practice medicine specializing in vascular surgery Des Moines, 1974—; chief surgery Broadlawns-Polk County Hosp., Des Moines, 1977-78; co-dir. peripheral vascular lab. Iowa Meth. Med. Ctr., Des Moines, 1977—, chief surgery, 1980-81, 88-91; co-dir. peripheral vascular lab. Iowa Luth. Hosp., Des Moines, 1980-88; dir. med. edn. Iowa Meth. Med. Ctr., Des Moines, 1994—; instr. surgery u. iowa, Iowa City, 1973, clin. asst. prof., 1981—; vis. prof. Gunderson Clinic, La Crosse, Wis., 1984, St. James' Hosp., London, 1985, Dublin, Ireland, 1987; cons. VA Med. Hosp., Des Moines, 1980—; dir. med. edn. Iowa Meth. Med. ctr., 1994—; sr. v.p. med. edn. & rsch. Cen. Iowa Health System, 1996—. Contbr. numerous articles to profl. and scholarly jours. Capt. USAR, 1967-77. Nat. Merit scholar, 1959. Fellow ACS (Iowa chpt. scholarship award com., credentials com., chmn. Iowa com. on applicants 1976—); mem. AMA, Naffziger Surg. Soc., Polk County Med. Soc. (councillor 1979-81, trustee 1981-83, pres.-elect 1983, pres. 1984), Iowa Med. Soc. (chmn. program com. sci. session 1982), Am. Trauma Soc., Iowa Acad. Surgery (program chmn. 1981, resident paper award com.), Midwest Surg. Assn. (councillor 1983-85, sec. 1985-88, pres. elect 1989-90, pres. 1990-91), Soc. Clin. Vascular Surgery, Internat. Soc. for Cardiovascular Surgery, Midwestern Vascular Surg. Soc. (membership com.), Soc. Non-Invasive Vascular Tech., Western Surg. Assn., Peripheral Vascular Surg. Soc., Phi Beta Kappa, Sigma Xi, Med. Libr. Club Des Moines (sec. 1989-90), Des Moines Club, Wakonda Club. Home: 5220 Waterbury Rd Des Moines IA 50312-1922 Office: Ste 100 1440 Pleasant St Des Moines IA 50314

DORNFEST, BURTON SAUL, anatomy educator; b. N.Y.C., Oct. 31, 1930; s. Irving and Yetta (Rosengarten) D.; BA, N.Y.U., 1952, MS, 1954, PhD, 1960; m. Eveline Drucker, June 13, 1954; children: Michael, Barry. Rsch. asst. dept. biostats. Sloan-Kettering Inst. and Meml. Hosp., N.Y.C., 1952-53; rsch. asst. dept. biology N.Y.U., 1953-54, 56-58, instr. gen. sci., 1958-63; instr. anatomy N.Y. Med. Coll., 1963-64; instr. anatomy SUNY Health Sci Ctr. at Bklyn., 1964-67, asst. prof., 1967-73, assoc. prof., 1973-91; cons. study sect. Nat. Heart and Lung Inst., 1975; adj. prof. Med. Sch. CUNY, 1974—; adj. prof. hematology sch. health scis. Hunter Coll., 1978-82, 90-91, anatomy Inst. Continuing Biomed. Edn., 1979-86, N.Y. Med. Coll., 1982-85, 91-96, Touro Coll. Ctr. Biomed. Edn., 1983-88, Einstein coll., Medicine, 1991—. NIH fellow, 1958-60, 61-63; Leukemia Soc., 1960-61; Nat. Inst. Arthritis and Metabolic Diseases grantee, 1964-71; Nat. Cancer Inst. grantee, 1973-75; Mildred Werner League for Cancer Research grantee, 1976-77; co-prin. investigator NIH Heart, Blood and Lung Inst., 1982-85. Served with U.S. Army, 1954-56. Mem. AAAS, N.Y. Acad. Scis., Am. Soc. Hematology, Am. Assn. Clin. Anatomists, Internat. Soc. Exptl. Hematology, Am. Assn. Anatomists, Sigma Xi. Jewish. Contbr. articles in field to profl. jours. Home and Office: 96 Everett Rd Demarest NJ 07627-1225

DOROUGH, H. WYMAN, toxicologist, educator, consultant; b. Notasulga, Ala., Dec. 23, 1936; s. J.D. and Audie Elise (Hendley) D.; m. Mary Davenport; children: Hendley, Kieth, Gary, Melissa, Melinda, Bradley (dec.). BS, Auburn U., 1959, MS, 1960; PhD, U. Wis., 1964. Asst. prof. Tex. A&M U., College Station, 1963-67, assoc. prof., 1967-68; assoc. prof. U. Ky., Lexington, 1969-70, prof., 1970-85, assoc. dean research grad. sch., 1974-76, dir. grad. ctr. toxicology, 1976-83; prof., head dept. biol. scis. Miss. State U., Starkville, 1985-91, prof. dept. biol. scis., 1991—; cons. toxicology to various indsl. and govtl. agencies including Internat. Atomic Energy Agy., Vienna, Austria, 1985—, Nat. Library Medicine, Bethesda, Md., 1985—. Co-author: Carbamate Insecticides, 1976; co-editor: Fate of Pesticides in Large Animals, 1977; contbr. over 125 articles to profl. jours. Mem. Entomological Soc. Am. (Bussart Research award 1981), Am. Chem. Soc., Soc. Toxicology, Soc. Environ. Toxicology and Chemistry (charter), Phi Kappa Phi, Sigma Xi. Home: 203 Greenbriar St Starkville MS 39759-4304 Office: Miss State U Dept Biol Scis Mississippi State MS 39762

DORPAT, THEODORE LORENZ, psychoanalyst; b. Miles City, Mont., Mar. 25, 1925; s. Theodore Ertman and Eda (Christiansen) D.; married; 1 child, Joanne Katherine. B.S., Whitworth Coll., 1948; M.D., U. Wash., 1952; grad., Seattle Psychoanalytic Inst., 1964. Resident in psychiatry Seattle VA Hosp., 1953-55, Cin. Gen. Hosp., 1955-56; instr. in psychiatry U. Wash., 1956-58, asst. prof. psychiatry, 1958-59, asso. prof., 1969-75, prof., 1976—; practice medicine specializing in psychiatry Seattle, 1958-64; practice psychoanalysis, 1964; instr. Seattle Psychoanalytic Inst., 1966-71, tng. psychoanalyt, 1971—, dir., 1984; chmn. Wash. Gov.'s Task Force for Commitment Law Reform; trustee Seattle Community Psychiat. Clinic; pres., trustee Seattle Psychoanalytic Inst. Contbr. numerous articles, revs. to profl. books and jours. Served to ensign USNR, 1943-46. Fellow Am. Psychiat. Assn.; mem. Am. Psychoanalytic Assn., AMA, Seattle Psychoanalytic Soc. (sec.-treas. 1965-67, pres. 1972-73), AAAS, Alpha Omega Alpha, Sigma Xi. Home: 7700 E Green Lake Dr N Seattle WA 98103-4913 Office: Blakely Bldg 2271 NE 51st St Seattle WA 98105-5713

DORR, RICHARD PAUL, urologist; b. Saginaw, Mich., Aug. 17, 1936; s. Paul Kenny and Monica Cecelia (Hogan) D.; m. Jane Frances Schmidt; children: Richard Joseph, Susan Jane Dorr-Gould, Mark Edward. BS, Mich. State U., 1957; MD, U. Mich., 1961. Diplomate Am. Bd. Urology. Intern Wayne County Gen. Hosp., Eloise, Mich., 1962, asst. resident surgery, 1965; resident in urology U. Mich., Ann Arbor, 1965-66; pres. Huron Valley Urology Assocs., P.C., Ann Arbor, Mich., 1974—; exec. v.p., CEO Mercy Alternative, Farmington Hills, Mich., 1985-87, pres., CEO, 1987-90; head dept. urology St. Joseph Mercy Hosp., Ann Arbor, 1974-80, 90-92; clin. instr. surgery U. Mich., Ann Arbor, 1968-74, clin. assoc. prof., 1974-80, clin. prof., 1980—; active staff Chelsea Cmty. Hosp., 1982—; courtesy staff McPherson Hosp., Howell, Mich., 1981—; cons. urology Beyer Meml. Hosp., Ypsilanti, Chelsea (Mich.) Cmty. Hosp., Saline (Mich.) Cmty. Hosp. Divsnl. bd. Catherine McAuley Health Ctr., Ann Arbor, 1980-82; chmn. bd. dirs. McAuley Health Plan, 1983-84, med. dir., 1984; cons. Catherine McAuley Health Ctr. for Programatic Devel., 1983—; alt. del. Physician's Adv. Coun., Sisters of Mercy Health Corp., 1981, mem. Project Partnership Task Force, 1984. Capt, M.C. U.S. Army, 1962-64. Fellow ACS; mem. AMA, Am. Urol. Assn. (exec. com. North Ctrl. sect. 1980-83, pres. Mich. br. 1980), Mich. Urol. Assn. (exec. com. 1977-80), Am. Fertility Soc., Scabbard and Blade, Tri Beta. Republican. Roman Catholic. Home: 2380 Gale Rd Ann Arbor MI 48105 Office: PO Box 994 Ann Arbor MI 48106-0994

DORR, ROBERT WILLIAM, osteopathic physician; b. Detroit, May 30, 1952; s. William Curtis and Laurel Jean (Thompson) D. BA, Albion Coll., 1974; DO, Mich. State U., 1977. Intern, Southeastern Med. Ctr., North Miami Beach, Fla., 1978; gen. practice osteo. medicine Jackson (Mich.) Northwest Clinic, P.C., 1978-86, Jackson Family Med. Care Clinic, P.C., 1986—; med. dir. Medistation Jackson P.C., 1982-87; chmn. credentials com. Jackson Osteo. Hosp., 1984-87, chmn. UR/QA Jackson Osteo. Hosp., 1982-89, vice chief of staff, 1980-82. Bd. dirs. Jackson YMCA, 1980-86; bd. advs. Jackson County chpt. MADD (Mothers Against Drunk Driving). Mem. Southcentral Osteo. Assn., Mich. Osteo. Assn. Physicians and Surgeons, Am. Osteo. Assn., Flying Physicians Assn., Am. Coll. Sports Medicine, Civil Aviation Med. Assn., So. Med. Assn., Jackson County Med. Soc., Am. Coll. Gen. Practicioners in Osteo. Medicine and Surgery, Osteo. Gen. Practitioners Mich. Home and Office: 4545 Eagle Dr Jackson MI 49201-2490

DORR, STEPHANIE TILDEN, psychologist; b. Orlando, Fla., Sept. 21, 1950; d. Luther Willis Tilden II and Lillian Murfee (Grace) Owen; m. Darwin Dorr, May 21, 1986. AA, El Camino Coll., 1975; BA, U. N.C., 1985; MA, Western Carolina U., 1991. Cons. psychologist Sylva (N.C.) Psychol. Assocs., 1991-92; staff psychologist Park Ridge Hosp., Naples, N.C., 1992, Blue Ridge Ctr., Asheville, N.C., 1991-93; pvt. practice psychology Asheville, 1991-93; project mgr. Sedgwick County Dept. Mental Health, Wichita, Kans., 1993-95; pvt. practice psychotherapy and psychol. assessment Counseling and Mediation Ctr., Wichita, Kans., 1995—; adj. faculty Kans. Newman Coll., Wichita, 1995—, Butler County (Kans.) Cmty. Coll., 1996—; presenter in field. Contbr. articles to profl. publs. Mem. APA, Internat. Rorschach and Projective Techniques Soc., Soc. for Personality Assessment, Soc. for Psychologists in Mgmt., Psychoanalytic Study Group (sec. 1989-93, award 1993), Western N.C. Psychol. Assn. (mem.-at-large 1985-93, pres.-elect 1993), Psi Chi, Pi Gamma Mu. Episcopalian. Office: The Counseling and Mediation Ctr Inc 334 N Topeka Wichita KS 67202

DORSEN, MICHAEL, physician; b. Sydney, Australia, June 25, 1945; came to U.S., 1974; s. Frederick and Gisela (Weissman) D.; divorced; children: Marcus, Matthew. MD, U. Sydney, 1969. Diplomate Am. Bd. Neurol. Surgery. Rotating intern Ryde Dist. Hosp., Sydney, 1969-70; resident in gen. surgery Baylor Coll. Medicine Affiliated Hosps., Houston, 1974-75, resident in neurosurgery, 1975-79; pvt. practice neurosurgery Denison, Tex., 1979, Austin, Tex., 1980—. Capt. Royal Australian Air Force, 1970-74. Fellow ACS, Am. Acad. Pediatrics. Jewish. Office: 2905 San Gabriel # 310 Austin TX 78705

DORSETT, ROSWELL BRANSON, III, neurologist; b. Akron, Ohio, Nov. 20, 1948; s. Roswell Branson Jr. and Sara Marie (Gallagher) D. BA, Coll. Wooster, 1970; D of Osteopathic Medicine, Kirksville Coll., 1975. Bd. cert. neurology. Commd. 2d lt. U.S. Army, 1975, advanced through grades to lt. col., 1985, retired, 1995; staff neurologist Kaiser Permanente, Akron, Ohio, 1995—; asst. prof. neurology Yonsei U., Seoul, Korea, 1979-80; assoc. prof. neurology Kirksville (Mo.) Coll. Osteo. Medicine, 1982—; clin. instr. U. Wash., Seattle, 1984-86. Recipient Mosby Med. Publs. Mosby Book award, 1975. Mem. Am. Osteo. Assn., Christian Med. Soc., Assn. Mil. Osteo. Physicians. Republican. Office: Kaiser Permanente 3090 W Market St Akron OH 44333

DORSEY, JAMES BAKER, surgeon, lawyer; b. Saratoga Springs, N.Y., Aug. 29, 1927; s. Francis Edward and Katherine (Baker) D.; m. Patricia Ann Walsh, June 10, 1950; children: Katherine, Mary Lee, Pamela, Suzanne, James B., Jr., Alison. BA, Brown U., 1949; LLB, Union U. Sch., 1952, JD, 1991; MD, N.Y. Med. Coll., 1957. Bar: N.Y. 1953, Mass. 1988, U.S. Supreme Ct. 1982; lic. physician, N.Y., Mass., Calif. Intern Greenwich Hosp., Conn., 1957-58; resident White Plains Hosp., N.Y., 1958-59, Lenox Hill Hosp., N.Y.C., 1961-64; chmn. dept. surgery Saratoga Hosp., Saratoga Springs, 1976-79, 85-87; cons. surgeon Wesley Nursing Homes, Saratoga Springs, 1964—. Bd. dirs. Saratoga YMCA, Saratoga Springs, 1971-72; pres. Saratoga Springs Hist. Soc., 1972-74. Diplomate Am. Bd. Surgery. Fellow ACS, Am. Coll. Legal Medicine; mem. Saratoga County Bar Assn., Saratoga County Med. Soc. (pres. 1982-85), Med. Soc. N.Y., Mass. Med. Soc., N.Y. State Bar Assn., Mass. Bar Assn., AMA. Republican. Roman Catholic. Lodge: Elks, K.C. Office: 112 S Broadway Adirondack Trust Bldg St 1 Saratoga Springs NY 12866

DORSEY, JEREMIAH EDMUND, pharmaceutical company executive; b. Worcester, Mass., Oct. 15, 1944; s. Jeremiah Edmund and Mary Theresa Dorsey; AB, Assumption Coll., Worcester, 1966; MBA, Fairleigh Dickinson U., 1978; m. Nadia S. Vidach, Dec. 6, 1970; children: Todd Edmund, Jaime Erin, Megan Elizabeth, Kelly Ann. With Johnson & Johnson, New Brunswick, N.J., 1969-88, nat. indsl. engring. mgr., 1975-76, supt. ops. and maintenance, from 1976, now dir. ops. and mem. mgmt. bd.; v.p. gen. mgr. sales Johnson & Johnson Dental Products Co.; exec. v.p. The Kaelin Group, Bridgeton, N.J.,1988, pres. Towle Housewares Co., Newburyport, Mass., 1988-90; pres., CEO Foster Med. Supply, Inc., Dedham, Mass., 1990-92, Carvel Hall Corp.; group pres., exec. v.p., COO West Co. Health Care Products, Lionville, Pa., 1992—, J.E. Dorsey Co, Carvel Hall Corp, Crisfield, Md.; corp. officer, bd. dirs. Schubert Seals Horsens, Denmark. Active N.J. Commn. for Discharge Up-grade, Appalachian Trail Conf.; mem. alumni bd. dirs. Assumption Coll.; mem. adv. com. U. P.R. Sch. of Pharmacy; mem. mil. acad. selection com. U.S. Senate; vice chmn. N.J. Vietnam Vets. Leadership Program; mem. Mercer County Pvt. Industry Coun. (N.J.), N.J. SR-92 Coalition; bd. dir. Schubert Seals, Horens, Denmark. Served with U.S. Army, 1966-69; Vietnam. Decorated Bronze Star with 2 oak leaf clusters, Purple Heart with 4 oak leaf clusters, Army Commendation medal, Air medal with oak leaf cluster; Medal of Honor, Gallantry Cross (Vietnam); recipient Corp. Affirmative Action award, 1981. named Mgr. of Yr., Johnson & Johnson, 1974-75. Mem. Sierra Club, Spl. Forces Assn., Smithsonian Assocs., DAV, Soc. First Div., Tiger Karate Soc. (Black Belt), K.C., Johnson & Johnson Mgmt. Club, Delta Epsilon Sigma. Roman Catholic. Editor: Spl. Forces Assn. News. Home: 30 Fox Ridge Dr Malvern PA 19355-2876 Office: PO Box 777 101 Gordon Dr Lionville PA 19341-0777

DORSEY, JOHN HENRY, JR., podiatrist; b. Portland, Maine, Sept. 23, 1946; s. John Henry and Jean (Logan) D.; m. Sarah C. Herrick, Aug. 15, 1992 (div.); children: Kirsten, Jill. BS, U. Maine, 1969; D in Podiatric Medicine, Pa. Coll. Podiatric Medicine, 1976. Diplomate Am. Bd. Podiatric Surgery. Resident Wash. Meml. Hosp., Turnersville, N.J., 1976-77; podiatrist Cumberland County Foot Care, South Portland, Maine; chief podiatry divsn. Mercy Hosp., Portland, 1986—; exec. com. Westbrook (Maine) Cmty. Hosp., 1996. 1st lt. U.S. Army, 1969-71, Vietnam. Mem. Am. Podiatric Med. Assn., Maine Podiatric Med. Assn. (pres.). Office: Cumberland County Foot Care 1486 Broadway South Portland ME 04106

DORSEY, WILLIAM OSCAR PARKS, III, ophthalmologist; b. Nashville, Aug. 20, 1948; s. William Oscar Parks Jr. and Tardiefay (Arvant) D.; m. Marilyn Patrice Palm, June 26, 1978; children: William Oscar Parks IV, Jon, Stephen. BA, Fisk U., 1973; MD, Meharry Med. Coll., 1977. Diplomate Am. Bd. Ophthalmology. Intern U. Tenn., Chattanooga, 1977-78; resident in ophthalmology VA Med. Ctr., Tuskegee, Ala., 1978-81; pvt. practice Chgo., 1981—. Bd. dirs. Friends of Hyde Park Pub. Schs., Chgo., 1987-91, Ancona Montessori Sch., 1989-95. Mem. Am. Acad. Ophthalmology, AMA, Ill. Med. Soc., Chgo. Med. Soc., Nat. Med. Assn., Frogs Club, Midwesterners Club, NAACP (bd. dirs. Chgo. chpt. 1992-95). Office: Hyde Park Eye-Dental Surg 1457 E Hyde Park Blvd Chicago IL 60615-3037 also: 7531 S Stony Island Ave Chicago IL 60649-3913

DORSHER, PETER T., physician; b. Chgo., May 21, 1958; s. Robert Peter and Mary Ruth (McGee) D.; m. Candace Burnette (div. Aug. 1994). BS in Biomed. Engring., Case Inst. Tech., 1980; MS in Biomed. Engring., Northwestern U., 1982; MD, Rush Med. Coll., 1985. Cert. Am. Bd. Phys. Medicine and Rehab. Sr. assoc. cons. Mayo Clinic, Rochester, Minn., 1989-91, Jacksonville, Fla., 1995—; physician Rehab. Medicine Cons. of La., Baton Rouge, 1991-95. Contbr. chpts. to books. Mem. Alpha Omega Alpha, Sigma Xi, Mortar Bd. Office: Mayo Clinic Jacksonville 4500 San Pablo Rd Jacksonville FL 32224

DORWORTH, THOMAS ROBERT, psychologist; b. Charleston, W.Va., July 6, 1941; s. John Dougherty and Faith Irene (Miller) D.; m. m. Judith Barr; 1 child, Christopher Erickson. AB magna cum laude, Marshall U., 1964, MA, 1966; PhD, U. Minn., 1971. Lic. psychologist, Fla. Social worker W.Va. Dept. of Welfare, 1964-65; instr. psychology Marshall U., Huntington, W.Va., 1966-68; from tchg. asst. to instr. U. Minn., Mpls., 1968-71; dir. Counseling and Testing Ctr., asst. prof. psychology U. Pitts., Johnstown, Pa., 1971-75; dir. Counseling Ctr. Fla. Atlantic U., Fla., 1975—; pvt. practice Boca Raton, Fla., 1976—. Lt. col. USAR, 1981—. Mem. APA, Am. Soc. Clin. Hypnosis, Psi Chi, Chi Beta Phi, Phi Eta Sigma. Home: 1873 Discovery Way Pompano Beach FL 33064-0903 Office: Fla Atlantic U Counseling Ctr Student Svc Bldg #8 Boca Raton FL 33431

DOS, SERGE JACQUES, surgeon, physiology researcher; b. Paris, Jan. 24, 1934; came to U.S., 1957; s. Octave Pierre Marie and Fernande Lucienne (Daire) D.; m. Rasma Kupers, Aug. 19, 1966; children: Soshana, Yasmin, Maiya. M.D., U. Paris, 1964; Ph.D. in Physiology, U. Minn., 1965. Diplomate Am. Bd. Surgery. Lab. instr. physiology U. Minn., Mpls., 1962-65; instr. in surgery Cornell U., N.Y.C., 1971-73; asst. prof. surgery SUNY-Stony Brook, 1973, asst. prof. clin. physiology, 1973-76; surgeon St. John's Episcopal Hosp., Smithtown, N.Y., 1978-89; Mercy Hosp., Rockville Centre, N.Y., 1989-91, Beth Israel Med. Ctr., N.Y.C., 1991—; research com. VA Hosp., Northport, N.Y., 1974-76. Contbr. chpt. to book. USPHS trainee., 1962-65; various research grants NIH; various research grants Am. Heart Assn.; various research grants pvt. labs.; Laureate (Silver Medal) Faculty of Medicine U. Paris, 1966. Fellow N.Y. Acad. Scis.; mem. Am. Fedn. Clin. Research, AAAS, Am. Physiol. Soc., Assn. Acad. Surgery. Current Work: Physiology, history. Subspecialties: Surgery; Cardiac surgery.

DOSEN, SUSAN GAIL, special education coordinator; b. Duluth, Minn., July 4, 1951; d. Oliver Gust and Dorothy (Kampa) Mackley; m. James Anthony Dosen, June 23, 1972; children: Jessica Ann, Anthony Oliver. BS, U. Minn., 1973, MA, 1975, PhD, 1992, EdAD, 1992. Cert. speech & lang. pathologist, early childhood spl. edn. tchr., dir. spl. edn., elem. and secondary prin., supt. Spl. needs cons. Project Head Start, Va., Minn., 1974-75; speech, lang. clinician Mid-Range Spl. Edn. Coop., Chisholm, Minn., 1975-78; coord. Mid-Range Spl. Edn. Coop., Chisholm, 1978-88, Minn. River Valley Spl. Edn. Coop., 1988-92; asst. dir. spl. edn. St. Paul Schs., 1993—; chair Scott County Interagency Early Intervention Com., 1989-91. Active Leadership St. Paul, 1995-96, St. Paul CTIC, 1993—. Mem. AAUW (br. pres. 1986-88, com. co-chair 1985-88), ASCD, Minn. Speech/Hearing Assn. (policy coun. 1984-86), Am. Speech, Lang. and Hearing Assn., Coun. Exceptional Children, West Metro Early Childhood Spl. Edn. Coords. (co-chair, sec. 1990-91), Reflective Leadership Inst., Ladies Klub, Elks (bd. dirs.).

DOSTER, ROBERT THOMAS, internist; b. Atlanta, Dec. 7, 1927; s. Robert Thomas and Dorothy (Turner) D.; m. Mary Bush Hammack, Dec. 21, 1949; children: Mary Leslie, Lisa Carole, Robert Thomas III. BA, Vanderbilt U., 1950; MD, U. Tenn., 1954. Diplomate Am. Bd. Internal Medicine. Internship Baptist Hosp., Nashville, 1954-55, residency internal medicine, 1955-56; internist pvt. practice Nashville, 1956—; bd. dirs. Mid-South Found. for Med. Care, Memphis, 1987-96; peer rev. adv. com. Medicaid of Tenn., Nashville, 1990-95. Cpl. U.S. Army, 1946-48. Fellow Am. Coll. Physicians; mem. Tenn. Soc. Internal Medicine (pres. 1990-92), Nashville Soc. Internal Medicine (sec.-treas.), Am. Soc. Internal Medicine, Tenn. Med. Assn., Nashville Acad. Medicine. Republican. Presbyterian. Office: 222 22nd Ave N Nashville TN 37203-1802

DOTSON, GERALD RICHARD, biology educator; b. Brownsville, Tex., Sept. 8, 1937; s. Jasper William and Mary Agnes (Courtney) D.; m. Rose Delores Gonzales; children: Roberta, Anna. BS, Coll. Santa Fe (N.Mex.), 1960; MS, U. Miss., 1966; PhD, U. Colo., 1974; postgrad., U. Tex., Loyola U. New Orleans, El Paso, 1960-61, Loyola U., New Orleans, 1962-63. Sci. tchr. Cathedral High Sch., El Paso, Tex., 1959-61; sci./math./music tchr. St. Paul's High Sch., Covington, La., 1961-62; sci./math./Spanish tchr. Christian Bros. Sch., New Orleans, 1962-63; sci. tchr., chmn. Hanson High Sch., Franklin, La., 1963-67; biology instr. Coll. Santa Fe (N.Mex.), 1967-69, U. Colo., Boulder, 1969-70, Community Coll. Denver, 1970-77; prof. biology and chmn. sci. Front Range Community Coll., Westminster, Colo., 1977—; mem. com. for teaching excellence FRCC in Westminster, 1988—, mem. curriculum devel. com., 1970—, mem. acad. standards com., 1980—. Reviewer biology text books, 1970—; contbr. articles to profl. jours. Mem. recreation dept. City of Westminster, 1971—. Avocations: fishing, hunting, camping, golf, bowling, walking, fly tying. Mem. Am. Microscopical Soc., Am. Soc. Limnology and Oceanography, Nat. Assn. Biology Tchrs., Nat. Sci. Tchrs. Assn. (regional sec. 1965), Human Anatomy and Physiology Soc., Eagles, KC (3rd and 4th deg.), Elks, Sigma Xi, Phi Sigma. Roman Catholic. Home: 8469 Otis Dr Arvada CO 80003-1241 Office: Front Range Community Coll 3645 W 112th Ave Westminster CO 80030-2105

DOTSON, JACK LEE, mental health nurse practitioner; b. Vancouver, Wash., July 12, 1954; s. Elmer Lee and Martha Rose (Gums) D.; m. Linh My Tong, Oct. 28, 1991; children: Bethani LeeAnn, Vy H. AAS in Nursing, Clark Coll., 1987; AAS, Ft. Steilcoom Coll., 1979; A in Health Tech., Ft. Stilcoom Coll., 1978. RN, Wash. Charge nurse Rose Vista Nursing Home, Vancouver, 1986-88; staff nurse cardiac unit Providence Med. Ctr., Portland, Oreg., 1988-90, Queens Med. Ctr., Honolulu, 1990-91, Madigan Army Hosp., Tacoma, Wash., 1991-92; charge nurse-charge of code team at night Western State Hosp., Tacoma, 1992—; personal fitness instr., Olympia, Wash., 1993—; testifying for health care Capitol Bldg., 1993-95. Author: The Evil of Time, 1994. Mem. 1199 Union-Wash. (delegate 1995), Wildlife Fedn. Democrat. Home: 3114 Chelsea Ct NW Olympia WA 98502 Office: Western State Hosp Steilcoom Blvd Tacoma WA

DOTSON, ROBERT LEE, retired psychologist; b. Caretta, W.Va., Mar. 9, 1924; s. Jasper Madison and Lucy Eunice (Gardner) D.; m. Virginia Ruth Burke, Nov. 4, 1950,. BA, W.Va. Wesleyan Coll., 1949; postgrad., Duke U.,

1949-50; BS in Edn., Concord Coll., 1952; MA, Marshall U., 1956; DSc, London Inst. Applied Rsch., 1973. Lic. psychologist, W.Va. House painter Olga Coal Co., Coalwood, W.Va., 1950, 52; asst. mgr. Time Fin. Co., Welch, W.Va., 1951; jr. and sr. high sch. tchr. McDowell County Bd. Edn., Welch, 1952-55, high sch. tchr. Big Creek High Sch., 1956-58; high sch. tchr. Edinburg (Ind.) Pub. Schs., 1955-56; chief clin. psychologist Mammoth Cave Area Mental Health-Mental Retardation Bd., Glasgow, Ky., 1967-68; counselor-psychologist W.Va. Rehab. Ctr., Institute, 1958-59, psychologist, 1959-88, ret., 1988—. Pres. Upper Vandalia Hist. Soc., Winfield, W.Va., 1992, pres., 1994-96; active Putnam County Landmark Commn., 1992-94. With U.S. Army, 1943-45, ETO. Mem. APA (assoc.), W.Va. Psychol. Assn. (treas. 1969-72), VFW (post comdr. Eleanor 1996—). Presbyterian.

DOTSON, RUTH GRIFFITH, exercise physiologist; b. Fayetteville, W.Va., Aug. 15, 1960; d. Vency Enos and Edith Diana (Cosner) Griffith; m. Donald Dotson, Sept. 16, 1989. BS, Bridgewater Coll., 1982; MS, Appalachian State U., 1989. Exercise specialist Ochsner Clinic, New Orleans, 1984-85; fitness dir. Charlotte (N.C.) Police Dept., 1985-86; program dir. cardiac rehab. Cannon Meml. Hosp., Banner Elk, N.C., 1987-89; adj. instr. Appalachian State U., Boone, N.C., 1989—, exercise coord. health promotion, 1992—. Mem. Am. Coll. Sports Medicine (cert. dir. health/fitness instr. exam 1991—, preventive and rehab. program dir.).

DOTTON, FRANCES JEAN, nursing educator; b. Niagara Falls, N.Y., Mar. 15, 1943; d. Dominic John and Martha Mary (Galante) Tedesco; m. James M. Sorge, Oct. 6, 1962 (div. 1975); children: Deborah, Patrick; m. Robert L. dotton, Apr. 23, 1994; children: Lisa, Michael. AAS, Niagara County C.C., 1970; BS, SUNY, Buffalo, 1975, MS, 1977; PhD, SUNY, 1993. Charge nurse emergency dept. Niagara Falls Meml. Med. Ctr., 1970-74; staff nurse dialysis Roswell Park Meml. Inst., Buffalo, 1974-75; staff nurse Deaconess Hosp., Buffalo, 1975; instr. Genesee C.C., Batavia, N.Y., 1975-77; assoc. prof. Niagara U., Lewiston, N.Y., 1977—; cons., dir. utilization mgmt. NOVA Health Care, Grand Island, N.Y., 1988—; profl. performance examiner Regents Coll. SUNY, Albany, 1994—. Contbg. author: Pediatric Nursing Nurse Test: A Review Series, 1992. Vol. ARC, Niagara Falls, 1988-93. Lt. col. USAR, 1979—. Decorated Army Achievement medal; named to Alumni Hall of Fame Niagara County C.C., 1993. Mem. AAUP, Speech Comm. Assn., N.Y. State Nurses Assn., Internat. Soc. Gen. Semantics, Sigma Theta Tau. Roman Catholic. Home: 110 Parkview Dr Grand Island NY 14072 Office: Niagara U Niagara University NY 14109

DOTTS, RANDALL JAMES, physician associate; b. Jacksonville, Fla., Aug. 29, 1955; s. William Bryan and Helen Jean (Schultz) D. BA, Furman U., 1977; BHS cum laude, Duke U., 1984; physician asst. cert., Fla. State U. Cert. physician asst. Urology technician Spinal Injury unit Lucerne Hosp., Orlando, Fla., 1980-82; adj. prof. sch. medicine U. Fla., Tallahassee, 1985; dir. night clinic, physician asst. Fla. State U., Tallahassee, 1984-86, physician asst., 1984-89; physician asst. Orlando Healthcare Group, 1990-95, Fla. Hosp. Psychiatry, Orlando, 1994—; lectr. in field. Inventor in field. Chmn. long range planning com. Fla. State U., Tallahassee, 1988, mem. physician peer evaluation com., 1987-88, quality control bd., 1986-89, pharmacy and therapeutics com., 1986-89. Sgt. U.S. Army Corpsman Ranger Battlion, 1977-80. Fla. State U. grantee, 1987-88. Mem. Am. Med. Students Assn., Fla. Acad. Physician Assts., Am. Acad. Physician Assts. Southern Baptist. Home and Office: 100 W Hillcrest St Altamonte Springs FL 32714

DOTY, ROBERT WILLIAM, neurophysiologist, educator; b. New Rochelle, N.Y., Jan. 10, 1920; s. Earle Birdsell and Ethel Laurette (Mack) D.; m. Elizabeth Natalie Jusewich, Aug. 30, 1941; children—Robert William, Mary E., Cheryl A., Richard M. B.S., U. Chgo., 1948, M.S., 1949, Ph.D., 1950. Postdoctoral fellow U. Ill., Chgo., 1950-51; asst. prof. U. Utah, Salt Lake City, 1951-56; from asst. to assoc. prof. U. Mich., Ann Arbor, 1956-61; prof. U. Rochester, N.Y., 1961—; vis. prof. U. Mex., 1975, U. Osaka, Japan, 1981; sci. adviser NIMH, Bethesda, Md., 1975-79, Yerkes Inst., Atlanta, 1975-78. Assoc. editor: Acta Neurobiologiae, Warsaw, 1971—, Behavioral Brain Research, 1981—; contbr. articles to profl. jours. Served to capt. U.S. Army, 1942-46. Recipient Javits award, Nat. Inst. Neurol. and Communicative Disorders and Stroke., NIH, 1986. Fellow AAAS; mem. Am. Psychol. Soc. (pres. div. 6, 1984), Internat. Brain Research Orgn., Current Anthropology (assoc.), Soc. for Neurosci. (pres. 1975-76, councilor 1970-74). Office: U Rochester Med Ctr Dept Neurobiology & Anatomy PO Box 603 Rochester NY 14642

DOTY, TIMOTHY JAMES, physician assistant, army officer; b. Carson City, Nev., Dec. 19, 1952; s. Stanley Paul and Mabel Gertrude (Quinn) D.; m. Martha Scott, Dec. 30, 1972; children: Ian Michael, David Stanley. BS, U. Nebr., Omaha, 1980. Physician asst. Mendocino County Indian Health Bd., Ukiah, Calif., 1980-83; physician asst. USAF, Offut AFB, Nebr., 1983-89, Kadena AFB, Japan, 1989-92; physician asst. and chief family practice clinic USAF, Eielson AFB North Pole, Alaska, 1992—. Home: 3489 Rosehip Dr North Pole AK 99705 Office: 354th Med Group Family Practice Clinic Eielson AFB AK 99702

DOUBEK, ALBERT E., health facility administrator. CRNA, Mayo Clinic; RN, Kahler Sch. Nursing, Rochester, Minn.; BA, Ottawa U. Asst. head nurse cardiac unit Worrall Hosp., Rochester, Minn., 1953-54; nurse anesthetist USAF, 1956-58; chief nurse anesthetist Meml. Hosp., Menomonie, Wis., 1958-63; staff anesthetist Sioux Valley Hosp., Sioux Falls, S.D., 1963-65; chief anesthetist Sioux Valley Hosp., Sioux Falls, 1965-80, adminstrv. dir. PAC, 1967—, adminstr. dir. same day surgery, 1978—, adminstr. dir. GI lab., 1979—, adminstr. dir. anesthesia, 1980—, adminstrv. dir. surgery (Main/CVOR), 1980—, adminstrv. dir. Pain Clinic, 1984—, adminstrv. dir. AM admissions, 1990—, adminstrv. dir. surg. svcs. info. sys., 1993—; mem. numerous coms. Sioux Valley Hosp. Mem. Am. Assn. Nurse Anesthetists (mem./chmn. planning com., program com., coun. on practice, bd. dirs., v.p.), S.D. Assn. Nurse Anesthetist (govt. rels. com., advisor to S.D. Nurses Assn., bd. dirs., pres.-elect, pres.), Upper Midwest Assembly Nurse Anesthetists (chmn. nominating com., bd. dirs., program chmn.). Democrat. Roman Catholic. Home: 1500 S Kiwanis Sioux Falls SD 57105 Office: Sioux Valley Hosp 1100 S Euclid Sioux Falls SD 57117-9884

DOUD, TINA MARIE, adult nurse practitioner; b. Mansfield, Pa., Aug. 2, 1967; d. Stephen Corwin and Nancy Jo (Sumner) D. BSN, Masnfield U. of Pa., 1991; MSN, Syracuse (N.Y.) U., 1994. RN, Pa. Per diem nurse Troy (Pa.) Cmty. Hosp., 1993-94; part time staff nurse Soldiers and Sailors Meml. Hosp., Wellsboro, Pa., 1991—; nurse practitioner Laurel Health Clinics, Elkland, Pa., 1996—. Vol. Am. Cancer Soc., 1993. Mem. Critical Incident Support Group, Sigma Theta Tau. Home: PO Box 153 Mansfield PA 16933 Office: Elkland Laurel Health 103 Forest View Dr Elkland PA 16920

DOUENIAS, ROBERT, urologist; b. N.Y.C., Aug. 21, 1958. BA, Boston U., 1980; MD, Wayne State U., 1985. Resident in gen. surgery L.I. Jewish Med. Ctr., New Hyde Park, N.Y., 1985-87, resident in urology, 1987-91; attending urologist Guthrie Clinic, Corning, N.Y., 1991—. Author chpts. in books. Mem. rotary. Office: Guthrie Clinic 130 Center Way Corning NY 14830-2255

DOUGHERTY, CHARLES HAMILTON, pediatrician; b. St. Louis, June 1, 1947; s. Charles Joseph and Suzanne Louise (Hamilton) D.; m. Mary Laverty Peckham, July 7, 1972; children: Bridget, Matthew, Erin, Kelly. BA in Biology, Coll. of the Holy Cross, 1969; MD, U. Rochester Sch. of Medicine, N.Y., 1973. Pediatric resident St. Louis Children's Hosp., 1973-76; pvt. practice pediatrics Primary Pediatric Care Group, St. Louis, 1976-86, Health Key Med. Group, St. Louis, 1986—. Fellow Am. Acad. Pediatrics; mem. Am. Coll. Sports Medicine. Roman Catholic. Office: Health Key Beacon Med Group 13131 Tesson Ferry Rd Saint Louis MO 63128

DOUGHERTY, JAMES, orthopedic surgeon, educator; b. Lawrence, Mass., July 31, 1926; s. James A. and Maude D. (Dillard) D.; m. Rita Buchman; children: James (dec.), Charles, Janice, Jonathan, Christopher. BS, Trinity Coll., Hartford, Conn., 1950; MD, Albany Med. Coll., N.Y., 1951. Diplomate, examiner and monitor Am. Bd. Orthopaedic Surgery, 1965-82. Intern U. Chgo. Clinics, 1951-52, resident, 1951-56, instr., 1955-56; chmn. divsn. orthop. surgery SUNY, Syracuse, 1958-60; prof. clin. surgery Albany Med. Coll., 1960-96, prof. emeritus, 1996—, 1996—; trustee Albany Med. Ctr., 1993-95; cons. Subacute Care Alternative Project, Washington. Mem. editl. bd. Techniques in Orthops.; contbr. articles to profl. jours. Mem. Bd. Edn. Ravena-Coeymans-Selkirk Ctrl. Schs., Ravena, N.Y., 1960-75; med. dir. N.Y. Sr. Games, 1986-89; trustee Schaeffer Meml. Libr., 1990-92, Albany Med. Ctr., 1993-95; bd. dirs. Inst. for Study of Aging, 1990—. Served with U.S. Army, 1944-46. Fellow Am. Acad. Orthopaedic Surgeons; mem. Crawford Campbell Soc. (founder, pres. 1978-88), U. Chgo. Surg. Soc., Northeastern Regional Assn. Sports Medicine (chmn. 1984-89), Albany Med. Coll. Alumni Assn. (trustee 1990—, pres. 1994-96, Meritorious Svc. award 1996), Internat. Platform Assn., Alpha Omega Alpha, Sigma Psi, Sigma Nu. Presbyterian. Home: 3510 Pine Fern Ln Bonita Springs FL 34134 Office: 1444 Western Ave Albany NY 12203-3421

DOUGHERTY, JOHN MICHAEL, psychology educator; b. Phila., Oct. 13, 1953; s. William Joseph and Helen Veronica (Logue) D.; m. Christine Irene Pulse, June 5, 1976; children: Jon-Michael, Stephen. BA, Concord Coll., 1975; MA, Radford U., 1977; PhD, Va. Poly. Inst. and State U., 1984. Lic. psychologist, marriage and family therapist, profl. counselor, N.C., Va., Pa., W.Va. Program specialist Ctr. for Human Devel., Roanoke, Va., 1977-79; coord., counselor Mental Health Svcs. of the Roanoke Valley, Roanoke, 1979-84; clin. asst. prof. psychiatry U. N.C., Chapel Hill, 1985-92, clin. assoc. prof., 1992—; adj. prof. child devel. and family rels. East Carolina U., Greenville, 1988-92, adj. asst. prof. psychology, 1989—. Mem. APA, Am. Assn. Marriage and Family Therapy, Autism Soc. Am., Am. Assn. Mental Deficiency. Home: 108 Woodhaven Ct Greenville NC 27834-6930 Office: South Hall Profl Ctr 108-D W Fire Tower Rd Winterville NC 28590

DOUGHERTY, STEVE HUDSON, surgery educator, researcher; b. L.A., Sept. 15, 1946; s. Clyde Hudson and Helen Virginia (Perdue) D.; m. Leah Diane Eberley, Mar. 12, 1976; children: Tobias, Alexis, Dane, Danforth. BA, Stanford U., 1969; MD, U. Calif., San Francisco, 1973. Diplomate Am. Bd. Surgery. Surg. intern U. Minn., Mpls., 1973-74, resident in surgery, 1974-80, fellow in surg. infections, 1980-82; instr. surgery Tex. Tech U., El Paso, 1982-84, asst. prof., 1984-89, assoc. prof., 1989-95, prof., 1995—, assoc. prof. microbiology, 1990-95; prof. microbiology Tex. Tech. U., El Paso, 1995—; chief staff R.E. Thomason Hosp., El Paso, 1995-96. Author: (monographs) Infections in Bionic Man, 1982, Biology of Surgical Drains, 1992. Fellow ACS; mem. Surg. Infection Soc., Western Surg. Assn. Office: Tex Tech U 4800 Alberta Ave El Paso TX 79905

DOUGLAS, DONALD DEAN, gastroenterologist; b. Waukegan, Ill., July 30, 1944; s. Donald B. and Regina (Rovelle) D.; m. Dorothy V. Early, June 7, 1969; children: Theresa A., David B., Virginia R. BS, Creighton U., 1966; MD, U. Md., 1970. Diplomate Am. Bd. Internal Medicine, Am. Bd. Gastroenterology. Intern Henry Ford Hosp., Detroit, 1970-71; resident Mayo Clinic, Rochester, Minn., 1973-75; fellow U. Wis., Madison, 1975-77; pres. Susquehanna Gastroenterology Assocs., Williamsport, Pa., 1977-88, Donald D. Douglas, P.C., Lewisburg, Pa., 1990—; head dept. medicine Evang. Community Hosp., Lewisburg, 1991-93. Inventor tubular sheath for endoscope, 1980; temperature, volume, pressure for insulfation device, 1991; gastric pacemaker, 1994. Lt. USN, 1971-73. Fellow Am. Coll. Physicians; mem. AMA, Am. Soc. Gastrointestinal Endoscopy, Am. Soc. Gastroenterology, Am. Gastrointestinal Assn. Republican. Roman Catholic. Home: The House at Turtle Creek RR 1 Box 443D Lewisburg PA 17837 Office: Brookpark Office Ctr 260 Reitz Rd Ste 1 Lewisburg PA 17837-9220

DOUGLAS, HOPE M., psychotherapist, forensic hypnotist; b. Marblehead, Mass., Jan. 14, 1947; d. W.I. and Beatrice B. Kenerson. BA in Psychology, Mich. State U., 1969, MA in Rehab. Counseling, 1970. Cert. mental health counselor, Fla.; cert. Ericksonian hypnotist. With Bur. Narcotics and Dangerous Drugs, U.S. Dept. Jusitce, Denver, 1971; with narcotics investigation, officer Glendale Police Dept., Denver, 1971-74; exec. dir., dir. edn., nat. speaker Child and Family Agy. of S.E. Conn., 1974-84; evidence technician, instr. homicide investigation Naples (Fla.) Police Dept., 1984-90; founder, exec. dir. wildlife rehab. svcs. and edn. Wind Over Wings, Inc., Clinton, Conn., 1990—; instr. wildlife rehab. Conn. Dept. Environ. Protection, 1991-92; adj. faculty Conn. Coll., Mitchell Coll. Contbr. articles to profl. jours. Mem. adv. bd. Child Welfare League Am. Recipient J. Edgar Hoover award for excellence, 1985. Mem. Conn. Wildlife Rehab. Assn. (pres. 1992), Internat. Wildlife Rehab. Coun. (v.p. 1993-94, acting exec. dir. 1995, bd. dirs. 1995-96, illustrator rehab. book series and disability book series 1995). Home: 22 Old Rd Clinton CT 06413-1855

DOUGLAS, JANICE GREEN, physician, educator; b. Nashville, July 11, 1943; d. Louis D. and Electa Green. BA magna cum laude, Fish U., 1964; MD, Meharry Med. Coll., 1968. Intern Meharry Med. Coll., 1968-71; NIH tng. fellow in endocrinology, instr. internal medicine Vanderbilt U., Nashville, 1971-73; sr. staff fellow sect. on hormonal regulation NIH, 1973-76; asst. prof. medicine Case Western Res. U. Sch. Medicine, Cleve., 1976-81, assoc. prof. medicine, 1981-84, prof. medicine, 1984—; dir. hypertension renal ambulatory care svc. Univ. Hosps. Cleve., 1976-80; dir. divsn. endocrinology and hypertension dept. medicine Univ. Hosps. Cleve. and Case Western Res. U., 1988-93, vice chair acad. affairs dept. medicine, 1991—, dir. divsn. hypertension dept. medicine, 1993—; mem. numerous grant rev. coms.; lectr., presenter in field; atteding physician in medicine and endicrinology U. Hosps., 1987; vis. prof. SUNY, Kings County Hosp. and Health Sci. Ctr., Bklyn., 1987, Med. U. S.C., 1989, Harlem Hosp., N.Y.C., 1993, N.Y. Med. Coll., Valhalla, 1994. mem. editl. rev. bd. Jour. Clin. Investigation, 1990—, Am. Jour. Physiology, Renal Fluid and Electrolytes, 1989-91; editl. bd. Hypertension, 1994—, Am. Soc Clin. Investigation, 1990—, Ethnicity and Disease, 1990—, Circulation, 1993—; guest editor Jour. Clin. Investigation, U. Calif., San Diego, 1992—; assoc. editor Jour. Lab. and Clin. Medicine, 1986-90; reviewer numerous manuscripts and abstracts.; contbr. numerous articles, abstracts to profl. publs., chpts. to books. Fellow High Blood Pressure Coun., Am. Heart Assn., 1993—. Mem. Assn. Am. Physicians, Cleve. Med. Assn., Am. Soc. Hypertension, Kidney Found. Ohio, Women in Endocrinology, Inter-Am. Soc. Hypertension, Women in Nephrology, Assn. for Acad. Minority Physicians, Am. Physiology Soc., Endocrine Soc., Ctrl. Soc. for Clin. Rsch., Internat. Soc. Hypertension in Blacks, Inst. Medicine of NAS, Internat. Soc. Nephrology, Am. Soc. Nephrology, Am. Soc. Clin. Investigation, Am. Fedn. Clin. Rsch., Am. Heart Assn., Phi Beta Kappa, Alpha Omega Alpha (pres. Meharry chpt. 1968), Beta Kappa Chi. Office: Case Western U Sch Medicine Divsn Hypertension Rm W 165 10900 Euclid Ave Cleveland OH 44106-4982

DOUGLAS, KATHLEEN MARY HARRIGAN, psychotherapist, educator; b. Boston, Apr. 24, 1950; d. John Joseph and Kathleen Margaret (Connolly) Harrigan; m. Dr. Robert E. Douglas, Feb. 24, 1977; children: David, Pamela, Elizabeth. Student, Uxbridge, England; BA in Psychology, Sophia U., Tokyo, 1972; MA in Counseling Psychology, Chapman U., Orange, Calif., 1983; PhD in Counselor Edn., U. Fla., 1990. Elem tchr. Marymount Prep Sch., Palos Verdes, Calif., 1973-75; pvt. practice Orlando, Fla., 1985-95; psychology prof. Valencia C.C., Orlando, Fla., 1989-93; prof. Fla. Inst. Tech., 1990-94; asst. prof., acad. advisor, clin internship supr. Troy State U., Orlando, Fla., 1993—; software developer of clinically oriented software Troy State U., 1994—; drug/alcohol counselor Ft. Belvoir, Va., 1981-82; counselor Orange County Mental Health Ctr., Winter Park, Fla., 1982-83; child abuse therapist Thee Door, Orlando. 1983-84; presenter in field. Author: The Therapeutic Superhighway, 1995. Counselor Winter Park Towers Nursing Home, 1985; vol. group counselor Hillcrest Halfway House, Orlando, 1985. 1st Lt. U.S. Army, 1976-80. Recipient Marion medal Cath. Ch., Boston, 1966, Civic award Spouse Abuse, Inc., Orlando, 1984. Mem. Am. Assn. for Counseling and Devel., Kappa Delta Phi, Pi Lambda Theta, Chi Sigma Iota. Roman Catholic. Home: 1781 Lake Berry Dr Winter Park FL 32789-5911

DOUGLAS, PAMELA SUSAN, physician. researcher, educator; b. New Brunswick, N.J., Dec. 2, 1954; d. Jocelyn Fielding and Rose Maria (Terrazzino) D.; m. Geoffrey Steven Ginsburg. AB, Princeton (N.J.) U., 1974; MD, Med. Coll. of Va., 1978. Asst. prof. U. Pa. Med. Sch., Phila., 1984-90; assoc. prof. Med. Sch. Harvard U., Boston, 1990—; chair med. control com. Triathlon-Fedn. U.S.A., Colorado Springs, Colo., 1989—; chair anti doping Internat. Triathlon Union, Vancouver, Can., 1989—. Author, editor: Heart Disease in Women, 1989; editor: Am. Jour. of Cardiology, 1986—, Cardiovascular Health and Disease in Women, 1993; mem. editl. bd. Jour. Am. Soc. Echocardiography, 1995—, AJC, 1986—, JACC, 1993—. Fellow Am. Coll. Cardiology (asst. sec., mem. bd. trustees 1995—, editl. bd. jour. 1994—), Am. Soc. Echo (dir. 1994—), Am. Heart Assn. (exec. com. coun. on clin. cardiology 1995—). Office: Beth Israel Hosp 330 Brookline Ave Boston MA 02215-5400

DOUGLAS, ROBERT GORDON, JR., physician; b. N.Y.C., Apr. 17, 1934; s. Robert Gordon and Alice (Lewis) D.; m. Ann Castle Moses, Dec. 22, 1956; children: Robert Gordon, 3d, Timothy Stuart, Catherine Lewis. AB, Princeton U., 1955; MD, Cornell U., 1959. Diplomate Am. Bd. Internal Medicine. Successively intern, asst. resident in internal medicine, resident N.Y. Hosp., 1959-61, 62-63; asst. resident Johns Hopkins Hosp., 1961-62; USPHS clin. assoc., clin. investigator Nat. Inst. Allergy and Infectious Disease, 1963-66; asst. prof. microbiology and medicine Baylor Coll. Medicine, Houston, 1966-70; mem. faculty Sch. Medicine and Dentistry U. Rochester, N.Y., 1970-82, prof. medicine and microbiology Sch. Medicine and Dentistry, 1974-82, head infectious disease unit Sch. Medicine and Dentistry, 1970-82, sr. assoc. dean edn. Sch. Medicine and Dentistry, 1979-82; prof., chmn. dept. medicine Med. Coll. Cornell U., 1982-90; physician in chief N.Y. Hosp., 1982-90; sr. v.p. medi. and sci. affairs Merck Sharp & Dohme Internat., 1990-91, pres. Merck Vaccine div., 1991-95; v.p. Merck & Co., Inc., Whitehouse Station, N.J., 1993-95; pres. Merck Vaccines, 1995—; cons. in field; adj. prof. medicine Cornell U. Med. Coll.; attending physician N.Y. Hosp., 1990—. Editor: Principles and Practices of Infectious Diseases, 1979, 2d edit., 1985, 3d edit., 1990; contbr. articles to profl. jours. Recipient Hawkins award Assn. Am. Pubs., 1980. Fellow ACP, Infectious Diseases Soc. Am. (pres. 1991-92, Feldman award); mem. Am. Soc. Microbiology, Am. Soc. Clin. Investigation, Assn. Am. Physicians, Am. Clin. Climatol. Assn., Nat. Vaccine Adv. Com., Inst. Medicine. Home: 11 Shadowstone Ln Lawrenceville NJ 08648-1026 Office: One Merck Dr PO Box 100 Whitehouse Station NJ 08889-0100

DOUGLAS, STEVEN DANIEL, immunologist, educator, director; b. Jamaica, N.Y., Feb. 28, 1939; s. Albert H. and Felice (Berner) D.; m. Mary Ann Forciea, Feb. 29, 1980; children: Hope Felice, Anne Genevieve. BA, Cornell U., Ithaca, N.Y., 1959; MD, Cornell U. Med. Sch., N.Y.C., 1963; MA (hon.), U. Pa., 1982. Intern Mt. Sinai Hosp., N.Y.C., 1963-64; resident Mt. Sinai Sch. Medicine, N.Y.C., 1966-67; staff assoc. NIH, Bethesda, Md., 1964-66; research fellow U. Calif.-San Francisco, 1967-69; from asst. prof. to assoc. prof. medicine Mt. Sinai Sch. Medicine, N.Y.C., 1969-74; from assoc. prof. to prof. medicine and microbiology U. Minn., Mpls., 1974-80; prof. pediatrics and microbiology U. Pa., Phila., 1980—; dir. allergy-immunology-pulmonology Children's Hosp., Phila., 1980-89, chief sect. immunology, 1989—. Editor-in-chief Clin. and Diagnostic Lab. Immunology, 1993—; editor Jour. Clin. Microbiology, 1983-93, Jour. Leukocyte Biology, 1980—; adv. bd. Diagnostic Immunology, 1984—; editorial bd. Jour. Immunology, 1984—, Clin. Immunology Immunopathology, 1975—, J. Clin. Lab. Analysis, 1988-93. Contbr. numerous articles in cellular and clin. immunology, particularly mononuclear phagocytes and immune deficiencies, to profl. publs. Served with USPHS, 1964-66. Recipient Career Devel. award NIH, 1969-74. Mem. Am. Assn. Immunologists, Am. Soc. Cell Biology, Am. Acad. Microbiology, Soc. Pediatric Research, Am. Pediatric Soc., Am. Soc. Clin. Investigation, Am. Soc. Hematology, Reticuloendothelial Soc. (sec. 1980-82, program chmn. 1981, councillor 1984-87, pres. 1988-89), Interurban Clin. Club (pres. 1994-95). Jewish. Home: 2122 Delancey Pl Philadelphia PA 19103-6512

DOUGLAS, ZACHARIAH HICKLIN, psychiatrist; b. Gainesville, Fla., Mar. 25, 1959; m. Jolanta Krazewska, June 26, 1985. BS, U. Fla., 1979; MD, Med. Coll. Wis., Milw., 1984. Diplomate Am. Bd. Psychiatry and Neurology. Intern Michael Reese Hosp., Chgo., 1984-86, resident, 1986-88, dir. inpatient unit, 1988-93; dir. cmty. psychiatry Rush Presbyn. Hosp., Chgo., 1993—; cons. Thresholds, Chgo., 1985—; HIV psychiatrist Komed Clinic, Chgo., 1994—. Named Tchr. of the Yr., Dept. Psychiatry, Rush Med. Sch., 1995. Mem. Am. Psychiat. Assn. Presbyterian. Office: Rush Presbyn St Lukes Med 1725 W Harrison Ste 744 Chicago IL 60612

DOUGLASS, JOHN MICHAEL, internist; b. Takoma Park, Md., Apr. 13, 1939; s. Jones All and Helen Louise D.; BA, Columbia Union Coll., Takoma Park, 1959; MD (Salutatorian), U. So. Calif., 1964; DPH Pacific West U., 1986; PhD Clayton U., 1987. m. Sue Nan Peters, May 15, 1962; children: Dina Lynn, Lisa Michele. Rotating intern Los Angeles County, U. So. Calif. Med. Ctr., 1964-65, resident internal medicine, 1965-67, home care physician, 1965-68; practice medicine specializing in internal medicine, Cin., 1968-70, L.A., 1970-91; physician Pasadena Emergency Ctr., 1965-68, Deaconess Hosp., 1968-70; postdoctoral fellow automobile safety and trauma rsch. UCLA, 1967-68, med. cons. Emergency Med. Svcs. Project, 1970-71; commd. officer USPHS, 1968, advanced through grades to comdr., sr. surgeon USPHS Res. 1982—, asst. sci. adviser injury control program ECA, Cin., 1968-69, med. specialities cons. Office Product Safety, FDA, 1969-70; internal medicine cons. East End Neighborhood Community Health Ctr. Cin., 1968-70, Hollywood Sunset Free Clinic, 1971-72; sr. med. cons. multidisciplinary hwy. accident investigation unit U. So. Calif., 1971-73; staff internist, coordinator health improvement service Kaiser Found. Hosp., L.A., 1970-92; instr. biomedical engring. course UCLA, 1968, sr. med. cons., assoc. sci. advisors, 1970—, instr. internal medicine, 1971-74; instr. internal medicine U. Cin. Sch. Medicine, 1968-70; instr. kinesthesiology, traumatic anatomy and head injury U. So. Calif., 1971-74, instr. foodstyle and lifestyle, 1977—; mem. med. adv. bd. Dominican Sisters of Sick Poor, 1969; traffic safety cons. Countywide Conf. on Emergency Med. Svcs., 1972; mem. nutrition council Las Virgenes Sch. Dist., 1977; coord. K-PMG Health Svc.; CFO Prepared Gormet, Inc.; engring. biomed. cons; tchr. anatomy and physiology. Active mgmt. devel. program Boy Scouts Am. Execs., 1966; bd. dirs. Calif. Assn. Pvt. Schs. and Colls., 1967, Coronary Club (adult jogging program), 1967-68; co-organizer Oriental rug exhibit Pacificulture Mus., Pasadena, Calif., 1973; v.p. L.A. Med. Milk Commn. Diplomate Nat. Bd. Med. Examiners, Am. Bd. Internal Medicine. Fellow ACP; mem. AMA, Am. Acad. Body Sculpting, Calif. Med. Assn., L.A. County Med. Assn., Am. Soc. Internal Medicine, Calif. Soc. Internal Medicine, L.A. Soc. Internal Medicine, Am. Assn. Automotive Medicine (exec. com. Western chpt. 1977-82), Am. Cancer Soc. (profl. edn. com., nutrition subcom.), Internat. Hajji Baba Soc., Decorative Arts Council, L.A. Mus. Art, Sierra Club, Phi Delta Epsilon, Alpha Omega Alpha, Phi Kappa Phi. Author: The Lost Language; contbr. over 100 articles to profl. jours.

DOUKAS, PETER G., banker; b. Athens, Mar. 26, 1952; s. George and Mary (Anastos) D. BA in Internat. Affairs, George Washington U., 1974; MA in Econs., NYU, 1976, PhD in Econs., 1982; MBA in Fin., Columbia U., 1979. Fgn. exch. market analyst, dealer and funding mgr. Citibank N.Y., 1979-85; corp. and investment banking head Citibank Athens/Greece, 1986-92, fin. markets, group head, 1994—; dep. minister of fin. Greek Govt., 1992-93. Home: 3 hronopoulou Str, Alimos 17455, Greece Office: Citibank, 4 Othonos Str, Athens 10557, Greece

DOULL, JOHN, toxicologist, pharmacologist; b. Baker, Mont., Sept. 13, 1922; s. John G. and Vivian (Kelling) D.; m. Vera Orsborn, Mar. 1, 1958; children: Ellen, John, James. BS, Mont. State U., 1944; MD, PhD, U. Chgo., 1953. From asst. to assoc. prof. U. Chgo., 1946-67, asst. dir. Toxicity Lab.; prof. Med. Sch. U. Kans., Kansas City, 1967—, dir. Ctr. for Environ. Health, 1985-89; chair com. on toxicology NRC/Nat. Acad. Sci., Washington, 1985—; mem. sci. adv. panel EPA, Washington, 1980-89. Editor: Textbook of Toxicology, 1975, 2d edit., 1980, 3d edit., 1986, 4th edit., 1991. With USN, 1944-46, PTO. Recipient Disting. Med. Alumni award U. Chgo., 1991. Mem. Am. Bd. Toxicology (pres. 1982-83), Soc. of Toxicology (pres. 1986-87). Office: U Kans Med Ctr Rainbow At 39th Kansas City KS 66103

DOUSKEY, THERESA KATHRYN, health facility administrator; b. New Haven, Conn., Nov. 30, 1938; d. Stanley Anthony and Wadia (Mekdeci) D. RN, Grace New Haven Sch. Nursing, 1959; BS in Nursing, So. Conn. State U., 1962; MPA in Health Care, U. New Haven, 1979. Various positions Yale New Haven Hosp., 1959-80; asst. dir. nursing Meriden (Conn.) Wallingford Hosp., 1980-81; nurse Regional Visiting Nurse Agy., North Haven, Conn., 1983-87; home care coord. Milford (Conn.) Hosp., 1990-93; case mgr., nurse Community Care, Inc., New Haven, 1988-90, 93-96; med. br. supr. Priority Care, Inc., East Haven, Conn., 1996—. Mem. Am. Nurses Assn., Conn. Nurses Assn. (nominating com. 1972-74), Conn. Assn. Continuity of Care, Sigma Theta Tau. Republican. Home: 412 Narrow Ln Orange CT 06477-3315

DOUTHAT, WALTER GUILLERMO, nephrologist; b. Santiago Delestero, Argentina, Mar. 2, 1964; s. Hector Eduardo and Rosario Antonia (Herrera) D.; m. Maria Guillerma, Jan. 6, 1990; children: Delfina, Augusto. Student, Nat. U. Cordoba, Argentina, 1982-87. Cert. surg. physician, nephrologist. Fellow Hosp. Clinicas, Cordoba, Argentina, 1989-92, Hosp. Privado, Cordoba, 1992, Unit Metabolic Bone Rrsch., Oviedo, Spain, 1992-94; staff dr. Hosp. Privado, Cordoba, 1994—; rschr. Conicor, Cordoba, 1995—. Co-author: (book chpt.) Avances en Nefrología y Urología, 1995; co-author: (jour.) Revista Portuguesa de Nefrologia, 1993 (Best Editl. of 1993); author: (monograph) Avances en Osteodistrofia Rena, 1995. With Argentine Army, 1988. Grantee Agua Mineral Besoya, 1993, Soc. Española Nefrologia, 1993, Eritropoyetina Soc. Española Nefrologia, 1993. Mem. Internat. Bone and Mineral Soc., Internat. Soc. Nephrology, Latin Am. Soc. Nephrology. Roman Catholic. Office: Hosp Privado, Naciones Unidas 346, 5016 Cordoba Argentina

DOW, DAVID SONTAG, ophthalmologist; b. Ann Arbor, Mich., Feb. 15, 1934; s. William Gould and Edna Lois (Sontag) D.; m. Gail Anita Bade, Feb. 11, 1961; children: Steven Michael, Bonnie Jean Dow Murphy, William Herbert, James Patrick. BS with distinction, U. Mich., 1956, MD, 1958, MS in Ophthalmology, 1964. Diplomate Am. Bd. Ophthalmology. Intern Denver Gen. Comm. Hosp., 1958-59; psychiat. wing profl. USAF Med. Svc., Wichita Falls, Tex., 1959-61; resident ophthalmology U. Mich. Med. Ctr., Ann Arbor, 1961-64; pvt. practice ophthalmology Scruggs, Dow, and Kannwischer ptnr., Waco, Tex., 1964-88, Cen. Tex. Eye Clinic, Waco, 1988—. Contbg. editor: Waco Tribune Herald, 1983—; author pamphlets in field. City coun. mem., mayor, Waco City Coun., 1977-81, 80-81; bd. dirs. Waco Symphony Assn., 1970-89, 94—, pres. 1982-83; bd. dirs. Tex. Med. Polit. Action Com., Austin, 1973-82; founding bd. mem., chmn. Greater Waco Arts Coun., 1986—, chmn. 1992, 94—. Capt. USAF, 1959-61. Mem. Am. Acad. Ophthalmology, Tex. Med. Assn., Waco Striders Club, Ridgewood Country Club, Rotary. Episcopalian. Home: 400 Ivy Ann Court Waco TX 76712 Office: Cen Tex Eye Clinic Ste 202 3115 pine Waco TX 76708

DOW, LOIS WEYMAN, physician; b. Cin., Mar. 11, 1942; d. Albert Dames and Elsie Marion (Krug) Weyman; m. Alan Wayne Dow, July 23, 1966 (div. Aug. 1979); children: Elizabeth Suzanne, Alan Wayne. BA summa cum laude, Cornell U., 1964; MD cum laude, Harvard U., 1968. Diplomate Am. Bd. Internal Medicine, Am. Bd. Hematology, Am. Bd. Oncology, Am. Bd. Pathology in Hematopathology. Intern Bronx Mcpl. Hosp. Ctr., N.Y.C., 1968-69; resident in internal medicine Presbyn. Hosp., N.Y.C., 1969-70; instr., research assoc. U. Tenn., Memphis, 1972-73, asst. prof., 1973-74; research assoc. in hematology and oncology St. Jude Children's Research Hosp., Memphis, 1974-77, asst. mem., 1977-80, assoc. mem., 1980-88; assoc. prof. pediatrics U. Tenn., Memphis, 1983-88; mem. staff St. Jude Children's Research Hosp., Bapt. Mem. Hosp., 1972-88, Med. Ctr. Del., Newark, 1988—; pvt. practice Newark, 1988—; dir. hematology lab. Med. Ctr., Newark, Del., 1993—; mem. staff Alfred I Dupont Inst., 1988—; assoc. prof., Jefferson Med. Coll., Phila., 1988—; cons., Nat. Cancer Inst. Contbr. articles to profl. jours. Fellow ACP; mem. Am. Soc. Clin. Oncology, Am. Fedn. Clin. Rsch., Am. Soc. Hematology, Am. Assn. for Cancer Rsch., Internat. Exptl. Hematology, Internat. Soc. Hematology, Am. Assn. Blood Banks, Am. Soc. for Blood and Marrow Transplantation, Cornell Club, Harvard Club. Office: Del Clin and Lab Physician 4745 Ogletown Stanton Rd Newark DE 19713-2070

DOW, THOMAS WENDELL, psychiatrist; b. Boston, Oct. 7, 1939; s. Wendell Adams and Elise Rose (Mullaney) D.; B.S., Boston Coll., 1961; M.D., U. Vt., 1965; postgrad. McGill U., 1968-71; m. Anne Campbell Shea, June 11, 1960; children: David Wendell, Abra Elise. Intern, Lakeland (Fla.) Gen. and Polk County (Fla.) hosps., 1965-66; resident psychiatry Douglas Hosp., Verdun, Que., 1968-69, Jewish Gen. Hosp., Montreal, 1969-71; practice medicine specializing in psychiatry Orlando, Fla., 1971—; mem. staffs Orlando Regional Med. Center, chmn. dept. psychiatry, 1983-85; clin. dir. West Lake Hosp., 1984—; mem. staff Fla. Hosp., Lucerne Gen. Hosp.; psychiat. cons. Orlando Regional Med. Center Community Mental Health Center, 1972-84, Cath. Social Services, 1973-77, Hillcrest Halfway House, 1971-73, Orange County Sch. System, 1977—; v.p. med. staff West Lake Hosp., Longwood, Fla., 1984-86, pres. 1986-88; clin. asst. prof. U. S. Fla. Coll. Medicine, 1978—. Mem. citizens advocacy com. Emotionally Disturbed Children of Central Fla., Orlando. Trustee, chmn. planning and evaluation com. Mental Health Bd. Central Fla., 1974-80; bd. dirs., chmn. profl. adv. com. Thee Door of Orange County Drug Abuse Program, 1971-74; bd. dirs. Orange County Mental Health Assn.; mem. Orange County Dem. Exec. Com., 1993—, del. Fla. Dem. Conv., 1995. Served to capt. M.C., USAF, 1966-68. Recipient Sir William Osler medal, 1965; diplomate Am. Bd. Psychiatry and Neurology. Fellow Am. Psychiat. Assn., So. Psychiat. Assn.; mem. Can. Psychiat. Assn., Am. Group Psychotherapy Assn., Am., So., Fla. med. assns., Orange County Med. Soc., Fla. Psychiat. Soc. (br. pres. 1975—), Am. Soc. Adolescent Psychiatry, Fla. Psychiat. Cons. (v.p.), Am. Acad. Child Psychiatry, Fla. Soc. Adolescent Psychiatry (pres. 1995-96). Unitarian. Club: Bay Hill Country. Home: 6083 Tarawood Dr Orlando FL 32819-4426 Office: 934 N Magnolia Ave Ste 200 Orlando FL 32803

DOW, TONY FARES, healthcare company administrator; b. Amman, Jordan, Apr. 1, 1947; came to U.S., 1975; s. Fares A. and Farha (Haddad) D.; m. May I. Mudarry, Dec. 25, 1976. BA in Bus. Adminstrn., Middle East Coll., Beirut, 1972; GCE advanced level, U. London, 1973-74. Sr. tech. rep. Scheing A.G. Berlin, Middle East, 1964-73; mgr. Ferrer Internat., 1973-76; cons. internat. bus. Whittier, Calif., 1976-81; chief exec. officer, pres. Lifecare Internat., Inc., Whittier, 1981—; cons. in field. Author: Damascus for the Tourist, 1965; translator: Round the World in Eighty Days, 1968; contbr. articles to profl. jours. Mem. Am. Cons. Assn., Am. Lebanese League (pres. 1982), Export Mgmt. Assn. Office: Lifecare Internat Inc 14831 Whittier Blvd Ste 103 Whittier CA 90605-1790

DOWBEN, ROBERT MORRIS, physician, scientist; b. Phila., Apr. 6, 1927; s. Morris and Zena (Brown) D.; m. Carla Lurie, June 20, 1950; children—Peter Arnold, Jonathan Stuart, Susan Laurie. AB, Haverford Coll., 1946; MS, U. Chgo., 1947, MD, 1949. Intern U. Chgo. Clinics, 1949-50; research fellow U. Oslo, 1950-51; fellow Johns Hopkins Hosp., 1951-52; resident in medicine U. Pa. Hosp., 1952-53; instr. medicine U. Pa. and dir. radioisotope unit VA Hosp., Phila., 1953-55; asst. prof. medicine Northwestern U. Med. Sch., 1957-62; asso. prof. biology M.I.T., 1962-68; lectr. medicine Harvard U. Med. Sch., 1962-68; prof. med. sci. Brown U., 1968-72; prof. biochemistry U. Bergen, Norway, 1972; prof. physiology and neurology, dir. grad. program in biophysics U. Tex. Health Sci. Center, Dallas, 1972-88; prof. neurology U. Tex. Health Sci. Ctr., Dallas, 1988-93; dir. Med. Cell Biology Lab. Baylor Rsch. Inst., Dallas, 1987-93; prof. physiology Brown U., Providence, R.I., 1993—; cons. neurologist Children's Hosp., Scottish Rite Hosp., Presbyn. Hosp., Baylor Hosp, all Dallas, 1972-93; mem. corp. Haverford (Pa.) Coll., 1979—, Marine Biol. Lab., Woods Hole, Mass., 1964-79; trustee Mt. Desert Island Biol. Lab., 1994—; bd. dirs. Greenhill Sch., Dallas, 1974-77. Author: Biol. Membranes, 1969, General Physiology, 1971, Cell Biology, 1972, also numerous articles; editor: Cell and Muscle Motility. Served to capt. M.C. USAF, 1955-57. Lalor fellow; recipient Disting. Service award Assn. Neuromuscular Diseases, 1964, Disting. Service award Alumni Assn. U. Chgo., 1980. Mem. Am. Physiol. Soc., Am. Soc. Biol. Chemists, Am. Chem. Soc., Soc. Exptl. Biology and Medicine, Biophys. Soc., Soc. Clin. Investigation, Central Soc. Clin. Research, Mass. Med. Soc., So. Med. Soc., Dallas County Med. Soc., Tex. Med. Assn., Biochem. Soc. London, Faraday Soc. (London), Phi Beta Kappa, Sigma Xi. Mem. Soc. of Friends. Office: Brown U Physiology Dept PO Box G-B3 Providence RI 02912-9007

DOWD, CAROLYN LAY, social worker; b. Hagerstown, Md., May 1, 1940; d. James S. Jr. and Emily Graham (Miller) Lay; m. William J. Dowd, Sept. 1, 1962 (dec.); children: William J. Jr., James P. AB, Meredith Coll., 1962; MSW, Catholic U., 1987. Cert. social worker, clin. social worker. Social work cons. Bethesda (Md.) Fellowship House, 1987-89; social worker Family Svcs. Agy., Gaithersburg, Md., 1987—, dir. svcs. for srs., 1991—, clin. dir., 1996—; pvt. practice Gaithersburg, 1991—; Presenter in field. Past mem. bd. dirs. Alzheimer's Assn. of Greater Wash. Mem. NASW (register of clin. social work, diplomate), Acad. Cert. Social Workers. Home: 21913 Foxlair Rd Gaithersburg MD 20882-1306 Office: 981 Russell Ave Gaithersburg MD 20879-3276 Other: The Family Svcs Agy Inc Ste A 640 E Diamond Ave Gaithersburg MD 20877

DOWD, KENNETH ROBERT, child counselor; b. N.Y.C., July 12, 1949; s. Robert Emmett and Mary (Rosko) D. A.B. magna cum laude, SUNY-Fredonia, 1971, M.S., 1972; M.L.S., Syracuse U., 1975; cert. advanced study, SUNY-Oswego, 1978, M.S., 1986; postgrad. Gesell Inst., Sheldon Inst. for Gifted, 1982, Omega Inst., 1985-87, Chautauqua Inst., 1986-87, 93; AS Onondaga C.C., 1986; BS SUNY, 1988. Tchr., Auburn (N.Y.) City Schs., 1971-72; tchr., curriculum devel., adminstrv. liaison West Genesee Central Sch., Camillus, N.Y., 1972-79; crisis counselor Contact-Syracuse, Inc., 1973-76; child counselor, human relations cons., leader parent effectiveness workshops, pupil retention study Oswego City Schs. (N.Y.), 1978—; cons. Syracuse City Schs., Fulton City Schs., Oswego County BOCES, Oswego Meth. Ch.; U.S. rep. Internat. Transpersonal Assn. Conf., Prague, Czechoslovakia, 1992. Bd. dirs. Central N.Y. Assn. for Learning Disabled, 1979-82; leader Parents Anonymous, Fulton, 1980-81. Named SUNY Coll. Pres.'s Scholar, 1971; Gen. Electric Corp. and Bristol Meyers Co. grantee, 1981; elected to N.Y. Acad. Scis., 1986. Mem. NEA, Am. Counseling Assn., Am. Sch. Counselor Assn., N.Y. State Counseling Assn., Assn. Humanistic Psychology (newsletter editor 1985-90), Transpersonal Psychol. Assn. (newsletter editor 1991—), Assn. Children With Learning Disabilities, Sierra Club, YMCA, Oswego Festival Chorus, May Meml. Unitarian Soc. (Syracuse), Syracuse Oratorio Soc., Syracuse Opera Guild, Kappa Delta Pi, Phi Delta Kappa. Club: Emerald Crest Country. Author: Changes: Managing Child Behavior, 1981, Computer Literacy, 1985, Social Problems Impacting on School Achievement: Bibliotherapy Guide, 1988, Gifted and Growing: A Guide for Parents of Able Children, 1996. Editor CNYALD News newsletter, 1980-82. Home: 828 Holly Dr Apt 38 Fulton NY 13069 Office: Oswego City Schs 233 W Utica St Oswego NY 13126

DOWDA, WILLIAM F., internist; b. Cobb County, Ga.. MD, Emory U., 1949. Intern Peter Bent Brigham Hosp., Boston, 1949-50; resident Barnes Hosp., 1950-51, 52-54; staff Piedmont Hosp., 1953-76; clin. assoc. prof. medicine Emory U., 1962-76; pvt. practice internal medicine, 1976—; pathology fellow, mem. staff Grady Meml. Hosp. Lt. med. corps USNR, 1950-52. Mem. ACP, AMA, Internat. Medicine-NAS, Soc. Med. Adminstrs. Address: 490 Peachtree St NE Atlanta GA 30308-3101*

DOWDELL, MICHAEL FRANCIS, critical care and anesthesia nurse practitioner; b. Cleve., June 5, 1949; s. Harry William and Dorothy May (McGivney) D.; 1 child, Michael Patrick. BSN, Ohio State U., 1975; MA in Counseling, Nat. U., San Diego, 1981; MSN, Calif. State U., Long Beach, 1991; diploma in nursing anesthesia, Kaiser Sch. Anesthesia, L.A., 1991; student, Case Western Res. U., 1996—. CCRN, CRNA, ARNP; cert. ACLS instr; cert. community coll. instr., Calif. Enlisted USN, 1968, commd. ensign, 1974, advanced through grades to lt. comdr., 1984, ret., 1988; resident nurse anesthesist Kaiser Sch. Anesthesia for Nurses, 1989-91; staff nurse anesthetist Kaiser Hosp., Panorama City, Calif., 1991-92, HCA Med. Ctr., Largo, Fla., 1992-93, Meml. Mission Hosp., Asheville, N.C., 1993—; vis. lectr. dept. anesthesia Makerere U., Kampala Uganda, 1995. Decorated Navy Achievement medal. Mem. AACN, NRA, Am. Assn. Nurse Anesthetists, Assn. Mil. Surgeons U.S., Ret. Officers Assn., Fleet Res. Assn., Am. Legion, Nat. Muzzle-Loading Rifle Assn., North-South Skirmish Assn. Republican. Home: 2 White Pine Cir Arden NC 28704-9553

DOWLING, JAMES KNOX, pediatrician; b. Omaha, Nebr., Nov. 3, 1934; s. Urban James and Dorothy Elston (Knox) D.; m. Dorothy Jean Mathews, Mar. 11, 1961; children: James Michael, Steven Matthew, Christopher Alan. Student, Tex. Tech. U., 1953-56; MD, U. Tex., 1960. Intern U. Okla. Hosp., Okla. City, 1960-61, resident in pediatrics, 1961-62, 63-65, chief resident in pediatrics, 1964-65; pvt. practice Denton, TX, 1965—; chief of staff Flow Meml. Hosp., Denton, 1978-79. Capt. U.S. Army, 1962-63. Fellow Am. Acad. Pediatrics; mem. AMA, Tex. Med. Assn., Tex. Pediatric Soc. Republican. Office: Childrens Clinic 1728 Scripture St Denton TX 76201-3811

DOWLING, JOHN ELLIOTT, biology educator; b. Pawtucket, R.I., Aug. 31, 1935; s. Joseph Leo and Ruth W. (Tappan) D.; children by previous marriage: Christopher, Nicholas.; m. Judith Falco, Oct. 18, 1975; 1 dau., Alexandra. A.B., Harvard U., 1957, Ph.D., 1961; M.D. (hon.), U. Lund (Sweden), 1982. Asst. prof. biology Harvard U., 1961-64, prof., 1971-87, Maria Moors Cabot prof. natural sci., 1987—; assoc. prof. Johns Hopkins Sch. Medicine, 1964-71. Author: The Retina: An Approachable Part of the Brain, 1987, Neurons and Networks: An Introduction to Neuroscience, 1992; contbr. numerous articles on vision to profl. jours. Recipient ann. award N.E. Ophthal. Soc., 1979, award of merit Retina Research Found., 1981, Prentice medal Am. Acad. Optometry, 1991, Von Sallman prize, 1992. Fellow Am. Acad. Arts and Scis., AAAS; mem. Am. Philos. Soc., Assn. Rsch. in Vision and Ophthalmology (Friedenwald medal 1970), Nat. Acad. Sci., Neurosci. Soc., Soc. Gen. Physiologists. Home: Master's Lodgings Leverett House 25 De Wolfe St Cambridge MA 02138 Office: Harvard U Biology Labs Cambridge MA 02138

DOWLING, JOSEPH LEO, JR., ophthalmologist; b. Providence, R.I., Sept. 11, 1926; s. Joseph Leo and Ruth Winifred (Tappan) D.; m. Sarah Agnes Trenkamp, July 28, 1962; children: Joseph III, Robert T., Charles T., Ruth T. AB, Brown U., 1947; MD, Tufts U., 1950. Diplomate Am. Bd. Ophthalmology. Ophthalmologist R.I. Eye Inst., Providence, 1957—; assoc. clin. prof. ophthalmology Brown U. Med. Sch., Providence, 1978—. Contbr. articles to profl. jours. Bd. chmn. Trinity Repertory Co., Providence, 1968-72; trustee Brown U., Providence, 1980-85, Butler Hosp., Providence, 1984-89. Lt. USNR, 1952-54. Recipient Best Original Presentation AMA Sect. on Ophthalmology, 1960. Fellow Am. Acad. Ophthalmology; mem. New Eng. Ophthalmol. Soc. (pres.). Office: RI Eye Inst 150 E Manning St Providence RI 02906-5109

DOWLING, ROBERT M(AXWELL), clinical psychologist; b. East Orange, N.J., Jan. 17, 1933; s. John Joseph and Margaret C. (Maxwell) D.; m. Vince Veltri, Feb. 5, 1955; children: Karen E., Robert D., Jennifer S., Thomas P., Michael J. AB, Gannon Coll., 1954; MS, U. Pitts., 1956; PhD, Clark U., 1962. Clin. psychologist DePaul Clinic, Rochester, N.Y., 1961-63; assoc. prof. Cath. U. Am., Washington, 1963-70; prof. psychology dept. Edinboro U. Pa., 1970-95; pvt. practice Psychology Assocs. Greater Erie, Pa., 1971—; spl. cons. in psychology Clin. Ctr., NIH, Washington, 1964-70; mem. adv. bd. Erie County Office Mental Health, Erie, 1972-75; mem., vice chmn., chmn. Erie County Commn. on Drug and Alcohol Abuse, 1973-79; mem., pres. N.W. Pa. Cleft Palate Inst., Erie, 1977—. Contbr. articles to sci. jours. 1st lt. U.S. Army, 1956-58. Fellow Pa. Psychol. Assn. (profl. stds. rev. com. 1975-80); mem. APA, Assn. for Applied Psychophysiology and Biofeedback, Am. Cleft Palate Assn., Behavioral Medicine and Biofeedback Soc. Pa., Nat. Register Health Svc. Providers in Psychology. Office: Psychol Assocs Greater Erie 2005 W 8th St Ste 202 Erie PA 16505

DOWLING, THOMAS JOSEPH, JR., orthopedist; b. N.Y.C.. BA, MD, Boston U., 1981. Diplomate Am. Bd. Orthop. Surgery. Resident surgery North Shore Univ. Hosp., Manhasset, N.Y., 1981-83; resident orthop. surgery SUNY, Stony Brook, 1983-87, U. Toronto, Ont., 1987-88; pvt. practice Smithtown, N.Y., 1988-92; orthop. spine surgeon L.I. Spine Specialists, P.C., Commack, N.Y., 1992—. Med. editor: Orthopaedic Index, 1985-88; contbr. articles to profl. jours., chpts. to books. Mem. transition team on health policy Gov. of N.Y., 1994-95. Fellow Am. Acad. Orthop. Surgeons, N.Am. Spine Soc.; mem. AMA, Suffolk County Med. Soc., N.Y. State Med. Soc., N.Y. State Soc. Orthop. Surgeons (dir. 1995—). Office: Long Island Spine Spec PC Ste 304 2171 Jericho Turnpike Commack NY 11725

DOWLING, W. LAINE, health medical products executive; b. Ann Arbor, Mich., June 11, 1966; s. William Laine and Sandra (Winsby) D.; m. Mary Margaret Eddy, May 23, 1992. BS in econs., Univ. Washington, 1988, M in health adminstrn., 1993. Mgr. Seattle Medical Care, Seattle, 1989-91; owner/cons. W. Laine Dowling Cons. Co., Seattle, 1990-93; sr. cons. Arthur Andersen LLP, Seattle, 1993-94; CEO Madrona Medical Group PS, Bellingham, Wash., 1995—. Contbr. article to profl. jours. Office: Madrona Medical Group PS 4370 Cordata Pkwy Bellingham WA 98226

DOWLING, WALTER JAY, psychology educator, researcher; b. Washington, Feb. 4, 1941; s. Walter James and Amrie (Donovan) D.; m. Caroline Monahan, June, 1963 (div. 1971); m. C. Darlene Smith, Jan. 1976; children: Calla Krista, Erica Lenée. BA, Northwestern U., 1963; MA, Harvard U., 1965, PhD, 1968. Asst. prof. UCLA, 1966-73, Calif. State U., L.A., 1973-75; asst. prof. U. Tex., Dallas, 1975-78, assoc. prof., 1978-89, prof., 1989—, chmn. psychology, 1987—, chmn. applied cognition and neurosci., 1990—; chmn. cognitive sci., 1992—; mem. adv. panel Internat. Conf. on Psychology and Arts, Cardiff, Wales, 1983. Co-author: Music Cognition, 1986; assoc. editor jour. Music Perception, 1995— Psychomusicology, 1981—; translater book The Perception of Music, 1988. Fellow Woodrow Wilson Found., 1963. Fellow Acoustical Soc. Am.; mem. Am. Psychol. Assn., Psychonomic Soc., Psi Chi, Sigma Xi. Democrat. Home: 804 Bristol Ct Richardson TX 75080-6913 Office: U Tex at Dallas Psychology Program Richardson TX 75083-0688

DOWNER, WILLIAM JOHN, JR., retired hospital administrator, consultant; b. Springfield, Ill., Sept. 29, 1932; s. William J. Sr. and Geraldine (Foster) D.; m. Wanda M. Parson, Oct. 3, 1953; children: William E., Lawrence R. BA, Mich. State U., 1954; M in Hosp. Adminstrn., U. Mich., 1961. Various mgmt. positions Blodgett Meml. Med. Ctr., Grand Rapids, Mich., 1961-74; pres., CEO Blodgett Meml. Med. Ctr., Grand Rapids, 1974-84; pres., chief exec. officer Columbus Hosp., Great Falls, Mont., 1985-95, sr. cons., 1995—; bd. dirs. First Interstate Bank, Great Falls. Contbr. articles to profl. jours. City commr. City of Gt. Falls, 1996—; hosp. divsn. chmn. United Way Kent County, Grand Rapids, 1969; elder Westminster Presbyn. Ch., Grand Rapids, 1968-85, 1st Presbyn. Ch., Great Falls, 1985—; mem. cmty. adv. bd. NW Mont. for Horizon Air, 1990—; bd. dirs. No. Rockies Easter Seals/Goodwill, 1995—; bd. dirs. Big Sky chpt. ARC, 1986-92, 96—. Lt. col. U.S. Army, ret. Fellow Am. Coll. Healthcare Execs. (life, regent for Mich. 1978-84, regent for Mont. 1986-89); mem. Am. Hosp. Assn. (life, mem. governing coun. sect. for met. hosps. 1991-94), Healthcare Forum, Mont. Hosp. Assn. (bd. dirs. 1987-90, chmn. 1989), Mich. Hosp. Assn. (bd. dirs. 1973-82, chmn. 1980-81, Homminga award 1982), Great Falls C. of C. (mem. exec. com. 1988, chmn. 1991-92), Rotary, Phi Kappa Phi, Beta Gamma Sigma. Home: 2719 Evergreen Dr Great Falls MT 59404-3635 Office: City of Great Falls Civic Ctr 2 S Park Dr Great Falls MT 59403-5021

DOWNES, JOHN J., physician, anesthesiologist; b. Pitts., Sept. 14, 1930; s. John Joseph and Lenore Marie (King) D.; m. JoAnn Carol Splon, June 14, 1956; children: Margaret, Katherine, John, Peter. BS, St. Louis U., 1952; MD, Loyola U., Chgo., 1956. Diplomate Am. Bd. Anesthesiology. Intern Indpls. Gen. Hosp., 1956-57; with div. Indian Health USPHS, 1957-59; resident dept. anesthesia U. Pa., Phila., 1959-63, fellow in clin. pharmacology, 1961-63, prof. anesthesia and pediatrics, 1973—; anesthesiologist-in-chief Children's Hosp. of Phila., 1972—. Contbr. chpts to books, articles to profl. jours.; mem. edit. bd. Anesthesiology, 1982-87. U.S. del. Internat. Standard, 1968—. Mem. Am. Soc. Anesthesiology, Soc. for Pediatric Anesthesia (bd. dirs. 1986-90), Soc. for Critical Care Medicine (founding mem., com. mem. 1988-90, Shubin-Weil award 1990), Physicians for Social Responsibility (nat. bd. dirs. 1995—). Office: Children's Hosp of Phila 34th St and Civic Ctr Blvd Philadelphia PA 19104

DOWNEY, JOAN CAROL, counselor; b. Waupun, Wis., Aug. 22, 1931; d. Lawrence Clarence and Johanna Gertude (VerMeer) Treffert; m. James Howard Downey, May 5, 1950 (dec. Mar. 1980); children: James, Linda, Roxe Ann, Jon. BS in Psychology cum laude, U. Wis.-Parkside, Kenosha, 1988. Cost acct. Twin Disc Corp., Racine, Wis., 1950-53; v.p. Treffert Trucking Inc., Racine, 1970-83; crisis counselor victim response unit Dist. Atty.'s Office, Racine, 1987—. Hospice vol., counselor St. Luke's Hosp., Racine, 1983-84; vol., counselor Women's Resource Ctr., Racine, 1986-87; gerontology researcher U. Wis., Kenosha, 1987-88; mem. campaign com. Rep. party, Racine, 1988; pres. PTA, Racine; mem. growth and fellowship com. First Reformed Ch.; mem. S.A.L.T. coun. Triad, Racine County Coun. Mem. U. Wis.-Parkside Alumni Assn., Psi Chi (pres. 1986-89, outstanding mem. 1986-89). Republican. Home: 941 Kentwood Dr Racine WI 53402-1955 Office: Harbor Med and Assocs 4810 Northwestern Ave Racine WI 53406

DOWNEY, JOHN ALEXANDER, physician, educator; b. Sept. 16, 1930. B.Sc. (Med.), U. Man., M.D. with honors, 1954; PhD, Oxford U., 1962. Diplomate Am. Bd. Phys. Medicine and Rehab. Intern, Vancouver Gen. Hosp., B.C., Can., 1953-54; resident phys. medicine and rehab. Columbia Presbyn. Med. Ctr., N.Y.C., 1954-56, resident, 1957-58; asst. resident internal medicine Peter Bent Brigham Hosp., Boston, 1956-57; asst. to med. dir., cons. phys. medicine Blythedale Children's Hosp., Valhalla, N.Y., 1957-59; research assoc. Columbia U. and vis. fellow Presbyn. Hosp., N.Y.C., 1958-59; sr. resident internal medicine Peter Bent Brigham Hosp., 1959-60; vis. worker Med. Research Council Group for Body Temperature Control, Oxford, Eng., 1960-62; asst. prof. rehab. medicine Columbia U. Coll. Physicians and Surgeons, 1962-64, assoc. prof., 1964-67, prof., 1967-74, Simon Baruch prof., 1974—, chair dept. rehab. medicine, 1974-90, asst. prof. medicine, 1963-64; asst. attending Presbyn. Hosp., N.Y.C., 1962-64, assoc. attending, 1964-68, attending, 1968—, dir. rehab. medicine svc., 1974-90; vis. prof. dept. human physiology and pharmacology U. Adelaide, Australia, 1969. Author: Stroke: Two to Recover, 1969, 2nd. edit. 1994; also articles. Co-editor: Physiological Basis of Rehabilitation Medicine, 1971, 2d edit., 1994; The Child with Disabling Illness: Principles of Rehabilitation, 1974, 2d edit., 1982; Bereavement of Physical Disability: Recommitment to Life, Health and Function, 1982; editorial bd. Brenneman's Practice of Pediatrics, 1974. Films: Rehabilitation: A Patient's Perspective, 1973; I Had a Stroke, 1978; Physiatry: A Physician's Perspective, 1981. Diplomate Am. Bd. Phys. Medicine and Rehab. Fellow Royal Coll. Physicians (Can.); mem. Inst. Medicine of NAS, AAAS, AMA, APA, Am. Congress Rehab. Medicine, Am. Acad. Phys. Medicine and Rehab., Assn. Acad. Physiatrists, Am. Rheumatism Assn., N.Y. Rheumatism Assn., N.Y. Acad. Scis., N.Y. Acad. Medicine, N.Y. Soc. Phys. Medicine and Rehab., Med. Soc. N.Y. State, New York County Med. Soc., Internat. Rehab. Medicine Assn., Internat. Med. Soc. of Paraplegia. Office: Columbia U Dept Rehab Medicine Coll Physicians New York NY 10032

DOWNEY, ROBERT M., respiratory therapist; b. Greeley, Colo., Aug. 9, 1958; s. Osborne Madison and Verna Mae (Hutt) D.; m. Cinthia Ann Bacon, June 5, 1977; children: Robert M. Jr., Bradley, Michael, Robin. Cert EMT, Colo.; registered respiratory therapist Nat. Bd. for Respiratory Care. EMT, Weld County (Colo) Ambulance, 1985-93; staff respiratory therapist St. Anthony Hosp., Denver, 1993-94; staff respiratory therapist No. Colo. Med. Ctr., Greeley, 1994—, profl. chmn. for respiratory svcs., 1995. Mem. Am. Assn. Respiratory Care, Colo. Soc. Respiratory Care. Home: 215 N 4th St La Salle CO 80645 Office: No Colo Med Ctr 1801 16th St Greeley CO 80631-5154

DOWNIE, PAMELA, psychologist; b. Chester, Calif., Dec. 1, 1954; d. William John and June (De La Mont) D. BA, Widener U., 1980; MS, Villanova U., 1985; PhD, U. So. Calif., 1995. Counselor, trainer Del. County C.C., Media, Pa., 1985-87; counselor, instr. New Beginnings, Media, Pa., 1986-87; tchg. asst. U. So. Calif., 1989-91, instr. practicum, 1991, psychol. intern. Student Counseling Ctr., 1991-93; staff psychologist U. San Diego, 1994-95; lectr. Calif. State U., Fullerton, 1995-96, asst. prof., 1996—. Mem. APA (student), NAFE, AACD, Am. Mental Health Coun. Assn., Assn. for Multicultural Counseling, Pa. Counselors Assn., Assn. for Specialists in Group Work, Assn. for Coun. Edn. and Supervision. Home: PO Box 660582 Arcadia CA 91066-0582 Office: Calif State U Fullerton Dept Counseling EC-105 Fullerton CA 91066

DOWNING, JACQY LESLEY HARRISON, nursing home administrator, educator; b. Stone, Stafford, Eng., July 17, 1941; d. J. Norman Standage and Murielle Mercer (Wood) Harrison; m. Robert Downing, Nov. 28, 1970; children: Russell John, Robert Gordon. AA summa cum laude, Barstow (Calif.) Coll., 1974; ASN, Grossmont Coll., 1978; BSN, Regents Coll., 1984; MBA, Nat. U., 1986. RN, Calif.; lic. nursing home administr., Calif. Nurse critical care transport unit Schaeffer Ambulance, San Diego; nursing supr., nurse emergency rm. Valley Med. Ctr., El Cajon, Calif.; nursing adminstr., quality assurance coord. Inland Valley Regional Med. Ctr., Wildomar, Calif.; health care adminstr. Golden State Manor Nursing and Rehab. Ctr., San Diego, to 1995, Las Villas del Norte Health Ctr., Escondido, Calif., 1995-96; coord. clin. quality mgmt. Found. Health Fed. Svcs., 1996—. Republican. Home: 13225 Alpine Dr Poway CA 92064-5716

DOWNING, JOHN EDWARD, ophthalmologist; b. Flippin, Ky., Aug. 3, 1937; s. J. Maurice and Isabel (Wallace) D.; m. Sheryl Magee, Feb. 14, 1978. BS in Biology, Baylor U., 1959; MD, U. Louisville Sch. Medicine, 1962. Diplomate Nat. Bd. Med. Examiners. Intern Parkland Meml. Hosp., Dallas, 1962-63; resident in ophthalmology Naval Hosp. and Wills Eye Hosp., Phila, 1966-69; flight surgeon USN, 1963-71; capt. USNR, 1971-85; staff mem. ophthalmology Greenview Hosp., 1972—; pvt. practice ophthalmology Bowling Green, Ky., 1971—; assoc. staff Med. Ctr. Bowling Green, Ky.; cons. staff Vets. Hosp., Nashville; asst. clin. prof. ophthalmology Vanderbilt U., U. Louisville. Fellow Am. Acad. Ophthalmology, ACS; mem. AMA, Am. Soc. Cataract and Refractive Surgery, Ky. Med. Assn., Tri-County Med. Soc. (pres. 1978), Ky. Acad. Eye Physicians and Surgeons (pres. 1982, legis. chmn. 1983-85, sec.-treas. 1994—), So. Med. Assn., Internat. Transactional Analysis Assn. Office: PO Box 20340 Bowling Green KY 42102-6340

DOWNING, RICHARD, surgeon; b. Stourbridge, West Midlands, U.K., Feb. 8, 1951; s. John Clifford and Greta Irene (Kelley) D.; m. Stella Elizabeth Kolada, July 24, 1976; children: Benjamin Louis, Thomas Kolada, Alice Elizabeth Gwendoline, Lily Anastazia. BSc in Physiology, Birmingham (Eng.) U., 1972, MB ChB in Pharmacology and Therapeutics with honors, 1975, MD, 1983. Lectr. in anatomy Birmingham (Eng.) U., 1976-77, lectr. in surgery, 1983-86, sr. lectr. in surgery, 1986-90; rsch. assoc. Washington U., St. Louis, 1977-78; registrar Ctrl. Birmingham Health Authority, 1979-80; registrar Worcester (Eng.) Royal Infirmary, 1980-83, cons. vascular surgeon, 1990—; advisor in surgery Internat. Hosps. Group, 1987-90. Mem. editl. bd. Internat. Jour. Care of the Injured, 1990-96; contbr. articles to profl. jours. Rsch. grantee Novo Labs., U.K., 1984, Diabetes Found., U.K., 1986-96, West Midlands RHA, U.K., 1993. Fellow Royal Coll. Surgeons of Eng. (examiner 1989-95, cert. in higher surg. tng. 1986), Assn. Surgeons Great Britain and Ireland; mem. Vascular Soc. Great Britain and Ireland, European Soc. Vascular Surgery. Home: 46 Lark Hill, Worcester WR5 2EQ, England Office: Worcester Royal Infirmary, Newtown Rd, Worcester WR5 1HN, England

DOWNING, SAMUEL WILLIAM, family practice physician; b. Phila., Apr. 5, 1959; s. Samuel william and Patricia Carolyn (Offutt) D.; m. Leigh Ann Hanscom, Apr. 28, 1984; children: Jeffrey Houston, Kathryn Leigh. BA, Colo. Coll., 1981; MD, U. Colo., 1985. Diplomate Am. Bd. Family Practice. Staff physician Prescott (Ariz.) Family Practice, 1989—; asst. med. dir. Meadowpark Care Ctr., Prescott, Ariz., 1990-94, med. dir., 1994-95; med. dir. Yavapai Med. Hospice, Prescott, Ariz., 1994—; med. dir. Prescott HIV Clinic, 1995—. Vol. physician Prescott Free Clinic, 1994—; bd. mem. Prescott Child Devel. Ctr., 1990-93, Drug Task Force, 1992-95. Fellow Am. Acad. Family Practice; mem. AMA, Alpha Omega Alpha. Democrat. Methodist. Office: Prescott Family Practice 999 Division St Prescott AZ 86301

DOWNING, WILLIAM MYRON, retired physician; b. Glouersville, N.Y., Sept. 2, 1907; s. William Henry and Madge (Gorton) B.; m. Evelyn W. Kirshbaum, Aug. 19, 1950 (div. 1974); children: Jill, Lee, Jeff, Greg; m. Janice Marie Mulkern, 1975. BA, U. Mich., 1931; MD, Boston U., 1937. Diplomate Am. Bd. Surgery. Surgeon Sturdy Meml. Hosp., Attleboro, Mass., 1949-84; pvt. practice Attleboro, 1984-94; ret., 1994. Capt. U.S. Army, 1942-46, ETO. Mem. ACS, Boston Surg. Soc., Mass. Med. Soc., Bristol North Dist. Med. Soc. Home: R-2 Box 311 Milo ME 04462-9633

DOWNS, AMY LOUISE, psychologist; b. Glen Cove, N.Y., Nov. 10, 1956; d. Chester and Hannah Jacqueline (Kaufman) Burger; m. Donald Allen Downs, June 27, 1993. BS, U. Iowa, 1979; MA, U. N.C., 1985, PhD, 1987. Lic. psychologist, N.C. Intern in clin. psychology W.S. Hall Psychiat. Inst., Columbia, S.C., 1984-85; staff psychologist John Umstead Hosp., Butner, N.C., 1987-90; sr. psychologist I in tng. Dorothea Dix Hosp., Raleigh, N.C., 1988; sr. psychologist Crossroads Mental Health, Yadkinville, N.C., 1991, cons., 1991-95. Mem. Am. Psychol. Assn., N.C. Psychol. Assn., Phi Beta Kappa.

DOWNS, BRIAN JEFFREY, family physician; b. Chgo., Feb. 18, 1958; s. Richard James and sylvia Patricia (Poley) D.; m. Marietta Abarca Quiros, June 16, 1994; 1 child, Brian Jeffrey Jr. ADN, Triton Coll., River Grove, Ill., 1983; BA, Northeastern Ill. U., Chgo., 1984; MBA, Rosary Coll., 1986; DO, Nova Southeastern U., 1996. RN, Ill.; cert. respiratory therapist. Respiratory therapist MacNeal Meml. Hosp., Berwyn, Ill., 1979-80; supr. respiratory care Children's Meml. Hosp., Chgo., 1980-83; clin. and classroom instr. respiratory care Triton Coll., River Grove, Ill., 1983-85; staff nurse ICU, CCU LaGrange (Ill.) Meml. Hosp., 1985-86; supr. respiratory ICU Holy Cross Hosp., Chgo., 1986-87; supr. neonatal ICU Kapiolami Med. Ctr., Honolulu, 1987-92; family practice resident Riverside Regional Med. Ctr., Newport News, 1992—. Nat. Health Svc. Corps scholar, 1992-96. Mem. AMA, Am. Osteo.. Assn., Am. Assn. Family Practitioners, Am. Assn. Osteo. Family Practitioners. Democrat. Home: 2417 Leyden Ave River Grove IL 60171

DOWNS, CORNELIA MARIE, nursing administrator; b. Bielefeld, Germany, Sept. 19, 1954; d. Gerhard Ralph and Margarete Louisa (Rosner) Heide; m. Christopher James Downs, Aug. 9, 1975; children: Erik Gerhard, Kiersten Heide. Attended, Elmira Coll., 1972-73, SUNY, Binghamton, 1973-74; diploma, Binghamton Gen. Sch. Nursing, 1977. Cert. gerontol. nurse. Coronary care nurse Binghamton Gen. Hosp., 1977-79; night supr. Sarnac Lake (N.Y.) Gen. Hosp., 1979-84; resident care coord. Good Shepherd Fairview Home, Binghamton, 1984-90; unit care coord., night supr. Ideal Nursing Ctr., Endicott, N.Y., 1990-94; asst. dir. nursing Hilltop Retirement Cmty., Johnson City, N.Y., 1994—. Recipient Professionalism award Endicott Woman's Club, 1972, Nurse of Yr. award Binghamton Gen. Sch., 1977. Home: RR Box 64A Tiffany Rd Friendsville PA 18818 Office: Hilltop Retirement Cmty 286 Deyo Hill Rd Johnson City NY 13760

DOWNS, KATHLEEN ANNE, healthcare consultant; b. Toledo, Sept. 20, 1951; d. Keith Landis and Cecelia Josephine (Wood) Babcock; m. Michael Brian Thomas, July 17, 1971 (dec. Oct. 1973); m. David Michael Downs, Aug. 8, 1981. Student, San Diego Mesa Coll., 1968-70; BS, Union Inst., 1989. Cert. med. staff coordinator. Sec. Travelodge Internat., Inc., El Cajon, Calif., 1970-73; intermediate stenographer City of El Cajon, 1973-77; adminstrv. asst. MacLellan & Assocs., El Cajon, 1977-78; sr. sec. WESTEC Services, Inc., San Diego, 1978; adminstrv. sec. El Cajon Valley Hosp., 1978-80; asst. med. staff Grossmont Dist. Hosp., La Mesa, Calif., 1980-83, coord. med. staff, 1983-87, mgr., 1987-94; mgr. med. staff Sharp Meml. Hosp., San Diego, 1994; dir. med. staff svcs. Sharp HealthCare, San Diego, 1994-96, sr. specialist med. staff svcs., 1996—; dir. med. staff svcs. Alvarado Hosp. Med. Ctr., San Diego, 1996—; tchr. The Vogel Inst., San Diego, 1986; mem. med. staff svcs. adv. com. San Diego Cmty. Dist.; adj. faculty Union Inst., 1991—, Chemeketa C.C., 1991-95; mem. credentials verification orgn. surveyor Nat. Com. Quality Assurance, Washington, 1996—. Mem. Nat. Assn. Med.. Staff Svcs. (edn. coun. 1989-93, chmn. 1991-93, bd. dirs. 1991-93, editl. bd. Over View 1993-96, lectr., spkr.), Calif. Assn. Med. Staff Svcs. (treas. San Diego chpt. 1984-86, pres. 1986-87). Office: Alvarado Hosp Med Ctr 6655 Alvarado Rd San Diego CA 92120

DOWNS, RICHARD TINSLEY, school counselor; b. Fort Clayton, Canal Zone, Panama, May 2, 1947; s. Richard Joseph and Lola Jean (Tinsley) D.; 1 child, Richard William. BS, U. Tex., 1975, ME, 1979. Lic. profl. counselor; registered profl. ednl. diagnostician. Spl. edn. tchr. El Paso (Tex.) Ind. Sch. Dist., 1975-79, ednl. diagnostician, 1979-81, spl. edn. counselor, 1981-90; elem. sch. counselor Hillsborough County Schs., Plant City, Fla., 1990—; mem. profl. bd. advisors El Paso Assn. Children with Learning Disabilities, 1986-90; bd. dirs. Trans. Pecos Assn. for Counseling and Devel., 1982-90. Co-author: Administrative Guide for Public Law 94-142, 1978, Texas Evaluation Model for Professional School Counselors, 1990; mem. editl. bd. Elem Sch. Guidance and Counseling, 1996—. Mem. Fla. PTA. Mem. DAV, Fla. Counseling Assn., Fla. Sch. Counselors Assn. (pres.-elect 1996—), Fla. Assn. Specialists in Group Work (exec. bd. dirs.). Home: 4939 Puritan Cir Tampa FL 33617-8356 Office: Bryan Elementary School Plant City FL 33567

DOWTY, MARTIN EUGENE, pharmaceutical researcher; b. Waukesha, Wis., Feb. 14, 1963; s. Eugene Thomas and Virginia Leigh (Klein) D.; m. Heather Vogel, June 18, 1994. BS in Pharmacy, U. Wis., 1986, MS in Pharmaceutics, 1988, PhD in Pharmaceutics, 1991. Author: (with others) Drug Delivery via the Oral Mucosa, 1989, Possible Mechanisms of DNA Uptake in Skeletal Muscle, 1994; contbr. articles to profl. jours. Mem. Sigma Xi. Office: Proctor & Gamble Co Miami Valley Labs PO Box 398707 Cincinnati OH 45239-8707

DOYLE, BRIAN BOWLES, psychiatrist; b. Boston, May 20, 1941; s. Joseph Bernard and Margaret (Kelley) D.; m. Margaret Mary Ready, Oct. 4, 1975; children: Mairin McCready, Cavan Kelley, Colin Calnan. BA magna cum laude, Harvard U., 1962; MD, McGill U. 1966. Diplomate Am. Bd. Psychiatry and Neurology. Resident in psychiatry Mass. Mental Health Ctr., Boston, 1967-70; clin. prof. psychiatry Georgetown Med. Sch., Washington, 1983—, dir. anxiety disorders program, 1993—; pvt. practice, Washington, 1972—. Maj. U.S. Army, 1970-72. Fellow Am. Psychiat. Assn. Democrat. Roman Catholic. Office: 1325 18th St NW Apt 209 Washington DC 20036-6511

DOYLE, CONSTANCE TALCOTT JOHNSTON, physician, educator; b. Mansfield, Ohio, July 8, 1945; d. Frederick Lyman IV and Nancy Jean Bushnell (Johnston) Talcott; m. Alan Jerome Demsky, June 13, 1976; children: Ian Frederick Demsky, Zachary Adam Demsky. BS, Ohio U., 1967; MD, Ohio State U., 1971. Diplomate Am. Bd. Emergency Medicine. Intern Riverside Hosp., Columbus, Ohio, 1971-72; resident in internal medicine Hurley Hosp., U. Mich., Flint, 1972-74; emergency physician Oakwood Hosp., Dearborn, Mich., 1974-76, Jackson County (Mich.) Emergency Svcs., 1975-95; core faculty St. Joseph Merch Hosp./U. Mich. Emergency Residency, Ann Arbor, 1995—; attending emergency physician St. Joseph Mercy Hosp., Ann Arbor, 1995—; cons. Region II EMS, 1978-79, disaster cons., co-chmn. emergency med. svcs. disaster com., 1983-95; St. Joseph Mercy Hosp., Ann Arbor, 1995—; survival flight physician helicopter rescue svc. U. Mich., 1983-91; course dir. advanced cardiac life support and chmn. advanced life support com. W.A. Foote Meml. Hosp., Jackson, 1979-85; clin. instr. emergency svcs., dept. surgery U. Mich., 1981—; faculty combined emergency medicine residency St. Joseph Mercy Hosp.-U. Mich., Ann Arbor, 1995—; instr. EMT refresher courses, Jackson County, Jackson C.C. Contbg. author: Clinical Approach to Poisoning and Toxicology, 1983, 89, May's Textbook of Emergency Medicine, 1991, Schwartz Principles and Practice of Emergency Medicine, 1992, Reisdorff Pediatric Emergency Medicine, 1993; contbr. articles to profl. jours. Fellow Am. Coll. Emergency Physicians (pres. Mich. disaster com. 1987-88, bd. dirs. Mich. 1979-88, chmn. Mich. disaster com. 1979-85, mem. nat. disaster med. svcs. com. 1983-85, chmn. 1987-88, cons. disaster mgmt. course Fed. Emergency Mgmt Agy. 1982, treas. 1984-85, emergency med. svcs. com. 1985, pres. 1986-87, councillor 1986-87, chair steering com. policy sect., 1994—, mem. disaster sect., 1995—), Nat. Assn. Coll. Emergency Physicians (vice chair sect. of disaster med. svcs. 1990-92, nat. disaster subcom. 1989-90, chair subsection psychol. rehab. svcs., disaster med. svcs. 1992-94, chair policy and legis. 1994—, task force on hazardous materials 1993—, steering com. sect. disaster medicine 1994—, exec. com. sect. disaster medicine 1995—, sec. sect. careers in emergency medicine); mem. ACP, Am. Med. Women's Assn , Am. Assn. Women Emergency Physicians, Mich. Assn. Emergency Med. Technicians (bd. dirs. 1979-80), Mich. State Med. Soc., Washtenaw County Med. Soc., Sierra Club. Jewish. Home: 1665 Lansdowne Rd Ann Arbor MI 48105-1052 Office: St Joseph Mercy Hosp Dept Emergency Medicine Ann Arbor MI 48109

DOYLE, GERTRUDE ILEENE, hospital administrator; b. Monon, Ind., Feb. 14, 1933; d. Samuel Elmer and Goldia Mae (Raines) Johns; m. Leo Francis Doyle, Apr. 16, 1955; children—Leo Edward, Phillip Wayne. R.N., Methodist Hosp., 1954; B.S.N., Ind. U., 1970, M.S., 1975. R.N., Ind. Office nurse, Indpls., 1954-55; asst. head nurse urology Meth. Hosp., Indpls., 1955-56; occupational health nurse Western Electric Co., Indpls., 1959-68; clin. instr. cardiovascular nursing Meth. Hosp., 1970-75, patient instr. and coord. cardiovascular rehab. program, 1975-82, program developer, ednl. coordinator noninvasive testing and edn. dept., 1982-86; adminstr. Meth. Hosp. Ind., 1986-93, coord. managed care, HCFA-CABG project, 1993—; cons. program devel., cardiac rehab. vol., past mem. exec. com., past chmn. bd. dirs. Marion County chpt. Am. Heart Assn., past bd. dirs. Ind. affiliate Am. Heart Assn., also instr. basic cardiac life support. Mem. U. Alumni Assn., Meth. Hosp. Council Cardiovascular Nursing Assn., Am. Heart Assn. (recipient Vol. Instr. CPR 5-Yr. award, 1981). Democrat. Roman Catholic. Clubs: St. Michael's Ladies Aux. (Greenfield); Our Lady of Fatima Ladies Guild (Indpls.). Author: (with Jack Hall) Manual of Cardiovascular Rehabilitation, 1975. Home: 3469 Ravenfield Blvd Greenfield IN 46140 Office: Meth Hosp 1701 N Senate Ave Indianapolis IN 46202-1239

DOYLE, JENNIFER, surgical educator, scholar; b. Milw., Aug. 23, 1952; d. Sylvester Edward and Ethel Anna (Axmann) D. BA, Mt. Mary Coll., 1974; MA, U. Wis., Milw., 1979; postgrad., Brown U., 1979-84. Grad. tchg. asst. U. Wis., 1977-79; fellow Brown U., Providence, 1979-80, grad. teaching asst., 1981-84; adj. instr. Bryant Coll., Smithfield, R.I., 1985; adj. instr. history R.I. Coll., Providence, 1986-90; residency coord. dept. family medicine Brown U., Providence, 1986-87, edn. coord. dept. surgery, 1987-90; assoc. surgery Harvard Med. Sch., Boston, 1990-92, lectr. in surgery, 1992—; asst. dir. surg. edn. Deaconess Hosp., Boston, 1990—. Dem. committeeman, Wauwatosa, Wis., 1976-78; mem. Big Sisters of R.I., Providence, 1980-88; co-organizer Providence Freeze Coalition, 1982. Recipient Charles Edison Meml. fellowship, 1974, Lucetta Bissell Meml. fellowship, 1978, univ. fellowship Brown U., 1979, Wayland Collegium fellowship Brown U., 1988. Mem. Am. Ednl. Rsch. Assn., Assn. Am. Med. Colls., Assn. Surg. Edn., Assn. Program Dirs. in Surgery (assoc.), Assn. of Women Surgeons (assoc.), Assn. for Study of Med. Edn. (U.K.), Generalists in Med. Edn., Am. Evaluation Assn., AAUW, Mass. Consort. on Faculty Devel. Home: 219 Willow St West Roxbury MA 02132-1326 Office: Deaconess-Harvard Surg Svc 110 Francis St Ste 3A Boston MA 02215

DOYLE, JOSEPH THEOBALD, physician, educator; b. Providence, June 11, 1918; s. Joseph Donald and Gertrude Harriet (Theobald) D.; m. Elizabeth Thompson, Dec. 26, 1944 (dec.); children: Shelagh Thompson, Michael Kedian; m. Joan Gleason Mastrianni, Dec. 30, 1976. A.B., Harvard U., 1939, M.D., 1943. Successively intern, asst. resident, chief resident in medicine Harvard Med. Service, Boston City Hosp., 1943-44, 47-49; Whitehead fellow in physiology, asst. in medicine and physiology Emory U. Med. Sch., 1950-52; assoc. in medicine Duke U. Med. Sch., 1952; mem. faculty Albany (N.Y.) Med. Coll., 1952—, prof. medicine, 1961—, head div. cardiology, 1961-84, dir. cardiovascular health center, 1952-90, head pvt. diagnostic clinic, 1957-82; cons. Albany VA Med. Center, 1962-1991. Author papers in field. Served as 1st lt. M.C. AUS, 1944-45. Fellow A.C.P., Am. Coll. Cardiology; mem. AMA, Am. Heart Assn. (chmn. council epidemiology 1969-71), Assn. Univ. Cardiologists, N.Y. Heart Assembly (pres. 1968-69), Med. Soc. County of Albany (pres. 1971-72). Presbyterian. Clubs: Ft. Orange, Schuyler Meadows. Home: 17 Lenox Ave Albany NY 12203-2005 Office: Albany Med Coll Albany NY 12208

DOYLE, JUDITH ANN, corporate executive, psychosocial consultant; b. L.A., Aug. 18, 1943; d. Raymond Ross Manley and Sarah Virginia (Fletcher) Manley Flint; life ptnr. Shelley Ann Doyle; children: Brennan Corey, Melody Rae. BA, Calif. State U.-Long Beach, 1975, MS, 1977. Registered hypnotherapist; ordained minister Universal Life Ch. Counselor Calif. State U., Long Beach, 1976-78; case mgmt. supr. Bridge/Boys Club, Wilmington, Calif., 1978-80, ElMonte Sr. Citizens Ctr., Calif., 1979-81; dir. counseling svcs. Gay/Lesbian Community Svc. Ctr., Orange County, Calif., 1985-88; owner, therapist Judith Doyle MFCC, Long Beach, 1978-90; cons. AIDS Response Program, Garden Grove, Calif., 1985-90; med. adv. bd. AIDS Svc. Found., Costa Mesa, Calif., 1985-88; exec. dir. One in Long Beach Inc., 1988-90; exec. dir. Marisol, Inc., 1990-92; with Doyle Enterprise, 1990—; exec. dir. Laguna Shanti, 1992-93; Golden mem. Long Beach Lambda Dem. Club, 1980—; chmn. So. Calif. Women for Understanding, L.A., 1981-85; active Orange County HIV Planning Adv. Coun., 1992-93; co-chair Orange County Regional LIFE Lobby, 1993; pres., bd. dirs. Long Beach Lesbian and Gay Pride, Inc., 1983-88; co-chair, founder AIDS Walk Long Beach, 1988-90; apptd. mem. Calif. State Commn. Econ. Devel. Task Force, 1984-85; trustee L. Diane Anderson Meml. Trust, 1984—. Recipient Woman of Yr. award Lambda Dem. Club, 1981, Christopher Street West, 1986, Disting. Community Leadership award, 1989, Spl. Person award Press/Telegram, 1985, Myra Riddell Svc. award So. Calif. Women for Understanding, 1985, Community Mentor award Orange County Blade Mag., 1993, Community Grand Marshal award 10th Annual Long Beach Lesbian & Gay Pride Parade, 1993. Mem. NAFE, ACLU, Calif. Assn. Marriage and Family Therapists (bd. dirs. 1981-85, pres. 1985-86, named Disting. Clin. Mem. 1988), Greenpeace, Human Right Campaign, Gay and Lesbian Assn. Against Defamation (mem. human rights campaign fund), Nat. Mus. of the Am. Indian, Smithsonian Instn., People for the Am. Way, Nat. Mus. Women in the Arts (charter). Avocations: dancing, theatre, volleyball, softball. Address: 11278 Los Alamito Blvd Ste 154 Los Alamitos CA 90720-3244

DOYLE, MICHAEL PATRICK, food microbiologist, educator, administrator; b. Madison, Wis., Oct. 3, 1949; s. Donald Vincent and Evelyn (Bauer) D.; m. Annette Marie Ripple, Dec. 27, 1971; children: Michael Patrick, Patrick Matthew, Kristen Anne. BS in Bacteriology, U. Wis., 1973, MS in Food Microbiology, 1975, PhD in Food Microbiology, 1977. Sr. project leader Ralston Purina Co., St. Louis, 1977-80; asst. prof. U. Wis., Madison, 1980-84, assoc. prof., 1984-88, prof., 1988-91; prof., dir. U. Ga., Griffin, 1991—; dept. head U. Ga., Athens, 1993—; mem. food and nutrition bd. Inst. Medicine, NAS, 1991—; mem. nat. adv. com. on microbiol. criteria for foods USDA, Washington, 1988-90, 94—; trustee Internat. Life Scis. Inst.-N.Am., Washington, 1992—, sci. advisor, 1987—; mem. Internat. Commn. on Microbiol. Specifications for Foods, 1989—;Wis. disting. prof. bd. regents U. Wis., Madison, 1988-91; James M. Craig meml. lectr. Oreg. State U., Corvallis, 1990; sci. lectr. Am. Soc. Microbiology Found., 1991-93; Peter J. Shields lectr. U. Calif., Davis, 1993; G. Malcolm Trout vis. scholar Mich. State U., Lansing, 1994. Editor: Foodborne Bacterial Pathogens, 1989; contbr. articles to Applied and Environ. Microbiology, Jour. Food Protection, Internat. Jour. Food Microbiology, Jour. Clin. Microbiology. Recipient Am. Agrl. Econs. Assn. award for profl. excellence, 1992. Fellow Am. Acad. Microbiology; mem. Internat. Assn. Milk, Food and Environ. Sanitarians (pres. 1992-93, Norbert F. Sherman article excellence award 1993), Am. Soc. for Microbiology (chmn. food microbiology divsn. 1987-89, P.R. Edwards award for outstanding career achievements 1994), Inst. Food Technologists (Fred. W. Tanner lectr. 1986, sci. lectr. 1987-90, Samuel Cate Prescott award for rsch. 1987, Nicholas Appert award for preeminence in and contbns. to field of food tech. 1996), Phi Kappa Phi, Gamma Sigma Delta. Roman Catholic. Office: U Ga Ctr Food Safety Quality Enhancement Ga Expt Sta 1109 Experiment St Griffin GA 30223

DOYLE, MICHAEL QUINN, physician; b. Detroit, June 9, 1945; s. Glenn Francis and Alice Aileen (Quinn) D.; 1 child, Brian Quinn; m. Elizabeth Ann Tacey, May 17, 1980; 1 child, Megan Eileen. BS, U. Dayton, 1967; DO, Kans. City Coll. Osteo. Med., 1972. Rotating intern Pontiac (Mich.) Osteo. Hosp., 1972-75, residency dir. emergency medicine, 1979—. Contbr. articles to profl. jours. Fellow Am. Coll. Emergency Osteo. Physicians, Am. Coll. Emergency Physicians; mem. Soc. Acad. Emergency Physicians. Roman Catholic. Office: Pontiac Osteo Hosp 50 N Perry St Pontiac MI 48342

DOYLE, PATRICK JOHN, otolaryngologist; b. Moose Jaw, Sask., Can., Nov. 17, 1926; s. William E. and Bertha L. (Fisher) D.; m. Irene Strilchuk, May 21, 1949; children: Sharon, Patrick, Robert, Barbara, Joseph, Kathleen. B.Sc., U. Alta., 1947, M.D., 1949. Diplomate Am. Bd. Otolaryngology (bd. dirs., v.p. 1986-88, pres. 1988-90). Intern U. B.C. Hosp., 1949-50; resident in medicine and pediatrics, 1950-51; resident in otolaryngology U. Oreg. Hosp., 1958-61; asst. prof., then assoc. prof. U. Oreg. Med. Sch., 1965-70; mem. faculty U. B.C. Med. Sch., 1963—, prof. otolaryngology, 1972-91, prof. otolaryngology emeritus, 1992—, head dept., 1972-91, program dir. residency tng. program, 1972-91; head div. otolaryngology St. Paul's Hosp., mem. numerous nat. med. coms. Author numerous articles in field; mem. editorial bds. profl. jours. Fellow Royal Coll. Surgeons Can., Am. Laryngol., Rhinol. and Otol. Soc. (v.p. western sect. 1988, pres. 1994), Am. Laryngol. Soc., Am. Acad. Otolaryngology-Head and Neck Surgery (v.p. 1984, bd. dirs. 1985-87), Am. Otol. Soc.; mem. Can. Soc. Otolaryngology-Head and Neck Surgery (pres. 1987), Pacific Coast Oto-Ophthal. Soc. (pres. 1977), Soc. Univ. Otolaryngologists, U. Oreg. Otolaryngology Alumni Assn. (pres. 1968-70), Am. Otological Soc., Centurion Club, Tinnitus Rsch. Found. Roman Catholic. Office: 150-809 W 41st Ave, Vancouver, BC Canada V5Z 2N6

DOYLE, SHEILA WITMER, optometrist; b. Ridley Park, Pa., Oct. 14, 1948; d. Clement J. and Madeleine (Groff) McGovern. BS in Human Ecology and Biology summa cum laude, U. Md., 1970; OD, Pa. Coll. of Optometry, 1978. Optometrist Norwalk, Conn., 1984—. Mem. Am. Optometric Soc., Conn. Optometric Soc., Nat. Homeopathic Soc., Beta Sigma Kappa. Home: 8 Fort Point St # 2 Norwalk CT 06855-1034 Office: 281 Connecticut Ave Norwalk CT 06854-1938

DOZIER, GLENN JOSEPH, medical, surgical products distribution executive; b. Lexington, Ky., Apr. 7, 1950; s. Emmitt and Henrietta Elsie (Geisler) D.; m. Paula Jean Cook, June 3, 1974; children: Laura Jean, Diana Leigh. BS in Indsl. Enging. and Ops. Rsch., Va. Poly. Inst., 1972; MBA, U. Va., 1975. Mfg. engr. Tex. Instruments, Dallas, 1972-73; fin. analyst Dravo Corp., Pitts., 1975-76, mgr. corp. fin. analysis, 1976-79, dir. corp. devel., 1980-82, dir. corp. planning and devel., 1982-83; v.p. fin. Dravo Constructors, Inc., Pitts., 1983-87; chief fin. officer, treas., asst. sec. AMF Bowling Internat. Inc. and AMF Bowling, Inc., Richmond, Va., 1987-90; v.p., chief fin. officer, treas. Owens and Minor, Inc., Richmond, 1990-93, sr. v.p. ops. and systems, chief fin. officer, 1991-92, sr. v.p. fin., chief fin. officer, 1992—. Author: Economic Development Finance, 1986. Mem. Colonies Civic Assn. Mem. Nat. Assn. Accts., Colonies Swim and Tennis Club, Phi Eta Sigma, Alpha Pi Mu, Phi Kappa Phi, Tau Beta Pi. Republican. Methodist.

DRAAYER, SHARI LYNN, sociologist; b. Clorinda, Iowa, Dec. 11, 1948; d. Gerald and Barbara (McGregor) D; children (adopted): Ryan, Randy, Rodney, Gregory, Halle, Marcy, George. BA cum laude, Eastern Coll., St. Davids, Pa., 1987; MA in Sociology summa cum laude, Temple U., 1989, postgrad. Hotline counselor, trainer Aware Shelter & Emergency Counseling Ctr., Inc., Jackson, Mich., 1978-83; adminstrv. assoc. Foote Hosp., Jackson, 1982-83; counselor, night mgr. Laurel House, Montgomery County, Pa., 1984-87; teaching asst. Temple U., Phila., 1987-92; rsch. intern Women's Ctr. Montgomery County, Norristown, Pa., 1987-92; lectr. in Sociology Chestnut Hill Coll., Phila., 1988-93; intern clin. and forensic sociology Walden Counseling and Therapy Ctr., Bryn Mawr, Pa., 1989; clin. sociologist, dir. McGregor Counseling and Therapy Assocs., King of Prussia, 1981—; foster care social worker and parent trainer Luth. Children and Family Svcs., Upper Darby, Pa., 1993-95; adj. prof. Ea. Coll., Pa., 1991-92; specialized foster parent adoption and foster care agys., Utah, Mich., Pa. Mem. Am. Sociol. Assn., Sociol. Practice Assn.(mem. sociology of children sect.), Eastern Sociol. Assn. Office: Defenders Assn Phila Child Advocate Unit 70 N 17th St Philadelphia PA 19103 also: McGregor Counseling & Therapy Assocs Valley Forge Towers N Ste 642 King of Prussia PA 19406-1145

DRACH, JOHN CHARLES, scientist, educator; b. Cin., Sept. 25, 1939; s. Charles Louis and Edrie B. (Braun) D.; m. Elda Jean Flamm, June 20, 1964; children: Laura J., Diane E. BS in Pharmacy, U. Cin., 1961, MS in Pharm. Chemistry, 1963, PhD in Biochemistry, 1966. Assoc. rsch. scientist Parke, Davis and Co., Ann Arbor, Mich., 1966-69, rsch. scientist, 1969-70; asst. prof. Dental Sch. U. Mich., Ann Arbor, 1970-74, assoc. prof., 1974-80, prof., 1980—, assoc. prof. Sch. Pharmacy, 1978-80, prof., 1980—, chmn. dept. oral biology Dental Sch., 1985-87, chmn. dept. biologic and materials scis. Dental

Sch., 1987-95; vis. prof. divsn. virology Burroughs Wellcome Co., Research Triangle Park, N.C., 1994; cons. Adria Labs., Am. Inst. Chem., Am. Pharm. Assn., AMA, Chartwell, Kimberly-Clark, 1976-83. Author: Clinical Pharmacology, 1986; contbr. numerous articles and revs. to profl. jours.; mem. editorial bd. Elsevier Sci. Pubs., 1984—; patentee antiviral drugs. NSF summer fellow, 1963; NIH grad. fellow, 1964-66; NIH grantee, 1970—. Mem. AAS, Am. Assn. Dental Rsch., Am. Assn. Dental Schs. (pres. oral biology sect. 1990-91), Am. Assn. Oral Biology, Am. Chem. Soc., Am. Soc. Microbiology (mem. editorial bd. 1982-91), Internat. Soc. Antiviral Rsch. (archivist 1992—), Sigma Xi, Rho Chi, Omicron Kappa Upsilon. Home: 1372 Barrister Rd Ann Arbor MI 48105-2875 Office: U Mich 1011 N University Ave Ann Arbor MI 48109-1078

DRACKER, ROBERT ALBERT, physician; b. Queens, N.Y., July 28, 1956; s. Albert Donald and Lee (Patruno) D.; m. Maria Elizabeth DiRubbo Dracker; children: Maria Lynn, Robert, Michael. BA in Biology, N.Y.U., 1978; MD, SUNY Health Sci. Ctr., 1982; MS in Health Svcs. Mgmt., New Sch. for Social Rsch., N.Y.C., 1995. Intern Dept. Pediatrics SUNY Health Sci. Ctr., Syracuse, 1982-83; resident Dept. Pediatrics, 1983-85, fellow Pediatric Hematology/Oncology, 1985-87, fellow Blood Banking/Transfusion Medicine, 1987-88, rsch. asst. prof. Dept. Pathology, 1988-89, dir. Dept. pathology, 1989-93; attending physician Am. Red Cross, 1994—; ptnr. North Area Pediatrics; med. dir. and founder Infusacare Med. Svcs., P.C.; rsch. scientist I Masonic Med. Rsch. Lab., Utica, N.Y., 1989—; med. dir. MetraHealth Ctrl. N.Y., 1995—; assoc. med. dir. POMCO, Syracuse, N.Y., 1994—; med. advisor, reviewer Ctrl. N.Y. Blue Cross/Blue Shield, Health Svcs. Adminstrn.; chmn. Ctr. N.Y. Divsn. Review Island Peer Review Orgn., 1988-90; physician reviewer N.Y. State Office of Med. Misconduct; physician reviewer for dispute resolution, Empire State Med. Scientific and Edn. Found.; consulting physician Jowonio Sch., 1983-85, Devillo Sloan Sch. for Handicapped, 1983-85, Walsh Med. Facility, N.Y. State Dept. Corrections, 1991—; Neonatal Transport Physician, 1983-86. Contbr. numerous abstracts, letters, presentations, articles to profl. jours. Recipient AMA Physicians' Recognition award 1989-92, 92-95, 95—, N.Y.U. Alumni award, The Dr. Charipper award, Pediatric Resident Teaching award; grantee Nat. Heart, Lung and Blood Inst, 1984-89, 88-90, Cutter Divsn.of Miles Labs., 1988-89, 90- 91, Pathology Med. Svc. Group SUNY Health Sci. Ctr., 1991-92, Hendricks Fund SUNY Health Sci. Ctr. at Syracuse, 1992. Mem. ARC, AMA, Ctrl. N.Y. AIDS Profl. Group, Vis. Nurse Assn. Ctrl. N.Y., N.Y. State Dept. Health, Ctrl. N.Y. Hosp. Assn., Just For Babies, St. Joseph's Hosp. and Health Ctr., Cmty. Gen. Hosp., Crouse Irving Meml. Hosp., Patients' Choice, Am. Assn. Blood Banks, Am. Acad. Pediatrics, Blood Bank Assn. N.Y. State, Am. Soc. for Apheresis, Med. Soc. N.Y. State, Onondaga County Med. Soc., Onondaga County Pediatric Soc., Internat. Soc. of Hematotherapy and Graft Engrng., Am. Soc. for Blood and Marrow Transplantation, Am. Acad. Pediatrics. Roman Catholic.

DRACOS, FRANK JONATHAN, orthopedic surgeon; b. Chester, Pa., Sept. 5, 1929; s. John J. and Stella (Pappas) D.; m. Patricia Morgan, July 1958; children: Diane, Frank Jonathan II, Ellen, William. BA, U. Pa., 1951, MD, 1956. Diplomate Am. Bd. Orthopedic Surgery. Intern, U.S. Naval Hosp. Great Lakes, Ill., 1956-57; resident Presbyn. Hosp., Phila., Univ. Pa. Hosp., Phila., 1960-64; practice medicine specializing in orthopedic surgery, East Stroudsburg, Pa., 1964—; mem. med. staff Pocono Med. Ctr., East Stroudsburg, 1964—, chief dept. orthopedic surgery, 1964—, sec.-treas. med. staff, 1970-73, dir., 1974-88, v.p., 1983-86, chmn. bd., 1986-88; bd. dirs. Buck Hill Falls Co., chmn. bd.; med. cons. Pocono Internat. Raceway, 1972-82, dir. Security Bank & Trust Co., Stroudsburg, 1970-85, chmn. bd., 1975-85; dir. United Penn Bank, 1986-90, Mellon Bank, N.E., 1991—; orthopaedic cons. Pa. Blue Shield, 1970-85. Served to lt. comdr. USNR, 1957-59. Fellow Am. Acad. Orthopaedic Surgeons, ACS; mem. Monroe County Med. Soc., Pa. Med. Soc., AMA, Eastern Orthopaedic Soc., Pa. Orthopaedic Soc., Am. Coll. Sports Medicine, Am. Orthopaedic Soc. Sports Medicine. Office: Pocono Ortho Consult Inc 447 Office Plz 100 Plaza Ct Ste C East Stroudsburg PA 18301

DRACUP, KATHLEEN ANNE, nursing educator; b. Santa Monica, Calif., Sept. 28, 1942; d. Paul Joseph and Lucy Elizabeth (Milligan) Molloy; children: Jeffrey, Jonathan, Joy, Jan, Brian. BS in Nursing, St. Xavier's Coll., Chgo., 1967; M of Nursing, U. Calif., L.A., 1974; D of Nursing Sci., U. Calif., San Francisco, 1982. Clin. nurse Little Co. of Mary Hosp., Chgo., 1967-70, UCLA Med. Ctr., 1970-74; asst. clin. prof. U. Calif., L.A., 1974-78, rsch. fellow dept. medicine, 1979-81, asst. prof. to prof., 1982—; clin. nurse U. Calif. San Francisco Med. Ctr., 1979; pvt. practice psychotherapist, 1980—. Editor Heart and Lung Jour., 1981-91, Am. Jour. Critical Care, 1991—; editor Critical Care Nursing Series; contbr. chpts. to books, articles to profl. jours. Disting. Practitioner Nat. Acad., Washington, 1987; Fulbright Sr. scholar, 1995. Fellow Coun. Cardiovascular Nursing, Am. Heart Assn., Am. Assn. Cardiopulmonary Rehab.; mem. Am. Nurses' Assn., Am. Assn. Critical Care Nurses (life), Sigma Theta Tau. Office: UCLA Sch of Nursing 10833 Le Conte Ave Los Angeles CA 90024

DRAELOS, ZOE D., dermalogist, consultant; b. Milw., Oct. 13, 1958; d. Dimitri Basil and Lorene June (Legan) Kececioglu; m. Michael Draelos, June 14, 1980; children: Mark, Matthew. BSME, U. Ariz., 1979, MD, 1983. Bd. cert. Am. Bd. Dermatology. Physician Ctrl. Carolina Dermatology, High Point, N.C., 1988—; cons., owner Dermatology Consulting Svcs., High Point, N.C., 1990—. Author: Cosmetics in Dermatology, 1995. Rhodes scholar, Oxford, Eng., 1979. Office: Ctrl Carolina Dermatology 624 Quaker Ln 302B High Point NC 27262

DRAGER, SHARON B., vascular surgeon; b. N.Y.C., June 23, 1946; d. Marvin and Lenore (Schwam) D.; children: Troy, Brooke. AB, Brown U., 1966; MD, NYU, 1970. Cert. Am. Bd. Surgery. Resident/fellow in surgery NYU, N.Y.C., 1970-78; pvt. practice San Pablo, Calif., 1978—; attending physician Brookside Hosp., San Pablo, 1978—, chief of staff, 1988; attending physician Doctors' Hosp. of Pinole, Calif., 1978—, chief of staff, 1994; attending physician Alta Bates Hosp., Berkeley, Calif., 1978—; asst. clin. prof. surgery U. Calif., San Francisco, 1981—. Fellow ACS; mem. Am. Med. Women's Assn., Assn. Women Surgeons, No. Calif. Vascular Soc., Internat. Soc. for Cardiovascular Surgery, East Bay Surg. Soc., Alameda Contra Costa Med. Soc., Alpha Omega Alpha. Office: 2089 Vale Rd San Pablo CA 94806

DRAGO, JOSEPH ROSARIO, urologist, educator; b. Jersey City, N.J., Oct. 28, 1947; m. Diane Lavacca; children: Andrea, Daniella, Denise. BS, U. Ill., 1968, MD, 1972. Diplomate Nat. Bd. Med. Examiners, Am. Bd. Urology; cert. Yag Laser, laparoscopic surgery. Intern in gen. surgery Pa. State U. Milton S. Hershey Med. Ctr., 1972-73, resident in urology, 1973-77, instr. urology, 1976-77; asst. prof. urology, dir. urology oncology U. Calif., Davis, 1977-79; asst. prof. urology, dir. urology oncology Milton S. Hershey (Pa.) Med. Ctr., 1979-80, assoc. prof. to prof. of surgery, dir. urologic oncology, 1980-85; assoc. staff Children's Hosp., Columbus, Ohio, 1985—; interim chief of staff elect, prof., dir. urologic oncology Ohio State U. Arthur G. James Cancer Hosp., Columbus, Ohio, 1990-92; with Easton Warren Urology, Easton, Pa., 1992-95; pvt. practice Washington, N.J., 1995—; editorial bd. In Vivo Jour.;advisor Internat. Urologic Svcs., Inc., 1987; cons. for various coms.; visiting professorship at over 30 univs. and hosps. Author 12 book chpts.; reviewer various profl. jours., 1979—; contbr. articles to profl. jours. Recipient various rsch. grants, 1978-81. Fellow Internat. Coll. Surgeons in Urology; mem. AMA, Am. Coll. Surgeons, Am. Fertility Soc., Am. Inst. Ultrasound in Medicine, Am. Soc. Andrology, Am. Urologic Assn., Assn. Academic Surgery, Assn. Surgical Edn., Hershey Surgical Soc. (sec.-treas. 1983-85), Pa. Med. Soc., Phila. Urologic Soc. and many more. Home: 3295 Beaufort Dr Bethlehem PA 18017-1955 Office: 10 Brass Castle Rd Washington NJ 07882 also: 224 Roseberry St Phillipsburg NJ 08865

DRAGON-DILILLO, MICHELLE ANNE, speech pathologist; b. Huntington, N.Y., May 6, 1963; d. Donald W. and Arlene C. (Gianquinto) Dragon; m. Douglas C. DiLillo, Apr. 25, 1987. BS, L.I. U., 1985; MS, Adelphi U., 1986. Speech-lang. pathologist East Islip (N.Y.) UFSD, 1986-87, Northport-East Northport (N.Y.) UFSD, 1987-89, East Meadow (N.Y.) UFSD, 1989—. Mem. Am. Speech-Lang.-Hearing Assn., N.Y. State United Tchrs. Assn. Home: 32 Bolan Dr Huntington Station NY 11746-2844 Office: Barnum Woods Elem Sch 500 May Ln East Meadow NY 11554

DRAIN, CECIL B., nurse anesthetist educator, retired army officer; b. Ft. Worth, Aug. 25, 1943; s. Harry Eugene and F. Colene (McDonald) D.; m. Cynthia M. Pfaff, Aug. 21, 1965; children: Timothy, Stephen, Kathryn. Diploma, St. Joseph Hosp. Sch. Nursing, Ft. Worth, 1967; BSN, U. Ariz., 1976, MS in Med.-Surg. Nursing, 1980, NS in Adult Pulmonary Nursing, 1980; PhD in Ednl. Curriculum and Instrn. in Higher Edn., Tex. A&M U., 1986. RN, Va., Tex.; cert. RN anesthetist. Staff nurse recovery room, head nurse psychiatry St. Joseph Hosp., 1967; commd. 2d lt. U.S. Army, 1968, advanced through grades to col.; chief nurse anesthetist 121st Evacuation Hosp., Seoul, 1972-73; ret., 1973; staff nurse anesthetist, chief respiratory therapy U.S. Gen. Leonard Wood Army Community Hosp., Ft. Leonard Wood, Mo., 1973-74; staff nurse anesthetist Tucson Med. Ctr., 1974-76, 78-80; staff nurse anesthetist Brooke Army Med. Ctr., Ft. Sam Houston, Tex., 1976-78, 86-89, spl. project officer, 1986-89; asst. program dir. U.S. Army-SUNY-Buffalo anesthesiology for ANC officers course U.S. Army Acad. Health Sciences, Ft. Sam Houston, 1980-83; program dir. program in anesthesia nursing U.S. Army-Tex. U.S. Army/Tex. Wesleyan U./Acad. of Health Scis., Ft. Sam Houston, 1989-92; program dir. U. Tex. Health Sci. Ctr. Houston/AMEDD Ctr. and Sch., Ft. Sam Houston, 1992-93; dir. anesthesia nursing program U.S. Army/U. Tex., Houston, 1992-93; prof. clin. nursing U. Tex. Health Sci. Ctr., Houston, 1992-93; prof. Med. Coll. Va., Richmond, 1993—, chmn. dept. nurse anesthesia, 1993-96, interim dean Sch. Allied Health Professions, 1996—; teaching asst. U. Ariz., 1979-80; clin. instr. family medicine U. Okla., 1983; adj. prof. Tex. Wesleyan U., 1989-92; guest lectr. Tex. A&M U., 1986-93; numerous presentations in field; mem. long-term civilian profls. Schooling Selection Bd., Alexandria, Va., 1988; reviewer Clin. Rev. Series in Critical Care Nursing, 1988—. Author: The Post Anesthesia Care Unit: A Critical Care Approach to Post Anesthesia Nursing, 3d edit., 1994; mem. editl. bd. Heart and Lung: Jour. Critical Care, 1977-92, Nurse Anesthesia, 1987-94, Am. Jour. Critical Care, 1992—, Jour. of Am. Assn. Nurse Anesthetists, 1980-83, 92—; contbr. articles, abstracts and book revs. to profl. jours., chpts. to books. Baseball commr., Ft. Sam Houston, 1980-81; bd. dirs. March of Dimes, San Antonio, 1981-83; umpire USTA, Bryan, Tex., 1985—. Decorated Legion of Merit, Meritorious Svc. medal with oak leaf cluster. Fellow Am. Acad. Nursing; mem. ANA, AACN (cert. of achievement 1980),Am. Assn. Nurse Anesthetists (jour. faculty 1982-83, bd. dirs. Ednl. and Rsch. Found. 1983-91, cert. of profl. excellence 1976), Am. Soc. Post Anesthesia Nurses (rsch. com. 1986-87), Tex. Assn. Post Anesthesia Nurses (life), 38th Parallel Nurses Soc. (pres. 1971), Ret. Officers Assn., Ret. Army Nurse Corps Assn. (assoc.), Order of Mil. Med. Merit, Sigma Theta Tau, Phi Delta Kappa, Sigma Epsilon Chi. Republican. Congregationalist. Home: 5511 W Bay Rd Midlothian VA 23112-2509 Office: Va Commonwealth U Med Coll Sch Allied Health Profs Richmond VA 23298

DRAKE, DIANNE ELIZABETH, internist; b. Payton, Ohio, May 3, 1946; d. Robert Mortimer and Jane Mardelle (Smith) D. BA, Harvard U., 1967; MD, Boston U., 1975. Diplomate Am. Bd. Internal Medicine. Resident Mt. Auburn Hosp., Cambridge, Mass., 1975-78; physician Harvard St. Neighborhood Health Ctr., Dorchester, Mass., 1978-81, med. dir., 1981-83; physician Roslindale (Mass.) Med. and Dental, 1983-85, Harvard U. Health Svcs., Cambridge, 1985—. Chmn. human rights com. Boston State Hosp., Dorchester, 1984-91; acolyte, Altar guild chair Ch. of the Advent, Boston. Mem. Am. Med. Women's Assn., Mass. Med. Assn. Home: 25 Chestnut St Boston MA 02108 Office: Harvard Univ Health Ctr 75 Mount Auburn St Cambridge MA 02138

DRAKE, LYNN ANNETTE, physician; b. Albuquerque, Aug. 4, 1949; d. Olen Lester and Lucille Susan (Henry) Drake; BA, Adams State Coll., 1966, MA, 1967; MD, U. Tenn., 1971. Instr. math. Adams State Coll., Alamosa, Colo., 1966-67; intern City of Memphis Hosp., 1971-72, resident in dermatology, 1972-75, chief resident, 1974-75; mem. faculty dept. medicine, div. dermatology U. Tenn. Ctr. Health Scis., also Med. Practice Group, Inc.; asst. prof. dermatology Emory U., Atlanta; chief dermatology VA Med. Ctr., Atlanta; chmn. chemosurgery tag group VA; instr. advanced cardiac life support Am. Heart Assn.; mem. emergency room com. St. Joseph Hosp. Vol., Am. Cancer Soc., 1973-75; dir. policy and planning dept. dep. chmn. dept. dermatology, Wellman Labs Photomedicine Harvard Med. Sch., Mass. Gen. Hosp., Boston, 1988—; mem. dermatology adv. panel FDA, 1985-89; U.S. del. to World Health Assembly, 1991-92; mem. nat. adv. bd. Nat. Inst. Musculoskeletal, Arthritis and Skin Diseases (NIH). Diplomate Am. Bd. Dermatology (chmn. com. health care quality assurance 1984-87, chair. 1987). Recipient Outstanding Achievement award Adams State Coll., 1988; Robert Wood Johnson Health Policy fellow, 1986-87. Bd. trustees Chapel Feur Chaplins. Fellow Am. Acad. Dermatology (bd. dirs. 1988-92); mem. AMA, ACP, Soc. for Investigative Dermatology, Am. Acad. Dermatology (com. on health planning, chmn. guidelines care com.), Women's Med. Assn. (sci. coun.), Ga. Dermatology Soc., Atlanta Dermatology Soc. (program chmn.), New Eng. Dermatology Soc. (program chair), Am. Assn. Med. Colls., Council Acad. Scis., Women's Dermatology Soc. (house staff liaison com., nominating com., pres. 1984-87), Dermatology Found. Mem. editorial bd. Skin and Allergy News. Home: One Longfelloe Pl 1 Longfellow Pl Apt 2418 Boston MA 02114-2422

DRAKE, PATRICIA EVELYN, psychologist; b. Lewiston, Maine, Feb. 9, 1946; d. Lewis and Anita (Bilodeau) D.; m. Colin Matthew Fuller, May 13, 1973 (div. Aug. 1983); children: R. Matthew, Meaghan Merry. Diploma, St. Mary's Sch. Nursing, 1967; BS, U. Nev., 1985; MA, Calif. Sch. Profl. Psychology, 1987, PhD, 1989. RN. Nurse Maine Med. Ctr., Portland, 1967-73, U. Calif. Sacramento Med. Ctr., 1973-78, Ben Taub Hosp., Houston, 1978-79; psychology intern Shasta County Mental Health Ctr., Redding, Calif., 1988-89, clin. psychologist, 1989-91, tng. dir., chief psychology, 1991—; psychologist pvt. practice, Redding, Calif., 1991—. Mem. AAUW, APA, Calif. Psychol. Assn., Shasta-Cascade Psychol. Assn., Phi Kappa Phi. Democrat. Roman Catholic. Office: Shasta County Mental Health 2640 Breslauer Way Redding CA 96001-4246

DRAKE, STEPHEN DOUGLAS, clinical psychologist, health facility administrator; b. Iola, Kans., Sept. 8, 1947; s. Harry Francis and Emojean (Price) D.; m. Rebecca Gonzalez. June 1, 1968; 1 child, Michael Paul. BA, U. Tex., 1970; PhD, U. North Tex., 1987. Lic. psychologist. Mental health worker Austin (Tex.) State Hosp., 1970-73; claims rep. Social Security Adminstrn., Galveston, Tex., 1974-77; ops. supr. Social Security Adminstrn., Dallas, 1977-79, staff asst., 1979-80; clin. psychologist Terrell (Tex.) State Hosp., 1987-89, Austin (Tex.) State Hosp., 1989-90; program dir. Austin State Hosp., 1990-92; cons. Tex. Rehab. Commn., 1992—. Contbr. articles to profl. jours. Vice-Chmn. bd. dirs. Galveston (Tex.) Island Mental Health/Mental Retardation Ctr., 1977; v.p. Grad. Assn. Students in Psychology U. North Tex., 1984, grad. rep. exec. com., 1984. Mem. APA, Assn. Advancement Behavior Therapy, Mensa, Phi Kappa Phi. Office: Tex Rehab Commn 6102 Oltorf St Austin TX 78704-1206

DRAKEMAN, DONALD LEE, biotechnologist, lawyer; b. Camden, N.J., Oct. 21, 1953; s. Fred J. and Jean (Faucett) D.; m. Lisa Natale Drakeman, Aug. 23, 1975; children: Cynthia, Amy. AB magna cum laude, Dartmouth Coll., 1975; JD, Columbia U., 1979; MA, Princeton U., 1984, PhD, 1988. Bar: N.J. 1979, U.S. Dist. Ct. N.J. 1979, N.Y. 1980, U.S. Supreme Ct. 1984. Assoc. Milbank, Tweed, Hadley & McCloy, N.Y.C., 1979-82; gen. counsel Essex Chem. Corp., Clifton, N.J., 1982-89, v.p., 1987-89; pres. Essex Med. Products, Clifton, 1988-89; pres., CEO Medarex, Inc., Princeton, N.J., 1987—; adj. prof. polit. sci. Montclair (N.J.) State Coll., 1984; rsch. cons. Lilly Found., Inc., 1989-90; lectr. dept. politics Princeton U., 1990-93, 95; bd. dirs. The Compass Capital Group, Edison, N.J., Immuno-Designed Molecules, Paris. Author: Church-State Constitutional Issues, 1990; coeditor Church and State in American History, 1986; contbr. articles to profl. jours. Chmn. Montclair Bd. Adjustment, 1984; bd. trustees Biotechnology Coun. N.J. Harlan Fiske Stone scholar, Columbia U., 1976-79. Mem. ABA, AAAS, Assn. Bar City N.Y., Nat. Coun. Chs. (religious liberty com.), Am. Arbitration Assn. (arbitrator), Am. Acad. Religion, Princeton Alumni Coun., John Maclean Soc., Princeton Club, Yale Club. Home: 49 Rolling Hill Rd Skillman NJ 08558-2319 Office: Medarex Inc 1545 Us Highway 22 Annandale NJ 08801-3059

DRANITZKE, RICHARD J., thoracic surgeon; b. L.I., N.Y., 1940. MD, Columbia U., 1966. Diplomate Am. Bd. Surgery, Am. Bd. Thoracic Surgery. Intern Columbia-Presbyn. Hosp., N.Y.C., 1966-67; resident in surgery Bellevue Hosp. Ctr., N.Y.C., 1969-73; resident in cardiothoracic surgery Albany, 1973-75; dir. surgery and chief thoracic and vascular surgery St. Charles Hosp., Port Jefferson, N.Y.; chief thoracic and vascular surgery J.T. Mather Meml. Hosp.; chief vascular surgery Brookhaven Meml. Hosp. Med. Ctr.; clin. instr. dept. surgery Stony Brook U. Hosp.; clin. instr. dept. surgery Stony Brook U. Hosp. Mem. ACP, ACS, AMA, Can. Med. Assn. Office: 635 Belle Terre Rd Port Jefferson NY 11777 also: 4 Phyllis Dr Patchogue NY 11772-2900

DRAPER, EDGAR, psychiatrist; b. St. Louis, Feb. 5, 1926; s. Neal McLain and Florence Mabel (Meyers) D.; m. Norma Jane Alexander, Mar. 16, 1949; children: Sue Draper Masteller, Anne Draper Klevay, Neal Edgar. AB, Washington U., 1946; BD, Garrett Biblical Inst., 1949; MD, Washington U. Med. Sch., 1953; grad., Inst. for Psychoanalysis, Chgo., 1966. Diplomate Am. Bd. Psychiatry and Neurology. Intern Washington U. Svc. City Hosp., St. Louis, 1953-54; resident psychiatry U. Cin., 1954-55, 57-59; sr. asst. surgeon USPHS, Ft. Worth, 1955-57; instr. U. Chgo., 1959-60, asst. prof., 1960-66, assoc. prof., 1966-68; co-dir. psychiat. outpatient dept., prof. psychiatry U. Mich., Ann Arbor, 1968, dir. psychiat. resident edn., 1968-74, prof. postgrad edn., 1970-75; prof., chmn. dept. psychiatry U. Miss. Med. Ctr., Jackson, 1975-93; prof. psychiatry U. Miss., Jackson, 1993-94; prof. emeritus, 1994—; cons. in field. Contbr. numerous articles to profl. jours. Named Vis. scholar U. Chgo., 1987, Fellow Soc. for Sci. Study of Religion, 1987, Man of Month Pastoral Psychology, 1970; recipient Physicians Recognition award, 1982-85, Cert. Appreciation Mental Health Assn. Hinds County, 1983, Plaque of Commendation Chgo. Acad. Religion and Mental Health, 1966-67. Fellow Am. Psychiat. Assn. (life), Am. Coll. Psychiatry (life), Am. Soc. Psychoanalytic Physicians, Soc. for Sci. Study of Religion (life), Am. Coll. Psychoanalysts (life), So. Psychiat. Assn.; mem. Miss. Psychiat. Assn. (past pres.), Miss. State Med. Soc., Mich. Psychiat. Soc., Washtenaw County Med. Soc., Mich. State Med. Soc., So. Psychiat. Assn., Mich. Psychoanalytic Soc. Office: 2500 N State St Jackson MS 39216-4500

DRAYER, JAN IGNATIUS, medical company executive, physician; b. Amsterdam, The Netherlands, Jan. 31, 1946; came to U.S., 1980; s. Roelof P. and Anna (De Swart) D.; m. Thea Van Kalmthout, July 3, 1971; children: Myke, Joris. MD, U. Nijmegen, The Netherlands, 1975. Intern St. Radboud Hosp., Nijmegen, The Netherlands, 1969-71; resident in dept. medicine U. Nijmegen (The Netherlands), 1971-75; instr. medicine N.Y. Hosp., Cornell U., N.Y.C., 1975-77; rsch. assoc. Cardiovascular Ctr., N.Y. Hosp., Cornell U., N.Y.C., 1975-77; internist Dept. Medicine, St. Radboud Hosp., Nijmegen, The Netherlands, 1977-80; assoc. prof. medicine U. Calif., Irvine, 1980-85; assoc. chief VA Med. Ctr., Long Beach, Calif., 1980-85; dir. clin. rsch. Boehringer Ingelheim Pharm., Inc., Ridgefield, Conn., 1985-88; v.p. mktg. support G. H. Besselaar Assocs., Princeton, N.J.; sr. v.p. G.M. Besselaar Assocs., Princeton, N.J., 1990-95; exec. v.p. gene therapy devel. Somatix Therapy Corp., Alameda, Calif., 1995—; cons, NIH Spl. Study Sect., 1984, Am. Coll. Chest Physicians, Sect. on Hypertension, 1985. Author numerous articles and book chpts. on drug devel. and hypertension, over 70 clin. rsch. abstracts; editor: Practical Clinical Guide Series, 1988, Drug Therapy in Hypertension, 1986; co-editor: Clonidine in Hypertension, 1985, Ambulatory Blood Pressure Monitoring, 1984, Mineralocorticoids in Essential and Secondary Hypertension, Clinical and Experimental Hypertension Vols. 9 and 10; contbr. over 100 articles to profl. jours. Fellow Am. Coll. Clin. Pharmacology, Coun. for High Blood Pressure Rsch., Am. Coll. Chest Physicians, Am. Coll. Cardiology; mem. Internat. Soc. Hypertension, Am. Soc. for Clin. Pharmacology and Therapeutics (nominating com. 1988, co-chair CME com. 1985, chair CME com. 1992—), Internat. Soc. Chronobiology, Am. Geriatrics Soc., Am. Soc. Hypertension (charter), Am. Fedn. for Clin. Rsch. Home: 5341 Golden Gate Ave Oakland CA 94618 Office: Somatix Therapy Corp 850 Marina Village Pky Alameda CA 94501

DRAZEN, JEFFREY MARK, medical educator, hospital administrator; b. St. Louis, May 19, 1946; s. Yale and Sylvia (Wainer) D.; m. Erica Coburn Drazen, July 27, 1969; children: David, Daniel. BS, Tufts U., 1968; MD, Harvard U., 1972. Diplomate Am. Bd. Internal Medicine, Am. Bd. Pulmonary Medicine. Parker B. Francis prof. Med. Sch. Harvard U., Boston, 1977—; chief pulmonary and critical care medicine divsn. Brigham & Women's Hosps., Boston, 1985—; mem. respiratory and applied physiology study sect. NIH, 1981-86, pulmonary disease adv. coun., 1988-92. NIH grantee, 1972—. Mem. Am. Soc. Clin. Investigation, Am. Thoracic Soc., Am. Physiology Soc., Am. Soc. Pharmacology and Exptl. Therapeutics, Assn. Am. Physicians. Office: Brigham & Women's Hosp 75 Francis St Boston MA 02115-6110

DREBORG, STEN KARL GUSTAV, pediatric allergologist; b. Södertälje, Sweden, Apr. 4, 1933; s. Karl-Erik and Dagmar Elvira (Dreborg) Johansson; m. Birgitta Kristina Wassberg, Aug. 24, 1958; children: Ingemar, Karin, Kerstin. MD, U. Uppsala, Sweden, 1961; PhD, U. Linköping, Sweden, 1987. Resident Ctrl. Hosp., Falcun, Sweden, 1961-65; cons. U. Hosp., Uppsala, 1965-69; head dept. pediatrics Ctr. Hosp., Boden, Sweden, 1969-79; med. dir. Pharmacia Diagnostics, Uppsala, 1979-85, med. advisor, 1985-89; asst. prof. pediatric allergology U. Hosp., Linköping, 1989-95; prof. pediatric allergology U. Oslo, Norway, 1996—. Asst. editor Pediatric Allergy & Immunology, 1989-94; editl. bd. Clin. Exptl. Allergy, 1989-93; contbr. articles to profl. jours. Fellow Am. Coll. Allergy & Clin. Immunology (disting. fellow), Am. Acad. Allergy and Immunology (corr. fellow); mem. European Soc. Pediatric Allergy and Clin. Immunology (hon. sec. 1989, treas. 1992, 1st v.p. 1995). Home: Box 68, S-44322 Lerum Sweden Office: Vokenstoppen, Ullveien 14, 0394 Oslo Norway

DREBUS, RICHARD WILLIAM, pharmaceutical company executive; b. Oshkosh, Wis., Mar. 30, 1924; s. William and Frieda (Schmidt) D.; m. Hazel Redford, June 7, 1947; children—William R., John R., Kathryn L. Berlin. BS, U. Wis., 1947, MS, 1949, PhD, 1952. Bus. trainee Marathon Paper Corp., Menasha, Wis., 1951-52; tng. mgr. Ansul Corp., Marinette, Wis., 1952-55; asst. to v.p. Ansul Corp., 1955-58, marketing mgr., 1958-60; dir. personnel devel. Mead Johnson & Co., Evansville, Ind., 1960-65; v.p. corporate planning Mead Johnson & Co., 1965-66, internat. pres., 1966-68; v.p. internat. div. Bristol-Myers Co. (merger Mead Johnson & Co. with Bristol-Myers Co.), N.Y.C., 1968-77, sr. v.p., 1977-78, v.p. parent co., 1978-85, sr. v.p. pharm. research and devel. div., 1985-89, ret., 1989. Past bd. dirs. Jr. Achievement S.E. Conn., Meriden Silver Mus.; past bd. dirs. Meriden-Wallngford United Way, chmn. fund raising drive, 1988-89; trustee emeritus Quinnipiac Coll. Served with AUS, 1943-45. Decorated Combat Inf. Badge, Purple Heart, Bronze Star. Mem. APA, N.Y. Acad. Scis., U. Wis. Bascom Hill Soc., Oshkosh Country Club, Oshkosh Power Boat Club, North Shore Country Club, Phi Delta Kappa. Home: 3720 Pau Ko Tuk Ln Oshkosh WI 54901-7332

DREESMAN, GORDON RONALD, biotechnology research administrator, immunologist; b. Marshalltown, Iowa, Nov. 28, 1935; s. Edwin Thomas and Mable Henrietta (Buskoni) D.; m. Dolores Rempe, Dec. 29, 1958 (div. June 1972); children: Kimberly Lynn, Thomas Lee, Andrea Beth; m. Margaret Carter Neville, Feb. 6, 1982. BA, Cen. Coll., 1957; MA, U. Kans., 1963; PhD, U. Hawaii, 1965. Postdoctoral fellow Baylor U. Coll. of Medicine, Houston, 1965-66; asst. prof. Sch. of Medicine St. Louis U., 1966-69; asst. to assoc. prof. Baylor Coll. of Medicine, 1969-79; prof. Baylor U. Coll. of Medicine, 1979-84; chmn. S.W. Found. Biomed. Rsch., San Antonio, 1984-88; sr. sci. dir. BioTech Resources, Inc., San Antonio, 1988-92; exec. v.p. D&B Techs., San Antonio, 1994—; mem. sci. advisors com. Am. Found. AIDS Rsch., 1986—; cons. in field. Author: (with others) HIV-1 Vaccines, 1987; contbr. over 185 articles to profl. jours. and books. Fellow Am. Acad. Microbiology, Sigma Xi; mem. Am. Found. for AIDS Rsch. (sci. adv. bd.), Am. Soc. Microbiology, Am. Assn. Immunologists. Republican. Presbyterian. Home: 10061 Rafter S Tr Helotes TX 78023-3815 Office: D and B Technologies Inc 18585 Sigma Rd Ste 100 San Antonio TX 78258-4204

DREILING, BERNARD JOSEPH, physician, educator; b. Victoria, Kans., Sept. 28, 1936; s. Joseph Francis and Josephine (Brungardt) D.; m. Jo Ann Swekosky; children: Karen, Elizabeth. BS in Biology, Rockhurst Coll., Kansas City, Mo., 1958; MD, St. Louis U., 1962. Rotating intern St. Louis City Hosp., 1962-63, resident in internal medicine, 1963-65, chief resident in internal medicine, 1965-66; fellow in hematology U. Miss. Med. Ctr., Jackson, 1969-70, asst. prof. medicine, 1970-75, assoc. prof., 1975-86, prof.,

1986—. Contbr. chpts. to books. Lt. comdr. USNR, 1966-69. Named Tchr. of Yr., Alpha Omega Alpha, 1987, 94, named Clin. Tchr. of Yr., 8 times. Fellow ACP; mem. Am. Soc. Hematology, Am. Fedn. Clin. Rsch., S.W. Oncology Group. Office: VA Hosp 1500 E Woodrow Wilson Dr Jackson MS 39216

DREISBACH, CRAIG DEWITT, physician; b. Detroit, June 22, 1953; s. Thomas Swope and Laurette Jean (Selmson) D.; m. Michele Authier, July 2, 1977; children: Erica, Christopher, Thomas. BS in Zoology, Mich. State U., 1975; MD, U. Mich., 1979. Resident Henry Ford Hosp., Detroit, 1979-84; attending physician Northeastern Vt. Regional Hosp., St. Johnsbury, 1984—; pres. med. staff Northeastern Vt. Regional Hosp., St. Johnsbury, 1993-94. Mem. Am. Acad. Orthopaedic Surgeons, Phi Beta Kappa. Home: PO Box 343 Saint Johnsbury VT 05819

DREIZIN, IVY J., neurologist, ophthalmologist; b. Newark, Jan. 25, 1948; d. David Harold and Estelle Barbara (Van Roon) D.; m. Frederick S. Edelman, Aug. 30, 1970; children: Joshua, Deborah. BA, Wellesley Coll., 1970; MD, Med. Coll. Pa., 1974. Bd. cert. diplomate am. Bd. Psychiatry and Neurology. Intern medicine Michael Reese Med. Ctr., Chgo., 1974-75, resident medicine, 1975-76, fellow neuro-ophthalmology, 1979-80; resident neurology Rush-Presbyn.-St. Lukes Med. Ctr., Chgo., 1976-79; staff neurologist, neuro-ophthalmologist Madison (Wis.) Neurol. Ctr.-Physicians Plus Med. Group, 1980—; clin. asst. prof. U. Wis. Med. Sch., Madison, 1980—. Mem. Am. Acad. Neurology, Am. Sleep Disorders Assn., N.Am. Neuro-Ophthalmology Soc., Upper Midwest Neuro-Ophthalmology Group, State Med. Soc. Wis. Office: Physicians Plus Neurology 20 S Park St #202 Madison WI 53715

DRELL, MARTIN J., psychiatrist, hospital administrator; b. Chgo., Dec. 18, 1948; s. Hyman Joseph and Muriel (Kadison) D.; m. Janice Melissa Lucas, May 11, 1975; children: David, Emily. BA in English, U. Ill., Urbana, 1970; MD, U. Ill., Chgo., 1974. Intern Louis Weiss Hosp., Chgo., 1974-75; resident in child psychiatry Boston Childrens/JBGC, 1975-77; resident in gen. psychiatry Cambridge (Mass.) Hosp., 1977-79; asst. prof. child psychiatry Baylor Coll. Med., Houston, 1979-87; dept. head child psychiatry La. State U. Med. Sch., New Orleans, 1987—, assoc. prof. psychiatry, 1987-95, prof., 1995—; clin. dir. New Orleans Adolescent Hosp., 1991—. Contbr. articles and book chpts. to profl. pubs. Mem. Soc. Prof. Child and Adolescent Psychiatry (pres. 1996—), Am. Assn. Dirs. Psychiatric Residency Tng. (treas. 1995-96), Am. Acad. Child and Adolescent Psychiatry (coun. 1992-95, newsletter editor 1995—). Office: La State U Med Sch 1542 Tulane Ave New Orleans LA 70112-2822

DRELL, STEVEN ALLEN, internist; b. Rockford, Ill., Apr. 29, 1951; s. Hyman Joseph and Muriel Ida (Kadison) D.; m. Sharon Frank; children: Amy Beth, Adam David, Lauren Stacie. BS, U. Ill., 1973, MD, 1976. Intern, resident U. So. Calif. Med. Ctr., L.A. County, 1976-79; chief resident U. So. Calif. Med. Ctr., 1979-80; pvt. practice Med. Group for Cardiology/Internal Medicine, Sherman Oaks, Calif., 1980—; chief of staff St. Joseph med. Ctr., Burbank, Calif., 1994—, chmn. patient care, 1990-91, chief of medicine, 1989-90. Mem. Am. Coll. Physicians, Am. Soc. Internal Medicine, Am. Diabetes Soc., Royal Soc. Medicine. Office: Med Group Cardio/Int Med 13320 Riverside #102 Sherman Oaks CA 91425

DRENNAN, FRANCES LASSITER, retired ooccupational health nurse; b. Scotland County, N.C., Nov. 30, 1923; d. John Winfree and Fannie (Anderson) Lassiter; m. James McLeod Drennan, May 5, 1950; children: Frances Lenora, Jimmie Ann, Robert Gaston. Diploma in nursing, High Point (N.C.) Meml. Hosp., 1944. RN, N.C., S.C. Operating room supr. Scotland Meml. Hosp., Laurinburg, N.C.; occupational health nurse Spring Mills, Inc., Laurel Hill, N.C., Ft. Mills, S.C.; ret., 1983. 1st lt. Nurse Corps, U.S. Army, 1945-46. Recipient Meritorious Svc. citation Am. Legion, 1965; named N.C. Occupational Nurse of Yr., 1981. Mem. Sand Hill Assn. Occupational Nurses (pres. 1976-78). Home: PO Box 103 Maxton NC 28364-0103

DRENNEN, D(ONALD) A(RTHUR), psychotherapist; b. N.Y.C., Aug. 8, 1925; s. William Michael and Anastasia (Kearney) D.; m. M. Eileen Connolly, Aug. 4, 1951; children: Maura, Deirdre, Susan, Eileen, Donald Reid, Maribeth. AB, Fordham U., 1947, MA, 1951, PhD, 1958; postdoctoral, Hebrew Union Coll., 1964, Am. U., Cairo, 1965, McGill U., 1967, Columbia U., 1970, Tallahassee Meml. Hosp., 1988. From asst. to assoc. prof. Marymount Coll., N.Y.C. and Tarrytown, N.Y., 1952-62; prof. Marist Coll., Poughkeepsie, N.Y., 1962-82; pvt. practice Carrabelle, Fla., 1985—; vis. scholar Columbia U., N.Y.C.,. 1965-66; vis. lectr. Cath. U. Am., Washington, 1966-67; pvt. practice psychol. counselor, Poughkeepsie, 1972-82; pastoral counselor Trinity Episcopal Ch., Apalachicola, Fla., 1987-89; cons. Editions de Paris, 1967-71, Ednl. Testing Corp., Princeton, N.J., 1968-71, Mid. States Assn. Sch. and Coll., N.Y.C., 1969-73, Ch. LDS, Blountstown, Fla., 1985—. Author, editor: Pastor's Referral Reference, 1988; contbr. articles to profl. jours. Rockefeller Found. grantee, 1952; recipient Carnegie Found. award, 1968, 69, Citation, Contemporary Authors, 1987. Mem. Assn. for Clin. Pastoral Edn. Home: Fairhaven Star Rte 36B Fairhaven Star Rte 36 Carrabelle FL 32322 Office: PO Box 1236 Lanark Village FL 32323-1236

DRESCHLER, WOUTER ALBERT, audiologist, educator, researcher; b. Amsterdam, The Netherlands, Sept. 19, 1953; s. Willem and Anna Maria (Pot) D.; m. Anne Marie Louise Overeem, June 7, 1974; children: Annemieke, Mark, Peter. EE, Tech. U., Delft, The Netherlands, 1977; PhD, Free U., Amsterdam, 1983. Rschr. Free U., 1977-80; head audiol. ctr. U. Amsterdam, 1980—, prof. clin. and experimental audiology, 1994—. Author: Relations Between Psychophysical Data and Speech Perception, 1983, (chpt.) Auditory Psychophysics: Spectro-temporal Representation of Signals, 1987. Fellow Internat. Collegium Rehab. Audiology, Acoustical Soc. Am., Dutch Soc. Audiology, Dutch Acoustical Soc. Dutch ENT Soc.; mem. Am. Auditory Soc., Am. Speech-Lang. Hearing Assn., Brit. Soc. Audiology, Internat. Audiology Soc., Dutch Soc. Clin. Physics. Home: Beemdgras 4, 1441 WB Purmerend The Netherlands Office: Acad Med Ctr, U Amsterdam PO Box 22700, 1100 DE Amsterdam The Netherlands

DRESKIN, ERVING ARTHUR, pathologist; b. Newark, Jan. 9, 1919; s. Harry and Sarah Molly (Krulvetsky) D.; m. Jeanet Irma Steckler, May 9, 1943; children—Richard Burgas, Stephen Charles, Jeanet Elizabeth, Rena Lynn. BS., Tulane U., 1940, MD, 1943. Diplomate Am. Bd. Pathology, subspecialty Blood Banking. Intern, Newark Beth Israel Hosp., 1943-44; resident in pathology, instr. pathology U. Ill. Coll. Medicine, Chgo., 1946-49, Am. Cancer Soc. fellow, 1949-50; asso. pathologist Grant Hosp., Chgo., 1949-50; chief pathologist, dir. labs. and Blood Bank, Greenville (S.C.) Hosp. System, 1950-85; med. dir. Carolina-Ga. Blood Center, 1980—; cons. pathologist to hosps.; clin. prof. pathology Med. U. S.C.; past pres., chmn., exec. com. Pathology Assocs., Greenville, Pa.; bd. dirs. United Way Greenville County, 1973-76; treas. Greater Greenville Community Found., 1980-81, bd. dirs., 1980-83, mem. exec. com., 1989—; pres. Temple of Israel, Greenville, 1966-68, Community Found. Greater Greenville, 1990-91, Greenville County Arts Commn., 1993, 95. Lt. M.C., USNR, 1944-46. Fellow Am. Soc. Clin. Pathologists, Coll. Am. Pathologists (S.C. regional commr. for lab. accreditation); mem. Am. Assn. Blood Banks (v.p. 1962, sec. 1963-65, pres. 1965-66), S.C. Soc. Pathologists (pres. 1957-59), AMA, S.C. Med. Assn., Alpha Omega Alpha. Clubs: Rotary, Poinsett. Home: 60 Lake Forest Dr Greenville SC 29609-5038 Office: Carolina-Georga Blood Ctr 515 Grove Rd Greenville SC 29605-4206

DRESSEL, IRENE EMMA RINGWALD, alcoholism and family therapist; b. Enderlin, N.D., Oct. 26, 1926; d. Albert William and Emma Anna Magdelena (Trapp) Ringwald; m. Clarence Irvin Dressel, Jr., Mar. 13, 1946 (div. Nov. 1972); 1 son, Keith Alan. Student pub. schs., Casselton, N.D. Cert. Master addiction counselor, N.D.; cert. chem. dependency counselor, Minn. Alcoholism counseling trainee Heartview Found., Mandan, N.D., 1974-75, family therapy intern, 1975-76, family counselor, 1976-77, supr. family mems. program, 1978; designer, supr. family program The Meadows, Wickenburg, Ariz., 1978-79; treatment programs cons., dir. consultation dept. Johnson Inst., Mpls., 1979-81; designer, assoc. dir. chem. dependency unit Presbyn. Hosp., Oklahoma City, 1981-83; designer, supr. adolescent program United Recovery Ctr., Grand Forks, N.D., 1983-85; dir. Irene Dressel Counseling, Grand Forks, 1985-89; designer, program dir. the Dressel Ctr., Fargo, N.D., 1989-90, ret., 1990; FDR/DIR Your Level Best, 1996; cons. S.W. Inst. Alcohol Studies, Norman, Okla., Kans. Alcoholism Counselors Assn., Okla. Assn. Alcoholism and Drug Abuse; lectr. U. N.D., Grand Forks, N.D. Sch. Alcohol Studies. Mem. N.D. Alcoholism Counselors Assn., Nat. Alcoholism and Drug Addiction Counselors Assn., Am. Assn. Counseling and Devel., Democrat. Lutheran.

DRESSLER, LINDA B., ophthalmologist; b. Stuttgart, Germany, Feb. 14, 1957; (parents Am. citizens); d. Samuel and Gorda (Dressler) Bubernak. m. Christopher Dressler Randolph, June 6, 1982; children: Brian Alexander. BA, U. Va., 1978; MD, Harvard Med. Sch., 1982. Intern St. Vincents Hosp., N.Y.C., 1983-84; resident in ophthalmology Manhattan (N.Y.) Eye, Ear & Throat Hosp., 1985-86; assoc., 1986-88; pvt. practice Fairfax, Va., 1987—. Office: Ste 305 12011 Lee Jackson Hwy Fairfax VA 22033-3310

DRESSLER, ROBERT MARK, nephrologist, educator; b. Oceanside, N.Y., Jan. 21, 1958. BA, Clark U., 1979; MD, Sackler Sch. Medicine, Tel Aviv, 1983. Intern, resident Montefiore Med. Ctr., Bronx, N.Y., 1983-86; fellow in nephrology Albert Einstein Coll. Medicine, Bronx, 1986-88, instr., 1988-89, asst. prof., 1989-91; asst. prof. Montefiore Med. Ctr., Bronx, 1991-92; pvt. practice Newark, Del., 1992—; asst. dept. medicine Med. Ctr. Del., Newark, 1994—, St. Francis Hosp., Wilmington, Del., 1992—; chairperson edn. com. Med. Ctr. Del., 1995—; mem. med. rev. bd. ESRD Network IV, Pitts., 1995—. Contbr. articles to profl. jours. Fellow ACP (exec. com. Del. chpt. 1994—); mem. Nat. Kidney Found., Am. Soc. Nephrology, Renal Physician Assn., Del. Med. Soc. Office: Nephrology Assocs PA Omega Profl Ctr Newark DE 19713

DREW, ALLAN PIERCE, forest biology educator; b. Chgo., Jan. 15, 1943; s. Freeman Pierce and Ruth Jessie (Knight) D.; m. Elizabeth Mary McTarnaghan, July 24, 1982; children, Katherine Elizabeth, William McTarnaghan. BS in Forestry, U. Ill., 1965; MS in Watershed Mgmt., U. Ariz., 1967; PhD in Forest Mgmt., Oreg. State U., 1974. Rsch. assoc. Yale U., New Haven, 1973-75, U. Ill., Urbana, 1975-77; asst. prof. Mich. Tech. U., Houghton, 1977-80; asst. prof. Coll. Environ. Sci. and Forestry, SUNY-Syracuse, 1980-84, assoc. prof., 1984-93, prof. 1993—, coord. internat. programs Faculty Forestry, 1991—; asst. conservator forests Dept. Forestry and Game, Malawi, Central Africa, 1967-69. Contbr. articles to profl. jours. Bd. dirs. Citizen Advocacy Onondaga County, 1983-84, Burnet Pk. Zoo, 1995—; mem. Park Ecosys. com. Coun. Pk. Friends; coordinator spl. adult program United Meth. Ch., 1982-95; bd. trustees Univ. United Meth. Ch., Syracuse, 1992—; officer Toastmasters Internat.; adv. Genesee House, 1981—. Weyerhaeuser fellow, 1970-72. Mem. AAAS, U.S. Poplar Council (exec. com. 1984-90), Ecol. Soc. Am., Internat. Soc. Tropical Foresters, Soc. Am. Foresters, Assn. Tropical Biology, Syracuse Chargers Track Club (bd. dirs. 1988-96), Sigma Xi (pres. Syracuse chpt. 1990-91). Avocations: photography; track and field. Office: SUNY Coll Environ Sci Syracuse NY 13210

DREW, NANCY MCLAURIN SHANNON, counselor, consultant; b. Meridian, Miss., Apr. 29, 1934; d Julian Caldwell and Emma Katherine (Sanders) Shannon; m. Thomas Champion III, Feb. 11, 1956; children: Thomas Champion IV, Julian C. Shannon. BA, Furman U., 1956; MEd, N.C. State U., 1968. Cert. sch. counselor; cert. supr. curriculum and instrn., N.C. Rsch. asst. N.C. State U., Raleigh, 1957-59; tchr. English Raleigh City Schs., 1959-60; dir. guidance program Millbrook Sr. High/Wake County Schs., Raleigh, 1969-77; guidance chmn. Daniels Middle Sch./Wake County Schs., Raleigh, 1977-84, guidance info. specialist, 1984-85; guidance supr. Wake County Pub. Schs., Raleigh, 1985-88; coord. model dropout prevention program Wake County Pub. Sch./State Dept. Pub. Inst., Raleigh, 1985-88; counseling chmn. Garner Middle Sch., Raleigh, 1988-96; presenter, cons. 1st and 2d Nat. Dropout Prevention Confs., Winston-Salem, N.C., 1986-87, Raleigh, 1986-88, N.C. Sch. Counselors Conf., Raleigh, 1986-88, Am. Pers. and Guidance Assn., 1976; presenter career workshops ParentScope 1996, speakers' staff ParentScope 1995-96. Contbr. articles to profl. jours. Vice chmn. bd. trustees Crossnore (N.C.) Sch., 1977—; mem. adv. bd. Tamassee DAR Sch., 1994—; sec., bd. dirs. Wake Teen Med. Svcs., Raleigh, 1978-88, Garner Edn. Found., 1991-95; mem. Wake County Bus. and Edn. Leadership Coun., 1992-96. Mem. AACD, NEA, DAR (area rep. spkrs. staff N.C. 1975-78, chmn. state DAR sch. com. 1985-88, state editor DAR News 1989-91, 94—, chpt. regent 1992-95, nat. house com 1992-94, nat. vice chmn. spl. svcs., state officer 1989-91, dir. dist. VI N.C. State DAR, N.C. Outstanding Jr. Mem. 1970), N.C. Edn. Assn., Am. Sch. Counselors Assn., N.C. Sch. Counselors Assn., Phi Delta Kappa, Delta Kappa Gamma (pres. chpt. 1985-88, state chmn. 1991-93, state com. chmn. 1994—). Democrat. Methodist. Home: 6000 Winthrop Dr Raleigh NC 27612-2142

DREW, SHARON LEE, sociologist; b. L.A., Aug. 11, 1946; d. Hal Bernard and Helen Elizabeth (Hammond) D.; children: Keith, Charmagne BA, Calif. State U., Long Beach, 1983; postgrad. Calif. State U., Dominguez Hills, 1988—. Clerical support Compton (Calif.) Unified Sch. Dist., 1967-78; case worker L.A. County Dept. Pub. Social Svcs., 1978—. Den mother Boy Scouts Am., Compton, 1971-72; employee vol. Dominguez Sr. H.S., Compton, 1972-73; project coord. Calif. Tomorrow's Parent Edn. Leadership Devel. Project, 1990; mem. L.A. Caregiver's Network, 1993-94; vol. Calif. State U., Dominguez Hill's Older Adult Ctr., 1994. Recipient cert. Calif. Tomorrow-Parent Edn. Leadership Devel. Project, 1990. Mem. Am. Statis. Assn. (So. Calif. chpt.), Internat. Soc. Exploration of Tchg. Alternatives, Calif. Sociol. Assn. (1st gov. at large grad. student 1990-91), Dominguez Hills Gerontology Assn. (chairperson 1990-91), Sociology of Edn. Assn., Alpha Kappa Delta (Xi chpt. treas. 1992-95) Home: 927 N Chester Ave Compton CA 90221-2105

DREWRY, MARCIA ANN, osteopath; b. St. Louis, Feb. 15, 1951; d. Owen and Annie Vernell (Smith) Palmer; m. Norman T. Drewry, Sept. 18, 1970 (dec. May 1978); 1 child, Tammy Robbins; m. David W. Worsdell Jr., Dec. 7, 1991. AS with honors, Forest Park Coll., 1989; DO, Kirksville Coll. Osteo. Med., 1993. Diplomate Nat. Bd. Osteo. Med. Examiners. Intern Riverside Hosp., Wichita, 1993-94, resident. 1994; med. transcriptionist Malcolm Bliss Mental Health, St. Louis, 1970-78; asst. adminstr. radiology Incarnate Word Hosp., St. Louis, 1977-79; grant writer molecular virology St. Louis (Mo.) U., 1977-79; med. transcriptionist Neurosurg. Assocs., Inc., St. Louis, 1979-87, Stat Transcription, St. Louis, 1987-88, PRN Transcription, St. Louis, 1988-90; physician Anthony (Kans.) Primary Care Ctr., 1994—; chief of staff Harper County Hosp. Dist. #6, 1995—; dir. credentials, emergency dept. and med. records Anthony (Kans.) Primary Care Ctr., 1995—. Capt. Operation Safe St., St. Louis, 1985-89; choir mem. Dover Place Christian Ch., St. Louis, 1986-93; mem Careers for Homemakers, St. Louis, 1987-89. Mem. Am. Coll. Osteo. Family Physicians, Am. Acad. Osteopathy, Am. Osteo. Assn., Kans. Assn. Osteo. Medicine, Bus. and Profl. Women, Beta Sigma Phi, Phi Theta Kappa (pres. 1988-89), Alpha Phi Omega (sec. 1990-91), Theta Psi (promotions asst. 1990-91). Home: 219 W Fanning Dr Anthony KS 67003 Office: Anthony Primary Care Ctr 1101 E Spring Anthony KS 67003

DREWRY, ROBERT HILL, internist; b. Oklahoma City; s. Ransom H. and Simmie Thelma (Hill) D.; m. Rita A. Dalle, June 17, 1959 (div. 1977); children: Ann Rene Chavez, Lisa Ann Ulrich. BS, Okla. U., 1956, MD, 1959. Diplomate Am. Bd. Internal Medicine. Pvt. practice internal medicine Lawton, Okla., 1965—. Capt. U.S. Army, 1962-63. Mem. Am. Soc. Internal Medicine, Am. Coll. Physicians, Okla. Med. Assn. Home: 3507 Ridgeroad Pl Lawton OK 73505 Office: 500 Montgomery Sq Ste 305 Lawton OK 73501

DREWS, JÜRGEN, pharmaceutical researcher; b. Berlin, Aug. 16, 1933; came to U.S., 1991; s. Walter and Charlotte (Schneider) D.; m. Helga Eberlein, July 24, 1963; children: Ulrike, Karoline, Bettina. MD, Free U. Berlin, 1959; Professorship, U. Heidelberg, Fed. Republic of Germany, 1973. Head chemotherapy Sandoz Rsch. Inst., Vienna, Austria, 1976-79, head of inst., 1979-82; head internat. pharm. rsch. and devel. Sandoz, Ltd., Basel, Switzerland, 1982-85; dir. pharm. rsch. F. Hoffmann-La Roche Ltd., Basel, 1985-86, chmn. rsch. bd., mem. exec. com., 1986-90; pres. internat. rsch. and devel., mem. exec. com. Hoffmann-La Roche Inc., Nutley, N.J., 1991-95; pres. global rsch., mem. exec. com. Hoffmann-La Roche Inc., Nutley, 1996—; prof. medicine U. Heidelberg, 1973—; mem. sci. adv. bd. (jour.) Infection, München, Fed. Republic of Germany, 1973—, Drug News & Perspectives, Barcelona, Spain, 1988—, Klinische Pharmakologie, München, 1989—; bd. dirs. Genentech, Inc., South San Francisco, 1990—; bd. dirs., internat. bd. advisors Basel Inst. Immunology, 1986—; mem. dean's coun. Yale U. Sch. Medicine, 1993—, chmn. sci. panel inter-company collaboration for AIDS drug devel., 1993-96, chmn. bd. participants inter-company collaboration for AIDS drug devel., 1996—; mem. adv. com. Mass. Gen. Hosp., Boston, 1994—; chmn. steering com. Sr. Adv. Group Biotech., 1994—. Author: Immunpharmakologie, Grundlagen und Perspektiven, 1986, Immunopharmacology, Principles and Perspectives, 1990; editor: (with others) Topics in Infectious Diseases, vol. 1, 1975, vol. 2, 1977; also over 200 articles. Office: Hoffmann-La Roche Inc Global Rsch 340 Kingsland St Nutley NJ 07110-1199

DREXLER, ELLEN DIANE, neurologist, educator; b. N.Y.C., Apr. 8, 1950; d. Arthur Stanley and Edith (Gelb) D.; m. Steven Jack Freimark, Dec. 24, 1972; children: Hannah, Emmi. BA summa cum laude, Queen's Coll., 1970; PhD, Columbia U., 1974; MD, SUNY, Bklyn., 1978. Diplomate Am. Bd. Psychiatry and Neurology. Intern St. Vincent's Hosp. and Med. Ctr., N.Y.C., 1978-79; resident in neurology Albert Einstein Coll. of Medicine (Bronx Mcpl. Hosp. Ctr.), Bronx, N.Y., 1979-82; assoc. attending neurologist Maimonides Med. Ctr., Bklyn., 1982—; assoc. prof. clin. neurology Health Scis. Ctr. at Bklyn. SUNY, 1982—. Mem. Am. Acad. Neurology, Am. Assn. Study Headache, Am. Acad. Clin. Neurophysiology. Office: Divsn Neurology Maimonide Med Ctr 4802 Tenth Ave Brooklyn NY 11219

DREYER, KRISTI LEIGH, oncology and medical nurse; b. Kokomo, Ind., Oct. 29, 1967; d. Dennis George and Jeffre Lynn (Butcher) D.; 1 child, Samantha Nikole Dreyer-Mathis. BSN, U. N.C., 1992. RN, N.C.; cert. BLS, ACLS. Nurse Durham (N.C.) VA Med. Ctr., 1992-93; clin. nurse in oncology and medicine 375th Med. Group, USAF, Scott AFB, Ill., 1993—. Vol. for blitz build Habitat for Humanity, East St. Louis, Ill., 1994. 2d lt. USAF, 1993—. Mem. Oncology Nurses Soc.

DREYFUSS, ELAINE EMILY, speech pathologist; b. Phila., Mar. 29, 1955; d. Gunter Arthur and Edith (Zinner) D. BA, Temple U., 1976; MS, Tchrs. Coll. of N.Y.C., 1979. Lic. speech pathologist, N.J., Pa. Pvt. practice speech pathology Cherry Hill, N.J., 1985—; speech pathologist Kennedy Meml. Hosp., N.J., Moss Rehab. Hosp., Phila., 1979-90, West Jersey Healthcare, N.J.; profl. adv. com. Camden County Vis. Nurse and Health Assn. Camden County, Olsten Kimberly Quality Care, Moorestown; vis. nurse, health assoc. Kennedy Meml. Home Health Care. Active Hadassah, N.J. Mem. Am. Speech Lang. Hearing Assn., Tri-County Speech Hearing Assn., Southeastern Pa. Speech Lang. Hearing Assn., N.J. Speech Lang. Hearing Assn., Pa. Speech Lang. Hearing Assn. Democrat. Jewish. Office: 661 Guilford Rd Cherry Hill NJ 08003-1406

DREYFUSS, ERIC MARTIN, allergist; b. Bad Homburg, Germany, July 11, 1930; came to U.S., 1934; s. Walter and Hedwig (Hertz) D.; m. Sandra Dale Gasul, June 16, 1957; children: Peter, Lisa. AB, Cornell U., 1953; MD, Chgo. Med. Sch., 1957. Diplomat Am. Bd. Allergy & Immunology. Allergist Allergy Assocs. Rochester (N.Y.), 1964—; asst. clin. prof. U. Rochester Sch. Medicine and Dentistry, 1970—. Capt. U.S. Army, 1960-62. Fellow Am. Acad. Allergy & Immunology, Am. Coll. Allergists, Am. Acad. Pediatrics. Office: Allergy Assocs Rochester 300 S Goodman Rochester NY 14607

DREZ, DAVID JACOB, JR., orthopedic surgeon, educator; b. Lake Charles, La., Aug. 21, 1938; s. David Jacob and Hester Adele (Bingham) D.; m. Judith Diane Wolfe, June 5, 1963; children: Susan Drez Joseph, Catherine Ann Self, David Jacob III. BS, Tulane U., 1959, MD, 1963. Diplomate Am. Bd. Surgery, Am. Bd. Orthopaedic Surgery. Intern Charity Hosp., New Orleans, 1963-64, resident in gen. surgery, 1964-68, resident in orthopaedic surgery, 1968-71; resident Scottish Rite Hosp., Atlanta, 1969, USPHS Hosp., New Orleans, 1970; pvt. practice Orthopaedic Assocs., Lake Charles, 1971-82; pvt. practice Orthopaedic and Sports Injury Clinic Knee and Sports Medicine Ctr., Lake Charles, 1982-94; pvt. practice Ctr. for Orthopaedics, Lake Charles, 1994—; staff Lake Charles Meml. Hosp., 1973—, bd. trustees, 1973, 80-82, sec.-treas., 1977, pres., 1981, chief surgery, 1984, 85; med. staff dept. orthopaedics Children's Hosp., New Orleans, 1988; La. state chmn. Orthopaedic Rsch. and Edn. Found., 1987, 90-92; network of orthopedic surgeons U.S. Gymnastics Fedn., 1988—; physician U.S. Soccer Assn., 1988—; examiner Am. Bd. Orthopaedic Surgery, 1989, 91, 92, bd. dirs.; vis. prof. numerous hosps. and univs.; speaker in field. Author: (with R. D'Ambrosia) Prevention and Treatment of Running Injuries, 1982, Prevention and Treatment of Running Injuries, 2d edit., 1989, (with D.W. Jackson) The Anterior Cruciate Deficient Knee-New Concepts in Ligament Repair, 1986, Orthopaedic Sports Medicine: Principles and Practice , 1994 (with Jesse DeLee); author 8 chpts. in books; editor Am. Jour. Sports Medicine, 1988—, Jour. Orthopaedic Techniques, 1993—; co-editor Operative Techniques in Sports Medicine jour., 1993—; mem. editorial bd. Orthopaedics, 1983—, Arthroscopy, 1984-89, Sports Medicine News, 1989—; author 5 video tapes, audio tape; mem. adv. bd. Clin. Update, Sports Medicine, 1983—, Clin. Orthopaedics and Related Rsch., 1987-93; con. rev. bd. Jour. Bone and Joint Surgeons, 1989—; contbr. over 35 articles to profl. jours. Team orthopaedist athletic dept. McNeese State U., Lake Charles, 1974—, pres. 100 Club, 1979; co-dir. Runner's Clinic, La. State U. Sch. Medicine, New Orleans, 1978-81; chief physician NAAU Boxing Championship, Lake Charles, 1979; mem. Gov.'s Coun. on Phys. Fitness and Sports, 1981; bd. dirs. Lake Area Runners, 1989-92. Maj. La. N.G., 1963-71. Named to La. Athletic Trainers Assn. Hall of Fame, 1989, McNeese State U. Hall of Honors, 1990. Mem. Acad. Orthopaedic Soc., Am. Acad. Orthopaedic Surgeons, Am. Acad. Sports Physicians, Am. Coll. Sports Medicine, Am. Coll. Surgeons, Am. Orthopaedic Assn., Am. Orthopaedic Foot Soc., Am. Orthopaedic Foot and Ankle Soc., Am. Orthopaedic Soc. Sports Medicine, Arthroscopy Assn. N.Am., Assn. Bone and Joint Surgeons, Assn. Sports Medicine Fellowship Dirs., Mid. Am. Orthopaedic Assn., Assn. Arthritic Hip and Knee Surgery, Australian-Am. Orthopaedic Soc., Calcasieu Parish Med. Soc., Clin. Orthopaedic Soc., European Soc. Knee Surgery and Arthroscopy, Herodicus Sports Medicine Soc. (past sec., v.p., pres.), Internat. Arthroscopy Assn., Internat. Soc. Knee, La. Orthopaedic Assn. (pres. 1992), La. State Med. Assn., Oscar Creech Surg. Soc., Orthopaedic Rsch. Soc., Soc. Internat. Chirurgie Orthopedique Traumatologie, Soc. Internat. Recherche Orthopedique Tramatologie. Office: Ctr for Orthopaedics 3rd Fl 1717 Oak Park Blvd Fl 3 Lake Charles LA 70601-8990

DRIEDGER, PAUL EDWIN, pharmaceutical researcher; b. Oak Park, Ill., May 7, 1948; s. Edwin Wilfred and Elinor (Kester) D. BS, MS in Chemistry, Tufts U., 1970; PhD in Pharmacology, Harvard Med. Sch., 1979. Chemist Kodak Rsch. Labs., Rochester, N.Y., 1970-73; v.p., dir. rsch. Lifesystems Co., Inc., Newton, Mass., 1979-80; pres. LC Svcs. Corp., Woburn, Mass., 1980-92, Alder Rsch. Ctr. Corp., Woburn, 1983-92; pres., CEO, chief sci. officer Procyon Pharm., Inc., Woburn, Mass., 1992—. Mem. AAAS, Am. Soc. Microbiology, Am. Chem. Soc. Office: Procyon Pharm Inc 165 New Boston St Woburn MA 01801-6201

DRIGGS, GUY KENNETH, retired surgeon; b. Driggs, Idaho, Sept. 18, 1921; s. Lewis Lynne and Margaret Gurney (Smith) D.; m. Maxine Daugherty, Feb. 14, 1944; children: Guy Kenneth Jr., Darryl Arlton, Dennis Lynne. Student, U. Ariz., 1939-42; MD, U. Md., 1946. Diplomate Am. Bd. Orthopedic Surgery. Intern U. Hosp., Balt., 1946-47; resident in surgery Meth. Hosp., Dallas, 1949-50; resident in orthopedic surgery VA Hosp., Dallas, 1950-52, Scottish Rite Hosp., Dallas, 1952-53; pres. staff Meth. Hosp., Dallas, 1970; asst. prof. anatomy Southwestern Med. Sch. U. Tex., Dallas, 1951-53, asst. clin. prof. orthopedic surgery, 1953-91, ret., 1991. Bd. dirs. YMCA-Oak Cliff, Dallas, 1966-70; pres. Mark Twain Sch. PTA, Dallas, 1965, hon. life mem. Tex. PTA. Capt. U.S. Army, 1947-49. Fellow Am. Acad. Orthopedic Surgery; mem. AMA, Tex. Med. Assn. (del. to ho. dels. 1965-87, del. Texpac 1962-72), Tex. Orthopedic Assn., So. Med. Assn., Western Orthopedic Assn. Mem. LDS Ch. Home: 1346 Rainbow Dr Dallas TX 75208-2626

DRINKWATER, DAVIS CLAPP, JR., surgeon, educator; b. Boston. BA, Harvard U., 1969; MD, U. Vt., 1976; MSc, McGill U., 1980. Diplomate Province of Que. Certification Gen. Surgery; diplomate Am. Bd. Surgery,

Am. Bd. Thoracic Surgery. Chief cardiothoracic surgery Wadsworth VA Hosp., West Los Angeles, 1984-95; asst. prof. surgery UCLA Sch. Medicine, 1984-90, assoc. prof. surgery, 1990—; dir. UCLA Pediat. Cardiac Transplant Program, L.A., 1993; assoc. med. dir. UCLA Perfusion and Assist Device Svc., L.A., 1995. Fellow Royal Coll. Physicians and Surgeons; mem. AMA, ACS, Am. Coll. Cardiology, Am. Assn. for Thoracic Surgery, Am. Heart Assn., Internat. Soc. for Heart and Lung Transplantation, N.Y. Acad. Scis., Physicians for Social Responsibility, Soc. Thoracic Surgeons, So. Calif. Transplant Soc., The Longmire Surg. Soc., Western Thoracic Surg. Assn. Office: UCLA Sch Medicine Cardiothoracic Surgery 10833 Le Conte Ave Los Angeles CA 90024

DRISCOLL, DAVID LEE, chiropractor; b. Storm Lake, Iowa, Aug. 3, 1954; s. Glenn Francis and Jeannine Ann (Layer) D.; m. Joan Marie Valle, Sept. 8, 1973; children: Jennifer Marie, Matthew Bryan. D Chiropractic, Logan Coll. Chiropractic, Chesterfield, Mo., 1978. assoc. instr. Internat. Biocranial Acad. Fellow Internat. Acad. Clin. Acupuncture; mem. Am. Chiropractic Assn., Colo. Chiropractic Assn., El Paso County Chiropractic Assn. Republican. Roman Catholic. Home: 813 Crownridge Dr Colorado Springs CO 80904 Office: Driscoll Chiropractic 1819 W Colorado Ave Colorado Springs CO 80904

DRISCOLL, DIANA SANDERSON, optometrist, consultant; b. Anderson, Ind., July 12, 1957. BA in Psychology, U. Tex., 1980; OD, U. Houston, 1985. Lic. optometrist, Tex. Ptnr. Vision Ctrs., Austin, Cedar Park,, Tex., 1988-91; pvt. practice San Antonio, 1988-95; ptnr. Total Eye Care, Colleyville, Tex.; pres., founder Practice Dynamics, Inc., San Antonio, 1988-92; ptnr. Profl. Cons., Lubbock, Tex., 1988-91; ptnr., founder Opticians Rev., Austin, 1988-92, Profl. Money Mgmt., Inc., 1992-94; guest radio and TV programs. Exec. program dir. Prevent Blindness, Austin, 1985, vol., 1988—; vol. Big Bros.-Big Sisters, San Antonio, 1991-93. Recipient Hydrocurve Contact Lens award Barnes-Hind, 1985, Found. of Excellence award Tex. Assn. Optometrists, 1983. Mem. Am. Optometrists Assn., Tex. Assn. Optometrists (Found. of Excellence award 1983), Tarrant County Optometric Soc., Soc. for Therapeutic Optometrists, Rotary Club. Republican. Office: Total Eye Care 5005 Colleyville Blvd Colleyville TX 76034

DRISCOLL, JEANNE WATSON, nurse; b. Bronx, N.Y., Aug. 23, 1949; d. Robert Ernest and Lorraine Jane (Rittereiser) Watson; m. David John Driscoll, Aug. 18, 1973; children: Lorraine, Kathleen. BS in Nursing, U. Del., 1971; MS, Boston Coll., 1975. Staff nurse New Eng. Deaconess Hosp., Boston, 1971-73; instr. Faulkner Hosp., Jamaica Plain, Mass., 1973-74, 77-78, Salem (Mass.) State Coll., 1976-77, Northeastern U., Boston State Coll., 1979-81; pvt. practice psychotherapy Boston, 1981—; clin. nurse specialist Brigham and Women's Hosp., 1981-89; v.p., co-founder Lifecycle Prodns., Inc., Newton, Mass., 1985—; childbirth educator Boston Hosp. for Women, 1979-81; founder Lacatation Assocs., Weston, Mass., 1981-93; adult psychomental health clin. nurse specialist. Author: Breastfeeding Your Premature Baby, 1986. Troop leader Girl Scouts U.S.A., Boston, 1985-88. Mem. NAFE, ANA (cert.), Mass. Nurses Assn. (clin. practice award 1983), Am. Assn. of Women's Health Obstet. Neonatal Nursing, Sigma Theta Tau. Roman Catholic. Office: Hestia Inst 12 Mila Ln Wellesley MA 02181

DRISKO, JAMES WINSHIP, clinical social worker; b. Yonkers, N.Y., June 7, 1950; s. Elliot Hillman and Elizabeth (Winship) D.; m. Marilyn Carey, Nov. 6, 1983; children: Ann Elizabeth, Meghan Lee. AB, Amherst Coll., 1972; MSW, Smith Coll., 1977; DSW, Boston Coll., 1983. Clin. social worker Marlborough Westborough Mental Health Clinic, Marlborough, Mass., 1977-79; chief clin. social worker Marlborough Pub. Schs., 1979-84; dir. children's svc. Mass. Dept. Mental Health, Lynn, 1984-87; clin. dir. O'Keefe Sch., Lynn, Mass., 1987-89; asst. prof. Smith Coll. Sch. Social Work, Northampton, 1989-95, chair rsch. sequence, 1992-94, assoc. prof., 1995—. Adj. asst. prof. Simmons Coll., 1983-85; rsch. adv. Smith Coll., Northampton, Mass., 1984-89; clin. cons. Mt. Tom Mental Health, Holyoke, Mass., 1995—. Contbr. articles to profl. jours. Bd. dirs. Greater Lynn Coun. for Children, vice chmn., 1987-89; bd. dirs. Greater Marlborough Council for Children. Mem. NASW, Boston Smith Coll. Sch. Social Work Alumni Assn. (treas. 1980-84), Am. Orthopsychiat. Assn., Child Group Psychotherapy Assn. Office: Smith Coll Sch Social Work Lilly Hall Northampton MA 01063

DROEGE, MARIE THERESE, hospital administrator; b. Washington, Mo., July 17, 1961; d. Firmin Francis D. BS in Biology, Chemistry, Quincy Coll., 1983; MHA, U. Mo., 1985. Adminstrv. fellow Mercy Hosp., Urbana, Ill., 1985-86, acting v.p. patient care services, 1986; ops. specialist Healthcor, Urbana, 1986-87; chief exec. officer Cen. Community Hosp., Clifton, Ill., 1987-90; sr. v.p. of ops. St. Mary Hosp., Quincy, Ill., 1990-93; exec. v.p. ops. and planning Our Lady of Bellefonte Hosp., Ashland, Ky., 1993—; bd. dirs. Our Lady of Bellefonte Hosp., MedTrac, Bellefonte Health Enterprises. Mem. Coll. Healthcare Execs., Ill. Hosp. Assn. (pres. region 3B 1990), Russell Rotary Club. Roman Catholic. Office: Our Lady of Bellefonte Hosp St Christopher Dr Ashland KY 41101

DRONBERGER, JAMES A., physical therapist, educator; b. Hutchinson, Kans., Sept. 16, 1953. BS, Kans. State U., 1975; cert. phys. therapy, U. Kans., 1975; MBA, Rockhurst Coll., 1986. Lic. phys. therapist, Kans., Mo. Staff phys. therapist Bethany Med. Ctr., Kansas City, 1976-78; dir. phys. therapy St. Mary's Hosp., Kansas City, 1978-84, dir. rehab. svcs., 1984-87, adminstr. family practice, 1987-88; instr. phys. therapy Rockhurst Coll., Kansas City, 1989-95, developer mentoring program with S.E. H.S., 1993, asst. prof., 1995—; mem. adv. bd. Penn Valley C.C., Kansas City, 1991—, Sanford-Brown Coll., Kansas City, 1995—. Vol. AIDS nursing home Hope Care Ctr., Kansas City, 1995; vol. home repair for fin. disadvantaged Christmas in Oct., Kansas City, 1992, 93; handicapped swimming instr. Bethany Med. Ctr., Kansas City, 1979. Mem. Am. Phys. Therapy Assn., Mo. Phys. Therapy Assn. (student liaision, com. chair 1994-95). Office: Rockhurst Coll 1100 Rockhurst Rd Kansas City MO 64110

DROPKIN, SHEREE A., clinical social worker; b. Dorchester, Mass., Jan. 23, 1959; d. Arthur L. and Concye A. (Patterson) Nelson; m. Kevin James Dropkin, Aug. 14, 1983. BA, R.I. Coll., 1980, MSW, 1989. Home care coord. Alternative Care, Warwick, R.I., 1980-81; admissions counselor Barrington (R.I.) Coll., 1983-84; behavior specialist Blackstone Valley Ctr., Pawtucket, R.I., 1984-85; unit coord. The Groden Ctr., Providence, 1985-89; psychiat. social worker Bradley Hosp., East Providence, R.I., 1989-93; sch. social worker Meeting St. Ctr., East Providence, 1993-95; clin. social worker Kent County Mental Health Ctr., Warwick, R.I., 1995—. Mem. NASW. Presbyterian. Home: 92 Abbott Ave Warwick RI 02886-8904

DROSS, CORNELIUS WILLIAM, dental surgeon, retired; b. Paterson, N.J., Apr. 25, 1915; s. Harry John and Jennie (Bandstra) D.; m. Catherine Scobie, Dec. 25, 1943; children: Harry, William, Walker. AB, U. Pa., Phila., DDS, 1939; postgrad., NYU, 1946. Diplomate Am. Dental Assn. of Oral Surgeons. Intern Med. Ctr., Jersey City, 1939-40; dental surgeon Teaneck (N.J.) Med. Group, 1941; dental dir. Hawthorne, N.J., 1941-73; dental surgeon Ridgewood, N.J., 1954-74; dental oral surgeon Gen. Hosp., Paterson, 1946-73, Valley Hosp., Ridgewood, 1953-78. Advisor erosion control Dept. Natural Resources, Broward County, Fla., 1974-91; chmn. Zoning Bd. Appeals, Pompano Beach, Fla., 1979-81, v.p. Civic Assn., Pompano Beach, 1974-80; mem. Am. Security Coun., 1970-91. Lt. col. USAAF, 1943-45, AUS Dental Corp, 1954-62. Grantee Proposed Beach Renourishment Project, City of Pompano Beach, 1983. Mem. Royal Soc. Health, Rotary (Paul Harris fellow), Elks, Masons, Delta Sigma Delta, Theta Chi. Republican. Presbyterian. Home: 111 N Pompano Beach Blvd Pompano Beach FL 33062-5712

DROSSMAN, DOUGLAS ARNOLD, medical investigator, educator, gastroenterologist; b. Bklyn., Mar. 20, 1946; s. Murray and Ruth (Cohen) D.; m. Deborah Risa Ducoff, June 3, 1970; children: David, Daniel. BA cum laude, Hofstra U., 1966; MD, Albert Einstein Coll., 1970. Diplomate Am. Bd. Internal Medicine, Gastroenterology. Resident N.Y.U.-Bellevue Med. Ctr., N.Y.C., 1972-73; fellow in psychosomatic medicine U. Rochester, N.Y., 1975-76; intern and resident U. N.C., Chapel Hill, 1970-72, fellow in gastroenterology, 1976-78, instr. in medicine, 1977-78, asst. prof. medicine and psychiatry, 1978-83, assoc. prof. medicine and psychiatry, 1983-90, prof. medicine and psychiatry, 1990—; mem. internship selection com. U. N.C., 1977—, housestaff-faculty com., 1980-84, chmn. selection com., 1983—; mem. com. for curriculum rev. III, subcom. on transition from basic scis. to med. scis. U. N.C. Med. Sch., 1981-83, mem. health promotion/disease prevention steering com., 1983, co-dir. med.-psychiat. liaison program faculty-resident study group in behavioral medicine, 1977—, liaison cons. to dept. medicine, 1977—, mem. com. to develop interviewing skills in dept. medicine, 1977—; vis. prof. over 50 med. ctrs. and univs. Author: (with others) Transfer Factor: Basic Properties and Clinical Applications, 1976, The Merck Manual, 14th edit., 1982, 15th edit., 1987, 16th edit., 1992, Functional Disorders of the Digestive Tract, 1983, Advances in Internal Medicine, 1983, Gastrointestinal Disease: Pathophysiology, Diagnosis, Management, 3d edit., 1983, 5th edit. 1993, Textbook of Gastroenterology, 1990, 2d edit., 1995, Manual of Psychiatric Consultation and Emergency Care, 1984, Clinical Problems in Ambulatory Care Medicine, 1985, Irritable Bowel Syndrome, 1985, Inflammatory Bowel Disease, 1988, Psychosocial Factors in GI Illness, others; editor: Manual of Gastroenterologic Procedures, 1982, 87, 92, Functional Gastrointestinal Disorders, 1994; mem. editorial bd. Behavioral Medicine Abstracts, 1985—, Stress Medicine, 1985—, Current Concepts Gastroenterology, 1986—, Jour. Clin. Gastroenterology, 1986—; editor gastroenterology sect. Merck Manual, 1990—; ad hoc reviewer over 15 profl. jours. including Jour. Annals of Internal Medicine, 1978, Gastroenterology, 1978, AMA, 1984—, Jour. Gen. Internal Medicine, 1985—, Jour. Clin. Gastroenterology, 1985—, Health Psychology, 1989—, Gut, 1990—; mem. adv. bd. Health Digest, 1986—, Merck Manual, 1988—; contbr. over 200 articles, book revs., abstracts to profl. jours., chpts. to textbooks. Maj. Med. Corps, USAF, 1973-75. Grantee S.S. Zlinkoff Found., 1979, Smith, Kline, Beckman, 1982, NIH, 1983-86, 91-95, Burroughts Wellcome Co. Inc., 1984-85, Core Ctr. for Diarrheal Diseases, U. N.C., 1986, Nat. Found. for Ileitis and Colitis, 1987-88, Bristol-Myers Pharm. Group, 1988-90, Procter & Gamble, 1991, Hoffman La Roche Co., 1991-92, NIMH, 1991-95, NIH, 1983-86, 95—, others. Fellow ACP (med. knowledge self-assessment program com. 1989-91), Am. Coll. Gastroenterology; mem. Am. Psychosomatic Soc. (councillor 1985-88, 90-92, 1986 program com. 1985-86, chmn. membership com. 1988-92, sec.-treas. 1992—, pres. 1996), Durham-Orange County Med. Soc., Am. Fedn. for Clin. Rsch., Am. Gastroenterol. Assn. (coun. on nerve gut interactions 1981-86, program selection com. 1985-86, program selection chmn., chmn. brain-guy rsch. group 1990-94), Am. Soc. for Gastrointestinal Endoscopy, So. Soc. for Clin. Investigation, Chmn. Functional Brain-Gut Rsch. Group. Office: U NC Div Digestive Diseases 420 Burnett Womack Clb # 7080 Chapel Hill NC 27599

DROUGHT, JAMES HENRY, healthcare business owner, exercise physiologist; b. Aurora, Ill., Mar. 29, 1957; s. James William and Lorna Beryl (Carlson) D. Student, U.S. Mil. Acad., 1975-77; BS in Sports Medicine, Rutgers U., 1980; MS in Clin. Exercise Physiology, Northeastern U., 1995. Comm. coord. Lake Placid (N.Y.) Olympic Organizing Com., 1980-81; dir. Rainmaker Prodns., Boston, 1982-85; health promotion mgr. City of Boston, 1986-87; owner Personal Trainers Strength & Conditioning Consulting, Boston, 1987—; cons. City of Boston, 1988-89, State of Mass., Boston, 1988-89, Lotus Devel. Corp., Cambridge, Mass., 1990-91; mem. (C.O.R.P.S.) nat. bd. Reebok Internat., Ltd., Stoughton, Mass., 1992—; articles cons. SHAPE mag., 1995—. Exec. editor Conditioning Instr., 1991-93; contbr. articles to profl. jours.; author Ask the Experts Column, Boston Globe, 1990-92. Mem. exec. com. Boston vs. Montreal Fitness Challenge, City of Boston, 1989. Mem. Am. Coll. Sports Medicine, Am. Coun. on Exercise, Nat. Strength and Conditioning Assn. (Mass. state dir. 1992—, task analysis com. 1992—, nat. conf. com. 1993-95, chmn. personal trainer com. 1991, exam devel. com., 1994—, Challenge Scholarship 1993, State Dir.'s award 1995, Agy. Appreciation award 1995). Home and Office: PO Box 15601 Boston MA 02215-0011

DROZDIS, MARIE TRESE, nurse; b. Scranton, Pa., Dec. 8, 1939; d. Stanley and Anna Mary (Rukas) Kwader; m. Anthony Alvin Drozdis, May 16, 1959 (div. Sept. 1986); children: Anthony, Diana, David. BSN magna cum laude, Marywood Coll., 1985. Bd. cert. emergency nurse. Instr. math. Internat. Correspondence Schs., Scranton, 1957-59; lic. practical nurse Community Med. Ctr., Scranton, 1977-85, RN, 1985-88; RN Thomas Jefferson U. Hosp., Phila., 1988—; cons. Home Health. Recipient Niemotko medal Marywood Coll. Mem. Emergency Nurses Assn., Internat. Soc. Philos. Enquiry, Intertel, Mensa Internat., Marywood Coll. Nursing Hon. Soc. (past v.p.), Human Ecology Action League, Kappa Gamma Pi, Delta Epsilon Sigma, Psi Chi. Democrat. Roman Catholic. Home: 605 Hummingbird Ln Bensalem PA 19020-4645 Office: Thomas Jefferson U Hosp 11th Walnut Philadelphia PA 19107

DROZDOWSKI, WIESLAW WLADYSLAW, neurologist, neurophysiologist, researcher; b. Goni—dz, Poland, Sept. 25, 1951; s. Antoni and Bronisława (Dziekońska) D.; m. Elizabeth Christina Kobus, Dec. 26, 1975; children: Magdalene, Martha. Physician, Med. Acad., Białystok, Poland, 1976, MD, 1982. Jr. asst. Neurology Clinic of Med. Acad. Białystok, 1976, asst., 1977-80, asst. lectr., 1981-83, lectr., 1984-93, asst. prof., 1994, head, 1995—, head Electromyographic Lab., 1978—. Contbr. articles to profl. jours. Mem. Solidarity Party, Białystok, 1980—. Mem. World Fedn. Neurology, Polish Neurol. Soc., Polish Neurophysiol. Soc. Roman Catholic. Office: Neurology Clinic Med Acad, 24A M Sklodowska-Curie St, 15-267 Białystok Poland

DRUCKER, BARRY JULES, environmental health specialist; b. St. Louis, Dec. 29, 1940; s. Morris Josef and Geraldine Drucker; m. Sandra Leta Lew, June 10, 1968; 1 child, Marlon. BA, So. Ill. U., 1969; MA, Webster U., 1976; MPH, St. Louis U., 1992. Registered sanitarian.; cert. profl. environ. health specialist. Chemist St. Louis City Health Dept., 1970-76; sr. research technician Washington U. Sch. Medicine, St. Louis, 1976-77; sanitarian Mo. Dept. Mental Health, St. Louis, 1977-79; sanitarian, supr. Mo. Dept. Health, St. Louis, 1979-82; program mgr. St. Louis County Health Dept., Clayton, Mo., 1982—; assoc. dir. Mo. Restaurant Assn., St. Louis, 1982—; mem. Mo. Food Adv. coun., Jefferson City, 1982—, St. Louis County Restaurant com., 1982; vice chmn. Mo. Bd. Certification for Sanitarians, Jefferson City, 1987-89, 90-91, mem., 1986-91; adj. faculty St. Louis U., 1992—; mem. Mo. State Milk Bd., Jefferson City, 1995—; mem. adv. bd. Sch. Pub. Health St. Louis U., 1996—. Peer reviewer Jour. of Environ. Health, 1995—; contbr. articles to profl. jours. With USAF, 1960-64. Mem. Mo. Environ. Health Assn. (pres. 1985-86, publ. awards 1986, 87, 88, 93, Sanitarian of Yr. 1987), St. Louis Area Pub. Health Assn. (pres. 1986-87, mem.-at-large 1992—), Mo. Pub. Health Assn. (bd. dirs. 1986-87, pub. award 1988, 93), Nat. Environ. Health Assn. (bd. dirs. 1984-86, Cert. of Merit 1987, Jour. Editor's award 1994). Home: 19250 River Ridge Ln Wildwood MO 63005-3818 Office: St Louis County Health Dept 111 S Meramec Ave Saint Louis MO 63105-1711

DRUCKER, MELVIN BRUCE, psychology educator; b. Phila., May 27, 1927; s. Maxwell Lionel and Sylvia (Layton) D.; m. Miriam Elizabeth Koontz, Feb. 3, 1925. BS in Psychology, Case Western Res. U., 1950; MA in Psychology, Ohio U., Athens, 1952; PhD in Psychology, Vanderbilt U., 1956. Diplomate Am. Bd. Profl. Psychology. Intern clin. psychology S.C. Mental Health Commn., Columbia, 1955-56; psychologist Fulton County Child Guidance Clinic, Atlanta, 1956-58; chief mental health planning, evaulation and rsch. Community Mental Health Svc., Ga. Dept. Pub. Health, Atlanta, 1958-61, chief psychologist, 1961-64; clin. and rsch. psychologist Chaplaincy Tng. Project Ga. Clinic, Atlanta, 1965-69, chief psychologist, 1969-70; chmn., assoc. prof. dept. mental health Ga. State U., Atlanta, 1970-77, chmn., prof. dept. mental health, 1977-80, prof. dept. mental health, 1980-89; prof. emeritus, 1990—; instr. psychology Fisk U., Nashville, 1952-53, U. S.C., Columbia, 1955-56; cons. St. Judes House for Addicted Persons, Atlanta, 1970-89; clin. psychologist South DeKalb Mental Health Ctr., Decatur, Ga., 1983-89; lectr. short term tng. program DeKalb Addiction Clinic, Atlanta, 1983—. NIMH grantee, Washington, 1978. Mem. APA, Southeastern Psychol. Assn., Ga. Psychol. Assn. Home: 424 Glendale Ave Decatur GA 30030-1922 Office: Ga State U University Plz Atlanta GA 30303

DRUCKER, MIRIAM KOONTZ, psychologist, educator; b. Mechanicsburg, Pa., Feb. 3, 1925; married. A.B., Dickinson Coll., 1947; M.A., Emory U., 1948; Ph.D., Peabody Coll., 1955. Counselor psychology Millsaps Coll., 1949-51; instr. Monticello Coll., 1951-52; asst. prof. psychology Agnes Scott Coll., Decatur, Ga., 1955-58, assoc. prof., 1958-62, prof., 1962-80, Charles A. Dana prof. psychology, 1981-90, prof. emeritus, 1990—, former chmn. dept. psychology. Mem. Am. Psychol. Assn. Home: 424 Glendale Ave Decatur GA 30030-1922

DRUCKREY, GERALD RICHARD, ophthalmologist; b. Long Beach, Calif., Jan. 9, 1933; s. Richard Adolph and Evelyn Alvina (Moede) D.; m. Marilyn Mae Sievert, June 11, 1955; children: Dawn Suzanne, Sara Joanne, Scot Richard. MD, Marquette U., 1957. Diplomate Am. Bd. Ophthalmology. Intern Tripler U.S. Hosp., Honolulu, 1957-58; resident ophthalmology Walter Reed Gen. Hosp., Washington, 1959-62; pvt. practice, Beloit, Wis., 1965—; past chmn. dept. surgery, past pres. med. staff, past chmn. instnl. rev. bd. Beloit Meml. Hosp.; past pres. med. staff Beloit Clinic. Maj. M.C. U.S. Army, 1957-65. Fellow Am. Acad. Ophthalmology; mem. Am. Soc. Cataract and Refractive Surgery, Wis. Acad. Ophthalmology. Office: Beloit Clinic 1905 Huebbe Pky Beloit WI 53511-1842

DRUDY, PATRICK, psychologist, human relations consultant; b. Reading, Pa., Apr. 6, 1943; s. Patrick J. and C. Violet (Chilcote) D. BA, Pa. State U., 1965; MEd, Temple U., 1971, PhD, 1978, MBA, 1988. Lic. psychologist, Pa. Nazareth Hosp., Phila., 1970-72; Clin. dir. Children's Home Burlington County, Mt. Holly, N.J., 1972-74; dir. specialized day programs N.E. Mental Health Ctr., Phila., 1974-78; exec. dir. Indiana County Guidance Ctr., Pa., 1978-79, Am. Inst. for Counseling, Roslyn, Pa., 1979—; ptnr. Alexander Assocs., Abington, 1984-85; pres. Applied Psychology Assocs., 1986-88; pres. Alliance for Wellness, 1988-90; pres. i/e Internat. Ltd., 1990-94; host radio show Sta. WCSD, 1980-82; exec. dir. Eugenia Day Treatment Ctr., Doylestown, Pa., 1993. Dir. clin. svcs. Cath. Charities, Wilmington, Del., 1995—. 1st lt. U.S. Army, 1965-67. Fellow Pa. Psychol. Assn.; mem. Am. Psychol. Assn., Eastern Psychol. Assn., Phila. Soc. Clin. Psychologists, Red Dragon Canoe Club (Edgewater Park, N.J.). Office: Catholic Chariites PO Box 2610 Wilmington DE 19805

DRUECK, CHARLES, III, surgeon, educator; b. Chgo., June 16, 1945; s. Charles Jr. Drueck; m. Jane Vincent; children: Amy Elizabeth, Laurie Catherine. BA, Northwestern U., Evanston, Ill., 1967; MD, Northwestern U., Chgo., 1971. Diplomate Am. Bd. Surgery; cert. am. trauma life support instr., provider and course dir. Intern Chgo. Wesley Meml. Hosp., 1971-72; resident in surgery Northwestern U. Med. Sch., Chgo., 1972-77, instr., 1976-77, assoc. in surgery, 1977-88; Coon fellow Brooke Army Med. Ctr., San Antonio, 1975-76; pvt. practice, Evanston; lectr. Cook County Grad. Sch. Medicine, Chgo., 1978—; asst. attending staff Evanston Hosp., 1977-79, assoc. attending staff, 1979-82, attending staff, 1982-88, sr. attending staff, 1988—, clin. dir. burn unit, 1977-79, dir. Grainger Burn Ctr., 1979-84, assoc. epidemiologist, 1984—, trauma dir., 1984—, surg. epidemiologist, 1985—, asst. prof. clin.. surgery, 1988—, pres.-elect profl. staff, 1992-93, pres., 1993-95. Deacon Northminster Presbyn. Ch., Evanston, 1986—. Recipient fire prevention achievement award Ill. Fire Insps. Assn., 1987. Fellow ACS; mem. AMA, Am. Burn Assn., Assn. for Acad. Surgery, Am. Soc. for Parenteral and Enteral Nutrition, Ill. Surg. Soc., Ill. Med. Soc. (ho. of dels. 1990—), Chgo. Surg. Soc., Chgo. Med. Soc. (med. practice com. 1985—, emergency medl care com. 1987-89, health care delivery com. 1990, presdl. adv. bd. 1990—, v.p. North Suburban br. 1988-90, pres. 1990-91). Office: Evanston Surgeons CTD 2500 Ridge Ave Evanston IL 60201

DRUGAN, ARIE, obstetrician, gynecologist, geneticist; b. Bucharest, Romania, Mar. 21, 1950; s. Alexander and Natalia (Shlesinger) D.; m. Aviva Tzeiler, Oct. 29, 1970; children: Roni, Shiri. MD, Hebrew U., Jerusalem, 1980. Resident in ob-gyn Rambam Med. Ctr., Haifa, 1979-85, coord. IVF program, 1985-87, cons. genetics MFM, 1990-95, vice chmn. dept. ob-gyn., 1995—; fellow divsn. genetics Hutzel Hosp., Detroit, 1987-89, Hutzel Hosp./Wayne State U., Detroit, 1988-90; cons. in genetics Sapir Med. Ctr., Kfar Saba, Israel, 1994-95; assoc. prof. ob-gyn. Wayne State U., Detroit, 1996. Editor: Maternal Genetic Disease, 1995. Lt. col. Israel Def. Forces, 1975-81. Recipient award Ctrl. Assn. Obstetricians and Gynecologists. Mem. ACMG, AIUM. Home: 11 A Baal Shem Tov St, Haifa Israel Office: Rambam Med Ctr Dept Ob-Gyn, PO Box 9602, Haifa 37096, Israel

DRUGAN, ROBERT CHARLES, psychology educator; b. Morristown, N.J., Jan. 26, 1957; s. Walter Thompson and Alice May (Leikam) D.; m. Constance Josephine Eppich, May 22, 1983; children: Kylee Jennifer, Timothy Robert. BA magna cum laude, Susquehanna U., Selinsgrove, Pa., 1979; MA in Psychology, U. Colo., 1981, PhD in Exptl. Psychology, 1984. Mead-Johnson rsch. fellow NIH, Bethesda, Md., 1985; posdoctoral fellow NIMH, Bethesda, 1986-88; asst. prof. psychology Brown U., Providence, 1988-95, U. N.H., Durham, 1995—; mem. radiation safety com. Brown U., Providence, 1991-94, U. N.H., Durham, 1995—. Contbr. articles to profl. jours., chpts. to books. Recipient Nat. Rsch. Svc. award NIMH, Bethesda, 1985-87; Alfred P. Sloan Found. rsch. fellow, N.Y.C., 1989-91. Mem. AAAS, Soc. Neurosci., Internat. Soc. Psychoneuroendocrinology. Office: U NH Dept Psychology 10 Library Way Durham NH 03824-3567

DRUMM-TOJINO, LORI LEE, physician, dental hygienist; b. St. Paul, July 25, 1961; d. Melvin Keith Drumm and Deanna Marie (Kiminki) Stephenson; m. Conrado Neri Tojino, Jr., May 22, 1994. AAS, Cuyahoga C.C., 1981; BS, Baldwin Wallace Coll., 1987; DO summa cum laude, U. Health Scis. Kansas City, 1994. Diplomate Nat. Bd. Med. Examiners. Dental hygienist Dr. Aros, Lorain, Ohio, 1981-83; also Dr. John Bostic, Brook Park, Ohio, 1981-83; dental hygienist Drs. Lipton & Knaus, Bridgeport, Conn., 1983-84, Drs. Ronald Arndt and Kurt Thomas, North Ridgeville, Ohio, 1984-87, The Cleve. Clin. Found., 1987-90, Drs. Miller, Laniauskas and Homitz, Shaker Heights, Ohio, 1989-91; intern Phila. Coll. Osteopathic Medicine, 1994-95; physician, gen. med. officer U.S. Navy, Groton, Conn., 1995—. Mem. Am. Osteopathic Assn., Pa. Med. Assn., Sigma Sigma Phi, Phi Sigma Alpha. Home: 10 Willow St Mystic CT 06355 Office: US Navy Hosp Acute Care PO Box 600 Groton CT 06349

DRURY, GERALD IRWIN, periodontist, educator; b. Chgo., July 23, 1944; s. Daniel and Dorothy (Chait) D.; m. Tineke Willy Ten Hagen, Dec. 25, 1970; children: Charles, Justin. BA, U. Ill., 1966; BSD, U. Ill., Chgo., 1970, DDS, 1972; MS, Med. Coll. Va., 1968; cert. in periodontics La. State U., 1979. Diplomate Am. Bd. Periodontology. Intern N.E. Fla. State Hosp., MacClenny, 1972-73; resident in anesthesiology VA Hosp., New Orleans, 1978; resident in medicine Charity Hosp., New Orleans, 1978, vis. resident periodontist, 1978-79; instr. La. State U. Sch. Dentistry, New Orleans, 1977-79; clin. asst. prof. dept. surg. scis. periodontics sect. U. So. Calif. Sch. Dentistry, Los Angeles, 1979, asst. prof. dept. surg. scis., 1979-81, clin. asst. prof. grad. div., 1981-85, clin. assoc. prof., 1985-92, clin. prof. advanced peridontics, 1992—; dir. predoctoral periodontal surgery clinic, 1980-81, course dir. current lit. rev. grad. periodontics, 1982—; mem. adv. com. Bryman Sch. Dental Assts., 1982—; pvt. practice dentistry, Fort Myers Beach, Fla., 1973-77, specializing in periodontics, Irvine, Calif., 1981, Hermosa Beach, Calif., 1981—; provisional med. staff Little Company of Mary Hosp., Torrance, Calif., 1986. Recipient cert. of appreciation U. So. Calif., 1981. Mem. Am. Acad. Periodontology (local arrangements com., fgn. relations com.), Internat. Acad. Periodontology, Am. Assn. Dental Rsch., Internat. Assn. Dental Rsch. (Rsch. award of excellence New Orleans chpt.), ADA, Western Soc. Periodontology (co-chmn. periodontal publs. com. 1977), Western Dental Soc. (membership com. 1981-90, mem. peer rev. com. 1992-95, ethics com. 1995—), Calif. Soc. Periodontists (regional leader 1991—). Home: 1100 Pacific Coast Hwy Apt F Hermosa Beach CA 90254 Office: U So Calif Sch Dentistry PO Box 77951 Los Angeles CA 90007-0951

DRURY, J. KEVIN, physician; b. Montreal, Que., Can., Oct. 28, 1949; came to the U.S., 1981; s. James T. and Thelma K. (Riley) D.; m. Joanna M. Langemeyer, Sept. 29, 1973; children: Paul C., Emily K. BSc, McGill U., Montreal, 1970, MDCM, 1976. Bd. cert. Am. Bd. Internal Medicine. Rsch. fellow Cedars-Sinai Med. Ctr., L.A., 1981-82, attending physician, 1982—; instr. medicine UCLA, 1982-84, asst. clin. prof. medicine, 1984—; pres. Internat. Retropertusion Soc., Austria, 1986-88; v.p. Cedar-Sinai Med. Group, L.A., 1993-95, L.A. Crettered Med. Group, 1996—. Fellowship Can. Heart Assn., 1981-83. Fellow Am. Coll. Cardiology; mem. Am. Heart Assn., Calif. Med. Assn., L.A. Calif. Med. Assn. Office: 8635 W Third #1050W Los Angeles CA 90048

DRURY, KENNETH CLAYTON, biological scientist; b. Madera, Calif., Mar. 27, 1945; s. Carma and Alice (Zollinger) D.; m. Sandra Rosemary hanlon, Apr. 28, 1972; children: Allison Hanlon, Vanessa Laura. BA,

Westmont Coll., 1967; PhD, U. Geneva, Switzerland, 1979. Cert. in andrology and embryology high complesicy lab. dir. Am. Bd. Bioanalysts. NIH fellow U. Calif., Berkeley, 1979-82; rsch. scientist Codon Corp., South San Francisco, Calif., 1982-84; sr. scientist Microgenics Corp., Concord, Calif., 1984-86; dir. U. Louisville, 1986-92, In Vitro Fertilization and Gamete Physiology Labs. U. Fla., 1992—. Contbr. articles to profl. jours. 1st Lt. U.S. Army, 1969-72, Vietnam. Mem. Am. Fertility Soc., AAAS. Office: U Fla Dept Ob-Gyn Div Reprod Endocrinology PO Box 100294 Gainesville FL 32610-0294

DRUSIN, LEWIS MARTIN, physician, educator; b. N.Y.C., Sept. 25, 1939; s. David and Gladys Margaret (Apfel) D. BS, Union Coll., 1960; MD, Cornell U., 1964; MPH, Columbia U., 1974. Med. intern 2nd medicine (Cornell div.) Bellevue Hosp., N.Y.C., 1964-65; jr. asst. resident in medicine Med. Ctr. Hosp. of Vt., Burlington, 1965-66; sr. asst. resident N.Y. Hosp., N.Y.C., 1968-69; fellow in medicine div. allergy and infectious diseases Cornell U. Med. Coll., N.Y.C., 1969-70; asst. prof. pub. health Cornell U., N.Y.C., 1970-77, asst. prof. medicine, 1972-79, assoc. prof. pub. health, 1977-84, assoc. prof. clin. medicine, 1979—, prof. clin. pub. health, 1984—; dir. dept. epidemiology The N.Y. Hosp., N.Y.C., 1970—, assoc. attending physician, 1979—; cons. The Rockefeller Univ. Hosp., N.Y.C., 1981—; regional dir. for N.Am. Internat. Union Against Venereal Diseases and Treponematoses, Leeds, Eng., 1986-95; liaison officer, UN for IUVDT, 1995. Contbr. book chpts., articles. Task Force Syphilis, N.Y. State Dept. Health, 1990-91. Sr. surgeon USPHS, 1966-68. Fellow ACP, Am. Coll. Preventive Medicine, Infectious Disease Soc. Am., N.Y. Acad. Medicine, Royal Soc. Medicine, Royal Soc. Tropical Medicine and Hygiene; mem. Am. Venereal Disease Assn. (pres. 1982), Soc. Hosp. Epidemiology Am., Med. Soc. Study of Venereal Diseases (hon. life), Phi Beta Kappa, Sigma Xi, Alpha Omega Alpha. Office: NY Hosp Cornell Med Ctr 520 E 68th St New York NY 10021-6342

DRUTZ, JAN EDWIN, pediatrics educator; b. Louisville, Jan. 8, 1942; s. Abe Morris and Lillian (Billig) D.; m. Anne Edwin Sussman, June 7, 1965; children: Jeffrey Benjamin, Lisa Michele, Dana Nicole. BA, U. Louisville, 1964, MD, 1968. Pvt. practice Houston, 1973-87; intern, then resident Baylor Coll. Medicine, Houston, 1968-71, clin. asst. prof., 1973-77, clin. assoc. prof., 1977-87, assoc. prof. clin. pediat., 1987-95, dir. pediat. continuity clinic, 1987—, assoc. prof. pediat., 1995—; pres. med. staff Tex. Children's Hosp., 1995. Maj. U.S. Army, 1971-73. Mem. AMA, Harris County Med. Soc., Tex. Pediat. Soc. (adv. com., mem. student preceptorship program 1995—), Houston Pediat. Soc. (sec. 1984-85, pres. 1988-89), Ambulatory Pediat. Assn. (chmn. continuity clinic spl. interest group 1990-95, edn. com. 1993—). Office: Baylor Coll Medicine Dept Pediatrics 1 Baylor Plz Houston TX 77030

DRYE, ROBERT CALDWELL, psychiatrist; b. N.Y.C., Oct. 1, 1927; s. John Wilson D. Jr. and Loraine Livingston (Caldwell) D.; m. Vivian Nevue, Sept. 10, 1955 (dec. Sept. 1979); children: Richard, David, Barbara, Robert Caldwell Jr., Caroline, Elizabeth, Loraine. BS, MIT, 1947; MD, NYU, 1951; postgrad., Chgo. Inst. Psychoanalysis, 1965. Intern Lenox Hill Hosp., N.Y.C., 1951-53; resident in psychiatry Army Med. Svc. Sch., Ft. Sam Houston, Tex., 1953, Ill. Rsch. and Edn. Hosp., Chgo., 1955-56, Michael Reese Hosp., Chgo., 1956-58; psychiatrist in student health U. Chgo., 1958-59; pvt. practice River Forest, Ill., 1959-70; chief Michael Reese Svc. Ill. State Psychiat. Inst., Chgo., 1959-61, asst. clin. dir., 1969-70; dir. edn. Ill. Dept. Mental Health, Chgo., 1961-69, dir. div. prof. svcs., 1964-65; mem. staff Western Inst. Group/Family Therapy, Watsonville, Calif., 1970-86; pvt. practice Carmel and Seaside, Calif., 1970-87; clin. dir. psychiatry dept. Oil City (Pa.) Area Health Ctr., 1987-90; pvt. practice Oil City, Pa., 1987-93; mem. adv. bd. Venango County Mental Health/Mental Retardation Svcs., Franklin, Pa., 1988—; med. dir. partial hosp. Venango County Counseling Ctr., Oil City, 1988-90; mem. NIMH psychiatry tng. com., 1967-71; lectr. dept. psychiatry Stanford U., 1970-87; clin. instr. Dept. of Psychiatry, U. Ariz., 1994—; instr. Keller Grad. Sch. of Mgmt., 1996—. Co-author: The Borderline Syndrome, 1968; contbr. articles to profl. jours. Pres. Oak Park and River Forest Com. for Human Rights, 1966-67. 1st lt. USAR, 1953-55. Life fellow Am. Psychiat. Assn.; mem. Internat. Transactional Analysis (bd. dirs. 1970-85), Chgo. Psychoanalytic Soc., Sigma Chi. Democrat. Presbyterian.

DUARTE, RAMON GONZALEZ, nurse, educator, researcher; b. San Fernando, Calif., Jan. 5, 1948; s. Salvador Revelez and Juanita (Gonzalez) D.; m. Sophia Constant Garabedian, Apr. 17, 1983; children: David Ramon, John Robert. AA in Nursing, Los Angeles Valley Coll., 1972; student, Calif. State U., Los Angeles, 1972-76. RN; Cert. Bd. Nephrology Examiners. Staff nurse hemodialysis unit U. So. Calif. Med. Ctr., L.A., 1971-75; charge nurse self care hemodialysis unit Kaiser Found. Hosp., L.A., 1976, Culver City (Calif.) Dialysis Svcs., Inc., 1981-82; adminstrv. head nurse hemodialysis unit Valley Presbyn. Hosp., Van Nuys, Calif., 1976-78; adminstrv. head nurse Kidney Dialysis Care Units, Lynwood, Calif., 1980-81; ind. nursing contractor Nursing Svcs. in Nephrology, Van Nuys and Santa Barbara, 1982-93; clin. instr., rschr. Nursing Svcs. in Nephrology, Santa Barbara, 1980—, dir. rsch., 1988—; pres., owner, mgr. DNA Nursing Svcs. Inc., Santa Barbara, 1993—; coord. clin. rsch. Valley Dialysis Assocs., Inc., Van Nuys, 1978-80; mem. rsch. com. Valley Presbyn. Hosp. Rsch.; founder, pres. Dialysis Mus. Coun., chmn. So. Calif. Dialysis Earthquake Preparedness Commn.; mem. coun. nephrology nurses and technicians, mem. allied profl. adv. com., chmn. allied health profl. rsch. grant com. Nat. Kidney Found., Inc.; mem. sci. adv. coun. Nat. Kidney Found. So. Calif.; coord. Airlift Armenia Dialysis Emergency Svcs.; team coord. Armenian Relief Soc. Editorial bd. Dialysis and Transplantation mag.; pubr., editor: Dialysis and the Earthquake Connection; contbr. articles to med. publs.; patentee biologicals. Founder Mus. Hope, Van Nuys; coord. Airlift Armenia, Armenia Relief Soc., 1988. Recipient Dedicated Svc. award Hemodialysis Found., 1976; named Allied Health Profl. of Yr., Nat. Kidney Found. So. Calif., 1986; scholar Am. G.I. Forum, 1966, 40 and 8, L.A. Valley Coll. Assoc. Students; grantee Santa Barbara Cottage Hosp., 1993. Mem. AACCN, Am. Assn. Artificial Internal Organs, Am. Assn. Nephrology Nurses and Technician, Am. Soc. Nephrology, N.Y. Acad. Scis. (cert.), Kidney Found. So. Calif., Ind. Nurses Assn., Nat. Assn. Patients on Hemodialysis and Transplantation Inc. Democrat. Roman Catholic. Home and Office: 3770 Torino Dr Santa Barbara CA 93105-4433

DUATTI, ADRIANO, chemist, radiochemist; b. Ostellato, Ferrara, Italy, May 17, 1952; s. Alvaro and Liliana (Ricci) D.; m. Maria Grazia Ghisini, Oct. 30, 1976; children: Francesca, Federica. PhD, U. Ferrara, 1976. Rsch. asst. U. Ferrara, 1978-81, sr. rsch. fellow, 1981-86, invited prof., 1990; assoc. prof. U. Bologna, Italy, 1986—. Contbr. articles to profl. jours.; patentee in field. Sgt. Italian Mil., 1976-77. Nat. Rsch. Coun. rsch. grantee, 1984. Mem. Soc. Nuclear Medicine, Italian Assn. Nuclear Medicine, N.Y. Acad. Scis. Office: U Bologna Phys Inorg Che, Viale Risorgimento 4, 40136 Bologna Italy

DUBAY, STEPHEN NEWTON, hospital administrator; b. Atlanta, Dec. 12, 1941; s. Charles Merrill and Katherine Cushing (Shultis) D.; m. Gloria Elizabeth Carver, July 16, 1972; children: Stephen Newton Jr., Sonya. BA in English, Clemson (S.C.) U., 1969; MPH, U. N.C., 1992. Asst. adminstr. Roanoke Rapids (N.C.) Hosp., 1971-72; assoc. adminstr. Huntersville (N.C.) Hosp., 1972-77, adminstr., 1977-81; assoc. dir. Charlotte (N.C.) Rehab. Hosp., 1982-83; adminstr. McCain (N.C.) Hosp., 1984—. Bd. dirs. West Charlotte Rotary Club, 1982-83; chmn. Nursing Home Adv. Com., Mecklenburg County, N.C., 1983. With U.S. Army, 1962-65. Recipient Vigil Honor, Boy Scouts Am., 1968, Silver Beaver award, 1984. Mem. Am. Coll. Healthcare Execs. Democrat. Episcopalian. Home: PO Box 1275 Southern Pines NC 28388-1275 Office: McCain Hosp Hwy 211 McCain NC 28361

DUBESA, ELAINE J., biotechnology company executive; b. Alton, Ill., July 26, 1943; m. Michael Dubesa, Oct. 28, 1967. BS in Med. Tech., Loyola U., New Orleans, 1966. Rsch. assoc. pesticides project U. Hawaii, Honolulu, 1968-69; field rep., pesticides project La. State U., New Orleans, 1970-71; lab. supr. Beaufort (S.C.) County Meml. Hosp., 1971-72; asst. supr. hematology Mayo Clinic, Rochester, Minn., 1973-75; edn. coord. Sherman Hosp., Elgin, Ill., 1975-78; sect. chief PCL (now Corning Clin. Labs.), Portland, Oreg., 1978-80; quality control supr. PCL-RIA, Inc., Portland, 1980-82; quality control mgr. Am. Bioclinical Inc., Portland, 1982-87; quality assurance mgr., regulatory affairs mgr. Epitope, Inc., Beaverton, Oreg., 1987-91, v.p. regulatory affairs, 1991-95, v.p. govt. affairs, 1995—. Active Troutdale (Oreg.) Hist. Soc. Mem. Am. Soc. Quality Control, Regulatory Affairs Profl. Soc., Am. Soc. Clin. Pathologists, Beta Epsilon Upsilon.

DUBIN, GARY ROGER, pharmaceutical company executive; b. Phila., Feb. 26, 1943; s. Joseph and Josephine G. (Garfunkel) D.; m. Maxine Lois Ostrow, Aug. 21, 1943; children: Rory, Michele. BS, U. Miami, 1963; MBA, Nova U., 1986. V.p., owner Generix Drug Sales (now Goldline Labs.), Hollywood, Fla., 1963-75; exec. v.p. Generix Drug Sales Corp., Hollywood, Fla., 1976-86, Bioline Labs., Bklyn., 1980-86; pres. Superpharm Labs., Islip, N.Y., 1982-85; v.p. Orlove Group, Ft. Lauderdale, Fla., 1986—; gen. ptnr. Lor-Max, Miami Springs, Fla., 1983—; trustee, owner O.J. Investments, Plantation, Fla., 1983—; gen. ptnr. Bull Moose Properties, Presque Isle, Maine, 1982—. V.p. planning Hillel Day Sch., North Miami, Fla., 1970-93; sponsor, life mem., dir. Diabetes Rsch. Inst., U. Miami, Coral Gables, 1980—; v.p. Project Transplant Juvenile Diabetes, North Miami, 1981-90; mem. U. Miami Pres. Coun., 1995—. Mem. Nat. Assn. of Pharm. Mfrs., Nat. Wholesale Druggists Assn. Clubs: Century, Cane (Coral Gables, Fla.). Office: Orlove Corp Group 1900 W Commercial Blvd Fort Lauderdale FL 33309-3018

DUBLIN, THOMAS DAVID, physician; b. N.Y.C., Jan. 18, 1912; s. Louis I. and Augusta (Salik) D.; m. Christina Macdonald Carlyle, June 3, 1939; children: Sarah Carlyle Dublin Slenczka, Barbara Dublin Van Cleve. A.B., Dartmouth Coll., 1932; M.D., Harvard U., 1936; M.P.H., Johns Hopkins U., 1940, Dr.P.H., 1941. Diplomate Nat Bd. Med. Examiners, Am. Bd. Preventive Medicine (dir. 1961-71, vice. chmn. for gen. preventive medicine 1965-71). Intern 2d Harvard med. service Boston City Hosp., 1936-38; asst. resident physician Hosp. Rockefeller Inst. for Med. Research, N.Y.C., 1938-39; epidemiologist-in-tng. N.Y. State Dept. Health, 1939-40, asst. dist. health officer, 1940, epidemiologist, 1941-42; instr. preventive medicine Johns Hopkins U. Med. Sch., 1940-41; instr. preventive medicine and public health Albany Med. Coll., 1942; lectr. epidemiology DeLamar Inst. Pub. Health, Coll. Physicians and Surgeons, Columbia U., 1942-45; assoc. prof., 1942-43; prof., exec. officer dept. preventive medicine/cmty. health L.I. Coll. Medicine, Bklyn., 1943-48; epidemiologist Kingston Ave. Hosp., Bklyn., 1943-48; exec. dir. Nat. Health Council, 1948-53; med. cons. Nat. Found. for Infantile Paralysis, 1953-55; med. dir. USPHS, 1955-76, Community Services Programs, Office of Dir., NIH, Bethesda, Md., 1955-60; chief epidemiology and biometry br. Nat. Inst. Arthritis and Metabolic Diseases, Bethesda, 1960-66; research adviser, health service Office Tech. Coop. and Research, AID, 1966-68; dir. Office Health Manpower, HEW, 1968-70; program planning officer Bur. Health Manpower, Health Resources Adminstrn., 1970-72, spl. asst. dep. dir. bur., 1972-76; cons. health manpower supply and edn., 1976-78; cons. div. med. edn. AMA and Coordinating Council on Med. Edn., 1976-78; cons. research and devel. Edn. Common. for Fgn. Med. Grads., 1978-86; mem. expert adv. panel pub. health adminstrn. WHO, 1954-80; mem. Nat. Adv. Com. Epidemiology and Biometry, 1956-60; chmn. com. on cert. Am. Bd. Med. Specialists, 1972-77. Contbr. articles on internat. health and health manpower to profl. publs. Fellow Am. Pub. Health Assn. (governing council 1954-60, chmn. research policy com. 1957-60), Am. Coll. Preventive Medicine (regent 1973-76), N.Y. Acad. Medicine; mem. AMA, AAAS, Am. Epidemiol. Soc., Assn. Tchrs. Preventive Medicine (sec. 1944-48), Internat. Epidemiol. Assn., Delta Omega. Home: 2949 Garfield Ter NW Washington DC 20008-3507 Office: 2938 Garfield St NW Washington DC 20008-3536

DUBNER, DANIEL WILLIAM, pediatrician; b. Newark, Apr. 18, 1947; s. Nathan M. and Sara K. (Kuskin) D.; m. Janet Lee, Oct. 5, 1975; children: Sarah, Jeffrey, Emily. BS, Rutgers U., 1969; MD, U. Pa., 1973. Intern, resident Childrens Hosp. Phila., 1973-76; pediatrician Med. Assoc., Chelmsford, Mass., 1978-88, Greater Lowell (Mass.) Pediatrics, 1988—. Author: The Pediatricians' Best Baby Plan for the First YEar of Life, 1994. Behavioral Pediatrics fellow U. Wash., Seattle, 1976-77, genetic counseling and birth defect edn. fellow Tufts U., Boston, 1977-78. Fellow Am. Acad. Pediatrics; mem. Mass. Med. Soc. Office: Greater Lowell Pediatrics 33 Bartlett St Lowell MA 01852

DUBNER, RONALD, neurobiologist; b. N.Y.C. Oct. 12, 1934; s. Louis and Matilda (Fox) D.; m. Mary Ann Pollack, June 22, 1958; children: Susan R., Andrew D., Julia P. BA, Columbia U., 1955, DDS, 1958; PhD, U. Mich., 1964. Intern USPHS Hosp., Balt., 1958-59; staff dentist Clin. Center, NIH, Bethesda, Md., 1959-61; research scientist Nat. Inst. Dental Research, NIH, 1961-68, chief neural mechanisms sect., 1968-73, chief neurobiology and anesthesiology br., 1973-95; prof., chmn. dept. oral and craniofacial biol. scis. U. Md. at Balt. Dental Sch., Balt., 1995—; vis. scientist dept. anatomy Univ. Coll., London, 1970-71; vis. assoc. prof. Howard U., 1968-80. Co-author: Oral Facial Sensory and Motor Mechanisms, 1971, The Neural Basis of Oral and Facial Function, 1978, Oral-Facial Sensory and Motor Functions, 1981, Current Topics in Pain Research and Therapy, 1983, Advances in Pain Research and Therapy, vol. 9, 1985, vol. 21, 1995, Pain Research and Clinical Management, vol. 3, 1988; mem. edit. bd. Jour. Pain, 1975—, chief editor in Americas, 1990—, Jour. Neurosci., 1980-87, Somatosensory Rsch., 1982-89, Brain Rsch., 1993—, Jour. Dental Rsch., 1995—; contbr. articles to profl. jours., chpts. in books. Recipient Meritorious service medal USPHS, 1975; Birnberg Research Columbia U., 1981; Carl A. Schlack award Assn. Mil. Surgeons U.S., 1985, Second Ann. award for disting. achievement in pain rsch. Bistol-Myers Co., 1989; named J.H. Wolstencroft Meml. lectr. Brit. Brain Research Assn., 1988; Disting. svc. medal USPHS, 1990. Mem. Internat. Assn. Study of Pain (coun. 1975-81, v.p. 1981-87, treas. 1989-93), Soc. Neurosci., Internat. Assn. Dental Research (pres. Neurosci. Group 1977), Am. Physiol. Soc., Am. Assn. Anatomists, AAAS, Am. Pain Soc. (dir. 1980-82, pres. 1987, F.W.L. Keer award lectureship 1992), Omicron Kappa Upsilon. Office: U Md Dental Sch Dept OCBS 666 W Baltimore St Baltimore MD 21201-1586

DUBOIS, ARTHUR BROOKS, physiologist, educator; b. N.Y.C., Nov 21, 1923; s. Eugene Floyd and Rebeckah (Rutter) DuB.; m. Roberdeau Callery, June 21, 1950; children: Anne R., Brooks, James E.F. Student, Harvard U., 1941-43; M.D., Cornell U., 1946. Intern in medicine N.Y. Hosp., 1946-47; med. research fellow U. Rochester, 1949-51; asst. resident Peter Bent Brigham Hosp., Boston, 1951-52; asst. prof. to prof. physiology and medicine U. Pa., 1952-74; prof. epidemiology and physiology Yale U., 1974—; dir. John B. Pierce Found. Lab., 1974-88. Author: The Lung, 3d ed. 1986, Body Plethysmography, 1969; contbr. articles to profl. jours. Served with USNR, 1947-49. Recipient Rsch. Career award NIH, 1963-74; Edward Livingston Trudeau medal Am. Lung Assn., 1989. Mem. Am. Physiol. Soc., Am. Soc. Clin. Investigation, Assn. Am. Physicians, Undersea Med. Soc. Democrat. Clubs: Harvard, Cosmos. Home: 370 Livingston St New Haven CT 06511-1336 Office: 290 Congress Ave New Haven CT 06519-1403

DUBOIS, DONNA MARIE, medical record services executive; b. Gary, Ind., Dec. 7, 1946; d. Steve and Danica (Arbutina) Bayus; m. Harvey M. Dubois, Jan. 1, 1982. AS in Med. Record Tech., Ind. U., Gary, 1981; BS in Med. Record Adminstrn., Ind. U., Indpls., 1986; MBA, U. Notre Dame, 1988. Registered record adminstrn., Ind. Asst. dir. med. record svcs St. Mary Med. Ctr., Hobart, Ind., 1973-87; dir. med. records St. Catherine Hosp., East Chicago, Ind., 1987-88; regional dir. health info. svcs. Lakeshore Health Sys., East Chicago, 1988—. Mem. Am. Health Info. Mgmt. Assn., Ind. Health Info. Mgmt. Assn. (disting. mem. 1993, pres. 1983-84), Notre Dame Club of the Calumet Region. Home: 2201 W 85th Ave Merrillville IN 46410-6134 Office: Saint Catherine Hospital 4321 Fir St East Chicago IN 46312-3049

DUBOIS, GERARD JEAN, public health medicine educator; b. St. Amand les Eaux, France, July 22, 1947; s. Jean and Marcelle (Barbieux) D.; m. Chantal Marie Debavelaere; children: Alexandre, Charles-Eric, Edouard. MPH, Johns Hopkins U., 1973; MD, Sch. Medicine, Lille, France, 1974. Prof. medicine Sch. Medicine, Lille, 1979-81; head preventive dept. French Social Security, Paris, 1981-90; gen. mgr. Screening Ctr. IPC, Paris, 1990-93; prof. medicine Sch. Medicine, Amiens, France, 1993—; chmn. Dept. Med. Evaluation, Amiens, 1995—; chmn. Nat. Com. Against Smoking, 1993—. Decorated Chevalier de l'Ordre Nat. du Mérite, 1996. Mem. French Soc. Preventive and Social Medicine (sec. 1985-95, chmn. 1995—). Office: Hosp Nord, Place V Pauchet, Svc d'evaluation medicale, 80054 Amiens France

DUBOIS, JEAN GABRIEL, pharmaceutical executive, pharmacist; b. Bethisy, Oise, France, Dec. 27, 1926; s. Rene Edmond and Isabelle Francoise (Chauvel) DuB.; m. Francoise Pradille, Sept. 7, 1945; children: Anne Frederique, Jean Christophe, Isabelle, Caroline. PhD in Pharmacy, Faculte de Pharmacy, Paris, 1951; postgrad., U. N.Mex., Albuquerque, 1951-52. Gen. mgr. Comptoir Pharmaceutique de Cambodge, Phnom Penh, Cambodia, 1955-61; quality control and mfg. mgr. Laboratoire Nativelle, Longjumeau, France, 1962-63; plant mgr. Laboratoire ANA, Paris, 1963-64; tech. dir. Pfizer Egypt, Cairo, 1966-68; tech. dir. Pfizer France, Orsay, 1969-88, gen. and quality assurance dir., 1988-91; pharm. mfg. cons. Dubois Conseil, Paris, 1992. Capt. French M.C., 1953-54, Vietnam. Office: Dubois Conseil, 220 bd Raspail, 75 016 Paris France

DUBOSE, HUGH HAMMOND, internist; b. Columbia, S.C., Aug. 14, 1922; s. Theodore Marion and Sarah (Hammond) DuB.; m. Katherine W. McCants, Sept. 15, 1947; children: Hugh H. Jr., Clarke W., Theodore B., Katherine Duvall. BS in Pre Medicine, U. N.C., 1943; MD, Med. U. S.C., 1950. Diplomate Am. Bd. Internal Medicine. Intern Phila. Gen. Hosp., 1950-51; resident Geisinger Med. Ctr., Danville, Pa., 1951-53, 1951-53; cardiology fellow N.C. Bapt. Hosp., Bowman Gray Sch. of Medicine, Winston-Salem, 1953-54; pvt. practice Columbia, S.C., 1954-91; v.p. med. staff affairs Providence Hosp., Columbia, 1989—. 1st lt. Air Corps, USMC, 1943-46. Mem. ACP, AMA, S.C. Med. Assn., Am. Coll. Physician Execs., Am. Coll. Cardiology, Columbia Med. Soc. (pres. 1969-70), Alpha Omega Alpha. Episcopalian. Home: 5001 Courtney Rd Columbia SC 29206-2908 Office: Providence Hosp 2435 Forest Dr Columbia SC 29204-2026

DUBOURG, OLIVIER JEAN, cardiology educator, researcher; b. Orleans, Loiret, France, Mar. 26, 1952; s. Jean Fortune and Arlette (Masson) D.; m. Sylvie Rolet, Sept. 21, 1979; 1 child, Benjamin. MD, U. Paris, 1981, Laureat, 1981. Cert. French Bd. Cardiology. Intern Salpetriere Hosp., Paris, 1975-76; resident in cardiology Pitie Hosp., Paris, 1977-81; fellow Ambroise Paré Hosp., Boulogne, France, 1981-89, prof. cardiology, 1989—; co-pres. med. com., mem. steering com., tech. com., pres. human rels. Ambroise Paré Hosp. Contbr. articles to med. jours. Fellow European Soc. Cardiology, Am. Coll. Cardiology, Am. Coll. Chest Physicians, French Soc. Cardiology; mem. Am. Soc. Echocardiography, Am. Fedn. for Clin. Rsch., Am. Inst. Ultrasound, French Soc. Pharmacology. Home: 8 rue Barye, 75017 Paris France Office: Ambroise Paré Hosp, 9 ave Charles de Gaulle, 92100 Boulogne 1, France

DUBOVSKY, EVA VITKOVA, nuclear medicine physician, educator; b. Prague, Czechoslovakia, 1933. MD, Charles U. Faculty Medicine, Prague, Czech Republic, 1957. Diplomate Am. Bd. Nuclear Medicine. Intern U. Hosp., Charles U., Prague, 1956-57, chief resident, 1961-63, fellow divsn. endocrinology & metabolism, 1963-65; rsch. fellow divsn. endocrinology U. Ala., Birmingham, 1968-70; clin. assoc. VA Med. Ctr., Birmingham, 1970-72; from instr. to prof. U. Ala., Birmingham, 1954—; vis. prof. U. Cin., 1987, Cleve. CLinic, 1987, VA Med. Ctr., Portland, Oreg.,1988, Columbia Coll. Physicians & Surgeons, 1989, Dartmouth Med. Ctr., 1989, William Beaumont Hosp., 1992, 94, Charles U., 1994, Baptist Med. Ctr. Okla., 1994, U. Louisville, 1994. Editor: Nuclear Medicine Technology Continuing Education Review, 1976, 2d edit., 1981; co-editor: Nuclear Medicine in Clinical Urology and Nephrology, 1985, Atlas of Nuclear Medicine and Imagine; contbr. chpts. to books and articles to profl. jours. Mem. AMA, Am. Coll. Nuclear Physicians, Soc. Nuclear Medicine, SECSNIM. Office: U Ala Hosp Divsn Nuc Medicine 619 19th St S Birmingham AL 35233*

DUBOVSKY, STEVEN LEW, physician, educator, researcher; b. Pueblo, Colo., July 12, 1944; s. Mortimer Herbert and Gladys (Levy) D.; m. Anne Lois Gallupe, May 27, 1972; children: Amelia, Elizabeth. BA, NYU, 1965, MD, 1969. Diplomate Am. Bd. Psychiatry and Neurology. Intern, Vancouver Gen. Hosp., B.C., Can., 1969-70; resident in psychiatry Colo. Psychiat. Hosp., Denver, 1970-73; mem. faculty Med. Sch. U. Colo., Denver, assoc. prof. psychiatry, 1979-83, assoc. dean acad. and faculty affairs, 1983—, assoc. prof. psychiatry and medicine, 1983-89, prof., 1989—; med. dir. Colo. Psychiat. Hosp., vice chmn. dept. psychiatry, 1987—; cons. psychiatry Fitzsimmons Army Hosp., Denver, 1978-96; external examiner King Saud U., Riyadh, 1982; vis. prof. U. Oreg., U. Man., U. Tex., U. W.Va., Kans. U.; examiner Am. Bd. Psychiatry and Neurology, 1978—; v.p. med. bd. U. Hosp.; pres. of faculty U. Colo. Med. Sch. Author: Clinical Psychiatry in Primary Care, 3rd edit., 1985, Psychotherapeutics in Primary Care, 1981, Concise Guide to Clinical Psychiatry, ; editor: Psychiatric Decision Making, 1984; numerous contbr. articles to profl. jours. Grantee NIMH, 1978-80, Bur. Health Manpower, 1979-81. Fellow Am. Psychiat. Assn.; mem. Group Advancement Psychiatry, Colo. Psychiat. Soc., Phi Beta Kappa. Office: U Colo Med Sch 4200 E 9th Ave Box C260 Denver CO 80262

DUBOW, JENNIFER ANN, social worker; b. Evergreen Park, Ill., July 24, 1964; d. Harry James and Roberta Marie (O'Neil) Mallory; m. Eric F. Dubow, Aug. 2, 1986; children: Daniel Steven, Mark Joshua. BSW cum laude, George Williams Coll., 1985; MSW, U. Mich., 1988. Lic. ind. social worker, Ohio. Social worker Jewish Family Svcs., Sylvania, Ohio, 1988—; social worker Dr. Tallman & Assocs., Maumee, Ohio, 1995—; cons. supervisor Greensprings (Ohio) Nursing Home, 1995—. Mem. Nat. Assn. Social Workers (recording sec. 1986-89, chair planning com. 1987-89, bd. dirs. 1987-88), Nat. Assn. of the Deaf. Office: Jewish Family Svc 6525 Sylvania Ave Sylvania OH 43560

DUBOWSKY, NATHAN, biology educator, museum administrator; b. Bklyn., Jan. 15, 1939; s. Jacob Jack and Miriam (Haber) D.; m. Linda Sue Sherman, Dec. 25, 1963; children—Jay, Scott. B.S., Bklyn. Coll., 1961; M.S., L.I.U., 1966; Ed.D., Columbia U., 1972. Tchr. Bkly. Bd. Edn., 1961-66; asst. prof. biology Westchester Community Coll., Valhalla, N.Y., 1966-72, assoc. prof., 1972-86, prof., 1986—; research assoc. Lamont-Doherty Research Lab., Palisades, N.Y., 1977-80; assoc. prof. SUNY-Purchase, 1976-84; dir. Westchester Mus. Natural History, Valhalla, 1984—; vis. prof. natural scis. Tchrs. Coll. Columbia U. Contbr. articles to profl. jours. Author lab. manual. Served with Army N.G., 1963-64. Grantee NSF, 1982, NEH, 1985. Mem. AAAS, Nat. Sci. Tchrs. Assn./Met. Assn. Coll. and Univ. Biologists (pres. 1981-83), Internat. Soc. Origin of Life, Brit. Soc. for History of Sci., Soc. Coll. Sci. Tchrs. (editor News and Views), Sigma Xi. Office: Westchester CC 75 Grasslands Rd Valhalla NY 10595-1636

DUBRIN, ANDREW JOHN, behavioral sciences, management educator, author; b. N.Y.C., Mar. 3, 1935; s. Albert Edward and Louise Theresa (Walsh) D.; m. Drew, Douglas, Melanie. A.B., Hunter Coll., 1956; M.S., Purdue U., 1957; Ph.D., Mich. State U., 1960. Diplomate: Am. Bd. Profl. Psychology; cert. psychologist N.Y. state. Psychologist Data Systems div. IBM, Kingston, N.Y., 1962-63; teaching asst., part-time instr. Purdue U., West Lafayette, Ind., 1956-57; psychol. cons. Clark, Cooper, Field & Wohl, N.Y.C., 1963-64; psychol. cons. Rohrer, Hibler & Replogle, N.Y.C., 1964-70, ptnr., 1964-70; assoc. prof. Rochester (N.Y.) Inst. Tech., 1970-72, prof. behavioral sci., 1972—, dept. head mgmt., 1982-84, prof. mgmt., 1984—; mem. N.Y. State Bd. Psychology, 1979—; cons. lectr. in field. Author: The Practice of Managerial Psychology, 1972, Women in Transition, 1972, The Singles Game, 1973, Fundamentals of Organization Behavior: An Applied Perspective, 1974, Survival in the Sexist Jungle, 1974, The New Husbands and How to Become One, 1976, Casebook of Organizational Behavior, 1979, Human Relations: A Job Oriented Approach, 1978, 5th edit., 1992, Fundamentals of Organizational Behavior: An Applied Perspective, 2d edit., 1978, Winning at Office Politics, 1979, Contemporary Applied Management, 1982, 4th edit., 1994, Essentials of Management, 1986, 4th edit., 1994, The Last Straw, 1987, Human Relations for Career and Personal Success, 3d edit., 1992, Management and Organization, 1989, 2d edit., 1992, Effective Business Psychology, 1980, 4th edit., 1994, Winning Office Politics: DuBrin's Guide for the '90s, 1990, Bouncing Back: How to Overcome Adversity in the Workplace, 1992, Your Own Worst Enemy: How to Prevent Career Self-Sabotage, 1992, Stand Out! 330 Ways to Gain the Edge with Superiors, Subordinates, Co-workers, and Customers, 1993, Getting It Done: The Transforming Power of Self-Discipline, 1995, The Reengineering Survival Guide, 1995, The Breakthrough Team Player, 1995; contbr. articles to profl.

jours. Served to capt. U.S. Army, 1960-62. Mem. Am. Psychol. Assn., Am. Mgmt. Assn., Acad. of Mgmt. Home: 2100 Clover St Rochester NY 14618-3209 Office: Rochester Inst Tech Coll Bus Rochester NY 14623-0887

DUC, THOMAS ALEXANDER, anesthesiologist; b. Charleston, S.C., Feb. 18, 1954; s. Thomas Alexander and Ann Veronica (Masche) D.; m. Lynn Christine Yeager, Dec. 29, 1989; children: Sarah, Laura, Whitney. BS, Auburn U., 1976; MD, Med. U. S.C., 1983. Diplomate Am. Bd. Anesthesiology. Staff anesthesiologist U.S. Navy, Charleston, S.C., 1986-89; assoc. prof. Med. U. S.C., Charleston, 1989—. Fire marshal City of Charleston, 1993—. Mem. AMA, Am. Soc. Anesthesiology, Am. Soc. Regional Anesthesia, S.C. Med. Assn. Roman Catholic. Home: 702 Whispering Marsh Dr Charleston SC 29412

DUCATMAN, ALAN MARC, physician; b. Plainfield, N.J., July 19, 1950; s. Fred Paul and Shirley (Buchman) D.; m. Barbara Steinmetz, June 18, 1978; children: Joseph, David, Samuel. BA, Columbia U., N.Y.C., 1972; MSc, CUNY, 1974; MD, Wayne State U., Detroit, 1978. Resident, fellow Mayo Clinic, Rochester, Minn., 1979-82; dir. occupational health Columbia Park Med., Mpls., 1982-83; dir. Environ. Med. Svcs. MIT, 1986-92; prof., dir. Inst. Occupational and Environ. Health W.Va. U., Morgantown, 1992—; adj. assoc. prof. Boston U. Sch. Medicine, 1990-92, U. Miss. Sch. Medicine, 1991—; adj. prof. medicine U. S.C., 1994; trustee Am. Bd. Preventive Medicine, 1994—. Contbr. articles to profl. jours. Comdr. USNR, 1983-86. Comdr. USNR, 1983-86. Fellow ACP, Am. Coll. Occup. and Environ. Medicine (chmn. toxicology com. 1987-92). Office: Inst Occupl & Environ Health WVa U/Sch Medicine Morgantown WV 26506-9190

DUCK, HOLLY JEAN, orthopaedic surgeon; b. Wilmington, Del., Apr. 4, 1958; d. Frederick Jean and Anne H. Duck. BS, U. Rochester, 1980, MD, 1985. Diplomate Am. Bd. Orthopedic Surgery. Gen. surgeon U. Medicine and Dentistry N.J., Newark, orthopaedic surgeon, 1985-90; orthopaedic surgeon U. Wis., Madison, 1990-91, Bone and Joint Surgery, Madison, 1991—. Fellow Am. Acad. Orthopedic Surgery; mem. AMA, Am. Med. Women's Assn., Ruth Jackson Orthopaedic Soc. (chair mentoring com. 1995—), Wis. Med. Soc. Office: Bone and Joint Surgery Asso 2704 Marshall Ct Madison WI 53705

DUCOS, JEAN BERNARD, immunology educator; b. Toulouse, France, Mar. 4, 1926; s. Louis and Emilie (Morere) D.; m. Lyliane Pecoul, July 19, 1951; children: Philippe, Bernard, Elisabeth. Lic. sci., U. Toulouse, France, 1953, MD, 1954. Attache rsch. Inserm, Toulouse, 1953-58; dir. U100 Inserm, Toulouse, 1973—; dir. gen. Ctr. Regional Transfusion, Toulouse; maitre de confs. agrege, faculty of medicine U. Toulouse, 1963-68, prof. immunology, 1969—; mem. Commn. Nat. Permanente Biol. Medicine, 1975-89; pres. Commn. Cons. Transfusion Sanguine, Paris, 1981-88; pres. 47th sect. com. Nat. Univs., 1983-94. Contbr. articles to Gen. Immunology, Immunopathology, Immunogenetics, Genetic Polymorphism of Immunoglosulins, Immuno-Hematology, Hemotypoloty, Forensic Medicine, Blood Transfusion. Adminstr. Ctr. Hosp. Regional, Toulouse, 1956-60; v.p. Caisse Primaire de Sécurité Sociale, Toulouse, 1955-62; pres. Ligue Midi-Pyrênées de Voile. Decorated officier Legion d'Honneur, officier des Palmes Academiques (France); officier Ordre de la Coronne (Belgium); recipient medaille d'Argent de la Jeunesse et des Sports, 1979. Mem. Soc. Francaise d'Hemapherese (pres. d'honneur 1985-86), Internat. Soc. Transplantation, French Nat. Acad. Medicine (corr.), Nat. Blood Transusion Soc. (pres. 1977-86), Nat. Soc. Immunology (v.p. 1975-78), Internat. Soc. Hematology. Home: 17 rue de l'Obélisque, 31500 Toulouse France

DUCRET, RENÉ PIERRE, physician; b. Langenfeld, Germany, Dec. 1, 1954; came to U.S., 1954; s. Dudley Vaughan and Doris (Klein) duC.; m. Susan Jeanne Roe, Jan. 12, 1983. AB cum laude, Princeton U., 1977; MD, U. Tex., 1982. With U. Minn. Health Ctr., Mpls. Mem. Am. Coll. Radiology, Am. Coll. Nuclear Physicians, Radiologic Soc. Am., Soc. Nuclear Medicine, Sigma Xi. Office: UMHC Dept Radiology Box 292 Harvard St at E River Rd Minneapolis MN 55455

DUDEK, FELICIA ANNE, rehabilitation counselor; b. Chgo., Aug. 30, 1947; d. Edmund and Bernice (Rak) Funk; m. John Dudek, Sept. 6, 1969; 1 child: Elizabeth. BS in Psychology, Ill. Inst. Tech., 1972, MS in Rehab. Counseling, 1974. Lic. clin. profl. counselor, Ill.; cert. rehab. counselor, alcohol and drug counselor. Alcoholism therapist Grant Hosp., Chgo., 1974-79, dir. alcoholism counselor tng. program, 1978-79; mem. adj. faculty Cen. YMCA Community Coll., Chgo., 1981-82; coord. substance abuse tng. Nat.-Louis U., Evanston, Ill., 1984—; pvt. practice Chgo., 1979—. Contbr. articles to profl. jours. Bd. dirs. Glenview Youth Svcs., 1984-86, Glenview Citizens for Alcohol and Drug Awareness, Glenview, 1984, Ill. Alcohol and Other Drug Abuse Profl. Cert. Assn., Inc., 1993—, pres., 1995. Mem. ACA (chair Ill. Alcohol/Drug Counselor Tng. Program Dirs.' consortium, 1989-92), Nat. Rehab Assn., Ill. Rehab. Assn., Ill. Alcohol and Drug Dependence Assn. Roman Catholic. Office: 30 N Michigan Ave Ste 1926 Chicago IL 60602-3605

DUDENHOEFER, PAUL ANTHONY, physician, retired; b. Milw., Sept. 7, 1927; s. Clarence William and Bernardine W. (Vogt) D.; m. Rosemary M. Longe, June 16, 1951; children: Barbara, Mary Kay, Paul Jr., Mark. BS in Medicine, Marquette U., 1947, MD, 1951. Diplomate Am. Bd. Phys. Medicine and Rehab. Intern Mercy Hsop., Janesville, Wis., 1951-52; resident in otolaryngology Milw. County Hosp., 1952-53; resident in phys. medicine and rehab. VA Ctr., Wood, Wis., 1953-56, chief phys. medicine and rehab. svc., 1958-60; pvt. practice, 1960-88; dir. phys. medicine St. Francis Hosp., 1960-86, chmn. in hosp. dept., 1974-78, exec. com., 1974-78, chmn. by laws com., 1979-81, chmn. impaired physician com., 1977-88, med. dir. dept. phys. medicine, 1972-86, chief of staff-elect, 1983-85, chief of staff, 1985-87; attending physician St. Joseph's Hosp., 1960-96, Deaconess Hosp., 1960-67, Mt. Sinai Hosp., 1963-66, St. Francis Hosp., Milw., 1960-86; founder, med. dir. Ctr. for Disability Evaluation, Milw., 1986-88; clin. instr. Marquette U. Sch. Medicine, 1955-59, asst. clin. prof., 1959-70, assoc. clin. prof., 1970-80; lectr. Marquette U. Sch. Nursing, 1974-84. Contbr. articles to profl. jours. Capt. U.S. Army, 1956-58. Recipient fellowship NIH, 1953-56. Fellow Am. Acad. Phys. Medicine; mem. AMA, Wis. State Med. Soc. (chmn. commn. on rehab. 1963-73, mem. Ho. of Dels. from Milw. 1974-84), Med. Soc. Milw. County, Pan Am. Med. Assn., Am. Congress of Rehab. Medicine, Nat. Rehab. Assn. (life), Chgo. Soc. Phys. Medicine, Mid Am. Soc. Phys. Medicine and Rahb., Wis. Soc. Phys. Medicine and Rehab., Am. Assn. Electromyography and Electrodiagnosis, Am. Soc. Clin. Hypnosis, Fla. State Med. Soc., Orange County Med. Soc., Elks. Roman Catholic. Home: 3756 Hasting Lane Clermont FL 34711

DUDIK, ROLLIE M., healthcare executive; b. Hartford, Conn., Sept. 29, 1935; s. Martin and Iola Maxine (Hamilton) D.; m. Nancy A. Slicner. PhD, Am. U., 1981. Gen. mgr. Freedman Artcraft Engring., Charlevoix, Mich., 1970-73; exec. v.p. Harrison Community Hosp., Cadiz, Ohio, 1973-77; dir. instl. rev. Dade Monroe PSRO, Miami, Fla., 1977-78; exec. dir. Fla. Keys Meml. Hosp., Key West, 1978-82; exec. v.p. Eisenhower Hosp., Colorado Springs, 1982-83; v.p. South Fla. Med. Mgmt., Inc., Miami, 1982—, Doctor's Health Systems Mgmt. Corp., Coral Gables, Fla., 1985-96, About Health, Inc., Rockville, Md., 1996—; pres. R.M. Dudik & Assocs., Inc., Miami, 1983—, Sydney, Australia, 1988—; med. projects cons. Orah Wall Med. Enterprises, Inc., San Antonio, 1985—; pres. Caribbean Diagnostic Ctrs., Inc., Coral Gables, 1986—; chief fin. officer Forenpsych Assocs., Inc., Coral Gables, 1990—. Served with U.S. Army, 1956-62. Mem. Am. Inst. Indsl. Engrs., Am. Acad. Med. Adminstrs., Am. Coll. Healthcare Executives, Hosp. Fin. Mgmt. Assn., Hosp. Mgmt. Systems Soc., Am. Soc. Law and Medicine, Nat. Assn. Flight Instrs., Nat. Assn. Accts., Nat. Counterintelligence Corps Assn., Assn. Former Intelligence Officers, Australian Intelligence Assn., Aerospace and Environ. Medicine Assn., Rotary, Kiwanis. Address: 2308 Floral Park Rd Clinton MD 20735-9657

DUDKIEWICZ, JAN, obstetrics and gynecology educator; b. Szczecno, Kielce, Poland, July 13, 1931; s. Stanislaw and Anna (Kozub) D.; m. Monika Samolewicz, Sept. 26, 1963; 1 child, Jan. Physician diploma, Silesian Sch. Medicine, Katowice, Poland, 1959, MD, 1964, D. Habilitation, PhD, 1974. Asst. human anatomy inst. Silesian Sch. Medicine, Katowice, 1955-64; asst., sr. asst., adj. 1st Clinic Ob-Gyn., Zabrze, 1959-64; sr. lectr. obs-gyn. clinic Silesian Sch. Medicine, Zabrze, 1964-73, lectr., head gynecological endocrinology dept., 1974-77; dir., chmn. obs.-gyn. inst. Silesian Sch. Medicine, Bytom, 1977-82; prof., head of chair obs.-gyn. Silesian Sch. Medicine, Zabrze, 1982—; cons. obs.-gyn., Katowice, 1974—. Author/co-author more than 300 articles in field. Fellow Internat. Acad. Cytology Que.; mem. Polish Assn. Clin. Cytology (v.p. 1972—), Polish Gynecological Assn. (v.p. Katowice region 1974-82), Polish Endocrinological Assn. Roman Catholic. Home: ul Bałtycka 58C, 40 778 Katowice Poland Office: Katedra i Klinika, Ginekologii Pl Traugutta 6, 41-800 Zabrze Poland

DUDLEY, ALDEN WOODBURY, JR., pathologist, educator; b. Lynn, Mass., May 15, 1937; s. Alden W. and Dorothy H. (Newth) D.; m. Mary E. Adams, Sept. 12, 1959; children: Raymond Adams, Eric C. AB, Duke U., 1958, MD, 1962. Diplomate Am. Bd. Anatomical and Neuropathology. Intern Duke U., Durham, N.C., 1963-64, resident, 1965-67, asst. prof. pathology, 1967-68; from asst. to assoc. prof. U. Wis., Madison, 1968-76; prof. U. So. Ala., Mobile, 1976-80, chmn. dept. pathology, 1976-77; neuropathologist Cleve. Clinic Foun., 1980-85; prof. Baylor Coll. of Medicine, Houston, 1985—; chief lab. svc. VA Med. Ctr., Houston, 1985—; cons. Nat. Biomed. Systems, Inc., Cleve., 1981-90; advisor Osler Inst., Terre Haute, Ind., 1983—; regional commr. pathology and lab. med. svc. all 20 VA facilities in Tex., 1994—; mem. adv. com. for pathology and lab. med. svc. Dept. VA, Washington, 1995—. Editor med. jours.; contbr. chpts. on muscles, toxicology to books and numerous papers on neuropathology to med. jours. Lt. comdr. USPHS, 1963-65. Recipient Golden Forceps award Armed Forces Inst. of Pathology, 1974, Prix de l'Inst. Muscle et Nerf, U. Marseilles, France, 1982. Fellow Am. Am. Soc. CLin. Pathology, Coll. Am. Pathologists; mem. AMA (com. physician rsch. and evaluation 1981—, com. tech. assessment 1986—), Am. Assn. Neuropathologists (com. chmn. 1975-81, 83-84). Group Rsch. in Pathology Edn. (pres. 1975-77), Am. Assn. Clin. Chemists, Neuropathology Internat. Scientific Exchs. (dir. 1990—). Republican. Home: 3759 Darcus St Houston TX 77005-3703 Office: VA Med Center Lab Service Houston TX 77030

DUDLEY, GEORGE WILLIAM, behavioral scientist, writer; b. Camden, N.J., July 18, 1943; s. Lester Allen and Dorothy Vernon (Hoopes) Boyd; m. Carol Ann Lorenzen, Sept. 14, 1968; 1 child, Suzanne Christine. BS, Baylor U., 1969; MS, N. Tex. State U., 1974. Dir. field testing, rsch. Southwestern Life Ins., Dallas, 1969-80; pres. Behavioral Scis. Rsch. Press, Dallas, 1980-92, chmn. bd. dirs., 1992-95, dir., 1995—; chmn. bd. dirs. Potentia Internat., Dallas, 1995—; discussant Southwestern Psychol. Assn., 1984. Editor: Handbook for Agent Selection in the Life Insurance Industry, 1980, Jour. Agt. and Mgmt. Selection and Devel., Dallas, 1984-87; co-author: The Psychology of Call Reluctance, 1986, Earning What You're Worth?, 1992 (rev. edit. 1995); contbr. articles to mgmt. publs. Cpl. USMC, 1961-65. Mem. Am. Psychol. Soc. Office: Behavioral Scis Rsch Press 12803 Demetra Dr Ste 100 Dallas TX 75234-6101

DUDRICK, STANLEY JOHN, surgeon, scientist, educator; b. Nanticoke, Pa., Apr. 9, 1935; s. Stanley Francis and Stephania Mary (Jachimczak) D.; m. Theresa M. Keen, June 14, 1958; children: Susan Marie, Paul Stanley, Carolyn Mary, Stanley Jonathan, Holly Anne, Anne Theresa. B.S. cum laude, Franklin and Marshall Coll., 1957; M.D., U. Pa., 1961. Diplomate Am. Bd. Surgery. Intern Hosp. of U. Pa., Phila., 1961-62, resident in gen. surgery, 1962-67; pvt. practice specializing in surgery Phila., 1967-72, 88-90, Houston, 1972-88, 90-94; chief surg. svcs. Hermann Hosp., Houston, 1972-80, surgeon in chief, dir. Ctr. Cardiovascular Disease, dir. nutritional support svcs., dir. Nutritional Sci. Ctr., 1990-94; prof. surgery U. Tex. Med. Sch., Houston, 1972-82, clin. prof. surgery, 1982-95, chmn. dept. surgery, 1972-80; cons. in surgery M.D. Anderson Hosp. and Tumor Inst., 1973-88, clin. prof. surgery, cons. to pres., 1982-88; sr. cons. surgery and medicine Tex. Inst. for Rehab. and Rsch., 1974-88; mem. Anatomical Bd., State of Tex., 1973-78; examiner Am. Bd. Surgery, 1974-78, bd. dirs., 1978-84, sr. mem. 1984—, also mem. and chmn. various coms.; chmn. sci. adv. com. Tex. Med. Ctr. Libr., 1974; mem. food and nutrition bd. NRC-Nat. Acad. Scis., 1973-75; mem. sci. adv. com. Nat. Found. for Ileitis and Colitis; mem. surgery, anesthesia and trauma study sect. NIH, 1982-86; chmn. dept. surgery Pa. Hosp., Phila., 1988-90, surgeon in chief, 1988-91, hon. surgery staff, 1991—, assoc. chmn. dept. surgery, 1994—; clin. prof. surgery U. Pa., 1988-93; dir. surgery program, 1994—, dir.. Med. Edn., 1995—, St. Mary's Hosp., Waterbury, Conn., 1994—; clin. prof. surgery, Yale, New Haven, Conn., 1995—. Editor: Manual of Surgical Nutrition, 1975, Manual of Preoperative and Postoperative Care, 1983, Current Strategies in Surgical Nutrition, 1991, Practical Handbook of Nutrition in Clinical Practice, 1994, Surgical Nutrition: Strategies in Critically Ill Patients, 1995; assoc. editor Nutrition in Medicine, 1975—; editorial bd. Annals of Surgery, 1975—, Infusion, 1978—, Nutrition and Cancer, 1980—, Nutrition Support Services, 1980-86, Jour. Clin. Surgery, 1980-83, Nutrition Research, 1981—, Intermed. Communications Nursing Services, 1981—, Postgraduate General Surgery, 1992—; others; contbr. chpts. to books, articles to profl. jours.; inventor of new technique of intravenous feeding and anti-cholesterol therapy. Bd. dirs. Found. for Children, Houston, Harris County unit Am. Cancer Soc., Phila. chpt., 1988-90; trustee Franklin and Marshall Coll., 1985—, mem. student life and trusteeship coms., 1986—, mem. overseers bd., 1986—, exec. com. 1986—, alumni programs and devel. com., 1991—, pres. regional adv. coun., 1992—, vice chmn. 1994—, John Marshall Soc., 1993—. Decorated knight Order St. John of Jerusalem Knights Hopitalier; recipient VA citation for significant contbn. to med. care, 1970; Mead Johnson award for rsch. in hosp. pharmacy, 1972; Seale Harris medal So. Med. Assn., 1973; AMA-Brookdale award in medicine, 1975; Great Texan award Nat. Found. Ileitis and Colitis, 1975; Modern Medicine award, 1977; Disting. Alumnus citation Franklin and Marshall Coll., 1980; WHO, Houston, 1980; Stinchfield award Am. Acad. Orthopedic Surgery, 1981; Bernstein award Med. Soc. State of N.Y., 1986, Alumni Svc. award U. Pa. Med. Sch., 1996; numerous others. Fellow ACS (vice chmn. pre and post operative com. 1975, gov. 1979-85, com. on med. motion pictures 1981-90, SESAP com. 1990—, co-chmn. multiple choice com. 1993—, mem. Conn. chpt.), Philippine Coll. Surgeons (hon.), Coll. Medicine and Surgery of Costa Rica (hon.), Am. Coll. Nutrition (Grace A. Goldsmith award 1982); mem. AMA (council on food and nutrition 1971-76, exec. com. 1975-76, council on sci. affairs 1976-81, Goldberger award in clin. nutrition 1970), AAAS, AAUP, Am. Surg. Assn., Am. Acad. Pediatrics (hon., Ladd medal 1988), Am. Pediatric Surg. Assn. (hon.), Am. Soc. Nutritional Support Services (bd. dirs. 1982-8ng Humanitarian award 1984) Soc. Univ. Surgeons (exec. council 1974-78), Assn. for Acad. Surgery (founders group), Internat. Soc. Surg., Internat. Fedn. Surg. Colls., Internat. Soc. Parenteral Nutrition (exec. council 1975—, pres. 1978-81), Internat. Fedn. Surgery Soc., So. Med. Assn. (chmn. surgery sect. 1984-85), Houston Gastroent. Soc., Houston Surg. Soc., Tex. Surg. Soc., Tex. Med. Assn. (com. nutrition and food resources), Tex. Med. Found., Harris County Med. Soc., New Haven (Conn.) County Med. Soc., Conn. Soc. Am. Bd. Surgeons, Am. Radium Soc., Am. Soc. Clin. Oncology, Am. Soc. Parenteral and Enteral Nutrition (pres. 1977, bd. advs. 1978—, chmn. bd. advisers 1978, Vars award 1982, Rhoads lectr. 1985, Dudrick Rsch. Scholar award named in his honor), Penn. Nutritionists Soc. (pres. 1985), Am. Gastroent. Assn., Soc. Surg. Oncology, James Ewing Soc., Ravdin-Rhoads Surg. Assn., Excelsior Surg. Soc. (Edward D. Churchill lectr. 1981), Soc. Laparoendoscopic Surgery, Soc. Surg. Chairmen, So. Surg. Assn., Southwestern Surg. Congress, Southeastern Surg. Congress, Surg. Biology Club II, Surg. Infection Soc. (chmn. membership com. 1987-90), Western Surg. Soc., Halsted Soc., Allen O. Whipple Surg. Soc., Am. Inst. Nutrition, Soc. Clin. Surgery, Am. Soc. Clin. Investigation, Soc. for Surgery of Alimentary Tract, Am. Trauma Soc. (founders group), Am. Assn. for Surgery of Trauma, Soc. Clin. Surgery, Am. Soc. Clin. Nutrition, Fedn. Am. Soc. Exp. Biology, Am. Burn Assn., John Marshall Soc., Coll. Physicians Phila., Phila. Acad. Surgeons, George Hermann Soc., Union League Phila., Med. Club Phila., Franklin Club Phila., Houston Doctors Club (gov. 1973-76), Nat. Alumni Coun. U. Pa. Med. Sch. (chmn. 1994—), Conn. United for Rsch. Excellence (bd. dirs. 1995—), Cosmos Club, Athenaeum, The Penn Club (charter), Phi Beta Kappa, Phi Beta Kappa Assocs., Sigma Xi, Alpha Omega Alpha. (sec.-treas. Houston chpt. 1982-83),. Home: 3050 Locke Ln Houston TX 77019-6202 Office: St Mary's Hosp Dept Surgery 56 Franklin St Waterbury CT 06706-1501

DUEHN, WAYNE DONALD, social work educator; b. Hector, Minn., Feb. 8, 1939; s. Donald R. and Dorothy (Jochens) D.; m. Barbara Mark, June 10, 1961; 1 child, Jennifer. BA, North Cen. Coll., 1961; MSW, Loyola U., Chgo., 1964; PhD, Washington U., St. Louis, 1970. ACSW, CSW-ACP, Tex.; Bd. Cert. Diplomate. Caseworker Chgo. State Hosp., 1963; rsch. asst. Ill. State Pediatric Inst., Chgo., 1964-65; social work supr. Inst. for Juvenile Rsch., Chgo., 1965-67; rsch. assoc. Masters & Johnson Inst., St. Louis, 1968-70; assoc. prof., chmn. clin. practice work Grad. Sch. Social Work, U. Tex., Arlington, 1970-75; dir., clinican Marriage and Family Counseling Assn., Arlington, 1970—; prof. U. Tex., Arlington, 1979—; adj. faculty U.S. Army Acad. Health Scis., Ft. Sam Houston, Tex., 1988—; cons. U.S. Army, USAF, San Antonio, 1985—; cons., trainer Tex. Dept. Human Svcs., Austin, 1984—. Author: Beyond Sexual Abuse, 1989. Bd. dirs. Grandfather Home for Children, Banner Elk, N.C., 1989—; cons. Big Bros./Big Sisters, Dallas, 1984-94. Named Disting. Vis. Prof. Wilford Hall U.S. Med., 1987, 89, Eighth U.S. Army Hosp., 1990. Fellow Am. Orthopsychiat. Assn.; mem. Am. Psychol. Assn., Nat. Assn. Social Workers, Am. Assn. for Marriage and Family Therapy, Assn. for Advancement of Behavior Therapy, World Congress of Med. Sexology (U.S. rep. 1987-89). Home: 2200 Wilson Dr Arlington TX 76011-3226

DUEL, WARD CALVIN, health care consultant; b. Fond du Lac, Wis., Mar. 13, 1924; s. Myrton M. and Matie Rose (Tidyman) D.; m. Madelyn Mae Kressin, Oct. 1, 1950; children: Ward Rick, Christine Selma, Roxanne Matie, Beth Dawn. BS, U. Wis., 1950; postgrad., Marquette U., 1955-57; MPH, U. Calif., Berkeley, 1959. Registered sanitarian, Ill., Calif., Nat. Environ. Health Assn. Sanitarian City of Kenosha (Wis.), 1951-59; br. office mgr. Lake County Health Dept., Waukegan, Ill., 1959-65; dir. health Skokie (Ill.) Dept. Health, 1965-68, McHenry County Health Dept., Woodstock, Ill., 1968-70; asst. dir. pub. and environ. health AMA, Chgo., 1971-81; chief environ. health City of Chgo., 1981-82; dir. Mid-Ohio Valley Dept. Health, Parkersburg, W.Va., 1982-83; dir. environ. health, pub. and mental health Choctaw Indians, Phila., 1984-85; cons. on environ. health to prisons, juv. detention ctrs. and mental hosps. in 44 states and D.C., 1985—; active Nat. Com. on Correctional Health Care; capt. U.S. Pub. Health Svc. Commn. Corps Res., 1958—; lectr. in field. Co-editor: Clinical Implications of Air Pollution Research; author monographs: Physicians Guide to Solid Waste, 1975, Physicians Guide to Air Pollution, 1973-80, Flood Area Health Guide, 1961; contbr. articles to profl. jours. Served in U.S. Army, 1945-46. Decorated Bronze Star for Heroism; recipient Theta award Defenders, 1969, Samuel J. Crumbine award Single Svc. Inst., 1963, Walter S. Mangold award nat. Environ. Health Assn., 1978, Outstanding Citizen award Ill. Dept. Edn., 1984, Jour. Environ. Health Editors award, 1979. Mem. ASME, ASHRAE, Nat. Environ. Health Assn. (pres. 1967-68), Wis. Environ. Health Assn. (pres. 1957-58), Ill. Environ. Health Assn. (pres. 1964-65), Am. Pub. Health Assn. (fellow 1967), Am. Correctional Assn., Am. Jail Assn. (nat. stds. com. 1993—). Lutheran. Home and Office: 4907 N West St Mc Henry IL 60050-7968

DUER, ELLEN ANN DAGON, anesthesiologist; b. Balt., Feb. 3, 1936; d. Emmett Paul and Annie (Sollers) Dagon; m. Lyle Jordan Millan IV, Dec. 21, 1963; children: Lyle Jordan V, Elizabeth Lyle, Ann Sheridan Worthington.; m. T. Marshall Duer, Jr., Aug. 23, 1985. AB, George Washington U., 1959; MD, U. Md., 1964; postgrad., Johns Hopkins U., 1965-68. Intern Union Meml. Hosp., Balt., 1964-65; resident anesthesiology Johns Hopkins Hosp., Balt., 1965-68, fellow in surgery, 1965-68; practice medicine specializing in anesthesiology Balt., 1968—; faculty Church Home and Hosp., Balt., 1969—; attending staff Union Meml. Hosp., Church Home and Hosp., Frankling Sq. Hosp., Children's Hosp., James Lawrence Kernan Hosp., Balt., 1982-94; co-chief anesthesiology James Kernan Hosp., 1983-94, med. dir. out-patient surgery dept., 1987-94; mem. med. exec. com. Kernan Hosp., 1988-94; affiliate cons. emergency room Church Home and Hosp., Balt., 1969—, mem. med. audit and utilizaions com., 1970-72, mem. emergency and ambulatory care com., 1973-74, chief emergency dept., 1973-74; cons. anesthesiologist Md. State Penitentiary, 1971; fellow in critical care medicine Md. Inst. Emergency Medicine, 1975-76; mem. infection control com. U. Md. Hosp., 1975—; instr. anesthesiology U. Md. Sch. Medicine, 1975—; staff anesthesiologist Mercy Hosp., 1978—, audit com., 1979-80, 82; asst. prof. anesthegiology U. Md. Med. Sch., 1989-94; mem. med. exec. com. Kernan Hosp., 1990-94, v.p. 1990, chief of staff, 1992—; mem. Tappahannock Family Practice, 1994-96, Rappahannock Gen. Hosp. Family Practice, 1996—; active staff Rappahannock Gen. Hosp., 1996—; med. examiner No. Neck of Va., 1996—; mem. Commonwealth of Va. Med. Bd. Mem. AMA, Am. Coll. Emergency Physicians, Met. Emergency Dept. Heads Am., Md. Soc. Anesthesiologists, Balt. County Med. Soc., Mid. Peninsula Med. Soc., No. Neck Med. Soc., Med. Soc. Va., Med. and Choir Faculty Med., Chirurgical Soc., Internat. Congress Anaesthesiologists, Internat. Anesthesia Rsch. Soc., Am. L'Hirondelle Club, Annapolis Yacht Club, Chesapeake Bay Yacht Racing Assn, Rappahannock River Yacht Club. Episcopalian. Address: Deep Creek Farm House RR 3 Box 463 Lancaster VA 22503-9803

DUERDEN, BRIAN ION, medical microbiology educator; b. Nelson, Eng., June 21, 1948; s. Cyril and Mildred (Ion) D.; m. Marjorie Hudson, Aug. 5, 1972. BSc in Med. Sci. with honors, Edinburgh (Scotland) U., 1970, MB, ChB., 1972, MD, 1979. House officer thoracic surgery City Hosp., Edinburgh, 1972-73, house officer infectious diseases, 1973; lectr. bacteriology Edinburgh U. Med. Sch., 1973-76; lectr. med. microbiology Sheffield (Eng.) U. Med. Sch., 1976-79, sr. lectr. med. microbiology, 1979-83, prof. med. microbiology, 1983-90; prof. med. microbiology U. Wales Coll. Medicine, Cardiff, 1991—; dir. Pub. Health Lab. Svc., Cardiff, 1991-95; dep. dir. Pub. Health Lab. Svc. Bd., Eng. and Wales, 1995—; mgr. South Glamorgan Microbiology Svc., Cardiff, 1991-95; mem. adv. com. on dangerous pathogens U.K. Dept. of Health, microbiology adv. com. Govt. of U.K. Chmn. Jour. Med. Microbiology, U.K., 1988—; author: Textbook of Microbial and Parasitic Infection, 1987, 93; author, editor: Topley & Wilson's Principles of Bacteriology, Virology and Immunity, 1990, Anaerobes in Human Disease, 1991; contbr. articles to profl. jours. Fellow Royal Coll. Pathologists (mem. coun. 1986-89, 90-93, mem. exec. com. 1990-93, chmn. exam. panel med. microbiology 1994—), Infectious Disease Soc. Am. (corr.); mem. Path. Soc. Gt. Britain and Ireland (editor, com. mem.), Soc. for Anaerobic Microbiology (chmn. 1989-93), Assn. Med. Microbiologists (mem. exec. com.), Nat. External Quality Assurance Panel. Office: U Wales Coll Medicine, Heath Pk, Cardiff CF4 4XN, Wales

DUERDEN, MARC EVAN, physician, educator; b. Provo, Utah, May 26, 1961; s. Noel Hatch and Ina (Norager) D.; m. Mary Ballstaedt, Aug. 4, 1984; children: Jonathan, Michael. BA, Purdue U., Indpls., 1985; MD, Ind. U., Indpls., 1989. Diplomate Am. Bd. Phys. Medicine and Rehab. Resident Northwestern U., Chgo., 1990-93; attending physician Hook Rehab. Ctr., Indpls., 1993—; asst. clin. prof. Ind. U., Indpls., 1993—; ptnr. Rehab. Assocs., Indpls., 1994—; mem. Residency Rev. Com. for Phys. Medicine and Rehab., Indpls., 1996—; exam. question writer Am. Bd. Phys. Med. and Rehab., 1994. Contbr. chpt. to book. Scoutmaster, asst. Boy Scouts Am., Chgo., 1991-93, orgnl. rep., Indpls., 1995—; mem. bishopric Ch. of Jesus Christ of Latter-day Saints, Indpls., 1995—. Fellow Am. Acad. Phys. Medicine and Rehab.; mem. AMA (Physician Recognition award 1994), Ind. State Med. Assn. (chmn. young physicians com. 1994—). Home: 10322 Swiftsail Ln Indianapolis IN 46256 Offce: Rehab Assocs 8202 Clearvista Pkwy Indianapolis IN 46256

DUERKSEN, DEAN FARISS, dentist; b. Chickasha, Okla., Feb. 14, 1931; s. Cornelius Arthur and Flossie (Fariss) D.; m. Carol Lynn Fraley, Mar. 23, 1952 (div. 1969); children: Michael D., Paul D., Joseph D.; m. Alice Leigh Tilton, Dec. 28, 1970; 1 child, Margaret Natalie. BA, Oklahoma City U., 1952; DDS, Baylor U., 1964. TV dir. WFAA TV, Dallas, 1953-63; pvt. practice dentistry Crane, Tex., 1964-67, Ft. Stockton, Tex., 1967—. Dir. TV documentary: Disaster Dallas, 1956-57; contbr. articles to profl. jours. Pres. Am. Cancer Soc., Ft. Stockton, 1974-75, dist. crusade chmn., Odessa, 1972-73; city councilman City of Crane, 1965-66; chmn. bd. dirs. First United Meth. Ch., 1984-85; dist. com. N.Mex. conf. United Meth. Ch., 1991—, bd. dirs. Emmaus program. Mem. Blue Key Soc., Phi Mu Alpha. Republican.

DUFF, RAYMOND STANLEY, pediatrics educator; b. Hodgdon, Maine, Nov. 2, 1923; s. Maurice Cameron and Ruth Myrtle (Barton) D.; m. G. Joyce London, Nov. 28, 1945; children: Jane, Carole, Lori. BS, U. Maine, 1948; MD, Yale U., 1952, MPH, 1959; hon. doctorate, U. Utrecht, The Netherlands, 1986. Diplomate: Am. Bd. Pediatrics. Intern Yale-New Haven Hosp., 1952-53, resident in pediatrics, 1953-55; dir. med. services New Haven Health Dept., 1955-56; instr. pediatrics and pub. health Yale U., New Haven, 1956-60, asst. prof., 1960-67, assoc. prof., 1967-78, prof. pediatrics, 1978—; advisor Louise Mellen Fellowship in Intensive Care Nursing, Cleve., 1978-83. Author: Sickness and Society, 1968; contbr. articles on moral and ethical issues in health care to profl. jours., chpts. in books. Mem. Woodbridge Democratic Town Com., 1972-75. Served to 2d lt. F.A. AUS, 1943-46. HEW research grantee, 1958-65; research grantee Robert Wood Johnson Found., 1973-79; Alpha Omega Alpha vis. prof. U. Hawaii, 1978. Fellow Am. Acad. Pediatrics; mem. AAAS, Am. Sociol. Assn. Home: 259 Newton Rd Woodbridge CT 06525-1246 Office: Yale U Sch of Medicine 333 Cedar St New Haven CT 06510-3206

DUFFIELD, MARK STUART, orthopaedic surgeon; b. Ypsilanti, Mich., Aug. 4, 1960; s. Holley G. and Donna J. Duffield. DO, Coll. Osteo. Medicine, Kirksville, Mo., 1987. Resident Mich. State U., 1993, fellow in sports medicine, 1994; pvt. practice Austell, Ga., 1996—. Office: 1668 Mulkey Rd Austell GA 30001

DUFFNER, LEE R., ophthalmologist; b. Milw., June 3, 1936; m. Alvina Bross, Aug. 31, 1957; children—Fay, Rachel, Tamar. B.S. in Engring., Purdue U., 1957; M.S. in Physiology, Marquette U., 1961; M.D., Med. Coll. Wis., 1962. Diplomate Am. Bd. Ophthalmology. Intern, Stanford U., 1962-63; resident U. Miami, Fla., 1966-69; practice medicine specializing in ophthalmology, Hollywood, Fla., 1969—; clin. prof. ophthalmology U. Miami Sch. Medicine, 1969—; dir. Am. Bd. Ophthalmology, 1995—. Pres. town council Town of Golden Beach, Fla., 1983-95. Served to capt. USAF, 1963-66. Fellow Am. Acad. Ophthalmology, ACS; mem. Miami Ophthal. Soc. (pres. 1983-84). Jewish. Avocation: racewalking. Home: 185 Ocean Blvd Miami FL 33160-2208 Office: 2740 Hollywood Blvd Hollywood FL 33020-4826

DUFFOO, FRANTZ MICHEL, nephrologist, director of medicine; b. Port-Au-Prince, Haiti, Mar. 5, 1954; came to U.S., 1970; s. Franck and Leonie (Narcisse) D.; m. Marcia Anne Sylvester, Dec. 18, 1982; 1 child, Brian Anthony. BS, CCNY, 1977; MD, Meharry Med. Coll., 1979. Diplomate Am. Bd Internal Medicine, Am. Bd. Nephrology. Resident in internal medicine Brookdale Hosp. Med. Ctr., Bklyn., 1979-82; clin. fellow in nephrology Montefiore Med. Ctr., Bronx, N.Y., 1982-83, rsch. fellow in nephrology, 1983-84; attending physician and cons. in nephrology Woodhull Hosp., Bklyn., 1984-92, chief nephrology svc., 1990-92, assoc. dir. medicine, 1990-92; dir. medicine St. Mary's Hosp. of Bklyn., 1992—; instr. dept. medicine SUNY Health Sci. Ctr., Bklyn., 1985-88, asst. prof. medicine, 1988—; adj. asst. prof. NYU Sch. Edn., 1990—; adj. clin. asst. prof. N.Y. Coll. Osteo. Medicine, Old Westbury, N.Y., 1993—; affiliate clin. assoc. prof. St. John's U., Jamaica, N.Y., 1993—. Sec. med. staff Woodhull Hosp., Bklyn., 1989, v.p. med. staff, 1990, pres., 1991; sec. med. bd. St. Mary's Hosp. Bklyn., 1992. Recipient City of N.Y. Cert. of Appreciation award Mayor Dinkins for the City of N.Y., 1993. Fellow ACP. Office: Saint Mary's Hosp of Bklyn 170 Buffalo Ave Brooklyn NY 11213-2421

DUFFY, CAROL I., cardiologist; b. Reading, Pa., Sept. 10, 1954; d. William Palm and Janet Lorraine (Wolf) Ibach; m. Michael G. Duffy, Aug. 7, 1977 (div.). BA in Biology and Psychology, U. Del., 1976; MEd in Counseling and Guidance, U. Ariz., 1978, MS in Biology, 1980; DO, Kirksville Coll. Osteo., 1994. Attending cardiologist Springfield (Vt.) Hosp., 1989-91; asst. staff Dartmouth Hitchcock Med. Coll., Hanover, N.H., 1990-91; Cleve. Clinic Found., 1991-93; asst. prof. Albany (N.Y.) Med. Coll., 1993—. Author: Echocardiography, 1995; contbr. articles to profl. jours. Fellow Am. Coll. Cardiology.

DUFFY, JOHN CHARLES, psychiatric educator, b. Cleve., June 19, 1934; s. John Joseph and Hannah (McIllwee) D.; grad. Boston Coll., 1956; MD, N.Y. Med. Coll., 1960; m. Francoise C. Antonini; children—Charles, Robert, John. Intern, Henry Ford Hosp., Detroit, 1960-61; resident Mayo Clinic, Rochester, Minn., 1963-67; practice medicine specializing in adult and child psychiatry; exec. dir. Tucson Child Guidance Center, 1971-74; commd. med. officer USPHS, 1974; prof., asso. chmn. Uniformed Services U. Sch. Medicine, Bethesda, Md., 1974-81; assoc. commr. health affairs FDA and cons. Surgeon Gen., Rockville, Md., 1981-88; asst. surgeon gen. USPHS, 1983-92, chief physician officer, 1983-88; dir. C. Everett Koop Inst. at Dartmouth, Hanover, N.H., 1992-94; prof. psychiatry Sch. Medicine La. State U., New Orleans, 1994—. Recipient Outstanding Service medal Bd. Regents Uniformed Services U., 1981, Surgeon Gen.'s medallion. Fellow Am. Psychiat. Assn., Aerospace Med. Assn. (assoc., Longacre medal); mem. Assn. Mil. Surgeons U.S., Sigma Xi. Roman Catholic. Author: Psychiatric Morbidity of Physicians, 1964; Psychiatric Issues in the Lives of Physicians, 1966; Child Psychiatry, 1972, 86; Psychiatric Reviews, 1976. Founding editor in chief Child Psychiatry and Human Devel., 1970-83; editor: Ship's Medical Chest, 1984; editor in chief Mil. Medicine; mem. editorial bd. M.D. mag., 1976-90; Office: LSU Med Ctr 1542 Tulane Ave New Orleans LA 70112-2825

DUFRESNE, CRAIG ROGER, plastic surgeon, educator; b. Newport, R.I., Sept. 20, 1951; s. Roger Joseph and Molly T. Dufresne; m. Katherine Ann Scrive, Aug. 11, 1978; children: Jacqueline Melissa, Elizabeth Ashley, Christopher Scrive. BA in Zoology summa cum laude, U. Vt., 1973; MD, Columbia U., 1977. Diplomate Am. Bd. Plastic Surgery. Intern Johns Hopkins Hosp., Balt., 1977-78, jr., then sr. resident in surgery, 1978-82; registrar in thoracic surgery Frenchay Hosp., Bristol, Eng., 1980-81; jr. res., then sr. resident in plastic surgery NYU Med. Ctr., N.Y.C., 1982-84, fellow in microvascular surgery, 1984, fellow in craniofacial surgery, 1985; asst. prof., dir. Ctr. for Reconstructive Surgery, Johns Hopkins U., 1985-89, dir. Cleft Lip and Palate Clinic, 1985-89, clin. asst. prof., 1989—; pvt. practice, Fairfax and Annandale, Va., 1989—, Chevy Chase, Md., 1989—; clin. instr. George Washington U., Washington, 1990-93; clin. assoc. prof. Georgetown U., Washington, 1994—; numerous presentations in field; chief plastic surgery svc. Loch Raven VA Med. Ctr., 1985-89; clin. assoc. in plastic surgery U. Md. Hosps., 1985-89; attending physician Md. Inst. for Emergency Med. Svcs. Ctr., 1985-89; mem. exec. com., and med. adv. bd. Internat. Craniofacial Found., 1990-92; co-dir. Ctr. for Facial Rehab., Fairfax Hosp., 1989—; vis. prof. U. Rochester, N.Y., 1992, Ea. Va. Med. Coll., Norfolk, 1993; cons. plastic surgery svc. Bethesda Naval Hosp. Co-editor: Complex Craniofacial Problems: Guide to Analysis and Treatment, 1992; contbr. numerous articles to med. jours., chpts. to books. Asst. scoutmaster troop 1449 Boy Scouts Am., Washington, 1994-95. Named One of Best 150 Drs. in Balt., Balt. Mag., 1986; One of Best REgional Breast Surgeons, The Washingtonian, 1986, One Best Plastic Surgeons in Washington Area, 1993, 95, also others; grantee AO/ASIF, Howmedica, Inc., Nat. Inst. Dental Rsch., Bowles Fund, Children's Hosp., Storz, Inc. Fellow ACS; mem. AMA, Am. Cleft Lip and Palate Assn., Am. Soc. Plastic and Reconstructive Surgeons (govt. rels. com. 1989—), Internat. Soc. Craniomaxillofacial Surgery, Am. Soc. Maxillofacial Surgeons (govt. rels. com. 1990—, best paper award com. 1993—), Plastic Surgery Rsch. Coun., John Staige David Soc., John M. Converse Soc., Northeastern Plastic Surgery Soc. (sci. program com. 1992-93), Southeastern Med. Soc., Pan-Pacific Plastic Surgery Assn., Fairfax Med. Soc., Nat. Capital Med. Soc., Montgomery Med. Soc., Johns Hopkins Med. and Surg. Assn. Office: Ctr for Plastic Surgery Ste 205 3700 Joseph Siewick Dr Fairfax VA 22033 also: Ctr for Plastic Surgery Ste 130 5550 Friendship Blvd Chevy Chase MD 20815 also: Ctr for Plastic Surgery 3299 Woodburn Rd Ste 490 Annandale VA 22003

DUGAN, CHARLES CLARK, physician, surgeon; b. Penn Yan, N.Y., Jan. 24, 1921; s. Charles Emanual and Wilhemia May (Clark) D.; m. Eugenie Alice Pounds, Aug. 12, 1944 (div. 1963); children: Charles Clark II, Douglas Craig, Timothy Gene; m. Ruth Louise Fugh, Dec. 3, 1965 (dec. 1983); adopted children: Dain Walters, Carl Jay. AA, Wentworth Mil. Jr. Coll., 1940; AB, Cornell U., 1942; MD, Jefferson Med. Coll., 1946; MPH, Naval Med. Sch. & Johns Hopkin, 1956. Diplomate Am. Bd. Dermatology, Am. Bd. Allergy and Immunology, Spl. Bd. Dermatopathology, Am. Bd. Cosmetic Plastic Surgery, Am. Bd. Preventive Medicine, Aviation Medicine and Pub. Health, Nat. Bd. Med. Examiners. Resident in psychiatry Pa. Psychiat. Hosp., Phila., 1945-46; rotating intern extended in gen. surgery Harrisburg (Pa.) Gen. Hosp., 1946-47; resident in dermatology U. Colo. Med. Ctr., Denver, 1956-57; resident in dermatology and allergy Henry Ford Hosp., Detroit, 1957-59; pvt. practice dermatology, allergy, cosmetic plastic surgery West Palm Beach, Fla., 1959—; physician mem. bd. Palm Beach County Environ. Control Hearing Bd., West Palm Beach, 1981-94; mem. staff Palm Beach Gardens (Fla.) Cmty. Hosp.; mem. Wellington Regional Med. Ctr., West Palm Beach; active staff Good Samaritan Hosp., West Palm Beach. Contbr. articles to profl. jours. Lt. col. USAF, 1947-56, ret. Recipient Cert. of Svc., Am. Cancer Soc., West Palm Beach, 1961; named Surgeon of Yr., Fla. Soc. Dematol. Surgeons, 1991. Fellow Am. Acad. Dermatology, Am. Coll. Preventive Medicine, Am. Coll. Allergy, Asthma and Immunology, Am. Acad. Allergy, Asthma and Immunology, Internat. Acad. Cosmetic Surgery, Am. Acad. Facial Plastic and Reconstructive Surgery, Am. Acad. Cosmetic Surgery, Am. Soc. Dermatol. Surgery (bd. dirs. 1980-83), Am. Soc. Dematopathology, Am. Soc. Cryosurgeons, Am. Soc. Cert. Allergists, Internat. Soc. Dematopathology, Noah Webster Dermatol. Soc., Fla. Soc. Dermatology (pres. 1973-74, Practitioner of Yr. award 1993), Fla. Soc. Dermatol. Surgeons (pres. 1980-83), and many others. Republican. Presbyterian. Office: M D Center 2600 Broadway West Palm Beach FL 33407-5431

DUGGAN, STEPHEN JOHN, physician; b. Phila., May 18, 1966; s. John and Theresa Angela (Comerford) D.; m. Lauren Nicole, May 20, 1995. BS, Villanova U., 1988; DO, Phila. Coll. Osteo. Medicine, 1992. Family medical physician Middletown, Del., 1995—. Recipient William Goldman Found. award, Phila., 1988-92. Mem. Am. Coll. Family Practice, AMA, Am. Osteo. Assn. Home: 221 Chestnut Way Middletown DE 19709 Office: 200 Cleaver Farm Rd Middletown DE 19709

DÜHMKE, ECKHART, radiation oncology educator; b. Berlin, July 22, 1942; s. Martin Walter and Christa Anna Luise (Horrer) D.; m. Eva Leopoldine Herta Bagge, Dec. 31, 1970; children: Anna Katharina, Elisa Maria, Rudolf Martin, Victoria Christina. MD, U. Kiel, Germany, 1969, Habilitation in Med. Radiology, 1980. Resident dept. radiology U. Kiel, 1970-74, specialist in radiology, 1975-80, specialist in radiotherapy, lectr., 1980-85; prof. radiation oncology, chmn. dept. radiotherapy U. Göttingen, Germany, 1985-93, provisional chmn. dept. diagnostic radiology, 1985-87, provisional chmn. dept. radiation physics and biology, 1987-91, dir. div. radiology, 1989-93; chmn. dept. radiotherapy and radiation oncology U. Munich, 1993—; vis. prof. dept. radiation oncology and nuclear medicine Hahnemann U., Phila., 1984. Co-author: Handbook of Medical Radiology, 1974; author: Medicinal Radiography with Fast Neutrons, 1980; co-editor, editor: Function Preserving Therapy of Laryngeal Carcinoma Proc., 1990-91; also numerous articles on diagnostic and therapeutic radiology. Mem. German Roengten Soc., German Cancer Soc., Am. Soc. Therapeutic Radiology and Oncology, European Soc. Therapeutic Radiology and Oncology, Am. Soc. Clin. Oncology. Lutheran. Office: Munich Dept Radiotherapy and Radiation Oncology, Marchioninistr 15, D-81377 Munich Germany

DUHRKOPF, RICHARD EDWARD, biology educator; b. Chgo., Oct. 11, 1949; s. Rodney Edward and Mildred Thelma (Walker) D.; m. Deborah Gay Adkins, May 26, 1984. BS, Ohio State U., 1971, MS, 1973, PhD, 1977. Vis. asst. prof. Bucknell U., Lewisburg, Pa., 1977-78; postdoctoral fellow Johns Hopkins U. Sch. Hygiene & Pub. Health, Balt. 1978-80; asst. prof. Grinnell (Iowa) Coll., Grinnell, 1980-84, Baylor U., Waco, Tex., 1984—. Editor jour. column The Am. Biology Tchr., 1987—. Mem. AAAS, Nat. Assn. Biology Tchrs., Soc. Study of Evolution, Sigma Xi. Methodist. Office: Baylor U Dept Biology Waco TX 76798

DUKE, LINDA RUTH WARREN, psychology educator, neuropsychologist; b. Richmond, Va., June 22, 1945; d. Ramon Eldridge and Ruth Elizabeth (Braudrick) W.; m. Robert Lee Duke, Jr. Apr. 29, 1978; children—Elizabeth Ruth, Kathryn Bernice. B.A., Duke U., 1967; Ph.D., U. Calif.-Berkeley, 1972. Clin. respecialization U. S.C. Asst. prof. Williams Coll., Williamstown, Mass., 1972-76; asst., then assoc. prof. psychology U. Ala., Birmingham, 1976—; intern U. Ala., Birmingham, 1988. NIH postdoctoral fellow, 1975-76. Mem. Am. Psychol. Assn., Gerontol. Soc., Soc. for Psychophysiol. Research, Psychonomic Soc. Contbr. articles to profl. jours. Home: 2417 Scepter Ln Birmingham AL 35226-2904 Office: U Ala Dept Psychology 1300 University Blvd Birmingham AL 35233

DUKER, NAHUM JOHANAN, pathologist; b. N.Y.C., Oct. 27, 1942; s. Abraham and Lillian (Sandrow) D.; m. Naomi Maisel, June 13, 1972 (div.); children: Eli Avishai, Joshua Jair, Jonathan Jacob, Ezra Aryeh; m Vita Khayyat, Apr. 12, 1992. BS, U. Ill., 1962; MD, U. Ill., Chgo., 1966. Diplomate pathologic anatomy and clin. pathology Am. Bd. Pathology. Intern Bellevue Hosp., N.Y.C., 1966-67; resident NYU Med. Sch., N.Y.C., 1970-76, instr., 1976-77; asst. prof. Temple U. Med. Sch., Phila., 1977-82, assoc. prof., 1982-87, prof., pathology, 1987—. Contbr. articles to profl. jours. Capt. U.S. Army, 1967-69. Recipient Career Devel. award, Nat. Cancer Inst., 1983. Mem. Agudath Israel of Phila. (treas. 1984-94, trustee 1994—). Republican. Jewish. Office: Temple U Med Sch 3400 N Broad St Philadelphia PA 19140-5196

DULBECCO, RENATO, biologist, educator; b. Catanzaro, Italy, Feb. 22, 1914; came to U.S., 1947, naturalized, 1953; s. Leonardo and Maria (Virdia) D.; m. Gulseppina Salvo, June 1, 1940 (div. 1963); children: Peter Leonard (dec.), Maria Vittoria; m. Maureen Rutherford Muir; 1 child, Fiona Linsey. M.D., U. Torino, Italy, 1936; D.Sc. (hon.), Yale U., 1968, Vrije Universiteit, Brussels, 1978; LL.D., U. Glasgow, Scotland, 1970. Asst. U. Torino, 1940-47; research asso. Ind. U., 1947-49; sr. research fellow Calif. Inst. Tech., 1949-52, asso. prof., then prof. biology, 1952-63; sr. fellow Salk Inst. Biol. Studies, San Diego, 1963-71; asst. dir. research Imperial Cancer Research Fund, London, 1971-74; dep. dir. research Imperial Cancer Research Fund, 1974-77; disting. research prof. Salk Inst., La Jolla, Calif., 1977—, pres., 1989-92; pres. emeritus Salk Inst., La Jolla, 1993—; prof. pathology and medicine U. Calif. at San Diego Med. Sch., La Jolla, 1977-81, mem. Cancer Ctr.,; vis. prof. Royal Soc. G.B., 1963-64, Leeuwenhoek lectr., 1974; Clowes Meml. lectr. Atlantic City, 1961; Harvey lectr. Harvey Soc., 1967; Dunham lectr. Harvard U., 1972; 11th Marjory Stephenson Meml. lectr., London, 1973, Harden lectr., Wye, Eng., 1973, Am. Soc. for Microbiology lectr., L.A., 1979; mem. Calif. Cancr Adv. Coun., 1963-67; mem. vis. com. Case Western Res. Sch. Medicine; adv. bd. Roche Inst., 1968-71, Inst. Immunology, Basel, Switzerland, others; esperto Italian Nat. Rsch. Coun.; trustee Am.-Italian Fedn. for Cancer Rsch.; mem. bd. dirs. Scientific Counselors Dept. Etiology NCI; cons. Nat. Rsch. Coun. ESPERTO, 1994—. Trustee La Jolla Country Day Sch., Am.-Italian Fedn. for Cancer Rsch.; bd. mem. sci. counselors dept. etiology NCI. Recipient John Scott award City Phila., 1958, Kimball award Conf. Pub. Health Lab. Dirs., 1959, Albert and Mary Lasker Basic Med. Rsch. award, 1964, Howard Taylor Ricketts award, 1965, Paul Ehrlich-Ludwig Darmstaedter prize, 1967, Horwitz prize Columbia U., 1973, (with David Baltimore and Howard Martin Temin) Nobel prize in medicine, 1975, Targa d'oro Villa San Giovanni, 1978, Mandel Gold medal Czechoslovak Acad. Scis., 1982, Via de Condotti prize, 1990, Cavaliere di Gran Croce Italian Rep., 1991, Natale Di Roma prize, 1993, Columbus prize, 1993; named Man of Yr., London, 1975, Italian Am. of Yr., San Diego County, 1978; hon. citizen City of Imperia (Italy), 1983, City of Arezzo, City of Sommariva Perno, City of Catanzaro, City of Torino; Guggenheim and Fulbright fellow, 1957-58; decorated grand ufficiale Italian Republic, 1981; hon. founder Hebrew U., 1931. Mem. NAS (Selman A. Waksman award 1974, com. on human rights), Am. Assn. Cancer Rsch., Internat. Physicians for Prevention Nuclear War, Am. Philos. Assn., Academia Nazionale dei Lincei (fgn.), Academia Ligure di Scienze e Lettre (hon.), Royal Soc. (fgn.), Fedn. Am. Scientists, Am. Acad. Arts and Scis., Comitato di Collaborazione Culturale (hon. mem.), Alpha Omega Alpha. Home: 7525 Hillside Dr La Jolla CA 92037-3941*

DULLY, FRANK EDWARD, JR., physician, educator; b. Hartford, Conn., Jan. 19, 1932; s. Frank Edward and Monica Theresa (Cooney) D.; m. Rebecca Sue Akers, Apr. 23, 1982; children: Kathleen, Ann, Margaret, David, Nancy, Tammy. BS, Coll. of Holy Cross, 1954; MD, Georgetown U., 1958; MPH, U. Calif., Berkeley, 1970. Diplomate Am. Bd. Preventive Medicine. Rotating intern D.C. Gen. Hosp., Washington, 1958-59; resident in family practice Bridgeport (Conn.) Hosp., 1959-60; resident in aerospace medicine Naval Aerospace Med. Inst., Pensacola, Fla., 1970-72; pvt. practice Shelton, Conn., 1960-64; commd. lt. USN, 1964, advanced through grades to capt., 1972; served with Destroyer Squadron 14, 1964-65; USN student flight surgeon, 1965-66; sr. med. officer USS Hornet, 1966-68, Naval Air Sta., Glynco, Ga., 1968-69; aerospace medicine resident USN, Pensacola Fla., 1970-72; sr. med. officer USS Enterprise, 1972-74; dir. tng. Naval Aerospace Med. Inst., Pensacola, 1974-77; sr. med. officer First Marine Aircraft Wing, 1977-78, Pacific Fleet Naval Air Force, 1978-82; commanding officer Naval Aerospace Med. Inst., 1982-85; instr. aviation safety Naval Postgrad Sch., Monterey, Calif., 1985-87; ret., 1987; field assoc. prof. Inst. Safety and Systems Mgmt. U. So. Calif., L.A., 1987-90, cons. aviation med., 1990-94; lectr. aviation safety worldwide, 1978—; tchr. safety N.W. Airlines, Mpls., 1988-90; cons. in aviation medicine U. So. Calif., 1990—. Co-editor: U.S. Navy Flight Surgeon Manual, 1976; contbr. over 40 articles on aviation medicine to med. jours. Decorated Legion of Merit, Air medal with oak leaf cluster, Meritorious Svc. medal. Fellow ACP, Am. Coll. Preventive Medicine, Aerospace Med. Assn.; mem. Internat. Acad. Aviation and Space Medicine, Soc. U.S.-Naval Flight Surgeons (pres. 1980, 81, 83), Internat. Soc. Air Safety Investigators, Am. Helicopter Soc., Am. Model Yachting Assn., St. Louis Admirals R/C Boat Club, Scale Ship Modelers Assn. N.Am., Tailhook Assn., Flight Safety Found., USS Enterprise Assn. Republican. Roman Catholic. Home: 2522 Briarcliff Dr Newburgh IN 47630-8604

DULTZ, LAWRENCE ROY, internist; b. Newark, Oct. 19, 1960; s. Norman and Thea Barbara (Brenner) D.; m. Margaret E. Pappas, May 20, 1990; children: Caroline Rebecca, Elizabeth Rachel. BA in Psychology with honors, Johns Hopkins U., 1982; MD, U. Medicine & Dentistry N.J., 1986. Diplomate Am. Bd. Internal Medicine. Transitional intern St. Barnabas Med. Ctr., Livingston, N.J., 1986-87; resident in internal medicine Morristown (N.J.) Meml. Hosp., 1987-89; house physician Chilton Meml. Hosp., Pompton Plains, N.J., 1989-90; pulmonary/critical care fellowship SUNY, Stony Brook, 1990-93; attending physician Burlington County Internal Medicine Assocs., Willingboro, N.J., 1993-96, AP & S Clinic Medicine Assocs., Terre Haute, Ind., 1996—. Fellow Am. Coll. Chest Phys.; mem. ATS. Office: AP & S Clinic Medicine Assocs 221 S 6th St Terre Haute IN 47808

DUMA, RICHARD JOSEPH, microbiologist, physician, pathologist, researcher, educator; b. Bethlehem, Pa., Apr. 2, 1933; s. Joseph Anthony and Helen Veronica (Bartek) D.; m. Mary Alyce Fridley, Apr. 18, 1957; 1 child, Scott. B.A., Va. Poly. Inst., 1955; M.D., U. Va., 1959; Ph.D., Va. Commonwealth U.-Med. Coll. Va., 1978. Diplomate Am. Bd. Internal Medicine. Intern, then resident in medicine U. Ala. Med. Center, Birmingham, 1959-60, 62-65; research fellow Harvard U. Med. Sch.-Mass. Gen. Hosp., 1965-67; mem. faculty Med. Coll. Va., Richmond, 1967-91; chmn. div. infectious diseases Med. Coll. Va., 1974-92, prof. medicine and pathology, 1975-92, prof. microbiology, 1977-92; mem. U. S. Pharmacopeia Adv. Panel on Hosp. Practices, 1971-82, chmn. subcom. rsch., 1976-82, clin. prof. medicine and infectious diseases Med. Coll. Richmond, 1992—; exec. dir. Nat. Found. for Infectious Diseases, 1991-94, v.p. bd. dirs., 1973-75, pres., 1975-91; chmn. Nat. Coalition for Adult Immunization, 1988-94; didr. infectious diseases Halifax Med. Ctr., Daytona Beach, Fla., 1995—. Served with M.C. USNR, 1960-62. Fellow ACP, Infectious Disease Soc. Am., Royal Soc. Tropical Medicine and Hygiene, Am. Soc. Tropical Medicine and Hygiene, Am. Soc. Rickettsiology; mem. AAAS, Am. Fedn. Clin. Rsch., Am. Soc. Microbiology, Va. Soc. Microbiology, Am. Soc. Internal Medicine, Va. Soc. Internal Medicine, Richmond Soc. Internal Medicine, So. Soc. Clin. Investigation, Am. Thoracic Soc., Royal Soc. Medicine, Med. Soc. Va., Richmond Acad. Medicine, Med. Assn. Fla., Volusia Med. Soc., Sigma Xi, Tau Beta Pi. Home: 407 Long Cove Rd Ormond Beach FL 32174-9241 Office: Halifax Medical Ctr PO Box 2830 303 N Clyde Morris Blvd Daytona Beach FL 32120

DUMANOWSKI, LINDA JANE, women's health nurse, educator; b. Warroad, Minn., Aug. 20, 1946; d. Joseph Raymond and Eva Louise (Quarstein) Lechleiter; m. James Earl Dumanowski, June 11, 1966; children: Lori Jane, Lisa Lynn. AA, Foothill Coll., 1966. Staff nurse Suburban Med. Ctr., Hoffman Estates, Ill., 1979-80, Alexian Bros. Hosp., Elk Grove Village, Ill., 1975-79; staff nurse, asst. head nurse El Camino Hosp., Mountain View, Calif., 1966-70; staff nurse O'Connor Hosp., San Jose, Calif., 1980-91; staff nurse high risk antepartum/perinatal svcs. unit Good Samaritan Hosp., San Jose, 1991—. Mem. Calif. Nurses Assn. Home: 5238 Barron Park Dr San Jose CA 95136-2808

DUMAS, RHETAUGH ETHELDRA GRAVES, university official; b. Natchez, Miss., Nov. 26, 1928; d. Rhetaugh Graves and Josephine (Clemmons) Graves Bell; m. A.W. Dumas, Jr., Dec. 25, 1950; 1 child, Adrienne. BS in Nursing, Dillard U., 1951; MS in Psychiat. Nursing, Yale U., 1961; PhD in Social Psychology, Union Grad. Sch., Union for Experimenting Colls. and Univs., Cinn., 1975; also various other courses; D Pub. Svc. (hon.), Simmons Coll., 1976, U. Cin., 1981; LHD (hon.), Yale U., 1989; LLD (hon.), Dillard U., 1990; LHD, U. San Diego, 1993. Instr. Dillard U., 1957-59, 61; research asst., instr. Sch. Nursing Yale U., 1962-65, from asst. prof. nursing to assoc. prof., 1965-72, chmn. dept. psychiat. nursing, 1972; dir. nursing Conn. Mental Health Ctr., Yale-New Haven Med. Ctr., 1966-72; chief psychiat. nursing edn. br. Div. Manpower and Tng. Programs, NIMH, Rockville, Md., 1972-76; dep. dir. Div. Manpower and Tng. Programs NIMH, 1976-79, dep. dir., 1979-81; dean U. Mich. Sch. Nursing, 1981-94; vice provost health affairs, Cole prof. Sch. Nursing U. Mich., 1994—, cole prof. sch. nursing; dir. Group Rels. Confs. in Tavistock Model; cons., speaker, panelist in field; fellow Helen Hadley Hall, Yale U., 1972, Branford Coll., 1972; dir. Community Health Care Ctr. Plan, New Haven, 1969-72; mem. U.S. Assessment Team, cons. to Fed. Ministry Health, Nigeria, 1982; mem. adv. com. Health Policy Agenda for the Am. People, AMA, 1983-86; cons. NIH Task Force on Nursing Rsch., 1984; mem. Nat. Commn. on Unemployment and Mental Health, Nat. Mental Health Assn., 1984-85; mem. com. to plan maj. study of nat. long-term care policy Inst. Medicine, 1985; mem. adv. com. to dir. NIH, 1986-87; mem. Sec.'s Nat. Commn. on Future Structure of VA Health Care System, 1990-91; mem. coun. on grad. med. edn. Nat. Adv. Coun. on Nurse Edn. and Practice Workgroup on Primary Care Workforce Projection, Divsn. Nursing, 1994. Author profl. monographs; contbr. articles to profl. publs.; mem. editorial bd. Community Mental Health Rev., 1977-79, Jour. Personality and Social Systems, 1978-81, Advances in Psychiat. Mental Health Nursing, 1981. Bd. dirs. Afro Am. Ctr., Yale U., 1968-72; mem. New Haven Bd. Edn., 1968-71, New Haven City Demonstrations Agy., 1968-70, Human Rels. Coun. New Haven, 1961-63, Nat. Neural Circuitry Database Com., Inst. Medicine, Nat. Acad. Scis.; mem. commn. on future structure of vets. health care U.S. Dept. Vets. Affairs, 1990. Named Disting. Alumna, Dillard U., 1966; recipient various awards, including cert. Honor NAACP, 1970, Disting. Alumnae award Yale U. Sch. Nursing, 1976, award for outstanding achievement and service in field mental health D.C. chpt. Assn. Black Psychologists, 1980, Pres. 21st Century award The Nat. Women's Hall of Fame, 1994. Fellow A.K. Rice Inst., Am. Coll. Mental Health Adminstrs. (founding), Am. Acad. Nursing (charter, pres. 1987-89); mem. Inst. Medicine NAS, Am. Nurses Assn., Nat. Black Nurses Assn., Am. Assn. Colls. Nursing (govtl. affairs com. 1990-93), Am. Pub. Health Assn., Nat. League Nursing (pres.-elect 1995—), Sigma Theta Tau Internat. (mentor award 1989), Delta Sigma Theta. Office: U Mich 3088 Fleming Adminstrn Bldg Ann Arbor MI 48109-1340

DUMMETT, CLIFTON ORRIN, dentist, educator; b. Georgetown, British Guiana, May 20, 1919; came to U.S., 1936; s. Alexander Adolphus and Eglantine Annabella (Johnson) D.; m. Lois Maxine Doyle, Mar. 6, 1943; 1 child, Clifton Orrin Jr. BS in Psychology, Roosevelt U., Chgo., 1941; DDS, Northwestern U., 1941, M.Sc.D., 1942, D.Sc. (hon.), 1976; M.P.H., U. Mich., 1947; Sc.D. (hon.), U. Pa., 1978. Diplomate Am. Bd. Periodontology, Am. Bd. Oral Medicine. Dean, and prof. periodontology Meharry Med. Coll., Nashville, 1945-49; chief dental service VA Hosp., Tuskegee, Ala., 1949-65, assoc. chief staff for research and edn., 1958-65; chief dental service VA Hosp., Chgo., 1965-66; dental dir., dir. ctr. Watts Health Ctr., Los Angeles, 1966-69; assoc. dean, chmn. dept. community dentistry Sch. Dentistry, U. So. Calif., L.A., 1969-75, prof., 1969-89, prof. emeritus, 1989—; adj. prof. Northwestern U. Dental Sch., 1989; vis. prof., cons. Sch. Vet. Medicine, Tuskegee Inst., 1962-65; vis. prof. Meharry Med. Coll., 1989—; trustee Am. Fund Dental Health, Chgo., 1968-78; chmn. devel. component rev. panel Calif. Regional Med. Programs, L.A., 1975-77; mem. Pres.'s Com. on Nat. Health Ins., 1977. Author: Community Dentistry, 1974, Afro-Americans in Dentistry: Sequence and Consequence of Events, 1977, Charles Edwin Bentley, 1982, Dental Education of Meharry Medical College: Origin and Odyssey, 1992, Culture and Education in Dentistry at Northwestern University, 1993; (editorial) Nor Yet the Last, 1962 (W.J. Gies award 1963), The Hillenbrand Era, 1986; editor Nat. Dental Assn., 1953-75; contbr. over 300 papers and articles to profl. jours., chpts. to books. Chmn. adv. bd. Econ. and Youth Opportunity Agy. Project Head Start, Tuskegee, Ala, 1964-65; mem. spl. health adv. com. Calif. Bd. Edn., Los Angeles, 1972-74; mem. Los Angeles regional hearing planning council, President's Com. on Health Edn., Los Angeles, 1973-74. Served to lt. col. USAF, 1955-58. Recipient Alumni award of Merit Northwestern U., 1971, Fones Gold medal

Conn. Dental Assn., 1976, Pierre Fauchard Gold medal Pierre Fauchard Acad., 1980. Fellow Internat. Coll. Dentists, Am. Coll. Dentists (Wm. J. Gies award 1992), Am . Pub. Health Assn. (John W. Knitson Disting. Svc. award 1992), Am. Pub. Health Assn. (v.p. for U.S., 1995-96), AAAS (chmn. dental sect. 1975-76, 87-88), Am. Acad. History of Dentistry (pres. 1982-83, Hayden and Harris award 1987); mem. ADA (hon.), Internat. Assn. Dental Rsch. (pres. 1969-70), Assn. Mil. Surgeons U.S. (life), Am. Assn. Dental Editors (editor 1963-72, pres. 1974-75, Disting. Svc. medal 1976), Nat. Acads. Practice (Disting. Practitioner 1987), Inst. Medicine Nat. Acad. Sci. (sr. mem.), Sigma Xi. Sigma Pi Phi, Alpha Phi Alpha, Omicron Kappa Upsilon (pres., founder Nashville chpt. 1947-49), Delta Omega. Democrat. Episcopalian. Home: 5344 Highlight Pl Los Angeles CA 90016-5119 Office: U So Calif Sch Dentistry PO Box 77006 Los Angeles CA 90007-0006

DUMONT, ALLAN ELIOT, physician, educator; b. N.Y.C., Oct. 8, 1924; m. Joan Auerbach, Oct. 1, 1949; children: Mark E., James A., David H. BA, Hobart Coll., 1945; MD, NYU, 1948. Diplomate Am. Bd. Surgery. Intern Bellevue Hosp., N.Y.C., 1948-49, resident, 1949-51, 53-54, chief resident, 1954-55; instr. surgery NYU, 1955-59, asst. attending surgeon Univ. Hosp., asst. vis. surgeon 3d and 4th surg. divs. Bellevue, 1955-60, asst. prof. surgery, 1959-62, assoc. vis. surgeon 3d and 4th surg. div. Bellvue, 1961-65; attending surgeon Manhattan VA Hosp., N.Y.C., 1958-67, cons. surgeon, 1967-90; assoc. attending surgeon Univ. Hosp. NYU, 1961-68, attending surgeon, 1968-90, assoc. prof. surgery, 1962-68, prof. surgery, 1968-73, Jules Leonard Whitehill prof. surgery, 1973-90, prof. emeritus, 1990—; clin. prof. surgery U. Conn. Sch. Medicine, 1991; career scientist N.Y.C. Health Research Council, 1959-62; univ. senate NYU, 1966-69; vis. surgeon Bellevue Hosp., 1965-90, assoc. dir. surg. service, 1975-90; cons. surgeon St. Francis Hosp., Hartford, 1990—. Editor: Lymphology. 1974-84. Served to lt (j.g.) USN, 1951-53. Recipient Research Career Devel. award USPHS, 1961-71, Purkinje medal, Czechoslovakia, 1977. Mem. Am. Coll. Surgeons, New Eng. Surg. Soc., Harvey Soc., N.Y. Surg. Soc. (pres. 1987-88), Am. Physiol. Soc., Soc. for Exptl. Biology and Medicine, Soc. Univ. Surgeons, Soc. for Surgery Alimentary Tract, Internat. Soc. Lymphology (pres. 1979-83), Transplantation Soc., Am. Surg. Assn.

DUMONT, ALLEN ANDRÉ, pyschotherapist, educator; b. N.Y.C., Nov. 17, 1942; s. Phillip J. DuMont and Gabrielle Dumas; m. Marilyn Sciacca, May 28, 1983; 1 child, James. BA, CUNY, Queens, 1965; MSW, Adelphi U., 1974; PhD, NYU, 1984. Cert. social worker, clin. social worker; bd. cert. diplomate Am. Bd. Examiners in Clin. Social Work; cert. psychoanalytic psychotherapy L.I. Inst. Mental Health. Clin. field instr. office staff devel. N.Y.C. Human Resources Adminstrn., 1985-89, psychotherapy supr., 1986—; sch. social worker N.Y.C. Bd. Edn., 1989—; child and family therapist L.I. Consultation Ctr., Rego Park, N.Y., 1985-90, St. Anthony's Guidance Clin., Mineola, N.Y., 1977-82; dir. spl. asst. for tng. office field svcs. Child Welfare Adminstrn., N.Y.C., 1980-84. Recipient Cath. Charities Svc. award, 1982; fellow L.I. Inst. Mental Health, 1979; grad. assistantship Adelphi U., 1973. Fellow Am. Orthopsychiat. Assn.; mem. NASW, N.Y. Soc. Clin. Social Work Psychotherapists (diplomate, 1st v.p., state treas., mem.-at-large Queen's chpt. pres.). Home and Office: 39-06 219th St Bayside NY 11361-2344

DUMONT, MARK ELIOT, biochemist, educator; b. N.Y.C., July 20, 1950; s. Allan Eliot and Joan (Auerbach) D.; m. Lynn Beth Mehlman, May 20, 1984; children: Anna Aline, Nora Matea. BA, Harvard U., 1972; MS, Western Wash. U., 1975; PhD, Johns Hopkins U., 1980. Postdoctoral fellow Yale U., New Haven, 1980-85; postdoctoral fellow U. Rochester, N.Y., 1985-89, asst. prof., 1989—. Office: U Rochester Sch Medicine Dept Biochemistry PO Box 607 Rochester NY 14642

DU MONT, NICOLAS, psychiatrist, educator; b. San Juan, P.R., Dec. 22, 1954; s. Joseph Henri and Isabel (Solano) Du M. Postgrad. adult psychiatry, Columbia U., 1990; MD, U. P.R., 1986; postgrad. child, adolescent psychiatry, Columbia U., 1992, postgrad. pub. cmty. psychiatry, 1993; PhD, LaSalle U., La., 1994. Assoc. prof. Polytech. U., San Juan, 1984-88, Inter-Am. U., San Juan, P.R., 1986-87; med. dir. Holistic Med. Ctr., N.Y.C., 1993-94; asst. prof. Albert Einstein Coll. of Medicine, N.Y.C., 1991—, Mt. Sinai Sch. of Medicine, N.Y.C., 1993—; asst. physician Elmhurst Med. Ctr., N.Y.C., 1993-94, Mt. Sinai Med. Ctr., N.Y.C., 1993—; v.p., CEO Engring. Med. Support, Inc., N.Y.C., 1992—; attending physician Westchester Jewish Med. Svcs., Hartsdale, N.Y., 1990—, Montefiore Med. Ctr., N.Y.C., 1991—, Albert Einstein Coll. Medicine, 1991—; vis. fellow N.Y. State Psychiat. Inst., 1992-93. Associate editor: Jour. Pagan Studies (N.Y. edit.), 1990—. Officer Am. Soc. for Minority Advocacy, N.Y.C., 1991—. Office: Engring Med Support Inc Ste 8F 200 W 70th St New York NY 10023

DUMONT, ROGER E., nursing home administrator; b. Lewiston, Maine; m. Nancy E. Dawe; children: Darren, Mary. BS in Acctg., Husson Coll., Bangor, Maine, 1969; MBA, N.H. Coll., 1990. Lic. nursing home adminstr., Maine. Auditor Peat Marwick Mitchell, Portland, Maine, 1969-72; contr. Sampson Supermarkets Inc., Auburn, Maine, 1972-83; mgr. retail acctg. Hannaford Bros. Co., Scarborough, Maine, 1983-84; v.p. extended care Sisters of Charity, Lewiston, 1984-94; adminstr. Maine Vets. Home, Scarborough, 1994—. With USAR, 1969-75. Office: Maine Vets Home 290 US Rt 1 Scarborough ME 04074

DUNBAR, BURDETT SHERIDAN, anesthesiologist, pediatrician, educator; b. Kewanee, Ill., Dec. 6, 1938; s. C. Marion and Marjorie LaVonne (Sweat) D.; m. Kathleen C. Empsucha, Aug. 12, 1989; children: Michael Eugene, Brian Randal, Alex Seaton, Bradley Hughes. BS cum laude, U. Ill., 1960, MD, 1963. Diplomate Am. Bd. Anesthesiology, Nat. Bd. Med. Examiners; lic. physician, Pa., Ill., D.C., Va., Tex. Intern Springfield (Ohio) City Hosp., 1963-64; resident U. Pa. Hosp., Phila., 1964-66; NIH fellow U. Pa., Phila., 1966-67; clin. asst. prof. anesthesiology U. Tex., San Antonio, 1968-69, prof. anesthesiology, 1986-89; asst. prof. U. Chgo., 1969-71; from asst. prof. to assoc. prof. anesthesiology George Washington U. Med. Ctr., Washington, 1974-80, prof., 1980-86; prof. anesthesiology and pediatrics Baylor Coll. Medicine, Houston, 1989—; clin. cons. Bexar County Hosp. Dist., San Antonio, 1968-69; assoc. attending physician Michael Reese Hosp. & Med. Ctr., Chgo., 1969-71; assoc. dir. spl. care unit George Washington U. Hosp., Washington, 1971-74, attending staff, 1971-86; assoc. chmn. anesthesiology Children's Hosp. Nat. Med. Ctr., Washington, 1974-83, acting chmn., 1983-85, sr. attending staff, 1974-86; attending staff Hermann Hosp., Houston, 1987-89; chief pediatric anesthesiology svc. Tex. Children's Hosp., Houston, 1989—. Author: (with others) Surgical Diseases of the Chest, 1974, The Practice of Clinical Engineering, 1977, Pediatric Trauma Surgery, 1979; contbr. numerous articles and abstracts to profl. jours. and newsletters. Emergency med. svcs. D.C. Dept. Health and Human Svcs., Washington, 1975-81, transp. safety com. 1981-84, vice-chmn. pub. info. com. 1983-85. Capt. USAF, 1967-69. Fellow Am. Coll. Anesthesiologists, Am. Acad. Pediatrics; mem. AMA, AAAS, AAUP, Am. Soc. Anesthesiologists (del. Ho. of Dels. 1979-85, alt. dir. 1985-86), Am. Bd. Anesthesiology (sr. assoc. examiner 1987—), Am. Soc. Anesthesiolgoists, Md./D.C. Anesthesiology Soc. (pres. 1985-86), Tex. Gulf Coast Anesthesia Soc., Tex. Med. Soc., Internat. Anesthesia Rsch. Soc., Harris County Med. Soc., Soc. Critical Care Medicine, Soc. Edn. Anesthesia, Soc. Ambulatory Anesthesia, Soc. Pediatric Anesthesia. Office: Tex Children s Hosp 6621 Fannin Mc 2 # 1495 Houston TX 77030

DUNBAR, JOSEPH CHATMAN, physiology educator; b. Vicksburg, Miss., Aug. 27, 1944; s. Joseph C. and Henrienne (Watkins) D.; m. Agnes Cecile Estorge, July 1, 1967; children: Andrea, Erica. BS, Alcorn State U., 1963; MS, Tex. So. Univ., 1966; PhD, Wayne State U., 1970. Rsch. asst. Tex. So. Univ., Houston, 1964-66, instr. biology, 1966-67; grad. tchg. asst. Wayne State U., Detroit, 1967-70, asst. prof., 1972-78, assoc. prof., 1978-85, prof., 1985—; postdoctoral diabetes trainee Sinai Hosp., Detroit, 1970-72, rsch. assoc., 1972-81; rev. bd. NIH, Washington, 1980-84, 92—; bd. sci. counselors Nat. Toxicology Program, 1980-82. Contbr. articles to profl. jours. Mem. Am. Physiology Soc., Am. Diabetes Assn., Soc. for Exptl. Biology. Office: Wayne State U 540 E Canfield St Detroit MI 48201-1928

DUNBAR-RICHMAN, ANNE CAMERON, pathologist; b. Bklyn., June 10, 1921; d. Robert Cameron and Alma (Kopriva) Dunbar; m. Robert Richman, July 14, 1950 (div. Apr. 1957); children: Robert Emmett, Carla Jeanne; m. Claude Lee Snider, Oct. 1, 1965 (dec. Dec. 1994). AB in Zoology, George Washington U., 1942; MA in Biology, Colo. Coll., 1944; MD, George Washington U., 1949. Diplomate Nat. Bd. Med. Examiners, Am. Bd. Pathology. Intern. Del. Hosp., Wilmington, 1949-50, resident, 1950-51; interim asst. supt. D.C. Gen. Hosp., Washington, 1952, med. officer, 1952-55; assoc. pathologist Drs. A.W. Freshman & Stanley K. Kurland, Denver, 1956-59; pathologist Ball Meml. Hosp., Muncie, Ind., 1958; assoc. pathologist Del. Hosp., 1958-59; jr. pathologist Armed Forces Inst. Pathology, 1959-61; assoc. pathologist Meth. Evang. Hosp., Louisville, 1961-75, 75-76, acting pathologist, 1975, assoc. pathologist, 1976-79; assoc. pathologist St. Joseph Inmfirmary Audubon Hosp., Louisville, 1976-80, Clin. Pathology Assocs., Louisville, 1977-85; med. dir. lab. Columbia Southwest Hosp. (formerly Humana Hosp. Southwest), Louisville, 1980—; asst. clin. prof. pathology U. Louisville Sch. Medicine, 1965-85, clin. instr., 1961-65; instr. Meth. Evang. Hosp. Sch. Med. Tech., 1963-76; med. dir. med. tech. lab. asst. program Jefferson C.C., 1976-92. Cardiology fellow George Washington U., 1952. Fellow Am. Assn. CLin. Pathologists, Coll. Am. Pathologists; mem. AMA, Ky. Med. Assn., Ky. Soc. Pathologists (pres. 1973, 88), Louisville Soc. Internists (sec.-treas. 1993-94, 1st v.p. 1994-95, pres. 1995-96), Delta Epsilon. Home: 5502 Hempstead Rd Louisville KY 40207 Office: Southwest Hosp. Louisville KY 40272

DUNCALF, DERYCK, anesthesiologist; b. York, Eng., Nov. 14, 1926; came to U.S., 1956; s. Hubert Claude and Anne Elizabeth D.; m. Mira Novakovic, July 23, 1978; children: Richard Michael, Tamara, Sharon. MB, ChB, U. Leeds, 1950. Diplomate Am. Bd. Anesthesiology. Resident in anesthesia St. James Hosp. and Gen. Infirmary, Leeds, 1950-54, Cardiff Royal Infirmary, Wales, 1954-56; fellow Faculty of Anaesthetists Royal Coll. Physicians and Surgeons, 1954; fellow in anesthesiology Mercy Hosp., Pitts., 1956-57, Montreal Children's Hosp., Que., Can., 1958-59; staff anesthesiologist Kings County Hosp., Bklyn., 1959-62; staff anesthesiologist Montefiore Med. Ctr., Bronx, 1962—, chmn. dept. anesthesiology, 1975-85; prof. anesthesiology Albert Einstein Coll. Medicine, Bronx, 1971—, vice-chmn. dept. anesthesiology, 1985-94; cons. Wyckoff Heights Hosp., Bklyn., 1966-85. Author: (with D.H. Rhodes) Anesthesia in Clinic Ophthalmolgy, 1963; contbr. articles to profl.jours. Fellow Am. Coll. Anesthesiologists; mem. Am. Soc. Anesthesiologists, N.Y. State Soc. Anesthesiologists, Pan Am. Med. Assn. (diplomate and hon. life mem. sect. anesthesiology), N.Y. Acad. Medicine, Assn. Univ Anesthetists, Ecuatoriano de Anesthesiologia (hon.). Home: 33 Ferncliff Rd Cos Cob CT 06807-1206 Office: Montefiore Med Ctr 111 E 210th St Bronx NY 10467-2490

DUNCAN, CONSTANCE CATHARINE, psychologist; b. Watertown, Wis., Nov. 2, 1948; d. Howard Burton and Mary Elizabeth (Fagan) Duncan; m. Allan Franklin Mirsky, July 4, 1986. BA, Northwestern U., 1970; AM, U. Ill., 1973, PhD, 1978. Sr. rsch. analyst Adolf Meyer Mental Health Ctr., Decatur, Ill., 1971-73; rsch. and teaching asst. Dept. Psychology, U. Ill., Champaign, 1974-78; postdoctoral fellow in neuroscis. Dept. Psychiat. and Behavioral Scis., Stanford U. Sch. Medicine, Palo Alto, 1978-81; rsch. psychologist VA Med. Ctr., Palo Alto, 1978-81; sr. staff fellow Lab. of Psychology & Psychopathology, NIMH, Bethesda, Md., 1981-88; chief unit on psychophysiology NIMH, Bethesda, Md., 1982-89, rsch. psychologist, 1988-89, rsch. specialist, 1989-93; pvt. practice psychology Bethesda, Md., 1981—; adj. assoc. prof. Johns Hopkins Sch. Hygiene and Pub. Health, Balt., 1987—; rsch. assoc. prof. uniformed svcs. U. Health Scis., 1993—. Assoc. editor Psychophysiology, 1987-91; cons. editor 15 sci. jours.; contbr. articles to profl. jours., chpts. to books. Found. assoc. Nat. Women's Econ. Alliance. Recipient Nat. Rsch. Svc. award, NIMH, 1978-81, Golden Anniversary Scholarship award, AAUW, 1974; USPHS fellow, 1970-74. Mem. APA (fellow 1992—), Soc. for Psychophysiol. Rsch. (dir. 1982-85, Disting. Sci. award for early career contbn. 1980, chmn. awards com. 1981-84, chmn. conv. com. 1983-87, chmn. program com. 1987, mem. Blue Ribbon panel on State of the Soc. in the Yr. 2000, 1990-93, chmn. enhancement com., 1992-93, chmn. early career award com. 1994—, sec., treas. 1996—), Soc. for Rsch. in Psychopathology (dir. 1986-88, membership com. 1987-88), Soc. for Neurosci., Internat. Neuropsychol. Soc., Am. Psychopathol. Assn., Mortar Bd., Shi-Ai, Sigma Xi, Phi Kappa Phi, Alpha Lambda Delta, Pi Mu Epsilon, Phi Beta Kappa. Home: 6204 Perthshire Ct Bethesda MD 20817-3348 Office: NIMH Lab Psychology & Psychopathology Bldg 10 Rm 4C110 10 Center Dr MSC 1366 Bethesda MD 20892-1366

DUNCAN, DAVID FRANK, community health specialist, educator; b. Kansas City, Mo., June 26, 1947; s. Chester Frank and Maxine (Irwin) D.; B.A., U. Mo., Kansas City, 1970; postgrad. Sam Houston State U., 1971; Dr.P.H., U. Tex., 1976; 1 foster son, Kevin Rheinboldt. Research asst. U. Kans. Bur. Child Research, 1967-68; supr. Johnson County Juvenile Hall, Olathe, Kans., 1968-70; asst. to warden Draper Correctional Center, Elmore, Ala., summer 1970; supr. Harris County Juvenile Hall, Houston, 1970-71; project dir. Who Cares, Inc. Drug Abuse Treatment Center, Houston, 1971-73; exec. dir. Reality Island Halfway House, Houston, 1974-75; research asso. Tex. Gov.'s Office, Austin, summer 1975; research asso. Inst. Clin. Toxicology, clin. toxicologist Ben Taub Gen. Hosp., Houston, 1975-76; asst. prof. health sci. SUNY, Brockport, 1976-78, asso. prof., 1978, acting chmn. dept. health sci., summer 1978; vis. prof. health environ. research U. Cologne, Fed. Republic Germany, 1986; prof. health edn., coordinator community health program So. Ill. U., Carbondale, 1978—; chmn. So. Ill. Health Edn. Task Force, 1979—; bd. dirs. Ill. Pub. Health Continuing Edn. Council; cons. to numerous health, edn. instns. Mem. Am. Public Health Assn. (past chmn. sect. mental health), Ill. Public Health Assn. (exec. council), Am. Coll. Epidemiology, Soc. Epidemiologic Research, AAAS, Ill. Acad. Sci., N.Y. Acad. Sci. Democrat. Methodist. Author: Drugs and the Whole Person, 1982, Health Education: A Transatlantic Perspective, 1987, Epidemiology-Basis for Disease Prevention and Health Promotion, 1988; contbr. articles to profl. jours.; editorial bd. Health Values, 1980—, also assoc. editor , Jour. Drug Edn., 1981—, Internat. Jour. Mental Health, 1982-83. Office: Brown U Ctr Alcohol & Addiction Studies Box G-BH Providence RI 02912

DUNCAN, ELIZABETH CHARLOTTE, marriage and family therapist, educational therapist, educator; b. L.A., Mar. 10, 1919; d. Frederick John de St. Vrain and Nellie Mae (Goucher) Schwankovsky; m. William McConnell Duncan, Oct. 12, 1941 (div. 1949); 1 child, Susan Elizabeth Duncan St. Vrain. BA, Calif. U., Long Beach, 1953; MA, UCLA, 1962; PhD, Internat. Coll., 1984. Cert. marriage and family therapist, Wash. Dir. gifted program Palos Verdes Sch. Dist., Calif., 1958-64; TV tchr., participant ednl. films L.A. County, 1961-64; dir. U. So. Calif. Presch., L.A., 1965-69, Abraham Maslow rsch. assoc., 1962-69; pvt. practice family counselor, Malibu and Ventura, Calif., Eastsound, Wash., 1979—, also, Seattle, pvt. practice in psychotherapy, West Seattle, 1994—; pub. spkr., lectr. comm.; cons. in field; psychotherapist Mentor Program Eastsound, 1992; bd. dirs. Children's Program North Sound Regional Support Network, 1992; resident psychologist for film series Something Personal, 1987—; mem. Rsch. Inst. of Scripps Clinic, La Jolla, Calif.; charter mem. Inst. Behav. Med., Santa Barbara, Calif.; TV performer: (documentary) The Other Side, 1985. Creator: Persephone's Child, 1988. Active Chryalis Ctr., L.A., 1984-86, Ventura County Mental Health Adv. Bd., Calif., 1985-86, United Way, L.A., 1985-92; mem. Menninger Found. San Juan County, Wash., 1992; adv. bd. North Sound Regional Support Network, 1992. Recipient Emmy award for best documentary Am. TV Arts and Scis., 1976, Child Adv. of Yr. Calif. Mental Health Adv. Bd., 1987. Mem. AACD (Disting. Svc. award 1990), Transpersonal Psychol. Assn., Calif. State Orgn. Gifted Edn. (sec. 1962-64), Internat. Platform Assn., Am. Assn. for Marriages and Family Therapy. Democrat. Avocations: swimming, plays, concerts, boating, political issues, especially women and child abuse. Office: 4505 44th Ave SW Seattle WA 98116

DUNCAN, GARY WILLIAM, neurologist; b. Nashville, Feb. 26, 1941; s. R. Dean and Willia (Gleaves) D.; m. Carol Ann Robinson, Aug. 2, 1962; children: Jennifer, Tim. BA, Vanderbilt U., 1963, MD, 1966. Resident in neurology Mass. Gen. Hosp., Boston, 1970-73, with Inst. Neurology, 1972-73; asst. prof. dept. neurology Vanderbilt U. Sch. Medicine, Nashville, 1985-78, assoc. prof., vice chair dept. neurology, 1978-81; pvt. practice Neurologic Cons., Nashville, 1981—; med. dir. Phi Beta Phi Rehab. Ins., Nashville, 1995—; med. dir. Rehab. Inst. Centennial Med. Ctr., Nashville, 1986—; prof., chief neurology Meharry Med. Coll., Nashville, 1994—, vice-chair internal medicine, 1995—; chmn. bd. trustees Centennial Med. Ctr., 1992-94. Author: Neurology for Psychiatrists, 1978. Capt. USAF, 1968-70. Fellow Am. Acad. Neurology; mem. Phi Beta Kappa, Alpha Omega Alpha. Roman Catholic. Office: Meharry Med Coll 1005 DB Todd Blvd Nashville TN 37208

DUNCAN, KIM FRASER, cardiothoracic surgeon; b. Toronto, Ont., Can., May 17, 1952; came to U.S., 1993; s. Neil Fraser and Eleanor Mary (Batcheller) D.; m. Valerie Jane Sept, Dec. 7, 1974; children: Brett, Cameron, Heather. B Med. Sci., U. Alta., Edmonton, Can., 1974, MD, 1976, MSc in Surgery, 1986. Diplomate Am. Bd. Thoracic Surgery; cert. gen. surgery, thoracic and cardiovasc. surgery. Jr. rotating internship Ottawa Civic Hosp., Ont., Can., 1976-77; gen. surgery residency U. Alberta Hosps., Edmonton, Can., 1977-82, thoracic surgery residency, 1983-84; pediatric cardiothoracic surgery fellowship Gt. Ormand St. Hosp. for Sick Children, London, 1984-85, Hosp. for Sick Children, Toronto, 1985-86; clin. instr dept. surgery U. Toronto, 1985-86; asst. prof. dept. surgery U. Man., Winnipeg, Can., 1986-93; assoc. prof. U. Nebr. Med. Ctr., Omaha, 1993—. Fellow ACS, Royal Coll. Physicians and Surgeons Can., Am. Coll. Chest Physicians; mem. Soc. Thoracic Surgeons. Office: U Nebr Med Ctr 600 S 42nd St Omaha NE 68198-2315

DUNCAN, MARGARET CAROLINE, physician; b. Salt Lake City, June 9, 1930; d. Donald and Margaret Aileen (Eberts) D.; m. N. Paul Arceneaux, Dec. 26, 1958; children—David Paul, Eleanor Anne, Stephen Louis, Andre. B.A., U. Tex., 1952, M.D., 1955. Intern Kings County Hosp., Seattle, 1955-56; resident in pediatrics John Sealy Hosp., Galveston, Tex., 1956-58; resident in neurology Charity Hosp., New Orleans, 1958-60; fellow child neurology Johns Hopkins Hosp., 1960-61; mem. faculty La. State U. Med. Center, New Orleans, 1961—; prof. neurology and pediatrics La. State U. Med. Center, 1973—. Chmn. La. Com. Epilespy and Cerebral Palsy, 1976-79. Fellow Am. Acad. Neurology, Am. Acad. Pediatrics; mem. Child Neurology Soc., Profs. Child Neurology, Alpha Omega Alpha. Episcopalian. Office: 1542 Tulane Ave New Orleans LA 70112-2825

DUNFEE, THOMAS P., nephrologist; b. South Bend, Ind., Jan. 15, 1940; s. Jack C. and Rosella M. (Barkley) D.; m. Gretchen Kay Dose, May 30, 1963; children: Jennifer A. Reynolds, Julie L. Dunfee, Alison K. Dunfee. AB, Ind. U., 1962, MD, 1965. Diplomate Am. Bd. Internal Medicine, Am. Bd. Nephrology. Co-dir. med. edn. St. Joseph's Med. Ctr., South Bend, Ind., 1972-92, co-dir. renal divsn., 1972-92; prof. medicine Ind. U., Indpls., 1973-92; adj. assoc. prof. biology Notre Dame U., South Bend, 1978-92; sr. phsycian nephrology Henry Ford Hosp., Detroit, 1992—, co-dir. nephrology fellowship, 1992—, dir. in-patient dialysis, 1992—; pres. End Stage Renal Disease Network, Indpls., 1980-82. Author: (with others) Clinical Disorders of Electrolyte Metabolism, 1994, Fluid, Electrolyte Acid Base Disorders, 1995. Fund raiser United Way, South Bend, Ind., 1980-92; bd. dirs. Med. Edn. Found., South Bend, 1975-92, Alcoholism Coun., South Bend, 1974-76; vol. Hunger Coalition, Ann Arbor, 1995—; bd. pres. South Bend Med. Found., 1978-80. Capt. USAF, 1966-68. Fellow ACP; mem. Internat. Soc. of Nephrology, Am. Soc. of Nephrology. Home: 9601 Wellington Plymouth MI 48170 Office: Divsn of Nephrology Henry Ford Hosp 2799 W Grand Blvd Detroit MI 48202

DUNGAN, JOHN RUSSELL, JR., anesthesiologist; b. Boston, Dec. 12, 1953; s. John Russell and Nancy Pauline (Beaton) D.; m. Nancy Elizabeth Perkins, July 12, 1986; children: Elizabeth Adelaide, Thayer Warren, Eleanor Grace Appleton. AB magna cum laude, Harvard Coll., 1977; EdM, Harvard U., 1978; DDS, Baylor U., 1984; MD cum laude, Creighton U., 1989. Diplomate Nat. Bd. of Anesthesiology (dir. 1989-92), Am. Acad. of Pain Mgmt. Attending staff anesthesiologist, residency instr. Boston City Hosp., 1986-89; anesthesiologist, chief Tobey Hosp., Wareham, Mass., 1989-91; chief of anesthesia Mary Lanning Meml. Hosp., Hastings, Nebr., 1991—; chief of surgery Mary Lanning Meml. Hosp., Hastings, 1995; pres. Hastings Anesthesiology Assoc., 1992—. Author: Angus Macdonald, The Kings of the Picts and Dial Riads, The Beatons; contbr. articles to profl. jours. Rschr. nat. trust Restoration of Celbridge Chapel and Cemetary, Kildare, Ireland, 1995. Nat. Merit scholar, 1971; Internat. fellow English-Speaking Union, 1971-72; John Harvard scholar; Harvard Coll. scholar. Mem. Phi Beta Kappa. Republican. Episcopalian. Home: Heartwell Park 923 North Elm Ave Hastings NE 68901 Office: Hastings Anesthesiology 608 W Sixth St Hastings NE 68901

DUNGAN, JOYCE M., nursing educator; b. Wadsworth, Ohio, Oct. 6, 1928; d. Berry and Lura R. (Kilpatrick) Garner; m. Kendrick W. Dungan, June 9, 1951; children: Laurel, Thomas, Jefferson. Grad., Jewish Hosp. Sch. Nursing, Cin., 1952; BSN, U. Evansville, 1955, MSN, 1975; EdD, Ind. U., 1984. RN, Ind. Asst. instr. Jewish Hosp. Sch. Nursing, 1952-54; instructional asst. U. Evansville (Ind.) Sch. Nursing, 1954-56; instr. St. Mary's Hosp. Sch. Nursing, Evansville, 1956-62; tchr. refresher course for returning inactive profl. nurses St. Mary's Hosp., 1968; with Sch. Occupational Health Evansville-Vanderburgh Sch. Corp., 1972; asst. prof. nursing U. Evansville Sch. Nursing, 1972, assoc. prof. nursing, 1980-83; dir. learning resource lab. Harlaxton Campus, Grantham, Eng., 1983-86; prof. nursing U. Evansville Sch. Nursing, 1986-88; assoc. prof. nursing U. Hawaii at Manoa, Honolulu, 1988-93; vis. prof. U. Evansville, 1994—; presenter in field; cons. in field. Author: Human Anatomy and Physiology Learning Guide, 1978, (with others) Neurological and Neurosurgical Nursing, 1982, Human Anatomy and Physiology, 1980, Perspectives on Building a Professional Staff, 1987, Critical Thinking and Nursing Process, 1989, Dungan Model of Dynamic Integration, 1990; contbr. articles to profl. jours. Vol. Boys Club Svc. League, Pennyrile Pony Club, 1978-79; active Mobile Health Unit, Heartbeat Health Festival, 1986; bd. dirs. Kunkini-at-Home, Youth Outreach, Wakiki Health Ctr. Mem. ANA, AAAS, Ind. State Nurses Assn., Hawaii Nurses Assn. (Nurse of the Yr. award 1992), N.Am. Nursing Diagnosis Assn., Nat. League for Nursing, Phi Beta Chi, Phi Kappa Chi (publicity chmn. 1982, 84, pres. 1985-86, sec. 1986-87), Sigma Theta Tau (Kupono award 1993). Office: U Evansville 226 Health Scis Bldg 1800 Lincoln Ave Evansville IN 47722

DUNHAM, PHILIP BIGELOW, biology educator, physiologist; b. Columbus, Ohio, Apr. 26, 1937; s. T. Chadbourne and Margaret (Bigelow) D.; m. Gudrun Bjarnarson, Mar. 9, 1985. B.A., Swarthmore Coll., 1958; Ph.D., U. Chgo., 1962. USPHS postdoctoral fellow Carlsberg Found., Copenhagen, 1962-63; asst. prof. zoology Syracuse U., 1963-67, assoc. prof., 1967-71, prof. biology, 1971—; rsch. prof. pharm. SUNY Health Sci. Ctr., Syracuse, 1990—; vis. assoc. prof. physiology Yale U. Sch. Medicine, 1968-70, vis. prof., 1986; vis. prof. medicine U. N.C., 1993-94; vis. scientist physiol. lab. Cambridge (Eng.) U., 1979, August Krogh Inst., Copenhagen, 1985-87; vis. prof. biochemistry U. Copenhagen, 1994; vis. honors examiner Swarthmore Coll., 1966-67, 74-76, mem. alumni coun., 1971-73; mem. exec. com. bd. trustees Marine Biol. Lab., Woods Hole, Mass., 1972-76; mem. physiology study sect. NIH, 1986-89; mem. review panel Am. Heart Assn., 1994-96. Assoc. editor Am. Jour. Physiology, 1984-87; contbr. over 100 rsch. publs. in field. Rsch. grantee NIH, 1965—; recipient Chancellor's Citation for Exceptional Acad. Excellence, Syracuse U., 1994-95. Mem. Soc. Gen. Physiologists (council 1967-69), Am. Physiol. Soc., Biophys. Soc. Home: 6402 Terese Ter Jamesville NY 13078-9430 Office: Syracuse U 130 College Pl Syracuse NY 13210-2819

DUNKLE, LISA MARIE, clinical research executive; b. Ann Arbor, Mich., Oct. 31, 1946; d. Robert Henry and Dorothy Rose (Heagstedt) D.; m. Richard James Scheffler, Dec. 28, 1972; children: Richard James Scheffler III, Margaret Dorothy Scheffler. AB, Wellesley Coll., 1968; MD, Johns Hopkins U., 1972. Cert. Nat. Bd. Med. Examiners, Am. Bd. Pediatrics, Pediatric Infectious Disease Soc. Intern pediatrics Washington U., St. Louis, 1972-73, resident pediatrics, 1973-74, fellow infectious diseases, 1974-76; asst. prof. pediatrics St. Louis U., 1976-79, assoc. prof. pediatrics, 1979-85, assoc. prof. microbiology, 1979-85, prof. pediatrics, 1985-89; dir. antiviral clin. rsch. Bristol-Myers Squibb, Wallingford, Conn., 1989-95, exec. dir. HIV clin. rsch., 1995—; dir. pediatric infectious diseases St. Louis U., 1976-89, dir. infectious diseases lab. Cardinal Glennon Hosp., St. Louis, 1976-89, dir. infectious control program, 1976-89. Mem. editorial bd. Pediatric Infectious Disease Jour., 1989-92; contbr. articles to profl. jours. Fundraiser Wellesley (Mass.) Coll., 1975-88, The Forsyth Sch., St. Louis, 1988-89. Scholar Johns Hopkins U., 1972; rsch. grantee Cystic Fibrosis Found., 1984. Fellow Infectious Disease Soc. Am.; mem. Soc. for Pediatric Rsch., Midwest Soc. for Pediatric Rsch. (sec. 1983-88, pres. 1989-90), Interscience Conf. on Antimicrobial Agts. and Chemotherapy (program com. 1992—). Republican.

Episcopalian. Office: Bristol Myers Squibb 5 Research Pky Wallingford CT 06492-1927

DUNKLE, SONDRA ELAINE, physical therapy educator; b. Geneva, Nebr., Jan. 29, 1945; d. Wesley A. and Doris E. (Motz) Lechtenberger. BS in Phys. Therapy, U. Calif., San Francisco, 1967; MEd in Health Occupations, U. Fla., 1976; EdD in Higher Edn., Nova S.E. U., 1985. Lic. State Bd. of Medicine, Calif., Idaho. Prof. phys. therapy program Calif. State U., Fresno, 1976-92; prof. phys. therapy dept. Idaho State U., Pocatello, 1992—; rep. on dept. environ. quality Citizen's Adv. Com., Am. Lung Assn., Pocatello, 1992-95; team leader, staff therapist Burger Rehab., Sacramento, 1989; per diem-on call therapist Fresno Cmty. Hosp., 1988-91, Beverley Enterprises Skilled Nursing Facility, Fresno, 1991, Gate City Phys. Therapy, Pocatello, 1992—, Madison Meml. Hosp., Rexburg, summer 1993, others; vacation relief therapist and cons. in field. Contbr. articles to profl. jours. Mem. Am. Phys. Therapy Assn., Idaho Phys. Therapy Assn. (organizer of bistate meeting, edn. com. 1993-96), Phi Kappa Phi. Office: Idaho State Univ Phys Therapy Dept MS #8002 650 Memorial Dr Pocatello ID 83209

DUNLAP, EDDIE RAY, nurse anesthetist; b. Ft. Worth, Oct. 16, 1953; s. Hershel Eugene and Mable Ray (Ragan) D.; m. Karen Lee Keitz, Apr. 8, 1978; children: Amanda Leigh, Brian Scott. BS, Stephen F. Austin State U., 1977; BSN, Tex. Woman's U., 1980; MSN, SUNY, Buffalo, 1985; diploma, Ft. Sam Houston Acad. Health, 1984. Cert. nurse anesthetist, ACLS instr. Staff anesthetist Comanche County Anesthesia Assocs., Lawton, Okla., 1986-88, William Beaumont Army Med. Ctr., El Paso, 1988—; coord. obstet. anesthesia Vista Hills Med. Ctr., El Paso; sole propr. Rio Grande Anesthesia, El Paso. Capt. U.S. Army, 1981-88. Decorated Army Commendation medal. Mem. Am. Assn. Nurse Anesthetists, Tex. Assn. Nurse Anesthetists (pres., past pres., fed. polit. dir., lectr. on bus. on anesthesia).

DUNLAP, JOE EVERETT, dentist, communications consultant, writer; b. Delaware, Ohio, May 11, 1930; s. Arthur Calvin and Mary Irene (Jones) D.; m. Mary Susan King, June 17, 1959; children: Marlene, Todd, David, Sherrie, Dru. Student, Ohio Wesleyan U., 1949-50; DDS, Ohio State U., 1959. With Fla. Instl. Dental Service, Gainesville, Ft. Myers, 1959-60; pvt. practice dentistry, Clearwater, Fla., 1961-81; gen. mgr. ops. corp. hdqrs. Sheppard Dental Ctrs., Tampa, Fla., 1981-84; cons. dental communications, 1986—; lectr. in field. Author: Surviving in Dentistry, The Beginning Dental Practice, Stress, Change and Related Pains, Keeping the Fire Alive, 10 Trends, Knowing The Numbers; editor PennWell Books, Tulsa, 1984-86; contbr. articles to dental jours., articles and photographs to regional publs. Served with Med. Service Corps, AUS, 1950-53. Mem. ADA, Fla. Dental Assn., West Coast Dist. Dental Assn. Home: 1816 Lombardy Dr Clearwater FL 34615-2235

DUNLAP, WALLACE HART, pediatrician; b. Wichita, Kans., Oct. 16, 1935; s. Fred Everett and Ermalea (Hart) D.; m. Judith Nell Gandner, Aug. 29, 1963 (div. 1974); children: Susan Margaret, John Gardner; m. Jane Stokley Davis, July 3, 1984; stepchildren: Hugh Wilson Raetzsch, Susan Stokely Raetzsch. BA in Zoology, Kans. U., 1957, MD, 1961. Intern U. Okla. Med. Ctr., Oklahoma City, 1961-62, resident in pediat., 1962-63; resident in pediat. Children's Med. Ctr., Dallas, 1963-64; pvt. practice Baton Rouge, 1966—. Bd. dirs. Baton Rouge Area Found., 1994—. Capt. U.S. Army Med. Corps, 1964-66. Fellow Am. Acad. Pediat. (pres. La. chpt. 1974-80, D.W. Van Gelder MD Disting. Svc. award 1994); mem. AMA, La. State Med. Soc. (chmn. coun. legis. 1984-93, bd. dirs. 1984-92). Presbyterian. Home: 3616 Willow Bay Dr Baton Rouge LA 70805 Office: The Pediat Clinic 888 Tara Blvd Baton Rouge LA 70806

DUNLEAVY, MARY THERESA, physician assistant; b. Scranton, Pa., Jan. 21, 1962; d. Nicholas George and Gertrude (Ann) Bolick; m. Patrick Joseph Dunleavy, July 18, 1989; children: Brian Patrick, Mark Lewis. AA, Keystone Jr. Coll., 1981; BS, King's Coll., 1984. Cert. physician asst. Med. physician asst. Dr. Walter Bloes, Jermyn, Pa., 1984-85; orthopedic physician asst. Pocono Orthopedic Cons., East Stroudsburg, Pa., 1985-88; surg. physician asst. St. Luke's Hosp., Bethlehem, Pa., 1988—. Mem. Am. Acad. Physician Asst. Democrat. Roman Catholic. Home: RR1 Box 7349 Moscow PA 18444 Office: St Luke's Hosp 801 Ostrum St Bethlehem PA 18015

DUNLOP, GEORGE RODGERS, surgeon; b. St. Peter, Minn., Mar. 31, 1906; s. George Crawford and Pearl (Rodgers) D.; m. Barbara Wallace, Apr. 3, 1939; children: Susan Dunlop Roberts, Madora Howell. B.S., U. Cin., 1927; M.D., Harvard U., 1931. Diplomate Am. Bd. Surgery. Intern Cin. Gen. Hosp., 1931-32; asst. resident in surgery N.Y. Hosp.-Cornell Med. Ctr., 1932-35; resident in surgery Worcester (Mass.) City Hosp., 1935-36; practice medicine specializing in surgery, 1935—; sr. surgeon, past chief surgery Worcester Meml. Hosp.; prof. surgery U. Mass. Med. Sch.; dir., past chmn. Mass. Blue Shield; bd. dirs., past chmn. bd. Nat. Assn. Blue Shield Plans; past dir. Med. Indemnity Am.; bd. commrs. Joint Commn. Accreditation Hosps., chmn. bd. coms.; mem. Pres.'s Commn. for Study of Ethical Problems in Medicine and Biomed. and Behavioral Rsch. Bd. dirs. Meml. Hosp. Found.; bd. dirs., past chmn. Mass. divsn. Am. Cancer Soc., also, Worcester Found. Exptl. Biology; bd. dirs. U. Mass. Med. Sch. Found., Med. Ctr. of Ctrl. Mass. Found.; past bd. dirs. Bancroft Sch., Worcester Boys' Club, Cmty. Chest. Served to lt. comdr. M.C. USNR, 1942-45. Fellow ACS (past pres.), Royal Australasian Coll. Surgeons (hon.); mem. AMA, New Eng. Surg. Soc. (past pres.), New Eng. Cancer Soc., Northwestern Med. Soc. (past pres.), Am. Surg. Assn., Boston Surg. Soc., Soc. Surgery Alimentary Tract (founder), Pan Am. Med. Assn. Club: Worcester. Home: 54 Massachusetts Ave Worcester MA 01602-2139 Office: 340 Main St Rm 356 Worcester MA 01608-1601

DUNMEYER, SARAH LOUISE FISHER, health care consultant; b. Ft. Wayne, Ind., Apr. 13, 1935; d. Frederick Law and Jeanette Blose (Stults) Fisher; m. Herbert W. Dunmeyer, Sept. 9, 1967; children: Jodi, Lisa. BS, U. Mich., 1957; MS, Temple U., 1966; EdD, U. San Francisco, 1983. Lic. clin. lab. technologist, Calif. Instr. med. tech. U. Vt., Burlington, 1966-67; instr. med. tech. Northeastern U., Boston, 1967-68, instr. lab. asst. program, 1968-70; educator, coord. sch. med. tech. Children's Hosp., San Francisco, 1970-73; dir. continuing edn. program Pacific Presbyn. Med. Ctr., San Francisco, 1974-82; project mgr., cons. Peabody Mktg. Decisions, San Francisco, 1983-87; sr. rsch. assoc. Inst. for Health and Aging, U. Calif., San Francisco, 1986-89; rsch. analyst student acad. svcs. U. Calif., San Francisco, 1991-94; external cons. Health Care Consulting Svcs., San Francisco, 1986-96; clin. lab. technologist Kaiser Hosp., San Francisco, 1989-96; seminar presenter Am. Assn. Blood Banks, San Francisco, 1976, Am. Soc. Clin. Pathologists, Miami Beach, Fla., 1977, Ann. Meeting of Am. Soc. Med. Technology, Atlanta, 1977; site surveyor Nat. Accrediting Agy. for Clin. Lab. Scis., Chgo., 1974-80. Contbr. articles to profl. jours.

DUNN, ADOLPHUS WILLIAM, orthopedic surgeon; b. Eden, N.C., Nov. 23, 1922; s. Adolphus William and Sally Grey (Ivie) D.; m. Doris Margery Nash, June 23, 1945 (div. 1975); children: John B.R., Adolphus W. III; m. Clara Delores Kelly, Sept. 3, 1977. BS, Wake Forest Coll., 1942; MD, Duke U., 1945. Diplomate Am. Bd. Orthopaedic Surgery. Commd. ensign USN, 1943, advanced through grades to capt., 1959, ret., 1965; intern Yale U. Hosp., New Haven, Conn., 1945; resident U.S. Navy Hosp., San Diego, 1948, Bethesda, Md., 1952-53; resident Children's Hosp., Boston, 1954; chmn. dept. orthopaedic surgery Ochsner Med. Instns., New Orleans, 1965-88; clin. prof. dept. orthopaedics sch. medicine Tulane U., New Orleans, 1965-88; ret., 1988. Contbr. numerous articles to profl. jours. Fellow Am. Acad. Orthopaedic Surgeons (emeritus); mem. Am. Orthopaedic Assn. (emeritus), Phi Beta Kappa. Republican. Home: One Kingfisher Cove Fripp Island SC 29920

DUNN, ADRIAN JOHN, neuroscientist; b. London, June 16, 1943; came to U.S., 1970; s. John Charles and Glendolyn Winifred (Gracie) D.; m. Glenda Susan Bradley, Oct. 6, 1973. BA, U. Cambridge, Eng., 1965, MA, 1966, PhD, 1968. Instr. biochemistry U. N.C., Chapel Hill, 1971-73, asst. prof., 1973; asst. prof. neurosci. U. Fla., Gainesville, 1973-77, assoc. prof., 1977-85, prof., 1985-88; prof., head pharmacology and therapeutics dept. La. State U. Sch. Medicine, Shreveport, 1988—. Author: Functional Chemistry of the Brain, 1974; editor: Peptides, Hormones and Behavior, 1984; assoc. editor: Hormones and Behavior, 1985—; mem. editl. bd.: Pharmacology, Biochemistry and Behavior, 1989—, Brain, Behavior and Immunity, 1990—, Neurosci. Rsch. Comm., Jour. Neurosci. Rsch., 1995—, NeuroImmunoModulation, 1995—. Alfred P. Sloan fellow Sloan Found., 1975. Mem. AAAS, Internat. Soc. for Neurochemistry, Am. Soc. Neurochemistry (various coms.), Soc. for Neurosci. (lectr. Albuquerque 1990), Am. Col. Neuropsychopharmacology, Collegium Internationale Neuro-Psychopharmacologicum, Sigma Xi. Office: La State U Sch Medicine Dept of Pharmacology 1501 Kings Hwy Shreveport LA 71103-4228

DUNN, BERNICE MARIE, retired women's health nurse; b. Danforth, Maine, Oct. 11, 1934; d. Henry Augustus Harding and Leah Orale (Gould) Crossman; m. Scott Andrew Dunn, Oct. 19, 1957 (div. Mar. 1984); children: Audrey M. Nutter, E. Lee Dunn Shirland, Janet L. Dunn Doucette, John E. II. Diploma in nursing, Ea. Maine Med. Ctr., Bangor, 1975. RN, Maine. Psychiat. aide to LPN, RN State of Maine, Bangor, 1953-76; aide, charge aide, charge LPN, med. nurse to supr. ob/gyn Ea. Maine Med. Ctr., 1976-95, ret., 1995. Vol. March of Dimes; organist, pianist, choir dir., Sunday Sch. tchr., Faith Bible Ch., Olamon, Maine, 1957-82. Mem. ANA, AWHONN (cert.), Maine State Nurses Assn., Nat. Assn. ACOG. Democrat. Baptist.

DUNN, CHARLETA JESSIE, retired psychology educator; b. Clarendon, Tex., Jan. 18, 1927; d. James A. Sisk and Ruby Roberta (Burcham) Sisk Rice; m. Roy E. Dunn; children—Thomas A., Roy E, III, Sharleta E. B.S., West Tex. U., 1951, Ed.M., 1954; Ed.D., U. Houston, 1966; postgrad. U. Tex.-Galveston, 1970. Tchr. Amarillo Pub. Schs., Tex., 1954-62; asst. prof. psychology U. Houston, 1966-69; psychologist Goose Creek Ind. Sch. Dist., Baytown, Tex., 1971-74; prof. Tex. Woman's U., Houston, 1974-90, prof. emeritus psychology dept., 1991—; pvt. practice psychology, 1971-95, ret., 1995; cons. pub. schs., Houston area, 1966-91. Author: Songs of Sharleta, 1969; World of Work, 1971; 5 monographs. Grantee Gusreda, 1965, Hogg Found. for Mental Health, 1966-69, Regional Edn. Svc. Ctr., 1978, ORGA, 1982-83. Mem. Am. Psychol. Assn., Tex. Psychol. Assn., Southwestern Psychol. Assn., Am. Assn. Marriage and Family Therapy, Nat. Register Mental Health Providers, Am. Bd. Med. Psychotherapists (diplomate). Avocations: reading, sewing, cooking, genealogy.

DUNN, DAVID HOWARD LESTER, physician; b. Baton Rouge, La., Oct. 10, 1959; s. Lester Treadway, Jr. and Janet (Bond) D.; m. Sylvia Ann Peacher, Nov. 7, 1992 (div. 1991); 1 child, Sarah Elizabeth. BS in Biology magna cum laude, Tulane U., 1981; MD, La. State U., 1985. Diplomate Am. Bd. Ob-Gyn. Resident, intern Parkland Meml. Hosp., Dallas, 1985-89; physician Browne-McHardy Clinic, Metairie, La., 1989—. Fellow Am. Coll. Ob-Gyn; mem. AMA, Greater New Orleans Ob-Gyn Soc., AAAS, La. State Med. Soc. Office: Browne-MC Hardy Clinic 4315 Houma Blvd Metairie LA 70006

DUNN, HELEN ASHLEY, dean. Dean of nursing La. State U. Med. Ctr., New Orleans. Office: LA State U Med Ctr Sch Nursing 1900 Gravier St New Orleans LA 70112-2223

DUNN, JAMES MICHAEL, physician, pharmaceutical company executive; b. Long Beach, Calif., May 8, 1937; s. Joseph Shelby and Mary Juanita (Fowler) D.; m. Carolyn Kay Olson, Oct. 23, 1971; children: Shannon, Lisa, Christopher, Kevin. BS, U. Oreg., 1958; MD, U. Calif., Irvine, 1962. Intern Sacred Heart Gen. Hosp., Eugene, Oreg., 1962-63; resident in ob-gyn Kaiser Found. Hosp., Oakland, Calif., 1965-67; practice medicine specializing in ob-gyn, Fairfield, Calif., 1967-75, asst. dir. clin. pharmacology Abbott Labs., 1975-76; asso. dir. clin. pharmacology, then dir. clin. research Wallace Labs., 1976-79; v.p. med. affairs Boots Pharms., Inc., 1979-80; pres. Verex Labs., Inc., Englewood, Colo., 1980-82, pres., chief exec. officer, chmn., 1982—; asst. prof. family medicine and pharmacology La. State U. Med. Sch., 1979-81. Author articles in field, also poems and short stories. Served as officer M.C., USAF, 1963-65. Fellow Am. Coll. Clin. Pharmacology, Fellow Am. Soc. Abdominal Surgeons, Fellow Royal Soc. Medicine, Internat. Coll. Physicians and Surgeons; mem. Am. Soc. Clin. Pharmacology and Therapeutics, AMA, N.Y. Acad. Sci., Am. Fertility Soc., AAAS, Western Soc. Ob-Gyn (a founder), Drug Info. Assn., Sigma Xi. Roman Catholic. Address: 14 Inermess Dr Ste D-100 Englewood CO 80155-3817

DUNN, JEFFREY EDWARD, neurologist; b. Shaker Heights, Ohio, Nov. 27, 1960; s. John Kenneth and Mary Margaret (O'Neill) D.; m. Sandra Lee Judy, Feb. 3, 1990; children: Caitlin Irene, Bronwyn Leigh, Colin John Donald. BA in French Lit., Haverford (Pa.) Coll., 1983; MD, Temple U., 1989. Diplomate Am. Bd. Psychiatry and Neurology. Molecular immunologist Fox Chase Cancer Ctr., Phila., 1984-85; intern Ea. Va. Grad. Sch., Norfolk, 1989-90; resident in neurology U. Wash., Seattle, 1990-93; attending physician Neurol. Assocs. of Wash., Bellevue, 1993—; clin. asst. prof. neurology U. Wash., Seattle, 1993—; founder, med. dir. Overlake Multiple Sclerosis Ctr., Bellevue, Wash., 1996—. Guest physician TV: MS Update, Denver, 1994, ALS Update, Seattle, 1995. Recipient Cert. of Excellence in MS Rx, Prodigy Online Com., 1995. Mem. Am. Acad. Neurology, Am. Neurol. Assn., World Congress Neurology, North Pacific Soc. of Psychiatry and Neurology, Puget Sound Neurol. Soc. Office: Neurol Assocs of Wash 1600 116th Ave NE Ste #302 Bellevue WA 98004

DUNN, KAREN K., mental health center executive, psychotherapist; b. Clovis, N.Mex., Dec. 10, 1944; d. Kent King II and Regina Catherine (Seitz) Chesnes; m. Thurman Stanley Dunn, Mar. 31, 1969; children: Michelle, Stan II. BS, E. N.Mex. U., 1966; MA, U. N.Mex., 1968; postgrad., U. Ariz., 1973-76, Denver Sem., 1995—. Employment counselor Ariz. State Employment Svc., Tucson, 1970-73; counselor, faculty mem. Pima C.C., Tucson, 1975-76; instr. psychology Cochise Coll., Sierra Vista, Ariz., 1976-78; pvt. practice Denver, 1979-81; pres., CEO Discovery Learning Ctr., Parker, Colo., 1981-85; mental health therapist Prince William County, Manassas, Va., 1988; substance abuse specialist Prince William County Schs., Manassas, Va., 1989; exec. dir., CEO KM Counseling and Resource Ctr., Parker, Colo., 1990—. Contbr. articles to profl. jours. Active Mile High United Way; v.p., pres. Parker Newcomers Club; health com. Douglas County Commnrs., Castle Rock, Colo., 1994-95; bd. dirs. Human Resource Coun., 1993-95, Douglas County Com. Youth and Families, 1995. Mem. Colo. Assn. Non-Profit Execs., Parker C. of C., Douglas County Srs. Home: 6281 S Netherland Way Aurora CO 80016

DUNN, MARIAN EISENBERG, psychotherapist; b. Bklyn., Apr. 7, 1937; d. Bernard Charles and Florence (Bloom) Eisenberg; m. Elliott Dranoff; children: Roarkm Darin, Jenny. BA, Bard Coll., 1960; MSW, Adelphi U., 1968; PhD, Inst. Advanced Study, San Francisco, 1980. Diplomate Acad. Cert. Social Workers. Pvt. practice Bklyn., 1972—; clin. asst. prof. psychiatry, dir. SUNY Downstate Med. Ctr., Bklyn., 1984-87, clin. assoc. prof., 1987—, dir. ctr. for human sexuality, 1987—; exec. bd. Soc. Sex Therapy & Rsch., 1986-89. contbr. articles to profl. jours. Fellow Am. Coll. Sexology; mem. Am. Assn. Sex. Educators, Counselors & Therapists, Soc. Sex Therapists & Researchers, Soc. for the Sci. Study Sex. Home: 15 Canopus Hl Putnam Valley NY 10579-1818 Office: SUNY 450 Clarkson Ave Brooklyn NY 11203-2012

DUNN, MARTIN JOSEPH, dentist; b. Apr. 23, 1935. AB, Boston Coll., 1957; DMD, Tufts U., 1961; PhD (hon.), Stonehill Coll., 1989, Northeastern U., 1993, Emmanuel Coll., 1993, Curry Coll., 1994. Diplomate, Am. Bd. of Oral and Maxillofacial Surgery, 1966. Intern in oral surgery Boston City Hosp., 1961-62, resident in oral surgery, 1962-63; prof. Forsyth Sch. of Dental Hygiene, 1979—; dir. facial pain and rehabilitaion ctr. Braintree (Mass.) Hosp., 1980—, med. dir. for cmty. programs; lectr., cons. in field; attended numerous mini-residencies throughout career. Author Dental Auxiliary Practice-Its Biological Basis and Clinical Application, 1975; co-author: Atlas of Orthognathic Surgery, Atlas of Preposthetic Surgery; contbr. numerous articles to various profl. jours. Mem. Mass. Bishop's Catholic Conf., Por Cristo (pres., exec. dir., recipient Distinguished Service in Ecuador award, 1980). Created knight Pres. of Ecuador, knighted Pope John Paul II, 1989; recipient Gold Medal Honor award Pres. of Ecuador, 1982, Man of Yr. award Archdiocese of Boston Holy Name Soc., Good Neighbor award ARC, Ron Burton Tng. Village Humanitarian of Yr. award, 1994, Humanitarian of Yr. award Kiwanis Club, 1994, Ignation award Boston Coll. H.S., 1990. Fellow Am. Coll. Oral and Maxillofacial Surgeons, Internat. Assn. of Oral Surgeons, Am. Dental Soc. of Anesthesiology (cert.), Internat. Soc. of Oral and Maxillofacial Surgeons (cert.). Am. Bd. Oral and Maxillofacial Surgeons (cert.); affiliate Nat. Faculty for Advance Life Support and Emergency Cardiac Care of Am. Heart Assn. (cert.), Am. Assn. Oral and Maxillofacial Surgeons, Am. Coll. Sports Medicine; mem. ADA, Mass. Dental Soc., New England Soc. of Oral Surgeons (program chmn, exec. com. 1972-73), Pan Am. Med. Assn., S. Eastern Metropolitan Dental Study Club (chmn 1974-75, 1977-78), Ea. Athletic Trainers Assn., Mass. Med. Soc. Com. (Sports Injuries com.), Boston Coll. Grad. Athletic Alumni Bd., Boston Coll. (Pres. Circle, Laetare Sunday Communion Breakfast, 1982), Boston Coll. Alumni Assn. (recipient Distinguished Pub. Service award, 1981). Home: 50 Brierbrook St Milton MA 02186-5252 Office: Milton Hosp Doctor Bldg 100 Highland Ave Milton MA 02186

DUNN, MICHAEL T., dean. Dean Med. Coll. Wis., Milw. Office: Med Coll Wis 8701 Watertown Planck Rd Milwaukee WI 53226*

DUNN, ROBERT HOWARD, nurse; b. Warren, Ohio, May 22, 1948; s. Robert and Doris Ruth (Dunlap) D.; m. Jill Marcia Taylor, May 22, 1977. BS in Agr., Ohio State U., 1971; ADN, Miami U., Oxford, Ohio, 1980. RN, Ohio. Vol. Peace Corps, Mali, 1972-74; inspector USDA and Ohio dept. Agr., Columbus, 1975-77; orderly Ft. Hamilton-Hughes Meml. Hosp. Ctr., Hamilton, Ohio, 1977-80, staff nurse psychology dept., 1980-81; nurse labor and delivery Ft. Hamilton-Hughes Meml. Hosp. Ctr., Hamilton, 1981-89, charge nurse labor and delivery, 1983-89; charge nurse adolescent psychology dept. Jewish Hosp., Cin., 1981-83, relief charge nurse labor and delivery, 1989-93; staff nurse Presbyn. Hosp., Albuquerque, 1993—, Charter Heights Hosp., Albuquerque; founder, chairperson Charge Nurse Group, 1985-88. Author: A Thought Full Collection, 1971, Elevage des Poulets de Chair aux Republique du Mali, 1973, Elevage des Ponduses aux Republique du Mali, 1974. Mem. NAACOG (cert. in-patient obstetrics), Nat. Perinatal Assn. Home: 7401 Armand Rd NW Albuquerque NM 87120-4948 Office: Presbyterian Hospital Albuquerque NM 87125

DUNN, RORY JAMES, hospital administrator; b. Pretoria, South Africa, Dec. 11, 1949; s. Hector Thomas and Joan Violet (Leck) D.; m. Melanie Ann Laidler, Feb. 10, 1979; children: Brett, Shaun. B.Com., U. South Africa, 1978, B.Com. with honors, 1985; MBA, Newport U., Calif., 1993, DBA, 1994. Fin. mgr. Burroughs, Johannesburg, South Africa, 1979-82; dir. Bus. Efficiency Appointments, Johannesburg, 1982-86; fin. mgr. Brenthurst Clinic, Johannesburg, 1986-89; dir. Kelmac Group, Johannesburg, 1989-92; lectr. Damelin Coll., Johannesburg, 1992; hosp. mgr. Rand Clinic, Johannesburg, 1992—. With South African Navy, 1968. Mem. JPM, SAIM, Internat. Hosp. Fedn. Home: 13 Goodman St, Rynfield Benoni 1501, South Africa Office: Rand Clinic, 33 Bruce St, Berea 2198, South Africa

DUNNE, HARRY POWERS, JR., marriage and family therapist, author; b. Morristown, N.J., Sept. 30, 1942; s. Harry Powers Sr. and Margaret (North) D.; m. Mary Louise Waggaman, June 25, 1977; children: Jenny Galvin, Brian Powers. BA, Mich. State U., 1965; MA, U. Conn., 1970; PhD, Union Inst., Cin., 1983. Lic. marriage and family therapist, Conn. Founder, dir. Youth Options Drug Abuse Prevention Network, various cities, Conn., 1972-77; cons. Xerox Employee Assistance Program, Stamford, Conn., 1980-84; pvt. practice Norwalk, Conn., 1977—; vis. prof. Grad. Sch. Psychology, U. Bridgeport, Conn., 1986-89, assoc. prof. marriage and family therapy, 1989-92; adj. prof. psychology and English, Sacred Heart U., 1993—; ptnr. Counseling Assocs. of Norwalk, 1989—; theme speaker Star Island Family Week. Author: (novels) Daughter of Darkness, 1981, The Dead of Autumn, 1990, The Stone Thrower, 1989, The Mooncusser, 1995; author: One Question That Can Save Your marriage, 1989; co-author: (psychology textbook) To Love and Work, 1986. Mem. AAUP, Am. Assn. for Marriage and Family Therapy (clin., supr.), Orthopsychiat. Assn., Authors Guild Am., Mystery Writers Am., Weston Field Club, Delta Tau Delta. Home: 61 Newtown Tpke Weston CT 06883-2110 Office: 147 East Ave Norwalk CT 06851-5723

DUNNER, DAVID LOUIS, medicine educator; b. Bklyn., May 27, 1940; s. Edward and Reichel (Connor) D.; m. Peggy Jane Zolbert, Dec. 27, 1964; children: Laura Louise, Jonathan Michael. AA, George Washington U., 1960; MD, Washington U., St. Louis, 1965. Diplomate Am. Bd. Psychiatry and Neurology. Intern Phila. Gen. Hosp., 1965-66; resident in psychiatry Barnes Renard Hosp. of Washington U., St. Louis, 1966-69; research psychiatrist N.Y. State Psychiat. Inst., N.Y.C., 1971-79; from asst. prof. to assoc. prof. clin. psychiatry Columbia U., N.Y.C., 1972-79; chief psychiatry Harborview Med. Ctr., Seattle, 1979-89, dir. outpatient psychiatry, 1989—; prof. psychiatry and behavioral scis. U. Wash., Seattle, 1979—, vice chmn. clin. svcs., 1989—; cons. Found. for Depression and Manic Depression, N.Y.C., 1974—. Editor-in-chief Comprehensive Psychiatry, 1997—; contbr. articles to profl. jours. Served to lt. comdr. USPHS, 1969-71. Fellow Am. Psychiat. Assn., Am. Psychopathol. Assn. (pres. 1986), Am. Coll. Neuropsychopharmacology, West Coast Coll. Biol. Psychiatry (charter, pres. 1987); mem. Psychiat. Research Soc. (pres. 1984). Office: U Wash Med Ctr 4225 Roosevelt Way NE Ste 306 Seattle WA 98105-6099

DUNNICK, N. REED, physician, radiologist, educator; b. Waukegan, Ill., Aug. 23, 1943; s. Paul A. and Marceil H. (Reed) D.; children: Cory, Amanda. BS, Purdue U., 1965; MD, Cornell U., 1969. Intern, resident U. Rochester, N.Y., 1969-71; resident Stanford U., Palo Alto, Calif., 1973-76; mem. staff NIH, Bethesda, Md., 1976-80; mem. faculty Duke U., Durham, N.C., 1980-92; chair dept. radiology U. Mich., Ann Arbor, 1992—. Author: Endourology, 1988, Textbook of Uroradiology, 1991. Served to lt. comdr. USPHS, 1971-73. Mem. Soc. Uroradiology (pres. 1990-91), Soc. Computed Body Tomography (pres. 1991-92), Am. Coll. Radiology, Am. Roentgen Ray Soc. (exec. coun. 1989-94). Office: U Mich Dept Radiology 1500 E Medical Ctr Dr Ann Arbor MI 48109-0030*

DUNNIHOO, DALE RUSSELL, physician, medical educator; b. Dayton, Ohio, June 8, 1928; s. John Russell and Hazel Nora (Roth) D.; m. Betty Lu Patterson, Sept. 1, 1950; children: Diana Lynn, John Russell, Dale Russell, Brian Michael, Janet Elizabeth. BS in Biology, Gannon U., 1949; MS in Zoology, U. Mich., 1950; MD cum laude, Washington U., St. Louis, 1956; PhD in Physiology, U. So. Calif., 1972. Diplomate Am. Bd. Obstetrics and Gynecology; lic. in medicine, Mo., Alaska, Calif., Miss., La. Asst. prof. biology Millsaps Coll., Jackson, Miss., 1950-52; intern straight medicine, resident in ob-gyn Washington U./Barnes Hosp., St. Louis, 1956-58, 61-63, fellow in oncology, 1963-64; commd. USAF, 1958, advanced through grades to col., 1978; fellow in maternal-fetal medicine U. So. Calif., L.A., 1969-72; dir. ob.-gyn. E.A. Conway Meml. Hosp., Monroe, La., 1980-88; prof. ob-gyn., prof. family medicine and comprehensive care La. State U., Shreveport, 1980-94, vice chmn. dept. ob-gyn, 1988-92; clin. prof. ob.-gyn. U. La. Med. Sch., Shreveport, 1994—; cons. to USAF Surgeon Gen., 1973-78; clin. asoc. prof. Tulane U., 1973-78; cons. Am. Jour. Ob-Gyn., 1980, 90-93, 95, 96, Ob-Gyn. Jour., 1990-95; cons. in Ob-gyn. Risk Mgmt. Divsn. State of La., 1994—; dept. chmn. and residency program dir. Keesler USAF Hosp., Biloxi, Miss., 1972-78, interim dep. commdr., 1975, 78; sec. med. staff E. A. Conway Meml. Hosp., 1984-85, vice chief of staff, 1985-86, chief of staff, 1986-87; adv. panel on ob-gyn. U.S. Pharmacopeial Conv., 1985-90; USAF reg. cons. Keesler USAF Med. Ctr., 1987-91; rep. to Assn. Am. Med. Colls., 1990-94. Author: Fundamentals of Gynecology and Obstetrics, 1990, 2d edit. 1992; contbr. numerous articles to profl. jours. Recipient tchr. of family practice award Am. Acad. Family Physicians, 1980-88, disting. alumni award Gannon U., 1990; named hon. citizen New Orleans, 1977; decorated meritorious svc. medal USAF, 1978. Fellow Am. Coll. Ob-Gyn. (chmn. Armed Forces dist. 1974-77, Appreciation award 1973, 77, 79, Kermit Krantz Cons. award Armed Forces dist. 1992, exec. bd. 1974-77, Continuing Med. Edn. award 1984-87, 87-90, 90-93, 93-96), ACS, Royal Soc. Medicine (London), Internat. Coll. Surgeons; mem. AMA (Physician's Recognition award 1984-87, 87-90, 90-93, 93-96), AAAS, Assn. Profs. Ob-Gyns., Gulf Coast Ob-Gyn. Soc. (founder, 1st pres.), So. Perinatal Assn., Soc. Air Force Clin. Surgeons, Miss. Ob-Gyn. Soc., Ctrl. Assn. of Ob-Gyns., La. Med. Soc., U.S. Power Squadron, St. Louis Gynecologic Soc., San Antonio Ob-Gyn. Soc., Am. Soc. Psychosomatic Ob-Gyn, Ouachita Parish Med. Soc., Masons, Shreveport Med. Soc., Lambda Chi Alpha (Hall of Fame 1996), Alpha Epsilon Delta, Phi Beta Pi. Episcopalian. Home: 1701 Parks Rd Benton LA 71006-4224

DUNSON, WILLIAM ALBERT, biology educator; b. Cedartown, Ga., Dec. 17, 1941; s. James Blake and Eleanor (Adams) D.; m. Margaret E.

Kvashay, Aug. 19, 1963; children: Mary Elizabeth, William Albert, David Brian. B.S. in Zoology with honors, Yale U., 1962; MS, U. Mich., 1964, Ph.D., 1965. Teaching fellow U. Mich., Ann Arbor, 1962-63; mem. faculty Pa. State U., University Park, 1965—, prof. biology, 1974—; adj. prof. biology U. Miami; Old Dominion U.; chief scientist various internat. oceanographic expdns.; collaborator Everglades Nat. Park. Author: The Biology of Sea Snakes, 1975, 125 rsch. papers. Queens marine sci. fellow, 1972, hon. Fulbright fellow, 1972; grantee NSF, U.S. Dept. Interior, U.S. Geol. Survey, U.S. EPA. Mem. Am. Soc. for Environ. Toxicology and Chemistry, Soc. for Study Amphibians and Reptiles (jour. editorial bd.), Am. Soc. Ichthyologists and Herpetologists, Herpetologists League, Ecol. Soc. Am., Atlantic Estuarine Rsch. Soc., Wetlands Soc., Fla. Acad. Sci. Home: 575 Brittany Dr State College PA 16803-1426 Office: Pa State U 208 Mueller Bldg University Park PA 16802

DUONG, THIEU, anesthesiologist; b. Hanoi, Vietnam, June 21, 1936; came to U.S., 1975; s. Phan T. and Thao T. (Pham) D.; m. Diep T. Nguyen; children: Anh T., Vi T., Mai T. MD, Saigon Med. Sch., 1962; MPH, Tulane U. Sch. Pub. Health, 1971. Diplomate Am. Bd. Anesthesiology. Intern Framingham (Mass.) Union Hosp., 1977-78; resident, fellow in anesthesiology Brigham and Women's Hosp., Boston, 1980-83; attending physician Cen. Hosp., Hue, Vietnam, 1966-67; chief Provincial Health Dept., Dalat, Vietnam, 1967-70; chmn. dept pub. health tng. Nat. Inst. Pub. Health, Saigon, Vietnam, 1971-75; anesthesiologist Boston U. Med. Ctr. Hosp., 1983—, assoc. clin. prof. in anesthesiology; sole proprietor AnesMED, Anesthesia Mgmt. Edn. and Design, Sharon, Mass. Contbr. articles to profl. jours. Mem. Mass. Soc. Anesthesiologists, Soc. Cardiovascular Anesthesia, Am. Coll. Physician Execs., Soc. Edn. in Anesthesia. Mem. Am. Soc. Anesthesiologists. Roman Catholic. Home: 18 Forge Rd Sharon MA 02067-2881 Office: Boston Med Ctr One Boston Med Ctr Pike Boston MA 02118

DUPAGNE, NESTOR L., gynecologist, oncologist, surgeon; b. Tillier, Namur, Belgium, June 29, 1922; s. Jules and Irma (LaFalize) DuP.; m. Lucy Chatelain, Dec. 26, 1948; children: Michel, Alan. MD, U. Liege, 1948, DDS, 1949. Intern St. Barnabas Hosp., Newark, N.J., 1953-54; resident in obstetrics Margaret Hague, Jersey City, 1954-55; resident in surgery Dr.'s Hosp., N.Y.C., 1955; resident in ob-gyn. Woman's Hosp., N.Y.C., 1955-59; gynecologist, oncology surgeon Brussels, Belgium, 1960—. Fellow ACS; mem. N.Y. Acad. Sci. Home and Office: 35 Blvd L Schmidt, Brussels 1040, Belgium

DUPONT, HERBERT LANCASHIRE, medical educator, researcher; b. Toledo, Nov. 12, 1938; s. Robert L. and Martha (Lancashire) DuP.; m. Margaret Wright, June 9, 1963; children: Denise Lorraine, Andrew Wright. BA, Ohio Wesleyan U., 1961; MD, Emory U., 1965. Diplomate Am. Bd. Internal Medicine. Resident U. Minn. Med. Ctr., Mpls., 1965-67; officer epidemic intelligence service, infectious disease fellow U. Md. Sch. Medicine, Balt., 1967-69; faculty, prof., dir. Ctr. for Infectious Diseases U. Tex., Houston, 1973-94, prof. Sch. Pub. Health, 1975—, prof. medicine M.D. Anderson Cancer Ctr., 1988—, Mary W. Kelsey prof. med. sci., 1988—, interim chmn. dept. internal medicine, 1987-89; chief internal medicine svc. and Baylor Coll. Medicine, H. Irving Schweppe chair in internal medicine St. Luke's Episcopal Hosp., Houston, 1995—; adj. prof. medicine and microbiology Baylor Coll. Medicine, Houston, 1977—; prin. investigator rsch. grants U.S. NIH, 1975—; mem. vaccines and related biologic products adv. com. U.S. FDA, 1989-93; sci. adv. com. Inst. Medicine, Nat. Acad. Scis., 1989-94; bd. sci. counselors Nat. Ctr. for Infectious Diseases, Ctrs. for Disease Control, 1992—; mem. standing sci. adv. com. Thrasher Rsch. Fund, 1993—. Author: various medical books; assoc. editor Am. Jour. of Epidemiology, 1978-81, Jour. of Infectious Diseases, 1983-88; editorial bd.: Clinical Infectious Diseases, 1990-95, Infectious Diseases in Clinical Practice, 1992—; contbr. articles to profl. jours. Served to lt. comdr. USPHS, 1967-69. Fellow ACP; mem. Am. Soc. Clin. Investigation, Infectious Diseases Soc. Am. (counselor 1978-81, sec. 1982-87, pres. 1989-90), Nat. Found. Infectious Diseases (bd. dirs. 1981—, v.p. 1994—), Am. Clin. and Climatol. Assn., Am. Epidemiology Soc., Assn. Am. Physicians, U.S.-Mex. Found. Sci. and Tech. (com. chair health 1994—), Internat. Soc. Travel Medicine (pres. 1991-93), Alpha Omega Alpha. Republican. Methodist. Home: 1111 Hermann Dr Apt 19F Houston TX 77004-6931 Office: St Luke's Episcopal Hosp 6720 Bertner St # 1-164 Houston TX 77030-2604

DUPONT, WILLIAM DUDLEY, biostatistician, educator; b. Montreal, Que., Can., Nov. 6, 1946; came to U.S., 1971; s. Charles Thomas and Jean White (Peters) Dupont; m. Susan Miller McChesney, July 20, 1974; children—Charles Thomas, Peter William. B.Sc., McGill U., 1969, M.Sc., 1971; Ph.D., Johns Hopkins U., 1976. Lectr., U. Md., Balt., 1976-77; asst. prof. biostats. Vanderbilt U. Sch. Medicine, Nashville, 1977-85; assoc. prof. 1986-92, prof., 1992—, dir. divsn. biostats., 1989—. Nat. Cancer Inst. grantee, 1980—. Mem. Am. Statis. Assn., Biometric Soc., Soc. Clin. Trials, Soc. Epidemiol. Research, Am. Assn. Advancement of Sci. Office: Vanderbilt U Med Sch Dept of Preventive Medicine A-1124 Med Ctr N Nashville TN 37232-2637

DUPRAT, JO ANN, pediatric rehabilitation nurse, consultant; b. Vallejo, Calif., May 21, 1948; d. Albert John Chester Jr. and Dorothy Marie (Anderson) Smith; m. Dennis Albert Duprat, May 14, 1966; children: Dana Marie, Daniel Gordon. ASN, Contra Costa Coll., San Pablo, Calif., 1982; BS in Health and Human Svcs., Columbia Pacific U., San Rafael, Calif., 1991, MS in Health and Human Svcs., 1992, postgrad., 1994—. RN, Calif.; CRRN, cert. rehab. nursing, UR/QA/discharge planning/risk mgmt. Learning Tree Univ. Staff nurse, adolescent Children's Hosp., Oakland, Calif., 1982-83, staff nurse med./surg. pediatric, 1983-84, pediatric rehab. nurse specialist, case mgr., 1984—; nursing supr. Adult Care Svcs., Walnut Creek, Calif., 1992-93; nurse cons. Regional Ctr. of East Bay, Emeryville, Calif., 1985—; panel nurse Calif. Children's Svcs., Sacramento, 1985—; clin. coord. Calif. Children's Svcs. Med. Therapy Unit, Del Norte and Humboldt Counties, 1996—. Author: Spina Bifida, Current Trends, 1991; Historical Perspectives and Attitudes Towards Women, Sexuality, Childbirth and Parenting, 1993. Supporting mem. San Pablo Little League, 1991-92. Mem. Spina Bifida of Calif., Assn. Rehab. Nurses, Children's Orthotics/Prosthetics Clinics, Nat. Neurofibramatosis Soc., Assn. for Syringomyelia, Simon Found., Alpha Gamma Sigma. Office: Children's Hosp 747 52nd St Oakland CA 94609-1809

DUPREY, THOMAS DONALD, pharmacist; b. Wyandotte, Mich., July 7, 1951; s. Donald Arthur and Laura Irene (White) D.; m. Cathryn Patricia Bell, June 29, 1974; children: Kimberly Christine, Stephen Thomas. BS in Pharmacy, Wayne State U., 1976; M in Pub. Adminstrn., U. San Francisco, 1985. Pharmacist West Outer Drive Med. Ctr., Lincoln Park, Mich., 1974-77; chief pharmacist CGM Enterprises, San Francisco, 1977-79; pharmacist Kaiser Permanente, Santa Clara, Calif., 1979-80; adminstrv. assoc. Kaiser Permanente, Oakland, Calif., 1980-81; asst. chief pharmacist Kaiser Permanente, Santa Clara, 1981; chief pharmacist Kaiser Permanente, Redwood City, Calif., 1981-93; rsch. utilization pharmacist Kaiser Permanente, Oakland, 1993—. Mem. Calif. Soc. Hosp. Pharmacists. Republican. Roman Catholic. Office: Kaiser Permanente 4th Fl 1814 Franklin St Oakland CA 94612

DUPUIS, SYLVIO LOUIS, optometrist, educator, administrator; b. Manchester, N.H., June 2, 1934; s. Arthur Edward Dupuis and Alma Lizotte; m. Cecile Marie Pellerin, July 14, 1956; children: Jeanne-Marie, Michelle, Marc, Mary Carol. Student, St. Anselm Coll., 1952-54; B.S., O.D., Ill. Coll. Optometry, 1957; L.H.D. (hon.), Notre Dame Coll., Manchester, N.H., 1975; D.Pub. Service (hon.), St. Anselm Coll., 1983; D of Ocular Sci. (hon.), New Eng. Coll. Optometry, 1993. Sr. ptnr. Dupuis/Michaud/Collins/Noury/Allard Assocs., optometry, Manchester, N.H., 1957-71; mayor City of Manchester, 1971-75; pres., CEO Cath. Med. Ctr., Manchester, 1975-83, 89-94; pres., CEO, prof. The New Eng. Coll. Optometry, Boston, 1985-89; pres., CEO Cath. Med. Ctr., Manchester, N.H., 1989-93; commr. health and welfare State of N.H., Concord, 1983-85, commr. ins., 1994-96; exec. dir. McLane, Grak, Raulerson and Middleton P.A., Manchester, N.H., 1996—; trustee Energy North Corp., Manchester, 1982—; dir. N.E. Healthcare Assembly, 1991—. Bd. dirs. Community Concert Assn., Manchester, 1978-89, Currier Gallery Art, Manchester, 1974-88, N.H. Performing Arts Ctr., Manchester, 1976-86, N.H. Charitable Fund, 1980-87, N.H. Assn. for Blind, 1987-90; bd. visitors U.S. Mil. Acad., West Point, N.Y., 1977-81; pres. United Health Systems Agy., Concord, 1981; trustee St. Anselm Coll., 1985—, Brewster Coll., 1985-90, N.H. Vision Plan, 1989—; pres. Palace Theatre Trust, 1990—; mem. Gov.'s Commn. on N.H. in 21st Century, 1990—; dir. N.H. Bus. Com. for Arts, Bus. and Industry Assn. Decorated D.S.M. Knight of Holy Sepulchre of Jerusalem; named State Citizen of Yr. Boy Scouts Am., Citizen of Yr. Manchester C. of C., 1979; recipient Fellowship award NCCJ, 1980, Granite State award U. N.H., 1975, Man of Vision award Nat. Soc. Prevention Blindness; Caroline Gross fellow Harvard/Kennedy Sch. Govt., 1995. Fellow Am. Acad. Optometry; mem. Am. Coll. Hosp. Adminstrs., Am. Optometric Assn. (trustee 1969-71), Am. Acad. Health Adminstrs., Nat. Health Coun. (bd. dirs. 1986-92), Nat. Assn. Ins. Commrs. (dir.), New England Coun. Optometrists (chmn. ann. congress, Disting. Svc. award 1984), N.H. Optometric Assn. (pres. 1969-70, Optometrist of Yr. award 1970), Nat. Soc. to Prevent Blindness (publs. rev. com. 1991—), Cath. Health Assn. (govt. rels. com. 1991—, bd. dirs. N.E. conf. 1991—), N.H. Bus. Com. for the Arts (bd. dirs. 1990-94), Bus. and Industry Assn. N.H. (bd. dirs.), Manchester C. of C. (chair 1993-94, past chair 1994—), Tomb and Key, Beta Sigma Kappa. Democrat. Roman Catholic. Home: 451 Coolidge Ave Manchester NH 03102-3214 Office: McLane Grak Raulerson and Middleton PA 900 Elm St Manchester NH 03105

DUQUETTE, ROBERT PAUL, optometrist, biologist; b. Fall River, Mass., Feb. 18, 1951; s. Joseph A. Duquette and Pauline O. Duquette Shurko; m. Marilyn Elizabeth Duquette. BS, U. Mass., North Dartmouth, 1971; OD, New Eng. Coll. Optometry, 1975. Pvt. practice, Swansea, Mass., 1975—. Bd. dirs. Little Theatre Fall River, Mass., 1985-95; bd. dirs. Sakonnet Players, v.p., 1981-95. Recipient cmty. svc. United Way, Fall River, 1980, award Charlton Meml. Hosp., Fall River, 1982, optometric recognition award Am. Optometric Assn., 1987, 90, ofcl. citation Mass. Senate and Ho. of Reps., 1993. Mem. New Eng. Coun. Optometrists (bd. dirs. 1992-93, 10 yr. tract award 1989), New Eng. Coll. Optometry (bd. corporators 1992-94), Mass. Soc. Optometrists (pres. 1991-92, chmn. bd. 1992-93), Lions (pres. Swansea 1985-86, 89-90, Lion of Yr. award 1988). Office: 1162 Grand Army Hwy Swansea MA 02777

DURA, KRZYSZTOF STANISLAW, surgeon; b. Cracow, Poland, Feb. 22, 1949; arrived in Spain, 1990; s. Stanislaw and Irena (Szelc) D.; m. Gloria Maria Perez Rodriguez, July 14, 1992; 1 child, Alejandro. Grad., Med. Acad. Cracow, 1977, MD, 1980. Cert. gen. & gastroenterology surgeon. Surgeon 1st dept. gen. surgery Jagiellonski U., Cracow, 1977-90; surgeon Pitie Salpetriere Hosp., Paris, 1979, 84; head surgeon gen. surg. dept. U. Hosp. Gafsa, Tunisia, 1987-89; head surgeon Bulawayo Group Hosp., Zimbabwe, 1989-90; cons. Sta. Maria del Pto, Cadiz, Spain, 1990-92; asst. lectr., gen. surg. chair Med. Acad, Cracow, 1972-83, lectr. prof., 1983-90. Contbr. articles to profl. jours. Recipient Health Min. award Ministry Health, 1977. Mem. Internat. Soc. Surgery, Internat. Gastrosurg. Club, European Assn. Endoscopic Surgery. Office: Cryomedsur Proctosurgery Clinic, Pza Elias Ahuja No 1-2 Pta 2, 11500 Cadiz Spain

DURACK, DAVID TULLOCH, physician, educator; b. Perth, Australia, Dec. 18, 1944; s. Reginald Wyndham and Grace Enid (Tulloch) D.; m. Carmen Elizabeth Prosser, July 25, 1970; children: Jeremy, Kimberley, Sonya, Justin. M.B., B.S., U. Western Australia, 1969; D.Phil., Oxford U., Eng., 1973. Diplomate Am. Bd. Internal Medicine, Royal Australasian Coll. Physicians, Royal Coll. Physicians U.K. Chief resident medicine, asst. prof. medicine U. Wash., Seattle, 1975-77; chief div. of infectious diseases and internat. health Duke U., Durham, N.C., 1977-94, prof. medicine, microbiology and immunology, 1982-94, cons. prof. medicine, 1994—; chmn. dept. medicine, chief divsn. infectious diseases Health Care Internat., Clydebank, Scotland, 1994-95. Co-editor: Infections of the Central Nervous Systems, 1991; contbr. articles to profl. jours. Rhodes scholar, 1969; NIH grantee, 1980, 86—, grantee R.J. Reynolds Co., 1983-88, Carnegie Corp., 1989-94, grantee Roche Labs., 1991-94. Fellow Royal Coll. Physicians U.K., ACP, Royal Australasian Coll. Physicians, Infectious Diseases Soc. Am., Am. Soc. Clin. Investigation, Am. Fedn. Clin. Research. Presbyterian. also: Duke U Med Ctr Medicine Divsn Infectious Diseases Box 3867 Durham NC 27710

DURAND, M. DOMINIQUE, biomedical engineering educator, researcher; b. Monbazillac, Dordogne, France, Oct. 19, 1951; came to U.S., 1973; s. Pierre and Simone Durand; m. Ellen Jo Mervis, Dec. 13, 1975; children: Lise, Remy. Diplome ingenieur, Ecole Nat. Superior Electronique, Toulouse, France, 1974; MSc, Case Western Res. U., 1975; PhD, U. Toronto, 1982. Clin. engr. Centre Hospitalier Universitaire, Laval, Que., Can., 1975; biomed. engr. Addiction Rsch. Found., Toronto, 1976-78, scientist, 1978-82; asst. prof. Case Western Res. U., Cleve., 1983-87, assoc. prof., 1987-95; prof. U. Cleve., 1995—; cons. Giner Inc., Boston, 1988-91; vis. prof. U. Toronto, Can., 1993. Author: Desynchronization of neural activity, 1994, Noyactu Stimulation of oxons, 1995, Generalized cable equation, 1995, Nonlinear Parameter estimation, 1996. French Fgn. Ministry scholar, 1974, Brit. Coun. scholar, 1979; grantee NSF, NIH; recipient Travel award Internat. Soc. Alcoholism, 1982, Presdl. Young Investigator award NSF, 1985, Wittlee Tching. award, 1991, Dickhoff Grad. Tching. award, 1994. Mem. AAAS, Soc. for Neurosci., Biomed. Engring. Soc. Roman Catholic. Office: Dept Biomed Engring Case Western Res U Cleveland OH 44105

DURDAHL, CAROL LAVAUN, psychiatric nurse; b. Crookston, Minn., Jan. 18, 1933; d. Elmer Oliver and Ovidia (Olson) Durdahl; m. Hans A. Dahl, May 22, 1956 (div. 1983); children: Hana Sorensen, Carla Pederson. RN, St. Lukes Hosp., Duluth, Minn., 1953; BA in Human Svcs., Met. State U., St. Paul, 1982. Staff nurse various hosps., Minn., 1953-59; human svcs. tech. Willmar (Minn.) State Hosp., 1970-74, supplemental tchr., 1974-83; staff nurse Rice Meml. Hosp., Willmar, 1983-86; utilization rev. various nursing homes, Willmar, 1985-86; tchr. Willmar Area Vocat. Tech. Inst., 1986; dir. nurses Glenmore Recovery Ctr., Crookston, Minn., 1986-88; shift supr. Golden Valley (Minn.) Health Ctr., 1988-92; with crisis dept. Hennepin County Med. Ctr., 1988—; managed care of psychiat. and substance abuse MCC Managed Behavioral Care, Mpls., 1992. Contbr. articles to profl. jours. Mem. AAUW, Bus. and Profl. Women, League Women Voters (pres. and state bd.), Federated Women, Does. Republican. Lutheran. Home: 6450 York Ave S Apt 403 Minneapolis MN 55435-2341 Office: Hennepin County Med Ctr 701 Park Ave Minneapolis MN 55415-1623

DURDEN, JIMMY DAVID, physician; b. Montgomery, Ala., May 23, 1945; s. Barney David and Avoleen (Lawrence) D.; m. Rebecca McShan, Feb. 8, 1969; 1 child, Meghan Leigh. BS, U. Ala., 1967; MD, U. So. Ala., 1978. Diplomate Am. Acad. Family Practice, fellow. Intern Carraway Meth. Med. Ctr., Birmingham, Ala., 1979, resident, 1981; chief of staff, 1985-87; dir. Community Hosp., Tallahassee, 1987—, also bd. dirs. Mem. AMA, Am. Acad. of Sports Medicine, So. Med. Assn., Elmore County Med. Soc. (pres. 1984-86), Ala. Med. Soc., Tallassee C. of C. (bd. dirs. 1987-88, 90-91). Home: 112 Bent Oak Ln Tallassee AL 36078-1110 Office: Cmty Med Arts Ctr 875 Friendship Rd Tallassee AL 36078-1247

DÜREN, METE, general surgeon; b. Istanbul, June 4, 1963; s. Erol and Mucella Hatice (Cokyuksel) D.; m. Ipek Halide Aktay, Aug. 30, 1990; 1 child, Selin. MD, Cerrampasa Med. Faculty, Istanbul, 1988. Cert. gen. surgeon. Attending surgeon U. Istanbul, Cerrahpasa Med. Faculty, 1993—. Author: (textbook) Textbook of Endocrine Surgery; contbr. articles to profl. jours. Doctor Marines, Turkey, 1992. Mem. Internat. Soc. Surgery, Turkish Assn. Endocrine Surgery, German Soc. Surgery. Home: Akatlar Maya Sitesi K 20, 80630 Istanbul Turkey

DURFEE, HERBERT ASHLEY, JR., medical educator; b. Burlington, Vt., Nov. 5, 1924; s. Herbert Ashley and Margaret Elizabeth (Spaulding) D.; m. Elizabeth Lea Dole, Sept. 18, 1947; children: Herbert Ashley III, Eleazer Lea Dole. BS, Yale U., 1948; MD, U. Vt., 1948. Diplomate Am. Bd. Ob-Gyn. Intern Lenox Hill Hosp., N.Y.C., 1948-50; fellow in pathology Free Hosp. Women, Brookline, Mass., 1950; resident in obstetrics Boston Lying-In Hosp., 1951; resident in surgery Faulkner Hosp., Jamaica Plain, Mass., 1953; resident in ob-gyn. Boston Lying-In Hosp. and Free Hosp. Women, Brookline and Boston, 1954-57; from instr. to assoc. prof. ob-gyn. U. Vt., Burlington, 1957-70, prof. ob-gyn., 1970-90, prof. emeritus ob-gyn., 1990—; assoc. chmn. Dept. Ob-Gyn., U. Vt., Burlington, 1965-90, acting chmn., 1961, 69, 76, 85; pres. med. staff Med. Ctr. Hosp. Vt., Burlington, 1985, 89, chmn. various coms. Capt. USAF, 1951-53. Mem. AMA, Am. Coll. Ob-Gyn. (Vt. sect. past vice-chmn., chmn.), N.Am. Ob-Gyn. Soc. (sec.-treas., 1980-90), Vt. State Med. Soc., N.E. Med. Assn., Baker-Channing Soc. Republican. Home: 25 Woodcrest Ln Burlington VT 05401-4151

DURHAM, NORMAN NEVILL, microbiologist, scientist, educator; b. Ranger, Tex., Feb. 14, 1927; s. Harold H. and Bernice (Griffith) D.; m. Jane Harriet Stovall, July 26, 1952; children: Susan Lynne, Janet Anne, Diane Elizabeth, Linda Jane. BS, N. Tex. State U., 1949, MS, 1951; PhD, U. Tex., 1954. Student instr., research asst. N. Tex. State U., Denton, 1947-51; research assoc., teaching asst. U. Tex., 1951-54; faculty dept. microbiology Okla. State U., Stillwater, 1954-66, prof., 1961-66, dean Grad. Coll., prof. microbiology, 1967—, asst. v.p. for rsch., 1989—, assoc. v.p. for acad. planning, 1991—, dir. Water Rsch. Ctr.; cons. biol. scis. communication project NASA, 1963—; vis. lectr. U. Okla. Sch. Medicine, 1963, Kans. State Tchrs. Coll., 1963, 65; program dir. molecular biology and cellular genetics U.S. AEC, 1966-67; evaluation team Nat. Council Accreditation Tchr. Edn., 1968—; mem. manpower adv. com. U.S. Office Edn., 1973—; mem. tech. adv. com. Fed. Energy Adminstrn., 1974—. Contbr. articles profl. publs. Served with USNR, 1944-45. Recipient Coll. Arts and Scis. award, 1963, Distinguished Alumni citation N. Tex. State U., 1970. Fellow Am. Acad. Microbiology, Okla. Acad. Sci. (pres. 1974-75); mem. Am. Soc. Microbiology (councilor 1961-65), Biochem. Soc., Soc. Gen. Microbiology, AAAS, AAUP, Stillwater C. of C. (pres. 1975), Sigma Xi, Pi Kappa Alpha, Phi Delta Kappa, Beta Beta Beta, Phi Kappa Phi. Presbyn. (elder). Clubs: Elk, Kiwanian. Home: Route 5 Box 138 Stillwater OK 74074

DURHAM, THENA MONTS, microbiologist, researcher, management executive; b. Bradenton, Fla., July 10, 1945; d. Turner Monts and Silverrene (Taylor) M.; m. Millard Durham, Aug. 30, 1969; children—Bryce Vincent-Barnard, Brittanie Yvonne. B.S., Fisk U., 1966; M.S. Purdue U., 1968. Research microbiologist Ctrs. for Disease Control, Atlanta, Ga., 1968-86, assoc. dir. for programs Nat. Ctr. for Prevention Svcs., 1988-95; program analyst Ctr. for Health Promotion and Edn., Office of the Dir., 1986-88; dir. exec. secretariat Ctr. Disease Control, Atlanta, 1995—; cons. FDA. Mem. NAACP, Neighborhood Planning Unit. Recipient Superior performance award Ctrs. for Disease Control and Prevention, 1972, 85, 86, 87, 88, 89, 90, 91, 92 and 93. Mem. Sci. Research Soc., AAAS, Am. Soc. Microbiologists, CDC Assn. of Exec. Women (founder, co-chair), Women in Sci. and Engring., Sigma Xi. Democrat. Author numerous tech. papers; contbr. articles to profl. jours.

DURHAM, THOMAS WESLEY, clinical psychologist, educator; b. Raleigh, N.C., Oct. 8, 1952; s. William Hicks Jr. and Rita (Kessler) D.; m. Anne Watts, Aug. 25, 1973; children: Brian Wesley, William Henry. BA summa cum laude, East Carolina U., 1973; MS, Fla. State U., 1975, PhD, 1977. Lic. psychologist, N.C. Clin. psychology intern St. Elizabeths Hosp., Washington, 1976-77; lect. East Carolina U., Greenville, N.C., 1977-79; asst. prof. East Carolina U., Greenville, 1979-85, assoc. prof., dir. clin. tng., 1985—; practicing psychologist Greenville Psychol. Assocs., 1978—; consulting psycholo gist Devel. Evaluation Clinic, Greenville, 1978-80, Tideland Mental Health Ctr., Washington, 1980—. Contbr. articles to profl. jours. Deacon Immanuel Bapt. Ch., Greenville, 1980—. Mem. APA, N.C. Psychol. Assn., South Ea. Psychol. Assn., N.C. Assn. for Advancement of Psychology. Democrat. Baptist. Home: 1204 Drexel Ln Greenville NC 27858-5225 Office: East Carolina U Psychology Dept Rawl Bldg. Greenville NC 27858

DURIGON, MICHEL LOUIS, pathologist, forensic medicine educator; b. Saint Cloud, France, Oct. 18, 1942; s. Ernest and Simonne (Etasse) D.; m. Geneviève Pascale Le Pont, May 13, 1971; children: Camille, Alice, Pauline. Physique biologie, Faculté Sciences, Paris, 1961; MD, U. Paris, 1969. Tng. in forensic medicine, Paris, 1969-72, tng. in pathology,, 1972-73; asst. Faculty of Médicine, Paris, 1974-77, asst. prof., 1977-84; prof., dept. head Hosp. R. Poincaré and Faculty of Medicine, Garches and Paris, France, 1985—; nat. expert Supreme Ct., Paris, 1986—; cons. ICPO, Lyon, France, 1982-91; coord. nat. edn. of forensic medicine, Paris. Author: Medecine Legale à Usage Judiciaire, 1979, Forensic Pathology, 1988, Forensic Clinical Medicine, 1994. Mem. Forensic Sci. Soc., Acad. Internat. de Medecine Légale, Soc. d'Anthropology, Soc. de Medecine Légale (sec. 1978-89, v.p. 1989—), Sevilla Working Party. Roman Catholic. Home: 39 cours du 14 Juillet, 78300 Poissy France Office: Hospital R Poincaré, 92380 Garches France

DURLING, SCOTT BRENT, trauma emergency nurse; b. Kirkland Lake, Ont., Can., Aug. 31, 1970; came to U.S., 1993.; s. Ronald Ray and Irene Ruth (Morrison) D. Associate degree, Georgian Coll., Barrie, Ont., Can., 1993. RN, Miss.; cert. in BLS. Camp RN Camp Lorraine, Cobalt, Ont., Can., 1991; LPN Grove Pk. Retirement, Barrie, Ont., Can., 1992-93; trauma nurse Clarkesdale, Miss., 1993—. Address: 109 Pine Knoll Dr Apt 280 Ridgeland MS 39157-1356

DURM, MARK WENDELL, educator; b. Winchester, Tenn., May 17, 1950; s. Darwin Lee and Edna Odell (Hatchett) D. AA, Martin Coll, 1970, BA, Middle Tenn. State U., 1972, MA, 1974; PhD, U. Miss., 1983. Dir. student affairs Martin Coll., Pulaski, Tenn., 1972-76; asst. prof. psychology Columbia State C.C., 1976-81; asst. prof. psychologist Athens State Coll., Ala., 1982-85, assoc. prof., 1985-89, prof. psychology, 1989—; adj. faculty Cumberland U., Lebanon, Tenn., 1984-86. Author: General Psychology Handbook, 1980-81. Contbr. articles to profl. jours. Mem. Exec. Com. Giles County, Pulaski, 1973-76; chmn. Young Dems., 1974-76; bd. dirs. Big Bros./Big Sis., Columbia, 1979-81. Home: 508 N Madison St Athens AL 35611-1750 Office: Athens State Coll Beaty St Athens AL 35611

DUROCHER, FRANCES ANTOINETTE, physician, educator; b. Woonsocket, R.I., Mar. 11, 1943; d. Armand D. and Teresa (Leverone) DuRocher. BA (with honors), Trinity coll., 1964; MS, Brown U., 1966; postgrad., Woman's Med. Coll., 1970. Med. resident Phila. VA Hosp. and Med. Coll. Pa., 1971-73; assoc. in internal med. Guthrie Clinic Ltd., Sayre, Pa., 1973-79, Annandale (Va.) Group Health Assocs., 1979-87; assoc. chair internal med. Annandale Group Health Assoc., 1986-87; pvt. practice, Fairfax, Va., 1987—; clin. asst. prof. med. and health svcs. George Washington U. Med. Sch., Washington, 1994—. Bd. dirs. Fairways of Penderbrook Homeowners Assn., 1993—, sec., 1995-96, pres., 1996—. Mem. AMA, Am. Med. Women's Assn. (exec. bd. br. I, 1985-91, pres. 1987-88), Med. Soc. Va., Am. Soc. Internal Medicine, Fairfax County Med. Soc. Office: 9926 Main St Fairfax VA 22031-3901

DUSANIC, DONALD GABRIEL, parasitology educator, microbiologist; b. Chgo., Dec. 15, 1934; s. Gabriel John and Harriet (Rojewski) D.; m. Roberta Leona Drost (dec. Feb. 1970); children: Donald, Robert; m. Jane Mitchell Haw, June 11, 1971; children: Belinda Conrad, Karla Conrad, Allan Conrad. BS, U. Chgo., 1957, MS, 1959, PhD, 1963. Instr. U. Chgo., 1963-64; asst. prof. U. Kans., Lawrence, 1964-68, assoc. prof., 1968-71, prof., 1971-72; prof. parasitology Ind. State U., Terre Haute, 1972—, dir. Interdisciplinary Ctr. for Cell Products and Techs., 1987—; prof. emeritus, 1995—; vis. prof. U. Philippines Sch. Medicine, Manila, 1964, Nat. Taiwan U. Sch. Medicine, Taipei, 1971, Nat. Sun Yat-sen U., Kaohsiung, Taiwan, 1991; adj. prof. Ind. U. Sch. Medicine, Terre Haute, 1982—. Contbr. numerous articles on biochemistry and immunology of schistosomes, nematodes, amebae, and trypanosomes to sci. jours., chpts. to books. Recipient rsch. and creativity award Ind. State, 1982, Coll. Arts and Scis. Disting. Prof. award, 1990; rsch. grantee NIH, NSF, Office Naval Rsch. Mem. Am. Soc. Parasitologists, Am. Soc. Tropical Medicine and Hygiene, Am. Soc. Protozoologists, Am. Assn. Immunologists, N.Y. Acad. Scis., Sigma Xi. Home: 5726 E Cougar Dr Terre Haute IN 47802-9804 Office: Ind State U Dept Life Scis Terre Haute IN 47809

DUSHANE, PHYLLIS MILLER, nurse; b. Portland, Oreg., June 3, 1924; d. Joseph Anton and Josephine Florence (Eicholtz) Miller; m. Frank Maurice Jacobson, Mar. 13, 1945 (dec. 1975); children: Karl, Kathleen, Kraig, Kirk, Karen, Kent, Krista, Kandis, Kris, Karlyn; m. Donald McLelland DuShane, July 21, 1979 (dec. 1989); stepchildren: Diane DuShane Bishop, Donald III. BS in Biology, U. Oreg., 1948; BS in Nursing, Oreg. Health Scis. U., 1968. R.N., Oreg. Pub. health nurse Marion County Health Dept., Salem, Oreg., 1968-77; pediatric nurse practitioner Marion County Health Dept., Salem, 1977-91, Allergy Assocs., Eugene, Oreg., 1979-89; mem. allied profl.

staff Sacred Heart Gen. Hosp., Eugene, 1979—. Named Oreg. Pediatric Nurse Practitioner of Yr., 1991. Mem. P.E.O., P.E.O. Sisterhood, Oreg. Pediatric Nurse Practioners Assn. (v.p. Salem chpt. 1977-78), Am. Nurses Assn., Oreg. Nurses Assn., Nat. Assn. Pediatric Nurse Assocs. and Practitoners, Am. Acad. Nurse Practitioners, Nurse Practitioners Spl. Interest Group, Salem Med. Aux. (sec. 1968), Oreg. Republican Women, Delta Gamma Alumni (v.p. 1979). Presbyterian. Home: 965 E 23rd Ave Eugene OR 97405-3074 Office: Oakway Pediatrics P C 465 Oakway Rd Eugene OR 97401-5405 also: Eugene Pediatric Assocs 1680 Chambers St Eugene OR 97402-3655

DUSTAN, HARRIET PEARSON, former physician, educator; b. Craftsbury, Vt., Sept. 16, 1920; d. William Lyon and Helen Gordon (Paterson) D. BS, U. Vt., 1942, MD, 1944, DSc (hon.), 1977; DSc (hon.), Med. Coll. Wis., 1986. Diplomate Am. Bd. Internal Medicine. Intern Mary Fletcher Hosp. U. Vt., Burlington, 1944-45; asst. resident medicine Royal Victoria Hosp., Montreal, Que., Can., 1945-46; asst. prof. Coll. Medicine U. Vt., 1946-48; rsch. fellow Cleve. Clinic, 1948-51, mem. staff rsch. dir., 1951-77, asst. dir., 1971-77; prof. medicine Sch. Medicine U. Ala., Birmingham, 1977-90; VA disting. physician Birmingham VA Med. Ctr., 1987-90; emeritus prof. medicine Sch. Medicine U. Ala., Birmingham, 1990—; mem. adv. coun. Nat. Heart, Blood, Lung Inst., Bethesda, Md., 1972-76; bd. regents Am. Coll. Physicians, Phila., 1979-84; mem. Am. Bd. Internal Medicine, Phila., 1973-79. Recipient Sci. Achievement award AMA, 1988. Fellow Am. Heart Assn. (pres. 1976-77, Lifetime Achievement award 1991); mem. Am. Coll. Physicians (master, John Phillips Meml. award 1994), Assn. Am. Physicians, Inst. Medicine. Home: 34 Lang Dr Essex Junction VT 05452-3379

DUSTIN, FRANK ARTHUR, neurologist; b. Pasadena, Calif., Sept. 4, 1962; s. Douglas Frank and Adelheid Gisela (Thiel) D.; m. Katherine Leydorf, June 24, 1989. BA, Stanford U., 1984; MD, Baylor Coll. Medicine, Houston, 1988. Diplomate Am. Bd. Psychiatry and Neurology. Intern Kaiser Med. Ctr.,, Oakland, Calif., 1988-89; resident U. Calif. David East Bay Program, Martinez, 1989-92, fellow, 1992-93; instr. U. Calif., San Francisco, 1993-94; pvt. practice Alameda, Calif., 1993—. Mem. Am. Acad. Neurology, Am. Assn. Electrodiagnostic Medicine (assoc.). Office: 947 Marina Village Pkwy Alameda CA 94501

DUTCHER, JANICE JEAN PHILLIPS, oncologist; b. Bend, Oreg., Nov. 10, 1950; d. Charles Glen and MayBelle (Fluit) Phillips; m. John Dutcher, Sept. 8, 1971 (div. 1980). BA with honors, U. Utah, 1971; MD, U. Calif., Davis, 1975. Diplomate Am. Bd. Internal Medicine, Am. Bd. Med. Oncology. Intern Rush-Presbyn. St. Luke's Hosp., Chgo., 1975-76, resident, 1976-78; clin. assoc. Balt. Cancer Rsch., Nat. Cancer Inst., 1978-81, sr. investigator, 1981-82; asst. prof. U. Md., Balt., 1982; asst. prof. Albert Einstein Coll. Medicine, N.Y.C., 1983-86, assoc. prof., 1986-92, prof., 1992—; course co-dir. Advances in Cancer Treatment Rsch. Albert Einstein Coll. Medicine, Manhattan, 1984—; chmn. biol. response mod. com. Ea. Coop. Oncology Group, Madison, Wis., 1989-95, mem. exec. com., 1995—; mem. data safety com. Nat. Heart Lung Blood Inst., Bethesda, Md., 1990-95; mem. biologic response modifier study sect. Nat. Cancer Inst., Bethesda, 1988, 90, 94, 96; mem. NIH Consensus Panel on Early Melanoma, 1992; mem. FDA Oncology Drug Adv. Bd., 1995—, NCI subcom. D for program project rev., 1995—. Editor: Handbook of Hematology/Oncology Emergencies, 1987, Modern Transfusion Therapy, 1990; sect. editor: Neoplastic Diseases of the Blood, 1996; mem. editl. bd. Jour. Immunotherapy, Med. Oncology, Jour. Clin. Oncology; contbr. articles to Blood, Leukemia, Jour. Clin. Oncology. Recipient Beecham award in Hematology So. Blood Club, 1983, Henry C. Moses Clin. Rsch. award Montefiore Med. Ctr., 1989, Outstanding Alumnus award U. Calif., Davis, 1989; named Outstanding Young Investigator Ea. Coop. Oncology Group, 1993; recipient numerous grants. Fellow ACP; mem. Am. Soc. Clin. Oncology (program com. 1988), Am. Assn. Cancer Rsch., Am. Soc. Hematoogy, Soc. for Biol. Therapy, Am. Radium Soc. (chair Jane Way com. 1995-96), Phi Beta Kappa (Presdl. scholar 1968), Alpha Lambda Delta, Phi Kappa Phi, Alpha Omega Alpha. Office: Albert Einstein Coll Med Montifiore Med Ctr 111 E 210 St Bronx NY 10467

DUTKA, ANDREW JOSEPH, neurologist, military officer; b. New Haven, May 24, 1951; s. Joseph John and Mary (McGillicuddy) D.; m. Ellen Shea, Nov. 11, 1978; children: Joseph, Michael. BS, Yale U., 1973; MD, Albert Einstein Coll., 1976. Diplomate Am. Bd. Psychiatry and Neurology. Commd. ensign USN, 1976; advanced through grades to capt., 1992; neurology resident Naval Hosp., Bethesda, Md., 1976-80; resident in neurology Naval Hosp., Bethesda, 1980-81; head EEG/EMG labs. Naval Hosp., San Diego, Md., 1981-83; head medicine div. diving medicine Dept. Naval Med. Rsch. Inst., Bethesda, 1983-91; chmn. neurology dept. NAT NAVAL MEDCEN, Bethesda, 1991—; prof. neurology Uniformed Svcs. U. Health Scis., Bethesda, Md., 1994—. Fellow Am. Acad. Neurology; mem. Am. Neurol. Assn., Undersea and Hyperbaric Med. Soc. Office: Nat Naval Med Ctr Neurology Dept Bethesda MD 20889

DUTT, KAMLA, medical educator; b. Lahore, Punjab, India; came to U.S., 1969; d. Gulzari Lal and Raj Bansi Dutt. BS with honors, Panjab U., Chandigarh, India, 1961, MS in Zoology with honors, 1962, PhD, 1970. Rsch. assoc. Harvard Med. Sch. Sidney Farber Cancer Ctr., Boston, Mass., 1972-76; rsch. assoc. Eye Inst. Retinal Fedn., Boston, 1977-80; sr. rsch. assoc. Yale Med. Ctr., New Haven, 1980-81, Emory U., Atlanta, 1981-82; asst. prof. Morehouse Sch. Medicine, Atlanta, 1983-89, assoc. prof., 1989—. Contbr. numerous articles to sci. jours.; author short stories (in Hindi); prodr., actor 3 maj. plays, Atlanta; actor 11 maj. plays, India. Bd. dirs. VSEI (vol. fundraising orgn. for edn. in India), 1973-78; v.p. Indian Am. Cultural Assn., 1985; podium spkr., participant King Week, 1990, 91, 93; spkr. Gandhi Day Celebration, 1984, 85; key participant Intercultural Conf., 1990; main participant joint document Women's Perspective; active human rights issues; stake holder Vision 20/20 Collaborative State of Ga., diversity and edn. coms., 1995. Hindu. Office: Morehouse Sch Medicine 720 Westview Dr SW Atlanta GA 30310-1458

DUTTON, PETER LESLIE, biochemist, educator; b. Ashton-Under-Lyne, Lancashire, U.K., Mar. 12, 1941; came to U.S., 1968; s. Arthur Bramwell and Mary (Drake) D.; mn. Julia R. Dwyer, July 19, 1965; children: Michael, Sara, Simon. BSc in Chemistry with honors, U. Wales, 1963, PhD in Biochemistry, 1967. Postdoctoral fellow with W. Charles Evans U. Wales, U.K., 1967; postdoctoral fellow Johnson Rsch. Found., U. Pa., Phila., 1968, asst. prof., 1971-75; assoc. prof. dept. biochemistry and biophysics U. Pa., Phila., 1976-80, prof. dept. biochemistry and biophysics, 1981—, acting chmn. dept., 1993-94, chmn. dept., 1994—, dir. Johnson Rsch. Found., 1991—; vis. prof. Imperial Coll., London, 1994, Univ. Coll., London, 1995. Author: Frontiers of Biological Energetics: From Electrons to Tissues, 1978, Protein Structure: Molecular and Electronic Reactivity, 1987; patentee in field; mem. editorial bd. Archives of Biochemistry, 1976-79; editor FEBS Letters, 1981-89; mng. editor Bioenergetics Revs. Sect. Biochimica et Biophysica Acta, 1981-96, Biochimica et Biophysica Acta, 1989-96. Mem. NIH adv. com. Molecular and Cellular Biophysics Study Sect., 1986-90; reserve mem. NIH Adv. Coms., 1990-94. Fellow Royal Soc. London. Office: Johnson Rsch Found B501 Richards Bldg Philadelphia PA 19104-6089

DUTZ-KOHOUT, ELFRIEDE, physician, educator; b. Vienna, Austria, June 23, 1926; came to U.S., 1974; d. Leopold and Valerie (Schiffer) Kohout; children: Peter, Micheal. MD, U. Vienna, 1952. Intern Miseri Cordia Hosp., Edmonton, Alta., Can., 1954-55; resident Nassau County Hosp., L.I., N.Y., 1956-58, Delafield Hosp., N.Y., 1958-59; fellow Columbia U., N.Y., 1959-60, Mt. Sinai Hosp.; from asst. prof. to prof. clin. pathology Pahlavi U., Shiraz, Iran, 1960-76; prof. pathology Med. Coll. Va., Richmond, 1974-94. Grantee NIH, 1964. Fellow Royal Soc. Pathology, Am. Soc. Pathology, Am. Soc. Clin. Pathology, Am. Soc. Microbiology, Am. Soc. Tropical Medicine. Home: 111 N 28th St Richmond VA 23223-7325

DUVAL, DAVID ROGER, anesthesiologist; b. Manchester, N.H., Jan. 5, 1960; s. Roger John and Lorraine Valerie (Pruneau) D. BS in Pharmacy, U. R.I., 1983; DO, U. New Eng., 1987. Diplomate Am. Bd. Anesthesiology. Intern Southeastern Med. Ctr., North Miami Beach, Fla., 1988; resident in anesthesiology Jackson Meml. Hosp., Miami, Fla., 1991; anesthesiologist Parkland Med. Ctr., Derry, N.H., 1991—; deans adv. com. UNECOM, 1995—; bd. dirs. N.E. Osteo. Consortium. Bd. dirs. N.H. Drug Utilization Rev. Bd., 1993-94. Mem. Am. Soc. Anesthesiologists, N.J. Osteo. Assn. (sec. 1994, pres. 1995-96), N.H.-Vt. Soc. Anesthesiologists. Office: Nutfield Anesthesia Assocs 1 Parkland Dr Derry NH 03038

DU VALL, BRENKA LYNN, telemetry nurse; b. Douglas, Ga., Oct. 31, 1953; d. Freddie La Vare and Ruby Lee (Walsh) Du V. BS in Elem. Edn., U. Ga., 1975; BSN, Ga. Coll., 1989, postgrad., 1990—. Cert. BLS, ACLS. Tchr. Laurens County Schs., East Laurens, Ga., 1975-76; supr. small display advt. Greensheet Advt. Paper, Houston, 1976-78; sec. BMC Software, Mobil Oil Corp., Houston, 1978-86; nurse USAFR, Warner Robins, Ga., 1989-92; telemetry nurse Oconee Regional Med. Ctr., 1992-93; gyn. nurse South Fulton Med. Ctr., Atlanta, 1993-95; psychiat. nurse Ga. Mental Health Inst., Atlanta, 1993-96. With USAFR, 1989-92. Whitehall scholar Whitehall Found., 1988-89; recipient Air Force Commendation medal. Mem. Nightingale Honor Soc., Sigma Theta Tau. Republican. Home: 3425-M North David Hills Rd Decatur GA 30033

DUVALL, CHARLES PATTON, physician; b. Evanston, Ill., June 16, 1936; s. Charles Fleming and Edith (Osgood) D.; m. Nancy Ash, June 21, 1958; children: Lawrence Charles, Stephen Rogers, Douglas Patton, Lauren Lynne. AB, Cornell U., 1958; MD, U. Rochester, N.Y., 1962. Diplomate Am. Bd. Internal Medicine, Am. Bd. Med. Oncology. Intern Yale New Haven Med. Ctr., 1962-63; resident in medicine U. Rochester, 1963-64; clin. assoc. Nat. Cancer Inst., NIH, Bethesda, Md., 1964-66; resident in medicine Georgetown U. Hosp., Washington, 1966-67, USPHS spl. fellow in hematology, 1967-68; physician Foxhall Internists, Washington, 1978—; clin. prof. medicine Georgetown U. Hosp., Washington, 1968—; vice chmn. dept. medicine Sibley Hosp., Washington, 1987-90, chmn., 1990-91; mem. emeritus staff Washington Hosp. Ctr., 1988—. Contbr. articles to profl. jours. Elder Bradley Hills Presbyn. Ch., Bethesda, 1974-77; mem. prof. edn. com. Am. Cancer Soc., D.C. chpt., 1978-79; chmn. bd. Blue Cross Blue Shield Nat. Capital area, Washington, 1986-94, Group Hospitalization Med. Svcs., Inc., Washington, 1986-94. Lt. comdr. USPHS, 1964-66. Recipient 5 Yr. Svc. award Am. Cancer Soc., 1978. Fellow ACP; mem. Am. Soc. Internal Medicine (pres. rsch. found. 1987-88, pres.-elect 1988-89, pres. 1989-90, speaker ho. of reps. 1991-95, Spl. Recognition award 1979-95), AMA (del. 1988-93, coun. on legislation 1991—, coun. on legislation vice chair 1995-96, chair 1996-97), D.C. Soc. Internal Medicine (pres. 1977), Spltys. and Svcs. Soc. (pres. 1990-91, sect. coun. IM), Coun. Internal Medicine (chmn. sect. 1987-88), Osler Soc. D.C. (pres. 1978-79), Clin. Pathologic Soc. (pres. 1995-96), Congl. Country Club, Bear Creek Club, Alpha OMega Alpha. Sigma Chi. Republican. Presbyterian. Home: 4 Hartman Ct Potomac MD 20854-4252 Office: Foxhall Internists 3301 New Mexico Ave NW Washington DC 20016-3622

DUVIVIER, ROGER, obstetrician, gynecologist; b. Jeremie, Haiti, July 15, 1945; came to U.S., 1964; s. Max Ulrick and Lily (Hilaire) D.; m. Edna Salguero, Apr. 6, 1968; children: Jacqueline, Jean-Paul, Julie-Marie. BS in Biology, St. John's U., Jamaica, N.Y., 1968; postgrad., L.I. U., 1970; MD, Albert Einstein Coll., 1974. Diplomate Am. Bd. Ob-Gyn. Instr. ob-gyn. Albert Einstein Dept. Ob/Gyn., Bronx, N.Y. 1978-79, asst. prof. in ob-gyn., 1979-83, dir. faculty practice, 1979-83; dir. faculty practice Winthrop U. Hosp., Mineola, N.Y., 1984-93, dir. gynecology, 1984-93, dir. ambulatory care, 1984-93; asst. prof. SUNY, Stony Brook, 1984-93; assoc. prof. AECOM, 1994—, dir. med. student edn. in ob/gyn., 1996; dir. gyn. Wyckoff Heights Med. Ctr., 1994-96; dir. gyn. and faculty practice Montefiore Med. Ctr., Bronx, N.Y., 1996—. Author: (with others) Infertility Surgery of Dr. Stangle, 1991; contbr. articles to profl. jours. Physician dir. Choice Care L.I., 1987-88; mem. Spl. Olympics, Bronx, 1983-84; bd. dirs. alumni bd. govs. Albert Einstein U., 1983—. Fellow Am. Coll. Ob-Gyn., Assn. of Profs. of Ob-Gyn., N.Y. Acad. of Medicine, N.Y. Acad. Scis., N.Y. Obstet. Soc.; mem. AMA (Physician Recognition 1986, 88, 90, 92, 94, 96), Am. Assn. of Gyn. Laparoscopists, Am. Fertility Soc., Am. Registry of Diagnostic Med. Sonographers. Office: Montefiore Med Ctr 111 E 210th St Bronx NY 10467

DUWELIUS, PAUL JUDE, orthopaedic surgeon; b. Des Moines, Mar. 25, 1955; s. Donald R. and Marilyn (Broderick) D.; m. Sarah E. Duwelius, June 7, 1987; children: Maureen, Connor, Margaret-Francis. Student, Notre Dame, 1973-75; BS, Creighton Coll., 1975-77, MD, 1979-82; FACS, ABOS, AAOS, U. Nebr., 1983-87. Resident in orthopaedics U. Nebr. (Omaha), 1983-87; fellow in orthopaedics U. Calif., Davis Sacramento, Calif., 1987-88; orthopaedic attending surgeon and assoc. prof. Oreg. Health Scis. Ctr., Portland, Oreg., 1988—. Contbr. articles to prof. jours. Volunteer inner city renewal projects, Christmas in Apr., Portland, 1989-94. Grantee Orthopedic Rsch. and Edn. Found., 1993, 95, Assn. for Osteosynthesis Internat. Fellow ACS, Am. Acad. Orthopedic Surgeons (bd. dirs.); mem. We. Orthopedic Assn. (bd. dirs. 1993), North Pacific Orthopedic Soc., Am. Assn. Hip and Knee Surgeons (bd. dirs.), Orthopedic Trauma Assn. (bd. dirs.), Notre Dame Club. Office: OHSC Orthopaedic Frac Clin Assoc Prof Orthopaedics 9155 SW Barnes Rd Ste 202 Portland OR 97225

DUXBURY, MITZI L., nursing educator. BS, U. Wis., 1966, MA, 1970, PhD, 1972. Staff nurse Victory Meml. Hosp., 1952, U.S. Army Hosp., 1953; head nurse non-acute med. unit War Meml. Hosp., 1953-54; staff nurse obstetrics D.C. Gen. Hosp., Washington, 1956-59; office nurse Fox Lake Med. Clinic, 1960, vol. office nurse, 1962-63; staff nurse Madison (Wis.) Gen. Hosp., 1963-64; instr. nursing Madison (Wis.) Area Tech. Coll., 1964; asst. prof., chmn. dept. maternal and child health nursing U. Wis., Oshkosh, 1971-72; asst. prof. nursing obstetrics U. Wis., Madison, 1972-73, prof. Sch. Nursing, 1989—; from assoc. prof. to prof. Sch. Nursing, U. Minn., Mpls., 1977-83, dir. grad. studies, 1977-78, asst. dean grad. studies, 1977-81, from assoc. prof. to prof. Sch. Pub. Health, 1979-83; dean Coll. Nursing, head dept. nursing sci., prof. maternal child nursing U. Ill., 1983-88, prof. health resources mgmt. Sch. Pub. Health, 1988-89; dir. clin. nurse scholar program Robert Wood Johnson Found., 1982-85; expert adv. panel nursing WHO, 1987-91; guest lectr. U. Minn., 1982-83, U. Ill., Chgo., 1984, 87-88; exch. sci. NAS, Poland, 1987; vis. prof. Sch. Nursing U. Wis., Madison, 1988-89; cons. J. L. Kellogg Grad. Sch. Mgmt. Northwestern U., Chgo., 1988, Rutgers U., New Brunswick, N.J., 1988. Contbr. articles to profl. jours. Rsch. grantee Nat. Found.-March of Dimes, 1977-80, 82, Dept. Health and Human Svcs., Health Svc. Adminstrn, Bur. Cmty. Health Svc., 1979-82, NIH, 1931-82, U. Minn. Computer Ctr., 1982-83, Robert Wood Johnson Found., 1982-84. Fellow Am. Acad. Nursing; mem. AAAS, APHA, NAS, ANA, Am. Soc. Law and Medicine, Am. Assn. Coll. Nursing, Soc. Behavior Medicine, N.Y. Acad. Sci. Office: U Wis Sch Nursing 600 Highland Ave Madison WI 53792*

DUZAN, FOSTER ALLEN, physician assistant; b. Paris, Ill., June 20, 1952; s. Robert Allan Duzan and Oma Jewell (Campbell) McCrocklin; m. Beth Ann Williamson, Jan. 24, 1987; children: Isaiah Bryan, Elisha William. AS, Danville (Ill.) C.C., 1976; BS in Biochemistry, U. Ariz., 1984, M in Sci. Clin. Pharmacy, 1988; B in Med. Sci., Alderson Broaddus Coll., 1987. Cert. physician asst. Commd. med. officer CIA, Nairobi, Kenya, 1990-93; physician asst. ER, ICU Sedan (Kans.) City Hosp., 1993-94; physician asst. rural health South Tex. Rural Health, Carrize Springs, 1994-95. Abilene (Tex.) Regional Med. Ctr., 1995—; clin. preceptor Baylor Coll. Medicine, Houston, 1995, Southwest Tex. Coll. Medicine, Dallas, 1996. Lt. USN/USPHS, 1988-90. Recipient Extreme Hazardous Duty award U.S. Dept. Justice, 1989, Isolation Duty award USPHS 1990, Purple Heart USN, 1993. Fellow Am. Assn. Physician Assts., Mil. Officers Assn. Republican. Office: Cisco Med Clinic PO Box 764 1621 Hwy 80 W Cisco TX 76437

DVORAK, ALLEN DALE, radiologist; b. Dodge, Nebr., Mar. 13, 1943; s. Rudolph Charles and Mildred B. (Misek) D.; m. Carol Ann Cockson, July 22, 1967; children: Kristin Ann, Andrea Marie, Ryan Allen. Grad., Creighton Coll. Arts and Scis., Omaha, Nebr., 1961-64; MD, Creighton Sch. Medicine, Omaha, Nebr., 1969. Intern Creighton Meml. St. Joseph Hosp., Omaha, 1969-70; resident Ind. U. Med. Ctr., Indpls., 1970-73; asst. prof. radiology Creighton U. Sch. Medicine, Omaha, 1973-83; diagnostic radiologist Nebr.-Iowa Radiology Cons., Papillion, Nebr., 1983—; staff radiologist Midlands Cmty. Hosp., Papillion, 1983—; mem. Nebr. State Bd. Health, 1995—, med. staff exec. bd., 1996-99. Author: (chpt.) Ultrasound, 1981; contbr. articles to profl. jours. Chmn. Midlands Area Health Adv. coun., State of Nebr., 1982-86; trustee Duchesne Acad., 1988-91, Boys Town Nat. Coun. Friends, 1989—; bd. dirs. Safety and health Coun. of Greater Omaha, 1990-91; mem. Gov.'s Blue Ribbon Coalition to Study Health Care in Nebr., 1991—; mem. Creighton Med. Sch. Alumni Adv. Bd., 1993—. Fellow Am Coll. Radiology; mem. AMA (alt. del. 1992—), Nebr. Radiol. Soc. (pres. 1980-81), Omaha Midwest Clin. Soc. (pres. 1982), Nebr. Assn. Nuclear Physicians (pres. 1976-78, del. 1984—), Met. Omaha Med. Soc. (exec. com. 1980—, pres. 1990), Nebr. Med. Assn. (del. 1986—, pres. elect 1996-97), Regency Lake and Tennis Club (bd. dirs. 1981-85, chmn. bd. 1983-85), Happy Hollow Country Club. Home: 9733 Brentwood Rd Omaha NE 68114-4970 Office: Nebr-Iowa Radiology Cons 401 E Gold Coast Rd Ste 102 Papillion NE 68128-4746

DVORAK, ANN MARIE TOMPKINS, pediatrician, pathologist, educator; b. Bangor, Maine, May 19, 1938; d. Lawrence Elwood and Laura Pauline (Sibley) Tompkins; m. Harold Fisher Dvorak, June 13, 1963; children: John Tompkins, Laura Ann Fisher, Jane Marie. BA, U. Maine, 1959; MD, U. Vt., 1963. Diplomate Am. Bd. Pediatrics, Am. Bd. Pathology. Resident pediatrics Boston Floating Hosp., 1963-65; pediatric pathology resident Children's Hosp., Washington, 1965-66; resident pathology Georgetown U. Hosp., Washington, 1966-67; resident pathology Peter Bent Brigham Hosp., Boston, 1967-69; postdoctoral fellow Harvard Med. Sch., Boston, 1969-71, asst. prof. pathology, assoc. prof. Tufts U. Sch. Medicine, Boston, 1971-75; assoc. prof. pathology Harvard Med. Sch., 1975-91, prof. pathology, 1991—; assoc. pathologist Mass. Gen. Hosp., Boston, 1975-79; pathologist Beth Israel Hosp., 1979-85, sr. pathologist, 1985—, head electron microscopy lab., 1979—; head electron microscopy lab Mass. Gen. Hosp., 1975-79, Contbr. articles to profl. jours. Fellow Am. Acad. Pediatrics; mem. Am. Assn. Immunologists, Am. Soc. Cell Biologists, Am. Assn. Pathologists, Collegium Internat. Allergologicum. Home: 27 Mason Rd Newton MA 02159-1505

DVORAK, CLARENCE ALLEN, microbiologist; b. Cedar Rapids, Iowa, July 6, 1942; s. Clarence Louis and Lily Ann (Duda) D. BS, Iowa State U., 1969. Microbiologist Penford Products Co., Cedar Rapids, 1969—, analytical chemist, 1970-81, sci. photographer. Mem. AAAS, TAPPI, Am. Soc. Microbiology, Soc. Indsl. Microbiology. Home: 1231 Sierra Dr NE Apt 10 Cedar Rapids IA 52402-6541

DVORAK, HAROLD F., pathologist, educator, scientist; b. Milw., June 20, 1937; s. Harold J. and Laura (Fisher) D.; m. Ann Marie Tompkins, June 13, 1962; children: John, Laura, Jane. AB, Princeton U., 1958; MD, Harvard U., 1963. Diplomate: Am. Bd. Pathology. Practice medicine specializing in pathology Boston; asst. prof. pathology Harvard Med. Sch., Boston, assoc. prof., prof., Mallinckrodt prof. pathology, 1979—; mem. staff Mass. Gen. Hosp., asst. pathologist, 1969-75, assoc. pathologist, 1975-78, head immunopathology unit, 1976-80; chief dept. pathology Beth Israel Hosp., Boston, 1979—; mem. study sect. pathology B NIH, 1978-82, Am. Cancer Soc., N.Y.C., 1982-86; chmn. merit rev. bd. immunology VA, Washington, 1982-84. Served to lt. comdr. USPHS, 1965-67. Mem. Am. Assn. Pathologists, Am. Assn. Immunologists, Am. Soc. Investigative Pathologists (v.p. 1996), Internat. Acad. Pathology, Pluto Club, Collegium Internat. Allergologicum, Phi Beta Kappa, Sigma Xi, Alpha Omega Alpha. Office: Beth Israel Hosp 330 Brookline Ave Boston MA 02215-5400

DVORAK, JOSEF CERMIN, endocrinologist; b. Prague, Czechoslovakia, July 20, 1945; came to U.S., 1969; s. Josef and Milena (Frankova) Dvorak; m. Vera Cermin, Sept. 26, 1970; children: Marek, Andrea. MD, Charles U., 1969. Intern Med. Coll. Va., 1970-71; resident U. Okla., 1971-74; rsch. fellow U. Pa., 1974-76; clin. asst. prof. medicine Georgetown U., 1977—; cons. in endocrinology and metabolism, Arlington, Va. Office: Ste 350 1635 N George Mason Dr Arlington VA 22205-3601

DVORAK, ROGER GRAN, health facility executive; b. St. Paul, Aug. 30, 1934; s. William Anthony and Evelyn Carolyn (Gran) D.; m. Gail Ann Peterson, Dec. 30, 1960; children: Karen, Mark. BBA, U. Minn., 1955, MHA, 1957. Asst. adminstr. Glenwood Hills Hosp., Mpls., 1958-61; asst. hosp. adminstrv. svcs. dir. Phila. Gen. Hosp., 1961-65; asst. dir. Presbyn. U. Pa. Med. Ctr., Phila., 1965-67, assoc. dir., 1967-72; adminstr. Symmes Hosp., Arlington, Mass., 1972-78; exec. dir. Lawrence Hosp., Bronxville, N.Y., 1978-86, pres., 1986—; Bd. dirs. Hosp. Underwriters Mutual, Latham, N.Y., No. Met. Hosp. Assn., Newburgh, N.Y., Hosp. Assn. N.Y. State, Albany; mem. bd. advisors Habitat for Humanity Northeast. 1st Lt. Med. Svcs. Corp., 1957-66. Fellow Am. Coll. Healthcare Execs. Presbyterian. Home: 11 Rolling Ridge Rd White Plains NY 10605 Office: Lawrence Hospital 55 Palmer Ave Bronxville NY 10708-3403

DVORKIN, RONALD ALAN, emergency physician; b. N.Y.C., May 1, 1945. BS in Chemistry, U. Rochester, 1966; MD, SUNY, Syracuse, 1970. Assoc. dir., dept. emergency medicine Lawrence Hosp., Bronxville, N.Y., 1982-87; assoc. dir., dept. emergency City Hosp. Ctr., Elmhurst, N.Y., 1987-88; chmn., dept. emergency svcs. St. John's Episcopal Hosp., Smithtown, N.Y., 1988—; asst. prof. medicine Mt. Sinai Sch. Medicine, 1988; asst. clin. prof. emergency medicine, SUNY, Stony Brook, 1990. Fellow Am. Coll. Emergency Physicians; mem. N.Y. Acad. Scis., Soc. for Acad. Emergency Medicine. Office: St John's Episcopal Hosp Rte 25A Smithtown NY 11787

DWORETZKY, MURRAY, physician, educator; b. N.Y.C., Aug. 18, 1917; s. Samuel and Frieda (Newhoff) D.; m. Barbara Ratner, June 11, 1943; children: Thomas Alan, Joan Mara. B.A., U. Pa., 1938; M.D., SUNY, Coll. Medicine, N.Y.C., 1942; M.S. in Medicine, U. Minn., 1950. Diplomate: Am. Bd. Internal Medicine (examiner allergy subbd. 1967-71), Am. Bd. Allergy and Immunology (founding mem., dir. 1971-74), Pan Am. Med. Assn. Intern City Hosp., N.Y.C., 1942-43; asst. resident pathology City Hosp., 1943, fellow in pathology, 1946-47; resident pathology U. Chgo., 1947-48; fellow in medicine Mayo Found., Rochester, Minn., 1948-50; practice medicine, specializing in internal medicine, allergy and clin. immunology N.Y.C., 1951—; asst. physician N.Y. Hosp., 1951, physician, 1951-56, asst. attending physician 1956-61, assoc. attending, 1961-66, attending physician, 1966—, physician-in-charge Allergy Clinic, 1961-88; asst. in medicine Cornell U. Med. Coll., 1951-52, instr. medicine, 1952-56, clin. asst. prof., 1956-61, clin. asst. prof. pub. health, 1957-62, clin. assoc. prof. medicine, 1961-66, dir. tng. program div. allergy and immunology, 1961-88, clin. prof. medicine, 1966—; attending physician Manhattan Eye, Ear and Throat Hosp., 1953-62; Med. dir.-at-large Asthma-Allergy Found. Am., 1963-64, bd. dirs., 1964-78, mem. exec. com., 1964-77; founding mem. bd. dirs. Am. Bd. Allergy and Immunology, 1971-74; examiner sub-bd. allergy Am. Bd. Internal Medicine, 1967-71. Contbr. articles to profl. jours. Served to capt., M.C. AUS, 1943-46. Recipient Frank L. Babbott M.D. Meml. award Alumni Assn. Coll. Med. SUNY, 1992. Fellow Am. Acad. Allergy and Immunology (past pres. 1968; Disting. Service award 1989), N.Y. Acad. Medicine, ACP; mem. N.Y. County Med. Soc., N.Y. Allergy Soc. (past pres., exec. com. 1958-94), Soc. Exptl. Biology and Medicine, Harvey Soc., Am. Fedn. Clin. Research, AMA (chmn. allergy sect. council 1974-77, mem. residency rev. com. for allergy and immunology 1980-85), Am. Assn. Immunologists, Sigma Xi. Home: 21 E 87th St New York NY 10128-0506 Office: 115 E 61st St New York NY 10021-8172

DWORKIN, HOWARD JERRY, nuclear physician, educator; b. Bklyn., Oct. 29, 1932; s. Joseph Henry and Mollie M. (Hodas) D.; m. Gina Gora; children: Rhonda Fran, Steven Irving, Paul J. BSChemE, Worcester Poly. Inst., 1955; MD, Albany Med. Coll., 1959; MS in Radiation Biology, U. Mich., 1965. Diplomate Am. Bd. Internal Medicine, Am. Bd. Nuclear Medicine. Intern Albany Hosp., N.Y., 1959-60; resident Rochester Gen. Hosp., N.Y., 1960-62; resident U. Mich. Hosps., 1962-65, asst. coord. nuclear medicine unit, 1963-66, instr., 1965-66; asst. prof. medicine U. Toronto, Ont., Can., 1966, assoc. prof., 1967; head dept. nuclear medicine Princess Margaret Hosp., Toronto, 1967; head nuclear medicine sect., radiology Nat. Naval Med. Ctr., Bethesda, Md., 1967-69; dir. sch. nuclear medicine tech. William Beaumont Hosp., Royal Oak, Mich., 1969—, chief dept. nuclear medicine, 1969—, dir. nuclear medicine resident tng. program, 1970—, chmn. CME com., 1993—; clin. asst. prof. dept. medicine Wayne State U. Med. Sch., Detroit, 1970—; asst. clin. prof. dept. radiology Mich. State U., East Lansing, 1976—; clin. prof. med. physics Ctr. for Health Scis., Oakland U., Rochester, Mich., 1977—; mem. Am. Bd. Nuclear Medicine, 1979—, treas., 1982-84. Author: (with N. Aspin and R.G. Baker) Clinical Use of Isotopes in the Physics of Radiology, 1969, Part Two, Clinical Prodedures in Radioisotope Laboratory Procedures, 1969; contbr. articles and chpts. to med. jours. and texts; patentee radioactive labeled protein material process and apparatus. Served with USN, 1967-69. Fellow ACP; mem. AMA, ACCME, Soc. Nuclear Medicine (trustee 1973-81, v.p. 1982, pres. 1986-87), Am. Fedn. Clin. Rsch., Am. Thyroid Assn., Endocrine Soc., Am. Coll. Nuclear Physicians (sec. 1974-75, pres. 1978-79). Office: William Beaumont Hosp Dept Nuclear Medicine Royal Oak MI 48073

DWORKIN, MARTIN, microbiologist, educator; b. N.Y.C., Dec. 3, 1927; s. Hyman Bernard and Pauline (Herstein) D.; m. Nomi Rees Buda, Feb. 2, 1957; children—Jessica Sarah, Hanna Beth. B.A., Ind. U., 1951; Ph.D. (NSF predoctoral fellow), U. Tex., Austin, 1955. NIH research fellow U. Calif., Berkeley, 1955-57; vis. prof. U. Calif., summers 1958-60; asst. prof. microbiology Ind. U. Med. Sch., 1957-61, assoc. prof., 1961-62; assoc. prof. U. Minn., 1962-69, dir. MD/PhD tng. program, 1990—, prof., 1969—; vis. prof. U. Wash., summer 1965, Stanford U., 1978-79; vis. scholar Oxford (Eng.) U., 1970-71; Found. for Microbiology lectr., 1973-74, 76-77, 81-82; Sackler scholar Tel Aviv U., 1992. Author: Developmental Biology of the Bacteria, 1985, Microbial Cell-Cell Interactions, 1991; contbr. numerous articles, revs. to profl. publs.; mem. editorial bd. Jour. Bacteriology, 1967-74, 86-88, Ann. Revs. Microbiology, 1975-79, The Prokaryotes, 2d edit. Alt. del. Democratic Nat. Conv., 1968; mem. Minn. Dem. Farm Labor Central Com., 1969-70. Served with U.S. Army, 1946-48. Recipient Career Devel. award NIH, 1963-68, 68-73; John Simon Guggenheim fellow, 1978-79. Mem. Am. Soc. Microbiology (vice chmn. div. gen. microbiology 1977-78, chmn. 1978-79, div. councillor 1980-82), Soc. Gen. Microbiology (Eng.). Home: 2123 Hoyt Ave W Saint Paul MN 55108-1314 Office: U Minn Dept Microbiology Minneapolis MN 55455

DWYER, DENNIS MICHAEL, microbiologist, consultant, educator; b. Passaic, N.J., Feb. 26, 1945; s. Alexander James and Julia (Sinkovitz) D.; m. Nancy Kinerson, Dec. 28, 1969; children—Jeffrey Scott, Matthew James. B.A. in Biology, Montclair State Coll., 1967; M.S. in Zoology, U. Mass., 1970, Ph.D. in Zoology, 1971. Postdoctoral fellow Rockefeller U., N.Y.C., 1971-73, asst. prof., 1973-76, adj. assoc. prof., 1976-81; research microbiologist lab. parasitic diseases Nat. Inst. Allergy and Infectious Diseases, NIH, Bethesda, Md., 1976-80, supr. microbiology, 1980-94, head cell Biology Scet. Lab. of Parasitic Disease Nat. Inst. Allergy and Infectious Diseases, 1994—; adj. assoc. prof. U. Mass., Amherst, 1978—; cons. WHO, Geneva, 1982—; sci. reviewer jours., books, grants, 1980—. Editorial bd. Jour. Protozoology, 1978-93, Infection and Immunity, 1981-88, Exptl. Parasitology, 1984—, J. Eukaryotic Microbiology, 1993—, Tropical Medicine Abstracts, 1990—. Contbr. numerous articles, chpts. to profl. publs., 1970—. Active PTA, Rockville, Md., 1980—, leader, Cub Scouts, Rockville, 1984-91, Boy Scouts Am., 1987—. Recipient Alumni Citation award Montclair State Coll., 1983, Dir.'s award NIH, 1987. Mem. Soc. Protozoologists, Am. Soc. Parasitologists, (Henry Baldwin Ward medal 1980); Am. Soc. Cell Biologists, Am. Soc. Tropical Medicine and Hygiene, AAAS, N.Y. Acad. Scis., Phi Kappa Phi. Democrat. Methodist. Avocations: down hill skiing; camping; fishing; hiking; jogging. Home: 13416 Bartlett St Rockville MD 20853-2938 Office: Nat Inst Allergy and Infectious Diseases Lab Parasitic Diseases Bldg 4 Rm 126 NIH Bethesda MD 20892-0425

DWYER, TERRENCE EDWARD, health association executive; b. Ft. Wayne, Ind., June 6, 1945; s. Michael Kenneth and Maxine Marie (Berkhimer) D.; A.B., Harvard U., 1967; M.P.A., U. Mich., 1968. Teaching fellow in polit. sci. U. Mich., 1968-72, research assoc. Sch. Public Health, 1973-74; research assoc. Pres.'s Adv. Council. on Exec. Orgn., White House, 1969-70; lectr. in polit. sci. Eastern Mich. U., 1972-73; assoc. dir. Mich. Profl. Standards Rev. Orgn. Support Center, East Lansing, Mich., 1974-76; exec. dir. Empire State Peer Rev. Orgn., Inc. (formerly Profl. Standards Rev. Orgn. Central N.Y.), Syracuse, 1976-87; exec. dir. Va. Health Quality Ctr., Richmond, 1987—; bd. dirs. Am. Med. Rev. Research Ctr., 1985-92, sec., mem. exec. com., 1985-86; bd. dirs. Am. HealthWatch, 1991-95, v.p., 1991-95. Mem. Am. Med. Peer Rev. Assn. (bd. dir., chmn. chief exec. officers sect. 1982-85), Am. Public Health Assn., Am. Soc. Public Adminstrn., Am. Polit. Sci. Assn., Am. Acad. Polit. and Social Scis., Acad. Polit. Sci. Republican. Clubs: Harvard of Va., Downtown of Richmond.

DYAR, STEPHEN CRAIG, pharmacist, pharmaceutical researcher; b. Abbeville, S.C., Oct. 5, 1961; s. Bobby Ray and Bobbie Jean (Brezeale) D.; m. Theresa Ann Warta, Nov. 26, 1984; children: Christina, William. BS in Biology, U. S.C., 1984; BS in Pharmacy, Med. U. S.C., 1987, postgrad. in Pharm. Scis., 1994—. Lic. pharmacist, S.C. Asst. to chmn. dept. pharm. scis. Med. U. S.C., Charleston, 1984-87; pharmacist-in-charge Revco, North Charleston, S.C., 1987-93; pharmacy mgr. Winn Dixie, Summerville, S.C., 1993-94. Fellow Am. Found. for Pharm. Edn.; mem. Am. Pharm. Assn., S.C. Pharm. Assn., Kappa Psi. Republican. Baptist. Home: 102 Pelican Ln Summerville SC 29485-6314 Office: Med Univ South Carolina 171 Ashley Ave Charleston SC 29407

DYAS, CHARLES LOUIS, plastic and reconstructive surgeon; b. Mobile, Ala., Aug. 23, 1949; s. Charles Louis and Olympia (Corte) D.; m. Joyce Click; children: Julie, Michael, Chez, Luke. BS, U. Ala., Tuscaloosa, 1971; MD, U. Ala., Birmingham, 1974. Diplomate Am. Bd. Plastic Surgery, Nat. Bd. Med. Examiners. Intern and resident Bapt. Med. Ctr., Birmingham, 1974-77; resident Med. Coll. Ohio, Toledo, 1977-79; fellow in hand surgery St. Vincent's Hosp. Med. Ctr., Toledo, 1979-80; pvt. practice Bay Area Plastic surgery Assocs., P.C., Mobile, Ala., 1980—; clin. instr. surgery Med. Coll. Ohio, Toledo, 1978-79, clin. assoc. faculty, 1979-80; clin. asst. prof. surgery U. South Ala., Mobile, 1980—; adv. bd. Mutual Assurance of Ala., Birmingham, 1989—. Mem. Ala. Soc. Plastic and Reconstructive surgery (pres. 1989). Office: Bay Area Plastic Surg Assoc 2860 A Dauphin St Mobile AL 36606

DYBELL, ELIZABETH ANNE SLEDDEN, clinical psychologist; b. Buffalo, Sept. 25, 1958; d. Richard Edward and Angela Brigid (Scimone) Sledden; m. David Joseph Dybell, Nov. 30, 1985. BA in Psychology summa cum laude, U. St. Thomas, Houston, 1980; PhD in Psychology, Tex. Tech. U., 1986. Lic. clinical psychologist, Tex. Rsch. asst. health sci. ctr. Tex. Tech. U., Lubbock, 1983-84, psychol. cons. health sci. ctr. neurology dept., 1982-84; psychology intern U. N.Mex. Med. Sch., Albuquerque, 1984-85; psychotherapist Katz & Assocs. P.C., Houston, 1985-88, Meyer Ctr. for Devel. Pediatrics Tex. Children's Hosp., Houston, 1988-92; pvt. practice Houston, 1990—. Author: (monograph) When Will Life Be Normal?, 1989; contbr. articles to numerous publs. choir mem. St. Thomas More Ch., Houston, 1974-87. Mem. Am. Psychol. Assn., Assn. for the Care of Childrens Health, Nat. Ctr. Clin. Infant Programs, Soc. Pediatric Psychology, Southwestern Psychol. Assn., Tex. Psychol. Assn., Houston Psychol. Assn., Am. Psychol. Soc. (charter). Roman Catholic. Office: 6001 Savoy Dr Ste 208 Houston TX 77036-3322

DYBKAER, RENÉ, clinical laboratory administrator; b. Copenhagen, Feb. 7, 1926; s. Ove and Kirsten Johanne (Nielsen) D.; m. Nanna Gjoel. MD, U. Copenhagen, 1951. Cert. specialist in clin. chemistry. Intern Sundby Hosp., Copenhagen, 1951-52, resident, 1952-54, 55; resident De Gamles By, Copenhagen, 1954-55, Frederiksberg Hosp., Copenhagen, 1955; reader Univ. Inst. Med. Microbiology, Copenhagen, 1959-70; head dept. med. microbiology Royal Dental Sch., Copenhagen, 1959-70; head dept. clin. chemistry De Gamles By, Noerre Hosp., Copenhagen, 1970-77, Frederiksberg Hosp., Copenhagen, 1977-96; cons. De Gamles By, Noerre Hosp., Copenhagen, 1959-69; mem. expert adv. panel Health Lab. Svc. WHO, 1992—. Author: Quantities and Units, 1967; editor: Good Practice in Decentralized Analytical Clinical Measurement, 1992, Continuous Quality Improvement in Clinical Laboratories--Guide for Latinamerica, 1994; contbr. numerous articles to profl. jours. Recipient award Commemorative Lecture Enrique Concustell Bas, 1988. Mem. Internat. Fedn. Clin. Chemistry (v.p. 1973-78, pres. 1979-84,past Pres. 85-90, Henry Wishinsky Disting. Internat. Svc. award 1993), European Community Bur. Ref. (chmn. cert. com. 1983-94), European Coun. Clin. Lab. Standardization (chmn. stand. act. com. good pract. decentr. clin. lab. 1984-92), European Confed. Lab. Med. (pres. 1994—), Nordkem (chmn. standardization lab. medicine 1992-94), Danish Soc. Clin. Chemistry (hon., chmn. 1991-93), Columbian Fedn. Clin. Lab. Specialists (hon.), Mex. Assn. Clin. Biochemistry (hon.), Austrian Soc. Clin. Chemistry (hon.), Israel Soc. Clin. Biochemistry (hon.), German Soc. Lab. Medicine (corr.), Italian Soc. Clin. Biochemistry (hon.). Office: Frederiksberg Hosp, Dep Clin Chem, Nordre Fasanvej 57, DK 2000 Frederiksberg Denmark

DYCK, GEORGE, psychiatry educator; b. Hague, Sask., Can., July 25, 1937; came to U.S., 1965; s. John and Mary (Janzen) D.; m. Edna Margaret Krueger, June 27, 1959; children: Brian Edward, Janine Louise, Stanley George, Jonathan Jay. Student, U. Sask., 1955-56; B. Christian Edn., Can. Mennonite Bible Coll., 1959; M.D., U. Man., 1964; postgrad., Menninger Sch. Psychiatry, 1965-68. Diplomate Am. Bd. Psychiatry and Neurology (added qualifications in geriatric psychiatry); cert. psychiatrist, Royal Coll. Physicians and Surgeons, Can. Fellow community psychiatry Prairie View Mental Health Center, Newton, Kans., 1968-70; clin. dir. tri-county services Prairie View Mental Health Center, 1970-73; prof. U. Kans., Wichita, 1973—; chmn. dept. psychiatry U. Kans., 1973-80; med. dir. Prairie View, Inc., 1980-89; dir. geriatric psychiatry U. Kans., 1993—; cons. Shenyang Psychiat. Hosp., People's Republic of China, 1990, Palestinian Mental Health Program, West Bank, 1990; mem. Kans. Hosp. Closure Commn., 1995. Bd. dirs. Mennonite Mut. Aid, Goshen, Ind., 1973-85, Chmn., 1982-85; bd. dirs. Mid-Kans. Community Action Program, 1970-73, Wichita Council Drug Abuse, 1974-76. Fellow Am. Psychiat. Assn. (pres. Kans. chpt. 1982-84, dep. rep. 1984-86, rep. 1986—, cert. in adminstrv. psychiatry 1984); mem. AMA, Kans. Med. Soc., Kans.-Paraquay Ptnrs. (treas. 1986-89). Mennonite. Home: 1505 Hillcrest Rd Newton KS 67114-1340 Office: U Kans Sch Medicine Wichita Dept Psychiatry 1010 N Kansas St Wichita KS 67214-3124

DYE, DAVID ALAN, industrial psychologist; b. Sharon, Pa., Dec. 28, 1956; s. James E. and Jane (Richmond) D.; m. Mary Jane De Sonia, Jan. 12, 1985; children: Katherine, Carol. BS, Bowling Green State U., 1979; MPhil, George Washington U., 1986, PhD, 1991. Mgmt. cons. Psychol. Svcs., Inc., L.A. and Washington, 1979-86; pers. rsch. psychologist U.S. Office of Pers. Mgmt., Washington, 1986—; cons. in field; faculty George Washington U., George Mason U., Am. U., all Washington, 1988—. Editorial bd.: Test Validity Yearbook, 1989; author: Biodata Handbook, 1991. Recipient Dirs. award U.S. Office Pers. Mgmt., 1990-93. Mem. APA, Soc. for Indsl. and Orgnl. Psychology (sci. affairs com. 1989-91), Internat. Pers. Mgmt. Assn. (bd. dirs. 1994—), Pers. Testing Coun. of Metro Washington (pres. 1985-86). Home: 9123 Lakeland Valley Ct Springfield VA 22153-4103 Office: US Office of Pers Mgmt 1900 E St NW Washington DC 20415-0001

DYE, FRANK JOHN, biology educator; b. Bronx, N.Y., Jan. 12, 1942; s. John Lester D. and Lucia Concetta (Del Pozzo) D.; m. Kathleen Susan Mauks, Aug. 5, 1967; children: John, Kathleen. B.S., Western Conn. State U., 1963; M.S., Fordham U., 1966, Ph.D., 1969. Prof. biology Western Conn. State U., Danbury, 1967—; Mellon vis. faculty fellow Yale U., New Haven, 1979-80, vis. fellow, 1981-87, 90-92. Fellow NIH, 1965-67, Nat. Inst. Dental Research, 1975-76; grantee Conn. State U., 1985-88, 91—, student-faculty collaborative grantee, 1990-91, 92—, Elias Howe Yankee ingenuity initiative high tech. grantee, 1990-91, 92-93, NSF, 1993—. Mem. Am. Soc. for Cell Biology, Soc. for Devel. Biology, Tissue Culture Assn., N.Y. Acad. Scis., Sigma Xi. Avocations: wildlife photography; bicycling; hiking; collecting amphibians. Office: Western Conn State U 181 White St Danbury CT 06810-6845

DYE, MICHAEL EDWARD, pharmacist; b. Bluefield, W.Va., Apr. 9, 1954; s. Lawrence Edward and Haseltine Mae (Barger) D.; m. Kim Marie Turner, Mar. 10, 1979; children: Emily Kathleen, Amelia Michelle. AS, Bluefield Coll., 1974; BS in Pharmacy, Med. Coll. Va., 1977. Lic. pharmacist, Va.; cert. firearms instr. Pharmacist in charge, co-owner New Graham Pharmacy, Bluefield, 1978—; clin. instr., preceptor Sch. Pharmacy Med. Coll. Va.; primary pharm. care provider for hospice care. Cons. speaker various sr. citizens housing projects, Bluefield and Pocahontas, Va., 1978—, Outstanding Young Men of Am., 1983; pres. Bluefield Downtown Devel. Corp., 1986-91; sponsor U.S. Shooting Team, 1990-91, 93; career speaker Bluefield Coll., 1991. Mem. NRA (life, benefactor), CCRKBA (life), GOA (life), Va. State Firle and Revolver Assn. (life), Bluefield Bus. and Profl. Assn. Office: New Graham Pharmacy 566 Virginia Ave Bluefield VA 24605-1729

DYE, TERRELL E., physician; b. Villa Rica, Ga., Oct. 27, 1942; s. William H. and Mary (Lane) D.; m. Donna Dye. BA, Kans. State U., 1966; MD, Univ. Kans., 1970. Pvt. practice Cardiovascular Surgery, Clearwater, Fla., 1977-78, Cardiovascular & Thoracic, San Jose, Calif., 1978-95, Cardiothoracic Surgery, Gulfport, Miss., 1996—. Fellow Am. Coll. Surgeons, Am. Coll. Cardiology; mem. Soc. Thoracic Surgeons. Office: 1110 Broad Ave Ste 800 Gulfport MS 39501

DYER, ALICE MILDRED, psychotherapist; b. San Diego, July 4, 1929; d. William Silas Cann and Louise Lair (Addenbrooke) Vaile; divorced; children: Alexis Dyer Guagnano, Bryan, Christine Dyer Morales; m. James Vawter, Dec. 26, 1972. BA, Calif. State U., Fullerton, 1965, MA, 1967; PhD, U.S. Internat. U., 1980. Coord., counselor Brea (Calif.)-Olinda High Sch., 1968-72; sch. psychologist Cypress (Calif.) Sch. Dist., 1972-86; instr. North Orange County Community Coll., Fullerton, 1975-77; pvt. practice ednl. psychology Long Beach and Fountain Valley, Calif., 1978—; pvt. practice marriage and family therapy Fullerton and Brea, Calif., 1979—; psychologist, cons. Multiple Sclerosis Soc. Orange County, 1986-95; facilitator adult mental health La Habra (Calif.) Comty. Hosp., 1988-89. Bd. dirs., officer, pres. Friends of Fullerton Arboretum, 1974-95; pres., bd. dirs. Fullerton Beautiful, 1987-88, Brea Ednl. Found., 1988-89; therapist Orange County Juvenile Connection Project, 1988—. Recipient Appreciation award Gary Ctr., La Habra, 1975, Multiple Sclerosis Soc. Orange County, 1987. Mem. Calif. Assn. Marriage and Family Therapists, Assn. for Children and Adults with Learning Disabilities (cons. 1970—, bd. dirs., facilitator), AAUW, Am. Bus. Women's Assn., Soroptomists (health chmn. Brea chpt. 1987-88). Republican. Unitarian. Office: Brea Mental Health Assocs PO Box 1688 Brea CA 92622-1688

DYER, DORIS ANNE, nurse; b. Washington, Jan. 14, 1944; d. William Edward and Helen Gertrude (Smith) Swain; m. Robert Francis Dyer, Jr., June 27, 1970; children: Robert Francis, William Edward, Anne-Marie Helen Sallie, Scott Robertson McGavin. RN cum laude, Sibley Nursing Sch., Washington, 1964; BS, Am. U., 1966, MEd, 1969. Mem. staff emergency medicine dept. George Washington U. Hosp., 1960-69, emergency specialist protective svcs. clinic, 1967-70, adminstr. asst. to dir. clinic, 1970-78; nurse cons., 1987—. Author: Say Ah, 1971; also articles. Patron Sibley Meml. Hosp. Chapel, 1992. Trinity Coll. scholar, 1960; Lucy Webb Hayes scholar, 1964; recipient Martha Washington award Md. Soc. SAR, 1977, Community Leaders award, 1979, Washington medal, 1984, Disting. Women of Washington award 1987; decorated Comdr. Order of St. Lazarus, 1984, medal of Merit, 1989; created dame Order of Sovereign Mil. Order, 1980, dame comdr., 1992; named Dame Grand Officier, 1992. Mem. Am. Nurses Assn., D.C. Nurses Assns., Am. Acad. Ambulatory Nursing Adminstrs., Washington Med.-Surg. Soc. Aux. (pres.), Am. U. Grads. Assn., DAR, Washington Assembly, Washington Club, Annapolis Yacht Club, Kenwood Golf and Country Club. Address: 5608 Albia Rd Bethesda MD 20816-3303

DYER, MARGARET ELLEN, clinical social worker; b. Waterville, Maine, July 4, 1951; d. Richard Nye and Ethel Fox (Moyer) D.; 1 child, Nathaniel. BA, Wells Coll., 1973; MSW, Smith Coll., 1975. Cert. social worker, N.Y. Grad. intern Berkshire Med. Ctr., Pittsfield, Mass., 1973-74, Med. Coll. U. Colo., Denver, 1974-75; clin. social worker Strafford Guidance Ctr., Dover, N.H., 1975-76; coord. Geriatric Svcs. Steuben County Elmira (N.Y.) Psychiat. Ctr., 1976-78; program supr. Tompkins County Mental Health, Ithaca, N.Y., 1978-81; program dir. outpatient svcs. Willard (N.Y.) Psychiat. Ctr., 1981-88; exec. dir. Suicide Prevention and Crisis Svc., Ithaca, 1988-89; pvt. practice Ithaca, 1989—; social work cons. Tioga County Health Dept., Owego, N.Y., 1989-92; mental health cons. Tompkin's County Mental Health, Ithaca, N.Y., 1989-93. Bd. dirs. S.E. Asian Refugee Com., Ithaca, 1985-87; bd. dirs. Ithaca Rape Crisis, 1986-89; sponsor Refugee Assistance Program, Ithaca, 1985—; com. chair Cayuga Heights Sch. PTA, Ithaca, 1989-90; community mem. HOMES, Ithaca, 1991—. Mem. NASW (qualified clin. social worker), Am. Orthopsychiat. Assn.

DYER, MOLLY ESTES, cardiac care nurse; b. Union City, Tenn., Jan. 10, 1963; d. Fred and Amie (Rinks) Estes; m. Stuart B. Dyer; 1 child, Gregory F. BS in Psychology and Sociology, Bethel Coll., 1985; BSN, U. Tenn., Memphis, 1993. RN, Tenn. Peer counselor psychology dept. Bethel Coll., McKenzie, Tenn., 1984; human svcs. eligibility counselor Dept. Human Svcs., Memphis, 1985-88; rehab. svcs. counselor Dept. Rehab., Memphis, 1988-91, rehab. svcs. supr., 1991-92; RN Bapt. Hosp. East, Memphis, 1993—. Mem. Sigma Theta Tau Internat. Presbyterian.

DYER, NORRIS WILLIAM, radiologist; b. Ft. Worth, Dec. 13, 1936; s. Herschel O'Dell and Mary Alta (Hiett) D.; m. Martha Ruth GAssei, Aug. 8, 1958 (div. Oct. 1982); dec. May 28, 1996; children: Jennifer Elizabeth, Mark Richard, John William, Stephanie Victoria, Susanna Mary; m. Dianne Rochelle Hays, June 6, 1984; stepchildren: Ronald Christopher Thompson. B in Music Edn., U. Tulsa, 1959; MD, U. Okla., 1969. Diplomate Am. Bd. Radiology. Radiologist Radioloy of Eastern Okla., Inc., Tulsa, 1976-82; pvt. practice Tulsa, 1982-87, Wheeling Med. Group, Tulsa, 1987-92, Met. Radiology, Tulsa, 1992—. Lt. comdr. USN, 1969-73. Mem. Tulsa County Med. Soc., Okla. State Med. Assn., AMA, N.E. Okla. Radiol. Soc., Okla. State Radiol. Soc., Am. Coll. Radiology, Radiol. Soc. N.Am. Republican. Home: 6530 E 106th St Tulsa OK 74133-7128 Office: Met Radiology 5215 E 71st Ste 400 Tulsa OK 74136-6345

DYER, ROBERT FRANCIS, JR., internist; b. Washington, Nov. 18, 1926; s. Robert Francis and Sallie Antoinette (Worley) D.; AB, U. Mich., 1951; MD, George Washington U., 1955; cert. Postgrad. Med. Sch. Harvard U., 1958; m. Doris Anne Swain, June 27, 1970; children: Robert Francis, William Edward, Anne-Marie Helen Sallie, Scott Robertson McGavin. Intern, George Washington U. Hosp., 1955-56; resident in medicine D.C. Gen. Hosp., 1956-57, VA Hosp., Washington, 1957-58; chief resident physician George Washington U. Hosp., 1958-59; chief of staff Herndon (Va.) Med. Ctr., 1960-61, U.S. Army Hosp., Ft. Lewes, Del., 1963-65; chief of medicine U.S. Army Hosp., Ft. Indiantown Gap, Pa., 1962-63, dep. comdr., 1964-65; practice medicine specializing in internal medicine, Washington and Chevy Chase, Md., 1965—; chmn. dept. medicine Sibley Hosp., 1986-89, vice-chmn. continuing edn. com., 1987—, dir. continuing edn., 1992—, chmn., 1992—; mem. staffs George Washington U. Hosp., Washington Hosp. Center, Drs. Hosp. (all Washington); dir. Rsch. Lab. on Eosinophil Effect of Heparin, Washington, 1959-71; asst. clin. prof. medicine George Washington U., 1963—; pres. Washington Coll. Occupational Medicine, 1982-84, dean; dir. clin. rsch. Police & Fire Clinic, Washington, 1964—, acting chief of medicine, 1970, clinic adminstr., 1973-75, clinic dir., 1973-80; mem. clin. faculty Georgetown U. Sch. Medicine, 1988—; dep. med. dir. Washington Nat. Airport, 1961; nat. med. dir. Emphysema Control Com., 1967-70; med. cons. bd. ARC, 1985—; med. cons. on Occupational Safety Act and Health Act of 1983, City of Washington; sr. internist med. rev. bd., D.C. Dept. Labor, 1983—; mem. D.C. Mayor's Adv. Bd. on Emergency Med. Svc., 1974-75; bd. dirs. ECG-VCG Corp., 1989; chmn. bd. Protective Svc. Physicians, Washington, 1973-80; lectr. U.S. Park Police Acad., Alexandria, Va., 1964-76, D.C. Fire Tng. Acad., 1964—; chief med. flight surgeon Met. Police, Washington, 1968—, U.S. Park Police Helicopter Corps, 1970—; cons. in medicine D.C. Gen. Hosp., Walter Reed Army Hosp., VA, George Washington U. Hosp. Cardiology Clinic. Bd. dirs. Bd. Police and Fire Surgeons, Washington, 1963-80, sec., 1964-71, chmn., 1973-80; founder, dir. Police and Fire Surgeons Library, 1976—; chmn. bd. dirs. D.C. Bd. Police and Fire Surgeons, 1973-80. With M.C., U.S. Army, 1945-47, to col., 1956-65, Korea. Decorated Knight Order of St. Lazarus, Cross of Merit, Knight of Grand Cross Internat. Order Templare, 1985; recipient E. H. Hill award U. Mich., 1950, Citizenship award Am. Legion, 1954, Osler award George Washington U., 1954; diplomate Nat. Bd. Med. Examiners. Fellow Internat. Coll. Angiology, Am. Coll. Angiology, Am. Geriatrics Soc., Royal Soc. Health, InterAm. Coll. Physicians, Am. Occupational Med. Assn., Am. Acad. Med. Dirs.; mem. AMA (Physician's Recognition award 1986, 90, 93, 94), Am. Coll. Occupl. and Environ. Medicine, Am. Soc. Clin. Rsch., Med. Soc. of Washington (governing bd. internal medicine sect. 1991—, ho. of dels. 1992—), George Washington U. Med. Soc., D.C. Med. Soc. (pres. sect. occupational medicine 1979—, inter-splty. bd. 1975, chmn. state com. on environ. and occupational health 1980—, pres.-elect, med. editor Metro-Intercom 1977-80, com. pub. health 1989), Nat. Capital (dir., exec. sec. 1979-80, v.p. 1980—, pres. occupational medicine sect. 1979—), Am. Soc. Internal Medicine, U.S. Assn. Mil. Surgeons, So. Med. Assn., Pan Am. Med. Soc. (pres. 1981-83), Am. Coll. Occupational and Environ. Medicine, Washington Coll Occupational Medicine (pres. 1982-84, dean 1991-92), Internat. Assn. Fire Chiefs (sec. med. sect. 1973-76), SAR (v.p. chpt. 1974-76, pres. 1976-77, state pres. 1976-78, surgeon gen. 1979—), Descs. Colonial Physicians (gov. gen. 1974—), Sons of Union Vets. (state comdr. 1980-81), Nat. Soc. Sons of Revolution (surgeon gen. 1991—, Disting. Fire Svc. Rsch. medal 1996), Washington Assembly, Am. Assn. Police Physicians and Surgeons (founder 1976), Washington Med. and Surg. 78, pres. 1978-79), Hippocrates-Galen Med. Soc. (chmn. bd. 1976-77), George Washington U. Faculty Club, Soc. Colonial Wars (gov. chpt. 1969-72, mem. resolutions com. 1972—, dep. gov. gen. 1978-81), D.C. Med. Soc. (ho. of dels. 1985—), Am. Legion (comdr. 1984), Sovereign Mil. Order of Temple U.S.A. (nat. pres. 1984-92), Delta Deuteron (pres. 1950), Phi Sigma Kappa (scholarship award 1950), Phi Chi (v,p. 1965, pres. 1977—). Clubs: Army and Navy (pres. Augustus Gardner Post Soc. 1983-84), Univ., Kenwood Golf and Country, George Washington U; Annapolis Yacht; Royal Health (London). Med. editor Met. Intercom Jour., 1973-80; contbr. articles to profl. jours. Home: Westwood 5608 Albia Rd Bethesda MD 20816-3303 Office: 5530 Wisconsin Ave Chevy Chase MD 20815-4404

DYER-COLE, PAULINE, school psychologist, educator; b. Methuen, Mass., Aug. 20, 1935; d. E. Dewey and Rose Alma (Des Jardins) Dyer; m. Richard Grey, Aug. 1, 1964 (dec. 1977); children: Douglas Richard, Christopher Lachlan, Heather Judith; m. Malcolm A. Cole, July 23, 1983. BS in Edn. and Music, Lowell State Coll., 1957; MEd, Boston State Coll., 1961; EdD, Clark U., 1991. Lic. psychologist; cert. sch. and ednl. psychologist. Supr. music and art Merrimac and W. Newburg (Mass.) Pub. Schs., 1957-59; music editor textbooks Allyn & Bacon, Inc., Boston, 1959-64; prof. music West Pines Coll., Chester, N.H., 1969-72; sch. psychologist Nashoba Regional H.S., Bolton, Mass., 1979—, chair SPED dept., 1995—; vis. lectr., then vis. prof. Framingham (Mass.) State Coll., 1980—; dir. psychol. testing Nashoba Regional Sch. Dist., Bolton, Mass., 1980—. Author: The Play Game Songbook, 1964. V.p., bd. dirs. Timberlane Devel. Ctr., Plaistow, N.H., 1970-73; founder Friends of Kimi Nichols Devel. Ctr., Plaistow, 1973; chmn. human svcs. St. Ann Parish, Southborough, Mass., 1974-77, active, 1973—; citizen amb. del. People to People, China, 1995; active The Regional Lab., Andover, Mass., 1993—. Frances L. Hyatt Sch. Psychology & Edn. fellow Clark U., 1977-79. Mem. NASP, Mass. Assn. Sch. Psychologists, Mass. Tchrs. Assn., CASE Sch. Psychologists Assn., People to People Internat. Roman Catholic. Home: 50 Framingham Rd Southborough MA 01772-1206 Office: Nashoba Regional Sch Dist 11 Green Rd Bolton MA 01740-1046

DYESS, STEPHEN JOSEPH, chiropractor; b. Lake Charles, La., May 1, 1952; s. Dalton Douglas and Melba Eugenia (Morrison) D.; m. Nancy Kay Austin, Mar. 10, 1979; children: Julie Stephenie, Lindsey Cynthia. AS in Respiratory Therapy, Houston C.C., 1976; D in Chiropractic, Tex. Chiropractic Coll., 1987. Dir. respiratory therapy Lexington-Henderson County (Tenn.) Hosp., 1978-79, City of Milan (Tenn.) Hosp., 1979-82; respiratory therapist Pasadena (Tex.) Bayshore Med. Ctr., 1982-87; pvt. practice Burke Rd. Chiropractic Clinic, Pasadena, 1988-89; staff chiropractor Beaumont (Tex.) Health Care Ctr., 1989; clinic dir. Chironetwork Health Care, Pasadena, 1989-91; pvt. practice Dyess Chiropractic Clinic, Pasadena, 1992-94; clinic chiropractor N.W. Healthcare and Rehab., Houston, 1994—. Mem. Tex. Chiropractic Coll. Alumni Assn., Tex. Chiropractic Assn. Baptist. Home: 2017 New Orleans Deer Park TX 77536 Office: NW Health Care Rehab Ctr 11251 NW Fwy Ste 240 Houston TX 77092

DYKEN, MARK LEWIS, JR., neurologist, educator; b. Laramie, Wyo., Aug. 26, 1928; s. Mark L. and Thelma Violet (Achenbach) D.; m. Beverly All, June 8, 1951; children: Betsy Lynn, Mark Eric, Julie Suzanne, Amy Luise, Andrew Christopher, Gregory Allen. B.S. in Anatomy and Physiology, Ind. U., 1951, M.D., 1954. Diplomate: Am. Bd. Psychiatry and Neurology. Intern Indpls. Gen. Hosp., 1954-55; resident in neurology Ind. U. Med. Center, 1955-58; clin. dir., dir. research New Castle (Ind.) State Hosp., 1958-61; asst. dept. neurology Ind. U., 1958-61, assoc. prof. neurology, 1964-69, prof., 1969—, chmn. dept. neurology, 1971—; dir. Ind. U. Cerebrovascular Disease Center, 1966—; chmn. profl. adv. council Nat. Easter Seal Soc., 1974-82; cons., chmn. panel on rev. neurol. devices subcom. FDA, 1979-83. Editor in chief Stroke, 1992—; contbr. numerous articles on topics including cerebral vascular disease, blood flow, epilepsy, electroencephalography, muscle disease, to profl. jours. Served with U.S. Army,

1946-48. Recipient numerous grants in cerebrovascular disease. Fellow ACP; mem. AMA, Am. Assn. Univ. Profs. Neurology (pres. 1986-88), Epilepsy Found. Am., Am. Heart Assn (chmn. stroke coun. 1984-86, v.p. for sci. couns. 1988-89), Ind. Neurol. Assn. (charter pres. 1966-68), Am. Acad. Neurology, Am. Neurol. Assn., Sigma Xi, Alpha Omega Alpha. Home: 7406 W 92nd St Zionsville IN 46077-9103 Office: Ind U Med Ctr Neurol Dept Emerson Hall-125 545 Barnhill Dr Indianapolis IN 46202-5112*

DYKERS, JOHN REGINALD, JR., family physician; b. Jacksonville, Fla., Sept. 25, 1935. BS in Biology and Chemistry, Davidson Coll., 1956; MD, U. N.C., 1960. Intern U.S. Naval Hosp., Pensacola, Fla., 1960; rsch. asst. dept. physicology U. N.C. Sch. Medicine, Chapel Hill, 1961; pvt. practice Siler City, N.C., 1964—; lectr. in field; asst. clin. prof. dept. family medicine U. N.C., Chapel Hill, 1975-87, Duke U., Durham, N.C., 1980—, East Carolina U., Greenville, N.C., 1981—; chmn. continuing edn. Chatham Hosp., Inc., chief med. staff, bd. trustees, dir. nurse midwifery svc., 1977-79; med. dir. Meadowbrook Manor, Siler City, 1983—; Chatham County med. examiner, 1969—; mem. EMT Examination Bd., 1991. Contbr. articles to profl. jours. Chmn. of physicians N.C. Driver's Lic. Med. Rev. Bd., 1986-91; mem. adv. bd. Ams. for a Sound AIDS/HIV Policy, 1990; mem. N.C. Humanities Coun., 1984-88; chmn. Chatham County Commn. for Developmentally Disabled, 1972-77; bd. dirs. Siler City Arts Coun., 1984; mem. N.C. Beef Cattle Improvement Program; mem. N.C. State Task Force on Substance Abuse and the Cts., 1993-95. With USN, 1961-64. Recipient Gov.'s Cert. of Appreciation in recognition of dedication and outstanding svc. to N.C., 1991, 94. Mem. AMA. Am. Acd. Family Practice, Am. Coll. Family Physicians, N.C. Med. Soc. (traffic safety com. 1991—), Chatham County Med. Soc. (past pres.), N.C. Acad. Family Physicians (chmn. edn. com. 1982-83, chmn. rev. course com. 1982-83), Siler City C. of C. (chmn. com. on health svc. 1983), N.C. Cattlemen's Assn. (mem. grading com.), Am. Internat. Charolais Assn., Siler City Rotary. Office: PO Box 565 Siler City NC 27344

DYKES, C. BARRY, healthcare administrator; b. Phila., Oct. 30, 1950; s. William W. and Edith (Rich) D.; m. Sandra S. Lewis, June 4, 1971 (dec. May 1985); 1 child, Ashley Elizabeth; m. Sue Ellen Surratt, Oct. 3, 1987. BBA, Temple U., 1972, MBA, 1976. Adminstrv. resident Med. Ctr. Del., Wilmington, 1974-76, asst. adminstr., 1976-84; adminstr. corp. ops. Kennedy Meml. Hosps.-Univ. Med. Ctr., Stratford, N.J., 1984-86; exec. v.p. Taylor Hosp., Ridley Park, Pa., 1986-88; pres. NPI/Sheffield Sch., Princeton, N.J., 1988-91; v.p. cons. svcs. Fulton, Longshore & Assocs., Plymouth Meeting, Pa., 1991-92; adminstr. Kennedy Meml. Hosp.-Univ. Med. Ctr., 1992—; chmn. bd. dirs. Stat Ambulance, Inc., Stratford, 1984-86, New Era Nursing, Inc., Cherry Hill, N.J., 1984-86; bd. dirs. South N.J. Perinatal Coop., Pennsauken, 1992—. Pres. bd. dirs. Cam-Glo div. Am. Heart Assn., Camden County, N.J., 1993-95. Mem. Am. Coll. Healthcare Execs., Am. Coll. Osteo Healthcare Execs. Office: Kennedy Meml Hosps-UMC Stratford Divsn 18 E Laurel Rd Stratford NJ 08084

DYKES, VIRGINIA CHANDLER, occupational therapist, educator; b. Evanston, Ill., Jan. 10, 1930; d. Daniel Guy and Helen (Schneider) Goodman; children: Ron Lee, Chuck Lee Chandler, James R. Jr. BA in Art and Psychology, So. Methodist U., 1951; postgrad. in occupational therapy Tex. Women's U., 1953. Occupational therapist Beverly Hills Sanitarium, Dallas, 1953-55; dir. occupational and recreational therapy Baylor U. Med. Ctr., Dallas, 1956-60, 68-89; pvt. practice, Dallas, 1989-92; dir. occupational and recreational therapy Fla. Hosp., Orlando, 1962-65; staff therapist Parkland Meml. Hosp., Dallas, 1965-68; cons. Arthritis Found., 1974-89, benefactor; Fanny B. Vanderkodi lectr. Tex. Women's U., 1993—. Mem. coordinating bd. allied health adv. com. Tex. Coll. and Univ. System, 1980-88; bd. dirs. Tex. Arthritis Found., chmn. patient svcs. com., 1985-89, exec. bd. sec.; sponsor Kimball Art Mus.; bd. dirs. Dallas Opera, also women's bd., CPA Wives, Theatre Ctr. Guild; women's bd. Dallas Arboretum; pres. Diana Dean Head Injury Guild, 1992-93. Named Tex. Occupational Therapist of Yr., 1985. Mem. Tex. Occupational Therapy Assn. (life mem. award), Am. Occupational Therapy Assn. (del. Fla. 1964, Tex. 1980-88), World Fedn. Occupational Therapists (participant 8th Internat. Congress, Hamburg, Germany, 1982, del. to 10th European Congress on Rheumatology, Moscow 1983), Chi Omega. Clubs: Boomerang (dir. 1971-88), Les Femmes du Monde, Pierian Lit. Club. Author: (manual) Lightcast II Splints, 1976; Adult Visual Perceptual Evaluation, 1981; contbr. articles to profl. jours. Home: 3203 Alderson St Dallas TX 75214-3059

DYKSTRA, DENNIS DALE, physiatrist; b. Lakewood, Ohio, Feb. 21, 1950; s. Gerald and Grace Maire (Thomas) D.; m. Mary Louise Kerker, May 16, 1992; children: Dorothy, Perry, Caitlin, Patrick. AB in Zoology summa cum laude, Ohio U., 1972; MD, U. Cin., 1976; PhD, U. Minn., 1988. Diplomate Am. Bd. Pediatrics, Am. Bd. Phys. Medicine and Rehab. Intern/resident Cin. Children's Hosp., 1976-81; instr. U. Minn., Mpls., 1981-88, asst. prof., 1988-92, assoc. prof. phys. medicine/rehab./pediatrics/urol. surgery, 1992—, head dept. phys. medicine/rehab., 1992—; assoc. chief staff for rehab. VA Med. Ctr., Mpls., 1994—. Author: Krusen's Handbook of Phys. Medicine and Rehabilitation, 1991; contbr. articles to profl. jours. Med. advisor Minn. Spasmodic Torticolits Soc., Duluth, Minn., 1991—. Recipient Phys. Med. and Rehab. Investigator award Phys. Med. and Rehab. Rsch. Found., 1984, 85; Spinal Cord Soc. grantee, 1990. Fellow Am. Acad. Phys. Med. and Rehab. (chair edn. com. 1994—), Am. Acad. Pediatrics, Am. Assn. Electrodiagnostic Medicine. Office: Univ of Minn 420 Delaware St SE Box 297 Mayor Bldg Minneapolis MN 55455

DYLAG, HELEN MARIE, healthcare administrator; b. Cleve., Oct. 14, 1950; d. Stanley John and Helen Agnes (Jarkiewicz) D. BSN, St. John Coll., Cleve., 1971; MS, Ohio State U., 1973. RN, Ohio. RN V.A. Adminstrn. Hosp., Brecksville, Ohio, 1971-72; clin. specialist, psychiat.-mental health nursing Marymount Hosp./Mental Health Ctr., Garfield Heights, Ohio, 1973-78, dir. consultation and edn. dept., 1978-84, dir. Ctr. for Health Styles, 1984-88; adminstrv. dir. Women's Healthcare Ctr./St. Luke's Hosp., Cleve., 1988-90; adminstrv. dir. dept. of psychiatry MetroHealth Med. Ctr., Cleve., 1990—. Contbg. author: Nursing of Families in Crisis, 1974, Distributive Nursing Practice: A Systems Approach to Community Health, 1977; producer and host "Health Styles" TV Talk Show, 1987-88; contbr. articles to profl. jours. Trustee The Stroke Assn. of Ohio, Cleve., 1990-91; mem. Women of Achievement com., Women's City Club, Cleve., 1989-91. Recipient award Greater Cleve. Hosp. Assn., 1981, Innovator award Am. Hosp. Assn./Ctr. for Health Promotion, 1985. Mem. Assn. Mental Health Adminstrs., Am. Coll. Healthcare Execs., Healthcare Adminstrs. Assn. of Northeast Ohio, Sigma Theta Tau. Home: 5709 Onaway Oval Cleveland OH 44130-1642 Office: Metro Health Med Ctr 2500 Metrohealth Dr Cleveland OH 44109-1900

DYM, MARTIN, medical educator; b. Montreal, Que., Can., Oct. 19, 1941; came to U.S., 1969; married; 3 children. BSc, Sir George Williams U., Montreal, 1964; MSc, McGill U., Montreal, 1966, PhD, 1969. Postdoc. fellow Harvard Med. Sch., Boston, 1970, instr., 1972-73, asst. prof., 1973-77, assoc. prof., 1977-81; prof., chmn. dept. cell biology Georgetown U. Sch. Medicine, Washington, 1981—; dir. med. gross anatomy, Georgetown U. Sch. Medicine, Washington, 1982-88, 95—; mem. reproductive biology study section NIH, 1988-92, mem. various other study sections, site visitor, grant reviewer; grant reviewer NSF, Med. Rsch. Coun. Can., others; presenter in field; vis. cons. Rsch. Inst. Family Planning, Beijing, 1991. Mem editl. bd. Micron, Anatomical Record, 1978—, Jour. Andrology, 1981-86, Biology of Reproduction, 1990—; manuscript reviewer various scientific jours; contbr. over 200 articles to profl. publs., chpts. to books. Grantee Population Coun., 1973-75, NSF, 1979-80, Office Naval Rsch., 1984-85, Mellon Found., 1982-86, 86-89, 90-93, NIH, 1971-92, 92-95, 92-96, others; fellow Rockefeller Found., 1973. Mem. Endocrine Soc., Am. Soc. Cell Biology, Am. Assn. Anatomists, Soc. Study Reproduction, Am. Soc. Andrology (exec. coun. 1979-83, chmn. publ. com. 1981-85, program. chmn. ann. meeting 1993), Peripatetic Club. Office: 3900 Reservoir Rd NW Washington DC 20007-2197

DYRLD, PETER ELDON, cardiothoracic surgeon; b. Mpls., Apr. 14, 1949; s. Amos Oliver and Ovidie Marie (Evenson) D.; m. Judith Lynn Kristan, July 19, 1980; children: Sarah, Leah, Paul, Hannah, Rebekah. BS summa cum laude, U. Minn., 1971, MD, 1975. Diplomate Am. Bd. Surgery, Am. Bd. Thoracic Surgery. Resident in gen. surgery U. Colo., Denver, 1975-80; resident in cardiothoracic surgery U. Wash., Seattle, 1982-84; cardiothoracic surgeon Park Nicollet Med. Ctr., Mpls., 1984—; cardiothoracic surgeon, clin. assoc. prof. U. Minn., Mpls., 1989—. Fellow ACS; mem. Soc. of Thoracic Surgeons, Twin Cities Thoracic Soc., Minn. Med. Assn., Hennepin County Med. Soc. Lutheran. Home: 4745 Goldenrod Ln N Plymouth MN 55442 Office: Park Nicollet Clinic Health Systems Minn 6490 Excelsior Blv Ste 200W Saint Louis Park MN 55426

DYSINGER, PAUL WILLIAM, physician, educator, health consultant; b. Burns, Tenn., May 24, 1927; s. Paul Clair and Mary Edith (Martin) D.; m. Yvonne Minchin, May 11, 1958; children: Edwin, Wayne, John, Janelle. B.A., So. Missionary Coll., 1951; M.D., Coll. Med. Evangelists, 1955; M.P.H., Harvard, 1962. Diplomate Nat. Bd. Med. Examiners, Am. Bd. Preventive Medicine. Intern Washington, 1955-56; sr. asst. surgeon USPHS; with Blackfeet Indians in Mont., Navajos of Ariz., 1956-58; physician, med. adviser Am. embassy, PhnomPenh, Cambodia, 1958-60; rsch. assoc. dept. preventive medicine Loma Linda (Calif.) U. (formerly Coll. Med. Evangelists), 1960-62, dir. field sta. Western Tanganyika, 1962-64, adminstrv. asst. div. pub. health, 1964-67, asst. to dean, chmn. dept. tropical health Sch. Pub. Health, 1967-69, asst. dean for acad. affairs and internat. health Sch. Pub. Health, 1969-71, assoc. dean for acad. affairs. 1971-79, dir. preventive med. residency Sch. of Medicine, 1983-88; pres., CEO, sr. health advisor Devel. Svc. Internat., Williamsport, Tenn., 1992—; med. cons. dept. Vocat. Rehab., Riverside, Calif., 1964-88; mother and child health cons. Ministry of Health, Tanzania, 1978-80; med. dir. Village Health Program, Punjab, Pakistan, 1980-81, tchr., cons., S.Am. and Caribbean, 1981-83; chief preventive medicine Pettis Meml. VA Hosp., Loma Linda, 1986-88; sr. health advisor Adventist Devel. and Relief Agy., 1988-92. Contbr. articles to med. publs. WHO fellow, Somalia, Ethiopia, India, Nepal and Burma, 1969. Fellow Royal Soc. Tropical Medicine and Hygiene, Am. Pub. Health Assn., Am. Coll. Preventive Medicine, Internat. Health Soc. (pres.); mem. AMA, Nat. Council for Internat. Health, Adventist Internat. Med. Soc. (pres. 1983-84), Delta Omega (nat. pres. 1977-78). Adventist. Home and Office: 684 Dry Prong Rd PO Box 210 Williamsport TN 38487-0210

DZELZKALNS, JANIS IVARS, ophthalmologist; b. Milw., Aug. 8, 1951; m. Kathryn Ann Sorenson, Aug. 20, 1978; children: Emma, Arnold. BS, U. Wis., 1975, MD, 1983. Diplomate Am. Bd. Ophthalmology. Ophthalmologist Neumann Eye Ctr., Deland, Fla., 1988-90, Miami Eye Ctr., Miami, 1990—. Contbr. articles to profl. jours. Fellow Am. Acad. Ophthamology; mem. Miami Ophthalmological Soc. Home: 13200 SW 69 Ave Miami FL 33156 Office: Miami Eye Ctr 619 NW 12 Ave Miami FL 33136

DZIEWANOWSKA, ZOFIA ELIZABETH, neuropsychiatrist, pharmaceutical executive, researcher, educator; b. Warsaw, Poland, Nov. 17, 1939; came to U.S., 1972; d. Stanislaw Kazimierz Dziewanowski and Zofia Danuta (Mieczkowska) Rudowska; m. Krzysztof A. Kunert, Sept. 1, 1961 (div. 1971); 1 child, Martin. MD, U. Warsaw, 1963; PhD, Polish Acad. Sci., 1970. MD recert. U.K., 1972, U.S., 1973. Asst. prof. of psychiatry U. Warsaw Med. Sch., 1969-71; sr. house officer St. George's Hosp., U. London, 1971-72; assoc. dir. Merck Sharp & Dohme, Rahway, N.J., 1972-76; vis. assoc. physician Rockefeller U. Hosp., N.Y.C., 1975-76; adj. asst. prof. of psychiatry Cornell U. Med. Ctr., N.Y.C., 1978—; v.p., global med. dir. Hoffmann-La Roche, Inc., Nutley, N.J., 1976-94; sr. v.p. and dir global med. affairs Genta Inc., San Diego, 1994—; lectr. in field U.S. and internat. confs. Contbr. articles to profl. publs. Bd. dirs Royal Soc. Medicine Found.; mem. alumni coun. Cornell U. Med. Ctr. Recipient TWIN Honoree award for Outstanding Women in Mgmt., Ridgewood (N.J.) YWCA, 1984. Mem. AMA, AAAS, Am. Soc. Pharmacology and Therapeutics, Am. Coll. Neuropsychopharmacology, N.Y. Acad. Scis., PhRMA. (vice chmn. steering com. med. sect., chmn. internat. med. affairs com., head biotech. working group), Royal Soc. Medicine (U.K.), Drug Info. Assn. (Woman of Yr. award 1994), Am. Assn. Pharm. Physicians. Roman Catholic. Office: Genta Inc 3550 General Atomics Ct San Diego CA 92121

DZWIERZYNSKI, WILLIAM WALTER, plastic and reconstructive surgeon; b. Chgo., Dec. 1, 1958; s. Walter and Stella Ann (Metych) D.; m. Christine Hucko, Sept. 7, 1991; 1 child, Elizabeth Grace. BSChemE with high honors, Ill. Inst. of Tech., 1980; MD, Chgo. Med. Sch., 1984. Diplomate Am. Bd. Surgery, Am. Bd. Plastic Surgery with added qualifications in Hand Surgery. Intern in gen. surgery Chgo. Med. Sch., North Chicago, Ill., 1984-89; resident in plastic and reconstructive surgery U. Mich., Ann Arbor, 1989-91; fellow in hand and micro surgery Med. Coll. of Wis., Milw., 1991-92, asst. prof. plastic and reconstructive surgery, 1992—, asst. prof. orthopedic surgery, 1992—; program com. chmn. Midwestern Assn. of Plastic Surgeons, 1995; adv. bd. Pharmacy and Therapeutic Com., Milw., 1995—, Clin. Resource Utilization Team, Milw., 1994—, Ergonomics Task Force, Milw., 1994—. Author: (with others) Mastery of Surgery-Plastic Surgery, 1994, The Foot, 1993, Hand Clinics, 1994; contbr. articles to profl. jours. Mentor, sponsor Boy Scouts of Am., Milwaukee County Coun., 1994. Fellow ACS; mem. Am. Soc. for Reconstructive Microsurgery, Plastic Surgery Rsch. Coun., Midwestern Assn. of Plastic Surgeons, Am. Soc. of Plastic and Reconstructive Surgeons, Am. Soc. Surgery of Hand, Am. Assn. for Hand Surgery, Reed O. Dingman Soc., Tau Beta Pi. Office: Med Coll of Wis 9200 W Wisconsin Ave Milwaukee WI 53226

EADS, DARWIN LEROY, management psychologist; b. Dodge City, Kans., July 16, 1949; s. Arthur Leroy and Rosalyn Irene (Way) E. BA in Psychology, Ottawa U., 1971; MS in Counseling, U. Kans., 1976, PhD in Counseling Psychology, 1980. Psychologist Miami County Mental Health Ctr., Louisburg, Kans., 1980, Osawatomie (Kans.) State Hosp., 1981; pers. cons. Marion Labs., Kansas City, Mo., 1981-85, dir. human resources, 1985-88; dir. orgn. devel. KV Pharm. Co., St. Louis, 1988-91; ceo, v.p., sec. Corp. Resource Group, Inc., Balt., 1991—; cons. Vocat. Rehab. Ctr., Topeka. Bd. dirs. Kans. Bapt. Conv., Topeka, 1968-70, Transitional Living Consortium, Kansas City, 1985-88, Ctrl. Bapt. Theol. Sem., Kansas City, 1985-88. Mem. APA, ASTD, Am. Compensation Assn., Soc. for Human Resource Mgmt., Md. Psychol. Assn. (lic.), Kans. Psychol. Assn. (cert.), Mo. Psychol. Assn. (lic.), Rotary, Phi Beta Kappa. Home: 4956 Lockard Dr Owings Mills MD 21117-6114 Office: Corp Resource Group 9145 Guilford Rd Ste 160 Columbia MD 21046-1896

EAGAN, MARIE T. (RIA EAGAN), chiropractor; b. Rockville Ctr., N.Y., June 17, 1952; d. John F. and Mary (Ebner) E. BA, Goddard Coll., 1975; D in Chiropractic Medicine, N.Y. Chiropractic Coll., 1983. Pvt. practice chiropractic medicine N.Y.C., 1983—; chiropractic examiner N.Y. State Bd. Chiropractic, 1995. Bd. dirs. Chalice Found., L.A., 1986. Fellow N.Y. Chiropractic Assn., Am. Chiropractic Assn., Internat. Chiropractic Assn. Democrat. Office: 231 W 21st St Apt B New York NY 10011-3119

EAGLES, DOUGLAS ALAN, neurophysiologist; b. New Britain, Conn., Feb. 22, 1943; s. Clyde Austin and Helen Frances (Sibley) E.; m. Joyce Pauline Juskalian, June 24, 1967; 1 child, Ross Brandon. BA, Lake Forest Coll., 1965; MA, U. Mass., 1968, PhD, 1972. Lectr. U. Mass., Amherst, 1970-71; postdoctoral fellow U. Iowa, Iowa City, 1971-73; asst. prof. biology Georgetown U., Washington, 1973—. Author: Your Weight, 1982, Nutritional Diseases, 1987, The Menace of AIDS: A Shdow on our Land, 1988; contbr. articles to profl. jours. Coach Prince William Soccer Inc., Prince William County, Va., 1980-90; judge sci. fairs Prince William County Schs. Mem. AAAS, Am. Soc. Biologists, Soc. for Neurobiology, Sigma (pres. Georgetown U. chpt. 1984-85, sec. Georgetown U. chpt. 1989—, chair mid-Atlantic region, nominating com. 1988—). Office: Georgetown U 37th O St NW Washington DC 20057

EAMES, WILMER BALLOU, dental educator; b. Kansas City, Mo., May 8, 1914; s. Prescott W. and Alice (Ballou) E.; m. Elma Elaine Bitter, July 2, 1939; children: Douglas, Alice. D.D.S., K.C.-Western Dental Coll., Kansas City, Mo., 1939. Practice dentistry Grand Junction, Colo., 1939-41, Denver, 1945-47, Glenwood Springs, Colo., 1947-61; prof. operative dentistry Northwestern U. Dental Sch., 1961-67, asso. dean, 1964-67; prof. operative dentistry, dir. div. applied dental materials Emory U. Sch. Dentistry, 1967-79, prof. emeritus, 1979—; clin. prof. U. Colo., 1980—; lectr. dental materials; research and publs.; lectr. on dental materials over 600 invitations. Contbr. over 100 articles to profl. jours. Served to maj., Dental Corps, USAAF, 1941-45. Recipient Golden Eagle award for Amalgam Films (2), 1965-66, Man in Dentistry award No. Dist. Ga. Dental Assn., 1978, Hinman Disting. Service medallion, Atlanta, 1981, Alumnus of Yr. award U. Mo., Kansas City, 1983, Alumni Achievement award 1990, Jerome and Dorothy Schweitzer Rsch. award Greater N.Y. Acad. Prosthodontics, 1979, Faculty Advisor award Alumni Assn. Student Clinicians and ADA, 1980, Disting. Svc. award U. Colo. Health Scis. Ctr., 1986, Dentist of Yr. award, Colo. Acad. Gen. Dentistry, 1982, Man of Yr. award Colo. chpt. Am. Coll. Dentists, 1985, Disting. Svc. award Bd. Regents U. Colo., 1986, Callahan Meml. award Ohio Dental Assn., 1989; others. Fellow Internat. Coll. Dentists, Am. Coll. Dentists (William Gies award 1986), Ga. Dental Assn. (Sci. Dentistry appreciation award), Acad. Gen. Dentistry (Albert L. Borish award 1983); mem. Internat. Assn. Dental Rsch. (Wilmer Souder award 1985), ADA, Am. Acad. Restorative Dentistry, Acad. Operative Dentistry (Hollenback Meml. prize 1979), Met. Denver Dental Soc. (Honus Maximus award 1990), Am. Dental Soc. Europe (hon.), Denver Acad. Clin. Dentistry (hon.), Sigma Xi, Omicron Kappa Upsilon, Alpha Omega, Wilmer B. Eames Study Club (hon.). Home: 3455 S Corona St Apt 531 Englewood CO 80110-2878

EARLE, JEAN BUIST, health and human services administrator; b. Newton, N.J., Oct. 5, 1951; d. Richardson and Jean (Mackerly) Buist; m. Terry Dean Earle, Mar. 4, 1989; children: Morgan, Abigail. AB, Cornell U., 1973; MEd, Coll. William and Mary, 1974; MBA, U. Pa., 1987. Mgr. The Korman Corp., Jenkintown, Pa., 1975-77; v.p. ops. Community Assn. Mgmt. Co., Havertown, Pa., 1977-78; adminstrv. asst. Albert Einstein Med. Ctr., Phila., 1978-83; assoc. adminstr. Meml. Hosp. Burlington County, Mt. Holly, N.J., 1983-87; v.p. Overlook Hosp., Summit, N.J., 1987-95; exec. dir. Summit (N.J.) Child Care Ctrs., Inc., 1995—. Fellow Am. Coll. Healthcare Execs; mem. Am. Hosp. Assn., Assn. for Health Svcs. Rsch., U. Pa. Wharton Sch. Alumni Assn., Cornell Club mem. bd. trustees family link of Union and Essex counties. Home: 31 Broadview Ter Chatham NJ 07928-1826 Office: Summit Child Care Ctrs Inc 14 Beckman Ter Summit NJ 07901

EARLEY, LAURENCE ELLIOTT, medical educator; b. Ahoskie, N.C., Jan. 23, 1931; s. Frank Claxton and Eleanor (Dilday) E.; m. Joanne Frances Sinclair, Sept. 5, 1953; children: Laurence Elliott Jr., Peter Hunter. BS, U. N.C., 1953, MD, 1956; MA (hon.), U. Pa., 1978. Diplomate Am. Bd. Internal Medicine (chmn. 1987-88). Asst. prof. Harvard Med. Sch., Boston, 1967-68; assoc. prof. U. Calif. Sch. Medicine, San Francisco, 1968-69, prof., 1969-73, chief of nephrology, 1968-73; prof., chmn. dept. medicine U. Tex. Health Sci. Ctr., San Antonio, 1973-77; chmn. dept. medicine, Frank Wister Thomas Prof. U. Pa., Phila., 1977-90, Francis C. Wood prof., 1993-95, sr. assoc.dean, 1992-95; clin. prof. medicine U. N.C., Chapel Hill, 1995—; mem. study sect. NIH, Bethesda, Md., 1969-77. Editor: Diseases of The Kidney; contbr. articles on Kidney desease and physiology to profl. jours. Chmn. sci. adv. bd. Nat. Kidney Found., N.Y.C., 1973-74. Sr. asst. surgeon USPHS, 1959-61. Recipient Kaiser award U. Calif. San Francisco, 1972, Disting. Svc. award U. N.C., 1976. Master ACP; mem. Assn. Profs. Medicine (pres. 1983-84), Am. Soc. for Clin. Investigation (pres. 1975-76), Am. Soc. Nephrology (pres. 1977-78), Inst. Medicine, Assn. Am. Physicians (pres. 1988-89), Phi Beta Kappa, Alpha Omega Alpha. Home: 209 Huntington Dr Chapel Hill NC 27514

EARLIE, WILLIE, pharmacist; b. Chgo., Nov. 25, 1947; s. Willie and Mattie (Kirksey) E.; children: Willie III, Jelani Jabar. BS in Pharmacy, Tex. So. U., 1970. Lic. phramcist, Tex. Staff pharmacist Osco Drugs, Chgo., 1970; staff and chief pharmacist Sav-Mor Pharmacy, Houston, 1971-80; owner, mgr. Kashmere Pharmacy, Houston, 1980—; owner Bay Pharmacy, 1994—; pharmacy preceptor Tex. So. U., Houston, 1975-93, mem. admissions com. Coll. Pharmacy, 1985-90; cons. Bayland Ctr., Houston, 1989; drug counselor Fight for Life, Houston, 1989; vice chmn. community adv. bd. Kashmere Multi-Svc. Ctr. Alt. del. Tex. Dem. Conv., 1984. Recipient William S. Apple Meml. award Am. Pharm. Assn., 1989, Outstanding Texan in Bus. award Legis Black Caucus; named to Wendell Phillips H.S. Acad. Hall of Fame. Mem. APHA, Nat. Pharm. Assn. (pres. 1987-88, Pharmacist of Yr. award 1989), Houston Pharm. Assn. (pres. 1984-85), Harris County Pharm. Assn., Tex. Pharm. Assn., Nat. Assn. Retail Druggists, Allied Pharmacy Network (pres. 1993—), Tex. So. U. Ex-Students Assn. (life), Tex. So. U. Pharmacy Alumni Assn. (pres. 1990-92), Nat. Coalition of Black Meeting Planners, Kappa Alpha Psi. Home: 8703 Brackley Ln Houston TX 77088-3303 Office: Kashmere Pharmacy 3513 Lockwood Dr # C Houston TX 77026-5441

EARLL, JERRY MILLER, internist, educator; b. Hawarden, Iowa, Aug. 15, 1928; s. Harry Ezra and Magdalene Anna (Miller) E.; m. Faith Anne Allbaugh, Sept. 14, 1956; children: Leslie Anne, Nikki Lee, Holly Magdalene. B.S., U. Nebr., 1950; M.D., U. Iowa, 1958; postgrad., U. Calif., 1965-66. Diplomate: Am. Bd. Internal Medicine, Am. Bd. Endocrinology, Am. Bd. Nuclear Medicine, Am. Bd. Geriatrics. Commd. 2d lt. U.S. Army, 1951, advanced through grades to col., 1972; intern Letterman Gen. Hosp., San Francisco, 1958; resident in internal medicine Letterman Gen. Hosp., 1959-62; chief endocrinology and metabolism William Beaumont Gen. Hosp., El Paso, 1963-65, Tripler Gen. Hosp., Honolulu, 1965-69, Walter Reed Army Inst. Research and Walter Reed Army Hosp., Washington, 1969-76; chief dept. medicine Walter Reed Army Hosp., 1976-79; cons. endocrinology Office Surgeon Gen.; asso. prof. medicine U. Hawaii, 1967-69; clin. prof. medicine Georgetown U., 1976-79; prof. medicine, vice chmn. dept. medicine Uniformed Services Univ. Health Scis., Washington, 1977-79; prof. and chief divsn. internal medicine Georgetown U., Washington, 1979-94; dir. geriatrics svc. Georgetown U. and Hosp., Washington, 1993—; med. dir. Washington Home, 1996. Decorated Legion of Merit, Army Commendation medal, Meritorious Service medal. Fellow ACP; mem. Am. Fedn. Clin. Rsch., Am. Diabetes Assn., Endocrine Soc., N.Y. Diabetes Assn., Assn. Mil. Surgeons, Acad. Medicine of Washington (Regional Laureate award of Am. Coll. of Physicians). Home: 8529 Brickyard Rd Potomac MD 20854-4834 Office: Georgetown U Hosp 3800 Reservoir Rd NW Washington DC 20007-2196

EARLY, AMES S., healthcare system executive; b. Allison, Iowa, Apr. 18, 1937; s. W.C. and F. Eva Early; m. Beryl J. Early; 1 child, Barbara. BA, Drake U., 1959; MHA, U. Iowa, 1961. Adminstrv. resident, adminstrv. asst. U. Minn. Hosp., Mpls., 1961-67; exec. dir. Mary Francis Skiff Meml. Hosp., Newton, Iowa, 1967-68; asst. adminstr. Mercy Hosp., Miami, Fla., 1968-76; pres. Scripps Meml. Hosp., La Jolla, Calif., 1976-91; exec. v.p., COO Scripps Instns. Medicine and Sci., ScrippsHealth, 1991-93; pres., CEO ScrippsHealth, San Diego, 1994—. Pres. So. Fla. Hosp. Assn., 1974-75, bd. dirs., 1971-76; bd. dirs. Fla. Hosp. Assn., 1974-76, Comprehensive Health Planning of So. Fla., 1974-76, Nat. Coun. Cmty. Hosp., 1974—, Hosp. Coun. San Diego and Imperial Counties, 1978-86, Calif. Polit. Action Com., 1979-85, Calif. Health Decisions, 1994—, Blue Cross/Hosp. Adv. Com., 1982, Vol. Hosp. Am. West, 1986-91; mem. peer rev. panel Fla. Blue Cross Assn., 1975-76; trustee Calif. Assn. Hosp. and Health Sys., 1984-92, mem. exec. com., 1984-90, mem. legis. com., 1985, mem. hosp. med. staff bylaws com., 1985-86, treas., 1987, chmn., 1989; mem. Healthcare Forum. Recipient Headline of Yr. in Healthcare San Diego Press Club, 1987. Mem. Am. Coll. Healthcare Execs., Am. Hosp. Assn., Am. Assn. Hosp. Planning. Office: ScrippsHealth 4275 Campus Point Ct San Diego CA 92121-1513

EARLY, GERALD LEE, cardiovascular and thoracic surgeon, educator; b. St. Joseph, Mo., June 10, 1947; s. Abram Lee and Arline Joyce (Stein) E.; m. Shauna R. Roberts, 1 dau., Jennifer Lynn. BA, Cen. Meth. Coll., Fayette, Mo., 1969; MD, U. Mo.-Kansas City, 1973; MA, U. Mo.-Columbia, 1975; cert. in sur. critical care, 1991. Diplomate Nat. Bd. Med. Examiners, 1974, Am. Bd. Surgery, 1980, Am. Bd. Thoracic Surgery, 1983. Intern, Kansas City Gen. Hosp. and Med. Ctr., 1973-74; resident in internal medicine Pensacola Ednl. Program, 1974-75; resident in surgery U. Mo.-Kansas City, 1976-79, in thoracic surgery Ohio State U., 1979-81; dir. dept. emergency medicine Pensacola (Fla.) Ednl. Program, 1975-76; dir. cardiovascular and thoracic surgery Truman Med. Ctr., Kansas City, Mo., 1982-83; clin. asst. prof. surgery U. Mo.-Kansas City, 1982-89; asst. prof. thoracic surgery U. Tenn., Memphis, 1989-91; with Heartland Hosp., St. Joseph, Mo. Recipient Meritorious Svc. award West Fla. Heart Assn., 1976; named Surgery Resident of Yr., Truman Med. Ctr., 1978, 79; USPHS Reproductive Biology Tng. grantee, 1970-71. Fellow Am. Coll. Surgeons, Am. Coll. Chest Physicians; mem. AMA, Buchanan County Med. Soc., Mo. Med. Assn., Soc. of Thoracic Surgeons, Methodist. Contbr. articles sci. jours. Office: 802 n rIVERSIDE sTE 310 Saint Joseph MO 64507

EARLY, GLEN ALAN, biology educator; b. Louisville, Oct. 5, 1948; s. Hubert Woodward and May Viola (Sparks) E.; m. Janice Lynn McGrath (div. Mar. 1981); 1 child, Douglas Arthur; m. Judy Florence Guy, Nov. 11, 1983; 1 child, Mark Alan. BS cum laude, U. Louisville, 1971, MS in Zoology, 1974. Biology tchr. St. Xavier High Sch., Louisville, 1971-72; lab instr. U. Louisville, 1972-74; staff biologist Miller/Wihry, Inc., Louisville, 1974-82; environ. planner Louisville Community Design Ctr., 1982; prof. Jefferson C.C., Louisville, 1983—, chmn. allied health div., 1986-92; cons., planner Blackacre Found., Louisville, 1985-87. Bd. dirs. Third Century, Louisville, 1981-83, chmn. environ. com., 1981-83. Mem. Am. Fisheries Soc., Ky. Acad. of Sci., Herpetologists League. Republican. Baptist. Office: Jefferson Community Coll 109 E Broadway St Louisville KY 40202-2005

EARNEST, TAMAR DEROY, physician; b. San Francisco, Dec. 16, 1940. BA, Temple U., 1964, MD, 1968. cert. Advanced Trauma Life Support Instr., Advanced Burn Life Support Instr., Pediat. Advanced Life Support Instr., Automatic External Defibrillator instr./med. dir., ACLS, Pediat. Advanced Life Support, CPR, Critical Incident Stress Mgmt. - Basic, Critical Incident Stress Debriefing and Post Trauma Syndromes-Advanced. Intern Abington (Pa.) Meml. Hosp., 1968-69; resident in surgery Springfield (Mass.) Hosp. Med. Ctr., 1969-70, Episcopal Hosp., Phila., 1970-71; resident in pediat. surgery St. Christopher's Hops. for Children, Phila., 1971; resident in surgery VA Hosp., Wilkes-Barre, Pa., 1971, Sacred Heart Hosp., Norristown, Pa., 1971-74; resident in pediat. cardiothoracic surgery St. Christopher's Hosp. for Children, Phila., 1973; fellow in peripheral vascular surgery Middlesex Gen. Hosp., New Brunswick, N.J., 1976-77; fellow in surg. critical care Johns Hopkins Hosp., Balt., 1988; physician Lehigh Valley Hosp., Allentown, Pa., 1974—, Good Shepherd Rehab. Hosp., Allentown, Pa., 1974—; clin. asst. prof. surgery Med. Coll. Pa. and Hahnemann U., 1988-96; clin. asst. prof. surgery Coll. Medicine of Pa. State U., Hershey, 1995—; co-chair Assn. Women Surgeons Found., 1992-94, bd. trustees, 1994—; mem. adv. bd. Burn Prevention Found., Allentown, 1995—; mem. steering com. Critical Incident Stress Mgmt. Team-Ea. Pa. EMS Region, 1989—, CISD team mem., 1990—; mem. med. exec. com. Good Shepherd Rehab. Hosp., Allentown, 1984-86, pres.-elect med. staff, 1986, pres. med. staff, 1986-87, bd. trustees, 1992—, CEO search com. 1996—; surg. edn. com. Lehigh Valley Hosp., Allentown, 1981-96, head sect. for pediat. trauma, divsn. trauma, 1992—, surgery dept. rep. to product review commn., 1993-96; pres., bd. dirs. Lehigh Valley Trauma Care Inc., Allentown, 1989-91, sec., bd. dirs., 1991-96; med. dir. Northwestern Ambulance Corps, New Tripoli, Pa., 1994-96, automated external defibrillator instr., 1995; treas. med. staff Sacred Heart Hosp., Allentown, 1983-84. Book reviewer: Abdominal Trauma, 1993. Past bd. trustees Jewish Fedn. Allentown. Fellow Am. Coll. Surgeons, Soc. Critical Care Medicine; mem. AMA, Am. Assn. for Automotive Medicine (life), Am. Burn Assn., Am. Med. Women's Assn. (life, del. nat. conv. 1990, state dir. Pa. 1990-94, Cmty. Svc. award 1994), Am. Soc. Gen. Surgeons (charter), Am. Trauma Soc., Assn. Women Surgeons (founding mem., life, v.p., treas. 1986-88, pres. 1988-90, past pres. 1990-92, chair devel. com. 1992, Disting. Mem. award 1994), Bus. and Profl. Women of Jewish Fedn. of Allentown, Delaware Valley Vascular Soc., Am. Coll. Emergency Physicians (disaster medicine sect.), Ea. Assn. for Surgery of Trauma, Internat. Assn. for Med. Assistance to Travelers, Internat. Critical Incident Stress Found., Lehigh County Med. Soc. (alt. del. to PMS 1991-96, del to PMS 1996—), Maimonides Soc. of Jewish Fedn. of Allentown, Med. Women of Lehigh Valley (founder, past chair, past membership chair) Pan Pacific Surg. Assn., Pa. Assn. Women Bus. Owners (chair nominations com. 1995-96, co-chair program com. 1995-96), Pa. Med. Soc., Peripheral Vascular Surgery Soc., Wilderness Med. Soc. (life, chair devel. com. 1989-96), World Assn. for Disaster and Emergency Medicine, Temple U. Med. Alumni Assn. (bd. dirs. 1989—, awards com. 1989—). Home: 2620 W Walnut St Allentown PA 18104-6231 Office: Ste 3100 1210 S Cedar Crest Blvd Allentown PA 19103

EASLEY, CHRISTA BIRGIT, nurse, researcher; b. Berlin, Apr. 30, 1941; came to U.S., 1966; d. Albert and Marianne (Uhlmann) Baldauf; m. Loyd Allen Easley, Oct. 23, 1964 (widowed Dec. 1993). Degree in nursing, Pawlow Coll. of Nursing, Aue, Fed. Republic of Germany, 1959; BS, NYU, Albany, 1978; MBA, Cen. Mich. U., 1979; EDS, Ctrl Mo. U., 1983; PhD, Kensington U., Glensdale, Calif., 1983. With placement sect. Sembach, A.B., Fed. Republic of Germany, 1972-73, suggestion program mgr., 1973-74; adminstrv. clk. Lajes Field, A.B., Terceira, Acores, Portugal, 1975-78, incentive awards and suggestion program mgr., 1978-79; intern Cen. Mo. State U., Warrensburg, 1980-81; instr. in bus. overseas campus Cen. Tex. Coll../Yokota, A.B., Japan, 1983; instr. Tokyo Ctr. for Lang. and Culture, 1981-83; tchr. dept. of def. Yokota Dept. of Def., Yokota AFB, Japan, 1981-84; tax examiner IRS, Austin, Tex., 1984-86; clin. rsch. coord. HealthQuest Rsch., Austin, 1987-94; v.p. Austin Clin. Rsch., 1994—. Treas. Am. Sch. System PTA, Acores, 1978-79; precinct chmn. Austin Rep. Com., 1988—. Mem. Assocs. of Clin. Pharmacology, Am. Assn. Translators, AAUW, Sigma Tau Delta. Methodist. Home: 12422 Deer Trak Austin TX 78727-5746 Office: Austin Clin Rsch Inc Creek Plaza # 202 8705 Shoal Creek Austin TX 78757

EASON, ROBERT GASTON, psychology educator; b. Bells, Tenn., May 15, 1924; s. William Bryant and Noba (Proctor) E.; m. Dorothy Jean Goodner, Sept. 5, 1952; children—Robert Gregory, Linda Joan. B.A., U. Mo., 1950, M.A., 1952, Ph.D., 1956. Postdoctoral fellow physiology UCLA, 1956-57; research psychologist Navy Electronics Lab., San Diego, 1957-67; asst. prof. San Diego State Coll., 1960-63, assoc. prof., 1963-66, prof., 1966-67; prof. U. N.C., Greensboro, 1967-70, Excellance prof., 1970-78, Elizabeth Rosenthal Excellence prof., 1978-94, prof. emeritus, 1994—, dept. head, 1967-80. Mem. editorial bd. Internat. Jour. Psychophysiology. Served with USAAF, 1943-46. Fellow Am. Psychol. Assn., Internat. Orgn. Psychophysiology; mem. AAAS, Am. Psychol. Soc., Eastern Psychol. Assn., Southeastern Psychol. Assn., Psychonomic Soc., Soc. for Neurosci., Soc. Psychophysiol. Research, Sigma Xi. Home: 115 Falkener Dr Greensboro NC 27410-5509

EASSON, WILLIAM MCALPINE, psychiatrist; b. Evanston, Ill., July 3, 1931; s. Alexander and Anne Meldrum (Watson) E.; m. Gwendolyn Bowen, May 31, 1958; children: Anne, Jane, David, Michael. M.B., Ch.B., U. Aberdeen, Scotland, 1954, M.D., 1967. Fellow in medicine and psychiatry Mayo Clinic, Rochester, Minn., 1956-59; resident in psychiatry U. Sask., 1959-60, instr. psychiatry, 1959-61; fellow in child psychiatry Menninger Clinic, Topeka, 1961-63; staff child psychiatrist Menninger Clinic, 1963-67; prof. psychiatry, chmn. dept. Med. Coll. Ohio, Toledo, 1967-72; prof., dir. div. child and adolescent psychiatry U. Minn. Med. Sch., Mpls., 1972-74; prof. psychiatry, head dept. La. State U. Med. Ctr., New Orleans, 1974-96, prof. emeritus, 1996—, head dept. psychiatry, 1974-82; prof. emeritus La. State U. Med. Ctr., New Orleans, Libya, 1974-96; prof. Sch. Grad. Studies, U. Riyadh, Saudi Arabia, 1980-81; U.S.-USSR health scientist, Moscow and Leningrad. Author: The Severely Disturbed Adolescent, 1969, The Dying Child, 2d edit., 1981, Psychiatry Exam. Rev., 5th edit., 1994, Psychiatry Patient Mgmt. Rev., 1977, (with N. Rock) Psychiatry Splty. Bd. Rev., 1991, The Management of the Severely Disturbed Adolscent, 1996; editor: Jour. Clin. Psychiatry, 1977-80. Carnegie fellow, 1956-58; Anderson fellow, 1956-58; WHO fellow, 1976. Fellow Am. Psychiat. Assn. (life), Royal Coll. Psychiatry. Home: 5218 St Charles Ave New Orleans LA 70115-4943

EAST, JACK MILTON, rehabilitation counselor, administrator, social worker; b. Little Rock, Jan. 7, 1950; s. James M. and Virginia (Price) E.; m. Nan Ellen Dickinson, May 27, 1979; step-children: Tyndall, Lee Butler, Edward. Student, U. Ark., Little Rock, 1969-72, 79-82; BS in Edn. and Rehab. Counseling, S.W. U., New Orleans, 1985, MA in Rehab. Counseling, 1988, postgrad., 1988—. Lic. social worker. Pres., founder Am. Amputee Found., Little Rock, 1975-77, exec. dir., 1977—; founder Life Care Mgmt. and Planning, 1985—; pres. Life Care Mgmt. and Planning, Little Rock, 1985—; del. Ark. Conf. on Disabled, White House Conf. on Disabled; adv. Ark. Rehab. Act of 1973; mem. planning com. and panel Atty. Gen.'s Conf. on Laws and Rights of Handicapped. Editor Nat. Resource Dir. for Amputees, 1984—, Ark. amputees referral program law, pub. sch. system drivers edn. program for handicapped, also articles and manuals; producer, dir. One Step at a Time, You're Not Alone; producer Winners, Arkansas Government: Close-Up, Hunger, Here and Now, That's A Good Boy, Ritchie, 12 Steps of Alcoholics Anonymous, Technologies for the Disabled in the 90's. Founder Am. Drug Abuse Prevention Found., Little Rock, 1980, Ark. Handicapped Athletic Assn. Rollin Razorbacks, 1980; co-founder Ark. Environ. Barriers Coun., Little Rock, 1980's; vol. Ark. Coalition for Handicapped, Am. Coalition for Citizens with Disabilities, Archtl. Barriers com. and Consumer Adv. coun. Ark. Spinal Cord Commn., Adv. coun. Ark. Div. Rehab., Nat. Orgn. Disability (chmn. Ark. chpt.). Recipient Gov.'s Vol. Activist award, Nat. Vol. Activist award, Citation award; named Outstanding Young Man of Am. Jaycees. Mem. Nat. Rehab. Assn., Nat. Rehab. Adminstrs. Assn., Internat. Soc. Prosthetist and Orthotist, Nat. Orgn. Disability, Nat. Spinal Cord Injury Assn., Rehab. Engring. Soc. N.Am. Republican. Methodist. Home: 11 Tanglewood Ln Little Rock AR 72202-1518 Office: Am Amputee Found Inc PO Box 250218 Little Rock AR 72225-0218

EASTER, DAVID EUGENE, II, business manager; b. Charleston, S.C., June 26, 1950; s. David Eugene and Doris Jean (McCorkle) E.; m. Elizabeth Layne Del Checcolo, May 27, 1977; 1 child, Sarah Elizabeth. Dipl., Interstate Bus. Coll., Portsmouth, Ohio, 1971; student, Marshall U., 1975-89. Land and lease mgr. Basic Mineral Industries, Huntington, W.Va., 1975-78; v.p. sales Whitten Coal and Land Co., Huntington, W.Va., 1978-83; registration supr. Cabell Huntington Hosp., 1983-88; bus. mgr. Huntington Anesthesiology Group, 1988—. With USN, 1971-74. Mem. Office Mgrs. Assn. Health Care Providers, Med. Group Mgrs. Assn., Anesthesia Adminstrn. Assembly, Huntington Area C. of C., W.Va. State C. of C. Democrat. Methodist. Home: 609 9th Ave Huntington WV 25701-2716 Office: Huntington Anesthesiology G 2828 1st Ave Ste 301 Huntington WV 25702-1236

EASTER, MARK E., osteopath; b. Phila., May 14, 1954; s. F.C. and Frances M. (Oeser) E.; m. Benna L. Yarrington, Mar. 27, 1976. BS, Graceland Coll., 1976; DO, UHS COM, Kansas City, Mo., 1981. Med. dir. F.O.C.U.S., Leon, Iowa, 1988—; v.p. med. staff Decatur City Hosp., Leon, Iowa, 1990—; med. examiner Decatur County, Leon, Iowa, 1990—; Editor Iowa Osteo. Jour., 1996. LDS Ch. Office: Decatur Medical Svcs 210 N Linden Lamoni IA 50140-1422

EASTERBROOK, JAMES ARTHUR, psychology educator; b. East Baudette, Minn., Apr. 10, 1923; s. William James and Bertha Lillian (Amorde) E.; m. Margaret Pamela Edith Evans, Nov. 19, 1944; children: Christine, Anthony, Pamela, Laurence, Margaret. B.A. with honors, Queen's U., Kingston, Ont., Can., 1949, M.A. (J. McBeth Milligan fellow), 1954; Ph.D., U. London, 1963. Mem. Canadian Def. Research Sci. Service, Churchill, Man., Edmonton, Alta., Halifax, N.S., 1950-57; research psychologist Burden Neurol. Inst., Bristol, Eng., 1959-61; mem. faculty medicine U. Alta. at Edmonton, 1961-67; prof. psychology U. N.B. at Fredericton, 1967-88, prof. emeritus, 1990—; mem. N.B. Bd. Examiners in Psychology, 1973-79, chmn., 1978-79. Served with RCAF, 1941-45. Mem. Brit. Psychol. Soc. Home: 749 Charters Settlement Rd, Charters Settlement, NB Canada E3C 1V8

EASTON, CAROL LEE, hospital official; b. Brockville, Ont., Can., Nov. 25, 1939; came to U.S., 1962; d. Robert Leroy and Luella Mae (Smith) Armstrong; m. J. Don Enterline, May 4, 1963 (dec. Apr. 1967); m. William Ivie Stevenson Easton, Apr. 15, 1972. Student, Brockville Bus. Sch., 1959; student med. records, Hotel Dieu Hosp., Kingstong, Ont. Registered record libr., Can. Asst. dir. med. records Kingstong Gen. Hosp., 1960-62; dir. med. records Kings View Hosp., Reedley, Calif., 1962-64, Community Hosp. Monterey Peninsula, Monterey, Calif., 1967—; mem. med. assisting adv. com. Monterey Peninsula Coll., 1987—. Mem. Am. Health Info. and Mgmt. Assn., Am. Med. Transcription Assn. (assoc.), Calif. Health Info. Assn., Calif. Med. Transcription Assn. (assoc.). Home: PO Box A Carmel CA 93921-0357 Office: Community Hosp Monterey PO Box Hh Carmel CA 93921-1840

EASTON, DEXTER MORGAN, physiology educator, neurophysiology researcher; b. Rockport, Mass., Sept. 13, 1921; s. Oscar Wallerius and Catherine Sophia (Bragner) E.; m. Jean Renfrew Mattoon, Dec. 18, 1953; children: Matthew, Andrew, Karl, Sylvia. PhD in Biology, Harvard U., 1947. Instr. dept. zoology U. Wash., Seattle, 1947-50, rsch. physiologist, from instr. to rsch. asst. prof., 1950-55; from asst. to assoc. prof. Fla. State U., Tallahassee, 1955-77, prof. biol. sci., 1978-82, svc. prof. biol. scis., 1982—; Author: Mechanisms of Body Function, 1963, 2d edit. 1974; contbr. over 70 articles to profl. jours. Porter fellow Harvard U., 1946; Fulbright scholar U. New Zealand, 1950-51; grantee NSF, NIH. Fellow AAAS; mem. Am. Physiol. Soc., Soc. for Neurosci., Biophys. Soc. Democrat. Home: 2908 Lasswade Dr Tallahassee FL 32312-2826 Office: Fla State U Dept Biological Science Tallahassee FL 32306

EASTON, J. DONALD, neurologist, educator; b. Saskatoon, Sask., Can., Apr. 1, 1938; s. John and Winnifred J. (Small) E.; m. Carol Anne May, 1959 (div. 1984); children: Erin, John, Murray; m. K. Von Gunten, May 19, 1985; children: Andrew, Alexander. BS in Zoology, Wash. State U., 1960; MD, U. Wash., 1964. Cert. Am. Bd. Psychiatry and Neurology (examiner, dir. 1984-92). From asst. to assoc. prof. U. Calif., San Diego, 1970-73; from assoc. prof. to prof. So. Ill. U. Sch. Medicine, Springfield, 1974-77; prof., chair neurology dept. U. Mo. Sch. Medicine, Columbia, 1977-82, U. Tex. Health Sci. Ctr., San Antonio, 1982-86, Brown U. Sch. Medicine, Providence, 1986—; pres. Neurology Found., Inc., Providence, 1990—. Author med. books; editor med. jours. Fellow Am. Heart Assn. Stroke Coun., 1971—, chmn., 1991-93, vol., Providence, 1986—. With USN, 1968-70. Fellow Am. Acad. Neurology; mem. Am. Neurol. Assn., Alpha Omega Alpha, Phi Beta Kappa. Presbyterian. Home: 7 Seaview Ave Jamestown RI 02835-1644 Office: RI Hosp Brown U 110 Lockwood St Providence RI 02903-4801

EATON, DORIS ARLENE, medical librarian; b. N.Y.C., Oct. 23, 1934; d. Walter Adam Randall and Elizabeth (Hoff) LoPinto; m. Keith Orval Eaton, Feb. 13, 1960 (div. Mar. 1981); children: Marifrances Abbott, Brian K., Terrence M. BA, Barry U., 1970; MA, U. Miami, 1973; MLS, Rutgers U., 1993. Cert. profl. libr., N.J., Acad. Health Info. Specialist. Sales profl. various orgns., N.J., 1978-88; pres. DA Eaton Constrn. Co., Long Branch, N.J., 1984-90; adj. prof. history Brookdale C.C., Lincroft, N.J., 1988-92; med. libr. Union (N.J.) Hosp., 1992—; mktg. dir. Info. Unltd. Inc., Summit, N.J., 1995-96. Candidate coun. Dem. Party, Little Silver, N.J., 1978. Mem. Med. Libr. Assn., N.J. Libr. Assn., Health Sci. Librs. N.J. (sec. 1994-96). Office: Union Hosp 1000 Galloping Hill Rd Union NJ 07083

EATON, GARY DAVID, physician; b. South Bend, Ind., Oct. 20, 1952; s. William Joseph and Virginia Lee (Dreibelbis) E.; m. Martha Marie Muir, Sept. 1973 (div. 1983); m. Margaret Jean Bell Eaton, Sept. 20, 1987 (div. 1996); children: Lynn, Heather, Brooke. AA in Fire Sci. Technology, Red Rocks C.C., Golden, Colo., 1978; BS in Biology, L.A. Coll. Chiropractic, Whittier, Calif., 1985, D Chiropractic Medicine, 1985; DO, U. Osteo. Med. and Health Sci., Des Moines, 1992. Diplomate Am. Acad. Disability Evaluating Physicans; cert. chiropractic physician, Utah, physician/surgeon, Mo., Tex. Firefighter, paramedic City of Aurora, Colo., 1976-82; chiropractic physician Pinehurst, Idaho, 1985-88; resident physician U. Ky., Lexington, 1992-94; staff physician, pvt. practice Tyler, Tex., 1994-95; resident U. Mo., Columbia, 1995-97. Mem. AMA, Internat. Spinal Injection Soc., Am. Acad. Phys. Medicine and Rehab., Physiatric Assn. of Spine, Sports and Occupl. Rehab. Republican. Home: PO Box 30697 Columbia MO 65205 Office: U Mo 5R01 One Hospital Dr Columbia MO 65212

EATON, MERRILL THOMAS, psychiatrist, educator; b. Howard County, Ind., June 25, 1920; s. Merrill Thomas and Dorothy (Whiteman) E.; m. Louise Foster, Dec. 23, 1942; children: Deirdre Ann, Thomas Anthony, David Foster. AB, Ind. U., Bloomington, 1941, MD, 1944. Diplomate: Am. Bd. Psychiatry. Intern St. Elizabeth's Hosp., Washington, 1944-45; resident Sheppard and Enoch Pratt Hosp., Towson, Md., 1948-49; pvt. practice medicine specializing in psychiatry Kansas City, Kans., 1949-60, Omaha, 1960—; dir. Nebr. Psychiat. Inst., 1968-85; assoc. in psychiatry Kans. U. Sch. Medicine, 1949-50, asst. prof., 1951-54, assoc. prof., 1954-60; assoc. prof. psychiatry U. Nebr. Coll. Medicine, 1960-63, prof., 1963-88, prof. emeritus, 1989—, chmn. dept. psychiatry, 1968-85; psychiatrist Immanuel Mental Health Ctr., 1986-88; pvt. practice cons. Omaha, 1989—. Author: Psychiatry, 1967, 5th edit., 1985, (with David Kentsmith) Treating Sexual Problems in Medical Practice, 1979. Served to capt. U.S. Army, 1945-47. Fellow ACP, Am. Psychiat. Assn.; mem. Group for Advancement Psychiatry (chmn. com. on mental health services 1970-73, chmn. publ. bd. 1976-83, cons. pub. bd. 1983—, bd. dirs. 1984-86), Nebr. Med. Assn., Nebr. Psychiat. Soc. (pres. 1973-75).

EATON, RICHARD GILLETTE, surgeon, educator; b. Forty Fort, Pa., Dec. 3, 1929; s. Walter L. and Ruth (Shaw) E.; B.A., Franklin and Marshall Coll., 1951; M.D., U. Pa., 1955; m. Du Ree Hunter, June 13, 1954; children: Bradford (dec.), Holly, Hillary. Intern U. Pa. Grad. Hosp., 1956; gen. surg. resident Peter Bent Brigham Hosp., Boston, 1957; orthopedic resident Children's Hosp. Med. Center, Mass. Gen. Hosp. and Peter Bent Brigham Hosp., Boston, 1959-62; hand surgery fellow J.W. Littler, Roosevelt Hosp., N.Y.C., 1962, now attending orthopedic surgery and reconstrn., chief hand surgery service; prof. clin. orthop. surgery Columbia Coll. Physicians and Surgeons, N.Y.C. Ruling elder Huguenot Presbyn. Ch., Pelham, N.Y. Capt., M.C., U.S. Army, 1957-59. NIH fellow, 1963-64. Diplomate Am. Bd. Orthopedic Surgeons. Mem. Am. Acad. Orthopedic Surgery, Am. Orthopaedic Assn., Am. Soc. Surgery of Hand, A.C.S., Interurban Orthopedic Club, N.Y. Acad. Medicine, J.W. Littler Soc., N.Y. Soc. Surgery of Hand. Author: Joint Injuries of the Hand, 1971; also articles. Home: 640 Ely Ave Pelham NY 10803-2402 Office: Roosevelt Hosp 1000 10th Ave New York NY 10019-1056

EBANKS, MARLON UDEL, health paraprofessional; b. Bklyn., Feb. 17, 1967; s. Udel Clifton and Austria Adrienne (Sanders) E. AA, Iona Coll., 1989. Seasonal office aide N.Y.C. Bd. of Edn., Bklyn., 1985, 86, provisional office aide, 1987, family assoc., 1987-90, health paraprofl., 1992—; family asst. pre-kindergarten program N.Y.C. Bd. Edn., Bklyn., 1988; owner, pres. Round Table Records, Nights at the Round Table Prodns. Songwriter, producer The Game, 1990, Feelings of Love, 1990. Vol. Woodhall Hosp., Bklyn., 1990; performer Kwanzaa Holiday Expo, Borough Manhattan Community Coll., 1990. Democrat. Episcopalian. Home: 964 Eastern Pky Brooklyn NY 11213-4612 Office: NYC Bd of Edn IS 391 790 E New York Ave Brooklyn NY 11203-1212

EBBELING, WILLIAM LEONARD, physician; b. Whitinsville, Mass., June 29, 1947; s. Titus Jr. and Agnes (Stienstra) E.; m. Dianne Wilder, Apr. 10, 1976; children: Jennifer Lynn, Daniel Wilder. BS, Wheaton Coll., 1969; MD, Wake Forest U. Sch. Medicine, 1974. Commd. ensign USN, 1974, advanced through grades to capt., 1988; resident Naval Med. Ctr., Portsmouth, Va., 1974-77; pediatrician Naval Med. Ctr., Naples, Italy, 1977-80; head ambulatory pediatrics, staff pediatrician Nat. NAval Med. Ctr., Bethesda, Md., 1981-85, head allery, immunology and clin. investigation dept., 1988-93; deputy chief med. corps, career planning Navy Bur. Medicine & Surgery, Washington, 1993-95; head direct med. care divsn. Naval Healthcare Support Office, San Diego, 1995—. Ch. coun., deacon Derwood (Md.) Bapt. Ch., 1988-95. Decorated Navy Commendation medal, Navy Achievement medal, Joint Svcs. Commendation medal, Meritorious Svc. medal; Duke U. Med. Ctr., Durham, N.C., 1985-88. Fellow Am. Acad. Allergy, Asthma & Immunology, Am. Acad. Pediatrics; mem. Am. Coll. Physician Execs., Southeastern Allergy Assn., Assn. Mil. Allergists (chair 1996—). Home: 10870 Autillo Way San Diego CA 92127 Office: HSO San Diego 34201 Wade Ave San Diego CA 92134-5288

EBERLE, PAUL GARRETT, respiratory therapist, educator; b. San Diego, Dec. 12, 1960; s. Orville Richard and Myrna (Garrett) E.; m. Jennifer James, Mar. 15, 1980 (div. May 1987); children: Adam, Matthew, Daniel (dec.); m. Lynda Fronk, Mar. 19, 1990; children: Ryan, Megan, Garrett, Hailey. BS, Weber State U., Ogden, Utah, 1984, MEd, 1993; postgrad., U. Chgo., 1985, U. Utah, 1995—. Registered respiratory therapist. Respiratory therapist McKay-Dee Hosp., Ogden, 1981—; asst. prof. Weber State U., Ogden, 1987—; home health cons. Olympus Med., Inc., Salt Lake City, 1995-96; presenter in field. Author: (case studies) Application of Mechanical Ventilation, 1996; cons. med.-surg. nursing Brunner & Washburn Pocket-Handbook, 1995; review editor Appleton-Lange Pubs., 1996. Mem. Am. Assn. Respiratory Care, Utah Soc. for Respiratory Care (v.p. 1996-97), Am. Lung Assn. Utah, Am. Cancer Soc. Republican. Mormon. Home: 3202 N Mountain Rd North Ogden UT 84414 Office: Weber State U 3904 University Cir Ogden UT 84408

EBERLI, FRANZ ROBERT, cardiologist; b. Sarmen, Switzerland, July 28, 1956; came to U.S., 1990; s. Franz Josef and Mama (Engel) E.; m. Ursula Kappeler; children: Tabea, Kayla, Dennis. Diploma, U. Zurich Med. Sch., 1981, MD, 1982. Asst. prof. medicine Boston U. Sch. Medicine, 1992—; assoc. dir. cardiac muscle rsch. lab., 1992—. Grantee Swiss NSF, 1988-90, Am. Heart Assn., 1993-95. Fellow Swiss Med. Soc., Swiss Soc. Cardiology; mem. Am. Heart Assn., Internat. Soc. Heart Rsch. Office: Boston U Sch Medicine 80 E Concord St W611D Boston MA 02118

EBERLY, ARTHUR LEE, JR., health facility administrator; b. Charleston, W.Va., Jan. 14, 1932; s. Arthur Lee and Ida Salome (Bernheim) E.; m. Jane Ellen Demaree, Sept. 30, 1961; children: Arthur L. III, John Brewer, Sarah Elizabeth. BS, Fla. So. Coll., 1955, DSc (hon.), 1993; MD, U. Miami Sch. Medicine, 1960. Diplomate Am. Bd. Family Practice, Quality Assurance, Utilization Review, Nat. Bd. Med. Examiners. Rotating intern Marion County Gen. Hosp., Indpls., 1960-61; pvt. practice Lighthouse Point, Fla., 1962-93; dir. med. edn. N. Broward Hosp. Dist., Ft. Lauderdale, Fla., 1993-94; med. dir. Fla. PCA Health Plans, Boca Raton, Fla., 1994—; bd. dirs. Fla. Task Force on Elderly Accesto Health Care, 1988-89, Sonshine Health Ctr., 1978-86, Am. Cancer Soc., 1972-76, v.p. Presenter in field; contbr. articles to profl. jours. Bd. trustees Fla. So. Coll., Lakeland, 1994—. With U.S. Army, 1952-54. Named Citizen of Yr. Pompano Star News, 1984; recipient Disting. Alumnus award U. Miami Sch. Medicine, 1996. Mem. Fla. Acad. Family Physicians (pres. 1981-82, Spl. Leader award 1992, Family Physician of Yr. 1988, Charter fellow 1972), Fla. Med. Assn. (pres. 1993-94, del. to AMA, sec. Fla. delegation to AMA 1995—), Royal Palm Yacht and Country Club. Republican. Methodist. Home: 3701 NE 30 Ave Lighthouse Point FL 33064 Office: PCA Family Health Plan Inc 301 Yamato Rd Boca Raton FL 33431

EBERLY, DONALD ALLEN, surgeon; b. Boston, Dec. 31, 1949; s. David Allen and Doris Ann (Holden) E.; m. Janice Kelley, June 14, 1980; children: Laura Ann, Nathan Allen. AB, Dartmouth Coll., 1971; MD, U. Fla., 1975. Diplomate Am. Bd. Surgery. Intern in surgery U. Vt., Burlington, 1975-76, resident in surgery, 1976-80; pvt. practice, New London, N.H., 1980—; staff surgeon New London Hosp., 1980—, trustee, 1988—. Fellow ACS; mem. AMA, N.H. Med. Soc. Home: 3 Meadowbrook Rd New London NH 03257 Office: New London Surg Assocs 280 County Rd Ste 8 New London NH 03257

EBERSOLD, MICHAEL JOHN, neurosurgeon; b. Wabasha, Minn., Nov. 2, 1944; s. John Roy and Sylvia (Michaels) E.; m. Janet Ray, May 17, 1947; children: Aimee, Annette, Ethan. BS, Riverfalls State U., 1966; MD, U. Wis., 1970. Diplomate Am. Bd. Neurologic Surgery. Intern Luth. Hosp., LaCrosse, Wis., 1970-71; resident in gen. surgery Luth. Hosp./Gundersen Clinic, LaCrosse, 1971-72; resident in neurologic surgery Mayo Grad. Sch., Rochester, Minn., 1972-76; neurosurgeon Midelfort Clinic, Eau Claire, Wis., 1976-79, Sacred Heart Hosp., Eau Claire, 1976-79; neurologic surgeon Mayo Clinic, St. Marys Hosp., Rochester Meth. Hosp., 1979—, joint appointment dept. orthopedics, 1995—; instr. neurosurgery Mayo Med. Sch., 1979-84, asst. prof. neurosurgery, 1984-89, assoc. prof. neurosurgery, 1989-96, prof. neurosurgery, 1996—; vis. prof., guest lectr. numerous orgns. including Wis. Acad. Family Physicians, Eau Claire, 1983-85, 87, 89, N.Y. State Soc. Anesthesiologists, N.Y.C., 1983, Acad. Hosp. Affiliates-Clin. Anesthesia, Keystone, Colo., 1985, 86, Minn. Soc. Neurol. Sics., 1985, 86, Gundersen Med. Found., 1986, 93. Mem. editl. bd. Clin. Neurosurgery, Neurosurg. Consultations, Neurosurgery, 1991—; book rev. contbr. Neurosurgery, Clin. Neurosurgery, Neurosurgery Update, Year Book of Orthopedics, 1988, Mayo Clinic Proceedings, Clin. Jour. Pain. Maj. USAR, 1970-80. Mem. AMA, Minn. Med. Assn., Zumbro Valley Med. Soc., Am. Assn. Neurol. Surgeons, Soc. Neurol. Surgeons, Minn. Neurol. Soc. (sec.-treas. 1993-95), Western Trauma Assn., Sigma Xi. Office: Mayo Clinic 200 2nd St SW Rochester MN 55905

EBERSTEIN, ARTHUR, biomedical engineering educator, researcher; b. Chgo., Apr. 23, 1928; s. Nathan and Sara (Estes) E.; m. Marion Apfel, Aug. 1, 1961; children—Sharon, Laura. B.S., Ill. Inst. Tech., 1950; M.S., U. Ill., 1951; Ph.D., Ohio State U., 1957. Asst. mem. Inst. for Muscle Disease,

N.Y.C., 1959-61; sr. scientist Am. Bosch Arma Corp., 1961-63; dir. biomed. engring. Lundy Electronics, Inc., Glen Head, N.Y., 1963-64; prof., dir. research dept. rehab. medicine NYU Med. Ctr, N.Y.C., 1964—. Co-author: Electrodiagnosis of Neuromuscular Disease, 1983. Served with U.S. Army, 1955-57. Fellow NSF, 1958, NIH, 1959. Mem. Am. Physiol. Soc., Biophys. Soc., Biomed. Engring. Soc. Am. Assn. Electrodiagnostic Medicine, Sigma Pi Sigma. Jewish. Office: NYU Med Ctr Dept Rehab Medicine 400 E 34th St New York NY 10016-4998

EBERT, GERALD DONALD, respiratory therapist; b. St. Paul, Apr. 24, 1957; s. William George and Helen Jean (Green) E.; m. Rebecca Ann Bush, Mar. 12, 1977; children: Sabrina Marie, Jill Ann, Jacklyn Lea. AAS in Respiratory Care, U. Minn., 1981. Respiratory therapist U. Minn. Hosp., Mpls., 1979-87; supr. respiratory care svc. Mpls. Childrens Med. Ctr., Mpls., 1987-89; tech. supr. respiratory care St. Paul Ramsey Med. Ctr., 1989-95, pulmonary rsch. tech., 1993-95; critical care specialist Childrens Healthcare, Mpls., 1995—; instr. Ramsey EMS, 1994—; adj. faculty St. Mary's Jr. Coll., Mpls., 1984-86; instr. Midwest Ctr. Health & Safety, St. Paul, 1990-95. Contbr. rsch. articles to profl. jours. EMT, firefighter, rescue capt. St. Paul Park Fire Dept., 1989—; sec. St. Paul Park Pub. Safety Com., 1992—, St. Paul Park Vol. Relief Assn., 1993—. Mem. Am. Assn. Respiratory Care, Minn. Soc. Respiratory Care. Home: 717 4th St Saint Paul Park MN 55071

EBERT, JAMES DAVID, research biologist, educator; b. Bentleyville, Pa., Dec. 11, 1921; s. Alva Charles and Anna Frances (Brundege) E.; m. Alma Christine Goodwin, Apr. 19, 1946; children—Frances Diane, David Brian, Rebecca Susan. AB, Washington and Jefferson Coll., 1942, ScD, 1969; PhD, Johns Hopkins U., 1950; ScD (hon.), Yale, 1973, Ind. U., 1975, Duke U., 1992; LL.D. (hon.), Moravian Coll., 1979. Jr. instr. biology Johns Hopkins U., 1946-49, Adam T. Bruce fellow biology, 1949-50, hon. prof. biology, 1956-86, hon. prof. embryology Sch. Medicine, 1956-86; instr. biology Mass. Inst. Tech., 1950-51; asst. prof. zoology Ind. U., 1951-54, assoc. prof., 1954-56, Patten vis. prof., 1963; dir. dept. embryology Carnegie Instn. of Washington, 1956-76, pres., 1978-87, trustee, 1987—; prof. biology Johns Hopkins U., 1987—, dir. Chesapeake Bay Inst., 1987-92; vis. scientist med. dept. Brookhaven Nat. Lab., 1953-54; Philips vis. prof. Haverford Coll., 1961; instr. in charge embryology tng. program Marine Biol. Lab., summers 1962-66, trustee, 1964—, pres., 1970-78, 91—, dir., 1970-75, 77-78; mem. Commn. on Undergrad. Edn. in Biol. Scis., 1963-66; mem. vis. com. for biol. and phys. scis. Western Res. U., 1964-68; Mem. panels on morphogenesis and biology of neoplasia of com. on growth NRC, 1954-56; mem. adv. panel on genetic and developmental biology NSF, 1955-56, mem. divisional com. for biology and medicine, 1962-66, mem. univ. sci. devel. panel, 1965-70, adv. com. for instl. devel., 1970-72; mem. panel basic biol. rsch. in aging Am. Inst. Biol. Sci., 1957-60; mem. panel on cell biology NIH, USPHS, 1958-62, mem. child health and human devel. tng. com., 1963-66; mem. bd. sci. counselors Nat. Cancer Inst., 1967-71, Nat. Inst. Child Health, 1973-77; mem. Com. on Scholarly Communication with People's Republic of China, 1978-81, chmn., 1989-95; chmn. Nat. Com. on Sci. Edn. Stds. & Assessment, 1992-93, chmn. Com. on Transportation and a Sustainable Environment, Transportation Rsch. Bd., 1995—; mem. vis. com. to dept. biology Mass. Inst. Tech., 1959-68; mem. vis. com. biology Harvard, 1969-75, Princeton, 1970-76; chmn. bd. sci. overseers Jackson Lab., 1976-80; mem. Inst. Medicine; bd. dirs. Baxter Internat., Transcend Therapeutics, Inc. (formerly known as Free Radical Sci., Inc.). Author: (with others) The Chick Embryo in Biological Research, 1952, Molecular Events in Differentiation Related to Specificity of Cell Type, 1955, Aspects of Synthesis and Order in Growth, 1955, Interacting Systems in Development, 2d edit., 1970, Biology, 1973, Mechanisms of Cell Change, 1979, This Our Golden Age, 1994; mem. editl. bd. (with others) Abstracts of Human Developmental Biology; editor: (with others) Oceanus; contbr. (with others) articles to profl. jours. Trustee Worcester Found. Lt. USNR, 1942-46. Decorated Purple Heart. Felow AAAS (v.p. med. scis. 1964), Am. Acad. Arts and Scis., Internat. Soc. Devel. Biology; mem. NAS (chmn. assembly life scis. 1973-77, v.p. 1981-93, chmn. Govt., Univ. and Industry Rsch. Roundtable 1987-92, chmn. on transp. and a sustainable environment 1994—), Korean Acad. Sci. and Tech. (hon. fgn. mem.), Am. Philos. Soc., Am. Inst. Biol. Scis. (pres. 1964, President's medal 1972), Am. Soc. Naturalists, Am. Soc. Zoologists (pres. 1970), Soc. Study Growth and Devel. (pres. 1957-58), Phi Beta Kappa, Sigma Xi, Phi Sigma. Home: 4100 N Charles St Baltimore MD 21218-1065 Office: Marine Biol Lab Pres Office Woods Hole MA 02543

EBERT, PAUL ALLEN, surgeon, educator; b. Columbus, Ohio, Aug. 11, 1932; m. Louise Joyce Parks, 1954; children: Leslie Ann, Michael Dean, Julie Ellen. BS, Ohio State U., 1954, MD, 1958. Diplomate Am. Bd. Surgery, Am. Bd. Thoracic Surgery. Intern in surgery Johns Hopkins Hosp., Balt., 1958-59, asst. resident surgeon, 1959-65, postdoctoral fellow Nat. Cancer Inst., 1962-63, chief resident, 1965-66; sr. asst. surgeon NIH, Bethesda, Md., 1960-62; asst. prof. surgery Duke U. Med. Ctr., Durham, N.C., 1966-68, assoc. prof. surgery, 1968-71; prof., chmn. dept. surgery Cornell U. Med. Coll., N.Y.C., 1971-75; surgeon in chief N.Y. Hosp., 1971-75; prof., chmn. dept. surgery U. Calif., San Francisco, 1975-86; dir. ACS, Chgo., 1986—. Mem. editorial bd. Am. Jour. Surgery, Annals Surgery, Cardiovascular Medicine, Internat. Dictionary Biology and Medicine, Surgery, Western Jour. Medicine; contbr. and co-contbr. over 200 med. articles. With USPHS, 1960-62. Mead-Johnson scholar ACS, 1964, Markle scholar Duke U. Med. Ctr., 1967. Fellow ACS, Royal Coll. Surgeons of Edinburgh (hon.), Royal Coll. Surgeons in Ireland (hon.); mem. Am. Assn. Thoracic Surgery (pres. 1987-88), Am. Coll. Cardiology (pres. 1983-84), Assn. for Acad. Surgery (pres. 1973), Soc. U. Surgeons (pres. 1975), Alpha Omega Alpha. Office: ACS 55 E Erie St Chicago IL 60611-2731

EBINGER, MARY RITZMAN, pastoral counselor; b. Reading, Pa., Nov. 23, 1929; d. Michael Erwin and Daisy Mae (Shaeffer) R.; m. Warren Ralph Ebinger, Aug. 11, 1951; children: Lee, Lori, Jonathan. BA, North Cen. Coll., Naperville, Ill., 1951; MS, Loyola Coll., Balt., 1981; grad. student, Wesley Theol. Sem., 1976, Cath. U., 1977. Cert. nat. counselor Dept. of Md. Health and Mental Hygiene, cert. nat. counselor Am. Assn. Pastoral Counselors. Elem. tchr. Naperville Washington Sch., 1952-54; dir. adult work Millian Ch., Rockville, Md., 1974-76; pastoral counselor Washington Pastoral Counselors, 1976-81; assoc. dir. Balt. Washington Conf. Pastoral Care and Counseling, Balt., 1990—; mem. adj. faculty psychology Frederick (Md.) C.C., 1982-87, Anne Arnold (Md.) C.C., 1988-90; pres. Wesley Guild Wesley Theol. Seminary, Washington, 1987-89; del. gen. conf. U. Meth. Ch., 1988, 92. Author: I Was Sick and You Visited Me, 1976, 2d edit., 1995, enlarged and reprinted, 1996, Does Anybody Care, 1978. Pres. Ch. Women United, Springfield, Ill., 1969-71; chmn. Episcopacy com. United Meth. Ch., Balt., 1988-90; del. gen. and jurisdictional conf. United Meth. Ch., 1988, 92. Recipient Disting. Alumnus award North Cen. Coll., 1990, Loyola Coll., 1991, Two Thousand Women of Achievement award Dartmouth Eng. Mus., 1969. Mem. Am. Assn. Counseling and Devel., Am. Assn. Pastoral Counseling (cert., Atlantic region chmn. theol. and social concerns 1988-92). Home: 6 Saint Ives Dr Severna Park MD 21146-1430 Office: Balt-Wash Conf Pastoral Care and Counseling United Meth Ch 5124 Greenwich Ave Baltimore MD 21229-2393

EBMEIER, PAMELA LEIGH, optometrist, educator; b. Ft. Polk, La., Aug. 3, 1966; d. Raymond Keith and Janet Kay (Spinner) E.; m. Christopher Dean Montmeny, Sept. 2, 1995. BS in Biology, U. Ill., 1988; OD, U. Mo., St. Louis, 1992. Pvt. practice, Boca Raton, Fla., 1992—; clin. asst. prof. Nova Southeastern U. Sch. Optometry, North Miami Beach, Fla., 1994—. Recipient excellence in clin. eyecare award Allergan, 1992. Mem. Am. Optometric Assn., Fla. Optometric Assn., Broward County Optometric Assn. Office: Aker Kasten Cataract and Laser Inst 1445 NE Boca Raton Blvd Boca Raton FL 33432-1610

ECCLES, SIR JOHN CAREW, physiologist; b. Melbourne, Australia, Jan. 27, 1903; s. William James and Mary (Carew) E.; m. Irene Miller, 1928; 9 children; m. Helena Táboríková, 1968. M.B., B.S., Melbourne U., 1925; M.A., Oxford U., 1929, D.Phil., 1929; LL.D., Melbourne U., 1965; D.Sc. (hon.), U. B.C., 1966, Cambridge U., 1960, U. Tasmania, 1964, Gustavus Adolphus, 1967, Marquette U., 1967, Loyola U., 1969, Yeshiva U., 1969, Charles U., Prague, 1969, Oxford U., 1974, U. Fribourg, 1981, U. Torino, 1983, Georgetown U., 1984, U. Tsukuba, Japan, 1986, U. Basel, 1990, U. Madrid, 1992, U. Ulm, 1993. Research fellow Exeter Coll., Oxford U., 1927-34; tutorial fellow Magdalen Coll., 1934-37; dir. Kanematsu Meml. Inst. Pathology, Sydney (Australia) Hosp., 1937-43; prof. physiology Otago U., Dunedin, New Zealand, 1944-51, Australian Nat. U., Canberra, 1951-66; mem. AMA/E.R.F. Inst. Biomed. Research, Chgo., 1966-68; disting. prof. SUNY, Buffalo, 1968-75, emeritus, 1975—. Author: (with others) Reflex Activity of the Spinal Cord, 1932; The Neurophysiological Basis of Mind: The Principles of Neurophysiology, 1953; The Physiology of Nerve Cells, 1957; The Physiology of Synapses, 1964; (with Ito, Szentagothai) The Cerebellum as a Neuronal Machine, 1967; The Inhibitory Pathways of the Central Nervous System, 1968; Facing Reality, 1970; The Understanding of the Brain, 1973; (with Karl Popper) The Self and Its Brain, 1977; (with others) Molecular Neurobiology of the Mammalian Brain, 1978, 2d edit., 1987; (with W. Gibson) Sherrington, His Life and Thought, 1979; The Human Mystery, 1979; The Human Psyche, 1980; (with D.N. Robinson) The Wonder of Being Human: Our Brain, Our Mind, 1984; Evolution of the Brain: Creation of the Self, 1989, How the Self Controls its Brain, 1993. Decorated knight bachelor, 1958, Gold and Silver Stars Order of the Rising Sun, 1986, companion Order of Australia, 1990; recipient Royal medal Royal Soc., 1962, Cothenius medal Deutche Akademie der Naturforscher Leopoldina, Nobel prize in physiology and medicine (with A. L. Hodgkin and A. F. Huxley), 1963, Gold medal Charles U., Prague, 1993. Fellow Royal Soc., 1941, Australia Acad. Sci. (pres. 1957-61); mem. Pontifical Acad. Scis., Am. Philos. Soc. (hon.), Accademia Nazionale del Lincei (fgn. hon.), NAS (fgn. assoc.), Am. Physiol. Soc. (fgn. hon.), ACP (hon.), Am. Acad. Arts and Scis. (fgn. hon.), Max Planck Soc. (hon.). Home: Ticino, CH-6646 Contra Switzerland

ECCLES, RALPH PARKER, osteopathic family medicine physician, educator; b. McMinnville, Oreg., Mar. 20, 1950; s. Julian Wright and Peggie (Parker) E.; m. Meredith Sue McKell, Mar. 15, 1974 (div. June 1983); children: R. David, Leah M., Robert M., Elizabeth; m. Carrie Atwell Ganong, Mar. 21, 1991. BA with honors, Brigham Young U., 1974; DO, Coll. Osteo. Medicine Pacific, 1982. Diplomate Nat. Bd. Osteo. Medicine. Adminstr. various nursing homes, Oreg., 1976-79; intern Rocky Mountain Hosp., Denver, N.D., 1982-83; pvt. practice Ellendale, N.D., 1984; gen. practice U.S. Army, Aurora, Colo., 1985-86; pvt. practice geriatrics Denver, 1986-89; pvt. practice gen. medicine Indian Health Svc., Eagle, 1990-91; attending in family practice Indian Health Svc., Phoenix, 1991-93; physician emergency dept. St. Anthony's Hosps., Denver, N.D., 1993; gen. practice Nat. Health Svc. Corps, Beulah, N.D., 1983-84; P/SL Health Care Ctr. Nat. Health Svc. Corps, Denver, 1994—; med. dir. Heritage Corp., Denver, 1987-89, Welcome Home Care, Arvada, Colo., 1995; asst. prof. family medicine Coll. Osteo. Med. Pacific, Pomona, Calif., 1995—. Author newsletter Health Care in a Nursing Facility, 1987-88; newspaper columnist Your Health, 1990. Recipient family practice tchr. recognition Good Samaritan Hosp., Phoenix, 1991. Mem. AMA, Am. Acad. Family Practice, Colo. Acad. Family Practice, Aircraft Owners and Pilots Assn. Home: 5090 S Boston St Greenwood Village CO 80111-1347 Office: PSL Health Care Ctr 4896 Chambers Rd Denver CO 80239

ECHAVARRIA, DAVID, psychologist; b. Bayamo, Cuba, June 26, 1950; came to the U.S., 1960; s. Lucas and Acacia (Tornes) E.; m. Adela Henriquez, July 4, 1975; 1 child, David. BA with honors, U. Fla., 1973; MS, Fla. Internat. U., 1975; PhD, Fla. Inst. Tech., 1983. Lic. psychologist, Fla. Counselor Fla. Div. Corrections, Miami, 1973-74; psychologist Waukesha (Wis.) Pub. Schs., 1975-76, Hillsborough County Pub. Schs., Tampa, Fla., 1976-86, Pathways Counseling Ctr., Tampa, 1986-88; area dir. Biodyne, Miami, 1988-90; pvt. practice, Miami, 1991—; health care mgr. Humana, Miami, 1989—. Named Merit Psychologist, Fla. Dept. Edn., 1980. Mem. APA. Roman Catholic. Home: 1250 Kane Concourse Miami FL 33154-1938 Office: 401 Miracle Mile Ste 204 Miami FL 33134-4924

ECHEVARRIA, EDDIE, medical technologist, biologist, career officer; b. Peñuelas, P.R., June 10, 1955; s. Miguel and Eva Echevarria. BS in Biology, U. P.R., 1977, postgrad., 1978-80; MA in Mgmt. Health Care Adminstrn., Ctrl. Mich. U., 1981; BSN, Howard U., 1995. RN, D.C., Md. Enlisted U.S. Army, Washington, 1980, advanced through grades to lt., 1995, biol. rsch. asst. Walter Reed Army Inst. Rsch., 1980-89, non-com. officer-in-charge Divsn. Biochemistry, 1992-93, staff nurse, 1995—. Contbr. articles to profl. jours. Mem. Am. Med. Technologists (cert.), Golden Key. Home: 8715 First Ave # 1516-D Silver Spring MD 20910 Office: Walter Reed Army Med Ctr Ward 57 Washington DC 20307

ECHOLS, CHARLES LITTLE, JR., physician; b. Covington, Va., Nov. 19, 1934; s. Charles Little and Elizabeth (Coleman) E.; m. Ann T. Echols, July 12, 1960; children: Charles Little III, Gray T., Anne Elizabeth. BA, Va. Mil. Inst., 1955; MD, U. Va., 1959. Internal medicine intern Bowman Gray Sch. Medicine, Winston-Salem, N.C., 1959-60, med. resident, 1960-61; resident in neurology U. Va., Charlottsville, 1961-64; chief, neurology svc. Valley Forge Gen. Hosp., Phoenixville, Pa., 1964-66; spl. fellow in neuropathology Air Force Inst. Pathology, Washington, 1966-67, Columbia U., N.Y.C., 1967-68; sr. neurologist Barrow Neurol. Inst., Phoenix, 1968—, chief cognitive disorders sect., divsn. neurology, 1990—. Capt. M.C., U.S. Army, 1964-66. Republican. Episcopalian. Home: 4948 E Rock Ridge Rd Phoenix AZ 85018

ECK, KENNETH FRANK, pharmacist; b. Alma, Kans., Feb. 4, 1917; s. Clarence Joseph and Rosa Barbara (Noller) E.; m. Ouida Susie Landon, July 2, 1938 (dec. Sept. 1986); children: Alan Grantland, Mark Warren, Dana Landon; m. Lorraine B. Wooster Rubottom, Apr. 14, 1989. BS in Pharmacy summa cum laude, Southwestern Okla. State U., 1950. Ptnr., mgr. Taylor Drug Store, Healdton, Okla., 1950-51, Taylor-Eck Drug Store, Healdton, 1951-59, Johnson-Eck Drug Store, Healdton, 1959-72; pres. Eck Drug Co., Inc., Healdton, 1972-87, cons., relief pharmacist, 1987—; cons., relief pharmacist Eck Drug and Gift, Waurika, Okla., 1987—; affiliate instr. pharmacy Southwestern Okla. State U., Weatherford, 1970-87, mem. dean's adv. com. Sch. of Pharmacy, early 1980's; bd. dirs. med. adv. bd. Dept. Human Svcs. Okla., Oklahoma City, 1990-91. Past mem. governing bd. Healdton Mcpl. Hosp.; mem. Okla. Profl. Responsibilty Tribunal of Okla. Bar Assn., 1983-88, vice chief master, 1988; past mem. bd. dirs. Carter County chpt. ARC, Ardmore, Okla.; bd. dirs. Healdton Oil Mus., 1993—; pres. bd. dirs. Okla. Pharmacy Heritage Found., 1994-95; mem. fin. com. Healdton br. Chickasaw Libr., 1993; bd. dirs. Healdton Econ. Devel., 1993—; deacon Ch. of Christ, 1945—. With USN, 1942-45, PTO. Recipient Achievement award Merck Sharp & Dohme, 1991, Bowl of Hygeia, 1985, outstanding svc. award Okla. Profl. Responsibility Tribunal of Okla. State Bar Assn.; named to Hall of Fame, Okla. Pharmacy Heritage Found., 1996. Mem. VFW (post comdr. Healdton 1974-78), Okla. Pharm. Assn. (pres. 1990-91, plaque 1991) Healdton C. of C. (bd. dirs. 1975—, pres. 1984-85), So. Okla. Devel. Assn. (coun. area agy. on aging adv. bd. 1987—, 1st v.p. 1994-95, pres. 1995-96), Nat. Assn. Retail Druggists (profl. affairs com. 1990-91), Am. Legion (post comdr. Healdton 1985—), Lions (eye bank bd. 1993-95, coord. campaign first sight 1993-94, pres. Healdton 1994-95). Democrat. Home: 1033 E Texas St Healdton OK 73438-3017

ECKELSON, ROBERT ALAN, orthodontist; b. Cleve., Feb. 2, 1947; s. Sam Robert and Frances (Kaplan) E.; m. Linda Goldstine, July 23, 1984. DDS, Ohio State U., 1971; postgrad., U. Ill., Chgo., 1971-73. Diplomate Am. Bd. Orthodontists. Pvt. practice Boca Raton, Fla., 1973—; mem. staff Boca Raton Community Hosp., 1978—. Bd. dirs. Boca Forum, Boca Raton, 1988-93, pres., 1992-93. Mem. So. Assn. Orthodontists, Fla. Dental Assn., Boca Raton Roundtable (pres. 1993-95), Rotary (pres. Boca Raton 1996-97). Office: 951 NW 13th St Ste 3B Boca Raton FL 33486-2337

ECKENHOFF, EDWARD ALVIN, health care administrator; b. Durham, N.C., Mar. 4, 1943; s. James Edward and Bonnie Lee E.; m. Judi G. Vicich, May 27, 1978. BA, Transylvania U., 1966; MA, U. Ky., 1968; MHA, Washington U., 1974. V.p., adminstr. Rehab. Inst. Chgo., 1976-82; pres., chief exec. officer Nat. Rehab. Hosp., Washington, 1982—; asst. prof. dept. community and family practice Med. Sch., Georgetown U., Washington, 1983-94; v.p. Medlantic Healthcare Group, 1987—; pres. Nat. Rehab. Services Corp., 1987-92; chmn. bd. NASCOTT, IBIS; instr. Med. Sch., Northwestern U., preceptor Grad. Sch. Bus.; mem. Ill. Commn. on Health Assistance Programs; mem. Ill. adv. com., chmn. exec. com. Internat. Yr. of Disabled; surveyor Commn. on Accreditation of Rehab. Facilities, bd. dirs., 1980-82; bd. dirs. Nat. Assn. Rehab. Facilities, 1982-83; mem. com. on accreditation and edn. Am. Phys. Therapy Assn. Contbr. articles to profl. jours. Bd. dirs. Am. Occupl. Therapy Found., Easter Seal Soc., Boy Scouts Am., Chgo. Area Coun., Nat. Area, 1987-87, Operation ABLE Chgo., Access Living of Met. Chgo., Am. Chamber Symphony, Chgo. Named Washingtonian of the Yr., Washingtonian Mag., 1989; recipient Citation for Disting. Svc., AMA, 1990. Fellow Inst. Medicine Chgo., Am. Coll. Hosp. Execs.; mem. Am. Hosp. Assn. (chmn. governing coun. for rehab. hosps. 1985, trustee 1991-93, chmn. policy com. 1993, mem. exec. com. 1993), Am. Congress Rehab. Medicine (chmn. policy and devel. com.), Chgo. Hosp. Coun. (chmn. com. rehab. 1978-82, exec. com. 1993—). Episcopalian. Home: 1658 35th St NW Washington DC 20007-2360 Office: Nat Rehab Hosp 102 Irving St NW Washington DC 20010-2921

ECKENSTEIN, RUTH ANN, nurse, educator; b. Guthrie, Okla, July 20, 1951; d. Ramon Richard and Juanita Ruth (McKenzie) McNulty; m. Ed Eckenstein, Dec. 31, 1986. B.S. in Health Edn., Central State U., Edmond, Okla., 1982, M.Ed. of Adult Edn., 1985; A.S. in Nursing, Okla. State U. Tech. Inst., Oklahoma City, 1976. R.N., Okla., Nebr. Staff nurse Okla. Teaching Hosp., Oklahoma City, 1976-77; dir. nurses Beatrice Manor (Nebr.), 1977-78, Good Samaritan Ctr., Wymore, Nebr., 1978-79; house supr. Logan County Health Ctr., Guthrie, Okla., 1979-82, Bapt. Med. Ctr., Oklahoma City, 1982-83; practical nurse instr. Francis Tuttle Vocat.-Tech. Ctr. Oklahoma City, 1983—; cons. Guthrie Nursing Ctr., 1979-80. Author: Team Teaching in Nursing Education, 1983; Computer Medical Terminology. Okla. Health Edn. Tching. Assn. (pres. 1995-96). Democrat. Roman Catholic. Home: 6604 Blue Spruce Ct Oklahoma City OK 73162-6722 Office: Francis Tuttle Vocat-Tech Ctr 12777 N Rockwell Ave Oklahoma City OK 73142-2710

ECKER, ARTHUR DAVID, neurologist; b. N.Y.C., Jan. 29, 1913; s. Murray and Olga (Edelstein) E.; m. Marcia Schlesinger, Sept. 15, 1935; children: Sandra Ecker Kaplan, Jonathan Ecker. AB, Dartmouth Coll., 1931; MD, Johns Hopkins, 1934; MS in Neurology, U. Minn., 1938, PhD in Neurology, 1938. Diplomate Am. Bd. Neurol. Surgery, Am. Bd. Psychiat. and Neurology. Intern Mary Hitchcock Meml. Hosp., Hanover, N.H., 1934-35; fellow neurology and neurosurgery Mayo Clinic, Rochester, Minn., 1935-39; pvt. practice Syracuse, N.Y., 1939-88; ret., 1988; sr. attending neurosurgeon Community Gen. Hosp., Crouse-Irving Meml. Hosp., Syracuse, 1955-57; founder Dept. Neurosurgery Med. Sch., Syracuse U., 1939; clin. prof. neurosurgery SUNY, 1955-57. Author: Normal Cerebral Angiography, 1951; (with others) Angiographic Localization of Cerebral Masses, 1955; contbr. over 115 articles to profl. jours. and publs. Major U.S. Army, 1942-45. Fellow ACS, Am. Acad. Neurology, Am. Assn. of Neurol. Surgeons, Assn. of Mil. Surgeons, N.Y. Acad. of Medicine. Home: 1301 Nottingham Rd Apt A208 Jamesville NY 13078-8703

ECKER, J(ACOB) ALDENE, former social services administrator, consultant; b. Waynesboro, Pa., May 1, 1916; s. Charles Leslie and Effie Pearl (Garnes) E.; m. Martha Elizabeth Andes, June 17, 1944; children: John Leslie, Janine Elizabeth Ecker Duffy. AB, Juniata Coll., 1938; MSW, Case Western Res. U., 1948; BDiv, Bethany Theol. Sem., 1948. Caseworker Ill. Dept. Pub. Welfare, Chgo., 1946-47; caseworker boys ct. svc. Ch. Fedn. of Greater Chgo., 1947-48, dir. boys ct. svc., 1948-52; dir. profl. svcs. family svcs. div. Salvation Army, Chgo., 1952-55; exec. dir. Fox Valley Mental Health Clinic, Elgin, Ill., 1955-82; cons. Ecker Ctr. for Mental Health (formerly Fox Valley Mental Health Ctr.), Elgin, 1982—. Vol. cons. Appalachia Habitat for Humanity, Robin, Tenn., 1986-91, Morgan-Scott Project for Christian Concern, 1987-95; organizing chmn. OEO for Kane County, Elgin, 1965; asst. dir. civilian pub. sc. Ch. of Brethren, Elgin, 1944-46. Recipient Agy. Exec. award Elgin United Way, 1980. Mem. NASW (vice chmn. Fox River Valley chpt. 1961-62, chmn. 1962-64), Mental Health Assn. Tenn. (rep. Cumberland County chpt. 1989-92). Home: 408 S McKendrie Ave Apt 344 Mount Morris IL 61054 Home: 408 S Mckendrie Ave Apt 344 Mount Morris IL 62054

ECKER, JEROME ALBERT, gastroenterologist; b. Cleve., Sept. 20, 1919; s. Albert and Leona (Gaspard) E.; m. Carolyn Wegat, July 25, 1945 (div. 1965); children: Laureen Lee, Shereen Kay, Maureen Anne; m. Isabel Darling, Mar. 3, 1965; 1 child, Jerome Albert Jr. BA with honors, Ohio Wesleyan U., 1941; MD with honors, Case Western Res. U., 1944. Intern Univ. Hosps., Cleve., 1944-46; resident in internal medicine Cleve. Clinic Found., 1948-51, staff gastroenterologist, 1951-54; staff gastroenterologist Magan Clinic, Covina, Calif., 1954, Santa Barbara (Calif.) Med. Clinic, 1954-76, Kerrville (Tex.) VA Med. Ctr., 1977-88; chief of medicine Santa Barbara Gen. Hosp., 1956-57, Santa Barbara Clinic, 1958-59; chief of medicine Santa Barbara Cottage Hosp., 1969-70, chief of staff, pres., 1974-75. Contbr. articles to profl. jours. Fellow ACP, Am. Coll. Gastroenterology (gov. for Calif. 1958-60, trustee 1960-74, v.p. 1968); mem. AMA, Am. Gastroenterol. Assn., Am. Soc. Gastrointestinal Endoscopy, Pacific Interurban Clin. Club, Kiwanis (local v.p. 1954). Republican. Presbyterian. Home: 1651 Beach Rd Unit 405 Englewood FL 34223-5832 Office: PO Box 1844 Englewood FL 34295-1844

ECKER, JONATHAN, psychiatrist; b. Syracuse, N.Y., Aug. 19, 1946; s. Arthur David and Marcia Muriel (Schlesinger) E.; m. Rosanne Orenstein; Diana, Laura. BA, Columbia Coll., 1966; MD, Yale U., 1970. Diplomate in psychiatry Am. Bd. Psychiatry and Neurology. Resident in psychiatry SUNY Health Scis. Ctr., Syracuse, 1970-74; Pvt. practice psychiatry Syracuse, N.Y., 1974-86; chair dept. behavioral medicine Health Svcs. Assn. Cen. N.Y., Syracuse, 1982—. Pres. Cen. N.Y. Civil Liberties Union, Syracuse, 1975, bd. dirs., 1988-94. Fellow Am. Psychiat. Assn. Home: 104 Downing Rd Syracuse NY 13214-1503 Office: 8280 Willett Pky Baldwinsville NY 13027-1306

ECKER, PAUL GERARD, physician, educator; b. Cleve., Dec. 28, 1919; s. Enrique Eduardo and Marie Josephine (van Reeth) E.; m. Henriette Juliette Dumas, Nov. 25, 1950; children: Hendrik Michel, Christian Paul. BS, Case Western Res. U., 1942, MD, 1944. Fellow Rockefeller Inst., N.Y.C., 1946-48; teaching fellow Med. Sch. Harvard U., Boston, 1948-49; instr. Columbia-Presbyn. Coll., N.Y.C., 1950-55; asst. prof. psychiatry U. Pa., Phila., 1955-60; chief functional disease svc. Hosp. U. of Pa., Phila., 1957-60; tng. analyst Inst. Phila. Assn. for Psychoanalysis, Phila., 1968—; cons. surgeon gen. USAF, USN, US Army, Washington. Mem. acquisitions com. Phila. Mus. of Art; benefactor Cleve. Mus. Art, Phila. Mus. Art., Mc Darcy Mus. Chgo. With USN, 1945-46, 52-54, capt. USNR. Decorated Legion of Merit. Fellow ACP, Am. Coll. Psychiatrists; mem. Am. Psychoanalytic Assn., Century Assn., Soc. Med. Cons. to Armed Forces (past pres.), Phila. Assn. for Psychoanalysis (past pres.), Royal Navy Club London, Sigma Xi. Roman Catholic. Home and Office: 631 St Georges Rd Philadelphia PA 19119-3341

ECKERLY, JEAN RUTH, internist; b. Chgo., June 25, 1937; d. Wilbur Joseph and Carrie Minnie (Wendorf) E. AA, Brainerd (Minn.) Jr. Coll., 1954; BS, U. Chgo., 1958, MD, 1962. Diplomate Am. Bd. Internal Medicine, Am. Bd. Chelation Therapy; cert. clin. nutritionist. Intern Mpls. Gen. Hosp., 1962-63; resident in internal medicine Hennepin County Gen. Hosp./U. Minn., 1963-66; asst. prof. U. Minn., 1966-70; med. dir. Hennepin County Outpatient Dept., Mpls., 1966-69, Pilot City Health Ctr., Mpls., 1969-73, Hennepin County Methadone Program, Mpls., 1974-81, Sacaris, Mpls., 1971-80; owner, med. dir. Preventive Medicine Assocs., Mpls., 1981—; mem. Minn. Health Adv. Bd., Mpls., 1970-72. Mem. Am. Med. Women's Assn., Am. Coll. Advancement Medicine (bd. dirs. 1984-87), Am. Acad. Environ. Medicine, Am. Coll. Nutrition, Gay-Lesbian Med. Assn. Office: Preventive Medicine Assocs Ste 350 10700 Old County Rd 15 Minneapolis MN 55441

ECKERT, RUTH MARIE, nursing administrator, oncological nurse; b. Chambersburg, Pa., July 18, 1956; d. Robert Daniel Sr. and Carolyn Ruth (Lucas) Boyer; m. Douglas Eckert, Aug. 4, 1979; 1 child, Dawn Andrea. Diploma, York Hosp. Sch. Nursing, 1977; BSN, Cath. U. Am., 1986; MS, U. Calif., San Francisco, 1991. Commd. 2d lt. USAF, 1978, advanced through grades to maj., 1989; staff nurse USAF Hosp., Scott AFB, Ill.; asst. charge nurse USAF Hosp., Andrews AFB, Md.; charge nurse USAF Travis AFB, Fairfield, Calif.; quality assurance coord. McConnel AFB, Kans. Decorated Air Force Commendation medal, Meritorious Svc. medal. Mem. Oncology Nursing Assn., Air Force Assn., Sigma Theta Tau. Office: 22d Med Group/SGQ 57950 Leavenworth Mc Connell AFB KS 67221

ECKHARDT, LAUREL ANN, biologist, researcher, educator; b. Palo Alto, Calif., Sept. 4, 1951; d. Joseph Carl Augustus Eckhardt and Ada Jane Williams Smith; m. Michael Warren Young, Dec. 27, 1978; children: Natalie Alice Eckhardt, Arissa Caroline Eckhardt. BA summa cum laude, U. Tex., 1974; PhD in Genetics, Stanford (Calif.) U., 1980. Damon Runyon-Walter Winchell postdoctoral fellow Albert Einstein Coll. Medicine, Bronx, 1980-83; asst. prof. Dept. Biol. Sci., Columbia U., N.Y.C., 1984-88, assoc. prof., 1989-92; prof. Dept. Biol. Sci., Hunter Coll. of CUNY, 1992—; reviewer immunobiology study sect. Dept. Rsch. Grants, NIH, Bethesda, Md., 1993-96; reviewer grand rev. com. Am. Heart Assn., N.Y.C., 1990-93. Contbr. articles to profl. jours. Rsch. grantee NIH-Inst. Allergy and Infectious Diseases, 1984-90, 90—, Am. Cancer Soc., 1990-95, NIH-Nat. Cancer Inst., 1994—. Mem. Am. Assn. Immunologists (program com. mem. 1995—), N.Y. Acad. Scis., Harvey Soc. Democrat. Office: Hunter College of CUNY Dept Biol Sci 695 Park Ave New York NY 10021

ECKHART, WALTER, molecular biologist, educator; b. Yonkers, N.Y., May 22, 1938; s. Walter and Jean (Fairrington) E. B.S., Yale U., 1960; postgrad., Cambridge U., Eng., 1960-61; Ph.D., U. Calif.-Berkeley, 1965. Postdoctoral fellow Salk Inst., San Diego, 1965-69, mem., 1970-73, assoc. prof. molecular biology, 1973-79, prof., 1979—, dir. Armand Hammer Ctr. for Cancer Biology, 1976—; adj. prof. U. Calif.-San Diego, 1973—. Contbr. articles on molecular biology and virology to profl. jours. NIH research grantee, 1967—. Mem. AAAS, Am. Assn. Cancer Rsch., Am. Soc. Microbiology, Am. Soc. Virology. Home: 951 Skylark Dr La Jolla CA 92037-7731 Office: Armand Hammer Ctr Cancer Biology Salk Inst for Biol Studies PO Box 85800 San Diego CA 92186-5800

ECKLER, MARIE ANN, gerontological nurse, educator, researcher; b. Boston, Aug. 24, 1947; d. Casimir Edward and Frances Marie (Radziszewski) E. Diploma, Boston City Hosp. Sch. Nursing, 1970; BS summa cum laude, Boston Coll., 1976, MS, 1977; gerontol./geriatric nurse cert., Boston U., 1977. Cert. clin. specialist in gerontology, rehab. RN. Staff nurse, ICU Boston City Hosp., 1970-74; clin. coord. Hebrew Rehab. Ctr. for Aged, Boston, 1974-78, asst. DON, 1978-79, clin. specialist, 1979—; rschr. clin. strategies program Brigham and Women's Hosp., 1994—. Recipient Jesse P. Baldwin medal for nursing excellence. Mem. Sigma Theta Tau. Home: 653 Ware St Mansfield MA 02048-3201

ECKLES, GEORGE LOVE, JR., surgeon; b. Nashville, Oct. 14, 1947; s. George Love and Caroline (Dunn) E.; m. Mary Ann Jones, Jan. 24, 1970; children: George L. III, Ryan Allen. BS in Biology, U. Memphis, 1969; MD, U. Tenn., 1973. Intern Emory U. Hosps., Atlanta, 1973-74, resident in surgery, 1974-78; pvt. practice Winchester, Tullahoma, Tenn., 1978-87; pvt. practice Murfreesboro (Tenn.) Med. Clinic, 1987—, also pres. bd. dirs.; chief of staff Meth. Hosp., Winchester, 1980-84, Middle Tenn. Med. Ctr., Murfreesboro, 1994, chmn. staff adv. com., 1995; mem. Medicare Carrier Adv. Bd., Nashville, 1994—. Chmn. Ctrl. Tenn. Solid Waste Bd., Murfreesboro, 1992—; alumnus Leadership Rutherford, Murfreesboro, 1993—; active United Way, Murfreesboro, 1992. Recipient Physicians Recognition award AMA, 1991, 92, 93, 94, 95. Fellow ACS, Southeastern Surg. Congress, SAGES; mem. Soc. for Laparoendoscopic Surgery, So. Med. Assn., Tenn. Med. Assn. (del., chair reference com. 1994-96, Disting. Svc. award 1991), Rutherford County C. of C. (dir. 1993—), Rotary, Moose, Alpha Omega Alpha. Home: 1619 Georgetown Ln Murfreesboro TN 37129 Office: Murfreesboro Med Clinic 1004 N Highland Ave Murfreesboro TN 37130

ECKSTEIN, EUGENE CHARLES, biomedical engineering educator; b. Bucyrus, Ohio, Oct. 31, 1946; s. Robert Frederick and Catherine C. (Pessefall) E.; m. Jane Foster Bernstein, Sept. 1, 1968; children: Matthew, Sarah, Adam. SB, MIT, 1970, SM, 1970, PhD, 1975. Assoc. in bioengring. Peter Bent Brigham Hosp./Harvard Sch. Medicine, Boston, 1974-75; asst. prof. mech. and biomed. engring. U. Miami, Coral Gables, Fla., 1975-81, assoc. prof., 1981-88, prof., 1988-92; J. R. Hyde Prof. Biomedical Engring., U. Tenn., Memphis, 1992—; cons. in field. Mem. ASME, Am. Inst. Med. & Biol. Engring., Internat. Soc. for Artificial Organs, Am. Soc. Artificial Internal Organs, Sigma Xi. Contbr. articles to profl. jours. Office: Univ Tenn Memphis Dept Biomed Engring 899 Madison Ave Ste 801 Memphis TN 38103-3405

ECKSTEIN, JOHN WILLIAM, physician, educator; b. Central City, Iowa, Nov. 23, 1923; s. John William and Alice (Ellsworth) E.; m. Imogene O'Brien, June 16, 1947; children: John Alan, Charles William, Margaret Ann, Thomas Cody, Steven Gregory. B.S., Loras Coll., 1946; M.D., U. Iowa, 1950. Asst. prof. internal medicine U. Iowa, Iowa City, 1956-60; assoc. prof. U. Iowa, 1960-65, prof., 1965-92, prof. emeritus, 1993; assoc. dean VA Hosp. affairs, 1969-70, dean coll. medicine, 1970-91, dean emeritus, 1993; chmn. cardiovascular study sect. NIH, 1970-72, Nat. Heart, Lung and Blood Adv. Couhn., 1974-78; mem. VA Manpower Study Group, 1988-92; mem. adv. com. to dir. NIH, 1990-95. Author papers and abstracts. Served with USAAF, 1943-45, U.S. Army Med. Corps., 1950-51. Rockefeller Found. postdoctoral fellow, 1953-54; Am. Heart Assn. Research fellow, 1954-55; Nat. Heart Inst. spl. research fellow, 1955-56; Am. Heart Assn. established investigator, 1958-63; recipient USPHS Research Career award, 1963-70, Disting. Alumni Svc. award U. Iowa, 1994, Disting. Alumnus award Loras Coll., 1994, Disting. Physician award Dept. VA, 1995;Eckstein Med. Rsch. Bldg. named in his honor, U. Iowa, 1988. Mem. Am. Heart Assn. (v.p. 1969, chmn. coun. on circulation 1969-71, pres. 1978-79), AMA (mem. health policy agenda panel 1982-86, governing coun. sect. on med. schs. 1985-92, mem. study sect. faculty and rsch. 1985-86, alt. del. Ho. of Dels. 1986-90, del 1990-92, Disting. Svc. award 1992), Am. Fedn. Clin. Rsch. (chmn. Midwestern sect. 1965), Ctrl. Soc. Clin. Rsch. (sec.-treas. 1965-70, pres. 1973-74), Am. Soc. Clin. Investigation, Am. Clin. and Climatol. Assn., Assn. Am. Physicians, Assn. Am. Med. Colls. (exec. coun. 1981-82, adminstrv. bd. 1980-82, 85-86), Inst. of Medicine of Nat. Acad. Scis., Assn. Acad. Health Ctrs. (mem. sci. policy study group 1988-93). Home: 1415 William White Blvd Iowa City IA 52245-4443 Office: U Iowa Hosps & Clinics Iowa City IA 52242-1101

ECKSTEIN, MARLENE R., vascular radiologist; b. Poughkeepsie, N.Y., Sept. 6, 1948; d. Marc and Lola (Charm) E.; A.B., Vassar Coll., 1970; M.D., Albert Einstein Coll. Medicine, 1973. Diplomate Nat. Bd. Med. Examiners; cert. Am. Bd. Radiology. Intern in medicine Yale-New Haven Med. Center, 1973-74, resident in diagnostic radiology, 1974-77; asst. radiologist, chief vascular radiology sect. South Nassau Communities Hosp., Oceanside, N.Y., 1977-78, asso. radiologist, chief vascular radiology sect., 1978-81, asst. dir. dept. radiology, chief vascular radiology sect., 1981-83; asst. prof. clin. radiology SUNY-Stony Brook Med. Sch., 1980-83; instr. radiology, Harvard Med. Sch., 1983-84, asst. prof., 1984—; asst. radiologist Mass. Gen. Hosp., 1983-87, assoc. radiologist, 1987—. Mem. exec. com. and hosp. chmn. United Jewish Appeal of Physicians and Dentists of Nassau County (N.Y.), 1981-83. Fellow Am. Coll. Angiology, Soc. Cardiovascular and Interventional Radiology; mem. Am. Coll. Radiology, Am. Inst. Ultrasound in Medicine, Mass. Radiol. Soc., Am. Assn. Women Radiologists, Am. Med. Women's Assn., AMA, Mass. Med. Soc., New Eng. Soc. Cardiovascular and Interventional Radiology (pres. 1985-86), Radiol. Soc. N.Am., Designer and developer line of vascular catheters. Avocations: writing poetry, exercising, video and electronic equipment, musical keyboard, computer. Home: 141 Fulton Ave Apt 312 Poughkeepsie NY 12603-2841 Office: Mass Gen Hosp Vascular Radiology Sect Boston MA 02114

EDDLEMAN, JANIE ANN, nurse; b. Vincennes, Ind., Nov. 30, 1945; d. Bub and Mary Elizabeth (Halter) Holscher; m. James Lewis Eddleman, June 25, 1966; children: Lisa, Lynda, Daniel. Diploma in nursing, St. Mary's Sch. Nursing, 1966. RN, Calif. Staff nurse critical care Valley Meml. Hosp., Livermore, Calif., 1970-74, nurse computer analyst, 1985-90; recreation specialist Livermore Area Park & Recreation Dist., 1973-77; tchr., dir. Wee Care Nursery Sch., Livermore, 1977-85, owner, 1977—; cancer care coord. Valley Health Sys., Livermore, 1990—. Bd. dirs. Hope Hospice, Dublin, Calif., 1991-94, pres., 1995—. Mem. Oncology Nursing Soc. (editor patient edn. spl. interest group 1995—, pres. Calif. East Bay chpt. 1994-95). Roman Catholic. Home: 2155 Westbrook Ln Livermore CA 94550 Office: Valley Care Health Libr#120 5575 W Los Positas Blvd Pleasanton CA 94588

EDDY, ARTHUR RICHARD, JR., chemist, biomedical engineer; b. Buffalo, Oct. 15, 1944; s. Arthur Richard and Ethel Aurellia (Stemler) E.; m. Judith Jean Kane, Oct. 4, 1969; children: Amy Renee, Jennifer Alison, Arthur Richard III. Student, Canisius Coll., 1962-65; BS in Chemistry, SUNY, Buffalo, 1969. Asst. scientist Ortho Diagnostics, Raritan, N.J., 1973-74; area supr. Buffalo Gen. Hosp., 1974-78; sr. assoc. research scientist Miles Labs., Elkhart, Ind., 1978-81; sr. chemist Graphic Controls, Buffalo, 1981-83, engr. quality assurance, reliability, 1983-86; sr. engr. Bard Critical Care, Lombard, Ill., 1986-90; dir. rsch. & devel. ConMed Corp., Rome, N.Y., 1990—; Faculty Sch. Med. Tech. Buffalo Gen. Hosp., 1974-78. Inventor in field. Vol. United Way, Buffalo, 1983-84, Haverhill, Mass. 1992-94. Mem. Am. Chem. Soc., Am. Assn. for Clin. Chemistry, Assn. for Advancement of Med. Instrumentation. Republican. Roman Catholic. Home: 32 Hayden Cir Hampton NH 03842 Office: Con Med Corp 5836 Success Dr Rome NY 13440

EDDY, ESTHER DEWITZ, retired pharmacist; b. Buffalo, 1926; d. Charles Frederick and Shirley Beulah (Sanderson) Dewitz; m. Russell Warren Eddy, June 8, 1948 (div. May 1977); children: Carl W., James R., Richard G. BS in Pharmacy, U. Buffalo, 1948. Community pharmacist various pharmacies, Buffalo, 1948-57; hosp. pharmacist Niagara Falls (N.Y.) Meml. Hosp., N.Y., 1964-68, Deaconess Hosp., Buffalo, 1968-69; staff pharmacist Children's Hosp. Buffalo, 1969-76, asst. dir. pharmacy, 1976-78, dir. dept. pharmacy svcs., 1978-91; adminstrv. dir. Western N.Y. Poison Control Ctr., 1978-91; ret., 1991; asst. clin. prof. Sch. Pharmacy SUNY, Buffalo, 1996—; mem. N.Y. State Bd. Pharmacy, 1984-93, chmn., 1988-89, extended mem., 1993—; part-time faculty Sch. of Pharmacy, SUNY, Buffalo, 1995—. Guest editor Pharmacy Law, 1995—. Recipient Phillip Melanchthon award for vol. svc. Luth. Coordinating Ministry, Buffalo, 1991; Willis G. Gregory award U. Buffalo Pharmacy Alumni Assn., 1992. Mem. Am. Soc. Hosp. Pharmacists, N.Y. State Coun. Hosp. Pharmacists (bd. dirs. 1974-76, Pharmacist of Yr. award 1991), Western N.Y. Soc. Hosp. Pharmacists (treas. 1968-69, pres. 1972), Pharmacy Assn., Western N.Y. (named to Hall of Fame 1989), Pharmacy Assn. of Western N.Y. Aux. (pres. 1995—).

EDDY, MARK JAMES, healthcare industry executive; b. Detroit, June 17, 1958; s. James Joseph and Sharon Lou (Nelson) E.; m. Wendy Mary Kohler, Aug. 8, 1980; 1 child, Matthew Mark. Student, U. Mich., Ann Arbor, 1976-78; BBA, Ea. Mich. U., Ypsilanti, 1980. CPA, Tenn. Intern Karpus & Karpus, Detroit, 1979; staff auditor, internal audit dept. HCA, Nashville, 1980-81, sr. auditor, 1981-82, audit supr., 1982-84, sr. audit supr., 1984-85, corp. and constrn. audit mgr., 1985-87; audit mgr. HealthTrust, Inc., Nashville, 1987-93, dir. internal audit, 1994-95; dir. internal audit Columbia/HCA, Nashville, 1995—. Mem. Am. Inst. CPAs, Tenn. Soc. CPAs, Am. Mgmt. Assn. Home: 413 Benton Ln Franklin TN 37067

EDELHEIT, LEWIS S., research physicist; b. Chgo., Aug. 24, 1942; m. Susan Wershkoff, 1965; children: David, Dena. BS, U. Ill., 1964, MS, 1965, PhD in Physics, 1969. Physicist GE R&D Ctr., Schenectady, N.Y., 1969-76; mgr. Applied Sci. Lab., GE Med. Sys GE Corp. R&D, Schenectady, N.Y., 1976-80, mgr. computed tomography prodn. engring., 1980-82, gen. mgr. dept. engring., 1982-83, gen. mgr. dept. computed tomography program, 1983-85; pres., CEO Quantum Med. Sys., 1985-91; mgr. electronics sys. rsch. ctr. Corp. R&D, Schenectady, N.Y., 1991-92; pres., CEO Quantum Med. Sys., 1985-91. Mem. NAE, Am. Physics Soc., Indsl. Rsch. Inst., Sigma Xi. Office: GE Corp R&D Ctr Bldg K1 Rm 5A1 PO Box 8 Schenectady NY 12301

EDELMAN, CORRINE R., retired hospital administrator; b. L.I., Nov. 4, 1940; d. Robert A. and Marie Louise (Schaal) Raggio; m. John R. Edelman, July 10, 1965; children: John R. Jr., Elisabeth W., Robert R. BA in English, Adelphi U., Garden City, N.Y., 1963; RRA, Grad. Hosp. U. Pa., 1963-64. Dir. med. records Lawrence Meml. Hosp., Medford, Mass., 1964-65; dir. health info. mgmt. Brandywine Hosp. and Trauma Ctr., Coatesville, Pa., 1972-95; ret. Mem. Am. Health Info. Mgmt. Assn., Montgomery County Hist. Soc., Chester County Hist. Soc. Republican. Roman Catholic.

EDELMAN, GERALD MAURICE, biochemist, educator; b. N.Y.C., N.Y., July 1, 1929; s. Edward and Anna (Freedman) E.; m. Maxine Morrison, June 11, 1950; children: Eric, David, Judith. B.S., Ursinus Coll., 1950, Sc.D., 1974; M.D., U. Pa., 1954, D.Sc., 1973; Ph.D., Rockefeller U., 1960; M.D. (hon.), U. Siena, Italy, 1974; DSc (hon.), Gustavus Adolphus Coll., 1975, Williams Coll., 1976; DSc Honoris Causa, U. Paris, 1989; LSc Honoris Causa, U. Cagliari, 1989; DSc, Georgetown U., 1989; DSc Honoris Causa, U. degli Studi di Napoli, 1990, Tulane U., 1991, U. Miami, 1995, Adelphi U., 1995. Med. house officer Mass. Gen. Hosp., 1954-55; asst. physician hosp. of Rockefeller U., 1957-60, mem. faculty, 1960-92, assoc. dean grad. studies, 1963-66, prof., 1966-74, Vincent Astor disting. prof., 1974-92; mem. faculty and chmn. dept. neurobiology Scripps Rsch. Inst., La Jolla, Calif., 1992—; mem. biophysics and biophys. chemistry study sect. NIH, 1964-67; mem. Sci. Council, Ctr. for Theoretical Studies, 1970-72; assoc., sci. chmn. Neurosciences Research Program, 1980—, dir. Neuroscis. Inst., 1981—; mem. adv. bd. Basel Inst. Immunology, 1970-77, chmn., 1975-77; non-resident fellow, trustee Salk Inst., 1973-85; bd. overseers Faculty Arts and Scis., U. Pa., 1976-83; trustee, mem. adv. com. Carnegie Inst., Washington, 1980-87; bd. govs. Weizman Inst. Sci., 1971-87, mem. emeritus; researcher structure of antibodies, molecular and devel. biology. Author: Neural Darwinism, 1987, Topobiology, 1988, The Remembered Present, 1989, Bright Air, Brilliant Fire, 1992. Trustee Rockefeller Bros. Fund., 1972-82. Served to capt. M.C. AUS, 1955-57. Recipient Spencer Morris award U. Pa., 1954, Ann. Alumni award Ursinus Coll., 1969, Nobel prize for physiology or medicine, 1972, Albert Einstein Commemorative award Yeshiva U., 1974, Buchman Meml. award Calif. Inst. Tech., 1975, Rabbi Shai Shacknai meml. prize Hebrew U.-Hadassah Med. Sch., Jerusalem, 1977, Regents medal Excellence, N.Y. State, 1984, Hans Neurath prize, U. Washington, 1986, Sesquicentennial Commemorative award Nat. Libr. Medicine, 1986, Cécile and Oskar Vogt award U. Dusseldorf, 1988, Disting. Grad. award U. Pa., 1990, Personnalité de l'année, Paris, 1990, Warren Triennial Prize award Mass. Gen. Hosp., 1992. Fellow AAAS, N.Y. Acad. Scis., N.Y. Acad. Medicine; mem. Am. Philos. Soc., Am. Soc. Biol. Chemists, Am. Assn. Immunologists, Genetics Soc. Am., Harvey Soc. (pres. 1975-76, Am. Chem. Soc., Eli Lilly award biol. chemistry 1965), Am. Acad. Arts and Scis., Nat. Acad. Sci., Am. Soc. Cell Biology, Acad. Scis. of Inst. France (fgn.), Japanese Biochem. Soc. (hon.), Pharm. Soc. Japan (hon.), Soc. Developmental Biology, Council Fgn. Relations, Sigma Xi, Alpha Omega Alpha. Office: Scripps Rsch Inst Dept Neurobiol SBR-14 10550 N Torrey Pines Rd La Jolla CA 92037-1027

EDELMAN, JERRY, physician; b. Bklyn., July 31, 1928; s. Samuel and Augusta (Cherwonsky) E.; m. Riva Kline, June 30, 1960; children: Laurie, Jeffrey, Hal. BA, NYU, 1950, MD, 1954. Cert. internal medicine. Intern, resident Montefiore Hosp., Bronx, N.Y., 1954-56; resident cardiology Phila. Gen. Hosp., 1959-60; resident medicine Trong Mem. Hosp., Rochester, N.Y., 1960-61; pvt. practice internal medicine Mamaroneck, Mameroneat, N.Y., 1961-95; examining physician Exec. Health Group, Stanford, Conn., 1995—; chief of medicine United Hosp. Portchester, N.Y., 1981-92, pres. med. staff, 1987-90; from instr. to asst. prof. Albert Einstein Coll. Medicine, Bronx, 1963-88. Capt. M.C., U.S. Army, 1956-58, Korea. Mem. ACP, Am. Heart Assn., Rochester Soc. Medicine. Home: 100 Hillair Cir White Plains NY 10605-4506

EDELMAN, JOEL, medical center executive; b. Chgo., Mar. 24, 1931; s. Maurice B. and Ethel J. (Newman) E.; m. Beth L. Sommers, July 31, 1955; children: Peter J., Ann Elizabeth, Deborah S. B.A. in Spl. Edn., U. Mich., 1952; J.D., DePaul U., 1960. Bar: Ill. 1961. Program dir. Chgo. Heart Assn., 1955-61; staff atty. Michael Reese Hosp. and Med. Center, Chgo., 1961-70; exec. v.p. Michael Reese Hosp. and Med. Center, 1971-73; dir. Ill. Dept. Pub. Aid, 1973-74; exec. dir. Ill. Legis. Adv. Com. on Pub. Aid, 1974-77; pres. Rose Med. Ctr., Denver, 1979-95; prin., sr. v.p. Frontier Holdings, Inc., Englewood, Colo., 1995—; asst. prof. dept. preventive medicine U. Colo.; U.; dir. office legal affairs Am. Hosp. Assn., 1970. Contbr. articles to profl. jours. Served with AUS, 1955. Mem. Soc. Hosp. Attys. (charter). Home: 3156 S Hills Ct Denver CO 80210-6830 Office: Frontier Holdings Inc 6312 S Fiddler's Green Cir Englewood CO 80111

EDELMAN, NORMAN H., medical educator, university dean and official; b. N.Y.C., May 21, 1937; s. Irving H. and Pearl Ruth (Solomon) E.; m. Ida Nadel, June 1959; children: David, Ruth, Deborah. AB, Bklyn. Coll., 1957; MD, NYU, 1961. Diplomate Am. Bd. Internal Medicine, Am. Bd. Pulmonary Diseases. Intern NYU Med. Sch., N.Y.C., 1961-62, resident, 1962-63; rsch. fellow NIH, Balt., 1963-65; vis. fellow Columbia U., Presbyn. Med. Ctr., N.Y.C., 1965-67; rsch. assoc. Michael Reese Med. Ctr., Chgo., 1967-69; asst. prof. medicine U. Pa. Sch. Medicine, Phila., 1969-72; prof. medicine, chief pulmonary medicine Robert Wood Johnson Med. Sch., U. Medicine and Dentistry of N.J., New Brunswick, N.J., 1972-96, dean, 1988-95; prof. medicine SUNY, Stony Brook, 1996—, v.p. univ. med. ctr., dean Sch. Medicine, 1996—; cons. for sci. Am. Lung Assn., N.Y.C., 1984—; mem. pulmonary disease adv. com. NIH, 1984-88. Contbr. articles, abstracts to profl. jours., chpts. to med. textbooks; mem. editorial bd. Jour. Applied Physiol., Am. Rev. Respiratory Diseases. Served as surgeon USPHS, 1963-65. Mem. Assn. Am. Physicians, Am. Soc. Clin. Investigation, Am. Thoracic Soc., Am. Physiol. Soc. Office: SUNYat Stony Brook Med Ctr Stony Brook NY 11794-8430

EDELMAN, STUART EDWARD, psychiatrist; b. N.Y.C., Mar. 14, 1947; s. Norman David and Mollie (Wollruch) E.; children: Joseph Jake, Kimberly Jean. BS cum laude, Trinity Coll., Hartford, Conn., 1968; MD, Columbia U., 1972. Diplomate Am. Bd. Psychiatry and Neurology. Resident in psychiatry Harvard U. Med. Sch., Boston, 1972-75; pvt. practice Wayland, Mass., 1975—; clin. instr. in psychiatry Harvard U. Med. Sch., Boston, 1975—; asst. clin. prof. psychiatry Sch. Medicine Boston U., 1993—; staff psychiatrist Trinity Mental Health Ctr., Framingham, Mass., 1975-80; chief dept. psychiatry, med. Eliot Cmty. Mental Health Ctr., Concord, Mass., 1980-90; supr. Erikson Ctr., Harvard U., Cambridge, Mass., 1982-90; guest spkr. TV program "Talking of the Mind: Adolescent Psychiatry", 1989. Contbr. articles to med. jours. Mem. Am. Psychiat. Assn., Mass. Psychiat. Assn., New Eng. Soc. for Adolescent Psychiatry (v.p.), Phi Beta Kappa. Office: 58 Glezen Ln Wayland MA 01778-1604

EDELSBERG, SALLY C., physical therapy educator and administrator; b. Rowno, Poland, Aug. 6, 1937; came to U.S., 1949; d. Joseph Luria and and Chana (Bebczuk) Comins; m. Warde C. Pierson, Oct. 8, 1968 (div. 1978); children: Nancy Pierson Beauchamp, Jeffrey Pierson; m. Paul Edelsberg, Feb. 2, 1979; 1 child, Tema. BS in Phys. Medicine, U. Wis., 1963; MS, Northwestern U., 1972. Lic. phys. therapist. Staff and supervisory phys. therapist Hines VA Hosp., Maywood, Ill., 1963-67; program dir. Health Careers Council of Ill., Chgo., 1967-70; instr., clin. edn. coordinator Programs in Phys. Therapy, Northwestern U. Med. Sch., Chgo., 1970-73, dir., assoc. prof., 1973—; pres. Phys. Therapy Ltd., Chgo., 1986—. Office: Northwestern U Med Sch Programs in Phys Therapy 345 E Superior St Rm 1323 Chicago IL 60611-3015

EDELSOHN, LANNY, neurologist; b. Camden, N.J., Aug. 23, 1941; s. Alan Edelsohn and Lena (Melamed) Cravitz; m. Michelle J. Labovsky; children: Andrew, Robert. BA, U. Pa., 1963; MD, Hahnemann Med. Coll., Phila., 1967. Diplomate Am. Bd. Neurology. Med. intern Hahnemann Med. Coll., 1967-68; residency in neurology Harvard U., Boston, 1970-73; pvt. practice Neurology Assocs., Wilmington, Del., 1973—; pres. med. staff Med. Ctr. Del., Wilmington, 1992-94, bd. dirs., 1992—. Bd. dirs. Grand Opera House, Wilmington, 1995—. Sr. asst. surgeon USPHS, 1968-70. Mem. Am. Acad. Neurology, Alpha Omega Alpha. Jewish. Office: Neurology Assocs 1228 N Scott St Wilmington DE 19806

EDELSON, RICHARD L., dermatology educator; b. Livingston, N.J., Dec. 19, 1944; s. Edmond and Merilyn Edelson; m. Ruth Cheris Edelson; children: Andrew, Ari. BA, Hamilton Coll., 1966; MD, Yale U., 1970. Intern U. Chgo., 1970-71; resident in dermatology Mass. Gen. Hosp., Boston, 1971-72; research assoc. in immunology NIH, Bethesda, Md., 1972-75; sr. resident in dermatology Columbia-Presbyn. Hosp., N.Y.C., 1975-76; asst. prof. Columbia U. Coll. Physicians and Surgeons, N.Y.C., 1976-78, assoc. prof., 1978-80, prof., assoc. dir. dermatol. rsch., 1980-85; prof., chmn. dept. Yale U. Sch. Medicine, New Haven, 1986—. Editor: Antigen and Clone Specific Immunoregulation, 1991. Trustee Yale-New Haven Hosp., 1994—. Mem. Dermatology Found. (exec. com. 1990—), Am. Acad. Dermatology, Assn. Profs. Dermatology, Interurban Club. Home: 75 Coleytown Rd Westport CT 06880 Office: Yale U Dept Dermatology 333 Cedar St New Haven CT 06510-3206*

EDELSTEIN, ROSE MARIE, nurse educator, consultant; b. Drake, N.D., Mar. 3, 1935; d. Francis Jerome and Myrtle Josephine (Merbach) Hublou; m. Harry George Edelstein, June 22, 1957; children: Julie, Lori, Lynn, Toni Anne. BSN, St. Teresa's of Avila's Coll., 1956; MA in Edn., Holy Names Coll., 1977; EdD, U. San Francisco, 1982, postgrad., 1987; postgrad. U. Ariz., 1985—; cert. pub. health nurse U. Calif., Berkeley, 1972. Dir., clin. supr. San Francisco Sch. for Health Professions, 1971-74, Rancho Arroyo Sch. of Vocat. Nursing, Sacramento, 1974-75; intensive care nurse Kaiser-Permanente Hosp., San Rafael, Calif., 1976-77; dir. inservice edn. Ross Hosp., Calif., 1977-78; assoc. dir. nursing, nursing edn. St. Francis Meml. Hosp., San Francisco, 1978-85; nursing cons., med.-surg. staff nurse met. hosps., San Francisco, 1985-90, St. Luke's Hosp., Duluth, 1990-91, St. Charles Hosp., New Orleans, 1992, UTMB, Galveston, Tex. 1992-94, staff RN family medicine faculty practice, 1992-94; med.-surg. nurse St. Anthony of Padua Hosp., Oklahoma City, 1994-95; RN medics and treatments Northgate Conv. Hosp., 1995—; RN, charge nurse Creekside Conv. Hosp., Santa Rosa, Calif., 1996, charge RN night, 1996—; RN, charge nurse medications, treatment and alzheimers unit, Fallon Cmty. Ctr., Nev., 1996; invited mem. People to People Nursing Edn. and Adminstrn., candidate to East Asia, Philosophy, 1985; postgrad. candidate U. Zurich, Switzerland, 1988. Candidate U.S. Senate Inner Circle, 1988, 89. Lt. col. USAR Med. Res. Mem. Calif. Nurses Assn., Am. Heart Assn., Sigma Theta Tau. Roman Catholic. Author: (with Jane F. Lee) Acupuncture Atlas, 1974; The Influence of Motivator and Hygiene Factors in Job Changes by Graduate Registered Nurses, 1977; Effects of Two Educational Methods Upon Retention of Knowledge in Pharmacology, 1981. Address: PO Box 580 Healdsburg CA 95448

EDEMEKA, UDO EDEMEKA, surgeon; b. Ndon Eyo, Akwa Ibom, Nigeria, Sept. 11, 1944; came to U.S., 1973; s. Buddie Udo and Dinah Buddie (Ekwere) E.; m. Iboro Udo David Akpan, May 18, 1973; children: Ubong, Dinah, Idara, David, Dennis, Donald. MB and BS, U. Ibadan, Nigeria, 1970; diploma in anesthesia, U. Lagos, 1972. Diplomate Am. Bd. Surgery, Am. Bd. Emergency Physicians. Instr. surgery Downstate Med. Ctr., Bklyn., 1974-80; attending physician Kings County Hosp. Ctr., Bklyn., 1980-91, Meth. Hosp., Bklyn., 1988—. Leverhulme Exchange scholar Lever Bros. U. Coll. Hosp., London, 1969. Fellow N.Y. Acad. Scis., Internat. Coll. Surgeons, Am. Coll. Emergency Physicians. Office: Meth Hosp 506 6th St Brooklyn NY 11215-3609

EDEN, ALVIN NOAM, pediatrician, author; b. Bklyn., Mar. 21, 1926; s. Emanuel M. and Rae (Taran) Edelstein; m. Elaine R. Jaffe, Nov. 20, 1952; children: Robert, Elizabeth. BA, Columbia Coll., 1948; MD, Boston U., 1952. Intern Bellevue Hosp., N.Y.C., 1952-53; resident in pediatrics Univ. Hosp., N.Y.C., 1953-55; practice medicine specializing in pediatrics, Forest Hills, N.Y., 1955—; assoc. clin. prof. pediatrics NYU Sch. Medicine, 1960-84, chmn., dir. dept. pediatrics Wyckoff Heights Hosp., Bklyn., 1959—; lectr. SUNY-Downstate Med. Ctr., Bklyn., 1984-86, assoc. clin. prof. pediatrics, 1986-90; assoc. clin. prof. pediat. Cornell Med. Coll., 1990—. Author: Growing Up Thin, 1975; Handbook for New Parents, 1978; Positive Parenting, 1980; Dr. Eden's Diet and Nutrition Program for Children, 1980 Pampers Parents' Handbook, 1986, Dr. Eden's Healthy Kids, 1987. Contbr. articles to profl. jours., author text and reference materials. Served to mate 2d class U.S.M., 1944-46. Mem. N.Y. Pediatric Soc., (pres. 1980-81), Queens Pediatric Soc. (pres. 1972-73), N.Y. Acad. Medicine (chmn. pediatric sect. 1985—), Am. Acad. Pediatrics (chmn. nutrition com. chpt. 2 1985-89). Avocation: tennis. Home: 710 Park Ave New York NY 10021-4944 Office: 10721 Queens Blvd Flushing NY 11375-4451

EDEN, JOHN, ophthalmologist; b. Germany, Apr. 30, 1933; came to U.S., 1938; s. Eric and Trudy (Geck) E. BA, NYU, 1953; MD, George Washington U., 1957. Diplomate Am. Bd. Ophthalmology. Intern Temple U. Med. Ctr., Phila., 1957-58, resident ophthalmology, 1958-61; attending ophthalmologist St. Lukes Roosevelt Med. Ctr., 1961-88, 88—; attending ophthalmologist Columbia Presbyn. Coll. Physicians & Surgeons, N.Y.C., 1961-88, attending ophthalmologist emeritus, 1988—. Author: The Eye Book, 1978 (PEN award 1978), The Physicians Guide to Cataracts,

Glaucoma and Other Eye Problems, 1994. Office: PO Box 173 Sagaponack NY 11962

EDER, HOWARD ABRAM, physician; b. Milw., Sept. 23, 1917; s. Samuel and Rebecca (Abram) E.; m. Barbara Straus, July 15, 1954; children—Rebecca (Susan, Michael. A.B., U. Wis., 1938; M.D., Harvard U., 1942, M.P.H., 1945; MD honoris causa, U. Linkoping, Sweden. Intern Peter Bent Brigham Hosp., Boston, 1942-43; asst. resident Peter Bent Brigham Hosp., 1943-44; research fellow in medicine Harvard Med. Sch., 1943-44, research fellow in biochemistry, 1945-46; asst. in medicine, asst. physician Rockefeller U. Hosp., 1946-50; asst. prof. medicine Cornell U. Med. Coll., N.Y.C., 1950-53; mem. staff Nat. Heart Inst., Bethesda, Md., 1953-55; asso. prof. medicine State U. N.Y., Downstate Med. Coll., Bklyn., 1955-57; asso. prof. medicine Albert Einstein Coll. Medicine, 1957-60, prof., 1960-88, prof. emeritus, 1989—; chmn. lipid metabolism adv. com. Nat. Heart, Lung and Blood Inst., 1978-80, mem. bd. sci. counselors, 1986-90, chmn., 1989-90; mem. diabetes and heart disease rev. panel NIH, 1995, 96. Editorial bd.: Am. Jour. Physiology, 1968-71, 79-82, Jour. Lipid Research, 1964—, Am. Jour. Medicine, 1976-80. Mem. Assn. Am. Physicians, Am. Soc. Clin. Investigation, Am. Soc. Biol. Chemists, Am. Physiol. Soc., Am. Heart Assn. (Disting. Accomplishment award 1985, mem. coun. on arteriosclerosis, Spl. Recognition award 1993), Inst. of Medicine NAS, Interurban Clin. Club (pres. 1971-72), Phi Beta Kappa, Alpha Omega Alpha. Home: 4465 Douglas Ave Bronx NY 10471-3525 Office: Albert Einstein Coll Medicine 1300 Morris Park Ave Bronx NY 10461-1926

EDERMA, ARVO BRUNO, consultant in occupational health, physician; b. Haapsalu, Estonia, May 13, 1928; came to U.S., 1949; s. Bruno Immanuel and Erika (Drake) E.; m. Miriam Maris Kikas, Sept. 25, 1954; children: Karin Erika, Tiina Inge, Erik Arvo. BA, Lenoir Rhyne Coll., 1952; M.S.P.H., U. N.C., 1953; MD, Bowman Gray Sch. Medicine, Winston-Salem, N.C., 1957. Diplomate Am. Bd. Gen. Preventive Medicine. Intern USPHS Hosp., Balt., 1957-58; med. officer in charge U.S. AEC, Germantown, Md., 1958-60; medi. cons. Fed. Employee Health Program, Washington, 1960-62; dep. chief Fed. Employee Health Program, Silver Spring, Md., 1962-65; asst. dir. Div. of Fed. Employee Health, Hyattsville, Md., 1965-75; dir. Div. of Fed. Employee Occupational Health, Hyattsville, 1975-84, Div. of Beneficiary Med. Programs, Rockville, Md., 1984-85; dep. dir. Gillis W. Long Hansen's Disease Ctr., Carville, La., 1985-90; acting dir. Regional Hansen's Disease Program, Carville, 1986-90; chmn. med. adv. bd. Estonian Am. Fund, Inc., 1990—; pub. health adv. bd. U.S. Baltic Found., 1991—; adj. assoc. prof. of preventive medicine and biometrics F. Edward Hebert Sch. Medicine, Uniformed Svcs. Univ., Bethesda, Md., 1978-87; cons. in occupational health OSHA, Washington, 1992—. Contbr. articles to profl. jours. Pres. PTA, Lewisdale Elem. Sch., Hyattsville, Md., 1968-69; pres., sec., council mem. St. Mark's Estonian Lutheran Ch., Washington, 1969-85. Capt. USPHS, 1957—. Recipient Disting. Alumnus award Lenoir Rhyne Coll., 1976, commendation medal USPHS, 1977, Meritorious Svc. medal USPHS, 1984, Outstanding Svc. medal USPHS, 1987, Outstanding Unit citation USPHS, 1988. Fellow Am. Occupational Med. Assn., Am. Coll. Preventive Medicine, Am. Acad. Occupational Medicine; mem. Commissioned Officer Assn. Republican. Lutheran. Home and Office: 10800 Kirkwall Ter Rockville MD 20854-2731

EDGAR, MARILYN RUTH, counselor; b. Springfield, Mo., Oct. 2, 1948; d. Donald LaVerne Sr. and Ruth Elenor (McClellan) Wilson; m. Robert Stephen Edgar, June 23, 1979; stepchildren: Terri, John, Shawna. BA in Psychology, Calif. State U., Sacramento, 1983, MS in Counseling, 1987. Lic. marriage, family, and child counselor, Calif. Counselor Sacramento Life Ctr., 1983-91; marriage and family therapist New Horizons Counseling Ctr., Carmichael, Calif., 1987—, exec. dir., supr. intern counselors, 1993—. Guest profl. therapist Faith in Crisis Group, Sacramento; mem. Warehouse Ministries of Sacramento, 1978—; mem. Arthritis Found., 1996. Mem. Calif. Assn. Marriage and Family Therapists (Valley chpt. 1992—), Capital City Motorcycle Club (pub. rels. officer 1994, sec., bd. mem. 1996). Republican. Office: New Horizons Counseling Ctr 3300 Walnut Ave Carmichael CA 95608-3240

EDGE, JAMES EDWARD, health care administrator; b. Anacortes, Wash., Apr. 29, 1948; s. Edward and Carol Marie (Lian) E.; m. Nellie Ruth Horton, Mar. 21, 1970; children: Elissa Marie, Gina Dawn. BS in Pharmacy, U. Wash., 1971; MPH, U. Hawaii, 1979. Registered pharmacist. Commd. USPHS, 1969—, advanced through grades to capt.; staff pharmacist USPHS Indian Hosp., Albuquerque, 1971-73; chief pharmacy, lab/x-ray S.W. Indian Poly. Inst., Albuquerque, 1972-73, Neah Bay Indian Health Ctr., Wash., 1973-75; svc. unit dir. Neah Bay Svc. Unit, Indian Health Svc., 1975-78, Western Oreg. Service Unit, Indian Health Svc., Salem, 1980—; cons. in field. Active Combined Fed. Campaign, Salem, 1985—. John Quick Pharmacy scholar, U. Wash., 1967, Health Professions scholar, 1969. Mem. APHA, Am. Coll. Healthcare Adminstrs., Am. Acad. Med. Adminstrs., Assn. Mil. Surgeons U.S., Mensa, Res. Officers Assn., Commd. Officer USPHS, Wash. Pharm. Assn., nat. Coun. Svc. Unit Dirs. (chmn. 1986-88). Office: PHS Indian Health Ctr 3750 Chemawa Rd NE Salem OR 97305-1119

EDGINGTON, THOMAS S., pathologist, educator; b. L.A., Feb. 10, 1931. BA in Biol. Scis., Stanford U., 1953, MD, 1957. Diplomate Am. Bd. Pathology, spl. cert. immunopathology. Intern Hosp. Univ. Pa., Phila., 1957-58; resident Ctr. Health Scis. UCLA, 1958-60; sr. postdoctoral fellow immunology Scripps Clinic & Rsch. Found., La Jolla, Calif., 1965-68, assoc. mem. dept. exptl. pathology, 1968-71, head dept. anatomic pathology & lab. medicine, 1968-74, prof. dept. immunology, dir. vascular cell molecular biology program, dir. immunology tng. program, 1971—; asst. prof., surg. pathologist dept. pathology Sch. Medicine UCLA, 1962-65; assoc. adj. prof. pathology U. Calif., San Diego, La Jolla, 1968-75, adj. prof., 1975—; lectr., vis. prof. Coll. de France, Paris, 1981; lectr. Nat. Blood Club, Washington, 1982; cons. Centocor, 1993-95, Eli Lilly, 1982-85, Becton-Dickinson, 1977-80; sci. advisor, bd. dirs. Inst. Biotech. & Advanced Molecular Medicine, Phila.; founder, bd. dirs. Corvas Internat.; bd. dirs. Apollon, Inc., CalBio Summit. Contbr. articles to profl. jours. Recipient John A. Lynch Molecular Biology award U. Notre Dame, 1992, Rous-Whipple prize Am. Soc. Investigative Pathology, 1995, Disting. Career award Internat. Soc. Thrombosis and Hemostatis, 1995. Mem. AAAS (electorate nominating com. sect. med. scis. 1994—), Fedn. Am. Socs. Exptl. Biology (pres., chmn. bd. 1990-91), Internat. Soc. Thrombosis & Haemostatis, Thrombosis Inst. (bd. sci. govs. 1995—). Office: Scripps Rsch Inst 10550 N Torrey Pines Rd La Jolla CA 92037*

EDIC-CRAWFORD, DARLENE MARIE, AIDS nurse; b. Las Vegas, Aug. 18, 1967; d. Robert Franklin and Belinda Lee (Brunning) E.; m. Robin Patrick Crawford, Dec. 1, 1990. BSN, U. Fla., 1990; MSN, U. Miami, 1996. Clin. nurse II in-patient AIDS unit Jackson Meml. Hosp., Miami, 1990-92; unit mgr. sub-acute AIDS unit Human Resources Health Ctr., Miami, 1992-95; adminstr. Jackson Meml. Hosp., Miami, 1995—. Mem. ANA (congl. dist. coord. 1991—), Fla. Nurses Assn. (state bd. dirs. 1995—), trustee PAC 1989—, pres. dist. 1993-96, newsletter editor 1991-96), Nat. League for Nursing, Fla. League for Nursing, Assn. Nurses in AIDS Care (nat. bylaws com. 1993—, treas. Miami chpt. 1993-94, pres. Miami chpt. 1995—). Republican. Home: 3057 E Rd Loxahatchee FL 33470 Office: Jackson Meml Hosp West Wing 105 1611 NW 12th Ave Miami FL 33142

EDIS, GLORIA TOBY, pediatrician; b. N.Y.C., Dec. 6, 1939; d. Murray Alvin and Anna G. (Goldstein) E.; m. Myron Royal Schoenfeld, June 14, 1959; children: Bradley, Glenn, Dawn, Melody. BA, Cornell U., 1960; MD, NYU, 1963. Intern Montefiore Hosp., N.Y.C., 1963-64; pediatric resident Columbia Presbyn. Med. Ctr., N.Y.C., 1966-68; pediatrician Scarsdale (N.Y.) Pediatric Assocs., 1967—; pediatric attending Albert Einstein Med. Coll., Bronx, 1968-70; pediatrician Barsky Med. Group, N.Y.C., 1970-80. Fellow Am. Acad. Pediatrics; mem. AMA, Westchester County Med. Soc., Cornell Alumni Assn. Office: Scarsdale Pediatric Assn 2 Overhill Rd Scarsdale NY 10583

EDISON, RICHARD B., plastic surgeon; b. Boston, Nov. 2, 1952; s. Robert G. and Louise R. (Wolf) E.; m. Nancy Letnes, July 19, 1984; children: Michele N., John D. BA, Pomona Coll., 1974; MD, U. Mass., Worcester, 1978. Diplomate Am. Bd. Plastic Surgery, Nat. Bd. Med. Examiners. Resident in gen. surgery Kaiser Found., L.A., 1978-81; resident in plastic surgery Med. U. S.C., 1981-84, Phoenix Plastic Surgery Residency, 1981-84; pvt. practice, Ft. Lauderdale, Fla., 1984—; commentator various TV programs, including Action Line, Speak Out. Contbr. articles to med. jours. and newspapers. Mem. Rep. Nat. Com., Washington, 1994—. Mem. AMA (physician's recognition award 1985, 88, 91, 94), Am. Soc. Plastic and Reconstructive Surgeons, Liposuction Soc. N.Am., So. Med. Assn., Fla. Med. Assn. Office: 3109 Stirling Rd Ste 100 Fort Lauderdale FL 33312

EDLAND, ROBERT WILLIAM, radiation oncology educator; b. Madison, Wis., Feb. 14, 1932; s. Alfred O. and Ella W. (Freund) E.; m. Carole F. McGinley, Sept. 17, 1955; children: Christopher, Anne, Christina, David. BS, U. Wis., 1953, MD, 1956. Diplomate Am. Bd. Radiology. Chmn. radiation oncology dept. Gundersen Clinic, La Crosse, Wis., clin. prof. radiation oncology U. Wis., Madison, 1978—, radiation oncology Med. Coll. Wis., 1983—. Contbr. articles to profl. jour. Served to lt. col. USMC, 1956-67. Fellow Am. Coll. Nuclear Medicine, Am. Coll. Radiology (bd. chancellors 1991—), Royal Soc. Health; mem. Am. Soc. Therapeutic Radiology and Oncology (pres. 1986-87). Home: 2200 Hickory Ln La Crosse WI 54601 Office: 1836 South Ave La Crosse WI 54601-5429

EDLICH, RICHARD FRENCH, biomedical engineering educator; b. N.Y.C., Jan. 19, 1939; married, 1961; 3 children. MD, NYU, 1962; PhD, U. Minn., 1973. From instr. to assoc. prof. U. Va. Sch. Medicine, Charlottesville, 1971-76, prof. plastic surgery and biomed. engring., 1976-82, disting. prof. plastic and maxillofacial surgery and biomed. engring., 1983-96, now Raymoon F. Morgan prof. plastic surgery and disting. prof. biomed. engring., 1996—; dir. Emergency Med. Svc. and Burn Ctr., 1974-85; physician tech. adviser Bur. Emergency Svc., HEW, 1974-79; cons. Divsn. Health Manpower and Nat. Ctr. Health Svc. Rsch., 1977-79. Recipient outstanding teaching award U. Va., 1989, Thomas Jefferson award, 1991, outstanding faculty award Commonwealth of Va. Coun. Higher Edn., 1989. Mem. ACS, Soc. Univ. Surgeons, Am. Assn. Surg. Trauma, Am. Burn Assn., Univ. Assn. Emergency Medicine, Am. Soc. Plastic and Reconstructive Surgeons, Soc. of Acad. Emergency Medicine, Coll. Emergency Physicians, Am. Surg. Assn. Office: U Va Sch Med Box 332 Med Ctr Charlottesville VA 22908-0001

EDMISTON, MARILYN, clinical psychologist; b. Lewiston, Maine, Dec. 9, 1934; d. Lewis Walter and Anne Mary (Nezol) Burgess; m. John Laing Edmiston (div. May 1969); children: John Laing, Eric James. BA, Fla. Atlantic U., 1967, MA, 1969; PhD, U. Ga., 1973. Lic. ind. practice psychologist, Calif., Fla. Staff psychologist children and adolescent unit Cen. Ga. Regional Hosp., Milledgeville, 1973-74, chief psychologist, 1974-75; clin. psychologist South Fla. State Hosp., Pembroke Pines, 1976-77; state psychol. cons. Office Vocat. Rehab., Fla. Dept. Health and Rehab. Svcs., Tallahassee, 1977-83; sr. psychologist forensic svcs. Fla. State Hosp., Chattahoochee, 1983-96, pres.-elect, pres. profl. clin. staff, 1990-94; pvt. practice Tallahassee, 1996—; expert witness Fla. cts., 1983-96. Mem. APA, Am. Bd. Forensic Examiners (diplomate), Nat. Register Health Svc. Providers in Psychology, World Fedn. for Mental Health, Internat. Coun. Psychologists. Democrat. Home: 2161 Shangri La Ln Tallahassee FL 32303-2360

EDMONDS, HARVEY LAWRENCE, neurologist; b. Cleve., Aug. 1, 1946; s. Albert Rosen and Doris (Rubinow) E.; m. Christine Patricia, June 1973 (div. 1982); children: Zachary, Oliver; m. Irma Corral, Mar. 27, 1983; children: Alexandra, Max. BS, U. Calif. Berkeley, 1968; MD, UCLA Sch. Medicine, 1972. Diplomate Am. Bd. Psychiatry & Neurology. Intern Harbor Gen. Hosp., Torrence, Calif., 1972-73; residency V.A. Hosp. Wadsworth, L.A., 1976-78; neurologist Fresno (Calif.) Neurol. Assocs Med. Group, 1978—. Mem. Am. Acad. Neurology, Am. Soc. Neuroimaging, Alpha Omega Alpha. Office: Fresno Neurol Assocs 6113 N Fresno Ste 101 Fresno CA 93710

EDMONDS, RICHARD, dean. Interim dean Albany (N.Y.) Med. Coll. Office: Albany Med Coll 47 New Scotland Rd Albany NY 12208*

EDMONDS, VELMA MCINNIS, nursing educator; b. N.Y.C., Feb. 17, 1940; d. Walter Lee and Eva Doris (Grant) McInnis; children: Stephen Clay, Michelle Louise. Diploma, Charity Hosp. Sch. Nursing, New Orleans, 1961; BSN, Med. Coll. Ga., 1968; MSN, U. Ala., Birmingham, 1980; postgrad. in doctoral nursing sci., La. State U., 1994—. Staff nurse Ochsner Found. Hosp., New Orleans, 1961-63, 1987—, clin. educator, 1987-89; staff nurse Suburban Hosp., Bethesda, Md., 1963-65; asst. DON svc., dir. staff devel. Providence Hosp., Mobile, Ala., 1967-70; staff nurse MICU U. So. Ala. Med. Ctr., Mobile, 1980-82, clin. nurse specialist, nutrition/metabolic support, 1982-84; instr., coord., BSN completion program Northwestern State Univ., Coll. Nursing, Natchitoches, La., 1984-86; head nurse So. Bapt. Hosp., New Orleans, 1986-87; instr. of nursing La. State U.Med. Ctr., New Orleans, 1989-91, asst. prof. nursing, 1991—; clin. coord. Transitional Hosp. Corp., 1994-95; gov.-appointed mem. La. State Bd. Examiners in Dietetics and Nutrition, 1990—, sec. treas. State Bd. of Examiners, 1996-97. Gov.'s appointee La. State Bd. Examiners in Dietetics and Nutrtion, sec.-treas. Recipient Excellence in Nursing group award Ochsner Fedn. Hosp., New Orleans, 1987, cert. Merit Tuberculosis Assn. Greater New Orleans, 1961. Mem. ANA, La. State Nurses' Assn. (dist. 7), Am. Soc. Parenteral and Enteral Nutrition, La. State Soc. Parenteral and Enteral Nutrition (program and edn. coms.), Assn. La. State Soc. Parenteral and Enteral Nutrition, Mobile Area Nonvolitional Nutrition Support Assn. (past pres.), Sigma Theta Tau.

EDMUNDS, CECELIA POWERS, health facility administrator; b. Dinwiddie County, Va., June 6, 1937; d. Charles Hardy and Maude Beatrice (Prosise) Powers; m. Thomas Fitzgerald Edmunds Jr., Apr. 5, 1956; children: Thomas Fitzgerald III, Anne Hardy, William McIlwaine, Cecelia Lynn, John Powers. RN, Johnston-Willis Hosp., Richmond, Va., 1957; BS in Health Sci., Chapman U., 1981; MS in Adminstrn. Health, Ctrl. Mich. U., 1996. RN, Va.; lic. nursing home adminstr., Va., adminstr. preceptor, Va. Staff nurse, head nurse Tucker Psychiat. Hosp., Richmond, 1957-59; pvt. duty nurse Johnston Willis Hosp., Richmond, 1959-65; head nurse Ctrl. State Hosp., Petersburg, Va., 1970-71; head nurse, instr. Petersburg Tng. Ctr., 1971-75; tng. coord., coord. ops., dir. nursing. Southside Va. Tng. Ctr., Petersburg, 1975-94, asst. dir. health svcs., 1994—; chairperson Dept. Mental Health Mental Retardation and Substance Abuse Svcs. Nursing Svcs. Group Commonwealth Va., Richmond, 1993-96. Mem. NAFE, Am. Coll. Health Care Adminstrs., Devel. Disabilities Nurses Assn. (charter). Republican. Presbyterian. Home: 8319 McKenney Hwy McKenney VA 23872 Office: Southside Va Tng Ctr PO Box 4110 Petersburg VA 23803

EDMUNDS, LELAND NICHOLAS, biology educator; b. Aiken, S.C., Apr. 21, 1939; s. Leland Nicholas and Elizabeth Hemphill (Grier) E.; children: Sunja Eve, Kira Beth, Alissa Lee. BS, Davidson Coll., 1960; MA, Princeton U., 1965, PhD, 1964. Instr. Princeton (N.J.) U., 1964-65; from asst. prof. to prof. anatomy SUNY, Stony Brook, 1965—, acting provost, head civ. biol. sci., 1975-76; vis. investigator Biol. Inst., Carlsberg Found., Copenhagen, 1972, Laboratoire du Phytotron, CNRS, Gif-sur-Yvette, France, 1978-79, Laboratoire des Membranes Biologiques, Université Paris VII, 1986; vis. prof. Dept. Human Genetics, Sackler Sch. Med., Tel Aviv U., 1983, Suzhou Med. Coll., People's Rep. China, 1994. Author: Cellular and Molecular Bases of Biological Clocks, 1988; editor: Cell Cycle Clocks (Marcel Dekker), 1984; editor jour. Chronobiology Internat. Endocytobiol. Cell Research; contbr. articles to profl. jours. Mem. AAAS, Am. Soc. Plant Physiologists, Group d'Etudes des Rythmes Biologiques, Internat. Soc. Chronobiology (bd. dirs. 1987-93, pres. 1993—), Internat. Soc. Endosymbiosis Cell Rsch. Home: Crystal Brook Park PO Box 390 Mount Sinai NY 11766-0390 Office: SUNY Sch Med Health Scis Ctr Dept Anatom Scis Stony Brook NY 11794

EDMUNDS, ROBERT THOMAS, retired surgeon; b. Toledo, Sept. 14, 1924; s. Marion Kenneth and Frances Ethel (McCauley) E.; widowed, 1983; children: Nancy, Priscilla, Elizabeth, Cynthia, Robert. BA, Harvard U., 1947; MD, Columbia U., 1951. Diplomate Am. Bd. Surgery. Intern St. Luke's Hosp., N.Y.C., 1951-52, asst. resident surgery, 1952-55, resident surgery, 1955-56, attending surgeon, 1956-78; clin. prof. surgery Columbia Coll. Physicians and Surgeons, N.Y.C., 1966-78; mini-residency in occupational medicine Inst. Environ. Health U. Cin. Coll. Medicine, 1983; med. dir. U.S. Steel Corp., Pitts., 1978-89; ret., 1989; prin. investigator Cen. Oncology Group, Madison, Wis., 1956-70. Contbr. articles to profl. jours. Lt. (j.g.) USNR, 1942-46. Fellow ACS; mem. Union Club. Republican. Congregationalist. Home: 40 E 89th St New York NY 10128-1220

EDNEY, JAMES AUGUSTINE, surgeon; b. Omaha, Dec. 16, 1948; s. John Anthony and Mary Jane (McGowan) E.; m. Patricia Ann McNamara, Sept. 11, 1971 (div. June 1986); m. Deborah Mertes; children: Michael, Christine, Daniel. BS, Creighton U., Omaha, 1971; MD, U. Nebr., 1975. Diplomate Am. Bd. Surgery. Resident gen. surgery U. Nebr. Med. Ctr., Omaha, 1975-80, asst. prof., 1981-90, assoc. prof., 1990—, residency program dir., 1984—; fellow surg. oncology U. Colo., Denver, 1980-81; attending surgeon Denver Gen. Hosp., 1980-81; chmn. bd. Nebr. Clinician's Group, Omaha, 1989-93. Contbr. chpts. to books. Mem. ACS, Southwestern Surg. Congress (sec.-treas. 1993-96), Western Trauma Assn. (program chmn., state chmn. 1993-95), North Ctrl. Cancer Treatment Group (co-chair surg. sect. 1995—). Republican. Roman Catholic. Office: U Nebr Med Ctr 600 S 42nd St Omaha NE 68198

EDSALL, DAVID W., anesthesiologist, computer systems consultant; b. Jan. 31, 1948; s. Walter S. Edsall. BA, U. Vt., 1970, Md, 1974. Diplomate Am. Bd. Anesthesiology. Chmn. dept. anesthesiology Burbank Hosp., Fitchburg, Mass., 1987—, Leominster (Mass.) Hosp., 1993—, Health Alliance Ctrl. Mass., 1994—. Contbr. chpt. to textbook. Maj. USAR, 1966-80. Office: Ste 16 326 Nichols Rd Fitchburg MA 01420-1914

EDSON, HERBERT ROBBINS, foundation and hospital executive; b. Upper Darby, Pa., Dec. 26, 1931; s. Merritt Austin and Ethel Winifred (Robbins) E.; m. Constance Anne Lowell, May 20, 1961 (div. Nov. 8, 1967); m. Rose Anne McGowan, July 25, 1970; children: Patricia Anne, David William, Merritt Austin III, Herbert Robbins Jr. BA, Tufts U., 1955; MBA, U. Pa., 1972. Commd. 2d lt. USMC, 1955, advanced through grades to major, 1967, adminstr., mgr., supr. various orgns., 1955-72; controller III Marine Amphibious Force and 3d Marine Div. USMC, Camp Butler, Japan, 1972-73; dir. acctg. Marine Corps Supply Activity USMC, Phila., 1973-75; ret. USMC, 1975; cons. acctg. Ardmore, Pa., 1975-77; CFO Mercy Meml. Hosp. Corp., Monroe, Mich., 1977-92, Mercy Meml. Hosp. Found., Monroe, 1986-92, Monroe Health Ventures Inc., 1986-92, Monroe Community Health Svcs., 1989-92, Byerly Hosp., Hartsville, S.C., 1992-95, Byerly Found., Hartsville, S.C., 1995—; assoc. Quorum Health Resources, Inc., Brentwood, Tenn., 1992-95. Co-pres. Custer Elem. Sch. Parent Tchr. Orgn., Monroe, 1985-87; v.p., trustee Christ Evang. Luth. Ch., Monroe, 1981-86; treas., chmn. Taylor Endowment Fund com. St. Paul's Evang. Luth. Ch., Ardmore, Pa., 1974-76, trustee, chmn. property com., 1976. Decorated Purple Heart, Navy Commendation medal, Combat Action ribbon. Mem. Am. Hosp. Assn., Healthcare Fin. Mgmt. Assn., Inst. Mgmt. Accts., Monroe County C. of C. (bd. dirs. 1982-84), NRA (life), U.S. Naval Inst. (life), Marine Corps Assn. (life), 1st Marine Div. Assn. (life), Edson's Raiders Assn. (hon. life 1st Marine Raider Bn.), Ret. Officers Assn. (life), Am. Assn. Ret. Persons, Nat. Geog. Soc., Edson Geneal. Assn., Marines Meml. Club, Hartsville Country Club, Army and Navy Club. Republican. Lutheran. Home: 1121 PineLake Hartsville SC 29550-7990 Office: Byerly Foundation PO Drawer 1925 Hartsville SC 29551-1925

EDSON, WAYNE E., dentist, consultant; b. Marinette, Wis., July 4, 1947; s. E.J. Edson and Anita (Pearson) Edson Sebero; m. Linda Mary Hullison, Apr. 3, 1971; children: William Earl, Erin Hullison, Thomas John. BS, U. Wis.-Madison/Milw., 1973; DDS, Northwestern U., 1977. gen. practice dentistry, Winnetka, Ill., 1982—. Pres. Kenilworth United Fund, 1983-84, bd. dirs., 1981—; com. mem. Kenilworth Baseball, 1978-83. Served with USN, 1965-72. Mem. Chgo. Dental Soc., Ill. State Dental Soc., ADA. Roman Catholic. Avocations: hunting; fishing, curling. Clubs: John Evans of Northwestern U., G.V. Black Soc. of Northwestern U., Kenilworth, Chgo. Curling Club. Home: 624 Exmoor Rd Kenilworth IL 60043-1021 Office: 450 Green Bay Rd Kenilworth IL 60043-1074 also: 1 E Delaware Pl Chicago IL 60611

EDWARDS, ADRIAN L., medical educator. MD, Harvard U., 1960. Prof. med. Med. Sch. Cornell U., 1968—. Mem. Inst. Medicine-NAS. Address: 135 E 71st St New York NY 10024*

EDWARDS, BERYL MARGARET, health science facility administrator; b. Hayes, Kent, Eng., May 3, 1932; came to U.S., 1962; d. Sidney McLuan and Florence Edith (Lister) Hunter; m. Bill Edwards, Dec. 25, 1979; 1 child, Michael David Hunter. BA in Nursing, U. London, 1953; BA in English, U. Hawaii, Honolulu, 1969; DD, U. Life Ch., Honolulu, 1978. RN, Eng. Squadron officer Women's Royal Air Force, Eng., 1953-61; med. record adminstr. Sunrise Hosp., Las Vegas, Nev., 1962-64; mgr. The Fronk Clinic, Honolulu, 1964-74; quality assurance coord. The Queen's Med. Ctr., Honolulu, 1974-87; health svc. analyst Desert Hosp., Palm Springs, 1988-89, quality improvement specialists, med. staff, 1989—; chmn. adv. com. Kapiolani Community Coll., Honolulu, 1965-74; cons. The Hunter Trust, Honolulu, 1968-87. Bibliographer: Book, A Study in Literary Romance 1968, The Life and Works of Oliver Onions 1971. Min. Weddings in Paradise, Honolulu, 1978-87. Mem. Cancer Soc. Hawaii Honolulu, Mental Health Assn. Honolulu Hawaii, Hawaii Med. Record Assn., Am. Med. Record Assn., Calif. Med. Record Assn., Hawaii Med. Record Assn. (pres. 1971-73, 85-87), Am. Record Mgmt. Assn., Hawaii Humane Soc., Hist. Hawaii Found. Democrat. Home: 62381 Belmont St Joshua Tree CA 92252-1314

EDWARDS, BRENDA FAYE, counselor; b. Hattiesburg, Miss., Apr. 3, 1945; d. Jack Howell and Annie C. (Sullivan) Zeigler; m. James A. Edwards Jr., June 5, 1962. BA, U. So. Miss., 1968; MEd, U. Ga., 1977. Registered catastropic rehab. supplier; lic. profl. counselor; cert. ins. rehab. specialist. Various positions Miss., 1968-70; tchr. Brunswick (Ga.) Coll., 1970-71; tng. coord. Coastal Ga. Regional Devel. Ctr., Brunswick, 1971-72; tchr. Glynn County Bd. Edn., Adult Edn. Ctr., Brunswick, 1972; social work tech. Gateway Ctr. for Human Devel., Brunswick, 1973; coord. consultation edn. and tng. Coastal Area Community Mental Health Ctr., Brunswick, 1979; rehab. counselor Div. Rehab. Svcs., Dept. Human Resources, Brunswick, 1973-78; supr. basic edn. dept. Brunswick Job Corp. Ctr., 1979-80; rehab. specialist Intracorp, Savannah, Ga., 1980-83; counselor, owner Southeastern Rehab. Svcs., St. Simons Island, Ga., 1983—. Pres. Citizens for Humane Animal Treatment, Brunswick, 1987-90, v.p. 1990-91; sec. Glynn County Animal Control Adv. Bd., Brunswick, 1987-88. Mem. ACA, Am. Mental Health Counselors Assn., Nat. Rehab. Assn., Ga. Rehab. Assn., Lic. Profl. Counselors Assn. Ga., Employee Assistance Profls. Assn., Brunswick Golden Isles C. of C. (chmn. drugs don't work com. 1995—), Internat. Coachmen Caravan, South Ga. Puddle Jumpers. Home: 135 Saint Clair Dr Saint Simons Island GA 31522-1036 Office: Southeastern Rehab Svcs 2483 Demere Rd Ste 103 Saint Simons Island GA 31522

EDWARDS, BRIAN SCOTT, emergency nurse; b. Columbus, Ohio, Nov. 29, 1959; s. Warren Graydon and Catherine (Walker) E.; m. Linda Marie Bohne, Nov. 18, 1989. BS in Chemistry and Biology, Ind. U., Indpls., 1987, BS in Nursing, 1990. RN, Ind. Rsch. asst. dept. endocrinology Ind. U., Indpls., 1988-89; clin. specialist Meth. hosp., 1990-92; emergency nurse Wishard Meml. Hosp., Indpls., 1992—; tech. advisor Boehringer Mannheim Corp., 1995—; prin. Sci. and Internat. Cons., Indpls., 1987—; ACLS instr. Contbr. to profl. pubs. Counselor Crossroads Rehab. Ctr., Indpls., 1973—; arbitrator Nat. Assn. Consumer Arbitrators, Indpls., 1986—; instr. ARC, 1990—; nurse Nat. Disaster Mgmt. Team, 1990—. 1st lt. USAR, 1991—. Eli Lilly scholar, 1989. Mem. Ind. State Nurses Assn. (legis. com. 1990-92). Republican. Office: Brilinco Inc PO Box 50212 Indianapolis IN 46250-0212

EDWARDS, CHARLES, neuroscientist, educator; b. Washington, Sept. 22, 1925; s. James Moses and Lola (Rosenthal) Edlavitch; m. Lois Bender, Aug. 12, 1951; children: Jan, James, Sally, David. AB, Johns Hopkins U., 1945, MA, 1948, PhD, 1953. Found. Infantile Paralysis postdoctoral fellow, asst. lectr. Univ. Coll., London, 1953-55; instr., asst. prof. physiol. optics Johns Hopkins U., Balt., 1955-58; asst. prof. physiology U. Utah, Salt Lake City, 1958-60; assoc. prof. physiology U. Minn., Mpls., 1960-65, prof., 1965-67; prof. biol. scis., dir. neurobiology research center SUNY, Albany, 1967-84, prof. emeritus biol. sci., 1986—; spl. asst. to sci. dir. Nat. Inst. Diabetes and Digestive and Kidney Diseases, NIH, 1984-88; prof. physiology, assoc. dean rsch. and grad. affairs U. South Fla. Coll. Medicine, Tampa, 1988-91; Grass lectr. CIEA del IPN, Mexico City, 1966; vis. prof. Karolinska Inst., 1975,

79, 84; mem. physiology study sect. NIH, 1971-75. Mem. editorial bd. Am. Jour. Physiology, 1967-73, Gen. Physiology Biophysics, 1983-95, Neurosci., 1979-92, Neurosci. Rsch., 1984-94. Mem. ACLU, Md. chpt., 1956-58, Utah chpt., 1959-60; mem. citizen adv. com. Sarasota Bay Nat. Estuary Program, 1994—. Lalor fellow, 1957, Lederle fellow, 1959-60; Nat. Acad. Scis. Chechoslovak Acad. Sci. Exchange fellow, 1980, 82, 84, 87, Japan Soc. Promotion of Sci. fellow, 1981, Naito Found.fellow, 1985; named to Johns Hopkins Univ. Soc. Scholars, 1987. Fellow AAAS; mem. AAUP (mem. coun. 1972-75), Am. Physiol. Soc., Marine Biol. Lab., Biophys. Soc., Japanese Physiol. Soc. (hon.), Soc. Gen. Physiology (sec. 1971-73).

EDWARDS, CHARLES CORNELL, physician, research administrator; b. Overton, Nebr., Sept. 16, 1923; s. Charles Busby and Lillian Margaret (Arendt) E.; m. Sue Cowles Kruidenier, June 24, 1945; children: Timothy, Charles Cornell, Nancy, David. Student, Princeton U., 1941-43; B.A., U. Colo., 1945, M.D., 1948; M.S., U. Minn., 1956; L.L.D. (hon.), Phila. Coll. Pharmacy and Sci.; L.H.D. (hon.), Pa. Coll. Podiatry, U. Colo.; LHD (hon.), U. Colo., 1993. Diplomate: Am. Bd. Surgery. Intern St. Mary's Hosp., Mpls., 1948-49; resident surgery Mayo Found., 1950-56; pvt. practice medicine specializing in surgery Des Moines, 1956-61; mem. surg. staff Georgetown U., Washington, 1961-62; also cons. USPHS; dir. div. socio-econ. activities A.M.A., Chgo., 1963-67; v.p., mng. officer health and sci. affairs Booz, Allen & Hamilton, 1967-69; commr. FDA, Washington, 1969-73; asst. sec. for health HEW, Washington, 1973-75; sr. v.p., dir. Becton, Dickinson & Co., 1975-77; pres. Scripps Clinic and Research Found., La Jolla, Calif., 1977-91; pres., CEO Scripps Insts. Medicine and Sci., La Jolla, 1991-93; bd. dirs. Bergen Brunswig Corp., Molecular Biosys., Inc., No. Trust Bank, IDEC Pharms.; trustee Scripps Rsch. Inst.; bd. regents Nat. Libr. Medicine, 1981-85; mem. Nat. Leadership Commn. on Health Care, 1986—; bd. govs. Hosp. Corp. Am., 1986-89. Trustee San Diego Hospice, San Diego YMCA. Lt. M.C. USNR, 1942-46. Mem. Inst. Medicine, Nat. Acad. Scis., Fairbanks Ranch Country Club, Princeton Club, La Jolla Country Club, La Jolla Beach and Tennis Club. Office: Scripps Rsch Inst 10666 N Torrey Pines Rd La Jolla CA 92037-1027

EDWARDS, CHARLES HENRY, JR., surgeon; b. Goldsboro, N.C., Dec. 22, 1920; s. Charles Henry and Lillie Estelle (Thornton) E.; B.A., U. N.C., 1940, postgrad. in Medicine, 1940-42; M.D., Thomas Jefferson U., 1944; m. Betty Shea, Mar. 11, 1950; children—Charles Henry, Christopher G. Intern, Pa. Hosp., Phila., 1944; resident in gen. surgery Halloran VA Hosp., S.I., 1947-51; surg. resident Martland Hosp., Newark, 1951-52; practice gen. and vascular surgery, Newark, 1951-55, Glen Ridge, N.J., 1955-71, Montclair, N.J., 1971—; mem. surg. staff St. Vincent's, St. James, United Hosp. of Newark, St. Barnabas, Riverside hosps.; med. dir. Riverside Hospice, Boonton, N.J., 1976-78; clin. asst. prof. surgery N.J. Coll. Medicine and Dentistry, Newark, 1966—; med. dir. Individual Freedom Found. Ednl. Trust, 1976—. Bd. dirs. Citizens Freedom Found. N.Y./N.J., 1980—. Served to capt., M.C., U.S. Army, 1944-47. Diplomate Am. Bd. Surgery. Fellow ACS; mem. AMA, N.J. State, Essex County med. socs. Lodges: Masons (32 deg.), Shriners. Office: 5 Roosevelt Pl Montclair NJ 07042

EDWARDS, CHRISTOPHER WATKIN, medicine educator; b. Irvinestown, Northern Ireland, Feb. 12, 1942; s. Thomas Watkin and Beatrice Elizabeth (Telfer) E.; m. Sally Amanda Kidd, Apr. 6, 1968; children: Adam, Kate, Crispin. BA, U. Cambridge, Eng., 1963, MA, 1967, MB, BChir., 1966, MD, 1974. House surgeon Norfolk & Norwich Hosp., 1966; house physician St. Bartholomew's Hosp., London, 1967, lectr. medicine, 1969-75, sr. lectr., 1975-80; house physician Brompton Hosp., London, 1968, Hammersmith Hosp., London, 1968; prof. clin. medicine U. Edinburgh, Scotland, 1980-95, dean faculty of medicine, 1991-95, provost, 1992-95; prof. medicine U. London, 1995—; prin. Imperial Coll. Sch. Medicine, 1995—; traveling fellow NIH, 1972-73; MRC sr. rsch. fellow, 1979-80, mem. coun., 1991-95, mem. sys. bd., 1988-91, chmn. grants com. A, 1990-91; mem. physiology and pharmacology panel Wellcome Trust, 1988-91; mem. chairs com. Brit. Heart Found., 1987-94. Editor: Essential Hypertension as an Endocrine Disorder, 1985, Endocrinology: Integrated Clinical Science, 1986, Davidson's Principles and Practice of Medicine, 1990. Fellow Royal Coll. Physicians (Nessie Ross lectr. 1984, Oliver Sharpey lectr. 1991), Royal Soc. Edinburgh. Mem. Ch. of Eng. Office: Imperial Coll Sch Medicine, Level 5 Siegfried Bldg, London SW7 2A2, England

EDWARDS, DAVID JOEL, biochemist; b. Durham, N.C., Dec. 5, 1943; s. Joseph Philip and Rebecca Josephine (Kornblut) E.; m. Mary Dawn Herring, Oct. 8, 1972; children: Leah Dianne, Rachel Rebecca. BA, Duke U., 1966; PhD, U. N.C., 1971. Postdoctoral fellow U. Pitts., 1971-73; asst. prof. U. Pitts. Sch. Medicine, 1973-79; asst. prof. U. Pitts. Sch. Dental Medicine, 1979-81, assoc. prof., 1981-88, prof., 1988—. Contbr. articles to Life Scis., Jour. Neurochemistry, Neuropharmacology; editor Greater Pitts. VHF Soc., 1991—. Mem. Soc. for Neuroscience, AAAS. Home: 6652 Ridgeville St Pittsburgh PA 15217-1315 Office: U Pitts 546 Salk Hall Pittsburgh PA 15261-1905

EDWARDS, GEORGE ALVA, physician, educator; b. Killeen, Tex., Oct. 19, 1916; s. John Clem and Maude May (Lam) E.; m. Winnie Belle Landes, Jan. 23, 1946; children—Karen Leigh, David Glen. B.A., Howard Payne Coll., 1939; postgrad., N. Tex. State Coll., 1946; M.D., U. Tex., Southwestern Med. Sch., 1950. Intern Johns Hopkins Hosp., Balt., 1950-51, resident, 1952-53; resident Duke Hosp., Durham, N.C., 1951-52, Firmin Desloge Hosp., St. Louis, 1953-54; asst. chief med. service VA, St. Louis, 1954-55; chief med. service VA Hosp, McKinney, Tex., 1955-59, Pitts., 1959-66; asst. chief med. service Dallas, 1966-68, chief of staff, 1972-84, assoc. chief staff for extended care, 1984-85; chief med. service Cin., 1968-72; asst. prof. Southwestern Med. Sch., U. Tex., Dallas, 1955-59, assoc. prof., 1966-68, prof. medicine, 1972-86, emeritus prof., 1987—, asst. dean, 1973-84; assoc. prof. U. Pitts., 1959-66; prof. U. Cin., 1968-72. Served with USAAF, 1940-46. Decorated Air medal. Fellow ACP; mem. Alpha Omega Alpha. Baptist. Home: 3630 Granada Ave Dallas TX 75205-2014

EDWARDS, IRENE ELIZABETH (LIBBY EDWARDS), dermatologist, educator, researcher; b. Winston-Salem, N.C., Mar. 17, 1950; d. Robert Dixon Edwards and Irene Octavia (Temple) Fisher; m. Clayton Samuel Owens, Apr. 19, 1985; 1 child, Sarah Tay. BS magna cum laude, Wake Forest U., 1972; MD, Bowman Gray Sch. Medicine, 1976; postgrad., N.C. Bapt. Hosp., 1979, U. Ariz., 1981, 84. Diplomate Nat. Bd. Med. Examiners, Am. Bd. Internal Medicine, Am. Bd. Pediatrics, Am. Bd. Dermatology. Intern N.C. Bapt. Hosp., Winston-Salem, 1976-78, resident in pediatrics, 1978-79; resident in internal medicine U. Ariz. Health Scis. Ctr., Tucson, 1979-81, resident in dermatology, 1982-84; instr. dermatology U. Ariz. Coll. Medicine, Tucson, 1984-85, asst. prof. dermatology, 1985-90; chief section dermatology Tucson VA Med. Ctr., 1984-90; chief dermatology Carolinas Med. Ctr., Charlotte, N.C., 1990—; clin. assoc. prof. dermatology Bowman Gray Sch. Medicine, Winston-Salem, 1993—, U. N.C., Chapel Hill, 1993—; nat. lectr. in field. Co-author: Genital Dermatology, 1994; contbr. chpts. to books, numerous articles to profl. jours. Reynolds scholar, 1969-72. Fellow Am. Acad. Dermatology, Am. Acad. Pediatrics; mem. Soc. Pediatric Dermatology, Internat. Soc. Tropical Dermatology, Soc. Investigative Dermatology, Women's Dermatologic Soc., Internat. Soc. for Study of Vulvovaginal Disease (exec. coun.), Charlotte Dermatological Soc., Phi Beta Kappa, Alpha Epsilon Delta. Home: 2409 Cuthbertson Rd Waxhaw NC 28173-8110 Office: Carolinas Med Ctr 1000 Blythe Blvd Charlotte NC 28203-5812

EDWARDS, JAMES BURROWS, university president, oral surgeon; b. Hawthorne, Fla., June 24, 1927; s. O.M. and Bertie R. (Hieronymus) E.; m. Ann Norris Darlington, Sept. 1, 1951; children: James Burrows Jr., Catharine Edwards Wingate. BS, Coll. of Charleston, 1950, LittD, 1975; DMD, U. Louisville, 1955, D Social Sci., 1982; postgrad. advanced correlated clin. scis., U. Pa. Grad. Med. Sch., 1957-58; LittD (hon.), Coll. Charleston, 1975; LLD (hon.), U. S.C., 1975, Bob Jones U., 1976, The Citadel, 1977; HHD (hon.), Francis Marion Coll., 1978, Bapt. Coll. Charleston, 1981; DS (hon.), Erskine Coll., 1982, Georgetown U., 1982; D of Social Sci. (hon.), U. Louisville, 1982; LLD (hon.), NEwberry Coll., 1986; others. Diplomate Am. Bd. Oral and Maxillofacial Surgery. Resident in oral surgery Henry Ford Hosp., Detroit, 1958-60; practice dentistry specializing in oral and maxillofacial surgery Charleston, S.C., 1960—; gov. State of S.C., 1975-79; U.S. sec. energy, 1981-82; pres. Med. U. S.C., Charleston, 1982—; bd. dirs. Phillips Petroleum Co., Bartlesville, Okla., SCANA Corp., Columbia, IMO Industries Inc., Lawrenceville, N.J., WMX Technologies, Inc., Nat. Data Corp., Atlanta, GS Industries, Inc., Charlotte, N.C.; mem. adv. bd. Norfolk-so. Corp., Va. Past bd. dirs. Coastal Carolina coun. Boy Scouts Am.; past trustee Charleston County Hosp., Greater Charleston YMCA, Coll. Preparatory Sch., Charleston, Baker Meml. Hosp., Charleston; chmn. Charleston County Rep. Party, 1964-69; del. to Nat. Rep. Convs., 1968, 72, 76, 80, 84, 88, 92l chmn. 1st Congl. Dist. Rep. Com., 1970; mem. S.C. State Senate, 1972-74; chmn. subcom. on nuclear energy Nat. Govs. Assn., 1978; chmn. So. Govs. Conf., 1978; founder, charter mem., chmn. bd. dirs. Oral Surgery Polit. Action Com., 1971-73; bd. dirs. Harry Frank Guggenheim Found., N.Y.C., Gaylord and Dorothy Donnelley Found., Chgo. With USNR. Fellow Internat. Coll. Dentists, Am. Coll. Dentists; mem. ADA, S.C. Dental Soc., Coastal Dist. Dental Soc. (past pres.), Chalmers J. Lyons Acad. Oral Surgery, Southeastern Soc. Oral and Maxillofacial Surgeons, Am. Soc. Oral and Maxillofacial Surgeons, Brit. Assn. Oral and Maxillofacial Surgeons, Internat. Soc. Oral and Maxillofacial Surgeons, Fedn. Dentaire Internat., S.C. Soc. Oral and Maxillofacial Surgeons (founder, charter mem., past pres.), Oral Surgery Polit. Action Com. (founder, charter mem., chmn. bd. dirs. 1971-73), Navy League U.S., Am. Hellenic Ednl. Progressive Assn., AHEPA (Plato chpt. # 4), Rotary, Masons, Pi Kappa Phi, Delta Sigma Delta, Omicron Delta Kappa. Office: Med U SC 171 Ashley Ave Charleston SC 29425-0001

EDWARDS, JOHN WESLEY, JR., urologist; b. Ferndale, Mich., Apr. 9, 1933; s. John W. and Josephine (Wood) E.; m. Ella Marie Law, Dec. 25, 1954; children: Joella, John III. Student, Alma Coll., 1949-50; BS, U. Mich., 1954; postgrad., Wayne State U., 1954-56; MD, Howard U., 1960. Internship Walter Reed Gen. Hosp., 1960-61, surg. resident, 1962-63, urol. resident, 1963-66; asst. chief urology Tripler Army Med. Ctr., 1966-69; comdr. 4th Med. Battalion, 4th Infantry Div., Vietnam, 1969; chief profl. svcs., urology 91st Evacuation Hosp., Vietnam, 1969-70; urologist Straub Clinic, Inc., 1970-74; pvt. practice, 1974—; v.p. med. staff svcs. Queen's Med. Ctr., Honolulu, 1993-94; v.p. physician rels. Queen's Health Sys., Honolulu, 1994-96; acting adminstr. Diagnostic Lab. Svcs., Inc., Honolulu, 1995-96, pres., 1996—; chief Dept. Surgery, Straub Clinic and Hosp., 1973; asst. chief Dept. Surgery Queen's Med. Ctr., 1977-79, chief, 1989-93; cons. in urology; chief Dept. Clin. Svcs., Kapiolani Women's and Children's Med. Ctr., 1981-83; clin. assoc. prof. U. Hawaii Sch. of Medicine; chmn. task force on phys. hosp. collaboration The Queens Health System, 1993—. Contbr. articles to profl. jours. Bd. dirs. Am. Cancer Soc., Honolulu unit, 1977-79, Hawaii Med. Svc. Assn., 1979-85, Hawaii Heart Assn., 1977-79, Hawaii Assn. for Physician's Indemnification, 1980-86; commr. City and County of Honolulu, 1990-91; mem. med. adv. bd. Nat, Kindey Found., Hawaii, 1994—; mem. adv. bd. MADD, Hawaii, 1992-96, bd. dirs., 1996—; bd. dirs. Neighborhood Justice Ctr., 1995—. Recipient Howard O. Gray award for Professionalism, 1988, Leaders of Hawaii award, 1983; named Hawaii African-Am. Humanitarian of the Yr. by Hawaii chpt. Links, Inc., 1991. Fellow ACS (sec.-treas. Hawaii chpt. 1980-81, gov.-at-large 1986-92); mem. AMA, NAACP, Am. Urol. Assn. (alt. del. Western sect. 1991-92, gen. chmn. Western sect. 56th ann. meeting 1980, exec. com. 1983-84, del. dist. 1 1985-86, gen. chmn. 63d ann. meeting 1987, pres. 1989-90, nom. com. 1990-93, chmn. nom. 1992-93), Am. Coll. Physician Execs., Nat. Med. Assn., Hawaii Urol. Assn., Hawaii Med. Assn., Surgicare of Hawaii (v.p. 1983-86), Alpha Phi Alpha, Chi Delta Mu, Alpha Omega Alpha. Office: Diagnostic Lab Svcs & Accupath 770 Kapiolani Blvd Ste 100 Honolulu HI 96813

EDWARDS, JULIE DIANE, maternity and staff nurse; b. Lewiston, Idaho, Jan. 4, 1958; d. William and Shirley Hinkley; adopted by Karl Frank and Margaret Esther (Carver) Stoehr, 1965; m. Raymond LeRoy Murphy, Jr., Mar. 19, 1977 (div. Mar. 1982); 1 child, Raymond LeRoy Murphy III; m. Monte Russell Edwards, Dec. 22, 1984; 1 child, Bryan James. AS with honors, Highline Cmty. Coll., Des Moines, Wash., 1982; AAS with honors, Mt. Hood Cmty. Coll., Gresham, Oreg., 1993. RN, Oreg.; cert. Neonatal Resuscitation Program. Staff nurse, maternity Woodland Pk. Hosp., Portland, Oreg., 1993—; staff on call nurse, maternity Providence Milwaukie Hosp., Milwaukie, Oreg., 1994-95. Mem. adv. bd. Adult Basic Edn., Pocatello, Idaho, 1982-85; VISTA vol., 1984-85; vol. Crisis Pregnancy Ctr., Portland, Oreg., 1990—; tchr. aide Good Shepherd Sch., 1992—; Sunday sch. tchr. Good Shepherd Cmty. Ch., 1984-91, 94—. With U.S. Army, 1976-79. Republican. Christian. Home: 304 NE 188th Portland OR 97230 Office: Woodland Park Hospital 10300 NE Hancock Portland OR 97220

EDWARDS, KENNETH JOHN, orthopedic surgeon; b. Roslyn, N.Y., Mar. 4, 1958; s. David E. and Nora M. (Kenny) E.; m. Wendy L. Redderoth, July 30, 1983; children: David, Jordan, Kathleen. BA, Coll. of Holy Cross, 1980; MD, SUNY Upstate Med. Ctr., Syracuse, 1994. Diplomate Am. Bd. Orthopedic Surgery. Commd. ens. USN, 1984, advanced through grades to lt. comdr., 1990; med. dept. head USS Coronado, 1985-86; gen. med. officer NAS Oceana, Virginia Beach, Va., 1986-87; orthopedic surgery resident Nat. Navel Med. Ctr., Bethesda, Md., 1987-91; staff orthopedic surgeon Naval Hosp. Great Lakes, Ill., 1991-93; resigned USN, 1993; orthopedic surgeon River Orthopedics and Sports Medicine, St. Joseph, Mich., 1993—; bd. dirs. Lakeland Care P.H.O., St. Joseph. Trustee Twin City Cath. Sch. Found., St. Joseph, 1993—. Fellow ACS, Am. Acad. Orthopedic Surgeons; mem. Mich. Orthopedic Soc., MidAm. Orthopedic Soc., Berrien County Med. Soc. (sec. 1995—, pres.-elect 1996), Phi Beta Kappa. Republican. Roman Catholic. Office: Riverview Orthopedics & Sports Medicine 4472 Sunnymeade Dr Saint Joseph MI 49085

EDWARDS, LARRY DAVID, internist; b. Macomb, Ill., June 20, 1937; s. Richard Marshall and Anna Louise (Hare) Edwards; m. Ann Leanor Will, Mar. 31, 1959; children: Elliott, Sharon, Beth. Pre-Med, U. Ill., 1961, MD, 1965. Diplomate Am. Bd. Internal Medicine, Am. Bd. Infectious Disease, Am. Bd. Geriatric Medicine, Nat. Bd. Medical Examiners, Am. Bd. Med. Mgmt., Am. Coll. Healthcare Execs.; cert. health exec. Rotating intern USPHS Hosp., Staten Island, N.Y., 1965-66, resident in internal medicine, 1966-68; fellow in infectious diseases Rush-Presbyn.-St. Luke's Med. Ctr., Chgo., 1968-70; instr. dept. internal medicine U. Ill. Coll. Medicine, Chgo., 1968-70; asst. prof. depts. internal medicine, preventive medicine, microbiology Rush Med. Coll., Chgo., 1972-74; assoc. prof. internal medicine U. Ill. Coll. Medicine, Rockford, 1974-80, prof., 1980-81; prof. internal medicine Oral Roberts U. Sch. Medicine, Tulsa, 1981-90; dir. div. infectious diseases Rockford Sch. Medicine, 1974-81, dep. head dept. biomed. scis., 1980-81; prof. internal medicine U. Va., Charlottesville, 1991-92; chief of staff VA Med. Ctr., Salem, Va., 1990-92; assoc. dean for acad. affairs VA, U. Va., Charlottesville, 1991-92; adj. assoc. prof. epidemiology, U. Ill. Sch. Pub. Health, 1977-81; affiliate dept. medicine, Abraham Lincoln Sch. Medicine, U. Ill., Chgo., 1980-81; dir. div. infectious diseases Oral Roberts U., 1981-84; assoc. dean clin. affairs Oral Roberts Sch. Medicine, 1981, 84, vice chmn. dept. internal medicine, 1981-83, chmn., 1983-86, chmn. preventive and internat. medicine, 1987-88, dean, 1984-90, v.p. for health affairs, 1987-90 and chief operating officer City of Faith Med. & Rsch. Ctr., 1989-90; med. dir. Cen. Bapt. Home for Aged, Norridge, Ill., 1968-74, Columbia County Homes, Wyocena, Wis., 1974-80; asst. dir. infectious diseases, hosp. epidemiologist, dir. infectious disease research Rush-Presbyn.-St. Luke's Hosp., Chgo., 1972-74, asst. sci. dept. microbiology, 1970-74; asst. med. dir. Mcpl. Contagious Disease Hosp., Chgo., 1970-74; cons. infectious diseases numerous other hosps. and med. ctrs.; med. dir. City of Faith Hosp., Tulsa, 1984-87, chmn. bd., 1989-90; bd. dirs. City of Faith Clinic, Tulsa, 1985-87; pres. Infectious Diseases Cons. Svcs., Inc., Barnhart, Mo., 1993—. Contbr. numerous articles to med. jours. Advisor resource com. Sch. Health Coalition of N.W. Ill., 1979-81; mem. med. adv. com. State of Ill. Refugee Health Services Program, 1980-81; mem. Ill. health services task force State of Ill. Dept. Pub. Health, 1980-81; mem. infectious disease adv. com. Tulsa City-County Health Dept., 1981-88; mem. physician manpower adv. com. Okla. Bd. Regents, 1984-88; mem. Oral Roberts U. Titan Scholarship Bd., 1985-87; v.p. World-Wide Med. Missions, Oral Roberts Evangelistic Assn., 1986-88, pres. 1989-90; mem. Leadership Roanoke Valley, 1991-92. Served with U.S. Army, 1955-58, with USPHS, 1965-70, lt. col. USAR, 1985, col. 1990—. Recipient Smith, Kline and French fellowship for study in Ethiopia, 1964; named Outstanding Faculty Mem. of Yr. Oral Roberts U. Sch. Medicine, 1982-83. Fellow ACP, Infectious Diseases Soc. Am., Am. Coll. Physician Execs., Am. Coll. Healthcare Execs.

EDWARDS, LESLIE ERROLL, retired physiology educator, researcher; b. Montesano, Wash., Dec. 26, 1914; s. Ive Oscar and Leah Fawn (Butler) E.; m. Carolyn Frances Trowbridge, Dec. 25, 1946; children: Patricia, Lucy, Keith. BS, Wash. State U., 1937, MS, 1939; PhD, U. Rochester, 1944. Instr. U. Rochester, N.Y., 1943-46; rsch. fellow Fels Rsch. Found., Phila., 1946; assoc. Med. Coll. Va., Richmond, 1947-49, asst. prof. physiology, 1949-51, assoc. prof., 1951-64, prof., 1964-78, prof. emeritus, 1978—, acting chmn. dept., 1966-67, 70-71, mem. faculty senate, 1978—, chmn. basic sci. faculty, 1970, ret., 1994. Contbr. articles to Jour. Nutrition, Growth, Proc. Soc. Exptl. Biology and Medicine, Jour. Cellular and Comparative Physiology. Pres. Oak Hall Ruritan, Sandston, Va., 1975, 87. Grantee NIH, 1957-62, 1959-65. Mem. AAUP, Am. Physiol. Soc., Soc. Gen. Physiology, Am. Inst. Biol. Scis., Am. Chem. Soc., N.Y. Acad. Scis., Va. Acad. Sci., Sigma Xi (past pres. Med. Coll. Va. chpt.). Republican. Home: 1990 Old Hanover Rd Sandston VA 23150-3419 Office: Med Coll Va Sta Dept Physiology Richmond VA 23298

EDWARDS, MARY ELLEN, social worker; b. Cleve., May 28, 1960; d. Walter H. and Delores Ann (Dillion) E. BSSW, BA in Journalism, Tex. Christian U., 1986; MSSW, U. Tex., Arlington, 1992. Social worker Women's Haven Tarrant County, 1986-88; with Tarrant County Mental Health Mental Retardation Svcs., Ft. Worth, 1988-90, mgr. community support and social club program, 1990-93; hospice social worker Am. Hospice, Inc., Dallas, 1993-94; case mgmt. coord., dir. social svcs. Charter Hosp., Ft. Worth, 1994; dir. therapy and social svcs. DFW Palliative Care Ctr., Bedford, Tex., 1995-96; psychotherapist Ctr. for Change, Discovery & Support, 1996—; staff therapist Samaritan Care Hospice, 1996—, New Horizons, 1996—. Vol., bd. dirs. Ft. Worth Counseling Ctr., AIDS Outreach Ctr., 1986-88; bd. dirs. TCLGA, 1993-95; pastoral care coord. Agape Met. Comm. Ch., 1995—. Mem. NASW. Home: 8809 Hornaday Cir S Apt 1309 Fort Worth TX 76120-3933

EDWARDS, MICHAEL HARPUR, surgeon, consultant; b. Birkenhead, Cheshire, Eng., Feb. 19, 1941; s. Ronald Frederick and Joan Worsley (Stelfox) E.; m. Catherine Elizabeth Davidson, Aug. 23, 1969; children: James, Joanne. MB BChir, Med. U. Liverpool, Eng., 1964. Lectr. Kings Coll. Hosp., London, 1970-72; sr. registrar U. Hosp. Wales, Cardiff, 1972-78; cons. surgeon Yorkshire (Eng.) Health Authority, 1978—; mng. dir. Scalpel Info. Sys., Darlington, Eng., 1992-96. Editor: (computer sys.) Satis-Fax Information for Patients; editor-in-chief: (surg. tng. program) Current Techniques in Surgery, 1995; patentee in field. Innovation grantee Dept. Trade and Industry, 1994. Fellow Royal Coll. Surgeons Eng. Home: 12 Staindrop Rd, Darlington DL3 9AE, England Office: Friarale Hosp, Northallerton England

EDWARDS, NEIL B., psychiatrist; b. Lake Ariel, Pa., Nov. 8, 1939. BS, Pa. State U., 1961; MD, Temple U., 1965. Chief resident Temple U. Health Scis. Ctr., Phila., 1970-71, asst. prof. psychiatry, 1971-73; asst. prof. psychiatry Hosp. U. Pa., Phila., 1973-77; assoc. prof. psychiatry and dir. clin. svcs. U. Tex. Med. Sch., Houston, 1977-79; assoc. prof. psychiatry U. Tenn., Memphis, 1979-84, prof. psychiatry, 1984—, acting chmn. psychiatry, 1983-85, chmn. dept. psychiatry, 1985—; cons. Tenn. Dept. Mental Health/ Mental Retardation to Select a Commr. of Mental Health, 1986; mem. master plan adv. com. Tenn. Psychiat. Assn./Tenn. dept. Mental Health/ Mental Retardation, Nashville, 1992; cons. Am. Psychiat. Assn. Task Force on Treatment of Psychiat. Disease, 1986; examiner Am. Bd. Psychiatry and Neurology, 1983-84, chief proctor written examination, 1983—, sr. examiner, 1984—; specialist site visitor psychiatry residency rev. com. Accreditation Coun. for grad. Med. Edn., 1990—. Contbr. numerous articles and abstracts to profl. jours.; editl. bd. Jour. behavior Therapy and Exptl. Psychiatry, 1979—; sci. advisor Jour. Clin. Psychiatry, 1990-93; book reviewer. Mem. mental health task force Memphis Coalition for the Homeless, 1987, pres., 1987-89; mem. bd. dirs., pres. Lowenstein House, Memphis, 1988-90; mem. City of Memphsi Mayor's Task Force for devel. of Police Crisis Intervention Team, 1988-89; adv. bd. alliance for Mentally Ill, 1988—, Green Spring of tenn., Chattanooga, 1994—. Decorated Bronze Star medal; recipient Nat. Alumni Assn. Alumni Pub. Svc. award, Knoxville, 1993, Golden Apple award for excellence in teaching, Class of 1995, Alumni Achievement award Dirs. Med. Alumni Assn. of Temple U., 1995. Fellow Am. Psychiat. Assn. (Cert. Recognition for Excellence in Med. Student Edn. 1992, Soc. Behavior Therapy and Rsch. (charter clin. fellow), Coll. Physicians of Phila. (assoc. fellow); mem. AAAS, AMA, Memphis and Shelby County Med. Soc., Acad. Psychosomatic Medicine, Memphis Neurosci. Soc., So. Assn. for Rsch. in Psychiatry (sec.-treas. 1990-91, pres. 1992-93), Am. Geriatric Soc., Am. Acad. Psychiatry in Alcoholism and Addictions, Soc. Biol. Psychiatry, Memphis Med. Seminar, Sigma Xi, Alpha Omega Alpha, Alpha Epsilon Delta (life, chpt. v.p. 1961). Office: U Tenn-Memphis Dept of Psychiatry Memphis TN 38163*

EDWARDS, NELSON GREY, optometrist; b. Clintwood, Va., May 16, 1952; s. Patsy E.; m. Cheryl Lee Sturner, Jan. 3, 1973; 1 child, Christopher Edwards. BS, Ferris State U., 1986, OD, 1987. Avionics tech USAF, Portsmouth, N.H., 1972-76; electronic tech Chrysler Corp., Highland Park, Mich., 1976-83; asst. prof. Ferris State U., Big Rapids, Mich., 1989-95; optometrist pvt. practice Fowlerville (Mich.) Family Eye Care, 1991—. Trip leader Voluntary Optometric, Haiti, 1989, Svc. to Humanity, Mexico, 1990, 92, 93, 94, Commonwealth of Dominica, 1995. Sgt. USAF, 1972-76. Mem. Am. Optometric Assn., Mich. Optometric Assn., Voluntary Optometric Svcs. to Humanity-Mich. (dir. 1995), Rotary Internat. (club pres. 1995). Republican. Office: Fowlerville Family Eyecare PO Box 618 136 E Grand River Fowlerville MI 48836

EDWARDS, PAMELA BALLANCE, nursing educator; b. Washington, Aug. 2, 1956; d. John Harding and Wana Irene (Tacy) Ballance; m. James Thomas Edwards, Apr. 2, 1988; children: James Thomas III. BSN, Atlantic Christian Coll., 1978; MSN, Villanova U., 1984; EdD, N.C. State U., 1989. Dir. health promotion Ephrata (Pa.) Community Hosp.; dir. nursing and mental health edn. Fayetteville (N.C.) Area Health Edn. Ctr.; asst. dir. continuing med. edn., affiliations Duke U. Med. Ctr., Durham, N.C., 1995—, dir. edn. svcs. Med. Ctr. and Health Sys., 1996—; consulting assoc. Duke U. Sch. Nursing; adj. asst. prof. East Carolina U. Sch. Nursing, U. N.C., Sch. Nursing. Mem. Sigma Theta Tau. Home: 113 Laurel Ridge Dr Clayton NC 27520 Office: Duke Univ Med Ctr Durham NC 27710

EDWARDS, RICHARD THOMAS, internist, educator; b. Roanoke, Va., Mar. 14, 1941; s. Richard Thomas Edwards and Augusta (Saul) Edwards Farrier; m. Evelyn Evans, Sept. 20, 1964; children: Chris, Clarissa, Jocelyn, Evans. AB, Washington and Lee U., 1963; MD, U. Va., 1967. Diplomate Am. Bd. Internal Medicine. Med. intern U. Va. Hosp., Charlottesville, 1967-68, resident in internal medicine, 1968-69, 71-73, cardiology fellow, 1972-73; pvt. practice, Roanoke, Va., 1973—; clin. assoc. prof. medicine U. Va. Sch. Medicine, 1975—; chief internal medicine Cmty. Hosp., Roanoke, 1977-78. Pres. Roanoke Valley chpt. Am. Heart Assn., 1978; bd. dirs. Planned Parenthood SW Va., Roanoke, 1984-88. Lt. comdr. M.C., USN, 1969-71. Fellow ACP; mem. AMA, Am. Soc. Internal Medicine (trustee 1988, v.p. 1990, pres. 1992-93), Med. Soc. Va. (del. 1989-93, health promotions com. 1992), Roanoke Acad. Medicine (trustee 1985-87), Phi Beta Kappa, Alpha Omega Alpha. Democrat. Lutheran. Home: 1901 Greenwood Rd SW Roanoke VA 24015-2821 Office: Roanoke Valley Med Clinic 1603 Franklin Rd SW Roanoke VA 24016-5208

EDWARDS, ROBERT HARRISON, pathologist; b. Gorgas, Ala., Oct. 26, 1927; s. Ellis Hewett and Lida Scott (McCarty) E.; m. Harriett Pauline Carlson, Feb. 7, 1959; children: Robert Scott, John Fergus, Andrew Ellis. AB, U. N.C., 1949; MD, Cornell U., 1953; PhD, U. Wis., 1970. Bd. cert. anatomic pathology and clin. pathology. Intern N.Y. Hosp., 1953-54; resident Presbyn.-St. Lukes Hosp., Chgo., 1954-59; commd. as capt. USAF, 1956, advanced through grades to col., 1969; pathologist, dep. comdr. Aeromed. Rsch. Lab., Holloman AFB, N.Mex., 1959-63; postdoctoral fellow genetics dept. U. Wis., Madison, 1963-67; pathologist Pediat. Hepatic Br. Armed Forces Inst. Pathology, Washington, 1967-72; chmn. dept. pathology Keesler AFB Hosp., Biloxi, Miss., 1972-76; ret. USAF, 1976; chmn. dept. pathology Children's Hosp. and U. Ala. Med. Sch., Birmingham, 1976-78; pathologist Eliza Coffee Meml. Hosp., Florence, Ala., 1978—; clin. prof. U. Ala. Med. Sch., Birmingham, 1976—. Fellow Coll. Am. Pathologists (chmn. USAF divsn. 1968-72), Am. Soc. Clin. Pathologists, U.S. and Can. Acad. Pathology, Am. Soc. Human Genetics; mem. Sigma Xi. Home: 914 Ridgecliff Dr Florence AL 35630 Office: ECM Hosp PO Box 818 Florence AL 35631

EDWARDS, SALLY ANNE, medical center administrator; b. Darlington, Wis., Feb. 28, 1945; d. Herbert C. and Marie M. (Smith) Wernke; m. H. Lynn Smith, June 20, 1964; children: Jeffrey L., Stacy A. Levinski; m. William E. Edwards, July 11, 1981 (dec. Nov. 1994). Accredited record technician. Clk. Marian Med. Ctr., Santa Maria, Calif., 1973-81, dir. med. records, 1981-95, cancer registry coord., 1995—; cancer registry coord. Valley Cmty. Hosp., Santa Maria, 1995—; health occupations advisor Hancock Jr. Coll., Santa Maria, 1993—; region advisor C/Net, Berkeley, Calif., 1996. Mem. Am. Health Info. Assn., Nat. Cancer Registry Assn., Calif. Cancer Registry Assn., Santa Maria Country Club, Med. Wives (pres. 1991). Home: 4321 Snowhill Ct Santa maria CA 93455 Office: Marion Medical Center 1400 E Church St Santa Maria CA 93454

EDWARDS, THOMAS ALLEN, orthopedic surgeon; b. Wrangell, Alaska, June 8, 1929; s. Ellis Hewitt and Lida Scott (McCarty) E.; m. Beata Cecilia Peterson, June 9, 1958; children: Barbara, Nancy, Mary, Thomas (dec.). BA, Williams Coll., 1950; MD, Cornell U. Med. Coll., 1954; MS, Oreg. State U., 1972. Diplomate Am. Bd. Orthopedic Surgery. Pvt. practice orthopedic surgery Salem, Oreg., Lafayette, Ind., Johnson City, Tenn., 1961-88; med. cons. Ins. Inst. Hwy. Safety, Washington, 1988-89; orthopedic surgeon Md., 1990-93; surgeon Alaska Native Hosp., Anchorage, 1993-94; clin. instr. Oreg. Med. Sch., Portland, 1962-75, Ind. Med. Sch., Indpls., 1976-79; assoc. clin. prof. surgery, East Tenn. Med. Sch., Johnson City, 1979-88. Capt. USAF, 1955-57. Fellow Am. Coll. Surgeons; mem. Am. Acad. Orthopedic Surgeons, Va. Med. Soc., Tenn. Med. Soc., Appalachian Trail Conf. Presbyn. Home: 5352 Sundance Rd Salem VA 24153

EDWARDS, VICKI LYNN, health facility administrator; b. Ashland, Ky., Aug. 19, 1955; d. James Russell and Myrtle (Stapleton) Fleming; m. John Arthur Edwards, Apr. 23, 1976. BBA cum laude, Ohio U., 1991. Lic. nursing home adminstr., Ky. Adminstr. King's Daus. & Sons, Ashland, Ky., 1983-87; dir. admissions Heartland of Riverview, South Point, Ohio, 1991-94; adminstr. Carter Health Care, Grayson, Ky., 1994-95, King's Daus. & Sons, Ashland, 1995—. Author: (short story) Shawnee, 1989. Mem. Am. Coll. Health Care Adminstrs. Democrat. Office: King's Daus & Sons 1100 Bath Ashland KY 41101

EDWARDS, WARD DENNIS, psychology and industrial engineering educator; b. Morristown, N.J., Apr. 5, 1927; s. Corwin D. and Janet W. (Ferriss) E.; m. Silvia Callegari, Dec. 12, 1970; children: Tara, Page. B.A., Swarthmore Coll., 1947; M.A., Harvard U., 1950, Ph.D., 1952. Instr. Johns Hopkins U., 1951-54; with Personnel and Tng. Research Center, USAF, Denver, 1954-56, San Antonio, 1956-58; research psychologist U. Mich., 1958-63, prof. psychology, 1963-73, head Engring. Psychology Lab., 1963-73; assoc. dir. Hwy. Safety Research Inst., 1970-73; prof. psychology and indsl. engring. Social Sci. Rsch. Inst. U. So. Calif., 1973-95, prof. emeritus, 1995—, dir. Social Sci. Rsch. Inst., 1973-93; pres. Wise Decisions, Inc., 1995—; cons. in field. Author: (with J. Robert Newman) Multiattribute Evaluation, 1982, (with D.V. Winterfeldt) Decision Analysis and Behavioral Research, 1986; editor: (with A. Tversky) Decision Making: Selected Readings, 1967; editor: Utility Theories: Measurements and Applications, 1992; contbr. to Ency. Social Scis., 1968. Served with USNR, 1945-46. Recipient Franklin V. Taylor award Soc. Engring. Psychologists, 1978, James McKeen Cattel Fellow award in applied psychology Am. Psychol. Soc., 1995. Fellow APA, Decision Scis. Inst.; mem. Western Psychol. Assn., Psychonomic Soc., Soc. Med. Decision-Making, Ops. Research Soc. Am. (Frank P. Ramsey medal 1988), Decision Analysis Soc. (pres. 1994-96), Inst. Mgmt. Scis. (pres. Coll. Managerial Problem Solving 1987-88).

EDWARDS, WARD EMIL, retired healthcare adminstrator; b. Mpls., Jan. 19, 1925; s. Ward Joseph and Amy T. Edwards; m. Donna Mae Knutson, Aug. 31, 1950; children: Terrie Pitts, Laurie Wilson, Scott. BA, U. Minn., 1949; MA in Hosp. Adminstrn., State U. Iowa, 1953. Asst. adminstr., purchasing agt. Middlesex Meml. Hosp., Middletown, Conn., 1954-56, asst. adminstr., 1956-57; asst. adminstr. Luth. Deaconess Hosp., Mpls., 1957-60, adminstr., exec. dir., 1960-73; dir. cmty. and edn. program Fairview Cmty. Hosp., Mpls., 1973-76; v.p. adminstrn. North Meml. Med. Ctr., Robbinsdale, Minn., 1976-84, v.p. found., 1985-87; exed. dir. Unity Cmty. Health Found., Fridley, Minn., 1985-87; cons. cmty. rels. North Meml. Med. Ctr., Robbinsdale, 1987—; bd. dirs. Meml. Blood Ctrs. of Minn., Mpls., 1965—, West Broadway Bus. Assn., Mpls., 1982—. Creator slide show and talk Living By Choice or Chance, 1983; founder various running events. Mem. coun. Trinity Luth. Congregation, Mpls., 1995—; loaned exec. United Way of Mpls. Area, 1988—; mem. com. Hennepin County Cmty. Health Adv. Com., Mpls., 1992—. Ensign USN, 1945, PTO. Fellow Am. Coll. Healthcare Execs. (life); mem. Am. Hosp. Assn. (life); mem. N.W. Sports and Health Club, Robbinsdale C. of C. (bd. dirs. 1980—). Home: 2474 Carman St Wayzata MN 55391 Office: North Meml Med Ctr 3300 N Oakdale Robbinsdale MN 55422

EDWARDS, WILLIE STANLEY, JR., physician; b. Washington, N.C., Nov. 27, 1954; s. Willie Stanley and Rosalyn Varn E.; m. Jennifer Burkett, June 6, 1987; children: William Burkett, Caroline Celeste. BA with honors, U. N.C., 1977, MD, 1981; Fellowship in Surgery, South Tex. Spinal Clinic, San Antonio, 1988. Fellow Am. Bd. Orthopaedic Surgery. Orthopaedic surgeon Pee Dee Orthopaedic Assocs., Florence, S.C., 1988—; pres. Bishopville Ford, LLP, S.C., 1995—; mem. Carolinas Hosp. System Adv. Bd., Florence, 1995—; prnter. Pee Dee Orthopaedic Assocs., Florence, 1988—. Mem. S.C. Orthopaedic Assn. (v.p. 1996-97), S.C. Spine Soc. (pres. 1996-97), Carolinas Hosp. System, N.Am. Spine Soc., So. Orthopedic Assn., S.C. Med. Assn., So. Med. Assn.

EDWARDSON, SANDRA, dean, nursing educator. Dean Sch. Nursing, U. Minn., Mpls. Office: U Minn Twin CitiesSch Nursing 6-100 Weaver-Defford 308 Harvard St Minneapolis MN 55455*

EDWARDS-TATE, LAURIE ELLEN, homecare services company executive, educator; b. San Diego, June 3, 1951; d. Donald Morgan and Doral (Erickson) Hurd; m. William James Tate Jr., Jan. 1, 1995. Student Calif. Poly. State U., 1977; BA, Nat. U., San Diego, 1978; postgrad. U. Calif., San Diego, 1982-84; MS, Chapman Coll., 1986. Founder, owner Am. Med. Claims, La Jolla, 1981-86; pres., founder At Your Home Svcs., San Diego, 1985—, At Your Home Family Care, 1996—; instr. bus. Palomar Coll., Mira Costa Coll., San Diego Community Colls., 1981—; lectr. in field. Mem. golden Triangle Chamber, Rancho Bernardo Chamber, Health Access of San Diego, San Diego Regional Coun. Quality Care, San Diego Coun. on Aging, North County Providers Coun., South Bay Providers Coun., Long Term Care Pub. Interest Ctr. Mem. NAFE, Calif. Assn. Health Svcs. at Home (past bd. dirs., steering com.), Rancho Bernardo C. of C., Nat. U. Alumni Assn. Avocations: photography, travel, exercising. Office: At Your Home Svcs 6540 Lusk BlvdSte C-266 San Diego CA 92121 also: At Your Home Family Care 16466 Bernardo Center Dr Ste 136 Rancho Bernardo CA 92128

EEG-OLOFSSON, ORVAR, pediatric neurologist; b. Boras, Sweden, Sept. 3, 1932; s. Ansgar Olof Cato and Sonja Anna Margareta (Samuelsson) Eeg-O.; m. Anne-Marie Enander, Aug. 31, 1963 (div. Sept. 1985); children: Jens, Mans, Mia; m. Karin Eva Kristina Edebol, May 19, 1990. MD, U. Lund, 1959; PhD, U. Goteborg, 1970. Head child neurology dept. U. Linkoping, Sweden, 1974-85; prof. pediatrics U. Kuwait, 1985-88; assoc. head clin. neurophysiology Nat. Ctr. Epilepsy, Sandvika, Oslo, Norway, 1988-90; prof., head child neurology dept. U. Uppsala, Sweden, 1990—; cons. Mubarak and Amiri Hosps., Kuwait, 1985-88; chmn. Swedish br. Pediatric Neurology and Rehab., 1994-95. Mem. editl. bd. Pediatric Neurology, 1991—, Devel. Brain Dysfunction, 1995—. Capt. Swedish Army, 1973-83. Mem. Rotary Internat. (sec. 1994-95, program mgr. 1995-96, incoming pres. 1996—).

EFFRON, CHARLES R., neurologist; b. Paterson, N.J., July 23, 1958. BA in Biology magna cum laude, Brown U., 1980, MD, 1983. Diplomate Am. Bd. Psychiatry and Neurology. Intern Beth Israel Hosp., N.Y.C., 1983-84; neurology resident Mt. Sinai Hosp., N.Y.C., 1984-87, attending in neurology, 1987—. Mem. Am. Acad. Neurology, Am. Acad. Clin. Neurophysiology, Sigma Xi. Office: 5 E 94th St New York NY 10128

EFFRON, DAVID, emergency medicine physician; b. Paterson, N.J., Feb. 12, 1954; s. Leonard and Bernice E. BA, Kenyon Coll., 1976; MD, U. Cin., 1980. Attending physician dept. emergency medicine Metro Health Med. Ctr., Cleve., 1983—; asst. prof. Case Western Res. U., Cleve., 1983—; med. dir. Bklyn. Emergency Med. Svcs., 1993—; exec. mgmt. com. Cuyahoga Emergency Disaster Com., Cleve., 1992—. Fellow Am. Coll. Emergency Physicians; mem. Northeast Ohio Emergency Physicians. Office: Metro Health Med Ctr 2500 Metro Health Dr Cleveland OH 44109

EFRAN, JAY STEVEN, psychologist; b. N.Y.C., Oct. 10, 1936; s. Sidney and Sylvia (Taylor) E.; m. Elsa Ann Rubin, Jan. 29, 1967; 1 child, Daniel Sidney. B.A., CCNY, 1958, M.S., 1959; Ph.D., Ohio State U., 1963. Asst. prof. psychology U. Rochester, 1963-68, assoc. prof., 1968-71; assoc. prof. Temple U., 1971-74, prof., 1974—, dir. clin. tng., 1971-80. Author: (with others) Language, Structure and Change: Frameworks of Meaning in Psychotherapy, 1990; contbr. chpts. to books and articles to profl. jours. Named. Tchr. Yr. Temple U., 1973; grantee in field. Fellow Am. Psychol. Assn., Am. Group Psychotherapy Assn., Pa. Psychol. Assn.; mem. Am. Cybernetic Soc., Delaware Valley Group Psychotherapy Soc. (past pres.), Phila. Soc. Clin. Psychologists. Office: Temple U Weiss Hall Philadelphia PA 19122

EGAN, BRIAN JOSEPH, osteopath; b. Joliet, Ill., Apr. 17, 1963; s. Bernard Joseph and Joan Helen (Boucher) E.; m. Diane Louise Nauert; 1 child, Kevin Joseph. BS, Quincy (Ill.) Coll., 1985; DO, U. Osteo. Med. & Health Scis., Des Moines, 1991. Diplomate Nat. Bd. Osteo. Med. Examiners. Intern Midwestern U. Chgo. Coll. Osteo. Medicine, 1991-92, resident, 1992-96, chief resident dept. ob-gyn., 1995-96. Mem. Am. Osteo. Assn., Am. Coll. Osteo. Obstetricians and Gynecologists (moderator midyear conf. 1993), Ill. Osteo. Physicians and Surgeons, Grad. Med. Edn. Soc. Office: Chgo Osteo Hosp 5200 S Ellis Ave Chicago IL 60615

EGAN, KENNETH J., dermatologist; b. N.Y.C., Feb. 2, 1956; m. Marcia Beth Robins, May 23, 1982; children: Heather, Daniel, Brian. BA, Franklin and Marshall Coll., 1978; MD, NYU, 1982. Bd. cert. Am. Acad. Dermatology. Resident internal medicine North Shore Univ. Hosp./Meml. Sloan-Kettering Hosp., Manhasset, N.Y., 1982-85; resident dermatology Albert Einsten Coll. Medicine, N.Y.C., 1985-88; pvt. practice Ridgefield, Conn., 1988—. Fellow Am. Acad. Dermatology; mem. AMA, Am. Soc. for Laser Medicine, Fairfield County Med. Assn. Office: 38B Grove St Ridgefield CT 06877

EGAN, LINDA LEE, nurse; b. Daretown, N.J., Mar. 25, 1947; d. John Joseph and Mary Elizabeth (Woodruff) E. A.S. in Nursing, Cumberland County Coll., 1972; B.S. in Nursing, Stockton State Coll., 1978. Cottage attendant Vineland (N.J.) State Sch., 1965-69, cottage supr., 1969-72, staff nurse, 1972-74, head nurse intensive care, 1974-75; staff nurse intensive care Cooper Med. Center, Camden, N.J., 1975-77, in-service clinician, 1977-78; dir. nursing Vineland State Sch. Hosp., 1978-79, instr. nursing insvc., 1979-82; rehab. specialist Staff Builders, San Diego, 1982-83; pvt. rehab. specialist, 1983-86; staff nurse Hemet Valley Hosp., Calif., 1986; nurse intensive care staff Tri-City Med. Ctr., Oceanside, Calif., 1986-87; adminstrv. supr. Pomerado Hosp., Poway, 1987-88; critical care unit staff nurse The Meml. Hosp. Salem County, 1988-90; critical care staff nurse Mother Francis Hosp., Tyler, Tex., 1990—; nursing care cons. (part-time) Am. Inst. for Mental Studies, 1980. Respiratory/circulatory emergency instr./multimedia first aide instr. ARC, Vineland, 1975-81. Recipient Instl. award N.J. Assn. for Retarded Children, 1969. Mem. AACN, Profl. Traveling Nurses Assn., South Jersey In-svc. Exchange, Am. Nurses Assn., Tex. Nurses Assn., Am. Nurses Found., Century Club. Roman Catholic.

EGAN, MICHAEL EUGENE, consultant; b. Denver, Oct. 24, 1945; s. Frank B. and Mary V. (Harris) E.; m. Abby S. Shapiro, Apr. 20, 1973 (div.); children: Matthew, Corey Edward. BA, U. Pa., 1967; PhD, U. Tex., 1973. Instr. U. Tex., Austin, 1973-74; faculty assoc. Princeton (N.J.) U., 1974-76; asst. prof. Lawrence U., Appleton, Wis., 1976-79; dir. mktg. R. P. Kincheloe Co., Dallas, 1979-90; pres. Zadall Systems Inc., Vancouver, B.C., Can., 1990; ptnr. Egan and Assocs., Dallas, 1990-95; v.p. InVivo Metrics, Inc., 1995—. Author: Human Function, 1979; contbr. articles to profl. jours. Bd. mem. Dallas Assn. Parent Edn., 1982-84, Am. Jewish Com., Dallas, 1987—; leader Boy Scouts Am., Dallas, 1988—; bd. mem. sci. fair adv. com. Dallas County Sch., 1990—. NIH fellow, 1973; recipient Institutional Sci. Edn. Program award NSF, 1975. Mem. AAAS, Am. Assn. Physicist Medicine, Radiol. Soc. N.Am. Home: 6016 Spring Flower Tr Dallas TX 75248 Office: InVivo Metrics Inc PO Box 797132 Dallas TX 75379

EGAN, SHIRLEY ANNE, retired nursing educator; b. Haverill, Mass.; d. Rush B. and Beatrice (Bengle) Willard. Diploma, St. Joseph's Hosp. Sch. Nursing, Nashua, N.H., 1945; B.S. in Nursing Edn., Boston U., 1949, M.S., 1954. Instr. sci. Sturdy Meml. Hosp. Sch. Nursing, Attleboro, Mass., 1949-51; instr. sci. Peter Bent Brigham Hosp. Sch. Nursing, Boston, 1951-53, ednl. dir., 1953-55, assoc. dir. Sch. Nursing, 1955-59, med. surg. coord., 1971-73, assoc. dir. Sch. Nursing, 1973-79, dir., 1979-85; cons. North Country Hosp., 1985-86; infection control practitioner, 1986-87; contract instr. Natchitoches Area Tech. Inst., 1988-90, Sabine Valley Tech Inst., 1990-91; coord. quality assurance Evangeline Health Care Ctr., 1991-92, asst. dir. nursing, 1992-93; coord. quality assurance Evangeline Health Care Ctr., Natchitoches, La., 1994-96; nurse edn. adviser AID (formerly ICA), Karachi, Pakistan, 1959-67; prin. Coll. Nursing, Karachi, 1959-67; dir. Vis. Nurse Service, Nashua, N.H., 1967-70; cons. nursing edn. Pakistan Ministry of Health, Labour and Social Welfare, 1959-67; adviser to editor Pakistan Nursing and Health Rev., 1959-67; exec. bd. Nat. Health Edn. Com., Pakistan; WHO short-term cons. U. W.I., Jamaica, 1970-71; mem. Greater Nashua Health Planning Council. Contbr. articles to profl. publs. Bd. dirs. Matthew Thornton health Ctr., Nashua, Nashua Child Care Ctr.; vol. ombudsman N.H. Council on Aging; mem. Nashua Service League. Served as 1st lt., Army Nurse Corps., 1945-47. Mem. Trained Nurses Assn. Pakistan, Nat. League for Nursing, Assn. for Preservation Hist. Natchitoches, St. Joseph's Sch. Nursing Alumnae Assn., Boston U. Alumnae Assn., Brit. Soc. Health Edn., Cath. Daus. Am. (vice regent ct. Bishop Malloy), Statis. Study Grads. Karachi Coll. Nursing, Sigma Theta Tau. Home: 729 Royal St Natchitoches LA 71457-5716

EGBERT, PETER R., ophthalmologist, educator; b. Indpls., Dec. 6, 1941. BA magna cum laude, DePauw U., Greencastle, Ind., 1963; MD, Yale U., 1967. Diplomate Nat. Bd. Med. Examiners, Am. Bd. Ophthalmology. Intern Cleve. Met. Gen. Hosp., 1967-68; resident in ophthalmology Yale U., New Haven, 1968-69, 71-73; acting asst. prof. surgery (ophthalmology Stanford (Calif.) U., 1973-74, dir. Ophthalmic Pathology Lab., 1973—, asst. prof. surgery, 1974-81; acting head divsn. ophthalmology Stanford U. Med. Ctr., 1980-82, assoc. prof. surgery, 1981-83, prof. ophthalmology 1988—, chmn. dept. ophthalmology, 1992—; vis. prof. ophthalmology Govt. Hosp., San Pedro Sula, Honduras, 1974, Noor Eye Hosp., Kabul, Afghanistan, 1975, U. West Indies Med. Sch., Kingston, Jamaica, 1976, Princess Marina Hosp. - The Ctrl. Govt. Hosp., Gadorone, Botswana, 1978, Grenfell Regional Health Svcs., St. Anthony, Nfld., 1981, Govt. Hosp., Western Samoa, 1982, Project Orbis, Ismir, Turkey, 1985, Bamako, Mali, 1983, San Jose, Costa Rica, 1986, Port-au-Prince, Haiti, 1987, King Khaled Eye Hosp., Rihayd, Saudi Arabia, 1985, Korle-bu Teaching Hosp., U. Ghana, Accra, 1987, Leicester Royal Infirmary, Eng., 1987, Esperanca Hosp., Santarem, Brazil, 1987, Chinese Med. Sch., Hong Kong, Inst. Ophthalmology, Canton, Peking Med. Coll., Beijing, 1988, Nepal-Trilovan Teaching Hosp., 1990. Recipient Bordon prize DePauw U., 1960. Mem. Am. Acad. Ophthalmology, Am. Assn. Ophthalmic Pathologists, Am. Intra-Ocular Implant Soc., Assn. for Rsch. in Vision and Ophthalmology, Michael Hogan Eye Pathology Soc., No. Calif. Soc. to Prevent Blindness, Peninsula Eye Soc., Verhoeff Ophthalmic Pathology Soc., Alpha Omega Alpha, Phi Beta Kappa. Office: Stanford U Sch of Medicine 300 Pasteur Dr Palo Alto CA 94304-2203*

EGDAHL, RICHARD HARRISON, surgeon, medical educator, health science administrator; b. Eau Claire, Wis., Dec. 13, 1926; s. Harry I. and Rebecca (Ball) E.; children: Scott, David, Bruce, Julie; m. 2d, Cynthia Taft, Apr. 1983. M.D., Harvard U., 1950; Ph.D., U. Minn., 1957. Intern U. Minn. Hosp., 1950-51, resident, 1956-57; prof. surgery Med. Coll. Va., 1957-64; prof., chmn. surgery Boston U. Med. Ctr., 1964-73, dir., 1973-96; dir. Health Policy Inst., Boston U.; Alexander Graham Bell prof. health care entrepreneurship Boston U.; bd. dirrs. Essex Investment Mgmt. Co. Inc., Health Payment Rev. Inc., Pioneer Family of Mut. Funds. Editor: Comprehensive Manuals of Surgical Specialties; mem. editorial bd. Am. Jour. Surgery. Lt. USNR, 1952-55. Mem. ACS, Soc. Univ. Surgeons (pres. 1970-71), Am. Surg. Assn. (1st v.p. 1980), Boston Surg. Soc. (pres. 1977), Soc. Med. Adminstrs., Endocrine Soc. (CIBA award 1961), Inst. Medicine NAS, Internat. Assn. Endocrine Surgeons (pres. 1981-83), Comml. Club, Brookline Country Club, Algonquin Club, Badminton and Tennis Club, The Registry Resort, Phi Beta Kappa, Alpha Omega Alpha. Home: 333 Commonwealth Ave Apt 23 Boston MA 02115-1931 Office: Boston U Health Policy Inst 53 Bay State Rd Boston MA 02215-2197

EGERTON, CHARLES PICKFORD, anatomy and physiology educator; b. Toronto, Ont., Can., Mar. 17, 1939; (parents Am. citizens); s. Matthew Davis and Margaret Swain (Pickford) E.; m. Carol Anne Carlson, Dec. 16, 1976; children: Matthew, Andrew, Victoria. BA in Zoology, Duke U., 1962; BS in Medicine, U. Okla., Oklahoma City, 1978; MS in Sci. Edn., U. So. Miss., 1981, PhD in Sci. Edn., 1991, MPH in Health Edn., 1994. Cert. physician asst. Nat. Commn. on Cert. Physician Assts. Commd. 2d lt. USAF, 1962, advanced through grades to maj., 1980, ops. officer, 1962-76; primary care med. officer USAF, Keesler AFB, Miss., 1978-88; ret., 1988; instr. anatomy and physiology Miss. Gulf Coast C.C., Gautier, 1992—; mem. Miss. Health Adv. Coun., Jackson, 1990—. Author: Student Study Guide for Anatomy and Physiology; editor: Physician Assistant Handbook, 1995; contbr. articles to profl. jours. Lectr. Miss. Inst. Drug-Free Sch., Hattiesburg, 1992; lectr. single parent-displaced spouse, Guatier, 1994; dir. smoking cessation Keesler AFB Med. Ctr., 1986-88; lay reader St. Luke's Anglican Ch., Gulfport, Miss., 1986-94. Mem. Am. Assn. Anatomists, Am. Acad. Physician Assts., Human Anatomy and Physiology Soc., Miss. Acad. Scis., Miss. Sci. Tchrs. Assn., Phi Delta Kappa, Eta Sigma Gamma. Democrat. Home: 6008 E Moreton Pl Ocean Springs MS 39564 Office: Miss Gulf Coast CC Box 100 Gautier MS 39553

EGGERS, GEORGE WILLIAM NORDHOLTZ, JR., anesthesiologist, educator; b. Galveston, Tex., Feb. 22, 1929; s. George William Nordholtz and Edith (Sykes) E.; m. Mary Futrell, Dec. 30, 1955; children: Carol Ann, George William Nordholtz III. BA, Rice U., 1949; MD, U. Tex., 1953. Diplomate Am. Bd. Anesthesiology. Instr. dept. anesthesiology, U. Tex., Galveston, 1956-59, asst. prof., 1959-61; assoc. prof. dept. anesthesiology, U. Mo., Columbia, 1961-67, prof., 1967—, acting chmn., 1969, chmn., 1970-94; prof. emeritus U. Mo., Columbia, 1994—; vis. instr. USAF Hosp., Lackland AFB, San Antonio, 1956-61; vis. research prof. dept. anesthesiology Northwestern U. Med. Sch., Chgo., 1968-69; research assoc. Space Sci. Research Ctr., Columbia, 1965-66. Contbr. over 50 articles to profl. jours. Mem. Am. Soc. Anesthesiology (bd. dirs. 1979-86, v.p. 1986-88, 1st v.p. 1989, pres.-elect 1990, pres. 1991), Am. Coll. Anesthesiology (bd. govs. 1965-74, chmn. bd. govs. 1973), Soc. Acad. Anesthesiology Chmn. (pres. 1971), Assn. Am. Med. Colls. (adminstrv. bd. council acad. socs. 1976-79), Mo. Soc. Anesthesiologists (pres. 1970), Tex. Gulf Coast Anesthesiology Soc. (v.p. 1960), Boone County Med. Soc. (pres. 1988), Am. Bd. Anesthesiology (assoc. examiner 1968, joint council with Am. Soc. Anesthesiology on in-tng. exams.), Acad. Anesthesiology (pres. 1994), Accreditation Council Grad. Med. Edn. (mem. residency rev. com. for anesthesiology 1989-94), Alpha Omega Alpha, Mu Delta, Sigma Xi. Republican. Roman Catholic. Home: 1509 Woodrail Ave Columbia MO 65203-0931 Office: Univ Mo Dept Anesthesiology 1 Hospital Dr Columbia MO 65201-5276

EGGERS, HANS JOACHIM, virology educator; b. Baumholder, Birkenfeld, Germany, July 26, 1927; s. Gustav and Margot (Finscher) E.; m. Gisela M.F. Hohmann, Apr. 10, 1954; children: Carsten, Jens, Susanne. MD, D. in Med. Biochemistry, U. Heidelberg, Fed. Republic Germany, 1953. Postdoctoral fellow virology Karolinska Inst., Stockholm, 1954; postdoctoral fellow neurology U. Nervenklinik, Cologne, Fed. Republic Germany, 1955-57, Children's Hosp. Rsch. Found., Cin., 1957-59; rsch. assoc. virology Rockefeller Inst., N.Y.C., 1959-61, asst. prof. virology, 1961-64; sect. head virology virus rsch. Max-Planck-Inst., Tuebingen, Fed. Republic Germany, 1965-66; prof. virology U. Giessen (Fed. Republic Germany), 1966-72; prof. virology U. Cologne, 1972-93, prof. emeritus, 1993—; mem. working group AIDS-Commn. of the European Communities, 1984-88, Senatskommission Deutsche Forschungsgemeinschaft, Sicherheitsfragen bei Neukombination von Genen, 1981-87. Mem. editorial Bd. Antiviral Rsch., 1981—; co-editor: Conditio Humana, 1969-74; contbr. approximately 250 virology articles to profl. jours. Pres. European Assn. against Virus Diseases, 1987-89. Mem. Am. Assn. Immunologists, Soc. for Exptl. Biology and Medicine, Am. Soc. for Microbiology, Deutsche Gesellschaft fuer Hygiene und Mikrobiologie (bd. dirs. 1969-87), Gesellschaft fuer Virologie (bd. dirs. 1990—), Deutsche Akademie der Naturforscher Leopoldina (senate 1990—), Akademie der Wissenschaften Goettingen (Fed. Republic Germany, external mem.), Goldenes Verdienstzeichen des Landes Salzburg, Internationale Stiftung Mozarteum, Salzburg (bd. dirs.). Office: Univ Koeln Inst fuer Virologie, Fuerst Pueckler Str 56, D-50935 Cologne Germany

EGGERS, JOAN FRANCES, dietitian; b. Iowa City, Mar. 11, 1934; d. Raymond Francis and Johanne Barbara (Kelsen) Dalbey; m. William Charles Eggers, Sept. 1, 1956; children: Michael, Deborah, Susanne, Steven. BS, U. Iowa, 1957. Registered dietitian; lic. dietitian, Kans. Clin. dietitian Iowa Meth. Med. Ctr., Des Moines, 1961-63; adminstrv. and clin. dietitian Iowa Luth. Hosp., Des Moines, 1963-65, Malcolm Bliss Mental Health Ctr., St. Louis, 1966-68; adminstrv. dietitian St. Louis State Hosp., 1968-70, Shawnee Mission (Kans.) Med. Ctr., 1982-85; cons. dietitian C.L. Gerwick & Assocs., Overland Park, Kans., 1975-82; chief dietitian Western Mo. Mental Health Ctr., Kansas City, 1985—. Mem. P.E.O., Am. Dietetic Assn., Am. Soc. Hosp. Food Svc. Adminstrs., Kans. Dietetic Assn., Kansas City Dietetic Assn., Mems. with Mgmt. Reponsibilites in Health Care Delivery Systems (DPG #41). Republican. Roman Catholic. Home: 10205 W 97th Ter Overland Park KS 66212-5235 Office: Western Mo Mental Health Ctr 600 E 22nd St Kansas City MO 64108-2620

EGGERT, LEONA LOUISE, nursing educator, researcher; b. Edmonton, Alta., Can., Dec. 30; d. Richard and Louise Eggert. Diploma, Vancouver Gen Hosp Sch Nursing, 1958; BSN, U. Wash., 1969, MA, 1970, PhD, 1984. Cert. sch. nurse, health edn. cons. Cons. Redmond, Wash.; sch. nurse, health edn. coord. Bellevue (Wash.) Pub. Schs.; asst. prof. U. Wash., Seattle, assoc. prof., prof., Spence Endowed prof. NIDA, NIMH and NINR grantee; recipient Award for Excellence, Interlake H.S. Interpersonal Rels. Program, Top Paper award Internat. Communication Assn. Mem. APHA, ANA, Nat. Assn. Sch. Nurses, Nat. Dropout Prevention Network, Soc. for Rsch. on Adolescence, Am. Assn. Suicidology. Office: U Wash Dept Psychosocial Box 357263 Seattle WA 98195

EGGLAND, ELLEN THOMAS, community health nurse, consultant; b. Canton, Ohio, Nov. 2, 1947; d. John Marron and Mary Mernabelle (Miller) Thomas; m. Gregory Hugh Eggland, Sept. 9, 1972; children: Karen, Ryan. BSN, Georgetown U., 1969; MN, Emory U., 1972. Staff nurse Cleve. Clinic Hosp., 1969-71; nurse clinician Univ. Hosps., Cleve., 1972-73; dir. nursing Med. Personnel Pool, Cleve., 1975-83; v.p. Healthcare Pers., Inc., Naples, Fla., 1984—; nursing cons., Ohio, Fla., 1983—; v.p. MedPad, Atlanta, 1991-93; mem. adv. bd. Springhouse (Pa.) Skillbuilder Series, 1991-92; vis. lectr. symposium Fla. Gulf Coast U., 1996; vis. lectr. U. South Fla., 1996. Author: Nursing Documentation Resource Guide, 1993, Nursing Documentation: Charting, Reporting and Recording, 1994; contbg. author: Better Documentation, 1992, Managing the Nursing Shortage, 1989, Community and Home Health Care Plans, 1990; contbr. articles to profl. nursing jours.; inventor computerized clin. record. Chmn. St. William Respect Life/Sr. Citizens, Naples, 1985-86; mem. health com. Naples C. of C., 1985-86; sec. Pelican Bay Incorporation Study Com., Naples, 1990-91; bd. dirs. Prevent A Care, Naples, 1986-87; bd. dirs., sec. Pelican Bay Found., Naples, 1993-96; bd. vis. Georgetown U. Sch. Nursing, 1993-96. Fed. grantee for edn. U.S. Govt., 1971; recipient Involved Mem. of Yr. award Greater Cleve. Nurses Assn., 1978, 5th Ann. Author's award U. South Fla., 1995. Mem. ANA, Fla. Nurses Assn., Nat. League Nursing, Master's Group, Greater Cleve. Hosp. Assn. (info. tech. and nursing com. 1991-95), Sigma Theta Tau. Democrat. Roman Catholic. Office: Healthcare Personnel Inc Ste 407 2335 Tamiami Trl N Ste 407 Naples FL 34103

EGLOFF, FRANK RATTRAY LILLIE, psychiatrist; b. Boston, July 7, 1925; s. William Chauncey and Margaret Crane (Lillie) E.; m. Nancy Ojerholm, Sept. 6, 1947; children: Frank, William, Christina, Elizabeth, Jennifer, Heidi. MD, Harvard U., 1947. Diplomate Am. Bd. Psychiatry and Neurology. Intern Faulkner Hosp., Boston, 1947-48; resident in psychiat. medicine Barnes Hosp., St. Louis, 1948-50; chief resident in psychiat. medicine Mass. Gen. Hosp., Boston, 1950-51; practice medicine specializing in psychiatry Falmouth, Mass., 1954—, Farmington, Conn., 1954-70; mem. courtesy staff Falmouth (Ma.) Hosp. Chmn. bd. dirs. Auburn Theol. Sem., N.Y.C., 1980—. Fellow Am. Psychiat. Assn. (life).

EGNATINSKY, JACK, anesthesiologist, medical director; b. Bklyn., Apr. 16, 1941; s. Sidney and Sarah (Sperling) E.; m. Judith Ellen Buchert, June 14, 1964; children: Wayne Andrew, Susan Beth, Roberta Louise. BS, Queens Coll., Flushing, N.Y., 1961; MD, SUNY, Syracuse, 1965. Diplomate Am. Bd. Anesthesiology. Commd. USN, 1963, advanced through grades to lt. comdr., 1969, resigned, 1971; intern St. Joseph's Hosp., Syracuse, 1965-66; resident in anesthesiology U.S. Naval Hosp., Phila., 1966-68; chief of anesthesiology U.S. Naval Hosp., Annapolis, Md., 1968-71; chief of anesthesiology Crouse Irving Meml. Hosp., Syracuse, 1974-82, attending anesthesiologist, 1971—; attending anesthesiologist Community Gen. Hosp., Syracuse, 1990-95; chief of anesthesiology Harrison Ctr. Outpatient Surgery, Syracuse, 1987-96, med. dir., 1987—; clin. prof. SUNY, Syracuse, 1972—. Contbr. articles to profl. jour. Coord. Ethiopia program Anesthesia Overseas, Inc., Washington, 1987-88; bd. edn. Temple Soc. Concord, Syracuse, 1978-82, trustee, 1978-83, Jewish Family Svc., Syracuse, 1979-89. Fellow Am. Coll. Anesthesiologists; mem. AMA, Am. Soc. Anesthesiologists, N.Y. State Soc. Anesthesiologists (bd. dirs. 1991—, chmn. com. govt. and legal affairs 1988—, Testimonial award 1986), Med. Soc. State of N.Y. Onondaga County Med. Soc. (exec. coun. 1991—, v.p. 1993, pres.-elect 1994, pres. 1995-96), Internat. Anesthesia Rsch. Soc., Soc. Ambulatory Anesthesia, Federated Ambulatory Surgery Assn. (bd. dirs. 1996—). Office: Harrison Ctr Outpatient Surgery 550 Harrison St Ste 230 Syracuse NY 13202-3096

EGNEW, THOMAS ROMINE, family medicine educator, counselor; b. Billings, Mont., Dec. 4, 1947; s. Charles Leaman and Dorothy Elizabeth (Hawk) E.; m. Kathleen Louise Cucciardi, July 25, 1968 (div. Feb. 1978); children: Danielle Marie, Aaron Thomas; m. Joan Elizabeth Halley, Mar. 21, 1992. BA, Rocky Mountain Coll., 1970; MA, U. Chgo., 1972; EdD, Seattle U., 1994. Social work officer Madigan Army Med. Ctr., Tacoma, 1972-75, behavioral scientist, 1975-77; clin. dir. Tacoma Girls' Club Children's Indsl. Home, 1978-79; behavioral scientist Tacoma Family Medicine, 1979—; adj. faculty Pacific Luth. U., Tacoma, 1975-82; pvt. counseling practice Tacoma, 1978-89; clin. asst. prof. U. Wash. Dept. Family Medicine, 1980—. Capt. U.S. Army, 1972-77. Mem. NASW (cert.), Soc. Tchrs. of Family Medicine. Episcopalian. Office: Tacoma Family Medicine 521 Martin Luther King Jr Tacoma WA 98405-4272

EGO-AGUIRRE, ERNESTO, surgeon; b. Lima, Peru, Dec. 16, 1928; came to U.S., 1956; s. Ernesto and Benjamina (Palma) E. B in Medicine, San Marcos U., 1947, MD, 1955; postgrad. in biometrics, Cornell U., 1965-66. Diplomate Am. Bd. Surgery. Intern in surgery Barnes Hosp. Washington U., St. Louis, 1956-57, resident asst. in surgery, 1957-60; asst. and sr. resident in surgery Ellis Fischel Cancer Hosp., Columbia, Mo., 1960-62; spl. fellow plastic and reconstructive surgery Meml. Sloan Kettering Cancer Ctr., N.Y.C., 1963-64, sr. resident, fellow in surgery, 1965-69; fellow in rsch. Sloan Kettering Inst., N.Y.C., 1964-69; attending in surgery N.Y. Infirmary, 1970-78, Doctors Hosp. (now Beth Israel Med. Ctr.-North), N.Y.C., 1978—. Contbr. articles to profl. jours. Fellowship grant Nat. Cancer Inst., 1965-68, Am. Cancer Soc., 1968-69; recipient 9 Triannual Continuous Med. Edn. awards AMA, 1969—. Mem. AMA, Am. Soc. Gen. Surgeons, Am. Statis. Assn., N.Y. County Med. Soc., N.Y. Med. Soc., N.Y. Acad. Scis., Vet. Corps. of Artillery (N.Y.), Mil. Order of the Loyal Legion, Sovereign Orthodox Order Knights Hospitallier of St. John, Seventh Regiment Rifle Club (N.Y.), Squadron A Assn., Down Town Assn. Republican. Roman Catholic. Home: 209 E 56th St New York NY 10022-3705 Office: 135 William St Fl 10 New York NY 10038-3805

EGORIN, MERRILL JON, physician; b. Balt., May 25, 1948; s. Nathan Anthony and Toba Rose (Rombro) E.; m. Karen Deborah Kantor, Aug. 6, 1969; children: Melanie Anne, Noah Michael. BA, Johns Hopkins U., 1969, MD, 1973. Intern Johns Hopkins Hosp., Balt., 1973-74, resident, 1974-75, instr. medicine, 1975-81, asst. prof. medicine, 1981—; clin. assoc. Balt. Cancer Rsch. Ctr./NCI, 1975-78, expert, 1978-81; asst. prof., dept. pharmacology U. Md. Sch. Medicine, Balt., 1982-83, assoc. prof., dept. pharmacology, 1983-90, prof. medicine, 1990—; cons. Duke U. Bone Marrow Transplant, Durham, 1982; organizer workshop in field; advisor City of Hope Fellowship Tng., Duarte, Calif., 1992—. Editor-in-chief: Cancer Chemotherapy and Pharmacology jour., 1991—; assoc. editor: Cancer Rsch. jour., 1990—; bd. editl. advisors, Jour. Nat. Cancer Inst. With USPHS, 1975-78. Grantee in field. Fellow Am. Coll. Physicians; mem. Am. Assn. Cancer Rsch., Am. Soc. Clin. Oncology, Am. Soc. Pharmacology and Exptl. Therapeutics, Am. Soc. Clin. Pharmacology and Therapeutics, European Orgn. for Rsch. and Treatment of Cancer. Democrat. Jewish. Home: 211 Bond Ave Reisterstown MD 21136 Office: U Md Cancer Ctr 655 W Baltimore St Baltimore MD 21204

EGUIGUREN-LEON, LUIS A., pediatrician; b. Quito, Ecuador, Feb. 17, 1955; s. Luis A. and Marta F. (Leon) Eguiguren; m. Cecilia Aspiazu, Apr. 4, 1979; children: Maria Cecilia, Juan Pablo. MD, U. Ctrl. Del Ecuador, Quito, 1980. Pediatric resident U. Fla., Jacksonville, 1984-87; clin. fellow in pediatric critical care Harvard Med. Sch., Boston, 1987-89; staff pediatrician Hosp. Metropolitano, Quito, 1989—, dir. neonatal ICU, 1992—; dir. pediatric ICU Hosp. Baca Ortiz, Quito, 1989-90; attending pediatric ICU Rockford (Ill.) Meml. Hosp., 1993-95. Contbg. editor: Pediatric Advanced Life Support (Spanish edit.), 1993; contbg. author: Manual de Procedimienzos y Prtocolos en Cuidado Intensivo Pediatrico, 1993; contbr. articles to profl. jours. Dir. Fundacion Natura, Quito, 1992-94; founding mem. Parents Against Lead, Quito, 1992-94. Home: Geovani Farina #430, Quito Ecuador Office: Hosp Metropolitano de Quito, Andrade Marin #167 y Almagr, Quito Ecuador

EHLE, ALBERT LAWRENCE, neurology educator; b. Seattle, July 16, 1940; s. Albert R. and Josephine (Matzger) E.; m. Virginia Forman, June 5, 1967; children: Gregory, Keri. BS, Wash. State U., 1962; MS in Physiology, MD, U. Wash., 1967. Diplomate Am. Bd. Psychiatry and Neurology, Am. Bd. Clin. Neurophysiology. Resident in neurology U. Calif., San Francisco, 1971-73; asst. prof. U. Ariz. Med. Sch., Tucson, 1973-76; assoc. prof. U. Tex. Health Sci. Ctr., Dallas, 1976-82, U. N.C. Sch. Medicine, Chapel Hill, 1982-91; prof. neurology Northwestern U. Med. Sch., Chgo., 1991—, vice chmn. dept., 1995—; mem. profl. adv. bd. Epilepsy Found. Greater Chgo., 1991—, bd. dirs., 1995—; mem. profl. adv. bd. Epilepsy Svcs. Northeastern Ill., 1992. Contbr. articles to med. jours., chpts. to books. Maj. M.C., U.S. Army, 1968-71. Fellow Am. Acad. Neurology, Am. EEG Soc., Am. Sleep Disorders Assn.; mem. AMA, Am. Epilepsy Soc., Am. Acad. Physician Execs., Alpha Omega Alpha. Office: Northwestern U Med Sch Dept Neurology 645 N Michigan Ave Rm 1058 Chicago IL 60611

EHLERS, EILEEN SPRATT, family therapist; b. Maynard, Mass., Feb. 28, 1948; d. Cyril J. and Irma A. (Wirkkanen) Spratt; m. Robert K. Ehlers, June 13, 1970; children: Robert (dec.), Edward, Erin, Katherine. BA, Boston Coll., 1970; MEd, Notre Dame Coll., Manchester, N.H., 1992. Social worker Cath. Med. Ctr., Manchester, 1991; grief counselor Hospice, Concord, N.H., 1992; program dir. Am. Cancer Soc., Bedford, N.H., 1992; pvt. practice family therapy Familystrength, Concord, 1993-96; coord. Worldwide Marriage Encounter, 1983-96; coord., supr. Mental Health Ctr. of Greater Manchester, N.H., 1996—; coord. Toward Marriage, Concord; regional dir., clin. supr. Family Strength, 1993-96; mem. Dist. Coun. for N.H. Health Care Reform; supr. Mental Health Ctr. Greater Manchester, 1996—. Mem. Mental Health Counseling Assn., Assn. for Counselor Edn. and Supervision, Internat. Assn. of Marriage and Family Counseling, Nat. Assn. for Family Based Svcs/. Democrat. Roman Catholic. Home: 14 Ardon Dr Hooksett NH 03106-1536 Office: Child and Adolescent Svcs 493 Beech St Manchester NH 03104-4209

EHLERS, WILLIAM HENRY, ophthalmologist, educator; b. Philip, S.D., Sept. 29, 1950; s. Marvin William and Bernadette Naomi (Hanson) E. BFA, U. Nebr., 1973; MD, U. Nebr., Omaha, 1985. Diplomate Am. Bd. Ophthalmology, Am. Bd. Med. Examiners. Resident in ophthalmology Eastern Va. Grad. Sch. Medicine, Norfolk, 1985-89; fellow in cornea and external disease U. Conn., Farmington, 1989-90; assoc. physician Eye Physician Assocs. of Hartford, West Hartford, Conn., 1990—; asst. clin. prof. medicine U. Conn. Med. Sch., Farmington, 1990—; chmn. Eye Injury Registry of Conn., Hartford, 1991—, bd. dirs. Comprehensive Eye Care Network. Contbr. articles to profl. jours. Vol. vision screener Conn. Soc. to Prevent Blindness, Hartford; bd. dirs. Comprehensive Eye Care Network. Fison's Corp. grantee for rsch. in contact lens sci. and immunology, 1990. Mem. AMA, Am. Acad. Ophthalmology, Assn. for Rsch. in Vision and Ophthalmology, Contact Lens Assn. Ophthalmologists (co-chmn. sci. post com. 1993-94, co-chmn. region contact lens courses 1995—, rev. staff jour. 1993—), Conn. Soc. Eye Physicians, Castroviejo Corneal Soc., Hartford County Med. Soc., Phi Chi. Home: 11 Winthrop Rd West Hartford CT 06110-1656 Office: Eye Physician Assocs Hartford 29 N Main St West Hartford CT 06107-1933

EHMANN, FRANK A., health care products executive; b. Chgo., Dec. 23, 1933; s. Henry E. and Victoria (Hengler) E.; m. Mary C. Corcoran; children: Victoria, Jean, Nancy. BA, Northwestern U., 1955, MBA, 1971. With Am. Hosp. Supply Corp., Evanston, Ill., 1957-85, pres., 1971-73, corp. v.p., pres. dental and pharm. groups, 1973-74, corp. v.p., pres. hosp. group, 1974-78; exec. v.p., pres. hosp. and pharm. bus. Am. Hospital Supply Corp., Evanston, Ill., 1978-80; v.p. hosp. bus. Am. Hosp. Supply Corp., Evanston, Ill., 1980-85, also bd. dirs., 1983—; pres., chief operating officer Am. Hosp. Supply Corp., 1985; exec. v.p., co-chief operating officer Baxter-Travenol Labs., Inc., Deerfield, Ill., 1985-86, also corp. dir., 1985-86; pres., chief oper. officer United Stationers, Inc., Des Plaines, Ill., 1987-90, Robertson Stephens Co., RCS Health Care Ptnrs., 1990—; bd. dirs. Genderm, Inc., Kinetic Systems, Inc., San Antonio, SPX Corp., Muskegon, Mich., Am. Health Corp. Inc., Nashville. With USN, 1955-57. Clubs: Chgo., Skokie Country, John's Island Country. Home: 864 Bryant Ave Winnetka IL 60093-1952

EHRENBERG, DARLENE BREGMAN, psychoanalyst; b. N.Y.C., Aug. 15, 1942; d. Samuel and Pauline (Gellman) Bregman; m. Bernard Ehrenberg, Nov. 26, 1970; children: Jonathan, Erica. BA magna cum laude, CCNY, 1963; MS, Yale U., 1965; PhD, NYU, 1970; cert. William Alanson White Inst. Psychiatry, Psychoanalysis and Psychology, 1973 . Intern Montefere Hosp., 1966-67; pvt. practice psychoanalysis and psychotherapy, N.Y.C., 1969—; tng. and supervising analyst faculty William Alanson White Inst. Psychiatry, Psychoanalysis and Psychology, N.Y.C., 1977—; tchg. faculty Chgo. Ctr. for Psychoanalysis, 1993—, Southeast Fla. Inst. Psychoanalysis and Psychotherapy, 1994—, N.W. Ctr. Psychoanalysis, Seattle, Portland, 1995—; supr. Inst. for Contemporary Psychotherapy, 1974-83; clin. instr. psychiatry Albert Einstein Coll. Medicine, 1968-69; conf. presenter. Author: The Intimate Edge: Extending the Reach of Psychoanalytic Interaction, 1992; editor: Contemporary Psychoanalysis, 1993-94, asst. editor, 1979-93; editorial bd., 1975-79, 94—; contbr. articles to profl. jours. Carnegie Teaching fellow CCNY, 1964, Harrison fellow Yale U., 1963, NIMH fellow NYU, 1964-66. Mem. APA, William Alanson White Psychoanalytic Soc., Phi Beta Kappa. Home and Office: 11 E 68th St New York NY 10021-4955

EHRENKRANTZ, DAVID, medical researcher; b. New Haven, Aug. 26, 1952; s. Harold Louis and Katherine (Russo) E. BA magna cum laude, U. Hartford, 1979; MSW, Adelphi U., 1982; MPH, N.Y. Med. Coll., 1987; ScD, U. Pitts., 1991. Cert. social worker, N.Y. Rsch. asst. U. Conn. Sch. Medicine, 1985; med. rsch. affiliate Genentech Corp., San Francisco; fellow in psychiatry Mt. Sinai Med. Ctr., N.Y.C., 1996—. Contbr. articles to sci. jours. Mem. Alpha Chi. Office: NY Med Coll Div Pediatric Endocrinology Munger Pavillion 1st Fl Valhalla NY 10595

EHRENPREIS, SEYMOUR, pharmacology educator; b. N.Y.C., June 20, 1927; s. William and Ethel (Balk) E.; m. Bella R. Goodman, June 30, 1953; children: Mark, Eli, Ira. B.S., CCNY, 1949; Ph.D., NYU, 1954. Mem. faculty dept. pharmacology Chgo. Med. Sch., prof., 1976—, chmn. pharmacology, 1976-85; prof. emeritus, 1985—; rsch. adj. prof. medicine Chgo. Med. Sch., 1992—; grants reviewer NSF, 1977-83, March of Dimes, 1983; vis. prof. Showa Med. Sch., Tokyo, 1985. Editor: Neurosciences Research, vols. 1-5, 1967-75, Revs. of Neurosci., vols. 1-3, 1974-77, Methods in Narcotics Research, 1974, Degradation of Endogenous Opoids, 1983; mem. editorial bd. Jour. Medicinal Chemistry, 1969-72, Jour. Clin. Pharmacology, 1991—. Served with USN, 1945-46. Recipient Meritorious Service award Coll. Pharm. Sci., Columbia U., 1976; recipient Parker award Chgo. Med. Sch., 1981, Vis. Prof. award Japan Soc. Promotion Sci., 1974, cert. of merit for research Showa Med. Sch., 1985. Fellow AAAS, Am. Coll. Clin. Pharmacology (editl. bd. Jour. Clin. Pharmacology 1991—), N.Y. Acad. Sci. (chmn. cholinergic mechanisms conf. 1966), Am. Inst. Chemists; mem. Am. Soc. Pharmacology and Exptl. Therapeutics, Sigma Xi. Office: Univ Health Sci Chgo Med Sch 3333 Green Bay Rd North Chicago IL 60064-3037

EHRET, JOSEPHINE MARY, microbiologist, researcher; b. Roswell, N.Mex., Feb. 26, 1934; d. Edward and Glenna (Memmer) E. BS, U. N.Mex., 1955. Med. technologist U. Colo. Health Scis. Ctr., Denver, 1956-75, rsch. microbiologist, 1956—; rsch. microbiologist Denver Dept. Health and Hosps., 1980—; instr. sch. medicine U. Colo., 1985—. Contbr. articles to profl. publs. Mem. Am. Soc. for Microbiology, Am. Soc. Med. Technologists (cert.), Am. Venereal Disease Assn., CACMLE. Democrat. Home: 1344 S Eudora St Denver CO 80222 Office: Denver Pub Health Dept 605 Bannock St Denver CO 80204

EHRICH, MARION, toxicologist, educator; b. Mobridge, S.D., June 28, 1945; d. J. Herman and Emma (Stangl) Fiedler; m. Roger W. Ehrich, Dec. 25, 1969; 1 child, Daniel. BS, S.D. State U., 1968; MS, U. Chgo., 1970; PhD, U. Conn., 1975. Diplomate Am. Bd. Toxicology; registered pharmacist. Rsch. assoc. Anaerobe Lab. Va. Poly. Inst. and State U., Blacksburg, 1976-80; asst. prof. Va.-Md. Regional Coll. Vet. Medicine, Blacksburg, 1980-83, assoc. prof., 1983-90, prof., 1990—; treas. Am. Bd. Toxicology, Washington, 1986-89. Contbr. articles to profl. jours. Fellow Am. Assn. Vet. Pharmacology and Therapeutics; mem. AVMA (assoc.), Soc. Toxicology (chmn. edn. com. 1989-91, sec. 1992-94). Home: Locust Ave Blacksburg VA 24060 Office: Va-Md Regional Coll Vet Med Blacksburg VA 24061

EHRIG, ULRICH, physician; b. Magdeburg, Germany, Apr. 30, 1938; came to U.S., 1965; s. Kurt A. and Rose (Hennig) E.; m. Karen S. Pollak, 1967 (dec.); children: Kirsten A., Kurt U.; m. Elke L. Haeusser, 1996. MD, Bonn U., 1963. Diplomate Am. Bd. Internal Medicine. Intern Marien Hosp. and St. Bonifatius Hosp., Marl and Lingen, Germany, 1963-64; intern then resident Monmouth Med. Ctr., Long Branch, N.J., 1965-66; jr. asst. resident New Eng. Deaconess Hosp., Boston, 1966-67, clin. fellow in medicine, 1967-68; sr. asst. resident in medicine Toronto (Ont.) Gen. Hosp., Can., 1958-70, Norman Urquhart fellow, 1970-71, assoc. physician, 1971-72; physician, cons. internal medicine Hale Hosp., Haverhill, Mass., 1972—; assoc. prof. medicine U. Toronto, 1971-72. Contbr. articles to profl. jours. Del. 1995 White House Conf. on Aging. Olin S. Pettingill scholar, 1973. Fellow ACP, Royal Coll. Physicians and Surgeons; mem. Am. Soc. Nephrology, Internat. Soc. Nephrology, Mass. Med. Soc., Essex County Dist. Med. Soc., Soc. Nuclear Medicine. Office: Pentucket Med Assocs Inc One Parkway Haverhill MA 01830

EHRLICH, FREDERICK, surgery consultant, orthopedist, rehabilitation specialist; b. Czernowitz, Bukowina, USSR, Mar. 23, 1932; came to Australia, 1947; s. Alexander and Klara (Schneider) E.; m. Shirley Rose Eastbourne, Sept. 26, 1959; children: Paul, Rachel, Simon, Adam, Miriam, Mark. M.B., B.S. (hons.), Med. Faculty, U. Sydney, 1955; B.A., Macquarie U., Sydney, 1970, Ph.D., 1979; Dip.Phys. and Rehab. Medicine, Australian Postgrad. Fedn. in Medicine, Canberra, 1974. Intern, Royal Newcastle Hosp., N.S.W., 1955, rotating resident, 1955-57; resident surg. officer Charing Cross and Fulham Hosp., Hammersmith, London, 1958-59; surg. registrar Royal Newcastle Hosp., 1959-63; dir. surg. svc. State Psychiat. Svc., Sydney, 1962-75; prin. advisor State Geriatric and Rehab. Svcs., N.S.W., 1975-77; pvt. practice cons. surgeon, Sydney, Australia, 1979—; hon. cons. Sydney Hosp., 1977—; cons. geriatrics and rehab. Hornsby Hosp., Sydney, 1977—, St. George Hosp., Sydney, 1990—, orthopaedic surgery Spastic Ctr. New South Wales; vis. gen. and orthpaedic surgeon Marrickville Dist. Hosp., Sydney, 1977—; prof. rehabilitation, aged and extended care U. New South Wales, also chmn. med. bd., Chatswood Community Hosp., Sydney, 1978—, Concord Hosp, 1987—. Cons. Subnormal Children's Welfare Assn., Multiple Sclerosis Soc., 1968-75. Author: Chronic Illness in New South Wales, 1977 and more than 40 monographs, papers; editor: The Demography of Disability, 1969; New Thinking on Housing for the Aging, 1973; Aging in a Metropolis, 1974; Rehabilitation and Geriatric Services; Report of a Task Force, 1978. Fellow Royal Coll. Surgeons Eng., Royal Coll. Surgeons Edinburgh, Australian Coll. Rehab. Medicine (found. mem.), Royal Coll. Psychiatrists, Australasian Faculty of Rehab. Medicine, Total Care Found. (hon. life), Adv. Council on Visually Handicapped (hon. life), Australia Assn. Gerontology (pres. New South Wales div.), New South Wales Council on Aging (chmn.). Jewish. Home: Box A2011, Sydney NSW 2000, Australia

EHRLICH, GEORGE EDWARD, rheumatologist, international pharmaceutical consultant; b. Vienna, Austria, July 18, 1928; came to U.S., 1938, naturalized, 1944; s. Edward and Irene (Elling) E.; m. Gail S. Abrams, Mar. 30, 1968; children: Charles Edward, Steven L. Abrams, Rebecca Sayles. A.B. cum laude, Harvard U., 1948; M.B., M.D., Chgo. Med. Sch., 1952. Intern Michael Reese Hosp., Chgo., 1952; resident Francis Delafield Hosp., N.Y.C., 1955, Beth Israel Hosp., Boston, 1956, New Eng. Center Hosp., Boston, 1957; fellow rheumatology NIH, Bethesda, Md., 1958, Hosp. for Spl. Surgery, N.Y.C., 1959-61; asst. attending physician Hosp. for Spl. Surgery, 1960-64; spl. fellow Sloan Kettering Inst., 1960-61; instr. medicine Cornell U., 1960-64; dir. Arthritis Center, chief rheumatology Albert Einstein Med. Center and Moss Rehab. Hosp., Phila., 1964-80; asst. prof. medicine Temple U., 1964-67, asso. prof. medicine, 1967-72, prof. medicine, 1972-80, asso. prof. rehab. medicine, 1964-74, prof., 1974-80; vis. lectr. U. Pa., 1964-80; prof. medicine, dir. div. rheumatology Hahnemann U., Phila., 1980-83; v.p. Anti-Inflammatory/Endocrine CIBA-Geigy Pharmaceuticals, Summit, N.J., 1983-86; head med. affairs CIBA-Geigy Ltd., Switzerland, 1987-88; pres. George E. Ehrlich Assocs., pharmaceutical cons.; adj. prof. clin. medicine NYU Med. Ctr., 1984—; lectr. in medicine U. Pa., 1989-91, adj. prof. medicine, 1992—; expert advisor, cons. Diabetes and Other Noncommunicable Diseases unit WHO, 1990—, chmn. Internat. Low Back Pain Initiative; rep. of pres. Internat. League Assns. of Rheumatology for Soft Tissue Rheumatisms; mem. arthritis adv. com. FDA, 1993-96, chmn., 1993-95; chmn. sci. adv. bd. Hochrheininstitut (Rheumatic Disease and Rehab. Rsch. Inst. of Upper Rhine in Germany, France and Switzerland for Treatment, Tchg., and Rsch.), 1993—; bd. dirs. Greenwich Inst. Am. Edn., 1994—; bd. dirs. sci. adv. bds., several U.S. and internat. socs. Author: Differential Diagnosis of Rhematoid Arthritis, 1972, Oculocutaneous Manifestations of Rheumatic Diseases, 1973, Total Management of the Arthritic Patient, 1973, Rehabilitation Management of Rheumatic Conditions, 1980, 2d edit., 1986, (with J. Fries) Prognosis, 1981, (with H.E. Paulus) Controversies in the Clinical Evaluation of Analgesic-Anti-Inflammatory-Antirheumatic Drugs, 1981; (with P. Utsinger, N. Zvaifler) Rheumatoid Arthritis, 1985, (with W. Simon) Medicolegal Consequences of Trauma, 1992; editor: Jour. Albert Einstein Med. Center, 1966-71; Arthritis and Rheumatic Diseases Abstracts, 1968-71; editorial bd.: Inflammation, 1974-88, Psychosomatics, 1977-83, Secual Medicine Today, 1977-84, Jour. Rheumatology, 1982—, Immunopharmacology, 1985-95, Med. Problems Performing Artists, 1985-92, Brazilian Jour. Rheumatology, 1992-95; contbr. articles to profl. jours. Pres. Ea. Pa. chpt. Arthritis Found., 1970-72; mem. Phila. Mayor's Sci. and Tech. Adv. Coun., 1972-81; chmn. ad hoc adv. com. Bur. Drugs, FDA, 1971; mem. subcom. on redefinition of disability Social Security Adminstrn., 1982-86. Served to comdr. M.C. USNR, 1953-55; Res. to 1975, ret. Recipient citations City Phila., 1969, 74, Distinguished Alumnus award Chgo. Med. Sch., 1969; decorated Cavaliere Order of Star of Italian Solidarity. Fellow ACP, Phila. Coll. Physicians, Am. Coll. Rheumatology (elected master, 1994, com. for publ. Arthritis and Rheumatism, 1977-79, mem. editl. bd. 1980-83), Rheumatism Socs. Ecuador, India (hon.); mem. AMA (editl. bd. Jour. 1972-82), Am. Soc. Clin. Pharmacology and Therapeutics, Assn. Mil. Surgeons (Philip Hench award 1971), Brit. Assn. Rheumatology and Rehab. (overseas mem., editl. bd. 1979-82), Alpha Omega Alpha. Club: Harvard (Boston, N.Y.C.). Home: 38 Holly Dr Loveladies NJ 08008-6119 Office: 1 Independence Plz 1 Independence Place #1101 Philadelphia PA 19106-3731

EHRLICH, GERALDINE ELIZABETH, food service management consultant; b. Phila., Nov. 28, 1939; d. Joseph Vincent and Agnes Barbara (Campbell) McKenna; m. S. Paul Ehrlich, Jr., June 20, 1959; children: Susan Patricia, Paula Jeanne, Jill Marie. BS, Drexel Inst. Tech. Nutrition cons., hypertension rsch. team U. Calif. Micronesia, 1970; regional sales dir. Marriott Corp., Bethesda, Md., 1976-78; dir. sales and profl. svcs. Coll. and Health Care div. Macke Co., Cheverly, Md., 1978, gen. mgr., 1978-79; v.p. ops., div., 1979-80, pres. Health Care div., 1980-81; regional v.p. Custom Mgmt. Corp., Alexandria, Va., 1981-83, v.p. mktg., 1983-87; v.p. mktg. and healthcare sales Morrison's Custom Mgmt., Mobile, Ala., 1987-88; v.p. sales ARA Svcs., Phila., 1988-93; v.p. bus. devel., ARAMARK, Phila., 1993-96; realtor Long & Foster, 1996—; cons. mktg. The Green House, Tokyo, 1987-88; chmn. bd. Mktg. Matrix, Falls Church, Va., 1984-88. Mem. Health Systems Agy. No. Va., 1976-77; chmn. Health Care Adv. Bd. Fairfax County Va., 1973-77; vice chmn. Fairfax County Cmty. Action Com., 1973-77; treas. Fairfax County Dem. Com., 1969-73; trustee Fairfax Hosp., 1973-77; bd. dirs. Tennis Patrons, Washington, 1984-88, Phila. Singers, 1993—, Physicians for Peace, 1994—. Mem. AAUW, Internat. Women's Assn., Am. Mgmt. Assn., Nat. Assn. Female Execs., Soc. Mktg. Profls. Home and Office: 6512 Lakeview Dr Falls Church VA 22041-1102

EHRLICH, IRA BERT, cardiologist; b. Chgo., Oct. 30, 1938; s. Joseph Charles and Corinne (Freed) E.; m. Sylvia Oseran, July 10, 1960 (div. 1976); children: David, Diana; m. Carolyn Jeanne House, Jan. 8, 1977. BA, Stanford U., 1960; MD, Harvard U., 1964. Diplomate Am. Bd. Internal Medicine, Am. Bd. Cardiology. Intern, resident in internal medicine UCLA Med. Ctr., 1964-67; fellow cardiology U. Calif., San Francisco, 1967-69; cardiologist Phoenix Cardiologists, 1969—; pres. med. staff St. Joseph's Hosp., Phoenix, 1988-92; trustee Mercy Healthcare of Ariz., Phoenix, 1994—. Trustee Mus. No. Ariz., Flagstaff, 1990-93, Herberger Theatre, Phoenix, 1993-96. Fellow Am. Coll. Cardiology, Am. Coll. Physicians, Am. Heart Assn. Coun. Clin. Cardiology (pres. Ariz. affiliate 1976); mem. Maricopa County Med. Soc., Phoenix Country Club, Forest Highlands Country Club. Republican. Office: Phoenix Cardiologists 500 W Thomas Rd Ste 900 Phoenix AZ 85013

EHRLICH, RICHARD MICHAEL, urologist, educator; b. N.Y.C., Mar. 12, 1938; s. Sydney and Hannah (Gottesman) E.; children: Cristina, Richard. BA, Cornell U., 1959, MD, 1963. Diplomate Am. Bd. Urology, Nat. Bd. Med. Examiners; lic. Calif., N.Y., Fla. Intern, resident N.Y. Hosp., Cornell Med. Ctr., N.Y.C., 1963-65; resident Columbia Presbyn. Med. Ctr., N.Y.C., 1965-69; from asst. prof. to prof. surgery/urology UCLA Med. Ctr., 1971—; Attending physician Wadsworth VA Hosp., 1971—, Sepulveda VA Hosp., 1971—, Harbor Gen. Hosp., 1971—, Cedars-Sinai Med. Ctr., 1981—, Santa Monica Hosp. Ctr., 1993—, Century City Hosp., 1995—; cons. St. John's Hosp., 1972—, Olive View Hosp., 1974—; lectr. in field. Contbr. chpts. in books, articles and abstracts to profl. jours. Mem. AMA, AAAS, ACS, Am. Urol. Assn. (we. sect.), Am. Acad. Pediatrics (pres.-elect 1992-93, pres. 1993-94, exec. com. 1995—), Soc. Pediatric Urology (exec. com. 1979-84, sec.-treas. 1986-88, pres.-elect 1989-90, pres. 1991-92), Internat. Soc. Urology, Am. Soc. Transplant Surgeons, Confedn. Am. Urologists, Am. Assn. Genitourinary Surgeons (historian 1987—), Urol. Soc. for Transplantation and Vascular Surgery, Soc. Genitourinary Reconstructive Surgeons (exec. com. 1989—), Soc. Minimally Invasive Surgery, Southwestern Pediatric Soc., Calif. Assn. Pediatric Surg. Subspecialties, Calif. Med. Assn., Calif. Soc. Transplant Surgeons, Soc. Univ. Urologists, Kidney Found. (So. Calif. Sci. Adv. coun.), So. Calif. Transplant Soc., L.A. County Med. Assn., L.A. Urol. Soc., L.A. Pediatric Soc. Office: UCLA Med Ctr 100 Medical Plz Ste 690 Los Angeles CA 90024

EHRLICH, S(AUL) PAUL, JR., physician, consultant, former government official; b. Mpls., May 4, 1932; s. Sol P. and Dorothy E. (Fiterman) E.; m. Geraldine McKenna, June 20, 1959; children: Susan P., Paula J., Jill M. B.A., U. Minn., 1953, B.S., 1955, M.D., 1957; M.P.H., U. Calif., 1961. Diplomate: Am. Bd. Preventive Medicine. Intern USPHS Hosp., S.I., N.Y.,

1958; resident epidemiology U. Calif., 1961-63; mem. grants and tng. br. Nat. Heart Inst., Bethesda, Md., 1959-60; chief field and tng. sta. div. chronic diseases Heart Disease Control Program, San Francisco, 1961-65; asst. chief program devel. Heart Disease Control Program, Arlington, Va., 1966-67; dep. chief Heart Disease Control Program of Nat. Center Chronic Disease Control, Arlington, 1967; asso. dir. bilateral programs Office Internat. Health of USPHS, Washington, 1967; dep. dir. Office of Internat. Health, Office of Sec., HEW, Washington, 1968-69; acting dir. Office of Internat. Health, Office of Sec., HEW, 1969-70, dir., 1970-77; also acting surgeon gen. USPHS, 1973-77, dep. surgeon gen., 1976-77; v.p. Am. Insts. Research, Washington, 1978-79; dep. dir. Pan Am. Health Orgn., Washington, 1979-83; sr. adviser Am. Assn. World Health, 1984-86; health cons., 1984—; adj. prof. internat. health U. Tex.; U.S. rep. exec. bd. WHO, 1969-74, 73-76, chmn., 1972. Contbr. articles to profl. jours. Bd. regents Uniformed Services U. Health Scis. Served to lt. USCG, 1958-59. Fellow Am. Coll. Preventive Medicine, Am. Pub. Health Assn.; mem. Assn. Mil. Surgeons (pres. 1977), Assn. Tchrs. Preventive Medicine, Nat. Coun. Internat. Health. Home: 6512 Lakeview Dr Falls Church VA 22041-1102

EHRLICH, WILLIAM WALLACE, physician; b. Detroit, May 21, 1952; s. William Gurney and Patricia Ann (Jones) E. ; m. Carrie Lynn Sundeck, May 30, 1992; children from previous marriage: Casey, Claire; children: Nicholas, James. BS in zoology, Univ. Mich., 1973, MD, 1979. Diplomate Am. Bd. Medicine, Diplomate Am. Bd. Opthalmology. Fellow orbital surgery Albany Medical Ctr., Albany, N.Y., 1984; preceptor in orbital surgery Moorfields Eye Hosp., London, 1984-85; clinical instr. in surgery Mich. State Univ., East Lansing, asst. clinical prof. in surgery; ptnr. Lansing Ophthalmology, East Lansing, 1987—; pres. Lansing Opthalmology, East Lansing, 1995-96; ptnr. Mich. Surgical Ctr., East Lansing, 1995—. Contbr. articles to profl. jours. Recipient Resident Rsch. award Henry Ford Hosp. Dept Ophthalmology, 1983, Williams Coll. Book award William Coll., 1970. Mem. AMA, Ingham County Medical Soc., Mich. State Medical Soc., Mich. Ophthalmologic Soc., Univ. Mich. Alumni Club (life). Office: Lansing Ophthalmology 2001 Coolidge East Lansing MI 48823

EHRMAN, LEE, geneticist; b. N.Y.C., May 25, 1935; m. Richard Ehrman, 1955; children: Esther, Judith. BS, Queens Coll., 1956; MS, Columbia U., 1957, PhD in Genetics, 1959; DSc (hon.), CUNY, 1989. Mem. faculty Barnard Coll., 1956-58; postdoctoral fellow in genetics Columbia U., N.Y.C., 1959-61; assoc. seminar on population biology Columbia U., 1981—; mem. faculty SUNY-Purchase, 1970—, prof. div. natural scis., 1972—; Disting. prof. biology SUNY, Purchase, 1995—; mem. spl. study sect. NIH, NIMH, 1979-80; vis. disting. prof. U. Miami, Coral Gables, Fla., 1981; vis. lectr. U. Puerto Rico, Rio Piedras, 1987; coordinator, panelist workshops, programs in field. Author: Behavior Genetics and Evolution, 2d edit., 1981, 2 other books; assoc. editor Evolution; assoc. editor for genetics and cytology Am. Midland Naturalist; co-editor: Behavior Genetics; assoc. editor, exec. com. Soc. Am. Naturalists, 1977-85, pres.-elect 1990; contbr. nearly 500 articles to profl. jours. Recipient Lit. Soc. Found. medal in German, 1956, Chancellor's award for excellence in teaching SUNY, 1977; Shirley Farr postdoctoral fellow, 1961-62; USPHS postdoctoral fellow, 1959-61; faculty exch. scholar, 1974—; NSF grantee, 1979-84; Sr. Scientist awardee Whitehall Found., 1987, 93; NIH gen. med. scis. grantee, 1987—; SUNY travel grantee, 1988, 93, 96. Fellow AAAS, Inst. Soc. Ethics and Life Scis; mem. AAUW (life), Am. Soc. Naturalists (pres. 1990), Behavior Genetics Assn. (pres. 1978, Dobzhansky award for lifetime resch. 1988), Soc. for Study of Evolution (exec. council 1986—), Phi Beta Kappa, Sigma Xi. Home: 2 Jennifer Ln Rye Brook NY 10573-1916 Office: SUNY Div Natural Scis Purchase NY 10577

EHRMAN, MADELINE ELIZABETH, government administrator; b. N.Y.C., July 4, 1942; d. Donald McKinley and Marie Madeleine (Brandeis) Ehrman. BA summa cum laude Brown U., 1964, MA, 1965; M of Philosophy, Yale U., 1967; PhD, The Union Inst., 1989. Sci. linguist U.S. Dept. State, Washington, 1969-73, regional lang. supr. U.S. Embassy, Bangkok, Thailand, 1973-75, lang. tng. supr. U.S. Dept. State, Washington, 1975-84, curriculum and tng. specialist, 1984-85, acting chmn. dept. Asian and African Langs., 1985, chmn. dept. Asian and African Langs., 1986-88, acting assoc. dean Sch. Lang. Studies, 1987-88, dir. rsch., evaluation and devel., 1989—. Author: The Meanings of the Modals in Present Day American English, 1966, Contemporary Cambodian, 1975, Indonesian Fast Course, 1982, Communicative Japanese Materials, 1984, Ants and Grasshoppers, Badgers and Butterflies: Qualitative and Quantitative Exploration of Adult Language Learning Styles and Strategies, 1989, Understanding Second Language Learning Difficulties: Looking Beneath the Surface, 1996; mem. editorial bd. Jour. Psychol. Type, 1991—. Mem., ESOL/HILT Citizen's Adv. Coun., Arlington County, Va., 1985-89; psychotherapist Meyer Treatment Ctr. Washington Sch. Psychiatry, 1989-94. Woodrow Wilson Found. fellow, 1964; NSF fellow, 1964-69; recipient Meritorious Honor award U.S. Dept. State, 1972, 83. Mem. Am. Psychol. Assn., Tchrs. of English to Speakers of Other Langs., Am. Assn. Asian Studies, Assn. for Psychol. Type, Am. Orthopsychiat. Soc., Phi Beta Kappa, Psi Chi. Avocations: reading, bicycling, gardening. Office: Fgn Svc Inst 4000 Arlington Blvd Arlington VA 22204-1586

EICH, WILBUR FOSTER, III, pediatrician; b. Tuskegee, Ala., June 26, 1938; s. Wilbur Foster and Lula Olivia (Dudley) E.; B.A., Huntingdon Coll., 1960; M.D., Tulane, 1964; m. Eugenia Glass Graves, May 31, 1963; children—Paul Foster, Mark Samuel, Donna Eugenia. Intern, Lloyd Noland Hosp., Fairfield, Ala., 1964-65; resident in pediatrics U.S. Naval Hosp., Portsmouth, Va., 1967-69; pediatrician Infants' and Children's Clinic, Florence, Ala., 1971—; pres. med. staff Eliza Coffee Meml. Hosp., 1980-81; ordained priest Episcopal Ch., 1981. Vol., Project Hope, Brazil, 1973; trustee Huntingdon Coll., Montgomery, Ala., 1977—. Served with USN, 1965-71. Diplomate Am. Bd. Pediatrics. Contbr. numerous articles and book revs. to med. and ch. jours. Fellow Am. Acad. Pediatrics, Am. Acad. Cerebral Palsy and Devel. Medicine; mem. AMA, So. Med. Assn., Med. Assn. Ala., Lauderdale County Med. Soc., Christian Med. Soc. Home: 120 Limerick Ct Muscle Shoals AL 35661-9741 Office: 421 W College St Florence AL 35630-5520

EICHELMAN, BURR SIMMONS, JR., psychiatrist, researcher, educator; b. Hinsdale, Ill., Mar. 20, 1943; s. Burr Simmons and Evelyn Cora (Budde) E.; children by previous marriage: Kathryn Elise, Andrew Burr; m. Anne del Carmen Hartwig; 1 child, Ian David. S.B. with honors, U. Chgo., 1964, M.D., 1968, Ph.D. in Biopsychology, 1970. Diplomate Am. Bd. Psychiatry and Neurology. Pediatric intern U. Calif.-San Francisco, 1969-70; resident, then fellow in psychiatry Stanford U., Calif., 1972-75, Kennedy fellow in medicine, law and ethics, 1975-76; asst. prof. psychiatry U. Wis.-Madison, 1976-79, assoc. prof., 1979-84, prof., 1984-88; chief psychiatry service, dir. lab. behavioral neurochemistry William S. Middleton Meml. VA Hosp., Madison, 1976-87; cons. Mendota Mental Health Inst., Madison, 1984-87; clin. dir. Dorothea Dix Hosp., Raleigh, 1987-90; prof. psychiatry U. N.C., 1988-90; prof., chmn. dept. psychiatry Temple U. Sch. Medicine, 1990—. Co-editor: Terrorism and Interdisciplinary Perspectives, 1983, Patient Violence and the Clinician, 1995; contbr. chpts. to books, articles to profl. jours. Elder, Presbyn. Ch. Served to lt. comdr. USPHS, 1970-72. Recipient A.E. Bennett award Soc. Biol. Psychiatry, 1972; Westerman prize (hon. mention) Am. Fedn. Clin. Research, 1976. Fellow Am. Coll. Neuropsychopharm. (chmn. ethics com. 1985-86, co-chair 1994-95, chmn. edn. com. 1990-91), Am. Psychiat. Assn. (Falk fellow 1973-75), Am. Psychol. Assn., Collegium Internat. Neuropsychopharmacologicum; mem. AAAS, Internat. Soc. Research on Aggression (co-chmn. ethics com. 1980-84, coun. 1988-90), Soc. Neurosci., Sigma Xi, Alpha Omega Alpha. Avocations: music (piano and voice); tennis; skiing. Office: Temple U Dept Psychiatry 3401 N Broad St Philadelphia PA 19140-5103

EICHENBAUM, JOSEPH WALTER, ophthalmologist; b. N.Y.C., Jan. 4, 1948; s. Irving and Renee (Cooperman) E.; m. Annette Tykocinski, Aug. 21, 1970; children: Gary, Kenneth. BA, AA, Yeshiva U., 1969; MD, Yale U., 1973. Diplomate Nat. Bd. Med. Examiners, Am. Bd. Ophthalmology. Asst. clin. prof. Mt. Sinai Hosp., N.Y.C., 1978—; asst. attending surgeon Manhattan Eye & Ear Hosp., N.Y.C., 1980—; assoc. adj. surgeon N.Y. Eye & Ear Hosp., 1993—; cons. in ophthalmology Beth Israel North Hosp., N.Y.C., 1980—, St. Vincent's Hosp., N.Y.C., 1979—. Editor: Treatment of Retinopathy of Prematurity, 1989; contbr. articles to profl. jours. Mem. bd. trustees Park Ave. Synagogue, N.Y.C., 1996—. Fellow ACS, N.Y. Acad. Medicine; mem. N.Y. County Med. Soc., N.Y. State Med. Soc. Office: 1050 Park Ave New York NY 10028

EICHENBERG, BARION KATHLEEN, nurse, psychotherapist; b. Washington, Nov. 11, 1942; d. Barnett Samuel and Iona Katherine (Hudson) E. MSID, U. Tex., Tyler, 1983; MSSW, U. Tex., Arlington, 1986. Nurse USAF, Vietnam; caseworker II Tarrant County Mental Health, Bedford, Tex.; clin. social worker Alpha and Omega Family Ctr., Ft. Worth; with Brookhaven Nursing Ctr., Ft. Worth, 1992-94; med. liaison S.I.L. Health Svcs. Home: 6231 Hott Springs Dr Arlington TX 76017-5052

EICHORST, GAIL SUSAN, nurse; b. Muskegon, Mich., Apr. 22, 1952; d. Franklin August and Leta Marie (Mendham) E. Student, Muskegon Community Coll., 1973, AA, 1986; BSN, Grand Valley State U., 1993. RN, Mich. LPN Brookhaven, Muskegon, 1973, Knollview Manor, Muskegon, 1973-74, English Hills, Grand Rapids, Mich., 1974, Sherman Oaks Nursing Home, Muskegon, 1975, St. John's Luth. Home, Butler, Pa., 1976-78, North Ottawa Hosp., Grand Haven, Mich., 1978-79. Med. Pers. Pool, Muskegon, 1974-80, Hackley Hosp., Muskegon, 1980-94; cashier Zody's Dept. Store, Butler, Pa., 1975; RN Riverside Nursing Ctr., Grand Haven, Mich., 1994-95, Interim Healthcare, Muskegon, 1995—. Rep. Del., Muskegon, 1986-89; singer, actress musical drama Bethlehem's Christmas Carol, Love's Finest Hour (Easter), 1986-89. Home: 913 Iroquois St Muskegon MI 49444

EICHSTÄDT, HERMANN WERNER, cardiology educator; b. Altenbuseck/Giessen, W. Ger., Feb. 15, 1948; s. Karl Heinz and Elisabeth Magdalena (Froese) E.; med. student U. Mainz, 1968; cand. med. U. Düsseldorf, 1971, M.D., 1974; children: Björn, Kerstin, Bastienne, Bernadette. Intern, Univ. Hosp., Düsseldorf, 1974, Augusta Hosp., Düsseldorf, 1974-75; researcher, Düsseldorf, 1972-74; resident cardiol clinic, Bad Krozingen, W. Ger., 1975-77; resident U. Tübingen (W. Ger.), 1977-79; lectr. dept. cardiology, cons. internal medicine Free U. Berlin, 1979—; mem. directory internal medicine and radiology Universitätsklinikum Charlottenburg, Berlin, 1981—, prof. cardiology, 1935—. Fellow Am. Coll. Chest Physicians, Internat. Coll. Angiology; mem. N.Y. Acad. Scis., German Soc. Internal Medicine, Profl. Assn. Internists, German Soc. Cardiology, European Soc. Cardiology (working group on isotopes), German Soc. Cardiovascular Surgery, German Heart Found. Roman Catholic. Contbr. numerous articles to English, French and German jours. Editor books and monographs. Home: 61 Konstanzerstrasse, 10707 Berlin Germany Office: Augustenburger Platz, D13353 Berlin Germany

EID, JEAN-FRANCOIS, urologist; b. Brussels, July 23, 1953; s. Pierre and Nadia E.; m. Isabelle Dieudonne, May 11, 1983; 1 child, Pierre Alexander. BS, Brown U., 1976; MD, Cornell U., 1982. From intern, resident surgery to asst. attending surgeon N.Y. Hosp./Cornell Med. Ctr., 1982—; dir. erectile dysfunction ctr. outpatient sexual clinic Burke Rehabilitation tr., White Plains, N.Y., 1989—. Author: Making Love Again—Regaining Sexual Potency Through the New Injection Treatment, 1993; contbr. articles to profl. jours. Mem. Am. Urol. Soc., Am. Fertility Soc., Am. Diabetes Soc., Am. Soc. Andrology, Soc. for Male Reproduction, Internat. Soc. for Impotence Rsch.. Office: NY Hosp/Cornell Med Ctr 525 E 68th St Box 29 New York NY 10021

EIDELHOCH, LESTER PHILIP, physician, educator, surgeon; b. N.Y.C., Jan. 7, 1932; s. Abraham David Eidelhoch and Ella (Sarah) Lovinger; m. Cecily Ruth Rosenberg, Apr. 28, 1963; children: Alison Marc, Arthur Mark, Meredith Marc. BA, Columbia U., 1952; MD, NYU, 1956. Diplomate Am. Bd. Med. Examiners. Intern Strong Meml. Hosp., Rochester, N.Y.; resident Harvard Surg. div. Boston City Hosp., 1958-62; pvt. practice New Hartford, N.Y., 1965—; med. dir. Walsh Med. Ctr., Rome, N.Y., 1991—; mem faculty SUNY. Bd. dirs. Jewish Fedn., Utica (N.Y.) Symphony, Charles T. Sitrin Home. Lt. comdr. USN, 1962-64. Recipient Lindner Surg. award NYU. Fellow ACS, Royal Coll. Medicine; mem. N.Y. Cen. Soc. Surgeons, Cen. N.Y. Acad. Medicine, Oneida County Med. Soc. Republican. Home and Office: 6 Old Willow Rd New Hartford NY 13413-2419

EIDELMAN, ARTHUR I., medical educator, pediatrician; b. Bklyn., Mar. 10, 1939; s. Julius and Edith (Kalmanowitz) E.; m. Arleen Sandra Pilzer, June 22, 1960; children: Aura, Yael, Ronain, Elie. BA, Yeshiva Coll., N.Y.C., 1959; BHL, Yeshiva U., N.Y.C., 1959; MD, Einstein Coll., N.Y.C., 1963. Chief resident pediatrics Yale U. Hosp., New Haven, Conn., 1966-67; nat. med. cons. Divsn. Med. Retardation, DHW, Washington, 1967-69; dir. neonatal ICU Bronx (N.Y.) Mcpl. Hosp., 1969-72; dir. newborn svcs. Hosp. Einstein Coll. of Medicine, Bronx, 1969-78 med. dir. Shaare Zetek Med. Ctr., Jerusalem, 1980-82, dir. neonatology, 1978—; assoc. prof. pediatrics Einstein Coll. of Medicine, Bronx, N.Y., 1976-88; prof. pediatrics Einstein Coll. of Medicine, Bronx, 1988—; vis. rsch. scholar Yale U. Sch. Medicine, New Haven, 1991—; assoc. prof. pediatrics Hebrew U. Med. Sch., Jerusalem, 1992—. Assoc. editor Israel Jour. Med. Scis., 1994—; internat. neonatology editor Jour. Perinatology, 1993—; editorial bd. Am. Journ. Diseases of Children, 1976-83, Obstetric Anesthesia Digest, 1980—. Lt. commdr. USPHS, 1967-69. Fellow Am. Acad. Pediatrics (E. Mead Johnson Rsch. award 1965-66); mem. European Soc. Pediatric Rsch., U.S. Soc. Pediatric Rsch., Israel Pediatric Soc., Israel Soc. Critical Care Medicine. Office: Shaare Zedek Med Ctr, POB 3235, Jerusalem 91031, Israel

EIFRIG, DAVID ERIC, ophthalmologist, educator; b. Oak Park, Ill., Jan. 4, 1935. BA, Carleton Coll., Northfield, Minn., 1956; MD, Johns Hopkins U., 1960. Diplomate Am. Bd. Ophthalmology. Mem. liaison svc. Johns Hopkins U. Hosp., Balt., 1957, mem. dept. pathology, 1958, mem. dog lab. dept. surgery, 1959-60; intern, then asst. resident Halsted Surg. Svc. Phipps Psychiat. Clinic, Johns Hopkins U. Hosp., Balt., 1960-62, resident in ophthalmology Wilmer Eye Inst., 1964-67; retinal fellow Jules Stein Eye Inst., UCLA, 1967-68; asst. prof. dept. ophthalmology U. Ky. Sch. Medicine, Lexington, 1968-70; asst. prof. dept. ophthalmology U. Minn. Sch. Medicine, Mpls., 1970-73, assoc. prof., 1973-77; prof. dept. ophthalmology U. N.C. Sch. Medicine, Chapel Hill, 1977—, Sterling A. Barrett prof., 1980—, chmn. dept. ophthalmology, 1977—; Z80 com. Am. Nat. Stds. Inst., 1980—, chmn. 1980—; mem. Med. Devices Stds. Bd., 1986—; mem. Internat. Stds. Orgn., 1986—; adv. bd. Am. Coll. of Surgeons, 1994—. Contbr. articles to profl. jours.; lectr. to profl. confs. With M.C. USNR, 1962-64. Recipient Schwentker medal for rsch. Johns Hopkins U., 1967. Fellow ACS; mem. AMA, Am. Acad. Ophthalmology, Assn. Rsch. in Vision and Ophthalmology, Assn. Univ. Profs. in Ophthalmology (trustee, pres. 1994-95), Durham-Orange County Med. Soc., Johns Hopkins Med. and Surg. Assn., N.C. Med. Soc., N.C. Soc. Ophthalmology, Retina Soc., Mensa, Order Ky. Cols. Home: 128 New Castle Dr Chapel Hill NC 27514-6545 Office: U NC Sch Medicine Dept Ophthalmology 617 Clinical Scis 229H Chapel Hill NC 27514

EIGEN, HOWARD, pediatrician, educator; b. N.Y.C., Sept. 8, 1942; s. Jay and Libbie (Kantrowitz) E.; m. Linda Hazzard; children—Sarah Elizabeth, Lauren Michelle. B.S., Queens Coll., 1964; M.D., Upstate N.Y. Med. Ctr., Syracuse, 1968. Diplomate Am. Bd. Pediatrics, Am. Bd. Pediatric Pulmonology, Am. Bd. Critical Care Medicine, Nat. Bd. Med. Examiners (mem. pediatric test com. 1986-90). Resident in pediatrics Upstate Med. Ctr., Syracuse, 1968-71; fellow in pediatric pulmonology Tulane U., New Orleans, 1973-76; asst. prof. pediatrics Ind. U., Indpls., 1976-84, prof., 1984—; assoc. chmn. of Pediatrics for Clin. Affairs, dir. pediatric intensive care, pulmonology sect. Riley Hosp. for Children, med. dir. ambulatory care, 1989—. Co-editor: Respiratory Disease in Children: Diagnosis and Management; assoc. editor Pediatric Pulmonology, 1984-91; contbr. articles to profl. jours. Served to maj. U.S. Army, 1971-73. Fellow Am. Acad. Pediatrics (pres. chest sect. 1983-85, pulmonology 1986—), Am. Thoracic Soc., Am. Bd. Pediatrics, Am. Lung Assn. (pres. Ind. 1984-85). Office: Ind U Dept Pediatrics 702 Barnhill Dr Rm 293 Indianapolis IN 46202-5128

EIGEN, MICHAEL, psychologist; b. Passaic, N.J., Jan. 11, 1936; s. Sol and Jeanette (Brody) E.; m. Betty Gitelman, Dec. 27, 1980; children: David Joshua, Jacob Paul. AB, U. Pa., 1957; PhD, New Sch. Social Rsch., N.Y.C., 1974. Lic. psychologist and psychoanalyst, N.Y. Past. dir. tng. Inst. for Expressive Analysis; supr., faculty New Hope Guild, 1972-91; assoc. clin. prof. of psychology NYU Postdoctoral Program in Psychoanalysis and Psychotherapy. Author: The Psychotic Core, 1986, Coming Through the Whirlwind, 1992, The Electrified Tightrope, 1993, Reshaping the Self, 1995, Psychic Deadness, 1996; co-editor: Evil: Self and Culture, 1984; contbr. numerous articles to profl. jours. Mem. Nat. Psychol. Assn. for Psychoanalysis. Office: 225 Central Park W Apt 101A New York NY 10024-6027

EIGHMEY, DOUGLAS JOSEPH, JR., hospital administrator; b. Cambridge, N.Y., Dec. 19, 1946; s. Douglas Joseph and Theresa E. (McGuire) E.; m. Karen S. Rife, Apr. 27, 1973; 1 child, Sarah Elizabeth. BS in Biology, SUNY, Cortland, 1968; MPH, U. Tenn., 1971. Pub. health cons. Ohio Dept. Health, Columbus, 1971-76, supr. cert. of need program Ohio Dept. Health, 1976-78; v.p. Cen. Ohio River Valley Assn., Cin., 1978-79, St. Francis-St. George Hosp., Inc., Cin., 1979-82; v.p., adminstr. Huber Heights Health Services Inc. (Ohio), 1982-84; pres., v.p. Children's Med. Ctr., Dayton, Ohio, 1984-89; sr. v.p. adminstrn. Kosair Children's Hosp., Louisville, 1989—; chmn. Montgomery County Mental Health Bd., 1986-89; mem. Montgomery County Human Services Levy Council, Children's Trust Fund; mem. Nat. Kidney Found. Bd., Ky. chpt., 1990; bd. dirs. Bingham Child Guidance Ctr., 1990—, Home of Innocence (bd. dirs.); mem. adv. bd. Dream factory; mem. tech. adv. com. for medicaid Cabinet for Human Resources, Ky. Recipient award USPHS, 1970. Mem. Am. Hosp. Assn., Am. Coll. Health Care Execs., Ohio Hosp. Planning Assn. (dir.-at-large 1980-82, pres. elect 1985, pres. 1986), Am. Soc. Hosp. Planning, Nat. Assn. Clock and Watch Collectors, St. Vincent DePaul Soc., Rotary, Elks. Roman Catholic. Office: Kosair Children's Hosps PO Box 35070 Louisville KY 40232-5070*

EIMERS, JERI ANNE, therapist; b. Berkeley, Calif., Jan. 20, 1951; d. Alfred D. Wallace and Marjorie E. (Nordheim) Stevens; m. Roy A. Neiman, June 12, 1969 (div. Aug. 1977); children: Lorien, Arwen; m. Richard A. Eimers, Mar. 2, 1996. AA, Palomar Jr. Coll., 1977; BA in Psychology with distinction, Calif. State U., Long Beach, 1979, MA in Psychology with distinction, 1981; postgrad. Human Sexuality Program, UCLA, 1991-92. Lic. marriage, family, child therapist, Calif.; cert. community coll. instr., counselor; cert. sex therapist. Rsch. asst. Calif. State U., 1978-82; tchr. Artesia (Calif.)-Bellflower-Cerritos Unified Sch. Dist., 1982-83; dir. Am. Learning Corp., Huntington Beach, Calif., 1983-85; social worker Los Angeles County Children's Protective Svcs., Long Beach, 1986-88; sr. social worker Orange County Social Svc. Agy., Orange, Calif., 1988-90; therapist Cypress Mental Health, Cypress, Calif., 1988—, cons., 1990—; cons., 1990—; group chair, leader Adults Abused as Children, Los Altos Hosp., Long Beach, 1991—, Coll. Hosp., Cerritos, 1993—; speaker, presenter in field. Mem. Child's Sexual Abuse Network, Orange, 1988—; mem. legis. com. Child Abuse Coun. of Orange County, 1988. Women's League scholar, 1980-81. Mem. AAUW, Am. Assn. Marriage, Family Therapists, Calif. Assn. Marriage, Family Therapists, Am. Profl. Soc. for Abused Children, Calif. Profl. Assn. for Abused Children, Phi Kappa Phi, Psi Chi. Republican. Methodist. Address: Huntington Group Ste 365 9191 Towne Centre Dr San Diego CA 92122

EIMON, PERRY LEROY, psychologist; b. Superior, Wis., Dec. 3, 1933; s. Perry Arthur and Deweyetta Beatrice (Dolysh) E.; m. Marilyn Carol Linnerson, June 16, 1961. BA, U. Minn., 1958, PhD, 1970. Lic. psychologist, Mass. Chief psychologist Hastings (Minn.) State Hosp., 1961-71; staff psychologist Brockton (Mass.)/West Roxbury VA Med. Ctr., 1971—; pvt. practice cons., Hastings, 1961-71, Brockton, 1971—. Contbr. articles to profl. jours. Fellow Mass. Psychol. Assn.; mem. Am. Psychol. Assn., Internat. Neuropsychol. Soc., New Eng. Psychol. Assn., N.Y. Neuropsychol. Group. Office: Brockton/West Roxbury VA Med Ctr 940 Belmont St Brockton MA 02401-5596

EIN, DANIEL, allergist; b. Liege, Belgium, Nov. 26, 1938; came to U.S., 1941; s. Max Motel and Sabine (Toeman) E.; m. Marion Hess, June 25, 1961 (div. 1978); children: Mark David, Jon Spencer; m. Marina Wallach, Apr. 10, 1988; stepchildren: Jacqueline A. Newmyer, Tory Newmyer. AB, Columbia U., 1959; MD, Albert Einstein Coll. Medicine, 1964. Diplomate Am. Bd. Internal Medicine, Am. Bd. Allergy and Immunology. Intern Bronx Mcpl. Hosp., N.Y.C., 1964-65; staff assoc. Nat. Cancer Inst., Washington, 1965-67, clin. assoc., 1967-68; asst. resident Mass. Gen. Hosp., Boston, 1968-69; sr. investigator Nat. Cancer Inst., Washington, 1969-71; pvt. practice Washington, 1971—; clin. prof. medicine George Washington U., Washington, 1982—, Georgetown U., Washington, 1996—; founder, pres. Capital Physicians Network, 1994. Contbr. articles to profl. jours. and newspapers. Fellow ACP, Am. Acad. Allergy (AMA del. 1994); mem. Med. Soc. of D.C. (pres. 1991), Greater Washington Allergy Soc. (pres. 1979), Cosmos Club. Jewish. Home: 4636 Kenmore Dr NW Washington DC 20007-1924

EINBECKER, MARK EDWARD, surgeon; b. Chgo., Sept. 10, 1953; s. Robert and Maureen Einbecker; m. Shelley Miller, May 31, 1986 (div. Feb. 1993); children: Kate, Brett; m. Janet Darlene Derington, Apr. 6, 1996. BJ, So. Ill. U., Carbondale, 1980; MD, Northwestern U., Chgo., 1985. physician rep. Cardinal Hill Rehab. Team, Lexington, 1993-96; cmty. outreach provider, Lexington, Ky., 1991-96. Author: Clinical Orthopedics and Related Research, 1990 (3rd pl. award 1990). Maj. U.S. Army, 1974-91. Recipient Christine M. Klienert fellowshipfor hand and microsurgery, Louisville, 1990. Fellow Am. Bd. Orthopedic Surgeons, Am. Acad. Orthopedic Surgeons; mem. AMA, Ky. Orthopedic Assn., Mid-Am. Orthopedic Assn., Fayette County Med. Soc. Republican. Office: Ky Orthopedic & Hand Surgeons 1780 Nicholasvill Rd # 501 Lexington KY 40509

EINSPRUCH, BURTON CYRIL, psychiatrist; b. N.Y.C., June 27, 1935; s. Adolph and Mala (Goldblatt) E.; B.A., So. Meth. U., 1956, Sc.B., 1958; M.D., Southwestern Med. Sch., Dallas, 1960; m. Barbara Standen Traeger, Oct. 9, 1960; children: Julia Moat, Alexander Louis, Robert Sands. Intern, Montefiore Hosp., N.Y.C., 1960-61; resident Nat. Hosp. Inst. Neurology, London, 1962, U. Tex., Dallas, 1961-64 (also fellow); sr. resident Parkland Meml. Hosp., Dallas, 1964; instr. psychiatry U. Pa., 1964-66; pvt. practice psychiatry, Dallas, 1966—; mem. staff Presbyn. and Parkland hosps., Timberlawn Psychiat. Hosp.; clin. asst. prof. U. Tex., Health Sci. Center, Dallas, 1966-70, dir. psychiat. div. Student Health Service, 1966-72, clin. assoc. prof., 1970—; dir. Southwestern Adult Psychiat. Clinic, Dallas, 1966-74; dir. psychiat. service Dallas Home for Jewish Aged, 1966-82, now cons. staff; research cons. Dallas Geriatric Research Inst., 1974-80; adj. prof. sociology N. Tex. State U., Denton, 1975-82; cons. staff Baylor U. Hosp., Golden Acres Hosp.; clin. assoc. prof. psychiatry U. Tex. Health Scis. Ctr., Dallas, 1971—; assoc. prof. psychiatry U. Tex. Southwestern Med. Ctr., Dallas, 1971—; clin. assoc. prof. psychiatry NYU Med. Ctr., N.Y.C., 1990; chmn., bd. dirs. Planned Behavioral Health Care, Inc., Dallas; affiliate Tex. Inst. Rsch. and Edn. on Aging, Health Sci. Ctr. Fort Worth; Mem. editorial bd. Tex. Medicine. Bd. dirs. Mental Health Assn. Dallas, 1960-69, Jewish Family Service, 1969-71, 73-75. Trustee Evans Fedn., N.Y.C., 1986—, St. Mark's Sch. Tex., 1987—, Jaffe Collection McDermott Libr., U. Tex., Dallas, 1987—; mem. exec. bd. libr. So. Meth. U., 1992—; adv. dir. Leonhardt Fedn., N.Y.C., 1990, Children of Alcoholics Fedn., 1991; arbitrator, N.Y. and Am. Exchs., N.Y.C., 1884—. Served to lt. comdr. M.C., USNR, 1964-66. Diplomate Am. Bd. Psychiatry and Neurology (examiner, 1974—). Fellow Am. Psychiat. Assn., Am. Coll. Psychiatrists, Am. Soc. Adolescent Psychiatry, N. Tex. Soc. Adolescent Psychiatry (past pres.); mem. Royal Coll. Psychiatry London, AMA, Tex. Med. Assn. Contbr. profl. jours. Home: 5411 Meaders Ln Dallas TX 75229-6651 Office: 8330 Meadow Rd Ste 117 Dallas TX 75231-3750

EINSTEIN, STANLEY, psychologist; b. N.Y.C., July 5, 1934; s. Abraham and Rebecca (Siskind) E.; m. Sarah Wenger, Aug. 31, 1958; children: Tamar Reva, Joshua Gregory. BA in Psychology cum laude, CCNY, 1957, MA in Social Psychology, 1958; MA in Clin. Psychology, U. Pa., 1960; PhD in Psychology, Yeshiva U., 1964. Staff psychologist Riverside Hosp., N.Y.C., 1960-63; psychologist, researcher dept. psychiatry, asst. prof. psychiatry N.Y. Med. Coll., N.Y.C., 1963-67; dir. N.Y. Council Alcoholism, N.Y.C., 1967-69; asst. dir. div. drug abuse, assoc. prof. Dept. Pub. Health N.J. Coll. Medicine, Newark, 1969-73; assoc. prof. dept. criminology Bar Ilan U., Ramat Gan, Israel, 1974-85; assoc. prof. dept. criminology, dept. psychology Hebrew U., Jerusalem, 1977-81; founder, dir. Jerusalem Ctr. Drug Misuse Intervention, 1976-84, Mid. Eastern Summer Inst. on Drug Use; pvt. practice psychology N.Y.C., 1964-73, Jerusalem, 1984—; presenter numerous lectures, workshops, seminars; cons. in field; creator, dir. Mid. Eastern Summer Inst. for the Study of Drug Use. Founder, editor-in-chief Internat. Jour. of the Addictions, Altered States of Conciousness, Drug Forum, Social

Pharmacology, Violence, Aggression and Terrorism, Decisions, Issues and Alternatives; weekly columnist Star Ledger, Newark, 1972, Newark News, 1973; author, editor, co-editor 14 books; contbr. articles to profl. jours. Recipient Pace Setter award Nat. Inst. Drug Abuse, 1979. Mem. Am. Psychol. Assn., Israel Psychol. Assn. Office: Mesidu, 113/41 E Talpiot, Jerusalem Israel

EISDORFER, CARL, psychiatrist, health care executive; b. Bronx, N.Y., June 20, 1930. B.A., NYU, 1951, M.A., 1953, Ph.D., 1959; M.D., Duke U., 1964; postgrad. in health systems mgmt., Harvard U., 1981. Lectr. in psychology Duke U. Med. Ctr., Durham, N.C., 1959-72, intern in medicine, 1964-65, psychiat. trainee, 1964-67, dir. tng., research coordinator Ctr. for Study Aging and Human Devel., 1965-70, prof. psychiatry and med. psychology, 1968-72, dir. med. studies behavioral scis. program, 1970-72, head div. med. psychology dept. psychiatry, 1970-72, dir. Ctr. for Study Aging and Human Devel.,, 1970-72; founding dir. Inst. on Aging, U. Wash., Seattle, 1977-79, prof., chmn. dept. psychiatry and behavioral scis. Sch. of Medicine, adj. prof. psychology, 1972-81; sr. scholar in residence Inst. Medicine, Nat. Acad. Scis., Washington, 1979-80; prof. psychiatry and neurosci. Albert Einstein Coll. Medicine, N.Y.C., 1981-85; chief exec. officer Montefiore Med. Ctr., N.Y.C., 1981-85; prof., chmn. dept. psychiatry U. Miami, Fla., 1986—; also dir. Ctr. on Adult Devel. and Aging U. Miami; chief div. mental health Jackson Meml. Med. Ctr., 1986—; coordinator Community Mental Health Services, Halifax County N.C., 1969-70; vis. prof. U. Calif., 1969-70, U. Calif.-Berkeley, 1969-70; H.T. Dozer vis. prof. geriatrics and psychiatry Ben Gurion U., Negev, Israel, 1980; cons. NIH, Bethesda, Md., Robert Wood Johnson Found., numerous others. Editor in chief Ann. Rev. Gerontology and Geriatrics, 1978—; cons. editor Ency. of Aging, 1984—; mem. editorial bd. Alzheimers Disease and Related Disorders-Internat. Jour., Aging and Human Devel., Western Jour. Medicine, Neurobiology of Aging: Exptl. and Clin. Research; contbr. numerous articles to profl. jours.; also books. Served with U.S. Army, 1954-56. Recipient Kesten award Ethel Percy Andrus Gerontology Ctr., U. So. Calif., 1976, Potamkin prize, 1982, Disting. Alumnus award Duke U. Sch. of Medicine, 1985. Fellow Soc. Behavioral Medicine, N.Y. Acad. Medicine, Am. Psychol. Assn. (chmn. div. adult devel. and aging 1970-71, task force on aging 1971-73, award for disting. contbns. 1981, award for contbns. on aging research 1985), Gerontol. Soc. Am. (pres. 1971-72, Robert W. Kleemeier award 1969, Joseph Freeman award div. clin. medicine 1979), Am. Geriatrics Soc. (Edward B. Allen award 1974, Edward Henderson Meml. award 1988), Am. Psychiat. Assn. (Jack Weinberg Meml. award 1984), Am. Coll. Psychiatrists, Am. Coll. Physicians (Menniger award 1990), AAAS; mem. Am. Soc. Aging (pres. 1980-82), Am. Fed. Aging Res. (pres. 1986-88), Sigma Xi, Alpha Omega Alpha. Office: U Miami Sch Medicine Dept Psychiatry D-28 PO Box 016960 # D28 Miami FL 33101-6960*

EISELE, JOHN EVANS, pediatrician; b. Madison, Wis., July 3, 1940; s. Edward Joseph and Dorothy Athalone (Evans) E. BS, U. Wis., Madison, 1962, MD, 1965. Diplomate Am. Bd. Pediatrics. Intern Children's Hosp., Oakland, Calif., 1965-66; resident in pediatrics U. Wis. Hosp., Madison, 1966-68; dir. phys. medicine U.S. Army Hosp., Denver, 1968-70; dir. rehab. Sharp Hosp., San Diego, 1970-78; dir. pediatric rehab. Johns Hopkins U., Balt., 1978-86, East Carolina U., Greenville, N.C., 1986-95; assoc. prof. East Carolina U., 1986-95, emeritus, 1995—; bd. dirs. Carolina Physicians Health Plan, Raleigh, N.C. Contbr. sci. articles to profl. jours. Maj. U.S. Army, 1968-70. Grantee NIH, 1973-86. Fellow Am. Acad. Pediatrics. Office: East Carolina U PO Box 6028 Greenville NC 27835-6028

EISEN, EUGENE J., genetics educator; b. N.Y.C., May 14, 1938; s. Abraham and Fay (Hantman) E.; m. Jacqueline Serxner, Aug. 27, 1960; children: Arri, Avram, Andrea. BSA, U. Ga., 1959; MS, Purdue U., 1962, PhD, 1965. Rsch. asst. Purdue U., West Lafayette, Ind., 1959-62; instr. Purdue U., West Lafayette, 1962-64; asst. prof. N.C. State U., Raleigh, 1964-67, assoc. prof., 1967-73, prof., 1973-88, William Neal Reynolds prof., 1988—; vis. assoc. prof. U. Calif., Davis, 1970-71; vis. prof. U. Edinburgh, Scotland, 1979-80; pres. Sigma Xi, N.C. State U., Raleigh, 1978-79, v.p., 1977-78. Contbr. more than 140 articles to profl. jours. Recipient Sigma Xi Rsch. award, 1972, Disting. Svc. award Gamma Sigma Delta, 1977; grantee NIMH, 1964-68, 79-81, N.C. Biotech., 1987-88, 90-91, Okla. State U., 1992-93, USDA, 1994—. Office: NC State U Dept Animal Sci Box 7621 Raleigh NC 27695

EISEN, HERMAN NATHANIEL, immunology researcher, medical educator; b. Bklyn., Oct. 15, 1918; m. Natalie Aronson, 1948; 5 children. AB, NYU, 1939, MD, 1943. Asst. in pathology Coll. Physicians and Surgeons, Columbia U., N.Y.C., 1944-46; NIH fellow Coll. Medicine, NYU, 1947-48, fellow in chemistry, 1948-49, asst. prof. indsl. medicine, 1949-53, assoc. prof., 1953-55; prof. medicine Sch. Medicine, Washington U., St. Louis, 1955-61; dermatologist-in-chief Barnes Hosp., St. Louis, 1955-61; prof. microbiology, head dept. Sch. Medicine Washington U., St. Louis, 1961-73; prof. MIT, Cambridge, 1973-82, Whitehead Inst. prof. immunology, 1982-89; prof. emeritus, 1989—; mem. adv. bd. Mass. Gen. Hosp., Yale Med. Sch., Harvard Sch. Pub. Health, Children's Hosp., Boston, Merck, Sharpe and Dohme Rsch. Labs., Roche Inst. for Molecular Biology, Howard Hughes Med. Inst., NAS (mem. editl. bd. Procs.), Am. Acad. Arts and Scis., Am. Soc. Clin. Investigation (v.p. 1963-64), Am. Assn. Immunologists (pres. 1968-69), Am. Soc. Biol. Chem., Inst. Medicine. Mem. NAS (editl. bd. Proceedings of the NAS), Howard Hughes Med. Inst., Am. Soc. Clin. Investigation (v.p. 1963-64), Am. Assn. Immunologists (pres. 1968-69), Am. Soc. Biol. Chem., Am. Assn. Physicians, Inst. Medicine, Am. Acad. Arts and Scis. Office: MIT Ctr Cancer Rsch B E 17R 128 Cambridge MA 02139-3594

EISEN, HOWARD JOEL, physician, researcher; b. Forest Hills, N.Y., May 25, 1956; s. Ezra Michael and Gertrude Margaret (Schmidt) E.; m. Judith Ellen Wolf, June 26, 1983; children: Jonathan Ezra, Miriam Sarah. BA in Biology, Cornell U., 1977; MD, U. Pa., 1981. Diplomate Am. Bd. Med. Examiners, Am. Bd. Internal Medicine, Am. Bd. Cardiovascular Diseases. Asst. prof. medicine U. Pa., Phila., 1990-93; assoc. prof. medicine and physiology Temple U., Phila., 1993—, dir. heart failure care unit, 1993—; med. dir. cardiac transplant program Temple U., 1993—; mem. cryptosporidiosis adv. com. Dept. Pub. Health, Phila., 1995—. Fellow Am. Coll. Cardiology, Am. Coll. Physicians, Am. Heart Assn. (clin. coun., mem. rsch. com. 1995—, chmn. peer-review com. 1996—, Established Investigatorship award 1996—, grant-in-aid, Dallas 1990—); mem. Am. Fedn. Clin. Rsch. (mem. nat. coun. 1992-95, H. Christian award 1993, ea. chmn. 1993-94), Internat. Soc. Heart and Lung Transplantation. Home: 507 Shortridge Dr Wynnewood PA 19096 Office: Temple U Sch Medicine 3401 N Broad St 9PP Philadelphia PA 19140*

EISEN, MARLENE RUTH, psychologist, educator; b. Chgo., Nov. 23, 1931; d. William and Sophia Maria (Brounwine) Friedlander; m. Lee B. Andalman, Aug. 2, 1963 (dec. July 1974); children: Martin Price, Dan Price, Robert; m. Sydney B. Eisen, June 6, 1979. Student, U. Wis., 1948-51; BA, Roosevelt U., Chgo., 1952; MA, U. Chgo., 1967, PhD, 1977. Tchr. Ravinia Nursery Sch., Highland Park, Ill., 1952-56; nursery sch. tchr. Country Schs., North Hollywood, Calif., 1958-61; kindergarten tchr. Sch. Dist. #65, Evanston, Ill., 1962-73; coord. early childhood program U. Chgo., 1974-75; coord. early childhood program, assoc. prof. Harper Coll., Palatine, Ill., 1976-84; pvt. practice cons. ednl. programs Evanston, 1972-86; assoc. faculty Ill. Sch. Profl. Psychology, Chgo., 1982—; pvt. practice psychotherapy Chgo., 1977—; mem. faculty tchr. edn. program Inst. Psychoanalysis, Chgo., 1984-95; cons. Evanston Sch. Dist. #65, 1967; chmn. adv. bd. early edn. program Harper Coll., Palatine, 1976-84; presenter papers and workshops at various confs., univs., community ctrs., parents groups, ednl. groups and profl. orgns. Contbr. articles to profl. jours. Fellow APA; mem. Soc. Clin. and Exptl. Hypnosis, Am. Soc. Clin. Hypnosis. Office: 1603 Orrington Evanston IL 60201-5000

EISENBAUM, ALLAN MELVIN, pediatric ophthalmologist, adult strabismologist; b. N.Y.C., Oct. 18, 1947; s. Morris C. and Jennie (Lubliner) E.; m. Sharon Jacqueline, Aug. 17, 1969; children: Joel Michael, Andrew Seth. B.A., George Washington U., 1969, M.D., 1972. Diplomate Am. Bd. Ophthalmology. Rotating intern Maimonides Med. Ctr., Bklyn., 1972-73; resident in ophthalmology George Washington U., Washington, 1975-78; fellow in pediatric ophthalmology and adult strabismus Nat. Children's Med. Ctr., Washington, 1978-79; chief ophthalmology service Children's Hosp., Denver, 1983—, Presbyn. Aurora Hosp., Colo., 1983-85; clin. asst. prof. dept. ophthalmology U. Colo. Health Scis. Ctr., Denver, 1984; chmn. med. adv. com. Aurora Pub. Schs., Colo., 1984-86; mem. med. adv. bd. Cherry Creek Schs., Colo., 1982, Listen Found., Englewood, Colo.; med. advisor Anchor Presch. for Blind, Littleton, Colo., 1982-86; mem. faculty sect. 6 basic and clin. sci. course Am. Acad. Ophthalmology; med. cons. Sturge-Weber Found., Aurora. Bd. dirs. Colo. Soc. To Prevent Blindness, 1979-86. Served to maj. USPHS, 1973-75, lt. col. Res. Trustees scholar George Washington U., 1966-68, Regents scholar State N.Y., 1965, Nat. Def. scholar, 1968-71. Fellow Am. Acad. Ophthalmology; mem. Am. Assn. Pediatric Ophthalmology and Strabismus. Jewish.

EISENBERG, BURTON L., surgeon; b. Hartford, Conn., Oct. 28, 1948; s. Samuel and Ruth (Herman) E.; m. Geraldine Eisenberg; children: Jamie, Corey. BA, U. Conn., 1970; MD, U. Tenn., 1974. Intern USAF Med. Ctr., San Antonio, 1974-75, resident in gen. surgery, 1975-79; resident in surg. oncology M.D. Anderson Hosp., Houston, 1978; fellow in surg. oncology Meml. Sloan-Kettering Cancer Ctr., N.Y.C., 1979-81; clin. asst. prof. surgery U. Tex. Health Sci. Ctr., San Antonio, 1981-87; clin. assoc. prof. U. Health Scis., Bethesda, Md., 1987—; chief surg. oncology USAF Med. Ctr., 1981-87; cons. to Surgeon Gen. in Surg. Oncology, 1981-87; acting chmn. dept. surgery Fox Chase Cancer Ctr., 1990-91, staff surgeon, 1987—, fellowship dir., 1991—, chmn. dept. surg. oncology, 1991—; assoc. prof. surgery Temple U. Sch. Medicine, Phila., 1987-92, chief sect. surg. oncology, 1991—, prof., 1992—. Contbr. articles to profl. jours.; reviewer Jour. Clin. Oncology, Jour. Cancer Rsch., Cancer Jour., Cancer; mem. editl. bd. numerous profl. jours. Fellow ACS; mem. Assn. for Acad. Surgery, Soc. Air Force Clin. Surgeons, Phila. Acad. Surgery, Soc. Surg. Oncology, Am. Soc. Clin. Oncology, Pa. Oncologic Soc., Soc. Head & Neck Surgery, Soc. for Surgery of Alimentary Tract, Am. Assn. for Cancer Rsch., Am. Radium Soc., Alpha Omega Alpha. Office: Fox Chase Cancer Ctr 7701 Burholme Ave Philadelphia PA 19111

EISENBERG, CAROLA, psychiatry educator; b. Buenos Aires, Sept. 15, 1917; came to U.S., 1945; d. Bernardo and Teodora (Kahan) Blitzman; m. Manfred Guttmacher, Oct. 11, 1946 (dec. 1966); m. Leon Eisenberg, Aug. 31, 1967; children: Laurence, Alan. B. in Social Work, Liceo de Senoritas; MD, U. Buenos Aires, 1945. Resident in psychiatry U. Md., 1946-48; fellow in child psychiatry Johns Hopkins Hosp., 1948-50; asst. prof. psychiatry and pediatrics Johns Hopkins Hosp., Balt., 1960-67; psychiatrist MIT, Boston, 1967-72, dean of students, 1972-78; dean student affairs Harvard Med. Sch., Boston, 1978-90, dir. internat. programs for students, 1990-92, lectr. psychiatry, 1970—; co-chmn. women in biomed. careers workshop Office on Women's Health, NIH, 1992, mem. adv. com. on rsch. and women's health, 1995-98; mem. com. on human rights ACP; mem. com. on women in sci. and engring. NAS, 1992-95. V.p. Physicians for Human Rights, Boston, 1987—; pres. Examiners Club, Boston, 1993—. Fellow Am. Psychiat. Assn. (com. on human rights), Am. Orthopsychiat. Assn. (life); mem. AAUP. Home and Office: 9 Clement Cir Cambridge MA 02138-2205

EISENBERG, DAVID E., physician; b. Scranton, Pa., Oct. 22, 1944. BA, Yeshiva U., 1966; MD, Albert Einstein Sch. Medicine, 1970. Diplomate Am. Bd. Ophthalmology. Pvt. pracitce Chelsea, Mass., 1976—. Capt. USAF, 1971-73. Mem. Lions. Office: 111 Everett Ave Chelsea MA 02150-2363

EISENBERG, HARRY VICTOR, plastic surgeon; b. Bklyn., May 8, 1945; s. Joseph and Faye (Simom) E.; m. Lya E. Chamikles, June 21, 1969; children: Davina, Erica. BA, Boston U., 1968, MD, 1968. Diplomate Am. Bd. Surgery, Am. Bd. Plastic Surgery. Surgical intern Maimonides Hosp., Bklyn., 1968-69, surgical resident, 1969-73; emergency room physician Orange Meml. Hosp., Orlando, Fla., 1973-75; plastic surgery resident Orange Meml. Hosp., Orlando, 1975-77; practice medicine specializing in plastic surgery Maitland (Fla.) Cosmetic Surgery Ctr., 1977—; chmn. dept. plastic surgery Fla. Hosp., Orlando, 1988-90. Contbr. articles to profl. jours. Bd. dirs. Fla. Symphony Orch., 1985—, pres., 1987-88; bd. dirs. So. Ballet Theater, 1990-93, pres.-elect, 1994, pres., 1995-96. Recipient Physicians Recognition award AMA, 1971, 74, 77, 80, 83, 86, 89, 92, 95. Fellow ACS; mem. Am. Soc. Plastic and Reconstructive Surgeons, S.E. Soc. Plastic and Reconstructive Surgeons, Fla. Soc. Plastics and Reconstructive Surgeons (sec.-treas. 1991-92, pres.-elect 1992-93, pres. 1993-94), Fla. Med. Assn., Lipoplasty Soc. N.Am., Am. Soc. for Aesthetic Plastic Surgery, Kiwanis (lt. gov. 1983-84, Kiwanian of Yr. award 1979). Republican. Jewish. Office: Maitland Cosmetic Surgery 451 N Maitland Ave Maitland FL 32751-4725

EISENBERG, HOWARD EDWARD, physician, psychotherapist, educator, consultant; b. Montreal, Que., Can., Aug. 5, 1946; s. Harold and Elsie (Goldbloom) E.; m. Nancy Roberta Jeffries, Jan. 10, 1976; children: Taryn Noelle, Jory Michael, Meredith Kate, Tessa Chloe. BSc with honors in Psychology, McGill U., 1967, MSc, 1971, MDCM, 1972. Intern Sunnybrook Med. Ctr., U. Toronto, 1973; research asst. psychology dept. McGill U., 1966-69, research asst. gerontology unit Alan Meml. Inst. Psychiatry, McGill U., 1968, clin. fellow Clarke Inst. Psychiatry, U. Toronto, 1973; lectr. Centre for Continuing Edn., York U., 1973-78, Sheridan Coll., Oakville, 1974-76; supr. individual directed study Faculty Environ. Studies, York U., 1975; lectr. dept. interdisciplinary studies U. Toronto, 1975; instr. ind. studies program, Innis Coll., U. Toronto, 1975-78, lectr. 1976-81, spl. conf. coordinator, 1977-79, 88-89, lectr. Sch. Continuing Studies, 1977-89; lectr. continuing edn. U. Vt., 1990-92, 95—; assoc. dir. edn. and growth opportunities program York U., 1975-76, dir. E.G.O. program, 1976-78; lectr. Sch. Adult Edn., McMaster U., 1980-89; instr. profl. and mgmt. devel. Humber Coll., 1982-85; pvt. practice psychotherapy and behavioral medicine, Toronto, Ont., 1973-91, Stowe, Vt., 1991—; assoc. prof. dept. family practice, Coll. Med. Univ. Vt., 1993—; cons. staff dept. medicine Copley Hosp., Vt., 1990-96; pres. Synectia Cons., Inc., Toronto, 1980-84, Syntrek, Inc., Stowe, Vt., 1989—, Synectia Prodns., Inc., Toronto, 1974—. Author: Inner Spaces, 1977, The Tranquility Experience, 1987, Stress Mastery for the Real World, 1991, Creative Thinking Tools for Innovation, 1994, Fundamentals of High Performance Teamwork, 1995; contbr. articles to profl. jours. McGill scholar, 1966-67; Quebec scholar, 1967-68; Earle C. Anthony fellow, 1967-68; Ont. Arts Council grantee, 1977. Mem. Ont. Med. Assn. (former chmn. sect. ind. physicians), Vt. State Med. Soc., Acad. Orgnl. and Occupational Psychiatry, Orgnl. Devel. Network, Am. Soc. for Tng. and Develop. Office: Syntrek Inc PO Box 1393 Stowe VT 05672-1393

EISENBERG, HOWARD MICHAEL, neurosurgeon; b. N.Y.C., May 4, 1939; s. Monroe L. and Regina (Fish) E.; children: Nancy M. Hoy, John A.; m. Janet Lee Campbell, Feb. 17, 1982. BA, Syracuse U., 1960; MD, SUNY, N.Y.C., 1964. Diplomate Am. Bd. Neurol. Surgery. Intern N.Y. Hosp., N.Y.C., 1964-65; resident, fellow Cornell U. Med. Sch., N.Y.C., 1964-66; resident in neurosurgery Peter Bent Brigham Hosp., Boston, 1966-70; surgery instr. Harvard U., Boston, 1972-75; assoc. prof. U. Tex. Med. Br., Galveston, 1975-80, prof., chief of neurosurgery, 1980-92; prof., head of neurosurgery, dir. med. svcs./Shock Trauma U. Md., Balt., 1992—, dir. med. svcs. Shock Truama Ctr., 1992—; chmn. neurology a study sect. NIH, Bethesda, Md., 1980-90; numerous vis. professorships and guest lectureships. Mem. editorial bd. Jour. Neurosurgery, 1989—; editor: The Cerebral Microvasulature, 1980, Neurobehavioral Recovery from Head Injury, 1987, Mild Head Injury, 1989, Neurosurgery Clinics of North America-Management of Head Injury, 1991, The Frontal Lobes, 1991; contbr. over 200 articles to profl. jours. Mem. devel. bd. Houston Grand Opera, 1989-92. Lt. comdr. USN, 1970-72. Recipient William Cavernes award Nat. Head Injury Found., 1994, Wakeman award, 1990, numerous grants in field. Mem. ACS (chair neurosurg. adv. coun.), Am. Bd. Neurol. Surgery (mem. bd. dirs., sec.-treas., bd. dirs. 1990—, chmn. 1995—), Soc. Neurol. Surgeons, Acad. Neurol. Surgeons, Am. Surgical Assn., Cosmos Club, Annapolis Yacht Club, N.Y. Yacht Club. Office: U Md Med Systems Divsn Neurosurgery 22 S Greene St Rm S10b11 Baltimore MD 21201-1544

EISENBERG, JOHN MEYER, physician, educator; b. Atlanta, Sept. 24, 1946; s. Irvin and Roslyn Furchgott (Karesh) E. AB magna cum laude, Princeton U., 1968; MD, Washington U., 1972; MBA with distinction, U. Pa., 1976. Intern, resident in medicine Hosp. of U. Pa., 1972-75, fellow, 1975-77; assoc. dir. med. affairs Nat. Health Care Mgmt. Ctr., 1976-78; asst. prof. medicine U. Pa., Phila., 1976-78, Sol Katz asst. prof. gen. medicine, 1978-81, Sol Katz assoc. prof., 1981-86, Sol Katz prof., 1986-92, chief sect. gen. internal medicine, 1978-92, interim chmn. dept. medicine, 1990-91; chmn. dept. medicine Georgetown U., Washington, 1992—, Anton and Margaret Fuisz prof. medicine, physician-in-chief, 1992—; cons. Nat. Ctr. for Health Svcs. Rsch., 1981-85; commr. Physician Payment Rev. Commn., 1986-95, chmn., 1993-95; program dir. Robert Wood Johnson Found. Generalist Physician Faculty Scholars Program, 1992—. Editor: The Physicians Practice, 1980; author: Doctors' Decisions and the Cost of Medical Care, 1986, Paying Physicians, 1992; mem. editorial bd. Pharmacoeconomics, Medicine, Am. Jour. Medicine; contbr. articles in field to profl. jours. Recipient Alumni Achievement award Wharton Sch., U. Pa., 1992; Robert Wood Johnson Found. clin. scholar, 1974-77; named Disting. Internist of Yr., Am. Soc. Internal Medicine, 1993. Fellow ACP (Master, bd. regents 1985-87, chmn. health care financing subcom. 1984-89), Coun. of Med. Socs. (chmn. 1985-87); mem. Soc. Gen. Internal Medicine (sec.-treas. 1978-80, pres. 1982-83, Glaser award 1995), Soc. Med. Decision Making (v.p. 1980-81), Assn. Program Dirs. Internal Medicine (coun. 1987-90), Am. Public Health Assn., Am. Fedn. Clin. Rsch., Assn. Health Svcs. Rsch. (sec. 1989-90, pres. 1991-92), Found. Health Svcs. Rsch. (pres. 1992-93, Alpha Ctr. bd. dirs., 1992-95), Am. Bd. Internal Medicine (bd. govs. 1987-93, exec. com. 1992-93), Inst. Medicine., Assn. Am. Physicians, Am. Soc. Clin. Investigation, Am. Soc. Internal Med., Am. Clin. and Climatological Assn, Washington Acad. Medicine, Interurban Club, Cosmos Club. Office: Georgetown Univ Med Ctr Dept Medicine 5-PHC 3800 Reservoir Rd NW Washington DC 20007-2196

EISENBERG, JOSEPH MARTIN, psychologist; b. Bklyn., June 19, 1944; s. David and Dora (Levine) E.; B.A. in Psychology magna cum laude, C. W. Post Coll., 1966; M.A. in Psychology, U. Alta., 1969, Ph.D. in Psychology, 1971; m. Susan Joan Kahn, Aug. 16, 1980; children: Ian, Lara, Jason, Davida. Psychol. diagnostician, counselor dept. psychology U. Alta. (Can.), 1969-70; field researcher Dept. youth Alta., 1967-69; assoc. dir. Toronto (Ont.) YMCA Centre for Counseling and Human Relations, 1970-71; counselor, cons. York Regional Sch. Nursing, Toronto, 1970-71; chief psychologist Salvation Army House of Concord, Toronto, 1971-72; dir. outpatient service St. Vincent Hosp. Community Mental Health Center, Erie, Pa., 1972-73; dir. Erie County Center for Learning Disabilities, 1973-74; pvt. practice psychology, Erie and Balt., 1972—; v.p. in charge personnel and communications Bridge Energy Corp., Balt., 1981—; pres. Reason House, Balt., 1981—; spl. cons. Md. Children and Family Services, Inc.; mem. profl. adv. bds. Balt. Assn. Children with Learning Disabilities, Feingold Assn.; cons. Mormac Ltd., 1979—; forensic cons. Howard County/Balt. County/Carroll County, Office of Public Defenders and Balt. City Solicitor's Office, 1977—. Chmn., Carroll County Child Abuse Consultation Com., 1978-80; dir. Psychol. Services for the Metabolic Nutrition Program, 1986-89; mem. profl. adv. bd. Catonsville Group Home, 1980-81. Recipient Richard P. Runyon award, 1966; cert., lic., Md.; cert. clin. hypnotherapist, Negotiation Inst. Mem. Am. Psychol. Assn., Md. Psychol. Assn., Assn. Advancement of Psychology, Balt. Psychol. Assn., Am. Bd. Profl. Disability Cons., Am. Bd. Cert. Managed Care Providers, Balt. County C. of C. (exec. dialogue program), Psi Chi, Phi Theta. Co-author computer software; contbr. articles to profl. jours. Office: 101 E Chesapeake Ave Ste 201 Baltimore MD 21286-5339

EISENBERG, KAREN SUE BYER, nurse; b. Bklyn., Mar. 11, 1954; d. Marvin and Florence (Beck) Byer; m. Howard Eisenberg, May 11, 1974; children: Carly Beth, Mariel Bryn. Diploma, L.I. Coll. Hosp. Sch. Nursing, 1973; BS in Nursing, L.I. U., 1976, M in Profl. Studies, 1977. Nurse recovery room and surg. intensive care unit Downstate Med. Ctr., Bklyn., 1973-75; utilization rev. analyst Bezallel Health Related Facility, Far Rockaway, N.Y., 1975-76; utilization rev. analyst, R.N. supr. Seagirt Health Related Facility, Far Rockaway, 1976; staff nurse neurosurg. and rehab. nursing Downstate Med. Ctr., Bklyn., 1978, nurse intensive care unit, 1978-79; asst. nursing dir. pathology, clin. rsch. assoc. Rsch. Found., Bklyn., 1979-90; instrl. support specialist pathology Health Sci. Ctr. SUNY, Bklyn., 1990-92; nurse practitioner pathology SUNY Rsch. Found., Bklyn., 1992-95; nurse rsch. coord. surgery SUNY Health Sci. Ctr., Bklyn., 1995—. Contbr. articles to profl. jours. Mem. Oncology Nursing Soc., Am. Nurses Assn., N.Y. State Nurses Assn., N.Y. Acad. Scis., L.I. Coll. Hosp. Alumnae Assn. Office: 450 Clarkson Ave Brooklyn NY 11203-2012

EISENBERG, LEON, psychiatrist, educator; b. Phila., Aug. 8, 1922; s. Morris and and Elizabeth (Sabreen) E.; m. Ruth Harriet Bleier, June 11, 1948 (div. 1967); children: Mark Philip, Kathy Bleier; m. Carola Blitzman Guttmacher, Aug. 31, 1967; children: Laurence, Alan. AB, U. Pa., 1944, MD, 1946; MA (hon.), Harvard U., 1967; DSc (hon.), U. Manchester, Eng., 1973, U. Mass., 1991. Diplomate: in child psychiatry and psychiatry Am. Bd. Psychiatry and Neurology. Intern Mt. Sinai Hosp., N.Y.C., 1946-47; instr. physiology U. Pa., 1947-48; resident psychiatry Sheppard-Pratt Hosp., Towson, Md., 1950-52; with Johns Hopkins, 1952-67, prof. child psychiatry Med. Sch., 1961-67; psychiatrist-in-charge children's psychiat. service Harriet Lane Home, 1958-67; prof. psychiatry Harvard U. Med. Sch., Boston, 1967—, Maude and Lillian Presley prof. psychiatry, 1975-80, chmn. exec. com. dept. psychiatry, 1973-80, Maude and Lillian Presley prof. social medicine, 1980-93, chmn. dept., 1980-91, prof. of social medicine emeritus, 1993—; psychiatrist-in-chief Mass. Gen. Hosp., 1967-74, mem. bd. consultation, 1974—; sr. assoc. in psychiatry Children's Hosp., Boston, 1974—; prof. emeritus, 1993—; Paley lectr. Cornell U., 1983; Schilder lectr. NYU, 1984; Eli Robins lectr. Washington U., St. Louis, 1985; vis. lectr. Yale U., 1987; R.W. Johnson vis. prof. U. Rochester, 1987; Carolyn Voorsanger lectr. Stanford U. Med. Sch., 1989; Willard Sears Simpkins lectr. Johns Hopkins U., 1989; William Potter lectr. Thomas Jefferson U., 1992; vis. prof. McMaster U., Can., 1991, Charles U. Prague; psychiat. cons. Crownsville (Md.) State Hosp., 1954-58, Rosewood State Tng. Sch., Owings Mills, Md., 1957-60, Balt. City Hosp., 1959-62, Children's Guild, Balt., 1954-61; cons. Sinai Hosp., Balt., 1963-67; Mapother-Lewis ann. lectr. Maudsley Hosp., London, 1977; Baan Meml. lectr. Netherlands Psychiat. Soc., Amsterdam, 1978; Royal Soc. Medicine vis. prof., London, 1983; mem. subcom. psychiat. nomenclature com. vital stats. USPHS; chmn. WHO Conf. Devel. Regulation, 1964-67; mem. Joint Commn. Mental Health of Children; cons. divsn. mental health WHO, 1974—, chmn. sci. group on evaluation of psychiat. treatment, 1989; mem. adv. com. to dir. NIH, 1977-80; lectr. Can. Royal Coll. Psychiatry, 1993, Italian Soc. for Biol. Psychiatry, Cagliari, Sardinia, 1994; Richard Goldbloom lectr. Dalhousie U., Halifax, N.S., Can., 1995; Wolfe Adler lectr. Sheppard-Pratt Hosp. Sys., Balt., 1995; spl. lectr. Health of the Child on the Eve of the Year 2000, Bologna, Italy, 1995. Editor Am. Jour. Orthopsychiatry, 1963-73; editorial bd.: Culture, Medicine and Psychiatry, Psychol. Medicine, Jour. Psychiat. Research. Capt. M.C., U.S. Army, 1948-50. Recipient Theobald Smith award Albany Med. Coll., 1979, Orton award Orton Soc., 1980, Disting. Alumnus award U. Pa., 1992, Presdl. Commendation Am. Psychiat. Assn., 1992, Agnes Purchell McGavin award, 1994, Camille Cosby World of Children award Judge Baker Children's Ctr., 1994, Salmon medal N.Y. Acad. Medicine, 1995, Mumford award and lecture, 1996. Fellow AAAS, Am. Psychiat. Assn. (life, trustee 1973-76), Am. Orthopsychiat. Assn. (life, Ittleson Meml. award 1996), Soc. Rsch. Child Devel., Royal Coll. Psychiatrists (hon., Eli Lilly lectr. 1986), Royal Soc. Medicine; mem. Inst. Medicine of NAS (coun. 1975-77, program and membership coms. 1979-82, bd. on health sci. policy 1989-91, Rhoda and Bernard Sarnat prize in mental health 1996), AAUP (past pres. Johns Hopkins chpt.), Am. Acad. Pediatrics (Aldrich award 1980, Dale Richmond lectr. 1989), Am. Pediatric Soc., Can. Pediatric Soc. (Queen Elizabeth II lectr. 1986), Assn. Rsch. Nervous and Mental Disease, Am. Psychopath. Assn., Md. Psychiat. Soc. (past pres.), Am. Acad. Arts and Scis. (communication sec. 1995—), Psychiat. Rsch. Soc. (past pres.), Soc. Neurosci., Mass. Med. Soc., Greek Soc. Neurology and Psychiatry (hon.), Ecuadorean Soc. Neurosci. (hon.), Johns Hopkins Soc. Scholars, Phi Beta Kappa (chpt. pres. 1958, volar 1994-95), I.O.M. (chair com. on planned childbearing 1993-95), Sigma Xi, Alpha Omega Alpha (lectr. Jefferson Med. Coll. 1994). Home: 9 Clement Cir Cambridge MA 02138-2205 Office: Harvard U Med Sch Dept Social Medicine Boston MA 02115

EISENBERG, RICHARD MARTIN, pharmacology educator; b. Weehawken, N.J., May 15, 1942; s. Herbert and Evelyn (Stecker) E.; m. Marsha Eisenberg, July 3, 1966; children: Marla, Aaron, Shana. BA, UCLA, 1963, MS, 1967, PhD, 1970; postgrad., U. Rochester, 1970-71. Asst. prof. pharmacology U. Minn., Duluth, 1971-76, assoc. prof., 1976-77, assoc. prof., acting dept. head, 1977-80, assoc. prof., dept. head, 1980-85, prof., dept. head, 1985—. Author-developer: (computer software) Mac Pharmacology, Mac MedVirology, Mac BrainLesion; presenter in field; contbr. articles to profl. jours. Recipient numerous rsch. grants Nat. Inst. Drug Abuse, 1978—, other instns., 1975—. Mem. Am. Soc. Pharmacology and Exptl. Therapeutics, Assn. Med. Sch. Pharmacology, Endocrine Soc., Western Pharmacology Soc., Coll. on Problems of Drug Dependence. Office: U Minn Duluth Sch Medicine Dept Pharmacology 10 University Dr Duluth MN 55812

EISENBERG, RONALD LEE, radiologist; b. Phila., July 11, 1945; s. Milton and Betty (Klein) E.; m. Zina Leah Schiff; 2 children. AB, U. Pa., 1965, MD, 1965. Diplomate Am. Bd. Radiology. Staff radiologist VA Med. Ctr., San Francisco, 1975-80; prof. and chmn. dept. radiology La. State U., Shreveport, 1980-91; chmn. dept. radiology Highland Hosp., Oakland, Calif., 1991—. Author: Gastrointestinal Radiology, 1982, 3d edit., 1996, Diagnostic Imaging in Internal Medicine, 1985, Diagnostic Imaging in Surgery, 1986, Clinical Imaging: An Atlas of Differential Diagnosis, 1987, Atlas of Differential Diagnoses, 1988, Radiology: An Illustrated History, 1992, others; contbr. over 70 articles to profl. jours. Maj. U.S. Army, 1971-73. Named Man of the Yr., Am. Physicians Fellowship, Boston, 1987. Fellow Am. Coll. Radiology; mem. Radiol. Soc. N.Am., Am. Roentgen Ray Soc., Assn. of Univ. Radiologists, Soc. for Gastrointestinal Radiology, So. Med. Assn., Am. Coll. Radiology, Ark-La-Tex Radiol. Soc. Office: Highland Hosp Dept Radiology 1411 E 31st St Oakland CA 94602-1018

EISENBERG, SIDNEY EDWIN, retired physician and cardiologist; b. New Britain, Conn., Jan. 15, 1913; s. Julius and Bertha (Kranowitz) E.; married; children: Emily Louise, Richard Alan. BA, Wesleyan U., Middletown, Conn., 1935; MD, U. Rochester, 1939. Diplomate Am. Bd. Internal Medicine. Intern New Britain Gen. Hosp., 1939-40; resident New Britan Gen. Hosp., 1940-42; sr. attending physician, cardiologist New Britain Gen. Hosp., 1950-88, dep. chief medicine, 1966-70; resident Yale New Haven Hosp., 1942-45; asst. clin. prof. Med. Sch. Yale U., New Haven, 1945-60. Contbr. articles to profl. jours. Fellow ACP; mem. Phi Beta Kappa, Sigma Xi. Home: 1 Del Pond Dr Apt 354 Canton MA 02021-2759

EISENBERG, TED STEVEN, plastic and reconstructive surgeon; b. Phila., June 21, 1952; s. Martin John and Mitzi (Singer) E.; m. Joyce Janet Kirschner, Sept. 1, 1973; children: Ben, Samantha. BS, Pa. State U., 1972; DO, Phila. Coll. Osteo. Medicine, 1976. Diplomate Nat. Bd. Examiners for Osteo. Physicians and Surgeons; Bd. cert. in Osteo. Plastic Surgery, Laser Surgery, Gen. Surgery; lic. physician, N.Y., Pa. Intern North Miami Beach Osteo. Gen. Hosp., 1976-77; resident in gen. surgery Met. Hosp., Phila., 1977-81; resident in hand surgery Hand Rehab. Ctr./Jefferson U., Phila., 1981; preceptee in plastic surgery Rolling Hill and Albert Einstein Med. Ctrs., Phila., 1983-85; practice plastic and reconstructive surgery Phila. area, 1985—; assoc. prof. Phila. Coll. Osteo. Medicine, 1991—; attending staff physician Grad. Hosp., John F. Kennedy Hosp., Northeastern Hosp., Suburban Genl. Hosp., others; cons. staff physician Delaware Valley Med. Ctr., Springfield Hosp.; lectr. in field. Contbr. numerous articles to profl. jours. Recipient numerous awards for sci. exhibits and publs. Fellow Am. Coll. Osteo. Surgeons; mem. Am. Acad. Aesthetic and Restorative Surgery (charter), Am. Osteo. Assn., Jefferson Hand Club (charter), Pa. Osteo. Med. Assn., Philadelphia County Osteo. Soc., Phila. Coll. Osteo. Medicine Alumni Assn. (life), Lambda Omicron Gamma (v.p. 1993-94). Office: 1331 E Wyoming Ave Ste 3050 Philadelphia PA 19124-3808

EISENBERGER, MARIO ALFREDO, oncology educator, physician; b. Rio de Janeiro, Mar. 16, 1949; came to U.S., 1973; s. Fritz Herbert and Anneliese (Lewin) E.; m. Johanna Jacomina Magdalena Hazenoot, Dec. 18, 1976. BS, Brazil-Am. Coll., 1966; MD, Fed. U. Rio de Janeiro, 1972. Diplomate Am. Bd. Internal Medicine, Am. Bd. Med. Oncology. Intern in medicine Michael Reese Hosp., Chgo., 1973-74, resident, 1974-75, fellow in hematology, 1975-76; fellow in oncology U. Miami (Fla.), 1976-78, asst. prof. hematology and oncology, 1980-82; pvt. practice Lauderdale Lakes, Fla., 1978-80; sr. investigator Nat. Cancer Inst., NIH, Bethesda, Md., 1982-84; asst. prof. medicine and oncology U. Md. Cancer Ctr., Balt., 1984-88, assoc. prof., 1988-93; prof. Medicine and Oncology, 1993; assoc. prof. oncology and urology Johns Hopkins U., 1993—; chief oncology sect. Balt. VA Hosp., 1984-87; participant nat. and internat. meetings; lectr. and researcher in field. Contbr. articles and abstracts to med. jours., chpts. to books. Mem. Am. Soc. Clin. Oncology (several grants/contracts), Am. Fedn. Clin. Rsch., S.W. Oncology Group (chairperson advanced prostate cancer com. 1988-94, vice chmn. genito-urinary com. 1990—). Jewish. Home: 4407 Bedford Pl Baltimore MD 21218-1002 Office: Johns Hopkins Oncology Ctr 600 N Wolfe St Rm 173 Baltimore MD 21205-2110

EISENBUD, MERRIL, engineer, scientist; b. N.Y.C., Mar. 18, 1915; s. Kalman and Leonora (Kopaloff) E.; m. Irma Onish, Jan. 22, 1939; children: Elliott, Michael, Fredrick. BSEE, NYU, 1936; ScD (hon.), Fairleigh Dickinson U., 1960; DHC, Cath. U., Rio de Janiero. Indsl. hygienist Liberty Mut. Ins. Co., 1936-47; faculty Inst. Environ. Medicine, NYU Med. Ctr., 1947-85, prof., dir. lab. environ. studies, 1959-84, prof. emeritus, 1984—; adj. prof. dept. environ. scis. and engring. U. N.C., 1985—; adminstr. N.Y.C. EPA, 1968-70; scholar-in-residence Duke U. Med. ctr., Durham, N.C., 1985—; dir. health safety lab. AEC, 1947-59; mem. Nat. Coun. Radiation Protection and Measurements, 1965-85, dir., 1971-76, hon. mem., 1985—; mem. expert panel on radiation hazards WHO, 1956-80, N.Y. State Health Adv. Coun., 1975-80. Author: Environment, Technology, and Health, 1979, Environmental Radioactivity, 3d edit., 1987, Environmental Odyssey, 1990. Mem. bd. mgrs. State Cmty. Aid Assn.; mem. adv. coun. Electric Power Rsch. Inst., Inst. Nuclear Power Ops. Recipient Gold medal AEC, 1974, Hermann Biggs medal N.Y. State Pub. Health Assn., Arthur Holly Compton award Am. Nuclear Soc., Power Division Life award Am. Inst. Elec. and Electronic Engrs., Disting. Achievement award Hudson River Environ. Soc., 1985. Fellow AAAS, N.Y. Acad. Scis. (hon. life mem., gov., v.p. 1979-80), N.Y. Acad. Medicine; mem. Nat. Acad. Engring., Health Physics Soc. (pres. 1965-66, Disting. Achievement award 1984), Am. Indsl. Hygiene Assn., Radiation Research Soc., Am. Bd. Health Physics, Brazilian Acad. Scis. (corr.). Club: Cosmos (Washington). Home: 340 Carolina Meadows Villa Chapel Hill NC 27514-7519

EISENMAN, RUSSELL, psychology educator; b. Savannah, Ga., Apr. 17, 1940; s. Abram and Georgia (Russell) E.; m. Frances Bradley, June 12, 1965 (div. Dec. 1972); children: David, Susan. Student, U. N.C., 1958; BA, Oglethorpe U., 1962; MS, U. Ga., 1963, PhD, 1966. Asst. to assoc. prof. Temple U., Phila., 1966-88; sr. clin. psychologist State of Calif., Norwalk, 1988-90; assoc. prof. psychology McNeese State U., Lake Charles, La., 1990—; vis. assoc. prof. U. Calif., Santa Cruz, 1972-73; rsch. assoc. Haverford (Pa.) Coll., 1970-71, Hahnemann Med. Coll. and Hosp., Phila., 1971-72. Author: From Crime to Creativity, 1991, Studies in Personality Social and Clinical Psychology, 1994, Political Issues and Social Problems, 1994, Contemporary Social Issues, 1994, Readings in Psychology, 1995, Readings for Introduction to Abnormal and Social Psychology, 1995; co-author: The New Families, 1972. Recipient Cert. of Merit, Kappa Alpha Psi. Mem. Nat. Assn. Creative Children and Adults, Southwestern La. Psychol. Assn. (pres. 1992), Internat. Assn. Correctional Tng. Pers., Soc. Advancement Social Psychology. Office: McNeese State U Dept Psychology Lake Charles LA 70609-1895

EISENMAN, TRUDY FOX, dermatologist; b. Chgo., Oct. 14, 1940; d. Nathan Henry and Bernice (Greenberg) Fox; student U. Ill. at Navy Pier, Chgo., 1958-60; M.D., U. Ill., 1964; m. Theodore S. Eisenman, Aug. 19, 1962 (div. 1985); children: Lawrence, Robert. Rotating intern Milw. County Gen. Hosp., 1964-65, med. resident, 1965-66; resident in dermatology Northwestern U. Med. Sch., Chgo., 1970-73, instr., 1973—; practice medicine specializing in dermatology, Chgo., 1973—; attending dermatologist Louis A. Weiss Meml. Hosp., Chgo., 1973—. Diplomate Am. Bd. Dermatology. Fellow Am. Acad. Dermatology; mem. Chgo. Dermatol. Soc., Am. Med. Women's Assn., AMA, Chgo. Med. Soc., Alpha Omega Alpha. Office: 4640 N Marine Dr Chicago IL 60640-5719

EISENSON, JON, psychologist, educator, writer; b. N.Y.C., Dec. 17, 1907; s. Abraham Eli and Sarah E.; m. Eileen Krinsky, Apr. 10, 1977; children by previous marriage: Elinore Lurie, Arthur M. B.S., CCNY, 1928; M.A., Columbia U., 1930, Ph.D., 1935. Lic. psychologist, Calif. Faculty; Bklyn. Coll., 1935-42; prof., dir. Speech and Hearing Ctr., Queens Coll., 1946-62; prof. speech and hearing sci. Stanford U., 1962-73, prof. emeritus, 1973—, disting. prof., 1973-81; pvt. practice communication consulting, Palo Alto, Calif., 1980—; lectr. Fromm Inst. Lifelong Learning U. San Francisco, 1982; Disting. prof., San Francisco State U., 1973-81. Author: The Psychology of Speech, 1983, Basic Speech, 1950, revised, 1975, Voice and Diction: A Program for Improvement, 1957, revised, 1996; (with J.J. Auer, J. Irwin) Psychology of Communication, 1963; Stuttering: A Symposium, 1958; Stuttering: A Second Symposium, 1975; Is My Child's Speech Normal?, 1976; Communicative Disorders in Children, 1983; Reading for Meaning, 1984; Aphasia and Related Disorders in Children, 1984, Adult Aphasia, 2d edit., 1984; A Special Zoo, 1985; Language and Speech Disorders in Children, 1986, Examining for Aphesia, 3d edit., 1995, How to Speak American English, 1996. Served to maj. U.S. Army, 1942-46. Fellow Am. Speech Lang. Hearing Assn., Am. Psychol. Assn; mem. Internat. Neuropsychology Soc., Am. Speech and Hearing Assn. (pres. 1958, Honors, 1962), Phi Beta Kappa. Home and Office: 82 Pearce Mitchell Pl Stanford CA 94305

EISENSTADT, J. MARVIN, clinical psychologist; b. N.Y.C., Oct. 26, 1936; s. Hyman and Anna (Granat) E.; m. Arlene Rosner, Jan. 28, 1962; children: Ellen, Felicia. BS, CCNY, 1959; PhD, Adelphi U., 1964. Lic. psychologist, N.Y., Calif. Staff clin. psychologist Modesto (Calif.) State Hosp., 1964-66; assoc. psychologist Creedmoor State Hosp., Queens Village, N.Y., 1966-71; clin. psychologist Mid-Nassau Community Guidance Ctr., Hicksville, N.Y., 1966-72; pvt. practice Syosset and Amityville, N.Y., 1965—; chief psychologist Cen. Nassau Guidance and Counseling Svcs., Hicksville, 1972-93; sr. psychologist South Oaks Hosp., Amityville, 1991—; cons. L.I. Lighting Co., Hicksville, 1981-84, Jour. Rsch. in Personality, 1982; faculty assoc. in psychology Hofstra U., Hempstead, N.Y., 1975-83, 86-90, Adelphi U., Garden City, N.Y., 1982-85, Yeshiva U., Bronx, N.Y., 1984-86; profl. adv. bd. doctoral program in profl. psychology L.I. U., Brookville, 1987-93. Author: Parental Loss and Achievement, 1989; editor L.I. Mental Health Clinician jour., 1987-93; contbr. articles to profl. jours. Fellow Am. Orthopsychiat. Assn.; mem. AAAS, APA, Nassau County Psychol. Assn. (exec. bd., pres. 1986-89), Suffolk County Psychol. Assn., Soc. Personality Assessment, Found. Thanatology, Am. Hist. Assn., N.Y. State Psychol. Assn. Office: South Oaks Hosp 400 Sunrise Hwy Amityville NY 11701-2508

EISENSTAT, THEODORE ELLIS, colon and rectal surgeon, educator; b. N.Y.C., Sept. 24, 1942; m. Sharon Diane Leonard, July, 1966; children: Maren Elise, Loren Aline. BA, Vanderbilt U., 1964; MD, NYU, 1968. Diplomate Am. Bd. Surgery, Am. Bd. Colon and Rectal Surgery, Nat. Bd. Med. Examiners; lic. surgeon Md., N.J., Pa. Rotating intern St. Vincent's Hosp., Worcester, Mass., 1968-69; resident in surgery Thomas Jefferson U. Hosp., Phila., 1969-71; chief resident in surgery Pa. Hosp., Phila., 1971-73; fellow in colon and rectal surgery Muhlenberg Hosp.-Robert Wood Johnson Sch. Medicine, N.J., 1977-78; dir. surg. endoscopy U. Md., 1975-80, dir. colon & rectal svc., 1976-80; asst. prof. surgery U. Md. Sch. Medicine, 1975-80; sr. attending surgeon Muhlenberg Regional Med. Ctr., Plainfield, N.J., 1979—, John F. Kennedy Med. Ctr., Edison, N.J., 1979—; clin. assoc prof. surgery U. Medicine and Dentistry of N.J., Newark, 1981—; clin. assoc. prof. surgery Robert Wood Johnson Med. Sch. U. Medicine and Dentistry of N.J., New Brunswick, N.J., 1979-91; clin. prof. surgery U. Medicine and Dentistry of N.J., New Brunswick, 1991—, dir. colon and rectal residency program, 1993—; cons. surgeon Lock Raven VA Hosp., Balt., 1975-80, U.S. Army, Kimbrough Army Hosp., Ft. Meade, Md., 1975-80; bd. dirs. ACS rep. Am. Bd. Colon and Rectal Surgery, 1990-96, pres., 1995-96; cons. Robert Wood Johnson U. Hosp., New Brunswick, N.J., 1984—; exhibitor and presenter in field; vis. prof. U. Md. Sch. Medicine, 1983, Abington (Pa.) Meml. Hosp., 1985, York (Pa.) Hosp., 1990, Pa. Hosp., Phila., 1990, others. Book reviewer: Colon and Rectal Surgery, 2d edit., 1989, Handbook of pharm. drugs for Am. Pharm. Assn., 1982—; contbr. articles to profl. jours. Maj. U.S. Army, 1973-75. Fellow ACS (adv. coun. colon and rectal surgery), Am. Soc. Colon and Rectal Surgeons (Walter A. Fansler award 1977, Purdue Frederick fellow 1977, 1st prize sci. exhibit 1979); mem. AMA, Soc. for Surgery of Alimentary Tract, Assn. for Acad. Surgery, Soc. Am. Gastrointestinal Endoscopic Surgeons (founder 1981, bd. govs. 1986-89), Am. Soc. Gastrointestinal Endoscopy, N.Y. Soc. Colon and Rectal Surgeons (mem. coun. 1983-85, sec.-treas. 1986-87, v.p. 1988-89, pres. 1990-92, 1st prize film 1978), Pa. Soc. Colon. and Rectal Surgeons, N.J. Soc. Colon and Rectal Surgeons (sec.-treas. 1983-85, pres. 1989-90), N.J. Soc. Gastroenterology, N.J. Soc. Gastrointestinal Endoscopy, Assn. Mil. Surgeons U.S., Soc. Surgeons N.J., Crohn's and Colitis Found. Am. Presbyterian. Office: Assoc Colon & Rectal Surgeons 1010 Park Ave Plainfield NJ 07060

EISENSTEIN, REUBEN, pathology educator; b. Bklyn., May 3, 1929; s. Abraham Baruch and Fanny (Rivlin) E.; m. Naomi Sobel, July 5, 1959; children: Eli Michael, Margaret Louise, Daniel Mark, Miriam Lisa. BS, Tulane U., 1949; MD, La. State U., 1959. From asst. prof. to prof. U. Ill., Chgo., 1957-68; prof. Rush Med. Coll., Chgo., 1968-75, Northwestern U., Chgo., 1975-80; prof. dept. pathology U. Wis., Milw., 1980—; pathologist Sinai-Samaritan Med. Ctr., Milw.; mem. study sect. NIH, Bethesda, Md., 1967-71, mem. breast cancer task force, 1986-88; cons. Leukemia Rsch. Found., Chgo., 1981-83. Contbr. over 100 articles to profl. publs. Capt. U.S. Army, 1955-57. Mem. Am. Assn. Pathologists, Am. Heart Assn., Internat. Acad. Pathology, Am. Soc. Clin. Pathology. Home: 718 E Daisy Ln Milwaukee WI 53217-3632 Office: Sinai-Samaritan Med Ctr 950 N 12th St Milwaukee WI 53233

EISENSTEIN, SAM, pediatric dentist; b. Montreal, Que., Can., Jan. 12, 1936; came to U.S., 1964; s. Isaac and Eva (Katz) E.; m. Esther Benjamin, June 24, 1962; children: Sandra Toby, Lana Rachel, Jeffrey Joshua. BSc, Sir George Williams Coll., 1957; MSc, McGill U., 1959, PhD, 1963; DMD, Tufts U., 1973. Rsch. asst. Royal Victoria Hosp., Montreal, 1962-64; postdoctoral trainee Wistar Inst., Phila., 1964-65; rsch. assoc. Albert Einstein Med. Ctr., Phila., 1965-66, Variety Children's Rsch. Found., Miami, Fla., 1966-69; dental resident Children's Hosp., Boston, 1973-75; pediatric dentistry fellow Harvard U. Sch. Dental Medicine, 1974-75; pvt. practice pediatric dentistry, South Weymouth, Mass., 1975-81, Miami, 1981—; clin. asst. in pedodontics Boston Children's Hosp., 1976-80; clin. instr. Harvard Sch. Dental Medicine, Boston, 1978-80, Tufts Sch. Dental Medicine, Boston, 1980-81; mem. attending staff Miami Children's Hosp., 1982—. Mem. ADA, Am. Soc. Dentistry for Children (cert. of merit 1973), Am. Acad. Pediatric Dentistry, Sigma Xi, Alpha Omega Delta, Omicron Kappa Epsilon. Jewish. Avocations: photography, model railroading, stamp collecting. Home: 5023 Grant St Hollywood FL 33021-5239 Office: 12333 NW 18th St # 4 Pembroke Pines FL 33026

EISENSTEIN, THEODORE DONALD, pediatrician; b. N.Y.C., July 4, 1930; s. Harry and Myra (Drexler) E.; married; children: Janet, Stephen. Student, NYU, 1948-49; A.B., Johns Hopkins U., 1952; M.D., Albany Med. Coll., 1956. Diplomate Am. Bd. Pediatrics. Pediatric intern Kings County Med. Ctr., Bklyn., 1956-57; resident in pediatrics N.Y. Hosp., N.Y.C., 1957-59; NIH vis. fellow in pediatric endocrinology Columbia-Presbyn. Med. Ctr., N.Y.C., 1961-62; practice medicine specializing in pediatrics West Caldwell, N.J., 1962—; full attending staff St. Barnabas Med. Ctr.; v.p. Pediatric Assos. West Essex, P.A.; asst. clin. prof. pediatrics Columbia U. Coll. Phys. and Surg., 1970—; clin. asst. prof. pediatrics N.J. Coll. Medicine and Dentistry, Rutgers U., 1970—. Research on pediatric endocrinology, human growth hormone. Mem. alumni coun. N.Y. Hosp.-Cornell Med. Ctr. Served with M.C., USAF, 1959-61. Fellow Am. Acad. Pediatrics; mem. AMA, Acad. Medicine N.J., Am. Diabetes Assn., AAAS, Soc. Practitioners Columbia-Presbyn. Med. Ctr., Albany Med. Coll. Alumni Assn., Am. Physicians Fellowship, N.J. Med. Sch. Faculty Orgn. Jewish. Home: 7 Byron Rd North Caldwell NJ 07006 Office: St Barnabas Med Ctr Old Short Hills Rd Livingston NJ 07039

EISLER, RONALD, biologist; b. N.Y.C., Feb. 23, 1932; s. Harry A. and Ann (Brand) E.; m. Jeannette Lustig, Aug. 29, 1963; children: David, Charles. BA, NYU, 1952; MS, U. Wash., 1957, PhD, 1961. Radiochemist U. Wash. Lab. Radiation Ecology, Seattle, 1958-61; fishery rsch. biologist U.S. Fish and Wildlife Svc., Highlands, N.J., 1961-66; bioscience advisor U.S. Fish and Wildlife Svc., Washington, 1979-84; sr. rsch. biologist U.S. Fish and Wildlife Svc./Nat. Biol. Survey, Laurel, Md., 1984—; rsch. aquatic toxicologist U.S. EPA, Narragansett, R.I., 1966-79; adj. prof. George Mason U., 1989—, Am. Univ., 1980-89, U. R.I., 1970-79; vis. prof. Hebrew U. of Jerusalem, 1972-73. Editorial advisor Marine Ecology Progress series, 1980—; assoc. editor: Transactions of the American Fisheries Soc., 1973-77; author: Trace Metal Concentrations in Marine Organisms, 1981; contbr. articles to profl. jours., chpts. to books in field. Cpl. AMEDS, 1953-55. Office: US Nat Biol Survey Patuxent Wildlife Rsch Ctr Laurel MD 20708

EISMAN, WAYNE BROOK, otolaryngologist; b. Springfield, Mass., Apr. 12, 1948; s. Sidney and Evelyn Pearl (Berger) E.; m. Susan Ellen Jaffe, May 22, 1977; children: Matthew, Jesse, Evan. BA, U. Mass., 1971; MD, Baylor U., 1975. Intern NYU, 1976-77; resident in otolaryngology Mt. Sinai Sch. Medicine, N.Y.C., 1977-80; pvt. practice Westchester Otolaryngology, White Plains, N.Y., 1983—; chmn. dept. otolaryngology White Plains Hosp., 1992—. Trustee, pres. Windward Sch., White Plains, 1987—. Mem. N.Y. State Med. Soc., Westchester County Med. Soc. (chmn. div. otolaryngology 1991—). Office: 79 E Post Rd White Plains NY 10601

EISNER, EUGENE M., ophthalmologist; b. Detroit, Oct. 23, 1942; s. Milton and Sophie (Tenner) E.; m. Karen Sue, Apr. 4, 1971; children: Brian, Lori. Student, U. Mich., 1963, MD, 1967. Intern Orange (Calif.) Gen. Hosp., 1967-68; resident Henry Ford Hosp., Detroit, 1968-72; ophthalmologist U.S. Navy, Bethesda, Md., 1972-74, Miami, 1974—, Ctr. for Excellence in Eye Care, Miami, 1996—. Home: 10250 SW 125th St Miami FL 33176 Office: 7800 SW 87th Ave Ste A100 Miami FL 33173 Also: Ctr Excellence Eye Care 8940 N Kendall Dr 4th Floor Miami FL 33176

EISNER, GEORG MICHAEL, ophthalmology educator; b. Basel, Switzerland, Apr. 8, 1930; s. Willy and Irma (Guggenheim) E.; m. Susanne Kartagener, Mar. 6, 1960; children: Daniel, Miriam, Simone. MD, U. Basel, 1959; postgrad., U. Eye Hosp., Bern, Switzerland, 1964. Docent U. Bern, 1971-75, prof. ophthalmology, 1975-93, dean faculty of medicine, 1989-91. Author: Biomicroscopy of Peripheral Fundus, 1973, Eye Surgery, 1980, 2d edit., 1990, Biomicroscopy of the Eye, 1994; inventor contact lenses for diagnostic purposes. Recipient Graefe prize German Ophthalmolog. Soc. Mem. Am. Acad. Ophthalmology, Am. Soc. Cataract and Refractive Surgery, Swiss Ophthalmol. Soc. (Vogt. prize), French Ophthalmol. Soc., Argentina Ophthalmol. Soc.

EISNER, THOMAS, biologist, educator; b. Berlin, June 25, 1929; s. Hans Edouard and Margarete (Heil) E.; m. Maria Lobell, June 10, 1952; children: Yvonne, Vivian, Christina. BA, Harvard U., 1951, PhD, 1955; DSc (hon.), U. Würzburg, Germany, 1982, U. Zürich, Switzerland, 1983, U. Göteborg, Sweden, 1989, Drexel U., 1992. Postdoctoral fellow Harvard U., 1955-57; asst. prof. biology Cornell U., Ithaca, N.Y., 1957-62; assoc. prof. Cornell U., 1962-66, prof., 1966-76, Jacob Gould Schurman prof. chem. ecology, 1976—, dir. Cornell Inst. for Rsch. in Chem. Ecology, 1992—; sr. fellow Cornell Ctr. for the Environ., 1994—; vis. scientist dept. entomology Sch. Agr., Wageningen, The Netherlands, 1964-65; vis. scientist Smithsonian Tropical Rsch. Lab., Barro Colorado Island, C.Z., 1968; sr. vis. scientist Max Planck Inst. für Verhaltensphysiologie, Seewiesen, Fed. Republic Germany, 1971, Disn. Entomology, CSIRO, Canberra, Australia, 1972-73; Rand fellow Marine Biol. Labs., Woods Hole, Mass., 1974; vis. rsch. prof. U. Fla., Gainesville, 1977-78; rsch. assoc. Archbold Biol. Sta., 1973—; vis. prof. Stanford U., 1979-80, U. Zürich, 1980-81. Co-author: Animal Adaptation, 1964, Life on Earth, 1973, and 4 other books; mem. editl. bd. Sci., 1970-71, Am. Naturalist, 1970-71, Jour. Comparative Physiology, 1974-80, Jour. Chem. Ecology, 1974—, Behavioral Ecology and Sociobiology, 1976—, Sci. Yr. World Books, 1979-82, Human Ecology Forum, 1981-85, Living Bird Quar., 1982-88, Experientia, 1982—, Quar. Rev. Biology, 1983-87; co-editor: Explorations in Chemical Ecology Series, 1987—; contbr. articles to profl. jours. Recipient Archie F. Carr medal, 1983, Procter prize Sigma Xi, 1986, Karl Ritter von Frisch medal, 1988, Centennial medal Harvard U., 1989, Tyler Environ. Achievement prize U. So. Calif., 1990, Esselen award, 1991, Silver medal Internat. Soc. Chem. Ecology, 1991, Nat. medal sci., 1994; Guggenheim fellow, 1964-65, 72-73. Fellow Am. Acad. Arts and Scis., Royal Soc. Arts, Animal Behavior Soc., Entomol. Soc. Am.; mem. NAS (rsch. opportunity in biology com. 1985, film com. 1986—, com. on human rights 1987-90), AAAS (chmn. biology sect. 1980-81, com. on sci. freedom and responsibility 1980-87, chmn. subcom. sci. and human rights 1981-87, judging com. sci. freedom and responsibility award 1985-87, Newcomb Cleveland prize 1967), Am. Philos. Soc., Explorers Club, Deutsche Acad. Naturforscher Leopoldina, Acad. Europaea, Zero Population Growth (bd. dirs. 1969-70), Nature Conservancy (nat. sci. adv. coun. 1969-74), Nat. Audubon Soc. (bd. dirs. 1970-75), Fedn. Am. Scientists (coun. mem. 1977-81), Ctr. on Consequences Nuclear War (steering com. 1983-90), World Wildlife Fund (sci. adv. coun. 1983-91), Am. Inst. Biol. Sci. (task force for 90s 1990—), Ctr. Plant Conservation (adv. bd. econ. potential rare and threatened plants 1992—), Am. Soc. Naturalists (pres. 1989-90), Monell Chem. Senses Ctr. (adv. coun. 1988-95), World Resources Inst. (adv. coun. 1988-95), Com. Concerned Scientists (nat. sponsor 1988—), Union Concerned Scientists (bd. dirs. 1993—), Xerces Soc. (sci. adv. com. 1990—, pres. 1992—, chmn. endangered species coalition 1994—). Office: Cornell U W347 Seeley Mudd Hall Dept Neurobiology & Behavior Ithaca NY 14853

EITNIER, CYNTHIA KAY, nurse, administrator; b. Lancaster, Pa., June 16, 1953; d. C. Quentin and Nancy Lee (Fisher) Martin. LPN, Willow State Vocat.-Tech. Coll., 1972; ASN, Harrisburg Area Community Coll., 1981; BSN, Millersville U., 1984; postgrad. U. Ariz., 1985; M in Nursing, U. S.C., 1988; MBA, Kennesaw State U., 1994. RN; cert. advanced nursing adminstrn.; lic. nursing home adminstr. Practical nurse Conestoga View, Lancaster, 1973-77, Polyclinic Med. Ctr., Harrisburg, Pa., 1977-81; nurse, 1981-85, St. Joseph Hosp., Tucson, 1985-86, mem. code team, pulmonary rehab. teams, 1985-86; nursing supr. Brian Ctr., Columbia, S.C., 1986-87, asst. dir. nursing, 1987-88, dir., 1990—, DON Rheems (Pa.) Nursing Ctr., 1988, Brian Ctr., Yanceyville, N.C., 1989-90, Brian Ctr., Jeffersonville, Ga., 1990—, Brian Ctr., Austell, 1990—; asst. v.p. clin. svcs. Atrium Mgmt. Co., Atlanta, 1992—; owner-pres. Ross Ventures. Mem. NAFE, Pa. Nurses Assn., NADONA. Democrat. Avocations: computers, swimming, hiking. Home: 166 Lancelot Way Lawrenceville GA 30245-4756

EKELAND, ARNE ERLING, surgeon, educator; b. Voss, Norway, Oct. 14, 1942; s. Magne and Birgit (Birkeland) E.; m. Synnove Godvik; 1 child, Magnus. MD, U. Oslo, Norway, 1967; PhD, U. Oslo, 1981. Lic. gen. surgeon 1984,, orthopedic surgeon 1988. Resident Aker Hosp., Oslo, 1971-74, lectr., 1974-76; rsch. fellow Rikhosp., Oslo, 1976-81; resident Ullevaal Hosp., Oslo, 1981-86, sr. orthopedic surgeon, 1987-90, 94-95, chief surgeon, 1990-94; dir., chief surgeon Martina Hansens Hosp., Berum, 1996—; prof. U. Oslo, 1990-96; resident Sophies Minde Orthopedic Hosp., Oslo, 1986-87. Editorial bd. Scandinavian Jour. for Medicine and Sci. in Sports, 1990—, Knee Surgery, Sports Traumatology and Arthroscopy, 1992—. With Norwegian Army. Mem. Surg. Assn. Oslo (sec. 1984-86), Internat. Soc. for Fracture Repair (founding mem.), ACL Study Group, Norwegian Soc. Sport Rsch. (bd. dirs. 1986-88), Internat. Soc. Skiing Safety (bd. dirs. 1981-89, v.p. 1989—). Office: Martina Hansens Hosp, Box 23, N-1355 Baerum Norway

EKHOLM, ROBERTA A., osteopath; b. Mobridge, S.D., Feb. 26, 1951; d. Otto Erle Ekholm and Florence Rose D'Amico; m. Thomas Wilson Pinney, July 4, 1987. BA in Biology, U. S.D., 1973; BS in Nursing, U. Miami, Fla., 1976; DO, Kirksville Coll. Osteo. Medicine, 1980. RN, Fla. quality assurance advisor Family Care, Portland, Oreg.; grief counselor Grief Recovery Inst., L.A.. advisor West Linn (Oreg.) Fire Dept.; pres. West Linn Bus. Group. Mem. Am. Osteo. Assn., Am. Coll. Family Practitioners (treas.), N. Clackamas C. of C.. Office: Ready Care 17070 SE McLoughlin Blvd Portland OR 97267

ELAM, KAREN MORGAN, food company executive, consultant; b. Watseka, Ill., Feb. 22, 1945; d. Howard Edgar and Margaret Lucille (Dilling) Johnson; m. Fred William Morgan, Jr., Aug. 26, 1967 (div. June 1974); 1 child, Todd Anthony; m. Rick Elam, Nov. 19, 1979; 1 stepchild, Paula Helene. B.S., Purdue U., 1967; M.S., Mich. State U., 1968; Ph.D., U. Mo., 1977. Instr. nutrition assessment and food policy research U. Mo., Columbia, 1973-74, grad. research asst., 1974-77, asst. prof., 1981-83, assoc. prof., 1983-86; asst. prof. Mich. State U., East Lansing, 1977-81; dir. consumer affairs Nabisco Brands, Inc., East Hanover, N.J., 1987-90; sr. dir. nutrition and consumer affairs Nabisco Foods Group, 1991—; cons. numerous food industries and pub. relation firms, 1979-87. Author: Nutrients in Foods, 1983; computerized nutrient data bank at Mich. State U., 1979 (yearly updates).

Editor Nutrition Data Bank Conf. Proc., 1980. Contbr. articles to profl. jours. Grantee USDA, HHS. Fellow Am. Coll. Nutrition; mem. Am. Inst. Nutrition, Nat. Acad. Scis. (com. foods additives survey data), Am. Agrl. Econs. Assn., Inst. Food Technologists, Am. Home Econs. Assn. Avocations: downhill skiing, reading. Office: Nabisco Foods Group Nutrition and Consumer Affairs 7 Campus Dr Parsippany NJ 07054-4407

ELAM, LLOYD CHARLES, psychiatrist; b. Little Rock, Oct. 27, 1928; s. Harry and Ruth D.; m. Clara Carpenter, Feb. 16, 1957; children: Gloria, Laurie. BS, Roosevelt U., 1950, LHD (hon.), 1974; MD, U. Wash., 1957; postgrad., U. Ill., 1957-58, U. Chgo., 1957-61; LLD (hon.), Harvard U., 1973. Staff psychiatrist Billings Hosp., Chgo., 1961; staff psychiatrist Hubbard Hosp., Nashville, 1961, asst. prof., chmn. dept. psychiatry, 1961-63, prof., chmn. dept. psychiatry, 1963; interim dean Meharry Med. Coll., Nashville, 1966, 6th pres., 1968-81, chancellor, 1981-82, Disting. Svc. prof. psychiatry, 1983—; bd. dirs. Merck & Co., Rahway, N.J., Pre Mark Internat., Dominion Bank, Nashville, South Cen. Bell Telephone Co., Nashville. Mem. Frontiers of Am., Nashville. Recipient Eleanor Roosevelt Key award Roosevelt U., 1972, Bus. and Profl. Leader of Yr. award Heritage of Am., 1974. Mem. AMA, Am. Psychiat. Assn., Nat. Med. Assn., Inst. Medicine, Nashville Acad. Medicine, R.F. Boyd Med. Soc. (pres.). Baptist. Office: Meharry Med Coll Dept of Psychiatry 1005 D B Todd Blvd Nashville TN 37208*

ELANDER, RICHARD PAUL, pharmaceutical company executive; b. Worcester, Mass., Sept. 17, 1932; s. Arthur Waldemar and Edith Alma Louise (Engstrand) E.; m. Barbara Ann Sudz, Feb. 8, 1958; children: Tracy, Richard, Ronald. BS with honors, U. Detroit, 1955, MS, 1956; PhD, U. Wis., 1960; postdoctoral, U. Minn., 1965-66. Rsch. scientist Eli Lilly and Co., Indpls., 1960-67; assoc. dir. Wyeth Labs., West Chester, Pa., 1967-72, Smith Kline and French, Phila., 1972-75; dir. fermentation devel. Bristol-Myers Squibb Co., Syracuse, N.Y., 1975-80, sr. dir. biotech. and rsch. devel., 1980-83, v.p. biotech., 1983—; lectr. Butler U., Indpls., 1965-66, Rensselaer Poly. Inst., 1983-88; rsch. prof. Syracuse U., 1983—; biotech. adv. bd., Dartmouth, MIT, Cornell. Mem. editl. bd. Biotech. Letters, 1985—, Jour. Indsl. Microbiology, 1985-94, Applied and Environ. Microbiology, 1974-83; contbr. articles to profl. jours., also chpts. to books in field; patentee in field. Recipient Charles Thom award Soc. Indsl. Microbiology, 1984. Fellow Am. Acad. Microbiology, Am. Inst. Chemists, Soc. Indsl. Microbiology (sec. 1968, pres. 1974); mem. AAAS, Am. Soc. Microbiology (chmn. div. 1977), Am. Chem. Soc., Lions (bd. dirs. 1970-73), Sigma Xi (v.p. Syracuse chpt. 1991, pres. Syracuse chpt. 1992). Republican. Home: 8376 Vassar Dr Manlius NY 13104-9425 Office: Bristol Myers Squibb Co Tech Operations Divsn PO Box 4755 Syracuse NY 13221-4755

ELBEIN, ALAN DAVID, medical science educator; b. Lynn, Mass., Mar. 20, 1933; s. Gersh and Golda (Stryer) E.; m. Elaine J. Brooks, June 21, 1953; children: Steven Conrad, Bradley Martin, Richard Craig. AB, Clark U., 1954; MS, U. Ariz., 1956; PhD, Purdue U., 1960. Rsch. assoc. in biochemistry Med. Sch. U. Mich., Ann Arbor, 1960-63; rsch. assoc. in biochemistry U. Calif., Berkeley, 1963-64; asst. prof., then assoc. prof. biology Rice U., Houston, 1964-69; prof. Health Sci. Ctr. U. Tex., San Antonio, 1969-90; prof., chmn. biochemistry dept. U. Ark. Med. Sci., Little Rock, 1991—; mem. study sect. NSF, 1972-75, NIH, 1983-87, 93—; mem. editl. bd. Jour. Biol. Chemistry, Arch. Biochem. Biophysics, Plant Physiology, Glycobiology, Jour. Bacteriology, Eur. Jour. Biochem. Editor: Swainsonine; contbr. articles, revs. to profl. jours. Mem. Am. Chem. Soc., Am. Soc. Plant Physiology, Am. Soc. Biol. Chem. and Molecular Biology. Jewish. Home: 23 Fontenay Cir Little Rock AR 72211-9569 Office: U Ark Med Scis Dept Biochem & Mol Biology 4301 W Markham St Little Rock AR 72205-7101

ELBEL, WARREN RAY, plastic surgeon; b. New Braunfels, Tex., 1952. MD, Baylor Coll. Medicine, Houston, 1978. Diplomate Am. Bd. Plastic Surgery. Resident in gen. surgery Baylor Coll. Medicine, 1979-83; resident in plastic surgery U. Ill., Chgo., 1983-85; pvt. practice, New Braunfels, Tex., 1985—; mem. staff McKenna Meml. Hosp., New Braunfels, N.E. Meth. Hosp., San Antonio. Mem. AMA, Tex. Med. Assn., Comal County Med. Soc. Office: 189 E Austin St Ste 103 New Braunfels TX 78130-4170

ELBERGER, ANDREA JUNE, medical educator, biomedical researcher; b. N.Y.C., Feb. 11, 1952; d. Jack and Helen (Perlman) E.; m. James Joseph Aschberger, May 7, 1978; children: Matthew Jared, Geoffrey David. BA, SUNY, Albany, 1972; PhD, SUNY, Stony Brook, 1977. Postdoctoral fellow U. Pa., Phila., 1977-80; asst. prof. U. Tex. Health Sci. Ctr., Houston, 1980-85; asst. prof. U. Tenn., Memphis, 1985-86, assoc. prof., 1986-93, prof., 1993—; reviewer NSF, Washington, 1985—, NIH, Bethesda, Md., 1987—. Contbr. chpts. in book Two Hemispheres - One Brain, 1986, Neural Plasticity, 1988. Mentor Tenn. Pre-Profl. Program, Memphis, 1988-90, Project Achieve, Memphis, 1990, 93, Young Memphis Scholars, 1993, 96, Grad. Achievement Program, 1993. NIH grantee, 1981-83, 84-87, 85-88, 90-93, 93-94. Mem. AAAS, Soc. for Neurosci., Assn. Rsch. in Vision and Ophthalmology, Rodin Remediation Found., Rsch. Soc. on Alcoholism. Office: U Tenn 855 Monroe Ave Memphis TN 38163

ELBERT, THOMAS RUDOLF, neuroscientist, educator. Diploma in physics, U. Munich, Germany, 1975; PhD in Psychology, U. Tubingen, Germany, 1978. Sci. fellow U. Tubingen, Germany, 1975-87; assoc. prof. Pa. State U., University Park, 1987; sci. fellow Stanford (Calif.) U., 1987-88; assoc. prof. U. Konstanz, Germany, 1989-91; prof. U. Münster, Germany, 1991-95, U. Konstanz, Germany, 1995—. Office: Univ Konstanz FG Psychologie, Postfach 5560-D23, D-78434 Konstanz Germany

ELBLE, RODGER JACOB, neurologist, researcher; b. Alton, Ill., Aug. 10, 1948; s. Rodger Jacob, Sr. and Blanche Dee (Baughman) E.; m. Suzanne Louise Marshall, Aug. 14, 1971; children: Rodger Jacob III, Joseph Marshall, Ann Elizabeth. BS in Aero. Engring., Purdue U., 1971; PhD in Physiology, Ind. U., 1975; MD, Ind. U., Indpls., 1977. Diplomate Am. Bd. Psychiatry and Neurology. Resident in neurology Washington U., St. Louis, 1978-81; asst. to assoc. prof. neurology So. Ill. U., Springfield, 1981-96, prof., 1996—, chair dept. neurology; dir. regional Alzheimer disease assistance ctr., So. Ill. U., Springfield. Co-author: Tremor, 1990; contbr. articles to profl. jours. Nat. Inst. Neurol. Disorders and Stroke grantee; Nat. Inst. on Aging grantee; The Whitaker Found. grantee, 1987—. Fellow Am. Acad. Neurology; mem. Am. Physiol. Soc., Soc. Neurosci. Office: So Ill U Sch Medicine PO Box 19230 Springfield IL 62794-9230

ELCHAHAL, SAMI, physician; b. Tripoli, Lebanon, Sept. 27, 1951; came to U.S., 1977; s. Samih and Hind (Afiouni) E.; m. Mouradi Baghdadi, Aug. 21, 1971; children: Samih, Roni, Farrah. MD, U. Montpellier, 1977. Intern Wayne State U., Detroit, 1979-82; dir. non-invasive cardiology U. Cmty. Hosp., Tampa, Fla., 1996—. Cardiology fellow Henry Ford Hosp., Detroit, 1982-85. Fellow Am. Coll. Cardiology; mem. N.Am. Soc. Pawing and Electrophysiology. Office: 3000 E Fletcher Ave #220 Tampa FL 33613

ELDER, JOHN BLANTON, psychologist, clergyman; b. Dallas, Dec. 27, 1926; s. Arthur Blanton and Inez (Staub) E.; m. Jeanine Copeland, June 9, 1950 (div. 1971); children: Nancy, Arthur, Jeanne; m. Thersia Dost, Sept. 21, 1974; 1 child, John Eric. BS, U. Tex., 1946; MDiv, Austin Sem., 1951; MA, U. Tex., 1966; PhD, U. Houston, 1974. Ordained to ministry Presbyterian Ch., 1951. Pastor Presbyn. chs., various locations, 1951-69; lectr. U. Md., College Park, 1976-88; clin. psychologist VA Med. Ctr., Grand Island, Nebr., 1989-90; clin. dir. Dept. of Army, Ft. Hood, Tex., 1990-91; pvt. practice Georgetown, Tex., 1991—; min. Leander (Tex.) Presbyn. Ch. Moderator Brazos Presbytery, Houston, 1969; bd. dirs. Nebraskans for Ind. Living, 1989. Lt. (j.g.) USN, 1944-47. Mem. APA. Home and Office: 1204 Power Rd Georgetown TX 78628-3145

ELDOR, JOSEPH, anesthesiologist; b. Tel-Aviv, Mar. 26, 1950; m. Nelly Eldor, Sept. 9, 1975; children: Elad, Nataly, Monica, Iddo, Loren, Sharon. MD, Hebrew U., Jerusalem, 1978; cert. in Anesthesiology, Hadassah Med. Ctr., Jerusalem, 1984. Anesthesiologist Hadassah Med. Ctr., Jerusalem, 1979-90, Misgav Ladach Gen. Hosp., Jerusalem, 1985—. Patentee in field. Home: 4 Hanayadot St, 97536 Jerusalem Israel Office: Misgav Ladach Gen Hosp, PO Box 12142, 91120 Jerusalem Israel

ELDRED, KENNETH MCKECHNIE, acoustical consultant; b. Springfield, Mass., Nov. 25, 1929; s. Robert Moseley and Jean McKechnie (Ashton) E.; m. Helene Barbara Koerting Fischer, May 31, 1957; 1 dau., Heidi Jean. B.S., MIT, 1950, postgrad., 1951-53; postgrad., UCLA, 1960-63. Engr. in charge vibration and sound lab. Boston Naval Shipyard, 1951-54; supervisory physicist, chief phys. acoustics sect. U.S. Air Force, Wright Field, Ohio, 1956-57; v.p., cons. acoustics Western Electro-Acoustics Labs., Los Angeles, 1957-63; v.p., tech. dir. sci. services and systems group Wyle Labs., El Segundo, Calif., 1963-73; v.p., dir. div. environ. and noise control tech. Bolt Beranek and Newman Inc., Cambridge, Mass., 1973-77; prin. cons. Bolt Beranek and Newman Inc., 1977-81; dir. Ken Eldred Engring.; mem. exec. stds. coun. Am. Nat. Stds. Inst., 1979-89, vice-chmn., 1981-83, chmn., 1985-87, bd. dirs., 1983-87; mem., past chmn. Acoustical Stds. Bd.; mem. com. hearing, bioacoustics and biomechanics NRC, 1963—; chmn. Internat. Stds. Orgn. Tech. Com. TC108 Mechanical Shock and Vibration, 1994—. Served with USAF, 1954-56. Fellow Acoustical Soc. Am. (stds. dir. 1987-93, past chmn. coordinating com. environ. acoustics, Silver Medal in Noise 1994); mem. NAE, Inst. Noise Control Engring. (pres. 1976, bd. dirs. 1987-91), Soc. Automotive Engrs., Soc. Naval Architects and Marine Engrs., Boothbay Harbor Yacht Club, Blue Water Sailing Club, Down East Yacht Club, Boothbay Harbor Yacht Club. Home: Meadow Cove East Boothbay ME 04544 Office: PO Box 501 East Boothbay ME 04544-0501

ELDREDGE, FRANK AUBREY, II, geneticist; b. Salt Lake City, Jan. 8, 1940; s. Frank Aubrey and Esther Edda (Rogers) E.; m. Birgitta Veronica Osterberg, Dec. 19, 1963; children: John William, Jennifer, Christine, Emilie Birgitta. Student, U. Utah, 1958-60, BA, 1965, MS, 1969, PhD, 1972. Teaching assoc. U. Utah, Salt Lake City, 1971; assoc. prof. biology Cen. Mich. U., Mt. Pleasant, 1972-79; exec. v.p. new product devel. Biomune Systems, Inc., Salt Lake City, 1995—. Contbr. research articles on plant cytogenetics and evolution to profl. jours. Active troop com. Lake Huron council Boy Scouts Am., 1973—. NIH genetics tng. fellow, 1967-72; faculty research and creative endeavors grantee, 1973-75, 77-79. Mem. AAAS, Am. Genetic Assn., Bot. Soc. Am., Smithsonian Assn., Amateur Radio Club, Sigma Xi, Beta Beta Beta, Phi Sigma, Phi Eta Sigma. Republican. Mormon. Office: Biomune Systems Inc 540 Arapeen Dr Ste 202 Salt Lake City UT 84108

ELDREDGE, LINDA GAILE, psychologist; b. Lubbock, Tex., Apr. 3, 1959; d. Jerry Greever and Madge (Harshbarger) Eldredge. BS, Howard Payne U., 1980; MA, Tex. Woman's U., 1981; EdD, Baylor U., 1989. Lic. psychologist, chem. dependency counselor, Tex.; cert. tchr. hearing impaired, sch. counselor, spl. edn. counselor, Tex.; lic. marriage and family therapist; cert. verbal self def. trainer; cert. eye movement desensitization and reprocessing. Tchr. hearing impaired Waco (Tex.) Ind. Sch. Dist., 1982-85, spl. edn. sch. counselor, cons. hearing impaired, 1986-87; doctoral teaching fellow Baylor U., Waco, 1985-87; dir. regional alcohol and drug abuse svcs. Heart of Tex. Coun. Govts., Waco, 1987; psychotherapist Houston, Tex., 1989-91; psychologist Houston, 1991-93; pvt. practice psychology Austin, 1993—; psychologist Tex. Sch. for the Deaf, Austin, 1993-95. Mem. APA, Nat. Assn. Alcoholism and Drug Abuse Counselors, Am. Deafness and Rehab. Assn., Am. Assn. of the Deaf-Blind, Gentle Art of Verbal Self-Defense Trainers Network, Tex. Assn. Alcoholism and Drug Abuse Counselors (sec.-treas. Waco chpt. 1988-89). Office: 5806 Mesa Ste 220 Austin TX 78731-3742

ELDRIDGE, MARK, physician assistant; b. Summit, N.J., Oct. 18, 1956; s. John B. and Barbara A. (King) E.; m. Linda A. Marchant, June 24, 1983; children: Justin Mark, Jennifer Marie. BS in Therapeutic Recreation, Green Mountain Coll., 1979; student, U. Ky., 1985. Cert. physician asst. Physician asst. VA Hosp., West Haven, Conn., 1985-87; paramedic Hunters Ambulance, Meriden, Conn., 1987-94; physician asst./EMS coord. emergency dept. VMMC, Meriden, Conn., 1987-94; physician asst. emergency dept. Wilson (N.C.) Meml. Hosp., 1994—. Tiger Cubs den leader Boy Scouts Am., Wilson, 1995-96; asst. and head soccer coach Wilson Recreation Dept., 1995-96. Fellow Am. Acad. Physician Assts., Conn. Acad. Physician Assts. Home: 4702 St Georges Dr Wilson NC 27896 Office: CES of the Carolinas 3708 Mayfair St Ste 300 PO Box 51997 Durham NC 27717

EL-DUWEINI, AADEL KHALAF, clinical pharmacologist, information scientist; b. Cairo, Dec. 26, 1945; Arrived in Can., 1988.; s. Atallah Khalaf El-Duweini and Flora Philobos Sedrah; m. Salwa Michael Rizk, Nov. 19, 1970; children: Salam, Hadi. BSc in Pharmacy, Cairo U., 1967, M Pharm. Sci., 1976; postgrad. in info. mtkg., Cath. U. Am., 1981; MBA, Am. U., 1981. Cert. pharmacist, Pharmacy Examining Bd. of Can. Bibliographer Nat. Info. and Document Ctr., Cairo, 1967-73, abstractor, indexer, 1974-76, staff coord., 1977-81; mgr. mktg., communications and sci. rels. Acad. Sci. Rsch. and Tech., Cairo, 1982-87; rsch. scientist Nat. Rsch. Ctr., Cairo, 1968-88; asst. to pharmacist Cumberland Drug, Dorval, Que., Can., 1988-92; pharmacist Groupe Cumberland, Dorval, Que., Can., 1992—, Shadia Fahim Pharmacy, St. Laurent, Que., 1994—, Pharmaprix, Cartierville, Que., 1996—, B.B. Levy, Pharmacien, St. Laurent, Que., 1996—; mktg. cons. Cow and Gate baby foods, Cairo, 1976-80; mgmt. cons. Bureau Joseph, Patents & Trade Marks Atty., Cairo, 1980-88; info. cons. Nat. Cancer Inst., Cairo U., 1983-88; instr. info. sci. Am. U. in Cairo, 1984-88. Co-author: The Infrastructure of an Information Society, 1984; contbr. articles to profl. jours. Mem. Ecumenical Youth Com., Cairo, 1970-88, PTA German Schs., Cairo, 1982-88; Sunday sch. coord. St. Mark Ch., Montreal, Que., Can., 1990—. Scholar Goethe Inst., Fed. Republic Germany, 1973, Internat. Agy. for Rsch. on Cancer, France, 1976, AID, 1980, 81, Brit. Coun., 1980-84. Mem. Egyptian Assn. Sci. and Tech. Librs. and Info. Ctrs. (founding sec. gen. 1985—), Ordre des Pharmaciens du Quebec, Egyptian Sci. Soc. for Group Tng. (coun. 1982—), Am. Soc. for Info. Sci., Libr. Assn. Gt. Britain, Egyptian Soc. for Pharmacology and Exptl. Therapeutics, Can. Pharm. Assn., Can. Cancer Soc., Egyptian Pharm. Assn., Coptic Orthodox. Home: 8 Oriole Dr, Kirkland, PQ Canada H9H 3X3 Office: Shadia Fahim Pharmacy, 3305 Côte Vertu, Saint Laurent, PQ Canada H4R 1Y5

ELEQUIN, CLETO, JR., retired physician; b. Antique, Philippines, Oct. 18, 1933; s. Cleto and Enriqueta (Tengonciang) E.; m. Nancy Johnson, May 14, 1958; children: Tracy, Thomas Kyle, Stuart Scott. M.D., Far Eastern U., Philippines, 1957. Rotating intern Good Samaritan Hosp., Lexington, Ky., 1957-58; gen. practice resident Central Bapt. Hosp., Lexington, 1958-59; psychiat. resident State Hosp., Danville, Pa., 1959-60, 61-62; psychiat. resident with child psychiatry State Hosp., New Castle, Del., 1962-63; staff physician Eastern State Hosp., Lexington, 1960-61, dir. Fayette County Project, dir. intensive treatment service, 1964-67, supt., 1969-71; dep. commr. Dept. Mental Health, State Ky., 1967-69; practice medicine, specializing in family practice Pecos, Tex., 1971-72, Austin, Tex., 1974-89; ret.; cons. psychiatrist Texas Youth Commn., Peyote, Tex., Permian Basin Cmty. Mental Health-Mental Retardation, Odessa, Tex., Pesde Ranch for Emotionally Disturbed Children and Adolescents, Ft. Davis, Tex., Dept. Mental Health-Mental Retardation State of Tex.; vis. lectr. in medicine and psychiatry Am. U. of the Caribbean, Plymouth, Montserrat; asst. dep. commr. Tex. Dept. Mental Health and Mental Retardation, Austin, 1973-74, dep. commr. mental health, 1974; pvt. practice family therapy and psychiatry, Austin, 1974-85; mem. attending staff Brackenridge Hosp., St. David Med. Ctr., Seton Med. Ctr., Shoal Creek Hosp.; med. dir. Mary Lee Sch. and Found., 1974-80, bd. trustees, 1980-85; attending psychiatrist U. Ky. Med. Ctr., 1964-71, Good Samaritan Hosp., 1969-71, Ctrl. Bapt. Hosp., 1966-71; cons. psychiatrist U. Ky. Student Health Svc., 1965-71, Peace Corps, 1966-68, Bur. Rehab. State Ky., 1965-71, Blue Grass Cmty. Care Ctr., 1967-71, Covington (Ky.) Cmty. Care Ctr., 1969-71, Hazard Cmty. Care Ctr., 1969-71, Danville (Ky.) Cmty. Ctr., 1969-71, Maysville (Ky.) Cmty. Care Ctr., 1969-71; clin. instr., asst. clin. prof. dept. psychiatry U. Ky. Med. Ctr., 1964-69, assoc. clin. prof., 1969-71; cons. psychiatrist Tex. Youth Commn. Tex. Dept. of MH-MR, State of Tex.; pvt. practice in psychiatry, Austin, 1974-85; mem. attending staff Brackenridge Hosp., St. David Med. Ctr., Seton Med. Ctr., Shoal Creek Hosp.; med. dir. Mary Lee Sch. and Found., 1974-80, mem. bd. trustees, 1980-85. Mem. Profl. Adv. Coun. Community Mental Health-Retardation Ctr., Lexington, 1967-71; mem. Lexington Hosp. Coun., 1969-71. Mem. AMA, Am. Psychiat. Assn., Am. Acad. Family Physicians (life), Assn. Med. Supts. Mental Hosps., Tex. Med. Assn., Travis County Med. Soc., Austin Psychiat. Soc. Home: 10101 Jupiter Hills Dr Austin TX 78747-1322

ELFTMAN, SUSAN NANCY, physician assistant, childbirth-lactation educator; b. Oakland, Calif., Apr. 3, 1951; d. Arthur Gerhardt Samuel and Ella Johanna (Nelson) E. AA summa cum laude, Chabot Coll., 1971; BA in Zoology, U. Calif., Berkeley, 1973; BS in Med. Sci. magna cum laude, Alderson-Broaddus Coll., 1980; MPH, UCLA, 1990. Bd. cert. physician asst., Calif. Physician asst. So. Calif. Permanente Group, San Diego, 1981-82, Mem. Med. Ctr., Long Beach, Calif., 1982-88, Harriman-Jones Med. Group, Long Beach, 1988-90, Pamela Kushner, MD, Long Beach, 1990—. Spkr. Am. Cancer Soc., Long Beach, Meml. Med. Ctr., Long Beach, March of Dimes. Fellow Am. Acad. Physician Assts., Calif. Acad. Physician Assts.; mem. Am. Soc. for Psychoprophylaxis in Obstetrics (cert. lactation and childbirth educator). Home: 275 Ximeno Long Beach CA 90803 Office: Pamela Kushner MD 2865 Atlantic Ave Ste 207 Long Beach CA 90806

ELGART, MERVYN L., dermatologist, educator; b. Bklyn., Aug. 12, 1933; s. Jacob and Sally R. E.; m. Sheila Ruth Cliff, June 13, 1954; children—Brian, George, Paul, Adam, James. A.B., Bklyn. Coll., 1953; M.D., Cornell U., 1957. Intern Buffalo Gen. Hosp., 1957-58; resident in dermatology Walter Reed Gen. Hosp., Washington, 1960-63; chief dermatology Andrews AFB Hosp., Washington, 1964-66; mem. faculty George Washington U. Med. Sch., 1967—, prof. dermatology, 1974—, chmn. dept., 1975—, prof. pediatrics, 1974—, prof. medicine, 1974—. Served as officer M.C. USAF, 1958-66. Fellow Am. Acad. Dermatology; mem. So. Med. Assn., Soc. Investigative Dermatology, Internat. Soc. Dermatology, Washington Dermatol. Soc., Am. Dermatol. Assn., Phi Beta Kappa, Alpha Omega Alpha. Roman Catholic. Office: George Washington Univ 2150 Pennsylvania Ave NW Washington DC 20037-2396

ELGEE, NEIL JOHNSON, retired internist and endocrinologist, educator; b. Oxford, N.S., Can., Apr. 3, 1926; came to U.S., 1946, naturalized, 1955; s. William Harris and Lucile (Nevers) E.; m. Leona Victoria Karlsson, Aug. 18, 1951; children—Joan, Susan, Laurie, Steve, Karen. B.Sc., U. N.B., Can., 1946; M.D., U. Rochester, 1950. Intern Peter Bent Brigham Hosp., Boston, 1950-51; resident Strong Meml. Hosp., Rochester, N.Y., 1951-52; fellow in endocrinology U. Wash., 1952-54; co-chief resident in medicine U. Wash., Seattle, 030, 1954-55; clin. prof. medicine U. Wash., Seattle, 1968-93, emeritus clin. prof. medicine, 1993—; practice medicine specializing in endocrinology Seattle, 1957-93; retired, 1993; pres. Ernest Becker Found., 1993—. Served as capt. USAF, 1955-57. Master ACP (gov. for Wash. and Alaska 1965-71, regent 1974-78); mem. Endocrine Soc., Inst. Medicine. Home: 3621 72nd Ave SE Mercer Island WA 98040-3330

ELGIN, GITA, psychologist; b. Santiago, Chile; came to U.S., 1968, naturalized 1987; d. Serafin and Regina (Urízar) Elguin; BS in biology summa cum laude, U. Chile, Santiago, DPs, 1964; PhD in Counseling Psychology, U. Calif., Berkeley, 1976; m. Bart Bödy, Oct. 23, 1971; children: Dio Christopher Károly, Alma Ilona Raia Julia. Clin. psychologist Barros Luco-Trudeau Gen. Hosp., Santiago, 1964-65; co-founder, co-dir. Lab. for Parapsychol. Rsch., Psychiat. Clinic, U. Chile, Santiago, 1965-68; rsch. fellow Found. Rsch. on Nature of Man, Durham, N.C., 1968; researcher psychol. correlates of EEG-Alpha waves U. Calif., Berkeley, 1972-76; originator holistic method of psychotherapy Psychotherapy for a Crowd of One, 1978; co-founder, clin. dir. Holistic Health Assos., Oakland, Calif., 1979—, Montclair Mediation Group, Oakland, 1994; lectr. holistic health Piedmont (Calif.) Adult Sch., 1979-80; hostess Holistic Perspective, Sta. KALW-FM, Nat. Public Radio, 1980. Author: (video documentary) Taking the Risk: Sharing the Trauma of Sexual & Ritualistic Abuse in Group Therapy, 1992. Lic. psychologist, Chile, Calif. Chancellor's Patent Fund grantee U. Calif., 1976, NIMH fellow, 1976. Mem. APA, Am. Holistic Psychol. Assn. (founder 1995—), Alameda County Psychol. Assn., Calif. State Psychol. Assn., Montclair Health Profls. Assn. (co-founder, pres. 1983-85), Sierra Club, U. Calif. Alumni Assn. Contbr. articles in clin. psychology and holistic health to profl. jours. and local periodicals. Presenter Whole Life Expo, 1986. Office: Montclair Profl Bldg 2080 Mountain Blvd Ste 203 Oakland CA 94611-2817

ELGORT, ANDREW CHARLES, school psychologist; b. N.Y.C., Mar. 27, 1953; s. George and Janet T. E.; m. Virginia B. Elgort, June 24, 1979; children: Mayan G., Ari N. BS, West Chester (Pa.) State Coll., 1975; MEd, U. Va., 1977; EdS, James Madison U., 1985; EdD, Coll. of William and Mary, 1992; postgrad., 1992. Nat. cert. sch. psychologist; cert. profl. counselor, Md., psychol. assoc., Md. Tchr. emotionally disturbed Greenbank Sch., Glenmore, Pa., 1975-76; asst. dir., project dir. TREES project Augusta County Pub. Schs., Fisherville, Va., 1977-78; tchr. emotionally disturbed City of Manassas (Va.) Pub. Schs., 1978-79, ednl. diagnostician, 1979-80; tchr. emotionally disturbed Albemarle County Pub. Schs., Charlottesville, Va., 1980-83; staff psychologist Child Devel. Ctr. James Madison U., Harrisburg, Va., 1984-85; sch. psychologist Henrico County Pub. Schs., Richmond, Va., 1985-93, Howard County Pub. Schs., Ellicott City, Md., 1993—; pvt. practice, 1994—; bd. dirs. Sir Moses Mantefiore Cemetery Corp., sec. 1992-93. Mem. edn. com. Rudlin torch Acad., Richmond, 1989-91, chmn. edn. com., 1989-90, v.p. adminstrn., 1991-92, sec., 1992-93; bd. dirs. Keneseth Beth Israel Synagogue, Richmond, 1987-93. Postgrad. scholar, 1992. Mem. NASP, Va. Psychol. Assn., Va. Acad. Sch. Psychologists, Md. Sch. Psychologists Assn., Acad. for Family Mediators. Office: Howard County Pub Schs 10910 State Route 108 Ellicott City MD 21042-6106

ELGUT, NOEL LORING, ophthalmologist; b. Bklyn., May 27, 1960; s. Malcolm Allen and Eileen (Witzer) E.; m. Kathleen Esther Donaldson; children: Daniel, Anne. BA, Rutgers U., 1982; MD, Temple U., 1986. Diplomate Am. Bd. Ophthalmology. Assoc. ophthalmologist Johnson Eye Inst., Zephyrhils, Fla., 1990-91; pvt. practice Ft. Lauderdale, Fla., 1991—; vice-chief surgery Cleve. Clinic Hosp., Ft. Lauderdale, 1995—, oper. rm. com., 1994-95. Henry Rutgers scholar Rutgers U., 1982. Fellow Am. Acad. Ophthalmology; mem. Alpha Omega Alpha. Republican. Roman Catholic. Office: Los Olas Eye Ctr 1820 E Las Olas Blvd Fort Lauderdale FL 33301

EL HAJJ, MARINA, healthcare services executive; b. Ain Delb, Lebanon, Jan. 20, 1962; d. Tanios and Salma (Arslan) El H. BS, Am. U., 1982; MD, Am. U. Med. Ctr., 1985; MBA, INSEAD, 1991. Rsch. assoc. Pitie-Salpetriere Hosp., Paris, 1989-90; med. info. mgr. Amgen SA, Paris, 1992-95; asst. dir. Am. U. Beirut Med. Ctr., 1995—. Mem. editorial bd. Biotech Medicine, 1993-95. Mem. Pharm. MBA Assn., Insead Alumni Assn., Lebanese Order of Physicians. Office: Hosp Administration Am U Beirut Med Ctr 850 3rd Ave New York NY 10022

EL-HUSBAN, TAYSEER KHALAF, internist, consultant; b. Hamamah, Mafraq, May 25, 1955; s. Khalaf Eyadeh and Kamayel (Hussein) El-H.; m. Angeleki Panayotis Dimakakou, May 20, 1987; children: Faris, Samir. BM, Athens (Greece) U., 1980. Cert. specialist in internal medicine. House officer St. Georg Hosp., Pireaus, Greece, 1980-81, St. Helen Hosp., Athens, 1981-85; med. specialist King Khalid Hosp., Riyadh, Saudi Arabia, 1985-87, Nat. Ins. Found., Athens, 1987-90; cons. State Hosp. Pireas, Greece, 1990-93, Elefsina Med. Ctr., Greece, 1993-95, Ippokratio Hosp. Diabetic Ctr., Greece, 1996—. Home: M Asias 51, 115-27 Athens Greece Office: Elefsis Med Ctr, Kimonos 12, 19200 Elefsina Attiki, Greece

ELIAKIM, MARCEL, physician, educator; b. Plovdiv, Bulgaria, June 2, 1921; arrived in Israel, 1949; s. Albert and Rosalie (Nachmias) E.; m. Caroline Sussman, Dec. 7, 1947; children: Abraham, Alon. MD, Hebrew U., Jerusalem, Israel, 1952. Intern Hadassah (Jerusalem) U. Hosp., 1951-52; instr. Hadassah Med. Sch. of Hebrew U., 1957-60, resident, 1954-59, sr. lectr., 1960-63, assoc. prof., 1963-68, prof., 1969—, head dept. medicine, 1969-89, dean. faculty medicine, 1985-88; head dept. medicine Bikur Holim Hosp., Jerusalem, 1989—; dir. Inst. Postgrad. Tng. Hebrew U., 1962-66; mem. com. for higher edn. Ministry Edn., Israel, 1976-79; ombudsman Israel Ministry of Health, 1994. Author: Recurrent Polyserositis, 1981; editor several books, Israel Journal of Medical Sciences, 1968-73. Recipient Hadassah award Hadassah Med. Orgn., Balt., 1987. Mem. Israel Med. Orgn., Israel Soc. Internal Medicine, Israel Med. Assn. (editorial bd. 1965—, Zwilling award 1965), Israel Assn. for Study Medicine (founder). Home: 14 Zabotinsky St, Jerusalem 92142, Israel Office: Bikur Holim Hosp, Jerusalem 91004, Israel

ELIAS, JACK ANGEL, physician, educator; b. Fayetteville, Ark., Apr. 10, 1951; s. Gabriel and Alma (Kowalsky) E.; m. Sandra Gross, Jan. 3, 1981; 1 child, Lauren Rachel. BA, U. Pa., 1973, MD, 1976. Intern internal medicine Tufts- New England Med. Ctr., Boston, 1976-77, resident internal medicine, 1977-78; sr. resident internal medicine Hosp. of U. Pa., Phila., 1975-79, joint fellow allergy and immunology, pulmonary and critical care medicine, 1979-82; prof., chief pulmonary and critical care medicine Yale U. Sch. Medicine, New Haven, 1990—; asst. prof. U. Pa. Sch. Medicine, Phila., 1979-82, 82-88, assoc. prof., 1988-90; mem. coun. Am. Lung Assn., 1992. Contbr. articles to Jour. Immunology, Jour. Clin. Investigation, others. Grantee Nat. Heart-Lung-Blood Inst./NIH, 1988—, 1991. Fellow Am. Coll. Chest Physicians; mem. Am. Soc. Clin. Investigation, Am. Thoracic Soc. (bd. dirs. 1992, pres. sci. assembly on allergy, immunology and inflammation 1990-91).

ELIAS, MAURICE JESSE, psychology educator; b. Bronx, N.Y., Dec. 1, 1952; m. Ellen Sue Rosen, Aug. 7, 1976; children: Sara Elizabeth, Samara Alexandra. BA in Psychology summa cum laude, CUNY, 1974; MA in Clin. Psychology, U. Conn., 1977, PhD in Clin. Psychology, 1980. Psychotherapist mental health svc. U. Conn., Storrs, 1977-78; prevention planning cons. Conn. Dept. Children and Youth Svcs., 1978-79; asst. prof. psychology Rutgers U., New Brunswick, N.J., 1979-85, assoc. prof., 1985—, coord. internship program in applied-community psychology, 1979—, field supr. psychol. clinic grad. sch., 1979—; mem. co-adj. faculty dept. psychiatry U. Medicine and Dentistry N.J.-Robert Wood Johnson Med. Sch., 1985, Schwartzman family parenting program Am. Jerusalem Acad. for Contemporary Judaic Studies, 1987—; cons. to numerous pub. sch. dists., pvt. schs., community groups, presenter in field. Author: (with J.F. Clabby) Teach Your Child Decision Making, 1986, Social Decision Making Skills: A Curriculum Guide for the Elementary Grades, 1989, (with S. Tobias) Problem Solving/Decision Making for Social and Academic Success: A School-based Approach, 1990, Social Decision Making & Life Skills Development: Guidelines for Middle School Educators, 1993, Social Problem Solving Interventions in the Schools, 1996, (with B. Friedlander) Personal Problem Solving Guide to Computer Software, 1995; contbr. articles to profl. jours. Treas., trustee Middlesex County Resources for the Menatlly Handicapped, Inc., 1981-83; bd. dirs. Nat. Orgns. Adv. Coun. for Children, 1981-85, Prevention Coalition N.J., 1990-92; mem. Interagy. Youth Devel. Consortium, 1982-86, Nat. Coalition Against TV Violence, 1979—; advisor Commn. to Deter Criminal Activity, 1988—; pres. religious sch. bd. edn. Highland Park Conservative Temple and Ctr., 1992—, trustee, 1992—; trustee Assn. for Children of N.J., 1992—; exec. com. Collaborative for Advancement of Social and Emotional Learning, 1995. Grantee Rutgers U., 1979-83, 84-85, 85-87, William T. Grant Found., 1982-90, NIMH, 1982-85, 88, Middlesex County Mental Health Bd. and Bd. Chosen Freeholders, 1984-87, Schumann Found. N.J., 1987-89, 90-93; Lilly Endowment grantee William T. Grant Found., 1991-94. Mem. ASCD, APA (Nat. Psychology award 1986, 88, Nat. Psychol. Cons. to Mgmt. award 1990, Disting. Contbn. to Practice award 1993), Nat. Assn. Sch. Psychologists, Phi Beta Kappa. Home: 139 N 5th Ave Highland Park NJ 08904-2924 Office: Tillett Hall Livingston Campus Rutgers U Dept Psychol New Brunswick NJ 08903

ELIAS, MERRILL FRANCIS, behavioral/cardiovascular epidemiology researcher; b. Apr. 17, 1938; m. Penelope K. Elias; children: Susan P., Eric J. and Benjamin J. BA, Allegheny Coll., 1960; MS, Purdue U., 1961, PhD, 1963; MPH, Boston U., 1996. Lic. psychologist, Maine. Asst. prof. Allegheny Coll., Meadville, Pa., 1965-68; asst. prof. med. psychology, coordinator aging research tng. program Duke U., Durham, N.C., 1971-72; assoc. prof. psychology W.Va. U., Morgantown, 1972-73, Syracuse (N.Y.) U., 1973-77; prof. psychology U. Maine, Orono, 1977—; adj. rsch. prof. medicine and pub. health Boston U., 1994—; dr. clin. tng. U. Maine, Orono, 1986—; vis. rsch. prof. medicine, vis. prof. pub. health Sch. of Medicine, Boston U., 1991-93; allied health scientist Maine Med. Ctr., Bangor, Maine, 1986—; vis. acad. U. Oxford, Eng., 1987, The Jackson Lab., Bar Harbor, Maine, 1968, 70, 74, 75; assoc. med. staff Bangor Mental Health Inst., 1977-79; instr. psychology Syracuse U., Mohawk Valley Community Coll., 1963-64; rsch. assoc. urdue U., 1960-63; cons. bd. sci. counselors Nat. Inst. on Aging, 1984, mem. animal adv. com., 1982—, evaluation panel animal resources prog., 1981-82, others. Contbr. articles to profl. jours.; speaker in field. Grantee, NSF, 1967-70, NIH, 1970-71, 73-75, 76-80, 82-84, 84—, NATO-Eng.-U.S. Rsch. Collaboration, 1986. Fellow APA, Am. Gerontol. Soc. (mem. coms.), Biol. Sci., Behavior and Social Sci., Soc. Behavioral Medicine; mem. Acad. Behavioral Med. Rsch., Am. Assn. Dental Editors, Am. Psychosomatic Soc. Home: PO Box 40 Mount Desert ME 04660-0040

ELIASOPH, IRA, ophthalmologist, educator; b. N.Y.C., Feb. 25, 1929; s. Benjamin and Ida (Endler) E.; m. Ann Patricia Levy Klein, Feb. 20, 1955 (div. July 1978); children: Jeffrey, Laura, Diane, Pamela; m. Margaret W. Alan, June 28, 1987. AB, Kenyon Coll., 1948; MD, NYU, 1952. Diplomate Am. Bd. Ophthalmology. Pvt. practice N.Y.C., 1958—; chief oculoplastic surgeon Beth Israel Hosp., N.Y.C., Bronx VA Hosp., N.Y.C.; assoc. attending ophthalmic surgeon Mt. Sinai Hosp., Manhattan Eye Ear and Throat Hosp., N.Y.C.; chief ophthalmology Jewish Home and Hosp. for Aged, N.Y.C.; assoc. clin. prof. Mt. Sinai Sch. Medicine, N.Y.C. Lt. (j.g.) USNR, 1953-55. Fellow Am. Acad. Ophthalmology, Am. Soc. Ophthalmic Plastic and Reconstructive Surgery, N.Y. Acad. Medicine. Office: 167 E 82d St New York NY 10028

ELIASOPH, JOAN, radiologist, educator; b. N.Y.C.; d. Samuel and Martha (Coe) Freeman. AB, Hunter Coll., 1946; MD, NYU, 1949. Diplomate Am. Bd. Radiology. Intern Mt. Sinai Hosp., N.Y.C., 1949-50, resident in radiology, 1951-53, radiology Columbia U., N.Y.C, 1953-55; instr. Columbia U., N.Y.C., 1953-55; asst. attending radiologist Mt. Sinai Hosp., N.Y.C., 1955-70, attending radiologist, 1982-85, 90; clin. asst. prof. Mt. Sinai Med. Sch., N.Y.C., 1970-77; assoc. prof. radiology U. So. Calif., L.A., 1977-82, Columbia U., N.Y.C., 1982-85; assoc. prof. Mt. Sinai Med. Sch., N.Y.C., 1985-90, Dartmouth Med. Sch., Hanover, N.H., 1990-92; attending radiologist Dartmouth-Hitchcock Med. Ctr., 1990-92; attending radiologist gastrointestinal and critical care imaging Kingsbridge VA Med. Ctr., 1992—; cons. Silver Hill Found., Conn., 1965-77, Stamford Hosp., Conn., 1970-77. Contbr. articles to profl. jours. Mem. Friends of Ballona Wetlands, Los Angeles, 1977-82. Heineman Pathology fellow Mt. Sinai Hosp., 1950-51, Radiology fellow, 1955-56. Fellow Am. Coll. Radiology, Am. Coll. Gastroent.; mem. Am. Roentgen Ray Soc., Am. Gastroent. Soc., Radiol. Soc. N.Am., Soc. Gastrointestinal Radiologists, N.Y. Roentgen Soc., Assn. Univ. Radiologists, Am. Ukiyo-E Soc. Avocations: environment, birding, Japanese prints. Office: Kingsbridge Vets Adminstrv Med Ctr Dept Radiology 130 W Kingsbridge Rd Bronx NY 10468

ELIASSON, SÖREN EDWARD, dentist; b. Boras, Sweden, Jan. 20, 1936; s. Justus Artur and Anna Viktoria (Hallin) E.; m. Kerstin Ulla Thomasson, Mar. 30, 1961; children: Peter, Thomas, Fredrik. DDS, Dental Sch., Stockholm, 1962, PhD, 1974. Asst. Dental Sch., Stockholm, 1962-70; pvt. practice Stockholm, 1962-74; assoc. prof. Dental Sch., Stockholm, 1970-74, prof., 1974—; chmn. Continuing Edn. Com., Stockholm, 1974-93; chmn. Edn. Bd., Stockholm, 1977-82, Rsch. Funds, Stockholm, 1994—. Contbr. articles to profl. jours. Capt. Swedish Army, 1963. Mem. Swedish Dental Soc. (bd. mem. 1974—, chmn. 1977-82), Dental Soc. Stockholm, Dental Soc. Helsingfors (hon.). Home: Brahegatan 29, 11437 Stockholm Sweden Office: Sch Dentistry, Box 4064, 14104 Huddinge Sweden

ELIASTAM, MICHAEL, physician; b. Springs, Republic of South Africa, Jan. 3, 1944; came to U.S., 1967; s. Theodore and Isa Eliastam; m. Suzanne Maynard, Dec. 31, 1983; children: Taylor, Jordan, Monet. MB B.Ch., U. Witwatersrand, Johannesburg, Republic of South Africa, 1966; MPA, Harvard U., 1972, MPP, 1973. Diplomate Am. Bd. Emergency Medicine, Am. Bd. Internal Medicine. Intern Rush Presbyn. St. Lukes Hosp., Chgo., 1967-68, resident, 1968-71; asst. prof. Stanford U., Stanford, Calif., 1974-83; dir. emergency svcs. Stanford U. Hosp., Palo Alto, Calif., 1974-90; assoc. prof. emergency medicine Stanford U., Palo Alto, 1983-90; deputy commr. for med. affairs, med. dir. Dept. of Health & Hosps. City of Boston, 1990-94; assoc. ptnr. Andersen Cons., Boston, 1994—. Editor: Manual of Emergency Medicine, 1989; contbr. articles to profl. jours. Fellow Am. Coll. Emergency Physicians, Am. Coll. Physicians; mem. Univ. Assn. for Emergency Medicine. Jewish. Office: Andersen Cons Admin 5 1 International Pl Boston MA 02110

ELIBOL, TARIK, physician; b. Turkey, Sept. 1, 1937; came to U.S., 1962, naturalized, 1970; s. Ismail Cemal and Nuriye (Tutkun) E.; M.D., U. Istanbul, 1962; m. Apr. 2, 1964; children—Kimberly, Lisa, David, Adam, John. Intern, Kenmore (N.Y.) Mercy Hosp., 1962-63; resident in internal medicine U. Buffalo, 1963-65; fellow in gastroenterology Cleve. Clinic, 1965-67; clin. asst. prof. medicine U. Buffalo, 1975—; practice medicine specializing in digestive diseases, Buffalo, 1969—; former chief of staff DeGraff Meml. Hosp.; mem. staff Erie County Med. Center, Kenmore Mercy Hosp. Fellow Am. Coll. Gastroenterology, Am. Coll. Physicians; mem. Western N.Y. Soc. Gastrointestinal Endoscopy (past pres.), Western N.Y. Gastrointestinal Liver Soc. (pres. 1980—), Western N.Y. Physician Found. (pres. 1980—); mem. ACP, Am. Soc. Internal Medicine, Erie County Med. Soc., AMA, Am. Soc. Gastrointestinal Endoscopy. Contbr. articles to profl. jours. Home: 55 Leicester Rd Buffalo NY 14217-2111 Office: 2949 Elmwood Ave Kenmore NY 14217-1356

ELINSON, JACK, sociology educator; b. N.Y.C., June 30, 1917; s. Sam and Rebecca (Block) E.; m. May Gomberg, July 5, 1941; children: Richard, Elaine, Mitchell, Robert. B.S., CCNY, 1937; M.A., George Washington U., 1946, Ph.D., 1954. Social sci. analyst Dept. Def., Washington, 1942-51; sr. study dir. Nat. Opinion Research Center, 1951-56; asst. prof. sociology U. Chgo., 1954-56; assoc. prof. adminstrv. medicine Columbia U., N.Y.C., 1956-64; prof. adminstrv. medicine Columbia U., 1964-68, prof. sociomed. scis. and sociology, 1968-86, prof. emeritus, 1986—; Service fellow Nat. Center Health Stats., 1977-81; vis. prof. behavioral scis. U. Toronto, 1969-77; Disting. vis. prof. Inst. Health Care Policy, Rutgers U., 1986-89, Disting. sr. scholar, 1990—; vis. prof. Robert Wood Johnson Med. Sch. (formerly Rutgers Med. Sch.), Univ. Medicine and Dentistry of N.J., 1986—; dir. program evaluation dept. patient care Harlem Hosp. Ctr., 1966-71; bd. dirs. Med. and Health Rsch. Assn., N.Y.C., 1977-89, Bergen County, N.J. To and Health Assn., 1960-65; mem. adminstrv. bd. Bur. Applied Social Rsch., Columbia U., 1970-75; co-dir. health care orgn. and adminstrn. track Program for Master's Degree in Pub. Health, Rutgers U.-U. Medicine and Dentistry of N.J., 1983-92. Author: (with R. E. Trussell) Chronic Illness in a Rural Area, 1959, (with J.J. Williams and R.E. Trussell) Family Medical Care under Three Types of Health Insurance, 1962, (with E. Padilla and M. Perkins) Public Image of Mental Health Services, 1967; editor: (with A.E. Siegmann) Sociomedical Health Indicators, 1979, (with A. Mooney and A. Siegmann) Health Goals and Health Indicators: Policy, Planning and Evaluation, 1977, (with N.K. Wenger, M.E. Mattson, and C.D. Furberg) Assessment of Quality of Life in Clinical Trials of Cardiovascular Therapies, 1984. Recipient nat. merit award Delta Omega Soc., 1982, Festschrift, spl. issue of Social Sci. and Medicine, 1989. Fellow Am. Sociol. Assn. (chmn. med. sociology, Leo G. Reeder award 1985), AAAS, APHA (1st award Assn. Social Scis. in Health 1984), Am. Assn. Pub. Opinion Rsch. (pres. 1979-80, Exceptionally Disting. Achievement award 1993); mem. Inst. of Medicine NAS, N.Y.C. Pub. Health Assn. (dir.), N.J. Pub. Health Assn. (exec. bd.Dennis J. Sullivan award 1990). Office: Rutgers Univ Inst Health Care Policy 30 College Ave New Brunswick NJ 08901-1245 Also: Columbia U Sch Pub Health Divsn Sociomed Scis 600 W 168 St New York NY 10032

ELION, GERTRUDE BELLE, research scientist, pharmacology educator; b. N.Y.C., Jan. 23, 1918; d. Robert and Bertha (Cohen) E. AB, Hunter Coll., 1937; MS, NYU, 1941; DSc (hon.), Hunter Coll., 1989, NYU, 1989; DMS (hon.), Brown U., 1969; DSc (hon.), U. Mich., 1983, N.C. State U., 1989, Ohio State U., 1989, Poly. U., 1989, U. N.C., Chapel Hill, 1990, Russell Sage Coll., 1990, Duke U., 1991, MacMaster U., 1992, SUNY, Stony Brook, 1992, George Washington U., 1969, Columbia U., 1992, Washington Coll., 1993, U. South Fla., 1993, U. Wis., 1993, East Carolina U., 1993, Wake Forest U., 1994, Utah State U., 1994; MD (hon.), U. Chieti, Italy, 1995; DHL (hon.), Rochester Inst. Tech., 1996; DSc (hon.), Phila. Coll. Pharmacy, 1996, Albany Coll. Pharmacy, 1996, Rensselaer Polytech. Inst., 1996. Lab. asst. biochemistry N.Y. Hosp. Sch. Nursing, 1937; rsch. asst. in organic chemistry Denver Chem. Mfg. Co., N.Y.C., 1938-39; tchr. chemistry and physics N.Y.C. secondary schs., 1940-42; food analyst Quaker Maid Co., Bklyn., 1942-43; rsch. asst. in organic synthesis Johnson & Johnson, New Brunswick, N.J., 1943-44; biochemist Wellcome Rsch. Labs., Tuckahoe, N.Y., 1944-50; sr. rsch. chemist Wellcome Rsch. Labs., 1950-55, asst. to assoc. rsch. dir., 1955-62, asst. to the rsch. dir., 1963-66, head exptl. therapy, 1966-83, sci. emeritus, 1983—; adj. prof. pharmacology and exptl. medicine Duke U., 1970, rsch. prof. pharmacology, 1983—; adj. prof. pharmacology U. N.C., Chapel Hill, 1973; chmn. Gordon Conf. on Coenzymes and Metabolic Pathways, 1966; mem. bd. sci. counselors Nat. Cancer Inst., 1980-84; mem. coun. Am. Cancer Soc., 1983-86; mem. Nat. Cancer Adv. Bd., 1984-91. Contbr. articles to profl. jours.; patentee in field. Recipient Garvan medal, 1968, Pres.'s medal Hunter Coll., 1970, Medal of Honor Am. Cancer Soc., 1990; Disting. Chemist award N.C. Inst. Chemists, 1981, Judd award Meml. Sloan-Kettering Cancer Ctr., 1983, Bertner award M.D. Anderson Hosp., 1989, Third Century award Fedn. for Creative Am., 1990, Discoverers award Pharm. Mfg. Assn., 1990, City of Medicine award Durham, N.C., 1990; co-recipient Nobel prize in medicine, 1988, Nat. Medal of Sci. NSF, 1991; inductee Hunter Coll. Hall of Fame, 1973, Nat. Inventors Hall of Fame, 1991, Nat. Women's Hall of Fame, 1991, Engring. and Sci. Hall of Fame, 1992; named Dame, Order of St. John of Jerusalem Ecumenical Found. (Knights of Malta) 1992. Fellow N.Y. Acad. Scis.; mem. AAAS, NAS (coun. 1994-97), Royal Soc. (fgn. mem.), Am. Chem. Soc., Am. Acad. Arts and Scis., Inst. of Medicine, Chem. Soc. London, Am. Soc. Biol. Chemists, Am. Assn. Cancer Rsch. (bd. dirs. 1981, 83, pres. 1983-84, Cain award 1984), Am. Soc. Hematology, Transplantation Soc., Am. Soc. Pharmacology and Exptl. Therapeutics. Home: 1 Banbury Ln Chapel Hill NC 27514-2504 Office: Glaxo Wellcome Inc 5 Moore Dr Research Triangle Park NC 27709

ELIOT, JOHN, psychologist educator; b. Washington, Oct. 28, 1933; s. Charles William and Regina (Dodge) E.; m. Sylvia Hewitt, July 3, 1959; children: John Cooper (dec.), Mary Ashley, Catherine Hewitt. AB, Harvard U., 1956, M of Art in Teaching, 1958; EdD, Stanford U., 1966. Asst. prof. Northwestern U., Evanston, Ill., 1967-69; assoc. prof. U. Md., College Park, 1969-77, prof., 1977—. Author: (with I. Smith) Spatial Tests, 1983, Models of Psychological Space, 1987; contbr. articles to profl. jours. Trustee Reservations, Milton, Mass., 1960—. Fellow Am. Psychol. Assn.; mem. Soc. Research Child Devel., Brit. Psychol. Soc., Soc. Internat. Psychologists. Democrat. Episcopalian. Home: 2705 Silverdale Dr Silver Spring MD 20906-5322 Office: U Md Inst Child Study College Park MD 20742

ELIOT, ROBERT SALIM, physician; b. Oak Park, Ill., Mar. 8, 1929; s. Salim and Ruth (Buffington) Elia; m. Phyllis Allman, June 15, 1957; children: William Robert, Susan Elaine. Student, Northwestern U., 1947-48; B.S., U. N.Mex., 1952; M.D., U. Colo., 1955. Intern Northwestern U., Evanston, Ill., 1955-56; resident U. Colo., Denver, 1956-58, fellow cardiology, 1958-60; clin. prof. medicine/cardiology U. Nebr. Coll. Medicine, 1983—; trainee cardiovascular pathology U. Minn., St. Paul-Mpls., 1962-63, instr., 1963-65, asst. prof., 1965-67; mem. faculty U. Fla., Gainesville, 1967-72, prof. medicine, 1969-72; chief div. cardiology VA Hosp., 1970-72; prof. medicine, dir. Cardiovascular Center U. Nebr. Med. Ctr., Omaha, 1972-81, dir. div. cardiology, 1972-80, chmn. dept. preventive and stress medicine, 1981-83; med. dir. Internat. Stress Found., 1977—; dir. Nat. Ctr. Preventive and Stress Medicine, 1984-87, Cardiovascular Inst., Swedish Med. Ctr., Denver, 1987-89; cardiol. cons. Cape Kennedy, 1971-77; cons. Kellogg Found., 1978; chmn. Nat. Goals and Objectives for Stress Mgmt. for Surgeon Gen. U.S., 1980—; dir. Inst. of Stress Medicine, Denver, 1989-90; chmn., dir. Inst. of Stress Medicine, Jackson Hole, Wyo., 1992—; dir. preventive and rehab. cardiology Heart Lung Ctr., St. Luke's Hosp., Phoenix, 1984-87; cons., lectr. Nat. Def. U., 1985—; adj. prof. Ariz. State U., nat. and internat. lectr. med. and sci. topics; pres. Alachua County Heart Div., 1969, 70; mem. adv. bd. stress and cardiovascular research center Eckerd Coll., St. Petersburg, Fla., 1980-83; chmn. Bethesda Conf. Com. on Prevention of Coronary Disease in the Occupational Setting, 1980-81; cons., lectr. in field to corps., pub. and profl. orgns. Author: Stress and the Major Cardiovascular Disorders, 1979, From Stress to Strength, How to Lighten Your Load and Save Your Life, 1994, (with D. Breo) Is It Worth Dying For?, 1984; editor: Cardiac Emergencies; mem. editl. bd. Heart and Lung; creator ednl. TV series Heartline to Health; contbr. articles to profl. jours. Served to capt. AUS, 1960-62. Recipient John P. McGovern medal Am. Med. Writer's Assn., 1985, Sci. and Art of Health award Inst. for Advancement of Health, 1989; grantee USPHS, Va, Fla. Heart Assn., Polk Family Charitable Fund, 1995, various pvt. sources. Fellow ACP, Clin. Council Am. Heart Assn., Am. Coll. Cardiology (mem. continuing edn. com., Mountain States coordinator for continuing edn., mem. long range planning com., mem. exec. com. gov. Nebr., vice chmn. bd. govs. 1976-77, chmn. bd. govs. 1977-78, trustee 1977-83, prevention com. 1987-91), N.Y. Acad. Scis.; mem. AMA, Ariz. Med. Assn., Colo. Med. Assn., Cen. Soc. Clin. Investigation, Biophys. Soc., Acad. Behavioral Medicine Research (charter), Soc. Behavioral Medicine (charter), Interstate Postgrad. Med. Assembly (pres. 1982), Alpha Omega Alpha, Phi Sigma, Phi Rho Sigma. Home: PO Box 279 Wilson WY 83014-0279

ELISCU, ANDREA TROCK, public relations executive; b. Chgo., Dec. 13, 1944; d. Harold and Natalie (Roussman) Trock; m. Edward H. Eliscu, Mar. 5, 1966; children: Adam, Alicia. BS with honors, Rollins Coll., Winter Park, Fla., 1981; postgrad., Yale U. Sch. Mgmt., 1988; cert. completition mgmt. program, Crummer Grad. Sch. Bus., 1991; RN, U. Ill., Michael Reese Hosp., 1966. RN, Mass., N.C., Fla. Med.-surg. nurse Mass. Gen. Hosp., Boston, 1966-68; intensive care nurse Beth Israel Hosp., Boston, 1968-69; recovery rm. nurse U.S. Naval Hosp., Orlando, Fla., 1973-74; float nurse Orlando Regional Med. Ctr., 1973-74; tennis pro shop mgr. Altamonte Racquet Club, Altamonte Springs, Fla., 1974-78; office nurse Bill Cheslock, MD, Orlando, 1978-79; fundraising project chair Orlando Regional Med. Ctr., 1983-84; pres., nat. cons. Med. Mktg., Inc., Winter Park, 1984—; mem. adv. bd. U. Ctrl. Fla. Coll. Health and Pub. Affairs, Orlando, 1988—; bd. dirs. Alliance for Healthcare Mktg. and Strategy, Chgo., 1995; health chmn. Goal 2000 Greater Orlando Chamber Cmty. Project, 1990, 1990-91; charter mem. adv. coun. Dept. Health Svcs. Adminstrn., U. Ctrl. Fla. for undergrad. and grad. programs; charter bd. mem. Coll. Health and Profl. Svcs., U. Ctrl. Fla.; mentor MBA program Crummer Sch. Bus., Rollings Coll.; bd. advisors Briefings on Practice Mgmt., Marblehead, Mass. Author: Position for Success!, 1995. Mem. Leadership Fla., Tallahassee, 1995; amb. Orlando World Cup Soccer, 1995; chmn. bd. Small Bus. Assn. Ctrl. Fla., 1994. Named Outstanding Woman in Bus. Women's Exec. Coun., Orlando, 1988, Ann. Friend of Medicine Orange County Med. Soc., Orlando, 1990; recipient Innovation award Small Bus. Assn. State of Fla., Tallahassee, 1986, Presdl. Citation for Svc., Am. Mktg. Assn., Chgo., 1993. Mem. Alliance for Healthcare Mktg. and Strategy (bd. dirs. at-large 1994—), Acad. Health Svcs. Mktg. (program com. 1991, bd. dirs. Orlando chpt.), Fla. C. of C. (bd. dirs., mgmt. corp. bd.), Greater Orlando C. of C. (exec. bd. dirs.). Office: Med Mktg Inc 1477 W Fairbanks Ave Winter Park FL 32789

ELKIN, MILTON, radiologist, physician, educator; b. Boston, Feb. 24, 1916; s. Philip and Rose (Dexter) E.; m. Gloria King, Nov. 12, 1943; children: Philip, Karen, Laura. A.B., Harvard Coll., 1937; M.D., Harvard U. Med. Sch., 1941. Diplomate Am. Bd. Radiology (trustee 1983-95). Assoc. radiologist Peter Bent Brigham Hosp., Boston, 1951-52; dir. radiology Cambridge (Mass.) City Hosp.; asst. radiologist New Eng. Med. Ctr., Boston, 1952-53; assoc. radiologist Cedars of Lebanon Hosp., L.A., 1953-54; prof., chmn. dept. radiology Albert Einstein Coll. Medicine, Yeshiva U., N.Y.C., 1954-86, prof., 1986—; dir. radiology Jacobi Med. Ctr., N.Y.C., 1954-86; attending radiologist Bronx Municipal Hosp. Center, N.Y.C., 1986—; spl. cons. radiology tng. com. Nat. Inst. Gen. Med. Scis., NIH, USPHS, 1966-70; cons. Gen. Med. Research Program-Project Com., 1970-72; radiology rep. to Council Med. Splty. Socs., 1976-81; mem. Residency Rev. Com. for Radiology, 1986-92. Author: Radiology of the Urinary System, 1980, Plain Film Approach to Abdominal Calcifications, 1983; Contbr. articles to profl. jours. Fellow Am. Coll. Radiology (bd. chancellors 1970-76, gold medal 1977); mem. AMA, Harvard Med. Soc., Am. Roentgen Ray Soc., Radiol. Soc. N.Am. (dir. 1975-82, chmn. bd. 1978-79, pres. 1980-81, Gold medal 1985), Assn. Univ. Radiologists, N.Y. Roentgen Soc. (pres.). Home: 13 Kingston Rd Scarsdale NY 10583-1148 Office: 1300 Morris Park Ave Bronx NY 10461-1926

ELKIND, BRANT A., health services administrator, consultant; b. Worcester, Mass., June 8, 1949; s. Melvin and Elinor (Gruber) E.; m. Lynda Davis, Oct. 16, 1983; 1 child, Sharon Halley. BA, Franklin Pierce Coll., Rindge, N.H., 1971; MS in Human Svc. Mgmt., Worcester State Coll., 1985. Regional adminstr. ARC Blood Svcs., Worcester, Mass., 1978-82; adminstr. dept. pathology U. Mass. Med. Ctr., Worcester, 1983-87; adminstr., COO Highwatch Rehab. Ctr., Effingham, N.H., 1987-91; asst. dir. univ. health svcs. for ops., fin., adminstrn. U. Mass., Amherst, 1991-94; regional adminstr. Cmty. Health Plan, Poughkeepsie, N.Y., 1994-95; prin. Monadnock Cons. Svcs., Keene, N.Y., 1987—; dir. brain injury svcs. Crotched Mountain Rehab. Ctr., Greenfield, N.H., 1996—; adj. faculty Franklin Pierce Coll., 1995—; cons. Ctrl. N.H. Head Injury Coun., Ossipee, 1987-93, Catskill Alliance of Physicians, Kingston, N.Y., 1994-95; dir. Monadnock Devel. Disabilities Coun., Keene, 1992—. Regional first aid advisor Nat. Ski Patrol, Worcester, 1978-80; pres. United Cerebral Plasy of Ctrl. Mass., 1982-83; co-chair advance giving United Way of Dutchess County, Poughkeepsie, 1995; mem. Hudson Valley Quality Coun., 1994-95. Recipient Shared Knowledge award ARC, Quincy, Mass., 1978, Alumni Achievement award Franklin Pierce Coll., 1971, 89. Mem. Masons, Scottish Rite, Shriners, Franklin Pierce Coll. Alumni Assn. (pres. 1976-78, 96—). Home: 108 Greenwood Ave Keene NH 03431 Office: Crotched Mountain Rehab Ctr 1 Verney Rd Greenfield NH 03047

ELKIND, DAVID, psychology educator; b. Detroit, Mar. 11, 1931; s. Peter and Bessie (Nelson) E.; children: Paul Steven, Robert Edward, Eric Allen. BA, UCLA, 1952, PhD, 1955; DSc (hon.), R.I. Coll., 1987. Diplomate: Am. Bd. Profl. Examiners in Psychology. Research asst. to David Rapaport, Austen Riggs Ctr., Stockbridge, Mass., 1956-57; staff psychologist Beth Israel Hosp., Boston, 1957-59; asst. prof. Wheaton Coll., Norton, Mass., 1959-61; asst. prof. med. psychology U. Calif. Med. Sch., Los Angeles, 1961-62; assoc. prof., dir. Child Study Ctr., U. Denver, 1962-66; prof., dir. grad. tng. in developmental psychology, dept. psychology U. Rochester, N.Y., 1966-78; chmn. Eliot Pearson dept. child study Tufts U., Medford, Mass., 1978-83, prof. child study, sr. resident scholar Lincoln Filene Ctr.; research dir. World of Inquiry Evaluation-NSF, 1970; project dir. Tng. of Early Childhood Specialists, U.S. Office Edn., 1970; psychol. cons. VA, 1962-74, Rochester Mental Health Center, 1966-74, Rochester Family Ct., 1967-73; headmaster Mt. Hope Sch., Rochester, 1974-77; co-host Lifetime TV series "Kids These Days". Author: (with H.J. Flavell) Studies in Cognitive Development, 1969, Children and Adolescents, 1974, A Sympathetic Understanding of the Child, 1974, (with I. Weiner) Child Development: A Core Approach, 1972, (with others) Psychology: An Introduction, 1973, Child Development and Education, 1976, (with D. Hetzel) Readings in Human Development: Contemporary Perspectives, (with I. Weiner) Development of the Child, 1978, The Child's Reality: Three Developmental Themes, 1978, The Child and Society, 1979, The Hurried Child, 1981, All Grown Up and No Place to Go, 1984, Miseducation: Preschoolers at Risk, 1987, Grandparenting: Understanding Today's Children, 1988; editor: Perspectives in Early Childhood Education, 1991, Parenting Your Teenager in the Nineties, 1993, Images of the Young Child, 1993, Understanding of Your Child, 1994, A Sympathetic Understanding of the Child Birth to Sixteen, 1994, Ties that Stress: The New Family Imbalance, 1994. NSF Sr. Postdoctoral fellow Geneva, 1964-65. Fellow Am. Psychol. Assn. (recipient Nicholas Hobbs Award div. 26), AAAS, Nat. Assn. Edn. of Young Children (pres. 1986-88). Home: 7 Lloyd Ln East Sandwich MA 02537-1225 Office: Tufts U Psychology Dept Medford MA 02155

ELKINS, JAMES PAUL, physician; b. Lincoln, Nebr., Mar. 20, 1924; s. James Hill and Antonia (Wohler) E.; MD, U. Va., 1947; m. May Hollingsworth Reynolds, June 15, 1946; children—Patricia May Elkins Riggs, Paulette Frances Elkins Phillips, James Barrington. Cert. Emergency Med. Svcs. Commn. Intern, DePaul Hosp., Norfolk, Va., 1947-48; resident in ob-gyn Alexandria (Va.) Hosp., 1948-49, Franklin Sq. Hosp., Balt., 1949-50, St. Rita's Hosp., Lima, Ohio, 1950, Tripler Army Hosp., Honolulu, 1953-54; practice medicine specializing in ob-gyn, Indpls., 1954-73; chief ob-gyn St. Francis Hosp., Beech Grove, Ind., 1965-66; mem. teaching staff Gen. Hosp., Indpls., 1954-73; dep. coroner Marion County, 1965-74; ret. med. cons. disability determination div. Ind. Rehab. Svcs.; ringside physician Ind. State Athletic Commn., Ind. Golden Gloves, Indpls. Pal Club, 1976-86; retired med. cons. Served with AUS, 1949-54. Recipient Fred Deborde Award Ind. Golden Gloves, 1985. Mem. Am. Coll. Ob-Gyn, Ind. State Med. Assn., Marion County Med. Soc., Indpls. Press Club (hon. life), Police League Ind., Fraternal Order Police, Nat. Sojourners, Ind. Sports Corp. (charter gold mem.), U.S. Auto Club (life), Phi Chi. Clubs: Ind. Pacers Booster (charter),

Thundering Herd Booster Indpls. Colts (charter mem.). Lodges: Masons, Shriners (life). Home: 11603 Boone Dr Indianapolis IN 46229-9610

EL KODSI, BAROUKH, gastroenterologist, educator; b. Cairo, Aug. 24, 1923; s. Moussa and Zohra (Aslan Cohen) El K.; came to U.S., 1957, naturalized, 1963; M.D., Cairo U., 1945; m. Marie Menasha, Mar. 26, 1960; children—Sylvia, Robert, Karen. Intern, Univ. Hosp. Cairo Sch. Medicine, 1946; resident in gen. medicine Jewish Hosp., Cairo, 1947-50, attending physician, 1950-57; intern, Miriam Hosp., Providence, 1958; resident in internal medicine, Boston City Hosp., 1959-61, chief resident, 1961-62, fellow in gastroenterology, 1962-64; asst. dir. medicine Union Hosp., Framingham, Mass., 1964-65; asso. dir. medicine Maimonides Med. Center, Bklyn., 1965-67, dir. gastroenterology, 1968—; chief gastroenterology Coney Island Hosp., N.Y.C., 1967-68; instr. Boston City Hosp., 1962-65; instr. Downstate Med. Center, SUNY, Bklyn., 1965-69, asst. prof. medicine, 1969-76, asso. prof., 1976—. Chmn. Bklyn. physicians com. United Jewish Appeal. Fellow Am. Coll. Gastroenterology, ACP; mem. Am. Fedn. Clin. Research, Am. Gastroent. Assn., Am. Soc. Gastrointestinal Endoscopy, Am. Soc. Study of Liver Disease, AMA, N.Y. Gastroenterologic Assn. (pres. 1985-86), Ostomy Club (mem. exec. council). Contbr. articles to profl. jours. Home: 118 Girard St Brooklyn NY 11235-3010 Office: 925 48th St Brooklyn NY 11219-2919

ELKOWITZ, LLOYD KENT, dental anesthesiologist, dentist, pharmacist; b. Bklyn., Jan. 26, 1936; s. Paul and Lillian (Applebaum) E.; m. Deanna A. Weinger; children: Sheryl, Andrew, Marc. BS in Pharmacy, Columbia U., 1956; DDS, Case Western Res. U., 1960, postgrad., 1961. Diplomate Am. Dental Bd. Anesthesiology. Resident in anesthesiology U. Ctr. Hosp, Pitts., 1961, fellow in anesthesiology, 1966; anesthesiologist Walson Army Hosp., Fort Dix, N.J., 1962-64; pvt. practice Great Neck, N.Y., 1964—; dir. divsn. dental anesthesiology dept. dentistry Nassau County Med. Ctr., East Meadow, L.I., 1975—; chmn. dept. dental anesthesiology Flushing (N.Y.) Hosp. Med. Ctr., 1989-95; pres. dental adv. coun. Adelphi U., Tufts U., Garden City, N.y., 1986—; adj. prof. dental biology Adelphi U., 1982—. Trustee Kings Point (N.Y.) Civic Assn., 1978-95. Capt. U.S. Army, 1962-64. Recipient Callahan Meml. award Ohio State Dental Assn., 1960. Fellow Am. Dental Soc. Anesthesiology, Acad. Gen. Dentistry, Am. Soc. for Advancement of Anesthesia in Dentistry; mem. ADA, Am. Pharm. Assn., N.Y. State Dental Assn., Queens Dental Assn., Queens County Dental Soc. (trustee 1995), Internat. Anesthesia Rsch. Soc., Am. Soc. Dentistry for Children, Queens Inst. for Continuing Dental Edn. (charter), Alpha Zeta Omega, Alpha Omega, Alpha Epsilon Delta. Office: 107 Northern Blvd Great Neck NY 11021-4309

ELKS, MARTHA LOUISE, endocrinology and internal medicine educator; b. Wilson, N.C., Jan. 6, 1954; d. Chester Arthur and Mary Louise (Taylor) E.; m. John W. Sawyer, Jr., May 15, 1982; children: Julia Marie, Karen Anne. AB, Duke U., 1974; MD, U. N.C., 1977, PhD, 1978. Diplomate Am. Bd. Internal Medicine, Am. Bd. Endocrinology. Intern, then resident Johns Hopkins U., Balt., 1978-80; clin. assoc. NIH/Nat. Heart, Lung, Blood Inst., Bethesda, Md., 1980-83, staff, 1983-85; prof. internal medicine/endocrinology Health Scis. Ctr. Tex. Tech. U., Lubbock, 1985-85, prof., 1995—. With USPHS, 1980-84. Fellow ACP, Am. Coll. Nutrition, Am. Coll. Endocrinology; mem. Endocrine Soc., Soc. of Gen. Internal Medicine, Am. Fedn. Clin. Rsch., Am. Diabetes Assn. Home: 3312 43rd St Lubbock TX 79413-3124 Office: Tex Tech U HSC 3601 4th St Lubbock TX 79430-0001

ELLENBERG, MAURY RUBEN, physician, educator; b. Cremona, Italy, Nov. 2, 1947; came to U.S., 1950; s. Mechel and Regina (Herzberg) E.; m. Joanna Miriam Gardin, June 8, 1976; children: Michael, David, Ari, Zev, Eliezer. BA in Chemistry, Wayne State U., 1969, MD, 1973. Diplomate Am. Bd. Internal Medicine, Am. Bd. Physical Medicine & Rehab., Am. Bd. Electrodiagnostic Medicine. Instr. in phys. medicine and rehab. Ohio State U., Columbus, 1976-78; clin. asst. prof. Wayne State U., 1991-95, clin. assoc. prof., 1995—; dir. phys. medicine and rehab. residency program Sinai Hosp., Detroit, 1990—; sr. assoc. attending physician Sinai Hosp., 1986—, assoc. dept. chair, 1991—, co-med. dir. rehab. unit, 1995—; provisional active staff Providence Hosp., Southfield, Mich., 1991—; med. dir. Functional Recovery Program of Mich., West Bloomfield, 1991—. Contbr. articles to profl. jours. Recipient RSVP grant Mich. Health Care Edn. and Rsch. Found., 1990. Fellow ACP; mem. AMA, Am. Acad. Phys. Medicine & Rehab. (Richard and Hinda Rosenthal Found. Lectureship award 1992, Disting. Clinician award 1995), Mich. Acad. Phys. Medicine & Rehab., Mich. State Soc., Wayne County Med. Soc., Am. Assn. Electromyography and Electrodiagnosis, Assn. Acad. Physiatrists, Am. Pain Soc., Am. Acad Pain Medicine, Physiatric Assn. of Spine, Sports and Occupational Rehab. Office: Rehab Physicians PC 6767 West Outer Dr Detroit MI 48235

ELLENBERGER, CARL, neurologist; b. Cleve., Mar. 31, 1939; s. Carl and Marguerite J. (McGuiness) E. BA, U. Rochester, 1961; MD, Yale U., 1965; MusD, Elizabethtown Coll., 1995. Asst. prof. medicine Pa. State U., Hershey, 1973-80; assoc. prof. neurology Case Western Reserve U., Cleve., 1980-86; med. dir. Lebanon (Pa.) Magnetic Imaging, 1989—. Mem. editl. bd. Neuro-Ophthalmology Jour., 1983—, Jour. Neuroimaging, 1991—. Bd. dirs. Pa. Chautauqua, Mt. Gretna, Pa., 1989-95; founder Music Festival Gretna, 1976-96, Music at Gretna, Mt. Gretna, Pa. Maj. U.S. Army, 1968-70. Fellow Am. Acad. Neurology; mem. Am. Neurol. Assn., Am. Soc. Neuroimaging, N.Am. Neuro-Ophthalmology Soc., Phi Beta Kappa. Office: Lebanon Magnetic Imaging 855 Tuck St Lebanon PA 17042

ELLENBERGER, DIANE MARIE, nurse, consultant; b. St. Louis, Oct. 5, 1946; d. Charles Ernst and Celeste Loraine (Neudecker) E.; RN, Barnes Hosp., St. Louis, 1970; BSN, St. Louis U., 1976; MSN, U. Colo., 1977. Staff nurse hosps., clin. nurse, St. Louis, 1973-76; nurse clinician, Sedalia, Mo., 1977-78; nurse clinician, educator Bothwell Hosp., Sedalia, 1977-78; clin. nurse specialist, coord. perinatal outreach edn. Cardinal Glennon Meml. Hosp. Children, St. Louis, 1978-80; instr. McKendree Coll., Lebanon, Ill., 1980; asst. prof. Maryville Coll., St. Louis, 1982-85; nurse cons. Carr, Korein, Tillery, Kunin, Montroy, & Glass, Attys. at Law, 1986—; owner, operator Diane Designs Needlepoint, St. Louis, 1981—. Served with Nurse Corps, USAF, 1970-72. Mem. Am. Nurses Assn., Nat. Perinatal Assn., Assn. Women's Health, Obstetric and Neonatal Nurses, Mo. Nurses Assn. (3d dist. sec. 1991-93, 1st v.p. 1993, pres. 1993-96, bd. dirs. 1995—, ANA del. 1996—), Mo. Perinatal Assn. (v.p. 1980), Sigma Theta Tau. Mem. Divine Sci. Ch. Contbr. articles profl. jours. Office: 412 Missouri Ave East Saint Louis IL 62201-3016

ELLENBERGER, THOMAS RICHARD, JR., internist; b. Johnstown, Pa., Nov. 24, 1952; s. Thomas Richard and Joan Agathe (Jackel) E.; m. Elisa M. Marziani, Mar. 26, 1977; children: Elisabeth, Laura, Ann, Mark. BS, Pa. State U., 1973; MD, Jefferson Med. Sch., 1975. Diplomate Am. Bd. Internal Medicine. Resident in internal medicine Lankenau Hosp., Phila., 1975-78; pvt. practice Johnstown, 1978—; active staff Lee Hosp., Johnstown, 1978—. Mem. Am. Soc. Internal Medicine, Pa. Soc. Internal Medicine, Alpha Omega Alpha. Presbyterian. Office: 321 Main St Ste 5D Johnstown PA 15901

ELLENBOGEN, CHARLES, internist; b. Winston-Salem, N.C., Feb. 10, 1939; s. Edward and Adele (Wilinsky) E.; divorced; children: Daniel, Jennie. SB, U. Chgo., 1960, MD, 1964. Intern USAF Med. Ctr., Lackland AFB, Tex., 1965-66, medicine resident, 1966-68, fellow infectious diseases, 1968-70; dir. internal medicine, lt. col. 483 USAF Hosp., Cam Rahn Bay, 1970-71; chief infectious disease USAF Med. Ctr., Lackland AFB, 1971-77; assoc. prof., vice-chmn. medicine U. Mo., Kansas City, 1977-80; dir. internal medicine Fayetteville (N.C.) Area Health Edn. Ctr., 1980—. Author: FAHEC Clinical Manual, 1990, 91; contbr. over 20 articles to profl. jours. Recipient Sustaining Membership award Air Force Assn., 1983, Commendation medal USAF, 1987. Fellow ACP, Infectious Disease Soc. Am.; mem. AMA, Cumberland County Med. Soc., N.C. Med. Soc. Office: Fayetteville Area Health Ed 1601 Owen Dr Fayetteville NC 28304-3425

ELLENBROEK, ALBERTUS ANTONIUS, neuroscientist, educator; b. Apeldoorn, The Netherlands, Mar. 22, 1958; s. Albertus Antonius and Anna (DeBoer) E.; m. Brigit Judith Hildegard Magnus, Dec. 13, 1985; children: Inessa, Arabella. BSc in Chemistry, U. Nymegen, The Netherlands, 1979, MSc in Chemistry, 1982, PhD cum laude, 1988. Lectr. King Saud U., Abha, Saudi Arabia, 1982-83; rsch. asst. Max Planck Inst., Gottingen, Germany, 1983-84; rsch. asst. Cath. U., Nymegen, The Netherlands, 1984-88, univ. lectr., 1988—. Contbr. articles to profl. jours. Recipient Sandoz Rsch. prize Interdisciplinary Soc. Biol. Psychiatry, 1989. Mem. European Neurosci. Assn., Am. Soc. Neurosci., N.Y. Acad. Scis. Office: U Nymegen Dept Pharmacology, PO Box 9101, Nymegen 6500 HB, The Netherlands

ELLENBURG, LUKE L., JR., ophthmologist; b. Greeneville, Tenn., Jan. 13, 1949; s. Luke L. Sr. and Katherine (Johnson) E.; m. Linda Blanton; 1 child, Ashley, Katherine, Jennifer, Matthew. MD, Vanterbilt U., 1975. Diplomate Am. Bd. Ophthalmology; lic. Tenn. Intern, resident Vanderbilt U. Hosp., Nashville, 1975-79; pvt. practice Greeneville, Tenn., 1979—; staff physician Laughlin Meml. Hosp., Greeneville, Takoma Adventist Hosp., Greeneville. Mem. Am. Acad. Ophthalmology, Tenn. Med. Assn., Greene County Med. Soc. Office: 801 E Church St Greeneville TN 37745

ELLENSOHN, KAROL KAYE, psychotherapist; b. Dubuque, Iowa, Sept. 14, 1942; d. Walter Alden and Winifred Mae (Putney) Roe; m. James Henry Mitchell, June 8, 1963 (div. 1984); 1 child, Jennifer Kaye; m. Edgar Ulrich Ellensohn, Sept. 27, 1989. AAS, RN, William Rainey Harper Coll., Palatine, Ill., 1977; BS, U. San Francisco, 1982; MS, U. La Verne, 1984; postgrad., Fielding Inst., Santa Barbara, Calif., 1984-86. RN, Calif., Ill.; MFCC; cert. community coll. tchr. Personnel dir. Mercy Hosp., Cedar Rapids, Iowa, 1963-64; personnel dir., exec. sec. to adminstr. Meml. Hosp., Colorado Springs, 1964-67; primary care and charge nurse oncology-hematology unit Evanston (Ill.) Hosp., 1977-78; adminstrv. asst. to interior designer Westlake Village, Calif., 1978-79; oncology nurse Vis. Nurses Assn., Ventura, Calif., 1979-81; contract therapist Caostal Radiation Oncology Med. Svcs., Inc., 1984—; art dealer, 1986—l contract chem. dependency therapy, 1983-84; pvt. practice as nurse therapist, Ventura County, Calif., 1979-83; quality assurance coord. Oxnard (Calif.) Cmty. Hosp., 1982, acting dir. nurses, 1982; part-time clin. instr. in psychology and neurology Ventura Coll., 1981-82; cons. in quality assurance Simi Valley (Calif.) Cmty. Hosp.; cons. Wellness Cmty., Westlake Village, 1988—, Palm Desert (Calif.) Art Assn., 1988—. Contbr. articles to local newspapers. Mem. lectr. staff Camarillo Women's Day.; vol., contbr. Bighorn Inst., Palm Desert, 1989—, AIDS Assistance Program, Palm Springs, 1993; contbr. McCallum Theatre for the Performing Arts, Palm Desert, 1993, Hospice of Valley, Scottsdale, 1996; vol. Phoenix Art Mus. Home Tour, 1996; counselor, developer Nat. Disting. Svc. Registry, 1989-90. Recipient award Danforth Found., 1956. Mem. AACD, Calif. Assn. Marriage and Family Therapists, Ill. Nurses Assn., ABA, Calif. Nurses Assn., So. Calif. Hospice Assn., Ventura County Hospice Assn. (lectr.), Ventura County Discharge Planners Assn., Nat. Assn. Quality Assurance Profls., Am. Cancer Soc. (vol. svc. and rehab. com., speaker's bur., facilitator coping with cancer therapy groups, co-facilitator understanding cancer course, bd. dirs., Midge Wilson award 1980, Order Golden Sword 1981, Outstanding Svc. 1983), Art Dealers Assn. Home: 55-801 Congressional La Quinta CA 92253-4754 Office: Le KAE Galleries 7175 E Main St Scottsdale AZ 85251

ELLER, M. EDWARD, JR., physician; b. Martinsville, Va., Oct. 20, 1954; s. Myron Edward and Clovis (Gregory) E. BA in Biology, U. Va., Charlottesville, 1977, MD, 1981. Diplomate Am. Bd. Family Practice. Chief resident dept. family practice U. Va., Charlottesville, 1983-84; pres. Commonwealth Family Physicians, Inc., Martinsville, Va., 1984—; med. dir. Blue Ridge Rehab., Martinsville, 1988-96; chmn. dept. family practice Meml. Hosp. Martinsville and Henry County, 1990-92. Home: 309 Thomas Heights Martinsville VA 24112 Office: Commonwealth Family Physicians Inc 445 Commonwealth Blvd Martinsville VA 24112

ELLFELDT, HOWARD JAMES, orthopedic surgeon; b. Kansas City, Mo., Feb. 11, 1937; s. Howard James and Peggy Maude (Bowen) E.; m. Dee Anne Park, June 18, 1960; children: Kimberly, Jeffrey, Kimela, Kent. AB, U. Kans., 1959, MD, 1963. Cert. Am. Bd. Orthopedic Surgery. Intern U. Kans., 1963-64, intern in orthopedic surgery, 1964-68; pvt. practice specializing in orthopedic surgery Kansas City, Mo., 1970—; team physician Kansas City King's Basketball Club, 1972-84, Kansas City Chief's Football Club, 1973-90; chief of staff Rsch. Med. Ctr., Kansas City, 1984-85, bd. dirs. 1986-92; bd. dirs. Rsch. Health Svcs., Kansas City, 1985-91; pres. Rsch. Comprehensive Health Care, Inc., 1985-91. Bd. dirs. K-Life, Shawnee Mission, Kans., 1983-86. Served to maj. U.S. Army, 1968-70, Vietnam. Fellow Am. Acad. Orthopedic Surgeons; mem. ACS (diplomate), Am. Orthopedic Soc. for Sports Medicine, Am. Coll. Sports Medicine, Alpha Omega Alpha. Republican. Episcopalian. Club: Mission Hills (Kans.) Country. Home: 5701 W 119th St Overland Park KS 66209-3722 Office: Kans City Bone and Joint Clinic 6420 Prospect Ave Ste 207T Kansas City MO 64132-4127

ELLINGER, RICHARD WAYNE, orthodontist; b. Columbus, Ohio, Mar. 28, 1945; s. Everett Carlton and Florence Margene (Bigony) E.; m. Linda Jane Hall, June 16, 1973; children: Erin Ruth, Lara Kathryn. BS cum laude, Muskingum Coll., New Concord, Ohio, 1967; DDS cum laude, Ohio State U., 1971; MS, U. Mich., 1976. Rotating dental intern Denver Gen. Hosp., 1971-72; clin. instr. operative dentistry Ohio State U., 1972-74; pvt. prac. family dentistry Worthington, Ohio, 1973; grad. instr. orthodontics U. Mich., 1975-76; pvt. practice Tiffin, Ohio, 1976—; trustee Mercy Hosp. Lay Adv., Tiffin, 1978-82. Mem. allocation com. Tiffin-Seneca United Way, 1978-86; bd. trustees Tiffin-Seneca Public Libr., 1993—; trustee Muskingum Coll. Alumni Adv. Bd., 1986-95. Mem. ADA, Am. Assn. Orthodontists, Ohio Dental Assn., North Ctrl. Ohio Dental Soc. (exec. bd. 1978-89, editor newletter 1978-84, past pres.), Elks, Kiwanis, Omicron Kappa Upsilon. Office: 6 Main St Tiffin OH 44883

ELLIOT, ELISA LOUISE, microbiologist; b. Mpls., Nov. 21, 1956; d. Arthur McAuley and Carol Ann (Brand) Elliot. Student, Tex. A&M U., 1974-76; BS in Microbiology, Tex. Tech U., 1977; PhD, U. Md., 1984. Med. technician, med. technologist Scott and White Clinic and Hosp., Temple, Tex., 1977-78; grad. teaching asst. U. Md., College Park, 1978-79, 82-84; asst. prof. seafood microbiology U. Alaska-Fishery Indsl. Tech. Ctr., Kodiak, 1984-87; rsch. microbiologist U.S. Dept. Agr. Food Safety and Inspection Svc., Beltsville, Md., 1987-89; part-time instr. Univ. Coll., U. Md., College Park, 1987-90; rsch. microbiologist FDA, Washington, 1989-92, sci. policy analyst, 1992—. Contbr. chpts. to books, articles to profl. jours. Bd. dirs. Kodiak Women's Resource and Crisis Ctr., 1986-87. NSF grantee, 1973; NSF grad fellow, 1979-82. Mem. Am. Soc. Microbiology (sec. Alaska br. 1985-87, councillor 1986-87), Nat. Shellfisheries Assn., Nature Conservancy, Alpha Lambda Delta, Phi Kappa Phi. Office: FDA HFS-22 Ctr for Food Safety & Applied Nutrition 200 C St SW Washington DC 20204-0001

ELLIOTT, CAROL HARRIS, nutrition counselor, dietitian; b. Chgo., Mar. 26, 1950; d. Ray Waymon and Lois Julia (Buendgen) Harris; m. Craig C. Elliott, Aug. 12, 1973; children: Stephen Craig, Diana Carol. BS in Dietetics, Mich. State U., 1972. Licensed dietitian, nutritionist, Fla. Dietetic intern Henry Ford Hosp., Detroit, 1972-73; chief therapeutic dietitian Seiler's Corp./N. Adams (Mass.) Regional Hosp., 1973-75; clin. dietitian Berkshire Med. Ctr., Pittsfield, Mass., 1975-78, Humana Hosp., Daytona Beach, Fla., 1979-81; faculty therapeutic dietitian Family Practice Ctr., Halifax Med. Ctr., Daytona Beach, 1982-83; pvt. practice nutrition counseling service, pres. Elliott Cons., Inc., Daytona Beach, 1980—; cons. Blind Svcs., 1983—, Conklin Ctr. Multihandicapped Blind, 1983—, Clyatt Meml. Ctr., 1984-88, 89—, Holiday Care Ctr., 1984—, Good Samaritan Ctr., 1984—, Daytona Beach Geriatric Ctr., 1984-88, 89-93, Huntington Sq. Convalariums, 1985-93, Act, Inc. Volusia County, 1985-88, Halifax Convalescent Ctr., 1987—, Atlantic Shores Hosp., 1987-88, Bishop's Glen, 1987—, Ormond in the Pines, 1987, 88-93, 95—, Daytona Manor, 1985-87, 88-91, Stetson U., 1990—; adj. instr., spkr. in field, Volusia County Head Start Program, 1993—, OutReach, Inc., 1993—. Author: ACLF Menu and Reference Guide, Long Term Care Quality Assurance Program Survey. Mem. Am. Dietetic Assn., Fla. Dietetic Assn., Fla. East Cen. Dietetic Assn. (numerous coms. 1979-95, legis. chair 1991-95), Cons. Nutritionists-Dietitians in Pvt. Practice, Fla. Health Care Assn. (assoc.), Am. Bus. Women's Assn., Delta Delta Delta. Lutheran. Home: 18 Lake Vista Way Ormond Beach FL 32174-6785 Office: 755A White St Daytona Beach FL 32114-1737

ELLIOTT, CHARLES HAROLD, clinical psychologist; b. Kansas City, Mo., Dec. 30, 1948; s. Joseph Bond and Suzanne (Wider) E.; 1 child, Brian Douglas. BA, U. Kans., 1971, MA, 1974, PhD, 1976. Cert. clin. psychologist, N. Mex. Asst. prof. E. Cen. Univ., Ada, Okla., 1976-79, U. Okla. Health Sciences, 1979-85; assoc. prof. Dept. Psychiatry U. Okla., 1983-85, Dept. Psychiatry U. N. Mex. Sch. Medicine, Albuquerque, 1985-87; adj. assoc. prof. dept. psychology U. N.Mex., Albuquerque, 1986—; faculty full appointment Fielding Inst., Santa Barbara, Calif., 1987—; consulting editor Jour. Clin. Child Psychology, 1987-89; ad hoc reviewer to profl. jours., 1983—; cognitive therapist NIMH Collaborative Study of Depression, Okla. City, 1980-85. Guest editor Psychiatric Annals, 1992; contbr. numerous articles to profl. jours. Mem. APA, Biofeedback and Behavioral Medicine Soc. N.Mex. (pres. 1988), Assn. for Advancement of Behavior Therapy, Assn. for Advancement Psychology, Soc. Behavioral Medicine, Soc. Pediat. Psychology, N.Mex. Psychol. Assn. Home: 2700 Vista Grande Dr NW Unit 83 Albuquerque NM 87120-1000 Office: 1400 Central Ave SE Ste 3200 Albuquerque NM 87106-4811

ELLIOTT, DAVID BRADLEY, optometrist, educator; b. Cottingham, Eng., Nov. 10, 1961; s. David Oliver and Valerie (Cook) E.; m. Mary McLaughlin, Sept. 23, 1990; children: Danny Patrick, Róisín. BS in Optometry with honors, U. Bradford, Eng., 1983, PhD in Optometry, 1988. Rsch. asst. prof. Sch. Optometry U. Waterloo, Can., 1991-93; asst. prof. Sch. Optometry U. Waterloo, 1993-95; sr. lectr., clin. dir. dept. optometry U. Bradford, 1995—; acting dir. Ctr. for Sight Enhancement, Waterloo, 1994-95. Contbr. chpts. to books and articles to profl. jours. Mem. Gt. Britain Students Rugby League Team, 1982-86, Profl. Rugby League, 1979-85, Bradford U. Colors, 1982. Fellow Am. Acad. Optometry; mem. Coll. Optometrists, Assn. for Rsch. in Vision-Ophthalmology, Vision Aid Overseas, Applied Vision Assn. Office: U Bradford Dept Optometry, Richmond Rd, Bradford BD7 1DP, England

ELLIOTT, DAVID PATRICK, pharmacist, educator; b. Edmonton, Canada, Mar. 16, 1956; came to the U.S., 1978; s. Clifford Albert and Lucia Catherine (Fuchs) E.; m. Anita Gertrude Lorenzo, Apr. 24, 1981; children: Matthew Paul, Sarah Anne, Mary Luisa. BS in Pharmacy, U. Manitoba, 1978; PharmD, U. Tex., 1981. RPh, W.Va., Tex. Resident in adult medicine U. Tex., Austin, 1980-81; asst. prof. pharmacy practice U. Ill., Chgo., 1981-84; asst. prof. clin. pharmacy W.Va. U., Charleston, 1984-90, assoc. prof., 1990—. Contbr. articles to profl. jours. Fellow Am. Soc. Cons. Pharmacists; mem. Am. Coll. Clin. Pharmacy. Roman Catholic. Office: W Va U 3110 Mac Corkle Ave SE Charleston WV 25304

ELLIOTT, GEORGE ALGIMON, pathologist, toxicologist, veterinarian; b. Trappe, N.D., June 6, 1925; s. George A. and Mattie Tileston (Sullivan) E.; m. Marguerite Van Zandt Hammond, Aug. 15, 1949; children: Kathleen, Elizabeth, Jennifer. DVM, U. Ga., 1953; MSc in Vet. Pathology, U. Pa., 1957. Diplomate Am. Coll. Vet. Pathologists. From instr. to asst. prof. U. Pa. Sch. of Vet. Medicine, Phila., 1955-60; asst. prof. comparative pathology Vanderbilt U. Sch. of Medicine, Nashville, 1960-62; rsch. scientist (sr. vet. pathologist, toxicologist) The Upjohn Co., Kalamazoo, Mich., 1962-90. Contbr. articles to profl. jours. With U.S. Navy, 1945-46 PTO. Mem. Am. Vet. Medicine Assn., Phi Kappa Phi, Sigma Xi. Democrat. Mem. Reformed Ch. of Am. Home: 4430 Romence Rd Portage MI 49002

ELLIOTT, KELLY ANN, women's health nurse, midwife; b. Leavenworth, Kans., Apr. 2, 1958; b. Robert Lee and Carol Geanne (Scott) Elliott; div.; children: Afton Leigh Cox, Shelby Ann. BA in Social Welfare, U. Ark., 1980; BSN, Kans. U., 1982; MSN, U. Hawaii; PhD, U. Kans., 1995—. CPR instr., ACLS; cert. nurse midwife; cert. women's health nurse practitioner. Nurse reviewer Tex. Med. Found., Tyler; staff nurse Med. Ctr. Hosp., Tyler; nurse cons. Aetna Life and Casualty Ins., Tyler; staff nurse U.S. Army, Honolulu; nurse midwife Women's Health Care Group. Cpt. USA, 1989-94. Mem. ANA, NAACOG, Am. Coll. Nurse Midwives, Tex. Nurses Assn. Home: 7893 W 153rd Terr Overland Park KS 66223-2700

ELLIOTT, LARRY PAUL, cardiac radiologist, educator; b. Manhattan, Kans., Oct. 16, 1931; s. Leonard Paul and Mary Elizabeth (Myers) E.; m. Betty Lou Hawkins, June 23, 1956; children—Laurie Lou, Mary Elizabeth, Larry Paul. B.S., U. Fla., 1954; M.D., U. Tenn., 1957. Intern John Gaston Hosp., Memphis, 1957-58; resident in pediatrics and pediatric cardiology U. Fla. Hosp., 1958-61; resident in cardiac pathology and cardiovascular radiology U. Minn. Hosp., 1961-65; asso. prof. cardiac radiology Washington U. Med. Sch., St. Louis, 1966-67; prof. cardiac radiology U. Fla. Med. Sch., 1967-76; prof. radiology, dir. div. cardiac radiology U. Ala. Med. Sch., Birmingham, 1976-81; prof., chmn. dept. radiology Georgetown U. Sch. Medicine, 1981—; chmn. Fac. Practice Group, 1989—. Author: The X-Ray Diagnosis Heart Disease, 1968, 79; editor: Radiology, 1967—, Cardiovascular and Interventional Radiology, 1979—, The Fundamentals of Cardiac Imaging in Infants, Children and Adults, 1990; assoc. editor cardiovascular sect. Taveras Radiology, 1986; contbr. articles to med. jours. Recipient Disting. Alumnus award U. Fla., 1981, Outstanding Alumna award U. Tenn. Med. Sch., 1993; grantee cardiac radiology Nat. Heart Inst., 1968-76, Allied Health Profl. Act, 1970. Fellow N.Am. Soc. Cardiac Radiology (pres. 1977-78), Am. Coll. Cardiology; mem. Radiol. Soc. N.Am., Soc. Cardiac Angiography, Am. Heart Assn., Soc. Thoracic Radiology (founding mem., pres. faculty practice group 1989-93). Home: 4420 Hadfield Ln NW Washington DC 20007-2033 Office: 3800 Reservoir Rd NW Washington DC 20007-2196

ELLIOTT, LARRY PHILLIP, biologist, educator, researcher; b. Fleming, Mo., Sept. 27, 1938; s. Melvin Jewell and Margaret Marie (Hedrick) E.; m. Wilma Lee Grove, Aug. 8, 1961; children: Kerri Lynn Elliott McDaniel, Kimberly Ann Elliott Dallas, Kelly Jo. BA, William Jewell Coll., 1960; MS, U. Wisconsin, 1962, PhD, 1965. From asst. prof. to prof. biology dept. Western Ky. U., Bowling Green, 1965—. Contbr. articles to profl. jours. Mem. Am. Assn. Southeastern Biologists, Am. Soc. Microbiologists, Ky. Acad. Sci. (bd. dirs., past pres.), Sigma Xi, Beta Beta Beta (faculty advisor 1972—). Republican. Baptist. Office: Western Ky U Biology Dept Bowling Green KY 42101

ELLIOTT, LESTER FRANKLYN, plastic surgeon; b. Macon, Ga., Oct. 18, 1950; s. Sewell and Mary Grace E.; m. Elizabeth Wilkinson, May 30, 1981; children: Mary Grace, Elizabeth Ballard. BA, Princeton U., 1972; MD, Vanderbilt U., 1976. Resident Vanderbilt U., Nashville, 1976-77, 77-78, Tulane U., New Orleans, 1978-80, 80-81, Emory U., Atlanta, 1981-83; instr. surgery La. State U., New Orleans, 1983-85, asst. clin. prof. surgery, 1985-87; clin. instr. srugery Emory U., 1987—; researcher in field. Contbr. articles to profl. jours. Bd. dirs. Atlanta Ballet, 1996—. Clin. orthopaedic fellow Sahlgranska Hosp., Gothenberg, Sweden, 1975. Fellow Am. Coll. Surgeons; mem. Am. Soc. Aesthetic Plastic Surgery, Am. Cleft Palate Assn., Am. Soc. Plastic and Reconstructive Surgeons, Am. Soc. Maxillo-Facial Surgeons (adv. coun.), Southeastern Soc. Plastic and Reconstructive Surgeons, La. State Med. Soc., Surg. Assn. La., Ga. Surg. Soc., Ga. Plastic Surgery Soc. (pres. 1994—), New Orleans Surg. Soc., Orleans Parish Med. Soc., Maurice J. Jurkiewicz Soc., Alton Ochsner Surg. Soc., Oneiro Travel Club, Cap and Gown Club, Kappa Alpha. Home: 3668 Tuxedo Rd Atlanta GA 30305 Office: Atlanta Plastic Surgery Ste 500 675 Johnson Fery Rd NE Atlanta GA 30342

ELLIOTT, MARK LOILLIAM, respiratory physician, consultant, educator; b. Rinteln, West Germany, Oct. 23, 1957; s. Derek Norman and Barbara Elsie (Pring) E.; m. Nicola Caroline Shelbourne, Oct. 30, 1982; children: Ruth, Katherine. BA, Cambridge U., England, 1979, MB BChir, 1982, MA, 1982, MD, 1993. Registrar Brompton Hosp., London, 1987; rsch. fellow Brompton and King's Coll. Hosp., London, 1988-90; sr. registrar King's Coll. Hosp., London, 1991-92, Brompton Hosp., London, 1992-93; cons. physician St. James' U. Hosp., Leeds, England, 1993—. Assocs. editor: Thorax, 1994—; co-author: (books) European Respiratory Society Educational Programme Lung Cancer, 1993, Pass the MRCP (U.K.)-All the Techniques You Need, 1996; contbr. chpts. to books in field. Mem. Am. Thoracic Soc., European Respiratory Soc. (sec. sect. non-invasive support), Royal Coll. Physicians, British Thoracic Soc. Office: St James Hosp, Beckett St, LS9 7TF Leeds England

ELLIOTT, MELINDA JEAN, neonatologist, researcher; b. Steubenville, Ohio, Oct. 26, 1958; d. Gene Luther and Carolyn Jane (Harvey) E.; m. William Frank Cassano, May 13, 1989. BS in Biology, Bethany (W.Va.) Coll., 1980; MD, W.Va. U., 1984. Diplomate Am. Bd. Pediatrics, sub-bd. of Neonatal-Perinatal Medicine. Intern, then resident in pediatrics U. Fla.,

Gainesville, 1984-87, chief resident in pediatrics, instr., 1987-88, clin. rsch. fellow div. neonatology, 1988-91; staff neonatologist Franklin Square Hosp., Balt., 1991—. Mem. Am. Acad. Pediatrics, Alpha Omega Alpha. Democrat. Methodist. Office: Franklin Sq Hosp Dept Pediatrics 9000 Franklin Square Dr Baltimore MD 21237-3901

ELLIOTT, ROBERT BETZEL, physician; b. Ada, Ohio, Dec. 8, 1926; s. Floyd Milton and Rose Marguerite (Betzel) E.; m. Margaret Mary Robichaux, Aug. 26, 1954; children: Howard A., Michael D., Robert Bruce, Douglas J., John C., Joan O. BA, Ohio No. U., 1949; MD, U. Cin., 1953. Diplomate Am. Bd. Family Practice. Intern Charity Hosp., New Orleans, 1953-54; resident in pathology Bapt. Meml. Hosp., Memphis, 1958-59; practice medicine specializing in family practice Ada, 1959—; mem. staff Ohio No. U. Health Service, Ada, 1960-70; coroner Hardin County, 1973-93. Mem. Ada Exempted Village Sch. Bd., 1960—, pres., 1966-69, 72—, v.p. 1971—. Named Ohio Family Physician of Yr., 1985. Mem. AMA, Ohio State Med. Assn., Hardin County Med. Soc. (pres. 1964), Am. Acad. Family Physicians, Ohio Acad. Family Physicians, Lima Acad. Family Physicians, Am. Coll. Health Assn. Democrat. Presbyterian. Lodges: Masons, Elks. Home: 4429 State Route 235 Ada OH 45810-9509 Office: 302 N Main St Ada OH 45810-1198

ELLIOTT, TIMOTHY RAYMOND, psychologist, educator; b. Montgomery, Ala., Nov. 7, 1956; s. B. Raymond and Virginia (Slaughter) E.; m. Nancy Mignon Hampton, Aug. 1979; children: Natalie Caitlin, Victoria Grace. BS, Freed-Hardeman U., 1979; MS, Auburn U., 1981; PhD, U. Mo., 1987. Asst. prof. psychology and rehab. medicine Va. Commonwealth U./Med. Coll. Va., Richmond, 1987-93; assoc. prof., psychologist Dept. Rehab. Medicine, U. Ala., Birmingham, 1993—; cons. Am. Press Inst., Reston, Va., 1989-93, McGuire VA Med. Ctr., Richmond, 1988-93; vis. prof. Randolph-Macon Coll., Ashland, Va., 1990-92. Editorial bd. Jour. of Counseling Psychology, 1994-96; assoc. editor Jour. of Social and Clin. Psychology, 1996—; contbr. articles to profl. jours. Grantee Nat. Inst. Disability Rehab. and Rsch., 1993—; recipient Wayne C. Hall Rsch. award Phi Kappa Phi, 1989. Fellow APA (early rsch. achievement award divsn. 22 1991, early career scientist practitioner award divsn. 17 1994); mem. Am. Assn. Spinal Cord Injury Psychologists (grantee 1989-90), Assn. for Advancement Behavior Therapy. Disciples of Christ. Home: 2054 Crestmont Dr Birmingham AL 35226-3211 Office: U Ala 530 Spain Rehab 1717 6th Ave S Birmingham AL 35233-1801

ELLIOTT-WATSON, DORIS JEAN, psychiatric, mental health and gerontological nurse educator; b. Caney, Kans., Dec. 6, 1932; d. Alva Orr and Mary Amelia (Boyns) Elliott; children Marsha Jean Watson, Sherwood Elliott Watson. BE, U. Miami, Fla., 1952, MEd, 1954; EdD, Pacific Western U., 1982; BSN, U. Kans., 1985; AS in Psychology, Kansas City (Kans.) C.C., 1989; AA in Music, Kansas City C.C., 1994. RN, Kans., Mo.; cert. clin. specialist gerontology nurse, gerontology nurse generalist, psychiat.-mental health nurse, med.-surg. nurse, ANCC; cert. elem. to jr. coll. tchr., Kans., Mo.; lic. adult care home adminstr., Kans. Tchr. learning disabled, gifted, emotionally disturbed Shawnee Mission, Kans., 1961-76; instr. hospitalized psychiat. and med.-surg. children U. Kans. Med. Ctr., Kansas City, 1979-82; pvt. practice, gerontol. nurse educator Bonner Springs, Kans., 1985—; libr. U. Miami, 1952, Kans. U., 1978; nurse ARC, Kansas City, 1985—; nurse educator Am. Heart Assn., Kansas City, 1985—; program designer mainstreaming spl. needs children into regular classrooms, 1969; specialist geriatric sexuality nursing homes, 1986. Editor Park Stylus, Parkville, Mo., 1952; author, speaker Kansas City area, 1950—. Tutor-organizer Tutoring Vol.Orgn. for Inner City Children, 1965-68; sustaining mem. Rep. Nat. Com., Washington, 1978—, rep. Congl. Com., 1978—, Rep. Senatorial Com., 1978—; pres. Young Reps., Kansas City, 1960; mem. Rep. Nat. Conv. Platform Planning Com., 1995; patron, charter mem. Kaw Valley Cmty. Choir, 1990-92; mem. Kansas City Cmty. Choir, 1992—, mem. tour of cathedrals Christ Ch., Oxford and King's Coll., Eng., 1993; mem. Mid. Am. Nazarene Coll. Cmty. Choir, 1993—, Leavenworth Cmty. Carnegie Choir, 1994—. Recipient Coast to Coast 2810 miles award Am. Running and Fitness Assn., 1994; inducted Rep. Nat. Hall of Honor, Rep. Nat. Conv., 1992. Mem. ANA (coun. on gerontol. nurses, coun. for cmty., primary care and long term care nursing practice, coun. for nursing rsch.), NEA (life, del. state conv. 1980, nat. conv. 1973), Kans. Nurses Assn., U. Kans. Alumni Assn., Bus. and Profl. Women, Order Ea. Star (Electra 1982, Martha 1994, Marshal 1995, Assoc. Conductress 1996), Order Rainbow for Girls (worthy advisor 1950), Am. Volkssport Assn. (Tri-Athlete 1993, 94, 95, 4500 Km Walking award 1993, 5500Km 1994, Sunflower State Games Athlete 1993, 94, 95, Sooner State Games Athlete award 1994, 95, Mid-Am. Walking Marathon 1994, 6500 Km Walking award 1995), Tiblow Trail-blazers Walking Club (pres. 1993—), Nat. Wildlife Fedn. (cert. backyard wildlife habitat 1994), Kappa Delta Pi, Pi Delta Epsilon, Phi Theta Kappa, Alpha Kappa Delta, Phi Alpha Theta. Home and Office: 231 Sheidley Ave Bonner Springs KS 66012-1410

ELLIOTT-ZAHORIK, BONNIE, nurse, administrator; b. Algona, Iowa. AAS, Coll. Lake County, Grayslake, Ill., 1979; student, U. Iowa; BS, Coll. St. Francis, Joliet, Ill., 1988; MSM, Nat. Louis U., Evanston, Ill., 1989; doctoral fellow, Walden U., Mpls., 1995—. RN, Ill.; CCRN; cert. nurse adminstr.-advanced; cert. critical care preceptor and instr. Evening nurse dir. Victory Meml. Hosp., Waukegan, Ill., 1991—; adminstrn./mgmt. doctoral fellow Walden U., Mpls., 1995—. Contbr. articles to profl. jours. Mem. AACN, Ill. Coun. Nurse Mgrs. (pres. Region 2B).

ELLIS, ALBERT, clinical psychologist, educator, author; b. Pitts., Sept. 27, 1913; s. Henry Oscar and Hettie (Hanigbaum) E.; life ptnr. Janet L. Wolfe. B.B.A., CCNY, 1934; M.A., Columbia U., 1943, Ph.D., 1947. Diplomate: Am. Bd. Profl. Psychology; in clin. hypnosis Am. Bd. Psychol. Hypnosis; Am. Bd. Med. Psychotherapists, Am. Bd. Sexology. Free-lance writer, 1934-38; personnel mgr. Distinctive Creations, 1938-48; sr. clin. psychologist N.J. State Hosp., Greystone Park, 1948-49; instr. psychology Rutgers U., 1948-49, adj. prof., 1971-83; instr. psychology N.Y. U., 1949; adj. prof. Union Grad. Sch., 1971-77, U.S. Internat. U., 1974-80, Pittsburg State U., 1978—; chief psychologist N.J. State Diagnostic Center, Menlo Park, 1949-50, N.J. Dept. Instns. and Agys., Trenton, 1950-52; pvt. practice psychotherapy and marriage and family therapy N.Y.C., 1943-68; exec. dir. Inst. for Rational-Emotive Therapy, N.Y.C., 1959-89; pres., 1989—; Cons. clin. psychology VA, 1961-67. Author: An Introduction to the Principles of Scientific Psychoanalysis, 1950, The Folklore of Sex, 1951, (with A.P. Pillay) Sex, Society and the Individual, 1953, The American Sexual Tragedy, 1954, Sex Life of the American Woman and the Kinsey Report, 1954, New Approaches to Psychotherapy Techniques, 1955, (with Ralph Brancale) The Psychology of Sex Offenders, 1956, How to Live With a Neurotic, 1957, Sex Without Guilt, 1958, What Is Psychotherapy, 1959, The Place of Values in the Practice of Psychotherapy, 1959, The Art and Science of Love, 1960, (with Robert A. Harper) A Guide to Successful Marriage, 1961, (with R.A. Harper) A Guide to Rational Living, 1961, (with Albert Abarbanel) The Encyclopedia of Sexual Behavior, 1961, Reason and Emotion in Psychotherapy, 1962, The Intelligent Woman's Guide to Manhunting, 1963, If This Be Sexual Heresy, 1963, Sex and the Single Man, 1963, The Origins and the Development of the Incest Taboo, 1963, Nymphomania, A Study of the Over-Sexed Woman, 1964, Homosexuality, 1965, Suppressed: Seven Key Essays Publishers Dared Not Print, 1965, The Case for Sexual Liberty, 1965, The Search for Sexual Enjoyment, 1966, (with others) How to Raise an Emotionally Healthy, Happy Child, 1966, (with Roger O. Conway) The Art of Erotic Seduction, 1967, Is Objectivism a Religion, 1968, (with John M. Gullo) Murder and Assassination, 1971, (with others) Growth Through Reason, 1971, Executive Leadership: A Rational Approach, 1972, The Civilized Couple's Guide to Extramarital Adventure, 1972, How to Master Your Fear of Flying, 1972, The Sensuous Person: Critique and Corrections, 1972, (with others) Sex and Sex Education: A Bibliography, 1972, Humanistic Psychotherapy: The Rational-Emotive Approach, 1973, (with Robert A. Harper) A New Guide to Rational Living, 1975, Sex and the Liberated Man, 1976, Anger How to Live With and Without It, 1977, (with Russell Grieger) Handbook of Rational-Emotive Therapy, 1977, (with W. Knaus) Overcoming Procrastination, 1977, (with E. Abrahms) Brief Psychotherapy in Medical and Health Practice, 1978, (with J.M. Whiteley) Theoretical and Empirical Foundations of Rational-Emotive Therapy, 1979, The Intelligent Woman's Guide to Dating and Mating, 1979, (with I. Becker) A Guide to Personal Happiness, 1982, (with M. Bernard) Rational-Emotive Approaches to the Problems of Childhood, 1983, (with M. Bernard) Clinical Applications of Rational-Emotive Therapy, 1985, Overcoming Resistance, 1985, (with Russell Grieger) Handbook of Rational-Emotive Therapy, Vol. 2, 1986, (with Windy Dryden) The Practice of Rational-Emotive Therapy, 1987, (with others) Rational-Emotive Treatment of Alcoholism and Substance Abuse, 1988, How To Stubbornly Refuse to Make Yourself Miserable About Anything-Yes Anything!, 1988, (with others) Rational-Emotive Couples Therapy, 1989, (with R. Yeager) Why Some Therapies Don't Work: The Dangers of Transpersonal Psychology, 1989, (with Windy Dryden) The Essential Albert Ellis, 1990, (with Patricia Hunter) Why Am I Always Broke: How to Be Sane about Money, 1991, (with Windy Dryden) A Dialogue with Albert Ellis: Against Dogma, 1991, (with Emmett Velten) What To Do When AA Doesn't Work For You: Rational Steps to Quitting Alcohol, 1992, (with Lidia Dengelegi and Michael Abrams) The Art and Science of Rational Eating, 1992, (with Arthur Lange) How to Keep People from Pushing Your Buttons, 1994, (with Michael Abrams) How to Cope with a Fatal Illness, 1994, Reason and Emotion in Psychotherapy Revised, 1994, Better, Deeper and More Enduring Brief Therapy, 1996, (with Jack Gordon, Michael Neenan nd Stephen Palmer) Stress Counseling: A Rational Creative Behavior Therapy Approach, 1996. Fellow APA (pres. divsn. cons. psychology 1961-62, exec. com. divsn. psychotherapy 1969-73, coun. reps. 1963-64, 72-74), AAAS, Am. Assn. Marriage and Family Therapists (exec. com. 1957-59), Soc. Sci. Study Sex (exec. com. 1957-58, pres. 1958-60), Am. Orthopsychiat. Assn., Am. Sociol. Assn., Am. Assn. Applied Anthropology; mem. ACA, Am. Assn. Sex Educators, Counselors and Therapists (bd. dirs. 1981-82), Nat. Acad. Practice, Soc. Psychotherapy Rsch., N.Y. Assn. Clin. Psychologists in Pvt. Practice (chmn. 1952-54), N.Y. Joint Coun. Psychologists on Legislation (exec. com. 1951-53), Am. Group Psychotherapy Assn., Am. Acad. Psychotherapists (exec. com. 1954-64, v.p. 1962-64), Mensa, Am. Assn. Advancement Psychotherapy, N.Y. State Psychol. Assn., Soc. Exptl. and Clin. Hypnosis. Office: Inst for Rational-Emotive Therapy 45 E 65th St New York NY 10021-6508

ELLIS, DANIEL SUMNER, physician; b. Bluefield, W.Va., Mar. 28, 1913; s. William Daniel and Emily (Jones) E.; m. Eloise Goodman, June 24, 1939; children: Daniel S. Jr., Carolyn H. Student, Duke U., 1930-33; MD, Harvard U., 1939. Diplomate Am. Bd. Internal Medicine, Am. Bd. Gastroenterology. Resident in medicine Wis. Gen. Hosp., Madison, 1941-42; instr., then assoc. clin. prof. medicine Med. Sch. Harvard U., Boston, 1946-83; ho. officer Mass. Gen. Hosp., Boston, 1939-41, sr. physician, 1942—; Note: CAR/career section has been revised per further information provided, however, style and order of information reflects our most current editorial guidelines. Maj., M.C., AUS, 1942-45. Decorated Bronze Star. Fellow ACP (gov., regent, mastership, Alfred Stengle award), Am. Gastroent. Soc.; mem. AMA, Mass. Med. Soc. Republican. Home: Fox Hill Village 10 Longwood Dr Westwood MA 02090-1123 Office: Mass Gen Hosp Fruit St Boston MA 02114

ELLIS, DAVID DALE, physician; b. Phoenix, Ariz., Feb. 8, 1952; s. B. Dale and Jean H. (Woodruff) E.; m. Jane Ellen Roberts, Jul. 9, 1976 (div. Jul. 1986); children: Daniel, Emily; m. Judy Kay Fulfer, Nov. 21, 1986; 1 child, Laura. BA, S. Meth. Univ., 1974; DO, Univ. North Tex., 1979; MPH, Univ. Wash., 1994. Diplomate Am. Bd. Family Practice. Family physician U.S. Army, Ft. Sill, Okla., 1982-85, Commerce, Tex., 1985-88; faculty team leader U.S. Army, Augusta, Ga., 1988-92; fellow U.S. Army, Seattle, 1992-94; dir. residency tng. U.S. Army, Honolulu, 1994-96, asst. chief dept. family practice, 1995-96; chief dept. family practice U.S. Army, Fort Sill, Okla., 1996—; chief of staff Citizens Hosp., Commerce, 1985-86; cons. Glen Oaks Psychatric Hosp., Greenville, Tex., 1985-87; dir. Hawaii Acad. Family Physicians, 1994-96. Contbr. articles to profl. jours. Dir. adult edn. Trinity Ch., 1995-96. With U.S. Army, 1979—. Decorated Kuwaiti Liberation medal Kuwaitt Govt., 1991, Army Commendation medal U.S. Army, 1985, 92, Meritorious Svc. medal, 1992, Southwest Asia medal, 1991. Fellow Am. Acad. Family Physicians; mem. Am. Military Surgeons of U.S., Christian Medical Soc., Soc. of Tchrs. of Family Medicine. Office: Reynolds Army Cmty Hosp Family Practice Dept Family Practice Fort Sill OK 73503

ELLIS, DAVID M., psychiatrist; b. Phila., Aug. 27, 1933; m. Adrienne, July 18, 1958. MD, Temple U., 1960. Diplomate Am. Bd. Psychiatry and Neurology. Program dir. adolescents Norristown (Pa.) State Hosp., 1965-67; dir. adolescent svc. Phila. Psychiat. Ctr., 1967-72; assoc. dir. adolescent svcs. Inst. of Pa. Hosp., Phila., 1978-95. Fellow Am. Psychiat. Assn., Am. Acad. Child and Adolescent Psychiatry. Office: 111 N 49th St Philadelphia PA 19139-2718

ELLIS, ELDON EUGENE, surgeon; b. Washington, Ind., July 2, 1922; s. Osman Polson and Ina Lucretia (Cochran) E.; BA, U. Rochester, 1946, MD, 1949; m. Irene Clay, June 26, 1948 (dec. 1968); m. Priscilla Dean Strong, Sept. 20, 1969 (dec. Feb. 1990); children: Paul Addison, Kathe Lynn, Jonathan Clay, Sharon Anne, Eldon Eugene, Rebecca Deborah; m. Virginia Michael Ellis, Aug. 22, 1992. Intern in surgery Stanford U. Hosp., San Francisco, 1949-50, resident and fellow in surgery, 1950-52, 55; Schilling fellow in pathology San Francisco Gen. Hosp., 1955; ptnr. Redwood Med. Clinic, Redwood City, Calif., 1955-87, med. dir., 1984-87; semi-ret. physician, 1987—; med. dir. Peninsula Occup. Health Assocs. (now Peninsula Indsl. Med. Clinic), San Carlos, Calif., 1991-94, physician, 1995—; dir. Sequoia Hosp., Redwood City, 1974-82; asst. clin. prof. surgery Stanford U., 1970-80. Pres. Sequoia Hosp. Found., 1983-92, bd. dirs.; pres., chmn. bd. dirs. Bay Chamber Symphony Orch., San Mateo, Calif., 1988-91; mem. Nat. Bd. of Benevolence Evang. Covenant Ch., Chgo., 1988-93; mem. mgmt. com. The Samarkand Retirement Cmty., Santa Barbara, Calif.; past pres. Project Hope Nat. Alumni Assn., 1992-94, bd. dirs., 1994—; med. advisor Project Hope, Russia Commonwealth Ind. States, 1992. Served with USNR, 1942-46, 50-52. Named Outstanding Citizen of Yr., Redwood City, 1987. Mem. San Mateo County (pres. 1961-63), Calif. (pres. 1965-66), Am. (v.p. 1974-75) heart assns., San Mateo Med. Soc. (pres. 1969-70), San Mateo County Comprehensive Health Planning Coun. (v.p. 1969-70), Calif., Am. med. assns., San Mateo Individual Practice Assn. (treas. 1984—), San Mateo, Stanford surg. socs., Am. Coll. Chest Physicians, Calif. Thoracic Soc., Cardiovascular Coun. Republican. Mem. Peninsula Covenant Ch. Club: Commonwealth. Home: 3621 Farm Hill Blvd Redwood City CA 94061-1230 Office: Peninsula Indsl Med Clinic 1581 Industrial Rd San Carlos CA 94070-4111

ELLIS, EUGENE JOSEPH, cardiologist; b. Rochester, N.Y., Feb. 23, 1919; s. Eugene Joseph and Violet (Anderson) E.; m. Ruth Nugent, July 31, 1943; children: Eugene J., Susan Ellis Renwick, Amy Ellis Miller. AB, U. So. Calif., L.A., 1941; MD, U. So. Calif., 1944; MS in medicine, U. Minn., 1950. Diplomate Am. Bd. Internal Medicine and Cardiovascular Diseases. Intern L.A. County Hosp., 1944, resident, 1946; fellowship Mayo Clinic, Rochester, Minn., 1947-51; dir. cardiology St. Vincent's Hosp., L.A., 1953-55; dir. dept. cardiology Good Samaritan Hosp., L.A., 1955-84; ret., 1984; prof. emeritus medicine U. So. Calif., 1984—; Mem. Med. Bd. of Calif., 1984-91; pres., 1988; pres. Div. of Med. Quality, State of Calif., 1985-89; exec. com. trustees U. Redlands, 1976-86. Lt. USN, 1944-46. Contbr. articles to profl. jours. Lt. USN, 1944-46. Mem. L.A. Country Club, Pauma Valley Country Club (bd. dirs. 1980-83), Birnam Wood Golf Club (bd. dirs. 1994-95), Valley Club of Montecito. Republican. Home: 450 Eastgate Ln Santa Barbara CA 93108-2248

ELLIS, FRANKLIN HENRY, JR., surgeon, educator; b. Washington, Sept. 20, 1920; s. Franklin Henry and Katherine (McClintock) E.; m. Mary Jane Walsh, Dec. 2, 1978; children: Katherine de Saulles (Mrs. Robert Manoff), Elizabeth Dunston (Mrs. Joseph Browning), Franklin Henry III, Margot McClintock (Mrs. Hugh Starkey), Laura Lawson (Mrs. David Milliken), Marie-Armide Longer (Mrs. Charles Storey), Hedrick Watson, Michael Garrison. A.B., Yale U., 1941; M.D., Columbia U., 1944; PhD, U. Minn., 1951. Diplomate: Am. Bd. Surgery, Am. Bd. Thoracic Surgery. Intern Bellevue Hosp., N.Y.C., 1944-45; fellow surgery Mayo Clinic, 1945-46, 48-52, fellow thoracic surgery, 1952-53, asst. to surg. staff, 1952-53, cons. surgery, 1953-70; mem. faculty Mayo Grad. Sch. Medicine, 1952-70, prof. surgery, 1964-70, chmn. thoracic surg. sect., 1966-70; chief cardiovascular surgery Lahey Clinic Found., Boston, 1970-75; chief thoracic and cardiovascular surgery Lahey Clinic Med. Ctr., 1975-86, sr. cons., 1986-90; chmn. dept. thoracic and cardiovascular surgery New Eng. Deaconess Hosp., Boston, 1971-90; lectr. surgery Harvard Med. Sch., 1970-74, asso. clin. prof. surgery, 1974-80, clin. prof. surgery, 1980-91, prof. emeritus, 1991—. Served with USNR, 1946-48. Mem. AMA (Billings Gold medal 1955), ACS, Am. Assn. Thoracic Surgery, Internat. Soc. Surgery, Boston Surg. Soc. (pres. 1985-86), New Eng. Surg. Soc., Soc. Clin. Surgery, Soc. Vascular Surgery (pres. 1971), Soc. Thoracic Surgeons (pres. 1977), Assn. Cardiothoracic Surgery Gt. Britain and Ireland (hon.), Am. Surg. Assn., European Assn. Cardiothoracic Surgery, European Soc. Thoracic Surgeons (corr.), Internat. Soc. Diseases of Esophagus (hon.). Home: 21 Fairmount St Brookline MA 02146-5905 Office: Deaconess Hosp Divsn Cardiothoracic Surg 110 Francis St Ste 2C Boston MA 02215-5501

ELLIS, HELENE RITA, social worker; b. St. Paul, Sept. 20, 1935; d. Moe and Cele (Sidletsky) Weisman; m. Bernard M. Ellis, Sept. 30, 1956; children: Miriam, Arienne, Elia, Evie. BS, U. Minn., 1956; MSW, Loyola U., 1974; PhD, Inst. Clin. Social Work, Chgo., 1996. Lic. clin. social worker, Ill.; bd. cert. diplomate. Tchr. Roosevelt High Sch., Mpls., 1957-58, Barrington (Ill.) High Sch., 1958-59; social worker Dist. #39 Schs., Wilmette, Ill., 1974—; lectr. Loyola U. of Chgo., 1996; chairperson Dist. 39 Health and Safety Curriculum Project, Wilmette, 1987-92. Mem. NASW, Am. Orthopsychiatric, N.Am. Soc. Adlerian Psychology, Ill. Assn. Sch. Social Workers, Pi Lambda Theta, Phi Beta Kappa, Alpha Sigma Nu. Home: 145 Euclid Ave Glencoe IL 60022-2106 Office: Dist 39 Schs 615 Locust Rd Wilmette IL 60091-2237

ELLIS, JAMES VAN NORWOOD, radiologist; b. Chattanooga, Feb. 11, 1951; s. James Chapman and Bennie Catherine (Sims) E.; m. Brenda Joyce Harris, May 27,1972; children: Courtney Elizabeth, James Van Norwood 11. BS in Chemistry, Worcester Poly. Inst., 1973; M.D., U. Tenn., Memphis, 1976. Diplomate Am. Bd. Radiology. Intern Naval Regional Med. Ctr., Porstmouth, Va., 1976-77; resident in radiology, than staff physician Naval Regional Med. Ctr., San Diego, 1977-81; fellow, then instr. radiology U. Tenn., Memphis, 1983-85, asst. prof., 1989-93; ptnr. Memphis Radiol. Profl. Corp., P.C., 1993—; pvt. practice Memphis Regional Profl. Corp., Meth. Hosps. of Memphis, 1993—; staff radiologist Health First Med. Group P.C., Memphis, 1985-88, Meth. Hosp., Memphis, 1993—. Contbr. articles to profl. jours. Officer M.C., USN, 1976-83. Baptist. Home: 8670 Tanoak Dr Germantown TN 38138-7335

ELLIS, JOHN TAYLOR, pathologist, retired educator; b. Lufkin, Tex., Dec. 27, 1920; s. John Taylor and Rowena (McCurdy) E.; m. Marian A. Caldwell, Dec. 26, 1942; children: Evelyn Floy, George Caldwell, John Taylor. BA, U. Tex., 1942; MD, Northwestern U., 1945. Diplomate Nat. Bd. Med. Examiners, Am. Bd. Pathology. Rotating intern St. Luke's Hosp., Chgo., 1945-46, asst. resident in pathology, 1946; rsch. asst. William Buchanan Blood Ctr. Baylor Hosp., Dallas, 1948; resident in pathology N.Y. Hosp., N.Y.C., 1948-49; prof., chmn. dewpt. pathology Emory U., N.Y.C., 1962-67; asst. in pathology Med. Coll. Cornell U., N.Y.C., 1948-49, instr. in pathology, 1949-50, asst. prof., 1950-56, assoc. prof., 1956-62, prof., chmn. dept. pathology, 1968-94, prof. emeritus, 1994—, David D. Thompson prof. emeritus; attending pathologist, pathologist in chief N.Y. Hosp., 1968-94; attending pathologist Meml. Sloan-Kettering Cancer Ctr., N.Y.C., 1973-94; chief pathology dept. pathology N.Y. Downtown Hosp., N.Y.C., 1991-94; attending pathologist N.Y. Hosp. Med. Ctr., Queens, 1994—; mem. adv. bd. Office of Chief Med. Examiner, N.Y.C., 1988—. Capt. USMC, 1946-48. Recipient Milton Helpern Meml. award. Milton Helpern Libr. Legal Medicine, 1989. Mem. AMA, Am. Soc. Investigative Pathology, Coll. Am. Pathology, Assn. Pathology Chmn., Internat. Acad. Pathology, Arthur Purdy Stout Soc., Harvey Soc., N.Y. Path. Soc. Democrat. Home: 276B James Trail West Kingston RI 02892-1700 Office: NY Hosp Med Ctr of Queens 56-45 Main St Flushing NY 11355-5095

ELLIS, KENT, radiologist, consultant; b. Grand Rapids, Mich., June 22, 1921; s. Luther Edward and Dorothy (Groman) E.; m. Barbara Janet Koehler, June 10, 1950; children—Stephen Mark, Karen, Kent Bradford. BS, Yale U., 1942, MD, 1950. Diplomate: Am. Bd. Radiology. Intern Walter Reed Army Hosp., Washington, 1950-51; resident radiology Columbia Presbyn. Med. Center, 1952-54, attending radiologist, 1955-92, cons. in radiology, 1992—; prof. radiology Columbia Coll. Physicians and Surgeons, 1958-92, prof. emeritus, 1992—; Cons. USPHS, Yale Med. Sch., Inter-Soc. Commn. for Heart Disease Resources, N.Y. Heart Assn. Contbr. articles to profl. jours. Served to lt. USNR, 1943-46. Fellow Am. Coll. Radiology, Radiol. Soc. N.Am.; mem. Med. Soc. State N.Y. (chmn. sect. radiology 1968-69), Assn. Univ. Radiologists, AAUP, N.Am. Soc. Cardiac Radiology (v.p. 1975-76, pres. 1976-77), N.Y. Roentgen Soc. (v.p. 1974-75, pres. 1975-77), Fleischner Soc. (sec. 1977-80, pres. 1981-82), Am. Heart Assn. (chmn. council on cardiovascular radiology 1980-82, dir. 1980-83), Am. Roentgen Ray Soc., St. Anthony Hall. Presbyterian. Home: 5 Sandburg Ct-Glenpointe Teaneck NJ 07666 Office: 622 W 168th St New York NY 10032-3702

ELLIS, LLOYD H., JR., emergency physician; b. Denver, Apr. 7, 1936; s. Lloyd Harris and Lura Lou (Wallace) E.; m. Nancy Kay Greenamyre, June 4, 1962 (div. June 1979); children: Peter, Amanda Hunt; m. Eva Marie Bevan, Sept. 1, 1984; children: Gwendolyn Ruth, David Bevan. BA, Yale U., New Haven, Conn., 1960, MA, 1961; MD, Case Western Reserve U., Cleve., 1970. Diplomate Am. Bd. Emergency Medicine. Farm mgr. Hastings, Nebr., 1961-62; vice consul Dept. of State, Lourenco Marques, Mozambique, 1963-64; intelligence analyst Dept. of State, Washington, 1965-66; dir. emergency dept. Univ. Hosps., Cleve., 1976-84, emergency physician, 1985-94; emergency physician Emergency Profl. Svcs., Chardon, Ohio, 1995—; instr. in surgery Case Western Reserve U., Cleve., 1976-78, asst. prof. surgery, 1979-94. Med. dir. Cleve. Emergency Svc., 1976-94; pres. Jeffrey Wallace Ellis Found., Hastings, 1993—. 1st Lt. Armor, 1956-59. Recipient Ford scholar Ford Found., New Haven, 1952-55. Mem. Am. Coll. Emergency Physicians, Am. Acad. Emergency Medicine. Republican. Episcopalian. Home and Office: 32250 Woodsdale Cleveland OH 44139

ELLIS, SUSAN GOTTENBERG, psychologist; b. N.Y.C., Jan. 24, 1949; d. Sam and Sally (Hirschman) Gottenberg; B.S., Cornell U., 1970; M.A., Columbia U., 1971; M.A., Hofstra U., 1975, Ph.D., 1976; m. David Roy Ellis, July 23, 1972; children: Sharon Rachel, Dana Michelle. Instr. health edn. Nassau Community Coll., Garden City, N.Y., 1971-73; sch. psychologist public schs., Somerville, N.J., 1976-77; clin. psychologist Somerset County Community Mental Health Center, Somerville, 1976-77; sch. psychologist, Pinellas County, Fla., 1977-78; instr. St. Petersburg (Fla.) Jr. Coll., 1978; clin. psychologist, Largo, Fla., 1977—; cons. Fla. Dept. Health and Rehab. Services, Med. Center Hosp., Largo, Morton Plant Hosp., Clearwater, Fla., 1978-79, N.Y. State Regents scholar, 1966-71; adj. prof. Eckerd Coll. St. Petersburg, 1988. Author: Interpret Your Dreams, 1987, A Dream Primer, 1988, Make Sense of Your Dreams, 1988. Mem. Am. Psychol. Assn., Fla. Psychol. Assn., Pinellas Psychol. Assn. (treas. 1978, polit. action chmn. 1979), Kappa Delta Pi. Club: Cornell U. Suncoast (v.p. 1979-80). Office: 3233 E Bay Dr Ste 100 Largo FL 34641-1900

ELLIS, W. FRANK, psychologist; b. Peabody, Mass., Oct. 14, 1952; s. William Henry and Mary Ann (O'Rourke) E.; m. Emily Martha Bufferd, June 22, 1980; children: Robert William, Matthew Joseph. BA, Merrimack Coll., 1974; PhD, U. S.C., 1983. Instr., adminstr. U. S.C., Columbia, 1981-83; dir. licensing, evaluation Maine Dept. Mental Health and Mental Retardation, Augusta, 1983-86; pvt. practice Auburn, 1985-92, 93—; coord. behavioral health svcs. Southeastern Alaska Regional Health Care, Auburn, 1992-93; adj. assoc. prof. U. Maine, Augusta, 1984—. Mem. Nat. Assn. Sch. Psychologists, Am. Psychol. Assn., Maine Psychol. Assn. Democrat. Home: 111 Pond Rd Lewiston ME 04240-1604 Office: One Auburn Ctr Ste 207 86 Main St Ste 306 Auburn ME 04210

ELLIS, WAYNE ENOCH, nursing educator, retired air force officer; b. Reno, Jan. 24, 1945; s. Willard Edward and Thelma Miriam (Patterson) E.; m. Robin Marie Mumme, Dec. 25, 1987; children: Wayne II, Sharon Peisel, Terri Lynn, Michael W., Melissa D., Rebekah J. Stube, Christopher H. Stube, Maria Noel Ellis, Peter Enoch Ellis, Stephen Charles. Diploma, L.S. Kaufmann Sch. Nursing, 1965; BS, Chapman Coll., 1982, MS, 1984; PhD in Edn., Tex. A&M U., 1990. Commd. 2nd lt. U.S. Army, 1966; trans. U.S. Air Force, 1980, advanced through grades col., 1992; ret., 1995; asst. operating room supr., instr. regional ctr. U.S. Army, Ft. Bragg, N.C., 1987; dir. inhalation therapy regional ctr. U.S. Army, Ft. Benning, Ga., 1970-72; chief anesthesia U.S. Air Force Hosp. U.S. Air Force, Edwards AFB, Calif., 1980-

83; asst. edn. dir. sch. anesthesia Wilford Hall Med. Ctr. U.S. Air Force, Lackland AFB, Tex., 1983-86; liaison officer Inst. Tech. U.S. Air Force, Wright Patterson AFB, Ohio, 1986-89; instr., coord. paramedical programs Cochise Coll., Sierra Vista, Ariz., 1975-79; pvt. practice Ellis Enterprises, Sierra Vista, 1972-79; chief nurse anesthetist Hobart (Ind.) Anesthesia Assocs., 1979-80; clin. dir. anesthesia program Sch. Nursing U. Tex. Health Sci. Ctr., San Antonio, 1989-93, advanced through grades to col., 1993-95, program dir., facilitator Sch. Nursing/USAF nurse anesthesia, 1990-93; dir. nurse anesthesia clin. tng. USAF David Grant Med. Ctr., Travis AFB, Calif., 1990-93; program dir., facilitator UTHSCSASN/USAF Nurse Anesthesia Major, 1993-95; dir. anesthesia nursing program Coll. Nursing, U. Iowa, Iowa City, 1995—; asst. prof. Coll. Nursing, dir. anesthesia nursing program U. Iowa, 1995—; asst. prof., dir. anesthesia nursing program U. Iowa Coll. Nursing, Iowa City, 1995—; chief cons. to USAF surgeon gen., 1992-94; cons., program coord. N.W. Anesthesia Seminars, Pasco, Wash., 1983—. Author tng. manual for respiratory therapy, emergency medicine; contbg. author Nurse Anesthesia Practice; contbr. articles to numerous publs. Decorated Legion of Merit; Cross of Gallantry with Palms (Vietnam). Mem. Am. Assn. Nurse Anesthetists, Am. Assn. Adult and Continuing Edn., Calif. Assn. Nurse Anesthetists (bd. dirs. 1990-93), Iowa Assn. Nurse Anesthetists, Air Force Assn. Nurse Anesthetists. Republican. Anglican. Office: Univ Iowa Coll Nursing Anesthesia Nursing Program 384 Nursing Bldg Iowa City IA 52242-1121

ELLIS, WILLIAM, ophthalmologist, educator; b. N.Y.C., Dec. 28, 1942; s. Benson and Pauline Ellis; m. Lucy Wiltshire Bugg, July 7, 1969 (div.); children: William Benson, Charles Edward. BS in Elec. Engring., U. Calif.-Berkeley, 1964; MD, Washington U., St. Louis, 1968. Diplomate Am. Bd. Ophthalmology. Intern Duke U. Med. Ctr., Durham, N.C., 1968-69; fellow Nat. Heart and Lung Inst., NIH, Bethesda, Md., 1969-71; resident in ophthalmology Stanford U. Med. Ctr., Calif., 1971-74, lectr. postgrad. ophthalmology meetings, 1972-74; practice medicine specializing in ophthalmology, Richmond, Calif., 1975-83, Pinole, Calif., 1974—, El Cerrito, Calif., 1983—; clin. asst. prof. ophthalmology U. Calif.-San Francisco, 1981-89; numerous TV and radio appearances on ophthalmology, 1983—; lectr. on refractive surgery, various internat. groups. Author: A Textbook of Radial Keratotomy and Astigmatism Surgery, 1985. Served with USPHS, 1969-71. Fellow Am. Acad. Ophthalmology, ACS; mem. AMA, Calif. Med. Assn., Alameda-Contra Costa Med. Assn., Keratorefractive Soc., Am. Intraocular Implant Soc., Pacific Coast Oto-Ophthalmol. Soc., Tau Beta Pi, Epsilon Kappa Nu, Nu Sigma Nu. Office: 6500 Fairmount Ave El Cerrito CA 94530-3623

ELLISON, CRAIG WILLIAM, psychology and urban studies educator, administrator, counselor; b. Springfield, Mass., Aug. 21, 1944; s. William Craig and Marilyn A. (Otto) E.; m. Sharon Roberta Andre, Sept. 20, 1969; children—Scott, Timothy, Jonathan. BA, The King'sColl., 1966; MA, Wayne State U., 1969, PhD in Social Devel. Psychology, 1972. Program coord. MacGregor Meml., Conf. Ctr., Wayne State U., Detroit, 1969-70; asst. prof. Westmont Coll. (Calif.), 1971-76, assoc. prof. psychology, 1977-78, dir. summer sessions, 1977, 78, dir. interterm, 1977-78; vis. prof. SUNY-Binghamton, 1973; prof. psychology and urban studies, chmn. dept. psychology, dir. summer inst. urban missions, adminstr. Simpson Cmty. Counseling Ctr., Simpson Coll., San Francisco, 1978-83; prof. urban studies and psychology Alliance Theol. Sem.-Nyack (N.Y.) Coll., 1983—; bd. dirs., founder, mem. adv. coun. Family Rsch. Coun. of Am., 1981—; western regional dir. Christian Assn. Psychol. Studies, 1973-83; cons. in urbanology Christian and Missionary Alliance, 1979-86, World Vision, 1982-84, Intervarsity, 1982-83, Evang. Presbyn. Ch., 1986; founder, dir. New Hope Counseling Ctrs., N.Y.C., 1993—. Author: The Urban Mission, 1974, 2d edit., 1983, Self-Esteem, 1976, Modifying Man: Implications and Ethics, 1978, Your Better Self, 1983, Saying Goodbye to Loneliness and Finding Intimacy, 1983, Healing for the City: Counseling for the Urban Context, 1992, From Stress to Well-Being, 1994; host Perspective on Personal Living, nationwide radio broadcast, 1981—; developer Spiritual Well-Being Scale; contbg. editor Jour. Psychology and Theology, 1989—; contbr. articles to profl. jours. Active Fairmede Alliance Ch., 1978-83. Mem. Simpson Meml. Ch., 1983—. Mem. Am. Psychol. Assn., Am. Assn. Christian Counselors, Christian Assn. Psychol. Studies (Disting. Mem. award 1986), Soc. Psychol. Study Social Issues. Office: Alliance Theol Sem 350 N Highland Ave Nyack NY 10960-1429

ELLISON, EDWIN CHRISTOPHER, physician, surgeon; b. Columbus, Ohio, Jan. 10, 1950; s. Edwin Homer and Molly (Scheeler) E.; m. Mary Pat Borgess, Dec. 23, 1978; children: Jonathon Scott, Eric Christopher. BS, U. Wis., 1972; MD, Med. Coll. Wis., 1976. Diplomate Am. Bd. Surgery. Resident surgery Ohio State U., Columbus, 1976-83, asst. prof. surgery, 1983-93, assoc. prof., 1993—; 1987-93; chief divsn. gen. surgery, bd. dirs. Ohio Digestive Disease Inst., Columbus, 1987-93; assoc. prof. surgery Ohio State U., 1993—, dir. divsn. surgery. Fellow ACS. Office: N-729 Doan Hall 410 W 10th Ave Columbus OH 43210

ELLISON, KATHERINE RUFFNER WHITE, psychologist, educator, minister; b. Charleston, W.Va., Jan. 17, 1941; d. Christian Streit and Katherine Ruffner (Hughey) White. BA, Agnes Scott Coll., 1962; PhD, CUNY, 1976; MDiv, New Brunswick Theol. Sem. Ordained to ministry Presbyn. Ch. Prof. Montclair State U., Upper Montclair, N.J., 1977—; cons. various law enforcement agys., 1973—. Author: Psychology & Criminal Justice, 1981, Stress & The Police Officer, 1983; contbr. articles to profl. jours. Mem. Am. Psychol. Assn. (sec.-treas. police psychology sect. 1989-93), Internat. Assn. Chiefs of Police, Phi Beta Kappa. Democrat. Office: Montclair State U Psychology Dept Upper Montclair NJ 07043

ELLISON, LOIS TAYLOR, physician, medical educator and administrator; b. Fort Valley, Ga., Oct. 28, 1923; d. Robert James and Annie Maude (Anderson) Taylor; m. Robert Gordon Ellison, Feb. 11, 1945; children—Robert Gordon, Gregory Taylor, Mark Frederick, James Walton, John Charles. B.S., U. Ga., 1943; M.D., Med. Coll. Ga., 1950. Fellow, Univ. Hosp., Augusta, Ga., 1950-51; mem. faculty Med. Coll. Ga., Augusta, 1951—; prof. medicine and surgery Med. Coll. Ga., 1971—, assoc. dean, 1974-75, provost, 1975-84, assoc. v.p. planning (hosps. and clins.), 1984—; attending VA Med. Ctr., Augusta; civilian cons. Eisenhower Army Med. Ctr., Fort Gordon, Ga.; mem. coal mine health research adv. council Nat. Inst. Occupational Safety and Health, 1972-75; bd. dirs. East Central Ga. Health Systems Agy., 1975-79, treas., 1979—; bd. dirs. Oak Ridge Associated Univs., 1978-84; mem. adv. council Univ. Systems Ga., 1975-84; mem. exec. com. Ga. Health Coordinating Council, 1980. Contbr. numerous articles to profl. jours. Bd. dirs. United Way Greater Augusta, 1975-78, chair div. hosp. and health, 1978, chair div. colls. and univs., 1980; mem. adminstrv. bd. Trinity-on-the-Hill United Methodist Ch., Augusta, 1974-77, mem. pastor-parish com., 1978—. NIH grantee, 1963-68. Fellow Am. Coll. Chest Physicians; mem. Am. Physiol. Soc., Am. Med. Women's Assn., AMA, Assn. Am. Med. Colls., Am. Lung Assn. (dir. 1967—, sec. 1982-85, pres.-elect 1985-86, pres. 1986-87), Am. Heart Assn. (pres. Ga. affiliate chpt. 1982-83, dir. 1979—), So. Soc. Clin. Investigation, Am. Lung Assn. of Ga. (pres. 1984-85), Ga. Heart Assn. Office: Med Coll Ga 1120 15th St Augusta GA 30912-5550

ELLISON, MADELINE MARIE, nursing home administrator; b. Glenville, W.Va., June 2, 1950; d. Anna Elizabeth (Smith) Stole. AA, Lorain County (Ohio) C.C., Elyria, 1983; BA in Social Work, Cleve. State U., 1988. Enlisted U.S. Army, 1970, advanced through grades to S/Sgt., ret., 1978; security officer Lorain County C.C., 1979-90; dir. social svc. Oak Ridge Home, Westlake, Ohio, 1990-95; adminstr.-in-tng. Oak Ridge Home, 1995-96; asst. exec. dir. Life Care Ctr. of Medina (Ohio), 1996—. Mem. Am. Coll. Health Care Adminstrs. Mem. Full Gospel Assembly. Office: Life Care Ctr of Medina 2400 Columbia Rd Medina OH 44035-5322

ELLISON, PATRICIA HURLBURT, neurologist; b. Madison, Wis., June 30, 1934; d. Virgil Lee and Julia (Knaff) Hurlburt; m. David L. Ellison, Aug. 1958 (div. 1983); children: David, Kim, Mark, Andrea. BA with distinction, Cornell U., 1956; MA, Columbia U., 1961; MD cum laude, U. Pitts., 1970. Diplomate Am. Bd. Pediatrics, Am. Bd. Neurology. Pediatric intern Children's Hosp. of Pitts., 1970-72; neurology resident Albany Med. Coll. and Hosp., 1972-74, pediatric neurology fellow, 1974-75; asst. prof. pediatrics and neurology Albany Med. Coll., 1975-79; dir. neonatal neurology, assoc. prof. pediatrics Med. Coll. of Wis., Milw., 1979-83; rsch. prof. Dept. Psychology, U. Denver, 1985-91; adj. prof. Dept. Pediatrics, U. Colo. Sch. Medicine, Denver, 1991—; part-time Drs. Levisohn & Finkel, Denver, 1985-89, Englewood and Littleton, Colo., 1989—; invited examiner Am. Bd. of Psychiatry and Neurology, 1979—. Author: The Infanib, A reliable Method for the Neuromotor Assessment of Infants, 1994; contbr. articles to profl. jours. Sr. internat. fellowship Fogarty Internat. Ctr., 1988. Mem. Am. Acad. of Pediatrics, Am. Acad. Neurology, Child Neurology Soc., Phi Beta Kappa, Alpha Omega Alpha. Office: Neurology in Colorado 5151 S Federal Blvd Littleton CO 80123

ELLISON, ROBERT GORDON, thoracic cardiac surgeon; b. Millen, Ga., Dec. 4, 1916; m. Lois Taylor, Feb. 11, 1945; children—Robert Gordon, Gregory, Mark, James, John. A.B., Vanderbilt U., 1939; M.D., Med. Coll. Ga., 1943. Diplomate Am. Bd. Surgery, Am. Bd. Thoracic Surgery (bd. dirs. 1971-81, chmn. 1979-81). Intern, resident in gen. surgery Univ. Hosp., Augusta, Ga., 1943-46; resident in thoracic-cardiac surgery Univ. Hosp., 1947-48, resident in pathology, 1949; resident in cardiopulmonary physiology Bellevue Hosp., N.Y.C., 1948; mem. faculty Med. Coll. Ga., 1947-87, chief sect. thoracic surgery, 1955-87, prof. surgery, 1959-87, Charbonnier prof. surgery, 1973-87, Charbonnier prof. surgery emeritus, 1987—; chief gen. thoracic surgery VA Med. Ctr., 1987-91; mem. surgery study sect. NIH, 1969-73; com. cardiovascular disease Ga. Regional Med. Program, 1971-74; cons. area hosps. Author 1 book, chpts. and, papers in field.; Editorial bd.: Annals Thoracic Surgery, 1965-79. Fellow A.C.S. (chmn. local credentials com. 1968-73, gov. 1973-78), Am. Coll. Chest Physicians, Am. Coll. Cardiology (past gov.), Southeastern Surg. Congress; mem. Am. Thoracic Soc. (councilor 1963-66), Soc. Thoracic Surgeons (pres. 1971, historian 1973-92), Thoracic Surgery Dirs. Assn. (exec. com., chmn. in-tng. exam. com. 1976-78), AMA, Soc. Univ. Surgeons, Am. Assn. Thoracic Surgery, Am. Surg. Assn., Am. Physiol. Soc., Am. Soc. Artificial Internal Organs, So. Thoracic Surg. Assn. (pres. 1963-64), So. Surg. Assn., So. Soc. Clin. Investigation, Ga. Heart Assn. (pres. 1974-75), Ga. Thoracic Soc. (pres. 1965-66), Ga. Tb Assn. (pres. 1959), Med. Assn. Ga., Ga. Surg. Soc. (pres. elect 1987, pres. 1988), Richmond County Med. Soc. (v.p. 1968), Richmond County Heart Assn. (trustee 1970—), Augusta Area Tb Assn. (pres. 1954), Augusta Coll. Alumni Assn. (trustee 1969-73, Most Outstanding Alumnus award 1962), Alpha Omega Alpha, Sigma Psi. Methodist. Office: 606 Wellesley Dr Augusta GA 30909

ELLMAN, ALEXANDER, physician, medical administrator; b. N.Y.C., Nov. 13, 1917; s. Abraham Isaac and Dina (Judevich) E.; m. Violet Mae Noe; children: Jonathan, Margery. BS, U. Ark., 1937; MD, Washington U., St. Louis, 1941. Rheumatologist Ctrl. Bklyn. Med. Group, 1947-94, med. dir., CEO, 1978—; chmn. Med. Group Coun. HIP, N.Y.C., 1989—, Md. Control Bd. HIP, N.Y.C., 1987—; chmn. bd. Group Coun. Mut. Ins. Com., N.Y.C., 1991—. Bd. dirs. HIP, 1987—. Recipient Nat. Brotherhood award NCCJ, 1992. Fellow Am. Coll. Rheumatology. Office: Ctrl Bklyn Med Group 345 Schermerhorn St Brooklyn NY 11217

ELLNER, PAUL DANIEL, clinical microbiologist; b. N.Y.C., May 2, 1925; s. George and Cele (Weis) E.; m. Estelle Ziswasser, 1948 (div. 1960); 1 child, Diane; m. Cornelia Johns, Jan. 15, 1965; children—David, Jonathan. B.S., L.I. U., 1948; M.S., U. So. Calif., 1952; Ph.D., U. Md. Coll. Medicine, 1956. Diplomate Am. Bd. Med. Microbiology; cert. clin. lab. dir. N.Y.C. Dept. Health. Clin. bacteriologist Los Angeles hosps., 1948-52; research asst. Mt. Sinai Hosp., N.Y.C., 1952-53; instr. microbiology U. Fla. Coll. Medicine, 1956-60; asst. prof. U. Vt. Coll. Medicine, 1960-63; asst. prof. Columbia U. Coll. Physicians and Surgeons, N.Y.C., 1963-66, assoc. prof., 1966-70, prof. microbiology, 1971-78, prof. microbiology and pathology, 1978-89, prof. emeritus, 1989, dir. clin. microbiology service, 1971-89; assoc. microbiologist Presbyn. Hosp., N.Y.C., 1966-70, attending staff, 1971-89; cons. in field; vis. prof. N.Y. Med. Coll., Valhalla, 1979; ASM Latin Am. vis. prof., Medellín, Colombia, 1982; Am. Bur. Med. Advancement in China vis. prof., Taiwan, 1982; regional coordinator Nat. Disaster Med. System; v.p. Am. BioSci. Cons. Author: Current Procedures in Clinical Bacteriology, 1978, Understanding Infectious Disease, 1992; editor: Infectious Diarrheal Diseases: Current Concepts and Laboratory Procedures, 1984; mem. editorial bd. Sexually Transmitted Diseases, 1982-84, European Jour. Clin. Microbiology, 1985-89; contbr. chpts. to books, numerous articles to sci. jours. Served with AC, USN, 1943-44; to capt. USPHS Res., 1956—; health project officer USCG, 1982-91. U.S. Navy research fellow, 1954-56. Fellow Am. Acad. Microbiology, Assn. Clin Scientists, N.Y. Acad. Medicine (assoc.), Infectious Diseases Soc. Am.; mem. AMA (spl. affiliate), Am. Soc. Microbiology (chmn. clin. divsn. 1980-81, Sonnenwirth Meml. award 1992), Acad. Clin. Lab. Physicians and Scientists, Am. Venereal Disease Assn., Sigma Xi. Republican. Jewish.

ELLSWORTH, DELBERT WARREN, psychology educator; b. Albany, Calif., Nov. 23, 1937; s. Heber M. and Mriam (Telford) E.; m. Mary Lou Holbrook, children: Kevin, Kristen, Carolyn, Joan Ellen, Lynne Ann, Sharon. BA, U. Calif.-Davis, 1962; MA, San Francisco State U., 1964; PhD, U. Calif.-Berkeley, 1977. Lic. psychologist, Pa. Assoc. prof. psychology Elizabethtown Coll., Pa., 1970-88, prof., 1988—, chmn. dept., 1972-75, 79-95, coordinator instl. research, 1973-76; dir. research and biofeedback Talbot Pl., Hummelstown, Pa., 1981-83. USPHS trainee, 1968-70. Mem. Pa. Soc. Biofeedback and Behavioral Medicine (pres. 1985-86), Coun. Undergrad. Psychology Programs (ea. coord. 1994-96), Am. Psychol. Assn., Am. Psychol. Soc., Eastern Psychol. Assn. Mormon. Home: 9 Donegal Pl Marietta PA 17547-1802 Office: Elizabethtown College Elizabethtown PA 17022

ELLSWORTH, RICHARD GERMAN, psychologist; b. Provo, Utah, June 23, 1950; s. Richard Grant and Betty Lola (Midgley) E.; BS, Brigham Young U., 1974, MA, 1975; PhD, U. Rochester (N.Y.), 1979; postgrad. UCLA, 1980-84; PhD, Internat. Coll., 1983; m. Carol Emily Osborne, May 23, 1970; children: Rebecca Ruth, Spencer German, Rachel Priscilla, Melanie Star, Richard Grant, David Jedediah. Cert. Am. Bd. Med. Psychotherapy, (fellow), Am. Bd. Sexology. Instr. U. Rochester, 1976-77, Chapman U., 1995—; rsch. assoc. Nat. Tech. Inst. for Deaf, Rochester, 1977; instr. West Valley Coll., Saratoga, Calif., 1979-80, San Jose (Calif.) City Coll., 1980; psycholinquist UCLA, 1980-81; rsch. assoc. UCLA, 1982-85; psychologist Daniel Freeman Meml. Hosp., Inglewood, Calif., 1981-84, Broderick, Langlois & Assocs., San Gabriel, Calif., 1982-86, Beck Psychiat. Med. Group, Lancaster, Calif., 1984-87, Angeles Counseling Ctr., Arcadia, Calif., 1986-89, Assoc. Med. Psychotherapists, Palmdale, Calif., 1988—; cons. LDS Social Svcs. Calif. Agy., 1981—, Antelope Valley Hosp. Med. Ctr., 1984—, Palmdale Hosp. Med. Ctr., 1984—, Treatment Ctrs. of Am. Psychiat. Hosps., 1985-86, Hollywood Cmty. Hosp., 1994—. Scoutmaster, Boy Scouts Am., 1976-79. UCLA Med. Sch. fellow in psychiatry, 1980-81. Mem. Am. Psychol. Assn., Am. Assn. Sex Educators, Am. Psychol. Assn., Counselors and Therapists, Assn. Mormon Counselors and Psychotherapists, Am. Soc. Clin. Hypnosis, Psi Chi. Contbr. articles to profl. jours. Office: 1220 East Ave S Ste A Palmdale CA 93550

ELLWEIN, LEON BURNELL, medical advisor; b. Roscoe, S.D., Dec. 21, 1942; s. Erwin E. and Cornelia (Mayer) E.; m. Sarah Ann Nelson, June 12, 1965; children: Charles E., Todd W. BSME with honors, S.D. State U., 1964, MS, 1966; PhD, Stanford U., 1970; cert. advanced mgmt. program, Harvard U., 1989. Assoc. engr. IBM Corp., Rochester, Minn., 1964-65; systems analyst Nat. Inst. Health, Bethesda, Md., 1966-72; sr. sci. Sci. Applications Internat. Corp., LaJolla, Calif., 1972-83; assoc. dean U. Nebr. Med. Ctr., Omaha, 1983-91; special advisor Nat. Inst. Health, Bethesda, 1991—; cons. Inst. Nacional de Oftalmologia, Lima, Peru, 1986-91, Sci. Applications Internat. Corp., LaJolla, 1983-91, The World Bank, Washington, 1992—, Lions Internat. 1990—. Contbr. articles to profl. jours. Vol. Fund Raising-Stanford (Calif.) U., 1972-77; mem. San Diego City Adv. Com., 1973-74; pres. LaJolla Luth. Ch., 1981-82, Pacific Hills Luth. Ch., Omaha, 1986; trustee Urol. Rsch. and Edn. Foudn., San Diego, 1978-94. Mem. Soc. for Risk Analysis, Soc. for Med. Decision Making, Ops. Rsch. Soc. Am., Inst. Mgmt. Sci., Assn. Health Svcs. Rsch., Am. Assn. Adv. Sci. Republican. Home: 5610 Wisconsin Ave Apt 1101 Bethesda MD 20815-4418 Office: Nat Inst Health 9000 Rockville Pike Bethesda MD 20892-2510

ELLWOOD, PAUL MURDOCK, JR., health policy analyst, consultant; b. San Francisco, July 16, 1926; s. Paul Ellwood and Rebecca May (Logan) E.; divorced; children: David, Cynthia, Deborah. B.A., Stanford U., 1949, M.D., 1953. Dir. Kenny Rehab. Inst., Mpls., 1962-63; exec. dir. Am. Rehab. Found., Mpls., 1963-73; dir. Inst. Interdisciplinary Studies, Mpls., 1970-73; pres. InterStudy, health policy analysis Excelsior, Minn., 1973-85; pres. Paul Ellwood & Assocs., Excelsior, 1985-87; chmn. bd. InterStudy, 1987-92; dir., mem. exec. com. Jackson Hole Ski Corp., Wyo., 1972—; clin. prof. phys. medicine and rehab., neurology and pediatrics U. Minn. Med. Sch.; cons. in health and delivery systems. Co-author: Assuring The Quality of Health Care, 1973; Co-editor: Handbook of Physical Medicine and Rehabilitation, 2d edit, 1971. Served with USNR, 1944-46. Recipient award Ministry Pub. Health, Republic Argentina, 1957; 1st award sci. exhibit Am. Acad. Neurology, 1958; citation President's Com. Employment Handicapped, 1962; Gold Key award Am. Congress Rehab., 1971; named Distinguished fellow Am. Rehab. Found., 1973. Mem. Inst. Medicine, Group Health Assn. Am. (dir. 1975-76), Nat. Health Council (dir. 1971-76), Assn. Rehab. Centers (pres. 1960-61, U.S. Healthcare Quality award 1991). Home: PO Box 57 Teton Village WY 83025-0057 Office: Jackson Hole Group PO Box 350 Teton Village WY 83025-0350

ELMAN, JOHN W., optometrist; b. Mpls., May 4, 1944; s. Harry M. and Bess F. (Falk) E.; m. Vicki Reece, Nov. 29, 1971 (div. Oct. 1985); 1 child, Shana. BS, L.A. Coll. Optometry, 1966; OD, So. Calif. Coll. Optometry, 1968. Diplomate Nat. Bd. Examiners in Optometry. Optometrist Dr. Erwin Rader, L.A., 1968-72; pvt. practice optometry Santa Monica, Calif., 1972—. Mem. Am. Optometric Assn. (charter contact lens sect.), Calif. Optometric Assn., Los Angeles County Optometric Soc., Malibu Rotary. Office: 2614 Pico Blvd Santa Monica CA 90405

ELMES, DAVID GORDON, psychologist, educator; b. Newton, Mass., Feb. 15, 1942; s. Leslie and Ruth (Adams) E.; m. Anne Louise Lawrence, June 7, 1963; children: Matthew David, Jennifer Anne. B.A., U. Va., 1964; M.A., U.Va., 1966; Ph.D., U. Va., 1967. Mgmt. trainee C & P of Va., 1963; asst. prof. psychology Washington and Lee U., Lexington, Va., 1967-71, assoc. prof., 1971-74, prof., 1975—, head dept. psychology, 1990—, co-dir. cognitive sci., 1987—; rsch. assoc. Human Performance Ctr., U. Mich., 1973-74; vis. fellow Univ. Coll., Oxford (Eng.) U., 1987; dir. rsch. in psychology at numerous undergrad. instns., 1995. Author: Readings in Experimental Psychology, 1978, Methods in Experimental Psychology, 1981, Research Methods in Psychology, 1989, Experimental Psychology: Understanding Psychological Research, 1996, Research Methods in Psychology, 1995; contbr. articles to profl. jours. Bd. dirs. Rockbridge Mental Health Clinic, 1968-73; ofcl., coach Little League Baseball and Basketball, 1969-77. Mem. Psychonomic Soc., Am. Psychol. Soc., Va. Acad. Sci., Coun. on Undergrad. Rsch. (chair psychology divsn.), Phi Beta Kappa, Sigma Xi. Home: 3 Westside Ct Lexington VA 24450-1970 Office: Dept Psychology Washington and Lee University Lexington VA 24450

ELMETS, CRAIG ALLAN, dermatologist; b. Des Moines, Aug. 16, 1949; s. Harry B. and Charlotte Irene (Musin) E.; m. Laurie Beth Melamed, June 30, 1985; children: Joshua Philip, Michael William, David Benjamin. BA, U. Iowa, 1967-71, MD, 1971-75. Intern U. Kans. Med. Ctr., Kansas City, 1975-76, resident internal medicine, 1976-78; resident dermatology U. Iowa Hosps., Iowa City, 1978-80; fellow immunodermatology U. Tex. Health Sci., Dallas, 1980-82; asst. prof. dermatology Case Western Res. U., Cleve., 1982-88, asst. prof. gen. med. scis., oncology, 1987-88, assoc. prof. gen. med. scis. oncology, dermatology, 1988-94, prof. gen. med. scis. oncology, dermatology, 1994—, assoc. prof. environ. health scis., 1991—; attending physician U. Hosps. Cleve., 1982—, chief immunodermatology svc., 1987—; attending physician Cleve. VA Med. Ctr., 1990—; chief photodermatology svc., 1994—; dir. Skin Diseases Rsch. Ctr. N.E. Ohio NIH; mem. rsch. adv. panel Rainbow Babies and Childrens Hosp., Cleve., 1990—. Editor: Photoimmunology, 1995; Mem. editorial bd. Photodermatology, Photoimmunology, Photmedicine, Jour. Investigative Dermatology, 1996—; sect. editor Experimental Dermatology; assoc. editor Photochemistry and Photobiology, 1994—, Jour. Immunology, 1995—; tech. adv. com. Edison Biotechnology Ctr.; rsch. adv. com. Diabetes Assn. Greater Cleve.; ad hoc reviewer gen. medicine study sect. NIH; contbr. articles to profl. jours. Recipient Frederic E. Mohs award Skin Cancer Found., 1986, New Investigator Rsch. award NIH, 1983-86, Rsch. Career Devel. award NIH, 1987-92. Mem. ACP, AAAS, Am. Acad. Dermatology (com. on occupational health, com. sci. and poster exhibits, chmn. com. on scientific and poster exhibits 1995—, EPA/NIEHS liaison com. 1995—), Soc. Investigative Dermatology (midwest chmn. 1986-89, mem. com. 1991-94, com. chmn. 1993-94), Am. Assn. Immunologists, Am. Soc. for Photobiology, Am. Assn. for Cancer Rsch., Ohio Dermatological Soc., Cleve. Dermatological Soc. Home: 3962 White Oak Trl Cleveland OH 44122-4722 Office: U Hosps Cleve 2074 Abington Rd Cleveland OH 44106-2602

ELMORE, ANDREW MONTEVERDE, psychologist; b. Seattle, Feb. 1, 1952; s. Robert Graham and Jane Charlotte (Monteverde) E.; m. Gail Eleanor Miers, Aug. 22, 1981; 1 child, Austen Chance. BA, Ill. Wesleyan U., 1974; PhD, SUNY, Stony Brook, 1979. Lic. psychologist, N.Y.; cert. biofeedback therapist, cognitive therapist. Psychologist pvt. practice N.Y.C., 1979—; asst. clin. prof. psychiatry Mount Sinai Sch. Medicine, N.Y.C., 1981—; staff psychologist Found. for Rsch. on Manic Depression, N.Y.C., 1981-91; psychol. dir. Tim. J. and Dental Phobia Clinic Mt. Sinai Hosp., N.Y.C., 1981—; staff psychologist L.I. Jewish/Hillside Med. Ctr., New Hyde Pk., N.Y., 1975—; dir. biofeedback clinic N.Y.C., 1979-88; chairperson Mount Sinai Hosp. Psychologists, N.Y.C., 1984-87; tng. faculty Biofeedback Cert. Inst. Am., 1993—; cons. Gracie Sq. Hosp., N.Y.C., 1984—. Author: (screenplay) The Master and Margarita, 1982, Goodboy, 1995; author: Introduction to Natural Psychology, 1992, A Pilgrim on the Road to Love, 1995. Recipient NIMH Predoctoral fellowship, 1976, Biomed. Rsch. fellowship SUNY at Stony Brook, 1978. Mem. APA, N.Y. Acad. Scis., Am. Assn. for Applied Psychophysiology and Biofeedback, Am. Assn. for Study of Headaches. Office: Andrew Elmore PhD 401 E 80th St New York NY 10021-0655

ELMSTROM, GEORGE P., optometrist, writer; b. Salem, Mass., Dec. 11, 1925; s. George and Emily Irene (Wedgwood) E.; grad. So. Calif. Coll. Optometry, 1951; m. Nancy DePaul, Apr. 29, 1973; children—Pamela, Beverly, Robert. Pvt. practice optometry, El Segundo, Calif., 1951—; mem. staff So. Calif. Coll. Optometry, 1951—; book cons. Med. Econs. Books, 1970—; instrument and forensic editor Jour. Am. Optical Assn.; comml. airplane and balloon pilot, 1968—. Served with U.S. Army, World War II. Decorated Silver Star; named Writer of Year, Calif. Optometric Assn., 1957, Man of Year, El Segundo, 1956; recipient spl. citation Nat. Eye Found., 1955. Fellow Am. Acad. Optometry, AAAS, Southwest Contact Lens Soc., Disting. Service Found. of Optometry, Internat. Acad. Preventive Medicine; mem. Am. Optometric Assn., Assn. for Research in Vision, Am. Soc. Ultrasonography, Am. Pub. Health Assn., Optometric Editors Assn., Assn. Research in Vision, Internat. Soc. Ophthalmic Ultrasound, Profl. Airshow Pilots Assn., Flying Optometrists Assn. Am., Beta Sigma Kappa, So. Calif. Coll. Optometry Alumni (pres. 1955-56). Author: Optometric Practice Management, 1963; Legal Aspects of Contact Lens Practice, 1966; Advanced Management for Optometrists, 1974; Modernized Management, 1982; mgmt. editor Optometric Monthly, 1973. Home: 484B Washington St Monterey CA 93940-3030 Office: PO Box S-3061 Carmel CA 93921-3061

ELSEA, WILLIAM ROBERT, preventive medicine physician; b. Kirksville, Mo., 1933. MD, Washington U., Saint Louis, 1959. Diplomate Am. Bd. Preventive Medicine. Intern Ea. Maine Gen. Hosp., Bangor, 1959-60; resident N.Y. State Pub. Health Svc., 1963-67; preventive medicine physician Grady Meml. Hosp., Atlanta; prof. preventive medicine Emory U., Atlanta. Mem. Assn. Pub. Health Adminstrs., Ga. Med. Assn. Office: 965 Winding Creek Tr Atlanta GA 30328*

ELSTER, ALLEN DEVANEY, radiologist, educator, scientific researcher; b. Houston, Jan. 26, 1954; s. Allen William and Martha Jo (Greene) E.; m. Jeanine Jones, June 6, 1980; children: Allen, Elizabeth, Martha, Patricia. BE, Vanderbilt U., 1976; MA, Oxford (Eng.) U., 1978; MD, Baylor Coll. Medicine, Houston, 1980. Diplomate Am. Bd. Radiology; lic. physician, Tex., N.C. Clin. fellow in surgery Harvard Med. Sch., Boston, 1980-83; resident in radiology U. Tex. Med. Sch., Houston, 1983-86; asst. prof. radiology Bowman Gray Sch. Medicine, Wake Forest U., Winston Salem, 1986-88, assoc. prof., 1988-91, prof., 1991—; dir. Ctr. for Magnetic Resonance

Imaging, Winston Salem, 1987—. Author: Magnetic Resonance Imaging, 1988, Cranial Magnetic Resonance Imaging, 1989, Questions and Answers in MR Imaging, 1993; editor Jour. Computer Assisted Tomography, 1995—; mem. editl. bd. 8 sci. jours.; contbr. articles to profl. jours. Sci. advisor Triplet Connection, Stockton, Calif., 1989—. Rhodes scholar, 1976; recipient numerous sci. rsch. grants from govt. and industry, 1989—. Mem. Radiol. Soc. N.Am. (Scholar award 1990), Am. Coll. Radiology, Am. Soc. Neuroradiology, Am. Soc. Rhodes Scholars. Office: Bowman Gray Sch Medicine Medical Center Blvd Winston Salem NC 27157

ELSTON, ROBERT C., medical educator. BA with honors, Cambridge (Eng.) U., 1955, diploma in agr., 1956, MA, 1957; PhD, Cornell U., 1959; postgrad., U. N.C., 1960. Asst. prof. U. N.C., Chapel Hill, 1960-62, assoc. prof., 1964-69, prof., dir. genetics lab. Sch. Pub. Health, 1969-79; sr. rsch. fellow biometric medicine U. Aberdeen, 1962-64; prof., head dept. biometry & genetics La. State U. Med. Ctr., New Orleans, 1979-95; prof. dept. epidemiology & biostats. Case Western Res. U., Cleve., 1995—; vis. prof. Yale U., 1965-66, London U., 1967, Cambridge U., 1970, Fourth Mil. Med. Coll. Xian, China, 1987, U. Calif., Irvine, 1988-89; dir. Ctr. Molecular & Human Genetics La. State U. Med. Ctr., 1991-95; mem. internat. adv. bd. Genetics Selection Evolution, 1992—; exec. com. mem. teaching of stats. in health scis. sect. Am. Stats. Assn., 1992-94, chair, 1993. Assoc. editor Biometrics, 1967-71, Am. Jour. Human Genetics, 1974-82; editl. bd. Thrombosis Rsch., 1972-76, Neuropsychobiology, 1975-78, Am. Jour. med. Genetics, 1977—, Genetic Epidemiology, 1984—; contbr. articles to profl. jours. Recipient Career Devel. award NIH, 1966-76, Rsch. Scientist award, NIMH, 1977-79, Hoch award Am. Psychopath. Assn., 1992, Wick R. Williams Meml. award Fox Chase Cancer Ctr., 1994, Leadership award Internat. Genetic Epidemiology Soc., 1995, William Allan Meml. award Am. Soc. Human Genetics, 1996; King George VI Meml. fellow, 1956-57, John Simon Guggenheim Meml. fellow, 1973-74; Coulthurst scholar, 1955-56, Cornell scholar, 1956-59. Fellow Am. Stats. Assn. Office: Case Western Res U Dept Epidemiology & Biostats 2500 Metrohealth Dr Rm R-258 Cleveland OH 44109*

ELTZ, ROBERT WALTER, bioprocess technologist; b. Callicoon, N.Y., June 22, 1932; s. Carl George and Adele (Markert) E.; m. Deborah Lee Kinkaid, Nov. 24, 1962; children: Karen, Kurt, Kirsten. BS in Biology/Chemistry, Rensselaer Poly. Inst., 1953; PhD in Microbiology, Cornell U., 1958. Rsch. microbiologist Chas. Pfizer & Co., Bklyn., also Groton, Conn., 1957-61, Sun Oil Co., Marcus Hook, Phila., Pa., 1961-70; biol. process devel. dir. E.R. Squibb & Sons, Inc., New Brunswick, N.J., 1970-80; tech. dir. Krause Milling Co., Milw., 1980-82; bioprocess devel. dir. Monsanto Co., St. Louis, 1982-90, bioprocess tech. dir., 1990-94; indsl. R&D mgmt. cons., 1994—; mem. Hungarian workshop on indsl. econs. Nat. Acad. Sci., 1991. Mem. Am. Chem. Soc. (chmn. div. biochem. tech. 1981-82, James M. Van Lanen Disting. Svc. award 1984), Am. Soc. for Microbiology, Sigma Xi. Home and Office: 727 Cedar Field Ct Chesterfield MO 63017-5727

ELWART, NANCY M., nursing administrator; b. Wausau, Wis., Dec. 10, 1939; d. Arthur and Stella Walker; m. Thomas G. Elwart, Feb. 15, 1960; children: Deborah L., James M. BSN, DePaul U., 1981, MS, 1983. RN, Ill.; lic. NHA, Ill.; cert. nursing adminstr. advanced ANCC. Staff nurse West Surburban Hosp., Oak Park, Ill., 1961-62; charge nurse surg. unit Loretto Hosp., Chgo., 1962-64; pvt. duty nurse Chgo., 1964-67; staff nurse coronary care unit St. Mary Nazareth Hosp., Chgo., 1967-69; evening supr. St. Anne's Hosp., Chgo., 1969-80; night supr. critical care Lutheran Gen. Hosp., Park Ridge, Ill., 1980-83; clin. dir. Edgewater Hosp., Chgo., 1983-88; assoc. v.p. nursing Swedish Covenant Hosp., Chgo., 1988-95, adminstr. extended care faculty, 1993—, v.p. nursing, 1995—. Mem. Am. Coll. Healthcare Execs., Ill. Orgn. Nursing Execs., Chgo. Met. Assn. Nurse Execs. (treas.), DePaul U. Nurses Alumni Assn. Roman Catholic. Office: Swedish Covenant Hosp 5145 N California Ave Chicago IL 60625-3642

ELWOOD, WILLIAM NORELLI, medical researcher; b. East Orange, N.J., Aug. 21, 1962; s. William Rogers and Frances Emma (Norelli) E. BS in Comm., U. Fla., 1985; MA in Human Comm., U. South Fla., 1989; PhD in Human Communication, Purdue U., 1992. Grad. teaching asst. U. South Fla., 1988-89; grad. teaching instr. Purdue U., 1989-91; asst. prof. Auburn (Ala.) U., 1992-94; rsch. assoc. Affiliated Systems Corp., Houston, 1994-96; adj. asst. prof. U. Tex. Sch. Pub. Health, Houston, Md., 1996—; co-prin. investigator Nat. Inst. on Drug Abuse, 1994-96; rsch. assoc. NOVA Rsch. Co., Bethesda, Md., 1995—; adj. asst. prof. Ctr. for Health Promotion Rsch. and Devel. U. Tex.-Houston Sch. of Pub. Health, 1996—. Author: Rhetoric in the War on Drugs, 1994, Public Relations Inquiry as Rhetorical Criticism, 1995; contbr. articles to profl. jours. Chmn. Grove St./Blossom Brook Neighborhood Improvement Project, Sarasota, Fla., 1990-92; poll sheriff Tippecanoe County, Ind. State Elections, 1990; precinct capt. Sarasota County, Fla., 1986-89. Recipient Alan H. Monroe Disting. Grad. scholar, and teaching award, 1990-91; Rsch. grantee, Auburn U., 1993. Mem. Houston Coun. on Substance Abuse Svcs., Tex. Drug Epidemiology Workgroup. Home: 402 Tuam Ave 1 Houston TX 77006

ELY, JOANN DENICE, health science facility administrator; b. Bay City, Mich., Dec. 18, 1951; d. Phillip C. Maurer and Elsie (Etherington) McGowan. AS, Eas. Mich. U., 1979; BS in Pharmacy, Mercer U., 1982, PharmD, 1983. Registered Pharmacist, Ga., Fla. Pharmacy intern Drs. Meml. Hosp., Atlanta, 1979-82; pharmacist Egleston Hosp., Atlanta, 1982-84; clin. specialist Lee Meml. Hosp., Ft. Myers, Fla., 1984-90; asst. clin. prof. U. Fla., 1989-90; clin. mgr. Beyer Hosp., Ypsilanti, Mich., 1991—. Lectr. Arthritis Found., Ft. Myers, 1984-91. Mem. Am. Soc. Hosp. Pharmacists, So. Gulf Soc. Hosp. Pharmacists (pres. 1988), Fla. Soc. Hosp. Pharmacists, Am. Soc. Parenteral and Enteral Nutrition, Phi Theta Kappa. Republican. Episcopalian. Home: 185 E Shore Dr Whitmore Lake MI 48189-9441

ELY, LAWRENCE ORLO, retired surgeon; b. Guthrie Center, Iowa, Dec. 13, 1919; s. John Ermerson and Luella Mabel (Knapp) E.; m. Dorothy Maxine Jenkins, Aug. 23, 1942; children: Patricia Anne, Lawrence Orlo, Stephen Craig, Bennett Knapp, Carolyn Elizabeth. BA, State U. Iowa, 1942, MD, 1943, MS, 1948, PhD, 1950. Diplomate Am. Bd. Gen. Surgery. Intern Mt. Carmel Mercy Hosp., Detroit, 1943-44; instr. dept. physiology Med. Sch., State U. Iowa, Iowa City, 1946-48, resident, instr. dept. surgery, 1948-52; pvt. practice gen. surgery Des Moines, 1952-85; mem. staff Iowa Luth. Hosp., Des Moines, 1952-85, Mercy Med. Ctr., Des Moines, 1952-85, Iowa Meth. Med. Ctr., Des Moines, 1952-86; cons. Iowa Blue Cross-Blue Shield, 1985-86, Iowa Found. for Med. Care, 1985-86. Sect. head United Campaign, Des Moines, 1958-60; mem. Des Moines Opera Bd., 1973—, pres., 1973-78; mem. Health Planning Coun. of Iowa Med. Corp., 1970-78; bd. dirs., pres. Ramsey Home, 1988-94; bd. dirs. Civic Music Assn. Des Moines, 1984—; mem. steering com. Friends of the Arts, Drake U., Des Moines. Capt. M.C., U.S. Army, 1944-46. Fellow ACS; mem. AMA, Iowa Med. Soc., Polk County Med. Soc. Republican. Mem. Disciples of Christ Ch. Home: 3500 Fleur Dr Des Moines IA 50321-2650

ELY, P. HAINES, dermatologist, educator; b. Washington, Sept. 19, 1945; s. Northcutt and Marica (McCann) E.; m. Elizabeth Magee, June 24, 1969; children: Sims, Rebecca, Meredith, Tess. AB, Stanford U., 1967; MD, U. So. Calif., 1971. Diplomate Am. Bd. Dermatology, Am. Bd. Pathology; lic. dermatologist, Calif. Intern in medicine U. So. Calif.-L.A. County Med. Ctr., 1971-72, resident, 1972-75; clin. prof. dermatology U. Calif., Davis, 1975—; bd. dirs. Nevada City Wineries. Mem. editl. bd. Calif. Physician, 1994—; manuscript reviewer Archives of Internal Medicine, 1988—, Annals of Internal Medicine, 1980—, Archives of Dermatology, 1977—; contbr. articles to med. jours. Fellow Am. Acad. Dermatology (asst. editor jour. 1988–94, manuscript reviewer 1994—), Am. Soc. Dermatopathology; mem. AMA, Internat. Soc. for Tropical Dermatology, Am. Fedn. for Clin. Rsch., Am. Soc. for Dermatologic Surgery, N.Am. Clin.. Dermatologic Soc., Calif. Med. Assn. (alt. del. 1995—, rep. to Calif. Telehealth/Telemedicine coord. project planning com. 1996—), Pacific Dermatologic Soc. (Nelson Paul Anderson Meml. Essay 1st pl. award 1979, Mini Presentation of Yr. award 1984), Noah Worcester Dermatol. Soc., Cutaneous Therapy Soc., Soc. Investigative Dermatology, Sacramento Valley Dermatol. Soc. (pres. 1990-91), Placer Nev. Med. Soc. (bd. dirs. 1978-79, 91-93, v.p. 1994, pres. 1995), Skin Cancer Found. (med. coun. 1987—), Tri-County Am. Cancer Soc. (bd. dirs. 1978-79, 91-92), Royal Soc. Medicine (London), Dermatology Found., Space Dermatology Found. (founding mem.), Shivas Irons Soc. (founding mem.). Office: Brunswick E # 7 10565 Brunswick Rd Grass Valley CA 95945

ELZAY, RICHARD PAUL, dental school administrator; b. Lima, Ohio, Dec. 6, 1931; s. Paul William and Edna Virginia (Moyer) E.; 1 child, Mark S. BS, Ind. U., Indpls., 1957, DDS with honors, 1960, M in Dental Surgery, 1962. Diplomate Am. Bd. Oral Pathology. Gen. practice dentistry Brownsburg, Ind., 1960-62; instr. dept. oral pathology Med. Coll. Va. Sch. Dentistry, Richmond, 1962-64; asst. prof. Sch. Dentistry Med. Coll. Va., Richmond, 1964-66, assoc. prof., 1966-69, prof., chmn. dept. oral pathology, 1969-86, asst. dean acad. affairs, 1970-74; prof., dep. v.p. for health scis., dean Sch. Dentistry U. Minn., Mpls., 1986—. Office: U Minn Sch Dentistry 515 Delaware St SE Minneapolis MN 55455-0343

ELZER, RUTH MARIE, nurse; b. Ottawa, Ill., Oct. 28, 1966; d. Frank Edward and Ann Veronica (Sagi) E. Diploma St. Francis Sch. Nursing, 1987; BSN, Gov.'s State U., 1994. RN, Ill.; cert. instr. CPR, Am. Heart Assn. Staff RN cardiovascular stepdown unit St. Joseph's Med. Ctr., Joliet, Ill., 1987-96, care coord. case mgmt., 1996—. Recipient Spirit of Nursing award Army Nurses Corp, 1995. Mem. AACN, Sigma Theta Tau. Roman Catholic.

EMANUEL, BEVERLY S., geneticist; b. Phila., Aug. 16, 1941. PhD, U. Pa., 1972. Cert. PhD med. geneticist, clin. cytogeneticist. Geneticist Children's Hosp., Phila.; prof. pediatrics and genetics U. Pa., Phila., 1988—. Mem. AAAS, ABMG, ASHG, HUGO. Office: Children's Hosp Phila 10th Fl Abramson Rsch Ctr Philadelphia PA 19104

EMANUEL, IRVIN, medical administrator, educator; b. Balt., Oct. 9, 1926; s. David and Dora (Hollander) E.; children—Gina Marie, Melissa Pauline; m. Christiane B. Hale. B.S., Rutgers U., 1951; M.A., U. Ariz., 1956; M.D., U. Rochester, 1960; M.S., U. Wash., 1966. Asst. prof. anthropology, asst. dir. U.S. Air Force anthropology project Antioch Coll., Yellow Springs, Ohio, 1953-55; anthropologist Aerospace Med. Lab., Dayton, Ohio, 1955-56; cons. Aerospace Med. Lab., 1956-60; intern Cleve. Met. Gen. Hosp., 1960-61; resident U. Wash., Seattle, 1961-62; sr. fellow depts. preventive medicine and pediatrics, 1962-66, asst. prof. depts. epidemiology, internat. health and pediatrics, 1966-70, assoc. prof., 1970-74, prof. epidemiology and pediatrics, 1974—; dir. Child Developmental and Mental Retardation Ctr., 1973-83, dir. Maternal and Child Health Program Sch. Pub. Health and Community Medicine, U. Wash., 1983-88, co-dir., 1988-94, assoc. dir., 1994—; guest investigator U.S. Naval Med. Research Unit 2, Taipei, Taiwan, 1964-66; mem. Harvard Peabody Mus. Solomon Islands Expdn., 1966; bd. dirs. Am. Assn. U. Affiliated Programs for Developmentally Disabled, 1977-80; vis prof. Dept. Clin. Epidemiology London Hosp. Med. Coll., 1987-88. Contbr. articles on phys. anthropology, pediatrics and epidemiology to profl. jours. Served with USNR, 1945-46. Recipient award Spl. Act Service Air Research Devel. Command USAF, 1961, research career devel. award Nat. Inst. Child Health and Human Devel., 1966-71; Fogarty Sr. Internat. fellow NIH, 1987-88. Mem. APHA, Soc. Epidemiol. Rsch., Am. Epidemiol. Soc., Phi Beta Kappa. Office: U Wash Dept Epidemiology Box 357236 Seattle WA 98195-7236

EMBREY, RICHARD PENN, pediatric cardiac surgeon; b. Lynchburg, Va., Dec. 3, 1957; s. Nelson Scales and Shirley Penn (Slaughter) E.; m. Denise Marlene Clark-Jones, Aug. 28, 1981 (div. Oct. 1990); children: Jillian Gail, Jenna Clark; m. Rebecca Lynn Angel, Mar. 9, 1991; 1 child, Pearce Thomson. Student, Tulane U. Sch. Engring., 1976-78; BA, Johns Hopkins U., 1980, MD, 1983. Diplomate Am. Bd. Surgery, Am. Bd. Thoracic Surgery. Intern in surgery Mass. Gen. Hosp., Boston, 1983-84, resident in surgery, 1984-88; resident in cardiothoracic surgery U. Ala., 1988-90, fellow in cardiothoracic surgery, 1990-91; asst. prof. surgery U. Iowa, 1991-95; dir. pediat. cardiac surgery Med. Coll. Va. Hosps., Richmond, 1995—. Contbr. chpt. to books: Pediatric Cardiac Surgery 2d. edit., 1994, Glen's Thoracic and Cardiovascular Surgery, 6th edit., 1995; editor: Yearbook of Cardiothoracic SUrgery, 1995. CV Mosby scholar, 1983. Fellow ACS, Am. Coll. Cardiology, Am. Coll. Chest Physicians; mem. Soc. Thoracic Surgeons, Internat. Soc. Heart and Lung Transplantation. Home: 6024 Abington Park Dr Glen Allen VA 23060 Office: Med Coll Va 1200 E Broad St Richmond VA 23298-0068

EMBRY, DENNIS DAVID, psychologist; b. Great Bend, Kans., Nov. 21, 1948; s. H. Herbert and Ruth Elizabeth (Gregory) E.; m. Lynne A. Haggarty, Aug. 21, 1971 (div. 1990). BA, U. Kans., 1972, MA, 1979, PhD, 1981. Lic. psychologist, Ariz. Dir. Curriculum and Instrn. Survey, Lawrence, Kans., 1969-72; rsch. asst. Dept. Human Devel., Lawrence, Kans., 1974-75; instr. Dept. Western Civilization, U. Kans., Lawrence, 1975-77; asst. rsch. dir. Early Childhood Rsch. Inst., Lawrence, 1977-79; pres. Circle Inst., Lawrence, 1979-82; sr. fellow Nat. Rsch. Adv. Coun., Wellington, N.Z., 1983-86; rsch. assoc. U. Kans., Lawrence, 1981-83, 84-87; pres. Quality Time, Inc., Tucson, 1987-91, Heartsprings, Inc., Tucson, 1991—; cons. Pentagon Family Policy/USAF, Washington, 1991—, Ctrs. for Disease Control, 1995—; dir. Tucson Children's Mus., 1991—; team leader Pathways to Resiliency Nat. Coalition, Tucson, 1992—; exec. dir. Project ME, Inc., Tucson, 1990—. Author six book series: Reunion: I'm Coming Home, 1991; two book series: Someone in my Family Went to Middle East, 1990; 6 book series: Safe Playing, 1981, 85, 87; author: I Play Creatively, 1991, I Help Build Peace, 1992, Peace Builders Violence Prevention Curriculum, 1993—; contbr. chpts. to books and articles to profl. jours. Designer Plan for FEMA Mental Health Response to L.A. Riots, Tucson, 1992; witness Senate Vets. Affairs Com., Washington, 1991; mem. Mayor's Task Force on Children's Mental Health, Tucson, 1990-91; founder Nat. Effort to Help Mil. Children in Gulf War, Tucson, 1990-91. Recipient Cert. of Appreciation U.S. Dept. Def., 1991, Desert Storm Bronze Coin 7th Army Germany, 1991; named Outstanding Community Contbr. 836th Davis Monthan AFB, Tucson, 1991. Mem. APA (task force on trauma response 1991—), Assn. for Behavior Analysis. Methodist. Office: Heartsprings Inc PO Box 12158 Tucson AZ 85732-2158

EMERSON, ANN PARKER, dietician, educator; b. Twin Lakes, Fla., Dec. 3, 1925; d. Charles Dendy and Gladys Agnes (Chalker) Parker; B.S., Fla. State U., 1947; M.S., U. Fla., 1968; m. Donald McGeachy Emerson, Sept. 22, 1950; children—Mary Ann, Donald McGeachy, Charles Parker, William John. Research dietitian U. Chgo., 1948-50; adminstrv. research dietitian U. Fla. Coll. Medicine, Gainesville, 1962-68, dir. dietetic edn., 1968-74, dir. dietetic internship program, 1968-75, dir. program in clin. and community dietetics, 1974-83; mem. Commn. on Dietetic Registration, 1974-77, Commn. on Accreditation, 1980-83. Pres., Gainesville chpt. Altrusa, Internat., 1977-78. VA Allied Health Manpower grantee, 1974-81; HEW Allied Health Manpower grantee, 1975-78, 78-81. Mem. Am., Fla. Dietetic Assns. Republican. Roman Catholic. Clubs: Jr. League, Altrusa.

EMERSON, DOROTHY VIRGINIA, retired medical and surgical nurse, administrator; b. Cumberland, Md., Apr. 17, 1923; d. Albert Herman and Lillian Marie (Rosser) Couter; m. Don Allen Emerson, Sept. 21, 1945; 1 child, Dian Margaret Emerson Williams. Diploma, Allegany Hosp. Sch. Nursing, Cumberland, 1945; student, Frostburg (Md.) State U. RN. Exec. dir. Allegany County League for Crippled Children, Cumberland, 1971-86; instr. med.-surg. nursing Meml. Hosp., Cumberland; nursing supr., head nurse med.-surg. Allegany Hosp. (now Sacred Heart Hosp.), Cumberland. Cadet nurse, 1944-45. Recipient numerous awards. Mem. ANA, Md. State Nurses Assn. (pres. Dist. 1 1962-64).

EMERSON, JAMES LARRY, beverage company executive; b. Garrett, Ind., Jan. 23, 1938; s. George Cary and Ellen A. (Bennett) E.; m. Madalyn Carol Brown, June 24, 1962; children: Todd Jeffrey, Kiersten Christine, Leisel Renee. Student in pre-vet medicine, Purdue U., 1958, MS, 1964, PhD, 1966; DVM, Ohio State U., 1962. Diplomate Am. Coll. Vet. Pathologists. Sr. rsch. specialist dept. pathology and toxicology Dow Chem. Co., Indpls., 1969-76; assoc. faculty mem. Ind. U., Purdue U., Indpls., 1972-76; mgr. dept. pathology Abbott Labs., North Chicago, Ill., 1976-79; mgr. life scis. Coca-Cola Co., Atlanta, 1979-81, assoc. dir. external tech. affairs, 1981-82, dir. sci. and regulatory affairs, 1982—, asst. v.p.; chmn. saccharin tech. com. Internat. Life Scis. Inst., Washington, 1984—, mem. editl. bd., 1983—; trustee Health and Environ. Scis. Inst., 1990—; hon. prof. U. del Salvador, Buenos Aires; v.p. Coca-Cola Internat. Bd. dirs. Jacquelyn McClure Lupus Found., Atlanta, 1984—. Fellow Royal Soc. Medicine; mem. AVMA, Indsl. Vet. Assn., Soc. Toxicology, Internat. Acad. Pathologists, Flavor and Extract Mfrs. Assn. (bd. govs. 1987—, chmn., sec. com. 1984—, pres. 1994-95). Methodist. Home: 290 Landfall Rd NW Atlanta GA 30328-1826 Office: Coca-Cola Co 1 Coca Cola Plz NW Atlanta GA 30313-2420

EMERSON, SHARON B., biology researcher and educator; b. Santa Monica, Calif., July 14, 1945. BA, U. Calif., Berkeley, 1966; MS, U. So. Calif., 1968, PhD, 1971. Rsch. assoc. Field Mus. Natural History, Chgo.; rsch. prof. Dept. Biology U. Utah; rsch. assoc. Field Mus. Nat. History, Chgo. Recipient John D. and Katherine T. MacArthur fellowship, 1995, award for excellence in environ. health rsch. Lovelance Inst., Albuquerque, 1995. Mem. Am. Soc. Zoology (elected chair divsn. vertebrate morphology). Office: U Utah Dept Biology Salt Lake City UT 84112

EMERY, MARCIA ROSE, psychologist, consultant; b. Phila., Mar. 19, 1937; d. David Gelfand and Naomi (Carner) Rose; m. Gordon M. Becker, 1970 (div.); m. James D. Emery, 1982; stepchildren: Stephen, Alicia, Jamie. B.A. in Psychology, Adelphi U., Garden City, N.Y., 1958; M.S. in Clin. Psychology, CCNY, 1960; M.A. in Social Psychology, New Sch. Social Rsch., 1964, Ph.D., 1968. Rsch. asst. Office Instl. Rsch., Hunter Coll., N.Y.C., 1959-62, Community Svcs. Soc., N.Y.C., 1962-65; lectr. psychology Hunter Coll., 1965-67; assoc. prof. psychology, chmn. M.A. program in community psychology Fed. City Coll., Washington, 1968-74; pvt. practice psychology counseling, Hollywood, Fla., 1981—; pres. Intuitive Mgmt. Cons. Corp.; adj. prof. bus. mgmt. Aquinas Coll., Grand Rapids; psychologist Renaissance Revitalization Ctr., Nassau, Bahamas, 1976-80; condr. workshops in whole brain thinking and intuitive mgmt. throughout U.S.; condr. corp. tng. programs in intuitive mgmt. skills and stress mgmt. Author: Marcia Emery's Intuitive Management Workout, Dr. Marcia Emery's Intuition Workbook: An Expert's Guide to Unlocking the Wisdom of Your Subconcious Mind, 1994, Intuition: How to Use Your Gut Instinct for Greater Personal Power, Nightingale Conant Audio Cassette Album, 1995. Grantee NIMH, 1992, Charlson Rsch. Found., 1991. Mem. APA, Assn. Humanistic Psychology, Assn. for Study of Dreams, Am. Soc. Psychical Rsch., Intuition Network, Assn. Past Life Rsch. and Therapy. Address: 1502 10th St Berkeley CA 94710

EMERY, PAUL EMILE, psychiatrist; b. Montreal, May 2, 1922; came to U.S., 1951; s. Esdras Fernand and Julia (Benoit) E.; m. Virginia Olga B. Kennick, July 27, 1979. BA, U. Montreal, 1942, MD, 1948. Diplomate in gen. psychiatry and forensic psychiatry. Staff psychiatrist Austen Riggs Ctr., Stockbridge, Mass., 1958-60; chief mental hygiene VA, Bridgeport, Conn., 1960-62; staff psychiatrist, chief of psychiatry VA, Manchester, N.H., 1988—; pvt. practice Concord, N.H., 1962-85; clin. dir. Ctr. for Stress Recovery, Brecksville, Ohio, 1985-87, dir., 1987-88; med. dir. forensic unit N.H. Hosp., Concord, 1980-82; cons. VA med. Ctr., Manchester, 1962-64, 82-85, pub. health State of N.H., Concord, 1962-71, St. Paul's Sch., Concord, 1971-78; mem. faculty Dartmouth Coll. Med. Sch., 1971—, Western Res. Sch. Medicine, 1985—. Contbr. articles to profl. jours.; author: Trauma Psychology Model of the Mind, 1993. Sec. adv. commn. health and welfare State of N.H., Concord. Capt. U.S. Army, 1953-55. Recipient Salutation plaque N.H. Program on Alcoholism, 1971. Fellow Am. Psychiat. Assn. (life); mem. N.H. Med. Soc. (cert. commendation 1972). Office: VA Med Ctr 718 Smyth Rd Manchester NH 03104-7004

EMERY, ROBERT WILLIAM, JR., cardiac surgeon; b. Springfield, Mass., July 22, 1947; s. Robert William and Ruth Eleanor (Brouillet) E.; m. Ann M. Emery, June 3, 1973; children: Kate, Liz, Christen, R.J. BS, Pa. State U., 1969; MD, Tufts U., 1973. Diplomate Am. Bd. Surgery, Thoracic Surgery; lic. Minn., Ariz. Intern U. Minn. Hosps., Mpls., 1973-74, resident, fellow, 1974-81; resident Brigham and Women's Hosp., Boston, 1981-82, Children's Hosp. Med. Ctr., Boston, 1983; asst. prof., assoc. prof. surgery U. Ariz. Health Scis. Ctr., Tucson, 1983-86; surgeon cardiovascular and thoracic Mpls. Heart Ins., St. Paul Heart and Lung Inst., 1987—; dir. cardiac transplantation Mpls. Heart Inst., 1987-89, dir. cardiothoracic transplantation, 1989—; dir. cardiac surgery Tucson VA Hosp., 1986; lectr. in field. Co-editor: Cardiothoracic Transplantation, 1988, Cardiothoracic Transplantation II, 1989, The Aortic Valve, 1991, Handbook of Cardiac Transplantation, 1995; contbr. numerous articles and abstracts to profl. jours. Office: 920 E 28th St Ste 420 Minneapolis MN 55407

EMERY, VIRGINIA OLGA BEATTIE, psychologist, researcher; b. Cleve., Apr. 9, 1938; d. Joseph P. and Antoinette Pauline (Misja) Kennick; m. Paul Hamilton Beattie Sr., 1960 (div. 1975); children: Tamsan Beattie Tharin, Paul Hamilton Beattie Jr.; m. Paul E. Emery, 1979. BA, U. Chgo., 1962, PhD, 1982; MA, Ind. U., 1973. Lic. psychologist, N.H., Ohio. Adj., clin. asst. prof. psychiatry Dartmouth Med. Sch., Lebanon, N.H., 1983-85; asst. prof. psychology Case Western Res. U., Cleve., 1986-89, asst. clin. prof. psychiatry, 1986-89; sr. faculty assoc. Ctr. on Aging and Health, 1986-89; clin. assoc. prof. psychiatry Dartmouth Med. Sch., Lebanon, N.H., 1989—; dir. Ctr. on Aging and Health, Inc. and Soc., Concord and Hanover, N.H., 1989—; mem. com. human devel. NIMH, Adult Devel. & Aging Traineeship, U. Chgo., 1974-76; sub-project dir. Case Western Res. U. Sch. Medicine, 1986-90; sec. women's faculty assn. Case Western Res. U., 1987-89; cons. Vets. Affairs Med. Ctr., Manchester, N.H., 1989—; sub-project dir. NIMH Mental Health Clin. Rsch. Ctr. Grant, Case Western Res. U. Sch. Medicine, 1986-90; mem. Dartmouth Coll. and Dartmouth Med. Sch. Neurosci. Group, 1990—. Author: Language and Aging, 1985, Pseudodementia: A Theoretical and Empirical Discussion, 1988; editor: Dementia: Presentations, Differential Diagnosis, and Nosology, 1994; contbr. articles to profl. jours. Bd. dirs. Frontiers of Knowledge Civic Trust, Concord, N.H., 1990—, pres. 1990-95. Recipient Adult Devel. and Aging grant/traineeship NIH/NIMH, 1974-76, Rsch. prize Am. Aging Assn., 1983, Havighurst prize for aging rsch. U. Chgo., 1984; named Frontiers of Knowledge Atlee Zellers lectr., 1994; rsch. grantee Western Res. Coll., 1986-87, NIMH Mental Health Clin. rsch. grantee, 1986-89. Fellow Gerontol. Soc. Am. (Disting creative contbn. award 1989), N.H. Psychol. Assn. (bd. dirs. 1991-93, chair com. acad. rsch. interests 1992-94, sec. 1994—, Riggs Disting. Contbn. award 1991); mem. AAAS, APA (student rsch. award 1984), AAUW, Internat. Psychiat. rsch. Soc., Internat. Psychogeriatric Assn. (2d place award for rsch. paper 1995, 2nd Pl. Rsch. award in psychogeriatrics for paper 1995, IPA/Bayer Rsch. award in psychogeriatrics 1995), Boston Soc. Gerontol. Psychiatry, Acad. Psychosomatic Medicine, N.Y. Acad. Scis. Home: 15 Buckingham Dr Bow NH 03304-5207 Office: Dept Psychiatry Box HB 7750 Dartmouth Med Sch Lebanon NH 03756

EMINI, EMILIO ANTHONY, research scientist; b. N.Y.C., Dec. 9, 1953; s. Emilio and Maria (Pescione) E.; m. Jacquelynn Ruby Cunliffe, Dec. 27, 1980; children: Emilia C., Alessandra J. BS, Manhattan Coll., 1975; PhD, Cornell U., 1980. Research fellow SUNY, Stony Brook, 1980-83; sr. scientist Merck Rsch. Labs., West Point, Pa., 1983-86, research fellow, 1986-89, assoc. dir., 1989-90, dir., 1990-92, sr. dir., 1992-94, exec. dir. dept. of antiviral rsch., 1994—; co-dir. AIDS vaccine and therapy rsch. programs; mem. NIH rsch. adv. coms.; adj. prof. microbiology Hahnemann U. Sch. of Medicine, Phila. Contbr. articles to profl. jours.; patentee in field. Fellow NSF, 1976, Am. Cancer Soc., 1980, NIH, 1981-82. Mem. AAAS, Am. Soc. Microbiology, N.Y. Acad. Sci., Phi Beta Kappa. Avocation: ancient history. Office: Merck Rsch Labs West Point PA 19486

EMMEL, JOHN EDWARD, family physician, educator; b. Pitts., Sept. 18, 1952; s. Thomas P. and Irene G. (Monson) E.; m. Deborah A. Gessert, June 14, 1975; children: John Trevor Gessert, Sean Tyler Gessert. AB in Biomed. Scis., Brown U., 1974, MD, 1977. Diplomate Am. Bd. Family Practice. Resident in family practice Med. U. S.C., Charleston, 1977-80, instr., 1980-81, clin. asst. prof., 1981-94; clin. assoc. prof. med. U. S.C., Charleston, 1994—; instr. doctoral candidates in phys. assessment Med. U. S.C., Charleston, 1981—; pvt. practice, Isle of Palms, S.C., 1981-90, Mt. Pleasant, S.C., 1990—; med. dir. Dept. Alcohol and Other Drug Abuse Svcs. Charleston County, 1980—; med. dir. Sandpiper Convalescent Ctr., Mt. Pleasant, 1985—, Manor Care Nursing Ctr., Charleston, 1993—; chief family medicine dept. East Cooper Cmty. Hosp., Mt. Pleasant, 1990-91. Fellow So. Assn. Geriatric Medicine (founder); mem. Am. Acad. Family Physicians, Am. Geriatric Soc., Am. Soc. Addiction Medicine (cert.), World Tae Kwon Do Assn. (bd dirs. southeastern region), Am. Med. Dirs. Assn. (cert., med.

dir. long-term care facility). Home: 204 Palm Blvd Isle Of Palms SC 29451-2143 Office: 1049B Anna Knapp Blvd Mount Pleasant SC 29464-3133

EMMERSON, BRYAN THOMAS, physician, educator; b. Townsville, Queensland, Australia, Sept. 5, 1929; s. Leonard Joseph and Thelma Ann (Thomas) E.; m. Elva Brett, Apr. 28, 1955; children—William Brett, Stephen Bryan. M.B.B.S., U. Queensland, 1952, M.D., 1962, Ph.D., 1973. Sr. lectr. in therapeutics U. Queensland, Brisbane, 1960-62, reader in medicine, 1963-73, prof. medicine, 1974-94, prof. emeritus, 1994—, chmn. dept. medicine, 1981-84; councillor Queensland Inst. Med. Research, 1978-94, Royal Australasian Coll. Physicians, 1979-86, Queensland Conservatorium of Music, 1981—; chmn. divsn. medicine Princess Alexandra Hosp., 1995-96; cons. emeritus Princess Alexandra Hosp. Author: Hyperuricaemia and Gout in Clinical Practice, 1983; mem. editorial bd. Nephron, Clin. and Exptl. Rheumatology; contbr. 160 articles to profl. jours. Bd. dirs. Australian Kidney Found., 1970—, chmn. med. and sci. adv. com., 1978-84; bd. dirs. Arthritis Found. Queensland, 1985—. Recipient Weinholt prize U. Queensland, 1950; Masonic Bursary, 1950; Parr prize, Australian Rheumatology Assn., 1966; USPHS fellow, 1967; hon. fellow St. John's Coll.; recipient Susman prize, Royal Australasian Coll. Physicians, 1978. Mem. Australasian Soc. Nephrology (life, pres. 1972-74), Australian Med. Assn., Australian Rheumatology Assn. (v.p. 1978-91, pres. 1992-93), Internat. Soc. Nephrology, Australian Soc. Clin. and Exptl. Pharmacology, Assn. Univ. Clin. Profs. Australia (chmn. 1979-81), Spina Bifida Assn. of Queensland (hon. life). Anglican. Clubs: Queensland, University. Office: Princess Alexandra Hosp, Ipswich Rd, Brisbane Queensland 4102, Australia

EMMERSON, DAVID A., radiologist; b. Honolulu, July 16, 1941; s. Joseph Othneil and Lila Mose (Goode) E.; widowed Sept. 1975; children; David A. II, Daniel A., Darla A., Darcie A. BA, Montana State U., 1964; MD, U. Guadalajara, 1970. Diplomate Am. Bd. Nuclear Medicine, Am. Bd. Radiology. Radiologist Kino Cmty. Hosp., Tucson, 1976-81, St. Joseph's Hosp., Tucson, 1982—; med. dir. radiology St. Joseph's Hosp., 1993—. Republican. Home: 8220 E Woodland Rd Tucson AZ 85749-9574 Office: St Josephs Hosp 350 N Wilmot Rd Tucson AZ 85711

EMMERT, ROBERTA RITA, health facility administrator; b. Buffalo, Aug. 28, 1953; d. Robert George and Rita Rose (Lambert) E. Diploma, St. Elizabeth Hosp. Sch. Nsg., 1974; BSN magna cum laude, SUNY, Utica, 1989; MS, Syracuse U., 1993, postgrad., 1993—. RN, N.Y., Calif. Charge nurse, staff nurse pediatrics St. Joseph Hosp. Health Ctr., Syracuse, N.Y., 1974-83; charge nurse spl. care pediatrics St. Joseph Hosp. Health Ctr., 1983-89; adminstrv. supr., nurse educator St Joseph Hosp. Health Ctr., Syracuse, N.Y., 1989—; instr. Am. Heart Assn. Mem. ANA (cert. pediat. nurse), NAFE, AAUW, Am. Orgn. Nurse Execs., N.Y. State Nurses Assn., Soc. Pediat. Nurses, Sigma Theta Tau. Home: 4750 Woodard Way Apt 9K Liverpool NY 13088-4621

EMMETT, MICHAEL, physician; b. Linz, Austria, Oct. 29, 1945; came to U.S., 1949.; s. Issac and Pearl (Gladstone) E.; m. Rachel Kozuch, Aug. 2, 1969; children: Mira, Daniel, Joshua. BS, Pa. State U., 1967; MD, Temple U., 1971. Diplomate Am. Bd. Internal Medicine, Am. Bd. Internal Medicine, Nephrology. Intern, then resident Yale U. Med. Ctr., New Haven, 1971-74; nephrology fellow Hosp. U. of Pa., Phila., 1974-76; clin. asst. prof. medicine U. Tex. Southwestern Med. Sch., Dallas, 1976-80, clin. assoc. prof. medicine, 1980-85, clin. prof. medicine, 1985—; Ralph Tompsett prof. medicine Baylor U. Med. Ctr., Dallas, 1986—, dir., nephrology/metabolism, 1986-96, dir. nephrology endocrinology labs, 1986—, chief of medicine, 1996—; cons. physician Parkland Hosp., Dallas, 1976—, Presbyn. Hosp., Dallas, 1976—. Contbr. articles to profl. jours. Fellow ACP; mem. Am. Fedn. Clin. Rsch., Dallas County Med. Soc., Tex. Med. Assn., So. Med. Soc., Am. Soc. Nephrology, Internat. Soc. Nephrology. Office: Baylor U Med Ctr 3500 Gaston Ave Dallas TX 75246-2045

EMMONS, BOBBI ANN, nursing educator; b. Gloversville, N.Y., Sept. 20, 1951; d. Maxwell and Hazel Ruth (Weiderman) Tomlinson; m. David Bennie Fincher, May 15, 1972 (div. 1974); m. Charles Wayne Emmons, July 19, 1974; children: Karen, Katherine, David, Katrina, Susan, Rebecca, Philip. AAS in Nursing, Alvin (Tex.) C.C., 1977; BSN, U. Tex. Health Sci. Ctr., 1984, MSN, 1991; student, Okla. State U., 1996. RN, Okla; cert. ACLS, Am. Heart Assn. ICU/CCU nursing technician St. Joseph's Hosp., Houston, 1972-75; ICU nursing technician Twelve Oaks Hosp., Houston, 1975-77; team leader, staff nurse, chair quality assurance in CVICU The Methodist Hosp., Houston, 1977-80; supr., charge nurse, staff nurse ICU/CCU Staff Temporary Agencies - 12 Hosps., Houston, 1980-88; asst. dir., curriculum cons. nursing Houston C.C. Sys., Houston, 1982-84; staff nurse ICU, inservice coord. Woman's Hosp. of Tex., Houston, 1985-88; staff nurse in ICU/CCU Meml. S.W. Hosp., Houston, 1988-91; instr. didactic and clin. nursing No. Okla. Coll., Tonkawa, Okla., 1991—; instr. anatomy and physiology Cowley County C.C., Arkansas City, Kans., 1994—; instr. in MEd. Terminology Pioneer Tech. Ctr., Ponca City, Okla.; spkr. Night Beat All Night C.E. Symposium, Houston, 1987; adv. Student Nurses Assn., Tonkawa, Okla., 1992—, pub. spkr., Tulsa, Edmond, Altus, Tonkawa, Okla., 1994-95; spkr. Okla. Nurses Assn., Enid, 1993. Contbr.: Nutrition and Nursing, 1994, Memory Notebook of Nursing, 1994. Grantee Rockefellar Found., 1969; Helene Fuld fellow Helene Fuld Found., 1970. Mem. AACN, ANA, Okla. Nurses Assn., NCLEX Test Item Writer, Sigma THeta Tau Internat. Republican. Mem. LDS Ch. Home: 98 Elmwood Ponca City OK 74601-3448 Office: No Okla Coll Div of Nursing Box 310 1220 E Grand Tonkawa OK 74653-0310

EMOND, LEONARD DAVID, orthopaedist; b. Greenville, N.H., Aug. 20, 1928; s. David Charles and Albina (Boulay) E.; m. Julienne M. Bolduc, June 19, 1955; children: Marc D., James A., Christopher J. BS, U. N.H., 1950; post grad., Laval U., 1956, U. Pa., 1957. Diplomate Am. Bd. Neurol. and Orthopedic Surgery. Intern Laval Univ. Hosp., Quebec City, Quebec, Can., 1956; resident gen. surgery Bradford (Pa.) Hosp., 1956-57; resident orthopaedic surgery Akron Gen. Hosp., Akron Children's Hosp., 1957-60; orthopedic surgeon Med. Assocs., Dubuque, Iowa, 1960-63, pvt. practice, Manchester, N.H., 1963—; cons. N.H. Retirement System, Concord, 1991—; pres. New Eng. Disability Evaluations, Manchester, 1991—; staff mem. Cath. Med. Ctr., Manchester, N.H., 1965—. Assoc. editor Jour. of Disability, 1990-93; contbr. articles to profl. jours. Tenor Nat. Opera Co., Que., 1954-55, Souhegan Valley Choral Soc., 1992—, Nashua Symphony Chorale, 1995—. Fellow Am. Acad. Neurol. and Orthopaedic Surgery, Am. Acad. Disability Evaluations (lectr. 1987—, bd. dirs. 1989—, chmn. clin. tng. program 1989-91); mem. N.H. Med. Soc., Hillsboro County Med. Soc., Am. Acad. Disability Evaluating Physicians (pres. 1994—), Appalachian Mountain Club (mem. 4000 footer club). Republican. Roman Catholic. Home: 110 Crestview Rd Manchester NH 03104-1842 Office: New Eng Disability Evals 20 Webster St Manchester NH 03104-2544

EMORY, EMERSON, psychiatrist, physician; b. Dallas, Jan. 29, 1925; s. Corry Bates and Louise (Linthecum) E.; m. Peggy Lillian Herald, Sept. 1, 1951; children—Sharon, Karon Hutchinson, Emerson, Jr. Student, Prairie View U., 1940-42; BA cum laude, Lincoln U., Pa., 1948; MD, Meharry Med. Coll., 1952. Cert. correctional healthcare profl. Intern St. Paul's Hosp., Dallas, 1952-53, resident in internal medicine, 1953-54; resident in internal medicine City of Hope, Duarte, Calif., 1954-55, VA Ctr., L.A., 1955-56; fellow in psychiatry U. Tex. Southwest Med. Sch., Dallas, 1966-69; staff physician VA Hosp., Dallas and McKinney, Tex., 1957-60; staff psychiatrist Terrell State Hosp., Tex., 1969-71; chief psychiatric svcs. Fed. Correctional Inst., Seagoville, Tex., 1971-72; vol. physician State Dept. AID program, Vietnam, 1966; pvt. practice medicine specializing in psychiatry and internal medicine Dallas, 1973—; psychiat. cons. Bridge Med. Group, 1990—; cons. Tex. Dept. of Human Svc. Adult Protective Svc.; mem. Sec. of Navy's adv. com. on retired pers., 1992—; dir. student health Paul Quinn Coll., Dallas. Editor, pub. weekly newspaper Freedom's Jour., 1979-81; host TV program Freedom Jour., 1985—. Ind. candidate for mayor City of Dallas, 1975, 77, Tex. State Legislature, 1974, 76. Recipient Humanitarian Svc. award AMA Com. of 100, 1966, Cert. Appreciation Vietnam govt., 1966. Fellow Acad. Psychiatry and Law; mem. Am. Coll. Forensic Examiners, Black Psychiatrists Am., Nat. Naval Officers Assn. (founder, past pres.), Washington-Lincoln Alumni Assn. (founder, past pres., Outstanding Alumni award Lincoln U. 1968), Prometheans Club (chaplain 1976-78), Pylon Salesmanship Club (pres. 1992—), Elks (asst. grand med. dir. 1961-81, exalted ruler 1985), KC. Roman Catholic. Home: 4931 W Mockingbird Ln Dallas TX 75209-5211 Office: Ste 355 2606 Martin Luther King Jr Blvste 216 Dallas TX 75215-6397

EMRICK, SISTER ANGELA MARIE, health corporation administrator; b. Venice, Calif., Dec. 11, 1929; d. William Henry and Lucille Mary Magdalene (Morgan) E. BA in English, U. San Francisco, 1963; MEd, U. Ariz., 1974, PhD, 1980. Cert. life secondary tchr., Calif.; secondary tchr., secondary/elem. prin., supr., supt., Ariz. Prin. Our Lady of Lourdes Sch., Salt Lake City, 1963-64, Beverly Hills (Calif.) Cath. Sch., 1965-70; co-adminstr. St. Cyril's Sch., 1970-76; asst. prof. secondary edn. U. Ariz., Tucson, 1979-83; dir. block program for full-time student teaching U. Ariz.; exec. dir. Ctr. for Human Empowerment, Mt. Carmel Health Ctr., Columbus, Ohio, 1987-91, sr. v.p. mission svcs., 1991-95; adminstrv. coord. healthcare A Room With a View Consultancy, 1995—; trustee St. Mary's Coll., Notre Dame, Ind. Regent in adminstrn. Ohio Hosp. Assn. Soc. Dirs. Vols.; trustee Mt. Carmel Coll. Nursing, Columbus, Ohio. Recipient Women of Yr. award for orgnl. empowerment Soroptimists Internat. Home and Office: 1750 Lane Rd Columbus OH 43220-3847

ENDERS, ALLEN COFFIN, anatomy educator; b. Wooster, Ohio, Aug. 5, 1928; s. Robert Kendal and Abbie Gertrude (Crandell) E.; m. Alice Hay, June 15, 1950 (div. Dec. 1975); children: Robert H., George C., Richard S., Gregory H.; m. Sandra Jean Schlafke, Aug. 5, 1976. AB, Swarthmore Coll., 1950; AM, Harvard U., 1952, PhD, 1955. From asst. prof. to assoc. prof Rice Inst., Houston, 1954-63; from assoc. prof. to prof. Washington U., St. Louis, 1963-75; prof., chmn. dept. human anatomy U. Calif., Davis, 1976-86, prof. cell biology and human anatomy, 1986—; cons. NIH, Bethesda, Md., 1964-68, 70-73, 76-80, 83-93. Author: (with others) Bailey's Microscopic Anatomy, 1984; editor: Delayed Implantation, 1964; contbr. numerous articles on anatomy and reproduction to profl. jours. Nat. pres. Perinatal Research Soc., 1981. Grantee NIH, 1959—. Fellow AAAS; mem. Am. Assn. Anatomists (v.p. 1980-82, pres. 1983-84), Soc. Study Reprodn., Am. Soc. Cell Biology. Home: 39707 Barry Rd Davis CA 95616-9415 Office: U Calif Sch of Medicine Cell Biology And Anato Davis CA 95616

ENDOH, RYOHEI, cardiologist; b. Omachi, Nagano, Japan, Apr. 1, 1954; s. Shinzi Endoh and Miharu Momose; m. Miki Kitahara, May 7, 1995. M of Medicine, Shinshu U., Matsumoto, Japan, 1981, MD, 1990. Intern Shinshu U. Hosp., Matsumoto, 1981-82, resident, 1983-84, cardiologist, 1985-87; intern Matsumoto Nat. Hosp., 1982-83; cardiologist Nagano Red Cross Hosp., 1984-85; head physician internal medicine Suwa Red Cross Hosp., 1987; head physician cardiology Showa Inan Gen. Hosp., Komagane, 1987-95; head physician internal medicine Nagano (Japan) Mcpl. Hosp., 1995—. Contbr. articles to Japan Circulation Jour., Artery, Japan Jour. Applied Physiology, Tex. Heart Inst. Jour. Fellow Japanese Soc. Internal Medicine, Japanese Circulation Soc., Japanese Assn. Acute Medicine; mem. Japanese Coll. Angiology. Office: Nagano Mcpl Hosp, 1333-1 Tomitake Nagano-shi, Nagano Japan 381

ENDRES, STEFAN J., immunologist; b. Augsburg, Fed. Republic Germany, June 17, 1957; s. Josef and Gabriele Endres; m. Elisabeth Dulme; children: Janina, Leopold. BA, Harvard U., 1980; MD, U. Munich, 1983. Resident Med. Sch., U. Munich, 1984-86, clin. fellow, 1988—; rsch. fellow Tufts U., Boston, 1987-88; researcher in immunology. Mem. Akademischer Ski Club. Home: Beltweg 26, 80805 Munich Germany Office: Medizinische Klinik, Ziemssenstr 1, 80336 Munich Germany

ENDSLEY, JANE RUTH, nursing educator; b. Harrisburg, Ill., Oct. 14, 1942; d. Clifford B. Bond and Haroldene (Malone) Miller; m. William R. Endsley, June 6, 1964. Grad., Deaconess Hosp. Sch. Nursing, Evansville, Ind., 1963; student, So. Ill. U., 1968; BSN cum laude, U. Evansville, 1978. RN, Ind., Ill. Staff nurse Deaconess Hosp., 1963-64; psychiat. nurse med.-surg. emergency room and obstetrics Ferrell Hosp., Eldorado, Ill., 1964-68, DON, 1969-70; DON, Good Shepherd Nursing Home, Eldorado, 1971-72; instr. nursing Southeastern Ill. U., Harrisburg, 1973—; cons. parents too soon Egyptian Pub. Health Dept., Eldorado, 1985. Vice chmn. Pvt. Industry Coun., Harrisburg, 1983-91; precinct committeeperson Harrisburg Dem. Com., 1986-90; donor chmn. ARC, Harrisburg, 1970—; instr. CPR to civic orgns. and students, 1980-87; pres. Peartree Antiques, Inc., 1995. Mem. AAUW, Ill. Nurses Assn. (nominating com. 1975), Southeastern Ill. Coll. Edn. Assn. (pres. 1988-91), Faculty Wives and Women Southeastern Ill. Coll. (sec.-treas. 1974-75), Sigma Theta Tau. Home: PO Box 345 1075 Shawnee Hills Rd Harrisburg IL 62946-4943

ENG, KARL TAT-KUEN, optometrist; b. Hong Kong, Oct. 12, 1965; came to the U.S., 1966; s. Yancey Yun Chee and Jenny Chun Yum E. BA in Biology, Boston U., 1987; OD, U. Houston, 1992. Lic. OD, N.Y., N.J., Tex. Pvt. practice Eye Dr. Rx, Paramus, Clifton, Totawa, N.J., 1992, Empire Eye Assocs., Bronx, N.Y., 1992-95, Stahl Eye Assocs., Garden City, N.Y., 1995; pvt. practice Lens Lab Express, Yonkers, N.Y., 1995, Bronx, 1995—, Paramus, 1996—. Mem. Am. Optometric Assn. (multidisciplinary practice sect. 1991—, contact lens sect. 1991—). Home: 10 Sylvan Ln New City NY 10956-6132 Office: 49 Tarrytown Rd White Plains NY 10607

ENG, KENNETH, surgeon, educator; b. N.Y.C., Jan. 6, 1943; s. Boy Hong and Bow Gee (Tow) E.; m. June Leong, May 21, 1966; children: Brian Douglas, Elizabeth Hope. B in Chemistry, Rensselaer Poly., Troy, N.Y., 1963; MD, NYU, 1967. Diplomate Am. Bd. Surgery. With NYU, 1972—; instr., 1972-74, asst. prof., 1974-78, assoc. prof., 1978-85, prof. of surgery, 1985—. Author: Anorectal, Presacral and Sacral Tumors, 1986. Fellow: Am. Coll. Surgeons; mem. Soc. Surgery Alimentary Tract. Home: 1111 Park Ave New York NY 10128-1234 Office: NYU Med Ctr 530 1st Ave New York NY 10016-6402

ENG, LAWRENCE FOOK, biochemistry educator, neurochemist; b. Spokane, Wash., Feb. 19, 1931; s. On Kee and Shee (Hue) E.; m. Jeanne Leong, Aug. 30, 1957; children: Douglas, Alice, Steven, Shirley. BS in Chemistry, Wash. State U., 1952; MS in Chemistry, Stanford U., 1954, PhD in Chemistry, 1962. Chief chemistry sect. lab. svc. VA Med. Ctr., Palo Alto, Calif., 1961—; rsch. assoc. dept. pathology Sch. Medicine Stanford (Calif.) U., 1966-70, sr. scientist dept. pathology Sch. of Medicine, 1970-75, adj. prof., 1975-82, prof. dept. pathology Sch. of Medicine, 1982—; mem. ad hoc neurol. sci. study sect. and neurology B study sect. NIH, 1976-79, mem. neurol. sci. study sect., 1978-83; mem. adv. bd. VA Office of Regeneration Rsch. Program, 1985-89; mem. VA Merit Rev. Bd. for Neurobiology, 1987-90; mem. Nat. Adv. Neurol. Disorders and Stroke Coun., 1991-94. Mem. editorial bd. Neurobiology, 1970-75, Jour. of Neurochemistry, 1978-85, Jour. of Neuroimmunology, 1980-83, Molecular and Chem. Neuropathology, 1982—, Glia, 1987—, Jour. for Neurosci. Rsch., 1991—, Neurochemical Rsch., 1993—. Capt. USAF, 1952-57. Mem. Am. Soc. for Neurochemistry (coun. 1979-83, 85-87, 93—, sec. 1987-93), Am. Soc. Biochemistry and Molecular Biology, Internat. Soc. for Neurochemistry, Soc. for Neurosci. Office: VA Med Ctr Lab Svc 3801 Miranda Ave Palo Alto CA 94304-1207

ENGEL, BERNARD THEODORE, psychologist, educator; b. Chgo., Apr. 18, 1928; s. Marvin I. and Hannah (Hollander) E.; m. Rae Goldberg, Mar. 10, 1951; children: Sandra E., Jeffrey P., Lauren C. BA, UCLA, 1954, PhD, 1956. Jr. rsch. psychologist UCLA, 1956; rsch. psychologist Inst. Psychosomatic and Psychiatric. Research and Tng., Michael Reese Hosp., Chgo., 1957-58; lectr. med. psychology, mem. sr. staff Cardiovasc. rsch. Inst., Sch. Medicine U. Calif., San Francisco, 1959-67; chief behavioral physiology sect., chief Lab. Behavioral Scis. Gerontology Research Center, Nat. Inst. Aging, NIH, Balt., 1967-95; assoc. prof. behavioral biology Johns Hopkins Sch. Medicine, Balt., 1970-82; prof. Johns Hopkins Sch. Medicine, 1982—. Contbr. 175 articles to sci. jours. Served in U.S. Army, 1950-52. Recipient award Pavlovian Soc., 1979. Fellow AAAS, Gerontol. Sci.; mem. Soc. Psychophysiol. Rsch. (pres. 1970-71), Assn. Applied Psychophysiology and Biofeedback (pres. 1981-82), Am. Psychosomatic Soc. (sec.-treas. 1981-85, pres. 1985-86), Pavlovian Soc., Gerontol. Soc. Am., Acad. Behavioral Medicine Rsch., Sigma Xi.

ENGEL, GEORGE LIBMAN, psychiatrist, internist, educator; b. N.Y.C., Dec. 10, 1913. B.A., Dartmouth Coll., 1934; M.D., Johns Hopkins U., 1938; M.D. (h.c.), U. Bern, Switzerland, 1980; ScD (h.c.), Med. Coll. Ohio, 1986. Rotating intern Mt.Sinai Hosp., N.Y.C., 1938-41; fellow in medicine Peter Bent Brigham Hosp., Boston, 1941-42; instr. and asst. prof. medicine and psychiatry U. Cin. Coll. Medicine, 1942-46; asst. prof., assoc. prof., prof. medicine and psychiatry U. Rochester Sch. Medicine and Dentistry, N.Y., 1946-84, prof. emeritus psychiatry and medicine, 1984—; lectr., vis. prof. numerous socs., hosps. and univs., 1959—, including U. Minn., U. Chgo., Albert Einstein Coll. Medicine, Columbia U., Univ. Coll. Hosp., London, SUNY-Bklyn., U. Pa., Albany Med. Coll., Monash U., Melbourne, Australia, U. Ariz., Mt. Sinai Hosp. and Med. Sch., U. Rochester Med. Center Alumni Assn., Tufts U., U. Calif.-San Francisco, U. Western Ont., London, Can., U. Mo., Case West Res. U., Temple U., U. So. Calif., U. Sask., Saskatoon, Can., SUNY-Syracuse, U. Ala., Johns Hopkins U., U. Colo., Beth Israel Med. Ctr., U. Ill., Urbana, Med. U. S.C., Mt. Sinai Med. Ctr., Milw., U. W. Va., Emory U., Brown U., N.Y. Med. Coll.; sci. adv. bd. Helen Dowling Inst. Biopsychosocial Medicine, Erasmus U., Rotterdam, Holland. Author: Fainting, 1950, 2d edit., 1962, Psychological Development in Health and Disease, 1962 (transl. into German, Japanese, Italian), (with W.L. Morgan) The Clinical Approach to the Patient, 1969 (transl. into Spanish, Italian and German), Interviewing the Patient, 1973; mem., former mem. editorial bd. Advances in Psychosomatic Medicine, Family Systesms Med., Jour. AMA, 1973-77, Jour. Psychiat. Research, Perspectives in Biology and Medicine, Psychoanalysis and Contemporary Thought, Psychosomatic Medicine; assoc. editor. Cin. Jour. Medicine; contbr. over 300 articles on psychosomatic medicine, internal medicine, EEG, clin. neurology, psychiatry, psychoanalysis, human devel. and med. edn. to profl. publs. Recipient Jacobi medal Mt. Sinai Hosp. and Med. Sch. Alumni Assn., 1972, gold medal U. Rochester Med. Ctr. Alumni Assn., 1972, student senate citation U. Rochester Sch. Medicine and Dentistry, 1983, exec. com. resolution, 1983, Albion O. bernstein Med. award Med. Soc. State of N.Y., 1989. Fellow AAAS; mem. Inst. Medicine NAS (sr.), Am. Coll. Psychoanalysts (charter), Am. Psychiat. Assn. (life; Vestermark award 1979, Presdl. citation 1988), Am. Psychoanalytic Assn., Am. Psychopathol. Assn., Am. Psychosomatic Soc. (pres. 1954), Am. Soc. for Clin. Investigation (emeritus), Assn. Am. Physicians, Chgo. Psychoanlytic Soc., Cin. Acad. Medicine, Internat. Soc. for Psychosomatic Medicine (founding mem.), N.Y. Acad. Scis., Rochester Acad. Medicine (award of merit 1976, Albert David Kaiser award 1988), Soc. Psychosomatic Research (London) (hon.), Western N.Y. Psychoanalytic Soc. (pres. 1969-71), Arbeitsgemeinschaft für Bio-Psycho-Sociale Medezin (Switzerland; hon.). Office: U Rochester Sch Medicine & Dentistry Rochester NY 14610-2833

ENGEL, JEROME, JR., neurologist, neuroscientist, educator; b. Albany, N.Y., May 11, 1938; s. Jerome and Pauline (Feder) E.; m. Catherine Margaret Lambourne, Feb. 26, 1967; children: Sean, Jesse, Anasuya. BA, Cornell U., 1960; MD, Stanford U., 1965, PhD in Physiology, 1966. Diplomate Nat. Bd. Med. Examiners, Am. Bd. Qualification in EEG, Nat. Bd. Psychiatry and Neurology. Intern in medicine Ind. U., Indpls., 1966-67; resident in neurology Albert Einstein Coll. Medicine, Bronx, N.Y., 1967-68, 70-72; resident in EEG Nat. Hosp. Nervous and Mental Disease Queen Sq., London, 1971, Maudsley Hosp., London, 1972; attending neurologist, dir. electroencephalography labs. Bronx Mcpl. Hosp. Ctr., Hosp. Albert Einstein Coll. Medicine, 1972-76; attending neurologist, chief of epilepsy, clin. neurophysiology UCLA Hosp. and Clinics, 1976—; assoc. investigator lab. nuclear medicine of Lab. Biomed. and Environ. Scis. UCLA Med. Ctr., 1981—; staff assoc. NINDS NIH Lab. Perinatal Physiology, San Juan, P.R.; vis. asst. prof. dept. physiology and biophysics U. P.R. Sch. Medicine, 1968-69, Lab. Neural Control, Bethesda, Md., 1969-70; asst. prof. neurology Albert Einstein Coll. Medicine, Bronx, 1972-76, asst. prof. neurosci., 1974-76; assoc. prof. neurology UCLA Sch. Medicine, 1976-80, assoc. prof. anatomy, 1977-80, prof. neurology, neurobiology (formerly anatomy and cell biology), 1980—; assoc. investigator Lab. Nuclear Medicine, Lab. Biomed. and Environ. Scis., 1981—; chmn. internat. and coop. projects study sect. NIH, 1989-90, mem. biomed. scis. study sect., 1985-89, chmn., 1988-89; vis. prof. dept. anatomy Sydney U., 1984. Author: Epilepsy and Positron CT, Clinical Relevance for Diagnosis of Epilepsy, 1985, Surgical Treatment of the Epilepsies, 1987, Seizures and Epilepsy, 1989, Surgical Treatment of Epilepsies, 1993, (with others) Neurotransmitters, Seizures and Epilepsy II, 1984, Neurotransmitters, Seizures and Epilepsy III, 1986, The Epileptic Focus, 1987, Fundamental Mechanisms of Human Brain Function, 1987, Clinical Use of Emission Tomography in Focal Epilepsy, Current Problems in Epilepsy, Vol. 7, 1990, Neurotransmitters in Epilepsy, 1992, Molecular Neurobiology and Epilepsy, 1992; contbr. over 100 chpts. to books including Functional Brain Imaging, 1988, Anatomy of Epileptogenesis, 1989, EEG Handbook, rev. series vol. 4, 1990, Comprehensive Epileptology, 1990, Generalized Epilepsy, 1990, Neurotransmitters in Epilepsy, Epilepsy Research (Supplement), 1992, Molecular Neurobiology and Epilepsy; contbr. over 550 articles to profl. jours. including, New Issues in Neurosci., Neurology, Jour. Neurosurg., Jour. Epilepsy, Epilepsia, Can. Jour. Neurol. Sci., Radiology, Jour. Cerebral Blood Flow Metabolism, Acta Neurochirugica, Jour. Clin. Psychiatry; chief editor Advances in Neurobiology of Epilepsy, 1989-91; assoc. editor Jour. Clin. Neurphysiology, 1983—, Epilepsy Rsch., 1985—, Epilepsy Advances, 1985-87, Brain Topography, 1990—, Epilepsia, 1994—. Active profl. adv. bd. Epilepsy Found. Am., 1979-87; chmn. organizing com. Workshop on Neurobiology of Epilepsy Internat. League Against Epilepsy, 1988-91. Lt. comdr. USPHS, 1968-70. Recipient N.Y. State Regents scholarship, 1956-60, NIH traineeship, summer 1962, predoctoral fellowship, 1964, postdoctoral fellowship, 1965-66, career devel. award 1972-76, Epilepsy Found. Am. award, 1963, Stiftung Michael prize, 1982; named Fulbright scholar, 1971-72, fellow in neurology Sch. Medicine Stanford U., 1965-66, Lab. Applied Neuophysiology, C.N.R.S., Marseilles, France, 1966, Dagan Lectr. Winter Conf. on Brain Rsch., 1981, John Guggenheim fellow, 1983-84, Hanna lectr. Case-Western Reserve, 1983, First Aird lectr. U. Calif. San Francisco, 1985, First Cox lectr. Albert Einstein Coll. Medicine, 1985, First Vaajasalo lectr. and award, Kuopio, Finland, 1987, Aring lectr. U. Cin. Med. Ctr., 1987, First Hans Berger lectr. Internat. Congress of EEG and Clin. Neurophysiology, 1990; Covy Williams lectr. Cleve Clinic, 1992; Hanslectr. Med. Coll. Va., 1993. Fellow Am. Acad. Neurology (self assessment epilepsy task force chair 1990—); mem. AAAS, Am. EEG Soc. (councillor 1984-87, chmn. rsch. fellowship com. 1988-91, pres. elect 1991-92, pres. 1992-93), Am. Epilepsy Soc. (sec. 1979-82, 2nd v.p. 1982-83, 1st v.p. 1983-84, pres. 1984-85, councillor 1985-86, v.p. to Internat. League Against Epilepsy 1990—, William G. Lennox lectr. 1990), Am. Neurol. Assn. (mem. program com. 1987-90), Am. Physiol. Soc., Internat. Brain Rsch. Orgn., Internat. Fedn. EEG and Clin. Neurophysiology Socs. (program com. 1988-90, chmn. com. on guidelines for long-term monitoring for epilepsy 1989—), Internat. League Against Epilepsy (program com. 1986-88, commn. on epilepsy surgery 1988—, chmn. commn. on neurobiology of epilepsy 1989—, amb. for epilepsy award 1991, treas. 1994—), Internat. Soc. Cerebral Blood Flow and Metabolism, Ea. Assn. Electroencephalographers (Kershman lectr. 1994), Nat. Assn. Epilepsy Ctrs. (bd. dirs. 1988—, treas. 1990-94), Soc. for Neurosci. (neurobiology of disease workshop organizing com 1989—), Australian Assn. Neurologists (hon.), Western Electroencephalography Soc. Home: 791 Radcliffe Ave Pacific Palisades CA 90272-4334 Office: UCLA Sch Medicine Reed Neurol Rsch Ctr # 1250 710 Westwood Plz Los Angeles CA 90024-8300

ENGEL, JOAN MARCIA, psychologist, canine behavior consultant; b. Boston, June 7, 1946; d. Morris and Thelma M. (Goldman) Lezar; m. Robert Lee Engel, Feb. 2, 1969 (div. 1982). BA, U. Mass., Boston, 1970; MA, New Sch. for Social Rsch., 1977; PhD, Fordham U., 1989. Asst. rsch. scientist NYU Med. Ctr., N.Y.C., 1988; adj. asst. prof. Coll. Mt. St. Vincent, Riverdale, N.Y., 1989-90, Lehman Coll., Bronx, N.Y., 1990, John Jay Coll., N.Y.C., 1990, Coll. of New Rochelle, N.Y., 1990; asst. prof. Marist Coll., Poughkeepsie, N.Y., 1990-91; statis. R&D Block Drug Co. Inc., Jersey City, 1991-94; canine behavior cons., Jersey City, 1994—. Author: Manual for Foster Parent Training, 1980. Mem. APA, Am. Psychol. Soc.

ENGEL, TIBOR, obstetrics and gynecology educator; b. Kosice, Czechoslovakia, Mar. 8, 1938; came to Mex., 1940, came to U.S., 1948, naturalized, 1954; married; 2 children, 2 stepchildren. BA, U. Tex., El Paso, 1957; MD, U. Tex., Galveston, 1961. Diplomate Am. Bd. Ob-Gyn. Intern Phila. Gen. Hosp., 1961-62; resident N.Y. Hosp. Cornell U. Med. Ctr., N.Y.C., 1962-65; fellow reproductive endocrinology Columbia U. Med. Ctr., 1967-69; clin. prof. ob-gyn Health Scis. Ctr. U. Colo., Denver; asst. dir. ob-gyn Denver Gen. Hosp., 1969-74, dir. gynecologic endocrinology service, past pres. med. staff; cons. in family planning Westinghouse Learning Corp., 1970-71; med.

dir. Rocky Mountain Planned Parenthood, 1973-74; editorial cons. Medcom Famous Teaching in Modern Medicine. Served to capt. M.C., U.S. Army, 1965-67. Fellow Am. Coll. Obstetricians and Gynecologists, Am. Fertility Soc.; mem. Colo. Gynecol. and Obstetrical Soc., Denver Med. Soc., Colo. Med. Soc., Am. Assn. Gynecol. Laparoscopists (nat. adv. com., editorial bd. Jour. AAGL), Endocrine Soc. Home: 220 S Eudora St Denver CO 80222-1137 Office: 4500 E 9th Ave Denver CO 80220-3900

ENGEL, TOBY ROSS, cardiology director, physiology educator; b. N.Y.C., Mar. 6, 1942; s. Fred and Pauline (Bienstock) E.; m. Loraine Barbara Rodney, Aug. 15, 1965; children: Joshua A., Jeffrey A., Benjamin E. BA in Chemistry cum laude, NYU, 1962, MD, 1966. Lic. physician Nebr., Pa; Diplomate Am. Bd. Internal Medicine, Sub-specialty Bd. Cardiovascular Disease, Nat. Bd. Med. Examiners. Intern, then resident Hosp. U. Pa., Phila., 1966-68; resident Ohio State U. Hosp., Columbus, 1970-71, fellow in cardiology, 1971-73; instr. medicine Ohio State U., 1971-73; from asst. prof. medicine to assoc. prof. medicine Med. Coll. Pa., Phila., 1971-80, prof. medicine, 1980-93; prof. medicine U. Nebr., Lincoln, 1985-93, fellow grad. faculty, 1986-93, prof. physiology, biophysics, 1989-93, chief cardiology sect., 1985-89, program dir. cardiology, 1989-93; prof. medicine med. br. U. Tex., Galveston, 1993-95; program dir. Divsn. Cardiology Miamonides Med. Ctr., Bklyn., 1995—; prof. medicine SUNY, Bklyn., 1995—; dir. med. intensive care unit Med. Coll. Pa., 1973-79, dir. electrophysiology lab., 1973-85, dir. heart sta., 1979-1985, assoc. dir. cardiac catheterization lab., 1973-85, assoc. dir. med. intensive care unit, 1980-85, mem. numerous coms.; mem. numerous coms. U. Nebr.; chmn. mortality com. Timolol, Encainide, Sotalol study Likoff Cardiovascular Inst. Hahnemann U.; cons. Bishop Clarkson Meml. Hosp., Cardiodata System, N.J., Great Plains Region Med. Ctr., N. Platte, Nebr., VA Hosp., Phila., 1973-85, Omaha, 1985—; vis. attending physician VA Hosp., Phila., 1973-85; attending physician VA Hosp., Omaha, 1985—; lectr. in field, presenter in field, mem. numerous panel discussions. Assoc. editor: Fundamentals of Internal Medicine, 1983, Internal Medicine for Dentistry, 1983, rev. edit., 1990, Annals Internal Medicine, 1978-85; mem. editorial bd. Clin. Pharmacology and Therapeutics, Clin. Advances Treatment Arrhythmia, Critical Reviews Cardiology; reviewer Am. Heart Jour., Am. Jour. Cardiology, Archives Internal Medicine, Audio Visuals On-Line-Nat. Library Medicine, Chest, Circulation, European Jour. Cardiology, Jour. Am. Med. Women's Assn., Jour. Electrocardiology, Medical Dialogues, Pacing and Clin. Electrophysiology; contbr. 11 chpts. to books in field; contbr. 62 articles to profl. jours. Mem. sci. sessions com. Am. Heart Assn., 1985—, fellow coun. clin. cardiology 1976, special investigator S.E. Pa. chpt. 1977. Capt. U.S. Army, 1968-70. Fellow ACP, Am. Coll. Cardiology (mem. editorial bd. jour.), Am. Coll. Clin. Pharmacology, Coll. Physicians Phila.; mem. AAAS, N.Am. Soc. for Pacing and Electrophysiology, Coun. Clin. Cardiology (bd. govs. S.E. Pa. chapt. 1976-79, 79-82, del. Pa. affiliate assembly 1976-85, mem. various coms., bd. dirs. Nebr. affiliate Douglas/Sarpy div. 1988-89, pres. 1987-88, mem. various coms.), Am. Soc. for Clin. Pharmacology and Therapeutics, Am. Fedn. for Clin. Rsch., Am. Assn. U. Profs., Cardiac Electrophysiology Soc., Cen. Soc. for Clin. Rsch., N.Y. Acad. Scis., Nebr. Cardiovascular Soc. (pres. 1987-88), Phila. Acad. Cardiology (program com.), Alpha Omega Alpha. Home: PO Box 177 Cornwell NY 12518 Office: Cardiology Division Miamonides Med Ctr 4802 Tenth Ave Brooklynn NY 11219

ENGEL-ARIELI, SUSAN LEE, physician; b. Chgo., Oct. 7, 1954; d. Thaddeus S. Dziengiel and Marion L. (Carpenter) Kasper; m. Udi Arieli. BA, Northwestern U., 1975; MD, Chgo. Med. Sch., 1982. Med. technician G.D. Searle, Skokie, Ill., 1972, 73, assoc. dir., 1983-84; dir. U.S. Regional Clin. Support G.D. Searle, 1984-86; rsch. editorial asst. U. Chgo., 1974; rsch. assoc. Loyola U., Maywood, Ill., 1977-78; intern Rush Presbyn. St. Lukes Hosp., Chgo., 1982-83; resident U. Chgo., 1983; mgr. hosp. products div. Abbott Labs., Abbott Park, Ill., 1986-87; bd. govs., dep. gov. Am. Biog. Inst. Rsch. Assn., 1988; vis. prof. Rush Presbyn.-St. Luke's Hosp., Chgo., 1985, faculty assoc., 1985; assoc. investigator, asst. prof. medicine King Drew Med. Ctr., UCLA, 1985-90; practical cardiology panel experts, 1988; Med. World News Rev. panel, 1988; bd. dirs. Am. Soc. Handicapped Physicians, acting v.p.; bd. dirs. fundraising, chmn. Vestibular Disorders Assn. Author: How Your Body Works, 1994, C-D Rom version, 1995; contbr. articles to profl. and scholarly jours. Bd. govs. Art Inst. Chgo., 1985—, mem. aux. bd., 1988—, mem. multiple benefit coms., 1984—, vice chmn. Capital Campaign, 1984-85; mem. pres. com. Landmark Preservation Coun., Chgo., 1984-90, chmn. multiple coms. polit. candidates, 1986; bd. dirs. Marshall unit Chgo. Boys Clubs, 1984—; mem. benefit com. Hubbard St. Dance Co. 10th Gala, 1988, Victory Garden's Theatre Ann. Benefit, 1988. Internat. Coll. Surgeons fellow, 1982. Mem. AMA, ACP, Am. Fedn. for Clin. Rsch., Southern Med. Assn., Ill. State Med. Soc., Chgo. Med. Soc., Am. Acad. Med. Dirs., Nat. Acad. Arts and Scis., Am. Soc. Handicapped Physicians (bd. dirs., v.p.), Vestibular Disorders Assn. (bd. dirs., pub. rels. com., co-chmn. fundraising).

ENGELBRECHT, MARY LOU, nurse; b. Mariemont, Ohio, Dec. 31, 1954; d. Arthur Robert and Marilyn Ruth (Van Ness) Meehan; m. Charles William Engelbrecht Jr., June 3, 1978; children: Jessica, William, Carol, Michael. BS in Biology, U. Albany, 1977; AAS in Nursing, Hudson Valley Community Coll., Troy, N.Y., 1980; BSN, Coll. Tech., Utica, N.Y., 1983; MS in Nursing, Syracuse U., 1989. RN, N.Y.; cert. alcoholism counselor, N.Y. Staff nurse Rome (N.Y.) Hosp., 1980-81; psychiatric nurse I McPike (Marcy) Alcoholism Treatment Ctr., Utica, 1981-85; vol. nurse Hospice Care, Inc., Utica, 1983-86; resource person Celiac Sprue Assn., Des Moines, 1984-88; nurse cons. in preventive health and addiction disorders West Leyden, N.Y., 1995—. Mem. Central N.Y. Human Ecology Action League, Syracuse, 1985—. Mem. N.Y. Coalition for Alternatives to Pesticides, Inner Wheel Rome (pres. 1984-85), Sigma Theta Tau. Roman Catholic. Home: RR 1 Box 20D West Leyden NY 13489-9707

ENGELHARDT, HUGO TRISTRAM, JR., physician, educator; b. New Orleans, Apr. 27, 1941; s. Hugo Tristram and Beulah (Karbach) E.; m. Susan Gay Malloy, Nov. 25, 1965; children: Elisabeth, Christina, Dorothea. B.A., U. Tex., Austin, 1963, Ph.D., 1969; M.D. with honors, Tulane U., 1972. Asst. prof. U. Tex. Med. Br., 1972-75, assoc. prof., 1975-77; mem. Inst. Med. Humanities, 1973-77; Rosemary Kennedy prof. philosophy of medicine Georgetown U., 1977-82; sr. research scholar Kennedy Inst. Center for Bioethics, Washington, 1977-82; prof. depts. internal medicine, community medicine and ob-gyn. Baylor Coll. Medicine, Houston, 1983—; mem. Ctr. for Ethics, Med./and Health Policy, Houston, 1983—; prof. dept. philosophy Rice U., Houston, 1983—; chmn. adv. panel on infertility prevention and treatment for office of tech. assessment of the U.S. Congress, 1986-87. Author: Mind Body: A Categorial Relation, 1973, The Foundations of Bioethics, 1986, rev. edit., 1996, Bioethics and Secular Humanism, 1991; co-author: Bioethics: Readings and Cases, 1987; assoc. editor Ency. of Bioethics, 1973-78, Jour. Medicine and Philosophy, 1974-84; mem. edit. adv. bd. Lit. and Medicine, 1982—, Bioethics, 1987—, Ethik in der Medizin, 1988—, Bioetica, 1993—; editor Jour. Medicine and Philosophy, 1984—, (series) Philos. Studies in Contemporary Culture, 1992—; co-editor Philosophy and Medicine series, 1974—, Clin. Med. Ethics, 1991—, Christian Bioethics, 1995—; editor: (with others) Evaluation and Explanation in the Biomedical Sciences, 1975, Philosophical Medical Ethics, 1977, Mental Health, 1978, Clinical Judgment, 1979, Concepts of Health and Disease, 1981, New Knowledge in the Biomedical Sciences, 1982, Scientific Controversies, 1987, The Use of Human Beings in Research, 1988, Sicherheit und Freiheit, 1990. Mem. bioethics com. Nat. Found. March of Dimes, 1975—. Fulbright fellow, 1969-70, Woodrow Wilson vis. fellow, 1988; fellow Inst. for Advanced Studies, Berlin, 1988-89. Mem. Am. Philos. Assn., European Acad. Scis. and Arts. Home: 2802 Lafayette Houston TX 77005-3038 also: HC 3 Box 1 New Braunfels TX 78132-4101 Office: Baylor Coll Med Ctr Med Ethics Med Health Policy Houston TX 77030

ENGELKEN, RENATE, speech pathologist; b. Emmeln, Niedersachsen, German, Oct. 25, 1951; d. Gerhardt and Veronika Weissensteiner Engelken; 1 child, Stella. Cert. children's nurse, speech pathologist. Governess Kindergarten, Berlin, 1975-83; nurse Oskar-Helene-Heim, Berlin, 1986-87; speech pathologist Max Buerger Zentrum, Berlin, 1987—; sec. Bundesverband für die Rehab. Aphasiker, Berlin, 1995—; advisor, tchr. swallowing disorder workshop; tchr. geriat. aphasia therapy classes. Mem. Deutsche Assn. for Logopädie, Deutsche Assn. for Neurotraumatologie & Klinishe Neuropsychology. Office: Max-Buerger-Zentrum Klinik Akutgeriatrie & Med Rehab, Sophie Chartottenstr 115, 14059 Berlin Germany

ENGELMAN, MELVIN ALKON, retired dentist, business executive, scientist; b. Waterbury, Conn., July 27, 1921; s. Herman B. and Marion (Halpern) E.; m. Muriel Phillips, Aug. 27, 1949; children: Curtis Land, Suzanne Ruth. AB, Ohio U., 1942; DDS, Western Res. U., 1944. Diplomate: Am. Bd. Oral Electrosurgery. Pvt. practice dentistry Wappingers Falls, N.Y., 1949-89; chmn. oral diagnosis and oral pathology sect., dir. oral diagnostic ctr. St. Francis Hosp., Poughkeepsie, N.Y., 1963-77, attending dentist, 1963-89, dir. dept. dentistry, 1967, 71-74, 78, hon. staff, 1989—; pres. Di-Equi Dental Products Inc., 1980—, Dentifax Internat. Inc., 1982—; observer Meml. Hosp. Cancer and Allied Diseases, N.Y.C., 1962-66; mem. adv. bd. Dutchess Community Coll., 1963-69, lectr. dental assts. program, 1960-63; dir. 1st regional sci. fair, Dutchess County, N.Y., 1960-61; project dir. USPHS community cancer demonstration project, St. Francis Hosp., 1963-66; asst. chief med. officer Dutchess County N.Y. CD, 1963-68; cons. Nat. Cancer Inst., mem. clin. cancer tng. com., 1968-71, Profl. edn. com. for cancer control, 1972-73; attending dentist Central Dutchess Nursing Home, 1970-85; cons. VA Hosp., Castle Point, N.Y., 1976-77, Lactona Corp., div. Warner Lambert, 1976-80; internat. lectr. on fixed prosthodontics, premedication, oral cancer, metallurgy. Co-author: Oral Cancer Examination Procedure, 16 edits., 1967-83; contbr. articles to profl. jours.; patentee for feeder bar, spruing assembly, and sprue pin. Chmn. Wappinger Red Cross Fund Drive, 1956; committeeman Troop 6, Boy Scouts Am., Chelsea, N.Y., 1963-67; pres. Dutchess County unit Am. Cancer Soc., 1969-71. From ensign to lt. Dental Corps, USNR, FMF PAC, 1942-46; lt. comdr. ret., 1986. Fellow AAAS (life), Royal Soc. Health (Eng.), Am. Pub. Health Assn., Acad. Gen. Dentistry; mem. ADA (life), Internat. Assn. Dental Research, Assn. Mil. Surgeons (life mem.), 9th Dist. Dental Soc. (life mem.), Dutchess County Dental Soc. (pres. 1965), Am. Acad. Dental Electrosurgery (pres. 1983), Wappinger Conservation Assn. (v.p. 1970-71), Wappingers Falls C. of C. (pres. 1952-54), Alpha Omega. Clubs: Masons (32 deg.), Shriners, B'nai B'rith (pres. So. Duchess lodge 1963-64). Address: Nutmeg Hill 76 Old State Rd Wappingers Falls NY 12590-3905

ENGELMAN, RICHARD MICHAEL, cardiac surgeon; b. N.Y.C., Oct. 18, 1938; s. Abraham and Dorothy (Feinbloom) E.; m. Jane Godwin, June 21, 1960; children: Daniel, Margery, Andrea. BA, Columbia U., 1959 MD, SUNY, 1963. Resident in surgery Yale U., New Haven, 1963-66, George Washington U., Washington, 1966-68; resident, then instr. cardiothoracic surgery NYU, 1968-75; assoc. prof. surgery U. Ill., Chgo., 1975-78; from asst. prof. to prof. surgery U. Conn., Farmington, 1978—; chief cardiac surgery Baystate Med. Ctr., Springfield, Mass., 1978—; adv. panelist Quest Med. Corp., Dallas, 1994—. Editor: A Textbook of Clinical Cardioplegia, 1982, A Textbook Clinical Cardioplegia for Difficult Clinical Problems, 1992. Grantee NIH, 1979—, Am. Heart Assn., 1977-82. Fellow ACS, Am. Coll. Cardiology; mem. Am. Surg. Assn., Am Assn. Thoracic Surgery, Soc. Vascular Surgery, Soc. Thoracic Surgeons. Office: Baystate Med Ctr 759 Chestnut St Springfield MA 01107

ENGELSEN, STEINAR J., pharmaceuticals company executive; b Oslo, Oct. 14, 1950; s. Steinar Engelsen. Cand. Sci., U. Oslo, 1980, MD, 1985. Bd. cert. MD, Norway. Dir. rsch. Nycomed, Oslo, 1989-91; sr. v.p. Nycomed, Linz, Austria, 1991-93, Nycomed Pharma, Oslo, 1994—. Contbr. articles to profl. pubis. Office: St Peter Str 25, 4020 Linz Austria

ENGLAND, ALBERT C., retired neurologist; b. Pittsfield, Mass., Mar. 6, 1912; s. Albert Charles and Aida Seiferth E.; m. Priscilla Stern; children: Albert Charles III, Michael Richard, Jean MacGregor. MD, Harvard U. Diplomate Am. Bd. Internal Medicine. Intern Peter Bent Brigham Hosp., 1938-40; resident in neurology Boston City Hosp., 1940-41; fellow EEG Mass. Gen. Hosp., Boston, 1954-56; physician Harvard Student Health Svc., 1952-56, MIT, Cambridge, Mass., 1956-60; neurologist Mass. Gen. Hosp., Boston, 1960-91; dir. M.G.H. Parkinson Clinic, 1960-91; neurologist Emerson Hosp., Concord, Mass., 1970-91. Democrat. Jewish. Home: 137 Old Concord Rd Lincoln MA 01773

ENGLAND, DAVID P., anesthesiologist, educator; b. Providence, Dec. 31, 1955; s. Norman A.W. and Edna C. (Vanasse) E.; m. Marty Jean Beck, May 29, 1987; children: Jozlyn, Addyson, Macy. Student, Providence Coll., summer 1976, U. Nebr., summer 1977; BS in Biology and Psychology, Creighton U., Omaha, 1978; MS in Physiology, Georgetown U., 1980; postgrad., No. Va. C.C., Alexandria, 1984; DO, U. Health Scis., Kansas City, Mo., 1989. Diplomate Nat. Bd. Osteopathic Med. Examiners. Intern Doctor's Hosp., Columbus, Ohio, 1989-90; resident Med. Coll. Va., Richmond, 1990-93, asst. prof. dept. anesthesiology, 1993-95; faculty No. Va. C.C., Annadale, 1983-84; emergency rm. physician Kenner Army Hosp., Ft. Lee, Va., 1991-95. Russell C. McCaughan scholar Nat. Osteopathic Found., E.F.N. Fed. scholar; Georgetown U. Nursing Sch. teaching fellow. Mem. Am. Soc. Anesthesiology, Ariz. Soc. Anesthesiology, Am. Osteo. Assn., Va. Osteo. Med. Assn., Psi Sigma Alpha, Sigma Sigma Phi, Ctrl. Va. Mustang Club. Office: Canyon State Anesthesiologists PC 4820 E McDowell Rd Ste 101 Phoenix AZ 85008

ENGLAND, DONALD LINKLATER, physician; b. Westimber, Oreg., Mar. 27, 1924; s. David Charles and Lillian Linklater (Gorrie) E.; m. Katherine Mowat Sutherland, Sept. 14, 1946; children: Janet Mowat, Barbara Joan, James David, John Mark. BA, U. Oreg., 1945, MD, 1997. Diplomate Am. Bd. Internal Medicine, added qualifications for geriatrics. Rotating intern St. Francis Hosp., Pitts., 1947-48; med. resident Md. Gen. Hosp., Balt., 1948-49, U.S. VA Hosp., Portland, Oreg., 1951-53; med. staff physician Eugene (Oreg.) Hosp. & Clinic, 1953-95; physician Peace Health Med. Group, Eugene, 1995—. Bd. mem. Oreg. State Bd. Med. Examiners, Portland, 1977-85; Oreg. rep. Fedn. State Med. Bds. Flex Test Com., Phila., 1978-86. Capt. U.S. Army, 1949-51. Fellow ACP; mem. AMA, Oreg. Med. Assn., Lane County Med. Soc. (pres. 1972). Presbyterian. Home: 2525 W 23rd Ave Eugene OR 97405 Office: Peacehealth Med Group 1162 Willamette St Eugene OR 97401

ENGLAND, JOHN DAVID, neurologist and educator; b. Clarksburg, W.Va., Jan. 20, 1954; s. John Draper and Imogene Lucille (Alexander) E.; m. Cathy Ann Drummond, Nov. 22, 1975. BA in Chemistry, W.Va. U., 1976, MD, 1980. Diplomate Nat. Bd. Med. Examiners, Am. Bd. Psychiatry and Neurology, Am. Bd. Electrodiagnostic Medicine; lic. physician, S.C., Pa., Colo., La. Intern Med. U. S.C., Charleston, 1980-81, resident in neurology, 1981-84; clin. neuromuscular fellow dept. neurology Hosp. of U. Pa., Phila., 1984-85, postdoctoral rsch. fellow dept. neurology, 1985-87; asst. prof. neurology U. Colo., Denver, 1987-92; assoc. prof. neurology La. State U., New Orleans, 1992—; attending physician U. Colo. Health Scis. Ctr., Denver, 1987-92, dir. electromyography lab., 1987-92; attending physician Med. Ctr. La., New Orleans, 1992—; lectr. in field. Contbr. numerous articles to profl. jours.; editl. cons. Muscle and Nerve, 1987—, Ann. Neurol., 1990—, Brain, 1993—. Recipient Koehler award in chemistry, Handbook award Chem. Rubber Co., Whitehall award of dept. chemistry; W.Va. U. Bd. Regents scholar, Masonic scholar, others; grantee Muscular Dystrophy Assn., 1985-87, NIH, 1987-88, Nat. Inst. Neurol. Disorders and Stroke, 1988-93, Nat. Inst. Aging, 1991-94, La. State U. Neurosci. Ctr. for Excellence, 1993-94, Dept. Def., 1993—. Mem. AMA, W.Va. U. Alumni Assn., Am. Assn. Electrodiagnostic Medicine (profl. practice com. 1988-91, spl. interest group com. 1992-93, tng. program com. 1993—), liaison rep. 1991-92), Am. Acad. Neurology, N.Y. Acad. Scis., Am. Soc. Neurol. Investigation, Soc. for Neurosci., Alpha Omega Alpha, Phi Kappa Phi, Phi Lambda Upsilon, Phi Beta Kappa. Democrat. Methodist. Office: Louisiana State U Med Ctr Dept Neurology 1542 Tulane Ave New Orleans LA 70112-2825

ENGLANDER, HAROLD ROBERT, dentist, biomedical research educator; b. Balt., Dec. 11, 1927; s. Samuel Harold and Elsie (Young) E.; m. Harriet Beecher; 1 son, Mark R. B.S., CCNY, 1943; student, Washington U., St. Louis, 1944; D.D.S., Columbia U., 1948, M.P.H., 1951. Diplomate: Am. Bd. Dental Pub. Health. Commd. lt. (j.g.) U.S. Navy, 1948, advanced through grades to lt. comdr., 1959; assigned U.S.S. Piedmont and U.S.S. Kearsarge, Korea, 1952-53; dir. naval dental research Inst. U.S. Naval Tng. Center, Gt. Lakes, Ill., 1953-58; sr. dental officer U.S.S. Pocono, Lebanon, 1959; prof. dentistry U. Ill. Dental Sch., 1959-62; commd. officer USPHS, 1962; dental dir., chief clin. and field trials Nat. Inst. Dental Research, ret., 1975; prof. dental public health Sch. Public Health, U. Tex., San Antonio, 1975—; vis. prof. Howard U., Johns Hopkins, U. Md.; adj. scientist SW Found. Research and Edn., 1977; cons. to govt., pvt. orgns. Served with AUS, 1942-44. Recipient Research Honor award ADA, 1975; Meritorious Service medal USPHS. Fellow Am. Coll. Dentists, Am. Pub. Health Assn., AAAS, Am. Assn. Pub. Health Dentists, Internat. Assn. Dental Research (sec., pres. Chgo. sect. 1958), Commd. Officers Assn., USPHS (del. 1967-68), Omicron Kappa Upsilon, Sigma Xi. Home: 11502 Whisper Bluff St San Antonio TX 78230-3704

ENGLANDER, RAYMOND NEAL, physician, neurologist; b. Indpls., Apr. 5, 1946; s. Imre Alan and Klari (Mandel) E.; m. Margot Ciampaglia, July 2, 1969 (div. Sept. 1976); m. Elizabeth Ann Thompson, Feb. 14, 1981; stepchildren: Hank Hart, Liz Hart. AB, Columbia U., 1968; MD, Ind. U., 1972. Diplomate Am. Bd. Psychiatry and Neurology. Resident Ind. U., Indpls., 1972-73; resident, chief resident U. Va., Charlottesville, 1973-76; neurologist Sacred Heart Med. Ctr., Eugene, Oreg., 1978—, mem. med. informatics com., 1994—, chief divsn. medicine, 1993-96; bd. dirs. N.W. Physicians Mut. Ins., Salem, Oreg. Mem. adv. bd. Epilepsy Assn., Portland, 1990—. Maj. USAF, 1976-78. Fellow Am. Acad. Neurology; mem. Am. Epilepsy Soc., Oreg. Med. Assn., Lorne County Med. Soc., Alpha Omega Alpha. Office: Neurology Assocs 1200 Hilyard St Ste S-420 Eugene OR 97401

ENGLE, CINDY, medical transcriptionist; b. Denver, Aug. 12, 1958; d. Wallace Clyde and Mary Margaret (Ingram) E. AA, Arapahoe C.C., 1979; BA in Kinesiology, U. No. Colo., 1992. Cert. paralegal; former cert. paramedic, Colo. EMT/paramedic Ambulance Svc. Co., Denver, 1978-80; pers. asst. payroll Burns Security Svc., Denver, 1980-82; part-time asst. mgr. Tokoyo Bowl Restaurant, Denver, 1982-85; paramedic Platte Valley Ambulance, 1982-85; part-time flight paramedic for Air Life North Colo. Med. Ctr., Greeley, Colo., 1986-91; paramedic Weld County Ambulance, Greeley, 1985-92; intern exercise svcs. Greeley (Colo.) Med. Clinic, 1992, med. transcriptionist, 1993-94; med. transcriptionist North Colo. Med. Ctr., Greeley, 1994—; part-time EMS/criminal justice instr. Aims C.C., Greeley, 1987—; founder The Human Factor, 1992—. Author ednl. game: The Reality Game, 1993. Office: The Human Factor 2626 23d Ave Greeley CO 80631

ENGLE, HOWARD A., pediatrician; b. Wis., Sept. 11, 1919; married; three children. BS, U. Wis., 1939, MS, 1941, MD, 1943. Diplomate Am. Bd. Pediatrics. Intern Michael Reese Hosp., Chgo., 1943, resident in pediatrics, 1943-44; pvt. practice Miami Beach, Fla., 1947—; assoc. clin. prof. U. Miami Sch. of Medicine, assoc. prof. pediatrics emeritus; sr. cons., past chmn. dept. pediatrics, Mount Sinai Med. Ctr., Miami Beach; com. mem., operation newborn U. Miami Sch. of Medicine; instr. dept. pediatrics U. Fla. Sch. of Nursing; pediatric preceptor Fla. Internat. U. Sch. Nursing; sr. cons. pediatrics Mount Sinai Med. Ctr.; courtesy staff Miami Childrens Hosp.; sr. attending pediatrics Jackson Mem. Hosp.; cons. Fla. Atlantic U. Dept. Spl. Edn., neuropediatrics, Childrens Home Soc. of Fla.; cons., lectr. Dupond de Nemours Found., State Miss.; cons. pediatric neurology Hope Sch.; dir. Symposium Cerebral Palsy, Miami; med. rep. Symposia Cerebral Palsy, State of Tex.; lectr. in field. Contbr. articles to profl. jours. Med. adv. bd. Easter Seal Soc., Dade County; com. mem. Edn. and Therapy for the Handicapped, Dade County Sch. Bd.; past med. dir. United Cerebral Palsy of Miami; cons. neuropediatrics United Cerebral Palsy of Fla.; past. mem. clin. adv. bd. United Cerebral Palsy; nat. del. World Commn. on Cerebral Palsy, Copenhagen, 1963; med. cons. divsn. exceptional student edn. Dade County Sch. Bd. Mem. Am. Acad. Pediatrics, Nat. Soc. of Pediatric Neurology, Am. Acad. of Cerebral Palsy (mem. exec. com.), Am. Acad. Neurology, Am. Assn. on Mental Retardation, Am. Population and Reproduction Assn., Inc. (pres., founder), Fla. Rehab. Assn., Internat. Soc. for Rehab. of the Crippled and Disabled, Am. Acad. of Phys. Medicine and Rehab., Internat. Soc. for Cerebral Palsy, Internat. Child Neurology Assn. (assoc.), Japanese Soc. Child Neurology, Dade County Med. Assn., Fla. Med. Assn., Fla. Pediatric Soc., Miami Pediatric Soc. (past pres.), Am. Acad. Pediatrics (Fla. chpt.), Southeastern Med. Assn., World Med. Assn., Internat. Population and Reproduction Com. (chmn. edn. programs, bd. dirs., past pres. 1981-82), Sigma Sigma, Alpha Omega Alpha. Office: 975 Arthur Godfrey Rd Miami FL 33140-3329

ENGLE, JEANNETTE CRANFILL, medical technologist; b. Davie County, N.C., July 7, 1941; d. Gurney Nathaniel and Versie Emmaline (Reavis) Cranfill; m. William Sherman Engle (div. 1970); children: Phillip William, Lisa Kaye. Diploma, Dell Sch. Med. Tech., 1960; BA, U. N.C., Asheville, 1976; postgrad., Marshall U., 1991—. Instr. Dell Sch. Med. Tech., Asheville, 1960-67; rotating technologist Meml. Mission Hosp., Asheville, 1967-68, asst. supr. hematology, 1968-71; supr. Damon Subs. Pvt. Clinic Lab., Asheville, 1971-73; chemistry technologist VA Med. Ctr., Durham, N.C., 1973-74, 75-76, supr., 1974-75; asst. supr. microbiology VA Med. Ctr., Salem, Va., 1976-79; supr. rsch. Med. Svc. Lab., Salem, 1979-90; flow cytometrist VA Med. Ctr., Huntington, W.Va., 1990-92, cons. to clin. lab. flow cytometry dept., 1992—; reviewer Jour. Club, Roanoke-Salem, Va., 1980-90. Author: (poem) Reflections on a Comet, 1984; contbr. numerous articles and abstracts on med. tech. to profl. jours., 1982—. Mem. The Acting Co. Ensemble. Democrat. Episcopalian. Home: 4775 Green Valley Rd Huntington WV 25701-9793

ENGLE, RALPH LANDIS, JR., internist, educator; b. Phila., June 11, 1920; s. Ralph Landis and Ruth (Enck) E.; m. Mary Allen English, June 7, 1945; children: Ralph Landis III (dec.), Marilyn Elizabeth Varela. BS, U. Fla., 1942; MD, Johns Hopkins U., 1945. Intern pathology N.Y. Hosp., 1945-46, intern medicine, 1948-49, asst. resident medicine, 1949-51, asst. attending physician, 1952-57, assoc. attending physician, 1957-69, attending physician, 1969-90, hon. staff, 1990—; Am. Cancer Soc. rsch. fellow anatomy Washington U. Med. Sch., St. Louis, 1951-52; chief div. med. systems and computer sci. dept. medicine N.Y. Hosp.-Cornell U. Med. Ctr., 1967-74; asst. prof. medicine Cornell U. Med. Coll., 1952-57, assoc. prof. medicine, 1957-69, prof. medicine, 1969-90, prof. emeritus, 1990—, prof. pub. health, 1973-90, prof. emeritus, 1990—, assoc. dir. Office Rsch. and Sponsored Programs, 1975-90; mem. com. sci. and tech. communications Nat. Acad. Scis.-Nat. Acad. Engring., 1967-70; chmn. Ad Hoc Task Group on Toxicol. Info., 1969-70; mem. toxicol. info. program com., div. med. scis., 1969-72, 76-78; mem. cancer clin. investigation rev. com. Nat. Cancer Inst., 1968-72, chmn. cancer control supportive svcs. rev. com., 1974-76, chmn. cancer control community activities rev. com., 1975, chmn. cancer control prevention, detection and pretreatment evaluation rev. com., 1976-78; mem. data rev. bd. statewide planning and rsch. coop. system State of N.Y. Dept. Health, 1990-92. Author: (with L.A. Wallis) Immunoglobulins, Immune Deficiency Syndromes, Multiple Myeloma and Related Disorders, 1969; also numerous articles. Served from 1st lt. to capt., M.C. AUS, 1946-48. Markle scholar in med. sci., 1952-57. Fellow ACP, N.Y. Acad. Medicine; mem. Internat. Soc. Hematology, Am. Soc. Hematology, N.Y. Soc. for Study Blood (past pres.), Soc. Exptl. Biology and Medicine, AAAS, AMA, Harvey Soc. (past sec.), Am. Clin. and Climatol. Assn., New York County Med. Soc. (past chmn. pub. health com.), Sigma Xi, Chi Phi, Nu Sigma Nu. Presbyterian. Home: 27213 Baileys Neck Rd Easton MD 21601-8503 Home (winter): 2451 Brickell Ave PH-A Miami FL 33129-2402

ENGLERT, JERRY FREDERICK, health, medical products company executive; b. Charleston, W.Va., Oct. 22, 1940; s. Ernest and Evelyn (Tyree) Dawson; m. Constance Chandler Englert, Oct. 17, 1987; children: Tina, Christina. BS, Morris Harvey Coll., 1963; LLD (hon.), U. Charleston, 1992. Sales rep., dist. mgr. Baxter Labs., Charlotteville, N.C., 1963-68; dir. corp. devel. IVAC, San Diego, 1968-72; pres. Cambridge Co., San Diego, 1972-87; chmn., pres., CEO Winfield Corp., San Diego, 1987—; vice chmn. Bank of Del Mar, Calif.; chmn. bd. Harvard Fair, San Diego. Office: Winfield Industries 9750 Distribution San Diego CA 92121-2310

ENGLISH, CHERYL ANN, medical technologist; b. West Palm Beach, Fla., Sept. 18, 1960; d. William Ernest III and Sandra (McLaren) Tydings; m. Gary Marvin English, Dec. 22, 1984; 1 child, Nathan Kyle. AAS, Southwestern Tech. Coll., Sylva, N.C., 1984. Cert. med. technologist, Am. Med. Technologists. Med. technologist Ridgecrest Hosp., Clayton, Ga., 1985-93, Stephens County Hosp., Toccoa, Ga., 1993—. Baptist. Home: Rt 2 Box 2292 Clayton GA 30525

ENGLISH, FRANCIS PETER, ophthalmologist, educator; b. Cairns, Australia, May 31, 1932; s. Peter Bede and Mona (Elliott) E.; m. Leonie Therese Jones, May 31, 1975; children: Lawrence, James. MB, BS, U. Queensland,

Australia, 1957. Glaucoma fellow Howe Lab., Harvard U., Cambridge, Mass., 1962-63; clin. asst. Moorfields Hosp., London, 1963-66; vis. prof. ophthalmology U. Okla., 1969; fellow retina svc. U. Tex., Houston, 1967-68; fellow in oculoplastic surgery Manhattan Eye and Ear Hosp., N.Y.C., 1969-70; fellow cornea svc. Retina Found., Boston, 1970-71; ophthalmic surgeon Repatriation Dept., Brisbane, Australia, 1972-88; instr. ophthalmology U. Queensland, 1972-88; cons. Australian Govt., 1979—; rsch. assoc. Queensland Inst. of Med. Rsch., 1989—. Author: Reconstructive and Plastic Surgery of the Eyelids, 1975; contbr. to Current Ocular Therapy (Fraunfelder), 1985, 4th edit. 1994, Techniques in Ophthalmic Plastic Surgery (Wesley), 1986; contbr. articles to profl. jours. Recipient ophthalmic study tour award Grenfell Found., Can., 1968. Fellow Internat. Coll. Surgeons, Royal Coll. Surgeons, Royal Australian Coll. Ophthalmologists; mem. Internat. Oculoplastic Soc. (bd. dirs. 1982—). Clubs: Tattersalls, United Svcs. Home: 41 Charlton St Ascot, Brisbane 4007, Australia Office: 113 Wickham Terr, Brisbane 4000, Australia

ENGLISH, JOSEPH THOMAS, physician, medical administrator; b. Phila., May 21, 1933; m. Ann Carr Sanger, Dec. 20, 1969; 3 children. AB, St. Joseph's Coll., 1954; MD, Jefferson Med. Coll., 1958. Intern Jefferson Med. Coll. Hosp., Phila., 1958-59; resident in psychiatry Inst. of Pa. Hosp., Phila., 1959-61, NIMH, Bethesda, Md., 1961-62; practice psychiatry, 1962—; psychiatrist Office of Dir., NIMH, 1964-65, asst. chief policy and program coordination, 1965-66, dept. chief office interagy. liaison, 1966; chief psychiatrist med. program div. Peace Corps, Washington, 1962-66; dep. asst. dir. health affairs OEO, Washington, 1966, asst. dir., 1966-68; adminstr. Health Services and Mental Health Adminstrn., HEW, 1968-70; pres. N.Y.C. Health and Hosps. Corp., 1970-73; chmn. dept. psychiatry St. Vincent's Hosp. and Med. Ctr., N.Y.C., 1973—; prof. psychiatry N.Y. Med. Coll., 1979—; also assoc. dean N.Y. Med. Coll., N.Y.C.; adj. prof. psychiatry Cornell U.; lectr. psychiatry Harvard U., 1978-89; vis. fellow Woodrow Wilson Nat. Fellowship Found., 1979—; chmn. interagy. task force emergency food and med. program for U.S. OEO-HEW, U.S. Dept. Agrl., 1968-69; chmn. Alaska Subcom. Fed. Health Programs Pres.'s Rev. Commn. Alaska, 1969-71; chmn. adv. com. on accessible environments for disabled Bldg. Rsch. Adv. Bd., Washington, 1974-76; chmn. exec. coord. panels on mental health svcs. delivery Pres.'s Commn. on Mental Health, 1977; mem. Health Adv. Coun. Gov. State N.Y., 1981; mem. profl. and tech. adv. com. for hosps. and accreditation program Joint Commn. Accreditation Hosps., 1984-86, vice chmn., 1986-88, chmn., 1988-89; mem. adv. panel on financing of psychiat. care NIMH, 1985-87; mem. commr.'s adv. com. N.Y.C. Dept. Mental Health, Mental Retardation and Alcoholism Svc., 1980-92; bd. dirs., chmn. nat. clin. adv. bd. Healthcare Svcs. Am., Inc., 1985-87. Author spl. reports on Peace Corps, other govtl. programs; editorial bd. The Psychiatric Times, 1985—; contbr. articles to profl. jours. Bd. dirs. Kennedy Child Study Ctr., 1975-93; trustee Menninger Found., 1993—, Sarah Lawrence Coll., 1986-90. Served to capt. USAF Res., 1958-63; sr. surgeon USPHS 1963-66. Named One of Outstanding Young Men of Year U.S. Jr. C. of C., 1964; recipient John XXIII medal Coll. New Rochelle, N.Y., 1966; Meritorious award for exemplary achievement pub. adminstrn. William A. Jump Meml. Found., 1966; Flemming award, also personal commendation Pres. of U.S., 1968. Fellow Am. Psychiat. Assn. (pres. 1992-93, chmn. coun. on econ. affairs 1983-85, chmn. task force on prospective payment 1983—, chmn. task force and strategic planning 1993—), N.Y. Acad. Medicine, Am. Coll. Psychiatrists, Inst. Medicine of Nat. Acad. Scis.; mem. AMA, N.Y. Psychiat. Soc., Hosp. Soc. N.Y., Assn. for Acad. Psychiatry, N.Y. State Med. Soc., Am. Assn. Gen. Hosp. Psychiatrists, Group Advancement Psychiatry, Am. Coll. Mental Health Adminstrs., Am. Hosp. Assn., Greater N.Y. Hosp. Assn. (chmn. mental health and substance abuse svcs. com. 1975—), Cath. Health Assn. (com. on govt. rels. 1984-87), World Psychiatric Soc. (chmn. sect. on religion and psychiatry 1994—), Alpha Omega Alpha, Kappa Beta Phi, Alpha Sigma Nu. Office: St Vincent's Hosp & Med Ctr 203 W 12th St New York NY 10011-7762

ENGLISH, JUJUAN BONDMAN, women's health nurse, educator; b. El Dorado, Ark., Dec. 16, 1947; d. Irvin Raymond and Ida Ruth (Payton) Bondman; m. Frederick J. English, Aug. 28, 1976; children: Michael, Christopher, Meagan. ADN, So. State Coll., Magnolia, Ark., 1970; BSN, U. Ark., 1988; MSN, U. Miss., 1992. Cert. childbirth educator. Charge nurse Union Med. Ctr., El Dorado; charge nurse Warner Brown Hosp., El Dorado, labor and delivery supr.; instr. nursing U. Ark., Monticello, asst.. prof. nursing, 1993-95; dir. nursing edn. Area Health Edn. Ctr.-South Ark., 1995—; coord. Parenting Coalition of South Ark. Mem. ANA, Ark. State Nurses Assn. (strategic planning com., sec. 1994—, exec. com., Outstanding Dist. Pres. 1994), Ark. Nursing Coalition (steering com., Salute to Nursing com. chair), So. Nursing Rsch. Soc. (rsch. reviewer for D. Jean Wood award 1993), Nat. League Nursing, Ark. League Nursing, So. Regional Heidegerian Hermeneutrical Inst., So. Ark. Breast Feeding Coalition (chair edn. com.), Sigma Theta Tau.

ENGLISH, MILDRED IONE, retired nurse supervisor; b. Moberly, Mo., May 28, 1916; d. Oscar and Lulu (Street) Oswalt; m. Deaver English, Apr. 9, 1955. RN, Jewish Hosp. St. Louis Sch. Nursing, 1942; BS, U. N.C., 1952. RN, Mo., Tex.; cert. pub. health nurse, Calif., sch. audiometrist, Calif. Nurse Nurse Corps USNR, 1943-46; comdr., pub. health nurse supr. Mo. Div. Health, Jefferson City, Mo., 1946-56; supervising pub. health nurse L.A. County Health Dept., 1957-67; sch. nurse Bonita Unified Sch. Dist., San Dimas, Calif., 1967-72; quality assurance coord. Moberly (Mo.) Regional Med. ctr., 1973-83; ret., 1983. Home: 1163 Fox Run Cir New Braunfels TX 78130-7200

ENGSTROM, PAUL F., oncologist, medical educator; b. St. Cloud, Minn., May 28, 1936; s. George F. and Lucile I. (Nelson) E.; m. Janet F. Johnson, Oct. 21, 1961; children: Karin Z. Engstrom Davis, Maria P. Engstrom Pharr, David W. BA, St. Olaf Coll., 1958; MD, U. Minn., 1962. Bd. cert. internal medicine, bd. cert. med. oncology. Intern, resident in internal medicine U. Minn. Hosp., Mpls., 1963-67; chief hematology and oncology sect. Tripler Army Hosp., Honolulu, 1967-70; attending physician medicine Am. Oncol. Hosp., Phila., 1970-72; chmn. dept. medicine Foxchase Cancer Ctr., Phila., 1972-84, v.p. population sci., 1984—; chmn., mem. intervention rev. com. divsn. cancer prevention and control NCI, Bethesda, Md., 1976-80, mem., chmn. bd. sci. comdrs., 1986-89; mem., chmn. sci. bd. Armed Forces Inst. of Pathology, Washington, 1980-84; mem. adv. com. Can. Ctrl. NCI Can., Toronto, 1992—; prof. medicine Temple U. Sch. Medicine, Phila., 1987-95. Editor, author: Advances in Cancer Control, 1983-90; author (editl.) Cancer Epidemiology Biomarkers and Prevention, 1993; contbr. chpts. to books. Chmn. bd. dirs. Paul's Run Retirement Com., Phila., 1988—. Maj. U.S. Army, 1967-70. Recipient Cancer Ctrl. award Am. Cancer Soc., Phila., 1989. Fellow ACP; mem. AMA, Am. Soc. Clin. Oncology, Am. Fedn. for Clin. Rsch., Am. Assn. for Cancer Edn., Am. Soc. Preventive Oncology, Alpha Omega Alpha. Office: Fox Chase Cancer Ctr 7701 Burholme Ave Philadelphia PA 19111

ENGUM, ERIC STANLEY, clinical neuropsychologist, lawyer; b. N.Y.C., Oct. 31, 1949; s. Silas H. and Gertrude (Brown) E. BS, Wagner Coll., Staten Island, N.Y., 1971; MS, Tulane U., 1973; PhD, U. S.D., 1977; JD, U. Tenn., 1982. Bar: Tenn. 1983, U.S. Dist. Ct. (ea. dist.) Tenn. 1983; U.S. Ct. Appeals (6th cir.) 1983; Diplomate Am. Bd. Forensic Examiners, Am. Bd. Profl. Disability Cons., Am. Bd. Med. Psychotherapists. Clin. intern U. Ala. Med. Ctr., Birmingham, 1977; clin psychologist Iowa Methodist Med. Ctr., Des Moines, 1977-79; dir. clin. psychology Ft. Sanders Regional Med. Ctr., Knoxville, Tenn., 1982-88; dir. clin. neuropsychology Lakeshore System Svcs., Inc., 1988-90; pvt. practice West Knoxville Neurol. Assocs., 1988-91, Behavioral Medicine Inst., 1991-92; neuropsychol. cons. Neuropsychol. Cons., Knoxville, 1992—; cons. in field. Mem. editorial review bd. Cognitive Rehab. Jour.; contbr. articles to profl. jours. Bd. dirs. Fed. Defender Svcs. for East Tenn. Recipient LeTourneau award Am. Coll. Legal Medicine, 1982, Chancellor's citation Univ. Tenn., 1982. Mem. ABA, Am. Psychol. Assn., Tenn. Bar Assn., Nat. Register Health Service Providers in Psychology, Psi Chi, Omicron Delta Kappa. Republican. Lutheran. Avocations: golf, tennis, scuba diving, billiards. Home: 706 Kempton Rd Knoxville TN 37909-2125 Office: Neuropsychological Cons Cross Park Plz-Ste D266 9111 Cross Park Dr Knoxville TN 37923-4506

ENHORNING, GORAN, obstetrician, gynecologist, educator; b. Birkdale, Eng., Mar. 18, 1924; came to U.S. 1986; s. Emil Augustin and Maria Rosina (von Haartman) E.; m. Louise Christina Carlberg, Apr. 16, 1955; children: Ulf, Dag and Peder (twins), Marianne. MD, Karolinska Inst., Stockholm, 1952, PhD in Physiology, 1961. Asst. prof. ob/gyn. Karolinska Inst., Stockholm, 1952-61; Fulbright scholar U. Utah, Salt Lake City, 1961-63, UCLA, 1963-64; assoc. prof. ob/gyn. Karolinska Inst., 1964-71; assoc. prof. ob/gyn. U. Toronto, Ont., Can., 1971-75, prof. ob/gyn., 1975-86; prof. ob/gyn. SUNY, Buffalo, 1986—. Contbr. articles to profl. jours. Home: 21 Oakland Pl Buffalo NY 14222-2008

ENLOW, DONALD HUGH, anatomist, educator, university dean; b. Mosquero, N.Mex., Jan. 22, 1927; s. Donald Carter and Martie Blairene (Albertson) E.; m. Martha Ruth McKnight, Sept. 3, 1945; 1 child, Sharon Lynn. B.S., U. Houston, 1949, M.S., 1951; Ph.D., Tex. A&M U., 1955. Instr. biology U. Houston, 1949-51; asst. prof. biology West Tex. State U., 1955-56; instr. anatomy Med. Coll. S.C., 1956-57; asst. prof. U. Mich. Med. Sch., Ann Arbor, 1957-62; assoc. prof. U. Mich. Med. Sch., 1962-67, prof. anatomy, 1969-72; dir. phys. growth program Center for Human Growth and Devel., 1966-72; prof., chmn. dept. anatomy W.Va. U. Sch. Medicine, Morgantown, 1972-77; Thomas Hill disting. prof., chmn. dept. orthodontics Case Western Res. Sch. Dentistry, Cleve., 1977-89, prof. emeritus, 1989—; asst. dean for rsch. and grad. studies Case Western Res. Sch. Dentistry, 1977-85, acting dean, 1983-86; adj. prof. U. N.C., 1992—; guest lectr. 27 fgn. countries, 1963—. Author: Principles of Bone Remodeling, 1963, The Human Face, 1968, Handbook of Facial Growth, 1975, 3d edit., 1990, Essentials of Facial Growth, 1996; contbr. chpts. to 26 books, numerous articles to profl. jours. Served with USCGR, 1945-46. Recipient Outstanding Research award Tex. Acad. Sci., 1952. Fellow Royal Soc. Medicine, Am. Assn. Anatomists, Internat. Assn. Dental Research; hon. mem. Am. Assn. Orthodontists (Mershon Meml. lectr. 1968, Spl. Merit award 1969, award for outstanding contbns. to orthodontia, 1984), Gt. Lakes Orthodontic Soc., Cleve. Dental Soc., Cleve. Orthodontic Soc., Omicron Kappa Upsilon. Republican. Methodist. Home: 36-A Martin Dr Whispering Pines NC 28327

ENNIS, GEORGE ELLIOTT, physician; b. Hickory, N.C., Aug. 10, 1933; s. Elliott Lee and Peggy (Deitz) E.; m. Doris Virginia Yount (div. 1973); children: Lee, Virginia, Kimberly; m. Frances Hahn; children: Kristi, George, Jr. AB, Lenoir Rhyne Coll., 1954; MD, U. N.C., 1958. Diplomate Am. Bd. Internal Medicine. Internship, residency U. Ala. Med. Ctr., Birmingham, 1958-61; fellowship in hematology Duke Univ. Ctr., Durham, N.C., 1961-62; physician, pvt. practice Hickory, N.C., 1965—; bd. dirs. So. Nat. Bank, Hickory, BB&T Bank, Hickory, Piedmont Health Alliance. Bd. dirs. Hickory Merchants Assn.; mem. bd. Hickory City Schs. Am. Disabilities Act Com. Capt. USAF, 1962-64. Mem. Am. Coll. Physicians, Am. Soc. Internal Medicine, AMA, So. Med. Assn., N.C. Med. Soc., Catawba County Med. Soc., Lake Hickory County Club (bd. dirs.), Elks, Moose. Republican. Lutheran. Home: 1805 2nd St NW Hickory NC 28601-1806 Office: 912 2nd St NE Hickory NC 28601-3851

ENOWITCH, BENNETT IRVING, psychiatrist, consultant; b. Middletown, Conn., Feb. 17, 1934; s. Elliot H. and Anne (Chester) E.; m. Elisa Cohen, July 14, 1965; children: Schalleen J., Boris I. BA, Wesleyan U., 1955, MALS in Comparative Lit., 1987; MPH, Yale U., 1959; MD, Basle (Switzerland) U., 1965, Geneva (Switzerland) U., 1966; MA in German Lit., U. Conn., 1987, postgrad., 1972. Diplomat Am. Bd. Psychiatry and Neurology, Am. Bd. Quality Assurance and Utilization Physicians. Pvt. practice Hartford, Conn., 1969—; cons. CIGNA, Hartford, 1973-94, Constitution Mental Health, Meriden, Conn., 1986-88, Health Care Inc, N. Haven, Conn., 1989—, Blue Cross-Blue Shield, Meriden, 1989—, Rocky Hill (Conn.) Sch. System, 1985-89, Rocky Hill Vets. Hosp., 1988—; attending psychiatrist Day-Kimball Hosp., Putnam, Conn., 1996—. With U.S. Army, 1956-57, Washington. Fellow Am. Psychiat. Assn.; mem. Phi Beta Phi. Office: 18 N Main St West Hartford CT 06107-1919

ENRIGHT, MICHAEL JOSEPH, radiologist; b. Richmond, Va., Mar. 27, 1955; s. Wliam Joseph and Margaret (O'Connell) E.l (div.); children: Kelly Ann, Margeaux Elizabeth; m. Susan Ross Lemon, June 29, 1991; 1 child, Darby Michelle. BS in Pharmacy, Ohio State U., 1978; MD, Ea. Va. Med. Sch., 1981. Diplomate Nat. Bd. Med. Examiners, Am. Bd. Radiology, Va. Bd. Pharmacy. Resident in radiology Ea. Va. Grad. Sch. Medicine, Norfolk, 1981-85; radiologist U.S. Navy, Charleston, S.C., 1985-88; body imaging fellow U. Va. Med. Ctr., Charlottesville, 1988-89; radiologist Radiology Assocs. of Roanoke, Va., 1989—; treas. Low Country Imaging Soc., Charleston, 1986-87; sect. head Body and Musculoskeletal Magnetic Resonance Imaging, Radiology Assn. Roanoke, 1993—. Author (exhibit) Scrotal Ultrasonography at Am. Roentgen Ray Soc. Meeting, 1989. Lt. commdr. U.S. Navy, 1985-88. Mem. AMA, Am. Coll. Radiology, Radiol. Soc. N. Am., Roanoke Soc. Medicine. Republican. Home: 4400 Kings Chase Dr Roanoke VA 24014-6530 Office: Radiology Assocs of Roanoke Ste 435 2037 Crystal Spring Ave SW Roanoke VA 24014-2441

ENRIQUEZ, CARLOS AMERICO, pediatrician; b. Mexico City, Mex., Dec. 21, 1945; s. Antonio and Louisa (Iglesias) E.; B.S. with honors, Seton Hall U., 1967; M.D., Boston U., 1971. Intern, U. Pa.-Children's Hosp. of Phila., 1971-72, resident in pediatrics, 1972-73; chief resident Children's Hosp., Phila., 1974; practice medicine specializing in pediatrics, Cherry Hill, N.J., 1975-95; med. dir. West Jersey Health Sys. Ctr. for Behavior Learning and Attention, Voorhees, N.J., 1995—; mem. staff West Jersey Hosp., Voorhees, N.J.; mem. faculty U. Pa., Hahnemann Med. Coll. Trustee Trenton State Coll. (N.J.). Diplomate Am. Bd. Pediatrics, Nat. Bd. Med. Examiners. Fellow Am. Acad. Pediatrics; mem. Phila. Pediatric Soc., N.J. Med. Soc., Camden County Med. Soc., So. N.J. PSRO, PRO of N.J. (trustee). Office: 100 Carnie Blvd Ste A-1 Voorhees NJ 08043

ENSENAT, LOUIS ALBERT, surgeon; b. Merida, Mexico, Oct. 24, 1916; s. Frank and Guadalupe F. (Ensenat) E.; B.S., Tulane U., 1938, M.D., 1941; M.Sc. in Medicine, U. Pa., 1953; m. Ruth Ogden, July 9, 1943; children—Gloria Louise, Tinita Ruth, Louis Albert, Rita Joan, Barbara Jean, Michael Monroe. Intern, Charity Hosp., New Orleans, 1941-42; resident surgery Charity Hosp., Monroe, La., 1942, Lakeshore Hosp., New Orleans, VA hosp., New Orleans, Batavia, N.Y.; fellow in surg. pathology Tulane U. Sch. Med.; preceptorship in surgery Biloxi (Miss.) VA Hosp.; staff surg. VA Hosp., Montgomery, 1946-52; pvt. practice surgery, Pasadena, Tex., 1952-63, New Orleans, 1963—; adminstr. Mercy Hosp. Pasadena, 1954-63, chief surgery, 1954-63; founder, dir. Gulf Coast Home Builders, Inc.; trustee Angiology Research Found., 1986—. Trustee, Big State Factors Corp. Served from lt. (j.g.) to lt. comdr. USN, 1942-46. Decorated Purple Heart, Bronze Star. Diplomate Am. Bd. Surgery, Am. Bd. Abdominal Surgery. Fellow French Soc. Phlebology, Am. Coll. Angiology (pres.); mem. Hawthorne Surg. Soc., Am. Soc. Abdominal Surgeons, N.Y. Acad. Scis., Am. Med. Writers Assn. Author articles in field. Home and Office: 7630 Jeannette St New Orleans LA 70118-4064

ENSLEY, NANCY JOY, orthopaedist; b. Arlington, Va., May 4, 1954; d. Bennett Dwight and Aline Mittie (Overton) E.; m. David Van Wyk, Feb. 6, 1993. BS, Ariz. State U., 1977; MS in Phys. Therapy, U. So. Calif., 1980; MD, Med. Coll. Va., 1984. Diplomate Am. Bd. Orthopaedic Surgery. Resident in orthopaedics U. Wash., Seattle, 1984-89; fellow in pediatric orthopaedics Vanderbilt U., Nashville, 1989-90; physician Children's Mercy Hosp., Kansas City, Mo., 1990-93; pvt. practice, Parkville, Mo., 1994—; clin. asst. prof. U. Mo., Kansas City, 1990-93. Fellow Am. Acad. Orthopaedic Surgeons, Pediatric Orthopaedic Soc. N.Am. Office: Parkville Med Ctr 8600 NW 64th St Ste 101 Parkville MO 64152

ENTE, GERALD, pediatrician; b. N.Y.C., July 18, 1930; s. Louis M. and Minnie (Lackfish) E.; m. Phyllis Warch, Aug. 27, 1995; children: Peter, William. BS, Union Coll., 1951; MD, NYU, 1955. Diplomate Am. Acad. Pediatrics. Intern Kings County Hosp., Bklyn., 1955-56, resident in pediatrics, 1958-59; resident in pediatrics Bronx Mcpl. Hosp., 1959-60; pvt. practice, 1960—; clin. instr. pediatrics Einstein Med. Sch., 1960-64; clin. instr. pediatrics Meadowbrook, 1960-65, asst. attending pediatrics, 1965-68, clin. assoc. dir. of newborn svcs., 1968-70; clin. dir neonatology Nassau County Med. Ctr., 1970-88, attending physician pediatrics, 1974—; assoc. clin. prof. pediatrics SUNY Med. Coll., Stony Brook, N.Y., 1985—; med. dir. Trya Hostel, 1974-77, Fellowship Med. Labs, 1974-80; pediatric cons. Project Headstart, 1972, Westbury med. dir., 1966-76; cons. staff physician SUNY Coll. at Old Westbury, 1971-82, physician in-charge, 1972-79; cons. Westinghouse Electric Co., 1971-72, GenTel Electric Co., 1972; mem. Westbury Health Coun., 1974-78; dir. neonatology Ctrl. Gen. Hosp., 1980-90, chmn. pediats., 1990-94; profl. adv. bd. L.I. Inst. for Tng. in the Psychotherapies, 1979-81; mem. rsch. panel Med. World News, 1979-81. Author: (with others) Handbook of Neonatology, 1974, Pediatricians Manual Vol. I & II, 1977, Management of Prader Willi Syndrome, 1988; contbr. numerous articles to profl. jours. Bd. dirs. Offspring Dance Group, 1976-92; chmn. L.I. physicians United Way, 1983-84. Capt. U.S. Army Res., 1956-58. Recipient Samaritan award N.Y. Assn. Brain Insured Children, 1968, Man of Yr. Fellow Am. Acad. Pediatrics (PREP fellowship award 1979-85, PREP awards 1980-86, 93, 96), Royal Soc. of Pediatrics, Royal Soc. of Health, Internat. Coll. Pediatrics, Nassau Acad. of Medicine; mem. AMA (Physicians Recognition award 1980-84, 86, 87, 89, 91, 93, 96), N.Y. State Med. Soc., Nassau County Med. Soc., World Med. Assn., Nassau Acad. Medicine (sect. on pediatrics), Pan Am. Med. Assn. (diplomate), Assn. Am. Soc. Photobiology, Internat. Transactional Analysis Assn., Am. Holistic Med. Assn., Nassau Acad. Medicine (bd trustees). Office: 530 Old Country Rd Westbury NY 11590-4500

ENTIAN, KARL-DIETER, microbiology educator; b. Mainz, Fed. Republic Germany, Oct. 4, 1952; s. Karl and Anneliese Mueller; m. Heike Grueter-Entian. Diploma in biology, TH Darmstadt, Fed. Republic Germany, 1977; postgrad., U. East Anglia, Norwich, Eng., 1978, U. Tuebingen, Fed. Republic Germany, 1985. Asst. U. Tuebingen, 1978-87, pvt. docent, Heisenberg scholar, 1987-88; prof. microbiology U. Frankfurt, Fed. Republic Germany, 1988—. Contbr. articles to profl. publs. Deutsche Forschungsgemeinschaft grantee, 1987. Mem. Soc. Biol. Chemistry Germany, Soc. Gen. and Applied Microbiology Germany, Am. Soc. Microbiol. Office: U Frankfurt Inst Microbiol, Niederurseler Hang, D-60439 Frankfurt Germany

EPEL, LIDIA MARMUREK, dentist; b. Buenos Aires, Argentina, Sept. 30, 1941; came to U.S., 1966; d. Israel and Ita Rosa (Sonabend) Marmurek; children: Diana, Bryan. BS, Buenos Aires U., 1959, DDS, 1964. Lic. dentist, N.Y. Gen. practice dentistry Argentina, 1965-66, Long Beach, N.Y., 1967-70, Lynbrook, N.Y., 1970-73, Rockville Centre, N.Y., 1973—. Bd. dirs. Rosa Lee Young Childhood Ctr., Rockville Centre, 1982-94, Rockville Centre Edn. Found., 1990—; mem. adv. com. on HIV/AIDS Bd. Edn. Rockville Centre Pub. Schs., 1994—; past pres. Queens-L.I. Women's Dental Study Group. Mem. ADA, Am. Assn. Gen. Dentistry, Fedn. Dentaire Internat., Nassau County Dental Soc. (bd. dirs., chair com. on pub. and profl. rels. 1990—, chairperson com. on health. 1989-92, chair membership com. 1993, treas. exec. com. 1993, sec. exec. com. 1994, v.p. 1995, membership task force 1994-95, pres-elect 1996), Overseas Dentists Assn. (pres. N.Y. chpt. 1968-72), Dental Soc. of State of N.Y. (coun. for pub. and profl. rels. 1990—, chair children's dental health month campaign 1991, chair mem. recruitment and retention), Hadassah Club (bd. dirs. Rockville Ctr. 1983-84, 92-93). Democrat. Jewish. Office: 165 N Village Ave Rockville Centre NY 11570-3701

EPP, DAVID L., optometrist; b. Hutchinson, Kans., July 15, 1958; s. Harold Donald and Lillian Rose (Schroeder) E.; m. Arlene Joyce Schmidt, July 31, 1982; children: Esther, Hannah, Rachel. BS, Tabor Coll., Hillsboro, Kans., 1980; OD, Northeastern State U., Tahlequah, Okla., 1990. Lic. optometrist, Okla. Tchr. math. Okla. Bible Acad., Enid, 1980-82; optician Browns Opticians, Enid, 1982-86; optometrist David Epp O.D. P.C., Sayre, Okla., 1990—. Task force chmn. Cert. Cities, Sayre, 1994—; bd. dirs. Planning and Zoning, Sayre, 1994-95. Mem. Am. Optometric Assn., Okla. Optometric Assn., Fellowship of Christian Optometrists, C. of C. (bd. dirs. 1991-92, 95—), Kiwanis (v.p. 1994-95, pres. 1995—). Republican. Baptist. Home: 10 Darla Dr Sayre OK 73662 Office: 104 E Main St Sayre OK 73662

EPPERSON, BRYAN KEITH, geneticist, educator; b. Fresno, Apr. 25, 1957; s. Edward Leo and Marianne (Schmall) E.; 1 child, Joseph Keith Epperson. BS, U. Calif., 1979, Phd, 1983. Postdoctoral assoc. U. Ga., Athens, 1983-84; postdoctoral geneticist U. Calif., Riverside, 1984-91, asst. rsch. geneticist, 1992-93; asst. prof. Mich. State U., 1994—; reviewer Princeton U. Press, 1992—; reviewer grant proposals for NSF, mem. panel, 1995; vis. prof. N.E. Forestry U. Harbin, China, 1995—. Reviewer for more than 20 jours.; author articles. Nat. merit scholar, 1975, Alumni scholar U. Calif., 1975, Calif. state scholar, 1975-79, Herbert-Kraft Meml. scholar, 1978; Jastro-Shields grad. rsch. fellow U. Calif., 1980; NIH grantee, 1993-96. Mem. European Soc. Evolutionary Biology, Soc. for the Study of Evolution, Genetics Soc. of Am., Nature Conservancy, Sigma Xi, Xi Sigma Pi. Office: Mich State U Dept Forestry East Lansing MI 48824

EPPINK, ANDREAS, psychologist; b. Gendringen, Gelderland, The Netherlands, Aug. 9, 1946; s. Jan and Henriette (Jansen Spittmann) E. BA in Sociology, U. Amsterdam, The Netherlands, 1968; BA in Psychology, U. Amsterdam, 1969, MA in Psychology, 1971, PhD, 1977, Psychoterapist, 1981. Social researcher U. Koln, Germany, 1972; tchr. Social Acad., Rotterdam, The Netherlands, 1972-77; dir. Averroes Stichting, Amsterdam, 1978-83, Psychologisch Buro, Hilversum, The Netherlands, 1983—; cons. Amsterdam, 1972-78; dir. Omroepadvies, Hilversum, 1990—, Dr. Eppink Adviesgroep, Hilversum, 1991—; expert Intergovernmental Com. European Migration, Geneva, 1978-79; forensic expert Dist. Ct., Amsterdam, 1979—. Author: Cultuurverschillen en Communicatie, 1981, Het Masker van de Pijn, 1990, Migrants and their Mental Health, 1992, Migranten byvoorbeeld, 1990, Gericht Solliciteren Wie Verdient beter?, 1994; editor: Kind Zijn in Twee Culturen, 1981, Cultuurcontact en Cultuurconflict, 1988. Fellow Assn. Francaise de Psychiatrie et de Psychopathologie Sociales; mem. Nederlands Inst. van Psychologen, Internat. Coun. Psychologists. Office: Dr Eppink Adviesgroep, PO Box 1599, 1200 BN Hilversum The Netherlands

EPPS, ANNA CHERRIE, immunologist, educator; b. New Orleans, July 8, 1930; d. Ernest and Anna L. (Johnson) Cherrie; m. Joseph M. Epps, Sr., Nov. 23, 1968. BS, Howard U., 1951, PhD, 1966; MS, Loyola U., New Orleans, 1959. Technologist clin. lab. dept. Our Lady of Mercy Hosp., Cin., 1953-54; asst. prof., acting chmn. dept. med. tech. Xavier U., New Orleans, 1954-60; technologist dept. medicine La. State U. Sch. Medicine, New Orleans, 1954-60; asst. prof. microbiology Coll. Medicine Howard U., Washington, 1961-69; fellow dept. medicine Sch. Medicine Johns Hopkins U., Balt., 1969; asst. prof., USPHS faculty fellow dept. medicine Tulane U. Sch. Medicine, New Orleans, 1969-71, assoc. prof., 1971-75, prof., 1975—, asst. dean student svcs., 1980—; dir. med. edn. reinforcement and enrichment program Tulane U. Med. Ctr., New Orleans, 1969—. Co-editor: Medical Education: Responses to a Challenge; mem. editorial bd. Jour. Med. Edn., 1980—; contbr. articles to med. jours. Trustee Children's Hosp., New Orleans, 1977-79; regent Georgetown U., Washington, 1975—; bd. dirs. Diabetes Assn. Greater New Orleans, 1978; mem. La. Bd. Health and Rehab. Svcs., 1972; mem. Kellogg Nat. Fellowship Program, 1981. Recipient award for meritorious rsch. Interstate Postgrad. Med. Assn. N.Am., 1966, Scroll of Merit, Nat. Merit Assn., 1980. Mem. Am. Soc. Clin. Pathologists (cert. in med. tech. and blood banking), Am. Soc. Med. Technologists, Am. Assn. Blood Banks (cert. in blood banking), Am. Soc. Tropical Medicine and Hygiene, AAUP, Musser-Burch Soc., Albertus Magnus Guild, Washington Helminthol. Soc., Am. Soc. Bacteriologists, Sigma Xi. Home: 3333 Annette St New Orleans LA 70122-2921 Office: Tulane U 1430 Tulane Ave New Orleans LA 70112-2699*

EPPS, CHARLES H., JR., medical educator, college dean; b. Balt., July 24, 1930. BS magna cum laude, Howard U., 1951, MD, 1955. Intern Freedmen's Hosp., 1955-56, resident, 1956-57, mem. staff, 1961—; resident D.C. Gen. Hosp., Washington, 1958-60, vis. staff, 1961—, orthopaedic med. officer for handicapped and crippled children's svc., 1961—; chief orthop. surgeon Howard U., Washington, instr. orthop. surgery, 1961-64, asst. prof., 1964-68, assoc. prof., 1968-73, prof., 1973—, chief divsn. orthop. surgery, 1968-88, dean Coll. Medicine, 1988—, exec. dean Coll. Medicine, 1994-95, v.p. health affairs, acting exec. dir., CEO, 1994—; assoc. prof. Johns Hopkins U., 1971; mem. staff VA Hosp., Washington, Cafritz Meml. Hosp., Providence Hosp.; cons. USN Med. Ctr., Bethesda, Md., Walter Reed Army Med. Ctr. Capt. M.C., U.S. Army, 1961-62. Fellow ACS; mem. AMA, Nat. Med. Assn., Ea. Orthop. Assn., Am. Orthop. Assn., Am. Acad. Orthop. Surgery. Office: Howard U 2041 Georgia Ave NW Washington DC 20060-0001*

EPPS, ROSELYN ELIZABETH PAYNE, pediatrician, educator; b. Little Rock, Dec. 11, 1930; d. William Kenneth and Mattie Elizabeth (Beverly) Payne; m. Charles Harry Epps, Jr., June 25, 1955; children: Charles Harry III (dec.), Kenneth Carter, Roselyn Elizabeth, Howard Robert. BS, Howard U., 1951, MD, 1955; MPH, Johns Hopkins U., 1973; MA, Am. U., 1981. Intern Freedmen's Hosp., Howard U., Washington, 1955-56, pediatric resident, 1956-59, chief resident, 1958-59; practice medicine specializing in pediatrics Washington, 1960; med. officer, pediatrics D.C. Dept. Pub. Health, Washington, 1961-64, dir. Clinic for Retarded Children, 1964-67, chief Infant and Pre-Sch. div., 1967-71, dir. children and youth project, 1970-71, dir. maternal and crippled children services, 1971-75; chief Bur. Clin. Services D.C. Dept. Human Services, Washington, 1975-80, acting commr. pub. health, 1980; instr., asst. research investigator Howard U. Coll. Medicine, Washington, 1960-61, prof. Dept. Pediatrics and Child Health, 1980—, chief div. child devel., 1985-89, dir. Child Devel. Ctr., 1985-89; rsch. assoc., vis. scientist smoking tobacco and cancer program, div. cancer prevention and control Nat. Cancer Inst. NIH, Washington, 1989-91; expert Nat. Cancer Inst. NIH, Pub. Health Applications Br., Bethesda, Md., 1991—; chmn. task force to prepare comprehensive child care plan for D.C. Dept. Human Services, 1973-74; mem. nat. task force on pediatric hypertension Heart, Lung and Blood Inst., NIH, 1975; chmn. rsch. grants rev. com. maternal and child health and crippled children's svcs. HEW, Rockville, Md., 1978-80; sec. Commn. Licensure to Practice Healing Arts, Washington, 1980; trustee med. svc. D.C. Blue Shield Plan Nat. Capital Area, 1980; chmn. sec.'s adv. com. on rights and responsibilities of women HEW, Washington, 1981; dir. high-risk young people's project Howard U. Hosp., 1981-85; Washington coord. Know Your Body Program Am. Health Found., N.Y.C., 1982-91; mem. bd. advs. Coll. Home Econs. Ohio State U., Columbus, Ohio, 1983-87; adv. com. Nat. Ctr. for Edn. in Maternal and Child Health Georgetown U., Washington, 1983-89; nat. steering com., subcom. chmn. Healthy Mothers, Healthy Babies Coalition, Washington, 1983-90, mem. nominating com., 1991; cons. sickle cell disease NIH, 1984-88, Govt. Liberia and World Bank, 1984, UN Fund for Population Activities, N.Y. and Caribbean, 1984, filmstrip Miriam Berg Varian/Parents Mag. Films, 1978; bd. dirs. Vis. Nurse Assn., Inc., Washington, 1983-89; pres. bd. dirs. Hosp. for Sick Children, Washington, 1986-90, bd. dirs., 1984-94; frequent guest lectr. Weekly columnist Your Child's Health, Afro-Am. Newspaper, Washington, 1960-63; contbr. articles syndicated column Nat. Newspaper Pubs. Assn., 1982, Nat. Newspaper Assn., 1986-87; co-author audiocassettes; exhibitor sci. program; contbr. over 70 articles to profl. jours. Trustee nat. bd. Palmer Meml. Inst., Sedalia, N.C., 1969-71, Ford's Theatre, Washington, 1973-79; U.S. trustee Children's Internat. Summer Villages, Casstown, Ohio, 1969-76, pres., 1974-75; bd. mgrs. YWCA of D.C., 1970-76, 77-83, vice chmn., 1975-76; v.p. Jack and Jill of Am., Inc., Washington, 1970-71; nat. bd. dirs. Ctr. Population Options, Washington, 1980-86, Alexander Graham Bell Assn. for Deaf, Washington, 1974-78; bd. dirs. Washington Performing Arts Soc., 1971-81, v.p., 1979-81, hon. dir., 1981—; nat. bd. dirs. Meridian House Internat., Washington, 1974-81, counselor, 1981—; bd. dirs. YWCA Nat. Capital Area, 1975-76, United Negro Coll. Fund D.C., 1981-85; nat. bd. dirs. Girls Inc. (Formerly Girls Clubs Am., Inc.), N.Y.C., 1984-95, asst. sec., 1986-88, sec., 1988-90, pres., 1990-92; bd. dirs. Nat. Assembly Vol. Health and Welfare Agys., 1985-90, exec. bd., 1986-90, sec., 1988-90; bd. dirs. Mut. of Am., 1992—. Recipient Leadership and Meritorious Service in Medicine award Palmer Meml. Inst., 1968, 14th Ann. Fed. Women's award CSC, Washington, 1974, Superior Performance award D.C. Govt., 1975, Meritorious Community Seraward Howard U. Sch. Social Work Alumni Assns. and vis. com., 1980, Cert. Commendation Mayor of D.C., 1981, Roselyn Payne Epps M.D. Recognition Resolution of 1983 Council D.C., 1983, Disting. Vol. Leadership award March of Dimes Birth Defects Found., 1984, Community Svc. award D.C. Hosp. Assn., 1990, Physician of Yr. award Women's Med. Assn. N.Y.C., 1990, 91; named Outstanding Vol. in Leadership category YWCA Nat. Capital Area, 1983; inducted into D.C. Women's Hall of Fame D.C. Commn. for Women, 1990; grantee Robert Wood Johnson Found., Princeton, N.J., 1982, div. maternal and child health HHS, Rockville, Md., 1986; honored Tribute Resolution of 1981 declaring Feb. 14 Dr. Roselyn Payne Epps Day, Council of D.C., 1981; recipient Ophelia Settle Egypt award Planned Parenthood of Met. Washington, 1991, Advocacy award Soc. Advancement Women's Health, 1996. Fellow Am. Acad. Pediatrics (alt. state chmn. D.C. 1973-75, exec. com. D.C. chpt. 1983-94, pres. D.C. chpt. 1988-91, sec. cmty. pediatrics sect. 1973-75, cert. appreciation 1979, mem. coun. of child and adolescent health, cmty. and internat. health sect., charter mem., exec. com. 1992-94); mem. Acad. Medicine, AMA (alt. del. Nat. Med. Assn. 1983-85), Am. Med. Women's Assn. (chmn. pub. health com. 1973-75, pres. br. 1 1974-76, sec. 1988, v.p. 1989, pres-elect nat. 1990, pres. 1991, found. founding pres. 1992, bd. dirs. 1992—, chmn. nominating com. 1993, Physician of Yr. award 1991, Cmty. Svc. award 1990, Elizabeth Blackwell award 1992), Women's Forum Washington, Med. Soc. D.C. (exec. bd. 1990, sec. 1990, pres.-elect 1991, pres. 1992, chair exec. bd. 1993, ann. Cmty. Svc. award 1982), Am. Pediatric Soc., D.C. Hosp. Assn. (Cmty. Svc. award 1990), Am. Pub. Health Assn. (action bd. 1977-79, joint policy com. 1978-79, gov. council 1978-81), Met. Washington Pub. Health Assn. (gov. council 1975-78, 81-83, ann. award 1981), Nat. Med. Assn. (chmn. pediatric sect. 1977-79, Ross Labs. award 1979, Outstanding Svcs. to Children during Internat. Yr. of Child award 1979, Meritorious Service Appreciation award 1979, W.M. Cobb co-lectr. 1985, mem. Coun. on Maternal and Child Health, 1974-92, chmn. 1979-89, ann. Roselyn Payne Epps Symposium 1994—, Grace Marilyn James award for Disting svc. Pediatric sect. 1991, Achievement award 1993), Am. Hosp. Assn. (maternal and child health sect. governing coun. 1989, 1992-94, maternal and child health nominating com. 1991), Alpha Omega Alpha, Delta Omega, Alpha Kappa Alpha. Mem. United Ch. of Christ. Clubs: Pearls (pres. 1984-86), Carrousels (corr. sec. 1978-80), Links (pres. Met. chpt. 1986-89) (Washington), Cosmos. Lodge: Zonta. Home: 1775 N Portal Dr NW Washington DC 20012-1014 Office: Nat Cancer Inst NIH DCPC/CCSP/PHARB/EPN-241 6130 Executive Blvd MSC7333 Bethesda MD 20892-7333

EPSTEIN, ANDREW ERNEST, cardiologist; b. N.Y.C., Nov. 30, 1950; s. Frederick Hermon Epstein and Ingeborg Luise (Gunther) Davenport; m. Judith Ann Mullen, Oct. 6, 1979 (div. 1980); m. Eileen Marie Dawson, Dec. 9, 1984; 1 child, Anne Elizabeth. BA in English, Amherst Coll., 1973; MD, U. Rochester, 1977. Diplomate Am. Bd. Internal Medicine; Cardiology, 1983; Nat. Bd. Med. Examiners, 1978. Intern Washington U. Burnes Hosp., St. Louis, 1977-78, resident, 1978-80; fellow U. Ala. at Birmingham, 1980-82; chief fellow Divsn. Cardiovascular Diseases, 1982-83; instr. U. Ala. at Birmingham, 1982-83, asst. prof. medicine, 1983-87, assoc. prof. medicine, 1988-91, prof. medicine, 1991—; advisor to many mfrs. cardiac rhythm mgmt. devices. Contbr over 90 articles, more than 106 abstracts to profl. jours., chpts. to 19 books in field. Vol. Am. Heart Assn., Birmingham and Dallas, 1983—, mem. Ala. cardiac care com., 1994—. Fellow Am. Coll. Cardiology, Am. Heart Assn. (clin. coun. 1983—, exec. com. 1992-95, chmn. com. on sudden death, 1992-95); mem. N. Am. Soc. Pacing and Electrophysiology, Cardiac Electrophysiology Soc. Home: 1616 Shades Crest Rd Birmingham AL 35226 Office: U Ala at Birmingham Divsn Cardiovascular Disease Univ Sta THT 321 Birmingham AL 35294

EPSTEIN, ARTHUR WILLIAM, physician, educator; b. N.Y.C., May 15, 1923; s. Jacob E. and Anne (Bass) E.; m. Leona Cruce, Mar. 2, 1955; children: David Byron, Nona Kathryn, Emily Vera, James Jacob. A.B., Columbia U., 1944, M.D., 1947. Intern Mt. Sinai Hosp., N.Y.C., 1947-48; resident Mt. Sinai Hosp., 1949-50; clin. asst. Norristown (Pa.) State Hosp., 1948-49; faculty Tulane U., New Orleans, 1954—; asso. prof. psychiatry and neurology, 1959-64, prof. Tulane U., 1964—; pvt. practice medicine, specializing in neuropsychiatry New Orleans, 1964—; prof. emeritus Tulane U., 1993—; vis. physician Charity Hosp., New Orleans, 1951—; cons. U.S. Army Hosp., New Orleans, 1958-64; mem. med. staff Tulane Med. Center Hosp., 1976—. Author: An Anatomist's Dream of Love, 1966, The Dissecting Room, 1978, The Lady and the Serpent, 1981, A Contemporary Religious Svc., 1987, Bridge Cross, 1989, Dreaming and Other Involuntary Mentation: An Essay in Neuropsychiatry, 1996; contbr. articles to profl. jours. Med. adviser Social Security Adminstrn., 1968-93; bd. dirs. Ednl. Rsch. and Treatment Ctr., New Orleans. Served with M.C. USNR, 1956-58. Named Psychiatrist of Yr. La. Psychiatric Assn., 1992. Fellow AAAS, Am. Psychiat. Assn. (life, leisure time and its uses com.), Am. Acad. Psychoanalysis (pres. 1987-88, Silverberg award 1985), Am. Acad. Neurology; mem. Soc. Biol. Psychiatry (v.p. 1979-80, pres.-elect 1980-81, pres. 1981-82), Am. Epilepsy Soc., Alpha Omega Alpha. Home: 1664 Robert St New Orleans LA 70115-4975 Office: 1430 Tulane Ave New Orleans LA 70112-2699

EPSTEIN, BARRY H., gastroenterologist; b. Bklyn., May 18, 1940; s. Morris Epstein and Esther (Cohen) Gelch; m. Evelyn Kramer, June 11, 1961; hcildren: Amy Lynn, Michael Adam. AB in Psychology, Columbia U., 1960; MD, Chgo. Med. Sch., 1964. Diplomate Am. Bd. Internal Medicine, Am. Bd. Gastroenterology. Fellow gastroenterology Mt. Sinai Med. Ctr., N.Y.C., 1967-69; chmn. gastroenterology P.G. Hosp. Ctr., Cheverly, Md., 1979-83; chmn. dept. medicine Prince Georges Hosp. Ctr., Cheverly, 1983-92; pvt. practice College Park, Md., 1971—; pres. med. staff Prince Georges Hosp. Ctr., Cheverly, 1994—; adj. prof. microbiology U. Md., College Park, 1990—; asst. prof. gastrointestinal/med. U. Md. Med. Sch., Balt., 1973-85; mem. exec. com. med. staff Prince Georges Hosp. Ctr., Cheverly, 1983-96. Contbr. articles to profl. jours., columns to newspapers. Bd. dirs. Doctors Hosp., Lanham, Md., 1980-84, Prince Georges Hosp. Ctr., Cheverly, 1992-96, Dimsusions Healthcare, Landover, Md., 1994-96. Maj. USAF, 1969-71. Fellow ACP, Am. Coll. Gastroenterology; mem. Am. Gastroent. Assn., Am. Soc. Gastrointestinal endoscopy, William Earl Clark Soc. (pres. 1976). Democrat. Jewish. Office: Epstein & Cohen 6201 Greenbelt Rd College Park MD 20740

EPSTEIN, DAVID LEE, ophthalmologist, surgeon, educator; b. Chgo., June 23, 1944. BA, Johns Hopkins U., 1965, MD, 1968. Diplomate Am. Bd. Ophthalmology. Intern King County Hosp. and Univ. Hosp., Seattle, 1968-69; fellow in ocular biochemistry Howe Lab. Ophthalmology and Mass. Eye and Ear Infirmary, Boston, 1973-75, glaucoma research fellow, 1975-76, mem. staff, asst. in ophthalmology, asst. dir. glaucoma cons. service, 1976—, assist. surgeon ophthalmology, 1980, dir. glaucoma cons. service, 1982-91, assoc. surgeon ophthalmology, 1984—, surgeon ophthalmology, 1987-91; prof., chmn. dept. ophthalmology Duke U. Med. Sch., Durham, N.C., 1992—; chmn. eye pharmacy com. Mass. Eye and Ear Infirmary, 1979-87; from instr. to assoc. prof. ophthalmology Harvard Med. Sch., 1981-91; prof. ophthalmology in residence U. Calif., San Francisco, 1991-92; mem. sci. adv. bd. Oakland U. Inst. Biol. Sci., Rochester, Minn., 1983—. Mem. editorial bd. Archives of Ophthalmology, 1985-94. Served as staff ophthalmologist and flight surgeon U.S. Sch. Aerospace Medicine, Brooks AFB, 1970-72. Recipient Ulmer award, 1970, Alcon Rsch. Inst. award, 1982, numerous hon. lectureships. Mem. Assn. Rsch. in Vision and Ophthalmology (pres. 1992-93, trustee 1988-93), New Eng. Ophthalmology Soc., Am. Acad. Ophthalmology (chmn. nat. com. on drugs 1984-89, honor award 1984), Internat. Soc. Eye Rsch., Glaucoma Soc. Internat., Phi Beta Kappa, Alpha Omega Alpha. Home: 9123 S Lowell Rd Bahama NC 27503-8757

EPSTEIN, DAVID NORTON, dentist; b. Elmira, N.Y., May 24, 1930; s. Norman charles and Edna (Voronoff) E.; m. Ellen Ruth Werman, Aug. 20, 1960; children: Karin Elise, Andrew Scott. BA, Cornell U., 1991; DDS, NYU, 1954. Intern Fitzsimmons Army Hosp., Denver, 1954-55; pvt practice dentistry Ithaca, N.Y., 1957-61, Dryden, N.Y., 1961-81; dental dir. The George Jr. Republic, Freeville, N.Y., 1961-81; staff dentist Gulf Coast Ctr., Ft. Myers, Fla., 1981-95; ret., 1995; mng. dir. Dad's Diversions, Ft. Myers, Fla., 1981—; tour escort Bell's Custom Travel, 1995—; adv. bd. Tompkins County Trust Co., dryden, 1979-81. Contbr. articles to profl. jours. Vice pres. Baden Powell coun. Boy Scouts Am.; vol. Barbara Mann Performing Arts Ctr.; mem. Abuse and Counseling Treatment Ctr. Fellow Acad. Gen. Dentistry; mem. Rotary (pres. Ithaca 1976, Ft. Myers 1986), So. Assn. Instnl. Dentists (pres. 1988).

EPSTEIN, JAY STUART, medical researcher; married; 2 children. BA cum laude, Harvard U., 1969; MD, Downstate Med. Coll., 1976. Resident internal medicine George Washington U. Hosp., Washington, 1976-79, clin. fellow infectious diseases, 1979-81; sr. staff fellow rsch. divsn. virology office biologics rsch. & review FDA, Rockville, Md., 1981-85, chief immunochemistry lab., 1984-86, chief retrovirology lab. divsn. transfusion sci., 1986-92, acting dept. dir., 1990-92, dir. divsn. transfusion transmitted diseases Office Blood Rsch. & Review, 1993-95, acting. dir., 1993-95, dir., 1995—; rsch. asst. Moffit Hosp., San Francisco, 1971-73; part time physician Potomac (Md.) Village Med. Ctr., 1981-83; part time house physician Capitol Hill Hosp., Washington, 1981-83. With USPHS, 1985-90. Nat. Merit scholar, 1965, Harvard Coll. scholar, 1965, N.Y. State Regents Medicine scholar, 1969. Mem. AAAS, Infectious Diseases Soc. Am., Greater Washington Area Infectious Diseaes Soc., Alpha Omega Alpha. Home: 1922 Foxhall Rd Mc Lean VA 22101 Office: HHS Office Blood Rsch & Review Ste 400 N HFM-300 1401 Rockville Pike Ste Rockville MD 20852-1448

EPSTEIN, JEFFREY MARK, neurosurgeon; b. Newark, Apr. 7, 1951; s. Herbert Joseph and Roberta Laura (Sank) E.; m. Ronit Adler. BA, Johns Hopkins U., 1973; MD, Autonomous U. Guadalajara, Mex., 1979. Diplomate Am. Bd. Neurol. and Orthopedic Surgery, Am. Bd. Pain Mgmt. 5th channel clerkship Newark Beth-Israel Med. Ctr., 1979-80; intern in surgery Muhlenberg Hosp., Plainfield, N.J., 1980-81; resident in neurosurgery SUNY-Downstate and Kings County Hosp. Ctr., Bklyn., 1981-85, chief resident neurosurgery, 1985-86; instr. neurosurgery SUNY-Downstate, 1986-87, asst. prof. neurosurgery, 1987-88; pvt. practice West Islip, N.Y., 1988—. Contbr. articles to Anesthesia Jour., 1985. Mem. N.Y. State Neurosurgery Soc., Med. Soc. State N.Y., Suffolk County Med. Soc., Magoun Landing Yacht Club, Alpha Epsilon Delta (v.p. 1973). Jewish. Office: 735 Montauk Hwy Ste A West Islip NY 11795-4931

EPSTEIN, LEON JOSEPH, psychiatrist; b. Jersey City, June 7, 1917; s. Irving and Sara (Pomerantz) E.; children: Lisa, David. A.B., Vanderbilt U., 1937, M.A., 1938; Ph.D., Peabody Coll., 1941; M.D., U. Tenn., 1949. Intern Wesley Meml. Hosp., Chgo., 1950; resident in psychiatry St. Elizabeths Hosp., Washington, 1951-54; staff psychiatrist St. Elizabeths Hosp., 1954-56; dep. dir. Calif. Dept. Mental Hygiene, Sacramento, 1956-61; prof. psychiatry, asso. dir. Langley Porter Inst. U. Calif. Sch. Medicine, San Francisco, 1961-83, interim chmn., dir., 1985-86, prof. psychiatry, emeritus, 1987-. Author books and articles in psychogerontology and psychopharmacology. Mem. San Francisco Crime Commn., 1969-71. Served to lt. comdr. USN, 1941-46. Recipient Sullivan award Peabody Coll., 1941; William A. White award St. Elizabeths Hosp., 1952, 53; J. Elliott Royer award U. Calif., 1976; Outstanding Achievement award Northern Calif. Psychiatric Soc., 1985. Mem. Am. Coll. Psychiatry, Am. Coll. Neuropsychopharmacology, Am. Psychiat. Assn., Am. Psychopath. Assn., Gerontol. Soc. Jewish. Home: 2251 Steiner St San Francisco CA 94115-2219 Office: 350 Parnassus Ave Ste 309 San Francisco CA 94117-3608

EPSTEIN, MARC CHARLES, optometrist; b. Bklyn., Mar. 2, 1948; s. Jack and Phyllis (Kleiger) E.; B.A., Cornell Coll., 1970; O.D., Mass. Coll. Optometry, 1975; m. Barbara Wolf, July 4, 1971; children—Adam, Brian, Scott. Practice optometry, Great Neck, N.Y., 1977—; attending staff dept. ophthalmology North Shore Univ. Hosp., Great Neck, 1976—, dir. low-vision and contact lense services, Cath. Med. Ctrs., 1987—; attending optometrist Fitzpatric Pavillion, Jamaica, N.Y., 1992—; low vision cons. Helen Keller Nat. Ctr., Sands Pt., N.Y., 1993—. Served with Army N.G., 1970-74. Recipient Irvin Borish award Am. Optometric Found., 1975, Kohnn award, 1975; HEW grantee, 1979-80. Diplomate Nat. Bd. Examiners in Optometry; cert. low vision specialist N.Y. Commn. for Blind, N.Y. Optometric Assn. Fellow Am. Acad. Optometry, N.Y. Acad. Optometry (v.p. 1979-81, pres. 1981-83); mem. Am. Optometric Assn., N.Y. Optometric Assn., Nassau Optometric Assn. (dir.). Inventor audible feed-back syringe for blind diabetics. Home: 14 Devon Rd Great Neck NY 11023-2317 Office: 23 Bond St Great Neck NY 11021

EPSTEIN, MEL H., neurosurgeon, educator; b. N.Y.C., Apr. 2, 1942; m. Lynn Chaikin; children: Kim, Darin, John. BA, Union Coll., 1961; AB, Johns Hopkins U., 1963, MD, 1966. Diplomate Am. Bd. Neurol. Surgeons. Asst. prof. Johns Hopkins U., Balt., 1972-78, assoc. prof., 1978-85; prof., chief, co-chmn. Brown U., Providence, 1985—; cons. NIH, Balt., 1969-71; exch. prof. Rheza Pahlavi Hosp., Tehran, Iran, 1975; vis. prof. neurol. surgery Tufts-New Eng. Med. Ctr., 1987. Author: Surgical Management of Hydrocephalus, 1983, Congenital Hydrocephalus, 1985, Myelomeningocele, 1988. Recipient citation EthiconAdv. Panel, 1979, Rsch. and Exch. award William and Flora Hewlitt Found., 1988; NSF fellow. Mem. AAAS, Soc. Neurol. Surgeons, Soc. Neurol. Surgeons, Congress Neurol. Surgeons. Office: Brown U RI Hosp 2 Dudley St Ste 505 Providence RI 02905

EPSTEIN, RICHARD SAUL, psychiatrist. BS, Yale U., 1960; MD, Washington U., St. Louis, 1964. Resident Johns Hopkins U., 1965-67; clin. assoc. NIMH, Bethesda, Md., 1967-79, cons. Suicide Prevention Project, 1969-78, cons. Borderline Personality Project, 1979-81; clin. adminstr. Hyperkinetic Child Study Project, Bethesda, 1968-69; cons. Nat. Inst. Dental Rsch., Bethesda, 1969-70; pvt. practice Bethesda, Md., 1969—; clin. prof., scientist trauma ctr. dept. psychiatry Uniformed Svcs. U. Health Scis., Georgetown U., clin. prof. dept. psychiatry Sch. Medicine. Author: Keeping Boundaries, 1994; contbr. articles to profl. jours. Sr. asst. surgeon U.S. Pub. Health Svc. 1967-69. Fellow Am. Psychiat. Assn. (chair ethics com. 1996—); mem. Washington Psychiat. Soc. (pres. 1994-95), Montgomery County Med. Soc. (chmn. mental health com. 1973-75), Am. Acad. Psychiatry and the Law (pres. Chesapeake Bay chpt. 1992-93). Office: 10401 Old Georgetown Rd Bethesda MD 20814-1911

EPSTEIN, ROBERT BERNARD, physician, oncologist, hematologist; b. Chgo., June 9, 1934; s. James and Faye (Winer) E.; m. Phyllis Joan Copper, Sept. 11, 1957; children: Scott, Ruth, Kenneth. BS, U. Ill., 1957, MD, 1959. Asst. prof. medicine U. Wash., 1967-70; clin. investigator VA Hosp., 1971-74, med. investigator, 1975-82, staff physician, 1982—; assoc. prof. medicine U. Ill., 1971-74, prof. medicine, 1974-82; prof. medicine Health Scis. Ctr. U. Okla., 1982—.

EPSTEIN, ROBERT MARVIN, anesthesiologist, educator; b. N.Y.C., Mar. 10, 1928; s. Nathan Batlan and Rebecca (Dickes) E.; m. Lillian Ray Cohen, Dec. 31, 1950; children: Judith Susan, Neal Myron, Charles Benjamin. B.S. with distinction, U. Mich., 1947, M.D. cum laude, 1951. Diplomate: Am. Bd. Anesthesiology (dir. 1972-84, pres. 1979-80). Intern U. Mich. Hosp., 1951-52; resident in anesthesiology Presbyterian Hosp., N.Y.C., 1952-53, 55-56; instr. in anesthesiology and fellow in medicine Columbia U., 1956-57, assoc., 1957-59, asst. prof., anesthesiology, 1959-65, assoc. prof., 1965-70, prof., 1970-72; prof. U. Va., Charlottesville, 1972-74, Alumni prof., 1974-87, Disting. prof., 1987-92, Harold Carron prof., 1992—; mem. anesthesiology tng. com. Nat. Inst. Gen. Med. Scis., NIH, 1966-69; mem. com. on anesthesia NRC, 1970-71; mem. Nat. Bd. Med. Examiners, 1982-90. Editor Anesthesiology, 1974-79; contbr. numerous articles to profl. jours. Bd. dirs., sec. U.Va. Health Svcs. Found., 1980-90, pres., 1990-93; trustee Ednl. Commn. for Fgn. Med. Grads., 1991-95, vice chmn., 1993-95. With U.S. Army, 1953-55. Guggenheim fellow Oxford (Eng.) U., 1966-67; N.Y. Heart Assn. fellow, 1956-57. Fellow Royal Coll. Anaesthetists (Eng.); mem. AAAS, Inst. Medicine NAS, Am. Physiol. Soc., Am. Soc. Anesthesiologists, Soc. Acad. Anesthesia Chmn. (mem. coun., rep. to Coun. Acad. Soc. Assn. Am. Med. Colls. 1984-91), Am. Soc. Pharmacy and Exptl. Therapeutics, Anaesthetic Rsch. Soc. (U.K.), Assn. Univ. Anesthesiologists (pres. 1973-74), Phi Beta Kappa, Sigma Xi, Alpha Omega Alpha. Office: U Va Hosp Jefferson Park Ave Charlottesville VA 22908

EPSTEIN, RUTH EVE, speech clinician; b. Ellenville, N.Y., Sept. 24, 1933; m. Joe M. Epstein, Feb. 16, 1985 (div. 1990). BS, Syracuse (N.Y.) U., 1954; MA, Appalachian State U., 1981. Lic. speech clinician, Fla. Speech clinician Bd. of Cooper Edn. Svcs., New Paltz, N.Y., 1964-74, Ellenville Cen. Schs., 1974, Union County Sch. System, Monroe, N.C., 1974-86, Palm Beach (Fla.) County Schs., 1986—. Mem. Am. Speech, Lang. and Hearing Assn. (cert. clin. competence). Jewish. Home: 61 Balfour Rd E Palm Beach Gardens FL 33418 Office: Lincoln Elem Sch Lincoln Elem Sch 1160 W 10th Ave Riviera Beach FL 33404

EPSTEIN, SAMUEL ERIC, physician, orthopedic surgeon; b. Harrisburg, Pa., Apr. 4, 1958; s. Irving and Marlene Ester (Finkel) E.; m. Judith Anne Epstein, Mar. 10, 1985; children: Aaron, Emily. BS, Swarthmore Coll., 1980; DO, Phila. Coll. Osteo. Medicine, 1984. Diplomate Am. Bd. Osteo. Orthopedic Surgeons. Mem. staff So. Ocean County Hosp., Manahawkin, N.J., 1992—, chmn. dept. surgery, 1993—. Mem. Am. Osteo. Assn., N.J. Osteo. Assn. Office: Stafford Orthopedics 56 Nautilus Dr Manahawkin NJ 08050

EPSTEIN, SANDRA GAIL, psychologist; b. Boston, July 19, 1939; d. Mischa and Frances (Greenfield) Schneiderman; 1 child, Suanne Charyl. AB, Boston U., 1962; MA, U. Conn., 1969, diploma, 1978, PhD, 1979. Sch. psychol. examiner various pub. schs., Conn., 1970-73, sch. psychologist, 1973—; staff psychologist Day Kimball Hosp. Mental Health Clinic, Putnam, Conn., 1971-74; psychologist Thompson (Conn.) Med. Ctr., 1973-80; staff psychiatry dept. Day Kimball Hosp., Putnam, 1983—; pvt. practice Woodstock, Conn., 1980-85, Farmington, 1983-93, Putnam, 1985—; instr. Annhurst Coll., Woodstock, Conn., 1971-76; cons. N.E. Area Regional Ednl. Svc., Wauregan, Conn., 1978-79, Capitol Region Ednl. Coun., West Hartford, Conn., 1980—, Ctr. for Interpersonal Rels., Putnam, 1985-88, Hebrew Acad. Greater Hartford, Bloomfield, Conn., 1983-89, Conn. Bur. Rehab. Svcs., Norwich, 1992—. Mem. Am. Psychol. Assn., Internat. Soc. Hypnosis, Internat. Psychosomatics Inst., N.Y. Acad. Sci., Conn. Psychol. Assn., Am. Soc. Clin. Hypnosis, Am. Acad. Pain Mgmt., N.Y. Acad. Sci. Office: PO Box 207 Woodstock CT 06281-0207

EPSTEIN, SIMON JULES, psychiatrist; b. Yonkers, N.Y., July 20, 1934; s. Joseph and Lillian (Shapiro) E.; m. Patricia E. Marlowe, June 23, 1957; children: Sharon, Joanne. BA, Yale U., 1956; MD, NYU, 1960. Diplomate Am. Bd. Psychiatry and Neurology. Psychiat. resident N.Y. Hosp., White Plains, 1964-66; assoc. med. dir. Child Guidance Clinic So. Conn., Stamford, 1978—; med. dir. New Eng. Ctr. for Psychiat. Treatment and Edn., Stamford, 1986—; clin. assoc. prof. psychiatry N.Y. Med. Ctr., Valhalla, 1975—; assoc. psychiatrist in chief Stamford Hosp., 1987—. Contbr. articles to profl. jours.; author Epstein Quar. Newsletter. Capt. U.S. Army, 1962-64. Fellow Am. Psychiat. Assn.; mem. Conn. Psychiat. Soc. (pres. 1985-86). Democrat. Jewish. Home: 60 Northwood Ln Stamford CT 06903-4333 Office: 91 Strawberry Hill Ave Stamford CT 06902-2762

EPSTEIN, STEVEN GUS, surgeon; b. Bklyn., Feb. 14, 1948; s. Morris and Dorothy Epstein; children: Tara, Scott. BSEE, Milw. Sch. Engring., 1969; MS in Biomed. Engring., Drexel U., 1972; MD with honors, U. Liege, 1980. Diplomate Am. Bd. Surgery. Intern, then resident in surgery N.Y. Med. Coll.-Westchester County Med. Ctr., Met. Hosp. Ctr., 1980-85; fellow in surg. critical care N.Y. Med. Coll., Valhalla, 1985-86; dir. surg. intensive care Bayfront Ned. Ctr., St. Petersburg, Fla., dir. Trauma Ctr.; pvt. practice, St. Petersburg; clin. instr. dept. family practice U. South Fla. Med. Sch.; asst. chief med. officer Fla.-3 DMAT, Tampa. Fellow ACS; mem. Eastern Assn. for Surgery of Trauma, Fla. Coll. Surgeons, Soc. Critical Care Medicine, So. Med. Assn. Office: Bay Area Surg Assocs PA 603 7th St S # 350 Saint Petersburg FL 33701

EPSTEIN, WILLIAM ERIC, health care executive; b. N.Y.C., Nov. 10, 1949; s. Felix Epstein and Betty Elizabeth Moses. BS in Indsl. Engring., Northeastern U., 1972; MBA, NYU, 1975. Sys. engr. Peter B. Brigham Hosp., Boston, 1969-72; sr. mgmt. cons. N.Y.C. Heath Hosp., 1972-76; asst. to v.p. planning Mt. Sinai Hosp., N.Y.C., 1976-80, asst. dir., 1980-82, adminstr., 1982-87, assoc. dir., 1987-91; asst. v.p. Hahnemann U., Phila., 1991-93, v.p. mgmt., regional v.p. corp. svcs., 1994-95; prin. Fineman & Assoc., Bronxville, N.Y., 1996—; preceptor Baruch Coll. CUNY, N.Y.C., 1984-91; adj. lectr. Mt. Sinai Sch. Medicine, N.Y.C., 1987-91; advisor, panel mem. healthcare adminstrn. program New Sch. for Social Research Grad. Sch. Mgmt., N.Y.C., 1988. Pres. Harmon Cove Condominium Assn., Secaucus, N.J., 1986-91; mem. campaign com. Young Leadership Nat. Bd.-State of Israel, 1991—. Fellow Am. Coll. Health Care Exec. (examiner, regents adv. coun.); mem. Health Care Infosystems Soc. (cert., sr. mem.), Hosp. Materials Mgmt. Soc. (sr. mem.), Health Care Mgmt. and Info. Systems Soc., Am. Hosp. Assn., NYU Alumni Assn. Grad. Sch. Bus. Home: Apt 1512 1 Franklin Town Blvd Philadelphia PA 19103-1247 Office: 15 Conever Ct Clifton NJ 07012

EPSTEIN, WILLIAM LOUIS, dermatologist, educator; b. Cleve., Sept. 6, 1925; s. Norman N. and Gertrude (Hirsch) E.; m. Joan Goldman, Jan. 29, 1954; children—Wendy, Steven. A.B., U. Calif., Berkeley, 1949, M.D., 1952. Mem. faculty U. Calif., San Francisco, 1957—; assoc. prof. div. dermatology U. Calif., 1963-69, prof. div. dermatology, 1969—, dir. dermatol. rsch., 1957-70, acting chmn. div. dermatology, 1966-69, chmn. dept. dermatology, 1970-85; cons. dermatology Outpatient Dept.; cons. various hosps. Calif. Dept. Public Health; cons. Food and Drug Adminstrn., Washington, 1972—, Dept. Agriculture, 1979; dir. div. research Nat. Program Dermatology, 1970-73; Dohi lectr., Tokyo, 1982; Beecham lectr., 1988-89; Nippon Boehringer Ingelheim lectr. 18th Hakone Symposium on Respiration, Japan, 1990. Mem. AAAS, AMA, Am. Soc. Cell Biology, Am. Acad. Dermatology and Syphilology (nominating com. 1984), Pacific Dermatologic Assn., Am. Fedn. Clin. Rsch., Soc. Investigative Dermatology (bd. dirs., pres. 1985), Am. Dermatol. Assn., Assn. Profs. Dermatology (sr. mem.), Dermatology Found. (pres. 1986-87), Phi Beta Kappa, Sigma Xi. Home: 267 Golden Hinde Passage Corte Madera CA 94925-1953

ERAKLIS, ANGELO JOHN, surgeon; b. Portland, Maine, Jan. 11, 1933; s. George and Georgia E.; m. Katherine Sferes, Sept. 13, 1959; children: Elaine, Marianna. AB, Bowdoin Coll., Brunswick, Maine, 1954; MD, Harvard U., 1958. Diplomate Am. Bd. Surgery, Am. Bd. Thoracic Surgery, Am. Bd. Pediatric Surgery. Intern in surgery Peter Bent Brigham Hosp., 1958-59, jr. resident in surgery, 1959-60; jr. resident in surgery Children's Hosp. Med. Ctr., 1960-61; chief resident in pediatric surgery Boston City Hosp., 1961-62; sr. resident in surgery Peter Bent Brigham Hosp., 1962-64; chief resident in surgery Children's Hosp. Med. Ctr., 1964-65, dir. office internat. affairs, 1995—; pvt. practice specializing in pediatric surgery Boston, 1965—; instr. in surgery to asst. prof. surgery Harvard Med. Sch., Boston, 1968-76; assoc. prof. surgery Harvard Med. Sch., 1976—; sr. surgeon Children's Hosp. Med. Ctr., 1968-92, dir. ambulatory surg. svcs., 1968-87, mem. staff Mt. Auburn Hosp., Newton-Wellesley Hosp.; vis. surgeon George Washington U., 1975, Northwestern U., 1975, St. Louis U., 1977, U. S.D., 1979; cons. in field, lectr. in field; founder, co-chmn. Health Care Internat. Ltd., Clydebank, Scotland; co-chmn. Ctr. Advanced Health Care. Contbr. articles to profl. jours. Mem. Boston Surg. Soc., Am. Pediatric Surg. Assn., Assn. Acad. Surgery, ACS (fellow), Am. Acad. Pediatrics, New Eng. Pediatric Soc., Mass. Med. Soc., Norfolk County Med. Soc., Phi Beta Kappa. Greek Orthodox. Home: 15 Day School Ln Belmont MA 02178-2030 Office: Children's Hosp Med Ctr 300 Longwood Ave Boston MA 02115-5724

ERB, BLAIR DILLARD, JR., cardiologist; b. Colorado Springs, Jan. 17, 1957. BA, Colo. Coll., 1979; MD, Vanderbilt U., 1983. Intern, then resident, then chief resident U. Calif., San Francisco, 1973-87; from fellow cardiovasc. diseases to chief fellow cardiology Vanderbilt U., Nashville, 1987-90; cardiologist Page-Campbell Cardiology Group, Nashville, 1990—. Fellow Am. Coll. Cardiology; mem. Am. Coll. Physicians, Am. Soc. Echocardiography, Alpha Omega Alpha. Office: Page-Campbell Cardio Group 4230 Harding Rd #900 Nashville TN 37205

ERBEL, RAIMUND, cardiologist educator; b. Baesweiler, Fed. Republic of Germany, Mar. 9, 1948; s. Peter and Maria (Loogen) E.; m. Hildegard Schürmann, Aug. 3, 1978; children: Susanne, Christian, Sebastian, Matthias. MD, U. Düsseldorf, 1974. Asst. St. Josef Krankenhaus, Leverkusen, 1973-74, U. Düsseldorf, 1974-75; stabsarzt Bundeswehrzentralkrankenhaus, Koblenz, 1975-77; asst. RWTH, Aachen, 1977-82; lectr. U. Mainz, 1982—, prof. internal medicine, 1983-93; dir. dept. cardiology U. Essen, 1993—. Co-editor: Bildgebende Verfahren in der Diagnostik von Herzerkrankungen, 1991, Transeohophageal Echo Cardiography, 1989, Tissue Doppler Echocardiography, 1994. Recipient Paul Beiersdorf award, 1983, award Dutch Soc. Cardiology, 1995. Fellow Am. Heart Assn., Am. Coll. Cardiology, European Soc. Cardiology; mem. Am. Soc. Echocardiography, German Soc. Biomedicine. Office: U Essen Divsn Internal Med, Dept Cardiology Hufelandstr 55, D-45122 Essen Germany

ERBER, WILLIAM FRANKLIN, gastroenterologist; b. N.Y.C., June 1, 1941; s. Sigmund and Marcia (Picard) E.; m. Ingrid Amelia Friedler, Dec. 25, 1967; children: Gregory, Karina, Jonathan, Joanna, Jeremy. BS, Muhlenberg Coll., 1963; MD, U. Health Sci., Chgo., 1967. Diplomate Am. Bd. Internal Medicine and Gastroenterology. Intern Maimonides Hosp., 1967-68, resident, 1968-69; fellowship in gastroenterology Albert Einstein Coll. of Medicine, 1973-75; rsch. fellow Hadassah Hosp., Jerusalem, 1971-72; clin. asst. prof. Health Sci. Ctr., Bklyn., 1975—; cons. Crohn's Colitis Found., N.Y.C., 1975—, H.I.P., N.Y.C., 1975—; attending gastroenterologist Maimonides Med. Ctr., Bklyn., 1975—. Author: Internal Medicine Review, 1979; contbr. articles to profl. jours. Maj. USAF, 1969-71. Fellow ACP, Am. Coll. Gastroenterology. Office: 591 Ocean Pkwy Brooklyn NY 11218

ERBICELLA-MARTIN, LINDA SUSAN, optometrist; b. Lower Merion, Pa., Oct. 14, 1957; s. Fred M. and Marie T. (Mazzei) E.; m. Barry C. Martin, June 12, 1993. BS in Biology, Widener U., Chester, Pa., 1984; OD, Pa. Coll. Optometry, Phila., 1987. Pvt. practice optometry Prospect Park, Pa., 1987-94, Aldan (Pa.) Optical, 1994—. Mem. Am. Optometric Assn. Office: Aldan Optical 20 Springfield Rd Aldan PA 19018-4028

ERDIL, MICHAEL, internist; b. N.Y.C., Apr. 18, 1952; s. Leo and Trudy Erdil; m. Elizabeth Glackin; 1 child, Rachel. BA in Chemistry magna cum laude, Queen's Coll., 1973; MD, SUNY Downstate Med. Ctr., 1977. Diplomate Am. Bd. Internal Medicine, Am. Bd. Preventive/Occupl. Medicine. Intern in internal medicine Kings County Med. Ctr., Bklyn., 1977-78; resident in internal medicine Bay State Med. Ctr., Springfield, Mass., 1978-80; staff physician, co-owner Emergency Physicians Inc., East Longmeadow, Mass., 1980-84; med. dir. Immediate Med. Care Ctr. Inc., Manchester, Conn., 1984-88, Holyoke (Mass.) Hosp. Occupl. Health Svc., 1988-90; dir. occupl. medicine Occupl. Medicine Svcs. of IMCC, Wethersfield, Conn., 1990—; Cons., assoc. med. dir. Health Direct, Farmington, Conn., 1992—; mem. adv. bd. chmn. Conn. Rd. Industry Surveillance Project, NIOHSH, 1992—; reviewer Agy. for Health Care Policy and Rsch., 1993-94, Oreg. Dept. Consumer and Bus. Svcs., Dept. Labor and Industries Treatment Guidelines for Carpal Tunnel Syndrome, 1994-95; reviewer State Calif. Indsl. Indemnity Treatment Guidelines for Work-Related Injuries and Illnesses, 1994-95; reviewer Am. Coll. Occpl. and Environ. Medicine, 1994-95. Editor: Cumulative Trauma Disorders, 1996; co-author videotape and tng. manual: The Exposure History: A Key to Better Care of Your Patients, 1991, The Environmental and Occupational Health Reference Guide, 1991; developer computer program: The Computer Assisted Diagnostic Aide for Diagnosis of Environmental Illness, 1991; contbr. articles to profl. jours., chpts. to books. Mem. gov.'s task force Conn. Environ. Health Project for Health Profls., 1991—; mem. adv. bd. Robert Wood Johnson Found., 1993-94. Grantee Conn. Dept. Health, 1991-93, VHA, Aetna Ins. Co., 1991—. Mem. Am. Coll. Occupl. and Environ. Medicine (mem. ad hoc com. on low back pain 1994-95, reviewer 1994-95), Assn. Occupl. and Environ. Clinics. Home: 3 Leonard St PO Box 344 Leeds MA 01053 Office: Occupl Medicine Svcs 12600 Silas Deane Hwy Wethersfield CT 06109

ERDMANN, JAMES BERNARD, educational psychologist; b. Springfield, Ill., Oct. 27, 1937; s. George C. and Emma (Hiltebrand) E.; m. Rebecca Susan Lindsay; children: Theodore Michael, Carolyn Louise, Christopher Joseph, Timothy James. cum laude, Pontifical Coll. Josephinum, 1959; MA, Loyola U., Chgo., 1964, PhD, 1966. Research asst. Psychometric Lab., Loyola U., Chgo., 1960-63, research asso., project dir., 1963-65, acting dir., 1965-66, asso. dir., 1967-69, instr. dept. psychology, 1964-66, asst. prof. measurement program, 1966-69; assoc. prof. Sch. Edn. and Sch. Human Medicine, evaluation coordinator Office Med. Edn., Research and Devel., Mich. State U., 1969-70; dir. div. ednl. measurement and research Assn. Am. Med. Colls., Washington, 1970-87; clin. assoc. prof. psychiatry and behavioral scis. George Washington U. Sch. Medicine and Health Scis., 1973-87; assoc. dean adminstrn. and spl. projects Jefferson Med. Coll. Thomas Jefferson U., Phila., 1987-89, assoc. dean adminstrn. and registrar, 1990—, prof. medicine (edn.) dept. medicine, 1993—. Mem. Am. Ednl. Research Assn., Nat. Council Measurement in Edn., Assn. Am. Med. Coll. Roman Catholic. Contbr. articles to profl. publs. Home: 408 Bickmore Dr Media PA 19086-6909 Office: 1025 Walnut St Philadelphia PA 19107-5083

ERDOES, LUKE STEPHAN, surgeon; b. L.A., Feb. 5, 1958; s. Frank Francis and Herta (Wernicke) E.; m. Vicky Leigh Cooke, June 9, 1989; 1 child, Grant Charles. BS in Chemistry, Stanford U., 1980; MD, Tufts U., 1984. Diplomate Am. Bd. Surgery added qualification in surg. critical care, added qualification in vascular surgery. Resident surgery U. Colo., Denver, 1984-89; fellow vascular surgery Ga. Bapt. Med. Ctr., Atlanta, 1989-90; staff surgeon St. Joseph Hosp., Denver, 1990-93; fellow vascular surgery U. Ariz., Tucson, 1993-95; vascular surgeon Pinehurst (N.C.) Surg. Clinic, 1995—; staff surgeon, clin. asst. prof. surgery Walter Reed Army Med. Ctr., Washington, 1991; clin. asst. prof. surgery Uniformed Svcs. U. of the Health Scis., Bethesda, Md., 1991—. Contbr. chpt. to book and articles to profl. jours. Maj. U.S. Army Med. Corps, 1991. Grantee Am. Heart Assn., 1994-95. Fellow ACS; mem. Periph Vasc Surg. Soc. Office: Pinehurst Surg Clinic PA One Memorial Dr Pinehurst NC 28374

ERENRICH, NORMAN HENRY, cardiologist; b. Toronto, Ont., Can., Aug. 20, 1952; came to U.S., 1978; s. Louis and Fay Erenrich; m. Carol Ungar, July 27, 1975; children: Rebecca, Daniel. SB, MIT, 1972; MD, U. Toronto, 1976. Med. intern St. Michael's Hosp., Toronto, 1976-78; med. resident Tufts-New England Med. Ctr., Boston, 1978-80; clin. cardiology fellow Mt. Sinai Med. Ctr., N.Y.C., 1981-83; clin. cardiology Cardiology Assocs. of Palm Beach, West Palm Beach, Fla., 1983—. Fellow Am. Coll. Cardiology, Royal Coll. Physicians of Can.; mem. Palm Beach County Med. Soc., AMA, Am. Heart Assn. (bd. dirs. Palm Beach County chpt. 1984—). Jewish. Office: 1401 Forum Way West Palm Beach FL 33401-2312

ERENSTEIN, ALAN, emergency room nurse, medical education consultant, aeromedical specialist. Grad., Aliquippa Hosp Sch. Radiology, Pa., 1974; student, Aliquippa Hosp. Sch. Radiology, New Wilmington, Pa., 1974; AA in Gen. Studies, LPN, Beaver County C.C., Monaca, Pa., 1977, AS in Nursing, RN, 1979. RN, Fla., Kans.; registered radiologic technologist. LPN Hamot Med. Ctr., Erie, Pa., 1977-78; team leader Trauma-Neuro ICU and Stepdown Unit Allegheny Gen. Hosp., Pitts., 1979-81, staff nurse Emergency Room, 1981; flight nurse LifeWATCH HCA Wesley Med. Ctr., Wichita, Kans., 1981-91, contigency and float pool, 1991-92, hyperbaric nurse, 1991-92; ER nurse, relief charge nurse, clin. coord., team leader JFK Med. Ctr., Atlantis, Fla., 1992-95; aeromed. specialist Bizjet Air Ambulance, West Palm Beach, Fla., 1994-95; med. edn. cons. Med. Edn. Cons. Am., Tampa, 1994—; with disaster team Cutler Ridge (Fla.) Field Hosp., 1992; response team Kans. Tornado Wesley Med. Ctr., Wichita, 1991; emergency rm./trauma nurse DelRay Cmty. Hosp., 1995—; paramedic clin. coord. Hutchinson (Kans.) C.C., 1989; skills lab coord. Advanced Trauma Life Support Course, HCA Wesley Med. Ctr., Wichita, 1989-92; lectr. various med. ctrs., univs. and confs. Author: Trauma in Pregnancy, 1990; co-author: LifeWATCH Transport Manual, 1988; author (Soc. Trauma Nursing course) Trauma Nursing: From Resuscitation through Rehabilitation, Module: The Pregnant Trauma Patient, 1996. Mem. Soc. Trauma Nurses, Nat. Flight Nurses Assn. Home: 308 Island Shores Dr West Palm Beach FL 33413-2105 Office: Delray Cmty Hosp 5352 Linton Blvd Delray Beach FL 33484

ERESHEFSKY, LARRY, psychopharmacologist, educator, consultant; b. Bklyn., Mar. 10, 1952; s. Sam and Claire (Geller) E.; m. Elke S. Weisburd, Sept. 1, 1974; children—Benjamin Jacob, Sabrina Hope. Pharm.D., U. So. Calif. 1976. Cert. psychiat. pharm. practice, Calif. Research asst. UCLA, 1970-73; clin. instr. U. So. Calif., 1976-77; asst. prof. U. Tex.-Austin, 1977-82, assoc. prof., 1982-88, Regents chair in psychopharmacology, 1985—, prof. pharmacology and psychiatry, Health Sci. Ctr., San Antonio, 1982—, program dir., 1983—, prof. clin. pharmacology, 1988—, chmn. postdoctoral tng., 1990—; cons. in field; adv. com. Sandoz, Inc., 1988-94, SmithKline Beecham, 1990-95, Janssen Pharmaceutica Inc., 1995—, Wyeth-Ayerst Labs., 1995—, others; mem. adv. com. on psychopharmacologic drugs FDA, 1992—; coord. clin. rsch. unit San Antonio State Hosp., 1992—. Editor Psychopharmacy Newsletter, 1990-94, Conf. Psychiat. and Neurologic Pharmacists Newsletter; section editor Psychopharmacology, Applied Therpeutics; mem. editorial bd. Am. Jour. Hosp. Pharmacy, 1988—, Drug Therapy Perspectives, 1990—, Primary Psychiatry, 1994—; contbr. articles to profl. jours. Mem. neurology and psychiatry panel U.S. Pharmacopieial Conv., 1985—; chmn. Conf. Psychiat. and Neurologic Pharmacists. Recipient award Wilford Hall USAF Med. Ctr. Fellow Am. Coll. Clin. Pharmacy (chmn. clin. practice affairs 1987-88, bd. regents 1989-94), Internat. Platform Assn.; mem. Am. Soc. Hosp. Pharmacists (SIG officer 1980-82, mem. council edn. affairs 1982-83, chmn. psychopharmacology 1982), AAAS, Am. Assn. Colls. of Pharm., N.Y. Acad. Sci., Phi Kappa Phi, Rho Chi. Avocations: sailing; snorkeling; hiking; reading. Office: U Tex Health Sci Ctr 7703 Floyd Curl Dr San Antonio TX 78284-6200

ERGIN, M.T., physician and surgeon; b. Istanbul, Turkey, Feb. 22, 1927; came to U.S., 1954; s. Sabri and Hacer (Daryal) E.; m. Flornece M. Roman; children: Meliha Ellen, Tahsin Mark, Tarik John, Turhan Michael (dec.). MD, U. Istanbul, 1950. Diplomate Am. Bd. Surgery; cert. in laser surgery, laparoscopic surgery, advanced laparoscopic surgery. Rotating intern J.J. McCook Meml. Hosp., Hartford, Conn., 1955-56, asst. resident in surgery, chief resident, 1956-57; resident in surgery Hartford Hosp., 1957-61; pvt. practice surgery Hartford; active staff dept. surgery Hartford Hosp., 1961—, sr. attending surgeon, 1976—; active attending surgeon U. Conn. Sch. Medicine, 1969—, clin. assoc., 1970-82, asst. clin. prof. surgery, 1982-89, assoc. clin. prof., 1989-92, clin. prof. surgery, 1992—. Recipient Presdl. Sports award, 1973; rsch. grantee Hartford Hosp., 1959, 59-65, U. Conn. Sch. Medicine/NSABP, 1985—, U.S. Dept. Health and Human Svcs./Nat. Cancer Inst., 1986, Yale U. Sch. Medicine/Nat. Cancer Inst., 1986, Hartford Hosp., 1990, 85-92. Fellow ACS (state chmn. commn. on cancer, cancer liaison program 1991—, com. on cancer Conn. chpt. 1991—, exec. com. 1991—, Recognition of Svc. award 1991), Royal Med. Soc. London (sec. on oncology); mem. Conn. Soc. Am. Bd. Surgeons, Conn. Med. Soc. (chmn. cancer coord. com. 1986-89), Hartford County Med. Assn., Hartford Med. Soc., New Eng. Cancer Soc., Pan Am. Med. Assn., Am. Cancer Soc. (bd. dirs. Hartford chpt. 1974-82, chmn. svc. com. 1977-80, mem. med. affairs com. 1988—, bd. dirs. Conn. divsn. 1986—, v.p. bd. dirs. 1989—, exec. com. 1986—, v.p. Conn. divsn. 1989-91, chmn. exec. com. 1991—, pres. Conn. divsn. 1991—, Conn. Divsn. Svc. award 1988, 90, Cert. of Merit, 1988, Leadership medal 1993, St. George Nat. Medal 1993), Internat. Soc. Lymphology, Conn. Oncology Assn., N.Y. Acad. Scis., Am. Radium Soc., Am. Soc. Clin. Oncology, Gastro Intestinal Tumor Study Group, Ea. Coop. Oncology Group. Office: 85 Seymour St # 511 Hartford CT 06106 also: 30 W Avon Rd Avon CT 06001

ERICH, LOUIS RICHARD, physician; b. Shanghai, China, Nov. 7, 1928; (parents Am. citizens); s. Otis G. and Julia A. (Cunningham) E.; m. Lillian Annie McFeters, June 7, 1951; children: Jonathan, Kevin, Timothy, Janine. MD, Loma Linda U., 1955. Diplomate Am. Bd. Ob-Gyn. Physician Sonora (Calif.) Med. Group, Inc., 1977—. Capt. U.S. Army, 1956-58. Fellow Am. Coll. Ob-Gyn. Office: Sonora Med Group Inc 4 S Forest Rd Sonora CA 95370

ERICKSON, CARLTON KUEHL, pharmacologist; b. Manistee, Mich., Apr. 6, 1939; s. Oscar Rudolph and Eleanor Lillian (Kuehl) E.; m. Eunice Mary Walloch, Aug. 14, 1965; children: Steig, Dirk, Annika, Hans-Peter. BS in Pharmacy, Ferris State Coll., Big Rapids, Mich., 1961; MS in Pharmacy, Purdue U., 1963, PhD in Pharmacy, 1965. Asst. prof. U. Kans., Lawrence, 1965-69, assoc. prof., 1969-74, prof., 1974-78; prof. U. Tex., Austin, 1978—; vis. rschr. Karolinska Inst., Stockholm, Sweden, 1973-74. AAAS fellow, 1988. Mem. Tex. Rsch. Soc. Alcoholism (pres., exec. dir. 1980-90), Nat. Rsch. Soc. Alcoholism (Disting. Svc. award 1991), Toastmasters Internat. (pres. 1992-94). Office: U Tex Coll of Pharmacy Austin TX 78712

ERICKSON, CAROL ANN, psychotherapist; b. Worcester, Mass., Dec. 26, 1933; d. Milton Hyland and Helen (Hutton) E.; m. Jean LaRue Barnes, Mar. 20, 1952 (div. Sept. 1962); children: Stephanie Free, Suzanne Hackett, Paul, Sandra Smith, Larry, Cynthia Baker. BS, Ariz. State U., 1964; MSW, Calif. State U., Fresno, 1977. Social worker Los Angeles County, 1964-83; pvt. practice psychotherapy Berkeley, Calif., 1977—; exec. dir. Erickson Inst., Berkeley, 1981—; adj. faculty U. Calif., Berkeley; adj. faculty Vermont Coll. San Francisco, 1986—. Co-writer, composer Deep Self Appreciation, 1983, Self-Hypnosis, A Relaxing Time Out, 1984, Natural Self Confidence, 1985, Deep Sleep and Sweet Dreams, 1989, Rapid Pain Control, 1989, Easy Enhanced Learning, 1989, Quick Stress Busters, 1990. Bd. dirs. YWCA, Torrance, Calif., 1981-83. Mem. Internat. Soc. Hypnosis, No. Calif. Soc. Clin. Hypnosis, So. Calif. Soc. Clin. Hypnosis, Calif. Assn. Marriage and Family Therapists (cert.), Soc. Clin. and Exptl. Hypnosis, Soc. Clin. Social Workers, Nat. Assn. Social Workers (cert.), AAUW, NOW, Phi Kappa Phi. Democrat. Office: Erickson Inst PO Box 739 Berkeley CA 94701-0739

ERICKSON, DONALD LESLIE, neurological surgery educator; b. St. Paul, Sept. 8, 1935; s. Gustaf Adolph and Elizabeth (Orlando) E.; m. Elaine Ann Kraakevik, May 25, 1958; children: Kristen, Steven, Brad, Tom. BS, U. Minn., 1958, MD, 1962. Diplomate Am. Bd. Neurosurgery. Pvt. practice, St. Paul, 1969-73, Mpls., 1973—; prof. neurol. surgery U. Minn., Mpls., 1973—; mem. editl. adv. com. Jour. Spine, 1980-86. Editor: Revascularization for the Ischemic Brain, 1988; contbr. over 50 articles to med. jours., chpts. to books. With USNR, 1952-60. Mem. Am. Assn. Neurol. Surgeons, Congress Neurol. Surgeons, Minn. Neurosurg. Soc. (pres. 1969), L.Am. Neurosurg. Soc. (hon.), Neurosurg. Soc. Argentina (hon.). Office: Univ Neurosurg Assocs 420 SE Delaware St SE Minneapolis MN 55455

ERICKSON, EDWARD LEONARD, biotechnology company executive; b. Chgo., Dec. 7, 1946; s. Leonard Gerald and Eleanore Antoinette (Picek) E.; m. Helen Leonora Masten, Dec. 29, 1979. BS in Math. and Physics, Ill. Inst. Tech., 1968, MS in Math., 1970; MBA in Gen. Mgmt., Harvard U., 1980. Mktg. rep. IBM, Miami, Fla., 1975-76; sr. systems engr. Advanced Tech., Inc., McLean, Va., 1976-78; cons. Bain & Co., Boston, 1979-80; sr. assoc. Resource Planning Assocs., Washington, 1980-82; dir. RPA Mgmt. Cons., London, 1982-83; dir. corp. devel. Amersham Internat. plc., Little Chalfont, Eng., 1983-86, gen. mgr. internat. ops., 1986-88; v.p. fin. ops. The Ares-Serono Group, Boston, 1988-90; pres. Serono-Baker Diagnostics (The Ares-Serono Group), Allentown, Pa., 1990-91; pres., chief exec. officer, dir. Cholestech Corp., Hayward, Calif., 1991-93; pres., CEO, DepoTech Corp., La Jolla, Calif., 1993—, also bd. dirs.; bd. dirs. Megabios Corp., Burlingame, Calif., BIOCOM/San Diego. Contbr. articles to profl. jours. Lt. USN, 1970-75. John L. Loeb fellow Harvard U., 1980, George F. Baker scholar, 1980, NASA fellow, 1968-70. Mem. Sigma Pi Sigma. Republican. Home: 6887 Tohickon Hill Rd Pipersville PA 18947-1415

ERICKSON, JAMES HUSTON, clergyman, physician; b. Omaha, Sept. 7, 1931; s. Paul Ferdinand and Naomi Marie (Berglund) E.; m. Shirley Arlene Nordling, Dec. 26, 1959; children: Jonathan, Sonja, Ingrid. AA, North Park Coll., 1950; AB, Stanford U., 1952; MD, U. Colo., 1959; MPH, U. Minn., 1975; MS, Loyola Coll., Balt., 1982. Ordained to ministry Evang. Covenant Ch., 1985; Diplomate Am. Bd. Preventive Medicine, Am. Bd. Med. Psycho Therapy. Intern Swedish Covenant Hosp., Chgo., 1959-60; resident in surgery VA Hosp., Hines, Ill., 1963; resident in gen. practice Swedish Covenant Hosp., Chgo., 1964-65; asst. minister Bethel Covenant Ch., Orange, Calif., 1960-61; commd. USN, 1960-63, 69-70, advanced through grades to commdr.; med. missionary Christian Med. Coll., Ludhiana, India, 1965; supply pastor Covenant and Presbyn. Chs., various locations, 1965-81; commd. USPHS, 1970—, advanced through grades to asst. surgeon gen., 1976, ret., 1993; chaplain Boy Scouts Am., Laurel, Md., 1977-81; dir. health svcs., prof. community health No. Ill. U., DeKalb, Ill., 1981-85; assoc. minister Hillcrest Covenant Ch., DeKalb, 1982-85; interim minister Community Covenant Ch., Springfield, Va., 1988-89, Bethany Covenant Ch., Bedford, N.H., 1993; dir. health svcs. and pastoral care Atlantic Fleet NOAA, Norfolk, Va., 1986-88; dir. health svcs. and pastoral care hdqrs. NOAA, Rockville, Md., 1988-93; dir. Memphis Space Ctr., 1995—; bd. dirs. The Holmstad, Batavia, Ill.; mem. commn. Christian action Evang. Covenant Ch., Chgo., 1984-90, ministerial ethics com., 1990-93; prof. family practice Uniformed Svcs. U., 1988-93; prof. pastoral care Memphis Theol. Sem., 1995—. Fellow Am. Coll. Preventive Medicine, Royal Soc. Health, Am. Acad. Family Physicians; mem. ACA, Aerospace Med. Soc., Memphis Ministerial Assn., Commd. Officers Assn. USPHS, Civil Air Patrol. Office: Memphis Space Ctr Atmospheric Adminstrn 650 E Parkway S Memphis TN 38104

ERICKSON, LEA ELLA, dental educator; b. Pocatello, Idaho, Aug. 28, 1947; d. Jerry C. and Deloris L. (Sayler) Sims; m. Richard D. Webb; children: Nicholas Richard, Janet Miesel, Amy Webb Riffe; m. John Robert Erickson, Mar. 26, 1983. AS, Idaho State U., 1969, BS, 1973; DDS, U. Md., Balt., 1978; MSPH, U. Utah, 1992. Cert. gen. practice residency 1979, fellow in geriatric dentistry 1991. Pvt. practice dental hygiene Pocatello, 1969-75; pvt. practice dentistry Sandy, Utah, 1979-89; clin. instr. U. Utah, Salt Lake City, 1982—; staff dentist and dir. geriatric dental edn. VA Med. Ctr., Salt Lake City, 1991—; adj. prof. Weber State Coll., Ogden, Utah, 1979-82; bd. dirs. Bethany Coll., Lindsborg, Kans.; cons. Wasatch Canyon Eating Disorders, Salt Lake City, 1985-89; mem. Utah State Bd. Dentists and Dental Hygienists, 1994—; speaker in field. Contbr. articles to profl. jours. Cons., Denture Access Program, Salt Lake City, 1980-89; mem. adv. com. Health Screening Ctr., Salt Lake City, 1981-86. Mem. ADA, Utah Dental Assn. (ho. of dels. 1988-91), Am. Soc. Geriatric Dentists (bd. dirs. 1992—, sec.-treas. 1993-94, v.p. 1994-95, pres. 1995—), Salt Lake Dist. Dental Soc. (bd. dirs. 1988-90). Lutheran. Home: 7165 S 2780 E Salt Lake City UT 84121-4152 Office: VA Med Ctr Dental Svc (160) Salt Lake City UT 84148

ERICKSON, ROLLAND PHILIP, physician; b. Fargo, N.D., Mar. 17, 1948; s. Oswald Philip and Jean Marie (Pitsenbarger) E.; m. Judy Wai Ching, Sept. 15, 1949; children: Steven, Lynn. BA, Concordia Coll., Moorhead, Minn., 1970; MD, U. Minn., 1974; postgrad., Mayo Grad. Sch. Medicine, 1980. Diplomate Nat. Bd. Med. Examiners, Am. Bd. Phys. Medicine and Rehab. Intern Hennepin County Med. Ctr., Mpls., 1974-75; resident in phys. medical and rehab. Mayo Grad. Sch. Medicine; pvt. practice Maui, Hawaii, 1975-77; instr. Mayo Med. Sch., Mayo Grad. Sch. Medicine, Rochester, Minn., 1981, asst. prof., 1981—; cons., staff physician Mayo Clinic, Rochester, 1981-88, Scottsdale, Ariz., 1988—; bd. examiner Am. Bd. Phys. Medicine and Rehab., 1987, 90, 93, 96. Recipient award Am. Congress Rehab. Medicine, 1979; named Tchr. of Yr., Mayo Fellows Assn., 1983, 85. Fellow Internat. Rehab. Medicine Assn., Am. Acad. Physical Medicine and Rehab.; mem. Minn. Physiatric Soc. (sec.-treas. 1981-83). Office: Mayo Clinic 13400 E Shea Blvd Scottsdale AZ 85259

ERICKSON-WEERTS, SALLY ANNETTE, dietetics educator; b. Phoenix, Oct. 18, 1952; d. Dennis Lee and Ann Marie (Conklin) E.; children: Matthew, Alexander, Kyle. BS, Mankato State U., 1973; MS, Kans. U., 1976. Registered dietitian, Minn. Clin. dietitian Saga Food Svc., Pitts., 1975-76; pub. health nutritionist Minn. Dept. of Health, Mpls., 1976-77; prof. Lakewood (Minn.) C.C., 1977-79; fed. nutritionist Indian Health Svcs./Pub. Health Svc., Anchorage, 1979-85; pvt. practice Mankato, Minn., 1986-89; pres. Dietary Care Systems, Inc., Mankato, Minn., 1989-92; asst. prof. Mankato State U., 1992—; cons. in field. Author: One Menu System, Nutritional Care System, Lite Weight, Diet Care Seminars, 1989-92. Mem. PEO, Am. Dietetic Assn. Office: Mankato State U Box 44/ PO Box 8400 Mankato MN 56002-0044

ERICSON, RUTH ANN, psychiatrist; b. Assaria, Kans., May 15; d. William Albert and Anna Mathilda (Almquist) E. Student, So. Meth. U., 1945-47; BS, Bethany Coll.; MD, U. Tex., 1951. Intern, Calif. Hosp., L.A., 1951-52; resident in psychiatry U. Tex. Med. Br., Galveston, 1952-55; psychiatrist Child Guidance Clinic, Dallas, 1955-63; clin. instr. Southwestern Med. Sch., Dallas, 1955-72; practice medicine specializing in psychiatry, Dallas, 1955—; cons. Dallas Intertribal Coun. Clinic, 1974-81, Dallas Ind. Sch. Dist., U.S. Army, Welfare Dept., Tribal Concerns, Alcoholism, Adv. Bd. Intertribal Coun. Fellow Am. Geriatrics Assn., Royal Soc. Medicine; mem. So. Med. Assn. (life), Tex. Med. Assn. (life), Dallas Med. Assns. (life), Am. Psychiat. Assn. (life), Tex. Psychiat. Assn., North Tex. Psychiat. Assn., Am. Med. Women's Assn., Dallas Area Women Psychiatrists, Alumni Assn. U. Tex. (Med. Br.), Navy League (life), Air Force Assn., Tex. Archaeol. Soc. (life mem.), Dallas Archaeol. Soc. (hon. life mem., pres. 1972-73, 82-84, 89-91, archival rschr.), South Tex. Archaeol. Soc., Tarrant County Archeol. Soc., El Paso Archeol. Soc., N.Mex. Archaeol. Soc., Paleopathology Soc., Internat. Psychogeriatric Assn. (Famous Women of the 20th Century), Alpha Omega Alpha, Delta Psi Omega, Alpha Psi Omega, Pi Gamma Mu, Lambda Sigma, Alpha Epsilon Iota, Mu Delta. Lutheran. Home: 4007 Shady Hill Dr Dallas TX 75229-2844 Office: 3026 Mockingbird Ln # 101 Dallas TX 75205-2323

ERIKSEN, MICHAEL, medical educator. ScD, Johns Hopkins U. Dir. preventive medicine and health edn. Pacific Bell, 1982-86; asst. prof. cancer prevention, dir. behavioral rsch. U. Tex. M.D. Anderson Cancer Ctr.; dir. office on smoking and health Nat. Ctr. Chronic Disease Prevention and Health Promotion, Atlanta. Bd. dirs. Ams. for Nonsmokers Rights. Mem. APHA, Soc. Pub. Health Edn. (nat. pres. 1988), Am. Cancer Soc. Office: Ctr Disease Control Prev Office Smoking and Health 4770 Buford Hwy NE Atlanta GA 30341-3724*

ERIKSON, CARL ANDERS, neurologist; b. Malmö, Skåne, Sweden, Apr. 16, 1944; s. Sten and Elsa (Svensson) E.; m. Ingegerd Malmer, Apr. 3, 1966

(div. 1981); children: Tobias, Anna, Ingemar. MD, U. Umeå, Sweden, 1970; PhD, U. Göteborg, 1986; docent, U. Umeå, 1992. Cert. physician; specialist in pediats. and child neurology. Chief physician dept. pediats. Boden (Sweden) Hosp., 1976-95; chief physician child neurology U. Hosp. No. Sweden, Umeå, 1995—. Contbr. sci. papers to profl. jours. Home: Skolgatan 119B, 90332 Umea Sweden Office: U Hosp No Sweden, Dept Pediats, Umea Sweden

ERIKSON, DAVID JUNKIN, JR., internist; b. Pitts., Mar. 15, 1935; s. David Junkin and Grace Erikson; m. Lois Anne Fowler, June 3, 1959; children: Susan, David (dec.), Kevin. BS, Denison U., 1955; MD, U. Pitts., 1959. Diplomate Am. Bd. Internal Medicine; lic. physician, Pa. Intern U. Pitts. Health Ctr., 1959-60; resident VA Hosp., San Francisco, 1960-62, U. Calif Hosp., San Francisco, 1962-63; pvt. practice Leisure World Med. Ctr., Laguna Hills, Calif., 1965-80; pvt. practice Laguna Hills, Calif., 1980-92, ret., 1992; mem. med. staff South Coast Med. Ctr., Laguna Beach, 1966-72, Mission Cmty. Hosp., Mission Viejo, Calif., 1972-90, Saddleback Meml. Med. Ctr. Hosp., Laguna Hills, Calif., 1972-96. Capt. M.C., U.S. Army, 1963-65. Mem. AMA, Calif. Med. Assn., Orange County Med. Assn. Home: 23871 Stillwater Ln Laguna Niguel CA 92677

ERIKSSON, ELOF, plastic surgeon; b. Backe, Sweden, June 8, 1943. MD, U. Goteborg, Sweden, 1969. Diplomate Am. Bd. Plastic Surgery. Intern U. Goteborg (Sweden) Hosp.-Vastervik Coll., 1972-73; resident in surgery Chgo. Affiliated Hosps., 1973-77; fellow in plastic surgery Med. Coll. Va., Va., 1977-79; active staff Meml. Med. Ctr., Springfield, Ill., 1982-86, Childrens Hosp., Springfield, Ill., 1986—, St. John's Hosp., Springfield, Ill., 1982-86; chief plastic surgery Brigham Women's and Children's Hosp., Boston, 1990—; prof. plastic surgery Harvard Med. Sch., Cambridge, Mass., 1990—; cons. surgery W. Roxbury (Mass.) VA Hosp., 1990—; courtesy staff Newton (Mass.)-Wellesley Hosp., 1990—. Mem. ACS. Office: Brigham Womens Hospital 75 Francis St Boston MA 02115

ERIKSSON, NILS ERIK, allergist; b. Bengtsfors, Dalsland, Sweden, Mar. 25, 1934; s. Gustaf and Signe Frideborg (Bryntesson) E.; m. Inger Egermark, July 6, 1958 (div. 1976); children: Anna, Tomas, Katarina, Per; m. Agneta Svennberg, Jan. 20, 1988. BMedicine, U. Lund, Sweden, 1965; MD, U. Göteborg, Sweden, 1977. Asst. physician Hosp. Karlstad (Sweden), 1965-66, Hosp. Halmstad (Sweden), 1966-70, Sahlgren's Hosp., Göteborg, 1971-73; chief physician Allergy Clinic, Dept. Medicine, Halmstad, 1974—; asst. prof. U. Göteborg, 1985. Author: Questions and Answers on Asthma, 1985, Asthma-Evaluation and Therapy, 1986, Asthma and Allergy in Practice, 1990; editor: Allergy and Other Kinds of Hyper-Sensitivity in Clinical Practice, 1992, Treacherous Meals-On Hypersensitivity Against Food and Drink, 1996; contbr. articles to profl. publs. Mem. Swedish Assn. for Allergy Rsch., Nordic Aerobiol. Assn., Internat. Solidarity Group. Mem. Swedish Assn. for Allergy Rsch., Nordic Aerobiol. Assn., European Acad. Allergology and Clin. Immunology, Internat. Solidarity Group, Amnesty Internat. Home: Gaggegatan 17 b, S-30237 Halmstad Sweden

ERIKSSON, SVEN-ERIK, neurologist; b. Stockholm, Dec. 22, 1949; s. Arne Erik and Kerstin Linnea (Jönsson) E.; m. Kristina Marianne Zackrisson, June 17, 1972; children: Emma, Jakob, Susanna. Degree in medicine, Karolinska Inst., Stockholm, 1971, MD, 1977; postgrad., Univ. Hosp., Linköping, Sweden, 1981. Intern Gävle (Sweden) Hosp., 1975-77; med. specialist tng. in neurology Univ. Hosp., Linköping, 1977-81, asst. physician dept. neurology, 1981-83, ward physician dept. neurology, 1983-84; chief doctor divsn. neurology dept. medicine Falu Hosp., Falun, Sweden, 1984-92, 1993—; chief doctor divsn. neurology dept. medicine Mälar-Hosp., Sweden, 1992. Contbr. articles to profl. publs. Mem. Swedish Soc. Medicine, Swedish Neurology Soc. Office: Falu Hosp, 791 82 Falun Sweden

ERK, FRANK CHRIS, biologist, educator; b. Evansville, Ind., Dec. 17, 1924; s. Carl Benjamin and Matilda (Schumacher) E.; A.B. magna cum laude, U. Evansville, 1948; Ph.D. in genetics, Johns Hopkins U., 1952; m. Ruth Parker Hobgood, June 12, 1948; children: Susan Patricia Erk Tierney, Elisabeth Carlene Erk Smith, Stephanie Diane Erk Lutostanski. Jr. instr. Johns Hopkins U., Balt., 1948-51, Adam T. Bruce fellow, 1951-52, Lalor faculty fellow, 1956; assoc. prof. biology, chmn. dept. Washington Coll., Chestertown, Md., 1952-57, dir. coll. choir, 1952-57; prof. biology SUNY, L.I. Center, Oyster Bay, 1957-61, chmn. div. sci. and math., 1958-59, chmn. dept. biology, 1958-61, dir. univ. choir, 1957-61; prof. biol. scis. SUNY, Stony Brook, 1962-81, prof. biochemistry and cell biology, 1981-90, prof. emeritus, 1990—, chmn. dept. biology, 1962-67, 76-78; vis. assoc. prof. biology, Carnegie intern in gen. edn. U. Chgo., 1954-55; research collaborator Masonic Med. Research Lab., Utica, N.Y., 1968-71; vis. investigator Poultry Research Centre, Agrl. Research Council, U. Edinburgh (Scotland), 1964-65, Genetics Inst., U. Milan (Italy), 1965, U. Sussex (Eng.), 1971-72, 85-86, Galton Lab. U. Coll. London, Eng., 1978-79, U. Edinburgh, 1979-80; vis. prof. U. Essex (Eng.), 1978-79; asst. examiner Internat. Baccalaureate Program, Geneva, 1977-82, cons., 1976-84; cons., writer Biol. Scis. Curriculum Study, Boulder, Colo., 1960-70, 85-90; chair Emeritus Faculty Assn. SUNY Stony Brook, 1990—, acting master honors coll., 1991-92; dir. Madrigal Singers, Stony Brook, 1963-71; mem. examining com. Advanced Placement Biology Coll. Entrance Exam. Bd., 1967-71, chmn., 1973-77. Served to 1st lt. USAAF, 1943-46, PTO. Mem. AAAS, AAUP, Am. Genetics Assn. (council 1978-81), Genetics Soc. Am., Soc. Genetics Can., Nat. Assn. Biology Tchrs., Am. Soc. Zoologists, Soc. for Study Evolution, Human Biology Council, SUNY Emeritus Faculty Assn. (chmn. 1990—), Sigma Xi, Phi Beta Chi, Omicron Delta Kappa. Author: (with others) Biological Science: Molecules to Man, 1963, 68; (with others) Biological Sciences: Interaction of Experiments and Ideas, 1965, 70, Biological Science: An Ecological Approach, 1987; editor: (with others) Evolution, Mammals and Southern Continents, 1972; exec. editor Quar. Rev. Biology, 1966-69; editor, 1969—; mem. editorial bd. Jour. Biol. Edn., London, 1976-90. Home: 33 Yorktown Rd Setauket NY 11733-1215 Office: SUNY Dept Biochemistry & Cell Biology Stony Brook NY 11794-5215

ERKELENS, DIRK WILLEM, medical educator; b. Rotterdam, The Netherlands, Oct. 11, 1941; s. Adriaan Dirk Erkelens and Ada Helena (De Byll) Nachenius; m. Eleonora S.C. Buttinger, Nov. 20, 1965; children: Gezina Wilhelmina, Charles Theodoor. MD, U. Leiden, The Netherlands, 1967. Intern, 1973; asst. St. Elizabeth Hosp., Curaçao, Netherlands Antilles, 1968-70; jr. fellow U. Hosp., Groningen, The Netherlands, 1970-75; sr. fellow U. Wash., Seattle, 1976-78; fellow U. Utrecht, The Netherlands, 1978-82, prof. medicine, 1982—, chmn. dept. medicine, 1986—; chamberlain to Queen of The Netherlands, 1994—. Author: Diagnosis in Internal Medicine, 1985; contbr. articles on lipid metabolism and diabetes to profl. jours. Pres. Provincial Utrecht Soc. for Arts and Scis., 1988-1990. 1st Fellowship of Postgrad. Medicine lecture, London, 1988. Mem. European Soc. Clin. Investigation (pres. 1985, hon. treas. 1981-84), European Assn. for Study of Diabetes (mem. coun. 1989-92), Dutch Soc. Scis., Haarlem. Liberal. Home: Wilhelminapark 29A, 3581 NG Utrecht The Netherlands

ERLEN, JUDITH ANN, nursing educator; b. Pitts., Dec. 6, 1943; d. William Andrew and Ruth Lucille (Lang) Fincke; m. Jonathon Erlen, Nov. 24, 1978. Student, Thiel Coll., 1961-63; BSN, U. Pitts., 1965; MSN, Wayne State U., 1967; PhD, Tex. Woman's U., 1979. Staff nurse Western Pa. Hosp., Pitts., 1965-66, 68; nurse trainee, 1966-67, 77-78; instr. Sch. Nursing, Duquesne U., Pitts., 1968-70; asst. prof. Sch. Nursing, Duquesne U., 1970-76; assoc. prof. Coll. Nursing Tex. Woman's U., Dallas, 1980-83; asst. prof. U. Pitts. Sch. Nursing, 1983-94, assoc. prof., 1994—, asst. prof. Sch. Health Related Professions, 1985-91, assoc. Ctr. for Med. Ethics, 1989—; assoc. dir. Ctr. Rsch. Chronic Disorders Sch. Nursing U. Pitts., 1994—. Co-author: Nursing Diagnosis, Nursing Process, Nursing Knowledge: Avenues to Autonomy, 1986. Contbr. articles to profl. jours. Choir dir. St. Paul Luth. Ch., Farmers Branch, Tex., 1977-83, Emmanuel Luth. Ch., Etna, Pa., 1990—. NEH fellow, 1981, 88-89; rsch. grantee U. Pitts., 1987-88, rsch. grantee Nat. Inst. Nursing Rsch., 1992-96. Mem. Am. Nurses Assn., Nat. League Nursing (chair-elect PLN area 6 1991-93, chair PLN area 6 1994-95), Assn. Care Children's Health (chmn. bylaws com., 1987—), Assn. Nurses in AIDS Care, Hastings Ctr., Soc. Health and Human Values (sec.-treas 1987-89, nursing and humanities sect., chair-elect 1991-93, chair 1994-95), Park Ridge Ctr., U. Pitts. Sch. Nursing Alumni Assn. (1st v.p. 1989-90, pres. 1990-91), Sigma Theta Tau (pres. Eta chpt. 1987-88, rsch. award Eta chpt. 1991-92, chmn. bylaws com. 1992-93, grad. counselor 1994-95, Leadership award in nursing rsch. 1994), PNA (nominating com. dist. 6 1995-96), Alpha Gamma Delta. Home: 123 Northview Dr Pittsburgh PA 15209-1021 Office: U Pitts 440 Victoria Bldg Pittsburgh PA 15261-2404

ERLENMEYER-KIMLING, L., psychiatric and behavior genetics researcher, educator; b. Princeton, N.J.; d. Floyd M. and Dorothy F. (Dirst) Erlenmeyer; m. Carl F. E. Kimling. B.S. magna cum laude, Columbia U., 1957, Ph.D., 1961. Sr. research scientist N.Y. State Psychiat. Inst., N.Y.C., 1960-69; assoc. research scientist N.Y. State Psychiat. Inst., 1969-75, prin. research scientist, 1975-78, dir. div. devel. behavioral studies, 1978—, acting chief med. genetics, 1991—; asst. in psychiatry Columbia U., 1962-66, rsch. assoc., 1966-70, asst. prof., 1970-74, assoc. prof. psychiatry and genetics, 1974-78, prof., 1978—; vis. prof. psychology New Sch. Social Research, 1971—; mem. peer rev. group NIH, 1976-80; mem. work group on guidance and counseling Congl. Commn. on Huntington's Disease, 1976-77; mem. task force on intervention Pres.'s Commn. on Mental Health, 1977-78; mem. initial rev. group NIMH, 1981-85; mem. adv. bd. Croatian Inst. Brain Rsch., 1991-93. Editor: Life-Span Research in Psychopathology, 1986; issue editor: Differential Reproduction, Social Biology, 1971, Genetics and Mental Disorders, Internat. Jour. Mental Health, 1972, Genetics and Gene Expression in Mental Illness, Jour. Psychiat. Rsch., 1992, Measuring Liability to Schizophrenia: Progress Report 1994, Schizophrenia Bull., 1994; mem. editorial bd. Social Biology, 1970-79, Schizophrenia Bull., 1978—, Jour. Preventive Psychiatry, 1980-84, Croatian Med. Jour., 1991—, Neurology/Psychiatry/Brain Research, 1991—, Neuropsychiat. Genetics, Am. Jour. Med. Genetics, 1992—. Recipient Merit award NIMH, 1989-96, William K. Warren Schizophrenia Rsch. award Internat. Congress on Schizophrenia Rsch., 1995; grantee NIMH, 1966-69, 71-96, Scottish Rite Com. on Schizophrenia, 1970-74, 84-87, 89-94, W.T. Grand Found., 1978-86, MacArthur Found., 1981, Stanley Found., 1995-96, NARSAD, 1996-97. Fellow APA, Am. Psychopath. Assn., Am. Psychol. Soc.; mem. AAAS, Am. Soc. Human Genetics, Behavior Genetics Assn. (mem.-at-large 1972-74, Theodosius Dobzhansky award 1985), Internat. Soc. Psychiat. Genetics, Soc. Study Social Biology (bd. dirs. 1969-84, 92-95, sec. 1972-75, pres. 1975-78), Scientists Ctr. for Animal Welfare, Phi Beta Kappa, Sigma Xi.

ERLICH, PHILIP, psychiatrist; b. N.Y.C., Feb. 24, 1924; s. Nathan and Rose (Klomberg) E.; m. Gloria Chasson, May 24, 1953; children: Julia L., Austin R. AB, Princeton U., 1944; MD, NYU, 1947. Diplomate, Am. Bd. Psychiatry and Neurology. Intern Bellevue Hosp., N.Y.C., 1947-48; resident U. Mich., Ann Arbor, 1948-51; instr. in psychiatry, Coll. Medicine U. Mich., 1951-53; pvt. practice psychiatry Princeton, N.J., 1955—; attending physician Med. Ctr. Princeton, N.J., 1957-75; chief, dept. psychiatry Med. Ctr. Princeton, 1975-80, sr. attending psychiatrist, 1975—; psychiat. cons. N.J. Div. Med. Assistance and Health Svcs., Trenton, 1983-86; chief psychiat. cons. N.J. Div. Med. Assistance and Health Svcs., 1987—; electroencephalographer, Med. Ctr. Princeton, 1957—; cons. in psychiatry, Trenton State Coll., 1956-71; preceptor in psychiatry, N.J. Neuropsychiat. Inst., Skillman, 1959-70. Bd. dirs., YMCA, Princeton, 1975-85. Capt. U.S. Army, 1953-55. Mem. Am. Psychiat. Assn., N.J. Psychiat. Assn. (sec. 1988-91, bd. dirs. 1982-91). Home and Office: 41 Littlebrook Rd Princeton NJ 08540-4038

ERMUTLU, ILHAN MEHMET, psychiatrist; b. Istanbul, Turkey, June 24, 1927; s. Sami and Ihsan Ermutlu; m. Karen Harper, Sept. 9, 1956; children: David S., Gary D. MD, Ankara (Turkey) U., 1952. Diplomate Am. Bd. Psychiatry and Neurology. Intern Knickerbocker Hosp., N.Y.C., 1954-55; resident in psychiatry Bellevue Hosp., N.Y.C., 1955-56, Hillside Hosp., N.Y.C., 1956-58; supt. Ga. Regional Hosp., Savannah, 1970-73; chief outpatient svc. William S. Hall Psychiatric Inst., Columbia, S.C., 1973-78; dir. DeKalb County div. Mental Health, Decatur, Ga., 1978-81; dir. Ga. div. Mental Health, Atlanta, 1981-83, med. dir., 1983-84; cons. Mental Health Hosp., Taif, Saudia Arabia, 1984-86, N. DeKalb Mental Health Ctr., Atlanta, 1986-90; cons. OBRA determination unit Atlanta Div. Mental Health, 1990-91; clin. dir. Ga. Mental Health Inst., Atlanta, 1991-92; cons. Metropolitan Atlanta Found. for Med. Care, 1993—; assoc. prof. U. S.C., Columbia, 1976-78, Emory U. Sch. Medicine, Atlanta, 1978-84. Contbr. articles to profl. publs. Lt., Turkish Army, 1952-54. Fellow AMA, Am. Psychiat. Assn., Ga. Psychiat. Physicians Assn. Moslem.

ERNE, PAUL JOSEPH ERWIN, cardiologist; b. Basel, Switzerland, Mar. 16, 1951; s. Paul and Anna Maria (Breitenmoser) E.; m. Doris Emmenegger, Sept. 12, 1980; 1 child, Susanne. Diploma in Chemistry, U. Basel, 1972; MD, U. Basel, 1978; privatdozent, U. Basel, Basel, 1972. Fellow in cardiology, medicine, hypertension U. Basel, Basel 1981-85; rsch. assoc. Postgrad. Med. Sch., London, 1986; guest prof. U. Nev. Med. Sch., Reno, 1987; rsch. assoc. Chiles Rsch. Found., Portland, Oreg., 1987-88; sr. registrar U. Hosp., Basel, 1988-90; head cardiology divsn. Kantonsspital, Lucerne, Switzerland, 1991—. Contbr. over 50 articles to profl. jours. Mem. Swiss Hypertension League (v.p. 1994-96). Roman Catholic. Home: Neumattstrasse 25, 6048 Horw Switzerland Office: Kantonsspital, Dept Cardiology, 6000 Lucerne Switzerland

ERNEST, J. TERRY, ocular physiologist, educator; b. Sycamore, Ill., June 26, 1935; married, 1965; 2 children. BA, Northwestern U., 1957; MD, U. Chgo., 1961, PhD in Visual Sci., 1967. Prof. ophthalmology U. Wis., 1977-79; prof., chmn. ophthalmology Ind. U., 1980-81; prof. ophthalmology U. Ill., 1981-85; prof., chmn. ophthalmology U. Chgo., 1985—; mem visual sci. A study sect., NIH, 1975-78, chmn. 1978-79, chmn. visual disorders study sect., 1979-80; rsch. prof. Rsch. to Prevent Blindness, Ind., 1981-84; mem. Vision Rsch. Program Com., 1982-84. Founding editor, Key, 1986-88; editor, Year Book of Ophthamology, 1982-88, Investigative Ophthalmology and Visual Sci., 1988-92. Recipient Rsch. Career Devel. award NIH, 1972. Mem. AAAS, Am. Ophthalmol. Soc., Am. Acad. Ophthalmology (Honor award 1982), Assn. Rsch. Vision and Ophthalmology. Office: University of Chicago Visual Sciences Ctr 939 E 57th St Chicago IL 60637-1454

ERNST, CALVIN BRADLEY, vascular surgeon, surgery educator; b. Detroit, May 12, 1934; s. Edward William and Irene Marie (Doelker) E.; m. Elizabeth Abbott, Dec. 21, 1957; children Lisa Anne, Matthew Abbott, David William, Susan Elizabeth. M.D., U. Mich., 1959. Diplomate Am. Bd. Surgery (bd. dirs. 1991—). Intern Ohio State U. Med. Ctr., Columbus, 1959-60; resident U. Mich. Med. Ctr., Ann Arbor, 1960-65; instr. surgery U. Mich., 1968-69, asst. prof., 1969-72, assoc. prof., 1972; assoc. prof. U. Ky., Lexington, 1972-74; prof. U. Ky., 1974-79; prof. surgery Johns Hopkins U., 1979-85, surgeon hosp., 1979-85; chmn. surg. scis. Balt. City Hosps., 1979-85; clin. prof. surgery U. Mich., Ann Arbor, 1985—; prof. surgery Case Western Res. U., Cleve., 1994—; head vascular surgery Henry Ford Hosp., Detroit, 1985—; cons. surgeon Loch Raven VA Hosp., Balt., 1979-85. Assoc. editor Jour. Vascular Surgery, 1986-91, editor, 1991—; mem. editl. bd. Archives of Surgery, 1983-93, Surgery, 1983-93; editor 6 vascular surgery textbooks; contbr. chpts. to books. Dir. Am. Bd. Surgery, 1991—. Served to capt. U.S. Army, 1966-68. Fellow ACS; mem. Soc. Vascular Surgery (sec. 1984-88, pres.-elect 1989-90, pres. 1990-910, Am. Surg. Assn., Internat. Cardiovascular Soc. (recorder 1977-82), So. Assn. Vascular Surgery (sec. treas. 1976-81, pres. 1982-83), Alpha Omega Alpha. Home: 860 Arlington Blvd Ann Arbor MI 48104-2730 Office: Henry Ford Hosp Divsn Vascular Surgery 2799 W Grand Blvd Detroit MI 48202-2608

ERNST, JOHN ALLAN, clinical neuropsychologist; b. Seattle, June 27, 1955; s. Gene Allan and Maxine Joan (Weedon) E. BA magna cum laude, U. Calif., San Diego, 1977; MS, San Diego State U., 1979; PhD, U. Mont., 1983. Diplomate Am. Bd. Clin. Neuropsychology, Am. Bd. Profl. Psychology; lic. psychologist, Calif., Wash., Queensland, Australia. Postdoctoral fellow U. Wash., Seattle, 1983-84; psychologist Western State Hosp., Tacoma, Wash., 1984-85; postdoctoral rsch. fellow Univ. Queensland, Brisbane, Australia, 1985-87; neuropsychologist St. Joseph Med. Ctr., Tacoma, Wash., 1987—; mem. Wash. State Examining Bd. of Psychology, 1995—. Contbr. approximately 20 articles to Behavioral Assessment, Psychology and Aging, others; mem. editorial bd. Rehab. Psychology, 1991—, SCI Psychosocial Process, 1994—. Mem. Am. Psychol. Assn. (cert. of appreciation rehab. divsn. 1991, 93), Am. Acad. of Clin. Neuropsychol., Nat. Register Health Svc. Providers in Psychology, Internat. Neuropsychol. Soc., Nat. Acad. Neuropsychology, Pacific N.W. Neuropsychol. Soc., many others. Office: St Joseph Med Ctr Dept Psychology PO Box 2197 Tacoma WA 98401

EROSS, ERIC JASON, osteopathic physician; b. Pitts., Sept. 9, 1968; s. Bela and Linda Lee (Dreher) E. BS in Neurobiology, Allegheny Coll., 1991; DO, Ohio U. Coll. Osteo. Medicine, 1996. Rsch. asst. dept. medicine U. Pitts., 1991-92; intern Western Pa. Hosp., Pitts., 1996-97. Pa. Osteo. Medicine Assn. scholar, 1995, 96. Mem. Am. Osteo. Assn. Home: 3817 Grove Rd Gibsonia PA 15044

ERRERA, PAUL, psychiatrist; b. Brussels, May 19, 1928; came to U.S. 1939; BS, Harvard Coll., 1949; postgrad., Columbia Med. Sch., 1949-51; MD, Harvard U., 1953; cert., Belgium Med. Cert., 1954. Intern in medicine Yale New Haven Hosp., 1953-54; resident in psychiatry Yale U. Sch. of Medicine, VA Hosp., Yale New Haven Hosp., New Haven, 1954-57, Yale Psychiat. Inst., New Haven, 1956-57; instr. dept. of psychiatry Yale U. Sch. of Medicine, New Haven, 1957-59, asst. prof., 1959-64, assoc. prof., 1964-70, prof., 1970-94, prof. emeritus, 1994—; dir. mental health and behavioral scis. svcs. VA Ctrl. Office, Washington, 1985-94; sr. clinician VA Med. Ctr., West Haven, 1994—; attending psychiatrist Yale New Haven Hosp., 1957—; mem. bd. permanent officers Yale U. Sch. of Medicine, 1970-94; mem. profl. standards bd. VA Med. Ctr., mem. resident rev. bd., mem. adv. com., mem. rsch. and edn. com., 1970-85, chmn., 1972-73, 83-85. Contbr. articles to profl. jours. Fellow Am. Psychiat. Assn. (life, Conn. dist. br.), Am. Coll. Psychoanalysts; mem. AMA, Western New England Psychoanalytic Soc. (chmn. membership com. 1974-85), Western New England Inst. for Psychoanalysis (trustee 1975-81), N.Y. Psychoanalytic Soc. and Inst., Am. Coll. Mental Health Adminstrn., Soc. of Med. Cons. to Armed Forces, Inst. of Medicine (mem. adv. coun. for homeless 1987—). Office: 182 VA Med Ctr 950 Campbell Ave West Haven CT 06516

ERSHLER, WILLIAM BALDWIN, biogerontologist, educator; b. Syracuse, N.Y., Jan. 13, 1949; s. Irving Leonard and Eunice (Baldwin) E.; m. Joan Lipstein, Nov. 6, 1971; children: Rachel Eve, Leah Rose. BA, Case Western Res. U., 1970; MD, SUNY Upstate Ctr., Syracuse, 1974. Diplomate Am. Bd. Internal Medicine, Am. Bd. Med. Oncology, Am. Bd. Hematology. Asst. prof. U. Vt., Burlington, 1980-85; assoc. prof. U. Wis., Madison, 1985-89, prof. medicine, 1989-96, dir. Inst. on Aging, 1989-96, head geriatrics, 1989-96; dir. geriatric rsch. Edn. and Clin. Ctr. William Middleton VA Hosp., Madison, 1991-96; prof. medicine, dir. Glennan Ctr. Geriatrics & gerontolog Eastern Va. Medical Sch., Norfolk, 1996—; editor Jour. of Gerontology, 1996—. Editor Jour. Gerontology; contbr. articles to profl. jours. Recipient Geriatric Leadership award NIH, 1990—; NIH grantee, 1989—. Fellow Gerontologic Soc. Am.; mem. Am. Geriatrics Soc., Am. Assn. Cancer Rsch., Am. Soc. Clin. Oncology, Am. Soc. Hematology, Assn. Dirs. Acad. Geriatrics (councilor). Jewish. Office: Glenn Ctr Geriatrics and Gerontology 825 Fairfax Ave Norfolk VA 23507

ERSKINE, JOHN MORSE, surgeon; b. San Francisco, Sept. 10, 1920; s. Morse and Dorothy (Ward) E. BS, Harvard U., 1942, MD, 1945. Diplomate Am. Bd. Surgery. Surg. intern U. Calif. Hosp., San Francisco, 1945-46; surg. researcher Mass. Gen. Hosp., Boston, 1948; resident in surgery Peter Bent Brigham Hosp., Boston, 1948-53; George Gorham Peters fellow St. Mary's Hosp., London, 1952; pvt. practice in medicine specializing in surgery San Francisco, 1954—; asst. clin. prof. Stanford Med. Sch., San Francisco, 1956-59; asst., assoc. clin. prof. U. Calif. Med. Sch., San Francisco, 1959—; surg. cons. San Francisco Vets. Hosp., 1959-73. Contbr. articles to profl. jours., chpts. to books. Founder No. Calif. Artery Bank, 1954-58, Irwin Meml. Blood Bank, San Francisco, commr., pres., 1969-74; bd. dirs. People for Open Space-Greenbelt Alliance, 1984—; chmn. adv. coun. Dorothy Erskine Open Space Fund. Capt. with U.S. Army, 1946-48. Fellow ACS; mem. San Francisco Med. Soc. (bd. dirs. 1968-72), San Francisco Surg. Soc. (v.p. 1984), Pacific Coast Surg. Soc., Am. Cancer Soc. (bd. dirs. San Francisco br. 1965-75), Calif. Med. Assn., Olympic Club, Sierra Club. Democrat. Unitarian. Home: 233 Chestnut St San Francisco CA 94133-2452

ERSKINE, KENNETH F., psychotherapist; b. N.Y.C., Nov. 9, 1919; m. Maria C., Feb. 23, 1952; children: Clarke, Lewis. B Social Svcs., CCNY, 1950; MSW, Columbia U., 1952. Cert. social worker; bd. cert. diplomate social work. Intake worker Vets Soc. Ctr., N.Y.C., 1946-50; social worker Family Svc. Bur., Newark, N.J., 1951-53, N.Y.C. Youth Bd., 1953-55; case worker, supr. U.S. VA, Bklyn., 1955-56, social wk. supr., 1956-62; asst. prof. casework Columbia U. Sch. Social Wk., N.Y.C., 1962-69, asst. dir. field work, 1969-74; asst. dir. social work psychiatry dept. Harlem Hosp. Affiliation with Columbia Med. Sch. and Hosp., N.Y.C., 1974-85; psychotherapist Edupsych Assocs., N.Y.C., 1971—; clin. supr./cons. N.Y. Urban League, Bklyn., 1987—. Bd. dirs. Man County Sch., Inwood Hts. Housing, others. With USAF, 1943-46. Mem. NASW, Assn. Black Social Workers, Am. Orthopsychiat. Assn. Office: Edupsych Assocs 224 Rsd # 2C New York NY 10025

ERVIN, BILLY MAXWELL, health care executive; b. Dante, Va., July 29, 1933; s. Willie Beldon and Ollie Lowel (Biggs) E.; m. Barbara Frances Walsh, June 27, 1971; 1 child, Honore McDonough; 1 stepchild, Kerry Thompson. BS, U.S. Naval Acad., 1955; grad., Navy Nuclear Power Training, 1961; M in Marine Affairs, U. R.I., 1971; MBA, U. Mass., 1989. Commd. ensign USN, 1955, advanced through grades to capt., 1975; chief engr. aircraft carrier USN, Pacific, 1969-70; destroyer capt. USN, Atlantic/Pacific, 1971-73; project mgr. USN, Washington, 1973-78, head logistics br., 1978-80, head rsch. and devel. br., 1980-82; insp. gen. Europe USN, London, 1982-85; ret. USN, 1985; adminstr. Baystate Eye Care, P.C., Springfield, Mass., 1986-88; mgr. engring. adminstrn. and planning Kaman Aerospace Corp., Bloomfield, Conn., 1990-92; chief oper. officer Conn. Orthopaedic and Sports Medicine Ctr., Vernon, CT, 1992—. Decorated Bronze Star; recipient Meritorious Svc. Medal award Pres. of the U.S., 1985. Mem. Naval War Coll. Found., Navy League, St. Andrew's Soc., Clan Irwin Assn., Bones Soc., Med. Group Mgmt. Assn. Home: 20 Magnolia Ter Springfield MA 01108-2512 Office: Conn Orthopaedic & Sports Medicine Ctr 428 Hartford Tpke Vernon Rockville CT 06066-4819

ERVOLINO, JOANNE MARIE, nurse; b. N.Y.C., Feb. 13, 1959; d. Sam Dominic and Dorothy Marie (Perry) E. BS in Nursing, Adelphi U., 1981. RN; cert. inpatient obstetrics. From staff nurse to nurse clinician NYU Med. Ctr., 1981-85, asst. clin. coord., 1985-87; nurse cons. Bower and Gardner Med. Malpractice Law Firm, N.Y.C., 1987-91, Jackson & Consumano, N.Y.C., 1991-96; founder, pres. MedSource, med.-legal cons., N.Y.C., 1996—. Bd. dirs., v.p., sec. Park Manor Condominium, Forest Hills, N.Y., 1989, pres., 1990. Mem. NAFE, Nat. Assn. Am. Coll. Ob-Gyn, Sigma Theta Tau. Democrat. Roman Catholic. Home: 10025 Queens Blvd Forest Hills NY 11375-2454 Office: MedSource 41 Wooster St Ste 2 New York NY 10013

ESACHINA, ANN MARIE, critical care nurse; b. Spangler, Pa., Jan. 14, 1957; d. Andrew A. and Mary Louise (Pavelko) Drahnak; m. Paul Edward Esachina, Aug. 16, 1980. Diploma, Ind. Hosp. Sch. Nursing, 1978; BSN, Pa. State U., 1983, Indiana U. of Pa., 1988; MS, Indiana U. of Pa., 1988. Rn, Pa. Staff nurse ortho.-critical care unit, emergency room Shadyside Hosp., Pitts.; staff nurse emergency room Latrobe (Pa.) Area Hosp., head nurse surg. floor, 1987-92; part time nursing instr. Westmore County Cmty. Coll.; part time nursing coord. utilization rev. dept. Latrobe Area Hosp. Mem. Sigma Theta Tau.

ESBORG, PATRICIA KEITH, mental health nurse; b. Santa Monica, Calif., Oct. 19, 1938; d. Robert David and Annie Elizabeth (Edmondson) Keith; m. Svend Esborg, Jan. 27, 1962; children: Julia, Kara Lynn, Erik. Diploma, Bishop Johnson Coll. Nursing, 1959; BS, Bowie (Md.) State U., 1982; MS, U. Md., Balt., 1984; PhD, U. Md., College Park, 1991. Pvt. practice clin. specialist Bowie, 1989—; orgnl. cons., Bowie, 1995—. Fellow NIH, 1989-91; grantee Nurses Ednl. Funds, Inc., 1989-90. Mem. Am. Assn. Marriage and Family Therapy (clin. mem.), Sigma Theta Tau. Home: 12808 Buckingham Dr Bowie MD 20715-2466

ESCASINAS, EDGAR RIVERA, nephrologist; b. Cebu City, Philippines, Feb. 2, 1953; came to U.S., 1982; s. Bienvenido Gomez and Filomena (Concecion) E.; m. Rosario Minoza; 1 child, John David. BS magna cum laude, U. San Carlos, 1972; MD, Cebu Inst. of Medicine, 1976. Diplomate Am. Bd. Internal Medicine, Am. Bd. Nephrology. Intern in internal medicine Wayne State U., Detroit, 1982-85; fellowship in nephrology U. Pitts., 1985-

87; pvt. practice St. Paul (Va.) Med. Ctr., 1988-90, Gladeville Med. Ctr., Wise, Va., 1990—; pres. med. staff Wise (Va.) Appalachian Regional, 1992-94, chief med. svcs., 1994—, mem. exec. com. 1992—. Mem. Am. Med. Soc., Am. Soc. Nephrology, Wise County Med. Soc. Roman Catholic. Office: ARH Gladeville Med Clinic Box B 10 Wise Cty Plaza Wise VA 24293

ESCHBACH, JOSEPH WETHERILL, nephrology educator; b. Detroit, Jan. 21, 1933; s. Joseph William and Marguerite (Wetherill) E.; m. Mary Ann Charles, June 16, 1956; children: Cheryl Louise, Ann Elizabeth, Joseph Charles. BA, BS, Otterbein Coll., 1955; MD, Jefferson Med. Coll., 1959. Practitioner nephrology and internal medicine Minor and James Med., Seattle, 1965—; dir. home dialysis U. Wash., Seattle, 1965-72, clin. asst. prof. div. nephrology, 1967-70, clin. assoc. prof. div. nephrology, 1970-75, clin. prof. div. nephrology, 1975-85, clin. prof. divs. nephrology and hematology, 1985—; cons. Ortho Pharm., Raritan, N.J., 1987-88, Amgen, Thousasnd Oaks, Calif., 1985-91. Co-editor: Erythropoietin: Molecular, Cellular and Clinical Biology, 1991; contbr. articles to jours. in field, chpts. to textbooks. Trustee First Ave. Svc. Ctr., 1976-86; pres. bd. trustees Northwest Kidney Ctr., Seattle, 1985-87 (Haviland award 1991). Recipient Disting. Svc. award Seattle Jaycees, 1979, Alumni Achievement award Otterbein Coll., 1991. Fellow ACP; mem. Inst. Medicine of NAS, AMA, Am. Soc. Nephrology, Internat. Soc. Nephrology, King County Med. Soc. (pres. 1987). Presbyterian. Home: 770 96th Ave SE Bellevue WA 98004-6502 Office: Minor & James Med 515 Minor Ave Seattle WA 98104-2138*

ESCHETE, MARY LOUISE, internist; b. Houma, La., Feb. 8, 1949; d. Marshall John and Louise Esther (Davis) E.; m. Lcrphy Joseph Bourque, July 7, 1979. BS, La. State U., 1970; MD, La. State U. Med. Ctr., Shreveport, 1974. Diplomate, Am. Bd. Internal Medicine. Resident in internal medicine La. State U. Med. Ctr., Shreveport, 1974-77; staff instr. La. State U. Med. Ctr., 1979, fellow in infectious disease, 1979; pvt. practice Houma, 1980-83; staff, dept. internal medicine South La. Med. Assocs., Houma, 1983—; chmn. infection control, Terrebonne Gen. Hosp., 1981—, South La. Med. Ctr., 1983—. Contbr. articles to med. jours. Bd. dirs. Houma Battered Women's Shelter, 1983-87, Houma YWCA, 1987-94; mem. Roche Nat. AIDS Adv. Bd., 1993; Triparish vol. activist, 1994. Named Citizen of Yr. Regional and State Social Workers, 1992. Mem. ACP, AAAS, AMA, Infectious Disease Soc., Am. Soc. Microbiology, So. Med. Assn. (grantee 1978), N.Y. Acad. Sci., La. State Med. Soc., Terrebonne Parish Med. Sco. (sec. 1982-83, v.p. 1993-94, pres. 1994-95), Krewe of Hyachinthians (pres. 1989-90, 94-95, bd. dirs. 1990-96), Houma Jr. Women's Club (reporter 1988-89, rec. sec. 1989—, pres.-elect 1991-93, pres. 1993-95), Alpha Epsilon Delta. Democrat. Roman Catholic. Home: 3387 Little Bayou Black Dr Houma LA 70360-2840 Office: South La Med Ctr 1978 Industrial Blvd Houma LA 70363-7055

ESCOBAR, HILDA LOPEZ, nurse practitioner, physician assistant; b. N.Y.C., Aug. 6, 1929; d. Eladio and Josephine (Justiniano) Lopez; m. John Louis Escobar, Sept. 10, 1949; children: Linda, Michael, Jean. AAS, Nassau Community Coll., 1967; BSN, C.W. Post U., 1975; cert. in nursing mgmt. Adelphi U., 1988. Cert. hemodialysis nurse, 1978; adult nurse practitioner, SUNY, Upstate Med. Ctr., Syracuse, 1978; cert. healthcare risk, diabetic educator. Staff nurse, South Nassau Community Hosp., Oceanside, N.Y., 1967-68; staff nurse Nassau Hosp., Mineola, N.Y., 1968-78, head nurse hemodialysis unit, 1976-78; adult nurse practitioner Community Health Program, New Hyde Park, N.Y., 1978—, nurse coord. dept. medicine and urgent visit dept., 1986-89. Mem. Am. Nurses Assn. (cert. adult nurse practitioner 1988), Am. Assn. Physician Assts. (cert. 1983), Am. Assn. Nephrology Nurses & Technicians (cert. 1976), Coalition Nurse Practitioners, Phi Theta Kappa, Sigma Theta Tau (exec. bd. dirs. Alpha Omega chpt. 1978—).

ESCOTT, SHOOLAH HOPE, microbiologist; b. Stamford, Conn., May 20, 1952; d. Robert R. and Fanny (Levy) E.; m. Joseph J. Sulmar, Sept. 6, 1992. Cert. med. tech., St. Vincent's Hosp., Bridgeport, Conn., 1974; BS, U. Conn., 1974; MS, Northeastern U., Boston, 1985. Cert. med. technologist. Clin. lab. scientist NCA, 1976; med. technologist St. Elizabeth's Hosp., Boston, 1976, Harvard U. Health Svcs., Cambridge, Mass., 1976-79; med. technologist microbiology lab. New England Deaconess Hosp., Boston, 1979-84; supr. microbiology Norwood (Mass.) Hosp., 1984-87; supr. microbiology lab. Meml. Hosp., Worcester, Mass., 1987-91; adminstrv. supr. microbiology labs. Med. Ctr. Ctrl. Mass., Worcester, 1991—. Named Nat. Merit Scholar, 1970; grantee, 1970. Mem. Am. Soc. Clin. Pathologists, Am. Soc. for Microbiology, Am. Soc. for Microbiology, N.E. Assn. for Clin. Microbiology and Infectious Disease (bd. dirs. Mass. chpt. 1989-91, treas. 1991-93, pres.-elect 1993-94, pres. 1994-95, past pres. 1995-96). Office: Med Ctr Cen Mass Microbiology Lab 119 Belmont St Worcester MA 01605-2903

ESHAM, RICHARD HENRY, internal medicine and geriatrics educator; b. Maysville, Ky., Oct. 6, 1942; s. Elwood and Ruth (Opfer) E.; m. Tamela Edwards; children: Ashley Ruth, Richard Henry II, Clay Hamlet. MD, U. Louisville, 1967. Resident in internal medicine U. Ala. Hosps. and Clinics, Birmingham, 1968-71, straight med. intern, 1967-68; pvt. practice Mobile, Ala., 1974-90; prof., dir. div. gen. internal medicine and geriatrics U. South Ala., Mobile, 1990-95, asst. to v.p. for med. affairs Coll. Medicine, 1994—, vice chmn. clin. programs dept. internal medicine, 1994—; instr. medicine U. Ala. Hosps. and Clinics, 1971-72; chmn. Bd. Med. Examiners, Montgomery Ala., 1992-94, Ala. Bd. Health, Montgomery, 1992-94. Contbr. med. articles to profl. jours. Bd. dirs. Arthritis Found., Mobile, 1974-81. Maj. U.S. Army, 1972-74. Fellow ACP; mem. Med. Assn. State of Ala. (officer, counselor, bd. censors 1984-94, vice chmn. 1991-92, chmn. 1992-94), Mobile Area C. of C. (bd. dirs. 1991-92, med. svcs. com. 1991—), Alpha Omega Alpha. Office: Health Svc Bldg USA Campus Mobile AL 36688-0002 also: PO Box 8569 Mobile AL 36689

ESHLEMAN, SILAS KENDRICK, III, psychiatrist; b. Gainesville, Fla., June 28, 1928; s. Silas Kendrick Jr. and Aileen Hope (McClamroch) E.; m. Judith Cooper, July 3, 1954; 1 child, Diane Eshleman Djordjevic. BS, U. Fla., 1949; MD, U. Pa., 1953. Diplomate Nat. Bd. Med. Examiners, Am. Bd. Psychiatry and Neurology, Am. Bd. Med. Psychotherapists, Am. Bd. Forensic Examiners. Mem. med. staff St. Joseph Hosp., Lancaster, Pa., 1959—, chmn. dept. psychiatry, 1968-88; mem. med. staff Lancaster Gen. Hosp., 1959—; $D $D, $D, $D; pvt. practice Lancaster, 1959—; cons. in psychiatry VA Med. Ctr., Lebanon, Pa., 1961-92, NIH Project, 1978—; mem. various med. staff coms. Contbr. articles to profl. jours. Capt. M.C., U.S. Army, 1955-57. Fellow Am. Psychiat.Assn. (life), Coll. Physicians of Phila.; mem. AMA, AAAS, Cliosophic Soc. (program chmn. Lancaster chpt. 1983-84), Torch Club. Episcopalian. Home: PO Box 306 Paradise PA 17562-0306 Office: 317 N Duke St Lancaster PA 17602-4915

ESKOW, ROBERT NORMAN, periodontist; b. Perth Amboy, N.J., Dec. 9, 1942; s. Jack Meyer and Theodosia (Katz) E.; m. Nancy Lynn Goldberg, June 29, 1969; children: Renee, Darren. DMD, U. Pa., 1967; MS in Dentistry, Boston U., 1969, cert. in Periodontology, 1969. Assoc. in periodontology Boston U., 1969-70; clin. asst. in periodontology Harvard U., 1971; clin. asst. prof. Fairleigh Dickinson U., Hackensack, N.J., 1972-79, clin. assoc. prof., 1979-88, clin. prof., 1988-90; clin. prof. dept. implant dentistry and surg. scis. NYU, 1992-93; chmn. Dentist Div. UJF, MetroWest, 1992-95; mem. dept. periodontics Univ. Hosp., Boston, 1969-72; attending St. Barnabas Med. Ctr., Livingston, N.J.; assoc. attending chmn. sect. periodontics Newark Beth Israel Med. Ctr.; chmn. sect. periodontics Hosp. Ctr. at Orange, N.J.; cons. staff Morristown (N.J.) Meml. Hosp. Mem. Am. Acad. Oral Medicine (treas. 1979-85, v.p. 1985-86, pres. 1987-88, pres. N.J. sect. 1977-79), Acad. Oral Diagnosis, Radiology and Medicine (exec. com. 1989-91), Alpha Omega. (pres. Newark Alumni chpt. 1979-80). Home: 11 Cornell Dr Livingston NJ 07039-5504 Office: 514 S Livingston Ave Livingston NJ 07039-4329

ESLAMI, HOSSEIN HOJATOL, physician; b. Tehran, Iran, July 30, 1927; s. Abul-Hassan and Assieh (Ghafari) E.; M.D., Tehran U., 1952; m. Jean Chinigo, Apr. 27, 1956; children: Darius, Cyrus. Intern, Jersey City Med. Center, 1955-56; resident in surgery Newark Beth Israel Med. Center, 1956-60, fellow in vascular surgery, 1960-61; practice medicine specializing in surgery and kidney transplantation, Newark, 1961-67; mem. faculty U. of Medicine and Dentistry of N.J., 1969—, dir. organ transplantation, 1968—, dir. surg. edn., 1967—, asso. prof. surgery, 1976—; chief surgery Newark Beth Israel Med. Center. Diplomate Am. Bd. Surgery. Fellow ACS, Acad. Medicine N.J.; mem. Essex County Med. Soc., Med. Soc. N.J., AMA, Am. Soc. Abdominal Surgeons Am. Soc. Artificial Internal Organs, Nat. Kidney Found., Transplantation Soc., Am. Soc. Transpolant Surgeons, N.J. Nephrology Soc. Research kidney and liver transplantations. Contbr. articles to profl. jours. Office: 62 Jefferson St Newark NJ 07105-2224

ESLAO, EDUARDO F., dentist; b. Baguio City, The Philippines, May 14, 1939; came to U.S., 1969; d. Martin Aspera and Sally (Flormata) E.; m. Leonor Capistrano, June 20, 1964; 1 child, Katherine. DDS, U. of East, Manila, 1961. Cert. Calif. Bd. Dental Examiners. lectr. in field. Treas. Philippine Progressive Group, L.A., 1987-88, Philippine Town Movement, L.A., 1988-89; bd. dirs. Philippine-Am. Cmty. Assn. Glassel Pk., L.A., 1988, St. Bernard Adult Choir, L.A., 1989—. Mem. So. Calif. Filipino Dental Soc. (bd. dirs., 1996—), Fedn. Calif. Dentists (chmn. continuing edn. program, 1996—), Nat. Assn. Filipino Dentists Am. (bd. dirs. 1989-90, v.p. 1990-91, sec. 1991-92, pres. 1993-94, outstanding mem. of yr. 1991, 95), Fedn. Calif. Dentists (pres. 1988-92), Am. Dental Assn., Calif. Dental Assn., So. Calif. Dental Soc. Home: 3658 Primavera Ave Los Angeles CA 90065 Office: 3120 W 6th St Los Angeles CA 90020

ESNAULT, VINCENT LOUIS MARIE, nephrologist, educator; b. Neuilly sur Seine, France, Oct. 26, 1959. Degree, Centre Hospitalier Universitaire, Nantes, 1983; PhD, Nantes U., 1991, degree in Rsch. Adminstrn., 1992. Intern Nantes (France) U. Hosp., 1983-87, asst. head clinic, 1987-89, prof. nephrology, 1992—; dir. rsch. group on ANCA positive systemic vasculitis, 1992; mem. clin. rsch. del. Sci. Commn., Nantes, 1993. Contbr. articles to profl. jours. Grantee Found. Med. Rsch., 1992, 93, Nephrology Svc., 1993, 94; recipient gold medal Acad. des Scis. inscriptions et belles lettres, Toulouse, 1995, Nurse of Distinction award St. Barnabas Hosp. N.Y. State Legis., 1995. Mem. Société Néphrologie, Internat. Soc. Nephrology, Am. Soc. Nephrology, European Dialysis and Transplantation Assn., European Soc. Clin. Investigation. Roman Catholic. Office: Hotel Dieu, Svc Nephrologie-Immunologie Clinique, 44035 Nantes France

ESOFF, COLLEEN ELIZABETH, critical care nurse; b. Bronx, N.Y., Nov. 12, 1970; d. Anthony Joseph and Winifred Mary (Snee) E. BS, Molloy Coll., Rockville Centre, N.Y., 1993. RN, N.Y.; cert. ACLS, BCLS. Staff nurse N.Y. Hosp., N.Y.C., 1993—; staff nurse Patient Care Technician Task Force, N.Y.C., 1994—. Mem. AACCN. Roman Catholic.

ESPADALER, JOSEP MARIA, neurologist; b. Barcelona, Catalunya, Spain, May 5, 1925; s. Ignacio L. and Pilar (Medina) E.; m. Montserrat Gamissans, Feb. 12, 1952; children: Josep M., Monte Serrat. MD, U. Barcelona, 1949. With Hosp. Clinico, 1945-50, Salpetriére, Paris, 1950; chief neurology Hosp. Clinic, Barcelona, 1958-62, Red Cross Hosp., Barcelona, 1960-87; gen. sec. X Internat. Congress, Barcelona, 1973; asst. prof. neurology Med. Sch., Barcelona, 1975-90; dir. emeritus Red Cross Hosp., Barcelona, 1986—; mem. Royal Acad. Drs. Catalunya, Barcelona, 1966—. Author: Cefaleas en la practica Medica, 1954, Enfermedades Neuromusculares, 1971, Diccionario Encielopedico de Cefaleas, 1988; editor: Neurology Proceedings, 1973. Ensign Spanish mil., 1950. Recipient prix Ramon y Cajal, 1957, Commendator Civil Order of Health, 1966, Paul Harris fellowship, 1990. Mem. Spanish Soc. Neurology (hon.), Am. Neurol. Assn., Soc. Francaise de Neurology (hon.), Soc. Belge de Neurology (hon.), Soc. Argentina de Neurologia (hon.), Academia Brasileira Neurology (hon.), Rotary (prs. 1990), Club Nautico el Balis Llavaneras. Home: Escuelas Pias 12, 08017 Barcelona Spain Office: Pvt Consultation, Gral Mitre 101, 08022 Barcelona Spain

ESPELAND, MARK ANDREW, biostatistics educator; b. St. Paul, May 16, 1952; s. Obert Leolfe and Esther Marie (Nelson) E.; m. Anne Marion Boyle, June 11, 1983; 1 child, Amos James Boyle. BS in Math., Ariz. State U., 1974; MA in Stats., U. Rochester, 1976, PhD in Stats., 1981. Asst. prof. U. Ill., Chgo., 1981-83; coord. biostats. and computing Eastman Dental Ctr., Rochester, N.Y., 1983-86; adj. asst. prof. U. Rochester, 1983-86; asst. prof. Bowman Gray Sch. Medicine, Winston-Salem, N.C., 1986-87, assoc. prof., 1987-94, head sect. biostats., 1993—, prof., 1994—; cons. NIH, Bethesda, Md., 1987—. Mem. editorial bd. AMA, 1992—; contbr. articles to profl. jours. Recipient Blood Pressure Rsch. grant Nat. Inst. on Aging, 1991—, Women's Health grant Nat. Heart Lung and Blood Inst., 1988-94. Mem. Am. Statis. Assn., Biometrics Soc., Soc. for Clin. Trials, Classification Soc. N.Am., Inst. Math. Stats. Office: Bowman Gray Sch Medicine Medical Center Blvd Winston Salem NC 27157*

ESPER, WALLACE JAMES, physician; b. Kirksville, Mo., Oct. 28, 1966; s. James Milhelm and Charlotte Jane (Steehler) E.; m. Eryn Nicole Smith, Aug. 24, 1996; 1 child, Cory. BA, Edinboro (Pa.) U., 1989; DO, U. Osteo. Medicine, Des Moines, 1994. Cert. physician, Pa. Physician, dir. ops. Westridge Med., Erie, Pa., 1995—; instr. Five Knuckle Bullet Karate, Berea, Ohio, 1991—. Appeared in Bad Influence, 1987, Talons of The Eagles, 1992, TC 2000, 1993, urban Legend, 1995. Recipient Nat. HUT Weight Champion, Profl. Karate Com., 1992-93, Nat. Middle Weight Runner-Up, 1993-94, Pa. State Middle Weight Champion, 1993-94. Mem. Am. Osteo. Assn., Pa. Osteo. Medicine Assn.

ESPINOSA, ENRIQUE, oncologist, researcher; b. Osnabrück, Germany, June 22, 1964; arrived in Spain, 1967; s. Jesus Maria and Manuela (Arranz) E.; m. Pilar Zamora. MD, U. Autonoma, Madrid, 1988, D in Medicine, 1993. Resident Hosp. La Paz, Madrid, 1989-92, mem. staff, 1993—; hon. tchr. U. Autonoma, Madrid, 1994. Co-editor: Prognostic Factors in Oncology, 1994, Palliative Care for Cancer Patients, 1995; contbr. articles to profl. jours. including Lung Cancer and Cancer Chemotherapy Pharmacology. Office: Hosp La Paz, Svc Med Oncology, Castellana 261, 28046 Madrid Spain

ESPINOSA, ROGER GONZALES, physician; b. Cebu City, Philippines, Feb. 16, 1956; s. Carlos and Nenita (Gonzales) E.; m. Maria Teresita Fuentes, Oct. 21, 1992. MD, Cebu Inst. Medicine, Cebu, Philippines, 1979. Diplomate Am. Bd. Internat Medicine, Am. Bd. Cardiology. Staff cardiologist Lake Hosp. System, Painesville, Ohio, 1986—. Fellow Am. Coll. Cardiology; mem. Am. Coll. Physician. Office: Lake Cardiology 124 Liberty St Painesville OH 44077

ESPINOZA, LUIS ROLAN, rheumatologist; b. Pisco, Peru, July 3, 1943; came to U.S.A., 1969; s. Luis R. and Luz Lelia (Bernales) E.; m. Carmen G. Gonzalez, Dec. 20, 1969; children: Luis M., Gabriela M. MD, Cayetano Heredia, Lima, Peru, 1969. Intern Jersey City (N.J.) Med. Ctr., 1969-70; resident Washington U., St. Louis, 1970-72, rheumatlogy fellow, 1972-73; rheumatlogy fellow McGill U., Montreal, Can., 1973-74, asst. prof., 1976-78; immunology fellow The Rockefeller U., N.Y.C., 1974-76; assoc. prof. U. South Fla., Tampa, 1978-83, prof. medicine, 1983-90; prof. medicine La. State U. Sch. Medicine, New Orleans, 1991—, also chief rheumatology sect. Editor: Infection in the Rheumatic Diseases, 1988, Psoriatic Arthritis, 1985, Immun Complexes, 1983; guest editor Infectious Arthritis Rheumatic Disease Clin. N. Am., 1993. Chmn. Lupus Found. Am., Tampa, 1979-90. Recipient Rsch. award NIH, Tampa, 1981, Arthritis Found., Tampa, 1990. Fellow ACP, Am. Coll. Rheumatology; mem. Am. Assn. Immunologists, So. Soc. for Clin. Investigation, Soc. for Clin. Rsch., Can. Soc. Rheumatologists, Can. Soc. for Clin. Investigation. Home: 1212 Conery St New Orleans LA 70115-3340 Office: La State U Med Ctr 1542 Tulane Ave New Orleans LA 70112-2825

ESPOSITO, ALBERTO J., health care administrator; b. N.Y.C., July 21, 1957; s. John and Josephine (Venditti) E.; m. Donna Lynne Gottesman, Nov. 11, 1985; children: Christopher, Melissa. BS in Health Care Adminstrn., St. Johns U., 1980; M of Pub. Health, L.I. U., 1987. ADM resident St. John's Hosp., Queens, N.Y., 1980—; mgr. emergency rm. and ambulatory care Brookdale Hosp. Med. Ctr., Bklyn., 1980-85; dir. emergency rm., EHS, and ambulatory care Woodhull Hosp., Bklyn., 1985-87; adminstrv. dir., trauma ctr., EMS and MD's PC St. Vincents Hosp. and Med. Ctr. of N.Y., N.Y.C., 1987-93; v.p. ops. U. Physicians Group of S.I. Univ. Hosp., 1993—; lectr. Hofstra U., N.Y. Assn. of Ambulatory Care, Am. Coll. of Health Care Execs., 1987—. Mem. Cmty. Bd., S.I., 1990—; chmn. budget com. S.I. Cmty. Bd., 1995—; mem. Sr. Citizen Adv. Coun. Mem. Am. Coll. of Health Care Execs. (diplomate, Health Exec. award 1995), Met. Health Adminstrs. Assn. (pres., v.p., treas., chair, coms.). Republican. Roman Catholic. Home: 252 Finley Ave Staten Island NY 10306 Office: Univ Physicians Group PC 1880 Hylan Blvd Staten Island NY 10305

ESPOSITO, JOHN CHARLES, physician; b. Phila., Jan. 1, 1927; s. Charles and Anna Sylvia (Primiano) E.; m. Janice J. Jerostic, Oct. 4, 1952; children: Suzanne, Nancy, Patricia. Student, Temple; MD, Georgetown U., 1951. Intern Phila. Gen., 1951-52, resident, 1952, 55-57; pvt. practice Springfield, Pa., 1958—; instr. Hahnemann Hosp., 1976—, Jefferson Hosp., 1981-86, Del. County Cmty. Coll., Media, Pa., 1983-90. Past comdr. Am. Legion. Capt. USAF, 1953-55. Mem. Am. Coll. Allergy and Immunology, Pa. Allergy Soc., Phila. Allergy Soc. Republican. Roman Catholic. Office: 226 E Springfield Rd Media PA 19064-3221

ESPOSITO, JOSEPH LOUIS, chiropractor, nutritionist; b. Jersey City, May 1, 1961; s. Joseph and Rose Marie (Zeier) E. BS in Nutrition, D of Chiropractic, LIFE, 1994. Lic. dietician., Ga. Chiropractor Health Plus, Marrietta; founder, CEO Health Plus, Inc., Marrietta, Ga., 1986—; lectr. in field. TV and radio host, 1981—; contbr. articles to profl. jours. Named one of Top 50 Bus. People in Atlanta, Cystic Fibrosis Found., 1996. Mem. Am. Acad. Pain Mgmt. (diplomate), Am. Chiropractic Assn., Ga. Chiropractic Assn. (coun. 1981—). Office: Health Plus 950 Cobb Pky Ste 190 Marietta GA 30062

ESPOSITO, SAL, physician; b. Palermo, Italy, Nov. 20, 1957; came to U.S., 1988; s. Rosario and Filomena (Passantino) E.; m. Jaclyn Phillips, Feb. 10, 1990; children: Patrick John, Mark Anthony. MD, Sch. Medicine, Palermo, 1984. Diplomate Am. Bd. Family Practice. House office in internal medicine Patologia Medica II, Palermo, 1987; house officer in neurosurgery Queen Elizabeth Hosp., Birmingham, Eng., 1988; resident in family practice St. Francis Hosp., Wilmington, Del., 1990-92, McAllen (Tex.) Med. Ctr., 1992-94; attending physician Family Clinic, Gainesville, Tex., 1994—; mem. med. adv. bd. Choice Home Health, Gainesville, 1994—. Recipient Burroughs Welcome Family Practice Resident scholarship Am. Acad. Family Physicians Found., 1993. Mem. AMA, Am. Acad. Family Practice, Tex. Med. Assn., Cooke County Med. Assn. Office: Family Clinic 1820 O'Neal St Ste 6 Gainesville TX 76240

ESQUENAZI, SALOMON, ophthalmologist; b. Bogota, Colombia, Sept. 29, 1961; s. Isidoro and Ketty (Tarragano) E.; m. Olga Bibas, June 7, 1986; children: Isi, Karina, Becky. MD, Rosario U., Bogota, 1985, postgrad., 1989. Diplomate Colombian Bd. Ophthalmology. Intern San Jose Hosp., Bogota, 1986-88, chief resident, 1988-89; ophthalmologist Barraquer Clinic, Bogota, 1989; instnl. mem. Fundacion Santa Fe, Bogota, 1989—; med. dir. Centro Oftalmologico, Bogota, 1993—. Contbr. articles to profl. jours. Mem. A.S.C.R.S., I.S.R.K., Soc. Ophthalmology Bogota. Liberal. Jewish. Office: Centro Oftalmologico Olsabe, Calle 120 #8-62, Bogota Colombia

ESQUIBEL, EDWARD VALDEZ, psychiatrist, clinical medical program developer; b. Denver, May 28, 1928; s. Delfino C. and Beatrice (Solis) E.; m. Elaine F. Telk (div. 1961); children: Roxanne, Cyndi, Allen, James; m. Lillian D. Robb, 1961; children: Amanda, Ramona. MD, U. Colo., 1958. Diplomate Am. Bd. Psychiatry and Neurology. Assoc. chief svc. Ill. State Psychiat. Inst., Chgo., 1964-66; dir. undergrad. program psychiatry, asst. prof. psychiatry Chgo Med. Sch., 1966-68; cons. and supr. group therapy Lake County Mental Health Clinic, Gary, Ind., 1968-72; pvt. practice Daytona Beach, Jacksonville, Fla., 1972-82; chief forensic svcs., dir. div. maximum security and inst. rsch. Colo. State Hosp., Pueblo, 1981; assoc. clin. prof. psychiatry Quillen-Dishner Coll. Medicine, Johnson City, Tenn., 1982-84; clin. psychiatrist VA Outpatient Clinic, Riviera Beach, Fla., 1984-86; mental health coord., supr. VA, Pensacola, Fla., 1986-88; assoc. chief staff, ambulatory care VA Med. Ctr., Ft. Lyon, Colo., 1988-90, Carl Vinson VA Med. Ctr., Dublin, Ga., 1990-91; staff physician VA Med. Ctr., Sheridan, Wyo., 1993—; chief psychiat. svcs. VA Med. Ctr., Lake City, Fla., 1993-94; contract physician Annashae Corp., Cleve., 1995—. Contbr. articles to profl. jours. Sgt. U.S. Army, 1952-58. Recipient Plaque Recognition award Southeastern Psychiat. Inst., 1964, Internat. Pers. Creative award, 1972, Key to City Daytona Beach, 1975, Hosp. Dirs. commendation VA, 1991. Mem. Am. Soc. Psychoanalytic Physicians. Home and Office: 801 Gospel Island Rd Inverness FL 34450-3592

ESSER, ARISTIDE HENRI, psychiatrist; b. Padalarang, Java, Indonesia, May 11, 1930; came to U.S., 1961; s. Samuel Jonathan and Anganita (Tawalujan) E.; m. Ada Reif; children: Jonathan Hendrik, Jessica. MD, U. Amsterdam, The Netherlands, 1955. Diplomate Am. Bd. Psychiatry and Neurology. Med. dir. N.S. Kline Inst., Orangeburg, N.Y., 1962-69; dir. research Letchworth Village, Thiells, N.Y., 1969-71; dir. Cen. Bergen Community Mental Health Ctr., Paramus, N.J., 1971-77; med. dir. Mission for Immaculate Virgin, S.I., N.Y., 1977-80; dir. quality assurance Bronx (N.Y.) Psychiat. Ctr., 1980-85; unit chief for supportive rehab. Rockland Psychiat. Ctr., Orangeburg, 1985-88, chief geriatrics div., 1988-90; psychiatrist St. Dominic's Home, Blauvelt, 1990—; attending psychiatrist Rye (N.Y.) Hosp. Ctr., 1990—, Good Samaritan Hosp., Suffern, N.Y., 1990—; rsch. prof. NYU Med. Ctr., N.Y.C., 1985-94. Co-author: Mental Illness: A Homecare Guide, 1989, Chi Gong: The Ancient Chinese Way to Health, 1990; co-editor: Behavior and Environment, 1971, Design for Communality and Privacy, 1978; editor Jour. Man-Environment Systems, 1969— (Internat. Design award 1973). Recipient travel grant City of Leyden, The Netherlands, 1960; Lederle Labs. fellow Yale U., 1961. Fellow AAAS, Am. Psychiat. Assn. (life); mem. Soc. for Biol. Psychiatry, Soc. for Gen. Systems Rsch., Am. Acad. Acupuncture (founding), Assn. for Study Man-Environment Rels. (founding). Home: 435 S Mountain Rd New City NY 10956-5731 Office: 337 N Main St Ste 2 New City NY 10956-4310

ESSEX, FRANCIS XAVIER, physician, educator; b. N.Y.C., July 17, 1931; s. John A. and Caroline H. (Weber) E.; m. Judith Ann McBride, July 11, 1959; children: Paul F., Anne C., Caroline E., Julia M. BS, Holy Cross Coll., 1953; MD, Creighton U., 1960. Diplomate Am. Bd. Internal Medicine. Commd. ensign USN, 1959, advanced through grades to comdr., 1969; regtl. surgeon 2d Marine div. FMF, FMF, Lant, 1960-61; staff med. officer U.S. Naval Hosp., Phila., 1963-65; from asst. to chief med. svc. U.S. Naval Hosp., Charleston, S.C., 1967-69; chief med. svc. U.S. Naval Hosp., Charleston, 1969-70; ret. capt. USNR, 1991; asst. prof. Med. Coll. of S.C., Charleston, 1969-70; from instr. to assoc. prof. U. Tex. Med. Br., Galveston, 1970—; pvt. practice, Galveston, 1970—; clin. assoc. prof. U. Tex. Med. Br., 1983—; chmn. internal medicine dept. St. Mary's Hosp., Galveston, 1984-85. Hon. adm. Tex. Navy, Galveston, 1985—; bd. dirs. Moody House Ret. Cmty., Galveston, 1970-71. Mem. AMA, Am. Soc. Internal Medicine, Tex. Med. Assn., Galveston County Med. Soc., Am. Coll. of Physicians. Home: 1203 Harbor View Dr Galveston TX 77550-3113 Office: Internal Medicine Assocs 1203 Harbor View Dr Galveston TX 77550

ESSEX, WANDA ELIZABETH, speech and language pathologist; b. Benham, Ky., Jan. 25, 1925; d. Nathaniel Otto and Elizabeth Marie (Ausmus) Irwin; children: Michael, Elane, Christopher. BS, U. Nebr., 1969, MA, 1973. Fingerprint classifier FBI, Washington, 1943-45; sec. Libr. of Congress, Washington, 1948-49; speech pathologist Ednl. Svc. Unit #6, Milford, Nebr., 1969, Fremont (Nebr.) Pub. Schs., 1969-92; pvt. practice speech pathology Lincoln, Nebr., 1993—; speech pathologist Meml. Hosp. Dodge County, Fremont, 1975-93, U. Nebr., Lincoln, 1994-96. Bd. dirs. Nebr. Stroke Found., sec. 1994. Recipient award of Excellence, Nat. Coun. for Better Hearing and Speech Month, 1988, 89. Mem. AAUW, Am. Speech-Lang. Hearing Assn. (continuing edn. award 1985, 89), Nebr. Speech-Lang. Hearing Assn. (chair better hearing and speech month 1993-96, chair Breakfast for Senators 1996, honors award 1985), Nat. Coun. Better Hearing and Speech Month (Nebr. co-chair 1988-95), Dodge County Stroke Club (project dir. 1987-94), Delta Kappa Gamma (v.p., pres.), Phi Delta Kappa.

ESSIN, EMMETT MOHAMMED, JR., obstetrician, gynecologist; b. Sherman, Tex., Jan. 2, 1920; s. Emmett Mohammed Sr. and Lela Priscilla (Tallent) E.; m. Margaret Cummings, Dec. 31, 1939; children: Emmett III, William Robert, Ellen Priscilla, Warren Namon. BA, Austin Coll., 1940; MD, U. Tex., Galveston, 1943. Intern U. Tex., John Sealy Hosps., Galveston, 1943-44, resident in ob./gyn., 1944-45; mem. med. staff Wilson

N. Jones Meml. Hosp., Sherman, Tex., 1946—; chief staff Wilson N. Jones Meml. Hosp., Sherman, 1976-77, chief ob-gyn., 1987-88; bd. dirs. Devel. Bd. Wilson N. Jones Meml. Hosp., Am. Bank, Sherman; ; founder, pres., ptnr. Essin Clinic, Sherman, 1946-89. Charter bd. dirs. Texoma Blood Bank, Sherman, 1975. Lt. USNR, 1945-46. Recipient disting. alumnus awards Austin Coll., 1987, Sherman H.S., 1993. Mem. Grayson County Med. Soc. (past pres.), Tex. Med. Assn., William R. Cooke Obstetrical & Gynecological Soc. (past pres.), Am. Coll. Ob-Gyn. (founding), So. Med. Soc., Am. Coll. Abdominal Surgery, Am. Soc. Fertility. Presbyterian. Home: 1430 Western Hills Dr Sherman TX 75092-5239 Office: Essin Med Bldg 600 N Highland Ave Sherman TX 75092-5646

ESSWEIN, ARTHUR JOSEPH, internist; b. Apr. 15, 1947; m. Vivian E. Esswein; children: Karen, Christine, Arthur, Carolyn, Katherine. BS, Fordham U., 1968; MD, Downstate Med. Ctr., 1972. Diplomate Nat. Bd. Med. Examiners, Am. Bd. Internal Medicine, Am. Bd. Gastroenterology; lic. physician, N.Y., Mass. Intern Nassau County Med. Ctr., East Meadow, N.Y., 1972-73, resident, 1973-75, fellow, 1975-76; fellow gastroenterology U. Mass., Worcester, 1983-85; assoc. attending physician Rochester (Mass.) Gen. Hosp., 1976-81, attending physician, 1981-83; assoc. attending physician Park Ridge Hosp., 1979-81, attending physician, 1981-83; instr. medicine U. Mass. Med. Ctr., 1984-85, assoc. attending physician, 1985-90; clin. instr. SUNY, Stony Brook, 1975-76; mem. provisional staff Falmouth Hosp., 1985, mem. active staff, 1986—, mem. libr. com., 1987-89, tissue and transfusion com., 1989-91, chmn., 1991—; treas. Falmouth Physicians, Inc., 1987-93; bd. mem. Falmouth Health Resources, 1987-93. Mem. fin. com. St. Ambrose Ch., 1981-83. Recipient Physicians Recognition award AMA, 1978, 82. Mem. Am. Soc. Internal Medicine, Am. Gastroent. Assn., Am. Soc. Gastrointestinal Endoscopy. Home: 105 Two Ponds Rd Falmouth MA 02540-2221

ESTABROOKS, LEWIS NORMAN, oral and maxillofacial surgeon; b. Laconia, N.H., Sept. 6, 1944; s. Eleanor Jean Reed, Apr. 15, 1963; children: Laurel, David. BS, U. Rochester, 1966; DMD, Tufts U., 1969, MS, 1972. Diplomate Am. Bd. Oral Surgery. Intern New Eng. Med. Ctr., Boston, 1969-70; resident oral surgery Boston City Hosp., 1970-72; maj. USAF, Minot, N.D., 1972-74; pvt. practice oral surgery South Portland, Maine, 1974—; bd. dirs. Blue Cross Blue Shield, Portland, 1974-84, med. adv. bd., 1988-94. Fellow Am. Assn. Oral and Maxillofacial Surgery, Am. Dental Soc. Anesthesia, Am. Coll. Oral and Maxillofacial Surgeons. Home: 20 Long Creek Dr South Portland ME 04106-2425

ESTERSOHN, HAROLD SYDNEY, retired podiatrist, educator; b. Trenton, N.J., Jan. 3, 1927; s. Mathew and Celia (Olitsky) E.; m. Mildred Evins, Dec. 25, 1949; children: Eileen Lisa, Michele Beth, Laura Rene. D of Podiatric Medicine cum laude, Dr. William M. Scholl Coll., Chgo., 1952. Diplomate Am. Bd. Podiatric Surgery. Resident Dr. William M. Scholl Coll. Podiatric Medicine, Chgo., 1952-53; dir. podiatry staff Daus. Israel Home for the Aged, Newark and West Orange, N.J., 1953-73; dir. podiatry residency programs and podiatry externship program St. Michael's Med. Ctr., Newark, 1974-86, established fellowship in lower extremity infectious diseases, 1984-86, dir. podiatric med. edn., 1986-88; assoc. dean podiatry div. Seton Hall U., South Orange, N.J., 1987-88; cons. Schering Corp., Union, N.J., 1964, Stryker Corp., Kalamazoo, 1972; adj. clin. instr. N.Y. Coll. Podiatric Medicine, Pa. Coll. Podiatric Medicine, Ohio Coll. Podiatric Medicine, Ill. Coll. Podiatric Medicine, Calif. Coll. Podiatric Medicine, 1974-86; podiatry staff South Amboy Meml. Hosp., West Essex Gen. Hosp., St. Vincent's Hosp.; dir. podiatry residency program Hadassah U. Hosp., Ein Karem, Israel, 1987-88; dir. podiatry staff St. Michaels Med. Ctr., 1972-86; staff Doctor's Hosp., Newark, 1958-68, West Essex Gen. Hosp., 1962-80, Newark Beth Israel Med. Ctr., 1963-73, Columbus Hosp. Newark, 1968-76, St. Michael's Med. Ctr., 1972-86, South Amboy Meml. Hosp., 1982-84, St. Vincent Hosp., 1974-80; lectr. in field. Co-author: Current Therapy in Podiatric Surgery, 1989; contbr. articles to profl. jours. Chmn. youth activities Young Israel Synagogue, Newark, 1961-63; podiatry adv. com. N.J. Dept. Instns. and Agys., Trenton, 1969-72; bd. dirs. N.J. affiliate Am. Diabetic Assn., 1975-83, lectr. on diabetic foot, 1974-82. Grantee Schering Corp., 1964, 66, Stryker Corp., 1972; recipient Astra award Astra Pharm. Products, Hershey, Pa., 1985. Fellow Am. Coll. Foot Surgeons (pres. ea. div. 1969-71); mem. Am. Podiatry Assn. (25 Yr. award 1977), N.J. Podiatry Assn. (pres. Ea. divsn. 1959-60, pres. 1967-68), N.J. Podiatry Soc., B'nai Brith (Svc. award 1956). Home: 210 Olive Ave Port Saint Lucie FL 34952-1348

ESTES, CARROLL LYNN, sociologist, educator; b. Fort Worth, May 30, 1938; d. Joe Ewing and Carroll (Cox) E.; A.B., Stanford U., 1959; M.A., So. Meth. U., 1961; Ph.D., U. Calif.-San Diego, 1972, D.H.L. (hon.) Russell Sage Coll., 1986; 1 child, Duskie Lynn Gelfand Estes. Research asst., asst. study dir. Brandeis U. Social Welfare Research Ctr., 1962-63, research assoc., 1964-65, project dir., 1965-67, vis. lectr. Florence Heller Grad. Sch., 1964-65; research dir. Simmons Coll., 1963-64; asst. prof. social work San Diego State Coll., 1967-72; asst. prof. in residence dept. psychiatry U. Calif.-San Francisco, 1972-75, assoc. prof. dept. social and behavioral scis., 1975-79, prof. 1979—, chair dept. social and behavioral scis., 1981-93, coordinator human devel. tng. program, 1974-75, dir. Aging Health Policy Research Center, 1979-85, dir. Inst. for Health and Aging, 1985—; U. Calif. faculty rsch. lectr., 1993. Mem. Calif. Commn. on Aging, 1974-77; cons. U.S. Senate Spl. Com. on Aging from 1976, Notch Commn. U.S. Commn. Social Security. Recipient Matrix award Theta Sigma Phi, 1964, award for contbns. to lives of older Californians, Calif. Commn. on Aging, 1977, Helen Nahm Research award, U. Calif., San Francisco, 1986; NIMH spl. fellow for research, 1970-72. Mem. Inst. Medicine of NA;, ACLU, Am. Sociol. Assn., Assn. Gerontology in Higher Edn. (pres. 1980-81, recipient Beverly award, 1993), Am. Soc. on Aging (pres. 1982-84, Leadership award 1986), Gerontol. Soc. Am. (Kent award 1992, pres. 1995-96), Soc. Study Social Problems, Alpha Kappa Delta, Pi Beta Phi. Democrat. Author: The Decision-Makers: The Power Structure of Dallas, 1963; co-author: Protective Services for Older People, 1972; U.S. Senate Special Committee on Aging Report, Paperwork and the Older Americans Act, 1978; The Aging Enterprise, 1979; co-author: Fiscal Austerity and Aging, 1983; Long Term Care of the Elderly, 1985, Political Economy, Health and Aging, 1984, 2d edit. 1987, Readings in the Political Economy of Aging, 1984, The Long Term Care Crisis, The Nation's Health, 1993; contbr. articles to profl. jours. Office: U Calif San Francisco Inst Health & Aging Box 0646 Ste 340 San Francisco CA 94143-0646

ESTES, EDWARD HARVEY, JR., medical educator; b. Gay, Ga., May 1, 1925; s. Edward Harvey and Veola (Jarrell) E.; m. Jean Anderson, Oct. 15, 1948; children: Sara Estes Malone, Susan Estes Jones III, Rebecca Estes Dunn, John, Elizabeth Estes Smith. B.S., Emory U., 1944, M.D., 1947. House officer, research fellow Grady Meml. Hosp., Atlanta, 1947-50; mem. faculty dept. medicine Duke U., 1952-90, Univ. Disting. Service prof., chmn. dept. community and family medicine, 1966-85, Univ. Disting Svc. prof. community and family medicine emeritus, 1990—, dir. family medicine div., 1985-88. Author: (with R.P. Grant) Spatial Vector Electrocardiography, 1950. Mem. AMA (ho. of dels. 1979-94, chmn. coun. sci. affairs 1992-94), ACP, Inst. Medicine, Am. Soc. Internal Medicine (Disting. Internist of Yr. award 1975), Am. Acad. Family Physicians, Soc. Tchrs. Family Medicine (bd. dirs. 1987-89), N.C. Med. Soc. (pres. 1977-78). Home: 3542 Hamstead Ct Durham NC 27707-5137*

ESTES, JACOB THOMAS, JR., pharmacist, consultant; b. Dallas, Sept. 2, 1944; s. Jacob Thomas and Burgenia Mae (Kelly) E.; m. Susan Jean Rader, Mar. 7, 1980; 1 child, Amy Dianne. BS in Pharmacy, U. Tex., 1967. Hosp. pharmacist St. Joseph Hosp., Ft. Worth; pharmacist Park Row Pharmacy, Arlington, Tex., Plaza Pharmacy, Ft. Worth; pharmacist in-charge, mgr. Whitten Pharmacy; pharmacist in-charge K-Mart Pharmacy, Ft. Worth, Pla. Pharmacy, Granbury, Tex.; owner Queen of Angels Cath. Books and Gifts, Ft. Worth; owner Ctrl. and North Ctrl. Tex. Relief Pharmacists, 1990—; cons. nursing homes, hospice; dist. intervenor Pharmacy Helpline for Impaired; dir. Tex. Bd. Pharmacy, Ft. Worth; ins. agt. N.Y. Life; pharm. cons. to surgery ctrs. in the Dallas and Ft. Worth areas. Bd. dirs. Mother and Unborn Baby, Ft. Worth, 1983—, Unborn Child Clinic Care, 1984—. Served to capt. USAFR, 1968-74. Mem. Am. Soc. Cons. Pharmacists, Tex. Pharm. Assn., Tarrant County Pharm. Assn., U. Tex. Ex Students Assn., Kappa Psi. Roman Catholic. Club: Holy Family Chor., Sierra Internat., Serra Club. Lodge: K.C. Avocation: golfing. Achievements include research in formulation and compounding for chemical peels with fruit acid and T.C.A. products; compounds formulated and compounds for local anesthetic gel to be used in conjunction with T.C.A. solutions; pharmaceutical compounding of new local anesthetics to be used in treatment of ears, of retinoic acid for reduction of wrinkles, of progesterone products for PMS syndrome in female patients, of special eye solutions, of ointment combinations for treatment of herpes simplex virus, of acne compound solutions, of sympathomimet compounds for urinary retention, of special ophthamologic allergy solutions; rsch. in formulation and compounding antibiotic topical preparations for infection; rsch. in formulation and compounding Azole preps for fungal infections and scopolanie topical gel for nausea and vomiting in cancer patients; animephylline ointment for psorlasis; antibiotic sprays for skin infections; topical application for skin cancers. Home: 5517 Wonder Dr Fort Worth TX 76133-2625 Office: K-Mart 4346 Pharmacy 1701 S Cherry Ln Fort Worth TX 76108-3601 also: Whitten Pharmacy 3700 E Rosedale St Fort Worth TX 76105-1701 also: Plz Pharmacy 800 8th Ave Fort Worth TX 76104-2601

ESTES, NATHAN ANTHONY MARK, III, cardiologist, medical educator; b. Newport, R.I., Aug. 20, 1949; s. Nathan Anthony Jr. and Ione (Lewis) E.; m. Noël Evangeline Thorbecke, June 22, 1974; children: Elise Thorbecke, N.A. Chace, Kathryn Elizabeth. BA cum laude, U. Pa., 1971; MD magna cum laude, U. Cin., 1977. Diplomate Am. Bd. Internal Medicine, Am. Bd. Cardiovascular Disease, Am. Bd. Cardiac Electrophysiology. Med. intern New Eng. Deaconess Hosp.-Harvard Med. Sch., Boston, 1977-78, med. resident, 1978-80; fellow in cardiology New Eng. Med. Ctr.-Tufts U., Boston, 1980-82; fellow in electrophysiology Mass. Gen. Hosp.-Harvard Med. Sch., Boston, 1982-83; dir. cardiac arrhythmia New. Eng. Med. Ctr. Svc., Boston, 1983-96, dir. heart station, 1983-91; assoc. prof. medicine Tufts U. Sch. Med., Boston, 1983-90, prof., 1990-96, chief New Eng. Cardiac Arrythmia Ctr., 1996—; ednl. cons., 1985-96; mem. internat. safety monitoring bd. 3M Pharms., Mpls., 1990-96; internat. tachycardia adv. bd. Telectronics Pacific, Denver, 1994-96; co-chmn. pubs. com. NIH, Bethesda, 1993-96. Contbr. over 100 articles to sci. jours.; contbr. over 30 chpts. to books; editor books, 1994-96; editl. bd. Jour. Interventional Electrophysiology, 1995—, Pacing and Cardiac Electrophysiology, 1995—. Vestry mem. St. Peters Ch., Newton, Mass., 1985-87; coach Baystate Tournament of Champions, Waltham, Mass., 1990-94; judge N.H. Racing Assn., Lincoln, 1993-95. Fellow Am. Coll. Cardiology; mem. Am. Heart Assn., N. Am. Soc. Pacing and Electrophysiology, New Eng. Electrophysiology Soc. (pres. 1994-96), Alpha Omega Alpha. Episcopalian. Office: New Eng. Med. Ctr. 750 Washington St Boston MA 02111

ESTES, STEPHEN ARTHUR, dermatologist; b. Rochester, N.Y., July 7, 1947; s. Cameron and Ruth (Madden) E.; m. Barbara Jane Carbary, May 29, 1977; children: Cameron, Jessica. BS, Purdue U., 1969; MD, U. Rochester, 1973. Diplomate Am. Bd. Dermatology. Intern Tucson Hosp., 1973-74; resident Johns Hopkins Hosp., Balt., 1974-77; instr. dermatology U. Ariz. Med. Ctr., Tucson, 1977-78; assoc. prof. U. Cin., 1978-85; pvt. practice Cin., 1985—. Contbr. more than 50 articles to profl. jours. Mem. Cin. Dermatol. Assn. (sec.-treas. 1994-96), Ohio Dermatology Assn. (trustee 1993-96). Home: 1227 Ridgecliff Dr Cincinnati OH 45215 Office: 800 Compton Rd # 28 Cincinnati OH 45231

ESTEVES, FRANCISCO ANTÂNIO, biomedical engineer, physicist; b. Ericeira, Lisbon, Portugal, Aug. 23, 1953; s. Francisco Braulio and Maria Nazaré Esteves; m. Marcia Anisia Freire, Apr. 30, 1979; 1 child, Francisco Freire. MS in Physics, U. Oporto, Portugal, 1976. Physicist-engr. Siemens, Lisbon, 1979-84; lectr., assoc. rschr. U. Oporto, 1976-81, U. Nove de Libre, Portugal, 1980-82; physicist, engr. GE, Lisbon, 1984-88; assoc. rschr. Hosp. Ejes Moiy, Lisbon, 1981-87; physicist, mgr. Toshiba, Lisbon, 1988-91; physicist, engr. Piclusa, Lisbon, 1991—. Author: Transfontanelar Ultrasound, 1984, Ultrasound-Technical Principles, 1985. Mem. Portuguese Soc. Physics (bd. cert.). Office: Piclusa Sistemas Médicos, Ave Almirante Reis 131 4F, 1150 Lisbon Portugal

ESTEVEZ, ROBERTO, cardiologist; b. Montevideo, Uruguay, Aug. 24, 1942; came to U.S., 1974; s. Alfonso and Alicia (Carmona) E.; m. Elizabeth Goodson, Oct. 31, 1967; children—Laura, Leonardo, Anahid. M.D., Montevideo Sch. Medicine, 1970. Diplomate Am. Bd. Internal Medicine. Intern Upstate Med. Ctr., Syracuse, N.Y., 1974-75; fellow cardiology Guthrie Clinic, Sayre, Pa., 1975; resident in internal medicine Guthrie Clinic and Robert Packer Hosp., Sayre, Pa., 1976-77; practice medicine specializing in cardiology, Amarillo, Tex., 1979—; mem. staff, dir. cardiac rehab. St. Anthony Hosp., Amarillo, chmn. dept. cardiology, 1986; chief of medicine North West Tex. Hosp., Amarillo, 1983-85. Fellow Am. Coll. Cardiology (cert.); mem. AMA, ACP. Home: 6402 Palacio Dr Amarillo TX 79109-5115 Office: 301 Amarillo Blvd W Suite 111 Amarillo TX 79107

ESTRADA, CARLOS ROBERTO, physician; b. Bayamo, Cuba, May 13, 1940; came to the U.S., 1970; s. Tomas Severino and Eduvigis (Fonseca) E.; m. Nieves A. Pereiro, Feb. 19, 1966; children: Lissette, Carlos Roberto Jr., Juan Manuel. BS, Pre-Univ., Bayamo, 1963; MD, Madrid U., 1970; postgrad., Tulane U., 1976. Diplomate Am. Bd. Internal Medicine. Chmn. credential com. Trumbull Meml. Hosp., Warren, Ohio, 1989-95; assoc. chief medicine Trumbull Meml. Hosp., Warren, 1992—; trustee Hillside Rehab. Hosp., Warren, 1994—. Mem. Ohio State Med. Assn., Trumbull County Med. Soc. (pres. 1994). Baptist. Office: 1405 E Market St Warren OH 44483

ETEFIA, FLORENCE VICTORIA, mental health professional, educator; b. Alton, Ill., Feb. 13, 1946; d. Esau and Pearl (Taylor) Anthony. BA, Mich. State U., 1968; MAT, Oakland U., Rochester, Mich., 1972; EdS, Wayne State U., 1977, MA, 1987, postgrad. Cert. tchr. mentally impaired, Mich.; spl. edn. supr., Mich.; cert. tchr. mentally impaired, learning disabled K-8 gen. edn., psychology, Mich. Special edn. tchr. Sch. Dist. of Pontiac, Mich. Mem. NEA, Mich. Edn. Assn., Pontiac Edn. Assn., Delta Sigma Theta. Home: 3035 Debra Ct Auburn Hills MI 48326-2044

ETESSAMI, RAMBOD, endonontist; b. Tehran, Iran, Mar. 20, 1960; came to U.S., 1977; s. Abdollah and Mahin E.; m. Pegah Etessami, Dec., 1991. BA in Math., Ind. U., 1980; DDS, Georgetown U., 1984; cert. in advanced endodontics, U. So. Calif., 1986. Head research & devel., chief sci. researcher, bd. dirs. Laseronics, Inc., Torrance, Calif., 1983—; assoc. clin. prof. endodontics U. So. Calif., L.A., 1986—; assoc. clin. prof. Sch. Dentistry UCLA, 1989—; pvt. practice L.A. and Beverly Hills, Calif., 1986—; lectr. Sch. Dentistry UCLA, 1995—. Chmn. Ind. U. chpt. United Jewish Appeal, 1978-79, chmn. Georgetown U. chpt., 1982-83; chmn. Young Dental divsn. Jewish Fedn. Coun.; bd. dirs. dental cabinet L.A. chpt.' 1987—; mem. Magbit Found.; bd. dirs. Iranian Jews Am., Washington, 1980-83, Am.-Israel Pub. Affairs Com., Washington, 1982-84; bd. dirs., chmn. Iranian immigration sect. Jewish Vocat. Svc., L.A., 1987-92. NIH grantee, 1978-79; B. Baj Bhussry fellow George U., 1981; Alpha Omega scholar, 1984. Mem. ADA (cert. Recognition and Appreciation 1984, 86), Am. Assn. Endodontists, Am. Dental Profls. Israel, Calif. Dental Assn., L.A. Dental Soc., B'nai Brith (bd. disr. Fred Matloob chpt. 1990-94), Study Club for Oral Facial Rsch. Jewish. Office: Beverly Sunset Med Bldg 9201 W Sunset Blvd Ste 908 West Hollywood CA 90069-3710

ETGES, FRANK JOSEPH, parasitology educator; b. Chgo., June 18, 1924; s. Joseph Peter and Anna Marie (Foss) E.; m. Ruth Camille Storkan, Sept. 20, 1948 (div. June 1984); children: Robert J., William J., Anne C., David J., Thomas J.; m. Lesta Judith Cooper-Freytag, July 6, 1985. AB, U. Ill., 1948, MS, 1949; PhD, NYU, 1953. Asst. prof. U. Ark., Fayetteville, 1953-54; asst. prof. U. Cin., 1954-59, assoc. prof., 1959-66, prof. parasitology, 1966-95; prof. emeritus, 1995—; rsch. assoc. U.S. Army Tropical Rsch. Med. Lab., San Juan, P.R., 1961-62; guest investigator London Sch. Tropical Medicine and Hygiene, 1971-72. Sgt. U.S. Army, 1943-46, ETO, PTO. NSF rsch. grantee, 1959-65; La. State U. Med. Sch. rsch. fellow, Santo Domingo, P.R., 1961-62, 64, 65, 67, 69; postdoctoral fellow NIH, London, 1971-72, WHO, Egypt, Sudan, Rhodesia, 1975. Mem. Am. Soc. Parasitologists (editorial com.), Am. Soc. Tropical Medicine and Hygiene, Am. Microscopical Soc. (v.p. 1970), Royal Soc. Tropical Medicine and Hygiene, Australian Soc. Parasitology, Soc. Protozoologists, Midwestern Parastiologists (pres. 1969), Sigma Xi. Home: 8284 Sunfish Ln Maineville OH 45039-9568 Office: U Cin Dept Biol Scis Cincinnati OH 45221

ETHEREDGE, EDWARD EZEKIEL, surgeon; b. Jacksonville, Fla., May 22, 1939; s. Ezekiel Yonce and Raymer Frances (Johnson) E.; m. Beverly Elizabeth Hooten, Aug. 26, 1961; children: Edward Ezekiel Jr., William Glenn. BA magna cum laude, Yale U., 1961, MD, 1965; PhD, U. Minn., 1974. Diplomate Am. Bd. Surgery. Intern U. Minn. Hosp., 1965-66, asst. resident, 1966-72, chief resident surgery, 1972-73; asst. prof. surgery Wash. U. Sch. Medicine, St. Louis, 1975-79, assoc. prof. surgery, 1979-84; prof. surgery Tulane U. Sch. Medicine, New Orleans, 1984—, dir. div. transp., 1984—; specialist site visitor residence rev. com. on surgery Accreditation Coun. Grad. Med. Edn., Chgo., 1989—; assoc. councillor United Network for Organ Sharing, Richmond, Va., 1991-93, councillor, 1993-95; pres. bd. dirs. La. Organ Procurement Agy., 1994—, End Stage Renal Disease Network # 13, 1995—. Editor, author (major, with others): Management Techniques in Surgery, 1986; contbr. articles to numerous sci. jours. Pres. Meml. Hall Found., New Orleans, 1990—; bd. dirs. Opera Theatre of St. Louis, 1979-83; pres., bd. dirs. La. Organ Procurent Agy., 1994—, End Stage Renal Disease Network # 13, 1995—. Lt. col. U.S. Army, 1973-75. Decorated Commendation medal. Fellow Am. Coll. Surgeons; mem. Am. Surg. Assn., Soc. Univ. Surgeons, Am. Soc. Transplant Surgeons, Am. Assn. Immunologists. Republican. Methodist. Home: 3313 Prytania St New Orleans LA 70115-3509 Office: Tulane U Sch Medicine SL-22 1430 Tulane Ave Ste 8207 New Orleans LA 70112-2699

ETHERIDGE, JOHN GREEN, pathologist; b. Macon, Ga., May 4, 1932; s. Hubert Calvin and Mary Lee (Aultman) E.; m. Anita Dawn Bruce, June 8, 1955; children: Debra Lynn, Bonnie Gay, John Bruce, Brian Dale. AB, Mercer U., 1954; MD, Med. Coll. Ga., 1958. Pathologist Med. Ctr. Ctrl. Ga., Macon, 1965—; chief of staff Med. Ctr. Ctrl. Ga., Macon, 1981; chmn. bd. Medcen Found., Macon, 1991-92. Capt. USN, 1959-61. Fellow Am. Soc. Clin. Pathologists (state counselor), Coll. Am. Pathologists; mem. So. Med. Assn., Ga. Med. Assn. (sec.), Med. Assn. Ga. (del.), Ocmulgee Med. Pathology Assn. (chmn. bd. 1982-96). Methodist. Home: 6848 Colaparchee Rd Macon GA 31201 Office: Med Ctr Ctrl Ga 777 Hemlock St Macon GA 31201

ETLINGER, JOSEPH D., biology educator; b. Albany, N.Y., Feb. 23, 1946; s. Murry and Rosaline (Spiegel) E.; m. Susan Ellen Neschis, July 12, 1970; children, Ari, Benjamin, Matthew. BS in Physics, Rensselaer Poly. Inst., 1968; PhD in Biophysics, U. Chgo., 1974. Rsch. fellow Harvard Med. Sch., Boston, 1974-77; asst. prof. anatomy and cell biology SUNY Downstate Med. Ctr., Bklyn., 1977-80, assoc. prof., 1980-85, dir. molecular and cellular biology, 1984-88, prof., 1985-87, prof., vice chmn., 1987-88; prof., chmn. cell biology and anatomy N.Y. Med. Coll., Valhalla, N.Y., 1988—; cons. Merck, Sharp and Dohme, Rahway, N.J., 1984-87, NIH, 1981-85, NASA, Ames, Calif., 1978-81. Author 70 jour. articles and chpts. in textbooks. Grantee NIH, NASA, Muscular Dystrophy Assn. Mem. AAAS, N.Y. Acad. Sci., Am. Heart Assn. (established investigator 1980-85), Am. Physiol. Soc., Am. Soc. Cell Biology. Office: NY Med Coll Dept Cell Biology & Anatomy Valhalla NY 10595

ETTENGER, ROBERT BRUCE, physician, nephrologist; b. Phila., Sept. 17, 1942; s.Ervin Earl and Sylvia (Goodstein) W.; m. Angela Joan Castellano Ettenger; children: Allison, Jessica. BA, U. Pa., 1964; MD, 1968. Maj. U.S. Army, El Paso, 1971-73; asst. prof. Pediatrics Children's Hosp. of L.A., 1976-80, U. Calif. L.A. Sch. Medicine, 1980-84; asst. prof. Pediatrics, 1984-89, prof. Pediatrics, 1989—; head Divsn. Pediatric Nephrology UCLA Dept. Pediatrics Sch. Medicine, 1990—; vice chmn. Clin. Affairs, 1990—; dir. Historcompatability lab. UCLA Med. Ctr., L.A., 1987—; mem., chair Sub bd. Nephrology Am. Bd. Pediatrics, Chapel Hill, N.C., 1986-91; cons. Immunosuppressive Adv. Com. Food and Drug Adminstrn., Bethesda, Md., 1994—, Biologics and Immune Response Modifiers, Food and Drug Adminstrn., Bethesda, Md., 1994—; mem. Biol. Scientific Adv. Com., U.S. Renal Data Sys., Ann Arbor, Mich., 1993—. Contbr. articles to profl. jours. Coach AYSO Soccer, Santa Monica, Calif., 1994—, Bobby Sox Softball, 1995—, YWCA Basketball, 1995—; mem. adv. bd. Nat. Kidney Found., L.A., 1993—. Recipient Ortho Biotech Lectureship Urologic Soc. for Transplantation, 1990, Robert Neerhaut Teaching award UCLA Dept. Pediatrics, 1981, Continuing Svc. award nat. Kidney Found., L.A., 1991, 92, 94. Fellow Am. Acad. Pediatrics, Am. Soc. Transplant Physicians, Am. Pediatric Soc., Transplantation Soc. Jewish. Office: UCLA Medical Ctr AZ-383 Dept Pediatrics 10833 LeCoute Ave Los Angeles CA 90095

ETTIEN, JAMES THOMAS, surgeon; b. Chattanooga, Mar. 23, 1941; s. Todd and Rosa Jane (Verheg) E.; m. Janey Cureton, Sept. 14, 1963 (div.); 1 child, James Keith. BA, U. of the South, 1963; MD, Med. Coll. Ga., 1971. Diplomate Am. Bd. Surgery. Intern Vanderbilt Hosp., Nashville, 1971-72; resident Med. Coll. Ga., Augusta, 1972-76, asst. prof. surgery, 1978-79; surgeon Gastonia (N.C.) Surg. Assocs., 1976-78; attending surgeon Diagnostic Clinic, Largo, Fla., 1979—; chief divsn. surgery Largo Med. Ctr. Hosp., 1985-86, liaision ACS com. on cancer, 1988—, chmn. cancer control com., 1993—; book reviewer JAMA. Author: (with others) Advances in Internal Medicine, 1981; editl. adviser Resident and Staff Physician, 1978—; contbr. articles to profl. jours. 1st lt. USAR, 1963-66. Recipient scholarship Mosby Book Co., 1971. Fellow ACS, Assn. Acad. Surgery, Internat. Coll. Surgeons; mem. SAGES, Undersea Med. Soc., Southeastern Surg. Congress, Alpha Omega Alpha. Episcopalian. Office: Diagnostic Clinic 1551 W Bay Dr Largo FL 34640

ETTINGER, HARRY JOSEPH, industrial hygiene engineer, project manager; b. N.Y.C., July 20, 1934; s. Morris and Pauline (Waxman) E.; m. June Kopf, June 14, 1958; children: Linda E., Steven E., Robert A. BCE, CCNY, 1956; MCE, NYU, 1958. Registered profl. engr., N.Mex.; cert. indsl. hygienist. Sanitary engr. USPHS, Bethesda, Md., 1958-61; staff mem. Los Alamos (N.Mex.) Nat. Lab., 1961-71, alt. group leader, 1971-74, group leader, 1974-80, program mgr., 1981-87; project dir. Occupational Safety and Health Adminstrn., Washington, 1987-89; tech. rsch. coord. Los Alamos (N.Mex.) Nat. Lab., 1989-91, program mgr., 1991-93; chief scientist environ., safety and health divsn., 1993—, acting dep. divsn. dir., 1995-96; cons. divsn. reactor licensing USAEC, 1970-71, cons. EPA, 1972-74, various industries, 1970—; cons. to adv. com. on nuclear facility safety DOE, 1990-91; mem. adj. faculty U. Ark., Little Rock, 1969-90, San Diego State U., 1981-86; vis. faculty Tex. A&M U., College Station, 1981—; faculty affiliate Colo. State U., Ft. Collins, 1983—; mem. exec. com. toxic substances rsch. and tchg. program U. Calif., 1984-90; mem. stds. steering group DOE Lab. Dirs. Environ. and Occupational Health, 1990-96. Contbr. jour. articles and tech. reports on indsl. hygiene, aerosol physics, respiratory protection. Chmn. Los Alamos County Utility Bd., 1970; vice chmn. Los Alamos County planning and Zoning Commn., 1974-76. Fellow Am. Indsl. Hygiene Assn. (editl. rev. bd. 1979-87, 90-91, 95—, bd. dirs. 1987-90, v.p. 1991-92, pres.-elect 1992-93, pres. 1993-94, Edward Baier award 1990); mem. Am. Acad. Indsl. Hygiene, Am. Assn. Aerosol Rsch., Am. Bd. Indsl. Hygiene (bd. dirs. 1979-85, chmn. 1983-85), Am. Conf. Govtl. Indsl. Hygiene (Meritorious Achievement award 1985), Internat. Soc. Respiratory Protection (bd. dirs. 1985-88, 95-98), Internat. Occupational Hygiene Assn. (bd. dirs. 1994-97). Democrat. Jewish.

ETTINGER, LAWRENCE JAY, pediatric hematologist and oncologist, educator; b. Bklyn., Dec. 17, 1947; s. Joseph and Blanche (Mittman) E.; m. Alice G. Renick. BA, Case Western Res. U., 1969, MD, 1973. Intern in pediatrics U. Md. Hosp., Balt., 1973-74, resident in pediatrics, 1974-75; resident in pediatrics Children's Hosp. Buffalo, 1975-76; fellow in pediatric hematology-oncology Roswell Park Meml. Inst. and Children's Hosp. Buffalo, 1976-78; asst. prof. pediatrics U. Rochester (N.Y.) Sch. Med. and Dentistry, 1978-81, U. So. Calif., L.A., 1981-84; assoc. prof. U. Medicine and Dentistry N.J., Robert Wood Johnson Med. Sch., New Brunswick; chief div. pediatric hematology-oncology U. Medicine and Dentistry N.J., Robert Wood Johnson Med. Sch., 1984—. Contbr. articles to profl. jours.; manuscript reviewer Cancer, Mayo Clinic Proceedings. Mem. adv. com. Sickle Cell Program, N.J., State Health Dept., Trenton, 1989, Pediatric Oncology Adv. Group, N.J. Commn. Cancer Rsch., 1986—; mem. State of N.J. Cancer Plan Task Force, 1991—; mem. med. adv. bd. Inst. for Children with Cancer and Blood Disorders, 1991—; field reader Office of Orphan Products Devel. FDA, 1988—; mem. spl. rev. com. NIH, 1992, 95; mem. cancer ad hoc com. Ocean County (N.J.) Health Dept., 1996—. Recipient Univ. Excellence award for patient care U. Medicine and Dentistry, N.J., 1991, Pride of N.J. award and Clara Barton Med. Svc. award Gov. of N.J., 1992, N.J. Pride award in health, 1993; grantee N.J. Commn. on Cancer Rsch., Trenton,

1987-89, Valerie Fund, Maplewood, N.J., 1985-90, The Upjohn Co., Kalamazoo, 1984-86, Wyeth-Ayerst Rsch., Phila., 1992—, Enzon Inc., Piscataway, N.J., 1992—, Amgen, Inc., Thousand Oaks, Calif., 1992—, Inst. for Children with Cancer and Blood Disorders, 1991—, Sanofi Winthrop, 1996; Jr. Faculty Clin. . Fellow Am. Cancer Soc., 1980-83. Fellow Am. Acad. Pediatrics; mem. AMA, Acad. Medicine N.J., Ea. Soc. Pediatric Rsch., Am. Assn. Cancer Rsch., Am. Soc. Clin. Oncology, Am. Soc. Hematology, Am. Soc. Pediatric Hematology-Oncology, Am. Cancer Soc. (svc. and rehab. com. N.J. divsn. 1985—, vice chmn. 1988-89, 92-94, chmn. 1994—, bd. trustees, exec. com. 1994—), Oncology Soc. N.J., Children's Cancer Group, Phi Beta Kappa. Office: U Medicine and Dentistry Robert Wood Johnson Med Sch New Brunswick NJ 08903

ETTINGER, VIRGINIA MILLER, respiratory therapist, educator; b. Tuscola, Ill.; d. George Bernard and Edith Mae (Baker) Miller; m. Glenn C. Wiprud, Dec. 16, 1955 (div. 1974); children: Barbara C., Valerie L.; m. Jerome Ettinger, Oct. 8, 1995. BS in Journalism, So. Ill. U., 1953; Cert. Respiratory Therapy, UCLA, 1973; MPH, Calif. State U., Northridge; 1983. Registered respiratory therapist, Calif. Women's editor Hollywood (Calif.) Citizen News, 1953-54; news writer L.A. Times-Mirror Co., 1954-56; promotion assoc. KOMO-TV, Seattle, 1956-57; promotions, pub. rels. writer L.A. Times, 1957-63; respiratory therapist UCLA Med. Ctr., 1973-76; respiratory care educator L.A. Valley Coll., Van Nuys, Calif., 1976—, program dir., 1995—; mem. Calif. Respiratory Care Examining Com., Sacramento, 1988—, vice chmn., 1989-90, chmn., 1991, v.p. Respiratory Care Bd., 1995. Author curriculum guide, editor syllabus. CPR instr. L.A. chpt. Am. Heart Assn. Grantee L.A. C.C. Dist., 1988-90, 92-93. Mem. Calif. Soc. Respiratory Care (pres. chpt. 4 L.A. 1986-87, state com. chair 1986-89), Am. Assn. Respiratory Care, Phi Kappa Phi, Pi Delta Epsilon, Sigma Sigma Sigma, Lambda Beta. Office: LA Valley Coll Dept Health Sci 5800 Fulton Ave Van Nuys CA 91401-4062

ETU, PAUL DAVID, psychologist; b. Glens Falls, N.Y., Sept. 26, 1954; s. James Lawrence and Cecelia Joan (Jordan) E.; m. Marcia Edna Mears, Aug. 13, 1977; children: Eric Mears, Joshua Jordan, Nathan Patrick. AAS, SUNY-Adirondack, Glens Falls, 1975; BA, SUNY, Oswego, 1977; MS, Marquette U., 1980; D in Psychology, SUNY, Albany, 1990. Cert. sch. psychologist, N.Y.; lic. psychologist, N.Y. Grad. dir. Ctr. Psychol. Svcs. Marquette U., Milw., 1978-80; psychologist, program coord. Cmty. Workshop, Inc., Glens Falls, 1980-83, supervising psychologist, 1995—; psychologist, program dir. Rehab. Support Svcs., Albany, 1983-85; psychologist N.Y. State Office Mental Retardation, Wilton, 1985-88, Glens Falls City Sch. Dist., 1988-94, Mental Health Assn. Warren and Washington counties, 1991; pvt. practice psychologist Glens Falls, N.Y., 1991—; mgr., Glens Falls Tennis and Swim Club, 1989.; sr. cons., Rape Crisis Ctr., Glens Falls, 1980-82. Author: Human Sexuality Curriculum, 1981; contbr. articles to psychol. jours. Coach, bd. dirs. Ft. Edward (N.Y.) Little League, 1970-82, Queensbury (N.Y.) Little League, 1985—, sec., 1989—; cub leader, com. mem. Mohican coun. Boy Scouts Am., 1988—. Grantee N.Y. State Office Mental Retardation, 1983-84, U.S. Dept. of Edn., 1988—. Mem. Am. Psychol. Assn., Tri-County Psychol. Assn. (sec.-treas. 1988—), Saratoga County Psychol. Assn., Nat. Assn. Sch. Psychologists, N.Y. State Assn. Sch. Psychologists, Glens Falls Tennis and Swim Club, Adirondack Computer Users Group (pres. 1985-87), Psi Chi, Pi Gamma Mu. Democrat. Roman Catholic. Home: 16 Sunset Dr Queensbury NY 12804-1126 Office: 498 Glen St Glens Falls NY 12801-2230

ETZEL, RUTH ANN, pediatrician, epidemiologist; b. Milw., Apr. 6, 1954; d. Raymond Arthur and Marian Dorothy (Neu) E. Student, St. Olaf Coll., 1972-73; BA in Biology summa cum laude, U. Minn., 1976; MD, U. Wis., 1980; PhD, U. N.C., 1985. Pediatrics resident N.C. Meml. Hosp., Chapel Hill, 1980-83; adj. asst. prof. pediatrics Emory U. Sch. Medicine, Atlanta, 1985-87; epidemic intelligence svc. officer Ctr. Environ. Health Ctrs. for Disease Control, Atlanta, 1985-87, med. epidemiologist Ctr. Environ. Health and Injury Control, 1987-90; chief air pollution and respiratory health br. Ctrs. for Disease Control and Prevention, Atlanta, 1991—; mem. preventive medicine and pub. health test com. Nat. Bd. Med. Examiners, 1992—; mem. U.S. Med. Licensing Exam. Step 2 Preventive Medicine and Pub. Health Test Material Devel. Com., 1992—; asst. dir. CDC Preventive Medicine Residency Program, 1992—. Contbr. articles to profl. publs. Robert Wood Johnson clin. scholar U. N.C., 1983-85, MacPherson scholar, 1972; recipient Arthur S. Flemming award D.C. Jaycees, 1991. Fellow Am. Acad. Pediatrics (com. on environ. hazards, CDC liaison 1986-92, chair sect. on epidemiology 1988-92, ex officio 1993—); mem. APHA, Ambulatory Pediatric Assn. (rsch. com. 1987—), Soc. for Pediatric Epidemiol. Rsch. (exec. com. 1988—), Physicians for Social Responsibility, Soc. for Pediatric Epidemiol. Rsch., Phi Beta Kappa, Delta Omega.

ETZIONI, AMITAI, sociologist, educator; b. Cologne, Germany, Jan. 4, 1929; s. Willi Falk and Gertrude Hannauer (Falk) E.; m. Minerva Morales, Sept. 14, 1965 (dec. Dec. 20, 1985); children: Ethan, Oren, Michael, David, Benjamin; m. Patricia Kellogg, Nov. 6, 1992. BA, Hebrew U., Jerusalem, 1954, MA, 1956; PhD in Sociology, U. Calif., Berkeley, 1958; LittD (hon.), Rider Coll., 1980, Gov.'s State U., 1987; LLD (hon.), U. Utah, 1991; LHD (hon.), Colo. Coll., 1994, Conn. Coll., 1994. Mem. faculty Columbia U., 1958-80; rsch. assoc. Inst. War and Peace Studies, 1961, prof. sociology, 1967, chmn. dept., 1969-78; dir. Ctr. for Policy Rsch., 1968—; guest scholar Brookings Instn., 1978-79; sr. advisor White House, 1979-80; univ. prof. George Washington U., Washington, 1980—, dir. Ctr. for Communitarian Policy Studies, 1995—; Thomas Henry Carroll Ford Found. vis. prof., grad. sch. bus. Harvard U., Cambridge, Mass., 1987-89; bd. dirs. Ctr. for Policy Rsch., Washington; mem. Econ. Forum The Conf. Bd., 1983-85; founder Ctr. for Comm. Policy Studies, George Washington U., 1995—; developed organizational analysis, a typology based on means used to control participants in orgns., how orgns. change, survive and are integrated into larger social units. Author: A Comparative Analysis of Complex Organizations, 1961, Modern Organizations, 1964, Political Unification, A Comparative Study of Leaders and Forces, 1965, Studies in Social Change, 1966, the Active Society, 1968, Genetic Fix, 1973, Social Problems, 1975, An Immodest Agenda, 1982, Capital Corruption, 1984, The Moral Dimension, 1988, The Spirit of Community, 1993; editor: The Responsive Community, 1990—; editorial bd. Sci. Mag., 1969-71; contbr. numerous articles to profl. jours. With Israeli Army. Social Sci. Rsch. Coun. faculty fellow, 1960-61, 67-68; fellow Ctr. for Advanced Study in Behavioral Scis., 1965-66; Guggenheim fellow, 1968. Fellow AAAS; mem. Am. Sociol. Assn. (pres. 1995), Soc. for the Advancement Socio-Econs. (founder 1989), The Communitarian Network (founder 1993), Inst. Medicine. Office: George Washington U 2130 H St NW Gelman Libr Rm 714 Washington DC 20052

ETZWILER, DONNELL DENCIL, pediatrician; b. Mansfield, Ohio, Mar. 29, 1927; s. Donnell Seymour and Berniece Jean (Meek) E.; m. Helen Brown Beard, Mar. 3, 1989; children from previous marriage: Nancy, Lisa, Diane, David. B.A. cum laude, Ind. U., 1950; M.D., Yale U., 1953. Intern dept. pediatrics Yale U. Sch. Medicine, New Haven, 1953-54; resident dept. pediatrics N.Y. Hosp. Cornell U. Med. Sch., N.Y.C., 1954-55, Nat. Inst. Arthritis and Metabolic Diseases fellow N.Y. Hosp., 1955-56, instr. pediatrics, 1956-57; mem. faculty Clin. Inst. U. Minn. Med. Sch., Mpls., 1957-74, clin. instr., asst. clin. prof. pediatrics, 1974-84, clin. prof. dept. pediatrics, 1985—, clin. prof. dept. family practice and community medicine, 1990—; pediatrician Nicollet Med. Ctr., 1957—; founder, pres., chief med. officer Internat. Diabetes Ctr., 1967—; instr. Project Hops, Trujillo, Peru, 1962; bd. dirs., pres. St. Louis Park Med. Ctr. Rsch. Found., 1969-71; mem. Nat. Commn. on Diabetes, 1975-77; dir. WHO Diabetes Collaborating Ctr. in Diabetes Edn., Translation & Computer Tech., chmn., 1988—; chmn. WHO Collaborating Ctr. for Diabetes, 1988-94; co-dir. Internat. Diabetes Programme, Russia. Author: Education and Management of the Patient with Diabetes Mellitus, 1967, 3d edit., 1992; editor: Learning to Live With Diabetes (in Russian), 1985, 2d edit., 91; also articles, reports. Bd. dirs. Minn. Soc. for the Blind, 1977-85, Diabetes Edn. and Rsch. Found., 1985—. With USNR, WWII. Recipient Good Neighbor award Sta. WCCO, 1977, 85, Park Nicollet Med. Ctr. Community award, 1987, Park Nicollet Med. Found. Rsch. award, 1991, Educator award, 1993. Fellow All India Inst. Diabetes; mem. AMA, Am. Diabetes Assn. (pres. 1976-77, Disting. Svc. Youth award 1976, Banting medal 1977, Becton-Dickinson award 1978, Upjohn Educator award 1983, Med. Alley Honor award 1988, hon., Russian award for peace efforts 1994), Am. Assn. Diabetes Educators (hon.), Internat. Diabetes Fedn. (exec. com., dir., bd. mgmt., chmn. internat. com. juvenile diabetes 1978-85, v.p. 1976-85), Soc. Pub. Health Educators, Am. Group Practice Assn., Am. Pub. Health Assn., Inst. of Medicine of NAS (camp dir. Minn. affiliate 1959-84, bd. dirs.), Am. Acad. Pediats., Am. Dietetic Assn. (hon.), Minn. Med. Assn., Internat. Soc. Pediat. and Adolescent Diabetes, European Assn. for Study of Diabetes. Presbyterian. Office: Internat Diabetes Ctr 3800 Park Nicollet Blvd Minneapolis MN 55416-2527

EUBANKS, MARY, biologist, anthropologist; b. Hattiesburg, Miss., May 21, 1947; d. Michael Joseph and Nell Elizabeth (Bass) E.; m. Thomas Patrick Settlemyre, May 31, 1967 (div. 1973); children: Dealey; m. Edward James Dunn, Mar. 3, 1974 (div. 1983); children: Laura Louise, Edward Wilkes. BA, U. N.C., 1970, MA, 1973, PhD, 1977; MS Vanderbilt U., 1987. Vis. scientist Harvard Bot. Mus., 1972; instr. U. N.C., Chapel Hill, 1975; research assoc. So. Meth. U., 1976-77, Tulane U. Middle Am. Research Inst., New Orleans, 1977-78, Vanderbilt U., Nashville, 1978-80; vis. scholar anthropology U. Cin., 1981-84; research assoc. biology Ind. U., Bloomington, 1984-85; teaching assist. biology Vanderbilt U., 1985-87; vis. asst. prof. genetics and crop sci. N.C. State U., 1987-88, cons., 1988—; rsch. scientist Duke U., 1992—. Research Corp. grantee, 1971-72; Nat. Geog. Soc. grantee, 1975-76. Fellow Am. Anthrop. Assn.; mem. Am. Med. Writers Assn., AAAS, Am. Inst. Biol. Scis., Soc. Econ. Botany, Am. Bot. Soc., Southeastern Archaeol. Conf., Sigma Xi. Contbr. articles on archaeology, genetics, toxicology, pharmacology and ethnobotany to profl. jours., monographs on neurobiology, agrl. chemicals and drug evaln.; patentee in field. Office: Duke U Dept Botany PO Box 90338 Durham NC 27708-0338

EUSTERMAN, VINCENT D., surgeon; b. Basin, Wyo., Feb. 24, 1954; s. George and Mary Cecilia (Cain) E.; m. Jane Dorsey Hochmuth; children: Matthew, Laura, Daniel. BS, Montana State U., 1973; DDS cum laude, Creighton U., 1978, MD cum laude, 1986. Otolaryngologist head, neck & skull base surgery U.S. Army, Washington, 1978-83, surgeon, 1983—. Home: 5454 S Idalin Way Aurora CO 80015

EUSTICE, DAVID C., pharmaceutical researcher; b. Wharton, N.J., Sept. 26, 1952; s. Clarence William and Helen (Hobbs) E.; m. Phylliss Paeth, Mar. 21, 1984 (div. Dec. 1994); children: Alexander, Shannon. BS, SUNY, Geneseo, 1974, MA, 1976; PhD, SUNY, Binghamton, 1980. Post doctoral fellow Dartmouth Med. Sch., Hanover, N.H., 1980-82, U. Rochester, N.Y., 1982-85; prin. investigator Dupont Co., Wilmington, Del., 1985-91; sr. rsch. investigator Bristol-Myers Squibb, Wallingford, Conn., 1991-94; sr. staff scientist Bayer Corp., West Haven, Conn., 1994—. Contbr. articles to sci. jours. Mem. Soc. Indsl. Microbiology, Soc. Biomolecular Screening. Home: 58 Middle Rd Guilford CT 06437

EUSTIS, LEOLA BARNHART, retired nursing educator; b. Nebo, Pa., Nov. 14, 1920; d. Herbert Wilson and Ada Pearl (Murphy) Barnhart; m. George Arthur Eustis, Nov. 3, 1942 (dec. Dec. 1981); children: Carole Ann, Sarah Ruth. Diploma in nursing, Washington Hosp. Sch. Nursing, Pa., 1942; BS in Nursing Edn. magna cum laude, U. Pitts., 1957, MEd, 1964. Staff nurse Washington (Pa.) Hosp., 1942-45, supr., 1945-52, assoc. dir., nursing svc., 1965-68, dir. pers. edn., 1968-74; instr. Washington Hosp. Sch. Nursing, 1952-60, 1974-83; private duty nurse Washington Hosp., 1960-65. Bd. dirs. Am. Cancer Soc., Washington County unit, 1958-70, Washington County Mental Health Assn., 1965-70; mem. Easter Seals Soc., 1960-91, Nat. Dem. Com., 1981-94, Nat. Wildlife Fedn., 1990-91; vol. Hospice of Washington County, Washington Hosp., Presbyn. Med. Ctr., Washington. Mem. Washington Hosp. Nurses' Alumnae Assn. (pres. 1947-49), Am. Assn. Retired Persons, AAUW (pres. Washington county br. 1972-73, Sigma Theta Tau. Methodist.

EVAGUES, KATHERINE ANN, nurse; b. Bay Shore, N.Y., Apr. 18, 1948; d. ARthur Robert and Katherine (Weber) Kirchner; m. Jeffrey Evagues, Oct. 5, 1991. AAS in Nursing, Suffolk County Community Coll., 1968; BS in Nursing, C.W. Post Coll., 1976; MA in Health Care magna cum laude, SUNY, Stony Brook, 1986. RN, N.Y.; credentialed alcoholism counselor. Staff nurse Southside Hosp., Bay Shore, 1968-69, staff nurse oper. rm., 1974-76, 81-89; insvc. instr. Boston Hosp. for Women, Brookline, Mass., 1969-70; staff nurse med.-surg. Newton Wellesley Hosp., Newton Lower Falls, Mass., 1970-71; nurse-in-charge Univ. Hosp., Boston, 1970-74; nursing team leader Straub Hosp., Honolulu, 1976-80; alcoholism counselor Lighthouse Counseling Ctr., Riverhead, N.Y., 1989-92; nursing care coord. Eastern L.I. Hosp., Greenport, N.Y., 1989-91; pub. health nurse Suffolk County Riverhead (N.Y.) County Ctr. Bur. Pub. Health Nurses, 1991-93; nurse Dept. Social Svcs., Med. Assessment Bur., Hauppauge, N.Y., 1993—. Assn. Oper. Rm. Nurses scholar, 1974; HEW grantee, 1975. Mem. N.Y. State Nurses Assn., N.Y. Fedn. Alcoholism Counselors. Lutheran. Office: Dept Social Svcs Med Svcs Bur PO Box 2000 Hauppauge NY 11788

EVANEGA, GEORGE RONALD, medical company executive; b. Cementon, Pa., Feb. 6, 1936; s. George and Helen A. (Cesanek) E.; m. Janet K. Roark, June 16, 1992; children: George C., Veronica A. BS in Engring., Lehigh U., 1957; MS, Yale U., 1958, PhD in Organic Chemistry, 1960. Rsch. scientist Union Carbide, Tarrytown, N.Y., 1962-69; mgr. Pfizer Cen. Rsch., Groton, Conn., 1969-75; dir. Biodynamics, Indpls., 1975-78; Hauptabteilungsleiter Boehringer Mannheim, Tutzing, Fed. Republic Germany, Germany, 1978-79; v.p. product devel. Boehringer Mannheim Diagnostics, Indpls., 1979-81, v.p. mktg. sales, 1981-84, v.p. tech., 1984-88; v.p., chief adminstrv. officer Miles Inc., Elkhart, Ind., 1988-91; pres., COO, Oncor Inc., Gaithersburg, Md., 1991-95; CEO, pres. Gull Labs., Inc., Salt Lake City, 1995—. NIH fellow, 1961. Mem. Am. Assn. Clin. Chemists, Am. Chem. Soc., N.Y. Acad. Sci.

EVANGELISTA, JESUS SORIANO, physician; b. Manila, Apr. 19, 1946; came to U.S., 1972; s. Feliciano Coronel and Cristina (Soriano) E.; m. Mary Ann Stancoven, May 6, 1978; children: Nicole Maria, Nathan Jess. BS in Zoology, U. Santo Tomas, Manila, 1966, MD, 1971. Diplomate Am. Acad. Family Physicians; diplomate, added certification in geriat. medicine Am. Bd. Family Physicians. Rotating intern St. Peter's Hosp., Albany, N.Y., 1972-73; family practice resident Washington Hosp., 1973-75; assoc. mem. staff Cohoes (N.Y.) Meml. Hosp., 1975-76; mem. active staff Washington (Pa.) Hosp., 1975—; mem. courtesy staff Canonsburg (Pa.) Gen. Hosp., 1985—; chmn. dept. family practice Washington Hosp., 1981-83. Chmn. exec. com. Washington Hosp., 1986-87. Fellow Am. Acad. Family Physicians, Am. Geriatrics Soc.; mem. AMA, Pa. Acad. Family Physicians, Washington County Med. Soc. (pres. 1989), Pa. Med. Soc., Cert. Am. Med. Dirs. Democrat. Roman Catholic. Home: 109 Trenton Cir Mc Murray PA 15317-3657 Office: 50 E Wylie Ave Washington PA 15301-2002

EVANS, BRADLEY DENNIS, psychiatrist, organizational consultant; b. Phila., June 17, 1950; s. Herman Harry Evans and Ida Evans-Swersky; m. Kristin Marie Updegrove, June 3, 1989; children: Jennifer, Katlyn. BS, Phila. Coll. Pharmacy and Sci., 1971; MD, Thomas Jefferson U., Phila., 1975. Diplomate Am. Bd. Psychiatry and Neurology; cert. Am. Soc. of Addiction Medicine, 1988; lic. psychiatrist, Ariz., Pa., N.J. Resident in psychiatry Thomas Jefferson U. Hosp., Phila., 1975-79, asst. prof. psychiatry, 1979-80; clin. asst. prof. psychiatry U. Pa., Phila., 1982-84; staff physician Phila. VA Med. Ctr., 1981-84; staff psychiatrist Carrier Found., Belle-Mead, N.J., 1984-90, dir. Addiction Recovery Svc. div., 1987-90; clin. asst. prof. psychiatry Rutgers Coll. Medicine, U. Medicine and Dentistry N.J., 1985-91; pvt. practice Tucson, 1991—; vis. faculty Ctr. for Alcohol Studies Rutgers U., Piscataway, N.J., 1989-91; cons. Thomas Jefferson U. Hosp. Drug and Alcohol Outreach Program, Phila., 1979-81. Contbr. numerous articles profl. jours. Recipient Earl D. Bond award dept. of psychaitry U. Pa., 1983. Fellow Am. Coll. Psychiatrists (Laughlin fellow); mem. AMA, Am. Psychiat. Assn.,Am. Soc. Addiction Medicine (cert.), Ariz. Med. Assn., PimaCounty Med. Soc., Ariz. Psychiat. Soc., Acad. of Organl. and Occupl. Psychiatry. Office: 2920 N Swan Rd Ste 206 Tucson AZ 85712-1255

EVANS, BRADLEY KEITH, physician; b. Columbus, Ohio, Nov. 8, 1954; s. Norman Edward and Carol (Smalley) E.; m. Diane Kaye Donley, Sept. 25, 1983; 1 child, Lillian Elizabeth. BSEE, Stanford U., 1976; MD, Baylor Coll., 1980. Diplomate Am. Bd. Neurology. Med. intern St. Luke's Hosp., Houston, 1980-81; resident, neurology Baylor Coll. Medicine, Houston, 1981-84; rsch. fellow Rockefeller U., N.Y.C., 1984-87; asst. prof. Sch. of Medicine U. Ala., Birmingham, 1987-93; chief of neurology Birmingham V.A. Med. Ctr., 1991-94. Contbg. author: AIDS and Neurology, 1991; contbr. articles to profl. jours. Mem. Alpha Omega Alpha. Office: 110 S Madison Traverse City MI 49684

EVANS, CAROL ROCKWELL, nursing administrator; b. New Orleans, Jan. 8, 1953; d. Daniel Raymond Sr. and Helen (Fischer) Rockwell; divorced; children: Nikki Elizabeth, Mimi Michelle. ADN, La. State Med. Ctr., 1990. RN, La.; cert. ACLS, BLS, cert. case mgr.; lic. life and health ins. agent. Life and health ins. agt. La. Ins. Agts. Assn., New Orleans, 1975-95; dir. case mgmt. and utilization rev. Associated Med. Rev. Svcs., Metairie, La., 1986-95; charge nurse med-surg. telemetry unit Elmwood Med. Ctr., Jefferson, La., 1990—; RN specialist III ICU St. Charles Gen. Hosp., New Orleans, 1993—; dir. med. mgmt. Nat. Health Resources, Inc., Metairie, La., 1995—. Lobby La. Health Care, Baton Rouge, 1991. Mem. ANA, Individual Case Mgmt. Assn., Assn. Rehab. Nurses Case Mgmt. Soc. Am., Assn. Respiratory Care, New Orleans Continuity Care, La. Managed Healthcare Assn., NAFE. Republican. Roman Catholic. Home: 6002 Mitchell Ave Metairie LA 70003-4254 Office: Nat Health Resources Inc Ste 800 3525 N Causeway Blvd Metairie LA 70002

EVANS, CASWELL ALVES, JR., dentist. BA, Franklin & Marshall Coll., 1965; DDS, Columbia U., 1970; MPH, U. Mich., 1972. Asst. prof. dentistry dept. dental ecology Sch. Dentistry, U. N.C., 1973-74; chief dental svc. and dir. rsch. and evaluation Healthco, Inc., 1973-74; clin. asst. prof. epidemiology and internat. health Sch. Pub. Health and Cmty. Med., Sch. Dentistry, U. Wash., 1974-85; asst. dir. health svc., dir. pub. health programs and svc. L.A. County Dept. Health Svc., 1985—; assoc. prof. cmty. medicine Charles R. Drew U. Med. and Sci., 1986—; chief dental svc. Seattle-King County Dept. Pub. Health, 1974-85, dir. ops., 1979; dir. King County Health Svc. Divsn., 1980-85; prin. investigator grant Nat. Cancer Inst.-NIH, 1986-91; co-prin. investigator, 1989-94; adj. prof. Sch. Dentistry, U. Calif., L.A., 1987—, Sch. Pub. Health, 1988—. Mem. APHA (pres. 1995), Inst. Medicine-NAS, Am. Assn. Pub. Health Dentistry. Office: LA County Dept Health Svcs 313 N Figueroa St Los Angeles CA 90012*

EVANS, CHARLES ALBERT, microbiology educator; b. Mpls., Feb. 18, 1912; s. Albert Grant and Susan Briery (Thompson) E.; m. Allie Ann Christman, Dec. 22, 1939; children: Nicholas J. (dec.), Susan Ethel, Thomas Charles, Carol Ann. BS, U. Minn., 1935, MD, 1937, PhD, 1943. Diplomate Am. B. Med. Microbiology. NRC fellow U. Rochester, 1941-42; rsch. supr. Minn. State Dept. Conservation, Mpls., 1942-43; asst. prof. dept. bacteriology U. Minn., Mpls., 1942-44, assoc. prof. dept. bacteriology, 1944-46; assoc. dir. Fred Hutchinson Cancer Rsch. Ctr., Seattle, 1971-75; prof. dept. microbiology U. Wash., Seattle, 1946-82, chmn., 1946-70, prof. emeritus, 1982—; mem. nat. cancer coun. USPHS, Bethesda, Md., 1958-59,64-67; chmn. rsch. adv. coun. Am. Cancer Soc., 1967-70. Contbr. over 100 articles to profl. jours. Recipient numerous rsch. grants from NIH and Am. Cancer Soc. Mem. Am. Soc. for Microbiology (hon., pres. 1959-60), Soc. for Infectious Diseases (emeritus), Am. Assn. for Cancer Rsch. (emeritus), Am. Acad. Microbiology (mem. bd. govs. 1959-65, chmn. 1960-61). Home: 7739 29th Ave NE Seattle WA 98115-4616 Office: U Wash Sch Medicine Dept Microbiology Seattle WA 98195

EVANS, DAVID A., plant geneticist; b. Apr. 9, 1952; m. Kitty Ann Reninger, Dec. 19, 1978. BSc in Plant Genetics, Ohio State U., 1973, MSc in Plant Genetics, 1975, PhD, 1977; MA in Mgmt. Devel., Harvard U., 1987. Rockefeller Found. postdoctoral fellow NRC/Prairie Regional Lab., Sask., Can., 1977-78; asst. prof. dept. biol. scis. SUNY, Binghamton, 1978-80; mgr. cellular genetics Campbell Inst. for Rsch. and Tech., Cinnaminson, N.J., 1981; v.p. tech. and prodn. devel. DNA Plant Tech. Corp., Cinnaminson, 1981-89, v.p. bus. devel., 1989—; adj. prof. divsn. biology grad. program plant scis. Rutgers U., New Brunswick, N.J., 1980—, bd. mgrs., 1992—; mem. bd. advisors coll. agriculture Ohoi State U., 1988—; mem. departmental vis. com. dept. botany U. Tex., 1989—. Co-author: Handbook of Plant Cell Culture, Vols. 1-6, 1983-89, Biotechnology of Plants and Microorganisms, 1986; contbr. articles to sci. jours. Office: DNA Plant Tech Corp 6701 San Pablo Ave Oakland CA 94608-1239

EVANS, DAVID MARK, cardiologist; b. Oakland, Md., Aug. 2, 1957; s. Dale Eugene and Shirley Jeanne E.; m. Felicia Ann Zelinsky; children: Tristan Mark, Aaron David, Gareth Zachary. BS, Frostburg State U., 1979; MD, Am. U. Caribbean, 1985. Diplomate Am. Bd. Internal Medicine & Cardiovasc. Disease. Resident in internal medicine Conemaugh Meml. Hosp./Temple U., Phila., 1985-88; fellow in cardiovasc. disease, interventional cardiology Hosps. of U. Pitts., 1988-91; pvt. practice interventional cardiology Johnstown, Pa., 1991—; clin. asst. prof. medicine Temple U. Sch. Medicine, 1993—; clin. instr. medicine U. Pitts. Sch. Medicine, 1996—. Fellow Am. Coll. Physicians, Am. Coll. Chest Physicians, Am. Coll. Cardiology. Office: Cardiology Assocs Johnstown 1127 Franklin St Johnstown PA 15905

EVANS, EDWIN CURTIS, internist, educator, geriatrician; b. Milledgeville, Ga., June 30, 1917; s. Watt Collier and Bertha Chambers E.; m. Marjorie Claire Wood, Nov. 27, 1945; children: Nancy, Edwin, Marjorie, Jane and Jill (twins), Carol. B.S., U. Ga., 1936; M.D., Johns Hopkins U., 1940. Diplomate: Am. Bd. Internal Medicine, also recertified. Intern Hartford (Conn.) Hosp., 1940-42; resident in medicine Balt. City Hosp., 1946-47; fellow in pathology Hosp. of U. Pa., Phila., 1947-48; practice medicine specializing in internal medicine Atlanta, 1948-87; dir. geriatrics Ga. Bapt. Med. Ctr., 1987-91; clin. assoc. prof. medicine Emory U. Sch. Medicine, 1972-87, clin. prof. emeritus medicine, 1987—; clin. prof. medicine Sch. Pharmacy, Mercer U., 1980-90; chief of staff Ga. Baptist Med. Center, Atlanta, 1973-79; pres. Atlanta Blue Shield, 1968-70. Contbr. articles to profl. jours. Served to maj. M.C. AUS, 1942-46. Fellow ACP (gov. Ga. 1972-76), Am. Coll. Chest Physicians; mem. Am. Geriatrics Soc., Diabetes Assn. Atlanta (pres. 1958), Ga. Diabetes Assn. (pres. 1965), Med. Assn. Atlanta (pres. 1973, many awards), Ga. Soc. Internal Medicine (pres. 1963), Am. Soc. Internal Med. (pres. 1972-73), So. Med. Assn. (pres. 1981-82, cert. appreciation 1979), Med. Assn. Ga. (cert. meritorious/disting. svc. 1990), AMA (physicians recognition award 1978, 81, 84, 86), Am. Heart Assn., Inst. Medicine Nat. Acad. Scis., Phi Chi (pres. Kappa Delta chpt. 1939). Republican. Methodist. Clubs: Cherokee Town and Country, Vinings. Home: 500 Westover Dr NW Atlanta GA 30305-3538

EVANS, ESSI H., research scientist; b. Bad-Schwalbach, W.Ger., Jan. 12, 1950; came to U.S., 1951, naturalized, 1957; d. John H. (b. Horst H. Jahn) and Jean E. (von Schwerin); m. Everett M. Turner, Jr., Aug. 16, 1974. BS in Agr. (James Harris scholar), U. Md., 1972; MS in Animal Sci., U. Guelph, 1974, PhD in Animal Sci., 1976. Polymer chemist Monarch Rubber Co., Balt., 1972; rsch. asst., teaching asst. U. Guelph (Ont., Can.), 1972-76; project dir. animal nutrition Can. Packers Inc., Toronto, Ont., 1976-85; tech. mgr. animal nutrition and animal health Can. Packers, Inc., Toronto, 1986-89, rsch. mgr., 1989-90, gen. rsch. and nutrition mgr. shur-gain div., 1990-93, mgmt. dir. 1993—; farm cons.; guest lectr. Hubbard Farms fellow, 1975-76; NRC Indsl. postdoctoral fellow, 1976-79; recipient Hamilton Milk Producers award, 1973, 74; Ont. Ministry of Agr. and Foods Provincial Lottery grantee, 1980-83. Mem. AAAS, Am. Soc. Animal Sci., Am. Dairy Sci. Assn., Ont. Comml. Rabbit Growers Assn., Am. Assn. Vet. Nutritionists, Coun. for Agrl. Sci. and Tech., Nat. Feed Industry Assn., Can. Feed Industry Assn. Republican. Contbr. to sci. publs. and confs. Home: 64 Scugog St, Bowmanville, ON Canada L1C 3J1 Office: Shur-Gain Div Maple Leaf Foods Inc, 2700 Matheson Blvd E Ste 600 E, Mississauga, ON Canada L4W 4V9

EVANS, FREDERICK JOHN, psychologist; b. Wollongong, Australia, Nov. 17, 1937; came to U.S., 1963; s. Frederick John and Phyllis Lurline (Wiffen) E.; m. Barbara Joan Marcelo, June 8, 1968 (div. 1990); children: Christopher Arthur, David Troy, Mark Fredrick, Diana Joy; m. Patricia E. Burns, Nov. 26, 1993. B.A. Honors Class I, U. Sydney, Australia, 1959, Ph.D., 1966. Teaching fellow U. Sydney, 1959-63; research psychologist Mass. Mental Health Center, 1963-64; from instr. psychology in psychiatry U. Pa. Sch. Medicine, Phila., 1965-66; to assoc. prof. psychiatry U. Pa. Sch. Medicine, 1972-81, assoc. prof. psychology, 1974-79; sr. research psychologist Unit for Exptl. Psychiatry Inst. of Pa. Hosp., Phila., 1964-79; vis. fellow psychology Yale U., 1970-71; trustee Inst. Exptl. Psychiatry, Boston, 1970-79; adj. prof. U. Medicine and Dentistry N.J.-Robert Wood Johnson Med. Sch., 1979-88; dir. rsch. divsn. Carrier Found., Belle Mead, N.J., 1979-88; v.p. Tex. Inst. Behavioral Medicine and Neurosci., 1989-96; pres.

Pathfinders, Cons. in Human Behavior; dir. Pain Mgmt. Behavioral Medicine Svcs., Reading, Pa. Adv. editor: Internat. Jour. Clin. and Exptl. Hypnosis, 1968-69, assoc. editor, 1969—; assoc. editor: Am. Jour. Clin. Hypnosis, 1986-91, 95—; cons. editor: Jour. Abnormal Psychology, 1979-87, assoc. editor, 1989-91; co-editor: Functional Disorders of Memory, 1979, Springer Series in Behavior Modification and Behavioral Medicine, 1980-86; contbr. chpts. to textbooks, articles to profl. jours. Served to capt. Australian Army, 1961-63. Fulbright grantee, 1963-66. Fellow AAAS, APA (divsn. 30 program chmn. 1972, sec-treas. 1973-75, pres. 1978-79), Am. Soc. Clin. Hypnosis (chmn. liaison com. 1975-77, 88-89, cert. cons. 1993—), N.J. Pshycol. Soc., Pa. Psychol. Soc., Soc. Clin. and Exptl. Hypnosis (co-chmn. sci. program 1970, chmn. rsch. workshop, 1971, 76, 79, 80, 87-90, sec. 1973-86, co-chmn. publs. com. 1975-77, v.p. 1979-81, pres. 1981-83, chmn. budget com. 1987-89); mem. Am. Pain Soc. (founding dir. 1977-80), Internat. Soc. Hypnosis (sec.-treas. 1973-79, co-chmn. 7th Internat. Congress Hypnosis 1976, vice chmn. bd. dirs. organizing com. 10th Internat. Congress 1985, pres.-elect 1986-88, pres. 1987-91, immediate past pres. 1991-94, chair nominations and election com. 1991-94), Nat. Pain Found. (pres. 1989-92), Royal Soc. Medicine, Internat. Soc. Inner Mental Tng. (v.p. 1993-96).

EVANS, GEORGE EDWARD CHARLES, psychiatrist; b. Cleve., June 14, 1930; s. Fred Charles and Laura Margaret (Knoll) E.; m. Kathleen Renata Grube, June 6, 1954; children: George E.C. II, Claudia Sue Evans Zale, Christie Lynn Evans Sturges, Stephanie Michelle Evans Hemdal. BS, Case Western Res. U., 1951; postgrad., Ohio State U., 1951-52; DO, Coll. Osteo. Medicine, Des Moines, Iowa, 1956. Diplomate Am. Bd. Psychiatry and Neurology. Intern Okla. Osteo. Hosp., Tulsa, 1956-57; gen. practice medicine Norwalk, Ohio, 1957-63; resident psychiatry Embreeville State Hosp., Coatesville, Pa., 1963-65; fellow in psychiatry Phila. Mental Health Clinic, 1965-67; pvt. practice psychiatry, 1967-79; supervisory psychiatrist Wernersville (Pa.) State Hosp., 1986-91; staff psychiatrist VA Med. Ctr., Lebanon, Pa., 1992—; clin. asst. prof. dept. psychiatry Milton S. Hershey Sch. Medicine, Pa. State U., 1994—. Capt. USN, 1979-84. NIMH grantee, 1965-67. Mem. Am. Coll. Neuropsychiatrists (sr.), Am. Psychiat. Assn., Psychiat. Physicians Pa., Assn. Mil. Surgeons U.S., Pennsy, N.Y. Acad. of Sci. Republican. Unitarian. Home: 19 Oak Cir Leesport PA 19533-9608 Office: VA Med Ctr Bldg 18 Lebanon PA 17042

EVANS, GEORGE LEONARD, microbiologist; b. Wilkes-Barre, Pa., Aug. 3, 1931; s. George Leonard and Anna M. (Check) E.; m. Joan Marie Snyder, Feb. 8, 1958; children: Paula Jean, Gregory Allen, Christopher Thomas. BS, King's Coll., 1954; MS, Fordham U., 1957; PhD, Temple U., 1962. Specialist microbiologist Am. Acad. Microbiology. Sr. scientist Warner-Lambert Pharm. Co., Morris Plains, N.J., 1961-64; rsch. virologist Univ. Labs., Inc., Highland Park, N.J., 1964-65; group chief Hoffmann-La Roche, Inc., Nutley, N.J., 1965-70; dir. diagnostic rsch. Schering Corp., Bloomfield, N.J., 1970-75; rsch. fellow Becton Dickinson & Co., Hunt Valley, Md., 1975—; chmn., advisor subcom. Nat. Com. Clin. Lab. Standards, Wayne, Pa., 1980—. Contbr. articles to Jour. Immunology, Jour. Reticuloendothelial Soc., Jour. Bacteriology, Am. Jour. Med. Tech., Jour. Clin. Microbiology. Mem. Am. Soc. Microbiology, Am. Assn. Clin. Chemistry. Office: Becton Dickinson 250 Schilling Cir Cockeysville Hunt Valley MD 21031-1103

EVANS, HAROLD WARREN, internist; b. Milton, Pa., Apr. 17, 1925; s. Charles Franklin and Edna Grace (Keil) E.; m. Jacqueline Mae Ranck, July 21, 1947; children: Ceanne Leslie, Joanne Louise, Charles David, Kenneth Franklin, Patricia Lynn. Student, Cornell U., 1943-45, MD, 1949; student, Columbia U., 1945; MS in Medicine, U. Minn., 1958. Diplomate Am. Bd. Internal Medicine. Med. intern Strong Meml. Hosp., Rochester, N.Y., 1949-50; med. asst. resident Strong Meml. Hosp., 1950-51; med. resident pulmonary VA Hosp., Batavia, N.Y., 1951-52; med. fellow Mayo Clinic, Rochester, 1955-58; specialist in internal medicine Grand Forks (N.D.) Clinic, 1958—; med. staff United Hosp., Grand Forks, 1958—; prof. medicine U. N.D. Sch. Medicine, Grand Forks, 1960—; bd. dirs. N.D. Health Care Rev., Inc., Minot, 1976—, Grand Forks Clinic, Ltd., 1965-73. Contbr. articles to profl. jours. Bd. dirs. Greater Grand Forks Sr. Citizens Assn., 1969-85; com. mem. N.D. Adv. Com. on Rehab. Svcs., Bismarck, 1969-80; bd. dirs. Blue Shield of N.D., Fargo, 1966-75; exec. com. Minn-Kota Area Health Edn. Ctr., Grand Forks, 1973-79; bd. dirs. N.D. Heart Assn., 1964-70, Fellows of the U. N.D., 1987—. Fellow ACP (gov. 1979-83, Laureate award 1986), Am. Coll. Chest Physicians (gov. 1967-75); mem. AMA, N.D. Med. Assn. (pres. 1978-79), Third Dist. Med. Soc. (pres. 1972-73), VFW, Am. Legion, Elks. Republican. Home: 293 Circle Hills Dr Grand Forks ND 58201-7958 Office: Grand Forks Clinic Ltd 1000 S Columbia Rd Grand Forks ND 58201-4032

EVANS, HARRY LAUNIUS, pathology educator; b. Mobile, Ala., June 11, 1948; s. Aurelius A. and Anne (Hathaway) E.; m. Cheryl J. Winfrey, June 6, 1970 (div. Dec. 1990); children: Thomas H., Sarah S. BS, Stetson U., 1970; MD, U. Fla., 1974. Diplomate Am. Bd. Pathology. Resident in pathology Vanderbilt U. Med. Ctr., Nashville, 1974-75; fellow in dermatopathology Mayo Clinic, Rochester, Minn., 1977-78; fellow in pathology U.Tex.-M.D. Anderson Cancer Ctr., Houston, 1975-77, asst. prof. pathology, 1978-82, assoc. prof., 1982-90, prof., 1990—. Contbr. articles to med. jours. Mem. U.S.-Can. Acad. Pathology, Arthur Purdy Stout Soc. Surg. Pathologists. Office: U Tex-MD Anderson Cancer Ctr Dept Pathology 1515 Holcombe Blvd Houston TX 77030-4009

EVANS, HOWARD MORGAN, acupuncturist; b. Phila., Dec. 4, 1943; s. Nathaniel Hathaway and Marjory Ada (Morgan) E.; m. Jennie Boyd Bull, Sept. 13, 1969 (div. June 1972); m. Vicki Cohn Pollard, Oct. 25, 1982; children: Tanya Louise, Justin Benjamin. BS in Civil Engring., Swarthmore (Pa.) Coll., 1965; MS in Environ. Engring. Sci., Johns Hopkins U., 1967. Research asst. Nat. Acad. Scis., Washington, 1966; high sch. dir. Am. Friends Service, Balt., 1968-71; dir. People's Community Clinic, Balt., 1971-73, Balt. Exptl. High Sch., 1972-77, Haystack Mountain Sch. of Crafts, Deer Isle, Maine, 1977-88; pres. Merlin Design, Blue Hill, Maine, 1988—; chair adv. bd. Worsley Inst. for Classical Acupuncture, Miami Lakes, Fla., 1995—; mem. Maine Arts Commn., Augusta, 1980-87; acunucturist, 1988—. Mem. Maine Assn. Acupuncture and Oriental Medicine (pres. 1990-93, 94-96). Mem. Soc. of Friends, Buddhist. Office: Traditional Acupuncture PO Box 838 Blue Hill ME 04614-0838

EVANS, HUGH E., pediatrician; b. N.Y.C., July 6, 1934; s. David and Geraldine (Krebs) E.; m. Ruth L. Orloff, June 5, 1960; children: Margo Lynn, Marc Douglas. A.B. cum laude, Columbia U., 1954; M.D., SUNY Downstate Med. Center, 1958. Intern Johns Hopkins Hosp., Balt., 1958-59; asst. resident Johns Hopkins Hosp., 1959-60; sr. asst. resident NIH, Bethesda, Md., 1960-62; chief resident outpatient dept. NIH, 1962-63; pvt. practice Bellaire, Ohio, 1963-66; assoc. dir. pediatrics Harlem Hosp. Center, N.Y.C., 1966-73; dir. dept. pediatrics Jewish Hosp. and Med. Center, Bklyn., 1973-85; prof. pediatrics U. Medicine and Dentistry of N.J., Newark, 1985—, prof. preventive medicine and community health, 1991—, chmn. dept. pediatrics, 1985-90; dir. dept. pediatrics U. Hosp., Newark, 1985-90, mem. attending staff, 1985—; assoc. clin. prof. pediatrics Columbia U., 1968-73; prof. pediatrics SUNY Downstate Med. Center, Bklyn., 1973-85; cons. Englewood (N.J.) Hosp., Hackensack (N.J.) Hosp.; trustee Bergen-Passiac County Lung Assn., 1973-85. Author: (with Leonard Glass) Perinatal Medicine, 1976, Lung Diseases of Children, 1979, 2d edit., 1985; editor: Hospital Care of Children and Youth, 1986, Jour. Perinatology, 1985—; contbr. articles to profl. jours., chpts. to textbooks. Served to sr. asst. surgeon USPHS, 1960-62. Mem. Soc. Pediat. Rsch., Harvey Soc., Am. Soc. Microbiology, Am. Acad. Pediat. (com. on hosp. care 1982-85, chmn. 1985-88, task force on pediat. AIDS 1987-92), Am. Thoracic Soc., Am. Pediat. Soc., Soc. Exptl. Biology and Medicine, N.Y. Pediat. Soc. (pres. 1982-83), Bklyn. Acad. Pediat. (v.p. 1976, pres. 1977), Infectious Diseases Soc., Med. Soc. N.J. (mem. spl. com. AIDS 1993-95), Alpha Omega Alpha. Home: 165 Serpentine Rd Tenafly NJ 07670-2739 Office: U Medicine and Dentistry NJ MSB-F586 185 S Orange Ave Newark NJ 07103-2714

EVANS, JOHN ROBERT, former university president, physician; b. Toronto, Oct. 1, 1929; s. William Watson and Mary Evelyn Lucille (Thompson) E.; m. Jean Gay Glassco, 1954; children: Derek, Mark and Michael (twins), Gillian, Timothy, Willa. MD, U. Toronto, 1952; DPhil (Rhodes scholar), Oxford U., 1955; LLD (hon.), Dalhousie U., McMaster U., McGill U., 1972, Queen's U., 1974, Wilfred Laurier U., 1975, York U., 1977, U. Toronto, 1980, U. Western Ont., 1982, Yale U., 1978; DSc (hon.), Meml. U., 1973, U. Montreal, 1977, Royal Mil. Coll., 1989; DHL (hon.), Johns Hopkins U., 1978; D Univ. (hon.), U. Ottawa, 1978, U. Limbourg, The Netherlands, 1980. Intern Toronto Gen. Hosp., 1952-53, chief resident physician, 1958-59; practice medicine specializing in cardiology Toronto, 1961-72; assoc. dept. medicine U. Toronto Med. Sch., 1961-65, prof., 1972—, pres. univ., 1972-78, pres. emeritus, 1995—; dir. population, health and nutrition dept. World Bank, Washington, 1979-83; chmn. Allelix Inc., Mississauga, Ont., 1983—; physician Toronto Gen. Hosp., 1961-65; dean Faculty Medicine McMaster U., Hamilton, Ont., 1965-72, v.p. health scis., 1967-72; chmn. Torstar Corp., Toronto, 1993—, Alcan Aluminium Ltd., Montreal, 1995—; bd. dirs. Allelix Inc., Torstar Ltd., Toronto, Royal Bank of Can., Alcan Aluminum Ltd., Montreal, MDS Health Group, Toronto, Connaught Labs., Inc., Toronto, Pasteur Merieux Serums and Vaccines, Lyon, France; hon. fellow London Sch. Hygiene and Tropical Medicine, Univ. Coll., Oxford, Eng. Trustee Rockefeller Found., N.Y.C., 1982-95, chmn., 1988-95; chmn. African Med. Rsch. Found., Can., 1986-90; trustee Walter and Duncan Gordon Charitable Found., Toronto, 1991—. Decorated companion Order of Can.; Order of Ontario, 1991; Markle scholar, 1960-65; recipient Gairdner Foundation Wightman Award, Gairdner Foundation, 1992. Fellow Royal Soc. Can., Royal Coll. Physicians and Surgeons Can., Royal Coll. Physicians (London); Master ACP. Home: 58 Highland Ave, Toronto, ON Canada M4W 2A3 Office: Torstar Ltd, 1 Yonge St, Toronto, ON Canada M5E 1P9

EVANS, JUDY ANNE, health center administrator; b. Elmira, N.Y., Mar. 29, 1940; d. Hugh Kenneth and Mary (Faul) Leach; m. Nolly Seymour Evans, Feb. 18, 1965; children: Samantha, Meredydd, Clelia, Nolly III. BS, Cornell U., 1962; MBA, Syracuse U., 1992. Fin. analyst Morgan Guaranty Trust Co., N.Y.C., 1962-66; bus. adminstr. SUNY Health Sci. Ctr., Syracuse, 1983-89, adminstr. dept. pediatrics, 1990—. Mem. allocations com. Children Miracle Network, Syracuse, 1990—; children's hosp. steering com. Crouse Irving/Univ. Hosp., Syracuse, 1990—; bd. dirs. Syracuse Friends of Chamber Music, 1983-89, Syracuse Camerata, 1982-88. Mem. Assn. Adminstrs. of Acad. Pediatrics. Home: 26 Lyndon Rd Fayetteville NY 13066-1016 Office: SUNY Health Sci Ctr 750 E Adams St Syracuse NY 13210-2306

EVANS, LOUISE, psychologist, investor, philanthropist; b. San Antonio; d. Henry Daniel and Adela (Pariser) E.; m. Thomas Ross Gambrell, Feb. 23, 1960. BS, Northwestern U., 1949; MS in Clin. Psychology, Purdue U., 1952, PhD in Clin. Psychology, 1955. Lic. Marriage, Family and Child Counselor Calif., Nat. Register of Health Svc. Providers in Psychology; lic. psychologist N.Y. (inactive), Calif.; diplomate Clin. Psychology, Am. Bd. Profl. Psychology (fellow), Am. Bd. Clin. Psychology. Intern clin. psychology Menninger Found.-Topeka (Kans.) State Hosp., 1952-53, USPHS-Menninger Found. postdoctoral fellow clin. child psychology, 1955-56; staff psychologist Kankakee (Ill.) State Hosp., 1954; head staff psychologist child guidance clinic Kings County Hosp., Bklyn., 1957-58; dir. psychology clinic Barnes-Renard Hosp., instr. med. psychology Washington U. Sch. Medicine, 1959; clin. rsch. cons. Episc. City Diocese, St. Louis, 1959; pvt. practice clin. psychology, 1960-92; fellow Internat. Coun. Sex Edn. and Parenthood, 1984; psychol. cons. Fullerton (Calif.) Community Hosp., 1961-81; staff cons. clin. psychology Martin Luther Hosp., Anaheim, Calif., 1963-70; nat., internat. lectr. clin. psychology schs. and profl. groups, 1950—; chairperson, participant psychol. symposiums, 1956—; guest speaker clin. psychology civic and cmty. orgns., 1950—. Elected to Hall of Fame, Central H.S., Evansville, Ind., 1966; recipient Svc. award Yuma County Head Start Program, 1972, Statue of Victory Personality of the Yr. award Centro Studi E. Ricerche Delle Nazioni, Italy, 1985; named Miss Heritage, Heritage Publs., 1965. Fellow APA (clin. divsn., psychology of women divsn., divsn. psychotherapy, cons. divsn., dir. exec. bd. 1976-79), Acad. Clin. Psychology, Am. Assn. Applied and Preventative Psychology (charter), Royal Soc. Health England (emeritus), Internat. Council of Psychologists (dir. 1977-79, sec. 1962-64, 73-76), AAAS (emeritus), Am. Orthopsychiat. Assn. (life), World Wide Acad. of Scholars of N.Z. (life), Am. Psychol. Soc. (charter); mem. AAUP (emeritus)L.A. Soc. Clin. Psychologists (exec. bd. 1956-67), Calif. State Psychol. Assn. (life, ins. com. 1961-65), L.A. County Psychol. Assn. (emeritus), Orange County Psychol. Assn. (charter founding mem., exec. bd. 1961-62), Orange County Soc. Clin. Psychologists (founder, exec. bd. 1963-65, pres. 1964-65), Am. Public Health Assn. (emeritus), Internat. Platform Assn., N.Y. Acad. Scis. (emeritus), Purdue U. Alumni Assn. (life, mem. pres. coun., dean's club pacesetters, Citizenship award 1975, Disting. Alumni award 1993, Old Master 1993), Center for Study of Presidency, Soc. Jewelry Historians USA (charter), Alumni Assn. Menninger Sch. Psychiatry, Soc. Sigma Xi Nat. Rsch. Hon. (emeritus), Pi Sigma Pi (pres. 1947-48, sec. 1946-47). Contbr. articles on clin. psychology to profl. publs. Achievements include development of innovative theories and techniques of clinical practice; acknowledged pioneer in devel. psychology as sci. and profession both nat. and internat., and pioneer in marital and family therapy. Office: PO Box 6067 Beverly Hills CA 90212-1067

EVANS, MARK RUSSELL, physician, researcher; b. London, July 21, 1957; s. Russell Wilmot and Pamela Muriel (Hayward) E. MB, ChB, U. Liverpool, Eng., 1982. House officer, sr. house officer Univ. Teaching Hosps., Liverpool, 1982-85; registrar Plymouth (Eng.) Hosps., 1985-87; sr. house officer in pediatrics Westminster Children's Hosp., London, 1988-89; clin. rsch. fellow St. George's Hosp., London 1989—. Recipient award for distinction in obstetrics and gynecology U. Liverpool, 1982. Fellow Royal Soc. Tropical Medicine and Hygiene; mem. Royal Coll. Physicians (diploma in tropical medicine and health, diploma in child health). Anglican. Office: CDU Jenner Wing SGHMS, Cranmer Ter, London SW17 0RE, England

EVANS, MARSHA JO ANNE, nursing administrator; b. Watseka, Ill., Aug. 18, 1951; d. Robert Lewis and Jane Eleanor (Orr) Niles; m. Larry E. Evans, Sept. 16, 1973; 1 child, Melinda Joy. BSN, So. Ill. U., 1973. Staff nurse Sevier County Hosp., Sevierville, Tenn., 1973-75; asst. DON Fair Oaks Nursing Home, Edward A. Utlaut Meml. Hosp., Greenville, Ill., 1975-76; insvc. coord., infection control nurse, nursing supr. Fayette County Hosp., Vandalia, Ill., 1976-83, quality assurance coord., 1983-88; infection control coord. St. Anthony's Meml. Hosp., Effingham, Ill., 1988-94, outpatient svcs. rep., 1994—. Office: St Anthony's Meml Hosp 503 N Maple St Effingham IL 62401-2006

EVANS, PAUL, osteopath; b. Nutley, N.J., May 23, 1950; m. Roxanne Romack. BS cum laude in Biology, U. Miami, 1972; DO, Phila. Coll. Osteopathic Med., 1979. Diplomate Am. Bd. Family Practice, Nat. Bd. Osteo. Examiners, Am. Acad. Pain Mgmt.; cert. Am. Osteo. Bd. Gen. Practice. Commd. 2d lt. U.S. Army, 1972, advanced through grades to col., 1995; asst. chief mil. pers. U.S. Army Med. Svc. Corps, Frankfurt, Fed. Republic Germany, 1972-75; intern Letterman Army Med. Ctr., San Francisco, 1979-80; resident in family practice Womack Army Community Hosp., Ft. Bragg, N.C., 1980-82; dir. family practice quality assurance Tripler Army Med. Ctr., Hawaii, 1984-86, dir. residency tng. dept. family practice, 1984-86; asst. prof. family practice, physician Uniformed Svcs. U. Health Scis., F. Edward Hebert Sch. Med., Bethesda, Md., 1986-92, clerkship dir., 1986-88, dir. continuing med. edn., 1987-91, asst. prof. mil. and emergency medicine, 1991-92; chief dept. family practice Reynolds Army Community Hosp., Ft. Sill, Okla., 1992-94, chief primary care, 1994-95, chief dept. family practice & cmty. medicine, 1994-95, chmn. rsch. com., dir. hosp. continuing med. edn., 1992-95, dir. physicians asst. tng. program, dir. quality improvement, 1992-94; tchg. chief dept. of family practice Madigan Army Med. Ctr., Tacoma, Wash., 1995—, dir. primary care, mem. exec. bd. dirs., exec. adv. coun.; clin. assoc. prof. of family medicine U. Wash., 1996—; presenter, lectr., cons. in field; mem. part-time clin. faculty, family practice residency DeWitt Army Hosp., Ft. Belvoir, Va., 1986-89, 91-92, Malcolm Grow USAF Med. Ctr., Andrews AFB, Md., 1989-91. Reviewer Am. Family Physician, Patient Care, Military Medicine, Family Medicine; contbr. articles to profl. publs. Asst. med. dir. Old Dominion 100 Mile Run, Front Royal, Va., 1990, med. dir., 1991; asst. med. dir. Am. Diabetes Assn. Youth, Honolulu, 1984, med. dir., 1985. USUHS grantee. Fellow Am. Acad. Family Physicians; mem. Uniformed Svcs. Acad. Family Physicians (chmn. edn. com. 1993—), Soc. Tchrs. Family Medicine (mem. genogram rsch. com. 1989—), Assn. Mil. Surgeons, Phila. Coll. Osteo. Medicine Alumni Assn. (life), Omicron Delta Kappa, Alpha Epsilon Delta. Home: 5802 63d Ave W Tacoma WA 98467

EVANS, PETER YOSHIO, ophthalmologist, educator; b. Tokyo, Dec. 19, 1925; came to the U.S., 1957; s. Paul Yuzuru Kawai and Vicki (Wichgraf) Evans; m. Helga Kemp, Sept. 19, 1953; children: Johannes, Marina, Michael, Andre, Thomas, Ursula, Christiane. MD, Innsbruck U., 1951. Resident Innsbruck (Austria) and Frankfurt (Germany) Univs., 1951-55; intern Sisters Charity Hosp., Buffalo, N.Y., 1957-58; chief dept. ophthalmology D.C. Gen. Hosp., 1958-63; fellow Georgetown U., Washington, 1958-59, program dir. div. ophthalmology, 1963-69, chmn., 1969-83, prof., 1973-92, prof. emeritus, 1992—; cons. D.C. Columbia Lighthouse for the Blind, 1959-63; sr. cons. D.C. Child and Maternal Welfare Dept., 1961-74; exec. v.p. Joint Commn. Allied Health Pers. in Ophthalmology, St. Paul, 1981-96. Author, producer scientific films; contbr. articles to profl. jours.; editor numerous jours. Fellow Am. Acad. Ophthalmology (Disting. Svc. award 1982), Austrian Ophthalm. Soc. (Ernst Fuchs Meml. Lectr. 1975), German Ophthalm. Soc., Am.-Austrian Soc. (pres. 1989-91), Cosmos Club D.C. Lutheran. Home and Office: 3113 Lewis Pl Falls Church VA 22042-2511

EVANS, R. MARK, pharmacologist; b. Omaha, Sept. 10, 1953; s. Ralph Matthew and Joan Elizabeth (Maddrix) E.; m. Mary Margaret Vaux, Oct. 19, 1979; children: Andy, Adam, Audrey. BS in Biology, Bates Coll., 1975; PhD in Pharmacology, SUNY/Roswell Park Meml. Inst., Buffalo, 1980. Rsch. asst. Brookhaven Nat. Labs., L.I., N.Y., 1974; postdoctoral fellow dept. cell biology Baylor Coll. Medicine, Houston, 1980-81; postdoctoral fellow dept. pharmacology U. Tex., Houston, 1981-83; sr. scientist Lorillard Rsch. Ctr., Greensboro, N.C., 1983; sr. scientist AMA, Chgo., 1983-86, dir. biotech., 1986-91; sci. editor divsn. consumer affairs Am. Med. TV and AMA, Chgo., 1992-94; dir. devel. multimedia interactive continuing med. edn. AMA, Chgo., 1995—; adv. com. Biol. Scis. Curriculum Study, Colorado Springs, 1991-92; sec. health policy agenda and ref. com., ho. dels. AMA, 1987-91. Contbg. author to 6th and 7th edits. AMA Drug Evaluations, articles to profl. jours. Mem. Hinsdale (Ill.) Village Caucus, 1990—; coach Am. Youth Soccer Orgn., Hinsdale, 1987—, Hinsdale Little League, 1990-94, Boy Scouts Am., 1991—. Mem. AAAS, N.Y. Acad. Sci. Republican. Methodist. Home: 712 S Bruner St Hinsdale IL 60521-4337 Office: Am Med Assn 515 N State St Chicago IL 60610-4320

EVANS, RAND BOYD, psychologist; b. Baytown, Tex., Feb. 20, 1942; s. William R. and Lacy J. (Mabe) E.; m. Mary Elizabeth Kubica, June 22, 1963; children: Victoria Anne, Karl M., Veronica M. BA, U. Tex., Austin, 1963, MA, 1964, PhD, 1967. Spl. lectr. U. Tex., Austin, 1967, asst. prof., 1967-72; assoc. prof. Wright State U., Dayton, Ohio, 1972-76, U. N.H., Durham, 1972-76; assoc. prof., prof., dept. head Tex. A&M U., College Station, 1976-87; dean., prof. U. Balt., 1987-90; prof., chmn. psychology East Carolina U., Greenville, N.C., 1990—; assoc. dir. history of psychology, U. N.H., 1972-76. Author: The Great Psychologists, 1991; editor: American Psychological Association, 1991, Making American Psychology, 1990. Fellow Am. Psychol. Assn. (divsn. 26 pres.), A., Psychol. Soc.; mem. Cheiron Soc. (exec. officer 1986-90), Scientific Instrumental Soc., Citizens Hist. Preservation (pres. 1979-87). Home: 1109 N Main St Tarboro NC 27886-3821 Office: East Carolina U Dept of Psychology Greenville NC 27886

EVANS, RANDOLPH WARREN, neurologist, educator; b. Houston, June 16, 1953; s. Richard Isadore and Zena Ann (Rubin) E.; m. Marilyn P. Diamond, June 13, 1976; children: Elliott, Rochelle, Jonathan. BA, Rice U., 1974; MD, Baylor Coll. Medicine, 1978. Diplomate Am. Bd. Psychiatry and Neurology. Intern Baylor Coll. Medicine, Houston, 1978-79, resident, 1979-82; pvt. practice, Houston, 1982—; clin. assoc. prof. dept. neurology U. Tex. Med. Sch., Houston, 1985—; chief neurology sect. Park Plaza Hosp., Houston, 1986—. Co-editor: Prognosis of Neurological Disorders, 1992; editor: Neurology and Trauma, 1996; contbr. numerous articles to med. jours. Fellow Am. Acad. Neurology; mem. Maimonides Soc. (chmn. Houston 1993-95). Jewish. Office: 1200 Binz # 1370 Houston TX 77004

EVANS, REX DUANE, physician assistant; b. Philipsburg, Pa., Jan. 16, 1957; s. Dewey Milton and Rachel Jean (Schoening) E.; m. Karen Elizabeth Mencer, Apr. 21, 1979; children: Margaret Jean, Miriam Elizabeth. BS in Biology, Fla. So. Coll., 1979; BS in Allied Health, Trevecca Nazarene Coll., 1983. Cert. physician asst. Physician asst. Lewis County Hosp., Hohenwald, Tenn., 1984-85; clinic/mission dir. God's Missionary Ch., Penns Creek, Pa., 1985—. Fellow Am. Assn. Physician Assts. Home: GMC MFI PO Box 15665 West Palm Beach FL 33416

EVANS, RICHARD, III, psychiatrist; b. Mpls., May 11, 1933; s. Richard; m. Kay Hamilton; children: Morgan, Leah. BA in Econs., U. Minn., 1958, postgrad., 1961-62, MD, 1967. Diplomate in psychiatry Am. Bd. Psychiatry and Neurology. Internship Bklyn.-Cumberland Med. Ctr., 1967-68; pvt. practice Wiscasset, Maine, 1968-70; resident in psychiatry Maine Med. Ctr., Portland, 1970-73; psychiatrist pvt. practice, Brunswick, Maine, 1973-92; staff psychiatrist VA Med. Ctr., Togus, Maine, 1992—. Office: VA Med Ctr Dept Psychiatry Togus ME 04330

EVANS, RICHARD MILNER, ophthalmologist; b. Sacramento, June 5, 1946; s. Robert Roy and Lois Joyce (Otta) E.; m. Janice Marie Lusty, Feb. 12, 1982; children: David, Elizabeth. BA, U. Tex., El Paso, 1968; MD, U. Tex., Galveston, 1971. Diplomate Am. Bd. Ophthalmology. Ophthalmologist Med. Ctr. Ophthalmology, San Antonio, 1980—. Methodist. Office: Med Ctr Ophthalmology 9150 Huebner Rd Ste 280 San Antonio TX 78240-1545

EVANS, ROBERT JOHN, retired biochemistry educator, researcher; b. Logan, UT, Mar. 18, 1909; s. Robert James and Alice Hazel (Stallings) E.; m. Alice Pugmire, Aug. 14, 1941 (dec.); children: Patricia Alice Evans Leavitt, Robert P. Student, Brigham Young U., 1929; BS, Utah State U., 1934, MS, 1936; PhD, U. Wisc., 1939. Instr. Carbon Coll., Price, UT, 1939-40; assoc. chemist Washington Agrl. Expt. Sta., Pullman, Wash., 1940-47; prof. Biochemistry Mich. State U., East Lansing, Mich., 1947-77; prof. emeritus Mich. State U., East Lansing, 1977—; vis. prof. Cambridge U., England, 1963-64, U. Edinburgh, Scotland, U. Coll. London, England, 1971, Rowett Rsch. Inst., Aberdeen, Scotland, 1971, Cambridge U., 1971. Contbr. articles to profl. jours. Active Boy Scouts Am., East Lansing, PTA, Lansing, Mich., Citizens Mich., Lansing. Recipient Rsch. Achievement award Poultry and Egg Nat. Bd., 1958, rsch. grants Nat. Inst. Health, 1963-75. Fellow AAAS; mem Am. Chem. Soc., Am. Inst. Nutrition., Poultry Sci. Assn. Mem. LDS Ch. Home: 760 Polk Ave Ogden UT 84404-5255

EVANS, ROBERT LEONARD, mathematical physiologist, educator; b. Duluth, Minn., May 30, 1917; s. John Leonard and Amy (Magnusson) E.; m. Frances Janet Bentley, Dec. 21, 1941 (dec. Nov. 1955); children: Amy Elizabeth, Thomas Randall, Julia May; m. Elsie Frances Hardy, Jan. 11, 1957. B of Chemistry, U. Minn., 1938, MS, 1939, PhD, 1951. Assoc. metallurgist U.S. Bur. Mines, Salt Lake City, 1940-44; rsch. assoc. Allegany Ballistics Lab., Cumberland, Md., 1944-45; from instr. math. and mechanics to asst. prof. physiology U. Minn., Mpls., 1945-63, assoc. prof. biometry and math. biology, 1963-70, lectr. physiology, 1970—. Author: Fall and Rise of Man If ...., 1973; editor, sect. author: Eight Writers Seeking Readers, 1985. Grantee Rockefeller Found., 1954-59, USPHS, 1958-68. Mem. AAAS (life), N.Am. Com. for Humanism, World Federalist Assn., Minn. Acad. Sci., Sigma Xi. Unitarian. Home and Office: Ste 503 2601 Kenzie Ter Minneapolis MN 55418-3262

EVANS, ROBERT TROY, respiratory therapist; b. Rome, Ga., June 14, 1967; s. Roy Lee and Judith Ann (Hancock) E. AS, Darton Coll.; BS, Med. Coll. of Ga. Pharmacy technician Palmira Park HCA Hosp., Albany, Ga., 1990-93; rsch. technician Med. Coll. of Ga., Augusta, 1993-95; staff therapist Phoebe Putney Meml. Hosp., Albany, 1995, 3-11 supr., 1995—. Mem. Ga. Sheriff's Assn., Stockbridge, Ga., 1989—. With Ga. Army N.G., 1985—. Mem. AARC. Home: 709 14th Ave Albany GA 31701

EVANS, THOMAS RONALD JEFFRY, oncology lecturer, consultant; b. Haverfordwest, Wales, July 15, 1961; s. Benjamin Wynford and Leila Price (Bevans) E. MBBS, U. London, 1984, MD, 1993. Cert. med. oncology. SHO in medicine St. Bartholomew's Hosp., London, 1986-87; registrar medicine Edgware Hosp., England, 1987-88; registrar medicine St. George's Hosp., London, 1988-89, rsch. registrar med. sch., 1989-91, lectr., sr. registrar med. sch., 1991-96; sr. lectr., cons. U. Glasgow, 1996—. Mem. Royal Coll. Physicians; mem. Brit. Assn. Cancer Rsch., Assn. Cancer Physicians. Mem. Welsh Bapt. Ch.

EVANS, WILLIAM LEE, biologist; b. Calvert, Tex., Aug. 28, 1924; s. James Herman and Lilly Australia (O'Neal) E.; m. Lillian Mary Madden, July 30, 1948; children: Kathy A., David C., Susan D. BA with honors, U. Tex., Austin, 1949, MA, 1950, PhD, 1955. Mem. faculty U. Ark., Fayetteville, 1955-89, prof. zoology, 1968-89, prof. emeritus, 1989, chmn. gen. biology, 1967-70; mem. health professions adv. com. Fulbright Coll. Arts & Scis., 1982-89, chmn. 1987-89. Author articles, lab. manuals. Capt. AUS, 1942-46; served with USAF, 1951-52. Decorated Air medal with oak leaf cluster; recipient award for classroom teaching Omicron Delta Kappa, 1959; grantee NSF, 1959-62; grantee NIH, 1960-63; grantee U. Ark. Found., 1979, Fulbright Coll. Arts and Sci., 1982. Mem. Ark. Acad. Sci. (treas. 1972-82, pres. 1984-85), Am. Philatelic Soc., Am. Numismatic Assn., Phi Beta Kappa, Sigma Xi, Phi Eta Sigma, Phi Sigma. Home and Office: 1916 Albany Ln Fayetteville AR 72704-5382

EVANSON, ROBERT VERNE, pharmacy educator; b. Hammond, Ind., Nov. 3, 1920; s. Evan and Dorothy (Gordon) E.; m. Helen Louise Wolber, June 29, 1947; children: Yvonne Louise Evanson Nash, Karen Denice Evanson Ivanson. B.S. in Pharmacy, Purdue U., 1947, M.S. in Indsl. Pharmacy, 1949, Ph.D. in Pharmacy Adminstrn., 1953. Apprentice pharmacist Physician's Supply Co., Hammond, 1946; grad. asst. pharmacy Sch. Pharmacy, Purdue U., 1947-48, mem. faculty, 1948—, prof. pharm. adminstrn., 1963-86, head dept., 1966-72; assoc. head dept. pharmacy practice, 1982-86, prof. emeritus, 1986—; cons. in field. Contbr. articles to profl. jours.; contbg. author: Central Pharm. Jour., 1964-72. Served with AUS, 1943-46. Recipient Lederle Faculty award, 1964; award for faculty excellence in pharmacy adminstrn. Nat. Assn. Retail Druggists, 1985. Fellow Am. Found. Pharm. Edn., Am. Pharm. Assn.; mem. Ind. Pharm. Assn., Am. Assn. Coll. Pharmacy (dir., Disting. Educator award 1982), Am. Assn. Coll. Pharmacy Council Faculties (chmn. 1985-86), Acad. Pharm. Scis., Acad. Pharmacy Practice, Soc. Preservation and Encouragement Barbershop Quartet Singing in Am., Sigma Xi. Mem. Fed. Ch. W. Lafayette. Home: 400 Lindberg Ave West Lafayette IN 47906-2032

EVATT, CLAY W., JR., ophthalmologist; b. Greenville, S.C., Apr. 16, 1931. BS, Davidson Coll., 1953; MD, Med. Coll. S.C., 1957. Diplomate Am. Bd. Ophthalmology. Intern Med. Coll. S.C., 1957-58; resident Wills Eye Hosp., Phila., 1959-61; pvt. practice North Charleston, S.C., 1962—; teaching fellow Wills Eye Hosp., 1961-62; clin. prof. Med. U. S.C.; mem. advisor S.C. Eye Bank. Contbr. articles to profl. jours. Bd. dirs. S.C. Commn. for the Blind; past bd. dirs. Trident Acad.; active Boy Scouts Am., Charleston Mus., Charleston Opera Co., The Footlight Players, Inc., Gibbes Art Gallery, Prevent Blindness, Soc. for Relief of Families of Deceased and Disabled Indigent Mems. of Med. Profession of S.C., Charles Webb Easter Seat Ctr. Mem. AMA, Am. Acad. Ophthalmology, Am. Assn. Ophthalmology, Am. Assn. workers for the Blind, Am. Intra Ocular Implant Soc., Am. Profl. Practice Assn., Assn. Am. Physicians and Surgeons, Assoc. So. Rwy. Sys., Charleston County Med. Soc. (health legis. com.), Charleston Ophthalmological Soc., Charleston Power Squadron, Charleston Trident C. of C., Med. U. S.C. Alumni Assn., Coll. Physicians of Phila., Coastal Med. Soc., Huguenot Soc. S.C., Med. Chirurgical Soc., Med. Soc. S.C., Nat. Rifle Assn., Physicians Edn. Network, Preservation Soc., Sons of Confederate Vets., S.C. Wildlife Assn., So. Med. Assn., Waring Libr. Soc., Wills Eye Hosp. Soc., Contact Lens Assn. of Ophthalmologists, Nat. Geog. Soc., Am. Soc. Contemporary Ophthalmology and Internat. Glaucoma Congress, Internat. Oceanographic Found., Am. Med. Polit. ActionCom., Southeaster Eye Bank Assn. Am. (past pres.), Eye Bank Assn. Am. (bd. dirs., med. and lay adv. bd.), Brigadier Club, Carolina Yacht Club, James Island Yacht club, Masons, Rotary, Seabrook Island Club, Kappa Sigma. Home: 617 N Shore Dr Charleston SC 29412 Office: 2741 Speissegger Dr #206 North Charleston SC 29405-8290

EVENS, RONALD GENE, radiologist, medical center administrator; b. St. Louis, Sept. 24, 1939; s. Robert and Dorothy (Lupkey) E.; m. Hanna Blunk, Sept. 3, 1960; children: Ronald Jr., Christine, Amanda. BA, Washington U., 1960, MD, 1964, postgrad. in bus. and edn., 1970-71. Intern Barnes Hosp., St. Louis, 1964-65; resident Mallinckrodt Inst. Radiology, St. Louis, 1965-66, 68-70; rsch. assoc. Nat. Heart Inst., 1966-68; asst. prof. radiology, v.p. Washington U. Med. Sch., 1970-71, prof., head dept. radiology, dir., 1971-72, Elizabeth Mallinckrodt prof., head radiology dept., 1972—, adj. prof. med. econs., 1988—; radiologist-in-chief Barnes Hosp., St. Louis, 1971—; radiologist-in-chief Children's Hosp., 1971—, pres., chief exec. officer, 1985-88; vice chancellor fin. Washington U., St. Louis, 1988—; mem. adv. com. on splty. and geog. distbn. of physicians Inst. Medicine, Nat. Acad. Scis., 1974-76, Hickey lectr., 1976, Carmen lectr. Calif. U., 1985, Kiewit lectr. Eisenhower Med. Ctr., 1986; Hornick lectr. U. Pitts., 1986; ann. orator Can. Radiol. Soc., 1984; Hodes lectr. Jefferson U., 1991—; Smith lectr. Royal Coll. Physicians, Edinburgh, 1992; Seaman lectr. Columbia Presbyn., 1992; dir. Boatmens Bank Inc., Mallinckrodt Group Inc., Right Choice Inc., Blue Choice, Inc.; chmn. bd. Med. Care Group St. Louis, 1980-86. Contbr. over 210 articles to profl. jours. Active Boy Scouts Am., 1975—; elder Glendale Presbyn. Ch., 1971-74, Kirkwood Presbyn. Ch., 1983-86. Served with USPHS, 1966-68. Advance Acad. fellow James Picker Found, 1970; recipient Disting. Svc. award. St. Louis C. of C., 1972; named Disting. Eagle Scout Nat. Coun., 1983. Fellow Am. Coll. Radiology (chair elect 1995); mem. AMA (editl. bd. JAMA), Mo. Radiol. Soc. (pres. 1977-78), Soc. Nuclear Medicine (trustee 1971-75), St. Louis Med. Soc., Mo. State Med. Assn., Soc. Chmn. Acad. Radiology Depts. (pres. 1979), Radiol. Soc. N.Am., Assn. Univ. Radiologists (pres. 1988), Am. Roentgen Ray Soc. (pres. 1989), Phi Beta Kappa, Alpha Omega Alpha (Sheard-Sanford award). Office: Washington U Mallinckrodt Inst Radiology 510 S Kingshighway Blvd Saint Louis MO 63110-1016

EVERETT, MARK ALLEN, dermatologist, educator; b. Oklahoma City, May 30, 1928; s. Mark Ruben and Alice (Allen) E.; 1 son, Howard Dean. B.A. in Polit. Sci., U. Okla., 1947, M.D., 1951; USAF intern in pub. health. Intern in pediatrics U. Mich. Med. Sch., 1951, resident in dermatology, 1954-57, instr. dermatology, 1956-57; intern in pub. health Tulane Med. Sch., 1951; mem. faculty U. Okla. Med. Sch., 1959—, chmn. dept. dermatology, 1964—, prof. dermatology, head dept., 1967—, adj. prof. pathology and anatomy, 1975—, prof., interim head dept. pathology, 1979-84, Regents prof., 1982—, chmn. faculty bd., 1974-90; chief staff Okla. Meml. Hosp., 1980-85; vice chmn. bd. Bone and Joint Hosp., Oklahoma City, 1976-85; chmn. Internat. Com. for Dermatopathology, 1980-86; bd. dirs. Am. Bd. Dermatology, 1985—, pres.-elect, 1994, pres., 1995. Author 200 articles in field, chpts. in books. Pres. Okla. Ballet Soc., 1973, 77-80, Oklahoma City Chamber Orch., 1979-81, Chamber Music Okla., 1989—; pres. bd. trustees Everett Found., 1961—; adv. bd. World Lit. Today, 1970—, Bizzell Libr. Soc., 1982—. With USAF, 1952-54. Recipient Bronze medal U. Okla. Fedn., Mayor's award for Lifetime Contbn. to Arts, Oklahoma City, 1989, Gov.'s Arts award, 1993; grantee Am. Cancer Soc., NIH. Mem. AMA, Am. Acad. Dermatology (chmn. long-range planning coun. 1975-80, dir. 1978-82, chmn. coun. on sci. assembly 1985), Assn. Profs. Dermatology (pres. 1976-78), Am. Soc. Dermatopathology (pres. 1980), Am. Assn. Cancer Rsch., Internat. Acad. Pathology, Am. Dermatol. Assn. (bd. dirs. 1990-95, pres. 1995-96), Am. Soc. Clin. Investigation, Soc. Investigative Dermatology, Radiation Rsch. Soc., Okla. Med. Soc., Coll. Physicians Phila., N.Y. Acad. Scis., N.Mex. Dermatol. Soc., Pacific Dermatol. Assn., South Ctrl. Dermatol. Soc., Austrian Dermatology Soc. (hon.), Polish Dermatology Soc. (hon.), Brit. Assn. Dermatology (hon.), RRC Dermatology RRC Dermapathology, Gougerot Soc., Sociètè Française de Dermatologie (hon.), Phi Beta Kappa. Democrat. Roman Catholic. Club: Lotos (N.Y.C.). Office: U Okla Health Sci Ctr Dept Dermatology 619 NE 13th St Oklahoma City OK 73104-5001

EVERETT, PATRICIA ROBERTSON, clinical psychologist; b. Tokyo, Japan, Nov. 2, 1957; came to U.S., 1959; d. William Henry Everett and Jean (Matthews) Halverson; m. Theodore Jacob Ellenhorn, Aug. 4, 1990. BA, Williams Coll., 1979; MA in Art History, Columbia U., 1982; MA in Psychology, NYU, 1985; MA, PhD in Clin./Sch. Psychology, Adelphi U., 1989. Dir. Barbara Mathes Gallery, N.Y.C., 1982-86; instr. Adelphi U., Garden City, N.Y., 1987-89; asst. psychologist Jewish Bd. Family & Children's Svcs., N.Y.C., 1989-90; pvt. practice Amherst, Mass., 1990—; psychotherapist Inst. for Contemporary Psychotherapy, N.Y.C., 1989-90; clin. psychologist Hampden Dist. Mental Health Clinic, Springfield, Mass., 1990-92; group practice, Keene, N.H., 1991—; adj. instr. U. Mass., Amherst, 1991—. Contbr. articles to profl. jour; editor: A History Of Having A Great Many Times Not Continued To Be Friends: The Correspondence Between Mabel Dodge and Gertrude Stein, 1996. Grantee Am. Coun. of Learned Socs., 1990. Mem. APA.

EVERETT, VIRGINIA SAUERBRUN, counselor; b. Newark, N.J., Mar. 24, 1939; d. Arthur Gordon and Elwyna (Van Allen) Sauerbrun; m. Chandler H. Everett, Sept. 14, 1963 (div. Feb. 1986); children: Chandler P., Alexander U. BA, Coll. Wooster, 1961; MS in Gen. Counseling, Seattle Pacific U., 1990. Cert. chem. dependency counselor I. Counselor South King County Drug & Alcohol Recovery Ctrs., Seattle, 1990—; counselor Seattle Mental Health Inst., 1988-89, King County Perinatal Treatment Program, 1992-93, King County Pub. Health Dept., 1991—. Treas. Pacific N.W. Ballet League, Seattle, 1983; chmn. publicity Seattle Opera Guild, 1984; mem. work com. Washington State Coalition on Women's Substance Abuse Issues, 1990. Mem. ACA, Nat. Assn. Alchoholism and Drug Abuse Counselors, Chem. Dependency Profls. Wash. Republican. Episcopalian. Home: 8408 NE 19th Pl Bellevue WA 98004-3236 Office: South King County Recovery Ctrs 15025 4th Ave SW Seattle WA 98166-2301

EVERHARD, MARTIN E., surgeon; b. Pitts., Jan. 28, 1933; s. Martin and Anna (Golaki) E.; m. Donna Ann Holden, July 30, 1988. BS, William & Mary Coll., 1953; PhD, U. Va., 1959; MD, NYU, 1967. mem. med. bd. Phelps Meml. Hosp., Tarrytown, 1989-94, dir., 1991. Contbr. articles to profl. jours. Bd. dirs., trustee Phelps Meml. Hosp. Lt. USN, 1953-59. Merit scholar NYU, 1963-67, Rubin scholar, 1963-67. Fellow ACS, Internat. Coll. Surgeons; mem. Westchester Surg. Soc. Office: Westchester Surg Group 8 Tarrow Ridge Rd Savannah GA 31411-3048

EVERLY, DON HAYES, JR., emergency room nurse; b. Bridgeton, N.J., Feb. 18, 1969; s. Don Hayes Sr. and Theresa Ann (Perticari) E. BS in Biology and Psychology, Ursinus Coll., 1991; AAS in Nursing and Bus. Adminstrn., Cumberland County (N.J.) Coll., 1993; BSN, Stockton State Coll., Pomona, N.J., 1995; postgrad., Widener U., Chester, Pa., 1995—. Cert. emergency nurse, cert. critical care nurse, cert. med.-surg. nurse, cert. clin. nurse specialist in emergency critical care; cert. ACLS, PALS, TNCC, CPR instr., others. Med./surg., ICU, emergency room nurse South Jersey Hosp. Sys.-Bridgeton (N.J.) Divsn., 1993—; clin. nurse III South Jersey Hosp. Sys.-Bridgeton Divsn., 1996—. Mem. AACN, Emergency Nurses Assn., N.J. Nurses Assn., Soc. Trauma Nurses, Intravenous Nurses Soc. Roman Catholic. Home: 161 Cocelli Dr Bridgeton NJ 08302 Office: Bridgeton Hosp 333 Irving Ave Bridgeton NJ 08302

EVERLY, GEORGE STOTELMYER, JR., psychophysiologist; b. Balt., May 31, 1950; s. George Stotelmyer and Kathleen Webster E.; children: Marideth, George III, Andrea. BS, U. Md., 1972, MA, 1974, PhD, 1978; postdoctoral tng., U. Miami, 1983-85, Harvard U., 1985-86. Lectr. U. Md., College Park, 1975-80; assoc. prof. psychology, dir. psychophysiology lab. Loyola Coll., Balt., 1980-85, prof. psychology, 1985—; dir. psychol. svcs. div. Homewood Hosp. Ctr. Johns Hopkins Health System, Balt., 1990-92; CEO Internat. Critical Incident Stress Found., Balt., 1992—, Inst. Advanced Studies Crisis & Disaster Mgmt., 1995—; vis. scholar Harvard U., 1985-87; vis. lectr. on medicine Harvard Med. Sch., 1987-88. Author: Occupational Health Promotion, 1985; The Nature and Treatment of the Stress Response, 1981, Psychotraumatology, 1995, Innovations in Disaster and Trauma Psychology, 1995; The Stress Mess Solution, 1980; co-author: Controlling Stress and Tension, 1979; Experiencing Health, 1985; Personality and Its Disorders, 1985, The Assessment of Human Stress, 1987, Clinical Guide to Treatment of the Human Stress Response, 1989; researcher, developer: The Everly Behavioral Survey, 1982. Recipient Cert. of Honor Balt. City Police Dept., 1981. Fellow Acad. Psychosomatic Medicine, Am. Inst. Stress (bd. trustees); mem. APA, Soc. Behavioral Medicine, Am. Acad. Behavioral Medicine.

EVERS, GARLOND EDWARD, hospital administrator; b. Richmond, Va., Feb. 14, 1923; s. Lester Edward and Lena Belle (Parham) E.; m. Rita Frances Yoss, Apr. 24, 1945 (div. June 1964); children: Rita Yvonne, Karen Frances; m. Anna Pauline Ridout, July 11, 1964; 1 daughter Anna Renee; 1 stepson, John A. Bradley. BA, U. Richmond, 1949; MHA, Va. Commonwealth U., 1959; cert., Cornell U., 1982, Harvard U., 1984. Administr. The Virginia Home, Richmond, 1959-63; hosp. adminstrn. specialist Vets. Adminstrn., Washington, 1974-76; dir. med. ctr. Vets. Adminstrn., Big Spring, Tex., 1978-80, Balt., 1980-81, Chillicothe, Ohio, 1981-86, Ohio, 1984-86; cmmdr. U.S. Power Squadron, Beaufort, S.C., 1990-91; gov. bd. Permian Basin Health Systems Agy, Midland, Tex., 1978-80; mem. state health coordinating coun., Columbus, Ohio, 1984-86; adj. prof., acad. advisor Webster U. Grad. Edn., Beaufort, S.C., 1987—. Contbr. author book Case Studies in Health Administration, 1978; mem. editorial bd. Owen's Modern Concepts Hospital Administration, 1962. Pres. Scioto Valley Arts Coun., Chillicothe, 1983; mem. Louisville St. Regis Park, (Ky.) City Coun., 1967. Lt. USN, 1942-45, ATO, ETO. A.D. Williams scholarship Sch. of Hosp. Adminstrn. Med. Coll. of Va., 1958, recipient Disting. Career award VA, 1986. Fellow Am. Coll. Health Care Execs.; mem. Am. Coll. Hosp. Adminstrs. (pres. D.C. 1974-75), Symposiarchs Club (Chillicothe) (pres. 1985-86), Rotary (v.p. Mich., Tex., Ohio 1964-86). Repubican. Methodist. Home: 614 Dolphin Anx Fripp Island SC 29920-9517

EVERS, MARTIN LOUIS, internist; b. Newark, Dec. 17, 1957; s. George and Eva (Auslander) E. BA in Biochemistry, Rutgers U., 1979; MD, U. Medicine and Dentistry N.J., 1985. Diplomate Am. Bd. Internal Medicine. Emergency medicine resident Hershey (Pa.) Med. Ctr., 1985-86; internal medicine resident Raritan Bay Med. Ctr., Perth Amboy, N.J., 1986-89; critical care fellow Presbyn. Hosp., Pitts., 1989; emergency room physician Shadyside Hosp., Pitts., 1989-90; assoc. program dir. St. Francis Med. Ctr., Trenton, N.J., 1990-94; program dir. internal med. residency Conemaugh Meml. Med. Ctr., Jonestown, Pa., 1995—; ACLS instr. Ctr.for Emergency Medicine, Pitts., 1990, St. Francis Med. Ctr., Trenton, 1991-94, Conemaugh Meml. Med. Ctr., 1995—. Fellow Acad. Medicine N.J., ACP; mem. AMA, Soc. Critical Care Medicine. Jewish. Office: Conemaugh Meml Med Ctr Dept Medicine 1086 Franklin St Johnstown PA 15963

EVERS, SEAN ROBERT, clinical psychologist; b. Jersey City, Apr. 18, 1949; s. John Robert and Katherine (Pilerci) E.; m. Anne Ellman, May 3, 1981; 1 child, Erin. BA in English, Marietta Coll., 1971; MA in Psychology, New Sch. for Social Rsch., 1977; PhD in Clin. Psychology, Fla. Inst. Tech., 1981. Diplomate Am. Bd. Psychotherapists, Internat. Acad. Behavioral Medicine and Psychotherapy, Am. Acad. Pain Mgmt., Am. Bd. Forensic Examiners, Forensic Medicine; profl. disability cons.; cert. addictions specialist; lic. psychologist, N.J. Tchr. Bricktown (N.J.) Bd. Edn., 1971-79; therapist/intern Bayshore Youth Svcs. Bur., Keyport, N.J., 1979-81; pvt. practice Brielle, N.J., 1981—; cons. N.J. Div. Mil. and Veterans Affairs, Trenton, N.J., 1989—. Fellow Am. Ortho Assn., Am. Bd. Vocat. Experts; mem. APA, Am. Orthopsychiat. Assn., N.J. Psychol. Assn., N.J. Acad. Psychology, Assn. Advancement of Psychology. Office: Brielle Hills Office Pk 2640 Highway 70 Ste 301 Manasquan NJ 08736-2609

EVERS, SHARON LEE, nursing educator, consultant; b. Rockford, Ill., July 15, 1951; d. William L. and Mary T. (Rossi) Sterner; m. John Warren Evers, July 3, 1982; 1 child, Amanda Colette. BSN, Marquette U., 1973; MSN, U. Wis., 1980. RN; clin. specialist. Emergency therapist Janet Wattles Mental Health Clinic, Rockford, 1985; instr. St. Anthony Hosp. Sch. Nursing, Rockford, 1973-87; dir. nursing Anchor Hosp., Atlanta, 1987-88, Charterbrook Hosp., Atlanta, 1988-89; dir. crisis team Charter Peachford Hosp., Atlanta, 1988; assoc. prof. Columbus (Ga.) Coll., 1989—; nursing cons. Northside Psychiat. Corp., Columbus, 1991-92, West Ga. Regional Hosp., La Grange, 1991-93, Charterbrook Hosp., Atlanta, 1988-89, H. Douglas Singer Zone Ctr., Rockford, 1985, Litigation Tech. Svcs., Atlanta, 1992—; nursing cons. Twin Cedars Youth Svcs., Columbus, 1994-95, nurse mgr., 1995—. Chmn. Arthritis Found., Evansville, Wis., 1986; bd. dirs. Coweta Hist. Soc., 1992-95, mem., 1992—; mem. Hist. Soc. Evansville, 1985-87. Recipient Mental Health Traineeship award DHEW, 1979-80. Mem. ANA, Ga. Nurses Assn., Sigma Theta Tau. Office: Columbus Coll Dept Nursing Columbus GA 31993-2399

EVERTON, MARTA VE, ophthalmologist; b. Luling, Tex., Nov. 12, 1926; d. T.W. and Nora E. (Eckols) O'Leavy; B.A., Hardin-Simmons U., 1945; M.A., Stanford U., 1947; M.D., Baylor U., 1955; postgrad. N.Y.U.-Bellevue Hosp., 1956-57; m. Robert K. Graham, Oct. 15, 1960; children: Marcia, Christie, Leslie Fox. Intern, Meth. Hosp., Houston, 1955-56; resident in ophthalmology Baylor Affiliated Hosps., Houston, 1957-59; clin. instr. ophthalmology Baylor U., 1959-60; asst. clin. prof. ophthalmology Loma Linda U., 1962-73; practice medicine specializing in ophthalmology, Houston, 1959-60, Pasadena, Calif., 1961-74, Escondido, Calif., 1974—. Mem. Calif. Med. Assn., Am. Acad. Ophthalmology, Alpha Omega Alpha. Home: 3024 Sycamore Ln Escondido CA 92025-7433 Office: 820 E Ohio Ave Escondido CA 92025-3421

EVETT, RUSSELL DOUGHERTY, internist, educator; b. Norfolk, Va., Feb. 1, 1932; s. Edward Hall and Elizabeth (Dougherty) E.; B.S., Randolph-Macon Coll., 1953; M.D., Med. Coll. Va., 1957; M.S. in Medicine, Mayo Clinic and U. Minn., 1963; m. Mary Gail Kirby, Aug. 18, 1956; children—Stephen, Anne, Gail, John. Intern, DePaul Hosp., Norfolk, 1957-58; fellow in internal medicine Mayo Clinic, Rochester, Minn., 1960-63; pvt. practice internal medicine, Norfolk, 1964—; pres. med. staff Leigh Meml. Hosp., Norfolk, 1970-72; chmn. dept. internal medicine Norfolk Gen. Hosp., 1972-74; asso. prof. medicine Eastern Va. Med. Sch., 1974—; mem. staff Med. Center Hosps., DePaul Hosp. Served with USNR, 1958-60. Diplomate Am. Bd. Internal Medicine. Fellow ACP; mem. Va. Gastroenterol. Soc. (pres. 1975-77), Norfolk Acad. Medicine (pres. 1976-77), Med. Soc. Va. (pres. 1994-95), AMA (alt. del. 1985-95, del. 1995—), So. Med. Assn., Phi Beta Kappa, Omicron Delta Kappa, Alpha Omega Alpha. Methodist. Clubs: Norfolk Yacht and Country, Harbor. Home: 6147 Studeley Ave Norfolk VA 23508-1044 Office: 530 Wainwright Bldg Norfolk VA 23510

EVEY, LOIS REED, psychiatric nurse; b. Burgettstown, Pa., Aug. 23, 1925; d. Harry Lemoyne and Willa Blanche (Miller) Reed; diploma Presbyn. Hosp. Sch. Nursing, Pitts., 1946; B.Nursing Edn., U. Pitts., 1959, M.Nursing Edn., 1963, postgrad., 1978; m. Raymond Cuervo, Sept. 1946; 1 son, Craig Dale; m. 2d, Kenneth George Evey, Aug. 20, 1959. Successively staff nurse, relief head nurse Women's Hosp., Pitts., 1946-53; staff nurse, then head nurse, asst. bldg. supr. Woodville (Pa.) State Hosp., 1953-59; med.-surg. nursing instr. St. Margaret Meml. Hosp., Pitts., 1959-61; psychiat. staff nurse Council House, Inc., Pitts., 1962-66, acting exec. dir., 1966, exec. dir., 1966-80; exec. dir. VA Med. Center, Pitts., 1979-95, coordinator in-patient psychosocial rehab. program, 1984-85; lectr. community mental health workshops; mem. nurse adv. bd. Pitts. Planned Parenthood; mem. Task Force to Establish Domiciliary Care, Community Human Service Center, Pitts.; mem. Greater Pitts. Rehab. Council; mem. Pitts. chpt. Gov.'s Com. Employment of Handicapped; mem. citizens council bd. St. Francis Gen. Hosp., Western Psychiat. Inst. and Clinics; bd. dirs. continuing edn. for nurses U. Pitts., Indiana U. of Pa., Carlow Coll. Author: (with others) Rehabilitating the Mentally Ill in the Community. Served with Cadet Nurse Corps, U.S. Army, 1943-46. USPHS grantee, 1961-63. Mem. Am. Orthopsychiat. Assn., Internat. Assn. Psycho-Social Rehab. Services (co-founder, dir.), Pa. Assn. Mental Health and Mental Retardation Service Providers, Nat. Council Therapy and Rehab. Through Horticulture, Am. Nurses Assn. (legis. com.), Pa. Nurses Assn., Nat. Assn. Mental Health Adminstrs., Pa. Assn. Mental Health Adminstrs., Am. Public Health Assn., Pa. Public Health Assn., United Mental Health, Nat. Assn. Retarded Citizens, Pa. Assn. Retarded Citizens, Western Pa. Aftercare Assn., Health and Welfare Planning Assn., Pitts. Exec. Women's Council (charter), U. Pitts. Alumni Assn., Presbyn. U. Hosp. Alumni Assn. (past pres.; life), Sigma Theta Tau, Alpha Tau Delta. Republican. Mem. United Ch. of Christ. Club: East Hills Pitts. (life). Home: 305 Lougeay Rd Pittsburgh PA 15235-4502

EVIATAR, LYDIA, pediatric neurologist; b. Bucharest, Romania, Apr. 7, 1936; came to U.S., 1966; d. Joseph and Ghitea (Scheinberg) Tamir; m. Abraham Eviatar, Oct. 9, 1956; children: Joseph, Daphne. BSc, Faculte des Scis., Strasbourg, 1954; MD, Hadassah Hebrew U., Jerusalem, 1961. Diplomate Am. Bd. Pediatrics. Intern and resident Tel Hashoner Hosp., Tel Aviv, 1961-65; U.C.P. fellow UCLA, 1966-67, fellow in pediatric neurology, 1967-69; pediatric neurologist Bronx (N.Y.) Lebanon Hosp., 1970-79; resident in neurology Montefiore Hosp. Med. Ctr., Bronx, 1973-75; pediatric neurologist L.I. Jewish Med. Ctr., 1979-86; chief pediatric neurology Schneider Children's Hosp., New Hyde Park, N.Y., 1986—; from assoc. prof. to prof. pediatrics and neurology Albert Einstein Coll. Medicine, Bronx, N.Y., 1989—. Co-author: (with others) Pediatric Neurology, 1988. Grantee Nat. Inst. Neurol. Disease and Blindness, 1970-77, Acad. Cerebral Palsy, 1980-81, Richmond award, 1981; recipient teaching award Am. Acad. Otolaryngology, 1983. Fellow Am. Acad. Pediatrics, Am. Acad. Neurology (cert. neurologist, child neurologist). Office: Schneider Children's Hosp New Hyde Park NY 11042

EVINS, STARLING CLAUDE, urologist; b. Danville, Ky., Aug. 6, 1944; s. Charles Parker and Bille (Early) E.; m. Mary Richard Shearer Pearce, June 29, 1968 (div. May 1985); children: Holly Elizabeth, Stephen Parker; m. Sarah Jeanne Kinnard, June 27, 1987; children: Tanner Kinnard, Cody Kinnard. BS, Davidson Coll., 1966; MD, U. Ky., 1970. Diplomate Am. Bd. Urology. Intern, resident in surgery Med. U. S.C., Charleston, 1970-72; served to maj. USAF, Patrick AFB, Fla., 1972-74; resident, then chief resident in urology Med. U. S.C., 1974-77, asst. prof. urology, 1977-78; pres., attending physician Franklin (Tenn.) Urol. Assn., 1978—; bd. dirs. Mid-Cumberland Cmty. Health Agy., Nashville, 1991-93. Bd. dirs. Cmty. Health Consortium, Nashville, 1989—, Harpeth Acad., Franklin, 1981-89; cub scout leader Boy Scouts Am., Franklin, 1988-89, webelow leader, 1989; bd. dirs., asst. coach Williamson County Baseball Assn., Franklin, 1990-91. Fellow Am. Coll. Surgeons; mem. Am. Urol. Assn., Southeastern Soc. Am. Urol. Assn., Tenn. Urol. Assn., Am. Assn. Clin. Urologist. Republican. Home: 7174 Fox Run Dr Brentwood TN 37027 Office: Franklin Urol Assn 100 Covey Dr Ste 309 Franklin TN 37067

EWALD, PAUL WILLIAM, biologist, educator; b. Evanston, Ill., Sept. 18, 1953; s. Arno Wilfred and Sara Jeanne (Hauke) E.; m. Christine Edith Bayer, Apr. 11, 1981; children: Sarah Elisabeth, Samuel Bennet. BS, U. Calif., Irvine, 1975; PhD, U. Wash., Seattle, 1980. Vis. asst. prof. dept. biol. scis., jr. fellow U. Mich., Ann Arbor, 1980-83; postdoctoral scholar NATO/NSF & Imperial Coll., U. London, 1984-85; asst. prof. biology Amherst (Mass.) Coll., 1983-89, assoc. prof. biology, 1989-94, prof. biology, 1994—; adj. asst., assoc. and prof. U. Mass., Amherst, 1985—; grant reviewer Am. Philos. Soc., Nat. Geog. Soc., H.F. Guggenheim Found., U.S.-Israel Binat. Found., NSF; sci. pub. reviewer Am. Naturalist, Animal Behavior, Am. Ornithologists' Union, Behavioral Ecology and Sociobiology, Condor, Ecology, others. Author: Evolution of Infectious Disease, 1994; contbr. articles to profl. jours. Sci. counselor UN AIDS Found., 1993-94. Recipient Amherst Coll. Faculty Rsch. award, 1988-89, 89-91, 91-92; grantee Audubon Soc., 1977-78, Frank M. Chapman Fund, 1977-78, NSF, 1977-79, 90, 84-85, 89-91, H.F. Guggenheim Found., 1980-82, NIH, 1983-85, 86-87, Wellcome Trust, 1985, Miner D. Crary fellowship, 1986-87, Amherst Coll. Trustees Faculty fellowship, 1987-88, Max and Etta Lazerowitz lectureship, 1989-90, George E. Burch fellowship, 1991-93, Leonard X. Bosack and Bette M. Kruger Found., 1993-96. Mem. AAAS, Am. Ornithologists' Union, Animal Behavior Soc., Cooper Ornithol. Soc., Wilson Ornithol. Soc. Office: Amherst Coll Dept Biology PO Box 5000 Amherst MA 01002-5000

EWIN, DABNEY MINOR, surgeon; b. New Orleans, Dec. 7, 1925; s. James Perkins and Lucille Havard (Scott) E.; m. Ethelyn Alexander Sherrouse, June 6, 1951 (div. 1968); children: Dabney Jr., Constance, Walton, Christopher, Leila; m. Marilyn Allison Abernathy, June 29, 1968. MD, Tulane U., 1951. Intern Jefferson-Hillman Hosp. U. Ala., Birmingham, 1951, resident, 1951-54; resident Ochsner Found. Hosp., New Orleans, 1954-56; chief resident Huey P. Long Charity Hosp., Pineville, La., 1956-57; pvt. practice, 1957—; staff surgeon Touro Infirmary, New Orleans, East Jefferson Gen. Hosp. Metairie, La., Charity Hosp. La., St. Jude Med. Ctr. (now called Kenner (La.) Regional Hosp.); clin. prof. surgery and psychiatry Tulane Med. Sch; clin. prof. psychiatry La. State U. Contbr. articles to profl. jours. Bd. dirs. Christ Sch., 1979-85; sr. class Sunday sch. tchr. Trinity Episc. Ch., 1960-66. Fellow ACS; mem. AMA, Am. Trauma Soc. (dir. 1975-79), Am. Burn Assn.,

Am. Occupational Medicine Assn. (spkr. Ho. of Dels., 1973-75), Am. Bd. Med. Hypnosis (past pres.), Am. Soc. Clin. Hypnosis (past pres.), La. State Med. Soc., Orleans Parish Med. Soc., Surg. Assn. La., New Orleans Surg. Soc., Alton Ochsner Surg. Soc. (past sec.), So. Med. Assn. (chmn. sect. on indsl. medicine and surgery 1966-67), La. Indsl. Med. Assn., La. Occupational Med. Assn. (past pres.), Soc. for Clin. and Exptl. Hypnosis, La. Psychiat. Assn. Republican. Office: 318 Baronne St New Orleans LA 70112-1606

EWING, DAVID LEON, radiation biologist; b. Shreveport, La., Aug. 20, 1941; s. Arlington B. and Mary Lenore (Bryant) E.; m. Mary Dessagene Crawford, Feb. 6, 1965 (div. Apr. 1991); children: Kelly Michelle, Scott Emlyn. BS in Physics, Centenary Coll., Shreveport, La., 1963; MS in Radiol. Health, U. Calif., Berkeley, 1965; PhD in Zoology, U. Tex., 1969. Radiobiologist NASA, Houston, 1965; rsch. scientist U. Tex., Austin, 1972-74, asst. prof., 1974-76; assoc. prof. Grad. Sch. and Med. Coll. Hahnemann U., Phila., 1976-82, prof., 1982—. Contbr. over 50 articles to profl. jours. Recipient Bell Telephone Sci. award 1959, Radiation Rsch. Soc. Travel awards, 1974, 79, Nat. Cancer Inst. Travel award, 1977; Centenary Coll. Freshman scholar, 1959-60, The Magale Found. fellow, 1960-63, AEC Health Physics fellow, 1963-64, USPHS grantee, 1964-65, Genetics Tng. grantee, 1965-69, NIH postdoctoral fellow, 1970-72. Mem. AAAS, The Radiation Rsch. Soc., Tex. Assn. Radiation Rsch., N.Y. Acad. Sci., Environ. Mutagen Soc., Soc. for Free Radical Rsch., Assn. for Radiation Rsch., Phila. Cancer Club, The Oxygen Soc., Alpha Sigma Pi. Home: 88 S Spring Ln Phoenixville PA 19460-2706 Office: MCPHU Dept Radiation Oncology/MS 102 Broad And Vine St Philadelphia PA 19102

EWING, JOHN ALEXANDER, psychiatrist; b. Fife, Scotland, Mar. 17, 1923; came to U.S., 1951, naturalized, 1959; s. James Anderson and Esther Stratton (Turner) E.; m. Janet S.G. Combe, Oct. 31, 1946; children: Christine, Ian James. M.B., Ch.B., U. Edinburgh, 1946, M.D., 1954; D.P.M., U. London, 1950. Intern, Royal Infirmary, Preston and Gogarburn Hosp., Edinburgh, 1946-47; resident in psychiatry U. Durham (Eng.) Hosp., 1947-50; sr. registrar Cherry Knowle Hosp., Sunderland, Eng., 1950-51; psychiatrist Alcoholic Rehab. Center, Butner, N.C., 1951-54; mem. faculty U. N.C. Med. Sch., Chapel Hill, 1954-84; prof. psychiatry U. N.C. Med. Sch., 1963-84, prof. emeritus, 1984—, chmn. dept., 1965-70, dir. Ctr. Alcohol Studies, 1970-84; cons., vis. lectr. in field. Author: Drinking to your Health, 1981; Co-editor: Drinking, 1978; Contbr. articles to profl. jours. Fellow Royal., Am. colls. psychiatrists, Am. Psychiat. Assn., Am. Acad. Psychoanalysis; mem. Am., Brit. med. assns., Am. Med. Soc. on Alcoholism, N.C. Med. Soc., N.C. Neuropsychiat. Assn. Home: 2311 Canterwood Dr Wilmington NC 28401-7300

EWING, MARY EILEEN, radiologic technologist; b. Morning Sun, Iowa, Aug. 26, 1926; d. Frank Leeman and Myrtle Marguerite (Mehaffy) Steele; m. Dean Willard Ewing, Mar. 29, 1952; children: John, Eileen, Diane, Denise. BS in Radiologic Tech., St. Louis U., 1948. Registered technologist. Staff technologist Mo. Pacific Hosp., St. Louis, 1948-52; staff technologist Blanchard Valley Hosp., Findlay, Ohio, 1968-69, asst. chief technologist, 1969-80, asst. dir. dept., 1980-90; clin. instr. Lima (Ohio) Tech. Coll., 1978-90; sec. N.W. Libr. Dist. Exec. Bd., 1988—. Library trustee McComb (Ohio) Pub. Libr., 1957—; pres. Libr. Bd., McComb, 1967—; elder ck. of session, 1994—. Mem. Am. Soc. Radiologic Techs., Ohio Soc. Radiologic Techs., World Orgn. China Painters, Internat. Porcelain Artists and Tchrs., Philomath Club (pres. 1958, 95), Mansfield China Painters, NSDAR (Ft. Findlay chpt. sec. 1993-94, regent 1995). Democrat. Presbyterian. Home: 103 W South St Mc Comb OH 45858

EWING, RUSSELL CHARLES, II, physician; b. Tucson, Aug. 16, 1941; s. Russell Charles and Sue M. (Sawyer) E.; m. Louise Anne Wendt, Jan. 29, 1977; children: John Charles, Susan Lenore. BS, U. Ariz., 1963; MD, George Washington U., 1967. Diplomate Am. Bd. Family Practice. Intern L.A. County-U. So. Calif. Med. Ctr., L.A., 1967-68; gen. practice medicine and surgery, Yorba Linda, Calif. and Placentia, Calif., 1970-90, Brea, Calif., 1990-96, Placentia, 1996—; mem. staff St. Judes Hosp., Fullerton, Calif., 1970—; mem. staff Placentia Linda Cmty. Hosp., 1972—, vice chief staff, 1977-78, chief staff, 1978-80, bd. dirs., 1974-81; sec., dir. Yorba Linda Med. Group, Inc., 1974-90; bd. dirs. Prospect Med. Group, 1984-93, Heritage Assoc. Physicians, 1995—, Western Empire Savs. & Loan Assn. (Calif.); bd. dirs., sec. St. Judes Med. Group, 1993—. Bd. dirs. Yorba Linda YMCA, 1973-88, pres., 1973-74, 81. With USN, 1968-70. Fellow Am. Acad. Family Practice; mem. AMA, Calif. Med. Assn. (house of del. 1978-90, 92—, trustee 1990-92), Orange County Med. Assn. (bd. dirs. 1983-90, pres. 1988-89). Republican. Episcopalian. Home: 9212 Smoketree Ln Villa Park CA 92667-2219 Office: Ste 5 1041 E Yorba Linda Blvd Placentia CA 92670

EWING-WILSON, DEBORAH LOUISE, neurologist; b. Seattle, Aug. 6, 1955; d. Edwin Stanley Ewing and Mary Alice Castleman; m. Fredrick Paul Wilson, Sept. 25, 1982; children: Victoria, Katherine. BA, Wellesley Coll., 1978; DO, Chgo. Coll. Osteo. Medicine, 1983. Diplomate Am. Bd. Psychiatry and Neurology, Am. Bd. Electrodiagnostic Medicine; added qualifications in clin. neurophysiology. Intern Brentwood Hosp., Cleve., 1983-84; resident Cleve. Clinic Found., 1984-87; staff section neurology Ohio Permanent Med. Group, Cleve., 1987—, chief neurology, 1992—; staff Cleve. Clinic found., 1992—, Metrohealth St. Luke's Med. Ctr., Cleve., 1992-94; clin. prof. neurology Ohio U., Athens, 1989—. Contbr. articles to profl. jours. Fellow Am. Assn. Electrodiagnostic Medicine; mem. AMA, Am. Acad. Neurology, Am. Osteo. Assn., Ohio Osteo. Assn., Cleve. Acad. Medicine, Epilepsy Found. N.E. Ohio, Cleve. (mem. profl. adv. bd. 1991—). Episcopalian. Office: Ohio Permanente Med Group 3733 Park East Dr Cleveland OH 44122-4311

EWY, GORDON ALLEN, cardiologist, educator; b. Brenham, Kans., Aug. 5, 1933; s. Marvin John and Hazel Miller (Allen) E.; m. Priscilla Ruth Weldon; children: Kim Elizabeth, Gordon Stuart, Mark Allen. BA, U. Kans., 1955, MD, 1961. Resident, house officer Georgetown U. Hosp., Washington, 1961-64, cardiology fellow, 1964-65; instr. in medicine Georgetown U., Washington, 1965-68, asst. prof., 1968-69; asst. prof. U. Ariz., Tucson, 1969-70, assoc. prof., 1970-75, prof. medicine, 1975—, chief cardiology, dir. cardiology fellowship program, 1982—, assoc. head dept. medicine, 1986-94, dir. Univ. Heart Ctr., 1991—. Editor: Cardiovascular Drugs and Management of Heart Disease, 1982, 93, Current Cardiovascular Drug Therapy, 1984; author 147 sci. publs., contbr. over 130 revs. to profl. jours.; chpts. to books. Lt. (j.g.) USNR, 1955-57. Fellow ACP, Am. Heart Assn. (mem. clin. coun., nat. faculty advanced cardiac life support 1982-84, chmn. nat. programs subcom. 1982, bd. dirs. Ariz. chpt. 1975-82, 84-89, teaching fellow 1970-75), Am. Coll. Cardiology (chmn. learning ctr. com. 1988-91, trustee 1992—), Alpha Omega Alpha. Republican. Office: Ariz Health Scis Ctr 1501 N Campbell Ave Tucson AZ 85724-0001

EYBERG, SHEILA MAXINE, psychology educator; b. Omaha, Dec. 31, 1944; d. Clarence George and Geraldine Elizabeth (Gilbert) E.; m. John Richard Graham-Pole, Nov. 10, 1985. BA, U. Omaha, 1967; MA, U. Oreg., 1970, PhD, 1972. Lic. psychologist, Fla. Intern in med. psychology Oreg. Health Scis. U., Portland, 1971-72, resident in pediatric psychology, 1972-74, asst. prof. med. psychology, 1974-81, assoc. prof., 1981-85, dir. child psychology outpatient clinic, 1974-85; prof. clin. and health psychology, pediatrics U. Fla., Gainesville, 1985—. Mem. editl. bd. Clin. Psychology: Sci. and Practice, 1994—, Jour. Pediatric Psychology, 1977—, Clin. Child Psychology & Psychiatry, 1995—, Jour. Clin. Child Psychology, 1982—, assoc. editor, 1992—; assoc. editor: Behavior Therapy, 1995—. Recipient Lee Salk award Disting. Svc. Pediatric Psychology, 1994. Contbr. articles to profl. jours. Fellow Am. Psychol. Assn. (pres. sect. 5, divsn. 12, 1984, sect. 1, divsn. 12, 1987, chair fin. com. divsn. clin. psychology 1993, sec. divsn. child, youth and family svcs., sec. divsn. child 1992-95); mem. Heritage Club, Alpha Lambda Delta, Phi Kappa Phi. Office: Dept Clin and Health Psychology U Fla Box 100165 HSC Gainesville FL 32610

EYMAN, RICHARD KENNETH, psychologist, educator; b. Joliet, Ill., Nov. 26, 1931; s. Robert Kennedy and Helen E. (Reick) E.; m. Vivian Kolodziej, Jan. 31, 1959. B.S., U. Ill., Urbana, 1954, M.A., 1955; Ph.D., U. So. Calif., 1966. Diplomate Am. Bd. Profl. Psychology. Personnel research specialist Gen. Motors, South Gate, Calif., 1955-56; asst. research psychologist U.S. Army Def. Human Research Unit, Ft. Bliss, Tex., 1956-58; with Pacific State Hosp., Pomona, Calif., 1958-73; research specialist III Pacific State Hosp., 1967-68; research specialist VA, 1968-73; chief research Pacific State Hosp., 1972-73; asso. research psychologist Pacific State Hosp. research group Neuropsychiat. Inst., UCLA, 1973-75, adj. asso. prof. III, 1975-76, adj. prof., 1976-80, prof.-in-residence, 1980—; research educationist UCLA, 1981; lectr. statistics and edn. U. Calif., Riverside, 1974-81, prof. edn., 1981—; cons. in field. Editorial cons. CHOICE, Assn. Coll. and Research Libraries div. ALA, 1968—, Am. Jour. Mental Deficiency, 1969—, Mental Retardation, 1971—, Hosp. and Community Psychiatry, 1974—, Sci, 1975—, Nature, 1975—; contbr. articles to profl. jours. Bd. dirs. Accreditation Council for Services for Mentally Retarded and Other Devel. Disabled Persons, Washington, 1982—. Served with U.S. Army, 1956-57. Calif. Dept. Mental Hygiene grantee, 1962-64; NIMH grantee, 1964-71; Nat. Inst. Child Health and Human Devel. grantee, 1976-81; Div. Developmental Disabilities Rehab. Services Adminstrn. grantee, 1972-75; Office Econ. Opportunity grantee, 1974-75. Fellow Am. Assn. Mental Deficiency (Research award 1986), Am. Psychol. Assn. (pres. div. 33, 1982-83); mem. Am. Acad. Mental Retardation (pres. 1974-75, research adv. bd. 1974—, award 1989), Am. Ednl. Research Assn., Am. Statis. Assn., Psychometric Soc., Western Psychol. Assn., Sigma Xi. Home: 20286 E Lorencita Dr Covina CA 91724-3833 Office: U Calif Sch Edn Riverside CA 92521

EYSTER, MARY ELAINE, hematologist, educator; b. York, Pa., Mar. 21, 1935; d. Charles Gable and March Viola (Schriver) E.; m. Robert E. Dye, Jan. 2, 1965; children: Robert E., Charles. AB, Duke U., 1956, MD, 1960. Intern. N.Y. Hosp.-Cornell Med. Coll., N.Y.C., 1960-61, resident in medicine, 1961-63, fellow in hematology, 1963-66, instr. medicine, 1966-67, asst. prof. medicine, 1967-70; asst. prof. medicine Milton S. Hershey Med. Ctr. Pa. State U., Hershey, 1970-73, assoc. prof. Milton S. Hershey Med. Ctr., 1973-82, prof. Milton S. Hershey Med. Ctr., 1982—, chief hematology div., dept. medicine Coll. Medicine, 1973—; bd. dirs. Hemophilia Ctr. Cen. Pa., 1973—, AIDS Clin. Trials Unit Pa. State U., 1987—; faculty rsch. assoc. Am. Cancer Soc., 1966-71; mem. State Hemophilia Adv. Com., 1973—, chmn., 1977-79, 1988-90; mem. policy bd. Coop. F VII inhibitor study Nat. Heart, Lung and Blood Inst., 1975-79; mem. med. and sci. adv. coun. Nat. Hemophilia Found., 1976-77, 82—, chmn. med. adv. com. Del. Valley chpt., 1979-82; co-investigator, mem. multi-agy. task force on AIDS HHS, 1982-83; mem. blood products adv. com. FDA, 1985-89; exec. com. NIH-NIAID Clin. Trials, 1988-90. USPHS grantee, 1976—. Fellow ACP; mem. Pa. Med. Soc., Am. Fedn. Clin. Rsch., World Fedn. Hemophilia, Am. Soc. Hematology, Am. Assn. Blood Banks, Internat. Soc. Thrombosis and Haemostasis, Insternat. Soc. Hematology, Pa. Soc. Hematology, Oncology (bd. dirs. 1982-85), Am. Heart Assn. Coun. on Thrombosis, Phi Beta Kappa, Alpha Omega Alpha. Office: Milton S Hershey Med Ctr PO Box 850 Hershey PA 17033-0850

EZAKI-YAMAGUCHI, JOYCE YAYOI, renal dietitian; b. Kingsburg, Calif., Mar. 18, 1947; d. Toshikatsu and Aiko (Ogata) Ezaki; m. Kent Takao Yamaguchi, Oct. 28, 1972; children: Kent Takao, Jr., Toshia Ann. AA, Reedley Coll., 1967; BS in Foods and Nutrition, U. Calif., Davis, 1969. Dietetic intern Henry Ford Hosp., Detroit, 1969-70, staff dietitian, 1970-71; renal dietitian Sutter Meml. Hosp., Sacramento, 1971-72; therapeutic dietitian Mt. Sinai Hosp., Beverly Hills, Calif., 1972-73; clin. dietitian Pacific Hosp., Long Beach, Calif., 1973-77; consulting dietitian Doctor's Hosp., Lakewood, Calif., 1976-77; clin. dietitian Mass. Gen. Hosp., Boston, 1977-78, Winona Meml. Hosp., Indpls., 1978-80; renal dietitian Fresno (Calif.) Community Hosp., 1980—. Author: (computer program) Dialysis Tracker, 1987; author: (with others) Cultural Foods and Renal Diets for the Dietitian, 1988, Standards of Practice Guidlines for the Practice of Clinical Dietetics, 1991. Mem. Nat. Kidney Found. (exec. com. coun. renal nutrition 1992—, region V rep. 1992-93, chair elect 1994-95, chair 1995-96, immediate past chair 1996—), Am. Dietetic Assn. (bd. cert. renal nutrition specialist, renal practice group 1993—), No. Calif/No. Nev. chpt. Nat. Kidney Found. (disting. achievement award coun. on renal nutrition 1993, co-chair-elect 1993, co-chair 1994, co-past chair 1995, treas., corr. sec.). Buddhist. Office: Cmty Hosps Ctrl Calif Fresno & R Sts Fresno CA 93715-2094

EZEH, UCHECHUKWU INNOCENT OSITA, obstetrician, gynecologist; b. Onitsha, Anambra, Nigeria, Jan. 19, 1958; s. Raphael and Louisa Ezeh; m. Nwamaka Nwanneka Onyekwuluje, 1992; 1 child, Uchechukwu Chibuzo. MBBS, U. Nigeria, Nsukka, 1982; postgrad., Nat. Postgrad. Coll. Nigeria, 1993—. Resident ob-gyn. U. Nigeria Tchg. Hosp., Enusu, 1976-91; postgrad. trainee in ob-gyn. Leicester/Lincoln, London, 1991-95; rsch fellow Jessop Hosp. for Women, Sheffield, Eng., 1995—. Inventor novel method of sterilization. With Nat. Paramil. Svc., Nigeria, 1982-83. Recipient scholarships Anambra State Govt. Nigeria, Double Sponsorship Programme. Mem. Internat. Soc. Gynecol. Endoscopy, Royal Coll. Obstetricians and Gynecologists. Office: Jessop Hosp for Women, Acad Dept Ob-Gyn, Sheffield, Canada

FABIANI, JEAN-NOEL, cardiovascular surgeon, educator; b. Paris, Dec. 23, 1947; s. Pierre Herve and Simonne (Hubert) F.; m. Francoise Anne Lunel; 1 child, Pierre-Alexandre. MD, U. Paris VI, 1977, cert. cardiac surgeon, 1978. Prof. cardiac surgery Hosp. Broussais, Paris, 1987—. Author: Cardioplegic Solution, 1977, La Cuisine de Vos Arteres, 1994, Vasoréactivity of Human Vessels, 1995, Vascular Surgery, 1995. Recipient Young Investigator award European Soc. Cardiology, 1981, Prix Athena, Paris Acad. Scis., 1986. Roman Catholic. Office: Hosp Broussais, 96 Rue Didot, 75014 Paris France

FABRICIUS, RICHARD NEIL, orthopedic surgeon; b. Albany, N.Y., Aug. 14, 1928; s. John and Janet Muir (Meekin) F; m. Janet Carrie Pitcher, Oct. 27, 1957. BS, Springfield (Mass.) Coll., 1949; MD, Vt. Coll. Medicine, 1953. Diplomate Am. Bd. Orthopedic Surgery, Nat. Bd. Med. Examiners. Intern Albany (N.Y.) Med. Ctr., 1953-54, surg. resident, 1956-57; orthopedic resident Ochsner Clinic, New Orleans, 1957-60, staff orthopedist, 1960-61; mem. med. staff Putnam Meml. Hosp., Bennington, Vt., 1961—, pres. med. staff, 1969-70, chief surgery, 1970-76; orthopedic surgeon Orthopedic & Hand Surgery P.C., Bennington; guest speaker Fla. Orthopedic, West Palm Beach, Fla., 1978. Lt. comdr. USN, 1954-56. Fellow Am. Acad. Orthopedic Surgeons (mem. Vt. coun. 1981-87), New Eng. Orthopedic Soc. (sec. 1990-94, pres. elect 1994-96). Home: 17 Fairview Rd Bennington VT 05201 Office: Orthopedic & Hand Surgery 332 Dewey St Bennington VT 05201-2225

FABRIKANT, CRAIG STEVEN, psychologist; b. Buffalo, Jan. 8, 1952; s. Benjamin and Laurine Miriam (Zucker) F.; B.A., Fairleigh Dickinson U., 1974, M.A., 1977; Ph.D., Fla. Inst. Tech., 1983; m. Carol Diane Golub, Nov. 6, 1977; children—Chad Adam, Carly. Intern in psychology N.J. Dept. Human Services, Trenton, 1977-78; clin. psychologist North Jersey Devel. Ctr., Totowa, 1978-85, Cedar Grove Residential Ctr.; chief psychologist Hackensack Med. Ctr., N.J., 1985—; adj. instr. Montclair State Coll., 1980-82; part-time instr. Fairleigh Dickinson U.; cons. psychology N.J. Dept. Labor and Industry, Newark, 1980—. Mem. Assn. Advancement Behavior Therapy, Am. Psychol. Assn., N.J. Psychol. Assn. Author profl. papers. Home: 750 Martin Ave Oradell NJ 07649-2300 Office: 106 Old Hook Rd Westwood NJ 07675-2421

FABRIZIO, KAREN, critical care nurse; b. Pottsville, Pa.. Diploma, Pottsville Hosp. Sch. Nursing, 1980; BSN, Kutztown (Pa.) Coll., 1983. MSN, Allentown Coll., 1990; post masters cert. in nursing adminstrn., Villanova U., 1995. RN, Pa.; cert. ACLS and CPR instr. Am. Heart Assn. Staff nurse step down unit Good Samaritan Hosp., Pottsville, 1983, staff nurse ICU and CCU, 1983-94, head nurse ICU and CCU, 1994—; instr. critical care nursing Pa. State U., 1994—; part-time coord. LPN program Pa. Schuylkill Tng. and Tech. Ctr., Frackeville, Pa., 1990-94. Mem. AACN, Am. Hosp. Assn., Am. Assn. Nurse Execs., Ea. Region Nurse Execs., Sigma Theta Tau. Home: 203 N 4th St Minersville PA 17954-1203

FABRIZIO, TUULA IRJA, physician, writer; b. Helsinki, Finland, May 13, 1931; d. Arne Valfrid Jokinen and Jenny Lydia Johansson; m. John A. Fabrizio, Aug. 4, 1962. MD, U. Helsinki, 1957, PhD, 1958. Orthopedist cen. hosp. U. Helsinki, 1960-62; attending physician emergency medicine dept. Park City Hosp., Bridgeport, Conn., 1964, Norwalk (Conn.) Hosp., 1966-69, Milford (Conn.) Hosp., 1973-77, St. Vincent's Med. Ctr., Birdgeport, 1977-1979; practice medicine specializing in occupational medicine Bridgeport, 1979—. Columnist Finnish Med. Jour., Nordisk Medicin mag., Health 2000; contbr. articles to profl. jours. Coordinator local state rep. campaigns, Norwalk, 1968-74. Recipient Medal award Finnish Med. Assn., 1980. Fellow Am. Coll. Preventive Med., Am. Acad. Family Physicians (charter); mem. AMA, Fairfield County Med. Assn., Conn. State Med. Soc., Am. Coll. Emergency Physicians, Am. Pub. Health Assn., Am. Assn. for Automobile Med., Internat. Coll. Pediatrics, Acad. Polit. Sci., Am. Med. Writers Assn., World Acad. N.Z. Home and Office: 42 Stevens St Norwalk CT 06850-3525

FABRY, THOMAS LESTER, gastroenterologist, educator; b. Budapest, May 30, 1937. BSc, St. Andrews Coll., Scotland, 1961; PhD, Yale U., 1963; postgrad., Albert Einstein Coll. Medicine, 1973-74. Instr. Yale U., New Haven, 1963-65; asst. prof. Columbia U., N.Y.C., 1965-69; intern and resident Mt. Sinai Hosp., N.Y.C., 1973-76, fellow in gastroenterology, 1976-78, asst. clin. prof., 1979, assoc. clin. prof., 1990—, assoc. attending, 1990—; cons. interactive edn. Am. Soc. Gastrointestinal Endoscopy; cons. endoscopic terminology European Soc. Gastrointestinal Endoscopy. Editor: Guide to Liver Transplantation. Fellow Am. Coll. Gastroenterology; mem. Am. Gastroent. Assn., Am. Soc. Gastrointestinal Endoscopy, N.Y. Soc. Gastrointestinal Endoscopy, Am. Assn. Study Liver Diseases. Office: 853 5th Ave New York NY 10021-5802

FACHADA, EDERITO PAUL, podiatrist, surgeon; b. Cumberland, R.I., Apr. 6, 1929; s. Ernesto J. and Julia Augusta (Loucas) F.; m. Vera Phillips; children: Paul, Peter, Mark. BS, Providence Coll., 1950; D Podiatric Medicine, Temple U., 1955. Instr. surgery R.I. Hosp., Providence, 1953-54, Temple U., Phila., 1954-55; intern, resident Phila. Gen. Hosp. and Temple U. Hosp., Phila., 1955-56; chmn. bd. Bd. Examiners, Concord, N.H., 1983—; staff mem. Chesire Med. Ctr., Maplewood Hosp. and Nursing Home; state del. Nat. Bd. Examiners, 1988. Mem. Keene (N.H.) Bd. Health; chmn. bd. dirs. Keene Sr. Ctr.; state chmn. Columbia Squires, Keene; staff mem. Cheshire Med. Ctr., Maplewood Hosp. and Nursing Home, Prospect Hill Home. Recipient Surgery award Temple Univ.; named by Track & Field Mag./U.S. Tennis Assn. 5th in Doubles, 20th in Singles Sr. Divsn., N.H. Sr. Singles Champ 1992, 93, 94, 95. Mem. Am. Podiatric Med. Assn., N.H. Podiatric Med. Assn. (pres. 1961-62). Home: 24A Stonehouse Ln Keene NH 03431-5241 Office: 112 Washington St Keene NH 03431-3104

FACKLER, MARTIN L(UTHER), surgeon; b. York, Pa., Apr. 8, 1933; s. Martin Luther and Naomi Dorcas (Gibbs) F.; m. Nancy Aleen Gray, Sept. 29, 1964. AB magna cum laude, Gettysburg Coll., 1955; MD, Yale U., 1959. Diplomate Am. Bd. Surgery. Enlisted USN, 1960, advanced through grades to col., 1976; intern U. Oreg. Med. Sch. Hosp., 1959-60; resident in gen. surgery U.S. Naval Hosp., Boston, 1961-65; resident in plastic surgery U.S. Naval Hosp., Bethesda, Md., 1966-67; staff surgeon NSA Hosp., DaNang, Socialist Republic of Vietnam, 1967-68, USN Hosp., Yokosuka, Japan, 1969-71; chief dept. surgery USN Hosp., Memphis, 1972-74; intersvc. transfer U.S. Army chief dept. surgery 2d Gen. Hosp., Landstuhl, Republic of Germany, 1975-80; chief dept. surgery U.S. Army Hosp., Ft. Carson, Colo., 1980-81; dir. wound ballistics lab. Presidio, San Francisco, 1981-91; ret. U.S. Army, 1991; tech. adv. Assn. Firearm and Toolmark Examiners, 1984—; adv. forensic sci. grad. sch. U. Calif., Berkeley, 1985-91; speaker on war surgery, wound ballistics, weapons effects; expert witness, cons. to various state, city and nat. law enforcement agys. and criminalistics labs.; appointed steering com. on devel. less-than-lethal weapons for law enforcement use Nat. Inst. Justice, 1986—; mem. of Can. Gen. Standards Bd. Com. on Police Ammunition, 1989—, FBI symposium on wound ballistics, 1987, 93; mem. adv. coun. on soft body armor U.S. Office Tech. Assessment, 1991-92; apptd. permanent mem. exam. jury wound ballistics, U. Marseille, France, 1993, vis. prof. wound ballistics faculty forensic medicine, U. Marseille, France, 1993—. Editor in chief Wound Ballistics Rev., 1990—; contbr. articles to profl. jours. Bd. dirs. ACLU, Gainesville area chpt., Fla., 1993—. Decorated Legion of Merit, Meritorious Svc. medal; recipient Commendation 2d Gen. Hosp., Landstuhl, 1981. Fellow ACS (reg. com. on trauma 1974-75, 84-91); mem. Internat. Wound Ballistics Assn. (pres. 1990—), French Wound Ballistics Soc. (hon. pres. 1995—), Am. Acad. Forensic Scis., NRA (life), Assn. Firearm and Toolmark Examiners (disting. life mem.), Phi Beta Kappa. Home: RR 4 Box 264 Hawthorne FL 32640-8043

FADEM, JEROLD JOSEPH, JR., physician; b. Columbia, Mo., Mar. 14, 1955; s. Jerold Joseph and Shirley (Cannon) F.; m. Carmen Lauda Fadem, June 5, 1987; children: Kal, Jess, Bronwyn. BA, Furman Univ., 1977; MD, Univ. Fla., 1981. Resident medicine Orlando Reg. Med. Ctr., Orlando, Fla., 1981-82; resident medicine ORMC, Orlando, Fla., 1982-83, chief resident medicine, 1983-84, asst. residency program, 1984-87, chief medical svc., 1987-92, program dir. internal medicine residency program, 1992—. Contbr. article to profl. jours. Recipient Sae scholarship, Furman U., 1977. Mem. Orange County Medical Soc., ACP, Assn. Program Direcions in Internal Medicine, ASIM. Home: 6062 Tarawood Dr Orlando FL 32819 Office: Orlando Regional Healthcare Sys Orlando FL 32806

FAGAN, MICHAEL CHARLES, internist; b. Chgo., Aug. 6, 1944; s. Arthur Joseph and Vivian Rose (Booth) F.; m. Marilyn Jean Faford, Mar. 16, 1968; children: Kimberly Ann, Tracy Marie. BS, Loyola U., 1966; MD, U. Ill., Chgo., 1970. Diplomate Am. Bd. Internal Medicine. Intern St. Joseph Hosp., Denver, 1970-71, resident, 1973-76, chief resident, 1975-76; pvt. practice internal medicine Aurora (Colo.) Internal Medicine Assocs., 1976—; mem. exec. com. Aurora (Colo.) Regional Med. Ctr., 1979-83, 90-91, trustee, 1980-83. Capt. USAF, 1971-73. Mem. ACP, Am. Soc. Internal Medicine, Colo. Med. Soc., Aurora-Adams County med. Soc. (sec.-treas.), Columbine Med. Group (bd. dirs., east region chief). Home: 5093 S Hannibal Way Aurora CO 80015 Office: Aurora Internal Medicine Assocs 1550 S Potomac Aurora CO 80012

FAGAN, PETER GAIL, occupational medicine physician; b. Big Spring, Tex., July 25, 1947; s. Joe Gail and Lura Juanita (Allison) F.; m. Susanne Brown, Mar. 18, 1966; children: Pamela Fagan Johnson, Paul Christopher. Md, U. Tex. Southwestern, 1972. Diplomate Am. Bd. Family Practice, Am. Bd. Occupl. Medicine. Physician Buffalo (Wyo.) Clinic, 1974-75, DeLeon (Tex.) Clinic, 1975-76; prof. family practice Tex. Tech. Sch. of Medicine, Amarillo, 1976-78; founder, physician Amarillo Indsl. Health Ctr., 1978-94; co-founder, v.p. OccuSystems, Inc., Dallas, 1985—; aviation med. examiner FAA, Washington, 1979—. Dir. Amarillo Bi-City County Health Dept., 1982-94. Fellow Am. Coll. Occupl. and Environ. Medicine. Home: PO Box 168 DeLeon TX 76444 Office: OccuSystems Inc 3010 LBJ Freeway Dallas TX 75234

FAGAN, THERESA BARLOW, geriatrics nurse; b. Shenandoah, Pa., Aug. 5, 1938; d. Walter and Tessie (Lazusky) Barlow; m. Thomas F. Fagan, Jr., July 17, 1961; children: E. Lynn, Thomas F. III, Timothy B., Leslie Nan, Lori Ann. Diploma in Nursing, Phila. General Hosp., 1959; BSN, Ga. Coll., 1991, MSN, 1994. Cert. Gerontol. Nurse, ANA. Staff nurse Tift Gen. Hosp., Tifton, Ga., 1962-70; nursing supr. Tift Gen. Hosp., Tifton, 1970-72; staff nurse Carl Vinson VA Hosp., Dublin, Ga., 1972-78; head nurse, gerontology Carl Vinson VA Hosp., Dublin, 1983—; York County Coun. Alcohol and Drug Abuse York County Alcohol and Drug Abuse, Rock Hill, S.C., 1980-82; nurse supr. Ebenezeer Convalescent Ctr., Rock Hill, 1982-83; CPR instr. Am. Heart Assn., Dublin, 1993—, spkr. in field. 2nd lt. Nurse Corps U.S. Army, 1959-61, PTO. Mem. Nat. Geriat. Nurses Assn., Sigma Theta Tau (nominating com.). Home: 803 Strawberry Crk Rd Dublin GA 31021

FAGAN, THOMAS KEVIN, psychology educator; b. Warren, Ohio, Feb. 25, 1943; s. Paul Francis and Ruth Ione Fagan; m. Susan Reuter; children—Shannon, Lance, Colleen. B.S. in Edn., Kent State U., 1965, M.A., 1966, Ph.D., 1969. Asst. prof., then assoc. prof. psychology Western Ill. U., Macomb, Ill., 1969-76; assoc. prof., then prof. U. Memphis, 1976—. Mem. Tenn. Assn. Sch. Psychologists, Nat. Assn. Sch. Psychologists. Republican. Roman Catholic. Lodge: Elks. Home: 1855 S Rainbow Dr Memphis TN 38107-3114 Office: U Memphis Psychology Dept Memphis TN 38152-6400

FAGAN, WILLIAM THOMAS, JR., urologist; b. Rutland, Vt., Sept. 21, 1923; s. William T. Sr. and Irene (Hevey) F.; m. Joy A. Lipman; children from previous marriage: Susan A. Barry, William T. III. BS, U. Vt., 1945,

MD, 1948. Diplomate Am. Bd. Urology. Intern Mary Fletcher Hosp., 1948-49; resident Med. Ctr. Hosp. Vt., Burlington, 1949-52, attending physician urology, 1952-86, emeritus attending, 1986—; assoc. prof. U. Vt., Burlington, 1954; chief urology dept. Fanny Allen Hosp., Winooski, Vt., 1956-86; cons. in urology Littleton Hosp., N.H., 1961-92, Cottage Hosp., Woodsville, N.H., 1981-92. Contbr. articles to profl. jours. Decorated Legion of Merit. Fellow ACS; mem. N.Y. Acad. Scis., Am. Urol. Assn., Am. Geriatric Soc., AMA, Royal Soc. Medicine, Assn. Mil. Surgeons U.S. Home and Office: PO Box 1508 Stowe VT 05672-1508

FAGELMAN, KERRY MARC, surgeon; b. Bklyn., Aug. 16, 1949; s. Jacob and Dorothy (Stogel) F.; m. Karen Marie Janovich, Jan. 15, 1977; 1 child, Jeremy. BA, NYU, 1970; MD, St. Louis U., 1974. Diplomate Am. Bd. Surgery. Resident in gen. surgery U. Va., Charlottesville, 1974-76, U. Louisville, 1976-80; resident pediat. surgery U. Miami, 1980-82; asst. prof. Rutgers U., New Brunswick, N.J., 1982-84; pvt. practice pediat. surgery Harrisburg, Pa., 1984—. Bd. dirs. Tri-county Soc. Children, Harrisburg, 1994—. Office: Pediat Surgery Ltd 2600 North 3d St Harrisburg PA 17110

FAGIN, CLAIRE MINTZER, nursing educator, administrator; b. N.Y.C.; d. Harry and Mae (Slatin) Mintzer; m. Samuel Fagin, Feb. 17, 1952; children: Joshua, Charles. BS, Wagner Coll., 1948; MA, Tchrs. Coll. Columbia, 1951; PhD, N.Y. U., 1964; DSc (hon.), Lycoming Coll., 1983, Cedar Crest Coll., 1987, U. Rochester, 1987, Med. Coll. Pa., 1989, U. Md., 1993, Wagner Coll., 1993, Loyola U., 1996; DHL, Hunter Coll., 1993; LLD (hon.), U. Pa., 1994. Staff nurse, clin. instr. Sea View Hosp., S.I., N.Y.; clin. instr. Bellevue Hosp., N.Y.C.; psychiat. nurse cons. Nat. League for Nursing, N.Y.C.; asst. chief psychiat. nursing svc. clin. ctr. NIH; rsch. project coord. dept. psychiatry Children's Hosp., Washington; instr., assoc. prof. psychiat.-mental health nursing NYU, N.Y.C., dir. grad. programs in psychiat. mental health nursing, 1965-69; chmn. nursing dept., prof. Herbert H. Lehman Coll., CUNY, N.Y.C., 1969-77; dir. Health Professions Inst., Montefiore Hosp. and Med. Ctr., 1975-77; Margaret Bond Simon dean sch. of nursing U. Pa., Phila., 1977-92, Leadership chair prof., 1992-96, interim pres., 1993-94, dean emeritus, prof. emeritus, 1996—; cons. in health care and orgnl. leadership to state, nat. and internat. coms. and profl. bds.; dir. Provident Mut. Ins. Co., mem. audit com., 1978—, chmn., 1985—, mem. exec. com., 1986—; dir. Salomon Inc., 1994—; mem. audit com. CMAC, 1994—; mem. compensation com., investment com., cons. to many pub. and pvt. univs. and health care agys.; spkr. at profl. confs., on radio and TV. Contbr. articles to profl. publs. Recipient Achievement award Wagner Coll., 1956, Achievement award Tchrs. Coll., 1975, Disting. Alumna award NYU, 1979, Founders award Sigma Theta Tau, 1981, Hon. Recognition award ANA, 1988, Woman of Courage award Womens Way, 1990, Alumni Merit award U. Pa., 1991, Trustee Coun. Pa. Women First Leadership award, 1991, Caring award Vis. Nurses Assn., 1992—, Hildegard Peplau award outstanding contbn. psych-nursing, 1994; Am. Nurses Found. Disting. scholar, 1984, Disting. Dau. Pa., 1994. Mem. Inst. Medicine of NAS (governing coun. 1981-83, chmn. bd. health promotion and disease prevention 1991-94), Am. Acad. Nursing (governing coun. 1976-78), Am. Orthopsychiat. Assn. (bd. dirs. 1972-75, exec. com. bd. dirs. 1973-75, pres. 1985-86), Nat. League for Nursing (pres. 1991-93).

FAHD, CHARLES F., II, hospital administrator; b. Albany, N.Y., June 15, 1949; s. Charles F. and Elizabeth (Bonville) F.; m. Susan Mary Del Costello, Aug. 5, 1984; children: Meaghan Anne, Jonathan Anthony, Francesca Maureen. Degree in Med. Lab. Tech., Hudson Valley C.C., Troy, N.Y., 1969; student, Albany Med. Coll., 1970; BA, Russell Sage Coll., Troy, 1984, MS, 1987. Cytotechnologist N.Y. State Dept. Health, Albany, 1970-73; cytotechnologist/supr. Nathan Littauer Hosp., Gloversville, N.Y., 1973-78, lab. mgr., 1978-84, dir. ancillary svcs., 1984-87; v.p. A.O. Fox Meml. Hosp., Oneonta, N.Y., 1987—, interim CEO, 1988—; vice chmn. Clin. Svcs. Adminstrs. Group of N.E. N.Y. Hosp. Coun., Albany, 1993-95. Bd. dirs. PTO, Oneonta, 1993—; mem. Downtown Oneonta Improvement Task Force, 1994-95. Mem. Am. Coll. Healthcare Execs., Healthcare Mgmt. Assn., Am. Soc. Clin. Pathologists, Upper N.Y. State Soc. Cytology (pres. 1975), Rotary, Elks. Republican. Roman Catholic. Home: 76 Spruce St Oneonta NY 13820 Office: A O Fox Meml Hosp 1 Norton Ave Oneonta NY 13820

FAHEY, CHARLES JOSEPH, priest, gerontology educator; b. Balt., Apr. 13, 1933; s. Charles J. and M. Elizabeth (Kelly) F. AB, St. Bernard's Sem., Rochester, N.Y., 1959, MDiv, 1982; MSW, Catholic U., 1963; LLD, St. Thomas U., Can., 1983; DD (hon.), St. Bernard's Inst., 1985; LLD, D'Youville Coll., 1987, LeMoyne Coll., Syracuse, N.Y., 1993. Ordained priest Roman Catholic Ch., 1959. Asst. pastor St. Vincent Ch., Syracuse, N.Y., 1959-61; asst. dir. Cath. Charities, Syracuse, N.Y., 1961-67, dir., 1967-79; dir. 3rd Age Ctr. Fordham U., N.Y.C., 1979—, Marie Ward Doty prof. of aging studies, 1980—; crw; chmn. Fed. Council on Aging, 1982; mem. faculty Salzburg Fellow Program, Austria, 1985. Contbr. articles to profl. jours. Fellow Am. Coll. Health Care Adminstrs., Gerontol. Soc.; mem. Inst. Medicine of Nat. Acad. Scis., Nat. Assn. Social Workers, Am. Pub. Health Assn., Am. Assn. Homes for Aging (pres. 1976-77), Nat. Conf. Cath. Charities (pres. 1979-81), Cath. Health Assn. (bd. mem.), Am. Fedn. Aging Rsch. (bd. dirs. 1982—), Am. Stroke Assn. (bd. mem. 1983—), N.Y. State Welfare Assn. (pres. 1975), Am. Soc. on Aging (pres.-elect 1990, pres. 1992, 93). Office: Fordham U 3d Age Ctr Bronx NY 10458-9998

FAHEY, JOHN LESLIE, immunologist; b. Cleve., Sept. 8, 1924. MS, Wayne State U., 1949; MD, Harvard U., 1951. Intern medicine Columbia-Presbyn. Hosp., N.Y., 1951-52, asst. resident, 1952-53; clin. assoc. Nat. Cancer Inst., NIH, 1953-54, sr. investigator metabolism, 1954-63, chief immunology br., 1964-71; prof. medicine, microbiology and immunology, chmn. dept. Sch. Medicine UCLA, 1971-81; dir. Ctr. Interdisciplinary Rsch. Immunological Diseases UCLA, 1978—. Recipient Abbott Laboratories award Am. Society for Microbiology, 1995. Mem. Assn. Immunologists, Assn. Am. Physicians, Am. Soc. Microbiology, Clin. Immunology Soc. (founding pres.), Clin. Immunology Com. (pres.), Internat. Union Immunological Socs., Am. Assn. Cancer Rsch. Office: UCLA Sch Medicine Dept Microbiology & Immunology Factor Bldg 12-262 Los Angeles CA 90095-1747

FAHIEN, LEONARD AUGUST, physician, educator; b. St. Louis, July 26, 1934; s. John Henry and Alice Katherine (Schubkegel) F.; m. Rose Marian Burmeister, June 21, 1958; children: Catherine Fahien Reuter, Lisa Fahien Uldrich, James. A.B., Washington U., St Louis, 1956; M.D., Washington U., 1960. Intern U. Wis., Madison, 1960-61; surgeon NIH, Bethesda, Md., 1964-66; asst. prof. dept. pharmacology U. Wis. Med. Sch., Madison, 1966-69; asso. prof. U. Wis. Med. Sch., 1969-74, prof., 1974—, asso. dean, 1979-83; vis. prof. Inst. Protein Rsch. Osaka U., Japan, 1991. Contbr. chpts. to books; contbr. articles to profl. jours. Served with USPHS, 1964-66. Numerous NIH grants, 1966—. Mem. Phi Beta Kappa, Sigma Xi. Lutheran. Home: 3212 Topping Rd Madison WI 53705-1435 Office: 426 S Charter St Madison WI 53715-1626

FAHN, STANLEY, neurologist, educator; b. Sacramento, Nov. 6, 1933; s. Ernest and Sylvia (Schumer) F.; m. Charlotte Zmora, June 21, 1958; children: Paul N., James D. BA, U. Calif.-Berkeley, 1955, MD, 1958. Diplomate Am. Bd. Neurology. Resident in neurology Neurol. Inst., N.Y., 1959-62; rsch. assoc. NIH, 1962-65; mem. faculty Columbia U., N.Y.C., 1965-68, prof. neurology, 1973-78, H. Houston Merritt prof., 1978—; mem. faculty U. Pa., Phila., 1968-73; dir. Dystonia Rsch. Ctr., 1981—; sci. dir. Parkinson's Disease Found., 1979—; chair adv. com. peripheral and ctrl. nervous sys. drugs FDA, 1987-89, 91-96. Editor Movement Disorders, 1985-95; assoc. editor Neurology, 1977-87. With USPHS, 1962-65. Grantee NIH, 1974-77, 80-82, 84-91, 92-95. Mem. Am. Acad. Neurology (chair edn. com. 1986-93, v.p. 1993—), Am. Neurol. Assn. (v.p. 1987-88, chair jour. oversight com. 1994—), Movement Disorder Soc. (pres. 1988-91). Home: 155 Edgars Ln Hastings Hdsn NY 10706-1107 Office: 710 W 168th St New York NY 10032-2603

FAHRIG, RUDOLF HINRICH HERMANN, geneticist; b. Hamburg, Germany, Nov. 22, 1940; s. Rudolf and Oda (Thies) F.; m. Brigitte Johanna Grunert, Dec. 18, 1969; children: Torsten, Rudolf. Diploma in biology, U. Giessen, 1967, Dr.rer.nat., 1968, habilitation, 1974. Departmental mgr. Ctrl. Labr. for Mutation Rsch., Freiburg, Fed. Republic Germany, 1969-80, Inst. for Toxicology, U. Tübingen, Fed. Republic Germany, 1981-82; departmental mgr., dep. dir. molecular biology Fraunhofer Inst. for Toxicology, Hannover, Fed. Republic Germany, 1982-95; prof. U. Hamburg, Germany, 1988; cons. Ministry Rsch. & Tech., Bonn, Fed. Republic Germany, 1978-79; cons. Fed. Health Office, Berlin, 1989—. Editor: Environmental Mutagens, 1990, Mutation Research and Genetic Toxicology, 1993; contbr. over 130 articles to sci. jours.; mem. editl. bd. several jours. in field. Recipient prize Fraunhofer Soc., 1987. Mem. Genetics Soc., Soc. for Environ. Mutation Rsch. (pres. 1988-94), Environ. Mutagen Soc. Home: Fritz-Goy-Weg 3, D-30657 Hannover Germany Office: Fraunhofer Inst Toxicology, Nikolai-Fuchs-Str 1, D-30625 Hannover Germany

FAILS, DONNA GAIL, mental health services professional; b. Harlingen, Tex., Apr. 27, 1958; d. Fred R. and L. Beth (Nicholson) F. BS, Phila. Coll. Bible, Langhorne, Pa., 1982; BA in Social Work, Rutgers U., Camden, N.J., 1984, MSW, 1985. Cert. social worker; lic. clin. social worker, N.J. Community resource specialist March of Dimes South Jersey, Mt. Ephraim, N.J., 1982-83; case mgr., liaison Guidance Ctr. Camden County, Cherry Hill, N.J., 1983-84; outpatient coord. CamCare Mental Health Ctr., Blackwood and Cherry Hill, N.J., 1984-86; dir. partial care Comhar Mental Health Ctr., Phila., 1986-87; cons. Callahan Cons. Group, Cherry Hill, 1987-88; dir. mental health svcs., adminstr. mental health svcs. Archway Programs, Inc., Atco, N.J., 1988-94; dir. program coordination Rainbow Healthcare Assocs., Glassboro, N.J., 1994—; chairperson Interagy. Assessment Team of Camden County, 1989-90. Author, cons. Simon for Pres., Cherry Hill, 1988; co-chair statewide tech. assistance team Children's Mental Health Svcs., N.J., 1992-94; mem. stds. com. Children's Assessment and Resource Teams, 1991-94, Children's Interagy. Assessment Coun., 1991-94; mem. exec. com. N.J. Children's Coordinating Coun., 1992-94. Mem. Nat. Assn. Social Workers, Nat. Network for Social Work Mgrs., Inc., N.J. Gerontological Inst. Mem. Free Ch. of Am. Home: 1232 Kohler Ave Deptford NJ 08096 Office: Rainbow Healthcare Assocs 17 S Delsea Dr Glassboro NJ 08028

FAINE, SOLOMON, microbiologist; b. Wellington, New Zealand, Aug. 17, 1926; s. John and Luba (Ketko) F.; m. Eva Rothschild, May 17, 1950; children: Miriam, Susan, Jonathan. B Med Sci, U. New Zealand, 1946, MB ChB, 1949, MD, 1958; PhD, Oxford U., 1955. Registered pathologist, microbiologist. Prof. microbiology Monash U., Melbourne, Australia, 1968-91, chmn. dept. microbiology, 1968-88, 89-90, prof. emeritus, 1992—; cons. WHO, Geneva, 1969—, various hosps., Melbourne, 1968—. Editor: Guidelines for the Control of Leptospirosis/WHO, 1982, Leptospira and Leptospirosis, 1993; contbr. articles to profl. jours./books. Recipient P Bancroft prize for rsch. U. Sydney, Australia, 1965, Sr. Stage award French Govt./ Inst. Pasteur, Paris, 1971-72, fellowships Australian-Am. Found., USA, 1978, German Acad. Exch., Fed. Republic Germany, 1978-79. Fellow Royal Coll. Pathologists, Australian Soc. Microbiology (hon. life mem., pres. 1969-70), Am. Acad. Microbiology (emeritus); mem. Internat. Union Microbiology Socs. (exec. bd. 1974-86, chmn. bacteriology 1978-82, Disting. Svc. medal 1986). Office: MediSci Cons, 2 Murray St, Armadale Victoria, Melbourne 3143, Australia

FAINGOLD, CARL LAWRENCE, pharmacologist, researcher; b. Chgo., Feb. 1, 1943; s. Charles and Ann Faingold; m. Carol Ann Baskin, June 21, 1964; children—Scott, Charles, Robert. B.S., U. Ill.-Chgo., 1965; Ph.D., Northwestern U., 1970. Postdoctoral fellow U. Mo., Columbia, 1970-72; asst. prof. pharmacology So. Ill. U., Springfield, 1972-76, assoc. prof., 1976—, acting chmn. dept., 1981-82. Contbr. articles to profl. jours. Grantee NIH, 1979-82, Deafness Research Found., 1985—, Am. Heart Assn., 1985—. Mem. Am. Soc. Exptl. Therapeutics, Soc. for Neurosci., Am. Epilepsy Soc., AAAS, N.Y. Acad. Sci., Sigma Xi. Home: 60 Danbury Dr Springfield IL 62704-5438 Office: So Ill Sch Medicine 801 Springfield IL 62708

FAINSTEIN, VICTOR, infectious disease physician; b. Mexico City, Sept. 18, 1949; came to U.S., 1977; s. David and Bertha (Domovska) F.; m. Deborah Margaret Brand, Sept. 1, 1979; children: Benjamin David, Karen Elizabeth. BS in Biology magna cum laude, Colegio Israelita de Mexico, Mexico City, 1967; MD summa cum laude, Autonoma Mexico, Mexico City, 1973; Internal Medicine Specialist, Inst. Nat. Nutrition, Mexico City, 1976. Intern Instituto Nacional Nutricion, 1974, resident, 1974-77; fellow Baylor Coll. Medicine, 1977-79, U. Tex./M.D. Anderson Hosp., 1979-80; infectious disease specialist Baylor Coll. Medicine, Houston, 1979; postgrad. fellow infectious disease U. Tex. M.D. Anderson Hosp., Houston, 1980; ptnr. Infectious Disease Assocs. of Houston, 1980—; chmn. infection control com. Meth. Hosp., Houston, 1988—, Vencor Hosp., 1990—, Tex. Orthop. Hosp., 1994—; dir. infectious disease fellowship M.D. Anderson Hosp., Houston, 1981-85; v.p. med. staff Vencor Hosp., Houston; cons. Pan Am. Health Orgn., 1981-88. Co-author 2 med. books; contbr. more than 160 articles to profl. jours. Bd. dirs. Amigos de las Americas, Houston, 1994—. Recipient Spl. award for suprerior performanace Nat. Pub. Health Svc., Mexico City, 1973, Physicians Recognition award AMA, 1980—, Meritorious Sci. Writing award Tex. Med. Assn., 1986; named Cons. of Yr. Inst. Rehab. and Rsch., Houston, 1994—. Mem. Tex. Infectious Diseases Soc. (pres. 1989). Jewish. Office: Infectious Diseases Assocs 6560 Fannin # 1540 Houston TX 77030

FAIRBANKS, JOEL KENT, psychologist, educator; b. Decatur, Ill., Mar. 5, 1956; s. James J. and Betty JoAnn (Spires) F.; m. Teresa Louise Toman, Oct. 12, 1985; children: Claire Elizabeth, Andrew Kent. BS in Psychology, U. Wis., 1978; MS in Mgmt., Troy State U., Pensacola, Fla., 1984; MA in Psychology, U. West Fla., 1986; PhD in Clin. Psychology, U.S. Internat. U., San Diego, 1990. Community outreach dir. Armed Svcs. YMCA, San Diego, 1987-89; mental health counselor Lakeview Ctr., Inc., Pensacola, Fla., 1986-87, staff psychologist, 1991-92, dir. youth residential svcs., 1992—; adj. faculty U. West Fla., Pensacola, 1991-93, Troy State U., 1991—. Mem., pres. Mil./Communities Task Team, San Diego, 1987-89; mem. San Diego County Commn. on Youth and Children, 1988; mem. children's case rev. com. Human Resource Svcs. Dist. I Fla., Pensacola, 1990—. Lt. USN, 1978-85. Mem. APA, Southeastern Psychol. Assn., Nat. Acad. Neuropsychology, Internat. Neuropsychol. Soc. (del.), Psi Chi. Home: PO Box 18487 Pensacola FL 32523-8487

FAIRBROOK, DAVID LYNN, physician; b. Arlington, Wash., Oct. 21, 1942; s. James Purdy and Selma Doris (Hall) F.; m. Cynthia Louise Sorensen, Nov. 15, 1968; children: Michelle Lynn, Aaron James. BA, Willamette U., 1965; MD, U. Wash., 1969. Intern Med. Ctr. Hosp. Vt., Burlington, 1968-69, resident in internal medicine, 1969-70; resident in internal medicine Mayo Clinic, Rochester, Minn., 1973-76; med. dir. Providence Mother Joseph Care Ctr., Olympia, Wash., 1991—. Lt. USN, 1970-71. Mem. ACP, Am. Geriatric Soc., Am. Med. Dirs. Assn. Office: Meml Clinic 500 N Lilly Rd Olympia WA 98502

FAIRCHILD, JOHN PHILLIP, physician; b. Washington, Dec. 25, 1918; s. Iler James and Vera Fae (Ward) F.; A.B., George Washington U., Washington, 1940, M.D., 1943; m. Julia Pearl Printz, Sept. 12, 1945; children: Jean Printz Fairchild DeTarnowsky, John Phillip, Jacqueline Patricia Fairchild Auxt, James Patrick, Jerome Paul, Jeffrey Preston. Enlisted U.S. Army, 1944, resigned, 1946, re-enlisted 1948, commd. 1st lt., 1944, advanced through grades to col.; intern Gallinger Mcpl. Hosp., Washington, 1943, resident pediatrics, 1948-50; chief pediatric svcs. U.S. Army Hosp. Ft. Bragg, N.C., 1950-53, Brooke Gen. Hosp., Ft. Sam Houston, Tex., 1953-58, Tripler Gen. Hosp., Honolulu, 1958-62, Walter Reed Gen. Hosp., 1963-66; dir. HEW U.S. Civil Adminstrn. Ryukyu Islands, 1966-69; dep. comdr. Walter Reed Hosp., 1969-71, ret., 1971; gen. practice medicine Garnett, Kans., 1946-48; dir. field svcs. div. Montgomery County (Md.) Health Dept., 1971-75; chief surgeon U.S. Soldiers and Airmen's Home Hosp., Washington, 1975-79; staff dept. pediatrics Regional Med. Clinic/Mountain Health Svcs., McDowell, Ky., 1979-85, chief of staff, 1986-88, active staff McDowell Appalachian Regional Hosp., 1979-88; asst. to assoc. clin. prof. pediatrics Baylor U., 1954-58; assoc. clin. prof. pediatrics Georgetown U., 1963-66, clin. prof., 1973-75; clin. prof. U. Louisville, 1981-89; cons. in field. Decorated Legion of Merit; recipient Supreme award Japanese Med. Assn., 1969. Mem. AMA, Med. and Chirurg. Faculty State Md., Ky. Med. Soc., Floyd County Med. Soc., Assn. Mil. Surgeons, Am. Public Health Assn., Sigma Chi. Presbyterian. Contbr. articles to profl. publs. Home: 9721 Inaugural Way Gaithersburg MD 20879-2104

FAIRFAX, LAURA MAY, pediatric psychologist; b. Otterville, Mo., Dec. 11, 1943; d. Hugh Reed and Lena Irene (Conrad) F. Ph.D., U. Mo., 1971. Lic. psychologist, Fla., Kans., Mo. Psychologist, Kansas City Mental Health Found., Mo., 1971-73; research psychologist Psychol. Corp. Wechsler Intelligence Scale for Children, 1974; community psychologist Western Mo. Area Health Edn. Ctr., Kansas City, Mo., 1973; pvt. practice clin. psychology Kansas City, 1972-74; cons. psychologist St. Johns River Psychiat. Hosp., Jacksonville, Fla., 1978—; rsch. psychologist Psychol. Corp. Wechsler Adult Intelligence Scale III, 1995; psychologist Mental Health Resource Ctr., 1995—, Flagler Hosp., 1996—; pvt. practice clin. psychology, Jacksonville, 1975—; rehab. evaluator Fla. Workers' Com., 1990—; asst. prof. dept. psychology U. N. Fla., 1974-79; guest prof. Stress Mgmt. Course, Jacksonville U., 1984; presenter mental health TV program Sta. WJCT-TV; speaker at mental health forums. Editor: Preschool Screening Handbook, Greater Kansas City Mental Health Found., 1973. Mem. Fla. State Atty.'s Youth Mediation Program (4th Jud. Circuit), 1985—; mem. legis. network Mental Health Assn. Jacksonville, 1976—; judge Kiwanis Ann. Sci. Fairs, 1976—. Fellow Menninger Found.; mem. Am. Psychol. Assn., Fla. Psychol. Assn. (membership chmn. 1977-79), Jacksonville Assn. Women in Psychology (charter mem.), Fla. Psychol. Assn. (Northeast chpt. pres.), Commn. on Cert. Work Adjustment and Vocat. Evaluation Specialists (cert.), Kappa Epsilon Alpha, Alpha Chi Omega (alumni adv. bd.), Jacksonville Alumnae Panhellenic Assn. (chmn. scholarship 1984-85, 95-96). Presbyterian. Clubs: Ponte Vedra Country (Fla.), Epping Forest Yacht. Avocations: tennis; swimming; jogging. Office: 2114 W University Blvd Jacksonville FL 32217-2018

FAIRLAMB, ALAN HUTCHINSON, molecular parasitology educator; b. Newcastle, Northumberland, Eng., Apr. 30, 1947; s. Alan H. and Margaret (Armstrong) F.; m. Christine Ann Williams, July 25, 1970 (div. Apr. 1986); 1 child, Saffron; m. Carolyn Strobos, Aug. 1, 1986; children: Zoë, Thomas. BSc in Med. Sci., U. Edinburgh, Scotland, 1968, MB,ChB, 1971, PhD, 1975. House officer Longmore & Western Gen. Hosps., Edinburgh, 1971-72; rsch. scholar faculty of medicine Edinburgh U., 1972-75; MRC travelling fellow U. Amsterdam, The Netherlands, 1975-76; rsch. fellow U. Edinburgh, 1976-80; rsch. fellow London Sch. Hygiene and Tropical Medicine, 1980-81, sr. clin. lectr., 1987-90, prof. of molecular parasitology, 1990—; asst. prof. Rockefeller U., N.Y.C., 1981-87; sci. advisor steering com. on integrated chemotherapy for African trypanosomiasis, Chagas disease and leishmaniasis WHO, Geneva, 1991-93. Recipient Frederic, Murgatroyd prize Royal Coll. Physicians, 1988; grantee Wellcome Trust, WHO. Fellow Royal Soc. Tropical Medicine and Hygiene, Linnean Soc.; mem. AAAS, Soc. Protozoologists, Am. Soc. Biochemistry and Molecular Biology (assoc.), Brit. Soc. Parasitology (C.A. Wright medal 1996), Biochem. Soc. Office: Wellcome Sci Inst, Dept Biochemistry, Univ Dundee, Dundee DD1 4HN, England

FAIRMAN, DAN S., internist; b. Toledo, Jan. 23, 1955; s. Ralph Charles and Ursula Annelisa (Sieber) F.; m. Melynda Kim Standlee, Mar. 5, 1986; children: Abigail, Connor. BA cum laude, Dartmouth Coll., 1977; MD, St. Louis U., 1982. Diplomate Am. Bd. Internal Medicine. Resident internal medicine U. Kans., 1985; staff physician USPHS, Glenns Ferry, Idaho, 1985-88; internist Wenatchee (Wash.) Valley Clinic, 1988-90, Assocs. in Medicine, Sun Valley, Idaho, 1990-93; emergency room physician St. Benedict Hosp., Jerome, Idaho, 1993—. Office: Wood River Med Ctr PO Box 86 Sun Valley ID 83353

FAJANS, STEFAN STANISLAUS, internist, retired educator; b. Munich, Mar. 15, 1918; came to U.S., 1936, naturalized, 1942; s. Kasimir M. and Salomea (Kaplan) F.; m. Ruth Stine, Sept. 6, 1947; children: Peter S., John S. B.S., U. Mich., Ann Arbor, 1938, M.D., 1942. Intern Mount Sinai Hosp., N.Y.C., 1942-43; resident U. Mich., 1947-49, research fellow, 1946-47, 49-51; mem. faculty U. Mich. Med. Sch., 1950—, prof., 1961-88, prof. emeritus, 1988—; chief divsn. endocrinology & metabolism Mich. Diabetes Rsch. and Tng. Ctr., 1973-87, dir., 1977-86; mem. endocrinology study sect. NIH, 1958-62, mem. diabetes and metabolism tng. grants com., 1966-70, mem. nat. diabetes adv. bd., 1987-91; chmn. Am. zone internat. sci. adv. com. Congresses Internat. Diabetes Fedn., 1977-79; Banting meml. lectr., 1978. Contbr. articles med. publns. Mem. career devel. com. VA Med. Rsch. Svc., 1987-91. Officer M.C., AUS, 1943-46. Research fellow in medicine A.C.P., 1949-50; fellow Life Ins. Med. Inst., 1950-51. Mem. Am. Diabetes Assn. (pres. 1971-72, Banting medal 1972, Banting Meml. award 1978), Endocrine Soc. (v.p. 1970-71, council 1967-71, 78-81), ACP (master), Am. Fedn. Clin. Research, Am. Soc. Clin. Investigation, Assn. Am. Physicians, Central Soc. Clin. Research, Nat. Acad. Sci. (sr. mem. inst. med.), Sigma Xi, Alpha Omega Alpha. Home: 2485 Devonshire Rd Ann Arbor MI 48104-2705 Office: Univ Mich Hosp Ann Arbor MI 48109

FAJVAN, JOHN, pediatrics nurse; b. Jersey City, N.J., Feb. 26, 1965; s. John and Lucy Marie (Koss) F. Diploma, Ann May Sch. Nursing, Neptune, N.J., 1993; student, U. State of N.Y., Albany, 1994—. RN, N.J. Staff nurse Clara Maass Med. Ctr., Belleville, N.J., 1993—; staff nurse Vis. Health Svcs. N.J., Totowa, 1995-96. Mem. ANA, Nat. League for Nursing, N.J. State Nurses Assn., N.J. League for Nursing, Nurses Strategic Action Team. Byzantine Catholic. Home: 57 Stelling Ave Maywood NJ 07607

FAKHARZADEH, FREDERICK F., surgeon; b. N.Y.C., July 2, 1955; s. Mehdi and Sigrun Kristin (Fridriksdottir) F.; m. Patricia Fleming, Sept. 3, 1983; children: Kristine, Stephanie, Daniel, Eric. BA magna cum laude, Cornell U., 1976; MD, Columbia U., 1980. Diplomate Am. Bd. Orthopaedic Surgery with added qualifications in surgery of the hand. Surg. intern Roosevelt Hosp., N.Y.C., 1980-81, surg. resident, 1981-82; orthopaedic surgery resident Columbia-Presbyn. Med. Ctr., N.Y.C., 1982-85; hand surgery fellow Thomas Jefferson U., Phila., 1985-86; pvt. practice hand surgeon Paramus, N.J., 1986—; asst. attending surgeon, Hackensack Med. Ctr., N.J., 1986—, Holy Name Hosp., Teaneck, N.J., 1986—; assoc. med. staff Pascack Valley Hosp., Westwood, N.J., 1986—; active med. staff, The Valley Hosp., Ridgewood, N.J., 1987—; clin. asst. prof.U. Medicine and Dentistry of N.J., Newark, 1990—. Contbr. articles to profl. jours. Coord. girl's basketball, Recreation League Grades 3, 4, 5,, Oradell, N.J., 1995-96, coach, 1993-96; asst. coach girl's softball, Oradell Little League, 1993-96. Fellow Am. Acad. Orthopaedic Surgeon; mem. Am. Soc. Surgery of the Hand, N.Y. Soc. for Surgery of the Hand, AMA, Med. Soc. of N.J., Bergen County Med. Soc. Office: 312 Forest Ave Paramus NJ 07652

FALCONE, ALFONSO BENJAMIN, physician and biochemist; b. Bryn Mawr, Pa., July 24; s. B. and Elvira (Galluzzo) F.; m. Patricia J. Lalim, Oct. 22; children: Christopher L., Steven B. AB in Chemistry with distinction, Temple U., 1944, MD with honors, 1947; PhD in Biochemistry, U. Minn., 1954. Diplomate Am. Bd. Internal Medicine subspecialty bd. endocrinology and metabolism. Intern Phila. Gen. Hosp., 1947-48, asst. resident, 1948-49; teaching fellow internal medicine U. Hosps., U. Minn., 1949-51; asst. clin. prof. medicine U. Wis., Madison, 1956-59, assoc. clin. prof., 1959-63, asst. prof. Inst. Enzyme Research, 1963-66, vis. prof., 1966-67; cons. in field; practice in endocrine/metabolic diseases, med.-legal cons. Fresno, Calif., 1968—; active staff mem. Fresno Community Hosp., chmn. dept. medicine, 1973; active staff mem. St. Agnes Hosp., Fresno; hon. staff Valley Med. Ctr., Fresno; sr. corr. Ettor Majorana Ctr. for Sci. Culture, Erice, Italy. Contbr. articles to profl. jours. with rsch. in mechanisms of energy transduction in biol. sys., mechanism of oxidative phosphorylation, mechanisms of enzyme action, mechanisms of drug action. Served with AUS, 1944-46; served to lt. comdr. M.C., USNR, 1954-56. NIH postdoctoral fellow, 1951-53; NIH research grantee, 1958-68. Fellow ACP; mem. AAAS, Am. Soc. Biochemistry and Molecular Biology, Cen. Soc. Clin. Rsch., Am. Fedn. Clin. Rsch., Am. Chem. Soc., Am. Assn. for Study of Liver Disease, Endocrine Soc., Am. Diabetes Assn., Assn. Acad. Excellence, U. Calif. Fresno Com., Fresno County Assn. for U. Calif. Campus, Archaeol. Inst. Am., Calif. Acad. Medicine, Sigma Xi, Phi Lambda Epsilon. Office: Metabolic and Endocrine Dis 2240 E Illinois Ave Fresno CA 93701-2118

FALK, RICHARD JAY, gynecologist, reproductive endocrinologist; b. N.Y.C., Oct. 27, 1940; s. Ernest H. and Mildred (Kranes) F.; m. Carole Portugal, Dec. 22, 1963; chidlren: Andrew, Hayley, Bradley. BA in Zoology, U. Vt., 1961, MS in Pathology, 1966, MD cum laude, 1966. Diplomate in og-gyn. and reproductive endocrinology Am. Bd. Ob-Gyn. Intern Bronx (N.Y.) Mcpl. Hosp., 1966-67; resident in ob-gyn. Mt. Sinai

Hosp., N.Y.C., 1967-68; rsch. assoc. NIH, Bethesda, Md., 1968-70; resident in pathology Georgetown U. Hosp., Washington, 1970-71, resident ob-gyn., 1971-73, asst. prof. reproductive endocrinology, 1974-78; dir. reproductive endocrinology Columbia Hosp. for Women, Washington, 1974—; assoc. prof. ob-gyn. Georgetown U., Washington, 1978-87, clin. prof. ob-gyn., 1987—. Assoc. editor Internat. Jour. of Fertility, 1987—; mem. editorial bd. (jour.) Endocrinology and Metabolism, 1995—; contbr. articles to profl. jours., chpts. to books. Surgeon USPHS, 1968-70. Recipient Purdue Frederick award, 1987. Fellow Am. Coll. Ob-gyn., Endocrine Soc.; mem. Soc. of Reproductive Endocrinologists, Soc. of Reproductive Surgery, Am. Soc. for Reproductive Medicine (chair practice com. 1995-98). Office: Columbia Hosp for Women 2440 M St NW Washington DC 20037

FALKNER, FRANK TARDREW, physician, educator; b. Hale, Eng., Oct. 27, 1918; came to U.S., 1956, naturalized, 1963; s. Ernest and Ethel (Letten) F.; m. June Dixon, Jan. 1948; 2 children. M.D., Cambridge U., 1945. Diplomate: Am. Bd. Clin. Nutrition. Intern London Hosp., 1945; resident Guys Hosp., London, 1947-48, Children's Hosp., Cin., 1948-50; practice medicine specializing in pediatrics U.K. and Paris, 1948-56, Louisville, 1956-70, Yellow Springs, Ohio, 1971—; chmn. dept. pediatrics U. Louisville, 1963-70; dir. Fels Research Inst., Yellow Springs, 1971-79; Fels prof. pediatrics, prof. obstetrics and gynecology U. Cin. Coll. Medicine, 1971-79; prof. child and family health U. Mich., 1979-81; prof. and chmn. maternal and child health U. Calif., Berkeley, 1981-89; prof. pediatrics U. Calif., San Francisco, 1981-89; prof. emeritus U. Calif., Berkeley, 1989—; San Francisco, 1989—. Editor-in-chief: International Child Health; syndicated columnist on children's and young people's health; contbr. articles to profl. jours. Fellow Am. Acad. Pediatrics, Royal Coll. Physicians; mem. NAS (sr. mem. Inst. Medicine), Am. Pediatric Soc., Brit. Paediatric Assn., Société Francaise de Pédiatrie. Home: 145 Forest Ln Berkeley CA 94708-1519 Office: U Calif Sch Pub Health Maternal and Child Health Berkeley CA 94720

FALLAT, MARY ELIZABETH, pediatric surgeon; b. Auburn, N.Y., May 1, 1953; d. George and Elizabeth (Sluty) F.; m. Ch. Thomas Walker, Jr., Dec. 16, 1989; children: Krista Penland Walker, Alexander Michael Walker, Andrew Colin Walker. BA, Northwestern U., 1975; MD, SUNY, Syracuse, 1979. Attending surgeon Kosair Children's Hosp., Louisville, 1987—, dir. trauma svcs., 1988—; asst. prof. surgery U. Louisville, 1987-93, assoc. prof. surgery, 1993—; mem. active staff U. Louisville Hosp. (formerly Humana Hosp.-U. Louisville), 1988—; mem. courtesy staff Audubon Regional Med. Ctr. (formerly Humana Hosp. Audubon), Louisville, 1987—; mem. prof. cons. staff Frazier Rehab. Ctr., Louisville, 1990—; bd. dirs. Ky. Organ Donor Affiliates, Louisville, 1989—; chmn. trauma com. Kosair Children's Hosp., 1988—. Contbr. articles to profl. jours. Crusade for Children grantee WHAS-TV, Louisville, 1989, Alliant Comty. Trust Fund grantee Alliant Health Sys., Louisville, 1990-93, 95, Emergency Svcs. Children Fed. grantee, 1992; named Outstanding Vol. Prof., Kosair Children's Hosp. and U. Louisville, 1990. Fellow ACS, Am. Acad. Pediats.; mem. Am. Trauma Soc., Assn. Acad. Surgery, Am. Assn. Surgery Trauma, Ea. Assn. Surgery Trauma, Brit. Assn. Pediat. Surgeons, Am. Pediat. Surg. Assn., So. Med. Assn., Ky. Med. Assn., North Am. Soc. Pediat. and Adolescent Gynecology, Am. Soc. Andrology. Roman Catholic. Office: Kosair Childrens Hosp PO Box 35070 Louisville KY 40232-5070

FALLAVOLLITA, JAMES A., cardiologist, educator, researcher; b. May 5, 1962. BS in Chemistry and Biology, U. Wash., 1983, MD, 1987. Diplomate Am. Bd. Internal Medicine. Intern and resident internal medicine Strong Meml. Hosp./ U. Rochester, N.Y., 1987-90; rsch./ clin. fellow cardiology SUNY, Buffalo, 1991-94; attending physician/ clin. asst., instr. emergency medicine Erie County Med. Ctr., Buffalo, 1990-93; rsch. asst. prof. medicine SUNY/ Buffalo Vets. Affairs Med. Ctr., 1994—; chief noninvasive sect. divsn. cardiology Buffalo Vets. Affairs Med. Ctr., 1994—; presenter in field. Manuscript reviewer Jour. Am. Coll. Cardiology, Am. Review Respiratory Disease, Am. Jour. Cardiac Imaging; contbr. articles to profl. jours. John C. Sable Meml. Heart Fund grantee, 1993; summer rsch. fellow Am. Cancer Soc., 1986. Mem. ACP, Am. Heart Assn. (coun. circulation, Clinician Scientist award 1996), Am. Coll. Cardiology (assoc., Young Investigator award 1994). Office: U Buffalo Divsn Cardiology Biomed Rsch Blsg Rm 345 3435 Main St Buffalo NY 14214

FALLECKER, ROSE MARIE, nurse; b. Butler, Pa., Oct. 25, 1955; d. Vincent Linus and Germaine Marie (Morin) F.; m. Daniel John Homison, Feb. 9, 1974 (div. Aug. 1990); children: Danielle Marie, Lisa Ann, BobbiJo Germaine, Mary Elizabeth, Jamie Rose. Diploma, St. Francis Sch. Nursing, New Castle, Pa., 1991; student, Slippery Rock (Pa.) U., 1993—. Staff nurse Butler VA Med. Ctr., 1992—. Democrat. Roman Catholic. Home: PO Box 473 523 Grant Ave East Butler PA 16029-0473

FALLER, JASON, physician; b. Rochester, Pa., Jan. 21, 1953; m. Karen; children: Avery, Morley, Ellery. BA, U. Pa., 1973, MD, 1977. Assoc., attending physician St. Luke's Roosevelt Hosp., N.Y.C., 1982—, chief, Arthritis Clinic, 1990—. Fellow ACP, Am. Coll. Rheumatology.

FALLETTA, JOHN MATTHEW, pediatrician, educator; b. Arma, Kans., Sept. 3, 1940; s. Matthew John and Norma (Luke) F.; m. Carolyn Ontjes, June 22, 1963; children: Elizabeth, Matthew. A.B., U. Kans., 1962, M.D., 1966. Diplomate: Am. Bd. Pediatrics, with subsply. hematology-oncology. Intern in mixed medicine Kans. U. Med. Ctr., Kansas City, 1966-67; surgeon Epidemic Intelligence Svc., Tex. Children's Hosp. USPHS, Houston, 1967-69; asst. instr. pediatrics Baylor Coll. Medicine, Houston, 1967-69, resident in pediatrics, 1969-71, chief resident Tex. Children's Hosp., 1971, postdoctoral fellow hematology-oncology, 1971-73, asst. prof. pediatrics, 1973-76; assoc. prof. pediatrics Duke U., Durham, N.C., 1976-83, prof. pediatrics, 1984—, chief divsn. hematology-oncology, 1976-94, dir. Clin. Pediatric Lab., 1976-95; chmn. transfusion com. Duke U. Med. Ctr., 1978—, mem. exec. com. med. staff, 1978—, instl. rev. bd. human rsch., 1979—, chmn., 1994—; mem. instl. rev. bd. human rsch. Baylor Coll. Medicine, 1974-76; mem. acad. coun. Duke U., 1982-86, 87—, exec. com., 1988, faculty compensation com., 1988, faculty com. on univ. governance, 1988, trustee-faculty com. to rev. pres., 1989, search. com. for pres., 1992; cons. pediatric hematologist-oncologist Charlotte (N.C.) Meml. Hosp., 1978—. Contbr. more than 105 articles to Nature, Am. Jour. Ophthalmology, Pediatrics, New Eng. Jour. Medicine, Clin. Pediatric Oncology, others. Cons. pediatric hematologist-oncologist Project Hope, Pediatric Inst., Krakow, Poland, 1979—; prin. investigator Pediatric Oncology Group, 1981-95, chmn. epidemiology com., mem. prin. investigator's exec. com., new agts. and pharmacology com.; chmn. prophylactic penicillin study I Nat. Heart, Lung and Blood Inst., NIH, 1982-86, chmn. study II, 1987-95; active Cancer Ctr. Support Rev. Com. Nat. Cancer Inst. NIH, 1986-90, NIH Reviewers Res., 1990—, Cancer Clin. Investigation Rev. Com., 1991-96, chmn., 1995-96; trustee Ronald McDonald Children's Charities, 1986—. Mem. Am. Assn. Cancer Rsch., Am. Acad. Pediatrics, Am. Pediatric Soc., Am. Soc. Clin. Oncology, So. Soc. Pediatric Rsch. (pres. 1981-82), Soc. Pediatric Rsch., N.C. Pediatric Soc., N.C. Med. Soc., Phi Beta Kappa, Alpha Omega Alpha. Office: Duke U Med Ctr PO Box 2916 Durham NC 27715-2916

FALLON, HAROLD JOSEPH, physician, pharmacology and biochemistry educator; b. N.Y.C., Aug. 13, 1931; s. Harold Joseph and Martha A. (Hansen) F.; m. Jo Ann Brouse; children—Thomas, Michael, Elisabeth, John. B.A., Yale U., 1953, M.D., 1957. Diplomate Am. Bd. Internal Medicine. Intern in medicine N.C. Meml. Hosp., Chapel Hill, 1957-58; asst. resident in medicine N.C. Meml. Hosp., 1958-59, chief resident in medicine, 1961-62; clin. assoc. NIH, 1959-61; postdoctoral fellow dept. biochemistry Duke U. Sch. Medicine, 1963-64; asst. prof. medicine U. N.C. Sch. Medicine, Chapel Hill, 1963-71; asst. prof. biochemistry U. N.C. Sch. Medicine, 1966-71, assoc. prof. medicine, 1967-70, chief div. clin. pharmacology, toxicology, environ. health, 1968-74, vice chmn. dept. medicine, 1968-71, assoc. prof. pharmacology, 1969-70, prof. medicine and pharmacology, 1970-74, assoc. prof. biochemistry, 1971-74, acting chmn. dept medicine, 1971-72; William Branch Porter prof. medicine, chmn. dept. medicine Va. Commonwealth U.-Med. Coll. Va., Richmond, 1974-93; dean, Sch. of Med. U. Alabama, Birmingham, 1993—; vis. scientist U. Utrecht, Netherlands, 1972-73; mem. numerous med. coms. and councils. Mem. editorial bd. Gastroenterology, Clin. Research, Hepatology; mem. adv. editorial bd. Jour. Lipid Research; mem. editorial com. Jour. Clin. Investigation, 1971-76; contbr. numerous articles to med. jours. Mem. exec. com. YMCA, Richmond, 1984—. Served with USPHS, 1969-62. Recipient Sinsheimer award, 1965-70, Research Career Devel. award, 1968, Burroughs-Wellcome award, 1974, Med. Coll. Va. Deans award, 1981; named Outstanding Affiliate appointee Sch. Basic. Scis., 1984; Yale U. Sch. Medicine research fellow, 1962-63. Fellow ACP (mem. sci. program com. 1982—); mem. Assn. Am. Physicians, Assn. Profs. Medicine (councillor chmn. Va. liaison com. 1982—), Am. Soc. for Clin. Investigation (v.p. 1972-75, councillor 1975-76), So. Soc. for Clin. Investigation (pres. 1976-77, councillor 1971-74), Am. Clin. Climatol. Assn., Am. Fedn. Clin. Research, Am. Gastroenterol. Assn. (mem. governing bd. 1978-82), Am. Liver Found. (bd. dirs. 1981), Am. Assn. for Study Liver Disease (pres. 1979, mem. publ. com. 1983—), Internat. Assn. for Study Liver Disease (councillor 1982-84), Gastroenterology Research Group (sec.-treas. 1973-74, mem. steering com. 1970-74), AAAS, Am. Soc. Pharmacology Exptl. Therapeutics, AMA, also numerous others. Presbyterian. Club: Commonwealth. Home: 5003 Applecross Rd Birmingham AL 35242-3917 Office: U Alabama Dean of Med Sch Birmingham AL 35294

FALLS, GERALD FLYNN, psychologist; b. Norfolk, Va., Sept. 27, 1949; s. John Thomas and Margaret Mary (Duffy) F.; m. Mary Louise Hodges, Dec. 16, 1972; 1 child, Patrick Joseph. BS, Old Dominion U., 1971; MS, U. Ga., 1975, PhD, 1980. Lic. psychologist Ala., Ga., Fla.; lic. marriage and family therapist Ga.; nat. cert. addiction counselor, clin. supr.; cert. group psychotherapist and hypnotherapist, cert. criminal justice specialist; diplomate Am. Bd. Forensic Examiners; master addiction counselor Nat. Assn. Alcoholism and Drug Abuse Counselors. Researcher Phila. Geriatric Ctr., 1974; asst. U. Ga., Athens, 1974-78; instr. Valdosta (Ga.) State Coll., 1983-86, 92—; pvt. practice Thomasville, Ga., 1987—; dir. psychology adult psychiat. svcs. Southwestern State Hosp., Thomasville, 1978—; chairperson Psychology Practice Coun., Southwestern State Hosp., Thomasville, 1981-83, 90—; program mgr. Gateway Dual Diagnosis Program-Southwestern State Hosp. U. Richmond fellow in psychology, 1971-72. Mem. APA, Am. Psychology Soc., Am. Assn. for Marriage and Family Therapy, Nat. Assn. Alcoholism and Drug Abuse Counselors, Ga. Addiction Counselors Assn., Ga. Psychology Assn., Ga. Assn. for Marriage and Family Therapy, Am. Group Psychotherapy Assn., Transpersonal Psychology Interest Group, Assn. Holotropic Breathwork, Internat. Assn. for Rsch. and Enlightenment, Am. Coll. of Forensic Examiners, Psi Chi, Phi Kappa Phi, Nat. Guild of Hypnotists, Sigma Nu. Democrat. Roman Catholic. Home: 7709 Bass Ridge Trl Tallahassee FL 32312-3603 Office: Southwestern State Hosp Adult Psychiat Svcs PO Box 1378 Thomasville GA 31799-1378

FALLS, WALDTRAUT MARGRETE GOETZE, medical librarian; b. N.Y.C., June 28, 1941; d. Otto Paul and Anna Irma (Zander) Goetze; AB, SUNY, Albany, 1963, MA (scholar), 1964; MS, Columbia U., 1967; m. John Allen Falls, Jr.; children: John Francis, Michael Gregory. Asst. advt. librarian Curtis Pub. Co., N.Y.C., 1964-65; libr. assoc. NYU Commerce Library, N.Y.C., 1965-67; libr., instr. N.Y.C. C.C., Bklyn., 1967-69, 70, 73-75; med. libr. Victory Meml. Hosp., Bklyn., 1975-87, clin. libr., U. Medicine and Dentistry N.J., Newark, 1987-88; info. mgr. otolaryngology Facial Plastic Surgery Assocs., 1988-95, coord. of outreach svcs. N.Y. Acad. of Medicine, 1995—. Mem. ALA, Med. Library Assn., N.Y. Libr. Assn., N.Y. Library Club (life). Home: 328 78th St Brooklyn NY 11209-3013 Office: NY Acad Medicine 1216 Fifth Ave New York NY 10029

FALOON, WILLIAM WASSELL, physician, educator; b. Pitts., July 6, 1920; s. Joseph Coulter and Martha Louise (Wassell) F.; m. Roberta Jane Emery, Sept. 11, 1948; children: Karen F. Durham, Nancy F. Dodd, William W. BA, Allegheny Coll., 1941; MD, Harvard U., 1944. Diplomate Am. Bd. Internal Medicine; cert. registered arbitrator; ordained as deacon Presbyterian, 1958, elder, 1963. Intern Pa. Hosp., Phila., 1944-45; asst. resident in medicine Albany (N.Y.) Hosp., 1945-46, resident in medicine, 1946-47; rsch. fellow in medicine Harvard Med. Sch., Thorndike Meml. Lab., Boston City Hosp., 1947-48; asst. prof. oncology, instr. medicine Albany Med. Coll., 1948-50; instr. medicine SUNY Coll. Medicine, Syracuse, 1950-51, asst. prof., 1951-56, assoc. prof., 1956-64, prof. medicine, 1964-68; program dir. Adult Clin. Rsch. Ctr., Syracuse, 1965-68; physician-in-chief, dir. clin. rsch. and edn. Santa Barbara (Calif.) Gen.-Cottage Hosps., 1968-69; prof. medicine U. Rochester (N.Y.) Sch. Medicine, 1969-92, emeritus prof. medicine, 1992—; mem. Univ. Senate, 1971-74; mem. staff Strong Meml. Hosp., Rochester; mem. staff Highland Hosp., 1969-90, chief medicine, 1970-80, dir. gastroenterology and nutrition, 1970-86; sr. attending physician The Genesee Hosp., 1990-91. Mem. editl. bd. Am. Jour. Clin. Nutrition, 1970-76; contbr. articles to profl. jours. Bd. mgrs. Camp Dudley YMCA, 1962-67, 69-74, chmn. bd., 1966-67, 71-73; bd. dirs. Onondaga County Met. Health Coun., Syracuse, 1959-61; mem. adv. com. Onondaga County Health Dept., 1966-68; bd. dirs. Am. Liver Found., 1982-92, pres. we. N.Y. chpt., 1982-83. Fellow ACP, Rochester Acad. Medicine (dir. 1979-82); mem. Am. Fedn. Clin. Rsch. (councillor 1956-59), AAAS, Onondaga County Med. Soc. (exec. com. 1964-66), Am. Assn. for Study Liver Disease, Am. Inst. Nutrition, Am. Soc. Clin. Nutrition, Endocrine Soc., Am. Gastroent. Assn., Western Soc. for Clin. Rsch., Med. Soc. Monroe County, Internat. Assn. for Study Liver, Assn. Program Dirs. Internal Medicine (councillor 1978-80), N.Y. State Dept. Health (bd. profl. med. conduct N.Y. State 1986—), Island Profl. Rev. Orgn. (cons. 1991-94), Nat. Health Lawyers Assn. (dispute resolver), Gt. Lakes Interurban (sec. 1977-84), Ea. Gut, Oak Hill Country Club (Rochester). Presbyterian. Home: 4 Whitecliff Dr Pittsford NY 14534-2926

FALSONE, JACK JOSEPH, physician; b. Queens, N.Y., Nov. 6, 1923; s. Joseph and Margaret (Cutelli) F.; A.B., Columbia Coll., 1944; M.D., L.I. Coll. Medicine, 1947; m. Anna Mandracchia, Dec. 23, 1945; children—Margaret, Catherine. Intern, Bklyn. Hosp., 1947-48, resident in internal medicine, 1948-51; attending physician Norwalk (Conn.) Hosp., 1953—, assoc. chief chest diseases, 1970-87, instr. Yale U. Coll. Medicine, 1955-61, asst. clin. prof. medicine, 1961-69. Served with AUS, 1943-46, USAF, 1951-53. Diplomate Am. Bd. Internal Medicine. Fellow ACP; mem. Norwalk Heart Assn. (pres. 1955), Norwalk Med. Soc. (pres. 1975), Am. Coll. Chest Physicians. Roman Catholic. Office: Beulah Hinds Ctr Norwalk Hosp Norwalk CT 06856

FALTER, RICHARD THOMAS, ophthalmologist; b. Reading, Pa., Sept. 26, 1938; s. Conrad Vincent and Doris Marie (Larzalere) F.; m. Jane Mary Falter, July 27, 1963; children: Jean, Richard, Heidi, Janie. AB, Kans. State U., 1963; MD, U. Kans., 1967. Diplomate Am. Bd. Ophthalmology. Intern U. Iowa, Iowa City, 1967-68, resident, 1970-74; staff Hutchinson (Kans.) Hosp.; pvt. practice Hutchinson (Kans.) Eye Physicians and Surgeons P.A., 1975—. Lt. USNR, 1968-70. Mem. ACS, AMA, Am. Acad. Ophthalmology, Am. Coll. Eye Physicians, Am. Soc. Cataract and Refractive Surgery, Cath. Physicians Guild, Internat. Soc. Refractive Keratoplasty, Iowa Eye Assocs., Kansas City Soc. Ophthalmology and Otolaryngology, Kans. Med. Soc., Kans. Ophthalmol. Soc., Kans. Acad. Family Physicians, Pan Am. Assn. Ophthalmologists, K.C. Roman Catholic. Home: 815 Bannock Burn Hutchinson KS 67502 Office: Hutchinson Eye Physicians 1708 E 23d St Hutchinson KS 67502

FAN, IAIN, radiologist; b. Hong Kong, Apr. 9, 1965; s. Robert and Mary (Lu) F.; m. Michelle Christiana Moy, Aug. 3, 1991; 1 child, Christopher. BS, N.Y. Inst. Technology, 1988; DO, N.Y. Coll. Osteo. Medicine, 1992. Intern Peninsula Hosp., Far Rockaway, N.Y., 1992-93; chief radiology resident St. Barnabas Hosp., Bronx, 1993-97. Mem. Am. Osteo. Coll. Radiology, Am. Ostopathic Assn., Am. Roentgen Ray Soc., N.y. State Radiol. Soc., Radiol. Soc. N. Am.

FANCHER, EDWIN CRAWFORD, psychologist; b. Middletown, N.Y., Aug. 29, 1923; s. Frank Dane and Elizabeth (McGarr) F.; student U. Alaska, 1941-42; B.A., New Sch. Social Research, 1949, M.A., 1951; m. Vivian Kramer, Nov. 8, 1969; children—Bruce Daniel, Emily Jill. Psychologist, Linden (N.J.) Mental Hygiene Clinic, 1955-58; co-founder, pub. Village Voice, N.Y.C., 1955-74; co-founder, clin. dir. Washington Sq. Inst. for Psychotherapy and Mental Health, N.Y.C., 1960-70; psychologist, Community Guidance Service, N.Y.C., 1958—; pvt. practice psychol. counseling, N.Y.C., 1958—; mem. faculty Am. Inst. Psychotherapy and Psychoanalysis, 1977—; mem. N.Y. Freudian Soc., 1985—; chmn. bd., mem. faculty N.Y. Sch. for Psychoanalytic Psychotherapy, N.Y.C., 1979—; dir. Orange County Telephone Co., Middletown, N.Y., 1946-60; cons. Plumsock Fund, Indpls., 1974—, pres. 1985—. Founder, past chmn N.Y. Neighborhoods Council on Narcotics Addiction. Served with U.S. Army, 1943-46. Decorated Bronze star. Mem. Am., N.Y. State psychol. assns., Am. Orthopsychiat. Assn., Council of Psychoanalytic Psychotherapists (past pres.), Internat. Psychoanalytic Assn. Democrat. Club: Gipsy Trail. Home: 40 Fifth Ave New York NY 10011-8843

FANCHER, ROBERT TRENOR, psychotherapist; b. Reno, Nev., Jan. 14, 1954; s. James Parkes and Margret Ewilda (Trenor) F. BA, Miss. Coll., 1975; MA, So. Ill. U., 1977; PhD, Vanderbilt U., 1980; cert. in psychotherapy, Blanton-Peale Grad. Inst., 1990. Project mgr. Vanderbilt Inst. Pub. Policy Studies, Nashville, 1982-84; program officer Twentieth Century Fund, N.Y.C., 1984-85; psychotherapist Blanton-Peale Counseling Ctr., N.Y.C., 1985-88, Washington Sq. Inst., N.Y.C., 1990-93; pvt. practice psychotherapy N.Y.C., 1988—; cons. TriSource Group, N.Y.C., 1988-93; adj. asst. prof. NYU, 1991-92, faculty The New Sch. for Social Rsch., 1995—. Author: Cultures of Healing: Correcting the Image of American Mental Health Care, 1995; co-author, co-editor: Against Mediocrity: The Humanities in America's High Schools, 1984; edtl. bd. Jour. Mental Health Counseling, 1991-94; contbr. to profl. jours. Henry Luce Found. scholar, 1980-81. Mem. AACD, Am. Mental Health Counselors Assn., Am. Philosophy Assn. Democrat.

FANCONI, SERGIO MARIO, pediatrician; b. Zürich, Switzerland, Oct. 3, 1949; s. Mario and Iginia (Binschädler) F.; m. Marta Meienhofer. Degree in experimental biology, U. Zürich, Switzerland, 1978, MD, 1979. Cert. in pediatrics. Intern U. Children's Hosp., Zürich; resident Inst. Med. Microbiology, Zürich, 1976-78, Pediatrics Triemlispital, Zürich, 1978-79, Childrens Hosp. U. Zürich, 1979-82; fellow intensive care unit Childrens Hosp., Bern, Switzerland, 1982-83, Hosp. for Sick Children, Toronto, Can., 1983-84; dir. ICU and neonatology Kinderspital, Zürich, 1984—; edit. bd. dirs. Current Opinion in Pediatrics. Contbr. articles to profl. jours. Mem. Swiss Soc. Intensive Care (sec. 1985-89, bd. dirs. 1985-95, pres. 1992-94), European Soc. Intensive Care (v.p. 1995—), Swiss Soc. Pediatrics, European Soc. Pediatric Intensive Care, European Soc. Pediatric Rsch. Office: Kinderspital, Steinwiesstrasse 75, 8032 Zürich CH, Switzerland

FANDEL, IVAR BARRY, pediatrician; b. N.Y.C., May 22, 1947; s. Samuel and Sally (Waxman) F.; m. Mona Mendelowitz; children: Sari, Shawn. BA, Queens Coll., 1967; MD, Med. Coll. Va., 1972. Diplomate Am. Bd. Pediatrics. Intern, resident in pediatrics Jackson Meml. Hosp., Miami, Fla., 1973-76; pediatrician in pvt. practice Cooper City, Fla., 1977—. Fellow Am. Acad. Pediatrics; mem. Fla. Med. Assn. Office: 9640 Griffin Rd Fort Lauderdale FL 33328

FANG, JING, epidemiologist, researcher; b. Chengdu, Sichuan, China, July 6, 1960; came to U.S., 1986; s. Duo Fang and Changxiang Tang; m. Jian Jiang, Nov. 30, 1986; 1 child, Yashu Jiang. MD, West China U. Med. Sci., Chengdu, 1982, MMs, 1986; MPH, U. Newcastle, Australia, 1989. Tchg. asst., resident West China U. Med. Sci., 1986-88, lectr., attending physician, 1989-93; rsch. assoc. dept. epidemiology Yeshiva U. Albert Einstein Coll. Medicine, Bronx, N.Y., 1993—. Contbr. articles to med. jours. Fellow Internat. Clin. Epidemiology Network.

FANGER, MARK, psychologist, psychotherapist, consultant; b. Boston, Dec. 6, 1943. AB in Polit. Sci., Syracuse U., 1965; EdM in Psychology, Boston State Coll., 1972; EdD in Counseling Psychology, Boston U., 1977; grad. Clin. Consultation Program, Boston Inst. for Psychotherapy, 1984. Lic. psychologist and Family Therapist, Mass., Nat. Register in Psychology; cert. social studies tchr., guidance counselor and dir., Mass.; diplomate Am. Bd. Family Psychology, Am. Acad. Behavioral Medicine. Clin. dir. Milford Assistance Program Community Mental Health Ctr., Milford, Mass., 1971-74; clin. cons. drug treatment program Boston City Hosp., 1975-77; staff psychologist Bay Area Psychiat. Assocs., Burlington, Mass., 1977-80, Suburban Counseling Assocs., Weston, Mass., 1977-80; clin. supr. Whiteman House, Survival, Inc., Quincy, Mass., 1982-84; pvt. practice psychotherapy, Newton Highlands, Mass., 1979—; mem. aj. faculty dept. counseling psychology Boston U., 1976-77, dept. psychology Boston State Coll., 1977-79; mem. adj. faculty Antioch's Inst. Open Edn., Cambridge, Mass., 1979-80; mem. adj. faculty, supr. family therapy Mass. Sch. Profl. Psychology, Newton, 1982-83; group psychotherapy cons. People for People, Inc., Framingham, Mass., 1990-92; mem. faculty group psychotherapy tng. program Northeastern Soc. for Group Psychotherapy, 1991-95; presenter in field; condr. workshops. Recipient Svc. of Self award Rotary Club, Franklin, Mass., 1974; grantee Mass. Gen. Hosp., 1975. Fellow Mass. Psychol. Assn.; mem. APA, Am. Group Psychotherapy Assn. (clin. mem.), Am. Mental Health Alliance New Eng. (charter), Internat. Acad. Behavioral Medicine, Counseling and Psychotherapy (diplomate in profl. psychotherapy and behavioral medicine), Psychologists for Social Responsibility, Soc. for Family Therapy and Rsch. (edn. com. 1984-87), Mass. Assn. Marriage and Family Therapy (clin. mem.), N.E. Soc. Study of Multiple Personality and Dissociation, Northeastern Soc. Group Psychotherapy (membership com. 1986-88, program com. 1988-94, faculty tng. program group psychotherapy 1991-95, bd. dirs. 1994—, inst. com. 1995-96, chair inst. com. 1996—), Consortium for Psychotherapy, Pi Lambda Theta, Phi Delta Kappa. Office: 4 Hartford St Newton MA 02161-1517

FANGER, MICHAEL W., medical educator; b. Ft. Wayne, Ind., July 3, 1940. BA in Chemistry and Zoology, Wabash Coll., 1962; PhD in Biochemistry, Yale U., 1967. NIH postdoctoral fellow Nat. Inst. Med. Rsch., London, 1967-68, U. Ill. Med. Sch., Chgo., 1968-70; asst. prof. microbiology Case Western Res. U., Cleve., 1970-76; faculty dept. immunology Middlesex Hosp., London, 1977-78; prof. microbiology and medicine Dartmouth Med. Sch., Lebanon, N.H., 1981—, chmn. dept. microbiology, 1992—, dir. immunology program, 1981-92; dir. immunology program Norris Cotton Cancer Ctr., 1984-92, dir. monoclonal antibody libr., 1984—; cons. Verax Corp., Lebanon, 1982-87, mem. sci. adv. bd., 1984-87; founder Medarex Inc., Annandale, N.J., 1987, dir., 1987—, chmn. sci. adv. bd., cons., 1987—. Contbr. numerous articles to profl. jours.; patentee in field. Mem. Am. Assn. Immunologists. Office: Dartmouth Med Sch Dept Microbiology 1 Medical Center Dr Lebanon NH 03756

FANN, MARGARET ANN, counselor; b. Pasco, Wash., July 16, 1942; d. Joseph Albert David and Clarice Mable (Deaver) Rivard; m. Jerry Lee Fann, June 13, 1986; children: Brenda Heupel, Scott Sherman, Kristin Johnson, Robert Lack III. AA, Big Bend C.C., Moses Lake, Wash., 1976; BA in Applied Psychology magna cum laude, Ea. Wash. U., 1977, MS in Psychology, 1978. Cert. mental health counselor, Wash.; cert. chem. dependency counselor II, nat. cert. addictions counselor II, cert. in chronic psychiat. disability. Intern counselor Linker House Drug Rehab., Spokane, Wash., 1976-78; drug counselor The House drug program, Tacoma, Wash., 1978-80; exec. dir. Walla Walla (Wash.) Commn. Alcohol, 1980-82; dir. Cmty. Alcohol Svcs. Assn., Kennewick, Wash., 1982-86; primary care coord. Carondelet Psychiat. Care Ctr., Richland, Wash., 1986-90; part-time instr. Ea. Wash. U., Cheney, 1981-88; instr. Columbia Basin Coll., Pasco, 1990-93; adminstr. Action Chem. Dependency Ctr., Kennewick, 1993—; bd. dirs. Benton-Franklin County Substance Abuse Coalition, Pasco, Kennewick, Richland, 1990—. Vol. Pat Hale for Senator, Kennewick, 1994. Mem. Am. Counselors Assn., Nat. Mental Health Counselors Assn., Wash. State Mental Health Counselors Assn., Tri-Cities Counselors Assn., Phi Theta Kappa. Office: Action Chem Dependency Ctr 552 N Colorado Ste 5525 Kennewick WA 99336 also: Benton-Franklin County MICA Detoxification Ctr 1020 S 7th St Kennewick WA 99336

FANNING, WALTER LEE, epidemiologist; b. Phila., June 15, 1944; s. Walter Lee and Ada (Wall) F.; m. Tosy Merk, July 6, 1970 (div. July 1993); children: Lori, Tony, Debbie, Shane; m. Claudia Green, Oct. 28, 1993. BS, Davidson Coll., 1966; MD, U. Va., 1970. Diplomate Am. Coll. Physicians. Intern U. Va. Sch. Medicine, Charlottesville, 1970-71; resident U. Wis., Madison, 1973-74; asst. prof. clin. medicine U. Mass. Med. Sch., Pittsfield, 1976-81; med. dir. dept. infectious disease & epidemiology Scottsdale (Ariz.) Meml. Hosps., 1982—, med. dir. outpatient antibiotic program, 1985—; med. dir. infectious disease & epidemiology Desert Valley Humana Hosp., 1985—; cons. in field.; mem. communicable diseases adv. coun. State of Ariz., 1988—. Contbr. articles to profl. jours. Lt. comdr. USCG, 1971-73. Infectious Disease fellow U. Vt., Burlington, 1974-76. Fellow Am. Coll. Physicians; mem. Am. Soc. Microbiology, Infectious Disease Soc. Am., Ariz.

Infectious Disease Soc., Maricopa County Med. Soc., Internat. Assn. Travel Medicine. Independent. Methodist. Home: 5331 E Sapphire Ln Paradise Valley AZ 85253 Office: 3501 N Scottsdale Rd #300 Scottsdale AZ 85251

FANOS, KATHLEEN HILAIRE, osteopathic physician, podiatrist; b. Bremerhaven, Germany, Aug. 18, 1956; came to U.S., 1957; d. Homer Dantangelo and Ilse Helmar (Ochs) F. AAS in Music, Nassau C.C., Garden City, N.Y., 1976; BS in Music Edn., Hofstra U., 1978, postgrad., 1978-79; D Podiatric Medicine, Coll. Podiatric Med. and Surg., Des Moines, 1987; DO, Coll. Osteo. Med. and Surg., Des Moines, 1994. Tchr. music McKenna Jr. High Sch. and Eastlake Elem. Sch., Massapequa, N.Y., 1978-79; musician numerous profl. orgns., N.Y., Iowa, 1979—; preceptorship in podiatry Bayshore, N.Y., 1987-88; pvt. practice podiatry Hyde Park, West Roxbury and Brookline, Mass., 1988-91; pvt. practice podiatry, Des Moines, 1991-92; resident in internal medicine Winthrop U. Hosp., Mineola, N.Y., 1994—; ins. med. examiner Portamedic, Burlington, Mass., 1988-91. Mem. AMA, Am. Coll. Physicians (assoc.), Am. Soc. Internal. Medicine, Am. Osteo. Assn., Am. Coll. Osteo. Family Physicians, N.Y. State Internal Medicine Soc., Phi Theta Kappa, Pi Kappa Lambda, Sigma Sigma Phi, Phi Delta Epsilon.

FARACLAS, WILLIAM G., medical educator, research evaluator; b. New Haven, Conn., June 10, 1950; s. George Nicholas and Helen Ethel (Basel) F.; m. Hanna Ian Curtis, May 2, 1977; children: Elias W., Christian W., Farah E., Azer W. BA, U. Conn., 1973; MPH, Yale U., 1975. Prof., chmn. dept. pub. health So. Conn. State U., New Haven, Conn., 1975—; doctorate prof. So. Conn. State U., New Haven, 1993; cons. in field. Author: None for the Road, 1984. Mem. Am. Pub. Health Assn., Am. Assn. Sec. Counselors & Therapists, Conn. Pub. Health Assn. (bd. dirs. 1990—). Office: Pub Health Dept So Conn State U 501 Crescent St New Haven CT 06515

FARBER, HARRISON W., critical care physician, medical educator; b. Ware, Mass., May 5, 1947; s. Seymour J. and Harriet W. (Wirtschafter) F. BS, Duke U., 1969; MD, George Washington U., 1977. Diplomate Am. Bd. Internal Medicine, Am. Bd. Pulmonary Diseases, Am. Bd. Critical Care Medicine. Intern Med. Coll. Va., Richmond, 1977-78; resident Med. Coll. Va., 1978-80, chief resident, 1980-81; fellow in pulmonary/critical care Boston U. Sch. Medicine, 1981-84, asst. prof., 1984-89, assoc. prof., 1989-94, prof., 1994—; staff physician Boston City Hosp., 1984—, med. dir. respiratory therapy, 1986—, dir. med. intensive care unit, 1985—; staff physician Univ. Hosp., Boston, 1984—; med. dir. respiratory therapy Mattapan Hosp., Boston, 1986—; Mem. spl. care unit adv. com. Boston City Hosp., chmn., 1992—, mem. code com., respiratory therapy com., diversion task force, com. on house officer performance, physicians comm. task force, clin. and edn. com., residency tchg. skills; spkr. numerous confs. in field. Contbr. over 100 articles and abstracts to profl. jours., chpts. to books; reviewer Am. Jour. Respiratory Cell and Molecular Biology, Am. Jour. Physiology, Jour. Cellular Physiology, Jour. Clin. Investigation, Circulation Rsch., Annals Internal Medicine, Chest, Endothelium, Am. Jour. Respiratory and Critical Care Medicine, Exptl. Eye Rsch. Active Nat. Youth Leadership Forum. Recipient Am. Lung Assn. Rsch. award, 1983-84, Career Investigator award, 1992—, Mass. Thoracic Soc. Rsch. award, 1984-85, NIH-NHLBI New Investigator award, 1985-88; biomed. rsch. grantee Univ. Hosp., 1984-85; rsch. grantee Am. Lung Assn.; 1986-88; program project grantee NIH-NHLBI, 1986-91; grantee Am. Heart Assn. Mass. Affiliate, 1989-91, NIH-NHLBI, 1992-96. Mem. AAAS, Am. Coll. Chest Physicians, Am. Thoracic Soc., Am. Heart Assn. (cardiopulmonary coun.), Am. Fedn. Clin. Rsch., Am. Physiologic Soc., Am. Soc. Cell Biology (congl. liaison com.), Am. Soc. Clin. Investigation. Office: Boston U Sch Medicine Pulmonary Ctr 80 E Concord St R-3 Boston MA 02118

FARBER, JERRY S., orthopedic surgeon; b. Chgo., Dec. 16, 1932; s. Albert H. and Cecelia (Shallat) F.; m. Sharon Iris Weisbach, Apr. 23, 1961; children: K. Allen, Lori, Daniel. BS, U. Ill., 1954; MD, U. Ill., Chgo., 1958. Internship Cook County Hosp., Chgo., 1958-59; residency Hines VA Hosp., Maywood, Ill., 1959-62, Shriners Hosp., 1962-63; pres. MOST, Silver Spring, Md., 1991-95; pvt. practice in orthopaedic foot and ankle Silver Spring, Md., 1995—. Author clin. paper. Capt. USAF, 1964-66. Fellow ACS, Am. Acad. Orthopedic Surgeons, Am. Foot and Ankle Soc. Jewish. Office: 2415 Musgrove Rd Silver Spring MD 20904

FARBER, NAOMI BETH, social work educator; b. New Orleans, July 13, 1956; d. Emmanuel and Ruth Wilma (Diamond) F.; m. Steven E. Grosby, Oct. 3, 1982; 1 child, Samuel I. AB, Grinnell Coll., 1978; MSW, U. Mich., 1980; PhD, U. Chgo., 1987. ACSW. Clin. social worker Lakehead Psychiat. Hosp., Thunder Bay, Ont., Canada, 1980-82; asst. prof. U. Wis., Madison, 1987-91, Bryn Mawr (Pa.) Coll., 1991—; rsch. fellow Murray Ctr. Radcliffe Coll., Cambridge, Mass., 1993-95; rsch. affiliate Inst. for Rsch. on Poverty, Madison, 1987—; grants reviewer HHS, Washington, 1995—; mem. adv. bd. Briarpatch Youth Svcs., Madison, 1987-89, Canadian Mental Health Assn., Thunder Bay, 1980-82. Contbr. articles to profl. jours. Rsch. grantee State of Pa. Dept. Edn., 1993-95, HHS, 1987-92, Ford Found., 1989-90. Mem. NASW, Coun. on Social Work Edn. Office: Bryn Mawr Coll 300 Airdale Rd Bryn Mawr PA 19010

FARBER, NEAL MARK, biotechnologist, molecular biologist; b. N.Y.C., Oct. 23, 1950; s. Sol Z. and Nettie (Handelman) F.; m. Varda E. Farber, Aug. 19, 1973; children: Dani, Arielle. BSc with honors, Hebrew U., Jerusalem, 1973; MA, Columbia U., 1975, PhD, 1979; postgrad., Harvard U., 1979. Rsch. fellow Harvard U., Cambridge, Mass., 1980-82; rsch. scientist Biogen, Inc., Cambridge, 1982, project leader, 1983-85, coord. new projects, 1986-87, mgr. bus. devel., 1988, product mgr., 1989-93; dir. bus. devel. T Cell Scis., Inc., Cambridge, 1993-95; v.p. corp. devel. Cubist Pharm., Inc., Cambridge, 1996—. Contbr. articles to profl. jours. Pres. SSDS Day Sch., Boston, 1989-91. Recipient Rsch. Svc. award NIH, 1975-78, Hammett award Columbia U., 1979; Helen Hay Whitney Found. fellow, Boston, 1980-82; Wexner Heritage Found. fellow, 1991-93. Mem. AAAS, N.Y. Acad. Scis., Licensing Execs. Soc., Sigma Xi.

FARBER, SAUL JOSEPH, physician, educator; b. N.Y.C.; s. Isodor and Mary (Bunim) F.; m. Doris Marcia Balmuth; children—Joshua M., Beth Mina Farber Loewentheil. A.B., NYU, 1938, M.D., 1942; Ph.D. honoris causa, Tel Aviv U., 1983. Diplomate Am. Bd. Internal Medicine. Intern Sinai Hosp., Balt., 1942-43; rsch. resident Goldwarer Meml. Hosp., N.Y.C, 1946-47; resident Bellevue Hosp., N.Y.C, 1947-48; fellow NYU, 1948-49; Instr., asst. prof. medicine NYU, N.Y.C., 1953-62, assoc. prof., 1962-66, prof., chmn. dept. medicine, 1966—, Frederick H. King prof. medicine, 1978—, dean for acad. affairs Sch. Medicine, 1978—, acting dean Sch. of Medicine, 1963-66, 79-81, 82—, provost, dean sch. medicine, 1987—; co-chmn. N.Y. State Health Adv. Council, 1975-80; chmn. Com. on Resource Requirements of VA Health Care Systems, NRC, 1974-77; mem. adv. com. on long term care chronic illness Robert Wood Johnson Found., 1979—, co-chmn. clin. nurse scholars adv. com., 1982—; mem. med. adv. bd. Hadassah; mem. adv. com. Harold C. Simmons Arthritis Research Ctr., U. Tex. Health Sci. Ctr., Dallas, 1983-86; organizing chmn. Fed. Council Internal Medicine, 1975, chmn., 1984-85; splty. advisor Naval Med. Command, Washington, 1985-86. Contbr. articles to profl. jours. Recipient Career Scientist award Health Rsch. Coun., N.y.C., 1960-65, Med. Alumni Achievement award NYU Sch. Medicine Alumni Assn., 1966, Gt. Tchr. award NYU Alumni Fedn., 1973, Alumni Assn. Achievement award Washington Sq. Coll. Arts and Sci., NYU, 1978, Alumni Meritorious Svc. award NYU Alumni Fedn., 1984, Wise medal Tel Aviv U., 1990, The Albert Gallatin medal NYU, 1993, The Abraham Flexner award for Disting. Svc. to Med. Edn., 1995. Recipient Career Scientist award Health Rsch. Coun., N.Y.C., 1960-65, Med. Alumni Achievement award NYU Sch. of Medicine Alumni Assn., 1966, Gt. Tchr. award NYU Alumni Fedn., 1973, Alumni Assn. Achievement award Washington Sq. Coll. Arts and Sci., NYU, 1978, Alumni Meritorious Svc. award NYU Alumni Fedn., 1984, Wise medal Tel Aviv U., 1990, The Albert Gallatin medal NYU, 1993. Fellow ACP (master 1975, pres. 1984-85, regent 1978-86, Disting. tchr. award 1986, Alfred Stengal Meml. award 1992); mem. Am. Soc. Internal Medicine (Disting. Internist of Yr. award 1976), Am. Soc. Clin. Investigation (sec.-treas. 1951-60, councillor 1960-63), Assn. Am. Physicians, Interurban Clin. Club, Inst. Medicine Nat. Acad. Scis., Am. Clin. and Climatol. Assn., Am. Physiol. Soc., Assn. Acad. Health Ctrs. (adv. com. 1981—), Sigma Theta Tau (hon.). Office: NYU Sch Medicine 550 1st Ave New York NY 10016-6481*

FARDON, DAVID F., orthopedic surgeon; b. Kansas City, Mo., June 25, 1940; s. Edgar Howard and Dorothy Jewell (Favreau) F.; m. Judith Gail Levitt, June 11, 1960; children: David Alexander, Amee Lyn, Joshua Edgar, Zachary Thomas. BA, Mo. U., 1960; MD, Kans. U., 1964. Physician and surgeon Knoxville (Tenn.) Orthopedic Clinic, 1970—. Author: Free Yourself From Neck Pain, Free Yourself From Back Pain, Osteoporosis. Fellow Am. Acad. Orthopedic Surgeons, Am. Orthopaedic Assn.; mem. N.Am. Spine Soc. (v.p. 1995-96). Office: Knoxville Orthopedic Clinic 1128 Weisgarber Knoxville TN 37909

FARGHALI, MOHAMED, surgeon; b. Alexandria, Egypt, Sept. 11, 1946; s. Mohamed Farghali Hanan and Wakika Abel-El-Gelil (Wakika) Ahmed;m. Nagure El-Sayed Mohamed, Aug. 21, 1975; children: Rane, Role. MB, ChB, Faculty Medicine, 1969. Cert. diplomate in surgery. House officer Al Moassat Hosp., Alexandria, 1969-70, resident surgery, 1971-74, asst. cons., 1975-80, cons. surgery, 1980—, resident orthopedics, 1981-82. Fellow Surg. Assn. Egypt; mem. Med. Assn. Egypt. Office: Al Moassat Hosp, Surg Dept, Alexandria Egypt

FARIA, EDWARD CYRINO, health care administrator; b. Peabody, Mass., Aug. 12, 1924; s. Celestino and Laura (Lucio) F.; student U. S.C., 1948-50, 1956-60, U.S. Armed Forces Inst., 1957-58, So. Ill. U., 1961-65; certificate USAF Sch. Aviation Medicine Air U., 1955; m. Gloria Jewel Harrison, Jan. 15, 1944; children—Gloria Dawn, Evelyn Celeste, Elizabeth Vermel. Served as enlisted man USAAF, 1942-46, USAF, 1950-67, advanced through grades to chief master sgt. USAF, 1960; med. adminstrv. specialist USAAF, 1942-46; chief storekeeper VA Regional Office, S.C., 1946-50; med. adminstrv. supt. Lawson AFB Hosp., Ga., 12th Air Force Surgeons' Office, Wiesbaden, Germany, Spangdahlem Air Base, Toul-Rosier Air Base, France, 1950-67; adjutant Spandahlem Air Base, 1951-54; exec. officer Mil. Air Transport Service, Scott AFB, Ill., 1961-62, chief adminstrv. services, 1965-66; asst. adminstr. Myrtle Beach (S.C.) AFB Hosp., 1966-67; sr. instr. med. adminstr. USAF Med. Service, USAF Med. Sch., Gunter AFB, Ala., 1954-60; ret., 1967; loan guarantee analyst VA Regional Office, Columbia, S.C., 1967; personnel statistician U.S. Army Hosp., Ft. Jackson Hosp., S.C., 1967-68; adminstr. Columbia (S.C.) Area Mental Health Center, 1968—; cons. in community mental health; instr. healthcare adminstrn., psychiat. residency Hall Psychiat. Inst., Columbia. Chmn. deacons Seventh Day Adventist Ch., Montgomery, Ala., 1957-58, supt. Sabbath Sch., Columbia, 1966-67, asst. supt. Sabbath Sch., Orangeburg, S.C., 1975-76, ednl. sec., 1975-76. Fellow Am. Acad. Med. Adminstrs.; mem. Adminstrv. Mgmt. Soc., Assn. Mental Health Adminstrs., Soc. Personnel Adminstrn., USAF Assn., S.C., Am. hosp. assns., Am. Cancer Soc., Heart and Lung Assn., Southeastern Statisticians, Smithsonian Inst. Assos. Clubs: Armed Forces, Am. Legion, DAV, VFW, Elks (hon.), Optimists (v.p. internat. 1971-72). Author: Medical Services Financial Management, 1959; Base Level Medical Checklist for Self Inspection, 1954, 3d rev. edit., 1956. Home: RR 2 Box 351 Saint Matthews SC 29135-9566 Office: 1618 Sunset Dr Columbia SC 29203-6513

FARICY, PATRICK OWEN, physician; b. Pueblo, Colo., Dec. 18, 1947; s. Robert Owen and Ceciliamae (Spitzer) F.; m. Kristine Kane, Dec. 27, 1969; children: Luke, Mark, Kathleen. BS, U. Colo., 1969, MD cum luade, 1969. Diplomate Am. Bd. Urology. Intern, resident surgery I U. Colo., 1973-74, intern, resident surgery II, 1974-75, intern, resident urology, 1975-77, chief urology resident, 1978; urologist No. Wyo. Urological Assocs., Sheridan, 1980-83, pvt. practice, Colorado Springs, Colo., 1983—; mem. healthcare bd., chmn. Penrose-St. Francis Health Care, Colorado Springs, 1989—. Maj. USAF, 1978-80. Mem. Am. Urological Assn., Am. Assn. Clin. Urologists, Rocky Mountain Urological Soc., El Paso County Med. Soc., Colorado Springs Clin. Club, Alpha Omega Alpha. Roman Catholic. Office: Urological Assocs 2170 Internat Cir Colorado Springs CO 80910

FARINA, MARK SERGIO, orthodontist; b. Newton, Mass., Feb. 25, 1966; s. Angelo Enrico and Luciana (Deluca) F.; m. Lissette Maria Martinez, May 19, 1990; 1 child, Stefano Marco. BS in Biology, Boston Coll., 1988; DMD, U. Pa., 1992; cert. in orthodontics, NYU, 1994. Pvt. practice, Tampa, Fla. St. Francis dental scholar, Boston, 1989; St. George oral cancer fellow, Phila., 1990. Mem. ADA, Am. Assn. Orthodontists, So. Soc. Orthodontists, Acad. Gen. Dentistry, Fla. Assn. Orthodontists, Hillsborough County Med. Soc., Omicron Kappa Upsilon. Republican. Roman Catholic. Home: 15210 Amberly Dr Apt 211 Tampa FL 33647 Office: 4700 N Habana Ave Tampa FL 33614

FARINELLA, CHARLES BERNARD, physician and surgeon; b. Newark, Feb. 4, 1924; s. Frank Paul and Mary (Calascibetta) F.; m. Blanche Elizabeth Sejen, Aug. 29, 1942; children: Ralph, Francis (dec.), Joyce, Philip, Mary, Laura. BSc, Seton Hall U., South Orange, N.J., 1948; MS, Fordham U., Bronx, 1950; MD, Georgetown U., 1954. Diplomate Am. Bd. Family Practice; lic. physician, Calif. Pvt. practice preventive medicine, gerontology Rancho Mirage, Calif., 1962—; adminstr. and owner Golden State Meml. Hosp., Newhall, Calif., 1962-84. Office: 69-730 Hwy 111 #106A Rancho Mirage CA 92270

FARKAS, CAROL GARNER, nurse, administrator; b. N.Y.C., Apr. 26, 1936; d. Charles Harry and Phyllis (Levine) Schotland; m. Theodore Arthur Garner, 1956 (dec. 1971); children: Charles Hugh Farkas Garner, Judi Beth Garner Farkas, Andrea Lee Garner Farkas Krupen; m. Robin Lewis Farkas, Oct. 17, 1972; adopted children: Bradford Lewis Farkas, Andrew Lawrence Farkas. BSN with distinction, Cornell U., 1976; MPH, Columbia U., 1980. Dir. Am. Inst. Life Threatening Illness & Loss, N.Y.C., 1980—; del. white House Conf. Aging, N.Y. State Gov.'s Conf. Aging; mem. N.Y. State Hospice Adv. Group, 1979-81; mem. adv. com. office health mgmt. N.Y. State Dept. Health, 1979-81; mem. select com. financing and licensure, com. legis. edn. Nat. Hsopice Orgn., 1980—, N.Y. task force on life and the law, 1994—; mem. Choice in Dying, 1991-92, Nat. Coun. Death and Dying, 1990-91, Soc. Right to Die, 1982-90; co-chair med. student conf. nursing com. Columbia Presbyn., N.Y.C., 1992. Co-editor: Nursing and Thanatology, 1982; contbr. articles to profl. publs. Bd. mem. N.Y. State Task Force on Life and the Law, 1994—. Mem. Sigma Theta Tau. Home: 730 Park Ave New York NY 10021-4945

FARKAS, PAUL STEPHEN, gastroenterologist; b. N.Y.C., 1952; s. Benjamin J. and Ellen (Tanner) F.; m. Esta Miriam Cantor, June 24, 1973; children: Melanie Sharon, Joshua David. AB magna cum laude with distinction in psychology, Brandeis U., 1972; MD, Tufts U., 1976. Diplomate Am. Bd. Internal Medicine, Am. Bd. Gastroenterology. Intern Baystate Med. Ctr., Sprinfield, Mass., 1976-77, resident in internal medicine, 1977-79; fellow in gastroenterology Albert Einstein Coll. Medicine, Bronx, N.Y., 1979-81; asst. clin. prof. medicine Tufts U., Boston, 1985—; med. advisor Med. Assist Program Springfield Tech. C.C., 1989—; co-dir. med. edn. Mercy Hosp., Springfield, 1990-95, chmn. dept. gastroenterology, 1995—, dir. libr., 1988—, mem. exec. com., 1995—; mem. adv. bd. VNA, Springfield, 1984-88; adj. asst. prof. clin. pharmacology Mass. Coll. Pharmacy, Boston, 1982—. Author: Diagnostic Diagrams Gastroenterology, 1985; contbr. book chpts., articles and revs. in field. Bd. dirs. B'nai Jacob Synagogue, Springfield, 1987-88, Com. for Longmeadow, Mass., 1989, Yeshiva, Longmeadow, 1994—. Fellow ACP; mem. AMA, Am. Coll. Gastroenterology, Am. Gastroent. Assn., Am. Soc. Gastrointestinal Endoscopy, New England Soc. Gastrointestinal Endoscopy. Office: 299 Carew St Springfield MA 01104-2301

FARLEY, DAVID RAY, surgeon; b. Portage, Wis., Aug. 1, 1960; s. George Michael and Rae Della (Turnbull) F.; m. Catherine Marie Belay, June 11, 1988; children: Thomas Anthony, Benjamin James. BS, U. Wis., 1983, MD, 1988. Resident in surgery Mayo Clinic, Rochester, Minn., 1988-94, cons. surgery, 1994—. Recipient Young Investigator award Internat. Pancreaticobiliary Soc., 1993, Resident award Minn. Surg. Soc., 1993. Mem. AMA, Minn. Med. Assn.

FARLEY, GARY LEE, optometrist; b. Williamson, W.Va.; m. Jackie Staley, May 20, 1978; children: Tommy, Katie, Jeffrey. BS in Chemistry and Math. summa cum laud, U. Richmond, 1978; OD summa cum laude, U. Ala., 1982. OD, Va. Pvt. practice Colonial Heights, Va., 1982—; mem. adv. bd. Innotec, Roanoke, Va., 1995—; cons. Va. Dept. for Visually Handicapped, Richmond, 1987—; bd. dirs. Va. Total Vision, Richmond, Va. EyeSite, Richmond. Councilman Colonial Heights City Coun., 1994—; mem. Colonial Heights Planning Commn., 1988-93. Named Outstanding Young Citizen of Colonial Heights Jaycees, 1990; recipient Builder award Masons, 1990. Fellow Va. Acad. Optometry; mem. Southside Optometric Assn. (pres. 1982—), Va. Optometric Assn. (chair coms.), Va. Svc. Plan (mem. adv. bd.). Methodist. Office: Drs Gilbert and Farley OD 3731 A Blvd Colonial Heights VA 23834

FARMER, CHARLES DUDLEY, nephrologist; b. Indpls., Nov. 22, 1933; s. Charles R. and Margaret (Shouse) F.; m. Lois Kay Poffenbarger, May 17, 1958; children—Stuart, Douglas, Randall, Suzanne. B.A., Ind. U., 1955, M.D., 1958; M.S., U. Minn., 1965. Diplomate Am. Bd. Internal Medicine. Intern, U. Calif. Hosp., San Francisco, 1959; resident in internal medicine Mayo Clinic, Rochester, Minn., 1961-65; practice medicine specializing in nephrology, Charlotte, N.C., 1966—; nephrologist Nalle Clinic Kidney Ctr., Charlotte, 1975—; dir. dialysis unit Charlotte Meml. Hosp., 1970-82; clin. prof. medicine U. N.C. Sch. Medicine, Chapel Hill. Bd. dirs. Charlotte Opera Assn., Meckenburg County Kidney Found, Community Concert Assn., Latta Place, Inc.; chmn. S.E. Kidney Coun. Served to capt. USAF, 1959-61. Mem. ACP, N.C. Med. Soc., Am. Soc. Nephrology, Am. Soc. Artificial Internal Organs, AMA, Phi Beta Kappa, Alpha Omega Alpha. Office: 928 Baxter St Charlotte NC 28204-2802

FARMER, JAMES LEE, genetics educator; b. South Gate, Calif., Aug. 8, 1938; s. James Ira and Ellen Eliza (Sheeks) F.; m. Gladys Clark, Jan. 27, 1967; children: Sarah, Clark, Rachel, Jared, Deborah. BS in Chemistry, Calif. Inst. Tech., 1960; PhD in Biology, Brown U., 1966. Instr. biophysics U. Colo. Med. Ctr., Denver, 1966-68; from asst. prof. to prof. zoology Brigham Young U., Provo, Utah, 1969—. Contbr. articles to profl. jours. Mem. AAAS, Genetics Soc. Am., Am. Soc. Human Genetics. Democrat. Mormon. Home: 222 E 4200 N Provo UT 84604-5043 Office: Brigham Young U 571 Widb Provo UT 84602-1049

FARMER, RICHARD GILBERT, physician, foundation administrator, medical advisor; b. Kokomo, Ind., Sept. 29, 1931; s. Oscar Irvin and Elizabeth Jane (Gilbert) F.; m. Janice Mae Schrank, Nov. 29, 1958; children: Amy Lynn, David Richard. Student, Ind. U., 1949-52; M.D., U. Md., 1956; M.S. in Medicine, U. Minn., 1960. Diplomate: Am. Bd. Internal Medicine, Gastroenterology. Fellow in internal medicine Mayo Clinic, Rochester, Minn., 1957-60; mem. staff Cleve. Clinic Found., 1962-91, chmn. dept. gastroenterology, 1972-82, chmn. div. medicine, 1975-91, mem. med. exec. com., 1975-91, bd. govs., 1974-79, mem. exec. com. bd. trustees, 1975-77; sr. med. advisor Bur. for Europe Agy. for Internat. Devel. U.S. Dept. State, Washington, 1992-94; cons. health care Eastern Europe and former Soviet Union, 1994—; assoc. clin. prof. medicine Case Western Res. U. Sch. Medicine, Cleve., 1980-91; clin. prof. medicine (gastroenterology) Georgetown U. Med. Ctr., Washington, 1992—; mem. nat. adv. bd. Nat. Commn. Digestive Diseases, 1977-79; mem. nat. sci. adv. bd. Nat. Found. Ileitis and Colitis, 1973-91; chmn. grants rev. com. Nat. Found. Ileitis and Colitis, 1981-85; mem. Council Subsplty. Socs. in Internal Medicine, 1978-85; mem. com. to assess quality care in Medicare program, Gen. Acctg. Office and House Ways and Means Com. U.S. Ho. of Reps., 1986-89. Editor 6 books; contbr. more than 260 articles to sci. jours., in books. Served as lt. comdr. USNR, 1960-62. Fellow ACP (gov. Ohio 1980-84, health and pub. policy com. 1982-91, chmn. 1986-88, chmn. med. tech. assessment com. 1985-86, regent 1985-91, chmn. clin. practice subcom. 1988-91, del. to AMA 1989-94, Spl. Presdl. citation 1984, master 1993), Am. Coll. Gastroenterology (pres. 1978-79, trustee, exec. com. 1975-80, master 1991); mem. Assn. Program Dirs. in Internal Medicine (founding pres. 1977-79, Founder's award 1993), Inst. Medicine of NAS (life), Am. Gastroent. Assn. (commn. on future 1973-74, tng. and edn. com. 1975-78, chmn. subcom. grad. edn. 1975-78), Interstate Postgrad. Med. Assn. (pres. 1983-84), Internat. Orgn. for Study Inflammatory Bowel Disease (dep. chmn. 1982-86). Democrat. Quaker. Home and Office: 9126 Town Gate Ln Bethesda MD 20817-4111

FARMER, THOMAS WOHLSEN, neurologist, educator; b. Lancaster, Pa., Sept. 18, 1914; s. Clarence R. and Laura (Wohlsen) F.; m. Phyllis McCormick, July 19, 1941; children: Pamela Farmer Henderson, Thomas Wohlsen. A.B., Harvard U., 1935, M.D., 1941; M.A., Duke U., 1937; postgrad., U. Copenhagen, 1957-58, U. Calif., San Diego, 1971-72. Diplomate: Am. Bd. Psychiatry and Neurology (dir. 1969—, pres. 1977). Intern Pa. Hosp., Phila., 1941-42; resident Boston City Hosp., 1942-43, Johns Hopkins Hosp., 1943-44, 46-47; mem. staff N.C. Meml. Hosp., Chapel Hill, 1952—; instr. medicine Johns Hopkins U., 1947-48; asst. prof. neurology Southwestern Med. Sch., U. Tex., Dallas, 1948-49; asso. prof. Southwestern Med. Sch., U. Tex., 1949-50, prof., 1950-52, prof. medicine, acting chmn. dept. medicine, 1951-52; prof. neurol. medicine, head div. neurology U. N.C., Chapel Hill, 1952—; Sarah Graham Kenan prof. medicine U. N.C., 1975—. Author: Pediatric Neurology, 1964, 3d edit., 1983, Neurologia Pediatrica, 1972. Served with USNR, 1944-46. Mem. Am. Acad. Neurology (nat. sec. 1955-57), Am. Neurol. Assn., Am. Acad. Neurology, ACP, AMA, Assn. Research Nervous and Mental Diseases, Child Neurology Soc. Home: 1304 Mason Farm Rd Chapel Hill NC 27514-4604 Office: U NC Sch Medicine Clin Scis Bldg Chapel Hill NC 27514

FARNHAM, JACK EDWIN, occupational medicine educator; b. Rutland, Vt. Sept. 26, 1931; s. Edwin John and Irma Louise (Kinney) F.; m. Anne Bertha Lyman, Sept. 8, 1956; children: Jean Louise, Carol Anne, James Edwin. AB, U. Vt., Burlington, 1953, MD, 1957; MPH, Harvard Sch. Pub. Health, 1992. Diplomate Am. Bd. Allergy and Immunology, Am. Bd. Preventive Medicine. Intern Henry Ford Hosp., Detroit, 1957-58; med. resident Lahey Clin., Boston, 1958-59, U. Vt. Med. Ctr., 1959-60, Henry Ford Hosp., 1962-63; clin. asst. medicine Mass. Gen. Hosp., Boston, 1968-94; lectr. in medicine Harvard U., Cambridge, Mass., 1993-94; physician Allergy-Immunology Assocs., Chelmsford, Mass., 1969-91; bd. dir. New Eng. Pollen Research, Chelmsford, 1981-90; cons. allergist Lowell Gen. Hosp. (Mass.), 1969-91; St. John's Hosp., Lowell, 1969-91, St. Joseph's Hosp., Lowell, 1969-91, Mass. Respiratory Hosp., Braintree, 1992-94; assoc. prof. occupl. medicine U. Tex. Health Ctr., Tyler, 1994—. Contbr. articles in field to profl. jours. Served to capt. M.C., USAF, 1960-62. Fellow Am. Acad. Allergy, Am. Coll. Allergy and Immunology; mem. AAAS, Am. Coll. Occupational and Environ. Medicine, Internat. Aerobiology Soc., Physicians for Social Responsibility, New Eng. Soc. Allergy, Mass. Allergy Soc. (sec. 1982-84, pres. 1987-88), Tex. Occupl. Medicine Assn., Tex. Allergy and Immunology Soc.. Methodist. Office: U Tex Health Ctr PO Box 2003 Tyler TX 75710

FARNSWORTH, CRAIG LEE, optometrist; b. Urbana, Ill., June 17, 1942; s. George Llelwyn and Gladys Fern (Kennedy) F.; m. Mary Ann DeLorenzo, Sept. 1982; children: Garrett Lawson, Karla Catherine. BS, Ind. U., 1962; DO, Ind. Sch. of Optometry, 1966. Pvt. practice Denver, 1968—; pres. Eye of a Champion, Inc., Lakewood, Colo., 1994—; adj. prof. U. Denver Dept. of Gerantology, Denver, 1994—; adv. mem. Acuvision Internat., Carlsbad, Calif., 1993—, U.S. Olympic Coms. Sports Medicine and Sci., Colorado Springs, 1986-88; profl. advisor Shooting Sports and Olympic Teams and Rsch. Coun., Colorado Springs, 1987-94. Author: Mastering Putting, 1996; inventor A-Lign, 1996; creator (game) Champions Challenge, 1995. Capt. U.S. Army, 1966-68. Mem. Am. Optometric Assn. (sports vision pres. 1984-86, Sports Vision Optometrist of Yr. 1991), Colo. Optometric Assn., European Acad. of Sports Vision (first pres. 1989-91). Office: Farnsworth & Politzer PC 550 S Wadsworth #201 Lakewood CO 80226

FARNSWORTH, ELLEN JANE, nursing educator; b. Boston, May 8, 1943; d. Edward Louis and Ellen Jane (McConnell) Lynsky; m. Richard Ransom Farnsworth, Dec. 16, 1967; children: Richard Edward, Ian Scott, Ellen Jane. Diploma in nursing, New England Bapt. Hosp., Boston, 1964; BSN, Boston U., 1968; MEd, Temple U., 1990; MS, Simmons Coll., 1996. Staff nurse Children's Hosp. Med. Ctr., Boston, 1965-67, New England Bapt. Hosp., 1964-65; clin. instr. New Eng. Bapt. Hosp., 1967-68; educator Lamaze childbirth Columbus (Ohio) Assn. Childbirth Edn., 1969-71; pvt. practice educator Lamaze childbirth Presque Isle, Maine, 1972-76, Haddonfield, N.J., 1977-82; clin. instr. Meth. Hosp., Phila., 1977-78; nurse Temple U. Health Svc., Phila., 1980-90; head nurse hosp. short procedure unit Temple U., Phila., 1990-92; asst. dir. continuing edn. health professions U. So. Maine, Portland, 1992-95; coll. health nurse Westbrook Coll., Portland, 1995—; co-founder, pres. Greater Camden Area Am. Soc.

Psychoprophylaxis Obstetrics Inc., Blackwood, N.J., 1979-81; regional trainer Am. Soc. Psychoprophylaxis Obstetrics, Washington, 1979-81; crew chief NCAA, 1987—, basic life support instr., 1992. V.p. Haddonfield Home Sch. Assn., 1979-81; dir. Peat Players, Phila., 1988-90. Recipient Mead Johnson award Nurses Ednl. Found., 1965; named Mass. Student Nurse of Yr., Mass. Student Nurses Assn., 1964. Mem. ANA, AAUW (v.p. Presque Isle chpt. 1974-76), Pa. Nurses Assn., Southea. Pa. Coll. Health Assn. (chairperson nominating com. 1986), Maine State Nurses Assn. (mem. govtl. rels. com.), Sigma Theta Tau, Eta Sigma Gamma.

FARON, JAMES F., optometrist; b. Chgo., Oct. 3, 1946; s. Frank and Rose A. (Podgorny) F.; m. Alice Odell, Dec. 5, 1971; children: Stephanie, Krista. BA, DePaul U., 1968; MA, Ohio State U., 1971; OD, Ill. Coll. Optometry, 1979. Tchr. St. Mary's Sch., Evanston, Ill., 1968-69; guidance counselor Greenville (S.C.) County Schs., 1971-74; optometrist Carle Clinic Assn., Urbana, Ill., 1979—. Mem. Am. Optometric Assn., East Ctrl. Optometric Soc. (pres. 1988), Ill. Optometric Assn., Champaign Apt. Assn. (pres. 1995). Home: 2014 Byrnebruk Rd Champaign IL 61821 Office: Carle Clinic 602 W University Urbana IL 61801

FARQUHAR, JOHN WILLIAM, physician, educator; b. Winnipeg, Man., Can., June 13, 1927; came to U.S., 1934; s. John Giles and Marjorie Victoria (Roberts) F.; m. Christine Louise Johnson, July 14, 1968; children: Margaret F., John C.M.; children by previous marriage: Bruce E., Douglas G. A.B., U. Calif., Berkeley, 1949; M.D., U. Calif., San Francisco, 1952. Intern U. Calif. Hosp., San Francisco, 1952-53; resident, 1953-54, 57-58, postdoctoral fellow, 1955-57; resident U. Minn., Mpls., 1954-55; research asso. Rockefeller U., N.Y.C., 1958-62; asst. prof. medicine Stanford (Calif.) U., 1962-66, asso. prof., 1966-73, prof., 1973—, C.F. Rehnborg prof. in disease prevention, 1989—; dir. Stanford Ctr. Research in Disease Prevention, 1973—; dir. collaborating ctr. for chronic disease prevention WHO, 1985—; prof. health rsch. and policy, 1988—; assoc. chief of staff for health promotion Stanford U. Hosp., 1994—; mem. staff Stanford U. Hosp.; chair Victoria Declaration Implementation com. Author: The American Way of Life Need Not Be Hazardous to Your Health, 1978, 2d edit., 1987, (with Gene Spiller) The Last Puff, 1990, The Victoria Declaration for Heart Health, 1992, The Catalonia Declaration: Investing in Heart Health, 1996; contbr. articles to profl. jours. Served with U.S. Army, 1945-46. Recipient James D. Bruce award ACP, 1983, Myrdal prize, 1986, Dana award for Pioneering Achievement in Health, Dana Found., 1990, Nat. Cholesterol award for Pub. Edn., Nat. Cholesterol Edn. Program of NIH, 1991, Rsch. Achievement award Am. Heart Assn., 1992, Order of St. George for Svc. to Autonomous Govt. of Catalonia, 1996. Mem. Inst. Medicine of NAS, Am. Soc. Clin. Investigation, Am. Heart Assn. (coun. epidemiology and prevention), Soc. Behavioral Medicine (pres. 1991-92), Gold Headed Cane Soc., Sigma Xi, Alpha Omega Alpha. Episcopalian. Office: Stanford U Sch of Medicine Ctr Rsch in Disease Prevention 1000 Welch Rd Palo Alto CA 94304-1825

FARQUHAR, MARILYN GIST, cell biology and pathology educator; b. Tulare, Calif., July 11, 1928; d. Brooks DeWitt and Alta (Green) Gist; m. John W. Farquhar, June 4, 1952; children: Bruce, Douglas (div. 1968); m. George Palade, June 7, 1970. AB, U. Calif., Berkeley, 1949, MA, 1952, PhD, 1955. Asst. rsch. pathologist Sch. Medicine U. Calif., San Francisco, 1956-58, assoc. rsch. pathologist, 1962-64, assoc. prof., 1964-68, prof. pathology, 1968-70; rsch. assoc. Rockefeller U., N.Y.C., 1958-62, prof. cell biology, 1970-73; prof. cell biology Sch. Medicine Yale U., New Haven, 1973-87, Sterling prof. cell biology and pathology, 1987-90; prof. pathology div. cell molecular medicine U. Calif., San Diego, 1990—, coord. div. cellular and molecular medicine, 1991—. Mem. editorial bd. numerous sci. jours.; contbr. articles to profl. jours. Recipient Career Devel. award NIH, 1968-73, Disting. Sci. medal Electron Microscope Soc., 1987. Mem. NAS, Am. Acad. Arts and Scis., Am. Soc. Cell Biology (pres. 1981-82, E.B. Wilson medal 1987), Am. Assn. Investigative Pathology, Am. Soc. Nephrology (Homer Smith award 1988). Home: 12894 Via Latina Del Mar CA 92014-3730

FARR, DAVID, cardiologist. BA, NYU, 1960, MD, 1964. Diplomate Am. Bd. Internal Medicine with subspecialty in cardiovascular disease. Rsch. fellow medicin/cardiology Harvard U., Boston, 1967-69; resident in cardiology Cleve. Clinic, 1969; pvt. practice Smithtown, N.Y.; dir. cardiology Southside Hosp., Bay Shore, N.Y., Cmty. Hosp. Western Suffolk, Smithtown; cons. cardiologist St. Francis Hosp., Roslyn, N.Y., Brookhaven Meml. Hosp., Patchoque, N.Y.; attending cardiologist St. John's Hosp., Smithtown, Good Samaritan Hosp., West Islip, N.Y.; asst. prof. clin. medicine SUNY-Stony Brook. N.Y. State Regents scholar, 1960. Fellow ACP, Am. Coll. Cardiology, Am. Coll. Chest Physicians, Phi Beta Kappa. Office: 48 Rt 25A Ste 209 Smithtown NY 11787-1448

FARR, JO-ANN HUNTER, psychologist; b. Brackenridge, Pa., Apr. 29, 1936; d. Francis Lytle and Dorothy (Colin) Hunter; m. William R. Hughes (div.); children: Cynthia Jo O'Hara, William Hunter, Christopher Eric, Michael Patrick, Amy Elizabeth; m. John E. Farr (div.); 1 child, John Herschel. BS in Psychology and Physiology, Pa. State U., 1970, MS in Psychology, 1971, PhD in Psychology, 1974. Diplomate Am. Bd. Sexology, Am. Acad. Clin. Sexologists (founding clin. fellow 1991); cert. sex therapist, supv. sex therapy, sex educator; cert. clin. hypnosis; cert. con. in clin. hypnosis. Dir., therapist Devel. Vision Ctr., State College, Pa., 1969-71; cons. Pk. Forest Nursery Sch., State College, Pa., 1970-71; in-take supr. psychol. clin. Pa. State U., University Park, 1972-73; cons. Centre County Youth Svc. Bur., State College, 1972-78, Juniata Tri-County Mental Health/Mental Retardation Adminstrn., Lewistown, Pa., 1974-76; asst. prof. of psychology Pa. State U., 1975-77; pvt. practice State College, 1977—; sponsored NIMH guest lectr. Kinsey Inst., Bloomington, Ind. Contbr. articles to profl. jours. Mem. Govs. Counsel for Sexual Minorities, Pa.; bd. dirs. Pa. Assoc. of Families, State Coll., Parents Without Ptnrs., State Coll. John W. White fellow Pa. State U., 1970-71, U.S. Pub. Health Svc. fellow Pa. State U., 1970-74; nominated Outstanding Pennsylvanian State Dept. of Health adn Welfare, 1986. Fellow Am. Acad. Clin. Sexologists (clin.); mem. APA, Sex Info. and Edn. coun. U.S. (assoc.), Assn. for Advancement of Behavior Therapy, Soc. for Sci. Study of Sex, Am. Soc. Sex Educators, Counselors and Therapists, Assn. Behavior Analysts, Pa. Psychol. Assn., Nat. Register Health Svc. Providers, Mental Health Profls. of Cen. Pa., Am. Soc. Clin. Hypnosis (cert. in clin. hypnosis, approved cons. in clin. hypnosis). Office: Jo-Ann Hunter Farr & Assocs 3490 W College Ave State College PA 16801-2505

FARR, LEE EDWARD, physician; b. Albuquerque, Oct. 13, 1907; s. Edward and Mabel (Heyn) F.; m. Anne Ritter, Dec. 28, 1936 (dec.); children: Charles E., Susan A., Frances A.; m. Miriam Kirk, Jan. 12, 1985. BS, Yale U., 1929, MD, 1933. Asst. pediatrics Sch. Medicine, Yale U., 1933-34; asst. medicine Hosp. of Rockefeller Inst. Med. Rsch., 1934-37, assoc. medicine, 1937-40; dir. research Alfred I. duPont Inst. of Nemours Found., Wilmington, Del., 1940-49; vis. assoc. prof. pediatrics Sch. Medicine, U. Pa., 1940-49; med. dir. Brookhaven Nat. Lab., 1948-62; prof. nuclear medicine U. Tex. Postgrad. Med. Sch., 1962-64, prof. nuclear and environ. medicine Grad. Sch. Bio-Med. Scis., U. Tex. at Houston, 1965-68; chief sect. nuc. medicine U. Tex.-M.D. Anderson Hosp. and Tumor Inst., 1962-67, prof. environ. health U. Tex. Sch. Pub. Health, Houston, 1967-68; head disaster health svcs. Calif. Dept. Health, 1968, chief emergency health svcs. unit, 1968-70, 1st chief bur. emergency med. services, 1970-73; Lippitt lectr. Marquette U., 1941; Sommers Meml. lectr. U. Oreg. Sch. Med., Portland, 1960; Gordon Wilson lectr. Am. Clin. and Climatol. Assn., 1956; Sigma Xi nat. lectr., 1952-53; guest scientist Institut fur Medizinder Kernforschungsanlage, Julich, Germany, 1966; Brookhaven Nat. Lab. lectr., 1990. Mem. NRC adv. com. Naval Med. Res., 1953-68; chmn. NRC adv. com. Atomic Bomb Casualty Commn., 1953-68; mem. adv. com. Naval Res. to Sec. of Navy and CNO, 1968-72; NRC adv. com. on medicine and surgery, 1965-66, exec. com., 1962-65; Naval Research Mission to Formosa, 1953; tech. adviser U.S. delegation to Geneva Internat. Conf. for Peaceful Uses Atomic Energy, 1955; mem. N.Y. Adv. Com. Atomic Energy, 1956-59; mem. cholera commn. SEATO Conf., Bangkok, 1960; mem. AMA Com. Nuclear Medicine, 1963-66; mem. com. med. isotopes NASA Manned Spacecraft Ctr., 1966-68; mem. expert adv. panel radiation WHO, 1957-79; mem. Calif. Gov.'s Ad Hoc Com. Emergency Health Service, 1968-69; mem. sci. adv. bd. Gorgas Meml. Inst., 1967-72; numerous other sci. adv. bds., panels; cons. TRW Systems, Inc., 1966-70, Consol. Petroleum Co., Beverly Hills, Calif., 1946-70. Mem. alumni bd. Yale, 1962-65, mem. alumni fund, 1966-76, agent alumni fund 1994—. With USNR, 1942-46; capt. (M.C.) USNR, ret. Recipient Mead Johnson award for pediatric research, 1940, Gold Cross Order of Phoenix, Greece, 1960, Verdienstkreuz 1st class Fed. Republic Germany, 1963; named Community Leader in Am., 1969, Disting. Alumni Yale U. Med. Sch., 1989. Diplomate Nat. Bd. Med. Examiners, Am. Bd. Pediatrics. Fellow AAAS, Royal Soc. Arts, Am. Acad. Pediatrics, N.Y. Acad. Scis., Royal Soc. Health, Am. Coll. Nuclear Medicine (disting. fellow); mem. Soc. Pediatric Research, Soc. Exptl. Biology, Harvey Soc., Am. Pediatric Soc., Soc. Exptl. Pathology, Am. Soc. Clin. Investigation, Radiation Research Soc., AMA (mem. council on sci. assembly 1960-70, chmn. 1968-70), Med. Soc. Athens (hon. mem.), Alameda County Med. Assn., Sigma Xi, Alpha Omega Alpha, Phi Sigma Kappa, Nu Sigma Nu, Alpha Chi Sigma. Club: Commonwealth (San Francisco). Author articles on nuclear medicine, protein metabolism, emergency med. services, radioactive and chem. environ. contaminants, environ. noise. Home: 2502 Saklan Indian Dr Apt 2 Walnut Creek CA 94595-3001

FARRAR, HENRY CHEAIRS, surgeon; b. Nashville, Dec. 20, 1926; s. Henry Cheairs and Nina Ellen (Mills) F.; m. Grace Angeline Johnson, Dec. 2, 1950; children: Paul, Martha, David, Henry III, Lee, Samantha. BA, U. Tenn., 1948, MS, 1950; MD, U. Tenn., Memphis, 1954; LLD, Harding U., 1973. Diplomate Am. Bd. Surgery. Intern Tampa (Fla.) Mcpl. Hosp., 1954-55; sr. asst. surgeon USPHS, Harlingen, Tex., 1955-57; resident in surgery Miners Meml. Hosp., Harlan, Ky., 1958-60; sr. surgery resident City Hosp., Winston Salem, N.C., 1960-62; surgeon Vets. Hosp., Johnson City, Tenn., 1962-64; missionary surgeon Nigerian Christian Hosp., Aba, Nigeria, 1964-67, 70-73, 83-84, Chimala Mission Hosp., Mbeya, Tanzania, 1979-80; surgeon Goodlark Hosp., Dickson, Tenn., 1967-69, White County Hosp., Searcy, Ark., 1973-82, Humana Hosp., Lebanon, Tenn., 1985-90; mem. Tenn. Med. Bd.; surgeon Carthage (Tenn.) Gen. Hosp., 1989—; vis. prof. surgery China Med. U., Shenyang, Liaoning Province, 1982-83. Trustee African Christian Hosps., Searcy, 1975—; founder Nigerian Christian Hosp., Aba, 1965. Christian Mobile Clinic, Kumba, Cameroon, Africa, 1968; elder Ch. of Christ, Lebanon, 1987—; trustee Harding U., 1993—; hon. trustee African Christian Schs., Nashville, 1993—. Recipient U. Tenn. Med. Sch. Verstandig award, 1954; named Outstanding Alumnus, Harding U., 1975. Fellow ACS (instr. advanced trauma life support 1989); mem. Tenn. Med. Assn., Phi Kappa Phi. Democrat. Home: 712 Spring Creek Rd Lebanon TN 37087-0356 Office: Carthage Gen Hospital Carthage TN 37030

FARRAR, LYNDA FAIVRE, optometrist; b. Reedsburg, Wis., Sept. 22, 1947; d. Everett Ernest and Kathleen (Page) F.; m. Dennis Edwin Farrar, Aug. 25, 1968; children: Erin, Erik, Elin. BS, Ill. Coll. Optometry, 1971, OD, 1971. Instr. Ill. Coll. Optometry, Chgo., 1971; optometrist Drs. Farrar & James, Oregon, Wis., 1971—; practice optometry Jackson Clinic, Madison, Wis., 1984—; instr. Madison Area Tech. Sch. 1978-82; mem. dept. licensing and regulation Wis. Optometry Examining Bd., Madison, 1984—, chair, 1991—; bd. dirs. Valley Bank of Oregon. Pres. Oregon Preschool Inc., 1980-81, 82-83. Mem. Am. Optometric Assn., Wis. Optometric Assn., Madison Area Optometric Soc., Epsilon Sigma Alpha. Methodist. Home: 298 Waterman St Oregon WI 53575-1553 Office: 185 W Netherwood Oregon WI 53575-1553

FARRAR, THOMAS CROWELL, emergency services physician; b. Memphis, Mar. 18, 1952; s. Dan Butler and Vivian Laura (Crowell) F.; m. Jean Louise Olsen, June 6, 1981; children: Allison Elise, Ryan Thomas. BA cum laude, Vanderbilt U., 1974; MD, U. Tenn. Ctr. Health, 1977. Diplomate Am. Bd. Emergency Medicine. Emergency dept. physician Edgefield Hosp., Nashville, 1983-91, Baptist Meml. Hosp., Memphis, 1991—; assoc. med. dir. Miller Med. Group, Nashville, 1986-91; vice chmn. emergency dept. east Baptist Meml. Hosp., 1996—. Fellow Am. Coll. Emergency Physicians (bd. dirs. Tenn. chpt. 1991-93), Am. Acad. Emergency Physicians; mem. AMA, Tenn. Med. Assn., Memphis-Shelby County Med. Soc. Home: 2292 Coathbridge Dr Germantown TN 38139

FARRÉ, JERÓNIMO JIMENEZ, cardiologist; b. Madrid, July 1, 1947; s. Fernando and Alicia (Muncharaz) F.; m. Rosa Buj, Oct. 23, 1972. MD, U. Complutense, Madrid, 1970; PhD, U. Autonoma, Madrid, 1988. Resident cardiology FJD, Madrid, 1970-74, staff cardiologist, 1975-77, dir. EP Lab., 1979-90, chief divsn. medicine, 1991-92, dir. coronary care unit and EP Lab., 1992—, assoc. chief cardiology, 1992-94, acting chief cardiology, 1994—; staff cardiologist H. LaPaz, Madrid, 1975; rsch. fellow Acad. Hosp Maastricht, 1977-78. Author: Cardiac Arrhythmias, 1992. Fellow European Soc. Cardiology. Office: Dept Cardiology, Fundacion Timenor Diaz, Avda Reyes Catolicos 2, 28040 Madrid Spain

FARRELL, BARBARA LOU, nursing consultant, resort owner; b. Bklyn., May 16, 1935; d. Edwin Linwood and Ada Louise (Bundrick) F. AA, Green Mountain Coll., 1955; BS, Columbia U., 1958, MA, 1966. Nursing supr., instr. Columbia-Presbyn. Hosp. Emergency Services, N.Y.C., 1958-62; commd. 2d lt. USAF, 1962, advanced through ranks to lt. col., resigned, 1976; asst. chief nurse for ambulatory care VA Med. Ctr., San Francisco, 1976-80, assoc. chief nursing services, 1980-83; pres. Timberhill Ranch Ltd., Timbercove, Calif., 1983—; cons. to surgeon gen. Aerospace Nursing, 1973-76; from med. augmentee to chmn. dept. nursing David Grant USAF Med. Ctr., Travis AFB, 1976-90. Advisor Redwood Coast Med. Svc., Stewart Point, Calif., 1983-85. Served to col. USAFR, 1980-90. Fellow Aerospace Med. Assn. (assocs., pres. flight nurses sect. 1975-76); mem. Am. Nurses Assn. Mem. Reformed Ch. Am. Home and Office: Timberhill Ranch 35755 Hauser Bridge Rd Cazadero CA 95421-9611

FARRELL, FRANCINE ANNETTE, psychotherapist, educator, author; b. Long Beach, Calif., Mar. 26, 1948; d. Thomas and Evelyn Marie (Lucente) F.; m. James Thomas Hanley, Dec. 5, 1968 (div. Dec. 1988); children: Melinda Lee Hanley, James Thomas Hanley Jr.; m. Robert Erich Haesche, June 3, 1995. BA in Psychology with honors, Calif. State U., Sacramento, 1985, MS in Counseling, 1986. Lic. marriage, family and child counselor, Calif.; nat. cert. addiction counselor. Marriage, family and child counselor intern Fulton Ct. Counseling, Sacramento, 1987-88; pvt. practice psychotherapist Sacramento, 1988—; instr. chem. dependency studies program, Calif. State U., Sacramento, 1985-94, acad. coord. chem. dependency studies program, 1988-90; trainee Sobriety Brings a Change, Sacramento, 1986-87; assoc. investigator, curriculum coord. Project S.A.F.E., Sacramento, 1990-91; presenter Sacramento Conf., ACA, 1986, 88, 89, 91, 92, Ann. Symposium on Chem. Dependency, 1993. Presenter (cable TV series) Trouble in River City: Charting a Course for Change, 1991. Mem. Nat. Coun. on Alcoholism, Calif. Assn. Marriage and Family Therapists, Calif. Assn. Alcoholism and Drug Abuse Counselors (bd. dirs. region 5, 1988-90), Phi Kappa Phi. Roman Catholic. Office: 2740 Fulton Ave # 100 Sacramento CA 95821-5108

FARRELL, GREGORY ALAN, biomedical engineer; b. Bklyn., May 12, 1942; s. Edmond William and Edna Florence (Williams) F.; BS in Mech. Engring., Cooper Union, 1964; MS in Biomed. Enggring., Columbia U., 1972, postgrad., 1972—; m. Mary Louise Lupiani, Sept. 3, 1966; children: Juliana Eden, Cristina Elizabeth. Mech. engr. Gen. Dynamics, San Diego, 1964-65, Rochester, N.Y., 1965-67; research asst. Columbia U. Med. Sch., N.Y.C., 1968-69; instr. pathology N.Y. Med. Coll., 1969-72; research engr. Technicon Instruments Corp., Tarrytown, N.Y., 1972-82; mgr. mech. engring. Baker Instruments Corp., Allentown, Pa., 1982-84, prin. mech. engr., 1984-86; prin. engr. Nat. Patent Devel. Corp., N.Y.C., 1986-87; project engr. Bayer Diagnostics (formerly Miles Diagnostics) (formerly Technicon Instruments), Tarrytown, N.Y., 1987-90, project mgr. 1990—. Patentee in field; achievements include product devel. of several automated clin. hematology and other instruments; contbr. articles to profl. jours. Democrat. Roman Catholic. Home: 447 Hillcrest Rd Ridgewood NJ 07450-1520 Office: Bayer Diagnostics 511 Benedict Ave Tarrytown NY 10591-5005

FARRELL, JOHN TIMOTHY, hospital administrator; b. St. Louis, Feb. 22, 1947; s. Michael James and Jane Frances (Lautenschlager) F.; m. Martha Anne Paynter, June 4, 1971; children: Kathleen Marie, Margaret Mary, Anne Elizabeth, John Timothy, Mary Ellen B.A. in Philosophy, Cardinal Glennon Coll., 1969; postgrad., U. Mo., 1969-71; M.H.A., St. Louis U., 1973. Adminstrv. resident St. John's Mercy Med. Center, St. Louis, 1970-72, 73, exec. v.p., chief operating officer, 1979-86; pres., chief exec. officer St. John's Mercy Med. Ctr., St. Louis, 1986-95; pres., chief exec. officer St. John's Mercy Hosp., 1986-95, chmn. bd. trustees, 1991-95; asst. exec. dir. St. Mary's Hosp., Richmond, Va., 1973-74, assoc. exec. dir., 1974-76; adminstr. St. Francis Mercy Hosp., Washington, Mo., 1976-78, exec. v.p., 1978-95; chmn. bd., pres., CEO St. John's Mercy Health Sys., 1994-95; cons. health care St. Louis, 1995-96; v.p. employee benefits Anheuser-Busch Cos., Inc., St. Louis, 1996—; adj. faculty mem., designated preceptor Grad. Program in Hosp. and Health Adminstrn., Xavier U., Cin., 1989; pres. Mercy Doctors Bldg., Inc., 1986-93, Mercy Health Ventures, Inc., Edgewood Program, Inc.; mem. health adv. bd. Sisters of Mercy of the Union, Province St. Louis, 1976-79, mem. personnel com., 1978-79; mem. Catholic health care facilities com. Mo. Cath. Conf., Jefferson City, 1976-82, chmn., 1979-82, mem. health affairs task force, 1977-82; mem. adv. com. med. records technician program St. Mary's Coll., O'Fallon, Mo., 1978-79; mem. subcom. on svcs. pediatric tech. adv. group Health Systems Agy., 1978-79; mem. mental health task force St. Louis-Jefferson-Franklin Counties, Devel. Mental Health Facilities, 1977-79; mem. steering subcom. Health Systems Agy. Local Impact Com., 1979; Mercy Physicians Partnership; mem. shared svcs. coun. Sisters of Mercy Health Sys., St. Louis; adj. instr. health care adminstrn. Washington U. Sch. Medicine, St. Louis, 1985—; pres. bd. dirs. Area Rescue Consortium of Hosp., St. Louis, 1988, 91-92, sec., bd. dirs., 1989-94, v.p., treas., 1990; mem. steering com. Greater St. Louis Healthcare Alliance, 1993-95, mem. exec. com., 1993-95, mem. quality measurement com., 1992; cons. com. St. Louis Regional Hosp., 1992-93; program com. Coun. Tchg. Hosps., 1993-94; bd. mgrs. Unity Health Network, 1994-95; bd. dirs. Mercy Med. Group; trustee Mercy Health Plan, 1994—. Mem. mgmt. adv. com. Washington (Mo.) Sch. Dist., 1976-79; bd. dirs. St. Francis Mercy Hosp., 1979-82, Mercy Health Conf., 1982-84, Family Planning Coun. St. Louis, 1979-81, mem. personnel com., 1979-81, budget com., 1980; bd. dirs. Mercy Hosp., Mansfield, Mo., 1983-87, St. John's Regional Hosp., Springfield, Mo., 1987-94, Affiliated Hosp. Dialysis Ctr., St. Louis, 1986—, Midwest Stone Inst., 1987-92; mem. CEO coun., corp. ethics com. Sisters of Mercy Health Systems, St. Louis, 1987-89; pres., bd. dirs. Cath. Outreach Cmty. Program, 1992; bd. dirs. United Way Greater St. Louis, 1995—, chmn. hosp. sect. campaign, 1988, chmn. Health Svcs., 1994, mem. area wide rels. com., 1995—; bd. dirs., chmn. postgrad. conf. St. Louis U. Alumni; mem. Parish Coun. St. Genevieve DuBois, St. Louis, 1989-92, pres., 1991-92; mem. Brotherhood/Sisterhood dinner com. NCCJ, St. Louis, 1990-94; bd. dirs. James Clinic Mercy Med. Group, Rolla, Mo., 1992-94, chmn. bd. dirs. Cath. Cmty. Svcs., 1992—; fundraising com. St. Louis County Police and Firefighter Meml., 1993; exec. com. Joint Hosp. Assn. Met. St. Louis and St. Louis Met. Med. Soc., 1991-93; bd. dirs. Priests Mutual Benefits Soc., 1996—. Mem. Am. Coll. Hosp. Adminstrs., Mo. Hosp. Assn. (chmn. bd. trustees 1993, chmn.-elect 1992, past chmn. 1994, trustee 1989, 91-95, chmn. coun. rsch. and policy devel. 1990, chmn. fin. and budget 1991, annual meeting com.), Hosp. Assn. Met. St. Louis (coun. on fin. 1979-81, chmn. environ. svcs. com. 1981-86, mem. coun. mgmt. svcs. 1981-86, physician rels. com. 1987-88, chmn. coun. on pub. policy and issues 1987-88, bd. dirs. sec. 1991, treas. 1992, vice chmn. 1993, chmn. 1994), Midwest Stone Inst. (pres. 1988-92, bd. dirs. 1988-93), St. Louis U. Sch. Pub. Health Alumni Assn. (pres. 1991-92), Shared Resources Enterprise (bd. dirs. 1990, treas. 1991, sec. 1992, vice chmn. bd. dirs. 1993, chmn. 1994), Mental Health Assn. (host Spirit of St. Louis com. 1990), Creve Coeur Squires. Home: 537 Meadow Creek Ln Saint Louis MO 63122-1656

FARRELL, KATHERINE PATRICIA MARY, physician, public health administrator; b. Cork, Ireland, Feb. 5, 1948; d. Vincent William and Ellen Margaret (Cronin) O'Connell; m. Bernard Patrick Farrell, Mar. 30, 1972; children: Jeannette, Maire, Deirdre. MB, BCh, BAO, Univ. Coll. Cork, Ireland, 1972; MPH, Johns Hopkins U., 1978. Resident in internal medicine South Balt. Gen. Hosp., 1973-74; med. dir. alcohol rehab. unit Crownsville (Md.) Hosp., 1975-76; resident in preventive medicine Md. Dept. Health and Mental Hygiene, Balt., 1976-78, divsn. chief environ. disease control, 1978-87; adminstr. Ctr. Environ. Health Md. Dept. Environ., Balt., 1987-88, asst. sec. for toxics environ. sci. and health, 1988-90; dir. cmty. health Anne Arundel County Health Dept., Annapolis, Md., 1990-92, dep. health officer for pub. health, 1993—; mem. adv. com. Pub. Health Residency U. Md., 1993—, Johns Hopkins Preventive Medicine, 1993—; mem. local planning bd. Anne Arundel County, 1993—; active Howard County Bd. Health, Columbia Md., Md. Occupl. Safety and Health Bd., Balt., Med. Ch. Faculty of Md.; adj. asst. prof. epidemiology and preventive medicine, U. Md. Contbr. articles to profl. jours. Recipient Woman Mgr. of Yr. Recognition cert. State of Md., 1981, 83. Mem. Delta Omega (hon.). Roman Catholic. Office: Anne Arundel County Dept Health 3 Harry S. Truman Pkwy Annapolis MD 21401

FARRELL, KENNETH HAYS, otolaryngologist; b. Washington, Oct. 23, 1942; s. George Raymond and Frances (Humphrey) F.; m. Jacqueline Maynard, Nov. 10, 1967; children: John, Jennifer. BS, U. Wis., 1963; MD, U. Ill., Chgo., 1967. Diplomate Am. Bd. Otolaryngology. Intern U. Ill. Hosp., Chgo., 1967-68; resident Mayo Clinic, Rochester, Minn., 1968-73; pvt. practice Ft. Lauderdale, Fla., 1975—; chief of surgery Broward Gen. Med. Ctr., Ft. Lauderdale, 1983-84; chief staff, 1984-86. Elder 1st Presbyn. Ch., Ft. Lauderdale, 1989-91. Comdr. M.C., USN, 1973-75. Fellow ACS, Am. Acad. Otolaryngology, Am. Rhinologic Soc.; mem. Broward County Med. Assn. (chmn. bd. censors 1982-84, sec. 1984-85), Royal Soc. Medicine. Democrat. Presbyterian. Office: 1112 E Broward Blvd Fort Lauderdale FL 33301-2012

FARRELL, PATRICIA ANN, psychologist, educator; b. N.Y.C., Mar. 11, 1945; d. Joseph Alexander and Pauline (Loth) F.; BA, Queens Coll., 1976; MA, N.Y. U., 1978, PhD, 1990. Diplomate Am. Bd. Forensic Examiners; lic. psychologist, N.J., Fla. Assoc. editor Pubs. Weekly Mag., N.Y.C., 1968-72; editor Bestsellers Mag., N.Y.C., 1972-73; assoc. editor King Features Syndicate, N.Y.C., 1973-78; staff psychologist, intake coord. Mid-Bergen Cmty. Mental Health Ctr., Paramus, N.J., 1978-84; instr. Bergen C.C., Paramus, 1978-94; adj. prof. The Union Inst., Cin., Walden U. cons. faculty. Thomas Edison State Coll.; resident clin. psychology Am. Inst. for Counseling, N.J., 1990-91; cons. Family Counseling Svc. of Ridgewood, N.J., 1984; clin. psychology intern Marlboro Psychiat. Hosp., N.J., 1984-85, staff psychologist, 1985-87; rsch. analyst Mt. Sinai Sch. of Medicine, 1987-88; account exec., sr. sci. writer Manning, Selvage and Lee, N.Y.C., 1988-90; sr. clin. psychologist, mem. med. staff Greystone Park (N.J.) Psychiat. Hosp., 1990-96; pvt. practice psychology, Englewood Cliffs, N.J.; health sci. editor Time Warner Cable, Channel 10 News, 1995—; cons. Intensive Weight Loss Program, Cath. Med. Ctr. Bklyn. and Queens; cons. pharm. clin. protocols; cons. to Thomas Edison State Coll. Distance Learning program; guest radio shows Sta. WWDJ, Hackensack, N.J., Montel Williams, Mark Walberg, Dini, Camilla Scott, USA Alive and Wellness with Carol Martin, News Talk, Maury Povich TV Show, The Carnie Wilson Show, Judge For Yourself TV Show, N.Y.C. Ten O'Clock News, WPIX-TV, N.Y., WWOR-TV News, WNRR-TV, In Your Interest, LTV, Channel 10 News, On Campus, Sta. WTTM, WSNJ, WHSI-TV, Common Concerns, WHSE-TV. Contbr. book chpt. to Innovations in Clinical Practice: A Source Book 15th edit., and articles to Writer's Digest, Real World, Postgrad. Medicine, Psychotherapy, New England Jour. Medicine, and newspapers, author manual Alzheimer's Disease Assessment Scale test. Mem. Bergen County Task Force on Crimes Against Children, Bergen County Task Force on Alcoholism and Drunken Driving, 1984; bd. dirs., chmn. med. liaison com. liaison to dept. psychiatry Bergen Pines County Hosp., Paramus, N.J., 1994-95. McDonald's rsch. grantee, 1994-95; recipient Good Citizen award DAR, Sci. award Rotary Club. Fellow Am. Bd. Disability Analysts; mem. AAAS, APA, Assn. for Advancement Psychology, Assn. for Indep. Video and Filmmakers, Prescribing Psychologists Inc. (chartered registrant), NYU/Bellevue Psychiatric Soc. Avocations: fitness, racquetball, kite-flying. Office: PO Box 1283 Englewood Cliffs NJ 07632

FARRELL, PAUL WILLIAM, cardiologist; b. Zanesville, Ohio, Apr. 12, 1946; s. Donald M. and Dorothy Hutcheson Burke; m. Karen Ann Hune, Sept. 19, 1970; children: Christina, Paul, Scott. BS, USAF Acad., Colo. Springs, 1969; MD, Ohio State U., 1973. Diplomate Am. Bd. Internal Medicine, Am. Bd. Cardiology. Chief cardiology USAF, Keesler AFB, Miss., 1979-82, chmn. dept. internal medicine, 1979-82, dir. internal medicine residency, 1979-82, cons. surgery, gen. internal medicine, cardiology, 1979-82; pvt. practice cardiology Fla. Cardiovasc. Cons., Jacksonville, 1982-94, Jacksonville Heart Ctr., 1994—. Pres. N.E. Fla. chpt. Am. Heart Assn., Jacksonville, 1986-88; pres. St. Matthew's Lutheran Ch., Jacksonville, 1990-

91, 96—; bd. dirs. Jacksonville Jaguar Youth Soc., 1988—. Named Disting. Grad. USAF Acad., 1969. Fellow ACP, Am. Coll. Cardiology, Am. Heart Assn.; mem. Soc. Air Force Physicians (bd. dirs. 1979-82), Alpha Omega Alpha. Lutheran. Office: Jacksonville Heart Ctr 836 Prudential Dr Ste 1700 Jacksonville FL 32207

FARRELL, PHILIP M., physician, educator, researcher; b. St. Louis, Nov. 26, 1943; m. Alice Yeakle; children: Michael Henry, David Sean, Bridget Mary. A.B., St. Louis U., 1964, M.D., 1970, Ph.D., 1970. Diplomate Am. Bd. Pediatrics. Asst. prof. dept. child health Washington U., Washington, 1975; asst. prof. dept. pediatrics U. Wis., Madison, 1977-78, assoc. prof. pediatrics, 1978-82, prof. pediatrics, 1982—, chmn. dept. pediatrics, 1985—, affiliate scientist Wis. Regional Primate Research Ctr., 1978, affiliate faculty dept. nutrition scis., 1978, dir. Pediatric Pulmonary Specialized Ctr. of Research, 1981—, co-dir. Cystic Fibrosis Ctr., 1983—, dean Med. Sch.; sr. investigator pediatric metabolism br. Nat. Inst. Arthritis, Metabolism and Digestive Diseases NIH, Bethesda, Md., 1974-75, chief sect. on devel. biology and clin. nutrition Neonatal and Pediatric Medicine br. Nat. Inst. Child Health and Human Devel., 1975, chief Neonatal and Pediatric Medicine br., 1975. Editor: Lung Development: Biological and Clinical Perspectives, 1982. Avalon Found. scholar, 1965-67, Thurston Meml. scholar, 1966-70; Fogarty Internat. fellow, 1985. Mem. Am. Chem. Soc., Am. Acad. Pediatrics, Soc. Pediatric Research, Am. Thoracic Soc., Soc. Exptl. Biology and Medicine, Am. Inst. Nutrition, Am. Soc. Clin. Nutrition, Wis. Assn. Perinatal Care, Sigma XI, Phi Beta Kappa, Alpha Omega Alpha. Home: 2783 Marshall Pky Madison WI 53713-1022 Office: Univ Wis Dept Pediatrics 600 Highland Ave Madison WI 53792-0001*

FARRINGER, JOHN LEE, III, dentist; b. Nashville, Dec. 13, 1947; s. John Lee Jr. and Mary Margaret (Smith) F.; m. Maribeth Ann West, June 20, 1970; children: Jennifer, John, Robert. BA, Vanderbilt U., 1969; DDS, U. Tenn., 1973. Pvt. practice Nashville, 1973—; mem. faculty Vanderbilt U. Med. Sch., Nashville, 1984-89; cons. St. Thomas Sleep Disorders Ctr., Nashville, 1985—. Pres. Vol. Study Club, Nashville, 1974; dist. chmn. Nashville area Boy Scouts Am. Recipient Silver Beaver award Boy Scouts Am., 1990. Mem. ADA, Am. Equilibraiton Soc., Am. Acad. Head, Neck, Facial Pain and TMJ Orthopedics, Tenn. Dental Assn., Tenn. CRANIO (sec.-treas. 1980, pres. 1982), Nashville Dental Assn., Rotary (treas. 1989, v.p. 1990). Roman Catholic. Office: 4205 Hillsboro Rd Nashville TN 37215-3336

FARRINGTON, BERTHA LOUISE, nursing administrator; b. Poteet, Tex., Jan. 20, 1937; d. Leonard Gilbert and Janie (Hernandez) Lozano; m. James Charles Farrington, Jan. 30, 1965; children: Mark Hiram, Robert Lee. BSN, Tex. Women's U., 1960; NP, U. Tex., 1984. RN, Tex. Charge nurse emergency rm. Parkland Meml. Hosp., Dallas; head nurse emergency rm./day surgery Bapt. Meml. Hosp., Pensacola, Fla.; asst. dir. health svcs. U. Tex. Southwestern Med. Ctr., Dallas, dir. student health svcs.

FARRIS, EDWARD THOMPSON, dentist, medical researcher, real estate developer and broker; b. Ft. Worth, Sept. 9, 1925; s. Chester Arthur and Bernice Boyd (Thompson) F.; m. Helen Dean Williams, Apr. 21, 1950 (div. 1976); children: Mark Alan, Glen Edward; m. Ethel Lynn Melnick, Dec. 10, 1984 (dec. Oct. 1993). AS, U. Tex., Arlington, 1944; BA in Biology, U. North Tex., 1948, MA in Biology, 1953; DDS, Baylor U., 1953. Lic. dentist, Tex., real estate broker. Dentist Dallas, 1953—; owner, pres., chmn. Celestial Ctr., Inc., Dallas, 1968—; pres. PEP II Ptnrs. Inc., Dallas, 1992-93, C.B.E., Inc., Sunshine Realty Co., Inc.; gen. ptnr. Edward T. Farris Co., Ltd. Producer: (ednl. film) Texas Our Texas, 1968; producer, pub.: Outdoor Plants of the Southwest, 1982; patentee in med./dental field, automotive safety systems. Active Circle Ten. coun. Boy Scouts Am., 1967-90; charter mem. Rep. Task Force, 1994—. Served as sgt. U.S. Army, 1944-46, ETO. Decorated Bronze Star. Recipient Award of Merit Boy Scouts Am., 1977, Silver Beaver award Boy Scouts Am., 1979. Mem. Beta Beta Beta (hon.), Omicron Kappa Upsilon (hon.). Baptist. Lodges: Shriners, Masons (32 degree). Home: 1928 Cobblestone Ln Garland TX 75042-4652 Office: Celestial Ctr Inc 4715 Greenville Ave Dallas TX 75206-4117

FARRON, ROBERT, physician, family practice; b. N.Y.C., May 17, 1947; s. Irving and Anne (Zavoznick) F.; m. Lorraine Herzberg, May 27, 1972; children: Cory, Eric, Jeffrey. BS, CCNY, 1968; DO, Kansas City Coll. Osteo. Med., 1972. Diplomate Am. Bd. Family Practice, Am. Osteo. Bd. Family Practice. Intern Interboro Gen. Hosp., Bklyn., 1972-73; practice medicine specializing in family practice Far Rockaway, N.Y., 1973—, Valley Stream, N.Y., 1978—; attending physician Peninsula Hosp. Ctr., Far Rockaway, N.Y., 1985—; asst. prof. family practice N.Y. Coll. Osteopathic Medicine. Recipient Physicians Recognition award AMA, 1983, 86, 89, 92, 95. Fellow Am. Acad. Family Physicians; mem. Am. Osteo. Assn., N.Y. Osteo. Soc., Am. Osteo. Coll. Family Practice, Mensa, N.Y. State Med. Soc., Queens County Med. Soc. Office: 2240 Mott Ave Far Rockaway NY 11691-3070 also: 201-5 E Merrick Rd Valley Stream NY 11580

FARROW, ROBERT CONVERSE, health care administrator; b. Greensville, S.C., Dec. 8, 1936; s. Willie and Azzle (Knuckles) F.; m. Violet Alice Brockenbrough, July 7, 1962; children: Robert Wayne, Trina Lynn Farrow-Ware. BA, Bklyn. Coll., 1970; MA, NYU, 1974; MPH, Columbia U., 1982. Cert. Am. Coll. Health Care Adminstrs.; cert. sch. counselor; cert. nursing home adminstr. Sch. counselor Salem (N.J.) Bd. Edn., 1970-71; asst. adminstr. Victory Lake Nursing Ctr., Hyde Park, N.Y., 1971-87; adminstr. Victory Lake Nursing Ctr., Hyde Park, 1987—; mem. Dutchess County Bd. Coop. Edn., Poughkeepsie, N.Y., 1974-83, Hospice, Poughkeepsie, 1986-89. With U.S. Army, 1960-64. Recipient Summer Excellence award U.S. Dept. Labor Summer Youth Employment, 1979, Gentleman Distinction award The Bykota Club, 1990. Mem. APHA, Am. Coll. Health Care Execs., Am. Coll. Health Care Adminstrs. (pres. N.Y. chpt. 1989-91), Nat. Notary Assn., Rotary Internat. Home: PO Box 307 Hyde Park NY 12538 Office: Victory Lake Nursing Ctr 419 N Quaker Ln Hyde Park NY 12538

FARY, DANIEL R.B., ophthalmologist; b. Hammond, Ind., Nov. 10, 1946. MD, Ind. U., 1974. Diplomate Am. Bd. Ophthalmology. Pvt. practice opthalmology Fort Atkinson, Wis., 1981—; clin. asst. prof. ophthalmology, vol. staff U. Wis., Madison, 1994—. Office: Spectrum Eye Ctr 512 Wilcox St Fort Atkinson WI 53538-1254

FASCETTI, CHRISTINA JOY, nursing educator; b. Kansas City, Mo., Dec. 26, 1944; d. Charles Anthony and Patricia Catherine (Slavin) Gialde; m. Phillip Fascetti, June 4, 1976; children: Michael, Phillip, Andrea. Diploma, St. Lukes Hosp., Kansas City, Mo., 1968; BSN, Gonzaga U., Spokane, Wash., 1987; MS, U. Portland, Oreg., 1990. Cert. med.-surg. nurse. Staff nurse, charge nurse L.A. County Gen. Hosp., 1968-69; staff nurse, asst. head nurse Rochester (Minn.) Meth. Hosp., 1969-71; staff nurse, charge nurse Sacred Heart Med. Ctr., Spokane, Wash., 1974-79, clin. instr., med.-surg. staff devel. coord., coord. edn., 1980—. Mem. ANA, Wash. State Nurses Assn., Inland Empire Nurses Assn. (pres. 1995-96), Am. Soc. Healthcare Edn. and Tng. (pres. Eastern Wash.-Idaho chpt. 1989), Sigma Theta Tau (Delta Chi chpt.), Alpha Sigma Nu. Home: 5502 N New York Ln Spokane WA 99212-1675

FASHING, NORMAN JAMES, biologist, educator; b. Walker, Minn., Aug. 14, 1943; s. Theodore Paul and Gladys Marion (Johnson) F.; m. Gisela Anna Krueger, Aug. 26, 1969; children: Peter James, Mark Alois, Maria Therese. AA, Lassen Jr. Coll., Susanville, Calif., 1963; BA in Biology, Calif. State U., Chico, 1965, MA in Biology, 1967; PhD in Entomology, Kans. U., 1973. Instr. biology Calif. State U., Chico, 1966-67; asst. prof. biology Coll. William and Mary, Williamsburg, Va., 1973-79, assoc. prof., 1979-89, prof., 1989—. Contbr. chpts. to books and articles to profl. jours. Grantee Sloan Found., 1978, NSF, 1984, Smithsonian Instn., 1986. Mem. Entomol. Soc. Am., Ctrl. States Entomol. Soc., Acarological Soc., Acarological Soc. Am. (governing bd. 1979-84, pres. 1982-83, 88-89), Va. Acad. Sci., Va. Natural History Soc. Democrat. Home: 104 Sherwood Dr Williamsburg VA 23185-5026 Office: Coll William and Mary Dept Biology Williamsburg VA 23185

FASNACHT, BETTY BEEGLE, retired nurse; b. Roaring Spring, Pa., May 19, 1931; d. Earl Ray and Mary Arminta (Myers) Beegle; m. Richard S. Fasnacht, June 14, 1952 (div. 1979); children: Richard II, Mary Jean, Mark Steven, Ruth Leslie, Raymon Lore. Diploma, Phila. Coll. Osteopathy Sch. Nursing, 1952; BA in Writing, U. Pitts., 1981. Operating room staff nurse Phila. Coll. Osteopathy Hosp., 1953-54, nursery staff nurse, 1955-56; operating room supr. Portland (Oreg.) Osteopathic Hosp., 1954-55; office nurse Dr. Richard Fasnacht, Bradford, Pa., 1960-69; county editor, writer The Bradford Era, 1969-72, city editor, 1972-75; free-lance author, pub. relations cons., 1975-84; psychiat. staff nurse Warren (Pa.) State Hosp., 1984-96; ret., 1996. Contbr. articles to Am. Oil and Gas Reporter. Mem. Romance Writers Am. Home: 30412 3rd Ave W Warren PA 16365

FASS, DANIEL ERIC, physician; b. N.Y.C., Aug. 26, 1959; s. Jerome Samuel and Joyce Barbbra (Liebowitz) F.; m. Jessica Carol Adler; children: Jacob, Sara. MD, Howard U., 1983. Resident NYU Med. Sch., N.Y.C., 1983-85, chief resident, 1985-86; fellow Meml. Sloan Kettering, N.Y.C., 1986-87, attending physician, 1986-92; asst. prof. Cornell Med. Sch., N.Y.C., 1989—; dir. radiation oncology Greenwich (Conn.) Hosp., 1992—. Contbg. author: Dental Clinics, NA, 1989. Fellow N.Y. Head and Neck Soc.; mem. Am. Soc. Therapeutic Radiology, N.Y. Met. Breast Group. Office: Greenwich Hosp 77 Lafayette Pl Greenwich CT 06830

FASS, ROBERT J., epidemiologist, academic administrator; b. N.Y.C., Feb. 23, 1939. BS in Chemistry, Biology, Tufts U., 1960, MD, 1964; MS in Med. Microbiology, Ohio State U., 1971. Diplomate Am. Bd. Internal Medicine; licensed physician, Ohio, N.Y., Pa. Intern in mixed medicine Montefiore Hosp., N.Y.C., 1964-65, resident in medicine, 1965-66; resident in medicine Ohio State U., Columbus, 1968-69, fellow in infectious diseases, rsch. asst. in med. microbiology, 1969-71, clin. instr. medicine, 1970-71, asst. prof. medicine, 1971-75, asst. prof. med. microbiology, 1971-76, assoc. prof. medicine, 1975-80, assoc. prof. med. microbiology, 1976-80, prof. internal medicine, medical microbiology and immunology, 1980—, Samuel Saslaw prof. infectious diseases, 1991—, dir. divsn. infectious diseases, 1987—; dir. infectious diseases fellowship tng. program Ohio State U., 1987-93, mem. task force on program evaluation Coll Medicine, 1973-75, search com. chmn. dept. med. microbiology, 1973-76, clin. cirriculum devel. project, 1875-77, profl. adv. com. to med. illustrations, 1975-85, vice chmn. practice plan com., 1979-85, trustee Med. Rsch. and Devel. Found., 1979-86, treas., 1979-85, assocs. medicine exec. com. dept. medicine, 1973-76, chmn., 1974-75, chmn. libr. com., 1973-78, bd. dirs. Dept. Medicine Found., 1987—, finance com., 1979-86, 91—, chmn., 1981-86, phase III module com. Med. Microbiology and Immunology divsn., 1973, 75, 76, 81, dir., 1976, 81, mem. infection control com. Univ. Hosp., 1972-77, exec. com., 1976-77, pharmacy and therapeutics com., 1981—, chmn. pharmacy and therapeutics antimicrobial com., 1984—, exec. com., 1984—; mem. infectious disease conf. Riverside Meth. Hosp., 1971-76; prin. investigator for Ohio State U. NIH AIDS Clin. Trials Group, 1987—, opportunistic info. com., 1987—, instl. evaluation com., 1989—; mem. internat. adv. bd. Bayer AG Auinolone Bd., 1985-93, Miles Inc. External Adv. Bd., 1988-93. Mem. editorial bd. Antimicrobial Agents and Chemotherapy, 1982-91, Quinolene Bulletin, 1989—; reviewer Am. Jour. Medicine, Am. Soc. Hosp. Pharmacists Drug Info., Antimicrobial Agents and Chemotherapy, Annals of Internal Medicine, Archives of Internal Medicine, Chest, Clin. Microbiology Revs., Jour. Infectious Diseases, Infectious Diseases in Clin. Practice, N.Y. State Jour. Medicine, Revs. Infectious Diseases, New England Jour. Medicine. Med. officer USAF, 1966-68. Fellow ACP, Infectious Diseases Soc. Am.; mem. AMA (reviewer AMA Drug Evaluations, Jour. AMA), Am. Fedn. Clin. Rsch., Am. Soc. for Microbiology, Am. Thoracic Soc., Ctrl. Soc. for Clin. Rsch., Inter-Am. Soc. for Chemotherapy, Brit. Soc. Antimicrobial Chemotherapy, Columbus Soc. Internal Medicine (sec.-treas. 1979, pres. 1980). Office: Ohio State U Med Ctr 4715 Univ Hosp Clinic 456 W 10th Ave Columbus OH 43210*

FASULA, VIVIAN KUDGERS, medical educator; b. Binghamton, N.Y., Apr. 13, 1955; m. Carmen R. Fasula; 4 children. BS, Coll. Mt. St. Vincent, 1976; MD, SUNY, 1980. Intern, resident Erie County Med. Ctr., Buffalo, N.Y.; clin. asst. prof. ophthalmology SUNY, Buffalo, 1984—; chief surgery Lockport (N.Y.) Meml. Hosp., 1995—. Fellow Am. Acad. Ophthalmology; mem. AMA, N.Y. State Ophthalmology Soc., N.Y. State Med. Soc., Niagara County Med. Soc., Buffalo Ophthalmological Soc. Office: 125 Professional Plz Lockport NY 14094

FATE, CAROL SUE, critical care nurse; b. Canton, Ill., Oct. 13, 1951; d. Eldon Jackson and Nelda Edith (Eyman) F.; m. Angela K. Boggs. ADN, Lincolnland C.C., Springfield, Ill., 1993; BSN, U. of Ill., Springfield, 1995. RN, Ill. CCU charge nurse Doctors Hosp., Springfield, 1993—. Vol. Dem. Hdqrs., Springfield, 1993, Ctrl. Ill. Cmty. Blood Bank, Springfield, 1993-94. Democrat. Christian.

FATHERREE, LARAINE CAUDELL, hospital administrator; b. Toccoa, Ga., Aug. 14, 1948; d. Dwain and Nell Marie (Smith) C. BS in Home Econs., U. Ga., 1970; MBA, U. South Ala., 1979. Cert. health exec. Tng. instr. Davis Bros., Inc., Atlanta, 1970-72; asst. to food svc. dir. West Paces Ferry Hosp., Atlanta, 1972-74; dir. food svcs. Drs. Hosp., Mobile, Ala., 1974-79; adminstrv. asst. Indian Path Hosp., Kingsport, Tenn., 1979-80, asst. adminstr., 1980-82; adminstr. Johnson City (Tenn.) Specialty Hosp. (formerly Johnson City Eye & Ear Hosp.), 1982—; food svc. cons., 1974-79; faculty mem. Ctr. for Health Studies, Nashville, 1979-87; bd. dirs. Tenn. Hosp. Assn., exec. com., 1988-91. Pres., bd. dirs., mem. exec. com. East Tenn. Regional Organ Procurement Agy.; Sunday sch. tchr. Colonial Heights Baptist Ch., 1980-82; adv. Experience Based Career Edn. Program, Murphy High Sch., 1977-79; bd. dirs. United Way Washington County, 1986-92, exec. com. 1988; bd. dirs. Washington County Am. Heart Assn.; pres. Upper East Tenn. Hosp. Dist., 1986-88; mem. fin. com. Munsey Meml. Meth. Ch., 1990-93, mem. mission com. Mem. AAUW (bd. dirs.), Am. Coll. Health Execs., Johnson City C. of C. (health svcs. coun., bd. dirs. 1987-92, v.p. 1988, 91), Johnson City Leadership 2000, U. Ga. Alumni Assn., U. South Ala. Alumni Assn., Christian Bus. and Profl. Women (bd. exec. com. 1987-88), Leadership Kingsport, 1995, Rotary (bd. dirs.). Home: 2228 Granite Ct Johnson City TN 37604-2170 Office: Johnson City Specialty Hosp 203 E Watauga Ave Johnson City TN 37601-4629

FATSIS, MICHAEL EVANGELOS, thoracic and vascular surgeon; b. Piraeus, Greece, Mar. 21, 1961; s. Evangelos Michael and Irene Stavros (Nicoladou) F.; m. Anastasia Christos Fotopoulou, May 9, 1987. Med. diploma, Med. U. of Patras, Patra, Greece, 1984. Resident in gen. surgery Nimts Gen. Hosp., Athens, Greece, 1985-88; resident in thoracic and vascular surgery Metaxas Cancer Hosp., Piraeus, Greece, 1988-92; sr. registrar dept. thoracic and vascular surgery 251 Hellenic Airforce and VA Gen. Hosp., Athens, 1992, 1st IKA Hosp., Athens, 1993—. Author: The Newer Data About The Surgical Treatment of Lung Cancer, 1991; contbr. 95 articles to profl. jours. Mem. Soc. Thoracic Surgeons, European Assn. Endoscopic Surgery, Internat. Assn. Study Lung Cancer, Hellenic Surg. Soc., European Soc. Parenteral and Enteral Nutrition, Hellenic Soc. Against Lung Cancer, Hellenic Soc. Vascular Surgery. Home: Psaron 9 Nikea, 18450 Piraeus Greece

FAUB, KENNETH JAMES, school nurse practitioner; b. Pitts., Sept. 5, 1942; s. Kenneth John and Emma L. (Morgan) F. Diploma, St. John's Gen. Hosp., Pitts., 1970; BSN, Carlow Coll., 1985; MSN in Nursing Edn., Duquesne U., 1995. Cert. ARC disaster nurse, emergency/primary care nurse practitioner, sexually transmitted disease specialist, AIDS educator, sch. nurse practitioner. Charge nurse emergency room St. John's Gen. Hosp., 1970-75, head nurse; nurse practitioner, sexually transmitted disease clinic Allegheny County Health Dept., Pitts., 1976-93; nurse practitioner Pitts. Bd. Pub. Edn., 1989—; pub. speaker on health-related topics. Instr. first aid, CPR and disaster health svcs., ARC; merit badge counselor Boy Scouts Am.; mem. human resource availability list Nat. Red Cross. Mem. Pitts. Sch. Nurse Orgn., Pa. Sch. Nurse Practitioners Orgn., Am. Acad. Nurse Practitioners, St. John's Gen. Hosp. Alumni Assn., Carlow Coll. Alumni Assn., Duquesne U. Alumni Assn., Sigma Theta Tau.

FAUCI, ANTHONY STEPHEN, health facility administrator, physician; b. Bklyn., Dec. 24, 1940; s. Stephen A. and Eugenia A. Fauci. AB, Coll. of Holy Cross, 1962; MD, Cornell U., 1966; DSc (hon.), Coll. Holy Cross, 1987, Georgetown U., 1990, Hahnemann U., 1990, Mt. Sinai Sch. Medicine, 1990, Universita di Roma, 1990, St. John's U., 1991, Long Island U., 1992, Med. Coll. Wis., 1993, Bard Coll., 1993, Bates Coll., 1993, SUNY, Farmingdale, 1994, U. Conn. Health Ctr, 1994, Duke U., 1995. Diplomate Am. Bd. Internal Medicine, Am. Bd. Allergy and Immunology (bd. dirs. 1984—), Am. Bd. Infectious Diseases. Intern N.Y. Hosp.-Cornell Med. Ctr., 1966-67, asst. resident in medicine, 1967-68, chief resident dept. medicine, 1971-72; clin. assoc. Nat. Inst. Allergy and Infectious Diseases-NIH, Bethesda, Md., 1968-70, sr. staff fellow, 1970-71, sr. investigator, 1972-74, head, clin. physiology sect., 1974-80, dep. clin. dir., 1977-80, chief Lab. Immunoregulation, 1980—, dir. Nat. Inst. Allergy and Infectious Diseases, 1984—; dir. Office of AIDS Rsch., NIH, assoc. dir. NIH for AIDS Rsch., 1988-94; cons. Naval Med. Ctr., Bethesda, 1972—. Contbr. numerous articles to med. jours. Served with USPHS, 1968—. Recipient meritorious svcs. award USPHS, 1979, Arthur S. Fleming award, 1983, Squibb award Infectious Diseases Soc., 1983, Commrs. spl. citation FDA, 1984, Clemons von Pirquet award Georgetown U. Med. Ctr., 1986, Disting. Clin. Educator award NIH Clin. Ctr., 1988, Leadership award Columbus Citizens Found., Inc., 1988, spl. award for rsch. in AIDS Nat. Hemophilia Fedn., 1989, Lee P. Brown Nat. Pub. Svc. award Nat. Acad. Pub. Adminstrn. and Nat. Soc. for Pub. Adminstrn., 1989, numerous awards Duke U., AMA, Children's Hosp., Nat. med. Ctr., Surgeon Gen., Am. Assn. Physicians for Human Rights, Nat. Health Coun., Nat. Found. Infectious Diseases, Helen Hayes award for med. rsch., 1989, Excellence in Pub. Svc. award Com. for Support of Pub. Svc., 1990, Lifetime Sci. award Inst. Advanced Studies in Immunology and Aging, 1990, Internat. Chiron prize, 1990, Pres. award N.Y. Acad. Sci., 1990, Thomas H. Ham-Louis R. Wasserman award Am. Soc. Hematology, 1992, Dr. Nathan Davis award AMA, 1992, Outstanding Achievement award Howard U., 1992, Humanitarian award Tiro a Segno Fedn., 1993, Cartwright prize Columbia U. Coll. Physicians and Surgeons, 1993, Commr. of Honor award SUNY, Farmingdale, 1994, Theobald Smith award Albany Med. Coll., 1995, many others. Fellow AAAS, ACP (Richard and Hinda Rosenthal award 1995), Am. Med. Writers Assn. (hon.), Am. Acad. Allergy, Am. Acad. Allergy and Immunology (hon.), N.Y. Acad. Med. (hon. 1991), Am. Acad. Arts and Scis.; mem. AAAS (Westinghouse award 1988), NAS, Am. Fedn. Clin. Rsch., Am. Assn. Immunologists (program chmn. 1982-85, Kober lectr. 1988), Am. Soc. Virology, Am. Soc. Cell Biology, Am. Fedn. Clin. Rsch. (pres. 1980-81), Internat. AIDS Soc., Commd. Officers Assn. USPHS (Pub. Health Leader of Yr. award), Infectious Diseases Soc. Am., Am. Soc. for Clin. Investigation, Assn. of Am. Physicians (recorder 1988-93, councillor 1993—), Inst. Medicine, Royal Danish Acad. Sci. and Letters (fgn.), Royal Acad. Medicine (Spain). Roman Catholic. Avocations: running; tennis. Home: 3012 43rd St NW Washington DC 20016-3547 Office: Nat Inst Allergy & Infectious Diseases 31 Ctr Dr MSC 2520 Bethesda MD 20892-2520

FAULCONER, ROBERT JAMIESON, pathologist, educator; b. Sedlescombe, Sussex, Eng., July 11, 1923; came to U.S., 1925, naturalized, 1932; s. Robert Hoffman and Gladys Alice (Jamieson) F.; m. Virginia Myrl Davis, Aug. 11, 1945; children: Anne Hurley, Elizabeth, Mary Waite, John. BS, Coll. William and Mary, 1943; MD, Johns Hopkins U., 1947. Diplomate Am. Bd. Pathology. Intern Johns Hopkins Hosp., 1948, fellow, 1948-49; resident Presbyn.-U. Pa. Med. Ctr., Phila., 1949-52; pathologist DePaul Hosp., Norfolk, Va., 1954-78; pathologist, dir. labs. DePaul Hosp., 1965-78; clin. prof. pathology Med. Coll. Va., 1972-79; prof. pathology Ea. Va. Med. Sch., 1974-94, chmn., 1978-93, prof. emeritus, 1994—; cons. pathologist U.S. Naval Hosp., Portsmouth, Va., VA Hosp., Hampton, Va., Children;s Hosp., Norfolk, Va. Beach Gen. Hosp. Med. editorial bd. Histology and Histopathology Jour.; contbr. articles on pathology to profl. publs. Pres. Va. div. Am. Cancer Soc., 1963-66, mem. nat. bd. dirs., exec. and sci. rev. coms.; mem. bd. visitors Coll. William and Mary, 1972-76, 79-87. With USNR, 1943-46, U.S. Army Med. Corps, 1952-54. Recipient J. Shelton Horsley award merit Va. div. Am. Cancer Soc., 1966, Alumni medallion Coll. William and Mary, 1985. Fellow AAAS; mem. AMA, Internat. Acad. Pathology, Am. Soc. Clin. Pathologists, Coll. Am. Pathologists, Am. Assn. Anatomists, Am. Soc. Clin. Oncology, Am. Assn. Phys. Anthropologists, Va. Soc. Pathology (pres. 1958-59), Norfolk Acad. Medicine (pres. 1964-65), Am. Assn. History of Medicine, Am. Assn. Pathologists, Assn. Pathology Chmn., Cypher Soc., Commonwealth Club (Richmond, bd. govs.), Sigma Xi. Episcopalian. Home: 1507 Buckingham Ave Norfolk VA 23508-1354 Office: Ea Va Med Sch Med Coll of Hampton Roads PO Box 1980 Norfolk VA 23501-1980

FAULK, WARD PAGE, immunologist; b. Ruston, La., Nov. 14, 1937; s. Clarence E. and Louise B. (Page) F.; m. Klára Barabás, 1994; children: Robin, Saskia, Josie, Holly. BS, U. South, 1959; MD, Tulane U., 1964; MRC, Royal Coll. Pathology, 1973, FRC, 1983. NIH fellow Netherlands Red Cross, Amsterdam, 1965-66; fellow Mayo Clinic, Rochester, Minn., 1966-67, U. Calif. Med. Ctr., San Francisco, 1967-69; mem. staff British Med. Rsch. Coun., London, 1973-76; prof. Med. U. S.C., Charleston, 1976-79; dir. Royal Coll. Surgeons, East Grinstead, England, 1979-81; prof., dir. Purdue U./Meth. Hosp., Indpls., 1986—; vis. prof. faculty medicine U. Nice, France, 1982-84, dept. obstetrics So. Ill. U., Springfield, 1984-85; cons. hematology and oncology Pembury (England) Hosp., 1982-96. Founder, coeditor: Immunological Obstetrics, 1992; contbr. articles to more than 350 publs.; co-editor for 11 jours. Med. officer WHO, Geneva, 1970-73; mem. NATO Advanced Study Group, Cordoba, Spain, 1988, 94, NIH Study Group, Bethesda, Md., 1990. Recipient award Calif. Trudeau Soc., 1965, Metchnikoff medal Bulgarian Acad. Scis., 1971. Fellow Royal Coll. Pathology, Fellow Nat.Inst. of Health; mem. Internat. Soc. for Immunology Reproduction, Am. Soc. Immunology Reproduction (Munksgaard award 1992), Internat. Soc. Heart and Lung Transplantation. Republican. Episcopalian. Office: Methodist Hosp 1701 Senate Blvd Indianapolis IN 46202-1239

FAUNCE, WILLIAM DALE, clinical psychologist, researcher; b. Lansing, Mich., Dec. 4, 1947; s. Lucius Dale and Wilhelmina (Hall) F. BA, Mich. State U., 1972; MA, Calif. State U., L.A., 1978; PhD in Clin. Psychology, U. So. Calif., 1983. Lic. psychologist, Alaska, N.C. Psychology intern Brentwood (Calif.) VA, 1981-82; clin. psychologist UCLA Neuropsychiat. Inst., Westwood, Calif., 1983, Coldwater Canyon Hosp., North Hollywood, Calif., 1983-84, So. Peninsula Community Mental Health Ctr., Homer, Alaska, 1984-86; pvt. practice Homer, Alaska, 1986-87; cons. Santa Cruz, Calif., 1987-90; clin. psychologist, program dir. Broughton State Hosp., Morganton, N.C., 1990—; mem. faculty Appalachian State U., Boone, N.C., 1992—. Co-author: (chpt.) Imagery, 1984; contbr. articles to profl. jours. Fellow NIMH; mem. APA, Union Concerned Scientists. Home: PO Box 241 Jonas Ridge NC 28641-0241 Office: Appalachian State U Dept Psychology Smith-Wright Hall Boone NC 28608

FAUST, DONALD CHARLES, surgeon; b. New Orleans, Feb. 8, 1951; m. Mary Kay Caire. BS in Biology, Loyola U., 1973; MD, La. State U., 1977. Intern Earl K. Long Meml. Hosp., New Orleans, 1977-78; resident in orthopaedic surgery La. State U. Med. Ctr., 1978-82; fellow hand surgery Daniel C. Riordan, New Orleans, 1982; fellow hand and microvascular surgery J.S. Gould, 1983; ptnr. Riordan, Saer and Williams, New Orleans, 1983-90; pvt. practice New Orleans, 1991—; bd. dirs. So. Hand Specialists, New Orleans. Chmn. bd. religious edn. St. Francis Xavier, 1983, active, 1985-89. Fellow Am. Soc. for Surgery of Hand, Am. Acad. Orthopaedic Surgery, ACS. Office: 2633 Napoleon Ave # 600 New Orleans LA 70115

FAUST, JERRY RUDOLPH, medical educator; b. Dallas, Mar. 10, 1948. BS in Chemistry, Stephen F. Austin State U., 1970; MA in Biochemistry, U. Tex., Arlington, 1974; PhD, Tufts U., 1991. Asst. prof. physiology Tufts U., Boston, 1991—. Reviewer profl. jours.; contbr. numerous articles to profl. jours. Robert A. Welch fellow, 1972-74; grantee NIH, 1991—, Pew Scholar, 1992-96, Harcourt Gen. Charitable Found., 1992-94, NSF, 1994—, U.S.-Israel Binat. Sci. Found., 1994—, Am. Heart Assn. Established Investigator, 1995—. Office: Tufts U Dept Physiology Physiology Dept Boston MA 02111

FAVA, DONALD ANTHONY, clinical psychologist; b. Paterson, N.J., Sept. 20, 1948; s. Michael A. and Josephine (Fusilli) F.; 1 child, Joshua. BA, Monmouth (Ill.) Coll., 1970; PhD, New Sch. Social Rsch., N.Y.C., 1978. Lic. psychologist N.Y., N.J. Rsch. asst. Calif. State U., Arcata, 1970-71; psychol. intern Dept. Spl. Svcs., Bd. Edn., Paterson, N.J., 1971-72; clin. psychol. trainee Kingsbrook Jewish Med. Ctr., Bklyn., 1972-73; grad. clin. supr. New Sch. Social Rsch., N.Y.C., 1974-76; clin. psychologist Passaic County Diagnostic Ctr., Paterson, N.J., 1973-78, sr. clin. psychologist, 1978-

80; adj. instr. psychology LaGuardia Coll., CUNY, N.Y.C., 1975-82, Seton Hall U., S. Orange, N.J., 1981-82; clin. dir. St. Francis Acad., Inc., Lake Placid, N.Y., 1984-92; founder, dir. Adirondack Inst. Mental Health, Lake Placid, 1984—; dir. No. N.Y. and Vt. Region, Inst. Forensic Psychology, Lake Placid, 1986—. Co-author monograph: Understanding Visual Metaphor, 1980. Past. bd. dirs. Community Svc. Bd., Elizbethtown, N.Y., Mental Health Bd. Essex County; chmn. Mental Health Com., Elizabethtown; mem. Profl. Adv. Bd. Greater Patterson Community Mental Health Ctr., 1975-77. New Sch. for Social Rsch. trustees scholar, 1972-76, teaching fellow, 1973-76. Mem. Am. Psychol. Assn., N.Y. Psychol. Assn., N.J. Psychol. Assn., N.Y. Soc. Clin. Psychologists, Southeastern Psychol. Assn. Home: Fawn Ridge Estates Lake Placid NY 12946 Office: Adirondack Inst Crestview Plz # 1108 Lake Placid NY 12946

FAVALE, STEFANO, physician, researcher; b. Bari, Puglia, Italy, Feb. 18, 1952; s. Donato Favale and Iolanda Maria Giannico; m. Angela Marie Leogrande, Oct. 1, 1979; 1 child, Donato. MD, U. Bari, Italy, 1976, cardiology specialty, 1979. Intern, resident U. Monpellier, France, 1977, Hammersmith Hosp., London, 1978, Duke U., Durham, N.C., 1982, Washington U., Seattle, 1989; rschr. U. Bari, Italy, 1980; aiuto universitario Inst. Cardiology, Bari, 1994—; prof. intensive care U. Bari, Italy, 1982—, prof. angiology, 1994—; aiuto univeristario Inst. Cardiology, Bari, 1994—, dir. implantable defibrillator sect., 1990—. Contbr. more than 200 articles to sci. jours. Mem. European Soc. Cardiology, Societa Itallana Cardiologia, Electrophysiology Soc. Home: Corso Degasperi 312/B, 70125 Bari Puglia Italy Office: U Bari-Inst Cardiology, Piazza G Cesare 11, 70124 Bari Puglia Italy

FAVARO, MARY KAYE ASPERHEIM (MRS. BIAGINO PHILIP FAVARO), pediatrician; b. Edgerton, Wis., Sept. 30, 1934; d. Harold Wilbur and Genevieve Catherine (Hyland) Asperheim; B.S., U. Wis., 1956; M.S., St. Louis Coll. Pharmacy, 1965; M.D., U. Wis., 1969; m. Biagino Philip Favaro, May 31, 1969; children—Justin Peter, Gina Sue. Instr. pharmacology St. Louis U. and St. Mary's Hosp. Sch. Practical Nurses, 1959-64; staff pharmacist U. Hosps., Madison, Wis., 1964-65; intern Albany (N.Y.) Med. Center, 1969-70, resident, 1970-71; resident in pediatrics U. S.C., Charleston, 1971-72, asst. prof. pediatrics, 1973-75; pvt. practice pediatrics, 1974—. Mem. A.M.A., Am. Med. Women's Assn. Roman Catholic. Author: Pharmacology, an Introductory Text, 1992; The Pharmacologic Basis of Patient Care, 1985. Home: 1866 Capri Dr Charleston SC 29407-7606 Office: 5390 Dorchester Rd Charleston SC 29418-5652

FAVAZZA, ARMANDO RICCARDO, psychiatrist, educator; b. N.Y.C., Apr. 14, 1941; s. Armando G. and Estelle (Barra) F.; divorced; children: Terence, Laura; m. Christine Woodland, 1994. BA, Columbia U., 1962; MD, U. Va., 1966; MPH, U. Mich., 1971. Intern Bon Secours Hosp., Grosse Pointe, Mich., 1966-67; resident U. Mich., Ann Arbor, 1967-71; prof. psychiatry dept. U. Mo., Columbia, 1973—. Author: Anthropological Themes in Mental Health, 1977, Themes in Cultural Psychiatry, 1982, Bodies Under Siege, 1987, rev. edit., 1996; editor in chief Dept. Psychiatry Jour., 1973-86. Served to lt. USNR, 1971-73. Recipient George B. Kunkel award Harrisburg Hosp., 1987. Fellow Am. Psychiat. Assn., Am. Coll. Psychiatrists, Am. Assn. for Social Psychiatry; mem. Mo. Psychiat. Soc. (pres. 1981-82). Home: 1304 Westview Ter Columbia MO 65203-5200 Office: U Mo Dept Psychiatry 3 Hospital Dr Columbia MO 65201-5276

FAWCETT, HOWARD HOY, chemical health and safety consultant; b. McKeesport, Pa., May 31, 1916; s. Harry Garfield and Ada (Deetz) F.; m. Ruth Allen Bogan, Apr. 7, 1942 (dec. Oct. 1986); children: Ralph Willard, Harry Allen. BS in Indsl. Chemistry, U. Md., 1940; postgrad. U. Del., 1945-47. Registered profl. engr., Calif. Rsch. chemist Manhattan project E.I. DuPont de Nemours & Co., Inc., Chgo., Hanford, Wash., 1944-45, rsch. and devel. chemist organic chemistry div., Deepwater, N.J., 1945-48; cons. engr. GE, Schenectady, N.Y., 1948-64; tech. sec. com. on hazardous materials Nat. Acad. Scis.-NRC, Washington, 1964-75; staff scientist, project mgr. Tracor Jitco, Inc., Rockville, Md., 1975-78; sr. chem. engr. Equitable Environ. Health, 1978-81; pres., sr. engr. Fawcett Consultations, Inc., 1981—; mem. adv. com. study on socio-behavioral preparations for, responses to and recovery from chem. disasters NSF, 1977-82; adj. prof. Fed. Emergency Mgmt. Agency Acad., 1983—; cons. to industry and govt. agys. Author Am.-Can. supplement Hazards in Chemical Lab., 1983, Hazardous and Toxic Materials, Safe Handling and Disposal, 1984, 2d edit., 1988; co-editor: Safety and Accident Prevention in Chemical Operations, 1965, 2d edit., 1982, (with others) Hazards in the Chemical Laboratory, 4th and 5th edits.; mem. editorial adv. bd. Jour. Safety Rsch., 1968—, Transp. Planning and Tech., 1972—; N.Am. regional editor Jour. Hazardous Materials, 1975—; guest editor: Jour. Hazardous Materials, 1994; also book chpt. Chief radiol. sect. Schenectady County CD, 1953-63; bd. dirs. Safety sect. Schenectady C. of C., 1957-64; tech. advisor Hazmat Emergency Response Team, Montgomery County, Md., 1988—. Deacon Warner Meml. Presbyn. Ch., Kensington, Md., 1990—. Recipient Disting. Svc. to Safety citation Nat. Safety Coun., 1966, Cameron award, 1962, 69, Profl. Svc. award, 1992. Fellow Am. Inst. Chemists; mem. Am. Chem. Soc. (sec. com. chem. safety, chmn. council com. on chem. safety 1974-77, chmn. div. chem. health and safety 1977-79, 91, vice-chair, 1990-91, chair, 1991—, councilor 1980-82, archivist, 1984—, author audio course on hazards of materials 1977, CHAS award 1993).; ASTM (membership sec. 1972—, sub-chmn. D-34 com.), Am. Inst. Chem. Engrs. (com. on occupational health and safety 1977—, editor newsletter 1988-89), Internat. Platform Assn., Am. Indsl. Hygiene Assn. (dir. Balt.-Washington chpt. 1975-77), Nat. Inst. Standards and Tech. (com. assistance 1993), Alpha Chi Sigma (contbr. video tapes on chemical hazards). Home and Office: PO Box 9444 12920 Matey Rd Wheaton MD 20906-4053

FAY, NANCY ELIZABETH, nurse; b. Fulton, N.Y., May 10, 1943; d. Harold and Jean (Junker) Sant; m. Ronald George Fay, July 30, 1966; step children: Rory Patrick, Ronald George Jr. R.N., Genesee Hosp., Rochester, N.Y., 1964. Cert. gerontology nurse practitioner; cert. physician's asst., cert. diabetes educator. N.Y. Head maternity nurse St. Luke's Hosp., Utica, N.Y., 1975-78, diabetes clinician, 1978-82, co-dir. diabetes out-patient clinic, 1980-82; nurse practitioner, physician's asst. Slocum Dickson Med. Group, Utica, 1982-86; gerontol. nurse practitioner Masonic Home, Utica, 1988-96; diabetes educator Upstate N.Y. Spl. Profl. Program Eli Lilly and Co., 1988—. Chair ann. Gerontol. Teaching Day Masonic Home, 1988-96, N.Y. State Physicians Diabetes Teaching Day A.D.A., 1983-90. Recipient Extra Mile award St. Luke's Hosp., 1979, Outstanding Citizenship award Am. Legion, Utica, 1982; Diabetes research grantee Diabetes Project, Ctr. Disease Control Utica, 1980-82, 21st Ann. Scroll award Cen. N.Y. Acad. Medicine. Fellow Acad. Medicine Cent. N.Y.; mem. Am. Diabetes Assn. (pres. Utica chpt. 1983-85, Outstanding Vol. of Yr. 1978, bd. dirs. N.Y. State affiliate 1983-95, 1st v.p. 1986-87, Program award 1985-86, profl. edn. chmn. 1983-92, chair patient and pub. edn. Upstate Affiliate, 1987-92, 1st v.p., 1988-89, applicant nat. com. patient and pub. and profl. edn. 1988-89, pres.-elect N.Y. State Affiliate 1987-89, pres. 1990-92, immediate past pres. 1992-94, Sp. Svc. award N.Y. Upstate Affiliate Am. Diabetes Assn., 1994), Am. Acad. Physician's Assts., Am. Assn. Diabetes Educators, Womens Health and Edn. Referral Service St. Luke's Hosp. (bd. dirs. 1987—), N.Y. State Coalition Nurse Practitioners. Republican. Methodist. Avocations: doll collecting, dancing, poetry, bike riding. Home: Valley Rd PO Box J Oriskany NY 13424-0710 Office: Masonic Home 2150 Bleecker St Utica NY 13501-1714

FAY, ROBERTA MARIE, nurse, educator; b. Boston; d. Nicholas and Catherine Shaughnessy; divorced; children: Mark, David, Karen. Diploma, Carney Hosp. Sch. Nursing, Boston; BS in Nursing Edn., Columbia U.; MS, St. John's U., N.Y.C.; postgrad., Tex. Women's U., 1984. From instr. to asst. prof. SUNY, Farmingdale, 1964-68; charge nurse med.-surg. unit Mercy Hosp., Rockville Centre, N.Y., 1964-68; mem. faculty Our Lady of Grace, Pitts., 1968-72; asst. prof. dept. nursing Bloomfield (N.J.) Coll., 1972-74, Morris County Coll., Randolph, N.J., 1974-76; asst. prof. Coll. Nursing Tex. Women's U., Denton, 1977-83; clin. care specialist Johnson & Johnson Home Health, Dallas, 1983-85; adminst., dir. nursing Collin County Home Health, Plano, Tex., 1985-86; acad. leader, internat. lectr. Nursing Inst.: Internat. Journeys, 1985—; med.-surg. cons. Martingale Rsch. Corp., 1986—; part-time psychiat. staff nurse Hosp. Corp. Am. Med. Ctr. (now Charter of Dallas), 1986—. Active Boy Scouts Am., Girl Scouts U.S., Safety Coun. and Recreational Adv. Council, Am. Field Svc., sr. citizen groups. Mem. AAUP, Am. Nurses Assn., Am. Rural Health Assn., Tex. Alcohol Rsch. Assn., Am. Heart Assn., Am. Cancer Soc., Oncology Nurses Soc., Assn. Clin. Care Specialists, Columbia U. Alumni Assn., St. John's of N.Y. Alumni Assn., Carney Hosp. Alumni Assn., Eta Sigma Gamma. Home: 1316 Auburn Pl Plano TX 75093-5046

FAZIO, SERAFINO, internist, educator; b. Napoli, Campania, Italy, Feb. 1950; s. Antonio and Anna Zara (Aliperti) F.; m. Gabriella Baratti, Mar. 29, 1979 (div. June 1987); children: Antonio, Giorgia, Valeria; m. Bernadette Biondi, June 17, 1988; 1 child, Federica. MD, U. Naples, Italy, 1974. Asst. U. Naples, 1976-80, rschr., 1980—, faculty medicine, 1987—. Contbr. articles to profl. jours. Lt. Italian Mil., 1975-76. Fellow Am. Coll. Angiology. Office: Federico II UnivMedical School, Via Sergio Pansini 5, 80131 Naples Campania, Italy

FAZIO, SERGIO, medical educator, researcher. MD in Medicine summa cum laude, U. Rome, 1983; PhD in Molecular Biology, U. Siena, Italy, 1989. Intern and resident in internal medicine U. Rome, Italy, 1983-86; resident svc. of emergency medicine Gen. Hosp. Udine, Italy, 1984-85; fellow in metabolism dept. medicine Univ. Hosp. U. Rome, 1986-88; postdoctoral fellow Gladstone Inst. Cardiovasc. Disease, San Francisco, 1988-91, staff rsch. investigator, 1991-93; rsch. fellow Cardiovasc. Rsch. Inst. U. Calif., San Francisco, 1988-93; asst. prof. medicine and pathology, dir. lipid lab. Vanderbilt U., Nashville, 1993—. Ad hoc reviewer Jour. Biol. Chemistry, Biochimica Biophysica Acta, Lipids, Arteriosclerosis and Thrombosis, Jour. of Lipid Rsch., Diabetes; contbr. to articles to profl. jours. Recipient Pilot Project and Young Investigator award CNRU, Established Investigatorship award Am. Heart Assn., 1996; grant-in-aid Am. Heart Assn., 1995; Joe C. Davies Found. scholar. Fellow Am. Heart Assn. (mem. coun. on arteriosclerosis); mem. Am. Fedn. for Clin. Rsch. Office: Vanderbilt U Sch Medicine Divsn Endocrinology 715 MRB II Nashville TN 37232

FAZIO, VICTOR WARREN, physician, colon and rectal surgeon; b. Sydney, Australia, Feb. 2, 1940; came to U.S., 1971; s. Victor Warren and Kathleen Eleanor (Hills) F.; m. Carolyn Kisandra Sawyer, Dec. 2, 1961; children: Victor, Jane, David. MB, BS, U. Sydney, 1965. Diplomate Am. Bd. Colon and Rectal Surgery (pres. 1991-92). Intern and resident St. Vincent's Hosp., Sydney, 1965-67, surgical registrar, 1969-71; lectr. anatomy U. NSW Med. Sch., Sydney, 1967; surg. registrar Repatriation Gen. Hosp., Concord, Australia, 1968; gen. surgeon Australian Surg. Team, Bien Hoa, Vietnam, 1971; fellow gen. surgery Lahey Clinic, Boston, 1972; fellow colorectal surgery Cleve. Clinic, 1973, staff surgeon colorectal surgery, 1974, chmn. dept. colon and rectal surgery, vice chmn. divsn. surgery, 1975—; bd. govs. Cleve. Clinic, 1990-95, exec. mem. bd. trustees, 1994-95. Author 320 manuscripts and book chpts.; editor: Current Therapy in Colon and Rectal Surgery, 1989; editor-in-chief Diseases of Colon and Rectum, Coloproctology, Ostomy Mgmt. 1995—. Fellow ACS, Royal Australian Coll. Surgeons, Am. Soc. Colon and Rectal Surgery (pres. 1995-96); mem. Soc. Pelvic Surgeons (exec. com. 1980), Soc. for Surgery Alimentary Tract, Ctrl. Surg. Assn., James IV Assn. Surgeons, Ohio Valley Soc. Colon and Rectal Surgeons (past pres.). Roman Catholic. Home: 17414 S Woodland Rd Cleveland OH 44120-1761 Office: Cleve Clinic 9500 Euclid Ave Cleveland OH 44195-0001

FEARON, RICHARD EUBANKS, internist; b. Bklyn., Apr. 7, 1935; s. Henry Dana and Frances Hudson (Eubanks) F.; m. Elizabeth Oravec, Aug. 4, 1962; children: Amy Hudson, Richard Eubanks Jr., William Fuller. BA, Williams Coll., 1957; MD, Harvard U., 1961. Diplomate Am. Bd. Internal Medicine; bd. cert. cardiovasc. disease. Attending staff in medicine Yale-New Haven Hosp., 1967—; asst. clin. prof. medicine Yale U., New Haven, 1971-81, assoc. clin. prof. medicine, 1982—; chmn. rsch. com. Conn. Heart Assn., Hartford, 1971-73. Contbr. articles to profl. jours. Mem. Woodbridge (Conn.) Bd. Edn., 1986-93; trustee Whitney Ctr., Hamden, Conn., 1988-94; mem. Emergency Med. Task Force, Woodbridge, 1995—. Fellow ACP, Am. Heart Assn. (Coun. Clin. Cardiology), Am. Coll. Cardiology; mem. AMA, Conn. State Med. Assn., New Haven County Med. Assn. Office: 2 Church St South New Haven CT 06519

FEATHERSTONE, BONNIE GALE, healthcare facility administratorr; b. Lawrenceburg, Tenn., Sept. 8, 1945; d. Charles Craig and Anna Pearl Featherstone; m. James Robert Riles, Mar. 7, 1969 (div. Apr. 1974); 1 child, Holli Ann. Grad. high sch., San Antonio. Accredited record technician Am. Med. Record Assn. Dir. med. records Meth. Hosp./Fayette, Somerville, Tenn., 1975-85; dir. med. records NHC-Healthcare, Somerville, 1985—, mem. adv. bd., 1987—, customer rels. trainer, 1990-94; cons. homecare med. records NHC-Healthcare, 5, 1990—, coord. quality assurance, 1995—. Mem. Am. Health Info. Mgmt. Assn., Tenn. Hosp. Assn., West Tenn. Health Info. Mgmt. Assn., Royal Order Women of Moose. Democrat. Methodist. Home: PO Box 638 Somerville TN 38068 Office: NHC Healthcare PO Box 550 308 Lake Dr Somerville TN 38068

FECZKO, WILLIAM ALBERT, radiologist; b. Homestead, Pa., May 27, 1937; s. Albert George and Rosalia Melania (Toth) F.; m. Margaret Ann Cloonan, July 8, 1961; children: Margaret Christine, William Martin. AB, St. Vincent Coll., Latrobe, Pa., 1959; MD, U. Pitts., 1963. Diplomate Am. Bd. Radiology. V.p. Almar Radiologists, Inc., Pitts., 1975-93, pres., 1993—; assoc. dir. St. Francis Med. Ctr., Dept. Diagnostic Radiology, Pitts., 1978-86; dir. radiology residence prog. St. Francis Med. Ctr., Pitts., 1980-86; med. dir. Imaging Ctr., Pitts., 1986—; pres. Imaging Ctr. Inc., 1986—; v.p. med. staff St. Francis Med. Ctr., 1988, pres., 1989, bd. dirs., chmn. exec. com., 1990. Contbr. articles to profl. jours. Capt. USAF, 1965-67. Fellow Am. Coll. Radiology; mem. Pitts. Roentgen Soc. (treas. 1984-85), Pa. Radiologic Soc. (bd. dirs. 1985-88), AMA, Allegheny County Med. Soc., Pa. Med. Soc., Radiol. Soc. N.Am., Am. Inst. Ultrasound in Medicine, Am. Roentgen Ray Soc. Republican. Roman Catholic. Home: 217 Highland Rd Pittsburgh PA 15238-2136 Office: Imaging Ctr 4221 Penn Ave # 102G Pittsburgh PA 15224-1389

FEDAK, BARBARA KINGRY, technical center administrator; b. Hazleton, Pa., Feb. 7, 1939; d. Marvin Frederick and Ruth Anna (Wheeler) Siebel; m. Raymond F. Fedak, Mar. 27, 1993; children: Sean M., James Goldey. BA, Trenton State Coll., 1961; MEd, Lesley Coll., Cambridge, Mass., 1986. Registered respiratory therapist. Dept. dir. North Platte (Nebr.) Community Hosp., 1974-75; newborn coord. Children's Hosp., Denver, 1975-79; edn. coord. Rose Med. Ctr., Denver, 1979-81; program dir. respiratory tech. program Pickens Tech., Aurora, Colo., 1981-86; mktg. rep. Foster Med. Corp., Denver, 1986-87; staff therapist Porter Meml. Hosp., Denver, 1987-88; dir., br. mgr. Pediatric Svcs. Am., Denver, 1988-90; dir. clin. edn. Pickens Tech., Aurora, Colo., 1991, divsn. chair health occupations, 1991—; site evaluator Joint Rev. Com. for Respiratory Therapy Edn., Euless, Tex. Met. coun. mem. Am. Lung Assn., 1987-91. Mem. Am. Assn. Respiratory Care (edn. sect. program com. 1992-96, abstract rev. com. 1993-96), Colo. Soc. Respiratory Care (dir. at large 1983-86, 90-92, sec. 1980-81, program com. 1982-92), Colo. Assn. Respiratory Educators (chair 1991—). Methodist. Home: 11478 S Marlborough Dr Parker CO 80134-7318 Office: Pickens Tech 500 Airport Blvd Aurora CO 80011

FEDDER, DONALD OWEN, pharmacist, educator; b. Balt., Nov. 20, 1926; s. William Samuel and Rose F.; student Western Md. Coll., 1944-47; Pharm. BS, U. Md., 1950; MPH, Johns Hopkins U., 1978, Dr.P.H., 1982; m. Michaeline R. Fedder; children: Debra M. Fedder Goren, Ira Louis. Staff pharmacist Pikesville (Md.) Pharmacy, 1950-51; chief pharmacist, owner Fedder's Pharmacy & Fedder Med. Svcs., Balt., 1951-74; pres. Med. Equipment & Supply Co., Inc., Balt., 1970-76; prof., dir. community pharmacy and pharmacy high blood pressure programs U. Md. Sch. Pharmacy, 1974—, prof. epidemiology and preventive medicine, 1992—; chmn. Md. Commn. on High Blood Pressure & Related Cardiovascular Risk Factors, 1984-91; chmn. hypertension com. Md. affiliate Am. Heart Assn., 1984-86, sec. bd. dirs., 1984-86, chmn. health care site com., 1987-92, New Initiatives Com., 1992-95; pres., CEO Bd. Orthotist Cert., 1984—; cons. in field. Bd. dirs. Dundalk Concert Assn., 1963-75; candidate Md. Legis., 1970. With U.S. Army, 1944-45. Recipient Order Double Star, Alpha Zeta Omega, 1972, 75; Beta chpt. award Phi Alpha, 1950; Bowl of Hygeia award, 1980, Vol. of Yr. award Md. Pub. Health Assn, 1988, Disting. Achievement award Md. Pharmacists Assn., 1988, Alumnus of the Yr. award Alumni Assn. Sch. of Pharmacy, U. Md., 1990. Fellow Acad. of Pharmacy Practice, Soc. Pub. Health Edn.; mem. Am. Pharm. Assn. (dir., chmn. 1976-77), Md. Pharm. Assn. (Pres.'s award 1971), Am. Assn. Colls. Pharmacy, Nat. Orgn. for Competency Assurance (sec.-treas. 1994-95), Md. Pub. Pub. Health Assn. (pres. 1995-96), Acad. Pharmacy Practice (pres. 1973-74), Balt. Met. Pharm. Assn. (pres. 1968, hon. pres. 1994), U. Md. Sch. Pharm. Alumni Assn. (honored Alumnus award 1990), Sigma Xi, Rho Chi. Democrat. Jewish. Club: Optimist (pres. local club 1963-64). Contbr. articles to profl. jours. Home: 136 Welcome Aly Baltimore MD 21201-2432 Office: 506 W Fayette St 2nd Fl Rm 240 Baltimore MD 21201-1083

FEDELE, CHARLES ROBERT, dermatologist; b. Somerville, N.J., June 8, 1942; s. Vincent Francis and Mary Lucille (Sanchini) F.; B.S. in Biology, Villanova U., 1964; M.D., Bologna (Italy) U., 1970; m. Kathleen Ann Fox, June 23, 1972; children—Charles Robert, Kerry Ann, David Vincent. Intern, No. Westchester Hosp., Mt. Kisco, N.Y., 1971-72; resident Univ. Hosps. of Cleve., Case Western Res. Med. Sch., 1972-75; dermatologist asso. Guthrie Clinic, Sayre, Pa., 1977-81, chief dermatology sect., 1981—; mem. staff Robert Packer Hosp., Sayre; assoc. clin. prof. dermatology SUNY, Syracuse. Served to maj. U.S. Army, 1975-77. Diplomate Am. Bd. Dermatology. Fellow Am. Acad. Dermatology; mem. Dermatology Found., AMA, Pa., Bradford County med. socs., Pa. Acad. Dermatology. Roman Catholic. Home: 114 S Pennsylvania Ave Sayre PA 18840-1014 Office: Guthrie Clinic Guthrie Sq Sayre PA 18840

FEDER, LEWIS MORRIS MONTGOMERY, dermatologist, cosmetic plastic surgeon; b. N.Y.C., Feb. 11, 1945; s. Abraham Al and Geraldine (Roselli) F. BA, Hobart Coll., 1964; MD, N.Y. Med. Coll., 1968. Cert. Am. Bd. Dermatology. Intern U.S. Pub. Health Svc. Hosp., S.I., N.Y.; resident USPHS, S.I., N.Y.; dermatologist N.Y. Hosp., Cornell Med. Ctr., 1970-72, chief resident, 1972-73; pvt. practice N.Y.C., 1973—. Author: About Face, 1989, The Fifth Avenue Doctors Video Guide to Dermatology and Cosmetic Surgery, 1989. Hon. N.Y.C. Commr. for Youth, 1977-85. Lt. USPHS, 1968-70. Fellow Am. Acad. Cosmetic Surgery, Am. Acad. Dermatology, Am. Soc. Dermatologic Surgery, Am. Bd. Dermatology; mem. Nat. Bd. Med. Examiners (diplomate), Internat. Soc. Aesthetic Surgery (dir., Tokyo). Republican. Universalist. Office: 965 5th Ave New York NY 10021-1709

FEDER, MARTIN ELLIOTT, biology researcher and educator; b. Newark, Mar. 14, 1951; s. S. and A. C. (Gerwin) F.; m. Juliana Helen Huta, Aug. 19, 1973; children: Jonathan R. L., Alison F. L. BA summa cum laude, Cornell U., 1973; PhD, U. Calif., Berkeley, 1977. Postdoctoral fellow U. Chgo., 1977-78, asst. prof., 1979-85, assoc. prof., 1985-89, master biol. scis. collegiate div., assoc. dean div. biol. scis., 1988-91, prof. dept. organismal biology and anatomy, 1989—. Author, editor: Predator-Prey Relationships, 1986, New Directions in Ecological Physiology, 1987, Environmental Physiology of the Amphibians, 1992; mem. editorial bd. jour. Physiol. Zoology, 1990—; contbr. over 60 articles to profl. jours. Undergrad. Edn. Initiative award Howard Hughes Med. Inst., 1989-94; NSF grantee, 1978—; Andrew Mellon Found. fellow. Mem. AAAS, Am. Physiol. Soc., Soc. Integrative Comparitive Biology, Soc. for Exptl. Biology, Phi Beta Kappa. Office: Univ Chgo Dept Organismal Biology and Anatomy 1027 E 57th St Chicago IL 60637-1508

FEDER, NAOMI E., social work educator; b. N.Y.C., May 19, 1932; d. Max Jacob and Malcha Gardner; m. Louis Feder, Jan. 7, 1962; children: Avi, David. MSW, Hunter Sch. Social Work, 1959. Lic. marriage counselor, N.J.; bd. cert. diplomate clin social work. Caseworker Jewish Family Svcs., N.Y.C.; supr. Catholic Family and Community Svcs., Paterson, N.J.; pvt. practice Englewood, N.J.; instr. Wurzweiler Sch. Social Work, N.Y.C.

FEDER, ROBERT ELLIOT, psychiatrist; b. Detroit, July 8, 1951; s. Norman W. and Helen (Kadushin) F.; m. Marsha Susan Cooper; children: Daniel, Elana. BS with high honors, U. Mich., 1972; MD, U. Wash., 1977. Diplomate Am. Bd. Med. Examiners, Am. Bd. Psychiatry and Neurology. Resident in psychiatry Yale U., New Haven, 1981; assoc. psychiatrist Elmcrest Psychiat. Inst., Portland, Conn., 1980-81; med. dir. inpatient psychiatry Beverly (Mass.) Hosp., 1981-83; chief psychiatrist Matthew Thornton Health Plan, Nashua, N.H., 1983-86; attending staff Nashua Meml. Hosp., 1983—; courtesy staff St. Joseph's Hosp., Nashua, 1984—, Cath. Med. Ctr., Manchester, N.H., 1988—; med. dir. Psychiatric Inst. Cath. Med. Ctr., Manchester, N.H., 1995—; dir. outpatient svcs. Charter Brookside Hosp., Nashua, 1986-95; assoc. med. dir. Brookside Hosp., Nashua, 1993-95; pvt. practice psychiatry Brookside Hosp., Nashua, N.H., 1995—; chmn. dept. psychiatry Nashua Meml. Hosp., 1988-93, chmn. credentials com., 1991-93. Contbr. articles in psychiatry to profl. jours. Recipient Exemplary Psychiatrist award Nat. Alliance for Mentally Ill, 1992, 94. Fellow Am. Psychiat. Assn.; mem. AMA, Am. Assn. Gen. Hosp. Psychiatrists, Physicians for Social Responsibility, N.H. Psychiat. Soc. (pres. 1995-96, chmn. pub. affairs, mem. exec. com. 1985—), Am. Psychiat. Assn. Arts Assn. (sec.-treas. 1985-87), Phi Beta Kappa, Phi Eta Sigma. Democrat. Office: 100 McGregor St Manchester MA 03102

FEDER, STUART, psychoanalyst; b. N.Y.C., May 7, 1930; s. Irving and Ida (Hendleman) F.; m. Carol F., May 15, 1961; children: Susanna, Adam. BA, Harvard U., 1953; MD, Albert Einstein Coll. Medicine, 1961. Diplomate Am. Bd. Psychiatry and Neurology. Editor: Psychoanalytic Exploration in Music, 1989, Psychoanalytic Explorations in Music, Second Series, 1993; author: Chances Ives: "My Father's Song," 1992. With U.S. Army, 1953-55. Fellow Am. Psychiatric Assn.; mem. APA. Office: 19 E 88th St New York NY 10128-0557

FEDERA, KLAUS OTTO, clinical psychologist, psychotherapist; b. Munich, Sept. 17, 1959; s. Otto Richard and Julia Anna (Ehrl) F.; m. Veronika Dorothea Dietrich, Mar. 9, 1990; children: Stella Laura, Elena Klara. Diploma in psychology, U. Paris, 1986. Clin. psychology diplomate. Clin. psychologist, psychotherapist Prof. Dr. Werner Thost, Psychologist, Stuttgart, Fed. Republic Germany, 1987-91; clin. psychologist/psychotherapist Rheumaklinik, Bad Wiessee, Germany, 1991-94, Clin. for Drug Addicts, Munich, Germany, 1994—. Mem. Pro Asyl. Mem. Orgn. German Psychologists, Internat. Rorschach Soc. Home: Mangfallstrasse 6, 85579 Neubiberg Bavaria, Germany

FEDERHAR, DAVID BERNARD, psychologist, educator; b. Tucson, Apr. 4, 1951; s. Richard Harvey and Doris (Lakritz) F.; m. Kristin Pedersen, Aug. 3, 1974; children: Peter Alexander, Lars Andreas. BA, U. Ariz, 1972, MA, 1975, PhD, 1983. Lic. psychologist, Ariz., sch. psychologist, Ariz., tchr. psychology, Ariz., Calif.; nat. cert. sch. psychologist. Program cons. Autism Program Tuscon Unifed Sch. Dist., 1975-77; sch. psychologist Tucson Unified Sch. Dist., 1977—; adj. faculty Pima C.C., Tucson, 1979—; prof. Embry-Riddle Aero. U., Tucson, 1982—, Park Coll., Tucson, 1983—; instr. Chapman Univ., Tucson, 1988—, Troy State U., Tucson, 1991—; faculty advisor Chapman Univ.; participant Tucson Nat. Soc. Autistic Children Group, 1975-80, Tucson Sudden Infant Death Syndrome Group, 1977-86, Pediat. Task Force U. Med. Ctr., Tucson, 1987-90; adj. prof. No. Ariz. U., 1985—. Author (reports to U.S. Gov. for Autism Program) Program for Autistic Children of Tucson, 1975-77. Pres. TV Edn. Fund, 1991-92, v.p., 1990-91, treas., 1992-93; pres. Van Horne PTA, Tucson, 1984-85; coach Am. Youth Soccer Assn., 1985-87; bd. dirs. Jewish Family Svc., Tucson, 1984-87, Tanque Verde Ednl. Enrichment Fund, 1989-95; active Vista Del Rio Homeowners Assn., 1980-85. Mem. APA, So. Ariz. Psychol. Assn. (v.p., sec., chmn. membership 1977-82), Nat. Assn. Sch. Psychologists. Democrat. Home: 12355 E Barbary Coast Rd Tucson AZ 85749-8446 Office: Tucson Unified Sch Dist #1 750 N Rosemont Tucson AZ 85719-5813

FEDERMAN, DANIEL DAVID, medical educator, educational administrator, endocrinologist; b. N.Y.C., Apr. 16, 1928; m. Elizabeth Buckley; children: Lise, Carolyn. BA, Harvard U., 1949, MD, 1953. Diplomate Am. Bd. Internal Medicine. Instr. to prof. Harvard Med. Sch., Boston, 1961-72, prof. medicine and dean for students and alumni, 1977-92, Carl W. Walter prof. medicine and med. edn., dean med. edn., 1992—; chmn. medicine Stanford Med. Sch., Palo Alto, Calif., 1972-77; Carl W. Walter prof. medicine, med. edn., dean med. edn., 1992—. Author: med. textbook Abnormal Sexual Development, 1967; editor: med. textbook Scientific American Medicine. Master ACP (pres. Phila. 1982-83). Home: 1 Evergreen Way Belmont MA 02178-2127 Office: Harvard Med Sch Office of Dean 25 Shattuck St Boston MA 02115-6027

FEDERMAN, JAY L., ophthalmologist; b. Grand Rapids, Mich., Dec. 28, 1937; s. Esther Federman; m. Davida Federman; children: Rebecca, Rachel; m. Sylvia R. Beck; children: Sarah, Erik. BS, Franklin & Marshall Coll., Lancaster, Pa., 1959; MD, Tufts U., Boston, 1963. Intern Phila. Gen. Hosp., 1963-64; resident Jefferson Med. Coll., Phila., 1967-70; fellow Wills Eye Hosp., Phila., 1970-73; physician Ophthalmic Subspecialty Cons., P.C., Wynnewood, Pa., 1974—. Capt. USAF, 1964-67. Office: Wills Eye Hosp 9th Walnut St Philadelphia PA 19107*

FEDERMAN, MICHAEL JOEL, medical educator; b. Detroit, July 9, 1940; s. Leo George and Estelle (Goldberg) F.; m. Marjorie Dee Hauser, Nov. 7, 1970; 1 child, Robert Jay. BS, Wayne State U., 1961, MD, 1965. Asst. attending Sinai Hosp., Detroit, 1969-73, co-chief med. intensive care, 1973-75, chief sect. infectious disease, 1975-76, chief infection control com., 1976-79; attending William Beaumont Hosp., Royal Oak, Mich., 1979—; attending Sinai Hosp., 1982-92, med. dir. ambulatory divsn., 1992-93; assoc. prof. medicine Wayne State U., Detroit, 1993—, dir. ambulatory devel., 1994—; v.p. managed care, adminstrv. divsn. Detroit Med. Ctr., 1995—; v.p. Ambulatory Detroit Med. Ctr., 1995—. Fellow Am. Coll. Physicians; mem. AMA, Am. soc. Microbiology, Am. Fedn. Clin. Rsch., Am. Coll. Physician Execs., Mich. State Med. Soc., Oakland County Med. Soc., Infectious Disease Soc. Office: Northwest Internal Medicine Group 26206 W 12 Mile #200 Southfield MI 48034

FEDERSEL, HANS-JÜRGEN, pharmaceutical company executive; b. Säter, Dalecarlia, Sweden, Mar. 16, 1949; s. Hans and Ilse Marie (Schild) F.; m. Sophie Linnéa Lovisa Åkergård, June 13, 1981; children: Christopher, Alexander, Lovisa Antonia. MSc, Royal Inst. Tech., Stockholm, 1973, PhD, 1980. Devel. chemist Astra Pharm. Prodn., Södertälje, Sweden, 1974-89, prin. devel. chemist, 1989-92; mgr. Astra Prodn. Chems., Södertälje, 1992-96, sr. mgr., 1996—; assoc. prof. Royal Inst. Tech., Stockholm, 1990—. Contbr. articles to profl. jours.; patentee in field. Mem. Swedish Chem. Soc., Drug Info. Assn., Internat. Soc. Heterocyclic Chemistry. Home: Igelkottsvägen 60, 16417/57 Stockholm-Bromma Sweden Office: Astra Prodn Chems, 151 85 Södertälje Sweden

FEDOR, JOSEPH JOHN, psychologist; b. Scranton, Pa., Jan. 21, 1955; s. Joseph Francis and Joan Matilda (Ott) F.; B.S. in Psychology, U. Scranton, 1977; M.A. in Gen. Psychology, Marywood Coll., 1980; postgrad., Temple U., 1980—, Structural Family Therapy Program, 1984-85. Cert. sch. psychologist, Pa. Psycho-ednl. assoc. Friendship House Childrens Ctr., Scranton, Pa., 1973-79; psychologist Hazleton/Nanticoke Mental Health Mental Retardation Center, Hazleton, Pa., 1979-85; psychotherapist comprehensive care Mercy Hosp., Wilkes-Barre, Pa., 1985-87; psychologist Broome Devel. Ctr., Binghamton, N.Y., 1987—; pvt. practice psychotherapy, Clark Summit, Pa., 1989—; psychodiagnostician Behavior Assocs., 1980-86; sch. psychologist Colonial Northampton I.U. # 20, 1992—. Treas., pres. bd. dirs. Daedalus-Community Enrichment Center, Scranton, 1977-79; bd. dirs. Lackawanna Area Epilepsy Unit, Scranton, 1979—, pres., 1986, cofounder self-help group, 1980—; pres. Family Assn. Allied Services, Scranton, 1981-82. Mem. Psi Chi. Democrat. Roman Catholic. Home: 235 Mountain Rd Scranton PA 18505-2648 Office: 6 Danforth Rd Easton PA 18045-7820

FEDOR-JOSEPH, STEPHANIE RAE, counselor, fitness educator; b. Milw., Jan. 9, 1956; m. David Barry Joseph, June 6, 1982. BS, U. Wis.-LaCrosse, 1977; MS, U. Wis.-Madison, 1981. Lic. profl. counselor; nat. cert. counselor, wellness educator. Job coach, asst. counselor LaCrosse Courthouse, Wis., 1976-77; counselor U. Wis.-Madison, 1979-84; fitness educator Harbor Athletic Club, Middleton, Wis., 1982-85; fitness educator SportPlex, 1986-88; mktg. rep. Munz Corp., Madison, Wis., 1984-85; cons. total fitness edn. Gov.'s Council on Phys. Fitness and Health and Wis. Park and Recreation Assn., Madison/Appleton, 1984; stress mgmt. cons. U. Wis.-Madison, 1980-85, Family Health Plan, Health Maintenance Orgn., Milw., 1981; counselor U. Ala., Birmingham, 1987-88, acting dir., 1988-89, dir., 1989-91; dir. sch. engring. Student Svcs. U. Ala, Birmingham, 1988-91; guest instr. U. Wis.-Madison, 1981; guest instr. mental health and stress mgmt. health edn. U. Ala., Birmingham; faculty advisor U. Ala. chpt. Nat. Soc. Black Engrs., 1987-91; mem. child care adv. bd. U. Ala., Birmingham, 1991—; contbr. to profl. jours; presenter in field; dancer, choreographer, tchr., performer Madison Jazz Dance Theatre, 1979-80; jazz dance instr. Kanopy Dance Theatre, 1981-82; mem. stress mgmt. personal counseling, wellness promotion/workshops Stress Counseling Svc., 1991—. Creator group program relaxation/dance exercise, 1981. Fitness educator vol. Am. Heart Assn., Madison, 1983; crisis phone vol., LaCrosse, Wis., 1977; CPR instr. ARC, 1985-90. U. Wis.-LaCrosse, 1985—; Alumni Assn. scholar, 1976-77; vol. facilitator parent support groups Exchange Club Ctr. Prevention Child Abuse, 1992-93. Named Client of the Year Small Bus. Devel. Svc. Corps Retired Execs., 1992. Mem. ACA, Nat. Bd. Cert. Counselors, Inc. (counselor 1984—), Aerobics and Fitness Assn. Am. (cons. 1983—cert.), Wis. Personnel and Guidance Assn., U. Wis.-Madison Student Personnel Assn., Am. Mental Health Counselors Assn., Ala. Assn. for Counseling and Devel. (jour. editorial bd. 1989—), Ala. Coll. Personnel Assn. (com. VIII wellness), Ala. Mental Health Counselors Assn. (exec. coun., co-chmn. membership com. 1990-92), Ala. Assn. for Humanistic Edn. and Devel. (exec. coun., newsletter editor 1989-90), Counseling Acad. and Profl. Honor Soc. Internat., Am. Assn. Religious and Value Issues Counseling, Nat. Career Devel. Assn., Am. Assn. Women Deans, Adminstrs. and Counselors, Ala. Assn. Specialists in Group Work, Ala. Career Devel. Assn., Hoover Recreation Ctr., Chi Sigma Iota. Avocations: dance; artwork, sewing; cooking; Nautilus. Office: South Point Bldg 1425 21st St Ste 203 Birmingham AL 35205

FEE, WILLARD EDWARD, JR., otolaryngologist; b. Portchester, N.Y., June 10, 1943; s. Willard E. and Jane Frances (Cromwell) F.; m. Caroline Fee, June 13, 1965; children: Heather, Adam. BS cum laude, U. San Francisco, 1965; MD magna cum laude, U. Colo., 1969. Intern Harbor Gen. Hosp., Torrance, Calif., 1969-70; resident in gen. surgery Wadsworth VA Hosp., L.A., 1970-71; resident in head and neck surgery UCLA Sch. Medicine, 1971-74; asst. prof. Stanford (Calif.) U. Med. Ctr., 1974-80, assoc. prof., chmn., 1980-86, prof., chmn. in otolaryngology, 1986—, Edward C. & Amy H. Sewall prof., 1996—; dir. Am. Bd. of Otolaryngology, Houston, 1985—; chmn. med. sch. faculty senate Stanford U., 1992-94. Editl. bd. Archives in Otolaryngology, Chgo., 1984-95; contbr. numerous articles to profl. jours. Mem. Collegium ORLAS-US (chmn. 1995—), Paul H. Ward Soc., Inc. (pres. 1988-89), Am. Soc. Head and Neck Surgery (pres. 1989-90), Am. Acad. Otolaryngology and Head and Neck Surgery, Calif. Soc. Otolaryngology (pres. 1995—), Alpha Omega Alpha. Home: 27299 Ursula Ln Los Altos CA 94022-3222 Office: Stanford Univ Med Ctr Divn Otolaryngology Edwards R135 300 Pasteur Stanford CA 94305-5328

FEELY, MALACHY PIO, community psychiatric nurse; b. Mullingar, Westmeath, Ireland, Nov. 3, 1959; arrived in Eng., 1987; s. Joseph John and Bridget Veronica (O'Callaghan) F.; m. Anne Mary McCormack, Sept. 20, 1985; 1 child, Stephen Noel. MA in Mental Health Studies, Portsmouth U., Eng., 1996. Registered psychiat. nurse; cert. in counseling; diploma in nursing. Staff nurse Midland Health Bd., Ireland, 1985-87, Chichester Priority Care Svcs., Eng., 1987-89; charge nurse Chichester Priority Care Svcs., 1989-91, clin. care coord., 1991-92, sr. charge nurse, 1992-94, sr. charge nurse comty., 1994—; mem. strategic planning group Chichester Priority Care, 1992-93, chmn. crisis svc. working group, 1994-95; mem. regional forum comty. Inter Agy., Eng., 1995. Contbr. articles to profl. jours. Roman Catholic. Home: St Melier Ashfield Rd, Midhurst GU29 9JX, England Office: Chichester Priority Care Sv, 9 College Ln, PO19 4PQ Chichester England

FEENEY, DON JOSEPH, JR., psychologist; b. Greenville, N.C., Jan. 17, 1948; s. Don Joseph Sr. and Louise (Saieed) F.; 1 child, Kelly Lynn. BA, Colgate U., 1971; MA, Gov.'s State U., 1973; PhD, Loyola U., Chgo., 1979. Registered psychologist, Ill., Ind.; cert. addictions counselor. Clin. dir. Champaign (Ill.) Coun. on Alcoholism, 1976-79; pvt. practice psychology, hypnotherapy, family services Downers Grove, Ill., 1979—; pvt. practice psychology, hypnotherapy and family svcs. Dangerous Drugs Com., Chgo., 1979-80; psychologist Tri-City Mental Health Ctr., East Chicago, Ind., 1980-82; psychologist alcohol treatment program Christ Hosp., Oak Lawn, Ill., 1982—; cons. Psychol. Cons. Svcs., Downers Grove, Ill., 1985—; chmn. adv. coun. on alcoholism Govs. State U., University Park, Ill., 1979-82; devel., presenter self-hypnosis and wellness programs on smoking, weight control and chem. abuse. Contbr. articles to profl. jours.; guest cons. to nat. talk shows, Oprah Winfrey, Jerry Springer, Jenny Jones, others. Fellow, Loyola U., 1976. Mem. APA, Ill. Psychol. Assn. Roman Catholic. Office: Psychol Cons Svcs 6900 Main St Ste 54 Downers Grove IL 60516-3455

FEENEY, DONALD PETER, urologist, surgeon; b. N.Y.C., Aug. 30, 1930; s. A. Edward and Madeline J. (Cusack) F.; m. Frances M. Clegg, Apr. 28, 1958; children: Carol, Laura, Douglas, Gregory. BS in Biology, Holy Cross Coll., Worcester, Mass., 1952; MD, Cornell Med. Coll., N.Y.C., 1956. Diplomate Am. Bd. Urology. Pvt. practice urology Rockford, Ill., 1964—. Capt. USAF, 1958-60, Japan. Democrat. Roman Catholic. Home: 511 Calvin Park Blvd Rockford IL 61107-4610 Office: Rockford Clinic 2300 N Rockton Ave Rockford IL 61103-3619

FEENEY, MARY KATHERINE O'SHEA, retired public health nurse; b. Niagara Falls, N.Y., July 10, 1934; d. James T. and Mary Elizabeth (Woodside) O'Shea; m. Gerald E. Feeney, Apr. 27, 1957; children: Patricia, Elizabeth, Susan, Kathleen. BSN, Niagara U., 1956; MS in Mgmt., SUNY, Binghamton, 1981. RN, N.Y.; hypnotherapist; Assessment Modified Reflexology for Nurses. Pub. health nurse Herkimer County (N.Y.) Pub. Health Nursing Svc.; ret.; past coord. Herkimer County Long Term Health Care; bd. dirs. Oneida/Herkimer Coalition for Tobacco Control. Home: RR 3 Box 329 Little Falls NY 13365-9556

FEGEN, JOSEPH PETER, JR., urologist, educator; b. Phila., Dec. 19, 1937; m. Carol Lee Huber, June 8, 1963; children: Katie, Joseph P. III. BS, John Carroll U., 1959; MD, Cornell U., 1963. Intern, resident Univ. Hosps. Cleve., 1963-65, 67-70; pvt. practice Cleve., 1970—; assoc. clin. prof. Case We. Res. U., Cleve., 1970—; chief urology sect. Fairview Gen. Hosp., Cleve., 1983—, St. John Westshore Hosp., Cleve., 1978-90. Capt. U.S. Army, 1965-67, Vietnam. Mem. Am. Urol. Assn. Inc. (North Ctrl. sect.), Am. Assn. Clin. Urologists, Cleve. Urol. Assn. (pres. 1976), Cleve. Acad. Medicine (bd. dirs.), Pasteur Club Cleve. (bd. censors). Office: North Coast Urology Inc 18099 Lorain Ln Cleveland OH 44111

FEHER, LESLIE, psychotherapist; b. N.Y.C., Mar. 6, 1944; s. Alexander and Elizabeth (Geller) F.; 1 child, Vanessa. BA, Pace U., 1967; MA, New Sch. Social Rsch., 1970; PhD in Clin. Psychology, Union Inst., 1990. Founder, Elizabeth Fehr Natal Therapy Inst., N.Y.C., 1974—; founder, exec. dir., pres. Assn. Birth Psychology, 1978—; pvt. practice psychotherapy, 1974—; assoc. prof. Kean Coll., 1991; prof. Touro Coll., 1993—. Mem. APA, Am. Orthopsychiat. Assn., Ea. Psychol. Assn., Am. Pers. and Guidance Assn., Authors Guild, Authors League. Author: The Psychology of Birth, 1980; contbr. articles to profl. jours.; founder, editor Birth Psychology Bull., 1979—. Home and Office: 444 E 82nd St New York NY 10028-5903

FEHLER, POLLY DIANE, neonatal nurse, educator; b. Harvard, Ill., Jan. 6, 1946; d. Arthur William and Charlotte (Stewart) Eggert; m. Gene L. Fehler, Dec. 26, 1964; children: Timothy, Andrew. AS, summa cum laude, Kishwaukee Coll., 1974; BSN, magna cum laude, No. Ill. U., DeKalb, 1977, MSN, summa cum laude, 1980. Cert. BLS, neonatal resuscitation instr. Ob-gyn. staff nurse Kishwaukee Hosp., 1977; community health nurse DeKalb County Health Dept., 1977-79; grad. teaching asst. No. Ill. Univ., 1978-80; adj. maternity instr. Auburn Univ., Montgomery, Ala., 1980-81; maternal/newborn nurse USAF Regional Hosp. Maxwell, Montgomery, Ala., 1980-81, nurse internship coord., 1981-83; edn. coord. USAF Hosp., Bergstrom, Austin, Tex., 1983-87; neonatal ICU & transport RN St. Mary's Hosp., Athens, Ga., 1988-90; nursing instr. Tri-County Tech. Coll., Pendleton, S.C., 1990—; EMT, course lectr. U. Tex., Austin, 1984-86; counselor, vol. Hospice, 1984-87; sec., v.p. Shared Resources for Nurses, Austin, 1984-87, high blood pressure instr.-trainer, 1986-87, home health staff nurse Interim Health Care, Anderson, S.C., 1991-94; expert witness St. Mary's Hosp., Athens, 1991-92; coord. NCLEX rev. course Health Edn. Systems, Inc., 1993—; lectr. on interculturalism in nursing, 1993—; mem. adv. bd. Tri-County Student Competencies, 1990—, mem. advising team, 1995—, mini grant sel. com., 1992-93, 95—. Nursing textbook reviewer Addison Wesley Pubs., 1993, Mosby Yearbook, 1995—. Nurse, med. evaluator Mass Casualty Exercises, Austin, 1984-87; tchr., sec. United Meth. Chs., Ill., Ala., Ga., S.C., 1970—; mem. alumni bd. No. Ill. Alumni, DeKalb, 1979-80; mem. Malta Dist. Bd. Edn., 1979-80; judge Austin Sch. Dist. Sci. and Math. Fair, Austin, 1983-84; S.C. Gov.'s Guardian ad Litem Vol., 1995—; vol. Oconee County Healthy Visions Task Force, 1996—, S.C. Good Health Appeal Coll. Campaign Mgr., 1996, Oconee County Humane Soc., 1996—. Capt. USAF, 1980-88. Decorated USAF Commendation medal with oak leaf cluster; recipient Sr. Nursing Class of Tri-County Tech. Coll. Instr. of the Yr. award, 1992, Nat. Inst. for Staff and Orgnl. Devel. Excellence award, 1995. Mem. AAUW, ANA, S.C. Nurses Assn., S.C. Assn. Perinatal Nurses, S.C. Tech. Edn. Assn., Nursing Faculty Orgn. (v.p. 1991-94), United Meth. Women, S.C. Internat. Ednl. Consortium, Delta Kappa Gamma, Sigma Theta Tau, Lambda Chi Nu. Meth. Home: 106 Laurel Ln Seneca SC 29678-2705 Office: Tri-County Tech Coll PO Box 587 Pendleton SC 29670-0587

FEHLER, VICKIE LYNN, nurse; b. Akron, Ohio, Oct. 31, 1948; d. Donald Leroy and Alice Rebecca (Baldwin) Irvin; divorced; children: Edward A. III, Lori Lynn; m. John Howard Fehler, Sept. 3, 1992. B in Nursing, U. Akron, Ohio, 1979. RN, Ohio; cert. case mgr. Staff nurse Akron City Hosp., 1979-80; psychiat. nurse A.E. Villalba, MD, Inc., Cuyahoga Falls, Ohio, 1979-83; staff nurse dialysis Greater Akron Dialysis Ctr., 1982-83; kidney transplant coord. Akron City Hosp., 1983; rehab. specialist, case mgr., hosp. bill rev. specialist Internat. Rehab. Assocs., Inc., Brecksville, Ohio, 1984-88; med. case mgr. Coordinated Rehab. Assn., Inc., Okemos, Mich., 1988-89; pres. Med. Evaluations and Cost Containment Assistance, Inc., Twinsburg, Ohio, 1989—; cmty. health cons. Parma (Ohio) Hosp., 1991-92. Mem. Sigma Theta Tau. Home: 3515 Courtland Rd Pepper Pike OH 44122 Office: Med Evaluations & Cost Containment Assistance Inc 8714 Tower Park Dr Twinsburg OH 44087

FEIGENBERG, MARVIN EDWARD, psychologist, consultant; b. Phila., July 2, 1932; s. Bernard and Jeannette (Heisman) F.; m. Evelyn Beer, July 1, 1956; children: Andrew, Sheri, Steven. BS in Edn., Temple U., 1954, MS in Edn., 1957; EdD, U. Sarasota, 1979. Cert. elem. tchr., Pa.; cert. sch. psychologist, Pa.; lic. psychologist, Pa. Elem. tchr. Sch. Dist. of Phila., 1954-58, sch. psychologist, 1958—; lectr. psychology Pa. State U., Upper Merion, 1968-75; cons. psychologist Pa. Bur. Vocat. Rehab., Phila., 1972—; staff psychologist Salvation Army Children's Home, Phila., 1972-79; cons. No. Home for Children, Phila., 1972-77. Author: Pre-screening Emotionally Disturbed Children, 1979. Mem. Internat. Assn. Sch. Psychologists, Pa. Psychol. Assn., Kappa Phi Kappa (pres. 1953, 54). Democrat. Jewish. Avocations: tennis; gardening. Home: 100 Red Rambler Rd Lafayette Hill PA 19444-2109 Office: Sch Dist Phila 21st And The Pky Philadelphia PA 19103-1031

FEIGIN, DAVID SIMON, radiology educator; b. N.Y.C.. AB, Cornell U., 1966; MD, NYU, 1970. Intern Bell Ctr., 1970-71; resident Johns Hopkins Med. Inst., 1971-74; fellow nuclear medincine Johns Hopkins Med. Inst., Balt., 1974; chief diagnostic radiology Armed Forces Inst. Pathology, 1975-78; instr., 1974-75; asst. prof. Johns Hopkins U., Balt., 1975-78; asst. prof. U. Calif.-San Diego, La Jolla, 1978-81, assoc. prof. radiology, 1981-87, prof. radiology, 1987—. Home: 8256 Caminito Lacayo La Jolla CA 92037-2208 Office: U Calif San Diego Dept Radiology # V-114 San Diego CA 92093

FEIGIN, JOEL STANLEY, physician, educator; b. N.Y.C., Sept. 1, 1951; s. Bernard Feigin and Ruth (Lerner) Harrison; m. Carolyn Ann Zerweck, 1987; children: Laura Alicia, Stephanie Erin. BA, Syracuse U., 1972; MD, SUNY, Syracuse, 1976. Diplomate Am. Bd. Family Practice. Resident in family practice U. Mass. Med. Ctr., Worcester, 1976-79, asst. prof., 1979-87; asst. dir. Barre (Mass.) Health Ctr., 1979-82; med. dir. Northhampton Health Ctr., Florence, Mass., 1982-84; pvt. practice Northhampton, Mass., 1984-87; mem. faculty family practice residency program U. Mass., Worcester, 1979-82; assoc. prof. Robert Wood Johnson Med. Sch., New Brunswick, N.J., 1987-94; assoc. dir. family practice residency Warren Hosp., Phillipsburg, N.J., 1987-94; clin. dir. Coventry Family Practice Assn., Phillipsburg, 1987-94; v.p., med. dir. Cigna Healthcare of No. N.J., Rockaway, 1994—. Mem. Am. Acad. Family Physicians, Mass. Acad. Family Physicians, N.J. Acad. Family Physicians, Soc. Tchrs. Family Medicine. Home: 1 Kenner Ct Flemington NJ 08822-2054 Offices: Coventry Family Practice Reo Sch Ln Phillipsburg NJ 08865 Office: Cigna Healthcare No NJ 100 Enterprise Dr Ste 610 Rockaway NJ 07866-2115

FEIGIN, RALPH DAVID, pediatrician, educator; b. N.Y.C., Apr. 3, 1938; s. Jack Bernard and Dorothy Phyllis (Strauss) F.; m. Judith Sue Zobel, June 26, 1960; children: Susan M., Michael E., Debra F. AB, Columbia U., 1958; MD, Boston U., 1962. Diplomate Am. Bd. Pediatrics, sub bd. for infectious diseases. Pediatric intern Boston City Hosp., 1962-63; pediatric resident Boston City Hosp. and Mass. Gen. Hosp., 1963-65; teaching fellow pediatrics Harvard U. Med. Sch., 1964-65; from asst. prof. to prof. pediatrics Washington U. Med. Sch., St. Louis, 1968-77; dir. divsn. infectious diseases dept. pediatrics Washington U. Med. Sch., 1973-77; prof. pediatrics, chmn. dept. Coll. Medicine Baylor U., Houston, 1977—, disting. svc. prof., 1990—, sr. v.p., 1992—; sr. v.p. Baylor Coll. Medicine, Houston, 1992-95, dean med. edn., 1994-95, pres., CEO, 1996—; physician-in-chief Tex. Children's Hosp., 1977—, exec. v.p., 1987-89; chief pediatric svc. Harris County Hosp. Dist., 1977—; pediatrician-in-chief Methodist Hosp., 1980—; mem. adv. ad hoc study group on spl. infectious disease problems U.S. Army Med. R & D Command, 1974-83; vis. prof., cons. in field; pres. Pediatris Rsch. Found., 1982—. Co-editor: Nutrition and the Developing Nervous System, 1975, Textbook of Pediatric Infectious Diseases, 1981, 3d edit., 1992, Roundsmanship, 1989-93, Practices and Principles of Pediatrics, 1989, 2d edit., 1993; mem. editorial bd. Pediatrics, 1978-90, consulting editor, 1993-94, assoc. editor, 1994—; mem. editorial bd. Jour. Pediatric Infectious Diseases; assoc. editor Jour. Infectious Diseases, 1984-88; editor-in-chief Seminars in Pediatric Infectious Diseases, 1990—; contbr. articles to med. jours., chpts. to books. With M.C., USAR, 1965-67. Recipient Rsch. Career Devel. award USPHS, 1970, Founders Day award Washington U. Med. Sch., 1977, Sr. Class Outstanding Tchr. award Baylor Coll. Medicine, 1978, 80, 81, 82, 83, 84, 85, 86, Minnie Stevens Piper Professorial award, 1984, John McGovern Outstanding Clin. Faculty award Baylor Coll. Medicine, 1986, 94, Disting. Alumnus award Boston U. Sch. of Medicine, 1989, Joseph St. Geme Jr. Leadership award in Pediatrics, Fedn. Pediatric Orgns., 1995, Disting. Faculty award Alumni Assn., Baylor Coll. of Medicine, 1994; named to Baylor Coll. Medicine Outstanding Tchr. Hall of Fame, 1984; Alumni Tchg. scholar Washington U. Med. Sch., 1975. Fellow AAAS, Am. Microbiology; mem. AMA, Am. Pediatric Soc. (pres.-elect 1996-97), Am. Acad. Pediat., Infectious Diseases Soc. Am., Pediatric Infectious Disease Soc. (Disting. Physician award 1996), Inst. Medicine of NAS, N.Y. Acad. Scis., Tex. Med. Assn., Tex. Pediatric Soc., Harris County Med. Soc., Houston Pediatric Soc., Soc. Pediatric Rsch. (pres. 1982-83), Assn. Med. Sch. Pediatric Dept. Chairpersons (pres. 1991-93). Office: Baylor Coll Medicine Dept Pediatrics 1 Baylor Plz Houston TX 77030-3411

FEIGON, JUDITH TOVA, ophthalmologist, surgeon, educator; b. Galveston, Tex., Dec. 2, 1947; d. Louis and Ethel (Goldberg) F.; m. Nathan C. Goldman; children: Michael G., Miriam G. AB, Barnard Coll., Columbia U., 1970; postgrad., Rice U. and U. Houston, 1970-71; MD, U. Tex.-San Antonio, 1976. Diplomate Am. Bd. Ophthalmology. Intern Mt. Auburn Hosp., Cambridge, Mass. Intern and clin. teaching fellow, Harvard U. Med. Sch., 1976-77; resident in ophthalmology, Baylor Coll. Medicine, Houston, 1977-80, fellowship in retina, 1980-82, clin. instr., 1982—; asst. prof. ophthalmology U. Tex. Med. Br., Galveston, 1982-85, clin. asst. prof., 1985-91, clin. assoc. prof., 1992—; pvt. practice medicine specializing in ophthalmology, vitreoretinal diseases and surgery, Houston, 1983—; physician advisor to Houston br. Tex. Soc. to Prevent Blindness, 1987-89, also bd. dirs.; mem. staff Meth., St. Lukes, Tex. Children's, John Sealy, St. Joseph's Hosp., Park Plaza. Contbr. articles to profl. publs. Mem. AMA, Assn. Am. Physicians and Surgeons, Am. Acad. Ophthalmology, Tex. Med. Assn., Tex. Opthal. Soc., Houston Opthal. Soc., Harris County Med. Soc., U. Tex.-San Antonio Alumni Assn., Harvard Med. Sch. Alumni Assn., Vitreous Soc. Office: 7515 Main St Ste 650 Houston TX 77030-4519

FEILD, JAMES RODNEY, physician, neurosurgeon; b. Memphis, Mar. 12, 1934; s. Roscoe A. and Georgia (Bledsoe) F.; m. Nancy Lee Tanner; children: Mary, Fred, Jamie, Alan, Glynn. Student, Rhodes Coll., 1952-54; MD, U. Tenn., 1957. Intern John Gaston Hosp., Memphis, 1958; pvt. practice Albany, Ky., 1959; resident in neurosurgery Bapt. Hosp., U. Tenn., Memphis, 1960-63; spl. fellow in neurology Mayo Clinic, Rochester, Minn., 1964; pvt. practice, Memphis, 1965—. Home: 3265 Burnt Pine Cove Destin FL 32541 Office: Mid-South Neurol Clinic 234 Germantown Bend Cv Cordova TN 38018-7237

FEIN, LINDA ANN, nurse anesthetist, consultant; b. Cin., Dec. 10, 1949; d. Joseph and Elizabeth P. (Kannady) Stofle; m. Thomas Paul Fein, Dec. 11, 1971. Nursing diploma, Miami Valley Hosp. Sch. Nursing, Dayton, Ohio, 1971, Wright State U., Dayton, 1969; postgrad. U. Cin. Med. Ctr., 1978. Nursing asst. Miami Valley Hosp., Dayton, 1969-71; staff nurse operating room Cin. Children's Hosp. and Med. Ctr., 1971, 73, Peninsula Hosp., Burlingame, Calif., 1972-73; staff nurse operating room and emergency room Doctors Hosp., San Diego, 1972; staff nurse emergency room Ohio State U. Hosps., Columbus, 1973-75, head nurse operating room, 1975-76; staff nurse anesthetist Bethesda Hosps., Cin., 1978-86; staff nurse anesthetist Mercy Hosp. of Fairfield, Cin., 1986-95; locum tenens anesthetist Good Samaritan Hosp., Dayton, Ohio, 1993—; staff nurse, anesthetist Fort Hamilton-Hughes Hosp., Hamilton, Ohio, 1995—. childbirth educator psychoprophylactic method, 1975—; critical care nursing cons. Med. Communicators & Assocs., Salt Lake City, 1985-89; ind. nursing cons., 1989—; co-owner Exec. Shops, Cin., 1982-85; speaker in field. Mem. search com. Cin. Gen. Hosp. Sch. of Anesthesia for Nurses, 1981-82; bd. dirs. YWCA, 1988-91, Children's Diagnostic Ctr., 1989-95, pres. bd. dirs., 1994, Planned Parenthood, 1992-95. Recipient Recognition of Profl. Excellence, First Nurse Anesthesia Faculty Assocs., 1982, Florence Nightengale awards, 1995. Mem. Miami Valley Hosp. Sch. of Nursing Alumni Assn., Cin. Gen. Hosp. Sch. Anesthesia for Nurses Alumni Assn., Nurse Anesthetists of Greater Cin., Ohio Assn. Nurse Anesthetists, Am. Assn. Nurse Anesthetists, Am. Assn. Operating Room Nurses, Am. Assn. Critical Care Nurses, Nat. Registry of Cert. Nurses in Advanced Practice (cert.), Ohio Coaliation of Nurses with Specialty Cert., Am. Soc. Critical Care Medicine, Am. Trauma Soc., NAFE, Altrusa Internat. (officer 1985-92). Republican. Methodist. Lodge: Eastern Star. Avocations: antiques, gourmet cooking, African violets, roses, swimming. Home: 650 History Bridge Ln Hamilton OH 45013-3659

FEIN, LOUIS IRA, speech pathologist; b. N.Y.C., Apr. 9, 1941; s. Saul N. and Sally F.; BA, L.I. U., 1966; MS, Bklyn. Coll., 1969; PhD, Elysion Coll., 1980; m. Carla Ginsburg, Apr. 25, 1965 (div.); children: Marc, Tracy; m. Angela Pyke; 1 child, Nicole. Sr. staff therapist Bklyn. Coll. Speech and Hearing Clinic, 1966-69; dir. speech pathology Miami Dade C.C., 1970-74; dir. South Miami Speech Clinic, 1970—; supr. speech clinic, instr. Grad. Sch. U. Miami, 1974-75, adj. asst. prof. dept. otolaryngology Med. Sch. U. Miami, 1975-83; exec. dir. United Testing Svc., Inc., 1976—. Cert. speech pathologist N.Y., Fla. Author: Berman-Fein Neurological Screening, Pre-Assessment for Scotopic Sensitivity, Releasing Your Child's Learning Power, , Fast: Fein Articulation Screening Test, Stop Stuttering: An Intensive Theraphy Program, Mem. Am. Speech Hearing Assn., Am. Counseling Assn., Fla. Speech and Hearing Assn., Fla. Cleft Palate Assn., Nat. Stutterers Found., Reading Assn., Nat. Reading Styles Inst. Office: 9485 Sunset Dr Ste A200 Miami FL 33173-3228

FEIN, RASHI, health sciences educator; b. N.Y.C., Feb. 6, 1926; s. Isaac M. and Clara(Wertheim) F.; m. Ruth Judith Breslau, June 19, 1949; children: Alan, Michael, Karen, Bena (dec.). Student, Bridgeport Jr. Coll., 1942-43; B.A., Johns Hopkins U., 1948, Ph.D., 1956; LittD (hon.), SUNY, 1996. Mem. staff Pres.'s Commn. on Health Needs, 1952; from lectr. to asso. prof. U. N.C., 1952-61; statistician Bur. of Census, 1958-59; sr. staff Pres.'s Council Econ. Advisers, 1961-63; sr. fellow Brookings Inst., 1963-68; prof. Harvard U., 1968—; Heath Clark lectr. London Sch. Hygiene and Tropical Medicine, 1980; chmn. med. assistance adv. council to sec. HEW, 1967-69; mem. adv. com. research and devel. Social Security Adminstrn., 1968-71; mem. Nat. Manpower Policy Task Force, 1967-79, Office Tech. Assessment, Health Adv. Panel., 1981-86; mem. spl. med. adv. group VA, 1987-91; mem. nat. adv. rsch. resources coun. NIH, 1995—. Author: Economics of Mental Illness, 1958, The Doctor Shortage: An Economic Diagnosis, 1967, (with Gerald Weber) Financing Medical Education: An Analysis of Alternative

Policies and Mechanisms, 1971, (with Charles Lewis and David Mechanic) A Right to Health: The Problem of Access to Primary Medical Care, 1976, Alcohol in America: The Price We Pay, 1984, Medical Care, Medical Costs: The Search for a Health Insurance Policy, 1986. Trustee Beth Israel Hosp., Boston, Hebrew Rehab. Home for Aged, Boston; bd. dirs. Harvard Cmty. Health Plan Found., 1980-87; mem. tech. bd. Millbank Meml. Fund, 1975-78, 86-90, bd. dirs., 1987-90. With USNR, 1944-46. Recipient John M. Russell award for advancement knowledge in medicine, 1971; Fellow Inst. History Medicine Johns Hopkins, 1951-52; traveling fellow WHO, 1971. Mem. Inst. Medicine of Nat. Acad. Scis., Am. Econ. Assn., AAUP, Am. Pub. Health Assn. Jewish. Office: 643 Huntington Ave Boston MA 02115-6019

FEIN, SEYMOUR HOWARD, pharmaceutical executive; b. N.Y.C., Oct. 28, 1948; s. Abner and Beatrice (Wolkoff) F.; m. Mary Louise Orizzonto, Apr. 1, 1979; children: Jessica Ann, David Thomas, Renee Elizabeth, Jonathan Parker. BA, U. Pa., 1970; MD, N.Y. Med. Coll., 1974. Intern Dartmouth-Hitchcock Med. Ctr., Hanover, N.H., 1974-75; resident in internal medicine Dartmouth-Hitchcock Med. Ctr., Hanover, 1975-77; fellow in hematology, oncology Beth Israel Hosp., Harvard Med. Sch., Boston, 1977-80; sr. rsch. physician Hoffmann-LaRoche, Nutley, N.J., 1980-83; dir. med. rsch. Miles Pharmaceuticals, West Haven, Conn., 1983-86, Rorer Pharmaceuticals, Fort Washington, Pa., 1986-87; v.p. med. rsch. Greenwich Pharmaceuticals, Fort Washington, 1987-88; dir. clin. rsch. and devel. Anaquest, Murray Hill, N.J., 1988-92; v.p. clin. rsch. and biostats. Oxford Rsch. Internat. Corp., Clifton, N.J., 1992-94; pres. Fein Consulting and Rsch. Svcs., New Canaan, Conn., 1994—; instr. medicine Harvard Med. Sch., 1979-80. Mem. Am. Soc. Clin. Oncology, N.Y. Acad. Scis., AAAS. Republican. Jewish.

FEIN, WILLIAM, ophthalmologist; b. N.Y.C., Nov. 27, 1933; s. Samuel and Beatrice (Lipschitz) F.; m. Bonnie Fern Aaronson, Dec. 15, 1963; children: Stephanie Paula, Adam Irving, Gregory Andrew. BS, CCNY, 1954; MD, U. Calif., Irvine, 1962. Diplomate Am. Bd. Ophthalmology. Intern L.A. County Gen. Hosp., 1962-63, resident in ophthalmology, 1963-66; instr. U. Calif. Med. Sch., Irvine, 1966-69; mem. faculty U. So. Calif. Med. Sch., 1969—, assoc. clin. prof. ophthalmology, 1979—; attending physician Cedars-Sinai Med. Ctr., L.A., 1966—, chief ophthalmology clinic svc., 1979-81, chmn. div. ophthalmology, 1981-85; attending physician Los Angeles County-U. So. Calif. Med. Ctr., 1969—; chmn. dept. ophthalmology Midway Hosp., 1975-78; dir. Ellis Eye Ctr., L.A., 1984—. Mem. editorial bd. CATARACT, Internat. Jour. of Cataract and Ocular Surgery, 1992—; contbr. articles to med. publs. Chmn. ophthalmology adv. com. Jewish Home for Aging of Greater L.A., 1993—. Fellow Internat. Coll. Surgeons, Am. Coll. Surgeons; mem. Am. Acad. Ophthalmology, Am. Soc. Ophthalmic Plastic and Reconstructive Surgery, Royal Soc. Medicine, AMA, Calif. Med. Assn., L.A. Med. Assn. Home: 718 N Camden Dr Beverly Hills CA 90210-3205 Office: 415 N Crescent Dr Beverly Hills CA 90210-4860 also: 8635 W 3d St # 390W Los Angeles CA 90048

FEINBAUM, GEORGE, internist; b. Samarkand, Uzbekistan, July 31, 1945; came to U.S., 1965, naturalized, 1972; s. Joseph and Cyrla (Szoken) F.; student Med. Acad. Wroclaw, Poland, 1963-65, Queens Coll., 1966-70; MD, Albert Einstein Coll. Medicine, 1973; 1 son, Livius. Diplomate Am. Bd. Internal Medicine. Intern, Met. Hosp. Ctr., N.Y.C., 1973-74, resident in internal medicine, 1974-76, fellow in endocrinology and metabolism, 1976-77; practice medicine, specializing in internal medicine, Bklyn., 1977—; asst. in medicine Brookdale Hosp. Med. Ctr., Bklyn. Fellow ACP; mem. Kings County Med. Soc., N.Y. Acad. Scis., Mensa. Office: 3245 Nostrand Ave Brooklyn NY 11220-3716 also: 934 Manhattan Ave Brooklyn NY 11222-1626

FEINBERG, ARTHUR IRWIN, surgeon; b. N.Y.C., June 29, 1940; s. William and Harriet (Abromowitz) F.; m. Gilda Jo, Apr. 11, 1981; children: Mark, Linda. MD, NYU, 1965. Diplomate Am. Bd. Surgery. Resident, chief resident Bellevue-NYU Med. Ctr., N.Y.C., 1961-70; surgeon Surgery Assocs., Hollywood, Fla., 1972—, mng. ptnr., 1987—; chief dept. surgery Hollywood Meml. Regional Hosp., 1991-95; asst. clin. prof. Miami (Fla.) Hosp., 1973—. Fellow Am. Coll. Surgeons, Am. Coll. Gastroenterology; mem. Am. Coll. Gastroenterological Surgery. Office: Surgery Assocs 1150 N 35 Ave Ste 490 Hollywood FL 33021

FEINBERG, DENNIS L., dermatologist; b. Bridgeport, Conn., June 10, 1951. AB, Cornell U., 1973; MD, SUNY, Syracuse, 1976. Diplomat Nat. Bd. Med. Examiners, Am. Bd. Internal Medicine, Am. Bd. Dermatology. Intern U. Miami (Fla.) Affiliated Hosps., 1976-77, resident, 1977-78; resident Johns Hopkins Med. Inst., Balt., 1978-80; dermatologist pvt. practice, Washington, 1981, Stratford, Conn., 1981—; assoc. attending Bridgeport Hosp., 1981—; attending St. Vincent's Med. Ctr., Bridgeport, 1981—, cons. Milford (Conn.) Hosp., 1982—; clin. instr. Yale U. Sch. Medicine, New HAven, Conn., 1985—. Fellow Am. Acad. Dermatology; mem. AMA, Am. Coll. Physicians, New Eng. Dermatological Soc., Conn. State Med. Soc., Fairfield County Med. Assn., Greater Bridgeport Med. Assn., Syracuse Med. Alumni Assn. Office: 2875 Main St Stratford CT 06497

FEINBERG, EDWARD BURTON, ophthalmologist, educator; b. Long Branch, N.J., May 24, 1945; s. Sidney and Marna (Reuckhaus) F.; m. Ruth Ann Eliasoph, Apr. 22, 1947; children: Daniel Ari, Rebecca Sara. BS, Lehigh U., 1966; MD, Mt. Sinai Sch. Medicine, 1971. Diplomate Am. Bd. Med. Examiners, Am. Bd. Ophthalmology. Intern U. Mich., Ann Arbor, 1971-72, resident in ophthalmology, 1974-77, fellow in retinal surgery, 1977-78; practice medicine specializing in ophthalmology Chattanooga, 1978—; chair dept. ophthalmology U. Tenn. Coll. Medicine Chattanooga Unit, Chattanooga, 1992-95; vice chief of staff Erlanger Med. Ctr., Chatanooga, 1992—; asst. prof. Clin. Edn. Ctr., Chattanooga, 1978—; chief ophthalmology W.D. Miller Eye Ctr., Chattanooga, 1986—; chief ophthalmology Erlanger Med. Ctr., Chattanooga, 1986, mem. bd. planning com., 1987—. Bd. dirs. Tenn. Diabetes Assn., 1984—; treas. St. Nicholas Sch., Chattanooga, 1985-87. Served to lt. M.C., USN, 1972-74. Fellow Am. Acad. Ophthalmology; mem. AMA, Hamilton County Med. Soc. Jewish. Office: Retina Assocs 979 E 3rd St Ste 708 Chattanooga TN 37403-3329

FEINBERG, JOEL AARON, podiatrist; b. Pitts., July 16, 1959; s. Harry and Barbara Kay F.; m. Sue Eileen Dalzell, Apr. 21, 1990; 1 child, Adam. BS, Allegheny Coll., 1981; DPM, Ohio Coll. Podiatric Medicine, 1985. Diplomate Am. Coll. Foot and Ankle Surgeons. Resident Elm Road Med. Ctr., Cortland, Ohio, 1985-86; pvt. practice podiatry Port Charlotte, Arcadia, Fla., 1986—. Fellow Am. Coll. Foot & Ankle Surgeons; mem. Am. Diabetes Assn., Am. Podiatric Med. Assn., Fla. Podiat. Med. assn., Charlotte County Med. Assn. Office: Gulf Coast Podiatry Inc 2101 D Tamiami Tr Port Charlotte FL 33948

FEINBERG, MICHAEL, psychiatry educator; b. Allentown, Pa., Apr. 30, 1942; s. Louis and Ruth (Austin) F.; children: Joshua, Ari. BSc, McGill U., Montreal, Que., Can., 1963; MD, Boston U., 1973, PhD, 1973. Diplomate Am. Bd. Psychiatry and Neurology. Asst. prof. psychiatry U. Mich., Ann Arbor, 1976-82, assoc. prof., 1982-86, adj. assoc. prof. psychology, 1983-88; assoc. prof. Med. Coll. of Pa., Phila., 1986-87, prof. psychiatry, 1988; prof. dept. psychiatry Hahnemann U., Phila., 1988—; sci. assoc. Mental Health Rsch. Inst., U. Mich., 1977-86. Author articles in field. Mem. AAAS, Am. Psychiat. Assn., Soc. Biol. Psychiatry, Am. Assn. Artificial Intelligence, Sigma Xi, Alpha Omega Alpha. Office: Hahnemann Univ Broad and Vine Sts # 360 Philadelphia PA 19102-1192

FEINBERG, RICHARD ALAN, clinical psychologist; b. Oakland, Calif., Aug. 12, 1947; s. Jack and Raechel Sacks (Hoff) F. BA, Calif. State U.-Hayward, 1969; MA in Clin. Psychology, Mich. State U., 1972, PhD, 1979; Nat. Register of Health Service Providers in Psychology, 1980. Instr., Merritt Coll., Oakland, 1975-76; clin. psychologist Highland Gen. Hosp., Oakland, 1976-79; asso. Lafayette Center Counseling and Edn., 1978-79; clin. psychologist Tri-City Mental Health Center, Fremont, Calif., 1979-81, dir., 1981-86; pvt. practice clin. psychology, 1976—; participant profl. conf. USPHS fellow, 1969-71. Mem. Am. Psychol. Assn., Calif. Psychol. Assn. Jewish. Office: 38950 Blaco Rd Ste D Fremont CA 94536

FEINBERG, SHELDON NORMAN, pediatrician; b. N.Y.C., Mar. 16, 1930; m. Maryellen Feinberg, Jan. 2, 1988; children: Lynn Ann, Bette Joan, Barbara Ellen, Paul Howard, John Joseph. MD, N.Y. Med. Coll., 1955. Diplomate Am. Bd. Pediat. Intern Bronx Mcpl. Hosp. Ctr., N.Y.C., 1955-56; resident Met. Hosp., N.Y.C., 1956-57; fellow pediatrics N.Y. Med. Coll., 1959-60; pediat. staff Passack Valley Hosp., Westwood, N.J., 1960-82; emergency physician various hosps., 1982-85; pediat. staff Hackensack (N.J.) U. Med. Ctr., 1985—; clin. asst. prof. pediat. U. Med. & Dentistry N.J., Newark, 1985—. Inventor infant scale guard, simple stool stain. Maj. USAF med. corps., 1957-59. Honor award Bergen County Med. Soc., 1965. Fellow Am. Acad. Pediat. (councillor); mem. AMA, N.J. Pediat. Soc. (pres. 1989-91, Honor award 1965). Home: 125 N Country Rd Mount Sinai NY 11766

FEINBERG, WILLIAM M., neurologist; b. Chgo., Apr. 21, 1952; s. Milton and Marjorie (Shafton) F.; m. Lois J. Loescher, May 13, 1984. BS, Stanford U., 1974; MD, U. Calif., San Francisco, 1978. Resident in internal medicine Ariz. Health Scis. Ctr., Tucson, 1978-81; fellow in cerebral blood flow and metabolism Mass. Gen. Hosp., Boston, 1984-85; resident in neurology U. Ariz., Tucson, 1981-84, asst. prof. neurology, 1985-92, assoc. prof. neurology, 1992—, dir. neurology tng., 1986-92, acting head of neurology, 1995. Contbr. to profl. publs. Grantee Am. Heart Assn., 1988-89, Ariz. Disease Control Rsch. Commn., 1988-90. Fellow Am. Heart Assn. (com. on sci. sessions programs 1991-94, exec. com. of stroke coun. 1991—); mem. AMA, Am. Acad. Neurology, Am. Neurol. Assn., Trout Unltd. (bd. dirs. Tucson chpt. 1987-91, pres. 1990). Office: Ariz Health Scis Ctr 1501 N Campbell Ave Tucson AZ 85724-0001

FEINDEL, WILLIAM HOWARD, neurosurgeon, consultant; b. Bridgewater, N.S., Can., July 12, 1918; s. Robert Ronald Feindel and Annie Swansburg; m. Dorothy Faith Roswell Lyman, July 28, 1945; children: Christopher, Alexander, Patricia, Janet, Michael, Anna. BA, Acadia U., Can., 1939, DSc (hon.), 1963; MSc, Dalhousie U., Can., 1942; MD, CM, McGill U., Can., 1945, DSc (hon.), 1984; DPhil in Neuroanatomy, Oxford U., Eng., 1949; LLD (hon.), Mt. Allison U., 1983, U. Sask., Can., 1986. Diplomate Am. Bd. Neurol. Surgery; licentiate Med. Coun. Can. Rsch. asst. Montreal (Can.) Neurol. Inst., 1942-44, fellow in neuropathology, 1944-45, dir. neuro-isotope lab., 1959-88, dir. inst., 1972-84; dir. gen., dir. profl. svcs. Montreal Neurol. Hosp., 1972-84; rsch. asst., demonstrator in anatomy Oxford U., Eng., 1946-49; demonstrator in neurosurgery McGill U., 1951-52, lectr. neurosurgery, 1952-55, William Cone prof. neurosurgery, 1959-88, chmn. dept. neurology and neurosurgery, 1972-77, dir. Cone lab. neurosurg. rsch., 1959-88; assoc. prof. surgery U. Sask., 1955-56, prof. surgery, 1956-59; co-ordinator rsch. in positron emission tomography Montreal Neurol. Inst. and Hosp., 1975-84, dir. brain imaging centre, 1984-87, dir. neuro history project, 1987—; chancellor Acadia U., 1991—; prin. investigator brain tumor project NIH, Bethesda, Md., 1986-89, co-investigator rsch., 1989—, mem.-reviewer neurol. disorders program project rev., 1983-88, external reviewer spl. programs, 1989-95; lectr. dept. history medicine and sci. U. B.C., 1976-78; neurol. cons. St. Paul's and City Hosps., Saskatoon, sask., 1955-59; cons. neurosurgeon Royal Victoria Hosp. and Catherine Booth Hos., Montreal, 1959-79, Sherbrooke (Que.) Gen. Hosp., 1964-85, Montreal Gen. Hosp., 1978—; cons. Champlain Valley Physicians Hosp., Plattsburgh, N.Y., 1973-85; neurosurgeon-in-chief Montreal Neurol. Hosp., 1961-72, sr. neurosurgeon, 1985—; neurologist and neurosurgeon-in-chief Royal Victoria Hosp., 1971-85, cons. neurosurgeon, 1985—; mem. sci. com. Found. for Study Ctrl. Nervous Sys. and Periphery, Geneva, 1983—; mem. expert panel on neurology WHO and Pan-Am. Health Orgn., 1976-94, cons. in neuroscis., 1996—. Author more than 400 articles on epilepsy, neurosurgery, brain imaging and history of medicine; editor: Memory, Learning and Language--The Physical Basis of Mind, 1960, The Anatomy of the Brain and Nerves by Doctor Thomas Willis, tercentenary edit., 1965; co-editor: Dynamics of Brain Edema, 1976, Brain Imaging and Metabolism, 1985. Mem. bd. curators Osler Libr., McGill U., 1963—, curator Penfield Archive, 1976—, hon. assoc. libr. Osler Libr., 1964-65; bd. govs. Acadia U., 1981-89, mem. exec. com., 1984-86. Decorated officer Order of Can., 1982; Rhodes scholar Oxford U., 1939. Fellow ACS, Royal Coll. Physicians and Surgeons Can., Royal Soc. Can.; mem. Am. Assn. Neurol. Surgeons, Am. Acad. Neurol. Surgeons (pres. 1976), Am. Neurol. Assn. (v.p. 1976), Am. Soc. Stereotactic and Functional Neurosurgery, World Soc. Stereotactic and Functional Neurosurgery, Can. Neurosurg. Soc. (pres. 1968), Montreal Medico-Chirurg. Soc. (pres. 1974), Osler Soc. McGill U. (pres. 1945, hon. pres. 1985-88, 90-95), Am. Osler Soc., Osler Club London (hon.), Univ. Club Montreal, Faculty Club McGill U., Indoor Tennis Club, Alpha Omega Alpha. Anglican. Office: Montreal Neurol Inst, 3801 University St # 110, Montreal, PQ Canada H3A 2B4

FEINER, JOEL S., psychiatrist; b. N.Y.C., July 14, 1938; s. Sol and Helen (Minkow) F. BA, Yale U., 1960; MD, Albert Einstein Coll. Medicine, 1964. Diplomate Am. Bd. Psychiatry and Neurology. Dir. dept. psychiatry Bronx (N.Y.) Psychiat. Ctr., 1985-87, devel. dir., 1987-92, pres. med. staff orgn., 1989-92; co-dir. residency tng. dept. psychiatry Albert Einstein Coll. Medicine, Bronx, 1979-83, dir. residency tng. dept. psychiatry, 1983-86, prof. dept. psychiatry, 1989-92, vis. prof. dept. psychiatry, 1992—, dir. div. social and community psychiatry dept. psychiatry, 1986-92, also chmn. Med. Sch. Minority Affairs Com.; prof. dept. psychiatry U. Tex. Southwestern Med. Sch., Dallas, 1992—; clin. and tng. dir. Mental Health Connections, 1992—; cons. in field; editl. adv. com. Family Sys. Medicine, 1983-92; vis. faculty Family Inst. Westchester, Mt. Vernon, N.Y., 1985-92. Recipient Profl. of Yr. award Dallas Alliance for Mentally Ill, 1993, Pamela Blumenthal award Dallas Mental Health Assn., 1994, Profl. of the Yr. award Tex. Alliance for Mentally Ill, 1995, Exemplary Psychiatrist award Nat. Alliance Mentally Ill, 1996; Career Tchg. fellow Albert Einstein Coll. Medicine, 1972-74. Fellow Am. Psychiat. Assn. (Mead Johnson fellow in pub. psychiatry selection com. 1986-89, Significant Achievmeent award 1995), Am. Family Therapy Assn. (charter); mem. Am. Orthopsychiat. Assn. (sect. 1987-90, prog. faculty chair 1985-86), Am. Acad. Child and Adolescent Psychiatry. Office: Southwestern Med Sch Mental Health Connections 5909 Harry Hines Blvd Dallas TX 75235-6209

FEINFELD, DONALD ALLEN, nephrologist, educator; b. N.Y.C., Nov. 12, 1944; s. Theodore and Anne (Reiken) F.; m. Daryl Drury, June 26, 1970; 1 child, Michael Jay. BA in Math., U. Rochester, 1965; MD, Columbia U., 1969. Diplomate Am. Bd. Internal Medicine. Dir. nephrology Harlem Hosp. Ctr., N.Y.C., 1978-86; assoc. prof. Columbia U., N.Y.C., 1984-86, Albert Einstein Coll. Medicine, Bronx, N.Y., 1986-89; co-dir. nephrology Nassau County Med. Ctr., East Meadow, N.Y., 1989—, dir. biomed. rsch. facility, 1991—; assoc. prof. SUNY Health Sci. Ctr., Stony Brook, 1990-95, prof., 1995—; cons. N.Y. Poison Control Ctr., N.Y.C., 1985—, L.I. Regional Poison Control Ctr., 1995—; chmn. institutional rev. bd. Harlem Hosp. Ctr., 1986. Author: (chpts.) Nephrotoxicity, 1989, Goldfrank's Toxicologic Emergencies, 1990, 94, Cardiovascular Pharmacotherapeutics, 1996, Clinical Management of Poisoning and Drug Overdose, 1996. Recipient rsch. fellowship Nat. Kidney Found., 1974-76. Fellow Am. Coll. Phys.; mem. Am. Soc. Nephrology, Am. Acad. Clin. Toxicology, European Renal Assn. (assoc.). Office: Nassau County Med Ctr 2201 Hempstead Tpke # 1175 East Meadow NY 11554-1859

FEINGLOS, MARK NEIL, endocrinologist; b. Syracuse, N.Y., Feb. 23, 1948; s. Clarence Robert and Berte F.; m. Susan Jean Goldman, July 4, 1971; children: Daniel, Rebecca. BS with distinction, McGill U., 1969, MD, 1973. Diplomate Am. Bd. Internal Medicine, Bd. in Endocrinology and Metabolism. Intern in medicine Duke U. Med. Ctr., Durham, N.C., 1973-74, jr. asst. resident, 1974-75, clin. fellow in endocrinology and metabolism, 1975-76, rsch. fellow in endocrinology and metabolism, 1976-77, assoc. in medicine, 1978-79, asst. prof. medicine, 1980-87, assoc. prof. medicine, 1987-93, prof. medicine, 1993—, asst. clin. prof. psychiatry, 1981-95, assoc. prof. psychiatry and behavioral scis., 1995—. Contbg. author: Diabetes mellitus: Theory and Practice Third Edition, 1982, Glipizide: A Worldwide Review, 1992, Clinical Endocrinology, 1986, Neuropsychological and Behavioral Aspects of Diabetes, 1989, Rational Therapeutics, 1990, Essentials of Surgery, 1993; contbr. numerous articles to profl. med. jours. Recipient scholarship Can. Inst. Mining and Metallurgy, 1967; named univ. scholar McGill U., 1970, 71, 72; grantee NIH, Eli Lilly & Co., Pfizer, Inc.; mineral Feinglosite named in his honor. Mem. Endocrine Soc., Am. Diabetes Assn., Am. Fedn. for Clin. Rsch., Soc. for Behavioral Medicine, Mineralogical Soc. of Am. Office: Duke U Med Ctr Box 3921 Durham NC 27710

FEINGOLD, DANIEL LEON, anesthesiologist; b. Boston, May 19, 1958; s. Macey Gerson and Hélène Sultana (Benlolo) F. BS with distinction, U. Ill., Chgo., 1980; MD, U. Health Scis., Chgo. Med. Sch., 1984. Intern Weiss Meml. Hosp., Chgo., 1984-85; resident in anesthesiology U. Ill. Hosps. and Clinics, Chgo., 1986-89; anesthesiologist Hosp. Anesthesia Group, Chgo., 1989—. Contbr. articles to profl. publs. Mem. AMA, AAAS, Am. Soc. Anesthesiologists, Am. Soc. Regional Anesthesia, Ill. State Med. Soc. Home: PO Box 577429 Chicago IL 60657-7429 Office: PO Box 25678 Chicago IL 60625-0678

FEINGOLD, DAVID SIDNEY, microbiology educator; b. Chelsea, Mass., Nov. 15, 1922; s. Louis Edward and Miriam (Young) F.; m. Batia Babette Haber, Nov. 15, 1949; children: Oded, Anat, Michele. B.S., MIT, 1944; Ph.D., Hebrew U., Jerusalem, Israel, 1956. Chemist Lucidol Corp., Buffalo, 1944; jr. research biochemist U. Calif. at Berkeley, 1957-60; asst. prof. biology U. Pitts., 1960-62, asso. prof., 1962-65, prof., 1965—; prof. microbiology Sch. Medicine, 1966-93, prof. emeritus molecular genetics and biochemistry, 1993—. Contbr. articles to profl. jours. Served with USNR, 1944-46. Recipient State of Israel prize in natural sci., 1957, Career Devel. award NIH, 1965-75. Fellow Infectious Disease Soc. Am.; mem. Internat. Endotoxin Soc., Am. Soc. Biol. Chemists, Am. Soc. Microbiology. Home: 6420 Bartlett St Pittsburgh PA 15217-1832

FEINGOLD, ELLEN, pediatrician, medical writer; b. N.Y.C., Oct. 8, 1942; arrived in Israel, 1981; d. Edward A. and Freida Magda (Zwillica) Weiss; m. Michael Feingold, June 14, 1964; children: Felicia Seaton, Barnett, Daniel, Joseph. BS, Cornell U., 1964; MD, SUNY, Bklyn., 1968; MPH, Hebrew U., Jerusalem, 1995. Rsch. coord. pregnant and drug addicts/neonates Downstate Med. Ctr., Bklyn., 1973-75; program dir. Physician's Asst. Program L.I. U. Hosp., Bklyn., 1976-78; physician in pvt. practice East Rockaway, N.Y., 1978-81, Jerusalem, 1981—; med. writer Hypermed, Jerusalem, 1995—; dir. rsch. in child labor Hadassah Med. Sch., Jerusalem, 1991—; rschr. Com. for Rsch. and Prevention in Occupl. Safety, Jerusalem, 1993-94; workshop coord. Hadassah Med. Sch. Design Implementation and Evaluation of Ednl. Programs to Reduce Risk of HIV Infection, 1991-94. Author: Handbook of Hebrew Verbs, 1991, Dictionary of Medical and Health Terminology, 1991; contbr. articles to profl. jours. Chmn. Overseas Fund Raising Com., Ramat Zion Synagogue, French Hill, Jerusalem, 1986-91. Rsch. grantee Com. for Rsch. and Prevention of Occupl. Safety and Health, 1993-94. Mem. Am. Pub. Health Assn., Israel Pub. Health Assn., Israel Med. Assn. Home: 87/7 Bar Kochbah St, Jerusalem Israel Office: 87/8 Bar Kochbah St, Jerusalem Israel

FEINGOLD, S. NORMAN, psychologist; b. Worcester, Mass., Feb. 2, 1914; s. William and Aida (Salit) F.; m. Marie Goodman, Mar. 24, 1947; children: Elizabeth Anne, Margaret Ellen, Deborah Carol, Marilyn Nancy. AB, Ind. U., 1937; MA, Clark U., 1940; EdD, Boston U., 1948; LLD, Edward Waters Coll., Saints Coll. Dir. vocat. service, also ednl. and vocat. dir. Hecht. Neighborhood House, Boston, 1940-43; exec. dir. Boston Jewish Vocat. Service and Work Adjustment Center, 1946-58; nat. dir. B'nai B'rith Career and Counseling Services, Washington, 1958-80; pres. Nat. Career and Counseling Services, 1980—, pvt. practice, 1980—; exec. adviser Rehab. Services, Boston, 1953-58; dir. ednl. and vocat. workshop United Cerebral Palsy of Greater Boston, Inc., 1957-58; cons. to Scholarships, Fellowships and Loans News Service, Social Security Adminstrn., 1962—; instr., spl. lectr. Boston U., 1951-58; profl. lectr. Am. U. Rehab. Counseling Adv. Panel, 1963-65; mem. Am. Bd. Counseling Services, 1962-65, 70—. Author: It Pays to Advertise, 1975, Occupations and Careers, 1969, The Vocational Expert in the Social Security Disability Program, 1969, A Counselor's Handbook, 1972, Counseling for Careers in the 80's, 1979, Whither Counseling, 1981, Making It on Your Own, rev., 1991, A Guide to Financial Success, 1981, rev., 1985, Emerging Careers: New Occupations for the Year Two Thousand and Beyond, 1983, The Professional and Trade Association Job Finder, 1983, Getting Ahead: A Woman's Guide to Career Sources, 1983, Scholarships, Fellowships and Loans, Vol. 8, 1987, New Emerging Careers: Today, Tomorrow, and in the 21st Century, 1988, Futuristic Exercises: A Work Book for Emerging Lifestyles and Careers in the 21st Century and Beyond, 1989, Where the Jobs Are: A Comprehensive Directory of 1200 Journals Listing Career Opportunities, 1989, The Complete Job and Career Handbook: 101 Ways to Get from Here to There, 1993; past editor Counselors Information Service. Chmn. Gov.'s Council on Aging, 1956-58, Washington Bus.-Industry Group, 1963-64; mem. Pres.'s Com. on Employment Handicapped, 1950—; mem. adv. com. Nat. Health Council; mem. Nat. Home Study Accrediting Commn.; chmn. human relations com. Dept. Agr. Grad. Sch.; mem. profl. adv. bd. Epilepsy Found. Served from pvt. to 1st lt. AUS, 1943-46, ETO and PTO. Recipient Community Service award B'nai B'rith, 1957, Brotherhood and Americanization award, 1958, Eminent Career award Nat. Capital Personnel and Guidance Assn. Fellow Am. Psychol. Assn.; mem. Greater Boston Personnel and Guidance Assn. (pres. 1952-53), Am. Personnel and Guidance Assn. (pres. 1974-75), Mass., Eastern psychol. assns., Nat. Vocat. Guidance Assn. (pres. 1968-69), Am. Assn. Adult Edn., Am. Assn. Marriage and Family Counselors (clin.), Internat. Coun. Psychologists, Nat. Press Club, Nat. Rehab. Assn., Torch Club, New Century Club (bd. dirs. 1954-58), Phi Delta Kappa. Home: 9707 Singleton Dr Bethesda MD 20817-2466 Office: 1511 K St NW Ste 541 Washington DC 20005-1401

FEINMAN, LARRY JAY, surgeon; b. Alhambra, Calif., Jan. 19, 1956; s. Michael and Bernice Fern (Stein) F.; m. Sheryl Nan Fiel, June 13, 1981; children: Matthew Scott, Alex Daniel, Michaela Chelsie. BS, Lebanon Valley Coll., Annville, Pa., 1977; DO, Phila. Coll. Osteo. Medicine, 1981. Diplomate Am. Osteo. Bd. Surgery. Gen. and vascular surgeon Parkview Hosp., Phila., 1987-89; pvt. practice gen. and vascular surgeon Seminole, Fla., 1989—; clin. asst. prof. U. Health Scis. Coll. Osteo. Medicine, Kansas City, Mo., 1992—; mem. faculty dept. surgery NOVA-Southeastern Coll. Osteo. Medicine, North Miami Beach, Fla., 1993—. Contbr. articles to profl. jours. bd. dirs. Pinellas County Jewish Day Sch., St. Petersburg, Fla., 1991-94. Mem. Am. Coll. Osteo. Surgeons (1st award cardiovascular surgery sect. 1989), Am. Osteo. Assn., So. Med. Assn., Fla. Osteo. Med. Assn., Pinellas County Osteo. Assn. (trustee 1994—). Jewish. Office: 9325 Seminole Blvd Seminole FL 34642

FEINMAN, SUSAN MARGARET ELLMANN, consultant, medical writer; b. Atlanta, Sept. 16, 1930; d. John. I. and Mary Florence (Smith) Ellmann; m. Philip S. Birnbaum, 1953 (div. 1970); 1 child, Mary Susan; m. David M. Feinman, Jan. 22, 1972; children: Abigail Gay, Elizabeth Bonnie. BA, Wellesley Coll., 1951; MS, George Washington U., 1952, PhD, 1969. Teaching fellow microbiol. dept. George Washington U., Washington, 1966-68; supervisory microbiologist D.C. Govt., Washington, 1969-69; postdoctoral fellow Nat. Inst. Allergy and Infectious Diseases, Bethesda, Md., 1969-71; program analyst Alcohol, Drug Abuse, and Mental Health Agy., Rockville, Md., 1971-74; microbiologist FDA, Rockville, 1974-79; supervisory biologist Ctr. Food Safety and Nutrition FDA, Washington, 1987-90, U.S. Consumer Products Safety Commn., Bethesda, Md., 1979-86; health scientist adminstr. Nat. Cancer Inst. NIH, Bethesda, 1990-93; author med. chpts. for dermatology and legal textbooks Office of Tech. and Assessment, U.S. Congress, 1995—. Author: Environmental Impact Statement on Low Level Antibiotics in Feed, 1978, Formaldehyde Sensitivity and Toxicity, 1988, Aspirin-Benefit and Risk, 1993; contbr. articles to profl. jours., chpts. for textbooks and reports. Pres. Toastmasters, Bethesda and Parklawn, Md., 1977, 86, Fed. Employed Women, Parklawn, 1976; pres. Grad. Women in Sci., Washington, 1994, nat. v.p., 1996—. Mem. Am. Coll. Toxicology, Am. Soc. Microbiology, Soc. of Toxicology, Grad. Women in Sci., Sigma Xi (pres. FDA chpt. 1978).

FEINSILVER, DAVID B., psychiatrist; b. Boston, Nov. 11, 1939; s. Oscar and Goldie (Gans) F.; m. Miriam Hoffman, Apr. 21, 1963; children: Ethan Joshua, Marissa Leah. BA, Brandeis U., 1961; MD, Tufts U., 1965. Intern Mt. Zion Hosp., San Francisco; resident Yale U., New Haven, Conn.; Grant program coord. NIMH, Chevy Chase, Md., 1969-71; staff psychiatrist Chestnut Lodge Hosp., Rockville, Md., 1971—. Editor: Towards a Comprehensive Model for Schizophrenic Disorders, 1986. Home: 2800 Mckinley Pl NW Washington DC 20015-1104 Office: Chestnut Lodge Hosp 500 W Montgomery Ave Rockville MD 20850-3892

FEINSILVER, STEVEN HENRY, physician, educator; b. N.Y.C., Oct. 27, 1952; s. Albert S. and Mildred C. (Weissman) F.; m. Margaret Caldwell Hall, July 4, 1982; children: Joseph, Samuel. ScB, Brown U., 1974, MD, 1977. Diplomate Am. Bd. Internal Medicine, sub-bds. pulmonary diseases and critical care medicine; cert. in sleep medicine; diplomate Nat. Bd. Med. Examiners; lic. physician, Mass., R.I., N.Y. Resident in internal medicine Univ. Hosp.-Boston U. Med. Ctr., 1977-80; fellow in pulmonary medicine Stanford U. Med. Ctr., 1980-82; from instr. to asst. prof. medicine Brown U., Providence, 1982-86; asst. prof. medicine SUNY, Stony Brook, 1986-92, assoc. prof., 1992—; mem. med. staff, dir. Pulmonary Function Lab. Winthrop-Univ. Hosp., Mineola, N.Y., 1986-94, dir. Sleep Disorders Ctr., 1986—. Contbr. articles to profl. jours. Pres. bd. dirs. Harbor Day Care Ctrs., New Hyde Park, N.Y., 1991-94. Fellow ACP, Am. Coll. Chest Physicians (nat. adv. com. on cardiopulmonary sleep disorders 1990, Nat. chair sec. of Sleep Disorders, ACCP, 1994—), Am. Sleep Disorders Assn.; mem. Am. Thoracic Soc., Clin. Sleep Soc., N.Y. State Med. Soc., N.Y. Trudeau Soc., L.I. Pulmonary Soc. (sec.-treas.), Steppingstone Sailing Club (commodore 1993-95), Sigma Xi. Office: Winthrop Pulmonary Assocs 222 Station Plz N Mineola NY 11501-3893

FEINSTEIN, ALVAN RICHARD, physician, educator; b. Phila., Dec. 4, 1925; s. Joel B. and Bella (Ukasz) F. B.S., U. Chgo., 1947, M.S. in Math, 1948, M.D., 1952; M.A. (hon.), Yale U., 1969. Intern, then resident Yale-New Haven Hosp., 1952-54; research fellow Rockefeller Inst., 1954-55; resident Columbia-Presbyn. Med. Center, N.Y.C., 1955-56; clin. dir. Irvington House, N.Y.C., 1956-62; instr., then asst. prof. N.Y. U. Sch. Medicine, 1956-62; chief clin. pharmacology VA Hosp., West Haven, Conn., 1962-64; chief clin. biostatistics VA Hosp., 1964-74; mem. faculty Sch. Medicine, Yale U., 1962—, prof. medicine and epidemiology, 1969—, dir. clin. scholar program, 1974—, Sterling prof., 1991—; chief Eastern Research Support Ctr. VA, 1967-74; pres. New Haven area chpt. Assn. Computing Machinery, 1968-69. Author: Clinical Judgement, 1967, Clinical Biostatistics, 1977, Clinical Epidemiology, 1985, Clinimetrics, 1987, Multivariable Analysis, 1996; editor Jour. Clin. Epidemiology; contbr. articles to profl. jours. Served with AUS, 1944-46. Recipient Francis G. Blake award for outstanding teaching Yale Med. Sch., J. Allyn Taylor Internat. prize, awards Soc. for Gen. Internal Medicine, U. Chgo., Ludwig Heilmyer Soc. (Europe). Gairdner Found. Internat. award 1993 (Can.). Master ACP (award); mem. AMA, Assn. Am. Physicians, Am. Soc. Clin. Investigation, Am. Epidemiol. Soc., Inst. Medicine, Am. Bd. Internal Medicine, Am. Fedn. Clin. Research, Am. Soc. Clin. Pharmacology Therapeutics, Am. Statis. Assn., Assn. Computing Machinery, Biometric Soc., Am. Assn. History Medicine, Alpha Omega Alpha. Home: 164 Linden St New Haven CT 06511-2400 Office: Yale U Sch Medicine 333 Cedar St New Haven CT 06510-3206

FEINSTEIN, ELENA, medical researcher; b. Moscow, Dec. 3, 1958; arrived in Israel, 1985; d. Lusian and Rachel (Labock) F.; m. Lev Birger, July 7, 1979; 1 child, Rachel. MD, Moscow Med. U., 1982; PhD, Weizmann Inst. Sci., 1993. Intern Moscow Clin. Pediatric Hosp., 1982-83; resident Moscow Clin. Hosp. for Infectious Diseases, 1983-85; staff scientist Weizmann Inst. Scis., Rehovot, Israel, 1985-87, postdoctoral fellow, 1992-95, scientist, 1995—. Contbr. articles to profl. jours. Spl. fellow Leukemia Soc. Am., 1995—. Office: Weizmann Inst Sci, Dept Molecular Genetics, 76100 Rehovot Israel

FEINSTEIN, PETER ALAN, orthopedic surgeon; b. N.Y.C., July 7, 1950; s. Gilbert Jean and Barbara (Cohen) F.; m. Jane Benovitz, June 7, 1977; children: Andrew, Eric, Ross. BA, Brown U., 1972, M Med. Sci., 1974, MD, 1975. Diplomate Am. Bd. Orthopedic Surgery, Arthroscopy Bd. N.Am.; cert. Am. Bd. Forensic Examiners. Surg. resident Albert Einstein Coll. Medicine, Montefiore Hosp., Bronx, N.Y., 1975-77; orthopedic resident Columbia Presbyn. Hosp. Coll. Physicians and Surgeons, Bronx, 1977-80; pvt. practice orthopedic surgery Wilkes Barre (Pa.) Gen. Hosp., 1980—, Mercy Hosp., Wilkes-Barre, 1980—, Nesbitt Meml. Hosp., Wilkes-Barre, 1980—; chmn. Orthopedic Rsch. and Edn. Found., Northeastern Pa., 1991-92; mem. test devel. com. Arthroscopy Bd. N.Am., 1990. Contbr. articles to profl. jours. Bd. dirs. N.E. Pa. Philharmonic, Wilkes Barre, 1982-90, Jewish Community Ctr., Wilkes Barre, 1982-90; bd. dirs. United Jewish Appeal, Wilkes Barre, 1982-92, mem. Nat. Young Leadership Cabinet, 1986-91, chmn. campaign, 1992. Fellow Am. Coll. Forensic Examiners; mem. ACS, AMA, Am. Acad. Orthopedic Surgeons, Arthroscopy Assn. N.Am., Ea. Orthopedic Assn., Pa. Med. Soc., Luzerne County Med. Soc. Office: Bone & Joint Assocs 35 W Linden St Wilkes Barre PA 18702-2619

FEINSTEIN, ROBERT P., dermatologist; b. N.Y.C., July 31, 1941; s. Jerome and May (Wolpin) F.; m. Diane Marla Gutstein, Oct. 25, 1969; children: Steven, Michelle, Suzanne, Gary, Lori. AB in Biology, NYU, 1963, MD, 1967. Diplomate Am. Bd. Dermatology. Intern Kings County Hosp. Ctr., Bklyn., N.Y., 1967-68; resident in dermatology Columbia U. Dept. Dermatology, N.Y.C., 1968-71; chief of dermatology, innoculations and phys. exams. Navy Regional Med. Clinic, Washington, 1971-73; pvt. practice in dermatology Mineola, Mineola and Smithtown, N.Y., 1973—. Author: (book) Dermatology, 1995; contbr. articles to profl. jours. Lt cmmdr. USNR, 1971-73. Fellow Am. Acad. Dermatology (mem. exec. com. of adv. bd., managed care com.), Am. Soc. for Dermatologic Surgery; mem. AMA, N.Y. State Soc. of Dermatology (pres. elect 1995), Long Island Dermatology Soc. (v.p. 1994-96, pres. 1996—), Suffolk County Dermatology Soc. (pres. 1982-84), Atlantic Dermatology Soc. (bd. dirs. 1995); N.Y. State Med. Soc. Office: Robert P. Feinstein MD PC 172 Mineola Blvd Mineola NY 11501

FEINSTEIN, SHELDON ISRAEL, molecular biologist, educator; b. Bklyn., Sept. 17, 1950; s. Harry George and Naomi T. (Weingarten) F.; m. Martha Louise Logan, May 15, 1983; children: Brian Isaac, Sarah Anne, Joseph Abraham, Elizabeth Gail, Matthew Dean. BA, Yeshiva U., 1971; MPhil, Yale U., 1974, PhD, 1977. Postdoctoral fellow Yale U., New Haven, 1977-80; vis. scientist Weizmann Inst., Rehovot, Israel, 1980-82; staff assoc. Columbia U., N.Y.C., 1983-84; asst. prof. Rockefeller U., N.Y.C., 1984-87; asst. prof. U. Pa., Phila., 1987-95, sr. rsch. investigator, 1995—. Patentee in field; contbr. articles to profl. jours. Grantee Am. Lung Assn., 1988-89, Life and Health Ins. Fund, 1988-91, Nat. Heart, Lung and Blood Inst., 1991—. Mem. Am. Heart Assn. (arteriosclerosis coun.; grantee 1988, 89, 88-91), John Morgan Soc. Home: 7661 Brookhaven Rd Philadelphia PA 19151-2023 Office: U Pa Sch of Medicine 1 John Morgan Bldg 36th St And Hamilton Walk Philadelphia PA 19104

FEIT, ALAN, cardiologist, internist, medical educator; b. N.Y.C., Sept. 24, 1946. BS, CCNY, 1968; MS, Syracuse U., 1971; MD, Columbia U., 1975. Diplomate Am. Bd. Internal Medicine, Am. Bd. Cardiovasc. Disease. Intern, resident, cardiology fellow Roosevelt Hosp., N.Y.C., 1975-80; pvt. practice N.Y.C., 1980-81; asst. prof. medicine Bklyn. VA Hosp., 1981-84; asst. prof. medicine SUNY Health Sci. Ctr., Bklyn., 1984-91, assoc. prof. medicine, dir. cardiac catheterization lab., 1991—, asst. dean for edn., 1994—. Contbr. over 30 articles to profl. jours. Trustee Tenafly (N.J.) Nature Ctr., 1984-86, 87-88. Fellow ACP, Am. Coll. Cardiologists. Office: SUNY Health Sci Ctr Box 1199 450 Clarkson Ave Brooklyn NY 11203

FEITELSON, JERALD STUART, molecular biologist; b. Peekskill, N.Y., Oct. 15, 1953; s. Herbert William and Evelyn Esther (Katz) F.; m. Eva Nagy, Oct. 27, 1985; children: Justine Hannah, Cory David. BS in Life Scis., MIT, 1975; PhD in Genetics, Stanford U., 1981. Rsch. asst. dept. biology MIT, Cambridge, 1974-75; rsch. asst. dept. genetics Stanford (Calif.) U., 1975-81; postdoctoral rsch. fellow dept. genetics John Innes Inst., Norwich, Eng., 1981-84; adj. prof. Waksman Inst. Rutgers U., Piscataway, N.J., 1984-88; sr. rsch. microbiologist Lederle Labs., Am. Cyanamid, Pearl River, N.Y., 1984-88; mgr. molecular biology dept. Mycogen Corp., San Diego, 1988-93, sci. fellow, 1993—; grant reviewer NIH, Bethesda, Md., 1986-93, NSF, Washington, 1987-88. Contbr. articles to profl. jours.; patentee in field. NIH Predoctoral Tng. grantee, 1975-81. NIH Postdoctoral Rsch. grantee, 1981-84. Mem. Am. Soc. Microbiology, Fedn. Am. Scientists, Planetary Soc., N.Y. Acad. Scis., Soc. for Invertebrate Pathology. Office: Mycogen Corp 5501 Oberlin Dr San Diego CA 92121-1736

FELCH, WILLIAM CAMPBELL, internist, editor; b. Lakewood, Ohio, Nov. 14, 1920; s. Don Harold Willison and Beth (Campbell) F.; m. Nancy Cook Dean, Aug. 4, 1945; children: Patricia, William Campbell, Robert Dean. B.A., Princeton U., 1942; M.D., Columbia U., 1945. Diplomate: Nat. Bd. Med. Examiners, Am. Bd. Internal Medicine. Intern St. Luke's Hosp., N.Y.C., 1945-46, resident in internal medicine, 1948-51; pvt. practice specializing in internal medicine Rye, N.Y., 1951-88; chief staff United Hosp., Port Chester, N.Y., 1975-77; med. dir. Osborn Home, Rye, N.Y., 1979-88; exec. v.p. Alliance for Continuing Med. Edn., 1978-91. Author: Aspiration and Achievement, 1981, Decade of Decision, 1989, Vision for the Future, 1992, The Secrets of Good Patient Care, Thoughts on Medicine for the 21st Century, 1996, Alliance for Continuing Medical Education: The First 20 Years, 1996; editor: The Internist, 1975-86, ACME Almanac, 1978-91, Journal of Continuing Education in the Health Professions, 1992-95; co-editor: Continuing Med. Edn.: A Primer, 2d edit., 1991. Trustee N.Y. Med. Coll., Valhalla, 1971-73. Served to capt. U.S. Army, 1946-48. Recipient award of merit N.Y. State Soc. Internal Medicine, 1976, Disting. Svc. award Alliance for Continuing Med. Edn., Founder's medal, 1995; named Internist of Distinction Internal Medicine Soc. N.Y. County, 1973. Mem. ACP, Alliance for Continuing Med. Edn. (exec. v.p. 1978-91), Am. Soc. Internal Medicine (pres. 1973-74), Inst. of Medicine of Nat. Acad. Scis., AMA (chmn. council on legislation 1977-79). Republican. Home: 26337 Carmelo St Carmel CA 93923-9133 Office: PO Box 222159 Carmel CA 93922-2159

FELDER, RICHARD EMERSON, physician; b. Fulton, Ind., July 30, 1918; s. Ernest Emerson and Ruth Anna (Adamson) F.; m. Blanche Taylor McCall; children: Marion Ruth, Virginia, William Richard, Sara Ann. AB, Emory U., 1940, MD, 1944. Asst. anatomy Emory U., Atlanta, 1941-42, instr. internal medicine, psychiatry, 1949-50, resident, 1950-53; psychiatrist Atlanta Psychiat. Clinic, 1953-95, pvt. practice, Atlanta, 1995—. Co-author: Experimental Psychotherapy: A Symphony of Selves, 1991. Capt. U.S. Army, 1942-47. Home: 8560 Swiss Air Rd Gainesville GA 30506 Office: 348 Mt Vernon Hwy Atlanta GA 30328

FELDHUSEN, JOHN FREDERICK, educational psychology educator; b. Waukesha, Wis., May 5, 1926; s. John C. and Luella Elsie (Gruetzmacher) F.; m. Hazel J. Artz, Dec. 18, 1954; children: Jeanne, Anne. B.A., U. Wis., 1949, M.S., 1955, Ph.D., 1958. Counselor Wis. Sch. for Boys, 1949-51; tchr. Northwestern Acad., Lake Geneva, Wis., 1951-54; instr. Madison Bus. Coll., 1955-58, U. Wis., Madison, 1958-59; asst. prof. U. Wis., Eau Claire, 1959-61, assoc. prof., 1961-62; assoc. prof. edn. psychology Purdue U., West Lafayette, Ind., 1962-65, prof., 1965-90, Disting. prof., 1990—, dir. Gifted Edn. Resource Inst., 1979—. Author: (with W. Krypsin) Writing Behavioral Objectives: A Guide for Planning Instruction, 1974, Developing Classroom Tests, 1974, (with D. Treffinger) Creative Thinking and Problem Solving in Gifted Education, 1985, (with others) Excellence in Educating the Gifted, 1989, Talent Identification and Development in Education, 1995; editor Ednl. Psychologist, 1966-69, Ednl. Psychology Series, 1976—, Gifted Child Quar., 1983-92, Gifted and Talented Internat., 1993—; contbr. articles to profl. publs. Served with AUS, 1944-45. Grantee U.S. Office Edn., 1967-71, Lilly Endowmen, 1985-88, Ind. Dept. Edn., 1981-93. Fellow APA; mem. Am. Ednl. Rsch. Assn., Nat. Assn. Gifted Children (pres.-elect 1981-83, Disting. scholar 1984), Coun. Exceptional Children, World Coun. for Gifted and Talented Children (gen. editor). Home: 2411 Trace 24 West Lafayette IN 47906-1887 Office: Purdue U LAEB 5116 West Lafayette IN 47906

FELDMAN, ARTHUR M., cardiologist; m. Susan Boochever; children: Emily Kate, Elizabeth Willa. BA, Gettysburg Coll., 1970; MD, U. Md., 1973, PhD, 1974; MD, La. State U., 1981. Diplomate Am. Bd. Internal Medicine, Am. Bd. Med. Examiners. Intern, resident, fellow in cardiology Johns Hopkins Hosp., Balt., 1981-86, from asst. prof. to prof. medicine, 1986—. Editl. bd. Heart Failure, Jour. Am. Coll. Cardiology, Journal Cardiac Failure, Joar. Cardivasc. Pharmacology & Therapeutics, Circulation Rsch., Heart Failure Rev. Grantee NIH, 1989-94, others. Fellow Am. Heart Assn., Am. Coll. Cardiology; mem. Am. Soc. Clin. Investigation, Internat. Soc. Heart Rsch., Assn. Subspecialty Profs., Assn. Profs. Cardiology, Heart Failure Soc. Am. Home: 140 Riding Trail Ln Pittsburgh PA 15215 Office: U Pitts Med Ctr S572 Scaife Hall 200 Lothrop St Pittsburgh PA 15213

FELDMAN, BERNARD ROBERT, physician; b. Bklyn., July 5, 1934; s. Maurice Sol and Florence (Wagner) F.; m. Clare Elizabeth Krameisen, July 3, 1960; children: David Lawrence, Janet Lynn. BS, Coll. William and Mary, 1955; MD, Chgo. Med. Sch., 1959. Intern Michael Reese Hosp. and Med. Ctr., Chgo., 1959-60, resident in pediatrics, 1960-62, fellow in allergy and immunology, 1962-63; fellow in allergy and immunology Columbia-Presbyn. Med. Ctr., N.Y.C., 1963-64; asst. prof. clin. pediatrics Columbia Coll. Physicians and Surgeons, N.Y.C., 1964-87, clin. prof. pediatrics, 1996—; assoc. clin. prof. pediatrics Columbia-Presbyn. Med. Ctr., N.Y.C., 1987—; cons. St. Mary's Hosp. for Children, Queens, N.Y., 1976—. Author: The Complete Book of Childhood Allergies, 1986. V.p. edn. Woodland Community Temple, White Plains, N.Y., 1985-87, trustee, 1983-85. Fellow Am. Acad Allergy and Immunology (cert.), Am. Acad. Pediatrics (cert.); mem. N.Y. Allergy Soc. (past pres., mem. exec. com.), N.Y. State Soc. Allergy and Immunology (treas. 1986-88, pres. 1988-91), Med. Soc. State N.Y. (chmn. sect. allergy and immunology 1982-83), Westchester Allergy Soc. Jewish. Office: Columbia-Presbyn Med Ctr 3959 Broadway Rm 107N New York NY 10032-1537 also: 7 Elmwood Dr New City NY 10956-5136 also: 280 N Central Ave Ste 308 Hartsdale NY 10530-1835 also: Columbia-Presbyn Westside 21 W 86th St New York NY 10000

FELDMAN, BRUCE ALAN, psychiatrist; b. St. Louis, Apr. 21, 1959; s. Jerome Stanley and Arlene (Greenberg) F.; m. Kathryn Matilda Estill, May 25, 1990. BA in Biology, U. Mo., Kansas City, 1982, MD, 1985. Diplomate Nat. Bd. Med. Examiners, Am. Bd. Psychiatry and Neurology. Resident in psychiatry So. Ill. U., Springfield, 1986-89, adminstrv. chief resident, 1988, geriatric psychiat. chief resident, 1989; pvt. practice Psychiat. Assocs., Springfield, 1990—; resident cons. psychiatrist Alzheimers Ctr. for Decatur, Ill., 1989, Alzheimers Ctr. and Memory Disorders Ctr., Springfield, 1989; cons. psychiatrist Taylorville (Ill.) Mental Health Ctr., 1990—, Country View Living Ctr., Decatur, 1990—, Jacksonville Terr. Nursing Home, 1990—, Walnut Ridge N.H., 1992—, Springfield Mental Health Ctr., 1992—; hosp. affiliate Drs. Hosp., 1990—, Meml. Med. Ctr., 1990—, St. Johns Hosp., 1990—, St. Vincent Meml. Hosp., 1990—, Passavant Hosp., 1990—; mem. utilization rev. com. Drs. Hosp., 1990-91, St. Johns Hosp., 1994—, pharm. & therapeutics com., 1992—; ltd. ptnr., owner Drs. Hosp., Springfield, 1990-94, Wentville, Mo., 1991—; bd. dirs. Ind. Physicians Network, Springfield; contbr. THA clin. studies SIU Alzheimers Clinic, 1989, Proscom Clin. Study, 1992. Mem. Jewish Fedn., Springfield, Ill., Temple Israel Synagogue, Springfield; exec. prodr., dir. Miss K.C. Pageant, 1981; mem. Nat. Rep. Congress com., 1988—, Rep. Nat. Candidate Trust, 1992—, Rep. Inner Circle, 1993—, Rep. Nat. Com., 1994—, Crescent Counties Found. for Med. Care, 1993—. Named to Rep. Nat. Hall of Honor, 1992; recipient Rep. Congl. Order of Liberty, 1993, Rep. Senatorial Medal of Freedom, 1994. Mem. AMA, Am. Psychiat. Assn., N.Y. Acad. Scis. (life), So. Med. Assn., Am. Assn. for Geriatric Psychiatry, Am. Geriatrics Soc., U.S. Senatorial Club, Bnai Brith (Emes chpt., former exec. bd. mem.), Delta Chi (past pres. Kansas City chpt. 1979, nat. v.p., chpt. advisor 1981-82, Alumnus of Yr. 1982). Republican. Office: Psychiat Assocs 1124 S 6th St Springfield IL 62703-2406

FELDMAN, BRUCE ALLEN, otolaryngologist; b. Washington, Mar. 22, 1941; s. Irvin and Miriam Thelma (Rothstein) F.; m. Sharon Lee Pearlman, Dec. 25, 1966; children: Kathryn Ellen, Michael Aaron. AB, Dartmouth Coll., 1962, B Med. Sci., 1963; MD, Harvard U., 1965. Diplomate Am. Bd. Otolaryngology. Intern Hosp. of U. Pa., Phila., 1965-66, resident in surgery, 1966-67; resident in otolaryngology Mass. Eye and Ear Infirmary-Harvard U., Boston, 1967-70; pvt. practice Washington, 1972—; clin. prof. surgery (otolaryngology), pediatrics/hlth. care George Washington U., Washington, 1990—; clin. prof. otolaryngology Georgetown U. Sch. Medicine, Washington, 1995—; pres. med. staff Children's Hosp. Nat. Med. Ctr., 1994-96. Contbr. articles to med. jours., chpt. to book. Lt. comdr. M.C., USNR, 1970-72. Mosby scholar, 1963; recipient Physician's Recognition award Children's Hosp. Washington, 1991. Fellow ACS, Am. Laryngol., Rhinol. and Otol. Soc. (Mosher award 1981), Am. Acad. Pediatrics; mem. AMA, Med. Soc. D.C., Jacobi Med. Soc. (pres. 1986-87), Washington Met. Ear, Nose and Throat Soc. (pres. 1978-79), Woodmont Country Club (Rockville, Md.), Phi Beta Kappa, Alpha Omega Alpha, Phi Delta Epsilon (pres. grad. club 1979-80). Jewish. Office: 1145 19th St Washington DC 20036

FELDMAN, EVA LUCILLE, neurology educator; b. N.Y.C., Mar. 30, 1952; d. George Franklin and Margherita Enriceta (Cafiero) F.; m. John Lawson Roberts, June 17, 1978; children: Laurel, Scott, John Jr. BA in Biology and Chemistry, Earlham Coll., 1973; MS in Zoology, U. Notre Dame, 1975; PhD in Neurosci., U. Mich., 1979, MD, 1983. Diplomate Am. Bd. Neurology; lic. med. practitioner, Mich. Instr. dept. neurology U. Mich., Ann Arbor, 1987-88, asst. prof. neurology, 1988-94, mem. faculty Cancer Ctr., 1992—, assoc. prof. neurology, 1994—; mem. faculty neurosci. program U. Mich., Mich. Diabetes Rsch. and Tng., Ann Arbor, 1988—. Author (book chpts.) Current Therapy in Neurological Disorders, 1993, Advances in Endocrinology Metabolism, 1994; contbr. articles to profl. jours. NIH grantee, 1989, 94; Juvenile Diabetes Inst. grantee, 1994, grantee Am. Diabetes Assn., 1995, Muscular Dystrophy Assn., 1996. Office: Dept Neurology U Mich 200 Zina Pitcher Pl Ann Arbor MI 48109-2206

FELDMAN, HERBERT ORVILLE, obstetrician, gynecologist; b. Detroit, July 9, 1929; s. William and Bessie (Dresser) F.; m. Charlotte Fay Schneider, June 20, 1954; children: Mark, Gary, Jeanette. BS in Chemistry, Wayne State U. (now Midwestern U.-Chgo. Coll. Osteopath Medicine), 1951, DO, 1956. Diplomate Am. Bd. Osteo. Ob-Gyn. Intern Garden City Hosp., 1956-57; resident in ob-gyn. Botsford Gen. Hosp., 1957-60, mem. staff, 1960-82; cons. Botsford Hosp., Farmington Hills, Mich., 1960-82, head dept. ob.-gyn., 1965-68; commd. comdr. USN, 1984; physician U.S. Naval Hosp., Corpus Christi, Tex., 1982-92, head dept. ob.-gyn., 1989-92; mem. faculty Portsmouth (Va.) Naval Hosp., 1992-94; staff Portsmouth Gen. Hosp., 1992-94; physician gynecology dept. Gt. Lakes Naval Tng. Ctr., North Chicago, Ill., 1994—; head gynecology divsn. Colposcopy Clinic-Recruit Tng. Ctr., 1994—; clin. prof. ob-gyn. Mich. State U., 1975-82; chaplain, Jewish rep. U.S. Naval Hosp., Corpus Christi, 1990-92; chmn. bd. Shifrin-Willens Jewelry Co., 1976-82;. Mem. AAAS, Am. Osteo. Assn., Mich. Assn. Osteo. Physicians and Surgeons, Am. Fellowship Israel Physicians, Am. Acad. Family Practice (sustaining sci. mem.), N.Y. Acad. Scis. Home: 205A F St Great Lakes IL 60088 Office: Gt Lakes Naval Hosp BMC # 1017 Gynecol Clinic Great Lakes IL 60088

FELDMAN, JACOB J., health facility administrator. Assoc. dir. analytical and epidemiology program Nat. Ctr. Health Stats., U.S. Dept. Health & Human Svc., Hyattsville, Md., 1988—. Office: HHS Nat Ctr Health Stats Analysis & Epidemiology Div 3700 E West Hwy Hyattsville MD 20782-2015*

FELDMAN, JEFFREY MARC, podiatrist; b. N.Y.C., Oct. 14, 1949; s. Abraham D. and Lilo (Mendelssohn) F.; m. Melanie Lewin, Oct. 21, 1985. BA in Psychology, Fairleigh Dickinson U., 1971; D of Podiatric Medicine, Ohio Coll. Podiatric Medicine, 1976. Pvt. practice Great Barrington, Mass., 1981—, Pittsfield, Mass., 1985—; mem. staff dept. surgery Fairview Hosp., Great Barrington; mem. courtesy staff dept. orthopedics Hillcrest Hosp., Pittsfield; mem. cons. staff dept. orthopedics Berkshire Med. Ctr., Pittsfield; chief podiatry svcs. Camp Eisner, Great Barrington, Camp Kingsmont, West Stockbridge, Mass.; asst. prof. dept. orthopedics U. Mass. Sch. Medicine, Worcester; cons., lectr. in field; forensic cons. Mass. State Police. Prodr, host: (TV program) Healthline, 1992—; multimedia editor: Berkshire Med. Jour. Editor Current Podiatric Medicine jour., 1984; editorial cons. Physicians & Computers jours., 1987; contbr. articles to profl. publs. Fellow Am. Soc. Podiatric Medicine (bd. cert., asst. sec. 1984-85, chmn. sci. seminar 1984-85, constitution com. 1985-86), Am. Coll. Podopediats. (bd. cert.), Am. Acad. Ambulatory Foot Surgery (bd. cert.); mem. Am. Acad. Podiatric Sports Medicine (assoc.), Am. Running and Fitness Assn.

FELDMAN, JEROME MYRON, physician; b. Chgo., July 27, 1935; s. Louis and Marian (Swichkow) F.; children: Karen Joy, Ellen Deborah, Mark Steven. B.S., Northwestern U., 1957, M.D. with distinction, 1961. Diplomate: Am. Bd. Internal Medicine. Mem. faculty Duke U. Med. Sch., 1968—, assoc. prof. medicine, 1972—, dir. diabetes clinic, 1970-73; assoc. dir. diabetes sect. Regional Med. Program N.C., 1967-70; clin. investigator Durham VA Hosp., 1971-74, chief endocrinology service, 1971—. Editor Jour. Clin. Endocrinology and Metabolism, 1983-89; contbr. articles to med. jours., chpts. to books. Served as officer M.C. USAR, 1965-67. Fellow A.C.P.; mem. Am. Diabetes Assn., Endocrine Soc., Am. Fedn. Clin. Research, So. Sugar Club, N.C. Diabetes Assn. (pres. 1973-74), Phi Beta Kappa, Sigma Xi, Alpha Omega Alpha. Home: 2744 Sevier St Durham NC 27705-5745 Office: Duke Univ Med Ctr PO Box 2963 Durham NC 27715-2963

FELDMAN, MARC DAVID, psychiatrist; b. Kingston, N.Y., Sept. 9, 1958. AB, Dartmouth Coll., 1980, MD, 1984. Diplomate Am. Bd. Psychiatry and Neurology, Am. Acad. Pain Mgmt, Nat. Bd. Med. Examiners. Resident in psychiatry Duke U. Med. Ctr., Durham, N.C., 1984-88; chief resident in psychiatry Durham VA Med. Ctr., 1987-88; asst. prof. Duke U. Med. Ctr., Durham, N.C., 1988-90; med. dir. Hill Crest Hosp., Birmingham, Ala., 1990-93; vice chair dept. psychiatry U. Ala., Birmingham, 1993—; med. dir. Ctr. for Psychiat. Medicine-U. Ala., Birmingham, 1993—; dir. divsn. adult psychiatry U. Ala., 1994—; med. dir. United Behavioral Sys., 1996—; pvt. practice, 1990-93; acting dir. psychosocial support program Duke Comprehensive Cancer Ctr., 1989-90. Contbr. articles to profl. jours. Laughlin fellow Am. Coll. Psychiatrists, 1988; Rufus Choate scholar Dartmouth Coll., 1977-79. Mem. AMA, So. Med. Assn., Am. Psychiat. Assn., Ala. Psychiat. Assn., Phi Beta Kappa. Office: Ctr for Psychiat Medicine 1713 6th Ave S UAB Sta Birmingham AL 35294-0018

FELDMAN, MICHAEL SAUL, cardiologist, educator; b. Phila., Dec. 25, 1941; s. Jack and Faye Leah (Romisher) F.; m. Nini R. Feldman. BS, Temple U., 1963; MD, Hahnemann U., 1967. Diplomate Am. Bd. Internat. Medicine, subspecialty in cardiovascular disease. Intern medicine Hahnemann U., Phila., 1967-68, resident in internal medicine, 1968-70, fellow in cardiology, 1970-72; clin. asst. prof. medicine dept. medicine U. Pa. Sch. Medicine, 1972-79, clin. assoc. prof. medicine dept. medicine, 1979—; prof. medicine Med. Coll. Pa. and Hahnemann U., 1996—; cons. in cardiology Dept. Medicine Meml. Hosp. Roxborough, Phila., 1972-80, Einstein So. Divsn., Phila., 1972-89, Met. Hosp., Phila., 1972-89; dir. non-invasive cardiac lab. Presbyn. Med. Ctr., Phila., 1972-80, Divsn. Cardiology Grad. Hosp., Phila., 1974-78; dir. electrocardiography and electrophysiology Mid-Atlantic Heart and Vascular Inst., Presbyn. Med. Ctr., Phila., 1980-84, dir. cardiology svcs., 1984-86, dir. atherosclerotic cardiovascular laser rsch., 1983-86; dir. cardiology svcs. Phila. Heart Inst., Presbyn. Med. Ctr., Phila., 1986-95; dir. atherosclerotic cardiovascular laser rsch. Phila. Heart Inst., 1986-91; investigator in field. Fellow Am. Coll. Cardiology, Am. Fedn. Clin. Rsch., Coun. on Cardiology, Coun. on Atherosclerosis, Coun. on Circulation, Laennec Soc., Am. Heart Assn.; mem. Phila. Acad. Cardiology (founder). Office: MCP/HU Bala Cardiac Care One Bala Plaza Ste 629 Bala Cynwyd PA 19004

FELDMAN, ROBERT GEORGE, neurologist, medical educator; b. Cin., Apr. 27, 1933; s. Jacob and Katie (Green) F.; m. Gail Poliner, Dec. 25, 1960; children—John, Elise. B.A., U. Cin., 1954, M.D., 1958. Diplomate Am. Bd. Psychiatry and Neurology, Am. Bd. Electroencephalography. Research asst. pharmacology U. Cin., 1949-54; jr. pharmacologist William S. Merrell Co., Reading, Ohio, 1951-56; fellow Nat. Assn. Mental Health, UCLA, 1957; intern Los Angeles County Hosp., 1958-59; resident neurology Yale-New Haven Med. Center, 1959-63, W. Haven VA Hosp., 1961; fellow metabolic diseases Yale Med. Sch., 1961-62; USPHS spl. fellow, 1962-63; practice medicine, specializing in neurology Boston, 1963—; neurologist-in-chief Univ. Hosp., 1969-96; co-investigator Environ. Hazards Ctr., Boston VA Med. Ctr., 1995—; chief neurology VA Med. Ctr., Boston; neurologist-in-chief Boston Med. Ctr., 1996—; mem. staff Boston City Hosp., Beth Israel Hosp.; vis. fellow Montreal (Can.) Neurol. Inst., 1962, Mayo Clinic and Found., Rochester, Minn., 1962; asso. electroencephalographer Yale-New Haven Med. Center, 1962-63; mem. faculty Harvard Med. Sch., 1963—, lectr., 1968—; lectr. Sch. Public Health, 1978—; mem. faculty Boston U. Sch. Medicine, 1963—, prof. neurology, 1970—, chmn. dept., 1969—, prof. pharmacology, 1977—; lectr. Tufts U. Sch. Medicine, 1977—; prof. environ. health Boston U. Sch. Pub. Health chief neurology services Boston VA hosps., 1966—; Mem. nat field adv. group Neurology VA, 1972-75; mem. sci. council Com. to Combat Huntington's Disease, 1972-75; chmn. Zone 1 Profl. Standards Rev. Orgn., 1973-78; mem. profl. adv. bd. Epilepsy Found.,

1976-85; mem. council sci. advisors Nat. Inst. Occupational Safety and Health, 1984-90. Editor-in-chief Jour. Club Neurology, 1982-85; contbg. editor Am. Jour. Indsl. Medicine, 1980—; mem. editl. bd. Jour. Clin. Neuropharmacology, 1986—, Jour. Occupl. Rehab., 1991—, Neurology Forum, 1990—, others. Bd. dirs. Postgrad. Med. Inst., 1973; bd. dirs. Norfolk County Med. Soc.; v.p. Mass. Med. Soc., 1973. Recipient Robbins award for excellence in teaching, 1987, Metcalf award for excellence in teaching, 1995. Fellow Am. Acad. Neurology (councillor 1979-84, v.p. 1989-91), Royal Acad. Medicine; mem. Am. Epilepsy Soc. (v.p. 1989—), Am. Assn. Electromyography and Electrodiagnosis (cert.), Am. Assn. Univ. Profs. Neurology, Boston Soc. Psychiatry and Neurology (pres. 1972-73), Am. Acad. Toxicology, Am. Neurol. Assn. (2d v.p. 1992-93), Eastern EEG Soc., Am. Med. EEG Assn., Am. Heart Assn. (fellow stroke coun.), AMA, Mass. Med. Soc., APHA, Assn. Am. Med. Colls. (rep. to coun. of acad. socs. 1991—), Am. Parkinson Disease Assn. Ctr. Advanced Rsch. (dir. 1993—), Boston U. Med. Ctr. Med. Dental Staff (pres. 1994-95). Home: 74 Rita Rd Braintree MA 02184-3904 Office: 80 E Concord St Boston MA 02118-2307

FELDMAN, RONALD ARTHUR, social work educator, researcher; b. Buffalo, Jan. 17, 1938; s. David Jacob and Clara (Spector) F.; m. Dina Cohen Feinstein, Dec. 23, 1962; children: Daniel, Deborah, Darrah. BA, U. Buffalo, 1960; MSW, U. Mich., 1963, PhD, 1966. Cert., Acad. Cert. Social Workers. Asst. prof. U. Calif., Berkeley, 1966-68; Fulbright lectr. Social Services Acad., Ankara, Turkey, 1968-69; assoc. prof. Washington U. Sch. Social Work, St. Louis, 1969-72, prof., 1972-86, acting dean, 1973-74; dir. Ctr. for Study of Youth Devel., Boys Town, Nebr., 1974-78, Ctr. for Adolescent Mental Health, St. Louis, 1983-87; assoc. dean Columbia U. Sch. Social Work, N.Y.C., 1985-86, prof., dean, 1986—, Ruth Harris Ottman Centennial prof., 1995—; cons. NIMH, Rockville, Md., 1980-91; bd. dirs. Ednl. Inst., Jewish Bd. Family and Children's Svcs., N.Y.C., 1986—, William T. Grant Found., Bd. Behavior and Mental Disorders, Inst. Medicine. Sr. author: Contemporary Approaches to Group Treatment, 1975, The St. Louis Conundrum: The Effective Treatment of Antisocial Youths, 1983, Children at Risk: In the Web of Parental Mental Illness, 1987; sr. editor: Advances in Adolescent Mental Health, vols. 1-4, 1986—. Citizen leader Clayton (Mo.) Bd. Edn., 1981-82; mem. profl. rev. bd. Mo. Dept. Metal Health, Jefferson City, 1981-86; trustee Wm. T. Grant Found., 1993—. Recipient Disting. Faculty award Washington U., St. Louis, 1984; research grantee NIMH, Rockville, Md., 1970-75, 80-84, Office of Human Devel. Services, Washington, 1983-87. Fellow NASW, Soc. for Rsch. in Child Devel.; mem. Coun. on Social Work Edn. (bd. dirs. 1992-95), Am. Sociol. Assn., Internat. Assn. Child and Adolescent Psychiatry and Allied Professions (v.p. 1995—). Office: Columbia U Sch Social Work 622 W 113th St New York NY 10025-7982

FELDMAN, TED, cardiologist; b. Lincoln, Nebr., Nov. 3, 1952. BA, Ind. U., 1974, MD, 1978. Diplomate Am. Bd. Internal Medicine, Am. Bd. Cardiology. Intern medicine Rush Med. Coll., 1978-79, resident, 1979-81, chief resident, 1981-82; fellow cardiology U. Chgo., 1982-85, asst. prof. medicine, 1985-92, assoc. prof., 1992—, dir. interventional cardiology, 1988—. Contbr. articles to profl. jours. Fellow Am. Coll. Cardiology, Soc. for Coronary Angiography and Intervention. Office: U Chgo Hosps 5841 S Maryland Ave MC 5076 Chicago IL 60637

FELDSCHUH, JOSEPH, physician, business executive; b. Vienna, Austria, June 10, 1935; came to U.S., 1938; s. Carl and Celia (Wildman) F.; m. Roxanne Cohen, Nov. 22, 1962 (div.); children: Jonathan, Stephen, Michael. BA, Columbia Coll., 1957; MD, N.Y. U., 1961. Diplomate Am. Bd. Internal Medicine, Am. Bd. Cardiovascular Diseases. Intern Montefiore Hosp. and Med. Ctr., N.Y.C., 1961-62, resident, 1962-65, mem. staff, 1966—; asst. prof. medicine N.Y. Med. Coll., 1966-78, asst. prof. pathology, 1969-83, assoc. prof. medicine, 1978-83; pres. Sci. Med. Systems, N.Y.C., 1969-74, Daxor Corp., N.Y.C., 1974—; clin. asst. prof. Cornell U., 1981-88, 1988—; cons. Cardio-Metabolic Lab. Met. Hosp., 1983—. Cons. editor Am. Jour. Medicine, 1983—; contbr. articles to profl. jours. Columbia U. fellow Bellevue Hosp., 1965-66; grantee Ortho Research Found. , 1972, Birnbaum Found., 1983; Regents scholar, 1957; recipient Am. Assn. Lab. Suprs. award, 1973. Fellow Am. Coll. Physicians, Am. Coll. Cardiology, N.Y. Heart Assn.; Mem. AMA, Am. Fertility Soc., Pan-Am. Med. Assn., N.Y. State Med. Soc., N.Y. Cardiological Soc., N.Y. Acad. Scis., Bronx County Med. Soc. Office: Idant Laboratory 350 5th Ave # 7120 New York NY 10118

FELICE, DENISE A. DOYLE, community health nurse; b. Flushing, N.Y., Apr. 3, 1958; d. Cornelius J. and Ida O. (Cassassima) Doyle; m. Paul J. Felice, May 7, 1978; children: April, Dana, Erin. ADN, SUNY, Stony Brook and Farmingdale, 1979; RN, BA, Fla. Atlantic U., 1992. RN, Fla. Infirmary nurse Little Flower Children's Ctr., Wading River, N.Y., 1983; staff nurse Skillman Emergency Ctr., Dallas, 1984-86; charge nurse, pediatrics West Boca Med. Ctr., Boca Raton, Fla., 1986-88; dir. health svcs. Lynn U., Boca Raton, Fla., 1988-94; cmty. nurse Coral Sunset Sch., Boca Raton, 1994—; nurse Boca Raton Cmty. Hosp., 1994-95; adminstrn. cons. bloodborne pathogen program Harid Conservatory, 1995—; chmn. security and safety task force, mem. disabled student com., sexual assault task force and safe ride program; area dir. Pine Tree Camps of Lynn U., 1988—; active Sch. Nurse Pilot Program and Comm. Health Focus Group, Boca Raton Comm. Hosp., 1994—. Mem. Girl Scouts Am., ARC; peer educator, safety instr. AIDS/STDS. Recipient Kiwanis Club L.I. MacArthur Airport Svc. award, Soroptimist Suffolk County Cmty. Svc. award, Boca Raton C. of C. Program award. Mem. Am. Coll. Health Assn., Fla. Coll. Health Nurses Assn.

FELICETTA, JAMES VINCENT, endocrinologist, educator; b. Seattle, Mar. 1, 1949; s. Vincent Frank and Alice Marie (Felton) F.; m. Susan Marie Roman, Aug. 3, 1985. BS, U. Wash., 1970, MD, 1974, postgrad., 1977-80. Intern U. Utah, Salt Lake City, 1974-75, resident, 1975-77; fellow in endicrinology and metabolism U. Wash., 1977-80; asst. prof. medicine U. Mich., Ann Arbor, 1980-84; chief endocrinology Wayne County Gen. Hosp., Westland, Mich., 1980-84; from asst. prof. medicine to vice chief endocrinology Wayne State U., Detroit, 1984-87; chief endocrinology VA Med. Ctr., Allen Park, Mich., 1985-87; chief medicine VA Med. Ctr., Phoenix, 1987—; assoc. clin. prof. medicine U. Ariz., Tucson, 1988-95, prof. clin. medicine, 1995—; adj. prof. Coll. of Liberal Arts, Ariz. State U., Tempe, 1991—. Contbr. many articles and abstracts to profl. jours. Fellow Am. Coll. Physicians; mem. Am. Fed. for Clin. Research, Am. Diabetes Assn., Am. Soc. Hypertension, The Endocrine Soc. Roman Catholic. Home: 5543 E Sheena Dr Scottsdale AZ 85254-2961 Office: VA Med Ctr 7th St Phoenix AZ 85034

FELKER, ALLYN CAROLINE, human services facility administrator; b. Tamaqua, Pa., May 5, 1962; d. Alfred F. and Santina M. (Jacobe) Benech. BS, Pa. State U., State College, 1984, MEd, 1986. Intern, rehab. therapist Harrisburg (Pa.) State Hosp., 1985; nurse's aid State Coll. (Pa.) Manor, 1985; supr., therapist, program specialist Turning Point, Pottsville, Pa., 1986-91; clin. therapist, casework supr. Concern Profl. Svcs. for Children, Youth and Families, Bethlehem, Pa., 1991—, asst. regional dir., 1993—. Home: 1857 Whitehall Ave Allentown PA 18104-1141 Office: Concern Profl Svcs for Children Youth Families 90 S Commerce Way Ste 300 Bethlehem PA 18017

FELKER, GARY VERNON, ophthalmologist; b. Ft. Worth, Feb. 5, 1943; s. Vernon Clisto and Romelia Vivenne (Bryant) F.; m. Joy Winona Jones, Aug. 28, 1966; children: Michael, Michelle, Kyle. BA, U. Ark., 1965; MD, U. Ark., Little Rock, 1969. Diplomate Am. Bd. Ophthalmology. Intern St. Francis Hosp., Wichita, Kans., 1969-70; resident U. Mo. Columbia Ophthalmology, 1970-73; pvt. practice Ft. Smith, Ark., 1973-76, Ophthalmology Clinic, Ft. Smith, Ark., 1976—; pres. The Eye Group, Ft. Smith, 1995—; dir. Ft. Smith Independent Physicians' Assn., 1994—, Health Point Physician Hosp. Orgn., Ft. Smith, 1994—; chief of staff Sparks Reg. Med. Ctr., Ft. Smith, 1982; bd. dirs. Mercy Health Plan west Ark., Ft. Smith. Fellow Am. Acad. Ophthalmology. Methodist. Office: The Eye Group 3000 Rogers Ave Fort Smith AR 72901

FELLBAUM, CHRISTIANE DOROTHEA, psychology and linguistics researcher; b. Braunschweig, Germany, Dec. 18, 1950; came to U.S., 1969; d. Hubert E. and Hanna E. (Hauser) F.; m. Elliott H. Lieb, Dec. 18, 1975. BA, Northeastern U., 1974; PhD, Princeton U., 1980. Assoc. prof. Rider U., Princeton, N.J., 1987—; rsch. staff psychology dept. Princeton U., 1987—; cons. Ednl. Testing Svc., Princeton, 1980-82; vis. scholar LADL, U. Paris 7, 1986. Contbr. articles to profl. jours. Mem. Linguistic Soc. Am. Office: Princeton U Psychology Dept Princeton NJ 08540

FELLER, RALPH PAUL, dentist, educator; b. Quincy, Mass., Aug. 31, 1934; s. Paul Frederich and Frances Elizabeth (Habert) F.; children: Lynne Anne Feller Grenier, Paul Herbert, Wendy Elizabeth. BS, Tufts U., 1956, DMD, 1964; MS, U. Tex., Houston, 1975; MPH, Loma Linda U., 1981. Diplomate Am. Bd. Prosthodontics. Asst. prof. Harvard U., Boston, 1965-71; assoc. prof. U. Tex. Med. Br., Houston, 1971-75; clin. investigator VA Med. Ctr., Houston, 1971-75; chief dental svc. VA Med. Ctr., Lyons, N.J., 1975-77, Loma Linda, Calif., 1977-95; assoc. prof. Fairleigh Dickinson U., Hackensack, N.J., 1975-77; prof., dir. clin. rsch. ctr. Sch. Dentistry Loma Linda U., 1995—; cons. Johnson & Johnson, East Windsor, N.J., 1980-85, Oral-B Labs., Inc., Redwood City, Calif., 1986-92, Richardson-Vicks, Shelton, Conn., 1988-92, Colgate-Polmolive Co., Piscataway, N.J., 1988—. Contbr. numerous articles to profl. jours. Col. USAR, 1960-95, ret. Mem. ADA (Achievement award 1995), Internat. Assn. Dental Rsch. (numerous offices 1964—), am. Coll. Prosthodontists, Am. Assn. Dental Schs., Calif. Dental Assn., Assn. Mil. Surgeons U.S., Rotary. Home: 225 Edgemont Dr Redlands CA 92373 Office: Loma Linda U Sch Dentistry Loma Linda CA 92350

FELLER, WILLIAM FRANK, surgery educator; b. St. Paul, Nov. 2, 1925; s. William and Eva Caroline (Nordstrom) F.; m. Margareta Elizabeth Helm, Sept. 5, 1964; children: William Frank III, Elizabeth Suzanne. BA magna cum laude, U. Minn., 1948, BS, 1952, MD, 1954, PhD, 1962. Diplomate Am. Bd. Surgery. Intern U. Minn., Mpls., 1954-55; asst. prof. Georgetown U., Washington, 1964-69, assoc. prof., 1969-92; ret.; ret., 1992. Contbr. articles to profl. jours. Warden St. John's Episc. Ch., Chevy Chase, Md., 1975-76. Recipient St. George's medal Am. Cancer Soc., 1987. Mem. AAAS, ACS, Am. Assn. Cancer Rsch., Am. Scandinavian Found. (chpt. pres. 1969-71), Med. Soc. D.C., Am. Cancer Soc. (D.C. divsn. pres. 1984-85, St. George's medal 1987), Washington Acad. Surgery (pres. 1982-83), Cosmos Club (Washington). Home: 7028 Barkwater Ct Bethesda MD 20817-4402

FELLNER, MICHAEL JOSEF, dermatologist; b. N.Y.C., Sept. 15, 1936; s. Stephen and Selma (Ehrlich) F.; m. Fredda Ginsberg, Aug. 27, 1961; children: Jonathan, Melinda. A.B. in Chemistry, Cornell U., 1956; M.D., U. Md., 1960. Diplomate: Am. Bd. Dermatology. Intern Kings County Hosp., State U. N.Y., Bklyn., 1960-61; resident Mt. Sinai Hosp., N.Y.C., 1961-63; NIH tng. fellow N.Y. U. Med. Center, N.Y.C., 1963-64; NIH research tng. fellow in allergy and immunology, dept. dermatology NYU, N.Y.C., 1964-66; Am. Allergy Found. fellow NYU, 1966-67; practice medicine specializing in dermatology N.Y.C., 1966—; dir. dermatology Bird S. Coler Hosp., N.Y.C., 1973-79, attending chief of dermatology, 1979-88; mem. staff Met. Hosp., 1973-88; asst. prof. dermatology NYU Sch. Medicine, N.Y.C., 1966-70, assoc. prof., 1970-72; prof. dermatology N.Y. Med. Coll., N.Y.C., 1973-88; clin. prof. dermatology Mt. Sinai Med. Sch., N.Y.C., 1988—; reviewer Archives of Dermatology, Jour. Am. Acad. Dermatology; attending dermatologist St. Vincent's Hosp., N.Y.C., 1985-93. Author: Immunology of Skin Diseases, 1980; editor, contbg. author: Unexpected Reactions to Drugs, 1986; contbr. numerous articles on immunology, allergy and dermatology to med. jours.; bd. editors: Internat. Jour. Dermatology, 1976—, corr. editor, 1976-81; mem. N.Am. editorial bd., 1981—. Recipient Fred Wise Meml. award N.Y. Acad. Medicine, 1963; Gold medal Am. Dermatol. Assn., 1967; award N.Y. State Med. Soc., 1973; NIH grantee, 1967-73; John A. Hartford Found. grantee, 1972-78. Mem. AAAS, Am. Acad. Dermatology, Am. Acad. Allergy, Dermatologic Soc. Greater N.Y. (Henry Silver award 1964), Am. Fedn. Clin. Rsch., Soc. Investigative Dermatology, Am. Dermatologic Soc. for Allergy and Immunology (founding mem., sec.-treas. 1977-79, pres. 1979-80), N.Y. Acad. Scis., N.Y. State Dermatology Soc., N.Y. County Soc. Medicine, Internat. Soc. Tropical Dermatology, Noah Worcester Dermatology Soc., Cornell Club. Office: 30 E 60th St New York NY 10022-1008

FELLNER, SUSAN K., nephrologist; b. Hartford, Conn.. BA, Smith Coll., 1958; MD, U. Fla., 1968. Faculty Emory U., Atlanta, 1971-83; prof. U. Chgo., 1983-96; clin. prof. U. N.C., Chapel Hill, 1996—.

FELLONE, CHRISTINA KATES, oncology nurse; b. Utica, N.Y., May 9, 1954; d. Harry H. and Frances M. (Voce) Kates; children: Jason Robert, Lori Diana, Frank Salvatore. AAS, Mohawk Valley C.C., 1985. RN, N.Y. Med.-surg. staff nurse Facton Hosp., Utica, 1985-88, staff nurse ambulatory med.-surg. oncology, 1988-90, 91-93, sr. staff nurse surg./orthopedics, 1993-94; nurse coord. Conpharma Home Healthcare, Utica, 1990-91; insvc. coord., supr. Cmty. Meml. Hosp., Hamilton, N.Y., 1994-95; regional infusion mgr. clin. practice Olsten Kimberly Quality Care, Syracuse, Utica, N.Y., 1995—; adj. instr. Mohawk Valley C.C., Utica, 1994—; mentor, preceptor Nursing Students from LPN, AAS, BSN Programs, Utica, 1987-93. Planner, participant teaching days and health fairs, Utica. 1988—, Cancer Survivors Day, Utica, 1994-96; participant Breast Cancer Awareness Am. Cancer Soc., Utica, 1991, 93, 95; vol. first aid Utica Boilermaker Road Race; planner, participant 1st Cancer Patients' Town Hall, New Hartford, N.Y., 1995. Mem. Oncology Nurses Soc. (chair nominating com. Grater Mohawk Valley chpt. 1988—), Nat. Nurse Staff Devel. Orgn., Intravenous Nurses Soc., NAFE. Home: 4972 Henderson St Whitesboro NY 13492-2429 Office: Olsten Kimberly Quality Care Regional Infusion Divsn 200 Elwood Davis Rd 2d Fl Liverpool NY 13088

FELLOWS, ROBERT ELLIS, medical educator, medical scientist; b. Syracuse, N.Y., Aug. 4, 1933; s. Robert Ellis and Clara (Talmadge) F.; m. Karlen Kiger, July 2, 1983; children—Kara, Ari. A.B., Hamilton Coll., 1955; M.D., C.M., McGill U., 1959; Ph.D., Duke U., 1969. Intern N.Y. Hosp., N.Y.C., 1959-60; asst. resident N.Y. Hosp., 1960-61, Royal Victoria Hosp., Montreal, Que., Can., 1961-62; asst. prof. dept. medicine Duke U., Durham, N.C., 1966-76; asst. prof. dept. physiology and pharmacology Duke U., 1966-70, assoc. prof. dept. physiology and pharmacology, asso. dir. med. scientist tng. program, 1970-76; prof., chmn. dept. physiology and biophysics U. Iowa Coll. Medicine, dir. med. sci. tng. program, 1976—, dir. physician sci. program, 1984—, dir. neurosci. program, 1984—; mem. Nat. Pituitary Agy. Adv. Bd.; mem. NIH Population Rsch. Com., 1981-86, VA Career Devel. Rev. Com., 1985-88; cons. NIH, NSF March of Dimes. Mem. editorial bd.: Endocrinology, Am. Jour. Physiology. Mem. AAAS, Am. Chem. Soc., Am. Fedn. Clin. Research, Am. Physiol. Soc., Am. Soc. Biol. Chemists, Am. Soc. Cell Biology, Assn. Chairmen Depts. Physiology, Biochem. Soc., Biophys. Soc., Endocrine Soc., Internat. Soc. Neuroendocrinology, N.Y. Acad. Scis., Soc. for Neurosci., Tissue Culture Assn., Assn. Neuroscience Depts. and Programs (pres. 1995—), Sigma Xi, Alpha Omega Alpha. Home: 15 Prospect Pl Iowa City IA 52246-1932 Office: 5-660 Bowen Sci Bldg Iowa City IA 52242

FELNER, JOEL MICHAEL, medical educator, dean; b. Bklyn., Sept. 15, 1942; s. Isidore Israel and Doris (Lavine) F.; m. Kay Ann Rubenstein; children: Eric Ian, Kevin Jay, Jennifer Kate. BA, Columbia Coll., 1963; MD, Cin. U., 1967. Intern Cin. Gen. Hosp., 1967-68, resident, 1968-69; resident Grady Meml. Hosp., 1971-72; fellow in cardiology Emory Univ. Sch. Medicine, 1972-74; asst. and assoc. prof. medicine Emory U. Sch. Medicine, Atlanta, 1974-80, prof. medicine cardiology, 1981—, assoc. dean, 1985—. Author: Echocardiography, 1974. Lt. comdr. USPHS, 1967-69. Fellow Am. Heart Assn. (Tchg. Scholar 1975-78), Am. Coll. Cardiology; mem. Alpha Omega Alpha. Office: 69 Eutler St Atlanta GA 30303

FELS, ROBERT ALAN, psychotherapist; b. Phila., Apr. 24, 1954; s. Joseph and Lenore F. BS, Pa. State U., 1974; MA, John F. Kennedy U., 1980. Lic. marriage and family therapist; cert. by the Biofeedback Cert. Inst. of Am. Probation officer Broward County Probation, Ft. Lauderdale, Fla., 1979; family counselor Child Protective Svcs., State of Fla., Plantation, Fla., 1981-84; psychotherapist Jewish Family Svc., Boca Raton, Fla., 1984-88, Ctr. for Psychol. Svcs., Boca Raton, 1987-90; dir. biofeedback svcs. Lake Hosp., Lake Worth, Fla., 1990-92; pvt. practice psychotherapy Boca Raton, Fla., 1990—; facilitator Stop Smoking Clinic, Am. Cancer Soc., Boca Raton, 1987-93. Fellow Am. Bd. Vocational Experts, Am. Acad Pain Mgmt.; mem. Am. Assn. for Marriage and Family Therapy, Assn. for Applied Psychophysiology and Biofeedback. Jewish. Office: 9045 La Fontana Blvd Ste C-12 Boca Raton FL 33434-5621

FELSENTHAL, GERALD, physiatrist, educator; b. N.Y.C., Aug. 27, 1941; s. Richard and Fay (Braunspiegel) F.; m. Diane Shretter, June 6, 1964; children: David, Steven, Suzann. BA, NYU, 1963; MD, Albany Med. Coll., 1967. Diplomate Am. Bd. Phys. Medicine and Rehab. (dir. 1993—), Am. Bd. Electrodiagnostic Medicine. Rotating intern USPHS Hosp., Seattle, 1967-68; resident in phys. medicine and rehab. Bronx Mcpl. Hosp. Ctr., Albert Einstein Coll. Medicine, 1970-73; assoc. physiatrist Sinai Hosp., Balt., 1973-76, assoc. chief, 1976-86, chief dept. rehab. medicine, 1986—; head div. rehab. medicine Levindale Hebrew Geriatric Ctr. and Hosp., Balt., 1983—; dir. residency tng. prog. in phys. medicine and rehab. Sinai Hosp.-Johns Hopkins U., 1986—; assoc. prof. U. Md. Coll. Medicine, Balt., 1987-92, prof., 1992—; assoc. prof. Johns Hopkins U. Sch. Medicine, 1989—. Editor of book Rehab of Aging and Elderly Patient and articles to profl. jours. Surgeon USPHS, 1967-70. Mem. Phys. Medicine and Rehab (residency review com. 1990, vice chmn. 1994, chmn. 1996—), Am. Assn. Electrodiagnostic Medicine (bd. dirs. 1990-93), AMA, Am. Geriat Soc., Am. Congress Rehab. Medicine, Am. Acad. Phys. Med. and Rehab., Assn. Acad. Physiatrists, Am. Coll. Physicians Execs. Office: Sinai Hosp Dept Rehab Med 2401 W Belvedere Ave Baltimore MD 21215-5216

FELTON, GARY SPENCER, clinical psychologist; b. San Francisco, Mar. 8, 1940; s. Jean Spencer and Janet Elizabeth (Birnbaum) F.; m. Lynn Ellen Sandell, Mar. 21, 1970; children: Colin Spencer, Megan Ariana. BA, Grinnell Coll., 1961; MS in Clin. Psychology, Calif. State U., 1966; PhD in Clin. Psychology, U. So. Calif., 1970. Lic. clin. psychologist, Calif. Coord. counseling svcs., co-dir. rsch. programs Student Devel. Ctr. Mount St. Mary's Coll., 1969-71; coord. human svcs. worker tng. program Brentwood VA Hosp., L.A., 1971-72; dir. allied health, coord. child health care worker tng. program U. Affiliated Program Childrens Hosp., L.A., 1972-75; dir. spl. edn. programs, assoc. prof. psychology L.A. City Coll., 1972-81; ptnr. Spectrum Psychol. Resources, L.A., 1986—; cons. Adult Back Clinic Orthopaedic Hosp., L.A., 1967-69; researcher, writer, Am. Heart Assn. program Calif. State U., San Francisco, 1965-66. Author: Up from Underachievement, 1977, The Record Collector's International Directory, 1980, The World of Phonecards, 1994, 4th edit., 1996; mem. editl. bd. Coll. Student Jour., Journ. Ednl. Psychology; contbr. articles to profl. jours. Bd. dirs. Pub. Advt. Council, L.A. Fellow UCLA, 1963. Mem. APA, Western Psychol. Assn., Calif. Psychol. Assn., L.A. County Psychol. Assn., L.A. Soc. Clin. Psychologists, Assn. Humanistic Psychology, Am. Humanist Assn., Am. Name Soc. Democrat. Office: Spectrum 10780 Santa Monica Blvd Ste 450 Los Angeles CA 90025-4749

FELTON, JEAN SPENCER, physician; b. Oakland, Calif., Apr. 27, 1911; s. Herman and Tess (Davidson) F.; m. Janet E. Birnbaum, June 27, 1937 (dec.); children: Gary, Keith, Robin; m. Suzanne E. Colvin, Sept. 2, 1990. AB, Stanford U., 1931, MD, 1935. Diplomate: Am. Bd. Preventive Medicine, Am. Bd. Indsl. Hygiene. Intern Mt. Zion Hosp., San Francisco, 1934-35; resident in surgery Mt. Zion Hosp., 1935-36, Dante Hosp., San Francisco, 1936-38; practice medicine San Francisco, 1938-40; guest lectr. indsl. sociology U. Tenn. at Knoxville, 1946-53; med. dir. Oak Ridge Nat. Lab., 1946-53; cons. dept. medicine, prof. dept. preventive medicine, pub. health U. Okla. Med. Sch., 1953-58; cons. indsl. hygiene Okla. State Dept. Health, 1953-58; past cons. VA, St. Louis area; prof. occupational health U. Calif. Schs. Medicine and Pub. Health, Los Angeles, 1958-68; dir. occupational health service Dept. Personnel, County Los Angeles, 1968-74; med. dir. occupational health Naval Regional Med. Center, Long Beach, Calif., 1974-78; clin. prof. community medicine U. So. Calif., 1968-82, clin. prof. emeritus, 1982—; clin. prof. medicine U. Calif., Irvine, 1975—; cons. occupational health NASA, USN, VA, AEC, USPHS, Social Security Adminstrn., 1955-62. Author: (with A. H. Katz) Health and Community, 1965, Man, Medicine, and Work, 1965, Occupational Medical Management, 1990; bd. dirs. Excerpta Medica, Sect. XXXV, The Netherlands; mem. editl. panel Occupational Medicine, London, 1994—; contbr. articles to med. jours. Past mem. youth svc. com. Oak Ridge Welfare Coun., 1946-53; past mem. Tenn. Commn. on Childen, Welfare Svcs. Dept.; chmn., mem. adv. bd. Oak Ridge; past mem. Gov.'s Com. on Utilization Physically Handicapped Pres.'s Com. on Employment People with Disabilities, 1947-94. Lt. col. M.C., 1940-46. Decorated Army Commendation Ribbon, 1946; recipient Citation for Excellence in Med. Authorship by Am. Assn. Indsl. Physicians and Surgeons, 1948; Knudsen award Indsl. Med. Assn., 1968; Physician of Yr. award Calif. Gov.'s Com. on Employment of Handicapped, 1979; Physician of Yr. award Pres.'s Com. on Employment of Handicapped, 1979. Fellow Am. Coll. Preventive Medicine (pres. 1966-67), Am. Acad. Occupational Medicine, Am. Occupational Med. Assn. (Meritorious Svc. award 1965, Health Achievement in Industry award 1983), Am. Pub. Health Assn., Collegium Ramazzini (coun. of fellows 1994—); mem. AMA (sec., vice chmn. sect. preventive and indsl. medicine and pub. health 1949-53, chmn. sect. 1953), Am. Indsl. Hygiene Assn., Nat. Rehab. Assn. So. Calif. (dir.), So. Calif. Ind. Hygiene Assn. (past pres.), Am. Coll. Occupational Medicine (Robert A. Kehoe award 1989), New Eng. Occupational med. Assn. (Harriet F. Hardy award 1989). Unitarian. Home: PO Box 246 45150 Cypress Dr Mendocino CA 95460 Office: U Calif Coll Dept Medicine Nelson Rsch Ctr Bldg Med Sci Complex Irvine CA 92717

FELTS, STEPHEN KAREY, internist; b. Pascagoula, Miss., Aug. 3, 1944; s. Alvin Lafayette and Irma Celestine (King) F.; m. Susan Elaine Smithwick, Aug. 28, 1971; children: Susannah Joy, Andrew Stephen. BS, Miss. State U., 1966; MD, U. Miss., 1968. Diplomate Am. Bd. Internal Medicine. Intern Vanderbilt U. Hosp., Nashville, 1968-69; resident U. Miss. Sch. Medicine, Jackson, 1969-70; fellow infectious diseases Vanderbilt U. Hosp., Nashville, 1970-72; officer epidemic intelligence svc. USPHS, Ctr. for Disease Control, Atlanta, 1972-74; acting state epidemiologist Ark. Dept. Health, Little Rock, 1973-74; pvt. practice Nashville, 1974—, Hermitage, Tenn.; vice-chmn. bd. trustees HCA Donelson (Tenn.) Hosp., 1990-91. Lt. comdr. USPHS, 1972-74. Fellow ACP; mem. Am. Soc. Internal Medicine, Nashville Acad. Medicine.

FELTS, WILLIAM ROBERT, JR., physician; b. Judsonia, Ark., Apr. 24, 1923; s. Wylie Robert and Willie Etidorpha (Lewis) F.; m. Jeanne E. Kennedy, Feb. 17, 1954 (div. 1971); children: William R. III, Thomas Wylie, Samuel Clay, Melissa Jeanne; m. Lila Mitchell Dudley, Feb. 14, 1987 (dec. 1993). BS, U. Ark., 1944, MD, 1946. Intern Garfield Meml. Hosp., Washington, 1946-47; resident in medicine Gallinger Mcpl. Hosp., Washington, 1949-51; resident in medicine George Washington U. Hosp., 1951-53, trainee in rehab. (rheumatology), 1955-57; asst. chief arthritis rsch. unit VA Hosp., Washington, 1953-54, adj. asst. chief, 1954-58, chief, 1958-62; cons. in rheumatology U.S. Naval Hosp., Bethesda, Md., 1959-70; mem. faculty dept. medicine George Washington U., instr., 1957-59, asst. prof., 1959-62, assoc. prof., 1962-80, prof., 1980-93, prof. emeritus, 1993—, dir. divsn. rheumatology, 1970-79, mem. univ. faculty senate exec. com., 1991-93; mem. Nat. Commn. on Arthritis and Related Musculoskeletal Diseases, 1975-76, Nat. Arthritis adv. bd., 1977-80, 90-93, nat. com. on health policy Project Hope, 1977, steering com. Health Policy Agenda for Am. People, 1982-87, nat. com. Vital and Health Stats., 1983-87, 88-91; mem. adv. com. on disabilities White House Conf. on Aging, 1995; mem. D.C. Health Planning Adv. Com., 1969-72, WHO Task Force on Rheumatology in Developing Countries, 1982, 84; mem. U.S. del. to 10th Revision Conf. Internat. Classification of Diseases; chmn. med. adv. com. D.C. chpt. Arthritis Found., 1963-85, vice chmn. of chpt. bd. dirs., 1983-94, chmn., 1992-96; bd. dirs. Symposium on Computer Applications in Med. Care, 1980-88, pres.-elect, 1982-83, pres., 1983-84; cons. health affairs and mem. profl. adv. bd. Control Data Corp., 1976-83, Nat. Ctr. for Health Stats., 1991-93. Author articles in field, especially med. socioecons.; mem. editorial adv. bd., cons. internal medicine Current Procedural Terminology, 3d edit., 1972-73; editorial adv. bd. Internal Medicine News, 1976-93. Bd. dirs. Nat. Capital Med. Found., 1979-84, pres., 1980-81. Served with AUS, 1943-46, 47-49. Recipient Disting. Svc. award AMA, 1996. Master Am. Coll. Rheumatology, 1992; fellow Am. Coll. Med. Informatics; mem. Nat. Acads. of Practice (pres. 1993-96), Nat. Acad. Practice in Medicine (chmn. 1991-93), Am. Soc. Internal Medicine (dir. 1968-78, pres. 1976-77), AMA (mem. coun. on legis. 1980-90, chmn. 1985-87, chmn. editl. adv. panel CPT-4 1980-92), Inst. Medicine of NAS, D.C. Med. Soc. (chmn. legis. com. 1972-76, 76-78), D.C. Soc. Internal Medicine (mem. exec. coun. 1975-78), So. Med. Assn. (sec. sect. internal medicine 1978-79, vice-chmn. 1979-80, chmn. 1980-81, assoc. councilor 1979-

81, 85-86), Rheumatism Soc. D.C. (pres. 1963-64), Internat. League Against Rheumatism (chmn. subcom. on classification and nomenclature 1982—, mem. epidemiology com. 1989-93), Alpha Epsilon Delta, Phi Chi, Kappa Sigma. Republican. Baptist. Home: 1492 Hampton Hill Cir Mc Lean VA 22101-6016 Office: 2150 Pennsylvania Ave NW Washington DC 20037-2396

FELZER, STANTON BERNARD, consulting psychologist; b. Phila., Nov. 6, 1928; s. Philip and Esther (Willig) F.; m. Stephanie Levick, Nov. 17, 1956; children: Andrea, Susan, Sharon. AB, Temple U., 1950, MA, 1951, PhD, 1954. Lic. psychologist, Pa. Sr. clin. psychologist Ea. Pa. Psychiat. Inst., Phila., 1956-59; assoc. prof. dept. psychiatry Sch. Medicine Temple U., Phila., 1961-69, asst. dir. Community Mental Health Ctr. Sch. Medicine, 1965-69, assoc. v.p. for planning Health Scis. Ctr., 1973-86; v.p. Woehr Assocs., Phila., 1959-61, 69-73; exec. v.p. Woehr Assocs., Haddonfield, N.J., 1986-91; pres. Felzer Assocs., Phila., 1991—; cons. NIMH, Rockville, Md., 1965-69. Pres. Abington (Pa.) Schs. Parent Coun., 1973-75; sec. bd. govs. Temple Hosp., 1975-86; cons. Phila. Mayor's Commn. on Health in 80's, 1982. With U.S. Army, 1954-56. NIMH grantee, 1965-69. Fellow Am. Psychol. Assn., Pa. Psychol. Assn. (pres. 1967-68); mem. Phila. Soc. Clin. Psychology (pres. 1963-64). Jewish. Home: 296 Ironwood Cir Elkins Park PA 19027-1336 Office: 1515 Locust St Ste 800 Philadelphia PA 19102-3711

FENCHEL, GERD H(ERMAN), psychoanalyst; b. Berlin, Mar. 29, 1926; arrived in U.S., 1940; s. Eric Otto and Rosa (Goldschmidt) F.; children: Karen Fenchel Spiler, Erich; m. Leslie Spitz, June 30, 1991. BSS, CCNY, 1949, MS in Edn., 1950; PhD, NYU, 1959; cert., Washington Sq. Inst., 1970. Cert. psychologist, N.Y., Pa. Pvt. practice psychoanalysis N.Y.C., 1949—; asst. dean Alfred Adler Inst., N.Y.C., 1955-73; psychotherapist, supr. and dir. group psychotherapy L.I. Cons. Ctr., Forest Hills, N.Y., 1953-60; mem. faculty Inst. for Analytic Psychotherapy, N.J., 1960-71; exec. dir., dean Washington Sq. Inst., N.Y.C., 1960—. Co-author: Development of Ego and Emergence of the Self in Group Psychotherapy, 1979; editor: Psychoanalysis at 100, 1994; contbr. articles to profl. jours. Fellow Coun. Psychoanalysts and Psychotherapists (pres. 1966-67); mem. Am. Psychol. Assn., Internat. Group Psychotherapy Assn. Office: Washington Sq Inst 41-51 E 11th St New York NY 10003

FENDERSON, CAROLINE HOUSTON, psychotherapist; b. East Orange, N.J., June 17, 1932; d. George Cochran and Mary Bullard (Saunders) Houston; m. Kendrick Elwell Fenderson, Jr.; 1 child, Karen Sibley. BA, Vassar Coll., 1954; MA, U. So. Fla., 1973. Lic. mental health counselor, Fla.; diplomate Am. Bd. Cert. Managed Care Providers; cert. Nat. Bd. for Cert. Clin. Hypnotherapists, Inc.; cert. trainer, devel. of human capacities Found. for Mind Rsch.; ordained to ministry of edn. Unitarian Universalist. Dir. of religious edn. Unitarian Universalist Ch., St. Petersburg, Fla., 1960-80; min. of religious edn. Unitarian Universalist Ch., Clearwater, Fla., 1981-83; counselor and staff devel. cons. Pinellas County (Fla.) Schools, 1973-83; pvt. practice Clearwater and Palm Harbor, Fla., 1983—. Author: Life Journey, 1988; (with Kendrick Fenderson Jr.) Magnets, 1961, Southern Shores, 1964; (with others) Man the Culture Builder, 1970, U.U. Identity, 1979; contbr. articles to profl. jours. Pub. affairs chmn. St. Petersburg Jr. League, 1960; founder Childbirth and Parent Edn. League of Pinellas County, 1960-70, pres., v.p., com. chair, tchr.; v.p. Child Guidance Clinic, St. Petersburg, 1960. Mem. ACA, Liberal Religious Edn. Dirs. Assn. (v.p. 1980-81), Assn. Transpersonal Psychology, Assn. Humanistic Psychology, Internat. Transpersonal Assn., Unitarian Universalist Assn. (com. mem. 1975-79), Phi Beta Kappa, Kappa Delta Pi. Home: 29 Freshwater Dr Palm Harbor FL 34684-1106 Office: 25 400 US 19 N Ste 172 Clearwater FL 34623

FENG, ALBERT S., science educator, researcher; b. Bandung, Java, Indonesia, Feb. 10, 1944; s. Shu-San and Yi (Chow) F.; m. Phoebe Lifei Wang, Oct. 14, 1974; children: Jeffrey Thomas, Jacqueline A. BSEE, U. Miami, 1968, MSc, 1970; PhD, Cornell U., 1975. Reliability engr. Singer Corp. Kearfott Div., Little Falls, N.J., 1970; asst. rsch. neuroscientist U. Calif. at San Diego, La Jolla, 1974-76; postdoctoral fellow Washington U., St. Louis, 1976-77; asst. prof. U. Ill., Urbana, 1977-83, assoc. prof., 1983-89, prof., 1989—, head dept. molecular and integrative physiology, 1992—; mem. adv. bd. Parmly Hearing Inst., Chgo., 1982-88; mem. review panel NSF, Washington, 1986-88; chmn. neurosci. program U. Ill., Urbana, 1987-90; mem. hearing rsch. study sect. NIH, Washington, 1991-95, chmn., 1993-95. Contbr. articles to profl. jours. including Jour. Neurophysiology, Jour. Comparative Physiology, Science, Jour. Comparative Neurology, Hearing Research. Fellow AAAS; mem. Assn. for Rsch. Otolaryngology, Internat. Soc. Neuroethology (treas. 1992—), Soc. of Neurosci., Acoustical Soc. Am. Home: 1209 Wilshire Ct Champaign IL 61821-6916 Office: U Ill 405 N Mathews Ave Urbana IL 61801-2325

FENG, GEN-SHENG, medical educator, researcher; b. Sept. 8, 1961. BSc in Biology, Hangzhou U., China, 1981; MSc in Immunology, 2d Med. Sch. of Army, Shanghai, China, 1984; PhD in Molecular Biology, Ind. U., 1990. Rsch. assoc. in molecular genetics 2d Med. Sch. of Army, Shanghai, China, 1985-86; assoc. instr. dept. biology Ind. U., Bloomington, 1987-90; postdoctoral fellow in molecular biology U. Toronto, 1990-94; with Rsch. Inst. The Hosp. for Sick Children, Toronto, 1990-91, Rsch. Inst. Mt. Sinai Hosp., Toronto, 1991-94; asst. prof. dept. biochemistry and molecular biology, dept. med. and molecular genetics, asst. mem. Walther Oncology Ctr. Ind. U., Indpls., 1994—. Ad hoc reviewer Jour. Biol. Chemistry, Jour. Cell Sci., Oncogene, Leukemia; contbr. articles to profl. jours.; reviewer of rsch. grants Internat. Human Frontier Sci. Program, 1994, 95, U.S. Vets. Affairs Med. Rsch. Sys., 1996; spkr. in field. Recipient Silver prize for Achievement of Health Sci. and Tech., China, 1986, Carrie E. Wolff award Am. Heart Assn. Ind. Affiliate, Inc., 1995. Mem. AAAS, Am. Diabetes Assn. (career devel. award 1995—), Am. Soc. Microbiology, Soc. Chinese Biologists Am. Office: Ind U Sch Medicine Dept Biochemistry and Molecular Biology 635 Barnhill Dr Rm 410 Indianapolis IN 46202-5122

FENICHEL, GERALD MERVIN, neurologist, educator; b. N.Y.C., May 11, 1935; s. Max I. and Sarah M. Fenichel; m. Barbara Ellen Ross, June 8, 1958; children—Amy Beth, Eric Ross, Adam Seth. A.B., Johns Hopkins U., 1955; M.D., Yale U., 1959. Diplomate Am. Bd. Neurology and Psychiatry. Intern in surgery Strong Meml. Hosp., Rochester, N.Y., 1959-60; research in neuropathology Nat. Inst. Neurol. Diseases and Stroke, Bethesda, Md., 1960-66; resident in neurology Nat. Inst. Neurol. Diseases and Stroke, Bethesda, 1961-63; instr. neurology George Washington U., 1964-67; asst. prof. Children's Hosp., Washington, 1967-69; prof., chmn. dept. neurology Vanderbilt U., Nashville, 1969—; dir. Jerry Lewis Neuromuscular Ctr., Nashville. Author: Neonatal Neurology; contbr. articles to profl. jours. Fellow Am. Acad. Neurology; mem. AMA, Am. Neurol. Assn., Child Neurology Soc. (pres. 1973-74), So. Clin. Neurol. Soc. (councilor 1984). Home: 234 Robin Hill Rd Nashville TN 37205-3535 Office: Vanderbilt U Dept Neurology 2100 Pierce Ave Nashville TN 37212-3162*

FENNELL, CHRISTINE ELIZABETH, health care consultant; b. Providence, July 14, 1948; d. Edmond John and Geraldine Mary (Goodenough) F. BS cum laude, Nat. Coll, Denver, 1983. Activity dir. Turtle Creek Convalescent Centre, Ft. Wayne, Ind., 1974-76; co-owner, operator Trail Ridge Welding, Estes Park, Colo., 1976-77; accounts mgr. Mayfair Women's Clinic, Denver, 1977-80; asst. adminstr. Ob-Gyn. Assocs., Aurora, Colo., 1980-82; admissions supr. St. Anthony Hosp. Sys., Denver, 1982-86; adminstr. Parkside Lodge of Colo., Thornton, 1986-89; ops./fin. mgr. Colo. Biodyne, Inc., Denver, 1989-90; adminstr. Kimberly Quality Care, Denver, 1990-93; br. mgr. Preferred Home Health Care, Inc., Lafayette, Ind., 1993-95; regional field cons. Arcadia Health Svcs., Inc., Southfield, 1995—; part-time instr. Nat. Coll., Denver, 1983-84. Contbr. articles to profl. jours. Bd. dirs. S.W. Denver Community Mental Health Svcs., 1986. Mem. Denver Bus. Women's Network (pres. 1986-87), Colo, Coun. Hosp. Admitting Mgrs. (v.p. 1985-86), Rotary Club. Office: Arcadia Health Svcs Inc 26777 Central Park Blvd Southfield MI 48076

FENNESSEY, PAUL VINCENT, pediatrics and pharmacology, educator, research administrator; b. Oklahoma City, Oct. 3, 1942; m. Susan Blackwell; children—Shirley, Karl, Shaun. B.S. in Chemistry, U. Okla., 1964; Ph.D. in Organic Analytical Chemistry, MIT, 1968. Research asst. U. Okla., Norman, 1963-64; predoctoral fellow MIT, Cambridge, 1964-69; asst. prof. pediatrics and pharmacology U. Colo. Health Sci. Ctr., Denver, 1975-81, co-dir. mass spectral ctr. 1980, assoc. prof. pediatrics and pharmacology, 1981-90, prof. ped. and pharmacology, 1990—, vice chair pediat., 1991—. Contbr. articles to profl. jours. Asst. program scientist Viking Project, Martin Marietta Corp., Denver, 1969-72, program scientist, 1972-74. Recipient NSF Undergrad. Research award, 1963-64; Merck award in Organic Chemistry, 1963; Woodrow Wilson Nat. fellow, 1964-65; NIH fellow, 1964-68. Mem. Am. Chem. Soc., Am. Soc. Mass Spectrometry, Nat. Acad. Clin. Biochemists, Soc. Inherited Metabolic Diseases, Am. Assn. Clin. Chemistry, AAAS, Am. Soc. Pharmacology and Exptl. Therapeutics, Internat. Soc. Study Xenobiotics, Sigma Xi. Home: 13009 S Parker Ave Pine CO 80470-9617 Office: U Colo Health Sci Ctr 4200 E 9th Ave # 232C Denver CO 80220-3706

FENNEY, NICHOLAS WILLIAM, retired pharmaceutical educator, consultant; b. New Haven, July 18, 1906; s. William Nicholas and Jennie Mary (Genovese) F.; m. Annamae Evangeline Dwyer, June 10, 1930 (dec. 1974); children: Nicholas William Jr., Barbara Jane; m. Anne Mary Manduck, Oct. 1, 1977; children: Nancy, Karen. Grad. in pharmacy, Columbia U., 1925; PhC, Conn. Coll. Pharmacy, 1930; BS in Pharmacy, U. Conn., 1942; MPH, Yale U., 1946. Lic. pharmacist, Conn. Instr. pharmacy Conn. Coll. Pharmacy, New Haven, 1925-35; asst. prof. U. Conn., Storrs, 1935-46, assoc. prof., 1946-50, prof., 1950-68, prof. emeritus, 1968—; pharm. and drug info. cons. Blue Cross and Blue Shield Conn., North Haven, 1968—. Author: Prescription Writing; also numerous articles. Recipient Sidney R. Rome award Conn. chpt. Alpha Zeta Omega, 1964, Disting. Faculty award from students U. Conn., 1965, Alumni award for disting. svc. in pharmacy to Conn. and nation, 1974, Bowl of Hygeia award A.H. Robins Co., 1969, Nat. Assn. Retail Druggists-Lederle Nat. Interprofl. Svc. award, 1969; established by Conn. Pharm. Assn. ann. Nicholas W. Fenney Scholarship at U. Conn., 1965. Mem. Conn. Pharm. Assn. (hon.), New Haven Pharm. Assn. (hon.), Hartford County Pharm. Soc. (hon.), Mortar and Pestle (hon.), Kappa Psi (grand regent 1953-55, editor Mask 1955-68). Roman Catholic. Home: 62 Broadfield Rd Hamden CT 06517-1503 Office: Blue Cross-Blue Shield Conn 370 Bassett Rd North Haven CT 06473-4201

FENNO, JAMES ROBERT, pharmacist, medical administrator; b. Milw., Aug. 10, 1943; s. Robert Ray and Loraine Emma Hazel (Hardtke) F.; m. Jane Helen Stenerson, Oct. 15, 1966; children: James Andrew, Lauri Jane. BS in Pharmacy, U. Wis., 1966. Registered pharmacist., Wis. Intern, staff mem. Peters Pharmacy, Milw., 1965-68; staff pharmacist Appleton (Wis.) Meml. Hosp., 1968-73; clin. cons. Pharm. Svcs., Appleton, 1973-74, pharmacist, 1976-77; resident, clin. specialist U. Wis. Med. Ctr., Madison, 1974-76; dir. pharmacy and clin. pharmacy svcs. St. Joseph's Hosp., Chippewa Falls, Wis., 1977—; owner, mgr. Profl. Consulting Svcs., Chippewa Falls, 1980—; pub. health officer City of Chippewa Falls, 1986—; reviewer U.S. Pharmacopeial Conv., Rockville, Md., 1986-89; prof. mem. Chippewa County Bd. Health, 1994—; presenter seminars; spkr. and lectr. in field. Bd. dirs. Chippewa County United Way, 1979-82, Chippewa Falls chpt. Am. Cancer Soc., 1980-83; cons. Parents Against Chem. Abuse, Chippewa County, 1983—. Recipient Chippewa/Eau Claire Leadership award WEAU Broadcasting Co., 1982, Pharmacy Leadership award Nat. Assn. Retail Druggists, 1983, Pharmacy Achievement award Merck Sharp & Dohme Labs, 1986, A.H. Robins Bowl of Hygeia award, 1988, citation of Merit, U. Wis., 1989. Mem. Wis. Pharm. Assn. (pres. 1983-84, 90—, Mortar & Pestal award 1986), Chippewa Valley Pharm. Assn. (pres. 1980-81), U. Wis. Pharmacy Alumni Assn. (pres. 1987-88), Am. Pharm. Assn. (del. 1983-85), Am. Inst. History of Pharmacy (author, photographer slide show 1976), Pres.'s Coun. (pres. 1990—). Home: 815 Dwight St Chippewa Falls WI 54729-1008 Office: St Joseph's Hosp 2661 County Trunk I Chippewa Falls WI 54729

FENSTER, HAROLD ALAN, surgeon; b. Miami Beach, Fla., Nov. 23, 1944; s. Moe and Claire (Krinitt) F.; m. Nicole Vandale, Oct. 26, 1968 (div. 1981); m. Cynthia J. Cannon, July 7, 1989; children: Annick, Donalee, Corinne. BA in Biology, Emory U., 1965; MEd, U. Fla., 1967; B.Dr.med., Free U. Brussels, Belgium, 1969; Dr.med., U. Miami, Fla., 1973. Diplomate Am. Bd. Surgery. Commd. 2d lt. U.S. Army, 1972, advanced through grades to lt. col., 1982; surg. intern Tripler Army Med. Ctr., Honolulu, 1973-74; resident in surgery Walter Reed Army Med. Ctr., Washington, 1978-82; staff surgeon, chief gen. surgery Nurnberg (Fed. Republic Germany) Army Hosp., 1982-84; resigned, 1984; staff surgeon Fish Meml. Hosp., New Smyrna Beach, Fla., 1984—; pvt. practice New Smyrna Beach, 1984—; asst. clin. prof. surgery Uniformed Svcs. U. of Health Scis., Bethesda, Md., 1982—; mem. Fla. State Com. on Trauma, Jacksonville, 1984—; diplomat U.S. Army War Coll., 1986, Command and Gen. Staff Coll., 1991; command 73rd Field Hosp., Ga., 1993-94, 345th Command Support Hosp., Jacksonville, Fla., 1994—. Contbr. articles to profl. jours. Col. USAR, 1985—, Operation Desert Shield and Desert Storm, Saudi Arabia, 1991. Decorated Army Commendation medal with oak leaf cluster; Am. Cultural Exch. scholar, Belgium, 1969-71. Fellow ACS, Southeastern Surg. Congress, Internat. Coll. Surgeons; mem. AMA, Fla. Med. Assn., Volusia County Med. Assn., Soc. Am. Gastroendoscopic Surgeons, Soc. Critical Care Medicine, Alpha Epsilon Delta. Democrat. Jewish. Office: 603 S Orange St New Smyrna Beach FL 32168-7320

FENSTERHEIM, HERBERT, psychologist, writer; b. Bklyn., July 22, 1921; s. Harry and Mollie (Feder) F.; m. Jean Baer, June 20, 1968 (dec.); m. Barbara Wiegand, Nov. 26, 1993. BA, NYU, 1941, PhD, 1958; MA, Columbia U., 1942. Diplomate Am. Bds. Behavioral Psychology, Profl. Psychology. Pvt. practice N.Y.C., 1952—; clin. assoc. prof. N.Y. Med. Coll., 1964-72; clin. assoc. prof. Med. Coll. Cornell U., N.Y.C., 1972-85, clin. prof. Med. Coll., 1985—; attending psychologist The N.Y. Hosp., 1985—; sports psychologist U.S. Olympic Fencing Team, 1981-85. Author: (with others) Don't Say Yes When You Want to Say No, 1975 (APA Media award), Behavioral Psychotherapy, 1983, Advances in Behavior Therapy, 1971, 72, Help Without Psychoanalysis, 1971, Stop Running Scared, 1977, Making Life Right When It Feels All Wrong, 1988; contbr. articles to profl. jours. Staff sgt. U.S. Army, 1942-45. Jewish. Home and Office: 151 E 37th St New York NY 10016-3157

FENTERS, JAMES DEAN, research institute administrator; b. Attica, Ind., Sept. 23, 1936; s. Noel Dean Fenters and Rose LaVerna (Wilkinson) Mountz. BS, Purdue U., 1958; MS, U. Iowa, 1961, PhD, 1962. Sr. rsch. virologist Abbott Labs., North Chicago, Ill., 1962-67; rsch. virologist IIT Rsch. Inst., Chgo., 1967-69; sr. virologist IIT Rsch. Inst., 1969-74, sci. advisor, 1974-85, sr. sci. advisor, 1985-89, dir. life scis. dept., 1989-92; dir. new bus. devel., 1992—; pres., Ill. Soc. Microbiology, Chgo., 1984-85; coun. mem. Midwest Soc. Toxicology, Chgo., 1986-88; editorial bd., Applied Microbiology Jour. Clin. Microbiology, 1967-82; mem., EPA Sci. Review Panel Health Rsch., 1981-89. Contbr. articles to profl. jours. Bd. dirs. Harbor Point Condo Assn. Bd., Chgo., 1988—; mem. Grant Park Assn., Chgo., 1989—. NIH fellow, 1959-62. Mem. Am. Soc. Microbiology, AAAS, Am. Acad. Microbiology, Soc. Toxicology, Sigma Xi. Home: Apt 5103 155 N Harbor Dr Chicago IL 60601-7326 Office: IIT Rsch Inst 10 W 35th St Chicago IL 60616-3799

FENTON, CLARENCE ASA, healthcare facility administrator; b. Warren, Ohio, Sept. 11, 1950; s. Calvin A. and Betty (Miller) F. AAS in Nursing, Youngstown (Ohio) State U., 1976; BS in Occupational Edn., U. So. Maine, 1988, postgrad., 1992—. RN, Maine, Ohio, Mass.; CNOR. Staff nurse operating rm. Mercy Hosp., Portland, Maine, preceptor operating rm.; clin. nurse educator Brighton Med. Ctr., Portland; dir. surg. svcs. Parkview Hosp., Brunswick, Maine, 1995—; mem. Nat. Cert. Bd. for Perioperative Nursing Inc., treas., 1995—. With USN, 1969-70. Mem. Maine Assn. Oper. Rm. Nurses (pres. 1992-94), Nat. Nursing Staff Devel. Orgn., Assn. Nurses in AIDS Care, Nursing Alumni Assn. Youngstown State U., Sigma Theta Tau, Kappa Zeta (cmty. counselor 1995—). Home: 705 Riverside St Portland ME 04103-1030

FENTON, WAYNE S., psychiatrist; b. Mar. 24, 1953. BA in Exptl. Psychology, Bard Coll., 1975; MD, George Washington U., 1979. Cert. Am. Bd. Medical Examiners, 1980; cert. Md., Conn., Va.; Diplomate in Psychiatry. Rotating internship, dept. internal medicine Norwalk Hosp., Conn., 1979-80; resident, post doctoral fellow psychiatry Yale U., 1980-83; fellow Inst. Social and Policy Studies, Yale U., 1983-84; staff psychiatrist Yale Psychiat. Inst., Yale U., New Haven, Conn., 1983-84, Chestnut Lodge, Rockville, Md., 1984-85; rsch. assoc. Chestnut Lodge Rsch. Inst., Rockville, Md., 1984-90; clin. adminstrv. psychiatrist Chestnut Lodge Hosp., Rockville, Md., 1985-90; dir. rsch. Chestnut Lodge Rsch. Inst., Rockville, Md., 1990—; asst. clin. dir. Chestnut Lodge Hosp., Rockville, Md., 1990—, med. dir., CEO, 1994—; assoc. clin. prof., psychiatry and behavior scis. George Washington U., D.C., 1990—; facualty Washington Sch. Psychiatry, D.C., 1991—; cons. Montgomery County Pub. Defender, Md., 1984—, McAuliffe House, Md., 1990—. Editl. cons. Schizophrenia Bulletin, 1986—, assoc. editor, 1994—; editl. cons. Jour. of Nervous and Mental Disease, 1986—, Am. Jour. Psychiatry, 1989—; contbr. to profl. jours. Recipient nat. rsch. svc. award USPHS, 1983-84, young investigator award NIH, 1989, Nat. Alliance for Rsch. in Schizophrenia and Depression, 1989, Gralnick award Am. Suicide Found., 1992, Md. Schizophrenia Sci. award, 1995. Mem. Am. Psychiat. Assn., Wash. Psychiat. Sopc., Nat. Alliance for Mentally Ill (exemplary psychiatrist 1996), NAPPH. Office: Chestnut Lodge Hospital 500 W Montgomery Ave Rockville MD 20850-3892

FEREKIDIS, ELEFTHERIOS, otorhinolaryngologist, educator, researcher; b. Istanbul, Turkey, Apr. 19, 1941; arrived in Greece, 1972; s. Antony and Elisabeth (Maioglou) F.; m. Angelika Karaviti, Jan. 21, 1973; 1 child, Elisabeth. MD, U. Istanbul, 1965. Diplomate in otorhinolaryngology. Intern Ear, Nose and Throat, Clinic State Hosp., Krefeld, Fed. Republic Germany, 1965-66, resident, 1966-71; chief resident Ear, Nose and Throat Clinic, U. Athens, 1972-81, lectr., 1981-88, assoc. prof., 1988—; prof. Mil. Nursing High Sch., Athens, 1978—; cons. Nat. Drug Orgn., Athens, 1986-89. Co-author: Manual of Otorhinolaryngology, 1989; author: Otorhinolaryngology for Nurses, 1989; contbr. over 130 articles to med. jours. Mem. Panhellenic Ear, Nose and Throat Assn. (pres. 1994-96), Greek Ear, Nose and Throat Assn. (v.p. 1984-86), German Ear, Nose and Throat Assn., Austrian Ear, Nose and Throat Assn., European Rhinologic Soc., Soc. for Med. Studies (cons. 1979—). Home: Antinoros 6-8, 116-35 Athens Greece Office: Hippokration Hosp, Vass Sofias Str 114, 115-27 Athens Greece

FERENCE, WAYNE, psychologist, human resources professional; b. Gary, Ind.; s. Andrew and Mary F. BA, UCLA, 1963; MA, U. So. Calif., L.A., 1965, PhD, 1970. Personnel rsch. psychologist City of Milw., 1971-74; personnel officer Chase Manhattan Bank, N.Y.C., 1974-76; pres. Ference Behavior Systems, Westwood, N.J., 1976-85; v.p. Exec. Search, Inc., Newark, 1985—. Contbr. to profl. publs. Mem. Am. Statis. Assn., Am. Psychol. Soc., N.J. Amateur Computer Group. Office: Exec Search Inc Ste 2600 Gateway One Newark NJ 07102

FERENCE-VALENTA, MARY JEAN, osteopath; b. Middletown, Pa., Nov. 26, 1969; d. Edward W. and Virginia J. (Dedik) Ference; m. Erik D. Valenta, Sept. 9, 1995. BS, St. Vincent Coll., 1992; DO, Chgo. Coll. Osteo. Medicine, 1996. Rsch. intern Pitts. Energy Tech. Ctr., 1991; chemistry analyst Allegheny Power Svc. Corp., Greensburg, Pa., 1992; intern St. Vincent Med. Ctr., Toledo, 1996—; med. edn. cmty. orientation participant, 1993. Grantee Chgo. Coll. Osteo. Medicine Alumni Assn., 1993-94, 94-95; scholar Pa. Osteo. Med. Assn., 1995; recipient Student Coun. Leadership award 1996. Mem. AMA, Am. Coll. Family Practitioners, Am. Osteo. Assn., Ill. Assn. Osteo. Physicians and Surgeons, Ill. State Med. Soc., Chgo. Med. Soc., Student Osteo. Med. Assn., Sigma Sigma Phi (sec.-treas. 1994-95, Am. Osteo. Assn. conv. rep. 1994).

FERENCZ, BARBARA J., health facility surveyor administrator; b. Toledo, Mar. 10, 1944; d. Roger Lee and Florence Elizabeth (Hudgin) Benham; m. Joseph R. Ferencz, July 3, 1965; 1 child, Ronald Lee. Diploma, Cleve. Met. Gen. Hosp., 1965; BA in Mgmt., Malone Coll., 1989; cert. primary health practitioner, Case Western Res. U., 1974. Cert. family nurse practitioner. Adminstrv. mgr., family nurse practitioner Eunice Carter M.D., Inc., Cuyahoga Falls, Ohio; family nurse practitioner Summit County Health Dept., Cuyahoga Falls; dir. health svcs. Hattie Larlham Found., Mantua, Ohio; supr. health facility surveyor Ohio Dept. of Health, Columbus, Ohio. Mem. ANA, Ohio Nurses Assn., Northeast Ohio Nurse Practitioner Assn. Home: 3507 E Prescott Cir Cuyahoga Falls OH 44223-3395

FERENCZ, CHARLOTTE, pediatrician, epidemiology and preventive medicine educator; b. Budapest, Hungary, Oct. 28, 1921; came to U.S., 1954; d. Paul Ferencz and Livia deFekete. BSc, McGill U., 1944, MD, CM, 1945; MPH, Johns Hopkins U., 1970. Cert. pediatrics Royal Coll. Physicians and Surgeons, Can., pediatric cardiology Am. Bd. Pediatrics. Demonstrator McGill U., Montreal, 1952-54; asst. prof. pediatrics Johns Hopkins U., Balt., 1954-58, U. Cin., 1959-60; asst. prof. SUNY, Buffalo, 1960-66, assoc. prof., 1966-73; assoc. prof. epidemiology and preventive medicine U. Md. Sch. Medicine, Balt., 1973-74, prof., 1974—, prof. pediatrics, 1985—; Prin. investigator population based study Etiology of Congenital Heart Disease, 1981-89; mem. epidemiology and disease control study sect. NIH, 1984-88; pres. Delta Omage Alpha chpt. Pub. Health Soc., 1990-92. Recipient M.E.S. Abbott scholarship McGill U., 1943-45, M.E.R.I.T. award Nat. Heart, Lung & Blood Inst., 1987, Fogarty Internat. Ctr. Health Sci. Exchange award NIH, 1988, Helen B. Taussig award Am. Heart Assn. Md. Affiliate, 1991, Achievement award Univ. Ctr. Life Scis., Balt., 1993. Fellow Am. Acad. Pediatrics (Spl. Achievement award Md. chpt. 1994), Am. Coll. Cardiology; mem. Teratology Soc. Democrat. Office: U Md Sch Medicine 660 W Redwood St Baltimore MD 21201-1596

FERET, ADAM EDWARD, JR., dentist; b. Newark, Mar. 5, 1942; s. Adam Edward and Bronislawa Anne (Szorc) F. BA (athletic scholar), Seton Hall U., 1963; DMD, U. Medicine & Dentistry of N.J., 1967. Pvt. practice Westfield, N.J., 1972—. With USNR, 1967-70. Fellow Am. Acad. Gen. Dentistry; mem. ADA, N.J. Dental Assn., L.D. Pankey Study Club, Soc. Oral Physiology and Occlusion, Quest Study Club, Internat. Coll. Oral Implantologists, Am. Soc. Oral Implantology, Central Dental Soc., Balloon Fedn. Am., Polish-Am. Guardian Soc., Polish Falcons of Am., Copernicus Soc. Am., Toastmasters, Psi Omega. Roman Catholic. Home and Office: 440 E Broad St Westfield NJ 07090-2124

FERGES, ROSE D., nursing educator; b. Balt., Feb. 8, 1930; d. Walker H. and Bessie E. (Dorsey) Dawson; m. Joseph H. Ferges Sr., Jan. 2, 1953; children: Frances, Toney, Joseph Jr., Paula. AA, Essex Community Coll., Balt., 1972; BS, U. Balt., 1979; MS, Coppin State U., 1991. Nursing supr. Highland Health Facility, Balt.; supr. Spring Grove Hosp., Balt.; supr. outpatient dept. & dialysis Veterans Adminstrn. Ft. Howard, Balt.; Instr. nursing edn., nursing informatic coord. Dept. Veterans Affairs, Balt. Chair Nurses Profl. Standards Bd.; equal employment opportunity counselor. Recipient Gov.'s citation for Outstanding Svc., Citizen citation for Dedication and Commitment from Mayor Kurt Schmoke, spl. contbn. award Dept. Vet. Affairs. Mem. Md. Nurses Assn., NAACP, Blacks in Govt. (rsch. com., sec. Ft. Howard br.), Toastmaster (charter; chair data validation com.).

FERGUSON, BILLY LEE, pediatrician; b. Haw River, N.C., Mar. 10, 1933; s. Bertram Lindsay and Ellen Flora (McCaskill) F.; m. Odessa Maxine Dale, Sept. 15, 1957; children: William Lee, Ann Michele Bishop; m. Sandra Helen Ritter, May 23, 1995. BS, Guilford Coll., 1954; MS in Pub. Health, U. N.C., 1955; MD, Bowman Gray Sch. Medicine, 1959. Diplomate Am. Bd. Pediat. Intern USAF Hosp., San Antonio, 1960-64; resident in pediat. N.C. Bapt. Hosp., Winston-Salem, 1964-66; commd. 2d lt. USAF, 1959, advanced through grades to maj., 1969; pvt. practice Greensboro, N.C., 1969—. Office: 614 Pasteur Dr Greensboro NC 27403

FERGUSON, CHARLES MASON, surgeon; b. Newton, Mass., Jan. 12, 1953; s. Ira Alfred and Anne (Mason) F.; m. Stacy Lark McCrary, Dec. 28, 1974; children: Ian Charles, Kate Clifford, Emily Tye. MD, Emory U. Sch. Medicine, 1976. Diplomate Am. Bd. Surgery. Intern in surgery Mass. Gen. Hosp., Boston, 1976-77; resident in surgery Mass. Gen. Hosp., 1977-82; sr. fellow in thoracic surgery Broadgreen Hosp., Liverpool, England, 1981; asst. prof. surgery Emory U. Sch. Medicine, Atlanta, 1984-90, Harvard Med. Sch., Boston, 1990—; assoc. vis. surgeon Mass. Gen. Hosp., Boston, 1990—, emergency ward task force com., 1991—, admission com., 1991—, clin. sys. adv. com., 1992—, exec. bd., 1993—, fin. com. comprehensive breast health ctr., 1993—. Edtl. bd. Videoscopic Surgery. Fellow Am. Coll. Surgeons (Ga. rep. 1987, com. on young surgeons 1987, liaison to commn. on cancer Grady Meml. Hosp. 1986-90, med. edn. com. Ga. chpt. 1986-90, review course coord. 1987, ann. mtg. program chmn. 19880; mem. Southeastern Surgical Congress (ednl. award 1992, gold medal forum com. 1988—, med. edn. and program com. 1990), Southeastern Surg. Soc. (edn. com. 1990-95),

Am. Bd. Surgery (advisor recertification exam 1991-94), Ga. Surg. Soc., So. Surgeons Club, Boston Surg. Soc., Soc. Surg. Oncology, Alpha Epsilon Upsilon, Alpha Omega Alpha. Office: Mass Gen Hosp 275 Cambridge St Ste 502 Boston MA 02114

FERGUSON, DONALD GUFFEY, radiologist; b. West Newton, Pa., July 19, 1923; s. Rutherford Hayes and Beulah Cristabel (Guffey) F.; BS, U. Pitts., 1944, MD, 1946; m. Anne Benedict Gallagher, Mar. 4, 1961. Intern, S. Side Hosp., Pitts., 1946-47; resident in radiology and radiation therapy Meml. Sloan-Kettering, N.Y.C., 1950-52; Am. Cancer Soc. fellow, staff radiologist Thomas Jefferson U. Hosp., Phila., 1952-55; attending radiologist Mercy Hosp., Pitts., 1955-57; sr. staff S. Side Hosp., Pitts., 1957—, St. Clair Meml. Hosp., Pitts., 1957—; clin. asst. prof. radiology U. Pitts., 1956—. Served with M.C., U.S. Army, 1948-50. Diplomate Am. Bd. Radiology, Am. Bd. Nuclear Medicine. Fellow Am. Coll. Radiology (dist. councilor 1972-78, pres. Pa. chpt. 1979-80); mem. Soc. Nuclear Medicine (chpt. pres. 1957-58), Pitts. Roentgen Soc. (pres. 1967-68), Am. Med. Assn. (ho. of del. 1987—), Pa. Med. Soc. (pres. 1992-93), Radiol. Soc. N. Am., Am. Roentgen Ray Soc., Allegheny County Med. Soc., Pitts. Athletic Assn. Presbyterian. Club: Masons (Shriner). Home: Hidden Valley Rd Canonsburg PA 15317 Office: 1000 Bower Hill Rd Pittsburgh PA 15243-1873

FERGUSON, DORIS LENA WAGNER, retired nurse educator; b. Ellinwood, Kans., Apr. 2, 1925; d. Charles and Frieda Augusta (Kasler) Wagner; m. Gerald E. Ferguson, Aug. 17, 1985 (dec. Dec. 1987). Diploma, Emanuel Hosp. Sch. Nursing, 1947; BS, U. Oreg., 1951; MS, Simmons Coll., 1955. Nursing supr. Tacoma (Wash.)-Pierce County Health Dept., 1955-60; asst. prof. nursing Pacific Luth. U., Tacoma, 1960-64; DON Marion County Health Dept., Salem, Oreg., 1964-67; chief nurse San Jose (Calif.) City Health Dept., 1967-68; asst. DON Santa Clara County Health Dept., San Jose, 1968-69; DON Harvard Community Health Plan, Boston, 1969-74; chief nurse Bur. Pub. Health Nursing Marion County Health Dept., Dept. Health and Hosp. Corp., Indpls., 1974-85; assoc. prof. Northwestern Okla. State U., Alva, 1985-91, dean sch. of nursing, 1991-96; ret., 1996. Mem. editorial team Blackwell Sci. Publ., 1983—; contbr. articles to profl. jours. Bd. dirs. Am. Jour. Nursing Co., N.Y.C., 1979-83; bd. mem. nursing unit ARC, Inddpls., 1982-85; v.p. Pond Creek (Okla.) C. of C., 1991. Recipient Pearl McIver award ANA, 1974, Community Svc. award Enid (Okla.) Toastmasters Club, 1987; named Nurse of Yr., Ind. Citizens League for Nursing, Indpls., 1979, Employer of Yr., Continuing Edn. Ctr., Ind. U., Purdue U., 1984. Fellow APHA, Am. Acad. Nursing; mem. Okla. Nurses Assn. (pres. dist. 1988-92, pres. cabinet of pres. 1989-91, Excellence in Community Health Nursing award 1988), Nat. League Nursing (editorial rev. bd. Nursing and Health Care 1983—), Assn. Community Health Nurse Educators, Sigma Theta Tau (Beta Delta chpt.), Delta Kappa Gamma (Kappa chpt.). Home: RR 2 Box 2 Pond Creek OK 73766-9601 Office: Northwestern Okla State U Alva OK 73717

FERGUSON, EMMETT BONLORE, occupational medicine consultant; b. Augusta, Ark., Feb. 12, 1933; s. Emmett Bonlore and Cora Dee (Fugate) F.; m. Hope Herrington, Dec. 27, 1957 (dec. Oct. 1986); children: William Bonlore, Becki Dale; m. Margarette Annette Plaster, Feb. 18, 1989. MD, U. Okla., Oklahoma City, 1959; MPH, Johns Hopkins U., 1965. Diplomate Am. Bd. Internal Medicine, Am. Bd. Emergency Medicine, Am. Bd. Preventive Medicine in Occupl. Medicine and Aerospace Medicine. Commd. 2d lt. USAF, 1960, advanced through grades to col., 1974; intern Orange Meml. Hosp., Orlando, Fla., 1959-60; resident in aerospace medicine USAF Sch. Aerospace Medicine, 1965-66; resident in bioastronautics USAF Eastern Test Range, 1966-69; resident in internal medicine USAF Med. Ctr., Keesler AFB, Miss., 1969-72; dir. flight medicine USAF Med. Group, Andersen AFB, Guam, 1962-64; dir. bioastronautics USAF Ea. Test Range, Patrick AFB, Fla., 1967-69; chief profl. svcs. USAF Hosp., Ramey AFB, P.R., 1972-73; chief evaluation function USAF Sch. Aerospace Medicine, Brooks AFB, Tex., 1973-74; comdr. USAF Hosp., Homestead AFB, Fla., 1974-77, Wiesbaden, Germany, 1977-80; comdr. USAF Med. Ctr., Wright-Patterson AFB, Ohio, 1980-83; ret., 1983; assoc. gen. mgr., dir. med. svcs. base ops. contract, Kennedy Space Center, Fla., 1983-94; occupl. medicine svcs. cons. Merritt Island, Fla., 1994—. Contbr. over 100 articles to med. jours., chpt. to book. Bd. dirs. Merritt Island Wildlife Assn., 1994—, Ctrl. Fla. dist. Boy Scouts Am., Orlando, 1994—. Decorated Legion of Merit with oak leaf cluster; named Fla. Occupl. Medicine Physician of Yr., Fla. Occupl. Health Nurses Assn., 1986; recipient pub. svc. medal NASA, 1991. Fellow ACP (component pres.), Aerospace Med. Assn. (Hubertus Strugholt award space medicine br. 1994), Am. Coll. Occupl. and Environ. Medicine (bd. dirs. 1992-96), Am. Coll. Emergency Physicians, Am. Coll. Preventive Medicine; mem. AMA, Soc. USAF Physicians (pres. 1977-78), Fla. Occupl. Medicine Assn. (pres. 1985-86), Fla. Coll. Emergency Medicine (pres. 1990-91), Brevard County Med. Soc. (pres. 1995-96), Nat. Eagle Scout Assn. Home and Office: 2945 Newfound Harbor Dr Merritt Island FL 32952

FERGUSON, JAMES EDWARD, II, obstetrician, gynecologist, maternal-fetal medicine specialist; b. Glendale, Calif., Oct. 25, 1951; m. Lynn Corpening, June 21, 1975; children: James Edward III, David Gregory, Joshua Scott. Student, USCG Acad., 1969-71; AB in History, Marquette U., 1973; MD, Wake Forest U., 1977. Diplomate Nat. Bd. Med. Examiners, Am. Bd. Ob/Gyn with a subspecialty in maternal-fetal medicine. Intern USPHS Hosp., San Francisco, 1977-78; resident ob/gyn Stanford (Calif.) U. Sch. Medicine, 1978-80, postdoctoral fellow ob/gyn, 1982-84; chief resident Bowman Gray Sch. of Medicine, Winston-Salem, N.C., 1980-81; clin. faculty Bowman Gray Sch. of Medicine, 1981-82; asst. prof. ob/gyn Stanford (Calif.) U. Sch. Medicine, 1984-87; asst. prof. ob/gyn U. Va. Sch. Medicine, 1987-90, assoc. prof., 1990-96; John Nokes prof. ob-gyn., 1996—; dir. prenatal diagnosis and treatment unit, ob/gyn U. Va. Sch. Medicine, 1989—, dir. Divsn. Maternal-Fetal Medicine, 1990—, John Nokes prof. ob/gyn., 1996—; attending staff U. Va. Hosp., 1987—, Va. Bapt. Hosp., 1996—, Stanford U. Hosp., 1982-87, Forsyth Meml. Hosp., Winston-Salem, 1981-82, Med. Park Hosp., Winston-Salem, 1981-82; assoc. staff Va. Bapt. Hosp., Lynchburg, 1992-96, Santa Clara Valley Med. Ctr., San Jose, Calif., 1982-87; cons. Mid-Coastal Calif. Perinatal Outreach Program, Stanford U., 1982-87, San Joaquin Gen. Hosp., Stockton, Calif., 1985-87; fellow Project Hope, maternal-fetal medicine program, Krakow, Poland, 1987, 89, others; mem. numerous coms. in field. Editl. referee Am. Jour. Ob-Gyn., Ob-Gyn. Jour., Clin. Chemistry Jour., Am. Jour. Human Genetics, Jour. Perinatology, Jour. Maternal-Fetal Medicine; obstet. editl. cons. Perinatal Continuing Edn. Program; contbr. articles to profl. jours., chpts. to books in field. Hon. chmn. March of Dimes Walkathon, U. Va. Health Scis. Ctr., 1990; active task force on smoking and pregnancy, Am. Lung Assn. of Santa Clara-San Benito Counties, 1983. Recipient numerous grants in field, including Dept. Mental Health, Retardation and Substance Abuse, Commonwealth of Va., 1992-93, Perinatal Nurse Liaison Contract, 1991-92, others. Fellow ACOG; mem. AAAS, Am. Gynecol. and Obstetrics Soc., Calif. Perinatal Assn., Peninsula Ob-Gyn. Assn., Peninsula Gynecol. Soc., Shufelt Soc., Soc. Perinatal Obstetricians, Frank Lock Soc., Assn. Profs. Ob-Gyn., Am. Inst. Ultrasound in Medicine, So. Ob-Gyn. Seminar, U. Va. Residents' Soc. (hon.), N.C. Ob-Gyn. Soc. (hon.), Am. Physiol. Soc., Phi Beta Kappa, Phi Alpha Theta. Office: U Va Sch Medicine Div Maternal and Fetal Medicine PO Box 387 Charlottesville VA 22908

FERGUSON, J(AMES) PAUL, neurological surgeon; b. Atlanta, July 21, 1937; s. James Alexander and Laura (Milton) F.; m. Catherine Blair, July 30, 1969; children: James Paul Jr., Andrew Milton. AB, Emory U., 1959, MD, 1963. Diplomate, Am. Bd. Neurol. Surgeons. Intern, then resident in neurosurgery Med. Coll. Va., Richmond, 1963-65, 68-71; fellow in neurophysiology Barnes Hosp., St. Louis, 1965-66; asst. prof., instr. neurosurgery U. N.C., Chapel Hill, 1971-73; assoc. Geisinger Med. Ctr., Danville, Pa., 1973-76; pres., chief exec. officer Harbin Clinic, Rome, Ga., 1976—, chmn. bd., 1995—; 1990—; bd. dirs., chmn. First Union Bank of Rome. Trustee, Rome YMCA, 1979-85; chmn. bd. trustees, Redmond Hosp., Rome, 1985-88; chmn. Rome-Floyd Drug Task Force, 1986-88; trustee, Berry Coll., Rome, 1984—. Capt. U.S. Army, 1966-68, Vietnam. Decorated Bronze Star medal, Air Medal, Combat Med. badge, Vietnamese Honor medal. Mem. Neurosurg. Soc. Am. (treas. 1988-91, pres. 1994-95), Am. Assn. Neurol. Surgeons, Congress Neurol. Surgeons, Ga. Neurosurg. Soc. (pres. 1987-88), Floyd-Polk Med. Soc. (pres. 1980-81), So. Neurosurg. Soc., Leadership Ga., Greater Rome C. of C. (v.p., bd. dirs. 1981-84), Rotary (bd. dirs. 1982-83, 85-86, 90-91, pres.-elect 1996—), Coosa Valley Tennis Assn. (bd. dirs.). Republican. Episcopalian. Office: Harbin Clinic 1825 Martha Berry Blvd Rome GA 30165

FERGUSON, JOHN BARCLAY, biology educator; b. Balt., July 5, 1947; s. John Miller and Helen (Sucro) F.; m. Jane Hough, June 28, 1970 (div. 1987); children: Hallam H., Gillian D.; m. Valeri J. Thomson, July 1, 1988; 1 child, Samantha T. BS, Brown U., 1969; PhD, Yale U., 1973. Asst. prof. Bard Coll., Annandale, N.Y., 1977-83, assoc. prof., 1983-92, prof., 1992—. Contbr. to 1 book and articles to profl. jours. Bd. trustees Ch. St. John Evangelist, Barrytown, N.Y., 1988—. NIH Postdoctoral fellow, 1974-76. Mem. AAAS, Am. Soc. Microbiology, N.Y. Acad. Scis., Sigma Xi. Home: RR 3 Box 305 Red Hook NY 12571-9425 Office: Bard Coll Dept Biology Annandale On Hudson NY 12504

FERGUSON, JOHN PATRICK, medical center executive; b. Weehawken, N.J., Jan. 22, 1949; s. Donald George and Margaret (Rienzo) F.; m. Gene Marie Promersperger, Jan. 16, 1971; children: Adam, David, Kate. BS in Econs., St. Peter's Coll., 1970; MBA in Hosp. Adminstrn., George Washington U., 1973. Sr. v.p. St. Vincent's Hosp., N.Y.C., 1972-81; v.p. ops. Hackensack (N.J.) Med. Ctr., 1981-85, sr. v.p., 1985, acting pres., chief exec. officer, 1985-86, pres., chief exec. officer, 1986—; mem. adj. faculty New Sch. for Social Rsch. Grad. Sch. Mgmt. and Urban Professions, N.Y.C., 1978—; pres. Met. Health Adminstrs., N.Y.C., 1977-78; vice chmn. bd. trustees Univ. Health Sys., New Brunswick, N.J., 1988-90; rep. to coun. on tchg. hosps. Assn. Am. Med. Coll., 1994-97; abstract presenter China-U.S. Conf. on Managing Hosps. in 1990s. Bd. govs. Ramapo Coll. Found., 1993—; trustee Univ. HealthCare Corp., 1994—; mem. exec. bd. Bergen coun. Boy Scouts am., 1993—; coun. rep. on tchg. hosps. of the Assn. of Am. Med. Colls., 1994-97. Recipient Man of Yr. award Tomorrow's Children's Fund, 1989, medal of merit Bergen C.C., 1993; named Man of Yr. Nat. Burn Victim Found., 1994; named One of Top 12 Up and Coming Healthcare Execs., Modern Healthcare mag., One of 50 People to Watch for the 1990's, N.J. Bus. Jour., Citizen of Yr., Meadowlands Regional C. of C., 1993. Fellow Am. Coll. Healthcare Execs. (regent, gov. dist. II 1994-98); mem. Am. Hosp. Assn., Cath. Hosp. Assn., Am. Heart Assn. (pres. Mid-Bergen div. 1992-93, bd. dirs. 1993-94). Office: Hackensack U Med Ctr 30 Prospect Ave Hackensack NJ 07601-1915

FERGUSON, MARK KENDRIC, physician, educator, researcher; b. Mpls., Jan. 10, 1951; s. David Lee and Shirley (Mark) F.; m. Phyllis Marie Young, July 8, 1989; 1 child, Benjamin. AB, Harvard U., 1973; MD, U. Chgo., 1977. Diplomate Am. Bd. Surgery, Am. Bd. Thoracic Surgery. Resident U. Chgo., 1977-81, chief resident gen. surgery, 1981-82, fellow cardiothoracic surgery, 1982-84, asst. prof., 1984-88, assoc. prof., 1988—. Fellow ACS, Am. Assn. Thoracic Surgery, Soc. Thoracic Surgeons, Soc. Surg. Oncology. Office: U Chgo Med Ctr 5841 S Maryland Ave Chicago IL 60637-1463

FERGUSON, SUSAN KATHARINE STOVER, nurse, psychotherapist, consultant; b. Warsaw, Ind., Mar. 11, 1944; d. Robert Eugene and Barbara Louise (Swaney) Stover; m. Philip Charles Ferguson, Oct. 2, 1965 (div.); children: Scott Duane, Shawn Alaine, Erin Kirsten. Diploma in nursing, Meth. Hosp., 1966; BA in Psychology, Purdue U., 1988; MSW, Smith Coll., 1991; advanced cert. in Psychoanalytic Psychotherapy, Psychoanalytic Psychotheraphy Ctr., 1993-94. Staff nurse, health hazard appraiser Meth. Hosp. of Ind., Indpls., 1966-68; staff nurse USPHS, Bethel, Alaska, 1968-70; instr. childbirth preparation Wabash, Ind., 1973-83; nurse Family Physicians Associated, Wabash, 1976-83; rsch. asst. Purdue U., Ft. Wayne, Ind., 1986-88; staff nurse, self-awareness seminar coord. Charter Beacon Hosp., Ft. Wayne, Ind., 1988-89; intern clin. social work Clifford Beers Guidance Ctr., New Haven, Conn., 1990-91; psychiat. nurse Yale-New Haven Hosp., 1990-91; pvt. practice Citadel Psychiat. Clinic, Ft. Wayne, Ind., 1991-93; dir. social svcs. Charter Northridge Behavioral Health sys., Raleigh, N.C., 1993-94; dir. social svcs., clinician adult psychiatry Charter Northridge Hosp., Raleigh, 1993-94; pvt. practice Raleigh, 1993—. Bd. dirs. Hoosiers for Safety Belts, Indpls., 1987-88, Ind. Med. Pol. Action Com., Indpls., 1986-87; coordinator, founder Safe Start Infant Safety Seat Loan Program, Wabash, 1981-87; participant in leadership devel. com. Wabash County C. of C., 1983; workshop leader Wabash County Hosp. Stop Smoking Program, 1982-83. Mem. NASW (family rels. coun.), Charles F. Menninger Soc., N.C. Psychoanalytic Soc., Kappa Kappa Kappa. Republican. Office: Atlantic Behavioral Health Systems Inc 2501 Atrium Dr Ste 400 Raleigh NC 27607

FERKO, ANDREW PAUL, pharmacologist; b. Trenton, N.J., Aug. 19, 1942; s. Andrew and Margaret M. (Rogaczewski) F.; children: Carolyn, Karen, Katharine. BS, Phila. Coll. Pharmacy, 1965; PhD, Hahnemann U., 1969. Instr. sch. medicine Hahnemann U., Phila., 1969-71, asst. prof., 1971-81, assoc. prof., 1981—. Author: (with others) Basic Pharmacology in Medicine, 3d edit., 1990, Warning: Drugs in Sports, 1995; co-editor: Basic Pharmacology in Medicine, 4th edit., 1994; contbg. editor: Basic Pharmacology in Medicine, 2d edit., 1982, Pharmacology-Pretest Self-Assessment and Review, 1995; contbr. articles to profl. jours. Recipient NIH training grant, 1965-68, Lindback Found. teaching award, 1981. Mem. Am. Soc. for Pharmacology and Exptl. Therapeutics, Toxicology Soc., Sigma Xi, Rho Chi. Office: Med Coll Pa and Hahnemann U Sch Medicine Dept Pharmacology Divsn Toxicology Broad & Vine St Philadelphia PA 19102-5087

FERLINZ, JACK, cardiologist, medical educator; b. Marburg, Austria, Feb. 18, 1942; came to U.S., 1957.; s. Anthony and Maria (Nachtigall) F. AB, Harvard U.; MBA, Northeastern U., 1965; MD, Boston U., 1969; doctorate (hon.), U. Maribor, Slovenia, 1990. Diplomate Am. Bd. Internal Medicine, Am. Bd. Cardiovascular Diseases. Intern. U. Hosp. Boston U., 1969-70; jr. resident M. Hitchcock Hosp. Dartmouth Med. Sch., Hanover, N.H., 1970-71; sr. resident Jackson Meml. Hosp., U. Miami, 1971-72; NIH rsch. fellow cardiology P.B. Brigham Hosp., Harvard U., Boston, 1972-74; dir. cardiac cath. lab., asst. chief cardiology V.A.M.C., Long Beach, Calif., 1974-82; asst. prof. medicine U. Calif., Irvine, 1975-81, assoc. prof. medicine, 1981-82; chmn. adult cardiology Cook County Hosp., Chgo., 1982-88; prof. medicine Chgo. Med. Sch., North Chicago, Ill., 1984-88; chmn. dept. of internal medicine Providence Hosp., Southfield, Mich., 1988-92; clin. prof. medicine Wayne State U. Sch. Medicine, Detroit, 1989-92; dir. med. edn. & rsch., prof. medicine & cardiology Hamad Med. Ctr., Doha, Qatar, 1992-94; chief dept. medicine Aleda E. Lutz VA Med. Ctr., Saginaw, Mich., 1994—; clin. prof. medicine Mich. State U. Coll. Human Medicine, 1994—; vis. prof. numerous U.S., Canadian and European med. schs., 1980—. Mem. editl. bds. Am. Jour. Cardiology, 1989—, Am. Jour. Noninvas Cardiology, 1987—, Jour. Am. Coll. Cardiology, 1984-88, 89-93; contbr. over 300 book chpts. and sci. papers. Named to Begg's Soc. Boston U. Sch. Medicine, 1969. Fellow Am. Coll. Cardiology, Am. Coll. Chest Physicians (chmn. coronary sect. 1983-85), Am. Heart Assn., Am. Coll. Physicians, Am. Coll. Angiology; mem. Am. Fedn. Clin. Rsch., Am. Soc. Clin. Pharm. Therapy. Office: VA Med Ctr 1500 Weiss St Saginaw MI 48602

FERLITA, THERESA ANN, clinical social worker; b. Pinar del Rio, Cuba, Sept. 8, 1944; came to U.S., 1945; d. Sam Marion and Maria (Garcia-Collia) F. AB in Sociology, Spalding Coll., Louisville, 1966; MS in Social Work, U. Louisville, 1972. Lic. clin. social worker, Fla. Various positions, 1966-70; sr. resource program developer Children's Bd. Hillsborough County, Tampa, Fla., 1990-92; supr. homefinding unit Ky. Dept. Child Welfare, Louisville, 1972-73; foster care worker Fla. Dept. Health and Rehabilitative Svcs., Tampa, 1974; homemaker supr. Family Counseling Ctr., Clearwater, Fla., 1974; sr. social worker, mem. intake team London Borough of Newham Social Svcs., 1976; clin. social worker Alcoholism Svcs. Hillsborough Community Mental Health Ctr., Tampa, 1977-78; clin. social worker The Children's Home, Inc., Tampa, 1978-80; case coord., coord. tng. and edn., supr. teen mother program The Child Abuse Coun., Inc., Tampa, 1980-90, clin. supr. Rainbow Family Learning Ctrs., 1989-90; pvt. practice family therapy, adults abused as children, 1991; social worker med.-surg. and trauma Tampa (Fla.) Gen. Hosp., 1992-95; mgr. family svcs. Hillsborough County Headstart Dept., Tampa, 1995—; adj. instr. Hillsborough C.C., Tampa, 1988; cons. The Spring Battered Spouse Shelter, Tampa, 1984; coord. Parents Anonymous Children's Group, Tampa, 1980-85; mem. state health adv. com. Redlands Christian Migrant Assn., Immokalee, Fla., 1982—; mem. policy coun. Hillsborough County Headstart, Tampa, 1986-89; mem. Cmty. Action Bd., Hillsborough County. Editor, compiler manuals for child abuse and neglect investigations, 1986, 87. Pres. Fair Oaks Condominium Assn., Tampa, 1990-91; past pres. Child Abuse Com., Fla., Inc.; bd. dirs., v.p. Centro Tampa, 1989-90. Mem. NASW (sec. Tampa Bay unit 1981-83, vice-chmn. 1990-91, Social Worker of Yr. award 1988, sec. Fla. chpt. 1986-88, del. assembly 1986-91), Acad. Cert. Social Workers, Nat. Network Social Work Mgrs. Democrat. Roman Catholic. Home: 3810 N Oak Dr Apt N-31 Tampa FL 33611-2574 Office: Hillsborough Co Headstart Dept County Ctr 801 E Kennedy Blvd Fl 13 Tampa FL 33602-4144

FERM, VERGIL HARKNESS, anatomist, embryologist; b. West Haven, Conn., Sept. 13, 1924; s. Vergilius T.A. and Nellie (Nelson) F.; m. Ruth Eleanor Rowe, June 5, 1948; children—Daniel W., David V., Judith N., Susan C. A.B., Coll. Wooster, 1946; M.D., Western Res. U., 1948; M.S., U. Wis., 1950, Ph.D., 1955; M.A. (hon.), Dartmouth, 1967. Asst. prof. Ind. U., 1955-57; asso. prof. U. Fla., 1957-61; asso. prof. pathology Dartmouth Med. Sch., Hanover, N.H., 1961-66, prof. anatomy and embryology, 1966-94, also chmn. dept. anatomy.; cons. on environ. effects of heavy metals. Mem. Am. Assn. Anatomists, Am. Soc. Human Genetics, Teratology Soc. Exptl. Pathology, Phi Beta Kappa, Sigma Xi. Home: 202 Dogford Rd Etna NH 03750-4307

FERNANDEZ-MARTINEZ, JOSE, physician; b. San Juan, P.R., Apr. 2, 1930; s. Telesforo and Luisa (Martinez) Fernandez; m. Carmen Dolores Noya, Dec. 26, 1954. BS, Villanova U., 1951; MD, U. Pa., 1955. Diplomate Am. Bd. Internal Medicine, Sub-Bd. Cardiovascular Diseases. Intern U. Pa. Hosps., Phila., 1955-56, resident in internal medicine, 1956-59, fellow in hypertension and cardiovascular diseases, 1956-57; practice medicine specializing in cardiovascular diseases Santurce, P.R., 1961—; attending physician in internal medicine San Juan City Hosp., 1961—; assoc. prof. medicine U. P.R., 1978-88, prof. Sch. of Medicine, 1988—. Served to capt. U.S. Army, 1959-61. Fellow ACP, Am. Coll. Cardiology; mem. P.R. Med. Assn. (pres. sci. coun. 1968), Alpha Omega Alpha. Office: Ashford Med Ctr Ashford & Washington Sts Ste 208 Santurce PR 00907

FERNANDEZ-POL, BLANCA DORA, psychiatrist, researcher; b. Buenos Aires, Mar. 5, 1932; came to U.S., 1967; d. Balbino Fernandez and Maria Remedios van Pol. MD, U. Buenos Aires, 1958. Diplomate Am. Bd. Psychiatry and Neurology. Intern N.Y. Polyclinic Med. Sch., 1967-68; resident in psychiatry UCLA/Brentwood Hosp., 1968-69, NYU/Bellevue Hosp., 1969-71; gen. practitioner Hosp. Espanol, Buenos Aires, 1959-62; forensic psychiatrist Criminoloy Inst., Buenos Aires, 1963-65; clin. attending psychiatrist Bellevue Psychiat. Hosp., N.Y.C., 1971-75; pvt. practice St. Petersburg, Fla., 1976-78; chief psychiat. svcs. USAF Hosp. Yokota, Tokyo, 1980, USAF Hosp., Homestead, Fla., 1981; chief continuing treatment program dept. psychiatry Bronx-Lebanon Hosp., Bronx, 1983—; prof. psychology U. Moran, Buenos Aires, 1962-67; asst. prof. psychiatry N.Y. Med. Coll., N.Y.C., 1972-74; clin. asst. prof. psychiatry Albert Einstein Coll. Medicine, Bronx, 1982—. Contbr. articles to profl. jours. Maj. USAF, 1978-81. Mem. Am. Psychiat. Assn., N.Y. Acad. Scis., Am. Acad. Psychiatrists in Alcoholism and Addictions, Res. Officers Assn. U.S., Assn. Mil. Surgeons U.S. Home: PO Box 21644 Brooklyn NY 11202-1644 Office: Bronx Lebanon Hosp 1285 Fulton Ave Bronx NY 10456-3401

FERNANDO, NEIL VERNON PATRICK, medical educator, academic administrator; b. Colombo, Sri Lanka, May 18, 1928; arrived in Malaysia, 1983; s. P. Nataniel and Rose Mabel (Wickramaratne) F.; m. Kalyani Gamage Haththotuwa, Oct. 22, 1957; children: Michael, Patrick, Kevin, Danny, Kenneth. B in Medicine and Surgery, U. Ceylon, Colombo, Sri Lanka, 1953; PhD in Pathology, U. Toronto, Ont., Can., 1963. Supernumerary pathologist Gen. Hosp. of Colombo, 1963-67; provincial pathologist Galle (Sri Lanka) Dept. of Health, 1967-69; pathologist U. Teaching Hosps., Kandy, Sri Lanka, 1970-76, Colombo, 1976-83; assoc. prof. Sch. of Med. Scis. U. Sains Malaysia, Kubang Kerian, 1983-93, head pathology dept., 1985-89; prof. pathology, internat. student advisor, dir. med. lab. technologists program St. Georges U. Sch. Medicine, Grenada, West Indies, 1993—, dir. Physician's Asst. and Med. Lab. Tech. Programme, 1996—. Social worker. Mem. Christian Ch. Office: St Georges U Sch Medicine, Dept Pathology, Saint George's Grenada

FERNANDO, RICARDO E., physician; b. Manila, May 16, 1929; s. Gregorio O. and Brigida G. (Garcia) F.; m. Elizabeth Z. Vitug, Apr. 5, 1958; children: Richard, Elizabeth Ann, Virginia Ruth. MD, U. Philippines, 1954. Diplomate Philippines Splty. Bd. Internal Medicine, Philippines Coll. Physicians, Philippines Soc. Endocrinology and Metabolism. Intern Philippine Gen. Hosp., 1953-54; resident in internal medicine Mary Johnston Hosp., 1954-59, physician diabetic clinic, 1957-87, head dept. medicine, 1960-72; med. dir., dir. med. edn. Mary Johnston Hosp., Tondo/Manila, 1972-87; from asst. prof. to assoc. prof., then head dept. med., dir. U. of the East - Ramon Maqsaysay Meml. Med. Ctr., 1962-86; head dept. medicine, pres. med. staff Capitol Med. Ctr., Quezon City, Philippines, 1970-72, physician diabetic clinic, 1970—. Author: Diabetes, 1974, 2nd edit., 1981, Understanding Diabetes, 1974, 2nd edit., 1980; editor: Diabetic Microangiopathies, 1978. Mem. Am. Assn. Diabetes Educators, Am. Diabetes Assn., European Assn. Study of Diabetes, Philippines Columbian Assn., Masons, Phi Kappa Mu. Office: St Lukes Med Ctr, E Rodriguez Ave, Quezon City The Philippines

FERNANDO, SONIA GABRIEL, neurologist; b. Manila, Jan. 2, 1954; d. Oscar Umali and Floradora (Gabriel) F.; children: Timothy Lewis, Benjamin Lewis. BS, U. Wis., 1974; MD, U. Philippines, 1979. Diplomate Am. Bd. Psychiatry and Neurology. Intern Booth Meml. Med. Ctr., Flushing, N.Y., 1980; resident Kings County Downstate Med. Ctr., Bklyn., 1981-83; pvt. practice neurology Farmington Hills, Mich., 1984—. Mem. Am. Acad. Neurology. Home: 3791 Kirkway Rd Bloomfield Hills MI 48302-1354 Office: 24381 Orchard Lake Rd Farmington Hills MI 48336-1917

FERNBACH, LOUISE OFTEDAL, psychiatrist; b. Fargo, N.D., Dec. 24; d. Sverre Johannes and Agnes Lenore (Halland) Oftedal; m. Henry Theodore Wensel (div.); children: Bertram, Olinda, David, Pamela, Theodore; m. Alfred Philip Fernbach, Nov. 29, 1986. BA, Wellesley (Mass.) Coll.; MD, George Washington U. Psychiatry resident UCLA, 1960; psychiatry fellow Johns Hopkins U., Balt., 1972; dir. mental health U. Fla., Gainesville, 1961-64, U. Ariz., Tucson, 1965-68; asst. prof. psychiatry Johns Hopkins Sch. Medicine, Balt., 1972-74; pvt. practice psychiatry Charlottesville, Va., 1985—; lectr. Physicians for Social Responsibility, 1980—. Author: Acupuncture in Medical Practice, 1980. Fellow Am. Geriatric Soc.; mem. AMA, Am. Med. Women's Assn. (Va. state dir. 1991—), Am. Psychiat. Assn. Unitarian. Home and Office: 11 Orchard Rd Charlottesville VA 22903-4728

FERNBACH, SANDRA KREPLICK, pediatric radiologist, educator; b. Revere, Mass., Aug. 18, 1949; d. Sumner and Elizabeth (Fitzgerlad) Kreplick; m. Eric Jay Russell; children: Gabrielle Russell, Meredith Russell. AB, Smith Coll., 1970; MD, Johns Hopkins U., 1975. Bd. cert. Am. Bd. Radiology. Surg. intern Montefiore Hosp. Med. Ctr., Bronx, N.Y., 1975-76; radiology resident Montefiore Hosp. Med. Ctr., Bronx, 1976-79, chief resident radiology, 1978-79; pediatric radiology fellow, chief resident Children's Hosp. Med. Ctr., Boston, 1979-80; attending radiologist Children's Meml. Hosp., Chgo., 1980—; instr. radiology Northwestern U. Med. Sch., Chgo., 1980-82, asst. prof. radiology, 1982-86, assoc. prof. radiology, 1986-95, prof. radiology, 1995—; voluntary attending, adj. staff Northwestern Hosp. and Med. Ctr., Chgo., 1988-89, assoc. attending staff, 1989—; attending staff Shriner's Hosp., Oak Park, Ill., 1992—; presenter in field. Mem. editl. bd. Am. Jour. Radiology; manuscript reviewer Am. Jour. Radiology, Radiology, Pediat. Radiology, RadioGraphics; contbr. chpts. to books and articles to profl. jours. Fellow Am. Coll. Radiology (com. on comms. and pub. info. commn. on mktg. comm. 1987-92, com. on mktg. and pub. rels. commn. on gen. radiology and pediat. radiology 1993-95, wrote std. on voiding cystourethrography in children 1995), Soc. Uroradiology; mem. Am. Assn. Women Radiologists (various coms. and positions including pres. 1987-88, chair fund raising com. 1988-89, newsletter editor, 1989-92, nominating com. 1989-90, chair pub. rels. com. 1989-92), Am. Roentgen Ray Soc. (awards com./sci. exhibits 1988), Radiol. Soc. N.Am. (local com. on credentials 1981, local com. on refresher courses 1985-86, 88-90, com. on comms. 1986-93, chair, 1991, 92, 93), Soc. for Pediat. Radiology (various coms. including com. on long range planning 1994-95, by-laws com. 1994—, program com. 1994—, long range task force 1994—, sec. 1995—, publs.

com. 1995—), Soc. Uroradiology (com. on stds. and pracice 1989-93, chair, 1993, program com. 1990, 92, 93, chair and course dir. 1994-95, core curriculum com. 1991, 92), Soc. Fetal Urology (coord. radiology for multi-instnl. study 1991—), Ill. Radiol. Soc. (alt. councilor 1994-95, by-laws com. 1994-95, membership com. 1995-96, nominating com. 1995-96), Chgo. Radiologic Soc. (nominating com. 1985-86, trustee 1986-87, 87-88, program com. 1987-90, dir. pediat. radiology sect. 1989-92, sec. treas./v.p. 1992-94, pres. 1994-95). Office: Childrens Meml Hosp 2300 N Childrens Plz Chicago IL 60614-3318

FERNEAU, ERNEST W., JR., psychologist. BS, Boston Coll., 1959; PhD, Boston U., 1973. Lic. psychologist, Mass.; cert. addiction specialist Am. Acad. Health Svc. Providers in the Addictive Disorders. NIMH fellow Mass. Gen. Hosp., Boston, 1964-65; psychologist Boston City Hosp., 1967-73, Lahey Clinic, Boston, 1973-80; prvt. practice Framingham, Mass., 1980—. 1st lt. U.S. Army, 1959-61. Mem. Vietnam Era Vets. (life), Cath. War Vets. Office: One Edgell Rd Framingham MA 01701

FERNIANY, ISAAC WILLIAM, hospital administrator; b. Mobile, Ala., Mar. 15, 1951; s. Joe Michael and Vivian Elizabeth (Farah) F.; m. Dana Brownell Hardy, Apr. 19, 1978; children: Dylan Hardy, Glennie Brownell. BS, U. Ala., 1973; MS, U. Ala., Birmingham, 1975, PhD, 1984. Asst. adminstr. Bryce Hosp., Tuscaloosa, 1975-77; dir. resource devel. S.W. Health Systems Agy., Mobile, 1977-79; owner Mgmt. Resources, Birmingham, 1981-83; faculty U. Ala., Birmingham, 1982-83; v.p. devel. Health Care Services Am., Birmingham, 1983-87; chief exec. officer Hill Crest Hosp., Birmingham, 1987-88; exec. adminstr. U. Ala., Birmingham, 1988-90, assoc. adminstr. strategic planning and market devel., 1990—; assoc. exec. v.p., pres. mktg. and strategic support U. Pa. Health System, Phila., 1992—; mem. faculty U. Ala., Birmingham, 1987-92, lectr., 1993—; adj. faculty Wharton Sch. Bus., 1993—; sr. fellow Leonard Davis Inst., 1993—. Author: Bay Area Directory, 1979. Mem. Am. Hosp. Assn., Alliance Healthcare Mktg. Episcopalian. Office: U Pa Health System 21 Penn Tower Philadelphia PA 19144-1407

FERNICOLA, NILDA ALICIA GALLEGO GÁNDARA DE, pharmacist, biochemist; b. Bahia Blanca, B.A., Argentina, Jan. 9, 1931; d. Francisco and Alicia (Gándara) Gallego; m. Lucio Fernicola, Jan. 2, 1964; 1 child, Pablo Francisco. BS in Pharmacy, U. Buenos Aires, Argentina, 1955, BS in Biochemistry, 1959, PhD in Pharmacy and Biochemistry, 1962. Analyst Nat. Chemistry Office, Buenos Aires, Argentina, 1957-67; instr. Coll Pharmacy & Biochemistry, U. Buenos Aires, 1962-75; prof. U. Sao Paulo, Brazil, 1976-82, prof. postgrad. courses environ. toxicology/health/environ., 1982-93; team leader Fundacentro, Sao Paulo, 1975-76; head toxicology divsn., agy. for environ. control. Companhia de Tecnologia de Saneamento Ambiental, Sao Paulo, 1976-82, head human toxicology, 1991-93; toxicology tech. asst. Companhia de Tecnologia de Saneamento Ambiental, Sao Paulo, Mexico, 1995—; toxicologist cons. PanAm. Health Orgn./WHO, Mex., 1982-91; mem. rsch. group Nat. Coun. Science, Tech., Rsch., Buenos Aires, 1967; short-term cons. PanAm. Health Orgn., Bogota, 1993-95. Co-author: Nociones Básicas de Toxicologia, 1985, Toxicologia Ocupacional , 1989; contbr. articles to profl. jours. Recipient award Argentina Congress, 1975. Mem. Argentinian Acad. Environ. Sci., Toxicology Soc. Panama (founder), Brazilian Toxicology Soc. (sec. Sao Paulo 1992-93). Home: Rua Joao Ramalho 586 Ap 31B, 05008001 São Paulo SP, Brazil Office: Ave Frederico Herman 345, 05489 São Paulo SP, Brazil

FERNSTROM, JOHN DICKSON, psychiatry educator, researcher; b. N.Y.C., July 9, 1947; s. Karl Dickson and Dorothy Weston (Bond) F.; m. Madelyn Jill Hirsch; children: Aaron, Lauren. SB, MIT, 1969, PhD, 1972. Research fellow Roche Inst. of Molecular Biology, Nutley, N.J., 1972-73; asst. prof. MIT, Cambridge, Mass., 1973-77; assoc. prof. MIT, Cambridge, 1977-82; assoc. prof. U. Pitts. Sch. of Medicine, 1982-87, prof. psychiatry, behavioral neurosci., 1987—; prof. pharmacology U. Pitts. Sch. Medicine, 1992—; mem. Nat. Inst. Neurol. and Communicative Disorders and Stroke/NIH Program Project Rev., Bethesda, Md., 1978-82, chmn., 1981-82; mem. NASA Life Scis. Adv. Commn., Washington, 1980-86, NIMH Neurosci. Br. Evaluation Panel, Rockville, Md., 1983, Nat. Adv. Coun., Monell Chem. Senses Ctr., Phila., 1987—; mem. nutrition program rsch. evaluation panel Nat. Inst. Childhood Diseases, 1989; Burroughs-Wellcome vis. prof. basic med. scis., 1993; mem. com. on mil. nutrition rsch., food and nutrition bd. NAS, 1994—. Contbr. articles to profl. jours. Recipient Rsch. Scientist Devel. award NIMH, Rockville, 1979-88, Alfred P. Sloan fellowship in neurochemistry A.P. Sloan Found., N.Y.C., 1974-76, Predoctoral fellowship NIH, Bethesda, 1970-72, Rsch. Scientist award NIMH, Rockville, 1989-94. Mem. Am. Soc. for Neurochemistry, Am. Soc. for Pharmacology and Exptl. Therapeutics, Am. Physiol. Soc., Am. Inst. Nutrition (chmn. nervous system sect., mem. publ info. com., mem. coun., Mead-Johnson award 1980), Endocrine Soc. Office: U Pitts Dept Psychiatry 3811 Ohara St Pittsburgh PA 15213-2593

FERRACCI, FRANCO, neurologist; b. S.Dona' di Piave Venice, Italy, Oct. 24, 1963; s. Giovanni and Anna (Barosco) F.; m. Carla Camana, Aug. 26, 1995. MD cum laude, Faculty Medicine, Bologna, Italy, 1988, degree in neurology cum laude, 1992. Internal medicine intern Ospedale S. Orsola-Malpighi, Bologna, Italy, 1986-87; resident Clinica Neurologica Ospedale SS. Annunziati/U. Chieti, Italy, 1988-92; chief resident dept. neurology Chieti, Italy, 1991-92; rschr. Ctr. Neurobiology & Behavior Columbia-Presbyn. Med. Ctr., N.Y.C., 1992; cons. neurologist reparto di neurologia Ospedale Civile di Belluno, Italy, 1993—. Author: Manuale Dei Poteziali Evocati, 1991; contbr. articles to profl. jours. Mem. Soc. Italiana Neurologia, Lega Italiana Contro Epilessia. Office: Reparto di Neurclogia, Viale Europa, 32100 Belluno Italy

FERRACCI, MARIE-ANGELE VINCENTI, pediatrician; b. Nice, France, July 29, 1948; d. Antoine and Paulette (Dumski) Vincenti; m. Jean-Paul Ferracci, Jan. 19, 1978; children: Marie-Pauline, Paul, Antoine. MD, Med. Univ., Marseilles, 1980. Intern Marseilles Hosp., 1974-80; resident in anesthesia Nice; practice medicine specializing in pediatrics Cannes, France, 1984—. Roman Catholic. Home: Au Beau Sejour, 06400 Cannes France Office: Les Iridees, 1 Rue des Phalenes, 06400 Cannes France

FERRACINI, ROMANO RODOLFO, pathologist, researcher; b. Bologna, Italy, Jan. 24, 1938; s. Carlo and Margherita (Fontana) F.; m. Maria Teresa Spaggiari, July 21, 1969. MD, U. Bologna, 1962. Fellow pathology U. Bologna, 1969-72; cons. pathologist Maggiore Hosp., Bologna, 1972-82, Bellaria Hosp., Bologna, 1982—; prof. neuro-oncology U. Ferrara, 1988; prof. neuropathology U. Bologna, 1996. Contbr. articles to profl. jours. Mem. Greenpeace, 1992, Amnesty Internat., 1992, WWF, 1972. Mem. Am. Assn. Pathologists, Can. Assn. Pathologists, Italian Soc. Neuropathology. Liberal Party. Roman Catholic. Home: Via Jussi 150/A, I-40068 San Lazzaro Savena Bologna, Italy Office: Bellaria Hospital, Dept Pathology, Via Altura 3, I-40139 Bologna Italy

FERRACUTI, STEFANO EUGENIO, forensic psychiatrist; b. Rome, June 2, 1958; s. Franco and Mirella (Garutti) F.; m. Lucia Fusco; children: Giorgia, Margherita. Cert. in teaching, Liceo Sperimentale, Rome, 1977; MD, U. Rome, 1985. Tchr. Istis Loiza Cordeiro for Blind, San Juan, P.R., 1977-78; resident dept. neurology U. Rome, 1985-90; fellowship in biol. psychol. psychopathology N.Y. Med. Coll., 1987-88; asst. prof. dept. psychiatry and med. psychology U. Rome La Sapienza, 1991—; fellow biol. psychiatry and psychopharmacology, N.Y. Med. Coll., 1987; active ednl. bd. Revista de Derecho Penal y Criminologia Quad. Psich. for Jour. Drug Issues; cons. in field, 1991—. Contbr. articles to profl. publs. Lt. Italian Army, 1986-87. Mem. Soc. Personality Assessment, N.Y. Acad. Sci., Italian Soc. Neurology, Am. Acad. Psychiatry and Law, Italian Soc. Criminology, Amnesty Internat. Home: Via Ugo Balzani 57, 00162 Rome Italy Office: U Rome Dept Psychiatry, Pzle A Moro 5, 00185 Rome Italy

FERRAIOLI, ARMANDO, biomedical company executive; b. Foggia, Italy, Mar. 19, 1949; s. Alfonso and Luisa (Taurino) F. m. Maria T. Kindjarsky-D'Amato, Aug. 30, 1976; children—Solange A.P., Naike M.L., Anika M.V. Dr. Ing., U. Naples, 1973; M.Sc. in Bioengring., U. Strathclyde, 1974; Ph.D., U. Southampton, 1981. Registered profl. engr., Salerno, Italy; chartered engr., Gt. Britain. Regional mgr. Gambro Soxil SpA, Bari, Naples, Italy, 1982-84; founder, gen. dir. A.G.A. Biomedica S.r.l., Cava dei Tirreni, Italy, 1985—; cons. Studio di Ingegneria Medica, Cava del Tirreni, 1984—; biomed. researcher, designer hosp. structures, Italy. Mem. adv. bd. Italian biomed. jours.; contbr. over 50 articles on biomed. engring. to profl. jours.; book review editor for various jours. Internat. Brit. Council grantee, 1974-78. Mem. IEEE, Instn. Elec. Engrs. Gt. Britain, Associazione Elettrotecnica Italiana, Biol. Engring. Soc. Gt. Britain, Association for the Advancement of Med. Instrumentation, Biomed. Engring. Soc., Associazione Italiana di Ingegneria Medica e Biologica, Centro Nazionale Edilizia e Tecnica Ospedaliera. Home: Via V Veneto 23/A, 84013 Cava dei Tirreni Italy Office: Corso Italia n 232, 84013 Cava dei Tirreni Italy

FERRARI, LINDA JOY, nurse; b. Wausau, Wis., Aug. 28, 1960; d. Joel Darwin and Sharron (Junghans) Walter; m. Louis A. Ferrari Jr., Oct. 28, 1989; 1 child, Louis A. III. ADN, Rochester (Minn.) C.C., 1982. Cert. BLS, ACLS, CCRN, Wis. RN Theda Clark Regional Med. Ctr., Neenah, Wis., 1982-88; RN Door County Meml. Hosp., Sturgeon Bay, Wis., 1988—, supr., 1992-95; supr. Dorchester Nursing Ctr., 1989—; staff nurse Baylake Outpatient Surgery Ctr., 1994—; entrepreneur LJ Mktg. and Promotions, 1996—; entrepreneur L.J. Mktg. and Promotions, 1996—.

FERRARO, CHARLES DOMENIC, psychologist, educator; b. Cleve., Apr. 12, 1913; s. Ross and Mary (Cundra) F.; m. Alice Carolyn Nimrichter, Dec. 30, 1939 (div. Dec. 1965); children: Diane, Linda; m. Donna Joan Gamble, Apr. 12, 1966. AB, Ohio U., 1936; BS, Case Western Res. U., 1938, MA, 1953, PhD, 1957. Lic. psychologist, Ohio. Chief counselor John Carroll U., University Heights, Ohio, 1949-51, lectr. psychology, 1951-70, 81-86, assoc. prof., 1970-74, prof., chmn. psychology dept., 1974-78; placement officer NASA-Lewis Research Ctr., Cleve., 1951-70; pvt. practice counseling psychologist Lakewood, Ohio, 1953—. Bd. dirs., chmn., governance com. Far W. Mental Health Ctr., Westlake, Ohio, 1979-85. Recipient Career Service award Cleve. Fed. Exec. Bd., 1969, Fed. Service award Am. Soc. Pub. Adminstrn., 1969, Commendation cert. Pres. Nixon, 1970. Mem. Am. Psychol. Assn. (life), Ohio Psychol. Assn. (life). Home: 1550 Cedarwood Dr Cleveland OH 44145-1811 Office: 1550 Cedarwood Dr Apt C Cleveland OH 44145-1811

FERRARO, RONALD LOUIS, health facility administrator; b. Washington, Pa., Apr. 14, 1943; s. Michael A. and Rose (Marino) F.; m. Lilyan McConomy, June 28, 1980; children: Suzanne Marie Schultz, Lynaia Lorraine Schultz. BA, Juniata Coll., 1965; MSW, W.Va. U., 1967. Diplomate Am. Bd. Examiners in Clin. Social Work; lic. social worker, Pa. Supr. social work Embreeville State Hosp., Coatesville, Pa., 1967-72; from chief social worker to dir. mental health The Consortium, Phila., 1972-88, dir. base svc. unit, 1988-91; asst. dir. Resources for Human Devel., Phila., 1991—. Bd. dirs. Big Bros./Big Sisters Bucks County, Doylestown, pa., 1986-91. Mem. NASW (bd. dirs. 1973-86), ACSW. Home: 40 New Pond Ln Levittown PA 19054-3822 Office: Resources for Human Devel 4333 Kelly Dr Philadelphia PA 19129-1723

FERRAZ, FRANCISCO MARCONI, neurological surgeon; b. Floresta, Pernambuco, Brazil, Aug. 14, 1951; came to U.S., 1976. Student, Colegio Nobrega, Recife-Brazil, 1967-69; MD, Faculdade de Medicine da Universidade Federal de Pernambuco-Brazil, 1975. Diplomate Am. Bd. Neurol. Surgery. Intern, Jamaica Hosp., N.Y.C., 1976-77; resident Georgetown U. Med. Ctr. and Affiliated Hosps., Washington, 1977-82; pvt. practice medicine specializing in neurol. surgery, Washington, 1982—; staff Georgetown U. Hosp., 1982—, Arlington Hosp., 1982—; chief div. neurosurgery, faculty clin. instr. Georgetown U. Sch. Medicine, 1988—; faculty clin. assoc. prof. George Washington Sch. Medicine; cons. in field. Contbr. articles to profl. jours. Mem. AMA, Am. Assn. Neurol. Surgeons, Pan Am. Med. Soc., D.C. Med. Soc., Arlington Med. Soc., Neurosurg. Soc. of D.C., Washington Medico Surg. Soc., Washington Acad. Neurosurgery, Congress of Neurol. Surgery.

FERRAZIN, ANTONIO RICCARDO, infectious diseases physician; b. Genova, Italy, Mar. 26, 1958; s. Luigino and Lilliana (Callegari) F.; m. Marina Rita Abisso, Sept. 25, 1993; children: Davide, Stefano. MD cum laude, U. Genova, 1984. Resident dept. infectious diseases U. Genova, 1989; asst. head physician dept. infectous diseases St. Martino Hosp., Genova, 1990—; tchg. prof. Sch. Tropical Medicine U. Genova, 1994-96; participant European Union-European Collaborative Study, U. London, 1988-96. Grantee Nat. Assn. for Fight Against AIDS, 1988. Roman Catholic. Home: Mura Delle Cappuccine, 16128 Genoa Italy Office: Clinica Malattie Infettive, Largo Rosanna Benzi 10, 16132 Genoa Italy

FERREE, CAROLYN RUTH, radiation oncologist, educator; b. Liberty, N.C., Jan. 29, 1944; d. Numer Floyd and Mary Isabel (Glass) Black; m. Bill K. Ferree, Aug. 17, 1968 (div. 1980). BA, U. N.C., Greensboro, 1966; MD, Bowman Gray Coll., Winston-Salem, 1970. Diplomate Am. Bd. Radiation Oncology. Intern medicine N.C. Bapt. Hosp., Winston-Salem, 1970-71, resident in radiation oncology, 1971-74; instr. radiation oncology Bowman Gray Sch. Medicine, Winston-Salem, 1974-75, asst. prof., 1975-80, assoc. prof., 1980-87, prof., 1987—. Contbr. articles to profl. jours. Mem., v.p. County Bd. of Pub. Health, Winston-Salem, 1985-92; bd. dirs. U. N.C.-Greensboro Excellence Found., 1988—; med. dir. Forsyth County chpt. Am. Cancer Soc., 1975—. Fellow Am. Coll. Radiology; mem. AMA (N.C. del. to AMA), Pediat. Oncology Group (radiotherapy coord.), N.C. Med. Soc. (2d v.p. 1990-91, sec.-treas. 1991-95, pres.-elect 1996), Am. Soc. Therapeutic Radiologists Orgn. Office: Bowman Gray Sch Medicine Med Center Blvd Winston-Salem NC 27157

FERREE, PATRICIA ANN, corporate managed care analyst, nurse; b. Middletown, N.Y., Oct. 5, 1947; d. William Harry and Florence Arlene (Sarr) Krenrich; m. Daniel Milton Ferree, Feb. 13, 1972; children: Patricia Ann, Daniel Milton Jr. AS, Cen. Fla. Community Coll., Ocala, 1969; BS in Nursing, Va. Commonwealth U., 1985. Cert. cardiac nurse therapist. Critical care nurse Fla. Hosp., Orlando, 1969-76, cardiac nurse therapist, 1976-80, head nurse cardiac rehab., 1980-82; nurse adminstrn., rsch. nurse Va. Heart Inst., Richmond, 1982-86; coord. health care cost containment Cir. City Stores, Inc., Richmond, 1986, mgr. health and safety, 1986-89, corp. mgr. workers' compensation and safety, 1989-93, corp. mgr. workers compensation, 1993-94, corp. sr. analyst for managed care unit in risk mgmt. dept., 1994—. Choir dir. Courthouse Rd. Seventh-Day Adventist Ch., Richmond, 1983-89, min. music, 1989-94; mem. curriculum com. Richmond Acad. Home and Sch. Leader; chmn. cardiovascular task force Am. Heart Assn., 1984-85. Recipient svc. plaque cardiology dept. Fla. Hosp., 1982; Peggy Gibson Meml. nursing scholar, 1967, Fla. Bd. Edn. nursing scholar, 1967-69. Mem. Am. Assn. Occupational Health Nurses, Am. Soc. Safety Engrs., Soc. Nursing Profls., Am. Assn. for Cardiovascular and Pulmonary Rehab. (founding), Richmond Met. Soc. for Cardiac Rehab. (founding), Phi Kappa Phi, Sigma Zeta. Republican. Office: Cir City Stores Inc 9950 Mayland Dr Richmond VA 23233-1463

FERRELL, DENNIS KEITH, psychologist; b. Nashville, Oct. 21, 1950; s. Guy Vernon and Phyllis Elizabeth F.; B.A., Wilkes Coll., 1972; M.A., Marywood Coll., 1974; m. Mary Lee Brennan, May 5, 1979. Human service counselor Nanticoke (Pa.) Mental Health Center, 1972-74; triage clin. diagnostician Hazleton (Pa.) Mental Health Center, 1974-75; dir. drug and alcohol abuse program Luzerne County Prison, Wilkes-Barre, Pa., 1975-80, dir. correctional psychology unit, 1981-87 , clin. dir. Cath. Social Services, 1987-89; pvt. practice, 1981—; exec. dir. Pa. Inst. Rational-Emotive Therapy, 1991—. Mem. Am. Psychol. Assn., Pa. Psychol. Assn., Northeastern Pa. Psychol. Assn. Home: 131 Laird St Wilkes Barre PA 18705-3818 Office: Ferrell & Assocs Inc 111 N Franklin St Wilkes Barre PA 18701-1401

FERRELLE, CHRISTINE BRUYETTE, pediatric nurse; b. St. Albans, Vt., Mar. 20, 1948; d. Davie Joseph and Evelyn Maude (Lefevre) Bruyette; m. William Middleton Ferrelle, Dec. 31, 1977; children: Britt, Alexandra, Scott; 1 stepchild, Kelly. RN, Jeanne Mance Sch. Nursing, 1970; BA, Med. U. S.C., 1975. RN, Ga. Nurse New Eng. Deaconess Hosp., Boston, 1970-72; supr. nurse Williamsburg County Hosp., Kingstree, S.C., 1972-73; nurse Williamsburg County Rural Health, Kingstree, 1973-74; physician asst. Franklin & Fetter Clinic, Charleston, S.C., 1975-77; pediatric nurse practitioner Westside Urban Health Ctr., Savannah, Ga., 1977—; foster care adv. bd. Dept. Family and Children, Savannah, 1980-84. Roman Catholic. Office: Westside Urban Health Ctr 2 Roberts St Savannah GA 31408

FERRENDELLI, JAMES ANTHONY, neurologist, educator; b. Trinidad, Colo., Dec. 5, 1936; s. Alex and Edna Ferrendelli; children—Elisabeth, Cynthia, Michael. AB cum laude in Chemistry, U. Colo., Boulder, 1958; M.D., U. Colo., Denver, 1962. Diplomate Am. Bd. Psychiatry and Neurology. Intern U. Ky. Med. Ctr., 1962-63; resident in neurology Cleve. Met. Gen. Hosp., 1965-68; research fellow in neurochemistry Washington U. Sch. Medicine, St. Louis, 1968-70, asst. prof. neurology and pharmacology, 1970-74, assoc. prof., 1974-77, prof., 1977-95, Seay prof. clin. neuropharmacology in neurology, 1977-95; prof., chmn. dept. neurology, prof. pharmacology U. Tex., Houston, 1995—, Kraft-Eidmann prof., 1995—. Contbr. numerous articles to profl. jours. Served to capt. M.C., U.S. Army, 1963-65. Recipient rsch. career devel. award USPHS, 1971-76, Founders Day award Washington U., 1981, Disting. Tchr. award, 1993, 94, Disting. Prof. of Yr. award, 1993, NIH grantee, 1971—. Mem. Am. Acad. Neurology, Am. Neurol. Assn., Am. Soc. for Pharmacology and Exptl. Therapeutics (Epilepsy award 1981), Am. Epilepsy Soc. (Lennox lectr. 1991). Office: U Tex-Houston Med Sch Dept Neurology 6431 Fannin St Ste 7044 Houston TX 77030

FERRERI, MICHAEL VICTOR, optometrist; b. Park Ridge, Ill., May 15, 1967; s. Samuel Joseph and Dolores Jean (Liebich) F.; m. Celaine Berenda Ward, Apr. 2, 1994; 2 children: Christopher, Anthony. BS in Biol. Scis., U. Calif., Irvine, 1989; OD, So. Calif. Coll. Optometry, 1993. Cert. therapeutic optometrist, Tex.; cert. optometrist, Calif. Extern Ctr. for the Partially Sighted, Santa Monica, Calif., 1992-93; pvt. practice Long Beach, Calif., 1993—; assoc. optometrist Antelope Valley Vision Ctr., Palmdale, Calif., 1995; color vision analysis cons. Dept. Health and Human Svcs., Long Beach, 1994-96; participating doctor Vision USA, Long Beach, 1995-96. Mem. Rep. Nat. Com., 1991-96; elder Grace Luth. Ch., Long Beach, 1996. Recipient Corning Low Vision award Corning Optics, Anaheim, Calif., 1993, Vision Therapy Enhancement cert. So. Calif. Coll. Optometry, Fullerton, 1993. Mem. Am. Optometric Assn. (contact lens sect.), Calif. Optometric Assn., Rio Hondo Optometric Soc., Fellowship of Christian Optometrists, Optometric Ext. Program (clin. assoc.). Office: Los Altos Med Ctr Ste 109 1777 Bellflower Blvd Long Beach CA 90815

FERRI, EVERETT LOUIS, JR., healthcare executive, former university official; b. Tampa, Fla., Apr. 12, 1945; s. Everett L. and Henrietta (Ferretti) F.; m. Suzanne Durand, Feb. 14, 1988. BS in Indsl. Engring., Columbia U., 1968; postgrad., Ohio State U., 1969, Temple U., 1973, U. Mich., 1977, U. Pa., 1992-93. Sys. engr. USAF Advanced Logistics Sys. Ctr., Wright-Patterson AFB, Ohio, 1968-70; mgr. programs Am. Medicorp Inc., Bala Cynwyd, Pa., 1970-73; sr. mgmt. analyst Hosp. of U. Pa., Phila., 1976-78; prin. E.L. Ferri-Health Facilities Planning, Phila., 1978-80; v.p. Health Facilities Design Inc., Phila., 1978-80; planning coord. Hahnemann U., Phila., 1973-76, asst. v.p. materials/facilities mgmt., 1980-94; v.p. facilities mgmt. The Valley Hosp., Ridgewood, N.J., 1994—; chmn. Built-Rite Constrn. Program, Phila., 1985-94, dir. Phila. Area Labor Mgmt. Com., 1986-94. Bd. dirs. Programs for Exceptional People, 1989-94; mem. bldg. com. United Way of Phila., 1990-94. Recipient Gov.'s Labor-Mgmt. Cooperation award State of Pa., 1988, Vol. Recognition awrd Emergency Aid of Pa., 1991. Mem. Am. Coll. Healthcare Execs., Assn. Phys. Plant Adminstrs., Soc. Coll. and Univ. Planners, Internat. Facilities Mgmt. Assn. Office: The Valley Hosp 223 N Van Dien Ave Ridgewood NJ 07450-2736

FERRIS, BENJAMIN GREELEY, JR., retired physician, environmental researcher, educator; b. Watertown, Mass., Jan. 24, 1919; s. Benjamin Greeley and Margaret (Wright) F.; m. Sarah Brooks Upham, Dec. 20, 1942 (dec. Oct. 13, 1979); children: Pamela Upham Barneby Farmer, Margaret Upham Zimmermann, Katharine Wright Goddard, Patience Brooks Sandrof, Sarah Elizabeth Di Monda; m. Stefana Puleo, Dec. 7, 1980. A.B., Harvard U., 1940, M.D., 1943; Dr. h.c., U. Bordeaux II, 1983. Diplomate: Am. Bd. Pediatrics, Am. Bd. Preventive Medicine. Rsch. fellow Harvard U., Boston, 1948-50; assoc. in physiology Harvard U., 1950-53, asst. prof., 1953-58, assoc. prof. environ. health and safety, 1958-71, prof., 1971-89, prof. emeritus, 1989—; dir. environ. health and safety Univ. Health Svc., 1958—, chief, 1988; cons. medicine Mass. Gen. Hosp.; cons. environ. health Children's Med. Center; sr. cons. internal medicine Lemuel Shattuck Hosp., Boston, 1955-56; vis. prof. U. B.C., Can., 1974-78; lectr. medicine Tufts U., Boston, 1965—. Editor emeritus Safety Report, Am. Alpine Club; contbr. articles to profl. jours. Served with M.C. U.S. Army, 1945-47. Fellow Am. Pub. Health Assn.; mem. AAAS, Am. Physiol. Soc., Am. Epidemiol. Soc., Royal Soc. Medicine (affiliate), Sigma Xi. Clubs: Am. Alpine, Appalachian Mountain, Harvard, St. Botolph. Home: Town House Rd Box 305 Weston MA 02193

FERRIS, FREDERICK JOSEPH, gerontologist, social worker; b. Troy, N.Y., June 2, 1920; s. John and Amelia (Deeb) F.; m. Ellen J. Walsh, June 12, 1965. BA cum laude, SUNY, Albany, 1942; MS, Columbia U., 1949, DSW, 1968. Head social studies dept. Heatly High Sch., Green Island, N.Y., 1946-47; sec. info. svc. Greater N.Y. Fund, N.Y.C., 1949-51; exec. sec. N. Met. div. United Community Svcs., Boston, 1951-53, mem. rsch. div. com., 1953-57; dir. community orgn., asst. prof. Boston Coll. Sch. Social Work, 1953-57; dean, prof. Nat. Cath. Sch. Social Svc. Cath. U. Am., Washington, 1960-69, mem. adv. com. Gerontology Conf., 1985-91; with AARP-Nat. Ret. Tchrs. Assn., Washington, coord. White House Conf. on Aging, 1970-72; dir. planning and rsch. dept. and adminstr. Andrus Found., 1970-86; adv. assoc. prof. Fordham U. Sch. Social Svc., 1957-60; lectr. Adelphi U., Rutgers U., 1959-60; social planning cons. Am. Found. for Blind, 1958-59; proposal reviewer NSF; cons. Inst. Community Studies, United Way Am., 1970, Psychiat. Inst. Found.; del. White House Conf. on Aging, 1971, resource person, 1981; tech. rev. panel Nat. Coun. on Aging; mem. commn. on svcs. to aging Archdiocese of Washington, 1971-76; vice chmn. Joint Legis. Com., Boston, 1954-57. Book reviewer Social Thought. Mem. exec. com. Nat. Vol. Orgns. for Ind. Living for the Aging, 1972-74, 77-82; mem. commn. on aging Cath. Charities U.S.A., 1972—, chmn., 1978-84; bd. dirs. Social Svc. Exch., Boston, 1955-57, Child Welfare League Am., 1966-70, Cath. Internat. Union Social Svc., 1967-72, Christ Child Soc. Washington, 1967-73; treas., bd. dirs. Nat. Conf. Cath. Charities, 1971-74; bd. dirs. Associated Cath. Charities, Archdiocese of Washington, 1976-83; chmn. Washington com. 13th Internat. Conf. Schs. Social Work, 1965-66; active Montgomery County Commn. on Aging, 1987, mem. pub. policy com., 1st and 2d vice chmn., 1988-92, mem. exec. com., planning com., chmn., 1992-93, nominating com., chmn. econ. security com., 1988-90; mem. Am. Task Force for Lebanon; mem. parish coun. Ch. of the Annunciation, Washington, 1968-70, chair ch. and comty. com., chair task force on self-study, chair nominating com., mem. nominating com., mem. task force for self-study; bd. dirs. Montgomery County Dept. Social Svcs., 1994—. Capt. U.S. Army, 1942-46, maj. Res. Recipient Lasker Doctoral fellowship Columbia U., 1957-58, Pres.'s Centennial medal Cath. U. of Am., 1988, Outstanding Citizenship award Albany County LWV, 1942. Mem. Nat. Assn. Social Workers (chpt. treas. 1956-57, task force on svcs. to aging 1973-75), Mass. Conf. Social Work (dir., chmn. nominating com. 1956-57), Alumni Assn. Columbia U. Sch. Social Work (chpt. chmn. 1954-55, dir. 1956-59), United Comty. Funds and Couns. Am. (nat. adv. com. health and welfare svcs. 1955-57, coun. planning execs. 1957-59), Nat. Assn. Hearing and Speech Agy. (nat. tng. adv. com. 1963-70), Acad. Cert. Social Workers, Coun. Social Work Edn. (deans adv. com. fed. welfare agys. 1962-64, 66-68, ho. of dels. 1977-86, adv. bd. gerontol. content in social work edn. 1983-86), So. Gerontol. Soc. (dir. 1981-86), Am. Soc. on Aging Assn. Gerontology in Higher Edn. (com. interorganizational rels., program com., Disting. Svc. Recognition award 1995), Gerontol. Soc., John Carroll Soc., Univ. Club, Club Washington. Home: 5101 River Rd Bethesda MD 20816-1512

FERRIS, JOHN ACKEL, JR., physician; b. Austin, Tex., Feb. 29, 1928; s. John Ackel and Frances Dean (White) F.; m. Sarah Jane Allen, June 12, 1953; children; Catherine, John III, Christopher, Martha, Paul, Elizabeth, Frank, Sarita, Jeanne, David. BS, Tulane U., 1950, MD, 1953. Diplomate Am. Bd. Family Practice, Am. Bd. Geriatric Medicine, Am. Bd. Med. Mgmt. Intern Denver Gen. Hosp., 1953-54; resident Parkland Meml. Hosp., Dallas, 1954-55; pvt. practice LaFeria, Tex., 1958-69; physician Valley Diagnostic Med. & Surg. Clinic, P.A., Harlingen, Tex., 1969—, pres., chmn., 1986-92; clin. prof. dept. family practice U. Tex. Health Sci. Ctr., San Antonio, 1976—; chief of staff Valley Bapt. Med. Ctr., Harlingen, 1984-85. Trustee Children's Heart Inst. of Tex., Corpus Christi, 1990-92. Maj. USAF, 1956-58, PTO. Fellow Am. Acad. Family Practice; mem. AMA.

Roman Catholic. Office: Valley Diagnostic Med and Surg Clinic 2200 Haine Dr Harlingen TX 78550-8549

FERRIS, THOMAS FRANCIS, physician; b. Boston, Dec. 27, 1930; s. Henry J. and Mildred M. (MacDonald) F.; m. Carol A. Connor, June 15, 1957; children—Richard C., Deirdre D., Thomas M., Claudia C. A.B., Georgetown U., 1952; M.D., Yale U., 1956. Intern Johns Hopkins Hosp., 1956-57; resident Yale—New Haven Hosp., 1951-53, fellow in renal diseases, 1961-63; fellow Linacre Coll., Oxford U., 1966-67; asst. prof. medicine Yale U. Med. Sch., 1964-67; prof. Ohio State U. Med. Sch., 1967-78; prof. medicine, chmn. dept. U. Minn. Med. Sch., Mpls., 1978—. Author articles on hypertension, renal disease. Served as officer M.C. AUS, 1957-59. Home: 1535 Hunter Dr Wayzata MN 55391-9661 Office: U Minn Hosps & Clinic Haward St At River Rd Minneapolis MN 55455

FERRONE, JOSEPH DANIEL, orthopaedic surgeon; b. Boston, July 20, 1936; s. Joseph Daniel and Elaine Antoinette (Poirier) F.; m. Patricia Wasack, Feb. 13, 1965; children: Joseph, Jennifer, Katherine, Christine, Stephanie, David. BA, U. Notre Dame, 1958; MD, Yale U., 1962. Intern Yale-New Haven Hosp., Boston, 1962-63; resident in gen. surgery Yale-New Haven Hosp., 1965-67, resident in orthopaedic surgery, 1967-70; clin. prof. orthopaedic surgery Tufts U. Sch. Medicine, Boston, 1970—. Lt. comdr. USNR, 1963-65. Recipient Jane des Forges Leadership award New England Med. Ctr., Boston, 1992. Fellow Am. Acad. of Orthopedic Surgeons. Roman Catholic. Office: New England Med Ctr #414 750 Washington St Boston MA 02111

FERTEL, DAVID JAY, cardiovascular and thoracic surgeon; b. Detroit, Sept. 10, 1960; s. Max Edward and Elaine Linda Fertel. BS, Mich. State U., 1982; DO, Kirksville Coll. Osteo., 1986. Intern Garden City (Mich.) Hosp., 1986-87, resident in gen. surgery, 1987-88, 92-95; dir. Southland Med. Ctr., L.A., 1988-91; fellow in cardiovascular/thoracic surgery Horizons Health Care, Warren, Mich., 1995—. Mem. Am. Coll. Osteo. Surgeons, Am. Osteo. Assn., Am. Osteo. Acad. Sports Medicine.

FESER, ROBERT JAMES, optometrist; b. Harlan, Iowa, Feb. 10, 1954; s. Charles John and Marcella Elizabeth (Bogler) F.; m. Jodi Layne Bandow; children: Christina, Michael, David, Daniel. BS, U. Iowa, 1976, Ill. Coll. Optometry, 1978; OD, Ill. Coll. Optometry, 1980. Pvt. practice Chariton, Iowa, 1980-83, Cherokee, Iowa, 1984—; pres., bd. dirs. Siouxland Ophthal. Labs. Den leader Boy Scouts Am. Mem. Nat. Youth Sports Coaches Assn., Am. Optometric Assn., Iowa Optometric Assn., Western Iowa Optometric Soc. (chmn. 1990-93), Pheasants Forever. Office: 208 W Bluff PO Box 278 Cherokee IA 51012

FESHBACH, SEYMOUR, psychology educator; b. N.Y.C., June 21, 1925; s. Joseph and Fannie (Katzman) F.; m. Norma Deitch, Aug. 16, 1947; children: Jonathan, Laura, Andrew. BS, Coll. City N.Y., 1947; MA, Yale U., 1948, PhD, 1951. Project dir. Army Attitude Assessment Br., 1951-52; from asst. prof. to asso. prof. U. Pa., Phila., 1952-63; prof. U. Colo., Boulder, 1963-64; prof. psychology UCLA, 1964—, chmn. dept., 1977-83, vice chair acad. senate, 1990-91, chair, 1991-92, spl. asst. to chancellor, 1992-95; dir. Fernald Sch., 1964-73; cons. CBS, Ednl. TV, 1972; vis. fellow Wolfson Coll., Oxford (Eng.) U., 1980-81. Author: Television and Aggression, 1970, Psychology, An Introduction, 1977; also others; co-author: Personality, 1982, Learning to Care, 1983; editor: Aggression and Behavior Change: Biological and Social Processes, 1979; cons. editor: Jour. Abnormal Psychology, 1973—; contbr. chpts. to books, articles to profl. jours. Served to 1st lt., inf. AUS, 1943-46, PTO. Recipient Ward medal Coll. City N.Y., 1947, Townsend Harris medal, Distinguished Alumnus award, 1972, Fellowship award Found. Fund Advancement of Psychiatry, 1980-81, Disting. Scientist award Calif. Psychol. Assn., 1983, Maurice and Fay Karpf Peace award UCLA, 1992; grantee NIMH, NSF. Fellow Am. Psychol. Assn.; mem. Western Psychol. Assn. (pres. 1976-77), AAAS, Soc. for Study of Social Issues (pres. 1988-89), Soc. for Rsch. in Child Devel., Internat. Soc. for Applied Psychology, Internat. Soc. for Study of Aggression (pres. 1984-86), Internat. Soc. for Study of Behavior Devel., ACLU, Phi Beta Kappa. Democrat. Jewish. Home: 743 Hanley Ave Los Angeles CA 90049-1926 Office: UCLA Dept Psychology 405 Hilgard Ave Los Angeles CA 90024-1301

FETCHERO, JOHN ANTHONY, JR., otorhinolaryngologist; b. Jeannette, Pa., June 4, 1951; s. John Anthony Sr. and Cleda (Byerly) F.; m. Wynona Ann Kestler, Feb. 26, 1982; children: John Anthony III, Christopher Jason, Dominic Vincent, Victor Thomas. BS in Biology, St. Vincent Coll., 1973; DO, Coll. Osteo. Medicine, Des Moines, 1976. Intern Des Moines Gen. Hosp., 1976-77; Flight surgeon Naval Aero. Med. Inst., Pensacola, Fla., 1977-78; resident Nat. Naval Med. Ctr., Bethesda, Md., 1980-84; otorhinolaryngologist, oro-facial plastic surgeon Am. Co. Osteo. Opthalmology and Otorhinolaryngology, 1987; otolaryngologist Am. Coll. Otolaryngology, Chgo., 1988; pvt. practice Orange Park, Fla., 1988—. Mem. Julington Creek (Fla.) Civic Assn., 1988—. With USNR, 1973—. Med. Sch. scholar USN, 1973-76. Mem. Fla. Osteo. Assn., Osteo. Acad. Otorhinolaryngology, Am. Acad. Otolaryngology, Am. Osteo. Assn., Fla. Med. Assn., Clay County Med. Soc. Republican. Roman Catholic. Home: 1474 Fruit Cove Forest Rd Jacksonville FL 32259-2811

FETTEROLF, DONALD EDWARD, physician executive, consultant; b. Scranton, Pa., Apr. 26, 1953; s. Donald James and Louise Ann (Pedrick) F.; m. Vicki Lynne Cochran. BA in Chemistry and Biochemistry, U. Pa., 1975, MD, 1979; MBA, U. Pitts., 1991. Diplomate Am. Bd. Internal Medicine, Nat. Bd. Med. Examiners, Am. Bd. Quality Assurance and Utilization Rev. Physicians, Am. Bd. Med. Mgmt. Intern and resident in internal medicine Hosp. U. Health Ctr. of Pitts., Presbyn. U. Hosp., 1979-82, fellow in occupational/environ. medicine, 1982-83; sole practice Pitts., 1982-88; group practice Allegheny Intermed, Ltd., Pitts., 1988-94; pres., chmn. St. Clair Hosp. LCO, Inc., Pitts., 1987-93; chmn. med. dir. Alpha Health Network, Pitts., 1990-93; sr. med. dir. Blue Cross Western Pa., Pitts., 1994—; dir. data chmn. Buy Right Coun. S.W., Pa., Pitts., 1988—; mem. staff Canonsburg (Pa.) Gen. Hosp., 1982-93, West Allegheny Hosp., Oakdale, Pa., 1985-86, Allegheny Medcare. Contbr. articles to profl. jours. Fellow Am. Coll. Utilization Rev. Physicians; mem. AMA, Pa. Med. Soc., Am. Coll. Physician Execs., Allegheny County Med. Soc. (mem. patient rels. com. 1986-88, chmn., 1988), Mensa. Home: 12 Laurel Hill Rd Mc Donald PA 15057 Office: 120 Fifth Ave Pl Ste 31213 Pittsburgh PA 15222

FETTGATHER, ROBERT, psychologist, special education educator; b. Seattle, May 3, 1951; s. Robert Paul and June Marie (Christensen) F.; children: Aaron, David. AS in Psychiat. Tech., West Valley Coll., Saratoga, Calif., 1976; BA in Psychology, San Jose U., 1979; MA in Edn., U. Santa Clara, 1981; PhD in Psychology, Calif. Coast U., 1985. Lic. psychologist, lic. learning handicapped specialist, psychiat. technician, Calif.; cert. stress mgmt. instr. Instr. psychology and spl. edn. Mission Coll., Santa Clara, Clif., 1979—; pvt. practice clin. psychology Los Gatos, Calif., 1991—; counselor Alexian Assocs., San Jose, Calif., 1987-91; program cons. Santa Clara Unified Adult Handicapped Program, 1984-90; spl. cons. Comprehensive Adult Student Assessment Sys. Project, Calif. Dept. Edn., 1983-84. Mem. Agnews Community Library Grant Adv. Bd., 1988. Mem. Am. Psychol. Assn., Calif. Psychol. Assn., No. Calif. Assn. Behavior Analysis, San Jose State Univ. Alumni Assn., Calif. Coast Univ. Alumni Assn. Democrat. Roman Catholic. Home: 14899 Payton Ave San Jose CA 95124-4335 Office: 15810 Los Gatos Blvd Los Gatos CA 95032

FETTO, JOSEPH F., orthopedic surgeon; b. Buffalo, N.Y., Jan. 11, 1947; s. Vincent D. and Grace (Hickler) F.; children: Joshua, Samara, Jordana. BS, SUNY, Buffalo, 1968; MD, N.Y. Med. Coll., 1974. Diplomate Am. Bd. Orthopedic Surgeons. Dir. orthop. N.Y. VA Med. Ctr., N.Y.C., 1979—; assoc. prof. NYU Med. Ctr., 1979—. Author: Sports Injuries to Lower Extremities, 1990; inventor in field; contbr. articles to profl. jours. Fellow Am. Acad. Orthop. Surgeons; mem. Internat. Soc. Tech. in Arthroplasty. Republican. Jewish. Office: NYU Med Ctr 530 1st Ave 5-B New York NY 10016

FEUER, ROBERT CHARLES, environmental biologist; b. N.Y.C., Feb. 23, 1936; s. Harry and Sara Gertrude (Bender) F.; m. Joan F. Colton, Mar. 29, 1969. BS, Cornell U., 1956; MS, Tulane U., 1958; PhD, U. Utah, 1966. Instr. Purdue U., Hammond, Ind., 1963-64; asst. prof. Phila. Coll. Pharmacy and Sci., 1964-74; sr. environ. analyst McCormick Taylor Assocs., Phila., 1975-76; sr. ecologist Louis Berger Assocs., East Orange, N.J., 1978; herpetologist LGL Environ. Rsch. Assocs., Muscatine, Iowa, 1980; cons. in environ. biology, Broomall, Pa., 1977—; columnist The Beachcomber, Ship Bottom, N.J., 1964-91; environ. specialist Phila. Suburban Water Co., Bryn Mawr, 1994—. Contbr. articles to profl. jours. Editor Bull. of Phila. Herpetological Soc., 1969-84, 96—, Phila. Grotto Digest, 1957-72. Chmn. Environ. Adv. Bd., Marple Twp., Pa., 1971-73, 84-89, 96—; flotilla comdr. U.S. Coast Guard Aux., Media, Pa., 1977. NSF fellow, 1960-61; Sigma Xi grantee, 1959-60; Karl P. Schmidt Meml. Fund grantee, 1960. Fellow Herpetologists League; mem. Am. Soc. Ichthyologists and Herpetologists, Soc. for Study Amphibians and Reptiles, Phila. Herpetol. Soc. (editor 1969-84, pres. 1990-94), Nat. Speleological Soc., Sigma Xi. Avocations: fishing; boating; reading; horticulture. Address: 102 S New Ardmore Ave Broomall PA 19008-2916

FIALKOV, MARTIN JEROME, psychiatrist; b. Capetown, Republic of South Africa, Feb. 1, 1944; came to U.S., 1977; s. Bertram and Rachel (Zieve) F.; m. Maureen Leibowitz, Jan. 2, 1969; children: Jonathan, Natasha, Joshua. BSc, U. Stellenbosch, Republic of South Africa, 1965, B. Medicine, B. Surgery, 1969. Diplomate Am. Bd. Psychiatry and Neurology, Child and Adolescent Psychiatry. Internship Frere Hosp., East London, Republic of South Africa, 1970; med. officer South African Med. Corps, Pretoria, Republic of South Africa, 1971-72; resident Karl Bremer Hosp., Bellville, Republic of S. Africa, 1972, Groote Schuur Hosp., Observatory, Republic of South Africa, 1973-76; fellow Washington U., St. Louis, 1977-78; asst. prof. U. Calif. at Davis, Sacramento, 1979, U. Pitts. Med. Sch., 1980-88. Contbr. various articles to profl. jours. 2nd Lt. Med. Corp, 1971-72. Fellow Am. Orthopsychiat. Assn.; mem. Am. Acad. Child and Adolescent Psychiatry, Am. Psychiat. Assn. Home and Office: 2174 Ramsey Rd Monroeville PA 15146-4838

FIALKOW, PHILIP JACK, academic administrator, medical educator; b. N.Y.C., Aug. 20, 1934; s. Aaron and Sarah (Ratner) F.; m. Helen C. Dimitrakis, June 14, 1960; children: Michael, Deborah. BA, U. Pa., 1956; MD, Tufts U., 1960. Diplomate: Am. Bd. Internal Medicine, Am. Bd. Med. Genetics. Intern U. Calif., San Francisco, 1960-61, resident, 1961-62; resident U. Wash., Seattle, 1962-63, instr. medicine, 1965-66, asst. prof., 1966-69, assoc. prof., 1969-73, prof. medicine, 1973—, chmn. dept. medicine, 1980-90, dean Sch. Medicine, 1990—, v.p. for med. affairs, 1992—; chief med. svc. Seattle VA Ctr., 1974-81; physician-in-chief U. Wash. Med. Ctr., Seattle, 1980-90; attending physician Harborview Med. Ctr., Seattle, 1965—; cons. Children's Orthopedic Hosp., Seattle, 1964—. Contbr. articles to profl. jours.; mem. editorial bds. profl. jours. Trustee Fred Hutchinson Cancer Research Ctr., Seattle, 1982-90. Recipient NIH Merit award, Mayo Soley award for achievement in research; NIH fellow, 1963-65; NIH grantee, 1965—. Fellow ACP; mem. AAAS, Am. Soc. Clin. Investigation, Assn. Am. Physicians, Am. Soc. Human Genetics (bd. dirs. 1974-77), Assn. Am. Med. Colls. (at large, coun. deans 1993—), Am. Soc. Hematology, Inst. Medicine, Alpha Omega Alpha. Office: U Wash Box 356350 1959 NE Pacific Seattle WA 98195-6350

FICARRA, BERNARD JOSEPH, retired surgeon, legal medicine and bioethics consultant; b. N.Y.C., Jan. 1, 1914; s. Humphrey and Rose Marie (D'Ambra) F.; B.A. magna cum laude, St. Francis Coll., 1935, Sc.B., 1936; M.D., Georgetown U., 1939; Sc.D., U. Steubenville, 1950; LL.D., St. Francis Coll., N.Y.; Ph.D., Minerva U., Milan, Italy, 1960; m. Jean Alice Augustine, Aug. 31, 1967; 1 son, Bernard Thaddeus. Diplomate Am. Bd. Surgery. Surg. intern Kings County Hosp. Med. Center, Bklyn., 1939-41, resident pathology, 1941-42, resident surgery, 1942-44; fellow surgery Lahey Clinic Found., Boston, 1946-48; practice medicine specializing in surgery, N.Y.C., 1948-60, Greenvale, N.Y., 1953-70; mem. vis. surg. staffs Kings County, St. Peters, Holy Family, St. Mary's hosps.; dir. surg. research Ficarra Found., Inc., 1949-69; prof. physiology St. Francis Coll., 1948-51; prof. research physiology St. John's U. Postgrad. Sch., 1951-61; professorial research asso. L.I. U., Postgrad. Sch., 1961-73; dir. Somerset Enterprises, Ltd., Doric Corp. Trustee L.I. Ednl. TV Council Inc., Sta. WLIW; pres. Cath. Acad. Scis. U.S.A. Fellow Am. Coll. Gastroenterology (com. for legal matters), Am. Coll. Legal Medicine (edn. com.), Am. Coll. Angiology (achievement honor award 1964-65); mem. AMA, N.Y. State Med. Soc., N.Y. Acad. Medicine, N.Y. Soc. Med Jurisprudence, Acad. Templars (Bologna, Italy), Greenvale C. of C., Lahey Clinic Alumni Assn. (mem. council), Cath. Acad. Scis. (U.S.)(pres.), Alpha Omega Alpha, Pi Alpha, Phi Chi. Lodges: Lions (honors: Knight of Malta, Knight Cmdr. of St. Gregory the Great), Equestrian Order of the Holy Sepulchre of Jerusalem (sect. rep. southeastern lieutenancy Washington, So. Md., No. Va., lt. mid. Atlantic lieutenancy Del., Md., Va., W.Va., Tenn., N.C., Washington, mil. svcs. of USA, Knight Grand Cross, lt. by grand magisterium). Author: Diagnostic Synopsis of Acute Surgical Abdomen, 1950; Emergency Surgery, 1953; Thyroid and Parathyroid Diseases, 1958; Surgical and Allied Malpractice, 1968; Medicolegal Handbook, 1983; Medicolegal Examination Evaluation and Report, 1986, Abortion Analyzed, 1989, Feudal Chateau, 1990, Church on The Hill, 1990; mem. adv. bd. jour. Med. Malpractice Prevention; mem. editorial bd. Jour. Contemporary Health Law and Policy; contbr. 250 articles to profl. jours. Named to Alumni Hall of Fame St. Francis Preparatory Sch., N.Y., 1990; received Silver Palm of Jerusalem, His Beatitude Archbishop Michele Sabbah, Latin Patriarch of Jerusalem, 1988, Gold medal for Svc. to Holy Land, His Patrimony Rev. Joseph Nazzaro, OFM Custos of the Holy Land, Jerusalem, 1993. Office: PO Box 9611 Washington DC 20016-9611

FICHTENBAUM, CARL JACK, physician, educator; b. New Haven, May 2, 1961; s. Leonard Joseph and Myrna (Levy) F.; m. Mary Beth Donica, June 8, 1986; children: Walter, Adrienne. BA, U. Mo., Kansas City, 1985, MD, 1985. Diplomate Am. Bd. Internal Medicine, Am. Bd. Infectious Diseases, Am. Bd. Pediatrics. Intern, then resident physician Bridgeport (Conn.) Hosp., 1985-89, chief med. resident, 1989-90; fellow Yale U., New Haven, 1990-91; fellow Washington U., St. Louis, 1991-94, instr. in medicine, 1993-96, asst. prof., 1996—. Contbr. articles to profl. jours. Mem. Parents Sch. Bd. Com., University City, Mo., 1995-96; mem. HIV/STD Planning Prevention Group, St. Louis, 1995—. Nat. Inst. on Drug Abuse rsch. grantee, 1996. Fellow Am. Acad. Pediatrics; mem. ACP, Infectious Diseases Soc. Am. (assoc.). Office: Washington U Box 8011 660 S Euclid Ave Saint Louis MO 63110

FIDEL, EDWARD ALLEN, clinical psychologist; b. Tyler, Tex., May 25, 1943. B.S.F.S., Georgetown U., 1966; Ph.D., Tex. Tech U., 1974. Lic. psychologist, La. Clin. instr. dept. neurology La. State U. Med. Ctr., New Orleans, 1973; staff clin. psychologist inpatient psychiatry VA Med. Ctr., New Orleans, 1974-79, coordinator clin. biofeedback program, 1979-87; staff clin. psychologist VA Mental Hygiene Clinic, New Orleans, 1979-87, VA Outpatient Clinic, Ft. Myers, Fla., 1987—; asst. prof. U. New Orleans, 1979. Mem. Am. Psychol. Assn., Biofeedback Soc. Am., Southeastern Psychol. Assn. Author research publs. Office: VA Outpatient Clinic 2070 Carrell Rd Fort Myers FL 33901-8009

FIDONE, LAURA PEEBLES, social worker; b. Little Rock, Nov. 30, 1962; d. L.M. and Tish (Maynard) Peebles; m. Jeff W. Fidone, Sept. 9, 1989. BA, Harding U., 1985, MSW, 1987. Lic. social worker, Ark., Tex., lic. cert. social worker, bd. cert. social worker, advanced clin. practitioner. Intern Ark. State Dept. Health, Little Rock, 1985-86; social worker intern Youth Home Inc., Little Rock, 1986-87; med. social worker VA Med. Ctr., Little Rock, 1987-91, Shreveport, 1991-94; med. social worker, discharge planning team leader Specialty Hosp., 1994—; dir. social work svc., group therapist for multi-family support group and multi-disciplinary team leader Splty. Hosp., 1994—; therapist bereavement support group Shiloh Ch. of Christ, Tyler, Tex.; co-chairperson Nat. Celebration of Social Work Month, Little Rock, 1988, 91, co-chairperson enrichment com., 1989-91; co-chairperson La. Celebration of Social Work Month, 1991, group therapist Cancer Support Group, 1990-91, Intensive Care Support Group, 1988-89, neurology multidisciplinary team leader, 1989-91, acute care medicine multidisciplinary team leader, 1991-94, vol. and student supr., 1991—. Vol. bereavement group therapist Shiloh Ch. of Christ. Fellow NASW; mem. Tex. Med. Alliance, Smith County Med. Alliance Soc. Mem. Ch. Christ. Office: VA Med Ctr Shreveport LA 71112

FIEDLER, CYNTHIA MARIE, nurse; b. Exeter, N.H., Aug. 31, 1957; d. David Charles Carr and Joan Elizabeth (Taylor) Carr Bruno; m. Dana Albert Fiedler; children: Joshua, Jared Ana. BS in Nursing, Fitchburg (Mass.) State Coll., 1979. RN, Fla., Calif., Mass. Staff, charge nurse Cardinal Cushing Hosp., Brockton, Mass., 1979-83, Santa Monica (Calif.) Med. Ctr., 1983-84; staff nurse Hosp. Staffing Services, Fort Lauderdale, Fla., 1984, Staff Builders, Boston, 1984—; staff, charge nurse Faulkner Hosp., Jamaica Plain, Mass., 1986—; staff nurse Milton (Mass.) Hosp., 1991-95. Recipient Nat. Cancer Soc. award, Fitchburg, Mass., 1979. Campaigner Walpole, Mass. town elections. Unitarian. Home: 320 Balcom St Mansfield MA 02048-1736

FIELD, BARRY ELLIOT, internist, gastroenterologist; b. Hartford, Conn., Apr. 21, 1947; s. Arnold and Selma (Nechrich) F.; m. Julie Farr, Jan. 6, 1991; 1 child, Rachel. B.A. (scholar), Harvard U., 1968; M.D., Albert Einstein Coll. Medicine, 1972. Intern in pediatrics Montefiore Hosp., Bronx, N.Y., 1972-73; intern medicine Met. Hosp., N.Y.C., 1973-74, resident in medicine, 1974-76; fellow in gastroenterology Harbor Gen. Hosp., Torrance, Calif., 1976-78; practice medicine specializing in internal medicine and gastroenterology, Pleasantville, N.Y., 1978—; dir. medicine Phelps Meml. Hosp., N. Tarrytown, N.Y. ; clin. instr. dept. medicine N.Y. Med. Coll., Valhalla. Mem. Am. Gastroenterol. Assn., Alpha Omega Alpha. Office: 777 N Broadway Ste 305 Tarrytown NY 10591

FIELD, E. MALCOLM, neurosurgeon; b. Brighton, Mich., Apr. 10, 1930. BS, U. Mich., 1951, MD, 1956, MSc, 1961. Diplomate Am. Bd. Neurol. Surgery. Neurol. surgeon Saginaw (Mich.) Valley Neurosurgery, 1962—; med. dir. Field Neurosci. Inst., Saginaw, 1986—. Fellow ACS, Internat. Coll. Surgeons, Royal Soc. Medicine London; mem. Am. Assn. Neurol. Surgeons, Soc. Critical Care Medicine, Am. Soc. Stereotactic and Functional Neurosurgery, Congress Neurol. Surgeons. Office: Saginaw Valley Neurosurgery 4677 Towne Centre Rd Saginaw MI 48604

FIELD, STEVEN PHILIP, medical educator; b. Newark, Feb. 21, 1951; s. Irving and Florence (Engel) F. BA, Yale U., 1973; MD, NYU, 1977. Diplomate Am. Bd. Internal Medicine, Am. Bd. Gastroenterology. Intern in internal medicine Bellevue Hosp., N.Y.C., 1977-78, resident in internal medicine, 1978-81; instr. in medicine Mt. Sinai Hosp., N.Y.C., 1981-83; instr. in medicine NYU Sch. of Medicine, N.Y.C., 1983—, clin. asst. prof. medicine, 1991—. Contbr. articles to med. jours., chpts. to med. textbooks. Recipient John Addison Porter Prize Yale U., 1973. Mem. Am. Gastroent. Assn., ACP, N.Y. Acad. Gastroenterology (v.p. 1995-96), N.Y. Soc. for Gastrointestinal Endoscopy (exec. com. 1989—), N.Y. State Med. Soc., Yale Club Ctrl. N.J. (alumni schs. com.), Alpha Omega Alpha. Office: 245 E 35th St New York NY 10016-4283

FIELDS, HENRY WILLIAM, college dean; b. Cedar Rapids, Iowa, Sept. 25, 1946; m. Anne M. Fields; children: Benjamin Widdicomb, Justin Riley. AB in Psychology, Dartmouth, Hanover, N.H., 1969; DDS in Dentistry, Univ. Iowa, Iowa City, 1973, MS in Pedodontics, 1975; MSD in Orthodontics, Univ. Wash., Seattle, 1977. Cert. dentistry Iowa 1973, N.C. 1978, Ohio 1991. Staff, Dept. Hosp. Dentistry Univ. Iowa Hosps., Iowa City, 1973; grad. supr. Muscatine (Iowa) Migrant Program, 1974; grad. instr., Undergrad. Pedodontic Clinic and Lab. Univ. Iowa, 1974-75; AFDH tchr. tng. fellow, Dept. Orthodontics Univ. Wash., 1975-77, clin. asst., Undergrad. Pediatric Dentistry Clinic and Seminars, 1977; active participant Dental Faculty Practice, Sch. Dentistry Univ. N.C., Chapel Hill, 1977-91, asst. prof., Depts. of Pediatric Dentistry and Orthodontics, 1977-82; with N.C. Meml. Hosp., Chapel Hill, 1978-91; assoc. prof., Depts. of Pediatric Dentistry and Orthodontics Univ. N.C., Chapel Hill, 1982-87, grad. program dir., Dept. Pediatric Dentistry, 1984-89, prof., Dept. Pediatric Dentistry and Orthodontics, 1987-91, acting dir. grad. studies, Sch. Dentistry, 1989, asst. dean acad. affairs, Sch. Dentistry, 1990-91; chair, Dept. Dentistry OSU Hosps., Columbus, Ohio, 1991—; adj. prof. of Orthodontics, Sch. Dentistry OSU Hosps., Columbus, 1992—; participant, Faculty Practice OSU Coll. of Dentistry, Columbus, Ohio, 1991—, prof. Dept. Orthodontics, 1991—, dean, 1991—; staff Columbus Children's Hosp., 1992—; mem. human subjects com. Sch. Dentistry, Univ. N.C., 1989-91, chmn. curriculum com., 1990-91, chmn. dirs. com. adv. edn. program, 1989-91, health promotion disease prevention task force, 1990-91; deans coun. computerization com. The Ohio State Univ., 1991—; bd. dirs. IADR-AADR Craniofacial Biology Group, 1988-90; cons. to com. to review grad. Pediatric Dentistry Univ. Pitts., 1991; co-chair cont. edn. com. Am. Acad. Pediatric Dentistry/ Am. Assoc. of Orthodontic, 1991—; cons. Callahan award commn., 1992; external examiner BDS and MDS programs Dept. Pediatric Dentistry and Orthodontics Univ. Hong Kong, 1991-93; course dir. and coord. for numerous grad. and undergrad. programs. Contbr. chpts. to books, articles to profl. jours. Recipient NIDR grantee, 1980-83, NIDR Inst. grantee, 1985-86, 1988-93. Home: 4066 Fenwick Rd Columbus OH 43220-4870 Office: Ohio State U Coll Dentistry 1159 Postle Hall Columbus OH 43210-1241

FIELDS, HOWARD LINCOLN, neurology and physiology educator; b. Chgo., Dec. 12, 1939; s. Charles and Mae (Pinkert) F.; m. Carol Margaret Felts, Dec. 31, 1966; children: Rima Tamar, Gabriel Charles. Research neurologist Walter Reed Research Inst., Washington, 1967-70; clin. fellow Harvard Med. Sch., Boston, 1970-72; asst. prof. U. Calif., San Francisco, 1973-78, assoc. prof., 1978-82, prof., 1982—; vice chmn. neurology, 1993—; cons. NIH, Bethesda, Md., 1979-84, Inst. of Medicine, Nat. Acad. Scis., Washington, 1985-86; vis. fellow Clare Hall Coll., U. Cambridge, Eng., 1979; vis. prof. Royal Soc. Medicine, 1988. Editor: (book) Recent Advances in Pain Research and Therapy, 1985, Core Curriculum for Professional Education in Pain, 1991, 2d edit., 1995; author: Pain, 1987, Pain Syndromes in Neurology, 1990, Pharmacotherapy of Pain, 1994; contbr. 160 articles to profl. jours. Recipient Research Career Devel. award NIH, Merit award. Mem. Internat. Assn. Study of Pain (program chmn. 1981-84, sec. 1990-93), Am. Soc. Clin. Investigation, Am. Acad. Neurology, Am. Neurol. Assn. (councillor 1991, program com. 1991), Soc. for Neurosci. Office: U Calif Dept Neurology PO Box 114 San Francisco CA 94143-0001

FIELDS, JAMES PERRY, dermatologist, dermatopathologist, allergist; b. Sherman, Tex., July 30, 1932; s. John Galloway and Alma (Goff) F.; m. Linda Hensley, May 30, 1958; children: Timothy Austin, Amy Elizabeth. BS, U. Tex., 1953, MS, 1957; MD, U. Tex., Galveston, 1958. Diplomate Am. Bd. Dermatology, Am. Bd. Allergy and Immunology, spl. competence cert. in dermatoapathology. Dir. dept. dermatology USPHS, S.I., N.Y., 1964-78; assoc. prof. medicine and pathology Vanderbilt U. Sch. of Medicine, Nashville, 1978-88; pvt. practice, Nashville, 1988—; dir. dermatopathology Lab. of the Mid-South, Nashville, 1988—; from instr. to assoc. clin. prof. dermatology and pathology Columbia-Presbyn. Hosp. and Coll. of Physicians and Surgeons, N.Y.C., 1968-88; assoc. clin. prof. medicine Vanderbilt U. Sch. Medicine, Nashville, 1988—. Author (with others): Mycobacterial Diseases, 1991; contbr. articles to profl. jours. Bd. dirs. Am. Leprosy Missions Internat., Greenville, S.C., 1974—; vol. med. missionary, United Meth. Vols. in Mission, 1984—. Capt. USPHS, 1958-79. Recipient citation for meritorious svcs. President's Com. on Employment of Handicapped, 1970, Meritorious Svc. medal USPHS, 1978. Fellow ACP, Am. Acad. Allergy and Immunology, Am. Acad. Dermatology, Am. Coll. Allergy and Immunology, Am. Soc. Dermatopathology, Am. Soc. for Dermatologic Surgery, N.Y. Acad. Medicine (sec. 1976-77, chmn. sect. on dermatology 1977-78). Home: 411 Lynwood Blvd Nashville TN 37205-3434 Office: 4301 Hillsboro Rd # 200 Nashville TN 37215-3314

FIELDS, KATHY ANN, dermatologist; b. Waukegan, Ill., May 14, 1958; d. Maynard Bernard and Blanche (Telson) F.; m. Garry Rayant, Aug. 10, 1991; 1 child, Richard. Student, Northwestern U., 1975-76; BS, U. Fla., 1979; MD, U. Miami, Fla., 1983. Diplomate Am. Bd. Dermatology. Intern in ob-gyn. Jackson Meml. Hosp., 1983-84; resident in dermatology Stanford (Calif.) U. Med. Ctr., 1984-87; laser specialist Sydney, Australia, 1987; pvt. practice San Francisco, 1988—; co-owner K-R Dermatologics, Inc.; creator Proactiv Solution. Fundraiser Am. Cancer Soc., San Francisco, 1988—, Child Abuse Prevention, United Jewish Appeal, Women's Young Leadership Cabinet, 1991—, mosaic counsel. Fellow Am. Acad. Dermatology; mem. AMA, Calif. Med. Assn., San Francisco Med. Soc., San Mateo Med. Soc. Office: 350 Parnassus Ave San Francisco CA 94117-3608

FIELDS, RICHARD STANLEY, anesthesiologist; b. Cleve., July 17, 1937; m. Carol Fields. BS, Yale U., 1959; MD, Albany (N.Y.) Med. Coll., 1963; JD, Pepperdine U., 1978. Diplomate Am. Bd. Anesthesiology. Pvt. practice Fullerton, Calif., 1970—. Mem. Airport Noise and Safety Com., Fullerton, 1983—, Airport Users Task Force, Fullerton, 1983—. Capt. USAR, 1966-68. Mem. Am. Soc. Anesthesiologists, Am. Coll. Legal Medicine, Calif. Soc. Anesthesiologists, Orange County Soc. Anesthesiologists. Office: Spring Anesthesia Group PO Box 22222 Los Angeles CA 90022

FIERER, JOSHUA, physician, educator; b. N.Y.C., Aug. 18, 1937; s. Sol F.; m. Norma Susan Damashek, Apr. 1960; children: Daniel, Adam, Emily. AB, Columbia Coll., 1959; MD, NYU, 1963. From asst. prof. to prof. U. Calif., San Diego, 1971-86, prof., 1986—; head divsn. infectious diseases U. Calif., San Diego, 1991—. Chmn. Universitywide Task Force on AIDS, Calif., 1994-96. Lt. col. USPHS, 1964-66. Fellow Infectious Disease Soc. Am.

FIERING, STEVEN, medical researcher; b. Aug. 28, 1951. BS in Geology with distinction, U. Mich., 1975; BS in Microbiology, Eastern Mich. U., 1985; PhD in Genetics, Stanford U., 1990. Ptnr. food processing bus. Soy Plant, Ann Arbor, Mich., 1975-83; teaching asst. microbiology Eastern Mich. U., 1982-84, lectr. microbiology, 1985; teaching asst. Med. Sch. Stanford U., 1986-89; rsch. group leader AFRC Ctr. Genome Rsch. U. Edinburgh, Scotland, 1990-91; postdoctoral fellow Hutchinson Cancer Rsch. Ctr., Seattle, 1991—. Contbr. articles to profl. jours. Scholar Am. Soc. Hematology, 1995. Mem. AAAS. Office: Fred Hutchinson Cancer Rsch Inst A3-025 1124 Columbia St Seattle WA 98104*

FIERMAN, LOUIS BEN, psychiatrist; b. Cleve., May 11, 1922; s. Benjamin and Rebecca (Ghidaleson) F.; m. Ella Yensen, Sept. 25, 1947; children: Daniel, Lauren. BS, Case Western Res. U., 1944, MD, 1946. Diplomate Am. Bd. Psychiatry and Neurology. Intern Cleve. Met. Hosp., 1946-47; resident in medicine VA Med. Ctr., 1949-50; resident in psychiatry Yale Dept. Psychiatry, New Haven, 1950-53; pvt. practice psychiatry Psychotherapy Assocs., New Haven, 1953—; cons. psychiatrist Yale New Haven Hosp., 1953—; cons. Conn. Valley Hosp., Middleton, 1968-89; sr. cons. Elmcrest Psychiatrist Inst., Portland, Conn., 1981—, med. dir., 1971-81. Editor: Effective Psychotherapy, 1965; contbr. articles to profl. jours. Capt. M.C., U.S. Army, 1947-49. Fellow Am. Psychiat. Assn. (life); mem. AMA, Conn. Psychiat. Soc., Conn. Med. Assn. Democrat. Home: 15 Enoch Dr Woodbridge CT 06525 Office: Psychotherapy Assocs 451 Orange St New Haven CT 06511

FIES, MARIE JOYCE, nurse; b. Reading, Pa., Dec. 17, 1939; d. Andrea Carmine and Josephine (Scimone) Torchia; m. Robert J. Fies, Feb. 17, 1962; children: Julie, Kathleen, Robert. BSN, Lebanon Valley Coll., 1981; RN, Reading Hosp. Sch. Nursing. RN. Exec. dir. Am. Cancer Soc., Berks County Unit, Reading, Pa., 1983-84; occupational health nurse Caloric Corp., Topton, Pa., 1985-87, NGK Metals Corp., Reading, Pa., 1987-88; pres. Nurses in Industry, Inc., Reading, 1988—. Mem. ANA, Am. Assn. Occupational Health Nurses (pres. Berks County chpt. 1989-92), Pa. Nurses Assn., Reading Hosp. Sch. Nursing Alumni Assn. Mem. United Ch. of Christ.

FIFE, TERRY D., neurologist; b. Ft. Wayne, Ind., Oct. 23, 1959. BS, U. Ariz., 1982; MD, Tex. A&M U., 1986. Resident U. Calif. Davis Med. Ctr., Sacramento, 1986-89; resident UCLA, L.A., 1989-92, clin. instr., 1992-93; cons. Barrow Neurol. Inst., Phoenix, 1993—, dir. balance ctr., 1994—; asst. clin. prof. neurology U. Ariz., Tucson, 1996—. Contbr. articles to profl. jours., chpts. to books. Recipient NIH Nat. Rsch. Svc. award, 1992. Mem. Am. Acad. Neurology, Am. Coll. Physicians. Office: Barrow Neurol Inst 222 W Thomas Rd Rm 401 Phoenix AZ 85013

FIGAZZOTTO, ANTHONY, analytical chemist; b. Phila., Oct. 18, 1962. BA in Chemistry, La Salle U., Phila., 1984; MS in Chemistry, Villanova U., 1994. Chemist The Upjohn Co., Kalamazoo, 1984-88; sr. chemist SmithKline Beecham Pharms., King of Prussia, Pa., 1988—. Office: SmithKline Beecham Pharms PO Box 1539 King Of Prussia PA 19406

FIGLEY, MELVIN MORGAN, radiologist, physician, educator; b. Toledo, Dec. 5, 1920; s. Karl Dean and Margaret (Morgan) F.; m. Margaret Jane Harris, Mar. 16, 1946; children: Karl Porter, Joseph Dean, Mark Thompson. Student, Dartmouth, 1938-41; MD magna cum laude (John Harvard fellow), Harvard, 1944. Diplomate: Am. Bd. Radiology (trustee 1967-72). Intern, then resident internal medicine Western Res. U., 1944-46; resident radiology U. Mich., 1948-51, instr., asst. prof., assoc. prof. radiology, 1950-58; practice specializing in radiology Seattle, 1958-86; prof. radiology, chmn. dept. U. Wash., 1958-78, prof. radiology and medicine, 1979-85, emeritus prof. radiology and medicine, 1986—; mem. radiation study sect. NIH, 1963-67; mem. com. on radiology Nat. Acad. Scis.-NRC, 1964-69, chmn., 1968-69. Editor: Am. Jour. Roentgenology, 1976-85; contbr. articles profl. jours. Bd. dirs. James Picker Found., 1970-80. Served to capt. M.C. AUS, 1946-48. John and Mary R. Markle scholar, 1952-57. Fellow Am. Coll. Radiology (Gold medal 1987), Royal Coll. Radiologists (hon., London), Royal Australian Coll. Radiologists (hon.); mem. Royal Soc. Medicine (hon.), Assn. Univ. Radiologists (pres. 1966, Gold medal 1983), Am. Roentgen Ray Soc. (exec. council 1970-88, pres. 1983-84, Gold medal 1986), N. Am. Soc. Cardiac Radiology (pres. 1974), Fleischer Soc. (pres. 1986-87), Radiol. Soc. N.Am. (Gold Medal 1986), AMA, Boylston Med. Soc., Wash. Heart Assn. (past trustee), Soc. Chmn. Acad. Radiology Depts. (exec. council 1969-71), Phi Beta Kappa, Sigma Xi, Alpha Omega Alpha, Sigma Alpha Epsilon. Episcopalian. Home: PO Box 10100 Bainbridge Is WA 98110-0100 Office: U Wash Dept Radiology Seattle WA 98195

FIGLIN, ROBERT ALAN, physician, hematologist, oncologist; b. Phila., June 22, 1949; s. Jack and Helen Figlin; m. Leslie Anne Figlin, 1 child, Jonathan B. BA in Chemistry, Temple U., 1970, postgrad., 1972; MD, Med. Coll. Pa., 1976. Diplomate Am. Bd. Internal Medicine, sub-bd. Med. Oncology; diplomate Nat. Bd. Med. Examiners; lic. physician, Calif. Med. intern, resident in medicine Cedars-Sinai Med. Ctr., L.A., 1976-79, chief resident in medicine, 1979-80; fellow in hematology-oncology UCLA, 1980-82; asst. prof. medicine UCLA Sch. Medicine, 1982-88, assoc. prof., 1988-94, prof. of medicine, 1994—; dir. Bowyer Oncology Ctr., dir. outpatient clin. rsch. unit Jonsson Comprehensive Cancer Ctr., 1990-92, dir. clin. rsch. unit, 1993—; prof. medicine, 1994—. Editor Interferons in Cytokines, 1988-90, Kidney Cancer Jour., 1993-94; affiliate editor Current Clin. Trials, 1992—; mem. editorial bd. UCLA Cancer Trials Newsletter, 1990—; author articles and revs. Mem. med. adv. bd. Nat. Kidney Cancer Assn., 1993—; FDA cons., 1990-92. Recipient numerous awards. Fellow ACP; mem. Am. Soc. Clin. Oncology, Am. Fedn. Clin. Rsch., Am. Assn. for Cancer Rsch., Soc. for Biologic Therapy, S.W. Oncology Group. Office: Ste 510-13 200 UCLA Med Plz Los Angeles CA 90095

FIGUERA, DIEGO, surgeon, educator; b. Algorta, Spain, Aug. 9, 1920; s. Jesus-Angel and Amelia (Aymerich) F.; m. Nieves Alvarez, Oct. 22, 1955; children: Angela, Isabel, Diego, Miguel, Pablo. MD, U. Madrid, 1949. Intern Hosp. Provincial, Madrid, 1946-50; assoc. prof. surgery U. Madrid, 1951-54; supernumerary thoracic surgeon Cardiff, England, 1955-56; head surgery Beneficiencia Provincial Madrid, 1959; prof. surgery Zaragoza Med. Sch., 1962-64; prof. surgery Madird Autonomous Med. Sch., 1966-91, emeritus prof., 1991—; surg. registrar San Carlos Teaching Hosp., 1949-53; head surg. dept., dir. Clinica Puerta de Hiervo, Madrid, head bd. cardiovascular surgery, 1967-68, dir., 1979-81, head dept., 1964-91. Contbr. articles to profl. jours. Recipient Grand Medal Order Civil de Sanidad, medal Fomento de la Invencion Cabrevizo Found., 1993; named to Order de Isabel la Catolice. Mem. ACS (gov. 1989-93), Soc. Espanola de Anyia Cardiovascular (pres. 1978-79), Soc. Espanola de Cardiologia (pres. cardiac transplant sect.), Soc. Espanola de Anestesia y Reanimacion (hon.), Assn. Espanola de Cirujanos (gold medal, hon.), Royal Acad. Medicine Madrid, Royal Acad. Medicine Seville (hon.). Roman Catholic. Home and Office: Ave Concha Espina 61, 28016 Madrid Spain

FIGUEROA-ROMAN, BETSY, medical records administrator; b. Ponce, P.R., Dec. 6, 1942; d. Flor Figueroa and Maria R. Roman. BS, Catholic U. P.R., 1965, med. records sci. diploma, 1967. Diplomate Am. Bd. Quality Assurance and Utilization Review. Dir. med. records adminstrn. Psiquiatric Hosp., Ponce, 1967-69, Univ. Hosp., Rio Piedras, P.R., 1969-74, Presbyn. Hosp., San Juan, P.R., 1975-77; peer review P.R. Found. for Med. Care Inc., San Juan, 1978-85; dir. med. records Clinica Espanola, Mayaquez, P.R., 1985-86, Tito Mattei Hosp., Yauco, P.R., 1986; profl. affairs dir. Dr. Pila Hosp., Ponce, 1986—. Mem. Puerto Rican Health Mgmt. Info. Assn. (pres. 1985). Roman Catholic. Home: Marginal 301 La Rambla 305 Ponce PR 00731

FIGUERRES, CYRIL IWAMURA AMOROZO, psychologist, educator; b. Lahaina, Maui, Hawaii, July 10, 1948; s. Cirilo Amoroso and Kimiko (Iwamura) F.; m. Aileen Chizuko Shitamoto, Jan. 14, 1972; children: Dawn Ayumi, Derek Shitamoto, Kevin Shitamoto. Student U. Hawaii, 1966-69, 71; BS, Brigham Young U., 1972, MA, 1974; PhD, Purdue U., 1977. Cert. tchr., Utah. Research assoc. Ch. of Jesus Christ of Latter-day Saints, Salt Lake City, 1978, mgr. research and evaluation, 1979—; adj. asst. prof. ednl. psychology U. Utah, Salt Lake City, 1979-91; mem. aux. faculty psychology Brigham Young U., Salt Lake City, 1979-83. Contbr. research articles to profl. jours. Active Boy Scouts Am., 1976-79; Bishopric, Ch. of Jesus Christ of Latter-day Saints, West Lafayette, Ind., 1976-78, high counselor, Salt Lake City, 1978-1984, Bishopric, Salt Lake City, 1986-91; mission pres. Japan Fukuoka Mission, 1991-94; mem. sch. bd. Fukuoka Internat. Sch., 1992-93. Ethnic minority doctoral fellow Purdue U., 1975-77; named Outstanding Young Man of Am., U.S. Jaycees, 1980. Mem. Internat. Soc. Intercultural Edn. Tng. and Rsch., Soc. Cross-Cultural Research. Republican. Avocations: martial arts, reading. Home: 2111 E Terra Linda Dr Salt Lake City UT 84124 Office: Church of Jesus Christ of Latter-Day Saints 50 E North Temple Salt Lake City UT 84150-0002

FIKRIG, EROL, rheumatologist, medical educator; b. Dec. 15, 1959. BA in Chemistry cum laude, Cornell U., 1981, MD, 1985. Diplomate Am. Bd. Internal Medicine, Am. Bd. Infectious Diseases. Resident in internal medicine Vanderbilt U. Hosp., 1985-88; fellow in infectious diseases and immunobiology Yale U., 1988-92, assoc. rsch. scientist in immunobiology, 1992, asst. prof. medicine sect. of rheumatology, 1992-96, assoc. prof. medicine sect. of rheumatology, 1996—. Contbr. articles to profl. jours.; ad hoc reviewer NIH study sect. Bacteriology and Mycology I, 1994; spkr. in field. Recipient Young Investigator award Nat. Found. Infectious Disease, 1991, award in vaccine devel. Infectious Disease Soc. Am., 1992, Young Investigator award Am. Heart Assn., 1993, Investigator award Arthritis Found., 1993, Apollo Kinsley award State of Conn., 1993, NIH First award, 1994, Goodyear award State of Conn., 1994, Established Investigator award Am. Heart Assn., 1996; NIH Clin. Investigation fellow, 1990, Daland fellow Am. Philos. Soc., 1990; pew scholar, 1993. Mem. Phi Beta Kappa. Office: Yale U Sch Medicine Dept Rheumatology 333 Cedar St New Haven CT 06520-8031

FILARDO, THOMAS WESLEY, physician; b. Alton, Ill., June 15, 1945; s. Vincent and Carmen Irene (Clagg) F.; m. Nora L. Zorich, Mar. 22, 1984; children: N.V. Wesley, T. Daniel. BS cum laude, U. Notre Dame, 1967; MD, U. Ill., Chgo., 1971. Diplomate Am. Bd. Family Practice. Asst. prof. U. Ill. Coll. Medicine, Urbana, 1978-87, dir. intro. to clin. medicine, 1979-87; med. dir. Nurse on Call, Norcross, Ga., 1990—; new terms editor Stedman's Med. Dictionary, 1995—. Author: (with others) Chronic Disease Management in the Homeless in Health Care of Homeless People, 1985, Medical Aspects of Homelessness in the Homeless Mentally Ill, 1984; contbr. articles to profl. jours. Founder Champaign-Urbana Physicians for Social Responsibility, Champaign, Ill., 1981. Lt. comdr. USPHS, 1975-78. Named Provider of Yr., Champaign County Health Care Consumers, 1986. Mem. Am. Acad. Family Practice, Alpha Epsilon Delta. Office: Nurse On Call 3080 Northwoods Cir Ste 110 Norcross GA 30071

FILER, ELIZABETH ANN, psychotherapist; b. N.Y.C., Oct. 16, 1923; d. Edwin and Edith Louise (Levy) Filer. B.S., Columbia U., 1944, M.A., 1945, M.S., 1954. Cert. bd. clin. social worker. Asst. tchr. to asst. dir. Mallay Nursery Sch., Bklyn., 1943-52; tchr., guidance staff N.Y. Sch. for Nursery Years, 1954-60; liaison social worker The Reece Sch., N.Y.C., 1954-60; cons. to schs. in N.Y.C., 1960-71; ednl. cons./therapist Ednl. Inst. for Learning and Research, N.Y.C., 1961-65; clin. social worker, psychotherapist in pvt. practice, N.Y.C., 1971—; cons. in field. Bd. dirs. Recreation Room and Settlement, N.Y.C., 1962-73; vol. Lenox Hill Hosp., N.Y.C., 1992—. Recipient Founders Day award and Bicentennial medal Columbia U., 1954. Mem. Nat. Assn. Social Workers, N.Y. State Soc. Clin. Social Work Psychotherapists, Nat. Inst. for Clin. Social Work Advancement, Soc. for Psychoanalytic Psychotherapy, World Fedn. for Mental Health. Avocations: swimming; sports; opera; reading; needlepoint; travel. Home: 240 E 79th St New York NY 10021-1257

FILION, DEAN THOMAS, orthopedist; b. Schenectady, N.Y., Sept. 20, 1965; s. Roger Ernest and Mary Alice (Cwicala) F. BS in Biology, Siena Coll., Loudonville, N.Y., 1987; DO, Phila. Coll. Osteo. Medicine, 1991. Diplomate Am. Acad. Phy. Medicine and Rehab. Resident dept. phys. medicine and rehab. Boston U. Med. Ctr., 1991-95; attending physician dept. orthop. and sports medicine Braintree (Mass.) Hosp., 1995—; head team physician U. Mass., Boston, 1995—, North Quincy (Mass.) H.S., 1995—; med. tent physician Boston Marathon/BAA, Boston, 1992—; assoc. clin. prof. dept. phys. medicine and rehab. Boston U. Med. Ctr., 1995—. Contbr. articles to profl. jours. Mem. Am. Coll. Sports Medicine, Am. Osteo. Acad. Sports Medicine, Nat. Acad. Sports Medicine. Republican. Roman Catholic. Home: 65 Ocean View Dr #11 Boston MA 02125 Office: Braintree Hospital Dept Orthop and Sports Medicine 250 Pond St Braintree MA 02184

FILITTI, MARTHA, psychiatrist; b. Geneva, Switzerland, Aug. 8, 1942; d. Octavian and Veturia Vladutiu; m. Don Filitti; 1 child, Gerard. MD, U. Bucharest, Romania, 1966, Specializaton in Neurology, Psychiatry, 1973, postgrad. studies with honors, 1976. Lic. MD, N.J., N.Y. Assoc. Regal Health Care Corp., N.Y.C., 1981-86; staff psychiatrist Bergen Pines County Hosp., Paramus, N.J., 1986—, West Bergen Med. Health Ctr., Ridgewood, N.J.; mem. adv. bd. Regal Healthcare Corps., N.Y.C., 1986—; cons. Dynamic Health Ins., Inc., Princeton, N.J., 1990—. Adv. bd. mem. Mid-Atlantic Polit. Action Com., Princeton, 1992; psychiatrist West Bergen Comty. Mental Health Ctr., 1993—. Recipient Cert. Recognition for Clin. Excellence, Med. Coll. Pa., 1990, Cert. Achievement in Medicine, Regal Healthcare Corp., 1992. Mem. Am. Psychiat. Assn., N.J. Psychiat. Assn., Boston Ashton Rsch. Group (scholar). Home: 206 E Glen Ave Ridgewood NJ 07450 Office: Bergen Pines County Hosp E Ridgewood Ave Paramus NJ 07652

FILLEY, CHRISTOPHER MARK, neurologist; b. Saranac Lake, N.Y., July 31, 1951; s. Giles Franklin and Mary Brown (Klinefelter) F. BA, Williams Coll., 1973; MD, Johns Hopkins U., 1979. Diplomate Am. Bd. Psychiatry and Neurology. Intern U. Conn., Farmington, 1979-80; resident in neurology U. Colo., Denver, 1980-83; behavioral neurology fellow Boston U., 1983-84; from instr. to asst. prof. neurology U. Colo. Sch. Medicine, Denver, 1984-91, assoc. prof. neurology, 1991—; prin. investigator studies in Alzheimers Disease NIH, Bethesda, Md., 1991-94. Author: Neurobehavioral Anatomy, 1995; contbr. articles to profl. jours. Health com. Denver Found., 1995—. Mem. Am. Acad. Neurology, Am. Neurol. Assn., Internat. Neuropsychol. Soc., Behavioral Neurology Soc., Colo. Soc. Clin. Neurologists. Office: Univ Colo Behavioral Neurology Sect 4200 E Ninth Ave Denver CO 80262

FILLMAN, JAMES, psychotherapist; b. Norristown, Pa., Jan. 29, 1951; s. James M. Sr. and Margaret Mary (Furey) F.; m. Sharon L. Klink, Aug. 30, 1969 (div. Jan. 1988); children: Shannon D., Joshua C. AS, Peirce Jr. Coll., Phila., 1971; student, Villanova U., 1972-75; BA, Allentown Coll. of St. Francis de Sales, 1988; MA, Rider Coll., 1991. Contr., acct. Pileggi & Sons, Inc., North Wales, Pa., 1973-88; pvt. practice in psychotherapy Levittown and Lansdale, Pa., 1990—; instn. and agy. wide trainer and presenter Rider U., Lawrenceville, N.J., Recovery Ctr., Wilmington, Del., Eagleville (Pa.) Hosp., N.J. Multi-Cultural Counselors Assn., N.J. Mental Health Counselors Assn., Northwestern Inst., Fort Washington, Pa. Spkr. Gay, Lesbian and Bisexual growth and interest orgns.; mem. Pride Therapy Network, Delware Valley, Bucks County Violence Prevention Task Force. Mem. Nat. Assn. of Lesbian and Gay Alcoholism Profls., Nat. Assn. of Drug and Alcohol Counselors, Alpha Sigma Lambda, Delta Delta. Democrat. Episcopalian. Home: 3627 Nancy Ward Cir Doylestown PA 18901-9041 Office: Ste 108 1400 New Rogers Rd Levittown PA 19055 also: 855 W Main St Lansdale PA 19446

FILLOY, BEVERLEE ANN HOWE, clinical social worker; b. Ogden, Utah, Mar. 11, 1926; d. Albert Herman Howe and Bernice Anna (Ewing) Howe Routt; m. Jose Antonio Filloy-Alvarez, Feb. 4, 1945 (dec. 1988); children: Richard Anthony, Emily Ann. BA with honors, U. Calif., Berkeley, 1947, MSW, 1954; PhD, Calif. Inst. Clin. Social Work, Berkeley, 1980. Bd. cert. diplomate clin. social work, sex therapist, clin. supr. Social caseworker Family Svc. Agy., Sacramento, Calif., 1959-63; cons. Stanford Lathrop Meml. Home, Sacramento, 1964-69; cons., supr. Arnold Homes for Children, Sacramento, 1968-71; pvt. practice social work Sacramento, 1963—; faculty Calif. Soc. Clin. Social Work, Sacramento, 1979—, Calif. State U., Sacramento, 1956-58, 90; sec. Nat. Registry Providers of Health Care in Clin. Social Work, 1983-85, bd. dirs., 1980-86, treas. Nat. Fedn. for Socs. for Clin. Social Work, 1981-86. Founder, bd. Planned Parenthood of Sacramento, 1964. Fellow Calif. Soc. for Clin. Social Work (pres. 1983-85, bd. dirs. 1969-87, Mem. of Yr. award 1990), Calif. Inst. for Clin. Social Worker (bd. trustees, sec.-treas. 1976-88, v.p. 1989-94); mem. Soc. for Sci. Study Sex, Amnesty Internat., Older Women's League, Am. Assn. Sex. Educators, Counselors, Therapists, Phi Beta Kappa. Democrat. Office: 3525 Watt Ave Ste 1 Sacramento CA 95821-2617

FILUT, JACK MORRIS, psychologist; b. Frankfurt, Germany, Feb. 19, 1949; s. Israel and Helen F.; B.S., N.Y. Inst. Tech., 1972; M.S., Eastern Ky. U., 1974; Ph.D. (Univ. scholar), Marquette U., 1976; m. Karen J. Kamler, June 4, 1972; children—Melissa B., Dara L. Grad. asst. Eastern Ky. U., 1973; intern in psychology Stanford (Ky.) Mental Health Center, 1974, Marquette U. Counseling Center, 1975-76; psychologist South Beach Psychiat. Center, Family Ct. Services Unit, S.I., 1977—; adj. prof. psychology N.Y. Inst. Tech., 1977—, St. John's U., 1984—. Recipient Behavioral Scis. Acad. Excellence award N.Y. Inst. Tech., 1972. Fellow Am. Orthopsychiat. Assn.; mem. Am. Psychol. Assn., N.Y. State Psychol. Assn. Home: 376 Cortelyou Ave Staten Island NY 10312-2403

FIMIAN, WALTER JOSEPH, retired biologist; b. N.Y.C., May 22, 1926; s. Walter Joseph and Christine (Magee) F.; m. Phyllis Ann Smith; children—Michael, Paul, Mark, John, James. A.B., U. Vt., 1950; M.S., U. Notre Dame, 1952, Ph.D., 1955; postgrad. Marquette U., 1954-55. Asst. prof. Boston Coll., Chestnut Hill, Mass., 1955-60, assoc. prof. biology dept., 1960-93, emeritus, 1993, dir. Radiation Biology Inst., AEC, NSF, 1962-72. Mem. AAAS, Radiation Research Soc. Democrat. Roman Catholic.

FINALDI, MELISSA ANN MARIE, occupational health nurse; b. Edison, N.J., June 28, 1971; d. Valerie Marie (Koval) F. ASN, U. Medicine and Dentistry N.J., 1993. Head psychiatry nurse Elizabeth (N.J.) Gen. Med. Ctr., 1993-94; mem. nursing staff Westfield (N.J.) Dermatology, 1994, Care Sta., Linden, N.J., 1994—. Mem. Am. Assn. Occupational Health Nurses. Republican. Roman Catholic. Home: 16 Birch St Port Reading NJ 07064 Office: 328 W St Georges Ave Linden NJ 07036

FINAZZO, JOSEPHINE JOANNE, osteopathic physician; b. Wyandotte, Mich., Mar. 17, 1966; d. John Joseph and Anna (Giaimo) F. BS in Physiology, Mich. State U.; DO, Kirksville Coll. Osteo. Med. Intern Horizon Health Sys., Mich., 1993-94, resident in radiology, 1994—; speaker in field. Cardiac arrest fund raiser Am. Heart Assn., Trenton, Mich., 1995; bd. dirs. Am. Heart Assn., Detroit, 1995—. Republican. Roman Catholic. Home: 3227 Van Alstyne Wyandotte MI 48192

FINBERG, LAURENCE, pediatrician, educator, dean; b. Chgo., May 20, 1923; s. Joseph and Anne (Malkow) F.; m. Harriet Levinson, June 17, 1945 (dec. Jan. 1994); children: Robert, Jeanne, James; m. Joann Quane, Mar. 17, 1995. BS, U. Chgo., 1944, MD, 1946. Diplomate: Am. Bd. Pediatrics (examiner 1969—, bd. dirs. 1974-79, 82-88 , pres. 1978, chmn. 1987). Intern U. Chgo. Clinics, 1946-47; asst. resident pediatrics Balt. City Hosps., 1949-50, resident in pediatrics, 1950-51; practice medicine specializing in pediatrics Balt., 1951-63, N.Y.C., 1963—; asst. chief pediatrician Balt. City Hosps., 1951-61, dir. pediatric out-patient dept., 1951-63, dir. premature nursery, 1951-59, assoc. chief pediatrics, 1961-63; pediatrician Harriet Lane Home, 1951-63; chmn. dept. pediatrics Montefiore Hosp. and Med. Center, Bronx, N.Y., 1963-80, prof., 1995—; chmn. dept. pediatrics SUNY Health Sci. Ctr., Bklyn., 1982-95, prof. pediatrics, 1982-95, prof. emeritus, 1995—, dean, 1988-91; prof. pediatrics U. Calif., San Francisco, 1995—; instr. pediatrics Johns Hopkins U., 1951-56; asst. prof., 1956-63; prof. pediatrics Albert Einstein Coll. Medicine, Yeshiva U., Bronx, 1963-82, chmn., 1968-80; cons. in field; mem. pediatric adv. com. N.Y.C. Dept. Health, 1970-94. Mem. editl. bd. Jour. Pediat., 1973-83, Am. Jour. Diseases of Children, 1984-94, named changed to Archives of Pediat. and Adolescent Medicine, 1994—, editor nutrition sect., 1995—. Served with USPHS, 1947-49. Recipient Bela Schick medal, 1992, Nutrition award Am. Acad. Pediatrics, 1992. Mem. AAAS, AMA (Goldberger Clin. Nutrition award 1993), Am. Pediatric Soc., Soc. Pediatric Research, Am. Acad. Pediatrics (com. on environ. hazards 1968-83, chmn. 1979-83, com. nutrition 1983-89—, chmn. 1984-89), Am. Coll. Nutrition, Am. Inst. Nutrition, Nat. Cholesterol Edn. Program Coordinating Com. (panel on children and adolescents 1989-93), Ambulatory Pediatric Assn., Am. Soc. Clin. Nutrition, Am. Fedn. Clin. Research, Sociedad Peruana de Pediatria, Sociedad Dominica De Peditria, Harvey Soc., N.Y. Acad. Medicine (past chmn. pediatric sec.), Phi Beta Kappa, Sigma Xi, Alpha Omega Alpha. Home: 152 Lombard St Apt 602 San Francisco CA 94111-1134 Office: U Calif San Francisco Dept Pediatrics Box 0110 San Francisco CA 94143

FINBERG, ROBERT WILLIAM, infectious diseases physician; b. Balt., Mar. 23, 1950; s. Laurence and Harriet Phyllis (Levinson) F.; m. Joyce Diane Fingeroth, July 4, 1971; children: Johanna Beth Fine, Sara Julie Fine, Leah Ann Fine. AB, U. Chgo., 1971; MD, Albert Einstein Coll. Med., 1974. Diplomate Am. Bd. Internal Medicine, Am. Bd. Infectious Diseases. Resident in internal medicine Bellevue Hosp., N.Y.C., 1974-77; rsch. fellow dept. pathology Harvard Med. Sch., 1977-79, asst. prof., 1980-82; clin. fellow infectious diseases Peter Bent Brigham Hosp., 1979-80; chief infectious diseases Dana Farber Cancer Inst., Boston, 1982—; prof. Harvard Med. Sch., Boston, 1996—; cons. Middlesex Scis., Norwood, Mass., 1994—; rsch. cons. Microwave Med. Mem. Alpha Omega Alpha. Office: 48 Spring Ln Canton MA 02021-1715

FINCH, CAROLYN BOGART, speech and language pathologist, kinesiologist; b. Mineola, N.Y., June 24, 1938; d. Harold Edwin and Ruth (Waring) Bogart; m. Gordon M. Finch (div. Oct. 1982); children: David Harold, Martha Louise; m. Donald Hill Hulme; children: Wendy Harriet Hulme, Allison Elizabeth Hulme. BS, Elmira Coll., 1965; MS, Western Conn. State U., 1972; postgrad., Nova U., 1982. Cert. speech and lang. pathologist, early childhood edn., elem. edn. and communication; cert. applied kinesiologist. Speech therapist Elmira (N.Y.) City Schs., 1963-65; supervision therapist Speech and Hearing Clinic Elmira Coll., 1966-67; speech therapist Greenshire Residential Sch., Cheshire, Conn., 1968-69; speech pathologist Danbury (Conn.) City Schs., 1970-73; owner, dir. Peter Piper Sch. and Learning ctr., Brookfield Center, Conn., 1973-88, Speech Pathology Assocs., Danbury, 1974-87; mem. adj. faculty Western Conn. State U., Danbury, 1974-86, prof., 1986-87; pres. Apples and Oranges; profl. spkr. Dunn & Brastreet Bus. Edn. Svcs.; organizer, chmn. bd. Liberty Nat. Bank, Danbury; freelance lectr., 1986-88; pres. nat. spkr. Bogart comm., Inc., Danbury; acct. exec. V.R. Bus. Brokers, R. Zemper Assocs.; pres. comm. Fitness Internat. divsn. Bogart Comm.; founder, dir. Candlewood Lake Seminars, 1995; nat. gender intercultural understanding; spkr. on body lang. and elctromagnetic. Author: (multisensory articulation program) Portraits of Sounds, 1969, (book and posters) Survival Sign System, 1982, Universal Handtalk, 1988, Socks Says!, 1993, Be Electrific. Dem. nominee Danbury Town Com., 1985; mem. adv. com. Fairfield County 4-H. Recipient Mayoral Proclamation for Survival Sign System, City of Danbury, 1986, Golden Apple Tchr. award, Danbury News Times; named Woman of Yr. Bus. and Prof. Women, 1990. Mem. Women in Comm., New Eng. Speakers Assn., Nat. Speakers Assn., Women in Comm., John Cosentino Singers. Home and Office: Bogart Communications Inc 51 Cedar Dr Danbury CT 06811-3302 Office: Treatment Office and Candlewood Lake Seminars 18 Old Rte 7 Brookfield CT 06804

FINCHER, JULIAN HAYES, pharmacist, educator; b. Union County, S.C., July 22, 1935; s. Robert Charles and Addie (Murphy) F.; m. Betty Jane Jarrell, June 2, 1966; 1 child, Timothy K. BS in Pharmacy, U. S.C., 1958; MS, U. Ga., 1962; PhD, U. Conn., 1964. Lic. pharmacist S.C., Ga., Miss. Instr. pharmacy U. S.C., Columbia, 1958-59, U. Ga., Athens, 1959-61; asst. prof. pharmacy U. Miss., University, 1964-67, assoc. prof. pharmacy, 1967-70, chmn. dept. pharmaceutics, 1970-72; prof. Coll. of Pharmacy U. S.C., Columbia, 1972—, dean Coll. of Pharmacy, 1972-96. Co-author: The History of Pharmaceutical Education at the University of South Carolina 1965-1978, 1982; editor-in-chief Dictionary of Pharmacy, 1986. Fellow Am. Found. Pharm. Edn.; mem. Am. Pharm. Assn., Am. Assn. Coll. Pharmacy (chmn. council deans 1981-82), Am. Assn. Pharm. Scientists, Am. Soc. Hosp. Pharmacists, Am. Inst. History Pharmacy, Rho Chi, Sigma Xi, Phia Lambda Sigma, Omicron Delta Kappa. Democrat. Baptist. Lodges: Kiwanis (pres. Oxford, Miss. 1968), Rotary. Home: 824 Gregg St Columbia SC 29201-3926 Office: U SC Coll of Pharmacy Columbia SC 29208

FINDER, ROBERT ANDREW, pharmaceutical company executive; b. Washington, Mo., Apr. 27, 1947; s. Richard Joseph and Jeanette Mary (Graser) F.; m. Sheryl Jean Johnson, Feb. 6, 1971. B in Chem. Engring., U. Detroit, 1970. Process engr. Monsanto-J.F. Queeny Plant, St. Louis, 1970-71, prodn. supr., 1975-79, project mgr., 1980-81; engring. supt. Monsanto-Trenton (Mich.) Plant, 1981-82; gen. supt. mfg., dir. Monsanto Chems., Ltd., Bangkok, 1985-89; chmn. bd., mng. dir. Rhone-Poulenc Thai Industries Ltd., Bangpoo Samutprakarn, Thailand, 1989-91; dir. mfg. Rhone-Poulenc Inc., Princeton, N.J., 1992-93; v.p. mfg. and process tech. Ecogen, Inc., Langhorne, Pa., 1995—; v.p. ops. Purepac Pharm., Inc. (Faulding, Inc.), Elizabeth, N.J., 1995—; mem. pres's. cabinet U. Detroit, 1988—. Life mem. World Wild Life Fund, Bangkok, 1988—. Lt. U.S. Army, 1971-74. Mem. AIChE, Am. Philatelic Soc., Bangkok Sports Club. Office: Purepac Pharm Inc (Faulding Inc) 200 Elmorea Ave Elizabeth NJ 07207

FINDLAY, RICHARD PAUL, psychologist; b. Brighton, Mass., June 29, 1956. BA in Psychology, Calif. State U., Long Beach, 1979; MA in Clin. Psychology, Western Carolina U., 1984; PhD, U.S. Internat. U., San Diego, 1989. Lic. clin. psychologist, Vt. Clin. psychology intern Western Carolina U., Cullowhee, N.C., 1984; sr. chem. dependency counselor Scripps Meml. Hosp., San Diego, 1984-86; predoctoral intern Elmcrest Psychiat. Inst., Portland, Conn., 1986-87; postdoctoral intern Family Therapy Assocs., Essex Junction, Vt., 1988-90, clin. psychologist, 1990-92; clin. psychologist and drug abuse program coord. Fed. Bur. Prisons, Montgomery, Pa., 1992—. Mem. APA. Office: PO Box 304 Lewisburg PA 17837

FINDLEY, JOHN SIDNEY, dentist; b. Bryan, Tex., Oct. 3, 1942; s. Sidney Albert and Leila Mae (Reading) F.; m. Patricia Ann Reep, June 10, 1967 (div. 1977); children: John Brett, Sidney Alan; m. 2nd Judith Ann Smith, May 22, 1981. Student USAF Acad., 1961-62, N. Tex. State U., 1963-65; DDS, Baylor U. Coll. Dentistry, 1970. Pvt. practice dentistry, Plano, Tex., 1970—; bd. dirs. Fin. Svcs. Inc. Contbr. articles to profl. jours. Formerly bd. dirs. Plano YMCA, United Way of Plano, Park Bd. City of Plano, Charter Rev. Commn. City of Plano; pres. Colleagues of the Plano Police, City of Plano; chmn. advancement com. North Trail Dist. Boy Scouts Am.; campaign chmn. Plano YMCA Fund Dr., 1978; councilman City of Cross Rds., Tex., 1988-89, mayor, 1992-94; chmn. bd. trustees Oak Grove United Meth. Ch.; gen. chmn. Dallas Midwinter Dental Clinic. Recipient Cert. of Recognition Am. Acad. Dental Radiology, 1970; Paul Harris fellow Rotary Internat., 1979. Fellow Am. Coll. of Dentists, Internat. Coll. Dentists; mem. ADA, Tex. Dental Assn. (chmn. coun. govt. affairs, Pres. award 1994, 95, pres.-elect 1996—), Dallas County Dental Soc. (bd. dirs., editor DDS News, gen. chmn. Dallas Mid-winter Dental Clinic 1992, pres.-elect 1992-93, pres. 1994, dentist of yr. 1995), Acad. Gen. Dentistry, Rotary (Plano, bd. dirs., pres. 1977-78). Methodist. Home: RR 3 Box 498 Aubrey TX 76227-9528 Office: 1410 14th St Plano TX 75074-6359

FINE, ALBERT SAMUEL, educator; b. Phila., Oct. 24, 1923; s. Max and Sylvia (Lerner) F.; m. Selma Joyce Skolnick, Mar. 29, 1959; 1 child, Martin. BA, Bklyn. Coll., 1950, MA, 1953; PhD, NYU, 1970. Rsch. chemist VA Hosp., Bklyn., 1956-70; chief dental rsch. VA Hosp., N.Y.C., 1970-88; assoc. prof. histology, cell biology and peridontics NYU Coll. Dentistry, N.Y.C., 1970—. With U.S. Army, 1942-46, ETO. Mem. Am. Chem. Soc., Am. Inst. Biol. Sci., Sigma Xi.

FINE, BETH ANNE, genetic counselor, educator; b. Bklyn., July 31, 1956; d. Charles Herbert and Marylln Rose (Klein) Fine; m. Daniel Steven Kaplan, Apr. 8, 1984; children: Joshua Fine, Aaron Fine. BS in Biol. Scis., Cornell U., 1978; MS in Biology, U. Nebr., 1982. Diplomate Am. Bd. Med. Genetics, Am. Bd. Genetic Counseling. Genetic counselor Boys Town Inst., Omaha, 1979-80, Children's Meml. Hosp., Omaha, 1980-84, Michael Reese Hosp., Chgo., 1984-88, Ill. Masonic Med. Ctr., Chgo., 1988-89; coord. grad program in genetic counseling, genetic counselor Northwestern U., Chgo., 1990—; asst. prof. ob-gyn. Northwestern U. Med. Sch., Chgo.; mem. adv. panel Office Tech. Assessment, U.S. Congress, Washington, 1991-93; mem. adv. panel Biol. Scis. Curriculum Study, Colorado Springs, Colo., 1992-93; bd. dirs. Am. Bd. Genetic Counseling, 1993—, v.p., 1996-97; bd. dirs. Am. Bd. Med. Genetics, 1992-93; mem. ethical, legal and social issues working group Human Genome Project, 1995—. Editor: Strategies in Genetic Counseling, 1984, 90; contbr. chpt. to book. Mem. aux. bd. Planned Parenthood Chgo., 1992-93; cultural arts chair Westmoor Sch. PTA, Northbrook, Ill., 1993-94. NIH/Nat. Ctr. for Human Genome Rsch. grantee, 1991-94. Mem. Nat. Soc. Genetic Counselors (bd. dirs. 1983-89, pres. 1986-87, chair edn. com. 1983-84), Am. Soc. Human Genetics (info. edn. com.). Office: Northwestern U Med Sch W143 Ward 18-171 303 E Chicago Ave Chicago IL 60611-3008

FINE, BOBBIE DEAN, JR., nephrologist; b. Rogers, Ark., May 11, 1959; s. Bobbie Dean and Lorene (Miller) F.; m. Georgia Ann Fuller, May 2, 1987; children: Sarah Katherine, Jonathan Colin, Tierney Elizabeth. BS cum laude, Oral Roberts U., 1981, MD, 1985. Diplomate Am. Bd. Internal Medicine, Am. Bd. Nephrology. Asst. clin. instr. U. Ill. Coll. Medicine, Peoria, 1985-86, 87-89, U. Okla. Med. Coll., Tulsa, 1986-87, U. Iowa Hosps., Iowa City, 1989-91; staff nephrologist Ark Nephrology Svcs., Hot Springs, 1991—. Med. adv. bd. Nat. Kidney Found. Ark., Little Rock, 1995—. Mem. AMA, Internat. Soc. Nephrology, Am. Coll. Physicians, Christian Med./Dental Soc. Republican. Mem. Assembly of God Ch. Office: Hot Springs Diagnostic 1900 Malvern Ave Ste 304 Hot Springs AR 71901

FINE, EDWARD JAY JUDAH, neurologist, educator; b. Cin., Jan. 18, 1941; s. Archie Aaron and Anne (Hoffman) F.; m. Debra Lee Kleiman, May 19, 1969. AB cum laude, Ohio U., 1962; MD, Ohio State U., 1966. Diplomate in neurology and clin. neurophysiology Am. Bd. Psychiatry and Neurology. Asst. prof. neurology Rutgers Med. Sch., Piscataway, N.J., 1974-78; fellow clin. neurophysiology Harvard Med. Sch., Boston, 1978-80; assoc. clin. prof. neurology Robert W. Johnson Med. Sch., New Brunswick, N.J., 1980-83; dir. clin. neurophysiology SUNY, Buffalo, 1983—, assoc. prof. neurology, 1995; med. dir. Niagara C.C., Sandbourn, N.Y., 1984—. Inventor in field; contbr. articles to profl. jours. Cmdr. USN, 1968-70. Fellow Am. Acad. Neurology (exec. com. History of Neurology sect. 1992—), Am. Assn. Electrodiagnostic Medicine; mem. Phi Delta Epsilon. Jewish. Office: SUNY Neurology Dept 3495 Bailey Ave Buffalo NY 14215

FINE, HERBERT LEON, dermatologist; b. N.Y.C., Aug. 18, 1935; s. Irving and Dora Fine; m. Theda Blitzer, Sept. 16, 1956; children: Leslie, Susan. MD, Chgo. Med. Sch., 1961. Diplomate Am. Bd. Dermatology. Intern Brookdale Med. Ctr., Bklyn., N.Y., 1961-62; resident NYU, 1964-67; resident in dermatology NYU, N.Y.C., until 1967; pvt. practice Westwood, N.J., 1967—. Home: 18 Emery Ln Woodcliff Lake NJ 07675 Office: Westwood Derm Group 390 Old Hook Rd Westwood NJ 07675

FINE, IRWIN HOWARD, eye physician, surgeon, educator; b. Syracuse, N.Y., Apr. 30, 1936; s. David William and Ann (Sobol) F.; m. Victoria Bond, June 16, 1963; children: William, Laura, Edward. BS, MIT, 1961; MD, Boston U., 1966. Diplomate Am. Bd. Ophthalmology. Intern St. Elizabeth's Hosp. of Boston, 1966-67; resident Boston U. Med. Ctr. & Affil. Hosps., 1967-70; pvt. practice Eugene, Oreg., 1970—; clin. assoc. prof. ophthalmology Oreg. Health Scis. U., Portland, 1987—. Author, editor: Clear Corneal Cataract Surgery and Topical Anesthesia, 1993, Phacoemulsification: New Technology and Clinical Application, 1996; author, assoc. editor Cataract Surgery: Technique, Complications and Management, 1995; designer 12 surg. instruments. With U.S. Army, 1959-60. Mem. AMA, Internat. Intraocular Implant Club, Am. Acad. Ophthalmology (quality of care anterior segment panel 1995-96, Honor award 1994), Am. Soc. Cataract and Refractive Surgery (sci. adv. bd. 1992-94, govt. rels. com. 1991—, Innovator's award 1994), Outpatient Ophthalmic Surgery Soc. (bd. dirs. 1990—), Am. Coll. Eye Surgeons (bd. dirs. 1993-96), Am. Bd. Eye Surgery (bd. dirs. 1996), Oreg. Acad. Ophthalmology, Oreg. Med. Assn. (med. peer review com.). Republican. Jewish. Office: I Howard Fine MD PC 1550 Oak Ste S Eugene OR 97401

FINE, JAMES STEPHEN, physician; b. St. Paul, June 14, 1946; s. Ralph Irving and Beverlee Lois (Rockler) F.; m. Meredith Ann Blehert, June 20, 1970; children: Zachary, Esther, Gabriel. BA in Math., U. Minn., 1968, MD, 1972, MS in Biometry, Health Info. Systems, 1977. Intern in medicine St. Paul-Ramsey Hosp., 1972-73; residency U. Minn., Mpls., 1973-77; assoc. prof., dir. info. and specimen processing div. U. Wash. Hosp., Seattle, 1977—; residency dir. Dept. of Lab. Medicine U. Wash., Seattle, 1981—. Editor: (videodisk) Videolibrary of Laboratory Medicine: Atlas of Hemotology, 1985, Acad. Clin. Lab. Physicians and Scientists Directory, 1977—. Mem. Am. Assn. Clin. Chemistry, Acad. Clin. Lab. Physicians and Scientists, Computer Soc. of IEEE. Office: U Wash Hosp SB10 Dept Lab Medicine Seattle WA 98195

FINE, JO-DAVID, dermatologist; b. Louisville, Apr. 9, 1950; s. Lewis and Bernice Rhea (Friedman) F.; m. Catherine Miles Evans, June 3, 1972; children: David, Jeffrey, Kenneth. BS in Chemistry, Yale Coll., 1972; MD with distinction, U. Ky., 1976; MPH in Epidemiology, U. N.C., 1992. Diplomate Am. Bd. Internal Medicine, Am. Bd. Dermatology (gen. and immunologic dermatology). Intern and jr. asst. resident Duke U. Med. Ctr., Durham, N.C., 1976-78; resident dermatology Harvard Med. Sch. and Mass Gen. Hosp., Boston, 1978-80; sr. resident dermatology Harvard Med. Sch. and Lahey Clin. Found., Boston, 1980-81; med. staff fellow dermatology br. Nat. Cancer Inst./NIH, Bethesda, Md., 1981-83; asst. prof. dermatology U. Ala. Sch. of Medicine, Birmingham, 1983-85, assoc. prof. dermatology, 1985-90; assoc. prof. dermatology U. N.C. Sch. Medicine, Chapel Hill, 1990-92, prof. dermatology, 1992—; clin. prof. epidemiology U. N.C. Sch. of Pub. Health, Chapel Hill, 1993—; prin. investigator Nat. Epidermolysis Bullosa Registry, Chapel Hill, 1986—; trustee Dystrophic Epidermolysis Bullosa Rsch. Assn. of Am., Inc., N.Y.C., 1989—; mem. med. sch. admission com. U. N.C. Sch. of Medicine, Chapel Hill, 1990-96; ad hoc reviewer grants NIH, 1986—. Editl. bd.: Clinical and Experimental Dermatology, London, 1994—; dep. editor: Jour. of Investigative Dermatology, 1992-93; editor/author: (book) Bullous Diseases, 1993; contbr. approximately 125 articles to profl. jours. Vice-pres. Yale Club of Ala., Birmingham, 1989; dir. cen. N.C. alumni schs. com., Yale U., New Haven, Conn., 1994—. Recipient Disting. Svc. award Dystrophic Epidermolysis Bullosa Rsch. Assn. of Am., N.Y.C., 1984, New Investigator Rsch. award, NIH, Bethesda, 1985, rsch. grants, 1985—, rsch. grants Vet. Adminstrn., Washington, 1984-88. Fellow Am. Acad. Dermatology, Am. Coll. Physicians, Royal Soc. of Medicine (London); mem. Soc. for Investigative Dermatology, Am. Fedn. for Clin. Rsch., Am. Pub. Health Assn. Jewish. Office: Univ NC Dept Dermatology 3100 Thurston CB #7287 Chapel Hill NC 27599

FINE, LEON GERALD, medical educator, administrator, researcher; b. Cape Town, South Africa, July 16, 1943; arrived in England, July, 1991; s. Matthew and Jeanette (Lipshitz) F.; m. Brenda Sakinovsky, Dec. 20, 1966; children: Michele, Dana. MB ChB, U. Cape Town, 1966. Diplomate Am. Bd. Internal Medicine. Instr. in medicine Albert Einstein Coll. of Medicine, N.Y.C., 1974-75, asst. prof. medicine, 1975-76; asst. prof. medicine U. Miami (Fla.) Sch. Medicine, 1976-78; chief divsn. nepnology UCLA, 1978-91, assoc. prof. medicine, 1978-82, prof. medicine, 1982-91; prof. medicine U. Coll. London, 1991—; head dept. medicine U. Coll., London, 1991-93; head joint dept. medicine UCL and Royal Free Med. Schs., 1994—. Editor: International Yearbook of Nephrology, 1988—, Experimental Nephrology, 1993—; contbr. numerous sci. articles to profl. jours. Recipient Rsch. Career Devel. award NIH, 1977. Fellow ACP, Royal Coll. Physicians U.K., Royal Coll. Physicians Glasgow, Athenaeum Club. Home: 17 Stanhope House, 38 Shepherd's Hill, London N6 5RR, England Office: U Coll London Med Sch, 5 University St, London WCIE 6JJ, England

FINE, MYRON GERALD, urologist; b. Newport News, July 26, 1929; s. Lawrence Stanley and Marjorie Vivian (Samuelson) F.; m. Brooke Bernice Rash, Sept. 2, 1956; children: Aim e Adashek, Lawrence, Joshua. BS, U. Tenn., 1950, MD, 1951. Diplomate Am. Bd. Urology. Intern Sinai Hosp., Balt., Md., 1951-52; resident in gen. surgery Kennedy Gen. VAMTG Hosp., Memphis, 1952-53; resident in urology Charity Hosp. La., New Orleans, 1955-58; pvt. practice Fine & Fine Urology Assocs., Dallas, 1958—; clin. prof. urology U. Tex./Southwestern Med. Sch., Dallas, 1994—. Contbr. articles and abstracts to profl. jours. Capt. U.S. Army, 1953-55. Fellow ACS; mem. AMA, Tex. Med. Assn., Dallas County Med. Soc., Am. Urol. Assn. (South Ctrl. sect.). Jewish. Home: 7108 Briar Cove Dallas TX 75240 Office: Fine & Fine Urology Assocs Barnett Twr Ste 1002 3600 Gaston Ave Dallas TX 75246-1800

FINE, ROBERT M., allergist, immunologist, dermatologist; b. Little Rock, Ark., Jan. 9, 1930. MD, Tulane U., 1955. Diplomate Am. Bd. Allergy & Immunology, Am. Bd. Dermatology. Intern Charity Hosp., New Orleans, 1955-56, resident, 1956-57, 59-61; with Dekalb Med. Ctr., Decatur, Ga., Vets Affairs Med. Ctr., Decatur, Ga.; prof. Emory U., 1986—. Mem. FAS-MOHSMicroS, Am. Acad. Allergy & Immunology, Am. Acad. Dermatology, Am. Coll. Allergy & Immunology, Am. Coll. Physicians, Am. Dermatological Assn. Office: Fine Derm Assoc 2675 N Decatur Rd Ste 601 Decatur GA 30033-6134

FINE, SAMUEL, biomedical engineering educator, consultant; b. Baranowiczach, Poland, Jan. 21, 1925; came to U.S., 1950; s. Abraham and Rose (Perlin) F. B.Applied Sci., U. Toronto, 1946, MD, 1957; SM, MIT 1953. Registered profl. engr., Ont., Can. Intern, E.G. Meyer Hosp., Buffalo, 1957-58; mem. staff rsch. lab. electronics MIT, Cambridge, 1951-53; biomed. engr. NIH, Bethesda, Md., 1958-59; rsch. assoc., assoc. in medicine Brookhaven Nat. Lab., Upton, N.Y., 1959-61; assoc. prof. elec. engring. Northeastern U., Boston, 1961-64; prof. biomed. engring., 1964—, chmn. dept., 1966-88, dir. biomed. engring., 1988—; Klein lectr., 1969; cons. Mass. Dept. Pub. Health, 1966—; cons. NIH, 1975-85; mem. exptl. cardiovascular scis. study sect. NIH, 1978-81; mem. Z136 com. Am. Nat. Stds. Inst., N.Y., 1972—; mem. U.S. adv. group tech. com. Internat. Electrotech. Commn., 1973-78; dir. Advanced Tech. Publs., Newton, Mass., 1968-81, Biometrics, Cambridge, 1968-72. Pres. New Eng. chpt. U. Toronto Alumni, 1968; mem. adv. bd. New Eng. Intercollegiate Sailing, Cambridge, 1981—, Combined Jewish Philanthropies Team, Boston, 1983—; trustee New England Coll. Optometry, 1975-80; cons. Inst. Svcs. Edn., Washington, 1970-75. Served as cadet Royal Can. Elec. and Mech. Engrs., 1945. Grantee NIH, NSF, U.S. Army, U.S. Air Force; recipient Am. Soc. Laser Medicine and Surgery award, 1986. Mem. IEEE (program com. N.E. region 1965-66, chmn. engring. in medicine and biology Boston chpt. 1969, prog. com. electro 1993—), Laser Industry Assn. (founding dir. 1967-71), Soc. Exptl. Pathology, Sigma Xi, Tau Beta Pi, Eta Kappa Nu, Phi Kappa Phi, Zeta Beta Tau (Disting. Service award 1984, faculty advisor). Jewish. Home: 16 Ware St Cambridge MA 02138-4034 Office: Northeastern U 360 Huntington Ave Boston MA 02115-5005

FINEBERG, HARVEY VERNON, physician, educator; b. Pitts., Sept. 15, 1945; s. Saul and Miriam (Pearl) F.; m. Mary Elizabeth Wilson, May 16, 1975; A.B., Harvard U., 1967, M.D., 1972, M.P.P., 1972, Ph.D., 1980. Intern Beth Israel Hosp., Boston, 1972-73; asst. prof. Harvard Sch. Pub. Health, Boston, 1973-78, assoc. prof., 1978-81, prof., 1981—; dean Harvard Sch. Pub. Health, 1984—; physician Harvard Street Health Ctr., 1976-84, East Boston Health Ctr., 1974-76. Co-author: Clinical Decision Analysis, 1980, The Epidemic That Never Was, 1983. Trustee Newton Wellesley Hosp., Mass., 1981-86; study sect. chmn. Nat. Ctr. Health Services Research, Rockville, Md., 1982-85; active Pub. Health Council, Mass., 1976-79; bd. dirs. Am. Found. AIDS Rsch., 1986—. Jr. fellow Harvard U., 1974-75; Mellon fellow, 1976. Mem. Inst. Medicine, Nat. Acad. Scis., Soc. Med. Decision Making (pres. 1980-81). Jewish. Home: 125 Shorneciffe Rd Newton MA 02158-2420 Office: Harvard Sch Pub Health 677 Huntington Ave Boston MA 02115-6028

FINEGOLD, DAVID NEAL, medical educator; b. Pitts., Oct. 5, 1947. BS in Physics, U. Pitts., 1968, MD, 1972. Bd. cert. Am. Bd. Pediat., Am. Bd. Pediat. Endocrinology. Intern and resident Children's Hosp. Pitts., 1972-75; postdoctoral rsch. fellow George S. Cox Med. Rsch. Inst., Hosp. U. Pa., Phila., 1975-77; JDF fellow Children's Hosp. Phila., 1977-78; rsch. assoc. dept. biochemistry and biophysics U. Pa., Phila., 1978-81, asst. prof. pediat. dept. pediat., 1979-81; asst. prof. pediat. dept. pediat. U. Pitts., 1981-88, asst. prof. medicine dept. medicine, 1981-88, assoc. prof. pediat. dept. pediat., 1989—, assoc. prof. medicine dept. medicine, 1989—; clin. assoc. dept. pediat. U. Pa., Phila., 1978-79; asst. physician dept. medicine, Divsn. Endocrinology and Diabetes, Children's Hosp. of Phila., 1978-81, animal rsch. and care com., 1986—, libr. com., 1986—, clin. lab. use com., 1988—, human rights com., 1990—; med. adv. bd. Biocontrol Tech., Inc., 1989—; lectr. and rschr. in field. Contbr. chpts. to books and articles to profl. jours. Mem. Am. Diabetes Assn. (bd. mem. Pa. affiliate 1990—, pres. Pa. affiliate 1990-91, vice chair-vol. devel. com. Pa. affiliate 1991—, chair affiliate rsch. com. 1992—, exec. bd. mem. western Pa. affiliate 1981-90, chmn. profl. edn. com. western Pa. affiliate 1982-86, v.p. western Pa. affiliate 1987-88, pres. western affiliate 1988-90, Recognition award), Am. Fedn. for Clin. Rsch., Am. Soc. Nephrology, Am. Assn. Diabetes Educators, Endocrine Soc., Soc. for Pediat. Rsch., Soc. for Inherited Metabolic Disease, Lawson Wilkins Pediat. Endocrine Soc. Office: Divsn Endocrinology Childrens Hosp Pitts 3705 Fifth at DeSoto St Pittsburgh PA 15213

FINEGOLD, IRA, immunologist, allergist; b. N.Y., June 29, 1938. MD, U. Chgo.-Pritzker Sch. Medicine, 1963. Diplomate Am. Bd. Internal Medicine, Am. Bd. Allergy & Immunology. Intern Bronx Mcpl. Hosp. Ctr., N.Y., 1963-64, resident medicine, 1964-65; resident medicine Montefiore Hosp., N.Y., 1967-68; resident allergy Roosevelt Hosp., N.Y., 1968-69; fellow immunology Nat. Cancer Inst.-NIH, Bethesda, 1965-67; assoc. attending physician St. Luke's Roosevelt Hosp., N.Y., 1994—, Beth Israel Med. Ctr., N.Y., 1994—; chief allergy sect. Roosvelt St. Lukes Med. Ctr., N.Y.C. Mem. AMA, Am. Acad. Allergy & Immunology, Am. Coll. Allergy & Immunology, Am. Coll. Physicians. Office: 25 Central Park West-1N New York NY 10023

FINESTONE, ALBERT JUSTIN, medical educator, dean; b. May 12, 1921; m. Alma Perch, 1951; children: Toby Gail Grubman, Jay David, Audrey Kanoff. AB, Temple U., 1942, MD, 1945, MSc in Internal Medicine, 1951. Diplomate Am. Bd. Internal Medicine. Intern Temple U. Hosp., Phila., 1945-46, resident in medicine, 1959-51, co-chmn. utilization com., 1964-74; fellow in pathology Georgetown U. Hosp., Washington, 1948-49; head metabolic svc. Episcopal Hosp. of Phila., 1954-72; asst. dean continuing med. edn. Sch. Medicine Temple U., Phila., 1972-79, chmn. biomed. scis. rev. com., 1973-81, prof., 1979, assoc. dean continuing med. edn., 1979-91, assoc. dean emeritus continuing med. edn., 1991, dir. Inst. on Aging, 1991—, additional qualification geriatrics, 1988, co-dir. geriatric edn. ctr., 1992—; geriatrics cons. Pa. Blue Shield, 1989—, mem. corp., 1988—. Mem. bd. editl. cons. Clin. Therapeutics, 1983; cons. editor Hosp. Medicine, Geriatrics, 1990; contbr. numerous articles to profl. jours. Capt. M.C., U.S. Army, 1946-48. Fellow ACP, Coll. Physicians of Phila.; mem. AMA (rep. med. schs. sect. 1988—), Am. Psychosomatic Soc., Am. Geriatrics Soc., Pa. Med. Soc. (commn. on accreditation 1984-90), Phila. County Med. Soc. (bd. dirs. 1978-84, 91-95, chmn. med. edn. com. 1978-84, 91-95, del. Pa. Med. Soc. 1980-95, sec. 1987-88), Med. Alumni Assn. Temple U. Sch. Medicine (Man of Yr. 1976), Soc. Med. Coll. Dirs. Continuing Med. Edn., Alliance for Continuing Med. Edn., Assn. Dir. Acad. Geriatric Medicine Programs, Alpha Omicron Alpha. Home: 606 Webb Rd Elkins Park PA 19027-2538 Office: Temple U Cancer Ctr Bldg 3322 110 Broad St Philadelphia PA 19140

FINGERHUT, ABE, surgeon; b. New Brunswick, N.J., Nov. 12, 1939; came to France, 1961; s. Samuel and Rose (Ranz) F.; m. Arlette Tomasini, Nov., 1970 (dec. May 1991); children: Anne, Stephane. BA, U. Pa., 1961; MD, U. Paris, 1975. Head surgeon Hopital Intercommunal, Poissy, France, 1975-90. Translator Gastroenterologie Clinique et Biologique, 1980, Annals of Vascular Surgery, 1983—; cons. editor World Jour. of Surgery, 1987. Mem. editorial adv. bd. Am. Jour. Surgery, 1990—, European Jour. Surgery, 1991. Avocations: mountaineering, ski mountaineering, alpinism. Home: 6 Clos Baron,, 78112 Fourqueux France Office: Centre Hospitalier Intercommunal,, 78303 Poissy France

FINK, ABEL KING, psychologist, educator; b. N.Y.C., Aug. 5, 1927; s. Max and Esther (Levy) F.; m. Billey Levinson, 1959 (div. 1990); children: Elias, Mira, Micah; m. Madeline Bondanza, 1993. BA, Bklyn. Coll.-CUNY, 1949; MA, Columbia U., 1950, EdD, 1956. Elem. tchr. Roosevelt Sch., Stamford, Conn., 1952-54; vis. prof. U. P.R., Rio Piedras, 1964-65; ednl. cons. N.Y.C., Buffalo, 1955—; from asst. prof. to prof. ednl. founds. Buffalo State U. Coll., 1956-95, emeritus prof., 1995—. Screenwriter: (films) Warm-up to Psychodrama, Generation Gap; (TV programs) The Importance of Feedback, Finding One's Place in a Group; contbr. articles to profl. jours. Co-dir. Citizens Coun. on Human Rels., Buffalo. SUNY Rsch. Found. grantee. Fellow Am. Soc. for Group Psychotherapy and Psychodrama; mem. APA, Inter-Am. Soc. of Psychology, Soc. for Psychol. Study of Social Issues, Psychol. Assn. Western N.Y. (pres. 1971, archivist), Torch Internat., Phi Delta Kappa. Office: Buffalo State U Coll Bacon Hall Buffalo NY 14222-1095

FINK, CHARLES AUGUSTIN, behavioral systems scientist; b. McAllen, Tex., Jan. 1, 1929; s. Charles Adolph and Mary Nellie (Bonneau) F.; m. Ann Heslen, June 1, 1955 (dec. June 1981); children: Patricia A., Marianne E., Richard G., Gerard A. AA, Pan-Am. U., 1948; BS, Marquette U., 1950; postgrad., George Washington Med. Ctr., Walter Reed Army Med. Ctr., 1969-70, No. Va. C.C., 1973, George Mason U., 1974; MA, Cath. U. Am., 1979. Journalist UP and Ft. Worth Star-Telegram, 1950-52; commd. 2d lt. U.S. Army, 1952, advanced through grades to lt. col., 1966, various positions telecommunications, 1952-56, instr., 1956-58, exec. project mgmt., 1958-62, def. analysis and rsch., 1962-65, fgn. mil. rels., 1965-67, def. telecommunications exec., 1967-69, chief planning, budget and program control office Def. Satellite Communications Program, Def. Communications Agy., 1969-72, ret., 1972; pvt. practice cons. managerial behavior Falls Church, Va., 1972-77; pres. Behavioral Systems Sci. Orgn. (and predecessor firms), Falls Church, 1978—; leader family group dynamics, 1958-67; home hemodialysis technician, 1969-81; pub (jour.) Circle, 1985—; computer program cons. Hubble Space Telescope Servicing Mission, NASA, 1993. Developer hierarchial theory of human behavior, 1967—, uses in behavioral, social and biol. sci. and their applications, 1972—, behavioral causal modeling research methodology, 1974—, computer-aided behavior systems coaching for persons and orgns., 1982—, telecoaching, 1989; microbiol. chromatographic profiling, 1989—; public domain Portable Personal Health Record, 1994; adv. for copyrighting computer graphics displays and multi-media communications in scis. Adv. bd. Holy Redeemer Roman Cath. Ch., Bangkok, Thailand, St. Philip's Ch., Falls Church, Va., 1971-73. Decorated Army Commendation medals, Joint Services Commendation medal; named to Fink Hall of Fame, 1982; recipient Behavior Modeling award Internat. Congress Applied Systems Rsch. and Cybernetics, 1980, Mission Pin award NASA, 1993. Mem. AAAS, Nat. Genealogical Soc., Internat. Soc. Systems Scis., Am. Soc. Cybernetics, Internat. Assn. Cybernetics, Internat. Network Social Network Analysis, Assn. U.S. Army, Ret. Officers Assn., Finks Internat. (v.p. 1981—), KC. Home: 3305 Brandy Ct Falls Church VA 22042-3705 Office: PO Box 2051 Falls Church VA 22042-0051

FINK, CHESTER WALTER, pediatrician, rheumatologist, educator; b. N.Y.C., May 6, 1928; s. Murray and Estelle (Halbfinger) F.; m. Dorothy Wiletts Crate, Dec. 3, 1955; children: Ellen L., Curtis M., Murray G. BA, Duke U., 1947, MD, 1951. Intern King's County Hosp., N.Y.C., 1952; resident in pediatrics Upstate Med. Ctr., Syracuse, N.Y., 1953, Univ. Hosp. Cleve., 1954, 57; from instr. to prof. pediatrics U. Tex. Southwestern Med. Sch., Dallas, 1957—; dir. pediatric rheumatology Tex. Scottish Rite Hosp. for Children, 1959—; chief pediatric rheumatology, Children's Med. Ctr., Dallas, 1987—. Contbr. articles to profl. jours. Served to capt. U.S. Army, 1954-56. Master Am. Coll. Rheumatology; mem. Am. Pediatric Soc., Soc. Pediatric Research, Internat. League Assns. Rheumatology (exec. com., chmn. pediatric standing com.), Sigma Xi. Home: 4432 Hockaday Dr Dallas TX 75229-2909 Office: U Tex 5323 Harry Hines Blvd Dallas TX 75235-7200

FINK, DAVID LEONARD, surgeon; b. St. Louis, June 6, 1936; s. Sidney Fink and Estelle Esses Goldstein; m. Frances Carole Bower, June 13, 1965; children: Dana Lynne, Denise Lysette. BA, Columbia Coll., 1957; MD, Cornell U., N.Y.C., 1961. Diplomate Am. Bd. Surgery. Resident in surgery St. Luke's Hosp. Med. Ctr., N.Y.C., 1961-64, U. Wis. Med. Ctr., Madison, 1964-66; pvt. practice, Paterson, N.J., 1970—; chief exec. officer Gen. Surgeons North Jersey, P.A., Paterson, 1970—; chief surgery Barnert Meml. Hosp., Paterson, 1982-86, pres. med. staff, 1988; assoc. clin. prof. surgery Seton Hall Postgrad. Sch. Medicine; asst. clin. prof. surgery U. Medicine and Dentistry of N.J. Maj. U.S. Army, 1966-70. Decorated Army Commendation medal. Fellow ACS, Soc. of Surgeons of N.J.; mem. Vascular Soc. N.J., Ea. Vascular Soc., Southeastern Surg. Soc., Cornell U. Med. Alumni Assn. (bd. dirs. 1986-89), Stuyvesant Yacht Club. Office: Gen Surgeons North Jersey 707 Broadway Paterson NJ 07514-1425

FINK, HOWARD DAVID, pediatrician; b. N.Y.C., Sept. 29, 1928; s. Frank E. and Eva (Tamor) F.; m. Marcia Klein, June 22, 1952; children: Andrea Hoogstraten, Susan Caplan. BA, U. Louisville, 1949, MD, 1954. Diplomate Am. Bd. Pediat. Rotating intern Kings County Hosp., Bklyn., 1954-55, intern in pediat., 1955-56, resident in pediat., 1956-57; chief of pediat. U.S. Army Med. Corps, Ft. Hood, Tex., 1957-59; pvt. practice, pediat. Milford, Conn., 1959—; assoc. clin. prof. pediat. Yale U. Sch. Medicine, New Haven, 1983—. Mem. Milford (Conn.) Bd. Health, 1962—, chmn. 1964-71. Fellow Am. Acad. Pediat.; mem. AMA, Conn. State Med. Soc., New Haven County Med. Soc., New England Pediatric Soc., Asantawae Lodge. Office: 75 New Haven Ave Milford CT 06460

FINK, JOEL CHARLES, dermatologist; b. Lebanon, Pa., June 29, 1922; s. Isadore Harry and Rose (Cohn) F.; m. Selma Florence Fink, Dec. 28, 1946 (dec. Dec. 1979); children: Ellen, Myles, Janet, Bruce, Paul; m. Carol Kaplan, Aug. 31, 1980. BS, U. Ala., 1943; MD, U. Md., 1947. Diplomate Am. Bd. Dermatology. Commd. 1st lt. U.S. Army, 1950, advanced through grades to maj., 1954, resigned, 1954; intern Walter Reed Army Hosp., Washington, 1947-48, resident, 1948-50; resident Brooke Army Hosp., San Antonio, 1952-53; pvt. practice Smithtown, N.Y., 1955-82, Phoenix, 1982--. Fellow Am. Acad. Dermatology; mem. Phoenix Dermatology Soc. (pres. 1987—), Southwestern Dermatology Soc. Republican. Home: 9760 E San Salvador Dr Scottsdale AZ 85258-5621 Office: Ste 100 4232 E Cactus Rd Phoenix AZ 85032-7615

FINK, LOUIS MAIER, pathologist, educator; b. Bklyn., Mar. 28, 1942; s. Jacob and Pauline (Kurtz) F. B.A., Boston U., 1961; M.D., Albany Med. Coll., 1965. Diplomate Am. Bd. Pathology. Intern U. Colo. Med. Ctr., 1965-66, resident, 1966-67; resident in pathology Coll. Physicians and Surgeons, Columbia-Presbyn. Hosp., Columbia U., N.Y.C., 1969-70, asst. prof., 1970; asst. prof. U. Colo. Med. Sch., 1972-77, 1977-81; prof. pathology Vanderbilt U., Nashville, 1981—, U. Ark. for Med. Scis., 1988—; chief lab. service John L. McClellan Meml. Veterans Hosp.-Med. Ctr., Little Rock. Mem. AAAS, Am. Assn. Cell Biology, Am. Assn. Pathologists, Coll. Am. Pathologists, Harvey Soc., Internat. Acad. Pathologists. Office: U Ark Sch Med Dept Pathology 4301 W Markham St Little Rock AR 72205-7101 also: J L McClellan VA Hosp 4300 W 7th St Little Rock AR 72205

FINKEL, MADELON LUBIN, epidemiology and public health educator; b. Mt. Vernon, N.Y., Oct. 11, 1949; d. Ralph H. and Lorraine (Alper) L.; m. David J. Finkel, Mar. 25, 1973; 1 child, Rebecca Anne. BA, NYU, 1971, MPA, 1973, PhD, 1980. Staff assoc. Columbia U. Sch. Pub. Health, N.Y.C., 1974-75; cons. Dept. Bio Statistics N.Y.C. Dept. Health, 1975-77; rsch. assoc. Cornell U. Med. Coll., N.Y.C., 1977-80, asst. prof., 1980-86, clin. assoc. prof., 1986-93, clin. prof. pub. health, 1993-95, prof. clin. pub. health, 1995—; pres., CEO Second Opinion Cons., Millwood, N.Y., 1986-93; v.p. MedSearch Network, Denver, 1991—; cons. Mobil Oil Corp, N.Y.C., 1979, Amalgamated Meat Cutters, Queens, N.Y., 1976-86, N.Y.C. Bd. Edn., Bklyn., 1976-80, Am. Coun. Sci. & Health, 1996—; commentator Nat. Pub. Radio, Washington, 1980. Author: Second Opinion Elective Surgery, 1981, Health Care Cost Management, 1985, 3d edit., 1996, Retiree Health Caree Benefits, 1988; editor, author: Delivery of Surgical Health Care, 1988, also others; contbr. numerous articles to profl. jours. Mem. Am. Coll. Epidemiology, Assn. Health Svcs. Rsch., Am. Pub. Health Assn., Internat. Epidemiol. Assn. Home: 292 Sarles Ln Pleasantville NY 10570-1947

FINKEL, MARTIN A., pediatrician, educator; b. Phila., Aug. 22, 1948; s. Harold H. and Ruth L. (Feldman) F.; m. Bonnie B. Bazilian. BS in Edn., Millersville State Coll., 1970; DO, Mich. State U., 1974. Diplomate Am. Bd. Osteo. Pediatrics. Asst. prof., assoc. prof. pediatrics U. Medicine and Dentistry N.J., Stratford, 1979-95, prof. clin. pediatrics, 1995—. Contbr. articles to profl. jours. Co-chair gov.'s task force on child abuse and neglect State of N.J., Trenton, 1989—. Recipient N.J. Pride award N.J. Monthly Mag., 1990, Commrs. award U.S. Dept. HHS, 1991, Humanitarian award Sunshine Found., 1986, Leadership award NASW, 1994. Fellow Am. Coll. Osteopathic Pediatrics (v.p.). Office: UMDNJ Ctr for Childrens Support 42 E Laurel Rd Ste 3400 Stratford NJ 08084

FINKELSTEIN, JACK, JR., biomedical company executive; b. Houston, Mar. 3, 1952; s. Jack and Carol Sue (Nathan) F.; m. Linda Marie Parisi, June 11, 1978; children: Laura, Emily. BBA, U. Tex., 1975. Pres. Brookstone Properties, Houston, 1978-82; v.p. Alpha I Biomedicals, Washington, 1982-84, pres., chief exec. officer, 1984—, also vice chmn. bd. dirs.; pres., chief exec. officer Viral Techs. Inc., 1986-89, also bd. dirs.; chief exec. officer Cryomedical Scis. Inc., Bethesda, Md., 1990—; also bd. dirs. Cryomedical Scis. Inc.; bd. dirs. Finkelstein Found., Houston.

FINKELSTEIN, JAMES DAVID, physician; b. N.Y.C., Oct. 16, 1933; s. Harry and Sylvia Z. (Bernstein) F.; m. Barbara Joan Eisenberg, Dec. 12, 1959; children—Donna Ilene, Laura Helene. A.B., Harvard U., 1954; M.D., Columbia U., 1958. Diplomate Am. Bd. Internal Medicine. Intern, resident in medicine Presbyn. Hosp., N.Y.C., 1958-61; fellow in gastroenterology Columbia U., N.Y.C., 1961-63. Chief med. service VA Med. Ctr., Washington, 1979—, chief gastroenterology, 1970-79, assoc. chief staff for research, 1975-79, med. investigator, 1970-75, clin. investigator, 1965-68, chief biochemistry research lab., 1965—; cons. Children's Hosp., Washington, 1968-85; prof. medicine George Washington U., 1969—; clin. prof. medicine Georgetown U., 1981—; prof. medicine Howard U., Washington, 1983—; mem. Nutrition Study sect. NIH, 1972-78. Contbr. articles biochemistry and nutrition of methionine to profl. jours. Served as surgeon USPHS, 1963-65. Recipient F.P. Gay Research award Columbia U., N.Y.C., 1956; Arthur S. Fleming award Jr. C of C., Washington, 1971; NIH grantee, 1966-95. Mem. Am. Soc. for Clin. Investigation, Am. Gastroent. Assn., Assn. of Am. Physicians, Am. Inst. Nutrition, Am. Soc. Clin. Nutrition, Am. Fedn. Clin. Research. Club: Harvard. Office: VA Med Ctr 50 Irving St NW Washington DC 20422-0001

FINKELSTEIN, SILVIO, medical educator. MD, U. Buenos Aires, 1958; MSc, Ohio State U., 1965. Aviation medicine physician Argentine Civil Aviation Air Base, 1958-63; resident in aerospace medicine Ohio State U., Columbus, 1963-66; sr. staff scientist Lovelace Found. for Med. Edn. and Rsch., 1966-71; aviation medicine officer Internat. Civil Aviation Orgn., 1971-75, chief, aviation medicine sect., 1975-94; vis. prof. in aviation medicine, Mex. Govt., 1966-70, vis. lectr. 1968-70; FAA aviation Med. examiner, 1966-70; cons. to med. dept. Iberia Airlines, Spain; observer Aviation Med. Rev. Bd., Ministry of Transport, Ottawa, Can., 1975—; liaison officer on internat. flight safety, WHO. Developer, supr., prof. first regional course in aviation medicine for designated med. examiners, Buenos Aires, and similar courses elsewhere. Recipient Gold medal Argentine Civil Aviation Official Air Base, 1972, Airlines Med. Dirs. Assn. Ann. award, Aerospace Med. Assn., 1992. Fellow Aerospace Med. Assn. (scientific program com., chair air transport medicine com. 1981-84, internat. activities com., v.p. 1976-77, John A. Tamislea award 1978, Harry G. Moseley award 1985, Eric Liljencrantz award 1995); hon. mem. Argentine, Can., Egyptian, Korean, and Mex. Aeromed. Assns.; mem. Internat. Acad. Aviation and Space Medicine (scholarship com., dir. 1984-87, 1st v.p. 1989-91, pres. 1991-93). Home: Ottawa, Canada

FINLEY, GORDON ELLIS, psychology educator; b. Evanston, Ill., July 30, 1939; married; 2 children. BA, Antioch Coll., 1962; MA, Harvard U., 1965, PhD, 1968. Asst. prof. U. B.C., 1967-69, U. Toronto, 1969-71; vis. asst. prof. U. Calif.-Berkeley, 1971-72; assoc. prof. psychology, Fla. Internat. U., Miami, 1972-76, prof., 1976—; exec. sec. U.S. and Can. Interamerican Soc. Psychology, 1974-76; sec. gen. XVI Interamerican Congress Psychology, 1976. Editor 2 books; contbr. articles to profl. jours., chpts. to books; consulting editor Jour. Cross-Cultural Psychology, 1974-90, Internat. Jour. Intercultural Rel., 1988—; editor Revista Interamericana de Psicologia/Interamerican Jour. Psychology, 1977-82, consulting editor 1983—; mem. bd. editorial commentators Behavioral and Brain Scis., 1978-82. Grantee U. Chgo., 1965, Ednl. Rsch. Inst. B.C., 1968-69, Can. Coun., 1969-71, Fla. Internat. U., 1972-76, NIMH 1975-76, Fla. Internat. U. Found., 1975-80, Nat. Inst. Aging 1977, Fla. Internat. U./Fla. Atlantic U., 1980-81, Fla. Internat. U. Latin Am. and Caribbean Ctr. 1981-84, Fla. Internat. U. Coll. Arts and Scis. 1981-92, AID, 1982-84, Southeast Fla. Ctr. for the Aging, 1985, William T. Grant Found., 1991-92. Mem. APA, InterAm. Soc. Psychology (v.p. for U.S. and Can. 1983-85), Internat. Assn. Cross-Cultural Psychology (treas. 1981-82), Soc. for Rsch. in Child Devel., Nat. Coun. on Family Rels. Office: Dept Psychology Fla Internat U Miami FL 33199

FINLEY, WAYNE HOUSE, medical educator; b. Goodwater, Ala., Apr. 7, 1927; s. Byron Bruce and Lucille (House) F.; m. Sara Will Crews, July 6, 1952; children: Randall Wayne, Sara Jane. BS, Jacksonville State U., 1948; MA, U. Ala., 1950, MS, 1955, PhD, 1958, MD, 1960; postgrad., U. Uppsala, Sweden, 1961-62. Cert. clin. cytogenetics Am. Bd. Med. Genetics, 1983. Sci. tchr. High Sch., Tuscaloosa, Ala., 1949-51; intern U. Ala. Hosps. and Clinics, 1960-61; from asst. prof. to assoc. prof. pediat. U. Ala. Sch. Medicine, 1962-70; prof., 1970—; from asst. prof. to assoc. prof. biochemistry U. Ala. Sch. Medicine, 1965-77; prof., 1977—; asst. prof. physiology and biophysics U. Ala. Sch. Medicine, 1968-75, assoc. prof., 1975—, prof. epidemiology, pub. health and preventive medicine, 1975—, adj. prof. biology, 1980—, dir. Lab. Med. Genetics, 1966-96; chmn. med. Student Rsch. Day, 1965-75, chmn. faculty coun. Sch. Medicine, 1977-78, 84-87; dir. med. genetics grad. program U. Ala. Sch. Medicine, 1983-96, dir. med. genetics program, 1978—; chmn. Carey Phillips Travel Fellowship, 1972—; nat. adv. rsch. resources coun. NIH-HEW, 1977-80; sr. scientist Comprehensive Cancer Ctr., Cystic Fibrosis Rsch. Ctr.; bd. dirs. Southeastern Regional Genetics Group; chmn. steering com. Reynolds Hist. Libr. Assocs., 1981—, Carmichael Fund for Grad. Students, 1989—; faculty rep. U. Ala. Sys. Bd. Trustees, 1995-96; senator U. Ala. Faculty Senate, 1995—. Contbr. articles on human malformations and clin. cytogenetics to tech. jours. With AUS, 1945-46, 51-53; lt. col. Res.; ret. Recipient Med. award Ala. Assn. Retarded Children, 1969, Turlington award, 1982, Disting. Faculty Lectr. award U. Ala. Med. Ctr., 1983, Wayne H. and Sara C. Finley chair in med. genetics U. Ala., Birmingham, 1986, Alumnus of Yr. award Jacksonville State U., 1989, Portrait Reynolds Libr., 1991. Fellow Am. Coll. Med. Genetics (founder, edn. com. 1993—, program dir. 1996); mem. AMA (Physicians Recognition award 1971, 75, 81, 84, 87, 90, 93), AAAS, N.Y. Acad. Scis., Soc. Exptl. Biology and Medicine, Am. Inst. Chemists, Am. Fedn. Clin. Rsch., Am. Soc. Human Genetics, So. Med. Assn., So. Soc. Pediat. Rsch., Med. Assn. Ala. (counsellor 1990—), Jefferson County Med. Soc. (maternal and child health com. 1975-79, chmn. 1976-77, pres. 1983), Jefferson County Pediat. Soc., Caduceus Club (pres. 1984-86), U. Ala. Sch. Medicine Alumni Assn. (pres. 1974-75, Disting. Alumni award 1978), Greater Birmingham Area C. of C. (bd. dirs. 1983-86), Newcomen Soc., Kiwanis (pres. Shades Valley 1973-74), Rotary, Sigma Xi, Kappa Delta Pi, Phi Delta Kappa, Alpha Omega Alpha, Phi Beta Pi, Omicron Delta Kappa. Baptist. Home: 3412 Brookwood Rd Birmingham AL 35223-2023 Office: U Ala Lab Med Genetics Univ Station Birmingham AL 35294-0017

FINN, ALBERT FRANK, physician; b. Huntington, N.Y., Sept. 30, 1956; s. Albert F. and Margaret F. (May) F.; m. Anna M. Cannella, July 19, 1982; children: Anastasia, Alexandria, Abigail. BS cum laude, St. John's U., 1980; MD cum laude, SUNY, Syracuse, 1984. Diplomate Am. Bd. Internal Medicine. Clin. asst. instr. SUNY, Stony Brook, 1985-91, cons. divsn. lab. medicine Med. Ctr., 1988-91, clin. asst. prof. medicine, 1991-92, head sect. on allergy, 1991-92; clin. asst. prof. medicine, microbiology and immunology Med. U. S.C., Charleston, 1992—; adj. asst. prof. St. John's U., N.Y.C., 1991-92. Contbr. articles to profl. jours. Mem. com. on advance cardiac life support Am. Heart Assn., Nassau County, N.Y., 1988-92; mem. Am. Lung Assn., S.C., 1992—. Mem. ACP (bd. rev. course allergy and immunology sect. 1992), Am. Acad. Allergy and Immunology (task force 1994), Am. Soc. Clin. Pathology (course dir. lyme borreliosis 1989-92). Office: Allergy & Asthma Ctrs of Charleston PA 9213-A University Blvd Charleston SC 29406

FINNBERG, ELAINE AGNES, psychologist, editor; b. Bklyn., Mar. 2, 1948; d. Benjamin and Agnes Montgomery (Evans) F.; m. Rodney Lee Herndon, Mar. 1, 1981; 1 child, Andrew Marshal. BA in Psychology, L.I. U., 1969; MA in Psychology, New Sch. for Social Rsch., 1973; PhD in Psychology, Calif. Sch. Profl. Psychology, 1981. Diplomate Am. Bd. Forensic Examiners, Am. Bd. Forensic Medicine, Am. Bd. Med. Psychotherapists and Psychodiagnosticians, Am. Bd. Disability Analysts; lic. psychologist, Calif. Rsch. asst. in med. sociology Med. Coll. Cornell U., N.Y.C., 1969-70; med. abstractor USV Pharm. Corp., Tuckahoe, N.Y., 1970-71, Coun. for Tobacco Rsch., N.Y.C., 1971-77; editor, writer Found. of Thanatology Columbia U., N.Y.C., 1971-76, cons. family studies program cancer ctr. Coll. Physicians &Surgeons, 1973-74; dir. grief psychology and bereavement counseling San Francisco Coll. Mortuary Scis., 1977-81; rsch. assoc. dept. epidemiology and internat. health U. Calif., San Francisco, 1979-81, asst. clin. prof. dept. family and community medicine, 1985-93, assoc. clin. prof., dept. family and community medicine, 1993—; chief psychologist Natividad Med. Ctr., Salinas, Calif., 1984—; profl. adv. coun. Am. Bd. Disability Analysts; asst. chief psychiatry svc. Natividad Med. Ctr., 1985—, acting chief psychiatry, 1988-89, vice-chair medicine dept., 1991-93, sec.-treas. med. staff, 1992-94; cons. med. staff Salinas Valley Meml. Hosp., 1991—, Mee Meml. Hosp., 1996—. Editor: The California Psychologist, 1988-95; editor Jour. of Thanatology, 1972-76, Cathexis, 1976-81. Mem. govs. adv. bd. Agnews Devel. Ctr., San Jose, Calif., 1988-96, chair, 1989-91, 94-95. Fellow Am. Bd. Med. Psychotherapists and Psychodiagnosticians (diplomate); mem. APA, Nat. Register Health Svc. Providers in Psychology, Calif. Psychol. Assn. (Disting. Svc. award 1989), Soc. Behavioral Medicine, Mid-Coast Psychol. Assn. (sec. 1985, treas. 1986, pres. 1987, Disting. Svc. to Psychology award 1993). Office: Natividad Med Ctr PO Box 81611 1330 Natividad Rd Salinas CA 93912-1611

FINNE, CHARLES OSVILLE, III, surgeon; b. Lynchburg, Va., Mar. 12, 1946; s. Charles Osville Jr. and Geraldine (Renfroe) F.; m. Rebecca Jane Schreckhise, Aug. 26, 1972; 1 child, Charles Osville IV. BA, Vanderbilt U., 1968; MD, U. Va., 1972; postgrad., U. Minn., 1981. Diplomate Am. Bd. Surgery, Am. Bd. Colon and Rectal Surgery. Intern Virginia Mason Med. Ctr., Seattle, 1972-73; resident in gen. surgery Brooke Army Med. Ctr., 1974-78; Clin. instr. U. Minn. Med. Sch., Mpls., 1984-89, clin. asst. prof., 1989—; surgeon Colon and Rectal Surgery Assocs., Mpls., 1983—; chief colorectal sect. dept. surgery VA Med. Ctr., Mpls., 1986-91; chmn. dept. surgery Abbott-Northwestern Hosp., Mpls., 1990-91, Fairview Ridges Hosp., Burnsville, Minn., 1995-96. Contbr. chpts. to books, articles to profl. jours. Lt. col. U.S. Army, 1971-83. Fellow ACS, Am. Soc. Colon and Rectal Surgeons; mem. Am. Soc. for Gastrointestinal Endoscopy. Home: 6900 W 105th St Bloomington MN 55438-2183 Office: Colon and Rectal Surg Assoc 2545 Chicago Ave # 507 Minneapolis MN 55404-4545

FINNEGAN, WALTER JAMES, orthopedic surgeon, lawyer; b. Orange, N.J., Aug. 11, 1944; s. James J. and Margaret M. (Kelly) F.; m. Eleanor Finnegan, Nov. 2, 1963 (div. Oct. 1976); children: Robert, Kathleen, Tracey; m. Peggy Ginter, Dec. 28, 1979; children: Sarah, Drew. BS in Chemistry, Seton Hall U., 1965; MD, Jefferson Med. Coll., 1969; JD, Nova U., 1986. Diplomate Am. Bd. Orthopedic Surgery. Med. intern Univ. Hosp., U. Mich., Ann Arbor, 1969-70; resident orthopedic surgery U. Pa., Phila., 1972-76, chief resident, 1975-76; pvt. practice Orthopaedic Assocs., Allentown, Pa., 1976-83, Allentown, 1986—; staff, mem. bylaws com. Sacred Heart Hosp., Allentown; courtesy staff, former mem. med. exec. com., chmn. credentials com. Lehigh Valley Hosp., Allentown; orthopaedic cons. Muhlenberg Coll., Allentown, 1977-83; former cons. Good Shepherd Rehab. Hosp., Allentown. Contbr. articles to med. jours. Lt. comdr. USPHS, 1970-72. Full tuition scholar Jefferson Med. Coll.; recipient DeForest Willard Outstanding Performance award Univ. Hosp., U. Pa. 1976. Mem. ACS, Am. Acad. Orthopaedic Surgeons, Eastern Orthopaedic Assn., Pa. Orthopaedic Soc., Lehigh Valley Orthopaedic Soc., Lehigh County Med. Soc., Internat. Back Pain Soc., Am. Coll. Legal Medicine, Alpha Omega Alpha, Delta Epsilon Sigma. Office: Kraynick and Finnegan MDs 40 S Cedar Crest Blvd Allentown PA 18104-5912

FINNERTY, FRANCES MARTIN, medical administrator; b. Asheville, N.C., Dec. 23, 1936; d. Robert James and Elizabeth Howerton (Babbitt) Martin; m. Richard Phillip Caputo, Sept. 23, 1961 (div. 1974); m. Frank A. Finnerty Jr., July 26, 1975; children: Jonathan, Robert, Richard. Student, Mary Washington Coll., 1954-55, Croft Coll., 1955-57. Dist. mgr. Bus. Census Dept. Commerce, Suitland, Md., 1969-71; program coord. Georgetown U. D.C. Gen. Hosp., Washington, 1972-76; clin. mgr. Hypertension Ctr. Washington, 1976-82; project dir. PharmaKinetic Clin. Rsch. Labs., Balt., 1983; dir. mktg. Classic Glass, Alexandra, Va., 1984-86; office adminstr. Frank A. Finnerty Jr., M.D., Washington, 1987—; cons. U.S. Census, U.S. Army, The Pentagon, Washington, 1969-70; cons. mapping ops. U.S. Census, Prince Georges County, Md., 1970; cons. paramedics pers. Merck Sharpe & Dohme, West Point, Pa., 1974. Contbr. articles to profl. jours. Recipient Cmty. Svc. award Dist. of Columbia, 1980. Mem. Am. Art League (Disting. Artist award 1993), Nat. Assn. Women in Arts, Dist. Med. Soc. Wives. Home: 519 E Front St New Bern NC 28560

FINNEY, BETTY JANE, psychology educator; b. N.Y.C., Apr. 11, 1926; d. James Phillip and Agnes Campbell (Fenwick) Mackey; m. Robert W. Finney, Dec. 16, 1948 (div. June 1971); children: Robbin L. Finney Hobbins, R. William Jr., Wendy, David C. BA, Flora Stone Mather Coll., 1946; MA, Western Res. U., 1958; PhD, Case Western Res. U., 1968. Tchr. pub. schs. Ohio, 1946-56; dean of girls Willoughby (Ohio)-Eastlake Jr. High Sch., 1956-58, asst. prin., 1958-63; instr. Cuyahoga Community Coll., Ohio, 1964-65; assoc. prof. psychology Millersville (Pa.) U., 1968-71, prof. psychology, 1971—; owner Psychol. Assocs., Pa., 1971-79; pvt. practice Lancaster, 1971—; rsch. cons. Lancaster Cleft Palate, 1969-71. Bd. dirs. Lancaster Coun. Alcohol and Drug Abuse, 1979-83, Hospice, Lancaster, 1979-83, Housing for People with AIDS, Lancaster, 1988—, United Way Lancaster, 1988-92. Mem. APA. Democrat. Episcopalian. Home: 416 Stonegate Ct Millersville PA 17551-2102 Office: Millersville U Byerly Hall Millersville PA 17551

FINNEY, ROY PELHAM, JR., urologist, surgeon, inventor; b. Gaffney, S.C., Dec. 7, 1924; s. Roy P. Finney Sr. and Mary Frances (Cannon) Woodard; m. Kay Harkness, Apr. 5, 1962; children: Wright C., James L., Joella R., Gray, Kevin. MD, Med. U. S.C., 1952. Diplomate: Am. Bd. Urology. Resident in urology Johns Hopkins U., Balt., 1952-57; prof. surg. urology U. South Fla., Tampa, 1972-84, dir. div. urology, 1972-84; ret. Designer and inventor implantable prostheses incontinence device inflatable penile prostheses treatment impotence, Double J ureteral stent, developer new surg. procedures treatment impotence; patentee in field. Fellow ACS; mem. Am. Urology Assn., Soc. Internationale D'Urologie, Internat. Continence Soc., Urodynamic Soc. Republican. Home: 4382 Cortez Blvd Spring Hill FL 34607-1201

FINSTERBUSCH, TAMMY JILL, physician assistant; b. Wilkes-Barre, Pa., Apr. 19, 1963; d. Murray Fischer and Harolyn Gay (Hertz) Thomas; m. Martin C. Finsterbusch, Jr., Sept. 5, 1993; children: Hannah Ruth, Emily Marie. BS in Health Scis., Touro Coll., 1985; cert. physician asst., Nat. Com. Cert. Physician Assts., 1986. Physician asst. neonatal intensive care Health Sci. Ctr. at Bklyn., 1985-88, Geisinger Med. Ctr., Danville, Pa., 1988-92, Meth. Hosp., Phila., 1992—; instr. CPR Meth. Hosp., Phila., 1994—. Literacy tutor Laubach Literacy Action, Danville, Pa., 1988-92. Jewish. Home: 650 Acer Ave Morton PA 19070

FIORI, MICHAEL J., pharmacist; b. Brunswick, Maine, Nov. 25, 1951; s. Columbus H. and Marie Alice (Pelletier) F.; m. Anna Marie Robinson, Dec. 25, 1980; 1 child, Michela. BA in Biology, Bowdoin Coll., 1974; BS in Pharmacy, Mass. Coll. Pharmacy, 1977; MBA, U. Maine, 1987; cert. exec. mgmt., Cornell U., 1992; PhD in Bus. Mgmt., LaSalle U., 1995. Notary Public, Justice of the Peace; lic. auctioneer. Rsch. student Rsch. Inst. Gulf Maine, 1974-75; pharmacy intern Newton-Wellesley (Mass.) Hosp., 1977; pharmacist Allen Drug Store, Brunswick, 1977-78; cons. pharmacist Allen Drug Store, Bangor, Maine, 1977-84; pres., chief operating officer Downeast Pharmacy, Inc.; pres., cons. Pharmacists of New Eng. Downeast Pharmacy, Inc., various cities, Maine, 1984—; pres. Guardian Healthcare Downeast Pharmacy, Inc., 1990—; commr. Maine Commn. Pharmacy, 1985-90; pres. and chief exec. officer Vector Assocs., Inc. dba ODV, Inc.; mem. dist. adv. coun. Small Bus. Adminstrn. Earle S. Thompson scholar, 1971-73, Charles Lowery scholar, 1974; named one of Outstanding Young Men Am., 1986; recipient Pres.' award for Svc. to Medicine Maine Med. Assn., 1993. Fellow Am. Soc. Cons. Pharmacists; mem. Am. Soc. for Pharmacy Law, Narcotic Enforcement Officers Assn., Internat. Assn. for Identification, Internat. Assn. Chiefs of Police, Nat. Assn. Bds. of Pharmacy, Maine Pharmacy Assn., Health Care Providers, Inc., Nat. Assn. Retail Druggists, Nat. Fedn. Indp. Bus. (guardian adv. coun.), Internat. Platform Assn., Mass. Coll. Pharmacy Alumni Assn., Bowdoin Coll. Alumni Assn., U. Maine Alumni Assn., Italian Heritage Soc., Gyro Internat., Maine Health Care Assn., NRA (life), KC, Elks, Beta Theta Pi (chpt. pres. 1972-73, ho. corp. pres. 1985—, ho. corp. dir. 1975—, dist. chief 1979-84, 88-89). Democrat. Roman Catholic. Home: 2079 Essex St Bangor ME 04401-2112 Office: Downeast Pharmacy Inc 4 Union St Bangor ME 04401-6457

FIORILLO, JOHN A(NTHONY), health care executive; b. N.Y.C., Jan. 20, 1943; s. John Albert and Matilda (Marotti) F.; m. Anita Daves Pitney, Dec. 6, 1969; 1 child, Alexandra. A.B., NYU, 1963; A.M., Brown U., 1965; postgrad., City U. of N.Y., 1972-74. Planning officer OEO, Washington, 1964-66; exec. asst. to commr. N.Y.C. Health and Hosps. Depts., 1966-68; sr. cons. Peat Marwick Mitchell and Co., N.Y.C., 1968-72; pres. Policy Planning Inc., N.Y.C., 1972-77; asst. v.p. Columbia U., N.Y.C., 1977-81; mng. dir. Am. Health Found., N.Y.C., 1981-82; pres. The Health Strategy Group, Inc., N.Y.C., 1982—; mgmt. cons. NIH, Bethesda, Md., 1979-86; founding dir. People's Med. Soc., Emmaus, Pa., 1982-84. Author: (with others) Art Work, No Commercial Value, 1972. Contbr. articles to profl. jours., chpts. in book. Mem. White House Task Force on Peace Corps, Washington, 1969, N.Y.C. Task Force on Employee Health Benefits, 1974-75; mem. advance team Sen. Robert Kennedy, 1964; asst. campaign dir. Congressman Jonathan Bingham, N.Y.C., 1964; bd. trustees Daytop Village Found., 1986—; bd. dirs. The Shaker Mus., 1995—. Served with USCG, 1965. Brown U. fellow, 1963-64. Avocations: tennis; carpentry; photography. Home: 275 Central Park West New York NY 10024-3019 Office: The Health Strategy Group Inc 920 Broadway New York NY 10010-6004

FIORINO, JOHN WAYNE, podiatrist; b. Charleroi, Pa., Sept. 30, 1946; s. Anthony Raymond and Mary Louise (Caramela) F.; m. Susan K. Bonnett, May 2, 1984; children—Jennifer, Jessica, Lauren, Michael. Student Nassau Coll., 1969-70; B.A. in Biology, U. Buffalo, 1972; Dr. Podiatric Medicine, Ohio Coll. Podiatric Medicine, 1978. Salesman, E. J. Korvettes, Carle Place, N.Y., 1962-65; orderly Nassau Hosp., Mineola, N.Y., 1965-66; operating room technician-trainee heart-lung machine L.I. Jewish-Hillside Med. Center, New Hyde Park, N.Y., 1967-69; pharmacy technician Feinmel's Pharmacy, Roslyn Heights, N.Y., 1969-70; mgr., asst. buyer Fortunoffs, Westbury, N.Y., 1972-73; bd. certified perfusionist L.I. Jewish-Hillside Med. Center, New Hyde Park, N.Y., 1973-74; clin. instr. cardiopulmonary tech. Stony Brook (N.Y.) Univ., 1973-74; operating room technician Cleve. Met. Hosp., 1975; lab. technician Univ. Hosp., Cleve., 1976-78; surg. resident Mesa Gen. Hosp., 1978-79; staff podiatrist, 1979—; pvt. practice podiatry, Mesa, 1979—; staff podiatrist Sacaton (Ariz.) Hosp., 1979—, Mesa Gen. Hosp., 1979, Valley Luth. Hosp., Mesa, 1985, Chandler Community Hosp., 1985, Desert Samaritan Hosp., Mesa, 1986, podiatrist U.S. Govt. Nat. Inst., Sacaton, 1980-87, Indian Health Services, Sacaton, 1980-87; cons. staff Phoenix Indian Med. Ctr., 1985. Served with USN, 1966-67. Mem. Am. Podiatry Assn., Ariz. Podiatry Assn. (treas. 1984-86), Acad. Ambulatory Foot Surgery, Am. Coll. Foot Surgeons (assoc.), Mut. Assn. Profls., Am. Acad. Pain Mgmt. (cert.), Pi Delta, Alpha Gamma Kappa. Home: 2624 W Upland Dr Chandler AZ 85224-7870 Office: 5520 E Main St Mesa AZ 85205-8793

FIRESTEIN, BETH ANN, psychologist; b. Houston, Nov. 20, 1957; d. Louis and Margaret (Furman) Firestein. BA, So. Meth. U., 1978; MA, U.

Tex., 1982, PhD, 1987. Lic. clin. psychologist, Colo., Mo., Ill. Coord. women's svcs. So. Ill. U., Carbondale, 1986-96, counseling psychologist, 1986-96; pvt. practice Psychotherapy Assocs., Carbondale, 1989—; programs chair exec. com. Women's Caucus, Carbondale, 1988-89, co-chair, 1989-90; vis. scholar Colo. State U., 1994; chair Presdl.-Mayoral Task Force on Sexual Assault, 1992-96. Editor: Bisexuality: The Psychology & Politics of an Invisible Minority. Named Univ. Woman of Dinstinction, So. Ill. U., 1996. Mem. APA (Outstanding Rsch. Women and Gender Rsch. prize 1987), Assn. Women in Psychology, Nat. Assn. Women's Ctrs., Phi Kappa Phi, Kappa Delta Pi, Phi Beta Kappa. Office: So Ill U Counseling Ctr Carbondale IL 62901

FIRMINGER, HARLAN IRWIN, pathologist, educator; b. Mpls., Dec. 31, 1918; s. Harry and Emily (Irwin) F.; m. Jane Ryder Hollings, Sept. 14, 1942; children: Ann Laura Firminger Howard, Carol Jean Firminger Feeney, Barbara Lynn. A.B., Washington U., St. Louis, 1939, M.D., 1943. Diplomate Am. Bd. Pathology. Intern Barnes Hosp., St. Louis, 1943; resident pathology Mass. Gen. Hosp., Boston, 1946-47; pathologist Nat. Cancer Inst., Bethesda, Md., 1948-51; practice medicine specializing in pathology Kansas City, Kans., 1951-57, Balt., 1957-75, Denver, 1975—; asst. prof., prof. pathology U. Kans., 1951-57; prof., chmn. dept. pathology U. Md., 1957-67, prof. pathology, 1967-75; dir. anatomic pathology Gen. Rose Meml. Hosp., Denver, 1975-76; prof. pathology U. Colo., 1975-89, prof. emeritus, 1989—; dir. Univs. Asso. for Research and Edn. in Pathology, 1964-71, scientist-asso., 1971-75; mem. sci. adv. bd. Armed Forces Inst. Pathology, 1965-70; mem. com. on pathology div. med. scis. Nat. Acad. Scis.-NRC, 1966-72. Editor Atlas of Tumor Pathology, 1966-75, mem. editorial adv. com., 1975-83; contbr. articles to profl. jours. Pres. Md. div. Am. Cancer Soc., 1967-68. Served to capt. M.C. AUS, 1943-46. Mem. Am. Soc. Investigative Pathology, Internat. Acad. Pathology, Am. Assn. Cancer Research, Soc. Mayflower Descs. (gov. Md. chpt. 1967-70), Md. Soc. Pathologists (pres. 1969-71), Colo. Soc. Clin. Pathology, Alpha Omega Alpha. Office: U Colo Health Scis Ctr 4200 E 9th Ave Denver CO 80220-3706

FIRST, MICHAEL BRUCE, psychiatrist, educator; b. Phila., Nov. 25, 1956; s. E. David and Reda Bell (Dissin) F.; m. Susan Beth Babkes, May 19, 1996. BS in Edn., Princeton (N.J.) U., 1978; MS in Computer Sci., U. Pitts., 1981, MD, 1983. Diplomate Am. Bd. Psychiatry and Neurology. Intern in medicine Shadyside Hosp., Pitts., 1983-84; resident in psychiatry Columbia-Presbyn. Hosp., N.Y.C., 1984-87; fellow in biometrics N.Y. State Psychiat. Inst., N.Y.C., 1986-88, rsch. psychiatrist, 1988—; pvt. practice Columbia-Presbyn. Hosp., 1987—; asst. prof. clin. psychiatry Columbia U., 1990—. Author: The Structured Clinical Interview for DSM-IV (SCID), OSM-IV Guidebook, DSM-IV Handbook; editor: DSM-IV Text and Criteria, 1990—. Mem. AMA, Am. Psychiat. Assn. Office: NY State Psychiat Inst 722 W 168th St New York NY 10032-2603

FIRTH, PAUL GERALD, physician; b. Troy, N.Y., May 29, 1953; s. Gerald Richmond and Doris (Yaddow) F.; m. Diana Murdoch, Dec. 4, 1956; children: Monica, Stephanie, Whitney, Stuart. BS, Washington and Lee Univ., 1975; MD, Med. Coll. Ga., 1979. Diplomate Am. Coll. Ob-Gyn. Intern ob-gyn. Med. Ctr. Cen. Ga., Macon, 1979-80, resident ob-gyn., 1980-83; quality assurance Ob-Gyn Med. Ctr., Macon, 1994-96; exec. com. Macon (Ga.) Northside, 1995—; ob-gyn. (capt.) BJACH, U.S. Army, Ft. Polk, La., 1983-85; chief ob-gyn. (major) WACH, U.S. Army, Ft. Stewart, Ga., 1985-87; vol. clin. instr. Mercer Med. Sch. Contbr. articles to profl. jours. Speaker ARC, Macon, 1987. Major U.S. Army, 1982. Decorated Army Commendation medal. Fellow Am. Coll. Ob-Gyn., Am. Fertility Soc.; mem. AMA, Ga. Med. Soc. Presbyterian. Office: 440 Charter Blvd Ste 2204 Macon GA 31210-4857

FISCH, CHARLES, physician, educator; b. Nesterov (Zolkiew), Poland, May 11, 1921; s. Leon and Janette (Deutscher) F.; m. June Spiegal, May 23, 1943; children: Jonathan, Gary, Bruce. AB, Ind. U., 1942, MD, 1944; Dr. Medicine (hon.), U. Utrecht, 1983. Diplomate Am. Bd. Internal Medicine, Am. Bd. Cardiovascular Medicine (mem. 1977-82). Intern St. Vincent's Hosp., Indpls., 1945; resident internal medicine VA Hosp., Indpls., 1948-50; fellow gastroenterology Marion County Gen. Hosp., Indpls., 1950-51; fellow cardiology Marion County Gen. Hosp., 1951-53; asst. prof. medicine Ind. U. Med. Sch., 1953-59, asso. prof., 1959-63, prof., 1963—, Distinguished prof., 1975, dir. cardiovascular div., 1963-90; dir. Krannert Inst. Cardiology, 1953-90; mem. cardio-renal adv. com. HEW-FDA, 1973-77, 79—, Am. Heart Assn. Connor lectr., 1980; chmn. manpower rev. com. Nat. Heart, Lung and Blood Inst., 1985-89. Author: Electrocardiography of Arrythmias, 1989; co-editor Digitalis, 1969, Cardiac Electrophysiology and Arrythmias, 1991; contbr. articles to med. jours.; mem. editorial bd. Am. Heart Jour., 1967—, Am. Jour. Electrocardiology, 1967—, Coeur et Medicine Interne, 1970—, Am. Jour. Medicine, 1973—, Circulation, 1977—, Am. Jour. Cardiology, 1967—; assoc. editor Am. Jour. Cardiology, 1977—. Served to capt. M.C. AUS, 1946-48. Recipient James Herrick award, Am. Heart Assn. Fellow ACP, Am. Coll. Cardiology (pres. 1975-77, dir., chmn. publ. com. 1988-94, Gifted Tchr. award 1993), World Congress Cardiology (v.p. 1986); mem. Am. Fedn. Clin. Research, Central Soc. Clin. Research, Am. Physiol. Soc., Assn. Univ. Cardiologists, Assn. Am. Physicians. Home: 7901 Morningside Dr Indianapolis IN 46240-2526 Office: Ind U Med Ctr Krannert Inst Cardiology 1111 W 10th St Indianapolis IN 46202-4800

FISCHBACH, GERALD D., neurobiology educator; b. New Rochelle, N.Y., Nov. 15, 1938; children: Elissa, Peter, Neal, Mark. AB, Colgate U., 1960; MD, Cornell U., 1965; MA (hon.), Harvard U., 1978. Intern U. Washington Hosp., Seattle, 1965-66; sr. surgeon, Pub. Health Svc., Lab. of Neurophysiology, Nat. Inst. Neurol. Diseases and Stroke NIH, Bethesda, Md., 1966-69; fellow Behavioral Biology Br. Nat. Inst. Child Health, 1969-73; assoc. prof. pharmacology Harvard Med. Sch., Boston, 1978-81, prof., 1978-81; Nathan Marsh Pusey prof. neurobiology, chair dept. neurobiology Harvard Med. Sch., Mass. Gen. Hosp., Boston, 1990—; Edison prof. neurobiology, chmn. dept. anatomy and neurobiology Washington U. Sch. Med., St. Louis, 1981-90; mem. exec. com. Program in Cell and Devel. Biology, Harvard Med. Sch., 1974-81; nonresident tutor Leverett House, Harvard Coll., 1974-77; clk. of corp. Marine Biol. Lab., Woods Hole, Mass, 1978-81, trustee, 1982—, exec. com., 1984-89; master Fuller Albright Acad. Soc., Harvard Med. Sch., 1979-81, faculty coun., 1980-81; chmn. Gordon Conf. on Molecular Pharmacology, 1983; dir. Ctr. for Cellular and Molecular Neurobiology, Washington U. Sch. of Med., 1983-90, dir. Jacob Javits Ctr. for Excellence in Neurosci., 1985-90, dir. Ctr. for Higher Brain Function, 1988-90, mem. Med. Ctr. Bd., 1989-90; dir. Neurosci. Ctr., Mass. Gen. Hosp., 1990—; mem. adv. bd. Nat. Spinal Cord Injury Assn., 1978—, Neurology B Study Sect., NIH, 1978-80, Alfred P. Sloan Found., 1984-89, Dept. Biology Adv. Coun., Princeton U., 1984-88, Fidia Rsch. Found., 1986—, McKnight Neurosci. Rsch. Awards Rev. Com., 1986—, Howard Hughes Med. Inst., 1988—, SUNY Health Sci. Ctr. at Bklyn, 1988—, Helen Hay Whitney Found., 1991, Children's Hosp., Boston, 1991; vis. prof. Dept. Pharmacology U. Calif. at San Francisco, 1978; lectr. Disting. Lecture Series in Pharmacology, U. Md. Sch. Medicine, 1978, 25th Ann. Bishop Lecture, Washington U. Sch. Medicine, 1980, Disting. Lecture Series, Dept. Zoology, U. Tex., 1981; invited speaker 5th Ann. Meeting European Neurosci. Assn., 1981 ; Alden Spencer lectr. Coll. Physicians and Surgeons, Columbia, U., 1981, Stephen W. Kuffler lectr. Harvard Med. Sch., 1990, numerous others; assoc. Neurosci. Rsch. Program, k1981—. Editor Jour. Cell Biology, 1985-86; assoc. editor Devel. Biology, 1974-78, Jour. Neurophysiology, 1975-81, 1989—, Jour. Neurobiology, 1986—; corr. editor Proc. Royal Soc., Series B, London, 1989—; contbr. articles to profl. jours. Recipient Polk award Cornell U., 1965, Mathilde Solowey award Found. for Advanced Edn. in the Scis., NIH, 1975, W. Alden Spencer award Coll. Physicians and Surgeons, Columbia U., 1981; N.Y.State Regents scholar, 1956-60, N.Y. State med. scholar, Cornell U., 1962-65; Salk Inst. non-resident fellow, 1990. Mem. Soc. for Neurosci. (llth ann. lectr., pres.-elect 1982-83, pres. 1983-84), Soc. Gen. Physiologists, Am. Soc. Cell Biology, Phi Beta Kappa. Office: Harvard Med Sch Dept Neurobiology 25 Shattuck St Boston MA 02115-6027

FISCHBARG, ZULEMA F., pediatrician, educator; b. Buenos Aires, Mar. 22, 1937; came to U.S., 1962; d. Naun and Esther (Pollner) Fridman; m. Jorge Fischbarg; children: Gabriel Julian, Victor Ernesto. MD, U. Buenos Aires, 1960. Pediatric intern Children's Hosp., Louisville, 1962-63, resident in pediatrics, 1963, chief resident in pediatrics, 1964; fellow hematology Michael Reese Med. Ctr., Chgo., 1964-66, Presbyn. St. Lukes Hosp., Chgo., 1966-67; fellow pediatric hematology Children's Meml. Hosp., Chgo., 1967-68; asst. clin. pediatrician U. Chgo., 1968-69; instr. in pediatrics Cornell U. Med. Sch., N.Y.C., 1970-72, asst. prof. in pediatrics, 1972-76, assoc. prof. pediatrics, 1978—; assoc. attending pediatrician N.Y. Hosp., 1979—; attending in pediatrics St. John's Hosp./Cath. Med. Ctr., N.Y.C.; med. specialist, sch. physician Bur. of Sch. Children and Adolescent Health, N.Y.C., 1994—; instr. in medicine Ill. U., Chgo., 1967-68; assoc. attending pediatrician, N.Y. Hosp., N.Y.C., 1972-76. Fellow Am. Acad. of Pediatrics, Queens Pediatric Soc. Democrat. Jewish. Home: 175 E 62nd St # 6D New York NY 10021-7626 Office: 125 Worth St Box 25 Rm 347 New York NY 10013

FISCHBEIN, CHARLES ALAN, pediatrician; b. Newark, June 5, 1945; s. Martin and Naomi (Litzky) F.; m. Ellen Ruth Niemtzow, Aug. 10, 1969; children: Melissa Paige, Neil Todd. BA in Biology, Case Western Reserve U., 1966; MD, SUNY, Buffalo, 1970. Diplomate Am. Bd. Pediatrics. Resident in pediatrics Children's Hosp. Med. Ctr., Cin., 1970-72; fellow in pediatric cardiology Children's Hosp. Med. Ctr., Boston, 1972-74; pvt. practice pediatrics, 1974—; pres. Pediatric Assocs. of Conn., Waterbury, 1982—; asst. clin. prof. U. Conn. Med. Sch., Farmington, Conn., 1974—, Yale U. Sch. Medicine, New Haven, Conn., 1974—; acting co-chief dept. pediatrics St. Mary's Hosp., Waterbury, Conn., 1995—. Fellow Am. Acad. Pediatrics; mem. AMA, Am. Coll. Sports Medicine. Office: Pediatric Assocs Conn PC 160 Robbins St Waterbury CT 06708

FISCHBEIN, JEROME WOLLISON, physician; b. N.Y.C., July 28, 1927; s. Nathan J. and Adeline (Meltzer) F.; m. Elizabeth Miriam Bell, May 17, 1953; children: Margery, Barbara, Nancy. AB magna cum laude, Harvard Coll., 1947, MD cum laude, 1951. Diplomate Am. Bd. Internal Medicine, Am. Bd. Gastroenterology. Intern in medicine Beth Israel Hosp., Boston, 1951-52, resident in medicine, 1952-53, chief med. resident, 1953-54; sr. resident gastroenterology Henry Ford Hosp., Detroit, 1954-56; instr. in medicine Harvard Med. Sch., Boston, 1956-58, asst. clin. prof. medicine, 1968-74, lectr. on medicine, 1974; assoc. clin. prof. medicine Boston U. Sch. Medicine, 1974; physician Beth Israel Hosp., Boston, 1956-88, cons. physician, 1990-96; assoc. physician Univ. Hosp., Boston, 1969-88. Contbr. articles to profl. jours. Mem. health care policy com. Boston U. Med. Ctr., 1974-77; mem. nat. campaign com. Harvard Med. Sch., Boston, 1985-95, nat. alumni com., 1985-95, com. ednl. evaluator, 1988-96. Lt. cmdr. USN, 1945-65. Mem. ACP (life), Am. Coll. Physician Execs., Mass. Med. Soc., Phi Beta Kappa, Alpha Omega Alpha. Home: 4791 Pineview Cir Delray Beach FL 33445

FISCHEL, EDWARD ELLIOT, physician; b. N.Y.C., July 29, 1920; s. Joseph L. and Lisa (Herman) F.; m. Pauline Dunieff, Dec. 26, 1943; children—Robert, Janet. B.A., Columbia U., 1941, M.D., 1944, Sc.D. in Medicine, 1948. Diplomate: Am. Bd. Internal Medicine. Intern Presbyn. Hosp., N.Y.C., 1944-45; asst. resident medicine Presbyn. Hosp., 1945-46; asst. in medicine Columbia U. Coll. Physicians and Surgeons, N.Y.C., 1947-50; asso. medicine Columbia U. Coll. Physicians and Surgeons, 1950-55, assoc. clin. prof. medicine, 1969-72, lectr. medicine, 1972-87; practice medicine specializing in internal medicine and rheumatology; asst. physician Presbyn. Hosp., N.Y.C., 1947-55; asso. clin. prof. medicine Albert Einstein Coll. Medicine, Yeshiva U., N.Y.C., 1957-69; prof. medicine Albert Einstein Coll. Medicine, Yeshiva U., 1972-80, vis. prof. medicine, 1980-81; dir. dept. medicine Bronx-Lebanon Hosp. Center, Bronx, N.Y., 1954-80; chief dept. medicine Mt. Sinai Hosp., Hartford, Conn. and prof. medicine U. Conn., 1980-83; chief of staff VA Med. Ctr., Northport, N.Y., 1983-91; prof. medicine, assoc. dean vet. affairs SUNY, Stony Brook, 1983-91, prof. medicine emeritus, 1991—; mem. exec. com. Health Rsch. Coun. City N.Y., 1966-75, chmn. allergy and infectious disease panel, 1968-75; mem. N.Y. State Coun. on Grad. Med. Edn., 1991-94. Fellow A.C.P., N.Y. Acad. Medicine (past v.p., trustee 1972-80), AAAS (past mem. coun.); mem. Am. Soc. Clin. Investigation, Am. Assn. Immunologists, Am. Coll. rheumatology (past pres.), Assn. Am. Med. Colls., Infectious Diseases Soc., Harvey Soc., Soc. Exptl. Biology and Medicine, Am.Fedn. Clin. Rsch., AMA, Bronx County Med. Soc., Am. Heart Assn. (past mem. rsch. com.), N.Y. TB and Health Assn. (past dir.), Phi Beta Kappa, Alpha Omega Alpha. Home: 220 Little Neck Rd Centerport NY 11721-1145

FISCHEL, NATHAN, pediatrician, educator, scientist; b. Munich, Germany, Dec. 2, 1955; came to U.S., 1983; s. Henry and Kitty (Lichtenstein) F.; m. Fariba Ghodsian, Nov. 25, 1983; children: David, Daniella. MD, Technion Sch. Medicine, Israel, 1981. Diplomate in pediatrics, pediatric hematology/oncology and clin. molecular genetics Am. Bd. Pediatrics. Rotating intern Hadassah Med. Ctr., Jerusalem, Israel, 1982-83; resident in pediatrics Harvard Med. Sch., Boston, 1983-85, fellow in pediatric hematology/oncology, 1987-88; rsch. fellow Oxford (Eng.) U., 1985-87; dir. molecular hematology Cedars-Sinai Med. Ctr., L.A., 1988—; assoc. prof. pediatrics UCLA Sch. Medicine, 1994—; founder, chief sci. officer GenoMed Pharms., Inc., Beverly Hills, Calif., 1995—; grant reviewer NIH, 1994—, Arthritis Found., 1994—; mem. bd. sci. counselors NIDCD, 1996—. Contbr. chpts. to books, numerous articles to profl. jours. NIH grantee, 1992—, 94—, 96—, Arthritis Found., 1994—. Fellow Am. Coll. Med. Genetics, Soc. for Pediatric Rsch., Assn. for Rsch. in Otolaryngology; mem. Am. Soc. Hematology, Am. Soc. Human Genetics. Jewish. Office: Cedars Sinai Med Ctr Dept Pediatrics 8700 Beverly Blvd Los Angeles CA 90048

FISCHELL, ROBERT ELLENTUCH, physicist; b. N.Y.C., Feb. 10, 1929; s. Philip and Julia (Ellentuch) F.; m. Marian Standard; children: David R., Tim A., Scott J.S. BSMechE cum laude, Duke U., 1951; MS in Physics, U. Md., 1953, ScD, 1996. Physicist U.S. Naval Ordinance Lab., Silver Spring, Md., 1951-56; prin. staff engr. Emerson Rsch. Labs., Silver Spring, 1956-60; various staff positions Applied Physics Lab., Johns Hopkins U., Laurel, Md., 1959—, prin. profl. physicist, 1962—, chief engr. space dept., 1972-80, chief tech. transfer space dept., 1978-88; pres., chmn. bd. MedInnovations, Inc., Dayton, Md., 1988-90, MedInTec, Inc., Dayton, Md., 1990—; chmn. bd., v.p. R & D Cathco, Inc.; chmn. bd., pres. IsoStent, Inc., Dayton, Md., 1993—; expert witness Brown and Bain, Palo Alto, Calif., 1992—; rsch. assoc. in medicine Johns Hopkins U. Sch. Medicine, 1983—, Yale U. Sch. Medicine, 1988—; mem. exec. panel Chief of Naval Ops., Washington, 1983-87; expert witness Fish and Neave, N.Y.C., 1986—; field reviewer for orphan products FDA, 1984—; mem. rsch. com. Md. affiliate Am. Heart Assn., 1985-87; mem. tech. com. on space guidance and control, AIAA, 1972-75, chmn. nat. conf., 1973; mem. space com. Internat. Fedn. Automatic Control, 1970-75; mem., chmn. photovoltaic specialities com. IEEE, 1959-72. Author 49 tech. publs.; assoc. editor AIAA Jour. Spacecraft and Rockets, 1972-75; holder 46 U.S. patents in field of biomed. engring, biomed. devices and spacecraft. Recipient Tech. Achievement award ASME, 1962, Outstanding Young Engr. award Washington Capitol Area, 1963, awards for most significant inventions Indsl. Rsch. mag., 1967, 70, 73, Inventor of Yr. award Intellectual Property Owners Assn., 1984, Gold medal for contbn. to aerospace sci. and tech. N.Y. Acad. Sci., 1987; NASA awards include Exceptional Engring. for MAGSAT satellite, 1980, Individual Achievement for human tissue stimulator, 1982, Exceptional Engring. medal, 1984, Space Act prize, 1984, Disting. Engring. Alumnus award Duke U., 1992; named Disting. Citizen of Yr. "M" Club U. Md., 1984; inducted into Space Technology Hall of Fame U.S. Space Found., 1988. Mem. NAE, Internat. Soc. for Artificial Organs, N.Y. Acad. Scis., Phi Beta Kappa, Tau Beta Pi, Pi Mu Epsilon, Sigma Pi Sigma, Pi Tau Sigma, Beta Omega Sigma. Office: Med Innv Tech Inc 14600 Viburnum Dr Dayton MD 21036-1247

FISCHER, A(LBERT) ALAN, family physician; b. Indpls., June 30, 1928; 4 children. MD, Ind. U., 1952. Diplomate Am. Bd. Family Practice. Intern St. Vincent Hosp., Indpls., 1952-53; pvt. practice, 1953-70; dir. family practice residency program St. Vincent Hosp., Indpls., 1969-75; prof. family medicine, chmn. dept. Ind. U., Indpls., 1974-90; med. dir. Lakeview Manor, 1970—; pvt. practice family medicine, 1953—. Mem. AMA, Inst. Medicine-NAS (mem. nat. joint practicing comm.), Am. Acad. Family Physicians (v.p. 1971-72, cert. mem. Am. Bd. Family Practice). *

FISCHER, CARL G., anesthesiologist; b. Cin., Dec. 4, 1937; s. Carl G. and Dorotha W. F.; m. Joyce D. BS, U. Cin., 1960; MD, U. Rochester, 1965. Diplomate anesthesia. Intern Christ Hosp., Cin., 1965-66; resident Yale U. Hosp., New Haven, 1969-71; fellow in pediat. anesthesia/ICU Pitts. Children's Hosp., 1971-72, staff anesthesiologist, asst. prof., 1972-77; staff anesthesiologist, from assoc. prof. to prof. U. Cin./Cin. Children's Hosp., 1977—; dir. anesthesia Shriners Burns Inst., Cin., 1989—. Lt. USN, 1967-69. Mem. Am. Soc. Anesthesia, Am. Acad. Pediatrics, Soc. Pediat. Anthesiology. Office: Shriners Burns Inst 3229 Burnet Ave Cincinnati OH 45229

FISCHER, CARL ROBERT, health care facility administrator; b. Rahway, N.J., Nov. 15, 1939; s. Robert Carlton and Elsie Marie (Wolfarth) F.; m. Lynn Eliane Ekstrand, Mar. 12, 1966; children: Kristen, Leslie, Meredith, Kelly. B.S. in Nursing, Wagner Coll., 1964; M.S., SUNY-Buffalo, 1966; M.P.H., Yale U., 1968. With Yale-New Haven Hosp., 1968-77, assoc. dir., 1975-77; exec. assoc. adminstr. U. Cin. Med. Ctr., 1977-80; exec. dir. clin. programs U. Ark. for Med. Scis., Little Rock, 1980-86; assoc. v.p. health scis. and exec. dir. Med. Coll. of Va. Hosps., Richmond, 1986—; active Univ. Hosps., Richmond, 1986—; active Univ. Hosp. Consorium Svcs. Corp., 1987, chmn. bd. dirs. 1988-89, chmn. supply and svcs. divsn., 1988-89, 96. Mem. Am. Assn. Med. Colls., Am. Hosp. Assn., Va. Hosp. Assn. (bd. dirs. 1986-91, chmn. coun. on adminstrn. and health planning 1988, coun. on assn. devel. 1987-88, physician liaison com. 1989-90), Univ. Health Systems Consortium (bd. dirs. 1981—, exec. com. 1983-96), Ctrl. Va. Health Planning Agy. (pres. 1991-93). Lutheran. Office: Med Coll Va Hosps Va Commonwealth U PO Box 980510 Richmond VA 23298

FISCHER, CONSTANCE TAYLOR, psychologist; b. Oahu, Hawaii, July 29, 1938; d. Milton Clay and Irene Elsie (Nelson) Taylor; 1 child, Michael Allen. BA, U. Okla., 1960; MA, U. Ky., 1963, PhD, 1966. Lic. psychologist, Pa. Asst. to full prof. Duquesne U., Pitts., 1967—; pvt. practice Pitts., 1970—; pres., dir. Pitts. Assessment & Cons. Ctr., P.C., 1985—. Author: Individualizing Psychological Assessment, 1985; co-editor: Duquesne Studies in Phenomenotogical Psychology, 1975, Client Participation in Human Services, 1978; contbr. articles to profl. jours. Bd. dirs. Children's Coun. Western Pa., Pitts., 1978-84. Recipient Disting. Svc. award Greater Pitts. Psychol. Assn., 1992, Disting. Svc. award Pa. Psychol. Assn., 1993. Fellow APA (pres. div. theoretical and philos. psychology 1985-86, coun. of reps. 1989-92), Pa. Psychol. Assn. (pres. 1985-86), Pa. Psychol. Found. (sec. 1990—). Home: 319 Garlow Dr Pittsburgh PA 15235-1918 Office: Ste 390 Med Ctr East 211 N Whitfield St Bldg 390 Pittsburgh PA 15206-3031

FISCHER, DANIEL EDWARD, psychiatrist; b. New Haven, Apr. 22, 1945; s. Alexander and Miriam (Kramer) F.; m. Linda Lee Bradford, June 12, 1969; children: Meredith Tara, Alexis Anne. B.A., Boston U., 1969, M.D., 1969; J.D., Coll. William and Mary, 1986. Bar: Va. 1986, U.S. Dist. Ct. (ea. dist.) Va. 1986, U.S. Ct. Appeals (4th cir.) 1986. Intern in medicine Baylor Affiliated Hosps., Houston, 1969-70; resident in psychiatry Washington U. Sch. Medicine, St. Louis, 1970-73; practice medicine specializing in psychiatry Virginia Beach, Va., 1975—; chmn. dept. psychiatry DePaul Hosp., Norfolk, Va., 1978-79, Bayside Hosp., Virginia Beach, 1980-81, 88-89, 1990-91; assoc. med. dir. adult in-patient svcs. rapid stabilization unit Tidewater Psychiat. Inst., Norfolk, 1989-94; med. dir. Norfolk (Va.) Psychiat. Ctr., 1995-96; pvt. practice in gen. psychiatry, 1996—. Contbr. articles to profl. jours.; patentee in field. Bd. dirs. Tidewater Pastoral Counseling Svc., Norfolk, 1976—, Kempsville Conservative Synagogue, Virginia Beach, 1982-86, Beth Chavarim, 1987-90; pres. Am. Investment Mgmt. Svcs., Inc., Virginia Beach, 1987—. Served as maj. U.S. Army, 1973-75. Decorated Army Commendation medal. Fellow Acad. Psychosomatic Medicine, Am. Psychiat. Assn.; mem. AMA, Va. Med. Soc., Va. Psychiat. Assn., Virginia Beach Med. Soc., Tidewater Acad. Psychiatry. Democrat. Jewish. Office: 621 Lynnhaven Pky Ste 366 Virginia Beach VA 23452-7300

FISCHER, DAVID SEYMOUR, internist; b. Bklyn., May 13, 1930; s. Simon and Charolotte Fischer; m. Iris Liquerman, June 1, 1958; children: Karen, Louise, Francie. AB, Williams Coll., 1951; MD, Harvard U., 1955. Diplomate Am. Bd. Internal Medicine, Am. Bd. Med. Oncology, Am. Bd. Hematology. Intern, Kings County Hosp., 1955-56; resident U. Utah, 1956-57, Montefiore Hosp., Bronx, N.Y., 1957-58; fellow U. Washington, Seattle, 1958-59, Yale U., 1962-64; attending physician Yale New Haven Hosp; emeritus attending physician, Hosp. St. Raphael; cons. Milford Hosp., Conn., 1970—, VA Hosp., West Haven, Conn., 1974—, Yale Comprehensive Cancer Ctr., New Haven, 1978—; clin. prof. medicine Yale U. Author: Cancer Chemotherapy Handbook, 4th edit., 1993, Follow-Up of Cancer, 4th edit. 1996; also articles; editor, author: Cancer Therapy, 1982. Pres., Conn. div. Am. Cancer Soc., 1981; pres. med. staff Hosp. St. Raphael, New Haven, 1980; pres. med. adv. bd. Jewish Home for Aged, 1983-85; med. adv. bd. Leukemia Soc. South Cen. Conn., 1984—; pres. Congregation Bikur Cholim Sheveth Achim, 1983-85; pres. Hebrew Congregation of Woodmont, 1995—. Capt. U.S. Army, 1959-61. Recipient Harris award Yale New Haven Hosp., 1974; Bronze medal Am. Cancer Soc., 1982. Fellow ACP; mem. AMA, Am. Soc. Hematology, Am. Soc. Clin. Oncology (chmn. pub. issues), Am. Fedn. Clin. Rsch., Am. Soc. Internal Medicine, Conn. State Med. Soc., Conn. Oncology Assn. (pres. 1979-80), New Haven County Med. Soc., New Haven Med. Assn. (pres. 1990-91). Jewish. Office: 37 Hilldale Ct Milford CT 06460-7706

FISCHER, EDMOND HENRI, biochemistry educator; b. Shanghai, Republic of China, Apr. 6, 1920; came to U.S., 1953; s. Oscar and Renée (Tapernoux) F.; m. Beverley B. Bullock. Lic. es Sciences Chimiques et Biologiques, U. Geneva, 1943, Diplome d'Ingenieur Chimiste, 1944, PhD, 1947; D (hon.), U. Montpellier, France, 1985, U. Basel, Switzerland, 1988, Med. Coll. of Ohio, 1993, Ind. U., 1993, U. Bochum, Germany, 1994. Pvt. docent biochemistry U. Geneva, 1950-53; research assoc. biology Calif. Inst. Tech., Pasadena, 1953; asst. prof. biochemistry U. Wash., Seattle, 1953-56, assoc. prof., 1956-61, prof., 1961-90, prof. emeritus, 1990—; mem. exec. com. Pacific Slope Biochem. Conf., 1958-59, pres., 1975; mem. biochemistry study sect. NIH, 1959-64, symposium co-chmn. Battelle Seattle Rsch. Ctr., 1970, 73, 78; mem. sci. adv. bd. Biozentrum, U. Basel, Switzerland, 1982-86; mem. sci. adv. bd. Friedrich Miescher Inst., Ciba-Geigy, Basel, 1976-84, chmn., 1981-84; mem. bd. sci. govs. Scripps Rsch. Inst., La Jolla, Calif., 1987—. Contbr. numerous articles to sci. jours. Mem. sci. council on basic sci. Am. Heart Assn., 1977-80, sci. adv. com. Muscular Dystrophy Assn., 1980-88. Recipient Lederle Med. Faculty award, 1956-59, Guggenheim Found. award, 1963-64, Disting. Lectr. award U. Wash., 1983, Laureate Passano Found. award, 1988, Steven C. Beering award, 1991, Nobel prize in Physiology or Medicine, 1992. Fellow Am. Acad. Arts and Scis.; mem. NAS, AAAS, AAUP, Am. Soc. Biol. Chemists (coun. 1989-93), Am. Chem. Soc. (adv. bd. biochemistry divsn. 1962, exec. com. divsn. biology 1969-72, monograph adv. bd. 1971-73, editl. adv. bd. Biochemistry, 1961-66, assoc. editor 1966-91), Swiss Chem. Soc. (Werner medal), Spanish Royal Acad. Scis. (fgn. assoc.), Venice Inst. Sci., Arts and Letters (fgn. assoc.), Japanese Biochem. Soc. (hon.). Office: U Washington Med Sch Box 357350 Seattle WA 98195-7350

FISCHER, JOSEF E., surgeon, educator; b. N.Y.C., May 7, 1937; s. Max and Molly (Ochs) F.; m. Karen Jean Down, Oct. 24, 1965; children: Erich, Alexandra. A.B. summa cum laude, Yeshiva Coll., 1957; M.D. magna cum laude, Harvard U., 1961; D.M. (hon.), Lund U., Sweden, 1990. Diplomate: Am. Bd. Surgery, Nat. Bd. Med. Examiners. Surg. intern Mass. Gen. Hosp., Boston, 1961-62; 3d asst. surg. resident Mass. Gen. Hosp., 1962-63, 2d asst. surg. resident, 1965-66, asst. resident surgery, 1966-68, chief resident, 1969-70, asst. in surgery, 1970-73, chief surg. physiology lab., 1970-78, chief hyperalimentation unit, 1972-78, asst. surgeon, 1973-76, asso. vis. surgeon, 1976-78; practice medicine, specializing in surgery Boston, 1970-78, Cin., 1978—; commd. med. officer USPHS, 1963; research assoc. lab. clin. sci. NIMH, 1963-65; teaching fellow in surgery Harvard U. Med. Sch., 1968-69, instr. surgery, 1970-72, asst. prof., 1972-75, assoc. prof., 1975-78; Christian R. Holmes prof., chmn. dept. surgery U. Cin. Med. Center, 1978—; surgeon-in-chief U. Cin. Hosp., Children's Hosp. Med. Center, Cin.; bd. dirs. Weston Med. Labs., Inc., 1973, Ethics Inst. Editor: Total Parenteral Nutrition, 1976, 2d edit., 1991, Internat. Jour. Artificial Organs, 1977—, Surgical Nutrition, 1983, Hepatic Encephalopathy in Chronic Liver Failure, 1984, Surgical Basic Science, 1993, Nutrition and Metabolism in the Surgical Patient, 2d edit., 1996, Mastery of Surgery, 3rd edit., 1996; editorial bd.; Jour. Surg. Research, 1976-84, AMA Archive of Surgery, Am. Jour. Surgery, Jour. Enteral and Parenteral Nutrition, Current Surgery; hepatology section editor Current Opinion in General Surgery; assoc. editor surg. gastroenterology Jour. ACS; contbr. articles to med. jours. Co-chmn. steering com. Seminarians; dept. Am. Decorative arts Boston Mus. Fine Arts, 1975-76; bd. dirs. Beacon Hill Nursery Sch., 1971-77, Maimonides Sch., 1973-78; chmn.

bd. dirs. Cin. Chamber Orch., 1983—. Recipient McCurdy-Rinkel award, 1971; James IV surg. fellow, 1974-75. Fellow Am. Surgery Bd. (bd. dirs. 1991—, vice-chmn. 1996—), ACS (vice chmn. exec. com., com. pre-op. and post-op. care 1987-89, vice chmn. surg. res. and edn. com. 1992-93, mem. exec. com. surg. res. and edn. 1991—, gov. 1992—, chmn. 1995—, chmn. med. liability com. bd gov. 1993—, exec. com. bd. gov. 1993—, pres.-elect Ohio chpt. 1990—, coun. 1987-90, pres. 1991-92); mem. Am. Assn. for Study Liver Disease, Am. Gastroent. Assn., Am. Soc. Clin. Investigation, So. Surg. Assn., Surg. Biology Club I (sec. 1989-92), Assn. for Acad. Surgery (exec. com. 1975, recorder 1976, surg. res. subcom.), Internat. Soc. Parenteral Nutrition, Soc. for Parenteral Alimentation, Am. Surg. Assn., Cen. Surg. Assn. (exec. coun. 1990—, treas. 1993-96), Ill. Surg. Soc. (hon.), Soc. Univ. Surgeons (chmn. com. social and legis. issues 1981-84, exec. coun. 1981-84), Soc. Surgery of Alimentary Tract (chmn. membership com. 1985-89, treas. 1996), Halsted Soc. (sec. 1991-93), Ohio Surg. Panel (pres. 1992—), Surg. Infection Soc. (treas. 1991-93, pres. 1995), Boston Inter-Hosp. Liver Group, Mass. Med. Soc., Boston Surg. Soc., N.Y. Acad. Scis., Chgo. Surg. Soc. (hon.), Ky. Surg. Soc. (hon.), Colombia Soc. Surgery (hon.), Cin. Surg. Soc., Acad. of Medicine of Cin., Soc. Surg. Chairmen, Med. Soc. Rome (Italy, hon.), Royal Coll. Surg. Edinburgh (Scotland, hon.). Office: U Cin Med Center Dept Surgery 231 Bethesda Ave Cincinnati OH 45267*

FISCHER, KURT WALTER, education educator; b. Balt., June 9, 1943; s. Kurt Wilhelm and Irmgaard-Louise (Funke) F.; m. Sandra Pipp (div.); 1 child, Seth; m. Jane Haltiwanger, Dec. 7, 1986; children; Johanna, Lukas, Kara. BA in Psychology summa cum laude, Yale U., 1965; MA in Soc. Rels., Harvard U., 1968, PhD in Soc. Rels., 1971. Asst. prof. Univ. Denver, 1972-78, assoc. prof., 1978-85, prof., 1985-87; prof. edn. Harvard U., Cambridge, Mass., 1986—, chair human devel., 1989-92, 94—; vis. scholar Univ. Geneva, 1978-79; vis. prof. U. Pa., Phila., 1985-86. Author: Cognitive Development, 1981, Levels and Transitions in Cognitive Development, 1983; co-author: (with P. Shaver and A. Lazerson) Psychology Today: An Introduction, 2d and 3d edits., 1972, 75; co-author: Human Development from Conception to Adolescence, 1984, Development in Context, 1993, Human Behavior and the Developing Brain, 1994, Self Conscious Emotions, 1995, Development and Vulnerability in Close Relationships, 1996; contbr. articles to profl. jours. Fellow James McKeen Cattell Fund, 1985-86, Ctr. for Advanced Study, Palo Alto, Calif., 1992-93; grantee Carnegie Found., Sloan Found., Rose Found., 1995—. Mem. Jean Piaget Soc. (pres. 1988-91), Phi Beta Kappa, Sigma Xi. Home: 29 Vincent Ave Belmont MA 02178-4418 Office: Harvard U Human Devel Grad Sch Edn Cambridge MA 02138

FISCHER, TIMOTHY LEE, osteopath, health facility administrator; b. Oak Park, Ill., Oct. 9, 1949; s. Glenn A. Fischer and Barbara A. (Mullen) Marley; m. Carol E. Benoit, June 14, 1971; children: Jonathan, Emily, Ian. BSS, Cornell Coll., Mt. Vernon, Iowa, 1980; DO, U. Osteo. Medicine Health Scis, Des Moines, 1987. Diplomate Am. Bd. Family Practice; cert. in addiction medicine by Am. Soc. Addiction Medicine. Pvt. practice Des Moines, 1989-92; adj. asst. prof. family practice U. Osteo. Medicine and Health Scis., 1990-92; med. dir. house calls Charter Cmty. Hosp., Des Moines, 1990-91; med. dir. Harold Hughes Recovery Ctrs., Des Moines, 1990-93; family practice and internal medicine residency supervisor in addiction medicine Des Moines Gen. Hosp., 1990-93; emergency med. staff Broadlawn's Med. Ctr., Des Moines, 1991-93; med. dir. Dawn Ctr., Orangeburg, S.C., 1993—; physician cons. Charleston (S.C.) Dept. Alcohol and Other Drug Abuse Svcs., 1996—; instr. BSN program S.C. State, 1995—; mem. Mount Vernon/Lisbon Bike Trail Com., 1980-82; mem. Lisbon Sch. Lunch/Nutrition Adv. Bd.; mem. Nat. Physical Fitness Adv. Bd. Amateur Athletic Union, 1990-93, lectr. S.C. Soc. Addiction Medicine, 1995—; mem. nat. adv. com. on reducing underage drinking through cmty. and state coalitions sponsored by the Robert Wood Johnson Found. and AMA. Rep. precinct chmn., Iowa, 1980-82, 1990-93, county ctrl. com., 1980-82, 1990-93; chmn. planning and zoning commn., Lisbon, Iowa, 1980-82; lobbyist Iowa Clean Indoor Air Coalition, 1990. Recipient Iowa Gov's. Vol. of the Yr. award, 1989. Mem. AMA, Am. Osteo. Assn., Am. Soc. Addiction Medicine (com. on practice guidelines 1993—, com. on membership 1993—, state chpts. com. 1995—), Am. Osteopathic Acad. Addiction Medicine, S.C. Soc. Addiction Medicine (founder, pres. 1995—), S.C. Osteo. Med. Assn., Nat. Wildlife Fedn., World Wildlife Found., Rails-to-Trails, Nature Conservancy, Nat. Parks and Conservation Assn. Republican. Roman Catholic. Home: 307 Church St Saint Matthews SC 29135 Office: Dawn Center PO Box 1166 Orangeburg SC 29116

FISCHHOFF, BARUCH, psychologist, educator; b. Detroit, Apr. 21, 1946; s. Henry and Shirley (Levine) F.; m. Andrea Marks, Dec. 22, 1968; children: Maya, Ilya, Noam. BS in Math., Wayne State U., 1967; MA in Psychology, Hebrew U., Jerusalem, 1972, PhD in Psychology, 1975. Rsch. assoc. Oreg. Rsch. Inst., Eugene, 1974-76, Decision Rsch., Eugene, 1976-85, Applied Psychology Unit Med. Rsch. Coun., Cambridge, Eng., 1981-82, Eugene Rsch. Inst., 1985-87; prof. Carnegie-Mellon U., Pitts., 1987—; vis. prof. U. Stockholm, 1982-83; mem. panels NRC; cons. in field. Author: Acceptable Risk, 1981; mem. editl. bd. Jour. Risk Uncertainty, Jour. Exptl. Psychology: Applied, Risk, others; contbr. numerous articles to profl. jours. Mem. Eugene Commn. on Rights of Women, 1975-81; pres. Eugene Human Rights Coun., 1979-81. Fellow APA (Disting. Sci. award 1981, psychology in Pub. Interest award 1991), Soc. for Risk Analysis (Disting. Achievement award 1991), Soc. Judgement and Decision-Making (mem. coun. 1988-91, pres. 1990-91), Inst. Medicine, Phi Beta Kappa. Home: 1437 Denniston Ave Pittsburgh PA 15217-1332 Office: Carnegie Mellon U Dept Engring & Pub Policy Pittsburgh PA 15213-3890

FISCHMAN, STUART LEE, oral medicine educator, dentist; b. Buffalo, Nov. 29, 1935; s. Ben and Lillian (Friedland) F.; m. Jane Ann Vogel, June 25, 1960; 1 child, Lisa. Student, Cornell U., 1953-56; DMD, Harvard U., 1960. Diplomate Am. Bd. Oral Pathology, Am. Bd. Oral Medicine. Resident Boston VA Hosp., 1960-61; prof. SUNY, Buffalo, 1961—; vis. prof. U. P.R., San Juan, 1974, Hebrew U., Jerusalem, 1981, 89. 96; cons. Cheseborough Ponds, Trumbull, Conn., 1965—, ADA, Chgo., 1975—, Unilever Rsch., Eng., 1985—; hon. prof. Nat. U., Paraguay, 1976; dir. dentistry Erie County Med. Ctr., Buffalo, 1973—. Contbr. numerous articles to profl. jours.; contbr. 3 textbooks. Named Disting. Alumnus, Harvard U., 1988. Fellow Am. Acad. Oral Pathology, Am. Coll. Dentists, Internat. Coll. Dentists. Jewish. Home: 255 Louvaine Dr Buffalo NY 14223-2757 Office: SUNY Buffalo 355 Squire Hall Buffalo NY 14214-3008

FISH, BARBARA, psychiatrist, educator; b. N.Y.C., July 31, 1920; d. Edward R. and Ida (Citrin) F.; m. Max Saltzman, Dec. 12, 1953; children: Mark, Ruth Saltzman Deutsch. B.A. summa cum laude, Barnard Coll., Columbia U., 1942; M.D., NYU, 1945. Diplomate Am. Bd. Psychiatry and Neurology, Am. Bd. child psychiatry. Intern Bellevue Hosp., N.Y.C., 1945-47, resident in pediatrics, 1948-49, resident in psychiatry, 1949-52; resident in pediatrics N.Y. Hosp., N.Y.C., 1947-48; practice medicine specializing in child psychiatry N.Y.C., 1952-65; instr. psychiatry Med. Coll Cornell U., N.Y.C., 1955-60; instr. pediatrics Cornell U., 1955-56, asst. prof. clin. pediatrics, 1956-60; child psychiatrist dept. pediatrics N.Y. Hosp.-Cornell Med. Center, 1955-60; mem. faculty William A. White Inst. Psychoanalysis, N.Y.C., 1957-66; assoc. prof. psychiatry sch. medicine N.Y. U., N.Y.C., 1960-70; prof. N.Y. U., 1970-72, adj. prof., 1972—, dir. child psychiatry med. ctr., 1960-72; prof. psychiatry and behavioral sci. UCLA, 1972-89, Della Martin prof. psychiatry and behavioral sci., 1989-91, Della Martin prof. psychiatry and behavioral sci. emeritus, 1991—; mem. advisory com. mental health services for children N.Y.C. Community Mental Health Bd., 1963-72; mem. profl. advisory com. on children N.Y. State Dept. Mental Hygiene, 1966-72; mem. com. cert. child psychiatry Am. Bd. Psychiatry and Neurology, 1969-77; mem. clin. program projects research rev. com. NIMH, 1976-78. Contbr. articles on the antecedents of schizophrenia and other severe mental disorders, and on the psychiat. diagnosis and treatment of children; mem. editorial bd.: Jour. Am. Acad. Child Psychiatry, 1966-71, Jour. Autism and Childhood Schizophrenia, 1971-74, Child Devel. Abstracts and Bibliography, 1974-82, Archives Gen. Psychiatry, 1975-84. Recipient Woman of Sci. award UCLA, 1978; NIMH grantee, 1961-72, 78-88, Harriett A. Ames Charitable Trust grantee, 1961-66, William T. Grant Found. grantee, 1977-83, Scottish Rite schizophrenia rsch. grantee, 1979-87. Fellow Am. Psychiat. Assn. (Agnes McGavin award 1987), Am. Acad. Child Psychiatry, Am. Coll. Neuropsychopharmacology (charter); mem. Am. Psychopath. Assn. (v.p. 1967-68), Assn. for Research in Nervous and Mental Diseases, Soc. Research in Child Devel., Psychiat. Research Soc. Home: 16428 Sloan Dr Los Angeles CA 90049-1157 Office: UCLA Neuropsychiat Inst 760 Westwood Plz Los Angeles CA 90024-8300

FISH, JAMES EDMOND, medicine educator; b. Ann Arbor, Mich., Nov. 29, 1945; s. Robert Gerard and Jeanne Elizabeth (Kenney) F.; m. Pamela Stecker, Apr. 26, 1985; children; James E., Cory O. BS, U. Notre Dame, 1967; MD, Northwestern U., 1971. Diplomate Am. Bd. Internal Medicine, Nat. Bd. Med. Examiners. Resident Duke U. Med. Ctr., Durham, N.C., 1971-73; rsch. assoc. in pulmonary disease Johns Hopkins Med. Insts., Balt., 1973-75; fellow in pulmonary diseases Northwestern U. Med. Sch., Chgo., 1975-76, assoc. in medicine, 1976-77, asst. prof. medicine, 1977-79; asst. prof. medicine Johns Hopkins U. Sch. Medicine, Balt., 1979-83; assoc. prof. medicine and environ. health sci. Johns Hopkins U., Balt., 1983-85; prof. medicine, dir. pulmonary medicine and critical care Jefferson Med. Coll., Phila., 1985—. Editor Respiratory Medicine, 1994—, Bronchial Asthma: Index and Reviews, 1995—; editorial bd. Am. Rev. of Respiratory Disease, 1981-86, Postgraduate Medicine, 1991-95; contbr. numerous articles to profl. jours. Bd. dirs. Am. Lung Assn. Phila., 1990-93. Comdr. USPHS, 1973-75. Walsh-Hudson-Cavanaugh scholarship, 1966-67; Am. Lung Assn. fellowship, 1975-76, Owen L. Coon Found. fellowship, 1975-76, Edward L. Trudeau fellowship, 1976-78; grantee NIH, 1976-78. Fellow ACP, Am. Coll. Chest Physicians, Phila. Coll. Physicians; mem. AAAS, AMA, N.Y. Acad. Sci., Am. Physiol. Soc., Am. Fedn. Clin. Rsch., Am. Thoracic Soc., Am. Thoracic Assn. Pulmonary Program Dirs. (pres. Eastern sect. 1989-92, trustee 1989-92), Am. Acad. of Allergy and Clin. Immunology, Pa. Thoracic Soc., Pa. Soc. for Pulmonay Physicians, Am. Sleep Disorders Assn., Pa. Med. Soc., Phila. County Med. Assn., Alpha Epsilon Delta, Alpha Omega Alpha. Home: 1526 Monticello Dr Gladwyne PA 19035-1246 Office: Jefferson Med Coll 1025 Walnut St Philadelphia PA 19107-5001

FISH, JEFFERSON MORRIS, psychologist; b. N.Y.C., Nov. 27, 1942; s. Morris and Doris (Levine) F.; m. Dolores Newton, Feb. 28, 1970; 1 child, Krekamey. BA, CCNY, 1963; MS, Columbia U., 1966, PhD, 1969; Postdoctoral diploma in Behavior Modification, SUNY, Stony Brook, 1969. Diplomate Am. Bd. Profl. Psychology, Am. Bd. Family Psychology, Am. Bd. Adminstrv. Pyschology, Am. Bd. Clin. Psychology; lic. psychologist, N.Y. Asst. prof. psychology SUNY, Stony Brook, 1969-70; dir. psychology dept. Suffolk (N.Y.) Psychiat. Hosp., 1970-71; asst. prof. Hunter Coll., CUNY, 1971-74; dir. edn. and tng. Manhattan Psychiat. Ctr., N.Y.C., 1977-78; dir. clin. psychology St. John's U., Jamaica, N.Y., 1978-81, chmn. psychology dept., 1981-84, prof. psychology, 1978—; asst. field assessment officer Peace Corps, Tunisia Tng. Program, 1966, field Assessment officer, Ethiopia Tng. Program, 1968; vis. prof. grad. program in clin. psychology Inst. of Psychology, Cath. U. of Campinas, Sao Paulo, 1974-76; cons. in field. Author: Placebo Therapy: A Practical Guide to Social Influence in Psychotherapy, 1973, Dimensoes da Empatia Terapeutica, 1976; co-editor Psychology: Perspectives and Practice, 1990, Culture and Therapy, 1996; contbr. articles to profl. jours.; mem. editl. bd. Jour. Mental Imagery, 1981—, Jour. Strategic and Systemic Therapies, 1982-92, Jour. Systemic Therapies, 1993—, Estudos de Psicologia, 1985—, Jour. Urban Psychiatry, 1982-84, Psychology and Marketing, 1983-92, Familia, 1987—; mem. editl. adv. bd. Jour. Personality and Clinical Studies, 1989—; spkr., lectr. in field. Pres. acad. divsn. N.Y. State Psychol. Assn., 1984-85. Postdoctoral fellow SUNY, Stony Brook, 1968-69; Fulbright scholar, Brazil, 1987; grantee Brazilian Nat. Sci. Found., 1990, 94. Fellow APA, Am. Psychol. Soc., Am. Assn. Applied and Preventive Psychology; mem. N.Y. Acad. Scis. (chair psychology sect. 1987), Ea. Psychol. Assn., Internat. Coun. Psychologists (treas. 1987-90), Am. Anthrop. Assn., Assn. Advancement Behavior Therapy, Am. Bd. Family Psychology (bd. dirs. 1987-91). Home: 17 Polo Rd Great Neck NY 11023-1014 Office: St Johns U Dept Psychology Jamaica NY 11439

FISH, JOHN RONALD, ophthalmologist; b. Salt Lake City, Apr. 13, 1945; s. John Henry and Anna Marie (Hieserman) F.; m. Donna Jean Caldwell, Aug. 23, 1969; children: Dianna Marie, Larry Alan. BA in Chemistry, Tex. Tech U., 1966; MD, U. Tex., Galveston, 1970. Internship Meth. Hosp., Dallas, 1970-71; resident in ophthalmology U. Tex. Health Sci. Ctr., 1973-76; pvt. practice Big Spring, Tex., 1976—; cons. VA Hosp., Big Spring, 1976—; assoc. clin. prof. Med. Sch. Tex. Tech U., 1991—. Designer ophthalmic surg. instruments; contbr. numerous articles on cataract surgery to profl. jours. Capt. USAF, 1971-73. Mem. AMA, Tex. Med. Assn., Tex. Ophthal. Assn. (bd. of councilors 1991), Am. Soc. Cataract and Refractive Surgery, Rotary. Home: 606 Hillside Dr Big Spring TX 79720-5342 Office: Fish Ophthalmology Clinic 207 E 7th St Big Spring TX 79720-2706

FISH, STEWART ALLISON, retired obstetrician and gynecologist; b. Benton, Ill., Nov. 4, 1925; s. Floyd Hamilton and Mary Vivian (Fish) F.; m. Patsy June Patterson, Apr. 24, 1957; children: Jayne, Jeffrey, Carolyn, Mary. Student, Va. Poly. Inst., 1943-44, U. Va., 1944-45; M.D., U. Pa., 1949. Intern Hosp. of U. Pa., 1949-50; resident obstetrics and gynecology Columbia-Presbyn. Med. Center, N.Y.C., 1950-53; chief resident gynecology Free Hosp. Women, Boston, 1953-54; asst. prof. obstetrics and gynecology Southwestern Med. Sch. of U. Tex., 1954-56; pvt. practice obstetrics and gynecology Dallas, 1956; asst. prof. U. Ark. Med. Sch., 1962-66; prof., chmn. dept. obstetrics and gynecology U. Tenn. Med. Sch., 1966-75; obstetrician and gynecologist in chief City of Memphis Hosps.; mem. staff Bapt. Meml. Hosp.; mem. active staff Nacogdoches (Tex.) Med. Ctr. Hosp., 1975-95; ret., 1995; cons. U.S. Naval Hosp., St. Joseph Hosp., Meth. Hosp. Contbr. to med. jours. Served to ensign USNR, 1943-46. Recipient Golden Apple award U. Ark., 1966, 75; Bicentennial Silver medal Columbia Coll. Phys. and Surg., 1968. Fellow ACS, ACOG; mem. ABA, Tex. Med. Assn., Ctrl. Assn. Ob-Gyns., Tenn. Ob-Gyn. Soc. (pres. 1972-73), Tex. Assn. Ob-Gyns. (coun.), So. Med. Assn., Sigma Xi, Sigma Chi, Phi Chi. Episcopalian. Home: 3975 Rolling Hills St Nacogdoches TX 75961-9569

FISHBANE, BRUCE MARC, orthopedic surgeon; b. N.Y.C., May 2, 1949; s. Stanley M. and Irene S. (Schwartz) F.; m. Marsha Joy Meyers, Aug. 29, 1970; children: Alissa, Meredith, Lauren. BS, Pa. State. Univ., 1965; MD, Jefferson Medical Coll., 1971. Diplomate Am. Bd. Orthopedic Surgery. Surgical intern Thomas Jefferson Univ. Hosp., Phila., 1971-72, resident in gen. surgery, 1972-73; resident in orthopedic surgery Johns Hopkins Univ., Balt., 1973-77; orthopedic surgeon St. Mary's Medical Ctr., West Palm Beach, Fla., 1977—, Good Samaritan Medical Ctr., West Palm Beach, Fla., 1977—. Fellow Am. Acad. Orthopedic Surgeons; mem. AMA, Fla. Medical Assn., Palm Beach County Medical Assn., Fla. Orthopedic Soc. Office: Palm Beach Orthopedic Assoc 603 Village Blvd West Palm Beach FL 33409

FISHBURNE, JOHN INGRAM, JR., obstetrician-gynecologist, educator; b. Charleston, S.C., Aug. 18, 1937; m. Jean Crawford, June 10, 1971; children: John Ingram III, Barron Crawford, Virginia Heyward. AB, Princeton U., 1959; MD, Med. Coll. S.C., 1963. Diplomate Am. Bd. Ob-Gyn. (sub. specialty maternal-fetal medicine). Surg. intern Duke U. Hosp., Durham, N.C., 1963-64; resident in ob-gyn. U. N.C., Chapel Hill, 1966-70, resident in anesthesiology, 1970-72, instr. dept. ob-gyn., 1970-71, asst. prof., 1971-74, assoc. prof., 1974-75, asst. prof. dept. anesthesiology, 1972-75; assoc. prof. dept. ob-gyn. Bowman Gray Sch. Medicine, Wake Forest U., Winston-Salem, N.C., 1975-78; prof. Bowman Grey Sch. Medicine, Wake Forest U., Winston-Salem, N.C., 1978-83, assoc. prof. anesthesiology, dept. anesthesiology, 1975-83; prof., chmn. dept. ob-gyn. U. Okla. Health Scis. Ctr., Oklahoma City, 1983—, adj. prof. dept. anesthesiology, 1983—, chmn. search com. for chair pathology dept., 1987-88, chmn. search com. for chair family medicine dept., 1993-94; dir. maternal-fetal medicine dept. ob-gyn. Forsyth Meml. Hosp., Winston-Salem, 1977-83; vis. prof. U. W.I., Kingston, Jamaica, 1973-74, African-Health Tng. Instns. Project Nairobi, Kenya, 1975; cons. devel. mission U.S. AID, Dacca, Bangladesh, 1980, Assn. Vol. Surg. Contraception World Fedn. Health Agys., Manila, 1984, Singapore, 1986, Zhordania Inst., Tbilisi, Republic of Georgia, 1992, 93, Ivanovo, Russia, 1994, Almaty, Kazakhstan, 1994, St. Petersburg, Russia, 1995, Khojand, Tahjikistan, 1995, Odessa, Ulraine, 1995, Checkeurox, Moldova, 1996, L'uiv Ukrania; chmn. Gov.'s Task Force on Perinatal Care, 1984-86; mem. steering com. Robert Wood Johnson Healthy Futures of Okla., 1988-92; trustee Am. Assn. for Gynecologic Laparascopists, 1980-81; presenter numerous sci. papers and lectures local, nat. and internat. profl. meetings. Author: (with others) The Prostaglandins, 1972, Endocrine-Metabolic Drugs, 1974, Gynecologic Laparoscopy: Principles and Techniques, 1974, Laparoscopy, 1977, Endoscopy in Gynecology, 1978, Clinics in Perinatology, 1982, Obstetric Anesthesia, 1982, Clinical and Diagnostic Procedures Obstetrics and Gyncecology, Part B, 1984, Advances in Clinical Obstetrics and Gynecology, Medical Economics Books, 1985, Clinical Obstetrics, 1987, Danforth's Obstetrics and Gynecology, 1994, Bonica's Obstetric Analgesia and Anesthesia, 1995; contbr. update series Am. Coll. Obstetricians and Gynecologists; editorial bd. Obstetrics and Gynceology, 1985-89; author self instructional programs in field; contbr. numerous articles to profl. jours. Capt. USAFR, 1964-66. Clin. fellow Am. Cancer Soc. U. N.C., 1968-69, clin. fellow obstet. anesthesia Pub. Health Svc. U. Hosps. Case Western Res. U., 1969; tng. rsch. grantee NIH Med. U. S.C., 1961-62. Fellow ACOG (spl. interest rep. for obstet. anesthesia 1974-78, learning resources commn. 1981-82, mem. PROLOG task force for obstetrics 1981-82, chair residency rev. com. Accreditation Coun. Grad. Med. Edn. 1994-96, vice chair residency rev. com. coun. of chairs), Am. Coll. Anesthesiologists (assoc. examiner 1974); mem. Am. Soc. Anesthesiologists, Soc. Perinatal Obstetricians (rep. liaison com. ob.-gyn. 1983-89, bd. dirs. 1981-84), S. Atlantic Assn. Assn. Obstetricians and Gynecologists (assoc.), Perinatal Rsch. Soc., Oklahoma City Ob-Gyn. Soc., Okla. County Med. Soc., Okla. Anesthesia Soc., Internat. Soc. Advancement Humanistic Studies in Medicine, Cen. Assn. Obstetricians and Gynecologists, Continental Gynecol. Soc., So. Med. Assn., Am. Gynecol. and Obstet. Soc., Med. Alumni Assn., Med. U. S.C. (Disting. Alumnus award 1989), Alpha Omega Alpha. Episcopalian. Home: 1717 Elmhurst Ave Oklahoma City OK 73120-1011 Office: U Okla Health Scis Ctr Dept Ob-Gyn/PO Box 26901 Oklahoma City OK 73190

FISHER, BERNARD, surgeon, educator; b. Pitts., Aug. 23, 1918; s. Reuben and Anna (Miller) F.; m. Shirley Kruman, June 5, 1947; children: Beth, Joseph, Louisa. BS, U. Pitts., 1940, MD, 1943; DSc (hon.), Mt. Sinai Sch. Medicine, CUNY, 1986. Diplomate Am. Bd. Surgery. Intern Mercy Hosp., Pitts., 1943-44, resident in surgery, 1944-48; fellow in surg. research, resident in gen. surgery Harrison Dept. Dept. Surg. Research U. Pa., Phila., 1950-52; fellow London Postgrad. Med. Sch. Hammersmith Hosp., 1955-56; teaching fellow in pathology U. Pitts., 1944-45, teaching fellow in surgery, 1945-47, assoc. prof., 1956-59, prof. surgery, 1959-86, Disting. Svc. prof., 1986—; med. surg. staff Presbyn.-Univ. Hosp., 1953—; mem. cons. staff Children's Hosp., Pitts., Magee-Women's Hosp., VA Hosp., Pitts.; chmn. Nat. Surg. Adjuvant Breast and Bowel Project, 1967-94, sci. dir., 1995—; chmn. Adjuvant Therapy Ctr., 1973-94, Breast Care and Diagnostic Ctr., 1980-93, Pitts. Cancer Inst., 1985—, Comprehensive Breast Care Ctr., 1992—; mem. spl. del. to China, 1977; mem. President's Cancer Panel, 1979-82, Nat. Cancer Adv. Bd., 1986-92, Inst. Medicine of NAS. Mem. editl. bd. Transplantation, 1966-71, Cancer, 1969-73, 75, Year Book of Cancer, 1973-85, Internat. Jour. Radiation Oncology Biology Physics, 1975-78, Cancer Clin. Trials, 1977, Invasion and Metastatis, 1981-85, Cancer Metastasis Revs., 1981-85, Jour. Clin. Oncology, 1982-87, Internat. Jour. Breast and Mammary Pathology, 1982-84, Cancer Rsch., 1976, Seminars in Oncology, 1979, Breast Cancer Rsch. and Treatment, 1980, 92—, Clin. and Exptl. Metastasis, 1980-94, Breast Diseases: Yr. Book Quar., 1989-95, Annals Surg. Oncology, 1993-96, Internat. Jour. Oncology, 1993-94, Advances in Oncology, 1992—, Breast Disease: Internat. Jour., 1993—, Cancer Jour., 1994—, Internat. Jour. Cancer, 1994—, European Jour. Cancer, 1995-97; contbr. over 500 articles to med. jours. Recipient Man of yr. award in medicine Pitts. Jr. C. of C., 1966, Philip Hench Disting. Alumnus award U. Pitts. Sch. Medicine, 1976, McGraw medal Detroit surg. Assn., 1978, Lucy Wortham James Clin. Rsch. award, 1981, Heath Meml. award, 1982, Joseph H. Morton Meml. award, 1983, Julia Hudson Freund Meml. award, 1983, Albert Lasker Med. rsch. award, 1985, Hammer Cancer prize 1988, Am. Cancer Soc. Medal of Honor, 1986, Milken Med. Found. Ctr. Rsch. award, 1989, Assn. Commn. Cancer Ctrs. award, 1990, Chancellors Dist. Rsch. award U. Pitts., 1992, Nat. Health Couns. Med. Rsch. award, 1992, Brinker Internat. Breast Cancer award 1992, Durham N.C. City of Medicine award, 1992, Dr. Josef Steiner Cancer Rsch. prize, 1992, GM Cancer Rsch. Found. Kettering prize, 1993, Susan Komen Found. Sci. Distinction award, 1988, Bristol-Myers Squib award, 1993, James Ewing Lectr. award SSO, 1993, Gottlieb Meml. award, 1993, Sheen award, 1993, Claude Jacquillet award, 1995, Lifetime Achievement award in Breast Cancer Rsch., Senologic Internat. Soc., 1996; Markle scholar in med. sci. John and Mary Markle Found., 1953-58; Alpha Omega Alpha, 1989, Fisher Breast Cancer lectureship established in his honor U. Pitts., 1989. Fellow AAAS; mem. AAUP, ACS, Assn. Cancer Edn., Am. Assn. Cancer Research (bd. dirs.), Am. Soc. Clin. Oncology (pres. 1992-93, bd. dirs., Karnofsky award 1980), Am. Physiol. Soc., Assn. Am. Med. Colls., Cell Kinetic Soc., Am. Surg. Assn. (v.p. 1996), N.Y. Acad. Scis., Soc. Surg. Oncology, Soc. Univ. Surgeons, Am. Socs. for Exptl. Biology, Pa. Med. Soc., Allegheny County Med. Soc. (Man of Yr. award 1983), Pitts. Acad. Medicine, Pitts. Surg. Soc. (pres. 1979), Peruvian Acad. Surgery (hon.), Italian Surg. Research Assn., Assn. Italiana per la Divulgaxione Sci. della Cancerologia Clinica, Internat. Assn. Breast Cancer Research, Am. Italian Fedn. Cancer Research, Phi Beta Kappa. Office: U Pitts Sch Medicine Rm 914 Scaife Hall 3550 Terrace St Pittsburgh PA 15213-2500

FISHER, BONNIE LEE MICHAELSON, psychologist; b. N.Y.C., Aug. 7, 1948; d. Robert and Lillian (Pecker) Barber; m. H. Edward Fisher, Aug. 23, 1986; 1 child, Rachel. BA cum laude, NYU, 1970; MA, Temple U., 1972, PhD, 1974. Lic. psychologist, Md., Del. Dir. counseling ctr. Washington Coll., Chestertown, Md., 1973—; clin. cons. Kent County Health Dept., Chestertown, 1974-87; clin. dir. Tressler Ctr., Dover, Delaware, 1985-90, Project 801 Aid-in-Dover, 1980-90. Mem. Am. Psychol. Assn. Home: 54 Bohemia Ln Earleville MD 21919-1116 Office: Washington Coll Counseling Ctr Chestertown MD 21620

FISHER, DAVID CLARENCE, optometrist; b. Detroit, Jan. 31, 1960; s. Edward Thomas and Bertha Lynn (Sanders) F. BS in Biol. Sci., U. Calif., Irvine, 1983; MPH in Epidemiology, UCLA, 1985; BS in Visual Sci., So. Calif. Coll. Optometry, Fullerton, 1987, OD, 1989. Lic. optometrist, Calif. Med. researcher U. Calif. Med. Ctr., Orange, 1982-83; epidemiologist Wadsworth VA Hosp., Brentwood, Calif., 1984-85; optometrist U.S. Indian Health Svc., Chinle, Ariz., 1988, Brentwood VA Hosp., 1989, Bellflower (Calif.) Med. Group, 1989-90, Rancho Calif. Vision Ctr., Temecula, Calif., 1990-93, Whittier (Calif.) Contact Lens Ctr., 1994-95; asst. prof. optometry, dir. Rural Eye Program Northeastern State U., Tahleguah, Okla., 1995—; optometrist Norton AFB, 1991-93, Geoge AFB, 1991-93, Whittier Contact Lens Ctr., 1993-94. Dep. sheriff Orange County Sheriff's Dept., Santa Ana, 1986-95. Libert U. scholar, 1978-80, USPHS scholar UCLA, 1983-85. Mem. APHA, Am. Optometric Assn., Orange County Optometric Assn., Okla. Optometric Assn., U. Calif.-Irvine Alumni Assn., So. Calif. Coll. of Optometry Alumni Assn., U. Calif.-L.A. Alumni Assn. Office: Rural Eye Program Coll Optometry Northeastern State Univ Tahlequah OK 74464

FISHER, DELBERT ARTHUR, physician, educator; b. Placerville, Calif., Aug. 12, 1928; s. Arthur Lloyd and Thelma (Johnson) F.; m. Beverly Carne Fisher, Jan. 28, 1951; children: David Arthur, Thomas Martin, Mary Kathryn. BA, U. Calif., Berkeley, 1950; MD, U. Calif., San Francisco, 1953. Diplomate Am. Bd. Pediatrics. Intern, resident in pediatrics U. Calif. Med. Center, San Francisco, 1953-55; resident in pediatrics U. Oreg. Hosp., Portland, 1957-58; from asst. prof. to assoc. prof. pediatrics Med. Sch. U. Ark., Little Rock, 1960-67, prof. pediatrics, 1967-68; prof. pediatrics UCLA, 1968-73; prof. pediatrics and medicine Med. Sch., UCLA, 1973-91, prof. emeritus, 1991—; chief, pediatric endocrinology Harbor-UCLA Med. Ctr., 1968-73, rsch. prof. devel. and perinatal biology, 1975-85, chmn. pediatrics, 1985-89, sr. scientist Rsch. and Edn. Inst., 1991—; dir. Walter Martin Rsch. Ctr., 1986-91; pres. Nichols Inst. Reference Labs, 1991-93; pres. Nichols Acad. Assocs., 1993-94, chief sci. officer, 1993-94; pres. acad. assocs., chief sci. officer Corning Nichols Inst., 1994—; cons. genetic disease sect. Calif. Dept. Health Svcs., 1978—; mem. organizing com. Internat. Conf. Newborn Thyroid Screening, 1977-88; examiner Am. Bd. Pediatrics, 1971-80, mem. subcom. on pediatric endocrinology, 1976-79. Co-editor: Pediatric Thyroidology, 1985, five other books; editor-in-chief Jour. Clin. Endocrinology and Metabolism, 1978-83, Pediatric Rsch., 1984-89; contbr. chpts. to numerous books; contbr. over 400 articles to profl. jours. Capt. M.C., USAF, 1955-57. Recipient Career Devel. award NIH, 1964-68. Mem. Inst. Medicine NAS, Am. Acad. Pediatrics (Borden award 1981), Soc. Pediatric Rsch. (v.p. 1973-74), Am. Pediatric Soc. (pres. 1992-93), Endocrine Soc. (pres. 1983-84), Am. Thyroid Assn. (pres. 1988-89), Am. Soc. Clin. Investigation, Assn. Am. Physicians, Lawson Wilkins Pediatric Endocrine Soc. (pres. 1982-83), Western Soc. Pediatric Rsch. (pres. 1983-84), Phi Beta Kappa, Alpha Omega Alpha. Home: 24582 Santa Clara Ave Dana Point

CA 92629-3031 Office: Corning Nichols Inst 33608 Ortega Hwy San Juan Capistrano CA 92690

FISHER, DONALD WAYNE, medical association executive; b. Pitts., Mar. 2, 1946; s. David H.W. and Jean K. F.; children by previous marriage—Kimberly Elizabeth, Jeffrey Wayne. A.A., Hinds Jr. Coll., 1966; B.S. in Biology and Chemistry, Millsaps Coll., 1968; M.S. in Anatomy, U. Miss., 1970, Ph.D. in Anatomy, 1973; postgrad. in assn. mgmt., U. Md., 1977-79. Cert. assn. exec. Instr. dept. chemistry and biology Hinds Jr. Coll., Raymond, Miss., 1968-74; instr. dept. anatomy U. Miss. Sch. Medicine, Jackson, 1973-74; co-dir. and exec. officer physician asst. program U. Miss. Sch. Medicine, 1972-74; asst. professorial lectr. George Washington U. Sch. Medicine, 1974—; exec. dir. Assn. Physician Asst. Programs, Arlington, Va., 1974-80, Am. Acad. Physician Assts., Arlington, 1974-80; CEO Am. Med. Group Assn., Alexandria, Va., 1980—; pres., CEO Am. Group Practice Corp., Inc., 1989, treas. polit. action com., 1980—; mem. Nat. Commn. on Allied Health Edn., 1977-80; mem. adv. com. for tng., devel. and utilization of physician extenders Systems Scis., Inc., 1975-80; pres. Am. Acad. Physician Assts. Ednl. and Rsch. Found., 1977-80; sec., treas. Am. Group Practice Found., 1980—; mem. Am. Express Health Care Faculty, 1985-88. Robert Wood Johnson Found. grantee, 1973-80. Mem. Am. Soc. Assn. Execs. (govt. rels. com. 1980—), Assn. Am. Med. Colls., AAAS, Am. Internat. Health Alliance (bd. dirs. 1992—, treas. 1995—), Greater Washington Soc. Assn. Execs., Fairfax County Hosp. Assn., Arlington (Va.) C. of C. Home: 3814 Ivanhoe Ln Alexandria VA 22310-2170 Office: Am Med Group Assn 1422 Duke St Alexandria VA 22314-3403

FISHER, EDWARD ABRAHAM, cardiologist, educator; b. Honolulu, Apr. 30, 1958; s. Hyman Wendell and Rosalie (Joseph) F.; m. Vivian Degenszejn, Mar. 27, 1993; children: Rebecca, Alexander. BA in Econs., U. Va., 1980; MD, Ea. Va. Med. Sch., 1984. Diplomate Nat. Bd. Med. Examiners, Am. Bd. Internal Medicine, Am. Bd. Cardiovascular Disease; lic. physician, N.Y. Intern Lenox Hill Hosp., N.Y.C., 1984-85, resident, 1985-87, adj. attending physician dept. medicine, 1987—; cardiology fellow Mt. Sinai Med. Ctr., N.Y.C., 1987-89, cardiology rsch. fellow, 1989-90, acting clin. asst. dept. medicine, 1990, asst. dir. echocardiography dept. medicine divsn. cardiology, 1990—; asst. attending Mt. Sinai Sch. Medicine, N.Y.C., 1990-92, asst. clin. prof., 1992—. Co-contbr.: The Menopause and Replacement Therapy: Facts and Controversies, 1991, Native Aortic Valve Endocarditis, Transesophogeal Echocardiography, 1995, Restrictive Cardiomyopathy, 1995; sect. editor Cardiovascular Rev. Reports, 1992-94; contbr. articles to profl. publs. and mags. Fellow ACP, Am. Coll. Cardiology, Am. Heart Assn. Office: 941 Park Ave New York NY 10028-0318 also: Mt Sinai Med Ctr Divsn Cardiology Box 1030 1 Gustave L Levy Pl New York NY 10029-6504

FISHER, EDWARD ALLEN, educator, physician, biochemist; b. N.Y.C., Nov. 5, 1950; s. Bernard S. and Renee (Nissim) F.; m. Catherine Williams, Jan. 20, 1977 (div. 1980); 1 child, Matthew; m. Jill F. Feltheimer, Nov. 3, 1985; children: Laura, Claudia. BA, Harpur Coll., 1971; MPH, U. N.C., 1978; MD, NYU, 1975; PhD, MIT, 1982. Diplomate Am. Bd. Pediatrics. Resident in pediatrics Duke U. Med. Ctr., Durham, N.C., 1975-77; fellow nutrition and metabolism Boston Children's Hosp., 1978-81; med. staff fellow NIH, Bethesda, Md., 1981-84; asst. prof. pediatircs U. Pa., Phila., 1984-87; asst. prof. biochemistry and medicine Med. Coll. Pa., Phila., 1987-91, assoc. prof. biochemistry and pediatrics, 1991-95; dir. lipoprotein rsch. Mount Sinai Cardiovascular Inst., 1995—. Contbr. articles to profl. jours. USPHS postdoctoral fellow, 1977-78, 78-81, 81-84; NIH grantee, 1989. Fellow Am. Heart Assn. (coun. arteriosclerosis), Am. Inst. Nutrition; mem. AAAS. Home: 188 Rock Creek Ln Scarsdale NY 10583 Office: Rockefeller U Box 4 Dept Biochemistry 1230 York Ave New York NY 10021

FISHER, GAIL FEIMSTER, government official; d. Maurice Blake and Sarah Estelle (Abell) Feimster; m. Eugene Joseph Fisher, Dec. 2, 1950 (dec.); children: Laurene Eugene, Robert Maurice. BA, U. Md., 1949, MA, 1951; PhD, U. N.C., 1976. Rsch. analyst Bur. of State Svcs., Dept. HHS, 1956-66; evaluation officer Bur. Health Svcs., Dept. HHS, 1966-68; planning officer Nat. Ctr. Health Stats.-Ctr. for Disease Control-Dept. HHS, Rockville, Md., 1968-93; assoc. dir. Nat. Ctr. Health Stats.-Ctr. for Disease Control-Dept. HHS, Hyattsville, Md., 1973—. Contbr. rsch. reports to profl. jours. and presentations. Home: PO Box 234 La Plata MD 20646 Office: DHHS-CDC-Nat Ctr Hlth Stats 6525 Belcrest Rd Hyattsville MD 27709

FISHER, HANS, nutritional biochemistry educator; b. Breslau, Silesia, Germany, Mar. 4, 1928; s. George and Johanna (Gottheiner) F.; m. Ruth Hirschberg, July 24, 1950; children: Deborah M. Joseph, David E. Fisher, Daniel Z. Fisher. MS, U. Conn., 1952; PhD, U. Ill., 1954. Cert. Am. Bd. Nutrition. Asst. prof. Rutgers U., New Brunswick, N.J., 1954-57, assoc. prof., 1957-62, prof., 1962-72, dept. chair, 1966-88, assoc. provost, 1988-90, disting. prof., 1972—; cons. food and pharm. industries, 1955—. Author: Rutgers Guide to Lowering Your Cholesterol, 1986; contbr. articles to profl. jours. Pres. Highland Park (N.J.) Temple Ctr., 1975-77; v.p. YMHA, Highland Park, 1958-70. Fellow AAAS, Am. Inst. Nutrition, N.Y. Acad. Scis.; mem. Am. Chem. Soc. Jewish. Home: 216 N 3rd Ave Highland Park NJ 08904-2412 Office: Rutgers U PO Box 231 New Brunswick NJ 08903-0231

FISHER, JAMES WILLIAM, medical educator, pharmacologist; b. Tucapau (now Startex), S.C., May 22, 1925; s. Ernest Amaziah and Mamie V. (Turner) F.; m. Carol Barbara Brodarick, June 5, 1947; children: Candis Loreen Fisher Smith, Patricia E., Richard W., William E., John C., Elaine Marie Fisher Spurr. B.S., U. S.C., 1947; Ph.D. in Pharmacology (USPHS fellow), U. Louisville, 1958. Devel. chemist Armour Pharm. Rsch. Labs., Chgo., 1950-53; pharmacologist Lloyd Bros. Pharm. Co., Cin., 1954-56; instr. pharmacology U. Tenn., 1958-60, asst. prof., 1960-62, assoc. prof., 1962-66, prof., 1966-68; prof., chmn. dept. pharmacology Med. Sch., Tulane U., 1968—; Regents prof. pharmacology Tulane U., 1987—, James W. Fisher Disting. Lectureship in Pharmacology, 1991—; vis. prof. U. Zambia, Lusaka, 1987, Keio U., Tokyo, 1987, U. Nairobi, 1993; external examiner U. W.I., Trinidad, 1992; vis. scientist Christie Hosp. and Holt Radium Inst., Manchester, Eng., 1963-64; dir. Tulane-Universidad Nacional del Nordeste, Corrientes, Argentina, Pan Am. Health Orgn. Physiol. Scis. Tng. Program, 1972-77; lectr. in field; mem. Nat. Heart, Lung and Blood Inst. (erythropoietin com. 1971-74), mem. NIH hematology tng. grants com., 1977; mem. Cooley's Anemia Nat. Rsch. Com., 1974; pres. So. Blood Club, 1975-77; mem. Wellcome Professorships Com., 1976, 93, 94, 95; mem. pharmacology com. Nat. Bd. Med. Examiners, 1988-92; mem. ad hoc group med. rsch. funding AAMC, 1990-93. Author: Readings on the History of Pharmacology; editor: Kidney Hormones, Vol. I, 1971, Vol. II, 1977, Vol. III, 1986, Renal Pharmacology, 1971, Handbook of Pharmacology: Blood and Blood Forming Organs, 1992; co-editor: Erythropoiesis, 1975, Erythropoietin and Erythropoiesis, 1981; cons. editor: Erythropoietin, 1968; mem. editl. bd. Proc. Soc. Exptl. Biology and Medicine, 1971-86; contbr. articles to profl. jours. Served to lt. (j.g.) USNR, 1943-46, PTO. Recipient rsch. career devel. award USPHS, 1960-65, Purkinje medal Czechoslovakia Med. Soc., 1975, Golden Sovereign award, 1976, Aspet Exptl. Therapeutics award, 1992; named Disting. faculty AOA Honor Med. Soc., 1993; Ann. Tulane Fisher Lectureship established in his honor, 1992. Mem. AAAS, AAUP, Am. Soc. Pharmacology and Exptl. Therapeutics (Sollman awards com. 1981, therapeutics award com. 1982, 94, alerting network 1986-90, ednl. affairs com. 1986-89, Krayer awards com. 1990, extpl. therapeutics award 1992, 94), Soc. Exptl. Biology and Medicine, Am. Soc. Nephrology, Am. Soc. Hematology (sci. affairs com. 1973-74, chmn. eythropoietin subcom. 1973), Assn. Med. Sch. Pharmacology (exec. com. 1979-82, chmn. nominating com. 1975, 86, 94, 96, chmn. essential knowledge base in pharmacology com. 1984-95, pres. 1990-92), N.Y. Acad. Scis., Sigma Xi. Home: 4025 S Pin Oak Ave New Orleans LA 70131-8449

FISHER, JEFFREY DAVID, cardiologist, educator; b. Bklyn., Jan. 11, 1951; s. Joseph and Marian (Traub) F.; m. Judy Essig, May 8, 1977 (div. June, 1981); m. Michelle Densen, Feb. 2, 1985; children: Katherine, James. AB, Cornell U., 1972; MD, Albert Einstein U., 1976. Intern, resident Bronx (N.Y.) Mcpl. Hosp. Ctr., 1976-79; fellow in cardiology Johns Hopkins Hosp., Balt., 1979-81; asst. prof. medicine Cornell U. Med. Coll., N.Y.C., 1981-87, assoc. prof. clin. medicine, 1987-89, clin. assoc. prof. medicine, 1989—; cons. cardiologist pvt. practice, N.Y.C., 1989—. Contbr. articles to Circulation, Am. Jour. Cardiology, Chest. Fellow ACP, Am. Coll. Cardiology; mem. Am. Heart Assn. (gov. clin. coun.). Office: 211 E 72d St New York NY 10021-4684

FISHER, JEFFREY ROBERT, physician assistant; b. Tiffin, Ohio, Nov. 5, 1960; s. David Robert and Majorie Ann (King) F. BS, Alderson Broaddus Coll., 1984; MS, Cen. Mich. U., 1992. Physician asst. Parsons Ave Med. Clinic, Columbus, Ohio, 1984-86, Diversified Physician Svcs., Columbus, 1986-90, Corp. Med. Affairs, Ashland Oil Co., Inc., Columbus, 1990-94; pres. Occupl. and Environ. Health Network; ops. mgr. DHCORP of Columbus; liaison physician asst. Medicare div. Nationwide Ins., Columbus, 1987-88; chmn. physician asst. adv. com. Ohio State Med. Bd., Columbus, 1987-91. Fellow Am. Acad. Physician Assts. (mem. conf. com. 1985-87), Ohio Assn. Physician Assts. (chmn. com. 1985, sec. 1986, v.p. 1987, 88, 89, pres.-elect. 1990, pres. 1991); mem. Am. Acad. Physician Assts. in Occupational Medicine. Roman Catholic. Home: 5332 Cosgray Rd Amlin OH 43002 Office: Ashland Oil Inc Corp Med Affairs 1299 Olentangy River Rd Columbus OH 43212

FISHER, JERID MARTIN, neuropsychologist; b. Houston, July 12, 1953; s. Seymour and Rhoda (Feinberg) F. BS magna cum laude, Duke U., 1975; MS in Psychology, U. Rochester, 1981, PhD in Clin. Psychology, 1981. Diplomate Am. Bd. Profl. Neuropsychology; lic. psychologist. Clin. dir. neuropsychiatry lab. U. Rochester, Rochester, N.Y., 1982-83; asst. dir. neuropsychiatry unit U. Rochester, Rochester, 1982-83, sr. instr. psychiatry and neurology, 1981-83; dir. Head Injury Ctr. at Highgate, Troy, N.Y., 1984; dir./developer Neurologic Ctr. at Highgate, Cortland, N.Y., 1985; pres., chief exec. officer Neurorehab Assocs., Inc., Rochester, N.Y., 1985-93; pres. Comprehensive Rehab Network, Inc., Rochester, N.Y., 1987-93, Brain Injury Consultants, Inc., Rochester, N.Y., 1993—; adj. asst. prof. SUNY, Albany, 1984—; clin. asst. prof. neurology U. Rochester Med. Sch., 1988—; developer brain injury rehab. program St. Mary's Hosp., Rochester, 1987-91, Our Lady of Victory Hosp., Buffalo, 1986-91. Contbr. articles to profl. jours. Adv. Compeer, Rochester, 1978—. Mem. APA, Internat. Neuropsychol. Soc., Nat. Acad. Neuropsychology, Am. Bd. of Profl. Disability Cons., Am. Congress Rehab. Medicine, Phi Beta Kappa. Republican. Jewish. Office: 1 Centennial Ct Fairport NY 14450-4113

FISHER, JOHN ANDRE, pharmacist; b. Wilsonville, Nebr., Sept. 24, 1931; s. Ralph Bailey and Maude Virgil (Andre) F.; m. Margaret Elsie Thomas, Sept. 9, 1951; children: Margaret Ruth Fisher Wood, Steven John, Anita Sue Holder. BS in Pharmacy, U. Nebr., 1954. Registered pharmacist, Nebr. Pharmacist Clin. Pharmacy, Valentine, Nebr., 1954, ptnr., 1956-73, owner, 1973-95; cons. pharmacist, Cherry County Hosp., Valentine, 1960-74, Pine View Manor Nursing Home, Valentine, 1978-85; preceptor, U. Nebr. Coll. of Pharmacy, Omaha, 1979-89. Mem. Valentine Vol. Fire Dept., 1960-80, fire chief, 1969-70; chmn. State Fire Marshalls Adv. Com., Lincoln, Nebr., 1971-75; organizer Cherry County Sheriff Res., Valentine, 1973-88. Recipient Bowl of Hygeia award, AH Robbins, 1979. Mem. Nebr. Pharmacists Assn. (pres. 1975-76), Nebr. Bd. Examiners in Pharmacy (chmn. 1984-86), Nat. Assn. Retail Pharmacists (nom. com. 1974), Nat. Assn. Bd. of Pharmacy (constitution and by-laws nom. com. 1985), Rotary, U. Nebr. Alumni Assn., Mason (Master 1964), Eastern Star (Worthy Patron 1966), Shrine. Republican. Presbyterian. Home: HC 15 Box 2 Valentine NE 69201-9302 Office: Clinic Pharmacy PO Box 176 Valentine NE 69201-0176

FISHER, JOHN D., ophthalmologist; b. Niagara Falls, Feb. 25, 1947; s. Malcolm Everett and Ruth Sanford (Hagerman) F.; m. Christie Winn Riddle, Dec. 27, 1969; children: Kathleen, Kevin, Lori. BA, Rice U., 1970, MEE, 1970, PhD, 1974; MD, U. Tex., San Antonio, 1977. Diplomate Am. Bd. Ophthalmology. Chief of ophthalmology VA, Temple, Tex., 1982—; assoc. prof. surgery Tex. A&M Med. Sch., College Station, 1982—; commrs. JCAHPO, Mpls., 1992—; field adv. com. on ophthalmology, VA, Washington, 1992—. Fellow Am. Acad. Ophthalmology; mem. Am. Acad. Ophthalmology Coun., Rotary. Methodist. Office: Vet Affairs Hosp 1901 S 1st St Temple TX 76524

FISHER, MARK JAY, neurologist, neuroscientist, educator; b. N.Y.C., Aug. 23, 1949; s. Ralph Aaron and Dorothy Ann (Weissman) F.; m. Janeth Godeau, Aug. 5, 1994. BA in Polit. Sci., UCLA, 1970; MA in Polit. Sci., U. S.D., 1972, BS in Medicine, 1973; MD, U. Cin., 1975. Diplomate Am. Bd. Psychiatry and Neurology. Intern UCLA Sepulveda VA Hosp., 1975-76; resident UCLA Wadsworth VA Hosp., 1976-79, chief resident, 1979-80; faculty mem. U. So. Calif. Sch. of Medicine, L.A., 1980—, prof. neurology, 1995—, dir. stroke rsch. program, 1980—; dir. residency tng. program U. So. Calif. Sch. Medicine, L.A., 1992-96. Editor: Medical Therapy of Acute Stroke, 1989. Recipient Tchr. Investigator award NIH, Bethesda, Md., 1984-89, Program Project grantee, 1994—. Mem. Am. Acad. Neurology, Am. Neurol. Assn., Am. Heart Assn. (stroke coun.), Nat. Stroke Assn., Internat. Soc. for Thrombosis and Haemostasis. Office: U So Calif Sch Medicine Dept of Neurology 1333 San Pablo St MCH 246 Los Angeles CA 90033

FISHER, MILDRED LUCILLE, retired nurse; b. Briggs, Tex., Feb. 12, 1919; d. Hubert W. and Zula (Stewart) Hall; m. Gordon Williams, Sept. 26, 1936 (div. 1979); children: Barbara Williams Drosche, Marilyn Williams Stone. Student, Tex. Woman's U.; grad., U. Houston, 1955. Lic. R.N., Tex. Pvt. office nurse Dr. Alan Lambert, Houston, 1955-56, 57-60, Dr. Victor Zima, Houston, 1956-57; nurse Galena Park Schs. (Tex.), 1960-74, Sam Houston Hosp., Houston, 1974-77; staff nurse med. unit Gen. Post Office, Houston, 1978-79; nurse, dir. health Leander Schs. (Tex.), 1979-85, ret. 1985. Campaign worker Senator Lloyd Doggett, Austin, Tex., 1981-83. Recipient Florence Nightingale award, 1955. Democrat. Methodist. Club: Byliners. Home: 1800 Junction Hwy Apt 1B Kerrville TX 78028

FISHER, ROBERT ANTHONY, transplant surgeon; b. San Antonio, Sept. 6, 1955; s. Robert William and Sofia Noy (Mata) F.; m. Joanne Nadine Hacha, Oct. 30, 1982; children: Ryan, Aaron, Alexander. BS, Tex. A&M U., 1976; MD, Baylor Coll. of Medicine, 1980. Diplomate Am. Bd. Surgery. Intern, gen. surgery resident Case Western Res. U. Hosps., Cleve., 1980-85; instr. in surgery U. Cin. Med. Ctr., 1989-91; surg. dir. liver transplant svc. Med. Coll. Va., Richmond, 1991-93, program dir. liver transplant program, 1993—, asst. prof. surgery and pediat., 1991-96, assoc. prof. surgery, 1996—; mem. spl. review com. NIH, Bethesda, Md., 1994—; mem. transplant ctr. bd. dirs. Med. Coll. Va., 1993—; surgeon to med. malpractice review panel Supreme Ct. Va., Richmond, 1993—; med. advisor LifeNet Ctrl. Va., Richmond, 1993—; guest faculty Joint Congress on Liver Transplantation Internat., London, 1995. Contbr. articles to profl. jours. Mem., rep. for Med. Coll. Va., United Network of Organ Sharing, Richmond, 1992—; mem., rep. for Med. Coll. Va., The Travelers Co., Richmond, 1992—; credentials com. Naval Hosp. Phila., 1985-87; liaison cancer control program Pa. Dept. Health, Phila., 1985-87. Lt. comdr. USN, 1985-89. Fellow Am. Coll. Surgeons; mem. Am. Soc. Transplant Surgeons, Med. Soc. Va., Richmond Acad. Medicine, Soc. Am. Gastrointestinal Endoscopic Surgeons. Office: Med Coll Va Sanger Hall Rm 8-012 1101 E Marshall St B Richmond VA 23298

FISHER, ROBERT DARRYL, cardiovascular and thoracic surgeon, lawyer; b. Wewoka, Okla., Sept. 18, 1939; s. R. D. and Lurine (Weir) F.; m. Orpha Lou Morrison, Aug. 19, 1961; children: Eric Scott, Laura Elizabeth. BS, East Cen. U., 1960; MD, U. Okla. Health Scis. Ctr., 1964; JD, Oklahoma City U., 1989. Diplomate Am. Bd. Surgery, Am. Bd. Thoracic Surgery. Surgical intern then resident Johns Hopkins Hosp., Balt., 1964-66; sr. and chief resident Johns Hopkins Hosp., 1969-73; clin. assoc. NIH, Bethesda, Md., 1966-68; rsch. fellow Harvard Med. Sch., Boston, 1968-69; assoc. prof. Sch. Medicine Vanderbilt U., Nashville, 1973-78; pvt. practice Oklahoma City, 1978—; chmn. bd. dirs. Pontotoc County Bank, Roff, Okla., 1989—; bd. dirs. Granite Reins. Co., Oklahoma City, 1988—. Contbr. articles to profl. jours. Recipient Disting. Alumnus award East Cent. U., 1980; Nat. Med. Scis. Tng. grantee., 1969-73. Mem. AMA, ABA, Am. Assn. for Thoracic Surgery, Soc. for Thoracic Surgery, So. Thoracic Surg. Soc., Soc. Univ. Surgeons, Okla. Med. Assn., Alpha Omega Alpha. Presbyterian. Office: Cardiac Surgeons of Oklahoma City Inc 3366 NW Expwy Ste 520 Oklahoma City OK 73112-4429

FISHER, ROBERT GEORGE, neurological surgeon, educator; b. Bound Brook, N.J., Jan. 6, 1917; s. F. LeRoy and Anna (Young) F.; m. Constance M. Sheehan, May 23, 1942; children: David, Carol, Robert. BS, Rutgers U., 1938; MD, U. Pa., 1942; PhD, U. Minn., 1949. Diplomate Am. Bd. Neurol. Surgery, v.p., 1974. Intern Hosp. of U. Pa., Phila., 1942-43; fellow in neurosurgery Mayo Clinic, Rochester, Minn., 1946-49; sr. resident, staff neurosurgeon Johns Hopkins Hosp., Balt., 1949-51; chief dept. neurosurgery Dartmouth Coll., Hanover, N.H., 1951-67, U. Okla., Oklahoma City, 1967-74, Rutgers U., New Brunswick, N.J., 1978-87; affiliated with dept. neurosurgery Dartmouth Coll., Hanover, N.H., 1987—. Contbr. articles to profl. jours., chpts. to books. Cubmaster Boy Scouts am., Hanover, 1961. Served to capt. AUS, 1943-46, PTO. Fellow ACS; mem. Congress Neurosurgery (editor 1955-58, sr. mem.), Am. Acad. Neurosurgery (v.p. 1973), Am. Assn. Neurosurgery (exec. com. 1973), Soc. Neurosurgeons, AMA. Republican. Home: 87 Shore Dr N Bristol NH 03222-9751

FISHER, ROBERT THOMAS, orthopaedic surgeon; b. Frederick, Md., July 14, 1951; s. Robert T. Sr. and Anne Calvert (Smith) F.; m. Elizabeth Collmus, Aug. 23, 1975; children: Robert III, James, Harrison, Elizabeth. BA, W.Va. U., 1973; MD, U. Md., 1977. Orthopaedic surgeon pvt. practice, Frederick, Md., 1982—; chief orthopaedics Frederick Meml. Hosp., 1986-88, chmn. dept. surgery, 1989-91, chmn. oper. rm./recovery rm., 1995—. Pres. Frederick Coalition Club, 1989. Pres. Frederick Cotillion Club, 1989. Fellow Am. Acad. Orthopaedic Surgeons; mem. Eastern Orthopaedic Assn., Md. ORthopaedic Soc., Frederick County Med. Soc. Democrat. Office: 52 Thomas Johnson Dr Frederick MD 21702

FISHER, SETH W., physician; b. Phila., Oct. 24, 1956; s. Seth Myles and Ruth E. (Miller) F.; m. Carolyn June Readler, June 13, 1987. BA, Bucknell U., 1978; MD, Hahneman U., 1982. Diplomate Am. Bd. Internal Medicine. Assoc. Geisinger Clin., Wilkes Barre, Pa., 1987—, med. dir. cardiac rehab., 1989—; vice-dir. dept. medicine Geisinger-Wyo. Valley Med. Ctr., Wilkes Barre, 1992—. Fellow Am. Coll. Cardiology; mem. Am. Coll. Physicians, Am. Heart Assn. Republican. Presbyterian. Office: Geisinger Clin 1000 E Mountain Dr Wilkes Barre PA 18711

FISHER, SEYMOUR, psychologist, educator; b. Balt., May 13, 1922; s. Sam and Jean (Miller) F.; married; children: Jerid, Eve. MA, U. Chgo., 1943, PhD, 1948. Chief psychologist Elgin (Ill.) State Hosp., 1949-51; rsch. psychologist VA Hosp., Houston, 1952-56; assoc. prof. Baylor Coll. Medicine, Houston, 1957-61; prof. SUNY Health Sci. Ctr., Syracuse, 1961—. Author: The Female Orgasm, 1973, Development and Structure of the Body Image (vols.1 and 2), 1986, Sexual Images of the Self, 1989; co-author (with Roger Greenberg): The Scientific Credibility of Freud's Theory and Therapy, 1977, The Limits of Biological Treatments for Psychological Distress, 1989. Mem. APA. Home: 7484 Armstrong Rd Manlius NY 13104-1418 Office: SUNY Health Sci Ctr 750 E Adams St Syracuse NY 13210-2306

FISHER, SEYMOUR, psychologist, educator; b. N.Y.C., Nov. 4, 1925; s. George and Fannie (Hesselson) F.; m. Carmen Eldridge, June 20, 1959; children: Mark, Andrew. BA, NYU, 1948; PhD, U. N.C., 1952; postgrad., Washington Sch. Psychiatry, 1954-55. Diplomate Am. Bd. Examiners in Psychol. Hypnosis. Clin. psychologist trainee VA Hosp., Roanoke, 1950, psychology trainee, 1952; intern Psychol. Clinic, U. N.C., Chapel Hill, 1950-51; supervising clin. psychologist Walter Reed Army Inst. Rsch., Washington, 1952-58; rsch. psychologist Psychopharmacology Svc. Ctr., NIMH, Bethesda, Md., 1958-60; chief spl. studies unit Psychopharmacology Rsch Br., NIMH, Bethesda, 1960-63; prof. psychiatry (psychology), dir. rsch. tng., dir. psychopharmacology lab., div. psychiatry Boston U. Sch. Medicine, 1963-78; prof. dept. psychiatry and behavioral scis., U. Tex. Med. Br., Galveston, 1978—, assoc. chmn. for rsch., 1978-80, rsch. advisor to chmn. dept., 1980-91, dir. Ctr. for Medication Monitoring, 1987—; vis. prof. Harvard U., Boston U., May to Nov., 1988; cons. NIMH, Chevy Chase, Md., 1964-66, mem. clin. psychopharmacology rsch. rev. com., 1973-77, mem. treatment devel. and assessment rsch. rev. com., 1979-83; cons. Office Naval Rsch., Washington, 1964-66, Mass. Dept. Mental Health, 1969-78, FDA, 1973-77; pres. Boston Mental Health Found., Inc., 1970-72; mem. Commn. on Community Care of Mentally Ill, chmn. tech. com. Hogg Found., 1987-90, planning com. for 50th anniversary rsch. conf., 1988-89. Editorial bd. Psychopharmacology Svc. Ctr. Bull., 1959-63; assoc. editor Psychol. Record, 1960-66; sr. editor vol. on clin. and biobehavioral aspects of cocaine, Oxford U. Press, 1987; contbr. numerous articles to profl. jours., chpts. in books. Recipient Disting. Alumnus award U. N.C., 1981, Donald E. Francke award for best paper Drug Info. Jour., 1987. Fellow Am. Coll. Neuropsychopharmacology (life, pres. 1984, asst. sec.-treas. 1974-77, chmn. hon. awards com. 1985-87, mem. other coms. 1973-87), Am. Psychol. Assn. (exec. coun. div. psychopharmacology 1979-82), Soc. Clin. and Exptl. Hypnosis, Internat. Coll. Psychosomatic Medicine, Collegium Internat. Neuro-Psychopharmacologicum; mem. AAAS, Am. Psychopathol. Assn. (exec. coun. 1970-72), Psi Chi, Sigma Xi, Beta Lambda Sigma. Office: U Tex Med Br Dept Psych Ctr for Med Monitoring Galveston TX 77555-0441

FISHER, STANLEY, psychologist; b. N.Y.C., June 7, 1927; s. Nathan and Fanny (Rosenthal) F.; m. May Wechsler, Nov. 25, 1951 (div. 1976); children: Paul G., Julia A.; m. Esther M. Margolis, Aug. 19, 1979. BS, CUNY, 1949; PhD, CUNY, 1977; MSW, Columbia U., 1952. Cer. psychologist, N.Y. Asst. mgr. Recording and Stat Corp., N.Y.C., 1957-63; dir. system programming Univac, N.Y.C., 1963-65; cons. TBS, N.Y.C., 1965-66; dir. corp. systems CCC, N.Y.C., 1966-67; dep. chief internat. computing ctr. UN, N.Y.C., 1967-68; research assoc. psychology and computer sci. CUNY, N.Y.C., 1968-74; assoc. research sci. Columbia U., N.Y.C., 1974—; pvt. practice N.Y.C., 1978—; lectr. in surgery Mt. Sinai Sch. Medicine, N.Y.C., 1984-88; vis. assoc. in surgery Albert Einstein Coll. Medicine, N.Y.C., 1983-91; cons. to numerous orgns. including Am. Heart Assn., N.Y. Hosp., U. P.R. Author: Discovering the Power of Self-Hypnosis, 1991; contbr. numerous articles to profl. jours. Active Heart Info. Services N.Y. Heart Assn. With USN, 1945-46. CUNY fellow, 1949-51. Mem. Am. Psychol. Assn., Am. Soc. Clin. Hypnosis, Soc. for Clin. and Experimental Hypnosis, Assn. for Computer Machinery, Psychoanalytic Soc. Jewish. Office: 220 E 63rd St New York NY 10021-7658

FISHER, TERRI L., intensive care nurse; b. Ames, Iowa, Apr. 7, 1970; d. Steven Carl and Paula Ann (Mayernick) F. BSN, Humboldt State U., Arcata, Calif., 1992; postgrad., Calif. State U., Sacramento. RN, Calif.; cert. BLS, ACLS, PALS. Med.-surg. staff nurse, shock-trauma ICU Mercy Med. Ctr., Redding, Calif., 1993—. Republican. Christian. Office: Mercy Med Ctr Clairmont Heights Redding CA 96049

FISHERMAN, NINA YARLOVSKY, nursing administrator; b. Flin Flon, Man., Can., Oct. 5, 1955; d. Vasyl Nicolov and Milka Georgi (Krehtinkoff) Yarlovsky; m. Jay Richard Fisherman, June 26, 1983 (separated 1991). BS, Roanoke Coll., 1977; postgrad., Autonomous U. Guadalajara, 1977-79; MS, Pace U. Grad. Sch. Nursing, 1982. Staff nurse oncology Yonkers (N.Y.) Gen. Hosp., 1982-83, Montefiore Med. Ctr., Bronx, N.Y., 1984-85; br. mgr., nursing supr. Staff Builders, Health Care Svcs., Inc., Flushing, N.Y., 1985-88; inpatient nurse mgr. Ritter-Scheuer Hospice, Bronx, 1988-90; supr. home care Jacob Perlow Hospice, Beth Israel Med. Ctr., N.Y.C., 1990; patient care mgr. Westmoreland Hospice, Greensburg, Pa., 1992-93; dir. clin. svcs. Olsten Kimberly Quality Care, Inc., White Plains, N.Y., 1993-94; utilization review supr. Staff Builders, Health Care Svcs., Inc., Washington, 1994-95; utilization rev. nurse ADP Integrated Med. Solutions, Bethesda, Md., 1996—; presenter AIDS conf. Mem. Nat. Hospice Orgn.

FISHMAN, ALFRED PAUL, physician; b. N.Y.C., Sept. 24, 1918; s. Isaac and Anne (Tinter) F.; m. Linda Fishman, Aug. 23, 1948 (dec.); children: Mark, Jay, Hannah Rae. AB, U. Mich., 1938, MS, 1939; MD, U. Louisville, 1943; MA (hon.), U. Pa., 1971. Diplomate Nat. Bd. Examiners, Am. Bd. Internal Medicine. Intern Jewish Hosp., Bklyn., 1943-44; Dazian Found. fellow pathology Mount Sinai Hosp., N.Y.C., 1946-47; asst. resident, resident medicine Mount Sinai Hosp., 1947-48; Dazian Found. fellow cardiovascular physiology Michael Reese Hosp., Chgo., 1948-49; Am. Heart Assn. research fellow Bellevue Hosp., N.Y.C., 1949-50; established investigator Am. Heart Assn. cardiopulmonary lab. Bellevue Hosp., 1951-55; Am. Heart Assn. research fellow physiology Harvard U., Boston, 1950-51; instr. physiology N.Y. U., 1951-53; assoc. in medicine Columbia Coll. Physicians and Surgeons, N.Y.C., 1953-55; asst. prof. Columbia Coll. Physicians and Surgeons, 1955-58, assoc. prof., 1958-66; prof. medicine U. Chgo., 1966-69; dir. Cardiovascular Inst., Chgo., 1966-69; dir. div. cardiovascular disease

Michael Reese Hosp., Chgo., 1966-69; prof. medicine U. Pa., 1969—, William Maul Measey prof., 1972—, assoc. dean Sch. Medicine, 1969-75, 90-91, dir. cardiovascular-pulmonary div., 1969-90, chmn. dept. rehab. medicine, 1990—; mem. steering com. of dept. chmn. U. Pa. Med. Ctr., 1992, mem. coun. on grad. med. edn., 1992-93; dir. Robinette Found., Clin. Cardiovascular Rsch. Center, U. Pa. Med. Ctr., 1969-82; mem. steering com. dept. chmn. U. Pa. Med. Ctr., 1992, coun. on grad. med. edn., 1992-93; dir. Specialized Center of Rsch. (Lung), 1973-81; attending physician Hosp. U. Pa., 1969—; sr. attending physician Phila. Gen. Hosp., 1970-78; physician Mass. Gen. Hosp., 1979; cons. to chancellor U. Mo., Kansas City, 1973-78; vis. prof. Harvard U., 1970, Oxford (Eng.) U., 1972, Washington U., St. Louis, 1973, Johns Hopkins U., 1974, Ben Gurion U., 1975, Emory U., Atlanta, 1976, U. Porto Alegra, Brazilia, Brazil, 1976, U. Zurich, Switzerland, 1978, Duke U., 1986, U. N.C., 1986; vis. scientist for NIH to Peking, China, 1980, to USSR, 1985; cons. Exec. Office Pres., 1961-69, U. Athens, Greece, 1980; mem. WHO Expert Panel, Geneva, 1973-76, Nat. Adv. Heart and Lung Council, NIH, 1968-71, 79-83, Steering Com. of Dept. Chmn U. Pa. Med. Ctrl, 1992, Coun. on Grad. Med. Edn. U. Pa. Med. Ctr., 1992-93; coun. mem. Coll. of Physicians of Phila., 1993—; chmn. Gov.'s Com. for Rsch. on Respiratory Diseases in Coal Miners, 1974-90, Internat. Conf. on Lung, Titisee, Germany, Florence, Italy, 1976, 84, Prague, Czeckoslovakia, 1986, 89; U.S. chief del. Internat. Union of Physiol. Scis., Helsinki, Finland, 1989; cons. N.Y. State Bd. Health, 1987-91, Cleve. Found., 1984—; vis. com. Case Western Res. Sch. Medicine, Cleve., 1987—, Lankenau Gen. Hosp., Phila., 1985; chmn. Scientific Edn. Partnership, U. Mo-U. Kans.-Merrill Dow, 1989—. Editor: (with D.W. Richards) Circulation of The Blood-Men and Ideas, 1964, (with H.H. Hecht) The Pulmonary Circulation and Interstitial Space, 1969, Handbooks of Respiratory Physiology, Am. Physiol. Soc., 1967-72, 79-87—, Physiology in Medicine, New Eng. Jour. Medicine, 1969-79, Jour. Applied Physiology, 1981-89, cons. editor, 1989—; editor: (with D.W. Richards) Circulation of the Blood Men and Ideas, 1982, Merck Manual, 1972-80, Ann. Rev. Physiology, 1977-81, Heart Failure, 1979, (with E. M. Renkin) Pulmonary Edema, 1979, Pulmonary Diseases and Disorders, 1979, 2d edit., 1988, 3d edit., 1995, Classics in Biology and Medicine, 1989—, The Pulmonary Circulation: Normal and Abnormal, 1990; contbr. articles to profl. jours.; reviewer Health Care Financing Adminstrn., 1995—. Bd. dirs. Polachek Found., Phila. Zool. Soc. Served to capt. M.C. U.S. Army, 1944-46. Recipient Disting. Alumni award U. Louisville, 1984. Fellow Am. Coll. Chest Physicians (hon.), Royal Coll. Physicians, ACP; mem. NAS (com. on sci., edn. and pub. policy 1987-90), Inst. Medicine of NAS (chmn. health scis. bd0, mem. health scis. bd. 1990—, com. on social and ethical impact of advances in biomedicine 1992—), Am. Physiol. Soc. (chmn. publs. bd. 1974-81, pres. 1983, editor handbook 1986, chmn. centennial celebration com. 1985-87), Am. Soc. Clin. Investigation, AAAS, Royal Soc. Medicine (London), Assn. Am. Physicians, Am. Heart Assn. (bd. dirs. 1988—, founder, chmn. council on cardiopulmonary disease 1972-74, rsch. coun. 1974-79, Disting. Achievement award 1980, sci. pub. com. 1986-88, chmn. 1988—, Merit award 1989, Gold Heart award 1992, scientific adv. com. 1992—), N.Y. Heart Assn. (pres. 1965-67), Internat. Union Physiol. Scis. (U.S. Nat. Com. 1982-89, chmn. 1986-89), Fedn. Am. Socs. for Exptl. Biology (exec. bd. 1983-85), Am. Coll. Cardiology (hon.), Interurban Clin. Club, N.Y. County Med. Soc., Coll. of Physicians of Phila. (coun. 1993—, pres.-elect 1994, pres. 1996), Heart Assn. Southeastern Pa. (bd. dirs.), Alpha Omega Alpha. Home: 2401 Pennsylvania Ave Apt 207A Philadelphia PA 19130-3001 Office: Hosp U Pa 3400 Spruce St Philadelphia PA 19104

FISHMAN, ARTHUR, urologist; b. Phila., Sept. 23, 1931; s. Edward and Sylvia Fishman; m. Barbara Bransdorf, June 15, 1959; children: James, Suzie, David. BA, Temple U., 1953, MD, 1957. Diplomate Am. Bd. Urology. Pvt. practice Ctrl. Ariz. Urology, Phoenix, 1964—. Contbr. articles to profl. jours. Bd. dirs. Phoenix Bapt. Hosp., 1990-96, exec. com., 1990-96. Capt. U.S. Army, 1957-59. Mem. Am. Urol. Soc. (western sect.), Maricopa Med. Soc., Galen Soc. Republican. Jewish. Home: 6040 N 22 Pl Phoenix AZ 85016 Office: Central Arizona Urology 1300 N 12th St Phoenix AZ 85006

FISHMAN, BRUCE ELIOT, physician, surgeon, consultant; b. Detroit, Apr. 30, 1952; s. Sheldon Russel and Marilyn Loraine (Goodman) F.; m. Elissa Patricia Adler, June 30, 1974; children: Nina Heather, Rachel Michelle. BS, Wayne State U., 1974, MD, 1979; JD, Whittier Coll., 1992. Orthopaedic surgery resident Henry Ford Hosp. Med. Ctr., Detroit, 1979-83; med./legal cons. EPA Consulting Inc., Calif., 1985-90; orthopaedic cons. West Oaks Urgent Care, Canoga Park, Calif., 1990—; med. dir. Encino (Calif.) Urgent Care Med. Ctr., 1992—. Fellow Am. Acad. Neurol. and Orthopaedic Surgeons, Am. Coll. Legal Medicine, Internat. Coll. Surgeons; mem. Am. Coll. Sports Medicine, Internat. Spinal Injection Soc., N.Am. Cervicogenec Headache Soc., Alpha Omega Alpha. Office: Encino Urgent Care Med Ctr 18065 Ventura Blvd Encino CA 91316-3517

FISHMAN, GLENN I., medical educator. BA in Chemistry cum laude, Cornell U., 1978; MD, Stanford U., 1983. Diplomate Am. Bd. Internal Medicine, Am. Bd. Cardiovascular Diseases. Rschr. Syntex Rsch., Palo Alto, Calif., 1979-81; resident in internal medicine Mass. Gen. Hosp., Boston, 1983-86; clin. fellow in cardiology Columbia-Presbyn. Med. Ctr., N.Y.C., 1986-88, asst. in clin. medicine, 1988-89; postdoctoral rsch. fellow sect. molecular cardiology Albert Einstein Coll. Medicine, Bronx, N.Y., 1988-90, asst. prof. medicine cardiology divsn., 1990-95, asst. prof. molecular genetics, 1991-95, assoc. prof. medicine cardiology divsn., assoc. prof. molecular genetics, acting dir. sect. molecular cardiology, 1995—. mem. editl. bd. Circulation Rsch., 1993—; contbr. articles to profl. jours. Recipient Physician Scientist award NIH, 1990, Louis Katz Basic Sci. Rsch. prize Am. Heart Assn., 1990, Established Investigator award, 1995. Fellow Am. Coll. Cardiology; mem. Phi Beta Kappa. Office: Albert Einstein Coll of Medicine 1300 Morris Park Ave Bronx NY 10461

FISHMAN, JACOB ROBERT, psychiatrist, administrator, educator, corporate executive, investor; b. N.Y.C., Aug. 6, 1930; s. Samuel and Fannie (Goldin) F.; A.B., Columbia U., 1952; postgrad. New Sch. for Social Rsch., 1951-52, N.Y.U., 1951-52; M.D., Boston U., 1956; m. Tamar Hendel, June 1, 1958; children: Marc Judah, Risa Esther Fishman-Kapit, Zalman Schneur, Rebecca Anne. Intern in medicine Einstein Coll. Medicine, Bronx, N.Y., 1956-57, resident psychiatry, 1957-59; research psychiatrist NIMH, Bethesda, Md., 1959-62; prof. psychiatry Howard U. Coll. Medicine, Washington, 1962-71; dir. Howard-D.C. Comprehensive Mental Health Center, 1966-68; chmn. bd., pres. Univ. Research Corp., Washington, 1968-78, Am. Health Services, Inc., 1971-78; pres. Ctr. for Human Services, 1968-74, Human Service Group, 1971-78, Horizon Mental Health Group, Inc., 1981-84, Cumberland Psychiat. Hosp., 1979-84; chmn. bd. dirs. Am. Mental Health Group, Inc., Am. Health Group Inc.; chmn. psychiatry So. Md. Hosp. Ctr., 1978-81; cons. fed. agys., U.S. Congress, numerous pvt. corps.; vis. lectr. Johns Hopkins, Northwestern Univ.; bd. dirs. Create Inc., Entertainment Concepts Inc., First Grafton Corp., Med. Services Corp., Inc., Am. Health Group, Inc., Md. Treatment Ctrs., Inc., Potomac Healthcare Found.; pres. Am. Healthcare Mgmt., LLC; mgmt. dir. Riverside Hosp., Washington. Bd. dirs. Webster Coll., Washington, 1971-75, Ctr. for Human Services, 1967-75, DePaul Hosp., New Orleans, 1973-78, St. Elizabeth's Hosp., Richmond, Va., 1971-78, Cin. Mental Health Inst., 1971-78, Nat. Capital Day Care Assn., 1966-68, founder; mem. D.C. Public Health Adv. Council, 1966-68; attending psychiatrist Freedman's Hosp., Washington Vets. Hosp., D.C. Gen. Hosp., 1962-68; dir. Am. Health Group, 1985—. Served with USPHS, 1959-61. Recipient Gold medal award Phi Lambda Kappa Med. Soc. Fellow Am. Public Health Assn., Am. Assn. Social Psychiatry; mem. Am. Psychiat. Assn., D.C. Psychiat. Soc., Potomac Psychiat. Assocs. (pres. 1978—), AAAS, D.C. Public Health Assn. (Disting. Service award), Am. Med. Soc. on Alcoholism and Other Addictive Drugs, Am. Council on Alcoholism, Nat. Assn. for New Careers in Human Svcs. (vice chmn. 1965-70), various others. Author numerous profl. articles and books. Bd. editors Nat. Jour. Research on Crime and Delinquency, 1965-71. Home: 1717 Poplar Ln NW Washington DC 20012-1135 Office: Md Treatment Ctrs Inc 3800 Frederick Ave Baltimore MD 21229-3618

FISHMAN, JOAN ROSLYN, clinical information analyst; b. Cambridge, Mass., Sept. 1, 1945; d. Joseph and Tilla (Gerson) F.; m. Stephan B. Abramson, June 8, 1969 (div. 1983). BA, Wheaton Coll., Norton, Mass., 1967; MS, U. So. Calif., 1978. Research asst. Harvard U. Med. Sch., Boston, 1967-69; pulmonary technologist Peter Bent Brigham Hosps., Boston, 1969-71, Framingham (Mass.) Union Hosp., 1971-74; chief pulmonary physiol. lab. Los Angeles County-U. So. Calif. Med. Ctr., 1975-79; dir. pulmonary diagnostic lab. White Meml. Med. Ctr., Los Angeles, 1979-84; asst. dir. respiratory care Pacific Med. Ctr., San Francisco, 1984-85; asst. product mgr. Gould Med. Products, Dayton, Ohio, 1985-86; installation analyst Health Data Scis., San Bernardino, Calif., 1987-93; sr. clin. info. analyst Dartmouth-Hitchcock Med. Ctr., Lebanon, N.H., 1993—; health profl. educator Am. Lung Assn., N.Y.C., 1977-78. Author: Programmed Gas Law for Cardiopulmonary Technology, 1979, Blood Gas Electrodes, 1984, (with others) Standards and Controversies in Pulmonary Function Testing, 1982. Mem. Nat. Soc. Cardiopulmonary Technology (regional dir. 1978-83), Nat. Bd. Respiratory Care (bd. dirs. 1983-92), Calif. Soc. Respiratory Care. Office: Dartmouth-Hitchcock Med Ctr Computer Svcs Lebanon NH 03756-0001

FISHMAN, LEN, state commissioner. Gen. counsel N.J. Assn. Non-profit homes for the Aging; commr. of health Dept. Health and Sr. Svcs., Trenton, N.J., 1994—; initiator Worlds Aids Day of Learning for Youth; supporter Electronic Birth Cert. Sys. in Hosps. Office: Dept Health and Sr Svcs CN 360 Trenton NJ 08625-0360

FISHMAN, MARVIN ALLEN, pediatrician, neurologist, educator; b. Chgo., Feb. 16, 1937; s. Joseph and Mary (Schneider) F.; m. Gloria Brenda Greenberg, Dec. 20, 1959; children: Bradley Steven, Patricia Ann. BS, U. Ill., 1959, MD, 1961. Diplomate Am. Bd. Pediatrics, Am. Psychiatry and Neurology. Intern, then resident in pediatrics Michael Reese Hosp. and Med. Center, Chgo., 1961-64; resident in neurology Mass. Gen. Hosp., Boston, 1966-67; fellow in pediatric neurology St. Louis Children's Hosp., 1967-70, dir. Birth Defects Ctr., 1971-79; prof. pediatrics, neurology and preventive medicine Washington U. Med. Sch., St. Louis, 1970-79; dir. Irene Walter Johnson Inst. Rehab. Washington U. Med. Sch., 1974-79; prof. pediatrics and neurology, dir. pediatric neurology tng. program Baylor Coll. Medicine, Houston, 1979—, vice chmn. dept. pediatrics, 1992—; chief neurology service Tex. Children's Hosp., Houston, 1979—; mem. residency rev. com. for neurology Accreditation Coun. for Grad. Med. Edn., 1991-96, chmn., 1995-96; bd. dirs. Am. Bd. Psychiatry and Neurology, 1991—, exec. com., 1995—, v.p., 1996—. Conbr. articles in field, chpts. in books; mem. editorial bd. Jour. Pediatrics, 1980-87, Jour. Child Neurology, Pediatric Neurology, Annals of Neurology; editor textbook. With USAR, 1964-66. Grantee HEW; Grantee Grant Found.; Grantee Ga. Warm Springs Found.; Grantee Nat. Found.-March of Dimes. Mem. Am. Soc. Neurochemistry (councilor 1977-79), Child Neurology Soc. (exec. com., councillor 1980-82, sec.-treas. 1984-86, pres.-elect 1986-87, pres. 1987-89, past pres. 1989-90), Houston Neurol. Soc. (pres.-elect 1989-90, pres. 1990-91), Am. Acad. Pediatrics, Am. Acad. Neurology, Am. Neurol. Assn., Am. Pediatric Soc., Soc. for Pediatric Rsch., Soc. for Neuroscis. Home: 1523-B Potomac Dr Houston TX 77057-1925 Office: Baylor Coll Med 1 Baylor Plz Houston TX 77030-3411

FISHMAN, NOEL HERBERT, surgeon, educator; b. Boston, 1934. MD, UCLA, 1960. Intern Phila. Gen. Hosp., 1960-61; resident in surgery Jefferson Med. Coll. Hosp., Phila., 1961-65; fellow U. Calif., San Francisco, 1965-66; pvt. practice Santa Cruz, Calif., 1988—; assoc. prof. surgery U. Calif. Med. Ctr., 1972-78, clin. prof. surgery, 1978-84; asst. chief cardiac surgery Mt. Zion Hosp., San Francisco, 1980-84; assoc. chief cardiothoracic surgery Carmel Hosp., Israel, 1984-88; dir. cardiac surgery Dominican Hosp., Santa Cruz, 1988—. Mem. Am. Assn. Thoracic Surgery, Soc. Thoracic Surgeons, Soc. Univ. Surgeons. Office: 1575 Soquel Dr Santa Cruz CA 95065

FISHMANN, ANDREW JAY, internist; b. Trenton, N.J., June 10, 1950; s. Marvin Louis and Blossom Alice (Bernstein) F.; m. M.E. Loree, Sept. 4, 1982; children: Megan Alix, Addie Lee. BA in Biology, Franklin & Marshall Coll., 1972; MD, Temple U., 1977. Diplomate Am. Bd. Internal Medicine, Pulmonary Disease, Critical Care Medicine. Resident Temple U. Hosp., Phila., 1977-80; fellow pulmonary U. Calif. San Diego, 1981-83; internist Calif. Lung Assocs., L.A., 1983—; internist Germantown Hosp., Phila., 1979; attending physician Temple U. Hosp., Phila., 1980-81, co-dir. respiratory therapy Hosp. Good Samaritan, L.A., 1991—; asst. dir. respiratory therapy St. Francis Med. Ctr., Lynwood, Calif., 1994—; cons. Cedars-Sinai Med. Ctr., L.A., 1989-92. Fellow ACP, Am. Coll. Chest Physicians; mem. L.A. Tennis Club, L.A. Athletic Club. Office: Calif Lung Assocs 1245 Wilshire Blvd Ste 514 Los Angeles CA 90017

FISK, DONALD ROBERT, general surgeon; b. Flandreau, S.D., June 18, 1945; s. Robert G. and Bette Mae (Porter) F.; m. Sandra S. Fisk, Aug. 15, 1969; children: Kristin L., Samuel G. GA, U. S.D., 1967, BS, 1969; MD, Northwestern U., 1971. Diplomate Am. Bd. Surgery. Surgeon, major USAF, Wurtsmith AFB, 1977-79; surgeon Galesburg, Ill., 1979-88, Arkansas City, Kans., 1988-90; pvt. practice surgeon Fisk Surg. Clinic, Galesburg, 1990—; pres. Surg. Clinics, Ltd., Galesburg, 1994—. Major, USAF, 1977-79. Fellow ACS; mem. AMA, Ill. State Med. Soc., Knox County Med. Soc. (pres., del. 1979—), Sunrise Rotary (pres. 1995—). Home: 1872 Patterson Drive Galesburg IL 61401 Office: Surgical Clinics Ltd 575 N Kellogg St Galesburg IL 61401

FISK, HARRIS RONALD, neurologist, educator; b. Phila., May 10, 1943. BA, Johns Hopkins U., 1963; MD, U. Chgo., 1967; PhD, Stanford U., 1971. Diplomate Am. Bd. Neurology and Psychiatry. Asst. clin. prof. neurology UCLA, 1984—; clin. chief neurology Cedars-Sinai Med. Ctr., L.A., 1990-93. Lt. comdr. USPHS, 1971-74. Mem. Am. Acad. Neurology (assoc.), Soc. Clin. Neurology. Office: 8631 W 3rd St Los Angeles CA 90048

FISKE, SANDRA RAPPAPORT, psychologist, educator; b. Syracuse, N.Y., Sept. 25, 1946; d. Sidney Saul and Helen (Lapides) Rappaport; B.S., Cornell U., 1968; M.Ed., Tufts U., 1969; M.A., Columbia U., 1971, Ph.D., 1974; m. Jordan J. Fiske, June 22, 1974. Supervising sch. psychologist St. Elizabeth's Sch., N.Y.C., 1971-76; instr. clin. psychology Tchrs. Coll., Columbia, N.Y.C., 1973, clin. asst. dept. psychology, 1975-76; adj. prof. Syracuse U., 1976; sch. psychologist Syracuse Bd. Edn., 1976-77; prof. psychology Onondaga Community Coll., Syracuse, 1976-87, prof. 1988—, chair social sci. dept., 1993—; pvt. practice psychology, Syracuse, 1976—. NIMH fellow, 1969-72. Mem. Am. Psychol. Assn., Psychologists of Central N.Y., Am. Orthopsychiat. Assn., Sigma Xi, Psi Chi. Home: 2 Signal Hill Rd Fayetteville NY 13066-9674 Office: Onondaga Community Coll Dept Psychology Syracuse NY 13215

FISS, HARRY, psychologist; b. Vienna, Apr. 15, 1926; came to U.S., 1939; s. Emil and Gertrude (Roemer) F.; m. Gerda May, Oct. 20, 1962; children: Karen, Naomi. BA, NYU, 1949, PhD, 1961. Diplomate in Clin. Psychology. Instr. Albert Einstein Med. Coll., Bronx, N.Y., 1960-63, dir. of tng., 1969-71; asst. prof. NYU, N.Y.C., 1963-69; prof. L.I. U., Bklyn., 1971-73; prof., chief psychologist U. Conn. Health Ctr., Farmington, 1973-92; prof. U. Hartford, Conn., 1993—. Contbr. chpts. in books and over 40 articles to profl. jours.; news editor Sta. KCBS, San Francisco, 1950. Bd. advisors Whiting Forensic Inst., Middletown, Conn., 1982-87. Corp. U.S. Army, 1944-46, ETO. Recipient Founders Day award NYU, 1961, rsch. grant NIH, Washington, 1967. Fellow Soc. for Personality Assessment; mem. Am. Acad. of Psychoanalysis (scientific assoc.), Assn. for the Study of Dreams (bd. dirs. 1986-90). Home: 75 Westmont St West Hartford CT 06117-2929

FITCH, COY DEAN, physician, educator; b. Marthaville, La., Oct. 5, 1934; s. Raymond E. and Joey (Youngblood) F.; m. Rachel Farr, Mar. 31, 1956; children: Julia Anne, Jaquelyn Kay. B.S., U. Ark., 1956, M.S., 1958, M.D., 1958. Diplomate: in internal medicine and endocrinology Am. Bd. Internal Medicine. Intern U. Ark. Sch. Medicine, 1958-59, resident, 1959-62, instr. biochemistry, 1959-62, asst. prof. medicine and biochemistry, 1962-66, asso. prof., 1966-67; dir. U. Ark. Sch. Medicine (Honors Med. Student Research Program), 1965-67; asso. prof. internal medicine and biochemistry St. Louis U. Sch. Medicine, 1967-73, prof. internal medicine, 1973—, prof. biochemistry, 1976—, head sect. metabolism, 1969-76, dir. div. endocrinology and metabolism, 1977-85; chief med. service St. Louis U. Hosps., 1976-77, vice-chmn. dept. internal medicine, 1983-85, acting chmn. dept. internal medicine, 1985-88, chmn. dept., 1988—; practice medicine, specializing in internal medicine Little Rock, 1962-67, St. Louis, 1969—; dir. Diabetic Clinic, U. Ark. Med. Ctr., 1962-67, head sect. metabolism and endocrinology, 1966-67; mem. nutrition study sect. div. research grants NIH, 1967-71. Asso. editor: Nutrition Revs., 1964; contbr. articles to profl. jours. Served from capt. to lt. col., M.C. AUS, 1967-69. Recipient Lederle Med. Faculty award, 1966-67; Russell M. Wilder-Nat. Vitamin Found. fellow, 1959-62. Fellow ACP (gov. Mo. chpt. 1995—); mem. Am. Fedn. Clin. Rsch., Am. Inst. Nutrition, Am., So. socs. Clin. Investigation, Am. Soc. Biol. Chemists, Ctrl. Soc. Clin. rsch., Phi Beta Kappa, Sigma Xi. Office: 1402 S Grand Blvd Saint Louis MO 63104-1004

FITCHETT, JUNE WISEMAN, health care facility administrator; b. Marion, N.C., May 29, 1942; d. Coy and Lena (Ellis) Wiseman; m. Bruce Harvey Fitchett, Jan. 19, 1963 (div. Aug. 1977); children: Alisa Michelle Fitchett Ashe, William Shawn. BA, Western Carolina U., 1968. Cert. activity dir., N.C. Tchr. English and remedial edn. Jackson County Pub. Schs., Sylva, N.C., 1966; tchr., counselor Asheville (N.C.) Buncombe Tech. Inst., County of Buncombe Neighborhood Youth Corp., 1971-75; coord. Buncombe County Title II County of Buncombe and City of Asheville, 1975—; job placement coord. of handicapped, orgn. devel. coord. Thoms Rehab. Hosp., Asheville, 1976-81; personnel dir., rehab. coord. Lions Industries for Blind, 1982-83; social worker food stamp office County of Buncombe Social Svcs., Asheville, 1984-85; res. svcs. assoc. Givens Estate Retirement Ctr., Asheville, 1985—; dir. resident activity therapy and volunteers Victoria Health Care Ctr., Asheville, 1986—; pres. Social Svcs. Coun., County of Buncombe, 1982-83; corr. Asheville Citizen Times. Recipient Outstanding Young Woman of Am. award, 1971, Outstanding Svc. to Handicapped award Asheville Area Mayor's Com., 1980. Mem. N.C. Activity Profls. (state bd. 1991-92, pres. western dist. 1991-92, writer state newsletter 1991-92, membership chair state bd.), Asheville Toastmistress Club (v.p. 1973), Beta Sigma Phi. Baptist. Home: 226 Forest Hill Dr Asheville NC 28803-2406 Office: Victoria Health Care Ctr 455 Victoria Rd Asheville NC 28801-4827

FITTI, REGINA MARY, retired psychiatrist; b. Bryn Mawr, Pa., June 22, 1925; d. Nicholas Saverio and Mary Louise (Vassallo) F. BS, Ursinus Coll., 1945; MD, Hahnemann Med. Coll., 1949, D Homeopathic Medicine, 1949. Intern Meml. Hosp., Wilmington, Del., 1940-50; resident St. Joseph's Infirmary, Louisville, 1950-51, Hahneman Hosp., Phila., 1951-52; fellow Hedgecroft Hosp., Houston, 1952; pvt. practice Ardmore, Pa., 1953-60; gen. psychiatry Norristown (Pa.) State Hosp., 1960-62; child psychiatrt fellow Phila. Child Guidance Clinic, 1962-64, staff psychiatrist, 1964-66; staff psychiatrist Media (Pa.) Child Guidance Clinic, 1966-93, clin. dir., 1977-80, child psychiatrist, 1980-93. Mem. Am. Psychiat Assn., Am. Orthopsychiat. Assn., Pa. Psychiatric Soc., Phila. Psychiatric Soc., Regional Coun. Child Psychiatry. Roman Catholic. Office: Media Child Guidance 600 N Olive St Media PA 19063-2418

FITZGERALD, DIANE CAROL, social worker; b. Keene, N.H., July 21, 1961; d. David I. and Beverly A. (Simeneau) S.; m. Michael Anthony Fitzgerald, Dec. 23, 1988; children: Kambrah Quin, Shelby Karen. BSW, Castleton State Coll., 1983; MSW, U. Ga., 1985. Social worker med Grady Meml. Hosp., Atlanta, 1986; social worker oncology South Fulton Hosp., East Point, Ga., 1985-86, Emory U. Hosp., Atlanta, 1986-89; social worker Home Health Care and Community Svc., Keene, N.H., 1989; social worker oncology Cheshire Med. Ctr., Keene, 1990—, Hospice of Menadnock Region, Keene, 1995-96; cons. Home Health Care and Cmty. Svc., Keene, 1990—, Leukemia Soc. Am., Atlanta, 1989; cons. Am. Cancer Soc., Bedford, N.H., 1990—, core team leader for cmty. cancer connection RIG chairperson-elect for N.H. chpt. svc. and rehab. com., vol. facilitator cancer prevention in cmty. practice; nominated to N.H. adv. panel Cancer and Chronic Diseases, 1996—. Counselor, Camp Sunshine, Atlanta, 1989. Mem. NASW, Nat. Assn. Oncology Social Workers. Democrat. Home: 44 Woodland Heights Dr East Swanzey NH 03446-2216

FITZGERALD, GARRET ADARE, medical educator; b. May 11, 1950; married; three children. MBBCh with honors, Univ. Coll., Dublin, 1974, MD, 1980; Diploma in Stats., Trinity Coll., Dublin, 1977; MS in Stats., U. London, 1979. FRCP/Ireland, FACP, RCP/U.K. Intern gastroenterology/therapeutics St. Vincent's Hosp., Dublin, 1974, intern, urology, 1975, intern, gen. surgery, 1975, sr. house officer, hematology/oncology, 1975-76; sr. house officer endocrinology/diabetes mellitus Mater Hosp., Dublin, 1976-77, rsch. register, endocrinology/diabetes mellitus, 1977; rsch. fellow Royal Postgrad. Med. Sch., London Clin. Pharmacology, 1977-79; rsch. fellow dept. internal medicine II U. Cologne, 1979-80; rsch. fellow to assoc. dir. Rsch. Ctr. Grant in Pharm. Scis. Vanderbilt U. Sch. Medicine, Nashville, 1980-91, chief. Divsn. Clin. Pharmacology, 1988-91, William Stokes prof. exptl. therapeutics, 1989-91; dir. Ctr. Cardiovascular Sci. U. Coll. Dublin/Mater Hosp., 1991-94; prof., chmn. dept. medicine and exptl. therapeutics U. Coll. Dubinlin/Mater Hosp., 1991-94; prof. medicine, pharmacology U. Pa., 1994—, chair dept. pharmacology, 1996—, dir. Clin. Res. Ctr., 1994—, Robinette Found. prof., dir. Ctr. Exptl. Therapeutics/Rsch., 1994—; lectr. in field, including vis. prof. clin. pharmacology Dalhousie U., Halifax, 1983, Med. Coll. Pa., Phila., 1985, U. Kans., 1986, U. B.C., Vancouver, 1987, Mario Negri Inst., Bergamo, 1987, U. Gotenburg, Sweden, 1988, U. Saskatchewan, Saskatoon, Can., 1988, Case Western Res. U., Cleve., 1988, N.Y. Med. Coll., 1990, U. Lond Med. Sch., 1994, Royal Coll. of Surgeons, Dublin, 1995, numerous others; served numerous coms. and advisory groups in field. Editl. bd.: Thrombosis News, 1987-91, Eicosanoid, 1991-92, Exptl. Nephrology, 1993-94, Jour. of Pharmacology and Exptl. Therapeutics, 1987—, Trends in Cardiovascular Medicine, 1990—, Atherosclerosis and Thrombosis, 1990—, Jour. Biol. Chemistry, 1993—, Circulation, 1993—, Jour. Cardiovascular Risk, 1994; contbr. numerous articles to profl. jours. and publs. Fellowship Nat. U. Ireland, 1977-80, Wellcome Clin. Rsch. fellow, 1977-79, Alexander von Humboldt Stiftung fellow, Germany, 1979-80; grantee in field. Mem. Assn. Physicians of Gt. Britain and Ireland, Am. Am. Physicians, Am. Soc. Clin. Investigation, Am. Fedn. Clin. Rsch., Am. Heart Assn. (exec. and long-range planning com. Thrombosis Coun. 1987-91), Am. Soc. Pharmacology and Exptl. Therapeutics, Am. Soc. Clin. Pharmacology and Therapeutics, AAAS. Office: 909 Biomed Rsch Bldg 422 Curie Blvd Philadelphia PA 19104

FITZGERALD, LYNNE MARIE LESLIE, family therapist; b. Berea, Ohio, Aug. 21, 1946; d. Glenn Willis and Blanche Marie (Monkosky) Leslie; m. J. Michael Fitzgerald, May 3, 1974; children: Joseph Glenn, Leslie Marie. BA, U. Miami, 1968; MS, St. Thomas U., 1983; PhD, Nova Univ., 1994. Lic. marriage and family therapist, Fla. Sml. group facilitator U. Miami Med. Sch., 1988; family therapist Family Life Ctr. of Fla., Inc., Coral Gables, 1985—; facilitator stress, depression and suicide prevention program Mental Health Assn., Charlottesville, Va., 1995—; facilitator Dade County Pub. Schs./Depression and Suicide Prevention, Miami, 1985-92, Mental Health Assn. Charlottesville/Albemarle/Depression and Suicide Prevention Program for Schs., 1996—; cons. Mediation Ministries, Miami, 1990—, Counseling Ctr., St. Louis Cath. Ch., Miami, 1990-92. Mem. Jr. League, Va., St. Anne's-Belfield Sch. parents aux. bd.; bd. dirs. The Vizcayans, Miami, 1979-83, Party Parade, Charlottesville, 1995, gen. chmn. 1995-96, pres. 1996—; active Marian Ctr. Aux., Miami. Named Woman of Yr., Kappa Kappa Gamma Alumnae Assn., Miami, 1973. Mem. Am. Assn. Marriage and Family Therapists (approved supr.), Am. Orthopsychiat. Assn., Am. Assn. Christian Counselors, Mental Health Assn Charlottesville (profl. bd. dirs. 1995—), Kappa Kappa Gamma (U. Va. house bd., 1995—, alumnae exec. bd. 1994—, Woman of Yr. 1973). Roman Catholic. Home: 888 Tanglewood Rd Charlottesville VA 22901-7817 Office: Family Life Ctr of Fla Inc 1550 Madruga Ave Miami FL 33146-3039

FITZGERALD, PAT, human services administrator; b. Augusta, Ga., Sept. 25, 1938; d. Perry L. and Pearl (Stevens) F. BA, Carson Newman Coll., Jefferson City, Tenn., 1960; MSW, Fla. State U., 1965. Cert. social worker, Ga.; cert. pub. mgr. Tchr. music Calhoun County (Fla.) Bd. Edn., 1960-61, Richmond County Bd. Edn., Augusta, Ga., 1962; pub. and child welfare worker Richmond County Div. Family and Children Svcs., Augusta, 1962-63, child welfare worker, 1965-67, casework supr. III, 1968-69, dep. dir., 1969-73; dir. Mental Health Ctr., 1973-75, Richmond County Dept. Family and Children Svcs., Augusta, 1975-96; instr. Augusta Coll., 1965, 68, Paine Coll., Augusta, 1970; cons. OEO, 1967, 68. Sr. companion Foster Grandparents, 1983-93, bd. dirs.; mem. child care adv. com. Augusta Tech., 1987-96; mem. adv. bd. Mental Health, Retardation and Sustance Abuse, 1985-93; mem. planning com. Job Tngf. Partnership Act, 1983-96; sec.-treas. bd. trustees Whole Life Ministries, 1984—, praise and worship leader; min.

music, soloist various Protestant chs.; mem. Golden Harvest Food Bank, Speech and Hearing Ctr., 1984-89; v.p. Augusta Coalition Children and Youth, 1985-93; bd. leadership Augusta, 1993-96. Mem. NASW, Am. Pub. Welfare Assn., Child Welfare League Am., Ga. County Welfare Assn.

FITZGERALD, ROBERT HANNON, JR., orthopedic surgeon; b. Denver, Aug. 25, 1942; s. Robert Hannon and Alyene (Webber) Fitzgerald Anderson; m. Lynda Lee Lang, Apr. 27, 1968 (div. 1984); children: Robert III, Shannon, Dennis, Katherine, Kelly; m. Jamie Kathleen Dent, Mar. 9, 1985; children: Brian, Steven. BS, U. Notre Dame, 1963; MD, U. Kans., 1967; MS, U. Minn., 1974, Magistri Artivum, U. Pa., 1995. Instr. orthop. surgery Mayo Med. Sch., Rochester, Minn., 1974-77, cons. orthop. surgery, 1974-89, asst. prof., 1977-82, assoc. prof., 1982-86 , prof., 1986-89, chief adult reconstructive surgery, 1987-89, dir. orthop. rsch., 1988-89; prof. chmn. dept. orthop. surgery Wayne State U. Sch. Medicine, 1989-95, Magnuson prof. orthop. surgery, 1996—; chief orthop. surgery Hutzel Hosp., 1989-95, Detroit Receiving Hosp., 1989-95; orthopaedist-in-chief Detroit Med. Ctr., 1989-95, chmn. coun., specialist-in-chief 1993-95; prof., chmn. dept. orthop. surgery U. Pa. Sch. Medicine, Phila., 1995—; chief orthop. surgery Hosp. U. Pa., Phila., 1995—; cons. Ctr. Disease Control, Atlanta, 1981—, NIH, 1987, chmn. orthop. study sect., 1989-91; bd. dirs. Hutzel Hosp., Detroit, 1989-95. Assoc. editor Jour. Orthop. and Traumatology, 1978—, Jour. Bone Joint Surgery, 1982-86, Clin. Orthop. and Related Rsch., 1988—; trustee Jour. Bone Joint Surgery, 1987-92, sec. 1988-92, Hutzel Hosp., 1989-95. Mem. bd. edn. St. John's Grade Sch./Jr. H.S., Rochester, 1983-87; mem. Bd. Devel. Mayo Clinic, 1984-87; mem. bd. devel. St. John's Ch., 1988-89; trustee Lourdes H.S. Devel. Bd., Rochester, 1982-88. Served to capt. USAF, 1968-70. Decorated Air Commendation medal; recipient Kappa Delta award for musculoskeletal rsch., 1983; . Fellow Am. Acad. Orthop. Surgeons; mem. Am. Orthopedic Assn., Rsch. Soc., AMA, Assn. Bone and Joint Surgeons, Internat. Soc. Microbiology, Zumbro County Med. Soc., Min-Da-Man Orthop. Soc., Minn. Orthopedic Soc., Am. Soc. Microbiology, N.Y. Acad. Scis., Am. Hip Soc. (Stinchfield award 1985, 95, Charnley award 1986, 95, pres. 1993-94), Internat. Hip Soc., Am. Orthop. Assn. (N. Am. travelling fellow 1974, Am. Brit. Can. traveing fellow, 1981), Surg. Infection Soc. (charter mem.), Clin. Orthop. Soc., Internat. Soc. Orthop. Surgery and Traumatology, Mid-Am. Orthop. Soc. (bd. dirs. 1989-93, 94—, pres. elect 1994, pres. 1996—), Detroit Acad. Orthop. Surgery, Mich. Orthop. Soc., Mich. State Med. Soc., Detroit Acad. Medicine, Phila. Orthop. Soc., Interurban Club, Sigma Xi, Kappa Delta, Alpha Epsilon Delta. Republican. Roman Catholic. Avocations: cross-country and downhill skiing. Home: 237 Ravenscliff Rd Saint Davids PA 19087 Office: II Silverstein Pavilion Hosp Univ Penn Philadelphia PA 19104

FITZGERALD, ROBERT JAMES, microbiologist, oral biologist; b. N.Y.C., Nov. 3, 1918; s. Maurice Edward and Anna Marie (Ledogar) F.; m. Dorothea Babbitt, June 20, 1945. BS, Fordham U., 1939; MS, Va. Tech. U., 1941; PhD, Duke U., 1948. Microbiologist Am. Cyanamid Corp., Stamford, Conn., 1941-45; sanitarian, ensign USPHS, Kansas City, Kans., 1945-46; lt. (j.g.) USPHS, 1948, advanced through grades to capt., 1963; rsch. microbiologist USPHS NIH, Bethesda, Md., 1948-69; ret. USPHS, 1969; rsch. career scientist U.S. Dept. Vets. Affairs, Miami, Fla., 1969-94; prof. microbiology Sch. Medicine U. Miami, 1969-88; rsch. prof. dentistry U. Fla., Gainesville, 1971-94; cons., advisor USPHS, Bethesda, 1970-94, Navy Dental Rsch. Inst., Great Lakes, Ill., 1972-94; cons. Merck Rsch., South Fla. Vets. Affairs Rsch. Found., 1994—. Contbr. 7 book chpts., 130 papers to scholarly and profl. books and jours. Recipient rsch. award Chgo. Dental Soc., 1968, Dental Rsch. prize Fedn. Dentaire Internat., Cologne, Fed. Republic of Germany, 1970, Sci. award Internat. Assn. Dental Rsch., Copenhagen, 1977, Undersec. for Health Honor award, 1994, Sec. of Vets. Affairs Exceptional Svc. award, 1994, Nat. Inst. Dental Rsch. Disting. Svc. award NIH. Fellow AAAS, Am. Soc. Microbiology.

FITZGERALD, THOMAS JOE, psychologist; b. Wichita, Kans., July 8, 1941; s. Thomas Michael and Pauline Gladys (Zink) F.; B.A., San Francisco State U., 1965; M.A., U. Utah, 1969, Ph.D., 1971. Dir. behavioral services programs VA Hosp., Topeka, 1971-73; pvt. practice as psychologist, Topeka, 1973-74, Prairie Village, Kans., 1974—; clin. instr. Menninger Sch. Psychiatry, Topeka, 1972-74; v.p. Preferred Mental Health Care Mgmt., Inc., 1986-90, pres., Preferred Mental Health, Inc., 1990—; sec.-treas. Kans. Bd. Psychologist Examiners, 1976-79, 79-80, chmn., 1980—, chmn. psychology examining com.; mem. Behavioral Scis. Regulatory Bd., 1980-82; pres. Psychol. Services Corp., Prairie Village, 1974—. Mem. Gov.'s Commn. on Criminal Adminstrn., 1974-76; vice-chmn. Gov.'s Com. on Med. Assistance, 1978-80; mem. Mid-Am. Health Systems Agy., 1979-82; mem. com. on utilization review orgns. Kansas Ins. Commr. Adv. Com., 1994—. Served with USMC, 1958-61. Mem. Kans. Psychol. Assn. (pres. 1980-81), Kans. Assn. Profl. Psychologists (pres. 1981-82, Outstanding Psychologist award 1979, 80, 81, 82), Greater Kansas City Soc. Clin. Hypnosis (pres. 1978-85). Office: Preferred Mental Health Inc 8220 Robinson St Overland Park KS 66204-3626

FITZGIBBONS, JOHN P., nephrologist; b. Boston, Dec. 3, 1938; s. John Patrick and Helen (Walsh) F.; m. Beverly Elizabeth Adams, June 6, 1964; children: Kathleen, Michael, Stacey, Matthew. BA, Coll. Holy Cross, 1960; MD, SUNY, 1964. Resident Boston City Hosp., 1964-66; rsch. fellow Mayo Clinic, Rochester, Minn., 1966-68; resident U. Calif., San Francisco, 1968-70; fellow in nephrology Tufts New Eng. Med. Ctr., Boston, 1970-73; nephrologist, chief nephrology Baystate Med. Ctr., Springfield, Mass., 1973-88; chair dept. medicine Lehigh Valley Hosp., Allentown, Pa., 1988—. Fellow Am. Coll. Physicians; mem. Internat. Soc. Nephrology, Am. Fedn. Clin. Rsch., Am. Coll. Physician Execs., Assn. Program Dirs. in Internal Medicine, Am. Soc. Nephrology. Office: Lehigh Valley Hosp Cedar Crest I-78 Allentown PA 18105-1556

FITZHARRIS, TIMOTHY P., scientist, corporation executive; b. N.Y.C., Oct. 31, 1944; s. Timothy P. and Mildred M. (Heim) F.; m. Linda L. Hummel, Nov. 4, 1945; children: Jeffrey Scott, Kelly Anne. BS, SUNY-Potsdam, 1966; MS, SUNY-Albany, 1969, PhD, 1971; postgrad. (postdoctoral fellow), U. Colo., 1971-72. Asst. prof. dept. anatomy Med. U. S.C., Charleston, 1972-77, assoc. prof., 1977-83, prof., 1983-84, prof., assoc. chmn. dept. cell biology and anatomy, 1992—, chmn. intellectual property & licensing, 1993—; assoc. dir. sci. and clin. affairs Litton Bionetics, Charleston, 1984-85, dir. clin. affairs, 1985-86; dir. R&D Organon Teknika Corp., Durham, N.C., 1985-92; affiliate marine scientist S.C. Wildlife & Marine Rsch. Ctr., Charleston, 1973-84; condr. workshops/seminars in field; established investigator Am. Heart Assn., 1980-84. Trustee Moultrie Sch. Dist. #2, 1980-84; bd. dirs. S.C. Heart Assn., 1983-87; co-chmn. fund drive Charleston chpt. S.C. Heart Assn., 1982-83; chmn. S.C. Heart Rsch. com., 1995—. NIH fellow, 1969; N.Y. State Regents scholar, 1962-66; NSF summer fellow, 1967, postdoctoral fellow, 1971; NIH grantee, 1974-77; Am. Heart grantee, 1979-82, 82-84; vis. exch. scientist Nat. Acad. Scis., Prague, Czechoslovakia, 1980. Fellow AAAS, (Biol. Scis. sect.); mem. S.C. Electron Microscopy Soc. (pres.), S.E. Electron Microscopy Soc. (pres.), Am. Soc. Cell Biology, Soc. Devel. Biology, Am. Assn. Anatomists, Sigma Xi (chmn. S.C. heart rsch. com. 1996—). Club: Dunes West Swim and Racquet. Contbr. articles to profl. jours. Home: 3427 Col Vanderhorst Circle Mount Pleasant SC 29464 Office: Medical University South Carolina 171 Ashley Ave Charleston SC 29425

FITZPATRICK, EDWARD FRANCIS, health facility administrator; b. Bangor, Maine, Dec. 8, 1954; s. Joseph Edward and Mary Elizabeth (Harding) F.; m. June Ann Gagnon, Oct. 26, 1953; children: Kristin, Kathryn. BS in Food and Nutrition, U. Maine, 1977; MBA, Husson Coll., 1990. Lic. long term care adminstr. Instr. nutrition H.O.M.E. Inc., Orlano, Maine, 1977-78; asst. dir. nutrition svcs. S.M.M.C., Biddeford, Maine, 1978-88; dir. micrographic project Creative Work Sys., Saco, Maine, 1988-90; dir. ops./adminstrn. River Ridge, Kennebunk, Maine, 1990-95; exec. dir. Sedgewood Commons, Falmouth, Maine, 1996—. Mem. Am. Coll. Health Care Adminstrs., Rotary. Roman Catholic. Office: Sedgewood Commons Northbrook Plz Falmouth ME 04105

FITZPATRICK, JOYCE J., dean, nursing educator. BSN, Georgetown U., LHD (hon.), 1990; MS in Psychiatric-Mental Health Nursing, Ohio State U.; PhD in Nursing, NYU; MBA, Case Western Reserve U., 1992. Elizabeth Brooks Ford prof. nursing Case Western Reserve U., Cleve., dean Frances Payne Bolton Sch. Nursing, 1982—; dir. WHO Collaborating Ctr. for Nursing Bolton Sch. Editor Applied Nursing Rsch.; co-editor Annual Rev. Nursing Rsch.; contbr. articles to profl. jours. Recipient Am. Jour. Nursing Book of Yr. awards, Midwest Nursing Rsch. Soc. Disting. Contrbn. to Nursing Rsch. award; Pub. Health Svc. Primary Care Policy fellow, 1995; Inst. Medicine/Am. Acad. Nursing/Am. Nurses Found. scholar, 1994-95. Fellow Am. Acad. Nursing; mem. N.Am. Nursing Diagnosis Assn. (chair taxonomy com.). Office: Case Western Res U 10900 Euclid Ave Cleveland OH 44106-4904

FITZPATRICK, LORRAINE ANNE, internist, educator; b. Joliet, Ill., Mar. 25, 1954; d. Thomas James and Ada Woodward (Flitcraft) F.; m. Kevin Elliott Bennet, May 24, 1980. AB, Wellesley Coll., 1976; MD, U. Chgo., 1980. Diplomate Am. Bd. Internal Medicine, Endocrinology and Metabolism. Intern, resident internal medicine Columbia-Presbyn. Hosp., N.Y.C., 1980-83; fellow in endocrinology and metabolism NIH, Bethesda, Md., 1983-87; asst. prof. U. Tex. Health Sci. Ctr., San Antonio, 1987-89; assoc. prof., prof. Mayo Clinic and Mayo Found., Rochester, 1989—; lectr. Rochester C.C., 1994—; mem. VA adv. merit, 1995—. Editor: Endocrinology, 1992—, editl. bd. mem., 1989-92; mem. editl. bd. Bone and Mineral, 1991-95. Mem. NIH (data and safety monitoring bd., chair study sect. 1995—), Am. Soc. Bone and Mineral Rsch. (Young Investigator award 1987), Endocrine Soc. (pub. comm. com. 1995—, chair 1996—). Office: Mayo Clinic & Mayo Found 200 1st St SW Rochester MN 55905

FITZPATRICK, M. LOUISE, nursing educator; b. South River, N.J., May 24, 1942; d. John Francis and Bettina (Galassi) F. Diploma in nursing, Johns Hopkins U., 1963; BSN, Cath. U. Am., 1966; MA, Columbia U., 1968, MEd, 1969, EdD, 1972; cert., Harvard U., 1985. Former assoc. prof., dept. nursing edn. Tchrs. Coll., Columbia U., N.Y.C.; dean, prof. Villanova (Pa.) U. Coll. Nursing, 1978—; cons. Mid. States Assn., Phila.; cons. to numerous univs., also univs. in USSR, Morocco, Egypt, Jordan, West Bank; cons., reviewer USPHS; bd. dirs. Nurses Ednl. Funds, Inc., N.Y.C. Author: The National Organization for Public Nursing, Development of a Practice Field, 1975; editor: Present Realities/Future Imperatives, 1977, Historical Studies in Nursing, 1978, Nursing in Society: A Historical Perspective, 1983; also 21 articles in profl. jours. Recipient Disting. Alumni award Columbia U. Tchrs. Coll., 1966, Cath. Univ. McManus medal, 1992; WHO fellow, Scandinavia and U.K., 1974; Am. Acad. Nursing fellow, 1978. Mem. Am. Nurses Assn. (past chmn. cabinet on nursing edn.), Am. Assn. Colls. Nursing, Nat. League for Nursing (bd. of govs.). Democrat. Roman Catholic. Home: 80 Woodstone Ln Villanova PA 19085-1425 Office: Villanova U Coll Nursing Villanova PA 19085

FITZPATRICK, ROBERT, psychologist; b. Cin., Aug. 26, 1924; s. John Joseph and Helen (Collins) F.; BS, U. Pitts., 1947, MS, 1948, PhD, 1953; m. Joanne Gehring Knauss, Aug. 12, 1952 (dec. Mar. 1970); children: John R., Janet E. Asbury, Jean A.; m. Dorothy May Gallagher, Jan. 31, 1976; 1 stepson, Matthew A. Kail. Project dir. Am. Inst. for Research, Pitts., 1948-54, program dir., 1954-59, 64-71; human factors unit supr. Boeing Co., Seattle, 1959-61; operational design group supr. System Devel. Corp., Lexington, Mass., 1961-62; mgr. psychol. dept., humetrics div. Thiokol Chem. Corp., L.A., 1963-64; pvt. practice indsl. psychology, Pitts., 1971—; dir. rsch. Psychol. Service, Pitts., 1976-78; lectr. U. Pitts., 1977-89; assoc. prof. St. Francis Coll., Pitts., 1979-85; grad. lectr. European div. U. Md., 1985-86. Served with USMC, 1943-46, 51-53. Mem. APA, Nat. Coun. Measurement in Edn., Pa. Psychol. Assn. Home: 100 Norman Dr Cranberry Township PA 16066-4236

FITZPATRICK, THOMAS BERNARD, dermatologist, educator; b. Madison, Wis., Dec. 19, 1919; s. Joseph J. and Grace (Lawrence) F.; m. Beatrice Devaney, Dec. 27, 1944; children: Thomas B., Beatrice, John, L. Scott, Brian. BA with honors, U. Wis., 1941; MD, Harvard U., 1945; fellow, Mayo Found., 1948-51; PhD, U. Minn., 1952; fellow, Commonwealth Fund, Oxford, 1958-59; DSc (hon.), U. Mass., 1987. Intern 4th (Harvard) Med. Service, Boston City Hosp., 1945-46; biochemist Army Med. Ctr., Md., 1946-48; asst. prof. dermatology U. Mich. Med. Sch., 1951-52; prof., head div. dermatology U. Oreg. Med. Sch., 1952-58; Edward Wigglesworth prof. dermatology Harvard Med. Sch., 1959-87, prof. emeritus, 1990—, head dept., 1959-87; chief dermatology svc. Mass. Gen. Hosp., Boston, 1959-87; Prosser White orator St. John's Dermatol. Soc., London, 1964; Dohi internat. exch. lectr. dermatology, Japan, 1969; spl. cons. USPHS, NIH; cons. in dermatology Brigham and Women's Hosp., Children's Hosp. Med. Ctr., Boston, 1962—; mem. sci. adv. bd. EPA, 1985; mem. climatic impact com., chmn. health effects NAS; pres. Dermatology Found., 1971, Internat. Pigment Cell Soc., 1978-81, Assn. Profs. Dermatology, 1983. Chief editor: Dermatology in General Medicine, 1971, 4th edit., 1993; mem. editl. bd. New Eng. Jour. Medicine, 1961-69; editor Year Book Dermatology, 1984—; editor-in-chief Fitzpatrick's Jour. Clin. Dermatology, 1993-95. Decorated Officer Order of Rising Gold Rays (Japan), 1986; recipient Mayo Found. Alumni Rsch. award, 1951, Outstanding Achievement award U. Minn. Bd. Regents, 1964, Myron Gordon award 6th Internat. Pigment Cell Conf., 1965, Disting. Svc. award Dermatology Found., 1989, U. Wis., 1983, award for discovery of PUVA photochemotherapy for psoriasis Nat. Psoriasis Found., 1993, Nat. Med. Rsch. award Nat. Health Coun., 1994, NAS Inst. Medicine, 1995, Am. Skin Assn., 1996. Fellow Am. Acad. Dermatology (hon., master, past bd. dirs.); mem. NAS (mem. inst. medicine 1994), Royal Soc. Medicine (hon.), Am. Acad. Arts and Scis., Assn. Am. Physicians, Soc. Investigative Dermatology (hon., pres. 1959-60, Stephen Rothman award, gold medal 1970, Am. Soc. for Clin. Investigation (emeritus 1965), Brit. Assn. Dermatology (hon.), South African Dermatol. Soc. (hon.), Med. Assn. Israel Dermatol. Soc. (hon.), St. John's Hosp. Dermatol. Soc. (London, hon.), Argentina, Danish, Italian, Finnish, German, Polish, Austrian dermatol. socs. (hon.), Pacific Dermatologic Assn. (hon.), French Soc. Dermatology and Syphiligraphy (fgn. corr.), Australasian Coll. Dermatologists, Alpha Omega Alpha. Home: 209 Newton St Weston MA 02193-2338 Office: Mass Gen Hosp Dermatology Svc 55 Fruit St Boston MA 02114-2620

FITZPATRICK, WILLIAM A., pharmacist; b. Edwardsville, Ill., Jan. 1, 1942; five children. Degree, St. Louis Coll. Pharmacy, 1965. Registered pharmacist, Mo., Ill. Pres. Fitzpatrick Pharmacy, Inc., Universal Packaging Sys., Inc.; v.p. Interlock Pharmacy Sys., Inc.; pres. Mo. State Bd. Pharmacy, 1992-96. Mem. Nat. Assn. Bds. Pharmacy (bur. vol. compliance com.), Am. Soc. Cons. Pharmacists, Am. Soc. Hosp. Pharmacy, Am. Pharms. Assn., Nat. Assn. Retail Druggists, Mo. Pharm. Assn., Mo. Hosp. Pharmacists Assn., St. Louis Pharmacist Assn., Acad. Gen. Practice Pharmacy, Mo. Found. Pharm. Care, Mo. League Nursing Home Adminstrs., Mo. Health Care Assn., Mo. Assn. Homes for the Aging, Am. Coll. Health Care Adminstrs., Kappa Psi, Kiwanis. Office: Fitzpatrick Pharmacy 15394 Manchester Rd Ellisville MO 63011

FITZSIMMONS, JOHN MICHAEL, physician, educator; b. Phila., Sept. 6, 1949; s. Johns Jospeh and Martha Catherine (McLouglin) F.; m. Sally Elizabeth Mauchly, June 13, 1970; children: Kathleen, Sara, Michael. BA in Math., LaSalle Coll., Phila., 1971; MD, Hahnemann Med. Coll., Phila., 1975; MBA, U. South Fla., Tampa, 1996. Diplomate Am. Bd. Ob/Gyn.; cert. maternal-fetal medicine physician. Intern Hershey (Pa.) Med. Ctr., 1975-76; resident Abington (Pa.) Meml. Hosp., 1976-78; attending physician Polyclinic Med. ctr., Harrisburg, Pa., 1978-79, 81-82; instr. ob/gyn. Jefferson Med. Coll., Phila., 1979-82, asst. prof., 1982-84; asst. prof. U. Wis., Madison, 1984-86; asst. prof. U. Wash., Seattle, 1986-89, asst. dean academic affairs, assoc. prof., 1989-92, assoc. prof. oby/gyn., 1992-95; assoc. prof. dept. ob-gyn. Med. Coll. Pa., Phila., 1995—; attending physician Hahnemann Hosp., Elkins Park Hosp., Med. Coll. Pa., Phila., 1995—; assoc. dir. perinatal svcs. Tacoma (Wash.) Gen. Hosp., 1992-95. Reviewer jours.; contbr. articles and abstracts to profl. jours. Mem. grant rev. com. Office of Substance Abuse Prevention, Washington, 1989-92; past S.W. region rep. Wash. State Perinatal Adv. Com.; past mem. Pierce County Perinatal Adv. Bd.; precinct officer Rep. Com., Tacoma, 1993, del. to county conv., 1994, del. to state conv., 1994; chmn. bd. dirs. Cmty. H.S., Phila. Mem. Am. Coll. Physician Execs., Am. Coll. Ob/Gyn., Am. Soc. Human Genetics, Soc. Perinatal Obstetricians, Rotary (Chestnut Hill). Republican. Roman Catholic. Home: 8030 Saint Martins Ln Philadelphia PA 19118-4101 Office: Med Coll Pa Dept Ob-Gyn 3300 Henry Ave Philadelphia PA 19129

FIUMARA, NICHOLAS JOHN, dermatologist; b. Boston, Oct. 31, 1912; s. John and Grace (Costa) F.; m. Sylvia G. Ponte, Dec. 24, 1944; 1 child, Sylvia Jean. AB, Boston Coll., 1934; MD, Boston U., 1939; MPH, Harvard U., 1947; DSc (hon.), Worcester State Coll., 1985. Intern Cambridge (Mass.) City Hosp., 1939-41; fellow in dermatology Mass. Gen. Hosp., Boston, 1953-55, Univ. Hosp. Boston, 1957-59; div. dir. communicable and veneral diseases Mass. Dept. Pub. Health, Boston, 1941-84; clin. prof. dermatology Boston U. Sch. Medicine, 1980—; prof. dermatology Tufts U. Sch. Medicine, Boston, 1959—; instr. dermatology Harvard Med. Sch., Boston, 1963—. Contbr. articles to profl. jours., chpts. to textbooks. Lt. USN, 1943-46. Recipient John D. Cromley award Mass. Health Officers Assn., 1972, award Alpha Omega Alpha, 1973, N.E. Regional Hadassah award Hadassah Soc., 1975, Ira Hirsch award N.E. Pub. Health Assn., 1979, Disting. Career award New Eng. Dermatol. Soc., 1985. Mem. Am. Veneral Disease Assn. (pres. 1959-60, 73-74, Thomas A. Panar award 1977), State and Territorial Epidemologists (pres. 1971-73). Republican. Roman Catholic. Home: 6 Gale Rd Belmont MA 02178-3938

FIUME, BARBARA PARENTY, social worker; b. N.Y.C., Nov. 19, 1949; d. Louis J. and Mary (Simonetti) Parenty; m. Orest Robert Fiume, Sept. 20, 1975; children: Christian Alexander, Michael Scott. BA, St. John's U., 1971; MSW, Fordham U., 1976. Bd. cert. diplomate in clin. social work; cert. English tchr., sch. social worker; lic. clin. social worker, N.J. Tchr. English Middletown (N.Y.) High Sch., 1971-73; social worker Pius XII, Middletown, 1973-75; social work therapist Family and Community Svcs., Fords, N.J., 1975-76; social worker Project Promise Presch., Belvidere, N.J., 1977-83, Project First Step, Washington, N.J., 1980-84; social work advocate Warren Assn. for Retarded Children, Washington, 1986-87; social work cons.; clin. social work therapist pvt. practice pvt. practice, Hackettstown, N.J., 1991—; adj. instr. Centenary Coll., Hackettstown, N.J., 1976-78; instr. Warren County Adult Edn. Mem. edn. input com. Lebanon Twp. Elem. Schs., Glen Gardner, N.J., 1988-90; mem. adv. bd. Arren CHADD. Mem. Nat. Assn. Social Workers, Acad. Cert. Social Workers. Roman Catholic. Home: 398 Penwell Rd Port Murray NJ 07865-3007

FIX, THOMAS HARRISON, dentist; b. Winston-Salem, May 14, 1951; s. Thomas Cooper and Jettie Mae Styers. BS in Dentistry, U. N.C., 1973, DDS, 1976. Dentist, lead dentist Mecklenberg County Health Dept., Charlotte, N.C., 1976-83; clin. instr. Ctrl. Piedmont C.C., Charlotte, 1976-80; assoc. Office of Dr. Bob Phillips DDS, P.A., Pineville, N.C., 1979-82; staff dentist Office of Drs. Edwards, Hensons & Lambeth, DDS, PA, Greensboro, N.C., 1982-93; lead dentist Piedmont Health Svcs., Inc., Chapel Hill, N.C., 1993—. Home: 3125 Jones Ferry Rd Chapel Hill NC 27516

FJERDINGSTAD, EJNAR JULES, retired biological scientist and educator; b. Copenhagen, Jan. 28, 1937; s. Einer Svend Aage and Else Emilie Sofie (Andersen) F.; m. Karen Madsen, Aug. 10, 1963; children: Svend Jules, Else Juliette. PhD, U. Copenhagen, 1962, U. Bergen, Norway, 1975. Asst. dept. zoology U. Copenhagen, 1961-67, 71-72; rsch. assoc. dept. biochemistry Duke U., Durham, N.C., 1967-68; rsch. assoc. dept. anesthesiology Baylor Coll. Medicine, Houston, 1968-69; asst. prof. biochemistry U. Tenn., Memphis, 1969-71; assoc. prof. anatomy U. Aarhus, Denmark, 1972-80, ret., 1980. Author: Cell Biology Perspectives, 1980; contbr., editor: Chemical Transfer of Learned Information, 1971; contbr. sci. articles to profl. jours. Mem. AAAS, Am. Cetacean Soc., Internat. Brain Rsch. Orgn., Planetary Soc., Jane Goodall Inst., Gorilla Found., Danish Mountain Club. Home: Svendgaardsvej 52, DK-8330 Beder Denmark

FLACH, FREDERIC FRANCIS, psychiatrist; b. N.Y.C., Jan. 25, 1927; s. George Raymond and Margaret (Donovan) F.; m. Patricia Anne Kane, June 23, 1951 (div. 1966); children: Frederica, Christopher, Geraldine, Andrew, Winifred; m. Joyce Elizabeth Rasmussen, Sept. 9, 1971. BA summa cum laude, St. Peter's Coll., Jersey City, 1947; MD, Cornell U., 1951. Diplomate Am. Bd. Psychiatry and Neurology. Intern second med. div. Bellevue Hosp., N.Y.C., 1951-52; from resident to chief resident psychiatry Payne Whitney Clinic, N.Y.C., 1953-58; pvt. practice N.Y.C., 1958—; attending psychiatrist Payne Whitney Clinic, N.Y. Hosp., N.Y.C., 1962—, St. Vincent's Hosp., N.Y.C., 1974—; adj. assoc. prof. psychiatry Cornell U. Med. Coll., N.Y.C., 1962—; program dir. Directions in Psychiatry, N.Y.C., 1981—. Author: The Secret Strength of Depression, 1974, Choices, 1976, Fridericus, 1980, Resilience, 1988, Rickie, 1990, Take Command, 1994, others. Lt. (j.g.) USNR, 1945-46. Fellow Am. Psychiat. Assn. (life). Roman Catholic. Office: 420 E 51st St New York NY 10022-8014

FLAGLE, CHARLES DENHARD, health policy and management educator, emeritus; b. Scottdale, Pa., Apr. 26, 1919; s. Charles David and Marie Elizabeth (Denhard) F.; m. Lois Hagaman, July 3, 1946 (dec. 1963); children—Charles Lawrence, Judith Ellen Flagle McClure, Douglas Anderson; m. Janet Sayward Waters Dryden, Mar. 27, 1965; 1 stepchild, Elizabeth Dryden Stephens. B.E., Johns Hopkins U., 1940, M.Sci, 1955, D.Engring., 1956. Devel. engr. Westinghouse Electric Co., Phila., 1940-46; analyst Henry C. Robinson and Co., Hartford, Conn., 1946-47; engr. Wayne Iron Works, Pa., 1947-50; successively research assoc., asst. prof., assoc. prof. Johns Hopkins U., Balt., 1950-60; prof. health policy and mgmt., prof. math. scis., head div. of ops. research Johns Hopkins U., 1961-84, prof. emeritus, 1984—; mem. adv. com. on occupational health, WHO Geneva, 1979-88; asst. to surgeon gen. USPHS, Washington, 1967-68. Editor: (with Huggins and Roy) Operations Research and Systems Engineering, 1960, Advanced Medical Systems, 1975; (with van Eimeren and Engelbrecht) System Science in Health Care, 1984, 88. Bd. dirs. Roland Park Pl. Life Care Residence, Balt., 1983-93, Vis. Nurse Assn., 1982-91; trustee Roland Park Country Sch., Balt., 1974-82. NIMH grantee, 1971-85. Fellow Am. Assn. for Med. Systems and Info. (founding mem., pres. 1974-75); mem. Inst. of Medicine of Nat. Acad. of Sci., Ops. Research Soc. (council 1975-78), Pavlovian Soc. (pres. 1981). Clubs: Johns Hopkins (exec. com. 1961-64), Hamilton St. (Balt.). Home: 1822 Circle Rd Baltimore MD 21204-6415 Office: Johns Hopkins U Dept Health Policy and Mgmt 624 N Broadway Baltimore MD 21205-1901

FLAHERTY, EMALEE GOTTBRATH, pediatrician; b. LaGrange, Ky., May 24, 1944; d. Frank Herman and Katherine Lee (Carothers) Gottbrath; m. Joseph Flaherty, Apr. 28, 1973 (div.); children: Joshua, Megan. BS, Purdue U., W. Lafayette, Ind., 1966; MD, Ind. U., Indpls., 1970. Resident, pediatrics U. Ill. Hosp., 1970-72, Columbus Hosp., 1972-73; med. dir. Outpatient Dept., Columbus Hosp., Chgo., 1984—, Columbus-Maryville Reception Ctr., Chgo., 1986-95; dir. ambulator pediatrics Columbus Hosp., Chgo., 1979-96; project dir. pediatric primary care tng. grant Columbus Hosp., 1989-95; med. dir. protective svc. team Children's Meml. Hosp., 1996—. Mem. Pediatric Primary Care Rsch. Grp. (steering com.), Pediatric Rsch. Office Setting (dist. coord.), Columbus Hosp. Woman's Bd. (exec. bd. 1988—). Office: Columbus Hospital 2520 N Lakeview Ave Chicago IL 60614-1804

FLAHERTY, LOIS T., psychiatrist, educator; b. Nashville, Apr. 28, 1942. BA, Wellesley Coll., 1963; MD, Duke U., 1968. Diplomate Nat. Bd. Med. Examiners. Intern D.C. Gen. Hosp., 1968-69; resident in psychiatry Georgetown U. Hosp., 1969-71; resident in child psychiatry Johns Hopkins Hosp., 1971-73; pvt. practice Cross Keys, Md., 1973-81; dir. tng. div. child and adolescent psychiatry U. Md., 1981-89, assoc. prof. med. sch. div. child and adolescent psychiatry, 1982—, dir. div. child and adolescent psychiatry, 1984-92; instr. depts. psychiatry and pediatrics Johns Hopkins U. Sch. Medicine, 1973-92; attending staff psychiatrist family, child and adolescent div. Sinai Hosp. Balt., 1974-77; staff child psychiatrist Walter P. Carter Ctr., 1977-78, dir. child and adolescent svcs., 1978-92, acting dir. impatient adolescent unit, 1979-80; clin. asst. prof. U. Md., 1977-81; cons. Northwest Drug Alert Sinai Hosp. Balt., 1971-72, St. Vincent's Child Care Ctr., 1973-78, Children's Guild, Inc., 1975-82, SSA, Balt., 1985, many others. Contbr. chpts. to books and articles and book revs. to profl. jours. NIMH grantee, 1983-86. Fellow Am. Psychiat. Assn., Am. Soc. for Adolescent Psychiatry; mem. Am. Acad. Child Psychiatry, Am. Assn. Dirs. Psychiat. Residency Tng. Programs, Md. Psychiat. Soc., Md. Regional Coun. for Child Psychiatry, Md. Soc. for Adolescent Psychiatry, Soc. Profs. Child Psychiatry. Office: U Md Sch Medicine Dept Psych Div Child Adolescent Psych 645 W Redwood St Baltimore MD 21201

FLAHERTY, SISTER MARY JEAN, dean, nursing educator. Dean, assoc. prof. Sch. Nursing, Cath. U. Am., Washington. Office: Cath U Am Sch of Nursing 620 Michigan Ave NE Washington DC 20064-0001*

FLAHERTY, SERGINA MARIA, ophthalmic medical technologist; b. Düsseldorf, Germany, Nov. 22, 1958; came to U.S., 1962; d. Austin W. and Evelyn (Kähl) F. Cert. ophthalmic med. technologist. Ophthalmic asst. U.S. Army, Ft. Rucker, Ala., 1978-82; ophthalmic technician Wiregrass Total Eye Care Clinic, Enterprise, Ala., 1983-86, Straub Hosp. and Clinic, Honolulu, 1986-90; ophthalmic technologist Eye Cons. of San Antonio, San Antonio, 1993-96, Stone Oak Ophthalmology, San Antonio, 1996—. Mem. Assn. Tech. Pers. in Ophthalmology, Ophthalmic Photographer Soc., Hawaii Ophthalmic Assts. Soc. (founding mem., sec. 1987-89, pres. 1989-90), Ophthalmic Pers. Soc. San Antonio (program dir. 1994-95, pres. 1996—). Home: 5650 Grissom Rd Apt 807 San Antonio TX 78238-2251 Office: Stone Oak Ophthalmology Ste 450 540 Stone Oak Med Bldg San Antonio TX 78258

FLAMM, EUGENE SOMER, neurosurgeon, educator; b. Bklyn., Jan. 1, 1937; m. Susan Flamm; children: Andrew, Douglas. AB, Princeton U., 1958; MD, U. Buffalo, 1962; MA (hon.), U. Pa., 1983. Diplomate Am. Bd. Neurol. Surgery. Intern dept. surgery Cornell Med. Ctr. N.Y. Hosp., N.Y.C., 1962-63, asst. resident dept. surgery Cornell Med. Ctr., 1963-64; clin. assoc. neurosurgery Nat. Inst. Neurol. Disease and Blindness NIH, Bethesda, Md., 1964-66; resident, chief resident dept. neurosurgery Sch. Medicine NYU, N.Y.C., 1966-70; attending neurosurgeon, chief neurosurgery sect. Manhattan VA Hosp., 1972-88, rsch. assoc., 1972-75; attending neurosurgeon Bellevue Hosp., 1975-88; asst. prof. neurosurgery Sch. Medicine NYU, N.Y.C., 1971-75, assoc. prof., 1975-81, prof. neurosurgery, vice chmn. dept. neurosurgery, 1981-87; co-dir. Neurosurg. Rsch. Labs. NYU Med. Ctr., 1972-74, dir. Neurosurg. Rsch. Labs., 1974-88; Charles Harrison Frazier prof. neurosurgery, chmn. divsn. neurosurgery U. Pa., 1988—; asst. physician Neurochirurgische Universitatsklinik Kantonsspital, Zurich, Switzerland, 1971-72; dir. Am. Bd. Neurol. Surgery, 1994—. Editorial positions with Neurosurgery, 1976-81, Neurological Rsch., 1977—, Stroke, 1980—, Neurosurg. Anesthesiology, 1988—. Recipient Wakeman award, 1990. Fellow Am. Coll. Surgeons, N.Y. Acad. Medicine, Coll. Physicians Phila.; mem. AAAS, AMA, Am. Acad. Neurol. Surgery (mem. various coms.), Am. Assn. Neurol. Surgeons, Am. Heart Assn. (fellow stroke coun.), Am. Neurol. Assn., Am. Bd. Neurol. Surgery (bd. dirs. 1994—), N.Y. Acad. Sci., N.Y. Soc. Neurosurgery (sec.-treas. 1975-80, pres. 1984-86), N.Y. Neurosurg. Soc. (dir. 1986-88), Pa. Neurosurg. Soc., Phila. County Med. Soc., Rsch. Soc. Neurol. Surgeons, Soc. Neurosci., Soc. Neurol. Surgeons. Assn. Rsch. Nervous and Mental Disease, Congress Neurol. Surgeons. Home: 1901 Walnut St Philadelphia PA 19103-4605 Office: Hosp of U Pa Divsn Neurosurgery 3400 Spruce St Philadelphia PA 19104

FLANAGAN, JOSEPH CHARLES, ophthalmologist; b. Phila., Feb. 7, 1938; s. John C. and Marie (Gable) F.; m. Catharine McHale, June 1, 1963; children: Katie, Joseph, Mimi. BA, LaSalle U., 1959; MD, Jefferson Med. Coll., 1963. Diplomate Am. Bd. Ophthalmology. Intern Fitzgerald Mercy Hosp., Darby, Pa., 1963-64; resident Wills Eye Hosp., Phila., 1964-67; Heed fellow ophthalmic plastic surgery Manhattan Eye & Ear Hosp., N.Y.C., 1967-68; ptnr. Annesley, Flanagan, Fischer, Stefanyszyn and Assocs., Phila., 1969—; prof. ophthalmology Jefferson Med. Coll., Phila., 1981; cons. Nat. Exam. Bd. Ocularists, MBF Computer Ctr., Phila.; dir. oculoplast dept. Wills Eye Hosp., 1981; chief dept. ophthalmology, Lankenaua Hosp., Phila., 1989. Author: Techniques in Ophthalmic Plastic Surgery, 1986, Current Therapy in Ophthalmic Surgery, 1989. Recipient fellowship grant Heed Found., Chgo., 1978, Freeman award Buffalo Ophthalmic Soc., 1986, Ruedemann Lecture award, 1986; named Wendell Hughes lectr. Am. Acad. Ophthalmology, 1992. Mem. Wills Eye Hosp. Soc. (sec. 1977-83, pres. 1988, Silver Tray award 1988), Am. Soc. Ophthalmic Plastic and Reconstructive Surgery (pres. 1983-84), Ophthalmic Club Phila. (sec. 1976-79), Phila. Country Club, Merion Cricket Club. Home: 1627 Lafayette Rd Gladwyne PA 19035-1117 Office: Annesley Flanagan Fischer Stefanyszyn & Assocs 256 Lankenau Med Wynnewood PA 19096

FLANAGAN, LATHAM, JR., surgeon; b. Pitts., Dec. 2, 1936; s. Latham and Elizabeth Lansing (Bunting) Kimbrough; m. Elizabeth Ruth Losaw, June 26, 1961 (dec. May 1971); 1 child, Jennifer Ruth; m. Mary Jane Flanagan, Mar. 28, 1975; children: Sahale Ann, David Nooroa. MD, Duke U., 1961, student, 1957, MD, 1961. Diplomate Am. Bd. Surgery. Intern U. Calif., San Francisco, 1961-62, resident in surgery, 1962-66, chief resident in surgery, 1965-66; pvt. practice surgery Sacred Heart Hosp., Eugene, Oreg., 1968-84, 85—; clin. sr. instr. in surgery Oreg. Health Scis. U., Portland, 1968-84; assoc. prof. surgery U. Otago, Dunedin (New Zealand) Pub. Hosp., 1984-85; nat. surgeon Cook Islands, 1985; founder Oreg. Ctr. for Bariatric Surgery, Eugene, 1993—. Contbr. articles to profl. jours. Founder White Bird Clinic, Eugene, 1969-71; mem. adv. com. Planned Parenthood of Lane County, 1979-84, Lt. comdr. USNR, 1966-68, Vietnam. Fellow ACS (pres. Oreg. chpt. 1991-92); mem. AMA, Oreg. Med. Assn., Lane County med. Soc. (com. chair 1970s), Am. Soc. Bariatric Surgery (chair ins. com. 1991-94, councillor 1994—), North Pacific Surg. Soc., Eugene Surg. Soc. (pres. 1981). Republican. Home: 31033 Foxridge Ln Eugene OR 97405-5305 Office: 655 E 11th Ave Ste 8 Eugene OR 97401-3621

FLANAGAN, ROGER M., ophthalmologist; b. Marshfield, Oreg., Feb. 10, 1920; s. John Winchester and Letitia (Howard) F.; m. Mary Lee Barnett; children: Thomas, Kathleen, James, John, David. BS, U. Oreg., 1942; MD, Oreg. Health Scis. Ctr., Portland, 1945. Resident in ophthalmology O.H.S.U.-Am. Bd. Ophthalmology, 1951; pvt. practice Coos Bay. Bd. dirs. and chmn. Coos Bay (Oreg.) Sch. Bd., 1970-79. Lt. col. Oreg. N.G., 1981—. Home: HC 52 Box 680B Coos Bay OR 97420 Office: 620 Commercial Coos Bay OR 97420-1846

FLANAGAN, ROSEMARY, psychologist, educator; b. Bklyn., Jan. 13, 1956; d. Patrick W. and Angela (Lauro) F. BS, St. Francis Coll., Bklyn., 1976; MA, New Sch. for Social Rsch., 1980, Hofstra U., 1982; PhD, Hofstra U., 1986; cert. advanced study, Queens Coll., 1989. Diplomate Am. Bd. Profl. Psychology; lic. psychologist, N.Y. Supr. labs. St. Francis Coll., Bklyn., 1977-81; psychologist West Hempstead (N.Y.) Union Free Sch. Dist., 1984-85, East Williston (N.Y.) Union Free Sch. Dist., 1985-86, Copiague (N.Y.) Union Free Sch. Dist., 1986-87, Baldwin (N.Y.) Union Free Sch. Dist., 1987—; asst. prof. Hofstra U., Hempstead, N.Y., 1989-91, St. John's U., Jamaica, N.Y., 1991-96, assoc. prof. 1996—; pvt. practice, Hempstead, 1988—. Fellow Am. Acad. Sch. Psychology, Inst. Rational Emotive Therapy (assoc.); mem. ASCD, APA, Am. Psychol. Soc., Assn. Advancement of Behavior Therapy, N.Y. State Psychol. Assn. (pres. sch. psychology divsn. 1992-93, sch. psychology rep. to governing coun. 1996-99), Am. Assn. for Applied and Preventive Psychology, Nat. Assn. Sch. Psychologists, Soc. Personality Assessment, Nassau County Psychol. Assn., Nassau County Psychol. Svcs. Inst. (trustee), Queens Psychol. Assn., N.Y. Assn. Sch. Psychologists, Sch. Psychology Educators Coun. of N.Y. State. Office: 230 Hilton Ave # 1 Hempstead NY 11550-8116

FLANDERS, DAVID JOSEPH, pathologist; b. Cleve., May 24, 1954; s. Raymond Michael and Mary Viola (Herr) F.; m. Susan Jane Ecroyd, May 16, 1981; children: Emily Meredith, William Alec. BA in Zoology cum laude, U. Iowa, 1975, MD, 1979. Diplomate Am. Bd. Pathology. Resident U. Iowa Hosps. & Clinics, Iowa City, 1979-83, clin. assoc./fellow surg. pathology, 1983-84; pathologist Associated Pathologists Ltd., Springfield, Ill., 1984-86, Peoria (Ill.)-Tazwell Pathology Group, 1986—; HyVee Found. scholar, Chariton, Iowa, 1972-76, Linn County Med. Soc. scholar, Cedar Rapids, Iowa, 1976, 78; chmn. pathology dept. Proctor Hosp., 1991-95, med. staff pres., 1997. Contbr. articles to profl. jours. Fellow Coll. Am. Pathologists; mem. U.S.-Can. Acad. Pathology, Ill. State Med. Soc., Ill. Soc. Pathologists, Peoria Med. Soc., Alpha Omega Alpha, Phi Beta Kappa. Office: Proctor Hosp Pathology Dept 5409 N Knoxville Ave Peoria IL 61614

FLANDERS, JAMES PRESCOTT, clinical psychologist; b. Cornwall, N.Y., Nov. 12, 1942; s. Dwight Prescott and Mildred Margaret (Hutchison) F.; m. Helen Juanita Hilderbrand, Dec. 29, 1966; children: Carl Prescott, Leah Teresa. BS with honors, U. Ill., 1964; MA, Vanderbilt U., 1966, PhD, 1968; clin. cert., U. Miami, 1981. Lic. psychologist, Wis., Miss. Asst. prof. psychology Bowling Green (Ohio) State U., 1970-72; assoc. prof. psychology Fla. Internat. U., Miami, 1972-85; pvt. practice Eagle River, Wis., 1985-90; clin. psychologist Vicksburg (Miss.) Clinic, 1990—; cons. Pastoral Dept., Episcopal Ch., Miami, 1983-85; book, manuscript reviewer various pubs., jours., 1970-87; speaker various civic groups, 1972—. Author: Practical Psychology, 1976; contbr. numerous articles to scientific and profl. jours.; creator: Hometown Project, 1989—. Leader Indian Guides for Boys, Miami, 1978; Sun. sch. tchr. various churches, Miami, 1978-84; bd. dirs. Tri-County Commn. on Domestic Violence, Rhinelander, Wis., 1988-90. Capt. USA, 1968-70. Vanderbilt U. fellow, 1964-65, NIMH Predoctoral fellow, 1966-68. Mem. APA, Nat. Register Providers in Psychology, Miss. Psychol. Assn., Psi Chi, Sigma Xi. Office: Vicksburg Clinic 1115 I 20 Frontage Rd Vicksburg MS 39182-0666

FLANNERY, ANN MARIE, pediatric neurosurgeon; b. Chgo., May 6, 1954; d. Edward and Dorothy Marie (Johnson) F.; m. Peter John Kobe, May 19, 1979; children: Caroline Brennan, Kathleen Teresa, Christopher Edward, Kimberly Elizabeth. BS in Biology with distinction, U. Ill., 1975; MD, Rush Med. Coll., Chgo., 1979. Diplomate Am. Bd. Neurol. Surgery. Intern Rush Presbyn.-St. Luke's Med. Ctr., Chgo., 1979-80, resident neurol. surgery, 1980-85; fellow pediatric neurol. surgery Children's Meml. Hosp., Chgo., 1985-87; instr. Rush Med. Coll., Chgo., 1983-85; provisional attending physician divsn. neurosurgery Children's Meml. Hosp., Northwestern U. Med. Sch., 1985-87; asst. prof. surgery (neurosurgery) and pediatrics Med. Coll. Ga., Augusta, 1987-92, asst. dean grad. med. edn., 1991—, assoc. prof. surgery (neurosurgery) and pediatrics, 1992—; women's liaison officer Am. Assn. Med. Colls., 1991—; mem. faculty senate exec. com. Med. Coll. Ga., 1989—. Edward J. James scholar U. Ill., 1972-75; recipient Academic Citation Am. Med. Woman's Assn., 1979; grantee Sterling-Winthrop Pharm. Rsch. Divsn., 1993-95. Fellow ACS; mem. Women in Neurosurgery (sec.-treas. 1996), Am. Assn. Neurol. Surgeons, Congress Neurol. Surgeons, Internat. Soc. Pediatric Neurosurgery, Ga. Neurosurg. Soc., Richmond County Med. Assn. Home: 815 Quail Ct Augusta GA 30909 Office: Med Coll Ga Dept Neurosurgery 1120 15th St BIW348B Augusta GA 30912

FLANNERY, WILBUR EUGENE, health science association administrator, internist; b. New Castle, Pa., June 19, 1907; s. Charles Francis and Mary Catherine (McGrath) F.; m. Ruth Iva Donaldson, June 27, 1929; children: Charles, John, Richard, Harry. BA, Dartmouth Coll., 1929; MA, Oberlin Coll., 1930; MD, Harvard U., 1935. Diplomate Nat. Bd. Medical Examiners. Minister Meth. Ch., New Castle, 1930-31; intern Cleve. City Hosp., 1935-36; resident physician Jameson Meml. Hosp., New Castle, 1936-37; fellowship Cleve. Clinic Found., 1937-40; practice medicine specializing in internal medicine New Castle, 1940—; med. dir. Hospice of St. Francis Hosp., New Castle, 1987—; chmn. bd. Pa. Blue Shield, Harrisburg, Pa., 1975-80. Contbr. numerous articles to med. jours. Pres. Bd. of Edn., New Castle, 1947-53; former trustee Knoville (Tenn.) Coll.; former pres. or chmn. Lawrence County chpt. ARC, Lawrence County chpt. Pa. Assn. for Blind, Lawrence County Mental Health Clinic, New Castle Exec. Club, Greater New Castle C. of C. Recipient Disting. Citizens award Optimists Club, 1974; named Boss of Yr., Am. Bus. Women's Assoc., 1987. Mem. AMA (del. 1953-63), Pa. Med. Soc. (pres. 1963-64), Lawrence County Med. Soc. (sec. 1954-55, pres. 1955-56), Am. Soc. Internal Medicine, Am. Med. Writers Assn., Acad. Hospice Physicians (pres. 1990), Internat. Hospice Inst., Internat. Coll. Hospice/Palliative Care, Internat. Platform Assn., Pa. Soc., New Castle Country Club, Univ. Club (Pitts.), Lawrence Club, Youngstown (Ohio) Club, Elks, Lions (pres. New Castle 1943-44, Disting. Svc. award). Republican. Presbyterian. Home: 106 E Hazelcroft Ave New Castle PA 16105-2133 Office: Hospice of St Francis 131 N Columbus Interbelt New Castle PA 16101-7401

FLAUM, MORRIS AARON, hematologist, oncologist; b. Fed. Republic of Germany, Jan. 29, 1947; came to U.S., 1949; s. Jacob S. and Sara (Sissiski) F.; children: Alisa, Geoffrey. BS, U. Pitts., 1969; MD, U. Miami, Fla., 1974; MBA, Tulane U., 1990. Diplomate Am. Bd. Internal Medicine and Hematology. Intern Yale-New Haven (Conn.) Hosp., 1974-75, resident, 1975-77; clin. assoc. NIH, Bethesda, Md., 1977-79; physician St. Petersburg (Fla.) Med. Clinic, 1979-81; physician Ochsner Clinic, New Orleans, 1981-92, bd. mgmt., fin. com., 1987-92; chmn. dept. internal medicine St. Joseph Mercy Hosp., Ann Arbor, Mich., 1992—; chmn. quality assessment com. Ochsner Med. Inst., New Orleans, 1987-92. Author: (with others) Transplantation, 1991. Bd. dirs. Am. Cancer Soc., New Orleans, 1982-89; trustee Leukemia Soc. Am., La., 1990-92. Recipient Best in Specialty (hematology) award Detroit Monthly, 1995. Fellow Am. Coll. Physicians, mem. Am. Soc. Hematology (practice com.), Am. Soc. Clin. Oncology, Am. Coll. Physician Execs., So. Assn. Oncology (founding mem. 1988), Beta Gamma Sigma, Phi Kappa Phi, Alpha Omega Alpha. Jewish. Office: St Joseph Mercy Hosp 5333 Mcauley Dr Ste R-3009 Ypsilanti MI 48197-1014

FLECHNER, STUART MARC, physician, researcher; b. N.Y.C., Oct. 23, 1950; s. Irving N. and Anne (Turbiner) F.; m. Susan Ann Richmond, July 1, 1972; children: Lawrence Martin, David Herman. BA, UCLA, 1971, MD, 1975. Diplomate Am. Bd. Urology. Surg. intern U. Calif.-San Francisco Moffitt Hosp., 1975-76, surg. asst., 1976-77, urology resident, 1977-80; fellow in transplantation Cleve. Clinic Found., 1980-81; asst. prof. U. Tex. Med. Sch., Houston, 1981-84, assoc. prof., 1985-86; assoc. prof. Stanford U. Sch. Medicine, Calif., 1986—, dir. div. transplantation, dept. surgery, 1986-93; Cleve. Clinic Found. Dept. Urology, renal transplantation, 44195. Contbr. over 150 articles, book chpts. to profl. publs. Fellow ACS; mem. Am. Urol. Assn. (program com. 1983, 88-90), Am. Soc. Transplant Surgeons, Soc. Univ. Surgeons, Urol. Soc. Transplantation and Vascular Surgery (pres. 1988), Phi Beta Kappa, Alpha Omega Alpha. Home: 2821 Stonebridge Ct Hudson OH 44236-2347 Office: Stanford U Med Ctr 300 Pasteur Dr Palo Alto CA 94304-2203 Office: Cleveland Clinic Foundation Dept Urology Sect Renal Tra 9500 Euclid Ave Cleveland OH 44195

FLECK, STEPHEN, psychiatrist; b. Frankfort-am-Main, Germany, Sept. 18, 1912; came to U.S., 1935; s. Georg and Anna (Beer) F.; m. Louise Harlan, Oct. 13, 1945 (dec. 1992); children: AnnaLou F.J. Singer, Stephen H., Carra Rockwood. Cand. Medicine, J.W. Goethe U., Frankfort, Fed. Republic of Germany, 1931-33; postgrad., U. Amsterdam, 1933-35; MD, Harvard U., 1940. Diplomate Nat. Bd. Med. Examiners, Am. Bd. Psychiatry and Neurology. Intern Beth Israel Hosp., Boston, 1940-42; clin. trainee Henry Phipps Psychiat. Clinic, Johns Hopkins Hosp., Balt., 1946-48, asst. internal medicine, Commonwealth fellow, 1948-49; asst. prof. psychiatry U. Wash., Seattle, 1949-53; psychiatrist-in-chief Psychiat. Inst., Yale U., New Haven, 1953-83, prof. psychiatry and pub. health Sch. Medicine, 1963-83, prof. emeritus, 1983—; psychiatrist-in-chief Conn. Mental Health Ctr., New Haven, 1969-83; cons. Bridgeport (Conn.) Mental Health Ctr., 1983-95; mem. adv. bd. Whiting Forensic Inst., Middletown, Conn. 1957; mem. Hamden (Conn.) Mental Health Commn., 1970-86. Served to maj. U.S. Army, 1942-46. Fellow Am. Psychiat. Assn. (life), Group for Advancement Psychiatry (life); mem. AMA, Am. Pub. Health Assn., Western New England Psychoanalytic Soc., Conn. Psychiat. Soc. (pres. 1966-67). Office: Yale U Sch Medicine 25 Park St Rm 608 New Haven CT 06519-1110

FLECKMAN, PHILIP HOWARD, dermatologist, cell biologist; b. Port Arthur, Tex., Apr. 27, 1946; s. Max and Jeanette (Lindenberg) F.; m. Star C. Leonard, Dec. 28, 1977; children: Mahri S. Leonard-Fleckman, Morgen L. Leonard-Fleckman. BA, U. Tex., 1968; MD, Washington U., St. Louis, 1973. Diplomate Am. Bd. Dermatology. Intern medicine Barnes Hosp., St. Louis, 1973-74; rsch. assoc. lab. of neurochemistry, NIMH, NIH, Bethesda, Md., 1974-76, med. officer rsch., 1976-78; resident dept. dermatology Yale U., New Haven, 1978-80; instr., 1980-81, asst. prof., 1981-82; asst. prof. med. dermatology U. Wash., Seattle, 1982-88, assoc. prof. dermatology, 1988—; cons. West Haven VA Hosp., Conn., 1980-82; staff physician Yale-New Haven Hosp., 1980-82, Univ. Hosp., Seattle, 1982—, Seattle VA Med. Ctr., 1994; prin. investigator Nat. Registry Ichthyosis and Related Disorders, 1994—. Contbr. articles to profl. jours. Served with USPHS, 1974-78. Recipient Clin. Investigator award NIH, 1980-83; Dermatology Found. fellow, 1980; grantee NIH, 1981—. Fellow Am. Acad. Dermatology; mem. Am. Soc. Cell Biology, Soc. Investigative Dermatology, Am. Fedn. Clin. Research, Fedn. Am. Scientists. Home: 5041 Ivanhoe Pl NE Seattle WA 98105-2832 Office: U Wash Divsn Dermatology Box 356524 Seattle WA 98195-6524

FLEG, JEROME LOUIS, physician, research cardiologist; b. Cin., June 15, 1945; s. Julian Francis and Elaine (Nelson) F.; m. Rosemarie T. Greyson, Sept. 20, 1977; children: Anthony, Jerome, Michael, Stephen. BS in Zoology, U. Cin., 1967, MD, 1970. Intern Balt. City Hosps., 1970-71; resident, internal medicine Barnes Hosp., St. Louis, 1973-75; fellow, cardiology Wash. Univ. Med. Sch., St. Louis, 1975-77; rsch. cardiologist Nat. Inst. Aging, Balt., 1977—, chmn., clin. evaluation com., 1986—. Editl. bd. Am. Jour. Cardiology, Jour. Gerontology, Cardiology in the Elderly, Jour Am. Geriatrics Soc.; contbr. over 100 articles to profl. jours. and chpts. to books. Capt. USAF, 1971-73. Fellow Am. Coll. Cardiology, Coun. on Geriatric Cardiology (v.p. 1988-90, pres. 1990-91); mem. Am. Heart Assn., Commd. Officers Assn., Am. Physiological Soc. Office: Gerontology Rsch Ctr Eastern Ave Baltimore MD 21224-2735

FLEISCH, JEROME HERBERT, pharmacologist, research advisor; b. Bronx, N.Y., June 6, 1941; s. Wolf and Miriam (Glaser) F.; m. Marlene L. Cohen, Aug. 8, 1976; children: Abby Faye, Sheryl Brynne. BS in Pharmacy, Columbia U., 1963; PhD in Pharmacology, Georgetown U., 1967. Rsch. fellow Harvard Med. Sch., Boston, 1967-68; rsch. assoc. NIH Nat. Heart and Lung Inst., Bethesda, Md., 1968-70, sr. staff fellow, 1970-74; sr. pharmacologist Lilly Rsch. Labs., Indpls., 1974-77, rsch. scientist, 1977-82, sr. rsch. scientist, 1982-86, rsch. advisor, 1986-93, Lilly rsch. fellow, 1993—. Contbr. articles to profl. jours. Patentee in field. Served to lt. comdr. USPHS, 1968-70. Mem. Am. Soc. Pharmacology Exptl. Therapeutics, Collegium Internationale Allergologicum, Soc. Exptl. Biology and Medicine, Am. Thoracic Soc., Inflammation Rsch. Assn. Office: Eli Lilly & Co. # 0520 Indianapolis IN 46285

FLEISCHAKER, GORDON HENRY, JR., pediatrician; b. Louisville, July 1, 1928; s. Gordon H. and Agnes Rose (Shatzen) F.; m. Barbara Lorraine Draeger, Aug. 15, 1954; children: Rachel, Judith, James. BA in Zoology, U. Louisville, 1949, MD, 1953. Intern Univ. Hosp., Madison, Wis., 1953-54; resident in pediatrics The Childrens Hosps., Denver, 1956-58; fellow in pediatric rheumatology State U. Iowa, Iowa City, 1958-60; practice medicine specializing in pediatrics Denver, 1960—; assoc. clin. prof. pediatrics U. Colo. Sch. of Med., Denver, 1960—; mem. active med. staff The Children's Hosp., Denver. Served to capt. MC, USAF, 1953-56. Fellow Am. Acad. Pediats.; mem. AMA, AAAS, Colo. Med. Soc., Clear Creek Valley Med. Soc. Office: G H Fleischaker MD 4485 Wadsworth Blvd Wheat Ridge CO 80033-3318

FLEISCHER, ALBERT GEORG, health facility administrator; b. Mineral Wells, Tex., Sept. 26, 1940; s. Albert Georg and Lilith Martesia (Boyd) F. AB, Austin Coll., 1962; MD, U. Tex., 1966. Fellow in spinal cord injuries Rusk Inst., N.Y.C., 1968, asst. prof., 1968-80; dir. rehab. medicine S.I. (N.Y.) Hosp., 1980-89; chair rehab. medicine S.I. U. Hosp., 1989-93; chmn. St. Vincent's Med. Ctr., S.I., 1993—, Bayley Seton Hosp., S.I., 1993—; asst. prof. Downstate Med. Ctr., Bklyn., 1985-95; assoc. clin. prof. phys. therapy divsn. Coll. S.I., 1991—; dir. rehab. medicine Luth. Med. Ctr., Bklyn., 1985-93. Mem. Mayor's Com. for Disabled, N.Y.C., 1980—, chairperson, 1990—; chair Borough Pres. Com. for Disabled, S.I., 1989—; med. dir. United Cerebral Palsy, N.Y.C., 1991—; pres. Tibetan Mus. Bd., 1993—; bd. dirs. Staten Island Ctr. for Ind. Living, 1983—; mem. N.Y. State Ind. Living Coun., N.J. State Brain Injury Coun., 1993—, N.Y. State Occupl.Therapy Licensure bd., 1990. Paul Harris fellow, 1989; named Humanitarian of Yr., N.Y. State Ctrs. for Ind. Living, 1993, Person of Yr., Salvation Army, S.I., 1994; recipient Nat. Spinal Cord Injury award 1996; torch bearer for 1996 Olympics. Mem. AMA, Am. Congress Rehab. Medicine, N.Y. Assn. Phys. Medicine and Rehab., Am. Assn. Phys. Medicine and Rehab., Am. Acad. Cerebral Palsy and Devel. Disabilties. Republican. Presbyterian. Office: St Vincent Med Ctr 355 Bard Ave Staten Island NY 10310-1664

FLEISCHER, LEE SCOTT, surgeon; b. N.Y.C., Sept. 5, 1960. AB, Washington U., St. Louis, 1982; MD, McGill U., Montreal, Can., 1987. Diplomate Am. Bd. Surgery. Intern in gen. surgery Beth Israel Med. Ctr., N.Y.C., 1987-88, resident in gen. surgery, 1988-91, chief resident in gen. surgery, 1991-92; attending surgeon Good Samaritan Hosp., Suffern, N.Y., 1992—. Fellow Am. Coll. Surgeons; mem. AMA, N.Y. State Med. Soc., Rockland County Med. Soc., Jr. Men's Honorary Soc., Sigma Alpha Mu. Office: Ramapo Valley Surg Assocs 100 Rte 59 Suffern NY 10901

FLEISCHER, LESLIE RAYMOND, cardiologist; b. Washington, Apr. 13, 1948; s. Ronald and Fanny (Heller) F.; m. Pamela Louise Roberts, July 2, 1970; children: Gillian Roberts, Darcy Elizabeth. BA in History, Duke U., 1969; MD, Creighton U., 1975. Pres. Conestoga Med. Assocs., Lancaster, Pa., 1985-92; with dept. cardiology Carle Clinic, Urbana, Ill., 1992—, dir. cardiac catherization labs., 1994—; chief cardiologist St. Joseph Hosp., Lancaster, 1988-92. Fellow Am. Coll. Cardiology, Soc. Cardiac Angiography, Am. Coll. Physicians; mem. Hamilton Club, Cornell Club (N.Y.C.), Princeton Club (N.Y.C).

FLEISCHHACKER, W. WOLFGANG, psychiatrist, educator, scientist; b. Baden, Austria, Apr. 29, 1953; s. Walter and Hedwig (Laschitz) F.; m. Astrid Fleischhacker, Aug. 29, 1987; children: Nicolas, Sebastian. MD, Innsbruck (Austria) U., 1978. Head dept. biol. psychiatry Innsbruck U. Clinics, 1993—; prof. psychiatry Innsbruck U., 1993—. Co-author: Pharmakotherapie in der Psychiatrie, 1991; editor: Kombinations therapie in der Psychiatrie, 1990, Die Behandlung der Schizophrenien: State of the Art; contbr. articles to profl. jours. Fulbright scholar Hillside Hosp. 1987-88. Mem. European Coll. Neuropsychopharmacology, Coll. Internat. Neuropsychopharmacology (v.p. 1995—), Austrian Schizophrenia Soc. (v.p. 1995—). Office: Dept Psychiatry, Anichstrasse 35, 6020 Innsbruck Austria

FLEISCHMAN, PAUL R., psychiatrist, writer; b. Newark, N.J., Aug. 4, 1945; s. Martin L. and Etta G. Fleischman; m. Susan K., June 15, 1974; 1 child, Forrest. BA, U. Chgo., 1967; MD, Albert Einstein Coll. Medicine, N.Y.C., 1971. Diplomate Am. Bd. Psychiatry & Neurology. Seminar leader in psychiatry & religion Yale U., New Haven, 1981-87; pvt. practice psychiatry Amherst, Mass., 1975—; keynote spkr. Highland Hosp., Asheville, N.C., 1992, Albany Med. Coll., Coll. St. Rose, Albany Jewish Family Svcs., 1993, Values in Psychotherapy conf. Nashville Inst. Psychotherapy, 1995; 31st Williamson lectr. in religion and medicine U. Kans., 1995; cons. in psychiatry, Amherst, 1975—; lectr., spkr. U. Mass., Amherst, Hampshire Coll., Smith Coll., Amherst Coll., 1989-92, Med. Group Rounds Albany Med. Coll., 1990, Beth Israel, Boston, 1994; cons. Smith Coll. Chapel, 1995. Author: Therapeutic Action of Vipassana Mediation, 1986, The Experience of Impermanence, 1990, The Healing Spirit, 1990, Spiritual Aspects of Psychiatric Practice, 1993; contbr. articles to profl. jours. Recipient Oskar Pfister award for important contbns. to spiritual & humanistic side of psychiatry Am. Psychiat. Assn., 1993. Mem. Phi Beta Kappa, Alpha Omega Alpha. Office: 1394 S East St Amherst MA 01002-3030

FLEISCHNER, ALOIS LEONARD, retired ophthalmologist; b. N.Y.C., Sept. 4, 1913; s. Otto and Frances (Goodman) F.; m. Jean Sokiran, May 1, 1938 (dec. Oct. 1978); children: Mark, Richard. BS, NYU, 1932, MD, 1935. Diplomate Am. Bd. Ophthalmology. Intern, househip eye-ear, nose and throat N.Y.C. Hosp., 1935-39; resident Queens Gen. Hosp., N.Y.C., 1939-40; pvt. practice N.Y.C., 1940-42, pvt. practice ophthalmology, 1946-88; ophthalmologist Bronx (N.Y.) Eye Infirmary, 1946-73, Montefiore Hosp. & Med. Ctr., Bronx, 1973—; cons. ophthalmologist Bronx-Lebanon Med. Ctr., 1946—. Capt. U.S. Army, 1942-46, ETO. Fellow ACS (pres. Bronx chpt. 1963); mem. Am. Acad. Ophthalmology, N.Y. Soc. Clin. Ophthalmology, N.Y. Acad. Medicine. Home: 3333 Henry Hudson Pky Bronx NY 10463-3224

FLEISHER, ARTHUR A., II, physician; b. Phila., Sept. 7, 1932; s. Oscar Teller and Beatrice Naomi (Rosenzweig) F.; m. Francine Queenth, June 26, 1955; children—Rebecca, Martin Q., Arthur III, Carolyn B. B.S., U. Miami, Fla., 1954, M.D., 1958. Diplomate Am. Bd. Obstetrics and Gynecology. Resident in obstetrics and gynecology Jackson Meml. Hosp., Miami, Fla., 1959-62; obstetrician/gynecologist So. Calif. Permanente Med. Group, Panorama City, Calif., 1962—, chief dept. ob-gyn, 1975-81; assoc. clin. prof. ob-gyn L.A. County/U. So. Calif. Med. Ctr., Los Angeles, 1972—, clin. prof. ; asst. clin. prof. ob-gyn UCLA, 1964-83. Fellow Am. Coll. Ob-Gyn,

ACS, Los Angeles Ob-Gyn Soc. Office: So Calif Permanente Med Group 13652 Cantara St Panorama City CA 91402-5423

FLEISHER, T. LAWRENCE, dermatologist; b. Phila., May 26, 1927; s. Nathan and Elizabeth F.; m. Feb. 21, 1953; children: Neil, Nancy. BS, Ursinus Coll., 1950; MD, U. Puerto Rico, San Juan, 1956. Diplomate Am. Bd. Dermatology. Prof. ad honorem U. Puerto Rico Sch. of Medicine, Rio Piedras, Puerto Rico, 1983—. With U.S. Army, 1950-52. Mem. AMA, Am. Acad. Dermatology, Puerto Rico Med. Assn., Soc. Dermatology Puerto Rico. Office: Ashford Med Bldg Ste 310 Santurce PR 00907

FLEISHER, THOMAS ARTHUR, physician; b. Rochester, Minn., Oct. 3, 1946; s. Gerard Adelbert and Gisela (Nolte) F.; m. Mary Frances Hopkins, Sept. 5, 1969; children: Jeffrey Alan, Jeremy Andrew, Matthew James. BS, U. Minn., 1969, MD, 1971. Diplomate Am. Bd. Pediatrics, Am. Bd. Allergy and Immunology. Staff physician bone marrow transplant svc. Naval Med. Rsch. Inst., Bethesda, Md., 1975-77; clin. assoc. metabolism br. Nat. Cancer Inst., NIH, Bethesda, 1977-80; asst. chief allergy clin. immunology svc. Walter Reed Army Med. Ctr., Washington, 1980-83; chief immunology svc. Warren G. Magnuson Clin. Ctr., NIH, Bethesda, 1983—; tng. program dir. clin. immunology svc. NIH, Bethesda, 1992—; bd. dirs. Am. Bd. Allergy and Immunology, Phila., 1991—, chair, 1996. Editor: Clinical Immunology, 1985-89, 93—, Immunology, 1983-86, Clin. Diag. Lab. Immunology, 1993—; contbr. over 75 articles to sci. jours. Bd. dirs. Bethesda Soccer Club, 1987-95; house capt. Christmas in April, Montgomery County, Md., 1991—; deacon, elder St. Mark Presbyn. Ch., Rockville, Md., 1983-88. With USPHS. Fellow Am. Acad. Allergy, Asthma and Immunology; mem. Am. Assn. Immunologists, Am. Fedn. for Clin. Rsch., Soc. for Pediat. Rsch., Clin. Immunology Soc., Internat. Soc. Analytic Cytology. Office: NIH 10/2C410 9000 Rockville Pike Bethesda MD 20892-1508

FLEISHMAN, PHILIP ROBERT, internist; b. Hartford, Conn., Apr. 17, 1935; s. Morris and Anna Lillian (Farber) F.; B.S., Trinity Coll., Harford, 1957; M.D., SUNY, Bklyn., 1961; m. Anita Rose Coopersmith, Oct. 18, 1964; children: David, Beth, Rachael. Practice medicine specializing in internal medicine, East Islip, N.Y., 1967—; attending physician, dir. medicine Southside Hosp., Bay Shore, N.Y., 1993—; attending physician Good Samaritan Hosp., W. Islip, Central Islip State Hosp.; v.p. med. bd. Southside Hosp., 1986-89, pres. 1989—; clin. asst. prof. SUNY Med. Sch., Stony Brook, 1967—, asst. dir. medicine, 1988—; dir. med. sch., 1993—; founder, co-dir. diabetic clinic Southside Hosp. Co-author, chmn. constn. and bylaws Pro-Arts Group Islips, 1979; asst. basketball coach Police Athletic League, 1979; v.p., pres., trustee Bay Shore Jewish Ctr., 1979—; pres.-elect, 1986-88, pres. 1988-90; coach CVO, 1980; active Bayshore Jewish Ctr. Theatre Group. Served to capt. M.C., U.S. Army, 1965-67. Diplomate Am. Bd. Internal Medicine. Fellow ACP; mem. AMA, Am. Diabetes Assn., N.Y. State Med. Soc., N.Y. State Soc. Internal Medicine (past chpt. pres.), Suffolk County Med. Soc. Contbr. articles med. jours. Office: 45 E Main St East Islip NY 11730-2502

FLEISIG, NORBERT, surgeon; b. Providence, Sept. 15, 1935; m. Jeanne C. Fleisig. BA magna cum laude, Brown U., 1957; MD, Yale U., 1961. Diplomate Am. Bd. Surgery. Intern surgery then resident surgery Yale Med. Ctr., New Haven, 1961-65; resident Univ. Hosp., Balt., 1965-67; assoc. prof. surgery R.I. Hosp., 1967, Brown Med. Ctr., Providence, 1968—; staff surgeon R.I. Hosp., Providence, 1967—, Roger Williams Hosp., Providence, 1968—; cons. surgery R.I. Med. Ctr., State R.I. U.S. Govt., Cranston, 1968—. Mem. ACS, AMA, Am. Soc. Bariatric Surgeons, Providence Surg., Providence Med. Soc., Sigma Xi, Phi Beta Kappa. Office: 1 Randall Sq Providence RI 02904-2709

FLEMING, ARTHUR WALLACE, physician, surgeon; b. Johnson City, Tenn., Oct. 1, 1935; s. Smith Goerge and Vivian (Richardson) F.; m. Dolores E. Caffey, Apr. 8, 1978; 1 child, Erik. Student, Ill. State U., 1953-54; BA, Wayne State U., 1958-61; MD cum laude, U. Mich., 1961-65. Diplomate Am. Bd. Surgery, Am. Bd. Thoracic Surgery. Intern Walter Reed Gen. Hosp., Washington, 1965-66, resident in gen. surgery, 1966-70, resident in thoracic and cardiovascular surgery, 1970-72; research tng. fellowship Walter Reed Army Inst. of Research, Walter Reed Army Med. Ctr., Washington, 1973-74, mem. staff dept. surgery, 1974-76, chief div. exptl. surgery, 1976-77, dir. dept. surgery, 1977-83; assoc. prof. surgery Uniformed Service U. of Health Scis., Bethesda, Md., 1978-83, clin. assoc. prof. surgery, 1983—; program dir. gen. surgery residency tng. program Martin L. King, Jr./Drew Med. Ctr., Los Angeles, 1983—, dir. trauma ctr., 1983—, chief surgery, 1983—; assoc. prof. surgery UCLA, 1983—; chmn. dept. surgery, assoc. prof. surgery Charles R. Drew Postgrad. Med. Sch., Los Angeles, 1983—. Contbr. numerous articles to profl. jours. Served with USN, 1954-62. Recipient Hoff Medal, 1974, Gold Medal for paper Southeastern Surg. Congress, 1977, Letter of Commendation Commanding Gen. U.S. Army Med. Research and Devel. Command, 1981, Surgeon Gen's. "A" prefix, 1981, Commendation Compton City Council, 1985, Recognition award King-Drew Hosp. Social Service, 1985. Mem. ACS., Nat. Assn. Minority Med. Educators (western region), Golden State Med. Soc., Nat. Med. Assn., Charles R. Drew Med. Soc., Am. Heart Assn., Soc. Surg. Chmn., Assn. Program Dirs. in Surgery, Soc. Thoracic Surgeons, Assn. Acad. Surgery, Am. Assn. Blood Banks, Southeastern Surg. Congress, Am. Fedn. Clin. Research, Assn. Mil. Surgeons. Democrat. Roman Catholic. Office: Charles R Drew Postgrad Med Hosp 12021 Wilmington Ave Los Angeles CA 90059-3019*

FLEMING, DUARD FRANCIS, JR. (FRANK FLEMING), neurologist; b. Charlotte, N.C., May 24, 1946; s. Duard F. Sr. and Lorene (Cress) F.; m. Mary Morgan, June 29, 1969; children: Elise, Emily. BS, Davidson Coll., 1968; MD, Wake Forest U., 1972. Diplomate Am. Bd. of Psychiatry and Neurology. Intern N.C. Bapt. Hosp., Winston-Salem, 1972-73, resident in neurology, 1973-76; chief neurologist Irwin Army Hosp., Ft. Riley, Kans., 1976-78; neurologist E. Carolina Neurol. Assn., Greenville, N.C., 1978—; clin. assoc. prof. medicine and pediatrics E. Carolina Sch. Medicine, Greenville, 1978—; active med. staff Pitt County Meml. Hosp., Greenville, 1978—; cons. med. staff Wayne County Meml. Hosp., Goldsboro, N.C., 1982—, Caswell Ctr., Kinston, N.C., 1986—. Maj. Med. Svc. Corps, U.S. Army, 1976-78. Recipient highest award Bowman Gray Sch. Medicine, Winston-Salem, N.C., 1972; Reynolds scholar, Bowman Gray Sch. Medicine, 1968. Fellow Am. Acad. Neurology; mem. AMA, Am. Soc. Neuroimaging (bd. dirs.), N.C. Med. Soc., Phi Beta Kappa, Omicron Delta Kappa. Lutheran. Office: E Carolina Neurol Assn 2501 Stantonsburg Rd Greenville NC 27834-7213

FLEMING, JAMES STUART, JR., pharmaceutial company manager; b. Buffalo, Sept. 1, 1936; s. James Stuart and Pauline (McClurg) F.; m. Marilyn Joyce Bartsch, June 7, 1960; children: Lois Vernette, James Stuart III. BA, Northwestern U., 1958; MS, U. Buffalo, 1962; PhD, Ohio State U., 1965; MBA, Syracuse U., 1983. Rsch. asst. Ohio State U., Columbus, 1962-65; rsch. scientist Bristol-Myers Co., Syracuse, N.Y., 1965-74, sr. rsch. scientist, 1974-82, mgr., 1982-85; assoc. dir. cardiovascular biology Bristol-Myers Co., Syracuse and Wallingford, Conn., 1985-90; assoc. dir. project planning Bristol-Myers Squibb Co., Wallingford, Conn., 1990—. Author: (with others) Platelet Aggregation Inhibitors, 1974-82; editor: Drugs and the Delivery of Oxygen to Tissues, 1989. Cons., tchr. Jr. Achievement, Wallingford, 1988-90. Mem. Am. Soc. Pharmacology and Exptl. Therapeutics, Am. Heart Assn. (coun. on thrombosis), Microcirculatory Soc., Internat. Soc. Oxygen Transport to Tissue, Am. Coll. Clin. Pharmacology, Beta Gamma Sigma. Office: Bristol-Myers Squibb Co 5 Research Pky Wallingford CT 06492-1927

FLEMING, JOHN ELLIOTT, physician's assistant; b. Augusta, Maine, Feb. 9, 1947; s. Stephen and Sybil Frances (Johnson) F.; m. Kathleen Beckett, June 14, 1969; children: Sean Michael, Sara Louise. BA, U. Conn., 1971; physician asst. cert., Albany-Hudson Valley Coll., 1975, Yale U.-Norwalk Hosp., 1983. Cert. physician's asst., Conn.; cert. Nat. Coun. Cert. Physician Assts. Physician's asst. Manchester (Conn.) Meml. Hosp., 1976-82, U. Mass. Med. Ctr., Worcester, 1983-85, Assoc. Urologists, Manchester, 1989-93, Johnson Meml. Hosp., Stafford Springs, Conn., 1989—, Westside Multi Care, Manchester, 1995—. Mem. Coventry (Conn.) Bd. Edn., 1986-87. Capt. U.S. Army, 1971-73. Fellow Am. Acad. Physician's Assts., Conn. Acad. Physician's Assts. Republican. Home: 50 Eric Dr Coventry CT 06238-1325

FLEMING, JUANITA W., nursing educator. BS, Hampton Inst., 1957; MA, U. Chgo., 1959; PhD, Cath. U. Am., 1969; D of Pub. Svc., Berea Coll., 1994. Form staff nurse to head nurseMed. Surg. Pediat. Unit Children's Hosp., Washington, 1957-58; pub. health nurse Bur. Pub. Health Nursing, 1959-60; instr. nursing children Sch. Nursing Freedmen's Hosp., Washington, 1962-65; cons. pub. health nursingdept. pediat.Child Devel. Clin. Howard U., 1965-66; from asst. prof. to assoc. prof. Coll. Nursing U. Ky., Lexington, 1969-73, prof. Coll. Nursing, 1973—, spl. asst. to pres. academic affairsctr. administrn., 1991—; mem. grad. faculty Coll. Nursing, U. Ky, 1971—, asst. dean grad. edn., 1975-81, assoc. dean, dir. grad. edn., 1982-86; prof. Coll. Edn. Edpt. Edn. Policy Studies and Evaln., 1979—; assoc. vice-chancellor acad. affairs Med. Ctr., 1984-91, spl. asst. to pres. for acad. affairs, 1991—; co. project dir. nursing care high risk infants State Maternal and Child Health Divsn., 1972; project dir. advanced nurse tng. grant divsn. nursing Dept. Health Edn. and Welfare, 1977-80, high tech home care chronically ill children Bur. Maternal Child Health, 1989-93; vis. prof. Case We. Res. U., Cleveland, 1984; Martin Luther King/Rosa Parks/Cesar Chavez vis. prof. U. Mich., Ann Arbor, 1989, Elizabeth Carnegie endowed vis. prof. Howard U., 1995. Prin. investor Am. Nurses Found., 1970-71. Recipient Ky. Nurses Assn. award, Marion E. McKenna leadership award, 1988, Disting. Svc. award ANA, 1994. Mem. Am. Acad. Nursing, Nat. Acad. Scis., Inst. Medicine. Office: U Ky 7 Adminstrn Bldg Lexington KY 40536-0032

FLEMING, MARILYN BROKERING, nurse, educator; b. Hart, Mich., Sept. 21, 1941; d. Harry Bernard and Miriam Irene (Slanker) Brokering; m. Thomas Charles Fleming, Aug. 24, 1963; children: Jon, Janine Allen, Juliana Pope, Charley, Skye, Lorraine. BSN, U. Pitts., 1963; MSN, U. N.Mex., 1981. Cert. Lamaze instr. Staff head, head nurse Columbia Presbyn. Hosp., N.Y.C., 1963-67; staff nurse Univ. Heights Hosp., Albuquerque, 1968-69; recovery room nurse Sinai Hosp. of Detroit, 1969-71; instr. Lamaze prepared childbirth Childbirth Without Pain Ednl. Assn., various cities, 1972-89; coordinator edn. and infection control S.W. Meml. Hosp., Cortez, Colo., 1986-87; orthopedic nurse clinician Four Corners Orthopedics, Cortez, 1987-95; vis. asst. prof. nursing U. Alaska, Anchorage, 1996—; faculty U. Albuquerque, 1981; asst. prof. U. N.Mex., Gallup, 1976-86; curriculum cons. San Juan Coll., Farmington, N.Mex., 1986-87, faculty, 1987-89; preceptor at various colls. and univs.; speaker in field. Contbr. articles to profl. journals. Active Telluride (Colo.) Town Coun., 1990-95, mayor pro tem, 1993-95. Mem. Am. Nurses Assn., Nat. League Nursing, N.Mex. League Nursing (bd. dirs. 1983-85), Nat. Assn. Orthopedic Nurses, Sigma Theta Tau.

FLEMING, THOMAS CRAWLEY, physician, medical director, former editor; b. Chgo., June 16, 1921; s. Frederic Sydney and Margaret A. (Moore) F.; m. Katherine Slaughter, Oct. 14, 1949; children—Sandra, Wendy, Margot, Frederic. Student, Calif. Inst. Tech., 1940-42; M.D., Columbia U., 1945. Intern St. Luke's Hosp., N.Y.C., 1945-46; instr. physiology. Coll. Physicians and Surgeons, Columbia U., N.Y.C., 1948-50; with dept. clin. research Hoffmann-LaRoche, Nutley, N.J., 1950-55, dir. med. info., 1955-56, product devel. mgr., 1956-57; dir. clin. research Mead Johnson & Co., Evansville, Ind., 1957-58, dir. product devel., 1958-59; med. dir. Warner-Chilcott Labs., Morris Plains, N.J., 1959-60; exec. v.p., med. dir. Robert E. Wilson Inc., N.Y.C., 1960-62; dir. med. edn., chief chronic medicine Bergen Pines County Hosp., Paramus, N.J., 1962-64; med. dir. Sudler & Hennessey, Inc., N.Y.C., 1964-73, sr. v.p., med. dir., 1982-88, med. cons., 1988—; med. dir. Little Hill-Alina Lodge, Blairstown, N.J., 1974-79, 84-89. Editor-in-chief Postgrad. Medicine, Mpls., 1979-82; contbr. articles to profl. jours. Served to capt. M.C., U.S. Army, 1946-48. Mem. Am. Soc. of Addiction Medicine. Home & Office: 159 Park St Montclair NJ 07042-3901

FLEMING, TIMOTHY, cardiologist; b. Pittsburg, Kans., Mar. 21, 1939; s. William Michael Fleming and Julia Charlotte (Carduazl) F.; m. Marilyn Ann Fleming; children: Jessica, Shannon, Jamie. BS, Ohio U., 1961; MD, U. Cin., 1961; postdoctoral, U. Wash., 1972. Diplomate Am. Bd. Cardiology. Cardiologist Mont. Heart Inst., Billings, 1987—; asst. prof. medicine U. Wash., Seattle, 1987—; cons. cardiology for interventional cardiology Mont. Heart Inst., Billings, 1987—. Fellow Am. Coll. Cardiology (gov. Wyo. 1989-94), Pi Kappa Epsilon, Alpha Omega Alpha. Office: Mont Heart Inst 1145 N 29th Billings MT 59101

FLEMING, WILLIAM P., physician assistant; b. Charlottesville, Va., July 23, 1959; s. Robert Jr. and Charlotte Beverly (Graham) F.; m. Deborah Ann Lanahan, Apr. 20, 1991; 1 child, William Patton, Jr. BS in Biology, Lynchburg Coll., 1981; BS, USAF/U. Okla. Health Sci., 1985. Cert. physician asst.; cert. ACLS instr., CPR instr. Physician asst. Va. Army Nat. Guard, Lynchburg, Va., 1985-87, Md. Army Nat. Guard, Balt., 1987—; physician asst. dept. anesthesiology/crit. care medicine Johns Hopkins Hosp., 1986—. Fellow Soc. Army Physicians Asst., Soc. Air Force Physician Assts. Office: Johns Hopkins Hosp Outpatient Ctr Rm 171 601 N Caroline St Baltimore MD 21287

FLEMING, WILLIAM WRIGHT, JR., pharmacology educator; b. Washington, Jan. 30, 1932; s. William Wright and Esme (Reeder) F.; m. Dolores D. Atchison, Sept. 1, 1952; children: Lisa Marie, Jennifer Amelia, David William. A.B. cum laude, Harvard U., 1954; Ph.D. (Procter fellow), Princeton U., 1957. Mem. faculty W.Va. U. Med. Ctr., Morgantown, 1960—, prof. pharmacology, 1966—, chmn. dept., 1966-86, Mylan Chmn. of Pharmacology and Toxicology, 1986—; vis. prof. U. Melbourne, Australia, 1969, St. George's Hosp. Med. Sch. U. London, 1978, Flinders U., Adelaide, Australia, 1985, 87, U. Adelaide, 1987; cons. Mead Johnson Rsch. Ctr., Evansville, Ind., 1970-77; mem. pharmacology-toxicology rsch. program. Nat. Inst. Gen. Med. Scis., NIH, 1973-77, chmn., 1975-77; mem. drug abuse rsch. rev. com. Nat. Inst. Drug Abuse, 1985-89; mem. pharmacology study sect., div. rsch. grants NIH, 1990-94. Mem. editl. bd. Jour. Pharmacology and Exptl. Therapeutics, 1966-85, Life Scis., 1978-90; contbr. articles to profl. jours. USPHS postdoctoral fellow Harvard U., 1957-60; Fogarty sr. internat. fellow, 1978; recipient P.L. MacLachlan award excellence in teaching W.Va. U. Med. Sch., 1964, 67, 78, 89, 92; named Outstanding Tchr., W.Va. U. Found., 1978. Mem. AAAS, Am. Soc. Pharmacology and Exptl. Therapeutics (councilor 1975-78, pres. 1981-82, chmn. bd publs. trustees 1984-90, Otto Krayer award 1986, Croker Meml. lectr. 1988), Assn. Med. Sch. Pharmacology (councilor 1977-79, treas. 1977-78, pres. 1986-88), Fedn. Am. Socs. for Exptl. Biology (dir. 1980-83), Internat. Union Pharmacology (del. 1980-83, 91-94, mem. internat. adv. com. for Congress of Pharmacology 1987, exec. com. 1994—). Home: 27 Citadel Rd Morgantown WV 26505-3612 Office: WVa U Health Scis Ctr Dept Pharmacology Morgantown WV 26506

FLEMMING, STANLEY LALIT KUMAR, family practice physician, mayor, state legislator; b. Rosebud, S.D., Mar. 30, 1953; s. Homer W. and Evelyn C. (Misra) F.; m. Marth Susan Light, July 2, 1977; children: Emily Drisana, Drew Anil, Claire Elizabeth Misra. AAS, Ft. Steilacoom Coll., 1973; BS in Zoology, U. Wash., 1976; MA in Social Psychology, Pacific Luth. U., 1979; DO, Coll. Osteopathic Med. Pacific, 1985. Diplomate Am. Coll. Family Practice; cert. ATLS. Intern Pacific Hosp. Long Beach (Calif.), 1985-86; resident in family practice Pacific Hosp. Long Beach, 1986-88; fellow in adolescent medicine Children's Hosp. L.A., 1988-90; clin. preceptor Family Practice Residency Program Calif. Med. Ctr., U. So. Calif., L.A., 1989—; clin. instr. Sch. Medicine U. So. Calif., L.A., 1989-90; clin. instr. Coll. Osteopathic Medicine Pacific, Pomona, Calif., 1989-90; clin. asst. prof. Family Medicine Coll. Osteopathic Medicine Pacific, Pomona, 1987—; exam. commr., expert examiner Calif. Osteo. Med. Bd., 1987-89; med. dir. Community Health Care Delivery System Pierce County, Tacoma, Wash., 1990—; mayor City of University Place, Wash.; clin. instr. U. Wash. Sch. Medicine, 1990—; bd. dirs. Calif. State Bd. Osteo. Physicians Examiners, 1989—, cons., 1989. Mayor, City of University Place, Wash. Col. M.C., U.S. Army, 1976—. Named Outstanding Young Man Am., 1983, 85, Intern of Yr. Western U. Health Sci. Coll. Osteo. Medicine of Pacific, 1986, Resident of Yr., 1988, Alumnus of Yr., 1993, Physician of Yr., 1993; recipient Pumerantz-Weiss award, 1985. Mem. Fedn. State Bds. Licensing, Am. Osteopathic Assn., Am. Acad. Family Practice, Soc. Adolescent Medicine, Assn. Military Surgeons U.S., Assn. U.S. Army (chpt. pres.), Soc. Am. Military Engrs. (chpt. v.p.), Calif. Med. Assn., Wash. Osteopathic Med. Assn., Calif. Family Practice Soc., Long Beach Med. Assn. (com. mem.), N.Y. Acad. Sci., Calif. Med. Review Inc., Sigma Sigma Phi, Am. Legion. Episcopalian. Home: 7619 Chambers Creek Rd W University Place WA 98467-2015 Office: Family Health Ctr Olympia WA 98504

FLETCHER, ANNE BOSSHARD, pediatrician; b. Worchester, Mass., Feb. 3, 1939; d. Heinrich Morant and Anne (Peter) Bosshard; m. John Raymond, June 16, 1963 (div. Dec. 1979); children: John Raymond, Stephen Dewitt, David Andrew; m. William James McSweeney, Mar. 8, 1985. AB, Clark U., 1960; MD, Wash. U., St. Louis, 1964. 1st yr. pediatric resident Strong Meml. Hosp., U. Rochester (N.Y.), 1964-65; 2d yr. pediatric resident R.H. Hosp., Brown U., Providence, 1965-66; 3d yr. pediatric resident Children's Hosp. of D.C., Washington, 1967-68, neonatology fellow, 1968-70, asst. prof. pediatrics, 1970-76; assoc. prof. pediats. Children's Nat. Med. Ctr., Washington, 1976-83, prof., 1983—, med. dir. newborn intensive care unit, 1975-93; chmn. dept. neonatology Children's Nat. Med. Ctr., Washington, 1991—. Co-author: (with R. Henig) Your Premature Infant, 1983; contbr. articles, abstracts and book chpts. to profl. publs. Alumni trustee Clark U., Worcester, 1980-82. Fellow Am. Acad. Pediatrics; mem. Am. Soc. Law and Medicine, Am. Soc. Parenteral and Enteral Nutrition, Hastings Soc., Phi Beta Kappa. Office: Children's Nat Med Ctr 111 Michigan Ave NW Washington DC 20010-2970

FLETCHER, IAIN GEORGE, radiologist; b. Carlisle, Cumbria, U.K., Oct. 24, 1943; s. Thomas and Mary Glen (Carlisle) F.; m. Angela Kathleen McElhinney, July 12, 1969; children: Jonathan, Clare. MB ChB, Edinburgh (Scotland) U., 1967, DMRD, 1971; diploma in health care mgmt., Inst. Pub. Adminstrn., Dublin, Ireland, 1994. Med. house officer Royal Infirmary, Edinburgh, 1967-68, surg. house officer, 1969; registrar radiology dept. Royal Infirmary, 1969-71; surg. house officer Kirkcaldy Infirmary, Scotland, 1968; sr. house officer Royal Hosp. for Sick Children, Edinburgh, 1968-69; sr. registrar Addinbrooke Hosp., Cambridge, Eng., 1971-75; cons. radiologist Wexford (Ireland) Gen. Hosp., 1975—. Fellow Royal Coll. Radiologists, Faculty of Radiologists; mem. Brit. Inst. Radiology, Radiologists Vis. Club, Rotary. Roman Catholic. Home: Bramble Hill Park, Wexford Ireland Office: Wexford Gen Hosp, Radiology Dept, Wexford Ireland

FLETCHER, JAMES WARREN, physician; b. Belleville, Ill., Oct. 6, 1943; m. Mary Bernadette Gatson; children: Michelle Marie, James W., Rebecca Lynn. MD, St. Louis U., 1968. Diplomate Am. Bd. Nuclear Medicine; lic. physician, Mo. Intern in internal medicine St. Louis U. Hosp., 1968-69, asst. resident in internal medicine, 1969-70, resident in nuclear medicine, 1970-71; clin. fellow in radiology Harvard Med. Sch., Boston, 1971-72; sr. resident in nuclear medicine Peter Bent Brigham and Children's Hosp. Med. Ctr., Boston, 1971-72; asst. prof. medicine dept. internal medicine St. Louis U., 1972-75, assoc. prof. medicine dept. internal medicine, 1976-83, assoc. prof. radiology dept. radiology, 1977-84, assoc. dir. divsn. nuclear medicine, 1978-85, prof. medicine dept. internal medicine, 1983—, prof. radiology, 1984—, acting dir. divsn. nuclear medicine, 1985-88, dir. divsn. nuclear medicine, 1988—; staff physician nuclear medicine svc. VA Med. Ctr., St. Louis, 1972-76, med. dir. nuclear medicine network, 1972-79, asst. chief nuclear medicine svc., 1976-79, chief, 1979—, med. dir. AMA nuclear medicine technologist tng. program, 1983—, dir. opers. NMR program project, 1983-88; staff physician St. Louis U. Hosps., 1972—, dir. nuclear medicine dept., 1988—, dir. PET imaging ctr., 1991—; dir., program official nuclear medicine svc., dept. medicine and surgery VA Adminstrn. Ctrl. Office, Washington, 1986-89; mem. tech. adv. com. to dir. nuclear medicine svc. VA Ctrl. Office, Washington, 1979-86, chmn. spl. interest user groups computer applications in nuclear medicine, 1984-85; spl. soc. liaison rep. Inst. Medicine Com. on Clin. Practice Guidelines, 1990-91; mem. residency rev. com. nuclear medicine Accreditation Coun. Grad. Med. Edn., 1992—, interag. NMR task force Office Health Tech. Assessment, 1982, Dept. Vet. Affairs Nat. Task Force on Tech. Assessment, 1992—. Contbr. articles to profl. jours. Second v.p. sch. bd., Mary Queen of Peace Elem. Sch., Webster Groves, Mo., 1981, treas., 1982. Lt. comdr. USNR, 1966-77. Recipient Spl. Commendation award Dept. Vets. Affairs, 1990. Fellow Am. Coll. Nuclear Physicians; mem. AAAS, AMA, Am. Coll. Radiology, Am. Bd. Nuclear Medicine (bd. dirs. 1990-93, vice chmn. 1992-93, chmn. 1994-95), Radiology Soc. N.Am., Soc. Nuclear Medicine (bd. trustees 1988-92, chmn. health care policy com. 1991-92, vice chmn. commn. health care policy 1996-97, v.p. elect 1996-97), Sigma Xi, Alpha Omega Alpha. Office: St Louis U Med Ctr PO Box 15250 3635 Vista Ave at Grand Blvd Saint Louis MO 63110-0250

FLETCHER, JEFFREY EDWARD, biochemist, researcher; b. Toledo, Mar. 11, 1948; s. John Harper and Eleanore (Jackson) F.; m. Marcia Ruth Miller, Mar. 21, 1970 (div. Mar. 1977); m. Jeanne Claire Untied, Aug. 22, 1981; children: Katherine Ann, Lindsay Nicole, Sarah Jeanne. AA, Mohegan C.C., 1974; BA, Conn. Coll., 1976; PhD, U. Conn., 1981. Resident rsch. assoc. NRC, Washington, 1981-83; sr. instr. dept. anesthesia Hahnemann U., Phila., 1983-85, asst. prof., 1985-90, assoc. prof., 1990-95, prof., 1995—. Mem. editl. coun. sci. jour. Toxicon, 1991—; contbr. articles to profl. jours. With USN, 1967-73, Vietnam. Conn. Coll. scholar, 1974-76. Mem. Am. Soc. Pharmacology and Exptl. Therapeutics, Internat. Soc. Toxinology, Am. Soc. Anesthesiologists, Am. Soc. Biochemistry and Molecular Biology, Soc. Exptl. Biology and Medicine, Soc. for Neurosci., Am. Chem. Soc., Biophys. Soc., Phi Beta Kappa, Sigma Xi, Rho Chi. Episcopalian. Office: Hahnemann U Dept Anesthesia Broad And Vine St Philadelphia PA 19104

FLETCHER, OSCAR JASPER, JR., college dean; b. Bennettsville, S.C., Oct. 18, 1938; s. Oscar Jasper and Virginia (Baskin) F.; m. Sybil Morrison, June 3, 1962; children: John, Gregg. BS, Wofford Coll., 1960; DVM, U. Ga., 1964, MS, 1965; PhD, U. Wis., 1968. Asst. prof. U. Ga. Coll. Vet. Medicine, Athens, 1968-74, assoc. prof., 1974-79, prof., 1979-89, assoc. dean, 1975-82, head dept. avian medicine, 1982-89; dean Coll. Vet. Medicine Iowa State U., Ames, 1989-92, N.C. State U., Raleigh, 1992—. Mem. Am. Coll. Vet. Pathologist (cert., pres. 1990). Methodist. Office: NC State U Coll Vet Medicine 4700 Hillsborough St Raleigh NC 27606-1428

FLICK, FERDINAND HERMAN, surgeon, prevention medicine physician; b. Bklyn., Feb. 19, 1925; s. Paul Albert and Elizabek Kath (Herz) F.; m. Marie T. Flick, Apr. 7, 1945; children: Paul, Ferdinand, Annette Flick Riddle. BS, Fordham U., MS; MD, Yale U., 1951. Diplomate Am. Bd. Preventive Medicine. Intern SUNY Downstate, 1951-52; resident Coll. Physicians & Surgeons, N.Y.C., 1952-54; asst. prof. Columbia U. Coll. Physicians and Surgeons, N.Y.C., 1959-62; surgeon 77th Divsn. USAR, N.Y.C., 1962-76; chief plant physician Fort Motor Co., Mahwah, N.J., 1976-80, Edison, N.J., 1980—; asst. prof. U. Calif., Berkeley, 1946-47; trauma lectr. Middlesex C.C., 1984-85. Contbr. articles to profl. jours. Mem. smoking intervention team Am. Cancer Soc., New Brunswick, N.J., 1993-95. Col. USAR, 1946-76. Mem. Am. Coll. Occupl. and Environ. Medicine, Am. Coll. Preventive Medicine, Am. Soc. Abdominal Surgeons, Sigma Xi (Yale chpt.). Home: 21 Miara St Parlin NJ 08859-1815

FLICK, GERVASE MEAD, surgeon; b. Boston, Feb. 21, 1936; s. Gervase Charles and Sarah Germain (Mead) F.; m. Anne Rene LaVasseur; children: Michelle, Lisa, Heather, Buff. AB, Colgate U., 1955, MA, 1956; DO, Kirksville Coll. Osteo., 1960; MD, U. Calif., Irvine, 1962; JD, McGeorge Law Coll., 1972; MPH, U. Hawaii, 1976. Diplomate Am. Bd. Forensic Medicine, Am. Bd. Forensic Examiners, Am. Bd. Legal Medicine. Chief of staff South Gate Cmty. Hosp., Sacramento, 1970-72; pvt. practice Sacramento, 1970-72; emergency physician Kona (Hawaii) Hosp., 1972-74; pvt. practice law and medicine Honolulu, 1974-80; pvt. practice law Sacramento, 1976-80; ship's surgeon U.S. Merchant Marine, 1980-88; emergency and occupl. medicine physician Kaiser Found. Hosp., Honolulu, 1989-92; occupl. medical physician, med./legal cons. Physorney Cons., Tacoma and Seattle, 1992—. Author: Medical Malpractice in Emergency Medicine, 1992; co-author: Hawaiian Calories, 1994, Head and Spinal Injury Problems, 1996. V.p. Hawaii Osteo. Med. Assn., Honolulu, 1988, pres., 1989. Capt. USAF (flight surgeon), 1962-68. Fellow Am. Coll. Legal Medicine, Am. Coll. Forensic Medicine, Am. Coll. Forensic Examiners. Republican. Mem. Soc. of Friends. Office: PO Box 1954 Tacoma WA 98401

FLICK, WILLIAM FREDRICK, surgeon; b. Lancaster, Pa., Aug. 18, 1940; s. William Joseph and Anna (Volkl) F.; m. Jacqueline Denise Phaneuf, May 21, 1966; children: William J., Karen E., Christopher R., Derrick W., Brian A. BS, Georgetown U., 1962, MD, 1966; MBA, U. Colo., 1990. Cert. Am. Bd. Surgeons, 1976. Self employed surgeon Cheyenne, Wyo., 1973-84; pres., surgeon Cheyenne Surgical Assocs., 1984-94; med. dir. Blue Cross Blue Shield of Wyo., Cheyenne, 1994—. Trustee Laramie County Sch. Dist. #1, Cheyenne, 1988-92. Maj., chief of surgery USAF, 1971-73. Fellow ACS; mem. Am. Coll. Physician Execs., Nat. Assn. Managed Care. Republican. Roman Catholic. Office: Blue Cross Blue Shield Wyo 400 House Ave Cheyenne WY 82007-1468

FLICKINGER, CHARLES JOHN, anatomist, educator; b. Bethlehem, Pa., July 13, 1938; s. Wilbur James and Verna (Diehl) F.; m. Agnes Elizabeth Dickel, Feb. 23, 1963; children: Laura Jill, David Paul. AB, Dartmouth Coll., 1960; MD, Harvard U., 1964. Research fellow dept. anatomy U. Colo., Denver, 1964-65, Harvard Med. Sch., Boston, 1965-66; research assoc. Inst. Developmental Biology, U. Colo., Boulder, 1966-67; asst. prof. Inst. Developmental Biology, U. Colo., 1967-70; assoc. prof. dept. anatomy Sch. Medicine, U. Va., Charlottesville, 1971-75; prof. Sch. Medicine, U. Va., 1975—, Harvey E. Jordan prof. anatomy, 1982—, chmn. dept. cell biology (formerly anatomy and cell biology), 1982—; mem. reproductive biology study sect. NIH, 1979-83; mem. anatomy test com. Nat. Bd. Med. Examiners, 1981-84. Author: (with Brown, Kutchai, Ogilvie) Medical Cell Biology, 1979; contbr. articles to profl. jours.; assoc. editor: Jour. Andrology, 1989-92; adv. editor: Internat. Rev. Cytology, 1975—; mem. editorial bd. Biology of Reprodn., 1986-89, Jour. Andrology, 1986-89, Anatomical Record, 1972—. NIH research career devel. award grantee, 1968-70. Mem. Am. Soc. Cell Biology, Am. Assn. Anatomists, Soc. Study Reprodn., Am. Soc. Andrology, Phi Beta Kappa, Alpha Omega Alpha. Home: 2009 Meadowbrook Rd Charlottesville VA 22903-1247 Office: University of Virginia Dept of Cell Biology Box 439 Health Scis Ctr Charlottesville VA 22908

FLIEGELMAN, MARTIN JULES, physician; b. Phila., Oct. 25, 1946; s. Norman H. and Ruth G. (Gerson) F.; m. Ellen Lee Sharon Fliegelman, Dec. 21, 1969; children: Alan D., Amy B. BA, Franklin & Marshall Coll., 1968; MD, Jefferson Medical Coll., 1972. Diplomate Am. Bd. Internal Medicine, Diplomate Am. Bd. Pulmonary Medicine, Critical Care. Physician Colorado Pulmonary Assocs., Denver, 1980—; chief internal medicine Mercy Hosp., Denver, 1988-91; chief pulmonary sect. Presby. St. Lukes, Denver, 1985—. With USPHS, 1973-75. Recipient CV Mosby prize Jefferson Medical Coll., 1972. Fellow Am. Coll. Chest Physicians; mem. Am. Thoracic Soc. Office: Colo Pulmonary Assocs 1721 E 19th Ave #366 Denver CO 80218

FLOCH, MARTIN HERBERT, physician; b. N.Y.C., July 24, 1928; s. Samuel and Jean (Scheinman) F.; m. Gladys Wisser, Nov. 24, 1954; children: Jeffrey Aaron, Craig Lawrence, Lisa Suzanne, Neil Robert. B.A., NYU, 1949; M.S., U. N.H., 1950; M.D., N.Y. Med. Coll., 1956. Diplomate: Am. Bd. Internal Medicine, Am. Bd. Gastroenterology Am. Bd. Nutrition. Intern Beth Israel Hosp., N.Y.C., 1956-57; resident in medicine Beth Israel Hosp., 1957-59; fellow in gastroenterology Seton Hall Coll. Medicine, South Orange, N.J., 1959-60; instr. medicine U. P.R., 1960-62; asst. attending physician Montefiore Hosp., N.Y.C., 1962-64; practice medicine specializing in gastroenterology Norwalk, Conn., 1962—; mem. staff Norwalk Hosp., 1964—, chmn. dept. medicine, 1970-94, chief gastroenterology and nutrition, 1970—; clin. prof. medicine Yale U., New Haven, 1976—; cons. staff Griffin Hosp., Hall-Brooke Hosp., Waveny Care Center; bd. dirs. Norwalk Bank, 1987. Editor Am. Jour. Gastroenterology, 1985-91, The Gastroenterologist, 1992—; asst. editor Am. Jour. Clin. Nutrition; contbr. articles in field to profl. jours. Trustee Aspetuck Valley Health Dist., 1974-76, Norwalk Hosp., 1972-78. Served with M.C. U.S. Army, 1960-62. Conn. Digestive Disease Soc. grantee, 1974-76, NIH grantee, 1975-78, U.S. Army Med. Rsch. grantee, 1964-67, Leslie Found. grantee, 1980, Ednl. Found. Am. grantee, 1989-92. Fellow ACP, Master Am. Coll. Gastroenterology (bd. trustees 1985-90), Am. Soc. Gastroendoscopy, Am. Coll. Nutrition; mem. Am. Soc. Clin. Nutrition, Am. Inst. Nutrition, Am. Gastroenterology Assn., Assn. Program Dirs. in Internal Medicine, Am. Soc. Internal Medicine, Am. Fedn. Clin. Rsch., Fairfield County Med. Soc., Conn. Med. Soc. (pres. gastroenterology sect. 1972-74), Assn. Am. Med. Coll., Conn. Digestive Disease Soc. (pres. 1972-74). Home: 32 Woody Ln Westport CT 06880-2259 Office: Norwalk Hosp Stevens St Norwalk CT 06856

FLOCH-BAILLET, DANIELE LUCE, ophthalmologist; b. Brest, France, Jan. 9, 1948; d. Herve Alexandre and Lucie (Henry) Floch; m. Gilles Pierre Baillet, Dec. 6, 1980; 1 child, Victoire-Amelie. MD, Med. U. Brest, 1972. Cert. in ophthalmology, 1975. Med. cons. ophthalmology Brest Hosp., 1976-85; gen. practice ophthalmology Landivisiau, France, 1977—; researcher ophthalmic bacteriology, 1985—. Author: (with P. Francois) Nosological Outlines from Coats, 1975, Exsudation from Coats, 1976. Mem. French Ophthalmologist Soc., European Contact Lenses Soc. Ophthalmologists, Nat. Syndicat French Ophthalmology, Contact Lens Assn. Ophthalmologists, Assn. Ophthalmologic Improvement from East-Paris. Roman Catholic. Home: 11 Rue Creach Joly, 29600 Morlaix France Office: 7 Rue Georges Pompidou, 29400 Landivisiau France

FLOERSH, JOHN ALEXANDER, osteopath; b. Nashville, Mar. 6, 1952; s. Frank Alexander and Helen Louise (Martin) F.; m. Tammie Lynn Davis, June 23, 1984; children: Helen, Joan, John. BS, East Tenn. State U., 1979; DO, U. Health Scis. Coll. Osteo., Kansas City, Mo., 1985. Intern Davenport (Iowa) Med. Ctr., 1985-86; primary care physician Rutherford (Tenn.) Clinic, 1986—; med. dir. Winfrey Ctr., Trenton, Tenn., 1987-95. Capt. USAR, 1982-93. Mem. Tenn. Osteo. Med. Assn. (v.p. 1990-91, 95-96). Office: Rutherford Clinic 104 Main St Rutherford TN 38369

FLOHR, HANS WERNER, neurobiologist; b. Bonn, Germany, Feb. 22, 1936; s. Hans Ernst and Gertrud (Richarz) F.; m. Ursula Klein, Sept. 27, 1967; children: Swantje, Dorothea, Niklas. MD, U. Bonn, 1962, Habilitation, 1969. Prof. physiology U. Bonn, 1977-76; chair neurobiology, dir. Brain Rsch. Inst., Bremen, 1977—. Editor: Lesion-Induced Neuronal Plasticity, 1981, Synergetics of the Brain, 1983, Post-Lesion Neural Plasticity, 1988, Emergence or Reduction, 1992. Fellow Royal Soc. Medicine London. Home: Scharrelmannweg 24A, 27726 Worpswede Germany Office: U Bremen, Brain Rsch Inst, 2800 Bremen Germany

FLOOD, DOROTHY GARNETT, neuroscientist; b. Sayre, Pa., Oct. 7, 1951; d. James Murlin and Dorothy Garnett (Dietrich) F.; m. Paul David Coleman, Feb. 26, 1983. BA cum laude, Lawrence U., 1973; student, U. Ill., 1972-73; MS, PhD, U. Rochester, N.Y., 1980. Sr. instr. in anatomy U. Rochester, 1980-83, asst. prof. neurology, neurobiology and anatomy, 1984-90, assoc. prof. neurology, neurobiology and anatomy, 1990-94; sr. sci. Cephalon, Inc., West Chester, Pa., 1994—. Contbr. to book chpts. and articles in field; editorial bd. Neurobiology of Aging, 1989—. Recipient Fenn award U. Rochester, 1980; grantee NSF, NIH, Office of Naval Rsch., 1979-94. Mem. Soc. Neurosci. Office: Cephalon Inc 145 Brandywine Pky West Chester PA 19380-4245

FLOOD, JOHN N., osteopath, orthopaedic surgeon; b. Cleve., Sept. 29, 1958; s. Dean and Dorothy (Ragan) F.; m. Pamela Jean Flood; children: Allison, Andrea, Melanie, Brandon, Meredith. BS, U. Akron, 1980; DO, Ohio U., 1984. Diplomate Am. Osteo. Bd. Orthopaedic Surgery. Resident in orthopaedic surgery, 1984-89; fellow in spinal surgery Mich. State U., East Lansing, 1993-94; pvt. practice, Ashtabula, Ohio, 1994—. Lt. comdr. M.C., USNR, 1989-93. Mem. Am. Osteo. Assn., Am. Osteo. Acad. Orthopaedics, Am. Coll. Osteo. Surgeons. Office: Lakeshore Orthopaedics 2825 Lake Ave Ashtabula OH 44004

FLORENCE, MICHAEL GLENN, medical educator; b. Atlanta, Sept. 15, 1949; s. Thomas James and Glenna Louise (Smith) F.; m. Gwen Yvonne Kawabata, Aug. 10, 1980; children: Jameson Michael, Kelsey Anne. BS, Washington and Lee U., 1971; MD, Emory U., 1975. Diplomate Nat. Bd. Med. Examiners, Am. Bd. Surgery; lic. physician, Wash. Intern then resident U. Wash., Seattle, 1975-80, acting instr., 1980-93, clin. assoc. prof. surgery, 1993—; mem. staff Providence Med. Ctr., Seattle. Swedish Hosp. Med. Ctr., Seattle; presenter and instr. in field. Contbr. numerous articles to profl. jours. Mem. AMA, ACS (program chmn. 1993, sec.-treas. 1994—), Wash. Med. Soc., King County Med. Soc. (membership com. 1982, 84-86), Seattle Surg. Soc. (trustee 1985, program chmn. 1986-89, sec. 1992-94), Henry Harkins Surg. Soc. (pres. 1990-91), North Pacific Surg. Soc., Pacific Coast Surg. Assn. Office: Arnold Pavilion 1221 Madison # 1411 Seattle WA 98104

FLORES, FRANK CORTEZ, health sciences administrator, public health educator; b. L.A., Mar. 13, 1930; s. Frank Chaves and Jane (Cortez) F.; m. Juliette Carmen Sotelo, Nov. 24, 1951; children: Patricia Marie, Marie Juliette, Frank Anthony, Gregory Steven, Mark Adam, Jon Eric, Aaron Michael. AA, East L.A. Coll., 1951; BS, U. So. Calif., L.A., 1955, DDS, 1957, MSEd, 1988, cert. in med. edn., 1988; cert. in risk mgmt., Golden Gate U., San Francisco, 1981; PhD Fellow in Higher Edn., Claremont (Calif.) Grad. Sch., 1991; MA and PhD, Claremont (Calif.) Grad Sch., 1992; MPH, Loma Linda U., 1996. Lic. dentist, real-estate broker, ins. broker. Dental care implementor Specialist Ctr. For Dental Therapy, Riyadh, Saudi Arabia, 1984-86; asst. clin. prof. Univ. So. Calif. Sch. Dentistry, L.A., 1987—; dentist Am. Dental Vols. for Israel, Jerusalem, 1987—; vis. fellow rsch. in higher edn. Claremont Grad. Sch., 1993. Fundraiser various colls. and univs., 1988—; 2nd v.p. Project Hosp. Ship Oceanic, Upland, Calif., 1986—. With USNR, 1947-52. Mem. AAUP, APHA, Am. Coun. on Edn., Am. Assn. Dental Schs., Am. Assn. Dental Examiners, Am. Coll. Healthcare Execs. Democrat. Office: PO Box 3729 San Dimas CA 91773-7729

FLORES, JOHN A., internist; b. Indio, Calif., Jan. 17, 1957; m. Gladys Dolores Flores; children: Angelina, Jacob, Matthew, Marisa, Lauren. BS in Biochemistry, U. Calif., Riverside, 1980, MS in Biochemistry, 1981; MD, U. Minn., 1986. Intern internal medicine San Fernando Valley Program UCLA, 1986-87, resident internal medicine San Fernando Valley Program, 1988-90; resident anesthesiology U. Kans. Med. Ctr., 1987-88; dir. Pain Mgmt. Clinic Beaver Med. Clinic, Redlands, Calif., 1990—, physician internal medicine, 1990—; mem. active staff Redlands Community Hosp., 1990—; instr. advanced coronary life support cert. San Fernando Valley program UCLA, 1988-89; mentor sci. ednl. enhancement svcs. health profl. mentor program Calif. Poly. State U., 1991—; preceptor med. student edn. Osteo. Sch. Medicine Coll. of Pacific, 1993-94; lectr. Med. Sch. U. Minn., 1982-84, San Fernando Valley program UCLA, 1988-89, Beaver Med. Clinic, 1992, Calif. Poly. State U., Pomona, 1992, Redlands Com. Hosp., 1994. Recipient Appreciation award Chicano/Latino Pre-Med. Student Assn. Calif. Poly State U., 1993, Appreciation award Beverly Manor Convalescent, 1993, Recognition award Coll. Osteopathic Medicine Pacific, 1993—. Mem. AMA, ACP (assoc.), Am. soc. Anesthesiologists, Am. Soc. Pain Mgmt., Am. Soc. Regional Anesthesia, Calif. Med. Assn. (alt. del. for San Bernardino County Med. Soc. 1993-94, tech. adv. com. on pain mgmt. 1994—), San Bernardino County Med. Soc. (young physicians com. 1992—, chmn. 1993—, exec. com. 1993—), Redlands C. of C. Home: 2 W Fern Ave Redlands CA 92373-5916

FLORES, JOSEFINA C., transplant coordinator; b. Manila, Feb. 28, 1953; d. Melchor V. and Felisa M. (Manigbas) Cerafica; m. Bernardino F. Flores, Jan. 7, 1977; children: Andrew Phillip, Austin Cody. BSN, U. St. Tomas, Manila, 1975. Cert. clin. transplant coord./Am. Bd. Transplant Coords. Nurse trainee Cagraray Emergency Hosp., Bicol, Philippines, 1975-76; staff nurse, head nurse U. St. Tomas Hosp., 1976-77; nurse technician, surg. ICU Howard U. Hosp., Washington, 1977-78, clin. nurse II, 1978-84; cons. nurse Howard U. Hosp. to U.S. V.I. Hosp., 1985-88; faculty, planning com. Howard U. Hosp., Washington, 1989-92. Contbr. articles to profl. jours. Cert. of Appreciation plaque, Gov. of U.S. V.I., 1985. Fellow Am. Assn. Minority Health and Transplant Profl.; mem. N.Am. Transplant Coords. Orgn. Roman Catholic.

FLORIN-CHRISTENSEN, JORGE, biologist; b. Buenos Aires, Jan. 25, 1951; came to the U.S., 1989; s. Vladimir and Nora (Christensen) Florin; m. Monica Ofelia Jacobsen, May 21, 1981; children: Nicholas, Anna. Degree, U. Buenos Aires, 1979, PhD, 1988. Fellow Nat. Rsch. Coun. Argentina, Buenos Aires, 1981-82, 86-89, ind. researcher, 1992—; fellow DANIDA, Copenhagen, Odense, Denmark, 1982-83; rsch. assoc. Natural Scis. Rsch. Coun., Odense, 1983-84; fellow EMBO, Munster, Germany, 1984; NIH-Fogarty postdoctoral fellow Yale U., New Haven, Conn., 1989-91; postdoctoral assoc. U. Cin., 1991-92. Contbr. chpt. to book; contbr. articles to TIBS Trends Biochem. Sci., Microbial Ecology, Jour. Biol. Chemistry, Biochem. Jour., Biochem. Biophys. Rsch. Comm. Recipient award Dansk-Argentinsk Kulturfond, 1984, 87,Erie of Martha Schneibel's Legat, 1984, Fogarty Internat. Rsch. Corp. award, 1993. Mem. Sigma Xi. Roman Catholic. Home: Calle 63 No 5628, 1653 Chilavert Argentina Office: U Buenos Aires, Pab II Piso 4 Ciudad Universitaria, 1428 Buenos Aires Argentina

FLOURNOY, DAYL JEAN, clinical microbiologist; b. San Antonio, Dec. 17, 1944; s. Dayl Jean Flournoy and Bonnie Allen; children: David, Michael, Michelle. BS, Southwest Tex. State U., 1965; AS, San Antonio Coll., 1966; MA, Incarnate Word Coll., San Antonio, 1968; PhD, U. Houston, 1973; postdoctoral fellow, St. Luke Episc. Hosp., Houston, 1975, U. Okla. Health Scis. Ctr., 1991. Cert. med. technologist, specialist in microbiology Am. Soc. Clin. Pathologists; cert. clin. lab. dir. Am. Bd. Bioanalysis. Med. tech. automated chemistry Santa Rosa Med. Ctr., San Antonio, 1966-69; teaching fellow Univ. Houston, Houston, 1969-72; med. tech., clin. lab. supr. St. Luke's Episc. Hosp., Houston, 1972-73, microbiologist, med. tech., 1974-75; dir. clin. microbiology/serology VA Med. Ctr., Oklahoma City, 1975—; prof. pathology Univ. Okla. Hlth. Sci. Ctr., Oklahoma City, 1987—; manuscript reviewer Lab. Medicine, Med. Sci. Rsch., Can. Jour. Med. Tech., Mil. Medicine, Am. Jour. Infection Control, Infection Control Hosp. Epidemiology. Contbr. articles to sci. jours. Head soccer coach Tri-City Athletic Assn., 1979-83; teenline vol. Okla. Dept. Mental Health, 1989-90. Fellow Am. Acad. Microbiology; mem. Am. Soc. Microbiology, Soc. Hosp. Epidemiologists Am., Southwestern Assn. Clin. Microbiology, Leadership 2000, Toastmasters Internat. Home: 2122 La Dean Dr Norman OK 73069-4255 Office: VA Med Ctr (113) 921 NE 13th St Oklahoma City OK 73104-5007

FLOWERS, CHARLES ELY, JR., physician emeritus medical educator; b. Zebulon, N.C., July 20, 1920; s. Charles Ely and Carmen (Poole) F.; m. Juanita Bays, Nov. 23, 1944 (dec.); children: Charles Ely III, Carmen Eva; m. Jaunzetta Shew, Sept. 25, 1972. B.S., The Citadel, 1941; M.D., Johns Hopkins U., 1944. Diplomate: Am. Bd. Ob-Gyn (assoc. examiner). Intern Johns Hopkins Hosp., 1944, resident, 1945-50; instr. SUNY, 1950-51, asst. prof., 1951-53; assoc. prof. U. N.C., 1953-61, prof., 1961-66; prof., chmn. dept. obstetrics and gynecology Baylor U. Med. Sch., 1966-69; prof., chmn. dept. ob-gyn U. Ala. Med. Center, Birmingham, 1969-85; chmn. emeritus U. Ala. Med. Center, 1985—, disting. prof., 1985—; obstetrician and gynecologist in chief U. Ala. Hosp., 1969-85; cons. NIH; mem. adv. com. oral contraceptives Internat. Planned Parenthood; mem. med. services adv. com. Nat. Found.; chmn. 6th World Congress Gynecology and Obstetrics, 1970. Mem. editorial bd.: Obstetrics and Gynecology. Served to capt. M.C., AUS, 1946-48. Recipient Disting. Service award U. N.C., 1970. Mem. AMA, Continental Gynecol. Soc., Am. Gynecol. and Obstet. Soc. (treas. 1981), Am. Assn. Obstetricians and Gynecologists (v.p. 1978-80), Central Assn. Obstetricians and Gynecologists, ACS, Am. Coll. Obstetricians and Gynecologists (chmn. com. obstetrics anesthesia and analgesia, v.p. 1983), Soc. Gynecologic Surgeons (pres. 1986), Internat. Coll. Anesthetists. Home: 3757 Rockhill Rd Birmingham AL 35223-1531

FLOYD, ALTON DAVID, cell biologist, consultant; b. Henderson, Ky., July 17, 1941; s. Frank and Queen Tina (Melton) F.; m. Barbara Wilson, Aug. 18, 1962; children: Fara Alison, Heather Lynn. BS, U. Ky., 1963; PhD, U. Louisville, 1968. From lectr. to asst. prof. U. Mich., Ann Arbor, 1967-72; from asst. to assoc. prof. Sch. of Medicine Ind. U., Bloomington, 1972-83; assoc. prof. Sch. of Medicine Ind. U., Indpls., 1983-84; sect. head cell biology Miles Sci., Inc., Naperville, Ill., 1984-85; sr. staff scientist Miles, Inc., Elkhart, Ind., 1985-89; pvt. practice cons. Edwardsburg, Mich., 1989—; assoc. dir. Ctr. Light Microscope Imaging and Biotech. Carnegie Mellon U., Pitts., 1991; bd. dirs. Endotech Corp., Indpls.; mem. subcom. immunohistochem. stains NCCLS, 1995-96; industry rep. adv. panel hematology and pathology devices FDA, 1996—. Mem. Am. Assn. Anatomists, Tissue Culture Assn., Soc. Analytical Cytology, Histochem. Soc., Soc. Quantitative Morphology, Biol. Stain Commn., Soc. Histotech., Biol. Stain Commn. Home and Office: 23126 S Shore Dr Edwardsburg MI 49112-9550

FLOYD, BRENDA CAROL, optometrist; b. Sacramento, Calif., Jan. 8, 1955; d. Louis Carrell and Catherine Louise (Hawkins) F.; m. Richard Joseph Brochetti, June 22, 1985. A.A. summa cum laude, Gaston Coll., 1973; B. in Chemistry summa cum laude, U. N.C.-Charlotte, 1975; B.S. in Physiol. Optics cum laude, U. Ala.-Birmingham, 1979, O.D. cum laude, 1981. Lic. optometrist, Tex. Research asst. U. Ala., Birmingham, 1977-79, researcher, 1980-81; optometrist Optical Clinic, Dallas, 1981-85; pvt. practice optometry, Lewisville, Tex., 1985—; clinician, intern Diabetes Hosp., Birmingham, 1980-81, Ctr. Devel. and Learning Disorders, Birmingham, 1980-81. Columnist eye care Lewisville Daily Leader. Sustaining mem. Republican Nat. Com., 1983—. Mem. Tex. Assn. Optometrists, Am. Optometric Found., Women in Optometry, Gamma Beta Phi. Baptist. Avocation: piano compositions. Home: 3920 Promontory Pt Plano TX 75075-3545 Office: 2410 S Stemmons Fwy Ste E Lewisville TX 75067-8785

FLOYD, HENRY BASCOM, IV, radiologist, nuclear medicine physician; b. Pensacola, Fla., Dec. 31, 1953; s. Henry Bascom III and Rubie Mae (Fore) F.; m. Kathryn Lee Betty, June 8, 1985. BS, U. Ala., Birmingham, 1976; MD, Am. U. of the Caribbean, Plymouth, Montserrat, Brit. W.I., 1981. Diplomate Am. Bd. Radiology, Am. Bd. Nuclear Medicine. Resident in anatomic pathology Deaconess Hosp., St. Louis, 1982-84; resident in nuclear medicine U. Ala.-Birmingham Hosp., 1984-86, chief resident, 1986; resident in diagnostic radiology Tulane U. Hosp., New Orleans, 1986-89; med. dir., radiologist, nuclear medicine physician Orlando (Fla.) Diagnostic Ctr., 1989-96. Mem. AMA, Am. Coll. Radiology, Radiol. Soc. N.Am., Am. Roentgen Ray Soc., Soc. Nuclear Medicine, Fla. Radiol. Soc., Fla. Med. Assn., Orange County Med. Soc. Office: Orlando Diagnostic Ctr 1717 S Orange Ave Ste 101 Orlando FL 32806

FLOYD, KAY CIRKSENA, medical technologist; b. Hastings, Nebr., Mar. 30, 1943; d. Frank H. and Mary Gertrude (Martini) Cirksena; m. Richard Clark Floyd, Jr., May 20, 1967; children: Scott, Matthew. BA, Hastings Coll., 1965. Registered med. technologist. Electrocardiogram technician Bishop Clarkson Meml. Hosp., Omaha, 1964-65, med. technologist, 1965-66; teaching med. technologist Rochester (N.Y.) Gen. Hosp., 1966-70; teaching technologist Presbyn. Hosp. Ctr., Albuquerque, 1970-71; asst. lab. supr. Anna Kaseman Hosp., Albuquerque, 1971-72; dir. govt. rels. Oklahoma State Sch. Bds. Assn., 1995—; dir. govt. rels. Okla. State Sch. Bds. Assn., 1995—. Traffic commr. Oklahoma City, 1980-85; PTA pres. Stonegate Elem. Sch., 1979-80, Hoover Mid. Sch., Oklohoma City, 1984-85; v.p., pres. Oklahoma City Bd. Edn., 1985-92 (v.p. 1987-88, pres. 1988-89); bd. dirs. Oklahoma City Pub. Sch. Found., 1990-91; active The Referral Ctr. for Alcohol and Drug Svcs., 1990—, v.p., 1994—; active Met. Area Projects Oversight, 1994—; grad. Leadership Oklahoma City, 1993. Mem. Am. Soc. Clin. Pathologists (assoc.), Okla. State Sch. Bds. Assn. (bd. dirs. 1985-92), Nat. Sch. Bds. Assn., Orch. League (bd. dirs. 1994), Okla. City Rep. Women's Club (2d v.p. 1994). Republican. Presbyterian. Home: 2401 NW 119th St Oklahoma City OK 73120-7407 Office: Okla State Sch Bds Assn 2801 N Lincoln Blvd Oklahoma City OK 73105

FLOYD, WILLIAM ANDERSON, psychology educator; b. Akron, Ohio, Dec. 5, 1928; married. A.B., Eastern Ky. U., 1949; M.A., U. Akron, 1953; B.D. with honors, So. Methodist U., 1956; D.Ed. in Counseling Psychology, North Tex. State U., 1962. Lic. psychologist, Ky.Asst. prof. psychology and religion Columbia Coll., 1959-61, assoc. prof. psychology, 1961-65, dir. Community Psychol. Service Ctr., 1959-65; assoc. prof. edn. and psychology Appalachian State U., 1965-68; prof. psychology Western Ky. U., Bowling Green, 1968—, prof. child devel. and family living, 1969-91, head dept. home econs. and family living, 1969-91, counseling psychologist VA, S.C. State and Baptist Hosps., S.C. Dept. Vocat. Rehab., Bowling Green Police and Fire Dept., numerous other instns. NIMH postdoctoral fellow U. Minn., 1967-68. Mem. Am. Assn. for Marriage and Family Therapy (clin. mem.; supr.), Am. Personnel and Guidance Assn. (life), Am. Psychol. Assn., Ky. Psychol. Assn., Nat. Vocat. Guidance Assn. (profl.), Soc. Police and Criminal Psychology, Phi Delta Kappa, Kappa Delta Pi, Phi Upsilon Omicron. Lodge: Masons. Author: A Definitive Study of Your Career As A Minister, 1969; contbr. chpts. to books, articles to profl. jours. Office: Cottage Psychol Clinic PO Box 1783 Bowling Green KY 42102-1783

FLUGMAN, MARK S., ophthalmologist; b. Bklyn., Feb. 10, 1952; s. Hyman G. and Bernice Flugman; 1 child, Pamela B. Greenfaden. BA, Hofstra U., 1974; MD, Automonous U. Guadalajara, Mex., 1978; DMed, NYU, 1979. Resident, chief resident in ophthalmology SUNY, Stony Brook, 1979-84, clin. instr. ophthalmology, 1984—. Recipient Outstanding Achievement award VA, 1984. Fellow ACS, Am. Acad. Ophthalmology. Office: 176 N Village Ave Rockville Centre NY 11570

FLUSSI, HARRY VALENTINE, former medical center administrator; b. Hilldale, Pa., Feb. 14, 1918; s. Sam and Josephine (Baldinucci) F.; m. Mary Martha Dinis, Apr. 8, 1944; children: Diane Marie (Mrs. John W. Gittinger, Jr.), Claire Denise (Mrs. Peter Jordan). B.A., U. Scranton, 1939; postgrad., Bucknell U., 1939-42. Social worker Pa. Dept. Pub. Assistance, 1939-41; officer mgr. SSS, Plains, Pa., 1941-43; with VA, 1946—; dir. VA Ctr., Togus, Maine, 1965-70, VA Med. Ctr., Lebanon, Pa., 1970-82; high sch. tchr. St. Thomas High Sch., Scranton, 1939. Chmn. U.S. CSC Interagy. Bd., Augusta, Maine, 1966-68, Combined Fed. Campaign for Maine, 1966—; mem. action panel USDA, 1968—; mem. regional health services com. Augusta-Gardiner Area Community Council, 1966—. Served with C.E. AUS, 1943-46. Recipient citations and awards of merit Am. Legion, VFW, Am. Vets., World War II; letters of commendation VA and other govt. agencies; VA Sustained Superior Performance award manager's commendation. Mem. Nat. Inter-Agy. Inst. Fed. Hosp. Adminstrs., U.S. Postoffice Mail Users Council, Lambda Alpha Phi. Address: 905 Aspen Dr # 8 Mountain Top PA 18707-9104

FLY, JAMES DOUGLAS, ophthalmologist; b. McComb, Miss., Feb. 7, 1949; s. Henry Edward and Velma (Crawford) F.; 1 child, Brett Douglas; m. Ruth Davis Conway, Apr. 12, 1980; children: Ann Elizabeth, Virginia Conway. BS, U. Miss., 1971, MD, 1974. Diplomate, Am. Bd. Ophthalmology. Resident in ophthalmology U. Miss. Hosp., Jackson, 1979; fellow in vitreous-retina disease Houston Eye Assocs., 1983-84; emergency physician St. John's Mercy Med. Ctr., St. Louis, 1975; mem. Houston Eye Assocs., 1979-83; practice medicine specializing in vitreo-retinal diseases Jackson, Miss., 1984—. Bd. dirs. Miss. unit Soc. to Prevent Blindness, 1985-88. Fellow Am. Acad. Ophthalmology, ACS; mem. AMA, So. Med. Assn., So. Retina Study Club, La.-Miss. Ophthal. and Otorlaryng. Assn., Jackson Ophthal. Soc. (pres. 1986-87), Vitreous Soc., Am. Diabetes Assn. (pres., chmn. bd. dirs. 1987-89), Miss. Eye, Ear, Nose and Throat Assn. (councillor 1985). Home: 3933 Stuart Pl Jackson MS 39211-6754 Office: 971 Lakeland Dr Ste 360 Jackson MS 39216-4607

FLYE, M. WAYNE, surgeon, immunologist, educator; b. Tarboro, N.C., June 23, 1942; s. Charlie A. and Martha E. (Bullock) F.; m. Phyllis Webb, June 7, 1964; children: Christopher Warren, Brandon Reid. BS, U. N.C., 1964, MD, 1967; MA in Immunology, Duke U., 1972, PhD in Immunology, 1980; MA (hon.), Yale U., 1985. Diplomate Am. Bd. Surgery, Am. Bd. Thoracic Surgery, Am. Bd. Vascular Surgery. Intern. surg. Case-We. Res. U., Cleve., 1967-68, res. gen. and cardio-thoracic surgery, 1968-75; instr., teaching scholar, vascular and transplantation surgery Duke U. Med. Ctr., Durham, N.C., 1975-76; sr. investigator , chief thoracic surg. svc. NIH, Bethesda, Md., 1977-79; chief vascular surgery U. Tex. Med. Br., Galveston, 1979-82, assoc. prof. surgery and microbiology, 1980-82; dir. div. organ transplantation and immunology, prof. transplantation, dir. sect. gen. surgery Yale U. Sch. Medicine, New Haven, Conn., 1983-85; prof. surgery, molecular microbiology and immunology Washington U. Med. Sch., St. Louis, 1985—; trustee New Eng. Organ Bank, Boston, 1984-85; com. mem. United Network Orgn. Sharing, Richmond, Va., 1986-89; mem. anesthesiology and trauma study sect. NIH Surgery, 1991—; merit rev. com. for surgery VA, 1994—, chmn., 1996—. Editor: Principles of Organ Transplantation, 1989, The Thymus: Regulator of Cellular Immunity, 1993, Atlas of Organ Transplantation, 1994; mem. editl. bd. Clin. Transplantation, 1986—, Prospectives in Gen. Surgery, 1988—, Transplantation, 1989—, Xanthus Intelligence Unit Reports, 1990—, Shock: Molecular, Cellular and Systemic Pathobiology of Injury, 1993—, Transplantation Sci., 1993—, Jour. Surg. Rsch., 1995—. Lt. col. U.S. Army, 1976-78. Recipient James W. McLaughlin medal U. Tex.-Galveston, 1982. Fellow ACP, So. Thoracic Surg. Assn. (Best Sci. Paper award 1980); mem. Am. Assn. Immunologists, Internat. Cardiovascular Soc., N.Y. Acad. Sci., Soc. Thoracic Surgeons, Am. Soc. Transplant Physicians, Am. Soc. Transplant Surgeons (program com. 1984-86, Ethics Com. 1994-95), Brit. Soc. Immunology, Transplantation Soc., Mid-Am. Transplant

Assn. (bd. dirs. 1986-89), Am. Fedn. Clin. Rsch., Royal Soc. Medicine, AAAS, Surg. Infection Soc., Reticuloendothelial Soc., Soc. Univ. Surgeons, Soc. Clin. Vascular Surgery, Brit. Transplantation Soc., So. Assn. Vascular Surgery, Am. Coll. Chest Physicians, Soc. Surg. Oncology, Am. Assn. Thoracic Surgery, Surg. Biology Club I, Am. Assn. Study Liver Diseases, Am. Surg. Assn., So. Surg. Assn., Cen. Surg. Assn., Soc. Internat. de Chirurgie, Midwestern Vascular Surg. Soc., Soc. Vascular Surg., World Ann. Hepato-Pancreato-Bilary Surg., Soc. Surgery of Alimentary Tract, Shock Soc., Sigma Xi, Alpha Omega Alpha., Chi Psi, Young Republicans N.C. Episcopalian. Office: Washington U Med Sch Ste 5108 1 Barnes Saint Louis MO 63110-1003

FLYER, JERROLD NEIL, surgeon; b. Bklyn., Sept. 23, 1954. BS summa cum laude, CUNY, 1976; MD, Albert Einstein Coll. Medicine, 1980. Bd. cert. Am. Bd. Surgery. Commd. 2d. lt. USAF, 1980, advanced through grades to lt. col., 1992; resident integrated surg. residency program Wright State U., Dayton, Ohio, 1980-85; chief gen. surgery USAF Hosp., Altus AFB, Okla., 1985-88; chief surg. svcs., comdr. 655 Tac Hosp. 475th Med. Group, Yokota Air Base, Japan, 1988-92; chief surg. svcs. 52d Med. Group, Bitburg Air Base, Germany, 1992-95; chief med. staff 355th Med. Group, Davis-Monthan AFB, Ariz., 1995—. Fellow ACS; mem. Air Force Soc. Clin. Surgeons, Alpha Omega Alpha, Phi Beta Kappa. Office: 355th Med Group 4175 S Alamo Ave Davis-Monthan AFB AZ 85707

FLYNN, FREDERICK VALENTINE, chemical pathology educator; b. Enfield, Middlesex, Eng., Oct. 6, 1924; s. Frederick Walter and Jane Laing (Valentine) F.; m. Catherine Ann Warrick, Sept. 25, 1955; children: David, Frances. MB, BS, U. Coll., London, 1946, Md, 1951. Registered med. practitoner, London. Obstetric house surgeon U. Coll. Hosp., London, 1947, rsch. registrar, trainee pathologist, 1947-60, cons. chem pathology, 1960-70; prof. chem. pathology U. Coll. London, 1970-89; chmn. panel examiners Royal Coll. Pathologists, London, 1972-82, dir. continuing med. edn., 1992—; assoc. clin. pathology Pepper Lab. Phila., 1954-55; cons. chem. pathology Royal Navy, 1978-92; chmn. Dept. Health Adv. Group on Sci. Computing, London, 1971-76; chmn. N.E. Thames Regional Health Authorities Rsch. Com., London, 1984-88. Editor: Socrates; Computing in Clinical Laboratores (6 vols.), 1978; contbr. articles to profl. jours. Trustee Sir Jules Thorn Charitable Trust, London, 1988—. Fellow Brit. Postgrad. Med. Fedn., 1954, Univ. Coll. London, 1974. Fellow Royal Soc. Medicine (v.p. pathology sect. 1971-73, 89-91), Royal Coll. Physicians, Royal Coll. Pathologists (v.p. 1975-78, treas. 1978-83, Disting. Svc. medal 1995); mem. Assn. Clin. Pathologists (pres. 1989-90). Home: 20 Oakleigh Ave, London Whetstone London N20 9JH, England Office: Royal Coll Pathologists, 2 Carlton House Terr, London SW1Y 5AF, England

FLYNN, JOHN THOMAS, physiologist, researcher; b. Chester, Pa., Mar. 14, 1948; s. Deward Belmont and Pauline (Dolski) F.; m. Harriet Yvonne Medwid, July 18, 1970; children: Susan Michelle, Mark Brian. BS, Widener U., Chester, 1970; PhD, Hahnemann U., 1974. Asst. prof. physiology Thomas Jefferson U., Phila., 1976-82, assoc. prof., 1982-87, prof., 1987—. Contbr. more than 85 articles to profl. jours. NIH grantee, 1981—. Mem. Am. Physiol. Soc., N.Y. Acad. Scis., Am. Fedn. for Clin. Rsch., The Shock Soc. (treas. 1988-92), Internat. Endotoxin Soc., Physiol. Soc. Phila. (coun. mem. 1984). Office: Thomas Jefferson U 1020 Locust St Philadelphia PA 19107-6731

FLYNN, MARGARET ALBERI, nutritionist, dietitian; b. Hurley, Wis., Nov. 22, 1915; d. Bernard and Anna (Chiado) Alberi; m. May 31, 1938 (dec. 1960); children: Phoebe, Timothy. BS, Coll. St. Caterine, St. Paul, 1937; MS, U. Iowa, 1938; PhD, U. Mo., 1960. Registered dietition; diplomate Am. Bd. Nutrition. Instr. Coll. St. Catherine, St. Paul, 1937-38; rsch. asst. pediatrics U. Iowa, Iowa City, 1939-40; instr. dietetics Levi Meml. Hosp., Hot Springs, Ark., 1942-46; teaching dietitian Holy Name Hosp., Teaneck, N.J., 1950-54; rsch. asst. pediatrics U. Mo., Columbia, 1961-63, asst. prof. nutrition and dietetics, 1966-69, assoc. prof. medicine, 1969-75, prof. medicine, 1975-86, prof. emeritus medicine, 1986—. Contbr. articles to profl. jours. Nat. Cancer Inst. grantee, 1977; Nat. Meat Bd./Wallace Genetic Found. grantee, 1978—; named Sesquicentennial Prof. U. Mo., 1989, Disting. Faculty awardee, 1988, Faculty Alumni award, 1976. Fellow Am. Coll. Nutrition; mem. Am. Soc. Clin. Nutrition, Am. Inst. Nutrition. Office: U Mo Sch Medicine 1 Hospital Dr Columbia MO 65201-5276

FLYNN, MICHAEL BURNETT, surgeon, educator; b. Bklyn., Aug. 30, 1938. BA, U. Dublin, Ireland, 1961; Bacclaureatus in Medicina, Chirurgia et Arte Obstetricia, U. Dublin, 1962. Diplomate Am. Bd. Surgery. Rotating intern Stamford (Conn.) Hosp., 1962-63; resident in gen. surgery U. Md. Hosp., Balt., 1965-69; surg. oncology fellow MD Anderson Hosp., Houston, 1969-70, head and neck surgery advanced sr. fellow, 1970-71; pvt. practice Surg. Oncology, Louisville, 1971-86; clin. instr. dept. surgery U. Louisville, 1971-72, asst. clin. prof. dept. surgery, 1971-78, assoc. clin. prof. dept. surgery, 1978-86, assoc. prof. dept. surgery, 1986-95, prof. dept. surgery, 1995—; dir. breast care ctr. J. Graham Brown Cancer Ctr., Louisville, 1987-94, assoc. dir. cancer control and cmty. rels., 1992—, med. co-dir. Ky. cancer program, 1990—. Author book chpt., 4 video tapes; contbr. articles to profl. jours. Recipient Cert. of Appreciation, Rep. of Vietnam Ministry of Health, 1968, Mike Hogg Travelling fellowship MD Anderson Hosp., 1971; named to Hon. Order of Ky. Cols., 1976. Fellow Am. Coll. Surgeons; mem. AMA (Humanitarian Svc. award 1968), Jefferson County Med. Assn., Ky. Med. Assn., Soc. Surg. Oncology, Soc. Head and Neck Surgeons (sec. 1988-92, v.p. 1992-93, pres.-elect 1993-94, pres. 1994-95). Office: James Graham Brown Cancer 529 S Jackson St Louisville KY 40202

FLYNN, THOMAS BROWN, neurosurgeon; b. Dyersburg, Tenn., Sept. 15, 1936; s. Thomas T. and Helen (Brown) F.; m. Joan Y. Kuebel, Dec. 19, 1959 (div. Dec. 1979); m. Pamela Noriea, July 25, 1980; children: Sean, Heidi, Rhys. BS, U. South, 1958; MD, Tulane U., 1962. Diplomate Am. Bd. Neurol. Surgeons. Straight surg. intern Charity Hosp. La., New Orleans, 1962-63; fellow neurol. surgery Ochsner Found., New Orleans, 1963-65; resident neurol. surgery Tulane U. Med. Sch., New Orleans, 1965-67, instr., 1967-68, asst. clin. prof. div. neurosurgery, 1979; chief resident neurol. surgery Charity Hosp. La. Tulane Service, New Orleans, 1966-67; practice medicine specializing in neurol. surgery, Baton Rouge, 1967—; assoc. prof. neurol. surgery La. State U. Med. Sch.; cons. neurol. surgery Karl K. Long Meml. Hosp., Baton Rouge; chief neurosurg. service Baton Rouge Gen. Hosp., 1974, 75, 76, chief surg. services, 1975, 76, 77, vice-chief staff, 1978-79, sec. staff, 1979-80, chief med. staff, 1980; vice-chief neurosurgery Our Lady of the Lake Hosp., 1982, chief neurosurgery, 1983, 93; chief neurosurgery Baton Rouge Gen. Hosp., 1983; mem. adv. council alcohol and drug abuse prevention program Baton Rouge Sch. System, 1981— . Contbr. articles to profl. jours. Fellow Internat. Coll. Surgeons, ACS; mem. Congress Neurol. Surgeons, Am. Assn. Neurol. Surgeons (continuing edn. award in neurosurgery 1976, 79), AMA (physician's recognition awards 1973-75, 75-78, 79-81, 82-84, 86—), Am. Soc. Stereotatic and Functional Neurosurgery, So. Med. Assn., So. Neurosurg. Soc., La. Neurosurg. Soc., (pres. 1977), La. State Med. Soc., Houston Neurol. Soc., Baton Rouge Surg. Soc. (pres. 1983), East Baton Rouge Parish Med. Soc. Home: 4555 Highway 966 Jackson LA 70748-7435 Office: 7777 Hennessy Blvd # 10000 Baton Rouge LA 70808

FLYNN, WILLIAM JOSEPH, JR., surgeon; b. June 21, 1955; m. Nancy Flynn. BS, St. Bonaventure U., 1977; MS, SUNY, Buffalo, 1979; MD, Northwestern U., 1983. Attending surgeon VA Med. Ctr., Louisville, 1990-91, Buffalo, 1991—; attending surgeon, dir. surg./trauma ICU Erie County Med. Ctr., Buffalo, 1991—; asst. prof. surgery SUNY, Buffalo, 1991—. Contbr. articles to profl. jours. and chpts. to books. Fellow ACS (assoc.); mem. Am. Burn Assn., ACS Regional Com. on Trauma, Am. Trauma Soc., Assn. Acad. Surgeons, Ea. Assn. for Surgery of Trauma, Med. Soc. Erie County, Microcirculatory Soc. Inc., N.Y. State Com. on Trauma, Shock Soc., Soc. Am. Gastrointestinal Endoscopic Surgeons, Soc. Critical Care Medicine, Surg. Infection Soc., Soc. VA Surgeons. Office: Erie County Med Ctr 462 Grider St Buffalo NY 14215

FOBBE, FRANZ CASPAR, radiologist; b. Thüngersheim, Bavaria, Fed. Republic Germany, Dec. 26, 1948; m. Doris Rummer-Löns, Mar. 10, 1989; children: Lukas, Lea. Student, Hansa Koll., Hamburg, Fed. Republic Germany, 1971-73, U. Glasgow, Scotland, 1979-80; MD, Med. Hochschule, U. Hannover, 1982; Habilitation, Freie U. Berlin, 1990. Asst. arzt. A.K. Barmbek, Chirurgie, Hamburg, 1981-83; asst. arzt. radiology U. Berlin, 1983-89, cons., 1974-79. Contbr. numerous articles to profl. jours and books. Recipient Röntgenpreis Deutsche Röntgengesellschaft, 1991. Office: Auguste-Viktoria Hosp Berlin Dept Diagnostic & Interventio, Rubensstr 125, 12157 Berlin Germany

FOCHT, MICHAEL HARRISON, health care industry executive; b. Reading, Pa., Sept. 16, 1942; s. Benjamin Harrison and Mary (Hannahoe) F.; m. Sandra Lee Scholwin, May 14, 1964; 1 child, Michael Harrison. Archtl. estimator Caloric Corp., Topton, Pa., 1964-65, cost acct., 1965-66, indsl. engr., 1966-68, mgr. wage rates and standards, 1968-70; indsl. engr. Am. Medicorp. Inc., Fort Lauderdale, Fla., 1970-71; exec. dir. midwest region Am. Medicorp. Inc., Chgo., 1977-78; asst. adminstr. Cypress Community Hosp., Pompano Beach, Fla., 1971-73, adminstr., 1975-77; adminstr. Doctor's Hosp. Hollywood, Fla., 1973-75; v.p. Medfield Corp., St. Petersburg, Fla., 1978-79; v.p. ops. hosp. group Nat. Med. Enterprises, Inc., Los Angeles, 1979-81; regional sr. v.p. hosp. group Nat. Med. Enterprises, Inc., Tampa, Fla., 1981-83; pres., chief exec. officer internat. group Nat. Med. Enterprises, Inc., Los Angeles, 1983-86, pres. chief exec. officer hosp. group, 1986-91; sr. exec. v.p., dir. ops. Nat. Med. Enterprises, Inc., 1991-93, pres., 1993-95; pres., COO Tenet Healthcare Corp., Santa Barbara, 1995—. Mem. Fedn. Am. Hosps. (bd. govs. 1983—), Fla. League Hosps. (bd. dirs. 1982-83). Republican. Roman Catholic. Home: PO Box 703 Santa Ynez CA 93460-0703 Office: Tenet Healthcare Corp 3820 State St Santa Barbara CA 93105

FODERA, FELICIA ANN, optometrist; b. Bklyn., Mar. 27, 1966; d. Joseph and Madeline (Piscitelli) F.; m. Thomas Richard Conrod, Oct. 30, 1993. BS, Fordham U., 1988; OD, New Eng. Coll. of Optometry, 1992. Resident optometrist St. Albans (N.Y.) VAECC, 1992-93; staff optometrist Health Drive, Meriden, Conn., 1993-94; staff optometrist, extern supr. FDR VA Hosp., Montrose, N.Y., 1994—. Contbr. chpt. to Ocular Pharmacology, 1995. Recipient Am. Optometric Student Assn. Svc. award Am. Optometric Assn., 1991. Fellow Am. Acad. Optometry; mem. Nat. Assn. VA Optometrists. Office: FDR VA Hosp Optometry Svc (123) Montrose NY 10548

FODOR, GUGLIELMO, radiologist; b. Pola, Istria, Croatia, Feb. 26, 1948; arrived in Italy, 1948; s. Alfred Fodor and Arianne Buttignoni; m. Tiziana Baldini, Feb. 4, 1984; 1 child, David. MD. Radiologist Hosp., Bolzano, Italy, 1974—; dir. ultrasound dept. Author: Hip Sonography Guide, 1991, Trattato Italiano di Elografia, 1992. Mem. SIRM. Office: Radiology, via L Böhler 5, 39100 Bozen Italy

FODY, EDWARD PAUL, pathologist; b. Balt., June 11, 1947; s. Edward Paul and Frances Dorothy (Schultz) F.; m. Nancy June Keipe, July 19, 1974. BS, Duke U., 1969; MS, U. Wis., 1971; MD, Vanderbilt U., 1975. Diplomate Am. Bd. Pathology. Resident in pathology Vanderbilt U. Hosp., Nashville, 1975-78; fellow in chemistry U. Tex. Med. Sch., Houston, 1979-80, asst. prof. pathology, 1980-81; chief lab. VA Hosp., Little Rock, 1981-87; assoc. prof. pathology U. Ark. Med. Sch. Little Rock, 1981-87; dir. pathology Bethesda Hosp., Cin., 1987—. Editor, author: Clinical Chemistry, 1984, chpt. to book. Mem. Cin.-Kharkov Sister City Project, 1990. Fellow Coll. Am. Pathologists, Am. Soc. Clin. Pathologists; mem. AMA, Am Assn. for Clin. Chemistry, Am. Soc. for Microbiology, Ohio Med. Assn., Cin. Acad. Medicine. Republican. Lutheran. Home: 7730 Coldstream Woods Dr Cincinnati OH 45255-5612 Office: Bethesda Hosp Dept Pathology 619 Oak St Cincinnati OH 45206-1613

FOEGE, WILLIAM HERBERT, public health administrator; b. Decorah, Iowa, Mar. 12, 1936; s. William August and Anne Erika (Ermisch) F.; m. Paula S. Ristad, Dec. 23, 1958; children: David, Michael, Robert. BA, Pacific Luth. U., 1957; MD, U. Wash., 1961; MPH, Harvard U., 1965. Intern USPHS Hosp., S.I., N.Y., 1961-62; epidemic intelligence svc. officer Communicable Disease Ctr., Atlanta, 1962-64; med. officer Immanuel Med. Ctr., Yahe, Nigeria, 1965-66; epidemiologist smallpox eradication/measles control program Nigeria, 1969-70; dir. smallpox eradication program Ctr. Disease Control, Atlanta, 1970-73; dir. Ctr. Disease Control, 1977—; med. epidemiologist smallpox program Southeast Asia Regional Office WHO, New Delhi, 1973-75; cons. WHO, Bangkok, Thailand, 1967, Kinshasha, Zaire, 1968; dep. field coord. Internat. Red Cross Joint Relief Action, Nigeria. Office: Dir Ctr for Disease Control 1600 Clifton Rd NE Bldg 1 Atlanta GA 30329-4018*

FOEHRING, MARY E., nursing administrator; b. New Brunswick, N.J., Jan. 17, 1960; d. Robert Anthony and Ruth (Shappert) F. BSN, U. Vt., 1982. RN, N.Y., Va. Nurse educator Elizabeth Lund Home, Burlington, Vt., 1982; staff nurse Lenox Hill Hosp., N.Y.C., 1982-87; asst. patient care dir. Fairfax Hosp., Falls Church, Va., 1987-89, coord. heart lung transplant, 1989-95, clin. practice specialist for transplant svcs., 1995—. Bd. dirs. Am. Heart Assn., Fairfax, 1993. Mem. AACN, Nat. Assn. Transplant Coords., Sigma Theta Tau. Office: Fairfax Hosp Transplant Ctr 3300 Gallows Rd Falls Church VA 22046

FOFT, JOHN WILLIAM, physician, educator; b. Los Angeles, May 13, 1928; s. Wilford L. and Mary E. (McMahon) F.; m. Marianne T. Deibler, Mar. 12, 1957; children—John, Christine. B.S., U. Nebr., 1951; M.D., 1954. Intern Mpls. Gen. Hosp., 1954-55; asst. prof. pathology, dep. dir. clin. chemistry U. Chgo., 1965-67; asso. prof. clin. pathology U. Ala., 1968-70, dir. pediatric-clin. pathology lab., 1968-70, dep. chmn. research clin. pathology, 1969-70, prof., chmn. dept. clin. pathology, 1970-77, clin. prof. dept. pathology, 1977-91; ret., 1991; chmn. dept. pathology Carraway Meth. Med. Center, 1977-91, Norwood Clinic, 1977-91. Served as capt. AUS, 1955-57; Served as capt. USAF, 1961-64. Nat. Heart Inst. fellow U. Minn. Hosps., 1959-61; Am. Cancer Soc. scholar Argonne Cancer Research Hosp., 1968. Mem. Am. Assn. Pathologists, Ala. Assn. Pathologists, Sigma Xi, Alpha Omega Alpha. Home: 3529 Spring Valley Ct Birmingham AL 35223-1467

FOGARTY, BRIAN KIRBY, psychologist; b. Hazleton, Pa., Nov. 13, 1948; s. Thomas Morris and Frances Regina (Salvador) F.; B.A. in Psychology, Indiana U. of Pa., 1970; M.Ed. in Counseling, Pa. State U., 1972; m. Cheryn Dianne Stoner, Nov. 24, 1973; children: Sean Patrick, Jason Kirby, Christopher Ryan. Tchr./counselor Exceptional Children, Inc., Mays Landing, N.J., 1971; asso. program dir. Yoke Crest, Inc., Harrisburg, Pa., 1973; dir. child and adolescent services Harrisburg Hosp. Mental Health Center, 1973-81, dir. quality assurance and clin. coordination, 1981-84; staff clin. psychologist Harrisburg Inst. Psychiatry, 1985-86; pvt. practice psychology and consultation, Commonwealth Affiliates, Harrisburg; staff psychologist Milton Hershey Sch., 1988—. Bd. dirs. Assos. for Children and Youth, 1977-81, v.p. 1980; bd. advs. Woodside Juvenile Detention Center, 1978-80; adv. bd. George Frey Center for Emotionally Disturbed Children, 1978-81, chmn. 1980-81; adv. com. Tri-County Headstart Program, 1976-80; bd. dirs. Tri County Mental Health Assn., 1982-87; profl. cons. Northwestern Mut. Life Ins. Co., 1983-84, Pa. Blue Shield, 1985—. Bd. dirs. West Shore Youth Soccer Club, 1986-88. Cert. clin. mental health counselor. Mem. Nat. Bd. Cert. Counselors, Nat. Acad. Cert. Clin. Mental Health Counselors, Pa. Psychol. Assn., Phi Kappa Phi. Democrat. Episcopalian. Home: 352 Futurity Dr Camp Hill PA 17011-8358 Office: Commonwealth Affiliates 2215 Forest Hills Dr Ste 38 Harrisburg PA 17112-1062

FOGARTY, HARRY WELLS, psychoanalyst; b. Sioux City, Iowa, Oct. 29, 1945; s. Charles Franklin and Wilma (Wells) F.; m. Aileen Koger, May 30, 1982; children: Mairin, Qiu Meng, Mei Lan. BA in Philosophy, Fordham U., 1968; MA in Econs., U. Wash., 1971; MDiv, STM with high distinction, Woodstock Coll., 1974; PhD, Union Theol. Sem., 1987. Ordained priest Roman Cath. Ch. Assoc. counselor Cath. Campus Ministry, Columbia U., N.Y.C., 1974-80; clin. assoc., tutor in psychiatry and religion Union Theol. Sem., N.Y.C., 1975-80; pvt. practice Jungian analysis N.Y.C.; instr. C.G. Jung Found. for Analytical Psychology, 1987—, bd. dirs. 1993-94; pres., mem. adv. bd. C.J. Jung Referral Svc., 1995—; bd. dirs., mem. faculty C.J. Jung Inst. N.Y., 1992, pres., 1994—; lectr. in field; mem. faculty Inst. of Religion and Health, 1991—; lectr. in psychiatry and religion Union Theol. Sem., N.Y.C., 1991—. Author: An Index of Concern: The United States Senate and Global Perspective, 1972; contbr. articles, book revs. to profl. publs. Mem. AACD, Nat. Assn. for Advancement of Psychoanalysis (past bd. dirs., past sec., chmn. assembly mem. insts.), N.Y. Assn. Analytical Psychology, Internat. Assn. Analytical Psychology (cert. Jungian analyst). Office: 7 W 96th St Apt 1E New York NY 10025-6514

FOGARTY, MICHAEL GARRETT, biologist; b. N.Y.C., May 14, 1933; s. Michael and Margaret (Cleve) F.; m. Dorothy Kennelly, Sept. 8, 1956; children: Michael, Kathleen, Patricia, Eileen. BS in Biology, Iona Coll., New Rochelle, N.Y., 1955; postgrad., Rutgers U., 1955-56, Columbia U., 1963. Group leader Johnson & Johnson, 1958-68; microbiologist Becton, Dickinson and Co., 1968-83; v.p. quality assurance/regulatory affairs Med. Sterilization Inc., Syosset, N.Y., 1983—; dir. course in Indsl. Sterization, Ctr. for Profl. Advancement, Princeton,. N.J. Editorial adv. bd., Medical Device and Diagnostic Industry. Mem. Assn. for the Advancement of Med. Instrumentation, Am. Soc. for Microbiology, Health Industries Mfg. Assn., Parenteral Drug Assn., Soc. for Indsl. Microbiology. Home: 642 N Meadow Dr Bound Brook NJ 08805-1417 Office: 225 Underhill Blvd Syosset NY 11791-3409

FOGARTY, THOMAS JAMES, surgery educator; b. Cin., Feb. 25, 1934; s. William Henry and Anna Isabella (Ruthemeyer) F.; m. Rosalee Mae Brennan, Aug. 28, 1965; children: Thomas James Jr., Heather Brennan, Patrick Erin, Jonathan David. BS in Biology, Xavier U., 1956; MD, U. Cin., 1960; D (hon.), Xavier U., 1987. Intern U. Oreg. Med. Sch., Portland, 1960-61, resident, 1962-65, instr. surgery, 1967-68; chief resident, instr. surgery divsn. cardiovascular surgery Stanford (Calif.) U. Med. Ctr., 1969-70, asst. prof. surgery, 1970-71, asst. clin. prof. surgery, 1971-73; cardiovascular surgeon pvt. practice, Stanford, 1973-78; pres. med. staff Stanford U. Med. Ctr., 1977-79; cardiovascular surgeon pvt. practice, Redwood City, Calif., 1978-93; dir. cardiovascular surgery Sequoia Hosp., Redwood City, Calif., 1980-93; prof. surgery Stanford U. Med. Ctr., 1993—; bd. dirs. Guided Med. Sys., Inc., Staellite Dialysis Ctrs., Inc.; co-founder, bd. dirs. Aneulx, Inc., Biopsys Med., Inc., Cardiac Pathways, Inc., Gen. Surg. Innovations, Inc., LocalMed, Inc., Physiometric, Inc., Vital Insite, Inc., Raytel Med. Corp., Cardiovascular Imaging Sys., Inc., Devices for Vascular Intervention, Inc., Hancock Labs., Imagyn Med., Inc., Physiometrix, Inc., Ventritex, Inc., Xenotech; mem. scientific adv. bd. Autogenics, BioLink Corp., Cardio Thoracic Sys., Inc., bd. dirs.; pres., founder Fogarty Engring., Inc.; co-founder, sr. ptnr. Three Arch Ptnrs.. Contbr. articles to profl. jours.; patentee in field. Fellow U. Cin. Coll. Medicine, Good Samaritan Hosp., 1961-62, Nat. Heart Inst. Surgery br., Bethesda, Md., 1965-67, rsch. fellow divsn. cardiovascular surgery Stanford Med. Ctr., 1968-69; recipient AstroLobe award Roger Bacon High Sch., 1974, Disting. Alumnus award U. Cin. Med. Sch., 1989; named Inventor of Yr., San Francisco Patent and Trademark Assn., 1980. Mem. AMA, Am. Assn. Thoracic Surgery, Am. Bd. Thoracic Surgery, Am. Coll. Physican Inventors, Am. Coll. Surgeons, Am. Heart Assn. (grantee), Am. Inst. Med. and Biol. Engring., Am. Med. Polit. Action Com., Am. Surg. Assn., Internat. Soc. Endovascular Surgery, Western Thoracic Surg. Soc., Calif. Med. Soc., Pacific Coast Surg. Assn., San Francisco Surg. Soc., San Mateo County Med. Assn., Santa Clara County Med. Assn. (Achievement award in medicine), Internat. Soc. Cardiovascular Surg. (N.Am. chpt.), Soc. Clin. Vascular Surgery, Soc. Vascular Tech., Soc. Thoracic Surgeons, Soc. Vascular Surgery (past pres. 1995), Copco Lake Sportsmen Assn., Santa Cruz Mountain Winegrowers Assn., South Skyline Assn., Sports Car Club Am., Rapley Trail Improvement Assn., Soc. Med. Friends of Wine. Republican. Office: 3270 Alpine Rd Portola Valley CA 94028

FOGEL, BARRY STEVEN, psychiatrist, educator; b. San Francisco, Jan. 23, 1952. MA in Math., U. Calif., Berkeley, 1970; MD, U. Calif., San Francisco, 1976. Diplomate Am. Bd. Psychiatry and Neurology. Intern in medicine Peter Bent Brigham Hosp., Boston, 1976-77; resident in neurology Peter Bent Brigham Hosp., Beth Israel Hosp. Childrens Hosp., Boston, 1977-79; resident in psychiatry Stanford (Calif.) U. Hosp., 1979-81; asst. prof. psychiatry Brown U., Providence, 1982-87, assoc. prof., 1987-92, prof., 1992—; assoc. dir. dept. Psychiatry R.I. Hosp., Providence, 1987-89; assoc. dir. Ctr. Gerontology and Health Care Rsch., Brown U., Providence, 1989—; v.p., treas. LTCQ, Inc., 1992—; bd. dirs. Health Care Review, Inc.; med. dir. psychiatry Eleanor Slater Hosp., Cranston, R.I., 1995-96; cons. in field; Sloan fellow MIT, 1996—. Editor: (with Alan Stoudemire) Principles of Medical Psychiatry, 1987, Medical Psychiatric Practice vol. 1, 1991, vol. II, 1993, vol. III, 1995, Psychiatric Care of the Medical Patient, 1993; (with A. Furino and G. Gottlieb) Mental Health Policy for Older Americans, 1990, (with Randolph Schaffer and Stephen Rao) Neuropsychiatry: A Comprehensive Textbook, 1996. Grantee NIMH, 1983-85, 91—; recipient Geriatric Mental Health Acad. award, 1985-88. Fellow Am. Psychiat. Assn. (coun. on aging 1991—, com. on long term care 1991—, chmn. 1995—, task force on geriat. psychiatry in pub. sector 1989-95, chmn. work group practice guidelines 1992-95, chmn. work group on pvt. long term care ins. 1992-95); mem. R.I. Psychiat. Soc. (councilor 1984-85, legis. rep. 1985—, chmn. ins. com. 1982-86), Am. Acad. Neurology, Assn. Acad. Psychiatry, Am. Neuropsychiat. Assn. (co-founder, exec. dir.), Am. Assn. Gen. Hosp. Psychiatrists, Am. Geriat. Soc., New Eng. Gerontology Acad. (pres. 1990—).

FOGEL, WILLIAM MARTIN, radiologist; b. Charleroi, Pa., July 6, 1939; s. Lewis and Celia (Silver) F.; m. Dolores Greenfield, July 1, 1962; children: Jonathan Tad, Hugh Alan. BA, Washington and Jefferson Coll., 1960; MD, Thomas Jefferson U., 1964. Diplomate Am. Bd. Radiology, Am. Bd. Nuclear Medicine. Intern York (Pa.) Hosp., 1964-65; intern in internal medicine Cleve. Clinic, 1965-66, resident in radiology, 1966-70; radiologist North Shore Hops., Miami, Fla., 1970-73; asst. prof. radiology U. Miami, 1973-74; chief of radiology Henrizo Doctors Hosp., Richmond, Va., 1974-80; pres. Home X-Ray Svc. of Richmond, 1976-92, X-Ray Med. Ctr. Inc., Richmond, 1983—; spkr. in field. Mem. bd. dirs. Jewish Cmty. Ctr., Richmond, 1975-80, Jewish Family Svcs., Richmond, 1975-80, Beth Israel Synagogue, Richmond, 1985-90. Recipient Spl. Svc. to Soviet Immigration award Jewish Family Svc., 1980. Mem. Am. Coll. Radiology, Am. Rocutgen Ray Soc., Am. Inst. Ultrasound. Home: 9312 Arrundel Rd Richmond VA 23229 Office: X-Ray Med Ctr Inc 8923 Three Chopt Rd Richmond VA 23229

FOGELMAN, ALAN MARCUS, internist; b. Bklyn., 1940. BA in Zoology, UCLA, 1962, MD, 1966. Diplomate Am. Bd. Internal Medicine. Intern UCLA Hosp., 1966-67, resident, 1967-68, 70-71, fellow cardiology, 1971-73, prof. medicine. With USN, 1968-70. Mem. ACP, Am. Coll. Cardiology. Office: UCLA Sch Medicine Rm 37-120 Ctr Health Scis 10833 Le Conte Ave Los Angeles CA 90024-1736

FOGELMAN, MORRIS JOSEPH, physician; b. Chgo., Feb. 27, 1923; s. Joseph and Tillie (Schwartz) F.; children—Evan, Joe, Margo. B.A., U. Ill., 1941; M.D., 1944, M.S., 1948. Diplomate: Am. Bd. Surgery. Intern Wayne County Gen. Hosp., Eloise, Mich., 1944-45; resident Parkland Hosp., Dallas, 1948-51; research fellow dept. clin. sci. U. Ill. Coll. Medicine, Chgo., 1947-48; asst. physiology U. Ill. Coll. Medicine, 1947-48; asst. in physiology and pharmacology Southwestern Med. Sch., Dallas, 1948-50; fellow in surgery Southwestern Med. Sch., 1948-52, instr. surgery, 1952-53, asst. prof. surgery, 1953, assoc. prof. surgery, 1953, prof. surgery, 1954-57, clin. prof. surgery, 1957—; practice medicine, specializing in surgery Dallas, 1952—; sr. attending surgeon Parkland Meml. Hosp., Dallas, 1953; cons. physician in surgery VA Hosp., Dallas, 1954; cons. surgeon Baylor Hosp., 1957, Parkland Meml. Hosp., 1952, Presbyn. Hosp., Dallas; pres. med. staff Presbyn. Hosp., U4Dallas, U71973, Morris J. Fogelman, M.D. & Assos., Dallas, 82, Windows & Walls, 1983. Author: Fluid Balance; Contbr. articles to various publs. Served to capt., M.C. AUS, 1945-47. Fellow Am. Assn. Surgery of Trauma; mem. Am. Assn. History of Medicine, A.C.S., AAAS, AMA, Dallas County Med. Soc., Dallas Soc. Gen. Surgeons, Am. Med. Writers Assn., N.Y. Acad. Sci., Tex. Med. Assn. Home and Office: 6921 Norway Pl Dallas TX 75230-4252

FOGELSON, DAVID LESLIE, psychiatrist, educator; b. Santa Monica, Calif., June 22, 1951. BA, U. Calif., Santa Cruz, 1972; MD, Harvard U., Boston, 1977. Diplomate Am. Bd. Psychiatry and Neurology. Internal medicine intern Faulkner Hosp., Jamaica Plain, Mass., 1977-78; resident in psychiatry Tufts/New Eng. Med. Ctr., Boston, 1978-79, UCLA, Belmont, Mass., 1979-81; pvt. practice, Santa Monica, 1982—; dir. Anxiety Disorders Clinic, UCLA, 1982-87, assoc. clin. prof. psychiatry, 1992—; pres. Pacific Psychopharmacology Rsch. Inst., Santa Monica, 1987—; bd. dirs. Obsessive Compulsive Disorders Found., New Haven, 1987-91. Contbr. articles to med. jours. Fellow Am. Psychiat. Assn.; mem. AMA. Office: 2730 Wilshire Blvd Ste 325 Santa Monica CA 90403

FOK, SHIU-KWAN, physiatrist; b. Macao, Portugal, May 2, 1943; came to U.S., 1970; s. Yat-Fung and Pui-Men Fok; m. Shawbong Fok, 1973. MD, Nat. Taiwan U., Taipei, 1969. Lic. physician, Maine, Calif. Intern Cath. Med. Ctr. of Bklyn. and Queens, N.Y.C., 1970-71; resident in physiatry and rehab. SUNY Downstate Med. Ctr./Kings County Hosp., Bklyn., 1971-72, UCLA/VA Sepulveda Med. Ctr., L.A., 1972-74; trainee, fellow in spinal cord injury VA Hosp., Long Beach, Calif., 1974-75; staff physiatrist Kaiser Permanente Hosp., Panorama City, Calif., 1976-87, Woodland Hills, Calif., 1988—; clin. lectr. dept. medicine UCLA Sch. Medicine, Sepulveda VA Hosp., L.A., 1985-90, asst. clin. prof., 1990-95, assoc. clin. prof., 1995—. Fellow Am. Bd. Electrodiagnostic Medicine, Am. Acad. Phys. Medicine and Rehab. Office: Kaiser Permanente Hosp & Med Group 5601 De Soto Ave Woodland Hills CA 91367

FOLEY, JAMES EDWARD, scientist, pharmaceutical company executive; b. Newburyport, Mass., Jan. 4, 1950; s. Everett James Foley and Jean Elizbeth (Wade) Doyle; m. Rosemary Ragozzine, June 3, 1972; children: Annarose, Ryan Seamus. BA in Biology, Merrimack Coll., 1972; PhD in Physiology, Dartmouth Med. Sch., 1976. Rsch. assoc. physiology and medicine Dartmouth Med. Sch., Hanover, N.H., 1976-77, postdoctoral fellow, 1977-79; guest scientist Panum Inst., Copenhagen, Denmark, 1979; lectr. physiology U. Århus, Denmark, 1979-80; rsch. asst., prof. medicine U. Tex., Phoenix, 1981; sr. staff fellow NIH/NIADDK, Phoenix, 1981-85; sr. scientist NIH, Phoenix, 1985-86; diabetes group leader Sandoz Rsch. Inst., E. Hanover, N.J., 1986, dir. diabetes, 1986-93, exec. dir. diabetes rsch., 1994-95, exec. dir. metabolic diseases rsch., 1995—. Contbr. articles to profl. jours. Mem. AAAS, Am. Diabetes Assn., N.Am. Assn. Study of Obesity, Am. Fedn. Clin. Rsch., Am. Jour. Physiology, European Assn. Study Diabetes, N.Y. Acad. Scis. Democrat. Roman Catholic. Home: 73 Seneca Lake Rd Sparta NJ 07871-2825 Office: Sandoz Pharms Corp RR 10 East Hanover NJ 07936

FOLEY, JOHN DONALD, physician; b. Rochester, N.Y., Jan. 2, 1944; s. J. Donald and Mary Margaret (Moran) F.; m. Patricia Susan Scaglione, June 6, 1970; children: Susan Mary, Karen Lynn. BS, U. Notre Dame, 1966; MD, SUNY, Buffalo, 1970. Diplomate Am. Bd. Pediats., Am. Bd. Adolescent Medicine. Intern in pediats. Buffalo (N.Y.) Children's Hosp., 1970-71, resident in pediats., 1971-73; asst. chief pediats. Eisenhower Army Med. Ctr., Augusta, Ga., 1973-82; chief of pediats. Martin Army Cmty. Hosp., Columbus, Ga., 1982-88; fellow in adolescent medicine William Beaumont Army Med. Ctr., El Paso, Tex., 1988-90, chief adolescent medicine, 1990-95; assoc. prof. pediats. Tex. Tech. U. Health Scis. Ctr., El Paso, 1995—. Contbr. articles to profl. jours. Fellow Am. Acad. Pediats., Soc. for Adolescent Medicine (treas. S.W. chpt. 1991—); mem. El Paso Pediat. Soc., Notre Dame Club of El Paso (treas. 1990—). Home: 5216 White Oak El Paso TX 79932 Office: Dept Pediats 4800 Alberta Ave El Paso TX 79905

FOLEY, KATHLEEN M., neurologist, educator, researcher; b. Flushing, N.Y., Jan. 28, 1944; d. Joseph Cyril and Catherine (Cribbin) Maher; m. Charles Thomas Foley, Aug. 10, 1968; children: Fritz, David. BA in Biology magna cum laude, St. John's U., N.Y.C., 1965, DSc (hon.), 1992; MD, Cornell U., 1969. Diplomate Am. Bd. Psychiatry and Neurology (examiner 1980—); lic. physician, N.Y. Intern, then resident in neurology The N.Y. Hosp., N.Y.C., 1969-74; asst. attending neurologist, neurology dept. Meml. Sloan-Kettering Cancer Ctr., N.Y.C., 1974-79, assoc. attending neurologist, 1979-88, chief-pain svc., 1982—, attending neurologist, 1988—; attending neurologist Manhattan (N.Y.) Eye & Ear Hosp., 1974-83; instr. in neurology, Med. Coll. Cornell U., N.Y.C., 1974-75, asst. prof., 1975-79, assoc. prof., 1979-89, assoc. prof. pharmacology, 1979-89, prof. neurology and neuroscience, 1989—, prof. clin. pharmacology, 1990—; rsch. assoc. lab. neurooncology Sloan-Kettering Inst. Cancer Rsch., N.Y.C., 1981-84; vis. asst. physician, cons. in neurology Rockefeller U. Hosp., 1975-79, vis. assoc. physician, 1979—; cons. Calvery Hosp., 1982—; assoc. mem. Meml. Sloan-Kettering Cancer Ctr., 1985-88, mem. 1988—. Editor Clinical Jour. Pain, 1985-87, Jour. Pain and Symptom Mgmt., 1987—, Palliative Medicine Jour., 1993—. Patient Svcs. Adv. Group, Am. Cancer Soc. Genetic Training grant NIH, 1970-71, Program for Pain Rsch. grant Bristol-Myers, 1988-92; Neuro-Oncology spl. fellow Meml. Sloan-Kettering Cancer Ctr., 1975-78; recipient Jr. Faculty award Am. Cancer Soc., 1975-78, Disting. Svc. award, 1992, Nat. Bd. award The Med. Coll. Pa., 1986, Willaim M. Witter award U. Calif. San Francisco, 1987, Annie Blount Storrs award Calvery Hosp., 1988, Balfour M. Mount award Am. Jour. Hospice Care, 1988, Disting. Oncologist award Dayton Oncology Soc., 1990, Tenth Barbara Bohen Pfeifer award Am. Italian Found. for Cancer Rsch., 1993; named Outstanding Women Scientist Women in Sci. Met. N.Y. Chpt., 1987, A. Soriano Jr. Meml. Lectr. The Andres Soriano Cancer Rsch. Found. Inc., 1992. Mem. AAAS, AMA (ad hoc adv. panel mgmt. chronic pain, DATTA reference panel), NAS (Inst. Medicine), Acad. Hospice Physicians, Am. Acad. Neurology (chmn. long range planning com. 1990—, scientific program com. 1990, and other coms.), Am. Fedn. Clin. Rsch., Am. Med. Womens Assn., Am. Neurological Assn. (mem. com. 1984-85, councilor 1984, 94), Am. Pain Soc. (bd. dirs. 1980-82, pres. 1984-85, bylaws com. 1986-87 long range planning task force 1989—), Am. Soc. Clin. Onocology (program com. 1991-92, com. on care at the end of life 1993—, and other coms.), Am. Soc. Clin. Pharmacology and Therapeutics, Assn. Rsch. in Nervous and Mental Diseases, Children's Hospice, Children's Hospice Internat., Cornell U. Med. Coll. Alumni Assn. (bd. dirs., nominating com.), Eastern Pain Assn. (John J. Bonica award 1986), Harvey Soc., Internat. Assn. Study Pain (councilor 1984-90, edn. com. 1986-93, and various coms.), N.Y. Acad. Scis. (USP adv. panel on neurology 1990—), Soc. for Neuroscience, Alpha Omega Alpha. Office: Meml Sloan-Kettering Cancer Ctr 1275 York Ave New York NY 10021-6007

FOLEY, MARY JOSEPHINE, nurse educator; b. Woburn, Mass., Feb. 22, 1936; d. Patrick Joseph and Catherine Agnes (Burke) F. BS magna cum laude, Boston Coll., 1957, MS, 1963; postgrad., NYU, 1969-71, Nova U., 1991. RN, Mass. Nurse Visiting Nurse Assn. Boston, 1957-61; instr. Simmons Coll., Boston, 1962-67, Holy Name Hosp. Sch. Nursing, Teaneck, N.J., 1979-81; asst. prof. SUNY, Buffalo, 1967-69; lectr. nursing Harlem Hosp. Sch. Nursing, N.Y.C., 1969-70; cons. test devel. Nat. League for Nursing, N.Y.C., 1971-78; asst. prof. Bunker Hill Community Coll., Boston, 1981-82, chmn. nurse edn. dept., 1982-88; dir. nursing edn. Youville Hosp. and Rehab. Ctr., Cambridge, Mass., 1988-92; assoc. prof. Mass. Bay Community Coll., Framingham, 1992-93; asst. div. dean for nursing Middlesex C.C., Lowell, Mass., 1993—; workshop cons. multiple choice testing, various cities, 1971-94. Mem. ANA, NLN (accreditation vis. 1987-88), Mass.-R.I. League for Nursing (v.p. 1989-93), St. Charles Alumnae Assn. (pres. 1962-63), Mother Cabrini Guild (v.p. 1960-61), Sigma Theta Tau. Democrat. Roman Catholic. Home: 13 Franklin St Woburn MA 01801-2937 Office: Middlesex Community Coll 44 Middle St Lowell MA 01852-1869

FOLINSBEE, LAWRENCE JOHN, physiologist, researcher; b. Vancouver, B.C., Can., Nov. 28, 1945; came to U.S., 1963; s. John Allan and Agnes Emily (Colpitts) F.; m. Jane Elizabeth Furchner, Aug. 24, 1969; children: John Alan, Emily Jane. BS, U. Oreg., 1967, MS, 1969; PhD, U. Calif., Davis, 1972. Rsch. assoc. U. Calif., Davis, 1969-72; postdoctoral fellow U. Toronto, Ont., Can., 1972-74, asst. prof., 1973-74; assoc. rsch. physiologist U. Calif., Santa Barbara, 1974-84; sr. scientist ABB Environ. Svcs., Chapel Hill, N.C., 1984-90; rsch. physiologist EPA, Research Triangle Park, N.C., 1990-95; chief environ. media assessment br. Nat. Ctr. Environ. Assessment, EPA, Research Triangle Park, N.C., 1995—; cons. Am. Petroleum Inst., Washington, 1983-84; mem. adv. bd. Electric Power Rsch. Inst., Palo Alto, Calif., 1987-93. Mem. editorial bd. Toxicology and Indsl. Health Jour., 1983-93; editor: Environmental Stress: Individual Human Adaptations, 1978; assoc. editor: Medicine and Science in Sports and Exercise; author chpts. in books; contbr. over 70 articles to profl. jours. Rsch. grantee NIH, EPA, Electric Power Rsch. Inst. Fellow Am. Coll. Sports Medicine; mem. Am. Physiol. Soc., Am. Thoracic Soc. Democrat. Episcopalian. Home: 227 Old Forest Creek Dr Chapel Hill NC 27514-5424 Office: EPA Nat Ctr Environ Assessment Mail Drop #52 Research Triangle Park NC 27711

FOLIO, LES ROGER, radiologist, military officer; b. Neubruecke, Germany, July 3, 1959; s. Joseph Roger and Martha (Pollard) F.; m. Jutta M. Frankfurter, June 5, 1993. BS in Radiologic Tech., Widener U., Chester, Pa., 1983; DO, Phila. Coll. Osteo. Medicine, 1987. Diplomate Am. Osteo. Bd. Radiology; lic. osteo. physician and surgeon, Pa., Calif., Utah; CPR provider; cert. flight instr., comml. pilot; designated FAA med. examiner. Intern Shenango Valley Med. Ctr., Farrell, Pa., 1987-88; resident Osteo. Med. Ctr. Phila., 1988-91; commd. USAF, 1989—, advanced through grades to maj.; chmn. radiology dept. 86th Med. Group, Ramstein AFB, Germany, 1991-93, 51st Med. Group, Osan AFB, Korea, 1993-94; dep. chief radiology dept. 77th Med. Group, McClellan AFB, Calif., 1994—; flight surgeon Army Aviation Support Group, Mather AFB, 1993-95; part-time phlebotomist Crozer Chester Med. Ctr., 1979-80; part-time radiologic technologist Osteo. Med. Ctr. Phila., 1982-83; med. technologist Hosp. of U. Pa., 1982. Contbr. articles to profl. jours. Vol. fireman East Whiteland Fire Co., 1977-79. Mem. AMA, Am. Assn. Osteo. Specialists, Am. Osteo. Assn., Am. Osteo. Coll. Radiology, Radiol. Soc. N.Am., Am. Soc. Radiologic Technologists. Home: 11258 Picture Rock Ct Gold River CA 95670 Office: 77th Medical Group/SGOAR 10535 Hospital Way Mather CA 95655-1200

FOLKENS, ALAN THEODORE, clinical and pharmaceutical microbiologist; b. Graceville, Minn., Oct. 26, 1936; s. Martin and Catherine (Laman) F.; m. Pearl June Putnam, July 29, 1961; children: Lee Alan, Kimberly Mae Folkens Anderson, Shannon Lee Folkens Tobin, Eric Martin. BA, Omaha U., 1962; PhD, U. S.D., 1971. Acting dir., dir. allied health professions Ill. State U., Normal, 1971-73; chief clin. microbiologist Peoria (Ill.) Tazewell Pathology Group, 1973-84; lab. dir. Delta Med. Ctr., Greenville, Miss., 1984-85; R&D clin. and pharm. microbiologist Alcon Labs., Inc., Ft. Worth, 1985—, assoc. dir., 1995—; vis. faculty E. Tenn. State U., Johnson City, 1978-86; adj. faculty U. Ill. Peoria Sch. Medicine, 1980-84, Ill. State U., Normal, 1973-84, U. N. Tex., Denton, 1992-94; presenter symposium in field. Contbr. chpt. to book and articles to profl. jours. Bd. edn., past pres. Blessed Sacrament Sch., Morton, Ill., 1978-81; chmn. sickle cell anemia screening Ill. State U., Normal, 1972; chmn. Tootsie Roll drive for retarded children, K.C., Morton, 1975. Trainee NIH, 1967. Mem. Am. Soc. Microbiology, Am. Soc. Clin. Pathology, Am. Acad. Microbiology (diplomate), Assn. Rsch. in Vision and Ophthalmology, Assn. Rsch. to Prevent Blindness, N.Y. Acad. Scis., Phi Sigma, Sigma Xi. Independent. Roman Catholic.

FOLKMAN, MOSES JUDAH, surgeon; b. Cleve., Feb. 24, 1933; s. Jerome D. and Bessie Folkman. BA, Ohio State U., 1953; MD, Harvard U., 1957; DSc honoris causa, Mt. Sinai Sch. Medicine, 1996. Intern, then asst. resident in surgery Mass. Gen. Hosp., Boston, 1957-60, sr. asst. resident in surgery, 1962-64, chief resident, 1964-65; chief resident in pediatric surgery Phila. Children's Hosp., 1969; instr. surgery Harvard U. Med. Sch., 1965-66, assoc. in surgery, 1967, prof. surgery, 1967—, Julia Dyckman Andrus prof. pediatric surgery, 1968—, prof. anatomy and cellular biology, 1989—; asst. surgeon Boston City Hosp., 1965-66; assoc. dir. Sears Surg. Lab., 1966-67; sr. surgeon Children's Hosp. Med. Ctr., Boston, 1968—. With M.C., USN, 1960-62. Recipient Career Devel. award NIH, 1966, Lila Gruber award Am. Acad. Dermatology, 1974, Gairdner Found. Internat. award, Toronto, Can., 1991, Christopher Columbus Commemorative Sci. medal U.S. Congress/NIH, Wolf award Wolf Found., Jerusalem, 1992, Lucian award Royal Coll. Surgeons Can., 1993, Steiner award Josef Steiner Found., Switzerland, 1994, Bristol-Myers Cancer Rsch. award, 1995. Fellow ACS (Sheen award 1989); mem. NAS, Am. Coll. Surgeons, Am. Surg. Assn., Assn. Acad. Surgery, Soc. U. Surgeons, Surg. Biology Club I, Am. Acad. Pediatrics, Allen O. Whipple Soc., Am. Pediatric Surg. Assn., N.Y. Acad. Scis., Mass. Med. Soc. Office: 300 Longwood Ave Boston MA 02115-5724

FOLLEZOU, JEAN-YVES, oncologist; b. Guingamp, France, July 8, 1948; s. Emile and Marie (Offret) F. Grad., Pitie Salpetriere, Paris, 1971, 77, Inst. Pasteur, Paris, 1974; PhD, Inst. Pasteur, Paris, 1992. Lic. MD. Intern Hosp. Assistance Pub., Paris, 1971-76; chief clin. U. Paris, 1977-85, maitre de conference, 1986; prin. Hosp. Salpetriere, Paris, 1987—; v.p. U. Paris 6, 1979-80; nat. bd. Health Ministry, France, 1982-86; nat. coun. Inserm, 1983-87, 91-95; nat. com. CNRS, 1987-91; gen. dir. Internat. Ctr. Lutte Against AIDS in Africa. Author: Cancer Chemotherapy, 1980—; contbr. 200 articles to profl. jours.; reviewer med. jour., 1980-96. Pres., Med. Help to Cambodia, Paris, 1979, France-S.U. Health Commn., 1988. Recipient medal, Town of Villejuif, 1980. Mem. N.Y. Acad. Scis., Amis de Charles Bukowski Club (pres. 1985), Amis Louis Aragon (adv. coun.). Home: 13 avenue de la Republique, Villejuif 94800, France Office: Hosp de la Salpetriere, 47 Bd de L'Hopital, Paris 75013, France

FOLTS, DAVID JACOB, occupational therapist, consultant; b. Buffalo, Sept. 19, 1958; s. Roger Allen and Eleanor Margaret (Chimeleski) F. BS cum laude, U. Buffalo, 1984. Occupational therapy supr. Western Res. Care System, Youngstown, 1987—; dir. occupational therapy Belmont Pines Hosp., 1990—; dir. Rehab. Med. Aid Inc., 1991—. Author: chpt. Social Skills Training, 1987, Treatment of the Chemically Dependent, 1988, Work Programs, 1993, Ergonomics, 1993, Industrial Rehabilitation Marketing, 1993. Choral mem. Youngstown Symphony Chorus, 1988—. Mem. Am. Occupational Therapy Assn., Ohio Occupational Therapy Assn. Home: 1466 Marlane Dr Girard OH 44420-1466

FOMBERSTEIN, BARRY JOSEPH, internist; b. N.Y.C., June 1, 1951; s. Louis and Golde (Feiner) F.; m. Deborah Sue Chayet, Oct. 12, 1980; 1 child, Kenneth Marc. BA, CUNY, 1973; MD, Albert Einstein Coll. Medicine, Bronx, 1976. Diplomate Am. Bd. Internal Medicine. Intern L.I. Jewish, 1976-77, resident, 1977-79, fellowship in rheumatology, 1979-81; chief divsn. rheumatology St. John's Episcopal Hosp., Far Rockaway, N.Y., 1983-92; chief rheumatology Our Lady of Mercy Med. Ctr., Bronx, 1992—, assoc. program dir., 1992-96, program dir., internal medicine, 1996—. Fellow ACP, Am. Coll. Rheumatology; mem. Phi Beta Kappa. Office: Our Lady of Mercy Med Ctr 600 E 233rd St Bronx NY 10466-2697

FONG, CAROLYN MAE, nursing educator; b. San Francisco; d. Albert and Mary Yee Jong; m. Wallace Fong; children: Tony, Suzy. BS, U. Calif., San Francisco, 1973, MS, 1974; PhD, U. Calif., Berkeley, 1984. RN, Calif.; cert. PNP, PALS. Asst. prof. U. Calif., San Francisco, 1974-78; nursing rsch. fellow U. Calif., Berkeley, 1980-84; assoc. prof. U. San Francisco, 1984-86; dir. health scis. San Joaquin Delta Coll., Stockton, Calif., 1986-88; prof. San Francisco State U., 1988—. Contbr. articles to profl. jours. Fulbright scholar U. Glasgow, Scotland, 1996. Mem. ANA, Nat. League Nursing, Transcultural Nursing Soc., Sigma Theta Tau. Home: 4465 Pinon Ct Concord CA 94521-4227

FONSECA, RAYMOND J., dental medicine educator. Prof. pathology and surgery Sch. Dentistry, U. Mich., until 1989; dean Sch. Dental Medicine, U. Pa., Phila., 1989—. Office: U Pa Sch Dental Medicine Philadelphia PA 19104*

FONTWIT, KATHRYN JACQUELINE, physician associate; b. Ingelwood, Calif., Oct. 17, 1956; d. Hyman and Elisa (Essrig) F. BA with honors, U. Calif., Santa Cruz, 1981; Physician Asst., Yale U., 1986. Cert. physician asst. Rsch. support specialist dept. reproductive endocrinology Cornell U., Ithaca, N.Y., 1981-84; physician asst. occupational medicine Danbury (Conn.) Hosp., 1986-87; clin. mgr., physician asst. urgent visit dept. Yale U. Health Svcs., New Haven, 1987—; sr. proctor NCCPA Cert. Exam. Yale U. Physician Asst. Program, New Haven, 1990-96, sr proctor physician asst. students in ambulatory rotation, 1989-96, clin. instr. phys. exam., 1993-95; summer intern NIH, Bethesda, Md., 1979. Fellow Am. Acad. Physician Assts.; mem. Conn. Assn. Physician Assts. Office: Yale U 17 Hillhouse Ave New Haven CT 06517

FOODEN, MYRA, psychologist, consultant, educator; b. N.Y.C., June 20, 1926; d. MAx and Bess (Cohen) Samit; m. Richard Fooden, Apr. 16, 1950; children: Madeleine (dec.), Bart, Melissa. BA, Hunter Coll., 1947; MS, Adelphi U., 1967; PhD, Yeshiva U., 1974. Lic. psychologist, N.Y. Assoc. prof. St. John's U., Jamaica, N.Y., 1969-70, 87-89; assoc. prof. St. John's U., 1987-88; asst. prof. Lehman Coll. CUNY, Bronx, 1970-74; asst. prof. Empire State Coll. SUNY, Old Westbury, N.Y., 1974-81; pvt. practice Great Neck, N.Y., 1975—; assoc. prof. L.I. U., Bklyn., 1980-86. Editor: Second X Women's Health, 1984; contbr. articles to profl. jours. NDEA fellow, 1971-73. Fellow Inst. Rational Living; mem. APA, Eastern Psychol. Assn.

FOON, KENNETH ALAN, oncologist; b. Detroit, Mar. 7, 1947; s. Alvin Nathan and Shirley Louise (Weiss) F.; m. Robecca Ann Garrett, Dec. 30, 1977; children: Melissa, Michele, Jeremy. BS, Wayne State U., 1968, MD, 1972. Diplomate Am. Bd. Internal Medicine, Am. Bd. Hematology, Am. Bd. Med. Oncology. Asst. prof. UCLA, 1980-81; head clin. investagion Nat. Cancer Inst. Biol. Response Modification Program, Frederick, Md., 1981-85; assoc. chief divsn. hematology & oncology U. Mich., Ann Arbor, 1985-87; chief clin. immunolgy, prof. Roswell Park Cancer Inst., Buffalo, 1987-91; assoc. dir. rsch. Green Cancer Ctr. Scripps Clinic & Rsch. Found., La Jolla, Calif., 1991-93; dir. Markey Cancer Ctr., chief divsn. hematology & oncology, prof. U. Ky., Lexington, 1993—. Assoc. editor Cancer Rsch., 1990—; editl. bd. Clin. Immunology, 1992—, Jour. Immunotherapy, 1982—. Fellow ACP; mem. Am. Soc. Hematology, Am. Soc. Clin. Oncology, Am. Assn. Cancer Rsch., Soc. Biol. therapy, Alpha Omega Alpha. Office: U Ky Markey Cancer Ctr 800 Rose St Rm 140 Lexington KY 40536

FOOS, K. MICHAEL, biology educator; b. Bellfontaine, Ohio, Jan. 16, 1943; s. Kenneth Boyd and Alberta (Storms) F.; m. Karen A. Adams, June 25, 1966 (div. 1990); 1 child, David Michael. BS in Edn., Ohio State U., 1965, MS, 1970, PhD, 1972. Sci. tchr. Ridgemont High Sch., Ridgeway, Ohio, 1965-66, Bowling Green (Ohio) High Sch., 1966-67, Jefferson Local Schs., Gahanna, Ohio, 1967-70; teaching assoc. Ohio State U., Columbus, 1970-72, vis. asst. prof., 1972-73; asst. prof. Lake Erie Coll., Painesville, Ohio, 1973-83; prof. Ind. U. East, Richmond, 1983—, div. chmn., 1985-95; program dir. Cleveland Clinic Lake Erie Coll., 1976-78. Editor Jour. of Coll. Sci. Teaching, 1988-91; contbr. articles to profl. jours. Mem. Mycological Soc. Am., British Mycological Soc., Nat. Sci. Tchrs. Assn., Soc. Coll. Sci. Tchrs., Nat. Assn. Biology Tchrs., Ind. Acad. Sci., Sigma Xi. Office: Ind U East 2325 Chester Blvd Richmond IN 47374-1220

FOOS, PAUL WILLIAM, psychologist, educator; b. Fremont, Ohio, Jan. 5, 1946; s. Clarence A. and Norma Ruth (Halm) F.; m. M. Cherie Clark, Sept. 7, 1977; 1 child, Arlo Clark-Foos. BA, Bowling Green State U., 1969, MA, 1973, PhD, 1975. Chairperson psychology Fla. Internat. U., Miami, 1985-91, U. N.C., Charlotte, 1991—. Author: Data Gathering, 1986; contbr. articles to profl. jours. Mem. Am. Psychol. Assn., Am. Psychol. Soc., Psychonomic Soc., Southeastern Psychol. Assn., Psi Chi, Sigma Xi. Home: 10709 Downpatrick Pl Charlotte NC 28262-9118 Office: U North Carolina Dept Psychology Charlotte NC 28223

FOOTE, WARREN EDGAR, neuroscientist, psychologist, educator; b. Boston, Nov. 5, 1935; s. Warren Edgar and Edith Irene (Landry) F.; B.A., Hamilton Coll., 1958; M.A., Boston U., 1960; Ph.D., Tufts U., 1965; m. Cynthia Sue Hall, July 21, 1973; children: Pamela Fowler, Sarah Canby, Julia Landry, Christopher Warren. Research assoc. Harvard U. Med. Sch., 1966-67, vis. asst. prof. psychology, 1970-73, asst. prof., 1974-83, assoc. prof., 1983—; USPHS postdoctoral fellow Yale, 1967-69; research scientist Norwich (Conn.) State Hosp., 1969-70; sr. Fulbright scholar Max-Planck Inst., Munich, Germany, 1973-74; assoc. psychologist Mass. Gen. Hosp., Boston, 1974—, psychologist, 1984-95, sr. psychologist, 1995—; cons. Gen. Foods Corp., 1970-74, Neurotech Corp., 1987-88. Served with M.C., AUS, 1959-60. Recipient McCurdy prize Mass. Soc. Research in Psychiatry, 1962; sr. Fulbright fellow, 1973-74; Nat. Inst. Neurol. Disease and Stroke grantee, 1974-77; NIMH grantee, 1970-73; Nat. Eye Inst. grantee, 1979—; Wayland Pub. Sch. Found. advisor, 1982—; Nat. Inst. Communicative Disorders and Stroke grantee, 1983—. Mem. AAAS, N.Y. Acad. Scis., Soc. Neurosci., Am. Psychol. Assn., Sigma Xi. Club: Harvard (Boston). Contbr. articles, revs. to profl. jours. Home: 5 Hilltop Park Wilbraham MA 01095-1753 Office: Mass Gen Hosp PO Box 70 Boston MA 02114

FORAND, ANGELA QUANTE, clinical psychologist, health administrator; b. Savannah, Ga., Jan. 25, 1956. BA, U. Ga., 1978, MS, 1981, PhD, 1984. Lic. clin. psychologist, S.C. Rsch. coord. psychology dept. U. Ga., Athens, 1982-84, instr. psychology dept., 1984-85; intern Psychology Internship Consortium, Albany, N.Y., 1985-86; staff psychologist William S. Hall Psychiat. Inst., Columbia, S.C., 1986-93, program dir. Dirs. Residential Treatment Ctr., 1993—; asst. prof. sch. medicine U. S.C., Columbia, 1989—; cons. New Hope Midlands, Columbia, 1989—. Bd. dirs. Ebenezer Luth. Ch., Columbia, 1990. Mem. APA, S.C. Psychol. Assn. (team leader Columbia chpt. 1990), Southeastern Psychol. Assn. Lutheran. Office: WS Hall Psychiatric Inst PO Box 202 Columbia SC 29202-0202

FORASTÉ, PAUL FRANCIS, ophthalmologist; b. N.Y.C., Nov. 23, 1940; s. Paul Louis and Anita (Schonbachler) F.; m. Annette Lareau, Apr. 2, 1943; children: Stephen, John, Laura, Michael, Kimberly. AB cum laude, Coll. Holy Cross, 1962; MD, Cornell U., 1967. Diplomate Am. Bd. Ophthalmology. Intern Rush Presbyn.-St. Luke's Med. Ctr., Chgo., 1967-68; resident in ophthalmology New York Hosp.-Cornell Med. Ctr., N.Y.C., 1970-73; pvt. practice Hyannis, Mass., 1973—; med. staff Cap Code Hosp., Hyannis, 1973—, chief of ophthalmology, 1990-93; mem. New Eng. Eye Ctr., Boston, 1996—. Capt. USAF, 1968-70. Fellow ACS, Am. Acad. Ophthalmology, Mass. Med. Soc.; mem. Mass. Soc. Eye Physicians and Surgeons, New Eng. Ophthal. Soc., Hyannis Yacht Club. Office: 100 Camp St Hyannis MA 02601

FORASTE, ROLAND, psychiatrist; b. N.Y.C., Mar. 1, 1938; s. Paul Foraste and Anita Schonbachler. AB honors cum laude, Coll. Holy Cross, 1960; cert. neurology, U. London, 1965; MD, SUNY, Downstate, 1965. Med. intern Jefferson Hosp., Phila., 1965-66; resident in psychiatry N.Y. Hosp., 1966-69, resident in child psychiatry, 1968-71, chief resident in adolescent psychiatry, 1970-71, asst. attending psychiatrist, 1973-86; med. dir. psychiatry U.S. Healthcare and Total Health, N.Y.C., 1986-90, cons., 1990—; clin. instr. psychiatry Cornell Med. Coll., 1967-73, clin. asst. prof. psychiatry, 1973-86; attending physician Gracie Sq. Hosp., N.Y.C., 1969—, Rye (N.Y.) Hosp. Ctr. Co-author: (audiotext) The Drug Syndrome and the Teacher, 1971; co-editor, contbr. Biology Jour. of Coll. of Holy Cross, 1957-58. Benefit chmn. Hosp. Audiences, Inc., N.Y.C., 1984; benefit com. Cultural Coun. Found., N.Y.C., 1984-86, Big Apple Circus, 1984-86, Five Men Named Moe, 1992; mem. Met. Mus. Art, Mus. Modern Art. Recipient Physicians Recognition award AMA. Fellow Am. Soc. for Adolescent Psychiatry (asst. continuing med. edn. officer 1989-90, continuing med. edn. officer 1990—); mem. Am. Acad. Child and Adolescent Psychiatry, N.Y. Coun. Child and Adolescent Psychiatry, N.Y. Soc. for Adolescent Psychiatry (bd. dirs. 1987-88, sec. 1988-90, pres.-elect 1990-91, pres. 1991-93, ex-officio 1993—), Am. Psychiat. Assn., Flying Physicians Assn. (instrument rated), N.Y. Hosp.-Cornell Med. Ctr. Alumni Assn., Aircraft Owners and Pilots Assn., Greenwich Boat and Yacht Club, Westchester Flying Club, Porsche Club Am., Westchester Country Club (mem. nominating com. 1987-88, membership com. 1987-88, 90-91, entertainment com. 1987-88, 90-93), U.S. Ski Assn., Wintergreen Club (dir.-trustee 1990-93, chmn. entertainment com. 1990-96), KC. Republican. Roman Catholic. Home and Office: 623 Steamboat Rd Greenwich CT 06830-7140

FORBES, GILBERT BURNETT, physician, educator; b. Rochester, N.Y., Nov. 9, 1915; s. Gilbert DeLeverance and Lillian Augusta (Burnett) F.; m. Grace Moehlman, July 8, 1939; children: Constance Ann (Mrs. Joseph F. Citro), Susan Young (Mrs. William A. Martin). B.A., U. Rochester, 1936, M.D., 1940. Intern Strong Meml. Hosp., Rochester, 1940-41; resident St. Louis Children's Hosp., 1941-43; practice medicine, specializing in pediatrics Los Alamos, 1946-47; instr. pediatrics Sch. Medicine, Washington U., St. Louis, 1943-46; asst. prof. Sch. Medicine, Washington U., 1947-50; prof. pediatrics, chmn. dept. Southwestern Med. Sch., Dallas, 1950-53; assoc. prof. pediatrics Sch. Medicine, U. Rochester, 1953-57, prof., 1957-68, prof. pediatrics, prof. radiation biology, 1968—, Alumni Disting. Service prof. pediatrics, 1978—, chmn. faculty council, 1969-70, acting co-chmn. dept. pediatrics, 1974-76; cons. Nat. Inst. Child Health and Human Devel.; mem. sci. adv. com. Nutrition Found., 1963-66; mem. Nat. Council on Radiation Protection; mem. com. infant nutrition, com. dietary allowances NRC, 1960-63; vis. research fellow U. Oxford, Eng., 1970-71. Author: Human Body Composition, 1987; assoc. editor: Am. Jour. Diseases Childhood, 1964-72; chief editor, 1973-82; asso. editor: Nutrition Revs, 1961-71; editor Pediatric Nutrition Handbook, 1985; contbr. numerous articles to profl. jours. Recipient Research Career award USPHS, NIH, 1962—, Borden award Am. Acad. Pediatrics, 1964, Alumni award to faculty U. Rochester, 1975; Albert David Kaiser award, Rochester Acad. Medicine, 1979. Mem. AAAS, AMA, Am. Pediatric Soc. (coun., v.p. 1975-76, John Howland award 1992), Soc.

Pediatric Research (past pres.), Am. Acad. Pediatrics (com. on nutrition 1974-80), U. Rochester Med. Alumni Assn. (past pres., Gold medal 1982), Rotary, Sigma Xi, Alpha Omega Alpha, Theta Chi. Home: 2021 Westfall Rd Rochester NY 14618-3113 Office: Univ of Rochester Dept of Pediatrics 601 Elmwood Ave Rochester NY 14642-0001

FORBES, JAMES, biology educator; b. Yonkers, N.Y., July 9, 1910; s. James and Annie Matheson (Innes) F.; m. Matilda Sophia Frank, June 19, 1937; 1 child, James. B.S., Fordham U., 1932, M.S., 1934, Ph.D., 1936. Mem. faculty Fordham U., N.Y.C., 1936—, prof. biology, 1966-79, emeritus, 1979—. Contbr. numerous articles to sci. publs. Assoc. editor, editor Jour. N.Y. Entomol. Soc., 1958-70. Served to capt. U.S. Army, 1943-47, PTO. Recipient numerous awards Fordham U. Mem. N.Y. Entomol. Soc., Entomol. Soc. Am., Council Biology Editors (treas. 1965-71), Sigma Xi. Presbyterian. Avocations: reading; music; gardening; travel. Address: 65 Shaw Dr Merrick NY 11566-1718

FORBES, MILTON LESTER, biology educator, writer; b. Aruba, Netherlands Antilles, Dec. 14, 1930; came to the U.S., 1945; s. Oliver Ferdinand and Hazel Alma (Walker) F.; m. Marcia June Boyer, Sept. 16, 1951; children: Pamella Diane Forbes Sullivan, James Alan, Stanley Lawrence, Brian Wayne. BA in Edn., U. No. Iowa, Cedar Falls, 1952, MA in Edn., 1953; PhD in Biol. Sci., Fla. State U., Tallahassee, 1962. Instr. biology Burlington (Iowa) High Sch., 1953-56, Ill. State U., Normal, 1956-57; assoc. prof. biology F. T. Nicholls State U., Thibodaux, La., 1960-63, Lamar U., Beaumont, Tex., 1963-70; prof. sci. U. of the Virgin Islands, St. Croix, 1970-91; writer Glenwood, Iowa, 1991—. Author: The Messiah, 1989, Out of the Mists of Time: Who Wrote the Bible and Why, 1992; contbr. articles to profl. jours. NSF grad. fellow, 1958-59. Mem. AAAS, Sigma Xi. Mem. Unitarian Universalist Ch.

FORCE, ELIZABETH ELMA, retired pharmaceutical executive, consultant; b. Phila., Sept. 6, 1930; d. Harry Elgin and Loretta G. (Werner) F. BA, Temple U., 1952; postgrad., U. Pa., 1965-67; MPh, George Washington U., 1972, PhD, 1973. Cons. sr. scientist Booz-Allen Hamilton, Bethesda, Md., 1967-68; rsch. cons. scientist GEOMET, Inc., Rockville, Md., 1968-70; profl. assoc. div. med. scis. NAS-NRC, Washington, 1970-74; mgr. clin. adminstrn. dept. clin. rsch. and devel. Wyeth Labs., Radnor, Pa., 1974-77; exec. dir. regulatory affairs Merck Sharp and Dohme Rsch. Labs., West Point, Pa., 1977-88; cons. Clin. Regulatory Systems, Sarasota, Fla., 1988-91; asst. professorial lectr. epidemiology and environ. health Sch. Medicine George Washington U., Washington, 1972-74; vis. assoc. prof. cmty. health and preventive medicine Med. Coll. Jefferson U., Phila., 1981-83. Editor Clin. Rsch. Practice and Drug Regulatory Affairs, 1983-85, Drug Info. Jour., 1984-88; contbr. 60 articles to profl. jours. Pres. Women's Resource Ctr., Sarasota, 1992-94, Sterling Lakes Owners Assn., Boynton Beach, 1996—; pres., bd. dirs. Siesta Tower Condominium Assn., Sarasota, 1990-92; vice chmn. Com. for Minority Contracts, Sarasota County, 1991; chmn. adv. coun. bd. trustees Ringling Mus. of Art, 1991-95, Coun. on Violence, Sarasota County, 1994. Ruhland Pub. Health fellow George Washington U. Sch. Medicine, 1971-73. Mem. Drug Info. Assn. (pres. 1986-87, Outstanding Dir. award 1985). Office: 7555 Northport Dr Boynton Beach FL 33437

FORD, ALLISON MILLER, physician; b. Saginaw, Mich., Sept. 23, 1961; d. Robert Frazier and Kay Wells (Miller) F. BS, Mich. State U., 1984, DO, 1989. Intern Pontiac (Mich.) Osteopathic Hosp., 1989—. Republican. Episcopalian. Home: 8221 San Simon Odessa TX 79765 Office: Westwood 4214 Andrews Hwy Midland TX 79703

FORD, ANN SUTER, family nurse practitioner, health planner; b. Mineola, N.Y., Oct. 31, 1943; d. Robert M. and Jennette (Van Derzee) Suter; m. W. Scott Ford, 1964; children: Tracey, Karin, Stuart. RN, White Plains Hosp. Sch. Nursing (N.Y.), 1964; BS in Nursing with high distinction, U. Ky., 1967; MS in Health Planning, Fla. State U., 1971, PhD, 1975; MSN, Fla. State U., 1992. Nurse, U. Ky. Med. Ctr., 1964-65, Tallahassee Meml. Hosp., 1968-69; guest lectr. health planning dept. urban and regional planning Fla. State U., Tallahassee, 1973-76, health planner and research assoc., 1974-76, vis. asst. prof., 1976-77, asst. prof. and dir. health planning splty., 1977-83, assoc. prof., 1982-83; health care analyst and policy cons., 1983-86; med., health program analyst Aging and Adult Svcs. for State of Fla., 1986-90; coordinator Fla. Alzheimer's Disease Initiative, 1986-90; family nurse practitioner Capital Area Physicians' Svcs., 1993-94; assoc. prof. nursing Fla. A&M U., 1994—; bd. dirs. Regional Fla. Lung Assn., 1986-91; mem. exec. com. human services and social planning tech. dept. Am. Inst. Planners, 1977-83. Author: The Physician's Assistant: A National and Local Analysis, 1975; contbr. numerous articles on health edn. and health planning to profl. jours.; contbr. chpts. to books; author rsch. reports. USPHS grantee, 1965-67; HEW grantee, 1978; Univ. fellow Fla. State U., 1971-72; recipient Am. Inst. Planners' Student award, 1975. Mem. Am. Planning Assn. (charter mem. human services and social planning tech. dept. 1976-83, chmn. health planning session Oct. 1978, 79, health policy liaison 1979-83, author assn. health policy statement), Am. Health Planning Assn., Fla. Nurses Assn., Phi Kappa Phi, Sigma Theta Tau. Home: 2602 Cline St Tallahassee FL 32312-3110

FORD, CHARLES VIRGIL, psychiatrist, author; b. Delano, Calif., Oct. 21, 1937; s. Clifford and Thelma May (Martin) F.; m. Edith Lillian Engel, July 26, 1961 (div. 1973); children: Charles Martin, Scott Timothy; m. Pamela Elaine Parker, Oct. 19, 1985; children: Katherine Evans, John Parker, Marc Barrett. BA in Zoology, U. Calif., L.A., 1959, MD, 1963. Diplomate Am. Bd. Psychiatry and Neurology. Head physician psychiat. liaison svc. Harbor Gen. Hosp., Torrance, Calif., 1969-77, dir. psychiat. residency tng. program, 1973-77; dir. geopsychiat. in-patient unit U. Calif., L.A., 1977-79; prof. psychiatry Vanderbilt U., Nashville, 1979-85; prof. psychiatry Med. Sch. UCLA, 1985-86; prof. psychiatry, vice chmn. edn. dept. U. Ark. Med. Scis., Little Rock, 1986-90; prof. psychiatry U. Ala., Birmingham, 1990—. Author: The Somatizing Disorders, 1983, LIes! Lies!! LIes!!!, 1996; co-author: books: asst. editor: Psychiat. Medicine, 1983-93, Psychosomatics 1985—; contbr. articles to profl. jours.. Lt. comdr. USN, 1964-69. NIMH grantee, 1975-77, 79-82. Fellow Am. Psychiat. Assn., Am. Coll. Psychiatrists, Acad. Psychosomatic Medicine (exec. coun. 1986, v.p. 1993-94, pres.-elect 1994-95, pres. 1995-96), Ala. Psychiat. Soc. (pres.-elect 1996-97). Republican. Office: U Ala Dept Psychiatry UAB Sta Birmingham AL 35233

FORD, EDWARD GREGG, surgery and pediatrics educator, pediatric surgeon; b. San Antonio, Sept. 14, 1953; s. Edward George and Eleonore Sabina (Büehl) F.; m. Karen Rae Johnson, Dec. 13, 1982; children: Edward Grant, Brittiney Rae, Austin Paul, Sean Christian. BA in Biology, S.W. Tex. State U., 1976, MS in Physiology and Biochemistry, 1982; MD, U. Tex., Houston, 1982. Diplomate Am. Bd. Surgery, Am. Bd. Pediatric Surgery, Am. Bd. Surg. Critical Carel; cert. BCLS provider, ACLS provider, advanced trauma life support inst., pre-hosp. trauma life support instr. Intern in family practice S.W. Meml. Hosp.-U. Tex. Affiliated Hosps., Houston, 1982-83; intern in surgery U. Tex. Affiliated Hosps.-U. Tex. Health Sci. Ctr., Houston, 1983-84, resident in surgery, 1984-88, instr. surgery, 1987-88; fellow in pediatric surgery Children's Hosp. L.A.-U. So. Calif., 1988-90; assoc. prof. surgery, dir. div. pediatric surgery Tulane U. Sch. Medicine, New Orleans, 1993-94, dir. program in extracorporeal membrane oxygenation, 1993-94; staff pediatric surgeon dept. surgery Scott and White Clinic and Hosps., Temple, Tex., 1994—; prof. surgery and pediatrics Tex. A&M U. Sch. Medicine, College Station, 1994—; clin. asst. prof. surgery Uniformed Svcs. Health Scis. U., Bethesda, Md., 1991-93, U. South Ala. Sch. Medicine, Mobile, 1992-93; cons. to surgeon gen, for pediatric surgery USAF, 1991-93; co-prin. investigator Pediatric Oncology Group, New Orleans, 1990-94, Temple, 1994—; presenter in field; mem. active cons. staff VA Med. Ctr., Biloxi, Miss., 1990-93; mem. active staff Tulane U. Med. Ctr. Hosp., 1993-94, Children's Hosp., New Orleans, 1993-94, Highland Park Hosp., Covington, La., 1994; mem. vis. staff Med. Ctr. La. at New Orleans, 1993-94; mem. provisional staff Huey P. Long Med. Ctr., Pineville, La., 1994, St. Tammany Parish Hosp., Covington, 1994; assoc. mem. dept. surgery Univ. Hosp., New Orleans, 1994. Editor: (with R. Andrassy) Pediatric Trauma: Assessment and Management, 1994; mem. editl. bd. Nutrition in Surg. Mgmt., 1988-90; abstractor Annals Surgery for Jour. Pediatric Surgery; contbr. numerous articles and abstracts to med. jours., chpts. to books. Officer M.C., USAF, 1990-93. Grantee Norwich Eaton Pharms., Inc., 1986, 87, NIH, 1987, Office Surgeon Gen. USAF, 1992, Ross Labs., 1994. Fellow ACS, Am. Acad. Pediatrics, Am. Coll. Nutrition; mem. Assn. for Acad. Surgery, Am. Assn. Surgerry of Trauma, Southwestern Surg. Congress, Soc. Critical Care Medicine, Am. Soc. Parenteral and Enteral Nutrition (pres. Miss. chpt. 1992-93), Soc. Air Force Clin. Surgeons, S.J. Dudrick Surg. Found., Tex. Med. Assn. Home: 410 N Main St Belton TX 76508 Office: Scott and White Clinic Dept Surgery 2401 S 31st St Temple TX 76508

FORD, GAIL W., nursing educator, family nurse practitioner; b. Charleston, S.C., Nov. 26, 1943; d. Lee Roy and Cecil (Daws) Watkins; m. Glenn Wells Dickson, Jr., Sept. 2, 1967 (div. Mar. 1987); 1 child, Glenn Wells III; m. John P. Ford, Jr., Nov. 26, 1994. BS in Nursing, U. S.C., 1966; MN in Nursing, Emory U., 1971, EdD in Health Edn. Adminstrn., 1990; cert. FNP, U. S.C., 1995. Cert. clin. specialist in med.-surg. nursing. Staff nurse VA Hosp., Charleston, S.C., 1966-67; staff nurse ICU S.C. Bapt. Hosp., Columbia, S.C., 1967; instr. Crafts-Farrow State Hosp., Columbia, 1967-68; instr. nursing Piedmont Hosp. Nursing, Atlanta, 1968-69; instr. U. S.C. Coll. Nursing, Columbia, 1971-74, asst. prof., 1974—; pres. Dickson & Assocs. Med.-Nursing Legal Cons., Columbia, 1984—; researcher Breast Cancer Screening, Columbia, 1984—. Reviewer video-ednl. Right to Die, 1989. Grantee Am. Cancer Soc., 1988, Alpha Xi, Sigma Theta Tau, 1988. Mem. Am. Nurses Assn., Oncology Nursing Soc., S.C. Nurses' Assn. (chmn legis. com. 1971—), Sigma Theata Tau (chmn. bylaws 1987-89), Crepe Myrtle Garden Club (pres. elect 1989—). Episcopalian. Home: 23 Swan Lake Dr Sumter SC 29150-4740 Office: Tucomey Family Health Ctr 100 W Liberty St Sumter SC 29150

FORD, GORDON BUELL, JR., English language, linguistics, and medieval studies educator, author, retired hospital industry financial management executive; b. Louisville, Sept. 22, 1937; s. Gordon Buell Sr. and Rubye (Allen) F. AB summa cum laude in Classics, Medieval Latin, and Sanskrit, Princeton U., 1959; AM in Classical Philology and Linguistics, Harvard U., 1962, PhD in Linguistics, 1965; postgrad., U. Oslo, 1962-64, U. Sofia, Bulgaria, 1963, U. Uppsala, Sweden, 1963-64, U. Stockholm, 1963-64, U. Madrid, 1963. Yeager, Ford, and Warren Found. Disting. prof. Indo-European, Classical, Slavic and Baltic linguistics, Sanskrit, and Medieval Latin Northwestern U., Evanston, Ill., 1965—; Lybrand, Ross Bros., and Montgomery Found. Disting. prof. English and linguistics U. No. Iowa, Cedar Falls, 1972—; sr. exec. v.p. for real estate fin. mgmt. Gorgay, Inc.-A Real Estate Co., Louisville, 1976-77; sr. exec. v.p. for reimbursement and rates accounting fin. mgmt. Humana, Inc., The Hosp. Co., Louisville 1978-93; dir. Southeastern Investment Trust, Inc., Louisville, 1978-93; ret. 1993; rsch. prof. Southeastern Investment Trust, Inc. Rsch. Found., Louisville, 1976—; rsch. prof. The Southeastern Investment Trust, Inc. Rsch. Found., Louisville, 1976—; vis. prof. Medieval Latin, U. Chgo., 1966—; vis. prof. linguistics U. Chgo., Downtown Ctr., 1966—; prof. English evening divs. Northwestern U., Chgo., 1968-69, prof. anthropology, 1971-72. Author: The Ruodlieb: The First Medieval Epic of Chivalry from Eleventh-Century Germany, 1965, The Ruodlieb: Linguistic Introduction, Latin Text with a Critical Apparatus, and Glossary, 1966, The Ruodlieb: Facsimile Edition, 1965, 3d edit. 1968, Old Lithuanian Texts of the Sixteenth and Seventeenth Centuries with a Glossary, 1969, The Old Lithuanian Catechism of Baltramiejus Vilentas (1579): A Phonological, Morphological, and Syntactical Investigation, 1969, Isidore of Seville's History of the Goths, Vandals, and Suevi, 1966, 2d edit. 1970, The Letters of Saint Isidore of Seville, 1966, 2d edit. 1970, The Old Lithuanian Catechism of Martynas Mazvydas (1547), 1971, others; translator: A Concise Elementary Grammar of the Sanskrit Language with Exercises, Reading Selections, and a Glossary (Jan Gonda), 1966, The Comparative Method in Historical Linguistics (Antoine Meillet), 1967, A Sanskrit Grammar (Manfred Mayrhofer), 1972; contbr. numerous articles to many scholarly jours. Appointed to Hon. Order Ky. Cols. (life). Mem. Linguistic Soc. Am. (life, Sapir life patron), Internat. Linguistic Assn., Societas Linguistica Europaea (charter, life), Am. Philol. Assn. (life), Classical Assn. Middle West and South (life), Medieval Acad. Am. (life), MLA (life), Am. Assn. Tchrs. Slavic and East European Langs., Am. Assn. Advancement Slavic Studies (life), Assn. for Advancement Baltic Studies (life), Inst. Lithuanian Studies (life), Tchrs. of English to Speakers of Other Langs. (charter, life), SAR (life), Princeton Club (N.Y.C., Chgo.), Princeton Alumni Assn. (Louisville), Harvard Club (N.Y.C., Chgo., Louisville, Lexington, Ky.), Pres.'s Soc. Bellarmine Coll. (life), Louisville Country Club, KC (life), Phi Beta Kappa (life). Baptist. Home: 3619 Brownsboro Rd Louisville KY 40207-1863 also: PO Box 2693 Clarksville Br Jeffersonville IN 47131-2693

FORD, JAMES HENRY, JR., hospital executive; b. Brownfield, Miss., May 25, 1931; s. James H. and Katie Sue F.; m. Peggy Simpson, Mar. 1959; children: Renee, James, Randy, Penny. B.S. in Acctg., Memphis State U., 1953; M.H.A., St. Louis U., 1969. Auditor Sears, Roebuck & Co., Memphis, 1955-60; adminstrv. asst. Meth. Hosp., Memphis, 1964-67; asst. adminstr. Druid City Hosp., Tuscaloosa, Ala., 1969-76, adminstr., from 1976, now pres.; pres. DCH Healthcare Authority, Tuscaloosa; past pres., now bd. dirs. West Ala. Emergency Med. Svcs.; past pres. West Ala. Hosp. Coun., 1974; treas. Ala. Vol. Hosps. Am., 1986-87. past pres. Phoenix House of Tuscaloosa, 1974; loaned exec. United Fund in Tuscaloosa County, 1974, 75; past chmn. adminstrv. bd. First Meth. Ch. of Tuscaloosa, 1973; bd. dirs. Blue Cross-Blue Shield Ala., 1986-92, 94—; mem. Black Warrior Coun. Boy Scouts Am., 1978—. Recipient William G. Follmar award, Robert H. Reeves award Hosp. Fin Mgmt. Assn., 1975. Mem. Ala. Hosp Hosp. Execs. (pres. 1981-82), Am. Coll. Adminstrs., Ala. Hosp. Assn. (trustee 1978-84, 88-94, chmn. 1993-94, gold medal 1991). Office: DCH Regional Med Ctr 809 University Blvd E Tuscaloosa AL 35401-2029

FORD, LANELLE BRIGANCE, psychotherapist; b. Plainview, Tex., Nov. 17, 1924; d. Albert Carroll and Eula Theresa (McPherson) Brigance; m. Dennis B. Ford, Sept. 11, 1943; children: B. Kathryn, Linda F. BBA, Tex. A&I U., 1948, MS, 1972; PsyD, Fielding Inst. Grad. Studies, 1978. Lic. profl. counselor, Tex.; lic. marriage and family therapist, Tex. Tchr. Olton (Tex.) High Sch., 1945-46; adminstrv. sec. Tex. A&I U., Kingsville, 1946-48, Tex. Tech. U., Lubbock, 1948-49; instr. air force West Tex. U., Canyon, 1951-52; exec. dir., counselor Family Guidance Svcs., Kingsville, 1973-78; staff psychotherapist Psychol. Svc. Ctr., Corpus Christi, Tex., 1978-80; pvt. practice Austin, Tex., 1980—. Contbr. articles to profl. publs. Leader Camp Fire Girls, Kingsville; program chairperson Kingsville Women's Club, 1969-70; pres. Tex. A&I Faculty Women, 1970-71. Mem. Am. Assn. Marriage and Family Therapists. Home: 21908 Briarcliff Dr Spicewood TX 78669-2490 Office: Ste 105A 1101 S Capital Of Tex Hwy Austin TX 78746-5437

FORD, LINCOLN EDMOND, physician, physiologist, educator; b. Boston, May 14, 1938; s. Johns Berchmans and Mary Margaret (Clark) F.; children: Catherine L., Gretchen A., Vanessa E., Emily W. BA, Harvard Coll., 1960, postgrad., 1960-61; MD, U. Rochester, 1965. Rotating intern Bassett Hosp., Cooperstown, N.Y., 1965-66; staff assoc. NIH, Bethesda, Md., 1966-68; NIH rsch. assoc. Peter Bent Brigham Hosp., Boston, 1968-70, resident, 1970-71; NIH rsch. fellow U. Coll. London, 1971-74; assoc. prof. medicine U. Chgo., 1974-96; prof. medicine U. Ind., 1996—; dir. VA Heart Failure Clinic, Am. Heart Assn. established investigator U. Chgo., 1975-80. chmn. rsch. coun. Chgo., Heart Assn., 1978-79. Adv. editor Jour. Muscle Rsch., 1979—; mem. editl. bd. Am. Jour. Physiology, 1981-87, Circulation Rsch., 1983-90. Contbr. numerous articles to profl. jours. Served with USPHS, 1966-68. Mem. Am. Physiol. Soc., Biophys. Soc., Soc. Gen. Physiologists. Clubs: Harvard (Boston), Quadrangle (Chgo.). Avocations: gardening; skiing. Office: U Ind Med Sch Krannert Inst Cardiology 1111 W 10th St Indianapolis IN 46202-4800

FORD, LINDA LOU, dietitian; b. Tipton, Okla., Aug. 14, 1948; d. Hulett Jasper and Wanda Ruth (Whitaker) Hooton; m. Gary Leroy Ford, Dec. 21, 1973; children: Temple Kaye, Tyler Jaye. AA, Altus (Okla.) Jr. Coll., 1968; BS summa cum laude, Harding U., 1970. Registered and lic. dietitian, Okla. Dietetic intern Okla. U. Health Scis. Ctr., Oklahoma City, 1970-71; therapeutic dietitian Comanche County Meml. Hosp. ARA Services, Inc., Lawton, Okla., 1971-72; traveling dietitian ARA Services, Inc., Okla. and Tex., 1972-73; mng. dietitian Sam Houston Hosp. ARA Services, Inc., Houston, 1973; asst. food service dir. Spring Branch Ind. Sch. Dist., Houston, 1973-74; dir. dietary dept. Jackson County Meml. Hosp., Altus, 1974-77; cons. dietitian Okla., 1975-86; nutritionist Women, Infants, Children program Okla. State Dept. Health, Altus, 1986-87, Chandler, Okla., 1988-89; Mangum, Okla., 1989—; instr. Okla. Dietetic Asst. Tng. Program, Altus, 1975, 77, 79; cons. food service Pioneer Manor, Frederick, Okla., 1975, 84-86; cons. instn. mgmt. Meml. Hosp., Frederick, 1975-81, 84-86; cons. dietitian B and K Nursing Ctr., Hobart, Okla., 1980-85; cons. nutrition Park Ln Manor, Altus, 1980-85. Active Thomas St. Ch. of Christ, Altus, 1959-87, Prague Ch. of Christ, Prague, Okla. 1988-89, Mangum Ch. of Christ; donor ARC, Altus, 1974-87; vol. Am. Heart Assn., Altus, 1971, Am. Cancer Soc., 1986. Mem. Am. Dietetic Assn., Okla. Dietetic Assn., Alpha Chi. Republican. Office: Greer County Health Dept 108 S Pennsylvania St Mangum OK 73554-4284

FORD, LORETTA C., retired university dean, nurse, educator; b. N.Y.C., Dec. 28, 1920; d. Joseph F. and Nellie A. (Williams) Pfingstel; R.N., Middlesex Gen. Hosp., New Brunswick, N.J., 1941; BS in Nursing, U. Colo., 1949, MS, 1951, EdD, 1961; DSc (hon.), Ohio State Med Coll.; LLD (hon.) U. Md., 1990; m. William J. Ford, May 2, 1947; 1 dau., Valerie. Staff nurse New Brunswick Vis. Nurse Service, 1941-42; supr., dir. Boulder County (Colo.) Health Dept., 1947-58; asst. prof., then prof. U. Colo. Sch. Nursing, 1960-72; dean Sch. Nursing, dir. nursing, prof. U. Rochester (N.Y.), 1972-86, acting dean Grad. Sch. Edn. & Human Devel., 1988-89; vis. prof. U. Fla., summer 1968, U. Wash., Seattle, 1974; mem. educators adv. panel GAO; dir. Security Trust Co., Rochester, Rochester Telephone Co.; internat. cons. in field. Bd. dirs. Threshold Alternative Youth Svcs., Easter Seal Soc., ARC, Monroe Community Hosp.; mem. adv. com. Commonwealth Fund Exec. Nurse Fellowship Program. Served with Nurse Corps, USAAF, 1942-46. Recipient N.Y. State Gov.'s award for women in sci., medicine and nursing, Modern Healthcare Hall of Fame award, 1994, Lillian D. Wald Spirit of Nursing award N.Y. Vis. Nurse Svc., 1994; named Colo. Nurse of Yr. Fellow Am. Acad. Nursing; mem. ANA, APHA (Ruth B. Freeman award), Nat. League Nursing (fellowship, Linda Richards award), Am. Coll. Health Assn. (Boynton award), NAS Inst. Medicine (Gustav O. Leinhard award, 1990). Author articles in field, chpts. in books. Office: U Rochester Med Ctr 601 Elmwood Ave Box SON Rochester NY 14642

FORDHAM, CHRISTOPHER COLUMBUS, III, university dean and chancellor, medical educator; b. Greensboro, N.C., Nov. 28, 1926; s. Christopher Columbus and Frances Long (Clendenin) F.; m. Barbara Byrd, Aug. 16, 1947; children: Pamela Fordham Richey, Susan Fordham Crowell, Betsy Fordham Templeton. Cert. in medicine, U. N.C., 1949; MD, Harvard U., 1951. Diplomate Am. Bd. Internal Medicine. Intern Georgetown U. Hosp., 1951-52; asst. resident Boston City Hosp., 1952-53; prof. medicine emeritus U. N.C. Sch. Medicine, 1993—; sr. asst. resident N.C. Meml. Hosp., Chapel Hill, 1953-54; fellow in medicine U. N.C. Sch. Medicine, 1954-55, instr. medicine, 1958-60, asst. prof., 1960-64, assoc. prof., asst. dean, Sch. Medicine, 1964-68, prof., assoc. dean, 1968-69; acting asst. sec. for health Dept. HEW, Washington, 1977; dean Sch. Medicine U. N.C., 1971-79; prof. medicine U. N.C. Sch. Medicine, 1971—, vice chancellor for health affairs, 1977-80, chancellor, 1980-88, chancellor emeritus and prof. medicine, 1988-93, chancellor emeritus, dean emeritus, prof. medicine emeritus, 1993—; prof. medicine, v.p. for medicine, dean Sch. Medicine, Med. Coll. Ga., Augusta, 1969-71; practice medicine, specializing in internal medicine Greensboro, N.C., 1957-58; chair Gov.'s Com. on N.C. Awards, 1993—. Bd. dirs. Royal Soc. Med. Found., N.Y.C., 1990-95; chmn. N.C. Awards Com., 1993—. Officer USAF, 1955-57. Fellow ACP, AAAS; mem. AAUP, AMA (spl. award 1990), Nat. Assn. State Univs. & Land Grant Colls. (chair coun. univ. governance 1990-91), N.C. Med. Soc., So. Soc. Clin. Investigation, Am. Soc. Nephrology, Am. Fedn. Clin. Rsch., Soc. Health and Human Values, Am. Assn. Med. Colls. (exec. coun. 1975-78, rep. liaison com. med. edn. 1977-79), Am. Assn. Med. Coll. So. Regional Deans (chmn. 1972-73, 75-76, chmn. nat. coun. deans 1977), N.Y. Acad. Scis., Inst. Medicine of Nat. Acad. Sci. (council 1985-90), Elisha Mitchell Sci. Soc., Order Golden Fleece, Sigma Xi, Alpha Omega Alpha. Office: Univ NC Sch Medicine Rm 5023 Clinic Wing Campus Box 7000 Chapel Hill NC 27514

FORDTRAN, JOHN SATTERFIELD, physician; b. San Antonio, Nov. 15, 1931; s. William M. and Josephine (Bell) F.; m. Jewel Evans, July 25, 1953; children: William, Bess, Josephine, Amy. Student, U. Tex., 1949-52; M.D., Tulane U., 1956. Internal medicine intern Parkland Meml. Hosp., Dallas, 1956-57; asst. resident internal medicine Parkland Meml. Hosp., 1957-58; research fellow gastroenterology Mass. Meml. Hosp., Boston, 1960-62; instr. internal medicine U. Tex. Southwestern Med. Sch., Dallas, 1962-63; asst. prof. internal medicine U. Tex. Southwestern Med. Sch., 1963-67, assoc. prof. internal medicine, 1967-69, prof., 1969-79, chief sect. gastroenterology, 1963-79; chief dept. internal medicine Baylor U. Med. Center, Dallas, 1979—; mem. attending staff Parkland Meml. Hosp., Dallas, 1963—; cons. gastroenterology Dallas VA Hosp., 1963—. Contbr. articlkes to profl. jours.; editorial bd. Jour. Clin. Investigation, 1968-73; editor Gastroenterology, 1977-81; co-editor: Gastrointestinal Disease, 5th edit., 1993. Served with USPHS, 1958-60. Recipient King Faisal prize in medicine Saudi Arabia, 1984. Mem. ACP, Am. Soc. Clin. Investigation (past pres.), Am. Gastroent. Assn. (Disting. Achievement award 1971, Kirsner prize 1990, Disting. Educator award 1991, Friedenwald medal 1993), Assn. Am. Physicians. Home: 3508 Hanover Ave Dallas TX 75225-7434 Office: Baylor U Med Ctr 3500 Gaston Ave Dallas TX 75246-2045

FORDTRAN, ROBERT L., III, cardiologist; b. Bishop, Tex., Jan. 24, 1931. BS, U. Tex., Galveston, 1952, MD, 1956. Diplomate Am. Bd. Internal Medicine. Pvt. practice physician internal medicine Corpus Christi, Tex., 1959-92; cardiologist Cardiology Assocs. Office: Cardiology Corpus Christi Ste 704 1521 S Staples Corpus Christi TX 78404

FORDYCE, JAMES GEORGE, physician; b. Detroit, Jan. 9, 1945; s. James Alexander and Stella Marie (Pakron) F.; m. Kathleen Marie Ray, June 17, 1967; children: James A., Jonathan A., Jared A. BS, Mich. State U., 1966, DVM, 1968; MD, Wayne State U., 1974. Diplomate Am. Bd. Pediats., Am. Bd. Allergy and Immunology. Intern, resident Children's Hosp. Mich., Detroit, 1973-76; fellow allergy and clin. immunology Henry Ford Hosp., Detroit, 1976-78; physician Dearborn (Mich.) Allergy and Asthma Clinic, PC, 1978—; cons. Metro Med. Group, Detroit, 1979-95. Author: Asthma in Clinical Pulmonary Medicine, 1992. Fellow Am. Acad. Pediats., Am. Acad. Allergy, Asthma and Clin. Immunology; mem. Mich. Allergy and Asthma Soc. (pres. 1991-92). Home: 45140 Brookside Ct Plymouth MI 48170 Office: Dearborn Allergy & Asthma Clinic PC 20200 Outer Dr Dearborn MI 48124

FORDYCE, THERESA ROSE, mental health nurse; b. Andrews AFB, Md., June 7, 1960; d. Robert David Sr. and Patricia Anne (Bahm) F. BA in Psychology, Belmont Abbey Coll., 1982; AAS, Mercer County Community Coll., Trenton, N.J., 1987. RN, N.J., S.C. Nurse supr. Trenton Psychiat. Hosp., 1987-88; staff nurse Greenville (S.C.) Hosp. Systems/Marshall Pickens, 1988-91, Chestnut Hill Psychiat. Hosp., 1991-92; RN supr. Magnolia Manor, 1992-94; nurse lead clin. staff Boys Home of the South, Belton, S.C., 1994-95. Home: 446 Emory Ave Trenton NJ 08611

FORE, WILLIAM WHATELY, internist, educator, administrator; b. Lynchburg, Va., May 27, 1936; s. William Henry and Rosalie (Reeves) F.; m. Judy O'Neal, Feb. 28, 1981; children—William Whately, Thomas Butler, Mary Tyler Reeves. Student Duke U., 1953-56, M.D., 1960. Diplomate Am. Bd. Internal Medicine, Am. Bd. Nuclear Medicine. Intern Osler med. service Johns Hopkins Hosp., Balt., 1960-61; jr. asst. resident in medicine, Duke U. Med. Ctr., Durham, N.C., 1961-62, sr. asst. resident in medicine, 1963-64; fellow in endocrinology and metabolism, 1962-63; practice medicine specializing in internal medicine and endocrinology, Greenville, N.C., 1966-84; instr. Lincoln Hosp., Durham, 1963-64; assoc. clin. prof. medicine East Carolina U. Sch. Medicine, Greenville, 1971-84; assoc. prof. medicine Sch. Medicine, E. Carolina U., Greenville, 1984-88; chief medicine Wyman Park Med. Assocs./Johns Hopkins Med. Svcs. Corp., Balt., 1988-93, asst. v.p. med. affairs, 1989-91; clin. assoc. prof. medicine Jefferson Med. Coll., Phila., 1993-96, clin. prof. medicine, 1996—, mem. divsn. endocrinology, diabetes, and metabolism, 1993—; dir. Joslin Ctr. for Diabetes at Wills and Jefferson, Phila., 1993-96; co-dir. Nuclear Medicine Lab., Pitt County Meml. Hosp., Greenville, 1966-80; former chmn. Heart Fund. Served to lt. comdr., M.C., USNR, 1964-66. Recipient Physician's Recognition award AMA, 1969, 75, 79, 83, 86, 89, 92, 95. Fellow ACP (pres. N.C. chpt. 1984, gov. for N.C. 1986-89), Am. Coll. Endocrinology; mem. AMA, Am. Coll. Physician Execs., N.C. Med. Soc. (2d v.p., chmn. sect. internal medicine, chmn. hosp. and profl. liaison com. task force third-party liaison commr., chmn. com. on practice variations), Pa. Med. Soc., Phila. Med. Soc., Pitt County Med. Soc.

(pres. 1981), N.C. Soc. Internal Medicine (pres. 1979-80, exec. council), Soc. Nuclear Medicine, Am. Diabetes Assn., (bd. dirs. Pitt County chpt., bd. dirs. Phila. chpt. 1994-96), Pa. Diabetes Acad. (vice chmn. 1995—). Republican. Methodist. Contbr. articles to profl. publs. Home: 513 William Ebbs Ln West Chester PA 19380 Office: Joslin Ctr for Diabetes at Wills & Jefferson Ste 600 211 S 9th St Philadelphia PA 19107

FOREMAN, HARRY, obstetrician, gynecologist, educator; b. Winnipeg, Manitoba, Canada, Mar. 5, 1915; came to the U.S., 1924; s. Monish and Fannie (Decter) F.; m. Billie Deane Smith, June 30, 1955; children: Matthew, Pamela. BS in Chemistry, Antioch Coll., Yellow Springs, Ohio, 1938; PhD in Biochemistry, Ohio State U., 1942; MD, U. Calif., San Francisco, 1947. Rsch. fellow, teaching asst. dept. physiol. chemistry Ohio State U., Columbus, 1939-42; asst. prof. biochemistry Oglethorpe U., Atlanta, 1942-43; intern Mt. Zion Hosp., San Francisco, 1947-48, resident in internal medicine, 1948-49; assoc. prof. sch. pub. health U. Minn., Mpls., 1962-73, assoc. dean office internat. programs, 1966-69, assoc. prof. ob.-gyn., 1966-69, dir. ctr. for population studies, 1969—, prof. ob.-gyn. and sch. pub. health, 1973—; staff mem. biomed. rsch. group Los Alamos (N.Mex.) Scientific Lab. U. Calif., 1951-62; postdoctoral fellow Crocker Radiation Lab. U. Calif., 1949-51; rsch. chemist Eldorado Oil Co., Oakland, Calif., 1943-44; mem. Atomic Safety and Licensing Bd. Panel; cons. family planning Office Econ. Opportunity, HEW. Contbr. articles to profl. jours. With U.S. Army, 1942-44. Fellow AAAS, Am. Pub. Health Assn.; mem. Am. Physiol. Soc., Am. Soc. for Pharmacology and Experimental Therapeutics, Health Physics Soc., Radiation Rsch. Soc., Population Assn. Am., Soc. for Experimental Biology and Medicine, Minn. State Soc. Obstetrics and Gynecology. Home: 1564 Burton St Saint Paul MN 55108-1301 Office: U Minn Minneapolis MN 55455

FOREMAN, THOMAS ALEXANDER, dentist; b. Tionesta, Pa., Oct. 24, 1930; s. James Aura and May (Lanson) F.; student Grove City Coll., 1948-50; BS, Allegheny Coll., 1952; DDS cum laude, U. Pitts., 1957, DMD, 1970; m. Dorothy Jean Wolf, June 12, 1953; children: Bonnie Jean, Julie Marie, Mary Aleta, Lloyd George. Gen. practice dentistry, Clarion, Pa., 1961—. Mem. Clarion Hosp. Assn., 1965—; mem. exec. bd. Colonel Drake Council Boy Scouts Am., 1969-72, mem.-at-large French Creek council, 1972-73, vice chmn. Indian Trails dist., 1971-73; mem. governing coun. Alpha Christian Acad. Sch., 1977-81. Served with Dental Corps, USAF, 1957-61. Fellow Pierre Fauchard Acad. Fellow Acad. Dentistry Internat., Am. Coll. Dentists, Internat. Coll. Dentists, Royal Soc. Health; mem. Am. Dental Assn., Pa. Dental Assn. (dir. 8th dist. 1964-87, 91—, pres. 1974-76, trustee 1987-91), Acad. Gen. Dentistry (mem. 1977, fellow 1984, master 1988), AMA (affiliate), Clarion County Dental Soc. (pres. 1983-87), S.A.R., (pres. Capt. Samuel Brady chpt. 1970-71, 77-80), Soc. Mayflower Descs., Pilgrim Edward Doty Soc., Fedn. Dentaire Internationale, Pa. Soc., Western Pa. Conservancy, Cook Forest Ctr. for Arts, Clarion County Hist. Soc., Phi Beta Phi, Omicron Kappa Upsilon, Delta Sigma Delta, Theta Chi. Presbyn. (pres. bd. trustees 1966-67, supt. Sunday sch. 1966-67, chmn. endowment trust fund dirs. 1980-84). Mason (Shriner). Home: 147 S 7th Ave Clarion PA 16214-2006 Office: 832 E Main St Clarion PA 16214-1156

FORFAR, JOHN OLDROYD, pediatrician educator; b. Glasgow, Scotland, Nov. 16, 1916; s. David and Edith Elizabeth (Campbell) F.; m. Isobel Mary Langlands Fernback, Sept. 5, 1942; children: Joan Langlands, David Oldroyd, John Colin. BSc, U. St. Andrews, 1938, MB, BChir, 1941, MD, 1955. House officer Perth Royal Infirmary, 1941-42; registrar, sr. registrar Dundee (Scotland) Royal Infirmary, 1946-48; sr. lectr. U. St. Andrews, Dept. Child Health, 1948-50; sr. cons., pediatrician Western Gen. Hosps. Edinburgh, 1950-64; prof. child life and health U. Edinburgh and Royal Hosp. for Children & Royal Infirmary, 1964-82. Editor: Textbook of Pediatrics, 1973, 78, 84, Pediatrics and Blood Tranfusion, 1980, Child Health in a Changing Society, 1988, History of the British Pediatric Association, 1989. Capt. Army, 1942-46, U.K., Europe. Recipient Mil. Cross, 1944; mentioned in Despatches. Fellow Am. Coll. Nutrition, Royal Soc. Edinburgh, Royal Coll. Physicians of Edinburg, Royal Coll. Physicians of London, Royal Coll. Physicians of Glasgow. Home: 110 Ravelston Dykes. 9 Ravelston Heights, Edinburgh EH4 3LX, Scotland Office: Univ Edinburgh, 17 Hatton Place, 20 Sylvan Pl, Edinburgh EH9 1UW, Scotland

FORGACS, JOSEPH, mycotoxicologist; b. Nokomis, Ill., Mar. 20, 1917; s. John and Elizabeth (Hallas) F.; B.S., U. Ill., 1940, M.S., 1942, Ph.D., 1944; m. Lillian Pearl Little, June 1, 1945; children—Theresa Maria, Joseph Alan, Lawrence David, Paul Axel, Lillian Pearl Maria. Dir. mycotoxicoses research Fort Detrick, Frederick, Md., 1944-54; sr. research fellow Am. Cyanamid Corp., Pearl River, N.Y., 1954-57; dir. lab. Spring Valley (N.Y.) Hosp., 1957-61; mycotoxicologist, staff microbiologist Good Samaritan Hosp., Suffern, N.Y., 1961-69; dir. clin. microbiology Ramapo Gen. Hosp. and Automated Biochem. Labs., Spring Valley, 1969-78. Cons. mycotoxicologist Agrl. Research Service, U.S. Dept. Agr., food and feed industries, 1957—; cons. microbiologist N.Y. State Dept. Mental Hygiene, Letchworth Village, Thiells, 1973-95. Served with AUS, 1944-46. Diplomate Am. Acad. Microbiology. Fellow Am. Acad. Microbiology, Inst. Food Technologists, AAAS; mem. N.Y. Acad. Scis., Am. Inst. Biol. Scis., N.Y. Med. Mycology Soc., Phi Sigma, Sigma Xi. Contbr. articles to profl. jours. Patentee in field. Home and Office: 302 Highland Ave Pearl River NY 10965-1005

FORIS-MILLER, CAROLYN M., histotechnologist; b. N.Y.C., Mar. 13, 1937; d. John Stephen and Caroline Bernice (Banoff) Foris; M. Herbert J. Miller. A.A., Thomas A. Edison Coll., 1979. Technician dept. Hosps. of City of NY., 1959-68; instr. histology Allen Sch. for Med. Tech.; supr. histology Wycoff Heights Hosp., 1968-70; adminstr. tissue pathology lab. Metpath, Inc., Teterboro N.J., 1970-84; coord., staff analyst anatomic pathology svcs. Woodhull Med. and Mental Health Ctr., Bklyn., 1985-86. Co-editor Golden Isles Newsletter, 1993-94. Coordinator legis. adv. bd. dirs. for chmn. health for N.Y. State, 1974-75; moderator of community discussion sessions on drug abuse, 1973; bd. govs. Mid Queens Regular Democratic Orgn., 1965-75, sec., v.p., also campaign coordinator for candidates of this orgn., editor newsletter. Co-editor Golden Isles newsletter; biographer Wavelength monthly publ. Recipient certs. Merit and Appreciation, N.Y. State Assemblymen. Mem. Nat. Soc. for Histotech. (charter mem. pub. relations com.), N.Y. Soc. for Histotech. (charter mem., co-editor newsletter 1975-76, editor 1984-85, chmn. membership com.), N.J. Soc. for Histotech. (charter mem.), Am. Soc. Clin. Pathology (assoc. and affiliate member). Roman Catholic.

FORKS, THOMAS PAUL, osteopathic physician; b. Great Lakes Naval Station, Ill., Apr. 15, 1952; s. Louis John and Rhoda Joan (Miles) F.; m. Sharron Elizabeth Wells, Dec. 15, 1979; 1 child, Joseph Miles. BA, St. Mary's U., 1975; MS, U. Tex., San Antonio, 1977; PhD, U. So. Miss., 1981; DO, U. Health Scis., Kansas City, Mo., 1988. Teaching asst., instr., then asst. prof. biology U. So. Miss., Hattiesburg, 1977-82; asst. prof. biology Wilkes Coll., Wilkes-Barre, Pa., 1982-83; intern Corpus Christi (Tex.) Osteo. Hosp., 1988-89; resident, then chief resident in family practice U. Miss., Jackson, 1989-91; emergency rm. physician Rush Hosp., Newton, Miss., 1989-91, Lackey Meml. Hosp., Forest, Miss., 1991—; physician N.E. Family Practice, San Antonio, 1992-93; family physician Morton, Miss., 1993—; lectr. in emergency med. mgmt. of snakebites. Contbr. articles to profl. publs. Charity physician Stewpot Free Clinic, Jackson, 1990-91; adv. bd. Cath. Charities, Jackson, 1990-91. Mem. AMA, AAFP, Am. Osteo. Assn., Miss. Acad. Sci., So. Med. Assn., Soc. for Study Amphibians and Reptiles, Chgo. Herpetological Soc. Republican. Roman Catholic. Home: 1809 Sarah Ln Jefferson City MO 65101

FORLINI, FRANK JOHN, JR., cardiologist; b. Newark, Mar. 30, 1941; s. Frank Sr. and Rose Theresa (Parussini) F.; m. Joanne Marie Horch, July 19, 1969; children: Anne Marie, Victoria, Frank III, Anthony. BS in Biology, Villanova (Pa.) U., 1963; MD, George Washington U., 1967. Diplomate Am. Bd. Internal Medicine, Am. Bd. Cardiovascular Disease. Intern Bklyn.-Cumberland Med. Ctr., N.Y., 1967-68, resident in internal medicine, 1968-70; fellow in cardiology Inst. Med. Sci. Pacific Med. Ctr., San Francisco, 1970-72; practice medicine specializing in cardiology Rock Island, Ill., 1974—; sr. ptnr. Forlini Med. Speciality Clinic, Rock Island, 1974—; owner Forlini Farm and Forlini Devel. Enterprises; assoc. prof. pharmacy L.I. U., Bklyn., 1969-70; pres., CEO U.S. Oil & Transp. Co., Inc., 1966-89; pres. Profl. and Execs. Ins. Assocs., 1973-89, Profls. Assocs., 1973-89; med. and exec. dir. Cardiovasc. Inst. Northwestern Ill., 1984—; exec. dir., owner Franksoft Pub., 1988—; Shelter for Abused Women and Children, Rock Island, 1992-94, pres., chmn., 1994, chmn. capital campaign com., 1994; bd. dirs. Rescue Missions and Christian Family Car Ctr., 1992-94, pres., 1994. Contbr. articles to profl jours. Chmn. D.C. Young Reps., 1965-66; mem. exec. com. Rep. Ctrl. Com., Washington, 1965-66; mem. nat. com. Coll. Young Reps., 1965-66; mem. exec. com. Young Rep. State Ctrl. Com., Washington, 1965-66; mem. Physicians for Reagen-Bush, 1980, 84; vice chmn. Rock Island Reps., 1985-90, precinct committeeman, 1985-90, 92-93; dep. registrar County of Rock Island, 1985—; trustee South Rock Island Twp., Rock Island County, 1987—; trustee Twp. Intergovtl. Agy., 1993—, Friends of Twp. Govt. of Rock Island County, chmn., 1995—; mem. exec. com. Rock Island County Rep. Ctrl. Com., 1992-94; del. Ill. State Rep. Conv., 1992; pres. parish coun., extraordinary min., eucharist min. Roman Cath. Ch. Maj. USAF, 1972-74. Nat. Inst. Heart Disease NIH-USPHS grantee, 1964-66, 70-72; Fellowship of Cath. Scholars, 1994—. Fellow Am. Coll. Cardiology, N.Am. Soc. Pacing and Electrophysiology; mem. AMA, Ill. State Med. Soc., Rock Island County Med. Soc. (chmn. com. on ins. 1990—), Western Ill. Ind. Physicians Assn. (bd. dirs. 1995—, mem. exec. com. 1996—, sec. 1996—), Rock Island County Twp. Assn. (v.p. 1994, pres. 1994-95, mem. exec. com. 1994—), Soc. Cath. Social Scientists, Univ. Faculty for Life, KC (3d deg. 1994—). Office: 2508 25th St Ste B Rock Island IL 61201-5419

FORLY, DOROTHY LYNCH, medical nurse, health facility administrator; b. Habre de Grace, Md., Feb. 10, 1943; d. Albert Jerone and Ruth Marie (Nelson) L.; children: David, Jim. Diploma in nursing, Mercy Hosp. Sch. Nursing, Balt., 1964. RN, La. Nurse Mercy Hosp., Balt., 1964-67; nurse Touro Infirmary, New Orleans, 1967-72, charge nurse, 1972-80, supr., 1980-90, nurse mgr., 1990-94; adminstr. Uptown Dialysis Ctr., New Orleans, 1994—. Den leader Cub Scouts of Am. pack 83, New Orleans, 1989-95; com. mem. Boy Scouts of Am. troop 35, New Orleans, 1995—. Mem. Am. Nephrology Diseases Assn., nat. Kidney Found. La. (fund raising com. 1994—), Am. Assn. Kidney Patients (bd. dirs. 1980—), Nat. Renal Adminstrs. Assn., S.E. Dialysis and Transplant Assn. (conf. com. 1996). Office: Uptown Dialysis Ctr 3434 Prytania St New Orleans LA 70115

FORMAAD, WILLIAM FRIEDBERGER, speech pathology educator; s. Samuel W. and Dora (Shonberg) F. BA, New Sch. Social Rsch., N.Y.C., 1949; MA, Columbia U., 1950, EdD, 1965. Lic. speech pathologist, N.Y. Speech improvement specialist N.Y.C. Dept. Speech Improvement, 1949-50; tchr. Latin, speech therapist Arlington (Va.) Speech Edn. Assn., 1950-51; dir. speech and hearing edn. Hamden (Conn.) Bd. Edn., 1951-57; dir. speech lab., asst. prof. So. Conn. State Coll., New Haven, 1953-57; assoc. prof. speech, coord. speech/hearing svc. William Paterson State Coll., Wayne, N.J., 1957-67; dir. speech pathology Mt. Carmel Guild Speech & Hearing Ctr., Newark, 1967-70; prof., dir. communication scis. Seton Hall U., South Orange, N.J., 1967-85, prof. speech improvement, phonology and oral communication, 1985-87, prof. emeritus, 1987—; vis. prof. NYU, N.Y.C., 1969-71, U. Catolica, Lisbon, Portugal, 1990-92; ltd. pvt. practice speech pathology and improvement, N.Y.C., 1965-86; head verbal comm. workshops John Molloy Dress for Success, N.Y.C., 1982-85. Author: Articulation Therapy, 1974; contbr. articles to profl. jours. Cpl. USMC, 1944-46. Fellow Am. Speech, Lang. and Hearing Assn.; mem. Am. Psychol. Assn. Home: 777 S Federal Hwy Apt C301 Pompano Beach FL 33062-5963

FORMAN, ALAN ROBERT, ophthalmologist; b. Cambridge, Mass., Aug. 24, 1945. AB, U. Vt., 1967; MD, Tufts U., Boston, 1971. Diplomate Am. Bd. Ophthalmology. Intern Albany (N.Y.) Med. Ctr., 1971-72; resident Georgetown U. Med. Ctr., Washington, 1972-75; pvt. practice Haddon Heights, N.J., 1977—; asst. clin. prof. Jefferson Med. Coll., Phila., 1978—; attending surgeon Wills Eye Hosp., Phila., 1978—; chief ophthalmology West Jersey Health Sys., Camden, N.J., 1992—. Contbr. articles to profl. jours. Maj. U.S. Army, 1975-77. Fellow ACS, Am. Acad. Ophthalmology; mem. Sigma Xi. Office: 200 White Horse Pike Haddon Heights NJ 08035

FORMAN, ARTHUR DAVID, neurologist, educator; b. Phila., Feb. 3, 1950; s. Philip Edward and Dorothy Jean (Alexander) F. BA, NYU, 1972; MD, Hahnemann Med. Coll., 1976. Diplomate Am. Bd. Neurology. Resident Hahnemann Hosp., Phila., 1976-79; resident neurology Mass. Gen. Hosp., Boston, 1979-84; fellow neuropathology Brigham & Women's Hosp., Boston, 1979-83; sr. registrar in neurology Radcliffe Infirmary, Oxford, Eng., 1983-84; asst. prof., assoc. prof. neurology MD Anderson Cancer Ctr. U. Tex., Houston, 1988—. Mem. AMA, Am. Acad. Neurology. Home: 1019 Barkdull St Houston TX 77006-6570

FORMAN, DONALD, orthopaedic surgeon; b. N.Y.C., June 18, 1934; s. Jack and Rose Forman; m. Esther Forman; children: Richard, Mark, Alan. MD, SUNY, Bklyn., 1958. Diplomate Am. Bd. Orthopedic Surgery. Intern Hosp. for Joint Diseases, N.Y.C., 1958-59, resident in orthopedics, 1959-63; attending orthopedic surgeon L.I. Jewish Hosp., New Hyde Park, N.Y., 1965—, North Shore U. Hosp., Manhasset, N.Y., 1967—, Little Neck (N.Y.) Cmty. Hosp., 1965—. Capt. USAF, 1963-65. Fellow ACS, Am. Acad. Orthopedic Surgeons, N.Y. Acad. Medicine, Ea. Orthopedic Assn., N.Y. Acad. Sci., Alpha Omega Alpha. Office: Mishkin Miller Forman PC 238-25 Hillside Ave Bellerose NY 11426

FORMAN, MARC ALLAN, child and adolescent psychiatrist, educator; b. Phila., Jan. 23, 1935; s. David E. and Ida Forman; m. Phillis Ann Taylor, Sept. 5, 1959; children: Robert, Vicki, William, Alyssa. AB, Haverford Coll., 1955; MD, U. Pa., 1959. Diplomate Am. Bd. Psychiatry and Neurology; cert. child psychiatrist. Intern Albert Einstein Hosp., Phila., 1959-60; resident Inst. Pa. Hosp., Phila., 1960-62; resident in child psychiatry St. Christopher's Hosp. for Children, Phila., 1964-66, dir. child psychiatry, 1970-85; prof. psychiatry and pediatrics Temple U. Sch. Medicine, Phila., 1970-85; prof. psychiatry and pediatrics Tulane U. Sch. Medicine, New Orleans, 1985—, dir. div. child and adolescent psychiatry, 1985—; cons. Hosps. Sarah-Brasilia, Salvador, Fortaleza, São Luis, Brazil. Co-author: On Behalf of Chilren, 1974, Psychiatric Hospitalization of School-Age Children, 1992; contbr. articles to profl. publs. Capt. USAF, 1960-62. Mem. Phi Beta Kappa, Alpha Omega, Alpha. Office: Tulane U Sch Medicine Dept Psychiatry Neurol New Orleans LA 70112

FORMAN, SUSAN GREENBERG, psychology educator; b. Bklyn., Dec. 28, 1948; d. George J. and Mildred (Weber) Greenberg. B.A., U. R.I., 1969, M.S., 1971; Ph.D., U. N.C., 1975. Sch. psychologist Washington pub. schs., 1971-72; dir. pupil personnel services Chapel Hill pub. schs., 1974-77; asst. prof. dept. psychology U. S.C., Columbia, 1977-82, assoc. prof. 1982-87, prof., 1987-92, assoc. provost, 1989-92; v.p. Rutgers U., 1992—. Ednl. and Profl. Devel. Act fellow 1970-71. Fellow Am. Psychol Assn.; mem. Nat. Assn. Sch. Psychologists (S.E. regional dir. 1981-83), S.C. Assn. Sch. Psychologists. Contbr. articles to profl. jours. Office: Rutgers U 105 Geology Hall New Brunswick NJ 08903

FORMBY, BENT CLARK, immunologist; b. Copenhagen, Apr. 3, 1940; naturalized, 1991; s. John K. and Gudrun A. (Dinesen) F.; m. Irene Menck-Thygesen, June 28, 1963 (div. May 1980); children: Rasmus, Mikkel; m. Florence G. Schmid, June 28, 1980. BA in Philosophy summa cum laude, U. Copenhagen, 1959, PhD in Biochemistry, 1968, DSc, 1976. Asst. prof. U. Copenhagen, 1969-73, assoc. prof., 1973-79, prof., 1979-83; vis. prof. U. Calif., San Francisco, 1979-84; sr. scientist, dir. lab. of immunology Sansum Med. Rsch. Found., Santa Barbara, Calif., 1984—; cons. Cell Tech., Inc., Boulder, Colo., 1989—, Immunex Corp., Seattle, 1989—; med. adv. bd. Biocellular Rsch. Orgn., Ltd., London, Childrens Hosp. of Orange County, Lautenburg Ctr. for Gen. and Tumor Immunology, Hebrew U., Hadassah Med. Sch., Jerusalem, 1993—, Loran Med. Sys., Inc. Editor: Fetal Islet Transplantation, 1988, 2d edit. 1995; contbr. articles to profl. jours.; patentee on non-invasive blood glucose measurement. Grantee Juvenile Diabetes Found., 1987, 88, E.L. Wiegand Found., 1993, Santa Barbara Cottage Hosp. Rsch., 1993-94, Breast Cancer Rsch. U. Calif., 1995—. Mem. N.Y. Acad. Scis., Am. Diabetes Assn. (grantee 1985, 86, 89, pres. Santa Barbara chpt. 1995), Am. Fedn. Clin. Rsch., European Assn. for the Study of Diabetes. Office: Sansum Med Rsch Found 2219 Bath St Santa Barbara CA 93105-4321

FORMICA, JOSEPH VICTOR, microbiology educator; b. N.Y.C., July 3, 1929; s. Joseph and Carmela (LaRosa) F.; m. Philomena Theresa Moretti, June 26, 1956; children: Diane, Jody Ann. BS, Syracuse U., 1953, MS, 1954; PhD, Georgetown U., 1967. Bacteriologist Biol. Warfare, Ft. Detrick, Frederick, Md., 1954-58; biochemist NIH, Bethesda, Md., 1958-63; asst. prof. dept. pediatrics Georgetown Med. Ctr., Washington, 1967-69; assoc. prof. dept. microbiology Med. Coll. Va., Richmond, 1969—, assoc. dean Sch. Basic Scis., 1977-81. Author: (chpt.) Pathobiology of Neoplasma, 1989; patentee in field; contbr. articles to profl. jours. With U.S. Army, 1946-48, Korea. Grantee Ctr. for Innovative Tech., Herndon, Va., 1986-89, NIH, 1970, 72, 78. Fellow Am. Acad. Microbiology; mem. Soc. Wine Educators (pres. 1985-87). Office: Va Commonwealth U MCV Sta Box 980678 Richmond VA 23298-0678

FORMICA, PETER FRANCIS, family physician, internist, psychiatrist; b. N.Y.C., Oct. 24, 1942; s. Philip and Carmela (Donato) F.; m. Elda Felicia Montanaro, Oct. 14, 1978; children: Philip, Peter, Marisa. BA, CUNY, 1964, MA, 1967; MD, U. Milan, 1974. Diplomate Am. Bd. Psychiatry and Neurology, Am. Bd. Family Practice. Intern Brookdale Hosp. and Med. Ctr., Bklyn., 1974-75, resident in Psychiatry, 1975-78; resident in family practice Downstate Med. Ctr., Bklyn., 1980-82; chief resident in psychiatry Brookdale Hosp. and Med. Ctr., Bklyn., 1977-78; fellow in psychosomatic medicine Downstate Med. Ctr, Bklyn., 1978-80, chief resident in family practice, 1981-82; pvt. practice medicine and psychiatry, Queens, 1982—; dir. psychiat. emergency room Woodhull Hosp. and Med. Ctr., Bklyn., 1985-87; med. dir. acute care South Beach Psychiat. Ctr., S.I., N.Y., 1987-88; chief psychiatrist Creedmore Psychiat. Ctr., Queens, N.Y., 1988—; founder, med. dir. Queens Counseling Ctr., Ridgewood, N.Y., 1989—. Author: The Immunology of Tumors, 1974. Fellow Am. Acad. Family Practice. Republican. Roman Catholic. Home: 84-46 63d Ave Middle Village NY 11379 Office: Queens Counseling Ctr 60-83 Myrtle Ave Ridgewood NY 11385-5908

FORNARI, VICTOR MASLIAH, psychiatrist; b. N.Y.C., June 20; s. Ermanno and Alice (Notrica) F.; m. Alice Johnson, Mar. 27, 1977; children: Eric, Amy, Marci. BS in Biology, Cornell U., 1974; MS in Human Nutrition, Columbia U., 1975; MD, SUNY-Downstate Med. Ctr., Bklyn., 1979. Diplomate Am. Bd. Psychiatry and Neurology, Am. Bd. Child and Adolescent Psychiatry and Neurology. Intern L.I. Coll. Hosp., Bklyn., 1979-80; resident in psychiatry Hosp. U. Pa., Phila., 1980-82; fellow in child and adolescent psychiatry L.I. Jewish Med. Ctr., New Hyde Park, N.Y., 1982-84; staff child psychiatrist Schneider's Children's Hosp./L.I. Jewish Med. Ctr., New Hyde Park, 1984-85; physician-in-charge Child Psychiatry Inpatient Unit/L.I. Jewish Med. Ctr., New Hyde Park, 1985-86; physician-in-charge, child psychiatry cons. liaison svc., eating disorders program North Shore-Cornell U. Hosp., Manhasset, N.Y., 1986-91, dir. tng./clin. svcs. div. child and adolescent psychiatry, 1991—; assoc. prof. psychiatry, pediatrics, Cornell U. Med. Coll., N.Y.C., 1991—. Fellow Am. Psychiat. Assn., Am. Acad. Child and Adolescent Psychiatry, Greater L.I. Psychiat. Soc. (pres. elect), Am. Assn. of Dirs. of Psychiat. Residency Tng., Soc. of Profs. of Child and Adolescent Psychiatry.

FORNATARO, KENNETH SAMUEL, health facility administrator; b. Long Branch, N.J., Sept. 15, 1958; s. John Carmen and Elizabeth Ann (Seeley) F. Student, Brown U., 1976-79, Northeastern U., 1982-83. Exec. chef Bloomingdale's, N.Y.C., 1984-87, Troutbeck, N.Y.C., 1987-88; coord. rsch. devel. Cmty. Rsch. Initiative, N.Y.C., 1988-89, dep. dir., 1989-90; exec. dir. AIDS Treatment Data Network, N.Y.C., 1991—. Author: The Experimental Treatment Guide, 1995, The Access Project, 1995, The Simple Facts Book, 1993; editor: The AIDS Clinical Trial Group: A Critique, 1991. Apptd. mem. steering com. N.Y. State Dept. Health HIV Uninsured Care Programs, 1993—, mem. clin. com., 1995—; active HIV Planning Coun. N.Y.C. Dept. Health, 1994—; bd. dirs. God's Love We Deliver, 1994—; chair cmty. adv. bd. Albert Einstein Sch. Medicine, Bronx, N.Y., 1993-94. Mem. Assn. of Nurses in AIDS Care. Democrat. Office: AIDS Treatment Data Network 611 Broadway Ste 613 New York NY 10012

FORNATTO, ELIO JOSEPH, otolaryngologist, educator; b. Turin, Italy, July 2, 1928; came to U.S., 1953; s. Mario G. and Julia (Stabio) F.; m. Mary Elizabeth Pearson, Dec. 17, 1960; children: Susan, Robert, Daniel. MD, U. Turin, Italy, 1952. Diplomate Am. Bd. Otolaryngology. Intern Edgewater Hosp., Chgo., 1956-57; resident U. Ill., Chgo., 1953-56; chief otolaryngologist Elmhurst (Ill.) Clinic, 1958—; sr. otolaryngologist Elmhurst (Ill.) Meml. Hosp., 1964—; med. dir. Chgo. Eye Ear Nose Throat Hosp., 1966-69; clin. asst. prof. Loyola U., Chgo., 1967-87; bd. dirs. DuPage County unit Am. Cancer Soc., 1977-94; chmn. Elmhurst Clinic, 1980-89. Founder Centurion Club, Deafness Research Found., N.Y.C., 1960—. Recipient Disting. Svc. award Elmhurst Meml. Hosp., 1994. Mem. AMA, Ill. Med. Soc., Am. Acad. Facial Plastic and Reconstructive Surgery, Am. Acad. Otolaryngologic Allergy, Am. Acad. Otolaryngology and Head and Neck Surgery. Roman Catholic. Home: 200 W Jackson St Elmhurst IL 60126-4807 Office: Elmhurst Clinic 172 Schiller St Elmhurst IL 60126-2816

FORNI, PATRICIA ROSE, nursing educator, university dean; b. St. Louis, Feb. 14, 1932; d. Harold and Glenda M. (Keay) Brown. B.S.N., Washington U., St. Louis, 1955, M.S. (USPHS trainee), 1957; Ph.D. (USPHS fellow), St. Louis U., 1965; postgrad. (USPHS scholar), U. Minn., summers 1968, 70. Staff nurse McMillan EENT Hosp., St. Louis, summer 1955, Renard Psychiat. Hosp., St. Louis, part-time 1955-57; rsch. asst. Washington U. Sch. Nursing, St. Louis, 1957-59, rsch. assoc., 1959-61, asst. prof., 1964-66, assoc. dean in charge grad. edn., assoc. prof. gen. nursing sci., 1966-68; assoc. prof. pub. health nursing Wayne State U., Detroit, 1968-69; asst. dir. for manpower and edn. Ill. Regional Med. Program, Chgo., 1969-71; project dir. Midwest Continuing Profl. Edn. for Nurses, St. Louis U., 1971-75; dean, prof. nursing So. Ill. U., Edwardsville, 1975-88; dean, prof. Coll. Nursing U. Okla., Oklahoma City, 1988—; grant proposal reviewer Divsn. Nursing, USPHS, 1972-79, 88, 91, NSF, 1978, U.S. Dept. Edn., 1980; active Ill. Implementation Commn. on Nursing, 1975-77, Okla. State Health Plan Adv. Com., 1994—. Mem. peer rev. panel Nursing Outlook, 1987-91; mem. editl. bd. Health Care for Women Internat., 1984—, Jour. Profl. Nursing, 1988-90. Chairwoman articulation of nursing programs task force Okla. State Regents for Higher Edn., 1990-91; bd. dirs. Greater St. Louis Health Sys. Agy., 1976-81, Adult Edn. Coun. Greater St. Louis, 1973-76, Edwardsville unit Am. Cancer Soc., 1981-88; mem. adv. com. Okla. Health State Plan, 1994—. Fellow WHO, Sweden, Finland, 1985. Mem. Nat. League for Nursing (accreditation site visitor 1979—, nominating com. Coun. Baccalaureate and Higher Degree Programs 1979-82, pub. policy and legis. com. 1981-85, bd. dirs. 1991-93, treas. 1991-93, mem. fin. com. 1991-95), Nat. League for Health Care (trustee 1991-93), Am. Nurses Assn. (chmn. continuing edn. publs. com. 1975-76), Mo. Nurses Assn. (chmn. edn. com. 1973-77), Greater St. Louis Soc. Health Manpower Edn. and Tng. (chmn. legis. com. 1974-75), Midwest Alliance in Nursing (1st governing bd. 1979-80, 93—, chmn. nominations com. 1980, 81, mem. fin. com. 1993-94, chair fin. com. 1994—, treas. 1994—), Am. Assn. Colls. Nursing (program com. 1978-82, mem.-at-large, bd. dirs. 1990-92, chair rsch. com. 1990-92), Ill. Coun. Deans/Dirs. Baccalaureate and Higher Degree Programs in Nursing (chmn. 1979-81), Am. Acad. Nursing (treas., chairwoman fin. com., mem. gov. coun. 1989-93, editor Newsletter 1982-87), Ill. Nurses Assn. (commn. on adminstrn. 1983-87, commn. on edn. 1987-89), Okla. Nurses Found. (pres. bd. trustees 1990-93), Sigma Theta Tau Internat. (charter mem. Epsilon Eta chpt. 1980). Office: U Okla Coll Nursing PO Box 26901 Oklahoma City OK 73126

FORNOS, PEDRO GENARO, internist; b. Havana, Cuba, Sept. 19, 1922; s. Pedro J. and Maria Angeles (Palencia) F.; came to U.S., 1965, naturalized, 1971; M.D., U. Havana, 1946; m. Caridad Lopez, Dec. 21, 1950; children—Pedro, Emma Maria. Intern, Univ. Hosp., Havana, 1947-49; resident Austin (Tex.) State Hosp., 1968-69, Meth. Hosp., Dallas, 1969-71; dir. pulmonary function dept. Univ. Hosp., Havana, 1961-65; dir. respiratory therapy dept., Bapt. Meml. Hosp. System, San Antonio, 1973—; pvt. practice internal medicine, San Antonio, 1971—. Diplomate Am. Bd. Internal Medicine. Fellow Am. Coll. Chest Physicians; mem. AMA, Tex., Bexar County med. assns., San Antonio Club Internal Medicine. Roman Catholic. Home: 3038 Oneida Dr San Antonio TX 78230-3431 Office: 201 Med Sq Med Bldg 311 Ca Antonio TX 78215

FORREST, ALEXANDER ROBERT, medical practitioner, forensic toxicologist; b. Glasgow, Scotland, July 5, 1947; s. Alexander Muir and Rose Ellen (Ringham) F.; m. Teresa Anne Booth, Apr. 14, 1979 (div. 1994);

children: Michael Robert, David Samuel. BSc with honors, Edinburgh U., 1970, MB ChB, 1973; LLM, U. Wales, Cardiff, 1993. Registered med. practitioner; chartered chemist; registered analytical chemist. Registrar in chem. pathology Addenbrooke's Hosp., Cambridge, Eng., 1976-79; sr. registrar in chem. pathology Royal Berkshire Hosp., Reading, 1979, Royal Infirmary, Glasgow, 1979-81; cons. in chem. pathology Royal Hallamshire Hosp., Sheffield, Eng., 1981—; lectr. forensic toxicology U. Sheffield, 1984—; med. adviser Claremont Hosp., Sheffield, 1989—; asst. dep. coroner South Yorkshire West, Sheffield, 1989—; clin. dir. lab. medicine Ctrl. Sheffield U. Hosps, 1992—. Contbr. papers to med. lit. Carnegie Trust scholar, 1971, Technicon scholar, 1978; Medicine-Gilliland fellow Royal Coll. Physicians, 1983. Fellow Royal Coll. Physicians, Royal Coll. Pathologists, Royal Soc. Chemistry (chmn. local area com. 1993-94); mem. Forensic Sci. Soc. (hon. sec.), Internat. Assn. Forensic Toxicologists, Royal Med. Soc. Quaker. Office: Royal Hallamshire Hosp, Glossop Rd, Sheffield S10 2JF, England

FORREST, DAVID VICKERS, psychiatrist, educator; b. N.Y.C., July 8, 1938; s. Melbourne Arthur and Cleo Florence (Garello); m. Lynne Putnam Stetson; children: Daniel Stetson, Susannah Nissly. AB summa cum laude, Princeton U., 1960; MD, Columbia U., 1964, cert. in psychoanalysis, 1974. Cert. in psychiatry Am. Bd. Psychiatry and Neurology. Intern in medicine St. Luke's Hosp., N.Y.C., 1964-65; resident psychiatry N.Y. State Psychiat. Inst., Columbia Presbyn. Med. Ctr., N.Y.C., 1965-68; chief psychiatric clinic 935th Med. Det. (KO) 93d Evacuation Hosp., Long Binh, Vietnam, 1968-69; chief psychiatric consultation Letterman Army Med. Ctr., San Francisco, 1969-70; pvt. practice psychiatry N.Y.C., 1970—; mem. psychiatry faculty Columbia U., N.Y.C., 1970—; dir. edn. ednl. rsch. dept. N.Y. State Psychiat. Inst., 1970-77; assoc. prof. clin. psychiatry Columbia U., Coll. Physicians and Surgeons, N.Y.C., 1984—; faculty psychoanalytic ctr. Columbia U., Coll. Physicians and Surgeons, 1974—, liaison psychiatrist neurology, 1977—; lectr. psychiatry U. Saigon Med. Sch., Vietnam, 1968-69; lectr. abnormal psychology Far East div. U. Md., Long Binh, Vietnam, 1969. Author: Selected American Expressions, 1974, 76, 82; co-author: Treating Schizophrenic Patients, 1983, (video cassette series) Electronic Textbook of Psychiatry, 1972-77; editor, pub. Spring: The Jour. of the E. E. Cummings Soc., N.Y.C., 1980—; editor: Neural Net News, N.Y. State Psychiat. Inst., 1989-91; contbr. articles to profl. jours., textbooks. Psychiat. cons. N.Y.C. Ballet Co., 1973; first aid instr. Boy Scouts Am., 1983—; NASA Outreach participant, 1991. Capt. USAF, 1968-70, Vietnam. Decorated Bronze Star; Gen. Motors nat. scholar. Fellow Am. Psychiat. Assn., Am. Coll. Psychiatrists, Am. Acad. Psychoanalysis (program chair), Am. Coll. Psychoanalysts (program chair 1987-89, bd. regents 1989-92, v.p. 1993, pres.-elect 1994, pres. 1995), Explorers Club; mem. Am. Acad. Neurology (assoc.), N.Y. Clin. Soc. (v.p. 1995, pres. 1996). Episcopalian. Office: 133 E 73d St Ste 211 New York NY 10021 also: 155 W 68th St Ste 1219 New York NY 10023

FORRESTER, ALFRED WHITFIELD, psychiatrist, educator; b. Springfield, Mass., May 15, 1953; s. Wallace Lomax and Alma Mae (Brooks) F. BA magna cum laude, Yale U., 1975; MD, Johns Hopkins U., 1979. Diplomate Nat. Bd. Med. Examiners, Am. Bd. Psychiatry and Neurology. Med. resident dept. medicine Mt. Auburn Hosp., Cambridge, Mass., 1979-82; psychiatry resident dept. psychiatry and behavioral scis. Johns Hopkins Med. Insts., Balt., 1982-85, research fellow, 1985-86, instr., 1986-93; clin. asst. prof. dept. psychiatry U. Md., Balt., 1987—; staff psychiatrist Cann Health Resources, Fallston, Md., 1987-88, The Sheppard and Enoch Pratt Hosp., 1988—; dir. psychiat. svcs. Chase-Breston Clinic, Balt., 1988-90, staff psychiatrist, 1990—; med. dir. Behavioral Sci. Assocs., Balt., 1993—; med. cons. Bon Secours Hosp., Balt., 1983-90; psychiat. cons. Shock-Trauma Ctr. U. Md. Hosp., 1987-90. Contbr. articles to profl. jours. Active Groton (Mass.) Sch. Bd. Govs., 1983-85, AIDS com., Med. and Chirurgical Faculty State of Md., 1988-91. Nat. Achievement scholar, 1971-75. Mem. Am. Coll. Physicians, Med. and Chirurgical Faculty State Md., AMA, Am. Psychiatric Assn., Md. Psychiatric Soc., Md. Psychiat. Liaison Assn., Yale Alumni Assn. (fundraiser 1975—), Greater Balt. Bus. Profl. Assn. Democrat. Episcopalian. Club: Mory's Assn. (New Haven), Yale (Md.). Home: 115 Saint Dunstans Rd Baltimore MD 21212-3311 Office: Sheppard & Enoch Pratt Hosp 6501 N Charles St Baltimore MD 21204-6819 also: Behav Sci Assocs 10751 Falls Rd Ste 255 Lutherville MD 21093

FORRESTER, DAVID ANTHONY, nurse educator; b. Ft. Worth, May 11, 1954; s. Billy Arthur and Alta Faye (Bateman) F. BS in Nursing, U. Tex., Ft. Worth, 1975; MS in Nursing, U. Tex., Arlington, 1979; PhD, NYU, 1985. R.N., N.J., N.Y. Asst. prof. Rutgers U. Coll. Nursing, Newark, 1979-85; assoc. clin. nurse specialist Univ. Hosp.-U. Medicine and Dentistry N.J., Newark, 1979-85; assoc. prof. Pace U. Sch. Nursing, N.Y.C., 1985-88; nurse Mt. Sinai Med. Ctr., N.Y.C., 1985—; prof. U. Medicine and Dentistry N.J., 1988—, assoc. dean acad. affairs and rsch., dir. ctr. for nursing rsch.; expert witness to priv. law firms, 1985—, N.Y.C. Commn. on Human Rights, 1988—. Rsch. grantee Rutgers U., 1982, Am. Jour. Nursing, 1982, Pace U., 1988, U. Medicine and Dentistry N.J., 1980. Mem. ANA, Am. Nurses Found. (charter), N.J. Nurses Assn., Emergency Nurses Assn., N.Y. Acad. Scis., Sigma Theta Tau. Democrat. Home: Buttonwood Cottage 27 1st St Califon NJ 07830-4316 Office: U Medicine and Dentistry NJ 65 Bergen St Newark NJ 07107-3001

FORSE, ROBERT ARMOUR, surgeon; b. Montreal, Dec. 25, 1950; came to U.S., 1989; s. Raymond Armour and Arlene Mabel (Burns) F.; m. Lynda Gail Kabbash, June 21, 1975; children: Alexander, Emily, James. BSc, McGill U., 1972, MD, 1976, PhD, 1982. Straight intern in surgery Royal Victoria Hosp., Montreal, 1976-77, jr. resident surgery, 1977-78, sr. resident in surgery, Surg. Nutrition Svc., 1978-80, sr. resident in surgery, Gen. Surg. Svcs., 1980-81, chief resident in surgery, 1981-82, asst. attending surgeon, attending surgeon surg. ICU, 1983-89, surg. program dir., 1986-89; attending surgeon, attending surgeon surg. ICU New England Deaconess Hosp., Boston, 1989—, chief surg. metabolism lab., 1989—, surg. dir. Deaconess Nutritional Mgmt. Ctrs., dir. program for surg. mgmt. of obesity, chief div. gen. surgery., 1991—; asst. prof. surgery Harvard Med. Sch., 1989-92, assoc. prof., 1992—; rsch. fellow McGill U., Montreal, 1972-73, 78-81; rsch. fellow med. rsch. Coun. Can., Coll. Physicians and Surgeons, Columbia U., N.Y., 1982-83; demonstrator dept. anatomy McGill U., Montreal, 1978-79, asst. prof. surgery, 1983-89, dir. surg. undergrad. edn., 1987-89; asst. prof. surgery Harvard Med. Sch., Boston, 1989—; asst. surgeon Reddy Meml. Hosp., Montreal, 1984-89; assoc. mem. McGill Nutrition and Food Sci. Ctr., McGill U., Montreal, 1984-89; attending surgeon Faulkner Hosp., Jamaica Plain, N.Y.; cons. staff in surg. oncology Dana Farber Cancer Inst., Boston, 1989—; mem. numerous coms. Royal Victoria Hosp., McGill U., New Eng. Deaconess Hosp., others; tchr., presenter in field. Contbr. chpts. to books and articles to profl. jours. Recipient Equipment grant Rsch. Inst., Royal Victoria Hosp., 1984, Operating grant, 1984-85, Equipment grant Med. Rsch. Coun. Can., 1985, Cedar Cancer Found., 1985, Operating grant Med. Rsch. Coun. Can., 1985-87, Med. Rsch. Coun. Can., 1987-89, 1989-91, NIH, 1990—, others. Fellow Royal Coll. Surgeons Can., Am. Coll. Surgeons, Am. Coll. Critical Care Medicine; mem. AAAS, Am. Soc. Parenteral and Enteral Nutrition, Assn. for Acad. Surgery, Can. Assn. Gen. Surgeons, Surg. Infection Soc., European Soc. for Parenteral and Enteral Nutrition, Can. Soc. for Clin. Investigation, Can. Soc. for Critical Care, Soc. Critical Care Medicine, Am. Soc. Bariatric Physicians, Can. Assn. for Med. Edn., N.Y. Acad. Scis., Assn. for Surg. Edn., Mass. Med. Soc., Cen. Surg. Assn., others. Office: Harvard Med Sch 110 Francis St # 3A Boston MA 02215-5501

FORSHA, ANITA LOUISE, health facility administrator; b. Williamsport, Pa., Aug. 26, 1950; d. Howard Monroe and June Eleanor (Turley) Fry; m. Frank Leroy Forsha, Nov. 15, 1974 (div. 1986). Cert., Mayer Sch. Fashion, N.Y.C., 1969; AA, Williamsport Community Coll., 1974; BA, Lycoming Coll., Williamsport, 1976; MBA, Bloomsburg (Pa.) U., 1985. Lic. nursing home adminstr., Pa. Asst. residence mgr., then residence mgr. Hope Enterprises, Inc. and Affiliates, Williamsport, 1973-76, caseworker, coord., 1977-78, dir. residential svcs., 1979-82, v.p. residential svcs., 1982-85, 86-91, acting pres., 1988-89; adminstr. Hampton House Nursing Home, Wilkes Barre, Pa., 1991—. Named Alumna of Yr. Williamsport Area Community Coll., 1989. Mem. Lycoming Assn. Retarded Citizens, Leadership Lycoming. Home: 401 N Courtland St East Stroudsburg PA 18301 Office: Hampton House Nursing Home 1548 Sans Souci Pky Wilkes Barre PA 18702-2028

FORSTOT, S. LANCE, ophthalmologist; b. N.Y.C., Aug. 19, 1943; s. Shepard and Edith Forstot; m. Lynne Rochelle Bitton, June 15, 1945; children: Michele, Jordan. AB, Princeton U., 1965; MD, Johns Hopkins U., 1969. Diplomate Am. Bd. Ophthalmology. Ophthalmologist Corneal Cons. of Colo., Denver, 1982—; ophthalmologist U. Colo. Sch. of Medicine, Denver, 1976-82, prof., 1982—. Contbr. articles to profl. jours. Recipient Honor award Am. Acad. Ophthalmology. Mem. Contact Lens Assn. of Ophthalmology (bd. dirs. 1985-87), Internat. Soc. Refractive Surgery (bd. dirs. 1995-96). Office: Corneal Cons of Colo 8381 Southpark Ln Littleton CO 80120

FORSUM, URBAN K., medical educator; b. Karlsborg, Sweden, Feb. 22, 1946; s. Rune and Maja F.; m. Elisabet K. Tornquist, Aug. 15, 1970; children: Gosta, Asa. PhD, Uppsala U., 1972, MD, 1973. Rsch. assoc. Uppsala U., Sweden, 1970-72; assoc. prof. Uppsala U., 1977-85; internship U. Hosp. Uppsala, 1972-73, resident, 1974-77; postdoctoral fellow Cornell U., Ithaca, N.Y., 1979-80; assoc. prof. Karolinska Inst., Stockholm, 1985-89; prof., chmn. dept. clin. microbiology Linkoping U., Sweden, 1990—; vis. assoc. prof., Rockefeller U., N.Y.C., 1989-90.

FORSYTH, REBECCA ELIZABETH, medical record administrator, consultant; b. St. Clair, Mich., Apr. 28, 1961; d. Frank James Jr. and Lucy Dolores (Webber) F. Student, St. Clair C.C., Port Huron, Mich., 1980, Memphis State U., 1981-83; BS, U. Tenn., Memphis, 1984. Work leader, tumor registry Cleve. Clinic Found., 1984-85, supr. data mgmt., 1985-86, supr. coding, 1986-87; corp. assoc. dir. Atlantic City (N.J.) Med. Ctr., 1987-89; dir. Dept. Med. Records St. Clair's Hosp. & Health Ctr., N.Y.C., 1989-92; dir. Dept. Health Info. Mgmt. Greenwich (Conn.) Hosp., 1992—; self-employed cons., 1987—. Missionary Children's Outreach Internat., Russia, 1995-96; Midnight Run vol. Stanwich Congl. Ch., Greenwich, 1992—, choir; past mem. Order Rainbow for Girls (faith, hope, charity, assoc. worth advisor, worthy advisor, grand rep. each 2 times, 1973-79, recipient grand cross 1976). Mem. Am. Health Info. Mgmt. Assn. (registered record administrator), Conn. Health Info. Mgmt. Assn., Health Info. Mgmt. Systems Soc., Health Info. Mgmt. Systems Soc. New Eng., Women's Healthcare Network, Meditech User's Sys. Exch. (assoc. peer group leader 1995-96), Order Ea. Star. Office: Greenwich Hosp 5 Perryridge Rd Greenwich CT 06830-4508

FORT, ARTHUR TOMLINSON, III, physician, educator; b. Lumpkin, Ga., Sept. 24, 1931; s. Thomas Morton and Gladys (Davis) F.; m. Jane Wilmer McClelland, June 15, 1957; children: Abby Lucinda, Arthur Tomlinson, Jr., Juliana Melody, Ernest Arlington, II. B.B.A., U. Ga., 1952; M.D., U. Tenn., 1962. Diplomate: Am. Bd. Ob-Gyn, Am. Bd. Family Practice. Intern, then resident in ob-gyn U. Tenn.-City of Memphis Hosp., 1962-66; asst. prof. U. Tenn. Med. Sch., 1966-70; prof. ob-gyn, head dept. Sch. Medicine La. State U., Shreveport, 1970-73; prof. maternal-child health and family planning, head program family health Sch. Pub. Health Tulane U., 1973-74; practice medicine specializing in rural family medicine Vacharie, La., 1974-79; prof. ob-gyn and family medicine, head dept. family medicine and comprehensive care Sch. Medicine La. State U., Shreveport, 1980—. Author articles in field. Adv. bd. mem. State of La. Dept. Health and Human Resources, 1986-88. With USAF, 1952-57. Recipient Golden Apple Teaching award Student AMA, 1969, Golden Apple Teaching award Western Interstate Commn. on Higher Edn., 1973. Fellow Am. Coll. Ob-Gyn, Am. Acad. Family Practice; mem. AMA. Office: PO Box 33932 Shreveport LA 71130-3932

FORT, GERALD MARSHALL, psychologist, consultant; b. Mitchell, S.D., Mar. 16, 1919; s. Lyman Marion and Mildred May (Dunsworth) F.; children: Michael Lyman, Sandra Mae. BA, Grinnell Coll., 1941; MA, U. Minn., 1948, PhD, 1960. Lic. psychologist, Wis., Minn. Assoc. prof. S.D. State U., Brookings, 1949-59; psychol. cons. Humber, Mundie & McClary, Milw., 1959-72; ptnr., mgr. Humber, Mundie & McClary, Mpls., 1972-84; bd. dirs. N. Cen. Career Devel. Ctr. Contbr. articles to profl. jours. Mem. coun. Mt. Zion Luth. Ch., Wauwatosa, Wis., 1966-72, Normandale Luth. Ch., Edina, Minn., 1974-80; mem. coun. Desert Hills Luth. Ch., Green Valley, Ariz., pres., v.p., 1985-90; chmn. Commn. Profl. Leadership, Minn. Synod, Mpls., 1976-82; bd. dirs. Samaritan Counseling Ctr., New Brighton, Minn., 1982-84; pres. Spearfish Canyon Owners Assn., 1988—, bd. dirs., 1986-92; tng. coord., pers. com., bd. dirs. Green Valley Recreation Assn., 1985—. Sgt. USAAF, 1941-45. Recipient Disting. Service award Greater Mpls. C. of C., 1984. Mem. Minn. Psychol. Assn. (life). Republican. Club: Edina Country (sec., bd. dirs. 1972-84). Lodge: Kiwanis, Elks. Home and Office: 1865 W Camino Estelar Green Valley AZ 85614-5402

FORT, PAVEL, physician; b. Prague, Czechoslovakia, Jan. 23, 1945; s. Miloš Fořt and Miloslava (Pivrncová) Fořtová; m. Susana Dutková, Dec. 13, 1970; children: Andrea, Pavel, Philip. MD, Charles U., Prague, 1969. Pediatric intern North Shore U. Hosp., Manhasset, N.Y., 1971-72, pediatric resident, 1972-74, pediatric fellow, 1974-75, pediatrician, 1975—; endocrinologist Hosp. Cornell U. Med. Coll., N.Y.C., 1975—; from instr. to assoc. prof. clin. pediatrics Cornell U. Med. Coll., N.Y.C., 1975—. Contbr. chpts. to books, articles to profl. jours.; numerous nat. orgn. meeting presentations. Med. dir. Long Island chpt. N.Y. Diabetes Assn., 1981-84, patients' svcs. com. mem. 1981—, profl. svcs. com. mem., 1984—; Long Island chpt. mem. Human Growth Found., 1978—; specialist in med. assistance program Children's Program of N.Y., 1986—. Named Outstanding Vol. Long Island chpt. Am. Diabetes Assn., N.Y., 1987, '92; Mineral Deficiencies During Growth grantee Kevin Kenny Found.; Coop Core Lab. and Clin. Nutrition Rsch. grantee NIH, Biomed Rsch. Support grantee NIH. Fellow Am. Acad. Pediatrics, Am. Coll. Nutrition; mem. AAAS, AMA, Am. Diabetes Assn., Am. Soc. Magnesium Rsch., Am. Inst. Nutrition, Am. Soc. Experimental Nutrition, Am. Soc. Clin. Nutrition, Internat. Diabetes Fedn., European Assn. Study of Diabetes, Eastern Soc. Pediatric Rsch., Nassau County Med. Soc., Nassau Pediatric Soc., N.Y. Acad. Scis., Lawson Wilkins Pediatric Endocrine Soc., Endocrine Soc., Soc. for Experimental Biology and Medicine.

FORTÉ, JOSEPH PATRICK, medical-surgical nurse; b. Decatur, Ga., Apr. 12, 1969; s. Rema Samuel and Sara BEll (McGarity) F.; m. Tina Dyan Donovan, Sept. 4, 1993. AD, Clayton State Coll., Morrow, Ga., 1993. RN, Ga. Dietary aide Henry Gen. Hosp., Stockbridge, Ga., 1985-87, nurse asst., 1987-93, med.-surg. nurse, 1993—. Baptist.

FORTES MAYER, KARL DAVID, consultant surgeon; b. Takoma Park, Md., July 26, 1942; came to Eng., 1960; s. Meyer and Doris (Yankauer) Fortes; m. Sarah Jane Bayliss, Aug. 15, 1965; children—Paul David, Thomas Herbert, Deborah Kate. B.A., Cambridge U. (Eng.), 1965, M.B., B.Chir., 1968, M.A., 1969. Registrar, Walsgrave Hosp., Coventry; Birmingham Children's Hosp., Eng., 1973-74, Queen Elizabeth Hosp., Birmingham, 1974-75; sr. registrar W. Midlands Regional Health Authority, Birmingham and Stoke-on-Trent, 1975-78; cons. surgeon Walsall Hosps., 1978—. Fundraiser Birmingham Bot. Gardens, 1981-82; active U.K. Cadet Nat. Com., London, 1984—. Mem. Brit. Med. Assn. (local chmn. 1983-85), Brit. Assn. Urol. Surgeons, Brit. Assn. Pediatric Surgery. Avocations: sailing; squash; computing. Home: 61 Vernon Rd, Edgraston, Birmingham B16 9SQ, England Office: St Elmo Chambers, 2A High Gate Rd Walsall, Edgraston, Birmingham B16 95Q England

FORTIER, ALEXANDER J., ophthalmologist; b. N.Y.C.; s. Normal L. and Gertrude A. (McLellan) F.; m. Carol L. Anderson, Aug. 9, 1969; 1 child, Lorna Ann. BS, Boston Coll., 1968; MD, McGill U., Montreal, Que., Can., 1972. Diplomate Nat. Bd. Med. Examiners, Am. Bd. Ophthalmology. Med. intern N.Y. Hosp./Cornell U., N.Y.C., 1973; resident in ophthalmology N.Y. Eye and Ear Infirmary, N.Y.C., 1973-76; pvt. practice ophthalmology Hartford, Conn., 1976—. Mem. Am. Acad. Ophthalmology, Conn. State Med. Soc., New Eng. Ophthalmol. Soc., Hartford County Med. Assn.

FORTIER, DANA SUZANNE, psychotherapist; b. Fresno, Calif., Jan. 15, 1952; d. Dan and Louise (Metkovich) Ninkovich; m. Timothy Fortier, Jan. 29, 1994. BA in Journalism summa cum laude, Calif. State U., Fresno, 1974; BSN, Calif. State U., 1979, MSW with distinction, 1986. Registered nurse, Calif; lic. social worker, Calif. Staff nurse Valley Med. Ctr., Fresno, 1980-81; pub. health nurse Fresno County Health Dept., 1981-83, therapist II Sierra Community Hosp., Fresno, 1986-87; women's svcs. coord. Turning Point Youth Svcs., Visalia, Calif., 1987-89; psychotherapist and cons. in pvt. practice Visalia, 1989—; instr. San Joaquin Valley Coll., 1994—; clins. cons. in field. Contbr. articles to profl. jours. Mem. Task Force on Pregnant Mothers, 1990—. Mem. Calif. Women's Commn. on Drugs and Alcohol, Calif. Advocacy for Pregnent Women, Soc. for Clin. Social Wk., Nat. Assn. Social Workers, Visalia Bus. and Profl. Women's Clubs. Republican. Office: 304 S Johnson St Visalia CA 93291-6136

FORTINA, ANTONIO FORMIA, orthopedic surgeon; b. Novara, Italy, July 29, 1952; s. Mario Boschi and Renata Vittonatto (Formia) F.; m. Michela Pesce Genta, June 3, 1978; children: Elisabetta, Giorgio. MD, U. Torino, Italy, 1977, degree in orthopedics, 1981, degree in physiotherapy, 1984. Prof. orthopedic diseases Regional Sch. Physiotherapy, Novara, 1988-89, 91-92, 94-95; asst. orthopedist Hosp. Novara, 1978-88, sub-chief orthopedics dept., 1989-95; in charge Integrated Orthopedic Activities Orgn., 1995—; lectr. in field. Contbr. to numerous sci. revs. and publs. including Encyclopedia Medica Italiana, 1987—. Chief med. staff Iris Oleggio Football Club, 1982-95. Recipient medal Nobile Collegio Caccia, 1977. Mem. Italian Soc. Orthopedics and Traumatology, Italian Soc. Phys. and Rehab. Medicine, Italian Soc. Sport Traumatology, Italian Soc. Medicine and Surgery Foot, Fedn. Medico-Sportiva Italiana, Club Italiano Chirugia del Ginocchio. Roman Catholic. Home: Viale Pasquali 15, 28100 Novara Italy

FORTMANN, STEPHEN PAUL, medical educator, researcher, epidemiologist; b. Burbank, Calif., Oct. 13, 1948; s. Daniel John and Mary (Van Halteren) F.; m. Lindy Barocchi, Mar. 11, 1984; children: Nicolas, Michele. AB, Stanford U., 1970; MD, U. Calif., San Francisco, 1974. Diplomate Am. Bd. Internal Medicine, Am. Coll. Epidemiology. Clin. instr. Stanford (Calif.) U. Sch. Medicine, 1979-83, asst. prof., 1983-90, assoc. prof., 1990—; advisor World Health Orgn., Geneva, 1980-86. Contbr. articles to profl. jours. Fellow ACP, Am. Heart Assn. (coun. on epidemiology and prevention), Am. Coll.Epidemiology, Soc. Behavioral Medicine. Office: Stanford U Sch Medicine 1000 Welch Rd Palo Alto CA 94304-1825

FORTNER, ROBERT DAVID, pharmacist; b. Sept. 24, 1949. AS, Enterprise State Jr. Coll., Ala., 1970; BS in Pharmacy, Auburn U., 1973; postgrad., U. Ala., Huntsville, 1981—. Lic. pharmacist, Ala., Ga. Intern Med. Coll. Ga., Augusta, 1974, clin. pharmacist, 1974-75; IV coord. Huntsville (Ala.) Hosp., asst. dir. pharmacy, 1976-89; retail pharmacist, bus. mgr. Buy Wise Drugs, 1989—; ednl. presentations at numerous institutions. Adminstrv. bd. mem., choir mem., treas. Methodist Men, Valley Meth. Ch.; soccer coach, referee and age div. coord., AYSO; vol. Panoply of the Arts Festival, Huntsville, March of Dimes Walk-a-Thon participator; pres. Huntsville-Madison County Auburn Club Bd., sec., treas. Mem. Madison County Pharm. Soc. (treas. 1978-79, v.p. 1980), Ala. Pharm. Assn. (vice chmn. acad. institutional practice, 1984-85), Am. Pharm. Assn., Am. Soc. Hosp. Pharmacists, Ala. Soc. Hosp. Pharmacists (program com. and quality assurance com.), Am. Assn. IV Therapists, Ala. State Dept. of Pub. Health (state tech. com. on drugs), Auburn Alumni Assn., Auburn Pharmacy Alumni Assn. Home: 1005 Bluefield Ave SE Huntsville AL 35801-3123

FORWAND, STANLEY A., cardiologist; b. N.Y.C., Apr. 8, 1935; s. Henry Lawrence and Hilda (Levy) F.; m. Ann, Aug. 7, 1972; children: Elizabeth, Amy. AB, Union Coll., 1956; MD, Columbia U. Coll., 1960. Diplomate Am. Bd. Internal Medicine, Am. Bd. Cardiology. Chief cardiology Mt. Auburn Hsop., Cambridge, Mass., 1967—. Capt. U.S. Army, 1965-67. Fellow Am. Coll. Cardiology. Office: Mt Auburn Cardiology Assoc 300 Mt Auburn St #312 Cambridge MA 02138

FOSCHINI, MARIA PIA, pathologist; b. Cotignola, Ravenna, Italy, June 17, 1960; d. Ennio and Maria Adele (Marangoni) F.; m. Ruggero Romano, July 24, 1988; children: Romano, Marco. MD, U. Bologna, Italy, 1985. Asst. prof. Ospedale Bellaria, Bologna, 1990—. Contbr. articles to profl. jours. Mem. Internat. Acad. Pathology (Biancifiori award 1988), European Acad. Pathology, Italian Assn. for Study of the Liver. Roman Catholic. Office: Anatomia Patologica, Osp Bellaria, Via Altura 3, 40139 Bologna Italy

FOSS, FREDERICK ALBERT, JR., surgeon, educator; b. Las Vegas, Nev., Feb. 15, 1955; s. Frederick Albert and Shirley Ann (Spinger) F.; m. Nancy Kunkel, June 20, 1981; children: Courtney, Sara, Charlotte, Alexander, Zachary. BS, U. Nev., 1978, MD, 1981. Diplomate Am. Bd. Surgery, Am. Bd. Surg. Critical Care, Nat. Bd. Med. Examiners. Commd. capt. USAF, 1981, advanced through grades to maj.; intern in surgery David Grant USAF Med. Ctr., Fairfield, Calif., 1981-82, resident, 1982-86; staff surgeon 401st TFW Hosp., Torrejon AFB, Spain, 1986-89, R.L. Thompson Stratetic Hosp., Carswell AFB, Tex., 1989-90; resigned, 1990; fellow Md. Inst. Emergency Med. Svc. Sys., Balt., 1990-91; pvt. practice, Englewood, 1991—; comdr. Flying Ambulance Surg. Trauma Team, Torrejon AFB, 1986-89; mem. staff Swedish Med. Ctr., Englewood, 1991—, Porter Meml. Hosp., Denver, 1991—, Littleton (Colo.) Hosp., 1991—; assoc. prof. family medicine, preceptor U. Colo. Med. Sch., Denver, 1993—. Pres. Rocky Mountain Rythmics Team Parents Club, Littleton, 1992-94, mem., 1994—. Fellow ACS, Southwestern Surg. Congress; mem. Am. Soc. Gen. Surgeons (charter), PanAm. Trauma Soc. (charter), Soc. Critical Care Medicine, Soc. Air Force Clin. Surgeons. Republican. Roman Catholic. Office: Summit Surg Assocs 601 E Hampden Ave Ste 340 Englewood CO 80110

FOSSEY, MARK DOUGLAS, psychiatrist; b. Pawnee, Okla., Feb. 6, 1950; s. William James Jr. and Helen Elizabeth (Haller) F. BA in English, Okla. State U., 1973; MD, U. Okla., Oklahoma City, 1977. Diplomate Am. Bd. Internal Medicine, Am. Bd. Psychiatry and Neurology. Resident internal medicine Tulsa Med. Coll. U. Okla., Tulsa, 1977-80; emergency physician Eastern Okla. Emergency Med. Assocs., Tulsa, 1980-81; resident in psychiatry U. Va., Charlottesville, 1981-84; fellow in rsch. psychiatry Med. U. of S.C., Charleston, 1984-85, instr. dept. psychiatry, 1984-86, asst. prof. dept. psychiatry, 1987-95; asst. prof. dept. psychiatry Med. Coll. of Ga., Augusta, 1986-87; staff psychiatrist VA Med. Ctr., Augusta, 1986-87, Charleston, 1990-95; assoc. clin. prof. depts. psychiatry and internal medicine U. Okla. Coll. Medicine, Tulsa, 1996—; med. dir. Post-Traumatic Stress Disorder Clin. Team VA Med. Ctr., Charleston, 1990-94, dir. consultation psychiatry svc., 1990-95; chief med. cons. Weight Mgmt.Ctr. Med. U. S.C., Charleston, 1989-95. contbr. articles to mags. Mem. AMA, ACP, Am. Psychiat. Assn.

FOSTER, ARTHUR LORNE, pastoral counselor; b. Thornloe, Ont., Can., Dec. 27, 1922; came to U.S., 1954; s. Arthur James and Elizabeth Ellen (Greer) F.; m. Iva May Hazzard, June 15, 1945 (div. Sept. 1978); children: Wendy, Janet, James, Catherine, Margaret; m. Marianne Stelting, Oct. 30, 1978. BA, McMaster U., Hamilton, Ont., 1945, BD, 1948; PhD, U. Chgo., 1964. Lic. psychologist, Mo.; registered marriage and family therapist, Kans.; diplomate Am. Assn. Pastoral Counselors (bd. dirs., editor 1969-73). Minister Glencairn Bapt. Ch., Toronto, Ont., 1945-50, Chatham (Ont.) Bapt. Ch., 1950-54, Normal Park Bapt. Ch., Chgo., 1954-57; counselor, psychotherapist YMCA Counseling Ctr., Chgo., 1956-58; instr. U. Chgo., 1958-59; asst. prof. Vanderbilt U., Nashville, 1959-62; assoc. prof. Meth. Theol. Sch., Delaware, Ohio, 1962-65; prof., acad. dean Berkeley (Calif.) Bapt. Div. Sch., 1965-68, Grad. Theol. Union, Berkeley, 1965-68; prof. Chgo. Theol. Sem., 1968-77; exec. dir., co-founder Counseling Ctr. for Human Devel., Kansas City, Mo., 1978-83; dir. pastoral assocs. Prairie View, Inc., Wichita, Kans., 1983-91; exec. dir., co-founder Counseling & Mediation Ctr., Inc., Wichita, 1991—; Editor: House Church Evolving, 1976. Pres. Delaware County Mental Health Assn., Delaware, 1963. Capt. Can. Army, 1951-54. Kent fellow Soc. for Values in Higher Edn., New Haven, 1956. Mem. Am. Assn. for Marriage and Family Therapy (clin. mem., approved supr.), Kiwanis (dir. 1983—). United Ch. of Christ. Office: Counseling/Mediation Ctr 334 N Topeka Wichita KS 67202

FOSTER, ASHLEY, retired psychologist; b. N.Y.C., Sept. 1, 1922; s. Isaac and Bella (Menes) F.; m. Jean Ray Goorman, Apr. 3, 1950 (wid. 1984); m. Carol Burnham Thomas, June 22, 1986; children: Robert H., David E. Fastovsky. BA, NYU, 1948, MA, 1949, PhD, 1952; MPH, U. Calif., Berkeley, 1966. Chartered psychologist, U.K. Psychologist Indian health USPHS, Anchorage, 1966-71; evaluation cons. Indian health USPHS, Portland, Oreg., 1971-76; asst. regional health adminstr. USPHS, Kansas City, Mo., 1976-79, health systems cons., 1979-83; ret. USPHS, 1983. Editor mag. articles; contbr. articles to profl. jours. Chmn. bd. Chamber Music Series, Eugene, Oreg., 1988-90; sec. bd. dirs., 1990—. Eugene City Club, 1994—. Home: 317 Spyglass Dr Eugene OR 97401-2092 Office: 825 Monroe St Eugene OR 97402-5176

FOSTER, CHRIS B., otolaryngologist; b. Glasgow, Ky., Nov. 8, 1932; s. Chris Benton Foster and Pearl (Poynter) Shannon; m. Kathleen Delores Goen, Apr. 30, 1957; children: Chris, Scott. MD, U. Louisville, 1957. Diplomate Am. Bd. Otolaryngology. Capt. USAF, Riverside, Calif., 1961-63; pvt. practice Glasgow, Ky., 1963-69, San Diego, 1969—; assoc. prof. dept. otolaryngology U. Calif. San Diego, 1975—; dir. Neurotology Lab., San Diego, 1970-95. Fellow Am. Coll. Surgeons, Am. Acad. Otolaryngology; mem. La Jolla Profl. Men's Soc., AMA. Republican. Disciples of Christ. Office: 8950 Genesee Ave Ste 650 La Jolla CA 92037

FOSTER, DANIEL W., medical educator; b. Marlin, Tex., Mar. 4, 1930; married, 1955; 3 children. BA, Tex. Western Coll., 1951; MD, U. Tex., 1955. Intern internal medicine Parkland Meml. Hosp., 1955-56, asst. resident, 1956-58, chief resident, 1958-59; fellow biochemistry U. Tex. Southwestern Med. Sch., 1959-60; investigator Nat. Inst. Arthritis and Metabolic Disease, 1960-62; from asst. prof. to assoc. prof. U. Tex. Southwestern Med. Sch., 1962-69; prof. U. Tex. Southwestern Med. Sch., Dallas, 1969-86, Jan and Henri Bromberg prof., 1986-89, chmn. dept. internal medicine, 1988—, Donald W. Seldin Disting. chair, 1989—; mem. metabolic study sect. NIH, 1968-70, chmn. sect., 1970-72; sr. attending physician Parkland Meml. Hosp. and Univ. Med. Ctr., Tex.; mem. Nat. Diabetes Adv. Bd., 1981-84; chair sci. adv. bd. Hartford Found.; cons. VA Hosp., Dallas, Presbyn. Hosp., Baylor U. Med. Ctr. Assoc. editor: Jour. Clin. Investigation, 1972-77, Jour. Metabolism, Clin. and Exptl., 1969-87; editor: Diabetes, 1978-83. Mem. AAAS, ACP, Inst. Medicine-NAS, Am. Soc. Clin. Investigation, Am. Diabetes Assn. (Banting medal 1984, Joslin medal 1984, Upjohn award 1988), Am. Fedn. Clin. Rsch., Am. Soc. Biol. Chemists, Assn. Am. Physicians. Office: U Tex Health Sci Ctr Dept Internal Medicine Dallas TX 75235-9030*

FOSTER, HELEN MONTAGUE, psychiatrist; b. Charlottesville, Va., Sept. 17, 1946; d. Edgar Allen and Nancy Montague (McCandlish) Prichard; m. Thomas Clark Foster, Aug. 31, 1968; children: Rebecca Robbins Foster Brown, Peter Montague. BA, George Mason U., 1969; MD, Med. Coll. Va., 1982. Diplomate Am. Bd. Psychiatry and Neurology. Resident psychiatry Med. Coll. Va., Richmond, 1982-85, chief resident psychiatry, 1985-86; psychiatrist Insight Physicians, P.C., Richmond, 1986—; asst. clin. prof. Med. Coll. Va., Richmond, 1988—. Vice chmn. program coun. First Unitarian Ch., 1992-93, co-chmn. mental health subcom., 1995—; mem. victim treatment subcom. Lt. Gov.'s Commn. for Reduction of Sexual Assault Victimization in the Commonwealth of Va., 1992. Mem. AMA, Am. Psychiat. Assn., Psychiat. Soc. Va. (pub. edn. coord. Richmond area 1990-93, rep. to Coalition for Mentally Disabled 1990—, legis. chmn. 1994—), Med. Soc. Va., Va. Psychoanalytic Soc., Richmond Psychiat. Soc. (sec. 1994-95, pres.-elect 1995-96, pres. 1996, councilor 1989-90), Richmond Acad. Medicine. Office: Insight Physicians 2006 Bremo Rd Ste 101 Richmond VA 23226-2438

FOSTER, HENRY WENDELL, medical educator; b. Pine Bluff, Ark., Sept. 8, 1933; s. Henry Wendell and Ivie (Hill Watson) F.; m. St. Clair Anderson, Feb. 6, 1960; children: Myrna Faye, Henry Wendell. B.S., Morehouse Coll., 1954; M.D., U. Ark., 1958. Am. Bd. Ob-Gyn. Chief ob-gyn John Andrew Hosp., Tuskegee, Ala., 1965-73; mem. faculty Meharry Med. Coll., Nashville, 1973—, prof., chmn. dept. ob-gyn; dir. maternal and infant care project Tuskegee Inst., Ala., 1970-73; sr. program cons. Robert Wood Johnson Found., Princeton, N.J., 1981-86; chmn. ob-gyn exec. com. Nat. Med. Assn., 1977-79. Mem. editorial bd.: Jour. Med. Edn., 1974-77. Bd. dirs. Planned Parenthood Assn. Am., 1975-81; bd. dirs. Alan Guttmacher Inst., N.Y.C., 1975-81. Served to capt. USAF, 1959-61. Fellow Am. Coll. Obstetricians and Gynecologists; mem. Alpha Omega Alpha. Democrat. Am. Baptist. Home: 4140 W Hamilton Rd Nashville TN 37218-1829 Office: Meharry Med Coll 1005 D B Todd Blvd Nashville TN 37208*

FOSTER, JAMES E., II, surgeon; b. Johnstown, Pa., Feb. 8, 1953; m. Donna K. Rosenberg, Aug. 20, 1977; children: Suzanne, Amanda, Betsy. BS, U.S. Air Force Acad., 1975; MD, Hahnemann Med. Coll., 1979. Diplomate Am. Bd. Surgery. From staff surgeon chief surg. svcs. USAF Hosp., Plattsburgh, 1984-86; fellow surgical gastroenterology U. Tex. Health Sci. Ctr., Houston, 1986-88; from attending surgeon to dir. residency tng. USAF Med. Ctr., Keesler AFB, Miss., 1988-95; assoc. dir. surg. edn. Roanoke (Va.) Meml. Hosps., 1995—. Fellow Am. Coll. Surgeons; mem. Assn. Acad. Surgery, Assn. Surg. Edn., Assn. Program Dirs. Surgery, Soc. Air Force Clin. Surgeons (Surgeon Gen.'s award 1988, Excalibur award 1995). Office: Carilion Roanoke Meml Hosp PO Box 13367 Roanoke VA 24033-3367

FOSTER, JAMES HOWARD, oral surgeon; b. Wharton, Tex., Apr. 30, 1947; s. Wallace Milton and Bessie Myrle (Hoover) F.; m. Donna Jean Ahlers, June 7, 1975; children: Jason Alan, Jessica Elaine, Jamie Michelle. BS in Biology/Chemistry, Sam Houston State U., 1969; DDS, U. Tex., Houston, 1973. Diplomate Am. Bd. Oral and Maxillofacial Surgery. Commd. 2d lt. USAF, 1970, advanced through grades to col., 1993; staff dental officer USAF, Myrtle Beach (S.C.) AFB, 1977-79; staff dental officer Hickam AFB USAF, Honolulu, 1979-82; resident in oral and maxillofacial surgery U. Tex. Dental Br., Houston, 1982-86; oral surgeon, chief profl. svcs., Chanute AFB USAF, Rantoul, Ill., 1986; also quality assurance coord., mem. resident teaching staff USAF, Rantoul; officer in charge oral surgery out-patient clinic, Lackland AFB Wilford Hall Med. Ctr., San Antonio; chmn. dept. oral surgery 3rd Med. Ctr., Elmendorf AFB, Alaska; comdr. 3rd Med. Ops. Squadron; dir. clin. ops. 3d Med. Group, 1994; mem. teaching staff oral and maxillofacial surgery residents Wilford Hall Med. Ctr., San Antonio. Mem. ADA, Am. Assn. Oral and Maxillofacial Surgery, Tex. Dental Assn., Alpha Tau Omega, Delta Sigma Delta. Republican. Roman Catholic. Home: 5530 H St # A Elmendorf AFB AK 99506-1218 Office: 3d Med Group Elmendorf AFB AK 99506

FOSTER, JILL ANNETTE, ophthalmologist; b. Madison, S.D., Nov. 26, 1960. AB, Augustana Coll., 1982; MD, U. Ill. Chgo., 1986. Intern Dept. Medicine U. Ill. Hosp., Chgo., 1986-87; resident ophthalmic plastic and reconstructive surgery U. Pa. Children's Hosp., Phila., 1987-90, fellow, 1990-90; staff physician Cleve. Clinic Found., 1992—. Fellow Am. Acad. Ophthalmology, Am. Soc. Ophthalmic Plastic and Reconstructive Surgeons. Office: Cleveland Clinic Found 9500 Euclid Ave Cleveland OH 44195

FOSTER, MARIETTA ALLEN, rehabilitation specialist; b. Greensboro, N.C., Feb. 10, 1934; d. Joseph Thomas and Marietta (Sowel) Allen; children: Thomas Allen, Michelle Jeanette. BS, U. N.C., Greensboro, 1956; MS, U. N.C., 1962; postgrad., N.C. State U., Raleigh, 1965-69, Macon (Ga.) Coll., 1982-83. Cert. ins. rehab. specialist, case mgr.; lic. profl. counselor, Ga. rehab. supplier. Home economist Duke Power Co., Greensboro, 1955-59, Wise Prefab Homes, Greensboro, 1961; rsch. spr. N.C. State U., Raleigh, 1962; social worker Woman's Prison, Raleigh, 1963-65, Alcoha Rehab. Clinic, Macon, Ga., 1979; caseworker DFCS Welfare Dept., Macon, 1980; cons. counselor Mid-Ga. Counseling Ctr., Macon, 1975-79; counselor Foster Clinic, Macon, 1973-82; logistics specialist Robins AFB, Ga., 1983-84; profl. counselor Macon, 1982—; rehab. counselor, supr. Gen. Rehab. Svcs., 1991-96; office owner, counselor Allen Women's Counseling Svcs., Macon, 1996—; rehab. specialist Intracorp, Macon, 1985-88. Contbr. articles to profl. jours. Recipient numerous scholarships. Mem. Nat. Rehab. Assn. (steering com. 1987-90), Ga. Rehab. Assn., Ga. Marriage and Family Therapists, Am. Legion. Methodist. Home: 1642 Wesleyan Hills Dr Macon GA 31210-1042

FOSTER, NORMAN LOUIS, neurology educator, researcher; b. Jacksonville, Ill., July 27, 1951; s. Louis Palmer and Evelyn Ann (Armstrong) F.; m. Carol Marvel, Nov. 19, 1977; children: Daniel Alexander, Sarah Elizabeth. BA, MacMurray Coll., 1973, DSc (hon.), 1995; MD, Washington U., St. Louis, 1977. Diplomate Am. Bd. Psychiatry and Neurology. Straight med. intern Jewish Hosp., St. Louis, 1977-78; resident in neurology U. Utah, Salt Lake City, 1978-81; med. staff fellow NIH, Bethesda, Md., 1981-84; asst. prof. neurology U. Mich., Ann Arbor, 1984-91, assoc. prof., 1991—, assoc. rsch. scientist Inst. Gerontology, 1995—. Contbr. over 150 articles to med. jours., chpts. to books. Office: U Mich Dept Neurology 1920 Taubman Box 0316 Ann Arbor MI 48109

FOSTER, RUTH MARY, dental association administrator; b. Little Rock, Jan. 11, 1927; d. William Crosby and Frances Louise (Doering) Shaw; m. Luther A. Foster, Sept. 8, 1946 (dec. Dec. 1980); children: William Lee, Robert Lynn. Grad. high sch., Long Beach, Calif. Sr. hostess Mon's Food Host of Coast, Long Beach, 1945-46; dental asst., office mgr. Dr. Wilfred H. Allen, Opportunity, Wash., 1946-47; dental asst., bus. asst. Dr. H. Erdahl, Long Beach, 1948-50; office mgr. Dr. B.B. Blough, Spokane, Wash., 1950-52; bus. mgr. Henry G. Kolsrud, D.D.S., P.S., Spokane, 1958—, Garland Dental Bldg., Spokane, 1958—. Sustaining mem. Spokane Symphony Orch. Mem. Nat. Assn. Dental Assts., DAV Aux., DAV Comdrs. Club, Wash. State Fedn. Bus. and Profl. Women (dir. dist. 6), Spokane's Lilac City Bus. and Profl. Women (past pres.), Nat. Alliance Mentally Ill, Wash. Alliance Mentally Ill, Internat. Platform Assn., Spokane Club, Credit Women's Breakfast Club, Dir.'s Club, Inland N.W. Zool. Soc., Pioneer Circle of Women Helping Women. Democrat. Mem. First Christian Ch. Office: Henry G Kolsrud DDS PS 3718 N Monroe St Spokane WA 99205-2850

FOSTER, SHARRON CECILE, internal medicine physician; b. Kingston, Jamaica, Nov. 6, 1963; arrived in U.S., 1977; d. Ken and Sheila Foster. BA, Rutgers Univ., 1985; MD, Rutgers Medical Sch., 1989. Intern, resident Robert Wood Johnson Univ. Hosp., New Brunswick, N.J., 1992; physician Richard Johnson M.D., West Palm Beach, Fla., 1992-94, Coastal Physicians Group, West Palm Beach, Fla., 1994-95; pvt. practice Sharron C. Foster M.D., P.A., Lake Worth, Fla., 1995—. Mem. AMA, Southern Medical Assn., RUJMS Alumni Assn. (class delegate 1989-92). Office: Sharron C Foster MD Ste 10 3918 Via Poinciana Lake Worth FL 33467

FOSTER, WILLIS ROY, physician; b. New Orleans, Dec. 8, 1928; s. Horace Frank and Callie Opal (Norman) F.; m. Delilah Stokes, July 1, 1957; children: Gregory Mark, Stuart David, Douglas Andrew. BA, La. State U., 1950, MS, 1957, MD, 1957. Rsch. assoc. George Washington U., Washington, 1957-58; postdoctoral fellow Johns Hopkins U., Balt., 1958-59; profl. assoc. Smithsonian Inst., Washington, 1959-63; assoc. dir. Smithsonian Sci. Info Exch., Washington, 1964-71; v.p. Smithsonian Sci. Info. Exch., Washington, 1972-76; tech. dir. Kappa Systems Inc., Arlington, Va., 1976-78; pres. Adv. Concepts Dev., Bethesda, 1978-83; expert cons. NIH, Bethesda, 1983-85, sr. staff physician, 1985—; cons. Metametrics, Inc., Washington, 1978-80, Pan Am. Health Orgn., Washington, 1976-78. Co-author: Human Nutrition, 1990; contbr. articles to profl. jours. Vol. ch. activities Cedar Lane Unitarian Ch., Bethesda. Mem. Washington Acad. Medicine. Home: 6711 Old Stage Rd Rockville MD 20852-4329

FOUGHT, SHARON GAVIN, nursing educator; b. Fort Dodge, Iowa, May 25, 1949; d. George F. and Velma E. (Smith) Gavin; m. Jeffrey R. Fought, Sept. 7, 1974. BS in Nursing, U. Md., Washington, 1971; MSN, U. Tex., Austin, 1974, PhD, 1983. Staff RN Walter Reed Army Hosp., Washington, 1971-73; head nurse ICU 121 Evac. Hosp., Seoul, Korea, 1973-74; clin. nurse specialist Brackenridge Hosp., Austin, 1976-78; clin. instr. U. Tex., Austin, 1978-79; asst. prof. U. Tex. Health Sci. Ctr., San Antonio, 1981-86; asst. prof. dept. physiol. nursing U. Wash., Seattle, 1986-92; assoc. prof., dir. nursing program U. Wash., Tacoma, 1992—. Contbr. articles to profl. jours. Lt. US Army Nurse Corps, 1971-74. WRAIN scholar, 1967-71; recipient Nursing Rsch. award Micromedex/ENA Best Original, 1989-90, ENA Rsch. award, 1990; NIDA/NIAAA faculty fellowship, 1989-92. Mem. ANA, AACN, Emergency Nurses Assn. (chair 1984-86, Nat. Com. Rsch. 1986-90, mem. spl. com. on trauma nat. faculty), Nat. League Nursing, Soc. Critical Care Medicine, Sigma Theta Tau. Home: 4613 144th Pl SE Bellevue WA 98006-3159 Office: U Wash Tacoma Security Bldg 917 Pacific Ave Tacoma WA 98402-4421

FOUNTAIN, ANDRE FERCHAUD, academic program director; b. Oklahoma City, Nov. 12, 1951; s. J. E. and Neaumatta Abilene (Edwards) F.; m. Linda K. Young. BS in Nursing, U. Okla., 1978. RN, Okla; cert. master hyrdotherapist, Kniepp Inst., Germany, massage therapist. Exec. dir. New Life Programs, Oklahoma City, 1981-87; dir. Praxis Coll. Health, Arts and Scis., Oklahoma City, 1988—; speaker in field. Author: A Psychoprophylactic Workbook, 1981; co-author: Psychological Reports, 1977. Found. Caucus for Men in Nursing, Norman, 1976. Recipient 1st Pl. award Internat. Sci. Fair Balt., 1970. Mem. Internat. Childbirth Edn. Assn. (state coord. 1982-84), Am. Soc. Psychoprophylaxis in Obstetrics, Body Workers and Wellness Therapies Assn., Okla. Sports Massage Assn., Masons. Office: Praxis Coll 808 NW 88 Oklahoma City OK 73114

FOUNTAIN, CAROL ELIZABETH, nursing educator; b. Boise, Idaho, Aug. 30, 1941; d. Richard Cash and Beryl Ruby (Headrick) F. AS, Boise Jr. Coll., 1964; BSN, U. Wash., 1966; M in Nursing, Mont. State U., 1972. Cert. orthopedic nurse. Staff St. Lukes Hosp., Boise, 1964, 66-67, Swedish Hosp., Seattle, 1964-66; assoc. prof. Boise State U., Idaho, 1967—; part-time staff St. Luke's Regional Med. Ctr., Boise. Mem. ANA, NLN (assoc. degree site visitor, mem. bd. rev.), Nat. Assn. Orthopedic Nursing, Sigma Theta Tau. Home: 906 Mckinley St Boise ID 83712-7339

FOUNTAIN, LINDA KATHLEEN, health science association executive; b. Fowler, Kans., Apr. 30, 1954; d. Ralph Edward and Ruth Evelyn (Cornelson) Young; m. Andre Fountain. BS in Nursing, Cen. State U., Edmond, Okla., 1976. RN, Okla. Staff nurse med./surg. and coronary care unit Presbyn. Hosp., Oklahoma City, 1976-79; mgr. nursing Hillcrest Osteo. Hosp., Oklahoma City, 1979-80; staff nurse, mgr. Oklahoma U. Teaching Hosp., Oklahoma City, 1981-82; pres. New Life Programs, Oklahoma City, 1981-88, Nursing Entrepreneurs, Ltd., Oklahoma City, 1988—; mgr. Internat. Health Supply, Oklahoma City, 1988—; coord. lactation cons. program State of Okla., 1981—, new life car seat rental program at various hosps., 1983-92, also speaker Success Co., Oklahoma City, 1984—; owner Rainbows Overhead Graphic Media, Oklahoma City, 1984-91; speaker in field. Founder Praxis Coll., Oklahoma City, 1988. Named Mentor of Yr., Okla. Metroplex Childbirth Network, Oklahoma City, 1984. Mem. Am. Nurses Assn., Internat. Lactation Cons. Assn., Internat. Platform Assn., Bodyworkers and Wellness Therapies Assn. Office: Nursing Entrepreneurs Ltd PO Box 75393 Oklahoma City OK 73147-0393

FOURAKER, BRADLEY DEAN, ophthalmology educator; b. Nov. 22, 1956. BA in Psychology, Vanderbilt U., 1978; MD, U. Fla., 1983. Diplomate Am. Bd. Ophthalmology. Intern in internal medicine Ochsner Found. and Clinic, New Orleans, 1983-84, resident in ophthalmology, 1984-87; also assoc. with U. South Ala., Mobile, 1984-87; fellow in corneal and external disease U. Okla. Dean McGee Eye Inst., Oklahoma City, 1987-89; instr. ophthalmology St. Louis U. Bethesda Eye Inst., 1989-90, asst. prof., 1991-92; asst. prof. U. South Fla., Tampa, 1992—; mem. staff Tampa Gen. Hosp., Ambulatory Surgery Ctr., Tampa; lectr. in field; former mem. Mo. Med. Adv. Bd.; former co-med. dir. eye divsn. Lupus Found.; former mem. Mid-Am. Eye and Issue Bank. Active various local civic orgns. Mem. AMA, Am. Acad. Ophthalmology (sci. referee Jour. 1993), Am. Eye Bank Assn., Am. Soc. Cataract and Refractive Surgery, Assn. for Rsch. in Vision and Ophthalmology, Castroviejo Soc., Contact Lens Assn. Ophthalmologists, Eye Bank Assn. Am., Internat. Soc. Refractive Keratoplasty, Fla. Soc. Ophthalmology, Hillsborough County Med. Assn., Ocular Microbiology and Immunology Group, St. Louis Ophthal. Soc., St. Louis Med. Soc., Sjogren's Syndrome Found., Tampa Bay Ophthal. Soc., Vanderbilt U. Alumni Assn. Home: 4905 Bay Way Pl Tampa FL 33609 Office: 12901 Bruce B Downs Blvd Tampa FL 33612

FOURNIER, ALBERT EDOUARD, nephrologist, medical educator; b. Calais, France, Nov. 26, 1938; s. Albert Pierre and Sabine (Six) F.; m. Jacqueline Catherine Kaponas, Apr. 14, 1973 (dec. Mar. 1988); children: Stephane, Alexandre, Sabine; m. Roxana Oprisiu, May 18, 1996. Student, Med. Sch. of Paris, Lille, France, 1957-62, Lycee Francais, London, 1957. Resident U. Hosp., Paris, 1964-68; asst. prof. U. Paris, $D; chief of clinic U. Hosp., Paris, 1969-72; prof. medicine 2nd class U. Picardie, Amiens, France, 1973—; chief of nephrology U. Hosp., Amiens, 1978—; prof. medicine 1st class U. Picardie, Amiens, 1987—. Author: Depletion Potassique, 1972, Rein et Hypertension, 1978, Vitamin D et maladie des os, 1984, also neurology textbook, hypertension textbook; contbr. articles to profl. jours. Mem. French, European, Am. and Internat. Socs. Nephrology and Hypertension. Office: Nephrology CHU, Hospital SUD, 80054 Amiens France

FOURNIER, ARNOLDO, plastic surgeon; b. San Jose, Costa Rica, Dec. 4, 1942; s. Enrique and Flora (Solano) F.; m. Maria-Isabel Gamboa, Aug. 14, 1970; children: Graciela, Adriana. MD, U. Costa Rica, 1967, Gen. Surgeon, 1970. Bd. cert. diplomate plastic surgeon, Costa Rica. Reconstructive plastic surgery staff Autonomous U. Mexico, Mexico City, 1970-72; with St. Luke's Hosp., Columbia U., N.Y.C., 1973; prof. plastic surgery U. Costa Rica, 1974-86. Mem. Soc. Plastic Surgery Costa Rica (founder 1975, pres. 1978-82), Am. Soc. Plastic Surgeons (corr. mem.), Internat. Confedn. Plastic Surgery, Lipoplasty Soc. N.Am. Roman Catholic. Office: Clinica Americana, 14 Ave Central & 1st St, 117-1002 San Jose Costa Rica

FOURNIER, DONALD FREDERICK, dentist; b. Phoenix, Oct. 16, 1934; s. Dudley Thomas and Margaret Mary (Conway) F.; m. Sheila Ann Templeton, Aug. 5, 1957 (div. 1972); children: Julia Marguerite, Donald Frederick, John Robert, Anne Marie Selin, James Alexander; m. Nancy Colleen Hamm, July 10, 1976; children: Catharine Jacinthe, Jacques Edouard. Student, Stanford U., 1952, U. So. Calif., L.A., 1952-54; BSc, U. Nebr., 1958, DDS, 1958. Pvt. practice restorative dentistry Phoenix, 1958—; pres. Hope Mining and Milling Co., Phoenix, 1970—; chief dental staff St. Joseph's Hosp., Phoenix, 1968; vis. prof. periodontology Coll. Dentistry U. Nebr., 1985; faculty Phoenix Coll. Dental Hygiene Sch., 1968-71; investigator Ariz. State Bd. Dental Examiners, 1978-89; mem. Meml. Dental Clinic Staff, 1968-70; dir. Canadian Am. Inst. Cariology, 1986—. Contbr. articles to profl. jours. Pres. bd. trustees Osborn Sch. Dist., Phoenix, 1976; dir. Lukesmen, Phoenix, 1978-81; patrolman Nat. Ski Patrol, Phoenix, 1974-79; pres. Longview PTA, 1969; mem. adv. bd. Phoenix Crime Commn., 1969-71, Phoenix Coll. Dean's Adv. Bd., 1968-75; mem. The Phoenix House Am. Indian Rehab., 1985-86. Lt. col. (retired) Ariz. Army Res. N.G., 1958—. USPHS fellow, 1956-57, 57-58. Fellow Am. Coll. Dentists, Internat. Coll. Dentists; mem. ADA, Ariz. State Dental Assn., Pacific Coast Soc. Prosthodontists, Am. Acad. Restorative Dentistry (pres. 1991-92), Am. Acad. Gold Foil Operators, Craniomandibular Inst. (dir.), Internat. Assn. Dental Rsch., Acad. Operative Dentistry (charter), U.S. Croquet Assn., Ariz. Croquet Club, Downtown Croquet Club (pres. 1993—), Phoenix Country Club, Am. Acad. Orofacial Pain (pres. 1988-89), Phi Delta Theta, Xi Psi Phi. Republican. Roman Catholic. Home: 86 E Country Club Dr Phoenix AZ 85014-5435 Office: 207 E Monterey Way Phoenix AZ 85012-2619

FOURNIER, JOSEPH ANDRE ALPHONSE, nurse, social worker, psychotherapist; b. Norwich, Conn., Jan. 11, 1942; s. Alphonse J. and Eva Marie (Duhaime) F.; children from previous marriage: Elizabeth A., Michael J., Michelle D.; m. Lorinda Bonnette, Dec. 29, 1990; 1 child, Eva M. AA, U. Md., 1977; BSN, Med. Coll. Ga., 1981; MSW, U. Ga., 1987. RN; cert. employee assistance profl.; cert. in marriage and family therapy; bd. cert. diplomate in clin. social work. Sr. staff nurse, psychiatry Med. Coll. Ga., Augusta, 1982-94; psychotherapist employee, faculty assistance program Med. Coll. Ga., 1988-92; mgr. homeless vets. program VA Med. Ctr., Augusta, 1987-88; psychotherapist Family Counseling Ctr. of CSRA, 1992—. Founder Comfort House, Inc. Recipient 79th Point of Light award Pres. George Bush, 1990, Vol. Svc. award Augusta chpt. ARC, 1995. Fellow Am. Orthopsychiat. Assn.; mem. NASW (Social Worker of Yr. award Augusta unit 1993, Ga. chpt. 1994), Employee Assistance Profl. Assn., Sigma Theta Tau. Home: 214 Taft Dr Evans GA 30809-9650

FOUTCH, RICHARD GEORGE, emergency physician; b. Alton, Ill., Aug. 1, 1950; s. Elmer Everett and Natalie Adelaide (Faulstitch) F.; m. Lynn Marie Knobloch, Aug. 2, 1993; 1 child, Zachary Richard. BA, Regis Coll., 1972; DO, W.Va. Sch. Osteo. Medicine, 1981. Diplomate Am. Bd. Emergency Medicine. Resident emergency medicine Madigan Army Med. Ctr., Tacoma, 1982-84; chief emergency treatment ctr. Irwin Army Cmty. Hosp., Ft. Riley, Kans., 1985-86; rsch. physician U.S. Army Rsch. Inst. of Environ. Medicine, Natick, Mass., 1987-89, Ft. Wainwright, Alaska, 1987-89; attending physician, faculty emergency medicine residency Madigan Army Med. Ctr., Tacoma, 1990-91; staff physician emergency dept. Providence Med. Ctr., Seattle, 1991—; clin. instr. emergency dept. U. Wash. Med. Ctr., Seattle, 1996—. Lt. col. U.S. Army, 1982-90. Fellow Am. Coll. Emergency Physicians. Office: Providence Med Ctr Emergency Dept 500 17th Ave Seattle WA 98124-1008

FOWLER, BRUCE ANDREW, toxicologist; b. Seattle, Dec. 28, 1945; s. Andrew and Dolores Yvonne F.; children: Glenn Andrew, Randall Bruce. BS in Fisheries, U. Wash., 1968; PhD in Pathology, U. Oreg., 1972. Staff fellow Nat. Inst. Environ. Health Scis., Research Triangle Park, N.C., 1972-74, sr. staff fellow, 1974-77, rsch. biologist, 1977-87, sr. scientist, 1978-86, head Metal Toxicology, 1986-87; dir. U. Md. Toxicology program, 1987; prof. pathology U. Md. Med. Sch., 1987—; dir. office collaborative studies on adaptive responses estuarine species U. Md., 1988; Meyer Bodansky lectr. Dept. of Pathology, U. Tex med. br., Galveston; adj. assoc. prof. pathology and toxicology curriculum U. N.C.; temporary adv. WHO; mem. work group Internat. Agy. Research Against Cancer; mem. Internat. Commn. on Occupl. Health, Sci. Com. on Toxicology of Metals (sec.); mem. Md. Gov.'s Coun. on Toxic Substances, 1988-93, chmn., 1990-93; chmn. Dahlem Workshop on Mechanisms of Cell Injury: Implications for Human Health, Berlin, 1985; mem. toxicology info. program com., com. on toxicology, chmn. com. on measuring lead in critical populations, com. on women in sci. and engring., com. on biologic markers in urologic toxicology NAS/NRC, 1989-93, com. on evaluation of viability of augmenting potable water supplies with reclaimed water; co-chmn. N.Y. Acad. of Scis. Conf. on Mechanisms of Chem.-Induced Porphyrinopathies, Rye, N.Y.; Swedish Med. Rsch. Coun. vis. prof. Karolinska Inst., 1994-95. Editor: Biological and Environmental Effects of Arsenic, 1983; Mechanisms of Cell Injury: Implications for Human Health; (with E.K. Silbergeld) Mechanisms of Chemical Induced Porphyrinopathies; mem. editorial bd. Chemico-Biol. Interactions, 1980-85, Environ. Health Perspectives, 1981—, Toxicology and Applied Pharmacology, 1985-96, Jour. Toxicology and Environ. Health, 1986—, Internat. Archives Environ. Health, 1986—, Renal Failure, 1988—, Internat. Jour. Occupl. and Environ. Health, 1994—; contbr. articles to profl. jours. and chpts. to books. Rsch. fellow Japanese Soc. for Promotion of Sci., 1990; Fulbright scholar Karolinska Inst., 1994. Mem. AAAS, APHA, Am. Soc. Pharmacology and Exptl. Therapeutics, Am. Assn. Pathologists, Soc. Toxicology (councilor mechanisms of toxicity sect., pres. metals specialty sect. 1996, councilor nat. capital area regional chpt. 1994-95), Am. Coll. Toxicology (councilor 1995—), Soc. for Occupational and Environ. Health (councilor 1988, v.p. 1993), N.Y. Acad. Sci., Profl. Assn. Diving Instructors, Sigma Xi. Office: U Md Program in Toxicology 5202 Westland Blvd TEC II Bldg Baltimore MD 21227-2349

FOWLER, CECILE ANN, nurse, professional soloist; b. Paterson, N.J., Feb. 14, 1920; m. Chester A. Fowler, Mar. 9, 1942. Grad., Passaic (N.J.) Gen. Hosp. Nursing Program, 1941. Nurse Beth Israel Hosp., Newark, 1941-42, Orange (N.J.) Meml. Hosp., 1942-50; asst. receptionist Dr. Stokes, Urologist, East Orange, N.J., 1943-44; nurse Mountainside Hosp., Montclair, N.J., 1960-69, head nurse, premature and newborns, 1966-67; profl. soloist, 1952-69; part-time nurse Upper Three Hosps., 1950-60; co-founder The Oratorio Soc. of N.J., Montclair, 1952; mem. quartet First Baptist Ch., Montclair. Active various coms. PTA, 1951-62; co-founder CD, Little Falls, N.J., 1967; sponsor Met. Opera Guild N.Y., 1977—; child sponsor World Vision, 1983—; mem. Rep. Presdl. Task Force, 1987; founder Challenger Ctr. for Math., Space and Sci. Edn., 1990—, Ptnrs. in Hope: St. Jude's Rsch. Ctr., 1991—; mem. Friends of Richard Tucker Music Found., 1987—. Recipient Vocal Accomplishment award Griffith Music Found., 1944, 45, medal of Merit, Pres. Reagan, 1988, Pres. Bush, 1990, Rep. Presdl. Legion of Merit, 1992. Mem. Lincoln Ctr. for the Performing Arts, Friends of Carnegie Hall, Friends of Richard Tucker Music Found., Am. Biog. Inst. Am. (rsch. bd. advs. 1989—, dep. gov., life mem., fellowship, Commemorative Medal of Honor 1991), Heritage Found. (U.S. English mem. 1986—), U.S. Senatorial (preferred mem.), Little Falls Woman's Club (edn. chmn. 1979-81), Montclair Operatta (various chairmanships 1943—, gov. 1990-92). Republican. Roman Catholic. Home: 9 Lotz Hill Rd Clifton NJ 07013-2312

FOWLER, CHARLOTTE ANN, occupational health nurse; b. Shreveport, La., June 10, 1954; d. William James Jr. and Erin Kathleen (Taylor) F. Student, N.E. La. U., 1973-74, La. State U., Shreveport, 1977-78; ADN, Northwestern State U., Shreveport, 1982. RN, La. RN in oper. rm. Schumpert Med. Ctr., Shreveport, 1982-85; RN in oper. rm. La. State U.

Med. Ctr., Shreveport, 1985-86, RN in recovery rm. and surg. ICU, 1986-87, RN in psychiatry, 1987-88, RN in recovery rm., 1988-89, RN in surg. ICU, 1989-90, RN clin. coord. dept. of surgery divsn. oral maxifacial surgery, 1990-93, nursing adminstrn. RN, house mgr., 1993—. Author: (with others) American Poetry Anthology, 1989. Dist. coord. La. Nurses' Network for Impaired Profls., 1987-90; bd. dirs., lay rep. Met. Cmty. Ch., Shreveport. Mem. ANA, Am. Assn. Occupl. Health Nurses, Critical Care Soc., La. State Nurses Assn., Shreveport Dist. Nurses Assn. Home: 625 Wilkinson Shreveport LA 71104 Office: La State U Med Ctr Occupl Health Clinic 1501 Kings Hwy PO Box 33932 Shreveport LA 71130-3932

FOWLER, GLENN W., pediatric neurologist; b. New Orleans, Feb. 8, 1934; s. John W. and Roxie L. (Breland) F.; m. Jane Meltzer, Aug. 15, 1965; children: Leslie, Joanna. BS, Tulane U., 1954; MD, La. State U., 1964. Diplomate Am. Bd. Psychiatry & Neurology. Instr. pediatrics, neurology Northwestern U., Chgo., 1969; prof. neurology and pediatrics U. Calif., Irvine, 1970—. Capt. U.S. Navy, 1954-59, Korea. Fellow Am. Acad. Neurology, Am. Acad. Pediatrics; mem. Nat. Tuberous Sclerosis Assn. (profl. adv. bd. 1978), Child Neurology Soc., Orange County Neurology Soc. (pres.). Office: Children's Hosp 455 S Main Orange CA 92668

FOWLER, JEFFREY MCCABE, physician, gynecologic oncologist, educator; b. Petosky, Mich., Oct. 13, 1958; s. James Harding and Barbara Ann (McCabe) F.; m. Leslie Mihalik, June 30, 1984; children: Kelsey, Jamie, John. BA, Kalamazoo Coll., 1981; MD, Northwestern U., 1985. Diplomate Am. Bd. Ob-Gyn. Resident in ob-gyn. Ohio State U., 1989; fellow in gynecologic oncology UCLA, 1991; assoc. prof. U. Minn., Mpls., 1991—. Fellow Am. Coll. Obstetric Gynecology, ACS; mem. Western Assn. Gynecologic Oncology, Soc. Gynecologic Oncology. Methodist. Office: U Minn 420 Delaware St 5F Minneapolis MN 55455

FOWLER, LINDA MCKEEVER, hospital administrator, management educator; b. Greensburg, Pa., Aug. 7, 1948; d. Clay and Florence Elizabeth (Smith) McK.; m. Timothy L. Fowler, Sept. 13, 1969 (div. July 1985). Nursing diploma, Presbyn. U. Hosp., Pitts., 1969; BSN, U. Pitts., 1976, M in Nursing Adminstrn., 1980; D in Pub Adminstrn., Nova U., 1985. Supr., head nurse Presbyn. Univ. Hosp., Pitts., 1969-76; mem. faculty Western Pa. Hosp. Sch. Nursing, Pitts., 1976-79; acute care coord. Mercy Hosp., Miami, 1980-81; asst. adminstr. nursing North Shore Med. Ctr., Miami, 1981-84, v.p. patient care, 1984-88, Golden Glades Regional Med. Ctr., Miami, 1988-89, Humana Hosp.-South Broward, Hollywood, Fla., 1989-91, assoc. exec. dir. nursing; v.p./CNO Columbia Regional Med. Ctr. at Bayonet Point, 1991-96; COO/CNO Greenbrier Valley Med. Ctr., 1996—; mem. adj. faculty Barry U., Miami, 1984—, Broward C.C., Ft. Lauderdale, 1984—, Nova U., 1986—; cons. Strategic Health Devel. Inc., Miami Shores, Fla., 1986—, So. Coll., Cleveland, Tenn., 1995-96. Bd. dirs. Pasco County Am. Cancer Soc., 1992-95. Dept. HEW trainee, 1976, 79-80. Recipient Pres.'s award Columbia Healthcare Corp., 1995. Mem. Am. Orgn. Nurse Execs. (legis. com. 1988-90), Fla. Orgn. Nurse Execs. (bd. dirs. 1986-88), South Fla. Nurse Adminstrs. Assn. (sec. 1983-84, bd. dirs. 1984-86), U. Pitts. Alumni Assn., Presbyn. U. Alumni Assn., Portuguese Water Dog Club Am. (bd. dirs. 1988-89), Ft. Lauderdale Dog Club (bd. dirs. 1981-82, 83-85, v.p. 1982-83), Am. Kennel Club (dog judge), Sigma Theta Tau. Lutheran. Home: 27 Potomac Crossway Lewisburg WV 24901-8917 Office: Greenbrier Valley Med Ctr PO Box 497 202 Maplewood Ave Ronceverte WV 24970

FOWLER, STANLEY, dean; b. Colo., Apr. 11, 1942; s. Aubrey O. and Margaret (Hazelwood) F.; m. Maryann Fowler, Sept. 7, 1968; children: Geoffrey, Kenneth. BA, Pomona Coll., 1964; PhD, Rockefeller U., 1969; postgrad., U. Louvain, Belgium, 1969-71, U. Wash., 1971-73. Asst. prof. dept. biochem. cytology Rockefeller U., N.Y.C., 1973-81, assoc. prof., 1981-82; prof. dept. pathology Sch. Medicine U. S.C., Columbia, 1982—, assoc. dean R&D, 1993—, assoc. dean rsch. & grad. studies, 1986-92; exec. mgr. S.C. Cancer Ctr./ Richland Meml. Hosp./ U. S.C., Columbia, 1992—. Contbr. articles to profl. jours. Fellow Helen Hay Whitney Found., 1969-72, NIH, 1973. Office: U SC Sch Medicine 6439 Garners Ferry Rd Columbia SC 29209

FOWLER, THOMAS JAMES, pharmacist, consultant; b. Pitts., Jan. 6, 1933; s. Charles T. and Clara Theresa (Zahren) F. BS in Pharmacy, Duquesne U., 1955; Diplomate Am. Bd. Pharmacy; m. Joan A. Craig, Sept. 2, 1961; children: Thomas M., John P., Michael C., Julie Ann. Pharmacist in community pharmacy, Pitts. and Kensington, Md., 1957-62; staff pharmacist Mercy Hosp., Pitts., 1962-66, chief pharmacist, 1964-66; dir. of pharmacy svcs. Sewickley Valley Hosp., Pa., 1966-94; pharmacist cons. D.T. Watson Rehab. Hosp., 1970-94; adj. instr. intern program Duquesne U. Sch. Pharmacy, Pitts., 1976-94; lectr. Sewickley Valley Hosp. Sch. of Nursing, 1966-94; owner Fowler Pharmacy Consulting Svcs., Pitts., 1989—; vice chmn. pharmacy adv. com. Hosp. Coun. Western Pa., 1978-80, chmn., 1981-82, chmn. intravenous sub-com., 1980-81, mem. value analysis steering com., 1982-83; mem. pharmacy task force Voluntary Hosps. Am.-Pa., 1985-89, chmn. task force, 1989-90; cons. Lifecare Home Svcs., 1989-94, Quad Pharms., 1989-90. Counselor, Allegheny Trails coun. Boy Scouts Am. With USN, 1955-57. Recipient Sister M. Gonzales award for outstanding mgmt. Hosp. Coun. of Western Pa., 1982, Merck, Sharp and Dohme Corp. Pharmacy Achievement award for mgmt., 1983, Alumni Achievement award Duquesne U., 1990. Fellow Am. Soc. Cons. Pharmacists, Am. Soc. Hosp. Pharmacists; mem. Western Pa. Soc. Hosp. Pharmacists (pres. 1970-71), Pa. Soc. Hosp. Pharmacists, Am. Pharm. Assn., K.C. Republican. Roman Catholic. Author: Incompatibilities of Some Intravenous Additives, 1971; contbr. articles on pharmacy to profl. publs. Home and Office: 104 Connie Dr Pittsburgh PA 15214-1218

FOWLER, VINCENT R., dermatologist; b. South Bend, Ind., Dec. 15, 1944; s. Vincent R. and Miriam Frances (Alwarn) F.; m. Madeline M. Fowler, Apr. 26, 1975; children: Debra, Michael, Peter. BA in Pscyhology, Calif. State U., L.A., 1969; MD, U. Autonoma Guadalajara, Mex., 1973. Diplomate Am. Bd. Dermatology; lic. Calif. Intern Long Beach (Calif.) Med. Ctr., 1974-75; resident in internal medicine SUNY Med. Ctr., Stonybrook, N.Y., 1975-78; resident in dermatology Letterman Army Med. Ctr., Praesido San Francisco, Calif., 1978-80; chief medicine/dermatology Reynolds Army Hosp., Fort Sill, Okla., 1980-82; chief dermatology W. L.A. Kaiser Med. Ctr., 1982—; asst. clin. prof. UCLA Sch. Medicine, 1984—. Major Army Med. Corps., 1978-82. Fellow Am. Acad. Dermatology; mem. L.A. Met. Dermatol. Soc. Office: Kaiser W LA Med Ctr 5971 Venice Blvd Los Angeles CA 90034

FOWLER, WAYNE LEWIS, SR., internist; b. Topeka, Kans., Jan. 5, 1923; s. Morrill George and Grace Anna (Carlson) F.; m. Violet June Ransom, Sept. 4, 1948; children: Wayne Jr., Deborah. BS, Washburn U., 1945; MD, U. Ind., 1947. Diplomate Am. Bd. Internal Medicine. Intern Kansas City (Mo.) Gen. Hosp., 1947-48, resident internal medicine, 1948-51; internist Galvin-Haughey Clinic, Concordia, Kans., 1953-95, NCK Med. Clinic, Concordia, Kans., 1995—; past pres. med. staff St. Joseph Hosp., Concordia Kans. Capt. US Air Force, 1951-53,. Fellow Am. Coll. Physicians (Laureate award Kans. chpt. 1994), Am. Coll. Chest Physicians; mem. AMA, Cl. County Med. Soc., Kans. Med. Soc., Am. Soc. Internal Medicine, Concordia Elks, Concordia Moose, Topeka Masonic Lodge # 17, Scottish Rite Bodies Topeka, ISIS Shrine alina. Republican. Episcopalian. Home: 332 W 8th St Concordia KS 66901 Office: NCK Med Inc 1010 3d Ave Concordia KS 66901

FOWLER, WESLEY C., JR., obstetrician, gynecologist; b. Dunn, N.C., Feb. 18, 1945. MD, U. N.C. Sch. Medicine, 1966. Diplomate Am. Bd. Ob-Gyn. Intern N.C. Maternity Hosp., Dunn, 1967; resident N.C. Maternity Hosp, Dunn, 1967-71; obstetrician-gynecologist U. N.C. Hosps., Chapel Hill, 1972—; prof., vice chmn. dept. ob.-gyn. U. N.C. Sch. of Medicine, Chapel Hill, 1972—. Mem. ACS, ACOG, AMA, Soc. Gynecologists and Obstetricians. Office: U NC Meml Hosp Dept Obstetrics Chapel Hill NC 27514*

FOWLER, WILEY DOUGLAS, surgeon; b. Shreveport, La., Nov. 15, 1938; s. Wiley Douglas and Abbie (Marston) F.; m. Sue McClendon, June 2, 1959; children: Doug III, Anne, Susan, Abigail, Mary. BS, La. State U., Baton Rouge, 1959; MD, La. State U., New Orleans, 1967. Diplomate Am. Bd. Surgery. Intern US Naval Hosp., Jacksonville, Fla., 1963-64; resident in gen. surgery Confederate Meml. Med. ctr., Shreveport, 1966-70; pvt. practice, Colquitt, Ga. Lt. comdr. M.C., USNR, 1963-68. Mem. ACS; mem. AMA, Ga. Med. Assn., Fla. Assn. Gen. Surgeons, So. Surg. Congress, So. Med. Assn. Republican. Office: 205 W Main St Colquitt GA 31737-1223

FOX, ALISSA BENIMOFF, dermatologist b. Cin., Sept. 20, 1954; d. Murray and Norma (Woldman) Benimoff; m. James A. Fox, May 29, 1977; children: Jonathan, Alexandra. AB, Smith Coll., Northampton, Mass., 1976; MD, NYU, N.Y.C., 1980. Diplomate Am. Bd. Dermatology. Med. intern Montions Hosp. Medicine, Bronx, N.Y., 1980-81; resident in dermatology N.Y. Hosp., Cornell U. Med. Ctr., N.Y.C., 1981-84; ptnr. Fox Skin & Allergy Assocs., Somerville, N.J., 1984—; mem. active staff Somerset Med. Ctr., Somerville, N.J., 1984—; mem. courtesy staff Hunterdon Med. Ctr., Flemington, N.J., 1984—. Recipient Vol. Leadership award Am. Cancer Soc., 1989, Physicians Recognition award AMA, 1994. Mem. Am. Acad. Dermatology, Med. Soc. N.J. Office: Fox Skin & Allergy Assocs 3461 US Hwy 22 Somerville NJ 08876

FOX, ARTHUR CHARLES, physician, educator; b. Newark, Sept. 16, 1926; s. Jacob and Mae (Bonda) F. Student, Harvard U., 1943-44. M.D., N.Y. U., 1948. Intern, asst. resident and chief resident in medicine Bellevue Hosp., N.Y.C., 1948-52; from asst. to prof. N.Y. U. Sch. Medicine, N.Y.C., 1954—; chief cardiology sect. N.Y. U. Sch. Medicine, 1969—; cons. Manhattan VA Hosp. Contbr. articles to profl. jours. Served with M.C. USAF, 1952-54. NIH fellow, 1954-56; grantee, 1956-80. Fellow ACP (gov. region 1981-86), Am. Coll. Cardiology; mem. Am. Fedn. Clin. Research, N.Y. Heart Assn. (pres. 1987-89), N.Y. Cardiologic Soc. (pres. 1992-93), Alpha Omega Alpha, AAAS, Sigma Xi. Home: 330 E 33rd St New York NY 10016-9466 Office: 550 First Ave New York NY 10016-6481

FOX, BERNARD HAYMAN, cancer epidemiologist, educator; b. N.Y.C., Dec. 26, 1917. BS, U. Mass., 1940; MS, Tufts U., 1947; PhD, U. Rochester, 1949. Teaching fellow U. Mass., 1941; asst. prof. George Washington U., Washington, 1949-56; chief exptl. rsch. Div. Accident Prevention, HEW, Washington, 1957-60, 62-67, assoc. chief rsch., neurol. and sensory disease control program, 1967-70; dir. lab. of exptl. psychology Cleve. Psychiat. Inst., 1960-62; asst. to chief perinatal rsch. program Nat. Inst. Neurol. Diseases and Blindness, NIH, Bethesda, Md., 1970-73, mgr. social sci., biometry br. Nat. Cancer Inst., 1973-82; prof. psychiatry Boston U. Sch. Medicine, 1983—; mem. sci. adv. coun. Inst. for Advancement of Health, 1982-90. Served to 1st lt. USAAC, 1942-46. Fellow APA; mem. Internat. Psycho-Oncology Soc. (bd. dirs. 1986-95). Co-editor: Alcohol and Traffic Safety, 1963; Minimal Brain Dysfunction, 1971; Cancer: The Behavioral Dimensions, 1976; Perspectives on Behavioral Medicine, 1981; Impact of Psychoendocrine Systems in Cancer and Immunity, 1984. Home: 99 Florence St Apt 320 Malden MA 02148-3955 Office: Boston U Sch Medicine 85 E Newton St Boston MA 02118

FOX, CLAUDE EARL, state health officer; b. Charleston, Miss., Nov. 8, 1946; s. Claude Earl Jr. and Shirley (Houston) F.; m. Carolyn Tedford, May 15, 1971; children: Stephanie Ryan, Victoria Crossley. BS with distinction, Miss. Coll., 1968; MD, U. Miss., 1972; MPH, U. N.C., 1975. Diplomate Am. Bd. Preventive Medicine, Am. Bd. Pub. Health; qualified Am. Bd. Pediatrics. Pediatric intern U. Miss. Med. Ctr., Jackson, 1972-73, pediatric resident, 1979-80; pediatric resident Johns Hopkins Hosp., Balt., 1978-79; with Miss. State Dept. Health, 1973-86; local health officer Charleston, 1973-74; dist. health officer Tupelo, Miss., 1975-78; chief Bur. Family Health Service Jackson, 1980-81, chief Bur. Personal Health Service, 1980-86; state health officer Ala. Dept. Pub. Health, Montgomery, 1986—; med. cons. N.C. Dept. Health, Chapel Hill, 1974-75, Rockwell Internat., Tupelo, 1976-78, Mo. Dept. Health, 1984; vis. tchr. maternal and child health U. Miss. Med. Ctr., 1980-86, mem. adv. council; vis. teaching staff Sch. Pub. Health and Sch. Medicine, U. Ala.; adv. group on prevention Sen. Com. Labor and Human Resources, Washington; mem. Ala. Statewide Health Coordinating Council; mem. Ala. State Child Abuse and Negelect Prevention Bd., Ala. Commn. on Aging, Ala. Youth Services Bd., Planning and Adv. Council for Devel. Disabilities, Pesticides Adv. Com., Ala. Bd. Examiners Nursing Home Adminstrs.; chmn. Ala. Task Force Prevention and Perinatal Health, Ala. Radiation Adv. Bd. Health; adv. com. Emergency Med. Services; past mem. work group to revise 1988 U.S. standard birth certificate Nat. Ctr. Health Stats., primary care work group Miss. Gov.'s Office; past chmn. infant mortality task force, adolescent pregnancy task force Gov.'s Council on Children and Youth. Mem. Ala. Resource Devel. Com.; bd. dirs. Montogmery chpt., bd. .dirs. Ala. div., med. adv. com. ARC.; mem external adv. com. Sch. Pub. Health U. Ala. Birmingham; mem. Ala. State Bldg. Commn. Recipient Sidney Chipman award for Outstanding Achievement in Maternal and Child Health U. N.C., 1982; named Pub. Citizen of Yr. Nat. Assn. Social Workers, Montgomery unit, 1987, Ala. chpt. 1987. Mem. Nat. Assn. Maternal and Child Health and Crippled Children's Dirs. (past steering com., legis. com., data com., pres-elect), Med. Assn. State Ala , Montgomery County Med. Soc., Am. Pub. Health Assn. (past Miss. del. Governing Council, Young Profl. Yr. award Maternal and Child Health sect. 1984), Ala. Pub. Health Assn., Assn. State and Terr. Health Officials (past forms revision com.), Am. Coll. Ob-gyn (past com. revision natality terminology). Baptist. Office: Disease Prevention & Health 200 Independence Ave SW Washington DC 20201

FOX, DAVID ALAN, rheumatologist, immunologist; b. Montreal, July 5, 1953; s. Lester L. and Zelda L. (Rothbart) F.; m. Paula L. Bockenstedt, July 10, 1977; children: Sharon Elizabeth, Michelle Caroline, Jonathan William. BS, MIT, 1974; MD, Harvard U., 1978. Diplomate Am. Bd. Internal Medicine, Am. Bd. Rheumatology. Intern. resident Brigham and Women's Hosp., Boston, 1978-81; fellow in rheumatology and immunology Harvard U. Med. Sch., Boston, 1981-85; asst. prof. U. Mich., Ann Arbor, 1985-90, assoc. prof., 1990-95; prof., 1995—; acting chief divsn. rheumatology U. Mich., Ann Arbor, 1990-91; chief, 1991—; dir. U. Mich. Multipurpose Arthritis Ctr., Ann Arbor, 1990—; trustee Mich. chpt. Arthritis Found., Southfield, Mich., 1993—. Author chpts. to books; contbr. articles to profl. jours. Mem. Am. Coll. Rheumatology, Am. Assn. Immunologists, Am. Soc. Clin. Investigation. Office: U MichMed Ctr Rackham Arthritis Rsch Unit 3918 Taubman Ctr Ann Arbor MI 48109

FOX, DONALD ALAN, science educator; b. Cleve., July 1, 1948; s. Hiram B. and Helen R. (Schwartz) F.; m. April Gail Genuth, Apr. 12, 1981; children: Mykal J., Hilary R. BS in Chemistry, Miami U., 1970; PhD in Toxicology, U. Cin., 1977. Asst. prof. U. Tex. Med. Sch., Houston, 1979-82; asst. prof. U. Houston, 1982-85, assoc. prof., 1985-93, prof. vision sci. and biochemistry, 1993—; cons. in field. Mem. AAAS, Assn. Rsch. and Vision in Ophthalmology, Soc. Toxicology (pres neurotoxicology sect. 1988-89), Soc. Neurosci. Office: U Houston Coll. Optometry 4901 Calhoun Houston TX 77204-6052

FOX, DONALD LEE, mental health counselor, consultant; b. Seymour, Ind., Sept. 9, 1948; s. John L. and Thelma P. (Engel) F.; m. Patricia L. Sain, Aug. 26, 1978; children: Ashley M., Aimee E. BA, Ind. U., Indpls., 1978; MS, Ind. State U., 1979. Cert. clin. social worker, social worker, marriage and family therapist. Coord. mental health Cath. Social Svcs., Indpls., 1979-85; coord. psychiat. assessment Valley Vista Hosp., Greenwood, Ind., 1985-86; clin. dir. Pathways, Speedway, Ind., 1986—; lectr., cons. Butler U., Indpls., 1988-89; adj. prof. U. Indpls., 1990—; cons. Wayne Twp Vol. Fire Dept., Indpls., 1984—, La Porte (Ind.) Child Welfare Dept., 1988—. Pres., CEO Five Stop of Ind.: A Program for Youth, Inc., 1987-92. Mem. APA (assoc.), AACD, Am. Mental Health Counselors Assn. (nat. conf. com. 1990), Ind. Assn. Counseling and Devel. (conf. chmn. 1989), Ind. Mental Health Counselors Assn. (pres.-elect 1989-91, pres. 1991-92, Outstanding Svc. award 1989), Soc. Personality and Social Psychology (assoc.). Roman Catholic. Home: 730 Greenlee Dr Indianapolis IN 46234-2237

FOX, EMILE, physician; b. Luxembourg, Jan. 4, 1953; s. Nicolas and Lucie (Waltzing) F. MD, U. Nancy (France), 1980, diploma in pub. health, 1982; MS in Tropical Medicine, London Sch. Hygiene, 1983. Registrar Cen. Hosp., Luxembourg, 1980-83; specialist physician Nat. Health Lab., Luxembourg, 1983-84; sr. med. officer Internat. Ctr. Med. Rsch., Lahore, Pakistan, 1984-85; lectr. medicine U. Papua New Guinea, 1985-86; staff epidemiologist USN Med. Rsch. Unit # 3, Cairo, 1986-90; med. officer WHO, Kigali, Rwanda, 1990-92; cons. WHO, 1993-94; med. officer and team leader WHO/GPA, Beijing, China, 1994-95; country program advisor UNAIDS, Beijing, 1996—; rsch. asst. prof. internat. health U. Md., Balt., 1984-90; hon. cons. Port Moresby Gen. Hosp., Papua New Guinea, 1985-86; team leader epidemiol. rsch. expeditons NAMRU-3, Republic Djibouti, 1987-90. Author: (with others) Tuberculosis in the Tropics, 1991; contbr. articles to profl. jours. Recipient Frederic Murgatroyd award London Sch. Hygiene, 1983. Fellow Royal Soc. Tropical Medicine and Hygiene; mem. Am. Soc. Microbiology, Am. Soc. Tropical Medicine and Hygiene, Am. Pub. Health Assn. Home: 16 rue Van Werveke, Luxembourg L-2725, Luxembourg

FOX, GERALD LYNN, retired oral and maxillofacial surgeon; b. Asheboro, N.C., Mar. 4, 1942; s. Clarence William and Jane Marie (Brock) F.; BS, U. Tenn., 1964, DDS, 1967; m. Ellen Carol Smith, Mar. 18, 1961; children: Angela Carol, Michael Lynn, Lisa Elaine. Diplomate Am. Bd. Oral & Maxillofacial Surgery. Rotating intern Wilford Hall USAF Hosp., San Antonio, 1968-69; intern and resident in oral surgery U. Tex. Med. Sch., San Antonio, 1974; mem. teaching staff U. Tex. Sch. Dentistry and VA Hosp., San Antonio; pvt. practice dentistry specializing in oral and maxillofacial surgery, retired; former mem. staff Holston Valley Hosp. and Med. Ctr., Indian Path Hosp., Tenn.; apptd. by gov. to Mal-Practice Rev. Bd., Tenn., 1975-81; pres. Sullivan County Chpt. Am. Cancer Soc., 1975-77; med. missionary, Honduras, 1980, 83, 85, 90; People-to-People amb. to Japan, Malaysia and Korea, 1985—. Contbr. articles to profl. jours. Capt. USAF, 1968-72. Recipient Marion Fuller award, 1967; award Am. Cancer Soc., 1977; award So. Bapt. Missionary Bd., 1980. Fellow Am. Coll. Oral and Maxillofacial Surgeons (founding master), Internat. Assn. Oral and Maxillofacial Surgeons (life), Am. Dental Soc. Anesthesia, Am. Assn. Oral and Maxillofacial Surgeons; mem. Am. Coll. Oral and Maxillofacial Surgeons (diplomate), Tenn. Dental Assn., Tenn. Assn. Oral and Maxillofacial Surgeons, S.E. Soc. Oral and Maxillofacial Surgery, Airplane Owners and Pilots Assn., Xi Psi Phi. Methodist.

FOX, HAROLD EDWARD, obstetrician/gynecologist, educator, researcher; b. East Orange, N.J., Feb. 19, 1945; s. Willis Edward and Elizabeth (Strathearn) F.; m. Rhea Keller, June 18, 1966; children: Harold Hamilton, Andrhea Alicia. BA, U. Rochester, 1967, MS, MD with honors, 1972. Diplomate Am. Bd. Ob-Gyn., Am. Bd. Maternal-Fetal Medicine. Intern, resident Strong Meml. Hosp., Rochester, N.Y., 1972-75; dir. Regional Perinatal Program, Rochester, N.Y., 1975-79; dir. obstetrics and maternal fetal medicine U. Rochester, 1977-79; dir. maternal fetal medicine Columbia U., N.Y.C., 1979-95, dir. obstetrics, 1985-88, vice chmn. ob-gyn., 1988-91, chmn. protem dept. ob-gyn., 1991-95; Oscar I. and Mildred S. Dodek prof., chmn. ob-gyn. The George Washington U., Washington, 1995—, exec. dir. ctr. of excellence for women's health, 1995—; chair primary care com. George Washington U. Med. Ctr., 1996—; chmn. women and infant transmission study NIH, 1988-93; mem. pediatric com. AIDS clin. trials group, 1988-91; organizing mem. women's com.; mem. obstet. adv. com. N.Y.C. Dept. Health; bd. midwifery N.Y. State Edn. Dept., 1994-95; chmn. N.Y. Acad. Medicine Ob-gyn. sect., 1993-94. Editor Pediatric AIDS, 1991—; contbr. articles to profl. jours. Grantee NIH, 1988-95, USPHS, 1991-95, March of Dimes. Fellow Soc. Gynecologic Investigation, Am. Coll. Ob-Gyn.; mem. Internat. AIDS Soc., Am. Inst. Ultrasound in Medicine, Perinatal Rsch. Soc., Washington Acad. Medicine, Washington Gynecol. Soc., Alpha Omega Alpha, Phi Beta Delta. Home: 4835 Foxhall Crescent Washington DC 20007 Office: The George Washington U ANCA 421 ob-gyn 2150 Pennsylvania Ave NW Washington DC 20037 also: Georgetown Sta PO Box 25526 Washington DC 20007

FOX, IRA MARTIN, podiatrist; b. Lancaster, Pa., Mar. 9, 1953; s. Leonard P. and Janice (Osipow) F.; m. Helen E. Yannelli, May 10, 1980; children: Julian P., Dara A., Dylan B. BA, Johns Hopkins U., 1975; D of Podiatric Medicine, Pa. Coll. Podiatric Medicine, 1980. From assoc. to asst. prof. surgery Pa. Coll. Podiatric Medicine, Phila., 1982-91; head sect. podiatric surgery Cooper Hosp., Univ. Med. Ctr., Camden, N.J., 1984—; clin. asst. prof. surgery divsn. orthopaedic surgery UMDNJ/Robert Wood Johnson Med. Sch., 1994. Contbr. articles to med. jours. Fellow Am. Coll. Foot and Ankle Surgeons (com. on trauma 1992—). Office: Cooper Hosp-Univ Med Ctr Dept Surg 3 Cooper Plz Ste 411 Camden NJ 08103

FOX, IRVING HARVEY, clinical researcher, medical products executive; b. Montreal, Que., Can., Dec. 7, 1943; came to U.S., 1976; s. Nathan and Phyllis (Maron) F.; m. Gloria Phyllis Godine, June 21, 1966; children: Caroline, Sharon, Joanna. BSC, McGill U., Montreal, 1965, MD, CM, 1967; student in rsch. tng. program, Duke U. Med. Ctr., 1969-70. Diplomate Am. Bd. Internal Medicine; lic. physician, Mich., Mass. Rotating intern Royal Victoria Hosp., Montreal, 1967-68, jr. asst. resident in medicine, 1968-69; rsch fellow div. rheumatic and genetic disease Duke U. Med. Ctr., Durham, N.C., 1969-71, sr. asst. resident in medicine, 1971-72; physician The Wellesley Hosp., 1972-76; assoc. dir. Clin. Rsch. Ctr. U. Mich. Hosp., 1976-77, acting program dir., 1977-78, program dir., 1978-90; interim div. chief in rheumatology U. Mich., 1986-88; v.p. med. affairs Biogen Inc., Cambridge, Mass., 1990—; clin. prof. medicine Harvard Med. Sch., Boston, 1991—; assoc. in gen. medicine Mass. Gen. Hosp., Boston, 1990—; asst. prof. medicine U. Toronto, Can., 1972-76; assoc. prof. internal medicine U. Mich., 1976-78, prof., 1978-90, asst. prof. biol. chemistry, 1976-80, assoc. prof., 1980-84, prof., 1984-90; advisor Henry Ford Hosp. clin. rsch. unit com., 1977; mem. fellowship subcom. Arthritis Found., 1977-80, AIDS and Related Therapy Study Sect. NIH, 1990-91, Nat. Inst. Arthritis and Musculoskeletal and Skin Diseases Task Force NIH, 1991—; ad hoc mem. Metabolism Study Sect. NIH, 1977, 78, site visit team Gen. Clin. Rsch., 1978, 81; cons. Warner Lambert/Park Davis Rsch. Labs., 1979-83, 85, Proctor and Gamble Rsch. Labs., 1982, Lily Rsch. Labs., 1983, Kenyon and Kenyon, Patent Lawyers, 1983-84, Pfizer, Inc., 1987-88, Nat. Cancer Inst. Nutrition Rsch. Lab., 1988; mem. com. for med. student rsch. U. Mich., mem. biomed. rsch. coun., 1977-80, mem. arthritis ctr. operating com., 1978-81, mem. molecular and cellular biology program com., 1983-85, postdoctoral rsch. tng. com., 1984, mem. v.p.'s budget priorities com., 1985-87, mem. exec. com. Sch. of Medicine, 1987-90; program dir. Gen. Clin. Rsch. Ctr., 1977-90; dir. core facilities, prin. investigator molecular subproject Multipurpose Arthritis Ctr., 1988—; active numerous other orgns. Author: (with others) Purine Metabolism in Man, 1974, Combined Immunodeficiency Disease and Adenosine Deaminase Deficiency: A Molecular Defect, 1975, Purine Metabolism in Man-II, 1977, Farmacologic Clinica e Terapia, 1978, Handbook of Experimental Pharmacology, 1978, Purine Metabolism in Man-III, 1980, Regulatory Function of Adenosine, 1983, 5th rev. edit. Nutrition and Gout, 1984, Purine Metabolism in Man IV, 1984, Physiology and Pathology of Electrolyte Metabolism, 1985, Metabolic Basis of Inherited Disease, 6th edit., 1986, Rheumatology and Immunology, 2nd edit., 1986, Primer on the Rheumatic Diseases, 1988, Textbook of Internal Medicine, 1st edit., 1989, Textbook of Rheumatology, 3rd edit., 1990, Purines in Cell Signaling, 1990; numerous others; contbr. articles to profl. jours. including Am. Jour. Med. Sci., Biochemistry, Molecular Pharmacology, Burns, Jour. Biol. Chemistry, New Eng. Jour. Medicine, Jour. Clin. Investigation, Am. Jour. Physiology, Clin. Chemistry, Archives Biochem. Biophys., Am. Jour. Medicine, Brain Rsch., Neurology, numerous others; mem. editorial bd. Jour. Rheumatology, 1974—, Clin. Rsch., 1978-81, Metabolism, 1979—, Jour. Lab. and Clin. Medicine, 1988—. Fin. v.p. Temple Beth Emeth, Ann Arbor, Mich., 1979-81, pres., 1981-83; treas. Genesis Bd. (St. Clare's Episcopal Ch. and Temple Beth Emeth), 1985-86, pres., 1986-87, sec. 1987-88. Named Frederick Smith Meml. scholar, 1966-67, postdoctoral fellow Med. Rsch. Coun. Can., 1969-71; grantee So. Med. Assn., 1971-72 and numerous other grants. Fellow in Medicine Royal Coll. Physicians; mem. ACP (chmn. rheumatology subsect. 1986-88), Am. Soc. Biol. Chemists, Am. Fedn. Clin. Rsch. (sec.-treas. Midwest sect. 1979-82, program com. 1980, 83, chmn. communications com. 1982-8 pub. policy com. 1983-84, chmn. Midwest sect. 1983-84), Am. Rheumatism Assn. (chmn. com. publ. of arthritis and rheumatism 1984-86, chmn. sci. program 1987 nat. meeting, rsch. coun. 1986-89, chmn. subcom. to define rheumatologic tng. 1986-87), Am. Soc. Clin. Investigation (mem. nominating com. 1984, sec.-treas. 1986-89), Inst. of Medicine (com. on addressing career paths for clin. rsch. 1991-93), Can. Arthritis and Rheumatism Soc., Can. Biochem. Soc., Can. Rheumatism Assn., Can. Soc. for Clin. Investigation, Cen. Soc. Clin. Rsch., Royal Coll. Physicians and Surgeons Can., Alpha Omega Alpha. Jewish. Office: Biogen Inc 14 Cambridge Ctr Cambridge MA 02142-1401

FOX, JAMES M., orthopedic surgeon; b. Milw., July 20, 1942; m. Ellen Fox. BS, U. Wis., 1964, MD, 1968. Diplomate Nat. Bd. Med. Examiners, Am. Bd. Orthop. Surgery. Intern Bronx (N.Y.) Mcpl. Hosp./Albert Einstein Coll. Medicine, 1968-69, surg. resident, 1969-70, orthop. surgery resident, 1970-72, chief resident orthop. surgery, 1972-73; asst. instr. orthop. surgery Albert Einstein Coll. Medicine, 1972-73; sports medicine fellow Nat. Athletic Health Inst., Inglewood, Calif., 1973-74, mem. med. adv. bd., 1974—; pvt. practice Sherman Oaks, Calif., 1976-81, So. Calif. Orthop. Inst., Van Nuys, Calif., 1981—; mem. staff Centinela Valley Cmty. Hcsp., Inglewood, 1973-74, Daniel Freeman Hosp., Inglewood, 1973-74, Videopark Hosp., L.A., 1973-74, Keesler Med. Ctr., Keesler AFB, Miss., 1974-76, Encino (Calif.) Hosp., 1976-81, Sherman Oaks Cmty. Hosp., 1976-83, Valley Presbyn. Hosp., 1981—; med. cons. sports medicine video cassettes VCI-Nat. Athletic Health Inst., 1974-76; cons. cmty. outreach program on emergency treatment of athletic injuries Sherman Oaks Cmty. Hosp., 1978-80; cons., presenter in field; cons. cons. Youth Soccer Mag.; orthop. cons. Vets. Hosp., Sepulveda, Calif., Denver Gold U.S. Football League, 1985; med. dir. Ctr. for Disorders of Knee, Van Nuys; mem. Ctr. for Sports Medicine, Calif. State U., Northridge, 1990; med. examiner State of Calif. Dept. Indsl. Rels., 1993-95. Mem. editl. bd. Jour. of Arthroscopy, 1989-93, video supplement, 1989, The Knee, 1994. Mem. Summer Olympics, 1984. Maj. Med. Corps USAF, 1974-76. Orthop. Rsch. Edn. Found. grantee, 1974-75. Fellow ACS; mem. AMA (Physician Recognition award in Continuing Med. Edn. 1972, 76), Am. Athletic Trainers Adv. Assn. and Cert. Bd., Inc. (mem. com.), Arthroscopy Assn. N.Am. (mem. rsch. com. 1986-89, bd. dirs. 1989-91, chmn. pub. rels. com. 1989, program chmn. 1993, sec. 1994), Calif. Med. Assn., Am. Med. Soccer Assn., U.S. Soccer Fedn. (med. adv. com.), Am. Assn. Rwy. Surgeons. Office: So Calif Orthop Inst 6815 Noble Ave Van Nuys CA 91405

FOX, JAMES W., ophthalmologist, ophthalmic surgeon; b. L.A., June 2, 1943. BA, Stanford U., 1965; MD, Duke U., 1969. Diplomate Am. Bd. Ophthalmology. Resident in ophthalmology U. Rochester, N.Y., 1981; asst. prof. ophthalmology U. Rochester, 1981—; pvt. practice ophthalmology, 1981—. Mem. AMA, Med. Soc. State N.Y., Am. Acad. Ophthalmology. Office: 1400 Portland Ave Rochester NY 14621

FOX, JOANE P., nurse; b. Rochester, N.Y., Nov. 23, 1950; d. Samuel and Mildred M. (Gunther) Pillar; m. Stuart W. Fox, June 8, 1975; children: Allison, Dana, Lindsay, Daniel. AA, Green Mountain Coll., Poultney, Vt., 1970; BS in Nursing, Columbia U., 1973. Registered nurse. Registered nurse N.Y. Hosp., N.Y.C., 1973-75, U. Mich. Med. Ctr., Ann Arbor, 1975-77, Morris Neurologic Assocs., Morristown, N.J., 1981—. Pres. Hadassah, Morristown, 1988-91, v.p., fundraising, 1985-87, No. N.J. region programming v.p., 1991-92, rec. sec., 1993—; mem. bd. edn. Morristown Jewish Cmty. Ctr., 1987—, chairperson youth activities, 1992—. Recipient Sabra Service award Nat. Hadassah, 1988, Woman of Yr. award, 1992. Home: 16 Mount Pleasant Rd Morristown NJ 07960-3367

FOX, LAWRENCE MICHAEL, infectious diseases specialist; b. Memphis, Oct. 25, 1949; s. Robert Franklyn and Claire (Reubin) F.; m. Lynn Saffer, Aug. 3, 1975 (div. 1984); m. Emilie Anne Cole, Sept. 10, 1989; children: Daniel Cole, Alexander Reuben, Amy Rachel. PhD, U. Miami, 1979; MD, N.J. Med. Sch., Newark, 1986. Diplomate Am. Bd. Pediatrics, Am. Bd. Internal Medicine. Rsch. asst. U. Miami (Fla.) Sch. Med., 1975-79, rsch. assoc., 1979-80; postdoctoral fellow Roche Inst. for Molecular Biology, Nutley, N.J., 1980-81; postdoctoral rsch. assoc. Hoffman-LaRoche, Nutley, 1981-82; rsch. cons. N.J. Med. Sch., Newark, 1982-83; resident physician Albert Einstein Med. Ctr., Phila., 1986-90; med. staff fellow NIH, Bethesda, Md., 1990-94; med. officer NIAID Divsn. AIDS, 1994—; comdr. USPHS, Bethesda, 1991—. Contbr. articles to Jour. Immunology, Jour. Biol. Chemistry, Antimicrobiol. Agts. Chemotherapy. Decorated Commendation medal USPHS, 1996; recipient Menin Humanitarian award, 1990, Price Humanitarian award, 1990. Fellow Am. Acad. Pediatrics; mem. AMA, ACP, Soc. Microbiology, Commd. Officers Assn., Sigma Xi. Jewish. Office: NIH NIAID Solar Bldg Rm 2C12 DAIDS Bethesda MD 20892

FOX, MAURICE SANFORD, molecular biologist, educator; b. N.Y.C., Oct. 11, 1924; s. Albert and Ray F.; m. Sally Cherniavsky, Apr. 1, 1955; children: Jonathan, Gregory, Michael. BS in Meteorology, U. Chgo., 1944, MS in Chemistry, 1951, PhD, 1951; Docteur Honoris causa, Université Paul Sabatier, Toulouse, France, 1994. Instr. U. Chgo., 1951-53; asst. Rockefeller Inst., 1953-55, asst. prof., 1955-58, assoc. prof., 1958-62; assoc. prof. MIT, Cambridge, 1962-66, prof., 1966-79, Lester Wolfe prof. molecular biology, 1979-96, head dept. biology, 1985-89. Served with USAAF, 1943-46. USPHS fellow, 1952-53; Nuffield Research fellow, 1957; Fogarty scholar, 1991. Fellow AAAS; mem. NAS, Am. Acad. Arts and Scis., Inst. Medicine. Office: MIT Dept Biology 77 Massachusetts Ave Cambridge MA 02139-4301

FOX, PETER DAVID, consultant; b. L.A., Mar. 28, 1940; s. John Samuel and Selma (Richman) F.; m. Beverly Alice Hanson, June 31, 1965 (div. Sept. 1959); children: David, Steven; m. Lynda Gebhart, Jan. 5, 1992. BA, Haverford Coll., 1961; MS, MIT, 1963; PhD, Stanford U., 1968. Sr. staff mem. office mgmt. and budget U.S. Govt., Washington, 1970-72; dir. office health policy analysis U.S. Dept. Health and Human Svcs., Washington, 1972-77, dir. office of policy analysis, health care fin. adminstrn., 1977-81; v.p. Lewin and Assocs., Washington, 1981-91; pres. PDF Inc., Chevy Chase, Md., 1991-96. Author: Health Care Cost Management, 1984, Determinants of HMO Success, 1987; editor: Chronic Care and Managed Care, 1996; contbr. articles to profl. jours.

FOX, POWELL G., JR., hospital administrator, urologist; b. Raleigh, N.C., Mar. 11, 1928; s. Powell G. and Shirley (Kingsbury) F.; m. Ann Herring, Apr. 21, 1990; 1 child, Sarah Wesley. BS, The Citadel, 1948; MD, Med. Coll. Va., 1952. Diplomate Am. Bd. Urology. Resident in urology Med. Coll. Va., Richmond, 1955-59; v.p. med. affairs Raleigh Cmty. Hosp., pres. bd. trustees, 1977-82; pres. local bd. dirs. United Carolina Bank, Raleigh, 1994-95. Med. rep. United Fund, Raleigh. Maj. M.C., U.S. Army, 1952-54; with N.C. N.G., 1954-62. Fellow ACS; mem. Carolina Urology Assn. (pres.), Raleigh Acad. Medicine (pres.), Carolina Country Club (pres. 1962), Sphinx Club (pres. 1994), Terpsichorean Club (pres. 1964). Home: 2700 Cambridge Rd Raleigh NC 27608 Office: Raleigh Cmty Hosp Wake Forest Rd Raleigh NC 27609

FOX, SAMUEL MICKLE, III, physician, educator; b. Andalusia, Pa., Feb. 13, 1923; s. Samuel Mickle, Jr. and Francenia Allibone (Randall) F.; m. Mary Alice Vann, June 25, 1949; children: Elizabeth Mickle, John MacRae, Samuel Mickle, Emily Randall Fox Conant. B.A., Haverford Coll., 1944; M.D., U. Pa., 1947. Intern, resident, fellow Hosps. U. Pa., Phila., 1947-50; commd. ensign USNR, 1942; advanced through grades to comdr. M.C. USN, 1957; acting chief gastroenterology (Nat. Naval Med. Center), Bethesda, Md., 1950-51; mem. staff, later chief cardiology service (Nat. Naval Med. Center), 1953-54; mem. staff (Office Naval Research, London, Hdqrs. Naval Forces Europe, Atlantic and Mediterranean), 1951-53; head dept. clin. investigation (U.S. Naval Med. Research Unit), Cairo, 1954-56; chief cardiology (U.S. Naval Hosp.), Portsmouth, Va., 1956-57; sr. staff sect. on cardiodynamics Nat. Heart Inst., NIH, Bethesda, 1957-58; co-chief, 1959-60, asst. inst. dir., 1961-62; dep. chief Heart Disease and Stroke Control Program, USPHS, 1962-65, chief, 1965-70; asst. clin. prof. medicine Georgetown U. Sch. Medicine, 1959-70, prof. medicine, 1975—, dir. preventive cardiology program, 1980-94; prof. medicine George Washington U. Sch. Medicine, 1970-75; vis. prof. medicine Ein Shams and Kasr-el-Aini Faculties Medicine, Cairo, 1955-56; chief Cardiac Out-patient Clinic, D.C. Gen. Hosp., 1959-62; med. monitor project Mercury NASA, 1960-64, mem. research adv. com. on biotech. and human research, 1964-67; mem. subcom. on altitude physiology U.S. Olympic Com., 1966-68; mem. Pres.'s Council on Phys. Fitness and Sports, 1970-82; organizer, mem. Nat. Research Com. on Phys. Activity and Heart Disease, 1964-78; mem. adv. com. Inter-Soc. Commn. on Heart Disease Resources, 1968-72, steering com., 1973-80; mem. subcom. on emergency services NRC, 1969-75; chmn. med. cert. policy rev. panel FAA, 1987-89, coord. Health Promotion for Older Adults, Office of Disease Prevention and Health Promotion, Dept. H.H.S., 1993-94; cons. USN, USAF, U.S. Army, NASA, VA, FAA, HHS, Dept. Transp., Dept. State, D.C. Gen. Hosp., Asian-Pacific Cardiol. Soc., WHO, Olympic Com., Nat. Jogging Assn., Nat. Ski Patrol, Alpha Omega Alpha. Mem. founders com. and adv. planning bd. Bethesda YMCA, 1960-62; nat. policy bd. YMCA Health Enhancement Program, 1976-84. Fellow Am. Coll. Cardiology (pres. 1972-73, Disting. fellow 1977), A.C.P., Am. Coll. Sports Medicine (v.p. 1976-77), AAAS; mem. Am. Heart Assn. (dir.), Inter-Am. Soc. Cardiology (exec. bd.), Internat. Soc. Cardiology (council), U.S. Naval Inst., Edgemoor Tennis Club (Bethesda), Causeway Club (SW Harbor, Maine). Home: PO Box 42 Mount Desert ME 04660-0042 Office: 3800 Reservoir Rd NW Washington DC 20007-2196

FOX, STUART IRA, physiologist; b. Bklyn., June 21, 1945; s. Sam and Bess F.; m. Ellen Diane Berley; 1 child, Laura Elizabeth. BA, UCLA, 1967; MA, Calif. State U., L.A., 1967; postgrad., U. Calif., Santa Barbara, 1969; PhD, U. So. Calif., 1978. Rsch. assoc. Children's Hosp., L.A., 1972; prof. physiology L.A. City Coll., 1972-85, Calif. State U., Northridge, 1979-84, Pierce Coll., 1986—; cons. William C. Brown Co. Pubs., 1976—. Author: Computer-Assisted Instruction in Human Physiology, 1979, Laboratory Guide to Human Physiology, 2d edit., 1980, 7th edit., 1996, Textbook of Human Physiology, 1986, 5th edit., 1996, Human Anatomy and Physiology, 1986, 4th edit., 1995, Perspectives on Human Biology, 1991, Laboratory Manual for Anatomy and Physiology, 1986, 4th edit., 1996; contbg. author: Biology, 4th edit., 1995, Synopsis of Anatomy and Physiology, 1997. Mem. AAAS, So. Calif. Acad. Sci., Am. Physiol. Soc., Sigma Xi. Home: 5556 Forest Cove Ln Agoura Hills CA 91301-4047 Office: Pierce Coll 6201 Winnetka Ave Woodland Hills CA 91371-0001

FOX, STUART WARREN, neurologist; b. Jersey City, N.J., Dec. 20, 1949; s. Alexander and Helen (Perl) F.; m. Joane Pillar, June 8, 1975; children: Allison, Dana, Lindsay, Daniel. BA, Cornell U., 1971, MD, 1975. House officer internal medicine U. Mich., Ann Arbor, 1975-78; resident in neurology Albert Einstein Coll. Medicine, Bronx, N.Y., 1978-81; fellow in clin. neurophysiology L.I. Jewish-Hillside Med. Ctr., New Hyde Park, N.Y., 1981-82; pvt. practice Morristown, N.J., 1982—; chmn. dept. neurosci. Morristown Meml. Hosp., 1991—; asst. clin. prof. medicine Columbia U., N.Y.C., 1990—. Bd. dirs. Morristown Jewish Ctr., 1993-95. Fellow ACP, Am. Acad. Neurology, Am. Coll. Electrodiagnostic Medicine, Neurol. Assn. N.J. (treas. 1994—), Phi Beta Kappa. Jewish. Office: Neurol Ctr No NJ 95 Madison Ave Morristown NJ 07960

FOX, WILLIAM RICHARD, retired physician; b. Bozeman, Mont., Oct. 12, 1915; s. William Edward Fox and Anah Grace Bump; m. Esther Viola Jorgenson, Aug. 15, 1948 (dec. 1985); 1 child, Susan Jane Fox. MD, U. Manitoba, Can., 1941. Intern St. Joseph Hosp., St. Paul, 1940-41; staff Good Samaritan Hosp, Johnson Clinic, 1941-85; pub. health officer Pierce County, 1948-85; surgeon Gt. No. Ry., 1950-70. Past pres. Rugby Econ. Devel. Assn. Recipient N.D. Physicians Community and Profl. Svc. award, 1984. Mem. Union Hills County Club (Sun City Ariz.), Mason (past master), Shriners, Elks.

FOZ, LIONEL DIAZ, health facility administrator; b. Manila, Philippines, Sept. 6, 1937; cmae to U.S., 1962; s. Antonio Ernesto and Dolores (Diaz) F.; m. Lucina Romillo, Feb. 10, 1962; children: Lionel R., Maria Lucina Foz Onderdonk, Lyle Anthony. MD, Far Eastern U., 1961. Diplomat Am. Acad. Pediatrics. Chmn. dept. pediatrics MCOC, Brick, N.J., 1974-87, Cmty. Med. Ctr., Toms River, N.J., 1989—; cons. in field. Home: 618 Rolling Hills Dr Brick NJ 08724 Office: Pediatric Med Group 1541 Rte 88 Brick NJ 08724

FRABLE, FRANK L., JR., surgeon; b. N.Y.C., Aug. 1, 1925; s. Frank L. and Geraldine (Stahl) F.; m. Thelma Jean Hyde, June 27, 1953; children: Pamela, Gordon, Rachel, Glenn, Guy, Garth, Amy. BM, Northwestern U., Chgo., 1950, MD, 1951. Diplomate Am. Bd. Surgery. Chief surgery Whitlatch Clinic, Milan, Ind., 1955-59; staff Dearborn County Hosp., Lawrenceburg, Ind., 1959—; chief surgery Dearborn County Hosp., Lawrenceburg, 1967, 73, 78, 83, 88, chief staff, 1970, 91, med. cons., bd. trustees, 1995—. Bd. edn. Aurora (Ind.) Schs., 1962, pres. bd. edn., 1963-67. With USN, 1944-46. Recipient Pres. award Dearborn County C. of C., 1993; Frank L. Frable Jr. Surg. Pavilion named in his honor Dearborn County Hosp., 1994. Home: 412 Sunnyside Ave Aurora IN 47001 Office: Dearborn County Hosp 370 Bielby Rd Lawrenceburg IN 47025

FRADE, PETER DANIEL, chemist; b. Highland Park, Mich., Sept. 3, 1946; s. Peter Nunes and Dorathea Grace (Gehrke) F.; m. Karen L. Kovich, Mar. 14, 1992. B.S. in Chemistry, Wayne State U., 1968, M.S., 1971, Ph.D., 1978. Chemist Henry Ford Hosp., Detroit, 1968-75; analytical chemist, toxicologist dept. pathology, div. pharmacology and toxicology Henry Ford Hosp., 1975-86, sr. clin. lab. scientist dept. pathology div. clin. chemistry and pharmacology, 1987—; research assoc. in chemistry Wayne State U., Detroit, 1978-79; vis. scholar U. Mich., Ann Arbor, 1980-90; vis. scientist dept. Hypertension Research, Henry Ford Hosp., Detroit, 1986-88; adj. prof. Coll. Pharmacy and Allied Health Professions Wayne State U., 1991—. Contbr. sci. articles to profl. jours.; peer reviewer for profl. jours., 1988—. Mem. Rep. Presdl. Task Force, 1984-88; organist St. John's Episcopal Ch., Royal Oak, Mich., 1995—. Recipient David F. Boltz Meml. award Wayne State U., 1977. Fellow Am. Inst. Chemists, Nat. Acad. Clin. Biochemistry, Assn. Clin. Scientists; mem. Am. Guild Organists, European Acad. Arts, Scis. and Humanities, Fedn. Am. Scientists, Am. Chem. Soc., AAAS, Am. Assn. Clin. Chemistry, Assn. Analytical Chemists, Mich. Inst. Chemists (treas. 1994—), N.Y. Acad. Scis., Detroit Hist. Soc., Am. Coll. Toxicology, Royal Soc. Chemistry (London), Titanic Hist. Soc., Bibl. Archaeology Soc., Virgil Fox Soc., Founders Soc., Detroit Inst. Arts, Sigma Xi, Phi Lambda Upsilon, Alpha Chi Sigma. Episcopalian. Home: 20200 Orleans St Detroit MI 48203-1356 Office: Henry Ford Hosp 2799 W Grand Blvd Detroit MI 48202-2608

FRAGER, MARC STEPHEN, endocrinologist; b. St. Louis, Feb. 20, 1949; s. Sidney Mayer and Gladys (Birenbaum) F.; m. Nancy Ellman, Sept. 12, 1977; children: Steven, Monica. BA, Northwestern U., 1971; MD, U. Mo., 1975. Diplomate Am. Bd. Internal Medicine, Am. Bd. Internal Medicine for Endocrinology and Metabolism, Am. Bd. Nuclear Medicine. Resident in internal medicine Wayne State U., Detroit, 1975-78; fellow in endocrinology and nuclear medicine U. Mich., Ann Arbor, 1978-81; pvt. practice, Boca Raton, Fla., 1981—. Editor several books; contbr. articles to med. jours. Fellow ACP; mem. AAAS, Endocrine Soc., Soc. Nuclear Medicine, Am. Diabetes Assn. Home: 17088 Northway Cir Boca Raton FL 33496-5905 Office: Endocrine-Diabetes Assocs 1500 NW 10th Ave Boca Raton FL 33486-1344

FRAGER, STANLEY R., psychologist, educator; b. St. Louis, Apr. 23, 1939; s. Alfred H. and Rose (Samuels) F.; (div.); children: Sarah, Joshua. BSBA, Washington U., St. Louis, 1961; MA, UCLA, 1966, PhD, 1969. Lic. psychologist, lic. family and child therapist. Postgrad. research educationist Ctr. for Study Evaluation UCLA, 1966-69; probation officer Los Angeles County Probation Dept., 1961-70, staff tng. officer, 1970-72; dir. continuing edn., assoc. prof. social work, dir. media services Kent Sch. Social Work U. Louisville, 1972-77, assoc. prof. Kent Sch. Social Work, 1972—, assoc. prof., dir. instructional resources and media tech. Coll. Urban and Pub. Affairs, 1977—; pres. Frager Assocs., Louisville, 1975—; talk show host Sta. WHAS, 1988—; adj. prof. Union Grad. Sch., 1977; sports psychologist basketball team U. Louisville, 1976—; ombudsman U. Louisville Student Grievance Office, 1978-81; dir. instructional rsch. Coll. Urban and Pub. Affairs, U. Louisville; mem. citizens adv. bd. coun. for social svcs. Dept. Human Resources Bur. Social Svcs., 1980-84; faculty advisor Alpha Phi Omega; amateur coll. and profl. sport psychologist; profl. cons. and speaker in field. Reviewer Film News mag., N.Y.C., 1973-81; producer, dir.: (documentary) How's School, Enrique?, 1970 (Creative Excellence award U.S. Indsl. Film Festival 1971, Blue Ribbon award Am. Film Festival 1971, Chris statuette Columbus Film Festival 1972, others); dir., writer: (film) Hand Line-Life Line, 1972 (Bronze Plaque award Columbus Film Festival 1973); dir.: (films) Buyer Beware, 1972, Previews, 1972; producer TV and radio commls. and programs; host (radio talk show) "Let's Talk with Dr. Frager); contbr. articles to profl. jours. Scoutmaster Boy Scouts Am.; bd. dirs., mem. speakers bur., mem. fin. com. Am. Cancer Soc., Ky.; active Jewish Community Fedn. Mem. Am. Psychol. Assn., Ky. Psychol. Assn., Am. Assn. for Counseling and Guidance, Nat. Acad. Counselors and Family Therapists Inc., Ky. Assn. Marriage and Family Counselors, Am. Film Assn., Info. Film Producers Am., Am. Soc. for Tng. and Devel. (past pres., bd. dirs.), Assn. for Ednl. Communication and Tech., Ky. Assn. for Communication and Tech., Am. Assn. Univ. Profs., United Ostomy Assn. (past pres.), Am. Assn. Coll. Baseball Coaches, Ky. Assn. for Specialists in Group Work, Assn. to Advance Ethical Hypnosis, North Am. Soc. for Psychology Sport and Physical Activity, Ky. Hypnosis Assn., Am. Soc. Clin. Hypnosis. Home: 7000 Chippenham Rd Louisville KY 40222-6611 Office: Frager Assocs 3906 Dupont Sq S Louisville KY 40207-4647

FRAHM, JOHN ALLEN, physician; b. Sioux Falls, S.D., Oct. 14, 1950; s. Hans Jacob and Agnes Louise (Langley) F.; m. Ruth Westra, June 10, 1973 (div. Feb. 1986); children: Jacob, Joseph; m. Vanessa Jean Grubb, May 27, 1989; stepchildren: Biran Paoli, Daniel Paoli. BA, Ctrl. Coll., Pella, Iowa, 1972; DO, Coll. Osteo. Medicine & Surg., Des Moines, 1975. Diplomate Am. Bd. Internal Medicine. Intern then resident Mt. Clemens (Mich.) Gen. Hosp., 1975-79; pvt. practice Mt. Clemens, 1979-85; staff physician VA Med. Ctr., Iron Mountain, Mich., 1985-89, chief med. svc., 1989-93, chief staff, 1993—. Mem. Am. Osteo. Assn., Am. Coll. Osteo. Internists. Home: 837 East B St Iron Mountain MI 49801 Office: VA Med Ctr 325 East H St Iron Mountain MI 49801

FRAIBERG, ELLIOT, gastroenterologist. MD, Wayne State U., 1969. Chief divsn. gastroenterology St Joseph Mercy Hosp., Pontiac, Mich., 1985—. Fellow Am. Coll. Physicians, Am. Coll. Gastroenterology, Am. Soc. for Laser Medicine and Surgery; mem. Am. Soc. Gastrointestinal Endoscopy, Bockus Internat. Soc. Gastroenterology. Office: Elliott N Fraiberg MS 888 Woodward Ave Ste 402 Pontiac MI 48341

FRAIR, WAYNE FRANKLIN, biologist, educator; b. Pitts., May 23, 1926; s. Herbert E. and Elizabeth M. (Greenawald) Gfroerer. BA, Houghton Coll., 1950; BS, Wheaton (Ill.) Coll., 1951; MA, U. Mass., 1955; PhD, Rutgers U., 1962. Tchr. sci. Ben Lippen Sch., Asheville, N.C., 1951-52; mem. faculty King's Coll., Briarcliff, N.Y., 1955—, prof. biology, 1967-93, prof. emeritus 1993—. Chmn. Heart Club, Phelps Meml. Hosp., Tarrytown, N.Y., 1979-80. With USN, 1944-46, PTO. Author: A Case for Creation, 3d edit., 1983; contbr. articles to profl. jours. Fellow AAAS, Am. Sci. Affiliation, Creation Rsch. Soc. (sec. 1974-84, v.p. 1985-86, pres. 1987-93); mem. Am. Inst. Biol. Sci., Am. Soc. Zoology, Evang. Theol. Soc., Sigma Xi (life). Baptist. Club: Saw Mill River Audubon Soc. (bd. dirs. 1963-66). Home and Office: 1131 Fellowship Rd Basking Ridge NJ 07920-2308

FRAIS, MICHAEL ALISTAIR, cardiologist; b. Liverpool, Eng., June 12, 1951; s. Montague Mark and Norah (Angelman) F. MB, ChB, Liverpool U., 1974, MD, 1981. Fellow Royal Coll. Physicians Can. From house officer to registrar Liverpool Area Health Authority, 1974-79; rsch. fellow in cardiology U. Calif., San Francisco, 1979-81; resident rsch., fellow in cardiology U. Calgary, Alberta, Can., 1981-83; rsch. fellow in cardiology U. Leeds, Eng., 1984-85; clin. project mgr. Pfizer Ctrl. Rsch., Sandwich, Eng., 1986-87; asst. prof. medicine U. Manitoba, Winnipeg, Can., 1987-91; assoc. prof. medicine U. Ark. for Med. Scis., Little Rock, 1991-93; cardiologist pvt. practice Albany (N.Y.) Assocs. in Cardiology, 1994-95, Soto Cardiology Assocs., Russellville, Ark., 1995—. Contbr. numerous articles to profl. jours. including Am. Jour. Cardiology, Brit. Heart Jour., Jour. Am. Coll. Cardiology, Jour. Clin. Pharmacology, European Jour. Clin. Pharmacology, Circulation, and others. Fellow Am. Coll. Cardiology, Royal Coll. Physicians Can.; mem. Royal Coll. Physicians (U.K.). Home: 2008 W 8th St Russelville AR 72801 Office: Soto Cardiology Assocs PO Box 1527 1660 W C Pl Russellville AR 72811

FRAKES, JAMES TERRY, physician, gastroenterologist, educator; b. Burlington, Iowa, Feb. 22, 1946; s. Harold Decatur amd Marjorie Marie (Kinnison) F.; m. Nancy Jean French, June 15, 1968; children: Sarah Jean Frakes Wallin, David Harold Frakes. BS, U. Ill., Urbana, 1968, MS, 1972; MD, U. Ill., Chgo., 1976. Diplomate Am. Bd. Internal Medicine, Nat. Bd. Med. Examiners; lic. Ill. Staff engr. Westinghouse Antinuclear Lab., Pitts., 1968-69; staff scientist Los Alamos (NMex.) Sci. Lab., 1970-71; intern, resident in internal medicine U. Mo. Med. Ctr., Columbia, 1976-78; fellow in gastroenterology U. N. Carolina Sch. Medicine, Chapel Hill, 1978-80; physician, gastroenterologist Rockford (Ill.) GE Assoc., Ltd., 1980—; clin. prof. medicine U. Ill. Coll. Medicine, Rockford, 1981—; dir. digestive disease unit Saint Anthony Med. Ctr., Rockford, 1983—; course dir. AGA/ASGE, 1996—; med. lectr., 1996—. Mem. bd. dirs. U. Ill. Alumni Assn., 1991—; mem. U. Ill. Found., Urbana, 1991—; mem. pres's coun. U. Ill. Found., Urbana, 1994—; mem. Ptnrs. in Prevention (drug edn.) County Med. Soc., Rockford, 1993. Fellow Am. Coll. Gastroenterology, Am. Coll. Physicians; mem. AMA, Am. Digestive Health Found. (numerous coms.), Am. Gastroenterological Assn. (nnumerous coms.), Am. Soc. Gastrointestinal Endoscopy (treas. 1980—). Republican. Office: Rockford Gastroeneterology Assocs Ltd 401 Roxbury Rd Rockford IL 61107

FRALEIGH, JOHN WALTER, psychotherapist, social worker; b. Grand Rapids, Mich., Oct. 21, 1945; s. John Duncan and Marie Cecilia (Furlong) F. BA, Mich. State U., 1968; MSW, Grand Valley State Coll., 1984; cert. in alcohol and drug abuse, Western Mich. U., 1988. Cert. social worker, Mich., addictions counselor, Mich., alcohol drug counselor-ICRC/ AODA. With prodn. staff Sta. WZZM-TV, Grand Rapids, 1969-87; social work intern Kent Oaks Psychiat. Unit, Grand Rapids, 1980-81; psychotherapist, grad. level practicum Diversities Counseling, Grand Rapids, 1981-86; crisis counselor Dwelling Pl. Inc., Grand Rapids, 1986-87; intern Glenbeigh of Kent Community Hosp., Grand Rapids, 1988; primary counselor adult intensive non-residential treatment program Glenbeigh Family Ctr., Grand Rapids, 1988-91; evaluation, assessment coord. Glenbeigh of Kent Community Hosp., 1990-93; pvt. practice, 1991-93; assessment specialist, site supr. Ctrl. Diagnostic and Referral Svcs., Inc., Alpena, Mich., 1994—; employee assistance counselor Occupl. Health Care Ctrs.-Am., 1995—; media cons. Grand Rapids Humane Soc., 1974-75; media producer West Mich. Burn Unit, 1975-76, Kent County Spay and Neuter Clinic; vol. Transitions Adult Aftercare Ctr., Grand Rapids, 1982; adj. faculty C.C. Health Svcs., Western Mich. U., 1993-95. Media cons. Grand Rapids Jaycees, 1975-77, recipient spl. award, 1977; pres. Mon. Night Rap Group, Grand Rapids, 1977-80; policy council mem. Mich. Orgn. Human Rights, Detroit, 1977, media producer, meetings coordinator, 1978, 82, v.p., 1982-84; mem. Human Sexuality Task Force for Mich. Ho. of Reps.; coord. Midwest planning session Lesbian-Gay March on Washington, 1979; asst. in founding many lesbian-gay orgns. in West Mich. and Grand Rapids area; sec. Grand Rapids AIDS Task Force, 1986; founding mem., advisor, counselor IME of Western Mich., 1988; part-time choir dir. Chapel Hill United Meth. Ch., Casnovia, Mich, 1974-79; adult edn. instr. Hackley Mus. Art, Muskegon, Mich., 1979. Mem. Calligraphic Soc. Grand Rapids, N.E. Mich. Artist's Guild. Home: 423 S 5th St # 3 Alpena MI 49707-2701

FRALEY, MARK STEVEN, physician; b. Indpls., Apr. 13, 1960; s. Carl D. and Ruby J. Fraley; m. Cheri L. Fraley, June 24, 1985; children: Megan L., Christa M. BS in Biology, Ind. U.-Purdue U. Ind., Indpls., 1983; DO, Ohio U., Athens, 1988. Diploamte Am. Bd. Osteo. Family Practice. Physician Dayton (Ohio) Family Practice, 1992-95, Express Care Plus, Colorado Springs, Colo., 1995—. Mem. Am. Osteo. Assn. Home: 2925 Terranove Ct Colorado Springs CO 80919

FRAM, ROBERT JAY, hematologist/oncologist; b. N.Y., May 20, 1949; s. Bennie Jacob and Esther (Torres) F.; m. Judith Margery Strymish, May 25, 1981; children: Sarah Elizabeth, Louis Michael, Julia Rose. AB, Harvard U., 1971; MD, Harvard Med. Sch., 1976. Diplomate Am. Bd. Internal Medicine. Intern, resident Columbia-Presbyn. Med. Ctr., N.Y.C., 1976-79; fellow in oncology/hematology Dana-Farber Cancer Inst., Boston, 1979-82; instr. medicine Harvard Med. Sch., Boston, 1982-84; from asst. prof. to assoc. prof. medicine and pharmacology U. Mass. Med. Sch., Worcester, 1984-92; oncologist, assoc. prof. medicine and oncology U. Md. Cancer Ctr., Balt., 1993-95; assoc. dir. oncology/immunology Knoll Pharm. Co., Parsippany, N.J., 1995—. Mem. Am. Assn. Cancer Rsch., Am. Soc. Clin. Oncology, Am. Coll. Physicians. Office: Knoll Pharm Co 199 Cherry Hill Rd Parsippany NJ 07054

FRAME, BARRY DEAN, cardiovascular and thoracic surgeon; b. Blytheville, Ark., May 12, 1945; m. Debra B. Frame; children: Jeffrey, Kathryn. BA in Chemistry Cum Laude, David Lipscomb U., 1967; MD, Tulane U., 1971. Diplomate Am. Bd. Surgery, Am. Bd. Thoracic and

Cardiovasc. Surgery. Straight surg. intern U. Tenn. and Affiliated Hosps., Memphis, 1971-72, resident in gen. surgery, 1974-78, resident in thoracic and cardiovasc. surgery, 1978-80; pvt. practice, Knoxville, Tenn., 1980—; clin. asst. prof. surgery U. Tenn., Knoxville; mem. staff St. Mary's Med. Ctr., East Tenn. Bapt. Hosp., U. Tenn. Med. Ctr., Ft. Sanders Regional Med. Ctr., Ft. Sanders Park West. Flight surgeon M.C., U.S. Army, 1972-74, Vietnam. Decorated Bronze Star. Mem. AMA, Knoxville Surg. Soc., Knoxville Acad. Medicine, Harwell Wilson Surg. Soc. Home: 3723 Oakhurst Dr Knoxville TN 37919 Office: St Mary's Profl Bldg 930 Emerald Ave Ste 719 Knoxville TN 37917

FRANCES, RICHARD JOSEPH, psychiatrist; b. N.Y.C., Mar. 3, 1946; s. Joseph and Julia (Levy) F.; 1 child, Jenny. BA, Columbia U., 1967; MD, NYU, 1971. Diplomate Am. Bd. Psychiatry and Neurology (added qualifications in addiction psychiatry, 1992). Resident and chief resident in psychiatry Albert Einstein Sch. Medicine, Bronx, N.Y., 1971-74; instr. in psychiatry Albert Einstein Sch. Medicine, Bronx, 1976; asst prof. New York Hosp., Cornell, White Plains, 1976-83; assoc. prof. psychiatry N.Y. Hosp., White Plains, 1983-86; prof. clin. psychiatry N.J. Med. Sch., Newark, 1986—; pvt. practice N.Y.C., 1976—; vice chmn. residency tng., 1986-93, AIDS grant review com. Nat. Inst. Drug Abuse; vice chair Coun. on Addiction Psychiatry; dir. psychiatry Hackensack Med. Ctr., 1993—. Author: Concise Guide to Addiction Treatment, 1989; editor: Self Assessment in Psychiatry, 1986, Clinical Textbook of Addictions, 1991. Lt. comdr. USN, 1974-76. Fellow Am. Coll. Psychiatrists, Am. Psychiat. Assn. (chmn. com. on alcoholism 1990); mem. Am. Acad. Psychiatrists on Alcoholism and Addictions (founding pres. 1985), Am. Assn. Gen. Hosp. Psychiatrists, Coun. on Addiction Psychiatry, Am. Bd. Psychiatry and Neurology Addiction (psychiatry exam. com.). Home: 200 E End Ave Apt 9B New York NY 10128-7891 Office: Hackensack Med Ctr 60 2nd St Hackensack NJ 07601-2029 also: 144 E End Ave New York NY 10028-7503

FRANCIOSA, JOSEPH ANTHONY, health care consultant; b. Easton, Pa., Apr. 24, 1936; s. Joseph and Letitia Beatrice (Cascioli) F.; m. Antonietta Battistoni, Feb. 8, 1964 (div. 1972); m. Barbara Ann Neilan, Aug. 3, 1973 (div. 1989); 1 child, Christopher David. BA, U. Pa., 1958; MD, U. Rome, 1963. Diplomate Am. Bd. Internal Medicine; lic. in Pa., Md., Ark. Intern USPHS Hosp., S.I., N.Y., 1964-65; resident Washington Hosp. Ctr., 1967-69; cardiology fellow VA Hosp.-Georgetown U., Washington, 1969-71; chief ICU, VA Hosp., Washington, 1971-73; asst. prof. medicine Georgetown U. Med. Sch., , 1971-73, assoc. dir. cardiovascular tng. program, 1973-74; dir. CCU VA Hosp., Mpls., 1974-76; asst. prof. medicine U. Minn., Mpls., 1977-79; chief cardiology VA Hosp., Phila., 1979-82; assoc. prof. U. Pa., Phila., 1979-82, adj. prof., 1987—; adj. prof. medicine Mt. Sinai Med. Sch., N.Y.C., 1989—; dir. cardiology div. U. Ark., Little Rock, 1982-86, prof., 1982-86; dir. cardio-renal drugs ICI Americas Inc., Wilmington, Del., 1986-88; v.p. rsch. & devel. Zambon Corp., East Rutherford, N.J., 1988-90; exec. dir. med. affairs Ciba-Geigy Pharm., Summit, N.J., 1990-91; exec. dir. med. svcs. Ciba-Geigy, 1992-95; health care/pharm. cons., N.Y.C., 1995—. Contbr. numerous articles to med. jours. Mem. med. rsch. com. Am. Heart Assn., Mpls., 1976-79, Phila., 1981-82. Lt. comdr. USPHS, 1965-67. VA grantee, 1974-84; U. Ark. grantee, 1982-83. Fellow ACP, Am. Coll. Cardiology, Am. Coll. Chest Physicians (chmn. hypertension com. 1981-83, gov. Ark. 1984-86), Am. Heart Assn. (circulation coun. 1978—, coun. high blood pressure rsch.1982—, clin. cardiology council 1984); mem. Am. Soc. Clin. Pharmacology and Therapeutics (vice chmn. cardiopulmonary com. 1981-89), Assn. Univ. Cardiologists. Avocations: computers, gardening, physical fitness.

FRANCIS, CHARLES K., medical educator; b. Newark, May 24, 1939. BA, Dartmouth Coll., 1961; MD, Jefferson Med. Coll., 1965. Med. intern Phila. Gen. Hosp., 1965-66; med. resident Boston City Hosp., Tufts U., 1969-70; clin. fellow cardiology Tufts Circulation Lab., 1970-71; clin. and rsch. fellow cardiology Mass. Gen. Hosp., 1971-72, sr. med. resident, 1972-73; chief cardiac catheterization lab. divsn. cardiology Martin Luther King Jr. Gen. Hosp., L.A., 1973-74, chief cardiology divsn., 1974-77; dir. cardiology divsn. Mt. Sinai Hosp., Hartford, Conn., 1980-83, assoc. dir. hypertension svc., 1980-87, dir. cardiac catheterization lab., 1983-87; dir. dept. medicine Harlem Hosp. Ctr., N.Y.C., 1987—; prof. clin. medicine Columbia U. Coll. Physicians and Surgeons, 1987—; clin. instr. medicine Sch. Medicine, Tufts U., 1970-71; tchg. fellow Harvard Med. Sch., 1971-72, clin. fellow, 1972-73; asst. prof. medicine Charles R. Drew Postgrad. Med. Sch. & Sch. Medicine, U. So. Calif., 1973-77; asst. prof. medicine, dir. Burgdorf Hypertension Clin., Med. Sch., U. Conn., 1977-80; mem. cardiac adv. comty. Nat. Heart, Lung & Blood Inst., NIH, 1977-79; asst. prof. medicine Sch. Medicine, Yale U., 1980-81, assoc. prof., 1981-87. Fellow Am. Coll. Cardiology; mem. Inst. Medicine-NAS, ACP, Am. Fedn. Clin. Rsch., Am. Heart Assn. Office: Harlem Hosp Ctr Rm 14101 506 Lenox Ave New York NY 10037*

FRANCIS, DAVID ANTHONY, radiologist; b. Wood River, Ill., Mar. 6, 1955; s. Lawrence J. and Gertrude J. (Militello) F. BA, Westminster Coll., 1977; MD, U. Ill., 1981. Resident Mt. Sinai Med. Ctr., Miami Beach, Fla., 1981-84, fellow, 1984-85; staff radiologist Cmty. Hosps., Miami, Fla., 1985-87, Mount Sinai Med. Ctr., Miami Beach, Fla., 1988—, Humana Health Care Sys., Ft. Lauderdale, Fla., 1989-94, Strax Inst., Lauderhill, Fla., 1994—, Physicians Outpatient Diagnostic Ctr., Plantation, Fla., 1995—; asst. prof. clin. radiology U. Miami Sch. Medicine, 1988-92. Contbr. articles to profl. jours. Mem. AMA, So. Med. Assn., Am. Coll. Radiology, Radiol. Soc. N.Am.

FRANCIS, IRENE DAISY, community health nurse; b. Tuskegee, Ala., Apr. 26, 1950; d. Richard Louis and DeWreathe Valores (Green) F.; divorced; 1 child, Nkechinyere Sarah Ezumah. Diploma nursing, Manhattan State Hosp., Ward's Island, N.Y., 1971; BSN cum laude, Syracuse U., 1974; student, N.Y.C. Community Coll., 1971; MA in Nursing Sci., NYU, 1984. Charge nurse Mercy Gen. hosp., Tupper Lake, N.Y.; pub. health nurse Franklin County, Tupper Lake, N.Y.; participant nurse's health study II Harvard Sch. Pub. Health. Chmn. bd. dirs. Alliance for Cmty. Svc., Inc., 1992-93; mem. High Peaks Hospice, Inc., Saranac Lake, N.Y., Bereavement Team for Tupper Lake, Nurses Svc. Org., Episc. Christian Women's Org., Tupper Lake, Altar Guild; mem. healing team St. Thomas Episc. Ch.; co-instr. in charge of Christian edn. for jr.-sr. high level, lay eucharistic minister, lay reader, lic., chalice bearer, Albany Episc. Cursillo, Ultreya convener, No. Adirondack Deanery West, Diocese of Albany, Diocesan Evangelism/renewal team, 1995; mem. com. Boy Scouts Am., com. chairperson Local Pack 220, Tupper Lake, bd. dirs.; active Franciscan Retreat Ctr., St. Anthony-on-Hudson, Rensselaer, N.Y., Bill Graham Evangelistic Assn., Capital Dist. Youth for Christ, Schenectady, N.Y.; vice-chair Break-A-Leg Prodns. theatre co., Tupper Lake, 1995—. Mem. NAFE, Nat. Assn. Fine Arts, Inst. Applied Behavior Analysis (assoc.), Friends Syracuse U., NYU Alumni Assn. (weekend planning com. 1994), Syracuse U. Alumni Assn., Syracuse U. Nurses Alumni Assn. Syracuse U. Black and Hispanic Alumni Assn., Smithsonian Inst. (nat. assoc. mem.), Libr. of Congress (assoc. charter), Woodrow Wilson Internat. Ctr. for Scholars (assoc.), Internat. Platform Assn., Mountain Artists of N.Y., Nat. Parks and Conservation Assn., Arts Coun. for the Northern Adirondacks, Coun. on the Arts for Clinton County.

FRANCIS, RICHARD IAN, anesthesiologist; b. Sheffield, Yorkshire, U.K., Jan. 13, 1951; s. Kenneth Henry and Muriel Mary (Ramsden) F.; m. Susan Blackmore, Mar. 5, 1977; children: Cathryn Elanor, Shelley Louise. M.B.Ch.B., U. Birmingham, U.K., 1975. Registrar in anesthesiology Ctrl. Birmingham Health Dist., 1979-82; sr. registrar Midland Anesthetic Tng. Scheme, U.K., 1982-86; cons. anesthesiologist Birmingham Heartland Hosp., 1986—; external examiner U. Ctrl. Eng., 1993—. Contbr. articles to profl. jours.; inventor endotracheal tube for tracheal and carinal resection, 1996; assoc. editor Brit. Jour. Pediatric Medicine and Surgery, 1994—; editor Midland Soc. Anesthetists Newsletter, 1989—. Mem. Midland Soc. Anesthetists (coun. mem. 1989—), Hosp. Cons. and Specialists Assn., Assn. Anesthetists of Gt. Britain and Ireland. Home: Northfield, 145 West Heath Rd, Birmingham B31 3HD, England Office: Birmingham Heartlands Hosp, Bordesley Green E, Birmingham B9 5SS, England

FRANCIS, TIMOTHY DUANE, chiropractor; b. Chgo., Mar. 1, 1956; s. Joseph Duane and Barbara Jane (Sigwalt) F. Student, U. Nev., 1974-80, We. Nev. C.C., 1978; BS, L.A. Coll. Chiropractic, 1982, Dr. of Chiropractic magna cum laude, 1984; postgrad., Clark County Community Coll., 1984-85; MS in Bio/Nutrition, U. Bridgeport, 1990. Diplomate Internat. Coll. Applied Kinesiology, Am. Acad. Pain Mgmt., Am. Naturopathic Med. Bd.; cert. kinesiologist, applied kinesiology tchr.; lic. chiropractor, Calif, Nev. Instr. dept. recreation and phys. edn. U. Nev., Reno, 1976-80; from tchng. asst. to lead instr. dept. principles & practice L.A. Coll. Chiropractic, 1983-85; pvt. practice Las Vegas, 1985—; asst. instr. Internat. Coll. Applied Kinesiology, 1990, chmn. exam review com., 1993, chmn. syllabus review com., 1994; adj. faculty The Union Inst. Coll. of Undergrad. Studies, 1993; joint study participant Nat. Olympic Tng. Ctr., Beijing, China, 1990. Charles F. Cutts scholar, 1980. Fellow Internat. Acad. Clin. Acupuncture, British Inst. Homeopathy (homeopathy diploma 1993); mem. Am. Chiropractic Assn. (couns. on sports injuries, mutrition, roentgenology, technic, and mental health), Nev. State Chiropractic Assn., Nat. Strength and Conditioning Assn., Gonsted Clin. Studies Soc., Found. for Chiropractic Edn. and Rsch., Nat. Inst. Chiropractic Rsch., Nat. Acad. Rsch. Biochemists, Phi Beta Kappa, Phi Kappa Phi (v.p. 1979-80, Scholar of the Yr. award, 1980), Delta Signa. Republican. Roman Catholic. Home 3750 S Jones Blvd Las Vegas NV 89103-2283

FRANCIS, WILLIE BRENARD, psychologist; b. Orangeburg, S.C.; s. David C. and Frances B. (Grant) F. BA, Morehouse Coll., 1977; MA, Kent State U., 1979, PhD, 1983. Lic. psychologist, La., Ga. Psychology intern Kent (Ohio) State U. Psychol. Clinic, 1977-80, Med. U. S.C., VA Med. Ctr., Charleston, 1980-81; staff psychologist VA Med. Ctr., La. State U. Med. Sch., Shreveport, 1983-87, VA Med. Ctr., Emory U. Sch. Medicine, Atlanta, 1987-94; chief psychology svc. dir. mental hygiene clinic, substance abuse program and PCT program VA Med. Ctr., Iron Mountain, Mich., 1994—; pvt. practice psychologist, Shreveport, 1983-87, psychol. cons., Atlanta, 1987-94. Mem. Am. Psychol. Assn., Nat. Orgn. Va. Psychologists, Southeastern Psychol. Assn., 100 Black Men of Am., Inc., Phi Beta Kappa. Office: VA Med Ctr H St Inn Mountain MI 49801

FRANCKE, GLORIA NIEMEYER, pharmacist, editor, publisher; b. Dillsboro, Ind., Apr. 28, 1922; d. Albert B. and Fannie K. (Libbert) Niemeyer; m. Donald Eugene Francke, Apr. 15, 1956. BS in Pharmacy, Purdue U., 1942; PharmD, U. Cin., 1971; postgrad. U. Mich., 1945; PharmD (hon.) Purdue U., 1988—. Pharmacist, Dillsboro Drug Store, 1943-44; instr. Sch. Pharmacy, Purdue U., Lafayette, Ind., 1943; asst. to chief pharmacist U. Mich. Hosp., Ann Arbor, 1944-46; assoc. editor Am. Jour. Hosp. Pharmacy, Washington, 1944-64; asst. dir. Div. Hosp. Pharmacy of Am. Pharm. Assn., Washington, 1946-56; exec. sec. Am. Soc. Hosp. Pharmacists, Ann Arbor, 1949-60; acting dir. dept. comms., Washington, 1963-64; drug lit. specialist Nat. Library Medicine, Bethesda, Md., 1965-67; clin. pharmacy teaching coord. VA Hosp., Cin., 1967-71; asst. clin. prof. clin. pharmacy Coll. Pharmacy, U. Cin., 1967-71; chief program evaluation br. Alcohol and Drug Dependence Svc., VA, Ctrl. Office, Washington, 1971-75; dir. Pharmacy Intelligence Ctr., Am. Pharm. Assn., Washington, 1975-85; mem. Roche Hosp. Pharmacy Adv. Bd., 1971-74; judge for ann. Lunsford Richardson Pharmacy awards, 1963, 64; mem. com. standards for drug abuse treatment and rehab. programs Joint Commn. Accreditation of Hosps., 1974-75. Author: (with D. E. Francke, C. J. Latiolais and N.F. H. Ho) Mirror to Hospital Pharmacy, 1964. Contbr. articles on hosp. pharmacy and clin. pharmacy to profl. jours. Recipient Harvey A.K. Whitney award Mich. Soc. Hosp. Pharmacists, 1953, Disting. Alumnus award Purdue U. Sch. of Pharmacy, 1985, Remington Honor medal, 1987, Career Achievement award Profl. Frat. Assn., 1991, Fedn. Internat. Pharm. Lifetime Achievement award, 1996; also various commendations. Mem. Internat. Pharm. Fedn., Am. Inst. History of Pharmacy (exec. sec. 1968-78), Tex. Soc. Hosp. Pharmacists (hon.), Am. Pharm. Assn. (hon. chmn. 1986, named the Gloria Niemeyer Francke Leadership Mentor award in her honor 1995), Am. Soc. Hosp. Pharmacists (Donald E. Francke medal 1995), Drug Info. Assn., Kappa Epsilon, Rho Chi. Presbyterian. Home and Office: 3900 Cathedral Ave NW # 208A Washington DC 20016-5201

FRANCKE, UTA, medical geneticist, genetics researcher, educator; b. Wiesbaden, Germany, Sept. 9, 1942; came to U.S., 1969; d. Kurt and Gertrud Müller; m. Bertold Richard Francke, May 27, 1967 (div. 1982); m. Heinz Furthmayr, July 27, 1986. MD, U. Munich, Fed. Republic Germany, 1967; MS, Yale U., 1985. Diplomate Am. Bd. Pediatrics, Am. Bd. Med. Genetics (bd. dirs. 1981-84). Asst. prof. U. Calif., San Diego, 1973-78; assoc. prof. Yale U., New Haven, 1978-85, prof., 1985-88; prof. Stanford (Calif.) U., 1989—; investigator Howard Hughes Med. Inst., Stanford, 1989—, mem. sci. rev. bd., Bethesda, Md., 1986-88; mem. mammalian genetics study sect. NIH, Bethesda, 1990—; bd. dirs. Am. Soc. Human Genetics, Rockville, Md., 1981-84. Profl. advisor March of Dimes Birth Defects Found., White Plains, N.Y., 1990, Marfan Assn., Port Washington, N.Y., 1991. Mem. Inst. Medicine of NAS (fgn. assoc.), Human Genome Orgn., Soc. for Pediatric Rsch., Soc. for Inherited Metabolic Disorders. Office: Stanford U Med Sch Howard Hughes Med Inst Beckman Ctr Stanford CA 94305*

FRANCO, KENNETH LAWRENCE, surgery educator; b. Hartford, Conn., Sept. 27, 1951; s. Nicholas Lawrence and Mary Elizabeth (LaRosa) F.; m. Jody Mazer, Oct. 10, 1981; 1 child, Jonathan Lawrence. BS, Fairfield U., 1973; MS, Georgetown U., 1975, MD, 1979. Surgical intern, resident Johns Hopkins Hosp., Balt., 1979-81; rsch. fellow Harvard Med. Sch., Boston, 1981-82; resident in surgery Georgetown U. Hosp., Washington, 1982-85, fellow in cardiothoracic surgery, 1985-86; fell in chest and cardiothoracic surgery Columbia-Presbyn. Med. Ctr., N.Y.C., 1986-88; asst. prof. cardiothoracic surgery Yale U. Sch. Medicine, New Haven, 1988-94, assoc. prof., 1994—, co-dir. heart and lung transplant program, 1988, dir. surg. rsch. labs., 1988—, dir. mech. assist device program, 1988—, dir. lung volume reduction surgery program, 1994—; reviewer Jour. Heart Transplant, 1989. Contbg. author: Critical Care Cardiology, 1986, Thoracic and Cardiovascular Surgery, 1990. Biorsch. grantee Harvard U. Med. Sch., 1981. Fellow ACS, ACCP, STS, ASAIO, ISAO, ASTS; mem. Internat. Soc. Heart Transplantation, Johns Hopkins Med. and Surg. Soc., Alpha Omega Alpha. Roman Catholic. Office: Yale U Sch of Medicine 333 Cedar St FMB 121 New Haven CT 06520

FRANCO, RICHARD ANTHONY, pharmaceutical company executive, pharmacist; b. N.Y.C., June 9, 1941; s. Vincent and Filomena (DeFeo) F.; m. Dianne Marie Pellecchia, Sept. 6, 1964; children: Richard, Danielle. BS in Pharmacy, St. John's U., N.Y.C., 1963. Registered pharmacist, N.Y., Vt. Community pharmacist Salisbury Pharmacy, Westbury, N.Y., 1963-68; pharm. sales rep. N.Y. area Eli Lilly and Co., Indpls., 1968-70, spl. sales rep., hosp. sales coord., 1970-73, dist. sales mgr., 1975-77, hosp. sales mgr., 1977-79, product mgr., 1979-81, group product mgr., 1981-84; mgr. N.Y. area Dista Products, Indpls., 1973-75; dir. mktg. Glaxo Inc., Research Triangle Park, N.C., 1984-86, v.p. mktg., 1986-88, v.p. comml. devel., 1988-91, v.p., gen. mgr. dermatology divsn., 1991-93, v.p., gen. mgr. Cerenex divsn., 1993-94; pres., CEO, dir. Trimeris Inc., Research Triangle Park, 1994—; dir. Entremed Inc. Mem. N.C. Edn. Forum, Raleigh, 1988, 89; judge N.C. Engrepreneur of Yr., Raleigh, 1990, 95; bd. dirs. United Way, Raleigh, 1990-93. N.Y. State scholar in engring. and nursing, 1959. Mem. Am. Pharm. Assn., Am. Mgr. Assn., Comml. Devel. Assn., Licensing Exec. Soc. Republican. Office: Trimeris Inc PO Box 13963 Research Triangle Park NC 27709

FRANCOIS, THEODORE VICTOR, psychoanalyst, psychologist; b. Bklyn., Sept. 10, 1938; s. Theodore Victor and Sylvia Antonia (Froix) F.; B.S., Manhattan Coll., 1960; M.A., Fordham U., 1968; M.Div., Woodstock Coll., 1970; M.A., NYU, 1975, Ph.D., 1977, postgrad., 1979-85. Intern clin. psychology NYU Med. Center, N.Y.C., 1973-75, research intern clin. psychology, 1975-76; clin. instr. SUNY Health Sci. Ctr. (formerly Downstate Med. Center), Bklyn., 1977-82, clin. asst. prof., 1983-92, clin. assoc. prof. psychiatry, 1992—, dir. tng. in clin. psychology, 1982—; sr. psychologist Kings County Hosp. Center, Bklyn., 1977-82, chief psychologist, 1982-88, dir. psychol. svcs., 1988—; pvt. practice psychotherapy, Bklyn., 1979—, psychoanalysis, 1985—; bd. dirs. N.Y. State Bd. Psychology, 1995—. Recipient Philip Zlatchin Clin. Psychology award N.Y. U., 1978; NIMH trainee, 1970-73. Mem. Am. Psychol. Assn., Assn. Black Psychologists, N.Y. Assn. Black Psychologists (dir. 1981—), N.Y. Soc. Clin. Psychologists, Psychoanalytic Soc. of NYU. Roman Catholic. Home: 507 Macon St Brooklyn NY 11233-1104 Office: Downstate-Kings County Med Ctr Dept Psychology 451 Clarkson Ave Brooklyn NY 11203-2054

FRANGER, ROBERT RICH, podiatrist; b. Buffalo, Feb. 17, 1954; s. Robert James and Lorraine (Rich) F.; m. Kristin Elizabeth Thompson, Aug. 18, 1990. BA, Hiram Coll., 1976; BS in Basic Sci., Calif.Coll. Podiatric Medicine, 1978, D Podiatric Medicine, 1980. Resident Doctors Hosp, Worcester, Mass., 1980-81; pvt. practice Shrewsbury, Mass., 1982—. Mem. Am. Podiatric Med. Assn., Mass. Podiatric Med. Assn. (div. treas. 1986—). Republican. Mem. United Ch. of Christ. Office: 626 Main St Shrewsbury MA 01545-5639

FRANK, AGNES T., medical librarian; b. Budapest, Hungary; d. Julius Furedi and Maria Szlovak; m. Neil Frank (div. 1971). MLS, Columbia U., 1964. Dir. med. library French & Polyclinic Med. Sch. and Health Ctr., N.Y.C., 1970-74, St. Vincent's Hosp. and Med. Ctr., N.Y.C., 1974—. Mem. Med. Libr. Assn. (cert.), Acad. Health Info. Practitioners (sr.). Home: 372 Central Park W Apt 16A New York NY 10025-8211 Office: St Vincent's Hosp Med Ctr 153 W 11th St New York NY 10011-8305

FRANK, ALLAN PAUL, physician, researcher; b. Toledo, Ohio, Sept. 30, 1963; s. Donald P. and Marilyn Frank. BS, Ea. Mich. U., 1985; MD, Wayne State U., 1990. Diplomate Am. Bd. Internal Medicine. Resident in internal medicine Northwestern Meml. Med. Ctr., Chgo., 1990-93; teaching/attending Cook County Hosp., Chgo., 1993-95; med. dir. Home Access Health Corp., Hoffman Estates, Ill., 1994—. Contbr. articles to profl. jours. Mem. ACP, AMA, ISMS. Office: Home Access Health Corp 2401 W Hassell Rd Ste 1510 Hoffman Estates IL 60195

FRANK, BARBARA BALIS, gastroenterologist, educator; b. Reading, Pa., Jan. 11, 1937; d. Irvin and Ruth Helen (Knoblauch) B.; m. Leonard Arnold Frank, Aug. 17, 1958; children: Michael Scott, Bradford Allan. BA magna cum laude, Smith Coll., 1958; MD, U. Pa., 1962. Diplomate Am. Bd. Internal Medicine and Gastroenterology. Intern, fellow gastroenterology Hosp. of U. Pa., Phila., 1962-63, 63-64, instr. internal medicine, 1966-69; resident internal medicine Bryn Mawr Hosp., Pa., 1964-66; clin. asst. prof. medicine Hahnemann U., Phila., 1973-75, clin. assoc. prof., 1975-85, clin. prof., 1985—, dir. div. gastroenterology Crozer-Chester Med. Ctr., Chester, Pa., 1968-89, attending gastroenterologist, 1989-94; cons. Sacred Heart Hosp., Chester, 1974-94; mem. sci. adv. com. Nat. Found. for Ileitis and Colitis, Phila., 1980—; mem. gastroenterology-urology devices panel FDA, 1988-90, chmn., 1990-92, cons., 1993-94; mem. Physician Payment Rev. Commn., Consensus Panel for Evaluation and Management Services, 1990; rep. for gastroenterology Pa. Medicare Carrier Adv. Com. Assoc. editor MKSAP in gastroenterology and hepatology 2; contbr. articles to profl. jours. Recipient History of Medicine prize U. Pa. Sch. Medicine, Phila., 1962; Legion of Honor award Chapel of Four Chaplains, Phila., 1978; U. Pa. research grantee, 1961-62. Fellow ACP, Coll. Physicians Phila., Am. Coll. Gastroenterology (ad hoc com. on women in gastroenterology 1989—, gov. ea. Pa. 1992—, regional councillor, bd. govs. 1994—, mem. ednl. affairs com. 1992—); mem. AMA, Delaware Valley Soc. for Gastrointestinal Endoscopy (pres. 1984-86, councillor, governing bd. dirs. 1986-88), Pa. Soc. Gastroenterology (councillor for Phila. 1982-84, 87-91, governing bd. dirs.), Am. Soc. for Gastrointestinal Endoscopy (councillor, governing bd. dirs. 1986-90, 92-94, pres. 1991-94, chmn. com. for ICD-9-CM revision 1986-89, mem. govt. relations com. 1987-88, sci. exhibits com. 1985-86, ann. sci. selection com. 1984-85, 90-91, nominating com. 1988-89, and many others), Am. Gastroenterol. Assn. (patient care com. 1986-88, tng. and edn. com. 1989-90, abstract selection com. 1990, nominating com. 1986-87, program evaluation com. 1981-85, mem. pub. policy com. 1992-93, mem. clin. svcs. task force 1994-95, chmn. nominating com. 1995-96, and many others), Bockus Internat. Soc. Gastroenterology, Internat. Assn. for the Study of the Liver, Am. Assn. Study Liver Disease, Am. Liver Found., Pa. Med. Soc., Phila. GI Tng. Group (pres. 1987-93), Phila. Gastrointestinal Research Forum, Delaware County Med. Soc., Israel Med. Assn., Gastroenterology and Urology Devices Panel, FDA, Alpha Omega Alpha, Sigma Xi, Alpha Phi, Kappa Psi, Phi Beta Kappa of Del. Valley (gov. coun. 1991-93, v.p. 1993-95, pres. 1995—). Democrat. Jewish. Avocations: sketching; dancing. Office: Divsn Gastroenterology Hahnemann U Sch Medicine Broad and Vine Sts MS 131 Chester PA 19102-1192

FRANK, ERICA, preventive medicine physician; b. Trenton, N.J., June 17, 1962. MD, Mercer U., 1988. Intern Cleve. Clin., 1988-89; resident in preventive medicine Yale U., New Haven, Conn., 1989-90; fellow in mass media Stanford U., 1990-92; asst. prof. Emory U. Sch. Medicine; Co-editor-in-chief Preventive Medicine. Recipient Clinician-Scientist award Am. Heart Assn., 1995-96. Office: Emory U 69 Butler St SE Atlanta GA 30303-3219

FRANK, HARVEY F., pediatrician; b. Newark, NJ, July 23, 1950; s. Bob and Zelda (Quinn); m. Rose Marvin, June 1996. BS, Temple U, 1971, MD, 1973. Diplomate pediatrics. From intern to resident to chief resident Children's Hosp. Pa., 1972-75; rsch. fellow Children's Hosp. Med. Ctr, Boston, 1975-76; rsch. dir. St. Jude Children's Rsch. Hosp., Memphis, 1977-79; chmn. pediatrics Valley Hosp., Ridgewood, NJ, 1980-86; chief pediatrics Overlook Hosp., Summit, NJ, 1986—; dir. leukemia rsch. programs. Author: You, Your Kids, and Your Doctor, 1991, Your Children Are Not Your Pets, 1993, The New Families: Some Are Extended, Some Are Abbreviated, 1996; Contbr. numerous articles to profl. jours. Am. Pediatrics Assoc., AMA. Democrat. Jewish. Office: Werik Profl Park Med Ctr 12 Nederlander Dr Ste 1066 Summit NJ 07904

FRANK, HERBERT LAWRENCE, anesthesiologist, educator; b. Bklyn., Sept. 22, 1932; divorced; children: Stephanie, Lisa, Erika, Erik, David. BS, Coll. of Gt. Falls, 1956; MD, U. Utrecht (The Netherlands), 1962. Diplomate Am. Bd. Anesthesiology. Intern Pittsfield (Mass.) Affiliated Hosps., 1963-64; resident in anesthesiology Montefiore Hosp. and Med. Ctr., Bronx, N.Y., 1964-66, fellow, 1966-67; fellow in anesthesiology Albert Einstein Coll. Medicine, Yeshiva U., Bronx, 1967-68, instr., assoc., asst. prof., 1967-1973; clin. fellow anesthesiology Bronx Mcpl. Hosp. Ctr., 1966-68; pvt. practice Harrisburg, Pa., 1973—; dir. anesthesiology Harrisburg Hosp., 1973-75; sr. staff anesthesiologist, 1975-96; retired, 1996; med. dirs. Harrisburg Area Sch. Anesthesia, 1973-75; assoc. clin. prof. anesthesiology Hershey Med. Ctr., Pa. State U., 1974—; presenter in field. Contbr. articles to med. jours. With USAF, 1952-55. Mem. Am. Soc. Anesthesiologists, AMA, Internat. Anesthesia Rsch. Soc., Netherlands-Am. Med. Soc., Pa. Med. Soc., Pa. Soc. Anesthesiologists, Dauphin County Med. Soc. Home: PO Box 6048 Harrisburg PA 17112-0048

FRANK, IRWIN NORMAN, urologist, educator; b. Rochester, N.Y., Mar. 24, 1927; s. Harry and Bess (Smalline) F.; m. Marilyn Ellowitch, June 13, 1954; children—Gary, Steven, Lawrence. B.A., U. Rochester, 1950, M.D., 1954. Diplomate Am. Bd. Urology. Intern Strong Meml Hosp., Rochester, 1954-55; asst. resident Strong Meml Hosp., 1955-58, Nat. Cancer Inst. trainee, 1957-59, chief resident urology, 1985-95, med. dir., 1985-95; asst. prof. urology U. Rochester, 1959-67, assoc. prof., 1967-74, prof., 1974—, acting chmn. dept. urology, 1967-69, sr. assoc. dean Sch. Medicine and Dentistry, 1985-95. Contbr. chpts., numerous articles to profl. publs. Med. adv. bd. Kidney Found. Upstate N.Y., Rochester. Served with USN, 1944-46; PTO. Am. Cancer Soc. fellow 1951. Fellow ACS, Am. Acad. Pediatrics; mem. Am. Urol. Assn. (bd. dirs. 1987-95), Am. Urol. Assn. N.E. (pres. 1983-84), N.Y. State Urol. Soc. (pres.), Irondequoit Country Club. Home: 221 Monteroy Rd Rochester NY 14618-1252 Office: U Rochester Med Sch 601 Elmwood Ave Rochester NY 14642-0001

FRANK, JEROME DAVID, psychiatrist, educator; b. N.Y.C., May 30, 1909; s. Jerome W. and Bess (Rosenbaum) F.; m. Helena Schneider, Dec. 4, 1932; m. Elizabeth Kleeman, Jan. 4, 1948; children: Deborah, David, Julia, Emily. A.B. summa cum laude, Harvard, 1930, A.M., 1932, Ph.D. in Psychology, 1934, M.D. cum laude, 1939; LHD honoris causa, SUNY, Binghampton, 1991. Rsch. assoc. group psychotherapy rsch. project VA, 1946-49; instr. Washington Sch. Psychiatry, 1947-49; clin. assoc. prof. Howard U., 1948-49; instr. Johns Hopkins Med. Sch., 1942-46, faculty, 1949—, prof. psychiatry, 1959-74, prof. emeritus psychiatry, 1974—; psychiatrist-in-charge psychiat. out-patient dept. Johns Hopkins Hosp., 1951-64; dir. clin. svcs. Henry Phipps Psychiat. Clinic, 1961-63, acting chief dept. psychiatry, 1960-61; staff mem. Ctr. Study Dem. Instns., 1966; adv. bd.

Patuxent Instn., 1954-78; mem. adv. coms. NIMH, 1951-55, 57-58, 59-61, 68-69, 74-78, mem. task force on homosexuality, 1967-69; mem. social sci. adv. bd. ACDA, 1970-73; mem. adv. com. psychiatry and neurology svc. Dept. Medicine and Surgery, VA Ctrl. Office, 1960-64; bd. dirs. Met. Balt. Assn. Mental Health, 1952—; bd. dirs. SANE, 1974-81, nat. bd. sponsors, 1983—; bd. dirs. Coun. for a Livable World, 1963-93; mem. nat. adv. bd. Physicians for Social Responsibility, 1980—, mem. nat. adv. bd. Psychologists for Social Responsibility, 1985—. Author: Persuasion and Healing: A Comparative Study of Psychotherapy, 1961, (with J.B. Frank), 3rd rev. edit., 1991, (with Florence Powdermaker) Group Psychotherapy: Studies in Methodology of Research and Therapy, 1953, Sanity and Survival: Psychological Aspects of War and Peace, 1967 (reissued as Sanity and Survival in the Nuclear Age, 1973), (with others) Effective Ingredients of Successful Psychotherapy, 1978, Psychotherapy and the Human Predicament: A Psychosocial Approach, 1978, also articles. Served to maj. AUS, 1943-46. Fellow Ctr. Advanced Study Behavioral Scis., Palo Alto, Calif., 1958-59; praelector in psychiatry Faculty Medicine, U. St. Andrews, Dundee, Scotland, 1967; H.B. Williams travelling prof. psychiatry Australia and N.Z., 1971; Litchfield lectr. Oxford U., 1977; Recipient Emil A. Gutheil award Assn. Advancement Psychotherapy, 1970, Kurt Lewin Meml. award Soc. for Psychol. Study Social Issues, 1972, Blanche Ittleson award Am. Orthopsychiat. Assn., 1979, Spl. Rsch. award Soc. for Psychotherapy Rsch., 1981, McAlpin Rsch. Achievement award Nat. Mental Health Assn., 1981, Oskar Pfister award Am. Psychiat. Assn., 1983, award for disting. contbn. to psychology in the pub. interest Am. Psychol. Assn., 1985, Salmon medal N.Y. Acad. Medicine, 1986, cert. Am. Counseling Assn., 1986, Harold D. Lasswell award Internat. Soc. Polit. Psychology, 1987, disting. and enduring contribution award APA divsn. psychotherapy, 1992, disting. svc. award Am. Coll. Psychiatrists, 1995, Great Mind award ACA, 1996, World Conf. honor, 1996. Fellow APA, Am. Psychiat. Assn., Soc. for Psychol. Study of Social Issues (pres. 1965-66), Am. Coll. Psychiatrists, Am. Group Psychotherapy Assn., Am. Assn. for Social Psychiatry (v.p. 1974), World Acad. Art and Sci., Royal Coll. Psychiatrists (hon.), Polish Psychiat. Soc. (hon.); mem. Am. Psychopath. Assn. (pres. 1963), Fedn. Am. Scientists (vice chmn. 1976-79, chmn. 1979), AAUP, Phi Beta Kappa, Sigma Xi, Alpha Omega Alpha.

FRANK, LAURIE, physician assistant; b. New Rochelle, N.Y., Apr. 2, 1963; d. Monroe and Gerry (Bloch) Adlman; m. Kevin Frank, Sr., June 13, 1982; children: Kevin, Jr., Katelyn. BMS, Emory U., 1985. Cert. physician asst. NCCPA. Physician asst. Dr. Benjamin Barnard, Vidalia, Ga., 1986, State of Ga./Dept. Corrections, Atlanta, 1989-90, Dr. Joseph Giles, Vidalia, 1993, Correctional Med. Systems, St. Louis, 1986-95, Prison Health Svcs., Del., 1995—. Mem. Am. Acad. of Physicians Assts. Home: 2009 Brenda Ln Vidalia GA 30474

FRANK, LUDWIG MATHIAS, psychiatrist; b. Phila., Apr. 16, 1920; s. Ludwig and Eleanore Emily (Saverwald) F.; A.B. maxima cum laude, LaSalle Coll., 1942; M.D., U. Pa., 1945; m. Marie T. Johnson, Sept. 21, 1946; children—Ludwig Matthew, Terri Frank Terni, Mary Ellen Frank Willsey; m. 2d, Hallie E. Moore, June 2, 1979. Intern, Fitzgerald Mercy Hosp., Darby, Pa., 1945-46; resident in psychiatry Mayo Found., Rochester, Minn., 1948-51; 1st asst. in psychiatry Mayo Clinic, 1948-52; clin. dir. Inst. Living, Hartford, 1952-55; pvt. practice medicine, specializing in psychiatry, West Hartford, 1955—; chief psychiatry St. Francis Hosp., 1955-75; clin. asso. U. Conn. Med. Sch., 1975—; cons. USAF, San Antonio, 1947—, Met. Tribunal, Hartford, St. Francis Hosp., 1987—; v.p., dir. Swiss Meadows Inc.; v.p., dir. Hatchetts Improvement Co. Mem. Sch. Bd. Archdiocese Hartford, 1969-74. Served to capt., M.C., AUS, 1946-48. Diplomate Am. Bd. Psychiatry. Fellow Am. Psychiat. Assn. (life), ACP (life); mem. Hartford Psychiat. Soc. (dir.; past pres.), AMA, Conn., Hartford County med. socs., Conn., Hartford psychiat. socs., Assn. Am. Med. Colls., N.Y. Acad. Sci., Piersol Anat. Soc., Mayo Clinic, Inst. Living, U. Pa. alumni assns. Contbr. to profl. jours. Home: 21 Walbridge Rd West Hartford CT 06119-1344 Office: 801 Farmington Ave Hartford CT 06119-1600

FRANK, MARY LOU BRYANT, psychologist, educator; b. Denver, Nov. 27, 1952; d. W.D. and Blanche (Dean) Bryant; m. Kenneth Kerry Frank, Sept. 9, 1973; children: Kari Lou, Kendra Leah. BA, Colo. State U., 1974, MEd, 1983, MS, 1986, PhD, 1989. Tchr. Cherry Creek Schs., Littleton, Colo., 1974-80; from grad. asst. to dir. career devel. Colo. State U., Ft. Collins, 1980-86; intern U. Del., Newark, 1987-88; psychologist Ariz. State U., Tempe, 1988-93; assoc., lead prof. psychology Clinch Valley Coll. U. Va., Wise, 1992-96, asst. acad. dean, 1993-95; head psychology dept., prof. North Ga. Coll., 1996—; instr. Colo. State U., Ft. Collins, 1981-82, counselor, 1984-85, 86-87; psychologist Ariz. State U., Tempe, 1989-92; assoc. prof. psychology Clinch Valley Coll. U. Va., 1992-96. Author: (program manual) Career Development, 1986; contbr. book chpts. on eating disorders and existential psychotherapy. Mem. APA, AACD, Phi Kappa Phi, Phi Beta Kappa, Pi Kappa Delta, Psi Chi. Office: North Ga Coll Psychology Dept Dahlonega GA 30597

FRANK, MICHAEL M., physician; b. Bklyn., Feb. 28, 1937; s. Robert and Helen (Prakin) F.; m. Ruth Sybil Pudolsky, Nov. 5, 1961; children: Robert E., Abigail B., Brice S.H. AB, U. Wis., 1956; MD, Harvard U., 1960. Intern Boston City Hosp., 1960-61; resident in pediatrics Johns Hopkins Hosp., 1961-62, 64-65; vis. scientist Nat. Inst. Med. Research, London, 1965-66; with NIH, 1967-90; chief lab. of clin. investigation, clin. dir. Nat. Inst. Allergy and Infectious Diseases, Bethesda, Md., 1977-90; prof., chmn. dept. pediatrics Duke U. Med. Ctr., Durham, N.C., 1990—. Mem. ACP, Assn. Am. Physicians, Am. Soc. Clin. Investigation, Soc. Pediatric Rsch., Am. Pediatric Soc., Infectious Diseases Soc., Am. Acad. Allergy, Am. Acad. Pediatrics.

FRANK, PAUL WILBUR, social worker; b. Amery, Wis., Oct. 5, 1947; s. Wilbur Raymond and Harriet Josephine (Sukow) F. BA magna cum laude, Augsburg Coll., 1969; MS in Social Work, U. Wis., 1975, MA in Pub. Policy and Adminstrn., 1975. Lic. ind. clin. social worker, Minn. Psychiat. aide Met. Med. Ctr., Mpls., 1972-73; social worker III Crow Wing County Social Svc. Ctr., Brainerd, Minn., 1976-78; supr. social svcs. Wright County Human Svcs. Agy., Buffalo, Minn., 1978-79; coord. tng. and placement Mo. Epilepsy Fedn., St. Louis, 1979-80; med. social worker Met. Med. Ctr., Mpls., 1980-82, counselor employee assistance program, 1981-87; mgr. employee assistance program Met.-Mt. Sinai Med. Ctr. (formerly Met. Med. Ctr.), Mpls., 1987-90, mgr. Behavioral Health Access Ctr., 1989-90; employee assistance program mgr. Health East St. Joseph's Hosp., St. Paul, 1990-93; employee assistance program counselor, mktg. rep. Behavioral Health Svcs., Inc., Mpls., 1993—. With U.S. Army, 1969. Grantee, scholar U. Wis., 1973-74. Mem. NASW, Acad. Cert. Social Workers, Employee Assistance Profls. Assn., Minn. Social Svc. Assn. (Minn. employer assistance program administrs. and counselors), Mental Health Assn. Minn. Home: 2548 83rd Ave N Brooklyn Park MN 55444-1504

FRANK, RICHARD ALAN, psychiatrist; b. Bklyn., Dec. 20, 1948. MD, Yale U., 1976. Resident in psychiatry McLean Hosp., Belmont, Mass., 1977-80, fellow in child psychiatry, 1978-81; staff psychiatrist Human Rels. Svc., Wellesley, Mass., 1981-84, South Shore Mental Health Ctr., Quincy, Mass., 1990-92; clin. asst. prof. Med. Coll. Wis., Milw., 1992—; clin. instr. Harvard Med. Sch. at Cambridge (Mass.) Hosp., 1984-92; clin. asst. prof. Tufts U. Sch. Medicine, 1989-92; mem. faculty Boston Psychoanalytic Inst., 1992—, Wis. Psychoanalytic New Tng. Facility, 1992—. Contbr. articles to profl. jours. Mem. Am. Psychoanalytic Assn., Am. Psychiat. Assn., Am. Acad. Child and Adolescent Psychiatry. Home: 5738 N Shore Dr Whitefish Bay WI 53217-4860 Office: 2577 N Downer Ave Milwaukee WI 53211

FRANK, RICK, public health officer. BA in Polit. Sci. and History, Purdue U., 1991. Intern Ind. State Senate, 1990; pub. inquires asst. Office of Gov. George V. Voinovich, 1993-94; sr. exec. asst., now exec. asst. to dir. Ohio Dept. Health, Columbus, 1994—; fin. asst. Voinovich/DeWine Campaign, 1990-91; intern Ohio State Lottery Commn., 1991; asst. press sec. DeWine for U.S. Senate Campaign, 1992. Home: 5347 Firebush Ln Columbus OH 43235 Office: Ohio Health Dept 246 N High St Columbus OH 43266-0588*

FRANK, ROBERT S., chiropractor; b. N.Y.C., Nov. 19, 1957; s. Edward and Bernice (Drucker) F.; m. Estelle Frank, Nov. 23, 1986; 1 child, Zachary M. BA, NYU, 1978; D in Chropractic, Cleve. Chiropractic Coll., Kansas City, Mo., 1982. Lic. chiropractor, N.Y., N.J. Pvt. practice Suffolk County, N.Y., 1982—; assoc. chiropractic dir. U.S Health Care, Blue Bell, Pa., 1995—. Mem. Masons. Home: 126 Carleton Ave Islip Terrace NY 11752-2639

FRANK, SANDERS THALHEIMER, physician, educator; b. Middletown, Conn., May 11, 1938; s. Harry S. and Pauline (Thalheimer) F.; B.A., Amherst Coll., 1959; M.D., N.Y. Med. Coll., 1963; children: Geoffrey Brooks, Susan Kimberly, Jonathan Blair. Intern, Sinai Hosp., Balt., 1963-64; resident Wilford Hall Med. Center, San Antonio, 1965-68; pvt. practice medicine, specializing in pulmonary disease, Monterey Park, Calif., 1971-92; dir. respiratory care Garfield Hosp., Monterey Park, 1974-92, Beverly Hosp., Montebello, Calif., 1975-78; assoc. prof. medicine U. So. Calif., L.A., 1972-90; pvt. practice, Zanesville, Ohio, 1992—. Served to maj. USAF, 1964-71. Decorated USAF Commendation medal; recipient Philip Hench award for demonstrating relationship of rheumatoid arthritis to lung disease, 1968; award of merit Los Angeles County Heart Assn., 1974. Fellow Royal Soc. Medicine (London), Am. Coll. Chest Physicians, A.C.P.; mem. Am. Thoracic Soc., Calif. Thoracic Soc., Nat. Assn. Dirs. Respiratory Care, Respiratory Care Assembly Calif., Alpha Omega Alpha. Contbr. articles in field to med. jours. Recorded relationship of ear-lobe crease to coronary artery disease, 1973.

FRANKEL, BARRY ROY, management consultant; b. Elizabeth, N.J., Nov. 16, 1950; s. Milton David and Celia (Nachman) F.; m. Karen Susan Laby, Apr. 22, 1979; children: Erin Danielle, Matthew David. BS in Indsl. Engrng., Rutgers U., 1972; MBA in Fin., U. Pa., 1974. Sr. rsch. officer CitiBank Investment Mgmt. Group, N.Y.C., 1974-77; mgr. strategic planning Pfizer Pharm., N.Y.C., 1977-79; group product mgr. Pfizer Pharms., N.Y.C., 1979-82; prin., pres. S.J. Weinstein Assocs., Inc., N.Y.C., 1982-93; mng. ptnr. The Frankel Group, Inc., N.Y.C., 1993—. Contbr. articles to profl. jours. Bd. dirs. 250 East 87th Owners Corp., N.Y.C., 1986—. James J. Slade scholar Rutgers U., 1972. Mem. Pharm. Advt. Coun., Med. Advt. Agy. Assn., Biomed. Mktg. Assn., Wharton Club N.Y., Rutgers Club N.Y., Tau Beta Pi, Beta Gamma Sigma. Democrat. Jewish. Home: Apt 24B 250 E 87th St New York NY 10128-3101 Office: The Frenkel Group Inc 475 Fifth Ave New York NY 10017

FRANKEL, DONNA LUCAS, rehabilitation physician, educator; b. Cleve., Feb. 1, 1947; d. Joseph and Dorothy (Helsir) Lucas; m. Eric C. Frankel, Jan. 24, 1970. BSc, Purdue U., 1968; M Nutrition Sci., Cornell U., 1970; MD, U. Md., 1977; M Rehab. Medicine, U. Wash., 1984. Diplomate Am. Bd. Internal Medicine, Am. Bd. Geriatrics, Am. Bd. Electrodiagnostic Medicine, Am. Bd. Phys. Medicine and Rehab.; registered dietitian. Floor dietitian St. Elizabeth's Hosp., Lafayette, Ind., 1968; pub. health nutritionist Bur. Maternal and Child Health, Cmty. Health/Hosp. Adminstrn, Washington, 1970-73; trainee in phys. medicine and rehab. George Washington U. Hosp., Washington, 1975; intern Washington Hosp. Ctr., 1977-78, resident in internal medicine, 1977-80; resident in phys. medicine and rehab. U. Wash. Affiliated Hosps., Seattle, 1980-82; instr. rehab. medicine U. Wash. Sch. Medicine, 1982-84; staff physician Pacific Health Assocs. of Seattle, 1984-87; med. dir. Restorative Care Ctr. Highline Cmty. Hosp., Burien, Wash., 1988-90; pvt. practice rehab. medicine Sequim, Wash., 1991—; nat. mgr. N.W. Nat. Rehab. Mgmt. Group, Inc., 1991-92; clin. asst. prof. rehab. medicine U. Wash. Sch. Medicine, 1988—; med. dir. Olympic Health Care Ctr., Sequim, 1994—; rehab. medicine cons. Group Health Coop. of Puget Sound, St. Cabrini Hosp., Seattle, 1987; mem. staff Olympic Meml. Hosp., Port Angeles, Wash., 1989—, Providence Med. Ctr., Seattle, 1987-92, Valley Med. Ctr., Renton, Wash., 1988, 90, Highline Cmty. Hosp., 1987-90, Seattle VA Hosp., 1987-89, St Cabrini Hosp., Seattle, 1987; assoc. med. staff mem. Univ. Hosp., Seattle, 1988-91, attending physician, 1982-84; cons., lectr., presenter workshops in field. Contbr. articles to profl. publs. Mem. adv. bd. Adult Action Ctr., Port Angeles, 1991—; mem. cmty. svcs. com. Puget Sound chpt. Nat. Multiple Sclerosis Soc., 1984-91, bd. dirs., 1985-87, mem. profl. adv. coun., 1983-87, chmn., 1986-87; mem. med. adv. bd. Cmty. Home Health Care, Seattle, 1988-90; mem. adv. coun. Dept. Vocat. Rehab., State of Wash., 1984-90, chmn., 1987-88; mem. anti-drinking and driving com. King County Med. Assn., 1985-86; vice chmn. profl. adv. coun. N.W. area Upjohn Home Health Care, 1985-86; chmn. profl. adv. coun. Resource Ctr. for the Handicapped, Seattle, 1983-85. Fellow Am. Assn. Electrodiagnostic Medicine (bd. dirs. 1994—), Am. Assn. Phys. Medicine and Rehab.; mem. AMA, Wash. State Med. Assn., Clallam County Med. Soc. (bd. dirs. 1995—), Am. Dietetic Assn., Am. Acad. Phys. Medicine and Rehab., Wash. State Soc. Phys. Medicine and Rehab., Am. Geriatrics Soc., Wash. Geriatrics Soc. (bd. dirs. 1989-91, editor newsletter 1990—), Am. Med. Dir.'s Assn., Sequim-Dungeness Valley C. of C., Phi Kappa Phi, Omicron Nu. Office: 777 N 5th Ave Sequim WA 98382

FRANKEL, ERIC HOWARD, clinical pharmacist, consultant; b. N.Y.C., Sept. 8, 1948; s. Albert and Helen Dorothy (Kirschenbaum) F.; m. Mariette Durack Edwards, Mar. 12, 1974 (div. Apr. 1988). BS in Psychology, CCNY, 1970, MS in Edn., 1972; BS in Pharmacy, Bklyn. Coll. Pharmacy, 1978; PharmD, Mercer U., 1979. Registered pharmacist, N.Y., Ga., Tex.; bd. cert. nutrition support pharmacist. Nutritional support pharmacist Crawford W. Long Meml. Hosp., Emory U., Atlanta, 1980-88; coord. nutritional support svc. St. Mary of the Plains Hosp., Lubbock, Tex., 1988-90, clin. coord., coord. nutritional support svc., 1990—; adj. assoc. prof. So. Sch. Atlanta, Mercer U., 1982-88; adj. clin. instr. Sch. Medicine, Emory U., 1983-88; adj. prof. Tex. Tech U., Lubbock, 1988—; cons. home parental nutrition various home care agys., Atlanta, 1983-85; cons. nutrition support Shallowford Community Hosp., Atlanta, 1985-88; del. U.S. Pharmacopeial Conv. Mem. med. bd. advisors Nutritional Support Svcs. Jour., 1986-88; contbr. articles to profl. jours.; patentee in field. Mem. Am. Pharm. Assn., Am. Soc. Hosp. Pharmacists, Am. Coll. Clin. Pharmacists, Am. Soc. for Parenteral and Enteral Nutrition, State and Local Hosp. and Gen. Pharm. Orgn., Atlanta Area Soc. for Parenteral and Enteral Nutrition (1st v.p. 1985-86, 1st past press. 1985-86), Sylvia Griffith Meml. Soc. for Parenteral and Enteral Nutrion West Tex. and E. N.Mex. (1st pres. 1991-92). Home: 509 N Genoa Ave Lubbock TX 79416-3331 Office: St Mary of the Plains Hosp 4000 24th St Lubbock TX 79410-1894

FRANKEL, GERALD J., urologist; b. Jersey City, N.J., Jan. 31, 1943; s. Abraham and Florence (Emmer) F.; m. Rhoda Frankel, Dec. 27, 1964; children: David, Michael. BA, Franklin Marshall Coll., 1964; MD, Hahnemann Med. Coll., 1969. Diplomate Am. Bd. Urology. Intern Abington (Pa.) Meml. Hosp., 1969-70; surg. resident Jeannes Hosp., Phila., 1970-71; urology resident Upstate Med. Ctr., Syracuse, N.Y., 1971-74; pvt. practice Indpls., 1974-84, Williamsport, Pa., 1984-85, McKinney, Tex., 1985—. Active Ad Hoc Baseball Com., Plano, Tex., 1996; candidate for Congl. Dist. 26 Dem. Ctrl. Com., Plano, 1996. Fellow Am. Urology Assn., ACS; mem. Tex. Med. Assn., Internat. Continence Soc. Hebrew. Office: Ctr for Bladded Prostate Disorders 1441 Redbud Blvd # 261 Mc Kinney TX 75069

FRANKEL, JACK, pediatrician, allergist; b. N.Y.C., Sept. 9, 1920; s. Max H. and Fanny F.; m. Ivene J. Frankel, Apr. 18, 1948; children: Barbara Meg, Judith Ann, Richard Harris, Carolyn, Joan Ellen. BS, Tulane U., 1941, MD, 1945. Diplomate Am. Bd. of Pediatrics; fellow Am. Coll. of Allergy. Pediatrician, allergist Manatee Family Physicians, Bradenton, Fla.; asst. prof. clin. pediatrics and allergy SUNY, Stony Brook, 1955-75, NYU, 1970-75; cons. Blake Meml. Hosp., Bradenton, Fla., 1970—, Manatee Meml. Hosp., Bradenton, 1977—. Capt. U.S. Army Med. Corps, 1946-48. Fellow Am. Acad. Pediatrics, Am. Coll. Allergy. Jewish. Home: PO Box 8452 Long Boat Key FL 34228 Office: Manatee Family Physicians 2010 59St W Bradenton FL 34209

FRANKEL, JUDITH JENNIFER MARIASHA, clinical psychologist, consultant; b. Bklyn., May 25, 1947; m. Anthony R. D'Augelli, Sept. 1, 1968 (div. 1985); children: Jennifer Hadley Frankel, Rebekah Lindsay Frankel. BA, New Coll. at Hofstra U., 1968; MA, U. Conn., 1971, PhD, 1972. Lic. psychologist, Pa. Rsch. psychologist Family Consultation Ctr., Roslyn, N.Y., 1968, Conn. State Dept. Mental Health, Hartford, 1969-71; staff intern VA Hosp., West Haven, Conn., 1971-72; asst./assoc. prof., dir. program devel. and evaluation Pa. State U., State College, 1972-81; pvt. practice psychology State College, 1976—; psychol. cons. PYRAMID Orgn., Walnut Creek, Calif., 1975-78, N.Y. Dept. Mental Health, 1976, Nat. Inst. Alcohol Abuse Prevention, Nat. Inst. Drug Abuse Prevention, Nat. Youth Alternatives Program, 1975-79, Meadows Psychiatric Ctr. Women's Program, 1993-95; v.p. Mental Health Profls., State College, 1978-80, pres., 1980-82; exec. bd. Ctrl. Pa. Psychol. Assn., 1989-90. Author: Decisions Are Possible, 1975, Communication and Parenting Skills, 1976, Helping Others, 1980; contbr. articles to profl. jours. Campaigner Stein for Rep., 1982, Wachob for Congress, 1984; chair cmty. action Congregation Brit Shalom, State College, 1985-87, coord. ednl. liaison, 1985-87; v.p. Jewish Cmty. Coun. Women, 1988-90, pres., 1990-93, bd. dirs. Congregation Brit. Shalom, 1985-87, 90-93; v.p. Hadassah, 1995—. USPHS fellow, U. Conn., 1969-71. Mem. APA (clin. psychology, psychology of women, ind. practice, & health psychology divsns.), Pa. Psychol. Assn., Ea. Psychol. Assn., Ctrl. Pa. Psychol. Assn. (exec. bd. 1989-90), Jewish Cmty. Coun. women (bd. dirs. 1990-94), Hadassah (v.p. programming 1995—), Phi Beta Kappa, Phi Kappa Phi. Democrat. Jewish.

FRANKEL, KENNETH MARK, thoracic surgeon; b. Bklyn., July 29, 1940; s. Clarence Bernard and Ruth (Rutes) F.; m. Felice Cala Oringel, Dec. 10, 1967; children: Matthew David, Michael Jacob. B.A., Cornell U., 1961; M.D., SUNY, Bkyln., 1965. Diplomate Am. Bd. Surgery, Am. Bd. Thoracic Surgery. Intern in surgery Yale New Haven Hosp., 1965-66; resident in surgery Kings County-SUNY Med. Ctr., Bklyn., 1966-67, 69-71, chief resident in gen. surgery, 1971-72, resident in thoracic surgery, 1972-73, chief resident thoracic and cardiovascular surgery, 1973-74; attending thoracic surgeon Mercy Hosp., Springfield, Mass., 1974—, Holyoke (Mass.) Hosp., 1974—, Providence Hosp., Holyoke, 1974—; pvt. practice medicine specializing in thoracic surgery Springfield, 1974—; chief thoracic surgery Baystate Med. Ctr., Springfield, 1977—; clin. prof. cardiothoracic surgery Tufts U. Sch. Medicine, 1978—; cons. in thoracic surgery Noble Hosp., Westfield, Mass., 1976—; cons. Shriners Hosp. for Crippled Children. Contbr. articles to profl. jours. Corporator Springfield (Mass.) Symphony Orch., Stage West, Springfield. Served to capt. U.S. Army, 1967-69. Decorated Bronze Star, Gallantry Cross (Republic of Vietnam). Fellow ACS, Am. Coll. Chest Physicians; mem. AMA, ACLU, Soc. Thoracic Surgeons, Am. Thoracic Soc., New Eng. Cancer Soc., Springfield Acad. Medicine (past pres.), Mass. Med. Soc. (councilor 1981-83), Hampden Dist. Med. Soc. (exec. com. 1990—, rep. to Blue Cross/Blue Shield Regional Health Care Improvement Coun.), Physicians for Social Responsibility, Maimonides Med. Club (past pres.), Amnesty Internat., Internat. Physicians for Prevention Nuclear War, Union Concerned Scientists, Cornell Club Western Mass., Porsche Club Am. Democrat. Jewish. Home: 202 Ellington Rd Longmeadow MA 01106-1510 Office: Baystate Med Ctr Office Bldg 2 Medical Center Dr Ste 304 Springfield MA 01107-1272

FRANKEL, MARK HENRY, psychiatrist; b. N.Y.C., Mar. 17, 1943; m. Jane Gould; children: Jessica, Joshua. BA, Washington & Jefferson U., 1964; MD, Ohio State U., 1968. Diplomate Am. Bd. Psychiatry and Neurology. Supr. med. student clerkship Brecksville (Ohio) VA Hosp., 1974-80; attending psychiatrist evening mental health clinic Cleve. Metro Gen. Hosp., 1974-78; asst. in psychiatry edn. Mt. Sinai Med. Ctr., Cleve., 1974-84, co-dir. sleep disorders ctr., 1976-91, dir. inpatient unit, 1981-84, asst. dir. dept. psychaitry, 1981-84; asst. dir. divsn. geriatric psychiatry Luth. Med. Ctr., Cleve., 1984-91; clin. dir. divsn. geriatric psychiatry Fairview Health Sys., Cleve., 1991—, chief of psychiatry, 1991—. Lt. comdr. USNR, 1970-72. Home: 1600 Oakwood Dr Cleveland Heights OH 44121 Office: Fairview Med Group 2609 Franklin Blvd Cleveland OH 44113

FRANKENHAEUSER, MARIANNE, psychology educator; b. Helsinki, Finland, Sept. 30, 1925; d. Tor and Ragni (Alfthan) von Wright; m. Bernhard Frankenhaeuser, Mar. 15 (dec. Nov. 1994). Dipl. in Psychology, Oxford U., 1947; BA, U. Helsinki, 1950; MA, U. Stockholm, 1954; PhD, U. Uppsala, 1959; D in Polit. Sci (hon.), U. Turku, Finland, 1990. Clin. psychologist Seraphimer Hosp., Stockholm, 1951-55; rsch. psychologist Karolinska Inst., Stockholm, 1955-60; asst. prof. U. Stockholm, 1960-63; rsch. fellow Swedish Coun. for Social Sci. Rsch., 1963-65; assoc. prof. Swedish Med. Rsch. Coun., 1965-69, prof., 1969-80; prof. psychology Karolinska Inst., Stockholm, 1980-92, head psychology div., 1982-92; mem. sci. adv. panel Swedish Nat. Bd. Health and Welfare, 1968-91; med. adv. bd. Swedish Tobacco Co., 1971-83; bd. dirs. Bank of Sweden Tercentenary Found., 1974-80, rev. com. on behavioral scis., 1974-80; vis. prof. psychiat. Stanford U., 1976; cons. U.S. Social Sci. Rsch. Coun. Com. on Life Course Perspectives in Middle and Old Age, 1978—; bd. dirs. Swedish Coun. for Mgmt. and Work Life Issues, 1981-91, Swedish Soc. for Mems. Parliament and Scientists, 1981—, many others in past. Mem. editl. bd. Acta Psychologica, European Jour. Psychonomic Sci., 1970-72, Jour. Human Stress, 1975-84, Motivation and Emotion, 1975-89, Internat. Jour. Psychology, 1976-80, Human Neurobiology, 1981-84, Plenum Series on Stress and Coping, 1985—, Stress Medicine, 1985—, New Trends in Exptl. and Clin. Psychiatry, 1986—, Jour. Orgnl. Behavior, 1987-94, Internat. Jour. Behavioral Medicine, 1992—, Jour. Gender, Culture and Health, 1994—; contbr. articles to profl. jours.; author: Stress - en del av livet, 1983, 4th edit. 1992, Women, Work and Health, 1991, Kvinnligt, Manligt, Stressigt, 1993, others. Sci. coun. Swedish Nat. Ency., 1987-96; mem. com. on human rights Nat. Acad. Scis., 1989—; mem. productivity commn. Swedish Govt., 1989-91; mem. work environ. coun. Swedish Govt., Dept. Labor, 1989-91; mem. Swedish Work Environment Fund Adv. Com. on Long Range Rsch. Investments, 1988-90; sci. coun. Swedish Inst. for Opinion Rsch. SIFO/Holen Network AB, 1988-90; com. on jobs in future soc. Swedish Employment Security Coun., 1986-89, others. Resident scholar Rockefeller Found. Study and Conf. Ctr., Bellagio, Como, Italy, 1980; Recipient Royal award The King of Sweden's medal of the 8th dimension with the ribbon of the Seraphimer Order, 1985, Swedish nat. award for zealous and devoted svc., 1986, Gold leaf award and hon. mem. Swedish Forum for Psychosocial Worklife Issues, 1988, Internat. Women's Forum award, 1989; named Woman of Yr. Am. Biog. Inst., 1994; Ctr. for Advanced Study in Behavioral Scis. fellow Stanford U., 1995-96. Mem. Swedish Psychol. Assn. (chmn. sci. coun. 1970-73), European Brain and Behavior Soc. (pres.), Academie Internationale de Philosophie des Scis. (corr. mem.), NAS (fgn. assoc.), Academia Europaea, N.Y. Acad. Scis., Finnish Soc. Scis. and Letters (fgn. mem.). Home: Vargardsvagen 75, S-133 36 Saltsjobaden Sweden 0000000 Office: U of Stockholm Psychology, Frescati Hagvag 14, 106 91 Stockholm Sweden

FRANKENTHALER, ROBERT ANDREW, surgeon; b. N.Y.C., Mar. 19, 1954; s. Norman Alfred and Bernice (Schlosser)F.; m. Roberta Diane Beller; children: Amy, Jill, Scott. BS, NYU, 1978; MD, Albert Einstein Coll Medicine, 1982. Diplomate Am. Bd. Otolaryngology; lic. surgeon N.Y., Tex., Mass. Resident Beth Israel Hosp., N.Y.C., 1982-84; resident otolaryngology Columbia Presbyn. Hosp., N.Y.C., 1984-87; fellow head and neck surgery U. Tex. M.D. Anderson Hosp., Houston, 1987-89, asst. prof., 1989-94; asst. prof. otology and laryngology Harvard U. Med. Sch., 1994—; dir. Langwood Ctr. for Head and Neck Cancer, 1994—; assoc. surgeon Brigham & Women's Hosp., Boston, 1994—, Beth Israel Hosp., Boston, 1994—; asst. surgeon Mass. Eye & Ear Infirmary, Boston, 1994—; adj. asst. prof. Baylor Coll. Medicine, Houston, 1994-95; courtesy staff Children's Hosp., Boston, 1994—, Dana Farber Cancer Inst., Boston, 1994—; resident selection com. Dept. Otolaryngology U. Tex. Med. Sch., Houston, 1993—; lectr. in field. Clin. Oncology fellow Am. Cancer Soc., 1988-89. Fellow ACS; mem. AMA, Am. Acad. Otolaryngology-Head and Neck Surgery (com. for head and neck surgery and oncology), Am. Soc. Head and Neck Surgery, Soc. Head and Neck Surgery, Am. Soc. Clin. Oncology. Office: Joint Ctr Otolaryngology 333 Longwood Ave Boston MA 02115

FRANK-FITZNER, FONTAINE LYNNE, geriatrics, medical and surgical nurse; b. Detroit; m. George H. Fitzner. AA with honors, Jackson Community Coll., Mich., 1984; BSN with honors, Ea. Mich. U., 1988; Assoc. in Geriatric Nursing Care, Ea. Mich. U.-Mich. State U., 1990. RN, Mich., Fla. Staff nurse Suncoast Hosp., Largo, Fla., 1988-89; charge nurse VA Hosp., Ann Arbor, Mich., 1989; infection control practitioner Med. Ctr. Hosp., Punta Gorda, Fla., 1992-93; health svcs. coord. Cigna Health Plan of Fla. Inc., Tampa, 1993-96; clin. rev. specialist Liberty Mut. Ins. Co., Tampa, 1996—. Mem. ANA, Fla. Nurses Assn., Nat. League of Nursing, Sigma Theta Tau.

FRANKL, WILLIAM STEWART, cardiologist, educator; b. Phila., July 15, 1928; s. Louis and Vera (Simkin) F.; m. Razelle Sher-, June 17, 1951; children: Victor S. (dec.), Brian A. B.A. in Biology, Temple U., 1951, M.D.,

1955, M.S. in Medicine, 1961. Diplomate: Am. Bd. Internal Medicine, Am. Bd. Cardiovascular Disease. Intern Buffalo Gen. Hosp., 1955-56; resident in medicine Temple U., Phila., 1956-57, 59-61; mem. faculty Temple U. (Sch. Medicine), 1962-68, dir. EKG sect. dept. cardiology, 1966-68, dir. cardiac care unit, 1967-68; prof. medicine, dir. div. cardiology Med. Coll. Pa., Phila., 1970-79; prof. medicine, assoc. dir. cardiology div. Thomas Jefferson U., Phila., 1979-84; physician-in-chief Springfield (Mass.) Hosp., 1968-70; practice medicine specializing in cardiology Phila., 1962-68, 70—; prof. medicine, co-dir. William Likoff Cardiovascular Inst. Hahnemann U., Phila., 1984-86, dir. William Likoff Cardiovascular Inst., dir. div. cardiology, 1986-92, Thomas J. Vischer Prof. medicine, chmn. dept. medicine, 1987-92; prof. medicine, dir. cardiovascular regional programs Allegheny U. of the Health Scis., 1992; dir. cardiovascular regional programs Allegheny Univ. Hosps., 1992—, v.p. cardiovascular program devel., 1995—; cons. cardiology Phila. Va Hosp., 1970-79; Fogarty Sr. Internat. fellow Cardiothoracic Inst., U. London, 1978-79; pres. Pa. affiliate Am. Heart Assn., 1985-86. Contbr. articles to profl. jours. Capt. Med. Corps, U.S. Army, 1957-59. Cardiovascular rsch. fellow U. Pa., Phila., 1961-62; recipient Golden Apple award Temple U. Sch. Medicine, 1967; award Med. Coll. Pa., 1972; Lindback award for distinguished teaching, 1975. Fellow ACP, Am. Coll. Cardiology (gov. Ea. Pa. 1986-89), Phila. Coll. Physicians, Am. Coll. Clin. Pharmacology (regent 1980-85, 93—), Coun. Clin. Cardiology of Am. Heart Assn. (coun. on arteriosclerosis); mem. AAUP, AAAS, N.Y. Acad. Scis., Am. Fedn. Clin. Rsch., Assn. Am. Med. Colls., Am. Heart Assn. (bd. govs. S.E. Pa. chpt. 1972-84, pres. 1976, Pa. affiliate pres. 1984-85), Am. Soc. Clin. Pharmacology and Exptl. Therapeutics, Philadelphia County Med. Soc. (pres. 1993-94). Home: 536 Moreno Rd Wynnewood PA 19096-1121 Office: Med Coll Pa Hosp 3300 Henry Ave Philadelphia PA 19129-1121

FRANKLAND, ALFRED WILLIAM, allergist; b. Bexhill, Sussex, Eng., Mar. 19, 1912; s. Henry and Rose (West) F.; m. Pauline Margaret Jackson, 1942; children: Penelope, Jenifer, Hilary, Andrew. BA, Oxford (Eng.) U., 1933, BM BCh, 1938, MA, 1946, DM, 1956. Cons. allergist St. Mary's, London, 1952-77, Guy's Hosps., London, 1977—. Contbr. articles to med. publs. Capt. U.S. Army, 1939-46. Anglican. Address: 46 Devonshire Close, London England

FRANKLIN, JAMES WILBERT, JR., physician assistant; b. Anoka, Minn., Dec. 21, 1954; s. James Wilbert Sr. and Mary Sue (Stone) F.; m. Cheryl Diane Wilson, Oct. 24, 1987; children: Megan Clarissa, James Alexander. BA in Microbiology, U. South Fla., 1977; B in Med. Sci. magna cum laude, Emory U., 1983. Cert. physician asst. Nat. Commn. of the Certification of Physician Assts.; lic. physician asst. Ga., Fla. Hon. assoc. prof. Emory U. Physician Assoc. Program, Atlanta, 1984; physician asst. Tifton (Ga.) Orthopedic Clinic, 1984-91, Tallahassee (Fla.) Orthopedic Clinic, 1991-95; adminstr., physician asst. So. Orthopedic Specialists, Bainbridge, Ga., 1995—; mem. Allied Health Profls. Credentialing/Policy and Procedures Com., Bainbridge Meml. Hosp., 1996. Pres. Harry L. Williams Student Soc., Emory U. Physician Asst. Program, Atlanta, 1982-83, pres. class of 1983, 1982-83. Recipient Meritorious Svc. award Peruvian Air Force-Med. Corps, Lima, 1994. Fellow Am. Acad. Physician Assts., Ga. Assn. Physician Assts., Fla. Acad. Physician Assts. Office: So Orthopedic Specialists 509 Wheat Ave Bainbridge GA 31717

FRANKLIN, KENNETH WILLIAM, cardiologist; b. Wantagh, N.Y., Jan. 8, 1952; s. Harold and Eleanor (Suess) F.; m. Carol Lee Schroeder, July 12, 1975. BA magna cum laude, Amherst Coll., 1974; MD, Harvard U., 1978. Med. intern, resident N.Y. Hosp.-Cornell Med. Ctr., N.Y.C., 1978-81; fellow cardiology Hosp. U. Pa., Phila., 1981-83, fellow cardiac catharization, 1983-84; attending physician, cardiologist Stamford (Conn.) Hosp., 1984-91; clin. instr. N.Y. Med. Coll., Valhilla, N.Y., 1987-91; clin. instr. Cornell U. Med. Sch., N.Y.C., 1986-91, clin. asst. prof. medicine, 1991—; clin. affiliate N.Y. Hosp.-Cornell Med. Ctr., N.Y.C., 1986-91, attending physician, cardiologist, 1991—; cons. cardiologist Olin Corp., Stamford, 1989-91; acting med. dir., physician GTE Corp., Stamford, 1989. Contbr. articles to profl. jours. Woodruff Simpson fellow Harvard Med. Sch., 1978-79; recipient cardiac rsch. fellowship, grant Am. Heart Assn., Pa. chpt., 1982-83. Fellow Am. Coll. Cardiology; mem. ACP, Am. Heart Assn. (coun. clin. cardiology). Office: 260 E 66th St New York NY 10021-6703

FRANKLIN, MORTON JEROME, emergency physician; b. Boston, Dec. 25, 1927; s. Jacob and Rose Ann (Borax) F. BA, Harvard U., 1949, MD, 1954. Diplomate Am. Bd. Emergency Medicine. Many positions as emergency physician various cities and states, 1955-94; emergency physician Noble Hosp., Westfield, Mass., 1994—. Lt. cmmdr. USN. Home: 20 Hammond Pond Pkwy # 1 Chestnut Hill MA 02167-2150

FRANKLIN, RANDALL MORROW, psychologist; b. Bloomington, Ind., May 13, 1947; s. Owen Ellsworth and Dicy Lou (Morrow) F.; B.A., U. Va., 1969; M.A., Temple U., 1976, Ph.D., 1979. Psychology intern Norristown (Pa.) State Hosp., 1973-74; clin. asst. Psychol. Services Ctr., Temple U., Phila., 1974-75; ward psychologist Phila. State Hosp., 1975-78, male forensic ward adminstr., ward psychologist, 1978-80, chief psychology services, male forensic ward adminstr., 1980-81, chief forensic psychologist, 1981, dir. regional forensic unit, 1981-88; dir. regional forensic psychiat. ctr. Norristown State Hosp., 1988-90; asst. supt. social and rehab. svcs. Norristown State Hosp., 1990—. Served with USNR, 1969-71. Mem. Am. Psychol. Assn., Pa. Psychol. Assn., Assn. Advancement Psychology, Am. Psychology-Law Soc., Phi Beta Kappa, Phi Sigma, Alpha Phi Omega. Home: 522 Hilaire Rd Saint Davids PA 19087-4413 Office: Norristown State Hosp Adminstrn Bldg # 19 1001 Sterigere St Norristown PA 19401-5300

FRANKS, CYRIL MAURICE, psychology educator; b. Neath, Wales, U.K., July 26, 1923; came to U.S., 1957; s. Harry and Cecelia (Zeiler) F.; m. Violet Greenberg, Mar. 29, 1952; children: Steven, Sharon. BSc, U. Wales, Swansea, 1943; MA, U. Minn., 1952; PhD, U. London, 1954. Lic. psychologist, N.J. Lectr. in sci. London Nautical Sch., 1947-50; lectr. in clin. psychology Inst. of Psychiatry U. London, 1954-57; dir. psychology Neuropsychiat. Inst. Princeton (N.J.) U., 1957-70; prof. Rutgers U., New Brunswick, N.J., 1970-74, disting. prof. Grad. Sch. Applied and Profl. Psychology, 1974—; prof. emeritus, 1992—; cons. clin. psychology Carrier Found., Belle Mead, N.J., 1957—. Author: Review of Behavior Therapy, 1973; founding editor Behavior Therapy, 1966-73, Child and Family Behavior Therapy, 1979—. Fellow APA (pres. div. 12 sect. III 1972-73), Brit. Psychol. Soc.; mem. Assn. for Advancement of Behavior Therapy (founder, 1st pres. 1966), Pavlovian Soc. N.Am. Jewish. Home: 315 Prospect Ave Princeton NJ 08540-5330 Office: Rutgers U Grad Sch Applied Profl Psychology Piscataway NJ 08855-0819

FRANKS, DAVID BRYAN, internist, emergency physician; b. Washington, D.C., Nov. 18, 1956; s. David Ardell and Erta Mae (Williford) F.; m. Deborah Ann Hayek, Jan. 31, 1987; children: Ariel Ann, David Henry, Theodore Gabriel. BS, U. Md., 1978, MD, 1980. Diplomate Am. Bd. Internal Medicine, Am. Bd. Emergency Medicine. Physician Temple U. Hosp., Phila., 1983-85, St. Joseph Health Ctr., St. Charles, Mo., 1985-87, Belleville (Ill.) Meml. Hosp., 1987—. Fellow Am. Coll. Emergency Physicians.

FRANKS, JOHN JULIAN, anesthesiology educator, medical investigator; b. Pueblo, Colo., Apr. 9, 1929; s. Frank Alec and Lila Ethelda (Ownbey) F.; m. Kathryne Jean Sammon, Dec. 27, 1951; children: John Alec, William Thomas, Margaret Lila, Elizabeth Ellen. BA, U. Colo., 1951, MD, 1954. Assoc. dir., dir. clin. rsch. ctr. U. Colo., Denver, 1969-81; assoc. chief of staff rsch. Denver VA Hosp., 1969-82, chief hematology div., 1983; resident in anesthesiology Vanderbilt U. Hosp., Nashville, 1984-86; prof., dir. rsch. div. Vanderbilt U., Nashville, 1987—, dir. div. organ transplant anesthesia, 1989—, interim chmn. dept. anesthesiology, 1993-94. Author chpts. in books; contbr. articles to Jour. of Gen. Physiology, Jour. of Clin. Investigation, New Eng. Jour. of Medicine, Anesthesiology and N.Y. Acad. Sci.; contbr. numerous articles to profl. jours. Col. USAF, 1955-63, 68-69. NIH grantee U. Colo., 1963-69, 64-82, Vanderbilt U., 1992—, U.S. VA grantee Denver VA Hosp., 1969-83. Mem. Am. Soc. Anesthesiologists, Am. Physiol. Soc., Cen. Soc. Clin. Rsch., Internat. Soc. Thrombosis Haemostosis. Home: 216 Vaughns Gap Rd Nashville TN 37205-3532 Office: Vanderbilt U Med Ctr Nashville TN 37232-2125

FRANKS, RONALD DWYER, university dean, psychiatrist, educator; b. Balt., Jan. 15, 1946; s. Wylie and H. Jeanette (Dwyer) F.; m. Vicky Ruth Vicklund; children: Aaron Matthew, Alexis Linda. Student, Albion Coll., 1964-67; MD with distinction, U. Mich., 1971. Intern Virginia Mason Hosp., Seattle, 1971-72; resident in psychiatry U. Colo. Med. Ctr., Denver, 1972-76; instr. psychiatry U. Colo. Sch. Medicine, Denver, 1976-77, asst. prof. psychiatry, 1977-83, assoc. prof., 1983-88, asst. dean student affairs, 1982-84, asst. dean student and curricular affairs, dir. inpatient svcs. dept. psychiatry, 1986-88; dean, prof. psychiatry U. Minn. Sch. Medicine, Duluth, 1988—. Contbr. numerous articles to profl. jours. Mem. AMA, Lake Superior Med. Soc., Am. Psychiat. Assn., Alpha Omega Alpha. Home: 300 Misquah Rd Duluth MN 55804-1860 Office: U Minn Duluth Sch Medicine 10 University Dr Duluth MN 55812

FRANKS, VIOLET, psychologist; b. N.Y.C., July 20, 1926; d. Joseph and Sarah (Chomsky) Greenberg; m. Cyril Maurice Franks, Mar. 29, 1952; children: Steven, Sharon. BS, Queens Coll., 1947; MA, U. Minn., 1950; PhD, U. London, 1959. Pvt. practice psychologist Princeton, N.J., 1970—; dir. psychology Carrier Found., Belle Mead, N.J., 1980—; pvt. practice psychologist Princeton Ctr. for Psychotherapy, 1984—; adj. prof. Rutgers U., New Brunswick, N.J., 1980—. Editor: Women and Therapy, 1974, Gender and Disordered Behavior, 1979, Stereotyping of Women, 1983. Fellow APA; mem. Clin. Psychology of Women (pres. 1990-91, bd. dirs. div. 12 1991-94), N.J. State Bd. Psychol. Examiners (vice chmn. 1975-80). Home: 315 Prospect Ave Princeton NJ 08540-5330 Office: Carrier Found Dept Psychology Belle Mead NJ 08502

FRANTZ, CECILIA ARANDA, psychologist; b. Nogales, Ariz., Aug. 6, 1941; d. Tomas Nävarro and Maria Guadalupe (Covarrubias) A.; m. Roger Allen Frantz, May 27, 1972; 1 child, Kimberly Marie Whelan. BA, U. Ariz., 1966; MA, Ariz. State U., 1972, PhD, 1975. Lic. clin. psychologist, Ariz., sch. psychologist, Va. Tchr. Wilson Sch. Dist., Phoenix, 1966-70; psychologist Child Evaluation Ctr., Phoenix, 1973-75; sch. psychologist Wilson Sch. Dist., Phoenix, 1975-78, spl. edn. dir., 1977-78, schs. supt., 1978-81; acting dir. Nat. Inst. Handicap Rsch. U.S. Dept. Edn., Washington, 1981-82, dep. asst. sec. dept. elm. and secondary edn., 1982-87; asst. dir. Bush's Nat. Steering Com. Campaign Hdqrs., Washington, 1987-88; pvt. practice Washington, 1988—; sch. psychologist Cath. Diocese of Arlington, Va., 1990-92; Arlington County Schs., Arlington, Va., 1992—; cons. U.S. Dept. Edn., Washington, 1987—. Mem. APA, Am. Assn Sch. Adminstrs., Ariz. State Psychol. Assn., Ariz. State Sch. Psychologists Assn., Maricopa Soc. Clin. Psychologists (sec. 1976-77). Republican. Roman Catholic. Home: 4501 Arlington Blvd Apt 609 Arlington VA 22203-2740

FRANTZ, DEAN LESLIE, psychotherapist; b. Beatrice, Nebr., Mar. 27, 1919; s. Oscar C. and Flora Mae (Gish) F.; m. Marie Flory, Aug. 31, 1940; children: Marilyn, Shirley, Paul. BA, Manchester (Ind.) Coll., 1942; MDIV, Bethany Theol. Sem., Oak Brook, Ill., 1945; Diploma, C.G. Jung Inst. Zurich, 1977. Assoc. prof. Bethany Theol. Sem., 1957-64; dir. ch. rels. Manchester Coll., North Manchester, Ind., 1964-72; pvt. practice Jungian analyst Ft. Wayne, Ind., 1977—. Author: Meaning for Modern Man in the Paintings of Peter Birkhauser; editor: Barbara Hannah: The Cat, Dog, and Horse Lectures, and the Beyond, 1992. Mem. Internat. Assn. Analytical Psychology, Assn. Grad Analytical Psychologists. Home: 3831 Evergreen Ln Fort Wayne IN 46815-4707

FRANTZIDES, CONSTANTINE THEMIS, general surgeon; b. Limassol, Cyprus, Nov. 6, 1950; came to U.S., 1983; s. Themistokles and Christothea (Papageorgeou) F.; m. Eleni Kasapi, May 8, 1981; children: Alexander, Marlena. MD, U. Athens, Greece, 1976; PhD, Med. Sch. Athens U., Greece, 1987. Chief resident Athens U., Greece, 1981-82; rsch. fellow Med. Coll. Wis., Milw., 1983-84, asst. clin. prof., 1984-85, vis. asst. prof., 1986-88, asst. prof., 1989-93, assoc. prof., 1993—; dir. minimally invasive surgery ctr. Med. Coll. Wis., 1995—; staff surgeon Milw. Regional Med. Ctr., 1989—, Froedtert Meml. Hosp., Milw., 1989—; com. mem. Laser Safety Com., Milw., 1990—, Adv. Com., Clin. Rsch., Milw., 1990—; sr. advidor Clin. Edn., Milw., 1990—. Author: Postcholecystectomy Syndrome, 1991, Laparoscopic and Thoracoscopic Surgery, 1995; contbr. over 95 articles to profl. jours. Recipient Shipley medal So. Surgical Assn., Hot Springs, Va., 1985; Physician's Recognition award AMA, Chgo., 1990; 1st Ind. Rsch. award NIH, 1986. Mem. ACS, Am. Gastroenterology Assn., Collegium Internat. Chirurgiae Digestivae, N.Y. Acad. Scis., Soc. Surgery Alimentary Tract, Soc. Univ. Surgeons, Colegio Brasilero de Cirurgia Digestiva (hon.), Sages, Soc. Laparoscopic Surgeons, Hellenic Surgical Assn. (hon.). Home: 3690 Emberwood Dr Brookfield WI 53005-2387 Office: Medical Coll Wisconsin 9200 W Wisconsin Ave Milwaukee WI 53226-3522

FRANTZVE, JERRI LYN, psychologist, educator, consultant; b. Huntington Beach, Calif., Sept. 9, 1942; d. Rolland and Marjorie (Ferrin) Weiland. Student, Purdue U., 1964-68; BA in Psychology and History, Marian Coll., 1969; MS in Organizational Psychology, George Williams Coll., 1976; PhD in Indsl. and Organizational Psychology, U. Ga., 1979. Case worker Marion County Welfare Dept., Indpls., 1970-71; sr. mktg. rsch. analyst Quaker Oats Co., Barrington, Ill., 1971-75; mgmt. cons. J.L. Frantzve & Assocs., Bklyn., 1978—; asst. prof. sch. of mgmt. SUNY, Binghamton, 1979-83; pers. rsch. and acad. affairs coord. Conoco/DuPont, Ponca City, 1983-86, dir. employee rels., 1986-88; cons. psychologist Mass., 1988-89; assoc. prof. psychology Radford (Va.) U., 1989-94; cons. Brooklyn, N.Y., 1994—; instrn. cons. USAF, Rome, N.Y., 1979-83; dir. Israel Overseas Rsch. Program, Ginozar, Israel, 1982, Japanese Overseas Rsch. Program, Tokyo, 1983; coord. rsch. Ctr. for Gender Studies, Radford U., 1989-94. Author: Behaving in Organizations: Tales from the Trenches, 1983, Guide to Behavior in Organizations, 1983; contbr. articles to profl. jours. Bd. dirs. Broome County Alcoholism Clinic, Binghamton, N.Y., 1980-83, bd. dirs. Broome County Mental Health Clinic, Binghamton, 1981-83; del. Dem. Caucus, Okla., 1985. Mem. APA (com. on women in psychology 1986-88), AAUW, Acad. Mgmt. (placement dir. Ea chpt. 1982), Internat. Pers. Mgmt. Assn., Assn. for Women in Psychology, Delta Sigma Pi. Home and Office: 1804 Glenwood Rd Brooklyn NY 11230-1816

FRANZ, JERRY LOUIS, cardiac surgeon; b. Decatur, Ind., Aug. 5, 1943; s. Lyle D. and Helen J. (Martin) F.; BS in Chemistry, Ohio No. U., 1965; MS in Bacteriology, U. Fla., 1967; MD, U. Ky., 1971; m. Jennie Rose Heim, June 20, 1970. Diplomate Am. Bd. Surgery, Am. Bd. Thoracic Surgery. Intern surgery U. Ky. Hosps., Lexington, 1971-72; jr. asst. resident surgery Bexar County Hosp., San Antonio, 1972-73, resident surgery, 1973-76, adminstrv. resident surgery, 1975-76, resident cardiothoracic surgery, 1976-78; surgeon, pvt. practice, San Antonio, 1978-88, Bristol, Tenn., 1988-93, Bowling Green, Ky., 1993-95, Milw., 1995—. Fellow Am. Coll. Surgeons, Am. Coll. Chest Physicians; mem. Am. Coll. Chest Physicians, Bexar County Med. Soc., AMA, Tex. Med. Assn., Assn. for Acad. Surgery, J. Bradly Aust Surg. Soc. (pres. 1983-84), Cooley Cardiovascular Soc., Soc. Thoracic Surgery, So. Thoracic Soc., Internat. Soc. Heart Transplantation. Contbr. articles to profl. jours. Home: 3123 N Lake Dr Milwaukee WI 53211-3123 Office: Milw Heart Surgery 3300 S 16th St Milwaukee WI 53215

FRANZBLAU, CARL, biochemist, consultant, researcher; b. Bklyn., Sept. 26, 1934; s. William and Fannie (Gerber) F.; m. Myrna Tucker, Aug. 24, 1958; children: William, Rachel. BS, U. Mich., 1956; PhD, Yeshiva U., 1962; DSc (hon.), Roger Williams Coll., 1988. Prof., chmn. dept. biochemistry Sch. Medicine, Boston U., 1978—, assoc. dean for grad. studies, 1989—; mem. coun. Nat. Heart, Lung and Blood Inst., Bethesda, Md., 1985-88; cons. study sects. NIH. Contbr. numerous articles to profl. jours.; patentee in field. Fellow Am. Heart Assn., Am. Thoracic Soc.; mem. Am. Assn. Biochemistry and Molecular Biology, Fedn. Am. Socs. of Exptl. Biology. Office: Boston U Sch Medicine 80 E Concord St Roxbury MA 02118-2307

FRANZBLAU, STEPHEN C., optometric physician; b. N.Y.C., July 10, 1934; S. Max Franzblau and Helene (Berkowitz) Muscarella; m. InaJean Meyer Londo, Apr. 15, 1962 (div. 1983); 1 child, Barry Alan; m. Ali Sherman Franzblau, June 1, 1986. OD, So. Coll. Optometry, 1966. Pvt. practice neuro-optometrist West Palm Beach, Fla., 1966—. Contbr. articles to profl. jours. With U.S. Army, 1954-56. Recipient Spurgeon B. Eure award Am. Optometric Found., 1974. Fellow Coll. Optometrists in Vision Devel.; mem. Am. Optometric Assn., Neuro-Optometric Rehab. Assn. Office: Family Vision Ctr 6802 Forest Hill Blvd West Palm Beach FL 33413

FRANZEL, JAMES RICHARD, emergency physician; b. Mpls., Apr. 11, 1955; s. Richard Martin and Dorothea (Holm) F.; m. Carol Elizabeth, Jan. 21, 1984; children: Christine, David, Julie. BA, St. Olaf, 1977; MD, U. Minn., 1982. Diplomat Am. Bd. Emergency Medicine. Emergency physician Burnett Med. Ctr., Grantsburg, Wis., 1990—, St. Luke's Hosp., Duluth, Minn., 1993—, Apple River Hosp., Amery, Wis., 1996—. Home: 2440 120th St Luck WI 54853

FRAPPIER, CARA MUNSHAW, school social worker; b. Grand Rapids, Mich., Feb. 13, 1942; d. Carroll Lambert and Ruth (Switzer) Munshaw; m. Calvin Leslie Frappier, July 30, 1966; 1 child, Arielle. BA, Mich. State U., 1963, MA, 1966, MSW, 1973. Lic. social worker, marriage and family counselor, Mich.; diplomate in clin. social work. Elem. tchr. Lansing (Mich.) Pub. Schs., 1963-65; sch. social worker Ingham Intermediate Sch. Dist., Mason, Mich., 1965—; bd. dirs. profl. staff assn. Ingham Intermediate Pub. Schs., 1981-85; founding mem. Family Therapy and Consultation Program for Sch. Social Workers. Mem. Nat. Assn. Social Workers, Am. Assn. Marriage and Family Counselors, Am. Orthopsychiat. Assn., Mich. Sch. Social Workers Assn. Democrat. Home: 5706 Bearcreek Dr Lansing MI 48917-1400 Office: Ingham Intermediate Sch Dist 2630 W Howell Rd Mason MI 48854-9329

FRARY, TIMOTHY NEIL, physician assistant; b. Omaha, Oct. 23, 1947; s. Vincent T. and Jacqueline M. (Hamilton) F.; m. Sue M. Frary, Dec. 5, 1969 (div. Apr. 1995); 1 child, Amy M.; m. Jennifer G. Frary, July 6, 1996. BS with high distinction, U. Nebr., 1975. Cert. physician asst. Instr. physician asst. edn. U. Nebr. Med. Ctr., Omaha, 1976-81; physician asst. rural Cedar Hills Family Practice, Newcastle, Wyo., 1981-87; physician asst. primary care McLoughlin Family Practice, Vancouver, Wash., 1987-90; physician asst. in emergency medicine Emergency Med. Physicians P.C., Casper, Wyo., 1990-93; physician asst., clinic mgr. Wyo. Med. Ctr., Casper, 1993—; mem. clin. skills com. Nat. Commn. on Cert. Physician Assts., Atlanta, 1985-87. Chmn. editl. bd. Jour. Am. Acad. Physician Assts., 1988-93; contbr. articles to profl. jours., chpt. to book. Staff sgt. USAF, 1968-72. Recipient Cert. of Appreciation Jour. Am. Acad. Physician Assts., 1992. Fellow Am. Acad. Physician Assts. (chmn. profl. practice coun. 1994—, Nat. Physician Asst. of Yr. 1986), Wyo. Assn. Physician Assts. (chief del. bd. dirs. 1990-95, Disting. Svc. award 1987). Office: Wyo Med Ctr 2233 E 2nd St Casper WY 82609

FRASCELLA, DANIEL WILLIAM, JR., scientist; b. New Brunswick, N.J., July 6, 1934; s. Daniel William Sr. and Jenny (Revere) F.; m. Mary Patricia Fitzpatrick, Sept. 2, 1956; children: Daniel III, Nancy, Thomas. BS in Pharmacy magna cum laude, Rutgers U., 1960, MS in Physiology, 1962, PhD in Physiology and Biochem., 1968. Jr. pharmacologist Carter-Wallace Pharm., Cranbury, N.J., 1960-61; rsch. assoc. U. Pa., Phila., 1962-63; rsch. fellow Rutgers U., New Brunswick, 1963-65, asst. prof., 1965-68; rsch. fellow Merck Inst. Med. Rsch., Rahway, N.J., 1968-69; asst.prof. St. John's U., Jamaica, N.Y., 1970-74; assoc. dir. Hoechst-Roussel Pharm., Somerville, N.J., 1974—; vis. assoc. prof. City U. S.I., N.Y., 1972-74; diabetes cons. Hoechst-Roussel, 1974-96, CE program devel., 1974-82; ind. med. mktg. cons. on diabetes; pres. Diabetologics, 1996—. Author: (with others) Secondary Diabetes, 1980. With USN, 1952-55. Recipient H.A.B. Dunning award Am. Pharm. Assn., 1986, Edn. award Calif. Pharm. Assn., 1985. Fellow Royal Soc. of Medicine; mem. AAAS, Am. Diabetes Assn. (profl.), Am. Coll. Clin. Pharmacology, N.Y. Acad. Sci., Sigma Xi. Republican. Roman Catholic. Home: 1006 Stanton Lebanon Rd Lebanon NJ 08833-3109 Office: Hoechst-Roussel Pharm Box 2500 Rt 202-206 North Somerville NJ 08876

FRASER, ELEANOR RUTH, radiologist, administrator; b. Woodlake, Calif., May 31, 1927; d. Morton William and Dorothy Jean (Harding) F. BA magna cum laude, Pomona Coll., 1949; MD, Stanford U., 1954. Diplomate Am. Bd. Radiology. Resident in radiology Los Angeles County Hosp., L.A., 1957; radiologist St. Joseph Hosp., Orange, Calif., 1957-61; pvt. practice Anaheim, Calif., 1961-78; radiologist Radiology Nuclear Med. Group, Bakersfield, Calif., 1978-85; dir. radiology Kern Valley Hosp., Lake Isabella, Calif., 1985—, chief of staff, 1992—. Mem. AMA, Calif. Med. Assn., Kern County Med. Assn., Soc. Nuclear Medicine, Kern Valley Exchange Club (sec. 1992-94), Phi Beta Kappa. Methodist. Home & Office: PO Box 1657 Lake Isabella CA 93240-1657

FRASER, ETTA WINIFRED, medical educator; b. Fairmont, W. Va.; d. Edward Watson and Grace Irene (Kibbe) Willis; divorced; Carlton, Christina, Paula. BS in Med. Technology, Wayne State U., 1955; MS in Biology, Microbiology, Incarnate Word Coll., 1971; ArtsD in Med. Tech. Edn., Cath. U. Am., 1986. Med. technologist Am. Soc. Clin. Pathologists. Med. technologist Receiving Hosp., Oscoda Clinic, Detroit, 1955-61; chief technologist Fairmount (W. Va.) Clinic, 1961-64; rsch. technologist S.W. Found. and Rsch. Edn., San Antonio, 1965-66; chief microbiologist Nix Hosp., San Antonio, 1971-74, Kent Gen. Hosp., Dover, 1974-75; asst. prof. biology Wesley Coll., Dover, 1975-79, assoc. prof., dir. med. technology program, 1980-83; assoc. prof., dir. med. technology program Ark. Coll., Batesville, 1984-90; assoc. prof. med. tech. med. branch, researcher U. Tex., Galveston, 1990—, mem. faculty Health Info. Sys. Simulation project, 1991—. Author: (software) 25 Case Studies for Medical Technology, 1988-89, (manual) Four Common Chronic Diseases of Elderly, 1992, (software) Simulation Immune Function in an AIDS Patient, 1993, (software) Virology Tutorial Medical Virology, 1995-96. Chair local unit ARC, Batesville, Ark., 1985-90, mem. adv. bd., Galveston, Tex., 1990—, chair AIDS com., 1990-96; svc. unit mgr. South Tex. Coun. Girl Scouts Am., Galveston, 1995-96. Mem. Am. Soc. Clin. Lab. Sci., N.Y. Acad. Scis., Mycol. Soc. Ams., Ctr. on Aging, Sigma Xi, Lambda Tau. Democrat. Methodist. Office: U Tex Med Branch 301 University Blvd Galveston TX 77555

FRASER, ROBERT GORDON, diagnostic radiologist; b. Winnipeg, Man., Can., June 30, 1921; s. William Gordon and Amy Dena (Rumball) F.; m. Joanne Elsa Williams, June 15, 1974; children by previous marriage: Richard S., Merrill A., John R., Nancy L. DS (hon. causa), McGill U., Can., 1994. Resident in radiology Royal Victoria Hosp., McGill U., 1948-51; radiologist-in-chief Royal Victoria Hosp., Montreal, Que., 1964-76; prof. diagnostic radiology McGill U. Med. Sch., Montreal, 1964-76; chmn. dept. McGill U. Med. Sch., 1971-76; prof. diagnostic radiology U. Ala. Med. Sch., Birmingham, 1976-89, prof. emeritus, 1989—; vis. prof. U.S. and fgn. univs. Sr. author: Diagnosis of Diseases of the Chest, 3rd edit., 4 vols., 1988-90; co-author: Synopsis of Diseases of the Chest, 2nd edit., 1993. Served with Can. Navy, 1945-46. Fellow Royal Coll. Physicians Can., Royal Coll. Radiologists (hon.), Am. Coll. Radiologists, Am. Coll. Chest Physicians (Ann. Gold medal 1972); mem. Fleischner Soc., Radiol. Soc. N.Am. (Gold medal 1990), Am. Roentgen Ray Soc. (Gold medal 1989), Can. Med. Assn. Office: 619 S 19th St Dept Diagnostic Radiology Birmingham AL 35233

FRASER, ROBIN, pathology educator; b. Melbourne, Australia, Dec. 20, 1933; arrived in N.Z. 1974; s. Malcolm and Kathleen Elizabeth (Gault) F.; m. Isabel Emily Gidney, Aug. 14, 1957 (div. 1976); children: Elizabeth Jean, Jane Caroline, Simon Hugh, Sarah Anne; m. Linda Marjorie Bowler, May 5, 1979; children: Kate Victoria, Rachel Lucille. BSc, U. Sydney, NSW, Australia, 1956, MB, 1958; PhD, Australian Nat. U., 1968; MD, U. Otago, 1987. Registered med. practitioner, N.Z. Resident Royal Prince Alfred Hosp., Sydney, 1958-59, sr. resident, 1959-60, registrar, 1960-61; gen. practice medicine Coonabarabran, Australia, 1961-66; postgrad. scholar John Curtin Sch. Med. Rsch., Canberra, Australia, 1966-68; USPHS fellow in pathology U. Chgo., 1969-70; sr. lectr. pathology U. Sydney, 1970-74; assoc. prof. pathology Christchurch (N.Z.) Sch. Medicine, 1974—, assoc. dean rsch., 1988-91; dir. project grants N.Z. Health Rsch. Coun., 1974—; elected inaugural patron of med. students Christchurch Sch. Med. Contbr. articles to internat. jours. Fellow Royal Coll. Pathologists Australia; mem. Sigma Xi. Home: 45 Kidson Terr, Christchurch 2, New Zealand Office: Christchurch Sch Medicine, Christchurch Hosp, Christchurch New Zealand

FRASIER, S. DOUGLAS, medical educator; b. L.A., Nov. 29, 1932; m. Robin D'Arvin; children: Karen Lynn, Eric Marc, Sara Leslie. BA, U. Calif., L.A., 1953; MD with highest honors, U. Calif., 1958. Diplomate Am. Bd. Pediat. Intern in pediat. Strong Meml. Rochester (N.Y.) Mcpl. Hosps.,

1958-59; asst. resident pediat. U. Calif. Hosps., L.A., 1959-61; postdoc. trainee U. Calif., L.A., 1963-65; from asst. prof. to prof. pediat. U. So. Calif. Sch. Medicine, L.A., 1965-86, prof. pediat., 1986—; attending physician Children's Mercy Hosp., Kansas City, Mo., 1962-63, L.A. county-Harbor Gen. Hosp., Torrance, Calif., 1965-67; endocrine cons. Pacific State Hosp., Pomona, Calif., 1965-69, tng. cons., 1965-70; med. adv. Human Growth Found. L.A. Chpt., 1967-74, chmn. adv. com., 1967-72, co-chmn. rsch. com., 1972-75; med. adv. bd. Nat. Pituitary Agy., 1971-74; chief divsn. pediat. endocrinology, L.A. County-U. So. Calif. Med. Ctr., 1967-86, physician, 1967-86, dir. pediat. endocrine and diabetic clinics., 1967-72; exec. asst. Calif. Student Health Project, L.A., 1967-68, faculty dir., 1968-69; coord. curriculum U. So. Calif. Sch. Medicine, L.A., 1969-76, assoc. dean student affairs, 1970-76, vice-chair dept. pediat., 1986—; assoc. attending physician divsn. endocrinology/metabolism children's Hosp. L.A., 1976-79, cons., 1979-82; cons. Calbiochem Corp., 1969-78, Hoechst-Roussel Pharmaceutical Corp., 1978-79, maternal and child health br. genetics disease sect. Calif. Dept. Health Scis., 1978—, Soreno Labs., Inc., 1979-94, growth hormone program Can. Med. Rsch. Coun., 1981, program on drugs AMA, 1985; endocrine cons. Lanterman State Hosp., Pomona, 1980-82; chief pediat. Olive View-UCLA Med. Ctr., Sylmar, Calif., 1986—; mem. med. staff UCLA Med. Ctr., L.A., 1986—; vis. lectr. Milwaukee Children's Hosp., 1977; vis. prof. U. Ariz. Sch. Medicine, 1978, Kapiolani/Children's Med. Ctr., Honolulu, 1983, U. Montreal/Hosp. Sainte-Justine, 1988, Australasian Pediat. Endocrine Group, 1990, Tripler Army Hosp., Honolulu, 1993; mem., chmn. various other hosp. coms. Mem. editl. bd. Jour. Pediat. Endocrinology; rev. Pediats., Jour. Pediats., Jour. Clin. Endocrinology and Metabolism, Am. Jour. Diseases Children, Pediat. Rsch., Med. Letter, Metabolism, Endocrine Revs. Capt. U.S. Army Med. Corps, 1961-63. Fellow U. Calif. Sch. Medicine, L.A., 1955-56, Cecil E. Vesy scholar, 1956-58; recipient Sheard-Sanford prize Am. Soc. Clin. Pathologists, 1958. Mem. L.A. Pediat. Soc., Am. Acad. Pediat., Western Soc. Pediat. Rsch. (chmn. nominating com. 1975-76), Endocrine Soc., Lawson Wilkins Pediat. Endocrine Soc. (membership com. 1971-74, chmn. membership com. 1973-74, dir. 1978-82, ad hoc com. uses human growth hormone 1981-87, 88-90, pres.-elect 1988-89, chmn. awards com. 1988—, pres. 1989-90, past pres. 1990-91, chmn. drug and therapeutic com., 1990-94), Soc. Pediat. Rsch., Am. Pediat. Soc. Home: 10428 Lorenzo Pl Los Angeles CA 90064 Office: Olive View UCLA Med Ctr 14445 Olive View Dr Sylmar CA 91342-1495*

FRAUMENI, JOSEPH F., JR., scientific researcher, medical educator, physician, military officer; b. Boston, Apr. 1, 1933; s. Joseph Francis and Pauline (Malta) F.; m. Patricia Welch D'Arcy, Apr. 23, 1977. AB, Harvard U., 1954; MD, Duke, 1958; ScM, Harvard U., 1965. Diplomate Am. Bd. Internal Medicine. Commd. lt. USPHS, 1962, advanced through grades to Capt., 1968; med. intern, resident Johns Hopkins Hosp., Balt., 1958-60; med. resident, chief resident Meml. Sloan-Kettering Cancer Ctr., N.Y.C., 1960-62; staff assoc. Nat. Cancer Inst., Bethesda, Md., 1962-65, assoc. chief, 1966-75, chief environ. epidemiology br., 1975-82, dir. epidemiology & biostats. program, 1979-95, dir. epidemiology & genetics divsn., 1995—; attending physician Clin. Ctr. NIH, Bethesda, 1966—; prof. epidemiology uniformed svcs. U. Health Scis., Bethesda, 1985—; adj. prof. Harvard U. Sch. Pub. Health, Boston, 1993—. Editl. bds. Jour. Nat. Cancer Inst., 1966-69, Teratology, 1974-78, Med. and Pediat. Oncology, 1974-78, Cancer Rsch., 1974—, Am. Jour. Indsl. Medicine, 1979, Oncology, 1980—, Cancer Investigation, 1980—, Preventive Medicine, 1982—, Genetic Epidemiology, 1984—, Cancer Causes and Control, 1989—, Cancer Epidemiology, Biomarkers and Prevention, 1990—, Cancer, 1991—, Internat. Jour. Oncology, 1992—; contbr. more than 600 articles to profl. jours. Recipient disting. svc. medal USPHS, 1983, Gorgas medal Assn. Mil. Surgeons U.S., 1989, W.W. Sutow award U. Tex. M.D. Anderson Cancer Ctr., 1992, disting. alumnus award Duke U. Med. Ctr., 1992, alumni award merit Harvard Sch. Pub. Health, 1993, Wick Williams meml. award Fox Chase Cancer Ctr., 1993, dir.'s award NIH, 1994, Charles Motl prize GM Cancer Rsch. Found., 1995, John Snow award APHA, 1995, Selikoff award Ramazzini Inst., 1996; vis. prof. GM Cancer Rsch. Found. Internat. Agy. Rsch. Cancer, 1990. Fellow AAAS, ACP, Am. Coll. Epidemiology (Lilienfeld award 1993, bd. dirs. 1985-89), Am. Coll. Preventive Medicine; mem. Inst. Medicine NAS, Am Soc. Preventive Oncology (Disting. Achievement award 1993, pres. 1981-83), Am. Assn. Cancer Rsch. (bd. dirs. 1983-87, Am. Cancer Soc. award rsch. excellence epidemiology, prevention 1993), Assn. Am. Physicians. Office: Nat Cancer Inst EPN/543 Div Cancer Epidemology & Genetics Executive Plz N Rm 543 Bethesda MD 20892

FRAUNFELDER, FREDERICK THEODORE, ophthalmologist, educator; b. Pasadena, Calif., Aug. 16, 1934; s. Reinhart and Freida Fraunfelder; m. Yvonne Marie Halliday, June 21, 1959; children—Yvette Marie, Helene, Nina, Frederick, Nicholas. BS, U. Oreg., 1956, MD, 1960, postgrad. (NIH postdoctoral fellow), 1962. Diplomate Am. Bd. Ophthalmology (bd. dirs. 1982-90). Intern U. Chgo., 1961; resident U. Oreg. Med. Sch., 1964-66; NIH postdoctoral fellow Wilmer Eye Inst., Johns Hopkins U., 1967; prof., chmn. dept. ophthalmology U. Ark. Health Scis. Ctr., 1968-78, 1978—; dir. Casey Eye Inst., 1989—, Nat. Registry Drug-Induced Ocular Side Effects, 1976—; vis. prof. ophthalmology Moorfields Eye Hosp., London, 1974. Author: Drug-Induced Ocular Side Effects and Drug Interactions, 1976, 4th edit., 1966, Current Ocular Therapy, 1980, 4th edit., 1994, Recent Advances in Ophthalmology, 8th edit., 1985; assoc. editor: Jour. Toxicology: Cutaneous and Ocular, 1984—; mem. editl. bd. Am. Jour. Ophthalmology, 1982-92, Ophthalmic Forum, 1983-90, Ophthalmology, 1984-89; contbr. numerous articles lens and eye toxicity rsch. to profl. jours. Served with U.S. Army, 1962-64. FDA grantee, 1976-86; Nat. Eye Inst. grantee, 1970-87. Mem. AMA, ACS, Am. Acad. Ophthaolmology, Assn. Univ. Profs. in Ophthalmology (pres. 1976), Am. Ophthalmol. Soc., Am. Coll. Cryosurgery (pres. 1977), Assn. Research in Ophthalmology. Lutheran. Clubs: Lions, Elks. Home: 13 Cellini Ct Lake Oswego OR 97035-1307 Office: Casey Eye Inst 3375 SW Terwilliger Blvd Portland OR 97201-4146

FRAZEE, BETTY LINDSAY, geriatrics nurse; b. Waynesboro, Pa., Apr. 28, 1929; d. Armour C. and Dorothy B. (Fetterhoff) Lindsay; m. Edgar L. Frazee; children: Curtis L., James R. Diploma in Nursing, Washington County Hosp., Hagerstown, Md., 1952. Cert. gerontologist. Staff nurse Chambersburg (Pa.) Hosp.; charge nurse South Mt. (Pa.) Restoration Ctr. Mem. ANA, Pa. Nurses Assn. Home: General Delivery Mont Alto PA 17237-9999

FRAZER, MARGARET NOLTING, physician, neurologist; b. Chgo., July 27, 1959; d. Henry F. and Dorothy H. (Wilson) Nolting; m. Jeffrey Marshall Frazer, June 11, 1988; children: Christine, Michelle, Amy, Sally. BS in Biology, Purdue U., 1980; MD, Ind. U., 1985. Internal medicine intern U. Iowa, Des Moines, 1985-86; resident in neurology Ind. U., Indpls., 1986-89; fellow in epilepsy Wake Forest U., N.C., 1990; neurologist Geisinger Clinic, Scranton, Pa., 1989-93, Hoosier Neurology, Indpls., 1994—; med. dir. Alzheimer's unit Carmel (Ind.) Care Ctr., 1995—; mem. speakers bur. Parke Davis, Sandoz, Dupont, 1993—; clin. prof. neurology Ind. U., 1995; mem. bd. examiners Am. Acad. Neurology, 1995-96. Mem. visioning com. Meth. Ch., Indpls., 1995; bd. dirs. Ind. chpt. Nat. Multiple Sclerosis Soc., 1995—. Mem. AMA, Am. Acad. Neurology, Ind. State Med. Soc. Republican. Home: 795 Grace Dr Carmel IN 46032 Office: Hoosier Neurology 1801 N Senate Blvd Indianapolis IN 46202

FRAZER, WENDY, nurse, physician assistant; b. Steubenville, Ohio, June 3, 1943; d. Richard William and Mary Elizabeth (Sliday) F. RN, Beaver Valley Gen. Hosp., New Brighton, Pa., 1964; AAS, Cuyahoga C.C., 1983. RN, Ohio, Pa. Pediatrics nurse Cleve. Clinic Found., 1964-65; asst. head nurse Cardiovascular Lab., 1965-73; surg. nurse clinician cardiothoracic surgery Cleve. Clinic Found., 1978-86, 88-91, gen. thoracic surgery nurse clinician, 1986-88, Brigham Women's Hosp., Boston, 1991-93; vascular surgery physician's asst. New England Deaconess Hosp. Vascular Surgery, 1994—; admissions officer Lakewood Hosp., 1984-85; instr. cardiovascular tech. program Cuyahoga C.C., Cleve., 1987-91, clin. preceptor surg. asst. program, 1984-87; mem. steering com. Master's Group of Phoenix Ctr., 1986-88; physician asst. membership com. Alumnus Assn., 1986. Assoc. founder, counselor Inst. Creative Living, 1976-80. Mem. Nat. Acad. Physician Assts., Surgical Assts. Assn., Boston Mus. Fine Arts. Republican. Baptist.

FRAZIER, ANDREA PETKER, nursing administrator; b. Trenton, N.J., Jan. 17, 1953; d. August Anton and Helen Jo Ann (Gaudy) Petker; 1 child, Melissa Colleen. ASN, St. Mary Coll., O'Fallon, Mo., 1983. RN, Mo. Nurse Barnes-St. Peters (Mo.) Hosp., 1980-89; from utilization rev. coord. to quality mgmt. analyst GenCare Health Sys. Inc., St. Louis, 1988-92, supr. quality mgmt., 1992—. Mem. Nat. Assn. Healthcare Quality (cert.), Met. St. Louis Quality Assurance Profls., Bus. and Profl. Womens Assn. (v.p. Mid-Rivers chpt. 1995-96, scholarship chmn. 1992-95). Republican. Roman Catholic. Home: 14 Wolfe Creek Trail Saint Peters MO 63376 Office: GenCare Health Sys Inc 969 Executive Pkwy Ste 100 Creve Coeur MO 63141

FRAZIER, HOWARD STANLEY, physician; b. Oak Park, Ill., Jan. 16, 1926; s. Cecil Austin and Harriet DeGolyer (Greenleaf) F.; m. Lenore Callahan, June 10, 1950; children—Mark C., Reid J., Anne K., Peter B. Ph.B., U. Chgo., 1949; M.D., Harvard U., 1953. Intern, then resident in medicine Mass. Gen. Hosp., Boston, 1953-55; postdoctoral fellow Harvard U. Med. Sch., 1955-56, Cambridge U., 1956-57, Case Western Res. U. Med. Sch., 1957-58; mem. faculty Harvard U. Med. Sch., 1958—, prof. medicine, 1978—; cons. NIH, Nat. Center Health Care Tech., Congl. Office Tech. Assessment. Author papers in field. Served with USNR, 1943-46. Mem. Am. Soc. Clin. Investigation, Am. Physiol. Soc., Am. Soc. Nephrology, Inst. Medicine. Office: 677 Huntington Ave Boston MA 02115-6028

FRAZIER, JEANETTE RENÉE, geriatrics nurse; b. Biloxi, Miss., Aug. 2, 1957; d. Monnie Graden and Jeanette Truet (Hopkins) Fields; children: Amy Yonish, Stephen Yonish, Timothy Yonish. ADN, San Hills C.C., Pinehurst, N.C., 1992. RN, N.C. Staff nurse Moore Regional Hosp., Pinehurst, 1992; nursing supr. St. Joseph of the Pines, Southern Pines, N.C., 1992—. Mem. Phi Theta Kappa. Home: PO Box 158 Quiet Oak Rd Lakeview NC 28350

FRAZIER, JOHN W., physiologist, researcher; b. Wilmington, Ohio. With Wright-Patterson AFB, 1956—, rsch. physiologist. Recipient Eric Liljencrantz award, 1996. Fellow Aerospace Med. Assn.; mem. SAFE (Sr. Scientist award, Pres. award), Aerospace Physiology Soc. (space medicine br., Paul Bert award), Aerospace Human Factors Assn. (life scis. & biomed. engrng. br.). Office: AL/CFBS 2245 Monahan Way Bldg 33 Wright Patterson AFB OH 45433-7008*

FRAZIER, SHERVERT HUGHES, JR., psychiatrist, educator; b. Shreveport, La., June 12, 1921; s. Shervert Hughes and Mary (Lowman) F.; m. Gloria Barger, July 20, 1947; children: Elise, Alan, Rosalie, Stephen. Student, Baylor U., 1936-39; B.S., U. Ill., Chgo., 1941, M.D., 1943; D.Sc. (hon.), U. Ill., 1986; M.S. in Psychiatry, U. Minn., 1957; cert. psychoanalytic medicine, Columbia Coll. Physicians and Surgeons, 1963; M.A. (hon.), Harvard U., 1972. Diplomate: Am. Bd. Psychiatry and Neurology (dir. 1965, pres. 1972), Am. Bd. Family Practice (by-laws com. 1979-80, exam. com. 1979-86, research and devel. com. 1979-80, chmn. patient mgmt. problem panel). Intern U. Ill. Research and Ednl. Hosp., 1943-44; fellow internal medicine Mayo Found., 1951-52, fellow psychiatry, asst. to staff, 1954-56; pvt. practice Harrisburg, Ill., 1946-50, 53; adminstr. Harrisburg Med. Found., 1948-51; cons. sect. psychiatry Mayo Clinic, St. Marys Hosp., also Meth. Hosp., Rochester, Minn., 1956-58; chief research scientist internal medicine N.Y. State Psychiat. Inst., 1958-61, dep. dir., 1968-72; asst. attending psychiatrist Presbyn. Hosp., N.Y.C., 1958-63; dir. inpatient cons. service in psychiatry, 1961-62; later attending psychiatrist; dir. Houston Psychiat. Inst., 1962-65; psychiatrist in chief Ben Taub Gen. Hosp., Houston, 1962-68; cons. VA Hosp., Houston, 1962-68; sr. attending psychiatrist Meth. Hosp., Houston, 1962-68; chief exec. officer, psychiatrist-in-chief McLean Hosp., Belmont, Mass., 1972-84; dir. NIMH Rockville, Md., 1984-86; gen. dir., psychiatrist-in-chief McLean Hosp., 1986-88; assoc. in psychiatry Columbia Coll. Phys. and Surg., Joske asst. prof. psychiatry, 1958-62, prof., 1968-72; prof. psychiatry, chmn. dept. Baylor U. Coll. Medicine, 1962-68; prof. psychiatry Harvard, Boston, 1972—; cons. Rice U., 1963-68; commr. Mental Health and Mental Retardation for Tex., 1965-67; pres. VI World Congress Psychiatry; mem. vis. com. Yale U. Med. Sch., 1977-81. Contbr. numerous articles to profl. jours. Served as officer, M.C. USNR, 1944-46, PTO. Recipient disting. alumnus award Mayo Found., 1983; Menninger award ACP, 1986. Fellow N.Y. Acad. Medicine (chmn. Salmon lecture com., trustee, mem. coun. 1987—); mem. AMA (council continuing physician edn. 1976-81), Mass. Med. Assn., Middlesex County Med. Soc., Am. Coll. Psychiatrists (regent 1972, v.p. 1977-79, pres. 1979-81), Am. Psychiat. Assn. (chmn. program com. 1965-68, chmn. joint commn. pub. affairs, sec. 1983-85), World Psychiat. Assn. (v.p. 1977-84), Central Neuropsychiat. Assn., Assn. Research Nervous and Mental Disease (pres. 1972, chmn. bd. 1976-78), Boston Psychoanalytic Soc. and Inst., Sigma Xi, Alpha Omega Alpha. Home: PO Box 79215 Waverley MA 02179-0215 Office: 115 Mill St Belmont MA 02178-1041

FRAZIER, TODD MEARL, health science adminstrator, epidemiologist; b. Lima, Ohio, Nov. 9, 1925; s. Todd M. and Gertrude (Blanks) F.; m. Barbara Welday, Sept. 28, 1946; children—Michael, Sarah, Nancy, David. A.B., Kenyon Coll., 1949; Sc.M., Johns Hopkins U., 1957. Dir. biostats. Balt. City Health, 1953-63; assoc. dir. planning and research D.C. Dept. Pub. Health, Washington, 1963-68; asst. dir. Harvard Ctr. Community Health and Med. Care, Harvard U., Boston, 1968-78; chief surveillance br. Nat. Inst. Occupational Safety and Health, Cin., 1978—; assoc. prof. Harvard Sch. Pub. Health, Boston, 1968-78; cons. WHO, Geneva, 1971-78. Served with USN, 1943-46, U.S. Army, 1950-51. Fellow Am. Pub. Health Assn.; mem. Sigma Xi. Home: 2164 Cablecar Ct Cincinnati OH 45244-4101 Office: Nat Inst Occupational Safety Robert A Taft Labs 4676 Columbia Pkwy Cincinnati OH 45226

FRAZIER, WILLIAM HENRY, plastic and reconstructive surgeon; b. Derby, Conn., Apr. 5, 1943; s. Donald Hart and Elizabeth (Hart) F.; m. Joan Francis Wrynn, Dec. 27, 1981; children: Robert J., Wilson F., Lucas T., William H. BA, Oberlin Coll., 1965; MD, Yale U., 1969. Diplomate Nat. Bd. Med. Examiners; cert. Am. Bd. Surgery, Am. Bd. Plastic Surgery. Intern surgery Yale-New Haven Hosp., 1969-70, asst. resident gen. surgery, 1970-72, asst. resident plastic and reconstructive surgery, 1972-73, chief resident gen. surgery, 1973-74, chief resident plastic and reconstructive surgery, 1974-75; cons. Nat. Ctr. Health Svcs. Rsch., HHS, Vero Beach, Fla., 1976—; instr. dept. surgeryYale U. Sch. Medicine, New Haven, 1973-74, assoc. dir. trauma program, 1975-77, dir. trauma program 1977-82, acting chief sect. plastic surgery, 1978-79, assoc. prof. plastic surgery, 1979-82; med. dir. emergency svcs. Yale-New Haven Hosp., 1975-82; attending surgeon W. Haven Vets. Admistrn., New Haven, 1975-82; faculty Ctr. for Study Health Svc., New Haven, 1976-82; dir. Yale Burn Svc., New Haven, 1978-82; cons. mediocolegal affairs Yale-New Haven Hosp., 1981-82. Contbr. articles to profl. jours. Cabinet mem. United Way, Vero Beach, Fla., 1988-89; bd. dirs. Indian River chpt. ARC, Vero Beach, 1987—. Capt. USAR, 1970-82. Grantee HEW, 1975, 1976-82, NIMH, 1978-82, John A. Hartford Found., 1982, Lederle Labs., 1982, Fund for Med. Edn., 1978-82, New Faculty Award Yale U., 1976, Purdue Frederick Co., 1976-78, Davis & Geck, 1976. Mem. Am. Assn. for Automotive Medicine, Am. Assn. for Med. Systems and Informatics, Am. Burn Assn., Am. Coll. Emergency Physicians, Am. Coll. Surgeons, AMA, Am. Pub. Health Assn. (accident and injury control sect.), Am. Soc. Plastic & Reconstructive Surgery, Am. Trauma Soc. (founding), Fla. State Med. Assn., Indian River County Med. Soc., New Eng. Soc. Plastic & Reconstructive Surgeons, N.Y. Regional Soc. Plastic & Reconstructive Surgery, Soc. Advanced Med. Systems, Soc. for Computer Medicine. Republican. Mem. United Ch. of Christ. Home: 131 Anchor Dr Vero Beach FL 32963-2941 Office: 31 Royal Palm Blvd Vero Beach FL 32960-5237

FREAS, GLENN CURTIS, emergency physician; b. Phila., Dec. 5, 1955; s. John Lewis and Eleanor (Tosh) F.; m. Melanie Montana, Oct. 8, 1982. BS magna cum laude, Ursinus Coll., 1977; MD, Jefferson Med. Coll., 1981; JD summa cum laude, Temple U., 1994. Asst. dir. emergency medicine Fitzgerald Mercy Hosp., Darby, Pa., 1982-89; mem. emergency medicine faculty Temple U. Hosp., Phila., 1989-91, asst. dir. emergency medicine, 1991-96; assoc. dir. emergency medicine residency Med. Coll. Pa./Hahnemann U., Phila., 1996—. Lt. comdr. USNR, 1977-92. Fellow Am. Coll. Emergency Medicine, Am. Acad. Emergency Medicine; mem. Soc. Acad. Emergency Medicine. Office: Hahnemann U Broad & Vine Sts Philadelphia PA 19146

FREDERICK, CLAY BRUCE, toxicologist, researcher; b. Hamlin, Tex., Oct. 29, 1948; s. Billy Bob and Mildred Lenora (Kemplin) F.; m. Anne Patricia Jones, Apr. 14, 1973; children: Scott Christopher, Erin Elizabeth. BS in Chemistry and Biology, Tulane U., 1971; PhD in Organic Chemistry, U. Tex., 1979. Diplomate Am. Bd. Toxicology. Chemist, asst. tng. coord. ICI U.S., Inc., Wilmington, Del., 1971-73; postdoctoral rsch. scientist Nat. Ctr. for Toxicol. Rsch., Jefferson, Ark., 1979-82; rsch. scientist Uniroyal Chem., Naugatuck, Conn., 1982-85; sr. rsch. fellow in biochem. toxicology Rohm and Haas Co., Spring House, Pa., 1985—; adj. assoc. prof. pathobiology dept. U. Pa. Sch. Vet. Medicine, Phila., 1990—. Contbr. articles to profl. jours. Mentor Project LABS, Spring House, 1989, 95; outside expert reviewer U.S. EPA, Washington, 1990, 93-95. Mem. Am. Assn. Cancer Rsch., Soc. of Toxicology, Soc. for Risk Analysis, Environ. Mutagen Soc., Phi Kappa Phi. Office: Rohm and Haas Co 727 Norristown Rd Spring House PA 19477

FREDERICK, KATHLEEN SUE, nurse clinician in otolaryngology; b. Greenville, Pa., Jan. 21, 1959; d. Robert Emilio and Marie Frances DeTullio; 1 child. BSN cum laude, Thiel Coll., 1993. RN, Ohio, Pa. Staff nurse, med. surg. Trumbull Meml. Hosp., Warren, Ohio, 1993-94; nurse clinician, otolaryngology Warren Otologic Group, Greenville, Pa., 1994—. Roman Catholic. Home: 88 & Haft N High St Greenville PA 16125

FREDERICKS, HAROLD EDWIN, orthodontist; b. Memphis, Dec. 30, 1952; s. Harold Irving and Katherine Marie (Mehrling) F.; m. Susan Pierce, Feb. 27, 1982; children: John Pierce, Katherine Ann, Benjamin Tate. BA, Vanderbilt U., 1973; DDS, U. Tenn. Ctr. for Health Scis., 1977, MS in Orthodontics, 1980. Pvt. practice orthodontist Nashville, 1980—; reviewer profl. manuscripts. Contbr. articles to profl. jours. Mem. Am. Assn. Orthodontics, Tenn. Assn. Orthodontics, So. Assn. Orthodontics. Office: Ste 111 4515 Harding Rd Nashville TN 37205

FREDERICKS, JOAN DELANOY, retired health science administrator; b. Dobbs Ferry, N.Y., Feb. 27, 1928; d. Robert Bert and Amelia (DeLanoy) F.; m. Stanley Whetstone, Mar. 20, 1993. BA, Skidmore Coll., Saratoga Springs, N.Y., 1949; MA, Syracuse U., 1954. Rsch. asst. C.F. Kettering Found., Yellow Springs, Ohio, 1949-50; rsch. tech. Syracuse (N.Y.) U. Med. Sch., 1950-54, Duke U. Med. Sch., Durham, N.C., 1954-58, NIH, Bethesda, Md., 1958-88; ret., 1988; chemist Nat. Inst. Arthritis and Metabolic Diseases, NIH, Bethesda, 1958-63, scientific grant asst. Nat. Inst. Heart, Lung and Blood Diseases, Bethesda, 1963-70, asst., program dir. Nat. Inst. Arthritis Metabolism and Digestive Diseases, 1970-81, exec. sec. div. Rsch. Grants, 1981-88; cons. in field. Vol. Sibley Meml. Hosp., Washington. Mem. Sumner Sq. Condominium Assn. (sec., v.p. 1988-92).

FREDERICKS, SHARON KAY, nurses aide; b. Grand Rapids, Mich., July 12, 1942; d. Leroy and Edith Luella (Crawford) F. Cert. in Interior Decorating, LaSalle U., 1975; AAS, Community Svc. Asst., Kalamazoo Valley Coll., 1982; assoc. paralegal studies, Internat. Corr. Schs., Scranton, Pa., 1991; AAS in Bus. Mgmt., Davenport Coll., 1994. Cashier Goodwill Industries, Battle Creek, Mich., 1963; dishwasher Woolworths, Kalamazoo, 1963; nurses aide Mary L. Bocher, Kalamazoo, 1964-69, Sisters St. Joseph, Nazareth, Mich., 1976—; kitchen aide Saga Foods, Kalamazoo Valley C.C., 1981-82, Saga Foods, Nazareth Coll., 1983-84. Vol. Portage Ctrl. Jr. and Sr. High Sch., 1961-62, Bronson Meth. Hosp., Kalamazoo, 1961-62; vol. nurse aide ARC, 1964-69, Bloodmobiles, 1970-75, Borgess Med. Ctr., 1977; sec.-treas. 3d Order St. Francis Secular, 1976-79, pres., dir. pres. pub. rels. and bulls., 1979-81; participant neighborhood watch Vine Neighborhood, Kalamazoo, 1985-88; vol. Cath. Family Svcs., 1991—; vol., adminstrv. aide, Kalamazoo, 1991—; vol. monitor Kalamazoo Women's Festival, 1991, 92. Thomas F. Reed Jr. scholar Davenport Coll.; recipient John Edgar Hoover gold medal, 1991; named vol. of month, Kalamazoo Regional Psychiat. Hosp., July 1976; named vol. of week Catholic Family Svcs., Sept. 13, 1993, Oct. 1995. Mem. Nat. Spl. Child Advocates. Roman Catholic. Home: 2310 Inverness Ln Apt 204 Kalamazoo MI 49001-1459

FREDERIKSEN, JAMES W., cardiothoracic surgeon; b. St. Louis, June 25, 1946; s. Stanley and Mary Ellen F.; m. Marilynn Elizabeth Connors, July 10, 1971; children: John Karl, Paul Stanley, Britt Louise. BA, Cornell Coll., 1968; MD, Harvard Med. Sch., 1972. Attending surgeon Northwestern Meml. Hosp., Chgo., 1980—; assoc. prof. surgery Northwestern Meml. Hosp., Chgo., 1985—; attending surgeon Columbus Hosp., Chgo., 1980-87, Vet. Adminstrn. Hosp. Lakeside Med. Ctr., Chgo., 1980—. Bd. dirs. Henry George Sch. Chgo. Fellow Am. Coll. Surgeons; mem. Am. Heart Assn., Am. Coll. Chest Physicians, Soc. Thoracic Surgeons. Home: 2002 W Devon Ave Chicago IL 60068 Office: Northwestern Meml Hosp 251 E Chicago Ave Chicago IL 60601

FREDERIKSEN, MARILYNN ELIZABETH CONNERS, physician; b. Chgo., Sept. 12, 1949; d. Paul H. and Susanne (Ostergren) Conners; m. James W. Frederiksen, July 11, 1971; children: John Karl, Paul S., Britt L. BA, Cornell Coll., 1970; MD, Boston U., 1974. Diplomate Am. Bd. Ob-Gyn., Am. Bd. Maternal-Fetal Medicine, Am. Bd. Clin. Pharmacology. Pediat. intern U. Md. Hosp., 1974-75, resident in pediat., 1975-76; resident in ob-gyn. Boston Hosp. for women, 1976-79; fellow in maternal fetal medicine Northwestern U., 1979-81, fellow clin. pharmacology, 1981-83; instr. ob-gyn. Northwestern U., Chgo., 1981-83, asst. prof. ob-gyn., assoc. clin. pharmacology, 1983-91, assoc. prof. ob-gyn., assoc. in clin. pharmacology, 1991—, sect. chief gen. ob-gyn., 1993—; mem. gen. faculty com. Northwestern U., Chgo., 1994—, mem. ob-gyn. adv. panel, 1985—, U.S. Pharm. Com. Revision, Rockville, Md., 1986—; del. U.S. Pharm. conv. Northwestern U. Med. Sch., 1990, 95; bd. dirs. Northwestern Med. Faculty Found., 1995—; mem. gen. clinic rsch. ctr. com. NIH, 1989-93, chairperson, 1992-93; mem. Task Force Working Group on Asthma in Pregnancy Nat. Heart, Lung and Blood Inst., 1991-92. Mem. editorial bd. Clin. Pharmacology & Therapeutics, 1993; contbr. numerous articles to profl. jours. Bd. dirs. Cornell Coll. Alumni Assn., Mt. Vernon, Iowa, 1986-90, Northwestern Med. Faculty Found., 1995—. Recipient Pharm. Mfrs. Assn. Found. Faculty Devel. award, 1984-86, Civil Liberties award ACLU, 1991. Fellow Am. Coll. Ob-Gyn.; mem. Soc. Perinatal Obstetricians, Ctrl. Assn. Obstetricians and Gynecologists, Am. Med. Womens Assn., Am. Soc. Clin. Pharmacology and Therapeutics (chmn. sect. pediat. and perinatal pharmacology 1993-96, bd. dirs. 1994—), Chgo. Gynecologic Soc. (treas. 1994—), Phi Beta Kappa. Republican. Episcopalian. Home: 2002 Devon Ave Park Ridge IL 60068-4306 Office: Northwestern U 680 N Lake Shore Dr Ste 1000 Chicago IL 60611-4402

FREDERIKSEN, MARY C. A., nurse educator; b. Columbus, Ohio, Jan. 9, 1951; d. Edward F. and Caroline A. (Kessler) Roubal; m. Glen A. Frederiksen, Nov. 13, 1976. BSN, Ohio State U., 1973; MEd, Calif. State U., 1984. Cert. pub. health nurse, diabetes educator. Nursing edn. instr. VA Wadsworth Hosp., L.A.; instr. Cencor Corp., San Bernardino, Calif.; nursing instr. Calif. Hosp. Sch. Nursing, L.A.; patient educator Kaiser Permanente Med. Ctr., Fontana, Calif., 1985-93, diabetes/health educator, 1993—. Mem. Am. Heart Assn. (chair nursing edn. com. 1986-87), Diabetic Teaching Nurses So. Calif. (pres. 1993-95).

FREDRICKSON, DONALD SHARP, physician, scientist; b. Canon City, Colo., Aug. 8, 1924; s. Charles Arthur and Blanche (Sharp) F.; m. Henriette Priscilla Dorothea Eekhof, Sept. 5, 1950; children: Eric Henderikus, Rurik Charles. Student, U. Colo., 1942-43; BS, U. Mich., 1946, MD, 1949; MD (hon.), Karolinska Institutet, 1977; DSc (hon.), U. Mich., 1977, Mt. Sinai Sch. Medicine, 1978, U. N.C., 1979, Georgetown U., 1981, Yeshiva U., 1981, N.J. U. Medicine and Dentistry, 1982, Med. U. S.C., 1985, George Washington U., 1985, U. Rochester, 1986. Intern Peter Bent Brigham Hosp., Boston, 1949-50; house staff mem., fellow Peter Bent Brigham and Mass. Gen. hosps., 1950-53; mem. sr. research staff lab. cellular physiology and metabolism Nat. Heart and Lung Inst., Bethesda, Md., 1955-61; clin. dir. inst. Nat. Heart and Lung Inst., 1961-66, dir. inst., 1966-68, chief molecular disease br. div. intramural research, 1966, dir. div. intramural research, 1968-74; pres. Inst. Medicine, Nat. Acad. Scis., 1974-75; dir. NIH, 1975-81; scholar-in-residence Nat. Acad. Scis., 1981-83; v.p. Howard Hughes Med. Inst., Bethesda, 1983, pres., chief exec. officer, trustee, 1984-87; scholar Nat. Library Medicine, 1987—; professorial lectr. medicine George Washington U. Sch. Medicine, 1956-84; lectr. preventive medicine Georgetown U. Sch. Medicine, 1963-84; pres. DS Fredrickson Assocs., 1987—; researcher Nat.

Heart, Lung and Blood Inst., 1987-90. Editor: (with others) The Metabolic Basis of Inherited Disease, 6th edit, 1989; Contbr. articles to profl. jours. Served with AUS, 1943-45. Recipient Internat. award James F. Mitchell Found. for Med. Edn. and Rsch., 1968, Disting. Achievement award Modern Medicine, Superior Svc. award HEW, 1970, Disting. Svc. award, 1971, McCollum award Am. Soc. Clin. Nutrition/Am. Inst. Nutrition, 1971, Modanina prize, 1975, Irving Cutter medal, 1978, Gairdner Found. ann. award, 1978, Purkinje medal Czechoslovakian Med. Soc., 1980, Fondazione Lorenzini medal, 1980, Disting. Pub. Svc. award HHS, 1981, Disting. Svc. award Miami Winter Symposium, 1985, Svc. to Sci. award Arthur M. Sackler Found., 1986, Sandoz Lifetime Achievement award, 1993. Fellow AAAS, ACP, Royal Coll. Physicians (London), Am. Coll. Cardiology (gold medal 1967, Disting. Svc. award 1983); mem. NAS, Am. Acad. Arts and Scis., Am. Philos. Soc., Am. Soc. Clin. Investigation, Assn. Am. Physicians, Harvey Soc. (hon.), Acad. Kingdom of Morocco, Med. Soc. Sweden, Phi Beta Kappa, Alpha Omega Alpha, Phi Kappa Phi.

FREDRICKSON, JOHN MURRAY, otolaryngologist; b. Winnipeg, Man., Can., Mar. 24, 1931; s. Frank S. and Beatrice (Rannveig) F.; m. Alix Gordon, June 8, 1956; children: Kristin, Lisa, Erik. BA, U. B.C., Vancouver, 1953, MD, 1956. bd. dirs. Am. Bd. Otolaryngology. Intern Vancouver Genl Hosp., 1957-58, resident in pathology, 1959-60; resident in gen. surgery Shaughnessy Gen. Hosp., Vancouver, 1958-59; resident in otolaryngology U. Chgo., 1960-63, instr. in otolaryngologic surgery, 1963-65; asst. prof. surgery Stanford U., Calif., 1965-68; assoc. prof. otolaryngology U. Toronto Gen. Hosp., 1968-77, asst. prof. physiology, 1969-82; lindburg prof., head dept. otolaryngology Wash. U. Sch. Medicine, St. Louis, 1982—. Co-editor: Advances in Oto-Rhino-Laryngology, 1973, Otolaryngology-Head and Neck surgery, 1983; editor Am. Jour. Otolaryngology, 1987-92; patentee implantable hearing aid, 1973, implantable voice box, 1981. Served to lt. RCAF, 1946-59. Mem. Am. Acad. Otolaryngology, Head and Neck Surgery, Soc. Univ. Otolaryngologists, Coll. Othrhinolaryngolica, Am. Laryngological Assn. (pres. 1992-93), Am. Otological Soc. Home: 12 Carrswold Dr Saint Louis MO 63105-2914 Office: Wash U Med Sch Campus Box 8115 517 S Euclid Ave Saint Louis MO 63110-1007

FREDRICKSON, WILLIAM ROBERT, trading company executive; b. Chgo., Sept. 2, 1960; s. Robert Arnold and Mary Eileen (Cleary) F. Student, Wabash Coll., Crawfordsville, Ind., 1979, Purdue U., West Lafayette, Ind., 1980-82, 90, Ind. U./Purdue U., Indpls., 1984, 87. Rschr. in amino acids Ind. U./Purdue U., Indpls., 1984-85; rsch. in HIV antivirals Fredrickson & Strecker Trading Co., Indpls., 1987—; cons. in fields of mktg. and mgmt. Author: The Tree of Life, 1994, Genesis, 1994; composer: (anthology of music) Believe, 1995; 1 patent pending. Republican. Home and Office: Fredrickson & Strecker 5461 N Illinois St Indianapolis IN 46208

FREEARK, ROBERT JAMES, surgeon, educator; b. Chgo., May 14, 1927; s. Ray H. and Lizette (Stauffer) F.; m. Ruth Nelson, June 24, 1950; children: Kris, Kim. BS, Northwestern U., 1949, MD magna cum laude, 1952; grad., Oak Ridge Inst. Nuclear Studies, 1953. Diplomate Am. Bd. Surgery (dir. 1980-86), Nat. Bd. Med. Examiners. Rotating intern, then resident in gen. surgery Cook County Hosp., Chgo., 1952-58; dir. surgery Cook County Hosp., 1958-68, attending physician, 1960-70, hosp. dir., 1968-70; research fellow Jerome D. Solomon Found. Chgo., 1953-54; mem. faculty Northwestern U. Med. Sch., 1960-70, prof. surgery, 1968-70; prof. surgery, chmn. dept. Loyola U.-Stritch Sch. Medicine, Maywood, Ill., 1970-95; surgeon-in-chief Loyola U.-Foster G. McGaw Hosp., 1970-95, cons. Hines VA Hosp., Ill., 1970-95, prof. emeritus, 1995—. Served with USMCR, 1945-46. Recipient Outstanding Clin. Prof. award Stritch Sch. Medicine, 1973, Alumni medal Northwestern U., 1980, Stritch medal Loyola U., 1981; named to Navy Pier Hall of Fame, Alumni Assn./U. Ill., Chgo, 1991. Fellow ACS (Surgeons award Nat. Safety Council 1987); mem. Am. Assn. Surgery Trauma (pres. 1982), Am. Surg. Assn., AMA, Am. Trauma Soc., Central Surg. Assn. (pres. 1980-81), Soc. Internat. de Chirurgie, Soc. Surgery Alimentary Tract, Soc. Surg. Chmn., Soc. U. Surgeons, Western Surg. Assn., Ill. Surg. Soc. (pres. 1983-84), Ill. Med. Soc., Midwest Surg. Soc. (pres. 1970), Chgo. Med. Soc., Inst. Medicine Chgo., Chgo. Surg. Soc. (pres. 1984), Alpha Omega Alpha, Omega Beta Pi. Congregationalist. Office: 2160 S 1st Ave Maywood IL 60153-3304

FREED, EDMOND LEE, podiatrist; b. Phila., Sept. 7, 1935; s. Frank and Jean D. (Schultz) F.; m. Judith Hope Falk (div. 1982); children: David Scott, Eric Corey. D of Podiatric Medicine, Temple U., 1960. Diplomate Am. Bd. Podiatric Surgery, Am. Bd. Podiatric Orthopedics. Pvt. practice Phila., 1960—; chmn. dept. podiatric surgery Met. Hosp., Phila., 1985-89, dir. podiatric residency program, 1983-89, co-chmn. limb salvage team, 1983—; mem. clin. faculty Pa. Coll. Podiatric Medicine, Phila., 1968—. Co-author booklets: Limb Salvage Concepts, 1984, Lower Extremity Ulcerations, 1985, Neurological Manifestations of Diabetes Mellitus, 1986. Fellow Am. Coll. Foot and Ankle Surgeons (Ea. div. pres. 1985-88), Am. Coll. Foot and Ankle Orthopedics, Am. Assn. Hosp. Podiatrists; mem. Am. Acad. Podiatric Sports Medicine, Phila. County Podiatry Soc., Am. Podiatric Med. Assn. Office: Graduate Hosp Med Bldg 520 S 19th St Ste 2 N Philadelphia PA 19146-1449

FREED, LINDA RAE, critical care nurse; b. Fond du Lac, Wis., Aug. 27, 1957; d. Donald J. and Patricia R. (Ingalls) Wegener; m. Frank A. Freed, Aug. 22, 1981; children: Stephanie P., Courtney R., Matthew F. AS in Nursing, Weber State Coll., 1981; BS in Nursing, U. Utah, 1985. Cert. critical care registered nurse. Nurse aide Weber Meml. Hosp., Roy, Utah, 1977-79; nurse aide, float pool McKay-Dee Hosp., Ogden, Utah, 1979-80; practical nurse McKay-Dee Hosp., Ogden, 1980-81, staff nurse, charge nurse med. monitoring unit, 1981-86, staff nurse cardiac intensive care unit, charge nurse, 1986-95, shift coord. critical care svc. line, 1995—; clin. faculty mem. Salt Lake C.C./Davis Applied Tech. Ctr., Kaysville, Utah, 1992—; preceptor in field. Mem. AACN (No. Utah chpt.), Sigma Theta Tau, Nu Nu. Home: 5832 Cedar Ln Ogden UT 84403-5253

FREED, RANDI ALISON, optometrist; b. Paterson, N.J., Jan. 28, 1958; d. Nathan and Selma Elaine (Stein) F.; m. Richard Palmesino, Mar. 30, 1985 (div. Dec. 1988); m. Keith Moskowitz, Aug. 23, 1991; children: Tori-Jean, Ariel Morgan. BS in Med. Tech. summa cum laude, Fairleigh Dickinson U., 1981, MS summa cum laude, 1986; OD, Pa. Coll. Optometry, 1993. Cert. optometrist, N.J. Med. technologist Barnert Hosp., Paterson, 1980-81, Nat. Health Labs., Cranford, N.J., 1981-85; asst. rsch. scientist Unigenes Labs., Fairfield, N.J., 1985-89; otometrist The Eye Inst., Phila., 1992-93, VA, Manchester, N.H., 1992-93; pvt. practice, Ft. Lauderdale, Fla., 1993, Secaucus, N.J., 1993—; sch. optometrist Secaucus Bd. Edn., 1994—. Mem. Am. Soc. Clin. Pathologists (cert. med. technologist), Am. Optometric Assn., N.J. Optometric Assn., Hudson County Optometric Soc., Kiwanis (lectr. Secaucus 1996). Republican. Jewish. Office: 1301 Paterson Plank Rd Secaucus NJ 07094

FREEDBERG, A. STONE, physician; b. Salem, Mass., May 30, 1908; s. Hyman and Rachel Leah (Freedberg) F.; m. Beatrice Gordon, Aug. 29, 1935; children: Richard Gordon, Leonard Earl. A.B., Harvard U., 1929; M.D., U. Chgo. (Rush), 1935. Diplomate: Am. Bd. Internal Medicine (cardiology). Intern Mt. Sinai Hosp., Chgo., 1934-35, Mass. Meml. Hosp., Boston, summer 1935; resident Cook County Hosp., Chgo., 1935-36; house officer pathology R.I. Hosp., 1936-37; practice medicine, specializing in internal medicine Boston, 1946—; asst. in medicine Beth Israel Hosp., 1938-40, jr. vis. physician, 1940-46, assoc. in med. research, 1940-50, assoc. vis. physician, 1946-48, vis. physician, 1949-63, assoc. dir. med. research, 1950-63, sr. Ziskind fellow, 1956, physician, 1964-84, acting physician-in-chief dept. medicine, 1973, dir. cardiology unit, 1964-69, bd. consultation, 1984-87, hon. bd. consultation, 1988—; research fellow medicine Med. Sch., Harvard U., 1941-42, asst. in medicine, 1942-46, instr. medicine, 1946-47, assoc. in medicine, 1947-50, asst. prof., 1950-57, assoc. prof., 1958-69, prof., 1969-74, prof. emeritus, 1974—, adminstrv. bd. faculty medicine, 1958-62; physician Harvard U. Health Svcs., 1974—; cons., com. mem. med. div. Oak Ridge Inst. Nuclear Studies, 1955-56; spl. cons. metabolism study sect. USPHS, 1956-60; mem. sr. cons. staff Nuclear Medicine Inst., 1966-67. Mem. editorial bd.: Circulation, 1956-60, 62-67; contbr. articles profl. jours. Guggenheim fellow Oxford U., 1967-68. Fellow Am. Heart Assn. (bd. dirs.; mem. council clin. cardiology); mem. Mass. Heart Assn. (dir., past pres., com. chmn.), Am. Thyroid Assn. (v.p.), Mass., Charles River Dist. med. socs., Am. Soc. Clin. Investigation, Am. Physiol. Soc., Assn. Am. Physicians, New Eng. Cardiovascular Soc. (pres. 1971-72), Assn. Profs. Medicine. Home: 111 Perkins St Boston MA 02130-4324 Office: 275 Longwood Ave Boston MA 02115-5704

FREEDBERG, IRWIN MARK, dermatologist; b. Boston, July 4, 1931; s. Arthur Harris and Sayde Ruth (Bixby) F.; m. Irene Sybil Lisman, July 4, 1954; children—Marjorie, Kenneth, Deborah. Student, Dartmouth Coll., 1949-52; M.D., Harvard U., 1956. Intern Beth Israel Hosp., Boston, 1956-57; resident in internal medicine Beth Israel Hosp., 1957-59; resident in dermatology Mass. Gen. Hosp., Boston, 1959-62; instr. to prof. dermatology Harvard U. Med. Sch., Boston, 1962-77; prcf., chmn. dept. Johns Hopkins Sch. Medicine, Balt., 1977-81; George Miller MacKee prof. and chmn. dept. dermatology, N.Y. U. Sch. Medicine, 1981—; adv. council Nat. Inst. Arthritis, Diabetes and Digestive and Kidney Diseases, 1984-86, musculoskeletal and skin diseases, 1986-87. Contbr. articles in field to profl. jours.; editor: Jour. Investigative Dermatology, 1972-77. Guggenheim fellow, 1969-70; NIH grantee, 1962—; Am Cancer Soc., Am. Contract Bridge League faculty research asso., 1965-70. Fellow AAAS; mem. Inst. Medicine of Nat., Acad. Sci.; mem. Coun. Biologic Editors, Am. Soc. Biol. Chemistry, Am. Soc. Clin. Investigation, Soc. Investigative Dermatology (pres. 1981-82), Harvey Soc., Am. Fedn. Clin. Rsch., Assn. Am. Physicians, Assn. Profs. Dermatology (pres. 1986-88), Am. Dermatologic Assn. (treas. 1987-92, dir. 1992—), Am. Soc. Cell Biology, Am. Bd. Dermatology (dir. 1984-94, v.p. 1992, pres. 1993), Am. Med. Assn. (Ho. of Dels. 1990—), N.Y. Acad. Medicine (sect. on dermatology 1986087, chmn. 1987-88), Am. Acad. Dermatology (dir. 1991-96), Soc. for Investigative Dermatoogy (pres. 1982), French Dermatology Soc. (hon.), Korean Dermatology Soc. (hon.). Home: 333 E 68th St New York NY 10021-5693 Office: 562 1st Ave New York NY 10016-6402

FREEDBERG, PAULINE D., nurse, educator; b. Bklyn., Mar. 15, 1946; d. Nunzio Frank and Antionette (LaMarca) DiGiovanna; m. Lawrence Elliot Freedberg, July 19, 1969; children: Kimberly, Jennifer Robin. BSN, U. Vt., 1968; MS in Nursing, U. Pitts., 1985. Sr. staff nurse U. Hosp., NYU Med. Ctr., N.Y.C., 1968-69; team leader Colo. Gen. Hosp., U. Colo. Med. Ctr., Denver, 1969-72; staff nurse Med. Personnel Pool, Denver, 1973-75; nursing instr. Westmoreland County C.C., Youngwood, Pa., 1981-94, asst. prof. nursing, 1995—. Writer, producer instructional videotapes: Respiratory Assessment in Nursing, 1985, Physical Examination of the Chest, 1989; instructional audio-cassette: Progressive Muscle Relaxation, 1984; also articles; guest lectr. presentations, nat. meetings, pulmonary related seminars. Westmoreland County Med. Auxiliary, Latrobe Area Hosp. Auxiliary. Named Univ. Scholar U. Pitts. Mem. ACCN, Assn. Clin. Nursing Specialists, Pa. NEA, Pa. Thoracic Soc. Sigma Theta Tau. Democrat. Roman Catholic. Avocations: walking, swimming. Home: 11 Saint Ives Dr Greensburg PA 15601-6203 Office: Westmoreland County # Cc Youngwood PA 15697

FREEDE, CATHERINE ANNETTE, nurse; b. Oklahoma City, Aug. 13, 1953; d. Henry James and Josephine W. (Lowe) F. BSN, U. Okla., 1975, BS in Phys. Assoc., 1993. RN, Pa., Okla. RN, PA Dr. H. J. Freede, Oklahoma City, 1971—; surg. RN, floor RN Mercy Hosp., Oklahoma City, 1973-86; surg. RN Bapt. Hosp., Oklahoma City, 1975—; orthopedic surgery RN Dr. David Flesher, Oklahoma City, 1982-84; plastic surgery RN Dr. William Dalton, Oklahoma City, 1983-84; DON, RN Roger Mills Hosp., Cheyenne, Okla., 1990—; mem., disaster RN ARC, Oklahoma City, 1975—; bd. mem. Allied Profl. Health Bd., Oklahoma City, Bapt. Hosp. Orthopedic Assoc. Bd. mem. Okla. Symphony, Oklahoma City, 1975—; mem. Ballet Okla., Oklahoma City, 1975—, Lyric Theater, Oklahoma City, 1983—. Mem. Am. Assn. Physician Assocs., Am. Quarter Horse Assn., Okla. Quarter Horse Assn.

FREEDLAND, JACOB BERKE, dentist, endodontist; b. Wilmington, N.C., Mar. 19, 1913; s. Morris and Molly (Burke) F.; m. Charlotte Soble, Sept. 7, 1939; children: Martin B., Leslie Ann Freedland Locke. Student, U. N.C.; DDS, Emory U., 1936; D of Pub. Svc. (hon.), U. N.C., Charlotte, 1990. Diplomate Am. Bd. Endodontists. Pvt. practice dentistry Charlotte, N.C., 1938—; adj. prof. U. N.C., Chapel Hill, 1963—; vis. lectr. Columbia, Pa., N.Y., 1970—; cons. lectr. U.S. Army Dental Corps, Walter Reed, 1964-86, USN Dental Corps, Nat. Naval Ctr., 1964-78, Area Health Edn. Ctrs., Charlotte; dir. dental programs Charlotte Area Health Edn. Ctr., Carolinas Med. Ctr., Charlotte; dir. program devel. AHEC, 1990. Contbr. articles to profl. jours. Bd. dirs. Charlotte Symphony, Mecklenburg Red Cross, Mecklenburg County Blood Bank; bd. visitors U. N.C., 1985-89. Maj. Dental Corps U.S. Army, 1941-45, ETO. Recipient Charlotte Dental Soc. award, 1965, Disting. Alumnus award U. N.C., 1979, Edgar D Collidge award, L.A., 1980, Disting. Practitioner award Nat. Acad. Dentistry, 1987, Thomas P. Hinman Disting. Svc. award, 1988, Louis Grossman Internat. award Soc. Francaise d'Endodontie, New Orleans, 1989, Achievement award Am. Fund Dental Health, Chgo., 1990, Disting. Svc. scroll N.C. Dental Soc., 1990, Distg. Philanthropist award Am. Rsch. and Endowment Found., Chgo., 1993; Jacob B. Freedland D.D.S. Conf. Rm. Spl. Care Dental Ctr., Huntersville Oaks Nursing Home named in his honor, 1990; Jacob B. Freedland Chair endowed in his honor U. N.C. Sch. Dentistry; Freedland Scholarship in endodontics established U. N.C. Sch. Dentistry, 1993. Fellow Am. Coll. Dentists, Internat. Coll. of Dentists, Am. Assn. Endodontists (1st Disting. Philathropist award Rsch. Edn. Found. 1993), Acad. Dentistry Internat. (named Internat. Dentist of Yr., 1994); mem. ADA (cons., comm. on accreditation, coun. on dental edn. 1964-86, del. to internat. profl. orgns. 1982, 86, 87, Presdl. citation 1988), Am. Assn. Endodontists (pres 1964-65), N.C. Dental Soc. (pres. 2nd dist. 1964-65), Am. Inst. Oral Scis. (pres. 1965-67), Am. Assn. Hosp. Dentists, Am. Fund Dental Health (trustee, adviser), Dental Found. N.C. (pres. 1975, bd. dirs.). Jewish. Home: 2633 Richardson Dr Charlotte NC 28211-3355 Office: 721 Doctors Bldg Charlotte NC 28283

FREEDLAND, RICHARD ALLAN, retired biologist, educator; b. Pitts., May 9, 1931; s. Milton and Gertrude (Davis) F.; m. Beverly Jane Pachefsky, June 22, 1958; children: Howard M., Judith L., Stephen J. BS, U. Pitts., 1953, MS, U. Ill., 1955; PhD, U. Wis., 1958. Research assoc. U. Wis., Madison, 1958-60; lectr. U. Calif., Davis, 1960-61, asst. prof., 1961-65, assoc. prof., 1965-69, prof. physiol. chemistry, 1969-74, prof., chmn. physiol. scis., 1974-93; Wellcome vis. prof. U. Ga., Athens, 1990-91. Author: A Biochemical Approach to Nutrition, 1977; mem. editorial bd. Archives Biochemistry and Biophysics, 1978—, Jour. Biol. Chemistry, 1985-91, Fedn. Am. Socs. for Exptl. Biology Jour., 1991-94; assoc. editor Jour. of Nutrition, 1984-88, editor, 1988-89. Fulbright scholar, Australia, 1987-83. Fellow AAAS; mem. Am. Soc. Biol. Chemists, Am. Inst. Nutrition. Office: U Calif Dept Physiol Scis Davis CA 95616

FREEDMAN, ALFRED MORDECAI, psychiatrist, educator; b. Albany, N.Y., Jan. 7, 1917; s. Jacob Abraham and Pauline Rebecca (Hoffman) F.; m. Marcia Irene Kohl, Mar. 24, 1943; children: Paul Harris, Daniel Sholom. AB, Cornell U., 1937; MD, U. Minn., 1941. Diplomate Am. Bd. Psychiatry and Neurology. Intern Harlem Hosp., N.Y.C., 1941-42; resident and fellow Bellevue Hosp., N.Y.C., 1948-51, sr. psychiatrist, 1951-54; asst. pediatrician Babies Hosp.-Columbia, N.Y.C., 1953-60; assoc. prof. psychiatry SUNY Downstate Med. Sch., Bklyn., 1955-60; prof. and chair psychiatry N.Y. Med. Coll., Valhalla, 1960-89, prof. psychiatry emeritus, 1989—; vis. prof. Harvard Med. Sch., Boston, 1988-93; hon. prof. Hunan Med. U., China, 1993; dir. psychiatry Westchester Med. Ctr., Valhalla, 1979-89; cons. WHO, Geneva, 1984, 89—; Roche vis. prof., Australia and New Zealand, 1988; S.Y. Mak vis. prof. U. Hong Kong, 1989; mem. awards jury Anna Monika Stiftung, Dortmund, Germany, 1983—; mem. Internat. Com. Prevention and Treatment of Depression, 1983—; sec.-treas. Ctr. for Comprehensive Health Practice Svc., N.Y.C., 1990—. Sr. editor textbook: Comprehensive Psychiatry, 1967-80; sr. editor book: Issues in Psychiatric Classification, 1986; editor-in-chief Polit. Psychology, 1981-90, Integrative Psychiatry, 1981—; contbr. articles to profl. jours. Mem. N.Y. State Commn. to Evaluate Drug Laws, Albany, 1970-73; founding trustee Ctr. for Urban Edn., N.Y.C., 1965-70; dir. Upper Park Ave. Boys Club of Am., N.Y.C., 1970-80; NGO rep. UN for World Psychiat. Assn., 1985-90, NGO rep. UN for World Assn. Psychosocial Rehab., 1990—; trustee N.Y. Acad. Medicine. Recipient Henry Wismer Miller award Manhattan Soc. Mental Health, 1964, Terence Cardinal Cooke medal N.Y. Med. Coll., 1985, Lapinlahti medal U. Helsinki, 1990, Wyeth Ayerst award World Psychiat. Assn., Athens, 1989, A.M. Freedman Ann. award Internat. Soc. for Polit. Psychology, 1990. Fellow Am. Psychiat. Assn. (pres. 1971-72, ethics appeals bd. 1993—, Rush medal 1974), Am. Psychopathol. Assn. (pres. 1971-72, Hamilton medal 1972), Am. Coll. Neuropsychopharmacology (pres. 1972-73), Am. Orthopsychiat. Assn. (dir. 1962-64), Academia Medicinae et Psychiatricae Found. (founding fellow, pres. 1990—); mem. N.Y. Psychiat. Soc. (pres. 1986-87), Nat. Com. on Confidentiality of Health Records (pres. 1976—). Home and Office: 1148 Fifth Ave New York NY 10128-0807

FREEDMAN, HERBERT N., ophthalmologist; b. N.Y.C., July 25, 1940; s. Theorore Raphael Freedman and Fay (Kaiser) Machlis; m. Erica Smilow, July 30, 1980. BS, Tufts U., 1962; MD, N.Y. Med. Coll., 196. Diplomate Am. Bd. Ophthalmology. Pvt. practice N.Y.C., 1973—. Capt. M.C., U.S. Army, 1967-73. Fellow Am. Acad. Ophthalmology. Office: 540 Park Ave Ste 425 New York NY 10021

FREEDMAN, JOEL D., social worker; b. Santa Monica, Calif., June 9, 1945. MSW, Fla. State U., 1969. Social worker VA Med. Ctr., Canandaigua, N.Y., 1969-94. Contbr. articles to profl. publs. Mem. Nat. Assn. Social Workers, Acad. Cert. Social Workers. Jewish. Home: 329 N Main St Canandaigua NY 14424-1229

FREEDMAN, JOSEPH MARK, optometrist; b. Bklyn., Jan. 28, 1951; s. Milton and Bernice (Lobele) F.; m. Lynn M. Gewant, Oct. 28, 1978; children: Rachel, Margot. BS summa cum laude, Bklyn. Coll., 1977; OD, SUNY, 1977. Lic. optometrist, N.Y., N.J. Dir. contact lens svc. Bronx, N.Y., 1977-83; pvt. practice North Shore Contact Lens Assocs. (name changed to North Shore Contact Lens & Vision Cons., P.C.), Roslyn, N.Y., 1983—; v.p. Vision Rsch. Tech., Inc., Great Neck, N.Y., 1985—; v.p., cons. for internat. health products Commack, N.Y., 1992—. Contbr. articles to profl. jours. Office: N Shore Contact Lens Assoc Flower Hill Ofc Bldg Ste 94 1025 Northern Blvd Roslyn NY 11576-1506

FREEDMAN, LAWRENCE RAPHAEL, medicine educator; b. N.Y.C., Dec. 1, 1927; s. Hyman and Hannah (Epstein) F.; m. Rina Esther Stahl, Apr. 3, 1955; children: Julia, Leora. BS, Yale U., 1947, MD, 1951. Diplomate Am. Bd. Internal Medicine. Intern in internal medicine, asst. resident Yale New Haven (Conn.) Hosp., 1951-532, chief resident in internal medicine, 1956-57; asst. in pathology Johns Hopkins Hosp., Balt., 1955-56; prof. medicine Yale U., New Haven, Conn., 1970-73; prof. medicine, chmn. dept. U. Lausanne, Switzerland, 1973-80; prof. medicine UCLA Sch. Medicine, 1980—; chief med. services VA Wadsworth Med. Ctr., Los Angeles, 1980-86, assoc. chief of staff for edn., 1986—. Author: Infective Endocarditis, 1982; contbr. articles to profl. jours. Served to 1st lt. U.S. Army, 1953-55. Mem. Société Suisse de Medecine Interne, Assn. Am. Physicians, Am. Soc. Clin. Investigation, We. Assn. Physicians, Sigma Xi, Alpha Omega Alpha. Jewish. Office: VA Wadsworth Med Ctr Wilshire And Santelle Blvd Los Angeles CA 90073

FREEDMAN, LOUIS MARTIN, dentist; b. Newark, Mar. 19, 1947; s. Morris and Sylvia (Swimmer) F.; m. Elizabeth Norine Palmer, June 17, 1978; children: Steven, Julie, Brian. Student, Emory U., 1963-66, DDS, 1970. Gen. dentist Freedman, Freedman & Weitman DDS, P.C., Atlanta, 1970—; clin. instr. Emory U. Dental Sch., Atlanta, 1970-77; team dentist Atlanta Hawks Basketball Team, 1971—, Atlanta Flames Hockey Team, 1979-80, Atlanta Knights Hockey Team, 1992, Atlanta Fire Ants Roller Hockey Team, 1994—. Mem. Exch. Club, Atlanta, 1970-73; mgr. Sandy Springs Youth Sports Little League Baseball, 1979—; head coach Sandy Springs United Meth. Ch. basketball program, 1991—. Mem. Alpha Epsilon Delta, Omicron Kappa Upsilon. Jewish. Office: Freedman Freedman & Weitman 3111 Piedmont Rd NE Atlanta GA 30305-2507

FREEDMAN, MERVIN BURTON, psychologist, educator; b. N.Y.C., Mar. 6, 1920; s. Eli and Rose (Weithorn) F.; m. Marjorie Ellingson, Feb. 16, 1952; children: Eric, Kristin, Rolf, Anne Marie. B.S., Coll. City N.Y., 1940; Ph.D., U. Calif. at Berkeley, 1950. Lectr. dept. psychology U. Calif. at Berkeley, 1950-53; research assoc. Mellon Found. for Advancement Edn., Vassar Coll., 1953-58; dir. Mellon Found., 1958-60; research assoc. Inst. for Study Human Problems Stanford U., 1962-63, asst. dean undergrad. edn. Stanford U., 1963-65; chmn. dept. psychology San Francisco State U., 1965-68, prof. psychology, 1968—; dean grad. sch. Wright Inst., Berkeley, 1969-79; sr. Fulbright research scholar U. Oslo, 1961-62; fellow Center for Advanced Study Behavioral Sci., 1960-61. Author: The College Experience, 1967; (with others) Search for Relevance, 1969, Academic Culture and Faculty Development, 1978, Human Development in Social Settings, 1983, Personality and Social Change, 1986, Americans and the Irrational, 1988; Assoc. editor: Polit. Psychology. Vice pres. San Francisco Am.-Scandinavian Found. Served with AUS, 1941-45. Decorated Bronze Star. Fellow Am. Psychol. Assn., Am. Psychol. Soc.; mem. Western Psychol. Assn., Internat. Soc. Polit. Psychology. Home: 866 Spruce St Berkeley CA 94707-2043 5105246815: San Francisco State U Dept Psychology San Francisco CA 94132

FREEDMAN, MICHAEL LEONARD, geriatrician, educator; b. Newark, Dec. 12, 1937; s. David Hyman and Alice Ella (Zwain) F.; m. Cora Ruth Singer, June 24, 1962; children: Lawrence Andrew, Deborah Lynn. AB with honors, Colgate U., 1959; MD cum laude, Tufts U., 1963. Diplomate Am. Bd. Internal Medicine, Am. Bd. Hematology, Am. Bd. Geriatric Medicine. Intern, then resident NYU/Bellevue Med. Ctrs., 1963-65, 68-69; rsch. assoc. lab physiology to staff investigator Nat. Cancer Inst., NIH, Bethesda, Md., 1965-68; asst. prof. NYU Med. Ctr., 1969-74, assoc. prof., 1974-77, prof., 1977—, firm chief, dir. geriatrics, 1979—; Diane and Arthur Belfer prof. geriatric medicine NYU, 1987—; cons. CBS, Inc., Bristol Meyers Corp., Kimberly-Clark Corp., Pfizer Corp., Nutrasweet Corp., Citicorp. Editor: Hematology in the Elderly, 1985; contbr. over 175 articles to profl. jours. Lt. comdr. USPHS, 1965-68. NIH rsch. grantee, 1969—; recipient Wholeness of Life award Hosp. Chaplaincy, 1988; named one of the Heroes of Bellevue, 1987. Fellow ACP, Am. Geriatrics Soc. (com. chmn. 1985—), Am. Soc. Hematology, Gerontol. Soc. Am. (com. chmn. 1984—); mem. Am. Soc. Clin. Investigation, Am. Soc. Hematology, AAAS, Am. Fed. Aging Rsch. (founder, mem. nat. adv. coun.), Alpha Omega Alpha. Democrat. Jewish. Office: NYU Med Ctr 550 1st Ave New York NY 10016-6481

FREEDMAN, ROBERT RUSSELL, psychology educator; b. Phila., Apr. 30, 1947; s. Bernard and Sarah (Lichtenstein) F.; m. Mary Ann Morris, July 12, 1981. BA in Psychology, U. Chgo., 1969; PhD, U. Mich., 1975. Lic. psychologist, Mich. Dir. behavioral medicine Wayne State U., Detroit, 1975—, adj. asst. prof. psychology, 1976-83, adj. assoc. prof. 1983-89, prof., 1989—, assoc. prof. psychiatry, 1983-90, prof. ob.-gyn., 1990—; cons. Nat. Inst. Drug Abuse, Washington, 1976-78, Nat. Inst. Mental Health, Washington, 1986—. Assoc. editor Biofeedback and Self-Regulation Jour., 1983—, editor, 1991—. Recipient NIH Merit award 1996; Nat. Heart, Lung, Blood Inst. research grantee, 1980—, Nat. Inst. Aging grantee, 1987—. Fellow Soc. Behavioral Medicine (Pres.'s citation 1983); mem. Soc. Psychophysiol. Rsch., Biofeedback Soc. Am. (publs. chmn. 1984—, Outstanding Paper award 1985), Assn. for Psychophysiol. Study Sleep, AAAS. Avocations: sailing, camping, music. Home: 605 Kellogg St Ann Arbor MI 48105-1675 Office: CS Mott Center 275 E Hancock St Detroit MI 48201-1415

FREEDMAN, STEPHEN ALAN, pediatrics educator, administrator; b. Bklyn., Aug. 17, 1942; s. Henry Theodore Freedman and Emily Kaplan; m. Denise J. Kaell, Dec. 14, 1981; children: Deborah, Lan, Melinda. BA, U. Fla., 1964, MA, 1966; PhD, Fla. State U., 1983. Acting dir. Children's Med. Svcs., Tallahassee, 1979-80, spl. asst. to dir., 1980; project dir. Dept. Health & Rehab. Svcs., Gainesville, Fla., 1980-83; project dir. U. Fla., Gainesville, 1983-85, asst. dir. pediatrics, 1983-88, assoc. prof., 1988—; pres. Family Health and Habilitative Svcs., Inc., Gainesville, 1984-94; dir. Inst. Child Health Policy, Gainesville, 1986—; sr. researcher Coll. Pub. Health U. South Fla., Tampa, 1990—; cons. Dept. Human Svcs., Little Rock, 1989; chair Supplemental Security Income Strategy Workshop, 1990-91; mem. task force on tech. dependent children HHS, Washington, 1987-88, task force on govt. financed health care State of Fla., Tallahassee, 1989. Author: (with others) Caring for Children with Chronic Illness, 1989. Bd. dirs. STOP Children's Cancer, Inc., Gainesville, 1989. Mem. APHA, Am. Acad. Pediatrics (hon., cons. 1989), Assn. for Care of Children's Health, Am. Health Planning Assn., Am. Soc. Law and Medicine. Democrat. Jewish. Office: Inst Child

Health Policy 5700 SW 34th St Gainesville FL 32608-5372 Address: 5623 NW 43rd Rd Gainesville FL 32606-4379

FREEDMAN, WILLIAM BERNIS, cardiologist; b. Rochester, N.Y., May 3, 1942; s. Jacob Philip and Phyllis (Sablowsky) F.; m. Lindsay Ann Scampole, July 10, 1971; 1 child, Daniel Jacob. BA, Cornell U., 1964; MD, U. Rochester, 1968. Bd. cert. internal medicine and cardiovascular disease Am. Bd. Internal Medicine. Intern medicine Strong Meml. Hosp., Rochester, 1968-69, resident medicine, 1969-70; resident medicine N.Y. Hosp., N.Y.C., 1970-72; fellow cardiopulmonary medicine North Shore U. Hosp., Manhasset, N.Y., 1972-73; cardiologist USAF Malcolm Grow Hosp., Andrews AFB, Md., 1973-75; fellow cardiology West Roxbury (Mass.) VA Hosp./Harvard, 1975-76; pvt. practice cardiology with C.D. Gosaynie MD, Inc., Venture, Calif., 1976-77, Cardiology Assoc. Med. Group Inc., Ventura, 1978-91, Charlottesville Cardiology Cons. Ltd., Va., 1991—; clin. asst. prof. medicine UCLA, Ventura, 1985-91; clin. assoc. prof. medicine U. Va., Charlottesville, 1991—; attending physician cardiac catheter lab. U. Va. Sch. Health Sci., 1991—. Major USAF, 1973-75. Fellow ACP, Am. Coll. Cardiology, Am. Heart Assn. (pres. Ventura County chpt. 1978). Office: Charlottesville Cardiology Cons Ltd 908 E Jefferson St Ste G-1 Charlottesville VA 22902

FREEHLING, DEBORAH JUNE, physician; b. Milw., Jan. 3, 1955; d. Frank Eugene and Betty June (Barfknecht) F. BS, U. Ill., 1977; MD, U. Ill., Chgo., 1981. Intern, then resident U. Calif. Davis Med. Ctr., Sacramento, 1981-83; resident in ear, nose and throat, otolaryngology Mass. Eye and Ear Infirmary, Boston, 1983-86; sr. physician, lectr. Kaiser Found. Hosp., Santa Clara, Calif., 1986-95; pvt. practice, 1995—; instr. med. students Harvard Med. Sch. Mass. Eye and Ear Infirmary, 1984-85, teaching asst. dissection course, 1985-86; discussant New Eng. Jour. Medicine, Boston, 1985-86; clin. faculty Stanford U. Med. Ctr., 1989—. Contbr. articles to profl. jours. Alpha Lambda Delta fellow, 1976. Fellow Am. Acad. Otolaryngology, Head and Neck Surgery (diplomate 1987); mem. Santa Clara County Med. Soc. Home: 250 S Balsamina Way Menlo Park CA 94028-7503 Office: 762 Altos Oaks Dr Ste 2 Los Altos CA 94024

FREELAND, ALAN EDWARD, orthopedic surgery educator, physician; b. Youngstown, Ohio, July 30, 1939; s. Harold Edward and Esther Amelia (Hanley) F.; m. Janis Ann Foerschl, Oct. 11, 1969; children: Matthew, Jennifer, Rebecca, Michael. BA, Johns Hopkins U., 1961; MD, George Washington U., 1965. Cert. hand surgery Am. Bd. Orthopaedic Surgery. Intern Church Home and Hosp., Balt., 1965-66; resident Johns Hopkins Hosp., Balt., 1967-70, Letterman Army Med. Ctr., San Francisco, 1973-75; prof. dept. orthopaedic surgery U. Miss. Med. Ctr., Jackson, 1978—; chief staff U. Med. Ctr., Jackson, 1986-87; chief surgery Miss. Meth. Rehab. Ctr., Jackson, 1991-93, pres. elect med. staff, 1994, pres. med. staff, bd. dirs., 1995—. Author: Stable Internal Fixation of the Hand and Wrist, 1986, The First Twenty-Five Years: History of the American Association for Hand Surgery, 1996; mem. editl. bd. Orthopedics, Slack, Inc., 1986—, Jour. Orthopaedic Trauma, Raven Press, 1993—. Mem. Fire Protection Dist., Brandon, Miss., 1990-93. Lt. col. U.S. Army, 1971-78. Fellow Am. Acad. Orthopaedic Surgeons, Am. Orthopaedic Assn.; mem. Am. Soc. Surgery of Hand (governing coun. 1989-92), Am. Assn. Hand Surgeons (parliamentarian 1994, historian 1995, mem. exec. com., bd. dirs. 1994—, treas. 1996), Internat. Fedn. Socs. for Surgery of Hand (chmn. bone and joint com. 1992—), Miss. State Orthopaedic Assn. (pres. 1986, pres. Jackson chpt. 1985). Home: 303 Swallow Dr Brandon MS 39042-6454 Office: 2500 N State St Jackson MS 39216-4500

FREEMAN, ARTHUR MERRIMON, III, psychiatry educator, dean; b. Birmingham, Ala., Oct. 10, 1942; s. Arthur Merrimon Freeman II; m. Linda Poynter; children: Arthur M. IV, Katherin Leigh, Edward Todd. AB in Philosophy, Harvard U., 1963; MD, Vanderbilt U., 1967. Diplomate Am. Bd. Psychiatry and Neurology; lic. psychiatrist, Ala., N.C., La. Asst. prof. dept. psychiatry and behavioral scis. Stanford (Calif.) U., 1974-77; prof., vice chmn. dept. psychiatry U. Ala., Birmingham, 1977-90; med. dir. Appalachian Hall Hosp., Asheville, N.C., 1990-91; prof., chmn. dept. psychiatry La. State U. Med. Ctr., Shreveport, 1991—, dean, 1993-96; regional med. dir. divsn. mental health La. Dept. Health and Hosps., 1992-94. Author: Psychiatry for the Primary Care Physician, 1979. Bd. dirs. Vols. of Am., Shreveport, 1993—, Shreveport Symphony, C. of C., 1993-96. Lt. comdr. M.C., USN, 1972-74. Nat. Merit scholar Harvard U., 1959-63; Biochemistry fellow Karolinska Inst., Stockholm, 1965, fellow in hepatic disease Royal Free Hosp., London, 1966. Fellow APA, Am. Coll. Psychiatrists (Laughlin fellow 1971), Acad. Psychosomatic Medicine, So. Psychiat. Assn.; mem. Am. Assn. Chmn. of Depts. of Psychiatry, Biomed. Rsch. Found. N.W. La. (bd. dirs. 1993-96). Home: 5929 E Ridge Dr Shreveport LA 71106-2423 Office: La State U Med Ctr Dept of Psychiatry 1501 Kings Hwy Shreveport LA 71103-4228

FREEMAN, CAROLYN RUTH, radiation oncologist; b. Kettering, Eng., Jan. 2, 1950; emigrated to Can., 1974, naturalized, 78; d. Ivor Thomas and Winifred Mary (Scotney) F.; m. J.C. Negrete, July 25, 1981. Student, King's Coll. London U., 1967-69; MB, BS, Westminster Med. Sch. London U., 1972. Prof., chmn. dept. radiation oncology, faculty medicine McGill U., Montreal, 1979—; radiation oncologist-in-chief McGill U. Hosps., Montreal, 1979—. Contbr. articles to med. publs. Fellow Royal Coll. Physicians (Can.); mem. Can. Assn. Radiol. Oncologists (pres. 1991-93), Am. Soc. Therapeutic Radiology and Oncology. Home: 4270 deMaisonneuve W, Montreal, PQ Canada H3Z 1K6 Office: 1650 Cedar Ave, Montreal, PQ Canada H3G 1A4

FREEMAN, DONALD CHESTER, JR., health care company executive; b. Haverhill, Mass., May 15, 1930; s. Donald C. and Isabelle (Brown) F.; m. Wilhelmina Lind, June 23, 1978; children: Robert M., Christopher B., Dorian M. B.S., Brown U., 1951; Ph.D., U. Md., 1955; postgrad., Duke U., 1960-61. Dir. tech. materials system div. Union Carbide Corp., Indpls., 1968-69; gen. mgr. instrument dept. Union Carbide Corp., White Plains, N.Y., 1969-71, dir. new bus. devel., 1971-78; pres. Davol, Inc., Providence, 1978-80; group v.p. C.R. Bard, Inc., Murray Hill, N.J., 1980-83; pres., CEO Xenotech Labs., Inc., 1984-87; pres. Intra-Sonix, Inc., 1988-93; ptnr. Grayson & Assocs., Denver, 1993—; bd. dirs. Medrad Inc. Contbr. articles to sci. jours.; patentee in field. Mem. Am. Phys. Soc., N.Y. Acad. Scis., Greater Providence C. of C. (dir. 1982), Sigma Xi, Alpha Tau Omega. Unitarian. Home and office: 23 Arborwood Dr Burlington MA 01803-3816

FREEMAN, ELLEN WOOD, research professor; b. Gloversville, N.Y., Aug. 8, 1935; d. John D. and Marion (Spicer) W.; m. David N., June 15, 1957; children: Jonathan K., Anne C., Gregory S. AB, Smith Coll., Northampton, Mass., 1957; MSS, Bryn Mawr Coll., 1973, PhD, 1976. ACSW, Pa. Asst./assoc. rsch. prof. Dept. OB/GYN and Psychiatry Sch. of Medicine U. Pa., Phila., 1977—. Contbr. articles to profl. jours. Office: Dept OB/GYN U Pennsylvania 3400 Spruce St Philadelphia PA 19104

FREEMAN, HUGH JAMES, gastroenterology educator; b. Edmonton, Alta., Can., June 9, 1947. BSc magna cum laude, Loyola U. of Montreal, Que., Can., 1968; MD, CM, McGill U., Montreal, 1972. Resident U. Alta. Hosp., Edmonton, 1972-74, gastroenterology fellow, 1974-76, MRC research fellow, 1974-75; MRC research fellow U. Calif., San Francisco, 1976-79; asst. prof. medicine U. B.C., Vancouver, 1979-81, assoc. prof. medicine, 1981-86, BCHRCF research fellow, 1979-83, head gastroenterology, 1981-93, prof. medicine, 1986—. Editor (book) Inflammatory Bowel Disease, 1988; contbr. articles to profl. jours. Medical Research Council Research fellow, Edmonton and San Francisco, 1974-75, 76-79; Queen Elizabeth scholar Province of Alta., 1965-72, B.C. Health Care Research Found. Research scholar, 1979-83. Fellow Royal Coll. Physicians and Surgeons Can., ACP; mem. Am. Soc. for Clin. Investigation, Can. Soc. Clin. Investigation, Am. Gasteroenterology Assn., Can. Assn. Gasterenterology. Office: U BC Hosp, 2211 Wesbrook Mall, Vancouver, BC Canada V6T 1W5

FREEMAN, MELVIN IRWIN, ophthalmic surgeon, educator, municipal official; b. Seattle, Mar. 17, 1935; s. Joseph and Rally (Arensberg) F.; m. Nanette Jean Dreyfuss, Feb. 17, 1979; children—Robert Eliot, Jacqueline Dreyfuss, Joseph Dreyfuss. B.S., U. Wash.-Seattle, 1957, M.D., 1960. Intern VA Hosp., Los Angeles, 1960-61; resident Washington U., St. Louis, 1961-66; fellow Retina Found., Boston, 1966-69, Mass. Eye and Ear Infirmary, Boston, 1967-69; head sect. ophthalmology The Mason Clinic, Seattle, 1969-95; dir. continuing med. edn. Virgina Mason Med. Ctr., Seattle, 1984-95; head contact lens clinic, clin. prof. ophthalmology U. Wash., Seattle, 1969—; cons. Madigan Gen. Hosp., U.S. Army, Tacoma, 1969-74; cons. to various mfrs. contact lenses; chmn. Tel-Med Trust of King County, Seattle, 1977-85; nat. commissionaire, nat. secretariat edn., pres. 1996—, The Joint Commn. on Allied Health Personnel in Ophthalmology, St. Paul, 1986—; sec., treas. exec. com. Alliance to Continuing Med. Edn., Northbrook, Ill., 1984—. Author, co-author numerous sci. papers, book chpts. and presentations. Mayor pro tempore, councilman Town of Yarrow Point, Wash., 1974-94; trustee, treas., v.p., pres. Temple De Hirsch Sinai, Seattle and Bellevue, 1976-94; trustee Virginia Mason Research Found., Seattle, 1978-84. Served to capt. M.C., U.S. Army, 1961-63. Fellow USPHS, 1957, 58, 59, NSF, 1959, Nat. Inst. Neurol. Disease and Blindness 1961, 64-69, Fight for Sight, 1966; recipient Williams prize in med. research U. Wash., 1960. Fellow ACS, Am. Acad. Ophthalmology (honors award 1984, sr. honors award 1995), Wash. State Acad. Ophthalmology (officer, trustee 1976—), Pacific Coast Oto-Ophthal. Soc., Seattle Surg. Soc. Club: Washington Athletic (Seattle). Home: 4625 Yarrow Point Rd Bellevue WA 98004-1336 Office: The Mason Clinic 1100 9th Ave Seattle WA 98101-2756

FREEMAN, MICHAEL LEONARD, radiation biologist; b. Boston, July 16, 1952; s. Michael S. and Corinne Freeman; m. Melanie H. Rutledge, June 1978; children: Carl, Scott, Mark. BS in Zoology, Colo. State U., 1974, PhD in Radiation Biology, 1978. Rsch. assoc. Radiol. Rsch. Lab. Coll. Physicians and Surgeons, Columbia U., N.Y.C., 1978-82; asst. prof. radiation oncology Vanderbilt U. Sch. Medicine, Nashville, 1983-89, assoc. prof. radiation oncology, 1990—, dir. quality assurance Ctr. Radiation Oncology, 1986-88; mem. com. for protection human subjects Vanderbilt Instnl. Rev. Bd., 1983-86; mem. steering com. Vanderbilt Free Electron Laser Use, 1987-91; bd. dirs. task force for new item devel. Am. Bd. Radiology; ad hoc reviewer Am. Cancer Soc., 1986; reviewer for program projects NIH-Nat. Cancer Inst., 1991, ad hoc reviewer, 1995, mem. radiation study sect. 1995-99; peer reviewer assessments program Dept. Energy, 1992. Author book chpt.; contbr. articles to profl. jours. Fire fighter, engr. Bellevue (Tenn.) Vol. Fire Dept., 1984-89, tng. officer, 1987-88, Pegram (Tenn.) Vol. Fire Dept., 1990-92; cub master Boy Scouts Am., 1990. Recipient grant Pub. Health Svcs.; NIH/Nat. Cancer Inst., 1984, 87, 92, 95, Shannon award, 1991; named Young Investigator, Symposium Cancer Therapy by Hyperthermia, Drugs, and Radiation, 1980, Internat. Congress of Radiation, 1983. Mem. AAAS, Radiation Rsch. Soc. (history com. 1985-87, site selection and policy com. 1986-92, chmn. 1988-91), North Am. Hyperthermia Soc., Am. Assn. Cancer Rsch. Office: Vanderbilt U Ctr Radiation Oncology B902 Vanderbilt Clinic Nashville TN 37232

FREEMAN, NATASHA MATRINA LEONIDOW, nursing administrator; b. Nyack, N.Y., June 12, 1958; d. Paul and Matrina (Butich) L.; m. Douglas Edward Freeman, Oct. 20, 1990; children: Alexandra, Mary. AAS, Rockland C.C., 1979; BS in Nursing cum laude, SUNY Coll. Technology, Utica, 1982; MS in Nursing magna cum laude, Syracuse U., 1985. RN, N.Y.; cert. nurse adminstr. Staff nurse Englewood Hosp., N.J., 1979-80; charge nurse Mary Imogene Bassett Hosp., Cooperstown, N.Y., 1980-82, nursing svc. coord., 1983-86, asst. dir. sys. devel., 1986-87; assoc. nursing practice coord. Strong Meml. Hosp.-U. Rochester, N.Y., 1987-88, asst. dir. nursing Bayfront Med. Ctr., St. Petersburg, Fla., 1988—. Translator: Excellence in Russian Language, 1976 (Otrada award). Served as 1st lt. USAFR, 1990-91, Persian Gulf War, Saudi Arabia. Mem. Fla. Orgn. Nurse Execs., Tampa Bay Orgn. Nurse Execs., Sigma Theta Tau. Office: Bayfront Med Ctr 701 6th St S Saint Petersburg FL 33701-4814

FREEMAN, PHILLIP, psychiatrist; b. Norfolk, Va., Jan. 16, 1954. BA, Princeton U., 1975; MS, U. Calif., Berkeley, 1977; DMH, U. Calif., San Francisco, 1980; MD, Columbia U., 1984. Diplomate Am. Bd. Psychiatry. Intern St. Vincents Hosp., N.Y.C., 1984-85; resident, clin. fellow psychiatry Harvard Med. Sch., McLean Hosp., Belmont, Mass., 1985-88; clin. instr. psychiatry Harvard Med. Sch., Boston, 1988—; asst. prof. psychiatry Boston U. Med. Sch., 1988—, assoc. dir. med. student program in psychiatry, 1988—; asst. attending psychiatrist McLean Hosp., Belmont, 1988—; asst. vis. physician Univ. Hosp., Boston, 1988—. Contbr. articles to profl. jours. including Jour. Nervous and Mental Disease, Psychiat. Annals. Mem. Am. Psychoanalytic Assn., Am. Psychiat. Assn., Mass. Psychiat. Assn., Boston Psychoanalytic Assn. Office: 720 Harrison Ave Ste 904 Boston MA 02118

FREEMAN, RICHARD J., medical products financial executive; b. Boston, Mar. 5, 1950; s. Richard T. and Helen E, (Leary) F.; m. Nancy Anne White, July 28, 1973; children: Adrienne M., Richard A. BA, Ohio Wesleyan U., 1973; MBA, Boston U., 1975. CPA, Ohio. Acct. Continental Ins. Co., Columbus, Ohio, 1975-76; sr. acct. Babcock and Wilcox, Lancaster, Ohio, 1976-79; accting. mgr. Babcock and Wilcox, Irvine, Calif., 1979-83; dir. accting. McCormick and Co./SETCO, Anaheim, Calif., 1983-87; v.p. fin. Sunrise Med./Quickie Designs, Fresno, Calif., 1987—. Auditor PTA, Fresno, 1989-91. Mem. Inst. Mgmt. Accts. (pres. Fresno chpt. 1991-92). Home: 3211 W La Costa Ave Fresno CA 93711-0227 Office: Sunrise Med/Quickie Designs 2842 N Business Park Ave Fresno CA 93727-1328

FREEMAN, TYLER IRA, physician; b. N.Y.C., Feb. 1, 1934; s. Jules and Mildred (Cohen) F.; m. Alice Fruchter, Dec. 22, 1957; children: Julie, Nancy. BA, Johns Hopkins U., 1955; MD, Chgo. Med. Sch., 1959. Intern L.I. (N.Y.) Coll. Hosp., 1959-60, resident in internal medicine, 1960-62; chief med. resident North Shore U. Hosp., Manhasset, N.Y., 1962-63; pvt. practice internal medicine, dir. Employee Health Svc., Mt. Sinai-Elmhurst Hosp., N.Y.C., 1965-75; asst. med. dir. Hoechst/Celanese, N.Y.C., 1975-78; med. dir. adminstrv. svcs. Consolidated Edison Corp., N.Y.C., 1978-81; corp. med. dir. Fielderest/Cannon Inc., Eden, N.C., 1981-88; med. dir. A.T. & T. Network Systems, Columbus, Ohio, 1988-90; pvt. cons. Bus. Health Mgmt., Cleve., 1990-94; dir. occupational and environ. medicine Charlotte/Mecklenburg Hosp. Assn., N.C., 1994-96; pres. Med. Evaluations Unltd., Charlotte, N.C., 1996—; MD cons. Health Ins. Plan-Greater N.Y., N.Y.C., Combustion Toxicity Task Group, Am. Textile Mfg. Assn.; pres. occupational med. com. Am. Indsl. Hygiene Assn., N.C. and S.C.; pres. Component Soc. Am. Coll. Del. steering com. Wellness Coun., Greensboro, N.C.; advisor Hospice Task Force, Rockingham, N.C.; bd. dirs. ARC, Eden. Capt. USAF, 1963-65. Fellow Am. Coll. Preventive Medicine, Am. Coll. Occupational Medicine; mem. AMA, N.Y. Acad. Sci., Am. Diabetes Assn., Am. Soc. Internal Medicine, Am. Pub. Health Assn. Jewish. Home: 12033 Delmahoy Dr Charlotte NC 28277-9635 Office: 1229 Greenwood Cliff Charlotte NC 28204

FREEMAN, WILLIAM EMMETT, dermatologist; b. Atlanta, Sept. 30, 1957; s. Hugh Lee and Sarah Frances (Wright) F. BA in Chemistry, Emory U., 1979; MD, Med. Coll. Ga., Augusta, 1983. Diplomate Am. Bd. Dermatology, Am. Bd. Laser Surgery. Intern Med. Coll. Ga. Hosps. and Clinics, Augusta, 1983-84, resident in dermatology, 1984-87; pvt. practice Warner Robins, Ga., 1987—; clin. instr. dept. dermatology Med. Coll. Ga., 1987-93; mem. staff Houston Med. Ctr., Warner Robins, 1987—. Contbr. articles to profl. jours. Fellow Internat. Soc. Dermatology, Am. Soc. for Dermatologic Surgery; mem. AMA, Am. Acad. Cosmetic Surgery (assoc.), Peachbelt Med. Soc., Med. Assn. Ga. Office: William E Freeman MD 136 S Houston Lake Rd Warner Robins GA 31088-6300

FREEMAN-LONGO, ROBERT EARL, psychotherapist; b. Harrison, N.Y., Sept. 26, 1951; s. Angelo Earl Longo and Shirley Mae (Shavenaugh) DeWalt; m. Patricial Lynn, Sept. 17, 1983. BA in Psychology, U. Fla., 1974, MA in Rehab. Counseling, 1976. Unit dir. North Fla. Evaluation and Treatment Ctr., Gainesville, 1979-81; mental health analyst Health and Rehabilitative Svcs., Gainesville, 1981-83; dir. Correctional Sex Offender Treatment Program, Salem, Oreg., 1983—; counselor The Human Ctr. Gainesville, Fla., 1978-79, The Gestalt Ctr., Gainesville, 1979-81; founder, pres. The Sexual Assault Rsch. Assn., Gainesville, 1981-83; adj. faculty Forensic Mental Healt Assn., Webster, Mass., 1982-88; part time faculty Santa Fe Community Coll., Fla. Police Acad., Gainesville, Eustis, Lake County Vocational-Tech. Community Coll., 1982; cert. Law Enforcement Instr. Fla., 1983-87, Oreg., 1983—; cons., lectr. and conductor of seminars nationwide. Co-author: (with L. Bays) Who Am I and Why Am I in Treatment, 1988; author: (with others) The Sexual Agressor: Current Perspectives on Treatment, 1983; contbr. numerous articles to profl. jours. Mem. Gov's. Task Force on Rape Prevention, Kans. City, Mo., 1980; bd. dirs. Oreg. Crime Victims Assistance Network, Salem, 1984-86; adv. staff Nat. Task Force on Adolescent Sex Offenders, Denver, 1987—; adv. bd. Office of Atty. Gen. Victims of Crime Act, Salem, 1989—. Assn. for the Behavioral Treatment of Sexual Abusers (founder and pres. 1984-86, bd. dirs. 1986-87), Am. Mental Health Counselors Assn., Pub. Offenders Counselor Assn., Am. Assn. for Counseling and Devel. Democrat. Presbyterian. Home and Office: Safer Soc Found Inc PO Box 340 Brandon VT 05733-0340

FREER, JOHN HERSCHEL, psychiatrist; b. Somerset, Ky., Jan. 3, 1938; s. Albert Herschel and Edith Evelyn (O'Dell) F.; m. Joyce Anita Simmons, Aug. 25, 1963; children: John Bryant, Ruth Evelyn. BS, Ky. Wesleyan Coll., 1960; MD, U. Ky., 1967. Diplomate Am. Bd. Psychiatry and Neurology. Intern U. Ky. Med. Sch., Lexington, 1968; resident in psychiatry Topeka VA Hosp., 1971-73; chief alcohol treatment VA Hosp., Lexington, 1973-74; psychiatrist pvt. practice Counseling and Psychotherapy Ctr., Lexington, 1974-89; pvt. practice Pikeville, Ky., 1990-91, Hopkinsville, Ky., 1992-93; staff Western State Hosp., Hopkinsville, 1991-92; dir. adult unit Cumberland Hall Hosp., Hopkinsville, 1992-93; staff Green River Comprehensive Care Ctr., 1991-92, Pennyroyal Comprehensive Care Ctr., 1992—; cons. staff Jennie Stuart Hosp., Hopkinsville, 1992—; cons. staff Cen. Bapt. Hosp., Lexington, 1975-87, Humana Hosp., Lexington, 1983-89; active staff St. Joseph Hosp., Lexington, 1975-89, Charter Ridge Hosp., 1982-89; active and courtesy staff Good Samaritan Hosp., Lexington, 1975-89; assoc. clin. prof. psychiatry U. Ky. Med. Sch., Lexington, 1974-89; mem. med. staff Meth. Hosp., Pikeville, 1990-91; staff psychiatrist Ky. River Community Care, 1990-91, Mountain Comprehensive Care, 1990-91; clin. dir. Pennyroyal Ctr., Hopkinsville, 1993—. Mem. AMA, Am. Psychiatric Assn., Christian Med. Soc., Ky. Med. Assn., Ky. Psychiatric Assn. Methodist. Office: 735 North Dr Hopkinsville KY 42240-2620

FREESE, ANDREW, neurosurgeon; b. Boston, July 4, 1959; s. Ernst and Elisabeth (Bautz) F.; m. Marcia Geary, June 14, 1986; children: John Alexander, Elisabeth Marguerite, Ernst Timothy. BA, Harvard U., 1981; MD, Harvard U., Boston, 1990; PhD, MIT, 1990. Lic. physican, Pa.; trauma cert. Rsch. assoc. NIH, Bethesda, Md., 1982-83; surg. intern U. Pa., Phila., 1990-91, neurosurgery resident, 1991-96, dir. Lab. Molecular Neurosurgery Grad. Hosp., 1994—, mem. Inst. Human Gene Therapy, 1994—; vis. scientist Wistar Inst., Phila., 1994-95; pres. Neurel, Inc., Boston, 1987-88, sci. dir., 1988-90; cons. Polykinetix, Inc., N.Y.C., 1993; exec. dir. Parkinson's Disease Gene Therapy Consortium. Editor: Biotechnology Processing, 1988, Neurological Disorders: Novel Experimental and Therapeutic Approaches, 1992; contbr. articles to profl. jours. Fellow Sigma Xi; mem. AMA, Internat. Brain Rsch. Orgn., Soc. Neurosci., Congress Neurol. Surgeons, Controlled Release Soc. Home: 18 Fawn Ln Haverford PA 19041-1116 Office: U Pa Divsn Neurosurgery 3400 Spruce St Philadelphia PA 19104 also: Lab of Molecular Neurosurgery Grad Hosp 415 S 19th St Philadelphia PA 19146

FREESE, BRIAN PAUL, consultant; b. Coronado, Calif., Feb. 3, 1969; s. Allen Paul and Gracia Marlene (Turman) F. BA, Coll. Charleston, 1991; M of Pub. Policy & Adminstrn., Miss. State U., 1995. Mgmt. intern City of Florence (S.C.), 1988-89, pub. safety telecommunicator, 1989; rep. bus. office Baker Hosp., North Charleston, S.C., 1989-92; acctg. analyst Magnolia Regional Med. Ctr., Corinth, Miss., 1992-93; dist. exec. Boy Scouts Am., Jackson, Miss., 1993-94; mgmt. intern City of Meridian (Miss.), 1994; grad. svc. asst. Miss. State U., 1995; rsch. asst. John C. Stennis Inst., Miss., 1995; mng. cons. Noreast Svcs. Co., Booneville, Miss., 1996—; guest lectr. Miss. Consortium Internat. Devel., Jackson, 1995; apptd. Programming Bd. FMC, Florence, 1988; rschr. in field. Sustaining mem. Rep. Nat. Com., 1990—, Boy Scouts Am., 1987—. Mem. Am. Coll. Health Care Adminstrn., Am. Soc. Pub. Adminstrn., Coll. Charleston Alumni Assn., Miss. State U. Alumni Assn., Phi Sigma Alpha, Omicron Delta Kappa. Mem. Ch. of Christ. Home: 540 Oblethorpe Ave #408 Athens GA 30606 Office: Noreast Svcs Co 408 W George Allen Dr Booneville MS 38829

FREESTONE, DAVID STANLEY, retired medical researcher, pharmaceutical physician; b. Derby, Eng., June 27, 1933; s. Stanley William and Nellie Swift (Machin) F.; m. Ellen Ada Izod, Jan. 15, 1958; children: Robin, Jonathan, Michael, Hugh. Student, Trent Coll., Derbyshire, Eng., 1946-51; MB, BS, St. Bartholomew's Hosp., London, 1956, diploma in laryngo-otology, 1960; diploma, Royal Coll. Ob-Gyn., London, 1961. Rsch. asst. Sandoz Lab., London, 1962-65, med. dir. rsch., 1965-69; clin. immunologist Wellcome Rsch. Labs., Beckenham, Eng., 1969-75, head dept. clin. immunology and chemotherapy, 1975-84, asst. dir. clin. and applied rsch. division, 1984-85, dir. med. scis., 1985-92; faculty Fellow of pharm. medicine Royal Colls. of Physicians, 1989. Contbr. over 50 med. papers to profl. jours. Fellow Royal Soc. Medicine; mem. Brit. Med. Assn. Anglican. Home and Office: The Paddocks Back Ends, Chipping Campden, Gloucestershire GL55 6AU, England Office: Wellcome Rsch Labs, Langley Ct, Beckenham England

FREI, EMIL, III, physician, medical researcher, educator; b. St. Louis, 1924; m. Elizabeth Smith (dec. Apr. 1986); children: Mary, Emil, Alice, Nancy, Judy; m. Adoria Smetana Brock, May 1987; stepchildren: Stephen, Francis, Peter, Vincent, John. M.D., Yale U., 1948. Diplomate Am. Bd. Internal Medicine, Am. Bd. Med. Oncology. Intern St. Louis U. Hosp., 1948-49; resident in pathology Barnes Hosp., St. Louis, 1952-53; resident in internal medicine St. Louis U., 1953-54, VA Hosp., St. Louis, 1954-55; chief gen. medicine br. Nat. Cancer Inst., Bethesda, Md., 1955-65; head devel. therapeutics, assoc. dir. M.D. Anderson Hosp. and Tumor Inst., Houston, 1965-72; dir., physician-in-chief Children's Cancer Research Found. (now Dana-Farber Cancer Inst.), Boston, 1972-91; physician-in-chief emeritus, chief div. cancer pharmacology Dana-Farber Cancer Inst., 1991—; prof. medicine Harvard U. Med. Sch., Boston, 1972—; Richard and Susan Smith prof. medicine Harvard U. Med. Sch., 1985; nat. cons. in internal medicine-oncology U.S. Air Force; mem. Eleanor Roosevelt internat. cancer fellowships com. Internat. Union Against Cancer; chmn. anti-neoplastic disease drug panel, drug efficacy study Nat. Acad. Scis.; mem. bd. sci. counselors Nat. Cancer Inst., 1986-90, mem. Presdl. Commn. for New Drugs for Cancer and AIDS, 1988-90. Served as lt. M.C. USNR, 1950-52. Recipient Lasker award 1972, Kettering prize GM, 1983, Hamao Umezawa award 1985, Armand Hammer Cancer Rsch. award 1989, Disting. Alumnus award NIH, 1990, Emil Frei III Professorship in Medicine, 1992. Fellow ACP; mem. AMA, Am. Assn. for Cancer Rsch. (past pres.), Am. Soc. Clin. Oncology (pres. 1968-69, Disting. Scientist award 1992), Am. Cancer Soc. (ann. Nat. award 1981), Am. Soc. Hematology, Am. Soc. Clin. Investigation, Assn. Am. Physicians, Inst. of Medicine, Nat. Acad. Medicine. Office: Dana Farber Cancer Inst 44 Binney St # 1562 Boston MA 02115-6013

FREIBOTT, GEORGE AUGUST, physician, chemist, priest; b. Bridgeport, Conn., Oct. 6, 1954; s. George August and Barbara Mary (Schreiber) F.; m. Jennifer Noble, July 12, 1980 (div.); children: Jessica, Heather, George; m. Arlene Ann Steiner, Aug. 1, 1982. BD, Am. Bible Coll., Pineland, Fla., 1977; BS, Nat. Coll. NHA, International Falls, Minn., 1978; ThM, Clarksville (Tenn.) Sch. Theology, 1979; MD, Western U., Phoenix, 1982; ND, Am. Coll., 1979; MsT, Fla. Sch. Massage, 1977. Diplomate Nat. Bd. Naturopathic Examiners; ordained priest Ea. Orthodox Ch., 1983. Chief mfg. cons. in oxidative chemistry Am. Soc. Med. Missionaries, Priest River, Idaho, 1976-88; mfg. cons. Oxidation Products Internat. div. ASMM, Priest River, 1974—; chemist/oxidative chemistry Internat. Assn. Oxygen Therapy, Priest River, 1985—; oxidative chemist, scientist, priest A.S. Med. Missionaries, Priest River, 1982—; massage therapist Fla. Dept. Profl. Registration, Tallahassee, 1977-91; cons. Benedict Lust Sch. Naturopathy; lectr. in field. Author: Nicola Tesla and the Implementation of His Discoveries in Modern Science, 1984, Warburg, Blass and Koch: Men With a Message, 1990, Free Radicals and Their Relationship to Complex Oxidative Compounds, 1991, Complex Oxidative Molecules: Their Implication in the Rejuvenation of the Human Cell, 1994, History of Naturopathy or Pseudomedicalism: Naturopathy's Demise?, 1990, 95; contbr. articles to profl. jours. Recipient Tesla medal of Scientific Merit, Benedict Lust Sch. Natural Scis., 1992. Mem. Am. Chem. Soc., Tesla Meml. Soc., Tesla Coil Builder's Assn., Internat. Bio-Oxidative Med. Found. (Disting. Spkr. award 1994), Brit. Guild Drugless Practitioners, Internat. Assn. for Colon Therapy, Am. Massage Therapy Assn., Am. Naturopathic Med. Assn., Am. Soc. Med. Missionaries, Am. Coll. Clinic Adminstrs., Nat. Assn. Naturopathic Physicians, Am.

Psychotherapy Assn., Am. Soc. Metals, Am. Naturopathic Assn. (trustee, pres.), Internat. Traders. Home and Office: PO Box 1360 Priest River ID 83856-1360

FREIDBERG, STEPHEN ROY, neurosurgeon; b. Bklyn., Oct. 16, 1934; s. Leslie Max and Bess Bernblum; m. Helen Deorsay, May 1, 1964; children: Michael, Jonathan. AB, U. Pa., Phila., 1956; MD, Albert Einstein Coll., 1960. Intern U. Okla. Hosp., 1960-61; resident King's County Hosp., Bklyn., 1964-68; fellow Nat. Hosp. Queen's Sq., London, 1965; staff physician Lahey Clinic Med. Ctr., Burlington, Mass., 1969—, chmn. divsn. surgery, 1995; chmn. dept. neurosurgery Lahey Clinic Med. Ctr., Burlington, 1984, bd. govs., 1978. Contbr. articles to profl. jours. Capt. U.S. Army, 1962-64. Mem. Am. Assn. Neurol. Surgeons, Congress Neurol. Surgeons, New Eng. Neurosurg. Soc. (pres. 1981-83), Mass. Med. Soc. Jewish. Office: Lahey Clinic Med Ctr 41 Mall Rd Burlington MA 01805-0001

FREIDLINE, JOSEPH LESTER, family physician; b. Chanute, Kans., Sept. 19, 1911; s. Oscar Charles and Myrtle Freidline; children: Clifford, Darla Jean, Glenn, Kenneth, Joseph, Sara. Student, Wichita U., 1932-33; DO, Kansas City Coll. Osteo. Med., 1938., 1943—; Pvt. practice Weatherford, Okla., Enid, Okla.; assoc. Hinton Gen. Hosp., Enid, Enid Gen. Hosp; med. examiner. Mem. Am. Osteo. Assn., Okla. Osteo. Assn., Rotary. Republican. Baptist. Home: 1533 Beverly Dr Enid OK 73703 Office: 915 E Garriott Rd Ste D Enid OK 73701-6153

FREIFELD, GERALD SHERMAN, neurosurgeon; b. N.Y.C., May 12, 1935; s. Isadore and Bessie (Dende) F.; m. Roberta Ellen Donde, Dec. 15, 1963; children: Brett, Mitchell, Andrea. BS, CCNY, 1956; MD, U. Lausanne, Switzerland, 1962. Diplomate Am. Bd. Neuro-Surgery. Intern Brookdale Med. Hosp.; resident in gen. surgery, neurology and neurol. surgery Kingsbridge VA Hosp./N.Y. Neurol. Inst.; assoc., ptnr. Regional Neurol. Surg. Group, P.C., Middletown, N.Y., 1963—; pres. Regional Neurol. Surg. Group, P.C., 1969—. Fellow ACS, Internat. Coll. Surgeons; mem. Am. Assn. Neurol. Surgeons, Congress Neurol. Surgeons, N.Y. State Soc. Surgeons, N.Y. State Neurosurg. Soc. Jewish. Office: Reg Neurol Surg Group Plc 12 Grove St Middletown NY 10940

FREIHOFER, HANS PETER MICHAEL, surgeon; b. Zürich, Switzerland, Feb. 8, 1937; arrived in The Netherlands, 1979; s. Hans Heinrich and Verena E. (Bertschinger) F.; m. Evelyn Louise Mann; children: Reto Henry, Bernhard Michael. DMD, U. Zürich, 1961, MD, 1965, PhD, 1978. Resident in ear, nose and throat U. Bern, Switzerland, 1965-66; resident in gen. surgery U. Basel, Switzerland, 1967-68; resident in maxillo-facial surgery U. Zürich, 1968-71; resident in cranio-facial surgery U. Paris, 1971-72; staff mem. dept. maxillo-facial surgery U. Zürich, 1972-79; prof. oral maxillo-facial surgery U. Nijmegen, The Netherlands, 1979—; cons. CWZ Hosp., Nijmegen, 1987—. Asst. editor: Jour. Maxillo-Facial Surgery, 1973-79; editor-in-chief: Jour. Cranio-Maxillo-Facial Surgery, 1980-92; contbr. articles to profl. jours. Mem. Swiss Assn. Maxillo-facial Surgery (founding), Swiss Workgroup on Oral-Maxillofacial Surgery (corr.), European Assn. Cranio-Maxillo-facial Surgery (founding, hon.), Dutch Assn. Maxillo-facial Surgery, French Assn. Maxillo-facial Surgery, German Assn. Maxillo-facial Surgery, Am. Oral Surgery in Europe (hon.). Office: Univ Hosp, Postbus 9101, 6500 HB Nijmegen The Netherlands

FREIMAN, ALVIN HENRY, cardiologist; b. N.Y.C., Jan. 26, 1927; s. Maurice and Beatrice (Freeman) F.; B.A., N.Y. U., 1947, M.D., 1953; M.S., U. Ill., 1949; m. Nadine Roehr, June 12, 1959; children—Audrey L., Gail L., Marshall A. Intern, Montefiore Hosp., N.Y.C., 1953-54; resident in medicine and cardiology Beth Israel Hosp., Boston 1954-56; fellow in cardiology Meml. Hosp., N.Y.C., 1956-58; individual practice medicine specializing in internal medicine and cardiology, N.Y.C., 1954—; attending physician Sloan-Kettering Inst., N.Y.C., 1995; prof. medicine Cornell U. Med. Coll., N.Y.C., 1995—; attending staff cardiology Meml. Hosp., N.Y.C., 1971—, dept. medicine Meml. Sloan-Kettering Cancer Center, N.Y.C., 1971—, dir. clin. info. center, 1974—. Served with USNR, 1945-46. Diplomate Am. Bd. Internal Medicine. Mem. Nat. Cancer Inst., A.C.P., Am. Coll. Cardiology, Am. Coll. Chest Physicians, Am. Coll. Angiology, AAAS, Am. Heart Assn., N.Y. Acad. Sci., Internat. Coll. Angiology, Alpha Omega Alpha, Sigma Xi. Contbr. articles to profl. jours. Home: 74 Homestead Rd Tenafly NJ 07670-1109 Office: 178 E End Ave New York NY 10128-7762

FREIMAN, HAL JEFFREY, gastroenterologist; b. Bronx, N.Y.C., May 23, 1954; s. Herbert Seymour and Irene Paula (Cheiken) F.; m. Ellen Louise Babin, Aug. 3, 1980; children: Marc, Rachel. BS cum laude, Rensselaer Poly. Inst., 1978; MD, Albany Med. Coll., 1978. Diplomate Am. Bd. Internal Medicine in internal medicine and gastroenterology. Resident internal medicine St. Vincent's Hosp. & Med. Ctr. N.Y., N.Y.C., 1978-81, attending physician, 1983—; fellow gastroenterology N.Y. Med. Coll., Valhalla, 1981-83; cons. physician Village Nursing Home, N.Y.C., 1990—. Fellow ACP, Am. Coll. Gastroenterology; mem. Am. Gastroent. Assn., Am. Soc. Gastrointestinal Endoscopy, N.Y. Acad. Gastroenterology. Home: 11 Magnolia Rd Scarsdale NY 10583-7445 Office: 59 W 12th St New York NY 10011-8563

FREIMUTH, VICKI S., health science association administrator. BS in Edn. with honors, Eastern Ill. U.; MA in Rhetoric and Pub. Address, U. Iowa; PhD in Comm. Theory and Rsch., Fla. State U. Former dir. health comm., prof. dept. speech comm. U. Md., College Park; now assoc. dir. comm. Ctrs. Disease Control and Prevention, Atlanta; cons. Nat. Cancer Inst., Nat. Heart, Lung and Blood Inst., Nat. Inst. Alcohol Abuse and Alcoholism, Agy. Internat. Devel., World Bank; dir. rsch. Porter Novelli and Assocs., Washington. Author: Searching for Health Information; co-editor: AIDS: A Communication Perspective; contbr. articles to profl. jours. Mem. Internat. Comm. Assn. (chair health comm. divsn.). Office: Ctr Disease Control & Prevention Bldg 1 1600 Clifton Rd NE Atlanta GA 30333

FREIREICH, EMIL J, hematologist, educator; b. Chgo., Mar. 16, 1927; s. David and Mary (Klein) F.; m. Haroldine Lee Cunningham, Mar. 13, 1953; children: Debra Ann, David Alan, Lindsay Gail, Thomas Jon. B.S., U. Ill., 1947, M.D. with honors, 1949, D.Sc. (hon.), 1982. Diplomate Am. Bd. Internal Medicine. Intern Cook County (Ill.) Hosp., Chgo., 1949-50; resident in internal medicine Presbyn. Hosp., Chgo., 1950-53; research asso. in hematology Mass. Meml. Hosp., Boston, 1953-55; sr. investigator, head Leukemia Service USPHS, Nat. Cancer Inst., Bethesda, Md., 1955-65; prof. medicine U. Tex. System Cancer Ctr., Houston, 1965—; chief research in hematology U. Tex. System Cancer Ctr., 1965-85, head dept. devel. therapeutics, 1972-83, chmn. dept. hematology, 1983-85, dir. Adult Leukemia Rsch. Program, 1985—; prof. medicine U. Tex. Health Sci. Ctr. (Sch. Medicine), 1973—, chief div. oncology, 1973-81; mem. faculty Grad. Sch. Med., Health Scis. Ctr., 1965—; mem. rev. com. drug. devel. div. cancer treatment NIH, 1975-80, Ruth Harriet Ainsworth chair in devel. therapeutics, 1980—. Assoc. editor Cancer, 1976—, Cancer Research, 1977-86; mem. editorial bd. Oncology News, 1975-90, Cancer Treatment Reports, 1976-80, Leukemia Research, 1976-87, Med. and Pediatric Oncology, 1974—, Leukemia 1987—; contbr. numerous articles on research in hematology and oncology to profl. jours. Recipient Albert Lasker Med. rsch. award, 1972, Charles F. Kettering prize Gen. Motors Cancer Rsch. Found., 1983, Outstanding Investigator award Nat. Cancer Inst., NIH, 1985-92, Alumnus award NIH, 1990; named Alumnus of Yr., U. Ill. Alumni Assn., 1974. Fellow ACP; mem. Internat. Soc. Hematology, Am. Soc. Hematology, Am. Fedn. Clin. Research, Am. Soc. Clin. Pharmacology and Therapeutics, Am. Soc. Clin. Oncology (David A. Karnofsky award 1976, pres. 1980-81), Am. Soc. Clin. Investigators, Am. Assn. Cancer Research, Leukemia Soc. Am. (pres. Gulf Coast chpt. 1968-70, trustee 1968-70, Robert Roesler DeVilliers award 1979, grant rev. subcom. 1986-89), Tex. Med. Assn., AMA (editorial bd. jour. 1973-83), Assn. Am. Physicians, Alpha Omega Alpha. Home: 810 Monte Cello St Houston TX 77024-4515 Office: M D Anderson Cancer Ctr 1515 Holcombe Blvd Houston TX 77030-4009

FREIS, EDWARD DAVID, physician, medical researcher; b. Chgo., May 13, 1912; 3 children. B.S., U. Ariz., 1936; M.D., Columbia, 1940. Intern, house physician Mass. Meml. Hosp., Boston, 1940-41; sr. intern, house physician Boston City Hosp., 1941-42; asst. resident Evans Meml. Hosp., 1946-47, resident fellow cardiovascular disease, 1947-49; adj. clin. prof. Georgetown U. Sch. Medicine, 1949-57, assoc. prof., 1957-63, prof., 1963—; sr. med. investigator VA Med. Ctr., Washington, 1959-87, asst. chief medicine, 1949-54, chief, 1954-59; instr. Boston U., 1947-49. Served with M.C. USAAF, 1942-45. Recipient Albert Lasker Med. Research award, 1971, Ciba award in hypertension, 1981, E. Fries award Nat. Conf. High Blood Pressure Coun., 1985, Spl. Achievement award Am. Soc. Hypertension, 1990. Office: VA Med Ctr 50 Irving St NW Washington DC 20422-0001

FREITAG, FREDERICK GERALD, osteopathic physician; b. Milw., Feb. 12, 1952; s. Frederick August and Shirley June (Siewert) F.; m. Lynn Nadene Stegner, Sept. 10, 1977; children: Crescentia Adella, Abigail Amadea, Genevieve Angelica. BS in Biochemistry, U. Wis., 1974; DO, Chgo. Coll. Osteopathic Medicine, 1979. Intern Brentwood Hosp., Warrensville Heights, Ohio, 1979-80, resident in family practice, 1980-81; dir., physician Twinsburg (Ohio) Family Clinic, 1981-83; assoc. prof. family medicine Coll. Osteo. Medicine, Ohio U., Warrensville Heights, 1982-83; mem. staff Diamond Headache Clinic, Chgo., 1983-86, assoc. dir., 1986—; attending staff mem. Louis A. Weiss Meml. Hosp., Chgo., 1983-93; attending staff Columbus Hosp., 1993—; mem. Janssen Rsch. Coun.; sec. Diamond Headache Rsch. and Edn. Found.; vis. lectr. dept. family medicine Chgo. Coll. Osteo. Medicine, 1985—; clin. assoc. dept. medicine Pritzker Sch. Medicine U. Chgo., 1989-93; editorial bd. Headache Quar., 1991—; chmn. instnl. rev. bd. Louis A. Weiss Meml. Hosp., 1991-93. Contbr. articles and abstracts to profl. jours., chpts. to books. Bd. dirs. Nat. Headache Found. Fellow Am. Assn. for Study of Headache; mem. AMA, Am. Coll. Gen. Practioners in Osteo. Medicine, Am. Osteo. Assn., Am. Soc. Clin. Pharmacology and Therapeutics (vice chmn. headache sect. 1995-96), Ill. Assn. Osteo. Physicians and Surgeons, Ill. Med. Soc., Internat. Assn. Study Pain, Am. Pain Soc., Nat. Headache Found., Chgo. Med. Soc. (speakers bur.), German Wine Soc. (past pres. Chgo. chpt.), U. Wis. Alumni Assn. Lutheran. Home: 931 Clinton Pl River Forest IL 60305-1503 Office: The Diamond Headache Clinic 467 Deming Pl Ste 500 Chicago IL 60614

FREITAS, LYNN GUERRA, social worker, therapist; b. Queens, N.Y., July 8, 1961; d. Joseph R. and Constance (Iuzzini) Guerra; m. Thomas M. Freitas, July 25, 1987. BA, Boston Coll., 1983, MSW, 1984; cert. family therapy, Ackerman Inst. Family Therapy, 1990. Lic. clin. social worker, N.Y.; cert. family therapist, N.Y., cert. in treatment of alcohol and drug abusing clients. Adolescent counselor South Boston (Mass.) Neighborhood House, 1984-85; social worker psychiatric in-patient unit St. Vincent's Hosp., N.Y.C., 1985-88, social worker out patient psychiatric clinic, 1988-93, coord. family component of alcoholism & addiction outpatient, 1993—; pvt. practice N.Y.C., 1990—. Mem. Acad. Cert. Social Workers, Am. Assn. Mental and Family Therapy (diplomate in social work). Home: 111 Hicks St Apt 7H Brooklyn NY 11201-1639

FRELINGER, JEFFREY ALLEN, immunologist, educator; b. Bklyn., July 16, 1948; s. John Edgar and Alice (Andersen) F.; m. A. Joy Vaughan, Apr. 4, 1970; children: Jacob Jeffrey, John Kees. BA, U. Calif., San Diego, 1969; PhD, Calif. Inst. Tech., 1973. Fellow U. Mich., Ann Arbor, 1973-75; from asst. prof. to prof. U. So. Calif., L.A., 1975-83; prof. U. N.C., Chapel Hill, 1983-88, leader immunology program Lineberger Cancer Ctr., 1983-91, Sarah Graham Kenan prof., 1988—; chmn. dept. micro immunology U. N.C., 1991—; cons. NIH, Bethesda, Md., 1978-83, VA, Washington, 1983-86, Nat. Inst. Gen. Med. Scis., Bethesda, 1986. Contbr. numerous articles to profl. jours. NIH grantee, 1978—; vis. fellow Trinity Coll., U. Oxford, 1989-90. Mem. AAAS, Am. Assn. Immunologists, Am. Soc. Microbiology, Sigma Xi. Office: U NC Cb 7290 Flob Chapel Hill NC 27599

FREMONT-SMITH, RICHARD, retired federal health care executive; b. Boston, Mar. 11, 1935; s. Maurice and Mary Dixon (Thayer) F.-S. Student, Harvard U., 1954-56; MBA, Columbia U., 1969; grad. cert., George Washington U., 1971; cert., Yale U., 1986. Enlisted USCG, 1956, advanced through grades to lt., 1966, served in Vietnam, 1965-66, resigned from active duty, 1966; advanced from lt. comdr. to capt USCGR, 1966-82; recalled to active duty USCG, 1982, dir. special projects Washington hdqrs., 1982-84, released from active duty, 1984, asst. chief med. adminstrn. Washington hdqrs., 1985-87, liaison officer to Asst. Sec. Defense, 1987-94; fed. account rep. Xerox Corp., Boston, 1970-71; stockbroker Paine, Webber, Jackson & Curtis, Boston, 1969-70; asst. dir. Peter Bent Brigham Hosp., Boston, 1972-75; assoc. dir. Bay State Profl. Stds. Rev. Orgn., Boston, 1975-78; v.p. Qualicare Inc., Boston, 1978-80, R.A. Wiegand and Co. Inc., Boston, 1980-81; dir. internal mgmt. controls directorate Office of Asst. Sec. Def., Washington, 1993-94; dir. spl. projects USCG Hdqtrs., Washington, 1994; ret., 1994. Contbr. articles to profl. jours. Bd. dirs. ARC, Boston, L.A., disaster relief officer nat. ARC staff, 1952—; chmn. ops. Boston chpt., 1980, vice chmn. disaster svcs., 1978-82, mem. exec. com., 1978-82, bd. dirs., 1972-82, chief asst. med. disaster officer Boston, chem. emergency med. svcs. transp. com. Boston, 1973-78. Decorated Bronze Star medal, and many others; fellow Kings Fund Coll., London, 1972. Mem. ARC Disaster Res., Mil. Order Loyal Legion (hon.). Home: 2401 E Las Olas Blvd Fort Lauderdale FL 33301-1572

FRENCH, BERTHA DORIS, medical, surgical and geriatrics nurse; b. Augusta Center, N.Y., Jan. 18, 1911; d. Charles Madison and Tillie (Hallenbeck) F. Diploma, Faxton Hosp. Sch. Nursing, Utica, N.Y., 1933. RN, N.Y., Tex. Pvt. duty nurse Brownsville, Tex.; dir. nurses Retama Manor Nursing Home, Brownsville, 1972, Valley Grande Manor Nursing Facility, Brownsville, 1973-76, PRN Home Health Agy., Brownsville; staff nurse Brownsville Med. Ctr.; relief dir. nursing svc. Village at Valley Inn, Brownsville, Brownsville Good Samaritan Ctr.; DON Ebony Lake Convalescent Ctr., 1990; nursing cons. Casa del Sol Adult Day Care Ctr., Brownsville, Harlingen, and San Benito, Tex., 1992-94; charge nurse, dir. Casa del Sol Adult Day Care Ctr. # 2 and #3, Brownsville, 1991—; adv. dir. J & J Home Health Agency; asst. Mary Lou Watkins, MD, PhD, 1994-95; cons. San Benito (Tex.) Adult Day Care Ctr., Happy Hearts Adult Day Care Ctr., Brownsville; guest spkr. LVN program Tex. Southmost Coll., 1990; pvt. duty for Gladys Porter; founder Gladys Porter Zoo, 1980. Recipient Recognition award Mayor of Brownsville, 1992. Home: 6070 Emilia Ln Brownsville TX 78520-9700

FRENCH, DANIEL LOGAN, residency administrator; b. Beckley, W.Va., Feb. 12, 1950; s. Charles Richard and Paula (Daniels) F.; m. Sharon Marie Prendergast, July 29, 1974; children: Rachael, Rebecca, Michael. BS, U. Tex., Arlington, 1971; MD, U. Tex., San Antonio, 1975. Diplomate Am. Bd. Family Practice. Resident in family medicine U.S. Army, Ft. Belvoir, Va., 1978-80; assoc. dir. Family Practice Residency, Ft. Benning, Ga., 1978-80; clin. asst. prof. primary care Emory U., Atlanta, 1978-80; assoc. dir. Family Practice Residency St. Elizabeth Med. Ctr., Edgewood, Ky., 1980-90, dir. Family Practice Residency, 1990—; assoc. prof. family practice U. Ky., Lexington, 1980—; bd. health No. Ky. Health Dept., 1986-88; chmn. AIDS Task Force of No. Ky., 1986-90. Founder, pres. Fairhaven Rescue Mission, Covington, Ky., 1983-91. Maj. U.S. Army, 1975-80. Fellow Am. Acad. Family Physicians; mem. Soc. Tchrs. of Family Medicine, Am. Geriatrics Soc. Office: St Elizabeth Family Practice Ctr 900 Medical Village Dr Edgewood KY 41017

FRENCH, LAURENCE ARMAND, education and psychology educator; b. Manchester, N.H., Mar. 24, 1941; s. Gerald Everett and Juliette Teresa (Boucher) F.; m. Nancy Picthall, Feb. 13, 1971. BA cum laude, U. N.H., 1968, MA, 1970, PhD, 1975; postdoctorate, SUNY, Albany, 1978; PhD, U. Nebr., 1981. Diplomate Am. Bd. Forensic Medicine, Am. Bd. Forensic Examiners; cert. psychologist, Ariz. Instr. U. So. Maine, Portland and Gorham, 1971-72; asst. prof. Western Carolina U., Cullowhee, N.C., 1972-77, U. Nebr., Lincoln, 1977-80; psychologist I N.H. Hosp., Concord, 1980-81; psychologist II Laconia (N.H.) State Sch., 1981-88; sr. psychologist N.H. Div. for Children & Youth Svcs., Concord, 1988-89; prof., chair dept. social scis. Western N.Mex. U., Silver City, 1989—; adj. assoc. prof. U. So. Maine, 1980-84; cons. N.C. Dept. Mental Health, 1972-77, Nebr. Indian Commn., Lincoln, 1977-80, Cherokee (N.C.) Indian Mental Health Program, 1974-77; cons. alcohol program Lincoln Indian Ctr., 1977-80. Author 7 books; contbr. articles to profl. jours. Commr. Pilsbury Lake Village Dist., Webster, N.H., 1985-90. With USMC, 1959-63. U. N.H. fellow, 1971-72, 72, Nebr. U. System fellow, 1978. Fellow APA; mem. NASP, Am. Soc. Criminology (life), Nat. Assn. Alcohol and Drug Abuse Counselors, N.Mex. Alcohol and Drug Abuse Counselors Assn., VFW, Phi Delta Kappa (treas. 1990-91, pres. 1991-92). Office: Western NMex U Dept Social Scis Silver City NM 88062

FRENCH, MICHAEL FRANCIS, non-profit education agency administrator; b. La Crosse, Wis., July 25, 1948; s. Albert Frank Jr. and Kathryn Patricia (MacKoske) F.; m. Janet Alan Streeter Head, Nov. 26, 1991. BS in Edn., U. Wis., 1972. Cert. emergency med. technician. Tng. coord. emergency med. svcs. Wis. Dept. Health and Social Svcs., Madison, 1975-80, tng. dir. emergency med. svcs., 1980-84, chief emergency med. svcs., 1984-90; co-dir. Mo. Rural AHEC Kirksville (Mo.) Coll. Osteo. Medicine, 1990—, adj. instr. community health, 1990—; emergency med. svcs. cons., Kirksville, 1984—; founding mem. Continuing Edn. Coordinating Bd. for Emergency Med. Svcs., Inc., Kirksville, 1992. Author: (tng. curriculum) EMS Instructor Training Course-U.S. Dept. Transportation, 1985; editor newsletter, editor-in-chief publs. Nat. Assn. Emergency Med. Technicians, 1983-91; author book chpts. V.p., pres. bd. dirs. Adair County Ret. Sr. Vol. Program, Kirksville, 1992-95. Recipient Lunda Trauma award Am. Trauma Soc., 1982, Svc. awards Nat. Coun. State EMS Tng. Coords., 1982, 83, A. Roger Fox Founders award Nat. Assn. Emergency Med. Technicians, 1989, others. Mem. ASTM, ASCD, ASTD, APHA, Nat. Rural Health Assn. (bd. dirs. 1995-96, pres.-elect 1996—), Mo. PEW Health Professions Partnership (chair exec. com. 1994-95), Mo. Pub. Health Assn., Wis. Emergency Med. Tech. Assn., Profl. Emergency Educators Assn., Mensa. Office: Mo Rural AHEC Program 800 W Jefferson St Kirksville MO 63501-1443

FRENCH, OLIVER (HAROLD), psychiatrist; b. Berlin, Germany, Sept. 3, 1921; came to U.S., 1957; s. Hermann Emil and Mathilde Charlotte (Cohn) Freund; m. Hannah Adler, Aug. 21, 1949 (dec. Nov. 1972); children: Deborah, Naomi, Jacqueline; m. Norma Prendergast, July 1, 1984. BA, Cambridge (Eng.) U., 1948, MB BChir, 1952, MA, 1987. Diplomate Am. Bd. Anesthesiology, Am. Bd. Psychiatry. Anaesthetic registrar Oxford U., England, 1955-57; anesthesiologist South Nassau Communities Hosp., Oceanside, N.Y., 1958-69; dir. anesthesiology South Oaks Hosp., Amityville, N.Y., 1969-74; assoc. dir. anesthesiology South Nassau Communities Hosp., Oceanside, 1964-69; assoc. clin. prof. U. Ky., Lexington, 1974-76; instr. psychiatry Rochester (N.Y.) U., 1977; chief psychiatrist Tompkins County Mental Health Svcs., Ithaca, N.Y., 1978-81, 90-95; med. dir. Dept. Psychiatry Tompkins Community Hosp., Ithaca, 1981-84, 90, psychiatrist in pvt. practice, 1981-95; cons. in field. Contbr. articles to profl. jours. Mem. Am. Psychiat. Assn., Am. Soc. for Clin. Hypnosis, Internat. Soc. for the Study of Multiple Personality. Democrat.

FRENI, D. RICHARD, general and thoracic surgeon, consultant, retired; b. Boston, Jan. 12, 1914; s. Louis and Pauline (Patti) F.; m. Dorothy A. Hannon, June 20, 1943; children: Richard Hannon, Donna Ann, Edward Christopher, Dorothy Hannon Freni Parker. AB, Harvard Coll., 1936; MD, Tufts U., 1942. Diplomate Am. Bd. Surgery, Nat. Bd. Med. Examiners. Intern dept. surgery Kings County Hosp., Bklyn., 1942-43; resident dept. surgery VA Hosp., West Roxbury, Mass., 1948-50, asst. chief of surgery, 1948-50; gen. surgery Lynn and Lynnfield, Mass., 1950-77; physician GE Dispensary, Lynn, Mass., 1939-42, 50-51; surg. cons. Raytheon, West Andover, Mass., 1974-76; surg. asst. West Roxbury VA Hosp. and affiliation with Mass. Gen. Hosp., Boston, 1946-48; asst. chief surgery West Roxbury VA Hosp., 1948-50; visiting surgeon Lynn (Mass.) Hosp., 1950, Union Hosp., Lynn, 1950; cons. surgeon Mary Alley Hosp., Marblehead, Mass., 1950, Danvers (Mass.) State Hosp., 1952; courtesy surgeon North Shore Children's Hosp., Salem, Mass., 1950; asst. surgeon in hand surgery VA Hosp., West Roxbury, 1950-56, VA Hosp., Jamaica Plain, Mass., 1950-62; asst. vis. surgeon Med. Sch. Tufts U., 1949-53; dir. teaching svcs. surgery Lynn Hosp.; assoc. chief surgery Lynn Hosp. 1961-69, Union Hosp., 1961-69; chief surgery Union Hosp., 1969-74, pres. med. staff, 1969-74, bd. trustees, 1969-84. Contbr. articles to profl. jours. Lt. USN Med. Corps, 1943. Fellow Am. Coll. Surgeons (trauma com.), Am. Geriatric Soc., Harvard Engring. Soc.; mem. AMA, Mass. Med. Soc. (coun. 1958-60), Boston Surg. Soc., Mass. Soc. Examining Physicians and Surgeons, New Eng. Surg. Soc., Essex Surg. Soc. (pres. 1968, 69), Govs. Island Club, Sr. Physicians Assn., Salem Country Club, Harvard Club Boston, Laconia Country Club. Roman Catholic. Home and Office: 1578 S Ocean Ln Apt 114 Fort Lauderdale FL 33316-3320

FRENKEL, KRYSTYNA, biochemist; b. Bialystok, USSR, Mar. 2, 1941; came to U.S., 1969; d. Henryk and Stefania (Szulc) F.; m. Nathan Julius Siegel, Feb. 13, 1977. MS, Warsaw U., 1964; PhD, NYU, 1974. Rsch. sci./organic chemistry instr. Warsaw (Poland) U., 1964-68; asst. rsch. scientist environ. medicine NYU Med. Ctr., 1969-74; staff assoc. Columbia U., N.Y.C., 1976-77; assoc rsch. scientist, asst. prof. pathology NYU Med. Ctr., 1977-88, asst. prof. environ. medicine, 1984-88, assoc. prof. environ. medicine and pathology, 1988-93, prof. environ. medicine and pathology, 1993—, dir. Lab. Oxidative Mech. in Carcinogenesis, 1990—; ad hoc mem. chem. pathology study sect. NIH, Bethesda, Md., 1990, mem., 1991-95; mem. reviewer res. NIH, 1995—; mem. study sect. Health Effects Inst., Cambridge, Mass., 1990; invited participant numerous nat. and internat. confs. Mem. editorial bd. Mutation Rsch.-DNA Repair, 1995—; contbr. articles to Cancer Rsch., Environ. Health Perspectives, Analytical Biochemistry, Carcinogenesis, Cancer Detection and Prevention, others. Recipient Young Environ. Sci. award Nat. Inst. Environ. Health Scis., 1979. Mem. Am. Assn. for Cancer Rsch., Am. Chem. Soc., The Oxygen Soc., N.Y. Acad. Scis., Internat. Soc. for Preventive Oncology. Office: NYU Med Ctr 550 1st Ave New York NY 10016-6481

FRENKEL, SALLY, research scientist, anatomy educator, researcher; b. N.Y.C., Oct. 24, 1949; d. David and Mina Rottenstreich; m. David Frenkel, June 23, 1970; children: Donny, Uri, Ronit. BA, Yeshiva U., 1971; MS, St. John's U., 1974; PhD, NYU, 1989. Instr. NYU Dental Sch., N.C.Y., 1983—, Albert Einstein Med. Sch., N.C.Y., 1988—; instr. anatomy City U., N.Y.C., 1983—; rsch. fellow Hosp. for Joint Diseases, N.C.Y., 1989, rsch. scientist in cell biology, 1990—; dir. cartilage repair rsch. Hosp. for Joint Diseases. Contbr. chpts. to books, articles to profl. jours. Rsch. grantee N.Y. Arthritis Found., 1991-92, 93-94, 95—, Musculoskeletal Transplant Found., 1992, 94, NIH, 1995-96, 96-97. Mem. AAAS, N.Y. Acad. Scis., Assn. Women in Sci., Orthopaedic Rsch. Soc., Soc. for Biomaterials.

FRENSILLI, FREDERICK JOHN, surgeon, urologist; b. Boston, Jan. 28, 1936; s. John Anthony and Teresa (Nardi) F.; m. Patricia Ann Parrott, Nov. 20, 1960 (div. 1984); children: Carol, Susan, Janet; m. Esme Maureen Dwyer, June 3, 1988. AB cum laude, Holy Cross Coll., 1957; MD, Georgetown U., 1961. Diplomate Am. Bd. Urology. Chief of urology Naval Hosp., Charleston, S.C., 1967-70; clin. assoc. U. S.C., Charleston, 1967-70; assoc. prof. urology George Washington Med. Sch., Washington, 1971-75, clin. prof. urology, 1975—; vice chmn. dept. urology Sibley Meml. Hosp., Washington, 1991-95, chmn. dept. urology, 1995—; pres. Georgetown Clin. Soc., Washington, 1980-81. Author: Medical Center's Introduction to Medical Terminology, 1978; contbr. nuymerous articles to profl. jours. Cmmdr. U.S.N., 1960-71. Fellow Am. Coll. Surgeons (pres. Washington chpt. 1986-87), Internat. Coll. Surgeons; mem. AMA, Am. Urology Soc., Soc. Univ. Urologists, Am. Fertility Soc. Republican. Roman Catholic. Office: Frederick Frensilli MD 5530 Wisconsin Ave Chevy Chase MD 20815-4404

FRENZ, DOROTHY ANN, cell and developmental biologist; b. New Rochelle, N.Y., Jan. 17, 1954; d. Anthony Joseph and Angelina Marie (Guida) Chiodo; m. Michael Richard Frenz, Sept. 15, 1974; children: Christopher, Elizabeth. BA summa cum laude, Iona Coll., 1978; MS, N.Y. Med. Coll., 1986, PhD, 1988. Postdoctoral fellow Albert Einstein Coll. Medicine, Bronx, N.Y., 1988-91; asst. prof. dept. otolaryngology Albert Einstein Coll. Medicine, Bronx, 1991—, asst. dir. rsch., 1993—, anatomy instr., 1991-92, asst. prof. anatomy and structural biology, 1993—; chairperson resident rsch. com. Albert Einstein Coll. Medicine, 1991—, senator faculty senate, 1991—. Contbr. chpts. in books and articles to profl. jours. Bd. dirs. New Rochelle YMCA, Songcatchers, Inc.; pres. Isaac E. Young Mid. Sch. PTA, 1992-93, mem. adv. coun., 1993-94; tchr., lectr. Blessed Sacrament Ch., New Rochelle, 1986—, parish bull. editor, 1988—, parish coun. rec. sec., 1990—, pa5rish trustee. Recipient Martha Pate award N.Y. Med. Coll., 1988, New Rochelle Interreligions Coun. award, 1995. Mem. Soc. for Cell Biology, N.Y. Acad. Sci., Assn. for Rsch. in Otolaryngology. Roman Catholic. Office: A Einstein Coll Medicine 1300 Morris Park Ave Bronx NY 10461-1926

FRENZ, JOHN A., neurosurgeon; m. Marie T. Frenz; children: John, Gretchen, David, Gary, Dale, Alexis, Jordan Marie, Jayne. BA, Ohio State U. Diplomate Am. Bd. Neurol. and Orthopaedic Surgery, Am. Bd. Clin. Neurosurgery, Am. Bd. Spinal Surgery. Intern Riverside Meth. Hosp., Columbus, Ohio, 1968-69, resident in neurosurgery, 1969-74; active staff Rankin Med. Ctr. Hosp., Brandon, Miss., 1980—. Lt. comdr. USN, Med. Corps Res., 1964-94. Mem. AMA, Am. Acad. Neurol. and Orthopaedic Medicine and Surgery, So. Med. Assn., Am. Physicians Assn., Miss. State Neurosurg. Soc., Miss. State Med. Assn., Cen. Miss. Med. Soc., Mid-Atlantic and Pa. Neurosurg. Soc., Ohio State Med. Assn., Miss. Neurosurg. Soc. Office: 346 Crossgates Blvd Brandon MS 39042

FRERE, ROBERT C., neurologist; b. Cleve., Nov. 24, 1953; s. Ralph Emil and Katherine (Gilbo) F.; m. Susan Cramer Gilliam, Oct. 17, 1981; children; Elizabeth, Garrett, Zachary, Olivia. BS, The Ohio State U., 1975, MD, 1984; MS, U. Mich., 1981. Diplomate Nat. Bd. Med. Examiners, Am. Bd. Psychiatry and Neurology, Am. Bd. Clin. Neurophysiology, Am. Bd. Electrodiagnostic Medicine. Secondary sci. tchr. in French The Peace Corps, Zaire, Africa, 1975-77; quality control analyst The Harshaw Chem. Co., Elyria, Ohio, 1978-79; rsch. asst. dept. neurology U. Mich. Med. Sch., 79-81; intern in internal medicine Ohio State U. Hosps., 1984-85; neurology resident Barnes Hosp., St. Louis, 1985-88; clin. neurophysiology fellowship Mayo Clinic, Rochester, Minn., 1988-89; staff neurologist, dept. medicine St. John's Mercy Med. Ctr., St. Louis, 1989—; mem. profl. adv. bd. Epilepsy Found. of St. Louis, 1995—. Fellow Am. Electroencephalographic Soc.; mem. Am. Acad. Neurology, Mayo Alumni Assn., Am. Epilepsy Soc., St. Louis Soc. Neurol. Scis., Am. Assn. Electrodiagnostic Medicine. Home: 346 Pebble Valley Dr Saint Louis MO 63141 Office: St Johns Mercy Med Ctr 621 S New Ballas Saint Louis MO 63141

FRESHWATER, MICHAEL FELIX, surgeon, educator; b. N.Y.C., Feb. 4, 1948; s. Jack and Rhonda F. BS magna cum laude, Bklyn. Coll., 1968; MD, Yale U., 1972. Diplomate Nat. Bd. Med. Examiners, Am. Bd. Plastic Surgery (cert. in surgery of hand). Asst. resident in surgery Yale New Haven Hosp., 1972-74; fellow in plastic surgery Med. Sch. Johns Hopkins U., Balt., 1974-77; resident, then chief resident in plastic surgery Jackson Meml. Hosp., 1977-78; Kleinert fellow hand and microsurgery U. Louisville, 1979; pvt. practice medicine specializing in hand surgery Miami, 1979—; pres., dir. Miami (Fla.) Inst. Hand and Microsurgery, 1980—; dir. hand and microsurgery Cedars Med. Ctr., 1985—, chief surgery, 1988-90, bd. dirs., 1990-92; faculty U. Miami Sch. Medicine, 1979—, Barry U. Sch. Podiatric Medicine and Surgery, 1989—; vis. prof. Javeriana U., Bogota, 1983-85, Centro Medico de los Andes, 1983-86; cons. Fla. Children's Med. Svc., Tallahassee, 1979—, Fla. Elks Crippled Children Soc., Orlando, 1983—, Fla. Dept. Bus. and Profl. Regulation, Tallahassee, 1984—, League Against Cancer, 1983—, Scientists Inst. for Pub. Info., 1985—, USCG, Miami Beach, 1992—. Contbr. chpts. to books and articles to profl. jours.; mem. bd. reviewers Plastic and Reconstructive Surgery, 1976—, Internat. Abstracts of Plastic Surgery, 1987—. Trustee Yale U. Med. Libr., New Haven, 1972-77, D.R. Millard Found., 1987—; bd. dirs. V and A Gildred Found., Miami, 1980-86; bd. dirs. Yale Sch. Medicine Fund, 1991—; active nat. campaign com. Yale Sch. Medicine, 1993—. Recipient Letter Commendation Gov. Bob Graham, 1984; Weinberger fellow NIH, 1974-76; Jonas Salk scholar CUNY, 1968-72. Fellow Internat. Coll. Surgeons; mem. AMA (Physicians Recognition award 1976, 79, 82, 85, 88, 90, 93, 96), Am. Assn. Hand Surgery, Am. Burn Assn., Am. Soc. Reconstructive Microsurgery, Internat. Soc. Reconstructive Microsurgery, Royal Soc. Medicine, Greater Miami Soc. Plastic and Reconstructive Surgeons (sec.-treas. 1987-88, pres.-elect 1988-89, pres. 1989-90), Am. Soc. Peripheral Nerve, Miami Assn. for Surgery of Hand (dir. 1991—), Yale Club (Miami, N.Y.), Grove Isle Club (Miami), Phi Beta Kappa. Office: Biscayne Med Arts Plaza Ste 201 21110 Biscayne Blvd Miami FL 33180-1228

FREUDENBERGER, HERBERT JUSTIN, psychoanalyst; b. Frankfurt, Germany, Nov. 26, 1926; came to U.S., 1938; s. Joseph and Jenny (Braunschweiger) F.; m. Arlene F. Somer, Dec. 24, 1960; children: Lisa, Marc, Lori. BA, Bkly. Coll., 1952; MA, NYU, 1953, PhD, 1956. Practice of psychoanalysis-group therapy, N.Y.C., 1954—; asst. prof. psychology N.Y.U., 1963-72; assoc. attending psychoanalyst Stuyvesant Hosp., 1961-67; cons. Haight Asbury Clinic, 1968-70, Mt. Vernon Drug Abuse Council, 1968-77, S.E.R.A. (hispanic drug therapeutic community), 1970-74, social actions program USAF, 1971-76, Tng. for Living Agy., 1972-76; staff trainor N.Y.C. Addiction Svcs. Agy., 1972-76; clin. tng. cons. Daytop Village, Covenant House, 1973-77; cons. drug abuse prevention N.Y. Archdiocese, 1973-89; cons. staff tng. Phoenix House, N.Y.C. Nat. co-chmn. Nat. Council on Grad. Edn., 1968-74. Mem. Mayor's Social Scientists Adv. Com., 1965-68, Dep. Mayor's Chem. Abuse Com., N.Y.C. Bd. dirs. Joint Council for Mental Health, 1968-71, Psychol. Svc. Ctr., 1965-68, Jewish Inst. for Blind, 1960-90; dir. psychol svcs. St. Marks Free Clinic, 1969-71. Recipient Psychologist of Yr. award Am. Soc. Psychologists in Ind. Practice, Disting. Psychologist award div. Am. Psychol. Assn. Fellow Am. Psychol. Assn. (dir. 1972-80, pres. div. psychotherapy 1980-82, pres. div. ind. practice 1982-84, Psychologist of Yr. award div. psychotherapy 1983, presdl. citation 1990, Karl F. Heiser APA-Spl. Presdl. award 1992, Disting. Prof. award 1993, Psychologist of Yr. award 1993). Fellow Clin. Psychology, Psychotherapy, Health and Addiction Psychology; mem. N.Y. Soc. Clin. Psychologist (dir. 1960-68, pres. 1965-67, 78-79), Nat. Assn. Psychoanalysts (dir. 1965-70, sr. mem. faculty 1960—), Nat. Acads. Practice (founding mem., sec. 1981-93), Internat. Council Alcohol and Addictions. Author: Burnout-The High Cost of High Achievement, 1981, Situational Anxiety, 1982, Women's Burnout, 1985; assoc. editor: History of Pshychotherapy: A Century of Change, Profl. Psychology, 1970-79, Jour. Psychotherapy, 1973—; exec. bd. Jour. Psychedelic Drugs, Jour. Selected Documents, 1975-80; contbr. articles to Fame mag., 1988-91. Office: 18 E 87th St New York NY 10128-0505

FREUND, CYNTHIA M., dean, nursing educator. BSN, Marquette U., 1963; MSN, U. N.C., 1973, FNP, 1974; PhD in Bus. and Health Adminstrn., U. Ala., 1981. Staff nurse McHenry (Ill.) Hosp., 1963, 64-65, VA Hosp., Wood, Wis., 1963-64; instr. Milw. County Instns., Wauwatosa, Wis., 1965-68, supr. Milw. County Rehab. and Chronic Disease Hosp., 1968-70; instr. Sch. Nursing U. Wis., Milw., 1972-73; dir. FNP program Area L Health Edn. Ctr., Tarboro, N.C., 1973-74; asst. prof., assoc. dir. FNP program U. N.C., Chapel Hill, 1974-78, assoc. prof., chair social and adminstrv. sys. dept., 1984-92, dean, prof. nursing, 1992—; asst. prof U. Pa., Phila., 1981-84, sr. rsch. assoc. Leonard Davis Inst. Health Econs., 1981-84, dir. MSN nursing adminstrn. program, PhD in nursing/MBA joint degree, 1981-84; mem. Gov. Advocacy Com. for Children and Youth State of Wis., 1973; mem. N.C. Med. Data Base Commn., N.C. Gen. Assembly, 1985-89; mem. nursing adv. panel P.E.W. Health Professions Commn., 1991-92; mem. nat. adv. com. for project future requirements for nurse practitioners and nurse midwives Dept. Health and Human Svcs., 1993-94, mem. joint adv. com. to project future requirements for primary care physicians, and others, Bur. Health Professions, 1994-95; cons., presenter in field. Author: (with D. del Bueno) Power and Politics in Nursing Administration, 1986 (Am. Jour Nursing Book of Yr. 1986), Nursing: A Kaleidoscopic View, 1991 (Am. Jour. Nursing Book of Yr. 1991); author chpts. to books; mem. editl. bd. Nursing Econs., 1982-84, manuscript reviewer, 1982—; manuscript reviewer Jour. Profl. Nursing, 1984—, Health Svc. Rsch., 1984—, Planning for Higher Edn., 1986; contbr. articles to profl. jours. Pub. Health Svc. Doctoral fellow Nat. Ctr. for Health Svcs. Rsch., 1980-81, Rsch. fellow Nat. Health Care Mgmt. Ctr., 1980-81; recipient Profl. Svc. Alumni award Marquette U., 1992. Fellow Am. Acad. Nursing; mem. ANA (vice-chair coun. FNP and clinicians 1977-78, cert. adult nurse practitioner 1977, Jessie M. Scott award 1990), Nat. League Nursing, Acad. Mgmt., Am. Orgn. Nurse Execs., Am. Hosp. Assn. Office: U NC Sch Nursing CB # 7460 Carrington Hall Chapel Hill NC 27599-7460*

FREUND, EMMA FRANCES, medical technologist; b. Washington; d. Walter R. and Mabel W. (Loveland) Ervin; m. Frederic Reinert Freund, Mar. 4, 1953; children: Frances, Daphne, Fern, Frederic. BS, Wilson Tchrs. Coll., Washington, 1944; MS in Biology, Catholic U., Washington, 1953; MEd in Adult Edn., Va. Commonwealth U., 1988; cert. in mgmt. devel. Va. Commonwealth U., 1975, supr. devel.; student SUNY, New Paltz, 1977, J. Sargeant Reynolds C.C., 1978. Cert. Nat. Cert. Agy. for Clin. Lab. Pers, supervisory devel., Va. Tchr. math. and sci. D.C. Sch. System, Washington, 1944-45; technician in parasitology lab., zool. div., U.S. Dept. Agr., Beltsville, Md., 1945-48; histologic technician dept. pathology Georgetown U. Med. Sch., Washington, 1948-49; clin. lab. technician Kent and Queen Anne's County Gen. Hosp., Chestertown, Md., 1949-51; histotechnologist surg. pathology dept. Med. Coll. Va. Hosp., Richmond, 1951—, supr. histology lab., 1970-88, mgr., supr. 1988—; cons. profl. meetings and workshops histotechnology, head infosvcs. Histo-Help; mem. exam. coun. Nat. Cert. Agy. Med. Lab. Pers. Asst. cub scout den leader Robert E. Lee coun. Boy Scouts Am., 1967-68, den leader, 1968-70. Co-author: (mini-course) Instrumentation in Cytology and Histology, 1985; editor Histo-Scope Newsletter. Mem. AAAS, NAFE, AAUW, Am. Soc. CLin. Lab. Sci. (rep. to sci. assembly histology sect. 1977-78, chmn. histology sect. 1983-85, 89-96), Va. Soc. Med. Technology, Richmond Soc. Med. Technologists (corr. sec. 1977-78, dir. 1981-82, pres. 1984-85), Va. State Soc. Histotechnology (pres. 1994—), Nat. Certification Agy. (clin. lab. specialist in histotech., clin. lab. supr., clin. lab. dir.), N.Y. Acad. Scis., Am. Assn. Clin. Chemistry (assoc.), Am. Soc. Clin. Pathologists (cert. histology technician), Nat. Geog. Soc., Va. Govtl. Employees Assn., Nat. Soc. Histotech. (by-laws com. 1981—; C.E.U. com. 1981—, program com. regional meeting 1984, 85, chmn. regional meeting 1987, program chmn. regional mtg. 1992), Am. Mus. Natural History, Smithsonian Instn., Am. Mgmt. Assn., Clin. Lab. Mgmt. Assn., Nat. Soc. Historic Preservation, Sigma Xi, Phi Beta Rho, Kappa Delta Pi, Phi Lambda Theta, Omicron Sigma. Home: 1315 Asbury Rd Richmond VA 23229-5305

FREUND, NORMAN LAWRENCE, colon and rectal surgeon; b. N.Y.C., Jan. 17, 1914; s. Morris and Sadie (Jacobson) F.; m. Mildred Weitzman, May 1, 1938 (dec. Sept., 1992); children: Diane Morgan, Sandra Mandell; m. Sylvia Barnett, Sept. 25, 1994. BS, N.Y.U., 1933; MD, U. Edinburgh, Scotland, 1938. Attending in charge proctologist Maimouides Hosp., Bklyn., 1941-94; preceptor Meyer Freund M.D., 1943-48; attending proctologist Kings Highway Hosp., Bklyn., 1943-94; cons. proctologist St. John's Hosp., Bklyn., 1960-68. With U.S. Army, 1944-45. Fellow Am. Soc. Colon and Rectal Surgeons, N.Y. Soc. Colon and Rectal Surgeons (sec. 1956-60, v.p. 1961-62, pres. 1963-64). Home: 4702 Fountains Dr S Lake Worth FL 33467

FREY, CHARLES FREDERICK, surgeon, educator; b. N.Y.C., Nov. 15, 1929; s. Charles N. and Julia (Leary) F.; m. Jane Louise Tower, July 20, 1957; children: Jane Elizabeth, Susan Ann, Charles Frederick, Robert Tower, Nancy Louise. BA, Amherst Coll., 1951; MD, Cornell U., 1955. Diplomate Am. Bd. Surgery. Intern Cornell Med. Ctr., N.Y.C., 1955-56, asst. resident, 1956-57, 59-61, 1st asst. resident, 1962, chief resident, 1963; instr. surgery U. Mich., Ann Arbor, 1964-65, asst. prof. surgery, 1965-68, assoc. prof., 1968-72, prof., 1972-76; prof. U. Calif., Davis, 1976—, vice. chmn. dept. surgery, 1976-81, exec. vice-chmn. dept., 1981-95; mem. staff VA Hosp., Martinez, Calif., chief surg. service, 1976-80; attending surgeon Sutter Hosps., Sacramento; surg. cons. U. Mich., 1966-76, VA, 1971—, Highway Safety Research Inst., 1973-76. Assoc. editor, mem. editorial bd. The Pancreas, Internat. Jour. of Pancreatology; mem. editorial bd. Western Jour. Medicine, Jour. Gastrointestinal Surgery; contbr. numerous articles to profl. jours. Served to capt. USAF, 1957-59. Fellow ACS (chief regional com. on trauma 1976-89, disaster preparedness com. 1978—, med. motion picutres com. 1981-91, allied health com. 1981-82, program com. No. Calif. chpt., 1981—, credentials com. No. Calif. chpt. 1982—, mem. bd. govs. 1989-94, gov. 1988-94, adv. com. on ambulatory surgery, chmn. ambulatory surg. care com. 1990-94, pres. No. Calif. chpt. 1995-96), Am. Assn. Surgery Trauma; mem. AMA, Calif. Med. Assn., El Dorado-Scarmento Med. Soc., Am. Fedn. Clin. Rsch., Am. Assn. Automotive Medicine (bd. dirs. 1970-74), Internat. Assn. Accident and Traffic Medicine, Am. Trauma Soc. (founding, standards devel. com. 1978—, v.p. Calif. divsn. 1979—, bd. dirs. 1980—), Calif. Trauma Soc. (trustee 1977—), Nat. Trauma Com. of ACS (chmn. membership com. 1980-84, exec. com. 1981-85), Assn. Acad. Surgery, Am. Surg. Assn., Brazilian Surg. Soc., Western Surg. Assn., Ctrl. Surg. Assn. (membership com. 1971-73), Pacific Coast Surg. Assn., Sacramento Surg. Soc. (pres. 1994), Assn. VA Surgeons (publs., program coms. 1981—), Soc. Univ. Surgeons, Soc. Surgery Alimentary Tract (constn. and by-laws com. 1969—, chmn. 1972-76, v.p. 1995-96), Internat. Assn. Pancreatology (mem. editl. bd. 1986, steering com.), Internat. Biliary Assn., Am. Gastroenterology Assn., Pancreas Club (chmn. 1975—). Home: 11450 Grinding Rock Pl Gold River CA 95670-7703 Office: U Calif Med Ctr Dept Surgery 4301 X St Sacramento CA 95817-2214

FREY, HARLEY HARRISON, JR., anesthesiologist; b. Toledo, Feb. 22, 1920; s. Harley Harrison and Mina Rosina (Wiedemann) F.; m. Jane Luceia Murray, Aug. 28, 1944 (dec. 1964); children: Richard E., Martha J., Thomas C.; m. Emma Jean Hamilton, Apr. 15, 1966; 1 stepchild, Rick A. Gregory. BS, U. Toledo, 1942; MD, U. Cin., 1945. Diplomate Am. Bd. Anesthesiology. Intern Akron City Hosp., Ohio, 1946-49; fellow anesthesia U. Minn., Mpls., 1950; hon. mem. staff St. Elizabeth Hosp. Med. Ctr., Lafayette, Ind., 1950—, Lafayette Home Hosp., 1950—. Bd. dirs. Lafayette Symphony Orch., 1952-54; counselor, committeeman Lafayette coun. Boy Scouts Am., 1955-63; ruling elder Presbyn. Ch., 1964-67, active deacon, 1991-94; bd. dirs. Lafayette Citizens Band, 1996—. Fellow Am. Coll. Anesthesiology; mem. Am. Soc. Anesthesiology (bd. dirs. 1965-74), Ind. Soc. Anesthesiology (pres., bd. dirs. 1961-74, Disting Svc. award 1992), Ind. State Med. Soc. (Cert. Distinction 1995), Tippecanoe County Med. soc. (pres. 1961), Rotary (bd. dirs. 1992-95) Lafayette Country Club (bd. dirs. 1963-65). Home and Office: 3513 Creek Ridge Lafayette IN 47905-5619 Office: 2323 Ferry St Ste 209 Lafayette IN 47904

FREY, JAMES L., ophthalmologist; b. Detroit, Mar. 15, 1920; s. J. Leonard and Jemima Ruth (Goudie) F.; m. Natalie Elizabeth Mattern, May 20, 1950; children: Kirk A., Eric D. BS, U. Chgo., 1942, MD, 1944. Diplomate Am. Bd. Ophthalmology. Intern U. Chgo. Clinics, 1945; resident Harper Hosp., Detroit, 1948-50, staff ophthalmologist, 1950-76; staff ophthalmologist William Beaumont Hosp., Royal Oaks, Mich., 1960-76, Providence Hosp., Southfield, Mich., 1962-76, Henry Ford Hosp., West Bloomfield, Mich., 1976—. Lt. USN, 1945-47, 52-54. Fellow ACS; mem. AMA, Am. Acad. Ophthalmology, Eye Study Club, Mich. State Med. Soc., Detroit Ophthalmological Club, Oakland County Med. Soc. (treas. 1960—). Home: 4316 Echo Rd Bloomfield Hills MI 48302 Office: Henry Ford Hosp 6777 West Maple Rd West Bloomfield MI 48322

FREYD, JENNIFER JOY, psychology educator; b. Providence, Oct. 16, 1957; d. Peter John and Pamela (Parker) F.; m. John Q. Johnson, June 9, 1984; children: Theodore, Philip, Alexandra. BA in Anthropology magna cum laude, U. Pa., 1979; PhD in Psychology, Stanford U., 1983. Asst. prof. psychology Cornell U., 1983-87, mem. faculty coun. of reps., 1986-87; assoc. prof. psychology U. Oreg., Eugene, 1987-92, prof., 1992—; mem. dean's adv. com. U. Oreg., 1990-91, 92-93, mem. exec. com. Ctr. for the Study of Women in Soc., 1991-93, mem. child care com., 1987-89, 90-91; fellow Ctr. for Advanced Study in the Behavioral Scis., 1989-90; elected mem. faculty coun. of reps. Cornell U., 1986-87; mem. dean's adv. com. U. Oreg., 1990—, exec. com. Ctr. for Rsch. Study of Women in Soc., 1991-92, Inst. of Cognitive and Decision Scis., 1991—. Author: Betrayal Trauma: The Logic of Forgetting Childhood Abuse, 1996; editl. bd. Jour. Exptl. Psychology: Learning, Memory, and Cognition, 1989-91; guest reviewer Am. Jour. Psychology, Am. Psychologist, others; contbr. articles to profl. jours. Recipient Graduate fellowship NSF, 1979-82, Univ. fellowship Stanford U., 1982-83, Presdl. Young Investigator award NSF, 1985-90, IBM Faculty Devel. award, 1985-87, fellowship Ctr. for Advanced Study in the Behavioral Scis., 1989-90, John Simon Meml. fellowship Guggenheim Found., 1989-90, Rsch. Scientist Devel. award NIMH, 1989-94; other rsch. funding. Fellow AAAS, APA, Am. Psychol. Soc.; mem. Psychonomic Soc., Sigma Xi. Office: U Oreg 1227 Dept Psychology Eugene OR 97403-1227

FREYMANN, JOHN GORDON, physician, educator; b. Omaha, Apr. 9, 1922; s. John Joseph and Marion (Wicks) F.; m. Ruth Ellen King, Dec. 16, 1950; children: Amanda, Martha, Sarah, Vance. BS, Yale U., 1944; MD, Harvard U., 1946; DSc, U. Nebr., 1982. Diplomate Am. Bd. Internal Medicine and Oncology. Asst. in medicine Mass. Gen. Hosp., Boston, 1954-59; dir. med. edn. Meml. Hosp., Worcester, Mass., 1959-65; gen dir. Boston Hosp. for Women, 1965-69; dir. edn. Hartford (Conn.) Hosp., 1969-75; pres. Nat. Fund for Med. Edn., Hartford, 1975-87; prof. dept. family medicine Sch. of Medicine U. Conn., Farmington, 1987—; pres. Ednl. Commn. for Fgn. Med. Grads., Phila., 1968-77; cons. div. manpower intelligence HEW, Washington, 1973-75; advisor nat. health ins. House Ways & Means Com., U.S. Congress, Washington, 1975. Author: American Health Care System, 1974 (Welch award 1975); author chpts. in books; contbr. numerous articles to profl. jours. Mem. Wayland (Mass.) Bd. of Health, 1957-69; treas. Farmington Land Trust Inc., 1978-94. Lt. USPHS, 1947-49, ETO. Commonwealth Fund grantee, 1970; recipient Welch Meml. award Nat. Assn. Blue Shield Plans, 1975, John E. Leonard award Assn. for Hosp. Med. Edn., 1981. Fellow ACP; mem. AMA (adv. com. grad. med. edn. 1969-75), Soc. Med. Adminstrs. (pres. 1980-81), Am. Assn. for History of Medicine, Alpha Omega Alpha, Phi Beta Kappa. Home: 2 Catalpa Ct Avon CT 06001-4510

FRIAS, JAIME LUIS, pediatrician, educator; b. Concepción, Chile, Mar. 20, 1933; came to U.S., 1970; s. Luis Humberto and Olga Ana (Fernandez) F.; m. Jacqueline May Steel, Apr. 8, 1961; children: Jaime Arturo, Juan Pablo, Patricio Andres, Maria Josefina. M.D., U. Chile, 1959. Diplomate Am. Bd. Pediatrics, Am. Bd. Human Genetics. Intern Hospital Regional, Concepcion, 1958-59; resident in pediatrics Calvo Mackenna Hosp., Santiago, Chile, 1960-62; clin. genetics and dysmorphology fellow U. Wis.-Madison, 1965-66, U. Wash., Seattle, 1966-67; asst. prof. pediatrics U. Concepcion, 1967-69, prof., 1969-70; asst. prof. pediatrics U. Fla. Coll. Medicine, Gainesville, 1970-74, assoc. prof., 1974-77, prof., 1977-86, chief div. genetics, 1977-86, chmn. med. sch. admissions com., 1983-86; prof. pediatrics U. Nebr. Med. Ctr., Omaha, 1986-91, chmn. dept. pediatrics, 1986-91; prof. pediatrics U. South Fla. Coll. of Medicine, chmn. dept. of pediatrics, 1991—, L.A. Barness prof. pediatrics, 1994—; chmn. Com. for Protection of Human Subjects, 1975-78; chmn. Fla. Com. on Prevention Devel. Disabilities, 1979-82, chmn. infant hearing screening adv. coun., 1982-86; cons. Spanish Collaborative Project on Congenital Malformation, Madrid, 1983—. Author chpts. to books; contbr. articles to profl. jours. Trustee All Children's Hosp; mem. exec. com. Assn. Med. Sch. Pediatric Dept. Chmn., 1993—. Named Tchr. of Yr. U. Fla. Coll. Medicine, 1978-79, Lewis A. Barness Endowed Chair Pediatrics, 1994. Mem. Am. Acad. Pediatrics (com. genetics 1995—), Am. Pediatric Soc., ACP (affiliate, W.K. Kellogg fellow 1965-67), Am. Soc. Human Genetics, Assn. Clin. Scientists, Tampa Yacht and Country Club, Tampa Club. Democrat. Roman Catholic. Office: U South Fla Dept Pediat 17 Davis Blvd Ste 200 Tampa FL 33606-3438

FRICK, OSCAR LIONEL, physician, educator; b. N.Y.C., Mar. 12, 1923; s. Oscar and Elizabeth (Ringger) F.; m. Mary Hubbard, Sept. 2, 1954. A.B., Cornell U., 1944, M.D., 1946; M.Med. Sci., U. Pa., 1960; Ph.D., Stanford U., 1964. Diplomate: Am. Bd. Allergy and Immunology (chmn. 1967-72). Intern Babies Hosp., Columbia Coll. Physicians and Surgeons, N.Y.C., 1946-47; resident Children's Hosp., Buffalo, 1950-51; pvt. practice medicine specializing in pediatrics Huntington, N.Y., 1951-58; fellow in allergy and immunology Royal Victoria Hosp., Montreal, Que., Can., 1958-59; fellow in allergy U. Calif.-San Francisco, 1959-60, asst. prof. pediatrics, 1964-67, assoc. prof., 1967-72, prof., 1972—, dir. allergy tng. program, 1964—; fellow immunology Inst. d'Immunobiologie, Hosp. Broussais, Paris, France, 1960-62. Contbr. articles papers to profl. publs. Served with M.C., USNR, 1947-49. Mem. Am. Assn. Immunologists, Am. Acad. Pediatrics (chmn. allergy sect. 1971-72, Bret Ratner award 1982), Am. Acad. Allergy (exec. com. 1972—, pres. 1977-78), Internat. Assn. Allergology and Clin. Immunology (exec. com. 1970-73, sec. gen. 1985—), Am. Pediatric Soc. Club: Masons. Home: 370 Parnassus Ave San Francisco CA 94117-3609

FRICKER, JOHN ARTHUR, pediatrician, educator; b. Detroit, Nov. 11, 1931; s. Franklin and Elizabeth Jane (Cossitt) F.; m. Patricia Alice Bedford, Sept. 10, 1955; children: Elizabeth Janet, Karen Paula. BA, Wayne U., 1956; MD, Western Res. U., 1961. Diplomate Am. Bd. Pediatrics (bd. mem. 1988—), Nat. Bd. Med. Examiners. Intern Yale-New Haven Med. Ctr., New Haven, 1961-62; asst. resident in pediatrics Yale-New Haven Med. Ctr., 1962-64, resident, 1964-65; pvt. practice pediatric and adolescent medicine L.A., 1965—; pediatrician, ptnr. So. Calif. Permanente Med. Group, L.A., 1965—; physician-in-charge Woodland Hills (Calif.) Clinic, 1977-83; pres. med. staff Kaiser Found. Hosp., Woodland Hills, 1985-86; instr. pediatrics Yale U. Sch. Medicine, 1964-65; clin. instr. pediatrics UCLA, 1968-72, clin. asst. prof., 1972-80, clin. assoc. prof., 1980-86, clin. prof., 1986—. Mem. diocesan coun. Episcopal Diocese L.A., 1976-84, 92-93, mem. standing com., 1980-84, 91-95, pres. standing com., 1993-94; dep. Gen. Conv. Episcopal Ch., New Orleans, 1982, L.A., 1985, Detroit, 1988, Phoenix, 1991, alt. dep., Indpls., 1994, Phila., 1997; hon. canon Cathedral Ctr. of St. Paul, 1993—; trustee The Ch. Div. Sch. of Pacific, Berkeley, Calif., 1992—. Recipient clin. teaching award dept. pediatrics UCLA, 1974, 78, 83, 84, 85, 91, 92, 93, 94, 95, 96, clin. tchg. award Kaiser Found. Hosp. Family Practice, 1996. Fellow Am. Acad. Pediatrics; mem. L.A. Pediatric Soc., Soc. for Adolescent Medicine. Democrat. Office: So Calif Permanente Med Group 5601 De Soto Ave Woodland Hills CA 91367-6701

FRIDAY, GILBERT ANTHONY, JR., pediatrician; b. Pitts., Apr. 16, 1930; s. Gilbert Anthony and Susan Dorothy (Kumer) F.; m. Christina Cecilia McShane, Sept. 12, 1959; children: Martin, Peter, Martha, Timothy, Amy, Anne, Robert. BS, Bucknell U., 1952; MD, Temple U., 1956. Diplomate Nat. Bd. Med. Examiners. Rotating intern Phila. Gen. Hosp., 1956-57; pediatric resident Children's Hosp. of Phila., 1960-62; pediatric resident Children's Hosp. of Pitts., 1962-63, asst. med. dir. ops., 1963-66, preceptorship in allergy/immunology, 1962-67; clin. instr. to asst. prof. U. Pitts., 1963-87, clin. assoc. prof., 1987, prof. pediatrics, 1987—; bd. dirs. Pa. Blue Shield, Camp Hill, 1979—, chmn. bd. dirs., 1992—. Contbr. articles to profl. jours., chpts. to books. Lt. comdr. USN MC, 1956-66. Wyeth Pediatric scholar. Fellow Am. Coll. Allergy, Asthma, and Immunology, Am. Acad. Allery, Asthma, and Immunology, Am. Acad. Pediats.; mem. AMA, Allegheny County Med. Soc. (pres. 1987), Pa. Med. Soc., Pa. Allergy Soc. (pres. 1975), Alpha Omega Alpha. Republican. Roman Catholic. Home: 1901 Highgate Rd Pittsburgh PA 15241-2210 Office: Children's Hosp of Pitts 3705 5th Ave Pittsburgh PA 15213-2524

FRIDLEY, JAMES OWEN, physician; b. Winchester, Va., July 30, 1941; s. Samuel Joseph and Ruby Virginia (Teets) F.; m. Marylin Lee Miller, June 14, 1967; children: Jason Davis, Joseph Owen, Laura Marie, Jonathan James. BS in Biology, W.Va. Wesleyan Coll., 1963; MD, W.Va. U., 1967. Intern Riverside Hosp., Newport News, Va., 1967-68; pvt. practice, Dunn, N.C., 1970-81; attending physician Betsy Johnson Meml. Hosp., Dunn, 1970-81, chief med. staff, 1973-74, chmn. coronary care com., 1973-80; attending physician Charles Parrish Meml. Nursing Ctr., Dunn, 1971-81; mem. Harnett County Bd. Health, Lillington, N.C., 1974-81; med. dir. E.A. Hawse Health Ctr., Baker, W.Va., 1982—, E.A. Hawse Continuous Care Ctr., Baker, 1985-90; med. advisor Wardensville (W.Va.) Vol. Rescue Squad, 1988—. Pres. Full Gospel Businessmen's Fellowship, Yellow Spring, W.Va., 1984-88. Capt. U.S. Army, 1968-70. Mem. AMA, Am. Acad. Family Physicians. Home: PO Box 67 55 Warden Circle Rd Wardensville WV 26851-0067 Office: E A Hawse Health Ctr PO Box 97 Baker WV 26801-0097

FRIED, BERNARD, parasitologist, biology educator; b. N.Y.C., Aug. 17, 1933; s. Harry and Anna (Bergstein) F.; m. Janet Avery, Aug. 25, 1959 (div.); 1 child, Neil; m. Grace Jean Evans, Jan. 31, 1969; 1 stepson, David. A.B., NYU, 1954; M.S., U. N.H., 1956; Ph.D., U. Conn., 1961. Postdoctoral fellow parasitology NIH, Emory U., Atlanta, 1961-63; asst. prof. Lafayette Coll., Easton, Pa., 1963-69, assoc. prof., 1969-75, Kreider prof. biology, 1975—; cons. thin-layer chromatography Ctr. Profl. Advancement, East Brunswick, N.J., Kontes Glassware, Vineland, N.J. Author: Thin Layer Chromatography, 1982, 3rd edit., 1994; contbr. over 300 articles to profl. jours. Recipient grants NIH, NSF, Research Corp. Mem. Am. Soc. Parasitologists (exec. council), Am. Micros. Soc., Helminthol. Soc. Washington, Pa. Acad. Sci. (pres. 1972-73), Internat. Soc. Chem. Ecology. Office: Lafayette Coll High St Easton PA 18042

FRIED, ELEANOR REINGOLD, psychologist, educator; b. Quantico, Va., Jan. 4, 1943; d. Morris and Eleanor (Wilson) R.; divorced, 1984; children: Joshua Mark, Noah Seth, Adam Lawrence. BS cum laude, Boston U., 1964; MS in Clin. Sch. Psychology, CUNY, 1971; postgrad. Fordham U., 1971-73; MA in Clin. Psychology, The Fielding Inst., 1980, PhD in Clin. Psychology, 1981. Lic. psychologist, N.J.; diplomate Am. Bd. Forensic Examiners. Psychology intern Roosevelt Hosp., N.Y.C., 1971-73; cons. Inwood House, N.Y.C., 1971-83; staff therapist Univ. Consultation Center Mental Hygiene, Bronx, N.Y., 1974-79, clin. instr., 1976-80; sr. clin. psychologist moderate security unit North Princeton Developmental Ctr., 1983—; cons. Early Childhood Learning Center, Paramus, N.J., 1978-80, Found. for Religion and Mental Health, Briarcliff Manor, N.Y., 1979-82, Inwood House, N.Y.C., 1981-83, prin. clin. psychologist Ewing Residential Ctr., Trenton, N.J., 1987-

88, Ind. Child Study Teams, East Orange, N.J; pvt. practice, Princeton, N.J.; expert witness in criminal cts. Mem. APA (assoc.), N.J. Psychol. Assn., Nat. Assn. Treatment Sex Offenders, Kappa Tau Alpha. Office: 601 Ewing St # C-20 Princeton NJ 08540-2757

FRIED, JEFFREY MICHAEL, health care administrator; b. Kansas City, Mo., Apr. 9, 1953; s. Harvey J. and SuEllen (Weissman) F.; m. Rosalyn Sue Matz. Student, Drake U., 1971-73; BGS, U. Kans., 1975; MHA, Washington U., St. Louis, 1979. Adminstrv. asst. Rsch. Med. Ctr., Kansas City, Mo., 1979-80; asst. to pres. Rsch. Health Svcs., Kansas City, 1980-81; asst. v.p. Sinai Hosp. Balt., 1981-83, Lancaster (Pa.) Gen. Hosp., 1983-85; v.p., chief oper. officer Lancaster (Pa.) Gen. Svcs. Corp., 1985-86, pres., 1986-88; sr. v.p. Lancaster Gen. Hosp., 1989-91, chief operating officer, 1992-94; pres., CEO Beebe Med. Ctr., Lewes, Del., 1994—; pres., bd. dirs. Lancaster Med. Equipment, Barge Ganse Vena Care; sec., bd. dirs. Preferred Health Care, Lancaster; bd. dirs. Lancaster Diagnostic Imaging, Inc.; v.p., bd. dirs., pres. Welsh Mountain Med. and Dental Ctr., Lancaster, 1989-94; mng. ptnr. Roherstown Imaging Assocs., Lancaster, 1986-94; part-time mem. faculty dept. health adminstrn. and devel. Pa. State U., 1988-94, Coll. of St. Francis, 1988-94; mem. bus. adv. coun. Goodwill Industries, 1989-94; asst. prof. Lebanon Valley Coll., 1994—; mem. MBA program adv. bd. Wilmington Coll., 1996—. Mem. Leadership Lancaster, 1987-88; pres. bd. dirs. Welsh Mt. Med. and Dental Ctr., 1989-94; pres. bd. dirs. Lancaster chpt. Nat. Commn. for Prevention of Child Abuse, 1986-89; treas., bd. dirs. Lancaster Jewish Fedn., 1986-89; bd. dirs. Lancaster Jewish Cmty. Ctr., 1989-94, Temple Shaarai Shomayim, Clinic for Spl. Children, 1991-94, Pa. Acad. Music, 1994—, Del. Hospice, 1996—. Fellow Am. Coll. Healthcare Execs. (com. on ethics 1991-93, credentials com. 1995-98); mem. Lancaster County Bus. Group on Health (legis. com. 1992-94), Ctrl. Pa. Health Care Adminstrs. Jewish. Home: A-12 Mariners Way Millsboro DE 19966 Office: Beebe Med Ctr 424 Savannah Rd Lewes DE 19958-1462

FRIED, JOSEF, chemist, educator; b. Przemysl, Poland, July 21, 1914; came to U.S., 1938, naturalized, 1944; s. Abraham and Frieda (Fried) F.; m. Erna Werner, Sept. 18, 1939 (dec. Nov. 1986); 1 dau., Carol Frances. Student, U. Leipzig, 1934-37, U. Zurich, 1937-38; Ph.D., Columbia U., 1941. Eli Lilly fellow Columbia U., 1941-43; research chemist Givaudan, N.Y., 1943; head dept. antibiotics and steroids Squibb Inst. Med. Research, New Brunswick, N.J., 1944-59; dir. sect. organic chemistry Squibb Inst. Med. Research, 1959-63; prof. chemistry, biochemistry and Ben May Lab. Cancer Research, U. Chgo., 1963—, Louis Block prof., 1973—, chmn. dept. chemistry, 1977-79; mem. med. chem. study sect. NIH, 1963-67, 68-72, chmn., 1971; mem. com. arrangements Laurentian Hormone Conf., 1964-71; Knapp Meml. lectr. U. Wis., 1958. Mem. bd. editors: Jour. Organic Chemistry, 1964-69, Steroids, 1966-86, Jour. Biol. Chemistry, 1975-81, 83-88; contbr. articles to profl. jours. Recipient N.J. Patent award, 1968, Roussel prize 1992, Gregory Pincus medal, 1994. Fellow AAAS, N.Y. Acad. Scis.; mem. NAS, Am. Acad. Scis., Am. Chem. Soc. (award in medicinal chemistry 1974, Alfred Burger award in medicinal chemistry 1996), Am. Soc. Biol. Chemists, Swiss Chem. Socs., Brit. Chem. Socs., Sigma Xi. Home: 5715 S Kenwood Ave Chicago IL 60637-1742

FRIED, MARVIN PETER, physician; b. N.Y.C., June 10, 1945; s. Otto and Leonore (Schwartz) F.; m. Rita Beth Hyfer, Jan. 25, 1970; children: Jaimie Lisa, Karen Lynn. BS, CUNY, 1961-65; MD, Tufts U. Sch. of Med., Boston, Mass., 1965-69. Am. Bd of Otolaryngology, 1975. Chief of otolaryngology Boston (Mass.) City Hosp., 1977-79; otolaryngologist Beth Israel Hosp., Boston, 1979-92; chief of otolaryngology Beth Israel Hosp., 1993—; otolaryngologist Brigham & Womens Hosp., Boston, 1979-92; chief otolaryngology Brigham & Womens Hosp., 1993—; otolaryngologist Childrens Hosp., Boston, 1979—, Mass. Eye and Ear Infirmary, Boston, 1979; Editorial bd., Ear, Nose & Throat Jour., 1988, Laryngoscope, 1992. Editor: Complications Of Laser Surgery Of The Head And Neck, 1986, Manual of Otolaryngology, 1992, The Larynx, 1995. Surgeon (CDR), U.S. Public Health Svc., Norfolk, Va., 1975. Recipient Fowler award, 1984, Mark award, 1994. Fellow Am. Acad. of Otolaryngology, Am. Coll. of Surgeons, Triologic Soc., Am. Laryngological Soc., Am. Bronchoesophagological Soc., Am Soc. for Laser Med. and Surgery (v.p. 1994), Phi Beta Kappa, Alpha Omega Alpha. Office: Joint Ctr Otolaryngology 333 Longwood Ave Boston MA 02115

FRIEDBERG, DAVID ZACHARY, pediatrician, cardiologist, educator; b. N.Y.C., Aug. 4, 1936; widowed; children: Jonathan, Daniel. BA summa cum laude, Williams Coll., 1958; MD cum laude, Harvard U., 1962. Diplomate Am. Bd. Pediats. Pediatric intern Strong Meml. Hosp. U. Rochester, N.Y., 1962-63, asst. resident pediatrics, 1963-64; heart disease control officer USPHS, San Juan, 1965-67; fellow in pediatric cardiology Children's Hosp. Med. Ctr., Boston, 1967-69, cardiologist, 1969-70; assoc. attending physician Milw. Children's Hosp., 1970-72, attending physician, 1972-75; pvt. practice Wauwatosa, Wis., 1975—; asst. prof. pediatrics Med. Coll. Wis., Milw., 1970-72; assoc. dir. Fairchild Cardiac Study Ctr. Milw. Children's Hosp., 1970-75; cons. Wis. So. Colony Tng. Sch.; project dir. Pediatric Cardiovascular Ctr. Wis.; assoc. prof. pediatrics Med. Coll. Wis., 1974-75, clin. prof., 1989—; attending physician Children's Hosp. Wis., Milw., 1975—, dir., chief pediatric cardiology, 1989-91; cons. So. Wis. Ctr. Developmentally Disabled, 1975—; dir. pediatric cardiology St. Joseph's Hosp., Milw. Hosp., 1982—. Editor Current Trends Pediat. Cardiovasc. Disease, 1972-75; contbr. articles to profl. jours. Fellow Harvard Med. Sch., 1964-65. Fellow Am. Coll. Cardiology; mem. Am. Acad. Pediatrics, Am. Heart Assn. (coun. cardiovasc. diseases in young), Midwest Pediatric Cardiology Soc., Milw. County Med. Soc., State Med. Soc. Wis., Wis. Heart Assn., Phi Beta Kappa. Office: 1000N 92nd St Wauwatosa WI 53226

FRIEDBERG, ERROL CLIVE, pathology educator, researcher; b. Johannesburg, South Africa, Oct. 2, 1937; s. Edward and Rena (Berman) F.; children: Malcolm, Andrew, Jonathan, Lawrence. BSc, Witwatersrand U., Johannesburg, 1957, MB BCh, 1961. Intern King Edward VIII Hosp./U. Natal, Durban, South Africa, 1962; resident pathologist Witwatersrand U., 1963-64, Cleve. Met. Gen. Hosp., 1965; postdoctoral fellow dept. biochemistry Case Western Res. U., Cleve., 1966-68; rsch. investigator divsn. nuclear medicine Walter Reed Army Inst. Rsch., Washington, 1969-70; asst. prof. pathology Stanford (Calif.) U., 1971-77, assoc. prof. pathology, 1977-84, prof. pathology, 1984-90; prof., chair dept. pathology U. Tex. Southwestern Med. Ctr., Dallas, 1990—, Senator Betty and Dr. Andy Andujar chair pathology, 1990-93, Senator Betty and Dr. Andy Andujar disting. chair pathology, 1993—; co-organizer symposia and confs. in field. Author: DNA Repair, 1984, Cancer Answers: Encouraging Answers to 25 Questions You Were Always Afraid to Ask, 1992, 93, (with others) DNA Repair and Mutagenesis, 1995; editor or co-editor: DNA Repair Mechanisms, 1978, DNA Repair: A Laboratory Manual of Research Procedures, Vol. 1, 1981, Vol. 2, 1983, Vol. 3, 1988, Cellular Responses to DNA Damage, 1983, Scientific American Reader: Cancer Biology, 1985, Mechanisms and Consequences of DNA Damage Processing, 1988; contbr. numerous articles to profl. publs. Rsch. fellow Andrew W. Mellon Found., 1973-76; recipient Rsch. Career Devel. award USPHS, 1974-79, Merit award USPHS, 1988—; Joshua Macy Jr. Found. faculty scholar, 1978-79. Fellow Royal Coll. Pathology. Office: U Tex Southwestern Med Ctr 5323 Harry Hines Blvd Dallas TX 75235-9072

FRIEDBERG, HAROLD DAVID, cardiologist; b. Johannesburg, Republic of South Africa, June 7, 1927; s. Samuel and Violet (Grodzen) F.; M.D., U. Witwatersrand, Johannesburg, 1949; postgrad. U. London (Eng.), 1949-54, U. Manchester (Eng.), 1956-58; m. P.A. Barnett, June 27, 1954 (div. 1986); children—Mandy V., Adrienne V., Richard C., Adam S.; m. Carol Gibson Glynn, June 14, 1986. Came to U.S., 1964. Intern, Baragwanath Hosp., Johannesburg, 1949-50; resident Royal Coll. Physicians Affiliated Hosps., London, 1950-54, Christie Hosp., Manchester, Eng., 1956-58; cons. cardiologist, Salisbury, Rhodesia, 1959-63; fellow medicine Johns Hopkins Med. Sch., Balt., 1964-65; mem. staff Milw. VA Hosp., chief cardiology, 1966-73, cons., 1973-79; cons. cardiology St. Luke's Hosp., 1968—, dir. coronary care unit and pacemaker clinic, 1972-79; cardiologist Sarasota Meml. Hosp., Fla., 1984—; asso. clin. prof. medicine Med. Coll. Wis., 1965-84; prof. medicine U. South Fla., Tampa, 1979—; sci. adviser to several med. tech. cos.; co-designer St. Jude Heart Valve, 1977, A.T.S. Med. Heart Valve, 1990. Fellow A.C.P., Am. Coll. Chest Physicians, Am. Coll. Cardiology, Am. Heart Assn. Council Clin. Cardiology, Royal Coll. Physicians (London); mem. AAAS, Am. Heart Assn. (dir. Wis. 1970-78, pres. 1973), N.Am. Soc. Pacing and Electrophysiology (founding mem.), Sociedad Argentina de Estimulacion Cardiaca (corr.), Lillehei Surg. Soc. Mem. editorial bd. Jour. Electrocardiology. Contbr. articles to profl. jours., chpts. to med. books. Office: 2540 S Tamiami Trl Sarasota FL 34239-4501

FRIEDBERG, MARK, ophthalmologist; b. N.Y.C., Feb. 2, 1960; s. George and Arlene Janice (Katz) F.; m. Ronda Gail Horowitz, June 8, 1985; children: Stacey Lauren, Lindsey Brooke. BSc, Brown U., 1982; MD, U. Pa. Sch. Medicine, 1986. Diplomate Am. Bd. Ophthalmology. Resident Wills Eye Hosp., Phila., 1987-90; vitreo-retinal fellow Washington Nat. Eye Ctr., 1990-91; ophthalmologist Midatlantic Ophthalmology, Red Bank, N.J., 1991—; lectr. in field. Editor, contbg. author: Wills Eye Hospital: Office and Emergency Room Diagnosis and Treatment of Eye Disease, 1991; contbr. articles to profl. jours. Mem. AMA, Am. Acad. Ophthalmologists, N.J. Acad. Ophthalmology, Retina Soc. N.J., Monmouth County Med. Soc. Office: MidAtlantic Ophthalmology 70 E Front St Red Bank NJ 07701

FRIEDBERG, RICHARD CHARLES, physician; b. Harare, Zimbabwe, Oct. 30, 1960; s. Harold David and Patricia Ann F.; m. Diane Michelow, Feb. 4, 1990; children: Oliver Simon, Joshua Jacob, Jenna Alexandra. BS, Stanford U., 1981; MD, Duke U., 1988, PhD, 1988. Diplomate in Pathology and Transfusion Medicine. Assoc. med. dir., blood bank U Ala., Birmingham, 1992—, asst. prof., pathology, 1992—; chief, pathology and lab. medicine VA Hosp., Birmingham, 1993—. Fellow Coll. of American Pathologists; mem. Am. Soc. Clinical Pathologists, Am. Assn. Blood Banks, Assn. Clin. Lab. Physicians and Scientists. Office: Univ Ala/Birmingham 619 S 19th E Birmingham AL 35233-7531

FRIEDE, SAMUEL A(RNOLD), health care executive; b. Starnberg, Fed. Republic Germany, Oct. 17, 1946; s. Simon and Faye F.; m. Andrea Mednick, Aug. 31, 1972; children: David, Rachel. AB, Columbia U., 1969; MBA, U. Chgo., 1975. Adminstrv. liaison to medicine Northwestern Meml. Hosp., Chgo., 1975-76; exec. adminstr. medicine Michael Reese Hosp. and Med. Ctr., Chgo., 1976-81; assoc. dir. patient care services Strong Meml. Hosp. of U. Rochester, N.Y., 1981-84; v.p. ops. Allegheny Gen. Hosp., Pitts., 1984-86; v.p. med. staff affairs and patient mgmt. services Shadyside Hosp., Pitts., 1986-94; cons. Hosp. Coun. of Warrendale, Pa., 1994—; sec., treas. Chgo. Health Execs. Forum, 1979, pres., 1980; mem. Alumni Council Exec. Com., Chgo., 1977-80, health adminstrn. program U. Chgo.; preceptor grad. program in hosp. adminstrn. U. Chgo., 1978-81. Sec. bd. dirs. Hyde Park-Kenwood Community Health Ctr., Chgo., 1980-81; v.p. bd. dirs. Congregation Rodfei Zedek, Chgo., 1981; bd. dirs. Beth El Congregation, Pitts., 1986-89. Fellow Am. Coll. Healthcare Execs., Health Exec. Forum Southwestern Pa. (sec. 1986, treas. 1987, v.p. 1988); mem. B'nai B'rith. Office: Hosp Coun of W Pa 400 Commonwealth Ave Warrendale PA 15086-7513

FRIEDELL, GILBERT HUGO, pathologist, hospital administrator, educator, cancer center director; b. Mpls., Feb. 28, 1927; s. Aaron and Naomi (Kepman) F.; m. Janet Newell Nelson; children: Mark Lowry, Benjamin Newell, Anne, James Gilbert, Sarah Jane. Student, Harvard Coll., 1943-45; B.S., U. Minn., 1947, M.B., 1949, M.D., 1950. Diplomate Am. Bd. Pathology. Intern Mpls. Gen. Hosp., 1949-50; resident in pathology Boston City Hosp., 1950-52, Free Hosp. for Women, 1952-53, Salem (Mass.) Hosp., 1953-54, Pondville Hosp., 1954-55; pathologist Mass. Meml. Hosps., 1958-61, New Eng. Deaconess Hosp., 1962-67, Boston City Hosp., 1967-69; chief pathology St. Vincent Hosp., Worcester, Mass., 1969-78, med. dir., 1978-82; dir. Lucille Parker Markey Cancer Ctr., Lexington, Ky., 1983-90, dir. cancer control program, 1990—; assoc.in pathology Boston U., 1958-61, assoc. prof. pathology, 1967-70; instr. Harvard U., 1962-67, lectr., 1967-69; prof. U. Mass., 1971-83, acting chmn. dept. pathology, 1973; prof. U. Ky., 1983—; mem. breast cancer task force Nat. Cancer Inst., 1968-72, dir. nat. bladder cancer project, Nat. Cancer Inst., 1971-84. Author: (with others) Carcinoma in Situ of the Uterine Cervix, 1960; contbr. numerous articles on cancer, cancer research and other pathologic-med. topics to sci. jours. Vice chmn. Mass. Com. on Medico-Legal Investigation, 1977-80. Served with USNR, 1955-57. USPHS spl. research fellow, 1961-62; grantee Nat. Cancer Inst., Am. Cancer Soc. Mem. Mass. Soc. Pathologists (pres. 1975-76, exec. com. 1974-77), Am. Urol. Assn., New Eng. Cancer Soc. (exec. com. 1975-78), Worcester Dist. Med. Soc. (exec. com. 1980-81), Mass. Med. Soc. (councillor 1980-81), Assn. Cmty. Cancer Ctrs. (trustee 1978-82), Ky. Med. Assn., Am. Assn. for Cancer Rsch., Am. Soc. Clin. Oncology, N.Am. Assn. Associated Ctrl. Cancer Registries (exec. bd. 1991-94), Athenaeum Club (London). Office: Lucille Parker Markey Cancer Ctr Lexington KY 40536-0098

FRIEDENBERG, RICHARD MYRON, radiology educator, physician; b. N.Y.C., May 6, 1926; s. Charles and Dorothy (Steg) F.; m. Gloria Geshwind, Jan. 22, 1950; children: Lisa, Peter, Amy. A.B., Columbia, 1946; M.D., L.I. Coll. Medicine, 1949. Diplomate Am. Bd. Radiology. Intern in medicine Maimonides Hosp., Bklyn., 1949-50; resident in radiology Bellevue Hosp., N.Y.C., 1950-51; Nat. Cancer fellow Bellevue Hosp., 1951-52; fellow radiology Columbia-Presbyn. Hosp., 1952-53; cons. radiologist 3d Air Force, London, Eng., 1953-55; asst. prof. radiology Albert Einstein Coll. Medicine, 1955-66, assoc. clin. prof. radiology, 1966-68; dir., chmn. dept. radiology Bronx Lebanon Hosp. Center, 1957-68; prof., chmn. dept. radiology N.Y. Med. Coll., 1968-80; dir. radiology Flower Fifth Ave Hosp., Met. Hosp. Ctr., Bird S. Coler Hosp., N.Y.C., Westchester County Med. Ctr., all 1968-80; prof., chmn. dept. radiol. scis. U. Calif., Irvine, 1980-92. Author: (with Charles Ney) Radiographic Atlas of the Genitourinary System, 1966, 2d edit., 1981; Contbr. (with Charles Ney) articles to profl. jours. Fellow Am. Coll. Radiology, N.Y. Acad. Medicine; mem. Assn. Univ. Radiologists, Radiol. Soc. N.Am., Am. Roentgen Ray Soc., N.Y. Acad. Scis., Assn. Am. Med. Colls., AMA, Soc. Chairmen Acad. Radiology Depts. (past pres.), N.Y. Roentgen Soc. (past pres.), Orange CTY Radiology Soc. (past pres.). Home: 18961 Castlegate Ln Santa Ana CA 92705-2801 Office: U Calif Dept Radiology San Diego CA 92103

FRIEDEWALD, WILLIAM FRANK, physician; b. St. Louis, June 3, 1912; s. William H. and Albertine (Eilers) F.; m. Mary L. Wright, May 29, 1937; children: William T., Jeannette A., James W., Richard W. B.S., St. Louis U., 1931, M.D., 1935. Intern, St. Louis City Hosp., 1935-36, asst. resident and resident in medicine, 1936-38; asst. in pathology and bacteriology Rockefeller Inst. for Med. Research, 1938-42; mem., staff Internat. Health div., Rockefeller Found., 1942-45; chmn. and prof. dept. bacteriology and immunology Emory U. Sch. Medicine, 1945-51, assoc. prof. medicine, 1945—; pvt. practice internal medicine, allergy, 1951-76; profl. cons. internal medicine to Surgeon 3d U.S. Army, 1958-68; chief of staff St. Joseph's Hosp., Atlanta, 1968-79; trustee St. Joseph's Hosp., 1969-82. Author articles on med. and bacteriol. subjects. Mem. Soc. Exptl. Biology and Medicine, AMA, Fulton County Med. Soc. Ga., Am. Soc. Exptl. Pathology. Home: 28 Vernon Glen Ct Atlanta GA 30338-5421

FRIEDEWALD, WILLIAM THOMAS, physician; b. N.Y.C., Mar. 7, 1939; s. William Frank and Mary Lucy (Wright) F.; m. Jacquline Jean Judd, Apr. 15, 1967; children: Laura Elizabeth, John Judd, Eric William. BS, U. Notre Dame, 1960; MD, Yale U., 1963; postdoctoral, Stanford U., 1968-69. Intern Yale-New Haven Hosp., 1963-64, resident, 1964-65, 67-68; commd. USPHS, 1965, advanced through grades to capt., 1983; officer Epidemiol. Intelligence Svc. Communicable Disease Ctr., Atlanta, 1965-67; med. officer Nat. Inst. Allergy and Infectious Diseases, NIH, Bethesda, Md., 1965-67, Nat. Heart, Lung and Blood Inst. and NIH, Bethesda, 1967-86; chief cons. sect. biomed. rsch. br. Nat. Heart, Lung and Blood Inst., NIH, Bethesda, 1971-76, br. chief clin. trials br., 1973-79, assoc. dir. clin. applications and prevention program and DHVD, 1979-84, div. dir. div. epidemiology and clin. applications, 1984-86; assoc. dir. Office Disease Prevention Office of Dir., NIH, Bethesda, 1986-89; chief med. dir. MetLife Ins. Co., N.Y.C., 1989-96, sr. v.p., 1991—, 1991—, chief med. Adv., 1996—. Democrat. Roman Catholic. Home: 326 W 71st St New York NY 10023-3502 Office: Met Life Ins Co One Madison Ave New York NY 10010

FRIEDHOFF, ARNOLD J., psychiatrist, medical scientist; b. Johnstown, Pa., Dec. 26, 1923; s. Abraham M. and Stella (Beiman) F.; m. Frances Wolfe, Feb. 24, 1946; children: Lawrence, Nancy, Richard. B.A., U. Pa., 1944, M.D., 1947. Diplomate: Am. Bd. Psychiatry and Neurology. Intern Western Pa. Hosp., 1947-48; resident psychiatry U.S. Army, 1952-53, Bellevue Hosp., N.Y.C., 1953-55; instr., to Menas S. Gregory prof. psychiatry Sch. Medicine, NYU, N.Y.C., 1956—, head psychopharmacology rsch. unit, 1956-63, co-dir. Ctr. for Study Psychotic Disorders, 1963-69, dir., 1970—, dir. Millhauser Labs., 1970—; mem. clin. projects rsch. rev. com. NIMH, 1970-74, mem., 1977-81; dir. MV/NIMH Mental Health Clin. Rsch. Ctr., 1981—; mem. Mayor's Com. on Prescription Drugs, N.Y.C.; mem. sci. coun. Nat. Alliance for Rsch. in Schizophrenia and Depression, 1986—; mem. rsch. scientist devel. award rev. com., NIMH, 1983-85, mem. nat. adv. mental health coun., 1987—; hon. prof. Basque U., Bilbao, Spain, U. Seoul, Republic of Korea. Co-editor: Yearbook of Psychiatry and Applied Mental Health, 1968-80; assoc. editor Biol. Psychiatry, 1989—, mem. adv. bd., 1969—; contbr. numerous reports on biochem. psychiatry, psychopharmacology. Served to 1st lt. M.C. U.S. Army, 1951-53. Recipient Research Scientist award NIMH, 1967—. Fellow Am. Coll. Neuropsychopharmacology (past councillor and past pres. 1978-79), Am. Psychiat. Assn., Am. Soc. Clin. Pharmacology and Therapeutics, Royal Coll. Psychiatrists (Gt. Britain); mem. Am. Chem. Soc., Internat. Soc. Neurochemistry, Assn. for Rsch. in Nervous and Mental Diseases (past asst. sec.-treas.), Am. Psychopath. Assn. (past pres., Samuel B. Hamilton award), Soc. Biol. Psychiatri (past pres., Gold medal 1989, Castilla del Pino Found. prize, Cordoba 1994). Office: NYU Med Ctr Millhauser Labs 560 1st Ave New York NY 10016-6402

FRIEDLAENDER, GARY ELLIOTT, orthopedist, educator; b. Detroit, May 15, 1945; s. Alex Seymour and Eileen Adrianne (Berman) F.; m. Linda Beth Krohner, Mar. 16, 1969; children: Eron Yael, Ari Seth. BS, U. Mich., 1967, MD, 1969; MA (hon.), Yale U., 1984. Diplomate Am. Bd. Orthopaedic Surgery. Intern, resident in surgery U. Mich., Ann Arbor, 1969-71; resident orthopaedics Yale New Haven Hosp., 1971-74; fellow in musculoskeletal oncology Mass. Gen. Hosp., Boston, 1983; dir. tissue bank Naval Med. Research Inst., Bethesda, Md., 1974-76; instr. surgery Yale U., New Haven, 1974, asst. prof., 1976-79, assoc. prof., 1979-84, prof., chief orthopaedics, 1984-86, prof. chmn. dept. orthopaedics and rehab., 1986—; mem. orthopaedics and musculoskeletal study sect. NIH, 1986-89, mem. nat. adv. bd. arthritis and musculoskelegal and skin diseases 1991-95, chmn., 1993-95; mem. blood products adv. com. FDA, 1995—. Mem. bd. cons. editors Jour. Bone and Joint Surgery, 1981—; mem. bd. assoc. editors Clin. Orthopaedics and Related Rsch., 1986—, Modern Medicine, 1988—; editor Rheumatology Digest, 1986-95; mem. editl. bd. Transplantation Scis., 1991—, Jour. Oncology, 1994—; contbr. articles to profl. jours., chpts. to books. Served to lt. comdr. USN, 1974-76. Recipient Kappa Delta Outstanding Rsch. award, 1982, Nicholas Andry award for Outstanding Orthopedic Rsch., 1995. Fellow ACS, Am. Acad. Orthopaedic Surgeons (chmn. com. biol. implants 1987-93); mem. AMA, NIH (orthopaedics and musculoskeletal study sect. 1986-89, Nat. Adv. Bd. arthritis and musculoskeletal and skin diseases 1991-95, chmn. 1993-95), Am. Assn. Tissue Banks (pres. 1983-85), Orthopaedic Rsch. Soc. (pres. 1994-95), Transplantation Soc., Musculoskeletal Tumor Soc., Am. Coun. on Transplantation (pres. 1983-85), Soc. for Surg. Oncology, Am. Soc. Transplant Surgeons, Am. Orthopaedic Assn., Assn. Bone and Joint Surgeons, Acad. Orthopaedic Soc. (pres. 1995-96). Jewish. Home: 15 Old Still Rd Woodbridge CT 06525-1101 Office: Yale U Dept Orthopedics & Rehab PO Box 208071 New Haven CT 06520-8071

FRIEDLAND, EDWARD CHARLES, orthopedic surgeon; b. N.Y.C., June 23, 1937; s. Solomon and Frances (Goldenberg) F.; m. Kathryn Amy Stern, Sept. 6, 1970; children: Steven Mark, Elizabeth Ann. AB, NYU, 1957; MD, SUNY, N.Y.C., 1961. Diplomate Am. Bd. Orthopedic Surgery. Intern Maimonides Hosp., Bklyn., N.J., 1961-62; resident in gen. surgery VA Hosp., Bklyn., 1962-63; resident in orthopedic surgery St. Joseph's Hosp., Paterson, N.J., 1966-68; pvt. practice Fair Lawn, N.J., 1968—; clin. asst. prof. Univ. of Medicine and Dentistry of N.J., Newark, 1970—; chmn. dept. orthopedic surgery Barnert Meml. Hosp., Paterson, N.J., 1974-75; attending orthopedic surgeon, Valley Hosp., Ridgewood, N.J., 1976—. Pres. Temple Beth Rishon, Wyckoff, N.J., 1991-93. Capt. USAF, 1963-65. Fellow Am. Coll. Surgeons, Am. Acad. Orthopedic Surgeons; mem. Ea. Orthopedic Assn., N.J. Orthopedic Soc., Bergen County Med. Soc., Zeta Beta Tau, AF&AM. Republican. Jewish. Office: 25-15 Fair Lawn Ave Fair Lawn NJ 07410-3404

FRIEDLANDER, ALAN MARC, biologist; b. Balt., Nov. 28, 1958; s. Henry Ephraim and Nancy Nessa (Merdler) F. BS in Biology, Roanoke Coll., 1980; MS in Oceanography, Old Dominion U., 1987; PhD in Zoology, U. Hawaii, 1996. Fisheries extension officer U.S. Peace Corps, Kingdom of Tonga, 1982-84; fisheries biologist U. Fla., Gainesville, 1987, Divsn. Fish and Wildlife, St. Thomas, V.I., 1988-90; marine biologist U.S. Nat. Park Svc., St. John, V.I., 1990-91. Contbr. articles to profl. jours. Mem. Am. Fisheries Soc., Gulf and Caribbean Fisheries Inst., Tropical Fisheries Scientists, Sigma Xi. Democrat. Jewish. Office: Univ Hawaii Dept Zoology 2538 The Mall Honolulu HI 96822-2233

FRIEDLANDER, BERNICE, federal agency administrator; b. Middletown, Conn., Aug. 25, 1943; d. Samuel Julius and Masha (Glazer) F. BA, Monmouth Coll., 1964; MA in Pub. Adminstrn., Harvard U., 1983. Legis. asst. Congressman James J. Howard, Washington, 1965-68; legis. rep. Action on Smoking and Health, Washington, 1969-70; adminstrv. asst. Congressman Edwin B. Forsythe, Washington, 1970-72; cons., freelance campaign mgr., 1973-78; pres. sec., sr. legis. asst. Congressman Eugene V. Atkinson, Washington, 1978-82; editor Washington Monitor, Inc., 1984-85; dir. legis. and pub. affairs Autism Soc. Am., Washington, 1985-87; dir. pub. affairs Women's Bur. US Dept. Labor, Washington, 1988-94; dir. US Office Consumer Affairs, Washington, 1994—; head U.S. delegation com. on consumer policy OECD, 1995, 96, vice chmn. com. on consumer policy. Dir. Claridge House Coop., Inc., Washington, 1988—, pres. 1992-95. Mem. Harvard Club, Women of Washington. Jewish. Home: 940-25th St NW Washington DC 20037 Office: US Office Consumer Affairs 750 17th St NW Ste 650 Washington DC 20006*

FRIEDLANDER, RALPH, thoracic and vascular surgeon; b. N.Y.C., Oct. 2, 1913; s. Samuel and Mollie (Drimmer) F.; m. Sybil Rainsbury, Apr. 10, 1950; children: Andrea Lynn, Beth Caryn. BA, Columbia Coll., 1934; MD, U. Chgo., 1938. Diplomate Am. Bd. Surgery, Am. Bd. Thoracic Surgery. Intern Bellevue Hosp., N.Y.C., 1938; intern surg. Michael Reese Hosp., Chgo., 1939, resident in surgery, 1940; resident in surgery Mt. Sinai Hosp., N.Y.C., 1941; sr. resident in surgery Michael Reese Hosp., Chgo., 1942; adj. surgeon Mt. Sinai Hosp., N.Y.C., 1946-50; chief surgery and thoracic surgery VA Hosp., Castle Point, N.Y., 1947-50, Ft. Hamilton, N.Y., 1950-53; dir. surgery Bronx-Lebanon Hosp. Ctr., N.Y.C., 1953-64, attending surgeon, cons. thoracic, vascular, gen. surgery, 1964—; attending surgeon, cons. thoracic and vascular and gen. surgery Union Hosp., N.Y.C., 1976—; attending surgeon thoracic and vascular surgery Beth Israel Hosp. North, N.Y.C., 1977—; cons. gen. and thoracic surgery Dept. of Health N.Y. State, 1963—; cons. thoracic and cardiovascular surgery Hebrew Hosp. for the Chronic Sick, N.Y.C., 1955-89, Hebrew Home for the Aged, Riverdale, N.Y., 1956—, Health Ins. Plan, N.Y.C., 1954—, Bur. Disability Determinations, State of N.Y., 1960—, City of N.Y. Med. Assistance Program, 1966—, Bronx County Supreme Ct., 1958-91; instr. anatomy Sch. Medicine NYU, 1946-49; assoc. clin. prof. surgery Albert Einstein Coll. Medicine, 1959-90. Contbr. articles to Diseases of the Chest, Tuberculosis, N.Y. State Jour. Medicine, Am. Jour. Gastroenterology, Clin. Rsch. Mem. med. bd. Bronx-Lebanon Hosp. Ctr., sec., v.p., pres., 1975-78. Major Med. Corps, U.S. Army, 1942-46, ETO. Alfred Moritz Michaelis fellow in physics Columbia U., 1934; grantee USPHS, 1960. Fellow ACS, N.Y. Acad. Scis., N.Y. Acad. Medicine; mem. AMA, Am. Heart Assn. (coun. on cardiovascular surgery), N.Y. Heart Assn., N.Y. County Med. Soc., N.Y. State Med. Soc., N.Y. Soc. for Thoracic Surgery, Am. Assn. for Thoracic Surgery, Harvey Soc., N.Y. Gastroent. Assn., Phi Beta Kappa, Alpha Omega Alpha. Home: 535 E 86th St New York NY 10028-7533

FRIEDLANDER, STEPHEN RICHARD, psychologist; b. Danbury, Conn., Sept. 17, 1944; s. Matt and Jacqueline (Sprayregen) F.; m. Lillian Goldstein, June 9, 1967 (div. 1975); children: Emil, Jesse; m. Ann Ruth Eisenberg, Sept. 2, 1992. Student, Yale U., 1962-65; BA, Ga. State U., 1972, MA, 1974, PhD, 1979. Diplomate in clin. psychology Am. Bd. Profl. Psychology. Cons. Human Devel. Inst., Atlanta, 1967-69, dir. program devel., 1969-71; asst. prof. U. Tenn., Knoxville, 1979; pvt. practice

Knoxville, 1980—; examiner Am. Bd. Profl. Psychology, 1989—; leadership devel. cons. Union Am. Hebrew Congregation, N.Y.C., 1990—; dir. studies Inst. Psychoanalytic Edn., Tng., N.Y.C., 1995—; founding dir. Ctr. Profl. Devel., Knoxville, Tenn., 1996—. Author: Discovering Spiritual Values, 1971; editor: Confronting the Challenges to Psychoanalysis, 1995; contbg. editor Clin. Studies: Internat. Jour. Psychoanalysis, 1995—; contbr. articles to profl. jours. Bd. mem. Union of Am. Hebrew Congregation, S.W. region, 1988-90, Arts Coun., Knoxville, Am. Cancer Soc., Knoxville, Child & Family Svcs., Knoxville, 1993—. Danforth Found. fellow, 1972. Fellow Acad. Clin. Psychochology, Soc. Personality Assessment; mem. Internat. Fedn. Psychoanalytic Edn. (pres. 1995), Found. for Psychoanalytic Edn. and Rsch. (pres. 1995), Inst. de Investigacon en Psciologia Clinicay Social, A.C., (hon.), Mex., 1996—, Assn. Yale Alumni (del. 1989-91). Office: 6025 Brookvale Ln Ste 120 Knoxville TN 37919

FRIEDLING, STEVEN PAUL, internist; b. N.Y.C., Dec. 23, 1943; s. Abe and Bella (Eichenholtz) F.; m. Carol Grosser; children: Melissa, Naomi, Lily. BA, NYU, 1964; MD, Downstate Med. U., 1968. Asst. prof. medicine Washington U., St. Louis, 1974-75; internist pvt. practice Smithtown, N.Y., 1975—; clin. asst. prof. medicine and microbiology SUNY, Stoneybrook, 1982—. With USPHS, 1969-71. Office: Branch Med 267 E Main St Smithtown NY 11787

FRIEDMAN, AARON LOUIS, pediatric nephrology educator; b. Bad Reichenhal, Germany, Oct. 29, 1948; came to U.S., 1949; s. Reuben and Sylvia (Zysman) F.; m. Sarah Seay Jones, June 17, 1971; children: Rebeccah, Robbin. BS, Cornell U., 1970; MD, SUNY, Syracuse, 1974. Resident pediatrics U. Wis., Madison, 1974-76, fellow pediatric nephrology, 1976-80, chief resident pediatrics, 1978-79; asst. prof. Duke U., Durham, N.C., 1980-81; asst. prof. U. Wis., Madison, 1981-86, assoc. prof., 1986-91, prof., 1991—, chair dept. pediatrics, 1996—; bd. dirs. U-Care HMO, Madison. Contbr. articles to profl. jours. Bd. dirs. 3-Wishes Day Care Ctr., 1987-88, U. Wis. Med. Found., 1995—. Named Best Doctor in Am. Am. Healthcare Mag., 1996. Fellow Am. Acad. Pediatrics; mem. Am. Soc. Pediatric Nephrology (sec./treas.), Am. Acad. Pediatrics, Soc. for Pediatric Rsch., Internat. Pediatric Nephrology Soc. Office: U Wis 600 Highland Ave Madison WI 53792-4108

FRIEDMAN, ALAN HERBERT, ophthalmologist; b. N.Y.C., 1937; BA in Chemistry with honors, Cornell U., 1959; MD (summer fellow NIH 1960, 62-63), NYU, 1963; m. Sandra Yasser, 1960; children: David, Jonathan, Lisa, Jennifer. Intern in medicine Bellevue Hosp., N.Y.C., 1963-64; resident in ophthalmology NYU Med. Ctr., 1966-69, fellow ophthalmic pathology, 1969-70; research fellow histochemistry Royal Postgrad. Med. Sch., London, 1972; practice medicine specializing in ophthalmology, N.Y.C., 1970—; attending ophthalmologist and pathologist Mt. Sinai Hosp.; attending ophthalmologist Beth Israel Med. Ctr.; clin. prof. ophthalmology and pathology, dir. eye pathology lab. Mt. Sinai Sch. Medicine; assoc. examiner Am. Bd. Ophthalmology; cons. in field. Contbr. numerous articles to profl. publs. With M.C., USAR, 1964-66. Diplomate Am. Bd. Ophthalmology. Fellow ACS, Royal Coll. Ophthalmologists London, Am. Acad. Ophthalmology (Sr. Honor award 1991), N.Y. Acad. Medicine, N.Y. Acad. Scis., Royal Soc. Medicine; mem. AMA, Am. Ophthal. Soc., French Ophthal. Soc., Assn. Rsch. Vision and Ophthalmology, Am. Assn. Ophthalmic Pathologists (pres. 1992—), N.Y. County Med. Soc., Med. Soc. State N.Y., Eastern Ophthalmic Pathology Soc., Pan Am. Assn. Ophthalmology. Address: Mt Sinai Sch Medicine 1 Gustave L Levy Pl # 1183 New York NY 10029-6574 also: 888 Park Ave New York NY 10021-0235

FRIEDMAN, ALLYN STANFORD, mental health executive, psychologist; b. Akron, Ohio, Jan. 24, 1942; s. Frank E. and Hilda (Rosenberg) F.; m. Natalie J. Goldberg, Oct. 14, 1969; children—Maria, Nicole. B.A., U. Akron, 1964, M.A., 1965; postgrad. Clark U., 1965-70. Lic. profl. counselor, marital and family therapist, nationally cert. counselor, nationally cert. mental health adminstr., real estate broker. Psychologist, Fallsview Mental Health Ctr., Cuyahoga Falls, Ohio, 1966, PMD Clinic, Worcester, Mass., 1968-70; psychologist, intern Worcester State Hosp., 1967-68; dir. Southwest Guidance Ctr., Oklahoma City, 1970-74, Red Rock Mental Health Ctr., Oklahoma City, 1974—; cons. Hosp. Corp. Am., Nashville, 1984—. Editor: Readings for General Psychology, 1965. NIMH fellow, 1965-68. Mem. Oklahoma City C. of C., Southwestern Psychol. Assn., Okla. Assn. Community Mental Health Ctrs. (sec. 1981-82, pres. 1983-84), Assn. Mental Health Adminstrs., Am. Soc. for Tng. and Devel., Soc. for Personality Assessment. Office: Red Rock Mental Health Ctr 4400 N Lincoln Blvd Oklahoma City OK 73105-5104

FRIEDMAN, ARNOLD CARL, diagnostic radiologist; b. Bronx, N.Y., Nov. 17, 1951; s. Isidore and Helen and (Lowenthal) F.; m. Wendy Sue Corn, June 8, 1975; children: Jeffrey, Jonathan. BA in Chemistry, Cornell U., 1972; MD, Albert Einstein Coll., 1975. Intern Mt. Sinai Hosp., Hartford, Conn., 1975-76; resident Montefiore Hosp., Bronx, N.Y., 1976-79; asst. prof. Uniformed Svcs. U., Bethesda, Md., 1979-83; assoc. prof. George Washington U., Washington, 1983-84; assoc. prof. Temple U., Phila., 1984-88, prof. radiology, 1989-92; prof. Med. Coll. Pa. Hahnemann U., Phila., 1992-96, acting chmn. radiology scis., 1992-93, chmn. radiology scis., 1993-95; dir. radiology rsch. Med. Coll. Pa. Hahnemann U., Phila., 1996—; chief radiology svcs. Med. Coll. Pa. Hosp., 1996—. Editor: Radiology of Liver, Spleen, Pancreas, Biliary Tract, 1987, Clinical Pelvic Imaging, 1990, Radiology of the Spleen, 1993, Radiology of the Liver Biliary Tract and Pancreas, 1993. Fellow Am. Coll. Radiology; mem. Radiologic Soc. N.Am., Am. Roentgen Ray Soc., Assn. Univ. Radiologists, Assn. Ultrasound in Medicine, Soc. Gastrointestinal Radiology. Home: 524 Hoffman Dr Bryn Mawr PA 19010-1745

FRIEDMAN, BERNARD, psychoanalyst; b. N.Y.C., Oct. 24, 1932; s. Harry and Evelyn (Singer) F.; m. Brenda Mytelka, Jan. 30, 1960 (div.); 1 child, Charles Kenneth. BA in Sociology, CCNY, 1958, MA in Criminology, 1962; MSW, NYU, 1971. Cert. social worker, N.Y. Caseworker N.Y.C. Bur. Child Welfare, 1959-63; probation officer N.Y. Dept. Probation, N.Y.C., 1963-71; supervising probation officer N.Y. Dept. Probation, 1971-89; pvt. practice psychoanalysis N.Y.C., 1979—; staff therapist, Bklyn. Ctr. Psychotherapy, 1971-74; field work supr. Columbia U. and Hunter Coll. Schs. of Social Work, N.Y.C., 1976-79; sr. staff therapist, Washington Sq. Inst. Psychotherapy, 1979—; peace officer trainer, N.Y. State Div. Probation, Albany; drug abuse trainer, N.Y. State Drug Abuse Control Commn., Albany. Cpl. U.S. Army, 1952-54, Korea. Fellow Acad. Cert. Social Workers; mem. Nat. Assn. Social Workers, Nat. Psychol. Assn. for Psychoanalysis (cert. 1971-79). Home and Office: 175 Adams St Brooklyn NY 11201-1850

FRIEDMAN, ELI ARNOLD, nephrologist; b. N.Y.C., Apr. 9, 1933; s. Israel and Ida (Gutman) F.; m. Mildred Barrett-Lennard, June 16, 1957; children: Amy Louise, Rebecca Alicia, Sara Jo. BS, Bklyn. Coll., 1953; MD, SUNY Downstate Med. Center, 1957; DSc (hon.), Maduri Kamaraj U., India, 1985, L.I. U., 1991. Intern in medicine Harvard Med. Sch., 1957-58; resident in medicine Peter Bent Brigham Hosp., Boston, 1960-61; Am. Heart Assn. rsch. fellow Harvard U., 1958-60; mem. faculty, chief divsn. renal disease Downstate Med. Ctr., Bklyn., 1963—; prof. Health Sci. Ctr. SUNY, Bklyn., 1972—, Disting. Tchg. prof., 1992—; bd. dirs. Am. Bur. Med. Aid to China, 1979—, Cleve. Found., 1979—, Bklyn. Nephrology Found., 1978—. Author: Acute Renal Failure, 1973, Strategy in Renal Failure, 1978, Diabetic Renal-retinal Syndrome, 1980, Diabetic Renal-retinal Syndrome 3 Therapy, 1986, Diabetic Nephropathy, 1986, Diabetic Renal-retinal Syndrome 4: Management Strategy, 1987; editor: Journal of Diabetic Complications, 1986—. Lt. comdr. USPHS, 1961-63. Recipient Hoenig award Nat. Kidney Found., 1986, Silver medal U. Bologna, 1988, Disting. Svc. to Black Kidney patients award Howard U., 1989, Physicians award Am. Assn. Kidney Patients, 1989, Alumni medal SUNY Downstate Med. Coll., William Dock Master Tchr. award Alumni Assn. SUNY Health Scis. Ctr., 1992, Recognition award N.Y. Regional Transplant Program, 1994, Am. Kidney Fund Nat. Torchbearer award, 1995, Juvenile Diabetes Found./Bklyn. award honoree, 1995, medal of excellence Am. Kidney Fund, 1996; grantee NIH, USPHS, N.Y. Kidney Found., N.Y. State Kidney Disease Inst., Am. Kidney Fund, Medal of Excellence award, 1996; named master ACP, 1996. Fellow Explorers Club (1st prize photo competition 1995); mem. ACP (Master 1996), Am. Soc. Nephrology, Internat. Soc. Nephrology, Am. Soc. Artificial Internal Organs (pres. 1987—, editor Transactions 1985—), Am. Soc. Immunology, Transplantation Soc., Assn. Am. Physicians, Internat. Soc. Artificial Organs (pres. 1986), Italian Soc. Nephrology (hon.), Royal Soc. Medicine Belgium (corres. mem.). Home: 1049 E 17th St Brooklyn NY 11230-4412 Office: 450 Clarkson Ave Brooklyn NY 11203-2012

FRIEDMAN, EMANUEL A., medical educator; b. N.Y.C., June 9, 1926; s. Louis and Pauline (Feldman) F.; m. E. Judith Salomon, June 6, 1948; children: Lynn Alice, Meryl Ruth, Lee Martin. AB, Bklyn. Coll., 1947; MD, Columbia U., 1951, ScD, 1959; MA, Harvard U., 1969. Diplomate Am. Bd. Ob-Gyn. Intern Bellevue Hosp., N.Y.C., 1951-52; resident Columbia-Presbyn. Hosp., N.Y.C., 1952-57; instr. Columbia Coll. Physicians and Surgeons, 1957-59, asst. prof., 1960-62, assoc. prof., 1962-63; prof., chmn. dept. ob-gyn Chgo. Med. Sch., 1963-69; chmn. dept. ob-gyn Michael Reese Hosp., Chgo., 1963-69; prof. ob-gyn Harvard U., 1969-90, prof. emeritus, 1990—; obstetrician-gynecologist-in-chief Beth Israel Hosp., Boston, 1969-90, obstetrician-gynecologist in chief emeritus, 1990—; prof. health scis. and tech. MIT, 1985-90; prof. ob-gyn Einstein, 1991—. Author: Labor: Clinical Evaluation and Management, 1967, 2d edit., 1978, Rh-Isoimmunization and Erythroblastosis Fetalis, 1969, Lymphatic System of Female Genitalia, 1971, Biological Principles and Modern Practice of Obstetrics, 1974, Blood Pressure, Edema and Proteinuria in Pregnancy, 1976, Pregnancy Hypertension, 1977, Uterine Physiology, 1979, Advances in Perinatal Medicine, 1981, 5th edit., 1986, Obstetrical Decision Making, 1982, 2d edit., 1987, Management of Labor, 1983, 2d edit., 1988, Gynecological Decision Making, 1983, 2d edit., 1987, Labor and Delivery Impact on Offspring, 1987, Legal Principles and Practice in Obstetrics and Gynecology, 1988, Vol. 2, 1990. Served with USNR, 1944-46. Recipient Joseph Mather Smith research prize Columbia U., 1958, Disting. Alumnus award Bklyn Coll., 1964, Bicentennial commemorative silver medallion award Columbia U., 1967. Fellow ACS, Am. Coll. Ob-Gyn, N.Y. Acad. Medicine; mem. N.Y. Acad. Scis., Soc. Exptl. Biology and Medicine, Soc. Gynecologic Investigation, AAUP, AAAS, Alpha Omega Alpha. Office: One Lincoln Pla New York NY 10023

FRIEDMAN, ERNEST HARVEY, physician, psychiatrist; b. Cleve., Jan. 8, 1931; s. Sol and Ann (Nittskoff) F.; m. Anita Rose Bogdanow, Oct. 26, 1962; children: Rachel Samantha, Sarah Ann, Eric Daniel, Jessica Emily. BS, Case Western Res. U., 1952; MD, Ohio State U., 1956. Diplomate Am. Bd. Psychiatry and Neurology. Intern U. Ill. Hosps., Chgo., 1956-57; psychiat. resident U. Hosps. of Cleve., 1957-60; clin. instr. Case Western Res. U., Cleve., 1974-86, asst. clin. prof., 1983—; vis. psychiatrist Mt. Sinai Hosp., Cleve., 1963-70, sr. vis. psychiatrist, 1970—; pvt. practice psychiatry, medicine Cleve., 1962—; owner, computer mfr. Voxaflex Co., East Cleveland, Ohio, 1986—; mem. courtesy staff Laurelwood Hosp., Willoughby, Ohio, 1991—; mem. courtesy staff Huron Hosp., East Cleveland, Ohio, 1971—; chmn. ad hoc com. on stress Am. Heart Assn., Cleve., 1977; cons. psychiatrist Nat. Exercise and Heart Disease Study, Washington, 1972-75. Mem. editorial bd. Heart and Lung, 1974-80; patentee computer software and hardware. Served as lt. comdr. M.C., USNR, 1960-62. Grantee-in-aid Am. Heart Assn., Cleve., 1964, 65, 75. Fellow Am. Psychiat. Assn. Jewish. Office: Voxaflex Co 1831 Forest Hills Blvd Cleveland OH 44112-4313

FRIEDMAN, GEORGE JAY, psychologist; b. N.Y.C., Oct. 15, 1945; s. Martin and Lee (Jones) F.; m. Patricia Ann Cole, June 9, 1969; 3 children. BA in Psychology, Rutgers U., 1969; MA in Psychology, U. Hawaii, 1972, PhD of Psychology, 1978. Lic. psychologist, Hawaii. Instr. dept. psychology U. Hawaii, Honolulu, 1972-78; intern clin. psychology Mercy Cath. Med. Ctr., Phila., 1978-79; psychologist Crozer-Chester (Pa.) Med. Ctr., 1980-86; dir. psychiat. svcs., chief planner cmty. mental health Am. Samoa Govt., Pago Pago, 1986-87; clin. psychologist State of Hawaii, Wailuku, 1987-91; pvt. practice Wailuku, 1991—; instr. dept. psychology Thomas Jefferson U., Phila., 1980-86; cons. Kula (Hawaii) Hosp., 1990-92, Maui Assn. Retarded Citizens, Wailuku, 1991-92, Baldwin H.S., Maui, Hawaii, 1987-91. Contbr. articles to profl. jours. Fellow NSF, 1970-74. Mem. APA, Hawaii Psychol. Assn., Maui Assn. Psychologists, Maui Mental Health Assn., Sigma Xi. Office: 2070 Vineyard St Wailuku HI 96793

FRIEDMAN, H. HAROLD, cardiologist, internist; b. N.Y.C., July 31, 1917; s. Morris and Sarah (Rudnitsky) F.; m. Charlotte Lostfogel, Mar. 7, 1943; children: Alan Edward, Marsha Lynn, Betsy Ellen. B.S., NYU, 1936, M.D., 1939. Intern Jewish Hosp., Bklyn., 1939-41; resident Jewish Hosp., 1941-42, 46, Bellevue Hosp., N.Y.C., 1947; practice medicine specializing in cardiology and internal medicine Denver, 1948—; attending physician, dir. electrocardiographic lab. Rose Med. Ctr., pres. med. staff, 1959; attending physician St. Joseph Hosp., Denver; fellow in medicine NYU Coll. Medicine, 1947; pres. med. staff Nat. Jewish Hosp., 1959; assoc. clin. prof. medicine U. Colo. Sch. Medicine, Denver, 1963-75, prof., 1975—; mem. Colo. State Bd. Med. Examiners, 1962-67. Author: Outline of Electrocardiography, 1963, Diagnostic Electrocardiography and Vectorcardiography, 1971, 3d edit., 1985; editor: Problem-Oriented Medical Diagnosis, 1975, 4th edit., 1987, 5th edit., 1991, 6th edit., 1996. Served to capt. M.C. AUS, 1942-46. Recipient Outstanding Clin. Faculty Teaching award U. Colo. Sch. Medicine, 1981-82, Outstanding Clin. Faculty Svc. award U. Colo. Sch. Medicine, 1991, Outstanding Clin. Faculty Acad. Pubs. award U. Colo. Sch. Medicine, 1992; Rose Med. Ctr. Physicians Recognition award for Excellence in Teaching Rsch., 1993. Fellow ACP, Am. Coll. Cardiology, Am. Coll. Chest Physicians, Council on Clin. Cardiology, Am. Heart Assn.; mem. AMA, Denver Med. Soc., Colo. Med. Soc., Phi Beta Kappa. Home: 442 Leyden St Denver CO 80220-5954 Office: 2005 Franklin St Denver CO 80205-5401

FRIEDMAN, HAROLD IRA, plastic surgeon, educator; b. N.Y.C., Oct. 22, 1946; s. Joseph and Dorothy (Asnin) F.; m. Clarke Emmons, Nov. 24, 1976. BS, Hobart Coll., 1967; PhD, U. Va., 1972, MD, 1974. Diplomate Nat. Bd. Med. Examiners, Am. Bd. Plastic Surgery. Intern surgery U. Va. Med. Center, Charlottesville, 1974-75; cell biologist gen. surgeon Letterman Army Inst. Research, San Francisco, 1975-78; resident gen. surgery U. Ariz. Med. Center, Tucson 1978-82; resident in plastic surgery U. Va. Med. Center, Charlottesville, 1982-84; prof. dept. surgery Sch. Medicine U. S.C., Columbia, 1984—, adj. assoc. prof. Coll. Health, 1986—; adj. assoc. prof. dept. biomed. engring. Clemson U., 1985—. Contbr. articles to profl. jours. Served to maj., M.C. U.S. Army, 1975-78; lt. col. M.C. USAR. Diplomate Am. Bd. Surgery, Recipient Van Winkle award U. Ariz., 1982; Upjohn Achievement award, 1982; decorated Army Commendation medal; recipient James Kembrough award for outstanding urologic research, 1976. Fellow ACS; mem. AMA, Am. Inst. Nutrition, Am. Assn. Clin. Nutrition, Am. Soc. Exptl. Biology, Am. Soc. Parenteral and Enteral Nutrition, Am. Soc. Plastic & Reconstructive Surgeons, Assn. Mil. Surgeons U.S., S.C. Soc. Plastic and Reconstructive Surgeons. Home: 22 Olde Springs Rd Columbia SC 29223-6043 Office: U SC Dept Surgery 3320 Medical Park Rd Ste 300 Columbia SC 29203-6806

FRIEDMAN, HARVEY MICHAEL, infectious diseases educator; b. Montreal, Quebec, Can., May 29, 1944; came to U.S., 1971; s. Sidney and Sybil (Garfinkle) F.; m. Cynthia Diane Mickey, Apr. 12, 1980; children: Lisa, Steven, Julie. BS, McGill U., 1965, MD, 1969. Intern, resident Jewish Gen. Hosp., Montreal, 1969-71; fellow in virology Wistar Inst., Phila., 1971-73; fellow in infectious disease U. Pa. Hosp., Phila., 1973-75; asst. prof., assoc. prof. Med. Sch. U. Pa., Phila., 1975-91, prof. Med. Sch., 1991—; med. dir. Clin. Virology Lab. Children's Hosp., Phila., 1975—; chief Infectious Diseases U. Pa. Hosp., Phila., 1990—. Contbr. numerous papers and book chpts. Grantee NIH, Found., 1978—. Fellow Infectious Disease Soc. Am.; mem. AAAS, Am. Soc. Clin. Investigation, Assn. Am. Physicians. Office: U Pa Med Sch 537 E Johnson St Philadelphia PA 19144

FRIEDMAN, IRA HUGH, surgeon; b. N.Y.C., July 17, 1933; s. Leonard Seymour and Ruth (Binder) F.; m. Erika Berger, Oct. 22, 1961; children—Richard Lawrence, Joanne Beth. B.A., NYU, 1953, M.D., 1957. Diplomate Am. Bd. Surgery, Nat. Bd. Med. Examiners. Intern, resident in surgery Beth Isreal Med. Ctr., N.Y.C., 1957-59, 61-63; surg. resident Bellevue Hosp., N.Y.C., 1959-60; practice medicine specializing in surgery N.Y.C., 1963—; attending surgeon Beth Israel Med. Ctr., pres. med. bd., 1981-82; assoc. clin. prof. surgery Albert Einstein Coll. Medicine; med. adv. to N.Y.C. dir. SSS, 1968. Contbr. articles to profl. jours. Bd. dirs. Union Orthodox Jewish Congregations Am., Am. Com. for Shaare Zedek Hosp. of Jerusalem, Yeshiva Sha-alvim, Isreal, P'Tach; co-chmn. bd. dirs. Yeshiva Chofetz Chaim, N.Y.C. Recipient Koach award Israel Bond Orgn., 1977; N.Y. Heart Assn. fellow, 1960-61. Fellow A.C.S., Am. Coll. Gastroenterology, Am. Soc. Colon and Rectal Surgeons, Royal Soc. Medicine; mem. AMA, N.Y. Acad. Medicine, N.Y. Surg. Soc., Soc. Surgery of Alimentary Tract, Soc. Am. Gastrointestinal Endoscopic Surgeons, Am. Gastroent. Assn., N.Y. Gastroent. Assn., N.Y. Cancer Soc., N.Y. Soc. Colon and Rectal Surgeons, Collegium Internationale Chirugiae Digestive, N.Y. State Med. Assn., N.Y. County Med. Assn. Home: 1175 Park Ave New York NY 10128-1211

FRIEDMAN, JAY SCOTT, internist; b. L.A., Dec. 11, 1956; s. Martin I. and Roberta (Glasser) F.; m. Marypat Gianotti, Feb. 9, 1986; children: Aaron, Adam. BA, UCLA, 1979; MD, U. Tex., 1983. Diplomate Am. Bd. Internal Medicine. Intern Good Samaritan Hosp. & Med. Ctr., Phoenix, 1983-84; resident St. Joseph's Hosp. and Med. Ctr., Phoenix, 1984-86; assoc. med. dir. Mercy Care St. Joseph's Hosp., Phoenix, 1986—; pvt. practice internal medicine, Scottsdale, Ariz., 1986—; med. dir. Hospice of the Valley, Phoenix, 1987—. Fellow Am. Coll. Physicians; mem. Ariz. Med. Assn., Maricopa County Med. Soc., assn. Physicians & Surgeons (bd. dirs. 1994—). Office: Adult Internal Medicine 10290 N 92d St Ste 300 Scottsdale AZ 85258

FRIEDMAN, JEFFREY ROBERT, psychiatrist, educator; b. Mpls., May 26, 1956; s. Harry Samuel and Gertrude (Rotenberg) F.; m. Laura Jean Weisblatt, July 14, 1985; children: Gabrielle Eve, Daniel Adam. BA, Yale U., 1978; MD, U. Chgo., 1982. Diplomate Am. Bd. Psychiatry and Neurology. Intern medicine Mt. Auburn Hosp., Cambridge, Mass., 1982-83; intern neurology Mass. Gen. Hosp., Boston, 1982-83; resident psychiatry McLean Hosp., Belmont, Mass., 1983-86, asst. psychiatrist, 1986-88, asst. clin. psychiatrist, 1988—; instr. psychiatry Harvard U. Med. Sch., Boston, 1986-88, clin. instr., 1988—, psychiatrist Harvard Community Health Plan, 1988—; assoc. residency dir. Harvard Longwood Psychiatry Residency, 1995—; candidate Boston Psychoanalytic Soc. and Inst., 1986—. Recipient Paul Howard award McLean Hosp., 1986; Group for Advancement Psychiatry Ginsburg fellow, 1984-86. Mem. Am. Psychiat. Assn. Office: 875 Massachusetts Ave Ste 51 Cambridge MA 02139-3067

FRIEDMAN, JOEL MATTHEW, oral and maxillofacial surgeon, educator; b. Chelsea, Mass., Sept. 20, 1942; s. Abraham and Theda (Epstein) F.; m. Gail Fishman, Dec. 18, 1965 (div. 1981); 1 child, Alison Beth; m. Carole Nadan, May 31, 1981 (dec.); m. Susan K. Shavin, Dec., 1990 (div. 1994); m. Marian G. Faytell, April 9, 1995. BA, Hofstra U., 1964; DDS, Columbia U., 1968. Diplomate Am. Bd. Oral and Maxillofacial Surgery. Intern, Bronx Mcpl. Hosp.-Albert Einstein Coll. Medicine, 1968-69, resident in oral and maxillofacial surgery, 1969-71; practice dentistry specializing in oral and maxillofacial surgery, Bronx, N.Y., 1971—, Yonkers, N.Y., 1986—; dir. oral and maxillofacial surgery Bronx Mcpl. Hosp., 1971-78, dir. house-staff edn., 1971-78, dir. oral and maxillofacial surgery, 1978-92; assoc. clin. prof. denistry Albert Einstein Coll. of Medicine, 1976—; asst. dir. oral and maxillofacial surgery Albert Einstein Coll. Medicine-Montefiore Med. Ctr., 1983-92; dir. oral & maxillofacial surgery Yonkers Gen. Hosp., 1988; vice-chmn. oral and maxillofacial surgery St. Johns Riverside Hosp., Yonkers; assoc. clin. prof. oral & maxillofacial surgery Columbia U. Sch. Dental & Oral Surgery, 1994—; assoc. attending Presbyn. Hosp., N.Y.C., 1994—. Contbr. articles to profl. jours. Chmn. Bronx Health Systems Agy. Bd., 1977-78, Montefiore Community Adv. Bd., 1977—; pres. MMC-CAB, 1981-84; bd. trustees Congregation B'Nai Jeshurun, N.Y.C., 1996—. Fellow Am. Dental Soc. of Anesthesiology, Am. Coll. Dentists, Am. Coll. Oral and Maxillofacial Surgeons, Internat. Coll. Dentists; mem. Bronx County Dental Soc. (treas. 1988-90, v.p. 1991-92, pres.- elect 1993-95, pres. 1995—), ADA, Am. Soc. Oral and Maxillofacial Surgeons, N.Y. State Dental Soc. Anesthesiology (pres. 1981), Am. Dental Soc. Anesthesiology (Heidbrink award com.), Riverdale Dental Study Group, Jarvie Soc., Riverdale Mental Health Assn. (bd. dirs. 1979—, asst. treas. 1987, profl. adv. com., 1973—), Nat. Young Judaea Alumni Assn. (pres. 1990-91), Hadassah Zionist youth commn. N.Y.C. Democrat. Jewish. Avocation: skiing. Home: 185 E 85th St 33B New York NY 10028 Office: 3333 Henry Hudson Pky W Bronx NY 10463-3224

FRIEDMAN, JONATHAN DAVID, athletic trainer, emergency medical technician; b. Bklyn., June 24, 1967; s. Phillip and Elaine R. (Brumberger) F. BS, East Stroudsburg U., 1989; postgrad., Rutgers U., 1989-90. Registered athletic trainer, emergency med. technician, N.J. Asst. athletic trainer East Brunswick (N.J.) Pub. Schs., 1989-90; dist. athletic trainer South River (N.J.) Pub. Schs., 1990-92, Long Branch (N.J.) Pub. Schs., 1992—; mem. N.J. State First Aid Coun., 1987—; lifeguard/EMS supr. Borough Monmouth Beach, N.J., 1994—; adminstrv. sec. East Brunswick Rescue Squad, 1992-93. Vol. EMT East Brunswick Rescue Squad, 1987—, Gen. Ambulance Corps., Stroudsburg, Pa., 1987-89, Eatontown (N.J.) First Aid Squad, 1994—. Recipient Heroism commendation N.J. Gov. Thomas Kean, 1985, Civilian Meritorious Svc. award East Brunswick Mayor William Fox, 1985, Bravery commendation Middlesex (N.J.) County Prosecutor Alan Rockoff, 1985. Mem. Nat. Athletic Trainers Assn., N.J. Athletic Trainers Assn., Phi Epsilon Kappa (v.p. 1988-89). Jewish. Home: 10 Ginger Ct Eatontown NJ 07724 Office: Long Branch Pub Schs 391 Westwood Ave Long Branch NJ 07740

FRIEDMAN, LEONARD ROBERT, physician, lawyer, medical legal consultant; b. Bklyn., Sept. 3, 1936; s. Jacob and Celia (Levine) F.; m. Doreen Kau, Feb. 3, 1962; 1 child, Amanda. AB, U. Chgo., 1956; MD, SUNY, Syracuse, 1960; JD, Harvard U., 1969. Diplomate Am. Bd. Psychiatry and Neurology, Am. Bd. Psychiatry and the Law. Pvt. practice Boston, 1969—. Capt. M.C., U.S. Army, 1964-66. Jewish. Office: 264 Beacon St Boston MA 02116-1236

FRIEDMAN, MARION, internist, family physician, medical administrator; b. Onley, Va., Aug. 15, 1918; s. Jacob and Bertha (Bernstein) F.; m. Esther Lerner, May 29, 1941; 1 son, Barry Howard. BS, U. Md., 1938, MD, 1942. Diplomate Am. Bd. Family Practice (charter). Rotating intern U.S. Marine Hosp., Norfolk, Va., 1942-43; asst. health officer Montgomery County (Kans.), 1943-44; health officer Cherokee County (Kans.), 1944-45; asst. health commr. St. Louis County (Mo.), 1945-46; resident internal medicine U.S. Marine Hosp., Balt., 1946-49; fellow medicine Johns Hopkins Sch. Medicine, Balt., 1948-49; individual practice medicine, specializing in family practice internal medicine, Balt., 1949-84; asst. medicine U. Md., Balt., 1954-72; chief dept. gen. practice Doctors Hosp., 1952-54; chief dept. family practice N. Charles Gen. Hosp., Balt., 1972-75, med. dir. ambulatory svcs., 1972-86, assoc. chief medicine, 1975-88, pres. med. staff, 1964, 68, chmn. med. exec. com., 1984-85, trustee, 1984-85, physician advisor, 1984-91; physician advisor Delmarva Found. for Med. Care, 1984-89; instr. Ctr. for Health Edn., 1985; lectr. Md. affiliate Am. Heart Assn., 1986-87; med. dir. Chesapeake Health Plan, 1991-92; task force on improving access to primary care Md.-DC AFL-CIO, 1993-94. Mem. profl. adv. bd. Patient Care, 1994—; contbr. numerous articles to sci. jours. Chmn. cultural com. Liberty Jewish Ctr., 1960-62; mem. Md. High Blood Pressure Coordinating Coun., 1980-82; mem. task force on family physicians Md. Health Resources Planning Commn., Md. State Legislature, 1983-84; trustee Jimmie Swartz Found., 1982—. Served with USPHS, 1942-49; maj. Md. Def. Force, 1995—. Fellow Am. Acad. Family Physicians (charter), Md. Acad. Family Physicians (chmn. comm. on health care svcs. 1978-83, 84-92, pres. 1983-84, prodn. editor 1984-86, editor 1986—, chmn. manpower adv. com. 1992—, Chpt. Publ. award 1991, 94); mem. AMA, Am. Acad. Family Physicians, Balt. City Med. Soc. (alt. del. 1978-82, 93-94, del. 1982-88, profl. edn. com. 1985-87, chmn. 1987-90, nominating com. 1992), Med. and Chirurg. Faculty Md. (lectr. 1983, legis. com. 1985-87, 90-93, pro com. 1989-94, standard benefits tech. adv. com. 1993-94, mem. editl. bd. Md. Med. Jour. 1994—, co-editor Nov. 1995, scientific activities com. 1995—), World Med. Assn., Pan-Am. Med. Assn., Md. Heart Assn., Md. Thoracic Soc. (mem. planning com. 1994—), Am. Thoracic Soc., Am. Heart Assn., Md. Taxpayers Assn. (bd. dirs. 1994—), Phi Kappa Phi (hon.Scholastic Soc., 1938). Democrat. First to suggest use of steroid in subacute deltoid bursitis in world lit., 1952. Home: 7906 Terrapin Ct Baltimore MD 21208-3126

FRIEDMAN, MARK TODD, pathologist; b. Augsburg, Germany, Oct. 22, 1963; s. Peter and Liselotte (Gebhard) F. BS magna cum laude, N.Y. Inst. Tech., 1987; DO, N.Y. Coll. Osteo. Medicine, 1990. Diplomate Am. Bd.

Pathology. Intern Humana Hosp. Palm Beaches, West Palm Beach, Fla., 1990-91; resident in pathology L.I. Jewish Med. Ctr., New Hyde Park, N.Y., 1991-95, chief resident in pathology, 1994-95; fellow in transfusion medicine N.Y. Blood Ctr., N.Y.C., 1995-96; dir. blood bank L.I. Coll. Hosp., N.Y.C., 1996—. Contbr. articles to profl. jours. Mem. AMA, Am. Osteo. Assn., Coll. Am. Pathologists, Am. Assn. Blood Banks. Office: LI Coll Hosp 340 Henry St Brooklyn NY 11201

FRIEDMAN, NAOMI, physician assistant; b. Bklyn., Oct. 16, 1955; d. Eugene and Claire (Papernick) F. BS, Bklyn. Coll., 1977; Physician Asst. Degree, L.I. U., Bklyn., 1987. Physician asst. Luth. Hosp., Bklyn., 1987-90, Downstate Med. Ctr., Bklyn., 1990-92, Cornell Med. Ctr., N.Y.C., 1992-95, St. Luke's Med. Ctr., N.Y.C., 1995—. Mem. Am. Acad. Physician Assts. Jewish. Home: 10 Amsterdam New York NY 10023 Office: St Luke's Hosp 1111 Amsterdam Ave New York NY 10025

FRIEDMAN, NATHAN BARUCH, physician; b. N.Y.C., Jan. 30, 1911; s. Emanuel David and Rose (Burgenicht) F.; widower; children: MaryLou, Emily. BS, Harvard U., 1930; MD, Cornell U., 1934. Intern Montefiore Hosp., 1936; resident U. Chgo., 1938-39; instr. Stanford U., L.A., 1941; dir. labs. Cedars Hosp., L.A., 1948-69, cons., 1970—; clin. prof. U. So. Calif., L.A., 1950—. Maj. AUS, 1942-46. Home: 15150 Mulholland Dr Los Angeles CA 90077 Office: Cedars-Sinai Med Ctr 8700 Beverly Blvd Los Angeles CA 90048

FRIEDMAN, NEIL RICHARD, urologist; b. Detroit, Sept. 24, 1948; s. Solomon Henry and Thelma Shaynee (Gootson) F.; m. Susan Hope Feit, May 25, 1980; children: Andrew Todd, Katherine Elizabeth. BS, U. Mich., 1970, MD, 1974. Diplomate Am. Bd. Urology. Resident Dartmouth U. Med. Ctr., Hanover, N.H., 1974-76, Washington U., St. Louis, 1976-79; pvt. practice Chgo., 1979—. Fellow Am. Urol. Assn. Office: 64 Old Orchard Ste 510 Skokie IL 60077

FRIEDMAN, NICHOLAS, physician; b. Port Elizabeth, South Africa, Dec. 2, 1958; came to U.S., 1979; s. Theodore Morris and Annette (Bengis) F.; m. Deborah Friedman; children: Elizabeth, Carolyn, Alexandra. BA, Emory U., 1983, MD, 1987. Diplomate Am. Bd. Nuclear Medicine. Resident in surgery Emory U., 1987-89; resident in nuclear medicine U. Conn., Hartford, 1991-93; clin. sect. chief nuclear medicine svc. Hines VA Hosp., Maywood, Ill., 1993—; asst. prof. radiology Loyola U. Med. Ctr., Maywood, Ill., 1994—. Contbr. articles to profl. jours. Mem. Soc. Nuclear Medicine (moderator Ctrl. chpt. 1996), Am. Congress of Nuclear Physicians (govt. rels. com. 1994). Home: 6023 Mill Bridge Ln Lisle IL 60532

FRIEDMAN, NORMAN, psychotherapist, writer, poet; b. Boston, Apr. 10, 1925; s. Samuel and Eva (Nathanson) F.; m. Zelda Nathanson, June 7, 1945; children: Michael, Janet. AB, Harvard U., 1948, AM, 1949, PhD in English, 1952; MSW, Adelphi U., 1978; grad., Gestalt Ctr. for Psychotherapy, 1978. Diplomate Am. Bd. Examiners in Clin. Social Work; cert. social worker, N.Y. From instr. to assoc. prof. U. Conn., Storrs, 1952-63; from assoc. prof. to prof. Queens Coll., CUNY, Flushing, 1963-88; pvt. practice Flushing, Manhattan, 1978—; dir. Gestalt Therapy Ctr. Queens, Flushing, 1984—; lectr. Fulbright Found., U. Nantes and Nice, France, 1966-67; faculty Gestalt Ctr. Psychotherapy and Tng., N.Y.C., 1995—. Author: E.E. Cummings: The Art of His Poetry, 1960, E.E. Cummings: The Growth of a Writer, 1964, Form and Meaning in Fiction, 1975; The Magic Badge: Poems 1953-84, The Intrusions of Love: Poems, 1992, Revaluing Cummings: Further Essays on the Poet, 1996. Lt. (j.g.) USNR, 1943-46, 48. Recipient Bowdoin Essay prize, Harvard U., 1948, Northwest Rev. Annual Poetry prize, 1963, Borestone Mountain Poetry awards, 1964, 67; grantee Am. Coun. Learned Socs., 1959, 60. Fellow N.Y. State Soc. Clin. Social Work Psychotherapists; mem. NASW, MLA, Phi Beta Kappa. Democrat. Jewish. Home and Office: Gestalt Therapy Ctr Queens 33-54 164th St Flushing NY 11358-1442

FRIEDMAN, PAUL JAY, radiologist, chest radiologist, educator; b. N.Y.C., Jan. 20, 1937; s. Louis Alexander and Rose (Solomon) F.; m. Elisabeth Clare Richardson, June 18, 1960; children: Elizabeth Ruth Coley, Deborah Anne Yeager, Matthew Alexander, Rachel Clare. B.S., U. Wis., 1955; postgrad., Oxford (Eng.) U., 1957-58; M.D., Yale U., 1960. Intern Einstein Med. Sch., N.Y.C., 1960-61; resident in radiology Columbia-Presbyn. Hosp., N.Y.C., 1961-64; fellow in pulmonary pathology Yale U., 1966-68; mem. faculty U. Calif. Med. Sch., San Diego, 1968—; prof. radiology U. Calif. Med. Sch., 1975—, assoc. dean acad. affairs, 1982-88, dean acad. affairs, 1989-95; cons. VA; vis. scholar Inst. Med./NAS, AAMC, 1988-89; mem. adv. com. on rsch. integrity DHHS, 1991-93; cons. 26th edit. Stedman's Med. Dictionary; specialist in thoracic radiology and rsch. ethics, tenure and retirement issues. Mem. editorial bd. Investigative Radiology, 1976-87, Am. Jour. Roentgenology, 1986-88; contbr. articles med. jours. Bd. dirs. La Jolla Symphony Assn., 1987-92. Lt. comdr. M.C., USNR, 1964-66. Markle scholar acad. medicine, 1969-74; Picker Found. advanced acad. fellow and scholar, 1966-69. Fellow Am. Coll. Chest Physicians, Am. Coll. Radiology; mem. Assn. of Am. Med. Colls., Coun. Acad. Socs. (adminstrv. bd. 1991—, chair 1995, chair com. on rsch. integrity 1994—), AAUP, Assn. Univ. Radiologists (rep. to coun. acad. socs. 1985—), Fleischner Soc. (pres. 1994-95), Calif. radiology Soc., Radiol. Soc. N.Am., San Diego radiology Soc., Roentgen Ray Soc., Soc. Med. Decision Making, Soc. Computer Applications in radiology, Phi Beta Kappa, Alpha Omega Alpha. Home: 5644 Soledad Rd La Jolla CA 92037-7048 Office: U Calif Sch Medicine Dept Radiology 200 W Arbor Dr San Diego CA 92103-8756

FRIEDMAN, PAUL SIGMUND, radiologist, educator; b. N.Y.C., Aug. 5, 1914; s. Lewis J. and Dorothy (Kantrowitz) F.; m. Elise Kohn; children: Ellen, Peter B., Steven L. AB, Columbia Coll., 1933; MD, NYU, 1937. Diplomate Am. Bd. Radiology. Intern, Bellevue Hosp., N.Y.C., 1937-38, Jewish Hosp., Phila., 1938-40; fellow, resident in radiology Jefferson Hosp. and Med. Coll., Phila., 1940-41; then asst. radiologist Episcopal Hosp.; instr. U. Pa. Grad. Sch., 1945; asst. radiologist Jewish Hosp., Phila., 1945-46, assoc. radiologist, 1946-49; radiologist Rush Hosp., 1949-60; cons. radiologist Valley Forge Gen. Hosp., 1949-70; from vis. prof. radiology to prof. radiology Hahnemann Med. Coll. and Hosp., 1980—; physician, pres. Radiology Assocs., Phila., 1980—; co-chmn. health div. Ben Gurion U.; cons. radiologist Malvern Inst. for Psychiat. and Alcoholic Studies. Contbr. articles to profl. jours. Mem. health issues adv. panel malpractice commn. HEW; bd. govs. Dropsie U., Nat. Jewish Coaltion, 1992—; bd. dirs. Phila. Jewish Community Relations Council, Montgomery County Library, Neighborhood Ctr., Temple Sinai, United Negro Coll. Fund, Hebrew Immigration Aid Soc., Phila. chpt. Am. Technion Soc., Mus. Am. Jewish History; Jewish Nat. Fund.; v.p., pres. Phila. chpt. Friends of Shaare Zedek Hosp. in Jerusalem; trustee Phila. State Hosp.; mem. nat. exec. com. Am. Jewish Com., chmn. Phila. chpt. Served with U.S. Army, 1941-45. Recipient Four Chaplains Legions of Honor award, 1978; named Goodwill Ambassador for City Phila., 1984; citation of honor Jewish Nat. Fund, 1984. Fellow Am. Coll. Radiology (emeritus); mem. AMA (legis. council, ho. of dels., nat. speakers bur.), Phila. Roentgen Ray Soc. (chmn. program com., econs. com.), Pa. Radiol. Soc. (v.p., bd. dirs., chmn. program com.), Pa. Med. Soc. (Speaker's award 1968), Phila. County Med. Soc., Pa. Med. Polit. Action Com., Am. Coll. Chest Physicians, Am. Coll. Legal Medicine, Am. Coll. Nuclear Medicine, Am. Heart Assn., Radiol. Soc. N.Am., Phila. Coll. Physicians, Vesper, Phi Beta Kappa, numerous others. Avocations: philosophy, photography, tennis, running. Office: Radiology Assocs Ste 715 1422 Chestnut St Philadelphia PA 19102-2509

FRIEDMAN, ROBERT, prosthodontist; b. Bridgeport, Conn., Jan. 23, 1928; s. Yale and Sarah (Mocher) F.; m. Elaine Manasevit; children: Dorian Randy, Amanda Pam, James Eric. BA, U. Bridgeport, 1950; DDS, Temple U., 1954. Pvt. practice dentistry Bridgeport, 1956-70, pvt. practice prosthodontics, 1970-88; pvt. practice prosthodontics Fairfield, Conn., 1989—; clin. assoc. prof. dental medicine, U. Conn., Farmington, 1972-75; vis. lectr., U. Pitts., 1973-80, Einstein Sch. Medicine, N.Y.C., 1977—, U. Pa., 1979-81; pres. New Eng. Found. Continuing Dental Edn., Durham, N.H., 1976-77. clin. assoc. prof. dental medicine U. Conn., Farmington, 1972-75; vis. lectr. U. Pitts., 1973-80, Einstein Sch. Medicine, N.Y.C., 1977—, U. Pa., 1979-81; pres. New Eng. Found. Continuing Dental Edn., Durham, N.H., 1976-77; mem. Northeast Regional Bd. Dental Examiners, 1994—; commr. Conn. State Dental Commn., 1994—. Fellow Internat. Coll. Dentists, Am. Coll. Dentists; mem. ADA, Am. Prosthodontic Soc., Am. Equilibration Soc., Bridgeport Dental Assn. (pres. 1987), Conn. State Dental Assn. (bd govs. 1983—, pres. 1990), So. New Eng. Acad. Practice Adminstrn. (pres. 1971-72), Birchwood Country Club (bd. govs. 1988) Hill and Dale Country Club. Republican. Jewish. Office: 111 Beach Rd Fairfield CT 06430-6668

FRIEDMAN, SELWYN MARVIN, biology educator; b. N.Y.C., May 17, 1929; s. Louis and Leah (Weinstein) F.; m. Rivka Teitelbaum, May 28, 1972. BS, U. Mich., 1951; MS, Purdue U., 1953, PhD, 1961. Postdoctoral fellow Case-Western Res. U., Cleve., 1961-62, Albert Einstein Coll. Medicine, N.Y.C., 1962-63; rsch. fellow Columbia U. Coll. Physicians and Surgeons, N.Y.C., 1963-66; asst. prof. Hunter Coll. of CUNY, N.Y.C. 1966-69, assoc. prof., 1969-91, full prof. biology. 1991—; vis. scientist dept. chemistry Columbia U., N.Y.C., 1973, Pub. Health Rsch. Inst., N.Y.C., 1991; U.S. coord. Japan Coop. Sci. Program, NSF, 1977; referee NSF and AEC Grant Proposals, 1976-87. Author: (with others) Thermophilic Microorganisms, 1992; editor: Biochemistry of Thermophily, 1978; contbr. articles to profl. jours. With U.S. Army, 1954-56. Rsch. grantee NIH, 1967-70, 75-78, CUNY Rsch. Award Program. 1971-95. Fellow N.Y. Acad. Scis. (chair microbiology sect., 1990-92); mem. Am. Soc. Microbiology, Sigma Xi. Democrat. Hebrew. Home: 340 E 64th St Apt 14L New York NY 10021-7517 Office: Hunter Coll CUNY 695 Park Ave New York NY 10021-5024

FRIEDMAN, SHELLY ARNOLD, cosmetic surgeon; b. Providence, Jan. 1, 1949; s. Saul and Estelle (Moverman) F.; m. Andrea Leslie Falchook, Aug. 30, 1975; children: Bethany Erin, Kimberly Rebecca, Brent David, Jennifer Ashley. BA, Providence Coll., 1971; DO, Mich. State U., 1982. Diplomate Nat. Bd. Med. Examiners, Am. Bd. Dermatology. Intern Pontiac (Mich.) Hosp., 1982-83, resident in dermatology, 1983-86; assoc. clin. prof. dept. internal med. Mich. State U., 1984-89, adj. clin. prof., 1989—; med. dir. Inst. Cosmetic Dermatology, Scottsdale, Ariz., 1986—. Contbr. aritcles to profl. jours. Mem. B'nai B'rith Men's Council, 1973, Jewish Welfare Fund, 1973. Am. Physicians fellow for medicine, 1982. Mem. AMA, Am. Osteopathic Assn., Am. Assn. Cosmetic Surgeons, Am. Acad. Cosmetic Surgery, Internat. Soc. Dermatologic Surgery, Internat. Acad. Cosmetic Surgery, Am. Acad. Dermatology, Am. Soc. Dermatol. Surgery, Frat. Order Police, Sigma Sigma Phi. Jewish. Office: Scottsdale Inst Cosmetic Dermatology 5206 N Scottsdale Rd Scottsdale AZ 85253-7006

FRIEDMAN, STANLEY MARCUS, psychiatrist; b. N.Y.C., May 19, 1925; s. Morris Albert and Celia (Walker) F.; children: Jennifer, Steven, William. BS, CCNY, 1946, MS, 1947; PhD, Case Western Res. U., 1950; MD, NYU, 1954. Rsch. cons. Port of N.Y. Authority, N.Y.C., 1951-58; pvt. practice N.Y.C., 1958—; with Mt. Sinai Hosp., N.Y.C., 1958—, clin. asst. prof. Sch. Medicine, 1975-81, clin. assoc. prof. Sch. Medicine, 1981—. Contbr. articles to profl. jours. Lt. (j.g.) USMS, 1943-46, USNR. Founds. Fund for Rsch. in Psychiatry grantee, 1958-59, NIMH grantee, 1954-65. Mem. Am. Psychiat. Assn., Am. Psychoanalytic Assn., N.J. Psychoanalytic Soc. Home: 53 Edgewood St Tenafly NJ 07670-2909 Office: 9 E 96th St New York NY 10128-0778 also: 53 Edgewood St Tenafly NJ 07670-2909

FRIEDMAN, SYDNEY M., anatomy educator, medical researcher; b. Montreal, Que., Can., Feb. 17, 1916; s. Jacob and Minnie (Signer) F.; m. Constance Aileen Livingstone, Sept. 23, 1940. B.Sc., McGill U., Montreal, Can., 1938, M.D., C.M., 1940, M.Sc., 1941, Ph.D., 1946. Med. licentiate, Que. Teaching fellow anatomy McGill U., Montreal, Que., Can., 1940-42, asst. prof. anatomy, 1944-48, assoc. prof. anatomy, 1948-50; prof., head dept. anatomy U. B.C., Vancouver, Can., 1950-81, prof. anatomy, 1981-85, prof. emeritus, 1985—; mem. panel on shock Def. Research Bd., Ottawa, Can., 1955-57; sci. subcom. Can. Heart Found., 1962-66, Am. Heart Assn., 1966-68, B.C. Heart Found., Vancouver. Author Visual Anatomy. Served as flight lt. RCAF, 1943-44. Recipient Premier award for rsch. in aging CIBA Found., 1955, Outstanding Svc. award Heart Found. Can., 1981, Disting. Achievement award Can. Hypertension Soc., 1987; Commemorative medal 125th Anniversary Can. Confedn.; Pfizer travel fellow Clin. Rsch. Inst., Montreal, 1971. Fellow Royal Soc. Can.; mem. Am. Anatomical Assn. (exec. com. 1970-74), Can. Assn. Anatomists (pres. 1965-66, J.C.B. Grant award 1982), Coun. High Blood Pressure Research, Internat. Soc. Hypertension, Am. Physiol. Soc., Royal Vancouver Yacht Club, Vancouver Club. Home: 4916 Chancellor Blvd, Vancouver, BC Canada V6T 1E1 Office: U BC Dept Anatomy, 2177 Wesbrook Mall, Vancouver, BC Canada V6T 1Z3

FRIEDMAN, WILLIAM FOSTER, pediatrician, cardiologist, educator; b. N.Y.C., July 24, 1936; s. Kadish and Lillian (Cohen) F.; m. Judith Serwer, Dec. 1957; children: Michael Ross, Jonathan Todd; m. Denise Willett, July 1976. A.B., Columbia Coll., 1957; M.D., State U. N.Y., Downstate, 1961. Intern, resident pediatrics Johns Hopkins Hosp., Balt., 1961-64; commd. med. officer USPHS, 1964; clin. asso. cardiology br. Nat. Heart and Lung Inst., Bethesda, Md., 1964-66, sr. investigator, pediatric cardiologist, 1966-68; prof. pediatrics and medicine, chief pediatric cardiology U. Calif., San Diego Sch. Medicine, La Jolla, 1968-79; J.H. Nicholson prof. pediatrics UCLA Sch. Medicine, 1979-85, chmn. dept. pediatrics, 1979-85; exec. chmn., 1985-94; sr. advisor clin. affairs UCLA Provost for Med.Scis., 1994—; also staff UCLA Med. Ctr., 1979—; chmn. sub-bd. pediatric cardiology Am. Bd. Pediatrics, 1984-85; mem. cardiology adv. com. NIH, 1987-92. Editor: Pediatric Research, 1983-88; mem. editorial bd.: Heart Bull, 1968-72, Circulation, 1970-75, 80-83, European Jour. Cardiology, 1972-80, Pediatric Annals, Cardiovascular Medicine, Am. Jour. cardiology, Jour. Am. Coll. Cardiology; guest editor various med. jours. Chmn. devel. study com. Am. Heart Assn., 1990-94. Fellow Am. Acad. Pediatrics, Am. Coll. Cardiology (bd. govs. So. Calif. chpt. 1988-93, chmn. pediatric cardiology com. 1986-90); mem. Am. Heart Assn. (coun. on clin. cardiology, nat. rsch. com. 1989-94, exec. com. coun. cardiovascular disease in young 1989-94), Am. Physiol. Soc., Am. Soc. Pharmacology and Exptl. Therapeutics, Soc. Nuclear Medicine, Am. Soc. Clin. Investigation, Am. Fedn. for Clin. Rsch., Internat. Study Group for Rsch. in Cardiac Metabolism, Soc. for Pediatric Rsch. (councillor, program chmn. cardiology sect., v.p. 1981), Am. Pediatric Soc., Am. Inst. Higher Studies (adv. bd.), Alpha Omega Alpha. Home 12050 Rose Marie Ln Los Angeles CA 90049-4033 Office: UCLA Sch Medicine 3754 MacDonald Rsch Labs 675 Circle Dr S Los Angeles CA 90024

FRIEDMANN, PAUL, surgeon, educator; b. Vienna, Austria, Dec. 2, 1933; came to U.S., 1938; s. Erich and Rochelle (Behar) F.; m. Janee Armstrong, Apr. 24, 1962; children: Pamela, Cynthia. BA, U. Pa., 1955; MD, Harvard U., 1959. Diplomate Am. Bd. Surgery, Am. Bd. Vascular Surgery. Chmn. dept. surgery Baystate Med. Ctr., Springfield, Mass., 1971—, sr. v.p. acad. affairs; prof. surgery Tufts U. Sch. Medicine, Boston, 1978—, chmn. ad interim dept. surgery, 1996—; mem. residency rev. com., 1985-91, chmn., 1989-91; chmn. RRC Coun., Accreditation Coun. for Grad. Med. Edn., 1989-91, mem., 1994—. Contbr. articles to profl. jours. Served to capt. USAF, 1961-63. Fellow ACS (bd. govs. 1978-84, 94—, pres. Mass. chpt. 1987); mem. Am. Surg. Assn., Assn. Program Dirs. in Surgery (sec. 1985-87, pres. 1987-89), Coun. Med. Specialty Socs. (bd. dirs. 1993—, sec. 1995—), New Eng. Soc. Vascular Surgery (recorder 1989-90, pres.-elect 1990-91, pres. 1991-92), New Eng. Surg. Soc. (treas. 1991-95, pres.-elect 1995-96), Accreditation Coun. for Grad. Med. Edn. (mem. exec. com. 1995—). Office: Baystate Med Ctr 759 Chestnut St Springfield MA 01199-1001

FRIEDMANN, PETER SIMON, dermatologist, educator; b. Johannesburg, South Africa, Nov. 18, 1943; arrived in Eng., 1949; s. Charles Aubrey and Atersia (Le Roux) F.; m. Bridget Ann Harding, Aug. 21, 1967; children: Adam, Kate. BA, Cambridge (Eng.) U., 1966, MB BChir, 1969, MD, 1971. Registrar in dermatology Kings Coll. Hosp., London, 1972-73; Wellcome rsch. fellow Royal Coll. Surgeons, London, 1973-77; lectr. in dermatology Newcastle U., Newcastle-upon-Tyne, Eng., 1977-81, sr. lectr., 1981-90; prof. dermatology U. Liverpool, Eng., 1990—. Editor book; author 80 sci. papers. Fellow Royal Coll. Physicians; mem. European Soc. for Dermatol. Rsch. (past sec. 1990-93, past pres. 1993-94), Brit. Soc. for Investigative Dermatology (chmn. 1989-90). Office: Liverpool U Dermatology, PO Box 147, Liverpool L69 JBX, England

FRIEDMANN, ROSELI OCAMPO, microbiologist, educator; b. Manila, Nov. 23, 1937; came to U.S., 1968; d. Eliseo Amio and Generosa (Campana) Ocampo; m. Emerich Imre Friedmann ; children: Maria Roseli, Rodolfo. BSc in Botany, U. Philippines, 1958; MSc in Biology, Hebrew U. of Jerusalem, 1966; PhD in Biology, Fla. State U., 1973. Rsch. assoc. Inst. Sci. and Tech., Manila, 1958-67; rsch. asst. Queen's U., Kingston, Ont., Can., 1967-68; teaching asst. Fla. State U., Tallahassee, 1968-73, rsch. assoc., 1973—; asst. prof. dept. biology Fla. A&M U., Tallahassee, 1975-84, assoc. prof., 1984-87, prof., 1987—. Contbr. articles to sci. jours. Recipient Resolution of Commendation, State of Fla., Tallahassee, 1978, Antarctic Svc. medal U.S. Congress, Tallahassee, 1981. Mem. Soc. Phycologigue France, Phycological Soc. Am., Planetary Soc., AAAS, U.S. Fedn. Culture Collections, Am. Soc. Microbiology, Assn. Women in Sci., Sigma Xi. Office: Fla A&M U Martin Luther King Blvd Tallahassee FL 32307

FRIEDMANN, THEODORE, physician; b. Vienna, June 16, 1935; s. Eric and Rochelle (Bewar) F.; m. Ingrid Anna Stromberg, Jan. 3, 1965; children: Eric, Carl. BA, U. Pa., 1956, MD, 1960, MA, 1994. Diplomate Nat. Bd. Med. Examiners. Staff scientist NIH, Bethesda, Md., 1965-68; asst. to full prof. pediatrics U. Calif. San Diego, La Jolla, 1970—; vis. scientist Salk Inst., La Jolla, 1968-70; Newton Abraham vis. prof., fellow Lincoln Coll., U. Oxford, Eng., 1994; mem. Congrl. Biomed. Ethics Adv. Com., U.S. Congress, Washington, 1989-92; mem. Exptl. Vriology Study Sect./NIH, Washington, 1986-90. Author: (monograph) Gene Therapy: Fact and Fiction, 1993; editor: (book series) Molecular Genetic Medicine, 1989—; patentee in gene therapy. Office: Univ Calif San Diego Pediatrics Dept La Jolla CA 92093

FRIEDMUTTER, MARTIN, psychologist; b. Bklyn., Jan. 14, 1947; s. David and Golda Friedmutter; m. Rena Ginsburg, Aug. 10, 1982; children: Jason, Rebecca. MA in Edn., NYU, 1981; MS in Edn., CUNY, 1982, Adv. Cert. in Edn., 1984; PhD, Yeshiva U., N.Y.C., 1987. Tchr. N.Y.C. Bd. Edn., 1981-88, sch. psychologist, 1988-90; pvt. practice, N.Y.C., 1989—; dir. Comprehensive Counseling Ctr., Queens, 1989—. With U.S. Army, 1968-70. Mem. Am. Psychol. Assn. Home: 68-37 18 St Forest Hills NY 11375 Office: 21615 Northern Blvd Flushing NY 11361-3458

FRIEDRICH, BRIAN GEORGE, osteopath; b. Camden, N.J., Nov. 18, 1961; s. Charles Philip and Lynne (German) F.; m. Carrie Lee Torma, Sept. 8, 1990; children: Andrew Steven, Michael Brian. BA, Gettysburg Coll., 1983; DO, Phila. Coll. Osteo. Medicine, 1987. Pvt. practice, Drexel Hill, Pa., 1991—; dir. occupl. health Crozer Keystone Ctr. for Occupl. Health, Springfield, Pa., 1992—. Mem. Am. Osteo. Assn., Am. Coll. Osteo. Internists. Republican. Episcopalian. Office: 5030 State Rd Ste 250 Drexel Hill PA 19026

FRIEDRICH, MARIOLA-ELZBIETA, physiologist, educator; b. Szczecin, Poland, May 26, 1948; d. Kazimierz and Janina Wielgorska (Wegner) Wielgorski; m. Stefan Friedrich, Sept. 25, 1971. MS, M.A. Mickiewicza U., Poznan, Poland, 1974; PhD, Agrl. U., Szczecin, 1983. Prof. animal physiology Agrl. U., 1974—. Contbr. articles to profl. publs. Lectr. Social U. for Elderly, Szczecin, 1989—. Mem. Polish Physiol. Soc., Polish Soc. Vet. Scis. Home: Łucznicza 19/2, 71-577 Szczecin Poland Office: Agrl U, Ul K Krolewicza 3, 71-550 Szczecin Poland

FRIEL, PATRICK BRENDAN, psychiatrist; b. Donegal, Ireland, May 16, 1925; s. Francis Coll and Cecelia F. (McAteer) F.; came to U.S., 1952, naturalized, 1962; grad. St. Eunans Coll., 1944; M.D. with honors, U. Coll., Dublin, 1950; m. Gerardine Martin, May 24, 1952; children—Daria, Sharon, Patrick F., Michael. Intern, St. Vincent's Hosp., N.Y.C., 1952-53; resident in psychiatry Norwich (Conn.) Hosp., 1953-58, Inst. of Living, 1955-56; staff psychiatrist Inst. Living, 1956-58; practice medicine specializing in psychiatry, West Hartford, Conn., 1958—; mem. psychiat. staff St. Francis, Hartford hosps.; dir. out-patient psychiat. clinic St. Francis Hosp., 1962-68, chmn., dir. dept. psychiatry, 1968-72; cons. psychotherapy Conn. Dept. Mental Health, 1962-68; clin. assoc. U. Conn. Sch. Medicine, 1972-86, assoc. prof. psychiatry, 1986—. Mem. Hartford Capitol Region Mental Health Planning Commn., West Hartford Mental Health Commn. Diplomate Am. Bd. Psychiatry and Neurology. Fellow Am. Psychiat. Assn., A.C.P., Royal Coll. Psychiatry, Royal Soc. Medicine; mem. Conn., Hartford (pres. 1968-69) psychiat. assns., AMA, Conn., Hartford med. socs. Contbr. articles to profl. jours. Home: 45 Kirkwood Rd West Hartford CT 06117-2832 Office: 801 Farmington Ave Hartford CT 06119-1600

FRIEND, HAROLD CHARLES, neurologist; b. Chgo., Nov. 28, 1946; s. Leonard Nathan and Sharlee (Friedman) F.; m. Joyce Friend; children: Reed, Chad. BA, U. Tex., 1968, MD, 1972. Diplomate Am. Bd. Neurology. Resident Upstate Med. Ctr., Syracuse, N.Y., 1972-73, Albert Einstein Coll. Medicine, Bronx, N.Y., 1973-75; mem. staff Boca Raton (Fla.) Community Hosp., 1975—; pres. Neurosci. Ctr., Boca Raton, 1984—; spl. expert witness Fla. Agy. for Health Care Adminstrn.; expert med. advisor divsn. workers compensation Fla. Dept. Labor and Employment Security; bd. dirs. So. Security Bankcorp.; pres. Puget Sound Yellow Taxi, Inc., 1994-95. Author: Territorial Marking, 1968, Bell's Palsy, 1975, Transient Global Amnesia, 1987. Bd. dirs. Boca Raton Children's Mus., 1989-92; dist. chmn., assoc. lodge advisor Boy Scouts Am., 1980-89, mem. exec. bd., v.p. Gulfstream coun., 1988-90, pres. coun., 1993-95, area I v.p., 1990-92, area IV v.p., 1993-95, area IV pres., 1995—, mem. so. region exec. bd., 1993—; exec. bd. United Way, Palm Beach County Agy. Rels. Com., 1992-95, mem. allocation com., 1990-92. Recipient Vigil Honor award Boy Scouts Am., 1983, Dist. Merit award, 1987, Silver Beaver award, 1990, Wood Badge, 1990, Disting. Commr. award, 1991, Disting. Eagle Scout, 1996; James West fellow, 1993. Fellow Am. Acad. Disability Evaluating Physicians, Am. Acad. Neurology, Am. Bd. Quality Assurance and Utilization Rev. Physicians; mem. Am. Soc. Neuroimaging (cert.), So. Clin. Neurol. Soc., Fla. Soc. Neurology, Am. Epilepsy Soc., Am. Med. EEG Assn., Am. Assn. Study Headache, N.Y. Acad. Scis. (life), Sierra Club (life), Palm Beach Med. Svc. (vice chmn. med./legal com.), Rotary (bd. dirs., pres. Boca Raton chpt., dist. world fellowship chmn. 1992-94, 96—, dist. found. chmn. 1994, chmn. dist. conf. 1995, gov.'s rep. 1994-95, 96-97, Paul Harris fellow, Dist. Svc. award 1992, 95, Pres. Salute Commendation 1993), Internat. Fellowship Running and Fitness Rotarians (internat. chmn. 1992-97), Internat. Fellowship Scouting Rotarians (N.Am. sect. chmn. 1995-96, internat. sec. 1996—), Boca Raton Road Runners Club (pres. 1992-93), Phi Beta Kappa, Phi Kappa Phi, Theta Xi, Alpha Phi Omega. Office: 1500 NW 10th Ave Ste 105 Boca Raton FL 33486-1344

FRIEND, KEVIN BURDETTE, medical center administrative assistant; b. Columbus, Ohio, Aug. 1, 1968; s. Robert B. and Reva J. (Clifton) F. BBA in Mgmt., U. Ky., 1990, B Health Adminstrn., 1991; MBA in Mgmt., Xavier U., Cin., 1992, M Health Adminstrn., 1993. Lic. nursing home adminstr., Ky. Adminstrv. intern Bourbon Gen. Hosp., Paris, Ky., 1990; adminstrv. resident Dayton (Ohio) VA Med. Ctr., 1993-94; health sus. specialist trainee VA Ctrl. Region Office, Ann Arbor, Mich., 1994-95; health sys. specialist Danville (Ill.) VA Med. Ctr., 1995—. Recipient scholarships Ky. Nat. Guard Foun., Frankfort, 1989, Bluegrass Pers. Assn., Lexington, 1990. Mem. Am. Coll. Healthcare Execs. (assoc.), Nat. Assn. Healthcare Quality, Soc. Healthcare Strategic Planning Mktg., Am. Mgmt. Assn., Lions Club (chmn. sight and sound com. 1996). Home: 705 Andover Village Dr Lexington KY 40509 Office: Danville VA Med Ctr HSS (002B) 1900 E Main St Danville IL 61832

FRIES, DAVID SAMUEL, chemist, educator; b. Manassas, Va., June 22, 1945; s. Basil L. and Ruby (Sperau) F.; m. Marjie Ann Strayer, May 1, 1964; children: Susan, Jane, Corey. BA in Chemistry, Bridgewater Coll., 1968; PhD in Medicinal Chemistry, Va. Commonwealth U., 1971. Prof. medicinal chemistry U. of Pacific, Stockton, Calif., 1973—, dean grad. sch.., 1993—; vis. rsch. prof. U. Groningen, The Netherlands, 1984-85, German Cancer Rsch. Ctr., Heidelberg, 1989-90; cons. on opioid drug addiction, 1975—. Contbr. articles to profl. jours. and chpts. to books. Rsch. grantee Nat. Inst. on Drug Abuse, NSF. Mem. Am. Chem. Soc., Am. Assn. Colls. Pharmacy, Sigma Xi, Phi Kappa Phi, Rho Chi, Phi Delta Chi. Office: U of Pacific Sch of Pharmacy Stockton CA 95211

FRIES, PETER DONALD, ophthalmologist; b. Chgo., May 10, 1955; s. Donald Eugene and Betty (Gordon) F.; m. Mary Pat O'Connell, May 8, 1982; children: Christopher, Patrick, Jamie. AA, Coll. DuPage, 1975; BA, Loyola U. Chgo., 1977; MD, Chgo. Med. Sch., 1981. Diplomate Am. Bd. Ophthalmology. Intern, resident Letterman Army Med. Ctr., San Francisco, 1981-85; fellow U. Calif., San Francisco, 1986-87, U. Pa., Phila., 1987-88;

chief ophthalmology svc. Letterman Army Med. Ctr., 1989-91; ptnr. Eye Surgeons Assocs., P.C., Davenport, Iowa, 1992—; adv. bd. Alcoa Advantage Med. Plan, Davenport, 1993—; asst. clin. prof. ophthalmology U. Calif., San Francisco, 1986-92. Decorated Meritorious Svc. medal U.S. Army, 1992, Col. Robert Shelton award, 1985. Fellow Am. Coll. Surgeons, Am. Acad. Ophthalmology, Am. Soc. Ophthalmic Plastic and Reconstructive Surgeons, Am. Acad. Facial Plastic Surgery. Republican. Roman Catholic. Home: 2829 E 44th Ct Davenport IA 52807 Office: Eye Surgeons Assocs 1351 W Central Park Davenport IA 52804

FRIESEN, WILLIAM GLENN, cardiologist; b. Hague, Can., June 27, 1937; s. Abram Jacob and Maria (Thiessen) F.; m. Barbara Neil Reilly, Oct. 18, 1978. MD, U. B.C., 1961. Diplomate Am. Bd. Internal Medicine. Asst. prof. medicine U. Alta., Edmonton, Can., 1969-72; clin. cardiologist Western Cardiology Assocs., Victoria, B.C., Can., 1972-94, Amarillo (Tex.) Diagnostics Clinic, 1994—; chief cardiology Victoria Gen. Hosp., 1973-88; chief medicine ICU/CCU North West Tex. Hosp., Amarillo, 1995—. Fellow Am. Coll. CArdiology, Royal Coll. Physicians & Surgeons (Can.); mem. Tex. Med. Assn., Randall-Potter County Med. Soc., Alpha Omega Alpha. Office: Amarillo Diagnostic Clin 6700 W 9th Ave Amarillo TX 79106

FRIESWYK, DAVID LYNN, physician assistant; b. London, Jan. 22, 1955; came to U.S., 1957; s. Henry and Marion A. (Armstrong) F.; married, May 28, 1982; children: Matthew, Nathan, Joanthan. BA, Carleton Coll., 1977; BS, U. Ala., 1984. Rsch. asst. CIA, Washington, 1974-75; nursing asst. Abbott Hosp., Mpls., 1977-79; rsch. technologist U. Minn., Mpls., 1980-82; physician asst. Cardiovascular Surgery, Evansville, Ind., 1984—; pres. physician asst. com. Ind. Health Profls. Bur., Indpls., 1994—. Treas., pres. meml. and spl. gifts. com. Bethlehem Ch., Evansville, 1995-96. Fellow Am. Acad. Physician Assts., Am. Acad. Surgeon Assts., Tristate Critical Care Soc., Assn. Physician Assts. Cardiovasc. Surgery; mem. Ind. Acad. Physician Assts. (pres. 1994-96). Office: Cardiovascular Surgery Inc 350 W Columbia St Ste 350 Evansville IN 47710

FRIOU, GEORGE JACOB, immunologist, physician, educator; b. Bklyn., Oct. 5, 1919; s. George Dyson and Lillian Edna (Ackerman) F.; m. Carolyn Anderson Bower, Jan. 18, 1947; children: Deborah, Linda, Sally, George; m. Hortense Joan Nichol, Mar. 29, 1972. B.S., Cornell U., 1940, M.D., 1944. Intern New Haven Hosp., 1945-46, asst. resident, 1946, chief resident in medicine, 1949-50; asst. prof. medicine Yale U., 1951-60; assoc. prof. medicine and microbiology U. Okla., 1961-64; assoc. prof. medicine U. So. Calif., 1964-68, prof., 1968-78; prof. medicine U. Calif., Irvine, 1978-91, prof. emeritus, 1991—; vis. investigator Med. Rsch. Coun., Rheumatic Disease Rsch. Lab., Taplow, Buckinghamshire, Eng., 1960; mem. hematology study sect., divsn. rsch. grants NIH, 1958-59; founding dir. clin. immunology and rheumatology rsch. and edn. program U. Okla., 1961-64. So. Calif., 1964-78, U. Calif., Irvine, 1978-91; cons. Arthritis Found., N.Y., 1962-64, Ctr. grants Comm., 1963—, Med. and Sci. Comm., 1962-64, Exec. Comm. 1964, Lupus Found. of Am., 1977-78, Council Mid-Winter Conf. Immunologists, 1965-70; mem. steering com. Calif. Gov.'s Conf. on Arthritis, 1967; mem. med. and sci. com. So. Calif. Arthritis Found., 1966—, chmn. med. and sci. com., 1977-78, bd. govs., 1977-78; NIH sr. rsch. fellow, hon. cons. dept. cell pathology, Med. Rsch. Coun., Clin. Rsch. Ctr., Harrow, Eng., 1975; cons. VA, mem. merit review bd. in immunology, 1972-74; hon. cons. immunology, Bloomsbury Health Dist., London, 1985-86; vis. scientist dept. immunology Middlesex Hosp. Med. Sch., London, 1985-86; rev. cons. specialized ctrs. research in arthritis divsn. rsch. grants NIH, 1987. Mem. editorial bd. Arthritis and Rheumatism, 1967-69; contbr. over 100 articles to profl. jours. and book chpts. Served with M.C. USNR, 1946-47, 52-53. James Hudson Brown Rsch. fellow Yale U., 1947-49. Fellow ACP, Infectious Disease Soc. Am. (charter fellow); mem. Am. Coll. Rheumatology (master 1991), Am. Soc. Clin. Investigation, Asociacion Rheumatologia de Columbia (hon. mem.), Am. Assn. Immunologists, Heberden Soc. (Gt. Britain Hon.), Brit. Soc. Immunology (hon.), Western Assn. Physicians, So. Calif. Rheumatism Soc. (pres. 1970), Ohio Rheumatism Soc. (hon. mem.), Los Angeles Acad. Medicine/. Home: 44 Canyon Island Dr Newport Beach CA 92660-5117 Office: U Calif Dept Medicine Med Scis Bldg 1 Irvine CA 92717

FRISHMAN, WILLIAM HOWARD, cardiology educator, cardiovasular pharmacologist, gerontologist; b. N.Y.C., Nov. 9, 1946; s. Aaron and Frances (Fishel) F.; m. Esther Rose Sandowsky, Mar. 11, 1971; children: Sheryl Renée, Amy Helene, Michael Aaron. BA, MD, Boston U., 1969. Diplomate Am. Bd. Internal Medicine, Am. Bd. Cardiovascular Medicine, Am. Bd. Critical Care Medicine, Am. Bd. Clin. Pharmacology, Am. Bd. Geriatrics, Am. Bd. Med. Mgmt. Med. intern Montefiore Hosp., Bronx, N.Y., 1969-70, resident in medicine, 1970-71; resident in medicine Bronx Mcpl. and Einstein Hosps., 1971-72; fellow in cardiology N.Y. Hosp.-Cornell U. Med. Coll., N.Y.C., 1972-74, instr., 1974-76; dir. noninvasive cardiac labs. Einstein Hosp. and Montefiore Hosp., 1976-80, dir. cardiology svc., 1980-82, Einstein Hosp./Montefiore Med. Ctr., 1981-91; prof. medicine and epidemiology, assoc. chmn. dept. medicine Albert Einstein Coll. Medicine Yeshiva U., Bronx, 1991—; expert cons. cardiorenal div. FDA, Bethesda, Md., 1987—; panel mem. U.S. Pharmacopeial Conv., Rockville, Md., 1990—. Author: Clinical Pharmacology of the Beta-Blocking Drugs, 1980 2d edit., 1984, Medical Management of Lipid Disorders, 1992; co-author: Calcium Channel Antagonists in Cardiovascular Disease, 1984, Therapy of Angina Pectoris, 1986, Current Cardiovascular Drugs, 1994, 2d edit. 1995, Beta-3 Adrenergic Agonism, 1995 also over 500 articles, revs. and chpts. in books; editor Yearbook of Medicine. Mem. fiscal affairs com. Village of Scarsdale, N.Y., 1991—. Lt. col. M.C., U.S. Army, 1969-90. Named to Boston Collegium of Disting. Alumni, Boston U., 1988, Disting. Alumnus sch. medicine, 1994; teaching scholar Am. Heart Assn., 1979-82; preventive cardiology acad. award Nat. Heart, Lung and Blood Inst., 1980-85. Fellow ACP, Am. Coll. Cardiology (bd. govs. 1987-91, pres. N.Y. State chpt. 1991), Am. Coll. Chest Physicians; mem. Am. Soc. for Clin. Pharmacology and Therapeutics (Mckeen Cattell award 1990), Am. Soc. for Clin. Rsch., N.Y. Cardiol. Soc. (v.p. 1994, pres. 1996—), Town and Village Club, Alpha Omega Alpha. Jewish. Home: 7 White Birch Ln Scarsdale NY 10583-7634 Office: Albert Einstein Coll Med 1300 Morris Park Ave Bronx NY 10461-1926

FRISHWASSER, EDWARD J., physician; b. N.Y., Sept. 7, 1916; s. Benjamin and Regina (Lowenthal) F.; m. Mary Houchmann, Apr. 16, 1993; children: Louise, Daniel. MD, U. Lausanne, Lausanne, Switzerland, 1942; MPH, Columbia Univ., 1949. Diplomate Am. Bd. Urology. Attending urologist Misericordia Hosp., N.Y., 1969-80; assoc. urologist Montefiore Hosp., N.Y., 1965—; asst. clinical prof. Coll. Medicine, N.Y., 1975—. Capt. U.S. Army, 1944-47. Fellow Am. Coll. Urology. Home: 219 Fox Meadow Rd Searsdale NY 10583

FRIST, RAMSEY HUDSON, biology educator; b. Meadville, Pa., Aug. 16, 1936; s. Joseph Osmond and Blanche (Ramsey) F.; m. Judith Nadolny, June 22, 1962 (div. Oct. 1979); children: Heidi, Jonathan, Erica. BS, Allegheny Coll., 1959; MS, U. Pitts., 1962, PhD, 1965. USPHS fellow Virus Rsch. Unit ARC, Cambridge, Eng., 1965-67; postdoctoral fellow U. Wis., Madison, 1967-69; assoc. prof. biology W.Va. U., Morgantown, 1969—; vis. prof. U. Pitts., 1991. Contbr. articles to sci. jours. Rsch. grantee. Mem. AAAS, Biophys. Soc., Am. Phytopath. Soc., Sigma Xi. Home: 633 Jones Ave Morgantown WV 26505-4722 Office: W Va U Biology Dept PO Box 6057 Morgantown WV 26506-6057

FRITSCH, DEREK ADRIAN, nurse anesthetist; b. Cuero, Tex., Sept. 12, 1957; s. Adrian Henry and Virginia Emma (Bernshausen) F.; m. Jacqueline Ann Joyce, June 8, 1985; children: Alexander Derek, Adrienne Joyce. AA, Wharton County Jr. Coll., Wharton, Tex., 1978; BSN, U. Tex. Health Sci. Ctr., 1980; CRNA, Harris County Hosp. Dist., Houston, 1983. Cert. registered nurse anesthetist. Anesthesia tng. Ben Taub Gen. Hosp., The Meth. Hosp., VA Hosp., others, Houston, 1979-88; staff anesthetist Anesthesia Specialists of Houston/The Woman's Hosp. Tex., Houston, 1988-94, 95—; freelance staff anesthetist Schick Shadel Hosp., Houston, 1990, Gulf Coast Regional Med. Ctr., Wharton, 1994-95; staff anesthetist, anesthesia specialists of Houston/The Woman's Hosp., Houston, 1995—. Colo. County emergency vol. Ambulance Corps, 1976-78; provider anesthesia internat. eye surgery team, Benovolent Missions Internat., Belize, Boliva, El Salvador, 1993-94, 93-95. Recipient Luth. Brotherhood scholarship, 1979, Rotarian scholarship, Houston, 1979, others. Mem. AANA, Tex. Assn. Nurse Anesthetists, Internat. Anesthesia Rsch. Soc., Gulf Coast Assn. Nurse Anesthetists (bd. dirs. 1987-89, pres. 1988-89), Greater New Eng. Acad. Hypnosis, Phi Theta Kappa (State Recognition award, chpt. pres. 1977-78), Sigma Theta Tau. Lutheran. Home: 410 Lake Bend Dr Sugar Land TX 77479-5804 Office: Anesthesia Specialists Houston 7800 Fannin Ste 101 Houston TX 77054

FRITTS, HARRY WASHINGTON, JR., physician, educator; b. Rockwood, Tenn., Oct. 4, 1921; s. Harry Washington and Hyder (Smith) F.; m. Helen Dyer Goodwin, Aug. 25, 1949; children: John Goodwin, Benjamin Carroll, Patricia Louise. Student, Vanderbilt U., 1941; B.S., Mass. Inst. Tech., 1943; M.D., Boston U., 1951. Diplomate: Am. Bd. Internal Medicine (mem.). Mem. research staff MIT, 1946-47; intern, then resident Univ. Hosp., Boston, 1951-53; vis. fellow Columbia Coll. Physicians and Surgeons, 1953-56, mem. faculty, 1956-73, prof. medicine, 1967-73, Dickinson W. Richards prof. medicine, 1972-73; prof., chmn. dept. medicine Sch. Medicine, State U. N.Y. at Stony Brook, 1973-87, Edmund D. Pellegrino prof. medicine, 1986-87; William Harris vis. prof. Nat. Med. Sch. Taiwan, 1987-88; vis. physician Bellevue Hosp., 1957-68, Presbyn. Hosp., N.Y.C., 1961-73; vis. physician, cons. Manhattan VA Hosp., 1957-68; vis. prof. U. London, 1982; bd. dirs., adv. council research N.Y. Heart Assn.; mem. sci. council Parker Francis Found.; mem. physiology study sect., mem. cardiovascular tng. com. USPHS; mem. council Nat. Heart, Lung and Blood Inst. Contbr. articles to profl. jours.; assoc. editor: Jour. Clin. Investigation; editorial bd.: Am. Rev. Respiratory Diseases. Served to lt. (j.g.) USNR, 1943-46. Guggenheim fellow, 1959-60. Fellow ACP; mem. Am. Physiol. Soc., Am. Soc. Clin. Investigation, Assn. Am. Physicians, Am. Clin. and Climatol. Soc., Alpha Omega Alpha. Home: 79 Bevin Rd Northport NY 11768-1133 Office: SUNY at Stony Brook Dept Medicine Stony Brook NY 11794

FRITTS, LILLIAN ELIZABETH, retired nurse; b. N.Y.C., July 19, 1923; d. William Franklin and Elzora Jane (Hodge) Bowen; A.D.N., R.N., Central Peidmont Community Coll., 1969; m. Thurman Luther Fritts, Aug. 5, 1944; children—William Luther, Franklin Lee, George Allen. Emergency room nurse Lexington (N.C.) Meml. Hosp., 1953-58; office nurse James T. Welborn, M.D., Lexington, 1958-60; staff nurse Haven Nursing Ctr., Lexington, 1960-61; pvt. duty nurse, 1961-63; owner, ptnr. Buena Vista Nursing Ctr., Lexington, 1964-91, ret., 1991; adult extension tchr. Davidson County Community Coll., 1978, adv. bd. nursing program, 1969-79; pres. Piedmont dist. Long Term Nursing Dirs., 1986-88, Long Term Care Piedmont Nurses Assn., 1987-89. Mem. Am. Nurses Assn., N.C. Nurses Assn., Lic. Practical Nurse Orgn. (state sec. 1958-60), N.C. Lic. Practical Nurse Assn., Dist. 9 Nurse Assn. N.C., N.C. Health Care Facilities Services Assn., Gideons Internat. Baptist. Home: 797 Hill Everhart Rd Lexington NC 27292-7102

FRITZ, JAMES STEPHEN, SR., managed care network development administrator; b. Versailles, Ky., Jan. 10, 1950; s. George Francis Sr. and Santina (Gormley) F.; m. Sandra Lynn Markland, Feb. 25, 1960; children: James Stephen Jr., William Markland. BS in Acctg., U. Ky., 1972, MBA, 1976. CPA, Ky. V.p. fin. Lexington (Ky.) Clinic, 1980-90; CEO Atlanta Med., 1990-93; sr. v.p. network devel. Columbia Park Healthcare Sys., Winter Park, Fla., 1994—; pres. One Source, NA, Winter Park, Fla., 1993—; pres. bd. dirs. MRI Joint Venture, Lexington, 1989-90. Active United Way, Lexington, 1985. Fellow Med. Group Mgmt. Assn., Ky. Soc. CPAs. Office: Columbia Park Healthcare 2111 Glenwood Dr Winter Park FL 32792

FRITZ, MICHAEL EDWARD, university dean, dentist; b. Boston, Feb. 26, 1938; s. Max and Jean (Meshon) F.; m. Suzanne Wine, Aug. 18, 1960; children: Allyson, Jason, Theron. Student Boston U., 1955-58. DDS, U. Pa., 1963, MS, 1965, PhD, 1967. Assoc. prof. and chmn. periodontology, Emory U., Atlanta, 1967-73, prof. and chmn. periodontology, 1973-82, dean Sch. Dentistry, Candler prof. sch. medicine, 1982—; cons. VA, Atlanta, 1967-90 , Ben Massell Dental Clinic, Atlanta, 1982-92 . Contbr. chpts. to books, articles to publs. Founder Paideia Sch., Atlanta, 1972; officer PTA, Atlanta, 1971-73; Little League coach, 1970-75. Nat. Inst. Dental Research research grantee, 1968-81, 88—. Fellow Am. Coll. Dentists, Ga. Dental Assn. (hon.); mem. ADA, Internat. Assn. Dental Research (officer 1973-75), Am. Acad. Periodontology (officer 1978—), Omicron Kappa Upsilon. Republican. Jewish. Avocations: sailing; tennis; reading; jogging. Home: 2057 Renault Ln NE Atlanta GA 30345-3442 Office: 3316 Piedmont Rd NE Ste 310 Atlanta GA 30305-1706

FRITZ, RONALD MATHEW, physician; b. Monrovia, Calif., Aug. 7, 1956; s. Walter and Edith Shirley (Quine) F.; m. Christine T. Tuzim, June 6, 1987; children: Allyson Brittney, Michael Mathew, Lauren Michelle. BS, UCLA, 1979; D of Osteopathy, U. Osteopathic Medicine and Health Scis., Des Moines, 1987. Intern Botsford Gen. Hosp., Farmington Hills, Mich., 1987-88; resident Cleve. Clinic Found., 1988-91; clin. assoc. cardiology Cleve. Clin. Found., 1991-92. Contbr. article to profl. publ. Cardiology fellow Cleve. Clin. Found., 1992-95. Mem. AMA, ACP, Am. Osteopathic Assn., Sierra Club, Green Peace. Home: 6004 Sundance Dr Coeur D Alene ID 83814 Office: 1607 Lincoln Way Coeur D Alene ID 83814

FRITZE, JULIUS ARNOLD, marriage counselor; b. Albuquerque, Dec. 30, 1918; s. Martin Herman and Mary (Staerkel) F.; m. Marion Caroline Becker, June 4, 1944; children: Christine, Timothy; m. 2d, Anita Carol Dozier, May 18, 1973. Student St. Paul's Jr. Coll., 1937-39; diploma Concordia Sem., 1944; B.A., in Edn., U. N.Mex., 1943; M.S., Central Mo. State Coll., 1969. Nat. cert. counselor; lec. marriage and family therapist, Tex. Ordained to ministry Lutheran Ch., 1944; pastor in Corpus Christi, Tex., 1944-48, Higginsville, Mo., 1948-57; exec. dir. Marriage and Parenthood Center, Dallas, 1957-59; pvt. practice marriage counseling, Dallas, 1959—; indsl. psychologist N. Am. Mktg., 1975-76; mgmt. cons. Concord Systems, Inc., 1978—; therapist Proctor & Gamble, Dallas, 1991—. Cons. Mo. Snyod, Luth. Ch., St. Louis, 1961, Tex. dist., 1976—; lectr. to profl. and laymen's insts., 1956—; lectr. Dallas County Jr. Coll. Bd. dirs. Dallas area Am. Lung Assn., 1976—. Lic. profl. counselor, Tex. Mem. Am. Assn. Marriage Counselors, Am. Personnel and Guidance Assn., Nat. Vocat. Guidance Assn., Nat. Council Family Relations, Am. Psychol. Assn., Southwestern Psychol. Assn., Tex. Psychol. Assn., Am. Orthopsychiat. Assn., Internat. Platform Assn. Author: The Essence of Marriage, 1969; Mini Manual for Ministers, 1978, The Essence of Life, 1990; contbr. series of articles to nat. mags. Home: 10531 Castlegate Dr Dallas TX 75229-5102 Office: 3198 Royal Ln Ste 100 Dallas TX 75229-3777

FRIZZELL, LINDA DIANE BANE, exercise physiologist; b. Council Bluffs, Iowa, May 6, 1950; d. Howard Austin and Dorothy (Eyberg) Bane; m. Richard J. Frizzell, Sept. 5, 1971; children: William, Michelle, Audra, Austin. Cert. athletic trainer, John F. Kennedy Coll., 1970; BA, Parsons Coll., 1972; postgrad., U. Iowa, 1973; MS, Bemidji State U., 1988; PhD, U. N.D., 1991. Lic. phys. edn. tchr., coach, adaptive phys. edn. tchr., Minn.; cert. auto mech., nursing asst.; trained medication aide; water safety instr.; life guard tng. instr.; cert. leisure profl.; qualified mental retardation profl.; cert. personal trainer, CPR, first aid instr. Mgr. swimming pool, dir. swimming lessons Town of Oakland (Iowa), 1971; head cross country, men and women's track and field, asst. coach women's basketball, dir. women's instramurals, phys. edn. instr. Parsons Coll., Fairfield, Iowa, 1972-73; mgr. parts and svc. head mech. Winebrenner Ford, Walker, Minn., 1974-76; tchr., coach Laporte (Minn.) Sch., 1976-81; coach Cass Lake (Minn.) Sch., 1981-85; grad. asst. coach men and women track and field Bemidji (Minn.) State U., 1987; community edn. instr., mem. adv. bd. Walker (Minn.)-Hackensack Schs., 1987-90; mgr. warranty parts and svc. Walker Electric & Hardware, 1987-90; recreation dir. Town of Walker, 1991; therapeutic recreation specialist Ah-Gwah-Ching (Minn.) SNF, 1987-91; grad. rsch. asst. Bureau Ednl. Svcs., U. N.D., Grand Forks, 1989-91; exec. dir. tng. facility developmentaly disable adults Deer River Hired Hands, 1991-92; cons. Bush Grant Study, U. N.D.; presenter at AAHPERD nat. conv. (conf. scholarship 1990, 91, 95); adj. prof. Bemidji State U., 1993—; ind. cons. excercise physiology, rehabilitative therapy, leisure edn., health edn., 1991—; tribal health planner. Leech Lake Reservation, 1993—; speaker for various nat. orgns. on adult aging, devel. and exercise, and innovations in health care and education for rural areas. Designed and copyrighted a wellness circuit for older adults; contbr. articles in field. Minn. rep. to Coun. on Aging and Adult Devel.; active mem. Nat. Minority Involvement Com.; mem. Gov.'s Task Force on Health Promotion and Phys. Fitness for Srs. Grantee Indian Health Svc.-Tribal Mgmt., 1994, State Minn. Cmty. Health Ctr., 1994, Bur. Primary Healthcare/Maternal & Child Health Sch. Based Health Clinic & Wellness Program, 1994. Mem. Am. Assn. Leisure and Recreation (mem. com. on aging), Am. Coll. Sports Medicine (profl., govt. affairs com., Minn. rep.), Nat. Assembly Sch. Based Health Ctrs. (co-chair health edn. sect., sect. rep. to exec. com.), Am. Assn. Health Edn. (govs. task force on health promotion and phys. fitness for srs.).

FROEDE, CRAIG BRIAN, internist; b. Balt., May 12, 1959; married. BS in Microbiology cum laude, U. Md., 1981, MD, 1986. Diplomate Am. Bd. Internal Medicine, Nat. Bd. of Med. Examiners. Intern in internal medicine Ea. Va. Grad. Sch. of Medicine, Norfolk, 1986-87, resident in internal medicine, 1987-89; staff attending physician Sentara Norfolk Gen. Hosp. and Sentara Leigh Hosp., 1989—; med. dir. Norfolk Health Care Ctr., 1990—; clin. adj. prof. Sch. of Nursing Old Dominion U., Norfolk, Va., 1995—, Dept. of Internal Medicine, Ea. Va. Med. Sch., 1995—; team physician Va. Wesleyan Coll., 1990—; co-team physician Tidewater Sharks Football Team, 1990-93; team physician Old Dominion U., 1993—; mem. IPA Primary Care com., 1992-94, critical care com., 1992-94, Sentara primary care planning com., physician practice/ambulatory care and computerized mem., patient record system evaluation com., 1995—, med. operating ctr. exec. coun., 1994—, standardization task force, 1995—; lectr. in field. Mem. ACP, Norfolk Acad. of Medicine, Seaboard Med. Assn., Omicron Delta Kappa, Phi Sigma, Psi Chi, Alpha Zeta, Alpha Lambda Delta, Sigma Alpha Omicron. Home: 1172 Lawson Cove Circle Virginia Beach VA 23455 Office: NDC Med Ctr 850 Kempsville Rd Norfolk VA 23502

FROHLICHSTEIN, ALAN, retinal angiographer; b. Fort Wayne, Ind., Oct. 31, 1953; s. Ben and Juliana Rose (Levey) F.; m. F. Diane Willett, Sept. 2, 1984. BFA, Ohio U., 1975; AS, Rochester (N.Y.) Inst. Tech., 1976, BS, 1977; cert. completion, Rsch. and Holographic Ctr., Chgo., 1983. Intern U. Chgo., 1976; med. photographer Luth. Gen. Hosp., Niles, Ill., 1977-80; cert. retinal angiographer Wilder & Vygantas MD, Ltd., Niles, 1980-84, C.M. Vygantas MD, Ltd., Des Plaines, Ill., 1984-89; pres. Retinal Angiography Svcs., Morton Grove, Ill., 1989—; adj. faculty Triton Coll., River Grove, Ill., 1988—; lectr. Joint Commn. on Allied Pers. in Ophthalmology; instr. Soc. of Ophthalmic Med. Assts. in Chgo. Ann. Rev. Course, 1991—. Contbg. editor: Jour. Ophthalmic Photography, 1988—; contbr. articles to profl. jours., jour. cover; inventor anaglyphic stereo projection sys. for ophthalmology. Recipient Med. Edn. award Biol. Photographic Assn., 1992. Fellow Soc. Ophthalmic Med. Assts. in Chgo.; mem. Ophthalmic Photographers Soc. (bd. dirs. 1994—, v.p. 1984-86, chmn. sci. exhibit 1988-89, ethics com. 1990—, cert. pres. Chgo. chpt. 1981—, workshop instr. 1983—), Fine Arts Rsch. and Holographic Ctr. Alumni Assn. (charter v.p. 1990—), Mensa, Am. Acad. Ophthalmology (Honor award 1993).

FROHMAN, LAWRENCE ASHER, endocrinology educator, scientist; b. Detroit, Jan. 26, 1935; s. Dan and Rebecca (Katzman) F.; m. Barbara Hecht, June 9, 1957; children: Michael, Marc, Erica, Rena. M.D., U. Mich., 1958. Diplomate: Am. Bd. Internal Medicine. Intern Yale-New Haven Med. Ctr., 1958-59, resident in internal medicine, 1959-61; asst. prof. medicine SUNY, Buffalo, 1965-69, assoc. prof., 1969-73; prof. medicine U. Chgo., 1973-81; dir. endocrinology Michael Reese Hosp., Chgo., 1973-81; prof., dir. div. endocrinology and metabolism U. Cin., 1981-92; chmn. Dept. Medicine U. of Ill. Chgo., 1992—; dir. Med. Svcs. U. of Ill. Hosp., Chgo., 1992—; dir. Gen. Clin. Rsch. Ctr., 1986-90; mem. sci. rev. com. NIH, Bethesda, Md., 1972-76; mem. sci. rev. bd. VA, Washington, 1979-82; mem. endocrine adv. bd. FDA, Washington, 1982-86; mem. adv. com. Nat. Inst. Diabetes, Digestive and Kidney Diseases, NIH, 1983-94, chmn., 1991-93; mem. sci. adv. bd. Edison Biotech. Inst., Ohio U. Editor: (with others) Endocrinology and Metabolism, 1995; editl. bd. 6 med. and sci. jours., 1970—; contbr. articles to profl. jours. NIH research grantee, 1967—, Endocrine Soc. Rorer Clin. Investigator award, 1991. Fellow ACP; mem. Endocrine Soc., Assn. Am. Physicians, Am. Soc. Clin. Investigation, Am. Diabetes Assn., Internat. Soc. Neuroendocrinology, Assn. Profs. Medicine, Pituitary Soc. Office: U Ill at Chgo Dept Medicine M/C 787 840 S Wood St Chicago IL 60612-7317

FROM, ARTHUR HARVEY LEIGH, cardiologist, educator; b. South Bend, Ind., Oct. 1, 1936; s. Irving and Sanda Ruth (Kornberg) F.; m. Suzanne Paine, May 1, 1962. AB, Ind. U., 1958, MA, 1960; MD, Ind. U., Indpls., 1961. Diplomate Am. Bd. Internal Medicine. Intern, resident in medicine U. Minn. Hosp., Mpls., 1961-64; NIH trainee in cardiovascular disease U. Minn. Hosp./C.T. Miller Hosp., St. Paul and Mpls., 1964-66; asst. prof. medicine U. Minn., Mpls., 1968-76, assoc. prof., 1976-88, prof., 1988—; cardiologist U. Minn. Health Sci. Ctr., Mpls., 1968-76, Mpls. VA Med. Ctr., 1976—. Contbr. articles to profl. publs. including Jour. Biol. Chemistry, Jour. Molecular and Cellular Cardiology, Biochemistry, Circulation Rsch. Sr. asst. surgeon, USPHS, 1966-68. Grantee NIH, 1976, 90, 91, 94, VA, 1977—. Mem. Internat. Soc. Cardiac Rsch., Am. Physiol. Soc., Am. Fedrn. Clin. Rsch., Am. Heart Assn., Soc. Gen. Physiologists, Phi Beta Kappa, Alpha Omega Alpha. Office: Mpls VA Med Ctr 1 Veterans Dr Minneapolis MN 55417-2300

FROM, GERALD, psychologist; b. N.Y.C., Dec. 6, 1942; s. Murray and Betty (Glassman) F.; m. Paula Goldstein, Oct. 26, 1971; children: Yisroel, Noam, Aron, Ahuva, Avi. BA, Yeshiva U., N.Y.C., 1964; MA, Columbia U., 1967; PhD, NYU, 1987. Cert. rehab. counselor, N.Y. Psychologist Albert Einstein Coll. Medicine, Bronx, N.Y., 1969-77, Misericordia Med. Ctr., Bronx, 1978-80, South Bronx Mental Health Council, 1981—; pvt. practice, N.Y.C., 1984—; cons. in field; chmn. community bd. Gouvernor Hosp., N.Y.C.. Contbr. articles to profl. jours. Mem. bd. visitors Manhattan Devel. Ctr., N.Y.C., 1980-84; co-chmn. Bronx Fedn. Rehab. Agys., 1979-84; bd. dirs. United Jewish Council, N.Y.C., 1978—. Named one of Outstanding Young Men of Am., 1974; recipient Jewish Meml. Found. grant, 1979-80. Mem. Am. Psychol. Assn., (profl.) Nat. Rehab. Counseling Assn., Nat. Rehab. Assn. Home: 2 Soland Rd Monsey NY 10952-1909 Office: S Bronx Mental Health Coun 781 E 142nd St Bronx NY 10454-1723 also: 1160 Fifth Ave New York NY 10029-6928

FROM, MARTHA ADELE, nursing educator, nurse; b. Suffern, N.Y., Sept. 5, 1944; d. Joseph Ezekiel and Genowefa (Grabowski) F.; divorced. Diploma in nursing, Englewood (N.J.) Hosp., 1965; BS, U. Pa., 1968, MS, 1972; EdD, Temple U., 1991. Instr. Lankenau Hosp., Phila., 1969-70; nurse Cmty. Home Health of Phila., 1972-74; asst. prof. nursing Hahnemann U., Phila., 1979-83, Temple U., Phila., 1982-86, Thomas Jefferson U., Phila., 1986-91, Widener U., Chester, Pa., 1992—; therapeutic touch practitioner, cons. in field; vis. nurse hospice Skilled Nursing, Inc., Phila., 1985-91. Tchr., chairperson edn. com. Childbirth Edn. Assn., Phila., 1974-82; writer health col. Weaver's Way Coop., Phila., 1981-88. Mem. ANA (commr. nursing edn. 1993—), Nurse Healers Profl. Group (parliamentarian 1982-86), U. Pa. Alumni Assn., Sigma Theta Tau. Democrat. Roman Catholic. Office: Widener Univ Sch of Nursing Old Main Rm 334 Chester PA 19013

FROME, DAVID HERMAN, dentist; b. Richmond, Va., Jan. 22, 1945; married; 3 children. Student, U. Md., 1962-64, 68; DDS, Georgetown U., 1968; MPH, Johns Hopkins U., 1973. Lic. dentist, Md., D.C. Pvt. practice Gaithersburg, Md., 1970—; clin. instr. dental materials Georgetown Sch. Dentistry, 1970-72; clin. instr. pediatric dentistry U. Md., 1970-73; dental dir. Group Health Assn., 1982-86, Md. State Dental Svc. Corp., 1980-81; cons. in field. Contbr. articles to profl. jours. Past pres. Layhill Village East Citizens Assn.; bd. dirs., trustee Hebrew Day Inst., pres., 1986-88; mem. adv. group FDA, 1985, 89-91. Capt. AUS, 1968-70, Vietnam. Nat. Inst. Dentistry rsch. grantee, 1967; Pub. Health fellow; decorated Purple Heart, Bronze Star, Vietnam Svc. Ribbon, Nat. Def. Svc. Ribbon. Master Acad. Gen. Dentistry; mem. ADA, Md. Dental Assn., So. Med. Dental Soc. Home: 8808 Wooden Bridge Rd Potomac MD 20854-2445 Office: 431 N Frederick Ave Gaithersburg MD 20877-2419

FROMHAGEN, CARL, JR., obstetrician and gynecologist; b. Tampa, Fla., 1926; s. Carl Frederick and Minnette Gertrude (Douglass) Von Fromhagen; children: Dana Lynn, Carol Leslie, Carl Scott. BS, U. Miami, 1950; student U. Utah, 1949; grad. mil. pilot tng. USAF, 1951; MS, U. Colo., 1952; MD, Emory U., 1955. Diplomate Am. Bd. Ob-Gyn. Intern, Baylor U., 1955-56, resident in ob-gyn, 1956-59; instr. Sch. Medicine U. Miami, Coral Gables, Fla., 1959-62, asso. prof., 1975—; obstetrician, gynecologist, specialist in aviation medicine, FAA sr. med. examiner, Clearwater, Fla., 1960—; pres.

Fromhagen Aviation Inc., 1969—; chmn. bd. Navigate Inc., 1970-73; med. cons. Planned Parenthood, 1963-67; chief of staff Clearwater Community Hosp., 1991-92. Mem. Fla. State Aviation Coun., 1966-67; mem. Com. of 100 Pinellas County, pres. Honduras Relief Soc., 1970; bd. dirs. Am. Cancer Soc., 1962-68; bd. dirs. Interprofl. Family Coun., 1967-68. Served to col. USAFR. Named outstanding resident Baylor U. Med. Sch., 1959; recipient award merit Res. Officers Assn., 1964; Silver Wings Frat. award of honor, 1981. Fellow ACOG, ACS, Am. Coll. Abdominal Surgeons, Internat. Coll. Surgeons; mem. Pan Am. Med. Assn., Fla. Soc. for Preventive Medicine (pres. 1968), Aerospace Med. Assn., Civil Aviation Med. Assn., Flying Physicians (v.p. 1967-68, dir., 1968-74, state pres. 1966-74), Res. Officers Assn. Fla. (Clearwater chpt. pres. 1963-67, state surgeon 1964), N.Y. Acad. Sci., Confederate Air Force, Clan Douglas Soc., Aviation Maintenance Found., U.S. Power Squadron (fleet surgeon), Iron Arrow, Omicron Delta Kappa, Pi Kappa Alpha, Beta Beta Beta. Clubs: Carlouel Yacht. Home: 1666 Robinhood Ln Clearwater FL 34624-6431 Office: 1745 S Highland Ave Clearwater FL 34616-1852

FROMM, DAVID, surgeon; b. N.Y.C., Jan. 21, 1939; s. Alfred and Hanna F.; m. Barbara Solter, June 13, 1961; children—Marc, Kenneth, Kathleen. B.S., U. Calif., Berkeley, 1960, M.D., 1964. Intern U. Calif. Hosp., San Francisco, 1964-65; resident in surgery U. Calif., San Francisco, 1965-71; asst. prof. surgery Harvard Med. Sch., Boston, 1973-77; asso. prof. Harvard Med. Sch., 1977-78; prof. chmn. dept. surgery SUNY-Upstate Med. Center, Syracuse, 1978-88; Penberthy prof., chmn. dept. surgery Wayne State U., 1988—; surgeon-in-chief Detroit Med. Ctr., 1988—; chief surgery Harper Hosp., Detroit, 1988. Author: Complications of Gastric Surgery, 1977; editor Gastrointestinal Surgery, 1985; contbr. articles to profl. jours. Trustee Karmanos Cancer Inst. With M.C., U.S. Army, 1971-73. NIH career devel. awardee, 1976-79; grantee, 1974—. Fellow ACS (gov. 1977-83); mem. Soc. Univ. Surgeons, Am. Gastront. Assn., Soc. Clin. Surgery, Assn. Acad. Surgery, Am. Physiol. Soc., Am. Surg. Assn., Halsted Soc., Soc. Surg. Alimentary Tract (sec. 1994—), Am. Bd. Surgery, Detroit Acad. Surgery. Office: 6C Univ Health Ctr 4201 Saint Antoine St Detroit MI 48201-2153

FROMM, HANS, gastroenterologist, educator, researcher; b. Hagenow, Germany, Aug. 1, 1939; s. Johannes C. and Irene (Biermann) F.; m. Sharon A. Kleiv, June 8, 1968; children: H. Chris, Martin T. MD, Albert Ludwig U., Freiburg, Fed. Republic Germany, 1964. Intern Meml. Hosp., Worcester, Mass., 1966-67; resident Lemuel Shattuck Hosp., Boston, 1967-68, Albany (N.Y.) Med. Ctr., 1968-69; fellow Mayo Clinic, Rochester, Minn., 1970-71; resident/fellow Medizinische Hochschule Hannover, Fed. Republic Germany, 1971-74; asst. prof. medicine U. Pitts., 1975-80, assoc. prof. medicine, 1980-84, prof. medicine, 1984; prof. medicine George Washington U., Washington, 1984—; dir. divsn. gastroenterology & nutrition George Washington Med. Ctr., Washington, 1984—; Mem. numerous grant review coms. including NIH, Med. Review Bd. Gastroenterology Med. Rsch. Svc. VA, Washington, 1984-87. Contbr. articles to profl. jours., chpts. to books; mem. editorial bds. Hepatogastroenterology, 1981-88, Hepatology, 1985-88, 1991—. Mem. Am. Soc. Clin. Investigators, Am. Gastroent. Assn. (chmn. com. on admissions 1990-91, vice chmn.-elect biliary sect. 1994—), Am. Assn. Study of Liver Diseases (chmn. pubs. com. 1988-90). Lutheran. Office: George Washington U Med Ctr Ste 705 2150 Pennsylvania Ave NW Washington DC 20037-2396

FROMM, STEFAN H., surgeon; b. Vienna, Austria, Dec. 24, 1936; s. Fritz W. and Ilse (Pflaum) F.; BS, U. P.R., 1955, MD, 1959; m. Shirley J. Burgy, June 25, 1960; children: Theresa, Stefan, Richard, Michael, Sandra. Intern, San Francisco Gen. Hosp., 1959-60; resident Wayne State U. program Detroit Gen. Hosp., 1961-62, 64-68; practice medicine specializing in surgery, Detroit, 1968-69, Hato Rey, P.R., 1969-78; asst. prof. surgery Wayne State U., 1968, VA Hosp., San Juan, P.R., 1969-71; attending surgeon Hamilton Meml. Hosp., Dalton, Ga., 1978—, chief surgery, 1982-85; asst. prof. surgery U. P.R. Sch. Medicine, Rio Piedras, 1969-76. Bd. dirs. Pee Wee Football League, 1974-77. Served with AUS, 1962-64. Diplomate Am. Bd. Surgery. Mem. A.C.S. (chmn. com. trauma 1975, sec. P.R. chpt. 1975), Christian Med. Soc., Whitfield-Murray County Med. Soc. (sec. 1985-88, pres. 1988), Med. Assn. Ga. (del. 1987, 88), AMA (del. 1976-78; Physician Recognition Award 1981, 84, 87), So. Med. Assn., Southeastern Surg. Congress, Alpha Omega Alpha. Home: 2235 Rocky Face Cir Dalton GA 30720-2941 Office: PO Box 1969 Dalton GA 30722-1969

FROMMELT, PETER, neurologist; b. Luebeck, Germany, Sept. 26, 1946; s. Heinz and Ursula (Statz) F.; m. Silvia Braun, Feb. 20, 1985; children: Jule, Marthe. MD, U. Freiburg, Germany, 1973. Internship Gen. Hosp., Kleve, Germany, 1974-75; residency Max-Planck Inst. of Systemic Physiology, Dortmund, Germany, 1975-76, Marien-Hosp., Dortmund, 1976-78, Johannes Hosp., Bielefeld, Germany, 1978-81; sr. neurologist Hosp. Lemgo, Germany, 1981-87; med. dir. Klinik Bavaria, Schaufling, Germany, 1987—. Editor: (with H. Grotzbach) Neurorehabilitation; contbr. articles to med. jours. Office: Klinik Bavaria, 8351 Schaufling Germany

FROMMER, ANN, health administrator; b. Coaldale, Pa.; m. Robert E. Frommer, Apr. 23, 1990. BS, Fairleigh Dickinson U., 1968, MA, 1975. RN. Cons. Custom Pers. Svc., Convent Station, N.J., 1978-80; coord. Gen. Hosp. Passaic, N.J., 1980-83; coord., mgr. Pocono Hosp., E. Stroudsburg, Pa., 1983-87; dir. utilization mgmt. Morristown (N.J.) Meml. Hosp., 1987—; critical path com., Cranberry, N.J., 1995-96, comparative data study com., Cranberry, 1995—, Quality Coun., 1996—, VHA, Cranberry, 1995-96, quality data com.; mem. quality and fin. data com. N.J. Hosp. Assn., Princeton, 1995-96; spkr. in field. Editor Alert News Mag.; contbr. articles to profl. jours. Mem. LWV, Nat. Healthcare Quality Profls., Am. Assn. Healthcare Execs., Am. Heart Assn. (bd. dirs. 1977-80), Healthcare Fin. Orgn. N.J., Healthcare Fin. Mgmt. Assn. N.J., Healthcare Quality Profls. N.J., Chatham Bd. Health. Home: 24 E Coleman Ave Chatham NJ 07928

FROMMER, PETER LESLIE, physician, medical institute administrator; b. Budapest, Hungary, Feb. 13, 1932; came to U.S., 1941, naturalized, 1947; s. Joseph Charles and Magda F.; m. Ellen Mills, June 27, 1953; children: Donald, Ann Frommer Ames, David, Stephen. B.S. in Elec. Engring, U. Cin., 1954; M.D., Harvard U., 1958. Intern, then resident in internal medicine U. Cin. Med. Center, 1958-59, 61-63; commd. officer USPHS, 1959-61, 73—, asst. surg. gen., 1981—; mem. staff Nat. Heart, Lung and Blood Inst., NIH, Bethesda, Md., 1959-61, 63—; asso. dir. cardiology div. heart and vascular diseases Nat. Heart, Lung and Blood Inst., NIH, 1972-78, acting chief devices and tech. br., 1973-75, cardiac diseases br., 1975-78, dep. dir. inst., 1978—, acting dir., 1981-82. Author. Recipient Disting. Alumnus award U. Cin. Coll. Engring., 1969, Disting Svc. medal USPHS, 1992. Fellow ACP, Am. Coll. Cardiology (Disting. Svc. award 1993); mem. AAAS, IEEE (chmn. joint com. engring. in medicine and biology 1964), Am. Physiol. Soc., Am. Fedn. Clin. Rsch., Am. Heart Assn., Am. Soc. Artificial Internal Organs, Biomed. Engring. Soc., Internat. Fedn. Med. and Biol. Engring. (v.p. 1969-71), Sigma Xi, Eta Kappa Nu, Tau Beta Pi. Home: 3 Old Club Ct Rockville MD 20852-4533 Office: Nat Heart Lung and Blood Inst 9000 Rockville Pike Bethesda MD 20892-0001

FROMSON, JOHN ADAM, psychiatrist; b. Forest Hills, N.Y., Dec. 22, 1953. BA, Hobart Coll., 1975; MD, N.Y. Med. Coll., 1979. Clin. med. fellow Dartmouth Med. Sch., Hanover, N.H., 1979-80; clin. fellow psychiatry Harvard Med. Sch., Boston, 1980-84, clin. instr. psychiatry, 1984—; dir. Physician Health Svcs., Waltham, Mass., 1986—. Fellow APA, Am. Acad. Child and Adolescent Psychiatry; mem. AMA, Am. Assn. Psychiatrists in Alcoholism and Addiction, Am. Psychiat. Assn., New Eng. Coun. Child and Adolescent Psychiatry, Mass. Med. Soc. Office: Mass Med Soc 1440 Main St Waltham MA 02154-1623

FRONEBERG, BRIGITTE, physician; b. Bevensen, Germany, May 3, 1945; d. Walter and Elisabeth Anna (Gandlau) F.; 1 child, Michael Chanan. MD, Georg-August-U., Göttingen, Fed. Republic Germany, 1974; postgrad., London Sch. Hygiene, 1976-77; diploma in tropical medicine, Bernhard-Nocht-Inst., Hamburg, Fed. Republic Germany, 1976; postgrad., Bayerische Acad. Arbeits, Munich, 1983-87, 89-91. Cert. in occupational medicine, phys. therapy, med. informatics, social medicine. Med. asst. Dist. Hosp. Wunsiedel-Selb, 1974-75; med. asst., asst. physician surgery Dist. Hosp. Wunsiedel-Marktredwitz, 1975-76; asst. physician internal medicine and tropical diseases Bernhard-Nocht-Inst. Tropenmedizin & Schiffkrankheiten, Hamburg, 1977; resident in occupational medicine Nat. Inst. Occupational Safety and Health, Cin., 1980-81, Inst. Environ. Health, U. Cin., 1981; med. epidemiologist Ministry of Health, Jerusalem, 1981-82; asst. physician Pvt. Hosp. for Multiple Sclerosis, Baiersbronn-Schonmunzach, 1982-83 asst. physician, documentation asst., occupational physician Fachklinik Enzensberg, Füssen, 1983-89; state occupational physician Bayerisches Landesinst. Arbeitsmedizin, Munich, 1990-93; group leader Fed. Inst. for Occupational Medicine, Berlin, 1993, dept. leader occupational health protection, 1993—; mem. epidemic intelligence svc. program Ctrs. for Disease Control, Am. Pub. Health Svc., Atlanta, 1979-81. Contbr. articles to profl. publs. Home: Pfeilstr 29, 13156 Berlin Germany Office: Bundesanstalt für Arbeitschutz und, Arbeitsmedizin, Postfach 5, 10266 Berlin 22, Germany

FRÖSNER, GERT G., virologist, educator, researcher; b. Tübingen, Germany, May 14, 1942; s. Herbert and Maria Anna (Schneider) F.; m. Helga Ruth Hannig, Jan. 18, 1969; children: Eva Katharina, Sebastian Gert. MD, U. Tübingen, 1967. Asst. prof. U. Tübingen, 1969-76; rsch. fellow Presbyn. St. Luke's Hosp., Chgo., 1972-73; assoc. prof. U. Munich, 1977-79, prof virology, 1980—. Home: Moostr 10, 85416 Langenbach Germany Office: Max von Pettenkofer Inst, Pettenkofer 9a, 80336 Munich Germany

FROST, DAVID, former biology educator, medical editor, consultant; b. Bklyn., Dec. 19, 1925; s. Charles and Regina (Sad) Feivlowitz; m. Ruthann Steinberg, Dec. 24, 1946; children: Michael Joseph, Jane Alice. BS, CCNY, 1945, MED, 1949; MS, NYU, 1952, PhD, 1960. Instr. in biology CCNY, 1946-49; instr. in sci. Rhodes Sch., N.Y.C., 1949-52; asst. prof. biology Rutgers U., Newark, N.J., 1952-59; adj. prof. biology Rutgers U., New Brunswick, N.J., 1960-78; sci. editor Squibb Inst. for Med. Rsch., Princeton, N.J., 1959-75; pvt. practice, Plainfield, N.J. Olmstedville, N.Y., 1975—. Pres. N.J. SANE, 1964-65; co-chmn. Plainfield Joint Def. Com., 1970-85; newsletter editor Cen. Jersey/Masaya, Nicaragua Friendship Cities Project, 1985—. Mem. Coun. Biology Editors (pres. 1982-83). Office: 1229 E 7th St Plainfield NJ 07062-1907 also: Box 41B RD1 Olmstedville NY 12857

FROST, ELIZABETH ANN MCARTHUR, physician; b. Glasgow, Scotland, Oct. 29, 1938; came to U.S., 1963; d. Robert Thomas and Annie M. (Ross) F.; m. Wallace Capobianco, Sept. 4, 1965 (dec. May 1988); children: Garrett, Ross, Christopher, Neil. MBChB, U. Glasgow, 1961. Diplomate Am. Bd. Anesthesiology, Royal Coll. Ob-Gyn., London. Intern in surgery Royal Infirmary, Glasgow, 1961-62; intern in medicine Victoria Infirmary, Glasgow, 1962; intern in obstetrics Royal Maternity Hosp., Glasgow, 1962-63; resident in internal medicine Englewood (N.J.) Hosp., 1963-64; resident in anesthesiology N.Y. Hosp., N.Y.C., 1964-66; instr. in anesthesiology Albert Einstein Coll. Medicine, Bronx, N.Y., 1966-68, asst. prof. to assoc. prof., 1968-81, prof. anesthesiology, 1981-91, mem. dept. history of medicine, 1973-91; prof., chmn. dept. anesthesiology N.Y. Med. Coll., Valhalla, N.Y., 1992—; dir. div. neuroanesthesia Albert Einstein Coll. Medicine and Affiliated Hosps. Book reviewer New Eng. Jour. of Medicine, 1983—; editor Preanesthetic Assessment, Anesthesiology News, 1984—, Gen. Surgery News, 1991; author/contbr. books; contbr. articles to profl. jours. Mem. N.Y. State Soc. Anesthesiologists, Am. Soc. of Anesthesiologists, Assn. of Univ. Anesthesiologists, Soc. of Neurosurg. Anesthesia and Neurologic Supportive Care, Am. Assn. of Neurol. Surgeons, Anesthesia History Assn., Internat. Trauma Anesthesia and Critical Care Soc. Office: NY Medical Coll Valhalla NY 10595

FROST, ELLEN ELIZABETH, psychologist, b. N.Y.C., July 16, 1947; d. John Joseph and Josephine Mary (Cornell) F.; m. Jerry Melnick, Jan 8, 1982; children: Mariel Frost, Matt James. B.A. magna cum laude, St. John's U., 1969; M.A. (N.Y. State regents fellow, 1969, USPHS fellow, 1969-72), Fordham U., 1981, Ph.D., 1982; candidate N.Y.U. Postdoctoral Program for Psychotherapy and Psychoanalysis, 1982-84. Clin. psychology intern Columbia-Presbyn. Psychiat. Inst., N.Y.C., 1972-73; asst. team leader, staff psychologist Bensonhurst inpatient unit, South Beach Psychiat Center, Bklyn., 1973-75, sr. psychologist, Bensonhurst outpatient dept., 1975-81, assoc. psychologist, supr., 1982-89; clin. supr. New Hope Guild, Bklyn., 1983—; faculty L.I. Inst. Mental Health, 1990—, supr., 1993—. Mem. Am. Psychol. Assn., Sigma Xi. Office: 200 E 33rd St # 25J New York NY 10016-4874

FROST, J. ORMOND, otolaryngologist, educator; b. Ireland, May 18, 1927; came to U.S., 1952, naturalized, 1963; s. James Patrick and Margaret (O'Loughlen) F.; m. Rita Robert, Oct. 1, 1955; 1 dau., Roberta. M.B.B.Ch., Univ. Coll. Dublin, 1952. House officer Mater Hosp., Dublin, Ireland, 1952; intern Loyola U. Mercy Hosp., Chgo., 1953; resident, asst., assoc. prof. Sch. Medicine NYU, N.Y.C., 1953-74, prof. clin. otolaryngology, 1974-89, clin. prof. otolaryngology, 1989—. Mem. AMA, N.Y. Otologic Soc. (pres. 1983-85), ACS, Am. Acad. Otolaryngology (bd. govs. 1985-88), Irish-Am Cultural Inst., Am. Otol., Rhinol. and Laryngol. Soc., Centurian of the Deafness Research Found., Amateur Comedy Club. Roman Catholic.

FROST, JAMES HAMNER, health facility administrator; b. Beaumont, Tex., Aug. 7, 1934; s. Harvey Newcomb and Velma Veda (Farmer) F.; children: Patricia Eileen, Kenneth Harvey; m. Mary Loonan, May 20, 1995. BA, U. Tex., 1957; MS, Trinity Univ., San Antonio, 1971. Asst. dir. Hermann Hosp., Houston, 1971-73; asst. adminstr. McAllen (Tex.) Gen. Hosp., 1973-75; chief support svcs. Whittaker Corp. Hosp. Tabuk, Tabuk, Saudi Arabia, 1975-77; hosp. dir. Almana Hosp., Al Khobar, Saudi Arabia, 1977-78; dir. med. svcs. corp. Bechtel Corp., Jubail, Saudi Arabia, 1979-83; chief exec. officer Al-Mutabagani Health Svcs., Riyadh, Saudi Arabia, 1983-86; hosp. dir. Asir Cen. Hosp., Abha, Saudi Arabia, 1987-90; dep. project dir. King Fahd Mil. Med. Complex, Dhahran, Saudi Arabia, 1990—, hosp. dir., 1990—; founder., sr. consulting officer J.H. Frost & Assocs., Beaumont, 1987—; founder, COO Paramedex Internat. Ltd., Lincoln, Eng., 1989—. Fellow Am. Coll. Healthcare Execs.; mem. Am. Businessmen's Assn., Internat. Fedn. Hosps., Am. Hosp. Assn., Tex. Hosp. Assn. Republican. Methodist. Home: 2809 Olympia Dr Grand Prairie TX 75052

FROST, JUANITA CORBITT, hospital foundation coordinator; b. Rockford, Ill., Aug. 4, 1926; d. Mervin Charles and Eva Marie (Moberg) Corbitt; m. Thomas Tapenden Frost, Jan. 3, 1954; children: Annamarie, Thomas Tapenden. Student, Little Rock U., Ark., 1959-61. Med. sec. asst. clinical pathology lab. VA, Whipple, Ariz., 1951-54; exec. dir. Camp Fire Girls, Temple, Tex., 1967-73; exec. sec. Scott & White Meml. Hosp. Found., Temple, Tex., 1973-82; hosp. found. coordinator, exec. asst. to bd. Scott & White Meml. Hosp., Scott Sherwood and Brindley Found, Temple, Tex., 1982—. Vestry mem. Episcopal Ch., Temple, Tex., 1985—, sr. warden, 1987, worship com., 1995—; active Com. on Bishops Address NW Region Diocese Episcopal Ch., Houston, 1988, Bell County Choral Group, Belton, Tex., 1988-92, Tchr. Literacy Coun., Temple, 1988-93. Mem. Am. Hosp. Assn. Exec. Assts. Home: 3001 Las Moras Dr Temple TX 76502-1643 Office: Scott & White Meml Hosp Found 2401 S 31st St Temple TX 76508-0001

FRUCHTMAN, STEVEN MARTIN, physician; b. N.Y.C., Apr 7, 1951; s. Harry and Anna (Rechstman) F.; m. Miriam Baker, Aug. 18, 1985; 1 child, Genna. BA, Cornell U., 1973; MD, N.Y. Med. Coll., 1977. Intern, then resident Downstate Med. Ctr., Bklyn., 1977-81; dir. sickle cell program Mt. Sinai Hosp., N.Y.C., 1986-90, assoc. prof. medicine, 1986—. dir. bone marrow transplantation, 1990—. Author Polychythemia Vera, 1991. Mem. ACP, Am. Coll. Hematology. Home: 25 Grandview Ter Tenafly NJ 07670-1120 Office: Mount Sinai Hosp 1 Gustave L Levy Pl New York NY 10029-6504

FRUMKIN, JUDITH ROGOFF, speech language pathologist; b. Cleve., Aug. 26, 1948; d. Bernard Daniel and Arlene (Cohen) R.; m. Michael Alan Frumkin, Aug. 22, 1971; children: Daniel Jed, Jeremy Rogoff. BA, Case Western Reserve U., 1970; MS, Syracuse U., 1971; Cert. Advanced Study Ednl. Adminstrn., SUNY, Oswego, N.Y., 1994. Lic. speech pathologist, N.Y. Speech and lang. pathologist presch. and infant deaf program Bd. Coop. Ednl. Svcs., Syracuse, N.Y., 1971-74; speech lang. pathologist communication disorders unit SUNY, Syracuse, 1974-77; speech and lang. pathologist UCP Pre-Sch. Lang. Disorders, Syracuse, 1980-81, UCP Enable Schneier Communication Unit, Syracuse, 1981-89; instr. Onondaga Community Coll., Syracuse, 1981-82; instr., lectr. Syracuse U., 1986-90; lectr. SUNY, Cortland, N.Y., 1989-90; speech lang. pathologist OCM BOCES, Syracuse, 1990—; pvt. practice speech pathology, Syracuse, 1989—; cons. Onondaga, Cortland and Madison Bd. Coop. Ednl. Svcs., Liverpool (N.Y.) Sch. Dsit., N.Y. State Office Health Sys. Mgmt., 1989—; adminstrv. intern Fabius-Pompey Sch. Dist., 1993—; prin. Sylvan-Verona Beach (N.Y.) Elem. Sch.; presenter lectures, seminars and workshops to profl. and local groups. Author computer software Magic Cymbals, 1986, Lang. Interaction Activities, 1988; contbr. numerous articles to profl. jours. Mem. ASCD, U.S. Soc. for Augmentative and Alternative Comm. (v.p. profl. affairs 1992-94), Internt. Soc. for Augmentative and Alternative Comm., Am. Speech, Lang. and Hearing Assn. (cert. clin. competence), N.Y. State Speech, Lang. and Hearing Assn. (chmn. com. on augmentative alternative comm. 1989-91, 91—, adv. 1988—), Ctrl. N.Y. Speech, Lang. and Hearing Assn. (pres. 1986-87, editor 1988-89), Rehab. Engring. Soc. N.Am.

FRUMKIN, ROBERT MARTIN, psychologist, behavioral and social sciences educator; b. Newark, Mar. 20, 1928; s. Solomon and Anna (Gruber) F.; m. Miriam Zisenwine, Dec. 30, 1950 (div. 1964); 1 child, Judith. BA, Upsala Coll., 1948; MA, Ohio State U., 1951, PhD, 1961; postgrad., Kent State U., 1969-74. Lic. psychologist, Ohio. Instr. U. Buffalo, 1954-57; from asst. prof. to assoc. prof. SUNY, Oswego, 1957-63; rsch. assoc. Benjamin Rose Inst., Cleve., 1964-65; rsch. dir. Community Action for Youth, Cleve., 1965-66, Cleve. Soc. for the Blind, 1966-67; assoc. prof. Kent (Ohio) State U., 1967-75; coord. rehab. counseling program, 1973-75; staff psychologist Northville (Mich.) State Hosp., 1976-77; assoc. prof. Shaw Coll., Detroit, 1977-81; staff psychologist Eastern Panhandle Mental Health Ctr., Martinsburg, W.Va., 1987-88; rsch. assoc. Shepherd Coll., Shepherdstown, W.Va., 1989-90; assoc. prof. Salem (W.Va.)-Teikyo U., 1990—; rsch. cons. Rsch. Experts Inc., Irvington, N.J., 1981-87. Rsch. editor Jour. Human Rels., Wilberforce, Ohio, 1958-70; author: The Measurement of Marriage Adjustment, 1954, The Nurse as a Human Being, 1956, Social Problems, Pathology & Philosophy, 1962, The Kent State Coverup, 3d edit., 1990; contbr. 200 papers profl. jours. Mem. ACLU, 1954—, Dem. Socialists Am., 1983—. With USN, 1946-47. Recipient John Ericsson sci. fellowship. Fellow AAAS, Soc. for Sci. Study Sex; mem. Am. Psychol. Assn., W.Va. Psychol. Assn., Am. Sociol. Assn. Office: Salem-Teikyo Univ Dept Social Scis Salem WV 26426

FRUSHOUR, SUSAN TYDINGS, hospital administrator; b. Washington, May 11, 1947; d. Richard Emmett and Marie Adele (Roversi) Tydings; m. Gerald Leon Frushour, June 15, 1968; children: David, Kelley, Matthew, Michael. Student, U. Md., 1965-68; BA in Psychology and Sociology, Mary Baldwin Coll., 1981; postgrad., Va. Commonwealth U., 1984-85. Medicaid tech. Dept. Welfare and Instns., Richmond, Va., 1970-72; social worker Western State Hosp., Staunton, Va., 1972-74, 76-85; admitting mgr. Western State Hosp., Staunton, 1985—, dir. admitting & health access, 1993—; social worker Community Residences, Staunton, 1974-76; owner Waynesboro (Va.) Athletic Ctr., 1984-85; bd. dirs. Waynesboro Dept. Social Svcs., 1991—; mem. Waynesboro CADRE, 1991; cons. Beauti Control Image, 1995—. Pres. Assn. Retarded Citizens, Waynesboro, 1980-81, bd. dirs., 1978-80; bd. dirs. Reality House Hotline, Waynesboro, 1972-80, v.p. bd., 1979; bd. dirs. Half Way Housing, Inc., Staunton, 1970-72; active Waynesboro Family Assessment & Planning Team, 1993, 1994—, Commn. for Alcohol & Drug Rehab. & Edn., 1993; chair Waynesboro Youth Commn., 1996—, Waynesboro ADA Disability Bd., 1996—; v.p. Youth Commn., 1994-95, chair, 1995; chair Western State Hosp. Critical Incident Stress Com.; critical incident stress debriefer Shenandoah Emergency Med. Svcs., 1990—;. Mem. Waynesboro Mental Health Assn., Waynesboro Assn. Retarded Citizens, Nat. Assn. Admitting Mgmt., No. Va. Alliance of Mentally Ill, Nat. Capital Area Health-Care, Delta Assn. Health Access Mgrs. (exec. bd./sec. 1994—). Democrat. Roman Catholic. Home: 828 Gwynne Ave Waynesboro VA 22980-3343 Office: Western State Hosp PO Box 2500 Staunton VA 24402-2500

FRUTH, BERYL ROSE, physician; b. Carey, Ohio, Mar. 27, 1952; d. Oscar W. and Alice (Arnett) Fruth. BA in Chemistry magna cum laude, Asbury Coll., 1973; MD, Ohio State U., 1977. Diplomate Am. Acad. Family Practice. Intern Grant Hosp., Columbus, Ohio, 1977-78, resident, 1978-79, chief resident, 1979-80; pvt. practice, Columbus, 1980-93; family physician Columbus Community Physicians, Inc., Grove City, Ohio, 1993—; asst. dir. family practice residency Grant Hosp., 1980-81; med. dir. Columbus Dispatch, 1983-93, St. Anthony Breast Evaluation Ctr., 1986—; lectr. Columbus Cancer Clinic, 1984; mentor family practice dept. Ohio State U., physician preceptor Sch. Medicine. Contbr. Ohio State U. Med. Sch. Learning Module in Alcoholism, 1983-84. Named Alumna of Yr., Vanlue Sch., Ohio. Fellow Am. Acad. Family Physicians; mem. AMA, Am. Med. Women's Assn., Acad. Family Practice. Office: 2041 Stringtown Rd Grove City OH 43123-2930

FRY, DONALD LEWIS, physiologist, educator; b. Des Moines, Dec. 29, 1924; s. Clair V. and Maudie (Long) F.; children—Donald Stewart, Ronald Sinclair, Heather Elise, Laurel Virginia. M.D., Harvard U., 1949. Rsch. fellow Univ Minn Hosp., Mpls., 1952-53; sr. asst. surgeon gen. NIH, Bethesda, Md., 1953-56; surgeon NIH, 1956-57, sr. surgeon, 1957-61, med. dir., 1961-80; prof. Ohio State U., Columbus, 1980—. Contbr. numerous articles and papers on physiology and biophysics of pulmonary mechanics, blood vascular interface, transvascular mass transport and the genesis of atherosclerosis to profl. jours., books. Mem. AAAS, Am. Physiol. Soc., Am. Soc. Clin. Investigation, Biophys. Soc., N.Y. Acad. Scis. Office: Ohio State U Coll Medicine 2025 Wiseman Hall 400 W 12th Ave Columbus OH 43210-1214

FRY, EDWARD IRAD, anthropology educator; b. Long Branch, N.J., Jan. 7, 1924; s. Wallace Cordiner and Abigail Elizabeth (Hidden) F.; m. Peggy June Crooke, Dec. 23, 1950. B.A., U. Tex., 1949, M.A., 1950; Ph.D., Harvard U., 1958. Cons. to U.S. Air Force; also asst. prof. Antioch Coll., 1955-56; asso. prof. U. Nebr., Lincoln, 1956-66; prof. anthropology So. Meth. U., Dallas, 1966-87, prof. emeritus, 1987—; anthropol. cons., 1987—. Author numerous publs. and papers on growth, body composition and forensic anthropology. Served with USAAF, 1942-45. Fulbright fellow N. Z. and South Pacific, 1953-54; Fulbright fellow Hong Kong U., 1963-64. Fellow AAAS (chmn. sect. anthropology 1980), Am. Anthrop. Assn.; mem. Soc. for Study Cranio-facial Biology, Internat. Assn. Human Biologists, Human Biology Council, Soc. for Study Human Biology, Am. Assn. Phys. Anthropologists (exec. com., sec.-treas., pres. 1973-75), Sigma Xi. Home: 3004 Fondren Dr Dallas TX 75205-1916

FRY, RANDY DALE, emergency medical technician, paramedic; b. Houston, Feb. 3, 1957; s. LeRoy D. Fry and Ardria Faye (Stegall) Boyd; m. Robbie Ruth Rippy, June 4, 1982. Paramedic Panola County Ambulance, Carthage, Tex., 1979-87; cardiac monitor tech. Bossier Med. Ctr., Bossier City, La., 1991—; instr. CPR, PALS Bossier Med. Ctr.; instr. EMS, coord. Panola Jr. Coll., Carthage. Home: Rt 1 Box 232 Joaquin TX 75954 Office: Bossier Med Ctr Bossier City LA 75954

FRY, ROBERT DEAN, surgeon; b. Beaver, Okla., Jan. 7, 1947; s. Donald D. and Elaine (Gregg) F.; m. Susan Marie Henninger. AB, Oklahoma City U., 1968; MD, Washington U., 1972. Diplomate Am. Bd. Surgery, Am. Bd. Colon and Rectal Surgery. Intern Jewish Hosp., St. Lois, 1972-73, resident, 1973-77; fellow in colorectal surgery Cleve. Clinic Found., 1977-78; instr. clin. surgery Washington U., St. Louis, 1980-84, asst. prof. clin. surgery, 1984-85, asst. prof. surgery, 1985-91, assoc. prof. surgery, 1991-93; prof. surgery Thomas Jefferson U., Phila., 1994—; chief divsn. colorectal surgery Thomas Jefferson U. Hosp., Phila., 1994—; program dir. divsn. colon and rectal surgery Jewish Hosp. St. Louis, 1980-93; assoc. examiner Am. Bd. Colon and Rectal Surgery, Arlington Heights, Ill., 1986-90. Contbr. articles to profl. jours. Louis M. Monheimer fellow, 1977; grantee Johnson & Johnson Products, Inc., 1984-85, U. Pitts., 1987-93. Fellow ACS (residency rev. com. colon and rectal surgery 1995), Am. Soc. Colon and Rectal Surgeons (pres., program dir. 1991-94); mem. AMA, Am. Gastroent. Assn., Union League Phila., Ctrl. Surg. Assn. (mem. com.). Office: Thomas Jefferson U Hosp 1100 Walnut St Ste 702 Philadelphia PA 19107

FRYER, GLADYS CONSTANCE, retired physician, medical director, educator; b. London, Mar. 28, 1923; came to U.S., 1967; d. William John and Florence Annie (Dockett) Mercer; m. Donald Wilfred Fryer, Jan. 20, 1944;

children: Peter Vivian, Gerard John, Gillian Celia. MB, BS, U. Melbourne, Victoria, Australia, 1956. Resident Box Hill Hosp., 1956-57; postdoctoral fellow Inst. of Cardiology, U. London, 1958; med. registrar Queen Victoria Hosp., Melbourne, Australia, 1958; cardiologist Assunta Found., Petaling Jaya, Malaysia, 1961-64; fellow in advanced medicine London Hosp., U. London, 1964; clin. research physician U.S. Army Clin. Research Unit, Malaysia, 1964-66; physician to pesticide program U. Hawaii, 1967-68; internist Hawaii Permanente Kaiser Found., Honolulu, 1968-73; practice medicine specializing in internal medicine Honolulu, 1973-88; med. dir. Hale Nani Health Ctr., Honolulu, 1975-89, Beverly Manor Convalescent Ctr., Honolulu, 1975-89; vis. pediatric cardiac depts. Yale U., Stanford U., U. Calif., 1958; asst. clin. prof. medicine John Burns Sch. Medicine U. Hawaii, 1968-89; vis. geriatrics dept. U. Capetown, 1990; med. cons. Salvation Army Alcohol Treatment Facility, Honolulu, 1975-81; physician to skilled nursing patients VA, Honolulu, 1984-88; preceptor to geriatric nurse practitioner program U. Colo., Honolulu, 1984-85; lectr. on geriatrics, Alzheimer's disease, gen. medicine, profl. women's problems, and neurosci., 1961—; mem. ad hoc due process bd. Med. Care Evaluation Com., 1982-88, Hospice Adv. Com., 1982-88; mem. pharmacy com. St. Francis Hosp. Clin. Staff, 1983-89, chmn. 1983-84. Contbr. articles to med. and sci. jours. Mem. adv. com. Honolulu Home Care St. Francis Hosp., 1974-87; mem. adv. bd. Honolulu Gerontology Program, 1983-89, Straub Home Health Program, Honolulu, 1984-87; mem. sci. adv. bd. Alzheimers Disease and Related Disorders Assn., Honolulu, 1984-89; mem. long term care task force Health and Community Svcs. Coun. Hawaii, 1978-84. Special Ops. Exec., War Office, London, 1943-44. Recipient Edgar Rouse Prize in Indsl. Medicine, U. Melbourne, 1955, Outstanding Supporter award Hawaii Assn. Activity Coordinators, 1987. Fellow ACP; mem. AAAS, AMA, Hawaii Med. Assn. (councillor 1984-89), Honolulu County Med. Soc. (chmn., mem. utilization rev. com. 1973-89), World Med. Assn., Am. Geriatrics Soc., N.Y. Acad. Sci. Episcopalian.

FRYER, WILLIAM NEAL, retired psychologist; b. Cin., Mar. 10, 1920; s. Roy Charles and Alice (Carson) F.; B.A., Harding Coll., 1948; M.A., Columbia U., 1953, Ed.D., 1965; m. Dorothy Elizabeth McClain, May 11, 1942; children—Bonnie Jean, Debra Lynn. Aircraft painter Aero. Corp. Am., Cin., 1937-39; salesman Sears, Roebuck & Co., Covington, Ky., 1940-41; minister Bklyn. Ch. of Christ, 1948-56; asst. prof. psychology Abilene (Tex.) Christian Coll., 1956-65, asso. prof., 1965-68, part-time tchr. psychology, 1968-70; chief psychologist Abilene State Sch., 1968-85. Mem. Mayor's Com. on Mental Retardation, Abilene, 1964-65; past mem. exec. com., profl. adviser Abilene Suicide Prevention Service. Bd. dirs., past mem. profl. adv. com. Abilene Assn. Mental Health, pres., 1958-59; past bd. dirs. Tex. Assn. Mental Health; vol. Christ's Prison Fellowship, 1989—. Served to capt. USAAF, 1941-46. Mem. Am., Southwestern, Tex., Abilene (pres. 1978-79) psychol. assns., AAAS, N.Y. Acad. Sci., Am. Assn. Mental Deficiency, Abilene Writers Guild (pres. 1990-91, 91-92), Phi Delta Kappa, Kappa Delta Pi. Mem. Ch. of Christ. Club: Kiwanis. Author: (with Orval Filbeck, Max Leach) College, Classroom, Campus, and You, 1959. Home: 833 E North 10th St Abilene TX 79601-4628

FRY-WENDT, SHERRI DIANE, psychologist; b. Clinton, Mo., Mar. 30, 1958; d. Charles Pierce and Norma Geraldine (Croft) Fry; m. Joseph Otto Wendt, May 24, 1980; children: Benjamin, Ethan, Nathaniel. BSE, Cen. Mo. State U., 1979, MS, 1981; PhD, U. Mo., 1989. Lic. psychologist, Mo. Mental health therapist Wyandot Mental Health Ctr., Kansas City, Kans., 1981-88; EAP contract psychologist Menninger Found., Topeka, 1988-89; contract psychologist Tri-County Mental Health Ctr., Kansas City, 1988-89; pvt. practice Kansas City, 1988—; tng. provider local and state level, 1985—; expert witness State of Kans., 1985—. Youth group sponsor Hillside Christian Ch., Kansas City, 1982-86, children's choir dir., 1983-87, deaconess, 1983-93, dir. vacation bible sch., 1992, 93; deaconess Fairview Christian Ch., co-chair Christian edn.; mem. ethics com. Kansas City region Christian Ch. (Disciples of Christ). Mem. APA, Internat. Soc. Study of Multiple Personality and Dissociation, Greater Kansas City Psychol. Assn., Phi Kappa Phi, Psi Chi. Office: 4901 Main St Ste 408 Kansas City MO 64112-2635

FUCHS, ELAINE V., molecular biologist, educator; b. Hinsdale, Ill., May 5, 1950; d. Louis H. and Viola L. (Lueck) F.; m. David T. Hansen, Sept. 10, 1988. BS in Chemistry with honors, U. Ill., Urbana, 1972; PhD in Biochemistry, Princeton U., 1977. Postdoctoral fellow dept. biology MIT, 1977-80; asst. prof. U. Chgo., 1980-85, assoc. prof., 1985-88, prof. dept. molecular genetics and cell biology, 1989—, Amgen prof. basic scis., 1993—, investigator, Howard Hughes Med. Inst., 1988—. Assoc. editor Jour. Cell Biology, 1993—; contr. numerous articles to profl. jours. Recipient R.R. Benesely award Am. Assn. Anatomists, 1988, Searle Scholar award Chgo. Cmty. Trust, 1981-84, Presdl. Young Investigator award NSF, 1984-89, NIH Merit award, 1993, Wm. Montagna award Soc. Investigative Dermatology, 1995. Fellow Am. Acad. Arts and Scis.; mem. NAS (elected mem.), Inst. Medicine of NAS, Am. Assn. Cell Biology (Keith Porter award 1996), Am. Assn. Biol. Chemists, Phi Beta Kappa. Office: U Chgo Howard Hughes Med Inst Dept Molecular Genetics 5841 S Maryland Ave Rm 314N Chicago IL 60637-1463

FUCHS, MICHAEL ALVIN, orthodontist; b. Hastings, Minn., Jan. 16, 1949; s. Conrad Albert and Elizabeth Ann (Leifeld) F.; m. Mary Elizabeth Swanson, Aug. 28, 1971; children: Ryan, Rick, Ann Marie. BA, St. John's U., Collegeville, Minn., 1971; DDS, U. Minn., 1974. Diplomate Am. Bd. Orthodontics. Practice dentistry specializing in orthodontics Huron, S.D., 1976—. Mem. Huron Bd. Edn., 1982—, pres. 1985-87; bd. dirs. Greater Huron Devel. Corp., 1986—; bd. dirs., pres. Our Home Inc., 1977-78. Named Outstanding Young Citizen, Huron Jaycees, 1985. Mem. ADA, S.D. Dental Assn. (trustee 1981-88, pres. 1996—), Am. Assn. Orthodontists, S.D. Orthodontic Soc. (pres. 1982-83), Midwestern Soc. Orthodontists (dir. 1986-92, pres. 1994-95), Minn. Orthodontic Soc. (affiliate). Lutheran. Lodge: Kiwanis (pres. Huron 1982-83). Home: 1860 Robin Ct Huron SD 57350-3432 Office: 530 Iowa Ave SE Huron SD 57350-2859

FUCHS, VICTOR ROBERT, economics educator; b. N.Y.C., Jan. 31, 1924; s. Alfred and Frances Sarah (Scheiber) F.; m. Beverly Beck, Aug. 29, 1948; children: Nancy, Fredric, Paula, Kenneth. BS, NYU, 1947; MA, Columbia U., 1951, PhD, 1955. Internat. fur broker, 1946-50; lectr. Columbia U., N.Y.C., 1953-54, instr., 1954-55, asst. prof. econs., 1955-59; assoc. prof. econs. NYU, 1959-60; program assoc. Ford Found. Program in Econ. Devel. and Adminstrn., 1960-62; prof. econs. Grad. Ctr., CUNY, 1968-74; prof. community medicine Mt. Sinai Sch. Medicine, 1968-74; prof. econs. Stanford U. and Stanford Med. Sch., 1974-95, Henry J. Kaiser Jr. prof., 1988-95, prof. emeritus, 1995—; v.p. research Nat. Bur. Econ. Research, 1968-78, mem. sr. research staff, 1962—. Author: The Economics of the Fur Industry, 1957; (with Aaron Warner) Concepts and Cases in Economic Analysis, 1958, Changes in the Location of Manufacturing in the United States Since 1929, 1962, The Service Economy, 1968, Production and Productivity in the Service Industries, 1969, Policy Issues and Research Opportunities in Industrial Organization, 1972, Essays in the Economics of Health and Medical Care, 1972, Who Shall Live? Health, Economics and Social Choice, 1975; (with Joseph Newhouse) The Economics of Physician and Patient Behavior, 1978, Economic Aspects of Health, 1982, How We Live, 1983, The Health Economy, 1986, Women's Quest for Economic Equality, 1988, The Future of Health Policy, 1993, Individual and Social Responsibility: Child Care Education, Medical Care, and Long-term Care in America, 1996.; contbr. articles to profl. jours. Served with USAAF, 1943-46. Fellow Am. Acad. Arts and Scis., Am. Econ. Assn. (disting.; pres. 1995); mem. Inst. Medicine of NAS, Am. Philos. Soc., Sigma Xi, Beta Gamma Sigma. Home: 796 Cedro Way Stanford CA 94305-1032 Office: NBER 204 Junipero Serra Blvd Stanford CA 94305-6072

FUCHS, WAYNE SCOTT, medical educator; b. N.Y.C., Sept. 4, 1954; married. BA magna cum laude, NYU, 1975; MD, Mt. Sinai Sch. Medicine, 1979. Intern U. Miami (Fla.) Hosps., 1979-80; resident Mt. Sinai Med. Ctr., N.Y.C., 1980-83, assoc. clin. prof., 1991—; treas. Profl. Offices, N.Y.C., 1994—; lectr. in field. Contbr. articles to profl. jours. V.p. Bay Ter. Jewish Ctr., Bayside, N.Y., 1994—; mem. med. adv. bd. Nat. Assn. Visually Handicapped, N.Y.C., 1989, Nat. Assn. Pseuduxan Thomal Elsaticum, Denver, 1989. N.Y. Hosp. Cornell Med. Ctr. fellow, 1983-84. Fellow Am. Acad. Ophthalmology; mem. AMA, N.Y. State Ophthalmological Soc., N.Y. County Med. Soc., Med. Soc. of State of N.Y., Vitreous Soc., Mt. Sinai Alumni Assn. (v.p. 1995—, treas. 1991-95), Alpha Omega Alpha, Phi Beta Kappa. Office: 121 E 60 St New York NY 10022

FUERST, DAVID JONATHAN, ophthalmologist, educator; b. Bklyn., Apr. 27, 1954; s. Adolph and Shirley Rita (Miller) F.; m. Marie Madeline Perrelli, Jan. 2, 1983; children: Jessica Lauren, Nicole Michelle, Jason Aaron. ScB, Brown U., 1975, MD, 1978. Diplomate Am. Bd. Ophthalmology. Intern in internal medicine L.I. Jewish-Hillside Med. Ctr., New Hyde Park, N.Y., 1978-79; resident in opthalmology U. Ill. Eye and Ear Infirmary, Chgo., 1979-82, asst. in ophthalmology, 1980-81, instr., 1981-82; fellow in cornea and external disease U. Calif. Proctor Found. for Rsch. in Ophthalmology, San Francisco, 1982-83, clin. instr., 1982-83; pvt. practice, L.A., 1983—; dir. cornea and external disease svc. White Meml. Med. Ctr., L.A., 1983—, dir. residency program, 1990-95; mem. faculty U. So. Calif., L.A., 1983—; mem. attending staff Cedars-Sinai Med. Ctr., L.A.; mem. courtesy staff Midway Hsop. Med. Ctr., L.A., St. Vincent Med. Ctr., L.A., West Anaheim (Calif.) Med. Ctr.; mem. provisional staff Little Company of Mary, Torrance, Calif., Anaheim Gen. Hosp.; mem. assoc. staff Queen of Valley Hosp., West Covna, Calif.; co-founder Pacific EyeNet; presenter, lectr. in field. Contbr. articles to med. jours., chpts. to books. Fellow Am. Acad. Ophthalmology; mem. Eye Bank Assn. Am., Internat. Soc. Refractive Surgery, Assn. Proctor Fellows, Calif. Med. Assn. (alt. del. 1988-89), Calif. Assn. Ophthalmologists (bd. dirs. dist. 4B 1996—, asst. v.p., v.p. 1988—), L.A. County Med. Assn. (precinct rep. 1986-88), L.A. Soc. Ophthalmology. Democrat. Jewish. Office: Pacific Eyenet Inc 5750 Wilshire Blvd Ste 285 Los Angeles CA 90036

FUERSTE, FREDERICK, physician, ophthalmologist; b. St. Louis, Dec. 9, 1921; s. Frederick and June (Brown) F.; m. Marion Skagen, Dec. 28, 1948; children—Nanette, Gretchen, Hunter, Rommel, Madelin, Garth. B.A., U. Iowa, 1953, M.D., 1945, postgrad. Northwestern U. Med. Sch., Chgo., 1948-49. Diplomate Am. Bd. Ophthalmology. Intern Cook County Hosp., Chgo., 1945-46; resident Milwaukee County Hosp., Wis., 1949-51; practice medicine specializing in ophthalmology, Dubuque, Iowa, 1953—; asst. in clin. ophthalmology eye dept. St. Louis City Hosp., 1952-53; asst. in clin. ophthalmology Washington U. Med. Sch., eye dept. McMillan Hosp., St. Louis, 1951-53. Served to lt. (j.g.) USNR, 1946-48. Mem. Dubuque County Med. Assn., Iowa Med. Assn., AMA, ACS, Am. Acad. Ophthalmology, Phi Beta Kappa, Alpha Omega Alpha. Home: 130 S Booth St Dubuque IA 52003-7203 Office: 2020 John F Kennedy Rd Dubuque IA 52002-3807

FUHRIMAN, PARKER JOHN, orthodontist; b. Glendale, Calif., May 11, 1940; s. David Hyrum and Maurine (Parker) F.; m. Rebecca Day, Oct. 17, 1967; children: Jennifer, Catherine, Diana, David. BA, Brigham Young U., 1967; DDS, U. Calif., San Francisco, 1967. Pvt. practice Portland, Oreg., 1969; cons. craniofacial disorders clinic Oreg. Health Scis. U., Portland, 1970—. Capt. U.S. Army, 1967-69. Mem. ADA, Oreg. Dental Assn., Am. Assn. Orthodontists, Oreg. State Soc. Orthodontists (past pres.), Edward H. Angle Soc. Orthodontists, Cedar HIlls Kiwanis Club, Omicron Kappa Upsilon. Mem. LDS Ch. Office: 1585 SW Marlow Ave Ste 200 Portland OR 97225

FUHRMAN, FREDERICK ALEXANDER, physiology educator; b. Coquille, Oreg., Aug. 13, 1915; s. Cyrus Jacob and Josie (Lyons) F.; m. Geraldine Jackson, Nov. 12, 1942. BS, Oreg. State Coll., 1937, MS, 1939; postgrad., Universität Freiburg im Breisgau, 1937-38, U. Wash., 1939-41; Ph.D., Stanford U., 1943. Univ. fellow in pharmacology U. Wash., 1939-41; research assoc. in physiology Stanford U., 1941-45, instr., 1945-49, asst. prof., 1949-52, assoc. prof., 1952-57, prof. physiology, 1957-61; dir. basic med. scis. labs. Stanford (Med. Sch.), 1959-70, prof. exptl. medicine, 1961-72; prof. physiology Stanford (Sch. Medicine), 1972-80, emeritus, 1981—; physiologist Hopkins Marine Sta., Pacific Grove, Calif., 1972-79; dir. Max C. Fleischmann Labs. of the Med. Scis., 1961-70. Author: Multidiscipline Laboratories for Teaching the Medical Sciences; assoc. editor: Ann. Rev. of Physiology, 1954-62; contbr. articles on metabolism, frostbite, hypothermia, animal toxins and marine pharmacology to profl. jours. Guggenheim fellow, labor of zoophysiology U. Copenhagen, 1951-52; sr. postdoctoral fellow NSF, Inst. Biol. Chemistry, U. Copenhagen and Donner Lab., U. Calif., 1958-59; Commonwealth Fund fellow, 1966-67. Fellow AAAS, N.Y. Acad. Scis.; mem. Am. Physiol. Soc., Am. Soc. Pharmacology and Exptl. Therapeutics, Sigma Xi, Phi Kappa Phi. Home: 2445 Sharon Oak Dr Menlo Park CA 94025-6828

FUJII, TATSUYA, child neurologist, pediatrician, researcher; b. Ikeda, Osaka, Japan, May 29, 1954; s. Mitsuharu and Michiko (Takahashi) F. MD, Kyoto U., 1979, PhD, 1990. Diplomate in pediatrics and child neurology. Pediatrician Niigata Ctrl. Hosp., Joetsu/Niigata, Japan, 1980-83; resident Kyoto (Japan) U., 1979-80, rsch. fellow, 1983-86, asst.prof., 1986-91; rsch. fellow Burke Med. Rsch. inst., White Plains, N.Y., 1991-92, Columbia U., N.Y.C., 1992-94; asst. prof. Kyoto U., 1994-95; doctor-in-chief Shiga Med. Ctr. for Children, 1995—. Contbr. articles to Annals of Neurology, Neurology, Jour. Pediatrics, others. Mem. AAAS, N.Y. Acad. Sci., Internat. Child Neurology Assn., Japanese Child Neurology Soc. Office: Med Ctr Children/Pediatrics, 120-6 Moriyama-cho, Shiga 524, Japan

FUJIKAWA, TOKUMI, medical administrator; b. Miyoshi, Hiroshima, Japan, Nov. 27, 1960. MD, Hiroshima U. Sch. Medicine, 1985, PhD, 1995. With Hiroshima U. Sch. Medicine, 1985-86, Saijyo (Japan) City Hosp., 1986-89, Hiroshima Seiyouin, 1989-90, Hiroshima Prefectural Hosp., 1990-92; chief of outpatient unit Hiroshima U. Sch. Medicine, 1992—. Contbr. articles to profl. jours. Grantee Sasakawa Found., 1993, Chiyoda Mental Health Found., 1994, Univer Found., 1994. Office: Hiroshima U Sch Medicine, Dept Psychiatry & Neurosci, Kasumi 1-2-3 Minami-ku, 734 Hiroshima Japan

FUJINAMI, ROBERT SHIN, neurology educator; b. Salt Lake City, Dec. 8, 1949. BA, U. Utah, 1972; PhD, Northwestern U., Chgo., 1977. Instr. microbiology and immunology Northwestern U., Chgo., 1973-76; rsch. fellow immunopathology Scripps Rsch. Found., La Jolla, Calif., 1977-80, rsch. assoc. immunopathology, 1980-81, rsch. immunopathologist, 1980-82, asst. mem. immunology, 1981-85, vis. investigator immunology, 1985-89, vis. investigator neuropharm., 1989—; assoc. prof. pathology U. Calif., San Diego, 1985-90; prof. neurology U. Utah, Salt Lake City, 1990—; adj. prof. pathology U. Utah, Salt Lake City, 1991—; mem. neurosci. steering com. U. Utah, 1992-96, chmn. biosafety and PRT coms., 1993-96. Contbr. chpts. to books, 84 articles to profl. jours. Recipient New Investigator award NIH, 1981-83; NIH scholar, 1989-96. Mem. Nat. Multiple Sclerosis Soc. (bd. dirs. Utah chpt. 1992—, Harry M. Weaver Neurosci. award 1982-86). Office: Dept Neurology U Utah 50 N Medical Dr Salt Lake City UT 84132

FUJISHIMA, SEITARO, pulmonologist, educator; b. Tokyo, Oct. 17, 1957; s. Seinosuke and Tomoko (Izumi) F.; m. Yumiko Fujishima, Nov. 22, 1986; children: Rie, Saki. MD, Keio U., 1982. Resident in internal medicine Keio U., Tokyo, 1982-84, instr. cardiopulmonary div., 1986-88; fellow in internal medicine Ise Keio Hosp., Tokyo, 1984-86; fellow pulmonary and critical care medicine Stanford (Calif.) U., 1988-91, fellow molecular biology and endocrinology, 1990-91; instr. dept. emergency medicine Keio U., 1991—. Contbr. articles to profl. jours. SAM fund fellow, 1988-91. Mem. AAAS, Am. Thoracic Soc., N.Y. Acad. Sci., Japanese Soc. Internal Medicine, Japan Soc. Chest Diseases, Japanese Soc. Immunology, Japanese Assn. Acute Medicine. Home: 11-8 Nanpeidai-cho, Shibuya-ku, Tokyo 150, Japan Office: Keio U, Dept Emergency Medicine, 35 Shinanomachi Shinjuku-ku, Tokyo 160, Japan

FUJIWARA, ISAO, biology educator; b. Hiroshima, Japan, May 24, 1921; s. Tsutomu and Yasuno Fujiwara; m. (Hotta) Yasuko Fujiwara. Degree, Hiroshima U., 1945. Asst. prof. Saga (Japan) U., 1955-68, prof., 1968-86, dean faculty edn., 1982-86; prof. Saga Jr. Coll., 1987-93; chief Environ. Protection Com., Saga, 1983-93. Contbr. articles to profl. jours. Home: 455-17 Honjio-machi, 840 Saga Japan

FUKUI, GEORGE MASAAKI, microbiology consultant; b. San Francisco, May 25, 1921; s. Tsunejiro and Kimiko (Wada) F.; m. Yuri Lillyn Kenmotsu, Sept. 23, 1944; children: Lisa Jo, Tenley Kay. BS, U. Conn., 1945, MS, 1948; PhD, Cornell U., 1952. Instr. bacteriology U. Conn., Storrs, 1948-49; lab. instr. Cornell U., Ithaca, N.Y., 1949-52, mem. adv. bd. microbiology dept., 1985-88; asst. br. chief U.S. Army, Frederick, Md., 1952-60; dir. microbiology and immunology Wallace Labs., Cranbury, N.J., 1960-77, Hazelton Labs., Vienna, Va., 1977-78; dir. microbiology Abbott Labs., North Chicago, Ill., 1978-79; rsch. microbiologist Abbott Labs., Irving, Tex., 1979-86; pres. Internat. Cons. in Microbiology, Irving, 1986—. Contbr. articles to sci. jours. Asst. scoutmaster troop 712, Boy Scouts Am., Topaz, Utah, 1943; recruiter Cornell U., Princeton, N.J., 1964-69. With U.S. Army, 1945-46. Recipient commendation Rsch. Soc. Am., 1959, medal for sci. achievement Hiroshima (Japan) U., 1973, Gran Amigo de Mex. commendation Nat. U. Mex., 1982, commendation Tohoku U., Sendai, Japan, 1983. Fellow Am. Acad. Microbiology (charter, diplomate); mem. Am. Soc. for Microbiology, Rutgers Soc. Japan (hon.), Phi Beta Kappa, Sigma Xi. Republican. Episcopalian. Home and Office: 3813 E Greenhills Ct Irving TX 75038-4819

FUKUI, YASUYUKI, psychology educator; b. Kyoto, Japan, July 8, 1934; s. Terutaro and Umeno (Okumura) F.; m. Terue Nakamura, Apr. 30, 1961; children: Miyuki, Hitoshi, Kaori. BS, Osaka (Japan) City U., 1959; MS, Kyoto (Japan) U., 1967, postgrad., 1967-69; researcher, Gestalt Inst., L.A., 1986. Student asst. Shinshyu U., Matsumoto, Nagano, Japan, 1959-62, Osaka (Japan) Ednl. Coll., 1962-65; tchr. Osaka High Sch., 1965-69; counselor Kanazawa U., Kanazawa, Ishikawa, Japan, 1969-76; assoc. prof. Ehime U., Matsuyama, Ehime, Japan, 1976-81; prof. Ehime U., Matsuyama, Ehime, 1981-96, Naruto (Tokushima) U. Edn., 1996—; counselor Shikoku Postal Svc. Matsuyama, Ehime, 1989—; dir. Shikoku Counseling Ctr., Matsuyama, Ehime, 1991—. Author: Anxiety and Growth in Adolescence, 1980, Psychology of Gazing, 1984, Psychology of Emotions, 1990; editor: Development of Group Approach, 1981; translator: Counseling Workbook, 1992. Com. mem. Japan Life Line Fedn., Tokyo, 1989—. Mem. Japanese Soc. Psychologist, Japanese Soc. Personality Psychology, Japanese Soc. Rsch. on Emotions, Japan Clin. Psychologist Assn., Japanese Assn. Humanistic Psychology. Home: 13-11 Tani Machi, Matsuyama Ehime 791, Japan Office: Naruto U Edn, 3 Bunkyo-Chyo, Takashima Naruto-Chyo, Naruto Tokushima 772, Japan

FUKUI, YOSHIO, biology educator; b. Shinagawa, Tokyo, Japan, Jan. 4, 1942; came to U.S., 1985; s. Shizuo and Momoko (Utsumi) F.; m. Yumiko Osawa, Mar. 12, 1978; children: Ibuki, Maya. BA, Internat. Christian U., 1966; MS, Osaka (Japan) U., 1969, PhD, 1972. Rsch. assoc. prof. Osaka U., 1972-74, asst. prof., 1974-77; rsch. assoc. Princeton (N.J.) U., 1977-78; assoc. prof. Osaka U., 1978-85; vis. assoc. prof. Northwestern U., Chgo., 1985-89, assoc. prof. cell, molecular, structural biology (tenured), 1989—; prof. cell biology, Yamada exch. scientist Yamada Sci. Found., Osaka, 1978; Yoshida exch. visitor Yoshida Chem. Found., Tokyo, 1983. Contbr. articles to profl. jours. including Nature, Jour. Cell Biology, Internat. Rev. Cytology. Recipient Matsunaga Rsch. award Matsunaga Meml. Found., Tokyo, 1976; rsch. grantee NIH, 1988—. Mem. Cooperation of Marine Biol. Lab. (Woods Hole, Mass.), Am. Soc. for Cell Biology, Soc. Advancement of Sci., N.Y. Acad. Scis. (elected), Japan Soc. for Cell Biologist (Tokyo). Office: Northwestern Med Sch 303 E Chicago Ave Chicago IL 60611-3008

FUKUSHIMA, AKIRA, psychiatrist, educator; b. Tokyo, Jan. 29, 1936; s. Masumi and Ei Fukushima; m. Hatsuko Inoue, Apr. 10, 1959; children: Hiroko Nakamura, Hikaru F., Makoto F. MD, Tokyo U., 1968, degree, Sch. Medicine, 1963. Psychiatrist Tokyo U. Hosp., 1963-66, Fuchuu Prison, Tokyo, 1966-69; assoc. prof. Tokyo Med. and Dental U., 1969-79; prof. psychology Sophia U., Tokyo, 1979—; lectr. Tokyo U. Sch. Medicine, 1976—, Tokyo Nat. U. Culture, 1988—; cons., Com. on Youth Problems, Prime Minister of Japan, 1981-83, Com. on Corection and Probation, Minister of Justice, 1993—. Author: Psychoanalysis of Genius, 1975, 2 vols., 1984, Study on Criminal Psychology, 1977, 2 vols., 1984, Love, Sex and Death, 1980, Psychology of Dependency, 1988, Psychoanalysis of Music and Musicians, 1990, Man Has Been A Hunter, 1991, Psychiatric Examination of Amphetamine Psychotic Criminals, 1994, Handbook of Criminology, 1995, Psychiatric Expert Testimony, 1995, Personality Disorders, 1995. Mem. Japanese Assn. Criminology (past pres.), Japanese Assn. Correctional Medicine (past pres.), Japanese Assn. Criminal Psychology (bd. dirs.), Japanese Assn. Pathography (pres.), Japanese Assn. Sex Edn. (bd. dirs.), Japanese Assn. Neurology and Psychiatry. Home: 27-2 Tsutsujigaoka, Aoba-ku Yokohama 227, Japan Office: Sophia U, 7-1 Kioi Chiyoda ku, Tokyo 102, Japan

FUKUSHIMA, MASAHIRO, oral pathologist; b. Tokyo, Feb. 11, 1940; s. Masuo and Chiyoko (Okada) F.; m. Michiko Harada, Mar. 30, 1970; 1 child, Shouchiro. DDS, Tokyo Med. and Dental U., 1965, PhD, 1969. Assoc. Sch. Dentistry Tokyo Med. and Dental U., 1969; asst. prof. Sch. Dentistry Niigata (Japan) U., 1969-72, assoc. prof., 1972—; lectr. Hokkaido U., Sapporo, Japan, 1976-77, Tokushima (Japan) U., 1980-81; internat. cons. Indian Jour. Dental Rsch., Bombay, 1986—. Author: Ane Structure of Cells and Tissues Electron Microscopic Atlas, 1971, (with others) Current Encyclopedia of Pathology, 1985, Oral Pathology, 1989, Illustrated Pathology, 1993. Mem. Japanese Soc. Pathology, Internat. Assn. Oral Pathologists (sec.-ten. 5th cons. 1990). Home: 6379-91 Ikarashi-1-No-Cho, Niigata 950-21, Japan Office: Niigata U Dept Oral Path, 5274 Gakko-Cho 2 Ban-Cho, Niigata 951, Japan

FUKUSHIMA, MASANORI, physician, biochemist, medical oncologist; b. Nagoya, Japan, Nov. 30, 1948; s. Jiro and Saeko Fukushima; m. Masae Fukushima, May 25, 1973; children: Kentaro, Mariko, Michiko. MD, Nagoya U., 1973; PhD, Kyoto (Japan) U., 1979. Asst. prof. Sch. Medicine Hamamatsu (Japan) U., 1976-78; sect. head Aichi Cancer Ctr., Nagoya, 1978—; vis. asst. prof. Baylor U. Coll. Medicine, Houston, 1980-81. Mem. editorial bd. Japanese J. Cancer Rsch., 1986—, Modern Medicine Japan Edition, 1986—, Cancer Therapy and Control, 1987—. Named One of Outstanding Young Persons of the World, Jr. Chamber Internat, 1986. Mem. Japanese Biochem. Soc., Japanese Cancer Assn. (Prize award 1985), Am. Assn. for Cancer Rsch., Am. Soc. Clin. Oncology. Home: Ji-yu-ga-oka 1-5-9, Nagoya 464, Japan Office: Aichi Cancer Ctr, Kanokoden 1-1 Chikusa-ku, Nagoya 464, Japan

FULCO, JOHN DOMINICK, diagnostic radiologist; b. Flushing, N.Y., Dec. 5, 1941; s. Vincent Carl and Lucy (Serpi) F.; m. S. Claire Bailey, Oct. 2, 1965; children—Vincent, Christie, Dana. B.A. in Biology, LIU, 1965, B.A. in Chemistry, 1965; Dr. Medicine and Surgery cum laude, U. Bologna, 1974. Diplomate Am. Bd. Radiology. Rotating intern, L.I. Jewish-Hillside Med. Ctr., New Hyde Park, N.Y., 1974-75, intern Queens Hosp. Ctr., Jamaica, N.Y., 1974-75; resident in radiology, 1975-78, chief resident, 1977-78, cons. interventional radiologist, 1979-81; fellow in cardiovascular and interventional radiology, Tufts-New Eng. Med. Ctr., Boston, 1978-79; attending radiologist, Ellis Hosp., Schenectady, 1979—; cons. diagnostic radiology Sunnyview Hosp., Schenectady, 1980—, chief of radiology, 1981—; mem. Schenectady Radiologists, P.C., 1979—; clin. instr. radiology Sch. Medicine SUNY, Stony Brook, 1976-80; asst. prof. diagnostic radiology Albany Med. Coll., 1985—; clin. instr. med. scis. N.Y. Sch. Med. and Dental Assts., Forest Hills, 1974-78; cons. Radiologic Tech. Adv. Com. Hudson Valley Community Coll., Troy, N.Y., 1980—, physician chmn., 1981—; house physician Doctors Hosp., Freeport, N.Y., 1976-78; cons. N.Y. Sch. Med. and Dental Assts., 1974-79; research assoc. dept. surgery, div. exptl. surgery, St. Vincent's Hosp. and Med. Ctr., N.Y.C., 1972-73; athletic physician Bellmore-Merrick Sch. Dist., Bellmore, N.Y., 1976-78; emergency rm. physician Lydia E. Hall Hosp., Freeport, N.Y., 1975-77. Abstract rev. staff Jour. Surgery, Jour. Ob-Gyn, 1977; contbr. articles to profl. publs.; presenter papers to profl. confs., U.S., Can., Japan. Bd. dirs. Sunnyview Hosp. and Rehab. Ctr., Schenectady, Am. Cancer Soc., Schenectady, 1986—; mem. profl. edn. com. Am. Cancer Soc., Schenectady, 1982—, mem. pub. edn. com., 1982—. Named Intern of Yr., L.I. Jewish-Hillside Med. Ctr., 1975; recipient award for sci. exhibit Can. Assn. Radiologists, 1978, spl. award for clin. research conducted outside Can., 1978. Fellow Cardiovascular 2d. Interventional Radiol. Soc. (diplomate 1987); mem. AMA, Radiol. Soc. N.Am. (cert. of merit 1977), Am. Coll. Radiology, Am. Inst. for Ultrasound in Medicine, Royal Soc. Health (London), N.Y. Acad. of Sci., New Eng. Roentgen Ray Soc., Med. Soc. State of N.Y. (v.p. 4th dist., councilor 1994—, awards in clin. research 1976, 77), Med. Soc. County of Schenectady (v.p. 4th dist. 1985-86, pres. elect 1986-87), Northeastern N.Y. Radiol. Soc. (pres. 1983-84), Mohawk Valley Health Plan, N.Y. Acad. Scis. (co-chmn.

Schenectady County com. Health Care Issues). Office: Schenectady Radiologists PC 2546 Balltown Rd Ste 100 Schenectady NY 12309-1079

FULD, GILBERT LLOYD, pediatrician; b. N.Y.C., Aug. 15, 1937; s. Arthur and Goldie (Kiss) F.; m. Alice Kinzler, Feb. 1, 1964; children: Rachel Anne, Sarah Elizabeth. AB, Hamilton U., 1958; MD, U. Pitts., 1962. Chief pediatrics Forbes AFB, Topeka, 1965-67; pvt. practice N.Y.C., 1967-71; staff pediatrician Lahey Hitchcock Clinic, Keene, N.H., 1971—. Bd. dirs. Elk Grove Village, 1992—. Mem. Am. Acad. Pediatrics. (chmn. N.H. chpt. 1977-82, alt. chmn. dist. I 1985-91, chair dist. I 1992—). Office: Lahen Hitchcock Clinic 590 Court St Keene NH 03431

FULD, ROBERT O'CONNOR, social worker; b. N.Y.C., Jan. 27, 1947; s. John Joseph Patrick O'Connor and Dorothea (Fuld) MacIntyre; m. Selene Letichevsky, Apr. 1970 (div. June 1979). BSc in Biology and Liberal Arts, Ill. Inst. Tech., Chgo., 1969; M in Social Svc. Adminstrn., U. Chgo., 1973; post master's cert. in social svc. adminstrn., Hunter Coll., 1985. Cert. social worker, N.Y., alcoholism counselor, N.Y. Tchr. physics and remedial scis. Chgo. Bd. Edn., 1968-73; tenant organizer Housing Conservation Coords., N.Y.C., 1974-75; social worker Henry St. Settlement House, N.Y.C., 1975-76; team leader, team IV, dir. youth employment programs Lower East Side Family Union, N.Y.C., 1976-83; dir. juvenile svcs. unit N.Y. Legal Aid Soc., N.Y.C., 1983-87; asst. dir. Stanley and Rita Kaplan Ctr., N.Y.C., 1987-88, social worker, 1989; therapist dept. psychiatry Outpatient Alcoholism Clinic Bellevue Hosp., N.Y.C., 1988-90; pvt. practice psychotherapy N.Y.C., 1989—; bilingual sch. social worker N.Y.C. Bd. of Edn., 1990—. Mem. PINS Adv. Bd. Mayor's Office, 1985-87; mem. Mayor's Youth Lit. Task Force, 1981-83. Mem. NASW, Acad. Cert. Social Workers, N.Y. Fedn. Alcoholism Counselors, Amnesty Internat. Home: 217 E 12th St Apt 4F New York NY 10003-9168 Office: 217 E 12th St Apt 1R New York NY 10003-9167

FULGENZI, WILLIAM RONALD, orthopedic surgeon; b. Detroit, Jan. 24, 1933; s. William Ronald and Rose Lucille (Ursini) F.; m. Carole Ann Dulcamara, Aug. 21, 1954; children: Kathleen Marie, Karen Ann, Kim Elizabeth, Kristina Lynn. BS in Chemistry, U. Detroit, Mich., 1954; MD, Wayne State U., Detroit, 1957. Intern St. Joseph Mercy Hosp., Detroit, 1957-58, resident in gen. surgery, 1958-59; resident in orthopedic surgery Wayne State U., Detroit, 1959-62; chief of staff St. Joseph Mercy Hosp., Detroit, 1970-72; instr. orthopedic surgery Wayne State U., Detroit, 1962—; pvt. practice in orthopedic surgery Grosse Pointe Orthopedic Assn., Detroit, 1974-81, Orthopaedic Clinic, Saint Clair Shores, Mich., 1981-96. Capt. U.S. Air Force, 1962. Fellow Am. Acad. Orthopedic Surgery, Mich. Orthopedic Soc., Detroit Acad. Orthopedic Soc.; mem. AMA, Mich. State Med. Soc., Wayne County Med. Soc. (coun. 1982-84). Office: Orthopaedic Clinic 22050 Greater Mack Farms Saint Clair Shores MI 48080

FULGHESU, ANNA MARIA, physician; b. Guspini, Cagliari, Italy, June 20, 1956; d. Giovanni F. and Antonietta Camba; m. Roberto Marco, June 10, 1988; 1 child, Giovanni Tommaso. MD, U. Degli Studi, Cagliari, 1982. Fellow in gynecol. endoscopy U. Cagliari, Italy, 1985, resident ob-gyn., 1983-87; fellow U. Sacred Heart, Rome, 1986-87, asst. prof., asst. Sterility Ctr., 1987-93, cons. in ultrasound, 1991—, rschr., dir. Sterility Ctr., 1993—. Editor: Major Advances in Human Female Reproduction, 1990; contbr. articles to profl. jours. State grantee, 1983. Mem. Gynecol. Endocrinology Soc., Soc. Ecografia Ginecologica. Roman Catholic. Office: U Sacred Heart Dept Ob-Gyn, Lgo Gemelli 8, 00168 Rome Italy

FULGHUM, ROBERT SCHMIDT, microbiologist, educator; b. Washington, Mar. 3, 1929; s. James Hooks and Frances (Witcraft) F.; m. Esther Marie Slagle, June 17, 1953; children: Robert Slagle, David James, Joseph Christopher. BS in Biology, Roanoke Coll., 1954; MS in Bacteriology, Va. Poly. Inst. and State U., 1959, PhD in Bacteriology, 1965. Approved cons. bacteriologist, Pa. Grad. asst. Va. Poly. Inst. and State U., Blacksburg, 1956-60; instr. Susquehanna U., Selinsgrove, Pa., 1960-63; asst. prof. Susquehanna U., Selinsgrove, 1963-64, N.D. State U., Fargo, 1964-68; asst. prof. Coll. Dentistry U. Ky., Lexington, 1968-71; dir. anaerobic products Robbin Lab. div. Scott Labs., Carrboro, N.C., 1971-72; assoc. prof. East Carolina U., Greenville, 1972-90, prof., 1990-96, asst. chair dept., 1989-96, prof. emeritus, 1996—; cons. Scott Labs., Fiskeville, R.I., 1972-73; cons., spkr. Norwich Eaton Pharm, Inc., 1987, Abbott Labs., Chgo., 1988, Otitis Media Rsch. Ctr. Children's Hosp., Pitts., 1988; program co-chmn. 3d ednl. strategies workshop tchg. microbiology and immunology Med. Students Assn., Med. Sch. Microbiology and Immunology Chairs, 1990, 4th ednl. stratgies workshop, 1992, 5th ednl. strategies workshop, 1994, 6th ednl. strategies workshop, 1996; mem. organizing com. Ednl. Strategies for Basic Scis. Workshop, Charleston, S.C., 1993. Regional editor newsletter The Anaerobist, 1973-75; contbr. articles to profl. jours. Troop committeeman, treas. Boy Scouts Am., Lexington, Ky., 1968-71, Greenville, 1981-83; bd. dirs. Wesley Found., Greenville, 1979-82; bd. dirs., fin. com. Greenville Community Shelter, 1989-91. With USAF, 1952-56. Rsch. grantee Nat. Inst. Dental Rsch., Washington, 1969, N.C. United Way, 1974, Deafness Rsch. Found., N.Y.C., 1979-88, Block Drug Co., N.J., 1991. Mem. Am. Soc. Microbiology (alternate councilor N.C. br. 1972, 83, ednl. rep. 1973-77, sec.-treas. 1978-81, 89-94, treas. 1994-96, v.p. 1983-84, pres. 1984-85, editor 1988—), Sigma Xi (Helms award 1982). Methodist. Home: PO Box 512 Greenville NC 27835-0512 Office: East Carolina U Medicine East Carolina U Dept Microbiology Greenville NC 27858

FULK, PAUL FREDERICK, chiropractor; b. Portsmouth, Ohio, Dec. 9, 1935; s. Raymond Tex Fulk and Lettie Marie (Tackett) Butler; m. Brenda Gail Yeary, May 22, 1987; children: Paul Jr., Robert E., Allan, Adam. Student, Olivet Nazarene U., 1954-57, Northwestern U., 1959, So. Meth. U., 1963; D Chiropractic, Palmer U., 1976. Founder, v.p. Liberty Am. Life Ins. Co., Columbus, Ohio, 1963-69; founder, pres., bd. dirs. Am. Liberty Investment Corp., Columbus, 1963-69; founder, chmn., pres., CEO Par Chem. Corp., Columbus, 1969-72; founder, chmn. bd. dirs., CEO Paratech Industries, Inc., Tulsa, 1992—; founder, pres., CEO Valley Chiropractic Ctr., Centerville, Ohio, 1977—; pres. Para Heath Foods, Inc., 1977—; founder Therasys, Inc., Orlando, Fla., 1996. Formulator nonphosphate indsl. cleaning product, 1969; inventor device to treat carpal tunnel syndrome, tarsal tunnel device. Mem. Nat. Coll. Applied Kinesiologists, Ohio Coll. Applied Kinesiologists, Ohio State Chiropractic Assn. Republican. Nazarene. Home: 6248 Rivercliff Ln West Carrollton OH 45449-3048 Office: Valley Chiropractic Ctr 7865 Paragon Rd Centerville OH 45459-4027

FULK, RONALD JON, health systems specialist; b. Clarinda, Iowa, Mar. 14, 1948; s. John L. and Leona M. (Bloomfield) F.; m. Kandy R. Fisher, Sept. 17, 1969; 1 child, Melissa. BS, U. Nev., 1975; MA, U. Iowa, 1987. Adminstrv. resident VA Med. Ctr., Iowa City, Iowa, 1987-88, adminstrv. officer, radiology, 1990-91; med. adminstrv. officer trainee VA Med. Ctr., Little Rock, 1988-89; med. adminstrv. officer VA Med. Ctr., Grand Junction, Colo., 1989-90; spl. asst. to dir. VA Med. Ctr., Grand Junction, 1991—. Sgt. USAF, 1968-72. Mem. Masons, Vietnam Vets of Am. (sec. 1994-96, bd. dirs. 1994-96). Methodist. Office: VA Med Ctr 2121 North Ave Grand Junction CO 81501

FULKERSON, FRED GROVER, social worker, priest, retired; b. Norman, Okla., Jan. 28, 1919; s. Boise Brown and Willie May (Reynolds) F.; m. Mary Jane Baile, Oct. 22, 1954; children: William Baile Fulkerson, Susan Fulkerson Gregory, Samuel Reynolds. BA in Social Work, U. Okla., 1941, MSW, 1946; postgrad., various univs. Lic. clin. social worker, Okla. Instr., Sch. Social Work Univ. Okla., Norman, 1945-50; area dir., immigration prog. Ch. World Svc., Munich, 1949-51; field supr., adminstr. E.D. Farmer Found., Episcopal Diocese, Dallas, 1951-53; exec. sec. dept. social welfare Ch. Fedn. of Greater Chgo., 1953-57; exec. sec. dpt. Christian social rels. Episcopal Diocese of Chgo., 1957-58; rector Ch. of Good Shepherd, Sapulpa, Okla., 1958-60; canon, priest-in-charge St. Paul's Cathedral, Oklahoma City, 1960-61; rector Grace Episcopal Ch., Muskogee, Okla., 1961-66; asst. prof. sociology East Cen. State U., Ada, Okla., 1966-68; social work supr., rsch. unit Stof Okla. Mental Health Dept., Norman, 1968-84; adj. prof. Rose State Coll., Midwest City, Okla., 1979—. Episcopalian. Home: 1510 Cinderella Ave Norman OK 73072-6029 Office: 2233 W Lindsey St Norman OK 73069-4054

FULLER, A. KENNETH, psychiatrist, researcher, author; b. Moultrie, Ga., Jan. 25, 1956; s. Arthur C. Fuller and Juanita (Jones) Thackston; m. Angela Deanna Edwards, Oct. 19, 1979; children: Jonathan Edwards, Angela Christina. BS in Edn., Valdosta (Ga.) State Coll., 1977; MD, Med. Coll. Ga., 1982. Diplomate Am. Bd. Psychiatry and Neurology. Resident U. Fla., Gainesville, 1983-86; staff psychiatrist Archbold Mental Health Ctr., Thomasville, Ga., 1987-90; chief of psychiatry Southwestern State Hosp., Thomasville, 1990—; clin. assoc. prof. U. Fla., Gainesville, 1987—. Coauthor: The Child Molester, 1989; contbr. numerous articles to profl. jours. Elder 1st Presbyn. Ch., Thomasville, 1990. Mem. AMA, Am. Coll. Psychiatrists (Laughlin fellow 1986), Am. Psychiat. Assn. Office: Southwestern State Hosp PO Box 1378 Thomasville GA 31799-1378

FULLER, BARBARA F., nursing educator; b. Chgo.. BA, U. Calif., Santa Barbara, 1956; MS, Cornell U., 1958, PhD, 1962; ADN, SUNY, Albany, 1980. Cert. family nurse practitioner, ANA. Instr. biology Case Western Res. U., Cleve., 1961-63; asst. prof. zoology Ohio State U., Columbus, 1964-67; lectr. biology U. Colo., Denver, 1968-69, assoc. prof. Sch. of Nursing, 1969-73, prof. Sch. of Nursing, 1973—; vis. assoc. prof. Sch. of Nursing, U. Colo., summer 1969; researcher, presenter and cons. in field. Edit. bd. Heart and Lung, 1983-91, Jour. Clin. Nursing Rsch., 1989—; contbr. over 65 articles to profl. jours. Office: U Colorado Sch Nursing 4200 E 9th Ave Denver CO 80220-3706

FULLER, MARGARET JANE, medical technologist; b. Park Rapids, Minn., Jan. 29, 1947; d. Rudolph Kenneth and Jean Ellen (Klenk) Haas; m. Phillip Fuller, Aug. 7, 1970; 1 child, Sharon Dawn. BS in Chemistry, Muhlenberg Coll., 1969; diploma in med. tech., Allentown (Pa.) Hosp., 1972; MPA, Angelo State U., 1988; MS in Microbiology, Tex. Tech. U., 1992. Lab. dir. San Angelo-Tom Green County Health Dept., 1984-89; outpatient lab. supr. Meth. Hosp., Plainview, Tex., 1995-96; lab. mgr. Highland Med. Ctr., Lubbock, Tex., 1996—; mem. med. adv. bd. Planned Parenthood West Tex., San Angelo, 1987-89; scientist-by-mail, assoc. Children's Mus. Houston, 1991-92; direct patient vol. Hospice of Lubbock, 1993—. Bd. dirs. El Camino coun. Girl Scouts U.S.A. Recipient Thanks Badge, El Camino coun. Girl Scouts U.S.A., 1986. Mem. Am. Soc. Microbiology, Am. Soc. Clin. Lab. Tech., Am. Soc. Clin. Pathologists (assoc., cert. med. technologist), Tex. Soc. Clin. Lab. Tech. (regional sec. 1985-87), Tex. Pub. Health Assn., Clin. Lab. Mgmt. Assn., Mensa, Beta Beta Beta, Sigma Theta Tau. Episcopalian.

FULLER, MARGARET VIRGINIA, nurse; b. Wynne, Ark., Dec. 28, 1948; d. Earnest B. and Irene (Robinson) Fowlkes; m. John Luther Fuller, Dec. 12, 1969; children: Johnny, Mary Virginia. Diploma, Meth. Hosp. Sch. of Nursing, Memphis, 1969. RN. Head nurse of diagnostic neurology Meth. Hosp., Memphis, 1975-77, head of patient mgmt. system, instr., 1977-81, coordinator of nursing info. system, 1981-85; mgr. patient care system Healthcare Internat., Austin, Tex., 1985-89; office nurse Austin Urology Assocs., 1989-90; owner Fuller & Assocs., Austin, Tex., 1990—; speaker in field. Mem. Am. Nurses Assn., Tex. Nurses Assn., Tenn. Nurses Assn. Republican. Baptist. Home: 11307 Jack Rabbit Austin TX 78750-1434 Office: Fuller & Assocs 10405 Lake Creek Pky Austin TX 78750-1225

FULLER, MARY KATHARINE, nursing administrator; b. Franklin, N.H., Nov. 28, 1948; d. Theodore Young and Martha Marie (Proulx) Gilchrist; m. David Earl Fuller, Aug. 29, 1970; children: Wendy K., Richard. Nursing diploma, St. Elizabeth's Sch. Nursing, 1969. RN, Mass., N.H. Staff nurse OR St. Elizabeth's Hosp., Brighton, Mass., 1969-70, Lakes Region Hosp., Laconia, N.H., 1970; staff nurse ICU Frisbie Meml. Hosp., Rochester, N.H., 1971; from staff nurse to mgr. quality assurance Franklin Regional Hosp., 1972-93, mgr. quality assurance, coord. med. staff, 1993—; bd. dirs. Vis. Nurse Assn., pres. Franklin bd., Franklin Outing Club Ski Patrol, pres., v.p. 1972—. Mem. Franklin City Sch. Bd., 1992—; city councilor, Franklin, 1986-88, city zoning bd. mem., 1989-92. Named Citizen of Yr. City of Franklin, 1981, Woman of Achievement Franklin Bus. and Profl. Women's Club, 1990. Mem. Nat. Assn. Healthcare Quality, N.H. Assn. Healthcare Quality (treas. 1991-95), N.H. Assn. Med Staff Svcs., N.H./Vt. Assn. Healthcare Risk Mgmt., Nat. Ski Patrol, Franklin Jr. Women's Club (Outstanding State Jr. 1983). Roman Catholic. Home: 200 Prospect St Franklin NH 03235 Office: Franklin Regional Hosp 15 Aiken Ave Franklin NH 03235

FULLER, ROSMARIE ANN, perinatal educator, neonatal nurse practitioner; b. Boston, Jan. 5, 1951; d. Kenneth Edward and Rosmarie Gertrud (Schwob) Fuller. BSN, Northeastern U., 1974; MSN, U. Ill., Chgo., 1982. RN; cert. neonatal nurse practitioner; cert. lactation cons. Staff nurse, rsch. assoc., tracheostomy specialist Rush Presbyn. St. Luke's Med. Ctr., Chgo., 1975-80, 82-85; civilian nurse, neonatal ICU 97th Gen. Hosp., Frankfurt, West Germany, 1985-88; childbirth educator, perinatal clinical nurse specialist Waltham (Mass.) Weston Hosp., 1989-90; neonatal nurse practitioner St. Margaret's Hosp., Boston, 1993-95; staff nurse, perinatal educator Beverly (Mass.) Hosp., 1991-93, 95—. Assoc. editor Jour. Human Lactation, 1995—; author articles. Mem. Internat. Lactation Cons. Assn., Nat. Assn. Neonatal Nurses, Assn. Women's Health, Obstet., Neonatal Nurses, Nat. Perinatal Assn., Ctr. for Biomed. Ethics. Office: Beverly Hosp Herrick St Beverly MA 01915

FULLMER, HAROLD MILTON, dentist, educator; b. Gary, Ind., July 9, 1918; s. Howard and Rachel Eva (Tiedge) F.; m. Marjorie Lucile Engel, Dec. 31, 1942 (dec. Apr. 1983); children: Angela Sue, Pamela Rose; m. Shirley Ford Davis, Mar. 28, 1987. B.S., Ind. U., 1942, D.D.S., 1944; hon. doctorate, U. Athens (Greece), 1981. Diplomate: Am. Bd. Oral Pathology. Intern Charity Hosp., New Orleans, 1946-47, resident, 1947-48, vis. dental surgeon, 1948-53; instr. Loyola U., New Orleans, 1948-49, asst. prof., 1949-50, assoc. prof. gen. and oral pathology, 1949-53; cons. pathology VA hosps., Biloxi and Gulfport, Miss., 1950-53; asst. dental surgeon Nat. Inst. Dental Research, NIH, Bethesda, Md., 1953-54; dental surgeon Nat. Inst. Dental Research, NIH, 1954-56, sr. dental surgeon, 1956-60, dental dir., 1960-70; chief sect. histochemistry Nat. Inst. Dental Research, 1967-70, chief exptl. pathology, 1969-70, cons. to dir., 1971-72; mem. dental caries program adv. com. HEW, 1975-79, chmn., 1976-79; dir. Inst. Dental Research; prof. pathology, prof. dentistry, assoc. dean Sch. Dentistry, U. Ala. Med. Center, Birmingham, 1970-87; prof. emeritus, 1987—; sr. scientist cancer research and tng. program, sci. adv. com. Sch. Dentistry, U. Ala. Med. Center (Diabetes Research and Tng. Center), 1977-87; mem. med. rsch. career devel. com. VA, 1977-81; mem. com. grants and allocations Am. Fund for Dental Health, 1977-83. Editor: (with R.D. Lillie) Histopathologic Technic and Practical Histochemistry, 1976; editor in chief, founder Jour. Oral Pathology, 1972-90, Tissue Reactions, 1976-88; assoc. editor Jour. Cutaneous Pathology, 1973-83, Oral Surgery, Oral Medicine, Oral Pathology, 1970. Served to capt. AUS, 1944-46. Recipient Isaac Schour award for outstanding research and teaching in anat. scis. Internat. Assn. Dental Research, 1973, Disting. Alumnus of Yr. award Ind. U. Sch. Dentistry, 1978; Disting. Alumnus of Yr. award, Ind. U., 1981; Disting. Faculty Lectr. award, U. Ala. Med. Ctr., Birmingham, 1989—, Disting. Scientist award Am. Assn. Dental Rsch, 1990. Fellow Am. Coll. Dentists, Am. Acad. Oral Pathology (v.p. 1984-85, pres.-elect 1985-86, pres. 1986-87), AAAS (chmn. sect. 1976-78, sec. sect. 1979-87), mem. ADA (cons. Coun. Dental Rsch. 1973-74), Internat. Assn. Dental Rsch. (v.p. 1974-75, pres. 1976-77, pres. Exptl. Pathology Group 1985-86), Am. Assn. Dental Rsch. (pres. 1976-77), Internat. Assn. Pathologists, Histochem. Soc., Nat. Soc. Med. Rsch. (dir. 1977-79), Biol. Stain Commn. (trustee 1977—), Commd. Officers Assn., Internat. Assn. Oral Pathologists (co-founder, 1st pres. 1979-81, 1st editor 1971-89), Soc. Oral Pathologists, Brit. Soc. Oral Pathologists (hon.), Exchange Club (Birmingham, pres. New Orleans 1952-53). Home: 3514 Bethune Dr Birmingham AL 35223-1418

FULLWOOD, ALTBURG MARIE, women's health nurse; b. Scharbeutz, West Germany, May 6, 1933; d. Hans F. and Cacilie A. (Bliesmer) Burmann; m. Marvin Fullwood, Sept. 6, 1963; children: Randal C., Renée M. Diploma, St. Georg Hosp., Hamburg, West Germany, 1953, Kleemann Sch., Kiel, West Germany, 1954; ADN, U. N.C., Wilmington, 1984. RN, N.C.; cert. psychiat./mental health nurse. Nurse German Social Security System, Hamburg; exec. sec. to dir. Fla. State U., Eglin AFB; civil service pers. Dept. of Army, Southport, N.C.; psychiat. nurse New Hanover Regional Med. Ctr., Wilmington.

FULMER, HUGH SCOTT, physician, educator; b. Syracuse, N.Y., June 18, 1928; s. Herbert C. and Emily (Price) F.; m. Zola M. Jones, July 12, 1952; children: James, Kim, Scott. A.B., Syracuse U., 1948; M.D., SUNY-Syracuse, 1951; M.P.H., Harvard U., 1961. Intern R.I. Hosp., 1951-52; resident internal medicine SUNY-Syracuse, 1954-57; fellow pulmonary medicine SUNY, Syracuse, 1957-58; asst. dir., rsch. assoc. Navajo-Cornell Field Health Research Project, 1958-60; instr. pub. health and preventive medicine Cornell U. Coll. Medicine, 1958-60; asst. prof. community medicine U. Ky. Coll. Medicine, 1960-64, assoc. prof., 1964-66, prof., 1966-68, dir. sr. med. student internat. cross-cultural program, 1964-68, dir. preventive medicine residency program, 1964-68; tech. cons. health Peace Corps, Malaysia, 1968-69; prof., chmn. dept. community and family medicine U. Mass. Med. Sch., 1969-77, asso. dean for clin. edn. and primary care, 1975-79, chief sect. gen. medicine, dept. medicine, 1978-83; dir. ambulatory and community svcs. Carney Hosp., Boston, 1983-88, dir. community-oriented primary care program, 1988-93, dir. preventive medicine residency, 1988-93; exec. dir. Ctr. for Cmty. Reponsive Care, Boston, 1991—, dir. preventive medicine residency & COPC fellowship program, 1991—; instr. pub. health and preventive medicine Cornell U. Coll. Medicine, 1958-60; adj. prof. socio-med. scis., cmty. medicine and pub. health Boston U. Sch. Medicine and Pub. Health, 1983-96. Served with M.C., USAF, 1952-54. Mem. AMA, APHA, Mass. Med. Soc., Soc. Gen. Internal Medicine, Assn. Tchrs. Preventive Medicine (past pres., Outstanding Tchr. award 1993), Am. Coll. Preventive Medicine (bd. regents 1988-94), Am. Coll. Physician Execs. Home: 61 Cherlyn Dr Northborough MA 01532-1135

FULOP, GEORGE, geriatric psychiatrist; b. Budapest, Hungary, Aug. 17, 1954; came to U.S. 1957; s. Albert and Irene (Hoffner) F.; m. Andrea Leigh Zuckerman; children: Douglas Ian, Kate Julia. BA, Columbia U., 1976; MD, Albert Einstein Coll. Med., Bronx, 1980; MS in Community Medicine, Mt. Sinai Med. Ctr., 1991. Diplomate Am. Bd. Psychiatry and Neurology, Am. Bd. Geriatric Psychiatry. Intern in medicine Montefiore Hosp., Bronx, 1980-81; resident in psychiatry Mt. Sinai Sch. Medicine, N.Y.C., 1981-84, faculty fellow gen. preventive medicine, 1984-86, from instr. to asst. prof. psychiatry, 1984-94, assoc. prof., 1994—; dir. disease mgmt. Merck-Medco Managed Care, Montvale, N.J., 1996. Reviewer Jour. AMA, Gen. Hosp. Psychiatry; contbr. 40 articles to profl. jours., 10 chpts. to books. NIMH grantee, 1989—. Mem. AMA, Soc. Liaison Psychiatry, Assn. Geriatric Psychiatry, Am. Geriatric Soc., Am. Psychiatric Assn. Office: Merck-Medco Managed Care 100 Summit Ave Mail Stop R2-21 Montvale NJ 07645 also: Mt Sinai Sch Medicine Box 1228 1 Gustave L Levy Pl New York NY 10029-6504

FULOP, MILFORD, physician; b. N.Y.C., Nov. 7, 1927; s. Herman and Adele (Karl) F.; m. Christine Lawrence, Aug. 4, 1957; children: Michael Alain, Tamara Ann. A.B., Columbia U., 1946, M.D., 1949. Intern, then resident in medicine Presbyn. Hosp., N.Y.C., 1949-51, 53-55; practice medicine specializing in internal medicine N.Y.C., 1955—; mem. faculty Albert Einstein Coll. Medicine, Bronx, N.Y., 1956—; prof. internal medicine Albert Einstein Coll. Medicine, 1968—, acting chmn. dept. medicine, 1975-80, vice chmn. dept. medicine, 1980—, disting. univ. prof. medicine, 1994—; mem. staff Bronx Mcpl. Hosp., Hosp. of Einstein Coll. Medicine. Served with M.C. USAF, 1951-53. Recipient Commendation medal. Master ACP (laureate N.Y. State chpt.); mem. Assn. Am. Physicians, Phi Beta Kappa, Alpha Omega Alpha. Home: 630 W 246th St Bronx NY 10471-3631 Office: 1300 Morris Park Ave Bronx NY 10461-1926

FULTON, ROBIN DENISE, clinical nurse specialist; b. Chgo., Mar. 25, 1954; d. Wilbert Gilbert and Margaret (Stigler) Wood; m. Sheldon Ray Fulton, Aug. 5, 1972 (div. 1976); children: Sheldon Ray Fulton, Jr., Craig Michael Fulton. AA in Liberal Arts, Loop Coll., Chgo., 1980; diploma in Nursing, Cook County Nursing Sch., Chgo., 1980; BSN, Gov's. State U., University Park, Ill., 1992; MSN, Govs. State U., 1995. Staff nurse Michael Reese Hosp., Chgo., 1981-82, Cook County Hosp., Chgo., 1981-84; staff nurse U. Ill. Hosp., Chgo., 1982-83, asst. head nurse, 1982—; co-investigator Clin. Rsch. Study U. Ill. Hosp., Chgo., 1991-93. Task force mem. Regional Action Project 2000, University Park, Ill., 1994—. Recipient Cert. Recognition for Successful Acad. Achievement African Am. Staff Caucus, Gov's. State U., 1993, Cmty. Svc. award, 1994-95, scholar, 1995, U.S. Achievement Acad. Collegiate award, 1993, Nat. award, 1995. Mem. Perinatal Assn. Ill., Profl. Nurse Orgn., Ill. Nurse Assn., Am. Diabetes Assn., Assn. Women's Health Obstetrics and Neonatal Nurses, Alumni Club Govs. State U. Alumni Assn., Sigma Theta Tau. Roman Catholic. Office: U Ill Hosp 1740 W Taylor St Chicago IL 60612-7232

FUNK, DOROTHEA, public health nurse; b. St. Louis, Oct. 26, 1916; d. John Arthur and Pearl M. (Dial) Johnson; m. Frank E. Funk, Jan. 3, 1941 (dec. Jan. 1996). Diploma, Leo N. Levi Meml. Hosp., Hot Springs Nat. Park, Ark. RN, Ark. Asst. dir. nursing svc. Helena (Ark.) Hosp.; nurse-investigator Little Rock Health Dept.; pub. health nurse Clark County Health Dept., Arkedelphia, Ark.; nurse coord. for health manpower recruitment Ark. State Nurses Assn.; patient-coord. and liaison nurse Medi-Ctr. of Am., Inc.; health manpower coord. Ark. Nursing Assn., Little Rock, 1970-73; trustee Ark. Nurses Found., Little Rock, 1996. Vol., field rep. Women's Meml.-Meml. Found. Ind., Arlington, Va.; mem. Ark. Gov.'s Commn. on Status of Women; mem. Spl. Task Force on Delivery of Health Care; active ARC, Ark. Red Cross. Lt. Nurse Corps, U.S. Army, World War II. Recipient Health Planning award in Ark., 1979, Jerome S. Levy award Ctr. Ark. Health Systems Agy., 1983, Lifetime Achievement award Ark. Nurses Coalition, 1994. Mem. ANA, Ark. State Nurses Assn. (pres. dist. 10 1971-73, state pres., state treas., chmn. pub. health nursing, trustee 1996-97), Ark. Pub. Health Assn. (hon. life mem.), Bus. and Profl. Women's Club (co-dir. S.W. Ark. Fedn., club pres.), Altrusa Internat. (club treas. 1969-71), Am. Bus. Women's Assn., North Little Rock Women's City Club. Home: Lakewood House 701 4801 North Hills Blvd North Little Rock AR 72116-7601

FUNK, JOEL DAVID, psychologist, educator; b. New Brunswick, N.J., May 25, 1946; s. Julius Jacob and Pearl (Wiseman) F.; m. Melody Rusomanis, Sept. 3, 1972; children: Rachel, Jeremy, Shoshana. BA, Rutgers U., 1967; MA, Clark U., 1974, PhD, 1977. Instr. to prof. Plymouth (N.H.) State Coll., 1975—. Contbr. articles to profl. jours.; editor/reviewer articles and books. Pres. Temple B'nai Israel, Laconia, N.H., 1987—. Mem. Assn. for Transpersonal Psychology, Internat. Assn. for Near-Death Studies, Soc. Rsch. Adult Devel., Phi Kappa Phi. Jewish. Home: 125 Quincy Bog Rd Rumney NH 03266-9707 Office: Plymouth State Coll Psychology Dept Plymouth NH 03264

FUNK ORSINI, PAULA ANN, health economist; b. Marietta, Ohio, May 16, 1956; d. James Corwin and Inez Aline (Smith) Funk; m. Michael Joseph Orsini, May 4, 1991. BS, Ohio State U., 1979, MS, 1986, PhD, 1992. Pharmacy resident Hosp. of U. Pa., Phila., 1979-80; staff pharmacist Nursing Ctr. Svcs., Hilliard, Ohio, 1984-85; mktg. rsch. assoc. Strategic Mktg. Corp., Bala Cynwyd, Pa., 1986; staff pharmacist Hahnemann U. Hosp., Phila., 1986-87, Mt. Carmel East Drugstore, Columbus, Ohio, 1987-91, Ohio State U. Hosps., Columbus, 1980-86, 87-91; asst. prof. U. Md., Balt., 1991-95; project mgr. health econs. State & Fed. Assocs., Alexandria, Va., 1995—; presenter in field. Author: (with others) Modern Medicine Dermatology Pocket Guide, 1982; reviewer Am. Jour. Hosp. Pharmacy, 1987; contbr. articles tp profl. publs., including Jour. Pharm. Mktg. and Mgmt., Am. Jour. Hosp. Pharmacy, Hosp. Pharmacy, Hosp. Formulary. Scholar in pharm. scis. IAPS-Am. Found. Pharm. Edn., 1988; Nat. Assn. Bds. Pharmacy-Am. Found. Pharm. Edn. fellow in pharmacy adminstrn., 1990, Albert B. Fisher Jr. PhD Citation fellow Am. Found. Pharm. Edn., 1989. Mem. Coun. Grad. Students in Pharm. Scis. (pres. 1990-91), Am. Assn. Pharm. Scientists, Am. Soc. Hosp. Pharmacists, Am. Pharm. Assn., Assn. for Consumer Rsch., Am. Mktg. Assn., Assn. for Health Svcs. Rsch., Rho Chi. Office: State & Fed Assocs 1101 King St Ste 600 Alexandria VA 22314

FURCHGOTT, ROBERT FRANCIS, pharmacologist, educator; b. Charleston, S.C., June 4, 1916; married, 1941; 3 children. BS, U. N.C., 1937; PhD in Biochemistry, Northwestern U., 1940; DM (hon.), Autonomous U., Madrid, 1984, U. Lund, 1984; DSc (hon.), U. N.C., 1989, U. Ghent, 1995; postdoctoral, Mt. Sinai Med. Sch., 1995. Rsch. fellow medicine Med. Coll. Cornell U., 1940-43, rsch. assoc., 1943-47, instr. physiology, 1943-48, asst. prof. med. biochemistry, 1947-49; from asst. prof. to assoc. prof.

pharmacology Med. Sch. Wash. U., 1949-56; chmn. dept. SUNY Health Sci. Ctr., Bklyn., 1956-83; prof. Health Sci. Ctr., Bklyn. State U., 1956-88, Univ. Disting. prof., 1988—, emeritus prof. pharmacology, 1990—; mem. pharmacol. tng. com. USPHS, 1961-64, mem. pharmacoltoxicol rev. com., 1965-68; Commonwealth fellow, 1962-63; vis. prof. U. Geneva, 1962-63, U. Calif., San Diego, 1971-72, Med. U. S.C., 1980, U. Calif., 1980; adj. prof. pharmacology Sch. Medicine, U. Miami, 1989—. Recipient Rsch. Achievement award Am. Heart Assn., 1990, Bristol-Myers Squibb award for achievement in cariovasc. rsch., 1991, Gairdner Fund Internat. award, 1991, medal N.Y. Acad. Medicine, 1992, Roussel Uclaf prize for rsch. in cell communication and signalling, 1994, Wellcome Gold medal Brit. Pharmacology Soc., 1995, ASPET award for exptl. therapeutics, 1996. Mem. AAAS, NAS, Am. Chem. Soc., Am. Soc. Biochemistry, Am. Soc. Pharmacology and Exptl. Therapeutics (pres. 1971-72, Goodman and Gilman award 1984), Harvey Soc., Polish Physiol. Soc. (hon.), Sigma Xi. Office: SUNY Health Sci Ctr Dept of Pharmacology 450 Clarkson Ave Box 29 Brooklyn NY 11203

FURCLOW, JOHN ROWE, internist; b. Kansas City, Kans., May 30, 1949; s. Michael Leo and Carolyn (Rowe) F.; m. Melisa Thomas, Dec. 18, 1971; children: Scott Michael, Samuel Christian Rowe. BA in Art, Rutgers U., 1971; MD, U. Ky., 1983. Diplomate Am. Bd. Internal Medicine, Am. Bd. Critical Care Medicine. Pvt. practice Prestonburg, Ky., 1986-95; staff physician Consol. Health Sys., Prestonburg, 1995—. Author: Handbook in Nutrition, 1980; film critic Lexington Herald-Leader, 1973-86. Fellow Am. Coll. Chest Physicians, Am. Coll. Rheumatology, Alpha Omega Alpha. Methodist. Office: Consol Health Sys US 23 North Prestonsburg KY 41653

FURIGAY, RODOLFO LAZO, surgeon; b. Bayom Bong, Nueva Vizcaya, Philippines, Aug. 24, 1938; came to U.S., 1963; s. Paulino Feril Furigay and Iluminada Mario Lazo; m. Margaret Josephine Reardon, Aug. 26, 1944; children: Paul Joseph, Tara Ann, Marc Damian. AA in Pre-Med. Studies, U. Santo Tomas, Manila, 1956, MD, 1961. Diplomate Am. Bd. Surgery; lic. in med. edn., Pa. Rotating intern Quincy (Mass.) City Hosp., 1963, resident in pathology, 1964, resident in gen. surgery, 1964-68; resident in cancer surgery Memorial Sloan-Kettering Hosp., N.Y.C., 1968-69; fellow gen. surgery Crouse-Irving Meml. Hosp., Syracuse, N.Y., 1969-70; mem. staff Windber (Pa.) Hosp., 1970—, chief of surgery, 1975—; Pres. Windber Hosp. Med. Staff, 1978. Fellow ACS, Am. Soc. Abdominal Surgeons, Am. Soc. Gen. Surgeons, Soc. Philippine Surgeons in Am.; mem. AMA, Cambria County Med. Soc. (bd. dirs. 1982-84, pres. 1984), Pa. Med. Soc. (del. 1985—), Pa. Blue Shield, Windber Country Golf Club (bd. dirs., pres. 1993-95). Roman Catholic. Office: Windber Hosp 609 Somerset Ave Windber PA 15963-1330

FURLONG, ROGER C., ophthalmologist; b. Edmonton, Canada, Oct. 2, 1960; s. Michael T. and Violet E. (Sawchuk) F.; m. Heidi L. Messer, July 7, 1990; children: Joshua, Katherine, Madison, Chase. BS, Stanford U., 1982; MD, U. Calif., San Francisco, 1986. Pvt. practice Rocky Mountain Eye & Ear, Missoula, Mont., 1990—; mem. faculty Am. Soc. Cararact/Refractive Surgeons, San Diego, 1995. Fellow Am. Acad. Ophthalmology (mem. faculty 1994, 95). Office: Rocky Mountain Eye and Ear 700 W Kent Missoula MT 59801

FURMAN, ERIC BERTRAM, pediatric anesthesiologist; b. Johannesburg, South Africa, Nov. 27, 1934; came to U.S., 1965, naturalized, 1976; s. Solomon and Milly (Dinkin) F.; m. June Elizabeth Abrams, Dec. 16, 1958; children: Terrence, Joanne Peta, Nicola Millicent. MB, BCh, U. Witwatersrand, Johannesburg, 1958; MS Adminstrv. Medicine, 1994. Intern in family practice, resident in anesthesiology U. Witwatersrand Hosps., Johannesburg, 1964; fellow in pediatric anesthesia Hosp. Sick Children, Toronto, 1965; fellow in anesthesiology, then instr. U. Vt. Hosps., 1965-68; dir. pediatric anesthesia Mass. Gen. Hosp., Boston, instr. anesthesia Harvard U. Med. Sch., Boston, 1968-71; prin. anesthesist Children's Hosp., Johannesburg, 1972-74; dir. anesthesia Children's Orthop. Hosp. and Med. Ctr., Seattle, 1974-87, dir. dept. anesthesia Cook-Fort Worth Children's Med. Ctr., 1987-95; dir. physician devel. Kaiser Permanente of Tex., 1995—; clin. assoc. prof. anesthesia/pediatrics U. Wash. Med. Sch., Seattle, 1974-86, prof. anesthesia, 1987; clin. prof. anesthesia U. Tex., San Antonio, 1988-90; clin. prof. U. Tex., Houston, 1990—; clin. prof. anesthesia Tex. Tech. U., 1988—. Trustee Bush Sch., Seattle, 1977-83, v.p., 1978; bd. dirs. Ft. Worth Symphony, Tarrent County Multiple Sclerosis Assn., 1988-91; bd. dirs. NCCJ, Jewish Fedn. Ft. Worth. Recipient African Oxygen Gold medal in anesthesia, 1963. Mem. Am. Soc. Anesthesiologists (chmn. com. pediatric practice 1978-81), Am. Acad. Pediatrics (chmn. sect. anesthesia 1980-82), AMA, Tex. Med. Assn., Tex. Soc. Anesthesiologists (treas. 1995—), Rotary Club (Ft. Worth). Jewish. Author articles in field; editor: International Anesthesia Clinics, 1975.

FURMAN, MARTIN JULIAN, psychiatrist, educator; b. Johannesburg, Republic of South Africa, Oct. 19, 1949; s. Koppel Isaac and Sarah Leah (Swartz) F.; m. Robyn Shelley Horwitz, Sept. 16, 1979; children: Michael Saul, Rachel Batsheva, Ruth Judith, Deborah Penina. BS, U. Witwatersrand, Republic of South Africa, 1970, MBA, 1972, MBBCh, 1978. Intern Baragwanath Hosp., Johannesburg, 1979; resident Butler Hosp./Brown U., Providence, 1980-82; chief resident Butler Hosp./Brown U., 1983, asst. unit chief, 1984-87, clin. asst. prof., 1986—, unit chief, 1988—. Mem. Am. Psychiat. Assn., Butler Hosp. Staff Assn. Jewish. Office: Butler Hosp 345 Blackstone Blvd Providence RI 02906-4861

FURMAN, ROBERT HOWARD, physician, educator; b. Schenectady, N.Y., Oct. 23, 1918; s. Howard Blackall and Jane Blessing (MacChesney) F.; m. Mary Frances Kilpatrick, Feb. 10, 1945; children: Carol K. Furman Lambert, Jane C. Furman Dougherty, Robert Howard, Hugh Patrick. AB, Union Coll., Schenectady, 1940; MD, Yale U., 1943. Diplomate Am. Bd. Internal Medicine. Intern, then asst. resident in medicine New Haven Hosp., 1944-45; asst. in medicine Yale U. Med. Sch., 1944-45; asst. resident physician, then resident physician Vanderbilt U. Hosp., 1948-50; from research asst. in medicine to asst. prof. Vanderbilt U. Med. Sch., 1946-52; assoc. prof., then prof. research medicine U. Okla. Med. Sch., 1952-70; prof. medicine Ind. U. Med. Sch., 1970-89, prof. emeritus, 1989—; head cardiovascular sect. Okla. Med. Research Found. and Hosp., 1952-70, assoc. dir. found., 1957-70; exec. dir. clin. research Eli Lilly and Co., Indpls., 1970-73, v.p. corp. med. affairs, 1976-83; v.p. Lilly Research Labs., 1973-76; clin. research cons. Walker Clin. Research, Indpls.; mem. vis. staff Wishard Meml. Hosp., Indpls., 1971; pres. Okla. Heart Assn., 1967-68; mem. cardiovascular study sect. Nat. Heart Inst., NIH, 1960-63, heart spl. projects com., 1963-66; bd. mgrs., sci. adv. com. Wistar Inst., 1972-78; sci. adv. com. Hormel Inst., Austin, Minn., 1973-83; mem. clin. scis. panel NRC, 1978-83; mem. clin. pharmacology adv. com. PMAF, 1977-83. Contbr. to med. jours.; mem. editorial bds. jours. Mem. council Inst. Adminstrn. and Mgmt.; mem. adv. bd. Union Coll., trustee, 1982-87; bd. dirs. Cathedral Arts, Indpls.; assoc. trustee U. Pa.; bd. dirs., exec. com. Indpls. Symphony Orch. Served to comdr., M.C. USNR, 1945-46, 55-57. Fellow Am. Coll. Cardiology, ACP, N.Y. Acad. Scis., Royal Soc. Medicine; mem. Am. Assn. World Health (dir. 1974-83), AAAS, Am. Clin. and Climatol. Assn., Am. Fedn. Clin. Research, Am. (fellow council arteriosclerosis, nat. bd. dirs., exec. and central coms.; chmn. research com. 1964-65), Ind. (dir.), Marion County heart assns.), Am. Physiol. Soc., Am. Soc. Clin. Pharmacology and Therapeutics, Am. Soc. Internal Medicine, Assn. Yale Alumni in Medicine, Cen. Soc. Clin. Research (council 1963-66), Endocrine Soc., Ind. Med. Assn., Marion County Med. Assn., Soc. Exptl. Biology and Medicine, So. Soc. Clin. Research, Nat. Audubon Soc., Garden of the Gods Club, Colorado Springs, Sigma Xi, Alpha Omega Alpha, Delta Upsilon. Home: PO Box 728 Green Valley AZ 85622-0728

FURMAN, SAMUEL ELLIOTT, dentist; b. Jersey City, Dec. 13, 1932; s. Sol T. and Cecilia (Berman) F.; m. Margaret Ann Gilardi, Feb. 27, 1971; children: Laurie, Jill, Sean, Ashley. AB, U. Pa., 1953, DDS, 1957. Diplomate Am. Bd. Quality Assurance and Utilization Rev. Physicians. Pvt. practice dentistry Tinton Falls, N.J., 1959—; sr. attending Monmouth Med. Ctr.; mem., pres. N.J. Bd. Dentistry; mem. N.E. Regional Bd. Dental Examiners. Capt. USAF, 1957-59. Fellow Acad. Gen. Dentistry, Internat. Coll. Dentists, Am. Coll. Dentists, Acad. Dentistry Internat.; mem. N.J. Soc. Dentistry for Children, Am. Prosthodontic Soc., Am. Assn. Dental Examiners, Acad. Osseointegration, Pierre Fauchard Acad., ADA, N.J. Dental Assn. (past trustee), Monmouth-Ocean County Dental Soc. (past pres.), B'nai B'rith, Omicron Kappa Upsilon, Alpha Omega. Home: 8 Woods End Rd Rumson NJ 07760-1040 Office: 1029 Sycamore Ave Eatontown NJ 07724-3131

FURNAS, DAVID WILLIAM, plastic surgeon; b. Caldwell, Idaho, Apr. 1, 1931; s. John Doan and Esther Bradbury (Hare) F.; m. Mary Lou Heatherly, Feb. 11, 1956; children: Heather Jean, Brent David, Craig Jonathan. AB, U. Calif.-Berkeley, 1952, MS, 1957, MD, 1955. Diplomate Am. Bd. Surgery, Am. Bd. Plastic Surgery (dir. 1979-85, sr. examiner 1986—), Royal Coll. Surgeons Found. (trustee 1995—). Intern U. Calif. Hosp., San Francisco, 1955-56, asst. resident in surgery, 1956-57; asst. resident in psychiatry, NIMH fellow Langley Porter Neuropsychiat. Inst. U. Calif., San Francisco, 1959-60; resident in gen. surgery Gorgas Hosp., C.Z., 1960-61; asst. resident in plastic surgery N.Y. Hosp., Cornell Med. Center, N.Y.C., 1961-62; chief resident in plastic surgery Cornell U. Svc., VA Hosp., Bronx, N.Y., 1962-63; registrar Royal Infirmary and Affiliated Hosps., Glasgow, Scotland, 1963-64; assoc. in hand surgery U. Iowa, 1965-68, asst. prof. surgery, 1966-68, assoc. prof., 1968-69; assoc. prof. surgery, chief div. plastic surgery U. Calif., Irvine, 1969-74, prof., chief div. plastic surgery, 1974-80, clin. prof., chief div. plastic surgery, 1980—; surgeon East Africa Flying Drs. Svc., African Med. and Rsch. Found., Nairobi, Kenya, 1972-73; plastic surgeon S.S. Hope, Nicaragua, 1966, Sri Lanka, 1968; mem. Balakbayan med. mission Mindanao and Sulu, The Philippines, 1980, 81, 82; overseas vis. prof. plastic surgery Ednl. Found., 1994. Contbr. chpts. to textbooks, articles to med. jours.; author, editor 6 textbooks; assoc. editor Jour. Hand Surgery, Annals of Plastic Surgery, Jour. Craniofacial Surgery. Expedition leader Explorer's Club Flag 171 Skull Surgeons of the Kisii Tribe, Kenya, Flag 44 Skull Surgeons of the Marakwet Tribes, Kenya, 1987. Capt. Med. Corps, USAF, 1957-59; col. Med. Corps., USAR, 1989-92, ret. Recipient Golden Apple award for teaching excellence U. Calif.-Irvine Sch. Medicine, 1980, Kaiser-Permanente award U. Calif.-Irvine Sch. Medicine, 1981, Humanitarian Service award Black Med. Students, U. Calif. Irvine, 1987, Sr. Research award (Basic Sci.) Plastic Surgery Ednl. Found., 1987; named Orange County Press Club Headliner of Yr., 1982. Fellow ACS, Royal Coll. Surgeons Can., Royal Soc. Medicine, Explorers Club, Royal Geog. Soc.; mem. AMA, Calif. Med. Assn., Orange County Med. Assn., Am. Soc. Plastic and Reconstructive Surgeons (bd. dirs. 1970-73), Am. Soc. Reconstructive Microsurgery, Soc. Head and Neck Surgery, Am. Cleft Palate Assn., Am. Soc. Surgery of Hand, Soc. Univ. Surgeons, Am. Assn. Plastic Surgeons (trustee 1983-86, treas. 1988-91, v.p. 1993-94, pres.-elect 1994, pres. 1995), Am. Soc. Aesthetic Plastic Surgery, Am. Soc. Maxillofacial Surgeons, Assn. Acad. Chairmen Plastic Surgery (bd. dirs. 1986-89), Assn. Surgeons East Africa, Assn. Plastic & Reconstructive Surgeons So. Africa (hon.), Pacific Coast Surg. Assn., Internat. Soc. Aesthetic Plastic Surgery, Internat. Soc. Reconstructive Microsurgery, Internat. Soc. Reconstructive Microsurgery, Internat. Soc. Craniomaxillofacial Surgery, Pan African Assn. Neurol. Sci., African Med. and Rsch. Found. (bd. dirs. U.S.A. 1987—), Muthaiga Club, Ctr. Club, Club 33, Univ. Club, Phi Beta Kappa, Alpha Omega Alpha. Office: U Calif Div Plastic Surgery Irvine Med Ctr 101 The City Dr S Orange CA 92668-3201

FURRY, DONALD EDWARD, health care executive; b. Cleve., Feb. 8, 1934; s. Cecil Earnest and Mary Letitia (Gallagher) F.; m. Anne Ross, Dec. 26, 1960; children: Elizabeth Anne, Joseph Donald. BS, John Carroll U., 1956, MS, 1957. Commd. lt. USN, 1959, advanced through grades to capt., 1982; commanding officer Naval Med. Rsch. & Devel. Com., Bethesda, Md., 1984-87; chmn. Health Facilities Authority, Pensacola, Fla., 1990—; pres. Med. Systems Cons., Pensacola, 1988—. Contbr. articles to profl. jours. Mem. Rep. Exec. Com., Escambia County, Fla., 1988-92, precinct com., 1988—; v.p., bd. dirs. Cath. Social Svcs., Pensacola, 1990-93, pres., 1993-96. Decorated Meritoris Svc. medal with gold star; Aerospaced Medicine fellow, Washington, 1979. Mem. Am. Mgmt. Assn., Aerospace Med. Assn., Aerospace Physiologist Soc., Ret. Officers Assn., Navy League. Republican. Roman Catholic. Home: 6802 Kitty Hawk Dr Pensacola FL 32506-5633 Office: Health Facilities Authority 120 S Alcaniz St Pensacola FL 32501-5907

FURST, ALEX JULIAN, thoracic and cardiovascular surgeon; b. Augusta, Ga., Aug. 21, 1938; m. George Alex and Ann (Segall) F.; m. Elayne Kobrin, Aug. 11, 1962; children: James Andrew, Jeffrey Michael, Joseph Robert. Student, U. Fla., 1963; M.D., U. Miami, 1967. Intern U. Miami Hosp., 1967-68, resident, 1968-72, clin. instr. dept. surgery, 1974-91; chief resident in thoracic and cardiovascular surgery Emory U. Hosp., Atlanta, 1972-73, sr. surg. registrar of thoracic unit, 1972-73; sr. surg. registrar of thoracic unit Hosp. for Sick Children, London, 1973-74; practice medicine specializing in thoracic and cardiovascular surgery Miami, Fla.; assoc. prof. surgery and cardiology, chief surg. svc. Miami VA Med. Ctr., 1991—, prof., surgery and medicine; chief thoracic surgery, pres. med. staff Mercy Hosp.; mem. staff Bapt. Hosp., South Miami Hosp., Doctor's Hosp. (all Miami), North Ridge Gen. Hosp., Ft. Lauderdale. Served with U.S. Army, 1958-60. Fellow Am. Coll. Cardiology, Am. Coll. Chest Physicians, A.C.S.; mem. Dade County Med. Assn., Fla. Med. Assn., Heart Assn. Greater Miami, Soc. Thoracic Surgeons, So. Thoracic Surg. Assn. Home: 8802 Arvida Dr Miami FL 33156-2302

FURST, ARTHUR, toxicologist, educator; b. Mpls., Dec. 25, 1914; s. Samuel and Doris (Kolochinsky) F.; m. Florence Wolovitch, May 24, 1940; children: Carolyn, Adrianne, David Michael, Timothy Daniel. A.A., Los Angeles City Coll., 1935; A.B., UCLA, 1937, A.M., 1940; Ph.D., Stanford U., 1948; Sc.D., U. San Francisco, 1983. Mem. faculty, dept. chemistry San Francisco City Coll., 1940-47; asst. prof. chemistry U. San Francisco, 1947-49, assoc. prof. chemistry, 1949-52; assoc. prof. medicinal chemistry Stanford Sch. Medicine, 1952-57, prof., 1957-61; with U. Calif. War Tng., 1943-45, San Francisco State Coll., 1945; rsch. assoc. Mt. Zion Hosp., 1952-82; clin. prof. pathology Columbia Coll. Physicians and Surgeons, 1969-70; dir. Inst. Chem. Biology; prof. chemistry U. San Francisco, 1961-80, prof. emeritus, 1980—, dean grad. div., 1976-79; vis. fellow Battelle Seattle Research Center, 1974; Michael vis. prof. Weizmann Inst. Sci., Israel, 1982; cons. toxicology, 1980—; cons. on cancer WHO; mem. com., bd. mineral resources NRC. Author: Toxicologist as Expert Witness, 1996; contbr. over 300 articles to profl. and ednl. jours. Bd. trustees Pacific Grad. Sch. Psychology. Recipient Klaus Schwartz Commemorative medal Internat. Toxological Congress, Tokyo, 1986, Profl. Achievement award UCLA Alumni Assn., 1992. Fellow Acad. Toxicological Scis. (diplomate), AAAS, Am. Coll. Nutrition, Am. Coll. Toxicology (nat. sec., pres. 1985), N.Y. Acad. Scis., Am. Inst. Chemists; mem. Am. Soc. Pharmacology and Exptl. Therapeutics, Am. Soc. Pharmacology and Exptl. Therapeutics, Am. Chem. Soc., Am. Assn. Cancer Research, Soc. Toxicology, Sigma Xi, Phi Lambda Upsilon. Home: 3736 La Calle Ct Palo Alto CA 94306-2620 Office: U San Francisco Inst Chem Biology San Francisco CA 94117-1080

FURST, SIDNEY CARL, social psychologist; b. N.Y.C., Dec. 11, 1925; s. Nathan and Anna (Levy) F.; student Princeton U., 1943; BA, U. Chgo., 1948; MA, Columbia U., 1950, postgrad. Bur. Applied Social Rsch., 1954; children-Anne Betsy, Carl Nathaniel. Project dir. mkt. rsch. Batten, Barton, Durstine & Osborn Inc., N.Y.C., 1952-58; sales presentation writer ABC, N.Y.C., 1958-59; pres. Furst Survey Rsch. Ctr., also Furst Analytic Ctr., 1959—; instr. Fairleigh-Dickinson Coll. Served with AUS, 1944-46. Author: Business Decisions That Changed Our Lives, 1964; Strategy of Change for Business Success, 1969. Home: 3 Washington Square Village New York NY 10012-1836

FURSTE, WESLEY LEONARD, II, surgeon, educator; b. Cin., Apr. 19, 1915; s. Wesley Leonard and Alma (Deckebach) F.; m. Leone James, Mar. 28, 1942; children: Nancy Dianne, Susan Deanne, Wesley Leonard III. A.B. cum laude (Julius Dexter scholar 1933-34); Harvard Club scholar 1934-35), Harvard U., 1937, M.D., 1941. Diplomate: Am. Bd. Surgery. Intern Ohio State U. Hosp., Columbus, 1941-42; fellow surgery U. Cin., 1945-46; asst. surg. resident Cin. Gen. Hosp., 1946-49; sr. asst. surg. resident Ohio State U. Hosps., 1949-50, chief surg. resident, 1950-51; limited practice medicine specializing in surgery Columbus, 1951—; instr. Ohio State U., 1951-54, clin. asst. prof. surgery, 1954-66, clin. assoc. prof., 1966-74, clin. prof. surgery, 1974-85, clin. prof. emeritus, 1985—; mem. surg. staff Mt. Carmel Med. Center, chmn. dept. surgery, 1981-85, dir. surgery program, 1981-82; mem. surg. staff Children's, Grant Med. Ctr., Univ., Riverside, Meth. Hosps., St. Anthony Med. Ctr., Park Med. Ctr. (all Columbus); surg. cons. Dayton (Ohio) VA Hosp., Columbus State Sch., Ohio State Penitentiary, Mercy Hosp., Benjamin Franklin Hosp., Columbus; regional adv. com. nat. blood program ARC, 1951-68, chmn., 1958-68; invited participant 2d Internat. Conf. on Tetanus, WHO, Bern, Switzerland, 1966, 3d, São, Paulo, Brazil, 1970, 4th, Dakar, Sénégal, 1975, 5th, Ronneby Brunn, Sweden, 1978, 6th, Lyon, France, 1981, 7th, Copanello, Italy, 1984, 8th, Leningrad, USSR, 1987, 9th, Granada, Spain, 1991; invited rapporteur 4th Internat. Conf. on Tetanus, Dakar, Sénégal, 1975; mem. med. adv. com. Medic Alert Found. Internat., 1971-73, 76—, bd. dirs., 1973-76; Douglas lectr. Med. Coll. of Ohio, Toledo; founder Digestive Disease Found. Prime author: Tétanos; Tetanus: A Team Disease; contbg. author: Advances in Military Medicine, 1948, Management of the Injured Patient, Immediate Care of the Acutely Ill and Injured, 1978, Anaerobic Infections, 1989, Procs. of Internat. Confs. in Switzerland, Brazil, Sweden, Sénégal, France, Italy, USSR, Current Therapy in Emergency Medicine, Surgical Infectious Diseases (4 edits.), Currenty Emergency Therapy, Surgical Infections, Current Diagnosis (multiple edits.), Current Therapy (multiple edits.), Surgical Infections, 5 Minute Clinical Consult, 3 edits., Medical Microbiology and Infectious Diseases, editor Surgical Monthly Review; contbr. articles to profl. jours. Mem. Ohio Motor Vehicle Med. Rev. Bd., 1965-67; bd. dirs. Am. Cancer Soc. Franklin County, pres., 1964-66. Served to maj., M.C. AUS, 1942-46, CBI, 1951-53. Recipient China Liberation medal, 2 commendations for surg. service in China U.S. Army; cert. of merit Am. Cancer Soc.; award for outstanding achievement in field clostridial infection dept. surgery Ohio State U. Coll. Medicine, 1984, Outstanding Service award, 1985; award for outstanding and dedicated service Mt. Carmel Med. Ctr., 1985; award for over 25 yrs. service St. Anthony Med. Ctr., U.S.A. Nat. Softball Champion for age group, 1992, 96. Mem. AMA, AAAS, APHA, Cen. Surg. Assn., Surgical Infection Soc., Internat. Biliary Assn., Shock Soc., Soc. Am. Gastrointestinal Endoscopic Surgeons (com. on stds. of practice, resident and fellow edn., com. legis. review), Soc. Surgery of Alimentary Tract, A.C.S. (gov.-at-large, chmn. Ohio com. trauma; nat. subcom. prophylaxis against tetanus in wound mgmt., Ohio chapter Disting. Service award 1987; regional credentials com.), Am. Assn. Surgery of Trauma, Ohio Surg. Assn., Columbus Surg. Assn. (hon. mem.; pres. 1983), Am. Trauma Soc. (founding mem., dir.), Ohio Med. Assn., Acad. Medicine Columbus and Franklin County (Award of Merit for 17 yrs. service, chmn. blood transfusion com., 50 Year Svc. award), Acad. Medicine Cin., Am. Med. Writers Assn., Grad. Surg. Soc. U. Cin., Robert M. Zollinger Surg. Ohio State U. Surg. Soc., Mont Reid Grad. Surg. Soc., Am. Geriatrics Soc., N.Y. Acad. Scis., Assn. Program Dirs. in Surgery, Assn. Physicians State of Ohio, Collegium Internationale Chirurgiae Digestivae, Assn. Am. Med. Colls., Internat. Soc. Colon and Rectal Surgeons, Soc. Internat. de Chirurgie, Am. Assn. Sr. Physicians, Sociēté Internationale sur le Tētanos, Am. Physicians Art Assn., China-Burma-India Vets., Assn. Columbus Basha (vice comdr. 1992-93, comdr. 1993-94, V-J Day coord., surgeon gen. 1994-96), Am. Legion NW Post # 443, Am. Med. Golfing Assn., Internat. Brotherhood Magicians, Soc. Am. Magicians, N.Y. Cen. System Hist. Soc., U.S. Squash Racquets Assn. (mem. ranking com.), Am. Platform Tennis Assn., Columbus Squash Racquets Assn. (bd. dirs.), Am. Legion. Presbyterian. Home and Office: 3125 Bembridge Rd Columbus OH 43221-2203

FURU, KAREN LEE, nurse, counselor; b. Ft. Riley, Kans., May 3, 1950; d. Jack Alvin and Mabel Lee (Zirk) Stanturf; m. Robert Llaird Furu, June 30, 1971; children: Robert B., Sandra R. Student Idaho State U., 1968-70, U. Idaho, 1970; grad. Walter Reed Army Inst. Nursing, 1972; BSN, U. Md., 1972; MEd in Counseling and Guidance, Mont. State U., 1981, postgrad., 1981-82. RN, Idaho, 1972, Mont., 1973; cert. chem. dependency counselor; lic. profl. counselor; cert. clin. mental health counselor. Head nurse U.S. Army Res. 396th Sta. Hosp., Helena, Mont., 1973-92, various positions including chief nurse, chief nursing edn. & tng., inactive, 1992—; ret., 1994; asst. dir. nursing Hillcrest Retirement Ctr., Bozeman, Mont., 1974-77; staff nurse, team leader/supr. Bozeman Deaconess Hosp., 1977-83; pub. health nurse Gallatin County, 1983-86; pvt. counselor, 1987—; tchr., cons. Mont. Law Enforcement Acad., Bozeman; mem. Gallatin County Driving Under Influence Task Force. Elder First Presbyn. Ch.; den leader Cub Scouts, Boy Scouts Am., 1981-83, cubmaster, 1983-84, troop leader Girl Scouts U.S.A. Served in U.S. Army, 1968-72, with Army Nurse Corps, 1972-73; to lt. col. USAR, 1973-94. Decorated Army Commendation medal with 2 oak leaf clusters. Mem. ACA, Res. Officers Assn., Mont. Counseling Assn., Mont. Mental Health Counselors Assn., Am. Mental Health Counselors Assn., Bozeman Bus. and Profl. Women (pres. 1993-95), Order Eastern Star, Alpha Omicron Pi (former chpt. advisor, former chpt. rels. advisor; honored alumnus 1982). Democrat. Presbyterian.

FURUYA, MASAKI, biologist; b. Tokyo, Apr. 9, 1926; s. Entei and Matsue (Nakamura) F.; m. Taeko Yamabe, Mar. 28, 1953; 1 child, Shoko. BSc, U. Tokyo, 1949, DSc, 1960; PhD, Yale U., 1962. Fellow Harvard U., Cambridge, Mass., 1962-63; asst. plant physiologist Brookhaven Nat. Lab., Upton, N.Y., 1963-65; assoc. prof. Nagoya (Japan) U., 1965-67; prof. U. Tokyo, 1968-87, dir. Botanic Garden, 1977-81; vis. prof. Nat. Inst. Basic Biology, Okazaki, Japan, 1981-87; head frontier rsch. program Riken Inst., Wako, Japan, 1986-92; cons. scientist Hitachi Ltd., Hatayama, Saitama, Japan, 1992—; pres. 15th Internat. Bot. Congress, Tokyo, 1993. Editor: Phytochrome and Photoregulation, 1987; editor-in-chief Plant and Cell Physiology, 1981-86. Mem. Am. Soc. Plant Physiology (corr.), Japan Assn. Photobiology (pres. 1985-86), Internat. Assn. Bot. and Mycological Socs. (pres. 1990-95). Home: 6-2-10 Kugahara Ota-ku, Tokyo 146, Japan

FUSARO, RAMON MICHAEL, dermatologist, researcher; b. Bklyn., Mar. 6, 1927; s. Angelo and Ida (Pucci) F.; m. Lavonne Johnsen, Nov. 6, 1971; children: Lisa Ann, Toni Ann; stepsons: Jeff, Scott. BA, U. Minn., 1949, BS, 1951, MD, 1953, MS, 1958, PhD, 1965. Diplomate: Am. Bd. Dermatology. Intern Mpls. Gen. Hosp., 1953-54, resident, 1954-57; instr. U. Minn., 1957-65, asst. prof., 1965-66, assoc. prof., 1966-70, dir. outpatient dermatology clinic, 1962-70; prof., chmn. dept. dermatology U. Nebr. Med. Center, Omaha, 1970-82, Creighton U., Omaha, 1975-87; dept. internal medicine Creighton U. Med. Sch., Omaha; prof. dermatology sect. dept. internal medicine U. Nebr. Med. Ctr., Omaha, 1982-91, acting chief sect. dermatology, 1991-94; prof. dept. pub. health and preventive medicine Hereditary Cancer Inst., Creighton U., 1984—. Contbr. over 250 articles to 97 profl. jours; also chpts. to books. With USN, 1944-46. Mem. Am. Acad. Dermatology, Soc. Investigative Dermatology, Am. Soc. Photobiology, Sigma Xi. Home: 908 Beaver Lake Blvd Plattsmouth NE 68048-4709 Office: U Nebr Med Ctr 600 S 42nd St Omaha NE 68105-1002 also: Creighton U Criss III Dept Preventive Medicine Omaha NE 68178

FUSCIARDI, KATHERINE, nursing administrator; b. Highland Park, Mich., Aug. 15, 1965; d. William Charles and Geraldine May (Revoldt) Freigruber; m. Antonio Fusciardi, July 11, 1987; children: Samantha Nicole, Michael Antonio. BSN, Oakland U., Rochester, Mich., 1987. Cert. BCLS instr., NALS instr. Staff nurse William Beaumont Hosp., Royal Oak, Mich.; staff nurse, head nurse Shady Grove Adventist Hosp., Rockville, Md.; staff nurse, asst. clin. mgr. St. Joseph's Mercy Hosp., Mt. Clemens, Mich.; staff nurse Mercy Hosp. South, Charlotte, N.C.; mem. clin. faculty Salisbury (Md.) State U., fall 1994; staff nurse Penninsula Regional Med. Ctr., Salisbury, 1995-96. Mem. NAACOG, Sigma Theta Tau.

FUSCO, JOSEPH J., internist; b. N.Y.C., Aug. 3, 1928; m. Isabell E. Porkolab, Oct. 11, 1956; children: Joseph M., John C., Frances, Joan G. BA, Columbia U., 1948; MD, NYU, 1952. Diplomate Am. Bd. Internal Medicine. Intern Cin. Gen. Hosp., 1952-53; resident Phila. Gen. Hosp., 1953-54, Hartford (Conn.) Hosp., 1956-58; attending physician Columbia Meml. Hosp., Hudson, N.Y., 1958—. Capt. USAF, 1954-56. Fellow Am. Coll. Chest Physicians; mem. ACP, N.Y. State Thoracic Soc. Office: 848 Columbia St Hudson NY 12534-2339

FUSELLA, JOSEPH PETER, physician; b. Amsterdam, N.Y., June 23, 1961; s. Joseph Peter and Joan (LoMaglio) F.; m. Loretta Giuliani, July 23, 1983; children: Nicholas, Michael. BS, Siena Coll., Loudenville, N.Y., 1983; DO, N.Y. Coll. Osteo. Medicine, Old Westbury, N.Y., 1987. Diplomate Am. Bd. Family Practice. Intern Suncoast Hosp., Largo, Fla., 1987-88; resident St. Clares Hosp., Schenectady, N.Y., 1988-91; pvt. practice Niskayuna Family Practice, Niskayuna, N.Y., 1991-93, The Primary Care Ctr., Schenectady, N.Y., 1993—. Mem. Am. Acad. Family Physicians, Am. Osteo. Assn., Am. Acad. Osteopathy, Am. Osteo. Dirs. Med. Edn. Office: 624 McClellan St Ste 601 Schenectady NY 12304

FUSTER, VALENTIN, cardiologist, educator; b. Barcelona, Spain, Jan. 20, 1943; s. Joaquin and Pilar Fuster; m. Angela-Maria Guals, Sept. 3, 1968; children: Pablo, Silvia. Baccalaurate, Colegio Jesuitas, Barcelona, 1961; MD, Barcelona U., 1967. Diplomate Am. Bd. Internal Medicine (mem. com. subsplty. bd. cardiovascular disease), Am. Bd. Cardiology. Intern Hosp. Clinico, Barcelona, 1967-68; research fellow U. Edinburgh, 1968-71; fellow in medicine and cardiovascular diseases Mayo Grad. Sch. Medicine, Rochester, Minn., 1971-74; asst. prof. medicine, Mayo Med. Sch., Rochester, 1974-77, assoc. prof. medicine, 1978-81, assoc. prof. pediatrics, 1980—, prof. medicine and cardiovascular diseases, 1981-82, cons., 1975-82; Arthur A. and Hilda M. Master prof. medicine Mt. Sinai Sch. Medicine, N.Y.C., 1982-91, chief div. cardiology, 1982-91; head cardiology unit Mass. Gen. Hosp., 1991-93; Mallinckrodt prof. medicine Harvard Med. Sch., Boston, 1991-93; dir. Cardiovascular Inst. Mt. Sinai Med. Ctr., N.Y.C., 1993—; mem. cardiology adv. com. NIH; mem. com. Am. Bd. Cardiology; hon. lectr. numerous orgns. Mem. editorial bd. Am. Jour. Cardiology, 1982, Arteriosclerosis, 1982, Internat. Jour. Cardiology, 1984, Jour. Exptl. and Applied Cardiology, 1985, Jour. The Am. Coll. Cardiology, 1987, Clin. Cardiology, 1988, Circulation, 1988; author of over 300 articles related to cardiovascular diseases. Recipient 17 rsch. and teaching awards including Gruntzig award Eur. Soc. Cardiology, 1992, Disting. Sci. award Am. Coll. Cardiology, 1993, Disting. Conner Lectr. award Am. Heart Assn., 1993. Fellow Am. Coll. Cardiology (Disting. Bishop Lectr. award 1994), Royal Coll. Physicians; mem. Am. Heart Assn. (chmn. pub. com., bd. dirs. 1994), Am. Soc. Clin. Investigations, European Soc. Clin. Investigation, Brit. Cardiac Soc. (corr.), French Soc. Cardiology (hon.), Columbian Soc. Cardiology (hon.). Office: Mt Sinai Med Ctr 1 Gustave L Levy Pl # 1030 New York NY 10029-6574

FUTCH, CHARLTON BUTLER, surgeon; b. Queens, N.Y., Apr. 1, 1941; s. Charlton Butler Futch and Agnes Story (Oliphant) Greenlaw; m. Helen Anne Morris, Aug. 12, 1962; children: Jeffery Butler, Jonathan Glynn, Jason Morris. BS, Hamilton Coll., 1962; MD, U. Va., 1966. Intern Columbia Presbyn. Hosp., N.Y.C., 1966-67, resident in surgery, 1967-72; pvt. practice Northshore Med. Group, Huntington, N.Y., 1972-74; attending Huntington Hosp., 1974, S.E. Ga. Regional Hosp., Brunswick, 1974—; attending Camden Med. Ctr. Hosp., St. Mary's, Ga., 1990—, Mercer Med. Ctr., Macon, Ga., 1984—; dir. Region IX Emergency Med. Svcs., Brunswick, 1976-84. Contbr. articles to profl. jours. Pres. Am. Cancer Soc., Brunswick, 1986—; affiliate faculty Am. Heart Assn., Atlanta, 1985—. Lt. comdr. USN, 1967-69. Office: Coastal Surgeons 3226 Hampton Ave Brunswick GA 31520

FUTRELL, JAMES WILLIAM, surgeon; b. Shreveport, La., Jan. 13, 1941; s. James Wilbur and Katherine Elizabeth (Brooks) F.; m. Anna Pickrell; children: Allison K., Kristin E. AB in English, Duke U., 1963; Grad., Med. Sch., Durham, N.C., 1967; postgrad., Case Western Res. U. Hosps., 1967-73, Johns Hopkins U. Med. Sch., 1973-75. Asst. prof. plastic srugery U. Va., Charlottesville, 1975-77, assoc. prof., 1977-79; prof. and chief plastic surgery U. Pitts. Med. Ctr., 1979—; co-founder PSX, Inc., Pitts., 1995. Editl. bd. Annals of Plastic Surgery, Yonsei Jour. Medicine, others. Active Third World Reconstructive Surgery team, Interplant, Inc., Vietnam, Thailand, Philippines, Peru, Korea, China, Russia, others. Lt. comdr. USN, 1969-71. Mem. Northeast Plastic Surgeons (pres. 1995-96), Southwestern Pa. Am. Coll. Surgeons (pres. 1989-90), Ivy Soc. (pres. 1990—). Presbyterian. Home: 1 Sweet Water Ln Pittsburgh PA 15238 Office: U Pitts Med Ctr 6-B Scaife Hall Pittsburgh PA 15261

FYLER, CARL JOHN, dentist; b. Spearville, Kans., May 14, 1921; s. John Henry and Helen Elsie (Parthie) F.; m. Marguerite E. Burris, Feb. 14, 1946. DDS, U. Mo., 1950. Practice dentistry Topeka, Kans., 1950-92; ret., 1992. Author: Staying Alive. Served to maj. USAF, 1942-46, ETO. Decorated Purple Heart, 5 Air Medals, Distinguished Flying Cross, E.T.O medal with 3 battle stars, Prisoner of War medal. Mem. ABA (life), Kans. Dental Assn., Shawnee County Dental Assn., Internat. Fedn. Dentists, Am. Ex-Prisoners of War (nat. dir. 1974-85, nat. jr. vice comdr. 1984-85), Kans. Ex-Prisoners of War (Gov.'s adv. com. 1978-86), 303d H.B.G. Assn. (pres. 1987-89), Eighth Air Force Hist. Soc. (bd. dirs. 1989-92, heavy bomb group), Mil. Order of World Wars (pres. Topeka chpt. 1996—), Distinguished Flying Cross Soc., Am. Legion, D.A.V., V.F.W., Am. Vets. Republican. Presbyterian. Home: 300 SW Yorkshire Rd Topeka KS 66606-2260

GAAB, MICHAEL ROBERT, neurosurgery educator, consultant; b. Landau, Germany, Mar. 11, 1947; s. Erich and Margarete (Hollinger) G.; m. Hannelore Sommer (div. 1972); 1 child, Marcus; m. Katharina Maria Weller, Sept. 28, 1974; children: Oliver, Jasmin, Florian. BS, U. Würzburg and U. Kiel, Germany, 1972; MD, PhD, U. Würzburg, 1973, U. Vienna., Austria, 1982, 83. House officer Knappschafts Hosp., Bochum, Germany, 1973; registrar, asst. neurosurgeon U. Hosp. Würzburg, Germany, 1974-79, sr. neurosurgeon, 1979-81, assoc. prof. neurosurgery, 1981-82; assoc. prof., head dept. pediatric neurosurgery U. Hosp. Vienna, 1982-84; assoc. prof. Med. Sch., U. Hannover, Germany, 1984-87, prof., 1987-92; full prof., head dept. neurosurgery Ernst Moritz Arndt U., U. Hosp. Greifswald, Germany, 1992—; cons. neurosurgeon City Hosp. Braunschweig, Germany, 1984-92. Author: Registratoin of Intracranial Pressure, 1981 (E.K. Frey award 1981); mem. editl. adv. bd. Brit. Jour. Neurosurgery, 1987-93; editl. bd. Neurosurg. Rev., 1995—; patentee device for intracranial pressure monitoring, in spondylodesis, devices for neuroendoscopy. Mem. Christian Dem. Union, Hannover, 1973—. German Rsch. Comty. grantee, 1981, 83, 95, German Ministry Rsch. and Tech. grantee, 1981, 82, German Cen. Nervous Sys. bd. trustees grantee, 1991, 92. Mem. German Neurosurg. Soc., Austrian Soc. Physicians, European Assn. for Pediatric Neurosurgery (sec. congress 1984), World Fedn. Neurosurg. Socs. (asst. treas. congress 1981), Bavarian Soc. Emergency Medicine, German Soc. Neuroendoscopy (bd. dirs.). Roman Catholic. Home: Senator-Bauer-Strasse 36, D-30625 Hannover Germany Office: U Hosp Ernst Moritz Arndt U, Sauerbruchstr 8 Dept Neurosurgery, D-17489 Greifswald Germany

GAAL, PETER GEORGE, surgeon; b. Chgo., July 24, 1930; s. George and Ethel (Friedman) G.; m. Aileen Sylvia Glassoff, June 14, 1952 (div. Dec. 1978); children: Eric, Linda, Ronald & Jennifer, Rebecca; m. Sandra Jane, June 16, 1979. BS, MD, U. Chgo., 1950, PhB, 1954. Diplomate Am. Bd. Surgery, Am. Bd. Thoracic Surgery. From asst. prof. to asst. clin. prof. surgery UCLA Med. Ctr., 1962-89; pvt. practice Santa Monica, Calif., 1965-82, Ventura, Calif., 1982—; chief surgery Ventura County Med. Ctr., 1987, Cmty. Meml. Hosp., 1988. Fellow Am. Coll. Surgeons; mem. Calif. Med. Assn., Ventura County Med. Assn. Office: 4080 Loma Vista Rd Ste D Ventura CA 93003-1811

GAARDER, MARIE, speech pathologist; b. New Britain, Conn., July 19, 1935; d. Nicholas and Clara (Sangeloty) Sarris; m. Kenneth R. Gaarder, Dec. 8, 1962; children: Jason, Galen. BS, U. Ill., 1957; postgrad. U. Md., 1962-63, Our Lady of Lake U. Grad. Sch. Social Work, San Antonio, 1976-77. Founder speech therapy program Flossmoor (Ill.) Sch. Dist. 161, 1957-59; speech pathologist Prince George's County (Md.) Bd. Edn., 1959-65, Sidwell Friend's Sch., Washington, 1966-67, St. Maurice Sch. for Learning Disabilities, Potomac, Md., 1968-69; pvt. practice speech therapy, Chevy Chase, Md., 1967—; adminstrv. officer Gaarder Med. Corp., Chevy Chase, 1977—. Pres., Prince George's chpt. Coun. for Exceptional Children, 1963-64; mem. Florence Crittenton Circle, 1966-69, Hospitality and Info. Svc. for Diplomats, 1967—; chmn. activities com. Jr. Teens, 1979-80; chmn. publicity YWCA Internat. Fair, 1977-79, chmn. entertainment, 1983, chmn. 1987-88; mem. internat. com. Woman's Nat. Dem. Club; co-chmn. Adv. Com. for Quality Integrated Edn. in Montgomery County, 1977-78; bd. dirs. D.C. br. YWCA, 1981-82, Washington Ctr. Chmn. oral history 65th Birthday Town of Chevy Chase; chmn. Mid-Atlantic regional adv. bd. Am. Found. for the Blind, 1984-85; founding mem. exec. bd. internat. adv. com. Very Spl. Arts, 1990-93. Recipient Appreciation cert. Opera Guild San Antonio, 1977, Outstanding and Dedicated Svc. to 1987 Internat. Fair Plaque YWCA of the Nat. Capital Area, Nat. Svc. Registry award, 1990, Disting. Svc. in Profession citation, Appreciation cert. Internat. Tng. in Communication, 1994. Mem. Am. Speech, Lang. and Hearing Assn. (advanced cert.), Md. Speech, Lang. and Hearing Assn., World Affairs Coun. of Washington, Soc. for Internat. Devel., Asia Soc., Soc. for Preservation of Greek Heritage, Capitol Speakers Club (sec. chpt. III 1983-84), Zeta Phi Eta. Greek Orthodox. Home and Office: 4221 Oakridge Ln Bethesda MD 20815-6058

GABAY, ELIZABETH LEE, infectious diseases physician; b. Milw., Oct. 20, 1951; d. George Gerald and Margaret Louise (Tracy) G.; m. Stephen K. Liu, June 29, 1974; children: Katherine Liu, Margaret Liu. BS, U. Wis., Milw., 1973; MD, U. Wis., 1976. Diplomate Am. Bd. Internal Medicine, Am. Bd. Infectious Diseases, Am. Bd. Geriatrics. Internal medicine physician FHP, Long Beach, Calif., 1981-90, chmn. infectious disease dept., 1990—. Contbr. articles to profl. jours. Fellow ACP; mem. Am. Soc. Microbiology. Roman Catholic. Office: PO Box 2607 Bellingham WA 98227

GABAY, JACK LEON, opthalmologist, medical association administrator; b. N.Y.C., Jan. 13, 1954; s. Albert and Mildred Gabay; m. JoAnne Gabay, June 19, 1983. MD, SUNY, Buffalo, 1980. Diplomate Am. Bd. Internal Medicine, Am. Bd. Ophthalmology. Pvt. practice Miami, Fla., 1986—; dir. South Fla. Ophthalmology Network, Miami, 1992—. Fellow Am. Ophthal. Assn.; mem. Miami Ophthal. Soc. Office: Ctr for Excellence in Eye Care 8930 N Kendall Dr Ste 400E Miami FL 33176

GABBAI, ALBERTO ALAIN, neurology educator, researcher; b. Cairo, May 19, 1953; arrived in Brazil, 1958; s. Maurizio and Farida (Sasson) G.; m. Miriam Benasayag Birmann, Sept. 21, 1978; children: Carolina, Lisa. Physician, Paulista Sch. Medicine, Sao Paulo, Brazil, 1976, MS, 1981, D in Medicine, 1986. Med. diplomate. Intern Paulista Sch. Medicine, 1977, resident in clin. neurology, 1978-80; rsch. fellow Tufts-New Eng. Med. Ctr., Boston, 1981-82; clin. and rsch. fellow Mass. Gen. Hosp.-Harvard U., Boston, 1987-89; asst. prof. Paulista Sch. Medicine, 1982-86, assoc. prof. medicine, 1989—; cons. Rsch. Found. State of Sao Paulo, 1991—. Contbr. articles on AIDS, HTLV and neuro-oncology to med. jours. Fellow Brazilian Acad. Neurology; mem. Am. Acad. Neurology (clin. assoc.), N.Y. Acad. Scis. Home: 203 Afonso Braz St, 04511 São Paulo Brazil Office: Paulista Sch Medicine, PO Box 20212, 04034 São Paulo Brazil

GABBE, STEVEN GLENN, physician, educator; b. Newark, Dec. 1, 1944; s. Charles Paul and Marcia May Gabbe; m. Jessica Gabbe, June 26, 1966 (div. 1980); children: Amanda, Daniel; m. Patricia Temple, July 26, 1981. BA, Princeton U., 1965; MD, Cornell U., 1969; MA (hon.), U. Pa., 1983. Diplomate Am. Bd. Ob-Gyn (examiner 1980—), Am. Bd. Maternal-Fetal Medicine (examiner 1979-89). Intern in medicine N.Y. Hosp., N.Y.C., 1969-70; rsch. fellow reproductive medicine Boston Hosp. for Women, 1970-71, resident in ob-gyn, 1972-74; rsch. fellow in biol. chemistry Harvard Med. Sch., Boston, 1970-71, clin. fellow ob-gyn., 1972-74; asst. prof. ob-gyn U. So. Calif., L.A., 1975-77; assoc. prof. U. Colo. Sch. Medicine, Denver, 1977-78; assoc prof. ob-gyn. and pediatrics U. Pa. Sch. Medicine, Phila., 1978-87, prof. radiology, 1987; prof. U. Pa. Sch. Nursing, Phila., 1982-87; prof., chmn. dept. ob-gyn Ohio State U. Coll. Medicine, Columbus, 1987—; mem. staff Hosp. of U. Pa., Phila., 1978-87, dir. Jerrold R. Golding div. fetal medicine, 1978-87, mem. med. bd. and numerous coms., 1984-87; vis. prof. ob-gyn King's Coll. Hosp., London, 1985-86; dir. maternal and infant care program Phila. Dept. Health, Disease Prevention and Health Promotion, 1982-87; mem. maternal and infant care adv. coun. Dept. Pub. Health, Phila., 1983-87; mem. subcom. on pregnancy and weight gain NRC, NAS, 1981; mem. internat. sci. bd. Reproductive Toxicology Ctr., 1984—; bd. dirs., med. adv. bd. Diabetes Treatment Ctrs. Am., 1984, others. Author: Clinical Obstetrics and Gynecology: Diabetes and Pregnancy, 1985, Clinical Obstetrics and Gynecology: Obstetric Ultrasound Update, 1988; (with J.R. Niebyl and J.L. Simpson) Obstetrics: Normal and Problem Pregnancies, 1986, 2d edit., 1991; contbr. numerous articles to profl. jours. and chpts. to books; editor i chief Am. Jour. Perinatology, 1983—; mem. numerous editorial bds. Mem. Pa. Diabetes Task Force, 1981-87, Ohio Diabetes Task Force, 1987—; bd. dirs. UNITE, Jeanes Hosp., 1980-87. Recipient Sr. Resident's award for Excellence in Tng., L.A. County Women's Hosp., 1976; grantee Juvenile Diabetes Found., 1981, HHS, 1984, 1985, Diabetes Treatment Ctrs. Am., 1986. Fellow Am. Coll. Obstetricians and Gynecologists (mem. PROLOG self assessment program task force 1981-82, chmn. 1986, mem. PROLOG subcom. 1986—); mem. Am. Gynecol. and Obstet. Soc., Am. Inst. Ultrasound in Medicine, Perinatal Rsch. Soc., Soc. Gynecologic Investigation, Soc. Perinatal Obstetricians (v.p. 1986, pres. 1987-38, bd. dirs. 1983-88, chmn. credentials, constn. and by-laws com. 1983-87), Am. Diabetes Assn. (mem. nat. rsch. bd. 1981-83, chmn. coun. on diabetes in pregnancy 1985, com. on food and nutrition 1976-80), Juvenile Diabetes Found. (mem. med. sci. rev. com., med. sci. adv. bd. 1981-83), Phila. Neonatal Soc., Obstet. Soc. Phila. (program chmn. 1986-87), Phila. Perinatal Soc. (pres. 1982-84), Columbus Ob-Gyn Soc., Pa. Diabetes Acad. (acad. steering com. 1986—, editorial rev. com. 1986—), Union League (Phila.), Phi Beta Kappa, Alpha Omega Alpha. Home: 2627 Haverford Rd Columbus OH 43220-4269 Office: Ohio State U Dept of Ob-Gyn 1654 Upham Dr Rm 505 Columbus OH 43210-1250

GABBIANI, GIULIO CESARE, pathology educator; b. Cremona, Italy, Mar. 19, 1937; s. Alceste and Rosita (Grisi) G.; m. Francoise Chatel, Sept. 20, 1963; children: Fabrizio, Francesca, Luca. MD, U. Pavia, 1961; PhD, U. Montreal, 1965; MD (hon.), U. Goteborg, Sweden, 1991. Rsch. asst. U. Montreal, Can., 1961-65, asst. prof., 1965-67, 68-69; rsch. assoc. Harvard Med. Sch., Boston, 1967-68; asst. prof. U. Geneva, 1969-75, prof., 1975-88, prof., chmn., 1988-90, prof., 1990—; sec. European Cytoskeletal Forum, 1982—. European editor: Arteriosclerosis, Thrombosis and Vascular Biology, 1995. Mem. European Tissue Repair Soc. (sec. 1990-95), European Vascular Biology Assn. (chmn. 1991-93). Office: Dept Path U Geneva CMU, 1 Rue Michel Servet, Ch-1211 Geneva 4, Switzerland

GABELNICK, HENRY LEWIS, medical research director; b. Boston, May 10, 1940; s. Murray and Lillian G.; m. Faith Schectman, June 17, 1962; children: Deborah Anne, Tamar Miriam; m. Clare Ann Donaher, May 22, 1987. BS, MIT, 1961, MS, 1962; PhD, Princeton U., 1966. Sr. chem. engr. Monsanto Co., Springfield, Mass., 1966-68; biomed. engr. NIH, Bethesda, Md., 1968-1986; dir. extramural rsch. CONRAD Program Ea. Va. Med. Sch., Arlington, 1986-89, dep. dir. CONRAD Program, 1989-90, dir. CONRAD Program, 1990—; tech. advisor World Health Orgn., Geneva, Switzerland, 1977—; tech. expert UN Devel. Program, Haifa, Israel, 1973. Editor: Rheology of Biological Systems, 1973, Drug Delivery Systems, 1976, Heterosexual Transmission of AIDS, 1990, Barrier Contraceptives, 1993, Biology, Pharmacology, and Clinical Applications of Androgens, 1996. Fellow Textile Research Inst.; mem. N.Y. Acad. Scis., Am. Chem. Soc., Controlled Release Soc., Sigma Xi. Home: 11612 Danville Dr Rockville MD 20852

GABER, ROBERT, psychologist; b. N.Y.C., Nov. 5, 1923; s. William and Freda (Harris) G.; m. Heidi Walters, Apr. 3, 1967 (div. Jan. 5, 1976) 1 child, Nathan. BA, NYU, 1949, MA, 1951; PhD, Columbia Pacific U., San Rafael, Calif., 1982. Psychotherapist Nat. Hosp. for Speech Disorders, N.Y.C., 1954-57; psychologist Indsl. Home for the Blind, N.Y.C., 1957-58; sch. psychologist Roosevelt Sch., Stamford, Conn., 1958-60; sr. clin. psychologist N.Y. State Dept. Mental Hygiene, Thiells, 1960-64; staff psychologist N.Y. Med. Coll., N.Y.C., 1965-66; cons. psychologist The Salvation Army, Phila., 1971-72; psychologist Md. Dept. Mental Hygiene, 1975-76, Dept. Corrections, Balt., 1979-80; CEO Axxiom De-Stress Ctrs., Balt., 1980—; dir. Ctr. for Stress Rsch., Norristown, Pa., 1994—; cons. Family Crisis Ctr. of Balt., 1973-74, Gov., Pa. Dept. Corrections, 1971; dir. mental health, nursery div. Dept. Welfare, N.Y.C., 1953-56. Author: Personality Traits and Behaviorisms of a Well-Adjusted Person, 1993, Federal Prisoners' Attitudes Toward Crime and Confinement, 1982, The Experience of Enlightenment, 1980; author booklet: Comprehensive Therapy Questionnaire, 1978; author articles, pamphlets on crime, human behavior and higher states of consciousness. With USAAF, 1942-46; PTO. Mem. Am. Psychol. Assn. Democrat. Office: Axxiom De-Stress Ctrs PO Box 22115 Baltimore MD 21203-4115 also: Ctr for Stress Rsch 207 Swede St Ste 102 Norristown PA 19401

GABLE, FRED BURNARD, pharmacist, author; b. Phila., June 30, 1929; s. Samuel and Mollie (Rayfield) G.; children: Tracy, Dana Jack. BS in Pharmacy, Temple U., 1951, MS in Pharmacy, 1953, M.A. in Sociology, 1959. Mem. faculty Temple U., Phila., 1955-80; prof. pharmacy Temple U., 1974-80, asst. dean, 1968-80; mem. pub. edn. com. Am. Cancer Soc., 1964-76; founding art curator Temple U. Sch. Pharmacy Art Collection, 1968-80. Author: Opportunities in Pharmacy Careers, 1964, rev. edits., 1969, 74, Opportunities in Pharmacy Careers, 1982, rev. edit., 1990, Psychosocial Pharmacy: The Synthetic Society, 1974; editor: The Temple Apothecary, 1959-80; contbg. critic Art Matters, 1991-95; contbr. articles to med. jours. With M.C. U.S. Army, 1953-55. Mem. Pharmacy Alumni Assn. Temple U. (life mem. bd. dirs.), Alumni Assn. Temple U., Phila. Mus. Art, Pa. Acad. Fine Arts, Sigma Xi, Rho Chi. Home: Ste 2703 1901 JFK Blvd Philadelphia PA 19103

GABOUREL, JOHN DUSTAN, retired pharmacology educator, legal consultant; b. San Francisco, Oct. 16, 1928; s. John Richard and Mary Josephene Gabourel; m. Carol E. Roberts, Aug. 5, 1951; children: Michele A., Linda S., Allison J., Candice M., John R. BS, U. Calif., Berkeley, 1950; MS, U. San Francisco, 1951; PhD, U. Rochester, N.Y., 1957. Instr. Stanford U. Sch. Medicine, Palo Alto, Calif., 1957-60, asst. prof., 1960-64; assoc. prof. pharmacology Oreg. Health Scis. U., Portland, 1964-71, prof., 1971-89, prof. emeritus, 1989-90; pvt. practice legal cons., Portland, 1971—; vis. scientist Walter and Eliza Hall Inst. of Med. Rsch., Melbourne, Australia, 1973-74. Contbr. numerous articles to profl. jours. Mem. rsch. com. Oreg. Heart Assn., Portland, 1976-82. Capt. U.S. Army, 1953-55. Mem. Am. Soc. for Pharmacology and Exptl. Therapeutics. Home: 6825 SW Raleighwood Way Portland OR 97225-1973 Office: Oreg Health Scis U Dept Pharmacology & Physiol 3181 SW Sam Jackson Pk Rd Portland OR 97201-3011

GABRIEL, EARL A., osteopathic physician; b. Phila., Aug. 13, 1925; s. John and Rose (Cohen) G.; m. Fredelle, Feldman, Dec. 19, 1948; children: Debra Mae, Barbara Lynn, Sheri Ann, Michael David. B.S., Muhlenberg Coll., 1950; D.O., Phila. Coll. Osteo. Medicine, 1954. Gen. practice osteo. medicine Allentown, Pa., 1955-78; chief of staff Allentown Osteo. Hosp., 1967-68, chmn. intern tng., 1956-58; prof., chmn. family practice medicine, assoc. dean clin. affairs Coll. Osteo. Medicine of Pacific, Pomona, Calif., 1978-88, assoc. dean clin. affairs for postdoctoral tng., 1983-88; med. dir. clinics, 1986-88, ret., 1988; pvt. practice gen. medicine Claremont, Calif., 1988-90, Rancho Cucamonga, Calif., 1990-94; dir. med. edn. San Bernardino (Calif.) County Med. Ctr., 1994—; mem. Pa. Gov.'s Sci. Adv. Com. on Health Care Delivery, 1970, 71; preceptor in gen. practice Phila. Coll. Osteo. Medicine; mem. ad hoc profl. group FDA, HEW, 1976-77; mem. Pa. Profl. Services Rev. Orgn. Council, 1977. Editorial adviser Family Practice News, 1976—, Data Centrum, 1984—. Fire surgeon Allentown Fire Dept.; trustee Community Services of Pa., Lehigh Valley Cancer Soc. Served with USNR and USMCR, 1943-46, PTO, CBI. Recipient cert. of honor Phila. Coll. Osteo. Medicine, 1981, Alumni Achievement award Muhlenberg Coll., 1983; elected Physicians Hall of Fame John Shankwiler Soc. Muhlenberg Coll., 1995. Fellow Am. Coll. Gen. Practice in Osteo. Medicine and Surgery (cert., pres. div. 1959, Disting. Svc. award, life mem. Pa. div. 1978); mem. Lehigh Valley Osteo. Soc. (pres. 1959-60), Pa. Osteo. Med. Assn. (pres. 1970, Disting. Svc. award 1975), Am. Osteo. Assn. (cert., ho. dels. 1966—, trustee 1970—, pres. 1975-76, cons. family gen. practice com. on osteo. colls. and bur. profl. edn. 1988), Osteo. Physicians and Surgeons of Calif. (trustee 1981—, pres. 1985), Calif. Bd. Osteo. Examiners, Phi Epsilon Pi (pres. 1950), Sigma Sigma Phi. Republican. Jewish. Clubs: Masons, Shriners, Jester, Lions (Host Pomona), Lehigh Valley. Address: 1551 Marjorie Ave Claremont CA 91711-3545

GABRIEL, JIŘÍ, chemist, research scientist; b. Liberec, Czechoslovakia, Apr. 5, 1963; s. Vratislav and Jiřina (Dvořáková) G.; m. Dagmar Štěrbová, July 9, 1988; children: Alena, Petr. Rerum Naturalium Doctorus, Charles U., Prague, Czechoslovakia, 1987; Candidatus Scientiarium, Inst. Microbiology, Prague, Czechoslovakia, 1992. Asst. Inst. Microbiology, 1986-87, rsch. scientist, 1992—, dep. head lab. biochemistry, 1994—; cons. environ. risks and monitoring dept. Ministry of Environ., Prague, 1994—; lectr. Charles U., Prague, 1995—; chmn. organizing com. Mini-Symposium on Microbial Degradations, Inst. Microbiology, 1993—. Contbr. articles to profl. jours.; patentee in field. Mem. Chamber of Elected Reps., Czechoslovak Acad. Scis., Prague, 1991-92. Recipient Global 500 award UN Environ. Programme, Nairobi, 1995. Mem. Czech Soc. Chemistry, N.Y. Acad. Scis., Czech Botan. Soc. Home: Trnkova 1773, 142 00 Prague Czech Republic Office: Inst Microbiology ASCR, Videnska 1083, 142 20 Prague Czech Republic

GABRIEL, MARK JOHN, internal medicine; b. Oak Park, Ill., Feb. 13, 1959; s. Joseph Martin Gabriel and Lillian Joyce (Opie) Malone; m. Carmell Caprice Dubose, Sept. 4, 1992; 1 child, Emily Anna. BA, U. Colo., 1987; DO, Coll. Osteo. Med. Pacific, Pomona, Calif., 1991. Diplomate Am. Bd. Internal Medicine. Intern in family medicine Presbyn./St. Luke's Med. Ctr., Denver, 1991-92; intern, resident in internal medicine Loma Linda (Calif.) U. Med. Ctr., 1992-95; chief resident internal medicine Riverside (Calif.) Gen. Hosp., 1995-96; cons. psychiatry Riverside Gen. Hosp., 1995-96. Mem. AMA, Am. Coll. Physicians, Am. Osteopathic Assn., Am. Coll. Osteopathic Internists. Office: Health Key Beacon Med Group 13131 Tesson Ferry Rd Saint Louis MO 63128

GABRIELSON, IRA WILSON, physician, educator; b. N.Y.C., Nov. 27, 1922; s. Benjamin and Lily (Baran) G.; m. Mary Putnam Oliver, Sept. 4, 1948; children: Deborah Anne, David Dwight, Hugh Wilson, Carl Oliver. BA, Columbia U., 1944, MD, 1949; MPH, Johns Hopkins U., 1959. Diplomate: Am. Bd. Pediatrics, Nat. Bd. Med. Examiners. Adminstrv. asst., asst. dir. Johns Hopkins Hosp., 1953-57; dir. community program retarded children New Haven, 1959-61; asst. attending pediatrician Yale-New Haven Community Hosp., 1959-68; asst. prof. public health Yale, 1961-68, exec. officer dept. epidemiology and public health, 1962-67; clin. prof. U. Calif., Berkeley, 1968-71; prof., chmn. dept. community and preventive medicine Med. Coll. Pa., 1971-89, prof. pediatrics, 1987-90, prof. emeritus, 1990—; adj. prof., exec. dir. physician asst. program Springfield (Mass.) Coll.; cons. in field. Editor Medicine Looks at the Humanities, 1987. With AUS. Fellow Nat. Found., 1958. Fellow Am. Acad. Pediatrics, Am. Public Health Assn., Coll. Physicians Phila. (pub. health com. 1976-90); mem. Phila. Pediatric Soc. (chmn. sch. health com. 1983-90—), Assn. Tchrs. of Preventive Medicine, Sigma Xi, Delta Omega. Club: Appalachian Mountain (Boston). Home: 85 Old Goshen Rd Williamsburg MA 01096-9707 Office: Med Coll Pa Dept Cmty and Preventive Medicine Philadelphia PA 19129

GABRIELSON, SHIRLEY GAIL, nurse; b. San Francisco, Mar. 17, 1934; d. Arthur Obert and Lois Ruth (Lanterman) Ellison; m. I. Grant Gabrielson, Sept. 11, 1955; children: James Grant, Kari Gay. BS in Nursing, Mont. State U., 1955. RN, Mont. Staff and operating room nurse Bozeman (Mont.) Deaconess Hosp., 1954-55, 55-56; staff nurse Warm Springs State Hosp., 1955; office nurse, operating room asst. Dr. Craft, Bozeman, 1956-57; office nurse Dr. Bush, Beach, N.D., 1957-58; pub. health nurse Wibaux County, 1958-59; staff and charge nurse Teton Meml. Hosp., Choteau, Mont., 1964-65; staff pediatric and float nurse St. Patrick Hosp., Missoula, Mont., 1965-70; nurse, insvc. dir. Trinity Hosp., Wolf Point, Mont., 1970-79; ednl. coord. Community Hosp. and Nursing Home, Poplar, Mont., 1979—; coord. staff devel. Faith Luth. Home, Wolf Point, 1980-81; CPR instr. ARC, Am. Heart Assn., Great Falls, Mont., 1979—; condr. workshops and seminars; program coord., test proctor for cert. nursing assts., 1989—; preceptor for student nurses in rural health nursing clin. U. N.D., 1993—. Author: Independent Study for Nurse Assistants, 1977. Former asst. camp leader Girl Scouts U.S.A.; former mother advisor, bd. dirs. Rainbow Girls; pres. Demolay Mothers Club, 1977; bd. dirs. Mont. div. Am. Cancer Soc., 1984-90, mem. awards com., 1986-89; founder Tri-County Parkinson's Support Group, N.E. Mont. Recipient Lifesaver award Am. Cancer Soc., 1987, Svc. award ARC, 1989, Health and Human Svcs. award Mont. State Dept., 1990, U.S. Dept. Health award, 1990, Outstanding award, U.S. HHS, Mont. Health Promotion award Dept. Health and Environ. Scis. Mem. ANA, Mont. Nurses Assn. (mem. commn. on continuing edn. 1977-91, chmn. 1984-86), Order Eastern Star (Worthy grand matron 1995—), Alpha Tau Delta (alumni pres. 1956). Presbyterian. Home: 428 Hill St Wolf Point MT 59201-1244 Office: Community Hosp-Nursing Home PO Box 38 Poplar MT 59255-0038

GABRILOVE, JACQUES LESTER, physician; b. N.Y.C., Sept. 21, 1917; s. Benjamin and Pauline (Levine) G.; m. Hilda R. Weiss, May 19, 1946; children: Sandra Leslie Saltzman, Janice Lynn Gabrilove Dirzulaitis. BS magna cum laude, CCNY, 1936; MD, NYU, 1940. Diplomate Am. Bd.

Internal Medicine. Intern Mt. Sinai Hosp., N.Y.C., 1940-41; rotating intern Mt. Sinai Hosp., 1941-43, vol. radiology, 1943, resident medicine, 1943-44, Blumenthal fellow medicine, 1946-48, research asst. medicine, 1949-51, asst. attending physician, 1952-60, assoc. attending physician, 1960-68, attending physician, 1969—; chief endocrine clinic, clin. prof. medicine Mt. Sinai Sch. Medicine, 1969-82, Baumritter prof., 1982-90, Baumritter prof. emeritus, 1990—, prof., 1995—, cting dir. divsn. endocrinology, 1985, assoc. dir. divsn., 1986—, dir. endocrine fellowship program, 1986—; Libman fellow in medicine Yale U., 1945; clin. asst. prof. SUNY Coll. Medicine, N.Y.C., 1957-59, clin. assoc. prof., 1959-66, clin. prof., 1966-69, professorial lectr., 1969—; cons. endocrinology VA Hosp., East Orange, N.J., 1958-66, Elizabeth A. Horton Hosp., Middletown, N.Y., 1961—, VA Hosp., Bronx, N.Y., 1969—, Norwalk (Conn.) Hosp., 1974—, Elmhurst (N.Y.) City Hosp., St. Francis Hosp., Port Jervis, N.Y.; mem. panel on metabolic and rheumatoid diseases U.S. Pharmacopeia, 1956; mem. spl. com. on rsch. tng. grants in diabetes, endocrinology and metabolism NIH, 1976-79, mem. com. on diabetes rsch. and tng. ctrs., 1977-79; Saltzman lectr. Mt. Sinai Hosp., Cleve., 1974; cons. Jour. Urology, 1984-89. Author, contbr. to books in field, also articles to med. jours.; mem. editl. bd. Mt. Sinai Jour. Trustee, v.p. area Jewish synagogue. Recipient Globus prize Mt. Sinai Jour.; J. Lester Gabrilove award established in his honor, 1988. Fellow ACP, Am. Coll. Endocrinology (Disting. Clin. Endocrinologist award 1996), N.Y. Acad. Medicine; mem. AMA, AAAS, Am. Assn. Clin. Endocrinologists, Am. Diabetes Assn., Harvey Soc., Endocrine Soc., Royal Soc. Medicine, Pan Am. Med. Assn. (v.p. N.Am. endocrinology), Peruvian Endocrine Soc. (hon.), N.Y. Acad. Scis., N.Y. County Med. Soc., N.Y. Diabetes Assn., Mt. Sinai Alumni Assn. (pres. 1970, Jacobi medallion), Lotos Club (bd. dirs.), Phi Beta Kappa, Phi Beta Kappa Assocs., Alpha Omega Alpha (prize). Home & Office: 25 E 86th St New York NY 10028-0553

GABRY, JEROME BENJAMIN, ophthalmologist; b. Bklyn., Sept. 28, 1949; s. Sol and Marsha (Deiches) G.; m. Mona J. Babbin, Aug. 13, 1983; children: Leora I., Shira A. BA, U. Pa., 1971; MD, Washington U., St. Louis, 1975. Diplomate Am. Bd. Ophthalmology; lic. physician, Md. Intern Pa. Hosp., Phila., 1975-76; resident Manhattan Eye Ear Hosp., N.Y.C., 1976-79; ophthalmologist in pvt. practice N.Y.C., 1979-93, Silver Spring, Md., 1993—; cons. ophthalmologist Hill Haven Nursing Home, Adelphi, Md., 1993—. Mem. med. adv. bd. Motor Vehicle Adminstrn., Glen Burnie, Md., 1995—. Fellow Am. Acad. Ophthalmology; mem. Montgomery County Med. Soc. Office: 9801 Georgia Ave # 221 Silver Spring MD 20902

GABRYS, KIRBY DEAN, nephrologist; b. Edmonton, Alta., Can., May 15, 1963; came to the U.S., 1965; s. Edward and Sylvia Milly (Pashniak) G.; m. Elaine Aloma Hart, Aug. 14, 1988; children; Lara Willow, Violet Skye, Forrest Reed. BS, Pacific Union Coll., 1985; MD, Loma Linda U., 1989. Bd. cert in nephrology and internal medicine. Intern and resident in internal medicine Wright State U./Kettering Meml. Hosp., Dayton, Ohio, 1989-92; fellowship in nephrology Vanderbilt U., 1992-94; nephrologist Renal Medicine Assoc., Albuquerque, 1994—. Seventh Day Adventist. Office: Renal Medicine Assoc 201 Cedar SE #604 Albuquerque NM 87120

GACHET, FRED SMITH, JR., gynecologist; b. Rochester, N.Y., June 1, 1932; s. Fred Smith and Clara Rebekah (DeShazo) G.; m. Shirley Crevda Fox, Sept. 14, 1991; children from previous marriage: Carl Christian Fred, Louise Willis, Catherine Chalmers; stepchildren: Debra Hedrick, Cheryl Bryant. AB, Duke U., 1953; MD, Johns Hopkins U., 1957. Diplomate Am. Bd. Ob-Gyn. Intern Pvt. Med. Svc. Johns Hopkins Hosp., Balt., 1957-58, jr. asst. resident, then resident in ob-gyn, 1958-62; pvt. practice ob-gyn Hickory, N.C., 1965; pvt. practice ob-gyn Woman's Clinic, Hickory, 1965-87, pvt. practice gynecology, 1987—. Pres. Hickory Symphony, 1969. Capt. U.S. Army, 1962-64. Fellow ACS, Royal Soc. of Medicine; mem. AMA, So. Med. Assn., Piedmont Ob-Gyn. Soc., N.Am. Gynecol. Soc., N.C. Ob-Gyn. Soc. Republican. Episcopalian. Office: Woman's Clinic 1205 N Center St Hickory NC 28601-3759

GACIOCH, GERALD MATTHEW, cardiologist; b. Syracuse, N.Y., Sept. 27, 1958; s. Michael Theodore and Marie Victoria Gacioch; m. Annette Rose, Aug. 7, 1982; children: Leah, Matthew, Rachel, Jonathan. BS in Biology, SUNY, Albany, 1980; MD, Johns Hopkins U., 1984. Diplomate Am. Bd. Internal Medicine, Am. Bd. Cardiology. Intern internal medicine Johns Hopkins Hosp., Balt., 1984-85, resident, 1985-87; fellow cardiology U. Mich., 1987-89, fellow interventional cardiology, 1989-90; physician Rochester (N.Y.) Cardiopulmonary Group, 1990—. Fellow Am. Coll. Cardiology; mem. AMA Coun. on Clin. Cardiology, Soc. Cardiac Angiography and Interventions, Rochester Acad. Medicine, Med. Soc. State N.Y., Med. Soc. Monroe County, Phi Beta Kappa. Office: Rochester Cardiopulmonary Group PC 1445 Portland Ave Ste 104 Rochester NY 14621

GADE, KAREN, physiatrist. BS, Appalachian State U., 1987; MD, Duke U., 1992. Resident Mayo Clinic, Rochester, Minn., 1992-96; pvt. practice physiatry Canton, Ohio, 1996—; gov. coun. Mayo Fellow Assn., Rochester, 1994-96. Mem. AMA, Am. Acad. Physical Medicine & Rehab., Minn. Med. Assn. (del. 1994-96), Zumbro Valley Med. Soc. Office: 3801 Whipple Ave NW Canton OH 44718

GADWAY, RONALD G., family physician; b. Danemora, N.Y., May 25, 1930; s. Orville Edward and Freda Irene (Bruso) G.; m. Dolores Estelle LaMountain, June 24, 1951 (div. May 1988); children: Cynthia Mae Gadway Morgan, Rhonda May Gadway Blaisdell; m. Judy Marie Colson, July 31, 1988; 1 child, Ronald Gene. Degree, Atlantic Union Coll., 1956; DO, U. of Health Scis., 1960. Pvt. practice family medicine South Royalton, Vt., 1961-73; pvt. practice family medicine, mgr. Med. Assoc., Inc., Bethel, Vt., 1973-90; physician clin. practice Gifford Family Health, Bethel, 1990—; pres. staff Gifford Med. Ctr., 1968-72. Chmn. Vt. Osteo. Licensing Bd., Montpelier, 1986-95; health officer Cities of Sharon, South Royalton and Tunbridge, Vt., 1960-95. Cpl. U.S. Army, 1951-53. Mem. Vt. State Assn. Osteo. Practitioners (pres. 1972-74, 86-88), Coll. Osteo. Family Practice. Republican. Seventh-Day Adventist. Home: Rt # 2 Box 40B South Royalton VT 05068

GAEDE, JAMES ERNEST, physician, medical educator; b. Calgary, Alta., Can., July 2, 1953; s. John Ernest and Florence Eleanor (Hilmer) G.; married, Dec. 23, 1994; children: Graham, Jason, Nikki, Mary Frances, Sydney. BA, Augustana Coll., 1975, MA, 1976; MD, U. S.D., 1980. Diplomate Am. Bd. Family Practice. Staff physician Queen of Peace, Mitchell, S.D., 1983—; chief of staff Queen of Peace, Mitchell, 1988, med. dir., 1988-89; med. dir. St. Joe's Med. Assn., Howard, S.D., 1988—, Women's Health Clinic, Mitchell, S.D., 1983—; assoc. prof. U. of S.D. Sch. Medicine; presenter U.S. Senate, Washington, 1991. Contbr. articles to profl. jours. Bd. dirs. Dakota Weslayan U., Mitchell, 1986-89, Dakota Mental Health, Mitchell, 1988-90; mem. Commn. 2000 S.D., Sioux Falls, 1988—; pub. health officer City of Mitchell, 1983—. Fellow Am. Acad. Family Practice (Active Tchrs. award 1984—); mem. AMA, S.D. Assn. Family Practice, S.D. State Med. Assn. (del. 1983—), Mitchell C. of C., Mayo Alumni Assn., Doctors Mayo Soc. Home: 210 N Harmon Dr Mitchell SD 57301 Office: Sixth Ave Family Practice 1200 E 6th Ave Mitchell SD 57301

GAETA-HARPER, THERESA, psychotherapist; b. Altoona, Pa., July 6, 1955; d. Joseph D. and Anna M. (Malfara) Gaeta; m. Kevin W. Harper, Oct. 16, 1982. BA in Psychology, St. Francis Coll., 1977; grad. cert., Roosevelt U., 1986, MA in Clin. Psychology, 1989. Clinically cert. substance abuse counselor. Clin. therapist Family Guidance Ctr., Chgo., 1985-86, counseling coord., 1986-87, dir., clin. therapist, 1987-89; pvt. practice psychotherapy Chgo., 1989-91; mgr. vol. dept., clin. therapist Howard Brown Health Ctr., Chgo., 1989-96; cons., psychotherapist Rush Presbyn.-St. Luke's Med. Ctr., 1995—; seminar and workshop trainer, educator Howard Brown Health Ctr., Chgo., 1989-96, nat. trainer and educator, 1991-94. Producer video Active Duty, 1992. Vol. Guild for the Blind, Chgo., 1990-94, Cris Radio, Chgo., 1987-88; bd. dirs. Lakeview Mental Health Ctr., Chgo., 1989-91. Recipient Friend for Life award Howard Brown Health Ctr., 1992, Hon. Recognition PWA Support award, 1991; finalist Internat. Health and Med. Film Festival, 1994. Mem. ACA, Am. Mental Health Counselors, Midwestern Psychol. Assn., Coalition Ill. Counselors. Democrat. Roman Catholic.

GAETHE, GEORGE, dermatologist; b. Chgo., Jan. 9, 1919; s. Rubin and Celia (Midlo) G.; m. Joy Rosenberg, Nov. 1, 1942; children: Gary, Gordon, Glenn. BS, La. State U., 1939; MD, La. State U., New Orleans, La., 1942. Diplomat, Am. Bd. of Dermatology 1950, Am. Coll. of Physicians 1962. Intern Charity Hosp. of La., New Orleans, 1942-43; resident med. sch. La. State U., 1946-49; pvt. practice Metairie, La., 1949—. Maj., Army of U.S., 1943-46, ETO. Mem. ACP. Office: 3939 Houma Blvd Ste 224 Metairie LA 70006-2923

GAEUMAN, JOHN VICTOR, physician, educator; b. Newberry Springs, Calif., Mar. 7, 1932; s. William F. and Marjorie Belle (Egley) G.; m. Ruth E. Farnsworth, Dec. 17, 1955; children: William, David, Suzanne, Dawn. AB, Oberlin Coll., 1954; MD, Ohio State U., 1958, MS, 1961. Diplomate Am. Bd. Internal Medicine, Am. Bd. Preventive Medicine, also cert. in aerospace medicine. Chief spl. env. medicine N.Am. Aviation, Downey, Calif., 1965-68; fellow pulomonary medicine U. So. Calif. Lavina Hosp., Altadena, 1968-69; resident in internal medicine Huntington Meml. Hosp., Pasadena, Calif., 1969-71; pvt. practice Sterling, Colo., 1971-79; dir. Giacomini Cardio Pulmonary Lab. High Plains Rehab. Facility, Sterling, 1971-79; assoc. prof. clin. preventive medicine and internal medicine Ohio State U., Columbus, 1979-95, med. dir. employee health svcs., 1995—. Fellow Am. Coll. Preventive Medicine; mem. ACP, Aerospace Med. Assn., Ctrl. Ohio Indsl. Hygiene Assn., Am. Coll. Occupational and Environ. Medicine. Office: Employee Health Svcs Rm 2110 UHC 456 W 10th Ave Columbus OH 43210

GAFFNEY, PAUL COTTER, retired physician; b. DuBois, Pa., May 12, 1917; s. John Charles and Anna Catherine (Cotter) G.; m. Lois G. Brown, Oct. 14, 1944; children: Louise A., Paul Cotter, William J., Maureen E., Mary Ellen, Frances J., Michael B. B.S. magna cum laude, U. Pitts., 1940, M.D., 1942. Intern St. Francis Hosp., Pitts., 1942-43; resident in pathology St. Francis Hosp., 1946-48; resident in pediatrics Children's Hosp., Pitts., 1948-50; mem. staff Children's Hosp., 1951-95, med. dir., 1978-81, trustee, 1981-95; ret., 1995; fellow hematology Children's Hosp., Detroit, 1950-51; practice medicine specializing in pediatrics and hematology, Pitts., 1951-63; mem. med. faculty U. Pitts., 1961-93, prof. emeritus pediatrics, 1993—; assoc. dean, dir. admissions U. Pitts. Sch. Medicine, 1977-78; exec. dir. Med. Alumni Assn. Sch. Medicine U. Pitts Sch. Medicine, 1980-90; mem. staff Magee-Women's Hosp., Pitts., 1951-80; mem. med. adv. com. Comprehensive Health Planning Assn. Allegheny County, 1968-76; bd. dirs. Cen. Blood Bank Pitts., 1969-76; med. dir. Childrens Hosp. Pitts., 1978-81; chmn. bd. trustees Cancer Support Network Pitts., 1992—. Served to maj., M.C. U.S. Army, 1943-46. Decorated Bronze Star with oak leaf cluster; named Man of Yr. in Medicine, Pitts. Acad. Medicine, 1978; recipient Phillip S. Hench Disting. Alumnus award U. Pitts. Sch. Medicine, 1980; Children's Hosp. of Pitts. established the Paul C. Gaffney Chair in Pediatric Hematology-Oncology, 1993. Fellow Am. Acad. Pediatrics; mem. AMA, Pa. Med. Soc., Allegheny Med. Soc. (dir. 1973-76, 81-84), Am. Pediatric Soc. (Golden Apple teaching award 1967, 71, 75), Pediatric Travel Club, Phi Beta Pi. Republican. Roman Catholic. Home: 5540 Elgin St Pittsburgh PA 15206-1433

GAFFNEY, THOMAS EDWARD, retired physician; b. East St. Louis, Ill., Nov. 5, 1930; s. John V. and Leola (Heisner) G.; m. Edith Ann Heitholt, June 12, 1954; children—John, David, Michael. A.B., U. Mo., 1951, M.S., 1953; M.D., U. Cin., 1957. Intern Harvard Med. Service of Boston City Hosp., 1957-58; resident medicine Mass. Gen. Hosp., 1958-59; instr. pharmacology, asst. medicine U. Cin., 1959-60; clin. assoc. Nat. Heart Inst., 1960-62; assoc. prof. pharmacology U. Cin., 1962-67, asst. prof. medicine, 1962, dir. div. clin. pharmacology, 1962-72, prof. pharmacology, 1967-72, prof. medicine, 1969-72; prof., chmn. dept. pharmacology, prof. medicine Med. Univ. of S.C., 1972-90, disting. prof., 1986-90; vis. scientist Merck Sharp & Dohme Rsch. Labs., Rahway, N.J., 1989-93; ret., 1993; mem. cardiovascular panel NAS Drug Efficacy Study, 1967-70; mem. pharmacology and exptl. therapeutics study sect. Nat. Heart Inst., 1967-69; mem. med. adv. bd. Coun. High Blood Pressure Rsch., 1969—; mem. Coun. on Basic Scis. of Am. Heart Assn., 1969—, mem. cardiovascular A study sect., 1972; mem. program rev. com. pharmacology and toxicology Nat. Inst. Gen. Med. Scis., 1971-75, chmn. 1973-75; mem. tech. adv. bd. S.C. Rsch. Authority, 1986-89. Mem. editorial bd. Jour. Pharmacology and Exptl. Therapeutics, 1965-77, Ann. Rev. Pharmacology and Toxicology, 1986-91. Served with USPHS, 1960-62. Recipient research career devel. award Nat. Heart Inst., 1962, 67, 72; Myrtle Wreath award for research Hadassah, 1980; NIH sr. rsch. fellow, 1989. Mem. Am. Fedn. Clin. Rsch., Am. Soc. Pharmacology and Exptl. Therapeutics, Ctrl. Soc. Clin. Rsch., Am. Soc. Clin. Investigation, Assn. Am. Physicians, Alpha Omega Alpha. Home: 348 Sugar Hollow Rd Fairview NC 28730-9560

GAGE, LOIS WAITE, nursing educator; b. Ipswich, Mass., Mar. 8, 1922; d. Roy Appleton and Mary Agnes (Surrette) Waite McGregor; children: Nancy Marie Gage-Lindner, John Barry. Diploma, St. Elizabeth Sch. of Nursing, Brighton, Mass., 1943; BS, Simmons Coll., 1949; MA, Columbia U., 1957; PhD, U. Mich., 1972. RN, Mass., Mich. Assoc. dir. primary care community medicine U. Mich., Ann Arbor, 1973-83; assoc. prof. Psychiatry-Mental Health Nursing Wayne State U., Detroit, 1963-73; supr. of pub. health nursing Health Dept., Pitts., 1952-55; prof. emerita Nursing U. Mich., Ann Arbor, 1991; cons. WHO, Pan-Am. Health Orgn., 1980, 85, 86, 87, 88. Contbr. numerous articles and rsch. to profl. jours. Lt. j.g. USNCR, 1944-46. Recipient Sarah Goddard Power award Acad. Women's Caucus, 1996. Fellow Am. Acad. Nursing, APHA (chmn. mental health sect., Mental Health Sect. award); mem. ANA, AAUP (steering com.), Mich. Nurses Assn., Nat. League for Nursing, Sigma Theta Tau (Excellence in Nursing award), Pi Lambda Theta, Kappa Delta Pi. Home: 423 Sumark Way Ann Arbor MI 48103-6613 Office: U Mich Sch Nursing #3342 400 N Ingalls Ann Arbor MI 48109-0482

GAGE, MARK DUDLEY, psychiatrist; b. Gardena, Calif., May 22, 1958; s. James Truby and Pegie Sue (Claypool) G.; m. Susan Gale Combs, Nov. 20, 1976; children: Christina Nicole, Brandon Levi. AAS, C.C. of the Air Force, Maxwell AFB, 1985; BA, Chapman U., 1985; DO, Coll. Osteo. Med. Pacific, 1991. Diplomate Am. Bd. Osteopathic Physicians & Surgeons. Internal medicine intern Tulsa Regional Med. Ctr., 1991-92; resident psychiatry Okla. U. Coll. Medicine, Tulsa, 1992-96, chief resident, 1994-95; med. dir. Ctr. for Geopsychiatry, Henryetta, Okla., 1996—; pres. Okla. Med. & Psychiat. Svcs., Inc., 1994—. Served in USAF, 1976-85. Mem. Am. Psychiat. Assn., Am. Osteopathic Assn., Am. Bd. Forensic Examiners, Oklahoma Psychiat. Assn., Okla. Osteopathic Assn., Tulsa Psychiat. Assn. Republican. Home and Office: 7506 E 91st Pl Tulsa OK 14133

GAGE, TOMMY WILTON, pharmacologist, dentist, pharmacist, educator; b. Stamford, Tex., Oct. 6, 1935; s. Carl and Mildred (Hughes) G.; m. Loyce M. Voss, June 2, 1956; children—Sharon, Stephen, Susan, Stacey. B.S., U. Tex., Austin, 1957; D.D.S., Baylor U., 1961, Ph.D., 1969. Gen. practice dentistry Munday, Tex., 1963-66; mem. faculty Baylor Coll. Dentistry, Dallas, 1969—; prof. pharmacology Tex. A&M U. Sys. at Baylor Coll. Dentistry, 1972—, chmn. dept., 1969-92, vice chmn. dept. oral and maxillofacial surgery and pharmacology, 1992—. Author papers in field, chpts. in books. Served with USAR, 1961-63. Nat. Inst. Dental Research postdoctoral fellow, 1966-69. Fellow Am. Coll. Dentists; mem. ADA, Am. Soc. Pharmacology and Exptl. Therapeutics, Am. Assn. for Dental Rsch., Internat. Assn. Dental Rsch., Am. Assn. Dental Schs., Tex. Dental Assn. (Cooley Trophy 1976), S.W. Soc. Oral Medicine, Dallas County Dental Assn., Rho Chi, Omicron Kappa Upsilon. Methodist. Office: 3302 Gaston Ave Dallas TX 75246-2013

GAGEL, BARBARA JEAN, health insurance administrator; b. Celina, Ohio, Nov. 19, 1943; d. Vincent James and Theresa Barbara (Goettermoeller) G. BA, Miami U., 1965; MBA, U. Chgo., 1977. Asst. dir. for internat. trade State of Ill., Chgo., Brussels, Hongkong and Sao Paulo, Brazil, 1973-76; dir. office of mgmt. and planning Office Human Devel. Svcs., Chgo., 1976-79; dep. regional adminstr. Health Care Financing Adminstrn., Chgo., 1979-82, regional adminstr., 1982-87; dir. bur. of prog. ops. Health Care Financing Adminstrn., Balt., 1987-92; dir. health stds. and quality bur. Health Care Fin. Adminstrn., Balt., 1992-96; pres., CEO AdminaStar, Inc., Indpls., 1996—. Recipient Presdl. Disting. Rank award 1988, 94, Presdl. Meritorious Rank award 1987, 92; named Fed. Exec. of Yr., 1987. Home: 10461 Spring Highlands Dr Indianapolis IN 46290 Office: AdminaStar Inc 6801 Hillsdale Ct Indianapolis IN 46250

GAGER, WALTER EDWARD, ophthalmologist; b. Madison, Wis., Mar. 31, 1932; m. Donna M. BS in Chemistry, Marquette U., 1959, MD, 1963. Diplomate Am. Bd. Ophthalmology. Intern Columbia Hosp., Milw., 1963-64; resident, asst. instr. dept. ophthalmology Marquette U. Sch. Medicine, Milw., 1964-67, asst. prof., 1968-70; clin. asst. prof. ophthalmology Med. Coll. Wis., 1970-72, assoc. clin. prof. ophthalmology, 1972-81, clin. prof. ophthalmology, 1981—; vice chief staff Waukesha Meml. Hosp., 1983-86, chief staff, 1987-89; mem. med. staff Columbia Hosp., Elmbrook Meml. Hosp., Froedtert Meml. Luth. Hosp., Children's Hosp. Wis., Milw. County Med. Complex, Sacred Heart Rehab. Hosp., VA Med. Ctr., Wood, Wis., Waukesha Meml. Hosp., Lakeside Hosp., St. Joseph's Hosp.; presenter in field. Contbr. articles to profl. jours. NIH fellow, 1967-68, ophthalmology fellow U. Miami Sch. Medicine, 1967-68. Mem. AMA, Am. Acad. Ophthalmology and Otolaryngology, Am. Assn. Ophthalmology, Am. Intra-Ocular Implant Soc., Am. Soc. Contemporary Ophthalmology, Am. Venereal Disease Assn., Nat. Found. Eye Care, Nat. Soc. Prevent Blindness, Upper-Midwestern Neuro-Ophthalmology Group, Wis. State Med. Soc., Wis. Soc. to Prevent Blindness, Wis.-Upper Mich. Soc. Ophthalmology, Milw. County Med. Soc. Milw. Ophthalmologic Soc. (treas. 1974, sec. 1975, v.p. 1976, pres. 1977), Waukesha County Med. Soc. (pres.-elect 1978-79, pres. 1979-80), Assn. Rsch. in Vision and Ophthalmology, Bascom Palmer Eye Inst. Alumni Assn., Waukesha C. of C. Office: Med Eye Assocs 102 E Main St Waukesha WI 53186 also: 9900 W Bluemound Rd Milwaukee WI 53226 also: 400 Bay View Rd Ste D Mukwonago WI 53149 also: 1500 Walnut Ridge Dr Hartland WI 53029

GAGNA, CLAUDE EUGENE, molecular biologist, biochemist, anatomist; b. N.Y.C., Sept. 16, 1956; s. Alexander and Leontina (Coda) G. BS, St. Peter's Coll., 1979; MS, Fairleigh Dickinson U., 1983; PhD in Basic Med. Scis., NYU, 1990. Teaching fellow NYU, N.Y.C., 1982-84, rsch. asst. in biochemistry basic med. scis., 1984-90, instr. human anatomy basic med. scis., 1988-91, instr. anatomy basic med. scis., 1991—, instr. biochemistry basic med. scis., 1991-93, postdoctoral fellow basic med. scis., 1991-93; rsch.-tchg. specialist dept. physiology/dept. ophthalmology U. Medicine and Dentistry Med. Sch., Newark, 1992—; biomed. cons. Herbert Law Firm, Palisades Park, N.J., 1990—. Author: Cellular and Molecular Aspects of Eye Research, 1990; contbr. articles to profl. jours. Recipient Leonardo Da Vinci award Leonardo Da Vinci Soc., 1976, First Author award Am. Assn. Anatomists, 1986, 89, 90. Mem. Internat. Soc. for Eye Rsch., Histochem. Soc., Am. Soc. Microbiology, Tissue Culture Assn. Home: 157 Morningside Ln Palisades Park NJ 07650-1917 Office: U Medicine and Dentistry-Med Sch 185 S Orange Ave Newark NJ 07103

GAGNEJA, GURCHARAN LOL, health facility administrator; b. Aug. 3, 1939; came to U.S., 1974; s. Balmukand and Ganga Devi (Nagpal) G.; m. Janet Graham Keirs Reid, Oct. 23, 1970 (div. July 1987); children: Sharan Devi, Anita Janet; m. Susan Romatz, May 23, 1992. BSc, Panjab U., 1958; MEng./BSc, Sheffield U., 1967; PhD, Heriot-Watt U., 1970; MSc in Microbiology, Detroit U., 1983; postdoctoral diploma in clin. biochemistry/lab. medicine, Windsor U., Can., 1976. Diplomate Am. Bd. Bioanalysis; cert. lab. dir. Mich. Dept. Pub. Health. Rschr. biotechnology U. Bath., Eng., 1970-73; asst. lab. dir. Bioanalytical Proc. Inc., Allen Park, Mich., 1974-78; lab. dir. Detroit Doctors, Livonia, Mich., 1978-85; pres. Sterling Biochems. Inc., Ferndale, Mich., 1985-91, Esquire Diagnostics, West Bloomfield, Mich., 1991-94, Clin. Lab. Hemet, Calif., 1994, Biotronic Diagnostics Inc., Hemet, 1996—; lab. dir. Diagnostic Rsch. Lab, Bloomfield, 1984-85; pres. Nuclear Diagnostics Inc., Troy, Mich., 1986-91. Fellow Royal Inst. Chemistry U.K., Nat. Acad. Clin. Biochemistry; mem. APHA, Am. Assn. Bioanalysis, Am. Assn. Clin. Chemists, Assn. Clin. Biochemists U.K., N.Y. Acad. Scis. Republican. Home: 2452 Uplong Dr West Bloomfield MI 48324 Office: Biotron Diagnostics Inc 850 E Latham Ave Hemet CA 92543

GAGNON, JOHN HARVEY, psychotherapist, educator; b. Derby, Conn., Dec. 16, 1946; s. Ernest John and Pauline Stella (Dziedulonis) G.; m. Eleanor Moser, Apr. 22, 1995; 1 child, Isabelle Eleanor. BS, Fairfield U., 1969; MS, Western Conn. State Coll., 1976; PhD, Union Inst., 1982. Diplomate Am. Bd. Med. Psychotherapists (fellow), Am. Bd. Psychotherapy; lic. marriage and family therapist, EMT, Conn.; cert. family life educator. Counselor in tng. Conn. Valley Hosp., 1972-73; counselor Whiting Forensic Inst., 1973; coord., dir. Danbury Hosp. Day Treatment Program, 1973-77; pvt. practice, 1977-80; psychotherapy intern Counseling Ctr. and N.Y. Inst. for Gestalt Therapy, 1981-83; pvt. practice, 1983—; rsch. cons. Newtown Counseling Ctr., 1987-89; instr. N.Y. Inst. for Gestalt Therapy, 1983-89; lectr. Yale U., 1983; adj. prof. Western Conn. State U., 1983-86, U. Bridgeport, 1988-90; adj. lectr. U. Conn., 1990-93; cons. dept. psychology Fairfield U., 1994-95. Author: Gagnon's Directory, 1986, Wounded Healer, 1993; contbr. articles to profl. jours. Ofcl. emergency sta. Am. Radio Relay League, 1992—; chmn. adult program Unitarian-Universalist Soc. North Fairfield County, West Redding, Conn., 1990-91, tchr. religious edn., 1984-86; judge sr. divsn. Conn. State Fair, 1986—; bd. trustees Unitarian-Universalist Ch. of Stamford, 1996—. Fellow Internat. Coun. for Sex Edn. and Parenthood; mem. ACA, AAUP, Assn. for Counselor Edn. and Supervision, Am. Soc. for Group Psychotherapy and Psychodrama, Am. Acad. Psychotherapists, Am. Assn. for Marriage and Family Therapy, Assn. for Humanistic Psychology, Internat. Assn. Marriage and Family Counselors, Nat. Coun. Family Rels., Phi Delta Kappa. Democrat. Home: 15 E Putnam Ave Ste 308 Greenwich CT 06830-5424 Office: 270 Greenwich Ave Ste # 26 Greenwich CT 06830

GAGNON, MONIQUE F., pediatrician; b. Detroit, Apr. 16, 1963; d. Alden George and Francine Marie-Paule (MArchand) G ; m. Tomas Jose Vietorisz, May 30, 1992. BA, Mt. Holyoke Coll., 1985; MD, Mt. Sinai Sch. Medicine, 1989. Diplomat Am. Bd. Pediatrics. Resident New Eng. Med. Ctr., Boston, 1989-92; pediatrician Stamford (Conn.) Hosp., 1993-94, pvt. practice, Stamford, 1994—. Fellow Am. Acad. Pediatricians; mem. Conn. Med. Soc., Soc. Adolscent Medicine. Office: The Pediatric Ctr 107 Glenbrook Rd Stamford CT 06902

GAHAGAN, THOMAS GAIL, obstetrician, gynecologist; b. Brush Valley, Pa., Apr. 14, 1938; s. Ben D. and Zula C. (Brown) G.; m. Mary A. Miller, Dec. 23, 1960; children: David, Diane, Kevin, Keith. BA, Washington and Jefferson Coll., 1960; MD, U. Pa., Phila., 1964. Diplomate Am. Bd. Ob/Gyn. Intern U. Ky., Lexington, 1964-65, resident in ob/gyn., 1965-68; group practice Dr. Jones and Kelch P.A., Newark, Ohio, 1970-71, Naples (Fla.) Ob/Gyn., 1971-85; pvt. practice Naples, 1985—. Capt. USAF, 1968-70. Fellow ACOG, Fla. Ob-Gyn. Soc.; mem. AMA, Am. Cancer Soc. (life, bd. dirs. Collier unit 1973-93, bd. dirs. Fla. div. 1976-91, pres. 1986-87, St. George medal 1990), Fla. Med. Assn., Collier County Med. Soc. (exec. com. 1989-94, pres.-elect 1991-92, pres. 1992-93). Republican. Presbyterian. Office: 700 2nd Ave N Ste 305 Naples FL 34102-5702

GAHAN, PETER BRIAN, cell biologist, researcher; b. London, Aug. 23, 1933; s. Desmond Edgeworth and Lily (Pam) G.; m. Viviane Maggi, Feb. 1963 (dec. 1974); m. Danielle France Carmignac; 1 child, Jonathan David Edgeworth. BS, U. London, 1960, PhD, 1964. Head biology Thames Poly., London, 1966-70; prof. Meml. U., Newfoundland, Can., 1970-74, Queen Elizabeth Coll., London, 1974-85; lectr. King's Coll. London, 1962-66, prof., 1985—; assoc. prof. U. Geneva, Switzerland, 1982-92. Author: Plant Histochemistry and Cytochemistry, 1984; co-author: Vascular Differentiation, 1988; editor: Autoradiography for Biologists, 1972. Fellow Inst. Biology (v.p. 1990-92), Royal Soc. Arts, Royal Microscopical Soc. (chmn. histochemistry 1976-80, coun. 1977-80); mem. Biochem. Soc., Soc. for Exptl. Biology (coun. 1984-86), Brit. Soc. of cell Biology. Office: King's Coll London, Campden Hill Rd, London W8 7AH, England

GAHM, NORMAN H., pediatric neurosurgeon; b. Washington, Apr. 7, 1935; s. Irvin George and Berenice (Gurbarg) G.; m. Ruthellen Chesler, June 15, 1957; children: Joshua Bernard, Sara-Jo. AB, Harvard U., 1957; MD, Tufts U., 1961. Diplomate Am. Bd. Neurol. Surgery. Intern Barnes Hosp., St. Louis, 1961-62; resident in neurosurgery Yale U., New Haven, 1962-67; neurosurgeon Neurosurgeons of Ctrl. Conn., Hartford. Office: Neurosurgeons of Ctrl Conn 100 Retreat Ave Hartford CT 06106

GAINES, HAZEL DIANNE, bureau director; b. Summit, Miss., Dec. 18, 1947; d. Willie and Emma Lee (Hill) Waterman, Jr.; m. Herman B. Gaines; children: Candace, Christina. Diploma, St. Dominic Sch. Nursing, Jackson, Miss., 1969; BS in Nursing, William Carey Coll., 1981; MS, U. So. Miss.,

1990. Charge nurse S.W. Miss. Regional Med. Ctr., McComb, Miss., 1969-70; staff nurse VA Hosp. Am. Lake, Tacoma, 1971-74; charge nurse recovery rm. S.W. Regional Med. Ctr., McComb, 1974-75; staff nurse Miss. State Dept. Health, McComb, 1975-80, home health coord., 1980-84; nurse cons. Miss. State Dept. Health, Jackson, 1984-91, dir. perinatal divsn., 1991-95, dir. Bur. Women's Health, 1995—; mem. Dept. Human Svcs. Foster Care Rev. Bd., Jackson, 1986-93. Mem. ANA, Miss. Nurses Assn. Miss. Perinatal Assn., Nat. Perinatal Assn., State Employees Assn. Miss., Nurses Assn. Am. Coll. Ob-Gyn. Office: Miss State Dept Health 2423 N State St Jackson MS 39216-4504

GAINES, JACQUELYN, public health facility administrator; b. Balt., Mar. 30, 1957; d. Herbert Van and Goldie Lorraine (Johns) Keyes; m. Charles Wesley Gaines, Dec. 18, 1977; children: Jennifer Nicole, Kimberley Michele. BSN, U. Md., 1980, MS, 1985. RN, Md. Staff nurse Johns Hopkins Hosp., Balt., 1980-82, head nurse gyn. surg. unit, 1982-84, clin. supr. ob.-gyn. outpatient svcs., 1984-85; dir. ednl. svcs., nurse practitioner Health Care for Homeless, Balt., 1987-89, pres., CEO, 1989—; bd. dirs. Md. Women's Health Coalition, 1988-91, Action for Homeless, 1990—; mem. Nat. Health Care for the Homeless Coun. Mem. Md. Pub. Health Assn., Nat. Assn. Community Health Ctrs., Mid-Atlantic Primary Health Care Assn. Democrat. Roman Catholic. Office: Health Care for Homeless 111 Park Ave Baltimore MD 21201

GAINES, KATHLYN ANNE, nursing specialist; b. Florence, Colo., Dec. 20, 1934; d. William Cody Gaines and Estelle May (Smith) Rizk. B.S. in Nursing, Syracuse U., 1962; M.Nursing, U. Fla., 1969; D.S. in Nursing, U. Ala., Birmingham, 1981. Coord. rehab. nursing workshops Ohio State U., Columbus, 1965-67; asst. prof. Western Carolina U., Cullowhee, 1969-73; clinician Duke U./Highland Hosp., Asheville, N.C., 1973-75; clin. specialist Bayfront Med. Ctr., St. Petersburg, Fla., 1976-77; mental health coordinator Vis. Nurses Assn., Cleve., 1980-81; chmn. nursing div. Carson-Newman Coll., Jefferson City, Tenn., 1982-86; clin. nurse specialist Lakeshore Mental Health Inst., Knoxville, Tenn., 1986-89, Broughton Hosp., Morganton, N.C., 1989-90; assoc. prof. Lincoln Meml. U., 1990-92; clin. nurse specialist Gaston Meml. Hosp., Gastonia, N.C., 1992-95; dir. psychiat. nursing Emerald Care, Inc., Gastonia, N.C., 1995-96, dir. performance improvement, 1996—; rehab. nursing cons. Ohio Dept. Health, Columbus, 1965-67, Orthopedic Hosp., Asheville, 1970-72; mental health nursing cons. Smokey Mountains Mental Health Ctr., Cullowhee, 1970-72, Highland Hosp., Asheville, 1970-72; mem. adv. council Your Home Vis. Nurse, Knoxville, 1982—. Mem. Friends of the Library, Jefferson City, 1982-95, Morganton, N.C., 1995—. Mem. AAUW, ANA (treas.dist. 29), North Am. Nursing Diagnosis Assn., Assn. Rehab. Nurses (reviewer), N.C. League for Nursing, Nat. League for Nurses, Sigma Theta Tau, Omicron Delta Kappa, Beta Sigma Phi. Episcopalian. Avocations: crocheting; reading; flower gardening; jigsaw puzzles. Home: 103 Shetland Ct Morganton NC 28655-8901

GAINES, MARLON DEAN, physician assistant, health administrator; b. Louisville, July 20, 1955; s. Joe D. and Mary Jean (Robison) G. B.Health Scis., U. Ky., 1980; MHA, Webster U., 1987. ACLS, BCLS, ATLS. Cost containment cons. Providian Corp., Louisville, 1985-88; dir. med. rev. Sentinel Med. Peer Rev., Louisville, 1988-89; physician asst. rehab. Rehab. Assocs., Louisville, 1989-95; physician asst./ENT Akin Med. Ctr., Louisville, 1992-93; physician asst. orthop. Sewell Orthop., Louisville, 1995-96; physician asst. VA Med. Ctr., Louisville, 1996—. Fellow Am. Acad. Physician Assts., Ky. Acad. Physician Assts. Home: 3641 Warner Ave Louisville KY 40207

GAINES, THURSTON LENWOOD, JR., retired surgeon; b. Freeport, N.Y., Mar. 20, 1922; s. Thurston Lenwood and Albertha R. (Robinson) G.; m. Jacqueline Eleanor Kelly, Feb. 26, 1944; children: Beverly Doreen, Terrell Lance, William Wesley. Student, Howard U., 1941-43; BA, NYU, 1948; MD, Meharry Med. Coll., 1953. Diplomate Am. Bd. Surgery. Intern, Meadowbrook Hosp., East Meadow, N.Y., 1953-54, resident, 1954-59; practice medicine specializing in surgery, Hempstead, N.Y., 1959-75; attending surgeon Mercy Hosp., Rockville Centre, N.Y., 1959-76, dir. surg. edn., 1969-74; assoc. attending in surgery Nassau County Med. Center, East Meadow, 1959-76; asst. prof. clin. surgery State U. N.Y., 1976-77; asst. dir. surgery Creedmoor State Hosp., Queens Village, N.Y.; dep. med. examiner Nassau County, 1962-77, aviation med. examiner, 1975-77; dir. profl. edn. and tng. South Nassau Community Hosp., Oceanside, N.Y., 1964-69; chief profl. svcs. Western Mass. Hosp., Westfield, 1977-79; med. dir. Holyoke (Mass.) Soldiers' Home, 1979-88. Author: (with others) Single Stage Treatment of Ano-Rectal Abscesses and Fistulas, 1958. Bd. Dirs. Nassau div. Am. Cancer Soc. 1966-74; pres. Hempstead Community Chest, 1965; trustee Cath. Hosp. Assn., 1973-76. Served as pilot USAAF, 1943-47. Decorated Air medals with 2 oak leaf clusters, Purple Heart. Fellow ACS, Internat. Coll. Surgeons, Am. Coll. Utilization Review Physicians (cert. 1977); mem. AMA, Nat. Med. Assn., Am. Coll. Utilization Review Physicians, Am. Acad. Med. Dirs., Nassau Acad. Medicine, Nassau Surg. Soc., Royal Soc. Medicine London (affiliate), Alpha Phi Alpha. Episcopalian.

GAINSFORD, SIR IAN, dental surgeon; b. Twickenham, Middlesex, Eng., June 24, 1930; s. Morris and Anne Freda (Aucken) Ginsberg; m. Carmel Liebster, June 13, 1957; children—Ann, Jeremy, Deborah. LDSRCS King's Coll., London U., 1955; BDS, London U., 1956; DDS with honors, Toronto (Can.) U., 1960; Fellow Dental Surgery Royal Coll. Surgeons, Eng., 1968, mem. Gen. Dental Surgery Royal Coll. Surgeons, Eng., 1979. Lectr., King's Coll. Hosp. Med. Sch., London, 1956-57, London Hosp. Med. Coll., 1957-60, sr. lectr., 1960-70; sr. lectr., cons. King's Coll. Med. Sch., London, 1970—, vice-dean dental studies, 1973-77, dean Faculty of Clin. Dentistry, dir. Clin. Dental Services, 1977-87, dean Kings Coll. Sch. Medicine and Dentistry, 1988—; examiner London U., Leeds U., Royal Coll. Surgeons, Hong Kong U. Author: Silver Amalgam in Clinical Practice, 1965, 3d edit. 1992; co-author film: Amalgam Restoration, 1967. Decorated knight HMH Queen Elizabeth II. Fellow Kings Coll., Royal Soc. Medicine (mem. council odontology sect. 1983, pres. 1993), Internat. Coll. Dentists; mem. Am. Dental Soc. London (past pres.), Am. Dental Soc. Europe (past pres.), Brit. Soc. Restorative Dentistry (past pres.), Am. Coll. Dentists, Gen. Dental Coun. (chmn. edn. com. 1990-94); hon. mem. ADA. Clubs: Carlton, Athenaeum. Home: 31 York Ter East, London NW1 4PT, England Office: King's Coll Sch Med and Dent, Denmark Hill, London SE5 8RX, England

GAIPA, NANCY CHRISTINE, pharmacist; b. Benton Harbor, Mich., Oct. 11, 1949; d. Frank Thomas and Anne Marie (Scardina) G. BS, Marygrove Coll., Detroit, 1971; BS in Pharmacy, Wayne State U., 1992; postgrad. in Cons. Pharmacy, Ferris State U., 1996. Registered pharmacist, Mich.; cert. secondary educator, Mich. Educator Regina High Sch., Harper Woods, Mich., 1971-88; staff pharmacist Perry Drugs, Northville, Mich., 1993, Meijers, Inc., Westland, Mich., 1993—. Vol. Detroit Welfare Reform Coalition, 1989-91, Maral, Southfield, Mich., 1991. State of Mich. scholar, 1967-71. Mem. NOW, Detroit Area Women's Network, Am. Pharm. Assn., Mich. Pharmacists Assn., Golden Key Nat. Honor Soc., Iota Gamma Alpha, Rho Chi. Office: Meijers Inc Westland MI

GAITHER, NEAL STREATER, cardiologist; b. Ft. Smith, Ark., Dec. 18, 1953; s. George Manney and Dorothy (Streater) G.; m. Lisa Marie Cudworth, Mar. 31, 1980; children: Christopher, Stephanie, Katherine. BA, Cornell U., 1976; MD, Med. Coll. Va., 1980. Diplomate Am. Bd. Internal Medicine, Nat. Bd. Med. Examiners. Commd. 2d lt. U.S. Army, 1980, advanced through grades to lt. comdr.; resident Tripler Army Med. Ctr., Honolulu, 1980-83; staff internist Ft. Knox (Ky.), 1983-87; cardiology fellow Walter Reed Army Med. Ctr., Washington, 1987-89, attending cardiologist, 1989-92; attending cardiologist Winchester (Va.) Med. Ctr., 1992—; consulting cardiologist City Hosp., Martinsburg, W.Va., 1994—; clin. tchg. asst. medicine John A. Burns Sch. of Medicine, U. Hawaii, 1982-83; assoc. clin. prof. medicine U. Louisville Sch. of Medicine, 1985-87; instr. in medicine F. Edward Hebert Sch. of Medicine, Uniformed Svcs. U. of Health Scis., Bethesda, Md., 1988-89, asst. prof. medicine, 1989-92. Contbr. articles to profl. jours. Fellow Am. Coll. Physicians, Am. Coll. Cardiology; mem. Am. Heart Assn. Episcopalian. Office: Panhandle Cardiovascular 2010 Oates Dr Ste 101 Martinsburg WV 25401-8896

GAITZ, CHARLES MILTON, geriatric psychiatrist; b. Victoria, Tex., May 7, 1922; s. Jacob and Evelyn (Gerson) G.; m. Celia Speer, Aug. 28, 1949 (dec. 1985); children: Jeffrey Preston, Debra Lynn, Ronald Steven; m. Arlene Fay LaVetter, Feb. 26, 1989. BA, Rice U., 1942; MD, U. Tex. Med. Br., 1946. Diplomate Am. Bd. Psychiatry and Neurology. Intern U. Chgo. Clinics, 1946-47; resident in psychiatry Phipps Clinic, Johns Hopkins U., Balt., 1949-52; clin. prof. Baylor Coll. Medicine, Houston, 1952-96, prof. emeritus, 1996—; head gerontology and geriatric psychiatry tng. and rsch. Tex. Rsch. Inst. Mental Scis., Houston, 1960-85, postdoctoral fellow in geriatric psychiatry and psychology, co-dir., 1979-85; clin. prof. U. Tex. Med. Sch., Houston, 1984—; med. dir. geropsychiatry AMI Bellaire Hosp., Houston, 1986-92; med. dir. psychiat. day treatment Sam Houston Hosp., Houston, 1992-94; cons. psychiatry Seven Acres Jewish Geriatric Ctr., Houston, 1956—; chief psychiatry St. Anthony Ctr., Houston, 1965-88; founding pres. Houston Internat. Hosp., 1972-74. Organizer, co-editor: Aging and the Brain, 1972, Aging 2000: Our Health Care Destiny, 1984; contbr. numerous articles to profl. jours. V.p. Jewish Community Ctr., Houston, 1977; bd. dirs. Sheltering Arms; chairperson Lou Lewis Meml. Symposium, Seven Acres, Houston, 1985—. Capt. U.S. Army, 1943-49. Recipient rsch. award Mental Health Assn. Houston-Harris County, 1984. Fellow Am. Coll. Psychiatrists, Gerontol. Soc. Am. (pres. 1976-77, Freeman award 1986), Am. Psychiat. Assn. (chmn. coun. on aging 1981-83, Jack Weinberg Meml. award 1995); mem. Group for Advancement Psychiatry (chmn. com. on aging 1978-83). Home: 121 N Post Oak Ln Apt 1101 Houston TX 77024-7712

GAJ, STANLEY THOMAS, pharmacist, computer business consultant; b. Meriden, Conn., Sept. 28, 1954; s. Stanley John and Dorothy Frances (Baigert) Gaj; m. Cecile Elisabeth Hanson Gaj, June 26, 1982. BS in Pharmacy, U. Conn., 1977; MBA, Western New England Coll., 1992. Registered Pharmacist. Pharmacist, mgr. Arthur Drug Stores, Hartford, Conn., 1977-83, Brooks Drug, West Hartford, Conn., 1983-84, CVS Pharmacy, Manchester, Conn., 1984-88; pharmacist western Mass. region CVS Pharmacy, 1988-93, pharmacist so. Conn. region, 1993—; owner Northeast Consultants Computer and Bus. Consulting Firm, Meriden, Conn.; pharmacy instr. U. Conn., Storrs, 1979-80, pvt. computer bus. cons., 1992—. Home and Office: 154 Thorpe Ave Meriden CT 06450

GAJDUSEK, DANIEL CARLETON, pediatrician, research virologist; b. Yonkers, N.Y., Sept. 9, 1923; s. Karl A. and Ottilia D. (Dobroczki) G.; children: Ivan Mbagintao, Josede Figirliyong, Jesus Raglmar, Jesus Mororui, Mathias Maradol, Jesus Tamel, Jesus Salalu, John Paul Runman, Yavine Borima, Arthur Yolwa, Joe Yongorimah Kintoki, Thomas Youmog, Toni Wanevi, Toname Ikabala, Magame Prima, Senavayo Anua, Igitava Yoviga, Luwi Ikavara, Iram'bin'ai Undae'mai, Susanna Undapmaina, Steven Malrui, John Fasug Raglmar, Launako Wate, Louise Buwana, Regina Etaugthaw Raglmar, Vincent Ayin, Daniel Sumal, Iyo Fanechigiy Raglmar John Clayton Harongsemal, Peter Paul Ffiran, Jason Sohorang, Edwina Wes Mugunbey, Brenda Gillippin, Carleton Kalikaipapadaua Mbagintao, Basil Talonu, Gideon Waiwaime, Okovi Yarao, Sesario Sigam Salalu. BS, U. Rochester, 1943; MD, Harvard U., 1946, DSc (hon.), 1987; NRC fellow, Calif. Inst. Tech., 1948-49; DSc (hon.), U. Rochester, 1977, Med. Coll. Ohio, 1977, Washington & Jefferson Coll., 1980, Hahneman Med. Coll., 1983, Med. and Dental Coll. of N.J., 1987; DHL (hon.), Hamilton Coll., 1977, U. Hawaii, 1986; LL.D. (hon.), U. Aberdeen, Scotland, 1980; Dr. honoris causa, U. Aix-Marseille, France, 1977, U. Lisbon, Portugal, 1991, U. Milan, Italy, 1992, U. Lodz, Poland, 1995, U. Las Palmas, Spain, 1995, U. Komenius, Bratislava, Slovakia, 1996. Diplomate Am. Bd. Pediatrics. Intern, resident Babies Hosp., Columbia Presbyn. Med. Center, N.Y.C., 1946-47; resident pediatrics Children's Hosp., Cin., 1947-48; pediatric med. mission Germany, 1948; resident, clin. and research fellow Childrens Hosp., Boston, 1949-51; research fellow pediatrics and infectious diseases Harvard U., 1949-52; rsch. virologist Walter Reed AMSGS, Washington, 1952-53; with Institut Pasteur, Teheran, Iran, 1954-55; vis. investigator Nat. Found. Infantile Paralysis, Walter and Eliza Hall Inst. Med. Research, Melbourne, Australia, 1955-57; dir. program for study child growth and devel. and disease patterns in primitive cultures and lab. slow, latent and temperate virus infections NINDS, NIH, Bethesda, Md., 1958—; chief Lab. Ctrl. Nervous System Studies, 1970—; chief scientist rsch. vessel Alpha Helix expdn. to Banks and Torres Islands, New Hebrides, South Solomon Islands, 1971; hon. prof. virology Hupei Med. Coll., Wuhan, China, 1986; hon. prof. neurology Beijing Med. U., 1987, Las Palmas de Gran Canaria, Spain, 1993; hon. faculty Med. Sch. U. of Papua New Guinea, 1980; vis. prof. Royal Soc. Medicine, London, 1987; Schulz lectr. Stanford U., 1995. Author: (book) Hemorrhagic Fevers and Mycotoxicoses in the USSR, 1951; contbr. over 45 articles to profl. jours. Recipient E. Meade Johnson award Am. Acad. Pediatrics, 1963, Superior Svc. award NIH, HEW, 1970, Disting. Svc. award HEW, 1975, Prof. Lucian Dautrebande prize in Pathophysiology Belgium, 1976, Nobel prize in Physiology and Medicine, 1976, Cotzias prize Am. Neurol. Assn., 1978, Huxley medal Royal Anthrop. Inst. Gt. Britain and Ireland, 1989, Gold medal Czechoslovak Med. Soc., 1989, Mudd award Internat. Union Microbiol. Socs., 1990, Gold medal, prize 3d. Internat. Congress on Alzheimers Disease, 1992, 2nd Pacific Rim Biotech. award, 1992, Gold medal Basque Acad. Med., 1993, Disting. Lectr. award Internat. Human Retrovirlogy, 1994, Disting. Scientist award Montefiore Hosp. Albert Einstein Sch. Medicine, 1995, Gold Medal Slovak Acad. Sci., Bratislava, 1996—; Dyer lectr. NIH, 1974, Heath Clark lectr. U. London, 1974, B.K. Rachford lectr. Children's Hosp. Research Found., Cin., 1975, Langmuir lectr. CDC, Atlanta, 1975, Withering lectr U. Birmingham, Eng., 1976, Cannon Elie lectr. Boston Children's Med. Center, 1976, Zale lectr. U. Tex., Dallas, 1976, Bayne-Jones lectr. Johns Hopkins Med. Sch., Balt., 1976, Harvey lectr. N.Y. Acad. Medicine, 1977, J.E. Smadel lectr. Infectious Disease Soc. Am., 1977, Burnet lectr. Australasian Soc. Infectious Disease, 1978, Mapother lectr. U. London, 1978, Disting. lectr. in medicine Mayo Clinic, 1978aiser Meml. lectr. U. Hawaii, 1979, Eli Lilly lectr. U. Toronto, 1979, Payne lectr. Children's Hosp. D.C., 1981, Ray C. Moon lectr. Angelo State U., Tex., 1981, Silliman lectr. Yale U., 1981, Blackfan lectr. Children's Hosp. Med. Ctr., Boston, 1981, Hitchcock Meml. lectr. U. Calif.-Berkeley, 1982, Nelson lectr. U. Calif.-Davis, 1982, Derick-MacKerres lectr. Queensland Inst. Med. Research, 1982, Bicentennial lectr. Harvard U. Sch. Medicine, 1982, Cartwright lectr. Columbia U., 1982, lectr. Chinese Acad. Med. Sci., 1983, Michelson lectr., prof., U. Tenn., Memphis, 1986, plenary lectr., Chinese Assn. Med. Virology, Yentai, 1986, returned Nobel Laureate, Karolinska Inst., Stockholm and U. Tromsö, Norway, 1986, Nobel Jubilee lectr. Karolinska U., Uppsala U., U. Trondheim, Norway, 1991, Rubbo Orator Australian Soc. Microbiology, 1992, Ashton Graybiel lectr. Naval Aerospace Med. Rsch. Lab, 1994. Mem. NAS, Am. Acad. Arts and Scis., Am. Philos. Soc., Deutsche Akad., Naturförscher Leopoldina, Russian Acad. Med. Sci., Australian Acad. Sci., Acad. Sci. Sakha Republic, Russian Acad. Sci., World Acad. Art and Sci., Acads. Nacionales de Medicina Mexico, Colombia and Argentina, Czechoslovak Acad. Scis., Third World Acad. Scis., Internat. Acad. Scis., Royal Coll. Physicians (Edinburgh), Royal Anthrop. Inst. Gt. Britain and Ireland, Soc. Pediatric Rsch., Am. Pediatric Soc., Am. Soc. Human Genetics, Am. Acad. Neurology (Cotzias prize 1979), Soc. Neurosci., Am. Epidemiol. Soc., Infectious Diseases Soc. Am., Soc. des Oceanistes, Paris, Papua and New Guinea Sci. Soc., Phi Beta Kappa, Sigma Xi.

GALABURDA, ALBERT MARK, neurologist, researcher, educator; b. Santiago, Chile, July 20, 1948; came to U.S., 1963; s. John and Eva (Drinberg) G.; m. Margaret S. Okun, July 27, 1969; children: Adam, Daniel, Laura, Julia, Michael. AB, Boston U., 1971, MD, 1971; MA (hon.), Harvard U., 1995. Intern Boston City Hosp., 1971-72, resident in internal medicine, 1972-74, resident in neurology, 1973-76; clin. fellow Boston U., 1971-74; clin. fellow Harvard U. Med. Sch., Boston, 1973-76, instr. neurology, 1976-80, asst. prof. neurology, 1980-84, assoc. prof., 1984—, prof. neurology and neurosci., 1994-95, Emily Fisher Landau prof. neurology and neurosci., 1995—; dir. dyslexia rsch. Beth Israel Hosp., Boston, 1980—, dir. div. behavioral neurology, 1993—; rsch. advisor Orton Dyslexia Soc., Balt., 1984—. Author: Cerebral Lateralization, 1985; editor: From Reading to Neurons, 1989, Neuropathology of Dyslexia, 1993; editorial bd. Neuropsychologia, 1987-89, Jour. Learning Disabilities, 1989—. Recipient Pattison prize in neurosci. Inst. Child Devel. Rsch., N.Y.C. Mem. AAAS (biol. sci. com. 1988—), Am. Acad. Neurology, Am. Neurol. Assn., Chilean Soc. Neurology and Psychiatry (hon.). Office: Beth Israel Hosp 330 Brookline Ave Boston MA 02215-5400

GALAMBOS, JOHN THOMAS, medical educator, internist; b. Budapest, Hungary, Oct. 29, 1921; came to U.S., 1947; m. Eva G. Cohn; children: Sharon Tobae Galambos McDuff, John Douglas, Michael Robert. BS, U. Ga., 1948; MD, Emory U., 1952. Diplomate Nat. Bd. Med. Examiners, Am. Bd. Internal Medicine, Am. Bd. Gastroenterology. Intern Barnes Hosp., St. Louis, 1952-53; resident U. Chgo. Clinics, 1953-55; dir. gastroenterology teaching program Emory U. Sch. Medicine, Atlanta, 1957-92, dir. gastroenterology labs., 1958-92, dir. div. digestive diseases, 1966-92; dir. Gastroenterology Clinic Grady Hosp., Atlanta, 1957-92; mem. adv. bd. Nat. Inst. Digestive Diseases, NIH, Washington, 1985-88. Author: Cirrhosis, 1979, Digestive Diseases, 1983; author or co-author 36 book chpts.; contbr. 165 articles to profl. jours. Fellow ACP, Am. Coll. Gastroenterology (pres. 1975), Am. Gastroenterol. Assn., Am. Assn. for Study Liver Diseases, Internat. Assn. for Study Liver Diseases, Alpha Omega Alpha. Republican. Jewish. Office: 95 Collier Rd NW Ste 4075 Atlanta GA 30309-1721

GALAN, VINCENT, anethesiologist; b. Havana, May 31, 1960; came to the U.S., 1962; s. Manuel Vincent and Alice (Riesgo) G.; m. Maureen Elizabeth Barbas, Mar. 24, 1990; children: Marissa Marie, Annalyse Isabel. BS in Chemistry cum laude; BS in Chemistry, Berry Coll., 1980; MD, U. Puerto Rico, 1984, MD with splty. in anesthesia, 1987; MD with pain subsplty., SUNY, Bklyn., 1988; MBA in Fin., Ga. State U., 1996. Diplomate Am. Bd. Anesthesia, Am. Acad. Pain Mgmt. Intern, resident Univ. P.R. Dist. Hosps., P.R., 1984-87; asst. instr. Downstate Med.-SUNY, Bklyn., 1987-88; vis. pain fellow Hermann Hosp., Houston, 1988; fellow in cardiac anesthesia Cleve. Clinic, 1989; co-dir. pain clinic So. Regional Med. Ctr., Atlanta, 1991—; contbg. test writer Am. Bd. Anesthesia, Hartford, Conn., 1995—. Contbr. articles to profl. jours.; abstract reviewer Pain Digest, 1995—. Mem. Am. Soc. Regional Anesthesia, Soc. Cardiovascular Anesthesiologists, Am. Acad. Pain Medicine, Am. Soc. Anesthesia, AMA, Ga. Med. Soc. Roman Catholic.

GALANDIUK, SUSAN, colon and rectal surgeon, educator; b. N.Y.C., Mar. 6, 1957; d. Joseph and Dora (Neu) G.; m. Hiram C. Polk Jr., Dec. 22, 1991. BS cum laude, SUNY, Albany, 1976; MD summa cum laude, Julius Maximilians U., Wuerzburg, Germany, 1982. Diplomate Am. Bd. Surgery, Am. Bd. Colon and Rectal Surgery. Surg. intern Chirurgische Univ. Klinik, Julius Maximilians U., Wuerzburg, Germany, 1982-83; surg. intern Cleve. Clinic Found., 1983-84, surg. resident, 1984-88; Price fellow in surg. rsch., dept. surgery U. Louisville, 1988-89, instr. dept. surgery, 1990-91, asst. prof. dept. surgery, 1991—, assoc. prof., 1996—; colon and rectal surgery fellow Mayo Clinic, Rochester, Minn., 1989-90; presenter in field. Author chpts. to books; contbr. articles to profl. jours. Chmn. fund raising com. ARC, Louisville, 1993; chair med. adv. com. Ky. chpt. Crohn's and Colitis Found. Am., Louisville, 1993—. William E. Lower Fellow Thesis prize Cleve. Clinic Found., 1986. Fellow ACS, Am. Soc. Colon and Rectal Surgeons (mem. rsch. found. young rschrs. com., mem. program com. 1994—); mem. AMA, Am. Med. Women's Assn., Am. Soc. Microbiology, Am. Soc. Univ. Profs., Assn. Acad. Surgery, Assn. Surg. Edn., Assn. Women Surgeons, Collegium Internat. Chirurgiae Digestivae, Jefferson County Med. Soc., Ky. Med. Assn. (mem. cancer com.), Louisville Surg. Soc., Hiram C. Polk Jr. Surg. Soc., Ohio Valley Soc. Colon and Rectal Surgeons, Priestly Soc., Soc. Surg. Alimentary Tract, Soc. Am. Gastrointestinal Endoscopic Surgeons, Soc. Surg. Oncology, Southeastern Surg. Congress, Surg. Infection Soc., Soc. of Univ. Surgeons, Am. Soc. Gastrointestinal Endoscopists, Ctrl. Surg. Assn. Greek Catholic. Office: U Louisville Dept Surgery 550 S Jackson St Louisville KY 40202-1622

GALANOPOULOS, KELLY, biomedical engineer; b. Athens, Greece, Jan. 4, 1952; came to U.S. 1970, naturalized, 1976; d. Panayotis and Catherine (Calas) G.; m. Dale S. Kruchten, Sept. 4, 1982; children: Catherine Roberta Kruchten, Stephanie Diane Kruchten. BA, CUNY, 1974; MS, Poly. Inst. N.Y., 1978, postgrad., 1982—; postgrad. L.I. U., 1982—. Dir. bio-med. engrng. Wyckoff Heights Hosp., Bklyn., 1980-83, Bronx Lebanon Hosp., N.Y.C., 1983-89; dir. clin. engrng. Mt. Sinai Med. Ctr., N.Y.C., 1991—; cons. Environ. Co., N.Y.C., 1980-85, Joint Purchasing, N.Y.C., 1980—; premier health alliance of N.Y. biomed. engrng. adminstrs., 1991—; lectr. in field. Mem. Am. Soc. for Hosp. Engrng. of Am. Hosp. Assn., Am. Coll. Clin. Engrs., Assn. Advancement Med. Instrumentation, IEEE, Soc. Women Engrs., N.Y. Acad. Scis. Office: Mt Sinai Med Ctr 1 Gustave L Levy Pl New York NY 10029-6504

GALANTER, EUGENE, psychologist, educator; b. Phila., Oct. 27, 1924; s. Max and Sarah (Honigman) G.; m. Patricia Anderson, Dec. 22, 1962; children: Alicia, Gabrielle, Michelle. A.B., Swarthmore Coll., 1950; A.M., U. Pa., 1951, Ph.D., 1953. From instr. to prof. psychology U. Pa., 1952-62; research fellow Harvard U., 1955-56, Center Advanced Study Behavioral Scis., 1958-59; chmn. dept. psychology U. Wash., 1962-64, prof., 1964-66; Joseph Klingenstein vis. prof. social psychology Columbia U., N.Y.C., 1966-67; prof. psychology Columbia U., 1967—; Cons. NIH, NSF, also to industry; in field. Mem. Council for Biology in Human Affairs; chmn. commn. on biology, learning and behavior Salk Inst. Author: Plans and Structure of Behavior, 1960, 2d edit., 1986, New Directions in Psychology, 1962, Textbook of Elementary Psychology, 1966, Kids & Computers: The Parents' Microcomputer Handbook, 1983, Kids & Computers: Elementary Programming for Kids in BASIC, 1983, Kids & Computers: Advanced Programming Handbook, 1984; editor: Handbook of Mathematical Psychology, 3 vols., 1963-64, Readings in Mathematical Psychology, 2 vols., 1963-65, Psych Tech Notes, 1988, version 2.1, 1994. Served with AUS, 1942-46. Fellow AAAS; mem. APA, Eastern Psychol. Assn., Acoustical Soc. Am., N.Y. Acad. Scis., Assn. Aviation Psychologists (pres. 1970-71), Human Factors Soc., Internat. Soc. for Psychophysics, Sigma Xi. Office: Columbia U 324 Schermerhorn Hall New York NY 10027

GALANTER, MARC, psychiatrist, educator; b. N.Y.C., Sept. 17, 1941; s. Jacob and Ada (Simms) G.; m. Wynne L. Roberts, June 7, 1964; children—Cathryn, Margit. B.A., Columbia U., 1963; M.D., Albert Einstein Coll. Medicine, 1967. Diplomate Am. Bd. Psychiatry and Neurology. Intern UCLA Hosp., 1967-68; resident in psychiatry Albert Einstein Coll. Medicine-Bronx Mcpl. Hosp. Ctr., 1968-71, fellow in community psychiatry, 1972-73, clin. instr., 1972-74, dir. Drug and Alcohol Cons. Service, 1972-75, career tchr. drug abuse and alcoholism Nat. Inst. on Alcohol Abuse and Alcoholism, Nat. Inst. Drug Abuse, 1973-76, asst. prof., 1974-78, dir. div. alcoholism and drug abuse, 1975-87, assoc. prof., 1978-83, prof. dept. psychiatry, 1983-87; prof. psychiatry, dir. div. alcoholism and drug abuse NYU Sch. Med., 1987—; rsch. scientist Collaborating Ctr. WHO, 1987—; clin. assoc. Lab. Clin. Psychopharmacology, NIMH, Washington, 1970-72; instr. psychiatry residency program St. Elizabeth's Hosp.; presenter at profl. confs. U.S., Can., Thailand, Germany, Japan, India, Kenya and Italy; chmn. Nat. Conf. on Alcohol and Drug Abuse Edn., 1977; program chmn. Internat. Conf. Med. Edn. in Alcohol and Drug Abuse, WHO and Assn. Med. Edn. and Rsch. in Substance Abuse, 1982, founder, pres., 1976-77; dir. Lab. Alcoholism and Drug Abuse WHO. Editor: Ofcl. Sci. Procs. of Nat. Coun. on Alcoholism, 1978—, Alcohol and Drug Abuse in Medical Education, 1980, (book series) Currents in Alcoholism, 1979, 80, 81, Recent Developments in Alcoholism; mem. editl. bd. Am. Jour. Drug and Alcohol Abuse, 1978—; assoc. editor jour. Alcoholism Clin. and Exptl. Rsch., Am. Jour. of Addictions, 1979, Jour. Substance Abuse Treatment, 1995—; co-editor: Advances in the Psychosocial Treatment of Alcoholism, 1984; editor-in-chief Substance Abuse Jour., 1978—; author: Network Therapy for Alcohol and Drug Abuse, 1993, Cults: Faith, Health and Coercion, 1989. Recipient Psychopharmacology award Am. Psychol. Assn., 1972; Career Tchr. award in drug abuse and alcoholism NIMN, 1973-77; ann. Book award Commonwealth Fund, 1978-82, Macarthur medal Assn. Med. Edn. and Rsch., 1994. Fellow Am. Psychiat. Assn. (chmn. panel on alcoholism, nat. task force on psychiat. treatment 1983—, mem. task force on cults 1977-80, mem. com. on alcoholism, chmn. com. on addiction edn. 1992—, chmn. com. on religion 1985-90, Gold Achievement award 1993); mem. AAAS, Am. Soc. on Addiction Medicine (bd. dirs. 1986—), Am. Bd. Psychiatry and Neurology (vice chair com. om added qualifications in addictino psychiatry), Rsch. Soc. on Alcoholism (sec. 1983-85), N.Y. Acad. Medicine (addiction com. 1985—), N.Y. State Task Force on Dual Psychiat. and Addictive Disorders (task force chmn. 1986-89, 93), N.Y. Psychiat. Soc., Am. Acad. Psychiatrists in Alcoholism and Addictions (v.p. 1987-89, pres. 1991-93), World Psychiat. Assn. (sect. drug abuse and alcoholism). Office: 285 Central Park W New York NY 10024-3006

GALAS, DAVID JOHN, molecular biology educator, researcher, administrator; b. St. Petersburg, Fla., Feb. 25, 1944; s. David Emanuel and Catherine Elizabeth (Filan) G.; div.; children: David John Jr., John Ryan. BA in Physics, U. Calif. Berkeley, 1967; MA in Physics, U. Calif. Davis, 1968, PhD in Physics, 1972; pres., chief scientific officer. Sr. scientist Lawrence Livermore Nat. Labs., Livermore, Calif., 1974-77; chargé de recherche dept. molecular biology U. Geneva (Switzerland), 1977-81; asst. prof. U. So. Calif., L.A., 1981-83, assoc. prof., 1983-86, prof., 1986—, dir. dept. molecular biology, 1986-90; dir. Health and environ. rsch. Dept. Energy, Washington, 1990-93; pres., CEO Darwin Molecular Corp., Seattle, 1993-95, exec. v.p., chief sci. officer, 1995—. Contbr. articles and revs. to profl. jours., chpts. to books. Capt. USAF, 1972-74.

GALASK, RUDOLPH PETER, obstetrician and gynecologist; b. Fort Dodge, Iowa, Dec. 23, 1935; s. Peter Otto and Adeline Amelia (Maranesi) G.; m. Gloria Jean Vasti, June 19, 1965. BS, Drake U., 1959; MD, U. Iowa, 1964, MS, 1967. Diplomate Am. Bd. Obstetrics and Gynecology. Research fellow in microbiology U. Iowa, Iowa City, 1965-67, resident in ob-gyn., 1967-70, asst. prof., 1970-74, asst. prof. microbiology, 1973-74, assoc. prof. obstetrics and gynecology microbiology, 1974-78, prof., 1978—; chmn. exec. com. Coll. Medicine, 1992-93; cons. various pharm. and diagnostic cos. Editor: Infectious Diseases in the Female Patient, 1986-89; contbr. numerous articles to profl. jours. Served to staff sgt. USNG, 1954-64. Recipient numerous grants to study the efficacy of various antibiotics and chemotherapeutics. Fellow Am. Gynecol. and Obstet. Soc., Am. Coll. Obstetricians and Gynecologists, Infectious Disease Am.; mem. AAAS, Cen. Assn. for Obstetricians and Gynecologists, Infectious Disease Soc. for Ob-Gyn. (pres. 1982-84, founding mem.), Soc. Gynecol. Investigation (coun. 1987-90), Queens Gynecol. Soc. (hon.), Tex. Assn. Obstetricians and Gynecologists (hon.), Am. Soc. Microbiology, Izaac Walton League, Ducks Unltd. Club (sponsor), Sigma Xi. Roman Catholic. Office: Univ Iowa Hosps Dept Ob-Gyn Iowa City IA 52242

GALASSIE, JOHN PERRY, medical supervisor; b. Appleton, Wis., Nov. 3, 1941; s. Philip Anthony and Lylase S. (Voit) G.; m. Dorothy Jean Bristol, Dec. 14, 1963; children: John Perry Jr., Angelina Maria. BS, U. Nebr., 1973. Cert. physician asst. Nat. Commn. on Certification of Physician Assts., 1975; lic. physician asst., Utah, 1990. Med. lab technician USAF, 1960-71, maj., physician asst., 1973-90; physician asst. FHP, Ogden, Utah, 1990-91; med. supr. Pharm. divsn. Bayer Corp., Ogden, 1991—. Fellow Utah Acad. Physician Assts. (Life Svc. award 1991), Soc. Air Force Physician Assts., Am. Acad. Physician Assts.; mem. Am. Legion, Am. Assn. Retired Persons. Home: 935 E 3000 N # 68 Layton UT 84040-6552 Office: Bayer Corp 3073 Harrison Blvd Ogden UT 84403

GALATIUS, SOREN, cardiologist; b. Copenhagen, Mar. 20, 1960; s. Frode and Helen Maria (Pedersen) Galatius-Jensen; m. Jette Stagsted Larson; 1 child, Emilie. MD, Copenhagen U., 1989. Resident Huidoure Hosp., Denmark, 1989-90, Hillerød Hosp., Denmark, 1991-93; rsch. fellow Rigs Hosp., Denmark, 1993-95; sr. resident Rigs Hosp., 1995—; instr. Danish Ski Assn. Fellow Danish Soc. Cardiology. Home: Weysesgade 53, DK 2100 Copenhagen Denmark Office: Rigs Hosp Dept Cardiology, Blegdam str 9, DK 2100 Copenhagen Denmark

GALBERSHTAD, SEMYON, biologist, neurophysiologist, researcher; b. Utena, Lithuania, Nov. 15, 1915; came to U.S., 1980; s. Chackel and Frida (Levin) G.; m. Khaya Mebelyte Galbershtad, Aug. 20, 1947; 1 child, Anna Halberstadt-Komar. D in Biol. Scis., Corresp. Moscow U., Lithuania, 1954. Tchr. gymnasiums, Vilnius, Kaunas, Lithuania, 1939-41; lab. asst. Vilnius U., 1945-48, sr. lectr., 1948-55, docent, 1955-67, prof., 1967-79; lectr. and author Russian Radio "Horisont", N.Y.C., 1980. Author: (in Lithuanian) Psyche and its Evolution, 1969, (in Russian) Nervous Regulation of Muscular Activity, 1975, (in English) New Aspects of Neural Regulation of Muscular Activity, 1991, (in English) The Knowledge of Science and the Wisdom of the Organism, 1993, Society of Naturalists, 1961, 63; contbr. numerous articles to sci. jours. Lt. Soviet Army, 1941-45. Mem. Jewish Assn. for the Aged (adv. com. 1982), Lithuanian Assn. Physiologists, Leningrad Assn. Naturalists, Leningrad Assn. Physiologists, Vilnius U. Chess Team (capt. 1955-79), N.Y. Acad. Scis., Assn. World War II Invalids (v.p. 1983-90, pres. 1992), Global Heritage Union (v.p., head dept. sci. 1989). Office: NY Acad Scis 2 E Sixty Third St New York NY 10021

GALBRAITH, GARY GENE, professor of psychology; b. DuQuoin, Ill., Feb. 6, 1934; s. Leonard and Edith Belle (Koenegstein) G.; m. Sandra Ann Salvaggiio, Mar. 18, 1966; children: Maury Scott, Cara Kirsten. BA, So. Ill. U., 1956; MA, Ohio State U., 1959, PhD, 1964; postgrad., U. Oreg. Med. Sch., 1978-79. Diplomate Am. Bd. Psychology; lic. psychologist, Wash. Instr. Ohio State U., Columbus, 1963-64; asst. prof. Pa. State U., State Coll., 1964-70; assoc. prof. Ariz. State U., Tempe, 1970-72; prof., dir. clin. tng. Wash. State U., Pullman, 1972—; resident U. Oreg. Health Sci. Ctr., Portland, 1978-79; postdoctoral fellow Chgo. Rehab. Inst., 1989; cons. VA, 1964-80; psychologist U.S. Army Hosp., Ft. Hood, Tex., 1960-63; dir. eastern br. Wash. Mental Illness Inst., 1990-91. Contbr. articles to profl. jours. cons. to developmental disabilities groups, Pullman, Wash., 1973-80. Capt. U.S. Army, 1958-63. Mem. Am. Psychol. Assn. Democrat. Office: Wash State U Pullman WA 99164

GALBRAITH, RICHARD FREDERICK, physician, neurologist; b. Seattle, Apr. 8, 1931; s. Maurice Frederick and Florence Evelyn (Smith) G.; m. Margaret Jean Patten, July 30, 1956; children: Deborah, Mark, Christine, Kevin. BS, Seattle U., 1952; MD, St. Louis U., 1956. Diplomate Am. Bd. Psychiatry and Neurology (examiner 1970-85). Intern St. John's Hosp., St. Louis, 1956-57; resident in medicine and neurology Mayo Grad. Sch. Medicine, Rochester, Minn., 1959-64; physcian, neurologist Mpls. Clinic Neurology, 1965—; pres., chmn. Found. Health Care, 1979-81. Served to lt. Med. Service Corps, USN, 1957-59. Fellow Am. Acad. Neurology, AMA, Hennipen County Med. Soc. Home: 6228 Sandpiper Ct Edina MN 55436-1926 Office: Mpls Clinic Neurology 4225 Golden Valley Rd Minneapolis MN 55422-4215

GALBRAITH, WILLIAM BRUCE, physician, educator; b. Romeo, Mich., Oct. 21, 1930; s. Bruce McKenzie and Helen Athelene (Stringham) G.; m. Jo Anne Fetterly Ames, June 27, 1953; children: Elise, Susan, Scott. BS, Ariz. State U., 1953; MD, George Washington U., 1957. Diplomate Am. Bd. Internal Medicine. Internship Good Samaritan Hosp., Phoenix, 1957-58; residency U. Iowa Hosps. and Clinics, Iowa City, 1958-61; internal medicine instr. Coll. Medicine U. Iowa, Iowa City, 1961-63, asst. prof. internal medicine, 1963-65, assoc. internal medicine, dir. gen. medicine, 1994-95; prof. clin. internal medicine, dir. gen. medicine tng. Coll.Medicine U. Iowa, Iowa City, 1995—; owner Internists P.C., Cedar Rapids, Iowa, 1965-93, pres., 1986-93; bd. dirs. Am. Bd. Internal Medicine, Phila., 1992-96. Fellow ACP (gov. for Iowa 1979-83, Laureate award 1988); mem. Iowa Clin. Soc. Internal Medicine (Internist of Yr. 1994), Am. Diabetes Assn., Soc. Gen. Internal Medicine, Alpha Omega Alpha. Office: U Iowa Hosps and Clinics 200 Hawkins Dr # BT 1036 Iowa City IA 52242-1009

GALDIERI, ANTHONY AUGUST, psychologist; b. Scranton, Pa., June 17, 1943; s. Christopher and Ann (Bocchino) G.; m. Judith Baldin, Oct. 2, 1960 (div. Feb. 1974); m. Mary Ellen Jordan, May 26, 1978; 1 child, Anthony. BS, U. Scranton, 1965, MS, 1966; PhD, Ohio U., 1971. Lic. psychologist, Pa. Cons. Scranton (Pa.) Sch. Dist., 1973-90, Friendship House Children's Ctr., Scranton, 1972—; pvt. practice psychology Scranton, 1972—; med. advisor Fed. Dept. Human and Health Svcs., Wilkes-Barre, Pa., 1986—. Fellow Pa. Psychol. Assn.; mem. APA, Nat. Register Mental Health Providers, Ea. Psychol. Assn. Home: 110 Gentilly Dr Clarks Summit PA 18411-1032 Office: Bank Towers 4th Fl 321 Spruce St Scranton PA 18503-1400

GALE, STANLEY WILLIAM, psychiatrist; b. Mpls., Apr. 30, 1947; s. Harvey and Florence (Lapp) G.; children: Shawna, Greg. BS, Yale U., 1970, JD, 1974, MD, 1975. Asst. psychiatrist N.Y. Hosp., N.Y.C., 1975-78; pvt. practice Providence, 1978—; mem. staff Butler Hosp., Providence, Miriam Hosp., Providence, Women's & Infant's Hosp., Providence, R.I. Hosp., Providence. Mem. Am. Psychiat. Assn., R.I. Med. Soc.

GALEF, HAROLD ROBERT, psychiatrist; b. N.Y.C., June 6, 1928; s. Joseph and Adelaide Irene (Obadiah) G.; m. Bernice Schutzer, May 26, 1983; m. Winifred Betty Kron, Sept. 17, 1950 (dec. 1969); children: Deborah, David. A.B., Syracuse U., 1948; M.A., Columbia U., 1949; M.D., Chgo. Med. Sch., 1953. Diplomate Am. Bd. Psychiatry. Intern, USPHS Hosp., S.I., N.Y., 1953-54; resident in psychiatry Hillside Hosp., 1956-57, Bronx Mcpl. Hosp. Ctr., 1957-59; practice psychiatry, N.Y.C., 1959—; clin. assos. prof. psychiatry Albert Einstein Med. Coll., Scarsdale N.Y., 1959—; supr., tng. analyst Westchester Ctr. for Psychotherapy and Psychoanalysis, White Plains, N.Y., 1978—, dir. 1995—. Served with USPHS, 1953-56. Fellow Am. Psychiat. Assn., Am. Acad. Psychoanalysis; mem. Am. Psychoanalytic Assn., Westchester Psychiat. Soc. (exec. coun. 1974-76), Westchester Psychoanalytic Soc. Avocations: chorale; foreign languages; etymology; reading; music. Home & Office: 15 Roosevelt Pl Scarsdale NY 10583-5909

GALEY, WILLIAM RALEIGH, JR., physiology educator; b. Boise, July 26, 1943; s. William Raleigh and Margaret Nancy (Sparkman) G.; children: Christina A., Scott A., Ryan W., Reid P. BS in Chemistry, Lewis and Clark Coll., 1965; PhD in Biochemistry, U. Oreg., 1969; postdoctoral biophysics, Harvard Med. Sch., 1971. Sr. biophysicist Alza Rsch. Corp., Palo Alto, Calif., 1971-72; asst. prof. physiology U. N.Mex. Sch. Medicine, Albuquerque, 1972-78, assoc. prof. physiology, 1978-84, prof. physiology, 1984—, dir. biomed. sci. grad. program, 1994—, asst. dean grad. studies, 1996—; cons. to trial lawyers; ednl. cons.; vis. prof. St. Georges U. Sch. Medicine, 1993-94; faculty mem. N.Mex. Jud. Tng. Program, 1992-94. Author/co-author numerous book chpts.; contbr. articles to profl. publs. Sr. judge N.Mex. Regional Sci. Fair, Albuquerque, 1975—; region dir. Basic Sci. Edn. Forum, 1990—; mentor H.S. Student Rsch. Apprenticeship Program, 1989—. Mem. Assn. of Am. Med. Colls. Home: 8 Crestwood Loop Dr Tijeras NM 87059 Office: U NMex Dept Physiology 915 Stanford Dr NE Albuquerque NM 87131

GALIE, FRANK D., sales executive; b. Norristown, Pa., Oct. 2, 1946; s. Peter J. and Mary M. (Schrader) G.; m. Mary M. Galie, Nov. 22, 1969; children: Jason, Stephen, Maegan. BS, Villanova U., 1974; MHA magna cum laude, St. Joseph's U., Phila., 1988. Coordinating mgr. support svc. dept. Wyoming Valley Hosp., Wilkes Barre, Pa., 1974-76, St. Agnes Med. Ctr., 1976-78; regional mgr. ServiceMaster, 1978-81, sr. survey engr., 1982-83; sr. mgmt. rep. ServiceMaster, Pa., N.J., 1983-91; sales mgr. ServiceMaster, Chgo., 1992-94; nat. sales exec. ServiceMaster, 1995—. V.p. bd. dirs. Methacton Sch. Dist., Fairview Village, 1992-95. With USMC, 1964-68, Vietnam. Mem. AM. Coll. Health Care Adminstrs., N.Y. Assn. Homes and Svcs. for Aging, Pa. Assn. Non-Profit Homes for Aging, N.J. Assn. Non-Profit Homes for Aging, Pa. Assn. Health Care Facilities, N.J. Assn. Health Care Facilities. Republican. Roman Catholic. Home: 7019 Cold Spring Dr Collegeville PA 19426

GALINSKY, DENNIS LEE, radiation oncologist, educator; b. Des Moines, Sept. 16, 1948; s. Sam and Joyce Geraldine (Givant) G.; m. Daryl Lee Goldstein, Nov. 9, 1975; children: Dana Lauren, David Lawrence. BS, Drake U., 1970; MD, U. Iowa, 1974. Diplomate Am. Bd. Radiology. Intern U. Ariz., Tucson, 1974-75, resident in radiation oncology, 1975-77; resident in radiation oncology U. Minn., Mpls., 1977-78; assoc. attending physician Evanston (Ill.) Hosp., 1978-80; dir. radiation oncology Copley Meml. Hosp., Aurora, Ill., 1980-89, U. Ill. Hosp., Chgo., 1991-93, DuPage Oncology Ctr., Winfield, Ill., 1993; assoc. prof. Rush U., Chgo., 1994—, 1994—; pvt. practice, Chgo., 1978; clin. assoc. Northwestern U., Evanston, 1978-80; co-dir. rev. course Osler Inst., Lisle, Ill., 1991; presenter Internat. Congress Radiology, 1989, European Soc. Radiation Oncology, 1990. Contbr. articles to med. jours. Bd. dirs. Congregation Beth Shalom, Naperville, Ill., 1984-85; mem. Dist. 27 Sch. Bd., Northbrook, Ill., 1990—. Graneee NSF, 1968. Mem. AMA, Am. Coll. Radiation Oncology (vice chmn. 1991-92), Chgo. Met. Area Radiation oncology Soc. (pres. 1987-88), Beta Beta Beta.. Office: Nuclear Oncology SC 6929 W Ogden Ave Berwyn IL 60402

GALIOTO, FRANK MARTIN, JR., pediatric cardiologist, educator; b. Newark, N.J., Sept. 6, 1942; s. Frank M. and Lucy M. A. (Cerami) G.; children: Frank Martin III, Anne Elizabeth; m. Lisa M. Crim. AB, Cornell U., 1964; MD, N.Y. Med. Coll., 1968. Diplomate Am. Bd. Pediat., Am. Bd. Cardiology. Intern N.Y. Med. Coll., 1968-69, resident, 1969-70; fellow Baylor Coll. Medicine, Houston, 1970-73; pediat. cardiologist Hartford (Conn.) Hosp., 1973-77; asst. prof. U. Conn., Farmington, 1973-79; assoc. prof. George Washington U., Washington, 1977-85, assoc. clin. prof., 1985-87; sr. attending physician Children's Hosp. Nat. Med. Ctr., Washington, 1977-89; prof. pediat. cardiology Georgetown U., Washington, 1987-94; clin. prof. pediat. Georgetown U., Washington, D.C., 1994—; pediat. cardiologist Child Cardiology Assocs., Annandale, Va., 1994—; clin. prof. pediat. U. Va., 1996—. Contbr. articles to profl. jours. Active Am. Heart Assn. Fellow Am. Coll. Cardiology, Am. Acad. Pediat.; mem. Am. Coll. Sports Medicine, N.Am. Soc. Pediat. Exercise Medicine (treas. 1986-91, pres. 1992-94). Republican. Roman Catholic. Office: 8318 Arlington Blvd Ste 250 Fairfax VA 22031

GALKIN, SAMUEL BERNARD, orthodontist; b. Newark, Feb. 9, 1933; s. Saul J. and Mollie (Kleinberg) G.; children from previous marriage: Jamie Michelle, Richard Stewart; m. Gail Beth Elkin, Feb. 26, 1972; children: Scott David, Seth Paul. Student, U. Conn., 1951-54; DDS, Temple U., 1958; MS in Histology, U. Ill., 1963, cert. grad. orthodontics, 1963; cert. in craniomandibular disorders, U. Medicine and Dentistry of N.J., 1989. Diplomate Am. Bd. Orthodontics. Group practice orthodontics Woodbridge, N.J., 1963—; staff orthodontist J.F.K. Community Hosp., Edison, N.J., 1966—, with cleft palate com., 1971—, dir. dental dept., 1979—; staff Woodbridge Health Ctr., 1967—, with dental adv. com., 1971—; dir. dept. dentistry John F. Kennedy Med. Ctr., Edison, 1979-81; staff orthodontist Perth Amboy (N.J.) Gen. Hosp., 1986—, dir. dept. dentistry, 1990—; staff orthodontist Rahway Hosp., N.J., 1986—; asst. prof. orthodontics N.J. Coll. Medicine and Dentistry, Jersey City, 1963-73; mem. panel physicians N.J. Crippled Children Program, 1971—; dentist Woodbridge Twp. Sch., 1989—. Chmn., Woodbridge Twp. Debutante Ball, 1970; bd. dirs. Woodbridge Twp. YMCA. Lt. Dental Corps, USN, 1958-61. Mem. ADA, Mid. Atlantic Soc. Orthodontists (chmn. clinics 1969-72), N.J. Dental Soc., Middlesex County Dental Soc., Am. Soc. Dentistry for Children, Am. Assn. Orthodontists, Am. Lingual Orthodontic Assn. (charter), Am. Assn. Dental Schs., Am. Acad. Head, Neck, Facial Pain and TMJ Orthopedics, N.E. Craniomandibular Soc., N.J. Craniomandibular soc. (charter), Am. Acad. Orofacial Pain, Am. Acad. Oral Medicine, Alpha Omega (chpt. v.p. 1969—), Omicron Kappa Upsilon. Home: 3 Dorset Rd Colonia NJ 07067-3101 Office: 711 Amboy Ave Woodbridge NJ 07095-3139 also: 233 Madison Ave Perth Amboy NJ 08861-4306

GALL, ERIC PAPINEAU, physician, educator; b. Boston, May 24, 1940; s. Edward Alfred and Phyllis Hortense (Rivard) G.; m. Katherine Theiss, Apr. 20, 1968; children: Gretchen Theiss Gall, Michael Edward. AB, U. Pa., 1962, MD, 1966. Asst. instr. U. Pa., Phila., 1970-71, post doctoral trainee, fellow, 1971-73; asst. prof. U. Ariz., Tucscon, 1973-78, assoc. prof., 1978-83, prof. internal medicine, 1983-94, prof. surgery, 1983-94, prof. family/community medicine, 1983-94, chief rheumatology allergy and immunology, 1983-93, dir. arthritis ctr., 1986-94; Herman Finch Univ. of Health Scis. prof. of medicine The Chgo. Med. Sch., North Chicago, Ill., 1994—, prof. microbiology and immunology, 1994—, chmn. dept. medicine, 1994—, chief rheumatology sect., 1994—, assoc. dean clin. affairs, 1996—. Author, editor: Rheumatoid Arthritis: Illustrated Guide to Path DX and Management of Rheumatoid Arthritis, 1988, Rheumatic Disease: Rehabilitation and Management, 1984, Primary Care, 1984; contbr. numerous articles to profl. jours. Chmn. med. and scientific com. Arthritis Found., Tucson, 1979-81. Maj. M.C., U.S. Army; Vietnam. Decorated Bronze Star; recipient Addie Thomas Nat. Svc. award Arthritis Found., 1988. Fellow ACP (coun. Ill. chpt. 1995—), Am. Coll. Rheumatology (founding chair ednl. materials com. 1986-89, bd. dirs. 1992-95, chmn. rehab. sect. 1992-95); mem. AMA (rep. sect. on med. schs. 1995—), Arthritis Health Professions Assn. (nat. pres. 1982-83), Am. Assn. Med. Colls., Am. Fedn. Clin. Rsch., Ctrl. Soc. Clin. Investigation, Arthritis Found. (nat. vice chmn. 1982-83, chmn. profl. edn. com. 1996—, chmn. ednl. materials com. 1991-96), Assn. Profs. Medicine, Ill. Med. Soc., Alpha Omega Alpha, Alpha Epsilon Delta, Sigma Xi. Office: The Chgo Med Sch Dept Medicine 3333 Green Bay Rd North Chicago IL 60064-3037

GALLAGHER, ABISOLA HELEN, psychologist, consultant; b. Chgo., Oct. 13, 1950; d. Lee Roy Gallagher and Lulla Mae (Granderson) Jointer. BA, Northeastern Ill. U., 1972; MA, U. Wis., Whitewater, 1974; EdD, Rutgers U., 1983. Lic. psychologist, N.J. Coordinator sickle cell anemia program Council for Bio-Med. Careers, Chgo., 1971-73; program coordinator, counselor U. Wis., Parkside, 1975-78; dir. residence hall Rutgers Coll. Rutgers U., New Brunswick, N.J., 1978-81, asst. dean Douglass Coll., 1981-85, asst. dean acad. svcs. Rutgers Coll., 1986-90; psychologist counseling & psychol. svcs. ctr. Jersey City (N.J.) State Coll., 1991—; mgmt. cons. Unlt. Potential, New Brunswick, 1985—; bd. dirs. Women's Resource Ctr., Summit, N.J. Martin Luther King scholar Rutgers U., 1979, 80. Mem. Am. Psychol. Assn., Assn. Black Psychologists, N.J. Psychol. Assn. (found. bd. dirs. 1994—), N.J. Assn. Black Psychologists (v.p. 1983-87, pres. 1989-91), N.J. Coalition of 100 Black Women (exec. bd. 1985), Eta Phi Beta (exec. bd. 1976-77). Home: 5 Roosevelt Pl #2G Montclair NJ 07042 Office: Jersey City State Coll Counseling & Psychol Svcs Ctr 54 College St Jersey City NJ 07305

GALLAGHER, MARY ANNE, maternal and child health nurse, administrator; b. N.Y.C., Nov. 20, 1956; d. Frederick M. and Margaret Theresa (Brennan) Gallagher. Diploma, Beth Israel Sch. Nursing, N.Y.C., 1977; BSN, Hunter Coll. CUNY, 1979; MA, NYU, 1984. RN, N.Y.; cert. BCLS provider, instr., neonatal resuscitation program instr. Staff nurse - medicine Beth Israel Med. Ctr., N.Y.C., staff nurse - pediatrics, pediatric spl. care, clin. nurse specialist - pediatrics, newborn intensive care, asst. DON maternal/child health; assoc. DON maternal/child health, Jack D. Weiler Hosp. Albert Einstein Coll. Medicine div. Montefiore Med. Ctr.; affiliate faculty Regional Emergency Svcs. Coun. N.Y., clin. adj. prof. CUNY, Hunter Coll.; nat. faculty BCLS Am. Heart Assn.; cons. (video series) Brady EMT-B Patient Assessment. rev. panel MCN, The Am. Jour. of Maternal/Child Nursing; contbr. article to profl. jour. nurse adv. com. March of Dimes, Greater N.Y. chpt. Mem. ANA (cert. pediatric nurse), AWHONN (sec./treas. Dist. II Downstate sect.), GNYNSONE, Am. Acad. Pediatrics (dist. II com. emergency svcs. for children), N.Y. State Perinatal Assn., N.Y. State Nurses Assn., N.Y. Counties RNS Assn., Am. Orgn. of Nurses Execs., N.Y. Orgn. of Nurse Execs., Beth Israel Nurse's Alumni Assn. (bd. dirs.), N.Y.U. Div. of Nursing Alumni, Sigma Theta Tau. Home: 21-32 38th St Astoria NY 11105-1802

GALLAGHER, ROBERTA, psychotherapist; b. Bklyn., May 15, 1940; d. Murray and Frances (Shukat) Kercheff; m. Victor Lescard, Apr. 1, 1994; children: Hayley Foster Higgins, Dori Morales. BA magna cum laude, U. Miami, 1972; MSW, Barry U., 1974. Cert. in clin. hypnosis, group therapy. Asst. prof. grad. div. marriage and family therapy St. Thomas U., Miami, Fla.; dir. family program addiction treatment South Miami (Fla.) Hosp.; clin. dir. Ctr. for Mind-Body Health and Inst. for Mind-Body Health, Miami; pvt. practice hypnotherapy and psychotherapy Miami; cons. and trainer in field. Jewish Fedn. scholar, 1972, U. Miami Honors scholar, 1970-72. Mem. Am. Assn. Mariage and Family Therapists (diplomate in clin. social work, supr.), NASW. Home: 90 Edgewater Dr Apt 501 Miami FL 33133-6916 Office: Ctr for Mind Body Health 1514 San Ignacio Ste 150 Coral Gables FL 33146

GALLAHER, WILLIAM MARSHALL, dental laboratory technician; b. Philipsburg, Pa., June 10, 1952; s. Marshall William and Florence Marie (Millner) G. Degree in Dental Tech., Hiram G. Andrews Ctr., 1971; BS, Rutgers U., 1979. Cert. dental technician in full dentures. Dental lab. technician to pvt. practice dentist Osceola Mill, Pa., 1971-72; dental lab. technician Profl. Dental Lab., South Amboy, N.J., 1972-79; instr. dental lab. tech. Union Tech. Inst., Neptune, N.J., 1979-84, Hiram G. Andrews Ctr., Johnstown, Pa., 1980-91; owner Gallaher's Dental Lab., Asbury Park, N.J., 1982-90; sr. dental lab. technician Denture Walk-In Ctr., Harrisburg, Pa., 1991—; adv. bd. Union Tech. Inst., 1984-90, Hiram G. Andrews Ctr., 1991-92; founder, pres. Person Enjoying New and Innovative Software User Group, Asbury Park, 1985-90. Author instrnl. manuals. Vol. deaf svcs. Monmouth County Deaf Group, Asbury Park, 1976-77; publicity chmn. Neighbor Preservation Program, Asbury Park, 1979-82. Mem. Nat. Dental Lab. Assn., Nat. Denturist Soc., N.J. Denturist Soc., Pa. Denturist Assn., Indian Tribal Denturity Assn., Internat. Brotherhood Magicians, Internat. Magicians Soc. (life), Masons (sr. master of ceremonies 1982—). Home: PO Box 2767 Harrisburg PA 17105-2767 Office: Denture Walk In Ctr 2023 N 2nd St Harrisburg PA 17102-2103

GALLANT, JOEL EMANUEL, physician; b. L.A., Jan. 23, 1958; s. Alfred Joseph and Donna Jean (McVey) G. BS in Biol. Scis., U. Calif., 1979, BA in Social Ecology, 1980, MD, 1985; MPH in Internat. Health, Johns Hopkins U., 1990. Intern, resident Yale-New Haven (Conn.) Hosp., 1985-88; chief resident and instr. Yale Univ. Sch. Medicine, New Haven, 1988-89; instr. emergency medicine Johns Hopkins Univ. Sch. Medicine, Balt., 1989-92, fellow infectious diesease, 1990-92, asst. prof. medicine, 1992—; dir. HIV clinic Johns Hopkins Hosp., Balt., 1992—; editorial bd. Jour. of the Gay & Lesbian Medical Assn., 1995—. Contbr. articles to profl. jours. Cmty. adv. bd. Md. State AIDS Adminstrn., Balt., 1996—, adv. com. HIV related clinical guidelines, 1995—. Recipient John C. Hume award Johns Hopkins Sch. Hygiene & Pub. Health, 1990. Mem. Am. Coll. Physicians, Infectious Disease Soc. Am., Gay and Lesbian Medical Assn., Am. Soc. Microbiology, Internat. AIDS Soc., Phi Beta Kappa, Delta Omega Alpha. Office: Johns Hopkins Univ Sch Medicine 600 N Wolfe St Carnegie 292 Baltimore MD 21287

GALLE, PHILLIP CHARLES, endocrinologist; b. Knoxville, Jan. 8, 1949; s. Fredrick Charles and Elisabeth Ann (NEvison) G.; m. Mary Abigail Gavigan, Apr. 7, 1979; children: Abigail, Elisabeth. BS in Zoology, Duke U., 1971; MD, Med. Coll. Ga., 1975. Intern N.C. Bapt. Hosp. and Bowman Gray Sch. Medicine, Winston-Salem, N.C., 1975-76, resident, 1975-80; asst. prof. ob-gyn. Med. Coll. Ga., Augusta, 1982-84; asst. reproductive endocrinology So. Ill. U. Sch. Medicine, Springfield, 1984-89, assoc. prof., 1989-92; reproductive endocrinologist pvt. practice, Springfield, 1992—; presenter in field. Contbr. articles to profl. jours. Reproductive endocrinology fellow U. Pa., Phila., 1980-82. Fellow Am. Coll. Ob-Gyn., Am. Soc. Reproductive Medicine (formerly Am. Fertility Soc., mem. sessions mgmt. com. 1980-84, 86-89, program com. meeting 1987); mem. AMA, Am. Fedn. Clin. Rsch., Am. Assn. Gunecologic Laparoscopists, Am. Inst. Ultrasound Medicine, N.Am. Menopause Soc., Ctrl. Assn. Ob-Gyn., Ill. State Med. Soc., Sangamon County Med. Soc., Frank Lock Soc., Soc. Reproductive Surgeons (charter), Soc. Reproductice Endocrinologists. Home: 1521 Wiggins Ave Springfield IL 62704 Office: Reproductive Endocrinology 340 W Miller Springfield IL 62702

GALLETTA, JOSEPH LEO, physician; b. Bessemer, Pa., Dec. 21, 1935; s. John and Grace (Galletta) G.; m. Teresita Suarez Soler, Feb. 19, 1961; children: John II, Angela, Eric, Christopher, Robert Francis, Michael Angelo. Student, U. Pitts., 1953-56; MD, U. Santo Tomas, Manila, 1962. Intern, St. Elizabeth Hosp., Youngstown, Ohio, 1963-64; family practice medicine, 29 Palms, Calif., 1967-77, Hemet, Calif., 1977—; chief of staff 29 Palms Cmty. Hosp., 1970-71, 73-76; vice chief of staff Hi-Desert Med. Center, Joshua Tree, Calif., 1976-77; chmn. dept. family practice Hemet Valley Hosp., 1981-83, med. dir. chem. dependency dept., 1985-88; med. dir. Loma Linda (Calif.) U. Behavioral Medicine Ctr. Recovery Svc., 1994—; pres. Flexisplint, Inc.; founding mem. Hemet Hospice; former cons. Morongo Basin Mental Health Assn.; mem. adv. com. on substance abuse Riverside County, 1995—. Hon. mem. 29 Palms Sheriff's Search and Rescue, 1971-77. Bd. dirs. 29 Palms Cmty. Hosp. Dist., Morongo Unified Sch. Dist. Served with M.C. USN, 1964-67. Diplomate Am. Bd. Family Practice. Fellow Am. Geriatric Soc. (founder West Coast chpt.), Am. Acad. Family Practice; mem. Calif. Med. Assn., Riverside County Med. Assn., Am. Holistic Med. Assn. (charter), Am. Soc. Addiction Medicine, Calif. Soc. Addiction Medicine (mem. exec. coun. 1995—), Am. Acad. Family Practice, Calif. Acad. Family Practice. Roman Catholic. Established St. Anthonys Charity Clinic, Philippines, 1965; inventor Flexisplint armboards. Home: 27691 Pochea Trl Hemet CA 92544-8180 Office: Westside Medical Pla 37020 Florida Ave Hemet CA 92545-3520

GALLETTI, PIERRE MARIE, medical science educator, artificial organ scientist; b. Monthey, Switzerland, June 11, 1927; s. Henri and Yvonne (Chamorel) G.; m. Sonia Aidan, Dec. 31, 1959; 1 son, Marc-Henri. BA in Classics, St. Maurice Coll., Switzerland, 1945; MD, U. Lausanne, Switzerland, 1951; PhD in Physiology and Biophysics, U. Lausanne, 1954; ScD (hon.), Roger Williams Coll., U. Nancy, France, U. Ghent, Belgium. Asst. prof. physiology Emory U., 1958-62, assoc. prof., 1962-66, prof., 1966-67, vis. prof., 1967-68; prof. med. sci. Brown U., 1967—, Univ. prof., 1991—, chmn. div. biol. sci., 1968-72, v.p. biology and medicine, 1972-91; pres. Found. for Biotech., Turin, Italy, 1991—; sci. adv. com. I-Stat, Princeton, N.J., 1984-90, Sorin Biomedica S.p.A., Turin, Italy, 1985—, Cardiopulmonics, Salt Lake City, 1988-93, Cytotherapeutics, Inc., Providence, 1989—, INCStar Stillwater, Minn., 1996—; bd. dirs. Sorin Biomedica, S.p.A., 1985—, chmn. bd., 1987-90; bd. dirs. Sorin Biomed., Inc., Irvine, Calif., 1993—; chmn. bd. dirs. INCStar, Stillwater, Minn., 1995—; chmn. Consensus Devel. Conf. NIH, chmn. devices and tech. br. task force; Hastings lectr. NIH, 1979; plenary lectr. World Biomaterials Conf., 1980, 88; McNeil Pharm. Sci. lectr., 1982; Whittaker lectr. Biomed. Engring. Sci., 1992; lectr. German Surg. Soc., 1987, Japan Soc. Artificial Organs, 1987-92; Jensen lectr. soc. Cardiac Anesthesiologists, 1992; trustee Morehouse Sch. Medicine, 1984—. Author: Heart-Lung Bypass: Principles and Techniques of Extracorporeal Circulation, 1962; contbr. chpts. to books, articles, abstracts to profl. jours. Trustee R.I. Philharm., 1988-93; bd. overseer Tufts U. Med. Sch., 1987—. Recipient John H. Gibbon award Am. Soc. Extracorporeal Technology, 1980, R.I. Gov. Sci. and Tech. award, 1987, Runzi prize, Switzerland, 1988, R.I. Commodore award, 1987; grantee NIH, 1962-91. Fellow Am. Coll. Cardiology, Am. Inst. Med. Biol. Engring. (v.p. 1991-93, pres.-elect 1993-94, pres. 1994-95); mem. AAAS, Am. Physiol. Soc., Swiss Physiol. Soc., Am. Soc. Artificial Orgns. (pres. 1969-70), Internat. Soc. Artificial Organs (trustee 1991—), Brussels Royal Acad. Medicine (fgn. assoc.), Swiss Acad. Med. Scis. (corr.), Acad. Medicine (Turin, Italy, fgn. assoc.). Office: Brown U PO Box G-b-393 Providence RI 02912

GALLIK, DONNA MARIE, cardiologist; b. Woonsocket, R.I., Feb. 16, 1961; d. Joseph and Barbara Evangeline (Gianco) G. ScB, Brown Univ., 1983, MD, 1987. Diplomate in internal medicine and cardiovascular diseases Am. Bd. Internal Medicine. Cardiologist West L.A. VA Hosp., L.A., 1994—; asst. dir. electophysiology UCLA Sch. Medicine, asst. prof. medicine. Contbr. articles to profl. jours. Fellow Am. Coll. Cardiology; mem. AMA, Greater L.A. Electrophysiology Soc. Office: West L A VA Medical Ctr Divsn Cardiology 11301 Wilshire Blvd Los Angeles CA 90073

GALLIN, JOHN I., clinical investigator; b. N.Y.C., Mar. 25, 1943; s. Nathaniel Mitchell and Hellen (Cohen) G.; m. Elaine Barbara Klimerman, June 23, 1966; children: Alice Jennifer, Michael Louis. BA (cum laude), Amherst Coll., 1965; MD, Cornell U. Med. Sch., 1969; ScD honoris causa, Amherst Coll., 1988. Diplomate Nat. Bd. Med. Examiners. Intern medicine Bellevue Hosp., N.Y.C., 1969-70, asst. resident, 1970-71; teaching asst., instr. in medicine NYU Sch. Medicine, 1970-74, 74-81; clin. assoc. lab. clin. investigation Nat. Inst. Allergy and Infectious Diseases, NIH, Bethesda, Md., 1971-74; sr. investigator lab. clin. investigation Nat. Inst. Allergy and Infectious Diseases, NIH, Bethesda, 1975-91; dir. div. intramural rsch. Nat. Inst. Allergy and Infectious Diseases, NIH, 1985-94, chief lab. of host defenses, 1991—; dir. NIH Warren Grant Magnuson Clin. Ctr., 1994—; assoc. dir. clin. rsch. NIH, 1994—; asst. surgeon gen.-rear admiral USPHS; guest lectr. and spkr. in field. Co-editor: Inflammation, Basic Principles and Clinical Correlates, 1988, 2d edit., 1992, Advances in Host Defenses, 1981—; contbr. more than 250 articles to profl. jours.; editl. bd. various profl. jours. Recipient Rsch. award Am. Fedn. for Clin. Rsch., 1984, Squibb award Infectious Diseases Soc. Am., 1987, Disting. Svc. medal USPHS, 1992. Fellow Infectious Diseases Soc. Am.; mem. Assn. Am. Physicians, Am. Soc. for Clin. Investigation, Am. Fedn. for Clin. Rsch., Internat. Immunocompromised Host Soc. (pres. 1992-94), Am. Assn. Immunologists, Soc. for Leukocyte Biology, Sigma Xi. Office: NIH Bldg 10/2C146 10 Center Dr MSC 1504 Bethesda MD 20892-1504

GALLINGER, LOIS MAE, medical technologist; b. Hibbing, Minn., Sept. 5, 1922; d. Clarence Adolph and Dorothy Mae (Stoller) Belanger; m. Ben Elton Gallinger, Sept. 1, 1956; children: Carol Elda, Gregory John. BS, U. Minn., 1946; Med. Tech. Intern, Coll. St. Scholastica, 1948-49. Cert. med. technologist. X-ray technologist Leigh Clinic, Grand Forks, N.D., 1946-47, Nicollet Clinic, Mpls., 1947-48; med. technologist Little Traverse Hosp., Petoskey, Mich., 1949-52; med. and x-ray technologist Lakeside Med. Ctr., Duluth, Minn., 1952-60; med. technologist St. Mary's Med. Ctr., Duluth, 1961-87; retired, 1987. Treas. Benedictine Health Ctr. Aux., Duluth, 1984—, Women's Assocs. Duluth Symphony, 1986—; cookie chmn. No. Pine Girl Scouts USA, Duluth, 1969; bd. dirs. St. Paul's Episc. Women's Club, Duluth, 1970s, greeter's chmn., 1970s, corr. sec., 1990-94, publicity chmn., 1994; vol. Am. Cancer Soc., 1993—, Am. Lung Assn., 1993. Mem. AAUW, Am. Soc. Med. Tech., Minn. Soc. Med. Tech. (regional historian 1969), Duluth Women's Club. Home: 364 Leicester Ave Duluth MN 55803-2203

GALLIS, HARRY A., physician/administrator; b. Atlanta, June 29, 1941; s. Anthony Henry and Frances (Skundale) G.; m. Sue Camlin, Aug. 27, 1966; children: Anthony Alexander, Sara Catherine. AB, Princeton U., 1963; MD, Duke U., 1967. Diplomate Am. Bd. Internal Medicine, Infectious Disease. Intern internal medicine Duke U. Med. Ctr., Durham, N.C., 1967-68, fellow in nephrology, 1970-71, resident in medicine, 1971-72, fellow in infectious diseases, 1972-74, assoc. prof. medicine, 1973-94; sr. asst. surgeon USPHS, NIH, Bethesda, Md., 1968-70; v.p., regional edn. Carolinas Health Care System, Charlotte, N.C., 1994—; mem. external CME adv. bd. Eli Lilly & Co., Indpls., 1990—; inerim dir. Charlotte Area Health Edn. Ctr., 1995—; cons. Upjohn Co., Kalamazoo, Mich., 1993—. Author: (book) The Complicated Medical Patient, 1984; contbr. articles to profl. jours. Sr. asst. surgeon, USPHS, 1968-70. Fellow Infectious Diseases Soc. of Am.; mem. Am. Soc. for Microbiology, N.C. Med. Soc. (mem. med. edn. com. 1995—), Alliance for Continuing Med. Edn. (program com. 1996—). Office: Carolinas Health Care System Hosp Authority PO Box 32861 Charlotte NC 28232-8610

GALLIVAN, WILLIAM RYAN, JR., orthopaedic surgeon; b. Arrington, U.K., Aug. 20, 1959; came to U.S., 1960; s. William Ryan Sr. and Nancy Jean (Mack) G.; m. Karen Elizabeth Daley, June 1, 1991; children: William Ryan III, Robert Emmet, Stephen Charles. BS in Biology, Loyola Marymount U., L.A., 1981; MD, Thomas Jefferson U., Phila., 1986. Lic. physician, Pa., Calif. Resident orthopaedic surgery Thomas Jefferson U. Hosp., Phila., 1990-91; fellow arthroscopy and sports medicine Inst. for Bone & Joint Disorders, Phoenix, 1991-92; pvt. practice Santa Barbara, Calif., 1992-94; ptnr. Peus, Smith, Birch, Kahmann & Gallivan, Santa Barbara, 1994—; chief orthopaedics St. Francis Hosp., Santa Barbara, 1993-95, Santa Barbara Cottage Hosp., 1996; physician Assn. Surfing Profls., 1995—. Contbr. articles to profl. jours. Fellow Am. Acad. Orthopaedic Surgeons, Am. Bd. Orthopaedic Surgeons; mem. Calif. Orthopaedic Assn. (bd. dirs. 1996); mem. Calif. Orthopaedic Assn. (bd. dirs. 1995—), Alpha Omega Alpha. Republican. Roman Catholic. Office: Peus Smith Birch Kahmann Gallivan 2324 Bath St Santa Barbara CA 93105

GALLOWAY, GLORIA M., neurology educator; b. Bklyn.. MD, St. Georges Univ. Sch. Medicin, 1987. Diplomate Am. Bd. Psychiatry and Neurology. Fellow clinical neurophysiology Univ. Iowa, Iowa City, 1991-92; fellow neurosurgery Univ. Pitts., 1992-93; neurologist Allegheny Gen. Space Ctr., Pitts., 1994-95; asst. prof. neurology La. State Univ. Medical Ctr., Shreveport, 1995—; asst. dir. neurology La. State Univ. Medical Ctr., 1995—; dir. EMB lab., 1995—. Contbr. articles to profl. jours. Internal Rev. Bd. La. State Univ. Medical Ctr., 1995—, bd. dirs., 1995—, medical sch. clinical com., 1995—. Mem. AMA, Am. Acad. Clinical Neurology, Am. Assn. Electrodiagnositc Medicine. Office: La State Univ Medical Ctr 1501 E Kings Hwy Shreveport LA 71130

GALLOWAY, JERRY EDWARD, ophthalmologist; b. Augusta, Ga., Mar. 27, 1954; s. James Edward and Marion (Moxley) G.; m. Evelyn Faye Cromer, Dec. 13, 1978; children: Daniel Ryan, Laura Ashley. BS in Chem. Engring., Clemson U., 1976; MD, Med. U. S.C., 1980. Resident Med. Coll. Ga., Augusta, 1981-84, W.Va. U. Sch. Medicine, Morgantown, 1984; ophthalmologist Greenwood (S.C.) Eye Clinic, 1984—. Mem. S.C. Soc. Ophthalmology, Kiwanis. Office: Greenwood Eye Clinic 210 Wells Ave Greenwood SC 29646

GALLOWAY, JOHN RUSSELL, surgeon; b. Atlanta, Sept. 22, 1955; m. Sharon Williams; children: Jennifer, Rachel. AB in Chemistry, Erskine Coll., 1977; MD, Emory U., 1981. Diplomate Am. Bd. Surgery. Intern Emory U. Affiliated Hosps., Atlanta, 1981-82, resident, 1982-87; attending physician Emory U. Hosp., Atlanta, 1987—, Crawford Long Meml. Hosp., Atlanta, 1987—, Grady Meml. Hosp., Atlanta, 1987—, VA Med. Ctr., Atlanta, 1994—. Fellow ACS; mem. Soc. Critical Care Medicine, Soc. Am. Gastrointestinal Endoscopic Surgeons, Assn. for Acad. Surgery, Soc. for Gen. Surgery. Office: Emory U Hosp 1364 Clifton Rd NE Atlanta GA 30322

GALLUP, BRUCE VALLE, oral and maxillofacial surgeon; b. Holyoke, Mass., Oct. 24, 1955; s. John Gardner and Paula Ellen (Burgee) G.; m. Mary Linda Pauszek, Aug. 1, 1981; children: John, Holly. BA in Psychology, DePauw U., 1978; DMD, Boston U., 1987. Diplomate Am. Bd. Oral and Maxillofacial Surgery. EMT, paramedic Myers Ambulance, Greenwood, Ind., 1978-80, McGanns Ambulance, South Bend, Ind., 1980-81, Riverview Hosp., Noblesville, Ind., 1981-83; intern VA Hosp., Manchester, N.H., 1987-88; resident U. Conn., Farmington, 1988-91; pvt. practice, Auburn, Maine, 1991—; active med. staff St. Mary's Hosp., Lewiston, Maine, 1991—, Ctrl. Maine Med. Ctr., Lewiston, 1991—; bd. dirs. Dental Task Force, Farmington, 1994—; pres. Maine Dental Forensics Team, Augusta, 1995—. Fellow Am. Coll. Oral and Maxillofacial Surgeons; mem. ADA, Am. Assn. Oral and Maxillofacial Surgeons, Am. Soc. Dental Anesthesia, Maine Dental Assn., Androscoggin Dental Soc. (past pres.), Omicron Kappa Upsilon. Home: RR 1 Box 1273 Turner ME 04282 Office: Ctrl Maine Oral Maxillofacial Surgery Assoc 405 Center St Auburn ME 04210

GALSTIAN, PAUL ROBERT, optometrist; b Forest Hills, N.Y., Apr. 12, 1965; s. Bob and Helen (Ponsolle) G.; m. Dawn Cecily Cannon, Apr. 22, 1995. BS in Fin., NYU, 1987; D Optometry, SUNY, 1991. OD. Optometrist Merrick (N.Y.) Optometrics, 1991-93; prof. optics N.Y. Eye and Ear Infirmary-Ophthalmic Tech. Program, N.Y.C., 1993—; optometrist Ophthalmic Cons., N.Y.C., 1993—. Mem. N.Y. State Optometric Assn. (N.Y.C. rep. 1995—), City of N.Y. Optometric Bd. (v.p. 1994—). Vol. Optometrists Serving Humanity, Am. Optometric Assn., City of N.Y. Optometric Assn. Office: Ophthalmic Cons Pc 310 East 14th St New York NY 10003

GALSTON, ARTHUR WILLIAM, biology educator; b. N.Y.C., Apr. 21, 1920; s. Hyman and Freda (Saks) G.; m. Dale Judith Kuntz, June 27, 1941; children: William Arthur, Beth Dale. B.S., Cornell U., 1940; M.S., U. Ill., 1942, Ph.D., 1943. Rsch. plant physiologist emergency rubber project Calif. Inst. Tech., 1943-44, sr. rsch. fellow, 1947-50, assoc. prof. biology, 1951-55; instr. Yale U., 1946-47, prof. plant physiology, 1955-65, prof. biology, 1965-76, Eaton prof. botany, 1973-90, emeritus prof., 1990, dir. div. biol scis., 1965-66, sr. rsch. biologist, 1990—, chmn. dept. botany, 1961-62, chmn. dept. biology, 1985-88; cons. ctrl. rsch. dept. E.I. duPont de Nemours & Co., 1956-78, Plant Resources Venture Funds, 1983-89, NASA, 1988-94; mem. divsn. biology and agr. NRC, 1963-66, 85-88, mem. com. on space biology and medicine, 1983-86; Einstein prof. Faculty Agr. Hebrew U., Jerusalem, 1980; vis. scientist Plant Breeding Inst., Cambridge, Eng., 1983; vis. fellow Wolfson Coll., Cambridge U., 1983; vis. scholar Riken Inst., Japan, 1988-89. Author: Life of the Green Plant, 1961, 3d edit. (with Peter J. Davies and Ruth L. Satter) 1980, (with James Bonner) Principles of Plant Physiology, 1952 (with Peter J. Davies) Control Mechanisms in Plant Development, 1970, Daily Life in People's China, 1973, Green Wisdom, 1981, Life Processes in Plants, 1994; mem. editorial adv. bd.: World Book Science Year, 1976-78, Pesticide Physiology and Biochemistry, 1978-88, Plant Growth Regulation, 1983-93, Chem. Engring. News, 1977-78, Environment, 1979-83; contbr. sci. articles. Served as ensign USNR, 1944-46; mil. govt. Okinawa. Guggenheim fellow Stockholm, Paris, Sheffield, Eng., 1950-51; Fulbright fellow Canberra, Australia, 1960-61; Sci. Faculty fellow NSF, London, 1967-68. Fellow AAAS (chmn. com. on meetings 1956-59, life mem.); mem. Am. Soc. Plant Physiologists (sec. 1955-57, v.p. 1957-58, pres. 1963-64), Internat. Assn. Plant Physiology (sec.-treas. 1961-67), Bot. Soc. Am. (editl. bd. 1959-61, 72-76, pres. 1967-68), Fedn. Am. Scientists (coun. 1973-76), Am. Soc. Biochemists, Molecular Biol., Am. Soc. Photobiology, Am. Inst. Biol. Scis., Am. Acad. Arts & Scis. Home: 307 Manley Heights Rd Orange CT 06477-3028 Office: Dept Biology Yale U New Haven CT 06520-8103

GALTERIO, LOUIS, healthcare information executive; b. N.Y.C., Apr. 20, 1951; s. Elio and Angelina (Mattina) G.; m. Elizabeth Anne Coddington, May 2, 1971; children: Jason, Heather. Student, CCNY, 1969-70, Baruch Coll., 1970-75; BS in Mgmt. summa cum laude, Mercy Coll., 1978; MBA in Fin., L.I. U., 1980. Asst. mgr. Mfrs. Hanover Trust, N.Y.C., 1971-82; v.p. Bankers Trust Co., N.Y.C., 1982-87; dir., tech. mgr. Mortgage Backed Securities Clearing Corp., N.Y.C., 1987-88; mgr. capital markets and mktg. Digital Equipment Corp., N.Y.C., 1988-90, integration exec., 1990-91; chief info. officer healthcare Health and Hosps. Corp. NYC, 1991-93; dir. clin. info. sys. Soc. of N.Y. Hosp., N.Y.C., 1993—; pres., mgmt. cons. Galterio Cons., N.Y.C., 1987—. Mem., sect. capt. Throgs Neck (N.Y.) Estates, 1988. Mem. IEEE (assoc.), Bankers Trust Alumni Orgn., Electronic mail and Messaging Assn., Am. Hosp. Assn., Coll. Healthcare Info. Mgmt. Execs., Healthcare Info. & Mgmt. Systems Soc., Alpha Chi. Republican. Home: 1417 Shore Dr Bronx NY 10465-1560 also: The NY Hosp 525 E 68th St # 151 New York NY 10021-4873

GALVIN, MATTHEW REPPERT, psychiatry educator; b. Seattle, July 24, 1950; s. Ralph B. and Virginia (Reppert) G.; m. Deborah Ann Chernin, Dec. 22, 1979; children: Joseph, Sarah. AB with honors, Ind. U., 1975, MD, 1979. Diplomate Am. Bd. Adolescent Psychiatry, Am. Bd. Psychiatry and Neurology. Asst. prof. Ind. U. Med. Ctr., Indpls., 1984-95, clin. assoc. prof., 1995—; staff psychiatrist Larue Carter Meml. Hosp., Indpls., 1984-88, assoc. dir. youth svcs., 1988, acting dir., 1988-90; child psychiatrist Riley Child Psychiatry Svcs., Indpls., 1990—; asst. dir. psychiatric svcs. children and adolescents Ind. U. Hosps. Author: Ignatius Finds Help, A Story About Psychotherapy, 1988, Otto Learns About Medicine, A Story About Grown-ups Helping Children, 1988, Clouds and Clocks, A Story for Children Who Soil, 1989; co-author: Sometimes Y, A Story for Families with Gender Identity Issues, 1993; contbr. articles to profl. jours. With M.C., U.S. Army, 1970-73, Vietnam. Fellow Am. Psychiat. Assn.; mem. Am. Acad. Child Adolescent Psychiatry, Am. Soc. Adolescent Psychiatry, Nat. Alliance Against Mental Illness (affiliate), Ind. Coun. Child and Adolescent Psychiatry (treas. Indpls. chpt. 1986-89, pres. elect 1989-90, pres. 1990-91). Office: Ind U Child and Adolescent Psychiatry Svcs 702 Barnhill Dr Indianapolis IN 46202-5128

GAMBACORTA, HUMBERT M., ophthalmologist; b. Boston, Aug. 12, 1926; s. Leopoldo and Adalgisa (Del Giacomo) G.; m. Esther Rose Giaimo, Oct. 25, 1952; children: Leo, Charles, Michael, John. BS, Seton Hall U., 1946; MD, U. Pa., 1950. cons. N.J. Commn. for the Blind and Visually Impaired, Newark, N.J., 1970-90. Capt. U.S. Army, 1955-56, Germany. Office: 2446 Church Rd Toms River NJ 08753

GAMBINO, S(ALVATORE) RAYMOND, medical laboratory executive, educator; b. N.Y.C., Oct. 13, 1926; s. Salvatore Benedict and Rose (Ragona) G.; m. Madeline Russo, Apr. 5, 1953; children: Catherine Rose Garroni, Stephen Raymond. BS, Antioch Coll., 1948; MD, U. Rochester, 1952. Diplomate Am. Bd. Pathology. Labs. dir. Englewood (N.J.) Hosp., 1961-68; prof. pathology Columbia U., N.Y.C., 1968-82; dir. chemistry labs. Presbyn. Hosp., N.Y.C., 1968-77; labs. dir. St. Luke's-Roosevelt Hosp., 1978-82; chief med. officer, exec. v.p. MetPath, Inc., Teterboro, N.J., 1983-94, exec. v.p., chief med. officer emeritus, 1994—; adj. prof. pathology Columbia U., N.Y.C., 1983—; mem. Corning (N.Y.) Mgmt. Group, 1984-94; bd. dirs. Ciba-Corning, 1988-94. Co-author: Beyond Normality, 1975; editor: (newsletter) Lab Report for Physicians, 1979—. Mem. Englewood Cliffs (N.J.) Sch. Bd., 1966-69. Served with USN, 1945-46. Mem. Am. Soc. Clin. Pathologists (editor check sample program 1968-93), Alpha Omega Alpha. Roman Catholic. Office: Corning Clin Labs One Malcolm Ave Teterboro NJ 07608

GAMBLE, RAYMOND WESLEY, marriage and family therapist, clergyman; b. East Orange, N.J., Feb. 11, 1933; s. Kenneth Nelson and Lillian Clare (Apgar) G.; m. Margaret Gamble, Sept. 11, 1954 (div. 1964); children: Karen F., Roy B.; m. Penelope Louise Hansen, Nov. 19, 1979; 1 child, Wesley B. BA, Houghton (N.Y.) Coll., 1956; MDiv, Union Theol. Sem., Richmond, Va., 1960; postgrad., Yale U., 1967; D Ministry, Columbia Theol. Sem., Decatur, Ga., 1990. Ordained to ministry Presbyn. Ch., 1960. Student chaplain Va. State Penitentiary, 1958-60; asst. pastor Immanuel Presbyn. Ch., Lake Park, Fla., 1960-62; founder, pastor Westminster Presbyn. Ch., Palm Beach Gardens, Fla., 1962-67; exec. dir. Mental Health Assn. Palm Beach County, West Palm Beach, 1967-73; pvt. practice marriage and family therapy, West Palm Beach, Stuart, Fla., 1973—; founder, sr. pastor Palm City (Fla.) Presbyn. Ch., 1984—; guest instr. Indian River Community Coll., 1978; cons., chaplain Lake Hosp., Lake Worth, Fla., 1973-75; chaplain Savannas Hosp., Port St. Lucie, Fla., 1986—; program dir., aftercare counselor narcotic addict rehab. program NIMH, West Palm Beach, 1969-73. Active numerous drug abuse rehab. programs, Palm Beach County; past mem. Com. for Mental Health Edn.; active Presbytery Tropical Fla., 1960—; mem. ch.-coll. coun. Montreat Coll., 1988—; past mem. bd. dirs. Alcohol and Drug Abuse Coun. Palm Beach County, North County Drug Abuse Bd., Boca Raton (Fla.) Drug Abuse Found.; past pres. Drug Abuse Rehab. Team, Inc. Mem. Am. Assn. for Marriage and Family Therapy (clin.), Am. Assn. Christian Counselors. Home and Office: 288 NE Alice St # 101S Jensen Beach FL 34957-6006

GAMBOA, GEORGE CHARLES, oral surgeon, educator; b. King City, Calif., Dec. 17, 1923; s. George Angel and Martha Ann (Baker) G.; m. Winona Mae Collins, July 16, 1946; children: Cheryl Jan Gamboa Granger, Jon Charles, Judith Merlene Gamboa Hiscox. Pre-dental cert., Pacific Union Coll., 1943; DDS, U. Pacific, 1946; MS, U. Minn., 1953; AB, U. So. Calif., 1958, EdD, 1976. Diplomate Am. Bd. Oral and Maxillofacial Surgery. Fellow oral surgery Mayo Found., 1950-53; clin. prof. grad. program oral and maxillofacial surgery U. So. Calif., L.A., 1954—; assoc. prof. Loma Linda (Calif.) U., 1958-94, chmn. dept. oral surgery, 1960-63; pvt. practice oral and maxillofacial surgery, San Gabriel, Calif., 1955-93; dir. So. Calif. Acad. of Oral Pathology, 1995—. Mem., past chmn. first aid com. West San Gabriel chpt. ARC. Fellow Am. Coll. Dentists, Am. Coll. Oral and Maxillofacial Surgeons (founding fellow), Pierre Fauchard Acad., Am. Inst. Oral Biology, Internat. Coll. Dentists, So. Calif. Acad. Oral Pathology; mem. Am. Assn. Oral and Maxillofacial Surgeons, Internat. Assn. Oral Surgeons, So. Calif. Soc. Oral and Maxillofacial Surgeons, Western Soc. Oral and Maxillofacial Surgeons, Am. Acad. Oral and Maxillofacial Radiology, Marsh Robinson Acad. Oral Surgeons, Profl. Staff Assn. Los Angeles County-U. So. Calif. Med. Ctr. (exec. com. 1976—), Am. Cancer Soc. (Calif. div., profl. edn. subcom. 1977-90, pres. San Gabriel-Pomona Valley unit 1989-90), Calif. Dental Soc. Anesthesiology (pres. 1989-94), Calif. Dental Found. (pres. 1991-93), Calif. Dental Assn. (jud. coun. 1990—), San Gabriel Valley Dental Soc. (past pres.), Xi Psi Phi, Omicron Kappa Upsilon, Delta Epsilon. Seventh-day Adventist. Home: 1102 Loganrita Ave Arcadia CA 91006-4535

GAMBONE, VICTOR EMMANUEL, JR., physician; b. Phila., Aug. 28, 1949; s. Victor Emmanuel and Eleanor Joyce (Porambo) G.; BS, Pa. State U., 1971, MD, 1975. Cert. Med. Dir. in Long Tern Care. Intern and resident in internal medicine U. South Fla., Tampa, 1975-78; practice medicine specializing in internal medicine and geriatrics, Dunedin, Fla., 1978—; coord. geriat. medicine curriculum Morton Plant Mease/U. South Fla. Family Practice Residency Program, 1996—; med. dir. Stratford Ct. Marriott Health Ctr., Palm Harbor, Fla., 1991—, St. Mark Village, Palm Harbor, 1993—, Mease Continuing Care, Dunedin, Fla., 1993—, Manor Care Nursing Ctr., Dunedin, 1994—, Spanish Gardens Nursing Ctr., Dunedin, 1994—, Gulfcoast Nursing Ctr., Clearwater, Fla., 1995—, Hospice Care, Inc., Pinellas County, 1982-86, Regency Oaks Nursing Ctr., Clearwater, 1996—, Bayside Nursing Pavillion, Clearwater, 1996—, Mariner Health of Clearwater, 1996—; chmn. dept internal medicine Mease Health Care, Dunedin, Fla., 1989. Diplomate Am. Bd. Internal and Geriatric Medicine. Mem. AMA, ACP, Am. Med. Dirs. Assn., Am. Geriatrics Soc., Am. Soc. Internal Medicine. Author: Post Operative Recall of Intra-Operative Events, 1975 (research award U. Miami Med. Sch.). Office: 601 Main St Dunedin FL 34698

GAMBRELL, RICHARD DONALD, JR., endocrinologist, educator; b. St. George, S.C., Oct. 28, 1931; s. Richard Donald and Nettie Anzo (Ellenburg) G.; m. Mary Caroline Stone, Dec. 22, 1956; children: Deborah Christina, Juliet Denise. BS, Furman U., 1953; MD, Med. U. S.C., 1957. Diplomate Am. Bd. Obstetrics and Gynecology, Diplomate Div. Reproductive Endocrinology. Intern Greenville Gen. Hosp., S.C., 1957-58, resident, 1961-64; commd. USAF, 1958, advanced through grades to col.; chmn. dept. ob-gyn, cons. to surgeon gen. USAF Hosp. USAF, Wiesbaden, Germany, 1966-69; chief gynecologic endocrinology Wilford Hall USAF Med. Ctr. USAF, Lackland AFB, Tex., 1971-78; ret. USAF, 1978; clin. prof. ob-gyn and endocrinology Med. Coll. Ga., Augusta, 1978—; practice medicine specializing in reproductive endocrinology Augusta, 1978—; fellow in endocrinology Med. Coll. Ga., 1969-71; mem. staff Westlawn Bapt. Mission Med. Clinic, San Antonio, 1972-78; assoc. clin. prof. U. Tex. Health Sci. Ctr., San Antonio, 1971-78; internat. lectr.; mem. ob-gyn. adv. panel U.S. Pharmacopeial Conv., 1986-90, sci. adv. bd. Nat. Osteoporosis Found., 1988-91. Co-author: The Menopause: Indications for Estrogen Therapy, 1979, Sex Steroid Hormones and Cancer, 1984, Unwanted Hair: Its Cause and Treatment, 1985, Estrogen Replacement Therapy, 1987, Hormone Replacement Therapy, 3rd edit., 1992, 4th edit., 1995, Estrogen Replacement Therapy Users Guide, 1989; mem. editl. bd. Jour. Reproductive Medicine, 1982-85, Maturitas, 1982—, The Female Patient, 1992—, Menopause: Jour. of the N.Am. Menopause Soc., 1995—; mem. editl. bd. Internat. Jour. Fertility, 1986-91, assoc. editor, 1988-91; contbr. articles to med. jours., chpts. to books. Deacon, Sunday sch. tchr. Baptist Ch., 1971—; mem. sci. adv. bd. Nat. Osteoporosis Found., 1988-91. Recipient Chmn.'s Best Paper in Clin. Rsch. from Teaching Hosp. award Armed Forces Dist. Am. Coll. Ob-Gyn., 1972, 88, Host award, 1977, Chmn.'s award, 1978, Purdue-Frederick award, 1979, Outstanding Exhibit award Am. Fertility Soc., 1983, Am. Coll. Obstetricians and Gynecologists award, 1983, Thesis award South Atlantic Assn. Ob-Gyn., Winthrop award Internat. Soc. Reproductive Medicine, 1985, Chmn.'s Best Paper award Pan Am. Soc. for Fertility, 1986, Outstanding Sci. exhibit award Am. Acad. Family Physicians, 1986, 87, 92, Outstanding Sci. Exhibit, Am. Acad. Family Physicians, Boston, 1994, Merit award ACS, 1994, Cert. of Appreciation for Sci. Exhibit, 1995. Fellow Am. Coll. Obstetricians and Gynecologists (subcom. on endocrinology and infertility 1983-86); mem. Pacific N.W. Ob-gyn Soc. (hon.), So. Med. Assn. (2d place Sci. Exhibit award 1992), Am. Fertility Soc., Ga. Obstetric and Gynecologic Soc., Tex. Assn. Ob-Gyn., Augusta Obstetric and Gynecologic Soc., San Antonio Ob-Gyn. Soc. (v.p. 1975-76), Chilean Soc. Ob-Gyn. (hon.), Soc. Obstetricians and Gynecologists of Can. (hon.), Internat. Family Planning Research Assn., Internat. Menopause Soc. (exec. com. 1981-84), Internat. Soc. for Reproductive Medicine (program chmn. 1980, pres. 1986-88), Am. Geriatric Soc. (editorial bd. 1981-83), Nat. Geog. Soc., Phi Chi, Alpha Epsilon Delta. Home: 3542 National Ct Augusta GA 30907-9517 Office: 903 15th St Augusta GA 30910-0192

GAMBUTI, GARY, hospital administrator; b. Paterson, N.J., Sept. 27, 1937; s. Archie and Edith (Santero) G.; m. Linda Lewis, Oct. 9, 1979. BA, Rutgers U., 1959; MA in Public Adminstrn., Cornell U., Ithaca, N.Y., 1961. Adminstrv. asst., asst. v.p. The Roosevelt Hosp., N.Y.C., 1961-67; assoc. v.p. St. Luke's Hosp. Ctr., N.Y.C., 1967-73, sr. adminstrv. v.p., 1973-75, exec. v.p., 1975-77, pres., 1977-79; pres. St. Luke's-Roosevelt Hosp. Ctr., N.Y.C., 1979-96; trustee St. Luke's-Roosevelt Hosp. Ctr., 1979-96; bd. dirs. Mid-Atlantic Health Congress, Princeton, N.J., pres., 1987-88; bd. dirs. Isabella Geriatric Ctr.; mem. Am. Coun. St. Luke's Internat. Med. Ctr., Tokyo; bd. commrs. Joint Commn. Healthcare Orgns. Assoc. officer Order St. John Jerusalem; chmn. AHA com. of commrs. for the Joint commn. Fellow Am. Coll. Hosp. Adminstrs., N.Y. Acad. Medicine (assoc.); mem. Hosp. Soc. N.Y., Soc. Health Svc. Adminstrs., Hosp. Assn. N.Y. State (chair 1984), Coun. Teaching Hosps. of AAMC (chair 1989), Greater N.Y. Hosp. Assn. (bd. dirs., chair 1980), League Voluntary Hosps. (bd. dirs.), Hosp. Adminstrs. Club N.Y. (chair bd. dirs. 1980). Office: St Luke's-Roosevelt Hosp Ctr 1111 Amsterdam Ave New York NY 10025

GAMELLI, RICHARD LOUIS, surgeon, educator; b. Springfield, Mass., Jan. 18, 1949; married; 3 children. AB in Chemistry magna cum laude, St.

Michael's Coll., Colchester, Vt., 1970; MD, U. Vt., 1974. Diplomate Nat. Bd. Med. Examiners, Am. Bd. Surgery (examination cons. 1988—, guest examiner 1993); lic. surgeon, Ill. Straight surg. intern. Med. Ctr. Hosp. Vt., 1974-75, surg. resident PG-II, PG-III, PG-IV, 1975-79; asst. prof. surgery U. Vt. Coll. Medicine, 1979-85, assoc. prof., 1985-89, prof., 1989-90, dir. surg. rsch. labs. dept. surgery, 1985-90, dir. house staff tng. program., 1985-89, vice chmn. dept. surgery, 1985-90, chmn. sect. gen. surgery, 1989; attending surgeon Med. Ctr. Hosp. Vt., 1979-90, dir., founder burn program, 1980-90, dir. nutritional support svcs., 1980-88, dir. resident teaching conf., 1983-90, assoc. surgeon-in-chief, 1985-89; prof. depts. surgery and pediatrics Strich Sch. Medicine, dir. Shock-Trauma Inst., chief burn ctr., dir. surg. rsch. Foster G. McGaw Hosp. Loyola U. Med. Ctr., Maywood, Ill., 1990—, now chmn, prof., dept. of surgery; chmn. quailty assurance com. burn ctr. Loyola U. Med. Ctr., 1990—, infection control com., 1990—, rsch. com. coun., 1990—, surg. rsch. com., 1991—, intensive care unit com., 1991—, EMS bldg. com., 1991—, med. chmn. nutrition com., 1992—, managed care tsck force, 1993—, commitment to teaching task force, 1993—; Dr John C. Hartnett lectr. St. Michael's Coll., 1983; mem. spl. study sect. NIH, 1991; mem. physicians adv. coun. Marianjoy Rehab. Hosps. and Clinics, 1993. Co-author: Trauma 2000, 1992, A Compendium of Slides on Surgical Infections, 1992; co-editor: Clinical Surgery, 1987, Early Care of the Injured Patient, 1990, Essentials of Clinical Surgery, 1991; mem. editorial bd., reivewer Jour. Trauma, 1984—, Essentials Clin. Surgery, 1988—, Clin. Surgery, 1990—, Shock, 1993—; reviewer Circulatory Shock, Surgery, Jour. Surg. Rsch.; contbr. 93 articles to profl. jours., 16 chpts. to books. Recipient Dr. James E. DeMeules 1st Annual Rsch. award U. Vt. Dept. Surgery, 1990; grantee NIH, 1981-84, 89-93, Ethicon, Inc., 1988-90, Genetech., Inc., 1988-89, Amgen, Inc., 1989-90, U. Ill., Chgo., 1991. Fellow ACS (vice chmn. Vt. state com. on trauma 1984-86, chmn. Vt. state com. on trauma 1986-91, sec.-treas. Vt. state chpt. 1987-90, subcom. on publs. 1987-90, exec. com. 1991-93, reviewer com. on trauma verification/consultaion program for hosps., 1991, 92, 93 chmn. audit com. 1992, 93, bd. dirs. 1992, cons., beta test site NTRACS, 1993); mem. Am. Burn Assn. (instr., dir. advanced burn life suuport course 1988—, regionalization com. 1992—, chair region V. 1992—, beta test site registry 1993), N.Am. Burn Soc. (pres. 1991), Shock Soc., Soc. for Leukocyte Biology, Soc. Univ. Surgeons (chmn. com. on social and legis. issues 1990-93, exec. com. 1990-93), Surg. Infection Soc. (edn. com. 1988—, chmn. fellowhsip com. 1990—), Surg. Biology Club III, Ea. Assn. for Surgery Trauma (exec. com. 1991-93, bd. dirs. 1992, chmn. audit com. 1992, 93), Internat. Soc. for Burn Injuries, John H. Davis Soc. (founding., bd. dirs. 1988—, coun. 1988-90, sec.-treas. 1990-92, pres. 1993—), New England Surg. Soc. Office: Loyola U Med Ctr Dept of Surgery 2160 S 1st Ave Maywood IL 60153-3304*

GAMMAITONI, CARLO JOHN, surgeon; b. Scranton, Pa., Oct. 28, 1964; s. Arnold Richard and Anita Louise (Contessa) G. BS in Biology magna cum laude, U. Scranton, 1986; MD, Pa. State U., 1990. Intern New Eng. Med. Ctr., Boston, 1990-91, resident, 1991-95; fellow R. Adams Coley Shock Trauma Ctr., Balt., 1995—. Contbr. articles to profl. jours. including Internat. Jour. Cardiology, Anesthesiology, Transplant Proceedings. Mem. AMA. Home: 320 Adams Ct Glen Burnie MD 21061

GAMMENTHALER, SAMMY ARNOLD, physician, cardiovascular disease consultant; b. Fredericksburg, Tex., July 25, 1950; s. Charles Allen and Esther Gammenthaler. BS, U. Ctrl. Fla., Orlando, 1972; MD, Loma Linda U., 1975. Diplomate Am. Bd. Internal Medicine, Sub-Bd. Cardiovascular Disease. Intern and resident Loma Linda (Calif.) U., fellow in cardiology; sr. staff cardiologist Scott and White Clinic, College Station, Tex., 1990—; asst. prof. medicine Tex. A&M U., College Station, 1990—; chmn. pharmacy and therapeutics com. St. Joseph Regional Med. Ctr., Bryan, Tex., 1993-95, Brazos Valley Med. Ctr., College Station, 1993-95. Active cmty. heart disease support group College Station Clinic, 1993-95. Fellow Am. Coll. Cardiology. Libertarian. Seventh-day Adventist. Office: Scott and White Clinic 1600 University Dr East College Station TX 77840-2642

GAMMILL, STEPHEN L., diagnostic radiologist; b. Bude, Miss., Jan. 1, 1936; s. Gurvis P. and Pauline B. G.; m. Mary Ann Perich, June 17, 1967; children: Marion Barbara, Stephen Lane. BA, U. Miss., 1957, BS, 1960, MD, 1962. Fellow in angiography U. Tex. Med. Ctr., Galveston, 1966-67; dir. angiography svc., assoc. prof. Charity Hosp./Tulane Med. Sch., New Orleans, 1967-73; assoc. prof. U. Tenn. Med. Sch., Memphis, 1973-75; diagnostic radiologist Mid South Imaging & Therapeutics, Memphis, 1975—. Author: A Prgorammed Introduction to Upper G.I. Radiology, 1977; contbr. articles to profl. jours. Fellow Am. Coll. Radiology. Home: 2935 Iroquois Rd Memphis TN 38111

GANCHROW, MANDELL I., surgeon; b. Bklyn., Feb. 6, 1937; s. Morris S. and Kate (Wallach) G.; m. Sheila Weinreb, Dec. 29, 1940; children: Marcia, Ari, Elliot. BA, Yeshiva U., 1958; MD, Chgo. Med. Sch., 1962. Intern Beth-el Hosp., Bklyn., 1962-63; surg. resident Montefiore Hosp., Bronx, N.Y., 1963-64, Brookdale Hosp., Bklyn., 1964-67; colon-rectal resident Ferguson Clinic, Grand Rapids, Mich., 1969-70; surgeon Good Samaritan Hosp., Suffern, N.Y., 1970—; cons. NYack (N.Y.) Hosp., 1970—; clin. assoc. prof. surgery N.Y. Med. Sch., 1984—. Contbr. articles to profl. jours. Pres. Hudson Valley Polit. Action Commn., Spring Valley, N.Y., 1982-94; pres. Adolph Schreiber Hebrew Acad., Monsey, N.Y., 1982-83, Cmty. Synagogue of Monsey, 1979-80, Union Orthodox Jewish Congregations of Am.; chmn. Inst. for Pub. Affairs; bd. dirs. Am. Israel Pub. Affairs Commn., Washington, 1985-90. Fellow Am. Coll. Surgeons, Am. Soc. Colon and Rectal Surgeons, Am. Coll. Gastroenterology, N.Y. Colon and Rectal Surgeons, N.J. Colon and Rectal Surgeons, Soc. Am. Gastroenterologic Endoscopic Surgeons. Home: 100 Route 59 Suffern NY 10901-4910 Office: Hudson Valley PAC 100A Schoolhouse Rd Spring Valley NY 10977

GANDER, BRUNO ALFRED, pharmacist; b. Switzerland, Feb. 27, 1955. Pharmacist, Sch. Pharmacy, Zürich, 1981; PhD, Sch. Pharmacy, Geneva, 1986. Rsch. scientist Zyma, Nyon, Switzerland, 1981-82; postdoctoral fellow U. Strathclyde, Glasgow, Scotland, 1986-87; sr. rsch. scientist Sch. Pharmacy, Geneva, 1987-89; assoc. prof. dept. pharmacy ETH, Zürich, 1989—. Author: Concepts in Vaccine Development, 1996; editor: Vaccine Delivery systems, 1996; contbr. articles to profl. jours.; patentee in field. Mem. Controlled Release Soc. Office: ETH, Dept Pharmacy, Winterthurerstrasse 190, 8057 Zürich Switzerland

GANDEVIA, BRYAN HARLE, physician; b. Melbourne, Australia, Apr. 5, 1925; s. Eric Neville Harle and Vera Brooking (Hannah) G.; m. Dorothy Virginia Murphy, Aug. 25, 1950; children: Simon Charles, Robin Harle. M.B., B.S., U. Melbourne, 1948, M.D., 1953. Intern, resident, Melbourne and London, Eng., 1950-57; sr. fellow occupational medicine U. Melbourne, 1958-63; assoc. prof. medicine U. New South Wales, Sydney, 1963-85; chmn. dept. respiratory medicine Prince Henry and Prince of Wales Hosps., Sydney, 1963-85; pvt. practice, Sydney, 1985—; occupational health cons. WHO, 1981-95. Author: Annotated Bibliography of History of Medicine in Australia, 1957; Tears Often Shed: Child Health and Welfare in Australia from 1788, 1978. Co-author: Annotated Bibliography of History of Medicine and Health in Australia, 1984. Chmn. editorial com.: BIBAM (Bibliography of Australian Medicine Project), 1983-89. Contbr. articles to profl. and hist. jours. Maj. Royal Australian Army Med. Corps, 1949-60. Mem. coun. Australian War Meml., Canberra, 1967-83. Decorated Order of Australia. Fellow Royal Coll. Physicians London (hon. faculty occupl. medicine), Royal Australasian Coll. Physicians (history of medicine libr. com. 1963-94, chmn. 1983—), Royal Australian Coll. Physicians, Faculty Occupl. Medicine; mem. Internat. Commn. Occupl. Health, Internat. Soc. History Medicine, Brit. and Australian Thoracic Soc. (hon.). Univ. & Schs. Club (Sydney). Avocations: History, wine and food, books. Office: 69 Arthur St, Randwick, Sydney 2031, Australia

GANDY, BONNIE SERGIACOMI, oncological and intravenous therapy nurse; b. Bridgeton, N.J., July 12, 1952; d. Albert A. and Jean (Goodwin) Sergiacomi; m.Robert H. Gandy, Aug. 15, 1981 (dec.); 1 child, Anthony Robert. BA, Glassboro (N.J.) State Coll., 1974; ADN, Cumberland County Coll., Vineland, N.J., 1985. RN, N.J., N.C.; cert. tchr., N.J.; cert. oncology nurse, intravenous nurse. Staff nurse, charge nurse William B. Kessler Meml. Hosp., Hammonton, N.J., 1985-86; supr. med. outpatient unit South Jersey Hosp. System-Millville (N.J.) Div., 1986-93; dir. home care nursing Med IV Home Health Svcs., Hickory, N.C., 1994—; IV nurse cons., IV therapist Am. Pharm. Svcs., Hickory, N.C., 1995—. Mem. Nat. Intravenous Therapy Assn., Oncology Nursing Soc., Phi Theta Kappa.

GANELES, JEFFREY, periodontist; b. Mountain Home, Idaho, Oct. 9, 1957; s. Ronald and Joyce (Kemins) G.; m. Lori Beth Berman, June 27, 1958; children: Caryn Elissa, Steven Aaron. BS, Cornell U., 1979; DMD, Boston U., 1983; cert. Advanced Grad. Study, U. Pa., 1987. Diplomate Am. Bd. Periodontology, 1993. Resident U. Pa. Hosp., Phila., 1983-84; rsch. assoc. U. Pa. Sch. of Dental Medicine, Phila., 1984-86; gen. dentist Springfield, Pa., 1984-87; asst. clin. prof. Sch. of Dentistry Georgetown U., Washington, 1987-89; pvt. practice dentistry specializing in periodontics Washington, 1987-89, Boca Raton, Fla., 1990—. Contbr. dental articles to sci. jours. Recipient Am. Coll. Dentists award, 1983, Acad. Operative Dentistry award, 1983; Alpha Omega scholarship, 1983. Mem. ADA, Am. Acad. Periodontology, Acad. Osseointegration, Fla. Dental Assn., Am-Jewish Appeals, Alpha Omega (pres. Boston U. chpt. 1982-83). Democrat. Jewish. Office: 327 Plaza Real Ste 321 Boca Raton FL 33432-3944

GANGAROSA, LOUIS P., SR., dentistry educator, dentist; b. Rochester, N.Y., June 8, 1929; s. Biagio and Carmella (Bellassai) G.; m. Clara A. Amalfi, Sept. 4, 1950; children: Michael, Louis Jr., Maria, Alyssa. BA with high distinction, U. Rochester, 1952, MS in Pharmacology, 1955, PhD in Pharmacology, 1961; DDS, U. Buffalo, 1955. Asst. prof., instr. U. Rochester, N.Y., 1965-66, asst. prof., 1966-68; assoc. prof. Med. Coll. of Ga., Augusta, 1968-71, prof., 1971-95, prof. emeritus, 1995—; chmn. OTC dentifrice and dental care agents panel FDA, Washington, 1972-78; cons. on iontophoresis Alza Pharm. Inc., Palo Alto, Calif., 1977-79, Iomed, Inc., Salt Lake City, 1980-84, Life Tech Inc., Houston, 1988-93; ad hoc cons. NIH, Washington, 1978-88. Co-author/editor: Pharmacotherapeutics in Dentistry, 1983, rev. 1987, 91, 95; contbr. numerous articles to profl. jours. Pres. St. James United Meth. Men's Club, Augusta, 1982-85; chmn. youth ministry St. James United Meth. Ch., Augusta, 1980-81. Fellow Am. Coll. of Dentists; mem. ADA, Am. Soc. for Pharmacology and Exptl. Therapeutics, Internat. Assn. for Dental Rsch. (pres. Southeastern sect. 1978-80), Am. Coll. Dentists.

GANGJEE, ALEEM, pharmacy educator and researcher; b. Calcutta, India, July 30, 1948; came to U.S., 1971; s. Asgarali A. and Sakina G.; m. Shameem Sultan, Aug. 7, 1972; children: Zia, Javed. BS, Indian Inst. Tech., Kharagpur, 1969, MS, 1971; PhD, U. Iowa, 1975. Postdoctoral fellow dept. biochemistry U. Iowa, Iowa City, 1975-76; postdoctoral fellow in med. chemistry SUNY, Buffalo, 1976-79; asst. prof. Sch. of Pharmacy Duquesne U., Pitts., 1979-83, assoc. prof. Sch. of Pharmacy, 1983-88, prof. Sch. of Pharmacy, 1988—, dir., prof. Grad. Sch. Pharm. Scis., 1990—. Contbr. articles to Jour. Medicinal Chemistry, Jour. Heterocyclic Chemistry. Mem. Am. Chem. Soc., Am. Assn. Pharm. Scientists, N.Y. Acad. Scis., Phi Lambda Upsilon, Rho Chi, Sigma Xi. Office: Duquesne U Sch of Pharmacy Mellon Hall Pittsburgh PA 15282

GANLEY, JAMES POWELL, ophthalmologist, educator; b. Altadina, Calif., Apr. 25, 1937; s. Joseph Harrington and Ruth Alice (Carr) G.; m. Anne Hay Hunter, Aug. 7, 1965; children: Anne Hay, Susan Powell, Katherine Carr, Elizabeth Pearson. BS in Biology, Mt. St. Mary's Coll., 1959; MD, Georgetown U., 1963; MPH, Johns Hopkins U., 1969, DPH, 1972. Diplomate Am. Bd. Med. Examiners, Am. Bd. Preventive Medicine (fellow), Am. Bd. Ophthalmology (fellow). Intern Washington Hosp. Ctr., 1963-64; resident in ophthalmology SUNY Upstate Med. Ctr., Syracuse, 1965-68; resident in preventive medicine Johns Hopkins U., Balt., 1969-71; sr. staff fellow Nat. Eye Inst., NIH, Bethesda, Md., 1971-74; asst. prof. ophthalmology U. Ariz. Med. Ctr., Tucson, 1974-80; assoc. prof., dept. head La. State U. Med. Ctr., Shreveport, 1980-82, prof., head dept., 1982—, asst. dean clin. affairs, 1981-87; mem. sci. adv. panel Onchocerciasis Control Program, WHO, Geneva, Switzerland, 1974-79; med. adv. bd. Internat. Eye Found., Bethesda, 1974-77; ophthalmic drugs adv. com. FDA, HEW, Rockville, Md., 1976-82; mem. epidemiol. and disease control study sect. NIH, 1982-86. Author: book chpts., procs.; editor Ophthalmic Epidemiology, 1993—; mem. editorial bd. Sightsaver, Nat. Soc. to Prevent Blindness, 1982-86. Bd. dirs. Northwest Lions Eye Bank, Shreveport, 1987. Lt. USN, 1964-65. Mem. Am. Coll. Preventive Medicine, Am. Acad. Ophthalmology (com. rsch. regulatory agys. and fed. sys. 1986-91, chmn. 1990-91), Internat. Soc. Geog. Ophthalmology (pres. 1982-88, treas. 1988—, exec. bd. 1988—), Am. Coll. Epidemiology, La. Assn. Blind (bd. dirs. 1980—, 1st vice chmn., sec. exec. bd. 1989-91, chmn. bd. 1992-93), Shreveport Med. Soc. (bd. dirs. 1990-94, 2d v.p. 1993, 1st v.p. 1994, pres. 1995), Assn. Rsch. in Vision and Ophthalmology (program planning com. 1993-96), Revs. Rsch. NIH. Republican. Roman Catholic. Office: La State Univ Med Ctr 1501 Kings Hwy Shreveport LA 71130-3932

GANNON, MARC JAY, optometrist; b. Cleve., Sept. 22, 1951; s. Leonard Justin and Norma S. (Falcovich) Goldstein; m. Cheryl Denise Congress, Aug. 4, 1974; children: Jennifer, Joshua. Student, Miami U., Oxford, Ohio, 1972; OD magna cum laude, Ill. Coll. Optometry, Chgo., 1976. Cert. optometrist, Fla. Intern, then resident Naval Regional Med. Ctr., Portsmouth, Va., 1976-78; pvt. practice Ft. Lauderdale, Fla., 1978—; pres. Oculon Vison Enhancement, Inc., Boca Raton, Fla., 1984-89; dir. Gannon Ctr. Low Vision. Patentee in field. Dist. exec. Lighthouse dist. Boy Scouts Am., 1980-82; pres. Kiwanis, Pompano Beach, Fla., 1981-82, Bus. Forum, Pompano Beach, 1982-83. Lt. comdre. USN, 1976-78. Mem. Am. Optometric Assn., Fla. Optometric Assn., Nat. Eye Rsch.Found., Broward County Optometric Assn., Tomb and Key Honor Soc. Home: 20827 Sonrisa Way Boca Raton FL 33433 Office: 1751 E Commercial Blvd Fort Lauderdale FL 33334

GANT, GERALD CHARLES, surgeon; b. Reedsburg, Wis., June 7, 1933; s. Willard Ray and Evelyn Lillian (Nissalke) G.; m. Helen Lydia Gade, June 16, 1956; children: Jennifer, Peter. BS, U. Wis., 1955, MD, 1958. Diplomate Am. Bd. Surgery. Intern St. Joseph's Hosp., Marshfield, Wis., 1958-59; resident U. Wis. Hosps., Madison, 1959-60, 62-65; instr. in anatomy U. Wis. Sch. Medicine, Madison, 1965-66; fellow surgery of trauma Downstate Med. Ctr., Kings County Hosp., Bklyn., 1966-67; pvt. practice gen. surgery Utica, N.Y., 1967—. Lt. comdr. USN, 1960-62. Fellow Am. Coll. Surgeons; mem. AMA, Ctrl. N.Y. Surg. Soc., Oneida County Med. Soc. (past pres.), Ctrl. N.Y. Acad. Medicine, Soc. Mil. Surgeons USA. Republican. Lutheran. Office: Gerald C Gant MD 95 Genesee St New Hartford NY 13413

GANTZ, BRUCE JAY, otolaryngologist, educator; b. N.Y.C., May 18, 1946; m. Mary Katherine DeJong; children: Ellen Katherine, Jessica Rose, Jay Alexander. BS in Gen. Sci., U. Iowa, 1968, MD, 1974, MS in Otolaryngology, 1980; fellow neurotology, U. Zürich, Zurich, 1981-82. Asst. prof. dept otolaryngology U. Iowa Coll. Medicine, Iowa City, 1980-84, assoc. prof., 1984-87, prof., 1987—; interim head dept. otolaryngology head & neck surgery U. Iowa Hosps. & Clinics, Iowa City, 1993-95, head dept. otolaryngology head & neck surgery, 1995—; mem. adv. bd. Deafness Research Found. Sci., 1988—. Mem. editl. bd. Am. Jour. Otology, Laryngoscope, Skull Base Surgery, Operative Techniques in Otolaryngology-Head and Neck Surgery, Anales De Otolarnolaringo-logica Mexicana; contbr. articles to profl. jours. Recipient Tchr.-Investigator Devel. award Pub. Health Svc., 1981-86, Program Project award NIH, 1985—; clin. rsch. ctr. grantee NIDCD, 1990, 95. Mem. AMA, Assn. for Rsch. in Otolaryngology (pres. 1995), Deafness Rsch. Found. (state chmn. 1985—), Am. Acad. Otolaryngology-Head and Neck Surgery, Soc. Univ. Otolaryngologists, Am. Neurotology Soc. (v.p. 1994-96, pres.-elect 1996—), Am. Otological Soc., Collegium Oto-Rhino-Laryngologicum Amictuae Sacrum. Office: U Iowa Hosps & Clinics 450 Newton St Iowa City IA 52242

GANZ, JOEL SIEGFRIED, psychiatrist; b. Bklyn., Dec. 19, 1935; s. Richard and Esther (Gallay) G.; m. Rhoda Ezrin, June 18, 1961; children: Jeri Lynn, Stefanie Joy, Jeffrey Steven, Stacy Joan. BS, Bethany (W.Va.) Coll., 1957; MD, George Washington U., 1963. Lic. physician, D.C., Md. Resident in adult psychiatry St. Elizabeth Hosp., Washington, 1964-66; resident in child psychiatry Children's Hosp., Washington, 1966-68. Home: 7 Hawthorn Ct Rockville MD 20850-2028

GANZ, LEONARD IRA, internist; b. Bklyn., May 4, 1962. BA, Harvard U., 1984, MD, 1989. Diplomate Am. Bd. Internal Medicine, Am. Bd. Cardiovascular Disease. Intern Brigham & Women's Hosp., Boston, 1989-90, resident, 1990-92, fellow, 1992-95, staff physician, 1995—. Contbr. chpt. to book: Intensive Care Medicine, 1996. Mem. AMA, ACP, Am. Coll. Cardiology, N.Am. Soc. Pacing and Electrophysiology. Office: Brigham and Women's Hosp Cardiovascular Divsn 75 Francis St Boston MA 02115

GANZ, WILLIAM I., radiology educator, researcher; b. Munich, Jan. 2, 1951; s. Lazar and Jean Ganz; m. Susan Rebecca Sirota, June 22, 1980; children: Tova, Debora, Harry. BA, Adelphi U., 1972; MS and MD, Albert Einstein Coll. Medicine, Medicine, 1979. Diplomate Am. Bd. Nuclear Medicine. NIH med. scientist trainee Albert Einstein Coll. Medicine, Bronx, N.Y., 1972-78, pharmacology rsch. fellow, 1978-79, NIH cardiovascular fellow, 1979-80, radiology resident, 1980-83; radiology/nuclear medicine fellow Barnes Hosp./Inst. Radiology, St. Louis, 1983-85; asst. prof. U. Miami Sch. Medicine, 1985-90, assoc. prof., 1990-93, coord. nuclear medicine teaching program, 1990—; radiation safety officer, coord. clin. nuclear medicine South Shore Hosp., 1994—; dir. nuclear medicine Animal Rsch. Lab., 1995—; prof. panel Pfizer Pharms., Miami, 1986-95; coord. Nuclear Medicine Tchg. Program; dir. Nuclear Medicine Animal Rsch. Lab. Exhibitor in field; contbr. articles to profl. jours. Recipient NIH Svc. awards 1975-78, NSF award 1976, others. Mem. AMA, Am. Coll. Nuclear Physicians, Am. Coll. Cardiology, Radiol. Soc. N.Am., Soc. Nuclear Medicine, Soc. Magnetic Resonance Imaging, Am. Soc. Orthodox Jewish Scientists. Democrat. Jewish. Home: 4333 Adams Ave Miami FL 33140-2927

GANZARAIN, RAMON CAJIAO, psychoanalyst; b. Iquique, Chile, Apr. 18, 1923; s. Eusebio Gastanaga and Maria Cajiao; m. Matilde Vidal Soto, Oct. 10, 1953; children: Ramon, Mirentxu, Alejandro. BS, St. Ignacio Coll., Santiago, Chile, 1939; MD, U. Chile, Santiago, 1947; postgrad., Chilean Psychoanalytic Inst., 1947-50, cert. tng. analyst, 1953. Assoc. prof. psychiatry U. Chile, Santiago, 1955-68, dir. dept. med. edn., 1962-68; prof. depth psychology, sch. psychology Cath. U., Santiago, 1962-68; dir. Chilean Psychoanalytic Inst., Santiago, 1967-68; tng. analyst Topeka Inst. Psychoanalysis, 1968-87; dir. group psychotherapy services The Menninger Found., Topeka, 1978-87; geog. tng. analyst Columbia U. Ctr. for Psychoanalytic Tng. and Research, Atlanta, 1987; assoc. prof. psychiatry Emory U., Atlanta, 1988—; tng. analyst Emory U. Psychoanalytic Inst., 1988—. Author: Fugitives of Incest, 1988, Objects Relations Group Psychotherapy, 1989; contbr. articles to profl. jours., chpts. to books. Fellow Am. Group Psychotherapy Assn.; mem. AMA, Internat. Assn. Group Psychotherapy (bd. dirs., exec. counselor 1986), Am. Group Psychotherapy Assn. (bd. dirs. 1984-87, 93-96), Internat. Psychoanalytic Assn., Am. Psychoanalytic Assn., Kans. Med. Soc., Topeka Psychoanalytic Soc. (pres. 1985-87). Roman Catholic. Office: Emory U Psychoanalytic Inst Dept Psychiatry PO Box AF Atlanta GA 30337-0503

GARBACZ, PATRICIA FRANCES, school social worker, therapist; b. Hamtramck, Mich., Nov. 26, 1941; d. Stanley and Frances (Harubin) G. BS, Siena Heights Coll., 1969; M. Pastoral Counseling, St. Paul U., Ottawa, Can., 1972; ThM, St. John Provincial Sem., 1983; MSW, Wayne State U., 1989. Cert. social worker Acad. Cert. Social Workers; cert. sch. social worker; lic. marriage and family therapists. Assoc. dir. vocations Archdiocese of Detroit, 1975-77; co-dir. of inst. for women Archdiocese of Lusaka (Zambia), 1977-78; pastoral minister Archdiocese of Detroit, 1979-80, assoc. dir. preformation, 1980-84; tchr., ministry coord. Bishop Borgess High Sch., Redford, Mich., 1984-86; tchr., dept. chair Aquinas High Sch., Southgate, Mich., 1986-88; therapist Community Coun. on Drug Abuse/Livonia (Mich.) Counseling, 1988-89; substance abuse therapist Oxford Inst., St. Clair Shores, Mich., 1989-91; sch. social worker Lakeshore Pub. Schs., St. Clair Shores, 1990—; therapist Macomb Child Guidance, 1989—. Mem. NASW, Am. Assn. Marriage and Family Therapists, Mich. Assn. Sch. Social Workers.

GARBER, ALAN MICHAEL, physician, educator, economist; b. Moline, Ill., May 7, 1955; s. Harry and Jean Garber; m. Anne Margot Yahanda, Oct. 9, 1988. AB in Econs. summa cum laude, Harvard Coll., 1976, AM in Econs., 1977, PhD, 1982; MD, Stanford U., 1983. Diplomate Am. Bd. Internal Medicine. Cons. Inst. Medicine, Washington, 1979-80; clin. fellow Med. Sch. Harvard U., Boston, 1983-86; rsch. fellow John F. Kennedy Sch. Govt. Harvard U., Cambridge, Mass., 1986; staff physician VA Palo Alto (Calif.) Health Care System, 1986—; rsch. assoc. Nat. Bur. Econ. Rsch., Palo Alto, Calif., 1986—; dir. health care program Nat. Bur. Econ. Rsch., Cambridge, 1990—; asst. prof. Stanford (Calif.) U., 1986-93, assoc. prof., 1993—; contractor Office Tech. Assessment, Washington, 1987-88, 89-92. Fellow NSF, 1976, Henry J. Kaiser faculty fellow Kaiser Found., 1989-92; grantee Robert Wood Johnson Found., 1988. Fellow ACP; mem. Soc. Med. Decision Making (trustee 1989-91), Am. Econ. Assn., Assn. Health Svcs. Rsch., Am. Fedn. Clin. Rsch. (nat. councillor 1991-96), Soc. Gen. Internal Medicine. Office: Stanford U Sch Medicine 204 Junipero Serra Blvd Palo Alto CA 94305-8006

GARBER, BETTY KAHN, social worker; b. Jersey City, May 22, 1950; d. Bernard and Rita (Dorn) Kahn; m. Dale J. Garber, June 17, 1973; 1 child, Amy. AB, Washington U., St. Louis, 1971, MSW, 1973. Lic. clin. social worker, Ill.; diplomate Am. Bd. Examiners in Clin. Social Work. Social worker E. Maine Sch. Dist., Des Plaines, Ill., 1973-78, Northbrook (Ill.)/Glenview Sch. Dist., 1986—; unit leader, asst. camp dir. Rogers Park Jewish Community Ctr., Chgo., summers, 1974, 75. Mem. sch. bd. W. Northfield Sch. Dist., Northbrook, 1983-95. Mem. NASW (bd. cert. diplomate, qualified clin. social worker, sch. social work specialist)., Acad. Cert. Social Workers. Office: Northbrook/Glenview Sch Dis 2500 Happy Hollow Rd Glenview IL 60025-1117

GARBER, EDWARD HENRY HAUSER, JR., surgeon; b. York, Pa., Dec. 12, 1950; s. Edward H.H. and Doris T. (Turnbull) G.; m. Judith Lauber, Aug. 19, 1972; children: Philip, Daniel, Elizabeth. BA, Valparaiso U., 1972; MD, Jefferson Med. Coll., 1976. Resident Polyclinic Med. Ctr., Harrisburg, Pa., 1976-80; active staff York Hosp., 1980—; chief divsn. gen. surgery York Hosp., 1993—. Bd. dirs. Am. Cancer Soc., York, 1985-91; active Christ Luth. Ch., 1981—. Office: 25 Monument Rd Ste 220 York PA 17403

GARBER, JOYCE STEINHARDT, psychiatrist; b. N.Y.C., Jan. 10, 1943; d. Herschel s. and Anna (Danenberg) Steinhardt; m. Nicholas Pernice, July 30, 1966, (div. 1972); m. David M. Garber, June 8, 1975; children: Ari, Sarah, Noah. BS cum laude, CCNY, 1963; MD, N.Y.U., 1967. Diplomate Am. Bd. Psychiatry and Neurology. Intern Jewish Hosp., St. Louis, 1968; resident in psychiatry U. Md. Hosp., Balt., 1970, SUNY Upstate Med. Ctr., Syracuse, N.Y., 1970-72; clin. asst. prof. psychiatry SUNY Upstate Med. Ctr., Syracuse, 1978—; asst. dir. Adult Psychiatric In-patient Unit, State U. Hosp., Syracuse, N.Y., 1972-78; pvt. practice Syracuse, 1978—. Fellow Am. Psychiat. Assn. (ethics chmn. Cen. N.Y. dist. br. 1980—, past pres.); mem. Innominate Club, Jacobsen Elsner Soc. Democrat. Jewish. Office: 120 E Washington St Syracuse NY 13202-4000

GARBER, MARY DIANE, physician assistant; b. Montreal; d. Geoffrey Vaughn and Mary Beatrice (Powell) Williams; m. Lawrence Lowell Garber, Jr. BFA, Concordia U., Montreal, 1979; M. Med. Sci., Emory U., Atlanta, 1993. Physician asst. Duke U. Med. Ctr., Durham, N.C., 1994-95, Collettsville (N.C.) Med. Clinic, 1995—. Mem. Am. Assn. Physician Assts., N.C. Assn. Physician Assts., Nat. Health Care Officers. Home: 206 Spruce Rd Blowing Rock NC 28605 Office: Collettsville Med Clinic PO Box 9 Collettsville NC 28611

GARBER, PERRY F., ophthalmologist, surgeon; b. Bklyn., June 12, 1943. BA in Chemistry, CUNY, 1964; MD, SUNY, Bklyn., 1968. Diplomate Nat. Bd. Med. Examiners, Am. Bd. Ophthalmology. Intern in medicine and surgery Kings County Hosp., Bklyn., 1968-69; resident in surgery Mount Sinai Hosp., N.Y.C., 1969-70; resident in opthalmology NYU Med. Ctr., N.Y.C., 1972-74, chief resident in opthalmology, 1974-75; fellow in ophthalmic plastic, reconstructive and orbital surgery N.Y. Eye & Ear Infirmary/Manhattan Eye & Ear Hosp., N.Y.C., 1975-76; assoc. clin. prof. ophthalmology and visual sci. Albert Einstein Coll. of Medicine, Bronx, N.Y., 1973—; attending physician L.I. Jewish Med. Ctr., New Hyde Park, N.Y.; sr. assoc. North Shore Univ. Hosp., Manhasset, N.Y. Maj. USAF, 1970-72. Recipient Svc. award Am. Acad. Ophthalmology, 1992. Office: Perry F Garber PC 1380 Northern Blvd Manhasset NY 11030

GARBER, SHELDON, hospital executive; b. Mpls., July 21, 1920; s. Mitchell and Esther (Amdur) G.; BA, U. Minn., 1942; postgrad. U. Chgo., 1952-53; m. Elizabeth Sargent Mason, May 16, 1949 (div. May 1983); children: Robert Michael, Daniel Mason, Sarah Sargent; m. Joellen Palmer Prullage, July 21, 1985. Reporter, editor U.P.I., Mpls., Chgo., Springfield, Ill., 1938-58; dir. media services U. Chgo., 1958-64; asso. dir. communication Blue Cross Assn., Chgo., 1964-69; pres. Sheldon Garber Assocs., Inc., 1969—; exec. v.p. Charles R. Feldstein & Co., 1969-73; v.p. philanthropy and communication Rush-Presbyn.-St. Luke's Med. Center, Chgo., 1973-88, sec. bd. trustees, 1976-92; exec. v.p. Orthopaedic Rsch. and Edn. Found., 1981-92, cons. Shedd Aquarium, Chgo., Cardinal Glennon Children's Hosp., St. Louis, Parkinson's Disease Soc. Am., Cook-Fort Worth (Tex.) Children's Med. Ctr., Univ. Chgo. Med. Ctr., Thoracic Surg. Found. Rsch., Edn., Chgo. Zool. Soc. (Brookfield Zoo), Dermatology Found., Commn. on Drug Safety, Joint Commn. for Accreditation of Healthcare Orgns., Ill. Math. and Sci. Acad., Great Books Found., Am. Assn. U. Programs in Hosp. Adminstrn., Am. Nurses Found., Am. Acad. Pediatrics, Sigma Theta Tau, Henry Ford Health Care Corp.; mem. faculty Inst. on Indsl. and Tech. Communications, Colo. State U., Fort Collins, 1970. Adv. bd. Internat. Inst. Edn.; trustee Citizens Information Service; mem. bd. Nat. Soc. Fund Raisers, 1974-77. Served to 1st lt. C.E., AUS, 1942-46, 50-52. Am. Soc. Hosp. Pub. Relations Dirs., AAAS, Nat. Assn. Sci. Writers, Am. Med. Writers Assn., Inst. Medicine Chgo., Sigma Delta Chi.

GARCIA, ALEXANDER, orthopedic surgeon; b. N.Y.C., July 3, 1919; s. Alexander and Pilar (Prieto) G.; m. Helen Ann Proskey, June 12, 1943; 1 son, Alexander, III. B.S., CCNY, 1940; M.D., L.I. Coll. Medicine, 1943. Diplomate: Am. Bd. Orthopaedic Surgery. Intern Syracuse (N.Y.) U. Med. Center, 1944, asst. resident in gen. surgery, 1944-45, chief resident, 1945-46; resident in gen. surgery Nassau Hosp., Mineola, N.Y., 1948; asst. resident in orthopaedic surgery N.Y. Orthopaedic Hosp., N.Y.C., 1948-50; resident, jr. Annie C. Kane fellow N.Y. Orthopaedic Hosp., 1950-51, acting dir. orthopaedic service, 1976-77, hosp. dir., 1977-83, dir. emeritus, 1983—; chief orthopaedic surg. sect. North Shore Hosp., Manhasset, N.Y., 1957-70, cons., 1970—; mem. faculty Columbia U. Coll. Phys. and Surg., 1952—, prof. orthopaedic surgery, 1972—, chmn. dept., 1977—, Frank E. Stinchfield prof., 1978-83, Frank E. Stinchfield prof. emeritus, 1983—; pres. med. bd. Presbyn. Hosp.-Columbia Presbyn. Med. Ctr., N.Y.C., 1979-82; cons. numerous area hosps. Mem. editoral bds. profl. jours. Served as officer M.C. AUS, 1946-48. Mem. Internat. Soc. Orthopaedic Surgery and Traumatology, A.C.S., AMA, Am. Acad. Orthopaedic Surgeons, Am. Assn. for Surgery of Trauma, Pan Am. Med. Assn., Assn. Bone and Joint Surgeons, Am. Orthopaedic Assn., N.Y. State Med. Soc., N.Y. Acad. Medicine, N.Y. Acad. Scis., N.Y. State Soc. Orthopaedic Surgeons, Soc. Ortopedia y Traumatologia Dominicana. Democrat.

GARCÍA, CELSO-RAMÓN, obstetrician and gynecologist; b. N.Y.C., Oct. 31, 1921; s. Celso García y Ondina and Oliva Menéndez (del Valle) G.; m. Shirley Jean Stoddard, Oct. 14, 1950; children: Celso-Ramón, Sarita Stoddard. BS, Queens Coll., 1942; MD, SUNY Downstate Med. Ctr., 1945; MA (hon.), U. Pa. Intern Norwegian Hosp., Bklyn., 1945-46; resident Cumberland Hosp., Bklyn., 1948-53, rsch. fellow in ob/gyn., 1949-50; rsch. fellow in gynecology Free Hosp. for Women, Brookline, Mass., 1955-57, asst. surgeon, 1958-61, assoc. surgeon, 1961-65; asst. prof. obstetrics and gynecology U. P.R., San Juan, 1953-55, assoc. in ob-gyn., 1953-54; asst. prof. ob-gyn. Sch. Medicine and Tropical Medicine, P.R., 1954-55; co-dir. Rock Reproductive Study Ctr.; asst. obstetrician and gynecologist Boston Lying-In Hosp.; assoc. surgeon Free Hosp. for Women, Brookline, Mass., 1955-65; sr. scientist, dir. tng. program in physiology reprodn. Worcester Found. for Exptl. Biology, Shrewsbury, Mass., 1960-62; asst. surgeon, chief Infertility Clinic, Mass. Gen. Hosp.; from asst., instr. to clin. assoc. ob-gyn Harvard Med. Sch., 195962-65; prof. obstetrics and gynecology U. Pa., Phila., 1965-92; William Shippen, Jr. prof. human reprodn. U. Pa., 1970-92, William Shippen, Jr. prof emeritus, 1992—, dir. reproductive surgery, 1987-95; extraordinary prof. U. San Luis Potosi, Mex., 1974; rapporteur com. of experts on clin. aspects oral gestogens WHO, Geneva, Switzerland, 1965; mem. ad hoc adv. com. contraceptive devel., contract program Nat. Inst. Child Health and Human Devel., 1971-75; mem. original team developing application of the first FDA approved progestagen-estrogen combinations for oral contraception (the Pill); developer, dir. first formal tng. program in physiology of reprodn. in U.S.; innovator surg. approach to infertility of women; cons. Pa. Hosp., 1973-94; asst. staff Faulkner Hosp., Jamaica Plain, Boston; courtesy staff Glover Meml. Hosp., Needham, Mass. Chmn. nat. med. adv. com. Planned Parenthood World Population, 1971-74; mem. nat. adv. child and human devel. coun. Nat. Inst. Child Health and Human Devel., 1981-84. Served with AUS, 1943-48. Recipient Carl G. Hartman award Am. Soc. Study of Sterility, 1961, MD Master Tchg. award Alumni Assn. SUNY, 1989, Recognition award APGO Wyeth-Ayerst, 1993, Frank L. Babbott award SUNY, 1995; Sidney Graves fellow in gynecology Harvard Med. Sch., 1955. Fellow ACS, ACOG, Royal Soc. Health, Coll. Physicians Phila.; mem. AMA, Am. Soc. Gynecol. Surgeons, Am. Gynecol. and Obstet. Soc., Am. Physiol. Soc., Assn. Planned Parenthood Physicians (past pres.), Soc. Reproductive Surgeons (founding pres.), Am. Fertility Soc. (bd. dirs., past pres.), Phila. Ostet. Soc., Miami Obstetrics Soc. (hon.), Fedn. Columbian Socs. Ob-Gyn. (hon.), Cuban Soc. Ob-Gyn. (in exile, hon.), Masons, Sigma Xi. Republican. Presbyterian. Home: 109 Merion Rd Merion Station PA 19066-1734 Office: 3400 Spruce St Philadelphia PA 19104

GARCIA, GEORGE EDWARD, ophthalmologist; b. Mendocino, Calif., May 2, 1930; s. Antonio J. and Zelmeda M. Garcia; m. Lois Ann O;Connor, Jan. 2, 1955; children: Suzanne Zell, Paul Anthony. BS, U. Calif., Berkeley, 1952, M of Optometry, 1953; MD, Boston U., 1961. Diplomate Am. Bd. Ophthalmology. Intern Mass. Meml. Hosp., Boston, 1961-62; fellow Howe Lab. of Ophthalmology Mass. Eye & Ear Infirmary, Boston, 1962-63, resident, 1963-66; asst. prof. ophthalmology Boston U. Sch. Medicine, 1966-72, asst. clin. prof., 1972-79; asst. clin. prof. ophthalmology Harvard Med. Sch., 1979—; assoc. chief ophthalmology Mass. Eye and Ear Infirmary, Boston, 1984-90, assoc. chief vis. staff, 1990-93; bd. dirs. Am. Bd. Ophthalmology, 1984-91. Contbr. articles to profl. jours. Mem. AMA, New Eng. Ophthal. Soc. (pres. 1994), Am. Assn. Ophthalmology (pres. 1981, mem. pub. info. com. 1980-83), Am. Acad. Ophthalmology (bd. dirs. 1981-91, pres. 1990). Office: 44 Washington St Brookline MA 02146-7130

GARCIA, GEORGE MASON, cardiologist; b. Tucson, May 25, 1962; s. Hector Lowrence Garcia and Ligia (Pazos) Padron. MD, U. Autonomous N. Mex., 1988. Diplomate Am. Bd. Internal Medicine, Am. Bd. Cardiology. From resident in internal medicine to fellow cardiology Oak Lawn (Ill.) Hosp., 1989-95; fellow interventional cardiology Temple (Tex.) Hosp., 1995—. Mem. Chgo. Coun. Fgn. Rels., Am. Colls. Physicians, Southern Med. Assn., N.Y. Acad. Scis., Am. Soc. Internal Medicine, Am. Coll. Cardiology. Republican. Roman Catholic. Home: 404 S Fryers Creek #1111 Temple TX 76504

GARCIA, GODOFREDO IGNO, physician; b. Manila, Dec. 14, 1958; s. Alberto and Rosita (Igno) G. BS cum laude, U. Philippines, 1979, MD cum laude, 1983. Physician Roane Gen. Hosp., Spencer, W.Va., 1991-92, Morgan County Hosp., W. Liberty, Ky., 1993-94, FHP/Greenfield Ctr., Mesa, Ariz., 1994-95, Bluegrass Regional Med. Ctr., Frankfort, Ky., 1995—. Mem. ACP, Ky. Med. Assn., Franklin County Med. Soc. Office: 107 Diagnostic Dr Frankfort KY 40601

GARCIA, HECTOR DAVID, toxicologist; b. Rio Grande City, Tex., Aug. 26, 1946; s. Toribio and Lilia Emma Garcia; m. Martha Rita Maldonado, Apr. 14, 1974; children: Mary Catharine, Christina, David. BA, U. St. Thomas, Houston, 1968; MS, U. Tex., Houston, 1975, PhD, 1979. Postdoctoral fellow Chem. Industry Inst. Toxicology, Reseach Triangle Park, N.C., 1979-81; rsch. scientist Philip Morris U.S.A., Richmond, Va., 1981-87; cons. Functional Mgmt. Inst., McLean, Va., 1987-89; v.p. Advanced Tech. Innovations, McLean, 1989-90; sr. rsch. scientist Krug Life Scis., Houston, 1990—; pres. Advanced Bus. Concepts, Houston, 1990—. Author: Banbury Report 13, 1982, Spacecraft Maximum Allowable Concentrations of Selected Airborne Contaminants, Vol. 1 and 2, 1994. Sgt. U.S. Army, 1969-71. Mem. KC (chancellor 1995—). Roman Catholic. Home: 8214 Buffalo Speedway Houston TX 77025 Office: Krug Life Scis 1290 Hercules Dr #120 Houston TX 77058

GARCIA, JANE DAVIS, medical management administrator, occupational health nurse; b. Mooresville, N.C., July 2, 1947; d. Charlie Moore and Colleen (Robbins) Davis; m. Ruben M. Garcia; children: Mikel Scott Hubbard, Julia Alicia Hubbard. ADN, Cen. Piedmont Community Coll., Charlotte, N.C., 1967; BS, Nova U., Ft. Lauderdale, 1987. Cert. adult nurse practitioner, occupational health nurse. Occupational health nurse practitioner Burlington Industries, Stonewall, Miss.; nurse practitioner otolaryngologist's office, Lansing, Mich.; DON EMSA Ltd. Partnership, Ft. Lauderdale. Mem. ANA, NPACE, Am. Assn. Occupational Health Nurses, Am. Acad. Nurse Practitioners, Fla. Nurses Assn., Emergency Nurses Assn. Home: 9140 Old Orchard Rd Davie FL 33328-5708

GARCIA, JOHN, psychologist, educator; b. Santa Rosa, Calif., June 12, 1917; married; 3 children. BA, U. Calif., Berkeley, 1948, MA, 1949, PhD, 1965. Teaching asst. U. Calif., Berkeley, 1949-51; psychologist U.S. Naval Radiol. Def. Lab., San Francisco, 1951-58; tchr. biol. sci. Oakland (Calif.) Pub. Schs., 1958-59; asst. prof. psychology Calif. State Coll., Long Beach, 1959-65; assoc. biologist, neurosurg. svc. Mass. Gen. Hosp., Boston, 1965-68; prof. psychology, chmn. psychobiology program SUNY, Stony Brook, 1968-71, chmn. dept., 1971-72; prof. U. Utah, Salt Lake City, 1972-73; prof. psychology and psychiatry UCLA, 1973-87, emeritus prof. psychology and psychiatry, 1987—. Fellow Soc. Exptl. Psychologists (Howard Crosby Warren medal 1978); mem. AAAS, APA (Disting. Sci. Contbn. award 1979, William James fellow), Nat. Acad. Scis., Am. Psychol. Soc., N.Y. Acad. Scis., Western Psychol. Assn. (pres. 1991—), Sigma Xi. Address: 1950-A Chilberg Rd Mount Vernon WA 98273

GARCIA, JOSE ANTONIO, obstetrician, gynecologist; b. San Juan, P.R., Jan. 12, 1954; s. Jose Antonio and Ana Maria (Saul) G.; m. Kathrine Warden Horn, Nov. 27, 1982; children: Ana Virginia, Jose Antonio, Kathrine Marie, Kelly Elizabeth. BS, U. P.R., 1973; MD, Duke U., 1977. Intern Duke U. Med. Ctr., Durham, 1977-78; resident Duke U. Med. Ctr., Durham, N.C., 1977-80, chief resident, 1980-81; obstetrician-gynecologist Peachtree Women's Clinic, Atlanta, 1981—, pres., 1989—; chmn. dept. obgyn Northside Hosp., Atlanta, 1991-93. Fellow Am. Coll. Ob-Gyn; mem. AMA, Am. Fertility Soc., Atlanta Ob-Gyn Soc., Carter Soc. Ob-Gyn, Atlanta Athletic Club. Roman Catholic. Office: Peachtree Women's Clinic Ste 220 980 Johnson Ferry Rd NE Atlanta GA 30342-1607

GARCIA, MARIA LUISA, biochemist; b. Valladolid, Spain, Oct. 9, 1953; came to U.S., 1979; d. Baldomero and Dolores (Garcia) G.; m. Gregory Kaczorowski, June 21, 1982. PhD, Autonoma U., Madrid, 1979. Sr. rsch. biochemist Merck & Co., Rahway, N.J., 1985-87; rsch. fellow Merck & Co., Rahway, 1987-91, sr. rsch. fellow, 1991—. Home: 5 Ashbrook Dr Edison NJ 08820 Office: Merck Rsch Labs PO Box 2000 Rahway NJ 07065

GARCIA, NELSON A., internist; b. Guayaquil, Ecuador, May 16, 1950; came to U.S., 1954; s. Nelson E. and Alicia S. (Sanchez) G.; m. Janice Renee Garcia, Nov. 4, 1989; children: Amanda, Alexandra, Alyssa. BS, U. Calif., Irvine, 1972; MD, U. Calif., San Francisco, 1976. Diplomate Am. Bd. Internal Medicine, Am. Bd. Infectious Disease. Instr. medicine U. Calif., Orange, Calif., 1982-83, asst. prof., 1984; pvt. practice in infectious diseases Whittier, Calif., 1985-92; staff physician, infectious diseases cons. Kaiser Found. Hosps., Bellflower, Calif., 1992—; advisor Orange County Med. Assn. AIDS Task Force, 1984; program dir. AIDS - Current Med. and Legal Aspects, 1986-88. Roman Catholic. Office: Kaiser Foundation Hosp Ste 3400 9400 E Rosecrans Bellflower CA 90706

GARCIA, RAYMOND LLOYD, dermatologist; b. Paterson, N.J., Jan. 24, 1942; s. Raymond and Ruth Elaine (De Graff) G.; m. Cynthia Ruth Towne (div.); m. Toy Ping Woo, Dec. 22, 1984; 1 child, Christopher Drew. BA cum laude, Drew U., 1963; MD, Temple U., 1967. Diplomate Am. Bd. Dermatology, Am. Bd. Dermatology-Pathology. Commd. Col. USAF, 1966; intern Wilford Hall USAF Med. Ctr., San Antonio, 1967-68; dermatology resident, 1969-72; vice-chmn. residency tng. program Wilford Hall USAF Med. Ctr., San Antonio, 1972-82; asst. chief aerospace medicine USAF Acad., Colorado Springs, Colo., 1968-69; chief dermatology Carswell USAF Hosp., Ft. Worth, 1982-86; pvt. practice Irving, Tex., 1986—; asst. prof. U. Tex. Med. Sch., San Antonio, 1972-82; assoc. prof. Tex. Coll. Osteo. Medicine, Ft. Worth, 1982-92; cons. to surgeon gen. USAF, 1979-86. Editor: Jour. the Assn. Mil. Dermatologists, 1978-86, Handbook of Dermatology, 1980; contbr. over 50 articles to profl. jours. Decorated Nat. Defense medal USAF, 1972, Meritorious Svc. medal 1982. Fellow Am. Acad. Dermatology (legis. liaison com. 1972-78); mem. Assn. Mil. Dermatologists (sec., treas. 1973-75, v.p. 1977-78, pres. 1980), Tex. Med. Assn., Tarrant County Med. Soc., Babcock Surg. Soc. of Temple U. Med. Sch., Tex. Dermatol. Soc., Biol. Honor Soc. of Drew U., Alpha Kappa Kappa, Beta Beta Beta. Republican. Baptist. Home: 1110 San Juan Ct Arlington TX 76012-2750 Office: Dermatology Center 2015 W Park Dr Irving TX 75061-2113

GARCIA, ROBERTO SIOSON, anesthesiologist, surgeon; b. Manila, Dec. 9, 1933; came to U.S., 1956; s. Vicente S. and Librada (Sioson) G.; m. Evelyn Colonna, Apr. 6, 1958; children: Robert C., Rebecca E., Melissa J. MD, U. Philippines, 1956. Diplomate Am. Bd. Anesthesiologists. Intern Ch. Home & Hosp., Balt., 1956-57, surg. resident, 1957-58; surg. resident South Balt. Gen. Hosp., 1958-61; anesthesia resident Johns Hopkins Hosp., Balt., 1961-63; instr. anesthesia Johns Hopkins Sch. Medicine, Balt., 1963-64; chief anesthesia dept. Balt. County Gen. Hosp., Randallstown, Md., 1964-89; cons. anesthesiologist N.W. Med. Ctr., Randallstown, Md., 1989-96.

GARCIA, SUSAN P., public health service officer. Legis. sec. Mich Ho. of Reps., Lansing, 1976-83, adminstrv. aide, 1983-85; adminstrv. asst. Mich. Dept. Transp., Lansing, 1985-88; dep. dir. Mich. Assn. for Local Pub. Health, Lansing, 1986-91; spl. asst. to dir. Mich. Dept. Pub. Health, Lansing, 1991-94, dir. fed./state rels., 1995-96; deputy dir. Assoc. of HMO's, Lansing, 1996—. Mem. Gov.'s Task Force on Children's Justice, 1991—, Lt. Gov.'s Commns. on Children, 1995—, ; bd. dirs. Children's Trust Fund, 1992—; adv. bd. Head Start State Collaboration, 1994—; mem. Mich. Children Policy Com., 1994—, Lt. Gov.'s Adoption Commn., 1992-93, Caring Arms Com., 1992-93; treas. Healthy Mothers, Healthy Babies, 1988-91; bd. dirs. Mich. Coalition for Children and Families, 1986-91. Recipient Nurse Adminstrs. Forum award Mich. Assn. for Local Pub. Health, 1991. Mem. Assn. of State and Territorial Health Ofcls. (mgmt. com. 1992—, legis. com. 1994—), Mich. Pub. Health Assn. (legis. chair 1988-91), Am. Pub. Health Assn. Office: Association of HMO's PO Box 19333 Lansing MI 48901-9333*

GARCIA-MALDONADO, MAURILIO, physician, medical director; b. Monclova, Mex., Sept. 11, 1955; came to U.S., 1983; s. Maurilio Garcia-Soberon and Leonor (Maldonado) Garcia; m. Patricia L. Gil-de-Garcia, Apr. 30, 1983; children: Maurilio and Daniel Garcia-Gil. MD, Autonomous U. Guadalajara, 1978. Diplomate Am. Bd. Internal Medicine, Am. Bd. Nephrology. Rsch. fellow in nephrology U. Calif. Davis, Sacramento, 1983-85; fellow in nephrology U. Okla., Oklahoma City, 1985-89, instr., 1987-93, asst. prof., 1993—; staff VA Med. Ctr., Oklahoma City, 1991—; med. dir. VA Clinic, Lawton, Okla., 1994—; affiliate faculty Am. Heart Assn., Oklahoma City, 1990—. Contbr. articles to profl. jours. mem. devel. com. Hospice of Okla. County, Oklahoma City, 1993. Recipient Leadership award Vet. Affairs program, Washington, 1993. Mem. Am. Soc. Nephrology, Am. Coll. Physician Execs., Am. Coll. Healthcare Execs., Okla. Acad. State Goals, Toastmasters (v.p. edn. 1992). Office: Lawton-Fort Sill VA OPC PO Box 33326 Fort Sill OK 73503

GARCIA-MUNOZ, MARIANELA, neuroscientist; b. San Jose, Mar. 9, 1949; d. Eugenio Garcia and Flora (Munoz) Antillon; m. J.G. Figueroa, Apr. 15, 1974 (div. 1985); children: Libertad, Samantha. Student, Nat. Univ. Mexico, 1967-70; MS in Neurophysiology, Edinburgh U., Scotland, 1975; PhD in Neuropharmacology, Edinburgh U., 1978. Rsch. prof. Nat. U., Mexico, 1980-86, prof. teaching, 1986; rsch. assoc. Div. Clin. Pharmacology Health Sci. Ctr. Colo., Denver, 1985, asst. prof., 1988; asst. prof. U. Calif., San Diego, 1988-93, assoc. prof., 1993—. Contbr. articles to profl. jours. Mem. Internat. Brain Rsch. Orgn., Internat Basal Ganglia Soc., Mex. Nat. Acad. Scis., Soc. for Neurosci., European Neurosci. Assn. Office: U Calif 9500 Gilman Dr La Jolla CA 92093-5003

GARCIA-RUBIRA, JUAN CARLOS, cardiologist; b. Tetuan, Marruecos, Spain, Aug. 9, 1957; s. Manuel and Gloria (Rubira) G.; m. Dolores Romero, Sept. 20, 1980; children: Maria Del Mar, Inés. MD, U. Sevilla, 1980, doctorate, 1986. Med. resident U. Hosp., Sevilla, 1982-86, cardiologist, 1987—. Contbr. articles to profl. jours. Sponsor Action Aid Spain, 1984-95; mem. Parents of Deaf-Blind Children, Spain, 1995. Mem. Sociedad Espanola de Cardiologia, European Soc. of Cardiology, N.Y. Acad. of Scis. Roman Catholic. Home: Santa Maria de Los Reyes, 8 130C, E-41008 Seville Spain Office: Unidad Coronaria Hosp, V Macarena, Avenida Doctor Fedriani, E-41009 Sevilla Spain

GARDENIER, EDNA FRANCES, nurse; b. Teaneck, N.J., June 30, 1935; d. Andrew Cairns and Edna Frances (Manney) O'Neil; diploma Newark Beth Israel Sch. Nursing, 1955; BS in Nursing, Seton Hall U., S. Orange, N.J., 1965; MEd, Tchrs. Coll. Columbia U., 1970; EdD SUNY, Albany, 1990; m. Harvey James Gardenier, Aug. 25, 1961; children: Andrew, William. Staff nurse N.J. hosps., 1955-65; pub. health nurse, 1965-70; mem. nursing faculty Dutchess C.C., Poughkeepsie, N.Y., 1970—, program chmn. nursing, 1971-83, acting head dept. health technologies, 1983-92, head nursing dept., 1983—; mem. overall nursing faculty N.Y. State Regents Coll., 1981-92; mem. nurse edn. com. SUNY; mem. Dutchess County chpt. Am. Heart Assn., 1974-90; nutrition adv. coun. Dutchess County Coop. Edn., 1970-79. USPHS trainess, 1968-70. Mem. Am. Assn. Women in Jr. and C.C.s, N.Y. Assn. Degree Nurse Coun., N.Y. State Nurses Assn., N.Y. State Two Year Coll. Assn., Sigma Theta Tau. Home: Rd 1 Box 85 Holsapple Rd Dover Plains NY 12522 Office: Dutchess C C Pendell Rd Poughkeepsie NY 12601

GARDIN, JOHN GEORGE, II, psychologist; b. Renton, Wash., Jan. 5, 1949; s. John George and Charlotte (Larabee) G.; m. Dana Rothrock, Oct. 22, 1986; children: Greg, Gina, Bret; 1 stepchild, Angie West. BS in Chemistry, Seattle U., 1971; BS in Psychology, U. Wash., 1972; MS in Psychology, Portland State U., 1975; PhD in Psychology, U. Tenn., 1986. Lic. psychologist. Clinician Luth. Family Svcs., Portland, Oreg., 1978-80; mental health specialist Probation Dept. Oreg. State, Roseburg, 1980-81; exec. dir. ADAPT, Roseburg, 1981-85; psychologist, ptnr. South Coast Psychol., Irvine, Calif., 1986-91; assoc. prof. psychiatry U. Calif. Irvine, Dana Point, Calif., 1988-90; med. dir. Chem. Dependency Charter Hosp., Corona, Calif., 1990-91; ptnr. LifeOne, Irvine, 1991-92; pvt. practice psychology Costa Mesa, Calif., 1985—; bd. dirs. Kangaroo Kids Ctr., Medically Fragile Children, 1992-94; cons. Real World TV Show, Bunim-Murray Prodns., 1993—, Flagship Healthcare, 1994-95, Orange County Youth Ctrs., 1996—. Pres. Alcohol/Drug Program Dirs. of Oreg., 1984; bd. dirs. Oreg. State Coun. on Alcoholism, 1983; mem. Counselors Credentials Task Force, Oreg., 1984. Mem. APA, Calif. State Psychol. Assn., Am. Athletic Union, Japan Karate-Do Fedn. Office: 2900 Bristol St Ste D-107 Costa Mesa CA 92626-5981

GARDIN, JULIUS MARKUS, cardiologist, educator; b. Detroit, Jan. 14, 1949; s. Abram and Fania (Toba) G.; m. Susan Deanne Kelemen, Dec. 19, 1982; children: Adam Lev, Tova Michal, Margot Anne. BS with high distinction, U. Mich., 1968, MD cum laude, 1972. Diplomate Am. Bd. Internal Medicine; cert. cardiovascular diseases. Intern then resident in medicine U. Mich., Ann Arbor, 1972-75; fellow in cardiology Georgetown U., Washington, 1975-77; dir. cardiology noninvasive lab., staff cardiologist Lakeside VA Med. Ctr., Chgo., 1977-79; staff cardiologist, asst. prof. Med. Sch. Northwestern U., Chgo., 1978-79; dir. cardiology noninvasive lab. Irvine Med. Ctr. U. Calif., Orange, 1979—, from asst. prof. to assoc. prof. Irvine Med. Ctr., 1979-89, prof., 1989—; chief cardiology U. Calif., Irvine, 1994—; acting chief cardiology Long Beach (Calif.) VA Med. Ctr., 1982-84. Co-editor: Textbook of Two-Dimensional Echocardiography, 1983; editor: Update on Cardiovascular Diagnostics, 1982; assoc. editor Am. Jour. Cardiac Imaging, 1985—; mem. editl. bd. Archives of Internal Medicine and Chest, 1978-88, Am. Jour. Noninvasive Cardiology, 1985-96, Am. Jour. Cardiology, 1987-94, Cardiovascular Imaging, 1988—, Echocardiography, 1985—, Jour. Am. Coll. Cardiology, 1990-94; cardiovasc. area editor Jour. Clin. Ultrasound, 1989-94, Jour. Am. Soc. Echocardiography, 1992—; contbr. articles to profl. jours. Maj. Med. Svc. Corps, USAR. Grantee Am. Heart Assn., 1980-82, 83-84, Nat. Heart Lung and Blood Inst., 1988—. Fellow ACP, Am. Coll. Cardiology (physician workforce adv., health care reform and electrocardiography coms.), Am. Heart Assn. (coun. clin. cardiology), Coun. Geriatric Cardiology (v.p. 1990-92, pres. 1992-93); mem. Internat. Cardiac Doppler Soc. (sec., bd. dirs., chmn. Pan-Am. sect. 1984—, v.p. 1988-90, pres. 1990-92), Am. Soc. Echocardiography (bd. dirs., treas. 1989-91, v.p. 1991-93, pres. 1993-95, chmn. nomenclature and stds. 1991-95), U. Mich. Med. Ctr. Alumni Assn. (bd. govs. 1979-81), Phi Beta Kappa, Alpha Omega Alpha, Phi Delta Epsilon. Jewish. Office: U Calif Irvine Med Ctr Div Cardiology 101 City Dr S Bldg 53 Rt 81 Orange CA 92668-2901

GARDNER, BERNARD, surgeon, educator; b. Bklyn., Oct. 1, 1931; s. Charles and Selma (Lovenberg) G.; m. Joan E. Mann., Dec. 18, 1954; children: Karen A., Pamela D., Robert A. AB cum laude, NYU, 1952, MD, 1956. Intern Bellevue Hosp. Ctr., N.Y.C., 1956-57; resident Mt. Sinai Hosp., N.Y.C., 1957-58, U. Calif. Med. Ctr., San Francisco, 1961-65; asst. prof. surgery SUNY Downstate Med. Ctr., Bklyn., 1965-68, assoc. prof., 1968-72, prof., 1972; prof. surgery, dir. Bklyn. Cancer Ctr., 1973—; prof. dir. divsn. surg. edn. U. Medicine and Dentistry of N.J., 1983—; dir. dept. surgery Hackensack Med. Ctr., 1983-92; cons. VA Hosp., Luth. Med. Ctr., Swedish Hosp., Meth. Hosp., Kingsbrook Med. Ctr., all Bklyn., VA Hosp., Newark, N.J. Univ. Hosp., Newark; dir. divsn. surg. oncology Kings County Hosp., 1971; mem. study sect. on cancer edn. Nat. Cancer Inst., 1981-83. Author: Emergency Surgery, 1974, 2d edit., 1986, Basic Surgery: Patient Oriented Text, 1978, 5th edit., 1995, Principles of Cancer Surgery, 1981. Capt. USAF, 1958-60. Fellow Am. Cancer Soc., 1965-68; Markle fellow, 1968-73; recipient numerous grants, 1962—. Fellow Soc. Surg. Oncology (pres. 1994—); mem. Am. Surg. Assn., Soc. Univ. Surgeons, Assn. Acad. Surgery (chmn. com. on issues 1971—), N.Y. Surg. Soc., N.Y. Cancer Soc., Soc. Exptl. Medicine and Biology. Office: U Medicine & Dentistry NJ MSB/G510 185 S Orange Ave Newark NJ 07103-2714

GARDNER, CHARLES CLIFFORD, JR., colorectal surgeon; b. Cleve., Dec. 19, 1946; s. Charles Clifford and Ann Julia (Marolt) G.; m. Martha Carroll Porter, Aug. 9, 1969; children: Tiffany Ann, Kelley Elizabeth. BA in Biology, St. Mary's U., San Antonio, 1972; MD, U. Tex. Health Sci. Ctr., 1976. Diplomate Am. Bd. Surgery, Am. Bd. Colon Rectal Surgery. Resident in gen. surgery Wilford Hall Med. Ctr., Lackland AFB, Tex., 1976-81; fellow colon rectal surgeon Cleve. Clinic, 1981-82; colorectal surgeon in pvt. practice Dayton, Ohio, 1987—; mem. colon rectal adv. bd. Ethicon, Inc., Cin., 1982-93; chmn. dept. surgery St. Elizabeth Med. Ctr., Dayton, 1994-95. Lt. col. USAF, 1972-87. Fellow ACS, Am. Soc. Colon Rectal Surgeons (self-assessment com. 1987-88); mem. AMA, Ohio Valley Colon Rectal Soc., Dayton Surg. Soc. (treas. 1987-88, pres. 1989-90), Alpha Omega Alpha. Republican. Roman Catholic. Office: Ste N 627 S Edwin C Moses Blvd Dayton OH 45408

GARDNER, CHARLES SPERRY, psychiatrist; b. New Haven, Aug. 10, 1949; s. Charles Wesley and Josephine Elizabeth (Sperry) G.; m. Janice Ann Cronin; children: Charles, Nora, Grace. Student, Choate Sch., 1964-67; AB, Columbia Coll., 1972; MD, U. Ky. Coll. of Medicine, 1979; cert. in psychoanalysis, Columbia U., 1990. Diplomate Am. Bd. Psychiatry and Neurology. Psychiat. resident N.Y. Hosp. Cornell Med. Ctr., White Plains, N.Y., 1979-83; instr. Cornell Med. Coll., N.Y.C., 1983-85, asst. clin. prof. psychiatry, 1985—; asst. attending psychiatrist N.Y. Hosp. Cornell Med. Ctr., N.Y.C., 1985—; attending psychiatrist Greenwich (Conn.) Hosp., 1987—; consulting psychiatrist Burke Rehab. Ctr., White Plains, 1983-85. Contbr. several articles to profl. jours. Mem. Am. Psychiat. Assn., Am. Psychoanalytic Assn., The Belle Haven Club (Greenwich). Home and Office: 409 Field Point Rd Greenwich CT 06830-7041

GARDNER, CLYDE EDWARD, health care executive, consultant, educator; b. Steubenville, Ohio, Oct. 8, 1931; s. Peter D. and Louella Mary (Gillespie) G.; m. Patricia Jackson, Oct. 4, 1953 (div. Dec. 1977); 1 child, Bruce Stephen. BA, San Francisco State U., 1969, MS, 1971. Adminstr. Gardner Convalescent Hosp., Napa, Calif., 1955-68; exec. dir. Haight Ashbury Free Med. Clinic, San Francisco, 1970-71; lectr. San Francisco State U., 1969-71; dir. planning and rsch. div. N. Country Com. on Area Wide

Health Planning, Canton, N.Y., 1971-77; prof. Gov.'s State U., University Park, Ill., 1977-83; sr. ptnr. Health Care Cons., Park Forest, Ill., 1983-86; exec. dir. Mahoning Shenango Area Health Edn. Network, Youngstown, Ohio, 1986-90; pres., chief exec. officer Mahoney Edn. and Tng. Network, Youngstown, Ohio, 1990-92; pres., CEO Health Sci. Assocs., Tucson, 1992—; bd. dirs. rec. sect. Mahoning Shenango Area Health Edn. Network, Youngstown, 1986-90; adj. prof. SUNY, Canton, 1975-76, Youngstown State U., 1987—; bus. rep. Apollo Coll., 1994-95. Author: Data Book for Health and Institutional Planning, 1981; author of numerous pub. health planning, health edn. studies and funded pvt., state and fed. health care grants, 1971-90. Pres. Found. I Ctr. for Human Devel., Harvey, Ill., 1978-83, U. Profls. of Ill., Chgo., 1982-83; bd. dirs. Blue Cross/Blue Shield Drug and Alcohol Benefit Study, Chgo., 1980-83. Recipient Recognition award Ill. Dangerous Drugs Commn., 1980, 81, Outstanding Svc. award U. Profls. Ill., 1983-84, Outstanding Svc. award Ill. Fedn. Tchrs., 1983. Mem. Disabled Artist Assn. (bd. dirs., chair resource devel. com.). Democrat.

GARDNER, HOWARD GARRY, pediatrician, educator; b. Gary, Ind., Oct. 5, 1943; s. Oscar and Anita (Arenson) G.; m. Judith (Green), June 21, 1986; children: Molly, Joseph. BA, Ind. U., 1965, MD, 1968. Intern, then resident St. Louis U., 1969-73; pvt. practice Hinsdale (Ill.) Pediatrics, 1973-79, DuPage Pediatrics, Darien, Ill., 1979—; attending staff Hinsdale Hosp., 1973—, Loyola U. Med. Ctr., Maywood, Ill., 1973—; courtesy staff Childrens Meml. Hosp., Chgo., 1988—; clin. prof. Dept. Pediatrics Loyola U. Sch. of Medicine, Maywood, 1983—; past-chmn. Dept. of Pediatrics Hinsdale Hosp., 1983-85; med. adv. bd. YMCA of the USA, Chgo., 1989—. Editorial adv. bd. Pediatric News, 1990—; contbr. articles to profl. jours. Co-chmn. med. adv. bd. DuPage Easter Seal Ctr., Villa Park, Ill.; bd. dirs. Loyola Ronald McDonald House; co-founder, past pres. Ill. Child Passenger Safety Assn.; pediatric program dir. Des Plaines Valley Health Ctr., Argo, Ill.; mem. med. adv. bd. Pathways Awareness Found.; officer, steering com. DuPage Interagy. Coun. on Early Intervention. Lt. USN, 1969-71. Recipient Outstanding Clin. Tchr. award Loyola Med. Sch., 1978, Tchr. of Yr. Hinsdale Hosp. Family Practice Residency, 1981, Chgo. Caring Physician's award Met. Chgo. Health Care Coun., 1987, Buckle Up Am.! award Ill. Coalition for Safety Belt Use, 1991, Parent and Child Edn. Soc. 20th Anniversary Achievement award, 1992. Fellow Am. Acad. Pediat. (past pres. Ill. chpt., mem. nat. nominating com., Pisani Pediatrician of Yr. award 1986); mem. Chgo. Pediat. Soc. (past pres., Archibald Hoyne Pediatrician of Yr. 1994), Ill. Maternal and Child Health Coalition (bd. dirs.). Democrat. Jewish. Office: DuPage Pediatrics 1306 Plainfield Rd Darien IL 60561-5038

GARDNER, J. H., physician; b. Corydon, Iowa, Dec. 12, 1928; s. William Hugh and Pauline (Baldwin) G.; m. Mary Bertha Pederson, 1956 (div. 1966); children: Anna Sarah, Hugh; m. Kathleen Amundson, Aug. 23, 1980; stepchildren: Kristine, Peter, Hans. BA, Drake Univ., 1951; MD, U. Iowa, 1957; MS, Drexel Inst. Tech., 1967. Diplomate Am. Bd. Family Practice. Pvt. practice Mrytle Point (Oreg.) Medical Ctr., 1958-64; medical cons. Am. Oncological Hosp., Phila., 1964-66; medical dir. diagnostic clinic for children Woodward (Iowa) State Hosp., 1966-68; student health svcs. Iowa State Univ., Ames, 1968-74, dir., team physician, 1971-74; emergency dept. dir. Trinity Regional Hosp., Ft. Dodge, Iowa, 1974-76; emergency dept. physician St. Lukes, Quad City, Ill., Iowa, 1976-83; family practice Coal Valley, Ill., 1980—; medical dir. Western Ill. IPA, Rock Island, 1990—, bd. dirs. Crescent Counties PRO, Chgo., 1996—. With USMC, 1946-48. Recipient First Beirring award U. Iowa, 1954, Phiger scholarship, U. Iowa, 1952-53, fellow U. Iowa, 1954-55, fellow NIH, 1964-66. Mem. Rock Island Co. Medical Soc. (pres. 1992-93), Valley Sunrise Rotary Club, Ill. State Medical Soc., AMA, Am. Family Practice, Phi Beta Kappa. Home: 101 McCellan Blvd Davenport IA 52803 Office: Coal Valley Clinic 104 W 18th Ave Coal Valley IL 61240

GARDNER, JAMES RICHARD, pharmaceutical company executive; b. Wellsville, N.Y., Nov. 18, 1944; s. James Myers and Adelaide (Stockman) G.; m. Linda Marie Cuomo, Oct. 14, 1967; children: Alexandra K., Mindy M. BS in Engring., U.S. Mil. Acad., 1966; M in Pub. Adminstrn., Princeton U., 1968, PhD, 1977; MBA, L.I. U., 1977; grad., U.S. Army War Coll., 1989. Commd. 2d lt. U.S. Army, 1966, advanced through grades to maj., 1976, resigned., 1977; staff asst. Office of U.S. Atty. Gen., 1973; asst. prof. U.S. Mil. Acad., West Point, N.Y., 1974-77; dir. agrl. planning Pfizer, Inc., N.Y.C., 1977-81, dir. corp. strategic planning, 1981-89, sr. dir. corp. strategic planning, 1989-94, v.p. corp. investor rels., 1994—; v.p. Pfizer Found., N.Y.C., 1985—; mem. faculty U.S. Army Command Gen. Staff Coll., 1986-92, U.S. Army War Coll., 1989; mem. adv. coun. Ctr. Internat. Studies, Princeton U., 1987—; mem. adv. coun. Dept. Astrophysical Scis. Princeton U., 1992—; head USAR polit. and mil. affairs div. Dept. Army, 1989-92. Author: (with others) American National Security, 1981, Business Competitor Intelligence, 1984; editor: Handbook of Strategic Planning, 1986; contbr. articles to profl. jours. Strategic planning com. United Way of Tri-State, N.Y.C., 1984-87; dir. adminstrn. Pfizer Inc. United Way campaign, N.Y.C., 1985-87; bd. dirs. Greater N.Y. couns. Boy Scouts Am., 1988—; N.Y.C. chmn. Nat. Eagle Scout Assn., 1989-92. Col. USAR, 1988-93, ret. Decorated Bronze Stars (3), Air medals, Rep. Vietnam Gallantry Cross with Silver Star; recipient George Washington medal The Freedoms Found., Valley Forge, Pa., 1970; recipient Silver Beaver award Boy Scouts Am., 1991, Disting. Eagle award, 1992. Mem. Planning Forum (pres. N.Y.C. chpt. 1985-86), N.Am. Soc. Corp. Planning (nat. v.p. 1984-85), West Point Soc. N.Y. (bd. dirs. 1984-91, v.p. 1986-88, pres. 1988-90), Nat. Investor Rels. Inst. (bd. dirs. N.Y.C. chpt. 1995—), U.S. Mil. Acad. Assn. Grads. (strategic planning com. 1992-96), Phi Kappa Phi. Republican. Roman Catholic. Home: 40 Brundige Dr Goldens Bridge NY 10526-1416 Office: Pfizer Inc 235 E 42nd St New York NY 10017-5703

GARDNER, JILL CHRISTOPHER, bioengineer, neuroscientist; b. Winchester, Mass., Dec. 23, 1948; d. Wallace Joseph Gardner and Lyna (Christopher) Mueller. BSc with 1st class honors, Dalhousie U., Halifax, N.S., Can., 1975, MS, 1977, PhD, 1981. Rsch. assoc. Dalhousie U., 1981-82; NSERC fellow MIT, Cambridge, 1982-85, NIH fellow, 1988-91; postdoctoral assoc. Children's Hosp., Boston, 1986-87; rsch. fellow in otolaryngology Mass. Eye and Ear Infirmary, Boston, 1987-91; specialist in neurophysiology Mass. Gen. Hosp., Boston, 1987-90; rsch. asst. prof. U. Wash., 1992—; owner Greg Fine Arts, 1992—. Contbr. articles to sci. jours., chpts. to books. Co-dir. Summer Village Camp, Marlboro, Mass., 1972; researcher Rockefeller for Pres. Com., N.Y.C., 1968; advance person Romney for Pres., N.H., 1968. Grantee Dalhousie U. R & D Fund, 1981, 81, Natural Scis. and Engring. Coun., 1983, 84, Royalty Rsch. Fund, 1994. Mem. Soc. Photo-Optical Inst. Engrs., Soc. for Neurosci., Assn. for Rsch. in Vision and Ophthalmology, Internat. Brain Rsch. Orgn., World Fedn. Neuroscientists, Brit. Brain and Behavior Soc., Phi Theta Kappa. Office: U Wash Dept Radiology Hlth Scis Box 357115 Seattle WA 98195

GARDNER, JOHN HOWLAND, III, neurologist; b. New Haven, Conn., Oct. 1, 1931; s. John Howland Jr. and Ruth (Huntley) G.; m. Anne Kates Larkin, Apr. 23, 1960; children: Elizabeth Larkin Gardner Milgram, Helen Douglass Gardner, Sarah Stewart Gardner Powell. BS, Harvard U., 1952; MD, Yale, 1956. Diplomate Am. Bd. Psychiatry and Neurology. Intern Stanford, 1956-57; asst. to assoc. resident in medicine Strong Mem. Hosp., Rochester, N.Y., 1957-59; resident in neurology Boston City Hosp., 1959-61; resident in neuropathology Strong Mem. Hosp., Rochester, N.Y., 1961-62; officer in charge in neurology USAF Hosp. Keesler AFB, Biloxi, Miss., 1962-64; asst. prof., asst. clin. prof. to assoc. clin. prof. Case Western Res. U. Sch. Med., Cleveland, 1964—; chief of neurology St. Luke's Hosp., Cleveland, 1967-85; neurologist U. Suburban Health Care Ctr., Cleveland, 1975—; bd. dirs., Greater Cleveland Chpt. Epilepsy Fdn. Am., 1973-75; chmn. Mediation Comm. Acad. Med. Cleveland, 1982-84. Vestryman, St. Paul's Episcopal Church, Cleveland Hts., 1980-82. Capt. USAF, 1962-64. Decorated Commendation Medal, USAF. Fellow Am. Acad. Neurology; mem. AMA, Acad. Med. Cleveland, Ohio State Med. Assn., Yale Alumni Assn. (v.p. Cleve. 1988—). Episcopalian. Office: U Suburban Health Care Ctr 1611 S Green Rd #203A South Euclid OH 44121

GARDNER, MURRAY BRIGGS, pathologist, educator; b. Lafayette, Ind., Oct. 5, 1929; s. Max William and Margaret (Briggs) G.; m. Alice E. Danielson, June 20, 1961; children: Suzanna, Martin, Danielson, Andrew. B.A., U. Calif., Berkeley, 1951; M.D., U. Calif., San Francisco, 1954. Intern Moffitt Hosp., San Francisco, 1954-55; resident in gen. practice Sonoma County Hosp., Santa Rosa, Calif., 1957-59; resident in pathology U. Calif. hosps., San Francisco, 1959-63; faculty U. So. Calif. Sch. Medicine, Los Angeles, 1963-81; prof. pathology U. So. Calif. Sch. Medicine, 1973-81; prof. pathology U. Calif., Davis Sch. Medicine, 1981—, chmn. dept. pathology, 1982-90. Contbr. chpts. to books, numerous articles in field to profl. jours. Served to lt. M.C. USNR, 1957-59. NIH grantee, 1968—. Mem. Coll. Am. Pathologists, Internat. Acad. Pathology. Home: 8313 Maxwell Ln Dixon CA 95620-9662 Office: U Calif-Davis Med Sch # Ms-1 Davis CA 95616

GARDNER, RICHARD ALAN, psychiatrist, writer; b. Bronx, N.Y., Apr. 28, 1931; s. Irving and Amelia (Weingarten) G.; m. Lee Robbins, Apr. 14, 1957 (div. Nov. 1984); children: Andrew Kevin, Nancy Tara, Julie Anne; m. Patricia Lefevere, July 4, 1987. AB, Columbia U., 1952; MD, SUNY Downstate Med. Ctr., 1956; cert. psychoanalysis, William A. White Psychoanalytical Inst., 1966. Diplomate Am. Bd. Psychiatry and Neurology, Am. Bd. Child Psychiatry. Intern Montefiore Hosp., N.Y.C., 1956-57, resident child psychiatry, 1959-60, 62-63; dir. child psychiatry U.S. Army Hosp., Frankfurt, Federal Republic of Germany, 1960-62; mem. attending staff Presbyn. Hosp., N.Y.C., 1963—; pvt. practice specializing in psychiatry, child psychiatry and psychoanalysis Cresskill, N.J., 1963—; instr. child psychiatry Columbia Coll. Physicians and Surgeons, N.Y.C., 1963-70, assoc. child psychiatry, 1970-72, asst. clin. prof. child psychiatry, 1972-76, assoc. clin. prof. child psychiatry, 1976-83, clin. prof. child psychiatry, 1983—; vis. prof. child psychiatry, U. Louvain, Belgium, 1981-83, U. St. Petersburg, Russia, 1994—; mem. faculty William A. White Psychoanalytic Inst., 1967-83. Author: The Child's Book about Brain Injury, 1966, The Boys and Girls Book about Divorce, 1970, Therapeutic Communication with Children: The Mutual Storytelling Technique, 1971, Dr. Gardner's Stories about the Real World, Vol. I, 1972, MBD: The Family Book about Minimal Brain Dysfunction, 1973, Understanding Children: A Parent's Guide to Child Rearing, 1973, Dr. Gardner's Fairy Tales for Today's Child, 1974, Psychotherapy with Children of Divorce, 1976, The Parent's Book about Divorce, 1977, Dr. Gardner's Modern Fairy Tales, 1977, The Boys and Girls Book about Stepfamilies, 1981, Family Evaluation in Child Custody Litigation, 1982, Dr. Gardner's Stories about the Real World, Vol. II, 1983, Separation Anxiety Disorder: Psychodynamics and Psychotherapy, 1984, Child Custody Litigation: A Guide for Parents and Mental Health Professionals, 1986, The Psychotherapeutic Techniques of Richard A. Gardner, 1986, Hyperactivity, The So-Called Attention Deficit Disorder and The Group of MBD Syndromes, 1987, The Parental Alienation Syndrome and the Differentiation between Fabricated and Genuine Child Sex Abuse, 1987, Psychotherapy with Adolescents, 1988, Family Evaluation in Custody Mediation, Arbitration and Litigation, 1989, The Girls and Boys Book about Good and Bad Behavior, 1990, Sex Abuse Hysteria: Salem Witch Trials Revisited, 1991, The Parents Book About Divorce, 2d edit., 1991, The Parental Alienation Syndrome: A Guide for Mental Health and Legal Professionals, 1992, Self-Esteem Problems of Children: Psychodynamics and Psychotherapy, 1992, The Psychotherapeutic Techniques of Richard A. Gardner, 2d edit., 1992, True and False Accusations of Child Sex Abuse: A Guide for Legal and Mental Health Professionals, 1992, Conduct Disorders of Childhood: Psychodynamics and Psychotherapy, 1994, Psychogenic Learning Disabilities: Psychodynamics and Psychotherapy, 1995, Testifying in Court: A Guide for Mental Health Professionals, 1995, Psychotherapy with Victims of Child Sexual Abuse: True, False, and Hysterical, 1995, Living Every Day of Your Life: A Psychiatrist's Treasury of Wise Quotes, 1996, Dream Analysis in Psychotherapy, 1996, Protocols for the Sex-Abuse Evaluation, 1995; editor in chief Internat. Jour. Child Psychothrapy, 1972-73. Capt. M.C., USAR, 1960-62. Fellow Am. Acad. Psychoanalysis, Am. Acad. Child and Adolescent Psychiatry, Am. Psychiat. Assn. (life). Home: 24 Mackay Dr Tenafly NJ 07670-2420 Office: 155 County Rd Cresskill NJ 07626-0522

GARDNER, RICHARD C., orthopedist, forensic medicine; b. Fall River, Mass., 1936. AB, Brown U., 1958; MD, Tufts U., 1962. Diplomate Am. Bd. Orthopaedic Surgery. Intern Hosp. for Joint Diseases and Med. Ctr., N.Y.C., 1962-63, resident, 1963-67; orthopaedic surgeon Jackson Park Hosp. and Med. Ctr., Chgo.; chief of orthopedic surgery USAF Hosp. Chanute, Rantoul; with Westchester Gen. Hosp., Miami, Fla. Contbr. articles to profl. jours. Served to capt. USAF, 1967-69. Mem. Assn. Mil. Surgeons, Soc. Air Force Clin. Surgeons, So. Med. Assn., So. Orthopedic Assn.

GARDNER, RODNEY EARL, health facility administrator, nurse; b. San Angelo, Tex., Dec. 16, 1953; s. W.C. and Betty (Jane) G.; m. Kaylan Sue Service, Apr. 1, 1980. AS in Nursing, Angelo State U., 1977. RN, Tex., Colo. Staff nurse West Coke County Hosp., Robert Lee, Tex., 1976-80; supr. ICU Eastland (Tex.) Meml. Hosp., 1980; dir. nursing Kimble Hosp., Junction, Tex., 1980-82, Crockett County Hosp., Ozona, Tex., 1982-86; emergency rm. nurse Shannon Med. Ctr., San Angelo, 1986-90, dir. emergency dept., 1990—. Mem. Emergency Nurses Assn. (pres. elect 1992-93). Baptist. Home: PO Box 671 Bronte TX 76933-0671 Office: Shannon Med Ctr 120 E Harris Ave San Angelo TX 76903-5904

GARDNER, SHEILA ANNE, medical technologist; b. El Paso, May 7, 1960; d. Eugene Anthony and Jeanne (Adam) Meyer; m. James L. Gardner, Aug. 1, 1981; children: Tara, Jennifer, Ashley. Diploma in Med. Lab. Rsch., Pikes Peak Inst. Med. Tech., Colorado Springs, 1988. Generalist med. technician San Juan Regional Med. Ctr., Farmington, N.Mex., 1980-90, Manulag Med. Ctr., Kotzebue, Alaska, 1990-92, Ketchikan (Alaska) Gen. Hosp., 1993—.

GARDNER, SHELDON FRANK, consulting clinical psychologist; b. Chelsea, Mass., Apr. 20, 1934; s. Phillip and Goldie (Stepansky) G.; m. Gwendolyn Ruth Stevens, Oct. 24, 1971; children: David, Loren, Stephen, Pamela, Angela. AB, Harvard U., 1956; PhD, U. So. Calif., 1963. Lic. psychologist, Conn. Dir. psychol. tng. Child Guidance Clinic, Pasadena, Calif., 1965-72; chief psychologist Psychiat. Clin. for Children, Long Beach, Calif., 1972-75; adminstrv. dir. Voorman Clinic, Pomona, Calif., 1975-78; staff psychologist St. Francis Mental Health Ctr., Cape Girardeau, Mo., 1978-82; chief psychologist Child Guidance Clinic, New London, Conn., 1983-90; pvt. practice cons. psychologist, Mystic, Conn., 1990—; pvt. practice clin. psychology, Asheville, N.C., 1964-65, Pasadena, 1970-74; clin. dir. Costa Mesa (Calif.) Psychiat. Svc., 1973-75. Co-author: Care and Cultivation of Parents, 1979, Women of Psychology, 1982, Red Vienna and the Golden Age of Psychology, 1991, Separation Anxiety and the Dread of Abandonment in Adult Males, 1993. Mem. APA, Rotary. Home and Office: 42 Denison Ave Mystic CT 06355-2728

GARDNER, STEPHEN RAY, neurosurgeon; b. Raleigh, N.C., Sept. 25, 1948; m. Leslie. BS, The Citadel, 1970; MD, La. State U. Sch. Medicine, 1974. Diplomate Am. Bd. Neurol. Surgery, 1989. Intern, resident Med. Coll. Va., Richmond, 1974-75, 79-84, fellow in head injury, 1981-82, fellow in pediat. neurosurgery, 1982; neurosurgeon Greenville (S.C.) Neurosurg. Group, 1984—; cons. neurosurgeon Shriners' Hosp. Crippled Children, 1987—; clin. assoc. prof. U. S.C. Sch. Medicine, 1992—. Served in USAMC, Italy, 1975-79. Mem. AMA, Am. Acad. Disability Evaluating Physicians, Am. Acad. Pain Medicine, Am. Assn. Neurol. Surgery, Am. Coll. Surgeons, Am. Med. Writers Assn., Am. Soc. Stereotactic & Functional Neurosurgery, Congress Neurol. Surgeons, Greenville County Med. Soc., Internat. Cerebral Hemodynamics soc., Internat. Coll. Surgeons, Internat. Soc. Mountain Medicine, N.Am. Skull Base Soc., N.Am. Spine Soc., Soc. Critical Care Medicine, S.C. Assn. Neurol. Surgeons, S.C. Med. Assn., So. Med. Assn., So. Neurosurg. Soc., Wilderness Med. Soc., World Soc. for Stereotactic & Functional Neurosurgery. Office: Greenville Neurosurg Group 27 Memorial Medical Dr Greenville SC 29605

GARDNER, WILLIAM ALBERT, JR., pathologist, medical foundation executive; b. Sumter, S.C., Aug. 2, 1939; s. William A. and Betty Lee (Kennedy) G.; m. Kathryn Ann Medlin, June 30, 1960; children: Mary Elizabeth, Kathryn Lee, William Dylan. B.S., Wofford Coll., 1960; M.S. in Anatomy, Med. Coll. S.C., 1963, M.D., 1965. Diplomate: Am. Bd. Pathology. Intern Johns Hopkins Hosp., Balt., 1965-66, asst. resident, 1966-67, fellow in pathology, 1965-67; asst. resident Duke U., Durham, N.C., 1967-68, chief resident, 1968-69, instr. pathology, 1968-69; chief lab. service VA Hosp., Charleston, S.C., 1969; asst. prof. pathology Med. U. S.C., 1969-72, assoc. prof., 1972-76; prof. pathology Vanderbilt U., Nashville, 1976-81, vice chmn. dept. pathology; chief lab. service VA Hosp., Nashville, 1976-81; prof., chmn. dept. pathology U. South Ala., Mobile, 1981—, pres. health svcs. found., 1988-91. Contbr. articles on oncology, urology, parasitology and pathology to profl. jours. Recipient Outstanding Teaching award Med. U. S.C., 1975, Disting. Alumnus award Med. U. S.C., 1988; named to Alumni Assn. Centennial Recognition list, 1992. Fellow Am. Soc. Clin. Pathologists, Coll. Am. Pathologists (del. for govtl. pathology); mem. AMA, Internat. Acad. Pathology (v.p., chair fin. com. 1994—, internat. councillor 1994—), U.S.-Can. Acad. Pathology (v.p., pres.-elect 1993-95, pres. 1995-96, mem. fin. com. 1996—), Acad. Clin. Lab. Physicians and Scientists, Ala. Med. Assn., Assn. Pathology Chmn. (coun., pres. 1992-94), Armed Forces Inst. of Pathology (mem. scientific adv. bd. 1996—), Alpha Omega Alpha. Methodist. Home: 1565 Fearnway St Mobile AL 36604-1311 Office: U South Ala Dept Path 2451 Fillingim St Mobile AL 36617-2238

GAREEBOO, HASSAM, physician; b. Port Louis, Mauritius, May 24, 1941; s. Abdool Gaffoor and Mahmooda (Soyfoo) G.; m. Khatijah Bibi Nahaboo, July 23, 1973; children: Mohammad Shafick, Zeenat, Sooraya, Nashreen, Mohammad Khalil. MB BS, London U., 1966. NCD project mgr. Ministry Health, Port Louis, Mauritius, 1969—; cons. internal medicine. Author: A Healthier Lifestyle for Mauritians, 1988. Fellow Royal Coll. Physicians (London); mem. Mauritius Med. Assn. Islam. Home: 58 Siv Virgile Naz St, Port Louis Mauritius

GARELL, DALE C., pediatrics educator, university dean; b. Salt Lake City, Oct. 31, 1935; s. Jack and Sara B. (Rosenblum) G.; m. Aggie Garell; children: Susan, Tracy, Scott, Cambria, Catia. MD, U. Colo., Denver, 1960. Diplomate Am. Bd. Pediat. Instr. pediat. U. So. Calif. Sch. Med., L.A., 1963-65, asst. prof., 1965-69, assoc. prof., 1969-74, clin. assoc. prof., 1978-85, clin. prof., 1985-89; assoc. dean curriculum U. So. Calif., L.A., 1989-93, exec. assoc. dean, 1990-93, sr. assoc. dean acad. affairs, 1993—; interim chmn. pediat. L.A., 1994—; clin. prof. U. Hawaii Sch. Pub. Health, 1986-89; provisional dir. child and adolescent planning Dept. Health Svc., L.A., 1982-84. Bd. dir. Pub. Health Found., L.A., 1989—; chmn. youth com. Fedn. Coordinated Couns., L.A., 1965-70; forum mem. White Conference on Children and Youth, 1970-72. Recipient Disting. Svc. award Children's Hosp. L.A., 1984, nat. recognition award Children's Hospice Internat., Washington, 1987. Fellow Am. Acad. Pediat., Soc. for Adolescent Medicine; mem. L.A. Pediat. Soc. Office: U So Calif Sch Med 1975 Zonal Ave Los Angeles CA 90033

GARELL, PAUL CHARLES, physician, family practice; b. Williamsport, Pa., July 18, 1930; s. Paul C. and Della Mary (Deime) G.; m. Teresa Ann Sullivan, Aug. 7, 1954; children: Ann, Della, Paula, P. Charles. BS in Biology, Villanova U., 1952; MD, Hahnemann U., 1956. Intern Williamsport Hosp., 1956-57; resident in aviation medicine USN Hosp., Pensacola, Fla., 1957-58; pvt. practice, Beacon, N.Y., 1960—; founder Park Med. Group, Beacon, 1970; dir. M.V.P. Health Plan, Poughkeepsie, N.Y., 1986-96. Lt. M.C., USN, 1957-60. Fellow Am. Acad. Family Physicians (chartr); mem. N.Y. State Acad. Family Physicians, Dutchess County Med. Soc. (pres. 1977-78). Office: Physicians Network 222 Fishkill Ave Beacon NY 12508-2014

GARELLA, SERAFINO, nephrologist, internist; b. Biella, Italy, Nov. 22, 1937; came to U.S., 1964; s. Luigi and Livia (Meneghesso) G.; m. Judith Queen, Nov. 19, 1961 (div. Dec. 1983); children: Elena, Richard; m. Judith Bromley, Dec. 31, 1983; stepchildren: Emily, Daniel. MD, U. Pisa, 1962. Diplomate Am. Bd. Internal Medicine with subspecialty in nephrology. Intern Miriam Hosp., Providence, 1964-65; resident R.I. Hosp., Providence, 1965-67; fellow NIH, 1967-69; sr. rsch. fellow in nephrology divsn. renal diseases R.I. Hosp., 1967-69, dir. divsn. renal disease, 1973-83; chief sect. nephrology Brown U., Providence, 1976-83, assoc. prof. medicine, 1977-83; assoc. chmn. medicine Michael Reese Hosp., Chgo., 1983-89, acting chmn. medicine, 1988-89; prof. medicine U. Chgo., 1983-90; dir. internal medicine residency program St. Joseph Health Ctrs. and Hosp., Chgo., 1989—, chmn. dept. medicine, 1989—; prof. clin. medicine Northwestern U. Med. Sch., Chgo., 1990—; founder, pres. CommunityHealth, Chgo., 1993—; project dir. tng. grant Dept. Health and Human Svc., Chgo., 1994—. Contbr. articles to profl. jours., chpts. to books. Pres. Am. Kidney Fund, Rockville, Md., 1986-90, bd. trustees, 1986-90; mem. policy com. Assoc. Program Dirs. in Internal Medicine, Washington. Maj. USAR, 1969-72. Recipient Sr. citation Brown U., 1978, Milton Hamolsky Teaching award R.I. Hosp., 1978, Russe award for Exemplary Compassion in Healthcare, 1996. Fellow ACP (laureate 1994); mem. Soc. Italian-Am. Nephrologists (pres. 1992-94), Assn. Program Dirs. Internal Medicine, Chgo. Soc. Internal Medicine (pres. 1995-96). Office: St Joseph Health Ctr 2900 N Lake Shore Dr Chicago IL 60657

GARFIELD, NANCY JANE, psychologist; b. N.Y.C., Oct. 24, 1947; d. William M. and Sue D. (Smalley) G. BA, Parsons Coll., 1968; MS, Western Ill. U., 1970; PhD, U. Mo., Columbia, 1975. Lic. psychologist, Kans. Counselor, career specialist Okla. State U., 1975-77; assoc. dean student life Wichita State U., 1977-80; staff psychologist Psychology Service VA Med. Ctr., Topeka, Kans., 1980—, dir. tng., 1981—, supr. counseling psychology sect., 1989—; cons. Nat. Ctr. Career Research and Devel., Dept. Def., Columbus, Ohio, 1981-83; psychology rep. Kans. Behavioral Scis. Regulatory Bd., 1983-88. Author: Career Exploration Groups, 1983; author, co-editor: Careers in Counseling and Human Development, Careers in Counseling and Human Services; assoc. editor Jour. Counseling and Devel., 1983-87; mem. editl. bd. JL Coll. Student Devel., 1990-95; contbr. articles to profl. jours., chpts. to books. Bd. dirs. Kans. Med. Credit Union, Topeka, 1980-84, Topeka AIDS project, 1987-89, also vice chair; vestry mem. St. David's Epis. Ch., 1988-90; co-coord. community coalition for AIDS edn. ARC, Topeka, Cath. Social Svc. Bd., mem., 1990-95, chair bd., 1991-92, planning com. Names Project (AIDS quilt), Topeka, 1992-93. Mem. APPIC (chair std. rev. com. 1995—), Am. Counseling Assn. (bd. dirs., media com.), Am. Coll. Pers. Assn. (senator, Presdl. Service award 1984), Am. Psychol. Assn. (site visitor 1982—, chair, dir. tng. divsn. 18, sect. 3), APPI (standards and rev. com. 1995—). Office: Psychology Service 116B 2200 SW Gage Blvd Topeka KS 66622-0001

GARG, RAM SWAROOP, neurologist; b. Rajasthan, Raj., India, Sept. 12, 1948; came to the U.S., 1981; s. Moti Lal and Kalawati Garg. MB, BChir, Jawaher Lal Nehru Med. Coll., Ajmer, India, 1970; postgrad., Med. U. S.C., 1988-91. Intern St. Francis Hosp., Evanston, Ill.; clin. assoc. in neurology Mich. State U., Lansing, 1991—; neurologist North Oakland Gen. Hosp., Pontiac, Mich., 1992—, St. Joseph Mercy Hosp., Pontiac, 1992—, Heritage Hosp., Taylor, Mich., 1992—, Riverside Hosp., Trenton, Mich., 1993—, Wyandotte (Mich.) Hosp., 1993—; con. neurologist various hosps., Detroit, 1992—. Mem. AMA, Am. Acad. Neurology. Office: 22997 Hall Rd Woodhaven MI 48183

GARGAN, THOMAS JOSEPH, plastic surgeon; b. Denver, Sept. 28, 1952; s. Thomas Joseph and Maria Augusta (Casagranda) G.; m. Nancy Lee Hall, Jan. 20, 1979; children: Daniel Thomas, John William. BA summa cum laude, Colo. Coll., 1974; MD, U. Colo., 1978. Diplomate Am. Bd. Plastic Surgery. Intern Presbyn. Med. Ctr., Denver, 1978-79, resident in surgery, 1978-79; resident in surgery Beth Israel Hosp., Boston, 1979-81, instr. gen. surgery, 1979-82, sr. resident in surgery, 1981-82, chief resident in plastic surgery, 1983-84; sr. resident in plastic surgery Cambridge (Mass.) City Hosp., 1982-83; resident in plastic surgery Children's Hosp. and Brigham and Women's Hosp., Boston, 1983, Newton-Wellesley Hosp., Mass., 1983; clin. fellow in surgery Harvard U. Med. Sch., Boston, 1979-84; clin. instr. plastic surgery U. Colo. Sch. Med., Denver, 1984; chief plastic surgery div. Rose Med. Ctr., 1987—; instr. plastic surgery Cambridge Hosp., Children's Hosp., and Beth Israel Hosp., Boston, 1982-84, Harvard Med. Sch., Boston, 1984. Contbr. articles to profl. jours. Bd. dirs. Rocky Mt. Adoption Exch., Lupis Found., Outward Bound Colo.; founder Plascicare for Kids Found. Recipient George B. Packard award for excellence in surgery U. Colo. Med. Ctr., 1978; Eagle Scout; Barnes Chemistry scholar Colo. Coll. Fellow ACS; mem. AMA, Denver Med. Soc. (pres. Gold Star award), Colo. Med. Soc., Am. Soc. Plastic and Reconstructive Surgeons, Rocky Mountain Hand Surgery Soc., Rocky Mountain Soc., Reconstructive Plastic Surgeons, Am. Soc. Aesthetic Plastic Surgeons, Order Hibernians in Am. Home: 10 Blackmer Rd Englewood CO 80110-6109 Office: 601 E Hampden Ave Englewood CO 80110-2764

GARGIULO, GERALD JOHN, psychoanalyst, writer; b. N.Y.C., Nov. 12, 1934; s. Fred Nunzio and Fanny Joy (Tarantino) G.; m. Julia Caldiero, Apr. 12, 1964; children: Paul Gerald, Connie Joy. BA in Philosophy, St. Bonaventure U., Orlean, N.Y., 1958; MA in Religious Studies, Washington Theol. Union, 1962. Mem. faculty Manhattan Coll., N.Y.C., Riverdale, 1962-70; pvt. practice N.Y.C., Greenwich, Conn., 1970—; dir. The Inst. N.P.A.P., N.Y.C., 1988-92, pres. tng. inst., 1992-96; assoc. editor The Psychoanalytic Review, N.Y.C., 1987—; pres. Coun. of Psychoanalytic Psychotherapists, N.Y.C., 1981-83; bd. dirs. N.Y. Ctr. for Psychoanalysis, 1973-75; mem. faculty Nat. Psychol. Assn. for Psychoanalysis, 1972—; lectr. in field. Contbr. over 50 articles to profl. pubs. Bd. dirs. Psychoanalysts Against Nuclear Weapons, 1982-85; com. mem. Greenwich Nuclear Freeze Orgn., 1987-90. Fellow Inst. for Psychoanalytic Tng. & Rsch. (bd. dirs. 1976), Coun. of Psychoanalytic Psychotherapists; mem. Internat. Fedn. for Psychoanalytical Edn. (bd. dirs. 1992—, pres.-elect 1996—), Internat. Psychoanalytical Assn., Nat. Psychol. Assn. for Psychoanalysis. Home: 11 Lafayette Ct Apt 1D Greenwich CT 06830-5307 Office: 158 Greenwich Ave Greenwich CT 06830-6548 also: 22 Shorewood Dr East Hampton NY 11937-3401

GARLAND, LINDA M., nursing care manager, consultant; b. New Orleans, Sept. 14, 1949; d. Richard Paul Coman and Lula June Tinker; children: Michelle Selvy, Nichole Rene. ADN with honors, Memphis State U., 1977; BSN cum laude, Maryville Coll., 1989. RN, Tenn. Tax examiner IRS, 1968-74; nurse clinician Bapt. Meml. Hosp., Memphis, 1977-83, postpartum unit supr., 1983-93; nurse case mgr., cons. Third Party Claims Mgmt., 1994—. Recipient award of merit Nat. Deans List, 1989. Mem. NAFE, Tenn. Nurses Assn. (One of Top 100 Nurses in Shelby County 1990), Golden Key Nat. Honor Soc., Alpha Lambda Delta. Home: 3787 Eddington Cv Memphis TN 38125-2108

GARMANY, GEORGE PARKER, neurologist; b. Detroit, Nov. 3, 1947; m. Catharine Doremus, June 12, 1970 (div. 1991); children: Richard, Jeffrey; m. Beverly Reeves, Apr. 8, 1995. BA, U. Va., 1969, MD, 1973. Diplomate Am. Bd. Psychiatry and Neurology. Intern medicine Emory U. Affiliated Hosps., Atlanta, 1973-74; resident neurology U. Colo. Med. Ctr., Denver, 1974-77; pvt. practice Associated Neurologists, Boulder, Colo., 1977—; cons. Jimmie Heuga Ctr., Avon, Colo., 1985—; pres. med. staff United Med. STaff, Boulder, 1986-87. Bd. mem. Nat. Multiple Sclerosis Soc., Colo. chpt., Denver, 1981—, chair profl. adv. com., 1992—, mem. nat. com. profl. adv. com. chairs, 1994—. Named Vol. Faculty of Yr. Denver Gen. Hosp., 1990, Over and Above award Nat. Multiple Sclerosis Soc., Denver, 1994. Mem. Am. Acad. Neurology, Colo. Soc. Clin. Neurologists (pres. 1988-90), Colo. Mayflower Soc. (capt. 1995—), Boulder Rotary. Office: Associated Neurologists 1000 Alpine Ste 291 Boulder CO 80304

GARN, STANLEY MARION, physical anthropologist, educator; b. New London, Conn., Oct. 27, 1922; s. Harry and Sadie Edith (Cohen) G.; m. Priscilla Crozier, Apr. 8, 1950; children: Barbara, William David. AB, Harvard U., 1942, AM, 1947, PhD, 1948. Rsch. assoc. chem. engring. Chem. Warfare Svc. Devel. Lab. MIT, 1942-44; tech. editor Polaroid Co., 1944-46; cons. applied anthropology, 1946-47; rsch. fellow cardiology Mass. Gen. Hosp., Boston, 1946-50; instr. anthropology Harvard U., 1948-52; anthropologist Forsyth Dental Infirmary, Boston, 1947-52; dir. Forsyth face size project Army Chem. Corps, 1950-52; chmn. dept. growth and genetics Fels Rsch. Inst., Yellow Springs, Ohio, 1952-68; fellow Ctr. Human Growth and Devel. U. Mich., Ann Arbor, also prof. nutrition and anthropology, 1968-92, prof. emeritus, 1993—; Raymond Pearl lectr. Human Biol. Coun., 1992—; E.B.D. Neuhauser lectr. Soc. Pediatric Radiology. Author: Human Races, 1970, Gain and Loss of Cortical Bone, 1970; also numerous articles; editorial bds. numerous jours. Recipient Disting. Svc. award U. Mich. Fellow AAAS, Am. Acad. Pediatrics (hon. assoc.), Am. Anthropol. Assn., Am. Acad. Arts and Scis., Human Biology Coun., Am. Inst. Nutrition; mem. NAS, Am. Assn. Phys. Anthropologists, Internat. Assn. Dental Rsch., Internat. Orgn. Study Human Devel., Am. Soc. Naturalists, Internat. Assn. Human Biologists (coun.). Home: 2410 Londonderry Rd Ann Arbor MI 48104-4016 Office: U Mich 300 N Ingalls St Ann Arbor MI 48109-2007

GARNER, LAFORREST DEAN, dental educator; b. Muskogee, Okla., Aug. 20, 1933; s. Sanford G. and Fannie (Thompson) G.; m. Alfreida Thomas, July 18, 1964; children: Deana Y., Thomas L., Sanford E. DDS, Ind. U., 1957, MSD, 1959; cert. orthodontics Ind. U., 1961. Diplomate Am. Bd. Orthodontics. Mem. faculty Sch. Dentistry Ind. U., Indpls., 1959-67, assoc. prof. dentistry, 1967-70, prof., chmn. orthodontics dept., 1970-87, assoc. dean, 1987—; assoc. dean minority student svcs., 1987; dir. grad. and post grad. dental edn. Sch. Dentistry Ind. U., Indpls, 1993—. Fellow Am. Coll. Dentists; mem. Am. Assn. Orthodontists, E.H. Angle Soc., Great Lakes Soc. Orthodontists, Internat. Assn. Dental Rsch., Am. Cleft Palate Assn., Ind. Dental Assn., Indpls. Dist. Dental Soc., Sigma Xi. Democrat. Presbyterian. Club: Nat. Boule (local pres. Indpls.). Contbr. articles to profl. jours. Home: 6245 Riverview Dr Indianapolis IN 46260-4239 also: 1121 W Michigan St Indianapolis IN 46202-5211 also: 2416 N Capitol Ave Indianapolis IN 46208-5712

GARNES, DELBERT FRANKLIN, clinical and consulting psychologist, educator; b. Lorain, Ohio, Jan. 13, 1943; s. Delbert Chauncey and Virginia (Scott) G.; m. Bertha J. Smith (div.); m. Joyce M. Roberts; children: Franklin Chauncey, Charles Deltre. BA, Ohio State U., 1969; MA, Xavier U., 1974; PhD, St. Louis U., 1980. Lic. clin. psychologist. Counselor Fairfield Sch. for Boys, Lancaster, Ohio, 1970-71; instr. Met. Coll., St. Louis, 1974-75; psychologist Narcotics Svc. Coun., St. Louis, 1974-75, Roxbury Ct. Clinic, Boston, 1975-77, Fuller Mental Health Ctr., Boston, 1976-77; asst. prof. psychology Tex. So. U., Houston, 1980-86, assoc. prof., 1986—; chmn. dept. counseling and psychology, 1990—; cons. Mass. Bar Assn., Boston, 1976-77, Mass. Parole Bd., Boston, 1977, Harris County Juvenile Probation, Houston, 1981—, Harris County Dept. Edn., Houston, 1988—. Judge, Internat. Sci. and Engring. Fair, 1982, Houston Sci. and Engring. Fair, 1983-85. Cpl. USMC, 1961-65. Recipient Disting. Svc. award Nat. Tech. Assn., 1985, Svc. award Student Nat. Pharm. Assn., 1987, Sam Houston Area coun. Boy Scouts Am., 1987; NIMH fellow, 1977; Boston U. Sch. Medicine teaching fellow, 1975. Mem. Houston Assn. Black Psychologists (pres. 1981-82), Am. Psychol. Assn., Nat. Assn. Black Psychologists, Am. Fedn. Tchr., Tex. State Tchrs. Assn. Office: Tex So U 3100 Cleburne St Houston TX 77004-4501

GARNETT, LINDA KOPEC, nurse, researcher; b. Springfield, Mass.; d. Frank J. and Anna (Paul) Kopec; m. Thomas R. Garnett, Oct. 6, 1990. BS in Nursing cum laude, Fitchburg (Mass.) State Coll., 1983; MS in Health Svcs. Adminstrn., Ctrl. Mich. U., 1996. RN. Nurse intern Med. Coll. Va. Hosps., Richmond, nurse clinician in neurosci. ICU; terr. mgr., patient care specialist Kinetic Concepts Therapeutic Svcs., Richmond; rsch. coord. dept. neurology Med. Coll. Va./Va. Commonwealth U., Richmond. Mem. Sigma Theta Tau.

GAROUTTE, BILL CHARLES, neurophysiologist; b. Absarokee, Mont., Mar. 15, 1921; s. Bernard Clark and Anna Kosir G.; m. Sally Jeter, July 18, 1948 (dec.); children—Brian, Susanna, David, Katherine; m. Rebecca Kasten, Mar. 22, 1989. Student, San Diego State Coll., 1939-42; A.B., U. Calif., Berkeley, 1943, M.D., 1945, Ph.D., 1954. With U. Calif. Med. Sch., San Francisco, 1949—; from lectr. to prof. anatomy and neurology U. Calif. Med. Sch., 1949-66, prof. emeritus, 1986—; vis. asst. prof. U. Indonesia, Jakarta, 1956-57; electromyography and electroencephalography U. Calif., San Francisco, 1953—; vis. investigator Brain Research Inst. U. Tokyo, 1963; external examiner anatomy Nat. U. Malaysia, 1978, Sci. U. Malaysia, 1984. Author: Survey of Functional Neuroanatomy, 1981, 3d edit., 1994, Neuromuscular Physiology, 1996. Lt. (j.g.) M.C., USNR, 1946-47. Fulbright scholar London, 1950-51. Mem. Western Inst. on Epilepsy (pres. 1962), Am. Assn. Anatomists, Am. Acad. Neurology, Am. Electroencephalography Soc., Western Electroencephalography Soc. (pres. 1961-62), Hist. Soc. Pa., San Francisco Neurol. Soc. (pres. 1969-70). Home: 1336 El Camino Real #245 Millbrae CA 94030-1411 Office: U Calif Box 0452 San Francisco CA 94143

GARRETT, CHARLES LEROY, JR., pathologist; b. Simpsonville, S.C., May 7, 1940; s. Charles Leroy Sr. and Iva Marie (Brown) G.; m. Susan Olga Spann, June 5, 1962 (dec. Oct. 1963); m. Mazie Antoinette Franklin, Dec. 26, 1964; 1 child, Edith Louise. BS, Wofford Coll., 1961; MD, Med. U. S.C., 1966. Diplomate Am. Bd. Pathology. Resident in pathology Med. U. S.C., Charleston, 1966-69, asst. prof. pathology, 1970-72; fellow in legal medicine Med. Coll. Va., Richmond, 1969-70; dep. chief med. examiner Dade County, Miami, Fla., 1972-74; pathologist Richland Meml. Hosp., Columbia, S.C., 1974-76; dir. labs. Onslow Meml. Hosp., Jacksonville, N.C., 1976-. Lt. comdr. USN, 1967-73. Fellow Coll. Am. Pathologists, Am. Soc. Clin. Pathologists, Am. Acad. Forensic Scientists; mem. AMA (del. 1995—), Nat. Assn. Med. Examiners (bd. dirs. 1981-86). Nemed Soc., Masons, Alpha Omega Alpha. Republican. Episcopalian. Home: 132 Dockside Dr Jacksonville NC 28546 Office: Onslow Meml Hosp 317 Western Blvd Jacksonville NC 28546-6338

GARRETT, LELAND EARL, nephrologist, educator; b. Spartanburg, S.C., Jan. 8, 1949; s. Leland Earl and Mary Lillian (Butler) G.; m. Sarah Anne Pryor, Aug. 13, 1970 (div. 1978); 1 child, Katherine; m. Nancy Jean Swenson, May 3, 1980; children: Christopher, Jennifer. BS, N.C. State U., 1971; MD, Med. U. S.C., 1976. Commd. 2d lt. USAF, 1971, advanced through grades to lt. col., 1985, ret., 1991; intern Wilford Hall, USAF Med. Ctr., 1976-77; resident USAF Med. Ctr., 1977-79; fellowship Duke U. Med. Ctr., 1979-81; pvt. practice Wake Nephrology Assocs., Raleigh, N.C., 1991—; assoc. clin. prof. medicine U. N.C., Chapel Hill, 1991—. Contbr. articles to profl. jours. Bd. dirs. South Tex. Organ Bank, San Antonio, 1984-86; data chair, bd. dirs. Southeastern Kidney Coun., Raleigh, 1993—, med. adv. chmn. N.C. affiliate Nat. Kidney Found., Charlotte, 1994—; med. dir. Open Door Clinic/Urban Ministries, Raleigh, 1996—. Named Physician of Yr. N.C. affiliate Nat. Kidney Found., 1995. Fellow ACP, Am. Soc. Nephrology, Internat. Soc. Nephrology. Lutheran. Office: Wake Nephrology Assocs 3604 Bush St Raleigh NC 27609

GARRETT, MARILYN RUTH, nurse; b. Columbia, Mo., Mar. 28, 1957; d. Charles Filmore and Mable Ruth (Rice) Pasley; m. Donald Burce Garrett, June 9, 1983 (div. Mar. 1994); children: Patrick Bryan, Christopher Ryan. ADN, Cen. Meth. Coll., 1985. Cert. psychiat. and mental health nurse. Staff nurse Fulton (Mo.) State Hosp., 1985, clin. nursing supr., 1989-91, overall nursing supr., 1991-92, nurse educator, nursing edn. and staff devel., 1992-94, psychosocial rehab. tng. specialist, 1994—; instr. CPR, 1987—; aggressive mgmt. tng. instr., 1990—; chair nurse recruitment and retention com., Mo., 1991-93. Mem. vol. task force team Callaway County unit Am. Cancer Soc.; mem. panel Smoking Cessation Group for County Health Svcs., 1993. Named Employee of the Month State of Mo., Dept. Mental Health, 1991. Home: 1015 Bluff St Fulton MO 65251-2320 Office: Fulton State Hosp 600 E Fifth St Fulton MO 65251-1753

GARRETT, ROBERTA KAMPSCHULTE, nurse; b. Amityville, N.Y., Aug. 15, 1947; d. Robert Henry and Gertrude Ann (Schweitzer) Kampschulte; m. Paul R. Garrett Jr., Nov. 26, 1977; children: Samantha Kristine, Kelly Nicole. BS, U. Fla., 1969. RN, Fla.; cert. in oncology nursing. Staff nurse Valley Hosp., Ridgewood, N.J., 1969-70; asst. head nurse Broward Gen. Hosp., Ft. Lauderdale, Fla., 1970-71; CCU nurse Grady Meml. Hosp., Atlanta, 1972-77; nurse to pvt. physician Orlando, Fla., 1977-94; case mgmt. Fla. Healthcare Svs., Orlando, 1996—. Republican. Lutheran.

GARRETT, SHIRLEY GENE, nuclear medicine technologist; b. Evanston, Ill., Apr. 19, 1944; d. Nathan and Emma Louise (Uecker) G. AA, Oakton C.C., 1977; AS in Nuc. Medicine, Triton Coll., 1980; BA, Northea. Ill. U., 1983; MA, Govs. State U., University Park, Ill., 1985. Cert. nuclear medicine technologist. Nuc. medicine technologist Chgo. Osteo. Hosp., 1980-88, Little Co. of Mary Hosp., Evergreen Park, Ill., 1989; nuclear medicine technologist Lutheran Gen. Hosp., Lincoln Park, Ill., 1989; nuc. medicine technologist Mt. Sinai Hosp., Chgo., 1990-92; technologist nuc. medicine Swedish Covenant Hosp., Chgo., 1992-93; pres. Providence Hosp. of Cook County, Chgo., 1994—. Contbr. articles to profl. jours. Vol. Ravenswood Hosp., Chgo., 1986—, Mt. Sinai Hosp., 1990-92, Congl. Health Ministry, Ch. of St. Lukes. Mem. Soc. Nuc. Medicine (mem. bylaws com. technologist sect. Ctrl. chpt. 1982-83, 85-86, 92—, mem. continuing edn. com. 1986-87, chmn. nominating com. 1987-88, 92-93, mem. edn. com. 1988-89, pres.-elect 1989-90, mem. bd. govs. 1990-92, pres. 1991-92, chmn. bylaws com. 1992-93), Assoc. and Tech. Affiliates Chgo. Area (coord. edn. 1981-84, mem. adv. bd. 1983-84, 87-88, pres. 1985-87, chmn. nominating com. 1987-89). Lutheran.

GARRETT, TRACY A., record administrator; b. Jackson, Tenn., Aug. 25, 1961; d. Lawrence Tyson and Virginia Louise G. BSBA, Union U., 1983; BS in Med. Record Adminstrn., U. Tenn., 1984. Registered record administr. Supr. med. records Bapt. Meml. Hosp., Memphis, 1984-87; prospective payment coord. Jackson-Madison County Gen. Hosp., Jackson, Tenn., 1987, asst. dir. med. records, 1987-88, 1989, dir. health info. mgmt., 1989—; quality assurance analyst Parkview Med. Ctr., Nashville, 1988; DRG coord. Parkview Med. Ctr., Nashville, 1988, interim dir., med. info. svcs., 1988-89. Mem. Am. Health Info. Mgmt. Assn., Tenn. Health Info. Mgmt. Assn. (pres.-elect 1992-93, pres. 1993-94, dir./past pres. 1994—, Outstanding New Profl. award 1989), West Tenn. Health Info. Mgmt. Assn. (pres. 1991).

GARRETT, WILLIAM ELWOOD, orthopedic surgeon; b. Person County, N.C., Apr. 23, 1949. MD, Duke U., 1976, PhD. Diplomate Am. Bd. Orthopedic Surgery. Intern, then resident Duke U. Med. Ctr.; prof. orthopedic surgery Med. Ctr. Duke U. Med. Ctr., Durham, N.C.; dir. sports medicine Duke U., Durham, N.C. Office: Duke U Med Ctr Sports Med Sect Science Dr Durham NC 27710

GARRISON, NORMAN EUGENE, biology educator; b. Mar. 25, 1943; m.; 2 children. BS, Mars Hill (N.C.) Coll., 1965; MA, Wake Forest U., 1967; MS, PhD, U. Mass., 1973. Teaching asst. biology Wake Forest U., 1965-67; instr. zoology Mars Hill Coll., 1967-68; asst. prof. human physiology, zoology, biology Madison Coll., 1968-70; teaching assoc. human physiology U. Mass., 1970-73; prof. molecular biology, physiology James Madison U., Harrisonburg, Va., 1971-73; acting head dept. biology James Madison U., Harrisonburg, Va., 1993-94, acting assoc. dean Coll. Letters and Sci., 1995, interim dean Coll. Sci. and Math., 1995—. Contbr. articles to profl. jours. Dorothy Van Dussen Updyke scholar; grantee NSF, 1966, 69-71, 78-79, 81-84, So. Regional Edn. Bd., 1976-78, Title VI-A, 1978-79. Mem. Va. Acad. Scis., Southeastern Devel. Biol. Conf., Sigma Xi, Phi Kappa Phi. Home: 470 Andergren Dr Harrisonburg VA 22801-4302 Office: James Madison Univ Coll Sci and Math Harrisonburg VA 22807

GARRISON, WILLIAM LLOYD, cemetery executive; b. Ridgway, Pa., Dec. 26, 1939; s. Lloyd and Mary Rebecca (Morrow) G.; m. Mary Jo Florio, May 30, 1964; children: David, Mark. BA in Psychology, Ohio Wesleyan U., 1962; postgrad., Garrett Theol. Sem., 1962-63, U. Pa., 1963-64; MSW, Fla. State U., 1967; MS in Mgmt., Case Western Res. U., 1976. Caseworker Mpls. Ct. Chgo., 1963-64, United Cerebral Palsy Assn., Phila., 1964-65; psychiat. social worker Bellefaire, Shaker Heights, Ohio, 1967-74; dir. pers. and tng. Ctr. Human Services, Cleve., 1974-81 dir. resource devel., 1981-83; exec. dir. Cleve. Soc. for the Blind, 1983-85, Cleve. Eye Bank, 1983-85; exec. v.p. Lake View Cemetery Assn., Cleve., 1985-87, pres., 1987—; v.p Lake View Cemetery Found., Cleve., 1988—; adj. prof. Sch. Applied Social Sci., Case Western Res. U., 1974-80; v.p. E.A. Mabry Inc., Akron, Ohio, 1970—; chmn. agri-bus. adv. com. Cleve. Pub. Schs., 1990—, bus. adv. directorate, 1991—. Dist. cub scout chmn. Boy Scouts Am., 1979-81, dist. chmn., 1981-84, scoutmaster, 1983-87, mem. exec. bd., 1981—, asst. coun. commr., 1984-87, v.p. Boy Scouting, 1987-89, scoutmaster to world jamboree in Australia, 1988, coun. commr., 1989-92, area v.p., 1992-95, area pres., 1995—, region exec. com., 1995—, mem. nat. coun., 1989—; mem. pers. com. Lake Erie coun. Girl Scouts U.S., 1982-89; mem. Big Bros., Cleve., 1968-73 pres. Mayfield Heights Homeowners Assn., 1974-84, Cuyahoga County Reach Out Counseling Svcs., trustee, 1977-95, pres., 1991-95; bd. dirs. Garfield Meml. United Meth. Ch., 1979-81; mem. del. assembly United Way Svcs. of Cleve., 1987-95; trustee Alta House Comty. Ctr., 1994, Ctr. for Families and Children, 1995—. Recipient Dist. award Merit Boy Scouts Am., 1980, Silver Beaver award, 1984, Silver Antelope award, 1994; Menninger Found fellow. Mem. NASW, Acad. Cert. Social Workers, Soc. Human Resource Mgmt., Pers. Accreditation Inst., Am. Cemetery Assn., Ohio Assn. Cemetery Supts. and Ofcls. (exec. bd. 1992—, v.p. 1993, pres.-elect 1994, pres. 1995—), Greater Cleve. Cemetery Assn. (pres. 1987-90), Nat. Eagle Scout Assn., Greater Cleve. Pers. Coun., Social Agys. Employee Union (pres. 1970-73), Greater Cleve. Growth Assn., St. Luke's Hosp. Assn., Cleve. U. Cir. Inc., Am. Field Svc., Cleve. Playhouse Club, Rotary (trustee Cleve. club 1993-96, v.p. 1996, pres.-elect 1996-97), Delta Tau Delta, Phi Mu Alpha. Office: Lake View Cemetery Assn 12316 Euclid Ave Cleveland OH 44106-4313

GARRITY, EDWARD R., internist, educator; b. Evanston, Ill., Dec. 14, 1951; s. Edward R. and Patricia (Purcell) G.; m. Linda A. Keipert, June 10, 1979; children: Jonathan R., Colin T. BS, U. Notre Dame, 1974; MD, Loyola U. Chgo., 1976. Diplomate Am. Bd. Internal Medicine, Pulmonary Disease, Critical Care. Intern, resident Foster G. McGraw Hosp., Maywood, Ill., 1976-79; physician Pub. Health Svc., Red Lake, Minn., 1979-81; fellow pulmonary U. Chgo., 1981-83; fellow rsch. Loyola U. Med. Ctr., Maywood, 1983-89, asst. prof., assoc. prof., 1989-96, prof., 1996—; bd. dirs. Am. Lung Assn. Metro Chgo., com. mem., 1984—; cons. UNR Asbestos Disease Claims Trust, North Aurora, Ill., 1988—. Contbr. chpts. in books and articles to profl. jours. Grantee NIH, 1981-83, Eli Lilly, Searle, Smith-Kline, Glaxo, 1984—. Fellow ACP, Am. Coll. Chest Physicians; mem. Am. Thoracic Soc., Internat. Soc. Heart and Lung Transplantation, Am. Soc. Transplant Physicians. Office: Loyola Univ Med Ctr 2160 S First Ave Maywood IL 60153

GARRITY, JAMES ANDREW, ophthalmologist; b. Moorhead, Minn., Mar. 18, 1954. BS in Biochemistry, U. Minn., 1976, MD, 1980. Diplomate Am. Bd. Ophthalmology. Intern Hennepin County Med. Ctr., Mpls., 1980-81; resident in opthalmology Mayo Clinic, Rochester, Minn., 1982-84; fellow in orbital surgery and neuro ophthalmology U. Pitts., Rochester, 1985-86; cons. in ophthalmology Mayo Found., Rochester, Minn., 1986—. Office: Mayo Clinic Rochester MN 55905

GARRITY, RODMAN FOX, psychologist, educator; b. Los Angeles, June 10, 1922; s. Lawrence Hitchcock and Margery Fox (Pugh) G.; m. Juanita Daphne Mullan, Mar. 5, 1948; children—Diana Daphne, Ronald Fox. Student, Los Angeles City Coll., 1946-47; B.A., Calif. State U., Los Angeles, 1950; M.A., So. Meth. U., Dallas, 1955; Ed.D., U. So. Calif., 1963. Tchr. elem. sch. Palmdale (Calif.) Sch. Dist., 1952-54; psychologist, prin. Redondo Beach (Calif.) City Schs., 1954-60; asst. dir. ednl. placement lectr., ednl. adviser U. So. Calif., 1960-62; asso. prof., coordinator credentials programs Calif. State Poly. U., Pomona, 1962-66; chmn. social sci. dept. Calif. State Poly. U., 1966-68, dir. tchr. preparation center, 1968-71, coordinator grad. program, 1971-73, prof. tchr. preparation center, 1968—, coordinator spl. edn. programs, 1979—; cons. psychologist, lectr. in field. Pres. Redondo Beach Coordinating Council, 1958-60; mem. univ. rep. Calif. Faculty Assns., 1974-76. Served with Engr. Combat Bn. AUS, 1942-45. Mem. Prins. Assn. Redondo Beach (chmn. 1958-60), Nat. Congress Parents and Tchrs. (hon. life), Am. Psychol. Assn., Calif. Tchrs. Assn. Democrat. Office: Calif State U Dept Special Edn Pomona CA 91768

GARROWAY, NEIL WARREN, internist, endocrinologist, geriatrician; b. Bklyn., Dec. 26, 1945; s. Solomon and Doris (Palley) G.; m. Cynthia Moeller, May 28, 1972; children: Nathan, Joshua, Jordan. AB, Cornell U., 1966; MD, SUNY, Buffalo, 1970. Intern in medicine Barnes Hosp., 1970-72; resident in medicine Vanderbilt U. Hosp., 1972-73, resident in endocrinology, 1973-75; med. dir. N.E. Med. Ctr., Rochester, N.Y., 1975-80; dir. ambulatory svcs. The Genesee Hosp., Rochester, 1981-94, sr. v.p. med. affairs, 1994—; pvt. practice internist, endocrinologist, geriatrician Rochester, 1975—; med. dir. Rochester (N.Y.) Primary Care Network, 1987—.

GARRUTO, RALPH MICHAEL, research biologist, educator; b. Binghamton, N.Y., Nov. 20, 1943; s. Ralph Anthony and Josephine Janet (DiMartino) G.; m. Judith Dryden Sharp, Apr. 19, 1969; children: Jessica Anne, Jason Michael, John Ralph. BS, Pa. State U., 1966, MA, 1969, PhD, 1973. Postdoctoral fellow NIH, Bethesda, Md., 1972-73, staff, then sr. staff fellow, 1973-78, sr. supervisory rsch. biologist, 1978—; adj. prof. med. genetics Coll. Medicine U. South Ala., Mobile, 1982—; adj. sr. scientist biol. anthropology Pa. State U., University Park, 1985—; participant anthropol. and biomed. fieldwork, Asia, Pacific Islands, L.Am., 1969—; mem., NIH rep. U.S. Nat. Com. U.S. Man and the Biosphere Program, 1993-95; founding mem. bd. trustees Nat. Mus. Health and Medicine Found., Washington, 1989-91; exec. sec. Commn. on Aging and the Aged, Zagreb, Yugoslavia, 1985-89; cons. WHO, 1987; chair selection com. Paul T. Baker Disting. lectr. in human biology and anthropology Pa. State U., 1986—. Co-editor: Biological Anthropology adn Aging: Perspectives on Human Variation over the Lifespan, 1994, Dermatoglyphics: Science in Transition, 1991; contbr. articles on neurodegenerative disorders, neurosci. and aging to profl. jours.; patentee bil. agts. Recipient Commendation for Rsch., Guam Legislature, 1987, Spl. Achievement award, 1990, Merit award NIH, 1991, Dir.'s award, 1993; Wenner-Gren Found. leadership grantee, 1986, grantee, 1993-95; Alumni fellow Pa. State U., 1987. Fellow Am. Coll. Epidemiology, Am. Dermatoglyphics Assn. (sec.-treas. 1981-82, pres. 1987-89, disting. achievement award 1995), Human Biology Assn. (pres./pres.-elect 1993-96, exec. com. 1991-93), Internat. Genetic Epidemiology Soc. (founding fellow); mem. Soc. for Neurosci., World Fedn. Neurology (rsch. com. on neurepidemiology).

GARSTEN, JOEL JAY, gastroenterologist; b. N.Y.C., Jan. 10, 1948; s. Richard Maxwell and Gertrude Ann (Perlberg) G.; m. Marion Susan Moscovitz, July 10, 1971; children: Bryan David, Lauren Roberta. BA in Biology, CUNY, 1968; MD, Georgetown U., 1973. Resident in internal medicine Cornell-Coop. Hosps. Program, N.Y.C., 1973-76; fellow gastroenterology Yale Affiliated Gastroenterology Program, New Haven and Waterbury, Conn., 1976-78; gastroenterologist Gastroenterology Assocs. of Waterbury, 1978-80; physican, mng. ptnr. Digestive Disease Ctr. of Conn., 1980—; dir. sect. of gastroenterology Waterbury Hosp. Health Ctr., 1990—; assoc. dir. Yale Affiliated GI fellowship program Waterbury Hosp. and Hosp. of St. Raphael, New Haven and Waterbury, 1990—; clin. instr. internal medicine Yale U. Sch. Medicine, New Haven, 1978, asst. clin. prof., 1981, assoc. clin. prof., 1987—; med. dir. Liberty Health Plan, Naugatuck, Conn., 1987-89, Physicians Health Plan, Trumbull, Conn., 1989-90, med. adv. bd., 1990—. Contbr. articles to profl. jours. Med. adv. chmn. Crohn's and Colitis Found., WTBY Satelite, Waterbury, 1990—; resource speaker Waterbury Celiac Group, Thomaston, Conn., 1990—, Am. Cancer Soc., 1991—; prin. investigator multiple drug trials. Fellow ACP; mem. Am. Soc. for Liver Disease, Conn. Soc. Internal Medicine (pres. sect. gastroenterology), Am. Soc. Internal Medicine, Am. Gastroenterology Assn., Am. Soc. Parenteral and Enteral Nutrition, others. Home: 47 Harvest Ct Cheshire CT 06410-1844 Office: Digestive Disease Ctr Conn 60 Westwood Ave Waterbury CT 06708-2460

GARTLAND, CHARLES JOSEPH, physician; b. Corpus Christi, Tex., Feb. 12, 1958; s. Charles Joseph and Margaret Regina (Martin) G.; m. Judith Doyne, Jan. 5, 1985; children: Sara, Melissa. BS in Pharmacy, Temple U., 1981; MD, Phila Coll. Osteopathic Medicine, 1984. Diplomate Am. Bd. Internal Medicine, Nat. Bd. Osteopathic Examiners. Pvt. practice Upper Darby, Pa., 1990-93; med. dir., physician Primary Care Assocs. Southeastern Pa., Darby, Pa., 1993-95; clin. asst. prof. medicine Med. Coll. Pa. Hahneman U., Phila., 1994-96. Home: 30 Fox Brook Ln Thornton PA 19373 Office: 1503 Landsdowne Ave Darby PA 19023

GARTLAND, JOHN JOSEPH, physician, writer; b. Phila., Nov. 16, 1918; s. John Joseph and Jane Madelyn (Lafferty) G.; m. Madelyn T. Duffy, Jan. 5, 1944; children: Lynn, Barbara, John Jr., Patricia, Mary Ellen. AB, Princeton U., 1941; MD, Jefferson Med. Coll., 1944. Diplomate Am. Bd. of Orthopaedic Surgery. Chief orthopaedic surgery Meth. Hosp., Phila., 1960-68, Lankenau Hosp., Phila., 1968-70; James Edward prof., chmn. dept. of orthopaedic surgery Jefferson Med. Coll., Thomas Jefferson U., Phila., 1970-85, dir. office departmental rev. Jefferson Med. Coll., 1986-89, univ. med. editor, 1990—. Author: Fundamentals of Orthopaedics, 1965, 4th edit., 1986, Medical Writing and Communicating, 1993; contbr. numerous articles to profl. jours. Trustee Thomas Jefferson U., 1996—. Served to capt. U.S. Army, 1945-47. NIH grantee, 1971-74. Fellow Am. Acad. Orthopaedic Surgeons (pres. 1979-80), Am. Orthopaedic Assn.; mem. Coun. Med. Splty. Socs. (pres. elect 1987, pres. 1988). Democrat. Roman Catholic. Clubs: Overbrook Golf (Bryn Mawr, Pa.); Atlantic City Country (Northfield, N.J.). Office: Thomas Jefferson U 624 Scott Bldg 1020 Walnut St Philadelphia PA 19107-5567

GARTLEY, LINDA ANN, speech-language pathologist; b. Pitts., Feb. 14, 1957; d. Theodore Joseph Sr. and Constance (Colatosti) Bienkowski; m. Robert James Gartley Jr., Sept. 1, 1979; children: Ryan Robert, Candace Christine. BS, Clarion U., 1979; MA, U. Pitts., 1983. Lic. speech-lang. pathologist, Pa.; cert. clin. competence; cert. tchr. Speech-lang. pathologist presch. program Valley Community Svcs., Cheswick, Pa., 1980-89, dir. speech-lang. dept., 1982-89; speech-lang. pathologist ICF/MR Program Individual Care Facility for Mentally Retarded, Cheswick, Pa., 1988-89; speech-lang. pathologist Easter Seal Soc. Allegheny County, Pitts., 1990-91; pvt. practice speech-lang. pathology Lower Burrell, Pa., 1986—; speech-lang. pathologist, cons. Valley Cmty. Svcs., Cheswick, 1989-93, United Cerebral Palsy Western Pa., Spring Ch., 1991-93, NovaCare, Inc., 1993—. Mem. Nat. Aphasia Assn. Home and Office: 537 Arizona Dr New Kensington PA 15068-3365

GARTNER, LESLIE PAUL, anatomy educator; b. Szolnok, Hungary, Mar. 18, 1943; came to U.S., 1956; s. Janos Gartner and Mary (Schwartz) Kramer; m. Roseann C. Kollar, 1971; 1 child, Jennifer. BA, Rutgers U., Newark, 1965; MS, Rutgers U., New Brunswick, N.J., 1968, PhD, 1970. Instr anatomy Dental Sch., U. Md., Balt., 1970-71, asst. prof., 1971-74, assoc. prof., 1974—; mem. test com. nat. bd. anatomic scis. ADA, Chgo., 1985-92, mem. test com. nat. bd. dental hygiene, 1995—; cons. Williams & Wilkins Pub. Co., Balt., 1985—; lectr. U.S. Army Dental Corps, Ft. Meade, Md., 1987—; editor Galileo Press, Sparks, Md., 1989—. Author: Textbook of Head and Neck Anatomy, 1987, Cell Biology and Histology, 2nd edit., 1994, Color Atlas of Histology, 2nd edit., 1994, Oral Histology and Embryology, 1989, Color Textbook of Histology, 1996. Soccer commr. Reisterstown (Md.) Recreation Coun., 1985-94. Mem. Am. Assn. Anatomists, Am. Assn. Dental Schs. (histology subcom. 1989—), Mid-Atlantic Assn. Drosophila Workers. Democrat. Jewish. Home: 119 Cherry Valley Rd Reisterstown MD 21136 Office: U Md Dental Sch Anatomy 666 W Baltimore St Baltimore MD 21201-1510

GARVEY, EVELYN JEWEL, mental health nurse; b. Carrizozo, N.Mex., Aug. 23, 1931; d. Everett E. and Jewel A. (Bullard) Bragg; m. Robert J. Garvey, July 10, 1949; children: Nancy, Annie, Catherine, Robert, Michael, Betty. AD, Ea. N.Mex. Coll., 1972. RN, N.Mex.; cert. EMT., N.Mex. Staff nurse N.Mex. Rehab. Ctr., Roswell, 1972; staff nurse Villa Solano State Sch., Roswell, 1972-79, DON, 1979-81; staff nurse Ft. Stanton (N.Mex.) Hosp., 1981-95, Sunset Villa Nursing Home, Roswell, N.Mex., 1995-96; ret., 1996.

GARVIN, GLENN, venture capitalist; b. Washington, Apr. 18, 1944; s. Hadden Glenn Garvin and Glenda (Dale) Kerr; m. Diane Evans; children: Christopher Galen, Jennifer Caye. BBA in Acctg., Stetson U., DeLand, Fla., 1966. V.p. investments Prudential/Bache, Ft. Lauderdale, Fla., 1968-79; sr. v.p. PaineWebber, Ft. Lauderdale, 1979—; sr. ptnr. TriLateral Trading, Ft. Lauderdale, 1980—, So. Fin., Ft. Lauderdale, 1982—; mem. adv. bd. Hanover Forum, Atlanta, 1995-96. Mem. NASD, Hanover Forum (bd. dirs. 1995-96), N.Y. Stock Exch. Republican. Episcopalian. Office: PaineWebber 1 E Broward Blvd # 1810 Fort Lauderdale FL 33301

GARVIN, PAUL JOSEPH, JR., toxicologist; b. Toledo, Nov. 16, 1928; s. Paul Joseph and Laura Mary (Blanchet) G.; m. Priscilla Ann Haines, Aug. 23, 1952; children: Peter, Thomas, Paul III, Peggy, Priscilla, Polly. BA, St. John's U., 1950; MS, U. Minn., 1958. Rsch. assoc. Sterling-Winthrop Rsch. Inst., Rensselaer, N.Y., 1954-58; sr. rsch. pharmacologist Baxter-Travenol Inc., Morton Grove, Ill., 1958-72, mgr. safety evaluation, 1972-77; dir. toxicology Amoco Corp., Chgo., 1977-88, sr. health sci. advisor, 1988-92; toxicology cons. pvt. practice, Mt. Prospect, Ill., 1992—; mem. adv. com. ctr. risk analysis Harvard U. Sch. Pub. Health, Boston, 1991-92; sci. adv. panel hazardous substance mgmt. rsch. ctr. U. Medicine and Dentistry, Newark, 1988-91, adv. panel ctr. alternatives to animal testing Johns Hopkins U. Sch. Hygiene and Pub. Health, Balt., 1990-92, scientific adv. com. CIIT, Research Triangle Park, N.C., 1986-88. Contbr. over 50 articles to profl. jours. Chmn. Mt. Prospect Bd. Health, 1960-70. Mem. AAAS, Am. Indsl. Hygiene Assn., Am. Soc. Pharmacology & Exptl. Therapeutics, N.Y. Acad. Sci., European Soc. Toxicology, Soc. Toxicology. Home and Office: 309 N Wille St Mount Prospect IL 60056

GARY, NANCY ELIZABETH, nephrologist, academic administrator; b. N.Y.C., Mar. 4, 1937; d. Walter Joseph and Charlotte Elizabeth (Sayer) G. BS, Springfield (Mass.) Coll., 1958; MD, Med. Coll. Pa., 1962. Diplomate Am. Bd. Internal Medicine, Am. Bd. Nephrology. Resident Nassau County Med. Ctr., East Meadow, N.Y., 1962-64; resident St. Vincent's Hosp. and Med. Ctr., N.Y.C., 1964-65, chief renal sect., 1967-74; fellow in nephrology Georgetown U. Med. Ctr., Washington, 1965-67; instr. medicine NYU Sch. Medicine, N.Y.C., 1968-74; asst. prof. U. Medicine and Dentistry of N.J.-Rutgers Med. Sch., Piscataway, 1974-76, assoc. prof., 1976-81, prof., 1981-88, assoc. dean, 1981-87, exec. assoc. dean, 1987-88; dean Albany (N.Y.) Med. Coll., 1988-90; sr. med. adv. to adminstr. health care financing HHS, Washington, 1990-92; clin. prof. medicine George Washington U. Sch. Medicine, 1991—; prof. medicine Uniformed Svcs. U. Health Scis., Bethesda, Md., 1992—; exec. v.p., dean Sch. Medicine Uniformed Svcs. U. Health Scis., 1992-95; clin. prof. Howard U. Coll. Medicine, Washington, 1992—; pres., CEO Ednl. Commn. Fgn. Med. Grads., Phila., 1995—. Contbr. chpts. to books, articles to profl. jours. Robert Wood Johnson Health Policy fellow NAS Inst. Medicine, 1987-88; recipient Joseph F. Boyle, M.D. award for Disting. Pub. Svc., Am. Soc. Internal Medicine, 1992. Mem. ACP (Master), AMA, Nat. Kidney Found., Alpha Omega Alpha. Office: Ednl Commn Fgn Med Graduates 3624 Market St Philadelphia PA 19104

GARZA, IRMA PEREZ, health care agency executive, elementary school educator; b. Benavides, Tex., Dec. 21, 1942; d. Roberto and Marina (Molina) Perez; m. Nestor Garza, July 26, 1959; children: Rene, Nestor III, Luis Roberto, Priscilla, David. BS in Edn., Tex. Agrl. & Indsl., 1976, M in Bilingual Edn.; postgrad., Sam Houston U. Office mgr. Duval Conservation Dist., Benavides, 1974-76; elem. libr. Benavides Ind. Sch. Dist., 1990-96; CEO, adminstr. First Rate Home Health, Inc., Pharr, Tex., 1993-96. Editor elem. yearbooks. Sponsor 4-H Fair, Benavides, County Fair, Benavides, Little League Baseball, Benavides; sponsor, vol. ARC, Benavides; chair sch. bd. & county elections, 1974-96. Home: PO Box 505 Benavides TX 78341

GARZIONE, JOHN EDWARD, physical therapist; b. Newburgh, N.Y., Jan. 3, 1950; s. John Edward and Della Elizabeth (Gentila) G.; m. Anita Louise Hirschman, Sept. 21, 1974; children: Adriana, Katrina. AAS Orange County Community Coll., Middletown, N.Y., 1970; BS, Ithaca Coll., 1973. Mem. staff phys. therapy Chenango Meml. Hosp., Norwich, N.Y., 1973-74; sr. phys. therapist N.Y. State Vets. Home, Oxford, N.Y., 1974-86; CEO Chenango Therapeutics, Norwich, 1975—; lic. examiner N.Y. State, 1976-86; cons. phys. therapy Broome Devel. Ctr., Binghamton, N.Y., 1985—, Upstate Home for Children, Milford, N.Y., 1986-88, Hospice Chenango County, Norwich, 1991—; adj. instr. Czenovia Coll., 1982-87. Ithaca Coll., 1993-94; presenter in field. Contbr. article sto profl. jours. Mem. Am. Phys. Therapy Assn., Am. Acad. Pain Mgmt. (clin. assoc.), N.Y. Acad. Scis., Lions (v.p. 1990). Home: Box 451 Cunningham Hill Rd Sherburne NY 13460 Office: Chenango Therapeutics Country Club Rd Norwich NY 13815-1613

GASCHO, JOSEPH ALVIN, physician; b. Grand Island, Nebr., Feb. 20, 1947; s. Alvin and Cora Irene (Garber) G.; m. Barbara Sue Brunk, July 27, 1968; children: Joseph Alvin II, Susan Loring. BA in Natural Sci., Ea. Mennonite Coll., 1968; MD, U. Va., 1973. Diplomate Am. Internal Medicine, Am. Bd. Cardiovascular Disease. Intern U. Va., Charlottesville, 1973-74, resident in medicine, 1974-76, fellow in cardiology, 1976-77; fellow in cardiology U. Iowa, 1977-80; asst. prof. medicine U. Va. Sch. Medicine, Charlottesville, 1980-84, assoc. prof. medicine, 1984-86; assoc. prof. medicine Pa. State U. Coll. Medicine, Hershey, 1986-92, prof. medicine, 1992—; dir. cardiology fellowship tng. program Pa. State U. Sch. Medicine, 1987—. Contbr. articles to profl. jours., books, monographs, publs. Chmn. local chpt. Am. Heart Assn., Charlottesville, 1984-85. Fellow Am. Coll. Cardiology, Am. Coll. Physicians, ; mem. Am. Heart Assn., Am. Fedn. Clin. Rsch., Am. Physiology Soc., Am. Soc. Echocardiology, Pi Mu Epsilon. Mennonite. Office: Hershey Med Ctr Hershey PA 17033

GASH, IRA ARNOLD, psychologist, educator; b. Newark, Nov. 19, 1930; s. Charles H. and Lillian (Schwam) G.; m. Sondra Regina Stetin, Mar. 30, 1958; children: Lauren Beth, Amy Leah. BA, NYU, 1952; MA, Columbia U., 1954, profl. diploma, 1958; PhD, Temple U., 1966. Rehab. counselor N.J. Rehab. Commn., Newark, 1956-59; project dir. Workman's Compensation Rehab., Trenton, N.J., 1959-60; psychologist Stevens Inst., Hoboken, N.J., 1965-69, Dept. VA Med. Ctr., Lyons, N.J., 1966-90; ind. cons. New Providence, N.J., 1968—; atending psychologist Essex County Guidance Ctr., East Orange, N.J., 1972-82; adj. faculty Seton Hall U., South Orange, 1990-94; instr. Farleigh Dickinson U., Rutherford, N.J., 1967-70; adj. lectr. Rutgers U., New Brunswick, N.J., 1968-70. Mem. Berkeley Heights (N.J.) Bd. Health; bd. dirs. Nova Psi, 1988-90. With U.S. Army, 1954-56. Mem. ACA, APA, Am. Bd. Profl. Disability Cons., Nat. Career Devel. Assn., Am. Rehab. Counselors Assn. Home: 82 Martins Ln Berkeley Heights NJ 07922-1713 Office: 82 Martins Ln Berkeley Heights NJ 07922 Also: 526 Water St Belvidere NJ 07823

GASKINS, WILLIAM DARRELL, ophthalmologist; b. Columbia, S.C., June 7, 1951; s. William and Virginia G. Herron; m. Cynthia Gaile Harper, Sept. 7, 1973; children: William Darrell Jr., Craig E., Trenton F. BS in Pharmacy, U. S.C., 1973; MD, Med. U. S.C., 1977. Diplomate Am. Bd. Ophthalmology. Intern in gen. surgery Med. U. S.C., Charleston, 1977-78; resident in ophthalmology U. Miss. Med. Ctr., Jackson, 1981-84; pvt. practice, Naples, Fla., 1984—. Capt. M.C., USAF, 1978-81. Paul Harris fellow Rotary Internat., 1986. Fellow ACS, Am. Acad. Ophthalmology; mem. AMA, Fla. Soc. Ophthalmology, Collier County Med. Soc. Presbyterian. Office: 2335 9th St N Ste 304 Naples FL 33940

GASKINS-CLARK, PATRICIA RENAE, dietitian; b. Ft. Sill, Okla., July 24, 1959; d. Jay Frank and Iwana (Robinson) Gaskins; m. Gene Martin Clark, June 6, 1986; children: Taylor Renae, Kyle Gene. BS, Cameron U., 1982; MS, Cen. State U., 1986. Cert. home econ.; registered dietitian. Nutrition specialist William E. Davis & Sons, Inc., Oklahoma City, 1985-87; dietitian intern Okla. Teaching Hosps., Oklahoma City, 1987; clin. dietitian Grady Meml. Hosp., Chickasha, Okla., 1987-89; chief clin. dietitian Presbyn. Hosp., Oklahoma City, 1989-90; mgr. nutrition svcs. Norman (Okla.) Regional Hosp., 1990—. Mem. Am. Dietetic Assn., Cameron U. Alumni Assn., Oklahoma City Dist. Dietetic Assn., Okla. Dietetic Assn., Cen. State U. Alumni Assn., Phi Upsilon Omicron. Republican. Baptist. Office: Norman Regional Hosp 901 N Porter Ave Norman OK 73071-6404

GASNER, WALTER GILBERT, retired dermatologist; b. N.Y.C., May 6, 1912; s. Charles and Gussie Gasner; m. Shirley M. Friedman, Dec. 31, 1937; children: Douglas, Jane, John, Mary. MD, Med. Coll. S.C., 1936. Diplomate in dermatology and syhilology. Assoc. prof. Albert Einstein Med. Sch., Bronx, N.Y., 1955-75; chief of dermatology Grasslands Hosp., Westchester County, N.Y., 1956-75. Contbr. articles to med. jours. Lt. col. USAF, 1936-54. Fellow ACP. Home: Harbor Pond Farm Block Island RI 02807-0391

GASPARINI, GIAMPIETRO, clinical oncologist; b. Ancona, Marche, Italy, Feb. 5, 1955; s. Mario Gasparini and Franca Folco-Gasparini; m. Daniela Mazzocco, June 18, 1989; 1 child, Gabriella. MD, U. Padua, 1980. Fellow Nat. Cancer Inst., Milan, 1981-84; med. asst. Centro di Riferimento Oncologico, Aviano, Italy, 1984-86; assoc. dir. Clin. Oncology/St. Bortolo Vicenza Hosp., Italy, 1987—; specialist in oncology U. Padua, 1980-83, clin. pharmacology, 1984-87, oncol. radiotherapy/U. Brescia, Italy, 1988-91; lectr. U. Tor Vergata, Rome, 1993—. Contbr. 120 articles to profl. jours. and publs.; mem. editl. bd. 4 internat. oncological jours.; reviewer oncology articles for several internat. med. jours.; pioneer of clin. applications of rsch. on angiogenesis for the management of cancer patients. Recipient L. Momigliano Sacerdote award Fondazione Italiana per la Ricerca Sul Cancro, Milan, 1993, grantee for projects on breast cancer, 1993—. Mem. Am. Soc. Clin. Oncol., Am. Assn. Cancer Rsch., European Soc. Med. Oncology, European Soc. Mastology, Assn. Italiana Oncol. Med. (Matilde Scalzi award 1987), Coll. Ital. Oncologi Medici. Office: St Bortolo Med Ctr Dept Oncology, Via Rodolfi, Vicenza 36100, Italy

GASS, GERTRUDE ZEMON, psychologist, researcher; b. Detroit; d. David Solomon and Mary (Goldman) Zemon; m. H. Harvey Gass, June 19, 1938; children: Susan, Roger. BA, U. Mich., 1937, MSW, 1943, PhD, 1957. Lic. clin. psychologist, Mich. Mem. faculty Merrill-Palmer Inst., Detroit, 1958-69, lectr., 1967; mem. faculty Advanced Behavioral Sci. Ctr., Grosse Pointe, Mich., 1969-72; pvt. practice clin. psychology Birmingham, Mich., 1972—; adj. prof. psychology U. Detroit, 1969-75; cons. Continuum Ctr. Oakland U., Rochester, Mich., 1961-77, Traveler's Aid, Detroit, 1959-75; pres. Shapero Sch. Nursing, Detroit, 1967-72, cons. 1958-78; psychol. cons. Physician's Ins. Co. of Mich., 1988—, mgt. Mich. Bell Telephone, 1979-82. Mem. Adv. Com Sch. Needs, 1954-56; trustee Sinai Hosp. Detroit, 1972—; bd. dirs. Tribute Fund United Community Services, 1955-67. Fellow Am. Assn. Marriage-Family, Am. Orthopsychiatric Assn. (v.p. 1975-76), Mich. Psychol. Assn.; mem. Am. Psychol. Assn., Psychologists Task Force (v.p. 1977-84), Mich. Inter-Profl. Assn. (pres. 1976-78), Mich. Assn. Marriage Counselors (1979-80, pres. 1979-80), Mental Health Adv. Svc., Blue Cross and Blue Shield of Mich., Phi Kappa Phi, Pi Lambda Theta. Office: 30200 Telegraph Rd Bingham Farms MI 48025-4502

GASSER, RICHARD CHARLES, radiologist; b. Sioux City, Iowa, Mar. 1, 1935; s. Charles Milton and Elsie Loretta (DeCooke) G.; m. Marilyn Louise Nystrom, June 21, 1958; children: Scott, Meri Robin, Robert. BA, Morningside Coll., Sioux City, Iowa, 1957; MD, U. Iowa, 1960; MS in Radiology, U. Minn., 1964. Diplomate Am. Bd. Radiology. Staff radiologist Radiology Assoc. of Tarrant County, Ft. Worth and Arlington, Tex., 1966—. Bd. dirs. Van Cliburn Piano Found., Ft. Worth, 1982—. Capt. USAF, 1964-66. Mem. Dallas Ft. Worth Radiology Soc. (pres. 1975), Tex. Radiol. Soc., Am. Coll. Radiology, AMA. Office: Radiology Assocs Tarrant Co 816 W Cannon St Fort Worth TX 76104-3146

GASTFRIEND, DAVID ROBERT, psychiatrist; b. Phila., Dec. 31, 1954; s. Edward and Marilyn (Weisman) G.; m. Jody Oppenheim, 1984; children: Eric Elias, Daniel Zev, Rebecca Sasha. BS, Haverford Coll., 1976; MD, Jefferson Med. Coll., 1980. Bd. cert. in psychiatry; cert. addictionologist. Med. dir. Revere (Mass.) Community Counseling Ctr., 1984-87; dir. Mass. Gen. Hosp. Psychopharmacology Info. System, Boston, 1985—; med. dir. Comprehensive Emergency Svcs., Chelsea, Mass., 1986-90; chief Mass. Gen. Hosp. Chem. Dependence Unit, Boston, 1987-91, Mass. Gen. Hosp. Addiction Svcs., Boston, 1991—; assoc. dir. alcohol and chem. dependence inpatient rehab. Spaulding Rehab. Hosp., Boston, 1990—; prin. investigator criterial validity study Am. Soc. Addiction Medicine, 1995—. Assoc. editor: Computers in Human Services 1985—; editor: Obtaining Medical Education in Alcohol & Drug Abuse, 1982, Directory of Clinical Training Sites in the Addictions, 1981; contbr. numerous articles to profl. jours. Recipient: Profl. Specialty Program Award, Am. Assn. for Med. Systems and Informatics, 1986, fellowship in hosp. and community psychiatry, Am. Psychiatric Assn . 1982. Mem. AMA, Am. Soc. Addiction Medicine (com. chmn. 1989-92), Am. Psychiat. Assn. Home: 30 Orient Ave Newton Center MA 02159-1426 Office: Mass Gen Hosp Addiction Svcs Acc # 812 Boston MA 02114

GASTL, GUENTHER ALOIS, hematologist, medical oncologist; b. Mieming, Tyrol, Austria, Nov. 7, 1952; s. Emil and Frieda (Rappold) G.; m. Sieglinde Maria Oberdorfer, Oct. 23, 1990. MD, U. Innsbruck (Austria), 1979. Resident U. Innsbruck Med. Sch., 1979-81, clin. fellow, 1981-85, asst. prof., 1985, assoc. prof., 1988; vis. assoc. prof. Cornell Med. Ctr., N.Y.C., 1989-93; with Tumor Biology Ctr., Freiburg, Germany, 1993-96; head dept. hematology, oncology U. Innsbruck, Austria, 1996—. mem. Austrian Soc. for Oncology and Hematology, German Cancer Soc., Internat. Soc. for Interferon Rsch., N.Y. Acad. Scis., Am. Assn. for Cancer Rsch. Office: Univ Innsbruck, Dept Hematology/Oncology, Anichstrasse 35, A-6020 Innsbruck Austria

GASTON, BENJAMIN MCTYEIRE, pediatrician, educator; b. Toronto, Ont., Can., Mar. 25, 1956; s. Benjamin McTyeire and Margery Andrews (Darling) G.; m. Susan Marie Boisvert, Nov. 23, 1985; children: Renee Margery, Daniel Benjamin, James Roger. BA, U. Va., 1979, MD, 1983. Diplomate Am. Bd. Pediatrics, Pediatric Pumonology. Intern, resident Nat. Naval Med. Ctr., Bethesda, Md., 1983-84, 86-88; head med. dept. USS Iwo Jima, Norfolk, Va., 1984-86; head pediatric dept. Naval Hosp., Camp Lejeune, N.C., 1988-90; fellow pulmonary medicine Boston Children's Hosp., 1990-93; cmdr., head pediatric pulmonary divsn. Naval Med. Ctr., San Diego, 1993—; asst. prof. pediatrics U. Calif. San Diego, 1994—. Contbr. articles to profl. jours. Fellow Soc. Cin., 1978, Readers Digest, 1982. Fellow Am. Acad. Pediatrics; mem. AAAS, Am. Thoracic Soc., Assn. Mil. Surgeons of U.S., Christian Med. Soc., Alpha Epsilon Delta (pres. local chpt. 1978-79). Democrat. Office: Dept Pediatrics Naval Med Ctr San Diego CA 92134

GASTON, MARILYN HUGHES, health facility administrator; b. Cin.; 2 children, Amy Marie, Damon Allen. AB in Zoology, Miami U., Oxford, Ohio, 1960; MD, U. Cin., 1964. Diplomate Am. Bd. Pediat. Intern Phila. Gen. Hosp., 1964-65; resident in pediat. Childrens Hosp. Med. Ctr., Cin., 1965-67, asst. dir. out-patient dept., 1967-68; asst. dir. out-patient dept. Convalescent Hosp. for Children, Cin., 1968-69; med. dir. Lincoln Heights (Ohio) Health Ctr., 1969-72; dir. Sickle Cell screening clinic Cin. Health Dept., 1972-76; med. expert Nat. Heart, Lung & Blood Inst./NIH, Bethesda, 1976-79; commd. 2d lt. USPHS, 1979-89; dir. divsn. medicine Bur. Health Professions, Rockville, Md., 1989-90; dir. Bur. Primary Health Care, Rockville, Md., 1990—; instr. pediat. U. Cin. Coll. Medicine, 1967-68, asst. clin. prof. divsn. cmty. pediat., 1968-70, asst. prof. pediat., 1970-76, assoc. prof. pediat., 1976-77; asst. clin. prof. pediat. Cin. Tech. Coll., 1974-76, Howard U. Coll. Medicine, 1978-91, Uniformed Svcs. U. the Health Scis., 1987—; attending pediatrician Childrens Hosp. Med. Ctr., 1969-76, attending pediatrician and clinician, 1969-76, dir. med. staff, 1969-76; attending pediatrician Bethesda Hosp., 1974-76; pediatrician Hosp. Albert Schweitzer, Deschapelles, Haiti, 1967; presenter, lectr. and spkr. in field. Author: A Bibliography: Comprehensive Sickle Cell Centers, 1977, (with C.L. Calhoun) 2d edit., 1981, Management and Therapy of Sickle Cell Disease, 1984, 88; (with others) Newborn Screening for Sickle Cell Disease and Other Hemoglobinopathies, 1989; contbr. articles to profl. jours. Med. advisor Sickle Cell Awareness Group, 1971-77, State Crippled Childrens Svcs., 1975-77; advisor Cin. Health Dept., 1971-76; co-chair Nat. Sickle Cell Dirs., 1974; chair black commd. officers retention subcom. USPHS, 1989—; bd. trustees Child Health assn., 1974-77; bd. dirs. U. Cin. Found., 1989—, George Washington U. Life Scis., 1993—, U. Md. Ctr. for Minority Rsch. External Adv. Bd., 1993—. Recipient Phyllis Wheatley award State of Ohio, 1975, Appreciation award Jack & Jill, Inc., 1975, Hildrus A. Poindexter award Pub. Health Svcs., 1990, Excellence award Pitts. Sickle Cell Soc. 1980, State of Ohio Govs. award, 1987, Disting. Alumnae award U. Cin., 1989, Pub. Health award D.C. Health Care for the Homeless Project, Inc.; named one of Outstanding Young Women in Am., 1973, Outstanding Black Women in Cin., 1974, Woman of Yr. in Medicine, Harriet Tubman Black Womens Dem., 1976, Woman of Yr., Cmty. Health Found., Fla., 1993; named to Temple Bible Coll. Hall of Fame, 1976, Ohio Womens Hall of Fame, 1990. Mem. AAAS, APHA, Am. Acad. Pediat., Nat. Assn. Med. Minority Educators, Nat. Med. Assn. (Lifing Legend award), Am. Soc. Hematology, Am. Pediat. Soc., Am. Med. Womens Assn., N.Y. Acad. Scis., Sigma Delta Epsilon, Alpha Kappa Alpha. Office: Pub Health Svc Bur 4350 East West Hwy Fl 11 Bethesda MD 20814*

GATELL, JOSE MARIA, physician; b. Brafim, Tarragona, Spain, Jan. 14, 1951; s. Jose and Maria (Artigas) G.; m. Rosa Gatell, Sept. 29; children: Mariano, Griselda, Violeta. MD, Med. Sch., Barcelona, 1976, PhD, 1981. From intern to resident Hosp. Clinic, Barcelona, 1976-80; rsch. fellow Mass. Gen. Hosp., Boston, 1982; chief infectious disease unit Hosp. Clinic, Barcelona, 1990—; assoc. prof. medicine Faculty of Medicine, Barcelona, 1982—. Author and editor of numerous books and articles on infectious diseases, AIDS. Mem. Am. Soc. Microbiology, Spanish Infectious Diseases Soc. (pres. elect 1992-96, pres. 1998-99), Nat. Geographic Soc., Spanish AIDS Soc. (vice chmn. 1990-94), Catalan Soc. Infectious Diseases (pres. 1992-94). Home: Santapau 62, Barcelona 08016, Spain Office: Hosp Clinic, Villarroel 170, Barcelona 08036, Spain

GATES, JOANNE FERRY, counselor; b. N.Y.C., Oct. 7, 1924; d. Joseph Rutherford and Constance (Riker) Ferry; B.A., Conn. Coll., 1946; M.A. in Counseling, St. Josephs Coll., 1981; DHL (hon.) Centenary Coll., 1987; m. Richard Judson Gates, Sept. 7, 1946; children: Pamela, Cynthia, Suzanne, Rebecca. Mem. exec. bd. Jr. League Hartford, 1957-64; bd. dirs. Inst. Living, 1968-69; counselor Counseling Center, Hartford Coll. Women. 1981-92; bd. dirs. Hartford Symphony, 1973-76, aux. v.p. nominating chmn., 1977; Greater Hartford Campus Ministry, 1981—; West Hartford Pastoral Counseling Ctr., 1985; trustee Childrens Mus. Hartford, 1970-73, West Hartford Sch. Music, 1962-83, Centenary Coll. for Women, N.J. 1968-86, trustee emeritus 1986—; pres. Jodik Found., 1977—; deacon 1st Ch. of Christ Congregational, 1977-79, tchr. religious edn., 1952-72, pres. women's guild, 1969-70; co-chmn. music and arts festival Trinity Coll., 1975; vol. Hartford Hosp., 1949-55, Meals on Wheels, 1977-80; v.p. women's bd., trustee, corporator Hartford Sem., 1978—; mem. alumnae exec. bd. capital fund drives Northfield (Mass.) Mt. Herman Sch.; sec., Smith Gates Corp., Farmington, Conn. Mem. Conn. Coll.,Forum, Northfield Mt. Herman Sch. alumnae assns., Seed and Weed Garden Club, Stonington Country Club, Musical of Hartford Club, Watch Hill Yacht Club, trustee Hartford Coll. For Women. Republican. Home: 108 Westmont St West Hartford CT 06117-2930

GATES, PHILIP DON, anesthesiologist; b. Canyon, Tex., Feb. 10, 1937; s. Charles Rufus and Thelma Coise (Wade) G.; m. Mary Alice Sweatt, May 7, 1966; 1 child, Randy Don Carr. Student, Tex. Tech Coll., 1955-58; MD, U. Tex. Med. Sch., 1962. Diplomate Am. Bd. Internal Medicine, Am. Bd. Anesthesiologists. Commd. 2d lt. USAF, 1962, advanced through grades to maj., resigned, 1971; intern in internal medicine Wilford Hall USAF Hosp., Lackland AFB, 1962-63; physician USAF, Ft. Walton Beach, Fla., 1962-71; practice medicine specializing in internal medicine Ft. Walton Beach, 1971-77; physician internal medicine White-Wilson Med. Ctr., Ft. Walton Beach, 1977-84; anesthesiologist Richland Meml. Hosp., Columbia, S.C., 1984-86, Humana Hosp., Ft. Walton Beach, 1986—. Contbr. articles to profl. jours. Mem. AMA, Am. Coll. Physicians, Am. Soc. Anesthesiologists, So. Med. Assn., Fla. Med. Assn. Republican. Methodist. Club: Ft. Walton Yacht. Home: 200 W Miracle Strip Pkwy # 1100 Fort Walton Beach FL 32548 Office: PO Box 3088 Fort Walton Beach FL 32547-0088

GATES, STEVEN LEON, physician; b. Newton, Kans., Aug. 13, 1954; s. Leon Martin and Mary Lorine (Adams) G.; m. Paula Ellen Banwart, Jan. 1, 1977; children: Stephanie, Scott, Jeffrey. BS in Pharmacy summa cum laude, S.W. Okla. State U., 1976; DO, Okla. State U., 1986. Diplomate Am. Bd. Internal Medicine; lic. pharmacist, Okla. Intern Osteopathic Med. Ctr. Tex., Ft. Worth, 1986-87; resident in internal medicine Dallas/Ft. Worth Med. Ctr., Grand Prairie, Tex., 1987-90; pharmacist M & D Star Drug Store, Okmulgee, Okla., 1976-80; pharmacist, mgr. Wal-Mart Pharmacy Div., Okmulgee, Okla., 1980-82; chief med. resident Ready Care Minor Emergency Ctr., Bedford, Tex., 1987-90; jail physician Tarrant County Sheriff's Dept., Ft. Worth, 1989-90; pvt. practice internal medicine Grand Prairie, 1990—; internal medicine physician and minor emergency physician Ready Care Med. Clinic, Bedford, Tex., 1990—; dir. med. edn. Dallas/Ft. Worth Med. Ctr.-Grand Prairie, 1990—; clin. asst. prof. dept. medicine Tex. Coll. Osteopathic Medicine, Ft. Worth, 1990—. Mem. AMA, Am. Coll. Osteopathic Internists (bd. cert.), Am. Osteopathic Assn., Tex. Osteopathic Med. Assn., Tex. Med. Assn., Tarrant County Med. Soc., Sigma Sigma Phi. Republican. Home: 3110 Sunny Meadows Ct Arlington TX 76016-5948

GATES, WILLIAM ALLMAN, III, lawyer, radiologist; b. Cin., Mar. 25, 1949; s. William Allman Jr. and Mary Patricia (Tuke) G.; m. Lynne Anne Mekus, Jan. 5, 1985. BS, U. Ky., 1971, MD, 1975, JD, 1986. Bar: Ky. 1986; Diplomate Am. Bd. Pediatrics and Am. Bd. Radiology. Resident in pediatrics U. Ky., Lexington, 1975-78, resident in radiology, 1978-81; practice medicine specializing in radiology Lexington and Louisville, 1981—; legal med. cons. Lexington, 1986—. Fellow Am. Coll. Legal Medicine; mem. Ky. Bar Assn., Ky. Med. Assn., Fayette County Med. Assn., Radiol. Soc. N.Am., Bluegrass Radiol. Soc., Phi Beta Kappa. Office: 237 S Ashland Ave Lexington KY 40502-1727

GATHRIGHT, JOHN BYRON, JR., colon and rectal surgeon, educator; b. Oxford, Miss., Sept. 29, 1933; s. J. Byron Sr. and Connie (Love) G.; m. Barbara Cooper, Sept. 19, 1959; children: John Byron III, Lin, John Miles, Peter C. BS, U. Miss., 1955; MD, Northwestern U., 1957. Diplomate Am. Bd. Colon and Rectal Surgery (pres. 1989-90). Intern Charity Hosp., New

Orleans, 1957-58, resident in gen. surgery, 1958-62; fellow in colon & rectal surgery Alton Ochsner Med. Found., New Orleans, 1962-63; mem. staff So. Bapt. Hosp., New Orleans, 1963-69; mem. staff Ochsner Found. Hosp., New Orleans, 1969—, chmn. colon and rectal surgery dept.; clin. prof. surgery Tulane U., New Orleans, 1991—; vis. surgeon So. La. Med. Ctr., Houma, 1977—; trustee, exec. com., bd. dirs. Alton Ochsner Med. Found., 1980—. Assoc. editor Diseases of the Colon and Rectum, 1977-93, Perspectives in Colon and Rectal Surgery, 1987—, Colon and Rectal Surgery Outlook, 1987—; mem. bd. editors Current Concepts in Gastroenterology, 1980-89. Fellow ACS (grad. edn. com. 1981-89, Am. Soc. Colon and Rectal Surgeons (pres. 1989-90), Soc. Coloproctology of Eng. and Ireland (hon.), Internat. Soc. Univ. Colon and Rectal Surgeons (sec. 1990—). Republican. Presbyterian. Office: Ochsner Clinic & Hosp 1514 Jefferson Hwy New Orleans LA 70121-2483

GATIPON, BETTY BECKER, medical educator, consultant; b. New Orleans, Sept. 8, 1931; d. Elmore Paul and Theresa Caroline (Sendker) Becker; m. William B. Gatipon, Nov. 22, 1952 (dec. 1986); children: Suzanne, Ann Gatipon Sved, Lynn Gatipon Pashley. BS magna cum laude, Ursuline Coll., New Orleans, 1952; MEd, La. State U., 1975, PhD, 1983. Tchr. Diocese of Baton Rouge, 1960-74, edn. cons. to sch. bd., 1974-78; dir. Right to Read program Capital Area Consortium/Washington Parish Sch. Bd., Franklington, La., 1978-80; dir. basic skills edn. Capital Area Consortium/Ascension Parish Sch. Bd., Donaldsonville, La., 1980-82; instr. Coll. Edn. La. State U., Baton Rouge, 1982-84; evaluation cons. La. Dept. Edn., Baton Rouge, 1984-85; dir. basic skills edn. Capital Area Basic Skills/East Feliciana Parish Sch. Bd., Clinton, La., 1985-86; program coord. La. Bd. Elem. and Secondary Edn., New Orleans, 1987-89; dir. divsn. of med. edn., dept. family medicine Sch. Medicine La. State U. Med. Ctr., New Orleans, 1989—; evaluator East Feliciana Parish Schs., 1982-86; presenter math. methods workshops Ascension Parish Schs., 1980-84. Author curriculum materials, conf. papers; contbr. articles to edn. jours. Curatorial asst. La. State Mus., New Orleans, 1987—; soprano St. Louis Cathedral Concert Choir, New Orleans, 1988—; chmn. Symphony Store, New Orleans Symphony, 1990—; lector St. Angela Merici Ch. Mem. Am. Ednl. Rsch. Assn., Assn. Am. Med. Colls., Midsouth Ednl. Rsch. Assn., La. Ednl. Rsch. Assn., Soc. Tchrs. Family Medicine, New Orleans Film and Video Buffs, Phi Kappa Phi, Phi Delta Kappa. Roman Catholic. Home: 105 10th St New Orleans LA 70124-1258 Office: LA State U Med Ctr Sch Medicine 1542 Tulane Ave New Orleans LA 70112-2825

GATSKI, ROBERT LAWRENCE, physician; b. West Hazelton, Pa., May 27, 1919; s. Peter Paul and Estella (Schlacky) G.; m. Betty Eileen Carey, June 29, 1942; children—Robert Lawrence, Charles P., Marsha E., Mark. Student, Bucknell U., 1942-44; M.D., Jefferson Med. Coll., 1948. Diplomate: Am. Bd. Psychiatry, Nat. Bd. Med. Examiners. Intern St. Josephs Hosp., Lancaster, Pa., 1948-49; resident Danville (Pa.) State Hosp., 1949-53; acting clin. dir. Gov. Bacon Health Center, Delaware City, Del., 1954-55; clin. dir. Danville (Pa.) State Hosp., 1954-55, supt., adminstr., 1955-77; ret., 1977; practice medicine specializing in psychiatry Danville, 1977—; med. dir. Cmty. Mental Health Clinic, Danville and Bloomsburg, Pa., 1977—; acting supt. Retreat State Hosp., 1965-67; psychiat. cons. Geisinger Med. Ctr., Bloomsburg Hosp., Muncy (Pa.) State Indsl. Home, Eastern Fed. Penitentiary, Lewisburg, Pa. Editor Pa. Psychiat. Quar., 1959-63, cons. editor, 1963-65. Mem. coun. on stroke Susquehanna Valley Regional Med. Program, 1971-72; mem. Pa. Drug Standardization Com. Recipient Alumni award Bucknell U., 1971. Mem. AMA, Am. Psychiat. Assn., Am. Coll. Hosp. Adminstrs. Address: 310 E Market St Danville PA 17821-2032

GATT, STEPHEN PAUL, anesthesiologist, intensivist; b. Floriana, Malta, Jan. 24, 1952; arrived in Australia, 1975; s. Henry John and Carmelina (Agius) G.; m. Alice Dingli, Sept. 16, 1975; children: Ian McAlister, Andrea Geraldine, Kristina Anne Teresa, Emma Kathleen Rachelle. MD, Royal U. Malta, 1975. Intern, resident Royal Prince Alfred Hosp., Camperdown, Sydney, Australia, 1976-77; gen. rotation resident and sr. resident St. Vincent's Hosp., Darlinghurst, Sydney, 1977-78, med. registrar, 1978-79; anesthetic and intensive care registrar Prince Henry/Prince of Wales Hosps., Randwick, Sydney, 1979-83; jr. cons., fellow in intensive care Prince of Wales Hosp., 1983; instr. anesthesia Harvard U. Med. Sch.-Brigham and Women's Hosp., Boston, 1983-85; clin. lectr. U. New South Wales, Kensington, Australia, 1985-89, sr. lectr., 1989—; dir. anesthesia Royal Hosp. for Women, Sydney, 1985-88, 91—, dir. anesthesia and acute care, 1988-91, established first free-standing obstetric intensive care unit, 1991; organizer numerous internat. and nat. confs. and symposia; reviewer Anesthesia and Intensive Care, 1988-95, Drugs, 1996. Mem. editl. bd. Obstetric Anesthesia, 1995—; editor-in-chief, prin. author Internat. Hypertextbook of Regional Anesthesia for Obstetrics, 1994—; contbr. numerous articles to profl. jours. Recipient Griffiths gold medal in surgery, 1975, Cachia Zammit prize in forensic medicine, 1975, Warrant Pres. of Republic of Malta, 1975, Matthew Spence medal, 1982, Shield, Jordanian Soc. Anesthesiology. Mem. Royal Coll. Surgeons, Royal Coll. Physicians England, Med. Def. Union, Med. Assn. Malta, Australasian Soc. Clin. Hypnotherapists, Australian Soc. Anesthetists, Australian Med. Assn., Australian and New Zealand Intensive Care Soc., Royal Australasian Coll. Surgeons, Smithsonian Inst. (assoc.), Am. Soc. for Edn. in Anesthesia (task force), Mensa, Brigham and Women's Hosp. Med. Staff Alumni Assn., Australian Soc. for Study of Hypertension in Pregnancy, Soc. Australasian Obstetric Anesthetists (chmn. ad hoc steering com.), Australian Salaried Med. Officer Fedn. (br. counselor), Obstetric Anesthesia Assn. Australian Soc. Anesthetists (founding, dep. chmn., sec.), Australian and New Zealand Coll. Anesthetists, Obstetric Medicine Group Australasia. Roman Catholic. Home: Kensington, A'Orangi 47 Balfour Rd, Sydney NSW 2033, Australia Office: Royal Hosp for Women, 188 Oxford Str, Paddington NSW 2021, Australia

GATTER, ROBERT ASHLEY, healthcare consultant, rheumatologist; b. Pitts., Pa., Aug. 4, 1931; m. Marilyn J. Craig, 1957; children: Anne, Robert Jr. BA, Johns Hopkins U., 1953; MD, U. Pitts., 1957. Diplomate Am. Bd. Internal Medicine, subspecialty rheumatology; lic. physician, Pa., N.Mex. Intern Western Pa. Hosp., Phila., 1957-60; resident internal medicine Phila. Gen. Hosp., 1960-62; trainee in rheumatology Hahnemann Med. Coll. and Hosp., Phila., 1962-63, instr. medicine, 1963-64, sr. instr., 1964-67, asst. prof., 1967, clin. asst. prof., 1967-71; clin. asst. prof. medicine U. Pa. Sch. Medicine, Phila., 1971-75, clin. assoc. prof., 1975-92; chief rheumatology Lovelace Med. Ctr., Albuquerque, 1992-95, med. dir. rehab. svcs., 1992-95, coord. chronic musculoskeletal pain mgmt., 1992-95; ind. healthcare cons. Livingston, Tex.; jr. attending in medicine Hahnemann Hosp., Phila., 1963-71; dir. X-ray Diffraction Lab. Hahnemann Med. Coll. and Hosp., Phila., 1963-67, dir. Gen. Arthritis Clinic, 1964-67, dir. Collagen Vascular Clinic, 1967-68; jr. attending dept. medicine Phila. Gen. Hosp., 1963-67; attending in rheumatology VA Hosp., Phila., 1964-66; cons. in rheumatology Landis State Hosp., Phila., 1967-68; coll. physician Beaver Coll., Glenside, Pa., 1967-68; dir. med. residency dept. medicine Abington (Pa.) Meml. Hosp., 1967-70, physician-in-chief sect. rheumatology, 1967-92, dir. Rheumatology Lab., 1967-85, dir. Arthritis Clinic, 1967-77, founder, dir. Arthritis Cmty. Outreach Program, divsn. rheumatology, 1975-92, dir. rheumatology fellowship program, 1982-83, chmn. rheumatic disease unit com., 1984-92, chmn. Osteoporosis Ctr. com., 1985-86; cons. rheumatology Doylestown (Pa.) Hosp., 1970-92, Chestnut Hill Hosp., Phila., 1971-91; asst. physician rheumatology Holy Redeemer Hosp., Meadowbrook, Pa., 1971-85, assoc. physician, 1985-92; attending physician dept. medicine Penn divsn. Phila. Gen. Hosp., 1971-75, sr. attending physician, 1975-77; dir. Ctr. Arthritis and Back Pain, Willow Grove, Pa., 1982-92; pres., founder Arthritis Ctrs. Am., 1987-92; mem. rev. panel Arthritis Ctr. Grants NIAMDD, NIH, Washington, 1977; reviewer rheumatology Edn. Materials Panel, Assn. Am. Med. Colls. and Nat. Libr. Medicine, 1977. Reviewer Jour. Rheumatology, 1985—, Arthritis and Rheumatism, 1990—; contbr. articles to profl. jours., chpts. to books. With USN, 1958-60. Named Physician of Yr. Ex-Residents Assn., Abington Meml Hosp., 1992. Fellow ACP, Am. Coll. Rheumatology (mktg. com. 1986-88, adminstrn. and evaluation group 1987-88, chmn. ad hoc com. on accreditation for joint fluid analysis 1988, rep. ACP 1989-92, chmn. ad hoc com. on office guidelines for joint fluid analysis 1991-93, exec. com. rehab. sect. 1994—), Coll. Physicians Phila.; mem. AMA, Arthritis Found. (mem. in charge film evaluation group visual aids subcom. profl. edn. com. 1969-74, mem. subcom. 1969-81, Russell Cecil nat. award 1965, patient svcs. com. N.Mex.-Western Tex chpt. 1994-95, award of appreciation Ea. Pa. chpt. 1983, Profl. Vol. of Yr. 1985), Nat. Soc. Clin. Rheumatologists (exec. com. 1981-82, future sites com. 1981-89, arrangements chmn. 1984, 86, historian 1984-91, chmn. future sites com. 1989-95, v.p. 1995—).

GAUDINO, MARIO, physician, pharmaceutical company executive; b. Buenos Aires, Argentina, May 22, 1918; came to U.S., 1946, naturalized, 1966; s. Nicolas M. and Maria Teresa (Ferrari) G.; B.A., U. Buenos Aires, 1934, M.D., 1944; Ph.D., N.Y. U., 1950; m. Ann Murray, Sept. 24, 1947 (div. Jan. 1983); children—David, Brian; m. 2d, Judith A. Jenkins, May 19, 1984. Asst., Inst. Histology and Embryology, U. Buenos Aires, 1936, asst., research asst. Inst. Physiology, 1937-42, chief of lab. biol. physics, 1944; resident, chief resident Ramos Mejia Hosp., Buenos Aires, 1941-44; Millet and Roux fellow Argentine Assn. for Advancement Sci., 1943; asst., attending physician Inst. Semiology, Nat. Clin. Hosp., Buenos Aires, 1944-46; fellow Argentine Nat. Cultural Commn., 1945; Sauberan fellow Argentine Assn. Advancement Sci., 1946; physiol. research fellow N.Y. U., U.S. State Dept., Dazian Found. Med. Research, 1946-49; asst. prof. Tex. U., 1949; chmn. dept. biol. physics U. La Plata, Argentina, 1950-51; attending physician Central Inst. Cardiology, Buenos Aires, 1950-51; asso. dir. med. writing and advt. Lederle Labs. div. Am. Cyanamid Co., N.Y.C., 1951-52; research asso., prof. dept. surgery N.Y. U., 1952-55, adj. asso. prof. surgery, 1955-57; established investigator Am. Heart Assn., N.Y.C., 1954-57; med. dir. Abbott Labs. Internat. Co., Abbott Universal Ltd., Chgo., 1957-61; asso. dept. medicine Northwestern U., 1959-61; asso. med. dir. Pfizer Internat., Inc., N.Y.C., 1962-67; asso. dir. advanced clin. research Internat. Merck Sharp & Dohme Research Labs., Rahway, N.J., 1967-70, dir., 1970-71, sr. dir. clin. research internat. med. affairs area, 1971-74; dir. med. compliance drug regulatory affairs CIBA-GEIGY Pharms., Summit, N.J., 1974-80, asso. dir. med. services med. affairs dept., 1980-89; dir. Med. Cons. Svcs. med. affairs dept., 1989—; clin. asst. prof. medicine Cornell U., N.Y.C., 1971-77. Fellow N.Y. Acad. Scis.; mem. Am. Physiol. Soc., Am. Acad. Clin. Toxicology, AMA, Am. Soc. Clin. Pharmacology and Therapeutics, Acad. Medicine N.J., Summit Med. Soc., Soc. for Exptl. Biology and Medicine, Am. Fedn. Clin. Research, Harvey Soc., Am., Internat. socs. nephrology, Microcirculatory Soc. Clubs: Jockey, Argentine Yacht., University, Buenos Aires Rowing. Home: 3 Brainerd Rd Summit NJ 07901-1410 Office: 556 Morris Ave Summit NJ 07901-1330

GAUDIO, MAXINE DIANE, biofeedback therapist, stress management consultant; b. Stamford, Conn., Oct. 7, 1939; d. Robert Fridolin and Doris (Altstadter) Goodman; m. Arthur Sebastian Gaudio, Oct. 7, 1962; 1 child, Dante Sebastian. Relaxation therapist The Biofeedback Clinic, New Canaan, Conn., 1970-73; chief EEG technologist St. Barnabas, Bronx, N.Y., 1973-75; biofeedback therapist Biofeedback Clinic, Stamford, Conn. and Winston-Salem, N.C., 1973—; clin. dir. Biofeedback Unltd. N.C., 1979—; clin. dir. Creative Mind Systems, Stamford, Conn., 1980—; tech. advisor Creative Mind Systems N.C., 1980-83; indsl. cons. major corps. U.S.A., 1976—; writer, creator stress video Hartley Prodns., Old Greenwich, Conn., 1984—; writer, creator, narrator Robert Gross Assocs., Stamford, Conn., 1984. Author, narrator video: Stress, 1984, Your Secret Energy Source, 1984; writer, dir. audio/visual package Captain Mind; creator, producer Stress and Relaxation, 1986-87; author, narrator book and tapes: Creative Union, 1980; author: Land Within the Shadow, 1980. Exec. dir. Friends of Children, Darien, Conn., 1985-87; dir. spl. projects Victim Svcs. Agy., N.Y.C., spl. events 1988-91; dir. pub. info. and devel. Louise Wise Svcs., N.Y.C., 1992-93; founder, chair bd. Kids with Kids, N.Y.C., 1991—; bd. dirs. cons. Childhope, N.Y.C., 1987-89. Mem. Am. Fed Press Women, Am. Soc. EEG Technologsts, Am. Assn. Advancement Tension Control, Biofeedback Soc. Am., Biofeedback Soc. N.C., Internat. Platform Assn., Internat. Reiki Alliance. Avocations: swimming; fencing; flying; metaphysics; astrology; piano. Club: Conn. Press. Home: 19 H Weavers Hill Greenwich CT 06831

GAUGHAN, KENNETH JOSEPH, social worker; b. Chgo., Nov. 13, 1953; s. Edward Francis and Margaret Catherine (Bonefas) G.; m. Linda Katherine Morrin, Sept. 26, 1987; 1 child, Ashlyn Elizabeth. BA, Northeastern Ill. U., 1974; MPA, Golden Gate U., 1982; MSW, Loyola U., Chgo., 1977. Lic. clin. social worker. Sch. social worker Grundy County Spl. Edn. Coop., Morris, Ill., 1977-80; sch. social worker Hillsborough County Pub. Schs., Tampa, Fla., 1980—, supervisor sch. social work svcs., 1989—. 1st chairperson Project LINK (Local Impact on Neighborhood Kids), Tampa, 1989-92. Mem. Acad. Cert. Social Workers. Roman Catholic. Home: 126 Hickory Creek Blvd Brandon FL 33511-8061 Office: Hillsborough County Pub Sch 1202 E Palm Ave Tampa FL 33605-3512

GAULDEN, GLORIA FRAN, dental hygiene educator; b. Monroe, La., Sept. 22, 1958; d. Frank Rials and Gloria (Tullous) G. BS in Dental Hygiene, N.E. La. U., Monroe, 1980; MA in Edn. Counseling, La. Tech. U., Ruston, 1988. Lic. La. State Bd. Dentistry. Pvt. practice dental hygienist Monroe, 1980-86; asst. prof. dental hygiene N.E. La. U., Monroe, 1986—; advisor Student Am. Dental Hygienists Assn., 1986—; recruitment chair Dept. Dental Hygiene, Monroe, 1990—, outcomes assessment chair, 1990—, quality assessment chair, 1990—. Contbr. articles to profl. jours. Mem. Acad. Advanced Studies, Am. Dental Hygienists' Assn. (v.p. 1980—), La. Dental Hygienists' Assn. (pres., sec. pub. rels. 1980-96, mandatory continuing edn. preceptorship 1989-90, expanded functions com. 1992), N.E. La. Dental Hygienists' Assn. (legis. chair 1981—), Sigma Phi Alpha. Republican. Baptist. Office: NE La U 700 University Ave Monroe LA 71209-0120

GAULT, THOMAS EMERSON, healthcare business executive, accountant; b. Cin., June 25, 1941; s. Emerson and Helen (Romer) G.; m. Patricia Ann Taylor, Sept. 25, 1965; children—Jeff, Sherri, Greg. B.B.A., U. Cin., 1965. C.P.A., Ohio. Supr. Coopers & Lybrand, Cin., 1965-72; contr. Garden Manor Extended Care Ctr., Middletown, Ohio, 1972-73; contr.-v.p. fin. Hyde Park Villa, Inc., Cin., 1973-80, pres., CEO, 1980-86; contr.-v.p. fin. Harrison House, Inc., Cin., 1973-80, pres., CEO, 1980—; pres., CEO Trine Technic, Inc., Cin., 1980—; CEO Day Share Ltd., Cin., 1993—; lectr. in field. Trustee St. Theresa Home for Aged, Cin., 1983—; mem. Nursing Home Ombudsman Steering Com., Cin., 1983—; instr. Referee Clinics, 1983-84; speaker IBM Exec. Health Seminar, 1982. Coach, mem. nominating com. Delhi Athletic Assn., Cin., 1979-84; mem. nat. referee com. U.S. Soccer Fedn., Chgo., 1991—; dir. instrn. Ohio South Soccer Assn., Dayton, Ohio, 1992—; mem. Soccer Assn. Youth Nat. Referee Council, Cin., 1983-84, chmn., chief referee, 1987—, treas., 1995-96; v.p., referee, coordinator Westside Soccer Club, Cin., 1983-84; pres. Western Area Soccer Assn., Cin., 1983; bd. dirs., coach, soccer coordinator St. Dominic Athletic Assn., Cin., 1978-84. Recipient Silver Ball award Soccer Assn. Youth, 1986; named to Hall of Fame St. Dominic Athletic Assn., 1989. Fellow Am. Coll. Health Care Adminstrs. (pres. Ohio chpt. 1994-96, Pub. Svc. award 1989); mem. Nat. Health Lawyers Assn. (assoc.), Nat. Fire Protection Assn. (health sect. 1994—), Ohio Health Care Assn. (chmn. dist. I 1980—, state bd. dirs./sec. 1984-85, chmn. reimbursement com. 1984, pres. 1987-89, v.p. Ednl. Found. 1994—, Pres.'s award 1984), Hosp. Fin. Mgmt. Assn. (advanced mem.), Am. Inst. C.P.A.s, Ohio Soc. C.P.A.s (dir. Cin. chpt. 1967—), Am. Health Care Assn. (conv. del. 1983-84, bd. dirs. 1987-89), Greater Cin. Nursing Home Assn. Republican. Roman Catholic. Club: St. Dominic Men's Soc. (pres. 1982-83) (Cin.). Office: Trine Technic Inc 2171 Harrison Ave Cincinnati OH 45211-8159

GAUNT, ALICE ADELLA, nurse practitioner; b. Coalinga, Calif., May 13, 1931; d. Alty Leslie and Margaret Lyda (Wolfe) Tully; m. James Robert Gaunt, Sept. 13, 1952. Diploma, Santa Clara County Nursing; AA, San Jose State U.; cert., U. Calif., Davis. RN, Calif. Nurse Cmty. Hosp., King City, Calif., 1952; office nurse John Green, M.D., King City, 1952-53, Richard Ames, M.D., King City, 1953-60; nursing supr. So. Monterey County Med. Group, King City, 1960-75, family nurse practitioner, 1975-92; family nurse practitioner Steven W. Harrison, M.D., King City, 1992—; CPR instr. Am. Heart Assn., King City, 1962-75. Mem. Calif. Coalition Nurse Practitioners, Calif. Cattlewomen. Home: 123 Carlson Ave King City CA 93930 Office: Steven W Harrison MD 400 Canal St Ste C King City CA 93930

GAUS, CLIFTON R., federal agency administrator. MA, U. Mich.; ScD, Johns Hopkins U. Mem. faculty Sch. Pub. Health Johns Hopkins U., Balt.; mem. faculty Med. Sch. Georgetown U., Washington; assoc. adminstr. policy, planning & rsch. Health Care Financing Adminstrn.; adminstr. Agy Health Care Policy & Rsch. USPHS HHS; co-founder, past. pres., bd. dirs. Assn. Health Svcs. Rsch. Office: HHS Agy Health Care Policy & Rsch 2101 E Jefferson St Rockville MD 20852-4908

GAUSS, KARL FREDERIK, internist, educator; b. Elmira, N.Y., July 19, 1956; s. Louis H. and Agnes L. (Yacubic) G.; m. Paula A. Tuite, Aug. 1, 1982; children: Erich Louis, Kurt William. BS in Biology summa cum laude, SUNY, Geneseo, 1981; MD with honors, SUNY, Syracuse, 1985. Diplomate Am. Bd. Internal Medicine (questions adv. panel 1992), Am. Bd. Geriatrics. Resident in internal medicine SUNY Health Sci. Ctr., Syracuse, 1985-88, asst. clin. instr. dept. internal medicine, 1988—; pvt. practice, Cortland, N.Y., 1988—; pres. PHI Aeromed. Cons., Inc., Cortland, 1989-95; clin. asst. prof. dept. medicine, 1995—; attending physician, mem. med. staff Cortland Meml. Hosp., 1988—, chmn. dept. internal medicine, 1989-93; dir., staff physician Moravia (N.Y.) Health Ctr., 1992-93; cons. physician Tully (N.Y.) Hill Drug and Alcohol Rehab. Ctr., 1990-92; aviation med. examiner Cortland County, 1988—; counselor in substance abuse Robert Wood Johnson Found., 1988—; profl. and sci. presenter in field. Exhibited photography in group shows Everson Art Mus., Syracuse, 1986, N.Y. State Fair, Syracuse, 1992. Fellow ACP; mem. Am. Geriatrics Soc., Flying Physicians Assn. (bd. dirs. 1994), N.Y. State Med. Soc. (Cortland county del. 1988—), Cortland County Med. Soc. (pres. 1992—), Aircraft Owners and Pilots Assn. Republican. Office: Cortland Internist Assocs 166 Madison St Cortland NY 13045

GAUTAM, SUBASH CHANDER, surgeon; b. Nathenal, Punjab, India, Jan. 3, 1948; s. Amar Nath and Kalish Liati (Sharma) G.; m. Gursarup Kler, Oct. 14, 1988; children: Siddarth, Vikrant. MBBS, Med. Coll., 1970. Sr. registrar King George Hosp., Oxford, Eng., 1974-79, cons., 1980-82; cons. Kuwait Hosp., Ajman, United Arab Republic, 1982-89; sr. surgeon, chmn. dept. surgery Fujiarah Hosp. (United Arab Republic), 1990—. Contbr. articles to profl. jours. Fellow Gastroentrology Divsn. Enirates; mem. Sirgery Adv. Com. Office: Fujeirah Hosp, PO Box 4848, Fujeirah United Arab Emirates

GAUTHIER, ANDRE PIERRE, gastroenterologist, educator; b. Brioude, France, Aug. 4, 1933; s. Marcel Antoine and Odette (Soulier) G.; m. Claude Marie Caire, Sept. 22, 1962; children: Pascale Michele, Pierre-Andre. MD, Med. Sch. Marseilles, 1960, Prof. Medicine, 1966. Intern, resident Marseilles Pub. Assistance, 1956-60, hosp. asst., 1960-62; chief of clinic Med. Sch. Marseilles, 1962-66, aggregation, 1966-76, prof., 1976-80, prof. 1st class, 1980—; chief of dept. Sainte Marguerite Hosp., Marseilles, 1973-82, La Conception Hosp., Marseilles, 1982—; adminstr. Marseilles Hosp., 1984-88, Observatoire Regional la Sante, Marseilles, 1985—. Author: Digestive Allergy, 1960, Intensive Care in Hepatology, 1984; contbr. numerous articles to profl. jours. Regional councillor Provence, France; city counsillor, Marseilles; mil. affairs and vets. attaché. With French Army, 1957-58. Roman Catholic. Home: 302 Rue Paradis, Marseilles France 13008 Office: Hopital la Conception, 147 Bd Baille, Marseilles France 13005

GAUTHIER, DAVID ADELARD, psychotherapist; b. Burlington, Vt., Mar. 27, 1952; s. Noel and Joan (Charette) G. MA in Counseling Psychology, U. No. Colo., 1978; BA in Psychology, Johnson State Coll., 1974. Cert. mental health counselor, Va.; cert. med. psychotherapist. Clinician Howard Mental Health Svcs., Vt., 1979-82, clinician Psychiat. Disabilities Svc., 1982-87; liaison Vt. State Hosp.; outpatient psychotherapist Pine St. Counseling Ctr., 1987-88; mental health counselor Mansfield Psychol. Assocs., Burlington, Vt., 1989—; counseling practicum supr., U. No. Colo., 1976; instr. Adolescent and Child Psychology Community Coll. Vt., 1979. Mem. APA, ACA, Vt. Psychol. Assn., Vt. Mental Health Assn., Vt. Mental Health Counselors Assn., Menninger Soc. Home: 41 Bishop Rd Shelburne VT 05482-7353 Office: Mansfield Psychology Assocs 177 Battery St Burlington VT 05401-5210

GAUZER, CHERYL, women's health nurse practitioner; b. Binghamton, N.Y., Aug. 4, 1948; d. Arthur John and Bernice Earlene (Badger) Calice; m. John Joseph Gauzer, July 3, 1971; children: Callie, Thomas. AS in Nursing, Monroe C.C., 1968; BSN, SUNY, Brockport, 1971; MS in Human Resource Adminstrn., U. Scranton, 1984; cert. ob.-gyn. nurse practitioner, U. Pa., 1992. Surg. staff nuse Our Lady of Lourdes Hosp., Binghamton, 1968-69; staff nurse Emergency Rm. Lakeside Meml. Hosp., Brockport, 1969-71; instr. med.-surg. nursing Highland Hosp. Sch. Nursing, Rochester, N.Y., 1971-73; instr. maternity nursing Binghamton Gen. Hosp. Sch. Nursing, 1973-76; perinatal nurse specialist SUNY-Upstate Med. Ctr., Syracuse, 1976-79; coord. perinatal nursing Wilson Meml. Hosp., Johnson City, N.Y., 1979-90; head nurse perinatal ctr. United Health Svcs., Johnsons City, N.Y., 1990—, nurse mgr. PNC, ob.-gyn. nurse practitioner, 1992—; nurse mgr. PNC Womens Health Connection, Johnsons City, N.Y., 1993—; vice chmn. advanced practice nursing United Health Svcs., Johnsons City, N.Y., 1994; profl. edn. com. Healthy Mothers/Healthy Babies, Binghamton, 1990—. Author: (hospital manuals) Perinatal Center Policy and Procedure Manual, 1986, In-Patient High Risk Obstetrical Policy and Procedure Manual, 1991. Mem. Assn. Women's Health Obstet. and Neonatal Nursing, N.Y. State Perinatal Assn., N.Y. State Nurses Assn. (dist. 5). Roman Catholic. Home: RR 1 Box 137 Chenango Forks NY 13746-9603 Office: United Health Svcs Perinatal Ctr 33-57 Harrison St Johnson City NY 13790-2143

GAVAZZI, ALADINO A., retired medical center administrator; b. Exeter, Pa., July 24, 1922; s. Guido and Ambrozina (Santoni-O'Brien) G.; m. Nancylee Ray, June 21, 1958; children: William A., Ann Marie, Lisa Kathryn, Alan Lee, Michael J. BS, Columbia, 1953, MS, 1955; PhD, U. Chgo., 1959. Adminstrv. officer VA br.-dist. office, N.Y.C., 1946-50; med. adminstrv. officer VA hosps., Bklyn., Bronx, N.Y., 1950-53; hosp. adminstrv. resident Bronx, Beth Israel and Presbyn. hosps., N.Y.C., 1953-54; hosp. adminstr. VA Hosps., Hampton, Va., 1955-57, Chgo. Rsch. Hosp., Dwight, Ill., 1957-59, 1960-61; hosp. adminstr. Mt. Alto VA Hosp., Washington, 1962-63; assoc. dir. hosp. cont. svc. VA Ctrl. Office, Washington, 1962-64; dir. VA Med. Ctr., Martinsburg, W.Va., 1964-68; exec. asst. to chief med. dir. and dir. adminstrn. Washington, 1968-71; dir. med. dist. and med. ctr. VA Med. Ctr., Washington, 1971-86; mem. State Health Coordinating Coun., Washington, 1971-86; health care cons., lectr., 1980-86; v.p. Adm. Arleigh Burke Pavilion Corp., McLean, Va., 1987-96; guest lectr. hosp. adminstrn. Med. Coll. Va., Richmond, Northwestern U., Chgo., U. Fla., U. Ala., Duke U., Cornell U., Columbia U., U. Sao Paulo, Brazil; adj. prof. internat. health Georgetown U.; bd. dirs. Vinson Hall Corp., McLean. Dist. chmn. Boy Scouts Am., W.Va., 1967-68; chmn. Combined Fed. Campaign for W.Va. for all fed. agys., 1966-68; mem. citizens bd. Providence Med. Ctr., Washington, 1976-90; bd. dirs., trustee U.S. Navy and Marine Coast Guard Residence Found., McLean, 1986-96; v.p. Adm. Arleigh Burke Pavilion, McLean, 1986-96. 1st lt. Armored Divsn. AUS, 1940-45; ret. Col. USAR, 1981—. Recipient Outstanding Performance awards VA, 1952, 56, 59, 63, 65, 70, 74, 80, Exceptional Service award, 1981; Disting. Career award 1986, Nat. Civil Servant of Year-Silver Helmet award Amvets, 1974. Fellow Am. Coll. Hosp. Adminstrs. (regent for D.C. 1965-69, mem. various commns.), Royal Soc. Health (London), Am. Hosp. Assn.; mem. Fed. Exec. Inst. Alumni Assn. (pres. 1974-75), Assn. Health Care Adminstrs. of Nat. Capital (founder, charter mem., pres. 1965). Home: 1541 Dahlia Ct Mc Lean VA 22101-3313

GAVELIS, JONAS RIMVYDAS, dentist, educator; b. Boston, Jan. 11, 1950; s. Mykolas and Janina (Povydis) G.; m. Bonnie Sylvester; children: Gregory, Nikolas. B.S., U. Mass., Amherst, 1971; D.M.D., U. Conn., 1975. Resident in dentistry Cabrini Health Care Center, N.Y.C., 1975-76; fellow in prosthetic dentistry Harvard U. Sch. Dental Medicine, Boston, 1976-78, instr., 1978-79; asst. prof. U. Conn. Sch. Dental Medicine, Farmington, 1979-82; practice dentistry specializing in prosthodontics Harvard Community Health Plan, Boston, 1982-92, Rockport, Mass., 1991—; asst. prof. Harvard Sch. Dental Medicine, 1982—. Contbr. articles on prosthetic dentistry to profl. jours. Fellow Acad. Gen. Dentistry (Vernon S. Johnson award 1981). Recipient Diamond award Harvard Community Health Plan, 1988. Mem. ADA, Northeast Prosthodontic Soc., Harvard Odontological Soc., Am. Acad. Crown and Bridge Prosthodontics, Am. Coll. Prosthodontists, Omicron Kappa Upsilon. Roman Catholic. Clubs: Southboro (Mass.), Rod and Gun, New Eng. Aquarium Dive (Boston), Southboro Rod and Gun, Cape Ann Sportsman's, Rotary. Home: 1238 Washington St Gloucester MA 01930-1056 Office: 23 Main St Rockport MA 01966-1512

GAVENCAK, JOHN RICHARD, pediatrician, allergist; b. Bklyn, June 21, 1949; m. Madeline Gavncak Aug. 12, 1972. BA, NYU, 1970; MD, N.Y. Med. Coll., Valhalla, 1974. Diplomate Am. Bd. Pediatrics, Am. Bd. Allergy and Immunology. Resident in pediats. Met. Hosp., N.Y.C., 1974-76, fellow in allergy and immunology, 1976-78; pediatric allergist pvt. practice, East Rockaway, N.Y., 1976—. Fellow Am. Coll. Pediatrics, Am. Coll. Allergy and Immunology.; mem. N.Y. Allergy Soc., Long Island Allergy Soc. Office: John R. Gavencak MD 400 Atlantic Ave East Rockaway NY 11518

GAVIN, MARY JANE, medical, surgical nurse; b. Prairie Du Chien, Wis., Sept. 1, 1941; d. Frank Grant and Mary Elizabeth Wolf; m. Alfred William Gavin, Nov. 9, 1963; children: Catherine Heidi Elizabeth, Carl Alfred Eric. Student, North Cen. Coll., Naperville, Ill., 1959-61; BS, RN, U. Wis., 1964; postgrad., Deepmuscle Tng. Ltd., 1980; postgrad. in deep muscle therapy. RN, Wis. Staff nurse U. Wis. Hosps., Madison; RN home response VA, Milw. Unit chair Badger Girls State, 1991—; mem. Wis. Am. Legion Aux.; mem. task force for handicapped Eastside Wis. Evang. Luth. Ch., Madison, 1993. U. Wis. scholar. Mem. Moncna Grove Am. Legion Aux. (pres. Unit 429). Home: 702 Fairmont Ave Madison WI 53714-1424

GAWLER, JEFFREY, neurologist consultant; b. London, July 17, 1945; s. Harry and Brenda (Webb) Gawler; m. Janet Mary Spinks, Dec. 19, 1970; children: Robert, Ruth, Susan, Sarah. MB BS (hons.), St. Bartholomew's Hosp., 1968. Con. neurologist St. Bartholomew's Hosp., London, 1976-88, dir. dept. neurology, 1988—; dir. dept. neurology Royal London Hosp., 1994—. Fellow Royal Coll. Physicians (sec. 1978-83); mem. British Med. Assn., Assn. British Neurologists. Office: Royal London Hosp, Whitechapel Rd, London E1 1BB, England also: 149 Harley St, London W1N 2DE, England

GAWLIK, GERALD M., hospital adminstrator, internist; b. Chgo., May 18, 1942; s. John Francis and Genevieve Victoria (Mysliwiec) G.; m. Maureen Bridget Egan, Apr. 4, 1970; children: Mary Therese, John Patrick, Jennifer Anne. BS in Biology, Loyola U., Chgo., 1964; MD, Loyola U., Maywood, Ill., 1969; MS in Mgmt. and Orgnl. Behavior, Ill. Benedictine Coll., 1996. Diplomate Am. Bd. Internal Medicine, Am. Bd. Hematology, Am. Bd. Oncology. Asst. prof. medicine Loyola U. Stritch Sch. Medicine, 1977-78, clin. asst. prof. medicine, 1978-90; pvt. practice hematology and oncology, Elmhurst and Carol Stream, Ill., 1978-90; med. dir. oncology Elmhurst Meml. Hosp., 1988-90, v.p. med. affairs, 1990-95, sr. v.p. for clin. affairs and network devel., 1995—; bd. dirs. Harmony Home Health Care, Winfield, Ill., 1984-88. Contbg. author: Hematology: Clinical Practice, 1991. Bd. dirs. Hospice Vols. DuPage, Lisle, Ill., 1981-85, pres., 1982-83. Lt. M.C., USNR, 1971-73. Mem. ACP (assoc.), Am. Soc. Internal Medicine, Am. Coll. Physician Execs., Am. Soc. Hematology, Assn. Cmty. Cancer Ctrs., Alpha Omega Alpha. Office: Elmhurst Meml Hosp 200 Berteau Ave Elmhurst IL 60126

GAWROŃSKI, MIECZYSŁAW, physician, pathomorphologist; b. Częstochowa, Katowice, Poland, July 23, 1933; s. Jan and Bronisława Juchnik and Urszula Gawrońska-Jędrowska, July 26, 1959; 1 child, Przemysław. Diploma, Med. Acad., Poznań, Poland, 1959, cert. pathology, 1965, MD, 1965. Student asst. dept. pathomorphology Med. Acad., Poznań, 1957-59, asst., 1959-62, head asst., 1962-65; sci. worker dept. pathology Free U., Amsterdam, The Netherlands, 1965-67; tutor dept. pathomorphology Med. Acad., Poznan, Poland, 1967-84, chief of prosectorium dept. clin. pathomorphology, 1970—, sr. lectr. dept. pathomorphology, 1983—; cons. Regional Lung Disease Control Ctr., Poznań, 1978—, Region Leszno, 1978—. Contbr. over 40 articles to profl. jours. Mem. Union Solidarity, Poznań, 1980. Mem. Polish Soc. Pathomorphologists, Polish Soc. of Cyto and Histochemistry. Roman Catholic. Home: Berestecka 5, Poznań Poland Office: Med Acad Dept Clin Pathomorphology, Przybyszewskiego 49, Poznań Poland

GAY, DENNIS FRANCIS, medical technologist; b. Washington, Oct. 29, 1941; s. Frank Gay and Clara Gai (De'Alessandro) Izzo; m. Elizabeth Hannon, Oct. 31, 1964 (div. Mar. 1974); children: Dennis F. Jr., John F., Lisa A.; m. Carol Frier, Mar. 1976 (div. Oct. 1991); 1 child, Jaime Lynn. Student, Monmouth Coll., 1965-70. Mechanic U.S. Army, Germany, 1960-63; med. tech. Ocean County Med. Lab., Laurelton, N.J., 1963-64, Princeton (N.J.) Med. Labs., 1964-65; med. tech. mgr. Dr. Jabush and Marasca, Lakewood, N.J., 1965-76; med. tech. supervisor Mease Hosp., Dunedin, Fla., 1976-77, Suncoast Hosp., Largo, Fla., 1977-78; clin. lab. supervisor Metro. Lab. Hosp., Pinellas Park, Fla., 1978-89, Univ. Gen. Hosp., Seminole, Fla., 1990-94; lab. supervisor various facilities, Largo, 1994—. Mem. Am. Med. Tech., Largo Jaycees (chaplain 1978-80). Republican. Home: 902 N Palm Dr SW Largo FL 34640

GAY, PETER CARL, physician; b. Saginaw, Mich., Nov. 9, 1938; s. Harold Howard and Catherine Louise (Barstow) G.; m. Sue Ellen MacDonald, June 6, 1964 (sep.); children: John, Brian, Karen, Kathleen, Melissa, Amy. BA, Albion Coll., 1961; MD, Wayne State U., 1964; MPH, U. Mich., 1969. Diplomate Am. Bd. Preventive Medicine and Occupl. Medicine. Intern Charity Hosp., New Orleans, 1964-65; occupl. medicine fellow U. Mich. Univ. Hosp., Ann Arbor; staff physician Dow Chem. U.S.A., Midland, Mich., 1970-72; staff physician Dow Chem. U.S.A., Freeport, Tex., 1972-78, med. dir. Oyster Creek divsn., 1978-82; med. dir. Oyster Creek divsn. Medicus PC, Wappingers Falls, N.Y., 1982—; cons. med. dir. N.Y. Power Authority, White Plains, 1988—; med. rev. officer various cos., 1990—; sr. airman med. examiner FAA, Oklahoma City, 1985—. Capt. USAR, 1965-67. Mem. Am. Coll. Occupl. and Environ. Medicine, Dutchess County Med. Soc., Brazoria County Med. Soc. (past pres.), Kiwanis (past pres.). Republican. Office: Medicus PC 1245 Route 9 Wappingers Falls NY 12590

GAY, RICHARD EDWIN, optometrist; b. Mt. Clemens, Mich., Nov. 16, 1964; s. George Edwin Gay and Barbara Ann (Pfeilsticker) Zada; m. Ann Marie Petroski, June 7, 1986; children: Amanda, Edwin, Natalie. Student, Mich. Technol. U., 1982-85; OD, Ferris State U., 1989. Lic. optometrist, Mich. 1989. Optometrist S.V.S. Vision, Mt. Clemens, Mich., 1989—. Home: 1229 Three Mile Dr Grosse Pointe Park MI 48230 Office: SVS Vision 140 Macomb Pl Mount Clemens MI 48043

GAY, SPENCER BRADLEY, radiologist, educator; b. Washington, June 12, 1958; s. Lendall Croxton and Claudine (Moss) G.; m. Debie Farris (div. Sept. 1982); 1 child, Colin Bradley; m. Marit Corinne Anderson; children: Chelsea Britt, Kristen Corinne. BS, U. Miami, Fla., 1973; MD, U. Va., 1983. Dir. Full Circle Farm, Somerset, Va., 1974-78; pres. Cen. Va. Title Agy., Orange, 1977-79; resident in radiology U. Va. Health Scis. Ctr., Charlottesville, 1983-87, fellow in radiology, 1987-88, asst. prof., 1988-94, assoc. prof., 1994—. Mem. Med. Soc. Va., Am. Roentgen Ray Soc., Radiol. Soc. N.Am. Episcopalian. Office: U Va Health Sci Ctr PO Box 170 Charlottesville VA 22902-0170

GAYLIN, NED L., psychology educator; b. Cleve., May 2, 1935; s. Harry C. and Fay I. G.; m. Rita Atran, June 30, 1957; children: Hilarie C., Ann E., Jed J., Daniel S. BA, U. Chgo., 1956, MA, 1961, PhD, 1965. Counselor Bellefaire Children's Home, Cleve., 1953, Sonja Shankman Orthogenic Sch., Chgo., 1954-56; group worker, supr. Jewish Community Ctrs. Chgo., 1957-60; grad. rsch. asst. Com. Human Devel., U. Chgo., 1959-60; intern Inst. Juvenile Rsch., Chgo., 1960-61, staff psychologist, 1965-68; intern Counseling and Psychotherapy Rsch. Ctr., U. Chgo., 1961-63; grad. teaching asst. dept. psychology U. Chgo., 1961-63; psychol. cons. State Ill., Rockford, 1961-64; psychotherapist, cons. Counseling and Psychotherapy Rsch. Ctr., U. Chgo., 1963-65, psychol. cons., lectr., 1965; lectr. dept. social sci. S.E. Jr. Coll., Chgo., 1965-66; psychol. cons. Peace Corps, No. Ill. U., DeKalb, 1966-68; chief psychologist S.W. Suburban Mental Health Assn., LaGrange, Ill., 1966-68; psychol. cons. Virginia Frank Child Devel. Ctr., Chgo., 1966-68; child clin. rsch. psychologist NIMH, Bethesda, Md., 1968-70; lectr., cons. Washington Sch. Psychiatry, 1968-72; chmn. dept. family and community devel. Coll. Human Ecology U. Md., College Park, 1970-77, prof., dir. family therapy tng. Coll. Health and Human Performance, 1977—; mem. rsch. com. Md. Community Coordinated Child Care, 1970-75. Contbr. articles in field to profl. jours. USPHS grantee, 1961-63; U. Chgo. fellow and scholar, 1954-56, 58-60; State Ill. edn. and tng. grantee, 1963-65. Mem. APA, Nat. Coun. on Family Rels., Am. Assn. Marriage and Family Therapy, Groves Conf. on the Family, Assn. for Devel. of Person-Centered Approach, Sigma Xi. Home: 4617 Norwood Dr Chevy Chase MD 20815-5348 Office: Univ Md 1204D Marie Mount Hall College Park MD 20742

GAYLIN, WILLARD, physician, educator; b. Cleve., Feb. 23, 1925; s. Harry C. and Fay (Baumgard) G.; m. Betty Schofer, June 15, 1947; children: Joan Deborah, Ellen Andrea. A.B., Harvard U., 1947; M.D., Western Res. U., 1951. Lic. psychiatrist, N.Y. Intern Cleve. City Hosp., 1951-52; resident psychiatry Bronx VA Hosp., 1952-54; faculty Columbia Psychoanalytic Sch., 1956—, clin. prof. psychiatry, 1972—; adj. prof. psychiatry Union Theol. Sem.; adj. prof. psychiatry and law Columbia Sch. Law, 1970; chmn. bd., founder The Hastings Ctr., Briarcliff Manor, N.Y., 1970—; vis. prof. Harvard U. Med. Sch., 1978. Author: The Meaning of Despair, 1968, In The Service of Their Country: War Resisters in Prison, 1970, Partial Justice: A Study of Bias in Sentencing, 1974, Caring, 1976, (with others) Doing Good: The Limits of Benevolence, 1978, Feelings: Our Vital Signs, 1979, The Killing of Bonnie Garland: A Question of Justice, 1982, The Rage Within: Anger in Modern Life, 1984, Rediscovering Love, 1986, Adam and Eve and Pinnocchio, 1990, The Male Ego, 1992; contbr. articles to profl. jours. Bd. dirs. Helsinki Watch., Nat. Bd. Planned Parenthood. Served with USNR, 1943-45. Recipient George E. Daniels medal of Merit for contbns. to psychoanalytic medicine, 1973; Elizabeth Cutter Morrow lectr. Smith Coll., 1970; Chubb fellow Yale U., 1972. Fellow Am. Psychiat. Assn.; mem. Inst. Medicine of NAS, Am. Psychoanalytic Assn., N.Y. Psychiat. Soc. Office: Hastings Center 255 Elm Rd Briarcliff Manor NY 10510-2207

GAYLOR, DONALD HUGHES, surgeon, educator; b. Bklyn., Apr. 17, 1926; s. Norman Hunter and Frances (Hughes) G.; m. Joan Winifred Power, Apr. 3, 1948; children: David, Christopher, Steven, Susan, Timothy. AB, U. Rochester, 1946, MD, 1949. Diplomate Am. Bd. Surgery, Am. Bd. Thoracic Surgery. Commd. lt. (j.g.) USN, 1949, advanced through grades to capt. M.C., 1966; intern U.S. Naval Hosp., Phila., 1949-50; student flight surgeon Sch. Aviation Medicine, Pensacola, Fla., 1950-51; flight surgeon U.S. Naval Sta., Trinidad, B.W.I., 1951-53; resident gen. surgery U.S. Naval Hosp., St. Albans, N.Y., 1953-57; postgrad. fellow surgery Royal Victoria Hosp., McGill U., Montreal, Can., 1957; resident thoracic surgery U.S. Naval Hosp., St. Albans, N.Y., 1957-59; resident cardiovascular surgery St. Francis Hosp., Roslyn, N.Y., 1958; staff thoracic surgeon U.S. Naval Hosp., Portsmouth, Va., 1959-64; surgeon U.S.S. Enterprise, 1964; staff thoracic surgeon U.S. Naval Hosp., Nat. Naval Med. Ctr., Bethesda, Md., 1964-65, chief thoracic and cardiovascular surgery, 1965-68; chief surgery, exec. officer U.S.S. Repose, 1968-69; exec. officer Naval Med. Sch., Bethesda, Md., 1969-72; ret., 1972; clin. assoc. surgery U. Pa. Sch. Medicine, 1976—; prof. clin. surgery Hahnemann U. Sch. Medicine, 1986—; chief surgery Allentown (Pa.) Hosp., 1972-90, Sacred Heart Hosp., 1973-76, Lehigh Valley Hosp. Ctr., 1974-90. Contbr. articles to profl. jours. Fellow ACS; mem. AMA, Am. Thoracic Soc., Am. Trauma Soc. (pres. Pa. divsn. 1979-83, treas. 1985-91), Soc. Thoracic Surgeons (founding), Pa. Assn. for Thoracic Surgery, Assn. Mil. Surgeons U.S., Am. Trauma Soc. (founding mem.). Roman Catholic. Home and Office: 3761 Devonshire Rd Allentown PA 18103-9628

GAYLOR, WALTER RALPH, endocrinologist; b. St. Louis, Jan. 31, 1924; s. Charles Sidney and Goldie (Shapiro) G.; m. Sylvia Katz, Aug. 8, 1968. AB, Washington U., St. Louis, 1947, MD, 1951. Diplomate Am. Bd. Internal Medicine. Intern U. Utah, Salt Lake City, 1951-52, resident, 1952-54; resident Duke U., Durham, N.C., 1954-55; pvt. practice Bristol, Tenn., 1955-94; prof. medicine Quillen Sch. Medicine, Johnson City, Tenn., 1977-80; clin. prof. medicine Quillen Sch. Medicine, Johnson City, 1980-89. With U.S. Army, 1943-46, PTO. Mem. AMA, ACP. Jewish. Home: 201 Sleepy Hollow Rd Bristol TN 37620-4830

GAYNOR, EDWARD BARRY, otolaryngologist; b. N.Y.C., Apr. 4, 1941; s. Norman N. and Mabel (Land) G.; m. Judith E. Greenberg, Apr. 15, 1968; children: Kenneth, Beth. AB, Adelphi U., 1962; MD cum laude, SUNY, Bklyn., 1966. Diplomate Am. Bd. Otolaryngology. Intern L.I. Jewish Hosp., New Hyde Park, N.Y., 1966-67, resident surgery, 1967-68; resident otolaryngology Temple U. Health Ctr., Phila., 1968-71; attending surgeon Temple U. Med. Ctr., St. Christopher's Hosp. Children, PHila., 1973-75; attending staff Park City Hosp., Bridgeport, Conn., 1985—, West Haven (Conn.) VA Hosp., 1980—; sr. attending surgeon Dept. Surgery, Sect. Otolaryngology, Norwalk, Conn., 1975—; mem. clin. faculty dept. otolaryngology Yale U. Sch. Medicine, New Haven, 1979—; asst. prof. otolaryngology Temple U., Phila., 1973-75. Contbr. articles to profl. jours. Bd. trustees, med. affairs com., laryngectomy group advisor Am. Cancer Soc., Fairfield County, 1979—. Maj. U.S. Army, 1971-73. Fellow ACS, Am. Acad. Otolaryngology (bd. govs.), Triological Soc., Pan Am. Soc. Otolaryngology, Am. Bronchoesophagologic Soc.; mem. Conn. State Med. Soc., Fairfield County Med. Soc., Conn. State Ear, Nose and Throat Soc. (pres. 1991—). Office: 40 Cross St Norwalk CT 06851-4647

GAYNOR, MARK LESLIE, clinical social worker; b. N.Y.C., July 9, 1950; s. Jules and Shirley (Rosenberg) G. BA in Sociology, CCNY, 1973; MSW, Columbia U., 1975; postgrad., New Hope Guild Tng. Program. Cert. social worker, N.Y., Conn.; lic. clin.social worker, Conn.; bd. cert. diplomate in social work. Treatment coord. dept. child and adolescent psychiatry Kings County Downstate Med. Ctr., N.Y., 1975-76; group therapist Epilepsy Found. Nassau County, Hempstead, N.Y., 1975-76; sr. social worker, clin. mgr. partial hospitalization Yale Psychiat. Inst., New Haven, 1977-80; pvt. practice New Haven, 1977—; therapist Student Counselling Ctr., Conn. Coll., New London, 1980-81; cons. Chapel Haven, New Haven, 1978-79, 83—, New Haven Halfway House, 1980-83; dir.devel. Mental Health Care Assocs., 1991-95; cons. for practice and orgn. devel., 1995—; presenter at profl. confs. Mem. NASW, Conn. Soc. Clin. Social Workers (past bd. dirs.), Conn. Soc. Psychoanalytic Psychologists. Office: 396 Orange St New Haven CT 06511-6405

GAZE, NIGEL RAYMOND, plastic surgeon; b. Leamington Spa, Warwick, Eng., Nov. 2, 1943; s. Raymond Ernest and Beatrice Maud (Caswell) G.; m. Heather Winifred Richardson, Aug. 6, 1966; children: Julia, Celia, Richard, Thomas, Mary, Harry. MB, ChB, Liverpool U., 1966; BMus, London U., 1986. House officer Whiston Hosp., Prescot, Lancashire, Eng., 1966-67, sr. house officer orthopaedics, 1967-68; sr. casualty officer Royal So. Hosp., Liverpool, Eng., 1969-70; surg. registrar Liverpool Regional Hosp. Bd., 1970-72; gen. surgery registrar Chester (Eng.) Royal Infirmary, 1972-73; registrar in plastic surgery Wordsley Hosp., Stourbridge, Worcs, Eng., 1973-75; sr. registrar plastic surgery Yorks Region Health Authority, Leeds, 1975-79; cons. plastic surgery Royal Preston (Lancashire) Hosp., 1980—. Contbr. med. articles to profl. jours.; composer choirs, organs, and solos. Condr. Elizabethan Singers, Preston; accompanist County Hall Singers, Preston, 1980—, Clitheroe Assn. Ch. Choirs, Preston, 1984—; assoc. organist Preston Parish Ch., Lancashire, 1980—. Fellow Trinity Coll. Music, Royal Coll. Organists. Fellow Royal Soc. Medicine, Royal Coll. Surgeons Edinburgh, Royal Coll. Surgeons; mem. Royal Acad. Music (licentiate), Brit. Acad. Experts, Brit. Inst. Organ Studies, Brit. Assn. Plastic Surgeons, Brit. Assn. Aesthetic Plastic Surgeons, Victorian Soc., Select Vestry Club, Assn. Brit. Choral Condrs. Mem. Conservative party; mem. Ch. of Eng. Home: Priory House, 35 Priory Ln Penwortham Lancashire, Preston PR1OAR, England Office: Fulwood Hall Hosp, Midgery Ln, Preston Lancashire PR1 OAR, England

GAZOO, ANTHONY ROBERT, hospital administrator; b. Scranton, Pa., Dec. 10, 1968; s. Anthony E. and Ann C. Gazoo. BS in Health Info. Mgmt., Temple U., 1992. Registered records adminstr. Rsch. analyst Lehigh Valley Hosp., Allentown, Pa., 1992; outpatient emergency room coder Marian Cmty. Hosp., Carbondale, Pa., 1993; dir. med. records Farview State Hosp., Waymart, Pa., 1993-96, Friendship House, Scranton, 19996—. Sec., mem. William R. Kramer Meml. Scholarship Com., Moscow, Pa., 1990—. Mem. Am. Health Info. Mgmt. Assn., Northeastern Pa. Health Info. Mgmt. Assn., Pa. Health Info. Mgmt. Assn.

GAZZILLO, FRANK LOUIS, JR., neurologist; b. Trenton, N.J., Mar. 24, 1946; s. Frank L. Sr. and Amelia (Jaworka) G.; m. Mary Ellen, Aug. 24, 1968 (div. Oct. 1994); 1 child, Lisa. BA, Rutgers U., 1968; MD, UMDNJ, 1972. Diplomate Am. Bd. Neurology. Intern Med. UMDNJ, Newark, 1972-73; resident UMDNJ, Newark, 1973-76; neurologist North Jersey Neurologic Assocs., Wayne, N.J., 1977—; chmn. bioethics com. Wayne Gen. Hosp., 1996—, Chilton Hosp., Pompton Plains, N.J., 1996—. Office: North Jersey Neurology Assn 220 Hamburg Turnpike Wayne NJ 07470

GE, NIELIN, microbiologist, researcher; b. Qianshan, Anhui, China, Aug. 13, 1962; came to U.S., 1991; s. Liangsong and Zhuanyong (Wang) G. MD, Wannan Med. Coll., China, 1984; MS in Med. Parasitology/Entomology, Jinan U., Guangzhou, China, 1987; Cert. in Immunoparasitology, Beijing Med. U., 1988; PhD in Pathobiology, Oklahoma State U., Stillwater, 1996. Lectr., asst. prof., sec. sci. rsch. program Jinan U. Sch. Medicine, Guangzhou, 1987-91; vis. scientist dept. vet. parasitology, microbiology Coll. Vet. Medicine, Okla. State U., Stillwater, 1991-92, vis. scientist dept. vet. pathology, 1992-93, rschr. dept. vet. pathology, 1993-96; rschr. dept. neurology Wayne State U. Sch. Medicine, Detroit, 1996—; lectr. in field. Contbr. articles to profl. jours. Recipient Rsch. Excellence award Okla. State U., 1996. Mem. Am. Soc. Microbiology, Soc. Neurosci., N.Y. Acad. Scis., Sigma Xi. Office: Wayne State U Sch Medicine Dept Neurology 124 Lande Bldg 550 E Canfield Detroit MI 48201

GEAGAN, THOMAS V., internist; b. Boston, May 31, 1939; s. Tholmas V. and Mary Margaret (McLaughlin) G.; m. Barbara Virginia Healey, May 21, 1966; children: Brian, Andrew, Daniel, Laura, Susan, Karen. BS, Boston Coll., 1961; MD, Tufts U. Sch. Medicine, 1965. Diplomate in internal medicine and geriatrics Am. Bd. Internal Medicine. Physician Tobey Hosp., Wareham, Mass., 1966—; asst. clin. prof. medicine Tufts U., Boston, 1988—; pres. Cape Geriatrics, Wareham, 1990—; bd. registration Nursing Home Adminstrn. Com. Mass., 1991—. Active Wareham Hist. Dist. Commn., 1991—. Mem. Mass. Med. Soc., Am. Geriatric Soc., Am. Coll. Physicians, Am. Soc. Internal Medicine. Home: Box 3070 Wareham MA 02571 Office: Wareham Med Ctr 194 Main St Wareham MA 02571

GEALT, MICHAEL A., molecular biologist, environmental microbiologist, educator; b. Phila., Nov. 27, 1948; s. Edward Leonard and Lillian Rose (Brenner) G.; m. Antonia Malandrucco, May 12, 1967 (div. 1977); children: Lillian, Benjamin: m. Maryjanet McNamara, Jan. 2, 1982; 1 child, Marina Rodriguez. BA, Temple U., 1970; PhD, Rutgers U., 1974. Research assoc. Med. Sch., Rutgers U., Piscataway, N.J., 1974-76; postdoctoral assoc. Inst. for Cancer Research, Phila., 1976-78; asst. prof. biol. scis. Drexel U., Phila., 1978-84, assoc. prof., 1984-90, prof., 1990—, dir. Environ. Studies Inst., 1994—. Contbr. articles to profl. jours. EPA grantee, 1983, 85, 89. Mem. Am. Soc. Microbiology (chair environ. & applied micro divsn. 1995), Am. Soc. Cell Biology, Am. Mycol. Soc., AAAS, Sigma Xi. Avocations: motorcycles; photography. Office: Drexel U Dept Biosci and Biotech 32D And Chestnut St Philadelphia PA 19104

GEARHART, JOHN PHILLIP, urologist; b. Lexington, Ky., May 24, 1949; s. J. Edwin and B. Jane (Underwood) G. Grad., Morehead State U., 1972; MD, U. Louisville Med. Coll., 1976. Diplomate Am. Bd. Urology. Instr. Johns Hopkins Sch. Medicine, Balt., 1984-86, asst. prof., 1986-91, assoc. prof., 1991-95, prof., 1995—; dir. pediatric urology Johns Hopkins Hosp. and Children's Ctr., Balt., 1993—; vis. prof. Royal Soc. Medicine, London, 1995. Contbr. articles to profl. jours. Fellow Am. Coll. Surgeons, Am. Acad. Pediatrics; mem. Brit. Urol. Soc., Masons. Methodist. Office: Johns Hopkins Hosp 600 N Wolfe St Baltimore MD 21205-2110

GEARY, PAUL, JR., surgeon; b. Plainfield, N.J., Sept. 10, 1935; s. Paul and Dorothy (Hecht) G.; m. Elizabeth Barwise, June 19, 1957 (div. 1970); children: Anne, Susan, Elizabeth, Peter, Robert. BA, Princeton U., 1957; MD, Johns Hopkins U., 1961. Diplomate Am. Bd. Surgery, Am. Bd. Thoracic Surgery. Intern, then resident Johns Hopkins Hosp., Balt., 1961-63; resident in gen. thoracic surgery Jackson Meml. Hosp., Miami, Fla., 1965-69; pvt. practice surgery Orlando, Vla., 1969-80, 83—; dir. burn unit Al Hada Hosp., Taif, Saudi Arabia, 1981-83. Capt. USAF, 1963-65. Republican. Presbyterian. Home: 1304 Windsong Rd Orlando FL 32809 Office: 1420 Lucerne Terr Orlando FL 32806

GEBBIE, KRISTINE MOORE, health science educator, health official; b. Sioux City, Iowa, June 26, 1943; d. Thomas Carson and Gladys Irene (Stewart) Moore; m. Lester N. Wright; children: Anna, Sharon, Eric. BSN, St. Olaf Coll., 1965; MSN, UCLA, 1968; DPH U. Mich., 1995. Project dir. USPHS tng. grant, St. Louis, 1972-77; coord. nursing St. Louis U., 1974-76, asst. dir. nursing, 1976-78, clin. prof., 1977-78; adminstr. Oreg. Health Div., Portland, 1978-89; sec. Wash. State Dept. Health, Olympia, 1989-93; coord. Nat. AIDS Policy, Washington, 1993-94; asst. prof. Sch. Nursing Columbia U., 1994—; assoc. prof. Oreg. Health Scis. U. Portland, 1980—; chair, U.S. dept. energy secretarial panel on Evaluation of Epidemioigic Rsch. Activities, 1989-90; mem. Presdl. Commn. on Human Imunodeficiency Virus Epidemic, 1987-88. Author: (with Deloughery and Neuman) Consultation and Community Orgn., 1971, (with Deloughery) Political Dynamics: Impact on Nurses, 1975; (with Scheer) Creative Teaching in Clinical Nursing, 1976. Bd. dirs. Luth. Family Svcs. Oreg. and S.W. Wash., 1979-84; bd. dirs. Oreg. Psychoanalytic Found., 1983-87. Recipient Disting. Alumna award St. Olaf Coll., 1979; Disting. scholar Am. Nurses Found., 1989. Fellow Am. Acad. Nursing; mem. Assn. State & Territorial Health Ofcls., 1988 (pres. 1984-85, exec. com. 1980-87, McCormick award 1988), Am. Pub. Health Assn. (exec. bd.), Inst. Medicine, N.Am. Nursing Diagnosis Assn. (treas. 1983-87), Am. Soc. Pub. Adminstrn. (adminstrn. award II 1983). Office: Columbia U Sch Nursing 630 W 168th St New York NY 10032-3702

GEBHARD, ROGER LEE, medical educator, researcher; b. Sioux City, Iowa, Jan. 30, 1945; s. Kenneth C. and Pauline E. (Glantz) G.; m. Gloria J. Brisson, Sept. 10, 1966; children: Kristin H., Roger K. BA, U. Minn., 1966, MD, 1969. Diplomate Am. Bd. Internal Medicine. Resident in medicine Columbia-Presbyn. Hosp., N.Y.C., 1969-71; clin. assoc. NIH, Bethesda, Md., 1971-73; med. resident Stanford (Calif.) U., 1973-74, fellow in gastroenterology, 1974-76; prof. medicine U. Minn. VA Hosp., Mpls., 1977—. Contbr. articles to profl. jours. Bd. dirs. Celiac Sprue Assn. U.S., Omaha, 1989—. Lt. comdr. USPHS, 1971-73. Grantee DVA, 1977—. Fellow ACP; mem. Am. Gastroenterologic Assn., Am. Soc. for Gastrointestinal Endoscopy, Am. Assn. Study Liver Disease, Am. Physiol. Soc. Office: Mpls VA Hosp One Vets Dr 111-D Minneapolis MN 55417

GEDGAUDAS, EUGENE, radiologist, educator; b. Lithuania, Oct. 7, 1924; came to U.S., 1963, naturalized, 1968; children: Kristina, Nora, Sandra. MD, U. Munich, 1948; D honoris causa, Acad. of Medicine, Kaunas, Lithuania, 1992. Diplomate: Am. Bd. Radiology. Intern St. Boniface Hosp., Winnipeg, Man., Can., 1953-54; resident in radiology St. Boniface Hosp., Winnipeg, 1954-58, U. Minn. Hosp., Mpls.; chmn. cardiac unit, asso. radiologist St. Boniface Gen. Hosp., Winnipeg, 1958-63; also dir. dept. radiology Misercordia Gen. Hosp., Winnipeg; asst. prof. radiology U. Minn., Mpls., 1963-67; assoc. prof. U. Minn., 1967-69, prof., 1969-86, prof. emeritus, 1986—, head radiology dept., 1969-86; chmn. council clin. scis. Med. Sch. Med. Sch., 1973-82, mem. dean's adv. council, 1973-83. Contbr. articles to profl. jours. Fellow Royal Coll. Physicians and Surgeons Can., Am. Coll. Radiology (emeritus), Royal Soc. Medicine; mem. AMA, Radiol. Soc. N.Am., Am. Roetgen Ray Soc. (pres. 1985-86, Gold medal 1991), Minn. Radiology Soc. (pres. 1975-76), Minn. Acad. Medicine, Assn. Univ. Radiologists. Home: 19850 Beach Rd Jupiter FL 33469 Office: Univ Hosps Box 292 Radiology Dept 420 Delaware St SE Minneapolis MN 55455-0374

GEE, STEPHEN S., ophthalmologist; b. Ames, Iowa, June 25, 1957. BS in Zoology and Computer Sci., Iowa State U., 1978; MD, U. Iowa, 1982. Diplomate Am. Bd. Ophthalmology. Resident, chief resident Med. Coll. Wis., Milw., 1983-86; fellow King Khalid Eye Specialist Hosp., Riyad, Saudi Arabia, 1986-87; staff ophthalmologist Kaiser Found., Honolulu, 1987-89; ophthalmologist Faulken Inst. for Eye Care and Surgery, Honolulu, 1989-95; pvt. practice ophthalmology Honolulu, 1995—; med. cons. PRAXIS, Honolulu, 1990—; presenter in field. Contbr. articles to profl. jours. Mission woeker Mission Cataract, Honolulu, 1991. Fellow Am. Acad. Ophthalmology; mem. AMA, Hawaii Ophthalmol. Soc., Internat. Soc. Refracture Surgery, Hawaii Med. Assn., Hawaii County Med. Assn., Phi Beta Kappa. Office: 1210 Ward Ave Honolulu HI 96814

GEE, VIRGINIA ANN (COX), hospice administrator; b. Lampasas, Tex., Oct. 29, 1953; d. Virgil E. Cox and Corine Roden; m. Patrick E. Gee. Cert. EMT, C.P.R. instr., cardiac care. Staff nurse Rolling Brook Hosp.,

Lampasas, 1975-76, Kerrville (Tex.) VA Hosp., 1982, Scott and White Hosp., Temple, Tex., 1984; supr. emergency room Shepperd Hosp., Burnet, Tex., 1985; dir. admissions Heart of Tex. Hospice, Temple, 1995; hospice mgr. Hospice Highland Lakes, Bwinet, Tex., 1996—. Mem. Burnet Emergency Med. Soc., North Burnet County Emergency Med. Soc. (pres.). Home: Rt 1 Box 2300 Kempner TX 76539-0005 Office: Hospice Highland Lakes PO Box 840 Hwy 2815 Bwinet TX 78611

GEELHOED, GLENN WILLIAM, surgeon, educator; b. Grand Rapids, Mich., Jan. 19, 1942; s. William and Alice (Stuk) G.; m. Sally Ryden (div. 1972); children: Donald W., Michael A. AB, BS cum laude, Calvin Coll., Grand Rapids, 1964; MD cum laude, U. Mich., 1968; DTMH, U. London, 1990; MA in Internat. Affairs, Elliott Sch. Internat. Affairs, Washington, 1991; MPH, George Washington U., 1992, MA in Anthropology, 1994, PhD in Human Scis. Intern Peter Bent Brigham Hosp., Harvard Med. Sch., Boston, 1968-69; resident in surgery Boston Children's Hosp. Med. Ctr., Boston, 1968-70; clin. investigator NIH, Bethesda, Md., 1971-73; prof. surgery George Washington U., Washington, 1973—; chmn. clin. rsch. Nat. Cancer Inst., 1972-73; editorial bd.: Factline, 1984—, Surg. Rsch. Communications, 1985—, Sound Surg. Collections, 1986, CINE-Med. Inc., 1986, Peptide Therapy: Index & Revs., 1989. Contbr. 500 articles to profl. jours. and chpts. to books. Chmn. med. adv. com. ARC, Washington, 1980—. Comdr. USN, 1970-73. Robert Wood Johnson Found. clin. scholar, 1975-78, James IV Surg. Assn. Traveling scholar, 1986, Sr. Fulbright scholar, 1996. Fellow ACS; mem. Acad. de Chirurgie, Wash. Acad. Surgery (pres. 1984), D.C. Med. Soc. (chmn. com. on blood sect., tissue transplant 1973-83), Washington Area Transplant Soc. (chmn. promotions and organ procurement com. 1975-85), So. Med. Assn. (spl. edn. sub-com. sect. surgery D.C. 1989-91), Southeastern Surg. Congress (councillor 1984-89). Republican. Mem. Christian Reformed Ch. Office: George Washington U 2150 Pennsylvania Ave NW Washington DC 20037-2396

GEERDES, MARY ELIZABETH, nurse, lawyer; b. Albuquerque, Nov. 6, 1947; d. Joseph John and Grace Garnet (Gladwin) Boyle; m. Franklin Geerdes, Oct. 12, 1985; children: David, Eric. BSN, U. N.Mex., 1969, MA in Edn., 1971; JD, Western States U., San Diego, 1994. RN; Bar: Calif. 1994. Staff nurse Presbyn. Hosp., Albuquerque, 1969-71; commd. lt. (j.g.) USN, 1971, advanced through grades to lt. comdr., 1981; clin. instr. Naval Hosp., Camp Pendleton, Calif., 1971-73, charge nurse, 1975-78; instr. Naval Sch. Health Scis., San Diego, 1973-75; charge nurse Naval Hosp., Okinawa, Japan, 1978-80; coord. emergency nursing Naval Hosp., Long Beach, Calif., 1983-86; coord. emergency nursing Naval Hosp., San Diego, 1980-83, clin. cons. emergency nursing, 1986-88, coord. command risk mgmt., 1988-91; ret., 1991—; lawyer pvt. practice, Chula Vista, Calif., 1994—; instr. advanced cardiac life support, 1983-89. Mem. Emergency Nurses Assn. (instr. trauma nurse care course 1987—), Profl. Assn. Diving Instrs. (emeritus), Calif. State Bar Assn., South Bay Bar Assn., Navy Nurse Corps Assn., Ret. Officers Assn. Republican. Roman Catholic. Office: Mary E Geeroes Attorney at Law 345 F St Chula Vista CA 91910

GEERTSMA, ROBERT HENRY, psychologist, educator; b. Chgo., July 22, 1929; s. Henry George and Ruth (Wren) G.; m. Nobuko Sakamoto, Apr. 8, 1956; children: Martin Alex, Phillip R., Francesca Ruth. A.B., U. Chgo., 1950, Ph.D., 1956. Diplomate: clin. psychology Am. Bd. Profl. Psychology. From instr. to asst. prof. psychiatry U. Calif. Med. Sch., Los Angeles, 1956-62; assoc. prof. med. communication U. Kans. Med. Sch., 1962-69, chmn. dept., 1964-69; prof., chmn. dept. med. edn. and communication, prof. psychiatry, also prof. Coll. Edn., U. Rochester (N.Y.) Sch. Medicine and Dentistry, 1969-86, clin. prof. psychiatry, 1986—; mem. N.Y. State Psychology Bd., 1985-94. Pres. Meridian Found., 1989—. Fellow Acad. Clin. Psychology. Home: 1 Mill Valley Rd Pittsford NY 14534-3903 Office: 120 Linden Oaks Rochester NY 14625-2833

GEEZE, DONALD STEPHAN, psychiatrist; b. N.Y.C., July 22, 1949; s. Walter Nelson and Margaret (Iuzzolini) G.; m. Mary Ann, Oct. 9, 1982; children: Donald Jr., Zachary, Mary Elizabeth. BA, Sam Houston State U., 1974; MD, U. Tex., 1980, MPH, 1995. Diplomate Am. Bd. Psychiatry and Neurology. Enlisted USAF, 1969, commd., 1976; flight surgeon Barksdale USAF Hosp., Bossier City, La., 1981-83; chief, mental health svcs. 313th Med. Group, Okinawa, Japan, 1986-89; chief, outpatient mental health Wilford Hall USAF Med. Ctr., San Antonio, 1989-90, chief inpatient psychiatry/assoc. dir. psychiat. residencies, 1990-91; dir. psychiatry residency program Wilford Hall USAF Med. Ctr., 1991-93; resident in aerospace medicine Brooks AFB, Tex., 1994—. Contbr. articles to profl. jours. Decorated Air medal (3), USAF, Vietnam. Mem. Soc. USAF Psychiatrists (pres. 1989-92), Okinawa Med. Soc. (sec. 1988-89), AMA, Assn. Mil. Surgeons U.S., Assn. Mil. Psychiatrists, Aerospace Med. Assn., Soc. USAF Flight Surgeons. Office: USAFSAM/AF Brooks AFB TX 78235-5123

GEFFEN, ABRAHAM, physician, radiologist, educator; b. Atlanta, Sept. 22, 1916; s. Tobias and Heni (Rabinowitz) G.; m. Ethel Petegorsky, Mar. 28, 1948; children: David Barry, Robert Joseph, Sara Jane Geller. BA, Emory U., 1937; MD, Columbia U., 1941. Diplomate Am. Bd. Radiology. Intern Beth Israel Med. Ctr., N.Y.C., 1941-42; resident Mt. Sinai Med. Ctr., N.Y.C., 1946-47; asst. radiologist Mt. Sinai Hosp., N.Y.C., 1948-49; attending radiologist Beth Isreal Med. Ctr., N.Y.C., 1949-55, dir. radiology, 1955-75, sr. radiologist, 1976-87, cons., 1987—; prof. clin. radiology Mt. Sinai Sch. of Medicine, 1968-94; clin. prof. emeritus Albert Einstein Coll. Medicine, 1994—. Conbtr. chpt. in book. Hon. v.p. Beth-El Synagogue, New Rochelle, N.Y., 1985—. Maj. U.S. Army, 1942-45. Fellow Am. Coll. of Radiology; mem. AMA, N.Y. State Med. Assn., N.Y. Roentgen Soc., N.Y. State Radiol. Soc., Beth Israel Alumni Assn. (Alumnus of Yr. 1989), Mt. Sinai Alumni Assn., Phi Beta Kappa, Alpha Omega Alpha. Democrat. Jewish. Home: 28 Disbrow Ln New Rochelle NY 10804-3209

GEFTER, WILLIAM IRVIN, physician, educator; b. Phila., Jan. 29, 1915; s. Samuel and Pauline (Bulmash) G.; m. Winnie Neiman, June 17, 1939; children: Sharon Gefter Greene, Warren, Gail Gefter Simon, Ellen. A.B., U. Pa., 1935, M.D., 1939. Diplomate Am. Bd. Internal Medicine. Intern, then resident medicine Phila. Gen. Hosp., 1939-43; mem. faculty Med. Coll. Pa., 1943-66, Mullen prof. medicine, 1959-66; prof. medicine Temple U. Sch. Medicine, 1966-74; chief medicine Phila. Gen. Hosp., 1959-66; dir. dept. medicine Episcopal Hosp., Phila., 1966-74; pres. med. bd. Episcopal Hosp., 1970-72; dir. profl. services St. Joseph Hosp., Stamford, Conn., 1974-77, dir. med. edn., 1977-92, dir. emeritus, 1992—; clin. prof. medicine N.Y. Med. Coll., 1975-92, prof. emeritus, 1992—. Author: Synopsis of Cardiology, 1965; also numerous articles. Served to capt. M.C., USAAF, 1943-46. Recipient Disting. Service citation Med. Coll. Pa., 1966, Disting. Service citation Phila. Gen. Hosp., 1964; named to Cultural Hall of Fame, So. High Sch., Phila., 1983. Fellow ACP, Coll. Physicians Phila., Am. Coll. Cardiology; mem. Am., Conn., Fairfield County med. assns. Home: West Ln and Toilsome Brook Rd Stamford CT 06905

GEHA, ALEXANDER SALIM, cardiothoracic surgeon, educator; b. Beirut, June 18, 1936; came to U.S., 1963; s. Salim M. and Alice I. (Hayek) G.; m. Diane L. Redalen, Nov. 25, 1967; children—Samia, Rula, Nada. BS in Biology, Am. U. Beirut, 1955, MD, 1959; MS in Surgery and Physiology, U. Minn.-Rochester, 1967; MS (privatum), Yale U., 1978. Asst. prof. U. Vt., Burlington, 1967-69; asst. prof. Washington U., St. Louis, 1969-73, assoc. prof., 1973-75; assoc. prof. Yale U., New Haven, 1975-78, prof., chief cardiothoracic surgery, 1978-86; prof., chief cardiothoracic surgery Case Western Res. U. and U. Hosp. of Cleve., 1986—; Jay L. Ankeney prof. cardiothoracic surgery Case We. Reserve U., 1994—; pres. Univ. Cardiothoracic Surgeons, Inc., Cleve., 1986—; cons. VA Hosp., West Haven, Conn., 1975-86, VA Hosp., Cleve., 1986—, Cleve. Met. Health Med. Ctr.,1986—, Mt. Sinai Med. Ctr., Cleve., 1990—, Waterbury Hosp., 1976-86, Sharon Hosp., 1981-86; mem. study sect. Nat. Heart Lung and Blood Inst., 1981-85. Editor: Glenn's Thoracic and Cardio-vascular Surgery, 4th edit. 1983, 5th edit. 1991, 6th edit. 1995; editor Basic Surgery, 1984. Bd. dirs. New Haven Heart Assn., 1981-85. Mem. AMA, Assn. Clin. Cardiac Surgery (chmn. membership com. 1978-80, sec.-treas. 1980-83, pres. 1988), Am. Heart Assn. (bd. dirs. 1981-85. councils on basic sci., cardiovascular surgery), Am. Coll. Chest Physicians (steering com. 1980-84), Am. Assn. Thoracic Surgery, Am. Coll. Cardiology, ACS (chmn. coordinating com. on edn. in thoracic surgery, chmn. 1992-95), Am. Lung Assn., Am. Physiol. Soc., Am. Surg. Assn., Assn. Acad. Surgery, Central Surg. Assn., Internat. Soc. Heart and Lung Transplantation, Internat. Soc. Cardiovascular Surgery, Lebanese Order Physicians, New Eng. Surg. Soc., Pan Am. Med. Assn., Halsted Soc., Soc. Thoracic Surgeons (govt. rels. com., manpower com., program com., edn. and resources com.), Soc. for Vascular Surgery, Soc. Univ. Surgeons, also others. Home: 17050 S Park Blvd Cleveland OH 44120-1644 Office: U Hosps Cleve 11100 Euclid Ave Cleveland OH 44106-1736

GEHL, RAYMOND HAROLD, psychiatrist, educator; b. Newark, Dec. 9, 1916; s. Philip Morris and Bertha (Schoenstadt) G.; m. Gita Rabin, Sept. 2, 1943; children: Richard, Leonard. BA, U. Mich., 1937, MD, 1940. Diplomate Am. Bd. Psychiatry and Neurology. Intern Kings County Hosp., Bklyn., 1940-42; resident in psychiatry VA Hosp., Lyons, N.J., 1946-48; trainee in psychoanalysis N.Y. Psychoanalytic Inst., N.Y.C., 1948-52; pvt. practice, West Orange, N.J., 1953—; adj. prof. Rutgers U. Sch. Social Work, New Brunswick, N.J., 1952-58; cons. VA Hosp., East Orange, N.J., 1954-84, Montclair (N.J.) Family and Child Agy., 1955-80; mem. bd. med. advisors Essex County Mental Hosp., Cedar Grove, N.J., 1972-79; clin. prof. psychiatry U. Medicine and Dentistry N.J., Newark, 1979—; clin. assoc. prof. psychiatry NYU Med. Sch., N.Y.C., 1980—, tng. analyst dept. psychiatry and psychoanalysis, 1969—. Co-author: The Graphomotor Projection Technique, 1954; contbr. articles to med. jours. Maj. M.C., USAAF, 1942-46, PTO. Recipient Disting. Teaching award U. Medicine and Dentistry N.J., 1982, 89-90. Fellow Am. Psychiat. Assn. (life); mem. AMA (life), Internat. Psychoanalytic Assn., Am. Psychoanalytic Assn. (pub. rels. com., exec. coun. 1961-63, 65-67), N.J.Psychoanalytic Soc. (founder, pres. 1960-61, 66-67, 72-74, 88-90, chmn. nominating com., by-laws com. 1990), N.J. Psychoanalytic Found. (pres.). Jewish. Home: Claridge House Apt 10N E Verona NJ 07044 Office: 111 Northfield Ave West Orange NJ 07052

GEHRING, GEORGE JOSEPH, JR., dentist; b. Kenosha, Wis., May 24, 1931; s. George J. and Lucille (Martin) G.; m. Ann D. Carrigan, Aug. 2, 1982; children: Michael, Scott. DDS, Marquette U., 1955. Pvt. practice dentistry, Long Beach, Calif., 1958—. Author: The Happy Flosser. Chmn. bd. Long Beach affiliate Calif. Heart Assn.; mem. Long Beach Grand Prix com. of 300; ind. candidate for pres. of the U.S., 1988, 92. Served with USNR, 1955-58. Fellow Internat. Coll. of Dentists, Am. Coll. Dentists; mem. Harbor Dental Soc. (dir.), Pierre Fauchard Acad., Delta Sigma Delta. Club: Rotary. Home: 1230 E Ocean Blvd Unit 603 Long Beach CA 90802-6908 Office: 532 E 29th St Long Beach CA 90806-1617

GEHRING, PERRY JAMES, toxicologist, chemical company executive; b. Yankton, S.D., Mar. 15, 1936; s. Rinold Lou and Bertha (Reiger) G.; m. Barbara Tennis, Aug. 8, 1959; children: Daniel, Matthew, Elizabeth, Heidi. B.S., D.V.M., U. Minn., 1960, Ph.D. in Pharmacology, 1965. Research asso. Iowa State U., 1960-61; with Dow Chem. Co., Midland, Mich., 1965-68, 70-89; dir. toxicology Dow Chem. Co., 1974-78, dir. health and environ. scis., 1978-81, v.p. agrl. chems. research and devel., dir. health and environ. sci., 1981-89; v.p. R & D DowElanco, Indpls., 1989—; asso. prof. pharmacology Mich. State U., 1968-70, adj. prof., 1970—; trustee Nutrition Found., 1981; chmn. sci. adv. panel Chem. Industry Inst. Toxicology, 1976-80; mem. safe drinking water subcom. organic contaminants Nat. Acad. Scis., 1975-76, mem. nat. center toxicol. research rev. com. 1976-77; participant internat. meetings. Asso. editor: Toxicology and Applied Pharmacology Jour., 1977-80; mem. editorial bds. profl. jours.; contbr. articles to profl. publs. Recipient Founders award Chem. Industry Inst. Toxicology, 1983; inducted into U. Minn. Athletic Hall of Fame, 1993; NIH fellow, 1961-65. Mem. Soc. Toxicology (pres. 1980-81, coun. 1975-77, Frank R. Blood award 1979, Merit award 1983), Internat. Union Toxicology (v.p. 1983-86, dir. 1981-83, pres. 1986-90), Am. Soc. Pharmacology and Exptl. Therapeutics, Am. Crop Protection Assn. (chmn. sci. regulatory oversight coun. 1989-93). Presbyterian (trustee 1983-86). Home: 3928 Kitty Hawk Ct Carmel IN 46033-4801 Office: DowElanco 9330 Zionsville Rd Indianapolis IN 46268-1053

GEIB, PHILIP OLDHAM, physician, retired naval officer; b. Verona, N.J., Oct. 6, 1921; s. Amos Philip and Ada Mae (Oldham) G.; m. Frances Parker, Nov. 5, 1949; children: Melanie, Philip John. B.S., Franklin and Marshall Coll., 1942; M.D., Temple U., 1945. Diplomate Am. Bd. Surgery. Commd. lt. U.S. Navy, 1945, advanced through grades to rear adm., 1972; intern Naval Hosp., Chelsea, Mass., 1945-46; med. officer Leyte and Samar, Philippines, 1946-47; mem. staff Naval Hosp., Portsmouth, Va., 1947-48; resident Naval Hosp., 1953-54, Phila., 1948-51; mem. staff Naval Hosp. Corpus Christi, Tex., 1950-51, Tripler Army Hosp., Pearl Harbor, Hawaii, 1951-53, Annapolis, Md., 1954-57; mem. staff U.S.S. Iowa, 1957-58; mem. staff Naval Hosp. Pensacola, Fla., 1962-64; chmn. dept. surgery Naval Hosp. Great Lakes, Ill., 1964-68; comdg. officer Naval Hosps. Yokosuka, Japan, 1968-71, Camp Lejeune, N.C., 1971-72; asst. chief research and mil. med. spltys. Bur. Medicine and Surgery, Navy Dept. Washington, 1972-74; fleet surgeon CINCLAN Fleet Norfolk, Va., 1974-76; med. tng. and readiness officer COMTRALANT Norfolk, 1976-77; ret., 1977; med. dir. Norfolk Shipbldg. and Drydock Corp., 1977-94; ret., 1994; asst. med. dir. Occupational Med. Svc. Ea. Va. Med. Sch., Portsmouth; mem. Sentara Norfolk Gen. and Sentara Leigh Meml. Hosps., Norfolk; asst. prof. Ea. Va. Med. Sch., Norfolk. Fellow ACS, Am. Coll. Chest Physicians; mem. Am. Occupational Med. Assn., AMA, Va. Occupational Med. Assn. (pres. 1986-88), Va. Surg. Soc., Va. Med. Soc. Home: 4309 Duke Dr Portsmouth VA 23703-4912 Office: 2700 London Blvd Portsmouth VA 23707-3647

GEIER, MARK ROBIN, obstetrical genetics and infertility physician; b. Washington, May 3, 1948; s. Charles S. and Clara (Shamon) G.; m. Anne Watson, Sept. 8, 1970; 1 child, David A. BS in Zoology, George Washington U., 1970, PhD in Genetics, 1973, MD, 1978; postgrad., Columbia U., 1970-71. Diplomate, Am. Bd. Med. Genetics. Med. researcher NIH, Bethesda, Md., 1969-70, 71-78, Inst. Cancer Rsch., N.Y.C., 1970-71; resident Johns Hopkins U., Balt., 1978-79; ptnr., physician Genetic Cons., Bethesda, 1980—; pres., lab. dir. Molecular Medicine, Inc., Bethesda, 1981—; pres. Genetic Counselling & Rsch., Inc., Balt., 1987—; pres. Geiers Child Devel., Inc., Adelphi, Med. 1972-92; prin. Med./Legal Cons., Silver Spring, Md., 1985—; asst. prof. Johns Hopkins U., Balt., 1979-82, U. Health Scis., Bethesda, 1984-90; expert witness. Contbr. med. rsch. articles to various publs. Mem. Am. Fertility Assn., Am. Soc. Human Genetics, Md. Tennis Assn. (ranking chmn. 1988—), U.S. Tennis Assn. (ranked #1 husband-wife team 1977), Am. Contract Bridge Leage, Sigma Xi. Democrat. Office: Genetic Cons 11125 Rockville Pike Ste 302 Rockville MD 20852-3142 also: Genetic Ctr 20 Crossroads Dr Owings Mills MD 21117-5419 also: Genetic Cons of Va 611 S Carlin Springs Rd Ste 106 Arlington VA 22204-1061

GEIGER, BRENDA HOUSTON, audiologist, speech pathologist; b. Phila.; d. William Cooper and Sarah (Hand) Houston; children: Erin Leigh, Shawn Ian. BS, U. Southern Miss., 1965, MS, 1966, PhD, 1968. Asst. prof. U. So. Alabama, Mobile, Ala., 1968-74; chief Audiology-Speech Pathoogy Svc. VA Med. Ctr., Tuskegee, Ala., 1974—; adj. prof. Auburn U., Ala., 1976—. Baptist. Office: VA Med Ctr Hospital Rd Tuskegee AL 36083-1541

GEIGER, H. JACK, medical educator; b Nov. 11, 1925; m. Nicole Schupf. Student, U. Wis., 1943; BA, U. Chgo., 1950; MD, Case Western Res. U., 1958; M in Sci. Hygiene, Harvard U., 1960; ScD (hon.), SUNY, Purchase, 1992. Intern Boston City Hosp. Harvard U., 1958-59, asst. resident in medicine, 1962-63, sr. resident in medine, 1963-64, clin. asst. in medicine, 1964-65; postdoctoral rsch. fellow social sci. and medicine Harvard U., 1959-61, instr. preventive medicine, 1961-62; asst. prof. pub. health, 1964-65; assoc. prof. Tufts U. Sch. Medicine, 1965-66; prof., 1966-71, chmn. dept. cmty. health and social medicine, 1969-71; dir. health ctrs. Columbia Point, Boston, Mound Bayou, Miss., 1965-71; project co-dir. SUNY, Stonybrook, 1971-73, prof., chmn. dept. cmty. medicine, 1971-77; Henry J. Kaiser sr. fellow Stanford U., 1983-84; Arthur C. Logan prof. chmn. cmty. health/social medicine CUNY Med. Sch., 1978—; vis. prof. medicine Harvard U., 1972-73. Mem. editorial Bd. Am. Jour Pub. Health; contbr. numerous articles to profl. jours. Recipient Disting. Svc. award Miss. Assn. Community Health for Poor, 1973, Nat. Health Achievement award in cmty. health Blue Cross and Blue Shield Assns. N.Am., 1979, Disting. Pub. Svc. award Nat. Assn. Cmty. Health Ctrs., 1981, Mass. League Community Health Ctrs., 1986, Robert H. Felix Disting. Svc. award St. Louis U. Sch. Medicine, 1986, Founders award Miss. Delta Health Ctr., 1990, Disting. Alumnus award of merit Harvard U. Sch. Pub. Health, 1992. Fellow AAAS (Inst. Medicine Mission to South Africa 1989, organizer conf. on health care for post-apartheid South Africa 1990), APHA (1st Ann. Excellence award 1972), Scientists Inst. Pub. Info.; mem. Inst. Medicine NAS (sr.), Am. Coll. Preventive Medicine, Internat. Edidemiol. Assn., Assn. Tchrs. Preventive Medicine, Assn. Behavioral Scis. and Med. Edn., Assn. Health Svcs. Rsch., Physicians for Human Rights (founding mem., pres., expert med. cons. to UN Human Rights Ctr. to Yugoslavia 1992, leader human rights missions to Yugoslavia 1993, Iraq and Kurdistan 1991, West Bank and Gaza Strip 1988, 90, and numerous others), Com. on Health in South Africa (nat. pres.), Physicians for Social Responsibility (founding mem.), Soc. Advancement of Ambulatory Care, Soc. Health and Human Value, Herman Biggs Soc. Office: CCNY Sch Medicine New York NY 10031

GEISELMAN, PAULA JEANNE, psychologist, educator; b. Ohio, June 30, 1944; d. Paul and Rosemary (Dawson) Parsley. AB in Psychology with honors, Ohio U., 1971, MS in Exptl. Psychology, 1976; PhD in Physiol. Psychology, UCLA, 1983. Adj. asst. prof. UCLA, 1986-91; dir. psychophysiol. rsch. UCLA Sch. Medicine, 1986-91; assoc. prof. dept. psychology La. State U., Baton Rouge, 1991—; adj. assoc. prof. Pennington Biomed. Rsch. Ctr. La State U., Baton Rouge, 1991—; lectr. in field. Reviewer for Sci. Jour., Am. Jour. Physiology, Physiology and Behavior, Brain Research Bulletin, Appetite: Determinants and Consequences of Eating and Drinking; contbr. numerous articles to profl. jours. Mem. Soc. Neurosci., AAAS, N.Am. Assn. Study of Obesity, Women in Neurosci., Assn. Acad. Women, Am. Psychol. Assn., Am. Psychol. Assn., Eastern Psychol. Assn., Western Psychol. Assn. (head of physiol. psychol., chair. Animal Feeding and Behavior paper session 1981), Assn. Advancement Psychology, Internat. Brain Research Orgn., World Fedn. Neuroscientists, Brit. Brain Research Assn. (hon.), European Brain and Behavior Soc. (hon.), N.Y. Acad. Scis., Sigma Xi, Psi Chi. Office: La State U Psychology Dept Pennington Biomed Rsch Ctr 6400 Perkins Rd Baton Rouge LA 70808-4124

GEISLER, CAROL JOY, psychologist, clinician, researcher, educator; b. N.Y., Mar. 3, 1948; d. Arthur H. and Sylvia (Bittner) G. BS in Math., MIT, 1968; MS in Math., NYU, 1970, MA in Psychology, 1973, PhD in Psychology, 1982. Lic. psychologist, N.Y. Psychologist, clinician, supr. Bklyn. Community Counseling Ctr., 1977—; pvt. practice psychologist N.Y.C., 1982—; researcher, educator, supr. Sch. of Social Work NYU, N.Y.C., 1983—; cons. in field. Mem. APA (mem. at large rsch. sect. div. psychoanalysis), Am. Orthopsychiat. Assn., Soc. Psychotherapy Rsch., N.Y. State Psychol. Assn., Assn. for Psychoanalytic Self-Psychology. Democrat. Jewish. Office: NYU Sch Social Work 1 Washington Sq N New York NY 10003-6635 also: 150 W 13th St New York NY 10011-7802

GEISLER, HANS EMANUEL, gynecologic oncologist; b. Ratibor, Germany, Apr. 5, 1935; came to U.S., 1938; s. Harry and Marianne C. (Barthel) G.; m. Margaret Ann Colglazier; children: Dorothy Marianne, Kathleen Marie, Stephan Harry, Suzanne Joan, John Patrick. HAB, Xavier U., 1955; MD, Loyola U., Chgo., 1959. Cert. Am. Bd. Ob-Gyn., Gynecologic Oncology. Pvt. practice specializing in gynecologic oncology and surgery Indpls., 1965—; asst. prof. ob-gyn. Ind. U. Med. Ctr., Indpls., 1967-84, dir. gynecol. tumor svc., 1967-70, clin. assoc. prof. ob-gyn., 1984-90, clin. prof. ob-gyn, 1990—; dir. gynecol. oncology Meth. Hosp., Indpls., 1970-72, 85-91; dir. gynecol. oncology div. St. Vincent Hosp., Indpls., 1972—, chmn. cancer com., 1985—, dir. oncology program, 1985-88. Contbr. articles to profl. jours. Mem. Marion County Cancer Soc., Indpls., profl. edn. com. Am. Cancer Soc., Indpls., Fire Merit Bd. Indpls., Com. to Select Police Chief, Indpls., 1975; pres. St. Luke Parish Coun., 1988-90; mem. Archdiocesan Pastoral Coun., 1991-94. Decorated knight Equestrian Order of Holy Sepulchre of Jerusalem; named Disting. Physician, St. Vincent Hosp. and Health Ctrs., 1996. Mem. AMA, Ind. Med. Soc., Med. Soc. Indpls., Am. Coll. Ob-Gyn., Soc. Gynecol. Oncologists, Ctrl. Assn. Ob/Gyn, Continental Gynecol. Soc. (pres.), Soc. Meml. Gynecol. Oncologists (pres.), Am. Assn. Pro-Life Ob/Gyn (bd. dirs.), Am. Assn. for Med. Ethics, European Soc. Gynecol. Oncologists, Internat. Soc. Gynecol. Oncologists. Republican. Roman Catholic. Home: 10609 Winterwood Carmel IN 46032-8258 Office: 8424 Naab Rd Indianapolis IN 46260-1954

GEISSLER, CURT JOHN, health facility administrator; b. Chippewa Falls, Wis., May 16, 1955; m. Dianne Marie Bruley; children: Adam, Laura. BS, U. Wis., 1977; M of Bus., Met. State U., 1996. RN, Minn. Dir. adminstrv. svcs. Met. Mt. Sinai Med. Ctr., Mpls., 1982-88; mgr. health care cons. Deloitte & Touche, Mpls., 1988-91; asst. adminstr. Lakeview Hosp., Stillwater, Minn., 1991—; bd. dirs. Common Health Clinic Stillwater. Mem. adv. bd. ARC, Mpls., 1990, Coon Rapids (Minn.) Mid. Sch., 1995. Mem. Am. Heart Assn. (bd. dirs. 1993-95), Stillwater Lions Club, Stillwater Rotary Club. Office: Lakeview Hosp 927 W Churchill St Stillwater MN 55082

GEISSLER, ERHARD, molecular biologist; b. Leipzig, Germany, Dec. 17, 1930; s. Johannes and Marianne (Hoell) G.; m. Ingrid Huebke, 1959 (div. 1982); children: Torsten, Cornelia; m. Renate Kindmann, Dec. 4, 1982; 1 child, Hans-Ulrich. Diploma biology, Karl-Marx U., Leipzig, 1955; D Natural Sci., Humboldt U., Berlin, 1959, Habilitation, 1964. Rsch. asst. Inst. Exptl. Cancer Rsch., Berlin, 1955-62, head dept. genetics, 1962-65; head inst. microbial genetics Rostock U., 1965-71; head dept. virology Ctr. Inst. Molecular Biology, Berlin, 1971-87, head peace rsch. group, 1988-91; head bioethical rsch. group Max-Delbrück-Ctr. for Molecular Medicine, Berlin, 1992—; cons. Stockholm Internat. Peace Inst., 1983—; vice chmn. Recombinant DNA Adv. Com. of German Democratic Republic, 1981-90. Editor: Darwin Today, 1983, Biological and Toxin Weapons Today, 1986, Prevention of a Biological and Toxin Arms Race, 1991, Control of Dual-Threat Agents: The Vaccines for Peace Programme, 1994, others; contbr. articles to profl. jours.; mem. editorial bd. ACTA Virologica, 1978-93, Biology and Philosophy, 1989—. Mem. presidium Urania, Berlin, 1972-90, pres., 1990-96; hon. pres. Neue Urania, 1995—. Mem. Biophys. Soc. Germany (chmn. 1968-72), Soc. Phys. and Math. Biology (chmn. 1972-74), Fedn. German Scientists (adv. bd. 1993—). Office: Max Delbruck Ctr, Ctr for Molecular Medicine, 13122 Berlin Germany

GEIST, FREDERICK STEWART, physician; b. Madison, Wis., May 23, 1923; s. Frederick Denkmar and Alice Mary (Stewart) G.; m. Mildred June Davis, June 25, 1944; children: Kathryn Ann Geist Voigts, Edward Davis. BS, Antioch Coll., 1945; MD, Case Western Res. U., 1947. Diplomate Am. Bd. Internal Medicine, Bd. Ins. Medicine. Intern Cleve. Met. Gen. Hosp., 1947-48, jr. asst. resident in internal medicine, 1948-49, asst. resident, 1949-50; resident VA Med. Ctr., Dallas, 1950-51, resident internal medicine, 1950-51, staff physician, 1951-52, 54-55; pvt. practice internal medicine Dallas, 1955-69; assoc. med. dir. Southwestern Life Ins. Co., Dallas, 1969-77, med. dir., 1977-87; med. dir. Optimum Reinsurance Co., Dallas, 1987—; clin. asst. prof. internal medicine U. Tex. Southwestern Med. Sch., Dallas, 1970—; dir. med. resident tng. program Meth. Med. Ctr., Dallas, 1958-62. Sect. coord. Neighborhood Crime Watch, 1980—. Capt. med. corps USAF, 1952-54. Mem. AMA, Dallas County Med. Soc., Tex. Med. Assn., Am. Acad. Ins. Medicine, Dallas Internist Club (pres. 1983-84). Episcopalian. Home: 6419 Malcolm Dr Dallas TX 75214-3186

GEISTFELD, RONALD ELWOOD, dental educator; b. St. James, Minn., Nov. 9, 1933; s. Victor E. and Viola (Becker) G.; m. Lois N. Tolzman Wilkens, June 15, 1955 (div. June 1974); m. Annette L. Swenson, Jan. 14, 1977; children: Shari, Mark, Steven, Ann, Leah, Erik. AA, Bethany Jr. Coll., 1952; BS, U. Minn., 1954, DDS, 1957. Pvt. practice dentistry Northfield, Minn., 1959-72; clin. asst. prof. dentistry U. Minn. Sch. Dentistry, Mpls., 1969-72, assoc. prof., 1972-82, chmn. dept. operative dentistry, 1978-87, prof., 1982—; dental cons. Hennepin County Med. Ctr., Mpls., 1975-96, VA Hosp., Mpls., 1977-96, VA Hosp., St. Cloud, Minn., 1978-96, Human Performance and Informatics Inst., Atama, Japan, 1990-95, K-9 Dental Sys. Quidnunc Australia Pty. Ltd., 1994-95, Metro Dental Group, Mpls., 1995—, VGM Expert Systems, 1996—, The Dentists Ins. Co., 1995—; mem. resource faculty for Bush faculty devel. program on excellence and diversity in teaching U. Minn., 1993-94. Pres. PTA, Northfield, 1965, Arts Guild, Northfield, 1968; bd. dirs., chairperson Rice County Health and Sanitation Bd., Faribault, Minn., 1966-74; bd. dirs. Northfield Bd. Edn., 1969-74; pres. Roseville Luth. Ch., 1987-88. Capt. U.S. Army, 1957-59. Am. Coll. Dentists fellow, 1972. Mem. Am. Dental Assn. (chairperson operative dentistry sect. 1979-80, curriculum cons. 1981-88, grants and spl. projects request evaluator 1988-92, Am. fund for Dental Health, edit. review bd. JADA 1992-96), Minn. Dental Assn. (ethics com. 1969-76, chairperson sci. and ann. sessions com. 1984-86, spkr. house del. 1992-96, del. to ADA 1992-96, bd. dirs. 1992-96), Mpls. Dist. Dental Soc. (program chairperson 1978-79, peer rev. com. 1988-92, bd. dirs. 1979-80, 87-89, MDA del. 1989-92), Minn. Acad. Restorative Dentistry (pres. 1979-80), Minn. Acad. Gnathological Rsch. (pres. 1986-87), Am. Assn. Dental Schs. (chairperson operative dentistry sect. 1984-85, edit. rev. bd. 1984-88), Acad. Operative Dentistry (exec. council 1978-81, rsch. com. 1987-89). Am. Acad. Gold Foil Operators, Northfield C. of C. (treas. and chairperson 1968-70), Delta Sigma Delta, Omicron Kappa Upsilon (Theta chpt.). Lodge: Rotary (pres. Northfield 1972-73). Home: 740 River Dr Apt 21D Saint Paul MN 55116-1037 Office: U Minn Sch Dentistry 8-450 Moos Tower 515 Delaware St SE Minneapolis MN 55455-0348

GEKOWSKI, KATHLEEN MARIA, infectious disease and internal medicine physician; b. Danville, Pa., Mar. 30, 1950; d. Raymond Frances and Dorothy (Lazarski) G. BS, Widener U., 1972; MD, Hahnemann, 1976. Diplomate Am. Bd. Internal Medicine, Am. Bd. Infectious Diseases. Head divsn. infectious diseases Cooper Hosp. U. Medicine & Dentistry N.J., Camden, 1982-94; clin. assoc. prof. medicine Robert Wood Johnson Med. Sch. U. Medicine & Dentistry N.J., New Brunswick, 1987—; adminstrv. dir. Mercer Area Early Intervention Svcs., Trenton, N.J., 1994-95; healthcare epidemiologist Mercer Med. Ctr., Trenton, N.J., 1995—; dir. AIDS activities Cooper Family HIV Ctr., Camden, 1991-94. Grantee NIH, 1994. Fellow ACP, Infectious Diseases Soc. Am.; mem. Soc. Healthcare Epidemiology, Internat. AIDS Soc., Infectious Disease Soc. N.J. (founding mem.), Phila. Coll. Medicine. Office: Mercer Med Ctr Floral Vale Blvd Yardley PA 19067

GELBART, S. SAMUEL, physician; b. Germany, Oct. 24, 1952; came to U.S., 1955; m. Mee Mee Wong; children: Chelsea, Claire. BS, Carnegie-Mellon U., 1974; MD, Howard U., 1978. Intern VA Wadsworth Hosp., L.A., 1978-79; resident U. Calif., San Francisco, 1979-82; physician pvt. practice, San Francisco, 1982—; chmn. dept. ophthalmology St. Mary;s Hosp., San Francisco, 1989-95; assoc. clin. prof. U. Calif., 1995—. Fellow U. Calif., San Francisco, 1982-83. Fellow Am. Acad. Ophthalmology. Office: Ste 640 490 Post St San Francisco CA 94102 also: Ste 448 595 Buckingham Way San Francisco CA 94132

GELBER, PHILIP MICHAEL, cardiologist; b. N.Y.C., June 14, 1946; s. Gabriel and Jeanne Gloria (Wagner) G.; m. Patricia A. Meyers, Sept. 16, 1972; children: Jacob, Toby, Jen. AB, U. Chgo., 1967, MD, 1971. Resident Montefiore Hosp., Bronx, 1971-73, NYU-Bellevue, N.Y.C., 1973-74; pres. Cardiovascular Cons. L.I., Hew Hyde Park, N.Y., 1976—. Contbr. articles to profl. jours. Mem. vis. com. U. Chgo., 1995. Cardiology fellow NYU-Bellevue, 1974-76. Mem. Am. Coll. Cardiology (com. info. tech. 1991—). Office: Cardiovascular Cons 3003 New Hyde Park Rd New Hyde Park NY 11042

GELDNER, PETER DAVID, plastic surgeon; b. Warsaw, Poland, Feb. 22, 1957; s. Michael M. and Barbara Geldner; m. Juliann Youngerman, Oct. 14, 1990; children: Nathan B., Aaron G. BA, Johns Hopkins U., 1979; MD, U. Wis., 1983. Resident in surgery U. Chgo., 1983-87; resident in plastic surgery Wayne State U., 1987-88, U. Tex., 1988-90; attending surgeon in plastic surgery Michael Reese Hosp., Chgo., 1990—, Ill. Masonic Hosp., Chgo., 1993—, Mercy Med. Ctr., Chgo., 1995—; asst. clin. prof. U. Ill., Chgo., 1990—; pvt. practice New Dimensions Ctr. for Cosmetic Surgery, Chgo., 1990—; mem. cons. com. Michael Reese Hosp., 1992—, dir. wound care clinic, 1993—, chief bio-ethics com., 1995—. Mem. AMA, Ill. Med. Soc., Chgo. Med. Soc. (mem. fee mediation com. 1994—), Am. Burn Assn. Jewish. Office: New Dimensions Ctr Cosmetic Surgery 60 E Delaware Pl Chicago IL 60611

GELEHRTER, THOMAS DAVID, medical and genetics educator, physician; b. Liberec, Czechoslovakia, Mar. 11, 1936; married 1959; 2 children. BA, Oberlin Coll., 1957; MA, U. Oxford, Eng., 1959; MD, Harvard U., 1963. Intern, then asst. resident in internal medicine Mass. Gen. Hosp., Boston, 1963-65; rsch. assoc. in molecular biology NIAMD NIH, Bethesda, Md., 1965-69; fellow in med. genetics U. Wash., 1969-70; asst. prof. human genetics, internal medicine and pediatrics Sch. Medicine Yale U., 1970-73, assoc. prof., 1973-74; assoc. prof. U. Mich., Ann Arbor, 1974-76; prof. internal medicine and human genetics U. Mich., 1976-87, dir. div. med. genetics, 1977-87, chmn. dept. human genetics, prof. human genetics and internal medicine, 1987—; Josiah Macy, Jr. Found. faculty scholar and vis. scientist Imperial Cancer Rsch. Fund Labs., London, 1979-80; vis. fellow Inst. Molecular Medicine; Keeley vis. fellow Wadham Coll., U. Oxford, Wellcome Rsch. Travel grantee, 1995. Mem. editl. bd. Jour. Biol. Chemistry, 1995—. Trustee Oberlin Coll., 1970-75. Rhodes scholar, 1957-59. Fellow AAAS, Am. Coll. Med. Genetics; mem. Am. Soc. Human Genetics (bd. dirs. 1994—), Am. Soc. Clin. Investigation, Am. Soc. Biochemistry and Molecular Biology, Assn. Am. Physics. Office: U Mich Med Sch Dept Human Genetics Box 0618 1500 E Medical Center Dr Ann Arbor MI 48109-0618

GELENBERG, ALAN JAY, psychiatrist, educator; b. Phila., May 2, 1944; s. Jacob and Mae R. (Gantman) G.; Sherry Ann Mullens, Sept. 17, 1972 (div.); children: Sara Ann, David Jesse Mullens, Rebecca Suzann. AB, Columbia Coll., 1965; MD, U. Pa., 1969. Diplomate Am. Bd. Psychiatry and Neurology. Intern in internal medicine Prebyn. U. Pa. Med. Ctr., Phila., 1969-70; fellow, then assoc. prof. Sch. Medicine Harvard U., Boston, 1970-89; resident in psychiatry Mass. Gen. Hosp., Boston, 1970-73, psychiatrist, 1970-89; med. dir. Erich Lindemann Mental Health Ctr., Boston, 1982-83; psychiatrist-in-chief The Arbour, Boston, 1983-89; prof., head dept. psychiatry U. Ariz., Tucson, 1989—. Author: Biological Therapies in Psychiatry; editor: Practitioners Guide to Psychoactive Drugs, 1983, 2d edit., 1990, 3d edit., 1991, Jour. Clin. Psychiatry, 1987—; contbr. to profl. publs. Recipient numerous grants, NIMH, pvt. industry and founds. Fellow AAAS, Am. Psychiatric Assn., Am. Psychopathological Assn. (chair rsch. on psychiatric treatments com.) ; mem. Am. Coll. Psychiatrists, Am. Soc. Clin. Psychopharmacy (bd. dirs.), West Coast Coll. Biol. Psychiatrists, Am. Assn. Chmn. Depts. Psychiatry, Pima County Med. Soc., Ariz. Med. Assn., Ariz. Psychiat. Soc., Tucson Psychiat. Soc. Jewish. Office: U Ariz Dept Psychiatry Health Scis Ctr Tucson AZ 85724

GELERNT, IRWIN M., surgeon, educator; b. N.Y.C., Sept. 27, 1935; s. Lipman and Ray (Samuels) G.; married, June 11, 1960; children: Lee, Alicia, Michelle. BS, CCNY, 1957; MD, SUNY, N.Y.C., 1961. Diplomate Am. Bd. Surgery. Intern Bellevue Hosp. Cornel Med. Svc.; attending surgeon Mt. Sinai Hosp., N.Y.C., 1962-67, pres. attending staff, 1985-87; clin. prof. of surgery Mt. Sinai Sch. Medicine, N.Y.C., 1987—, dean for hosp. and med. affairs; pres. med. bd. Mt. Sinai Hosp. Contbr. articles to profl. publs., chpts. to books. Trustee Manhattan Country Sch., N.Y.C., 1978-84. Named Physician of Yr., Nurses Assn. of Mt. Sinai Hosp., 1991. Fellow ACS, Am. Coll. Gastroenterology; mem. Found. Ileitis and Colitis (Man of Yr. 1983), Phi Beta Kappa, Alpha Omega Alpha. Office: 25 E 69th St New York NY 10021-4925

GELFAND, MARTIN DAVID, gastroenterologist; b. N.Y.C., Dec. 27, 1936; s. Maxwell L. and Grace (Albert) G.; m. Ann Gelfand, Oct. 6, 1962; children: Andrew, Carolyn, Jane. BA, Harvard U., 1958; MD, Johns Hopkins U., 1962. Diplomate Am. Bd. Internal Medicine, Am. Bd. Gastroenterology. Intern Bellevue Hosp., N.Y.C., 1962-63, resident in internal medicine, 1964-65; fellow in gastroenterology Yale-New Haven Hosp., 1965-67; gastroenterology staff Virginia Mason Clinic, Seattle, 1969—; sect. head Virginia Mason Clinic, Seattle, 1977-89. Contbr. articles to profl. jours. Trustee The Bush Sch., Seattle, 1976-82; pres. Pacific N.W. Gastroenterology Soc., 1978. Capt. USAF, 1967-68. Named Premier Physician, Cron's & Colitis Found., 1993. Mem. Am. Coll. Gastroenterology (trustee 1988—), Am. Gastroenterological Assn. (councillor 1994—). Office: Virginia Mason Clinic 1100 Ninth Ave Seattle WA 98101

GELINAS, MARC ADRIEN, healthcare administrator; b. Springfield, Mass., Aug. 25, 1947; s. Marcel Joseph and Jeanette (Couture) G.; m. Mary Lillian Smith, Mar. 3, 1984; 1 child, Alexander Joseph Marcel. BS in Zoology, U. Mass., 1969; Cert. in Phys. Therapy, Duke U. Med. Ctr., 1970; MHA, Duke U., 1978; D (hon.) Hamburgerology, McDonald's Hamburger U., Oak Brook, Il., 1988. Acting dir. patient svcs. div. U. Mass. Health Ctr., Amherst, 1975-76, mgr. clin. support svcs., 1976; adminstr. Health Care Systems, Inc., Durham, N.C., 1978; dir. gen. support svcs. Burlington County Meml. Hosp., Mt. Holly, N.J., 1978-80; v.p. facilities and program devel. Nexus Healthcare Corp., Mt. Holly, 1980-82; adminstr. Burlington Geriatric Ctrs., Inc., Mt. Holly, 1982-84; regional v.p, northeast Vol. Hosps. of Am., Inc., Irving, Tex., 1984-86, v.p. bus. devel., 1986-88; pres., owner LSG Bus. Devel. Group, Colleyville, Tex., 1988-93; v.p. strategic devel. Harris Meth. Health System, Ft. Worth, 1993-95; v.p. product mgmt. Harris Meth. Health Plan, Arlington, Tex., 1995—. Commr. Planning and Zoning Commn., Colleyville, 1987-89; com. mem. Woodland Hills Homeowners Assn., Colleyville, 1986-87; scoutmaster Boy Scouts Am., 1995—. 1st lt. U.S. Army, 1970-71; capt. USAR, 1971-76. Fellow Am. Coll. Healthcare Execs.; mem. Am. Hosp. Assn., Ctr. for Entrepreneurial Mgmt., Am. Coll. Nursing Home Adminstrs., Colleyville C. of C. (bus. retention com. mem. 1989, planner leadership course 1988-89, bd. dirs. 1993-94), Las Colinas Sports Club. Democrat. Roman Catholic. Office: Harris Meth Health Plan Ste 900 600 Ryan Plaza Arlington TX 76011

GELL, GUNTHER, medical educator; b. Leoben, Austria, Sept. 10, 1941; s. Karl and Herma (Kolitsch) G.; m. Ingrid Stengg, Dec. 22, 1967; children: Georg, Barbara. PhD, U. Graz, Austria, 1967. Scientific asst. dept. theoretical physics U. Graz, 1966-67, asst. dept. applied math., 1968-70, asst. dept. radiology, 1970-84, assoc. prof., 1984-89, prof., chmn. dept. med. informatics, 1989—. Office: U Graz Dept Medical Informatics, Auenbruggerplatz 9/III, 8036 Graz Austria

GELLER, ANDREW L., social worker; b. N.Y.C., Mar. 18, 1954; s. Lee William and Judith (Behr) G. BA, Antioch Coll., 1979; MSW, Yeshiva U., 1989. Diplomate in clin. social work; credentialled alcoholism counselor, substance abuse counselor. Dir. tng. Areba Casriel Inst., N.Y.C., 1978-79; tng. dir., re-entry Il Porto, Torino, Italy, 1983-84; adminstr. Areba Casriel Inst., N.Y.C., 1984-87, clin. supr., 1987-89, dir. social svcs., 1989-94, clin. dir., 1990-94; exec. dir. First Steps to Recovery, N.Y.C., 1994—; cons. CAP Behavioral Assocs., N.Y.C., 1989—. Mem. NASW, ACSW (diplomate). Home: 1628 2nd Ave # 3E New York NY 10028-4470 Office: 330 W 58th St Ste 609 New York NY 10019

GELLER, JOSEPH JEROME, psychiatrist; b. Elizabeth, N.J., Feb. 19, 1917; s. Samuel A. and Sarah (Zabriskie) G.; m. Janice G. Clack, Feb. 28, 1938; children: Robert, Anne, Elizabeth. ScB in Biology, Rutgers U., 1937; MD, NYU, 1941. Diplomate Am. Bd. Psychiatry and Neurology. Intern Elizabeth (N.J.) Gen. Hosp., 1941-42; resident Ctrl. Islip State Hosp. and N.Y. State Psychiat. Inst., 1948-50; psychoanalytic tng. William Alanson White Inst. of Psychiatry, N.Y.C., 1946-51, faculty, 1951-80; preceptor in psychiatry St. Vincent's Hosp. & Med. Ctr., N.Y.C., 1964-80; dir. in-patient psychiatry Jersey City Med. Ctr., 1984-86; clin. psychiatrist Greystone Park (N.J.) Psychiat. Hosp., 1986—; med. dir. West Bergen Mental Health Ctr., Ridgewood, 1988-96. Major U.S. Army, 1942-46. Fellow AMA, Am. Psychiat. Assn., Am. Acad. Child and Adolescent Psychiatry, Am. Assn. on Mental Retardation, Am. Group Psychotherapy Assn., Am. Acad. of Psychoanalysis. Home and Office: 307 Chatterson Dr Raleigh NC 27615

GELLER, NICOLE FAERMAN, obstetrics and gynecology nurse; b. N.Y.C., Oct. 3, 1970; d. Stephen Elliot and Frieda (Faerman) G.;. BSN, Georgetown U., 1993. RN, Washington, Md. Intern in social work Meml. Sloan-Kettering, N.Y.C., 1989, student nurse, 1991; pre-sch. aide Georgetown Montessori Sch., Washington, 1990; student nurse Sint Elizabeth Hosp., Curacao, Netherlands Antilles, 1992; clinical nurse Holy Cross Hosp., Silver Spring, Md., 1993—. Vol. Kraam Kliniek Rio Canario, Curacao, 1986, Monseignor Verriet, Caracao, 1987; sch. coord. Princeton (N.J.) Red Cross, 1986-89; tutor St. James AME Ch., Highstown, N.J., 1987-89, Higher Achievement Program, Washington, 1993-94; counselor DC Rape Crisis Ctr., 1993-94. Mem. Am. Women's Health, Obstet. and Neonatal Nurses. Jewish. Home: 1400 20th St NW #215 Washington DC 20036

GELLER, RONALD GENE, health administrator; b. Peoria, Ill., Jan. 15, 1943; s. Harold H. and Rose G.; m. Lois S. Geller, Sept. 5, 1971; children—Andrea, Steven, Lauren. B.S. in Zoology, U. Wis., 1964, Ph.D. in Physiology, 1969. Spl. research fellow Nat. Heart Inst. NIH, Bethesda, Md., 1969-71, sr. staff fellow Nat. Heart, Lung and Blood Inst., 1971-72, grants assoc., 1972-73, asst. chief, chief hypertension and kidney diseases br. Nat. Heart, Lung and Blood Inst., 1973-78, assoc. dir. extramural and collaborative programs Nat. Eye Inst., 1978-86, acting dir. div. program analysis Office Program Planning and Eval., 1986, dir. div. program analysis, 1987-89, dir. div. extramural affairs Nat. Heart, Lung and Blood Inst., 1989—; instr. Found. for Advanced Edn. in Sci.; USPHS trainee, 1966-67. Contbr. articles to profl. jours. Wis. Heart Assn. fellow, 1967-69. Mem. Am. Heart Assn. (mem. med. adv. bd. coun. for high blood pressure rsch.), Am. Physiol. Soc. Home: 14960 Dufief Dr North Potomac MD 20878-2593 Office: NIH Rockledge Bldg 2 Rm 7100 Bethesda MD 20892-7922

GELLER, STEPHEN ARTHUR, pathologist, educator; b. Bklyn., Apr. 26, 1939; s. Sam John and Alice (Podber) G.; m. Kate Eleanor DeJong, June 24, 1962; children: David Phillip, Jennifer Lee. BA, Bklyn. Coll., 1959; MD, Howard U., 1964. Diplomate Am. Bd. Pathology, Nat. Bd. Med. Examiners. Intern Lenox Hill Hosp., N.Y.C., 1964-65; resident in pathology Mt. Sinai Hosp., N.Y.C., 1965-69; chief lab. Naval Hosp., Beaufort, S.C., 1969-71; asst. prof. pathology Mt. Sinai Med. Ctr., N.Y.C., 1971-75, assoc. prof., 1975-78, prof., 1978-84; chmn. dept. pathology Cedars-Sinai Med. Ctr., L.A., 1984—; prof. pathology UCLA, 1984—. Co-author: Histopathology, 1989; contbr. articles to profl. jours. Recipient Excellence in Teaching award CUNY, 1974. Fellow Coll. Am. Pathologists, Am. Soc. Clin. Pathologists; mem. Am. Assn. Study of Liver Diseases, Hans Popper Hepatopathology Soc. (sec. 1989—), Calif. Soc. Pathologists (sec. 1989—), L.A. Soc. Pathologists (v.p. 1989—), N.Y. Pathol. Soc., Alpha Omega Alpha. Democrat. Jewish.

GELLER, STEVEN ANDREW, internist; b. Bronx, N.Y., June 15, 1959; s. Louis Benjamin and Bernice Ruth (Shapiro) G.; m. Beth Marcy Cohen, May 12, 1985; children: Kaitlin, Erin, Meredith. BS summa cum laude, Union Coll., Schenectady, N.Y., 1981; MD, Johns Hopkins U., 1985. Diplomate Am. Bd. Internal Medicine. Internist Primary Care Specialists MD PA, Ellicott City, Md., 1988—; asst. chmn. dept. medicine Howard County Gen. Hosp., Columbia, Md., 1994-95; sec.-treas. profl. staff Howard County Gen. Hosp., 1996—, bd. trustees, mem. fin. com., 1996—, mem. ops. com., 1994-95. Mem. ACP, Am. Soc. Internal Medicine. Office: Primary Care Specialists 9501 Old Annapolis Rd Ellicott City MD 21042

GELLHORN, ALFRED, physician, educator; b. St. Louis, June 4, 1913; s. George and Edna (Fischel) G.; m. Olga Frederick, Aug. 4, 1939; children—Martha, Anne, Christina, Maria, Edna. Student, Amherst Coll., 1930-32, DSc (hon.), 1969; MD, Washington U., St. Louis, 1937; DSc (hon.), CCNY, 1979, SUNY, 1984, Albany Med. Coll., 1986, U. Pa., 1992. Diplomate Am. Bd. Internal Medicine. Gen. surg. tng. Barnes Hosp., St. Louis, 1937-39; gynecology trainee Passavant Meml. Hosp., Chgo., 1939-40; fellow Carnegie Instn. of Washington, Balt., 1940-43; instr., later asst. prof. physiology Coll. Physicians and Surgeons, Columbia U., N.Y.C., 1943-45, asst., then assoc. prof. pharmacology, 1945-48, assoc. prof. clin. cancer research dept. medicine, 1948-52, assoc. prof. medicine, 1952-58, prof. medicine, 1958-68; prof. medicine and pharmacology, dean Sch. Medicine, also dir. Med. Ctr. U. Pa., Phila., 1968-73; dir. Ctr. Biomed. Edn., City Coll., v.p. for health affairs CUNY, 1974-79, emeritus, 1979—; dir. med. affairs N.Y. State Dept. Health, Albany, 1983—; sr. cons. Commonwealth Fund, N.Y., 1979-80, Aaron Diamond Found., 1987—; vis. prof. Harvard Sch. Pub. Health, 1980-83; physician Francis Delafield Hosp., N.Y.C., 1949-52, chief med. service, 1952-68; vis. prof. medicine Albert Einstein Med. Sch.; dir. Inst. Cancer Research, Columbia; bd. regents Nat. Library Medicine. Mem. ACP, Coll. Physicians Phila., Soc. for Clin. Investigation, Assn. Am. Physicians, N.Y. County Med. Soc., Am. Assn. Cancer Research (pres. 1962-63), Am. Soc. Pharm. and Exptl. Therapeutics, Inst. Medicine, Am. Soc. Biol. Chemistry. Office: State NY Dept Health Empire State Pla Rm 910 Albany NY 12237*

GELLIN, GERALD ALAN, dermatologist; b. Bklyn., May 24, 1934; m. Lucille E. Gellin. AB, U. Pa., 1954; MD, NYU, 1958. Diplomate Am. Bd. Dermatology. Chief sect. dermatology VA Hosp., Bklyn., 1964-67; clin. prof. U. Calif. Med. Ctr., San Francisco, 1969—; chief dermatology divsn. VA Hosp., Bklyn., 1963-67, San Francisco Gen. Hosp., 1969-73, Calif. Pacific Med. Ctr., 1986—. Contbr. articles to profl. jours. With USPHS, 1967-69. Fellow ACP. Office: 3838 California St San Francisco CA 94118-1522

GELLIS, SYDNEY SAUL, physician; b. Claremont, N.H., Mar. 6, 1914; s. Morris Aaron and Minnie (Bernstein) G.; m. Matilda Lichter, March 6, 1939; children: Beth Louise Gellis Crocker, Stephen E. AB magna cum laude, Harvard U., 1934; MD, Harvard Med. Sch., 1938. Diplomate Am. Acad. Pediatrics. Resident in pediatrics Yale-New Haven Hosp., 1938-39, Children's Hosp., Cin., 1939-41; chief resident in pediatrics Johns Hopkins Hosp., Balt., 1941-42; captain armed forces epidemiol. bd. M.C., epidemiology bd. U.S. Army, ETO, 1942-46; asst. prof. pediatrics Harvard Med. Sch., Boston, 1946-55; chief outpatient and emergency Children's Hosp., Boston, 1946-53; prof., chmn. pediatrics Boston U. Med. Sch., 1955-65, dean, 1963-65; pediatrician-in-chief Boston City Hosp., 1955-65; prof., chmn. dept. pediatrics Tufts U. Med. Sch., Boston, 1965-83; prof. pediatrics New Eng. Med. Ctr., Boston, 1965—, pediatrician-in-chief, 1965-83. Editor: Yearbook of Pediatrics, 1952-85, Pediatric Notes, 1977—; contbr. articles to profl. jours. Fellow Am. Acad. Pediatrics (Jacobi award and lifetime Med. Edn. award, 1993); mem. Am. Pediatric Soc. (John Howland medal award 1994), Pediatric Rsch. Soc. (sec.-treas. 1946-52, pres. 1972); corr. mem. Acad. Pediatrics (France), New Zealand Pediatric Soc. Home: 77 Alderwood Rd Newton MA 02159-1226 Office: Tufts-New England Med Ctr 750 Washington St Boston MA 02111-1533

GELMAN, ELAINE EDITH, nurse; b. Bklyn., Feb. 16, 1927; d. Michael Levi and Shirley (Drezner) Rodkinson; m. David Graham Gelman, Apr. 6, 1952; children: Eric, Andrew, Amy. BS, CUNY, Queens, 1946; RN, NYU, 1948. Cert. PNP. Mem. oper. rm. staff, supr. Queens Gen. Hosp., Bellevue, Beth-El Hosp., N.Y.C., 1948-61; mem. labor and delivery rm. staff, supr. Georgetown Hosp., Washington, 1962-66; pub. health nurse N.Y.C. Dept. Pub. Health, 1966-72; PNP Roosevelt Hosp., N.Y.C., 1972-82; pvt. practice N.Y.C., 1982-95. Mem. Dem. County Com., N.Y.C., 1984—; apptd. mem. N.Y. State Bd. Nursing, 1990—, exec. dir. N.Y. State Coalition Nurse Practitioners, Inc., 1996—. Named Nurse of Distinction N.Y. State Legis., 1991; recipient Spl. Presdl. award N.Y. State Coalition of Nurse Practitioners, 1991. Fellow Nat. Assn. PNPs (legis. chmn. 1986-88, cert. of recognition 1986, 87), Coalition of Nurse Practitioners, Inc. (pres. 1984-85, 87-88). Jewish. Home: 229 W 78th St New York NY 10024-6604

GELMAN, MARTIN L., nephrologist; b. Chgo., Nov. 3, 1943; s. Irving and Esther G.; m. Rosemary Carroll; children: David, Matthew. AB, Ind. U., 1964, MD, 1968. Diplomat Am. Bd. Internal Medicine, Am. Bd. Nephrology. Asst. prof. medicine nephrology Tufts U. Sch. Medicine, Boston, 1976—; med. dir. Hopedale Dialysis Ctr., Mass., 1987—, Metro. North Hosp. Dialysis Ctr., Everett, Mass., 1993—, Dialysis Svc. Inc., Everett, Mass., 1994—; pres. Greater Boston Med. Assocs., 1994—. Pres. Nat. Med. Rsch. Found., Boston. Maj. U.S. Army, 1971-73. Recipient Purple Heart U.S. Army, 1973. Mem. Am. Soc. Nephrology. Office: Greater Boston Med Assocs 280 Washington St Brighton MA 02135

GELMANN, EDWARD PAUL, hematologist, oncologist, educator; b. N.Y.C., May 31, 1950; m. Connie Sommers; children: Lauren R., Elyssa R., Emily B. BS magna cum laude, Yale U., 1972; MD, Stanford U., 1976. Diplomate Nat. Bd. Med. Examienrs, Am. Bd. Internal Medicine; lic. physician, Ill., Md., D.C. Intern then resident U. Chgo. Hosps., 1976-78; med. staf fellow Nat. Cancer Inst., Bethesda, Md., 1979-83, sr. investigator, 1983-88; adj. assoc. prof. microbiology Georgetown U., Washington, 1986-88, prof. medicine and cell biology, 1988—, chief med. oncology divsn., 1988-93, chief hematology/oncology divsn., 1993-95; dir. urologic oncology program Lombardi Cancer Rsch. Ctr., 1990-93, dir. prostate cancer program, 1993—. Mem. editorial bd. jour. Blood, 1985-90; ad hoc reviewer jours.; contbr. 125 articles to profl. jours. Sr. surgeon USPHS, 1978-88. Grantee Nat. Cancer Inst., 1990—. Fellow ACP; mem. AAAS, Am. Soc. Clin. Investigation, Am. Assn. Cancer Rsch., Am. Soc. Clin. Oncology. Office: Georgetown U 3800 Reservoir Rd NW Washington DC 20007-2196

GELPI, JOSE ANGEL, physician; b. Sdetanamo, Cuba, Aug. 2, 1933; came to U.S., 1960; s. Juan and Josefa (Cabreja) G.; m. Yolanda Rivas; 1 child, Juan. BA, Institotodel Vedado, Habana, Cuba, 1951; MD, Universidad de Salamanca, Spain, 1963; MSc, Ohio State U., 1967. Intern Charleston (W.Va.) Gen. Hosp., 1963-64; resident Milledgeville (Ga.) Hosp., 1964-65, Ohio State U., 1966-67; staff psychiatrist Springfield Hosp. Ctr., 1991—; asst. prof. U. Md., Balt., 1980—. Author: (with others) The Forensic Hospital, 1988. Bd. dirs. Cirwb Cubano, Balt., 1985. Fellow Am. Psychiat. Assn. Republican. Roman Catholic.

GELTZEILER, JULES M., urologist; b. Newark, June 17, 1955; m. Linda Geltzeiler, May 24, 1996; children: Mathew N., Mara N. BS magna cum laude, Wilkes Coll., 1979; MD, Hahneman Med. Coll., 1979. Diplomate Am. Bd. Urology, Nat. Bd. Med. Examiners. Surg. intern Monmouth Med. Ctr., Long Branch, N.J., 1979-80, asst. resident in surgery, 1980-81; resident in urol. surgery George Washington U. Hosp., Washington, 1981-83, chief resident in urol. surgery, 1983-84; urologist Shore Urology P.A., Long Branch, 1984—; attending urologist Jersey Shore Med. Ctr., 1984, Monmouth Med. Ctr., 1994; asst. attending urologist Riverview Med. Ctr., 1991. Recipient 1st prize Washington D.C. Urologic Resident's Day Competition, 1983, 2d prize, 1984. Fellow ACS, Acad. Medicine N.J., Am. Soc. for Laser Medicine and Surgery; mem. Am. Urol. Assn., Am. Fertility Soc., Am. Assn. Clin. Urologists, N.J. State Med. Soc., Monmouth County Med. Soc., Urol. Soc. N.J. Office: Shore Urology PA 279 3d Ave Ste 101 Long Branch NJ 07740

GELZER, JUSTUS, secretary general; b. Basel, Switzerland, Nov. 8, 1929; s. Heinrich and Charlotte (Ludecke) G.; m. Antoinette Miescher, Sept. 29, 1960; children: Adel, Samuel, Anna. MD, Basel Med. Sch., 1954. Bd. Cert. Pediatrics. MD, biologist, Biol. Rsch. Labs. CIBA Ltd., Basel, 1964-67; dir. Microbiology Subdiv., dept. dir. Biology Rsch. CIBA Pharm. Ltd., Summit, N.J., 1967-70; rsch. head biology Pharm. div. CIBA-GEIGY Ltd., Basel, 1970-80, head strategic rsch. planning med. dept. Pharm. Div., 1985—; mem. Ciba Pharma Mgmt. Com., 1993. Contbr. articles to profl. jours. Exec. com. mem., sec.-gen., and senate Swiss Acad. med. Scis.; exec. com. mem. Swiss chpt. Mother Child Internat. Assn. for Maternal and Neonatal Health. Maj. Swiss Med. Corps., ret. Mem. AMA, Swiss Med. Assn., Swiss Pediatric Soc., Swiss Soc. Microbiology. Home: Munsterplatz 6, CH-4051 Basel Switzerland Office: Swiss Acad of Med Scis, Petersplatz 13, CH-4051 Basel Switzerland

GEMELLI, BERNARD NATALE, JR., health services administrator; b. Phila., July 26, 1948; s. Bernard Natale Gemelli Sr. and Florence Muriel (Davis) Podbevsek; m. Sylvenia Gemelli, Aug. 1, 1966; 1 child, Sylvenia Kathleen. BA in Bus. Adminstrn., Flagler Coll., St. Augustine, Fla., 1986. Fin. mgr. McDill AFB, NCO Club, Tampa, 1980-81; grants and spl. projects coord. City of St. Augustine, Fla., 1986-89; program devel. dir. Fla. Spl. Olympics, Tallahassee, 1989-91; human svcs. counselor III Fla. Dept. Corrections, Raiford, 1991-93, health svcs. adminstr., 1993-94, sr. health svcs. adminstr., 1994—; grants cons. Lightner Mus., St. Augustine, 1986-87; nat. unified sports com. U.S. Sply. Olympics, N.Y.C., 1990-91. Mem. adv. bd. Cmty. Devel. Block Grant, City of Gainesville, Fla., 1990. With U.S. Army, 1966-79, Vietnam. Decorated Bronze Star for valor, 3 Purple Hearts, Cross of Gallantry. Mem. DAV (treas. 1987-88), VFW. Democrat. Roman Catholic. Home: 2426 NW 52nd Pl Gainesville FL 32605 Office: Union Correctional Instn PO Box 221 Raiford FL 32083

GEMMA, FRANK E., physician; b. Clarksburg, W.Va., Aug. 28, 1934. BA, W.Va. U., 1956, BS, 1958; MD, Med. Coll. of Va., 1960. Diplomate Am. Bd. Surgery. Physician U.S. Army, 1962-84, pvt. practice, Killeen, Tex., 1985—; Pres. Bell County Med. Soc., Bell County, Tex., 1992, Cor-Bell Unit Am. Cancer Soc., Bell County, 1992. Fellow ACS; mem. AMA, Am. Soc. Gen. Surgeons, Tex. Med. Assn., Soc. Laparoendoscopic Surgeons. Office: 2301 S Clear Creek Rd #106 Killeen TX 76542

GEMMELL-AKALIS, BONNI JEAN, psychotherapist; b. Lansing, Mich., Mar. 11, 1950; d. James Stewart Gemmell and Alpha Alice (Hackenberg)

Vanden Bosch; m. Thomas Joe Akalis, Dec. 14, 1974 (div. Sept. 94); children: Scott Aaron, Ty Alexander, Zachary Alan. BS, Ctrl. Mich. U., 1972, MA, 1974. Ltd. lic. psychologist, Mich.; cert. social worker, Mich. Clin. psychologist, sr. mental health therapist Lincoln Ctr. for Emotionally Disturbed Children & Youth, Lansing, 1974-77; outpatient psychologist Grand Rapids (Mich.) Child Guidance Clinic, 1978-81; pvt. practice Grand Rapids Psychiat. Svcs., 1981-88; pvt. practice Associated Therapists, Inc., Grand Rapids, 1988—, pres., 1989-90. Grad. fellow Ctrl. Mich. U., 1972-73. Mem. Mich. Psychoanalytic Coun., Mich. Women Psychologists, Mich. Assn. Profl. Psychologists, Am. Group Psychotherapy Assn. (founder nat. registry 1996), Grand Rapids Area Psychology Assn., Psi Chi. Home: 632 Duxbury Ct SE Grand Rapids MI 49546-9605 Office: Psychol Svcs 1025 Spaulding Ste B Grand Rapids MI 49546

GEMSA, DIETHARD, immunologist; b. Berlin, Aug. 9, 1937; s. Hans and Hedwig (Reinhard) G.; m. Inken Fischer, Apr. 11, 1968; children: Jan Ulrich, Kerstin Friederike, Meike Charlotte. MD, U. Freiburg, 1968; Pvt. Dozent, U. Heidelberg, 1974. Rsch. fellow U. Wash., Seattle, 1965-67; resident U. Mainz, Germany, 1968-70; rsch. assoc. in internal medicine U. Calif., San Francisco, 1970-73; asst. prof. Inst. Immunology, U. Heidelberg, 1974-82; assoc. prof. Med. Sch. Hannover, 1983-84; prof. head Inst. Immunology, Philipps U., Marburg, 1985—. Editor German Textbook of Immunology; contbr. over 180 articles to med. jours.; editor-in-chief Immunobiology, 1978—. Mem. Am. Assn. Immunologists, German Soc. Immunology (councillor 1980—), German Soc. Cancer Rsch. Liberal Party. Roman Catholic. Office: Inst Immunology, U Marburg, Robert-Koch-Str 17, Marburg D-35037, Germany

GENCO, CHRISTOPHER MICHAEL, cardiothoracic surgeon; b. Fort Dix, N.J., Feb. 6, 1958; s. Victory Anthony and Lilly Ann (Gauvin) G.; m. Paulette Lollias, Apr. 20, 1991; children: Christopher, Caroline Rose. BS, U. Notre Dame, 1980; MD, SUNY, 1984. Diplomate Am. Bd. Gen. and Thoracic Surgery. Intern, resident surgery SUNY, Stony Brook, 1984-89; fellow cardiothoracic rsch. New Eng. Med. Ctr., Boston, 1989-90, resident cardiothoracic, 1990-92; cardiothoracic surgeon Great Lakes Cardiovasc. Surgery PC, Saginaw, Mich., 1993—. Contbr. articles to profl. jours. Fellow ACS (assoc.), Am. Coll. Cardiology, Am. Coll. Chest Physicians; mem. AMA, Mich. Soc. Thoracic Surgeons, Mich. State Med. Soc., Saginaw County Med. Soc. Office: Great Lakes Cardio Surgery 4701 Towne Ctr Rd #301 Saginaw MI 48604

GENCO, ROBERT JOSEPH, scientist, immunologist, periodontist, educator; b. Silver Creek, N.Y., Oct. 31, 1938; s. Joseph A. and Santa (Barone) G.; m. Sandra Clarke, Sept. 14, 1957; children: Deborah Genco Powell, Robert M., Julie Clarke Alford. DDS cum laude, SUNY, 1963; PhD, U. Pa., 1967. Asst. prof. dept. oral biology Sch. Dental Medicine SUNY, Buffalo, 1967-69, assoc. prof., 1969-72, prof., 1972—, chmn. dept., 1977—, Disting. Univ. Prof., 1990—. Editor Jour. Periodontology, 1988—. Recipient Gold medal ADA, 1991. Fellow AAAS (chmn. dental sect. 1980); mem. Am. Assn. Dental Researchers (pres. 1985), Inst. Medicine, Internat. Assn. Dental Researchers (pres. 1991-92), Am. Acad. Periodontology, Am. Assn. Immunology. Office: SUNYat Buffalo Periodontal Disease Rsch Ctr Foster Hall Buffalo NY 14214*

GENDER, ALOMA RUTH, health facility administrator; b. Richmond, Va., May 23, 1943; d. Roy Casper and Norma Eugenia Pauline (Peterson) Shriber; m. John Edmond Gender, Jan. 22, 1966; children: Jamine Noelle, Jordana Pauline. Diploma in nursing, Mercy Coll. Nursing, 1965; BSN, U. San Diego, 1979; MS in Nursing Systems Adminstrn., San Diego State U., 1988. Cert. rehab. RN. Asst. head nurse Sharp Rehab. Ctr., San Diego, 1973-74, 78-79, head nurse, 1974-78, liaison nurse and outpatient supr., 1979-80, liaison nurse, 1980-81, rehab. nursing mgr., dir. IV, 1981-85, rehab. nursing mgr., dir. V, 1985-87, rehab. mgr./PCS, 1987-88; asst. adminstr., dir. of nursing San Diego Rehab. Inst., 1988-96, COO, 1996—; mem. adv. coun. Bradenton Rehab. Hosp., Sarasota, Fla., 1992. Author: The Specialty Practice of Rehabilitation Nursing: A Core Curriculum, 1993, Rehabilitation Nursing, 1995, Nursing Management in the New Paradigm, 1996; contbr. articles to profl. jours. Mem. chpt. svcs. com. Multiple Sclerosis Soc., San Diego. Mem. Assn. Rehab. Nurses (pres. 1991-92, chair cert. bd. 1989-90), Rehab. Nursing Found. (trustee 1992-93), Sigma Theta Tau (2d v.p. Zeta Mu chpt. 1995—). Republican. Lutheran. Home: 11320 Trebol St San Diego CA 92126 Office: San Diego Rehab Inst 6645 Alvarado Rd San Diego CA 92120

GENDZWILL, JOYCE ANNETTE, retired health officer; b. Milw., Aug. 8, 1927; d. Felix Vincent and Antoinette Marie (Borske) G.; m. Lauren E. Trombley, June 13, 1952 (div. Jan. 1960); children: Regan Eve Trombley Kovacich, Eugene Vincent, Paul Quentin. BS, U. Mich., 1949, MD, 1952, MPH, 1961. Cert. pub. mgr., Ala. Internship USPHS, Detroit, Cleve., 1952-53; dir. extern edn. Beyer Meml. Hosp., Ypsilanti, Mich., 1953-54; resident in radiology St. Luke's Hosp., Denver, 1954-55; health officer Dickinson-Iron Dist. Health Dept., Stambaugh, Mich., 1959-76; dir. bur. local health svc. Ala. Dept. Pub. Health, Montgomery, Ala., 1976-81; asst. state health officer Ala. Dept. Pub. Health, Montgomery, 1981-91; ret., 1991. Mem. AMA, So. Med. Assn., Mensa, Phi Beta Kappa, Delta Omega, Phi Kappa Phi. Home: 6580 Thorman Rd Port Charlotte FL 33981-5579

GENEL, MYRON, pediatrician, educator; b. York, Pa., Jan. 6, 1936; s. Victor and Florence (Mowitz) G.; m. Phyllis Norma Berkman, Aug. 25, 1968; children: Elizabeth, Jennifer, Abby. Grad., Moravian Coll., 1957; MD, U. Pa., 1961; MA (hon.), Yale U., 1983; DSc (hon.), Moravian Coll., 1995. Diplomate: Am. Bd. Pediatrics. Intern Mt. Sinai Hosp., N.Y.C., 1961-62; resident in pediatrics Children's Hosp. Phila., 1962-64; trainee pediatric endocrinology Johns Hopkins Hosp., Balt., 1966-67; instr. pediatrics U. Pa. Sch. Medicine, 1967-69, assoc. in pediatrics, 1969-71; trainee in genetics, inherited metabolic diseases Children's Hosp. Phila., 1967-69, assoc. physician, 1969-71; attending physician Yale-New Haven Hosp., 1971—; mem. faculty Yale U. Sch. Medicine, New Haven, 1971—, dir. pediatric endocrinology, 1971-85, program dir. Children's Clin. Rsch. Ctr., 1971-86, prof., 1981—, assoc. dean, 1985—, dir. Office Govt. and Cmty. Affairs, 1985—; mem. genetic adv. bd. State of Conn., 1979-82; cons. subcom. investigations, oversight com. sci. and tech. U.S. Ho. of Reps., 1982-84; mem. adv. bd. New Eng. Congenital Hypothyroidism Collaborative; cons. Hosp. St. Raphael, Milford Hosp., Norwalk Hosp., Stamford Hosp., Danbury Hosp.; chmn. transplant adv. com. Office of Commr., Conn. Dept. Income Maintenance, 1984-92; health policy fellowship bd. Inst. Medicine, 1989-95. Contbr. articles to profl. jours. Served as capt. U.S. Army, 1964-66. Robert Wood Johnson Health Policy fellow Inst. Medicine NAS, Washington, 1982-83; recipient ann. award Conn. Campaign Against Cooley's Anemia, 1979, Ann. Comenius Alumni award Moravian Coll., 1990. Mem. APHA, AAAS, AMA (med. schs. sec. 1985—, alt. del. governing coun., med. schs. sec. 1995—, coun. on sci. affairs, 1994—, Task force on fin. grad. med. edn. 1995), Am. Acad. Pediatrics (task force organ transplants, coun. on govt. affairs), Am. Coll. Nutrition, Am. Diabetes Assn. (co-recipient Jonathan May award 1979), Am. Fedn. Clin. Rsch., Am. Pediatric Soc., Am. Soc. Bone and Mineral Rsch. Assn. Am. Med. Colls. (mem. adminstrv. bd. coun. acad. socs. 1987-92, chmn.-elect coun. acad. socs., 1989-91, mem. exec. coun. 1989-92), Assn. Health Svcs. Rsch., New Haven County Med. Assn. (bd. govs. 1990-96), Assn. Program Dirs. (pres.-elect 1980-81, pres. 1981-82), Nat. Assn. Biomed. Rsch. (bd. dirs. 1990-93, exec. com. 1991-93), Conn. Endocrine Soc., Conn. United for Rsch. Excellence (chmn. steering com. 1989-90, pres. 1990-93, chmn. bd. dirs. 1993-94), Endocrine Soc., Soc. Pediat. Rsch., Conn. Acad. Sci. and Engring., Sigma Xi. Jewish. Home: 30 Richard Sweet Dr Woodbridge CT 06525-1126 Office: PO Box 3333 New Haven CT 06510-0333

GENGLER, NORMAN JOHN, anesthesiologist, consultant; b. Oak Park, Ill., May 22, 1924; s. Michael Joseph and Adeline Emma (Oldenburg) G.; m. Faith Rita Larkin, Aug. 30, 1947 (dec. Jan. 1974): children: Pamela J. Gengler Fuss, Michael J.; m. Myrle Pierce, Aug. 7, 1974. BS in Medicine, Northwestern U., 1946, BM, 1947, MD, 1949. Diplomate Am. Bd. Anesthesiology. Postdoctoral fellow in anesthesiology U. Minn. Hosps., Mpls., 1949-51; staff St. Francis Hosp., Evanston, Ill., 1953-65; staff Sarasota (Fla.) Meml. Hosp., 1965-85, chief of staff, 1973-74; physician surveyor Joint Commn. for Accreditation of Hosps., Chgo., 1985-86; cons. staff VA Hosp., Asheville, N.C., 1990-92. Lt. USNR, 1951-53. Mem. AMA, AM. Soc. Anesthesiologists, Fla. Soc. Anesthesiologists (pres. 1972-73), Country Club of Asheville. Republican. Lutheran. Home: 511 Cokesbury Ln Asheville NC 28803

GENKINS, GABRIEL, physician; b. Berlin, Mar. 20, 1928; came to U.S., 1940, naturalized, 1945; s. Arkady and Tamara (Schlesinger) G.; children: Karen Lee Genkins Fairbank, Steven M., Amy E. B.S., NYU, 1949, M.D., 1952. Diplomate Am. Bd. Internal Medicine, Diplomate Am. Bd. Cardiology. Intern, resident Mt. Sinai Hosp., N.Y.C., 1952-57; practice medicine specializing in cardiology N.Y.C.; clin. prof. medicine Mt. Sinai Med. Ctr., N.Y.C., 1973—, chief myasthenia gravis clinic and rsch. labs., 1972—; attending physician in cardiology Mt. Sinai Hosp., N.Y.C., 1973—; v.p. bd. dirs. Myasthenia Gravis Found., 1973—, mem. nat. med. adv. bd., 1956—. Contbr. articles to profl. jours., chpts. to books. Served with airborne inf., U.S. Army, 1945-46. Democrat. Office: 30 E 60th St New York NY 10022-1008

GENNARI, F(RANK) JOHN, medical educator; b. Jersey City, May 18, 1937; s. Frank and Amelia (Sargia) G.; m. Emily Hewson Michie, Sept. 15, 1958; children: John Hewson, Jennifer Meade, Amelia Sargia. BS cum laude, Yale U., 1959, MD, 1963. Diplomate Am. Bd. Internal Medicine, Am. Bd. Nephrology. Intern U. Va. Hosp., Charlottesville, 1963-64, resident in medicine, 1964-66; fellow in nephrology Tufts-New Eng. Med., Boston, 1968-71; asst. prof. Sch. Medicine, Tufts U., Boston, 1971-75, assoc. prof., 1975-79; prof. medicine Coll. Medicine, U. Vt., Burlington, 1979—, dir. nephrology, 1979—, assoc. chair dept. medicine, 1987-92, 96; interim chair dept. medicine, 1993; mem. Nephrology bd. Am. Bd. Internal Medicine, 1994—. Co-author: Acid-Base, 1981, Acid-Base Disorders, 1987; contbr. articles to profl. publs., chpts. to books. Mem. exec. com. Vt. Heart Assn., 1982-85; mem. exec. com. Vt. Kidney Assn., 1980—, pres., 1984-86; mem. merit rev. bd. VA, Washington, 1989-92. Capt. Med. Corps, USAF, 1966-68. Grantee NIH, 1971-91, Fogarty Internat., 1991. Fellow ACP; mem. Am. Fedn. Clin. Rsch., Am. Soc. Clin. Investigation, Am. Soc. Nephrology, Am. Physiol. Soc., Internat. Soc. Nephrology. Democrat. Office: U Vt Coll Medicine D305 Given Bldg Burlington VT 05405

GENNARO, JOHN NICHOLAS, optometrist; b. Hazleton, Pa., Dec. 1, 1926; s. Joseph Anthony and Emma (Martini) G.; m. Pitzie Leona Gabriel, July 25, 1950 (dec. Feb. 5, 1987); children: Jean, Laurie, Gabriel. BS, U. Scranton, 1950; BS in Optometry, Ill. Coll. Optometry, 1951, OD, 1954. OD, Minn. Regional dir. Ventilation Air Contact Lens Corp., Mpls., 1954-69; doctor of optometry Park Nicollet Med. Ctr., St. Louis Park, Minn., 1985-87; doctor of optometry pvt. practice Coon Rapids, Minn., 1969—. Developer of Volume Method of Contact Lens Fit, 1956, Now To Truncate Bevel Contact Wens Without Warping, 1960. Mem. Eye Rsch. Found., Chgo., 1956-69, Coon Rapids (Minn.) Lions, 1970-74; bd. mgmt. YMCA, Mpls., 1970-74. Staff sgt. U.S. ARmy, 1945-46. Mem. Am. Optometric Assn., Minn. Optometric Assn., Minn. Assn. Optometrists and Opticians, Coon Rapids Am. Legion (comdr. and all chairs 1963—), VFW. Republican. Roman Catholic. Home: 3517 Mississippi Dr NW Coon Rapids MN 55433 Office: Dr John N Gennaro 11441 Osage St NW Coon Rapids MN 55433

GENOVESE, MARIO NICHOLAS, podiatrist; b. Bklyn., July 3, 1960; s. Anthony and Catherine Genovese; m. Agnes Paula DeLuca, July 24, 1982; children: Matthew, Christina, Nicole. BS cum laude, SUNY, Albany, 1982; DPM, N.Y. Coll. Podiatric Medicine, 1986. Pvt. practice Bklyn., 1989—; cons. N.Y. Hotel Coun., N.Y.C., 1988-96; lectr. Bklyn. Pub. Libr., 1989-92. Mem. Am. Podiatric Med. Assn., N.Y. State Podiatric Med. Assn. Office: 7715 Fourth Ave Brooklyn NY 10306

GENOVESI, ANTHONY DENNIS, geneticist, plant tissue culturist; b. Muskogee, Okla., June 20, 1944; s. Louis Antonio and Wilma Dell (Melton) G.; B.S., U. Tex.-Arlington, 1967; M.S., Tex. A&M U., 1975, Ph.D., 1978. Post doctoral fellow U. Ky., Lexington, 1978-81; cellular geneticist Dekalb Genetics Corp., 1981—. Co-author several sci. publs. Served to capt. U.S. Army, 1967-70. Mem. Soc. Invitro Biology, Internat. Assn. Plant Cell Tissue Cultures, Am. Soc. Agronomy, Sigma Xi, Phi Kappa Phi, Phi Sigma, Gamma Sigma Delta. Democrat. Baptist. Avocations: tropical fish, sports, jogging. Office: De Kalb Genetics Corp 3100 Sycamore Rd De Kalb IL 60115-9621

GENT, DONALD HERBERT, psychiatrist; b. Binghamton, N.Y., Dec. 8, 1926; s. Thomas Wilfred and Cora Dorothea (Tripp) G.; m. Myrtle Gertrude Miller, June 25, 1949; children: Donna Helene, Douglas Harlan, Rebecca Ann, Kathryn Leigh, David Leslie. BA, Hamilton Coll., 1949; MD, Columbia U., 1952. Diplomate Am. Bd. Psychiatry and Neurology. Resident surgery and internal medicine Robert Packer Hosp., Sayre, Pa., 1953-57; pvt. practice internal medicine Binghamton, N.Y., 1957-64; resident in psychiatry Warren (Pa.) State Hosp., 1964-67; asst. clin. prof. health sci. U. Ill., Urbana, 1968-70; county mental health dir. Montgomery County Mental Health Clinic, Amsterdam, N.Y., 1970-72; asst clin. prof. psychiatry Albany (N.Y.) Med. Coll., 1970-72; staff psychiatrist, dir. adolescent prog. Fair-Oaks Hosp., Summit, N.J., 1972-76; clin. asst. prof. psychiatry Coll. Medicine & Dentistry, N.J. Rutgers Med. Sch., Piscataway, 1972-76; clin. dir. dept. psychiatry and pvt. practice Hanover (Pa.) Gen. Hosp., 1976-88, pvt. practice, 1988-93; cons. Adams-Hanover Counseling Ctr., 1995—; mem. adv. bd. York/Adams Mental Health and Retardation Program, 1983-91; chmn. dept. medicine Hanover Gen. Hosp., 1988-90. Vice pres. Citizens for Decency through Law, Hanover, 1983-88. With U.S. Army, 1944-46. Fellow Am. Psychiat. Assn. (life); mem. AMA, Psychiat. Physicians Pa., Cen. Pa. Psychiat. Soc. (pres. 1982-83), Christian Med. and Dental Soc. (pres. Psychiat. sect. 1987-89, 93-95), Pa. Med. Soc., York County Med. Soc. Republican. Baptist. Home: 303 Deguy Ave Hanover PA 17331-1395

GENTILE, DIANA PALAZZO, physician assistant, nurse; b. N.Y.C., Apr. 24, 1951; d. Philip Anthony and Lydia Grace (Buracchio) Palazzo; m. Robert Gentile, Sept. 13, 1987. BS, SUNY, Bklyn., 1973; MS, CUNY, Bronx, 1979; BS, Touro Coll., Dix Hills, N.Y., 1986. RN, N.Y. Staff nurse pediatric ICU, surgery Downstate Med. Ctr., Bklyn., 1973-77; head nurse psychiatry Bronx Children's Hosp., 1977-78; clin. instr. nursing Misericordia Sch. Nursing, Bronx, 1978-83; asst. prof. nursing Columbia-Presbyn., N.Y.C., 1983-86; physician asst. St. Barnabas and Union Hosp., Bronx, 1989—; lectr. in field. NIMH grantee, 1977-79. Mem. Am. Acad. Physician Assts., N.Y. State Soc. Physician Assts., Amnesty Internat. Democrat. Home: 110 Cox Ave Yonkers NY 10704 Office: St Barnabas/Union Hosp 260 E 188th St Bronx NY 10458

GENTILE, J. RONALD, educational psychology educator; b. Pottsville, Pa., Apr. 14, 1941; s. Joseph and Evelyn Marie (Warfield) G.; m. Patricia Koch, Sept. 7, 1963 (div. 1973); 1 child, Douglas Alan; m. Kay Burgher Johnson, Aug. 30, 1979. BS, Pa. State U., 1963, MS, 1964, PhD, 1967. Rsch. psychologist Walter Reed Army Inst. Rsch., Washington, 1967-69; prof. SUNY, Buffalo, 1969—, chair dept. ednl. psychology, 1971-72, 81, master Internat. Coll., 1977-79, dir. ednl. psychology programs, 1991-94; dir. UNESCO and SUNY (Buffalo) program, Owerri, Nigeria, 1976-81. Author: (textbook) Educational Psychology, 1990, (children's book/cassette) Great Horse and Greater Horses, 1989, (cassette) Genteel Songs and Poems for Genteel People, 1991, (monograph) Instructional Improvement: A Summary and Analysis of Madeline Hunter's Essential Elements of Instruction and Supervision, 1993; contbr. over 50 articles to profl. jours. Capt. U.S. Army Med. Corps, 1967-69. Recipient Chancellor's award for excellence in teaching SUNY, 1991. Mem. Am. Psychol. Soc., Am. Ednl. Rsch. Assn., Am. Fedn. Musicians. Office: SUNY at Buffalo 409 Baldy Hall Buffalo NY 14260

GENTILE, ROBERT DALE, optometrist, nutritionist; b. Pottsville, Pa., Oct. 24, 1946; s. Joseph and Evelyn Marie (Warfield) Gentile; m. Patricia Diane Fernsler, June 20, 1969; 1 child, Heather Ly Luxon. BA in Sci., Pa. State U., 1968; BS in Optometry, Pa. Coll. of Optometry, Phila., 1974, OD, 1977; MA in Human Resources, Webster U., 1985. Bd. cert. Am. Acad. Optometry. Advanced through ranks to lt. col. AUS, 1968-94; chief optometry 9th Gen. Dispensary, Aschaffenburg, Germany, 1977-80; optometrist Brook Army Med. Ctr., Ft. Sam Houston, Tex., 1980-82; chief eye sect., medicine and surgery Acad. Health Scis., Ft. Sam Houston, Tex., 1982-84; chief optometry Dunham Army Health Clinic, Carlisle Barracks, Pa., 1984-88, Med. Dept. Activity, Berlin, 1988-91, 121st Evacuation Hosp., Seoul, Korea, 1991-93; optometry cons. 18th Med. Command, Seoul, 1991-93; chief optometry Raymond W. Bliss Army Cmty. Hosp., Ft. Huachuca, Ariz., 1993-94; optometrist Naval Hosp., Camp Pendleton, Calif., 1994-96; nutritionist New Vision Internat., Escondido, Calif., 1996—; adj. prof. U. Houston Coll. Optometry, 1980-84, Pa. Coll. Optometry, 1980-84, New Eng. Coll. Optometry, Boston, 1980-84. Decorated Legion of Merit, Meritorious Svc. medal with 3 Oak Leaf Clusters, Army Commendation medal with 4 Oak Leaf Clusters. Fellow Am. Acad. Optometry; mem. Am. Optometric Assn., Armed Forces Optometric Assn., Calif. Optometric Assn., Berlin Internat. Med. Soc., 38th Parallel Med. Soc., Silver Caduceus Soc. of Korea. Home and Office: 2241 Canyon View Glen Escondido CA 92026

GENTRY, GREGG THORNTON, hospital executive; b. Meridian, Miss., Oct. 20, 1957; s. Robert Arlie and Ernestine (Null) G.; m. Pamela Starr Smith, Oct. 29, 1988. BA in Psychology, U. Ala., 1979, MBA, 1982. Cons. Arthur Andersen & Co., Atlanta, 1982-83; systems analyst Ga. Power Co., Atlanta, 1983-84; ESP/ESOP coordinator Ga. Power Co., 1984, pension coordinator, 1985, group ins. coordinator, 1986-89; dir. compensation and benefits Erlanger Med. Ctr., Chattanooga, 1989—; asst. instr. Dale Carnegie. Mem. Ga. Power Employee Forum (pres. 1986), Ga. Power Toastmasters, Tenn. Soc. Healthcare Human Resources Adminstrs., Chattanooga Area Soc. for Healthcare Human Resources Adminstrn., Club of Hearts (bd. dirs. 1989). Republican. Methodist. Home: 3704 Lerch St Chattanooga TN 37411-4528 Office: Erlanger Med Ctr 975 E 3rd St Chattanooga TN 37403-2112

GENTRY, LINDELL R., radiologist; b. Somerset, Ky., Feb. 7, 1951; s. Otis Ray and Hazel Evylene (Boyatt) G.; m. Phyllis Sue Kyle, Dec. 18, 1971; children: Tyler, Rachel, Nathan. BS, Western Ky. U., 1973; MD, U. Ky., 1978. Diplomate Am. Bd. Radiology. Neuroradiologist U. Iowa Hosp. & Clinics, Iowa City, 1983-85, U. Wis. Hosp., Madison, 1985—. Mem. Am. Soc. Neuroradiology, Am. Soc. Head & Neck Radiology, Alpha Omega Alpha. Republican. Home: 5491 Maves Rd Madison WI 53711

GENUNG, SHARON ROSE, pediatrician; b. Williamsport, Pa., Oct. 6, 1951; d. Joseph Patrick and Jeanette (Mossendew) Lynch; m. Norman Bernard Genung, June 9, 1973; children: Jeffrey, Sarah. BS in Microbiology cum laude, Mich. State U., 1973; MS in Clin. Microbiology, U. Ark., 1979, MD, 1984. Lic. physician, Wash., Ark. Clin. resident in pediatrics Wright State U./Children's Med. Ctr., Dayton, Ohio, 1987; dir. pediatrics USAF Hosp. Fairchild, Spokane, Wash., 1987-88, dir. med. svcs., 1988-91; pvt. practice in pediats. Kapstaffer, Maixner & Genung, Spokane, 1991—; instr. in pediatric advanced life support, neonatal resuscitation. Contbr. articles to profl. jours. Maj. USAF M.C., 1980-91. Fellow Am. Acad. Pediatrics; mem. So. Med. Assn., Wash. State Soc. Pediatrics, Spokane Med. Soc., Spokane Pediatric Soc., Spokane Women's Assn. Physicians, Alpha Omega Alpha. Office: Kapstaffer Maixner & Genung 105 W 8th Ave Ste 318 Spokane WA 99204-2318

GENYK, RUTH BEL, psychotherapist; b. Los Angeles, Apr. 5, 1955; d. John Douglas Bel and Ella Adiline (Lips) Medeiros; m. Edward A. Genyk, Aug. 8, 1983; children: Steven, Timothy, Devlon, Suzanne. Student, U. Copenhagen, 1975; BA, BSW, Whittier Coll., 1977; MA, U. Detroit, 1979; MSW, U. Mich., 1987. Mich. cert. Soc. Worker, lic. Marriage and Family Therapist, Mich. Social worker, community liaison Family Service, Whittier, Calif., 1976-77; social worker Children's Group Home, Detroit, 1977, Family Group Homes, Ann Arbor, Mich., 1977; probation officer Dept. Corrections, Detroit, 1978-86; cons. Cath. Social Svcs., Jackson, Mich., 1986-87; pvt. practice psychotherapy Jackson, Mich., 1987—, Chelsea, —, 1993—. Mem. Jr. League. Mem. AAUW, Am. Corrections Assn., Mich. Corrections Assn., Nat. Assn. Social Workers. Democrat. Unitarian. Office: 1 Jackson Sq Ste 910 Jackson MI 49201-1446 also: 114 N Main St Ste 11 Chelsea MI 48118-1514

GEOPPINGER, JAMES CARL, pharmacist; b. Cin., Aug. 3, 1940; s. Edwin John and Catherine Teresa (Tallon) G.; m. Judy Delle Lansdowne, Aug. 1, 1964; children: Carl E., John R., Teresa M., Catherine L. BS in Pharmacy, U. Cin., 1968. Registered pharmacist, Ohio, Ky., Ind. Staff pharmacist SuperX Drugs, Cin., 1968-69, store mgr., 1969-79, pharmacist, dist. supr., 1979-89; ops. mgr. Hook-SuperX, Inc, Cin., 1989-94; P.A.L. trainer Revco Drugs, 1994, regional pharmacy supr., 1995—; clin. instr. U. Cin. Coll. Pharmacy, 1987-94. Dir. Crimestoppers Greater Cin., 1981-90, treas., 1981-84. Named Citizen of Day Sta. WLW, 1981, Kentucky Col., 1987. Mem. Am. Pharm. Assn., Ohio State Pharm. Assn. (legis. com. 1990-94), Hamilton County Pharm. Assn. (treas. 1987, pres. 1990), Nat. Assn. Retail Druggists (Leadership award 1991), U. Cin. Alumni Assn. (trustee 1990—, v.p. 1993, pres. 1994-95). Roman Catholic. Office: 13 Mary St Cincinnati OH 45216

GEORGE, ALFRED L., JR., medical educator, researcher; b. Batavia, N.Y., June 14, 1956. BA in Chemistry, Coll. of Wooster, Ohio, 1978; MD, U. Rochester, 1982. Diplomate Am. Bd. Internal Medicine, Am. Bd. Nephrology. Intern and resident in internal medicine Vanderbilt U. Hosps., Nashville, 1982-86; chief resident in medicine St. Thomas Hosp., Nashville, 1985-86; instr. medicine Vanderbilt U. Sch. Medicine, Nashville, 1985-86, asst. prof. dept. medicine nephrology and pharmacology, 1992-95; assoc. prof. medicine and pharmacology Vanderbilt U., Nashville, 1995—; postdoctoral fellow in clin. nephrology renal-elctrolyte sectl dept. medicine Hosp. of U. Pa., Phila., 1986-87; rsch. fellow dept. medicine and dept. biochemistry and biophysics U. Pa., Phila., 1988-91, rsch. assoc. dept. medicine and Inst. Neurol. Scis., 1991-92; vis. postdoctoral fellow Inst. Suisse de Recherches Experimentales sur le Cancer, Lausanne, Switzerland, 1987-88. Mem. editl. bd. Am. Jour. Physiology, 1996—; jour. reviewer Neuron, Nature Genetics, Jour. Membrane Biology, Jour. Biol. Chemistry, Kidney Internat., Jour. Physiology. Mem. AAAS, Am. Soc. Nephrology, Am. Heart Assn. (mem. coun. on kidney disease, established investigator award 1996), Biophys. Soc. Office: Vanderbilt U Med Ctr Nephrology Divsn S-3223 MCN 21st and Garland Aves Nashville TN 37232

GEORGE, DAVID ALAN, biologist; b. Laurel, Miss., Aug. 17, 1961; s. Bill M. and Helen Ann (Dougherty) G.; m. Amy Marie, Dec. 22, 1992. BS in Biology, U. Tex., 1995. Cert. ACLS instr., Pediat. Advanced Life Support instr. Rougheck Keydril, Houston, 1981-82; electrician Safeway Electric, Jonestown, Tex., 1982-86; paramedic MedStar, Ft. Worth, 1986-92. Mem. Am. Coll. Emergency Physicians, Am. Osteo. Assn., Tex. Coll. Emergency Physicians (student mem. emergency svc. com. 1994—).

GEORGE, GLADYS, hospital administrator; b. 1946. With Lenox Hill Hosp., N.Y.C., 1973—, pres., 1989—. Office: Lenox Hill Hosp 100 E 77th St New York NY 10021-1882*

GEORGE, JOHN ANTHONY, health corporation executive; b. New Kensington, Pa., July 11, 1948; s. Moses and Veronica (Raymond) G.; BS, Duquesne U., Pitts., 1970; MBA, U. Pitts., 1973; MS in Taxation, Robert Morris Coll., Pitts.; cert. fin. planner; m. Leah Diane Vota, Oct. 30, 1971 (div. 1992); children: Jessica, Cara, John. Asst. adminstr. mental health and mental retardation program Western Psychiat. Inst. and Clinic, Pitts., 1971-72; adminstrv. dir. Latrobe Area Hosp., Latrobe, Pa., 1973-76; asst. dir. Presbyn. Univ. Hosp., Pitts., 1976-80; owner, prin. George-Anstey Food Distributing Corp., Pitts., 1978-81; mgmt. cons. Arthur Young & Co., Pitts., 1980-82; exec. dir. Eastern Allegheny County Health Corp., 1982-85; pres. Alpha Health Network, 1985-88; pres., bd. dirs. Intergroup Service Corp., 1988—; mng. ptnr. Med. Benefit Svc., 1991—; bd. dirs. ARC southwestern Pa. chpt.; lectr. in field. Contbr. articles to profl. jours. Mem. Am. Coll. Health Care Execs., Am. Hosp. Assn., Healthcare Fin. Mgmt. Assn., Assn. Managed Healthcare Orgns. (adv. bd. dirs., regional bd. dirs., editorial bd. Jour. of AAPPO), Assn. Healthcare Providers (bd. dirs., pres.), Inst. Cert. Fin. Planners. Roman Catholic. Home: 930 Saint James St Pittsburgh PA 15232 Office: 300 Penn Center Blvd Ste 722 Pittsburgh PA 15235-5507

GEORGE, JOSEPH PAUL, surgeon; b. Michigan City, Ind., Apr. 14, 1920; s. Elias Solomon and Matilda Beshara (Massad) G.; m. Beatrice McKnight Porter, June 6, 1953; children: Joseph Jr., Michael, Stephen, Lisa, Carla, MaryAnne. BS, U. Miami, Fla., 1949; MD, Georgetown U., 1953.

Diplomate Am. Bd. Surgery. Pvt. practice surgery Miami, 1959—. Staff sgt. USAAF, 1942-45, ETO. Fellow ACS. Roman Catholic. Home and Office: 5705 SW 114th Ter Miami FL 33156-5026

GEORGE, PETER T., orthodontist; b. Akron, Ohio; s. Tony and Paraskeva (Ogrenova) G.; BS Kent State U., 1952; DDS, Ohio State U., 1956; cert. in orthodontics Columbia U., 1962; children: Barton Herrin, Tryan Franklin. Pvt. practice orthodontics, Honolulu, 1962—; cleft palate cons. Hawaii Bur. Crippled Children, 1963—; asst. prof. Med. Sch., U. Hawaii, Honolulu, 1970—; lectr. in field. Mem. Hawaii Gov.'s Phys. Fitness Com., 1962-68; mem. Honolulu Mayor's Health Coun., 1967-72; mem. med. com. Internat. Weightlifting Fedn., 1980-84; chmn. bd. govs. Hall of Fame of Hawaii, 1984; bd. dirs. Honolulu Opera Theatre, 1986-91, chmn. bd. Hawaii Internat. Sports Found., 1988-91. Served to capt. Dental Corps, U.S. Army, 1956-60. Olympic Gold medallist in weightlifting, Helsinki, 1952, Silver medallist, London, 1948, Melbourne, 1956; six times world champion; recipient Disting. Service award Hawaiian AAU, 1968; Gold medal Internat. Weightlifting Fedn., 1976; named to Helms Hall of Fame, 1966; named mem. 100 Golden Olympians, 1996. Diplomate Am. Bd. Orthodontics. Fellow Am. Coll. Dentistry, Internat. Coll. Dentistry; mem. Hawaii Amateur Athletic Union (pres. 1964-65), U.S. Olympians (pres. Hawaii chpt. 1963-67, 80—), Am. Assn. Orthodontists, Honolulu Dental Soc. (pres. 1967-68), Hawaii Dental Assn. (pres. 1978), Hawaii Soc. Orthodontists (pres. 1972). Editor Hawaii State Dental Jour., 1965-67. Inventor appliance to prevent sleep apnea. U.S. weightlifting coach USSR, 1979, asst. coach Olympic weightlifting team, 1980. Home and Office: 1441 Kapiolani Blvd Ste 520 Honolulu HI 96814-4403

GEORGE, RONALD BAYLIS, physician; b. Zwolle, La., Nov. 17, 1932; s. Ronald Lee and Theodora Virginia (Baylis) G. B.A., U. Ala., 1954; M.D., Tulane U., 1958. Diplomate: Am. Bd. Internal Medicine. Intern Charity Hosp., New Orleans, 1958-59; resident internal medicine Charity Hosp., 1959-60, 62-64; fellow pulmonary diseases Tulane U., New Orleans, 1964-66, asst. prof. medicine, 1966-71; asso. prof. medicine, head pulmonary diseases sect. La. State U. Med. Center, Sch. Medicine, 1972-74, prof. medicine, 1974—, dep. head dept. medicine, 1978-92, chmn. dept. medicine, 1992—; chief med. service Shreveport VA Med. Center, 1978-82. Served to capt. M.C. USAF, 1960-62. Fellow ACP, Am. Coll. Chest Physicians; mem. Am. Thoracic Soc., Alpha Omega Alpha. Home: 1821 Willow Point Dr Shreveport LA 71119-4109 Office: PO Box 33932 Shreveport LA 71130-3932

GEORGE, STEPHEN CARL, healthcare reinsurance expert, educator, consultant; b. Miami, Fla., July 11, 1959; s. Joseph P. and Beatrice P. George; 3 children. BS in MIS, Fla. State U., 1983; MBA in Health Adminstrn., U. Miami, Fla., 1986. Provider rels. spec. Travelers Health Network, Phila., 1995—; prin. Tyler & Co., Atlanta, 1989-93; risk mgmt. cons. John Alden - Provider Group, Miami, 1994; pres. Provider Risk, Inc., Miami, 1995—; instructor U. Miami, 1995—. Contbr. articles to profl. jours. Worker Habitat for Humanity, Miami, Fla., 1995—. Mem. Am. Assn. of Physician Hosp. Orgns. (regional dir. 1995—), Soc. for Healthcare Planning and Mktg., Am. Coll. of Health Care Execs. (mem. regents adv. coun. 1995—), Toastmasters International (CTM), South Fla. Exec. Forum, Alpha Kappa Psi. Office: Provider Risk Inc 9761 SW 123 St Ste 1000 Miami FL 33176

GEORGE, WILLIAM DAVID, surgery educator; b. Reading, Berkshire, Eng., Mar. 22, 1943; s. William Abel George and Peggy Eileen Godden; m. Helen Marie Moran (dec. June 1986); children: Sarah Louise, Caroline Sorcha, Katherine Elizabeth, William Thomas; m. Pauline Mooney, Dec. 22, 1989. MB BChir, London U., 1966, MS, 1977. Various jr. surg. positions London, 1966-69; surg. registrar St. Andrews Hosp., 1969-74, Hammersmith Hosp., 1971-73; lectr. in surgery Manchester U., 1973-77; sr. lectr. in surgery Liverpool U., 1977-81; prof. surgery U. Glasgow, Scotland, 1981—; chmn. Scottish Breast Cancer Trials Group, 1990—; mem. U.K. Breast Cancer Trials Coordinating Subcom., 1992—; organizer Glasgow Internat. Surg. Forum, 1990—. Contbr. numerous articles to peer-reviewed med. jours. Recipient multiple grants from rsch. couns., charities, and industry. Fellow Royal Coll. Surgeons Eng., Royal Coll. Surgeons Glasgow, Royal Coll. Physicians and Surgeons Glasgow (coun. mem. 1991-93); mem. Brit. Assn. Surg. Oncology. Home: 21 Kingsborough Gardens, G12 9NH Glasgow Scotland Office: Dept Surgery, West Infirmary, G11 9NT Glasgow Scotland

GEORGE-LEPKOWSKI, SUE ANN, echocardiographic technologist; b. Altoona, Pa., Sept. 17, 1948; d. Charles Frederick and E. Anita (Haller) G.; m. Walter Lepkowski. AS, BS in Agronomy, Pa. State U., 1968, 70, MEd in Agronomy, Biol. Scis., Edn., 1972; PhD, Columbia & Columbia Pacific U., 1980; DS, Columbia Pacific U., 1981. Internship echocardiology West Pa. Hosp., Pitts., 1979-80; echocardiology tech. Bronson Meth. Hosp., Kalamazoo, 1981-82; echocardiographic technologist Nalle Clinic, Charlotte, 1983-85; tech. dir. Carolina Cardiology, Asheville, N.C., 1985-86; chief echocardiolographic technologist Candler Gen. Hosp., Savannah, Ga., 1986-88; echocardiography, clin. specialist, technical spl. edn. specialist, chief technologist Self Meml. Hosp., Greenwood, S.C., 1988—; cons., rschr., lectr. in field. Contbr. articles to profl. jours.; co-author: Clinical 2-D Echocardiography. Mem. choir Carolina Mountain Brass, Gospell Quartet; percussionist Images; edn. chmn. Greenwood Lupus Group, pres.; edn. chmn. S.C. Lupus Found. Recipient ACP award, Berkeley-Whittinger award for rsch. and acad. excellence. Mem. Am. Soc. Ultrasonic Tech. Specialists, Am. Inst. Ultrasonic Medicine, Soc. Diagnostic Med. Sonographers, Am. Registry Diagnostic Med. Sonographers (registered diagnostic med. sonographer, registered diagnostic cardiac sonographer), Altoona/Pa. State U. Alumni Assn., Columbia Pacific U. Alumni Assn., Altoone High Alumni Assn., IPTAY, S.C. Ultrasound Soc., N.C. Ultrasound Soc., Am. Soc. Echocardiography, Pa. State Carolina Club, USGA, PGA, LPGA, Rollings Platform Assn., Phi Epsilon Phi. Mem. Dutch Reformed Ch. Home: 531 Willson St Apt 3 Greenwood SC 29649-1560 Office: Self Meml Hosp 1325 Spring St Greenwood SC 29646-3860

GEORGES, ROBERT AUGUSTUS, emeritus professor, researcher, writer; b. Sewickley, Pa., May 1, 1933; s. John Thomas and Pauline Pantzis G.; m. Mary Virginia Ruth, Aug. 11, 1956; 1 child, Jonathan Gregory. BS, Ind. U. of Pa., 1954; MA, U. Pa., 1961; PhD, Indiana U., 1964. Tchr. Bound Brook (N.J.) High Sch., 1954-56, Southern Regional High Sch., Manahawkin, N.J., 1958-60; asst. prof. U. Kans., Lawrence, 1963-66; asst. prof. UCLA, 1966-70, assoc. prof., 1970-76, prof., 1976-94; prof. emeritus, 1994—; vice chmn. Folklore and Mythology Program UCLA, 1966-82, chmn. 1983-86. Author: Greek-American Folk Beliefs and Narratives, 1980; co-author: People Studying People: The Human Element in Fieldwork, 1980, American and Canadian Immigrant and Ethnic Folkore: An Annotated Bibliography; co-author: Folkloristics: An Introduction, 1996; editor: Studies on Mythology, 1968; translator: Two Studies on Modern Greek, Folklore by Stilpon P. Kyriakides, 1968; contbr. numerous articles to folklore periodicals. With U.S. Army, 1956-58. NDEA fellow, 1962-63, Guggenheim fellow, 1969-70. Fellow Am. Folklore Soc.; mem. Calif. Folklore Soc. Home: 906 Fiske St Pacific Palisades CA 90272-3841

GEORGESON, PAMELA ANNE, allergist; b. Detroit, Dec. 2; d. Peter E. and Tula (Athens) G. BA, Albion Coll., 1978; DO, Chgo. Coll. Osteo. Medicine, 1983. Allergist, physician Grosse Pointe Allergy and Asthma Ctr., East Pointe, Mich., 1989—. Greek Orthodox. Office: Grosse Pointe Allergy Ctr 21300 Kelly Rd Eastpointe MI 48021

GEORGIADE, NICHOLAS GEORGE, physician; b. Lowell, Mass., Dec. 25, 1918; s. George Nicholas and Stephanie (Englisch) G.; m. Ruth Katherine Sauer, Sept. 21, 1942; children—Gregory Stephen, Robert Charles, Nancy Jeanne. Student, Fordham U., 1937-40; DDS, Columbia U., 1944; MD, BS in Medicine, Duke U., 1950. Diplomate: Am. Bd. Plastic Surgery (vice chmn. 1974-75), Am. Bd. Oral Surgery. Intern Kings County Hosp., N.Y.C., 1944; intern surgery Med. Center, Duke U., Durham, N.C., 1949-50; resident gen. surgery, plastic maxillofacial recon. surgery Med. Center, Duke U., 1950-54; mem. faculty Med. Center, Duke U. (Sch. Medicine), 1953—, assoc. prof. plastic, maxillofacial, oral surgery, 1957-61, prof., 1961—; prof. div. plastic, maxillofacial and oral surgery; mem. staff Duke Hosp., 1981—, chmn. div. plastic, maxillofacial and reconstructive surgery. Co-author: Textbook of Plastic and Reconstructive Surgery, 1964, Textbook on Burns, 1965; editor: Plastic and Maxillofacial Trauma Symposium, 1969, Aesthetic Breast Surgery, 1983, Cleft Lip-Palate Symposium, 1973, Reconstructive Breast Surgery, 1976, Reconstructive Surgery Following Mastectomy, 1979; co-editor: Pediatric Plastic Surgery, 1983, Essentials of Plastic Maxillofacial and Reconstructive Surgery, 1987, Textbook of Plastic, Maxillofacial and Reconstructive Surgery, 1987, 2nd edit., 1992, Aesthetic Surgery of the Breast, 1990; internat. editor: Cleft Palate Jour, 1970-79, assoc., editor Jour. Internat. Soc. Aesthetic Plastic Surgery; contbr. numerous articles to profl. jours. Served with AUS, 1944-46. Recipient Disting. Alumnus award Duke U. Sch. Medicine. Fellow A.C.S. (chmn. plastic and maxillofacial adv. com. 1972-73), So. Surg. Assn.; mem. Am. Soc. Maxillofacial Surgeons (pres. 1962-63), AMA (vice chmn. sect. plastic and maxillofacial surgery), Am. Assn. Plastic Surgeons (v.p., nat. sec., pres. 1977-78), Am. Soc. Plastic and Reconstructive Surgeons (exec. com., chmn. postgrad. edn. com. Ednl. Found.), Am. Soc. Plastic Surgeons (recipient jr. rsch. award 1955, 1st prize sr. rsch. paper 1972, Dieffenbach Outstanding Contributions in Plastic Surgery award 1992), Soc. Head and Neck Surgeons, Plastic Surgery Rsch. Coun., Internat. Surg. Soc., Internat. Soc. Aesthetic Surgery (sec. N.Am. 1979—, internat. sec.-gen. 1984-90), So. Surg. Assn., Am. Burn Assn., Tissue Culture Assn., Sigma Xi, Alpha Omega Alpha. Home: 2523 Wrightwood Ave Durham NC 27705-5829 Office: Duke U Med Ctr PO Box 3098 Durham NC 27715-3098

GEORGITIS, JOHN, allergist, educator; b. Columbus, Ohio, June 19, 1950; s. William James and Mary Helen (Wyman) G.; m. Marilyn Georgitis; children: Nancy Lynn, Kathryn Mary, Matthew Walter. BA, Bowdoin Coll., Brunswick, Maine, 1972; MD, U. Vt., 1976. Diplomate Am. Bd. Pediatrics, Am. Bd. Allergy and Immunology. Resident in pediatrics James Whitcomb Riley Hosp., Indpls., 1976-78, pulmonology fellow, 1978-79; allergy fellow SUNY, Buffalo, 1979-81, rsch. asst. prof., 1981-84; assoc. prof. Bowman Gray Sch. Medicine, Winston-Salem, N.C., 1984-94, prof., 1994—; dir. allergy and immunology tng. program Bowman Gray Sch. of Medicine, Winston-Salem, 1987—. Office: Bowman Gray Sch of Medicine Med Ctr Blvd Winston Salem NC 27157

GEORGITIS, WILLIAM JOHNSON, endocrinologist, medical educator; b. Bangor, Maine, Aug. 7, 1947; p. William James and Mary Helen (Wyman) G.; m. Betsy Comeau; children: Jonathan, Elizabeth, Kate, Emily. AB in Chemistry magna cum laude, Bowdoin Coll., 1969; MD, Boston U., 1973. Diplomate Am. Bd. Internal Medicine; diplomate Am. Bd. Endocrinology and Metabolism. Intern Maine Med. Ctr., Portland, 1973-74, resident internal medicine, 1974-76; staff Mid-Maine Med. Ctr., 1976-79; endocrinology fellow Fitzsimons Army Med. Ctr., Aurora, Colo., 1979-81; asst. chief endocrine svc. Brooke Army Med. Ctr., San Antonio, 1981-84; staff endocrinologist Fitzsimons Army Med. Ctr., Aurora, Colo., 1984-87; asst. chief endocrine svc. Fitzsimons Army Med. Ctr., Aurora, 1987-91, 91—; asst. chief medicine svc. 21st Evacuation Hosp., Ft. Hood, Tex., 1991; asst. clin. prof. U. Colo. Health Scis. Ctr., Denver, 1984-91, assoc. clin. prof., 1991—; physician instr. Maine Med. Ctr., Portland, 1976; courtesy staff Mid-Maine Med. Ctr., 1979-84; attending staff Ctrl. Maine Family Practice Residency Program, 1976-79; preceptor Boston U. Sch. Medicine, Cmty. Medicine Diagnosis, 1978, U. Vt. Med. Ctr., Cmty. Preceptorship Program, 1979; cons. Ctrl. Maine Med. Edn. Consortium Program, 1977-79; clin. instr., clin. asst. prof. U. Tex. Health Sci. Ctr., San Antonio, 1982-84; cons. San Antonio (Tex.) State Chest Hosp., 1982-84, DOD Region III USA MEDDAC's endocrinology, 1984—; presenter in field. Contbr. chpts. to books and articles to profl. jours. Col. USAR, 1979-84, U.S. Army, 1994—. Decorated Army Commendation medal, 1987, with oak leaf cluster, 1991, Army Achievement medal, 1988, S.W. Asia Svc. ribbon, 1991, Liberation of Kuwait medal, 1991; named Golden Ball honoree Am. Diabetes Assn.-Colo. Affiliate, 1994; recipient Peter Forsham award for academic contbns. to mil. endocrinology, 1995. Fellow ACP; mem. Am. Thyroid Assn., Endocrine Soc., Am. Diabetes Assn., Colo. Soc. for Endocrinology and Metabolism, Soc. Uniformed Endocrinologists (sci. program dir. 1992-93). Home: 7938 S Pontiac Way Englewood CO 80112-3115

GERACI, ANTHONY CHARLES, internist; b. Flushing, N.Y., Nov. 26, 1963; s. Richard Robert and Ann Catherine Geraci; m. Marcy Hope Speiser, May 25, 1992. BS in Life Scis., N.Y. Inst. Tech., 1988; DO, N.Y. Coll. Osteo. Medicine, 1991. Diplomate Am. Bd. Internal Medicine, Osteo. Medicine. Rotating intern St. Michael's Med. Ctr., Newark, 1991-92; specialty track internal medicine intern Sch. Grad. Med. Edn. Seton Hall U., Newark, 1992-94; internist, med. dir. Blue Cross Blue Shield Health Ctr., Eatontown, N.J., 1994—; physician emergency rm. Saint James Hosp., Newark, 1994—; sch. physician Lakeside Sch., Orange, N.J., 1994—; chairperson Physician Group Practice Assocs., Newark, 1994—; pres. house staff St. Michael's Med. Ctr., Newark, 1993-94. Contbr. articles to profl. jours. Mem. ACP, AMA, Am. Coll. Physicians Execs., Am. Osteo. Assn. Roman Catholic. Office: Blue Cross Blue Shield Ctr 274 Hwy 35 S Eatontown NJ 07724-2105

GERAGHTY, PATRICK JAMES, organ recovery coordinator; b. Evanston, Ill., June 23, 1971; s. Martin Patrick and Maureen (Ganey) G.; m. Diana Lee Stanton, June 17, 1995. BS, George Washington U., 1993. Nationally registered emergency med. technician-paramedic, cert. procurement transplant coord. Paramedic/firefighter Bethesda (Md.)/Chevy Chase Rescue Squad, 1991—, sgt., ALS svcs. coord., 1994-96; organ recovery coord. Washington Regional Transplant Consortium, Falls Church, Va., 1993-96; procurement coord. Lifenet Transplant Svcs., Richmond, Va., 1996—. Rep. EMS Com., Montgomery County, Md., 1993-96. Office: Lifenet Transplant Svcs 3001 Hungary Spring Rd #F Richmond VA 23229

GERALD, BARRY, radiology educator, neuroradiologist; b. Greenville, Miss., Feb. 10, 1934; s. Louis Elmo and Eula (Mitchell) G.; m. Marjorie Brown, Aug. 6, 1955; children: Lucy Gerald Cook, Lee, Paul. Student, U. Miss., Oxford, 1951-54; MD, U. Miss., Jackson, 1958. Diplomate Am. Bd. Radiology. Intern Hermann Hosp., Houston, 1958-59, resident in radiology, 1959-62; fellow in pediatric radiology Children's Hosp. Med. Ctr., Cin., 1962-64; mem. faculty dept. radiology U. Ark., Little Rock, 1964-65, 67-69; dir. radiology dept. Children's Hosp. Med. Ctr., Oakland, Calif., 1965-66; mem. faculty dept. radiology U. Tenn. Coll. Medicine, Memphis, 1969—, prof., chmn. dept., 1979-95; fellow in neuroradiology Tufts-New Eng. Med. Ctr., Boston, 1971-72; dir. radiology dept. Le Bonheur Children's Hosp., Memphis, 1983-88, 91—; acting dir. radiology dept. St. Jude Children's Rsch. Hosp., Memphis, 1985-87; trainee Nat. Cancer Inst., 1960-62. Contbr. articles to med. jours., chpts. to books. Fellow Am. Coll. Radiology; mem. Am. Soc. Neuroradiology, Soc. for Pediatric Radiology, Radiol. Soc. N.Am. (councillor 1980-85), Am. Roentgen Ray Soc., Southeastern Neuroradiologic Soc. (founder, pres. 1977-78), So. Radiologic Conf. (pres. 1975-76). Home: 694 Clanlo Dr Memphis TN 38104-5067 Office: U Tenn Dept Radiology 800 Madison Ave Memphis TN 38103-3400

GERALD, MICHAEL CHARLES, pharmacy educator, college dean; b. N.Y.C., Nov. 20, 1939; s. Tobias Gerson and Ruby Rose (Weinstock) G.; m. Gloria Elaine Gruber, Jan. 31, 1965; children—Marc Jonathan, Melissa Suzanne, B.S. in Pharmacy, Fordham U., 1961; Ph.D., Ind. U., 1968. Registered pharmacist, N.Y. Postdoctoral fellow USPHS, U. Chgo., 1968-69; asst. prof. Coll. Pharmacy Ohio State U., Columbus, 1969-74, assoc. prof., 1974-80, prof., 1980-93, prof. and assoc. dean., 1984-93; dean, prof. Sch. Pharmacy U. Conn., Storrs, 1993—; cons. WHO, Geneva, 1983-84; mem. adv. panel U.S. Pharmacopeia Com. Revision, Washington, 1980-85. Author: Pharmacology: An Introduction to Drugs, 2d edit. 1981, Nursing Pharmacology and Therapeutics, 2d edit. 1988, The Poisonous Pen of Agatha Christie, 1993; (co-author) The Nurse's Guide to Drug Therapy: Drug Profiles for Patient Care, 1984, Editor: Instruction in Pharmacology: New Approaches and New Faces, 1979. Mem. FDA Drug Abuse Adv. Com., 1993—. Served to 1st lt. USAF, 1963-65. USPHS fellow Ind. U., 1965-68; Gustavus A. Pfeiffer Meml. Research fellow Am. Found. Pharm. Edn., 1983-84. Fellow Acad. Pharm. Scis. (sect. sec. 1975-77, sect. v.p. 1978-79). (sect. sec. 1975-77, sect. v.p. 1978-79); mem. Am. Assn. Colls. of Pharmacy (bd. dirs. 1980-82), Am. Soc. Pharmacology and Exptl. Therapeutics, N.Y. Acad. Scis., Soc. Neurosciences. Avocations: photography, reading, music, walking, cycling.

GERARD, GARY, neurologist; b. N.Y.C., Apr. 16, 1949; s. Victor and Sylvia G.; m. Pauline Judd, May 27, 1971; 1 child, Michael. BA, NYU, 1971; MD, Hahnemann U., 1975. Diplomate Am. Bd. Neurology and Psychiatry. Intern medicine Brookdale Med. Ctr., Bklyn., N.Y., 1975-76; resident in diagnostic radiology Mt. Sinai Med. Ctr., N.Y.C., 1976-78; resident in neurology L.I. Jewish Med. Ctr., New Hyde Park, N.Y., 1978-81; chief of neurology Winthrop U. Hosp., Mineola, N.Y., 1984-89; assoc. prof. neurology and radiology, dir. cerebrovascular lab. Med. Coll. Ohio, Toledo, 1990-94, vice chmn. neurology, 1991-94; med. dir. Neurology Ctr. Ohio, Toledo, 1994—, dir., 1994-96. Contbr. chpts. to books; guest editor: (jour.) Seminars in Neurology, 1986. Bd. dirs. Nat. Rsch. Found., Toledo, Ohio, 1994-96. Fellow AHA (stroke coun.); mem. Am. Acad. Neurology, Am. Pain Soc., Am. Acad. Pain Mgmt., Am. Assn. Study of Headache, Am. Soc. Neurorehabilitation, Nat. Headache Found., Soc. Nuclear Medicine (brain imaging coun.). Democrat. Jewish. Home: 4724 Corey Rd Toledo OH 43623

GERARD, MAYER J., physician; b. Buenos Aires, Argentina, Nov. 8, 1942; Came to the U.S., 1968.; s. Ludwig and Yvonne (Moritz) Mayer; m. Nicole Paulette Wolf, July 23, 1971; children: Daniella, Marc. BA, Saint Andrews Scots Sch., Olivos, Argentina, 1960; MD, U. Buenos Aires, 1967. Diplomate Am. Bd. Pediatrics. Intern pediatrics Michael Reese Hosp., Chgo., 1968-69, resident in pediatrics, 1969-70; resident in pediatrics Montefiore Med. Ctr., Bronx, N.Y., 1970-71, Strong Meml. Hosp., U. of Rochester, N.Y., 1971-72; fellow in pediatrics St. Christopher's Hosp. for Children, Phila., 1972-74; attending physician Montefiore Hosp., Bronx, 1974—, North Central, Bronx, 1976—; pvt. practice Yorktown Heights, N.Y., 1985—; head pediatric emergency Montefiore-NCB, Bronx, 1978-83; head pediatric primary care North Central Bronx Hosp., 1978-85; attending physician No. Westchester Hosp., Mount Kisco, N.Y., 1986—. Fellow Am. Acad. Pediatrics. Home: 60 Old Aspetong Rd Katonah NY 10536 Office: 1974 Maple Hill St Yorktown Heights NY 10598

GERBA, CHARLES PETER, microbiologist, educator; b. Blue Island, Ill., Sept. 10, 1945; s. Peter and Virginia (Roulo) G.; m. Peggy Louise Scheitlin, June 6, 1970; children: Peter, Phillip. BS in Microbiology, Ariz. State U., 1969; PhD in Microbiology, U. Miami, 1973. Postdoctoral fellow Baylor Coll. Medicine, Houston, 1973-74, asst. prof. microbiology, 1974-81; assoc. prof. U. Ariz., Tucson, 1981-85, prof., 1985—; cons. EPA, Tucson, 1980—, World Health Orgn., Pan Am. Health Orgn., 1989—; advisor CRC Press, Boca Raton, Fla., 1981—. Editor: Methods in Environmental Virology, 1982, Groundwater Pollution Microbiology, 1984, Phage Ecology, 1987; contbr. numerous articles to profl. and sci. jours. Mem. Pima County Bd. Health, 1986-92; mem. sci. adv. bd. EPA, 1987—. Named Outstanding Research Scientist U. Ariz., 1984, 92, Outstanding Rsch. Team, 1994. Fellow AAAS (environ. sci. and engring.), Am. Acad. Microbiology, Am. Soc. Microbiology (divsn. chmn. 1982-83, 87-88, pres. Ariz. chpt. 1984-85, councilor 1985-88); mem. Internat. Assn. Water Pollution Rsch. (sr. del. 1985-91), Am. Water Works Assn. Home: 1980 W Paseo Monserrat Tucson AZ 85704-1329 Office: U Ariz Dept Microbiol & Immunol/Water & Soils Tucson AZ 85721

GERBA, CONNIE LOUISE, nurse; b. Sharon, Pa., Dec. 1, 1950; d. Robert Lee and Helen Louise (Erb) Richardson; m. Terry Allan Gerba, Nov. 26, 1994. Diploma, Trumbull Meml. Hosp. Sch., 1971; BS, Youngstown State U., 1974; MS, Columbia Pacific U., 1984; quality mgmt. cert., Learning Tree U. Ext., Calif., 1995. RN, Pa., Ohio. Staff nurse Shenango Valley Osteo. Hosp., Farrell, Pa., 1971-72; staff nurse, asst. head nurse St. Joseph Riverside Hosp., Warren, Ohio, 1972-74; dir. edn. Greenville (Pa.) Regional Hosp., 1975-87; assoc. DON St. Joseph Riverside Hosp., Warren, 1987-90; DON Belmont Pines Hosp., Youngstown, 1990-91; staff devel. coord. Youngstown (Ohio) Osteo. Hosp., 1991; unit mgr. Salem (Ohio) Cmty. Hosp., 1991-92, staff devel. coord., 1992-94; quality improvement mgr. Dacas Nursing Support Sys., Youngstown, 1994—; co-dir. Continuing Edn. Assn., Youngstown, 1985-91. Contbr. chpts. to books. Mem. AACN, Northeastern Ohio chpt. AACN (life, CCRN, pres., bd. mem.), Assn. for Profls. in Infections Control and Epidemiology. Office: Dacas Nursing Support Sys Ste 204 250 Federal Plaza E Youngstown OH 44503

GERBER, DONALD ALBERT, medical educator; b. N.Y.C., Apr. 10, 1932; s. J. August and Isabel (Globus) G.; m. Marica Lynn Getz, June 13, 1964; children: Susan E., Andrew J. AB, Columbia Coll., 1953; MD, Columbia U., 1957. Diplomate Am. Bd. Internal Medicine. Intern Osler Med. Svc. Johns Hopkins Hosp., Balt., 1957-58, asst. resident Osler Med. Svc., 1958-59; asst. resident in medicine Columbia Presbyn. Med. Ctr., N.Y.C., 1959-60; fellow in rheumatology Coll. Physicians and Surgeons Columbia U., N.Y.C., 1960-63; instr. SUNY Health Sci. Ctr., N.Y.C., 1963-64; asst. prof. SUNY Health Sci. Ctr. Bklyn., N.Y.C., 1964-69, assoc. prof., 1969-95; prof. clin. medicine SUNY Health Sci. Ctr. Bklyn., 1995—; clin. asst. dean SUNY Health Sci. Ctr., 1991—; chief arthritis clinic King's County Hosp., N.Y.C., 1972—; attending physician State U. Hosp., N.Y.C., 1966—; asst. to chmn. for ednl. affairs SUNY Health Sci. Ctr./Bklyn. Med. Sch., N.Y.C., 1980-93, adminstrv. course co-dir. 3d yr. medicine, 1993—; spl. investigator Arthritis Found., 1963-66; prin. investigator rsch. grants NIH, 1966-78, 82-85; career scientist Health Rsch. Coun. City of N.Y., 1965-75, prin. investigator, 1963-75. Contbr. articles to profl. jours. Fellow ACP, Am. Coll. Rheumatology; mem. Am. Fedn. for Clin. Rsch., N.Y. Rhematism Assn. (v.p. 1976-77), N.Y. Arthritis Found. (med. and sci. com. 1971-74), Alumni Coll. of Physicians and Surgeons Columbia U. (co-chmn. class fund raising 1983-87, chmn. class fund raising 1987—, mem. alumni coun.), Alpha Omega Alpha. Office: SUNY Health Sci Ctr Bklyn 450 Clarkson Ave # 42 Brooklyn NY 11203-2098

GERBER, FREDERIC HANFORD, health service administrator, medical educator; b. Reno, Nev., Mar. 8, 1936; s. Joseph H. and Freda (Guzman) G.; m. Zenta Zebergs, Feb. 22, 1958; children: David H., Michael H. AB, Cornell U., 1957; MD, Duke U., 1965. Diplomate Am. Bd. Radiology, Am. Bd. Nuclear Medicine. Intern Oak Knoll Naval Hosp., Oakland, Calif., 1965-66; resident in radiology Oak Knoll Naval Hosp., Oakland, 1968-71; fellow in nuc. medicine U. Wash. Hosps., Seattle, 1971-72; nuc. physician Nat. Naval Med. Ctr., Bethesda, Md., 1973-76; chmn. dept. radiology Balboa Naval Hosp., San Diego, 1976-82; med. dir. diagnostic imaging Pacific Med. Ctr., Seattle, 1982—; clin. assoc. prof. nuc. medicine U. Wash., 1984—; dir., chmn. Pacific Health Assocs., Seattle, 1985-88; vice-chair Wash. State Radiological Tech. Adv. com., Olympia, 1988-94; med. adv. U.S. Nuc. Weapons Testing Program, Dept. Energy, Las Vegas, 1984-95; dir. Pacific Med. Ctr., Seattle, 1992-95. 1st lt. USMC, 1957-60; Capt. USN, 1964-82. Fellow Am. Coll. Nuc. Physicians (regent 1989-95), Am. Coll. Radiology (coun. 1979); mem. Soc. Nuc. Medicine, Am. Roetegen Ray Assn. Democrat. Office: Pacific Med Ctr 1200 12th Ave S Seattle WA 98144

GERBER, GWENDOLYN LORETTA, psychologist, educator; b. Calgary, Alta., Can.; came to U.S., 1958; d. Ernest and Alma (Tesky) G. AB, UCLA, 1961, MA, 1964, PhD, 1967; cert. in psychoanalysis, NYU, 1970. Lic. psychologist, N.Y. Clin. psychologist Hillside Hosp., Glen Oaks, N.Y., 1970-73; asst. prof. psychology John Jay Coll. of Criminal Justice CUNY, N.Y.C., 1973-77, assoc. prof. psychology, 1977-90, prof., 1991—; pvt. practice in psychotherapy N.Y.C., 1970—. Contbr. chpts. to books and numerous articles to profl. jours. USPHS fellow, 1962-63, 66-67, NIMH fellow, 1967-69; CUNY grantee, 1989-92, 45 Found. grantee, 1991-96. Mem. APA (bd. dirs. divsn. 39 sect. III 1988-92, 94-95, sec., mem. exec. coun. divsn. 39 sect. VI 1991-96, exec. com. divsn. 35 1989-96), N.Y. State Psychol. Assn. (pres. acad. divsn. 1989-90, coun. rep. 1991-96, William Wundt award 1993, disting. svc. award 1996), N.Y. Acad. Sci. (chair psychology adv. com. 1992-94), Phi Beta Kappa, Chi Delta Pi. Office: John Jay Coll CUNY 445 W 59th St New York NY 10019-1104

GERBER, HENRY WALLACE, neurosurgeon; b. Gilmore City, Iowa, Apr. 11, 1937. BA, U. Iowa, 1958, MD, 1961. Diplomate Am. Bd. Neurol. Surgery. Pvt. practice, Spokane, Wash., 1969—. Office: Neurosurg Assocs Sacred Heart Doctors Bldg 105 W 8th Ave Ste 124 Spokane WA 99204-2318

GERBER, LINDA MAXINE, epidemiology educator; b. N.Y.C., Apr. 12, 1953; d. Kenneth K. and Hilda (Butschowitz) S.; m. Michael Leit, Feb. 27, 1982; children: Benjamin Kenneth Leit, Rachel Joanna Leit. BA, SUNY, Binghamton, 1973; MA, U. Colo., 1976, PhD, 1978. Rsch. assoc. Inst. Behavioral Sci., U. Colo., Boulder, 1978; rsch. assoc. Cornell U. Med. Coll., N.Y.C., 1979-81, asst. prof. pub. health, 1982-84, 87—, preceptor dept. pub. health, 1980-84, 87-95; rsch. scientist, epidemiologist Nassau County Dept. Health, Mineola, N.Y., 1984; clin. asst. prof. pub. health Cornell U. Med.

Coll., N.Y.C., 1984-86; dir. office epidemiology Nassau County Dept. Health, Mineola, 1985-86; asst. prof. clin. community and preventive medicine SUNY Sch. Medicine, Stony Brook, 1985-87; asst. prof. epidemiology in medicine and pub. health Cornell U. Med. Coll., N.Y.C., 1987-95, assoc. prof. pub. health, 1995—; rsch. intern East-West Population Inst., East-West Ctr., Honolulu, 1976-77; cons. Inst. Behavioral Sci. U. Colo., Boulder, 1974; mem. institutional rev. bd. Fordham U., N.Y.C., 1980—; presenter numerous confs.; organizer symposia. Author: Relationship of Body Fat Distribution to Blood Pressure Level, 1990; guest editor Am. Jour. Human Biology, Vol. 7, 1995; contbr. articles to profl. jours. Mem. N.Y. Heart Assn., N.Y.C., 1980-88. Post-doctoral fellow Pub. Health Svc., Cornell U. Med. Coll., 1979-81, Fleischmann fellow U. Colo., 1978, NIMH predoctoral fellow U. Colo., 1975-78. Fellow Am. Phys. Anthropologists (career devel. com.), Human Biology Assn. (chair membership com.), Am. Heart Assn. (coun. on epidemiology), Am. Soc. Hypertension. Office: Cornell U Med Coll Dept Pub Health 411 E 64th St New York NY 10021-4873

GERBER, MICHAEL LEWIS, cardiac surgeon; b. Pitts., Mar. 25, 1938; s. Max H. and Fay F. G.; m. Barbara Schulman, Feb. 23, 1963; children: Michael L., Laurel E., Andrew D. BS, U. Pitts., 1959, MD, 1963, JD, 1990; LLM Georgetown U. Law Ctr., 1992. Intern, Ind. U. Med. Center, 1963-64; resident U. Pitts. Med. Ctr., 1964-68, Allegheny Gen. Hosp., 1968-69; resident plastic surg. EVMC, 1993-94, UMMC, 1994-95; clin. instr. surgery U. Pitts. With USAR, 1963-69. Diplomate Am. Bd. Surgery, Am. Bd. Thoracic Surgery. Mem. ACS, Soc. Thoracic Surgeons, AMA, Am. Coll. Chest Physicians, Pan-Pacific Surg. Assn., Am. Heart Assn., Am. Assn. for Thoracic Surgery, Pitts. Thoracic Surg. Soc. (past pres.). Republican. Home: 1535 El Paso Real La Jolla CA 92037

GERBER, SAMUEL DAVID, orthopaedic surgeon; b. Meriden, Conn., Feb. 19, 1954; s. Abraham and Diane Beatrice (Zimmerman) G.; m. Lori A. Gerber, May 4, 1980; children: Alyson Rebecca, Caroline Lauren, Adam Joshua. BA, Yale U., 1976; MD, Harvard U., 1980. Cert. Am. Bd. Othopaedic Surgery. Resident surgery Mass. Gen. Hosp., Boston, 1980-82, chief resident, 1986, fellow sports medicine, orthopaedic surgery, 1986; resident Harvard Combined Orthopaedic Program, Boston, 1982-86; staff orthopaedic surgeon Lowell (Mass.) Gen. Hosp. and St. Meml. Med. Ctr., 1987—. Fellow ACS, Am. Acad. Orthopaedic Surgeons, Arthroscopy Assn. N.Am., Internat. Arthroscopy Assn.; mem. Mass. Orthopaedic Assn. (dir. 1995-96), Mass. Orthopaedics and Sports Medicine Assn. (dir. 1995-96). Office: 222 Merrimack St Lowell MA 01852

GERBI, SUSAN ALEXANDRA, biology educator; b. N.Y.C.; Mar. 13, 1944; d. Claudio and Jeannette Lena (Klein) Gerbi; m. James Terrell McIlwain, Apr. 10, 1976. BA, Barnard Coll., 1965; MPhil, Yale U., 1968, PhD, 1970. NATO and Jane Coffin Childs Fund fellow Max-Planck Institut fur Biologie, Tubingen, Fed. Republic Germany, 1970-72; asst. prof. biology Brown U., Providence, 1972-77, assoc. prof., 1977-82, prof., 1982—, dir. grad. program in molecular and cell biology, 1982-87, asst. dir. grad. program in molecular biology, cell biology and biochemistry, 1987-89, vice-chair sect. molecular, cellular and devel. biology, 1991-93, chair dept. molecular biology, cell biology and biochemistry, 1994—; vis. assoc. prof. Duke U., Durham, N.C., 1981-82; mem. genetics research grants rev. panel NSF, 1979-80; mem. genetic basis of disease com. NIH, 1980-84. Contbr. articles to profl. jours. Dist. commr. Palmer River Pony Club, 1973-75. N.Y. State Regents scholar, 1965; NIH fellow, 1966-70; NIH research grantee, 1974—, research career devel. award, 1975-80. Mem. Assn. Am. Med. Colls. (pub. policy com. 1994—), Fedn. Am. Socs. Exptl. Biology (pub. policy com. 1994—), Am. Soc. for Cell Biology (program chair 1986, council mem. 1988-90, pub. policy com. 1991—, pres. 1993), Soc. for Devel. Biology, Genetics Soc., Sigma Xi (nat. lectr.). Office: Brown Univ Biomedical Divsn Providence RI 02912

GERBIE, ALBERT BERNARD, obstetrician, gynecologist, educator; b. Toledo, Nov. 20, 1927; s. Louis and Fay (Green) G.; m. Barbara Hirsch, June 29, 1952; children: Gail Diane, Stephen Ralph. MD, George Washington U., 1951. Intern Michael Reese Hosp., Chgo., 1951-52; preceptorship in Ob-Gyn under Drs. R.A. Reis, J.L. Baer, E.J. DeCosta, Chgo., 1952-55; practice medicine specializing in Ob-Gyn Chgo., 1955—; mem. faculty Northwestern U. Med. Sch., Chgo., 1952—; prof. Ob-Gyn Northwestern U. Med. Sch., 1972—, dir. continuing grad. edn., 1975—; mem. staff Northwestern Meml. Hosp., 1955—; chief divsn. ob-gyn. Children's Meml. Hosp.; v.p., dir. Am. Bd. Ob-Gyn, 1976—, chmn. 1988—, pres. 1990; chmn. liaison com. for ob-gyn., 1989. Author textbooks; assoc. editor Surgery, Gynecology, and Obstetrics, Am. Jour. Ob-Gyn.; editor ACOG Current Jour. Rev.; contbr. chpts. to books, articles to profl. jours. Served with U.S. Army, 1946-47. Mem. Am. Gynecol. Soc., Am. Assn. Obstetricians and Gynecologists, Am. Gynecol. and Obstet. Soc., ACS (bd. govs.), Am. Coll. Obstetricians and Gynecologists (chmn. learning resources commn.), Am. Coll. of Sports Medicine, Central Assn. Ob-Gyn, Soc. Human Genetics, AMA, Chgo. Gynecol. Assn. (pres. 1977-78). Office: 707 N Fairbanks Ct Ste 500 Chicago IL 60611-3042

GERBINO, PETER GEORGE, II, orthopedist, educator; b. Boston, July 23, 1955; s. Peter G. and Adeline (Marino) G.; m. Christine Agel, Oct. 20, 1984. BA, Stanford U., 1977, MS, 1980; MD, U. Pitts., 1986. Rsch. assist., assoc. Children's Hosp., Boston, 1977-82; physician USN, 1986-94; fellow sports medicine Children's Hosp., Boston, 1994-95; asst. prof. orthopedic surgery U. Cin., 1995—, dir. performing artists medicine. Physician Boston Ballet, 1994-95, Boston Marathon, 1995, 96, Pitts. Marathon, 1984-86. Travelling fellow Clin. Orthopedic Soc., 1996; recipient Nat. Merit Commendation, 1973. Fellow Am. Acad. Orthopedic Surgery; mem. AMA, Am. Coll. Sports Medicine, Am. Soc. Mil. Orthopedic Surgeons. Office: Univ Cin Dept Orthopedics PO Box 670212 Cincinnati OH 45267

GERBITZ, LOIS LYNN, medical association administrator; b. Madison, Wis., Sept. 13, 1954; d. Alfred Arnold and Lorena Christina (Marotz) G. Med. Asst. Diploma, Madison Area Tech. Coll., 1973, student in Acctg., 1994—. Med. asst. U. Wis. Family Practice Clinic, Verona, 1973-75; deli mgr. The Vineyard, Escondido, Calif., 1976-77; claims supr. Wis. Physicians Svc., Madison, 1977-81; new bus. clk. Lincoln Nat. Life, Madison, 1981-83; office mgr. Employers Health Ins., Madison, 1984—. Mem. NAFE, Am. Bus. Women's Assn. Lutheran. Home: 408 Morningside Ave Madison WI 53716-1735 Office: Employers Health Ins 2800 Royal Ave Ste 305 Madison WI 53713-1518

GERDING, THOMAS GRAHAM, medical products company executive; b. Evanston, Ill., Feb. 11, 1930; s. Louis Henry and Helen Frances (Graham) G.; m. Beverly Ann Starnes, June 18, 1955; children: Mark, David, Gail, Gene Ann. Student, U. Notre Dame, 1948-49; BS in Pharmacy, Purdue U., 1952, MS, 1954, PhD, 1960. Registered pharmacist, Ind. From instr. to asst. prof. Purdue U., West Lafayette, Ind., 1956-61; dir. product devel. Pitman-Moore divsn. Dow Chem., Indpls., 1962-64; tech. dir. new products Glenbrook Labs., N.Y.C., 1964-66; dir. product devel. Sterling-Winthrop Rsch. Inst., Rensselaer, N.Y., 1966-70; v.p. rsch. and devel. Calgon Consumer Products, Rahway, N.J., 1970-77; v.p., dir. rsch. and devel., quality assurance, consumer affairs, engring. Johnson & Johnson Products Inc., New Brunswick, N.J., 1977-88; pres. Thomas G. Gerding, Inc., Georgetown, Tex., 1988—; dir. Drug Dynamics Inst. U. Tex., Austin, 1988-95; pres., CEO Newform Devel. Labs., Inc., Georgetown, Tex., 1993—; deans adv. coun. Purdue U. Sch. Pharmacy. Sgt. U.S. Army Med. Svc. Corp, 1954-56. Recipient Disting. Alumni award Purdue U., 1984. Mem. Am. Chem. Soc., Am. Assn. Pharm. Scientists, Nonprescription Drug Mfrs. Assn. (assoc.), Union League Club (Chgo.), Berry Creek Country Club. Republican. Roman Catholic. Home: 355 Logan Ranch Rd Georgetown TX 78628-1209 Office: Newform Devel Labs Inc PO Box 52 Georgetown TX 78627-0052

GEREIGE, RANI SIMON, physician; b. Kousba, Lebanon, Nov. 24, 1964; came to U.S., 1989; s. Simon Georges and Wadad (Saba) G. BS in Biology with distinction, Am. U. Beirut, 1985, MD, 1989; postgrad. in Pub. Health, U. South Fla., 1994—. Diplomate Am. Bd. Pediat. Intern in pediat. All Children's Hosp., U. South Fla., St. Petersburg, 1991-92, resident in pediat., 1992-94, chief resident in pediat., 1994-95, faculty gen. acad. pediat., 1995—; tchr. med. students and residents All Children's Hosp., 1994—; clin. asst.prof. pediat. U. South Fla. Recipient scholarship Fares Found., Lebanon, 1989, scholarship Am. U. Beirut, 1983-89. Fellow Am. Acad. Pediat.; mem. Pinellas County Med. Soc. Office: All Childrens Hosp Univ South Fla 801 6th St S Saint Petersburg FL 33731

GERGESHA, EDWARD ALEX, health services administrator, pediatrician; b. East Chicago, Ill., July 29, 1940; s. Alex and Anne (Deja) G.; m. Mary Elizabeth Noel, Sept. 16, 1963; children: Catherine Marie, Carol Anne, Deborah Jean. AB in Chemistry, Ind. U., 1962, MD, 1965, MPA, 1990. Diplomate Am. Bd. Med. Mgmt. Resident in pediat. Ind. U. Sch. Medicine, Indpls., 1968; fellow in pediatric infectious disease U. Colo. Med. Sch., Denver, 1971; pvt. practice pediatrician South Bend (Ind.) Clinic, 1971-80, Michiana Pediat., Ind., South Bend, 1980-90; exec. dir. physicians svcs. St. Joseph's Care Group, South Bend, 1990-94, v.p. Horizon Group Enterprises, 1994-95, v.p. outcomes mgmt. and managed care, 1996—; cons. women's and children's svcs. St. Joseph's Care Group, South Bend, 1988-90; bd. dirs. Sagamore Health Network, Indpls., 1987—; pres med. staff St. Joseph's Med. Ctr., South Bend, 1984-86; mem. adj. faculty Ind. U., South Bend, 1996, asst. clin. prof. pediat. sch. medicine, Indpls., 1980—. Bd. dirs. past pres. Madison Ctr. Found., South Bend, 1986-96, CANCO, Inc., South Bend, 1973—, Am. Lung Assn. North Ind., 1978—. Major U.S. Armu, 1968-70. Fellow Am. Acad. Pediat.; mem. AMA, ISMA, Am. Coll. Healthcare Execs., Am. Acad. Pediat., Am. Coll. Physician Execs., St. Joseph County Med. Soc. Methodist. Office: St Joseph's Care Group 801 E La Salle PO Box 1935 South Bend IN 46634

GERGITS, FRANKLYN ROBERT, III, otorhinolaryngologist; b. Allentown, Pa., Sept. 10, 1964; s. Franklyn Robert Jr. and Mary Ann (Duda) G.; m. Katherine Ruth Nicolin, Jan. 7, 1989; children: Franklyn IV, Nicole. BA, W.Va. U., 1986; MS, Lehigh U., 1988; DO, Phila. Coll. Osteo. Medicine, 1992. Intern Pontiac (Mich.) Osteo. Hosp., 1992-93; resident otorhinolaryngology Phila. Coll. Osteo. Medicine, 1993—. Local pres. Students Osteo. Med. Assn., Phila., 1989, nat. region I coord., 1990, co-founder environ. awareness com., 1990. Edward D. Amstutz fellow Lehigh U., Bethlehem, Pa., 1988; named to Oustanding Young Men of Am., 1989; scholar SOMA-ICI Pharms., Chgo., 1989, 90. Mem. AMA, Am. Acad. Otolaryngology-Head and Neck Surgery, Am. Osteo. Coll. Otolaryngology and Ophthalmology, Am. Osteo. Assn., Pa. Osteo. Med. Assn., Pa. Med. Assn. Office: Phila Coll Osteo Medicine 4190 City Ave Philadelphia PA 19131

GERHARDSSON, LARS GERHARD, environmental scientist; b. Stockholm, May 21, 1952; s. Gideon and Runa Margareta (Rönnmark) G. MD, Med. U., Stockholm, 1979; cert., Ednl. Commn. Fgn. Med. Grad., Stockholm, 1979; PhD, U. Umeå, Sweden, 1986 postgrad., Northwestern U., Chgo., 1991-92. Registrar physician Hosp. Skellefteå, Sweden, 1977-79; resident dept. medicine U. Hosp., Umeå, 1979-84, resident dept. occupl. medicine, 1984-85, specialist dept. occupl. medicine, 1985-89, assoc. prof., cons. dept. occupl. medicine, 1989-90; assoc. prof., cons. dept. occupl. and environ. medicine U. Hosp., Lund, Sweden, 1990—. Contbr. sci. handbooks and articles to profl. jours. Active Amnesty Internat., Lund, 1992—; choir mem. All Saints Ch., Lund, 1992—. Capt. Swedish Army Svc. Corps. Mem. Swedish Soc. Medicine, Swedish Med. Assn., Swedish Soc. Occupl. and Environ. Medicine, Internat. Soc. for Trace Element Rsch. in Humans. Home: Kulgränden 15A, S 226 49 Lund Sweden Office: Univ Hosp, Dept Occupl and Environl Medicine, S 221 85 Lund Sweden

GERHARDT, PHILIPP, microbiologist, educator; b. Milw., Dec. 30, 1921; s. Philipp W. and Agnes (Daigh) G.; m. Vera Mary Armstrong, Feb. 24, 1945; children: Ellen Daigh, Stephen Philipp, Doris Mary. Ph.B. with honors, U. Wis., 1943, M.S., 1947, Ph.D., 1949. Diplomate: Am. Bd. Med. Microbiology. Faculty microbiology Oreg. State U., 1949-51, Med. Sch., U. Mich., Ann Arbor, 1953-65; prof., chmn. dept. microbiology and pub. health Colls. Natural Sci., Human Medicine, Osteo. Medicine, Vet. Medicine and Agr. Expt. Sta. Mich. State U., East Lansing, 1965-75, prof., assoc. dean for research and grad. study Coll. Osteo. Medicine, 1975-87, prof. dept. microbiology and pub. health, 1987-91, prof. emeritus, 1992—; adj. sr. sci. Mich. Biotech. Inst., 1985—; dir. Ribi Immuno Chem Research Inc., 1985—; cons. various univs. and corps. Editor in chief: Manual of Methods for General Bacteriology, 1981, Methods for General and Molecular Bacteriology, 1993. Served with AUS, 1943-46, 51-52. Wis. Alumni Rsch. Found, fellow, 1946-47; NIH rsch. fellow, 1947-49; recipient Disting. Faculty award Mich. State U., 1982, Pasteur award Ill. Soc. Microbiology, 1993. Fellow AAAS, Am. Acad. Microbiology (charter, bd. govs. 1970-76); mem. Am. Soc. Microbiology (hon., sec. 1961-67, v.p. 1973-74, pres. 1974-75, coun. and coun. policy com. 1961-67, 74-76), Brit. Soc. Gen. Microbiology, Internat. Union Microbiol. Socs. (v.p. 1978-82, pres. 1982-86, exec. bd. 1978-90), Internat. Coun. Sci. Unions (steering com. internat. bioscis. network 1985-91, pres. com. biotech. 1987-89), Polish Med. Soc. (hon.), Phi Beta Kappa, Sigma Xi. Home: 529 Woodland Dr East Lansing MI 48823-3273 Office: Mich State Univ Dept Microbiol East Lansing MI 48824

GERHART, GLENNA LEE, pharmacist; b. Houston, June 11, 1954; d. Henry Edwin and Gloria Mae (Mrnustik) G. BS in Pharmacy, U. Houston, 1977. Registered pharmacist, Tex. Staff pharmacist Meml. City Med Ctr., Houston, 1977-84, asst. dir. pharmacy, 1984—. Mem. Am. Pharm. Assn., Am. Soc. Hosp. Pharmacists, Tex. Pharm. Assn., Tex. Soc. Health-System Pharmacists, Harris County Pharm. Assn., Plumeria Soc. Am., U. Houston Alumni Orgn. (life), Houston Cat Club, Nat. Cougar Club, Slavonic Benevolent Order of Tex., Greentrails Ladies Club, Kappa Epsilon. Republican. Methodist. Home: 19811 Cardiff Park Ln Houston TX 77094-3031 Office: Meml City Med Ctr 920 Frostwood Dr Houston TX 77024-2312

GERHOLD, NANCY HARRIS, hospital information administrator, marketing executive; b. Ft. Pierce, Fla., Aug. 4, 1948; d. Leland Louis and Olive Joan (Merritt) Harris; m. Charles Henry Gerhold Jr., July 4, 1974 (div. Sept. 1984); children: Merritt Elizabeth, Jennifer Hayden, Charles Henry III. BS, Med. Coll. Ga., 1970. Cert. RRA. Dir. health info. mgmt svcs. Charter Peachford Hosp., Atlanta, 1977—; owner Merritt Mktg., Marietta, Ga., 1995—. Mem. Am. Health Info. Mgmt. Assn., Ga. Health Info. Mgmt. Assn., Greater Atlanta Health Info. Mgmt. Assn. Home: 3631 Lassiter Rd NE Marietta GA 30062-4119

GERINGER, ALAN, urologist; b. N.Y.C., Oct. 5, 1950; s. Joseph and Edith (Frackman) G.; children: Jason, Elizabeth. AB, Boston Univ., 1972; MD, Medical Coll. Wis., 1976. Resident in urology Columbia Presbyn. Hosp., 1977-81, fellow in pediatric urology, 1981-82; clinical instr. urology Johns Hopkins Hosp., Balt., 1987-96; physician Balt., 1983—. Mem. Am. Urologic Assn., Am. Soc. Reproductive Medicine, Am. Assn. Clinical Urologist, AMA, Soc. Study of Male Reproduction, AUA (mid atlantic sect.). Office: Ste 204 5601 Loch Raven Blvd Baltimore MD 21239

GERMAN, BERNARD, psychiatrist; b. Newark, July 31, 1914; s. Nathan and Yetta (Maltz) G.; m. Charlotte Marie Kimberg, Aug. 19, 1951; children: Steven, Amy German Levinsohn, Susan. AB summa cum laude, Harvard U., 1936, MD cum laude, 1940; Cert. Psychoanalytic Med., Columbia U., 1956. Diplomate, Am. Bd. Psychiatry and Neurology, Nat. Bd. Med. Examiners, Am. Bd. Pediatrics. Asst. prof. psychiatry N.J. Coll. Medicine & Dentistry, Newark, 1956-86; asst. in pediatrics Columbia U. Coll. Physicians and Surgeons, N.Y.C., 1947-62; collaborating psychoanalyst Columbia U. Ctr. Psychoanalytic Tng. and Research, N.Y.C., 1970—. Contbr. articles to profl. jours. Maj. U.S. Army M.C., 1943-46; ETO. Fellow Am. Psychiat. Assn.; mem. Internat. Psychoanalytical Assn., Am. Psychoanalytic Assn. (cert. in adult psychoanalysis), N.J. Psychoanalytic Soc. (past pres.), Alpha Omega Alpha. Home: 261 Dale Dr Short Hills NJ 07078-1513 Office: 206 Main St # 21 Millburn NJ 07041-1158

GERMAN, RONALD STEPHEN, health care facility administrator; b. Jersey City, May 26, 1946; s. Steve and Eleanor (Gruttke) G.; m. Diana Lynn Jones, Dec. 3, 1972 (div. 1983); m. Cheryl Dunbar Gardner, Apr. 26, 1985; children: Scott James Gardner, Brian Dunbar Gardner. BSBA cum laude, U. Tenn., 1974; MBA summa cum laude, Bristol U., 1991. With Bankers Trust Co., N.Y.C., 1969-70; dir. employee tng. and devel. personnel dept. U. Tenn., Knoxville, 1975-78; mgr. East Tenn. Orthopaedic Ctr., Knoxville, 1978—; bd. dirs. Knoxville Acad. Medicine Med-Staff Placement Inc. Mem. First United Meth. Ch., Knoxville 1987—. Served with USAF, 1965-69. Mem. Med. Group Assn. (pres. 1982), Nat. Orthopaedic Mgrs. Assn., Profl. Assn. Health Care Office Mgrs., Am. Mgmt. Assn., Am. Coll. Med. Group Adminstrs., Knoxville Med. Group Mgrs. Assn. (pres. 1992), Tenn. Valley Pers. Assn. (treas. 1987-88, sec. 1989), Knoxville Rotary. Republican. Home: 420 Dixieview Rd Knoxville TN 37922-2609 Office: East Tenn Orthopedic Ctr 2701 Kingston Pike Knoxville TN 37919-4619

GERMANN, BARBARA STARCEVICH, school nurse; b. Canton, Ill., Jan. 2, 1947; d. Angelo Joseph, Jr. and Elizabeth (Urbanc) Starcevich; m. Carl Clark Germann; children: Carl, Hans. Diploma in Nursing, St. John's Hosp. Sch. Nursing, Springfield, Ill., 1968; BA, Sangamon State U., 1975, MA, 1994. Cert. sch. nurse, Ill. Pediatric office nurse; pediatric and mental health nursing experience, sch. nurse Springfield Pub. Schs., 1984—; staff nurse in psychiatry and pediat.; sch. nurse Springfield Public Schs., 1984—; Mem. sch. district med. adv. com. Founding mem. Chatham Area Libr. Dist., regional supr. and bd. of gov.'s U.S. Pony Clubs, Inc. Home: 11477 Gordon Dr Chatham IL 62629-9731 Office: Lee Sch 1201 Bunn Ave Springfield IL 62703

GERMINO, VICTOR HUGO, physician assistant; b. Durham, N.C., June 11, 1938; s. Hugo Louis and Catherine May (Barbee) G.; m. Susan Andrews, Oct. 1957 (div. Sept. 1960); 1 child, Greg Anthony; m. Barbara Susan Brod, June 6, 1965; children: Michael Andrew, Laura Julianna. Physician's Assoc., Duke U., Durham, N.C., 1967; BA, Columbia (Mo.) Coll., 1977; MPA, Golden Gate U., San Francisco, 1978. Cert. physician's asst. Bd. Med. Examiners of N.C.; controlled substances registration cert. Physicians asst. Duke U. Med. Ctr., Durham, 1967-72, Student & Employee Health Svc., N.C. Meml. Hosp., Chapel Hill, 1972-74; medic and camp mgr./physician's asst. Fairweather, Inc., Prudhoe Bay, 1981-82; physician's asst./surg. rsch. lab. coord. VA Med. Ctr., Durham, 1982-85; physician's asst./med. adminstr. dept. diagnostic radiology Duke U. Med. Ctr., 1985-87; rsch. physician's asst. Ctr. for Health Rsch., Rsch. Triangle Inst., Research Triangle Park, N.C., 1987-89; physician's asst. Coastal Govt. Svcs./Cherry Point USMC Air Sta., Havelock, N.C., 1988-93; physician's asst./asst. to project safety engr. Gilbane Bldg. Co., Durham, 1989-91; program dir. employee health svcs. City of Durham, 1991-92; fed. officer/physician's asst. Fed. Correctional Instn., Butner, N.C., 1992; clin. regulatory compliance auditor ClinTrials, Inc., Research Triangle Park, 1992-93, Pharm. Product Development, Research Triangle Park, 1993; physician asst./asst. to project safety engr. Gilbane Bldg. Co., Durham, 1993—; adj. faculty U. N.C. Sch. Nursing, Chapel Hill, 1972-74; project med. officer NSF, Internat. Antarctic Inspection Team, 1980. mem. emergency med. svcs. com. for Orange County, Triangle J. Coun. og Govts., Research Triangle Park, 1985—, critical incident stress debriefing team, 1990—; mem. Gov.'s Com. on Environ. Affairs, Orange County, N.C., 1986-90. With USCG, 1974-81. Home: 107 Forest Ridge Dr Chapel Hill NC 27514 Office: Gilbane Bldg Co 2030 Ellis Rd Durham NC 27703

GERNER, EDWARD WILLIAM, medical educator; b. N.Y.C., Nov. 8, 1940; s. David and Anne (Robbins) G.; m. Judith E. Delbaum, June 5, 1983; 1 child, Danielle. BA magna cum laude, Clark U., 1961; MD, NYU, 1965. Diplomate Am. Bd. Ophthalmology, Am. Bd. Neurology. Intern Presbyn. U. Pitts. Hosp., 1965-66; resident Hosp. U. Pa., Phila., 1967-69; instr. dept. neurology U. Pa. Sch. Medicine, Phila., 1967-69, instr. dept. ophthalmology, 1972-74; attending neurologist Tulane U. Sch. Medicine, New Orleans, 1969-71; asst. surgeon Wills Eye Hosp., Phila., 1981-88, assoc. surgeon, 1988—; asst. prof. dept. neurology T. Jefferson U. Sch. Medicine, Phila., 1978-88, asst. prof. dept. ophthalmology, 1982-88, assoc. prof., 1988—; bd. dirs. Pa. Physicians Healthcare Plan, Harrisburg. Contbr. chpts. to books and articles to profl. jours. Lt. comdr. USPHS, 1969-72. N.Y. State Regent scholar N.Y. State Bd. Regents, 1957-61; Jones fellow Mayo Clinic, Rochester, Minn., 1965. Fellow Am. Acad. Ophthalmology, Am. Acad. Neurology; mem. Royal Soc. Medicine (affiliate), Phi Beta Kappa. Office: 834 Chestnut St (T-160) Philadelphia PA 19107

GERNSBACHER, MORTON ANN, psychology educator; b. Ft. Worth, Nov. 22, 1955; d. Larry Morton and Phyliss (Berwald) G.; m. H. Hill Goldsmith, Aug. 12, 1983. BS, U. North Tex., 1976; MS, U. Tex., Dallas, 1980; PhD, U. Tex., 1983. High sch. tchr. Richardson (Tex.) Ind. Sch. Dist., 1976-80; rsch. and tech. asst. U. Tex., Austin, 1980-83; asst. prof. U. Oreg., Eugene, 1983-88, assoc. prof., 1989-91, prof., 1991-92; prof. U. Wis., Madison, 1992—, Sir Frederic C. Bartlett prof. psychol., 1994—; ad hoc reviewer for Jour. Memory and Lang., Cognitive Psychology, Jour. of Exptl. Psychology, Psychol. Rev., Cognitive Sci. Soc., NSF, Air Force Office of Sci. Rsch., NIH, NIMH, Natural Scis. and Engring. Rsch. Coun. of Can.; speaker First NSF Korea-US Coop. Conf. on Cognitive Sci., Seoul, 1991, First Evan L. Brown Meml. lectr., U. Nebr., Omana, 1991, Third Annual CUNY Conf. on Human Sentence Processing, 1990, 68th Annual Meeting Western Psychol. Assn., 1988, among others. Author: Language Comprehension as Structure Building, 1990, Handbook of Psycholinguistics, 1994, Fundamentals of Psycholinguistics, 1995; mem. editl. bd. Jour. Explt. Psychology; contbr. articles to profl. jours. Recipient Rsch. Career Devel. award NIH, 1989, Ersted award for Disting. Univ. Teaching U. Oreg., 1986; Fulbright Rsch. scholar 1989; grantee NSF 1985-85, Air Force Office of Sci. Rsch., 1989-90, 90-91, 91-92, Nat. Inst. Neurol. and Communication Disorders and Stroke, 1989-94, 91-96. Mem. APA (Edwin B. Newman Excellence in Rsch. award 1982), AAAS, Am. Psychol. Soc., Western Psychol. Assn., Psychonomic Soc., Cognitive Sci. Soc., Soc. for Computers in Psychology, Linguistic Soc. Am., Found. for Behavioral Rsch., Phi Kappa Phi, Psi Chi. Office: U Wis Madison Dept Psychology 1202 W Johnson St Madison WI 53706-1611

GEROFSKY, DEBORAH L. DITON, speech and language pathologist; b. Bklyn., Oct. 19, 1959; d. Irving Leo and Charlotte (Abelson) Diton; m. Brian Sholom Gerofsky, Aug. 27, 1983; children: Evin Samuel, Alexander David. BA, Brandeis U., 1981; MA, NYU, 1984. Cert. clinical competence Am. Speech-Lang.-Hearing Assn.; lic. speech-lang. pathology, N.Y. Traineeship Manhattan VA Hosp., N.Y.C., 1982; clinical practicum St. Vincent's Med. Ctr., N.Y.C., 1982-83, NYU Para-Educator Ctr., N.Y.C., 1983; speech-lang. pathologist Mount Sinai Hosp. Communication Disorders Ctr., N.Y.C., 1984-87; pvt. practice Huntington Station, N.Y., 1987—; cons. Commack Communication Disorders Ctr., Commack, N.Y., 1987-89, Nassau and Suffolk County preschools; itinerant speech-lang. pathologist Suffolk County Bd. of Edn., Hauppauge, N.Y., 1990—. Mem. Am. Speech-Lang.-Hearing Assn., South Huntington Jewish Ctr. Democrat. Jewish. Home and Office: 8 Kingston Pl Huntington Station NY 11746-3807

GERONEMUS, DIANN FOX, social work consultant; b. Chgo., July 4, 1947; d. Herbert J. and Edith (Robbins) Fox; BA with high honors, Mich. State U., 1969; MSW, U. Ill., 1971; 1 dau., Heather Eileen. Diplomate Am. Bd. Clin. Social Work; lic. clin. social worker, marriage and family therapist, Fla.; cert. case mgr.; bd. cert. diplomate clin. social work. Social worker neurology, neurosurgery and medicine Hosp. of Albert Einstein Coll. Medicine, 1971-74; prin. social worker ob-gyn and newborn infant service Rush-Presbyn.-St. Luke's Med. Center, Chgo., 1974-75; social worker neurology, adminstr. Multiple Sclerosis Treatment Center, St. Barnabas Hosp., Bronx, N.Y., 1975-77, socio-med. researcher (Nat. Multiple Sclerosis Soc. grantee), dept. neurology and psychiatry, 1977-79, dir. social service, 1979-80; field work instr. Fordham U. Grad. Sch. Social Service, 1979-80; preceptor, social work program Fla. Atlantic U., Fla. Internat. U.; mem. edn. com., med. adv. bd., program cons. Nat. Multiple Sclerosis Soc., 1980-83, area service cons., 1983-86 ; pvt. practice psychotherapy; social work cons.; cons. in gerontology, rehab. and supervision, 1980—. Mem. Ombudsman Coun., 1992-94, vice chmn. 1993-94. Mem. NASW, Acad. Cert. Social Workers, Registry Clin. Social Workers, Am. Orthopsychiat. Assn. Jewish. Contbr. articles to profl. jours. Home: 833 NW 81st Way Fort Lauderdale FL 33324-1216

GERRARD, NANCY KAY, health information services administrator; b. St. Anthony, Idaho; d. Walter Arthur and Lucille Bernice (Schaat) Schroeder; m. John M. Gerrard, Nov. 17, 1989; children: Staci, Shawn, Jeremy, Stephanie. AA, U. Nev., Las Vegas, 1968. Sec. respiratory therapy So. Nev. Meml. Hosp., Las Vegas, 1966-72; dir. health info svcs. Cassia Regional Med. Ctr., Burley, Idaho, 1982—; cons. Canyon View Hosp., Twin Falls, Idaho, 1990-93. Chmn. Minicassia Health Fair, Burley, 1994, 95, 96, Raft River Health Fair, Malta, Idaho, 1995, 96. Mem. Am. Health Info. Mgmt. (cert. accredited records technician), Idaho Health Info. Mgmt. Home: PO

Box 1043 Burley ID 83318 Office: Cassia Regional Med Ctr 1501 Hiland Ave Burley ID 83318

GERRY, DEBRA PRUE, psychotherapist; b. Oct. 9, 1951; d. C.O. and Sarah E. Rawl; m. Norman Bernard Gerry, Apr. 10, 1981; 1 child, Gisele Psyche Victoria. BS, Ga. So. U., 1972; MEd, Armstrong State U., 1974; PhD, U. Ga., 1989. Cert. Ariz. Bd. Behavioral Health Examiners. Spl. edn. tchr. Chatham County Bd. Edn., Savannah, Ga., 1972-74; edn. and learning disabilities resource educator Duval County Bd. Edn., Jacksonville, Fla., 1974-77; ednl. resource counselor spl. programs adminstr. Broward County Bd. Edn., Ft. Lauderdale, Fla., 1977-81; pvt. practice Scottsdale, Ariz., 1990—. Contbr. author coll. textbooks; contbr. articles to profl. jours. Vol., fundraiser, psychol. cons., group leader Valley AIDS Orgns., Phoenix, 1990-96; fundraiser Hosp. Health Edn. Programs, Scottsdale, 1992-93; mem. com. for women's issues Plz. Club, Phoenix, 1992-93; pres. Laissez Les Bon Temps Rouler, Wrigley Club, Phoenix, 1993-96. Recipient Rudy award Shanti Orgn., 1991. Mem. APA, NOW, Am. Counseling Assn., Nat. Assn. Women Bus. Owners, Assn. for Multicultural Couns., Assn. for Specialists in Group Work, Mensa, Phi Delta Kappa, Kappa Delta Epsilon, Sigma Omega Phi, Kappa Delta Pi.

GERS, SEYMOUR, psychiatrist; b. Bklyn., June 11, 1931; s. Harry and Lottie (Timianski) Gerskovich; m. Joan J. Kessler, June 2, 1956 (div. 1982); children: Glenn J., Melissa D. Gers Rodriguez. BS cum laude, Bklyn. Coll., 1952; MD, SUNY, Bklyn., 1956. Diplomate, Am. Bd. Psychiatry and Neurology. Intern Bklyn. Hosp., 1956-57; resident in psychiatry Kings County Hosp., Bklyn., 1957-58, Hillside Hosp. Glen Oaks, Queens, N.Y., 1960-62; pvt. practice Bklyn., 1962-63, N.Y.C., 1963—; supr., acting dir. mental hygiene dept. Kings County Hosp. Ctr., Bklyn., 1962-65; dir. psychiatry Kings County Hosp. Ctr., 1971-78; candidate in tng. N.Y. Psychoanalytic Inst., N.Y.C., 1962-70; cons. psychiatrist dept. pulmonary medicine Triboro Hosp. div. Queens (N.Y.) Gen. Hosp., 1970-71; dir. acute care, dept. psychiatry Harlem Hosp., N.Y.C., 1973-83; dir. post-traumatic stress disorder unit FDR VA Med. Ctr., Montrose, N.Y., 1983-84; admitting svc. psychiatrist Rockland Psychiat. Ctr., Orangeburg, N.Y., 1984-85; dir. med. edn. Manhattan Psychiat. Ctr., N.Y.C., 1985-91, admitting psychiatrist, 1991-94, dir. med. student edn., 1991—, psychiatrist rsch. ward, 1995—; tchr., cons. in psychiatry, dept. medicine, Bklyn.-Caledonian Hosp., 1987-91. Contbr. to profl. publs. Capt. M.C., U.S. Army, 1958-60. Fellow Am. Psychiat. Assn. (Warren Williams award 1984), Am. Soc. Psychoanalytic Physicians (pres. 1989-90); mem. AMA, Am. Acad. Clin. Psychiatrists, Med. Soc. State of N.Y., Med. Soc. County of King, Bklyn. Psychiat. Soc. (del. to Am. Psychiat. Assn. 1975—), Alpha Omega Alpha. Democrat. Jewish.

GERSH, WAYNE DAVID, psychologist, cognitive behavior therapist; b. Bklyn., Sept. 7, 1949; s. Paul and Florence (Gelfand) G.; m. Barbara Marilyn Schwab, Apr. 20, 1981; children: Robert Schwartz, Jonathan Schwartz. BS, SUNY, Oneonta, 1971; MA, Calif. State U., Fresno, 1975; PhD, Adelphi U., 1977; postdoctoral clin. fellow, Inst. Behavior Therapy, 1981. Lic. psychologist, N.Y. Staff psychologist Suffolk Devel. Ctr., Melville, N.Y., 1978-81, Nassau Ctr. for Behavior Therapy, Massapequa, N.Y., 1980-81; clin. dir. Westchester Ctr. for Behavior Therapy, White Plains, N.Y., 1981—; psychol. cons. Am. Cancer Soc., White Plains, N.Y., 1991—, Four Winds Hosp., Cross, N.Y., 1993—, Almay Cosmetics Health Watch Coun., 1992—. Author: Psychological Treatment of Cancer Patients-A Cognitive Behavioral Approach, 1992; contbr. articles to profl. jours. Mem. APA, Westchester Psychol. Assn., Assn. for the Advancement of Behavior Therapy. Office: Westchester Ctr for Behavior Therapy 77 Tarrytown Rd White Plains NY 10607-1620

GERSHENGORN, MARVIN CARL, physician, scientist, educator; b. N.Y.C.. M.D., NYU, 1971. Diplomate Am. Bd. Internal Medicine. Intern Strong Meml. Hosp., Rochester, N.Y., 1971-72, asst. resident in medicine, 1972-73; asst. prof. medicine NYU Sch. Med., 1976-80, assoc. prof., 1980-83; prof. medicine Cornell U. Med Coll., N.Y.C., 1983—; Abby Rockefeller Mauze disting. prof. Cornell U. Med Coll. Office: Cornell Univ Med Coll 1300 York Ave New York NY 10021-4805

GERSHENSON, DAVIS MARC, oncology educator, university administrator; b. Mt. Vernon, Ill., Feb. 10, 1946; s. David Abraham and Lucille Clara (Cunningham) G.; m. Jo Anne Vaughan, Aug. 2, 1969 (div. May 1977); m. Michelle Renacci; children: Rebecca, Rachel, Hannah. BA, U. Penn., 1967; MD, Vanderbilt U., 1971. Diplomate Am. Bd. Ob-Gyn, Am. Bd. Gynecologic Oncology, Nat. Bd. of Med. Examiners. Assoc. prof. gynecology, assoc. surgeon U. Tex. M.D. Anderson Hosp. and Tumor Inst., Houston, 1984-87; assoc. prof. U. Tex. M.D. Anderson Hosp., Houston, 1987-88, clin. assoc. prof. gynecologic oncology, 1987-88, assoc. v.p. for patient care, 1989-92, prof., dep. chmn. dept. gynecology, 1988—; ext. reviewer Ob-Gyn Hudzel Hosp., Detroit, 1995—. Editor Clin. Consultations in Ob-Gyn, Gynecologic Oncology, 1990—; assoc. editor Ob-Gyn Clin. Alert, 1989—. Maj. USAF, 1975-77. Recipient Favorite Son award So. Ill. Med. Assn., 1995. Mem. Soc. of Gynecol. Oncologists (pres. 1996-97, President's award), Felix Rutledge Soc., Houston Gynecologic and Obstet. Soc., Alpha Omega Alpha. Office: U Tex MD Anderson Cancer Ct 1515 Holcombe Ave Houston TX 77030

GERSHON, ELLIOT SHELDON, psychiatrist; s. David and Ann (Pohorille) G.; m. Faye Deborah Saltman, Nov. 4, 1967; children: Ari Andrew, Ethan Daniel. A.B., Harvard U., 1961, M.D., 1965. Intern Mt. Sinai Hosp., N.Y.C., 1965-66; teaching fellow psychiatry Harvard U. Med. Sch., Cambridge, Mass.; also resident in psychiatry Mass. Mental Health Ctr., Boston, 1966-69; cons. Peter Bent Brigham Hosp., Boston, 1968-69, Prince George's County (Md.) Health Dept., 1969-70; clin. assoc. lab. clin. sci. NIMH, Bethesda, Md., 1969-71, unit chief, sect. psychogenetics, biol. psychiatry br., 1974-78, sect. chief, 1978-84, chief clin. neurogenetics br., 1984—; dir. office sci. Alcohol, Drug Abuse and Mental Health Adminstrn., Rockville, Md., 1986-87; dir. research Jerusalem (Israel) Mental Health Ctr., 1971-74; mem. faculty Washington Sch. Psychiatry, 1976-86; sci. adv. bd. Israel Ctr. Psychobiology, 1972-74; sr. surgeon USPHS, 1969-71, 75-80, med. dir., 1980—; Mem. sci. adv. bd. Am. Friends of Jerusalem Mental Health Center, 1978—. Author: Impact of Biology on Modern Psychiatry, 1977, Genetic Research Strategies for Psychobiology and Psychiatry, 1981, Relatives at Risk for Mental Disorders, 1988, Genetic Approaches to Mental Disorders, 1994, also articles; mem. editorial bd. Jour. Affective Disorders, 1978—, Psychiatry Research: An Internat. Jour. for Rapid Communications, 1978—, Psychiat. Devels., 1982-88, Jour. Psychiat. Rsch., 1983-93, Behavior Genetics, 1983-87, Psychiat. Genetics, 1989—, Advances in Neuropsychiatry and Psychopharmacology, 1989—, Neuropsychiatry in Genetics, 1992—. Recipient Anna Monika Found. prize, 1979; USPHS Commd. Officer's Commendation medal, 1984, 92, Meritorious Svc. medal, 1987. Fellow Am. Coll. Neuropsychopharmacology; mem. AAAS, Am. Psychiat. Assn., Am. Psychopath. Assn. (v.p. 1989-90, pres. elect 1990-91, pres. 1991-92), Nat. Depressive and Manic Depressive Assn. (sci. adv. bd. 1986-93, 95—, Gerald L. Klerman Lifetime Rsch. awad 1994). Jewish. Office: NIMH Bldg 10 Room 3N218 Bethesda MD 20892-1274

GERSHON, MICHAEL DAVID, anatomist, educator; b. N.Y.C., Mar. 3, 1938. AB with distinction, Cornell U., 1958, MD, 1963. Predoctoral fellow USPHS for rsch. and teaching, 1960-61; rsch. fellow USPHS, N.Y.C., 1963-64; fellow, instr. Cornell U. Med. Coll., 1963-65; asst. prof. anatomy Cornell U. Med. Coll., N.Y.C., 1966-69, assoc. prof., 1969-75, prof., July 1975-Sept. 1975; rsch. assoc. and rsch. fellow USPHS Oxford (Eng.) U. Dept. Pharmacology, 1965-66; prof., chmn. dept. anatomy and cell biology Columbia U. Coll. of Physicians and Surgeons, N.Y.C., 1975—; mem. neurol. disorders program project rev. com. NIH, 1973-75, Neurology A study sect., 1980-84; Grass Found. vis. prof., 1981. Mem. editorial bd. Anat. Record, Jour. Comparative Neurology, Jour. of Gastrointestinal Motility, Synapse, Jour. Neurobiology, Am. Jour. Physiology; contbr. articles to profl. jours. Recipient Borden Undergrad. rsch. prize, 1963 , N.Y.C. Health Rsch. Coun. Career Scientist award, 1970, Jacob Javits award NIH, 1985, Camilio Golgi medal Fidia Rsch. Found. 1986, medal of Francis I Coll. de France, 1990; Markle Found. scholar acad. medicine, 1968; grantee NIH. Mem. Am. Assn. Anatomists (pres. 1995-96), Assn. Anatomy Chmn. (pres. 1985-86, Tousimis prize for outstanding rsch. and contbns. to field of anatomy), Am. Gastroenterol. Assn. (State of the Art Lecture award 1986, 96), Am. Soc. for Cell Biology, Am. Physiol. Soc., AAAS, Endocrine Soc., Soc. Neurosci., N.Y. Soc. Electron Microscopists (pres. 1977-78), N.Y. Acad. Sci., Internat. Soc. Devel. Neurosci., Am. Soc. for Pharmacology and Exptl. Therapeutics, Harvey Soc., Soc. for Developmental Biology, Phi Beta Kappa, Sigma Xi, Alpha Epsilon Delta, Phi Kappa Phi, Alpha Omega Alpha. Office: Columbia U Coll Physicians & Surgeons Dept Anatomy & Cell Biology 630 W 168th St New York NY 10032-3702

GERSON, CAROL ROBERTS, pediatric otolaryngologist; b. Phila., Jan. 28, 1948; d. Milton and Lillian (Becket) Roberts; m. Gary Gerson, Oct. 12, 1969; children: Jordana, Jessica. BA, U. Pa., 1969, MD, 1976. Diplomate Am. Bd. Otolaryngology. Tchr. deaf children Bet Shemesh Sch., Israel, 1969-70; counselor retarded children Wood Sch., Langhorne, Pa., 1970; instr. dept. otolaryngology Northwestern U. Med. Sch., Chgo., 1982-84, assoc. prof. otolaryngology, 1984; provisional attending surgeon Children's Meml. Hosp., Chgo., 1982-83, attending surgeon otolaryngology, 1983-84, active assoc., 1984—; cons. Parenthesis Child-Parent Ctr., Oak Park, Ill., Nat. Found. Ectodermal Dysplasia. Contbr. articles to profl. jours. Recipient Cancer Bioassay fellowship U. Pa. Med. Coll., 1974-75, Academic Excellence award Am. Women's Med. Assn., 1976. Fellow ACS, Am. Acad. Pediatrics (mem. com. early childhood, adoption and dependent care 1984—, program chmn. 1986, 89); mem. AMA, Am. Bronchesophol. Assn., Am. Acad. Otolaryngology, Head and Neck Surgery, Am. Soc. Pediatric Otolaryngology, Soc. Univ. Otolaryngologists, Head and Neck Surgeons, Am. Med. Womens Assn., Am. Physicians Fellowship, Alpha Omega Alpha.

GERSON, LOWELL WALTER, epidemiologist, educator; b. N.Y.C., Sept. 26, 1942; s. Jack J. and Sylvia (Berliner) G.; m. Francine Linda Goldstein, Aug. 16, 1964; children: Stacey, Jeremy. BA, Western Res. U., 1964, MA, 1966; PhD, Case-Western Res. U., 1970. Asst. prof. sociology John Carroll U., University Heights, Ohio, 1968-70; asst. prof. med. sociology Meml. U. Newfoundland, St. John's, Can., 1970-74, assoc. prof. epidemiology, 1975; assoc. prof. epidemiology McMaster U., Hamilton, Ont., Can., 1975-78; assoc. prof. epidemiology Northeastern Ohio U. Coll. Medicine, Rootstown, 1978-82, prof., assoc. dir. divsn. cmty. health, 1982—; standing chair on pub. policy Can. Pub. Health Assn., Ottawa, Ont., 1974-78; mem. Mayor's Adv. Bd. for Emergency Med. Svcs., 1979-82. Author: Profiles of Nursing Care, 1975; editor: Patterns of Health: Rural and Urban, 1975; contbr. articles, papers, abstracts to profl. publs. Trustee Weathervane Playhouse, Akron, Ohio, 1981-90; adv. bd. Adolescent Svcs. Network, Akron, 1985—. Grantee So. Australia Health Commn., 1986, Robert Wood Johnson Found., 1989-90, 90-91, Bruce A. Mansfield Found., 1990-91, John A. Hartford Found., 1993. Mem. AAAS, APHA, Ohio Pub. Health Assn. (governing coun. 1992—, chair planning com. 1993 annual meeting), Assn. Tchrs. Preventive Medicine, Internat. Epidemiology Assn., Soc. Epidemiologic Rsch., Ohio Acad. Family Practice (rsch. com. 1982—), Soc. for Acad. Emergency Medicine (geriatric emergency medicine task force 1991—, pub. health and edn. com. 1994—). Home: 7385 Lacosta Dr Hudson OH 44236-1804 Office: Northeastern Ohio Univ Coll Medicine PO Box 95 Rootstown OH 44272-0095

GERSON, MYRON CRAIG, cardiologist, researcher; b. Cleve., Oct. 27, 1947; s. Gerald and Estelle Anita (Fogelman) G.; m. Joanne Steiner, June 21, 1969; children: Craig Alan, Linda Deborah. BA in Med. Scis., U. Wis., 1969; MD, Ind. U., Indpls., 1972. Diplomate Am. Bd. Internal Medicine. Intern in internal medicine Ind. U. Sch. Medicine, Indpls., 1972-73; resident Ind. U. Hosp., 1972-75, fellow in cardiology, 1977-79; prof. medicine and radiology, dir. cardiac exercise lab. U. Cin., 1979—. Editor: Cardiac Nuc. Medicine, 2d edit., 1991; editl. adv. bd. Jour. Nuc. Cardiology, 1993—, editl. bd., 1996—; contbr. articles to profl. jours. V.p. Ohio Cardiac Coun., Columbus, 1987-90. Maj. USAF, 1975-77. NIH grantee, 1989-92. Fellow Am. Coll. Cardiology, Am. Heart Assn. (coun. clin. cardiology, coun. rep. Ohio 1989-92, trustee Ohio chpt. 1994-96, grantee 1980-87, 92-94); mem. Am. Soc. Nuclear Cardiology (founder). Office: U Cin Divsn Cardiology PO Box 670542 Cincinnati OH 45267

GERSON, THEODORE FREDERICK, gynecologist; b. Phila., Sept. 17, 1920; s. Larry Aaron and Mollie Esther (Rosenbaum) G.; m. Josephine Parkinson, June 30, 1951; children: Mark, Larry. BA, Temple U., 1942, MD, 1945. Diplomate Am. Bd. Ob.-Gyn. Rotating intern Einstein Med. Ctr., Phila., 1945-46; resident in ob.-gyn. Sibley Meml. Hosp., Washington, 1948-49; resident in ob./gyn. Hahnemann U. Hosp., Phila., 1949-51; pvt. practice West Palm Beach, Fla., 1951-93; ret., 1993; hon. staff Palm Beach Regional Hosp./J.F.K. Hosp., 1951—. Capt. U.S. Army, 1946-48. Mem. Am. Coll. Ob.-Gyn., Am. Assn. Gynecologic Laparoscopists, Palm Beach Med. Soc., Fla. Med. Assn., Fla. Ob-Gyn. Soc, Palm Beach Ob-Gyn. Soc. Home: 367 Glenbrook Dr Lake Worth FL 33462-1009 Office: Comprehensive Ctr Womens Health 3537 Forest Hill Blvd West Palm Beach FL 33406-5816

GERSONY, WELTON MARK, physician, pediatric cardiologist, educator; b. Syracuse, N.Y., Nov. 19, 1931; s. Irving and Ann (Cohen) G.; m. Susan; children: Neal, Anne, Richard, Deborah. A.B., Syracuse U., 1954; M.D., SUNY, Syracuse, 1958. Diplomate Am. Bd. Pediatrics, Sub Bd. Pediatric Cardiology. Intern Cleve. Met. Gen. Hosp., 1958-59, resident in pediatrics, 1959-61; resident in pediatrics Babies and Childrens Hosp., Cleve., 1959-61; fellow in cardiology Harvard U., 1963-65; asst. prof. pediatrics U. Tex., Dallas, 1965-68; asst. prof. pediatrics Columbia U., 1968-71, assoc. prof., 1971-74, prof., 1974—; dir. div. pediatric cardiology Columbia-Presbyn. Med. Ctr.; vis. dir. pediatric cardiology Gt. Ormond St. Hosp. Sick Children, London, 1984-85; organizer 2d World Congress Pediatric Cardiology, N.Y.C., 1985; chmn. steering com. World Congress Pediatric Cardiology and Cardiac Surgery, 1989—; mem. Sub.-bd. Pediatric Cardiology, 1976-83, chmn., 1981-83, com. ofcl. examiners, 1983—; cons. in drug evaluation AMA, 1985—; cons. Extramural Affairs div. Nat. Heart Lung and Blood Inst., 1988—; James Overall vis. prof. pediatrics Vanderbilt U., 1991; lectr. Brit. Heart Found., 1991, Toby Keenan Meml. Symposium U. Md., 1994; Gladys Fashena lectr. Southwestern Med. Ctr. Dallas, 1994; Jerome D. Solomon Meml. lectr. Nat. Ctr. Advanced Med. Edn., Chgo., 1994. Author: Nelson's Textbook of Pediatrics, 1983, 3d edit., 1991; mem. editl. bd. Pediatric Cardiology, 1978-90, Jour. of Pediatrics, 1986-93, Jour. Am. Coll. Cardiology, 1990-94, Cardiology in the Young, 1990—, Progress in Pediatric Cardiology, 1991—, Circulation, 1993—; contbr. revs. to profl. jours., chpts. to books. Prin. investigator NIH grants; mem. internat. com., bd. dirs. Internat. Cardiology Found., 1993—; mem. program com. Internat. Kawasaki Disease Chmn. Cardiology Symposiu, 1989, 92, 95. Capt. M.C., U.S. Army, 1961-63. Falkner fellow U. Sydney, Australia, 1983. Fellow Am. Coll. Cardiology, Am. Acad. Pediatrics; mem. AMA (accreditation coun. for grad. med. edn. 1994—), Soc. Pediatric Rsch., Am. Pediatric Soc., Am. Heart Assn. (pres. coun. cardiovascular disease in the young 1988-90), Am. Fedn. Clin. Rsch., Harvey Soc., Assn. European Paediatric Cardiologists (corr.), Internat. Soc. for Adult Congenital Heart Disease, Am. Contract Bridge League (life master). Office: Columbia U 630 W 168th St New York NY 10032-3702

GERST, PAUL HOWARD, physician; b. Sept. 24, 1927; s. David and Hilde (Werbel) G.; m. Elizabeth Carlsen, Aug. 3, 1957; children—Steven R., Jeffrey C., Andrew L. A.B., Columbia U., 1948, M.D., 1952. Diplomate: Am. Bd. Surgery, Am. Bd. Thoracic Surgery. Intern Columbia Presbyn. Med. Center, N.Y.C., 1952-53; resident Columbia Presbyn. Med. Center, 1956-62, mem. staff, 1962—; instr. physiology U. Pa., 1955-56; practice medicine specializing in surgery N.Y.C., 1962—; asst. clin. prof. surgery Columbia U., 1964-72; prof. surgery Albert Einstein Coll. Medicine, 1972—; dir. surgery Bronx-Lebanon Hosp. Center, N.Y.C., 1964—. Contbr. articles to profl. jours. Served to 1st lt. U.S. Army, 1953-55. USPHS postdoctoral fellow, 1955-56; Recipient Research Career Devel. award, 1964-65. Fellow A.C.S.; mem. Am. Physiol. Soc., N.Y. Soc. for Thoracic Surgery, N.Y. Surg. Soc., N.Y. Soc. for Cardiovascular Surgery, Am. Heart Assn. Home: 141 Tekening Dr Tenafly NJ 07670-1218 Office: Bronx Lebanon Hosp Ctr 1650 Grand Concourse Bronx NY 10457-7606

GERST, STEVEN RICHARD, healthcare director, physician; b. N.Y.C., Oct. 20, 1958; s. Paul Howard and Elizabeth (Carlsen) G.; m. Isabelle Sylvie Meier, Apr. 21, 1987 (div.); 1 child, Chantal Elizabeth. BA, Columbia U., 1981, MD, 1986, MPH, 1987. Lic. ins. broker, N.C. Med. affairs coord. Sun Health Care Plans, Charlotte, N.C., 1987-88, cons., 1988-90; asst. v.p., dir. Preferred Provider Orgns. Crawford & Co., Atlanta, 1994, Preferred Provider Arrangements Crawford & Co., Atlanta, 1990-94; v.p. Imaginative Devices Inc., Atlanta, 1993-94, Columbia/HCA Healthcare Corp., Nashville, Tenn., 1994-95; pres., CEO Health Advantage Network, Orlando and Atlanta, Fla., 1994—, Woodland Hills, Calif., 1994-95; sr. cons. Coopers & Lybrand, Atlanta, 1995—; interviewer Columbia Coll., N.C., 1987. Editor-in-chief: Handbook Coll. Physicians and Surgeons (Alumni award), 1983, Columbian (Robert Shellow Gerdy award), 1981. Vol. Presbyn. Hosp., N.Y.C., 1979-81, St. Lukes Hosp., N.Y.C., 1978-79. Mem. AMA, Am. Acad. Med. Dirs., Am. Coll. Med. Staff Affairs, Am. Coll. Physician Execs., Am. Coll. Health Care Execs., Am. Assn. Physician-Hosp. Orgns., Am. Assn. Preferred Provider Orgns., Andover Alumni Soc. N.Y. (dir. 1986-87), Alliance Francaise (v.p. Charlotte, N.C. chpt. 1987-88). Home: 5450 Glenridge Dr NE Apt 372 Atlanta GA 30342-4921 Office: 1155 Peachtree Rd Atlanta GA 30309

GERSTEIN, ALAN R., pulmonologist; b. Springfield, Mass., Aug. 20, 1935; s. Morris Kibble and Mae (Dunn) G.; m. Bette Gerstein, Mar. 3, 1974; children: Moshe, Meir, David. BA, Wesleyan U., 1957; MD, Albert Einstein Coll. Medicine, 1961. Diplomate Am. Bd. Internal Medicine. Dir. renal unit Springfield Hosp., 1967-69; pvt. practice Maple Med. Assoc., Springfield, 1969-95; pulmonologist Valley Pulmonary & Med. Assoc., Springfield, 1996—. Capt. USAF, 1965-67. Fellow Am. Coll. Physicians. Office: Valley Pulmonary & Med Assn 222 Cavan St Springfield MA 01104

GERSTMAN, HUBERT LOUIS, healthcare risk manager, speech and language pathologist, audiologist, otolaryngology educator; b. Buffalo, Feb. 20, 1934; s. Sidney and Lillian (Ruben) G.; m. Nanci Rebeckah Wintrub, June 7, 1959; children—Evana Rachel, Gavriella, Joshua Michael. B.S., SUNY-Geneseo, 1955; M.Edn., Pa. State U., 1960, D. Edn., 1962. Clinician Pa. State U., University Park, 1960-62; psychologist St. Elizabeth Hosp., Washington, 1962-63; asst. prof. speech U. Akron, Ohio, 1963-65; instr. Tufts Sch. Dental Medicine, Boston, 1967-87; assoc. prof. Tufts Sch. Medicine, Boston, 1965-87; chief speech, hearing and lang. ctr. New Engl. Med. Ctr. Hosp., Boston, 1965-87; assoc. prof. surgery SUNY, Stony Brook, 1989-93; risk mgr., ins. investment, Seattle, 1993—; cons. in field; pres. Acoustic Corp. Am., Boston, 1971-78, Gerstman Cons., Natick, Mass., 1965-87; adj. prof. Emerson Coll., Boston, 1971—. Contbr. chpts. to books. Chmn. adv. bd. Boston Vis. Nurse Assn., 1978-87; advisor Mass. Dept. Pub. Welfare, 1969-76, Model Cities Program, 1968-73; organizer Citizens for Humphrey, 1968. Served with U.S. Army, 1955-57. Recipient 1st Gerstman award Mass. Hearing Soc., 1976. Fellow Am. Speech Lang. Hearing Assn. (various bds. and coms., chair prof. svcs. bd. 1986-87); mem. Assn. Service Programs (pres. 1981—), Nat. Alliance Stuttering (pres. 1987-88), Acoustic Soc. Am., Am. Cleft Palate Assn. Jewish. Lodge: B'nai B'rith. Avocations: theatrical producing, magician, tuba. Home and Office: 11234 NE 146th St Kirkland WA 98034

GERTEIS, MARGARET, health services administrator, writer; b. Arlington, Va., Nov. 3, 1945; d. Louis Howard and Helen (Saxton) G.; m. Richard Samuel Brown IV, Dec. 22, 1982; 1 child, Katherine Saxton Brown. BA, Antioch Coll., 1968; MA, Tufts U., 1975, PhD, 1985. History instr. Tufts U., Medford, Mass., 1972-76, Wheaton Coll., Norton, Mass., 1973, Univ. Lowell, 1975; rsch. assoc. Harvard Sch. Pub. Health, Boston, 1976-86, dep. dir. Ctr. Health Comm., 1986-89; dir. comm. and edn. The Picker Inst., Boston, 1994—; instr. Harvard Med. sch., Boston, 1995—; mem. adv. bd. Issues & Outcomes Ctr. Case Mgmt., Natick, Mass., 1994—; cons. THe Commonwealth Fund, N.Y.C., 1989-90, U.S. Dept. Health & Human Svcs., Washington, 1985-86. Author, editor: Through the Patient's Eyes, 1993; contbr. chpt. to book, articles to profl. jours. Home: 39 Garfield St Cambridge MA 02138 Office: The Picker Inst 1295 Boylston St Ste 100 Boston MA 02215

GERTLER, MENARD M., physician, educator; b. Saskatoon, Sask., Can., May 21, 1919; came to U.S., 1947, naturalized, 1953; s. Frank and Clara (Handelman) G.; m. Anna Paull, Sept. 4, 1943; children—Barbara Lynn, Stephanie Jocelyn, Jonathan Paull. BA, U. Sask., 1940; MD, McGill U., 1943, MS, 1946; DSc, NYU, 1960. Intern Royal Victoria Hosp., Montreal, Que., Can., 1943-44; resident Mass. Gen. Hosp., Boston, 1947-50; also research fellow in medicine Mass. Gen. Hosp., Harvard Med. Sch., 1947-50; dir. cardiology Francis Delafield div. Columbia Presbyn. Med. Ctr., N.Y.C., 1950-54; spl. research fellow NIH, NYU Dept. Biochemistry, 1954-56; prof. Sch. Medicine, dir. cardiovascular research Rusk Inst. NYU Med. Ctr., 1958-71; sr. med. examiner FAA, 1975; med. dir. Sinclair Oil Corp., 1958-68; dir. Washington Fed. Savs. & Loan Assn., 1972-83; internat. cons. cardiovascular diseases, social and rehab. svcs. HEW, Washington, 1968-92. Author: Coronary Heart Disease in Young Adults, 1954, Coronary Heart Disease, 1974; Contbr. articles to profl. jours. Pres. Friends of McGill U.; mem. dean's com. McGill U. Med. Sch. With M.C., Royal Can. Army, 1940-43. Recipient Founders Day award NYU, 1959, medal of honor McGill U., 1993, award of merit McGill U., 1993. Mem. Gallatin Assocs. NYU, Cosmos Club (Washington), Harvard Club (Boston), Univ. Club. Home: 1000 Park Ave Apt 2C New York NY 10028-0934 Office: NYU Med Ctr Rusk Inst 400 E 34th St New York NY 10016-4901

GESUMARIA, DONNA BEATRICE, pharmacist; b. Newark, July 22, 1955; d. Cosmo Lincoln and Nancy (Cassese) Rossi; children: Robert Cosmo, Anthony Samuel. BA in Biology and Chemistry, Kean Coll. N.J., 1977; BS in Pharmacy, U. Colo., 1986. Lic. pharmacist, Colo. Research scientist dept. biochemistry and drug metabolism Hoffman-La Roche, Inc., Nutley, N.J., 1977-78, research scientist dept. toxicology, 1978-80; research scientist dept. toxicology Rohm & Haas Co., Spring House, Pa., 1981-82; pharmacy intern, pharmacist Drug Systems Pharmacy, Commerce City, Colo., 1986; pharmacist Don's Prescription Shop, Inc., Wheatridge, Colo., 1986-89; clin. pharmacist The Children's Hosp., Denver, 1989-90, Luth. Med. Ctr., Wheatridge, Colo., 1990-92; home infusion pharmacist Home-Care, Inc., 1992-96. Mem. Golden (Colo.) Landmarks Assn. Mem. Colo. Soc. Hosp. Pharmacists, Am. Soc. Hosp. Pharmacists, Rho Chi (Sec. 1985-86), Lambda Alpha Sigma.

GETER, RODNEY KEITH, plastic surgeon; b. Baton Rouge, La., Nov. 13, 1946; s. Argless William and Jewel Alma (Rudolph) G. BA in Chemistry with honors, U. Mo., 1975, MD, 1979. Resident in gen. surgery U. Mo., Columbia, 1979-83, fellow in microvascular surgery, 1983-84, resident in plastic surgery, 1984-86; pvt. practice Springfield (Mo.) Clinic, 1986—; chmn. dept. surgery St. John's Regional Health Ctr., Springfield, 1992-94, chmn. two hosp. coms., 1994—. Contbr. articles to profl. jours. Pres. Springfield Music Found., 1989—; leader troop 210 Boy Scouts Am., Springfield, 1995—. Sgt. U.S. Army, 1968-71, Vietnam. Mem. Am. Soc. Plastic and Reconstructive Surgeons, Greene County Med. Soc., Mo. State Med. Assn., Phi Beta Kappa, Phi Lambda Upsilon. Office: Springfield Clinic 3231 S National Springfield MO 65807

GETNICK, RICHARD ALAN, ophthalmologist; b. Bklyn., Jan. 31, 1943; s. George Sherry and Helen Schrier Getnick; m. Paula Beth Hamar, Aug. 19, 1967; children: Pamela Ellen, Geoffrey Scott, Emily Lynn. AB magna cum laude, Princeton U., 1964; MD, Yale U., 1968. Diplomate Nat. Bd. Medical Examiners, Am. Bd. Ophthalmology. Pvt. practice Waterbury, Conn., 1974-80; ophthalmologist Eye Assocs. Waterbury, 1980-87, OptiCare, Waterbury, 1988—; asst. clin. prof. surgery U. Conn. Med. Ctr., John Dempsey Hosp., Farmington, 1978—; attending surgeon St. Mary's Hosp., Waterbury, 1977—, Waterbury Hosp., 1977—. Contbr. articles to profl. jours. Undergrad. schs. com. Princeton U., 1985—. Fellow ACS, Am. Acad. Ophthalmology; mem. New Eng. Opthalmol. Soc., Conn. Soc. Eye Physicians, New Haven County Med. Assn., Waterbury Med. Assn., Wills Eye Hosp. Soc., Princeton Club Cen. Conn., Phi Beta Kappa. Jewish. Office: OptiCare 87 Grandview Ave Waterbury CT 06708-2514

GETTMAN, JENNIFER E., nursing home administrator; b. Kansas City, Mo., June 8, 1960; d. Bobbie Randall and Norma Jean (Sorrell) Bears; m. Randall Jack Gettman, June 14, 1980; children: Gregory Randall, Samuel Grant. BSBA, Lindenwood Coll., 1986, MS in Gerontology, 1995. NHA, Mo. With Digital Equipment Corp., St. Louis, 1979-86; nursing home adminstr. LTC Corp., Bridgeton, Mo., 1986-87, Hillhaven Corp., Des Peres, Mo., 1987-91, NHC Health Care, Maryland Heights, Mo., 1991—; adv. bd. for geriatric program, Lindenwood Coll., St. Charles, Mo., 1996—. Seniors sponsor, St. Charles First Assembly of God, Mo., 1996—; adv. ethics bd. St.

Charles Children's Outreach, 1995; tchr. Jr. Achievement, Des Peres, 1990-91. Mem. Am. Coll. Health Care Adminstrs. (treas. Mo. chpt. 1995-96, pres. St. Louis sub-chpt. 1995, 96, Adminstr. of Yr. award 1995), C. of C., Rotary. Office: NCH Health Care 2920 Fee Fee Rd Maryland Heights MO 63043

GETTYS, THOMAS WIGINGTON, medical researcher. BS in Biology, Lander Coll., 1978; PhD in Nutrition, Clemson U., 1984. Grad. rsch. asst. animal sci. dept. Coll. Agriculture Clemson (S.C.) U., 1979-84; rsch. assoc. Howard Hughes Med. Inst., Dept. Molecular Physiology and Biophysics Vanderbilt U. Sch. of Medicine, Nashville, 1985-87; rsch. assoc. divsn. gastroenterology Dept. Medicine Duke U. Med. Ctr., Durham, N.C., 1987-90, rsch. asst. prof. divsn. gastroenterology Dept. Medicine, 1990—, rsch. asst. prof. dept. cell biology, 1992-93; assoc. prof. medicine Med. U. S.C., Charleston, 1993—, assoc. prof. biochemistry & molecular biology, 1995—. Contbr. articles to profl. jours., chpts. to books. Predoctoral Rsch. fellow Clemson U., 1981-82; NIH/NIDDK grantee, 1990, 94, 96; recipient Rsch. award Am. Diabetes Assn., 1996. Mem. Am. Soc. Biochemistry and Molecular Biology, Sigma Xi. Office: Med U SC 751 Basic Sci Bldg 171 Asley Ave Charleston SC 29425

GETZ, GODFREY SHALOM, dean, pathology educator; b. Johannesburg, S. Africa, June 18, 1930; came to U.S., 1963; naturalized, 1971; s. Judah Nathan and Fay (Lakofski) G.; m. Millicent Lorraine Cohen; children—Edwin A., Andrew R., Keith S., Jonathan D. B.Sc., Witwatersrand U., Johannesburg, 1952, B.Sc. Hons. 1955, M.B., B.Ch., 1954; Ph.D., Oxford U., 1963. Lectr. Witwatersrand U., 1956, 59-63; Nuffield demonstrator Oxford U., Eng., 1956-59; research assoc. Harvard Med. Sch., Boston, 1963-64; asst. then assoc. prof. U. Chicago., 1964-72, prof., 1972—, now dean, U. Chicago Pritzker Sch. Med. Home: 5523 S Kimbark Ave Chicago IL 60637-1618 Office: U Chicago Pritzker Sch. Med. Office of the Dean Chicago IL 60637-1470

GETZ, MORTON ERNEST, medical facility director, gastroenterologist; b. Bklyn., May 22, 1930; s. Jacob Michael and Regina (Kohn) G.; m. Carol Washer, Aug. 12, 1956; children: Jacob Michael, Deborah Etta. AB, Emory U., 1950; MS, Purdue U., 1952; MD, Wake Forest U., 1956. Intern Jackson Meml. Hosp., Miami, Fla., 1956-57; resident in medicine Jackson Meml. Hosp., 1957-58; sr. surgeon NIH, Atlanta and Bethesda, Md., 1958-60; chief resident in medicine Jackson Meml. Hosp., 1960; NIH fellow in gastroenterology U. Miami, 1960-61; pvt. practice internal medicine and gastroenterology Coral Gables, Fla.; mem. courtesy staff South Miami Hosp.; attending physician Cedars Med. Ctr. Contbr. articles to profl. jours. With USPHS, 1958-60. Mem. Miami Fla. Gastroenterologic Soc., Dade County Soc. Internal Medicine, Am. Soc. Internal Medicine, So. Med. Assn., Fla. Med. Assn., Dade County Med. Assn., AMA, Ind. Acad. Scis., N.C. Acad. Sci., Phi Rho Sigma. Democrat. Jewish. Office: # 370 14100 Palmetto Frontage Rd Miami Lakes FL 33016

GEUMEI, AIDA M., physician; b. Alexandria, Egypt, Dec. 26, 1930; d. Mohamed Geumei and Amina (Bassuni) G.; m. Ahmed H. Khalifa, Sept. 22, 1955; children: Soumaya, Amina, Anwar. MB, ChB, U. Alexandria, 1955, diploma in physiology, 1957, diploma in pharmacology, 1959, diploma in medicine, 1960, PhD in Pharm, 1965. Instr., lectr. U. Alexandria, 1956-69; asst. dept. internal medicine Southwestern Med. Sch., Dallas, 1969-71; fellow in cardiovasc. divsn. Meth. Hosp.-U. Tex., Dallas, 1971-73, fellow in pulmonary divsn., 1973-75; asst. prof. internal medicine U. Tex., Dallas, 1975-77, clin. asst. prof. internal medicine, 1978—; med. dir. pulmonary clin. rsch. Meth. Hsop., Dallas, 1976-79; dir. pulmonary divsn. Henderson (Tex.) Meml. Hosp., Dallas, 1978—. Author: Chron. Obst. Pulm. Disease, 1978, Vasoactive Intes. Pept., 1982. Fellow ACP, Am. Coll. Chest Physicians; mem. Am. Thoracic Soc., Tex. Med. Soc., Rusk County Med. Soc. Office: 701 N High Ste # 3 Henderson TX 75652

GEWANTER, HARRY LEWIS, pediatric rheumatologist; b. Bklyn., Oct. 29, 1950; s. Aaron Philip and Ruth (Bleishewitz) G.; m. Cynthia Louise Gardner, Nov. 30, 1975; children: Nathan Paul, Neil Philip, Noah Michael, Naomi Louise. BS cum laude, Duke U., 1972; MD, Wayne State U., 1976. Diplomate Am. Bd. Pediatrics, Pediatric Rheumatology. Resident in pediat. U. Rochester (N.Y.)-Strong Meml. Hosp. Med. Ctr., 1976-79, gen. pediat. acad. fellow, rheumatology, 1979-81, asst. dir. pediat. rheumatology clin., 1981-83; pediatrician Anthony L. Jordan Health Ctr., Rochester, 1981-83, McGuire Clinic, Richmond, Va., 1983-85; dir. pediat. rheumatology Children's Hosp., Richmond, Va., 1983-94, asst. med. dir., dir. pediat. rheumatology, 1986-94; pediatrician, pediat. rheumatologist Richmond Pediat. Assocs., 1995—; bd. dirs. Arthritis Found. Tri-City chpt., Richmond, 1984-93; clin. dir. Pediatric Rheumatology Programs Children's Splty. Svcs., Va., 1986-94; mem. adv. bd. Cen. Va. chpt. Lupus Found. Am., Richmond, 1986—; bd. dirs. Parent-to-Parent, 1986-91, bd. for Rights of Virginians with Disabilities, 1987-91; chmn. health Com. bd. for Rights of Virginians with Disabilities, 1989-91, Va. Bd. People with Disabilities, 1992— (chair Monitoring and Evaluation com. 1992-93); mem. Va. Coun. on Coordinating Prevention, 1990-93. Author: Primary Pediatric Care, 1987, 91, 96; contbr. articles to profl. jours. Bd. dirs. Genesee chpt. ACLU, Rochester, 1980; active Downs Syndrome Assn., Richmond, 1985—. Recipient Gen. Pediatrics Acad. Fellow Robert Woods Johnson Found., Easter Seals Soc., 1979-81. Fellow Am. Acad. Pediatrics (exec. bd. dirs. rheumatology 1991-94, sect. on rheumatology 1986—, sect. on children with disabilities 1991—, chmn. pediatric rsch. in office settings Va. chpt. 1986-95, liaison mem. com. children with disabilities 1989—), Am. Coll. Rheumatology (pediatric rheumatology sect. 1986—, Sr. Rheumatology award 1981); mem. Ambulatory Pediatrics Assn., Physicians for Social Responsibility. Office: Richmond Pediat Assocs 2821 N Parham Rd Ste 203 Richmond VA 23294-4412

GEWERTZ, BRUCE LABE, surgeon, educator; b. Phila., Aug. 27, 1949; s. Milton and Shirley (Charen) G.; children: Samantha, Barton, Alexis. BS, Pa. State U., State Coll., 1968; MD, Jefferson Med. Coll., Phila., 1972. Diplomate Am. Bd. Surgery. Surg. resident U. Mich., Ann Arbor, 1972-77; asst. prof. U. Tex., Dallas, 1977-81; assoc. prof. U. Chgo., 1981-87, prof. surgery, 1988—, faculty dean med. edn., 1989-92, Dallas Phemister prof., chmn. dept. surgery, 1992—; teaching scholar Am. Heart Assn., Dallas, 1980-83; pres. Assn. Surg. Edn., 1983-84. Author: Atlas of Vascular Surgery, 1989; editor Jour. Surg. Rsch., 1987—; patentee removable vascular filter. Recipient Jobst award Coller Surg. Soc., 1975, Coller award Mich. chpt. Am. Coll. Surgeons, 1975. Mem. Soc. Vascular Surgery, Midwestern Vascular Soc. (pres. 1994-95), Soc. Clin. Surgery, Soc. Univ. Surgeons, Chgo. Surg. Soc. (treas. 1989-92), Am. Surg. Assn., Point O'Woods Club (Benton Harbor, Mich.). Office: U Chgo MC 5029 5841 S Maryland Ave Chicago IL 60637-1463

GEWIRTZ, ANDREW ELLIS, ophthalmologist; b. N.Y.C., Apr. 26, 1954. BA, U. Pa., 1975; MD, Chgo. Med. Sch., 1978. Diplomate Am. Bd. Ophthalmology, Am. Bd. Pediatrics. Ophthalmologist fellow Manhattan Eye, Ear and Throat, N.Y.C., 1992-94; clin. practice ophthalmology N.Y.C., also Syosset, N.Y., 1984—; chmn. dept. ophthalmology East Nassau Med. Group; tchr. residents in glaucoma, L.I. Jewish Med. Ctr., New Hyde Park, N.Y., 1990—, Nassau County Med. Ctr., East Meadow, N.Y., 1993—. Fellow Am. Coll. Surgeons, Am. Acad. Pediatrics, Am. Acad. Ophthalmology; mem. Am. Coll. Eye Surgeons. Home: 519 Beach 133d St Belle Harbor NY 11694 Office: 175 Jericho Tpke Syosset NY 11791

GEWIRTZ, HAROLD, plastic surgeon, educator; b. Burlington, Vt., Mar. 19, 1950; s. Julius Gaius and Sylvia Gewirtz; m. Joan Helen Torpey, July ll, 198l; children: Charles, Alexandra. BA, U. Pa., 197l; MD, Johns Hopkins U., 1975. Diplomate Am. Bd. of Plastic and Reconstructive Surgery; cert. additional qualifications in hand surgery. Resident in surgery UCLA, 1975-79, chief resident, 1979-80; resident in plastic surgery NYU, N.Y.C., 1980-8l, chief resident, 198l-82; pvt. practice Stamford, Conn., 1982—; attending plastic surgeon St. Joseph Med. Ctr., Stamford, 1982—, chief plastic surgery, 1986—; attending plastic surgeon Stamford Hosp., 1982—; chief plastic surgery, 1992—; asst. clin. prof. plastic surgery N.Y. Med. Coll., Valhalla, 1988—; cons. plastic surgeon Greenwich Hosp.; plastic surgeon Kingstown Gen. Hosp. Plastic surgeon for Armenian earthquake victims Americares, New Canaan, Conn., 1980. Fellow ACS; mem. Am. Soc. Plastic and Reconstructive Surgeons, New Eng. Soc. Plastic and Reconstructive Surgeons, Conn. Soc. Plastic and Reconstructive Surgeons, Conn. Med. Soc., Rotary, Phi Beta Kappa. Office: 70 Mill River St Stamford CT 06902-3725 also: 2 1/2 Deerfield Dr Greenwich CT 06830

GEWIRTZ, JOAN (LUBAN), psychotherapist; b. Seattle; d. Joseph and Sarah (Gann) Luban; m. Arthur Gewirtz; children: Shelly Ruth, Laurence Paul, Jerry Martin. BA magna cum laude, Bklyn. Coll.; MSS, Bryn Mawr Coll., 1964; postgrad., Columbia U. Lic. psychotherapist; bd. cert. diplomate. Psychotherapist, supr. Irving Schwartz Inst. Phila., 1964-72; field instr. clin. practice grad. sch. Bryn Mawr (Pa.) Coll., 1967-72; co-leader tng. seminars in adult individual psychotherapy for psychologists, psychiatrists and interns, 1967-72, leader tng. seminars in adult group psychotherapy for psychologists, 1967-72; pvt. practice psychotherapist individuals and families, personal growth and devel., treatment chronic fatigue syndrome Bala Cynwyd, Pa., 1968—; psychiat. cons. schs., supr. interns Irving Schwartz Inst. Phila., 1970-72; cons. North Am. Publ. Co., 1977-78; mem. advanced profl. study groups psychiat. lit. and diagnosis/treatment pvt. practice cases. Contbr. articles to profl. jours. Recipient Chapel of Four Chaplains Legion of Honor award, 1987; scholar grad. sch. Bryn Mawr Coll., Columbia U. Mem. Am. Group Psychotherapy Assn., Am. Orthopsychiat. Assn., Am. Assn. Sex Educators, Counselors and Therapists, Alpha Kappa Delta. Home and Office: 405 Bala Cir Bala Cynwyd PA 19004-2616

GEWIRTZ, MINDY L., organizational and human relations consultant; b. N.Y.C., Mar. 19, 1951; d. Martin and Miriam (Altman) Lebovicz; m. Gershon C. Gewirtz, Sept. 7, 1971; children: Yussy, Henoch, Sora Leah, Adina, Doniel. MPS, N.Y. Inst. Tech., 1977; MSW, SUNY, Albany, 1981; PhD in Orgnl. Sociology, Boston U., 1995. Lic. ind. clin. social worker; diplomate Am. Bd. Clin. Social Workers. Project coord. Ringel Inst. Gerontology SUNY-Albany, 1980-82; coord. sr. adult dept. Jewish Family Svcs., Albany, 1983-84; dir. eldercare connection long distance caregiving svc. Jewish Family and Children's Svc., Boston, 1984-93; pres. Strategic Bus. Solutions, Boston, 1988—; postgrad. fellow orgnl. devel. & human resources cons. Boston Inst. Psychotherapy, 1990; adj. asst. prof. Boston U. Sch. Social Work; cons. Ibis Cons. Group, Cambridge, 1990—; orgn. and mgmt. cons. Boston Digital Equipment Corp., Boston, 1988-92; orgnl. cons. Malden Mills, Lawrence, Mass., 1992—. Author: (with E. and N. Newman) Elderly Criminals, 1984; assoc. author: Human Dilemmas in Work Organizations, 1994; contbr. articles to profl. jours. and pubs. Mem. Boston Work and Family Forum, New England Human Resources Assn., Greater Boston Orgnl. Devel. Network. Recipient Max Siporin Social Work fellow. Mem. NASW, ACSW (bd. cert. diplomate), Am. Assn. Bus. Women (career advancement fellow), Phi Beta Kappa. Home: 23 Browne St Brookline MA 02146-3804

GEWIRTZMAN, GARRY BRUCE, dermatologist; b. Albany, N.Y., Mar. 26, 1947; s. Benjamin Joseph and Mary (Lebowitz) G.; m. Sheila Ellen Cuba, July 4, 1971; children: Beth Lauren, Aron Jeffrey. BA, Rutgers U., 1969; MD, Albany Med. Coll., 1973. Diplomate Am. Bd. Dermatology. Intern U. Miami (Fla.), 1973-74; resident in dermatology SUNY-Buffalo, 1974-77; practice medicine specializing in dermatology; attending staff Humana Hosp., Plantation (Fla.) Gen. Hosp.; pres. Arbet Enterprises Inc. Author: Smooth as a Baby's Bottom, Skin Care Tips and Skin Sense; contbr. articles to profl. jours. Fellow Am. Acad. Dermatology; mem. AMA, Fla. Med. Assn., Broward County Med. Assn., Fla. Soc. Dermatology. Soc. Dermatol. Genetics, Broward Bus. and Profl. Assn. (pres.), Broward County Dermatol. Soc. Office: Bennett Med Park 201 NW 82nd Ave Plantation FL 33324-7808

GEYMAN, JOHN PAYNE, physician, educator; b. Santa Barbara, Calif., Feb. 9, 1931; s. Milton John and Betsy (Payne) G.; m. Eugenia Clark Deichler, June 9, 1956; children: John Matthew, James Caleb, William Sabin. A.B. in Geology, Princeton U., 1952; M.D., U. Calif., San Francisco, 1960. Diplomate: Am. Bd. Family Practice Intern L.A. County Gen. Hosp., 1960-61; resident in gen. practice Sonoma County Hosp., Santa Rosa, Calif., 1961-63; pvt. practice specializing in family practice Mt. Shasta, Calif., 1963-69; dir. family practice residency program Community Hosp. Sonoma County, Santa Rosa, 1969-71; assoc. prof. family practice, chmn. div. family practice U. Utah, 1971-72; prof., vice chmn. dept. family practice U. Calif., Davis, 1972-77; prof., chmn. dept. family medicine U. Wash., 1977-90, prof. family medicine, 1990-93; prof. family medicine emeritus, 1993—. Author: The Modern Family Doctor and Changing Medical Practice, 1971, Family Practice: Foundation of Changing Health Care, 1980, 2d edit., 1985; editor: Content of Family Practice, 1976, Family Practice in the Medical School, 1977, Research in Family Practice, 1978, Preventive Medicine in Family Practice, 1979, Profile of the Residency Trained Family Physician in the U.S, 1970-79, Funding of Patient Care, Education and Research in Family Practice, 1981, The Content of Family Practice Current Status and Future Trends, 1982, Archives of Family Practice, 1980, 81, 82; founding editor Jour. Family Practice, 1973-90; editor Jour. Am. Bd. Family Practice, 1990—; co-editor: Behavioral Science in Family Practice, 1980; editor: Family Practice: An International Perspective in Developed Countries, 1983. Served to lt. (j.g.) USN, 1952-55, PTO. Recipient Gold-headed Cane award U. Calif. Sch. Medicine, 1960. Mem. AMA, Am. Acad. Family Physicians, Soc. Tchrs. Family Medicine, Inst. Medicine of Nat. Acad. Scis., Royal Soc. Medicine. Unitarian. Home: 4909 Hannah Rd # C Friday Harbor WA 98250-9422 Office: U Wash Sch Medicine Dept Family Medicine Inter Island Med Ctr Friday Harbor WA 98250

GFELLER, DONNA KVINGE, clinical psychologist; b. Chgo., Jan. 15, 1959; d. Milton Melvin and Doris Ann (Chapman) Kvinge; m. Jeffrey Donald Gfeller, Aug. 2, 1986. BS in Biol. Scis., Ill. State U., 1980, MS in Clin. Psychology, 1984; PhD in Clin. Psychology, Ohio U., 1987. Lic. psychologist. Staff psychologist Cardinal Glennon Children's Hosp., St. Louis, 1986-87, sr. psychologist, 1988-89, dir. dept. psychology, 1990—. Mem. APA (divsn. clin. psychology, sect. on clin. child psychology), Soc. Pediatric Psychology, World Wildlife Fund. Office: Cardinal Glennon Children's Hosp 1465 S Grand Blvd Saint Louis MO 63104-1003

GHALI, ANWAR YOUSSEF, psychiatrist, educator; b. Cairo, May 30, 1944; came to U.S., 1974, naturalized, 1980; s. Youssef and Insaf Wahba (Soliman) G.; m. Violette Fouad Saleh, May 23, 1968; 1 child, Susie. MD, Cairo U., 1966, DPM, 1970, DM, 1971. Diplomate Am. Bd. Psychiatry and Neurology; cert. adminstrv. psychiatry. Registrar in psychiatry Woodilee Hosp., Glasgow, Scotland, 1973-74; resident in psychiatry N.J. Med. Sch., Newark, 1974-77, instr., 1977-78, clin. asst. prof., 1978-79, asst. prof., 1979-83, clin. assoc. prof., 1983—; chief Outpatient Dept.-Community Mental Health Ctr., N.J. Med. Sch., Newark, 1978-86; dir. Emergency Psychiat. Svcs. Univ. Hosp., U. Medicine and Dentistry of N.J., Newark, 1986-87; med. dir. Profl. Counsel Ctr., Westfield, N.J., 1984-87; med. chief ambulatory psychiat. svcs. Elizabeth (N.J.) Gen. Hosp., 1987-89; dir. psychiat. tng. VA Med. Ctr., East Orange, N.J., 1989—, asst. chief psychiatry, 1990-91, assoc. chief psychiatry, 1991—. Contbr. articles to profl. jours. Recipient Exceptional Merit award Coll. Medicine & Dentistry, Newark, 1981. Mem. AMA, Christian Med. Soc., Am. Psychiat. Assn., N.J. Psychiat. Assn., N.Y. Acad. Scis. Republican. Presbyterian. Home: 22 Benvenue Ave West Orange NJ 07052-3202

GHATE, VIJAY RAMKRISHNA, physician, educator, consultant; b. Nasik, India, Oct. 14, 1937; s. Ramkrishna V. and Manorama R. (Moghe) G.; m. Sunanda V. Patankar, June 5, 1966; children: Sujata, Jayashiri. MB, BJ Med. Coll., U. Poona, 1960; MS in Otolaryngology, U. Bombay Grant Med. Coll., 1964; postgrad. Coll. Physicians and Surgeons, Bombay, 1964. Intern, Sassoon Hosp., Poona, India, 1960-51, resident, 1961-62; resident MGM Hosp., Bombay, 1962-65, D.Dix Hosp., Raleigh, N.C., 1971-74; ear, nose, throat surgeon M.G.M. Hosp., Bombay, India, 1965-67; staff physician Central State Hosp., Petersburg, Va., 1967-69, D. Dix Hosp., Raleigh, N.C., 1969-71; clin. dir. Wilson Green Mental Health Ctr., Wilson, N.C., 1974—; chmn. dept. psychiatry Wilson Meml. Hosp. (N.C.); pvt. practice medicine specializing in psychiatry, Wilson, 1974—; clin. asst. prof. psychiatry East Carolina U., Greenville, 1977—; cons. disability div. State of N.C., Raleigh, 1982—. Recipient Shankarseth prize, Urankan prize U. Poona. 1960. Diplomate Am. Bd. Psychiatry and Neurology. Mem. N.C. Neuropsychiat. Assn., Am. Psychiat. Assn. (cert. in adminstrv. psychiatry).

GHEBREHIWET, BERHANE, immunologist, educator; b. Asmara, Eritrea, Sept. 28, 1946. D.V.M., Sch. Vet. Medicine, Warsaw, Poland, 1971; MVSc, Ecole Nationale Vétérinaire D'Alfort, France, 1973; DSc, U. Paris VII, 1974. Rsch. assoc. dept. molecular immunology Scripps Clinic and Rsch. Found., La Jolla, Calif., 1974-79; asst. prof. medicine SUNY, Stony Brook, 1979-85, asst. prof. pathology, 1983-85, assoc. prof. medicine and pathology, 1985-92, prof. medicine and pathology, 1992—; vis. scientist Oxford U., 1991-92, 95; mem. immunology, virology, pathology study sect. NIH, 1992-96. Contbr. articles to profl. jours. Fogarty Internat. sr. fellow, Oxford, Eng., 1991-92, Burroughs Wellcome Rsch. fellow, Oxford U., Eng., 1995. Mem. AAAS, Am. Assn. Immunology, Am. Tissue Culture Assn., Am. Fedn. Clin. Rsch., N.Y. Acad. Sci., Am. Chem. Soc., Am. Assn. Vet. Immunology, Clin. Immunology Soc., Soc. Leukocyte Biology, The Planetary Soc., Sigma Xi. Coptic Orthodox. Office: SUNY Stony Brook HSC T-16 Rm 040 New York NY 11794-8161

GHERARDI, GHERARDO J., pathologist; b. Lucca, Italy, July 1, 1921; came to U.S., 1933; s. Mario E. and Maria (Gilli) G.; m. Celeste Tranfaglia, Sept. 16, 1957; children: Roberta, Ronald, Mark, Peter. BA, Princeton U., 1942; MD, Columbia U., 1945. Diplomate Am. Bd. Pathology. Pathologist in charge, assoc. prof. pathology Tufts N.E. Med. Ctr., Boston, 1954-70; assoc. prof. pathology Tufts Med. Sch., 1954-70; sr. pathologist Farmingham (Mass.) Union Hosp., 1970-93; assoc. prof. pathology Boston U. Sch. Medicine, 1970—. Capt. AUS, 1945-48. Fellow Coll. Am. Pathologists; mem. N.E. Soc. Pathologists (past pres.).

GHERTNER, JOHN LORY, physician; b. Nashville, May 4, 1949; s. Leonard C. and Jean (Bloom) G.; m. Nancy Ghertner; children: Asher, Robin, Zoe. BA, Colby Coll., 1971; MD, U. Tenn., Memphis, 1974. Pvt. practice, Williamson, N.Y.; med. dir. Myers Cmty. Hosp., Sodus, N.Y., 1985—, Blossomview Nursing Home, Sodus, 1985—, Wayne County Pub. Health Dept., Lyons, N.Y., 1994—. Office: Williamson Med PC 4418 Ridge Rd Williamson NY 14589-9375

GHODSE, ABDOL HAMID, psychiatry educator; b. Shahrood, Iran, Apr. 30, 1938; arrived in Eng., 1968; s. Abdol Rahim Ghods and Batool Daneshmand; m. Barbara Bailin, June 30, 1973; children: Amir Hossein, Nassrin, Ali Reza. MD, U. Tabriz, Iran, 1965; PhD, U. London, 1976. Diploma psychol. medicine, Eng. Rsch. psychiatrist Inst. Psychiatry, London, 1971-74; cons. psychiatrist St. Thomas' Hosp., London, 1978-88, St. George's Hosp., London, 1978—; chmn. dept. addictive behavior St. George's Med. Sch., London, 1987—; dir. Regional Drug and Alcohol Svcs., 1987—; mem. Faculty Pub. Health Medicine; mem. Internat. Narcotics Control Bd., 1992—, pres., 1993-95; mem. expert adv. panel WHO, 1979—; dir. European Collaborating Ctr. in Addiction Studies, 1992—. Co-author: Misuse of Drugs, 2d edit., 1991, supplement, 1993; author: Drugs and Addictive Behavior - A Guide to Treatment, 2d edit., 1995; editor: Psychoactive Drugs - Improving Prescribing Practices, 1988 (translated into 8 other langs.); inventor pupillometer for measurement of anisocoria. Lt. Health Corps Iranian armed forces, 1965-67. Named McLeod Prof., South Australia, 1990. Fellow Royal Coll. Psychiatrists (chmn. sustance abuse sect. mem. coun. and ct. electors), Royal Coll. Physicians; mem. Assn. Profs. Psychiatry (coord.), Athenaeum Club. Moslem. Office: St George's Hosp Med Sch, Cranmer Terr, London SW17 0RE, England

GIAMBRONE, ANGELA C., psychologist; b. Scranton, Pa., Oct. 9, 1960; d. Alfonzo William and Ann Marie (Ellis) G. BS, Marywood Coll., 1983, MA, 1986. Child care worker Keystone City Residence, Scranton, 1983-85; from social rehab. counselor to psychol. assoc. trainee Northeast Tri-County Mental Health/Mental Retardation Ctr., Carbondale, Pa., 1985-87; masters clinician Scranton Counseling Ctr., 1987-93; psychol. cons. Pa. Bur. Disability Determination, Wilkes-Barre, 1993-94; psychol. svcs. assoc. State Correctional Inst. Waymart-Pa. Dept. Corrections, 1993-96, psychologist, 1996—; tng. com. Pa. Dept. Corrections, 1995—, cert. suicide prevention trainer, 1994—, critical incident stress mgmt. team, 1994—. Mem. Pa. Psychol. Assn. Democrat. Roman Catholic. Office: State Correctional Inst Waymart PO Box 256 Waymart PA 18472

GIANAKOS, PATRICIA ANN, social worker; b. Warren, Ohio, Oct. 14, 1948; d. Jimmie Lambros and Julie (Mougianis) G. BA in Pre-Profl. Social Work, Kent State U., 1970. Lic. social worker. Aid for aged workers Trumbull County Human Svcs. Dept., Warren, 1970-71, social svc. worker, 1971-88, adult svcs. worker, 1988—, mem. excellence com., 1991, 93, contbg. editor County Line newsletter, 1991—, mem. awards com., 1991-93, chmn. awards com., 1993—; mem. Trumbull County Task Force on Wellness in Later Yrs., Warren, 1991-92. Vol. St. Demetrios Festival, Warren, 1979—; mem. Dem. Nat. Com., Warren, 1992—, Ladies Philoptochos Soc., Warren, 1979—; co-founder, adviser Sr. Citizens Orgn. St. Demetrios Ch., Warren, 1979—. Mem. ACA, NASW, Am. Bus. Women's Assn., Assn. for Adult Devel. and Aging, Nat. Com. for Prevention of Elder Abuse. Greek Orthodox. Home: 1786 Dodge Dr NW Warren OH 44485-1823 Office: Trumbull Cou Human Svcs 150 S Park Ave Warren OH 44481-1018

GIANCOTTI, FILIPPO GIUSTO, cell and molecular biologist; b. Rome, Mar. 25, 1958. MD, U. Torino, Italy, 1981, PhD, 1987. Diplomate Italian Bd. Hematology/Oncology. Intern and resident Dept. Hematology-U. Torino Sch. Medicine, 1979-83; sr. rsch. fellow LaJolla (Calif.) Cancer Rsch. Found., 1987-91; asst. prof. Sch. of Medicine, NYU, 1991—; spkr. in field. Ad hoc reviewer NIH Biol. Scis., 1994—; contbr. articles to profl. jours. including Cell, European Molecular Biology Orgn. Jour., Jour. of Cell Biology, Molecular Biology of The Cell. Sr. postdoctoral fellowship European Molecular Biology Orgn., 1987-89, postdoctoral fellowship European Orgn. for Rsch. and Treatment Cancer and Nat. Cancer Inst., 1987-89; postdoctoral fellowship Am. Cancer Soc., 1989-90, Arthritis Found., 1990-93, Whitehead Presdl. fellowship, 1992-93; recipient Lucille P. Markey Charitable Trust award, 1992—, Established Investigatorship award Am. Heart Assn., 1996. Mem. AAAS, ASCB. Office: Kaplan Comprehensive Cancer Ctr MSB 548 NYU Sch Medicine 550 First Ave New York NY 10016*

GIANGOLA, GARY, surgeon; b. N.Y.C., Feb. 2, 1955; s. John and Elena (Zollo) G.; m. Joan Evelyn Feierabend, Aug. 20, 1977; children: Gary, Vincent, Paul. BA, NYU, 1976, MD, 1980. Diplomate Am. Bd. Surgery. Intern in surgery NYU Med. Ctr., N.Y.C., 1980-81, resident in surgery, 1981-85, fellow in vascular surgery, 1985-86, asst. prof. surgery, 1986—, attending surgeon, 1986—; attending surgeon Bellevue Hosp. Med. Ctr., N.Y.C., 1986—; svc. chief, vascular surgery Manhattan VA Med. Ctr., N.Y.C., 1990—; chief vascular surgery Manhattan VA Med. Ctr., N.Y.C., 1990—. Fellow Am. Coll. Surgeons; mem. Peripheral Vascular Surgery Soc. (pres. elect 1995, pres. 1996—), Internat. Soc. Cardio Vascular Surgery, Ea. Vascular Surg. Soc., N.Y. Cardiovascular Surg. Soc. Office: NYU Med Ctr 530 1st Ave New York NY 10016-6402

GIANINI, GLENN DAVID, osteopathic physician; b. New Haven, Apr. 13, 1957; s. Joseph Jr. and Ann Virginia (Maffeo) G.; m. Deborah Mary Garabedian, June 11, 1983; children: Gerard Andrew Malo, Lucas Henry Malo, Denise Andrea. BS in Biology, Fairfield U., 1979; DO, U. New Eng., 1983. Diplomate Am. Bd. Ob-Gyn. Intern Osteo. Hosp. of Maine, Inc., Portland, 1983-84; resident in Ob/Gyn David Grant USAF Med. Ctr., Travis AFB, Calif., 1987-91; officer USAF, 1984, advanced through grades to maj.; chief ob-gyn. svcs. 39th Tactical Group Hosp., Incirlik Air Base, Turkey, 1991-93; resigned, 1993; pvt. practice, Augusta, Maine, 1993—; mem. assoc. clin. staff Kennebec Valley Med. Ctr., Augusta, 1993—. Fellow ACOG (treas. Maine sect. 1995—); mem. Am. Osteo. Assn., Maine Osteo. Assn. Roman Catholic. Office: Kennebec Valley Ob-Gyn 5 Caldwell Rd Augusta ME 04330

GIANNINI, A. JAMES, psychiatrist, educator, researcher; b. Youngstown, Ohio, June 11, 1947; s. Matthew and Grace Carla (Nistri) G.; children: Juliette Nicole, Jocelyn Danielle. B.S., Youngstown State U., Ohio, 1970; M.D., U. Pitts., 1974; postgrad., Yale U., 1974-78, Goldsmiths Coll., U. London. Diplomate Nat. Bd. Med. Examiners. Intern St. Elizabeth Med. Ctr., Youngstown, 1974; resident dept. psychiatry Yale U., New Haven, 1975-78, chief resident, 1977-78; assoc. psychiatrist Elmcrest Psychiat. Inst., Portland, Conn., 1976-78; acting ward chief Conn. Mental Health Ctr., New Haven, 1977; assoc. dir. family medicine, psychiatry St. Elizabeth Med. Ctr., Youngstown, 1978-80; asst. prof. N.E. Ohio Med. Coll., 1978-80, program dir., 1980-88, assoc. prof. dept. psychiatry, 1980-84, prof., 1984-90, vice chmn., 1985-89; assoc. clin. prof. dept psychiatry Ohio State U., 1983-89, clin. prof., 1989—; chmn. depts. psychiatry and toxicology Western Res. Care System Hosp., 1985-87, med. dir. toxicology, 1987; examiner in psychology LaTrobe U., Bundoora, Australia, 1988-89; sr. cons. Fair Oaks Hosp., Summit, N.J., 1979, Regent Hosp., N.Y.C., 1981—, chmn. Nat. Adv. Council Prevention and Control of Rape, NIMH, Rockville, Md., 1983-86; mem. drug abuse clin., behavioral and rsch. rev. com. Nat. Inst. Drug Abuse, Rockville, Md., 1987-88; chief forensic psychiatrist Mahoning County Prosecutor, 1989—; Am. Participant USIA Drug Abuse program to Cyprus, Italy, Can., Barbados, St. Lucia and Yugoslavia, 1990—; cons. Smith-Kline Labs., McNeil Labs., Excerpta Medica Pubs., Amino Labs., Fund for Am. Renaissance; dir. clin. rsch. Princeton Diagnostic Labs., South Plainfield, N.J., 1987-89; med. dir. med. adv. bd. Neurodata Inc., 1987-89, pres., 1989—, med. dir. Chem. Abuse Ctrs. Inc., 1987; spl. reviewer initial review group, 1995—, health, behavior and prevention review com. NIH, Rockville, Md.; corp. med. dir. Chemical Abuse Ctrs., Inc., 1987—; mem. ethics com. Mahoning County Mental Retardation Bd., Youngstown, Ohio, 1995—. Author: (with Henry Black) Psychiatric, Psychogenic, Somatopsychic Disorders, 1978; (with Robert Gilliland) Neurologi and Neuropsychiatric Disorders, 1983; (with Andrew Slaby) Overdose and Detoxification Emergencies, 1983; Biological Foundation of Clinical Psychiatry, 1988, (with Andrew Slaby and Mark Gold) Drugs of Abuse, 1989, 2d edit., 1996, Comprehensive Laboratory Services in Psychiatry, 1986, (with Philip Jose Farmer) Red Orc's Rage, 1991, (with Andrew Slaby) The Eating Disorders, 1993; contbr. numerous articles to profl. jours. Vice chmn. Mahoning County (Ohio) Mental Health Bd., 1982-84, chmn. 1984-86; councilor Nat. Italian Am. Found. Recipient James Earley award U. Pitts., 1974, Upjohn Research prize Upjohn Co., 1974; recipient Fair Oaks Research award Fair Oaks Hosp., 1979, Bronze award Brit. Med. Assn, 1983, Outstanding Leadership award Mahoning County Mental Health Bd., 1986; Entrepreuner of Yr. nominee Inc. Mag., 1989, Silver Rose award Assn. Italiano Donati d'organo, Milan, Italy, 1990. Recipient Physician's Recognition award, 1978—. Fellow Royal Soc. Am., Royal Acad. Medicine (Eng.), Acad. Medicine, Am. Coll. Clin. Pharmacology (sec.-treas. Ohio chpt. 1990—, mem. steering coun. and exec. com. Ohio chpt. 1990, 91—), Am. Psychiat. Assn.; mem. Soc. Neurosci., Brit. Brain Soc., European Neurosci., Royal Coll. Medicine, N.Y. Acad. Scis., Am. Psychiat. Assn., Acad. Clin. Psychiatry, Youngstown C. of C. (vice chmn. health com. 1986-89, chmn. 1989—), Yale Club (Cleve, Pitts.), Youngstown Club, Atrium Club (Warren, Ohio), Poland Club (Ohio), Swim and Racquet Club, Sigma Xi. Republican. Roman Catholic.

GIANNINI, MARGARET JOAN, pediatrician; b. Camden, N.J., May 27, 1921; married; four children. MD, Hahnemann Med. Coll., 1945. Diplomate Am. Bd. Pediat. From assoc. prof. to prof. pediat. N.Y. Med. Coll., 1948-79; dir. Univ. Affiliate Mental Retardation Inst., 1950-79, Nat. Inst. Handicapped Rsch., Washington, 1979-81; dir. rehab. devel. VA, Washington, 1981-91, dep. asst. chief medicine, dir. prosthetics and rehab., 1988-91; ret., 1991; cons. Bur. Handicapped Children, N.Y. Health Dept., 1960—; mem. state wide planning com. mental retardation N.Y. State Dept. Mental Hygiene, 1964; mem. adv. bd. Mental Retardation Sect., Headstart Project, Massive Econ. Neighborhood Devel.; bd. dirs. Avard Learning Ctr.; mem. adv. coun. Assn. Help Retarded Children; chmn. Internat. Seminar Mental Retardation; chmn. mental retardation task force State Wide Planning Vocat. Rehab. Svc., N.Y. State Dept. Edn. Fellow Am. Acad. Pediat.; mem. Inst. Medicine-NAS, Assn. Univ. Affiliate Facility Rsch. *

GIANNOTTA, STEVEN LOUIS, neurosurgery educator; b. Detroit, Apr. 4, 1947; s. Louis D. and Betty Jane (Root) G.; m. Sharon Danielak, June 13, 1970; children: Brent, Nicole, Robyn. Student, U. Detroit, 1965-68; MD, U. Mich., 1972. Diplomate Am. Bd. Neurol. Surgeons. Surg. intern U. Mich., Ann Arbor, 1972-73, neurosurg. resident, 1973-78; asst. prof. neurosurgery UCLA, 1978-80; asst. prof. neurosurgery U. So. Calif., Sch. Medicine, L.A., 1980-83, assoc. prof. neurosurgery, 1983-89, prof. neurosurgery, 1989—; sec. Congress Neurol. Surgeons, Washington, 1986-89, v.p., 1993; pres. L.A. (Calif.) Soc. Clin. Neuroscis., 1992-93. Fellow ACS, Am. Heart Assn. (stroke coun., rsch. grantee 1980, 84), So. Calif. Neurol. Soc. (pres. 1993-94). Democrat. Roman Catholic. Office: Dept Neurosurgery Box 239 1200 N State St Los Angeles CA 90033

GIAROLI, JOHN NELLO, oral and maxillofacial surgeon; b. Memphis, Feb. 14, 1928; children: Cindy, John, Eddie, Linda, Nancy, Mark. BS, Memphis State U., 1950; DDS, U. Tenn., Memphis, 1953. Diplomate Am. Bd. oral and Maxillofacial Surgery; lic. physician, Tenn., Miss., La. Resident in oral surgery Charity Hosp., New Orleans, 1955-59; pvt. practice Memphis, 1953—; asst. prof. oral and maxillofacial surgery U. Tenn., 1960-64, assoc. prof., 1964-76, prof., 1976—; chief dental svc. St. Francis Hosp., Memphis, mem. various coms; lectr. in field; cons. LeBonheur Children's Hosp., Bapt. Meml. Hosp. Ctr., Bapt. Meml. Hosp. East, St. Joseph Hosp., Meth. Hosp. North, Meth. Hosp. Ctrl.; instr. Loyola U. New Orleans, 1955-56; hosp. staff City of Memphis Hosps., LeBonheur Children's Hosp., Bapt. Meml. Hosp. Ctrl., Bapt. Meml. Hosp. East, St. Joseph Hosp., St. Francis Hosp., Meth. Hosp. Ctrl., Eastwood Hosp. Mem. Unico Nat. Fellow Am. Coll. Dentists; mem. ADA, AAUP, Tenn. Dental Assn. (fellow, med. malpractice rev. bd., del. 1973—, v.p.), Memphis Dental Soc. (v.p. 1975, treas. 1976-77, sec. 1977-78, pres. 1979-80), Dental Legion of Tenn. (sec. 1963, v.p. 1964, pres. 1965), Am. Soc. Oral and Maxillofacial Surgery, Am. Soc. Dentistry for Children, Tenn. Soc. Dentistry for Children, Memphis Soc. Dentistry for Children, Am. Acad. Oral Medicine, Am. Dental Soc. of Anesthesiology, Fedn. Dentari Internationale, Shelby County Dental Soc., Tenn. Soc. Oral and Maxillofacial Surgery, Southeastern Soc. Oral and Maxillofacial Surgery, Memphis Soc. Oral and Maxillofacial Surgery, Internat. Fedn. Dental Anesthesiology, Am. Coll. Oral and Maxillofacial Surgeons, Internat. Assn. Maxillofacial Surgery, Delta Sigma Delta, Omicron Kappa Upsilon, R.D. and M.T. Dean Hon. Odontological soc., Pierre Fouchard Acad, KC (3rd and 4th degrees). Office: 4515 Poplar Ave Memphis TN 38117

GIBALDI, MILO, university dean; b. N.Y.C., Dec. 17, 1938; s. Ignatius and Angela G.; m. Florence D'Amato, Dec. 26, 1960; 1 dau., Ann Elizabeth. B.S., Coll. Pharmacy, Columbia U., 1960, Ph.D., 1963. Asst. prof. pharmacy Columbia U., N.Y.C., 1963-66; asst. prof. pharmaceutics SUNY, Buffalo, 1966-67, assoc. prof., 1967-70, prof., 1970-78, chmn. dept., 1970-78; prof. pharmaceutics U. Wash., Seattle, 1978—, dean Sch. Pharmacy, 1978—; cons. Bur. Drugs, FDA, 1970-72, VA, Washington, 1971-72; vis. prof. U. Rochester, 1972-74; program dir. clin. pharmacokinetics and biopharmaceutics NIH, 1973-78, mem. pharmacology study sect., 1976-80; mem. sci. adv. bd. G.D. Searle & Co., 1978—. Author: (with Donald Perrier) Pharmacokinetics, 1976; contbr. (with Donald Perrier) articles to profl. jours. Fellow Acad. Pharm. Scis., AAAS; mem. Am. Chem. Soc., Am. Pharm. Assn., Acad. Soc. Clin. Pharmacology, Am. Soc. Pharmacology and Exptl. Therapeutics, N.Y. Acad. Scis., Am. Assn. Colls. Pharmacy, Nat. Acad. Scis. (mem. Inst. Medicine 1986), Health Scis. U. Wash. (assoc. v.p. 1983), Sigma Xi, Rho Chi. Office: U Wash Sch Pharmacy Dept Pharmaceutics Box 357610 Seattle WA 98195-7610*

GIBB, JAMES WOOLLEY, pharmacologist; b. Magrath, Can., Apr. 19, 1933; s. James Lye and Arla (Wolley) G.; m. LaVon Robinson, Sept. 14, 1956; children: Kathryn A., J. Mark. BS, U. Alberta, 1958, MS, 1961; PhD, U. Mich., 1965. Rsch. assoc. in pharmacology NIH, Bethesda, Md., 1965-67; from asst. prof. to prof. pharmacology U. Utah, Salt Lake City, 1967—; vis. rsch. prof. U. Innsbruck, Austria, 1973-75, U. London, 1974; assoc. corp. office sci. & tech. Johnson & Johnson, New Brunswick, N.J., 1995-96; drug abuse adv. com. FDA, Rockville, Md., 1975-79. Mem. Am. Soc. Pharmacology & Exptl. Therapeutics (sec. treas. 1993-94), Am. Soc. Clin. Pharmacology & Therapeutics (pub. bd. 1993—). Office: U Utah Dept Pharmacology Salt Lake City UT 84112

GIBBAS, DONNA LEE, rheumatologist; b. May 23, 1942. BS, U. Md., 1964, MD, 1969. Diplomate Am. Bd. Pediatrics, Am. Bd. Pediatric Rheumatology; lic. physician, Ga. Intern, resident pediatrics Emory U., Atlanta, 1969-72; chief resident Henrietta Egleston Hosp. for Children, Atlanta, 1972-73; instr. pediatrics Emory U., Atlanta, 1973-75, asst. prof. pediatrics, 1975-87, clin. assoc. prof. pediatrics, 1987—; clin. assoc. prof. Mercer U., Atlanta; dir. pediatric arthritis ctr. Grady Meml. Hosp., 1973-87, attending physician, 1973-87; chief Pediatric Rheumatology Clinic Scottish Rite Hosp. for Children, 1982-88, 90—; cons. Emory U. Clinic, 1975-83; cir. Atlanta Regional Pediatric Rheumatology Ctr., 1983—. Contbr. articles to profl. jours. Grantee Levi Strauss and Lupus Erythematosus Found., Atlanta chpt., 1979—, U.S. Dept. Health and Human Svcs., 1983—, 84; Pediatric Rheumatology Ctr., 1984—, 87, Boots Pharm., 1984—, 87, Smith, Kline and French, 1984—, 87. Fellow Am. Acad. Pediatrics, Ga. Acad. Pediatrics; mem. Am. Coll. Rheumatology, Collaborative Pediatric Rheumatology Study Group, So. Soc. Pediatric Rsch., Ga. Rheumatism Assn., Greater Altanta Pediatric Soc., Met. Atlanta Rheumatology Soc., U. Md. Med. Alumni Assn., Emory Pediatrics Alumni Assn. Office: Atlanta Regional Pediatric Rheumatology Ctr 1740 Century Cir NE Ste 14 Atlanta GA 30345

GIBBONS, EDWARD FRANCIS, psychobiologist; b. Bronx, N.Y., Dec. 25, 1949; s. Edward Francis and Mary Theresa (Westervelt) G. BS, SUNY, Stony Brook, 1977, PhD, 1986. Dir. ctr. for sci. and tech. Briarcliffe Coll., Woodbury, N.Y., 1992—. Series editor: SUNY Press Series on Endangered Species, 1986-95, Naturalistic Environments in Capitivity for Animal Behavior Research, 1994, Conservation of Endangered Species in Captivity: An Interdisciplinary Approach, 1995; contbr. articles to profl. jours. Sgt. USAF, 1970-74. Grantee Inst. Mus. Svcs., 1988-90, N.Y. State Dept. Edn., 1993-95. Mem. Animal Behavior Soc., Soc. Behavioral Medicine, L.I. Soc. Women in Sci. and Tech. (bd. dirs., founder), Sigma Xi. Roman Catholic. Home: 33 Warren St Brentwood NY 11717-1531 Office: Briarcliffe Coll 250 Crossways Park Dr Woodbury NY 11797-2015

GIBBS, DENIS LAUREL, radiologist; b. Wayne, Mich., Mar. 6, 1945; s. Laurel Pierce and Alwyn Marie (Larson) G.; m. Paula Kay Lynn, Sept. 6, 1974 (div. Aug. 1988); children: Jeremy Paul, Matthew Ryan, Kevin Christopher, Denis Patrick; m. Kathleen Marie DeLaFuente, July 9, 1989; 1 child, Andrew Zachery. BS, Andrews U., Berrien Springs, Mich., 1967, postgrad., 1967-69; DO, Kansas City Coll. Osteopathic Medicine, 1974. Bd. cert. radiology, bd. cert. nuclear medicine Am. Osteo. Coll. Radiology. Intern, radiology resident Doctors' Hosps., Columbus, Ohio, 1974-78, staff radiologist, 1978; chmn. dept. radiology Rocky Mountain Hosp., Denver, 1978-88, vice chief of staff, 1982, chief of staff, 1983, 84; chmn. dept. radiology Colo. Plain Med. Ctr. Regional Trauma Ctr., Ft. Morgan, 1988—, vice chief of staff, 1992; med.-legal cons., Colo., Calif., Fla., 1979—; consulting radiologist East Morgan Hosp., Luth. Health Sys., Brush, colo., 1988—; CEO IRS Radiology Cons., P.C., Ft. Morgan, 1988—. Med. reviewer Post Grad. Medicine. Acad. booster Fort Morgan H.S./Morgan C.C. Mem. Am. Osteopathic Assn., Am. Osteopathic Coll. Radiology, Nat. Assn. Seventh-Day Adventist Osteopaths, Colo. Med. Soc., Colo. Osteopathic Soc., Ft. Morgan Med. Soc. Republican. Home: PO Box 1243 Fort Morgan CO 80701 Office: IRS Radiology Cons PC 1000 Lincoln Fort Morgan CO 80701

GIBBS, JOHN PATRICK, physician, educator; b. Tecumseh, Nebr., Mar. 17, 1948; s. Leonard Keith and Mary Myrtle (Murphy) G.; m. Elise Marie Buras, Aug. 30, 1973; 1 child, Caroline Michelle. BS in Chem. Engring. with high distinction, U. Nebr., 1970; MD, U. Tex., Galveston, 1976. Diplomate Am. Bd. Preventive Medicine, Nat. Bd. Med. Examiners. Rsch. engr. Shell Oil Co. div. Shell Devel. Co., Houston, 1970-73; resident in internal medicine U. Okla. Health Ctr., Oklahoma City, 1976-77; contract energency physician Houston, 1980-90, Pasadena, Tex., 1981-91; plant med. dir. Ethyl Corp., Pasadena, 1981-88, asst. corp. med. dir., 1988-91; corp. med. dir. Kerr-McGee Corp., Oklahoma City, 1990-95; v.p. health mgmt. Kee-McGee Corp., Oklahoma City, 1995—. Mem. planning com. community awareness and emergency response Chem. Mfrs. Assn., Harris County, Tex., 1987-89, health programs task group, 1991—; mem. occupational health com. Am. Mining Congress, 1991—. Lt., flight surgeon USMC, USNR, 1977-80. Fellow Am. Coll. Occupational Medicine (sec., treas. Tex. chpt. 1987); mem. AMA (Physicians Recognition award 1981, 85), Okla. State Med. Assn., Tex. Med. Assn. Home: 2201 Augusta Ave Edmond OK 73034-3016 Office: Kerr-McGee Corp PO Box 25861 Oklahoma City OK 73125-0861

GIBBS, MARTIN, biologist, educator; b. Philadelphia, Penn., Nov. 11, 1922; s. Samuel and Rose (Sugarman) G.; m. Svanhild Karen Kvale, Oct. 11, 1950; children: Janet Helene, Laura Jean, Steven Joseph, Michael Seland, Robert Kvale. BS, Phila. Coll. Pharmacy, 1943; PhD, U. Ill., 1947. Scientist Brookhaven Nat. Lab., 1947-56; prof. biochemistry Cornell U., 1957-64; Abraham S. and Gertrude Berg prof. biology, chmn. dept. Brandeis U., Waltham, Mass., 1965-93; cons. NSF, 1961-64, 69-72, NIH, 1966-69; mem. corp. Marine Biol. Lab., Woods Hole, Mass., 1970, RESA lectr., 1969; NATO cons. fellowship bd., 1968-70; mem. Coun. Internat. Exch. of Scholars, 1976-82; chmn. adv. com. selection Fulbright Scholars for Eastern Europe; adj. prof. Bot. Inst., U. Munster, Fed. Republic of Germany, 1978, 80, 87; adj. prof. dept. botany U. Calif., Riverside, 1979-89. Author: Structure and Function of Chloroplasts, Crop Productivity-Research Imperative, Revisited, Hungarian-USA Binational Symposium on Photosynthesis; editor in chief Plant Physiology, 1963-92; assoc. editor: Physiologie Vegetale, 1966-76, Ann. Rev. Plant Physiology, 1966-71. Recipient Charles Reid Barnes award, 1984, Adolph E. Gude award, 1993, Martin Gibbs medal, 1993. Mem. NAS, AAUP, Am. Soc. Plant Physiologists, Japanese Soc. Plant Physiologists, Russian Soc. Plant Physiologists (hon. life mem.), Am. Acad. Arts and Scis., Am. Soc. Biochem. Molec. Biology, Can. Soc. Plant Physiologists (hon. life mem.), Acad. Scis. France. Home: 32 Slocum Rd Lexington MA 02173-5622

GIBBS, RAYMOND WELDON, surgeon; b. Boston, Aug. 1, 1920; s. Raymond T. and Elizabeth (Weldon) G.; m. Dorothy Dawson; children: Virginia, Raymond W., Janet. SB, Boston U., 1943; MD, N.Y. Med. Coll., 1951. Instr. surgery Yale Med. Sch., 1953-54; sr. clin. instr. surgery Tufts Med. Sch., 1960-70; instr. Harvard Med. Sch., 1961-89; surgeon Harvard U. Dept. Athletics, 1957-90; surgical cons. Boston, 1957—. Fellow ACS, Am. Coll. Sports Medicine, Am. Burn Asn., Boston Surgical Soc., Mass. Med. Soc. Home: 67 Vermont St West Roxbury MA 02132-2502 Office: State House Boston MA 02133

GIBBS, RICHARD ANTHONY, medicinal chemist; b. Long Beach, Calif., July 31, 1961; m. Barbara Schuster, Aug. 11, 1990. BA, Johns Hopkins U., 1983; PhD, U. Calif., Riverside, 1988. Postdoctoral fellow Pa. State U., University Park, 1988-91; asst. prof Wayne State U., Detroit, 1992—. NSF fellow, 1988; grantee Pharm. Mfrs. Assn. Found., 1993, Nat. Cancer Inst., 1995, Am. Cancer Soc., 1996. Mem. AAAS, Am. Assn. Colls. Pharmacy, Am. Chem. Soc. Office: Wayne State U Dept Pharm Scis Coll Pharmacy & AHP Detroit MI 48202

GIBBS, RONALD STEVEN, obstetrician-gynecologist; b. Phila., Mar. 31, 1943. MD, U. Pa., 1969. Intern Hartford (Conn.) Hosp., 1969-70; resident ob.-gyn. U. Pa. Hosp., Phila., 1970-74; fellow maternal-fetal medicine U. Tex. Health Ctr., San Antonio, 1976-78; obstetrician-gynecologist Univ. Hosp. U. Colo., Denver, 1980—; prof., chmn. dept. ob.-gyn. U. Colo., Denver, 1980—. Mem. ACOG, AMA, Am. Genito-Obstetric Soc., IDSA, IDSOG, SGI. Soc. Profs. Obstetrics. Office: U Colo Health Sci Ctr 4200 E 9th Ave Box B-198 Denver CO 80262-0001*

GIBBS, SYDNEY ROYSTON, health facility administrator; b. West Plains, Mo., June 15, 1934; s. Wallace Pemberton and Leila Mary (Royston) G.; m. Clarice Ellen Smith, Dec. 28, 1958; children: Sydney Royston Jr., Julie Gibbs Erwin. BS with honors, U. Ala., 1955; MD, U. Tenn., 1958. Diplomate Am. Bd. Surgery. Intern U. Tenn. Hosps., Knoxville, 1959; pvt. practice Roberta, Ga., 1960; jr. asst. surgery resident U. Ala. Hosps., Birmingham, 1961; ptnr. Drs. Clinic and Hosp., Bessemer, Ala., 1963-66; jr. surgery resident Lloyd Noland Hosp., Birmingham, 1967-68, sr. surgery resident, 1969; pvt. practice Bessemer, 1970-88; med. dir. ACIPCO Health Svcs., Birmingham, 1989—; pres. med. staff Bessemer Carraway Med. Ctr., 1982-83, mem. bd. trustees, 1982-83, chief of surgery, 1974-75. Contbr. articles to profl. jours. Witness on employer mandate/health security act U.S. Ho. of Reps., 1994; active deacon bd. Shades Mountain Bapt. Ch., 1980; med. missionary Antigua, West Indies, 1975, 78. Major U.S. Army, 1962. Fellow ACS, Southeastern Coll. Surgeons; mem. Am. Coll. Physician Execs., Birmingham Acad. Medicine. Office: ACIPCO Health Svcs 2930 N 16th St Birmingham AL 35202

GIBBY, DIANE LOUISE, physician, plastic surgeon; b. Miami, Feb. 5, 1957; d. John and Mabel (Kunce) G.; m. Rodney J. Rohrich. BS, Duke U., Durham, N.C., 1975; MD, U. Miami, 1980. Diplomate Am. Bd. Gen. Surgery, Bd. Plastic and Reconstructive Surgery. Clin. asst. prof. U. Tex. Southwestern, Dallas, 1987—; pvt. practice plastic surgery Med. City Dallas, 1987—; founder Women's Ctr. for Plastic and Reconstructive Surgery, 1992. Fellow Am. Coll. Surgeons; mem. Am. Soc. Plastic and Reconstructive Surgeons, Am. Med. Soc., Tex. Soc. Plastic Surgeons, Dallas Soc. Plastic Surgeons, Aesthetic Soc. Office: 7777 Forest Ln C820 Dallas TX 75230

GIBBY, MABEL ENID KUNCE, psychologist; b. St. Louis, Mar. 30, 1926; d. Ralph Waldo and Mabel Enid (Warren) Kunce; student Washington U., St. Louis, 1943-44, postgrad., 1955-56; B.A., Park Coll., 1945; M.A., McCormick Theol. Sem., 1947; postgrad. Columbia U., 1948, U. Kansas City, 1949, George Washington U., 1953; M.Ed., U. Mo., 1951, Ed.D., 1952; m. John Francis Gibby, Aug. 27, 1948; children—Janet Marie (Mrs. Kim Williams), Harold Steven, Helen Elizabeth, Diane Louise (Mrs. Roderick Rohrich), John Andrew, Keith Sherridan, Daniel Jay. Dir. religious edn. Westport Presbyn. Ch. Kansas City, Mo., 1947-49; tchr. elementary schs., Kansas City, 1949-50; high sch. counselor Arlington (Va.) Pub. Schs., 1952-54; counselor adult counseling services Washington U., 1955-56; counseling psychologist Coral Gables (Fla.) VA Hosp., 1956—; counseling psychologist Miami (Fla.) VA Hosp., 1956—, chief counseling psychology sect., 1982-86; sr. psychologist Office Disability Determination Fla. Hdqrs., 1987-94. Sec. bd. dirs. Fla. Vocat. Rehab. Found. Recipient Meritorious Service citation Fla. C. of C., 1965, President's Com. on Employment of Handicapped, 1965; commendation for meritorious service Com. on Employment of Physically Handicapped Dade County, 1965, named Outstanding Rehab. Profl., 1966, 81; named Profl. Fed. Employee of Year, Greater Miami Fed. Exec. Council, 1966; Outstanding Fed. Service award Greater Miami Fed. Exec. Council, 1966; Fed. Woman's award U.S. Civil Service Commn., 1968, Community Headliner award Theta Sigma Phi, 1968, Outstanding Alumni award Park Coll., 1968, Freedom award The Chosen Few, Korean War Vets. Assn., 1986; certificate of appreciation Bur. Customs, U.S. Treasury Dept., 1969, Fla. Dept. Health and Rehab. Services, 1970. Mem. Am., Dade County (past sec.) psychol. assns., Nat., Fla. (past dir. Dade County chpt.) rehab. assns., Nat. Rehab. Counseling Assn. (past sec.). Patentee in field. Home: 7107 Aberdeen Ave Dallas TX 75230-5406

GIBBY-SMITH, BARBARA, psychologist, nurse; b. Woodburn, Oreg., Dec. 13, 1938; d. Chester Clifton and Marvel Elizabeth (Hill) Gibby; m. Roy Milton Smith, June 2, 1957 (div. June 1990); children: Thomas Clifton, Jeffery Shawn, Mark Anderson. ADN, Chemeketa C.C., Salem, Oreg., 1972; BS, SUNY, Albany, 1980; MS, Western Oreg. State Coll., 1982; D of Psychology, Pacific U., Forest Grove, Oreg., 1993. Diplomate Am. Bd. Profl. Disability Cons.; cert. disability specialist. Adminstr. Birch St. Manor, Dallas, Oreg., 1973-81; disability determination specialist State of Oreg. Workers' Compensation Dept., Salem, 1983-85; counselor Women's Crisis Ctr., Salem, 1986-88; rehab. counselor Employer Rehab. Svcs., Portland, Oreg., 1985-87; therapist, counselor Pacific U., Hillsboro, Oreg., 1988-89, Forest Grove, 1989-91; intern in psychology Portland State U., 1991-92, Kaiser-Permanente, Salem, 1991-92; resident in psychology Tillamook (Oreg.) Counseling Ctr., 1993-95; group therapy counselor Women's Crisis Ctr., Dallas, 1982-83; eating disorders group therapy facilitator, Salem, 1986-88. Active Women's Coalition Orgn., Salem, 1988—. Mem. APA (clin. neuropsychology divsn. 40), Am. Coll. Forensic Examiners (diplomate), Oreg. Psychol. Assn., Prescribing Psychologist Assn. Democrat. Office: Mountain View Counseling Ctr Ste 500 1911 Mountain View Ln Forest Grove OR 97116 also: Mountain View Med Ctr Ste 200 1909 Mt View Ln Ste 200 Forest Grove OR 97116

GIBERT, CYNTHIA LIVINGSTONE, infectious diseases physician; b. Washington, Oct. 25, 1941; d. Kenneth Mackay and Anna Champion (Taliaferro) L.; m. Stephen Pierre Gibert; children: Christopher, Jennifer. BA in French, Sweet Briar Coll., 1963; MS in Phys. Chemistry, Cath. U. Am., 1974; MD, Howard U., 1984. Diplomate Am. Bd. Internal Medicine with subspecialty infectious diseases, Nat. Bd. Med. Examiners; lic. physician D.C., Va. Intern in medicine Washington Hosp. Ctr., 1984-85, resident in medicine, 1985-87, fellow in infectious diseases, 1988-89; fellow in infectious diseases Dept. Vets. Affairs Med. Ctr., Washington, 1987-88, clin. dir. and attending in infectious diseases, 1989-92, asst. chief sect. infectious diseases, 1992—; asst. prof. medicine Georgetown U., Washington, 1990—; mem. Fed. Consensus Panel for Devel. Treatment Improvement Protocol for Screening of Infectious Diseases in Substance Abusers, Substance Abuse and Mental Health Svcs. Adminstrn., Ctr. for Substance Abuse Treatment, Rockville, Md., 1991-93; grant reviewer NIH, Nat. Inst. Allergy and Infectious Diseases, AIDS Clin. and Epidemiology Rsch. Rev. Br., 1994, sml. bus. tech. transfer program NIH, 1995; cons. Johnson, Bassin and Shaw, 1991-94, Battelle/Human Affairs Rsch. Ctrs., 1992-93; lectr. in field. Contbr. numerous articles and abstracts to profl. jours. Bd. visitors Nat. Cathedral Sch., Washington, 1996—. Mem. ACP, Infectious Diseases Soc. Am., Greater Washington Infectious Diseases Soc., Internat. AIDS Soc., Am. Med. Women's Assn. (D.C. chpt. pres. 1995—). Episcopalian. Home: 6530 Sunny Hill Ct Mc Lean VA 22101 Office: VA Medical Ctr Sect Infectious diseases 50 Irving St NW Washington DC 20422

GIBLETT, ELOISE ROSALIE, hematology educator; b. Tacoma, Wash., Jan. 17, 1921; d. William Richard and Rose (Godfrey) G. B.S., U. Wash., 1942, M.S., 1947, M.D. with honors, 1951. Mem. faculty U. Wash. Sch. Medicine, 1957—, research prof., 1967-87, emeritus research prof., 1987—; asso. dir., head immunogenetics Puget Sound Blood Center, 1955-79, exec. dir., 1979-87, emeritus exec. dir., 1987—; former mem. several research coms. NIH. Author: Genetic Markers in Human Blood, 1969; editorial bd. numerous jours. including Blood, Am. Jour. Human Genetics, Transfusion, Vox Sanguinis; Contbr. over 200 articles to profl. jours. Recipient fellowships, grants, Emily Cooley, Karl Landsteiner, Philip Levine and Alexander Wiener immunohematology awards, distinguished alumna award U. Wash. Sch. Med., 1987. Fellow AAAS; Mem. Nat. Acad. Scis., Am. Soc. Human Genetics (pres. 1973), Am. Soc. Hematology, Am. Assn. Immunologists, Brit. Soc. Immunology, Internat. Soc. Hematologists, Am. Fedn. Clin. Research, Western Assn. Physicians, Assn. Am. Physicians, Sigma Xi, Alpha Omega Alpha. Home: 6533 53rd Ave NE Seattle WA 98115-7748 Office: Puget Sound Blood Ctr Terry and Madison Sts Seattle WA 98104

GIBLIN, MARY ELLEN, mental health professional; b. Warsaw, N.Y., July 31, 1943; d. William Marcy and Mary Agnes (Conroy) Hurlburt; m. Robert Paul Giblin, Aug. 27, 1966; 1 child, Darlene Mary. BA in Psychology, SUNY Empire State Coll., Albany, 1975; MS in Pub. Adminstrn., Russell Sage Coll., 1978; PhD in Urban and Environ. Studies, Rensselaer Poly. Inst., 1991. Residential supr., tng. and edn. coord., transp. coord Eleanor Roosevelt Devel. Svcs., O.D. Heck Devel. Ctr., Schoharie, N.Y., 1974-81; policy analyst bur. program design Office of Mental Retardation and Devel. Disabilities, Albany, N.Y., 1981-83, statewide community residence coord. bur. residential svcs., 1983-84, asst. dir. bur. operational design, program evaluation, 1984-87, supr. design and evaluation unit bur. program design, 1987-90, asst. dir. bur. consumer and family supports, 1990—; instr. pub. policy grad. program SUNY Empire State Coll., 1992—. Contbr. articles to profl. jours. Mem. adv. coun. Schenectady (N.Y.) County Office for the Aging, 1994-96. Mem. ASPA (coun. rep. 1992-94, co-chair Ann. Inst. 1990-91, 93-94, treas. 1995-96), Empire State Coll. Bd. Govs. (sec. 1993-96, pres. 1996—), Empire State Coll. Alumni-Student Assn. (chair phonothon 1992, 95-96, Alumni of Yr. 1993), Am. Assn. on Mental Retardation. Office: Office Mental Retardation & Devel Disabilities 44 Holland Ave Albany NY 12229

GIBOFSKY, ALLAN, medical educator, law educator, physician, lawyer; b. N.Y.C., Sept. 7, 1949; s. Louis and Sally (Levy) G.; m. Karen Beth Sussman, June 5, 1982; children: Lewis Marshall, Esther Rachel, Laura Aimee. BS, Bklyn. Coll., 1969; MD, Cornell U., 1973; JD, Fordham U., 1985. Bar: N.Y. 1986, N.J. 1986, D.C. 1987; diplomate Am. Bd. Internal Medicine, Am. Bd. Legal Medicine; bd. cert. rheumatology 1980, legal med., 1987. Intern N.Y. Hosp., N.Y.C., 1973-74; resident in internal medicine N.Y. Hosp., 1974-77, fellow, 1977-79; asst. prof. medicine Cornell U. Med. Coll., N.Y.C., 1979-85; assoc. prof. medicine, asst. prof. pub. health Cornell U. Med. Coll., 1985-90, assoc. prof. pub. health, 1990-94, prof. medicine, pub. health, 1994—; adj. assoc. prof. law Fordham U., N.Y.C., 1986-95, adj. prof. law, 1995—; v.p. med. and sci. affairs N.Y. Arthritis Found., 1984-89, pres., 1989-93; bd. govs. N.Y. Arthritis Found., trustee, 1995—; bd. govs. Am. Bd. Legal Medicine, 1990—. Editor: Manual of Orthopedics and Rheumatology,

1981; contbr. articles to med. sci. and legal jours. Arthritis Found. rsch. grantee, 1975—; NIH rsch. grantee, 1977-82. Fellow ACP, Am. Coll. Legal Medicine (bd. govs. 1989—, treas. 1991-93, pres. 1994-95), Am Coll. Rheumatology, N.Y. Acad. Medicine; mem. Nat. Health Lawyers Assn., N.Y. Rheumatism Assn. (sec.-treas. 1985—), Soc. Salk Scholars CUNY (v.p. 1986-93, pres. 1992—). Home: 425 E 79th St New York NY 10021-1037 Office: Hosp for Spl Surgery 535 E 70th St New York NY 10021-4892

GIBRALTER, RICHARD PAUL, ophthalmologist; b. N.Y.C., Feb. 25, 1951; s. Marshall and Barbara Gibralter; m. Susan Gibralter, Aug. 6, 1975; children: Daniel, Michael. BA, Amherst Coll., 1972; MD, Mt. Sinai Med. Sch., 1976. Pvt. practice in ophthalmology N.Y.C., 1981—; surgeon dir. dept. ophthalmology Manhattan Eye Ear and Throat Hosp., N.Y.C., 1992—; dir. cornea fellowship Manhattan Eye Ear and Throat Hosp., 1985—; mem. med. adv. bd. N.Y. Eye Bank for Sight Restoration, 1986-95, sec., 1994-95; prin. investigator FDA Clin. Trials, 1992—. Orgnl. mgr., coach Multiple Civic Youth Baseball, Basketball and Football Teams, Scarsdale, N.Y., 1989—. Fellow Am. Acad. Ophthalmology, Am. Coll. Surgeons; mem. Manhattan Ophthal. Soc. Office: Cataract and Cornea Assoc 154 E 71st St New York NY 10021

GIBSON, ALOIS EUGENE, orthopedic surgeon; b. Muncie, Ind., June 21, 1934; s. Walter Eugene and Hugoline Josephine (Knecht) G.; m. Jean Laura Weeke, Jan. 18, 1958; children: Mark, Karen, Susan, David, Daniel, Paul. AB, Ind. U., 1955, MD, 1958. Orthopedic surgeon Park Miller Gibson, Richmond, Ind., 1963-77, Orthopedic Surgeons Richmond, 1977-92; pvt. practice Indpls., 1992—. Named physician of yr. Disability Awareness Coun., 1989; inducted Ind. Football Hall of Fame, 1994. Fellow Am. Acad. Orthopedic Surgeons; mem. Am. Orthopedic Soc. Sports Medicine, Ind. Orthopedic Soc., Indpls. Med. Soc. Roman Catholic. Office: 8424 Naab Rd 1-K Indianapolis IN 46260

GIBSON, BARBARA ARLENE, nurse, writer; b. Port Jefferson, N.Y., July 6, 1942; d. David M. and Marion G. (Nyman) Ramos; m. Robert R. Gibson, Feb. 10, 1979; children: Joan M. Gunther, Karen L. Mullins. AAS, Suffolk County C.C., 1976. RN, Fla. Team leader Tarpon Springs (Fla.) Gen. Hosp., 1977-80; office mgr. Bob's Concrete Pumping Svc., Clearwater, Fla., 1980-89; nurse team leader St. Anthony's Hosp., St. Petersburg, Fla., 1981-89; founder Fibromyalgia Network Greater Tampa Bay, Fla., 1989-90; lectr. on fibromyalgia syndrome, 1989—; freelance writer. Author, pub.: The Fibromyalgia Handbook, 1990, 2d edit., 1995, Fibromyalgia: Exploring the Possibilities, Vol. I, Sumatriptan, 1994; freelance writer; former med. columnist Suncoast CFIOS Support Group Newsletter. Home: 1443 Mission Dr W Clearwater FL 34619-2744 Office: Gemini Press PO Box 4546 Clearwater FL 34618-4546

GIBSON, DAVID M., dean; b. Phila., Apr. 13, 1940; s. Robert Allen and Rose Frances (Morris) G.; m. Margaret M. Reilly, Apr. 15, 1945; children: Geoffrey, John. BA, St. Charles Borromeo Seminary, Phila., 1964; attended, St. Charles Borromeo Seminary, 1968; MA, Seton Hall U., 1983, EdD, 1992. Ordained to ministry, 1968. Exec. v.p. Gar Raymnod Co., Inc., Lafayette Hill, Pa., 1970-75; exec. asst. dean U. Medicine and Dentistry N.J., Newark, 1975-79, asst. dean, 1979-85, assoc. dean, 1986-89, acting dean, 1989-92, dean, 1992—; cons. Suez Canal U., Ismalia, Egypt, 1992-95, 1st Med. Faculty Charles U., Prague, Czech Republic, 1994. Contbr. articles to profl. jours., chpts. to books; artist medical illustration Jour. Neurosurgery, 1985. Pres., bd. edn. Our Lady of Sorrows Sch., South Orange, N.J., 1980-84; pres. doctoral assn. Seton Hall, South Orange, 1986-89; mem. bd. health, South Orange, 1989-92; mem. task force N.J. Dept. Labor, Trenton, 1992-96. Grantee Multi-Lab Stillman Trust Fund, 1993; recipient Excellence award Nat. Assn. State Mental Health Program Dirs., 1995, Gov. award N.J., 1982-83. Mem. Northea. Deans (chair), Assn. Schs. Allied Health Profs. (chair gov. rels. com.), Task Force on Basic Skills, Am. Health Info. Mgmt. Assn. (mem. gov. rels. com. 1993, chair 1995), N.J. Soc. Allied Health Profs. (pres.-elect 1995-96). Office: U Medicine & Dentistry NJ 65 Bergen St Newark NJ 07107-3001

GIBSON, EDGAR THOMAS, surgeon, educator; b. Phila., Mar. 23, 1915; s. Albert and Mabel (Cave) G.; m. Helen Tomlinson, Nov. 7, 1943; children: Ann Peluso, Barbara, Jeanne Rollins, Helen Tucker. BS, Villanova U., 1938; MD, Jefferson Med. Coll., 1942; postgrad., U. Pa., 1947-48. Resident surgery Cleve. Clinic, 1943-44, West Jersey Hosp., Camden, N.J., 1948-50; resident thoracic surgery Phila. Gen. Hosp., 1952-54; pres. staff Camden County Chest Hosp.; chmn. dept. surgery West Jersey Hosp. Group, 1975-78; staff mem. Our Lady of Lourdes Hosp., Camden, N.J.; instr. surgery Jefferson U., Phila. Pres. Camden County Heart Soc., 1960. Capt. U.S. Army, 1944-46, ETO. Fellow AMA, ACS, Am. Bd. Surgery, N.J. Soc. Surgeons; mem. Camden County Med. Soc. (pres.). Republican. Home: Grandview Rd Newagen ME 04552

GIBSON, ERNEST L., III, healthcare consultant; b. Baton Rouge, Oct. 29, 1945; s. Ernest L. Jr. and Ethel (Dunning) G.; m. Susan R. Wilson, Aug. 29, 1970; children: E. Lee, Elizabeth K. BS in Pharmacy, U. of the Pacific, 1968, PharmD, 1969. Resident hosp. pharmacy U. Tex. Med. Br., Galveston, 1972; assoc. dir. pharmacy U. Calif. Med. Ctr., Sacramento, 1970-78; dir. pharmacy mgmt. Svc. Master Industries, Downers Grove, Ill., 1978-82; exec. v.p. DOSE Sys., 1982-93, Capital Solutions Group, Plano, 1992; pres. HealthCare Solutions Group, Plano, 1992—; lectr. Sacramento Jr. Coll., 1975-78. Stephens min. Custer Rd. United Meth. Ch., Plano, Tex., adminstrv. bd. dirs., 1984-87. Mem. Health Info. Mgrs. Soc., Am. Soc. Hosp. Pharmacists, Tex. Soc. Hosp. Pharmacists (bd. dirs. 1976-77, chmn. legal affairs com.), Sacramento Valley Soc. Hosp. Pharmacists (prs. 1975), Jaycees (state chmn. drug abuse campaign 1976). Republican. Home: 4549 Miami Dr Plano TX 75093-5511 Office: Healthcare Solutions Group 4549 Miami Plano TX 75093

GIBSON, FRANCES, nurse; b. Junction, Tex., Sept. 28, 1936; d. August and Juanita (Corpus-Garcia) Rehwoldt; m. Richard Gibson, July 4, 1954 (dec. July 25, 1962); childreN; Kenneth, René, Allison. AA, East Los Angeles Coll. Lic. vocat. nurse, 1969; registered nurse 1976, operating room technician, 1971; cert. adult edn. tchr., paralegal. Instr., profl. expert East Los Angeles Coll., Monterey Park, Calif., 1971-74; hostess talk show (in Spanish) Sta. KMEX-TV, Los Angeles, 1970-76; tchr. adult edn. Garvey Sch. Bd., Rosemead, Calif., 1976-77; clin. nurse L.A. County/U. So. Calif. Med. Ctr., 1981-89; case mgr. AIDS Healthcare Found., L.A., 1991-93; AIDS clinician Los Angeles County/U. So. Calif. Med. Ctr., 1993; vol. nurse Lung Assn., L.A., 1970-76, ARC, L.A., 1969—; instr. health classes ARC, also instr. Spanish to ARC pers., mgr. info. booths at health fairs and convs., provider first aid at various gatherings, immunization clinics, chmn. adv. bd., 1971-72, bd. dirs., 1972-75, 89-82; med. editor, legal asst. Ivie & McNeill, L.A., 1986—. Author: Spanish for English-Speaking Personnel, 1972. Recipient Spotlight award ARC, 1972, Clara Barton award, 1976, Associate Womens Students award, 1969; named one of Ten Prettiest Chicanas in East Los Angeles, 1970. Mem. Nursing Edn. Associates, Chicana Nurses Assn., AFL CIO, ACLU, Alpha Gamma Sigma. Democrat. Home: 2241 Charlotte Ave Rosemead CA 91770-3624

GIBSON, GEOFFREY ERIC, gastroenterologist; b. Adelaide, Australia, Feb. 28, 1942; s. Eric Ambrose and Marjorie Alice (Nicholls) G.; m. Diana Helen Gibson, Jan. 6, 1966; children: Hamish, Lachlan, Alistair. MB, BS, U. Adelaide, Australia, 1965. Fellow in gastroenterology U. Iowa Clinics, 1970-73; cons. gastroenterologist U. Adelaide, Royal Adelaide Hosp., 1973—; vis. specialist Royal Adelaide Hosp., 1989—. Fellow Royal Australian Coll. Physicians; mem. Am. Gastrolent. Assn. Home: 251 Stanley St, North Adelaide 5006, Australia Office: 266 Melbourne St, North Adelaide 5006, Australia

GIBSON, JAMES EDWIN, toxicologist; b. Des Moines, Aug. 22, 1941; s. Donald Edwin and Lorene Jane (Faris) G.; m. Karen Rae Hasselquist; children: Debra Rae, Bradley James, Mark Alan. BA, Drake U., 1964; MS, U. Iowa, 1967, PhD, 1969. Prof. pharmacology Mich. State U., East Lansing, 1969-76; v.p., dir. rsch. Chem. Industry Inst. Toxicology, Durham, N.C., 1976-89; dir. toxicology affairs Dow Chem. Co., Midland, Mich., 1989-90; global dir., regulatory, toxicology and environmental affairs Dow Elanco, Indpls., 1990-95; dir. rsch. and devel. Dow Elanco N.Am., Indpls., 1995—; vis. prof. U. Mainz, Fed. Republic Germany, 1975-76; adj. prof. U. N.C., Chapel Hill, 1984-90, Duke U., Durham, 1985-90, N.C. State U., Raleigh, 1985-90, Purdue U., West Lafayette, Ind., 1992—, Ind. U., Indpls., 1992—. Editor: Formaldehyde Toxicity, 1983; co-editor: Formaldehyde, Toxicology, Epidemiology and Mechanisms, 1983; contbr over 100 articles to profl. jours. Bd. dirs. Triangle Youth Hockey Assn., Durham, 1986-89. Recipient Alexander von Humboldt Sr. U.S. Scientist Award Univ. Mainz, 1976. Fellow Acad. Toxicol. Scis.; mem. AAAS, Soc. Toxicology (pres. 1986—, Achievement award 1977), Internat. Union of Toxicology (sec.-ten. 1986—), Soc. for Risk Assessment, Teratology Soc. Home: 1106 E 82nd St Indianapolis IN 46240-2388 Office: Dow Elanco Zionsville Rd Indianapolis IN 46268

GIBSON, JEANNETTE LOUISE, quality assurance professional; b. Warren, Ohio, Jan. 13, 1947; d. Roy M. and Evelyn M. (Smith) Meister; m. George R. Gibson, Aug. 13, 1976; children: Christopher, Erica. AA, N.Mex. State U., 1979; BS in Health Arts, Coll. of St. Francis, 1993. Cert. utilization review, Interqual. Patient care coord. Nathan Adelson Hospice, Las Vegas, 1988; utilization review coord. Med. Mgmt. Svcs., Las Vegas, 1989-90; psychiat. nurse Monte Vista Hosp., Las Vegas, 1988-89, 89-92; med. rev. coord. Valley Hosp., Las Vegas, 1990-95; admission coord. subacute unit Corner Stone Health Mgmt. Lake Mead Medical Ctr., Las Vegas, Nev., 1995—.

GIBSON, JOANN MARIE, psychotherapist, consultant, personal mentor; b. Watertown, N.Y., Sept. 11, 1942; d. Guy and Doris (D'Angelo) G.; divorced; Mark Mawby, Jeannean Mawby. AD in Nursing Sci., Gwynned-Mercy Coll., 1967; BS in Nursing Edn., Temple U., 1971; postgrad., U. Pitts., 1984-86; PhD in Health Psychology, Union Inst., 1990. RN, Pa.; cert. mental health nurse. Psychiat. nurse instr. Phila. State Hosp., 1967-71; asst. dir. nursing svc. Crownsville (Md.) State Hosp., 1971-72; dir. counseling Phila. Family Planning, 1972-73; group therapist Eagleville (Pa.) Rehab. Ctr., 1973-75; tng. and program devel. forensic divsn. St. Elizabeth's Hosp., Washington, 1975-76; owner Gibson Assocs., Phila., 1976-80; prodr. Filmadelphia, Phila., 1980-83; exec. dir. Planned Parenthood of Cambria/Somerset, Johnstown, Pa., 1983-84; pvt. practice Phila., Pa., 1984—; adj. faculty psychology dept. Montgomery County C.C., 1990, Chestnut Hill Coll., Phila., 1992; adj. faculty Divsn. Alternative Edn. and Grad. Studies, Vt. Coll.; patient care coord. Belmont Ctr., Phila., 1977. Mem. ASTD, Inst. Noetic Scis., Fetzer Inst. for Advancement of Holistic Health. Home: 6123 Wayne Ave Philadelphia PA 19144-6103

GIBSON, KATHLEEN RITA, anatomy and anthropology educator; b. Phila., Oct. 9, 1942; d. Keath Pope and Rita Irene (Shewell) G. BA, U. Mich., 1963; MA, U. Calif., Berkeley, 1969, PhD, 1970. Teaching assoc. U. Calif., Berkeley, 1965-69; lectr., adj. assoc. prof., then adj. prof. Rice U., Houston, 1973—; asst. prof. U. Tex. Health Sci. Ctr., Houston, 1970-73, assoc. prof., 1973-80, prof., 1980—; mem. com. on parenting behavior Social Sci. Rsch. Coun., N.Y.C., 1980-89; mem. fellowship rev. panel NSF, 1992-95; vis. fellow Cambridge U., 1993; vis. scholar Oxford U., 1996. Editor: (with M. Thames and K. Molokon) Genealogy and Demography of the West Main Cree, 1989, (with S. Parker) Language and Intelligence in Monkeys and Apes, 1990, 94, (with A. Petersen) Brain Maturation and Cognitive Development, 1991, (with Tim Ingold) Tools, Language and Intelligence in Human Evolution, 1993, 94, (with Paul Mellars) Modelling the Early Human Mind, 1996; contbg. editor Anthropology Newsletter, 1990-93; contbr. articles, commentaries and abstracts in profl. jours. Conf. grantee Wenner Gren Found., 1990, Sloan Found., 1985, travel grantee NSF, 1984, 86, Brit. Soc. Devel. Biology, 1982. Fellow Am. Assn. Phys. Anthropologists, Am. Assn. Anthropologists; mem. AAAS, Am. Assn. Anatomists, Internat. Primatol. Assn., Am. Assn. Dental Schs. (chmn. sect. anatomical scis. 1990), Am. Anthropol. Assn. (chmn.-elect biolog. anthropology sect. 1994-96, co-chmn. com. on ethics, 1994-95), Lang. Origins Soc., Am. Assn. Primatologists (publs. com. 1987-89). Office: Dept Basic Scis U Tex Health Sci Ctr Houston TX 77225

GIBSON, MELVIN ROY, pharmacognosy educator; b. St. Paul, Nebr., June 11, 1920; s. John and Jennie Irene (Harvey) G. B.S., U. Nebr., 1942, M.S., 1947, D.Sc. (hon.), 1985; Ph.D., U. Ill., 1949. Asst. prof. pharmacognosy Wash. State U., Pullman, 1949-52; assoc. prof. Wash. State U., 1952-55, prof., 1955-85, prof. emeritus, 1985—. Editor: Am. Jour. Pharm. Edn, 1956-61; editorial bd., co-author: Remington's Pharm. Sci, 1970, 75, 80, 85; editor, co-author: Studies of a Pharm. Curriculum, 1967; author over 100 articles. Served as arty. officer AUS, 1942-46. Decorated Bronze star, Purple Heart; sr. vis. fellow Orgn. for Econ. Cooperation and Devel., Royal Pharm. Inst., Stockholm, Sweden and U. Leiden (Holland), 1962; recipient Rufus A. Lyman award, 1972, Wash. State U. Faculty Library award, 1984; named Wash. State U. Faculty Mem. of Yr., 1985. Fellow AAAS; assoc. fellow Am. Coll. Apothecaries; mem. AAUP, APHA, N.Y. Acad. Scis., Am. Pharm. Assn., Am. Soc. Pharmacognosy (pres. 1964-65), Am. Assn. Coll. Pharmacy (exec. com. 1961-63, bd. dirs. 1977-79, chmn. coun. faculties 1975-76, pres. 1979-80, Disting. Educator award 1984), U.S. Pharmacopeia (revision com. 1970-75), Am. Found. Pharm. Edn. (hon. life, bd. dirs. 1980-85, exec. com. 1981-85, vice chmn. 1982-85), Acad. Pharm. Sci., Fedn. Internat. Pharm., Am. Inst. History of Pharmacy (sponsor mem.), Am. Acad. Polit. and Social Sci., U. Nebr. Chancellor's Club, U. Nebr. Pres. Club, Sigma Xi, Phi Kappa Phi, Omicron Delta Kappa, Rho Chi, Kappa Psi (Nat. Svc. citation 1961). Democrat. Presbyterian. Home: 707 W 6th Ave Apt 41 Spokane WA 99204-2813

GIBSON, PETER JEREMY, company executive; b. Bishops Hartford, Hertfordshire, Eng., May 5, 1946; s. Alan Frank and Judith (Cresswell) G.; m. Denise Patricia Oliver, July 22, 1972; children: Hannah Jane, Ruth Charlotte, Elizabeth Claire. BA (hons.), Hull U., Eng., 1969. Gen. mgr. Devoro Lurefilm, Window, Eng., 1978-80; mng. dir. Zimmer Ltd., Window, Eng., 1980-83, internat. v.p., 1983-85; chmn., mng. dir. Corin Med. Ltd., Eng., 1985-94; chmn. Corin Ltd., Cirewlester, Gloucestershire, Eng., 1994—.

GIBSON, RAY ALLEN, obstetrician, gynecologist; b. Webster County, Ky., Jan. 15, 1941; s. Curtis Ray and Mildred J. (Allen) G.; B.S., Berea Coll., 1962; M.D., U. Louisville, 1968; m. Nancy Sue Bailey, Nov. 28, 1963; 1 dau., Rachel Janel. Intern, U. Louisville Hosps., 1968-69, resident in obstetrics and gynecology, 1969-72; sr. obstetrician-gynecologist Howard Clinic, Glasgow, Ky., 1974-82; chief of staff T.J. Samson Hosp., Glasgow, 1976-77, dir. med. edn., 1976-83. Deacon, Glasgow Bapt. Ch.; bd. dirs. Ky. div. Am. Cancer Soc., 1983-84. Served with U.S. Army, 1972-74. Diplomate Am. Bd. Obstetrics and Gynecology. Mem. Ky. Med. Assn., Barren County Med. Soc., Am. Coll. Obstetricians and Gynecologists, Am. Fertility Soc., So. Seminar Obstetrics and Gynecology, Ky. Ob-Gyn Soc. (pres. 1983-84), Glasgow C. of C. Club: Masons (32 deg). Home: 530 Horton Rigdon Rd Cave City KY 42127-9310 Office: 120 State Ave Glasgow KY 42141

GIBSON, SAM THOMPSON, internist, educator; b. Covington, Ga., Jan. 1, 1916; s. Count Dillon and Julia (Thompson) G.; m. Alice Chase, Oct. 31, 1942 (dec. Jan. 1971); children: Lena S., Stephen C. (dec.), Judith Gibson Hammer, Lucy Gibson Simpson; m. Madge L. Crouch, Sept. 20, 1986. BS in Chemistry, Ga. Inst. Tech., 1936; MD, Emory U., 1940. Diplomate: Am. Bd. Internal Medicine. Med. house officer Peter Bent Brigham Hosp., Boston, 1940-41, asst. resident medicine, 1946-47, asst. medicine, 1947-49; rsch. fellow medicine Harvard Med. Sch., 1941-42, spl. rsch. assoc., 1943, Milton fellow medicine, 1947-49; assoc. medicine George Washington U. Med. Sch., also George Washington U. Hosp., 1949-63, asst. clin. prof. medicine, 1963—, clin. asst. prof. medicine, Uniformed Svcs., Univ. Health Scis., 1980—; asst. med. dir. ARC Blood Program, 1949-51, assoc. med. dir., 1951-53, assoc. dir., 1953-56, dir., 1956-66; sr. med. officer ARC, 1957-67; asst. dir. div. biologics standards NIH, 1967-72; asst. dir. Bur. of Biologics, FDA, Bethesda, Md., 1972-74; asst. to dir. Bur. Biologics, FDA, Bethesda, Md., 1974-77, dir. div. biologics evaluation, 1977-83; dir. div. biol. product compliance Ctr. for Drugs and Biologics, 1983-85; assoc. dir. sci. and tech. Office of Compliance, Ctr. Drugs and Biologics, FDA, 1985-88; dir. sci. and tech. Office of Health Affairs FDA, Rockville, Md., 1988-89; cons. 1990-; Naval Med. Sch., Nat. Naval Med. Center, Bethesda, 1950-63; mem. med. adv. bd. CARE-Medico, 1962-70, cons., 1970-89; chmn. U.S. com. for tranfusion equipment for med. use Am. Standards Assn., 1954-66, tech. adv. group transfusion equipment for med. use Nat. Commn. Clin. Lab. Standards/Am. Nat. Standards Inst., 1975-89; adviser orgn. blood transfusion services League Red Cross Socs., 1955-66. Contbg. editor: Vox Sanguinis Jour. Blood Transfusion, 1956-65; mem. adv. bd., 1965-76. Served from lt. (j.g.) to comdr., M.C. USNR, 1941-46; capt. Res. ret. Mem. AMA, AAAS, Internat., Am. socs. hematology, Nat. Health Coun. (dir. 1957-60, 61-64), Internat. Soc. Blood Transfusion (regional counselor 1962-66), Am. Fedn. Clin. Rsch., N.Y. Acad. Scis., Delta Tau Delta, Alpha Kappa Kappa, Alpha Chi Sigma, Tau Beta Pi, Phi Kappa Phi, Omicron Delta Kappa, Alpha Omega Alpha. Home: 5801 Rossmore Dr Bethesda MD 20814-2229

GIBSON-SCHULTZ, ARTHUR CHARLES, dietary manager; b. Bklyn., Sept. 30, 1944; s. Joseph John Schultz and Dorothy Cecilia (Strahle) Gibson. Cert. dietary mgr. Dietary Mgrs. Assn., 1994; cert. food mgr. Internat. Food Svc. Execs. Assn., 1996; cert. food svc. mgr. City of Chgo. Dept. Health; cert. sanitation State Ill. Dept. Health. V.p., sec. Protech Fin. Svcs., Foster City, Calif., 1974-77; pres., CEO Key Svcs. Corp., Burlingame, Calif., 1977-80; chef, owner Occidental (Calif.) Seafood Co., 1980-81; chef Bungalow Resort, Clearlake Oaks, Calif., 1980-82, Broadway Properties, Chgo., 1982-91; dietary IV U. Ill. Hosp., Chgo., 1990-92; cert. dietary mgr. Instnl. Mgrs. Approved Home, Chgo., 1992—. Mem. Am. Coll. Health Care Adminstrs. Home: 5445 N Sheridan Rd #3511 Chicago IL 60646

GIDDINGS, HERMAN, physician; b. Aug. 28, 1944; came to U.S., 1963; s. Morsteny and Harmon (Evelyn) G.; divorced; children: Lisa, Andrea, Loren, Lesley Ann, Trent. MD, Mehoney Med. Coll., Nashville. Diplomate Am. Bd. Internal Medicine, Am. Bd. Endoscopy.

GIDDINGS, LUCILLE CASSELL, nurse; b. Port Chester, N.Y., Jan. 30, 1947; d. Curtis Emmitt and Rose (Lucente) Cassell; R.N., St. Clare's Hosp., N.Y.C., 1969; B.A., Coll. Mt. St. Vincent, Bronx, N.Y., 1979; M.P.A., NYU, 1982; m. William Alfred Giddings, Apr. 2, 1977. Staff nurse hosps. in N.Y. State, 1969-71; elem. sch. nurse Port Chester-Rye Town Bd. Edn., 1971-82; dir. interdepartmental svcs. Our Lady of Mercy Hosp. Med. Center, Bronx, N.Y., 1982-83, dir. admissions, 1984-86, asst. adminstr., 1986-87; v.p. med. support svcs., 1987-89; dir. patient registration Greenwich (Conn.) Hosp. Assn., 1989-91, asst. v.p. patient support svcs., 1991, v.p. ambulatory care, 1991-96; health svcs. mgmt. cons. New Dimensions in Leadership, Inc., 1983-84; pres., CEO Nantucket Cottage Hosp., 1996; chmn. Port Chester br. ARC, 1978. Mem. community adv. bd. Jr. League of Greenwich; mem. first selectman's com. for people with spl. needs, domestic abuse com. Town of Greenwich; mem. needs assessment com., planning com. United Way of Greenwich.; Citizen Amb. Program del. to China, 1992. Recipient Rev. Mother Jean Marie award, 1969, Shepard award United Way, 1992, Bravo award YWCA, 1992. Mem. Soc. Ambulatory Care Profl., NYU Alumni Assn., Coll. Mt. St. Vincent Alumni Assn. Home: 23 Vesper Lane Nantucket MA 02554 Office: 57 Prospect St Nantucket MA 02554

GIDDINGS, WOOSTER PHILIP, surgeon, retired; b. Boston, Jan. 27, 1913; s. Harold Girard and Mildred Day (Potter) G.; m. Elizabeth Fisk, May 24, 1941; children: Robert F., Deborah, David G., James P. AB, Amherst Coll., 1934; MD, Harvard U., 1938. Diplomate Am. Bd. Surgery. Intern, asst. resident Mass. Gen. Hosp., Boston, 1938-42; resident, 1946; asst. in surgery Mass. Gen. Hosp, Boston, 1947-50, Harvard Med. Sch., Boston, 1947-50; asst. prof. surgery Albany (N.Y.) Med. Coll., 1950-54; surgeon Putnam Meml. Hosp., Bennington, Vt., 1950-75; bd. dirs. emeritus First Vt. Bank, Brattleboro, Vt.; trustee Bennington Mus., 1960-88, trustee emeritus, 1988—. Assoc. editor: Surgery in World War II, 1955. Maj. M.C. AUS, 1942-46. Decorated Purple Heart, Bronze Star. Fellow Am. Coll. Surgeons; mem. New Eng. Surg. Soc., Excelsior Surg. Soc., Vt. State Med. Soc., Mass. Med. Soc. Home: 4219 Wake Robin Dr Shelburne VT 05482-7577

GIDDON, DONALD B(ERNARD), psychologist, educator; b. Newark, May 1, 1930; s. William and Ruth (Franklin) G.; m. Phoebe L. Rothman, Aug. 28, 1955; children: David, Kenneth, Joanna, James. A.B., Brown U., 1952; M.A., Boston U., 1953; D.M.D., Harvard U., 1959; Ph.D. in Psychology, Brandeis U., 1961. Lectr. psychology Brandeis U., 1954-71, 82-84, lectr. physical edn., 1985-89; prof., chmn. dental ecology Harvard U., 1972-75, vis. prof., 1976-89, lectr., 1989—, lectr. health services adminstrn. Sch. Pub. Health, 1972-75, asst. dean adminstrn. Sch. Dental Medicine, 1973-75; assoc. staff New Eng. Med. Center, 1964-73; assoc. prof., chmn. dept. social dentistry Tufts U., Boston, 1964-67, prof., chmn. dept. social dentistry, 1967-72, asst. dean, 1967-69, assoc. dean, 1969-71; dean NYU Dental Ctr., 1975-78, prof. behavioral sci. and community health, 1976—; prof. psychology Grad. Sch. Arts and Scis., prof. anesthesiology NYU Med. Center, 1976-80; prof. Faculty of Medicine, U. Groningen, The Netherlands, 1980-81; cons. Astra Pharm. Products, Inc., 1960—; cons. dept. medicine and surgery VA, 1966-69, med. rsch. cons., 1988—, Peter Bent Brigham Hosp., 1975-76, Meml. Sloan-Kettering Cancer Ctr., 1976-78; vis. staff physician (surgery) NYU Med. Ctr., 1976—, Brookdale Hosp. Med. Ctr., 1977—, Goldwater Meml. Hosp., 1977-80; cons. psychologist dept. anesthesiology Brigham and Women's Hosp., 1979—; vis. prof. U. Gothenburg, Sweden, 1971, Royal Dental Coll., Aarhus, Denmark, 1972, U. Pa., 1972, McGill Med. U., 1981-83; vis. prof. psychology Mass. Coll. Pharmacy and Allied Health Scis., 1984-89; lectr. Brown U., 1985-89, clin. prof., 1989—; clin. prof. psychology U. Ill., Chgo., 1994—; founding dir. Rsch. Inst., Royal Victoria Hosp., Montreal, Can., 1981-82. Contbr. articles to profl. jours. Bd. dirs. Mass. Health Coun., 1965-70, pres., 1968-69; pres. Hamilton sch. PTA, Newton Lower Falls, Mass., 1963-64; trustee Emerson Coll., 1991—; mem. Com. on Univ. Resources, bd. overseers Harvard U., 1991—. Fulbright scholar, 1971. Fellow AAAS, APA, Am. Pub. Health Assn., Am. Coll. Dentists, Internat. Coll. Dentists, Internat. Coll. Psychosomatic Medicine, Royal Soc. Medicine; mem. AAUP, Am. Statis. Assn., Internat. Assn. Study Pain, Am. Psychosomatic Soc., Am. Coll. Sports Medicine, Am. Dental Soc. Anesthesiology (assoc. editor 1965-72, chmn. ethics com. 1979-81), Behavioral Sci. in Dental Rsch. (pres. 1976-77), Internat. Assn. Dental Rsch. (pres. Boston sect. 1965-66), Am. Pain Soc. (dir. 1977-79), Soc. Behavioral Med., Soc. Psychophys. Rsch., Soc. Clin. and Experimental Hypnosis, Sigma Xi. Office: 277 Linden St Wellesley MA 02181-5920

GIDEON, WILLIAM P(ATRICK), obstetrician, gynecologist, educator; b. Oklahoma City, June 16, 1943; s. A.C. and Catherine Rose (McCormack) G. BS, Okla. State U., 1964; MD, U. Okla., 1969, MPH in Health Adminstrn., 1991. Diplomate Am. Bd. Ob-Gyn. Intern, resident in ob-gyn St. John's Hosp., Hillcrest Hosp., 1969-73; chief ob-gyn USPHS Hosp., Claremore, Okla., 1973-75; chief med. officer USPHS Hosp., Oklahoma City, 1985-88, maternal and child health cons., 1975-95; asst. prof. ob-gyn. U. Okla.-Tulsa Med. Ctr., 1978—. Capt. USPHS, 1973-95. Decorated Disting. Svc. Medal, USPHS Commendation medal. Fellow ACS, ACOG; mem. APHA, Ctrl. Assn. Ob-Gyn., Okla. Med. Assn., Royal Soc. Health, Royal Soc. Medicine. Roman Catholic. Office: PO Box 721988 Norman OK 73070-8513

GIEGERICH, PAUL RAYMOND, podiatrist; b. Queens, N.Y., Dec. 31, 1953; s. Edmund William and Mary J. (Cicione) G.; m. Nancy Jeanne Cooper, Aug. 20, 1977. BS in Biology, SUNY, Geneseo, 1976; D of Podiatric Medicine, Ill. Coll. Podiatric Medicine, 1980. Diplomate Am. Bd. Podiatric Surgery. Resident podiatric surgery Md. Podiatric Residency Program, Balt., 1980-82; podiatric physician self-employed Washington, 1982—; sec., treas. Parkwood Podiatric Residency Program, Clinton, Md., 1984-88; teaching staff Capitol Hill Hosp. Podiatric Residency Program, Washington, 1989—, podiatric residency program Washington Hosp. Ctr., 1992—. Podiatric physician Dept. Health & Mental Hygiene, Md., D.C., 1980—, med. lectr., 1980—. Recipient Dedicated Svc. award Kappa Tau Epsilon, 1980. Fellow Am. Coll. Foot and Ankle Surgeons; mem. Durlacher Nat. Podiatric Honor Soc., Am. Podiatric Med. Assn., D.C. Podiatric Med. Assn., Am. Diabetes Assn. Roman Catholic. Office: 3230 Pennsylvania Ave SE Washington DC 20020-3722

GIELEN, UWE PETER, psychology educator; b. Berlin, Aug. 15, 1940; s. Alfred and Ursula (Hackemesser) G. MA in Psychology, Wake Forest U., 1968; PhD in Social Psychology, Harvard U., 1976. Asst. prof. psychology York Coll./CUNY, N.Y.C., 1977-80; assoc. prof. St. Francis Coll., Bklyn., 1980-87, chmn., dept. psychology, 1980-90, prof., 1987—. Co-author: The Kohlberg Legacy for the Helping Professions, 1991; sr. editor: Psychology in International Perspective, 1992; co-editor: Cross-cultural Topics in Psychology, 1994, Advancing Psychology and Its Applications: International Perspectives, 1994; founding editor World Psychology, 1995; mem. editl. bd.

Moral Edn. Forum, 1988-95; contbr. articles to profl. jours. Del. to UN Internat. Coun. Psychologists, N.Y., 1985-92. Recipient rsch. grants H.F. Guggenheim Found., N.Y., 1986-88, Pacific Cultural Found., Taipei, Taiwan, 1986-87. Mem. Internat. Assn. Cross-cultural Psychology, Internat. Coun. Psychologists (pres.-elect 1993-94, pres. 1994-95, past pres. 1995-96, mem. exec. bd.), N.Y. Psychol. Assn. (Kurt Lewin award 1993), N.Y. Acad. Scis. (adv. bd. psychology sect.), Bklyn. Psychol. Assn. Office: St Francis Coll Psychology Dept 180 Remsen St Brooklyn NY 11201-4398

GIEM, ROSS NYE, JR., surgeon; b. Corvallis, Oreg., May 23, 1923; s. Ross Nye and Goldie Marie (Falk) G.; student U. Redlands, Walla Walla Coll.; BA, MD, Loma Linda U.; children: John, David, Paul, James, Ross Nye, Matthew, Julie. Intern, Sacramento Gen. Hosp., 1952-53; resident in ob-gyn, Kern County Gen. Hosp., Bakersfield, Calif., 1956-57, in gen. surgery, 1957-61; practice medicine specializing in gen. surgery, Sullivan, Mo., 1961-70; staff emergency dept. Hollywood Presbyn. Med. Center, 1971-73, Meml. Hosp., Belleville, Ill., 1973-87, St. Elizabeth Hosp., Belleville, Ill., 1973-90; St. Luke Hosp., Pasadena, Calif., 1973-89, Doctors Hosp., Montclair, Calif. 1990-93, Harriman Jones Med. Group, Long Beach, Calif., 1993—; instr. nurses, physicians, paramedics, emergency med. technicians, 1973-91. Served with AUS, 1943-46. Diplomate Am. Bd. Surgery. Fellow ACS, Am. Coll. Emergency Physicians; mem. AMA, Ill. Med. Assn., Pan Am. Med. Assn., Pan Pacific Surg. Assn., Royal Coll. Physicians (Eng.)

GIENAPP, JOHN CHARLES, accreditation organization administrator; b. Milw., Feb. 3, 1939; s. John Henry and Anne Marie (Bahde) G.; m. Katie Ann Berg, Aug. 22, 1964; children: Anne Aileen, John William. BA, Concordia Sr. Coll., Ft. Wayne, Ind., 1961; MDiv, Concordia Sem., Clayton, Mo., 1965; PhD, U. Kans., 1970. Ordained to ministry Luth. Ch., 1968. Asst. prof., then assoc. prof. Concordia Sr. Coll., 1968-77; vis. asst. prof. U. Ill., Champaign-Urbana, 1977-78; asst. dir. AMA, Chgo., 1978-81; exec. dir. Accreditation Coun. for Grad. Med. Edn., Chgo., 1981—. Office: ACGME 515 N State St Ste 2000 Chicago IL 60610

GIER, KARAN HANCOCK, counseling psychologist; b. Sedalia, Mo., Dec. 7, 1947; d. Ioda Clyde and Lorna (Campbell) Hancock; m. Thomas Robert Gier, Sept. 28, 1968. BA in Edn., U. Mo., Kansas City, 1971; MA Teaching in Math/Sci. Edn., Webster U., 1974; MA in Counseling Psychology, Western Colo. U., 1981; MEd Guidance and Counseling, U. Alaska, 1981; PhD in Edn., Pacific Western U., 1989. Nat. cert. counselor. Instr. grades 5-8 Kansas City-St. Joseph Archdiocese, 1969-73; ednl. cons. Pan-Ednl. Inst., Kansas City, 1973-75; instr., counselor Bethel (Alaska) Regional High Sch., 1975-80; ednl. program coord. Western Regional Resource Ctr., Anchorage, 1980-81; counselor U. Alaska, Anchorage, 1982-83; coll. prep. instr. Alaska Native Found., Anchorage, 1982; counselor USAF, Anchorage, 1985-86; prof. U. Alaska, Anchorage, 1982—; dir. Omni Counseling Svcs., Anchorage, 1984—; prof. Chapman Coll., Anchorage, 1988—; workshop facilitator over 100 workshops on the topics of counseling techs., value clarification, non-traditional teaching approaches, peer-tutor tng. Co-author: Coping with College, 1984, Helping Others Learn, 1985; editor, co-author: A Student's Guide, 1983; contbg. author developmental Yup'ik lang. program, 1981; contbr. photographs to Wolves and Related Canids, 1990, 91; contbr. articles to profl. jours. Mem. Am. Bus. Women's Assn., Blue Springs, Mo., 1972-75, Ctr. for Environ. Edn., World Wildlife Fund, Beta Sigma Phi, Bethel, Alaska, 1976-81. Recipient 3d place color photo award Yukon-Kuskokwim State Fair, Bethel, 1978, Notable Achievement award USAF, 1986, Meritorious Svc. award Anchorage Community Coll., 1984-88. Mem. Coll. Reading and Learning Assn. (editor, peer tutor sig leader 1988—, Cert. of Appreciation 1986-93, bd. dirs. Alaska state, coord. internat. tutor program, Spl. Recognition award 1994-95), AACD, Alaska Assn. Counseling and Devel. (pres. 1989-90), Alaska Career Devel. Assn. (pres.-elect 1989-90), Nat. Rehab. Assn., Nat. Rehab. Counselors, Greenpeace, Human Soc. of U.S. Wolf Haven Am., Wolf Song of Alaska. Home and Office: Omni Counseling Svcs 8102 Harvest Cir Anchorage AK 99502-4682

GIERSON, EUGENE DOBSON, physician; b. L.A., Oct. 7, 1940; s. Hyman William and Sylvia Gierson. BA, Occidental Coll., 1962; MD, U. So. Calif., 1966. Diplomate Am. Bd. Surgery. Instr. in surgery NYU, 1967-71; resident in surgery NYU Hosp., 1967-71, Bellevue Hosp., N.Y.C., 1967-71; asst. prof. surgery UCLA, 1971-74; asst. clin. prof. surgery UCLA-Harbor, Torrance, Calif., 1974-80, U. Calif., Irvine, 1981-83; mem. surg. staff Valley Hosp., Van Nuys, 1984—; oncologic surgeon The Breast Ctr., Van Nuys, 1984—. Fellow ACS. Office: 320 Superior Ave Ste 360 Newport Beach CA 92663-2742

GIESSER, BARBARA SUSAN, neurologist, educator; b. Bronx, N.Y., Jan. 21, 1953; d. David and Evelyn (Cohen) G.; m. Philip D. Kanof, June 17, 1979; children: David, Marisa. BS, U. Miami, 1972; MS, U. Tex., Houston, 1974; MD, U. Tex., San Antonio, 1978. Diplomate Am. Bd. Psychiatry and Neurology. Intern Montefiore Hosp., Bronx, 1978-79; resident Bronx Mcpl. Hosp. Ctr. (Albert Einstein Coll. Medicine), 1979-82; asst. prof. neurology Albert Einstein Coll. Medicine, Bronx, 1983-91; med. dir. Gimbel MS Comprehensive Care Ctr., Teaneck, N.J., 1985-90, Rehab. Inst. of Tucson, 1991-95; assoc. prof. clin. neurology Ariz. Health Scis. Ctr., Tucson, 1993—. Author: Neurology Specialty Board Review, 3d edit., 1986, 4th edit., 1996; contbr. articles to profl. publs. Dean's Tchr. scholar Ariz. Health Scis. Ctr., 1995. Fellow Am. Acad. Neurology; mem. Nat. Multiple Sclerosis Soc. (rsch. grant 1989, mem. profl. adv. com. Desert S.W. chpt. 1994—, bd. dirs. 1994—). Office: Ariz Health Scis Ctr 1501 N Campbell Tucson AZ 85724

GIESSER, NANCY LYNNE, nursing educator; b. Cleve., Apr. 4, 1942; d. Robert Raymond and Blanche Bernice (Buchholzer) G. BA, Baldwin Wallace Coll., 1966; MEd, Kent State U., 1971. Staff nurse Fairview Gen. Hosp., Cleve., 1963-66, head nurse orthopedic unit, 1966-68, instr. Sch. Nursing, 1968-78, coord., 1975-78; asst. dir. nursing Lorain (Ohio) Community Hosp., 1978-80; instr. pediatric nursing Cleve. Met. Gen. Hosp. Sch. Nursing, 1980, lead instr. medicine and surgery, 1980-82, asst. dir., curriculum coord., 1982-85; dir. Sch. Nursing MetroHealth Med. Ctr., 1985, Cleve.; instr. continuing edn. Cleve. State U., 1976-79. Mem. adv. com. Project Ladders in Nursing Careers, 1988-93; chair steering com. Access in Nursing N.E. Ohio Nursing Articulation Project. Mem. ANA, Nat. League for Nursing, Ohio Citizens League Nursing (bd. dirs. 1988—), Nursing Edn. Coun., Ohio Coun. Hosp. Based Sch. Nursing, Greater Cleve. Nursing Roundtable (sec.-treas.), Greater Cleve. Hosp. Assn. (exec. nursing com.), N.E. Ohio League for Nursing (pres. 1995—). Republican. Home: 25118 Carey Ln North Olmsted OH 44070 Office: Met Health Med Ctr Sch Nursing 1803 Valentine Ave Cleveland OH 44109-1930

GIESY, JERRY DONALD, urologist; b. Portland, Oreg., July 16, 1933; s. Ralph Griffiths and Evelyn Lucille (Hulse) G.; m. Barbara Ann Peterson, Aug. 24, 1957; children: Julie, Jan. BA, Stanford U., 1955; MD, U. Oreg., 1959. Intern, resident urology U. Oreg. Med. Sch., Portland, 1960-64; physician The Urology Clinic, Portland, 1964—; pres. med. staff Emanuel Hosp., Portland, 1986, Legacy Portland Hosps., 1993. Fellow Am. Coll. Surgeons. Office: The Urology Clinic 501 N Graham Portland OR 97227

GIFFEN, LAWRENCE EVERETT, SR., family physician, anesthesiologist, historian; b. Jefferson City, Mo., Jan. 30, 1923; s. Fred Lemon and Angeline Henrietta (Patterson) G.; m. Mary Opal McKnight, Oct. 15, 1947 (div. Mar. 1950); 1 child, Lawrence Everett Jr.; m. Jerena East, June 17, 1955; children: Michael Gregory, Jerena Ann. DO, Kirksville Coll. Osteo Medicine, 1945; BS in Biology, Lincoln U., 1960; BA in History, U. Md., 1981; MS in Criminal Justice, Cen. Mo. State U., 1980; MA in History, Lincoln U., 1987; postgrad., U. Mo. Diplomate Am. Osteo. Bd. Anesthesiology, Am. Bd. Family Practice. Intern Brighton Med. Ctr., Portland, Maine, 1945-46; practice gen. medicine Chamois, Mo., 1946-50; resident in anesthesiology Art Ctr. Hosp., Detroit, 1950-51; practice gen. medicine and anesthesiology Jefferson City, Mo., 1951-80, 83—; med. examiner Jefferson City, 1968-80. Contbr. articles to profl. and hist. jours. Comdr. USNR, 1980-83; ret. 1991. Fellow Am. Osteo. Coll. Anesthesiologists (pres. 1962), Am. Osteo. Coll. Surgeons (hon.), Am. Acad. Family Physicians; mem. AMA, Mo. State Med. Soc., U.S. Naval Inst., Am. Assn. History Medicine, Am. Hist. Assn., Orgn. Am. Historians, Masons. Republican. Presbyterian. Home and Office: 1606 Hayselton Dr Jefferson City MO 65109-1212

GIFFIN, MARY ELIZABETH, psychiatrist, educator; b. Rochester, Minn., Mar. 30, 1919; d. Herbert Ziegler and Mary Elizabeth (Nace) G. BA, Smith Coll., Northampton, Mass., 1939; MD, Johns Hopkins, 1943; MS, U. Minn., 1948. Diplomate Am. Bd. Psychiatry and Neurology. Cons. in neurology and psychiatry Mayo Clinic, Rochester, 1949-58; med. dir. Josselyn Clinic, Northfield, Ill., 1958-89; pvt. practice psychiatry Northfield, 1989—; mem. faculty Inst. for Psychoanalysis, Chgo., 1963-89. Contbr. numerous articles to profl. jour. Mem. Ill. Psychiat. Soc., Am. Acad. Child Psychiatry. Republican. Mem. Am. Bapt. Ch. Home: 1190 Hamptondale Ave Winnetka IL 60093-1812 Office: 1 Northfield Plz Ste 300 Northfield IL 60093-1214

GIFFORD, GEORGE E., immunology and medical microbiology educator; b. Mpls., Dec. 6, 1924; s. Ernest Wilbur and Hulda Victoria (Widen) G.; m. June Marie Pirila, Dec. 29, 1956 (dec. Nov. 1977); children: Charles Stephen, Sheryl Dianne. BA cum laude, U. Minn., 1949, MS, 1953, PhD, 1955. Instr. U. Minn. Sch. Medicine, Mpls., 1955-56; asst. prof. U. Fla. Coll. Medicine, Gainesville, 1957-64, assoc. prof., 1964-68, prof. immunology and med. microbiology, 1968-93, acting chmn., 1972-73, 82-83, prof. emeritus, 1993—; vis. prof. Hebrew U.-Hadassah Med. Sch., Jerusalem, 1984, Fraunhofer Inst. Toxicology, Hannover, Fed. Republic Germany, 1985; assoc. dean for grad. edn. Univ. Fla. Coll. Medicine, 1990-93. With USN, 1943-45. Recipient Faculty Rsch. award Sigma Xi, Gainesville, Fla., 1975, Grants, USPHS, Am. Cancer Soc., 1968-93. Fellow AAAS, Am. Acad. Microbiology; mem. Am. Assn. Microbiology, Soc. Gen. Microbiology, Tissue Culture Assn., Am. Inst. Biol. Scientists, Am. Assn Immunology, Sigma Xi. Republican. Lutheran. Home: 132 Turkey Crk Alachua FL 32615-9571

GIFFORD, NATALIE EVE, obstetrical and gynecological nurse; b. Live Oak, Fla., Nov. 7, 1966; d. Augmond Jackson and Madeleine Francois (Derédec) Voyles; m. Alan Nye Gifford, Nov. 6, 1987. ADN, Fayetteville (N.C.) Tech. C.C., 1993. Mem. gynecological/antenatal nursing staff Cape Fear Valley Med. Ctr., Fayetteville, N.C., 1993-94. Home: 533 Lake Vernon Rd Leesville LA 71446

GIFFORD, RAY WALLACE, JR., physician, educator; b. Westerville, Ohio, Aug. 13, 1923; s. Ray Wallace and Alma Marie (Wagoner) G.; m. Frances Anne Moore, Jan. 13, 1973; 1 son, George; children by previous marriage: Peggy, Cynthia, Susan. BS, Otterbein Coll., 1944, ScD (hon.), 1986; M.D., Ohio State U., 1947; M.Sc., U. Minn., 1952. Diplomate: Am. Bd. Internal Medicine. Intern Colo. Gen. Hosp., Denver, 1947-48; resident in internal medicine Mayo Clinic, Rochester, Minn., 1949-52; practice medicine specializing in hypertension and nephrology; asst. prof. medicine, cons. sect. medicine Mayo Clinic, Mayo Found., 1953-61; staff mem. dept. hypertension and nephrology Cleve. Clinic Found., 1961-67, head dept. hypertension and nephrology, 1967-85, sr. physician dept. hypertension and nephrology, 1986-93, acting chmn. dept. hypertension and nephrology, 1991-92, cons. dept. hypertension and nephrology, 1994—, bd. govs., 1973-78, vice chmn., 1977-78, vice chmn. div. medicine, 1978-93, chmn. regional health affairs, 1986-93, 94—; prof. internal medicine Ohio State U. Coll. Medicine, Columbus, Ohio, 1993—; asst. attending physician U.S. Congress, 1954-56; chmn. hypertension task force Intersoc. Commn. on Heart Disease Resources, 1979-81; mem. nat. high blood pressure coordinating com. Nat. Heart, Lung and Blood Inst., 1978—; mem. 2d, 3d, 4th and chmn. 5th joint nat. coms. on detection, evaluation and treatment of high blood pressure, 1979-80, 83-84, 87-88, 91-92; mem. Congl. Commn. on Drug Approval Process, 1981-82; mem. adv. com. to dir. NIH, 1982-86; mem. Joint Commn. on Accreditation of Healthcare Orgns., 1989-90; mem. Forum on Drug Devel., Inst. Medicine, 1990-94. Author: (with William Manger) Pheochromocytoma, 1977, 96; contbr. numerous papers to med. jours.; editl. bd. Stroke Jour., 1971-74, Am. Jour. Cardiology, 1973-78, Geriatrics, 1974—, Hypertension Rsch., 1994—, Jour. Cardiovasc. Rsch., 1994—. Mem. Rochester (Minn.) City Coun., 1960-61, Rep. precinct committeeman, Cleveland Heights, Ohio, 1966-70. Lt. comdr. M.C., USNR, 1954-56. Recipient Alumni Achievement award Ohio State U., 1962, Alumni medal, 1989; Disting. Sci. Achievement award Otterbein Coll., 1970, Spl. Achievement award, 1992; individual achievement award high blood pressure edn. programs Nat. Heart, Lung and Blood Inst., 1989, Bristol Myers lifetime achievement award Am. Heart Assn., 1992; spl. achievement award Cleve. Clinic Alumni Assn., 1994; Ray W. Gifford, Jr. endowed chair in hypertension established at Cleve. Clinic, 1994. Fellow ACP (master), Am. Coll. Cardiology (bd. trustees 1969-70, gov. Ohio chpt. 1970-73), Am. Coll. Chest Physicians (chmn. com. on hypertension 1970-72, Simon Rodbard Meml. award 1982); mem. AMA (coun. on sci. affairs 1976-85, vice chmn. 1981-83, chmn. 1983-85, trustee 1986-90), Am. Heart Assn. (bd. dirs. 1969-72, chmn. stroke coun. 1970-72), Am. Soc. Clin. Pharmacology and Therapeutics (pres. 1976-77, Oscar B. Hunter Meml. award in Therapeutics 1979, Henry W. Elliott award Disting. Svc. 1995), Ctrl. Soc. Clin. Rsch., Internat. Soc. Hypertension, Internat. Soc. Hypertension in Blacks, Interstate Postgrad. Med. Assn. (pres. 1976-77), Interam. Soc. Hypertension, Coun. on Geriatric Cardiology (bd. dirs. 1989-92), Ohio State U. Alumni Assn. (bd. dirs. 1990-95). Methodist. Home: 3479 Glen Allen Dr Cleveland OH 44121-1503 Office: Cleve Clinic Found 9500 Euclid Ave Cleveland OH 44195-0001

GIFT, JAMES J., toxicologist. BA in Biology, Harvard U, 1964; MA in Environ. Sci., Rutgers U., 1968, PhD in Environ. Sci., 1970. Lab. rsch. dir. Ichthyological Assocs., Brigentine, N.J., 1970-75; sr. v.p., dir. sci. and tech. EA Engrng., Sci. & Tech. Inc., Md., 1975—; ž. Mem. Soc. Environ., Toxicology and Chemistry, Water Environ. Fedn., Am. Fisheries Soc. Office: EA Engrng Sci & Tech Inc 11019 Mccormick Rd Cockeysville MD 21031-1423

GIGANTELLI, JAMES WILLIAM, ophthalmic plastic surgeon; b. Dover, N.J., Sept. 3, 1959. BS, U. So. Calif., 1981; MD, Vanderbilt U., 1985. Diplomate Am. Bd. Ophthalmology. Resident Vanderbilt U., Nashville, 1985-86, Baylor Coll. Medicine, Houston, 1986-89; fellow Duke U., Durham, N.C., 1989-90; staff Alton Ochsner Med. Found., Baton Rouge, 1990-94; asst. prof. U. Mo., Columbia, 1994—. Fellow Am. Acad. Ophthalmology; mem. AMA, Assn. for Rsch. in Vision and Ophthalmology, Mo. State Med. Assn. Office: U Mo Mason Eye Inst One Hospital Dr Columbia MO 65212

GIGLI, IRMA, physician, educator, academic administrator; b. Cordoba, Argentina, Dec. 22, 1931; d. Irineo and Esperanza Francisca (Pons de Gigli) G.; m. Hans J. Muller-Eberhard, June 29, 1985. B.A., Liceo Nacional Manuel Belgrano, Cordoba, 1950; M.D., Universidad Nacional de Cordoba, 1957. Intern Cook County Hosp., Chgo., 1957-58; resident in dermatology Cook County Hosp., 1958-60; fellow in dermatology NYU, 1960-61; mem. faculty Harvard Med. Sch., 1967-75, asso. prof. dermatology, 1972-75; chief dermatology service Peter Bent Brigham Hosp., Robert B. Brigham Hosp., 1971-75; prof. dermatology and exptl. medicine N.Y. U. Med. Center, N.Y.C., 1976-82; mem. Irvington Houst Inst. N.Y. U. Med. Center, mem. faculty N.Y. Grad. Sch. Med. Scis., dir. Asthma and Allergic Disease Center for Immunodermatology Studies, 1980-91; prof. medicine, chief div. dermatology U. Calif.-San Diego, 1983-95; prof. medicine and dermatology, vice chair medicine for sci. U. Tex. Health Sci. Ctr., Houston, 1995—; vice-chair medicine for sci. Health Sci. Ctr., Inst. Molecular Medicine for Prevention of Human Diseases U. Tex., Houston, 1995—; chmn. study sect. Allergy and Immunology Inst., NIH; Guggenheim Found. Western Hemisphere and Phillippines Com. of Selection; adv. bd. NIH Fogarty Internat. Ctr., 1984—. Contbr. articles to profl. jours. Recipient Stephen Rothman Meml. award Soc. for Investigative Dermatology, 1996, rsch. award Am. Cancer Soc., 1970-72, NIH, 1972-76; Guggenheim Found., grantee, 1974-75. Mem. Am. Soc. Clin. Investigation, Am. Assn. Immunologists, Am. Acad. Dermatology, Soc. Investigative Dermatology, Am. Acad. Allergy, Assn. Am. Physicians, Am. Dermatol. Assn., Soc. for Investigative Dermatology (prs. 1990-91), Inst. Medicine/NAS. Office: U Tex Health Sci Ctr Inst Molecular Medicine 2121 W Holcombe Blvd Houston TX 77030

GIGLIO, FRANCIS A., gynecologist; b. Beaumont, Tex., Dec. 29, 1928; s. Charles Samuel and Antoinette Cecilia (Cuchia) G.; m. Marcia May Frey, June 25, 1955; children: Joan Marie, Suzanne. BA, U. Tex., 1950; MD, U. Tex., Galveston, 1955. Diplomate Am. Bd. Ob-Gyn. Intern Providence Hosp.; resident U. Ala. Med. Ctr., asst. prof. Dept. OB-GYN, 1963-65; pvt. practice Beaumont, 1965—; cons. St. Elizabeth, Bapt. Hosps., Beaumont Med. and Surg. Hosp.; clin. asst. prof. Tex. U. Med. Br., 1979-92. Patentee rectal med. suppository, urethral insert, 1992; contbr. articles to profl. jours. Adv. bd. vol. Bur. Beaumont, 1966; chmn. crusade Am. Cancer Soc. North Jefferson County, pres., 1967-68. Lt. col. M.C., USAR, Operation Desert Shield/Desert Storm. Decorated Army Commendation medal. Fellow Am. Coll. Obstretricians and Gynecologists (chair sect. membership com.); mem. AMA, Am. Fertility Soc., Ctrl. Assn. Obstetricians and Gynecologists, Tex. Assn. Obstetricians and Gynecologists, Am. Assn. Gynecol. Laparascopists, Am. Soc. Colposcopy and Cervical Pathology, Soc. Reproductive Surgeons, Inc., Beaumont C. of C., Mu Delta. Roman Catholic. Home: 1265 Nottingham Ln Beaumont TX 77706-4315 Office: 3560 Delaware St Ste 402 Beaumont TX 77706-3060

GIGLIO, NICKI SUE, critical care nurse, administrator; b. Terre Haute, Ind., Apr. 2, 1951; d. James Dean and Doris Marie (Campbell) G. Student, Ind. U., 1969-71, Ind. State U., 1971-74; diploma, St. Anthony Hosp. Sch. Nursing, Terre Haute, 1974. Cert. emergency nurse, ACLS. Clinician, emergency dept. Humana Hosp., San Antonio, 1983-84; staff nurse emergency dept. Mary Immaculate Hosp., Newport News, Va., 1985-87, St. Mary's Hosp., Richmond, Va., 1987-88; house supr. Iroquois Meml. Hosp., Watseka, Ill., 1988—. Mem. ANA, ARC, Emergency Nurses Assn., Ill. Coun. Nurse Mgrs., Bus. and Profl. Women's Assn., Watseka Bus. and Profl. Women's Orgn., Delta Theta Tau. Home: 559 N 6th St Watseka IL 60970

GIKAS, PAUL WILLIAM, medical educator; b. Lansing, Mich., July 23, 1928; s. John and Minnie (Neumann) G.; m. Lois Suzanne Haglund, Dec. 27, 1952; children—Sandra Jane, Sarah Elizabeth, Paula Suzanne. A.B., U. Mich., 1950, M.D., 1954. Diplomate: Am. Bd. Pathology. Chief lab. service VA Hosp., Ann Arbor, Mich., 1960-68; mem. faculty U. Mich. Med. Sch., Ann Arbor, 1959—; assoc. prof. pathology U. Mich. Med. Sch., 1966-69, prof., 1969-95, prof. emeritus, 1995—, faculty rep. to Big Ten Intercollegiate Conf., Nat. Collegiate Athletic Assn., 1982-88, asst. dean for admissions, 1990—, prof. emeritus of pathology, 1995—; cons. Armed Forces Inst. Pathology, 1966-74. Author: The Accident Problem, 1976, Uropathology, 1976, Forensic Aspects of the Highway Crash, 1983; co-editor: The Prevention of Highway Injury, 1967. Mem. adv. com. traffic safety HEW, 1966-68; mem. Gov. Mich. Spl. Commn. Traffic Safety Mich., 1964; chmn. bd. dirs. Pub. Citizen, Inc., 1971—; co-trustee Center Study Responsive Law, Washington, 1969-71. Served to capt. M.C. AUS, 1956-58. Recipient Auto Safety award Med. Tribune, 1966-67, Distinguished Service award U. Mich., 1965. Fellow Coll. Am. Pathologists; mem. N.Y. Acad. Scis., U.S. and Can. Acad. Pathology, Alpha Omega Alpha, Nu Sigma Nu. Lutheran. Home: 1900 Mershon Dr Ann Arbor MI 48103-5939

GIL, DAVID GEORG, social policy educator; b. Vienna, Austria, Mar. 16, 1924; came to U.S., 1953; s. Oskar and Helene (Weiss) Engel; m. Eva Aviva Breslauer, Aug. 2, 1947; children: Daniel W. and Gideon R. (twins). BA, Hebrew U., 1957; MSW, U. Pa., Phila., 1958, DSW, 1963. Lic. social worker, Mass.; lic. ind. clin. social worker. Farmworker, laborer Sweden and Palestine, 1939-43; counselor, tchr. Home for Dependent, Neglected and Delinquent Children, Tel-Mond, Palestine, 1943-45; probation officer Dept. Social Welfare, Palestine and Israel, 1945-53; fellow UN, Phila., 1953-55; asst. dir. Youth Probation Svc., Jerusalem, 1955-57; family counselor Jewish Family Svc., Phila., 1957-59; supr., rsch. assoc. Assn. Jewish Children, Phila., 1959-63; rsch. dir. Soc. to Prevent Cruelty to Children, Boston, 1963-64; from asst. to prof. social policy Brandeis U., Waltham, Mass., 1964—; dir. Ctr. for Social Change, Heller Grad. Sch., Brandeis U., Waltham, 1984—; Kenneth L. Pray lectr. U. Pa., Phila., 1991; vis. prof. George Washington U. Sch. of Social Work, 1973—. Author: Violence Against Children, 1970, Unravelling Social Policy, 1973, 76, 81, 90, 92, The Challenge of Social Equality, 1976, Beyond the Jungle, 1979, editor: Child Abuse and Violence, 1979; co-editor: Toward Social and Economic Justice, 1985, The Future of Work, 1987; chair faculty senate Brandeis U., 1989-92. Rep. bd. trustees Brandeis U., 1990-94; co-chair Socialist Party, 1995—. Rsch. grantee U.S. Children's Bur., Washington, 1965-73, project grantee Levinson Found., Boston, 1983, 85. Mem. NASW (del. assembly 1987-90), Assn. Humanist Sociology (pres. 1981), Am. Orthopsychiat. Assn. (bd. mem. 1990-93). Office: Heller Sch Brandeis U Waltham MA 02254-9110

GILBERG, ARNOLD L., psychiatrist and psychoanalyst; b. Chgo., Sept. 11, 1936; s. Jack and Anne (Schwartz) Gilberg; children: Suzanne, Jonathan. MD, U. Ill., Chgo., 1961; PhD, So. Calif. Psychoanalytic Inst., 1971. Diplomate Am. Bd. Psychiatry and Neurology; cert. in psychoanalysis Am. Psychoanalytic Assn. Practice medicine specializing in adult psychiatry, psychoanalysis Beverly Hills, Calif., 1965—; assoc. clin. prof. psychiatry UCLA Sch. Medicine; pres. So. Calif. Psychoanalytic Inst., Beverly Hills, 1990-92; tng. and supervising psychoanalyst So. Calif. Psychoanalytic Inst.; mem. bd. govs. Sinai Temple, L.A., 1993—. Contbr. articles to profl. jours. Apptd. by 3 govs. to Med. Bd. of Calif., (Med. Quality Rev. Com.), 11th Dist., 1982-91. Fellow APA, Am. Coll. Psychoanalysts; mem. Am. Psychoanalytic Assn., Internat. Psychoanalytic Assn. Jewish. Office: 9915 Santa Monica Blvd Beverly Hills CA 90212-1606

GILBERT, JO, psychologist; b. L.A., July 25, 1949; d. Joseph Raymond and Rochelle Rose (Burdman) G.; divorced; 1 child, Branden Christopher Smale. BA in Psychology cum laude, UCLA, 1972; postgrad., U. Houston, 1971-72, William Marsh Rice U., 1972-77; PhD in Clin. Psychology, Calif. Sch. Profl. Psychology, 1980. Lic. psychologist, Calif.; qualified med. evaluator. Psychol. intern, researcher, then counselor Olive St. Bridge, Fresno, Calif., 1978-80; registered psychologist FCEOC Project Pride, Fresno, 1980-82; psychologist Fox, Pick and Assocs., Napa, Calif., 1982-85; pvt. practice Napa, 1985—; ptnr. Napa-Solano Psychotherapy Svcs., 1993—; adj. faculty in forensic psychology Calif. Sch. Profl. Psychology, Berkeley, 1987; faculty U. San Francisco, 1987-88; presenter at profl. confs.; mem. Sacramento County panel ct.-appointed psychologists, Yolo County panel ct.-appointed psychologists, Solano County panel ct.-appointed psychologists. Contbr. articles to profl. publs. Mem. APA, Calif. Psychol. Assn. (assoc. sec. 1994-95), Napa Valley Psychol. Assn. (past pres.), Soc. Personality Assessment. Democrat. Jewish.

GILBERT, JOHN HUMPHREY VICTOR, audiologist, speech scientist, educator; b. Bath, Somerset, Eng., Mar. 19, 1941; s. Daniel and Nancy (Johns) G.; divorced; children: Eliot Daniel, Oliver Gaius. Grad., U. London; Ph.D., Purdue U., 1966. Asst. prof. U. B.C., 1966-69, assoc. prof., 1969-74, prof., 1974—, Med. Research Council postdoctoral scholar, 1969-74, head div. audiology and speech sci., dir. Sch. Audiol. Speech Sci., 1980-88, acting dir. Sch. Rehab. Medicine, 1985-88; coord. health scis. Univ. B.C., Vancouver, Can., 1995—; mem. study sect. NIH, 1981; mem. senate U. B.C., 1984-87, 93—; chmn. adv. com. B.C. Med. Svcs. Found., 1981—, chmn., pres. com. lectures, 1986-90; mem. health and welfare com. Vancouver Found. Mem. editl. bd. Cambridge U. Press, Clin. Phonetics and Linguistics, J. Child Lang. Fulbright scholar Purdue U., 1963-66; David Ross Rsch. fellow, 1965-66; recipient Killam Tchg. prize U. B.C., 1995; named Outstanding Alumnus, Purdue U., 1993. Mem. Can. Assn. Audiologists and Speech Lang. Pathologists (pres. 1984-85, chmn. com. on examinations 1986-88, medal for outstanding profl. achievement 1988), Internat. Assn. Child Lang. (exec. coun. 1983—), Point Grey Golf and Country Club, Vancouver Club. Home: 3350 W 37th Ave, Vancouver, BC Canada V6N 2V6 Office: Univ BC Health Sci Office, RM 400 IRC 2194 Health Mall, Vancouver, BC Canada V6T 1Z3

GILBERT, LIANE MARIE, research scientist executive; b. Long Branch, N.J., June 20, 1949; d. Charles Wilson and Edith Doris (Johnson) Case; m. Roger William Gilbert, July 17, 1971; children: David Aaron, Charles Paul. BA in Psychology, Monmouth U., West Long Branch, N.J., 1972; MA in Teaching, Trenton State Coll., 1979. Cert. tchr. of handicapped, N.J. Tchr. spl. edn., dir. afternoon program S.E.A.R.C.H., Ocean, N.J., 1972-74; tchr. spl. edn. Jackson (N.J.) Twp. Sch. System, 1974-79; exec. dir. Otologic Edn., Inc., Shrewsbury, N.J., 1980-88; dir. clin. rsch. Nat. Patent Analytical Systems, Inc., Roslyn Heights, N.Y., 1983-86, v.p. rsch., 1986-88; pres. Westerman Rsch. Assocs., Inc., Shrewsbury, N.J., 1988—; participant numerous convs., profl. organs. and spl. interest groups, U.S.A., Israel and The Netherlands, 1974—; software devel. expert to knowledge engr. for Visual Perceptual System, 1984—; v.p. Otologic Edn., Inc., Shrewsbury, 1988—. Co-contbr. articles and chpts. to profl. publs.; U.S. and Can. patentee computer-aided drug-abuse detection. Fundraiser Am. Heart Assn., 1991; active MADD; activist Nat. Audubon Soc. Mem. Internat. Regulatory Affairs Profls. Soc., Nat. Graphic Soc., Assn. Clin. Pharmacologists, Regulatory Affairs Profls. Soc., Monmouth County Assn. Children with Learning Disabilities, Psi Chi, Sigma Xi. Office: Westerman Rsch Assocs Inc 499 Broad St Shrewsbury NJ 07702-4003

GILBERT, NEIL ROBIN, social work educator, author, consultant; b. N.Y.C., Sept. 18, 1940; s. Alan and Ida (Bedzin) G.; m. Barbara Diane Feinstein, June 2, 1963; children: Evan Mallory, Jesse Arthur. BA, Bklyn. Coll., 1963; MSW, U. Pitts., 1965, PhD, 1968. Caseworker Interdepartmental Service Ctr., N.Y.C., 1963; dir. research Mayor's Com. on Human Resources, Pitts., 1967-69; prof. sch. social welfare U. Calif., Berkeley, 1969—, chmn. doctoral program, 1983—, acting dean sch. social welfare, 1986, Milton and Gertrude Chernin prof. social welfare and social svcs., 1989—; advisor Jour. Social Policy, 1982—. Author: Clients or Constituents, 1970, Capitalism and the Welfare State, 1983, (with others) Dimensions of Social Welfare Policy, 1974, 2d rev. edit., 1986, Dynamics of Community Planning, 1978, (with Barbara Gilbert) The Enabling State, 1989, Protecting Young Children from Sexual Abuse, 1989, Practical Program Evaluation, 1990, (with Jill Berrick) With the Best of Intentions, 1992, Welfare Justice, 1995; editor Social Welfare Series, 1977-83, Social Worker and Social Welfare Series, 1977—. Trustee Head Royce Sch.; chair bd. dirs. Seneca Ctr. Fellow NIMH, 1966, U.N. Research Inst. for Social Devel., 1975; Fulbright scholar, U.S. Info. Agy, 1981; Fulbright Research fellow, London, 1981, Fulbright Western European scholar, 1987; recipient Medallion of Distinction U. Pitts., 1987. Mem. Nat. Assn. Social Workers, Assn. Pub. Policy Analysis and Mgmt. Office: U Calif Sch Social Welfare Haviland Hall Berkeley CA 94720

GILBERT, NORMAN SUTCLIFFE, research physician; b. Butte, Mont., July 8, 1919; s. Norman Sutcliffe and Naomi (Robinson) G.; m. Andrea Pearce Armbruster, Apr. 23, 1949; children: Andrea Naomi, Carolyn Sutcliffe. BS, La. State U., 1939, MD, 1943. Diplomate Am. Bd. Internal Medicine. Intern Charity Hosp., New Orleans, 1943; resident in Internal Medicine La. State U., New Orleans, 1946-48; intern Charity Hosp., New Orleans, 1943; instr. to prof. emeritus sch. medicine La. State U., 1950-75, assoc. dean, 1964-70; dir.Nat. Spinal Cord Injur Ctr. Charity Hosp., New Orleans, 1966-75; head Dept. Rehab. Charity Hosp., 1966-75; research physician Naval Biodynamics Lab., New Orleans, 1976-93; med. rating specialist VA Regional Office, New Orleans, 1993—; vis. prof. U. Costa Rica Sch. Medicine, San Jose, 1963-64; med. cons. La. State Dept. and Vocat. Rehab., New Orleans, 1965—; chmn. combined deans com. VA Hosp., 1965-75; mem. Acad. Health Affairs Com., VA Dist. #1, 1974-76. Contbr. articles to profl. jours. Bd. dirs. Greater New Orleans Cancer Assn., 1962-71, St. Bernard United Way, 1960-70. Served to capt. M.C., 1944-46. Mem. La. Rehab. Assn., Orleans Parish Med. Soc., La. State Med. Soc., New Orleans Acad. Internal Medicine, Academic Health Affairs Comm. Republican. Episcopalian. Home: 1800 Bayou Rd Saint Bernard LA 70085-9748

GILBERT, ROBERT PETTIBONE, retired physician, educator; b. Chgo., Sept. 29, 1917; s. Newell Clark and Charlotte Louise (Pettibone) G.; m. Anne Cribben Heneage, June 5, 1943 (div. 1964); children: Robert P., Diane H., Nancy C., Anne E., m. Brenda Drake, Oct. 2, 1964; children: Jane D., Newell C. BA, Haverford Coll., 1938; MD, Northwestern U., 1942. Diplomate Am. Bd. Internal Medicine. Cardiology fellow Stanford U. Med. Sch., San Francisco, 1947-48; instr. to assoc. prof. of Medicine Northwestern U. Med. Sch., Chgo., 1949-65; rsch. assoc. in Physiology U. Minn., Mpls., 1956-57; dir. edn. and rsch. Evanston (Ill.) Hosp., 1957-65; assoc. dean Jefferson Med. Coll., Phila., 1965-72, assoc. prof., 1965—; clin. prof. of Medicine and dir. student health Thomas Jefferson U., Phila., 1981-90. Contbr. articles to profl jours. Lt. USNR, 1943-46, PTO. Markle scholar Markle Found. and Northwestern U., 1952-57. Fellow Am. Coll. Physicians. Republican. Presbyterian. Home: 304 Keithwood Rd Wynnewood PA 19096-1224

GILBERT, THOMAS TIBBALS, family physician, epidemiologist; b. Boston, Jan. 8, 1947; s. Carl Joyce and Helen (Homans) G.; m. Margaret Ray, June 28, 1968; children: Carolyn, Daniel. BA, Stanford U., 1968; BS in Med. Scis., Dartmouth U., 1972; MD, Harvard U., 1974, MPH, 1987. Diplomate Am. Bd. Family Practice. Resident in family practice Highland Hosp., Rochester, N.Y., 1974-77; attending physician Island Med. Ctr., Stonington, Maine, 1977-80; asst. prof. family medicine U. Colo., Denver, 1980-82, Meml. Hosp., Brown U., Pawtucket, R.I., 1982-86; with epidemic intelligence service ctr. disease control N.H. Div. Pub. Health, Concord, 1987-89; med. epidemiologist R.I. Dept. Health, Providence, 1989-91; clin. asst. prof. family medicine Brown U., Providence, 1991—; pvt. practice East Providence, R.I., 1991—. USPHS grantee, 1984, Nat. Ctr. for Health Svcs. Rsch. fellow, 1986-87. Mem. Am. Acad. Family Physicians, Undersea Med. Soc., Soc. Tchrs. Family Medicine, Am. Pub. Health Assn.

GILBOA, NISAN, physician; b. Balachna, Russia, Feb. 12, 1945; came to U.S. 1973; s. Schmuel and Mina (Lapp) G.; married, 1967; children: Amit, Noam, Keren. MD, Hebrew U., Jerusalem, 1973. Resident U. Oreg. Med. Sch., Portland, 1973-75; fellow U. Colo. Med. Sch., Denver, 1975-77; asst. prof. Union U. Med. Sch., Albany, N.Y., 1977, to 1990; assoc. prof. medicine U. Pitts., 1990—; cons. Genentech Co., San Francisco, 1985; peer rev. com. Am. Heart Assn., 1985-89. Referee, reviewer med. and sci. jours.; contbr. articles to profl. jours. Am. Heart Assn./Am. Kidney Found. grantee, 1980-91. Office: Children's Hosp 3705 5th Ave Pittsburgh PA 15213-2524

GILBREATH, ROY EARL, III, physician; b. Melbourne, Fla., Oct. 6, 1953; s. Roy Earl Jr. and Carolyn Nell (Mock) G.; m. Heidi Monroe Molick, Aug. 27, 1987; 1 child, Carolynn Jewell. BS, U. Fla., 1975; MD, U. Miami, 1979; MBA, U. Nev. Diplomate Am. Bd. Internal Medicine, Am. Bd. Quality Assurance Utilization Rev. Physicians. Intern, resident internal medicine Walter Reed Army Med. Ctr.; chief internal medicine U.S. Army Hosp., Bremerhaven, Germany, 1982-85; med. informatics Tricity Hosp., Dallas, 1993-95; med. dir. Primary Care Concepts/Alliance Health Providers, Ft. Worth, 1995—; prin. Virtual Healthcare, Dallas, 1993—. Contbr. articles to prof. jours., chpts. to books. Maj. U.S. Army, 1979-85. Fellow ACP; mem. Healthcare Info. Sys. Soc., Am. Med. Info. Assn., Soc. med. Decision Making, Dallas County Med. Soc., Tex. Med. Assn., Am. Coll. Physician Execs., Am. Soc. Internal. Medicine. Office: Alliance Health Providers 5601 Bridge St Ste 410 Fort Worth TX 76112

GILCHREST, BARBARA A. D., dermatologist; b. Port Chester, N.Y., 1945. MD, Harvard U., 1971. Cert. dermatology, internal medicine. Intern Boston City Hosp., 1971-72, resident internal medicine, 1972-73, resident dermatology, 1973-76; fellow photobiology Harvard U., Boston, 1974-75; chief dermatology U. Hosp., Boston, Boston City Hosp.; prof., chmn. dermatology Boston U. Sch. Medicine, 1985—. Mem. AAAS, Am. Acad. Dermatology, Assn. Am. Physicians, Am. Soc. for Clin. Investigation, Soc. for Investigative Dermatology. Office: Boston U Sch Medicine Dermatology 80 E Concord St Boston MA 02118-2394

GILDENBERG, PHILIP LEON, neurosurgeon; b. Hazleton, Pa., Mar. 15, 1935; s. Samuel and Ida (Kline) G.; m. Patricia O'Neill Franklin; children: Susan, Steven, Ronald, Laura, Alexandra. AB in Zoology with honors (Edward Pendleton scholar 1952-55), U. Pa., 1955; MD, MS in Exptl. Neurology (Pa. Senatorial scholar 1955-59), Temple U., 1959, PhD in Neurophysiology (Nat. Inst. Neurol. Diseases and Blindness 1966-67, spl. fellow 1967, NIH grantee 1966), 1970. Diplomate Am. Bd. Neurol. Surgery. Intern Grace Hosp., Detroit, 1959-60; resident in surgery Temple U. Hosp., 1962, resident in neurosurgery, 1962-67, lectr. neurosurgery Sch. Nursing, 1963-67, lectr. neurosurgery Philippine Nurse Exchange Program, Health Scis. Ctr., 1965-67; research fellow neurophysiology Max Planck Inst. Brain Research, Frankfurt, Fed. Republic of Germany, 1968; staff neurosurgeon Cleve. Clinic Found., 1968-72, head clinician neurosurg. research, 1969-72; prof., chief div. neurosurgery Med. Ctr., U. Ariz., Tucson, 1972-75, Med. Sch., U. Tex., Houston, 1976-82; clin. prof. neurosurgery Med. Sch. U. Tex., Houston, 1982-94, clin. prof. psychiatry and behavioral medicine, 1988-94; co-dir. pain clinic Med. Sch., U. Tex., Houston, 1975-83; chief neurosurg. service Hermann Hosp., Houston, 1975-82, 90-91; clin. prof. neurosurgery Tex. A & M. Med. Sch., College Station, 1992-94; clin. prof. neurosurgery, clin. prof. radiology Baylor Med. Coll., 1994—; adj. asst. prof. Case Western Res. U., Cleve., 1970-72; vis. prof. Temple U. Med. Sch., 1978, 80, 94, Hahnemann Med. Sch., Phila., 1980, U. Fla. Med. Sch., 1981, U. Pa. Med. Sch., 1985, Wayne State Med. Sch., Detroit, 1988, U. Ariz. Med. Sch., 1995; dir. Houston Stereotactic Ctr., Houston; cons. Tucson VA Hosp., 1972-74; mem. numerous nat. med. coms. and study groups. Author numerous articles in field.; Editor: Applied Neurophysiolcgy, Pain and Headache, Stereotactic and Functional Neurosurgery; mem. editorial bds. profl. jours. Dir. Houston Stereotactic Ctr., 1993—. Recipient Research award U. Ariz. Med. Sch., 1973, Fan Kane Research award, 1974; grantee NIH. Fellow ACS; mem. World Soc. Stereotactic and Functional Surgery (pres. 1993—), Am. Soc. Stereotactic and Functional Surgery (sec.-treas. 1972-93), Am. Assn. Neurol. Surgeons, Congress Neurol. Surgeons, Soc. Neurol. Surgeons, Am. Physiol. Soc., Soc. U. Neurosurgeons, Research Soc. Neurol. Surgeons, Soc. Neurosci., Internat. Assn. Study Pain (a founder), Houston Neurol. Soc., Am. Trauma Soc. (a founder), Am. Acad. Neurology (assoc.), Harris County Med. Soc., Rocky Mountain Neurosurg. Soc., So. Neurosurg. Soc., Neuroanesthesia Soc., Nat. Pain Found. (bd. dirs. 1987-92), Coun. Biology Editors (bd. dirs. 1989-93), Am. Assn. Pain Medicine. Republican. Jewish. Home and Office: 6624 Fannin St # 1620 Houston TX 77030-2707

GILDER, RICHARD EARL, operating room nurse, researcher; b. Dallas, July 21, 1955; s. Elbert Earl Jr. and Mary Francis G.; m. Mary Ann Meier, Apr. 26, 1975; children: Stephen Earl, David Andrew, Katherine Rose. AS in Nursing, El Centro Coll., Dallas, 1974; BS cum laude in Nursing, Tex. Woman's U., 1996. RN, Tex.; cert. oper. rm. nurse. Staff nurse emergency dept. Parkland Hosp., Dallas, 1974-81; chem. engring. cons. Kool-X-Co., Dallas, 1981-82, Hon Mining Co., Laguna Hills, Calif., 1981-82; owner, pres. Gilder Co., Dallas, 1983—; staff nurse, clin. nurse III Presbyn. Hosp., Dallas, 1986—; instr. rifle, pistol & shotgun, 1984. Sustaining mem. Republican Nat. Com., 1980—; asst. scout master Boy Scouts Am., Dallas, 1985—; founder United Nurses Internat.; asst. moderator Microsoft Nursing Network Forum. Mem. AAAS, Assn. Oper. Rm. Nurses (Dallas chpt. rsch. com. chair 1992—), Am. Soc. Ophthalmil Registered Nurses, Tex. Astron. Soc., Golden Key Nat. Honor Soc., Gamma Beta Phi. Republican. Home and Office: Gilder Co 13318 Mt Castle Dallas TX 75234

GILES, CONRAD LESLIE, ophthalmic surgeon; b. N.Y.C., July 14, 1934; s. Irving Samuel Giles and Victoria Ampole; m. Marilyn Toby Schwartz, June 20, 1955 (div. 1978); children: Keith Martin, Suzanne Speer, Kevin William, Brian Alan; m. Lynda Fern Schenk, Nov. 26, 1978; stepchildren: Jared Schenk, Jamie Schenk. MD, U. Mich., 1957, MS, 1961. Diplomate Am. Bd. Ophthalmology. Clin. assoc. NIH, Bethesda, Md., 1961-63; clin. asst. prof. Wayne State U. Sch. Medicine, Detroit, 1965-72, clin. assoc. prof. ophthalmology, 1973-89, clin. prof. ophthalmology, 1989—; chief ophthalmologist Children's Hosp. Mich., 1985—. Contbr. articles to med. jours. Active Jewish Welfare Fedn., Detroit, 1981-86, pres. 1986-89; bd. govs. Jewish Agy. for Israel, 1995-96, Fellow Am. Acad. Ophthalmology; mem. AMA, Mich. State Ophthal. Soc., Coun. Jewish Fedns. (v.p. 1992-95, treas. 1995-96, pres. 1996—), United Jewish Appeal (nat. vice chmn. 1992—), Mich. Jewish Conf. (pres. 1992-95). Avocations: golf, tennis, skiing. Home: 6300 Westmoor Rd Bloomfield Hills MI 48301-1359 Office: 4400 Town Ctr Southfield MI 48075-1601

GILES, JACKSON THERMAN, ophthalmologist; b. Griffin, Ga., June 23, 1946; s. Jackson Therman and Jeanne (Mann) G.; m. Pamela Adele King, June 10, 1972; children: Jackson T. III. Ashley Adele, Brian Reeves. BA, Emory U., 1968, MD, 1972. Intern Wash. Sch. Medicine, Seattle, 1972-73; resident U. Colo. Sch. Medicine, Denver, 1975-78; ptnr. PAPP Clinic, Newnan, Ga., 1978—; chief of staff Newnan Hosp., 1986, bd. dirs., 1993—. Pres. Newnan Country Club, 1990-92, Coweta County Med. Soc., Newnan, 1984-85. Lt. USN, 1973-75. Fellow Am. Acad. Ophthalmology; mem. Am. Soc. Cataract and Refractive Surgery, Ga. Med. Assn., Ga. Soc. Ophthalmology. Home: 19 Woodlane Dr Newnan GA 30263 Office: PAPP Clinic 15 Cavender St Newnan GA 30263

GILES, LYNDA FERN, clinical psychologist; b. Detroit, May 18, 1943; d. Samuel and Shirley (Finkelstein) S.; m. David Reuven Schenk, Sept. 5, 1965 (div. July 1975); children: Jared, Jamie; m. Conrad Leslie Giles, Nov. 26, 1978. BA, U. Mich., 1965, PhD, 1989; MSW, Wayne State U., 1977; PhD in Edn.-Psychology, U. Mich., 1989. Cert. social worker, clin. social worker. Clin. psychologist Counseling Assocs. Inc., Southfield, Mich., 1977—. Mem. com. on identity and affiliation Jewish Welfare Fedn., Detroit, 1985-88, com. on univ. rels., 1987—, com. on edn., 1987—, v.p. Ag. Jewish edn., 1995—. Mem. APA, Counseling Assocs. (chmn. Southfield gifted and talented program 1979-81), Mich. Soc. Clin. Social Workers. Democrat. Club: Franklin Country. Home: 6300 Westmoor Rd Bloomfield Hills MI 48301-1359 Office: Counseling Assocs Inc 25835 Southfield Rd Southfield MI 48075-1827

GIL-EXTREMERA, BLAS, internist, educator; b. Campillo De Arenas, Jaen, Spain, Dec. 6, 1943; s. Blas and Isabel (Extremera-Milla) Gil-Garcia; m. Trinidad Ruiz-Vico, Mar. 10, 1973. Physician, Medicine, Granada, 1968, MD, 1973, Prof., 1981. Resident Univ. Hosp., Granada, Spain, 1968-71; postdoctoral fellow U. Tex., Houston, 1974-75, 76-77; asst. prof. Dept. Medicine, Granada, Spain, 1968-77, assoc. prof., 1978-90, prof., 1991—, head dept., 1986-93; vice-rector Univ., Granada, Spain, 1993-96; chief internal medicine Univ. Hosp., Granada, 1980, chief hypertension unit, 1990; dir. Rsch. Group "Trace Elements", Spain, 1990. Author: Hipertension Arterial, 1991, Autoevaluacion en Medicina, 1992; editor Actualidad Medica, 1988; mem. editl. bd. (jour.) Medicine (Madrid), 1996, (jour.) Anales de Medicina Interna (Madrid), 1996. Spanish Ministry of Edn. fellow, 1970-73. Mem. Andalousian Soc. Internal Medicine (pres. 1994-96), Am. Soc. Hypertension, Nat. Commn. on Pharmacology, N.Y. Acad. Scis., Acadèmico Numerario, Acadèmico Numerario Instituto, Academias de Andalucia, Andalousian Hypertension Soc. (pres. 1994—), Spanish Soc. Internal Medicine (exec. coun. 1994—), The World Ctrs. of Excellence Club. Roman Catholic. Home: Alminares del Genil 4, 18006 Granada Spain Office: Dept de Medicina, Avenida de Madrid 11, 18012 Granada Spain

GILFILLAN, ALADSAIR MITCHELL, biomedical researcher; b. Perth, Scotland, Aug. 2, 1956; came to U.S., 1982; s. Alex and Sheena (Mitchell) G.; m. Corinne Min Hew, Feb. 20, 1981. BS, U. Strathclyde, 1977; MS, U. Manchester, 1979, PhD, 1981. Assoc. Yale U., New Haven, Conn., 1982-85, assoc. rsch. scientist, 1985-87; sr. scientist Hoffmann-LaRoche, Nutley, N.J., 1987-89, assoc. rsch. investigator, 1989-92, rsch. investigator, 1992—. Mem. editl. bd. Jour. Pharm. Exptl. Therappy. Mem. Am. Soc. Biochemistry and Molecular Biology, Am. Soc. Cell Biology, Royal Pharm. Soc. Gt. Brit. Office: Hoffmann-LaRoche Nutley NJ 07110

GILFOIL, JAMES HENRY, psychiatrist; b. Vicksburg, Miss., Oct. 8, 1946; s. James H. III and Annie Rose (Wyly) G.; m. Claudia M. Moller, Oct. 12, 1968; children: Chelsea, Ryan, Caroline. BS, La. State U., 1968; MD, Vanderbilt U., 1972. Diplomate Am. Bd. Psychiatry and Neurology, Diplomate Am. Bd. Adolescent Psychiatry. Intenr Phila. Gen. Hosp., 1972-73; resident Hosp. of U. Pa., Phila., 1972-75; clin. assoc. dept. psychiatry U. Pa. Hosp., Phila., 1975-95; clin. assoc. Jefferson Med. Coll., 1995—; sr. attending psychiatrist dept. psychiatry Bryn Mawr (Pa.) Hosp., 1987—; attending staff mem. Inst. of Pa. Hosp., Phila., 1975—. Mem. APA, Am. Soc. for Adolescent Psychiatry, Phila. Soc. for Adolescent Psychiatry (membership chmn. 1984—, v.p. 1990, pres. 1992-94). Office: 864 County Line Rd Bryn Mawr PA 19010-2516

GILFRICH, JOHN VALENTINE, chemist; b. Springfield, Mass., Sept. 14, 1927; s. John Valentine and Irene Frances (Connery) G.; m. Nancy Jane Tucker, Jan. 23, 1954; children: John T., N. Lynn, Beth Ann, Robert H., Georgia Ann. BA, Am. Internat. Coll., 1949; postgrad., George Washington U., 1954-56. Analytical chemist Nat. Bur. Stds., Washington, 1948-51; phys. chemist Nat. Bur. Stds., 1951-52; analytical chemist Naval Ordnance Lab., Silver Spring, Md., 1952-60; phys. chemist Naval Ordnance Lab., 1960-66; research chemist x-ray optic br. Naval Research Lab., Washington, 1966-71; head spectrochem. analysis sect. Naval Research Lab., 1971-77, cons., 1977-81, assoc. head condensed matter physics br., 1981-82; ret.; part-time cons. Condensed Matter Physics Br., 1983-87; cons. research chemist Bethesda, Md., 1987—. Editor-in-chief X-Ray Spectrometry jour., 1986—; mem. editorial adv. bd. Spectroscopy and Spectral Analysis (Chinese) jour., 1990—; mem. editorial bd. Trace and Microprobe Techniques 1982—; contbr. articles to profl. jours. With USAAF, 1946-47. Recipient Meritorious Civilian Svc. award Naval ORdnance Lab., USN, 1958, Birks award in X-ray Spectrometry 45th Ann. Denver X-ray Conf., 1996. Fellow Am. Inst. Chemists (cert. profl. chemist), ACS (emeritus), Am. Crystallographic Assn., Microbeam Analysis Soc., Soc. for Applied Spectroscopy, Sigma Xi. Address: 8710 Lowell St Bethesda MD 20817-3218

GILINSON, PHILIP JULIUS, JR., retired laboratory administrator; b. Lowell, Mass., July 28, 1914; s. Philip Julius and Anna (Turnquist) G.; m. Hulda Einarsdottir, July 6, 1943; 1 child, Robert Alan. BS, MIT, 1936, MS, 1952. Registered profl. engr., Mass. Jr. engr. Heinze Electric Co., Lowell, 1936-38; engr. Pacific Mills Inc., Lawrence, Mass., 1938-40, Doelcam Corp., Newton, Mass., 1946-48; assoc. dir. C.S. Draper Labs., Cambridge, Mass., 1948-80; sr. cons. People's Republic China, Beijing, 1980-90; ret., 1990. Coauthor: Magnetic and Electric Suspensions, 1974. Pres., bd. dirs. Scholarship Fund, Chelmsford, Mass., 1964. Lt. col. USAAF, 1940-46, ETO. Mem. Masons (master 1963-64), Sigma Xi. Luthran. Home: 8 Fuller Rd Chelmsford MA 01824-1818

GILL, BENJAMIN FRANKLIN, physician; b. Boston, Nov. 28, 1917; s. Howard Belding and Isabelle Virginia (Kendig) G.; m. Erna Maria Fredrike Hoffner, Mar 24, 1956; children: Nancy Maria, Lucia Franklin. BS, Harvard Coll., 1940, MD, 1943. Diplomate Am. Bd. Internal Medicine, Am. Bd. Psychiatry and Neurology. Intern Peter Bent Brigham Hosp., Boston, 1944, asst. resident, 1947; resident Cushing VA Hosp., Framingham, Mass., 1947-49; resident in psychiatry Cushing VA Hosp. and Boston VA Hosp., 1951-53; fellow in psychiatry Beth Israel Hosp., Boston, 1953-55; asst. clin. prof. psychiatry Harvard Med. Sch., Boston, 1977—; hon. psychiatrist Mass. Gen. Hosp., Boston, 1987; assoc. psychiatrist Beth Israel Hosp., Boston, 1984—; ret., 1987; pvt. practice psychoanalysis and analytic psychotherapy, 1952-88; psychotherapy supr. consultation and outpatient psychotherapy Mass. Gen. Hosp., 1955-88, Beth Israel Hosp., 1955-88. Contbr. papers to profl. jours., 1959-61. Served to capt. M.C., AUS, 1944-46. Fellow Am. Psychiat. Assn.; mem. Am. Psychoanalytic Assn., Mass. Med. Soc., Boston Psychoanalytic Soc. and Inst. (pres. 1982-84), U.S. Power Squadron. Home and Office: 168 Homer St Newton MA 02159-1518

GILL, CARL CARTER, cardiothoracic surgeon; b. Kansas City, Mo., Dec. 21, 1943; s. Winston Carter Gill and Opal Lee (Peery) Gill-Pursley; m. Diane Ruth Miner, July 25, 1965; children: Mallory Anne, Erin Elizabeth, Hudson Carter. BA, Westminster Coll., 1965; MD, U. Okla., 1969. Diplomate Nat. Bd. Med. Examiners, Am. Bd. Surgery, Am. Bd. Thoracic Surgery. Intern in surgery U. Okla. Health Scis. Ctr., 1969-70, asst. resident in surgery, 1970-71; fellow in cardiovascular rsch. Duke U., 1971-72; asst. resident in surgery U. Okla. Health Scis. Ctr., 1972-73, sr. resident in gen. surgery, 1973-74, sr. resident in thoracic surgery, 1974-75; fellow in cardiac surgery Mayo Clinic, 1975-76; asst. prof. surgery U. Okla. Health Scis. Ctr., 1976-77; head sect. congenital surgery dept. thoracic surgery cardiac The Cleveland Clinic Found., 1977-87; med. dir. Cleveland Clinic Fla., 1987-88, CEO, 1988—; chmn. bd. govs. Cleveland Clinic Fla., chmn. info. svcs. com., chmn. adminstrv. coun., mem. Fla. Mgmt. Team; bd. trustees Cleveland Clinic Hosp.; vice-chmn. bd. govs. Cleveland Clinic Found. Contbr. over 90 articles to profl. jours. Mem. Broward Workshop, Mus. Art, Broward Econ. Devel. Coun., Bylobs. Recipient Alumni Achievement award Westminster Coll., 1995. Mem. AMA, Am. Coll. Cardiology, Am. Coll. Surgeons (Fla. chpt.), Am. Heart Assn., Broward County Med. Assn., Cleveland Acad. Medicine, Cleveland Surg. Soc., Fla. Med. Assn., Fla. Soc. Thoracic and Cardiovascular Surgeons, Ohio State Med. Assn., Okla. State Med. Assn., Soc. Thoracic Surgeons, Southwestern Surg. Congress, Ft. Lauderdale C. of C. (trustee). Office: Cleveland Clinic Fla 3000 W Cypress Creek Rd Fort Lauderdale FL 33309

GILL, DIANE LOUISE, psychology educator, university official; b. Watertown, N.Y., Nov. 7, 1948; d. George R. and Betty J. (Reynolds) G. BS in Edn., SUNY, Cortland, N.Y., 1970; MS, U. Ill., 1974, PhD, 1976. Tchr. Greece Athena High Sch., Rochester, N.Y., 1970-72; asst. prof. U. Waterloo, Ont., Can., 1976-78; asst. prof. U. Iowa, Iowa City, 1979-81, assoc. prof., 1981-86; assoc. prof. sport & exercise psychology U. N.C., Greensboro, 1987-89; prof. U. N.C., Greenboro, 1989—; assoc. dean U. N.C., Greensboro, 1992—. Author: (book) Psychological Dynamics of Sports, 1986; editor Jour. of Sport and Exercise Psychology, 1985-90; editorial bd. Jour. of Applied Sport Psychology, 1988—; contbr. articles to profl. jours. Fellow AAHPERD (rsch. consortium pres. 1987-89), APA, Am. Psychol. Soc., Assn. for Advancement of Applied Sport Psychology, Am. Acad. Kinesiology and Phys. Edn.; mem. N.Am. Soc. for Psychology of Sport and Phys. Activity (pres. 1988-91). Democrat. Office: U NC Dept Exercise and Sport Sci Greensboro NC 27412

GILL, GORDON N., medical educator; b. Dec. 19, 1937. BA in Chemistry/Lit., Vanderbilt U., 1960, MD, 1963. Diplomate Am. Bd. Internal Medicine with subspecialty in endocrinology and metabolism. Intern in internal medicine Vanderbilt U. Hosp., Nashville, 1963-64; resident Yale-New Haven Hosp., 1964-66; fellow postdoctoral fellow metabolism/endocrinology NIH/Yale U., 1966-68; spl. postdoctoral rsch. fellow NIH/U. Calif., San Diego, 1968-69; asst. prof. medicine U. Calif., San Diego, 1969-73, assoc. prof., 1973-78, prof. medicine, 1978—, chief divsn. endocrinology dept. medicine, 1971-83, chief divsn. endocrinology/metabolism, 1983-95, assoc. chair sci. affairs, 1992-95, chmn. faculty basic biomed. scis., 1995—; chmn. endocrinology study sect. NIH, 1979-80, chmn. task force on endocrinology, 1978, dir. tng. grant on exptl. endocrinology and metabolism, 1978—; prin. investigator interdisciplinary program to study macromolecules regulating growth and oncogenesis U. Calif., San Diego, 1988-95; chmn. Gordon Conf. on Hormone Action, 1979, Gordon Conf. on Peptide Growth Factors, 1990; mem. sci. adv. bd. BioCryst, 1990—; sci. and med. adv. bd. chair Whittier Inst., 1991-95; sci. adv. bd. Liver Ctr., U. Calif., San Francisco, 1991-95, Charles E. Culpepper Found., 1992—, Coun. for Tobacco Rsch. USA, 1991—, ICN Pharms., 1992—; internat. adv. bd. dept. molecular and structural biology U. Grenoble, France, 1993—; S. Richardson Hill vis. prof. U. Ala., Birmingham, 1991; Berlin lectr. Northwestern U. Sch. Medicine, 1994. Editl. bd. Jour. Cyclic Nucleotide and Protein Phosphorylation Rsch., 1974-84, Endocrinology, 1978-82, Am. Jour. Physiology, Cell Physiology, 1981-87, Jour. Biol. Chemistry, 1983-88, Jour. Cellular Biochemistry, 1984-89, Ann. Rev. Medicine, 1986-91, Analytical Biochemistry, 1980-92; editor Molecular and Cellular Endocrinology, 1974-92; cons. editor Jour. Clin. Investigation, 1992—; sect. editor: Endocrinology, Best and Taylor Physiological Basis of Medical Practice, 11th and 12th edits., Endocrinology and Metabolism, Cecil's Textbook of Medicine, 20th edit. Bd. dirs. Med. Rsch. and Edn. Found., The Agouron Inst., 1985—; mem. biochemistry and endocrinology sci. adv. com. Am. Cancer Soc., 1989-91; adv. com. Markey Charitable Trust, 1990—; peer rev. com. Am. Heart Assn., 1991—;. Helen Hay Whitney Found. fellow, 1969-73; NIH Rsch. Career Devel. awardee, 1969-73, Merit award. Fellow ACP, Am. Acad. Arts and Scis.; mem. AAAS, Assn. Am. Physicians, Am. Fedn. Clin. Rsch., Am. Soc. Clin. Investigation, Am. Soc. Biol. Chemistry and Molecular Biology, Endocrine Soc., Western Assn. Physicians, Western Soc. for Clin. Investigation, Am. Soc. for Cell Biology, Phi Beta Kappa, Alpha Omega Alpha. Office: Univ of California 9500 Gilman Dr La Jolla CA 92093

GILL, KEVIN, orthopedic surgeon; b. Abilene, Tex., Mar. 29, 1955; s. Robert and June (Scott) G.; m. Cindy Whitehurst, Dec. 23, 1977; children: Allison, Jonathan. BA, U. Tex., Austin, 1977; MD, Baylor U., 1980. Diplomate Am. Bd. Orthopedic Surgery. Physician, orthopedic surgeon U. Tex., Dallas, 1980-85, U. Vt., Burlington, 1986, London Hosp., 1985-86; physician, orthopedic surgeon S.W. Orthopedic Inst., Dallas, 1986—, med. mgmt., 1993—; fouding dir., pres. S.W. Med. Inst., Dallas, 1989—. Atuhor: (with others) Management of Treatment Falures After Decompressive Surgery, 1995, Discography, 1995. med. dir. Maple Ave Cmty. Ctr. Clinic, Dalls, 1994-95. Mem. ACP Execs., Am. Orthopaedic Assn., Am. Acad. Orthopaedic Surgery, Internat. Soc. Study Lumbar Spine, Tex. Spine Soc. (pres. 1988—), Dallas County Med. Soc. (bd. dirs. 1995—), Cervical Spine Rsch. Soc. Presbyterian. Office: 5820 Forest Park Rd Ste 560 Dallas TX 75235

GILLENWATER, JAY YOUNG, urologist, educator; b. Kingsport, Tenn., July 27, 1933; s. Jay King and Ann Marion (Young) G.; m. Shirley Joyce Brockman; children: Linda, Ann, Jay. BS, U. Tenn., 1954, MD, 1957.

Diplomate Am. Bd. Urology (pres. 1988). Intern U. Pa. Grad. Hosp., 1958-59, resident, 1959-60, 62-65; asst. prof. U. Va. Med. Sch., Charlottesville, 1965-67, prof., chmn. urology dept., 1967-95; prof., 1995—; mem. coun. Nat. Inst. Diabetes and Digestive and Kidney Diseases, NIH, 1987-93; pres. AUA, 1991-92. Editor: Adult and Pediatric Urology, 1987, 91, 95; editor Urology Yearbook, 1978-94; assoc. editor Jour.Urology, 1985-93, editor, 1994—. Capt. U.S. Army, 1960-62. Mem. Am. Urol. Assn. (exec. com. 1987—, Hugh Young award, 1989, Mary Scott Hughes edn. award 1985, pres. 1991-92), Health Svc. Found. (pres. 1980-91), Am. Bd. Urology (pres. 1988), Am. Found. Urol. Diseases (pres. 1992—). Republican. Methodist. Home: 648 Dry Bridge Rd Charlottesville VA 22903-7630 Office: U Va Hosps Dept Urology Box 422 Charlottesville VA 22908

GILLER, ROBERT MAYNARD, physician; b. Chgo., Sept. 14, 1942; s. Edward M. and Lillian (Katz) G. Student, U. Ill., 1960-63, MD, 1967; postgrad., Columbia U., 1979—. Intern U. Ill., 1967-68; resident in internal medicine Cornell Hosp., N.Y.C., 1968-69, pvt. practice medicine specializing in preventive medicine, 1974—; mem. faculty New Sch. Social Rsch., 1975—. Author: A Guide for Health, 1982, Medical Makeover, 1986, Maximum Metabolism, 1989, Natural Prescriptions, 1994. With U.S. Army, 1969-71. Fellow Am. Coll. Preventive Medicine, Internat. Acad. Preventive Medicine, Am. Acad. Family Physicians; mem. AMA (Physician Recognition award 1982, 90, 96). Office: 960 Park Ave New York NY 10028-0325

GILLESPIE, ANITA WRIGHT, nursing administrator; b. S.C., Jan. 3, 1953; d. Ernest L. and Thelma G. Wright; m. Howard Gillespie Jr., Aug. 4, 1973; children: Christopher, Howard III. BSN, N.C. A&T State U., 1974. Cert. CPR instr., ACLS cert., cert. neonatal resusitation. Nursing instr. Norfolk (Va.) Community Hosp., 1975-76, staff nurse emergency dept., 1976-79; asst. nurse mgr. emergency dept. Mercy Hosp., Cin., 1979-83; evening dir. Mercy Hosp. Anderson, Cin., 1983-95; staff nurse emergency dept. Bethesda Oak Hosp., Cin., 1995—; staff nurse labor and delivery maternity dept. Mercy Hosp. Anderson, Cin., 1996—; mem. stds. com., employee activities com., med. records com., forms com., chairperson clin. nurse practice com. Mercy Hosp. Mem. ANA, NAFE, Nat. Coun. Negro Women, N.C. A&T Alumni Assn., Alpha Kappa Alpha (mem.-at-large, chair health com.). Home: 2290 Lauren Close Cincinnati OH 45244-2668 Office: Mercy Hosp Anderson 7500 State Rd Cincinnati OH 45255-2439

GILLESPIE, EDWARD MALCOLM, hospital administrator; b. Mpls., Oct. 19, 1935; s. Harold Livingston and Alice May (Thompson) G.; children: Karin, Timothy, Kenneth. BS, U. Minn., 1957, MPA, 1959, MHA, 1962. Engaged in refugee adminstrn. Linz, Austria, 1958-60; asst. adminstr. Luth. Med. Ctr., Denver, 1962-66; asst. gen. sec. Meth. Bd. Health and Welfare Ministries, Evanston, Ill., 1966-69; adminstr. Meth. Hosp., Rochester, Minn., 1969-74; adminstr. Univ. Hosp., Augusta, Ga., 1974-91, pres. Health Advance, 1991-92; bd. dirs. Augusta Area Mental Health, Augusta Speech and Hearing Ctr., St. John's Towers, CSRA Blood Assurance; chmn. hosp. divsn. certification coun. Meth. Health and Welfare. Bd. dirs. local United Way, Boy Scouts Am., Blue Cross Ga., Bankers First; chmn. Augusta Resource Ctr. on Aging, Brandon Wilde. Fellow ACHA; mem. Am. Hosp. Assn., Ga. Hosp. Assn. (chmn.), Rotary Internat. (bd. dirs. Augusta chpt.). Methodist. Home and Office: Health Advance 12 Indian Creek Rd Augusta GA 30909

GILLESPIE, GARRETT GREGORY, neurologist; b. Winthrop, Mass., Aug. 12, 1935; s. Frederick Garrett and Aline theresa (Keleher) G.; m. Elizabeth Lowell Barton (div. Sept. 1984); children: Meredith, Melanie, Garrett Jr.; m. Vicki Lynn Miller, Oct. 27, 1984. BA, Yale U., 1955; MD, Tufts U., 1959. Diplomate Am. Bd. Neurol. Surgery, Profl. Disability Cons., Nat. Bd. Med. Examiners. Intern Bellevue Hosp., N.Y.C., 1959-60; resident New Eng. Med. Ctr., Lahey Clinic, 1960-64; pres., owner Hillsborough Neurol. Assocs., Nashua, Manchester, N.H., 1964—; staff physician Cath. Med. Ctr., Manchester, St. Joseph Hosp., Nashua, So. N.H. Med. Ctr., Nashua, Elliott Hosp., Manchester. Fellow ACS, Am. Acad. Neurol. and Orthopedic Surgery; mem. AMA, Am. Assn. Neurol. Surgeons (sports medicine sect., pediatric neurol. surgery sect., pain sect., disorders of spine and peripheral nerves sect., joint sect. of neurotrauma and critical care), Soc. Examining Physicians, Am. Arbitration Assn., Am. Soc. Law and Medicine, Congress Neurol. Surgeons, N.E. Neurol. Soc., New Eng. Pain Assn., Am. Assn. for Study of Headache, Am. Geriatric Soc., Am. Physicians Fellowship of Israel Med. Soc., N.H. Med. Soc., Hillsborough County Med. Soc., Vesper Country Club, Pipers' Landing Country Club, Oyster Harbors Country Club. Episcopalian. Office: 168 Kinsley St Ste 18 Nashua NH 03060

GILLESPIE, GARY DON, physician; b. Jackson, Mich., Apr. 23, 1943; s. Harold Don and Marion Estella (Diemer) G.; m. Nancy Bliven Hinkle, June 29, 1969 (div. July 1980; children: Brian James, Julie Elizabeth; m. Elaine Marie Beard, July 25, 1984. BS, U. Mich., 1966, D of Medicine, 1971. Diplomate Am. Bd. Family Practice. Intern Edward W. Sparrow Hosp., Lansing, Mich., 1971-72, resident in family practice, 1971-74; physician Dept. Family Practice, USN Med. Corps., Orlando, Fla., 1974-76; pvt. practice Okemos, Mich., 1976—; chmn. continuing edn., dept. family practice Edward W. Sparrow Hosp., 1976-91; asst. clin. prof. dept. family practice Mich. State U. Coll. Medicine, East Lansing, 1981—. Lt. comdr. USN, 1974-76. Mem. AMA, Am. Acad. Family Physicians, Am. Bd. Family Practice, Mich. Acad. Family Physicians (treas. Capitol chpt. 1982-92). Republican. Office: 1745 Hamilton Rd # 340 Okemos MI 48864-1810

GILLESPIE, IAIN ERSKINE, surgeon; b. Glasgow, Scotland, Sept. 4, 1931; s. John and Flora (MacQuarrie) G.; m. Mary Muriel, Sept. 5, 1957; children: Rhona Kirstine, Gordon McIntosh. MB, Ch.B., U. Glasgow, 1953, MD with honors, 1963; MSc, U. Manchester, 1972. Med. officer Royal Army Med. Corps, Eng., 1954-56; sen. H.O. Orthopaedics Western Infirmary, Glasgow, 1956-57, M.R.C. Grantee, 1957-59; lectr. surgery U. Sheffield, 1958-64; sr. lectr., reader, prof. U. Glasgow, 1964-70; prof. surgery U. Manchester, 1970-92; ret., 1992; office bearer numerous surg./gastroenterol. socs., 1961-85; dean med. sch. U. Manchester, 1983-86; med. com. U. Grants Commn., Eng., 1975-86; univ. and polytech. grants com., Hong Kong, 1984-89. Contbg. author book in gastroenterology. Recipient William H. Rorer prize So. Calif. Soc. Gastroenterology, 1962; postdoctoral rsch. fellow UCLA, 1961-62. Fellow Royal Coll. Surgeons London, Royal Coll. Surgeons Edinburgh, Royal Coll. Physicians and Surgeons Glasgow; mem. Assn. Surgeons Gt. Britain and Ireland (mem. coun. 1970-76), Brit. Soc. Gastroenterology (coun. 1972-75), Surg. Rsch. Soc. Gt. Britain and Ireland (coun. 1975-80), Assn. Profs. of Surgery (treas. 1970-81). Mem. United Reformed Ch. of Eng. Home: 27 Athol Rd, Cheshire, Bramhall SK7 1BR, England

GILLESPIE, JACQUELYN RANDALL, psychologist; b. Paris, France, Oct. 10, 1927; came to U.S., 1932; d. John Roberts and Hazel Maurine (Hammel) Hunter; m. Thomas Gilbert Gillespie, Apr. 27, 1947 (dec. May 1995); children: Thomas Randall, Catherine Claire Gillespie Laroche. AB, Calif. State U., Long Beach, 1959; MS, Calif. State U., Fullerton, 1965; PhD, Calif. Grad. Inst., L.A., 1977. Lic. psychologist, psychoanalytic psychotherapist, Calif. Guidance cons. Lowell Sch. Dist., Whittier, Calif., 1963-69; psychologist Fullerton (Calif.) High Sch., 1969-82; pvt. practice Orange, Calif., 1976-90; assoc. prof. Calif. Grad. Inst., L.A., 1978-90. Author: Projective Use of Mother-and-Child Drawings, 1994; co-author: (reading text) Diagnostic Analysis of Reading Errors, 1981; contbr. articles to profl. jours. Grantee State of Calif., 1979; rsch. award Calif. Assn. Sch. Psychologists, 1972. Mem. APA (assoc.), Calif. Assn. Lic. Ednl. Psychologists (pres. 1983). Episcopalian. Home: 421 Meadowlark Ln # A Naples FL 33942-2459

GILLESPIE, PENNY HANNIG, business owner; b. Schenectady, N.Y., June 4, 1954; d. William Armand and Freda (Penney) H.; m. Kenneth Scofield Keyes, Jr., Sept. 2, 1984 (div. Aug. 1992). Student, U. Ariz., 1972-74. Cert. EMT, Ariz., N.Y.; completion in skills tng. for profls. in Hakomi psychotherapy, Oreg. Co-founder Ken Keyes Coll., Coos Bay, Ore., 1982-91; pvt. practice counseling Eugene, Ore., 1991-95; founder, pres. The Wellness Network, Eugene, Oreg., 1994—. Co-author: Gathering Power Through Insight and Love, 1986, Handbook to Higher Consciousness: The Workbook, 1989; editor: How to Enjoy Your Life in Spite of It All, 1980, The Hundredth Monkey, 1982, Your Heart's Desire, 1983, Your Life Is a Gift, 1987, Discovering the Secrets of Happiness, 1988, PlanetHood, 1988, The Power of Unconditional Love, 1990. Bd. dirs. Living Love Ch., 1980-91, sec., v.p.; founding bd. dirs., sec., sec.-treas., v.p. The Vision Foundation, Inc., 1982-91; founding bd. dirs., sec., sec.-treas. Cornucopia, The Living Love Ch. of Ky., 1982-91; vol. Victim Advocate Lane County Dist. Attys. Victim/Witness Svcs. Program, Oreg., 1993. Recipient peace award Coalition for Justice and Peace, Ariz. State U. and the Inst. Peace Edn., 1989; award as site mgr. for Anne Frank exhibit Jewish Fedn. Lane County, Ore., 1993. Home: PO Box 21942 Eugene OR 97402-0413

GILLETT, PATRICIA, pulmonary clinical nurse specialist; b. Mass., Jan. 2, 1948; d. Clyde and Estelle (Carter) Gleason; m. Warren Gillett, July 1968; children: Michael, James. ADN, Berkshire Community Coll.; BSN, U. N.Mex.; MSN, U. Tex., El Paso. Nursing instr. U. Albuquerque, Albuquerque T-VI; critical care edn. coord. St. Joseph Med. Ctr., Albuquerque. Mem. ANA, AACN (Outstanding Cricital Care Educator 1989), Am. Heart Assn. (edn. com. local chpt.), N.Mex. Nurses Assn. (award for clin. excellence 1994), Coun. Clin. Nurse Specialists, Sigma Theta Tau.

GILLETTE, EDWARD LEROY, radiation oncology educator; b. Coffeyville, Kans., May 21, 1932; s. Harold R. and Laura Belle (McLaughlin) G.; m. Carol J. Peterson, June 2, 1956 (div. Oct. 1981); children: William R., Jeffrey S., Timothy E., Jennifer L.; m. Sharon L. McChesney, Nov. 26, 1988. BS, DVM, Kans. State U., 1956; MS, Colo. State U., 1961, PhD, 1965. From instr. to prof. radiology and radiation biology Colo. State U., Ft. Collins, 1959-72, prof., 1972—, dir. comparative oncology, 1974—, chmn. dept. radiol. health scis., 1989—; adj. prof. dept. radiation Duke U. Med. Coll., Durham, N.C.; bd. dirs. The Children's Hosp. Kempe Rsch. Ctr., Denver, 1984-90; vis. scientist M.D. Anderson Cancer Ctr. U. Tex., 1988. Assoc. editor Radiation Rsch., 1986-90, Internat. Jour. of Radiation Oncology Biology and Physics, 1990-95, editor 95—; contbr. articles to profl. jours. Bd. dirs. Colo. State Sci. Fair, 1984-90. 1st lt. U.S. Army, 1956-58. U. Tex. fellow 1968-69; recipient Outstanding Svc. to the Vet. Profession, Am. Animal Hosp. Assn., 1984, Ralston-Purina rsch. award, 1988. Mem. AVMA, Am. Coll. Vet. Radiology (cert., pres. 1973-74), Am. Coll. Vet. Internal Medicine, Oncology (cert.), Am. Cancer Soc. (mem. exec. com. Colo. divsn. 1978-82, bd. dirs. Colo. divsn. 1984-90, pres. Larimer County chpt. 1977-81), Vet. Cancer Soc. (pres. 1982-84), Radiation Rsch. Soc. (councilor 1988-91), Am. Soc. Therapeutic Radiology and Oncology, Am. Assn. Cancer Rsch., Colo. State U. Alumni Assn. (Honor Alumnus award 1985). Republican. Office: Colo State U Dept Radiol Health Sci Fort Collins CO 80523

GILLETTE, ETHEL, medical and surgical nurse, educator; b. Plainfield, N.J., Jan. 23, 1923; d. Herbert and Sarah (Sutterlin) Perry; m. John Gillette, Oct. 16, 1943; children: John, Susan. AD, St. Petersburg Jr. Coll., 1975; BA in Psychology magna cum laude, St. Leo's Coll., 1977. Cert. tchr. Insvc. instr. Met. Gen. Hosp., Pinellas Park, Fla.; lectr., speaker in field. Author: Good Night Nurse (Pub. award); editor books; contbr. articles to profl. jours.; columnist Jour. Nursing Care, 1980-82 (consumer advocate nursing homes, fellowship fine arts 1978, writers award 1987, contracts news America syndicate award 1987-88). Mem. Am. Nurses Found. Century Club. Home: 4409 58th Ave N Saint Petersburg FL 33714-1016

GILLETTE, JOYCE LYNNE, nursing administrator; b. Youngstown, Ohio; d. Frederick T. Gillette and Eleanor (Kulow) G. BS in Nursing, U. Rochester; MA in Edn., Kent State U., 1980; MS in Nursing Adminstrn., Calif. State U., L.A., 1993. RN. Asst. coord. edn. St. Francis Med. Ctr., Lynwood, Calif., 1980-83; nurse educator Daniel Freeman Hosp., Inglewood, Calif., 1983-86; clin. instr., acting dir. edn. Anaheim (Calif.) Meml. Hosp., 1986-88; med./surg. nurse educator UCI Med. Ctr., Orange, Calif., 1988-90; regional ambulatory nursing edn. mgr. FHP, Inc., Long Beach, Calif., 1990-91; home health care nurse St. Mary Med. Ctr., Long Beach, 1992-93; client svcs. area coord. Hosp. Home Health Care of Calif., Torrance, 1993; nursing supr. Long Beach Meml. Med. Ctr. Home Health Care Agy., 1993—; affiliate faculty for BLS Am. Heart Assn. Orange County, Calif., 1988-94. Editor: CEN Rev. Manual, 1984. Mem. Am. Soc. Healthcare Edn. and Tng. (treas. Orange County chpt. 1988), Sigma Theta Tau (pres. chpt. 1991-93, fundraising chair 1995—). Office: Long Beach Meml Med Ctr Home Health Care Agy 450 E Spring St Ste 5 Long Beach CA 90806-1624

GILLETTE, PAUL CRAWFORD, pediatric cardiologist; b. Winston-Salem, N.C., Dec. 1, 1942; s. Crawford Paul and Eileen Marie (O'Rourke) G.; m. Vicki Lynn Zeigler, 1992; 2 children. B.A. in Chemistry, U.N.C., 1965; M.D., Med. Coll. S.C., 1969. Intern, then resident in pediatrics Baylor U. Coll. Medicine, Houston, 1969-71, fellow in pediatric cardiology and cell biophysics, 1971-74, mem. faculty, 1974-84, assoc. prof. exptl. medicine, 1977-84, prof. pediatrics, 1980-84; prof. pediatrics Med. U. S.C., Charleston, 1984-96, chmn. promotions com., dept. pediatrics, 1989-96; dir. S.C. Children's Heart Ctr., Charleston, 1984-96; med. dir. Cook Children's Cardiology, 1996—, Cook Childrens Cardiac Ctr., Fort Worth, Tex., 1996—; dir. electrophysiology and electrocardiography Tex. Children's Hosp.; co-dir. Palmetto Heart Inst., 1988-96; chmn. rsch. peer rev. com. S.C. chpt. Am. Heart Assn., 1989, chmn. rsch. com., 1990. Co-author: A Guide to Pediatric Cardiac Dysrhythmias, 1980, Pediatric Cardiac Dysrhythmias, 1981, A Practical Guide to Cardiac Pacing, 1986, Pediatric Electrophysiology, Arrythmia and Pacing, 1990, Pediatric Cardiac Pacing, 1995; edtl. bd. Circulation, Am. Heart Jour., Pediatric Cardiology, Jour. Am. Coll. Cardiology; contbr. articles to profl. jours. Mem. sports com., treas. St. Thomas More Sch., Houston; bd. dirs. Toler's Cove Homeowners Assn. Charleston, 1989-94; mem. tng. grant manpower rev. com. Nat. Heart, Lung and Blood Inst., 1989-93, chmn., 1992-93. Nat. Heart, Lung and Blood Inst. grantee; named Disting. Alumni, Medical Univ. S.C., 1991; recipient Rsch. award So. Med. Assn., 1994. Fellow Am. Acad. Pediatrics (exec. com. cardiology sect. 1979, ednl. grantee 1970, Young Investigator award 1975, trustee 1987—, chmn. rsch. rev. com. 1987-88 S.C. chpt.), Am. Coll. Cardiology (trustee 1984-90, learning ctr. com. 1984-88, strategic planning com. 1986-90, long range planning com. 1987-88, chmn. pacemaker com. 1990-95, mem. rsch. com. 1990—); mem. Soc. Pediatric Rsch., So. Soc. Pediatric Rsch., Southeastern Pediatric Cardiology Soc. (pres. 1987), N.Am. Soc. Pacing and Electrophysiology (pres. 1986-87, trustee 1987-90, program com. 1987), Am. Heart Assn., Tex. Pediatric Soc., Harris County Med. Soc., Houston Cardiology Soc., Houston Pediatric Soc., S.C. Med. Soc., Charleston County Med. Soc., S.C. Heart Assn. (researcher of the yr. 1991), Alpha Omega Alpha, Phi Chi. Republican. Roman Catholic. Office: Cook Childrens Cardiac Ctr 8017th Ave Fort Worth TX 76104-2796

GILLETTE-BAUMANN, MURIEL DELPHINE, nurse; b. Pasadena, Calif., Nov. 10, 1945; d. Edwin and Jean Helen (Fremont) Gillette; m. Larry Houston Potter, Dec. 31, 1971 (dec. 1979); children: Melissa Darlene Genevieve Potter Stephens, Bryan Scott; m. Robert George Baumann Jr., Aug. 18, 1980; 1 child, Robert George III. Student, Western Coll. for Women, Oxford, Ohio, 1963-65; BSN, UCLA, 1968; M of Nursing, Oreg. Health Scis. U., 1991. Sch. nurse, health tchr. Hawthorne (Calif.) Intermediate Sch., 1969-70; nurse St. John's Hosp., Santa Monica, Calif., 1969-71; camp nurse L.A. Girl Scout Coun., 1969-71; nurse UCLA Med. Ctr., 1967-70; ICU/CCU/pediatrics nurse Mercy Med. Ctr., Roseburg, Oreg., 1971-79; nurse Umpqua Valley Community Hosp., Myrtle Creek, Oreg., 1981-91; health edn. dir. City of Myrtle Creek, 1986-91; nurse practitioner Umpgua Nat. Forest, Roseburg and Glide, Oreg., 1991-93; camp nurse, health coord. Oreg. Trail Boy Scout Coun., Roseburg, 1991—, Western Rivers Girl Scout Coun., Roseburg, 1984-90. Musician quartet, orch., soloist; artist in oils; poet. Bd. dirs. River 'N Dell Day Care Ctr., Myrtle Creek, 1983-85; trustee Augusta Bixler Farms, Inc., Stockton, Calif., 1976—; mem. Douglas County Cancer Screening Com. Capt. USAF, 1970-89. Umpqua Valley Hosp. Aux. scholar, 1989; L.A. Watercolor Soc. traveling art collection award, 1963. Mem. UCLA Alumni Assn., Umpqua Valley Hosp. Aux., Oreg. Health Sci. U. Alumni Assn., OES, Delta Zeta. Republican. Presbyterian. Home: PO Box 668 Myrtle Creek OR 97457-0104

GILLIAM, M(ELVIN) RANDOLPH, urologist, educator; b. Elliott County, Ky., Jan. 5, 1921; s. Adolphus and Grace (Thornsberry) G.; m. Sara Dee Rainey, May 15, 1948; children: Elizabeth Neal, Virginia Dee, Bryan Randolph, Frank Stuart, Grace Carroll. Student Centre Coll. of Ky., 1938-41; MD, U. Louisville, 1944. Diplomate Am. Bd. Urology. Intern Norfolk (Va.) Marine Hosp., 1944-45; resident in urology Nichols VA Hosp., Louisville, 1947-50; pvt. practice medicine specializing in urology, Lexington, Ky., 1950—; ptnr. Commonwealth Urology, P.S.C., Lexington, 1971—; clin. prof. urology, U. Ky. Med. Sch., 1964—; chief of urology Good Samaritan Hosp.; mem. staff Central Baptist Hosp., St. Joseph's Hosp. Capt. U.S. Army, 1945-47. Mem. AMA, Ky. Med. Assn., Fayette County Med. Soc. (past pres.), Am. Urology Assn. Republican. Methodist. Home: 1244 Summitt Dr Lexington KY 40502-2273 Office: 1760 Nicholasville Rd Lexington KY 40503-1471

GILLIAM, PAUL EDWIN, JR., surgeon; b. Washington, Oct. 13, 1952; s. Paul Edwin and Winifred Love (Conrad) G.; m. Marlene Ruth Mailman; children: Katie, Matthew. BS, USAF Acad., 1974; MD, U. Md., 1978. Diplomate gen. surgery Am. Bd. Surgery with added qualification in surg. critical care. Commd. 2d lt. USAF, 1974, advanced through grades to col., 1996; surg. intern Keesler Med. Ctr., Biloxi, Miss., 1978-79, resident in surgery, 1979-83; staff surgeon USAF, Incirlik, Turkey, 1983-85, Wiesbaden, Germany, 1985-88, Ft. Walten Beach, Fla., 1988-91; fellow in trauma and critical care USAF, Houston, 1991-92; chief of surgery USAF, Dayton, Ohio, 1992-96; chief hosp. svcs. USAF, Albuquerque, 1996—. Lutheran. Home: 8705 Vineyard Ridge NE Albuquerque NM 87122

GILLILAND, CHARLES DONALD, internist; b. Mercer, Pa., Feb. 25, 1945; s. Charles Jonathan and Delilah (Snyder) G.; m. Irene Lydia Chodan, Mar. 24, 1974 (div. 1990); children: Amy Irene, Charles Michael, Robert Matthew; m. Cheryl Sykes Holcomb, 1992. AB, Bucknell U., 1967; MD, Temple U., 1971. Diplomate Am. Bd. Internal Medicine. Residency Temple U. Hosp., Phila., 1975; internist pvt. practice Roanoke, Va., 1975—; clin. assoc. prof. U. Va., Charlottesville, 1977—; chief internal medicine Community Hosp. of Roanoke, 1978-86. Editor, author: Handbook of Medical Emergencies, 1976. Bd. dirs. Am. Heart Assn., Roanoke, 1980, First Presbyn. Ch., Roanoke, 1986-88. Mem. AMA, Am. Soc. Internal Medicine, Am. Coll. Physicians, Roanoke Acad. Medicine. Republican. Presbyterian. Home: 6768 Corn Tassel Ln Roanoke VA 24018-5628 Office: 1802 Braeburn Dr Salem VA 24153-7306

GILLILAND, MARCIA ANN, nurse clinician, infection control specialist; b. Kansas City, Mo., Sept. 15, 1949; d. Robert Joseph and Mary Agnes (Paup) Caton; m. John Lee Gilliland, Mar. 28, 1974 (dec. Oct. 1983); children: Marcella Lyn, John Patrick, Devon Marie. ADN, Kansas City C.C., 1979; BSN, Webster U., 1990. RN, Kans. Staff nurse U. Kans. Med. Ctr., Kansas City, 1979-84, infection control coord., 1984—, facilitator HIV/AIDS wellness group, 1991—; community health nurse Cath. Charities, Kansas City, 1980-82; pres., owner Kansas City Total Image, Overland Park, Kans., 1981-83. Active Rep. Committeewoman, Overland Park, Kans., 1994; Rep. candidate Overland Park City Coun., Kans., 1995. Mem. Nat. Speakers Assn., Assn. Profls. in Infection Control and Epidemiology (pres. Kansas City chpt., 1993-94), Assn. Nurses in AIDS Care. Republican. Home: 9430 Riggs St Overland Park KS 66212-1443 Office: U Kans Med Ctr 3901 Rainbow Blvd Kansas City KS 66160-0001

GILLILAND, MARY MARGARETT, healthcare consultant; b. Leland, Miss., Dec. 23, 1942; d. Lindon Edward and Allie Earlene (Saulters) Palmore; m. Carl Ralph Gilliland, Jan. 12, 1963; children: Carl Ralph, Gini Lynn. Diploma in Nursing, Greenwood Leflore, 1963; B of Healthcare Adminstrn., East Tex. State U., 1976; M of Human Rels. and Mgmt., Abilene Christian U., 1978; BS, Tex. Woman's U., 1991, MS, 1993. RN, Tex. Staff nurse Sunflower County Health Dept., Indianola, Miss., 1965-66; asst. dir. nursing Presbyn. Hosp. Dallas, 1966-80, assoc. dir. nursing, 1980-87, assoc. exec. dir., 1987-91; healthcare cons. G&S Healthcare Cons., Allen, Tex., 1991—; adj. faculty Tex. Woman's U., Denton. Contbr. articles to profl. jours. Mem. ANA, Am. Orgn. Nurse Execs., Tex. Orgn. Nurse Execs., Tex. Nurses Assn. (continuing edn. com, Great 100 Nurses 1991), Nurses Alumni Assn. (sec.) Sigma Theta Tau, Phi Kappa Phi. Home: 2101 Rigsbee Dr Plano TX 75074-4913 Office: G&S Healthcare Cons Raceway Profl Bldg I 200 Boyd Pl Allen TX 75002-2560

GILLION, JEAN FRANCOIS, surgeon; b. Nogent Le Rotrou, Eure et Loir, France, Apr. 16, 1953. Resident Paris, 1978-84, sr. resident, 1984-86; MD Mondor Hosp., Paris, 1987—. Mem. French Assn. Surgery, French Soc. Digestive Surgery, French Soc. Endoscopic Surgery. Office: Clinique Du Sud, 112 Avenue de General De Gaulle, 94320 Thiais France

GILLIS, JOHN SIMON, psychologist, educator; b. Washington, Mar. 21, 1937; s. Simon John and Rita Veronica (Moran) G.; m. Mary Ann Wesolowski, Aug. 29, 1959; children: Holly Ann, Mark, Scott. B.A., Stanford U., 1959; M.S. (fellow), Cornell U., 1961; Ph.D. (NIMH fellow), U. Colo., 1965. Lectr. dept. psychology Australian Nat. U., Canberra, 1968-70; sr. psychologist Mendocino (Calif.) State Hosp., 1971-72; asso. prof. dept. psychology Tex. Tech U., Lubbock, 1972-76; prof. psychology Oreg. State U., Corvallis, 1976—, chmn. dept. psychology, 1976-84; cons. VA, Ciba-Geigy Pharms., USIA, UN High Commn. for Refugees; commentator Oreg. Ednl. and Pub. Broadcasting System, 1978-79; Fulbright lectr., India, 1982-83, Greece, 1992; vis. prof. U. Karachi, 1984, 86, U. Punjab, Pakistan, 1985, Am. U., Cairo, 1984-86. Contbr. articles to profl. jours. Served with USAF, 1968-72. Ciba-Geigy Pharms. grantee, 1971-82. Mem. Am. Psychol. Assn., Western Psychol. Assn., Oreg. Psychol. Assn. Roman Catholic. Home: 7520 NW Mountain View Dr Corvallis OR 97330-9106 Office: Oreg State U Dept Psychology Corvallis OR 97331

GILLISS, CATHERINE LYNCH, nursing educator; b. New Britain, Conn., Apr. 18, 1949; d. James A. and Lorraine (Balocki) Lynch; m. Thomas P. Gilliss, June 6, 1970. BS in Nursing, Duke U., 1971; MS in Nursing, Cath. U. Am., Washington, 1974; D of Nursing Sci., U. Calif., 1983; cert. adult nurse practitioner, U. Rochester, 1979. Staff and charge nurse Duke U. Med. Ctr., Durham, 1971, VA Hosp., Washington, 1971-72; asst. prof. U. Md., Balt., 1974-76, The Cath. U. Am., 1976-79; assoc. prof. U. Portland, Oreg., 1979-83; lectr. in nursing Sonoma State U., Rohnert Park, Calif., 1983-84; prof., chmn. dept. family health care U. Calif., San Francisco, 1984—; mem. NIH, Nat. Inst. Nursing Rsch. Study Sect., 1995—. Co-author: Toward a Science of Family Nursing, 1989, The Nursing of Families, 1993; editl. bd. mem. Families, Systems and Health, 1994—; contbr. articles to profl. jours. Recipient Disting. Alumna award Duke U., 1991; Pres.'s fellow U. Calif., 1983; Primary Care Policy fellow USPHS, 1993; Regent U. Portland, Oreg., 1994—. Fellow Am. Acad. Nursing; mem. ANA, Am. Heart Assn., Nat. Coun. on Family Rels., APHA, Nat. Orgn. Nurse Practitioner Faculty (pres. 1995), Soc. for Tchrs. Family Medicine, Primary Care Fellowship Soc. (pres. 1996-98), Duke U. No. Calif. Exec. Leadership Bd. Office: U Calif San Francisco Sch Nursing San Francisco CA 94143-0606

GILLMAN, ARTHUR EMANUEL, psychiatrist; b. N.Y.C., June 6, 1927; s. Hyman David and Sadie Ruth (Ornstein) G.; m. Barbara E. O'Connell, June 29, 1961 (div. 1980); children: Elizabeth Waite Mazei, Abigail Tenedorio, Theodore Jones, Sarah Ann. BS, U. Vt., 1947; MD, N.Y. Med. Coll., 1950. Diplomate Am. Bd. Psychiatry and Neurology, Child and Adolescent Psychiatry. Intern State U. Iowa Hosps., Iowa City, 1950-51; asst. resident in neurology Montefiore Hosp., Bronx, N.Y., 1951-52; asst. resident in psychiatry Bellevue Hosp., 1952-53; resident in psychiatry Hillside Hosp., Glen Oaks, N.Y., 1953-54; fellow in child psychiatry Child Guidance Inst., Jewish Bd. Guardians, N.Y.C., 1954-56; clin. fellow in child psychiatry Bronx Mcpl. Hosp. Ctr./Albert Einstein Coll. Medicine, 1955-56; pvt. practice Larchmont, N.Y., 1956-95; clin. dir. community svcs. Rockland Children's Psychiat. Ctr., Orangeburg, N.Y., 1985-95; chief physician child adolescent svcs. Bronx Lebanon Hosp., 1995—; asst. prof. psychiatry Albert Einstein Coll. Medicine, N.Y.C., 1995—; asst. clin. prof. Columbia U., 1989-95; asst. prof. Albert Einstein Coll. Medicine, 1995—; cons. psychiatrist, dir. evaluative studies, dir. rsch. devel., then dir. rsch. N.Y. Assn. for Blind, 1966-85; dir. curriculum in child psychiatry Montefiore Hosp., 1968-69; vis. lectr. Manhattanville Coll., Purchase, N.Y., 1974-76; dir. psychiat. clinic Jewish Guild for Blind, 1962-66; presenter at profl. confs. Contbr. articles to profl. publs. Fellow Am. Psychiat. Assn. (life), Am. Orthopsychiat. Assn. (life), Am. Acad. Child and Adolescent Psychiatry (life); mem. AMA. Office: 34 Pryer Manor Rd Larchmont NY 10538-3437 also: Bronx Lebanon Hosp Child Adolescent Svcs 1842-44 Webster Ave Bronx NY 10457

GILLMAN, KAREN LEE, clinical psychologist; b. Wichita, Kans., Sept. 16, 1937; d. Raymond H. and Myra Ruth (Hudson) Hein; m. Louis Charles

Thomason, Dec. 21, 1958 (div. 1980); children: Debra Lynn Roelke, Sandy River; m. Richard Earl Gillman, June 18, 1983. Student, Phillips U., 1955-58; BS, Okla. State U., 1959; MS, Va. Polytech. Inst., Blacksburg, 1974; PhD, SUNY, Albany, 1985. Lic. clin. psychologist, Maine, N.Y. Tchr. Washington Elem., Stillwater (Okla.) Jr. High Sch., Ponca City, 1959-64, West Hurley (N.Y.) Elem. Sch., 1971-72; therapist Family Svc. Ctr., Kingston, N.Y., 1974-77; sr. counselor Readiness Tng. Project Ulster County Community Coll., Stone Ridge, N.Y., 1978-79; clin. dir. Greene County Mental Health Clinic, Cairo, N.Y., 1979-84; dir. student assistance program Rens. County Dept. Mental Health, Troy, N.Y., 1984-86; dir. intensive day treatment St. Lawrence Psychiat. Ctr., Ogdensburg, N.Y., 1986-89; pvt. practice Dover-Foxcroft, Skowhegan & Winslow, Maine, 1989—; adj. prof. St. Lawrence U., Canton, N.Y., 1986; cons. Project Readiness Arbor Hill Dept. Labor, Albany, 1978, Overlook Pre-sch. Ctr., Woodstock, N.Y., 1974; vol. tchr. Ulster Acad., Kingston, 1974; music tchr. Headstart, Woodstock, 1970-71. newspaper columnist The Apple Polisher. Dir. Cmty. Vacation Ch. Sch., Woodstock, 1967-70; Head of Day Family of Woodstock, Inc., 1974-77; Ulster County townsman. Fellow NSF, 1961. Mem. APA, LWV (bd. dirs., editor 1967-69) Am. Assn. Marriage & Family Therapists, Soc. Psychologists in Addictive Behaviors, Maine Psychol. Assn. Democrat. Home: RR 5 Box 5215 Winslow ME 04901 Office: Garland Rd Winslow ME 04901

GILLMOR, ROGENE GODDING, medical technologist; b. El Dorado, Kans., Jan. 25, 1939; d. Marc Antone and Verda May (Bogue) Godding; m. Charles Stewart Gillmor Jr., Nov. 28, 1964; children: Charles Stewart III, Alison Bogue. AA in Liberal Arts, Cottey Coll., 1958; BA in Biology, Stanford U., 1960; postgrad., Wesleyan U., U. Hartford, Foothills Coll. Rsch. asst. genetics Joshua Lederberg lab. Stanford U., 1960-62; assoc. scientist space biology/medicine Lockheed Missiles & Space Co., Palo Alto, Calif., 1962-64; rsch. asst. biology Princeton (N.J.) U., 1965-66, Wesleyan U., Middletown, Conn., 1967-69; lab. technician immunochemistry Hartford (Conn.) Hosp., 1978-84, instr. immunology clin. lab. edn. program, 1985-89, lab. supr. proteins/immunology dept. pathology and lab. medicine, 1986—; rschr. various labs, France and Switzerland, 1984-85. Contbr. articles to profl. jours. Leader Girl Scouts U.S., 1977-85; trustee, deacon Higganum (Conn.) Congl. Ch., 1980—. Recipient Achievement award Girl Scouts U.S., 1985. Mem. Am. Assn. Clin. Chemistry, Am. Soc. Clin. Pathologists (cert. immunology specialist), Am. Soc. Clin. Lab. Sci., Wesleyan Potters (pres. 1982-84), Haddam, Conn. Hist. Soc. (sec. 1970-72), PEO Sisterhood. Home: 29 Spencer Rd Higganum CT 06441-4034 Office: Hartford Hosp Dept Pathology & Lab Medicine 80 Seymour St Hartford CT 06102

GILLOTEAUX, JACQUES JEAN-MARIE ANTHIME, cell biologist, researcher; b. Mons, Hainaut, Belgium, July 9, 1944; came to U.S., 1976; s. Anthime A. and Victoire M. (Pierrard) G.; m. Christiane Marie-Pierre Lenaerts, June 28, 1972; 1 child, Laurent C. MS in Biol. Zoology, Cath. U. Louvain, Belgium, 1966, DSc, 1974, MS in Edn. Prof. scis. Coll. Nivelles, Uccle, Brussels and Liege, Belgium; postdoctoral fellow in cancer INSERM, Lille, France, 1975-76; lectr. in cell biology SUNY, Stony Brook, 1976; asst. prof. physiology SUNY, Syracuse, 1977-79; asst. and assoc. prof. anatomy and urology Northeastern Ohio U. Coll. Medicine, Rootstown, 1979-95; prof. anatomy and cell biology Lake Erie Coll. Osteo. Medicine, Erie, 1995—. Contbr. articles to profl. jours.; guest editor: Microscopy Rsch. and Tech. Named hon. prof. Alpha Omega Alpha, 1994; grantee Am. Heart Assn., 1980—, Am. Cancer Soc., 1981, Akron City, 1985—, Summa Health Sys. Found., 1988—, NATO Internat. Collab. Rsch., 1994-96; fellow Belgian U. Found., 1974-75, European Molecular Biology Orgn., 1975. Mem. Am. Soc. Cell Biology, Am. Assn. Anatomists, Histochem. Soc., French Soc. Cell Biology and Electron Microscopy, Belgian Soc. Zoology, Soc. Ultrastructural Pathology, Microscopy Soc. Am. (invited editor Microscopy Rsch. & Tech.), Federative Com. Anat. Terminology. Office: Lake Erie Coll Osteo Med 1858 W Grandview Blvd Erie PA 16509-1025

GILL THOMPSON, NORMA N., home healthcare executive; b. Akron, Ohio, June 26, 1920; Richard Nottingham and Esther (Mullennax) Day; m. Edward Grover Gill, Sept. 5, 1938 (dec. 1974); children: Marilyn A., David E., Sally J. Thompson; m. Herbert George Thompson, Oct. 1, 1983. Cert. in enterostomal therapy, Cleve. Clinic Found., 1958. Dir. R.B. Turnbull Jr., M.D. Sch. Enterostomal Therapy Cleve. Clinic Found., 1961-78, coord. enterostomal therapy, 1978-81; v.p. Worldwide Home Health Care Ctr., Inc., Akron, 1981—, Worldwide Home Health Ctr., Akron, 1996—; cons. Akron City Hosp., St. Thomas Hosp. Med. Ctr., Children's Hosp. Med. Ctr. Akron, Cuyahoga Falls (Ohio) Gen. Hosp.; lectr. on ostomy care; cons. in establishing enterostomal therapy schs., Eng., Australia, Germany, France, Sweden, India, Japan, Brazil, Argentina, Peru, Chile; 1st dir. Rupert B. Turnbull Sch. of Enterostomal Therapy, Cleve. Clinic Found., 1961; lectr. to colon-rectal surgeons and enterostomal therapy nurses, Tokyo, Shanghai, China, Hangzhou, China, 1994-95; spkr. in field. Author: Ostomy Series, 1990, rev. 1995 and ednl. materials; contbr. numerous articles on ostomy-related topics to various publs.; editor World Coun. of Enterostomal Therapists Jour., 1982-84, 84-86; editl. bd. Am. Urol. Assn., 1982-83, 83-85. Recipient Rupert B. Turnbull Spl. Recognition award Cleve. Clinic Found., 1988. Mem. Internat. Ostomy Assn. (profl. adv. bd. 1980-83, 83-85), Wound, Ostomy and Continence Nurses (hon.; Pres.'s aard 1993), United Ostomy Assn. (enterostomal therapist 1990-91), Akron Ostomy Assn., Am. Urol. Assn., Ileitis and Colitis Found., French Assn. Stoma Therapy (hon. pres.), World Coun. Enterostomal Therapists (founder 1975, hon. 1984, Norma N. Gill Found. established 1980). Democrat. Methodist. Office: Worldwide Home Health Ctr 926 E Tallmadge Ave Akron OH 44310-3562

GILLUM, PATRICIA ANN, emergency room nurse; b. Madill, Okla., Dec. 28, 1953; d. Benjamin Franklin Spicer and Betty Jean (Kenedy) Higgs; m. Terry Lynn Gillum, Oct. 17, 1970; children: Michael Alan, Anthony Paul. AAS, Murry State Coll., Tishomingo, Okla., 1991. RN, Okla., Tex.; cert. ACLS, TNCC. Nurse's aide Healdton (Okla.) Mcpl. Hosp., 1988-90; mem. nursing staff, charge nurse Meml. Hosp. So. Okla., Healdton, 1990-94, pharmacy tech., 1992; emergency room nurse Meml. Hosp. So. Okla., Ardmore, 1990-94; staff nurse ICU St. Anthony's Hosp., Oklahoma City, 1993. Democrat. Southern Baptist. Home: HC 75 Box 138 Wilson OK 73463 Office: Meml Hosp So Okla at Healdton 918 SW 8th Healdton OK 73438

GILMAN, ALFRED GOODMAN, pharmacologist, educator; b. New Haven, July 1, 1941; s. Alfred and Mabel (Schmidt) G.; m. Kathryn Hedlund, Sept. 21, 1963; children: Amy, Anne, Edward. BS, Yale U., 1962; MD, PhD, Case Western Res. U., 1969; DSc (hon.), U. Chgo., 1991, Case Western Res. U., 1995. Pharmacology research assoc. NIH, Bethesda, Md., 1969-71; from asst. prof. to assoc. prof. pharmacology U. Va., Charlottesville, 1971-77, prof., 1977-81, dir. med. sci. tng. program, 1979-81; prof. pharmacology, chmn. dept. U. Tex. Southwestern Med. Ctr., Dallas, 1981—, Raymond Willie prof. molecular neuropharmacology, 1987—; mem. pharmacology study sect. NIH, 1977-81, mem. nat. adv. gen. med. scis. coun., 1992-95; bd. sci. counselors Nat. Heart, Lung & Blood Inst. NIH, 1982-86; sci. adv. com. Am. Cancer Soc., N.Y.C., 1982-86; adv. com. Lucille P. Markey Charitable Trust, Miami, Fla., 1984-96; sci. rev. bd. Howard Hughes Med. Inst., Bethesda, 1986-93; dir. Regeneron Pharmaceutics, 1989—, Eli Lilly and Co., Inc., 1995—. Editor: The Pharmacological Basis of Therapeutics, 1975, 80, 85, 90; contbr. over 200 articles to profl. jours. Recipient Poul Edvard Poulsson award Norwegian Pharmacology Soc., 1982, GairdnerFound. Internat. award, Can., 1984, Albert Lasker Basic Med. Rsch. award, 1989, Passano Sr. award Passano Found., 1990, Waterford Biomedical Sci. award Scripps Clinic and Rsch. Found. 1990, Basic Sci. Rsch. prize Am. Heart Assn., 1990, Steven C. Beering award Ind. U., 1990, City of Medicine award, Durham, N.C., 1991, CIBA-GEIGY Drew award, 1991, Nobel Prize in Physiology or Medicine, 1994. Mem. Am. Soc. Pharmacology & Exptl. Therapeutics (John J. Abel award in pharmacology 1975, Louis S. Goodman and Alfred Gilman award 1990), Am. Soc. Biol. Chemistry, Nat. Acad. Scis. (Richard Lounsbery award 1987), Am. Acad. Arts and Scis., Inst. Medicine of NAS. Office: U Tex Southwestern Med Ctr Dept Pharmacology 5323 Harry Hines Blvd Dallas TX 75235-9041*

GILMAN, NANCY ELLEN HELGESON, medical and surgical nurse; b. Ill., July 5, 1934; d. Elmer Theodore and Florence Fleda (Powell) Helgeson; m. William O. Gilman, July 20, 1955; children: Anita Leihy, Leeanne Gilman White, Jerilyn Szalonek. Diploma, Copley Meml. Hosp., Aurora, Ill., 1955; BSN, Fla. So. Coll., 1989. Cert. med.-surg. nurse. Staff nurse Community Meml. Hosp., La Grange, Ill., 1958-60, 63-68; staff nurse physician's office, Downers Grove, Ill., 1968-75, office mgr., 1975-80; staff nurse Meml. Hosp. of DuPage County, Elmhurst, Ill., 1980-82; nurse, multi-skilled surg. practitioner Lakeland (Fla.) Regional Med. Ctr., 1982—, multi-skilled team leader, 1991-94. Home: 5750 El Dorado Ave Lakeland FL 33809-4218

GILMAN, SID, neurologist; b. L.A., Oct. 19, 1932; s. Morris and Sarah Rose (Cooper) G.; m. Carol G. Barbour. B.A., UCLA, 1954; M.D., 1957. Intern UCLA Hosp., 1957-58; resident in neurology Boston City Hosp., 1960-63; from instr. to assoc. in neurology Harvard Med. Sch., 1965-68; from asst. prof. to prof. neurology Columbia U., N.Y.C., 1968-76; H. Houston Merritt prof. neurology, 1976-77; prof., chmn. dept. neurology U. Mich., Ann Arbor, 1977—; cons. VA Hosp., Ann Arbor, 1977—; mem. peripheral and ctrl. nervous sys. drugs adv. com. FDA, 1983-85, 86-87, 90-94, chmn., 1996—; adj. attending neurologist Henry Ford Hosp., Detroit; mem. chronic disease adv. com. Mich. Dept. Pub. Health, 1988-94; mem. neurol. sci. rsch. and tng. com. NIH, mem. neurol. disorders program project B com., mem. sci. programs adv. com. Nat. Inst. Neurol. Diseases, Communicative Disorders and Stroke, 1982-84, mem. nat. adv. neurol. disorders and stroke coun., 1994—; dir. Mich. alzheimer's Disease Rsch. Ctr., 1991—; mem. rsch. adv. coun. United Cerebral Palsy Found.; mem. sci. adv. coun. Nat. Ataxia Found., Nat. Amyotrophic Lateral Sclerosis Found., Inc.; mem. profl. adv. bd. Epilepsy Found. Am.; mem. rsch. adv. com. Nat. Multiple Sclerosis Soc., 1986-90; mem. exec. bd. Nat. Coalition for Rsch., 1989-95, Nat. Found. for Brain Rsch., 1989-95; mem. rsch. adv. com. Dana Alliance. Author: (with J.R. Bloedel and R. Lechtenberg) Disorders of the Cerebellum, 1981, (with S.W. Newman) Manter and Gatz's Essentials of Clinical Neuroanatomy and Neurophysiology, 9th edit., 1996, (with J.C. Mazziotta) Clinical Brain Imaging: Principles and Applications, 1992; mem. editl. bd. Exptl. Neurology, Current Opinion in Neurology and Neurosurgery, Neurology, Annals Neurology, Jour. Neuropathology and Exptl. Neurology, Neurobase Arbor Pub. Co.; editor-in-chief Contemporary Neurology Series, 1995—, Neurology Network Commentary, 1996—; contbr. articles to profl. jours. With USPHS, 1958-60. Recipient Lucy G Moses prize Columbia U., 1973, Weinstein Goldenson award United Cerebral Palsy Assn., 1981, UCLA Alumni Profl. Achievement award, 1992, UCLA Med. Alumni Profl. Achievement award, 1992. Mem. AAAS, Am. Neurol. Assn. (1st v.p. 1985-86, pres.-elect 1987-88, pres. 1988-89), Mich. Neurol. Assn. (pres. 1987-88), Soc. Clin. Investigation, Am. Physiol. Soc., Am. Assn. Neuropathologists, Soc. Neurosci., Am. Acad. Neurology (vice chmn. geriatric neurology subcom. 1992—, chmn. 1994-96, chmn. Decade of Brain com. 1990-95), Am. Epilepsy Soc., Assn. Rsch. in Nervous and Mental Disease, Inst. Medicine, Nat. Acad. Scis., Phi Beta Kappa, Alpha Omega Alpha. Home: 3411 Geddes Rd Ann Arbor MI 48105-2518 Office: U Mich Dept Neurology Ann Arbor MI 48109

GILMAN, SUSAN CHERNOW, psychiatrist, consultant; b. N.Y.C., Dec. 22, 1948; d. William and Sylvia (Stein) Chernow; m. Peter M. Gilman, Feb. 3, 1979; children: Andrew, Jonathan, Benjamin. BA in Psychology cum laude, Beloit (Wis.) Coll., 1969; MD, Albert Einstein Coll. Medicine, 1974. Intern in family practice Montefiore Hosp., Bronx, N.Y., 1974-75; resident in psychiatry St. Lukes, N.Y.C., 1978-80; resident in psychiatry Thomas Jefferson U., Phila., 1980-81, clin. asst. prof. psychiatry, 1985—; dir. geriatric svcs. Charter Fairmount Inst., Phila., 1981-92; neuropsychiatry cons. Chestnut Hill Hosp., Phila., 1985-92; med. dir. partial hosp. program Villas of Brandy Wine Belmont Care Ctr., West Chester, Pa., 1992-94; attending psychiatrist Friends Hosp., Phila., 1995; attending psychiatrist geropsychiatry Presbyn. Hosp. of U. Pa. Health Sys., Phila., 1995—; cons. Pauls Run Nursing Home, Phila., 1984-88, Cen. Pk. Lodge Nursing Home, Phila., 1988-92, Fairview Care Ctr., Phila., Twp. Line Manor, Elkins Patch, Pa., Martin's Run, Newtown Square, Pa., Brandywine Care Ctr., West Chester, Pa. Lt. comdr. USPHS, 1975-78. Mem. Am. Psychiat. Assn., Am. Soc. Geriat. Psychiatrists, Phi Beta Kappa. Democrat. Jewish. Home: 27 Wiltshire Rd Wynnewood PA 19096-3644 Office: Presbyn Hosp Univ Pa Health Sys 3910 Powelton Ave Philadelphia PA 19104

GILMARTIN, RAYMOND V., health care products company executive; b. Washington, Mar. 6, 1941; m. Gladys Higham; 3 children. BS in Elect. Engring., Union Coll., 1963; MBA, Harvard U., 1968. Sr. cons. Arthur D. Little Inc., 1968-76; v.p. corp. planning Becton Dickinson & Co., Paramus, N.J., 1976-79, pres. Becton Dickinson div., 1979-87, group pres., 1982-83, sr. v.p., 1983-86, exec. v.p., 1986-87; pres. Becton Dickinson & Co., Franklin Lakes, N.J., 1987-94, chief exec. officer, 1989-94, also bd. dirs.; chmn., pres., CEO Merck, White House Station, NJ, 1994—; bd. dirs. Providian Corp., Pub. Svc. Enterprise Group. Chmn. Valley Hosp., Ridgewood, N.J.; bd. dirs. Ethics Resource Ctr., Project HOPE, Coll. Fund/United Negro Coll. Fund, Pharm. Rsch. and Mfrs. Am.; chmn.-elect Healthcare Leadership Coun.; bd. dirs., bd. assocs. Harvard Bus. Sch.; mem. Bus. Coun., Bus. Roundtable, Conf. Bd., Union Coll., Com. Econ. Devel. Mem. N.J. C. of C. (bd. dirs.). Office: Merck & Co 1 Merck Dr Whitehouse Station NJ 08889

GILMORE, DAVID SCHNEITER, administrator; b. St. Louis, Nov. 27, 1951. BS in Psychology, S.E. Mo. U., 1974, MA in Psychology, 1981. Bd. cert. pyschotherapist; cert. hypnotherapist. Chief psychologist State of Mo., Farmington, 1975-80; pvt. practice Farmington, 1978-80; prof. State of Mo., Flat River, 1978-80; rehab. cons. Ft. Myers, 1980-85; adminstr., dir. Ctr. for Pain Control, Ft. Myers, 1985-91; adminstr. Bayshore Workplaces, Ft. Myers, 1990-91, Vocat. and Rehab. Svcs., Ft. Myers, 1980—; prin. The Gilmore Clinic, Ft. Myers, Sarasota, St. Petersburg, Orlando, St. Louis, Miami, Fla., 1986—. Mem. Am. Psychol. Assn., Fla. Rehab. Assn. (pres. S.E. chpt.). Office: Vocat and Rehab Svcs 3660 Broadway Fort Myers FL 33901-8005

GILMORE, H. WILLIAM, college dean, dentistry educator. DDS, Ind. U., 1958, MSD, 1961. Now dean Sch. Dentistry, Ind. U.-Purdue U., Indpls., -1996; also prof. operative dentistry Sch. Dentistry, Ind. U.-Purdue U. home: 8960 Camby Rd Camby IN 46113 Office: Ind U-Purdue U Sch of Dentistry 1121 W Michigan St Indianapolis IN 46202-5211*

GILMORE, JOHN VAUGHN, JR., clinical psychologist; b. Boston, Aug. 6, 1948; s. John Vaughn and Eunice Chandler (Crocker) G. MDiv, Gordon-Conwell Sem., 1976; MTh, Princeton Theol. Sem., 1977; PhD, Mich. State U., 1984. Lic. psychologist, Calif. Clin. chaplain intern Princeton (N.J.) U. Med. Ctr., 1976-77; counseling intern Personality Dynamics, Southfield, Mich., 1978-79; psychologist Profl. Psychol. Cons., East Lansing, Mich., 1980-81, Los Angeles County Dept. Mental Health, L.A., 1984-85; clin. psychology intern Psychol. Ctr., Pasadena, Calif., 1981-82; adminstr. dir. I-Can Program, Pasadena, 1982-84; supervising psychologist Pacific Clinics, Pasadena, 1985-87; pres. John V. Gilmore Psychology Corp., Covina, Calif., 1988-89; forensic psychologist Taunton Secure Care Program, 1989—. Ednl. Testing Svc. rsch. grantee, 1976. Fellow Mass. Psychol. Assn.; mem. Am. Psychol. Assn., Am. Soc. for Psychology and Law. Office: Taunton State Hosp Chambers Blvd Taunton MA 02780

GILMORE, JUDITH MARIE, physician; b. Houston, Dec. 28, 1942; d. Howard Ray and Mary Gardner (Currier) G.; m. Richard E. Kelley, July 21, 1974 (div. 1981); 1 child, Lisa Kelley. BA, U. Maine, 1965; MA, NYU, 1968; MD, Woman's Med. Coll., 1972. Diplomate Am. Bd. Internal Medicine, Am. Bd. Endocrinology. Resident St. Vincent's Hosp., N.Y.C., 1972-74; fellow in endocrinology St. Raphael's Hosp., New Haven, 1974-75, West Haven VA-Yale Hosp., New Haven, 1975-76; pvt. practice Bridgeport, Conn., 1976-80, Cranston, R.I., 1986—; mem. staff St. Joseph's Hosp., Providence, 1986—; mem. cons. staff Newport (R.I.) Hosp., 1986—; mem. courtesy staff Roger Williams Hosp., Providence, 1994—, R.I. Hosp., Providence, 1995; mem. staff St. Joseph's Hosp., Providence, 1986—; mem. consulting staff Newport (R.I.) Hosp., 1986—; mem. courtesy staff Roger Williams Hosp., Providence, 1994—, R.I. Hosp., Providence, 1995. Lt. comdr. USN, 1980-86. Mem. ACP, AMA, Am. Assn. Edn., Am. Diabetes Assn., R.I. Endocrine Assn. Office: 725 Reservoir Ave Ste 2 Providence RI 02910-4450

GILMORE, LOUISA RUTH, retired nurse, retired firefighter; b. Pitts., Oct. 31, 1930; d. Albert Leonard and Bertha Christina (Birch) Huber; m. William Norman Kemp, May 27, 1950 (div. 1975); children: Janyce Louise Kemp Lipson, Barbra Lea Kemp Bilharz, Robert William, Paul Lee, Charles Albert; m. Robert James Gilmore, Sept. 1, 1989. Diploma in nursing, San Bernardino C.C., Needles, Calif., 1983. Office nurse Santa Fe Clinic, Needles, 1953-57; spl. duty nurse Needles Cmtys. Hosp., 1957-62; nurse supr. Santa Fe Clinic, 1962-79; staff nurse in surgery Needles Desert Cmtys. Hosp., 1979-90; ind. distbr. Cell Tech, Temple, Tex., 1991-95; instr. CPR Needles Desert Cmtys. Hosp., 1987-90; med. officer San Bernardino County Fire Dept., Needles, 1980-83, pub. info. officer, 1983-85, vol. fire fighter, 1983-90; ind. distbr. Reliv Products, 1991-95, Cell Tech., 1996—. Mem. Calif. State Fireman Assn., Needles Firefighters Assn. (treas. 1987, 88), Beta Sigma Phi-Zeta Gamma (treas. 1966, sec. 1967, v.p. 1968, pres. 1969, named Sweetheart Queen 1969), Order of Rose (life).

GILMORE, MICHAEL CLINTON, health services executive; b. Lafayette, Ind., Sept. 26, 1954; s. John William and Betty Ruth (Hollis) G.; m. Terrie Lynn Schreiver, Apr. 28, 1984. Cert. nursing with honors, Ind. Vocat. Tech. Coll., 1982. LPN, Ind. Staff nurse St. Vincent Hosp. and Heathcare Ctr., Indpls., 1982-87, chief orthop. technologist, 1987-90; patient rep. Thera-Kinetics, Inc., Mt. Laurel, N.J., 1990-91; pres. Health Tech. Assocs., Indpls., 1991—; rsch. asst. total joint patient edn. program St. Vincent Hosp. and Healthcare Ctr., Indpls., 1990-91. Sponsor, Explorer Post 384, Boy Scouts Am., Indpls. With U.S. Army, 1972-75. Mem. ASTM (com. F-32 on search and rescue), Nat. Assn. Orthopedic Technologists (mem.-at-large), Nat. Assn. Orthopaedic Nurses, Nat. Assn. for Search and Rescue, Zulu Land Search and Rescue Assn. (dir.), Ind. Search and Rescue Assn. (exec. dir.). Presbyterian. Office: Health Tech Assocs PO Box 68805 Indianapolis IN 46268

GILMORE, ROBIN L., physician, medical educator, researcher, consultant; b. Dayton, Ohio, July 8, 1950; d. Charles Bronson and Dorris (Lake) G.; m. Dennis Ira Nedelman, Dec. 23, 1974 (div. Oct., 1981); 1 child, Cassandra; m. Peter Nash Colonnese, Oct. 14, 1989. BS in Chemistry summa cum laude, U. Cin., 1972; MD in Surgery with honors, Ohio State U., 1975. Diplomate Am. Bd. Clin. Neurophysiology, Am. Bd. Psychiatry and Neurology, Am. Sleep Disorders Assn. Intern dept. neurology Coll. Medicine U. Fla., Gainesville, 1975-76, resident dept. neurology Coll. Medicine, 1976-78, chief resident dept. neurology Coll. Medicine, 1978-79, fellow dept. neurology Coll. Medicine, 1979-80, assoc. prof. dept. neurology, 1990-95, prof. dept. neurology Coll. Medicine, 1995—; asst. prof. medicine Coll. Medicine East Tenn. State U., Johnson City, 1980-82; asst. prof. dept. neurology Coll. Medicine U. Ky., Lexington, 1982-90; vis. scientist Cleve. Clinic Found., 1990. Contbr. articles to profl. jours. Mem. bd. Epilepsy Found. Fla., Gainesville, 1990-91. Recipient Clin. Investigator Devel. award NIH, 1985-90. Fellow. Am. Acad. Neurology, Am. Clin. Neurophysiology Soc. (sec. 1995—); mem. Am. Epilepsy Soc., So. EEG Soc. (sec. 1984-87, Caton award 1980), Am. Bd. Clin. Neurophysiology (bd. mem.), Alpha Omega Alpha. Office: U Fla Coll Medicine PO Box 100236 Gainesville FL 32610-0236

GILMOUR, EDWARD ELLIS, psychiatrist; b. Schenectady, May 6, 1930; s. William Ellis and Adeline (Campbell) G. B.Engring., Yale, 1952, M.A. in Philosophy, 1957; M.D., Boston U., 1961. Intern St. Luke's Hosp., N.Y.C., 1961-62, resident in medicine, 1962-64, resident in psychiatry, 1964-66, child psychiatry, 1966-68, asst. attending, child psychiatry, 1968-80, asso., 1980—; cons. community psychiatry, 1973-75, supr. residents, 1968—; individual practice medicine, specializing in adult, child and adolescent psychiatry and psychoanalysis, N.Y.C., 1968-82, Falmouth, Mass., 1982—; psychoanalytic tng. William Alanson White Inst., N.Y.C., 1969-74; attending psychiatrist Columbia U. Health Service, N.Y.C., 1969-74; staff psychiatrist Ittleson Center Child Research, Riverdale, N.Y., 1976-82; staff Falmouth Hosp., 1982—; mem. provisional staff St. Vincent Hosp., Santa Fe, 1995—; asst. clin. prof. N.Y.U., 1979—. Diplomate Am. Bd. Psychiatry and Neurology with subspltys. in adult and child psychiatry. Fellow Am. Acad. Psychoanalysis Am. Acad. Child Psychiatry; mem. Am. Psychiat. Assn., AMA, Mass. Med. Soc., William Alanson White Psychoanalytic Soc., Soc. Adolescent Psychiatry, Mass. Psychiat. Home: PO Box 10108 Santa Fe NM 87504 Office: 2025 S Galisteo Santa Fe NM 87505

GILPATRICK, ELEANOR, health sciences educator; b. N.Y.C., Oct. 29, 1930; d. Murry and Essie (Hirsch) Gottesfocht. BA, CUNY, 1951; MA, New Sch. for Social Rsch., 1959; PhD, Cornell U., 1964. Instr. Cornell U., Ithaca, N.Y., 1963-64; rsch. asst. prof. U. Ill., Urbana, 1964-66; sr. rsch. assoc. Skill Advancement Inc., N.Y.C., 1966-67; dir. Health Svcs. Mobility Study, N.Y.C., 1966-78; assoc. prof. Hunter Coll. Sch. of Health Scis., N.Y.C., 1968-81, program dir. allied health svcs. adminstrn., 1982—; prof. Hunter Coll. Sch. of Health Scis., 1981—. Author: Grants for Non-profit Organizations, 1989, The Occupational Structure of N.Y.C. Municipal Hospitals, 1970, Structural Unemployment and Aggregate Demand, 1966; contbr. articles to profl. jours. Home: 302 W 12th St New York NY 10014-6025 Office: Hunter Coll 425 E 25th St New York NY 10010-2547

GILPIN, RICHARD WILLIAM, microbiologist; b. Detroit, Sept. 3, 1940; s. Watson A. and Vera Catherine (Gray) G.; m. Ann D. Domine, Apr. 23, 1943 (div. 1983); children: Todd Watson, Sara Edith; m. Adele Marleen Kaplan, Oct. 21, 1948; 1 child, Claire Elizabeth. BA in History, U. Mich., 1963; MS in Biology, Wayne State U., 1966; PhD in Microbiology, Mich. State U., 1970. NIH postdoctoral fellow U. Rochester Sch. Medicine, 1970-72; asst. prof. microbiology Med. Coll. Pa., Phila., 1972-79; assoc. prof. microbiology Med. Coll. Pa., 1979-85; pres. Core Strategies, Willow Grove, Pa., 1985-86; research/devel. mgr. Becton Dickinson & Co., Cockeysville, Md., 1986-88; pres. pvt. practice, Reisterstown, Md., 1988—; biosafety officer Johns Hopkins Instns., Balt., 1989—; adj. scientist Franklin Rsch. Ctr., Phila., 1977-82; adj. asst. prof. environ. health scis. Sch. Hygiene and Pub. Health, Johns Hopkins U., 1991-93, asst. prof. occupational medicine Sch. Medicine, 1994—. Contbr. articles to profl. jours. Pres. Marple Twp. Environ. Adv. Bd., Broomall, Pa., 1980-82; mem. Marple Twp. Planning Commn., 1977-82. Grantee NIH, 1972, Whitaker Found., 1979, Ben Franklin Partnership, 1983, U.S. Army R&D Command, 1994. Mem. Am. Soc. Microbiology, Am. Biol. Safety Assn. (pres. Chesapeake chpt. 1986—), Am. Soc. Safety Engrs. Republican. Home: 12 Folly Farms Ct Reisterstown MD 21136-5932 Office: Johns Hopkins Instn 2024 E Monument St Baltimore MD 21205-2223

GILSON, GRETA MELISSA, nursing administrator; b. Columbus, Ga., Apr. 9, 1957; d. John Clayton and Anna (Agnew) G. RN, Gordon Coll., Barnesville, Ga., 1978; BS in Health Scis., Columbus Coll., 1983, MS in Health Adminstrn., 1992. Staff nurse Univ. Hosp., Augusta, Ga., 1978-83; med. sales rep. Support Systems Internat., Inc., Charleston, S.C., 1984-89; mgr. clin. svcs. Support Systems Internat., Inc., Charleston, 1989-94; implementation specialist Ventech Sys., Inc., Louisville, 1994—; asst. dir. clin. svcs. Pegasus Airwave, Inc., Deerfield Beach, Fla., 1994—, Boca Raton, Fla., 1994—; with CareCentric Solutions, Duluth, Ga., 1996—. Author: (video tape/workbook series) Modern Wound Management, 1991, Topical Agents for Open Wounds, 1992, Local Aspects of Diabetic Foot Ulcer Care: Assessment, Dressings and Topical Agents, 1992, (with others) The Diabetic Foot, 1991. Mem. Internat. Assn. Enterostomal Therapist, Wound Healing Soc., Wound, Ostomy, Conf. Nurses, Dermatol. Nurses Soc. Republican. Methodist. Office: Pegasus Airwave Inc 5300 Broken Sound Blvd Ste 100 Boca Raton FL 33487

GIMBRONE, MICHAEL ANTHONY, JR., research scientist, pathologist, educator; b. Buffalo, Nov. 16, 1943; married, 1971; 3 children. AB, Cornell U., 1965; MD, Harvard U., 1970. Intern, resident fellow Mass. Gen. Hosp., Boston, 1970-72; staff assoc. Nat. Cancer Inst., Bethesda, Md., 1972-74; resch. assoc. Harvard Med. Sch., Boston, 1974-76, from asst. prof. to assoc. prof., 1979-85, Elsie T. Friedman prof. pathology, 1985—; cons. Nat. Heart, Lung and Blood Inst., NIH, 1976—; established investigator Am. Heart Assn., 1977-82; head Vascular Pathophysiol. Rsch. Lab., 1977-85; dir. vascular rsch. div. Brigham and Women's Hosp., 1985—. Mem. AAAS, Am. Heart Assn. (Basic Rsch. prize 1993), Am. Soc. Cell Biologists, Tissue Culture Assn., Am. Soc. Hematology, Am. Assn. Pathologists (v.p. 1991-92), Am. Soc. Invest. Pathology (pres. 1992-93), Am. Assn. Physicians, Fedn. Am. Socs. for Exptl. Biology (Exptl. Pathologist award 1982, bd. dirs. 1990-94), N.Am. Vascular Biology Orgn. (founding pres. 1994—). Office: Brigham and Womens Hosp Vascular Rsch Div Dept of Pathology Boston MA 02115

GIMENEZ, LUIS FERNANDO, physician, educator; b. Antofagasta, Chile, Mar. 3, 1952; came to U.S., 1979; s. Luis Sr. and Nelly (Basulto) G.; m. Diane Marie Salazar, Sept. 20, 1957; children: Luis Andres, Pilar Elizabeth, Nicholas Miguel. MD, U. Chile, Valparaiso, 1976. Diplomate Am. Bd. Internal Medicine, Am. Bd. Nephrology. Intern U. Chile Sch. Medicine, Valparaiso, 1975-76; resident U. Concepcion Sch. Medicine, Chile, 1976-77, U. Chile Sch. Medicine, Valparaiso, 1977-79; research fellow in nephrology Johns Hopkins U. Sch. Medicine, Balt., 1979-81; intern Johns Hopkins Hosp., Balt., 1981-82, resident, 1982-84, clin. fellow nephrology div., 1984-85; instr. Johns Hopkins U. Sch. Medicine, Balt., 1985-86, asst. prof. medicine, 1986—; dir. dialysis unit The Good Samaritan Hosp., Balt., 1985—, chief renal div., 1990; mem. med. adv. bd. Am. Kidney Found., Balt., 1987—. Contbr. articles to profl. jours. Recipient Outstanding Civic Svc. award Chilean Med. Assn., Valparaiso, 1974. Mem. Am. Fedn. for Clin. Research., Am. Soc. Nephrology, Am. Coll. Physicians, Internat. Soc. Nephrology, Internat. Soc. Peritoneal Dialysis, Am. Coll. Clin. Pharmacology. Office: Johns Hopkins Hosp Renal Divsn 720 Rutland Ave Baltimore MD 21205-2109

GINDIN, R. ARTHUR, neurosurgeon; b. Perth Amboy, N.J., Sept. 10, 1934; m. Sara Roberson, 1971. Undergrad., U. Richmond, 1955; MD, Va. Commonwealth U., Richmond, 1959. Diplomate Am. Bd. Neurological Surgery. Intern U. Okla. Hosp., Oklahoma City, 1959-60; resident Montreal (Can.) Neurol. Inst., 1963-65, Med. Coll. Va., 1965-67; assoc. prof. neurological surgery Med. Coll. Ga., Augusta, 1967-78; practice medicine specializing in neurological surgery. Mem. Am. Assn. Neurol. Surgery. Office: 133 Morrison Dr #9 Princeton WV 24740

GINGERICH, NAOMI R., emergency room nurse; b. Linwood, Mich., Sept. 18, 1945; d. Leroy and Mary Alice (Driver) G. Diploma in Nursing, Kansas City (Mo.) Gen. Hosp., 1967. RN, Pa., Md., Fla.; cert. advanced trauma life support. Charge nurse emergency rm. Kansas City (Mo.) Gen. Hosp. and Med. Ctr., 1967-70, oper. rm. nurse, 1971-74; charge nurse emergency rm. Univ. Med. Ctr., Kansas City, Kans., 1970-73; oper. room charge nurse Lancaster (Pa.) Gen. Hosp., 1974-79, charge nurse emergency rm., 1979-88; staff nurse emergency room Preferred Nursing Pool, Balt., 1988-90; with home health care, emergency room Norrell Health Care, Sarasota, Fla., 1990-91; office nurse Landisville Family Practice, 1991-92; on-call night nurse Hospice of Lancaster County, 1992—. Home: 13 Hilltop Rd Lititz PA 17543-8625 Office: Hospice Lancaster County PO Box 4125 685 Good Dr Lancaster PA 17604-4125

GINGOLD, BRUCE STEPHEN, surgeon; b. N.Y.C., Mar. 21, 1944; s. Henry and Evelyn (Glazer) G.; m. Miriam Ann Rubin, Aug. 24, 1968; children: Rachel, Eric. BSEE, CCNY, 1965; MD, Jefferson Med. Sch., 1970. Diplomate Am. Bd. Surgery, Am. Bd. Colorectal Surgery. Surg. intern St. Vincent's Hosp. and Med. Ctr., N.Y.C., 1970-71, resident in surgery, 1971-75; fellow colorectal svc. Cleve. Clinic Found., 1975-76; attending surgeon St. Vincent Hosp., N.Y.C., 1976—, Beth Israel Hosp., N.Y.C., 1982—; chief colorectal svc. St. Vincent Hosp. and Med. Ctr., N.Y.C., 1993—. Contbr. chpts. to books and articles to profl. jours. Capt. U.S. Army, 1970-76. Fellow ACS, Am. Soc. Colorectal Surgeons, N.Y. Surg. Soc.; mem. N.Y. Colorectal Soc. (pres. 1994-96), N.Y. Cancer Soc. Office: 36 7th Ave New York NY 10011

GINGOLD, WILLIAMS, psychologist, researcher, educator, administrator; b. Warsaw, Poland, Sept. 20, 1939; s. David and Lilliam (Weintal) G.; m. Phyllis Kay Shapiro, Aug. 22, 1964; children: Steven, Shara, Tamara, Jason. BS, U. Wis., Milw., 1963; MS, U. Wis., Madison, 1966, PhD, 1971; MHA, U. Minn., Mpls., 1974; post doctorate, UCLA, 1976, 77. Lic. psychologist, Minn.; cert. sch. supt., tchr., spl. edn. dir., Wis., Minn., N.D., Ill. Tchr. regular and spl. edn. Milw. and Madison Pub. Schs., 1963-67; dir. spl. edn. CESA #3, Gillett, Wis., 1967-70; chmn. dept. spl. edn. and rehab. svcs. Moorhead (Minn.) State U., 1971-72; exec. dir. Mental Health and Retarded Ctr., Fargo, N.D., 1972-81; chief exec. officer, dir. Devel. Services Ctr., Champaign, Ill., 1981-87; pres. Twin Cities WMG, Inc., Champaign, Ill., 1987—; dir. rsch., clin. asst. prof., family practice U. Ill. Coll. of Medicine, Urbana, Ill., 1988—; v.p. clin./physician svcs. United Samaritans Med. Ctr., 1993—; asst. clin. prof. U. N.D. Med. Sch., Fargo, 1975-81; pres., CEO Disabled Children's Found., Champaign, 1982-87; v.p., sec. Champaign Chem. Corp., 1985-87; pres., CEO Active Senior Options, Inc., 1990. Author: (tests) Magic Kingdom, 1976, (tng. materials) Individualizing of Instruction, 1972, Geriatric Curriculum, 1981, Watch Me Grow, 1985, Mental Retardation Systems, 1985, Sage for Aging: An Expert Clinical Support System. Mem. Pres. Commn. for Children's Mental Health, Washington, 1979; chairperson Minn. State Adv. Council on Child Care, Mpls., 1971; trustee The neuropsychiatric Inst. and Hosp., Fargo, 1978-81. Served with USAR, 1958-66. Recipient honor scholarship U. Wis., 1985, project assistantship Office Edn./HEW, 1970; grad. fellow Rehab. Svcs. Adminstrn./HEW, 1965. Mem. Am. Assn. Mental Retardation (treas. 1985), Nat. Coun. Community Mental Health Ctrs. (treas. 1979-80), Am. Assn. Healthcare Execs., Coun. Exceptional Children (pres. 1969-70, N.E. Wis. award 1970), Am. Ednl. Rsch. Assn., Kiwanis. Jewish. Office: U Ill Coll of Medicine 190 Medical Sciences Urbana IL 61801

GINN, JOSEPH M., pharmacist; b. Idabel, Okla., May 18, 1964; s. James H. and Maxine (Garcia) G. BA in Biol. Sci., Okla. State U., 1987; BS in Pharmacy, Southwestern Okla. State U., 1990. Registered pharmacist, Okla., Tex. Staff pharmacist Palace Drug Store, Idabel, 1990-91; relief pharmacist Palace Drug, Idabel, 1990—; staff pharmacist McCurtain Meml. Hosp., Idabel, 1991, pharmacy dir., pharmacy and therapeutics sec., 1991—, mem. quality assurance team, 1991—. Dir. Sunday sch. Regional Bapt. Ch., 1994-95; mem. Idabel Arts and Humanities Coun., program coord., 1995—. Mem. Masons. Democrat. Office: McCurtain Meml Hosp 1301 Lincoln Rd Idabel OK 74745

GINSBERG, BARRY HOWARD, physician, researcher; b. Bklyn., May 9, 1945; s. Emanuel and Ruth (Friedman) G.; m. Marjorie Ellen Kanef, Aug. 20, 1967; children: Susan, David. BA, SUNY, Binghamton, 1965; PhD, Albert Einstein Coll., 1971, MD, 1972. Intern Beth Israel Hosp., Boston, 1972-73, resident in internal medicine, 1973-74; fellow in endocrinology NIH, 1974-77; asst. prof. U. Iowa, Iowa City, 1977-82, assoc. prof. medicine, biochemistry, 1979-87, prof. medicine, biochemistry, 1988-90, assoc. dir. Diabetes-Endocrinology Research Ctr., 1982-84, dir. 1984-86; co-dir. Diabetes Control and Complications Trial, Iowa City, 1984-86, dir. 1986-90; med. dir. Worldwide Diabetes Healthcare Becton Dickenson and Co.; adj. prof. medicine Robert Wood Johson Coll. Medicine. Contbr. chpts. to profl. books. Served to comdr. USPHS, 1974-77. Mem. Am. Fedn. Clin. Research, Endocrine Soc., AAAS, Central Soc. Clin. Research, Am. Diabetes Assn. (pres. Iowa chpt. 1982-84, bd. dirs. 1982-85), N.J. Soc. to Prevent Blindness. Avocation: computer programing. Office: Becton Dickinson and Co 1 Becton Dr Franklin Lakes NJ 07417-1815

GINSBERG, HAROLD SAMUEL, virologist, educator; b. Daytona Beach, Fla., May 27, 1917; s. Jacob and Anne (Kalb) G.; m. Marion Reibstein, Aug. 4, 1949; children: Benjamin Langer, Peter Robert, Ann Meredith, Jane Elizabeth. AB, Duke U., 1937; MD, Tulane U., 1941, DSc (hon.), 1995. Resident Mallory Inst. Pathology, Boston, 1941-42; intern, asst. resident Boston City Hosp., 4th Med. Service, 1942-43; resident physician, assoc. Rockefeller Inst., 1946-51; assoc. prof. preventive medicine Western Res. U. Sch. Medicine, 1951-60; prof. microbiology, chmn. dept. U. Pa. Sch. Medicine, 1960-73; prof. microbiology, chmn. dept. Coll. Phys. and Surg. Columbia, 1973-85, prof. microbiology and medicine, dir. section molecular pathogenesis of infection, 1986—; part time expert scientist NIH, Rockville, Md., 1993—; mem. commn. acute respiratory diseases Armed Forces Epidemiological Bd., 1959-73; cons. NIH, 1959-72, 75—, Army Chem. Corps, 1962-64, NASA, 1969-73, Am. Cancer Soc., 1969-73, mem. coun. on rsch. and pers., 1976-80; v.p. Internat. Com. on Nomenclature of Viruses, 1966-75; mem. space sci. bd., chmn. panel microbiology Nat. Acad. Sci., 1973-74; chmn. microbiology exam. com. Nat. Bd. Med. Examiners, 1974-79; mem. microbiology and infectious disease com. Nat. Inst. Allergy and Infectious Disease, NIH, 1976-81, chmn., 1979-81; co-chmn. Inst. Medicine, NAS Roundtable: AIDS: Modern Approaches Vaccines and Anti-Viral Drugs, 1989-92; mem. U.S. Nat. Com. for Internat. Union of Microbiological Socs. (USNC/IUMS), Nat. Rsch. Coun., 1992—. Contbr. textbooks; co-author: Microbiology, 1967, 4th edit., 1990, Virology, 2d edit., 1988, Vaccines 88-95, Modern Approaches to New Vaccines, Including Prevention of AIDS; mem. editorial bd. Jour. Infectious Diseases, Jour. Immunology, Jour. Exptl. Medicine, Jour. Virology and Bacteriological Revs., Jour. Acquired Immune Deficiency Syndromes; editor: Jour. Virology, 1979-84, Cancer Research, 1978-82. Served to lt. col. M.C. AUS, 1943-46. Decorated Legion of Merit; Fogarty scholar NIH, 1993-94; recipient Disting. Svc. award Coll. Physicians and Surgeons, Columbia U., 1991, Acad. medal N.Y. Acad. Medicine, 1994, Bristol-Myers Squibb award for Disting. Achievement in Infectious Disease Rsch., 1994, Outstanding Alumnus award Tulane Sch. Medicine, 1995. Fellow AAAS; mem. NAS, Inst. Medicine of NAS., Assn. Am. Physicians, Am. Acad. Microbiologists (chmn. bd. govs. 1971-72, bd. govs. 1993—), Am. Soc. Clin. Investigation (councillor 1958-60), Am. Assn. Immunologists, Am. Soc. Microbiology (chmn. virology div. 1961-62, councillor div. 1977-81), Soc. Exptl. Biology and Medicine, Assn. Med. Sch. Microbiology Chairmen (pres. 1972-73), Harvey Soc. (pres. 1984coun. 1985-88), Cen. Soc. Clin. Research, Am. Soc. Biol. Chemists, Am. Soc. Virology (pres. 1983), Alpha Omega Alpha. Home: Apt 1313S 5225 Pooks Hill Rd Bethesda MD 20814 Office: Columbia U Coll Phys and Surg Dept Medicine 650 W 168th St New York NY 10032-3702

GINSBERG, MARK ALAN, psychologist; b. Bklyn., Sept. 23, 1944; s. Mac and Sophie (Rubin) G.; m. Pauline E. Speiglman, Nov. 24, 1974; children: Peter Kipp, Daivd Kipp, Matthew Kipp. BS, CCNY, 1966; MA, So. Ill. U., 1971, PhD, 1975. Lic. psychologist, N.Y. Counseling psychology intern Iowa State U., Ames, 1972-73; clin. pschology intern Health and Scis. Ctr. U. of Manitoba, Winnipeg, Can., 1973-74; program dir. CVS CYS Hutchings Psychiat. Ctr., Syracuse, N.Y., 1974-79; program dir. Adult Svcs. Hutchings Psychiat. Ctr., Syracuse, N.Y., 1979-81, dir. Psychology tng., 1981-90, chief psychologist, 1990—; pvt. practice psychologist, Syracuse, 1977—; adj. asst. prof. psychiatry Health Scis. Ctr. SUNY, 1975—; adj. assoc. prof. Syracuse U., 1979—. Bd. dir. Alt. Route Inc., Syracuse, 1977-79; v.p. Madison County Community Svcs. Bd., Wampsville, N.Y., 1988—. Mem. Am. Psychol. Assn., N.Y. State Psychol. Assn., Cen. N.Y. Psychol. Assn. (sec. 1987-88), Eastern Evaluation Rsch. Soc. Democrat. Jewish. Home: PO Box 27 Canastota NY 13032-0027 Office: Hutchings Pschiat Ctr 620 Madison St Syracuse NY 13210-2319

GINSBERG, PHILLIP CARL, physician; b. Fairbanks, Alaska, June 1, 1954; s. Richard and Sondra (Soble) G.; m. Judith Carson, June 19, 1977; 1 child, Rachel Hope. BS in Biology, Villanova U., 1976; MS, Phila. Coll. Osteopath, 1985, DO, 1980; JD, Temple U., 1995. Diplomate Nat. Bd. Osteopathic Examiners; Am. Bd. Osteopathic Surgeons; cert. urological surgery. Intern Hosp. Phila. Coll. Osteopathic Medicine, Phila., 1980-81; resident Albert Einstein Med. Ctr., Phila., 1981-82; resident in urologic surgery Hosp. Phila. Coll. Osteopathic Medicine, Phila., 1981-85; pvt. practice Phila., 1985—; clin. assoc. prof. Phila. Coll. Osteopathic Medicine; med. dir. Urodiagnostics, Inc., Del. Valley Continence Ctr.; chmn. div. of urology, Phila. Geriatric Ctr., 1988, Albert Einstein Med. Ctr., 1989, Albert Einstein Med. Ctr.; cons. Nat. Cancer Inst. Contbr. numerous articles to profl. jours. Mem. AMA, ABA, Am. Coll. Legal Medicine, Am. Osteo. Assn., Pa. Osteol. Assn., Pa. Med. Soc., Pa. Urology Assn., Am. Fertility Assn., Am. Urol. Assn., Mid Atlantic Urol. Assn., Phila. Urol. soc., Lambda Omicron Gamma. Home: 118 Righters Mill Rd Narberth PA 19072-1313 Office: Albert Einstein Med Ctr 5401 Old York Rd Philadelphia PA 19141-3030

GINSBERG, RONALD LAWRENCE, gastroenterologist; b. Balt., Nov. 16, 1947; s. Benjamin Daniel and Sylvia Pauline (Chinn) G.; m. Karen Joyce Datnoff, Mar. 25, 1947; children: Michael Elliott, Ellen Debra. BA cum laude, Johns Hopkins U., 1968, MD, 1972. Diplomate Am. Bd. Internal Medicine, Am. Bd. Gastroenterology. Intern medicine Johns Hopkins Hosp., Balt., 1972-73; clin. assoc. NIH, Nat. Inst. Arthritis, Metabolism and Digestive Disease, Phoenix, 1973-75; resident medicine Balt. City Hosps., 1975-76, fellow in gastroenterology, 1976-78; pvt. practice cons. gastroenterologist, 1978—; staff Northwest Hosp. Ctr., Sinai Hosp., Balt., Carroll County Gen. Hosp., North Arundel Hosp., Union Meml. Hosp., Franklin Square Hosp.; chief div. gastroenterology and med. endoscopy Northwest Hosp. Ctr.; pres. Northwest Health Alliance; bd. dirs. M.D. Health Network. Contbr. articles to profl. jours. Lt. comdr. USPHS, 1973-75. Fellow ACP; mem. AMA, AAAS, Am. Gastroenterol. Assn., Am. Soc. Gastrointestinal Endoscopy, Am. Coll. Gastroenterology, Am. Soc. Internal Medicine, Md. Soc. Gastrointestinal Endoscopy, Balt. City. Med. Soc., Baltimore County Med. Assn., N.Y. Acad. Scis., Phi Beta Kappa, Alpha Omega Alpha. Republican. Jewish. Office: 19 Walker Ave Ste 302 Baltimore MD 21208-4006

GINSBERG, STANLEY ARTHUR, urologist, consultant; b. N.Y.C., Aug. 29, 1933; s. William and Ruth (Mutterperl) G.; m. Suaun Judith Kabran, Aug. 20, 1967; children: Marnie, Jodi. BA, Amherst Coll., 1955; MD, Columbia U., 1959. Diplomate Am. Bd. Urology. Dir. urology Peninsula Hosp. Ctr., Far Rockaway, N.Y., 1964—; acting dir. urology St. John's Episc. Hosp., Far Rockaway, 1964—; cons. Long Beach (N.Y.) Hosp., 1964—. Home and Office: 704 Empire Ave Far Rockaway NY 11691

GINSBERG-FELLNER, FREDDA, pediatric endocrinologist, researcher; b. N.Y.C., Apr. 21, 1937; d. Nathaniel and Bertha (Jagendorf) Ginsberg; m. Michael J. Fellner, Aug. 27, 1961; children: Jonathan R., Melinda F. Bramwit. AB, Cornell U., 1957; MD, NYU, 1961. Diplomate Am. Bd. Pediatrics, Am. Bd. Pediatric Endocrinology. Intern Albert Einstein Coll. Medicine, N.Y.C., 1961-62, fellow in pediatrics, 1962-63, 64-65, 66-67, resident in pediatrics, 1963-64, 65-66, clin. instr. pediatrics, 1967; assoc. in pediatrics Mt. Sinai Sch. Medicine, N.Y.C., 1967-69, asst. prof., 1969-75, assoc. prof., 1975-81, dir. div. pediatric endocrinology, 1977—, prof. pediatrics, 1981—. Mem. med. scis. rev. com. Juvenile Diabetes Found., 1985-88, mem. scis. adv. bd., 1991-95; mem. N.Y. State Coun. on Diabetes, Albany, 1988-89; chmn. Camp NYDA for Diabetic Children, Burlingham, 1977-89. Recipient Humanitarian award, Juvenile Diabetes Found., 1994; grantee NIH, 1977—, Am. Diabetes Assn., 1978, March of Dimes, 1983-87, Juvenile Diabetes Found., 1982-88, 93-95, Wm. T. Grant Found., 1985-89. Fellow Am. Acad. Pediatrics; mem. Am. Diabetes Assn. (chmn. 1992-94, Outstanding Contbns. award 1991, Svc. award 1994), Soc. Pediatric Rsch., Am. Pediatric Soc., Endocrine Soc., Lawson Wilkins Pediatric Endocrine Soc., N.Y. Diabetes Assn. (pres.-elect 1985-87, pres. 1987-89, Svc. award Camp NYDA 1989, Max Ellenberg Profl. Svc. award 1993). Office: Sinai Med Ctr Dept Pediats Box 1659 1176 Fifth Ave New York NY 10029-6504

GINSBURG, ARTHUR, urologist; b. Bklyn., Aug. 23, 1933; s. Archie and Rose (Hecker) G.; m. Davida White, May 29, 1960; children ira Allan, Lee Mark, Beth Anne. BA, Cornell U., 1954; MD, N.Y. Med. Coll., 1958. Diplomate Am. Bd. Urology. Pvt. practice Morristown, N.J., 1965—; mem. exec. com. Morristown Meml. Hosp., 1982-90, pres., 1988-89. Capt. U.S. Army, 1960-62. Fellow ACS, Acad. Medicine N.J. (pres. urology sect. 1987); mem. AMA, Am. Urol. Soc. (N.Y. chpt.), N.J. State Med. Soc., Morris County Med. Soc. (pres. 1983-84, exec. com. 1975-90), Phi Beta Kappa, Alpha Omega Alpha. Office: Adult & Pediatric Urologist 261 James St Ste 3 A Morristown NJ 07960

GINSBURG, DANIEL ALAN, healthcare administrator; b. Pitts., Sept. 21, 1961; s. Sidney David and Sandra (Rothman) G.; m. Laura Ann Lechner, Aug. 23, 1986; children: Eric Charles, Katharine Elizabeth. AB magna cum laude, Havard Coll., 1983; MBA, Harvard U., 1987. V.p. ops. Systems Analysis Svcs., Inc., Auburndale, Mass., 1980-81, exec. v.p., 1981-83; assoc. Boston Cons. Group, Inc., 1983-85, cons., 1987-90, mgr., 1990-94; assoc. Aeneas Group Harvard Mgmt. Co., Boston, 1986; COO Mass. Gen. Physicians Orgn., Mass. Gen. Hosp., Boston, 1994—. Contbr. articles to profl. jours. Office: Mass Gen Physicians Orgn Mass Gen Hosp Fruit St Boston MA 02114

GINSBURG, DAVID, human genetics educator, researcher; b. Newburgh, N.Y., Aug. 11, 1952; s. Leonard and Ruth Helena Henrietta (Falkson) G.; m. Maureen Rose Kushinsky, June 7, 1981; children: Daniel William, Leah Beth. BA magna cum laude, Yale U., 1974; MD, Duke U., 1977. Diplomate Am. Bd. Internal Medicine, Am. Bd. Med. Oncology, Am. Bd. Hematology. Resident in pathology Presbyn. Hosp., San Francisco, 1977-78; intern, resident in internal medicine Peter Bent Brigham Hosp., Boston, 1978-81; fellow tng. program in hematology and med. oncology Brigham and Women's Hosp., Harvard Med. Sch., Boston, 1981-84, instr. medicine, 1984-85; asst. prof. dept. medicine U. Mich., Ann Arbor, 1985-89, assoc. prof. with tenure, 1989-93, assoc. prof. human genetics, 1989-93; asst. investigator Howard Hughes Med. Inst. Howard Hughes Med. Inst., Ann Arbor, 1985-89, assoc. investigator, 1989-93; prof. medicine and human genetics, 1993—, dir. divsn. molecular medicine and genetics, dept. medicine, 1993—; investigator Howard Hughes Med. Inst., 1993—. Contbr. numerous articles to profl. jours. Recipient Jerome W. Conn award Dept. Medicine, U. Mich., 1987-88, Frank E. Trobaugh Hematology Young Investigator award Midwest Blood Club, 1988; Med. Scientist Tng. Program scholar Duke U., 1974-77. Mem. AAAS, ACP, Am. Fedn. for Clin. Rsch., Am. Soc. Human Genetics, Am. Soc. Hematology, Am. Heart Assn. (thrombosis coun.), Assn. Am. Physicians, Am. Soc. for Clin. Investigation, Alpha Omega Alpha. Jewish. Office: Howard Hughes Med Inst 1150 W Medical Center Dr Ann Arbor MI 48109-0726

GINSBURG, IONA HOROWITZ, psychiatrist; b. N.Y.C., Dec. 2, 1931; d. A. Eugene and Gertrude (Seidman) Horowitz; m. Selig M. Ginsburg, Aug. 15, 1954 (div. 1984); children: Elizabeth, Jessica. AB, Vassar Coll., 1953; MD, Columbia U., 1957. Diplomate Am. Bd. Psychiatry and Neurology. Pvt. practice N.Y.C., 1961—; instr. psychiatry Columbia U., N.Y.C., 1961-81, asst. clin. prof. psychiatry, 1981-95, assoc. clin. prof. psychiatry, 1995—; psychiatrist student health svc. NYU, N.Y.C., 1978—; cons.-liaison psychiatrist Columbia Presbyn. Med. Ctr., N.Y.C., 1982—. Contbr. articles to profl. jours. Med. adv. bd. Nat. Psoriasis Found. Recipient Josie Bradbury Travel award Psoriasis Assn. Gt. Britain. Mem. Am. Soc. Adolescent Psychiatry, N.Y. Soc. Adolescent Psychiatry (pres. 1986, cert. of appreciation 1986), Am. Psychiat. Assn., Am. Psychosomatic Soc., Met. Coll. Mental Health Assn. (pres. 1980), Assn. Psychocutaneous Medicine N.Am. (sec.-treas. 1994-95, v.p. 1995—).

GINTAUTAS, JONAS, physician, scientist, administrator; b. Justinava, Lithuania, Oct. 3, 1938; came to U.S., 1967; s. Jonas and Elena (Zaveckaité) Sinsinas; m. Kristina Zebrauskaite, June 13, 1970; children: Pasaka, Vadas. PhD, Northwestern U., 1976; MD, U. Juarez, Mex., 1984; MBA, Century U., 1996. Assoc. prof. Tex. Tech. U., Lubbock, 1975-77; assoc. prof. and dir. rsch. Tex. Tech. U. Health Scis. Ctr., Lubbock, 1979-82; dir. basic and clin. rsch., prof. neurology The Brookdlae U. Hosp. Med. Ctr., N.Y.C., 1985—; cons. Amtorg Corp., N.Y.C., 1987-94, Ralex Internat. Co., Boston, 1988-91, Arrow Biomed Inc., Metuchen, N.J., 1988—. Editorial cons. Jour. Aphasia Agnosia Apraxia, 1979—; contbr. articles on pharmacology, anesthesia and surgery to profl. jours. Charter mem. Rep. Presdl. Task Force, Washington, 1982—; mem. Nat. Rep. Senatorial Com., Washington, 1984—, U.S. Senatorial Club, Washington, 1984—; nat. campaign advisor Nat. Rep. Senatorial Com., Washinton, 1995—. Recipient Gold medal for rsch. in med. sci. Am. Biog. Inst., medal of honor Rep. Presdl. Task Force, 1982; rsch. grantee various pvt. and govtl. agys. Fellow Internat. Coll. Physicians and Surgeons (hon.); mem. Am. Biog. Inst. (dep. gov. 1987—), U.S. Senatorial Club (preferred). Roman Catholic. Home: 84-19 107th St Richmond Hill NY 11418-1140 Office: The Brookdale Univ Hosp Med Ctr Linden And Rockaway Brooklyn NY 11212

GINZBERG, ELI, economist, emeritus educator, government consultant, author; b. N.Y.C., Apr. 30, 1911; s. Louis and Adele (Katzenstein) G.; m. Ruth Szold, July 14, 1946 (dec. Aug. 1995); children: Abigail, Jeremy, Rachel. Student, U. Heidelberg, U. Grenoble, 1928-29; AB, Columbia U., 1931, AM, 1932, PhD, 1934, LittD, 1982; LittD, Jewish Theol. Sem., 1966; LLD, Loyola U., Chgo., 1969; LHD, Rush U., 1985; DHL, Kirksville Osteo. Sch., 1993; LLD, Phila. Coll. Osteo. Medicine, 1994; DHL, State Coll. of Optometry, N.Y., 1995. Dir. rsch. econs. and group behavior Columbia U., N.Y.C., 1939-42, 48-49, faculty, 1935—, A. Barton Hepburn prof. econs. Grad. Sch. Bus., 1967-79, prof. emeritus, spl. lectr. Grad. Sch. Bus., 1979—, dir. conservation human resources project, 1950-90, dir. Eisenhower Ctr. for Conservation Human Resources, 1990—; dir. Revson fellows program on future City of NY, 1979—; adj. prof. health and society Barnard Coll., 1980-88; spl. lectr. health and soc., Sch. Pub., Health, Columbia U., 1989—; hon. faculty mem. Indsl. Coll. Armed Forces, 1957-71; chmn. bd. Manpower Demonstration Research Corp., 1974-82, chmn. bd. emeritus, 1982—; Spl. asst. to chief statistician U.S. War Dept., 1942-44; spl. asst. to dir. hosp. div. U.S. War Dept. (Surgeon Gen.'s Office), 1944, dir. resources analysis div., 1944-46; cons. Dept. Army, 1946-70, Dept. State, 1953, 56, 65-69, Dept. Labor, 1954-82, Dept. Def., 1964-71, Dept. Commerce, 1965-66, 79-80, GAO, 1973-82, Exec. Office Pres., 1942; mem. med. adv. bd. to Sec. War, 1946-48; U.S. rep. 5 power Conf. Reparations for Non-Repatriable Refugees, 1946; dir. N.Y. State Hosp. Study, 1948-49; mem. Com. on Wartime Requirement for Sci. and Specialized Personnel, 1942; med. cons. Hoover Commn., 1952; adviser Commn. Chronic Illness, 1950-53; mem. adv. council NIMH, 1959-63; chmn. com. on studies White House Conf. on Children and Youth, 1960; dir. staff studies Nat. Manpower Council, 1951-61; chmn. Nat. Manpower Adv. Com., 1962-74, Nat. Commn. for Manpower Policy, 1974-79, Nat. Commn. for Employment Policy, 1979-82; mem. Nat. Adv. Allied Health Council, 1968-72; mem. sci. adv. bd. USAF, 1969-73; chmn. taskforce manpower rsch. Dept. Def., 1970-71; mem. Inst. Medicine, Nat. Acad. Scis., 1972—; mem. Office of Sci. and Engring. personnel adv. com. Nat. Acad. Scis., 1984-91; advisor Internat. Inst. Mgmt. Sci. Ctr., Berlin, 1982-89; mem. ORT Acad. Adv. Council, 1984-91, chmn., 1991—; mem. Econ. Policy Coun. UN Assn. USA, 1984-87; co-chair adv. com. Job Creation Project Nat. Com. for Full Employment, 1984-86; mem. Mayoral Commn. to Consider Future of Child Health in N.Y.C., 1987-88; mem. med. adv. bd. Hadassah-Hebrew U., 1988—; bd. dirs. Found. Biomed. Rsch., 1988—; mem. Mayoral Commn. to Rev. Health and Hosps. Corp., 1991-92. Author: The House of Adam Smith, 1934, The Illusion of Economic Stability, 1939, Grass on the Slag Heaps: The Story of the Welsh Miners, 1942, The Unemployed, 1943, The Labor Leader, 1948, A Pattern for Hospital Care, 1949, Agenda for American Jews, 1950; Occupational Choice, 1951, The Uneducated, 1953, Psychiatry and Military Manpower Policy, 1953, What Makes an Executive, 1955, The Negro Potential, 1956, Effecting Change in Large Organizations, 1957, Human Resources, 1958, The Ineffective Soldier, 3 vols., 1959, The Nation's Children, 3 vols., 1960, Planning for Better Hospital Care, 1961, The Optimistic Tradition and American Youth, 1962, The American Worker in the Twentieth Century, 1963, The Troublesome Presence, 1964, Talent and Performance, 1964, The Negro Challenge to the Business Community, 1964, The Pluralistic Economy, 1965, Keeper of the Law: Louis Ginzberg, 1966, Life Styles of Educated Women, 1966, Educated American Women-Self-Portraits, 1966, Manpower Strategy for Developing Countries, 1967, The Middle Class Negro in the White Man's World, 1967, Manpower Strategy for the Metropolis, 1968, Business Leadership and the Negro Crisis, 1968, Men, Money and Medicine, 1969, Urban Services-The Case of New York, 1971, Career Guidance, 1971, Manpower for Development, 1971, Manpower Advice for Government, 1972, New York Is Very Much Alive, 1973, Corporate Lib: Women's Challenge to Management; editor, 1973, Federal Manpower in Transition, 1974, The Great Society: Lessons for the Future, 1974, The University Medical Center and the Metropolis, 1974, The Future of the Metropolis, 1974, The Manpower Connection: Education and Work, 1975, Jobs for Americans, 1976, The Human Economy, 1976, Regionalization and Health Policy, 1977, The Limits of Health Reform, 1977, The House of Adam Smith Revisited, 1977, Health Manpower and Health Policy, 1978, Good Jobs, Bad Jobs, No Jobs, 1979, American Jews: The Building of a Voluntary Community (in Hebrew), 1979, Employing the Unemployed, 1980, The School/Work Nexus, 1981, Technology and Employment: Concepts and Clarifications, 1986, Medicine and Society, 1987, The Skeptical Economist, 1987, Executive Talent, 1988, The Financing of Biomedical Research, 1989, Bridges to Work, 1989, Physicians, Politicians, and the Public, 1989; editor: The Delivery of Health Care: What Lies Ahead, 1982, The Coming Physician Surplus: In Search of a Public Policy, 1983, Home Health Care: Its Role in the Changing Health Services Market, 1983, Beyond Human Scale: The Large Corporation at Risk, 1985, American Medicine: The Power Shift, 1985, The U.S. Health Care System: A Look to the 1990s, 1985, Understanding Human Resources: Perspectives, People, and Policy, 1985, From Health Dollars to Health Services: New York City 1965-85, 1986, From Physician Shortage to Patient Shortage: The Uncertain Future of Medical Practice, 1986, Medicine and Society: Clinical Decisions and Societal Values, 1987, The Skeptical Economist, 1987, Young People at Risk: Is Prevention Possible, 1988, Executive Talent: Developing Tomorrow's Leaders, 1988, The Financing of Biomedical Research, 1989, My Brother's Keeper , 1989, Does Job Training Work: The Clients Speak Out, 1989, The Medical Triangle, 1990, Health Services Research: Key to Health Policy, 1991, The Eye Of Illusion, 1993,

The Economics of Medical Education, 1993, The Road to Reform: The Future of Health Care in America, 1994, Medical Gridlock and Health Reform, 1994, The Changing U.S. Labor Market, 1994, The Financing of Medical Schools in an Era of Health Reform, 1995, Tomorrows Hospitals, 1996, Improving Healthcare of the Poor: A New York Perspective, 1996, Urban Acualur Health Centers, 1996. Dir. research United Jewish Appeal, 1941; bd. govs. Hebrew U., Jerusalem, 1953-59. Fellow AAAS, Am. Acad. Arts and Scis.; mem. Am. Econ. Assn., Indsl. Rels. Rsch. Assn., AAUP, N.Y. Sci. Policy Assn. of N.Y. Acad. Scis., Soc. Med. Cons. to Armed Forces (assoc.), Allen O. Whipple Surg. Soc., AOA (hon.), Phi Beta Kappa, Beta Gamma Sigma. Home: 845 W End Ave New York NY 10025-8435 Office: Columbia U Eisenhower Ctr 475 Riverside Dr Ste 248 New York NY 10115-0122

GIOIELLA, EVELYN, dean, nursing educator. BS in Nursing with distinction, Cornell U., 1959; MA in Pub. Health Nursing, NYU, 1963, PhD in Nursing, 1977. Cmty. health instr. Sch. Nursing Lenox Hill Hosp., 1963-73; asst. prof., curriculum coord. Sch. Nursing CCNY, 1976-78, assoc. prof., dir. curriculum & curriculum rsch. Sch. Nursing, 1978-89, acting dean, assoc. prof., 1979-80, dean, prof. nursing, 1980-83; dean, prof. nursing Hunter-Bellevue Sch. Nursing, N.Y.C., 1983—; cons. Russell Sage Coll., N.Y.C., U. P.R., St. Anselm Coll., N.H., U. Fla., St. Louis U., U. Wis., Madison, Dept. Health, Taiwan, Taipei City Nurses Assn. Homecare Unit, Taipei Coll. Nursing, Kaochsiong U., Tien Med. Ctr.; vis. prof. Shanghai Med. U., 1991-94; presenter in field. Editor: The History of the Lenox Hospital School of Nursing, 1973, Nursing Care of the Aging Client, 1985 (AJN Book of Yr. award 1985), Gerontology in the Professional Nursing Curriculum, 1986; contbr. chpts. to books and articles to profl. jours. Recipient Disting. Alumnus award Cornell U.-N.Y. Hosp. Sch. Nursing Alumni Assn.; named one of YWCA Acad. Women Achievers; grantee Diamond Found., 1989-95, Helene Fuld Health Trust, 1989-90, Astor Found., 1994. Fellow Am. Acad. Nursing (panel on aging 1991—); mem. ANA (coun. nurse rschrs. nurse rep. 1984—, coun. gerontol. nursing), N.Y. State Nurses Assn. (bd. com. strategic planning 1991-93, geriatric nurse practice group, coun. edn. 1985-88), Assn. Am. Colls. Nursing (sec. 1986-90, mem. edn. stds. task force 1987-91), Nat. League for Nursing, Sigma Theta Tau (v.p. Upsilon chpt. 1983-87, mem. Alpha Phi chpt. 1986—, charter mem. Cornell chpt., disting. educator award 1978). Office: Hunter Bellevue Sch Nursing 425 East 25th St New York NY 10010*

GIORDAN, ANDRE JEAN PIERRE HENRI, biologist researcher; b. Nice, France, Nov. 7, 1946; s. Francois and Laurence (Abbo) G.; 1 child, Severine. D of Physiology, U. Nice, France, 1970; Postmaster of History of Scis., U. Paris, 1974; D on Didactic and Epistemology of Scis., U. Paris V "Sorbonne", 1976. Physiologist researcher U. Nice, France, 1968-71; tchr. Ministry of Edn., France, 1971-80; sci. didactic researcher Nat. Inst. Edn., Paris, 1972-76, rsch. dir., 1976-80; extraordinary prof. U. Geneva, Switzerland, 1980-83; rsch. dir. U. Paris VII, 1978—; prof. U. Geneva, 1983—; LDES dir.; pres. ednl. scis. sect. 1992—; rsch. dir. Nat. Ctr. for Sci. Rsch., Paris, 1976-80; environ. cons. UNESCO and UNEP, 1976-87; CECSI network dir., 1980—; sci. and tech. communication cons. OCDE, 1993—, CCE, 1993—; chmn. Geneve Edn. Sci. Com., 1991—. Author: Une pedogogie pour les sciences experimentales, 1978, Quelle education scientifique pour quelle societe, 1978, L'education relative a l'environment, 1986, Histoire de la biologie, 1987, Les origines du savoir scientifique, 1987, L'enseignement scientifique, 1989, Psychologie genetique et didactique des sciences, 1989, Maitriser l'information scientifiques et medicale, 1990, L'education pour l'environnement, 1991, Maitriser les methodes de travail, 1994, Conceptions et connaissances, 1994, Comme un poisson rouge dans l'homme, 1995; contbr. articles to profl. jours. Recipient Grameyer award U. Louisville, 1988, Cage a mouche award, Nice, 1989. Mem. Swiss Soc. Edn., Internat. Network in Scis., Tech., Edn., Internat. Union Biol. Scis., Commn. Biol. Edn. (vice chmn. 1994—), Assn. for Devel. Rsch. on Didactic Scis., Pansemiotic Assn., European Soc. Didactic Biology (v.p. 1990—), Comm., Edn., Culture Sci. and Tech. Network (pres. 1988—), DIRES (chmn. 1990—), Batelum de le Scis. (chmn. 1993—). Home: Benoit Bunico 3, F-06300 Nice France Office: LDES, FPSE, 9 Rt de Drize, 1227 Carouge Geneva Switzerland

GIORDANO, CATHERINE KOWKABANY, nurse; b. Bklyn., Feb. 18, 1956; d. Emil and Madeline (Asmar) Kowkabany; m. William Lawrence Giordano, Feb. 2, 1985; 1 child, Lawrence William. ADN, L.I. Coll., 1978; BS in Adminstrn. cum laude, St. Francis Coll., Bklyn., 1982. RN, N.Y.; cert. apheresis nurse. Educator Downstate Med. Ctr., Bklyn., 1979-84; counselor ARC, Bklyn., 1981-84; head apheresis nurse Coney Island Hosp., Bklyn., 1982—. Office: Coney Island Hosp 2601 Ocean Pky Brooklyn NY 11235-7791

GIORDANO, JAMES JOSEPH, neuroscientist, educator; b. Staten Island, N.Y., Sept. 22, 1959; s. James and Gloria (Timpone) G.; m. Ginger Heathman. BS, St. Peter's Coll., Jersey City, 1981; MA, Norwich U., 1982; MPhil, CUNY, 1985, MS, PhD cum laude, 1986. Diplomate Am. Acad. Pain Mgmt. Rsch. asst. Einstein Med. Coll., Bronx, N.Y., 1983-86; rsch. fellow Johns Hopkins U., Balt., 1986-88; asst. prof. neurosci. Drake U., Des Moines, Iowa, 1988-92; dir. pain rsch. Iowa Meth. Hosp., Des Moines, 1990-92; commd. lt. USN, 1992; divsn. officer USN, Pensacola, Fla., 1992-93; dept. head aerospace physiology USN, Cherry Point, N.C., 1993-95; neurology prof. Lamar U., Tex., 1996—; coord. pain mgmt. S.E. Tex. Med. Ctr., 1996—; vis. prof. dept. neurology U. Tex. Med. Br., Galveston, 1996—. Textbook author; contbr. numerous articles to profl. jours. Recipient Presdl. Point of Light award Pres. George Bush, 1991. Fellow Am. Coll. Sports Medicine; mem. Acad. Sports Medicine, Soc. Neurosci., Soc. USN Flight Surgeons.

GIORDANO, LAURA ANN, quality management professional; b. Bronx, N.Y.; d. Joseph P. and Viola N. (Seymour) Morrissey; m. Joseph P. Giordano. BS in Nursing, Molloy Coll., Rockville Centre, N.Y., 1978; MBA, Adelphi U., Garden City, N.Y., 1985. RN, N.Y., Ariz.; cert. profl. in health care quality. Staff nurse Winthrop U. Hosp., Mineola, N.Y., 1978-79; staff nurse nursing supr. alcohol treatment ctr. Creedmoor Psychiat. Ctr., Queens, N.Y., 1979-80, asst. adminstr., cen. systems coord. acute admissions div., 1980-84, asst. dir. edn. and tng., 1984-85; community program rep. Office Community Behavioral Health Ariz. Dept. Health Svcs., Phoenix, 1985-87; clin. quality assurance coord. Ariz. State Hosp., Ariz. Dept. Health Svcs., Phoenix, 1987-90; dir. quality mgmt. svcs. div. behavioral health svcs. Ariz. Dept. Health Svcs., 1990-93; health outcomes project mgr., coop. projects specialist Health Svcs. Adv. Group Inc., Phoenix, 1994—. Mem. Am. Coll. Med. Quality, Ariz. Assn. for Healthcare Quality, Nat. Assn. for Healthcare Quality, Sigma Theta Tau, Delta Mu Delta.

GIORDANO, PATRICIA J., radiation therapist; b. Phila., Aug. 2, 1945; d. Anthony Michael and Louise (Testa) G. AS, Gwynedd-Mercy Coll., 1977, BS, 1981; MS, Beaver Coll., 1985. Staff radiographer Nazareth Hosp., Phila., 1965-66; from staff radiation therapist to asst. program dir., instr. Temple Univ. Hosp., Phila., 1967-84; from asst. program dir. to program dir., asst. prof. Gwynedd-Mercy Coll., Gwynedd Valley, Pa., 1986—; adv. bd. Franklin Learning Ctr., Phila., 1987-92. Mem. Am. Soc. Radiol. Techs. (edn. del. region 7, joint rev. com. on edn. in radiol. tech., site visitor team chair radiation therapy 1986—), European Soc. Therapeutic Radiologists and Oncologists. It was unclear where, in career section, "asst. dept. head, clin. supr." is to appear. Please resubmit this info. showing exact placement. Office: Gwynedd-Mercy Coll Sumneytown Pike Gwynedd Valley PA 19437

GIORDANO, SONDRA, nursing educator, medical and surgical nurse; m. Ralph Giordano; children: Lori, Daniel. BS, Adelphi U., 1965; MS, Russell Sage Coll., 1981. RN, N.Y. Head nurse Maimonides Hosp. Ctr., Bklyn.; clin. instr. Kings County Hosp. Sch. Nursing, Bklyn.; prof. Dutchess C.C., Poughkeepsie, N.Y. Mem. ANA, N.Y. State Assn. Two-Year Colls., Sigma Theta Tau. Home: 8 North Rd Tillson NY 12486-1000

GIOSCIA, NICOLAI, psychiatrist; b. Anzi, Basilicata, Italy, June 14, 1903; came to U.S., 1909; s. Rocco and Serafina (Belletiere) G. MD, Middlesex Coll. Medicine and Surgery, 1933. Intern Swedish Hosp., Bklyn., 1932-34; psychiat. intern St. Johns Hosp., Bklyn., 1935-36; psychiatric intern N.Y. State Mental Health, Harlem Valley, 1935-59; sr. psychiatrist Manhattan State Hosp., 1935-59; asst. dir. Creedmoor State Hosp., 1960-61, 62-63; dir. mental health svcs. Nassau County Mental Health Bd., N.Y., 1959-65; dir. psychiatric svcs. V.I., St. Croix, St. Croux, 1966-70; visiting cons. St. Lukes-Roosevelt Hosp., N.Y.C., 1975—. Maj. M.C., U.S. Army, 1942-47. Named Doctor of Yr., Nassau County, 1966. Fellow Am. Psychiatric Assn., Nassau County Med. Soc.; mem. Am. Med. Soc., Phi Sigma Delta, Alpha Sigma. Home: 4100 Galt Ocean Dr Fort Lauderdale FL 33308-6002 Office: 116 Central Park S New York NY 10019-1559

GIOVACCHINI, PETER LOUIS, psychoanalyst; b. N.Y.C., Apr. 12, 1922; s. Alex and Therese (Chicca) G.; m. Louise Post, Sept. 29, 1945; children: Philip, Sandra, Daniel. BS, U. Chgo., 1941, MD, 1944; postgrad., Columbia U., 1939; cert., Chgo. Inst. Psychoanalysis, 1954. Diplomate Am. Bd. Psychiatry and Neurology. Intern Fordham Hosp., N.Y.C., 1944-45; resident U. Chgo. Clinics, 1945-46, resident and research fellow, 1948-50; candidate Chgo. Inst. Psychoanalysis, 1949-54, clin. assoc., 1957—; clin. prof. U. Ill. Coll. Medicine, 1961-92, prof. emeritus, 1992—; chief cons. psychodynamic unit Barclay Hosp., Chgo., 1979-81; cons. Wilmette (Ill.) Family Svc. Ctr. and United Charities, Boyer-Marin Lodge, Marin County, Calif., 1986—, Mario Martin Inst. for Psychotherapy, 1989—, Psychoanalytic Ctr. Calif., L.A., 1990—; vis. prof. Smith Coll., Mass.; tng. and supervising analyst Chgo. Ctr. for Psychoanalytic Studies, 1994—. Author: (with L.B. Boyer) Psychoanalytic Treatment of Schizophrenia and Characterological Disorders, 1967, Psychoanalytic Treatment, 1971, also several books on character structure, primitive mental states, psychopathology and psychoanalytic technique, psychoanalysis; also articles.; Co-editor: Annals of Adolescent Psychiatry, 1972-80. Capt. M.C AUS, 1946-48. Fellow Am. Psychiat. Assn., Am. Orthopsychiat. Assn. (bd. dirs. 1979-83), Am. Coll. Psychoanalysts; mem. Am. Soc. Adolescent Psychiatry, Chgo. Soc. Adolescent Psychiatry (pres 1972-73), Internat. Psychoanalytic Soc. (chmn. standing com. on rsch. in psychosis 1994—). Am. Psychoanalytic Soc., Chgo. Psychoanalytic Soc. Home: 270 Locust Rd Winnetka IL 60093-3609 Office: 505 N Lake Shore Dr Chicago IL 60611-3427

GIPSON, GAYLE, medical, surgical nurse; b. Scottsbluff, Nebr., Apr. 1, 1950; d. Raymond C. and Darline (Rohrick) Hartley; m. Mike S. Gipson, Jan. 4, 1971; children: Shawn, Kacey. AS, Ky. Wesleyan Coll., 1982; BSN, Coll. of Misericordia, 1992. Staff nurse orthopedics unit St. Joseph Hosp., Providence; staff nurse med. unit Oliver C. Anderson Hosp., Maryville, Ill.; nurse mgr. med.- surg. orthopedics & pediatrics, hosp. nurse recruiter Tyler Meml. Hosp., Tunkhannock, Pa.; instr. trainer CPR. Mem. Am. Heart Assn., Northeastern Pa. Assn. Health Care Recruiters, Nightingale Soc., Sigma Theta Tau.

GIPSTEIN, MILTON FIVENSON, psychiatrist, lawyer; b. Schenectady, N.Y., Aug. 31, 1951; s. Milton and Evelyn (Mannes) G.; m. Carol Grace Zippin, July 21, 1974; children: Steven Mark, Richard Seth. BA, Columbia U., 1972; MD, SUNY, Syracuse, 1976; JD, U. N.C., 1981. Bar: Mass., 1982; diplomate Am. Bd. Psychiatry and Neurology. Resident psychiat. U. N.C., Chapel Hill, 1976-79; practice medicine specializing in psychiat. Dept. Corrections N.C., Raleigh, 1979-81; med. dir. Brockton (Mass.) Dist. Ct. Clinic, 1981-86, Bridgewater (Mass.) St. Hosp., 1985-87, Charter Hosp. of Aurora, Colo., 1988-91; med. dir. of forensic svcs. Columbine Psychiatric Hosp., Littleton, Colo., 1991-96; cons. med.-legal N.C. Legal Aid Soc., Raleigh, 1978-79, forensic Mass. Treatment Ctr. Sexually Dangerous, Bridgewater, 1981-88, psychiat. La. Gov.'s Task Force Mental Health, Baton Rouge, 1982; med.-legal cons. Med. Evaluators, Inc. Denver, 1991-96; legal counsel indigent clients mental health Com. Pub. Counsel Svcs., Boston, 1982-86; lectr. mental health legal advisors com. Law and Mental Health for Mass. Supreme Ct., Boston, 1986. Cons. Pub. Health Adv. Com. Town of Sharon, Mass., 1983-84, Mental Health Legal Advisors Com. Mass. Supreme Ct., Boston, 1985-86; v.p. community affairs Heights Elem. Sch. PTA, Sharon, 1983-84; adv. com. gifted and talented Cherry Creek H.S., 1992—, Campus Middle Sch., 1993—. Mem. ABA, Mass. Bar Assn., Am. Profl. Practice Assn. Office: 4660 S Yosemite St # 9062 Englewood CO 80111-1227

GIRARD, LOUIS JOSEPH, ophthalmologist; b. Spokane, Mar. 29, 1919; s. Harry and Agnes (Cain) G.; m. Bonita Crossnay, Mar. 31, 1945; children: Hilaire Michelle (Mrs. Cliff Richey), Bryan, Suzanne (Mrs. R. Thackston), Christina Ann (Mrs. E.J. Hudson, Jr.), Michael Sanford (dec.), Hugh Ashley, Gabrielle Inez; m. Loraine McMurrey, June 30, 1967; 1 son, Louis McMurrey; m. Louise Bell, June 14, 1975. BA, Rice U., 1941; MD, U. Tex., 1944; postgrad., NYU, Med. Sch., 1947-48. Diplomate: Am. Bd. Ophthalmology. Intern Jersey City Med. Ctr., 1944-45; assoc. to Dr. Conrad Berens, N.Y.C., 1947-49, 51-53; resident ophthalmology N.Y. Eye and Ear Infirmary, 1949-51; asst. surgeon, 1951-53, dir. chronic infection project, 1949-52, assoc. dir. dept. rsch., 1951-53; assoc. prof., assoc. chmn. dept. ophthalmology Baylor Coll. Medicine, Houston, 1953-57, prof., chmn. dept., 1957-70, clin. prof., 1971—; asst. attending St. Clare's Hosp., 1948-53, Willard Parker Hosp., 1949-53, N. Country Community Hosp., 1951-53, Nassau Hosp., 1951-53; cons. ophthalmologist Southside Hosp., 1951-53; attending ophthalmologist Jefferson Davis Hosp., 1953-59, VA Hosp., Houston, 1954-58, Tex. Children's Hosp., 1954—, St. Luke's Episcopal Hosp., 1954-61, Meth. Hosp., 1955—; cons. Montgomery County Hosp., 1955—, Tex. Children's Hosp., 1957—, VA Hosp., Houston, 1958—, St. Luke's Episcopal Hosp., 1961—, St. Joseph's Hosp., 1965—; sr. attending Ben Taub Gen. Hosp., 1959—, Meth. Hosp., 1959—; chief ophthalmology, co-chief surgery Ctr. Pavilion Hosp., 1970-76; coord. grad. course ophthalmology N.Y. U. Postgrad. Med. Sch., 1948-49, instr., 1951- 53; clin. asst. prof. U. Tex. Postgrad. Sch. Medicine, 1953-57, lectr., 1957—; assoc. mng. dir. Ophthal. Found., N.Y., 1951-55, cons., 1957; founder Tex. Med. Ctr.-Lions Eye Bank, 1953; cons. Meth. Hosp., St. Luke's Hosp.; founder, exec. dir. Inst. Ophthalmology, Tex. Med. Ctr., 1958—; mem. Am. Orthoptic Council, 1962-72; pres. Internat. Eye Film Library, 1967-71; mem. med. adv. bd. Internat. Eye Bank, 1965-70; Pres. IX Pan Am. Congress Ophthalmology, 1972. Author: Advanced Techniques in Ophthalmic Microsurgery, Vol. I: Ultrasound Fragmentation for Intraocular Surgery, 1979, Vol. II: Corneal Surgery, 1981; author, editor. over 7 books, 400 sci. pubs., 1200 sci. presentations; prodr. 70 films.; editor: Corneal Contact Lenses, 1964, 2d edit., 1971, Corneal Scleral Contact Lenses, 1957; mem. editorial bd. Ophthalmologia, 1965-72, Annals of Ophthalmology, 1968-74; cons. Highlights Ophthalmology, 1972. Recipient Alfred H. Bond award for rsch. in ophthalmology, 1950, Prof. Ignacio Barraquer Meml. award Inst. Barraquer, 1965, 2d prize Internat. Eye Film Festival, 1966, 1st prize, 1970, 1st prize, 1972, Golden Eagle award Internat. Film Festival Nantes, France, 1970, 71, Alumnus award Baylor U., 1984, First Disting. Alumnus award N.Y. Eye and Ear Infirmary, 1984, Disting. Alumnus award Rice U., 1985, Disting. Alumnus award U. Tex. Med. Br. at Galveston, 1991; named to Hall of Fame, Alcon Labs., 1990. Fellow ACS (bd. govs. 1966-72); mem. Am. Acad. Ophthalmology and Otolaryngology (2d pl. award sci. exhibits 1960, Honor award, Sr. Honor award), Pan Am. Assn. Ophthalmology (1st pl. award sci. exhibits 1960, 62, vis. prof. 1967, v.p. 1972), Assn. Research Ophthalmology, N.Y. Acad. Medicine, N.Y. Acad. Sci., Nassau, Houston ophthal. socs., French Soc. Ophthalmology, Houston Neurol. Soc., Jules Gonin Club, Tex. Opthal. Assn., Alumni Assn. N.Y. Eye and Ear Infirmary, Am. (certificate of merit sci. exhibit 1961), So. med. assns., Nat. Med. Found. Eye Care, Assn. Am. Physicians and Surgeons, Am. Assn. Ophthalmologists, Nat. Med. Found. Eye Care, Tex. Rehab. Assn., Harris County Med. Soc., Am. U. Profs. Ophthalmologists, Med. Research Found. Tex., Contact Lens Soc. Ophthalmologists (Exceptional Merit award 1968), Inst. Horacio Ferrer (corr.), Am. Eye Study Club (pres.). Home: 59 Tiel Way Houston TX 77019-1509

GIRARD, MARC PAUL, pharmaceutical consultant; b. Laval, Mayenne, France, Jan. 15, 1955; s. Joseph and Genevieve (Simion) G.; children: Genevieve, Olivier, Sebastien, Aude. Baccalaureat, Lycee, Laval, France, 1971; MS in Math., U. Orsay, France, 1976; MD, U. Paris, 1983. Researcher Lab. Etudes et Recherche Synthelabo, Paris, 1982-87; cons. Marc Girard Conseil, Paris, 1987—; cons. in drug monitoring and pharmacoepidemiology. Author: Grimm's Tales: A Psychoanalytical Reading, 1990, La Passion de Charles Bovary, 1995; contbr. articles to profl. jours. Fellow Royal Soc. Medicine; mem. Brit. Assn. Psychopharmacology, Assn. European Psychiatrists, Assn. Française de Psychiat. Biologique. Office: Marc Girard Conseil, 1 Blvd de la République, 78000 Versailles France

GIRDLEY, JAMES D., psychologist; b. Osceola, Ark., Apr. 3, 1931; s. Russell and Ada (Montgomery) G.; m. Delores Ann Grayson, June 6, 1953; 1 child, Steven James (dec.). MA, Harding U., 1974; MS, Ea. Ill. U., 1982; DMin, Luther Rice Secm., 1988; PhD, Emmanuel Bapt. U., 1991. Cert. pastoral counselor, reality therapist, hypnotherapist. Commd. 2d lt. USAF, 1959, advanced through grades to major, retired, 1979; job developer, cons. Correctional Employment Svc., Champaign, Ill., 1980-83; counselor Huntsville, Huntsville, Ala., 1984-86; minister of counseling Beltline Ch. of Christ, Decatur, Ala., 1987-89; dir., counselor Counseling and Enrichment Ctr., Athens, Ala., 1990—. Mem. Internat. Acad. Behavioral Medicine, Psychotherapy and Counseling (diplomate), ACA, Am. Assn. Christian Counselors, Nat. Guild of Hypnotists. Republican. Home: PO Box 386 Athens AL 35611-0386 Office: Athens Counseling & Enrichment Ctr 110 Thomas St Athens AL 35611

GIRITSKY, ALEXANDER SERGE, cardiothoracic surgeon; b. Shanghai, China, Aug. 27, 1948; s. Serge Nicholas and Tatiana Joachim (Kroupenin) G.; m. Susan Rae McCanna, May 6, 1984. AB in Biology, Stanford U., 1968; MD, Stanford Sch. Medicine, 1972. Diplomate Am. Bd. Surgery, Am. Bd. Thoracic Surgery. Fellow internal medicine Johns Hopkins Hosp., Balt., 1972-73; resident in cardiac surgery Stanford (Calif.) U. Hosp., 1973-74; rsch. fellow Stanford U., 1974-75; resident in thoracic, gen., and vascular surgery Stanford U. and affiliated hosps., Palo Alto, Calif., 1975-78; chief resident cardiac surgery Stanford U., Stanford, 1978-79, chief resident in gen. surgery, 1979-80; sr. staff cardiac surgery Scripps Meml. Hosp., La Jolla, Calif., 1980—; head dept. cardiothoracic surgery Scripps Meml. Hosp., La Jolla, 1987-91; mem. cardiology adv. bd. Scripps Instns. of Sci. and Medicine, La Jolla, 1991—. Contbr. articles to profl. jours. Bay Area Rsch. fellow Am. Heart Assn., Stanford, 1974-75. Fellow ACS, Am. Coll. Chest Physicians, Am. Coll. Cardiology; mem. Soc. of Thoracic Surgeons, Western Thoracic Surgery Assn. Office: LaJolla Cardiovasc and Thoracic Surgeons 9850 Genesee Ave Ste 560 La Jolla CA 92037

GIRLING, BETTIE JOYCE MOORE, home health executive; b. Midlothian, Tex., Feb. 10, 1930; d. Robert and Florence Irene (Shaw) Moore; BS in Edn., Daniel Baker Coll., 1952; MSSW, U. Tex., Austin, 1956; m. Robert George William Girling, III, Sept. 2, 1960; children: Robert George William IV, Maria Julia Anastasia, Samuel Marcus Shaw, Katherine Susan Jane. Tchr., Clairemont (Tex.) Ind. Sch. Dist., 1952-53; caseworker Tex. Dept. Public Welfare, 1953-57, licensing supr., Dallas, 1960; caseworker Austin State Sch. for Mentally Retarded, 1957-60; with adoption intake Edna Gladney Home, Ft. Worth, 1961-65; rschr. Child Welfare League Am., N.Y.C., 1966; organizer, exec. dir. Girling Home Care, Austin, 1967-69; asst. dir. agy. programs Girling Health Care, Inc., ex-v.p., COO multi-state, Tex., La., N.Y., Okla., Tenn., comprehensive health care agy., 1967—; owner, operator child care facility, 1973-75; mem. long range planning com. Grad. Sch. Social Work, Bd. U. Tex.-Austin Sch. Nursing; mem. home health services adv. council Tex. Dept. Health; organizer, coord. profl. workshops; mem. adv. bd. U. Tex. Sch. Social Work, Austin, 1996. Mem. NASW, Tex. Hosp. Assn., Tex. Home Health Agys., Nat. Assn. Home Health Agys., Women's Symphony League of Austin, Austin Symphony Orchestra Soc. (bd. dirs.), Austin Womens Club, Austin Country Club (co-chair Austin Lyric Austin Ball 1988, 89), Daniel Baker Ex-Students Assn. Tex. Recipient Ida Mae Hebert award Tex. Assn. for Home Care, 1994, Disting. Alumni award Daniel Baker Coll. Ex-Students Assn., 1988. Democrat. Baptist. Office: Girling Health Care Inc PO Box 4294 Austin TX 78765-4294

GIRLING, MARTIN T., podiatrist; b. Suffern, N.Y., Sept. 28, 1956; s. George W. and Catherine T. (Fay) G.; m. Sue Anna Conway, Aug. 9, 1986; children: Martin Conway, Max T. BA in Biology, SUNY, Potsdam, 1978; DPM, Ohio Coll. Podiatric Medicine, 1985. Diplomate Am. Bd. Podiatric Surgery. Pvt. practice Bretshire Med. Clinic, Houston, 1986-88, Foot and Ankle Ctr., Trenton, N.J., 1988-90, Foot Health Ctr., Plant City, Fla., 1990—, Wauchala (Fla.) Podiatric Ctr., 1995—; adj. clin. faculty Pa. Coll. Podiatric Medicine, Phila., 1988-93; instr. Berlington C.C., N.J., 1989-90. Committeeman Dem. Party, Dist. 9, 1976-81; mem., sec. Lions Club, Haverstraw, N.Y., 1978-81. Fellow Am. Coll. Foot and Ankle Surgeons; mem. Am. Diabetes Assn., Am. Podiatric Med. Assn. (Surg. award 1986), Fla. Podiatric Med. Assn., Hillsborough County Podiatric Med. Assn. (pres. 1990), Rotary Club. Roman Catholic. Office: Foot Health Ctr 1408 W Reynolds Plant City FL 33566 also: Wauchula Podiatry Ctr 406 S Sixth Ave Wauchula FL 33873

GIROD, FRANK PAUL, retired surgeon; b. Orenco, Oreg., Aug. 13, 1908; s. Leon and Anna (Gerig)úG.; m. Nadine Mae Cooper, Aug. 26, 1939; children: Judith Anne, Janet Carol, Franklin Paul, John Cooper. AB, Willamette U., Salem, Oreg., 1929; MD, U. Colo., 1938. Diplomate Am. Bd. Family Practice. Tchr. physics and chemistry, athletic coach Cortez High Sch., Colo., 1929-34; intern U. Colo., Denver, 1938-39; resident surgeon U.S. Marine Hosp., Balt., 1939-41; pvt. practice specializing in family practice and surgery Lebanon, Oreg., 1946-95; ret., 1995; bd. dirs. Lebanon Hosp., 1960—, pres. med. staff. Trustee, sec. Blue Shield Ops., Oreg., 1950-60; grand marshal Lebanon Strawberry Festival, 1988; mem. bd. Coun. of Govts. Sr. Svcs., 1991, 92. Maj. Army Med. Corp, 1942-45. Decorated Bronze Star; recipient Disting. Svc. First Citizen award Lebanon, Oreg., 1989; Frank P. Giron Med. Scholarship named in his honor. Mem. AMA, Oreg. Med. Assn. (trustee), Am. Acad. Family Practice, Kiwanis (pres. 1947-48). Republican. Methodist. Home: 625 E Rose St Lebanon OR 97355-4544

GIROLAMI, JAMES PAUL, podiatrist; b. Washington, Nov. 27, 1953; s. Andrew Joseph and Maria Regina (Caporaletti) G. BS, U. Md., 1975; D Podiatric Medicine, Ohio Coll. Podiatric Medicine, 1980. Diplomate Am. Bd. Podiatric Surgery. Resident in podiatric surgery Md. Podiatric Residency Program, Balt., 1980-82; pvt. practice, Washington, 1982—; dir. podiatric residency edn. program Parkwood Hosp., Clinton, Md., 1984-88; mem. teaching staff residency program Capitol Hill Hosp., Washington, 1989—, Washington Hosp. Ctr., 1991—; podiatrist, lectr. Dept. Health and Mental Hygiene, Balt., 1980-82. Clin. dir. City Mission Clinic, Cleve., 1978-79. Fellow Am. Coll. Foot Surgeons (sec./treas. region II 1993—); mem. Am. Podiatric Med. Assn., D.C. Podiatric Med. Assn. (v.p. 1990-93, pres. 1993-95), Am. Diabetes Assn., Pi Delta, Phi Sigma. Office: Ste 215 3230 Pennsylvania Ave SE Washington DC 20020-3722

GIROTTI, ROBERT BERNARD, medical and surgical nurse; b. New London, Conn., Dec. 10, 1962; s. Alfred E. and Patricia (Turello) G. BS, U. Conn., 1985, MS in Nursing, 1995. RN, Conn.; cert. med.-surg. nurse; cert. CPR. Staff nurse respiratory unit Lawrence Meml. Hosp., New London, 1985-90, staff nurse float pool, 1990—. Contbr. articles to nursing newsletters. Mem. Cath. Nurses Assn., Conn. Nurses Assn., U. Conn. Sch. Nursing Alumni Assn. (exec. bd. dirs. 1985—), U. Conn. Alumni Assn. (S.E. chpt. bd. dirs. 1994—), Lawrence Meml. Alumnae Assn., Sigma Theta Tau, Phi Kappa Phi. Home: 5 Charles Ave Quaker Hill CT 06375-1604

GIROUARD, JIMMY JOHN, III, medical products executive; b. Port Arthur, Tex., Jan. 5, 1947; s. David Mines and Mary Louise (Arceneaux) G.; children: Wendy Lynn Girouard, Cindi Chrystal Attaway, Jimmy John Girouard II. Degree Civil Engring., Lamar U., Tex., 1970. Ship fitter Burton Ship Bldg., Port Arthur, Tex., 1965-68; staff prodn./process Texaco Chemical Co., Port Neches, Tex., 1968-85; owner Colon Therapeutics, Groves, Tex., 1979—; mem. bd. cons./examining Colon Therapeutics Rsch. Inst., Groves, 1980—. Patentee in field. Mem. Internat. Assn. for Colon Therapy, Am. Holistic Med. Found. Republican. Roman Catholic. Home and Office: 2909 Main Ave Groves TX 77619

GIROUARD, SHIRLEY ANN, nurse, policy analyst; b. New London, Conn., Jan. 16, 1947; d. Maxime Albert Girouard and Irene Barbara (Arnold) Reid. BA in Sociology, Ea. Conn. State Coll., 1972; MA in Sociology, U. Conn., 1974; MSN, Yale U., 1977; PhD in Policy Analysis, Brandeis U., 1988. Nurse Woodstock (Conn.) Pub. Health Assn., 1968-70; staff nurse Clinton (Conn.) Convalescent Ctr., 1970-72; ins. edn. coord. Middlesex Meml. Hosp., Middletown, Conn., 1973-75; clin. nurse specialist Dartmouth Hitchcock Med. Ctr., Hanover, N.H., 1977-83; staff nurse Dartmouth Hitchcock Med. Ctr., Hanover, 1983-84; legis. cons., lobbyist N.H. Nurses Assn., Concord, 1985-87; program officer Robert Wood Johnson Found., Princeton, N.J., 1987-92; exec. dir. N.C. Ctr. Nursing,

1992-93, Am. Nurse's Assn., 1993-94; health policy and nursing cons. pvt. and pub. sector orgns., Washington, 1994-95; dir. child health planning & Evaluation Nat. Assn. Children's Hosps. and Related Instns., Alexandria, Va., 1995—; pvt. practice cons., 1983-87; profl. devel. cons., Lebanon, N.H., 1983-87; health policy and nursing cons. Author: (chpt.) Health Policy and Nurse Services, 1989; mem. editorial bd. Clin. Nurses Specialist Jour., 1986—; contbr. articles to profl. jours. State rep. N.H. Legislature, Concord, 1982-84; counselor City of Lebanon Coun., 1984-87. Fellow Am. Acad. Nursing; mem. ANA (project dir. 1986), N.C. State Nurses Assn., Sigma Theta Tau. Democrat. Office: Nat Assn Childrens Hosps & Related Instns 401 Wythe St Alexandria VA 22314

GIRVIN-QUIRK, SUSAN, nursing administrator; b. Owensboro, Ky., Dec. 9, 1950; d. William Fred and Anna (Tillotson) G.; m. Thomas Michael Quirk; 1 child, Thomas Matthew. BSN, U. Ky.; MS in Nursing, Ind. U. Adminstr. Am. Transitional Hosps., Indpls. Mem. ANA, Am. Assn. Neurosci. Nurses, Am. Mgmt. Assn., Sigma Theta Tau.

GISOLF, AART CORNELIS, physician; b. Haarlem, Netherlands, Sept. 10, 1937; arrived in Germany, 1986; s. Jacob H. and Elisabeth B. (Venema) G.; 1 child, Louise. MD, U. Amsterdam, 1965. Gen. practitioner Amsterdam, 1965-69; dir. audiovisual ctr. Erasmus U., Rotterdam, 1969-82; broadcaster NOS-TV, Hilversum, 1972-86; tech. corr. Algemeen Dagblad, Rotterdam, 1973—; produce med. program Sta. SDR-TV, Stuttgart, 1986—; prof. Film and TV Acad., Amsterdam, 1978-86. Mem. Dutch Med. Assn., Dutch Assn. Cinematographers (former pres., hon.), Internat. Sci. Film Assn. (former pres. 1984-90). Home: Zandpad 7, NL1054GA Amsterdam Netherlands also: Werder Str 17, D68165 Mannheim Germany Office: Studio Mannheim, Suddeutscher Rundfunk, D68165 Mannheim Germany

GITELMAN, DARREN ROSS, neurologist, educator; b. Bklyn.. BA, Washington U., St. Louis, 1981, MD, 1985. Med. lic. Ill., N.Y., Mass. Intern, resident Columbia Presbyn. Med. Ctr., N.Y.C., 1985-88; fellow brain imaging N.Y. State Psychiat. Inst., N.Y.C., 1988-89; resident neurology Mass. Gen. Hosp., Boston, 1989-92; fellow behavioral neurology Beth Israel Hosp., Boston, 1992-94; asst. prof. neurology and radiology Northwestern U., Chgo., 1994—. Fellow Am. Acad. Neurology; mem. AMA, ACP, Soc. Neurosci. Office: Northwestern Univ 320 E Superior St # 11-470 Chicago IL 60611

GITLER, BERNARD, cardiologist and critical care specialist; b. Munich, Fed. Republic Germany, Aug. 14, 1950; came to U.S., 1957; s. Abe and Lola (Greenberg) G.; m. Ellen Spielman, Aug. 4, 1974; children: Stefanie, Cynthia, Bryan. BS in Chemistry, MIT, 1972, BS in Life Scis., 1972; MD, Cornell U., 1976. Diplomate Am. Bd. Internal Medicine, Nat. Bd. Med. Examiners, Am. Bd. Internal Medicine-Cardiovascular Diseases. Am. Bd. Internal Medicine-Critical Care Medicine. Resident in internal medicine Bronx Mcpl. Hosp. Ctr., Albert Einstein Coll. Medicine, Bronx, N.Y., 1976-79; cardiology fellow Montefiore Med. Ctr., Albert Einstein Coll. Medicine, Bronx, 1979-81, chief fellow, 1980-81; clin. instr. Albert Einstein Coll. Medicine, 1981-84; asst. clin. prof. medicine AECOM, Bronx, 1984-92, assoc. clin. prof. medicine, 1992—; assoc. attending cardiologist Montefiore Med. Ctr., Bronx, 1993—; attending cardiologist New Rochelle Hosp. Med. Ctr., New Rochelle, N.Y., 1991—; pvt. practice cardiology New Rochelle, 1981—; asst. attending cardiologist Columbia-Presbyn. Med. Ctr., N.Y.C., 1992—; asst. prof. clin. medicine Columbia U., N.Y.C., 1992—; physician cons. Island Peer Rev. Orgn., N.Y., 1985-88; faculty senator Albert Einstein Coll. Medicine, 1987-89, co-dir. cardiology curriculum New Rochelle Hosp. Housestaff, 1985-92; attending cardiologist dept. electrocardiology Montefiore Med. Ctr., Bronx, 1983—. Referee Am. Heart Jour., 1983-95, Jour. Am. Coll. Cardiology, 1987-89, N.Y. State Jour. of Medicine, 1990-91; contbr. articles to profl. jours. Fellow ACP, Am. Coll. Cardiology, Am. Coll. Chest Physicians, Am. Heart Assn., N.Y. Cardioil. Soc.; mem. AMA, Am. Soc. Echocardiography, Soc. Critical Care Medicine, Am. Med. Athletic Assn., Am. Fedn. Clin. Rsch., Phi Beta Kappa, Phi Lambda Upsilon. Democrat. Jewish. Office: 150 Lockwood Ave New Rochelle NY 10801-4916

GITMAN, PAUL, internist; b. Bklyn., Dec. 30, 1940; s. Leo and Rose (Bluttal) G.; m. Gail Donna Yaeger, June 8, 1963; children: Robin Jane, Linda Beth, Michael David. BA, Columbia U., 1962; MD, Boston U., 1966. Diplomate Am. Bd. Internal Medicine. Intern Univ. Hosp., Boston, 1966-67, resident, 1967-68; resident L.I. Jewish Hosp., New Hyde Park, N.Y., 1968-70; staff physician L.I. Jewish Hosp., New Hyde Park, 1970-81, attending physician Med. Ctr., 1981—; faculty L.I. Jewish Med. Ctr., med. dir. quality and resource mgmt., drs. chmn. United Hosp. Fund for L.I. Jewish Hosp., 1980-85; asst. clin. prof. medicine SUNY, Stony Brook, 1972-89, asst. prof. medicine Albert Einstein Coll. Medicine, 1995—; bd. dirs. Advance Biofactors Corp., 1988—; co-chmn. N.Y. State Medicare Physician Adv. Com., 1992—; chmn. criteria norms stds. com. Island Peer Rev. Com.; mem. Physician Discipline Evaluation Panel. Maj. USAF, 1970-72. Fellow ACP (pres. Queens divsn. 1984-86, mem. liaison com. N.Y. state chpt. 1984-86, health and pub. policy com. N.Y. state chpt. 1991—, governing coun. 1993—), Am. Coll. of Med. Quality (cert., treas. N.Y. chpt. 1988-94, pres. N.Y. chpt.); mem. AMA, Am. Soc. Internal Medicine (mem. clin. lab. com., 1991-95), Med. Soc. State N.Y. (sec. governing coun. hosp. med. staff sect. 1990-92, vice chmn. 1992-96, chmn. 1996—), Staff Soc. L.I. Jewish Hosp. (pres. 1980-81), Queens Soc. Internal Medicine (pres. 1987-91), N.Y. State soc. Internal Medicine (bd. dirs. 1988—, sec. 1992-93, treas. 1993-94, pres. elect 1994-95, pres. 1995—). Jewish. Office: 167 Executive Dr New Hyde Park NY 11040-1052

GITTELMAN, MARTIN, clinical psychiatry educator; b. N.Y.C., Sept. 24, 1930; s. Philip and Frieda Gittelman; m. Lourdes Publico; children: Michelle, Maya Sofia. PhD in Clin. Psychology, Columbia U., 1966. Prof. clin. psychiatry N.Y. Med. Coll., Lincoln Health and Mental Health Ctr., Bronx, 1984—; cons. WHO, China, 1988, 90, 91, 92, 94, Philippines, 1988, 90, West Africa, 1991, Vietnam, 1990, Korea, 1995, med. com. human rights nat. sec., 1965; dir. Advanced Inst. Psychol. Rehab. Fgn. editor: Hosp. and Community Psychiatry; editor-in-chief: Internat. Jour. Mental Health. Fellow Acad. Medicine and Psychiatry; mem. APHA (mem. governing coun. 1982-84, 87-88, chair mental health sect. 1986), World Psychiat. Assn. (mem. edn. com.), World Assn. Psychosocial Rehab. (pres. 1991-93), Psy Sans Frontieres (pres. 1993—), Assn. Advancement Behavior Therapy (co-founder 1965), Am. Assn. Psychosocial Rehab. (pres. 1989-91), Internat. neuropsychol. Soc. (co-founder 1964). Office: NY Med Coll Dept Psychiatry 234 E 149th St Bronx NY 10451-5589

GITTES, RUBEN FOSTER, urological surgeon; b. Mallorca, Spain, Aug. 4, 1934; s. Archie and Cicely Mary (Foster) G.; m. K.S. Zipf, June 10, 1955; m. Rita R. Drum, Feb. 21, 1976; m. Vera Gomes, Feb. 9, 1996; children: Julia S., Frederick T., George K., Robert F. Grad., Phillips Acad., Andover, Mass., 1952; A.B., Harvard U., 1956, M.D., 1960. Intern, then resident in surgery and urology Mass. Gen. Hosp., Boston, 1960-67; asst. prof. UCLA Med. Sch., 1968-69; assoc. prof., then prof., chief urology U. Calif. at San Diego Med. Sch., 1969-75; prof. urol. surgery Harvard U. Med. Sch., chmn. Harvard program urology Longwood area, 1975-87; chmn. dept. surgery Scripps Clinic and Rsch. Found., La Jolla, Calif., 1987—; mem. study sects., task forces NIH, 1973—. Author, editor publs. in field. Served with USPHS, 1963-65. NIH grantee, 1969—. Mem. AAAS, Endocrine Soc., Soc. Univ. Surgeons, Soc. Univ. Urologists, Am. Assn. Genito-Urinary Surgeons, Clin. Soc. Genito-Urinary Surgeons, A.C.S., Am. Surg. Assn., Am. Urol. Assn., Am. Soc. Transplant Surgeons, Soc. Ancient Numismatics, Phi Beta Kappa, Alpha Omega Alpha. Office: Scripps Clinic & Rsch Found 10666 N Torrey Pines Rd La Jolla CA 92037-1027

GITTESS, RONALD MARVIN, dentist; b. Nyack, N.Y., Nov. 10, 1937; s. David and Mildred (Levin) G.; m. Carol May Block, Apr. 6, 1963; children: Robert Andrew, Leslie Ellen. B.S., Columbia, 1959, D.D.S., 1963; postgrad., U. Pa., 1964-66. Diplomate Am. Bd. Endodontics. Intern Mt. Sinai Hosp., Miami, Fla., 1963-64, attending dental surgeon, chief of endodontics, 1989—; pvt. practice dentistry specializing in endodontics Miami, 1966—; mem. staff Variety Children's Hosp., VA Hosp., Miami, Mt. Sinai Hosp.; cons. Dade County Dental Research Clinic; ann. guest lectr. dental div. Pan Am. Med. Conf., 1983—. Asst. coordinator dental div. United Fund Campaign, 1968. Recipient certificate of recognition Jarvie Honor Soc., 1961; USPHS fellow, 1962-63. Mem. ADA, Am. Assn. Endodontics, AAAS, Fedn. Dentaire Internationale, Fla., Miami, Miami Beach, South Dade, East Coast dental socs., So. Endodontic Study Group, Alpha Omega. Home and Office: 7400 N Kendall Dr Ste 312 Miami FL 33156-7721

GIUDICE, GIOVANNI (GIUSEPPE), biology educator; b. Palermo, Sicily, Italy, Sept. 24, 1933; s. Vito and Eleonora (La Bua) G.; m. Anna Maria Amore, June 27, 1961; children: Silvia, Elisa. MD, U. Palermo, 1956. Prof. biology U. Palermo, 1971—, dean faculty sci., 1973-76, dir. dept. cell and devel. biology, 1983-89, 93—; dir. Inst. Devel. Biology NRC, Palermo, 1980-94; pres. Istituto Gramsci Sicil, 1992—; vice rector Univ. Palermo, 1993—; mem. sci. coun. Istituto Superiore di Sanita, Rome, 1977-83; corp. mem Marine Biol. Lab., Woods Hole, Mass., 1966—; mem. Academia Nat. Lincei, Rome, 1988—. Author: Developmental Biology Sea Urchin, 1973, The Sea Urchin Embryo, 1985, others; contbr. articles to profl. jours. Senator, Italian Parliament, Rome, 1973-79, dep., 1979-83. With Italian Health Svc., 1959-60. Named Hon. Citizen, Tenn. Gov., 1963. Mem. European Molecular Biology Orgn., European Cell Biology Orgn. (bd. dirs., treas. 1968-83), Internat. Cell Rsch. Orgn. (bd. dirs. 1988—), Italian Soc. Reprodn. Devel. (pres. 1973-83), Italian Assn. Biol. Cellular Sviluppo (pres. 1986-90), Internat. Marine Ctrs. (pres. sci. bd. 1988—).

GIUFFRA, LAWRENCE JOHN, hospital administrator, medical educator; b. N.Y.C., Oct. 13, 1923; s. Lawrence A. and Eugenia (Rossi) G.; m. Yolanda Girulli, Apr. 12, 1947 (dec.); children: Lawrence, Marie, Barbara. MD, L.I. Coll. Medicine, 1946. Diplomate Am. Bd. Internal Medicine. Pathology fellow Mt. Sinai Hosp., 1950-51; chief med. svcs. U.S. Army Hosp., Ft. Monmouth, 1951-53; pvt. practice, 1953—; clin. instr. medicine L.I. Coll. Medicine and Dentistry, 1962—; chmn. dept. medicine St. Francis Hosp., Jersey City, 1988—. Contbr. articles to med. jours. Capt. U.S. Army, 1951-53. Fellow Am. Coll. Gastroenterology. Home: 175 Highfield Ln Nutley NJ 07110 Office: 2787 Kennedy Blvd Jersey City NJ 07306

GIULIANO, ROBERT PAUL, pharmacist; b. N.Y.C., Mar. 7, 1943; s. Salvatore Anthony and Marie Rita (LoScalzo) G.; BS in Pharmacy, Fordham U., 1965; MS in Hosp. Pharmacy Adminstrn., L.I. U., 1970; m. Maja Hreljanovic, July 2, 1966; children: Christopher Robert, Kenneth Paul. Clin. pharmacist Columbia-Presbyterian Med. Center, N.Y.C., 1965-70; dir. pharmacy dept. St. Barnabas Hosp., N.Y.C., 1970-71; dir. dept. pharm. scis. Misericordia Hosp. Med. Center, N.Y.C., 1971-78, adminstrv. dir. materiel mgmt., 1978-79, asst. adminstr. Misericordia Hosp. Med. Center, 1979-81; pres. Apotheke Assos. Ltd., N.Y.C., 1980-81; pres., dir., chief exec. officer U.S. Home Health Care Corp. and Steri-Pharm subs., 1981-91; chmn. bd. U.S. Health Care Corp. & Steri-Pharm. Subs., 1981-91; mem. Tech. Adv. Svc. for Attys., 1988—; pres. RPG Assoc., 1991—, pres. dir.; chmn. bd. Bryce Lab. Inc., 1995— con. Welieda Internat., 1991-92; affiliated clin. instr. St. John's U., 1971-81; cons. Healix Health Care, 1992—, Rye Beach Pharmacy, 1992—, Champlain Valley Physicians Hosp., 1993-94, Columbia Presbyn. Med. Ctr., 1984—, Transworld Home Health Corp., 1991-93, N.Y. Med. Coll., 1992-95, ROR Group, 1992-93, Geneva Gen. Regional Hosp., 1994-95; home health care cons. Alternative Care Svcs. Inc., 1988-90, Robert Wood Johnson Found., 1985; mem. clin. pharmacy adv. bd., 1971-81; mem. exec. com., Bronx Emergency Med. Services Council, 1975-80, chmn. tng. com., 1975-79, chmn. council, 1979-80; sr. emergency med. technician instr./coordinator N.Y. State Dept. Health, Bur. Emergency Med. Services, 1975-81; speaker's bur., CPR instr. Am. Heart Assn., 1975-81; CPR instr. Westchester Heart Assn., 1977-80; speaker's bur. Misericorida Hosp. Med. Center, Westchester County Soc. Hosp. Pharmacists. Asst. Cub Scout master, Eastchester, N.Y., 1976-78; coach youth baseball T.Y.A., Eastchester, 1975-83. Certified Am. Bd. Diplomates in Pharmacy, Nat. Registry Emergency Med. Technicians. Mem. Am. Pharm. Assn., Italian Pharm. Assn., Am. Soc. Cons. Pharmacists, Am. Soc. Hosp. Pharmacists, N.Y. State Council Hosp. Pharmacists, Nat. Assn. Sr. Emergency Med. Technician Instrs., Nat. Assn. Emergency Med. Technicians (founding), Am. Soc. Parenteral-Enteral Nutrition, League IV Therapists, Nat. IV Therapy Assn., Nat. Assn. of Retail Druggists, Mem. Pharmacy Compounding Ctr. Am. mem. Internat. Acad of Compounding Pharmacists, Fordham U. Pharmacy Alumni Assn. (dir. 1982—, 1st v.p. 1990-91, pres. 1992-95). Republican. Roman Catholic. Club: N.Y. Athletic. Author: (with others) RX Technician Manual, 1994; editor Misericorida Hosp. Pharmacy Newsletter, 1971-78. Home: 157 Oakland Ave Tuckahoe NY 10707-1403 Office: PO Box 1 Tuckahoe NY 10707-0001

GIVEN, KENNA SIDNEY, surgeon, educator; b. Charleston, W.Va., Nov. 22, 1938; s. Virgil and Chessie Given; m. Charlene K. Given; children: Kari, Patrick, Amy. BA, W.Va. U., 1960; MD, Duke U., 1964. Diplomate Am. Bd. Surgery, Am. Bd. Plastic Surgery (chairperson-elect 1996-97, bd. dirs. 1992—). Intern Ind. U. Med. Ctr., Indpls., 1964-65; resident, then chief resident gen. surgery Grady Meml. Hosp./Emory U. Hosp., Atlanta, 1965-69; asst. resident, then chief resident plastic surgery Duke U. Med. Ctr., Durham, N.C., 1975-77; clin. instr. surgery Emory U., Atlanta, 1972-74; chief surgery Lanier Meml. Hosp., Langdale, Ala., 1974; prof., chief divsn. plastic surgery Med. Coll. Ga., Augusta, 1977—, med. dir. oper. rm., 1989-90; assoc. dir. burn unit Med. Coll. Ga. Hosp.; cons. Augusta Correctional and Med. Instrn.; plastic surgery dir. Children's Med. Svc., 1981—; mem. Residency Rev. Commn. for Plastic Surgery, 1991—, chmn., 1994-96; chmn. residency rev. com. ACGME, 1994-96; lectr. in field. Contbr. articles to profl. jours. Pres. Med. Rsch. Found. Ga., 1985-88; trustee Plastic Surgery Edn. Found., 1994-97; bd. dirs. Augusta Country Day Sch.; bd. dirs. Augusta Prep. Day Sch., 1988, trustee, 1989-90. Fellow ACS; mem. AMA, Am. Assn. Plastic Surgeons (trustee 1994-97), Assn. Acad. Chmn. in Plastic Surgery (pres. 1996-97, bd. dirs. 1985-88, 93—), Southeastern Plastic and Reconstructive Surgery (chmn. CME com. 1987, bd. dirs. 1992-95), Am. Soc. Plastic and Reconstructive Surgery (bd. dirs. 1988), Am. Assn. Hand Surgery, Am. Cleft Palate Assn., Am. Soc. Aesthetic Plastic Surgeons, Internat. Soc. Clin. Plastic Surgeons, Ga. Plastic Surgery Soc. (pres. 1985), Med. Assn. Ga., Richmond County Med. Soc., Southea. Surg. Congress., So. Med. Assn. Baptist. Home: 748 Tripps Ct Augusta GA 30909-1816 Office: Med Coll Ga Divsn Plastic Surgery HB-5040 Augusta GA 30912

GIVHAN, EDGAR GILMORE, physician; b. Montevallo, Ala., Aug. 6, 1935; 7. AB in German Lit., Washington & Lee U., 1956; MD, Washington U., St. Louis, 1960. Diplomate Am. Bd. Internal Medicine. Intern Vanderbilt U., 1960, resident in internal medicine, 1965, instr. in hematology, 1965-66; instr. in hematology Auburn U. Sch. Lab. Tech., 1967-85; co-owner Commercial Garden Design, Montgomery, Ala., 1982—; pres. med. staff Montgomery Bapt. Hosp., 1974-75; cons. physician Ala. Medicaid Program, 1982-86; bd. dirs., cons. Humana Hosp. East Montgomery; med. dir. Humana Ins. Co. Ala.; horticulture lectr. Author: (guide and video) How to Grow Great Southern Gardens, 1992, Flowers for South Alabama Gardens, 1980, (with others) Heritage Gardens, 1992; contbr. articles to profl. jours. Chmn. bd. South Montgomery YMCA, 1973; bd. dirs. ARC, Montgomery, 1970-73, med. dir. blood processing ctr., Montgomery, 1973-80; bd. dirs. Montgomery Symphony Orch., Blue Cross and Blue Shield Ala., 1979-85, Montgomery C. of C., 1980-84; bd. vis. for the humanities Auburn U. Capt. USAF, 1962-64. Vanderbilt U. fellow, 1965-66. Fellow ACP; mem. AMA, Ala. Soc. Internal Medicine, Montgomery Soc. Internal Medicine (pres. 1970), Montgomery County Med. Soc. (pres. 1976), Ala. Soc. Clin. Oncology (v.p. 1982), Am. Soc. Hematology, So. Garden History Soc. (pres., bd. dirs.), Phi Beta Kappa. Office: 6912 Winton Blount Blvd Montgomery AL 36117

GIZZI, MARTIN SHERMAN, neurophysiologist; b. Yonkers, N.Y., Jan. 1, 1957; s. Vincent George and Laura (Cronkhite) G.; m. Norka Suarez, Sept. 17, 1988. PhD, NYU, 1983; MD, U. Miami, Fla., 1985. Diplomate Am. Bd. Psychiatry and Neurology. Med. intern New Rochelle (N.Y.) Hosp., 1985-86; resident in neurology Mt. Sinai Hosp., N.Y.C., 1986-89; asst. prof. neurology Mt. Sinai Sch. Medicine, N.Y.C., 1989-92; assoc. prof. neurosci. Seton Hall U. Sch. Grad. Med. Edn., 1992—. Recipient Physician Scientist award Nat. Eye Inst., 1989. Mem. Am. Acad. Neurology, Soc. Neurosci. Democrat. Office: JFK Med Ctr 65 James St PO Box 3059 Edison NJ 08818

GLADFELTER, JOHN HENRY, psychotherapist, educator; b. Tomahawk, Wis., Oct. 17, 1926; s. Elmer Sylvester and Dora (Marten) G.; m. Rose Ellen Wilhelm, Oct. 26, 1946. B.S., U. Houston, 1951, M.A., 1953, Ph.D., 1957. Lic. psychologist, Tex. Clin. assoc. prof. Southwest Med. Sch., Dallas, 1955-78; coordinator Fielding Inst., Dallas, 1974—; faculty mem. Southwest Law Enforcement Inst., Dallas, 1968-88. Contbg. author chpt. in book. Fellow Am. Group Psychotherapy Assn.; mem. Southwestern Group Psychotherapy Soc. (pres. 1965-66), Dallas Group Psychotherapy Soc. (pres. 1965-74), Am. Psychol. Assn., Internat. Transactional Analysis Assn., Tex. Assn. Magicians (pres. 1965-66). Avocations: magician; photograpy; computer programming. Office: 3300 West Mockingbird St #530 Dallas TX 75235

GLADFELTER, WILBERT EUGENE, physiology educator; b. York, Pa., Apr. 29, 1928; s. Paul John and Marea Bernadette (Miller) G.; m. Ruth Isabelle Ballantyne, Jan. 26, 1952; children: James W., Charles D., Mary A. AB magna cum laude, Gettysburg (Pa.) Coll., 1952; PhD, U. Pa., 1960. NSF fellow U. Pa., Phila., 1956-58, NIH fellow, 1958-59, asst. instr., 1954-56; instr. physiology W.Va. U., Morgantown, 1959-61, asst. prof., 1961-69, assoc. prof., 1969-96, prof. emeritus, 1996—. Contbr. articles to profl. jours. Treas., Monongalia County chpt. W. Va. Heart Assn., 1976-95. With USN, 1946-48. NSF fellow, 1956-58. Mem. Am. Physiol. Soc., Soc. Neurosci., Am. Soc. Zoologists, Sigma Xi, Phi Beta Kappa, Beta Beta Beta. Lutheran. Home: 70 Pine Tree Ln Morgantown WV 26505-9118 Office: WVa U Health Sci Ctr Dept Physiology Morgantown WV 26506

GLADNEY, JOHN DAVIDSON, surgeon; b. Homer, La., May 3, 1952; s. James Frank and Margaret Gray (Ford) G. BA in Religion/Philosophy (distinction), Southwestern U. at Memphis, 1974; MD, La. State U. Med. Ctr., Shreveport, 1979. Diplomate Am. Bd. Surgery with added qualifications in surg. critical care. Intern La. State U.-Shreveport Affiliated Hosps., 1979-80, resident in gen. surgery, 1980-84; fellow in thoracic surgery Baylor U. Hosp., Dallas, 1985-86; fellow in thoracic and cardiovascular surgery Meth. Hosp., Dallas, 1985-86; pvt. practice Shreveport, 1986—; past asst. prof. surgery La. State U., Shreveport, now asst. clin. prof. surgery; former staff gen. surgeon VA Med. Ctr., Shreveport; past cons. E.A. Conway Meml. Hosp., Monroe, La.; v.p. surg. staff Physicians and Surgeons Hosp., Shreveport; active staff Schumpert Med. Ctr., Shreveport, Bossier Med. Ctr., Bossier City, La., La. State U. Med. Ctr., Shreveport. Contbr. articles to profl. jours. Bd. trustees Rhodes Coll., Memphis, 1996—, amb. Charles E. Diehl Soc., 1996; founder Gladney Fund to Support Faculty Teaching of the Man in Light of Hisstory and Religion course at Rhodes Coll., 1994; founder Drs. James and Pat Gladney Fund to Support Practice of Medicine in rural La., 1994. Mem. ACS, Surg. Assn. La., Soc. Critical Care, La. Thoracic Soc., La. State U.-Shreveport Surg. Soc., Omicron Delta Kappa (chpt. pres. 1974-75). Presbyterian. Home: 850 Monrovia Shreveport LA 71106 Office: Drs Brown Eddleman Gladney & Goldman 1801 Fairfield # 306 Shreveport LA 71101

GLADSTONE, LEE, psychiatrist, addictionist; b. Chgo., May 22, 1914; s. Maurice and Sadie (Siegel) G.; m. Gertrude Hope Fremmel; children: Evan-Lorna. Student, U. Ill., 1936; BS, MD, Chgo. Med. Sch., 1940. Cert. by Am. Soc. Addictive Medicine, 1986. Intern Meml. Hosp., Harvey, Ill., 1940-42; resident psychiatry Northwestern Meml. Hosp., 1967-70; pvt. practice Chgo., 1946—; dir. McHenry Med. Group and Hosp., McHenry, Ill., 1947-67; dir. psychiat. day hosp. Northwestern Meml. Hosp., Chgo., 1971-72, dir. alcoholism treatment program Inst. of Psychiatry, 1975-80, med. dir. chem. dependence program Inst. Psychiatry, 1988-90; med. dir. Amethyst Group, Chgo., 1988—; assoc. Northwestern U. Chgo., 1972—, prof. emeritus, 1990—; dir. Foxfire Partial Hosp. Program, Summit, Ill., 1974—; dir. Martha Washington Hosp., Chgo., 1982-88. Contbr. articles to profl. jours. Med. adv. bd. Ill. Dept. Alcoholism and Substance Abuse, 1986—; mem. HEW's Nat. Adv. Coun. on Alcohol Abuse and Alcoholism, 1980-83; adv., bd. Alcoholism Treatment Licensure Program Ill. Dept. Mental Health, 197780; bd. dirs. Head Start, McHenry, Ill., 1966-67; founder, bd. dirs. McHenry Hosp., 1958-71. With U.S. Army, 1941-46. Recipient Francis J. Gerty award Ill. Dept. Mental Health, 1978; fellow Dingleton (Scotland) Hosp., 1970; Lee Gladstone Fellowship in Addiction Medicine named in his honor Northwestern Med. Sch., 1992. Mem. Am. Soc. Addictive Medicine (nat. com. nicotine cessation 1989—), Ill. Med. Soc. (impaired physicians com. 1982-85), Am. Acad. Clin. Psychiatrists, Am. Psychiat. Assn., Wilderness Soc., Sierra Club, Nature Conservancy. Office: The Amethyst Group 233 E Erie St Chicago IL 60611-2926

GLADUE, BRIAN ANTHONY, psychologist, researcher; b. Norwich, Conn., Nov. 30, 1950; s. William Raymond and Julia (Boako) G.; m. Lynn D. Jordan, Jan. 7, 1984; children: Garrett William, Samantha Lynn. BA, Northeastern U., 1973; PhD, Mich. State U., 1979; postdoctoral studies psychiatry, SUNY, Stony Brook, 1979-81. Research assoc. L.I. Research Inst. of SUNY, Stony Brook, N.Y., 1981-84; asst. prof. psychiatry SUNY, Stony Brook, 1982-84; asst. prof. N.D. State U., Fargo, 1984-89, assoc. prof., dir. human sexuality program, 1989—; chairperson instnl. rev. bd. N.D. State U., 1985-90; vis. lectr. Rutgers U., New Brunswick, N.J., 1983-84. Contbr. chpts. to book Human Sexuality, also over 40 articles to profl. jours. Grantee NSF, 1986, 89-91; recipient Nat. Research Service award Nat. Inst. Mental Health, 1979-81. Mem. Internat. Soc. for Human Ethology, N.Y. Acad. Scis., Internat. Acad. Sex Research, Endocrine Soc., Sigma Xi.

GLASAUER, FRANZ ERNST, neurosurgeon; b. Khoau, Czechoslovakia, Feb. 19, 1930; s. Rudolf and Marie (Eckert) G.; m. Elizabeth A. Garofalo. M.D. magna cum laude, U. Heidelberg, Germany, 1955. Diplomate Am. Bd. Neurosurgery. Intern St. Mark's Hosp., Salt Lake City, 1955-56; resident in surgery, neurosurgery New Eng. Med. Ctr., Boston, 1957-61; asst. in neurosurgery Tufts U. Sch. Medicine, Boston, 1960-61; asst. prof. neurosurgery SUNY, Buffalo, 1965-69; assoc. prof. SUNY, 1969-72, prof., 1972—, acting chmn. dept. neurosurgery, 1983-85; clin. dir. neurosurgery Erie County Med. Ctr., Buffalo, 1983; attending neurosurgeon Buffalo Gen. Hosp.; trustee Found. for Internat. Edn. in Neurol. Surgery Inc., 1981—, 1st vice chmn., 1991. Author: (with Louis Bakay) Head Injury, 1980; contbr. articles to med. jours. Served with USNR, 1961-63. Mem. ACS, Congress Neurol. Surgeons, Am. Assn. Neurol. Surgeons, Cervical Spine Rsch. Soc., Found. Internat. Edn. Neurol. Surgery, N.Y. State Neurosurg. Soc. (dir. 1971-73), Internat. Med. Soc. of Paraplegia. Office: 462 Grider St Buffalo NY 14215-3075

GLASBERG, H(ERBERT) MARK, psychiatrist; b. N.Y.C., Oct. 11, 1939; s. Joseph and Elsa (Haber) G.; m. Paula Drillman, June 19, 1960; children: Scot Bradley, Hilary Jennifer. BA, Yeshiva U., 1953; MS, Columbia U., 1954; MD, SUNY, 1958. Diplomate Nat. Bd. Med. Examiners, Am. Bd. Psychiatry and Neurology. Intern Maimonides Hosp. N.Y.C., 1958-59; resident in psychiatry Kings County Hosp., N.Y.C., 1959-60; resident in internal medicine Kingsbridge VA Hosp. of Columbia U. Coll. Med. Program, N.Y.C., 1960-61; resident Payne Whitney Psychiat. Clin., N.Y. Hosp., 1963-65, fellow, 1965-66; spl. rsch. fellow Nat. Inst. Mental Health, 1966-68, Cornell U. Med. Sch., N.Y. Hosp.; pvt. practice medicine specializing in psychiatry, N.Y.C., 1968—; attending physician dept. of psychiatry Columbia U. Coll. of Physicians & Surgeons; instr. Cornell U. Med. Sch., 1966-68; assoc. prof. psychiatry Mt. Sinai Sch. Medicine, 1968-80; dir. psychiat. outpatient svcs. Beth Israel Hosp., N.Y.C., 1968-74, assoc. attending physician, 1968-74, chief psychiat. emergency and cons. svcs., 1974-75; attending psychiatrist and clin. prof. psychiatry Coll. Physicians and Surgeons Columbia U. Coll. of Physicians and Surgeons, 1986—, neurosurgery, 1992, clin. assoc. prof. neurosurgery, 1990. Examiner Am. Bd. Psychiatry & Neurology, 1988—. Cons. mem. panel of ind. psychiatrists N.Y.C. Mental Health Info. Svc., 1968—. Mem. Manhattan physicians com. United Jewish Appeal, 1970—; mem. com. admission selection Cornell U. Med. Coll., Ctr. Alumni Assn. N.Y. Hosp. Lt. col., M.C., AUS, 1961-63. Fellow ACP, Am. Psychiat. Assn. (internat. platform com. 1980—); mem. N.Y. Acad. Scis., N.Y. Acad. Medicine, APA, AAAS, Am. Psychosomatic Soc., Soc. for Adolescent Psychiatry, Internat. Platform Assn. Office: 14 E 73rd St New York NY 10021-4128

GLASCO, WAYNE, chiropractor; b. Oklahoma City, July 26, 1965. AS, Oklahoma City C.C., 1986; BS, Logan Coll. Chiropractic, St. Louis, 1990; D of Chiropractic, Logan Coll. Chiropractic, 1991. Cet. chiropractic sports physician. Pvt. practice Oklahoma City, 1993-96. Office: Glasco Chiropractic Clinic 11639 S Western Oklahoma City OK 73170-5802

GLASER, GILBERT HERBERT, neuroscientist, physician, educator; b. N.Y.C., Nov. 10, 1920; s. Burnard Richard and Sidelle (Rogers) G.; m. Morfydd Mai Pugh, Mar. 17, 1946; children: Gareth Evan, Sara

Elizabeth. A.B., Columbia, 1940, M.D., 1943, Med. Sc.D., 1951; M.A. (hon.), Yale, 1963. Diplomate: Am. Bd. Psychiatry and Neurology. Intern Mt. Sinai Hosp., N.Y.C., 1943-44; resident neurology N.Y. Neurol. Inst., 1944-46; research asst. to assoc. neurology Columbia Coll. Physicians and Surgeons, 1948-52; research scientist N.Y. Psychiat. Inst., 1948-50; head. sect. neurology Sch. Medicine Yale U., 1952-71, chmn. dept. neurology Sch. Medicine, 1971-86, asst. prof. neurology Sch. Medicine, 1952-55, assoc. prof. Sch. Medicine, 1955-63, prof. neurology Sch. Medicine, 1963-91, prof. neurology emeritus, 1991—; Commonwealth Fund vis. prof. neurology U. London, Eng., 1965-66; cons. West Haven (Conn.) VA Hosp., 1955—; vis. prof. neurology Nat. Hosp., London, 1972, Park Hosp., Oxford, Eng., 1973-86, Hunan Med. Coll., Peoples Republic of China, 1986, U. Niigata, Kyoto, Japan, 1989; Fulbright Disting. prof. neurology Zagreb U., Yugoslavia, 1981; vis. scholar Green Coll. Oxford U., Eng., 1987-88; mem. neurology research adv. com. USPHS, 1956-60, 68-72, spl. cons., 1973, epilepsy adv. com., 1974-77, chmn. basic sci. subcom., 1977-80; mem. neurobiology rev. com. VA, 1975-78, chmn., 1977-78. Author: EEG and Behavior, 1963; Editor: Epilepsia, 1958-76; adv. editor, 1976-86; editor: Recent Advances in Clinical Neurology, 1978, 81, 84, Antiepileptic Drugs: Mechanisms of Action, 1980; mem. editorial bd.: Jour. Nervous and Mental Diseases; Contbr. articles to profl. jours. Capt. M.C. AUS, 1946-48. Recipient Janeway prize Columbia U., 1943, Bicentennial medal award, 1968, Book award Commonwealth Fund, 1975. Fellow Royal Soc. Medicine, ACP; mem. Am. Neurol. Assn. (1st v.p. 1977-78), Am. Acad. Neurology (pres. 1973-75), Am. Epilepsy Soc. (pres. 1963, Lennox lectr. 1985), Am. Electroencephalographic Soc. (council 1958-61, bd. qualifications), Eastern Assn. Electroencephalographers (pres. 1958), EEG Soc. (Gt. Britain), Assn. Brit. Neurologists, Soc. for Neurosci., Epilepsy Found. Am. (med. adv. bd.), Myasthenia Gravis Foundation (med. adv. bd. chmn. 1964-65), Multiple Sclerosis Soc. (chmn. research programs com. 1973-74, med. adv. bd.). Club: Athenaeum (London). Home: 205 Millbrook Rd North Haven CT 06473-4334 Office: Yale U Sch Medicine 333 Cedar St New Haven CT 06510-3206

GLASER, JOEL STEPHEN, ophthalmologist, educator; b. N.Y.C., Mar. 1, 1938; s. Benjamin and Roberta (Richman) G.; m. Irena Sterbinsky, Nov. 28, 1978; children: Larah, Benjamin, Jacob. AB, Duke U., 1959, MD, 1963. Diplomate Am. Bd. Ophthalmology. Prof. ophthalmology, neurology and neurosurgery U. Miami (Fla.) Sch. Medicine, 1970—; faculty mem. Mercy Neurosci. Inst., Miami, 1995—. Author: (textbook) Neuro-Ophthalmology, 1978, 90; contbr. numerous articles to profl. jours. Lt. comdr. USPHS, 1967-69. Recipient Franceschetti prize German Ophthalmol. Soc., 1991. Mem. Am. Acad. Ophthalmology (Sr. Honor award 1990), N.Am. Neuro-Ophthalmology Soc. (bd. dirs. 1975-90). Jewish. Home: 4121 Crawford Ave Coconut Grove FL 33133 Office: Mercy Neurosci Inst 3661 S Miami Ave Ste 209 Miami FL 33133

GLASER, KURT, psychiatrist; b. Vienna, Austria, Feb. 16, 1915; came to U.S., 1939; s. Richard and Hedwig (Gans-Schiller) G.; m. Susanne Stein, Jan. 1, 1923; children: Richard, Benjamin, David, Dan. Student, U. Vienna, 1933-38; MD, U. Lausanne, Switzerland, 1939; MS, U. Ill., Chgo., 1949. Emeritus assoc. prof. Sch. Medicine U. Md., Balt., 1988—; clin. dir. Rosewood Hosp. Ctr., Owings Mills, Md., 1961-72; asst. prof. pediatrics and psychiatry Med. Sch. Johns Hopkins U., Balt., 1972-81, emeritus asst. prof. pediatrics and psychiatry Med. Sch., 1981—; dir. adolescent svcs. Springfield Hosp. Ctr., Sykesville, Md., 1972-81; staff psychiatrist Sheppard Pratt Hosp., Towson, Md., 1981-85; hon. cons. pediatrics and psychiatry Sinai Hosp., Balt., 1959—; cons. J.F. Kennedy Inst., Balt., 1976-92, Harbel Cmty. Mental Health Clinic, Balt., 1986—; psychiat. cons. Social Security Adminstrn., Balt., 1985—; spkr. numerous presentations in profl. and lay orgns. Author: Learning Difficulties, 1974; contbr. 60 articles to profl. jours. Fellow Am. Acad. Pediatrics (emeritus), Am. Psychiat. Assn. (life), Am. Soc. for Adolescent Psychiatry (life), Md. Soc. for Adolescent Psychiatry (life, pres. 1972-73), Mountain Club Md., Sigma Xi. Home: 7200 3rd Ave # C-101 Sykesville MD 21784-5201

GLASER, PAUL RUSSEL, podiatric surgeon; b. Bklyn., June 23, 1945; s. Paul R. and Mary Margaret (Hopkins) G.; m. Carolyn Winnifred Kane, Aug. 10, 1968; children: Paul R. II, Alana Lee. BS, L.I. U., 1968; D in Podiatric Medicine, Ill. Coll. Podiatric Medicine, 1972. Diplomate Am. Bd. Podiatric Surgery, Am. Bd. Podiatric Orthops., Am. Nat. Bd. Podiatry Examiners. Resident in surgery Ohio Coll. Podiatric Medicine, Cleve., 1972-73, N.Y. Coll. Podiatric Medicine, N.Y.C., 1973-74; pvt. practice Huntington, N.Y., 1974—; cons. Diabetes Assn. L.I., Melville, N.Y., 1985—, N.Y. Athletic Club, N.Y.C., 1983—, N.Y. State Supreme Ct. Arbitration, Riverhead, 1983—; co-dir. dept. surgery L.I. SurgiCtr., 1988—; ofcl. Meadowlands Vitalis Invitational Track, 1985-91. Fellow Am. Coll. Foot Surgeons, Suffolk Acad. Medicine; mem. Am. Coll. Podopediatrics, Suffolk County Podiatric Med. Soc. (pres. 1985-87). Republican. Roman Catholic. Office: 3208 Oleander Dr Wilmington NC 28403-9999

GLASER, ROBERT JOY, physician, foundation executive; b. St. Louis, Sept. 11, 1918; s. Joseph and Regina G.; m. Helen Louise Hofsommer, Apr. 1, 1949; children: Sally Louise, Joseph II, Robert Joy. SB, Harvard U., 1940, MD magna cum laude, 1943; DS (hon.), U. Health Scis.-Chgo. Med. Sch., 1972, Temple U., 1973, U. N.H., 1979, U. Colo., 1979; LHD, Rush Med. Coll., 1973; DS, Mt. Sinai Med. Sch., 1984; DS (hon.), Washington U., 1988, Thomas Jefferson U., 1991. Med. intern Barnes Hosp., St. Louis, 1944, asst. resident physician, 1945-46, resident physician, 1946-47, asst. physician, 1949-57; asst. resident physician Peter Bent Brigham Hosp., Boston, 1944-45; NRC fellow med. scis. Wash. U. Med. Sch., 1947-49, instr. medicine, 1949-50, asst. prof., 1950-56, asst. dean., 1947, 53-55, assoc. prof., 1956-57, assoc. dean, 1955-57; dean, prof. medicine Med. Sch. U. Colo., 1957-63, v.p. for med. affairs, 1959-63; vis. physician Washington U. Med. Service, St. Louis City Hosp., 1950, chief service, 1950-53, cons., 1953-57; attending physician Colo. Gen. Hosp., Denver, 1957-63; prof. social medicine Harvard U., Boston, 1963-65; pres. Affiliated Hosps. Ctr., Inc., 1963-65; v.p. med. affairs, dean Sch. Medicine, prof. medicine Stanford U., 1965-70, acting pres., 1968, cons. prof., 1972—; bd. dirs. Henry J. Kaiser Family Found., 1970-83, pres., chief exec. officer, 1972-83; attending physician Columbia-Presbyn. Med. Ctr., N.Y.C., 1971-72, clin. prof. medicine, 1971-72; dir. for med. sci. Lucille P. Markey Charitable Trust, 1984—, trustee, 1989—; bd. dirs. Alza Corp., Hanger Orthopedic Group, Nellcor Inc., DCI, Pharmagenesis; cons. medicine VA Hosp., Denver, 1957-63, Fitzsimons Army Hosp., Aurora, Colo., 1957-63, Lowry AFB, Denver, 1957-63; mem. nat. adv. council NIMH, 1970-72, Harvard Fund Council, 1953-56, Harvard Med. Alumni Council, 1956-59; assoc. mem. streptococcal commn. Armed Forces Epidemiologic Bd., 1958-61; chmn. com. study nat. needs biomed. and behavioral research personnel Nat. Acad. Scis.-NRC, 1974-77; mem. vis. com. Med. Sch. Harvard U., 1968-74, Sch. Pub. Health, 1971-77; bd. visitors Charles Drew Postgrad. Med. Sch., 1972-79; mem. com. on med. affairs Yale U., 1969-82, adv. bd. Sch. Orgn. and Mgmt., 1976-84; vis. com. Tufts Med. Sch., 1974-84. Editor: Pharos, 1962—; contbr. articles to sci. jours. and chpts. to books. Bd. regents Georgetown U., 1976-78; bd. dirs. Kaiser Found. Hosps., Kaiser Found. Health Plan, 1967-79, Council on Founds., 1974-79, Packard Humanities Inst., 1987—; trustee Commonwealth Fund, 1969-88, v.p., 1970-72; trustee David and Lucille Packard Found., 1984-96, Pacific Sch. Religion, 1972-77, Washington U., St. Louis, 1979-87, 88—; mem. Sloan Commn. on Govt. in Higher Edn., 1977-79. Fellow AAAS, Am. Acad. Arts and Scis. (exec. bd., v.p. 1972-76); mem. Am. Clin. and Climatological Assn. (pres. 1982-83), Am. Fedn. Clin. Research (chmn. midwestern sect. 1954-55), Central Soc. Clin. Research (councillor 1955-58), Am. Soc. Clin. Investigation, Assn. Am. Med. Colls. (asst. sec. 1956-60, chmn. com. edn. and research 1958-63, mem. exec. council 1959-63, 76-79, v.p. 1963-64, chmn. exec. council and assembly 1968-69), Assn. Am. Physicians, Western Assn. Physicians (councillor 1960-63), Am. Soc. Exptl. Pathology, Nat. Inst. Allergy and Infectious Disease (tng. grant com. 1957-60), Inst. Medicine, Nat. Acad. Sci. (mem. exec. com. 1971-73, chmn. membership com. 1970-72, acting pres. 1970-71), Harvard Med. Sch. Alumni (pres. 1993-1994), Harvard Club (N.Y.C.), Century Club, Sigma Xi, Alpha Omega Alpha (bd. dirs. 1963-77). Office: 525 Middlefield Rd Ste 130 Menlo Park CA 94025-3447

GLASGOLD, ALVIN I., physician; b. N.Y., Apr. 28, 1936; s. Jeanne (Brown) Ovis; m. Joyce Padrusch; children: Mark, Ellen, Robert. MD, N.Y. Med. Coll., 1961. Diplomate Am. Bd. Facial Plastic and Reconstructive Surgery, Am. Bd. cosmetic Surgery, Am. Bd. Otolaryngology-Head and Neck Surgery. Intern Beth Israel Hosp., N.Y.C., 1961-62; resident Bronx Vet.'s Hosp. and Columbia U. Coll. Physicians and Surgeons, 1962-66; chmn. Dept. Otolaryngology-Head and Neck Surgery St. Peter's Med. Ctr., New Brunswick, N.J., Robert Wood Johnson Univ. Hosp., New Brunswick; attending physician Manhattan Eye, Ear and Throat Hosp., N.Y.C. assoc. clin. prof. surgery, chief divsn. otolaryngology Robert Wood Johnson Med. Sch., New Brunswick, N.J.; chmn. Facial Plastic sect. N.J. Acad. Ophthalmology and Otolaryngology, 1980-88; chmn. ann. facial plastic symposium N.J. Acad. Ophthalmology and Otolaryngology, 1983-88; co-chmn. external rhinoplasty course Manhattan Eye, Ear and Throat Hosp., AAFPRS, 1989, 90; instr. rhinoplasty Mt. Sinai Hosp., 1986-88; mem. bd. govs. Am. Acad. Ophthalmomogy and Otolaryngology, 1981-84. Author: (book) Application of Biomaterials in Facial Plastic Surgery, 1991. Fellow Am. Acad. Facial Plastic and Reconstructive Surgery, Am. Acad. Cosmetic Surgery (pres., bd. dirs. Facial Plastic Surgery Info. Svc., Inc., credentials com.), Am. Coll. Surgeons, Am. Acad. Otolaryngology-Head and Neck Surgery (instr. revision rhinoplasty-external approach 1990, bd. govs. 1981-84), Am. Soc. Head and Neck Surgery, Am. Soc. Liposuction Surgery. Home: 31 River Rd Highland Park NJ 08904-1731

GLASGOW, AGNES JACKIE, social welfare administrator, therapist; b. El Paso, Tex., July 23, 1941; d. Carl Lecota Pace and Henrietta Ford (Cozart) Robertson; m. Morgan Walton, Sept. 20, 1958 (div. 1979); children: Scotty Gene, Carley Earlene Walton DeVore; m. Phillip Sidney Glasgow, Aug. 9, 1986. Lic., Trinidad State Jr. Coll., Colo., 1968; AAS, Met. State Coll., Denver, 1979, BS, 1980; MPA, U. Colo., Denver, 1987. Cert. substance abuse counselor, Colo., Tenn. Pvt. practice Life Counseling Ctr., Denver, Memphis, 1980—; coord. masters program for substance abuse Met. State Coll., Denver, 1980-81; exec. dir. Concord Commons Counseling Ctr., Decatur, Ill., 1981-82; child care specialist Adams Community Mental Health Ctr., Commerce City, Colo., 1982-84; adolescent family counselor Parkside Lodge Colo., Thorhton, Colo., 1984-86; family therapist Charter Lakeside Hosp., Memphis, 1986-87; counselor, coord. Shelby State Community Coll., Memphis, 1987-88; supr. adolescent and young adult program Meth. Outreach, Memphis, 1988-90; sr. mental health specialist dual diagnosis unit Meth. Hosp. Cen., 1990—, relapse prevention specialist, 1994—; cons., part-time instr. Shelby State C.C., Memphis. Contbr. articles to profl. jours. Com. mem. Youth Suicide Task Force, Memphis, 1988—. Recipient Vol. of Yr. award United Way, Decatur, Ill., 1982, Cmty. Svc. award scholarship Mental Health Soc., 1983, Outstanding Svc. award, 1989, Disting. Svc. award Sheriff Dept., Memphis, 1988; nominated Diamond award Memphis Mental Health Assn., 1994. Mem. Nat. Orgn. Human Svc. Workers, Nat. Orgn. Substance Abuse Counselors, Surrender Al Anon (group rep.), Am. Assn. Counseling & Devel., Psi Chi (treas. 1979-80). Republican. Methodist. Office: 10 Thomas 1265 Union Ave Memphis TN 38104-3415 also: 1835 Union Ave Ste 203 Memphis TN 38104-3900

GLASKOWSKY, ELIZABETH POPE, nutritionist, dietitian; b. Sarginer, Ala., Jan. 13, 1924; d. Hubert Collins and Amanda Elizabeth (Alston) Pope; m. Nicholas Alexander Glaskowsky Jr., June 13, 1953; children: Peter Nicholas, Alexandra Elizabeth. BS with honors, U. Montevallo, 1945. Lic. dietitian, nutritionist, Fla.; registered dietitian. Dietetic internship Brooke Army Med. Ctr., San Antonio, 1945-46; 2d lt., 1st lt., hosp. dietitian Oliver Gen. Hosp., Augusta, Ga., 1946-49; asst. prof. home econs. U. Montevallo, Ala., 1949-51; 1st lt., capt. U.S. Army, 1951-54; chief dietitian Camp Breckenridge, Ky., 1951-52; instr. dept. adminstrn. Med. Field Svc. Sch., Fort Sam Houston, Tex., 1952; chief ward food svc., nutrition instr. Letterman Army Hosp., San Francisco, 1952-54; asst. dir. Stern Dining Hall, dir. Encina Hall Stanford (Calif.) U., 1954-55, 55-57; head dietitian Masonic Hosp.-U. Minn., Mpls., 1958-59; consulting nutritionist, dietitian Dade County (Fla.) Pub. Health Dept., 1978-87, 87—. Mem., 2d officer Old Cutler Women's Rep. Club, Dade County, 1980—; del. Rep. Sate Conv., 1990-91, 95; mus. guide Vizcaya Mus., Date County, 1981—. Mem. Am. Dietetic Assn., Fla. Dietetic Assn., Miami Dietetic Assn. Republican. Episcopalian. Home: 13421 SW 69th Ct Miami FL 33156-6943

GLASS, BURTON JOEL, physician, general surgeon; b. N.Y.C., Aug. 26, 1945; s. Charles and Lucille (Krisberg) G. BA, NYU, 1967; MD, U. Md., Balt., 1971. Diplomate Nat. Bd. Med. Examiners. Intern pediatrics Nassau County Med. Ctr., 1971-72, resident in pediatrics, 1972-73, resident in gen. surgery, 1973-77; physician, gen. surgeon Burton J. Glass MD, P.C., Rockville Centre, N.Y., 1979—; cons. Island Peer Review Orgn., Lake Success, N.Y., 1990-94. Fellow ACS, Nassau Acad. Medicine; mem. Nassau County Med. Soc. (bd. censors 1991—, chmn. membership ins. com. 1995—, chmn. hosp. liaison com. 1996—, mem. exec. com. 1996—, mem. comms. and media com. 1996—), N.Y. State Med. Soc., Nassau Surg. Soc. Office: Burton J Glass MD PC 24 Maple Ave Rockville Centre NY 11570-4259

GLASS, CHRISTOPHER KEVIN, physician; b. Oakland, Calif., Aug. 13, 1955; s. William Charles and Arden Barbara (Raysor) G.; m. Renee Fitzmorris; children: Erin Rose, Bryan James, Megan Christine, Sean William. BA Biophysics, U. Calif., Berkeley, 1977; MD, U. Calif. San Diego, 1984, PhD Biology, 1984. Intern dept. medicine Brigham & Women's Hosp., Boston, 1984-85, resident dept. medicine, 1985-86; fellow div. endocrinology U. Calif. San Diego, La Jolla, 1986-89, asst. prof. medicine, 1989-95, assoc. prof. medicine, 1995—; cons. Parke-Davis, Ann Arbor, Mich., 1994-95, Ligand Pharms., San Diego, 1994-95. Contbr. articles to profl. jours. Recipient Wilson S. Stone award M.D. Anderson, Houston, 1989, Lucille P. Markey scholarship, Lucille P. Markey Trust, Miami, 1987. Fellow Am. Heart Assn. (Established Investigator award 1995); mem. Endocrine Soc., FASEB. Office: U Calif San Diego 9500 Gilman Dr La Jolla CA 92093-0651*

GLASS, DAVID CARTER, psychology educator; b. N.Y.C., Sept. 17, 1930; s. Samuel and Dorothy (Braunstein) G.; m. Kathleen Kehoe, May 15, 1982. AB, NYU, 1952, MA, 1954, PhD, 1959, postdoctoral fellow, 1959-62. Mem. staff social psychologist Russell Sage Found., N.Y.C., 1963-71; assoc. prof. psychology Rockefeller U., N.Y.C., 1966-68; prof. psychology N.Y.U., N.Y.C., 1968-72; chmn., prof. dept. psychology U. Tex., Austin, 1972-75; vis. scholar Russell Sage Found., 1975-76; prof. psychology, dir. Lab. Biobehavior, CUNY Grad. Ctr., N.Y.C., 1976-82; prof. psychology and psychiatry SUNY, Stony Brook, 1982-94, vice provost for research and grad. studies, 1982-86, spl. advisor to provost, 1987-89, vice provost for rsch., 1990-93, prof. emeritus psychology, 1994—; vis. prof. psychology Inst. Health, Rutgers U., New Brunswick, N.J., 1994-96; cons. in field. Author: Behavior Patterns, Stress and Coronary Disease, 1977; co-author: (with J.E. Singer) Urban Stress: Experiments in Noise and Social Stressors, 1972 (AAAS prize 1971); contbr. articles to profl. jours. Fellow Am. Psychol. Assn., AAAS; mem. Am. Psychosomatic Soc., Soc. Psychophysiol. Research, Soc. Exptl. Social Psychology, Acad. Behavioral Medicine Research (pres. 1981-82), Sigma Xi, Phi Kappa Phi. Home: 330 E 33rd St Apt 11J New York NY 10016-9437 Office: Rutgers U Inst Health 30 College Ave New Brunswick NJ 08901-1245

GLASS, DONALD DAVID, anesthesiologist; b. Johnston, Pa., May 1, 1942; s. Donald S. and Meriel L. Glass; m. Bonnell W. Glass, Sept. 5, 1965 (div. Nov. 1992); children: David J., Jennifer J. Student, U. Pitts., 1960-62; MD, W.Va. U., 1966. Diplomate Am. Bd. Anesthesiology (chmn. CCM examination com. 1988—, asst. sec.-treas. 1991-94, chair com. on Americans and Disabilities Act 1991, chair credentials com. 1992, sec.-treas. 1994-96, pres. 1996-97); cert. spl. qualifications in critical care medicine, cert. continued demonstration of qualifications; lic. anethesiologist Miss., N.H. Rsch. assoc. dept. surgery W.Va. U., 1965-66; intern in surgery U. Pitts., 1966-67, resident in surgery, 1969-70; asst. resident in anesthesia Mass. Gen. Hosp., Boston, 1970-71, chief resident in anesthesiology, 1971-72; clin. fellow Harvard U., 1972; dir. edn. dept. anesthesiology, dir. cardiovascu. anesthesia U. Miss. Med. Ctr., Jackson, 1972-77, asst. dir. inhalation therapy, 1972-77, asst. prof. anesthesia, 1972-76, med. dir. ICU, 1975-77, assoc. prof. anesthesiology and surgery, 1976-77; assoc. prof. surgery and medicine Med. Sch., Dartmouth Coll., Hanover, N.H., 1977-84, prof. surgery and medicine, 1984-88, prof. anesthesiology and medicine, 1988—; med. dir. adult unit ICU Dartmouth-Hitchcock Med. Ctr., Hanover, 1977-87, chief sect. anesthesiology, 1983-89, chmn. dept. anesthesiology, 1989; mem. house staff com. U. Miss. Med. Sch., 1972-77, senator faculty senate, 1975-77, chmn. ad hoc com. on blood utilization, 1975-77; chmn. intensive care com. Dartmouth-Hitchcock Med. Ctr., 1977—, vice-chmn. med. mgmt. adv. com., 1980—, staff bd. govs., 1986—, various search coms.; mem. surgery, anesthesia and trauma study sect. NIH, 1980; del. Am. Bd. Med. Specialists, 1988, mem. nominating com., 1991; assoc. examiner Am. Coll. Anesthesiology, 1976-85, examiner, 1975; guest lectr. McGill U., Montreal, 1983, U. Calif.-San Diego, 1985, Profl. Seminars, Vail, Colo., 1986, Fla. Soc. Univ. Anesthesiologists, Gainesville, Fla., 1987, C-V Anesthesiologists, Montreal, 1986, New Eng. Soc. Anesthesiologists, Basin Harbor, Vt., 1987, many others; vis. prof. Mass. Gen. Hosp., Boston, 1980, 87, U. Pitts. Health Ctr. Hosps., 1980, Willford Hall Hosp., San Antonio, 1981, SUNY Downstate Anesthesiology, 1982, Mayo Clinic Sch. Medicine, 1982, U. Pa., Phila., 1983, U. Miami, Fla., 1983, 93, Cornell U. Med. Ctr., 1984, 93, C.H.U. Pitie-Salpetriere, Paris, 1985, 86, 89, 90, 92, McGill U., Montreal, 1986, Mt. Sinai Med. Ctr., N.Y.C., 1986, Wake Forest U., Winston-Salem, N.C., 1987, Duke U., Durham, N.C., 1988, Tulane Med. Ctr. Sch. Medicine, New Orleans, 1989, Washington U., St. Louis, 1993, Maimonides Med. Ctr., N.Y.C., 1994, and numerous others; disting. vis. prof. U. Wis., 1978; Ellis Gillespie lectr. ann sci. meeting Royal Australasian Coll. Surgeons and Faculty Anesthesiologists, Wellington, New Zealand, 1990; William P. Hust Meml. lectr. Ga. Bapt. Med. Ctr.-U. Ga., Atlanta, 1991; invited lectr. State of Russia Soc. of Anesthesiologists, 1992; presenter in field. Co-editor: (with M.P. Yeager) Anesthetic Management of the Vascular Surgical Patient, 1990; contbr. chpts. to books including Rhoads Textbook of Surgery, 1976, Intensive Care Therapeutics, 1980, Cardiac Anesthesia, 1987, Anesthesia in Vascular Surgery, 1989; contbr. numerous articles to med. jours. Lt. USNR MC, 1967-69. Recipient Lange Med. Publs. award, 1966. Fellow Am. Coll. Anesthesiology, Am. Coll. Chest Physicians, Faculty of Anesthesiologists of Royal Australian Coll. Surgeons; mem. Am. Soc. Anesthesiologists (U. Miss. preceptorship com. liaison 1974, coord. ICU workshop 1976, chmn. com. on sci. papers 1986, vice chmn. ann. meeting 1987, chmn. ann. meeting 1988, chair ABA-ASA joint select com. on recertification 1988), Internat. Anesthesia Rsch. Soc., Soc. Critical Care Medicine, Assn. Cardiac Anesthesiologists (elected), Assn. Univ. Anesthesiologists, Assn. Critical Care Anesthesiologists, N.H./Vt. Soc. Anesthsiologist. Acad. Anesthesia Chairmen, Alpha Omega Alpha. Home: RR 1 Box 142 Lyme NH 03768 Office: Dartmouth Hitchcock Med Ctr Dept Anesthesiology Medical Center Dr Lebanon NH 03756*

GLASS, DOROTHEA DANIELS, physiatrist, educator; b. N.Y.C.; d. Maurice B. and Anna S. (Kleegman) Daniels; m. Robert E. Glass, June 23, 1940; children: Anne Glass Roth, Deborah, Catherine Glass Barrett, Eugene. BA, Cornell U., 1940; MD, Woman's Med. Coll. Pa., 1954; postgrad., U. Pa., 1960-61; DMS (hon.), Med. Coll. Pa., 1987. Diplomate: Am. Bd. Phys. Medicine and Rehab. (guest bd. examiner 1978, 89). Intern Albert Einstein Med. Center, Phila., 1954-55, clin. asst. dept. medicine, 1956-59, attending phys. medicine and rehab., 1968-70, chmn. dept. phys. medicine and rehab., sr. attending, 1971-85; chief rehab. medicine VA Med. Ctr., Miami, Fla., 1985-95; clin. prof. dept. orthopaedics and rehab. U. Miami Sch. Medicine, 1985—; Lois Mattox Miller fellow preventive medicine Woman's Med. Coll. Pa., 1955-56, instr. preventive medicine, 1956-59, instr. medicine, 1960-62; resident phys. medicine and rehab. VA Hosp., Phila., 1959-62, chief phys. medicine and rehab., 1966-68, cons., 1968-82; asst. clin. dir. Jefferson Med. Coll. Hosp., Phila., 1963-66, Camden County Stroke Program, Cooper Hosp., Camden, N.J., 1963-66; gen. practice medicine, Phila., 1956-59; asst. med. dir., chief rehab. medicine and rehab. Moss Rehab. Hosp., Phila., 1968-70, med. dir., 1971-82, sr. cons., 1982—; mem. active staff Temple U., Phila., 1968—, asso. prof. rehab. medicine, 1968-73, prof., 1973—, dir. residency tng. rehab. medicine, 1968-82; program dir. Rehab. Research and Tng. Center, 1977-80, chmn. dept. rehab. medicine, 1977-82; staff physician Hosp. Med. Coll. Pa., Phila., 1955-59, vis. assoc. prof. neurology, 1973-79, clin. prof., 1977-82, vis. prof., 1982-96; mem. cons. staff Frankford Hosp., Phila., 1968-82, Phila. Geriatric Center, 1975-82; mem. active staff Willowcrest-Bamberger Hosp., Phila., 1980-82; asso. phys. medicine and rehab. U. Pa. Sch. Medicine, Phila., 1962-66; asst. prof. clin. phys. medicine and rehab., 1966-68; asst. clin. dir. dept. phys. medicine and rehab. Jefferson Med. Coll., Phila., 1963-66. Contbr. articles to profl. jours. Mem. profl. adv. com. Easter Seal Soc. Crippled Children and Adults Pa., 1975-82; active Goodwill Industries Phila., 1973-82, Cmty. Home Health Svcs. Phila., 1974-82, Ea. Pa. chpt. Arthritis Found., 1968-82. Recipient humanitarian svc. cert. Gov.'s Com. on Employment Handicapped, 1974, Outstanding Alumnae award Commonwealth of Pa. Bd., Hosp. Med. Coll. Pa., 1975, humanitarian award Pa. Easter Seal Soc., 1981, John Eiselie Davis award Am. Kinesiotherapy Assn., 1988, Carl Haven Young svc. award, 1994. Mem. AMA, Am. Acad. Med. Dirs., Am. Acad. Phys. Medicine and Rehab. (disting. clinician award 1995), Am. Assn. Electromyography and Electrodiagnosis (assoc.), Am. Assn. Sex Educators, Counselors and Therapists, Am. Burn Assn., Am. Coll. Antiology, Am. Coll. Utilization Rev., Am. Congress Rehab. Medicine (bd. govs., pres. 1986-87, gold Key award 1989), Am. Heart Assn. (coun. on cerebrovascular disease), Am. Lung Assn. Phila. and Montgomery County (bd. dirs. 1977-79), Am. Med. Women's Assn., Assn. Acad. Physicatrists, Assn. Med. Rehab. Dirs. and Coordinators, Coll. Physicians Phila., Emergency Care Rsch. Inst., Gerongol. Soc., Internat. Assn. Rehab. Facilities, Internat. Rehab. Medicine Assn., Pan Am. Med. Assn., Fla. Med. Assn., Fla. Soc. Phys. Medicine and Rehab. (pres. 1975-77), Pa. Med. Soc. (phys. medicine and rehab. adv. com. 1975-82), Pa. Thoracic Soc., Martin County Med. Soc., Delaware Valley Hosp. Coun. Forum, Phila. Med. Soc., Phila. PSRO (bd. dirs. 1975-82), Phila. Soc. Phys. Medicine and Rehab. (pres. 1968-69), Laennec Soc. Phila., Martin County Med. Assn., Royal Soc. Health, Alpha Omega Alpha.

GLASS, JOEL BENNETT, psychiatrist; b. Phila., Dec. 23, 1942; m. Ellen Bloom, 1980; children: Alexandra, Claire. BS, Muhlenberg U., 1964; MD, U. Pa., 1968. Intern Michael Reese Hosp., Chgo., 1968-69; resident in psychiatry U. Pa., Phila., 1969-72; pvt. practice psychiatry, 1972—; assoc. in psychiatry West Jersey Health Sys., 1995—; clin. assoc. profl. psychiatry U. Medicine and Dentistry of N.J., 1982—; asst. clin. prof. psychiatry U. Pa., Phila., 1975-81, assoc. in psychiatry, 1982-85; mem. exec. com. Cooper Hosp./U. Med. Ctr., Camden, 1985-90; psychiat. cons. Family Counseling Svcs., Camden, A Welcome Change, Westmont, N.J., Genesis Counseling Ctr., Collingswood, N.J.; pastor counselor, Cherry Hill, N.J. Author several papers. Mem. AMA, Am. Psychiat. Assn., Am. Coll. Forensic Psychiatry, Am. Assn. for Geriatric Psychiatry, am. Soc. for Adolescent Psychiatry, Am. Family Therapy Assn., Am. Inst. Wine and Food, Assn. for Study of Headache, N.J. Psychiat. Assn., Camden County Med. Soc., Lombard Swim Club (exec. com. 1987—), Omicron Delta Kappa. Office: Greentree Commons Ste 8004-E Rt 73 and Greentree Rd Marlton NJ 08053

GLASS, KATHLEEN ZILLNER, nurse; b. Lackawanna, N.Y., June 26, 1957; d. Frederick Max and Margaret Agnes (Herr) Z.; m. James T. Glass, June 25, 1994. Nursing Diploma, Sister's Hosp. Sch., Buffalo, N.Y., 1978; postgrad., Daemen Coll., 1983-85, Buffalo State Coll., 1988-89. RN, N.Y.; cert. PRI screener; cert. ACLS. Staff nurse in neurology Millard Fillmore Hosp., Buffalo, 1978-81; case mgr. Rehab. Coordinators, Inc., Phila., 1981-82; nursing supr. Hamlin Terrace Health Care, Buffalo, N.Y., 1981-83; admission, discharge coord. 24 R.I. St., Inc., Buffalo, 1984-85; instr. Stratford Sch., Buffalo, 1985-86; nursing supr. Ridgeview Manor Home, Buffalo, 1986-87, St. Francis Home, Williamsville, N.Y., 1988-89, Sheehan Meml. Hosp., Buffalo, 1989-95; emergency room nurse Tri-County Meml. Hosp., Gowanda, N.Y., 1995—. Mem. Rep. Com., Evans, 1995-96. Regents scholar N.Y. Edn. Dept., 1975-78. Mem. N.Y. State Nurses Assn., Neurosurg. Nurses Assn. Roman Catholic. Office: Tri-County Meml Hosp 100 Memorial Dr Gowanda NY 14070

GLASS, NEAL R., surgeon; b. N.Y.C., May 18, 1946; s. Harry and Bernice Glass; children: Darren, Laura, Janine; m. Laveda K. Kirkpatrick; stepchildren: James Goen, Julie Goen, Tammy Robinson. BA in Exptl. Psychology, NYU, 1968; MD, SUNY, Bklyn., 1972. Diplomate Nat. Bd. Med. Examiners, Am. Bd. Surgery. Physician SUNY Downstate Med. Ctr., Bklyn., 1973-78, U. Wis. Hosp., Madison, 1978-85, Lubbock (Tex.) Gen. Hosp., 1985-89; co-dir. abdominal organ transplantation St. Louis U. Med. Ctr., 1989-90; prof. surgery, dir. organ transplantation Our Lady of Lourdes Med. Ctr., Camden, N.J., 1990-92; gen. surgen and physician Pike Cmty. Hosp., Waverly, Ohio, 1992—. Contbr. over 60 articles to profl. jours. Mem. Pike County Bd. of Health, Rotary. Office: Neal R Glass MD Inc 100 Dawn Ln Ste 2 Waverly OH 45690

GLASS, PAUL JASON, ophthalmologist; b. Bridgeport, Conn., Sept. 5, 1953; s. William Isaac and Miriam (Kenigsberg) G. BA, Harvard U., 1975; MD, Cornell U., 1979. Diplomate Am. Bd. Ophthalmology. Med. resident

Northwestern U. Hosps., Chgo., 1979-80; ophthalmology resident Yale U. Hosps., New Haven, Conn., 1980-83; corneal fellow Emory U. Hosps., Atlanta, 1984-85; pvt. practice ophthalmology Atlanta, 1986—; cons. Ga. Med. Care Found., Atlanta, 1990—. Recipient Physician's Recognition award AMA, Chgo., 1996. Fellow Am. Acad. Ophthalmology; mem. DeKalb County Med. Soc., Med. Assn. Ga. Jewish. Office: 2163 Northlake Pky Ste 102 Tucker GA 30084-4102

GLASS, SARAH ELIZABETH, health services executive, educator; b. Sugarland, Tex., Aug. 21, 1958; d. Edward Alvin and Dorothy Ann (Talafuse) Andrejczak; m. Tracy Scott Glass, Feb. 15, 1975; children: Travis Wayne, Crystal Ann. AAS in Med. Record Tech., Wharton (Tex.) Co. Jr. Coll, 1983; BS in Health Info. Mgmt., U. Tex., Galveston, 1994. Pvt. practice rschr., typist Wharton, 1975-81; tutor Wharton County Jr. Coll., 1981-83; accredited records technician El Campo (Tex.) Meml. Hosp., 1983; dir. med. records Tex. Dept. Corrections, Jester Units I & II, Richmond, 1984-87; dir. health info. mgmt. Gulf Coast Med. Ctr., Wharton, 1987—; instr. Wharton County Jr. Coll., 1986—; cons. Riceland Regional Mental Health Authority, Wharton, 1989-93; chmn. Wharton County Jr. Coll.-Health Info. Tech. Adv. Bd., Wharton, 1994—; presenter in field. Mem. Citizen Amb. Program, Spokane, Wash., 1995—, del. to People's Republic of China, 1995. Charlsie Jennings Meml. award scholar Wharton County Jr. Coll., 1982. Mem. Am. Health Info. Mgmt. Assn. (registered records adminstr.), Tex. Health Info. Mgmt. Assn., Houston Area Health Info. Mgmt. Assn., Phi Theta Kappa. Home: 615 Lake Shore Dr Wharton TX 77488 Office: Columbia Golf Coast Med Ctr 1400 Hwy 59 Bypass Wharton TX 77488

GLASSCOCK, STEPHEN GREGORY, psychologist, researcher; b. Hartselle, Ala., Feb. 19, 1953; s. William Gregory and Ruth Ellen (Davis) G.; m. Dianne Frances Hanafee, July 30, 1983; children: Erin Frances, James Davis, John Gregory. BS, Lambuth Coll., 1975; MA, Middle Tenn. State U., 1977; PhD, U. Kans., 1987. Lic. clin. psychologist, Tenn., Ky. Rsch. assoc. Rutherford County Guidance Ctr., Murfreesboro, Tenn., 1976-77; psychiatric technician Jackson (Tenn.) Mental Health Ctr., 1977; psychiatric tchr./counselor Cumberland House Sch., Nashville, 1977-82; intern behavioral pediatrics U. Kans. Med. Ctr., Kansas City, Kans. 1984-86; NIH postdoctoral fellow in behavioral pediatrics Vanderbilt U. Med. Ctr., Nashville, 1987-89; dir. children's svcs. Pennyroyal Ctr., Hopkinsville, Ky., 1989—; dir. psychology Cumberland Hall Psychiatric Hosp., Hopkinsville, 1989—; dir. Western Ky. Internship Consortium. Contbr. articles to profl. jours. Recipient NIH fellowship Vanderbilt Med. Ctr., 1987-89; grantee Vanderbilt Med. Ctr., 1987. Mem. Am. Psychol. Assn., Nat. Register of Health Svc. Providers in Psychology. Episcopalian. Home: 238 Oxford St Hopkinsville KY 42240-5149

GLASSE, DOROTHY, child and family therapist; b. Bklyn.; d. Manuel Wolvington and Lillyan Dorothy (Shaffer) G.; m. Geoffrey Smith (div. 1980). BA, Adelphi U., 1953; MEd, MA, Columbia U., 1985. Cert. addiction counselor. Crisis intervention counselor Sexual Trauma Clinic Psychiatric Inst., N.Y.C., 1979-82; life skills educator Pratt Inst., Bklyn., 1982-87; coord. aftercare svcs. Outreach House Adolescent Rehab., Queens, N.Y., 1987-90; clin. coord. intensive outpatient clinic St. John's Episcopal Hosp., Queens, 1990-92; child & family therapist high risk intervention Franklin Mental Health Clinic, Louisburg, N.C., 1992—; founder N.Y. Women Against Rape rape crisis hotline, N.Y.C., 1971-82. Mem. Nat. Assn. Alcohol & Drug Addiction Counselors, N.Y. Fedn. Addiction Counselors. Office: Franklin Mental Health Ctr VGFW Area Mental Health Franklin NC 27549

GLASSER, STEPHEN PAUL, cardiologist; b. N.Y.C., Feb. 29, 1940; s. Leo and Ada G.; children: Laurie Jeanne, Julie Anne Student, U. Miami, 1957-60, MD, 1964. Diplomate Am. Bd. Internal Medicine, Am. Bd. Cardiology, Am. Bd. Clin. Pharmacology. Intern Letterman Gen. Hosp., San Francisco, 1964-65; resident Tripler Gen. Hosp., Honolulu, 1965-68; resident Walter Reed Gen. Hosp., Washington, 1968-69, asst. in cardiology, 1969-70; dir. critical care unit William Beaumont Gen. Hosp., El Paso, Tex., 1970-73; asst. chief cardiology Sch. of Medicine La. State U., Shreveport, 1973-76, dir. CCU, 1973-76; assoc. prof. U. So. Fla. Coll. Medicine, Tampa, 1976-80, prof., 1980—, dir. Noninvasive Lab., 1976-89, dir. divsn. cardiology, 1978-90, dir. cardiovasc. unit for rsch. and edn., 1990—, dir. lipid disorders clinic, 1991—; vis. prof. Med. Sch. U. Minn., 1995—; spl. cons. U.S. FDA, 1994—. Author: The Clinical Approach to Exercise Testing, 1980, A Casebook of Electrocardiographic Tracings, 1982, Case Physician's Guide, 1982, Noncardiac Surgery in the Cardiac Patient: Management and Assessment, 1983; editorial bd. Am. Jour. Cardiology, Jour. Non Invasive Cardiology, Jour. Clin. Pharmacology; contbr. more than 200 articles to profl. jours. Pres. N.W. unit, v.p. phys. edn. com., bd. dirs. Am. Heart Assn., Shreveport, 1974-76, mem. coun. on clin. cardiology, other offices; chmn. med. student admissions com. U. So. Fla., 1982-83. Fellow ACP, Am. Coll. Cardiology, Am. Coll. Clin. Pharmacology (mem. bd. regents 1992—); mem. Va. Cardiovasc. Assn., Am. Soc. Echocardiography. Office: Univ Profl Ctr 3500 E Fletcher Ave Ste 218 Tampa FL 33613-4712

GLASSMAN, GEORGE MORTON, dermatologist; b. N.Y.C., Sept. 7, 1935; s. Oscar and Jeanette (Bitterbaum) G.; m. Carol Beth Frankford, July 10, 1960; children: Keith F., Laurie C. BA cum laude, Brown U., 1957; MD, NYU, 1962. Diplomate Nat. Bd. Med. Examiners. Rotating intern Greenwich (Conn.) Hosp., 1962-63; resident in dermatology NYU Med. Ctr., N.Y.C., 1963-66; chief dermatology U.S. Navy, St. Albans, N.Y., 1966-68; pvt. practice White Plains, N.Y., 1968—; clinical asst. prof. Albert Einstein Coll. Medicine, Bronx, N.Y., 1970-75, N.Y. Med. Coll., Valhalla, N.Y., 1975-87; assoc. attending dermatologist Westchester County Med. Ctr., Valhalla, 1974-87, St. Agnes Hosp., White Plains, 1978—; attending dermatologist White Plains Hosp., 1977—. Contbr. articles to profl. jours. Lt. comdr. USN, 1966-68. Mem. Am. Acad. Dermatology (Continuing Med. Edn. award, 1980—), Internat. Soc. Tropical Dermatology, Dermatology Found., Westchester County Med. Soc., Westchester Acad. Medicine (pres. dermatology sect., 1990-91), N.Y. State Soc. Dermatology, AMA (Physician's Recognition award, 1980—), World Med. Assn., N.Y. Acad. Scis., Am. Soc. Dermatologic Surgery, Soc. for Pediatric Dermatology, Dermatologic Radiotherapy Soc. Home: 268 Stuart Dr New Rochelle NY 10804-1423 Office: George M Glassman MD PC 1 Old Mamaroneck Rd White Plains NY 10605-1703

GLASSMAN, LAWRENCE S., plastic surgeon; b. June 20, 1953. BA, Johns Hopkins U., 1975, MD, 1978. Diplomate Am. Bd. Surgery, Am. Bd. Plastic Surgery. C.A.Q. hand surgeon Columbia Presbyn. Med. Ctr., N.Y.C., 1978-83; plastic surgeon Montefiore Med. Ctr. and Albert Einstein Coll. of Medicine, Bronx, N.Y., 1983-85; prof. plastic surgery Albert Einstein Coll. Medicine, 1985—; plastic surgeon, dir. Inst. Aesthetic and Reconstructive Surgery, Pomona, N.Y., 1985—; plastic surgeon Good Samaritan Hosp., Suffern, N.Y., 1985—, Nyack (N.Y.) Hosp., 1985—, Chilton Meml. Hosp., Pompton Plains, N.J., 1985-89. Contbr. articles to profl. jours. Fellow ACS; mem. AMA, Am. Soc. Plastic and Reconstructive Surgery, Am. Assn. Surgery of the Hand, Med. Soc. Rockland County, Phi Beta Kappa, Alpha Omega Alpha. Office: 978 Rt 45 Pomona NY 10970

GLASSMAN, RICHARD DEAN, plastic surgeon; b. Chgo., Aug. 2, 1949; m. Lisa M. Sandford; children: Sienna, Gabriela. AA Santa Fe Jr. Coll., 1973; MD, U. Michoacan, 1981. Diplomate Am. Bd. Plastic & Reconstructive Surgeons;. From assoc. prof. to prof. U. Fla., Jacksonville, 1989—. Mem. AMA, Am. Soc. Maxillofacial Surgeons, Am. Soc. Plastic & Reconstructive Surgeons, Fla. Plastic Surgery Soc., Fla. Med. Assn. Home: 4270 Point La Vista Jacksonville FL 32207 Office: Baptist Med Ctr Pavilion 836 Prudential Dr #1603 Jacksonville FL 32207

GLASSNER, JAMES R., ophthalmologist; b. Milw., May 15, 1955; s. David M. and Nancy Lou (Heinemann) G.; m. Rebecca Abram; children: Kristen, Sarah. BA, U. Wis., 1977; MD, Vanderbilt U., 1981. Intern Mercy Hosp. and Med. Ctr., San Diego, 1981-82; resident U. Ala. Birmingham Eye Found. Hosp., 1982-85; pvt. practice Montgomery (Ala.) Eye Physicians, 1985—. Fellow ACS; mem. Montgomery Med. Soc. (bd. dirs.), Lions. Office: Montgomery Eye Physicians 2752 Zelda Rd Montgomery AL 36106

GLASSON, LINDA, hospital security and safety official, healthcare consultant; b. Nassawadox, Va., July 2, 1947; d. William Robert and Doris (Savage) G.; m. Charles William Lemon, Jr., Mar. 21, 1969 (div. 1973). Student Eastern Shore Br. U. Va., 1965-67, J. Sargent Reynolds C.C., 1976-80, Old Dominion U., 1981, Va. Wesleyan Coll., 1985. Cert. ambulance emergency med. technician. Clk.-typist G.L. Webster Co., Inc., Cheriton, Va., 1962-70; tchrs. aide Cape Charles High Sch., Va., 1970-72; dir. recreation and infirmary asst. United Meth. Children's Home, Richmond, Va., 1972-73; stockroom mgr. Flair Clothing Store, Richmond, 1973-74; with med. record dept. Richmond Meml. Hosp., 1974-75, asst. utilization rev. coord., 1975-80, hosp. police sgt., 1977-80; dir. safety and security Maryview Hosp., Portsmouth, Va., 1980—, chmn. hosp. safety com., 1980—, mem. disaster com., 1980—, chmn., 1986—. Contbg. author tng. manuals; contbr. articles to profl. pubis. Instr. first aid and personal safety ARC, 1970-85, multimedia first aid instr., 1983-88, first aid chmn. bd. dirs. Henrico chpt., 1979-80, vol. emergency med. technician ambulance state fair annually 1974—. Mem. Internat. Assn. Hosp. Security (sr., chmn. Region III 1985, v.p., sec. 1985-88, spl. appointee to bd. 1988-89), Am. Soc. Indsl. Security (mem. nat. standing com. healthcare security 1979-84, v.p. 1983-84), Internat. Assn. Healthcare Security & Safety (pres.-elect 1990, pres. 1991-92, past pres. 93—), Internat. Healthcare Security and Safety Found. (pres. 1994-95). Baptist. Avocations: golf, softball, swimming, reading, classical music. Office: Maryview Hosp 3636 High St Portsmouth VA 23707-3236

GLATHE, JOHN PARSONS, psychiatrist; b. Bklyn., Nov. 22, 1926; s. Henry Bernhard and Alice Elizabeth (Parsons) G.; m. Jean-Karlin Johnson, Dec. 26, 1953 (div. Jan. 1973); children: Jeffrey, Susan, Caroline. AB, Stanford U., 1949, MD, 1953. Diplomate Am. Bd. Psychiatry and Neurology. Intern U. Hosp., Ann Arbor, Mich., 1952-53; resident Max Found., Rochester, Minn., 1957-60; practice medicine specializing in psychiatry Palo Alto, Calif., 1960—; clin. prof. dept. psychiatry Stanford (Calif.) U., 1960—; bd. dirs. Found. Med. Care of Santa Clara County, San Jose, Calif. Served to capt. USAF, 1953. Fellow Am. Psychiat. Assn. (life); mem. Calif. Med. Assn., Biofeedback Soc. Am., Med. Friends of Wine, Sigma Chi, Nu Sigma Nu. Home: 13801 La Paloma Rd Los Altos CA 94022-2627 Office: 900 Welch Rd Palo Alto CA 94304-1516

GLATT, AARON ELI, physician, medical educator; b. Bklyn., Oct. 25, 1958; s. Joseph and Anna (Deberg-Kahn) G.; m. Marjorie Bell Korn; children: Ephraim, Ari, Chavi, Chezki. BA, Yeshiva U., 1979; MD, Columbia U., 1983. Diplomate Am. Bd. Infectious Diseases and Internal Medicine. Asst. chief infectious disease Nassau County Med. Ctr., L.I., N.Y., 1988-92; chief infectious diseases Cath. Med. Ctr., Queens and Bklyn., 1992—; co-dir. dept. of infection control and environ. health Albert Einstein Coll. Medicine, Bronx, N.Y., 1992—; assoc. prof. medicine Albert Einstein Coll. Medicine, Bronx, 1992—; cons. in field. Editor: Infection Disease Clinics of North America, 1994; contbr. articles to profl. jours. Recipient Rsch. prize-1st place Ortho Diagnostics, 1992, Faith and Medicine award Nat. Inst. of Healthcare Rsch., 1996. Fellow ACP, Infectious Disease Soc. Am., Am. Coll. of Chest Physicians; mem. AMA (Physician Recognition award), L.I./Queens Infectious Disease Soc. (pres. 1996—), Infectious Diseases Soc. of Am., Am. Soc. of Microbiology, others. Jewish. Office: Cath Med Ctr Divsn Infectious Disease 88-25 153 St Jamaica NY 11432

GLATTER, KATHLEEN MARY, medical/surgical nurse; b. Albion, Nebr., June 6, 1959; d. James M. and Mary Catherine (Clinch) McQuillan; m. Mark Andrew Glatter, June 9, 1984; children: Melissa Rae, Jessica Ann, Casey James, Mary Kaitlyn (dec.). BSN, Marymount Coll., 1981. RN, Nebr. Nurse's aide St. John's Hosp., Salina, Kans., 1980, Greeley (Nebr.) Care Home, 1977, 78, 79; med.-surg. nurse Good Samaritan Hosp., Kearney, Nebr., 1981-87; oper. rm. nurse Good Samaritan Hosp., 1988—. Mem. Assn. Oper. Rm. Nurses. Home: 610 E 36th St Kearney NE 68847-3109

GLAZER, GARY MARK, radiology educator; b. Feb. 13, 1950; children: Daniel I., David A. AB, U. Mich., 1972; MD, Case Western Res. U., 1976. Intern in internal medicine U. Calif., San Francisco, 1976-77, resident in diagnostic radiology, 1977-80, clin. instr., fellow in diagnostic radiology, 1980-81; asst. prof. radiology, dir. div. body computed tomography U. Mich., Ann Arbor, 1981-84, assoc. prof. radiology, 1984-87, dir. divs. magnet resonance imaging and body computed tomography, 1984-89, assoc. prof. cancer ctr., 1986-87, prof. radiology, prof. cancer ctr., 1987-89; prof., chmn. dept. radiology Stanford (Calif.) Sch. Medicine, 1989—. Cons., assoc. editor, reviewer Radiology; cons., reviewer Jour. Computer Assisted Tomogrphy; cons., chmn., reviewer, mem. editorial bd. Radiographics; contbr. articles to profl. pubis. Fellow Am. Cancer Soc., 1980-82, Clarence Heller Found., 1980-81. Mem. Am. Roentgen Ray Soc., Radiology Soc. N.Am., Soc. Magnetic Resonance in Medicine, Fred Jenner Hodges Soc., Soc. Magnetic Resonance Imaging, Alpha Omega Alpha. Office: Stanford Sch Med Dept Radiology Stanford CA 94305

GLAZER, ROBERT ARNOLD, health facility administrator; b. Mineola, N.Y., Mar. 22, 1954; s. Ben and Dorothy (Camhi) G.; m. Randee Rae Kessler, Oct. 7, 1984; children: Emma Beth, Jonathan Samuel. BSBA, State U. Plattsburgh, 1976; MPA in Health Care, NYU, 1980. Grants specialist NYU Med. Ctr., 1976-80, sr. acct., 1980-83, spl. asst. to contr., 1984-85; dir. adminstrn. Columbia Presbyn. Med. Ctr. Fund, N.Y.C., 1986-88; treas. Presbyn. Hosp., N.Y.C., 1989-93; sr. dir. fin. and bus. devel. United Hosp. Med. Ctr., Port Chester, N.Y., 1993—. Office: United Hosp Med Ctr 406 Boston Post Rd Port Chester NY 10573-4703

GLEASON, JOHN RUSSELL, JR., nephrologist; b. Louisville, Ky., Jan. 24, 1960; s. John R. Sr. and Marion U. (Cecil) G.;m . Carolyn Banks, Nov. 14, 1987. BA, U. Ky., 1982; MD, U. Louisville, 1986. Diplomate Am. Bd. Nephrology, Am. Bd. Internal Medicine. Intern then resident U. Louisville Hosp., 1986-89, fellow, 1989-92; nephrologist Nephrology Assocs. Kentuckiana, Louisville, 1992—. Author: (with others) High Efficiency and High Flux Dialysis, 1992; contbr. articles to profl. jours. Mem. ACP, Ky. Med. Assn., Jefferson County Med. Soc. Office: Nephrology Assocs 224 E Broadway Louisville KY 40202

GLEATON, HARRIET E., retired anesthesiologist; b. Altoona, Pa., Aug. 25, 1937; d. Munsey Sinclair and Anna Morgan (Scofield) G. BA, Franklin & Marshall Coll., 1959; MD, Temple U., 1962. Diplomate Am. Bd. Anesthesiology. Intern Mt. Sinai Hosp., N.Y.C., 1962-63; resident in anesthesiology Hosp. U. Pa., 1963-65; fellow Hosp. U. Pa., Phila., 1965-66, instr. anesthesiology, 1966-69; clin. anesthesiologist Michael Reese Hosp., Chgo., 1969-71; assoc. prof. U. Okla., Oklahoma City, 1971-81; clin. anesthesiologist Jane Phillips Episcopal Meml. Med. Ctr., Bartlesville, Okla., 1981-92; pvt. practice, 1992. Mem. AMA, Am. Soc. Anesthesiologists, Nature Conservancy, World Wildlife Fedn., Environ Def. Fund, Sierra Club.

GLEEKMAN-GREENBERG, HILARY AMY, internal medicine physician; b. Boston, May 28, 1963; d. Wallace Joseph and Barbara Ann (Zonis) Gleekman; m. William Jay Greenberg, Nov. 19, 1994. BA, Wellesley Coll., 1985; MD, Mt. Sinai Sch. Medicine, 1989. Diplomate Am. Bd. Internal Medicine, Nat. Bd. Med. Examiners. House staff officer dept. internal medicine Mt. Sinai Med. Ctr., N.Y.C., 1989-92; attending physician dept. emergency Montefiore Med. Ctr., Bronx, N.Y., 1992-94, primary care physician-AIDS ctr., 1994-95; staff physician Exec. Health Group/Life Ext. Inst., N.Y.C., 1995—. Mem. AMA, Am. Coll. Physicians.

GLEESON, GEORGE HENRY, physician, geriatric consultant; b. Pitts., July 24, 1949; s. George H. and Mary Elizabeth (Edwards) G.; m. Janice Lignoski, Sept. 3, 1977; children: Catherine, Edward, Margaret. BS, U. Pitts., 1971; MD, Hahnemann U., 1975. Diplomate Am. Bd. Internal Medicine. Intern, resident in internal medicine St. Francis Med. Ctr., Pitts., 1975-78; clin. asst. prof. medicine U. Pitts., 1988—; vice chmn. dept. medicine St. Francis Med. Ctr., Pitts., 1990—, med. dir. ambulatory svcs., 1994—; pres. med. staff St. Francis Med. Ctr., 1994, chmn. med. exec. com., 1995; med. dir. St. Francis Nursing Home, Cranberry, Pa., 1994—. Fellow Am. Coll. Physicians; mem. AMA, Assn. Program Dirs. in Internal Medicine, Pa. Med. Dirs. Assn., Pa. Med. Soc., Western Pa. Geriatric Soc. (pres. 1996). Office: St Francis Med Ctr 45th St and Penn Ave Pittsburgh PA 15201

GLEIS, LINDA HOOD, physician; b. Louisville, Jan. 28, 1952; d. Edgar Pete Hood and Joan Ray (Brenner) Hulsey; m. Gregory Eric Gleis, Aug. 18, 1973; children: Eric, Matthew, Kevin, Anna. BA cum laude, Bellarmine Coll., 1974; MD, U. Louisville, 1978. Diplomate Am. Bd. Phys. Medicine and Rehab. Lic. physician Ky., Ind. Resident Frazier Rehab. Ctr., Louisville, Ky., 1978-81, mem. med. staff, 1982—, dir. residency tng., 1985-95; asst. clin. prof. of medicine U. Louisville, Louisville, Ky., 1985—; chief phys. medicine and rehab. VA Med. Ctr., Louisville, Ky., 1985—; mem. med. staff VA Med. Ctr., Louisville, 1986—; founding ptnr. Rehab. Assoc.-PSC, Louisville, Ky., 1986—; bd. dirs. Republic Bank and Trust Co.; cons. Baptist Hosp. East, Clark Meml. Hosp., Humana Hosp. Audubon, Humana Hosp. Southwest, Humana Hosp. Suburban, Jewish Hosp., Kosair Children's Hosp., Meth. Evangelical Hosp., Norton Hosp., Sts. Mary and Elizabeth Hosp., Southern Ind. Rehab. Hosp., U. Louisville Hosp.; spkr. numerous med. confs. in U.S. and internationally. mem. U. Louisville Med. Alumni Bd., 1986-91, v.p., 1989-90, pres., 1990-91; mem. bd. overseers Bellarmine Coll, 1989-95; mem. adv. bd. Jefferson County Office for Women, 1990—; mem. Health Care Task Force Louisville C. of C., 1991-92; marriage sponsor Archdiocese of Louisville Holy Spirit Parish Couple to Couple Program, 1991—, Salute to Cath. Alumni Steering Com., 1991—, chmn., 1993-94; dir. JCMS Outreach Program, Inc., 1991—; trustee Spalding U., 1992—, vice chair, 1994—, chair com. Acad. and Student Affairs, 1995—, Spalding U./Presentation Acad. Com., 1995—, Devel. Com., 1994-95; mem. adv. panel The Physicians Inc., 1993—; bd. dirs. mem.-at-large U. Louisville Alumni Assn., 1993—; mem. Leadership Louisville Class of 1992, hon. chair scholarship campaign, 1994; judge exec. Jefferson County Small Bus. Growth Coun., 1992-93; mem. cabinet Metro United Way, 1992-94; bd. dirs. Louisville Cmty. Found., 1992—; mem. med. adv. group Home of the Innocents Pediatric Convalescent Ctr., 1993—; mem. adv. coun. Louisville Forum, 1995—. Recipient 1st Ann. Salute to Cath. Schs. Disting. Alumni award Archdiocese Louisville, 1990, Disting. Alumni Svc. award U. Louisville, 1991, Bellarmine Coll. Outstanding Alumnus of Yr., 1991, Assumption H.S. Outstanding Alumna award, Louisville, 1993, Order of Merit U. Louisville Alumni Assn., 1993; honored with Tribute to Linda Gleis, M.D. Modern Day Heroine Congl. Record, 1992; featured testimonial in Women Physicians Leading Change, Jour. Ky. Med. Assn., 1995. Fellow Am. Acad. Phys. Medicine and Rehab.; mem. AMA, Am. Med. Womens Assn., Am. Assn. Electrodiagnostic Medicine, Assn. Acad. Physiatrists (sec./program chmn. residency program dirs. coun., v.p. 1994-95, pres. 1995—, mem. grad. med. edn. com. 1995—), Ky. Med. Assn. (com. sch. health, phys. edn. and med. aspects of sports 1988—, physician orgn. study com. 1993—, task force on domestic violence 1992—), Ky. Acad. Phys. Medicine and Rehab. (sec.-treas. 1988—), Jefferson County Med. Soc. (found. bd. dir. 1990—, del. to Ky. Med. Assn. 1993—, treas., 1990-91, 1st woman pres. 1991-92, chmn. bd. dirs. 1992-93, physicians Metro United Way campaign chair 1990-94, bd. dirs. outreach program 1993—, 1st v.p. bd. dirs. 1994—). Catholic. Office: Rehab Assoc PSC 250 E Liberty St Ste 800 Louisville KY 40202-1537

GLENDAY, MARIANNA CATHRYN, health education and environmental consultant; b. Stillwater, Okla., Feb. 3, 1957; d. George Alexander and Mary Elizabeth (Kontra) G.; m. Robert Addison Allen III, July 9, 1983 (div. Jan. 1989). BA in Psychology, U. Calif., San Diego, 1980; MPH, U. Tex., Houston, 1989; MA in Clin. Psychology, Calif Inst. Integral Studies, 1995, PhD Candidate in Clin. Psychology, 1995—. Phone counselor employee assistance program U. Tex., Houston, 1987-88; project mgr. Ctr. for Health Promotion Rsch. and Devel., Houston, 1988-89; sr. rsch. asst. dept. family medicine Coll. Medicine Baylor Coll. Medicine, Houston, 1989-90; pvt. practice health edn. cons. Redwood City, Calif., 1990-91; rsch. dir. Found. for Glaucoma Rsch., San Francisco, 1991-92; cmty. substance abuse svcs. evaluation epidemiologist Mayor's Cmty. Partnership Substance Abuse Prevention Program, San Francisco Dept. Pub. Health, 1992-93; adj. faculty integral health Calif. Inst. Integral Studies, 1995; pre-doctoral psychology intern OMI-Family Ctr., 1995-96; trainer in group facilitation for Networks Empowering Women, San Jose, Calif., 1991-93; lay chaplain Unity Ch., 1993—; presenter, cons., rschr. in field.; project mgr. smoke exposure project U. Tex.-Houston; meta-analysis rsch. asst. U.S. Preventive Medicine Task Force. Contbr. articles to profl. publs.; reviewer Guide to Clinical Preventive Svcs., 1989. Facilitator Houston Ctr., 1990, Casa de Clara Emergency Shelter, San Jose, Calif., 1990. Mem. Alpha Omicron Pi. Home: 1 Carmel Ave Apt 1 Pacifica CA 94044-2549

GLENN, DANETTE LYNN, nurse; b. Denver, June 26, 1955; d. Charles Fredrick Glenn and Karen Lynn (Thomas) Davenport. BS, So. Coll. of SDA's, 1977; MS, U. Colo., 1987. RN, Colo. Staff nurse Porter Meml. Hosp., Denver, 1977-88; head nurse Rose Med. Ctr., Denver, 1988-90; mgr. Porter Care Hosp., Denver, 1990—. Victoria Crossing Condominium Assn., Aurora, 1994-96. Mem. Assn. Seventh-Day Adventist Nurses (treas. 1980-82), Assn. Rehab. Nurses, Colo. Nurses Assn., Colo. Fedn. Nursing Orgns. (task force on nurse practice act 1990-95). Democrat. Office: Porter Care Hosp 2525 S Downing St Denver CO 80210

GLENN, FRANCES BONDE, dentist; b. Tampa, Fla., Nov. 29, 1933. Student, U. Fla., 1951-52; DDS, U. Pa., 1956. Resident Children's Hosp., Washington, 1956-57; pvt. practice dentistry Miami, 1957—; vis. lectr. U. Miami, 1959—, Miami Dade Sch. of Dental Hygiene, 1979; cons. D.C. Tng. Ctr. for the Retarded and Handicapped, 1956-57; lectr. Lindsey Hopkins Vocat. Sch., 1981, U.S. and other countries; bd. overseers U. Pa. Sch. Dental Medicine; rschr. Pediat. Dent. Ortho. Contbr. articles to Lady's Home Jour., Parents Mag., Chicago Tribune Newspaper, Med. and Dent. Jour. Active Dade County Welfare and Planning Coun., 1959-61; vol. dentist Cerebral Palsy Clinic, 1959-63; advisor, cons. Crippled Children's Soc., 1976—; dental clinic staff mem. Coral Gables Jr. Women's Club, 1959-61. Recipient Alumni award merit U. Pa. Sch. Dental Medicine, 1984. Fellow Am. Acad. of Pedodontics; mem. Am. Orthodontic Soc. (diplomate of bd., Moore Disting. Svc. award 1994), Fla. Soc. Dentistry for Children, Am. Assn. Women Dentists. Office: 7741 SW 62d Ave Miami FL 33143-4908

GLENN, GUY CHARLES, pathologist; b. Parma, Ohio, May 13, 1930; s. Joseph Frank and Helen (Rupple) G.; m. Lucia Ann Howarth, June 13, 1953; children: Kathryn Holly, Carolyn Helen, Cynthia Marie. BS, Denison U., 1953; MD, U. Cin., 1957. Intern, Walter Reed Army Med. Center, Washington, 1957-58; resident in pathology Fitzsimons Army Med. Center, Denver, 1959-63; commd. 2d lt. U.S. Army, 1956, advanced through grades to col., 1977; demonstrator pathology Royal Army Med. Coll., London, 1970-72; chief dept. pathology Fitzsimons Army Med. Center, Denver, 1972-77; pres. med. staff St. Vincent Hosp., Billings, Mont.; past mem. governing bd. Mont. Health Systems Agy. Diplomate Am. Bd. Pathology, Am. Bd. Nuclear Medicine. Fellow Coll. Am. Pathologists (chmn. chemistry resources com., chmn. commn. sci. resources, mem. budget program and review com., council on quality assurance, chmn. practice guidelines com., bd. govs., chmn. nominating com.), Am. Soc. Clin. Pathology, Med. Cons. to Armed Forces (chair legal and legis. com.), Midland Empire Health Assn. (past pres.), Rotary (bd. dirs. local chpt.). Contbr. to profl. jours. Home: 3225 Jack Burke Ln Billings MT 59106-1113

GLENN, JAMES FRANCIS, urologist, educator; b. Lexington, Ky., May 10, 1928; s. Cambridge Francis and Martha (Morrow) G.; m. Gale Brooke Morrison, Dec. 29, 1948; children: Cambridge Francis II, Sara Brooke, Nancy Carrick, James Morrison Woodworth. Student (Yale Regional scholar), Univ. Sch., Lexington, 1946; B.A. in Gen. Sci. (Bausch and Lomb Nat. Sci. scholar), U. Rochester, 1949; M.D., Duke U., 1952. Diplomate: Am. Bd. Urology (mem.), Nat. Bd. Med. Examiners. Intern Peter Bent Brigham Hosp., Boston, 1952-54; asst. resident urology Duke U. Med. Ctr., 1956-58, resident, 1958-59; instr. urology Duke U., 1958-59, prof., chief div. urology, 1963-80; asst. prof. Yale U., 1959-61; assoc. prof. Bowman Gray Sch. Medicine, Wake Forest Coll., 1961-63; practice medicine specializing in urology New Haven, 1959-61, Winston-Salem, N.C., 1961-63, Durham, N.C., 1963-80; prof. surgery, dean Med. Sch., Emory U., 1980-83; pres. Mt. Sinai Med. Ctr., 1983-87; prof. surgery U. Ky. Coll. Medicine, Lexington, 1987—; CEO Markey Cancer Ctr., 1989-93; chief staff Univ. Hosp., Lexington, 1993-95, chmn. dept. surgery, 1996—; sci. dir. Coun. for Tobacco Rsch. U.S.A., 1987-91, chmn. bd., 1991—. Contbg. author: Renal Neoplasia, 1967, Urodynamics, 1971, Textbook of Surgery, 1972, Plastic and Reconstructive Surgery of The Genital Area, 1973, Current Operative Urology, 1975, Campbell's Urology, 1977; author, editor: Diagnostic Urology, 1964, Ureteral Reflux in Children, 1966, Urologic Surgery, 1969, rev. edit., 1975, 84, 90; contbr. numerous articles to profl. jours. Served to capt. M.C., USAF, 1954-56. Mem. Am. Assn. Genitourinary Surgeons (pres. 1992-93), Am. Surg. Assn., ACS, AMA (sec. sect. urology 1972-73, chmn. 1975-77), Assn. Am. Med. Colls., Internat. Urol Soc. (v.p. 1985-91, pres. 1991-94), Clin. Soc. Genito-Urinary Surgeons (pres. 1990-91), N.Y. Acad. Medicine, Soc. Pediatric Urology, Soc. Pelvic Surgeons (pres. 1980-81), Soc. Univ. Surgeons, Soc. Univ. Urologists (pres. 1971-72), Royal Coll. Surgeons (hon. fellow 1987), German Urol. Assn. (hon.), Australasian Urologic Soc. (hon.), Brit. Assn. Urologic Surgeons (hon.). Home: Glenninish Farm 2600 Basin Springs Rd Winchester KY 40391-9724 Office: Univ Ky Med Ctr Hosp Adminstrn 800 Rose St Lexington KY 40536-0001

GLENN, JUDY CAROLE, nurse, naval officer; b. Birmingham, Ala., July 2, 1946; d. Talmadge William and Maude Elizabeth (Steading) G.; diploma in nursing Univ. Hosp., Birmingham, 1967; BSN, Samford U., 1975; MSN in Cardiovascular Nursing, U. Ala., Birmingham, 1978; postgrad. Calif. Coast U. Staff nurse Univ. Hosp., 1967-68; charge nurse CCU, Lloyd Noland Found., Fairfield, Ala., 1968-70; charge nurse Bessemer (Ala.) Carraway Med. Center, 1970-75, unit coordinator, 1975-76, cardiovascular clin. specialist, 1978-80; commd. lt. USNR, 1979; asst. charge nurse intermediate intensive care Naval Regional Med. Center, San Diego, 1981-83, staff nurse, charge nurse med. ward Naval Hosp., Long Beach, Calif., 1983-85; promoted to lt. comdr., 1984; chief nurse clin. investigation Naval Med. Rsch. Unit 3, Cairo, 1985-88; head edn. and tng. dept. Naval Med. Clinic, Quantico, Va., 1988-91; served on USNS Comfort, Persian Gulf, 1990-91, U.S. Naval Hosp. Subic Bay, Republic of the Philippines, 1991-92, div. officer Cubi Clinic, 1992, head edn. dept. Naval Hosp., Millington, Tenn., 1992-95; ret. USN, 1995; dir. edn. Comanche County Meml. Hosp., 1995-96; RN Patient First Home Health, 1996—; affiliate faculty AHA CPR; instr. ARC CPR, ACLS, corpsman cardiology course; mem. regional area CPR com. Ala. Heart Assn., 1979-80, CPR regional course coordinator, 1977-78. Camp nurse Assembly of God Ch., Montgomery, Ala., 1968, 77, 78; lectr. WHO/EMRO AIDS Tng. Workshop, Cairo, 1986-88. Decorated Kuwait Liberation medal, S.W. Asia medal; recipient citation Ala. Heart Fund, 1975; USPHS Title II trainee, 1977-78. Mem. Am. Nurses Assn., Am. Heart Assn. (council on cardiovascular nursing, instr. CPR), Am. Assn. Critical Care Nursing (tech. assistance panel 1978-79). Republican. Office: Patient First Home Health 311 W Blakely Rush Springs OK 73082

GLENN, WILLIAM WALLACE LUMPKIN, surgeon, educator; b. Asheville, N.C., Aug. 12, 1914; s. Eugene Byron and Elizabeth Elliot (Lumpkin) G.; m. Amory Potter, May 15, 1943; children: William Amory Lumpkin, Elizabeth Glenn McLellan. B.S., U. S.C., 1934; M.D., Jefferson Med. Coll., 1938; M.A. (hon.), Yale U., 1962; M.D. (hon.), U. Cadiz, 1981. Diplomate Am. Bd. Surgery, Am. Bd. Thoracic Surgery. Intern Pa. Hosp., Phila., 1938-40; surg. resident Mass. Gen. Hosp., Boston, 1940-42, 45-46; asst. physiology Harvard Sch. Pub. Health, 1941-43; asso. surgery Jefferson Med. Coll., Phila., 1946-48; mem. faculty Yale Med. Sch., 1948—, prof. surgery, 1962-74, Charles W. Ohse prof. surgery, 1974-85, Charles W. Ohse prof. emeritus surgery, 1985—, chief cardiovascular surgery, 1948-76, sr. rsch. scientist, 1985-87; hon. staff Yale-New Haven Hosp.; cons. Surgeon Gen. Com. Environ. Medicine, 1962-64. Co-editor: Thoracic and Cardiovascular Surgery, 1962, 75, editor, 1983; co-editor: Complex Surgical Problems, 1981; mem. editorial bd. numerous jours.; cons., editor: Cardiac Pacemakers, 1964; contbr. articles to profl. jour. Mem. com. cardiovascular systems NRC, 1955-56; bd. dirs. Charles E. Culpeper Found., 1976-85. Served to maj., M.C. AUS, World War II, ETO. Mem. Am. Heart Assn. (pres. 1970-71), Internat. Soc. Surgery (v.p. U.S. sect.), Internat. Surg. Group (pres. 1964, hon. 1994), Am. Surg. Assn., ACS (chmn. Conn. adv. com. 1963-66, gov. 1967-72), Soc. Univ. Surgeons, New Eng. Surg. Soc. (pres. 1983-84), So. Surg. Assn., New Eng. Soc. Vascular Surgeons (pres. 1979-80), Am. Assn. Thoracic Surgery, Vascular Surg. Soc., Halstead Soc., Soc. Thoracic Surgeons (hon.), Morys' Assn. (New Haven), Yale Club of N.Y., Sigma Xi, Alpha Omega Alpha. Episcopalian. Home: 685 Forest Rd New Haven CT 06515-2520

GLENNER, RICHARD ALLEN, dentist, dental historian; b. Chgo., Apr. 14, 1934; s. Robert Joseph and Vivian (Prosk) G.; BS, Roosevelt U., 1955; BS in Dentistry, U. Ill., 1958, DDS, 1959; m. Dorothy Chapman, July 13, 1957; children: Mark Steven, Alison, Scott Jay. Gen. practice dentistry, Chgo., 1962—; cons. on dental history to Smithsonian Instn. Nat. Mus. Dentistry, ADA, various corps., libraries, univs., museums, dental jours., Dr. Samuel D. Harris Nat. Mus. Dentistry; dental rschr. Nat. Park Svc., Nat. Mus. Health and Medicine, 1993—. lectr. in field. Served to capt. AUS, 1960-62. Mem. ADA, Ill. Dental Assn., Chgo. Dental Soc., Assn. Mil. Surgeons U.S., Am. Acad. History of Dentistry (historian 1984, chmn. Smithsonian Instn. adv. group 1987, Hayden-Harris award 1983, columnist The Bull. of the History of Denistry 1989—, editorial bd. The Bull. of the History of Dentistry, 1993—, hist. display com. 1993—, pub. com., 1993—, Hayden-Harris award com. 1995-96), Fed. Dentaire Internationale, Lindsay Soc. Great Britain, Ill. State Dental Soc. (history com.), The Pierre Fauchard Acad., Am. Med. Writers Assn., Sci. Instrument Soc., Jewish War Vets. U.S.A, Alpha Omega. Author: The Dental Office: A Pictorial History; coauthor The American Dentist: A Pictorial History, A Visit to the Dentist: Then & Now; appeared in PBS video Scientific American Frontiers; cons. editor A Bicentennial Salute to Am. Dentistry, 1976; contbr. articles on dental history to profl. jours.; film maker The Dental Office. Home: 6715 N Lawndale Ave Lincolnwood IL 60645-3711 Office: 3414 W Peterson Ave Chicago IL 60659-3447

GLESER, GOLDINE COHNBERG, psychologist; b. St. Louis, June 15, 1915; d. Julius and Lena (Goldberg) Cohnberg; m. Sol Morris Gleser, June 4, 1936; children: Leon Jay, Malcolm Anthony, Judith Augusta. AB, Washington U., 1935, MS in Math., 1936, postgrad., 1936-38, PhD in Psychology, 1950. Instr. math. Washington U., St. Louis, 1947-49, rsch. asst. psychol. svcs., 1949-50; rsch. asst. to assoc. Washington U. Coll. Medicine, St. Louis, 1950-54; asst. to assoc. prof. U. Cin. Coll. Medicine, 1956-64; rsch. asst. to assoc. prof. U. Ill., Urbana, 1957-63; prof. psychology U. Cin., 1964-79, dir. psychol. div. dept. psychiatry, 1967-79, prof. emerita, 1979—; cons. Dept. Edn., U. Ill., 1951-55, Malcolm Bliss Rsch. Lab., Washington U., 1954-56, Traumatic Stress Study ctr., U. Cin., 1981-91; cons. on evaluation Shiawassee County Community Mental Health Ctr., Ososso, Mich., 1972-85; mem. adv. com. on clin. drug evaluation NIH, Washington, 1960-61, reviewer devel. behavioral sci. rsch. grants, 1972-75; mem. joint com. to revise edn. and psychol. test standards APA/AERA, 1981-83. Author: (with Cronbach) Psychological Tests and Personnel Decisions, 1965, (with Gottschalk) Measurement of Psychological States, 1969, (with others) The Dependability of Behavioral Measurements, 1972, Prolonged Psychosocial Effects of Disaster, 1981, (with Ihilevich) Evaluating Mental-health Programs: The Progress Evaluation Scales, 1982, Defense Mechanisms: Their classification, correlates and measurement with the Defense Mechanisms Inventory, 1986, Defenses in Psychotherapy: The Clinical Application of the Defense Mechanisms Inventory, 1991, The Defense Mechanisms Test, 1968, others. Grantee Found. Fund for Rsch. in Psychiatry, U. Cin., 1959-65, NIMH, 1975-77; recipient Rieveschl award U. Cin., 1979, Lifetime Achievement award Ohio Women in Psychology, 1988, award for Traumatic Stress Studies, 1990. Fellow APA (rep. to coun. 1976-78, award 1985), Am. Statis. Assn., Am. Psychol. Soc., Ohio Psychol. Assn.; mem. Midwest Psychol. Assn., Cin. Psychol. Assn. (pres. 1957-58, 65-66, award 1988), Psychometric Soc. (trustee 1966-69), Soc. of Multivariate Exptl. Psychology (pres. 1977-78). Home and Office: 3604 Lansdowne Ave Cincinnati OH 45236-3008

GLICHOUSE, ERIC SCOTT, family physician; b. Lynn, Mass., Mar. 2, 1960; s. Myron Woodrow and Barbara Jean (Barry) G.; m. Debra Michelle Glichouse, Nov. 5, 1989. BA, Clark U., 1982; DO, U. Health Scis., 1987. Diplomate Am. Osteo. Bd. Gen. Practice. Intern Tulsa Regional Med. Ctr., 1987-88; resident Coll. Osteo. Medicine, Okla. State U., 1988-90; pvt. practice Glenpool, Okla., 1990-96; chief of staff Fairfax Meml. Hosp. Mem. Am. Osteo. Assn., Okla. Osteo. Assn., Tulsa Dist. Osteo. Soc. (bd. dirs. 1990—). Jewish. Office: 212 N Main St Fairfax OK 74637

GLICK, BRAD PETER, dermatologist, family physician; b. Bklyn., Nov. 3, 1961; s. Merton and Vivian (Schwartz) G.; m. Mona Susan Kaminsky, July 12, 1987; 1 child, Lauren Alexandra. BA in Chemistry, Emory U., 1983, MPH, 1984; DO with honors, Nova-Southeastern U., 1989. Diplomate Am. Osteo. Bd. Dermatology, Am. Osteo. Bd. Family Practice. Rsch. assoc. AIDS Program-CDC, Atlanta, 1983-84; intern Humana South Broward, Hollywood, Fla., 1989-90; family physician Wellington Regional Med. Ctr., West Palm Beach, Fla., 1990-92; staff physician urgent care medicine First Med, Inc., Tamarao, Fla., 1991—; staff physician dept. dermatology Mt. Sinai Med. Ctr., Miami Beach, Fla., 1996—; pvt. practice Margate, Fla., 1995—; rsch. investigator Quality Rsch. Group, Inc., Miami beach, 1993—; adminstr. Comprehensive Med. Care, Inc., Plantation, Fla., 1984-85; lectr. in field. Contbr. articles to profl. jours. Mem. Gold Coast Bus. Coun., Coral Springs, Fla., 1995—. Recipient Morton Terry Internal Medicine award Nova-Southeastern U., 1989. Mem. AMA, Am. Osteo. Assn., Am. Osteo. Coll. Dermatology, Am. Acad. Dermatology, Fla. Osteo. Med. Assn., Broward County Osteo. Med. Assn. Home: 6536 NW 99th Ln Parkland FL 33076 Office: 5800 Colonial Dr #304 Margate FL 33063

GLICK, GINA PHILLIPS MORAN, physician; b. Chgo., Dec. 6, 1931; d. Edward Langan Moran and Virginia Louise Phillips; m. L. Michael Glick, Feb. 9, 1957; children: Mark Michael, Celeste Michele, Felicia Michele, Matthew Michael. Student, Mundelein Col., Chgo., 1949-52; MD, Loyola U., Chgo., 1956. Diplomate Am. Bd. Anesthesiology. Intern Mercy Hosp., Chgo., 1956-57; resident in anesthesia Chgo. Wesley Mem. Hosp., 1957-59; pvt. practice anesthesia Cumberland, M.D., 1959-83; clin. instr. anesthesia U. Md., Balt.; chmn. dept. anesthesia Sacred Heart Hosp., Cumberland, 1967-83; asst. prof. anesthesia U. Tex. S.W. Med. Ctr., 1985—; dir. Jenkins Anesthesiology Libr. Recipient gold, silver and bronze medals Md. chpt. Am. Heart Assn., Community Achievement award Sta. WCBC, 1981, St. Benedict medal St. Scholastica High Sch., Chgo., 1978. Mem. Am. Soc. Anesthesiologists, Tex. Soc. Anesthesiologists, Dallas County Soc. Anesthesiologists, Dallas County Med. Soc. Roman Catholic. Office: U Tex Sci Med Ctr Dept Anesthesiology 5323 Harry Hines Blvd Dallas TX 75235-7200

GLICK, JOHN H., oncologist, medical educator; b. N.Y.C., May 9, 1943; s. Arthur W. and Sybil (Goldman) G.; m. Jane Mills, May 25, 1968; children: Katherine, Sarah. AB magna cum laude, Princeton U., 1965; MD, Columbia U., 1969. Diplomate Am. Bd. Med. Oncology, Am. Bd. Internal Medicine (sec. subspecialty com. med. oncology 1976-83, mem. subspecialty bd. med. oncology 1983-87, chmn. 1987-89, cert. examination com. 1986-88, bd. govs. 1987-89). Intern in medicine Presbyn. Hosp., N.Y.C., 1969-70, asst. resident in medicine, 1970-71; commd. surgeon, clin. assoc. medicine br. Nat. Cancer Inst., USPHS, Bethesda, Md., 1971-73; postdoctoral fellow in med. oncology Stanford (Calif.) U., 1973-74; asst. prof. medicine U. Pa., Phila., 1974-79, Ann B. Young asst. prof. cancer rsch., 1974, assoc. prof., 1979-83, prof., 1983—, Madlyn and Leonard Abramson prof. clin. oncology, 1988—; dir. clin. trials U. Pa. Cancer Ctr., Phila., 1977-79, assoc. dir. for clin. rsch., 1980-85, dir. Cancer Ctr., 1985—; mem. numerous acad. coms., dept. medicine coms., hosp. coms., 1974—; attending physician Hosp. of U. Pa., 1974—, dir. Hematology-Oncology Clinic, 1974-76; cons. Phila. VA Hosp., 1974—; mem. NIH clin. trials rev. com., 1980-83, radiosensitizer/radioprotector working group, radiotherapy devel. br., 1980-85, chmn. consensus devel. panel conf. adjuvant therapy for breast cancer, 1985, all Nat Cancer Inst., NIH; mem. com. accreditation med. oncology tng. progams, 1983—, mem. appeals panel, 1987-94, Accreditation Coun. Grad. Med. Edn.; prin. investigator Ea. Coop. Oncology Group, U. Pa. Mem. editorial bd. Am. Jour. Clin. Oncology, 1983-89, Blood jour., 1983-86, Jour. Clin. Oncology, 1986-88, Jour. Cancer Rsch. and Clin. Oncology, 1987-93; bd. editors Internat. Jour. Radiation Oncology, Biology and Physics; assoc. editor Cancer Rsch. jour., 1984-88; contbr. more than 100 original papers to profl. jours. Recipient Am. Cancer Soc. Faculty Rsch. award, 1982-86; rsch. grantee Nat. Cancer Inst., Eastern Coop. Oncology Group, Am. Cancer Soc., others. Fellow ACP (various splty. coms. 1983-85), Coll. Physicians and Surgeons; mem. Am. Soc. Clin. Oncology (chmn. program com. 1983-84, nominating com. 1983-84, pub. issue com. 1984-85, bd. dirs., pres. 1995-96), Am. Assn. Cancer Edn., Am. Assn. Cancer Rsch., Am. Radium Soc. (exec. com. 1986-87), Am. Soc. Hematology, Am. Fedn. Clin. Rsch., John Morgan Soc. U. Pa., Phi Beta Kappa, Alpha Omega Alpha. Office: U Pa Cancer Ctr 3400 Spruce St Philadelphia PA 19104

GLICK, RICHARD STEPHEN, internist, rheumatologist; b. Pitts. May 18, 1947; s. William and Ruthe (Scher) G. B.A. cum laude, U. Pa., 1969, M.D., 1973. Diplomate Am. Bd. Internal Medicine (also subsplty. bd. rheumatology). Intern, U. Mich. Hosp., Ann Arbor, 1973-74, resident, 1974-77; fellow in rheumatology U. Pa., 1977-78, Albany Med. Coll. Hosp., 1978-79; practice medicine specializing in rheumatology and internal medicine, Ft. Lauderdale, Fla., 1979—. Mem. AMA, Am. Coll. Rheumatology, Fla. Med. Assn., Fla. Soc. Rheumatology. Contbr. articles to profl. jours. Office: 6405 N Federal Hwy Ste 105 Fort Lauderdale FL 33308-1414

GLICK, SHIMON MICHAEL, medical educator; b. Paterson, N.J., June 30, 1932; arrived in Israel, 1974; m. Oct. 1956; six children. AB magna cum laude, NYU, 1951; MD, SUNY, Bklyn., 1955. Diplomate Nat. Bd. Med. Examiners, Am. Bd. Internal Medicine, Am. Bd. Internal Medicine Subspeciality Endocrinology Bd.; cert. specialist internal medicine, Israel, cert. specialist endocrinology, Israel; lic. N.Y., Conn., Pa., Israel. Intern Maimonides Hosp., Bklyn., 1955-56; asst. resident internal medicine Yale U., Grace New Haven (Conn.) Hosp., 1956-57; chief outpatient dept. and med. clinic USAR Army and Navy Hosp., Hot Springs, Ark., 1957-59; asst. resident internal medicine Mt. Sinai Hosp., N.Y.C., 1959-60; trainee in diabetes and metabolic disorders USPHS Jewish Chronic Disease Hosp., Bklyn., 1960-61; spl. rsch. fellowship USPHS VA Hosp., Bronx, 1961-63, clin. investigator, 1963-64; assoc. dir. divsn. metabolism and endocrinology Maimonides Med. Ctr., 1964-74; prof. medicine Ben-Gurion U. of the Negev, Faculty of Health Scis., Beer-Sheva, Israel, 1974—; dean Ben-Gurion U. of the Negev, Faculty of Health Scis., Beer-Sheva, 1986-90; head internal medicine Soroka U. Hosp., 1974—; chief div. metabolism and endocrinology Coney Island Hosp. of Maimonides Med. Ctr., 1964-69, chief med. svcs., 1967-74, vis. physician, 1967-74; clin. asst. prof. medicine SUNY, Downstate Med. Ctr., 1965-68, clin. assoc. prof., 1968-72, clin. prof., 1972-74; attending physician Maimonides Med. Ctr., 1967-74; chmn. divsn. medicine Ben-Gurion U. of the Negev and Soroka U. Hosp., 1974-83; established investigator Israel Ministry of Health, 1978-81, mem. nat. health coun., 1995—; vis. scientist NIH, 1983-84; chmn. faculty of health scis. Ctr. for Med. Edn., Ben-Gurion U. of the Negev, 1990—. Editorial bd.: Jour. Clin. Endocrinology and Metabolism, 1971-74; assoc. editor: Israel Jour. Med. Scis., 1978—. Mem. nat. adv. com. on human experimentation Ministry of Health, Israel, 1985—; head health svcs. Negev region, Kupat Holim (Sick Fund) of Gen Fedn. of Labor, 1986-90, chmn. med. coun., 1986-90. Fellow ACP; mem. Israeli Soc. for Med. Ethics (coun. 1989—), Endocrine Soc., Assn. Orthodox Jewish Scientists (pres. 1965-67), Israel Soc. Internal Medicine, Israel Diabetes Assn., Soc. Urban Physicians (pres. 1969), Am. Soc. for Clin. Investigation, Com. of Concerned Scientists (co-chmn. med. sci. sect. 1973-74), Israel Endocrine Soc. (pres. 1979-82), Phi Beta Kappa, Alpha Omega Alpha (pres. sch. chpt. 1954-55). Office: Ben Gurion U of the Negev, PO Box 653, 84105 Beersheva Israel

GLICK, THOMAS HARTER, neurologist; b. N.Y.C., May 15, 1939; s. Milton Bachrach and Evelyn (Harter) G. m. Georgia Sherman, May 28, 1966; children: Steven, Sharon. AB magna cum laude, Harvard U., 1961; MD cum laude, Harvard U., Boston, 1966. Diplomate Am. Bd. Psychiatry and Neurology. Intern Columbia Presbyn. Med. Ctr., N.Y.C., 1966-67; epidemic intelligence svc. officer USPHS, Ctrs. for Disease Control, Atlanta, 1967-69; resident in neurology Mass. Gen. Hosp., Boston, 1969-72; chief neurology Cambridge (Mass.) Hosp., 1972—; from instr. to assoc. prof. neurology Harvard Med. Sch., Boston, 1972—; chmn. sci. adv. bd. Nat. Reye's Syndrome Found., Ohio, 1983—; mem. clin. neurology task force Nat. Bd. Med. Examiners, 1996. Author: Process of Neurologic Care, 1984, Neurologic Skills: Examination and Diagnosis, 1993, Problem-Based Neuroscience: A Casebook and Curricular Guide, 1996; contbr. articles to profl. jours. Lt. USPHS, 1967-69. Sheldon Travelling fellow, 1961-62. Fellow Am. Acad. Neurology (mem. undergrad. edn. com. 1994—); mem. Boston Soc. for Neurology and Psychiatry, Physicians for Social Responsibility. Office: Cambridge Hosp Dept Medicine 1493 Cambridge St Cambridge MA 02139

GLICKENHAUS, SARAH BRODY, speech therapist; b. Mpls., Mar. 8, 1919; d. Morris and Ethel (Silin) Brody; BS, U. Minn., 1940, MS, 1945; m. Seth Morton Glickenhaus, Oct. 23, 1944 children: James Morris, Nancy Pier. Speech therapist Davison Sch. Speech Correction, Atlanta, 1940-42; speech pathologist U. Minn., Mpls., 1945-46; speech therapist Queens Coll., N.Y.C., 1946-48; speech therapist VA, N.Y.C., 1949-50; pvt. practice, New Rochelle, N.Y., 1950-71; speech therapist Abbott Sch. United Free Sch. Dist. 13, Irvington, N.Y., 1971-79; pvt. practice, Scarsdale, N.Y., 1979—; tutor learning disabled children New Rochelle Public Schs., 1968-71. Mem. AAAS, Am. Speech Hearing & Lang. Assn., N.Y. State Speech &Hearing Assn., Westchester Speech & Hearing Assn. Club: Harvard (N.Y.C.). Jewish. Home and Office: 100 Dorchester Rd Scarsdale NY 10583-6051

GLICKMAN, FRANKLIN SHELDON, dermatologist, educator; b. Bklyn., Dec. 14, 1929; s. Arthur Zachary and Hilda (Kurtz) G.; m. Leatrice Sallie Alter, Mar. 29, 1953; children: Todd Scott, Jeff Bret. BA cum laude, Hofstra Coll., 1950; MD, SUNY-Bklyn., 1954; MS in Health Care Mgmt., NYU, 1990. Diplomate: Am. Bd. Dermatology. Intern Flushing (N.Y.) Hosp., 1954-55; resident in dermatology Kings County Hosp., Bklyn., 1957-58, Bronx VA Hosp., 1958-60; practice medicine specializing in dermatology Bklyn., 1960-94; mem. faculty dermatology dept. SUNY-Bklyn., 1960—, clin. prof., 1982—; dir. med. edn. Wyckoff Heights Med. Ctr., Bklyn., 1990—, chmn. dept. grad. med. edn., 1992—. Author: General Dermatology, 1978, Fundamentals of Dermatology: A Study Guide, 1990; contbr. articles to profl. jours. Served to capt. M.C. USAF, 1955-57. Fellow N.Y. Acad. Medicine, ACP; mem. Am. Acad. Dermatology, Bklyn. Dermatol. Soc. (pres. 1970-72), N.Y. State Med. Soc., Kings County Med. Soc., AMA, N.Y. State Soc. Dermatology (pres. 1983-85), N.Y. Acad. Scis. Home: 33 Farm Ln Roslyn Heights NY 11577-2603 Office: 122 Avenue A Brooklyn NY 11236-1203

GLICKMAN, RANDOLPH DAVID, ophthalmology educator, researcher; b. N.Y.C., Aug. 24, 1949; s. Stanley Irwin and Ruth Marion (Kaiser) G.; m. Pauline Po-Ling Leung, July 12, 1985. AB, Columbia U., 1971; PhD, U. Toronto, Ont., Can., 1978. Postdoctoral fellow Harvard U., Cambridge, Mass., 1978-79; rsch. fellow Schepens Eye Rsch. Inst., Boston, 1979-81; assoc. rsch. scientist Technology, Inc., San Antonio, 1981-86; rsch. scientist KRUG Life Scis., San Antonio, 1986-92; assoc. prof. U. Tex. Health Sci. Ctr., San Antonio, 1992—; assoc. dir. Ctr. for Environ. Radiation Toxicology. Guest editor: Neurosci. and Biobehavioral Revs., 1993; reviewer Lasers in Surg. Med.; contbr. chpt. to book, articles to profl. jours. Bd. dirs. Terra-Genesis, San Antonio, 1993—, pres., 1994—; adv. bd. Lions Sight and Tissue Found., San Antonio, 1985-89. Recipient U. Toronto open fellowship, 1972, U. Toronto Mary H. Beatty fellowship, 1972-73, Nat. Rsch. Coun. Can. postgrad. fellowship, 1973-76, Nat. Eye Inst., postdoctoral fellowship, 1978-81. Mem. AAAS, Soc. Neuroscience (Alamo chpt. v.p. 1992-93, pres. 1993-94), Assn. Rsch. in Vision and Ophthalmology, Internat. Brain Rsch. Orgn., Oxygen Soc., Sigma Xi. Office: U Tex Health Sci Ctr Dept Ophthalmology 7703 Floyd Curl Dr San Antonio TX 78284-6200

GLICKMAN, ROBERT MORRIS, physician, educator; b. Bklyn., June 23, 1939; s. David B. and Sally G.; m. Mary Holahan, June 20, 1961; children; Jonathan, Michael. B.A. magna cum laude, Amherst Coll., 1960; M.D. cum laude, Harvard U., 1964. Diplomate Am. Bd. Internal Medicine. Intern Harvard U. Med. Services, Boston City Hosp., 1964-65, asst. resident in medicine, 1965-66; research fellow in medicine Med. Sch., Harvard U., Boston, 1966-68, instr. medicine, 1970-72; asst. prof. Harvard Med. Sch., Boston, 1972-77; assoc. prof. Med. Sch., Harvard U., Boston, 1977; clin. and research fellow in medicine Mass. Gen. Hosp., Boston, 1966-68, asst. in medicine, 1970-74, asst. physician, 1974-75; chief div. gastroenterology, asst. physician Beth Israel Hosp., Boston, 1975-77; chief div. gastroenterology Coll. Physicians and Surgeons, Columbia U., N.Y.C., 1977-84, chmn. gastrointestinal sect. abnormal biology, 1978-84, assoc. prof., 1977-81, prof., 1981-82, Samuel Bard prof. medicine, chmn. dept. medicine, 1982-90; dir. med. svc. Presbyn. Hosp., N.Y.C., 1982-90, attending physician, 1981-90; Herrman L. Blumgart Prof. Med. Harvard Med. Sch., Boston, 1990—; physician-in-chief Beth israel Hosp., 1990—; mem. Nat. Digestive Diseases Adv. Bd., 1985—. Mem. editorial bd. Jour. Lipid Research, 1978-79, Jour. Clin. Investigation, 1979-84, Am. Jour. Medicine, 1981—; contbr. articles to med. jours. Served to maj. M.C. U.S. Army, 1968-70. Fellow ACP; mem. Am. Fedn. Clin. Rsch. (councillor Eastern sect. 1975-79, sec.-treas. 1976-79), Am. Gastroent. Assn. (v.p. 1985-87, pres. elect 1987, pres. 1988), N.Y. Acad. Medicine, Harvey Soc., Interurban Clin. Club, Assn. Am. Physicians (councillor 1992), Nat. Found. Ileitis and Colitis (mem. sci. adv. bd. 1978), Am. Soc. Clin. Investigation (councillor 1981-84, pres. elect 1983, pres. 1984-85), Assn. Profs. Medicine (councillor 1989-94, pres. 1992-93), Am. Bd. Internal Medicine (sub-splty. bd. on gastroenterology 1989-95), Harvard Soc., Phi Beta Kappa, Sigma Xi, Alpha Omega Alpha. Office: Beth Israel Hosp YA-419 330 Brookline Ave Boston MA 02215-5400

GLICKSMAN, ARVIN S(IGMUND), radiologist, physician; b. Bklyn., Mar. 14, 1924; s. Charles and Myrtle (Fetner) G.; m. Bernice R. Grobstein, Jan. 30, 1956; children: Jonathan, Jane Ellen, Merrylee, Caroline, Jeanette. M.B., M.D., Chgo. Med. Sch., 1949. Intern Kings County Hosp., Bklyn., 1948-50; AEC postdoctoral research fellow Duke U., 1950-51; postgrad. research fellow Brookhaven Nat. Labs., Upton, N.Y., 1951-52; resident in medicine Meml. Hosp., N.Y.C., 1952-54; clin. asst. physician in medicine Meml. Hosp., 1955-64, asst. attending radiation therapist, 1964-65; research fellow Sloan-Kettering Inst., N.Y.C., 1954-60; asso. Sloan-Kettering Inst., 1960-65; mem. med. research inst. Michael Reese Hosp., Chgo., 1964-65; asso. chmn. dept. radiation therapy Michael Reese Hosp., 1965-67; dep. dir. radiotherapy Mount Sinai Hosp., N.Y.C., 1967-73; prof. radiotherapy Mount Sinai Sch. Medicine, 1971-73; dir. radiation oncology R.I. Hosp., Providence, 1973-84, chmn. dept. radiol. medicine and biol. rsch., 1984-89; prof. med. scis. Brown U., 1973-95, prof. emeritus, 1995—; chmn. dept. radiation oncology Roger Williams Med. Ctr., 1989-95; practice medicine specializing in radiation oncology; hon. med. cons. NIH, Royal Marsden Hosp.; mem. cancer clinic, investigation rev. com. Nat. Cancer Inst., 1975-79, mem. radiation oncology com., 1976-86, mem. cancer intervention study sect., 1991-94. Editor: (with others) Computers in Radiotherapy, 1970, 73; contbr.: numerous articles to profl. jours. Mem. exec. com. Am. Cancer Soc., R.I., 1987—, pres., 1987-89, nat. bd. dirs., 1990-93; chmn. radiotherapy com. Cancer and Leukemia Group B.; dir. Quality Assurance Rev. Ctr., R.I. Cancer Control Bd., 1980—, chmn. task force info. sys., mem. exec. com.; co-chmn. exec. com. ASSIST Program Nat. Cancer Inst./Am. Cancer Soc., 1991—. Dillon fellow Royal Marsden Hosp., Surrey, Eng., 1961-62; Rsch. Career Devel. awardee NIH, 1962-64; Fulbright sr. scholar, 1986-87; recipient St. George medal Am. Cancer Soc., 1991. Fellow Am. Coll. Radiology; mem. New Eng. Soc. Radiation Oncologists (pres. 1975-76), N.Y. Roentgen Ray Soc. (chmn. sect. therapeutic radiology 1972-73), Am. Soc. Clin. Oncology, Am. Assn. Cancer Edn., Am. Assn. Cancer Research, Am. Radium Soc., Am. Soc. Therapeutic Radiologists, Brit. Inst. Radiology. Home: Old Blackstone Rd Uxbridge MA 01569 Office: Quality Assurance Rev Ctr Providence RI 02908

GLICKSMAN, MICHAEL LEWIS, psychologist; b. N.Y.C., Mar. 15, 1941; s. William and Julia (Wachs) G.; m. Marcia Spence, Feb. 4, 1979; 1 child, Noah Stafford. BA, Hofstra U., 1962; MA, U. Toledo, 1964; postgrad., NYU, 1968. Psychologist Narcotic Addiction Control Commn., N.Y.C., 1967-71; clin. asst. prof. psychiatry SUNY Downstate Med. Ctr., Bklyn., 1971-74; psychologist Office Mental Retardation and Devel. Disabilities, Bklyn., 1977-80, Rockland Children's Psychiat. Ctr., Goshen, N.Y., 1980-82, Middletown (N.Y.) Psychiat. Ctr., 1982-94, Mid-Hudson Psychiat. Ctr., New Hampton, N.Y., 1994—; cons. Crystal Run Village, Inc., Middletown, N.Y., 1991—. Contbr. articles to profl. jours. and hobby-related periodicals. NIMH fellow, 1963-64. Mem. Internat. Steamboat Soc., Aquatic Gardeners Assn., Hudson Valley Antique Radio and Phonograph Soc. (bd. dirs.), Messerschmitt Owners Club. Democrat. Jewish. Home: 147 Highland Ave Middletown NY 10940-4729 Office: Mid-Hudson Psychiat Ctr New Hampton NY 10958

GLICKSTEIN, ARTHUR F., psychologist; b. Bklyn., Nov. 18, 1927; s. Samuel and Esther (Beckman) G.; m. Beverly Florence Teitelbaum, Nov. 13, 1953; children: Susan, Lisa and Karen (twins). BA, Bklyn. Coll., 1948; MA, U. Ky., 1951, PhD, 1959. Lic. psychologist, Conn.; lic. marriage and family therapist, Conn. Clin. psychology trainee VA Hosp., Lexington, Ky., 1951-52; clin. psychology officer U.S. Army Mental Hygiene Clinics, Ft. Polk, Ft. Riley, La., Kans., 1952-56; staff psychologist Norwich (Conn.) State Hosp., 1957-61; dir. psychol. dept. Newington (Conn.) Childrens Hosp., 1961-68; pvt. practice Newington, 1957—; cons. South Windsor (Conn.) Pub. Sch.,

1968-89, Newington Police Dept., 1979—, Southfield Project, Newington, 1980—. Pres. Temple Sinai, Newington. 1st lt. Med. Svc. Corps, 1952-56. Mem. APA, Am. Assn. Marriage and Family Therapists, Nat. Register Health Svc. Providers in Psychology, Conn. Psychol. Assn. (former pres.), Conn. Assn. Marriage and Family Therapists (former bd. dirs.). Democrat. Jewish. Home: 70 Dover Rd Newington CT 06111-1014 Office: 1268 Main St Ste 107 Newington CT 06111-3043

GLIDEWELL, JOHN CALVIN, psychology educator; b. Okolona, Miss., Nov. 5, 1919; s. Henry Clay and Jessie Kate (Jones) G.; m. Frances Lee Reed, Sept. 12, 1941; children: Pamela Lee, Janis Lynn. M.A., U. Chgo., 1949, Ph.D., 1953. Diplomate Am. Bd. Profl. Psychology. Dir. psychol. services Meridian Pub. Schs., Miss., 1949-50; dir. research-devel. St. Louis County Health Dept., Clayton, Mo., 1953-67; assoc. prof. psychology Washington U., St. Louis, 1953-67; prof. psychology U. Chgo., 1967-81; prof. psychology Vanderbilt U., Nashville, 1981-90, prof. psychology emeritus, 1990—. Editor: (books) Parental Attitudes and Child Behavior, 1961, Social Context Development and Learning, 1975, Corporate Cultures: Implications for Human Resource Development, 1986, Impossible Jobs in Public Management, 1990; author: Choice Points, 1970, (with others) Nurses, Patients, Social Systems, 1968; editor Am. Jour. Community Psychology, 1976-87. Served to maj. USAF, 1942-46, 50-52. Fellow Am. Sociol. Assn., Am. Psychol. Assn. (award for disting. contbn. div. 27, 1975); mem. Sigma Xi. Home: 101 Longwood Pl Nashville TN 37215-1926 Office: Vanderbilt Univ Peabody Box 512 Nashville TN 37203-0512

GLIJANSKY, ALEX, psychiatrist, psychoanalyst; b. Caracas, Venezuela, Oct. 6, 1948; came to U.S., 1975; s. Natalio and Ghenea (Rechtman) G.; m. Belinda Matyas, Aug. 12, 1973; children: Ghena, Avi. MD, Universidad Cen. de Venezuela, 1971, MS, 1974. Resident in psychiatry Hahnemann U., Phila., 1978; med. dir. Fishtown/Lower Kensington Mental Health Ctr., Phila., 1978-82; assoc. psychiatrist dept. psychiatry Abington (Pa.) Meml. Hosp., 1982—; asst. prof. dept. Mental Health Scis., MCP-Hahnemann Sch. Medicine, Phila., 1978—. Fellow Am. Psychiat. Assn.; mem. Pa. Psychiat. Soc., Phila. Psychiat. Soc., Phila. Assn. for Psychoanalysis, Am. Psychoanalytic Assn. Office: 8302 York Rd Ste 9 Elkins Park PA 19027

GLIKLICH, JERRY, physician, educator; b. Jelenia Góra, Poland, May 6, 1948; came to U.S., 1958; s. Henry and Henia (Gotajner) G.; m. Jane Salmon, Sept. 12, 1976; children: David, Benjamin. AB, Columbia U., 1969, MD, 1975. Intern N.Y. Hosp., N.Y.C., 1975-76, resident, 1977-78; fellow in cardiology Presbyn. Hosp., N.Y.C., 1978-81, attending physician, 1981—, assoc. clin. prof., 1991—; asst. prof. medicine Columbia U., N.Y.C., 1981-91; cons. in field. Contbr. articles to profl. jours. Mem. ACP, Am. Coll. Cardiology, N.Am. Soc. Pacing & Electrophysiology, Phi Beta Kappa. Office: Presbyn Hosp 161 Fort Washington Ave New York NY 10032-3713

GLIMCHER, MELVIN JACOB, orthopedic surgeon; b. Brookline, Mass., June 2, 1925; s. Aaron and Clara (Fink) G.; m. Geraldine Lee Bogolub, June 22, 1946; children: Susan Deborah, Laurie Hollis, Nancy Blair. Student, Duke U., 1943-44; B.S. in Mech. Engring. with highest distinction; B.S. in Physics with highest distinction, Purdue U., 1946; M.D. magna cum laude, Harvard, 1950; postgrad., Mass. Inst. Tech., 1956-59. Intern surgery Strong Meml. Hosp., Rochester, N.Y., 1950-51; 3d asst. resident surgery Mass. Gen. Hosp., Boston, 1951-52; 2d asst. resident Mass. Gen. Hosp., 1952-53, asst. resident orthopedic surgery, 1954-55, chief resident, 1956, chief orthopedic service, 1965-71, chmn. dept. orthopedic surgery, 1968-71; asst. resident orthopedic surgery Children's Med. Center, Boston, 1953-54; jr. resident Children's Med. Center, 1955-56; mem. faculty Harvard Med. Sch., 1956—, Edith M. Ashley prof. orphopedic surgery, 1965-71, Harriet M. Peabody prof., 1971—; also chmn. dept.; orthopedic surgeon-in-chief Children's Hosp. Med. Center, Boston, 1971-81, dir. Lab. for Study of Skeletal Disorders and Rehab., 1980—. Trustee Forsyth Dental Infirmary, New England Sinai Hosp. With USMCR, World War II. Recipient Soma Weiss award Harvard Med. Sch., 1950, Borden Research award, 1950; Kappa Delta award, 1959; Internat. Assn. Dental Research award, 1964; Ralph Pemberton award Am. Rheumatism Soc., 1969; Bristol-Meyers/Zimmer instl. grant for excellence; Disting. Achievement in Orthopaedic Research award Orthopaedic Research Edn. Found. Fellow Am. Acad. Arts and Scis., Am. Acad. Orthopaedic Surgeons (Silver anniversary Kappa Delta prize 1974), Am. Orthopedic Assn.; mem. Orthopedic Research Soc. (past pres.), Assn. Bone and Joint Surgeons (Nicholas Andry award 1978), Internat. Soc. for Study Lumbar Spine (Volvo award 1983), Societe Internationale de Chirurgie Orthopedique et de Traumatologie. Office: 300 Longwood Ave Boston MA 02115-5724

GLITSCH, HELFRIED GÜNTHER, physiologist, educator; b. Berlin, Sept. 2, 1937; s. Günther and Margarete (Rahlfs) G.; m. Hanne Will, Aug. 3, 1963; children: Johannes, Verena, Angela. MD, Ruprecht-Karls-U., Heidelberg, 1963. Postdoctoral fellow I. Physiol. Inst., U. Heidelberg, 1963-64; intern Hosp. Schwetzingen, 1965, Med. U. Hosp., Heidelberg, 1966; asst. prof. Pharmakolog. Inst. of U. Mainz, 1967-69, Inst. Cell Physiology, Ruhr-U. Bochum, 1969; rsch. fellow German Rsch. Coun., Cambridge, Eng., 1972-73; prof. and head Arbeitsgruppe Muskelphysiologie Ruhr-U. Bochum, 1973—; vis. prof. Rockefeller U., N.Y.C., 1982. Contbr. articles to profl. jours. With German Mil., 1966-67. Mem. Physiol. Soc., German Physiol. Soc., German Pharmacology Soc. Office: Arbeitsgruppe Muskelphysol, Ruhr Univ Bochum, Unversitätsstr 150, 44780 Bochum Germany

GLOCK, MARVIN DAVID, retired psychology educator; b. San Jose, Ill., Nov. 19, 1912; s. David William and Lydia (Gruensfelder) G.; m. Elva Ruth Snell, Apr. 13, 1941; children—Carol Sue, Sandra Kay. Student, Blackburn Coll., 1930-32; A.B., U. Nebr., 1934; M.S., U. Ill., 1935-38; Ph.D., State U. Iowa, 1947. Tchr. Edison (Nebr.) High Sch., 1934-36; prin. Mason City (Ill.) Community High Sch., 1936-41; asst. prof. edn. Mich. State U., 1947-49; prof. ednl. psychology Cornell U., Ithaca, N.Y., 1949-83, prof. emeritus, 1983—; cons. in communication skills; cons. in communications skills. Author: (with J.S. Ahmann and Helen Wardeberg) Evaluating Elementary School Pupils, 1960, (with J.S. Ahmann) Evaluating Pupil Growth: Principles of Tests and Measurements, 6th edit, 1980, Readings in Educational Psychology, 1971, Measuring and Evaluating Educational Achievement, 2d edit, 1975, PROBE: An Audiotutorial College Reading Program, 3d edit, 1984, PROBE II: An Audio tutorial Reading Program, 1978; author numerous sci. papers. Lt. USN, 1942-45. Fulbright fellow Sri Lanka, 1962-63; recipient numerous research grants. Fellow Am. Psychol. Assn.; mem. Sigma Xi, Phi Kappa Phi. Presbyterian. Home: 101 Homestead Ter Ithaca NY 14850-6217

GLOETZNER, FRANK LUDWIG, hospital executive, educator; b. Berlin, Oct. 20, 1938; s. Karl Michael and Ingeborg (Fiedler) G.; m. Gisela Emli Herms, May 16, 1969; children: Tilman, Juliane, Sebastian, Ulrike, Charlotte, Maximilian, Marietta. MD, Julianum/Helmstedt, Niedersachsen, Germany, 1958. Intern U. Göttingen (Germany), 1964-66, Free U. Berlin, 1964; resident in neurology and psychiatry U. Munich, 1968-71; asst. prof. neurol. surgery U. Wash., Seattle, 1971-73; lectr. U. Würzburg (Germany), 1973-82, assoc. prof. neurology, 1982; head neurology dept. Rummelsberg Hosp., Schwarzenbruck, Germany, 1982—. Contbr. articles to profl. jours. V.p. Parents Coun. Leibniz Gymnasium Altdorf, 1984—; mem. bd. Bavarian Parents Coun., Munich, 1991—. Capt. German Navy, 1967-68. Mem. AAAS, Lions. Home: Zum Wiesengrund 1, D90592 Schwarzenbruck Germany Office: Krankenhaus Rummelsberg, Postfach 1162, D-90588 Schwarzenbruck Germany

GLOGAU, RICHARD G., dermatologist; b. Camden, N.J., Dec. 28, 1947; m. Pamela Ann Baj, June 11, 1977; 1 child, Gordon. AB, Dartmouth Coll., 1969; BMS, Dartmouth Med. Sch., 1971; MD, Harvard U., 1973. Intern Pa. Hosp., Phila., 1973-74; resident in dermatology U. Calif., San Francisco, 1974-77, chief resident, 1977-78, fellow in dermatologic surgery, 1978-79; pvt. practice, 1979—; lectr. in field. Co-author: Basics of Dermatologic Surgery, 1982, Flaps and Grafts, 1988, Cosmetic Dermatologic Surgery, 2d edit., 1989; co-editor: Dermatologic Surgery Year Book, 1991, 92, 93, 94; contbr. chpts. to books and articles to profl. jours. Fellow Am. Acad. Dermatology, Am. Dermatol. Assn., Am. Acad. Facial Plastic and Reconstructive Surgery, Am. Coll. Mohs' Micrographic Surgery and Cutaneous Oncology, Am. Soc. for Dermatol. Surgery, Am. Soc. for Dermatopathology, Am. Acad. Cosmetic Surgery, Am. Soc. Liposuction Surgery, N.Am. Soc. Phlebology; mem. Dermatology Found. Leaders Soc., San Francisco Dermatol. Soc., San Francisco Med. Soc., San Mateo County Med. Soc. Office: Dermatology 350 Parnassus Ave S 400 San Francisco CA 94117

GLOOR, PATRICIA ANN, critical care nurse, disaster nurse; b. Hawthorne, N.J., Aug. 15, 1942; d. Emil A. and H. Eileen (Garehan) G. Diploma in nursing, St. Luke's Hosp., 1966; student, Columbia U., N.Y.C., 1967-75; BA in Sociology, Marymount Manhattan Coll., 1983; cert., Inst. of Theology, 1987. Cert. in quality assurance and utilization rev. Health nurse Meadowmount Sch. of Music, Westport, N.Y.; relief nurse Juilliard Sch. of Music, N.Y.C.; staff nurse AIDS unit St. Luke's Hosp., N.Y.C. Mem., instr. ARC, 1976—, vol. com. for nursing ARC, 1978-79, del.-at-large disaster nursing steering com., 1989—, RN, phlebatomist N.Y. blood program, 1983-86, disaster nurse, 1976—. Mem. Am. Heart Assn., Internat. Platform Assn., N.Y. State Nursing Assn. Home: 448 E 20th St Apt 7F New York NY 10009-8235

GLOTH, F(RED) MICHAEL, III, physician; b. Balt., May 20, 1956; s. Fred Michael Jr. and Mary Jane (Prosser) G.; m. Maybian Pruet, Oct. 14, 1989; children: Anna, Mary Kate. BS, Coll. William & Mary, 1979; MD, Wayne State U., 1984. Diplomate in internal medicine and geriatrics Am. Bd. Internal Medicine. dir. rsch. dept. medicine Union Meml. Hosp., Balt., 1993—; guest rschr. Nat. Inst. on Aging, NIH, Balt., 1989—; asst. prof. medicine Johns Hopkins U., Balt., 1990—; med. dir. Carroll Hospice, Westminster, Md., 1992—; chief geriatrics Union Meml. Hosp., Balt., 1993—, dir. geriat. fellowship program, 1996—; clin. asst. prof. medicine U. Md., Balt., 1994—; cons. Merck & Co., West Point, Pa., 1995—, Ortho-McNeil Pharm., Raritan, N.J., 1995—, Purdue-Frederick, Norwalk, Conn., 1994—. Membership com. Ctr. Club, Balt., 1988—; bd. dirs. Carroll Hospice, 1996—. Fellowship Am. Fedn. for Aging Rsch., 1990, Internat. Life Sci. Inst.-Rsch. Foun., 1990; recipient New Investigator award Am. Geriatric Soc., 1993. Fellow ACP, Am. Geriatric Soc.; mem. Balt. Bone Club (pres. 1990—), Internat. Coll. of Hospice/Palliative Care, Gerontol. Soc. Am., Am. Soc. for Bone/Mineral Rsch. Office: Union Meml Hosp Divsn of Geriatrics 201 E University Pkwy Baltimore MD 21218

GLOVER, JOHN ERIC, medical educator; b. Melbourne, Victoria, Australia, Apr. 5, 1947; s. Thomas Allison and Dorothy Joan (Churcher) G.; m. Lesley Alice Anderson, May 4, 1974; children: Bronwyn, Cameron. BEd, U. Melbourne, 1982, MSc, 1996. Radiographer trainee, supr. Box Hill Hosp., Melbourne, Australia, 1969-76; lectr. Royal Melbourne Inst. Tech., 1976—. With RAAF, 1973-96. Fellow Kellogg Found., 1983-84. Fellow Australian Inst. Radiography; mem. Australian Coll. Edn. Home: 33 Hamilton Dr, Ringwood Victoria 3134, Australia Office: Med Radiations Sci, 124 Latrobe St, Melbourne Victoria 3000, Australia

GLOWCZEWSKIE, FRANK PATRICK, JR., medical researcher, medical facility administrator; b. Wood River, Ill., Nov. 15, 1943; s. Frank Patrick and Marilyn Ann (Walters) G.; m. Jeanette Harper, Nov. 1964 (dec. Mar. 1987); children: Frank Patrick III, Morfydd Marie Glowczewskie Gum. AD in Radiation Physics, Ocala (Fla.) C.C., 1969; degree in edn., U. Fla., 1973. Tchr. Marion County Bd. Edn., Ocala, 1971-78; rsch. surg. assist., labs. U. Fla., Gainesville, 1978-91, asst. in orthops., dir. bone bank, 1991-92, asst. orthops. rsch. faculty, 1992—; co-dir. G & G Techs., Gainesville, 1994—. Author (fifth-grade textbook) Organ and Tissue Transplantation, 1990; created tchg./instrn. video Tissue and Bone Recovery Edn., 1991. Mem. pub. edn. forum, Am. Coun. Transplantation, 1985-90. With AUS, 1961-64. Mem. Am. Assn. Tissue Banks, N.Am. Transplant Coords. Orgn., Orthop. Rsch. Soc., U. Fla. Orthop. Assn. (hon.). Home: PO Box 1496 Alachua FL 32616 Office: Univ Florida Tissue Bank Box J246 Gainesville FL 32610

GLUCKMAN, JEAN-CLAUDE, immunology educator; b. Jan. 23, 1940; m. Eliane Gluckman; 1 child, Philippe. MD, Faculty Medicine, Paris, 1968; PhD, U. Paris, 1977. Intern Hosp. Paris, 1964-68; lectr. physiology Paris Med. Sch., 1966-68; asst. prof. nephrology U. Paris 5, 1969-72, U. Paris 6, 1974-79; assoc. prof. nephrology Pitié-Salpêtrière Med. Sch., Paris, 1980-87, prof. immunology, 1987—; chief immunology lab. Pitiè-Salpêtrière Hosp., Paris, 1988—; rsch. fellow U. Wash., Seattle, 1988—; head transplantation immunology lan Pitiè-Salpêtrière Med. Sch., 1974-86; dir. CRNS Lab. Unite de Recherche Associèe 1463, 1991-94; dir. d'Etudes EPHE, 1991—; mem. various French Govt. coms. on AIDS, 1985-90; mem. sci. coms. Internat. Confs. on AIDS, 1987-96, project leader European Cmty. Concerted Action on Immunology and Immunopathology of HIV Related Diseases, 1987-92. Author (with others): AIDS, Proceedings of the International Conference of AIDS, Paris, 1986, Elsevier, Amdsterdam, 1987, SIDA et infection par VIH, 1989, Modern Pathology of AIDS and Other Retroviral Infections, 1990, Morphological and Functional Aspects of Accessory Cells in HIV and Other Retroviral Infections, 1991; mem. editl. bd. AIDS, 1987—; contbr. numerous AIDS rsch. articles, 1983—. Mem. French Immunology Soc., French Hematology Soc., French Transplantation Soc., Internat. AIDS Soc. (regional sec. Europe and Israel). Office: Biologie & Genetique Des, Deficits Immunitaires, 83 Bld De L'Hopital, 75634 Paris France

GNARRA, DAVID JOSEPH, hematologist; b. Aliquippa, Pa., Dec. 3, 1943; s. Tony and Mary Theresa (Galzerano) G.; m. Elaine C. Gonzior, June 9, 1971; children: Rosanne M., Michael D. BS, U. Pitts., 1964, MD, 1968. Diplomate Am. Bd. Pediatric Hematology/Oncology. Intern, resident Charity Hosp. La. State U., Baton Rouge, 1968-70; resident pediatric hematology/oncology U. Ill. Hosp., Chgo., 1970-71, Cin. Children's Med. Ctr., 1973-74; asst. dir. pediatric hematology/oncology Children's Hosp. Med. Ctr., Cin., 1974-75; dir. pediatric hematology/oncology Childrens Meml. Hosp., Omaha, 1977—; clin. assoc. prof. pediatrics U. Nebr. Sch. Medicine, 1982—; assoc. prof. Creighton U. Sch. Medicine, Omaha, 1990—, asst. prof. 1975-77; dir. pediatric hematology/oncology St. Elizabeth Cmty. Health Ctr., Lincoln, Nebr., 1992—. Contbr. articles to profl. jours. Mem. Am. Soc. Pediatric Hematology/Oncology, Am. Soc. Clin. Oncology, Nebr. Med. Soc., Greater Omaha Med. Soc., Omaha Mid-West Clin. Soc., Am. Cancer Soc. (bd. dirs. Nebr. divsn., profl. edn. com. Nebr. divsn. Republican. Roman Catholic. Office: Childrens Meml Hosp Pediatric Hematology/Oncol 8301 Dodge St Omaha NE 68114

GNIADECKA, MONIKA, dermatologist; b. Warsaw, Poland, Mar. 29, 1967; d. Kazimierz and Barbara Gajkowscy; m. Robert Gniadecki, Oct. 20, 1990. MD, Warsaw Med. Sch., 1991; PhD, Copenhagen U., 1994. Resident dermatology dept. dermatology Warsaw U., 1992-94; rsch. fellow dept. dermatology Copenhagen U., 1994—. Co-author: Handbook of Non-Invasive Methods and the Skin, 1995; contbr. articles to profl. jours. Grantee LEO Pharm. products, 1992-93, 96, Gerda and Aage Haensch Found., 1993, 95, Sigvaris Ganzoni, 1995. Roman Catholic. Office: U Copenhagen Dept Dermatology, Bispebjerg Bakke 23, 2400 Copenhagen Denmark

GNIADECKI, ROBERT, dermatologist, researcher; b. Wroclaw, Poland, Apr. 9, 1967; arrived in Denmark, 1992; s. Jan and Walentyna (Morgunowicz) G.; m. Monika Gajkowska, Oct. 20, 1990. MD, Warsaw (Poland) Med. Sch., 1991; PhD, U. Copenhagen, 1994. Sr. house officer dept. endocrinology Warsaw Med. Sch., 1991-92; rschr. dept. dermatol. rsch. Leo Pharm. Products, Denmark, 1993-95; registrar dept. dermatology U. Hosp., Copenhagen, 1995—. Author: In Vivo Examination of the Skin, Electron Microscopy in Dermatology; contbr. articles to profl. jours. Recipient Acad. Achievement award Ministry Health, 1989-90; grantee Haensch Found., Bangs Found., 1992, 94-95. Home: Frederiksberg Alle 29 3tv, 1820 Frederiksberg Denmark Office: Nat U Hosp Dept Dermatology, Blegdamsvej 9, 2100 Copenhagen Denmark

GOATES, DELBERT TOLTON, child psychiatrist; b. Logan, Utah, Apr. 14, 1932; s. Wallace Albert and Roma (Tolton) G.; m. Claudia Tidwell, Sept. 15, 1960 (div. Apr. 1994); children: Jeanette, Byron, Rebecca Lynn, Alan, Paul, Jonathan Phillip, Kendra, Michelle, George Milton; m. Julie Anderson Headley, Dec. 29, 1994. BS, U. Utah, 1953, MD, 1962; postgrad., U. Nebr., 1965, 67. Intern Rochester (N.Y.) Gen. Hosp., 1962-63; resident Nebr. Psychiat. Inst., Omaha, 1963-67; pvt. practice medicine specializing in child psychiatry Omaha, 1963-67, Albuquerque, 1967-71, Salt Lake City, 1971—; dir. psychiatry Riverdell Psychiat. Ctr., 1986-92, staff psychiatrist, 1992—; asst. prof. child psychiatry U. N.Mex., 1967-71, dir. children's svcs., 1967-71, asst. prof. pediatrics, 1969-71; clin. dir. Children's Psychiat. Ctr., Primary Children's Med. Ctr., Salt Lake City, 1971-77; med. dir. Life Line, 1990-93, Brightway Adolescent Psychiat. Hosp., 1992—; pres. Magic Mini Maker, Inc., Salt Lake City, 1972-78; chmn. bd. Intermountain Polytex, Inc. Bishop Ch. Jesus Christ Latter-day Sts., 1968-71; bd. dirs. Utah Cancer Soc., Great Salt Lake Mental Health. Served with MC, AUS, 1953-55. Mem. AMA, Orthopsychiat. Assn. Am., Utah Psychiat. Assn., Intermountain Acad. Child Psychiatry (pres. 1974-76), Pi Kappa Alpha, Phi Kappa Phi. Home: 4187 Abinadi Rd Salt Lake City UT 84124-4001 Office: 404 E 45th S #B-38 Salt Lake City UT 84109-0531

GOBAR, GAIL TAMARA, nurse; b. Bronx, N.Y., Nov. 4, 1940; d. Jack Arthur and Anne (Schussler (dec.)) Ossin; m. Seymour Gobar, Nov. 10, 1962; children: Bonnie Deborah, Tammy Dana. RN, N.y. Med. Coll. and Flower and Fifth Ave. Hosp., 1961; EdD (hon.), Rhyme U., Buffalo, 1985. RN. Head nurse of cardiology Flower and Fifth Ave. Hosp., N.Y.C., 1960-62; head nurse, supr. Jersey Shore Med. Ctr., Neptune, N.J., 1963-67; surg. asst. Dr. M. Levbarg DDS, Bricktown, N.J., 1978-81; supr. Medictr. of Am., Lakewood, 1967-68; adminstr. for handicapped programming Family YMCA's of Ocean County, Lakewood, N.J., 1981-87, also bd. dirs.; freelance writer Penfield, N.Y., 1987-93, Lakewood, N.J., 1993—; part-time nurse Jersey Shore Med. Ctr., Neptune, 1967-70, psycho-geriatric unit Rochester (N.Y.) Psychiat. Hosp., 1988-93, orthopedic diagnostic nurse, 1994—; part-time sch. nurse Fairport (N.Y.) Sch. Sys., 1989-93; part-time staff nurse Medictr. of Am., Lakewood, 1986-70; govs. appointee Juvenile Alcohol Prevention Adv. Bd., Ocean County, 1982-84. Columnist for weekly newspaper, Ocean County, 1978-81; editor Flower-Fifth Ave. Hosp. Alumni Newspaper; poet: (poem included in anthology) The Best Poems of the 90's, 1996. Mem. Lakewood Bd. Edn., 1975-78, 84-86, pres.; coord. Parents Against Forced Busing, Lakewood, 1972-75; troop leader Ocean County Girl Scouts, Lakewood, 1972-77; coord. Pop Warner Girls Activities, Lakewood, 1975-80; mayor's appointee Civil Defense Adv. Bd., 1977-79; mem. Ocean County Bd. of Elections, 1976-83, 95; campaign chairperson Sen. Robert Singer, 1995. Recipient Ocean County Girl Scouts Hidden Heroine award, 1976, Assistance to Handicapped award N.J. Dept. of Human Services, 1984. Mem. N.J. Sch. Bds. Assn., Sisterhood Ahavat, Shalom (bd. dirs. Lakewood 1964-70, v.p. congress Dov'v' Schmuel, 1994—), FFAH Nursing Alumni Assn., Rotary (recipient Speakers award 1985, Lakewood). Republican. Jewish.

GOBLE, JOHN LEWIS, pediatric ophthalmologist; b. Delaware, Ohio, July 18, 1926; s. John Lester and Esther Pauline (Freese) G.; m. Elise Joan Hollenberg, Oct. 4, 1956; children: John Robert, Michael William. AB, Ohio Wesleyan U., 1948; MD, U. Rochester, 1952. Diplomate Am. Bd. Ophthalmology. Intern U. Va. Hosp., Charlottesville, 1952-53; resident in Ophthalmology Columbia Presbyn. Hosp., N.Y.C., 1956-58; practice medicine San Mateo, Calif., 1959—; instr. ophthalmology Stanford U., 1960-68, Am. Acad. Ophthalmology, 1970-74; pres. Peninsula Eye Soc., Calif., 1973-74; chief ophthalmology Mills Hosp., San Mateo, 1974-75, 90-92. Author: Visual Disorders in the Handicapped Child, 1984. Served to lt. U.S. Army, 1953-55. Fellow Am. Coll. of Surgeons, Am. Acad. for Cerebral Palsy, Am. Acad. of Ophthalmology; affiliate fellow Am. Acad. of Pediatrics; charter mem. Am. Assn. for Pediatric Ophthalmology, Peninsula Club. Republican. Unitarian. Home: 2007 New Brunswick Dr San Mateo CA 94402-4012 Office: Goble & Goble Inc 100 S Ellsworth Ave Ste 507 San Mateo CA 94401-3929

GOBLIRSCH, DEAN EDMUND, otolaryngologist; b. Little Falls, Minn., Nov. 14, 1934; s. Edmund Conrad and Hyacinthe Evangeline (Felix) G.; m. Leila Joyce Kissel, Dec. 29, 1956; children: David, Cynthia, Dean II, Constance. BS, St. John's U., Collegeville, Minn., 1955; DO, Kirksville Coll. Osteo. Medicine, 1959. Practice osteo. medicine specializing in otolaryngology Milw.; mem. staff Lakeview Hosp., Milw., chmn. dept. otolaryngology, 1979-94, chmn. dept. surgery, 1982-87; mem. staff Elmbrook Hosp., Lakeview hosp., Milw.; chmn. dept. otolaryngology NW Gen. Hosp., Milw., 1981-86. Fellow Osteo. Coll. of Otolaryngology Head and Neck Surgery, Am. Acad. Otolaryngology Head and Neck Surgery, Am. Acad. Otolaryngology (cert.), Osteo. Coll. Otolaryngology (mem. Bd. Examiners 1982-92); mem. Am. Osteo. Assn. (hosp. insp. residency in otolaryngology 1980-94), Wis. Osteo. Assn., Milw. Osteo. Assn., Milw. Head and Neck Soc., Am. Osteo. Assn., AMA, Wis. State Osteo. Assn., Wis. Med. Soc., Milw. Dist. Osteo. Assn., Milw. County Med. Assn. Roman Catholic. Home: 830 Shadow Lawn Dr Elm Grove WI 53122-2164 Office: 9900 W Bluemound Rd Milwaukee WI 53226-4339

GODAGER, JANE ANN, social worker; b. Blue River, Wis., Nov. 29, 1943; d. Roy and Elmyra Marie (Hood) G. BA, U. Wis., 1965; MSW, Fla. State U., 1969. Lic. clin. social worker. Social worker III State of Wis. Dept Corrections, Wales, 1965-71; supervising psychiat. social worker I State of Calif., San Bernardino, 1972-75, La Mesa, 1975-77; psychiat. social worker State of Calif., San Bernardino, 1978-85; supr. mental health services Riverside (Calif.) County Dept. Mental Health, 1985-86; mental health counselor Superior Ct. San Bernardino County, 1986—; mem. adv. bd. Grad. Sch. Social Work Calif. State U., San Bernardino, Mental Health Assn. Mem. Nat. Assn. Social Workers, Acad. Cert. Social Workers (diplomate), Kappa Kappa Gamma Alumnae Assn. Office: Office Mental Health Counselor 700 E Gilbert St Bldg 1 San Bernardino CA 92415-0920

GODARD, JOSEPH EDWARD, radiologist; b. Clinton, Mass., June 3, 1942; s. William Horace and Isabel (Crossman) G.; m. Nancy Coleman, Jan. 28, 1984; children: Andrew, Michael. AB, Brown U., 1964; MD, U. Vt., 1968. Diplomate Am. Bd. Radiology, Am. Bd. Nuclear Medicine. Radiologist Bert Fish Med. Ctr., New Smyrna Beach, Fla., 1974-96; ptnr. New Smyrna Radiology Assocs., 1977-96; cons., 1996—. Lt. cmdr. U.S. Navy, 1970-72. Mem. AMA, Am. Coll. Radiology, Am. Coll. Nuclear Physicians, Radiol. Soc. N.Am., Fla. Radiol. Soc., Soc. Nuclear Medicine. Home: 4387 S Sea Mist Dr New Smyrna Beach FL 32169

GODBEY, FRANK ROBERT, JR., hospital administrator; b. Charleston, W.Va., Mar. 24, 1959; s. Frank Robert and Marlene Rose (Lambert) G.; m. Vicki Lynn Register, Aug. 15, 1980; children: Michael Cory, Courtney Leigh. BA in Bible, Bob Jones U., 1981. Painting supr. Carolina Painting Co., Easley, S.C., 1980-84; mgr. Eckerd Drugs, Greenville, S.C., 1984-93; adminstr. W.J. Barge Meml. Hosp., Greenville, 1993—; ins. com. Bob Jones U., 1993—. Deacon Northside Bapt. Ch., 1993—. Republican. Baptist. Home: 200 Wendfield Dr Travelers Rest SC 29690 Office: WJ Barge Meml Hosp 1700 Wade Hampton Blvd Greenville SC 29614

GODDARD, FRANCES BYRD, social worker; b. Greensboro, N.C., Aug. 11, 1935; d. Henry Davis and Blanche Leavell Blake; m. Anthony Edward Goddard, Oct. 10, 1964; 1 child, Caroline Stuart. BA in Sociology with honors, Converse Coll., 1961; MSW, U. N.C., 1963. Lic. social worker; diplomate Nat. Assn. Social Workers. Social worker Children's Home Soc., Richmond, Va., 1964-71; supr. of svcs. Coun. of Culpeper, Va., 1971-74; dir. Culpeper Mental Health, 1974-76, Culpeper Family Counseling, 1976—; exec. dir. Am. Assn. State Social Work Bds., Culpeper, 1989-94; bd. dirs. Va. Mental Health Assn.; adv. bd. PCU Sch. Social Work, Richmond. Author studies in field. NIMH traineeship NIMH. Mem. Holloway-Amiss-Leave II Soc. (sec./treas. 1990—), Nat. Clearinghouse on Licensure, Enforcements and Regulations, Nat. Orgn. of Competency Assurance, am. Soc. Assn. Exec., Va. Commonwealth U. Social Work Adv. Bd. (past chmn.), numerous others. Episcopalian. Office: Culpeper Family Counseling Ste A 400 South Ridge Pkwy Boston VA 22713

GODDY, LEONARD ALAN, surgeon; b. Pitts., Feb. 26, 1933; s. Abe and Jeanette (Fineman) G.; m. Lynn Francis Cassen, Aug. 24, 1955; children: David, Karen, Suzanne. AB, Washington and Jefferson Coll., 1954; MD, U. Louisville, 1958. Diplomate Am. Bd. Orthopedic Surgery. Asst. clin. prof. orthopedic surgery U. Louisville Sc. Medicine, 1970—, asst. clin. pediatric surgery, 1980—; mem. med. advisory Ky. Commn. for Children with Spl. Healthcare Needs, Louisville, 1993—. Lt. col. U.S. Army, 1967-69, Vietnam. Office: Goddy Leob Maurey PSC Ste 402 225 Abraham Flexner Way Louisville KY 40202-1846

GODFRAIND, THEOPHILE JOSEPH, pharmacologist educator; b. Bande, Belgium, Feb. 18, 1931; m. De Becker Anne, July 12, 1957; children: Pierre, Catherine. MB, U. Libre de Bruxelles, Belgium, 1951; MD, U. Catholique de Louvain, Belgium, 1955; Cert., Inst. de Med. Tropicale, Anvers, Belgium, 1958; PhD, U. Catholique de Louvain, Belgium, 1958.

Prof. U. Lovanium, Leopoldville, Congo, 1958-65, Université Catholique de Louvain, Brussels, 1965—; fellow Royal Acad. Medicine, Brussels, 1974-88, v.p., 1988-91, pres., 1991—; sec. gen. Internat. Union Pharmacology, 1987-94, pres., 1994—. Recipient Lauréat du Concours des Bourses de Voyage, 1955, Lauréat du Prix Spécia, 1955, Lauréat du Priz J.F. Heymans, 1967, Lauréat du prix Quinquennal des Sciences Thérapeutiques, 1973, Lauréat du Prix Smith Kline, 1982, Peter Debye prize U. Limburg, 1987, Lauréat du Prix de la Fondation de Physiopathologie Prof. Lucien Dautrebande, 1988, ASPET award, 1991. lMem. Acad. Royale de Médecine de Belgique, Acad. Nat. de Médecine de France, Acad. Nat. de Pharmacie de France, Acad. Europaea, Assn. des Physiologist, Deutsche Pharmakologische Gesellschaft, Biochem. Soc., Brit. Pharmacol. Soc., Physiol. Soc., N.Y. Acad. Scis., Am. Soc. for Pharmacology and Exptl. Therapeutics. Home: Rue du Bémel 19, B 1150 Brussels Belgium Office: Lab de Pharmacologie UCL 5410, Av Hippocrate 54, B-1200 Brussels Belgium

GODFREY, GEORGE CHEESEMAN, II, surgeon; b. Atlantic City, Oct. 15, 1926; s. William M. and Elizabeth (Uzzell) G.; m. Evelyn Fry, Sept. 20, 1952; children: Cheryl Lynn, George Cheeseman III. Student St. Bonaventure Coll., 1944, U. Ky., 1945; AB, Colgate U., 1948; MD, Jefferson Med. Coll., 1952. Intern, Atlantic City Hosp., 1952-53; resident in gen. surgery U.S. VA Hosp., Ft. Howard, Balt., 1953-57; practice medicine specializing in surgery, Somers Point, N.J., 1957—; chief gen. and trauma surgery, dir. dept. surgery Shore Meml. Hosp., Somers Point, 1973-76, dir. surgery, 1982-87; instr. surgery Jefferson Med. Coll., Phila., 1958-84; cons. in orthopedics and neurology N.J. Div. Disability Determinations, N.J. Rehab. Program, 1960—; physician FAA Tech. Center, part-time, 1977—, med. mgr., 1982-85; pres. Shore Surg. P.A., Atlantic Indsl. Med. Assocs. Contbr. article to profl. jours. Pres. Linwood (N.J.) Bd. Edn., 1972-73; mem. Atlantic County United Way, Atlantic County YMCA, Atlantic Performing Arts. Served with U.S. Army, 1944-46. Recipient Disting. Service award N.J. Jr. C. of C., 1960, Maroon Citation, Colgate U. Diplomate Am. Bd. Surgery, Am. Coll. Forsenic Medicine, Nat. Bd. Med. Examiners. Fellow ACS; mem. AMA, Am. Trauma Soc., Am. Soc. Abdominal Surgeons, Aerospace Med. Assn., Am. Coll. Occupational and Environ. Medicine, N.J., Atlantic County Med. Socs., Atlantic Indsl. Med. Physicians (pres.), Chainede Rotesseurs, Atlantic City Country Club, Marriott Seaview Country Club, Resorts Internat. Racquet Club, Kiwanis, Masons, Shriners, KT, Phi Kappa Tau, Phi Beta Pi. Methodist. Home: 112 Glenside Ave Linwood NJ 08221-2424 also: 5550 N Ocean Dr West Palm Beach FL 33404-2552 also: 674 Shore Rd Somers Point NJ 08244 also: 1616 Pacific Ave Atlantic City NJ 08401-6939 also: 705 White Horse Pike Absecon NJ 08201

GODFREY, HENRY GEORGE, surgeon; b. May Pen, Clerendon, Jamaica, Feb. 10, 1945; came to U.S., 1974.; MB, BS, U. W.I., Jamaica, 1973. Diplomate Am. Bd. Surgery. Intern Columbia Coll. Phys. and Surg./Harlem Hosp. Ctr., N.Y.C., 1974-75, resident in gen. surgery, 1975-79, fellow in gastrointestinal endoscopy, 1979-80; dir. surgery North Gen. Hosp., N.Y.C., 1989—; cons. Breast Exam. Ctr. Harlem, N.Y.C., 1984—; mem. Harlem exec. bd. N.Y.C. divsn. Am. Cancer Soc., 1995—. Recipient cert. of appreciation Nat. Black Leadership Initiative on Cancer, 1992. Fellow ACS. Office: North Gen Hosp 1879 Madison Ave New York NY 10035

GODFREY, MAURICE, biomedical scientist; b. Addis Ababa, Ethiopia, June 11, 1956; s. Robert and Liliana (Gandolfi) G.; m. Matilde Elena Almeida, July 5, 1985; children: C. Maximilian, R. Alessandro, D. Guillermo. BS, Monmouth Coll., 1977; MS, Columbia U., 1980, M in Philosophy, 1983, PhD, 1986. Postdoctoral fellow Oreg. Health Sci. U., Shrine Hosp., Portland, 1986-89; assoc. prof. pediatrics, dir. connective tissue lab. U. Nebr. Med. Ctr., Omaha, 1990—. Author: (with others) McKusick's Heritable Disorders of Connective Tissue, 1993, The Metabolic Basis of Inherited Disease, 1995; contbr. articles to profl. jours. Recipient grant-in-aid Am. Heart Assn., 1989, 93; Basil O'Connor scholar March of Dimes, 1991; established investigator Am. Heart Assn., 1995. Mem. AAAS, Am. Soc. of Human Genetics, Am. Fedn. for Clin. Rsch., Basic Sci. Coun. of the Am. Heart Assn. Office: U Nebr Med Ctr 600 S 42nd St Omaha NE 68105-1002*

GODLASKI, THEODORE MICHAEL, health facility administrator, researcher, educator; b. Cleve., Sept. 7, 1946; s. Edward James and Regina (Truszczynski) G.; m. Janice Emanuele, Oct. 17, 1975; children: Adam Paul, Aaron John, Leah Claire. BA, Borromeo Coll., 1968; MDiv, St. Mary's Theol. Sem., 1972; MA, John Carroll U., 1973. Dir. alcoholism treatment Bluegrass Bd. Mental Health/Mental Retardation, Inc., Lexington, Ky., 1975-82; dir. chem. dependency treatment Charter Ridge Hosp., Lexington, 1982-92, dir. adult treatment, 1992-94; cons. Growth Resources, Lexington, 1979-82; guest lectr. dept. psychiatry U. Ky., Lexington, 1982-94, prof. psychiatry Sch. Medicine and dir. comty. treatment rsch. Multidisciplinary Rsch. Ctr. on Alcohol and Drug Rsch., 1994—; mem. clin. faculty dept. nursing and allied health professions Ea. Ky. U., Richmond, 1986—. Contbr. articles to profl. jours. Mem. Gov.'s Task Force on Welfare Reform, Frankfort, Ky., 1985; mem. panel on human problems United Way, Lexington, 1989; mem. Mayor's Adv. Task Force on Addiction, Lexington, 1990—. Mem. Am. Coll. Addiction Treatment Adminstrs., Profl. Counselors Cert. Assn. (bd. govs. 1989-92). Home: 310 S Main St Winchester KY 40391-2458

GODSEY, WILLIAM COLE, physician; b. Memphis, Dec. 11, 1933; s. Monroe Dowe and Margaret Pauline (Cole) G.; m. Norma Jean Wilkinson, June 18, 1958; children: William Cole, John Edward, Robert Dowe. B.S., Rhodes Coll., 1955; M.D., U. Tenn., 1958. Diplomate Am. Bd. Psychiatry and Neurology. Intern John Gaston Hosp., Memphis, 1958-59; resident in psychiatry Gailor Meml. Hosp., Memphis, 1960-63; practice medicine specializing in psychiatry and neurology; asst. supt. Memphis Mental Health Inst., 1965-74; supt. Cen. State Hosp., Nashville, 1974-75; med. dir. Whitehaven Mental Health Ctr., Memphis, 1975-84, St. Joseph Hosp. Life Ctr., 1984-88; pres. Civilian Material Assistance, Memphis, 1988—; mem. staff St. Joseph Hosp., Eastwood Hosp.; asst. prof. U. Tenn. Coll. Medicine, 1965-74, Coll. Pharmacy, 1972-75; chief of staff Lakeside Hosp., Memphis, 1976-77; songwriter, pub.; pres. Memphis Country Music, Inc. Fellow Am. Psychiatric Assn. (past pres. West Tenn. chpt.); mem. Tenn. Psychiat. Assn. (exec. coun., past pres.), Tenn. Med. Assn., So. Med. Assn., Memphis and Shelby County Med. Soc., Nat. Rifle Assn., Moose. Methodist. Office: 5118 Park Ave Ste 323 Memphis TN 38117-5711

GODSON, GODFREY NIGEL, molecular geneticist, educator; b. London, June 20, 1936; s. Godfrey Edward and Elsie Louise (Harrington) G.; m. Barbara Cohen, Aug. 9, 1969; children: Rebecca Charlotte, Vanessa Alexandra. B.S., London U., 1957, Ph.D., 1961, D.Sc. (hon.), 1984. Research fellow Calif. Inst. Tech., 1964-67; staff scientist Nat. Insts. Med. Research, Med. Research Council, Mill Hill, London, 1968-69; asst. prof., assoc. prof. radiobiology Yale Med. Sch., New Haven, 1969-74, 1974-80; prof./chmn. dept. biochemistry NYU Med. Sch., N.Y.C., 1980—; mem. biochemistry sect. Nat. Bd. Med. Examiners, 1985-89; chmn. NIH, 1988-89; mem. tropical medicine and parasitology study sect. NIAID, 1985-90. Editor: Gene jour., 1984-96, Jour. Cell and Molecular Biology, 1984-86; contbr. chpts. to books, articles to profl. jours. Mem. Am. Soc. for Biochemistry and Molecular Biology, N.Y. Acad. Scis. Office: NYU Med Sch 550 1st Ave New York NY 10016-6481

GODWIN, BRUCE WAYNE, nurse corps officer; b. Del Rio, Tex., June 28, 1954; s. Owen Wilson and Thelma Jean (Dill) G.; m. Barbara Houston; 1 child, Brandon Bosworth. BS, Austin Peay, 1976; MSA, Cen. Mich., 1985; BSN, St. Louis U., 1990. RN, BLS instr., ACLS. Supply corps officer USN, 1976-90, nurse corps officer, 1990—. Lt. cmdr. USN, 1976—. Recipient Navy Achievement medal USN, 1994. Mem. Am. Assn. Nurse Anesthetists, Am. Soc. Post-Anesthesia Nurses, Internat. Anesthesia Rsch. Soc., Navy Nurse Corps. Assn. Home: 1519 B Carswell Circle Washington DC 20336 Office: Navy Med Ctr San Diego ASU SWA PSC 451 Med Dept FPO AE 09834-2800

GODWIN, SARA MOAK, retired medical research laboratory administrator; b. Phila., Miss., Jan. 26, 1924; d. Conway Columbus and Katie Elizabeth (Bridges) Moak; m. John Thomas Godwin, Mar. 5, 1948; children: Elizabeth, Thomas Adams, Patricia. BS, Miss. State Coll. Women, 1945. Cert. med. technologist. Med. technologist Touro Infirmary, New Orleans, 1945-48; chemist Meml.-Sloan Kettering Cancer Ctr., N.Y.C., 1948-49; mgr. med. lab. Med. Diagnostic and Rsch. Lab., Atlanta, 1965-90, ret. Mem. found. Ga. Rep., Atlanta, 1989. Mem. Am. Soc. Clin. Pathology (assoc.), Med. Assn. Atlanta Aux. (bd. dirs., treas. 2 yrs.), Med. Assn. Ga. Aux. (bd. dirs., treas. 1955), Atlanta Hist. Soc. (charter patron), Atlanta Bot. Gardens (founder), Ga. Trust for Hist. Preservation, Rose Garden Club, Emory U. Women's Club, Ga. Tech. Faculty Women's Club. Methodist. Home: 4691 Sentinel Post Rd NW Atlanta GA 30327-3915

GODWIN, WINSTON YUVAWN, JR., surgeon; b. Manning, S.C., Sept. 11, 1952; s. Winston Yuvawn and Mary (Hodge) G.; m. Kimberly Ann Thompson, Aug. 11, 1979; children: Ashley, Anna, Courtney, Kimberly, Amy, Mary-Chase. BS in Biology, The Citadel, 1974; MD, Med. U. S.C., 1978. Diplomate Am. Bd. of Surgery. Surgeon in pvt. practice Cheraw, S.C., 1983-85; ptnr. Randolph Surg. Assn., Charlotte, N.C., 1985—; mem. faculty Advanced Laparoscopic Tng. Ctr., Marietta, Ga., 1990-91, Carolinas Med. Ctr., Charlotte, 1995—. Bd. dirs. Chesterfield (S.C.) County Bd. Edn., 1984-85; exec. bd. dirs. Am. Cancer Soc., Mecklenberg, Charlotte, N.C., 1988—. Fellow ACS; mem. N.C. Med. Soc., Mecklenberg Med. Soc. Republican. Baptist. Office: Randolph Surg Assocs 2300 Randolph Rd Charlotte NC 28207

GODZIK, CATHLEEN A., orthopaedic surgeon, hand surgeon, educator; b. Mass., Apr. 4, 1954; d. Francis John and Jeannette Barbara Godzik. BA in Biology cum laude, Coll. of Holy Cross, 1976; MD, N.Y. Med. Coll., 1981. Diplomate Am. Bd. Orthopaedic Surgery, Am. Bd. Surgery of Hand; qualified med. evaluator, Calif.; cert. added qualification surgery of hand Fellow in immunology Rockefeller U., N.Y.C., 1976-77; intern Brown U. Sch. Medicine, Providence, 1981-82, resident in gen. surgery, 1982-83; resident in orthopaedic surgery U. Conn. Sch. Medicine, Hartford, 1983-86; Joseph Boyes fellow in hand surgery U. So. Calif., L.A., 1986-87, clin. assoc. prof.; chief hand svc. Orthopaedic Hosp., L.A., 1988—; dir. Inst. Hand and Upper Extremity Surgery, L.A., 1993—; dir. internat. vol. children's program, Calexico, Calif. and Mexicali, Mex., 1988—. Contbr. articles to med. jours. Chmn. support group for congenital upper extremity anomalies Children's Hosp. LA. Mem. Am. Acad. Orthopaedic Surgeons, Am. Soc. for Surgery of Hand, Western Orthopaedic Assn., Calif. Orthopaedic Assn., AO Alumni Assn., Phi Beta Kappa, Delta Sigma Mu. Republican. Office: Inst Hand and Upper Extremity Surgery 2300 S Hope St Ste 200 Los Angeles CA 90007

GOE, ERIC ALBERT, physician; b. N.Y.C., Jan. 21, 1948; s. George and Frieda H. (Zisca) G.; m. Carole A. Ryan, June 7, 1969; children: Deirdre, James, Siobhan. BS, Rensselaer Polytech. Inst., 1969; MD, Albany Med. Coll., 1973. Diplomate Am. Bd. Family Practice; cert. added qualifications in geriatrics. Intern U. Miami Affil Hosps., Coral Gables, 1973-74, resident Afful Hosp., 1974-76; pvt. practice Orlando, Fla., 1976-87; clin. instr. Fla. Hosp. Family Practice Residency, Orlando, 1976-91; asst. clin. prof. U. South Fla., Tampa, 1976-91; clin. dir. Park Care Cmty. Health Ctr., Orlando, 1987-90; med. dir. Cmty. Health Plan, Glens Falls, N.Y., 1990—; clin. assoc. faculty Grad. Program Nursing Sage Grad. Sch., 1995—; clin. asst. prof family practice Albany Med. Coll , 1996—; dir. Fla. Acad. Family Physicians, 1987-90; grant reviewer Am. Acad. Family Physicians Found. Mem. editorial rev. bd. Family Practice Rsch. Jour., 1987-94. Named Preceptor of Yr., Fla. Hosp., Orlando, 1987-88. Fellow Am. Acad. Family Physicians; mem. Warren County Med. Soc., Med. Soc. State of N.Y., N.Y. State Acad. Family Physicians. Office: Cmty Health Plan 747 Upper Glen St Queensbury NY 12804-2018

GOEBEL, MARISTELLA, retired clinical psychologist, educator; b. Racine, Wis., Sept. 10, 1915; d. James Nicholas and Henrietta Marie (Rademacher) Goebel. BS, Edgewood Coll., 1944; MA, Cath. U. Am., 1946, PhD, 1966. Diplomate Am. Bd. Clin. Biofeedback. Mem. Dominican Sisters; tchr. English Cathedral High Sch., Sioux Falls, S.D., 1946-47, Heart of Mary High Sch., Mobile, Ala., 1947-49; assoc. prof. edn. Rosary Coll., River Forest, Ill., 1949-61, prof. psychology, 1966-91, prof. emeritus, 1991—; clin. psychologist Hines VA Hosp., Ill., 1970-92; cons. Sinsinawa Dominican Sisters, Wis., 1966—. Author, editor tchr. guides Southeastern Curriculum Com., vols. Kindergarten-grade 8. Contbr. numerous articles to profl. jours. Mem. task force ch. related hypertension project Chgo. Heart Assn., 1979-92, NHLBI Hypertension Investigation Pooled Project, 1982-86. Citizens Ambassador Del. to China, 1987. Recipient NIH awards, 1962-63, 65-66, 82-84, Outstanding Achievement in Psychol. Research, Ill. Psychol. Assn., 1982; Performance award Hines VA Hosp., 1983. Clin. fellow Am. Assn. Biofeedback Clinicians, Des Plaines, Ill., 1983. Mem. AAAS, Am. Psychol. Assn., Assn. for Applied Psychophysiology and Biofeedback (cert.), Soc. Clin. and Exptl. Hypnosis, Internat. Soc. Hypnosis, Biofeedback Soc. Ill. (bd. dirs.), Soc. Behavioral Medicine. Avocations: gardening, knitting, bicycling. Home: 7900 Division St River Forest IL 60305-1066

GOEDKEN, ANN MARY, psychotherapist; b. Dubuque, Iowa, Feb. 28, 1949; d. Earl M. and Ruth A. (Evers) Wessels; m. Dennis D. Goedken, June 5, 1970; children: Eric, Jill. Diploma in nursing, Mercy Med. Ctr., Dubuque, 1970; BA, U. Wash., 1979; MS, Winona (Minn.) State U., 1989. RN, Wis.; approved psychotherapy provider, Wis.; cert. ind. clin. social worker, Wis., profl. counselor, Wis. Staff nurse, counselor to adolescents Mercy Med. Ctr., 1976-77; rsch. asst. U. Wash., Seattle, 1979; staff nurse, therapist St. Francis Med. Ctr., La Crosse, Wis., 1980, La Crosse Luth. Hosp., 1980-81; staff nurse, therapist Trempealeau County Health Care Ctr., Whitehall, Wis., 1981-89, psychotherapist, educator, 1989—. Mem. ACA, Assn. Specialists in Group Work, Internat. Assn. Marriage and Family Counselors, Nat. Honor Soc. Home: RR 3 Box 222 Osseo WI 54758-9367

GOEHLE, JOHN JEFFREY, healthcare executive, accountant; b. Buffalo, N.Y., Aug. 5, 1960; s. Ronald Kenneth and Betty Ann (Rhote) G.; m. Marlene Kay Jenner, May 16, 1987; children: Jenna Kristen, Kristen Nicole. BS, Ithaca Coll., 1982. CPA, N.Y. Sr. acct. Peat, Marwick, Mitchell and Co., Rochester, N.Y., 1982-86; mgr. KPMG Peat Marwick, Rochester, 1986-90; pres. The Eden Group, Rochester, 1990—; CFO, adminstr. Lattimore Community Surgicenter, Rochester, 1990—; ptnr., treas. Westfall Health Care Ctr., Rochester, 1990-96; mem. faculty St. John Fisher Coll., Rochester, 1993—; bd. dirs. Federated Ambulatory Surgery Assn., 1995—; mem. fin. devel. com. Monroe County chpt. ARC; mem. no. Subarea coun. Finger Lakes Health Sys. Agy., Rochester, 1991-95; mem. profl. adv. com. Monroe County Dept. Health, Rochester, 1991—. Treas. Montgomery Neighborhood Ctr., Rochester, 1985-96; leader disaster team ARC, Rochester, 1992—. Mem. AICPA, N.Y. Soc. CPA, Healthcare Fin. Mgmt. Assn., Am. Hosp. Assn., Soc. for Ambulatory Care Profls., Am. Mgmt. Assn., Am. Coll. Healthcare Execs., N.Y. State Assn. Ambulatory Surgery Ctrs. (past pres.). Republican. Lutheran. Home: 64 Lansmere Way Rochester NY 14624-1166 Office: Lattimore Surgicenter 125 Lattimore Rd Rochester NY 14620-4155

GOEHNER, ELAINE DALKE, nursing administrator, educator; b. Newport, Wash., June 23, 1943; d. Henry Unruh and Edna Sylvia (Nafziger) Dalke; m. Delbert M. Goehner, Aug. 2, 1963; children: Jewellyn C. Goehner Forrest, Darin Morris. Diploma, L.A. County Gen. Hosp. Sch. Nursing, 1964; BSN, L.A. State Coll., 1966; MSN in Med.-Surg., Pediat., Nursing Edn., Calif. State U., L.A., 1975; PhD in Edn., Claremont (Calif.) Grad. Sch., 1992. RN, Calif.; cert. child adolescent nurse. Instr. med.-surg. nursing and pharmacology L.A. County Gen. Hosp. Sch. Nursing, 1966-68; charge nurse, surg. specialties (ENT) L.A County U. So. Calif. Med. Ctr., 1968-72; instr. pediatric nursing Calif. State U., L.A., 1972-75; prof. pediatrics, med.-surg. nursing, nursing adminstrn. Azusa (Calif.) Pacific U., 1975—; asst. dir. nursing Childrens Hosp. L.A., 1984-90; dir. nursing ops. Glendora (Calif.) Cmty. Hosp., 1990-92; dir. profl. practice devel. Huntington Meml. Hosp., Pasadena, Calif., 1992—. Mem. Orgn. Nursing Execs., Nat. Assn. Pediatric Nurses Assocs. and Practitioners, Rsch. in Nursing (charter mem.), N.Am. Nursing Diagnosis Assn., So. Calif. Nursing Diagnosis Assn., Philathian Honor Soc., Phi Kappa Phi, Sigma Theta Tau. Home: 2950 Lombardy Rd Pasadena CA 91107

GOELLNITZ, GERHARD-CARL, medical educator; b. Güstrow, Germany, Apr. 28, 1920; s. Carl-Alrik and Anna-Marie (Schroeder) G.; m. Hildegard Henriette Röhr, Aug. 29, 1947; children: Gabriele, Ulrike. MD, Rostock (Germany) U., 1945. Resident in neurology, psychiatry and child neuropsychiatry Rostock U., 1945-51, head physician Clinic Psychiatry and Neurology, 1952, lectr. faculty medicine, 1953, prof. dept. child neuropsychiatry, 1958, prof. emeritus faculty medicine, 1985—, dir. dept. child neuropsychiatry, 1958-85. Author, editor: Manual About Child and Adolescent Neuropsychiatry, 1st edit., 1970, 5th edit., 1991; editor 11 textbooks about child neuropsychiatry, 1955-90; contbr. 130 sci. articles to European and U.S. profl. jours., 1947-91. With M.C. German mil., 1941-44. Recipient Austrian Hon. Cross 1st class for Sci. and Art, Pres. Fed. Rep. of Austria, Vienna, 1990. Mem. Austrian Soc. Child and Adolescent Neuropsychiatry and Psychology (hon.), Hungarian Psychiat. Soc. (hon.), German Soc. Child and Adolescent Psychiatry and Psychotherapy (hon.). Home: Strandweg 5, D-18119 Rostock-Warnemuende Germany

GOEPP, ROBERT AUGUST, dental educator, oral pathologist; b. Chgo., Nov. 3, 1930; s. Charles August and Ernestine Josephine (Mertz) G.; m. Iraida Pineiro, July 9, 1960; children—Robert C., Heidi M., Myra J. B.S. in Biology, Loyola U.-Chgo., 1954, D.D.S., 1957; M.S. in Pathology, U. Chgo., 1961, Ph.D. in Pathology, 1967. Instr. to assoc. prof. Sch. Medicine, U. Chgo., 1961-75, prof. dentistry and pathology, 1975-96, prof. emeritus, 1996—; med. Med. Radiation Adv. Coun. FDA, 1979-82; mem. Nat. Coun. Radiation Protection, Washington, 1976-94. Contbr. articles to profl. jours. Recipient Career Devel. award USPHS, 1970. Fellow Am. Coll. Dentists, Internat. Coll. Dentists, Am. Acad. Oral Pathology, Am. Acad. Dental Radiology (pres. 1974), Ill. Soc. Oral Pathologists (pres. 1977-78), Inst. Medicine Chgo., Odontographic Soc. Chgo. (bd. dirs., treas. 1993—); mem. ADA (chmn. coun. dental rsch. 1981-82). Roman Catholic. Office: U Chgo Zoller Dental Clinic 5841 S Maryland Ave Chicago IL 60637-1463

GOETCHEUS, JOHN STEWART, orthopaedic surgeon; b. Cin., May 14, 1938; s. Lester Frederick and Elizabeth (Gibson) G.; m. Janice Berg, July 13, 1963; children: Amy, Gregory. BA, DePauw U., 1960; MD, Case Western Res. U., 1964. Cert. Nat. Bd. Examiners, Am. Bd. Orthopaedic Surgery. Surgeon USAF, Edwards, Calif., 1966-68; resident orthopaedic surgery Yale New Haven Hosp., Yale Sch. Medicine, 1968-71; pvt. practice orthopaedic surgery Essex, Conn., 1971—; cons. orthopaedic surgery West Haven (Conn.) Vets. Hosp., 1970—; clin. instr. orthopaedic surgery Yale Med. Sch., New Haven, 1970—. Elected mem. regional Dist. 4 Bd. Edn., Essex, Deep River, Chester, 1983-89; mem. bd. visitors DePauw U., Greencastle, Ind., 1990-93. Fellow Ea. Orthopaedic Assn. (bd. dirs. 1991, 94—, treas. 1994—); mem. Am. Acad. Orthopaedic Surgeons. Republican. Home: 14 Partridge Ln Essex CT 06426-1428 Office: PO Box 697 Essex CT 06426-0697

GOETTSCHE, DENISE STALLINGS, physician; b. Walnut Creek, Calif., Aug. 19, 1961; d. Dale Grow and Reane (Hunter) Stallings; m. Jeffrey Lynn Goettsche, July 26, 1986; 1 child, Shannon Renae. BS, Brigham Young U., 1984; DO, Coll. Osteo. Medicine Pacific, Pomona, Calif., 1989. Diplomate Am. Bd. Family Practice. Intern San Bernardino County Med. Ctr., 1989-90, resident, 1990-92; physician Yorba Park Med. Group, Orange, Calif., 1992—. Ch. music singing instr. children LDS Ch., Anaheim, Calif., 1994. Mem. Calif. Med. Assn., Orange County Med. Assn. Republican. Office: Yorba Park Med Group 2501 E Chapman Ave Orange CA 92669

GOETZ, KENNETH LEE, cardiovascular physiologist, research consultant; b. Java, S.D., Jan. 7, 1932; m. Shirley Anne Caldwell, July 14, 1962; children: Gregory Earl, Anne Katherine. PhD, U. Wis., 1963; MD, U. Kans., 1967. Instr., asst. prof. dept. physiology U. Kans. Med. Ctr., Kansas City, 1963-69; med. intern St. Luke's Hosp., Kansas City, 1969, head, div. of exptl. medicine, 1970-91, dir. rsch., 1980-91; adj. prof. dept. physiology U. Kans. Med. Ctr., 1976-92; vis. prof. U. Kuopio, Finland, 1985, 91, U. Munich, 1992; vis. scientist German Inst. Aerosapce Medicine, Cologne, 1993-94. Recipient Alexander von Humboldt award, 1992. Fellow Am. Phys. Soc. (circulation sect.); mem. Am. Physiol. Soc., Alexander von Humboldt Assn. of Am. Home: 4856 Black Swan Dr Shawnee Mission KS 66216-1237

GOETZKE, GLORIA LOUISE, social worker, income tax specialist; b. Monticello, Minn.; d. Wesley and Marvel (Kreidler) G. BA, U. Minn., 1964; MSW, U. Denver, 1966; MBA, U. St. Thomas, 1977. Cert. enrollment to practice before IRS. Social worker VA Med. Ctr., L.A., 1980—; master tax preparer and instr. H&R Block, Santa Monica, Calif.; clin. instr. UCLA Grad. Sch. Social Welfare; adj. prof. Calif. State U., Long Beach Grad. Sch. of Social Work. Mem. Nat. Assn. Social Workers (cert.). Lutheran.

GOFF, CHRISTOPHER WALLICK, pediatrician; b. Phila., Jan. 24, 1948; s. Donald Heiserman and Jean Christman Wallick G.; m. Holly Lynn Housner, Aug. 1970; children: Heather Elizabeth, Rebecca Ann, Abigail Christine. BA in Psychology, Yale U., 1970; MD, U. Pa., 1974. Diplomate Am. Bd. Pediatrics, Pediatric Endocrinology, Nat. Bd. Med. Examiners. Intern, then resident in pediatrics Yale-New Haven (Conn.) Hosp., 1974-76, chief resident in pediatrics, 1977; pvt. practice specializing in pediatrics Wildwood Pediatrics, Essex, Conn., 1977—; alternate dir. Health Town of Essex, 1980-81, dir. Health, 1981—; co-dir. Child Diagnostic Assocs., Essex, 1983—; assoc. staff Yale-New Haven Hosp., 1977-80, attending staff, 1980—; clin. instr. Pediatrics Yale U. Sch. Med., 1977-79, clin. asst. prof., 1979—; bd. dirs. Wildwood Med. Ctr. Assn., 1986-89, treas. 1988—; co-med. adviser Mt. St. John Sch., Deep River, Conn., 1977—, Oxford Acad., Westbrook, Conn., 1990-95; acting med. adviser Essex Elem. Sch., 1981—; med. adviser Old Saybrook Sch. sys., 1992—. Reviewer Clinical Pediatrics; clin. reactor Contemporary Pediatrics; contbr. articles to prof. jours. Chmn. prof. adv. com. Visiting Nurses Lower Valley, 1980—; devel. bd. Tri-Town Youth Svc. Bur., 1987-88; mem. Sexual Abuse Prevention Task Force, 1987-95, Tri-Town Substance Abuse Task Force, 1988—, Westbrook Sexual Abuse Prevention Task Force, 1988-93, Shoreline Child Protection Team, 1988—, Tri-Town Sexual Abuse Response Team, 1990-91; vestryman St. John's Episcopal Ch., Essex., 1978-79, sr. warden, 1979-83, coord. Youth Ministry program, 1986—, treas. 1994—; lector 1989—; pres. Marlins Parents Club, 1989-91; bd. dirs. Lower Valley Cmty. Health Svcs., 1979-80, Essex Ambulance Assn., 1985-89, Cougar Aquatic Team, 1992—, v.p. 1992-93, treas. 1993-94. Recipient Joel Gordon Miller award, 1974. Fellow Am. Acad. Pediatrics; mem. AMA, N. Am. Soc. Pediatric and Adolescent Gynecology, New England Soc. Clin. Hypnosis, Conn. State Med. Soc. (malpractice claims rev. bd., 1981-84), New Haven County Med. Soc., Lawson Wilkins Pediatric Endocrine Soc. Republican. Office: Wildwood Pediatrics and Adol Med 1 Wildwood Medical Center Essex CT 06426

GOFF, ROBERT EDWARD, health plan executive; b. Worcester, Mass., Nov. 19, 1952; s. Julius Lewis and Doris (Katz) G.; m. Jinny Sue Yaver, June 30, 1985; 1 child, Blake Adam. BBA with honors, Northeastern U., Boston, 1976; MBA with honors, Babson Coll., 1978; cert., Cornell U., 1981. Adminstrv. dir. Adirondack PSRO Inc., Glens Falls, N.Y., 1977-80; v.p. No. Met. Hosp. Assn., Newburgh, N.Y., 1980-83, Good Samaritian Hosp., Suffern, N.Y., 1983-85; exec. dir., chief exec. dir. WellCare N.Y., Inc., Newburgh, 1985—; pres. Wellcare Leasing Corp., Newburgh, N.Y., 1990-96, Well Care Med. Mgmt. Inc., 1992-96; exec. v.p. Well Care Mgmt. Group, Inc., 1992—; bd. dirs. Wellcare Mgmt. Group Inc.; pres. Wellcare Med. Mgmt.; cons. in field. Bd. dirs. Hospice Care, Inc., Hospice of Orange Inc. Recipient Vigil Honor award Order Arrow, 1969, Eagle Scout award Boy Scouts Am., 1970. Mem. Hudson Valley Hosp. Exec. Assn. (pres., bd. dirs. 1982-85), Healthcare Fin. Mgmt. Assn., Am. Coll. Hosp. Adminstrs., Beta Gamma Soc. Home: 93 Old Castle Point Rd Wappingers Falls NY 12590-9801 Office: Wellcare of NY Park West Hurley Ave Ext PO Box 4059 Kingston NY 12401

GOFMAN, JOHN DAVID, physician, ophthalmologist; b. San Francisco, May 28, 1947; s. John William and Helen (Fahl) G.; m. Betty S. Lawrence, Sept. 5, 1993. BA, U. Calif., Berkeley, 1969; MD, Stanford U., 1974. Intern in internal medicine U. Wash., Seattle, 1974-75, resident in ophthalmology, 1976-79; dept. chief ophthalmology U.S. Pub. Health Hosp., Seattle, 1979-81, Pacific Med. Ctr., Seattle, 1981-89; assoc. clin. prof. ophthalmology U. Wash., Seattle, 1979—; ptnr. Eye Clinic of Bellevue, Wash., 1989—. Recipient Alumni scholarship award Stanford U., 1979. Fellow Am. Acad. Ophthalmology; mem. Phi Beta Kappa. Office: Eye Clinic of Bellevue 1300 116th Ave NE Bellevue WA 98004

GOGAN, CATHERINE MARY, dental educator; b. Buffalo, Feb. 9, 1959; d. John Francis and Mary Louise (Solomon) G. BA, SUNY, Buffalo, 1981,

DDS, 1985, MS, 1995. Resident Erie County Med. Ctr., Buffalo, 1985-86, attending dentist, 1986—, dental residency coord., 1987—, dental dir. skilled nursing facility, 1989—; pvt. practice Buffalo, 1986—; clin. instr. SUNY, Buffalo, 1987-88, asst. prof., 1988—. Editor mag. UB Dental Report, 1989-94 (Golden Scroll award); contbr. articles to profl. jours. Fellow Am. Assn. Hosp. Dentists; mem. ADA, Am. Assn. Dental Schs., Orgn. Tchrs. Oral Diagnosis, Acad. Dentistry for Persons with Disabilities, Am. Soc. Geriatric Dentistry, U. Buffalo Dental Alumni Assn. (sec. 1988-89, v.p. 1989-90, pres. 1990-91), Mt. Mercy Acad. Alumni Assn. (bd. dirs. 1990-91), Omcicron Kappa Upsilon (v.p., pres.-elect Lambda Lambda chpt., pres. Lambda Lambda chpt. 1996-97). Roman Catholic. Office: SUNY at Buffalo Dept Oral Diagnostic Scis 355 Squire Hall Buffalo NY 14214

GOISMAN, ROBERT MICHAEL, psychiatrist; b. Milw., Nov. 5, 1947; s. Max Marvin and Shirley Ruth (Levings) G.; m. Jeanne M. Traxler, Aug. 31, 1975; children: Matthew Abraham Traxler Goisman, Jacob Isadore Traxler Goisman. BA with honors, U. Wis., 1970, MD, 1974. Diplomate Am. Bd. Psychiatry and Neurology. Resident psychiatry U. Cin. 1977; instr. psychiatry U. Cin. Coll. Medicine, 1977-79; instr. psychiatry Harvard Med. Sch., Boston, 1979-93, asst. prof. psychiatry, 1993—; pvt. practice psychiatry Boston, 1979—; dir. phobia clinic Mass. Mental Health Ctr., Boston, 1985—; clinic dir. Brighton-Allston Mental Health Clinic, Brighton, Mass., 1988-90; med. dir. Continuing Case Svc. Mass. Mental Health Ctr., Boston, 1991-92, dir. outpatient tng. and rsch., 1992—, dir. med. student edn., 1994—; vis. prof. dept. psychiatry U. Cin., 1988. Contbr. articles to profl. jours. Bd. trustees Temple Israel, Boston, 1982-85. Summer fellow NIMH, 1971, Ginsburg fellow Group for the Advancement Psychiatry, 1976-78. Fellow Am. Psychiat. Assn.; mem. Anxiety Disorders Assn., Assn. for Advancement of Behavior Therapy, Am. Assn. Cmty. Psychiatry (Mass. state rep. 1989-92, nat. bd. dirs. 1992-96). Jewish. Office: Mass Mental Health Ctr 74 Fenwood Rd Boston MA 02115-6196

GOLAB, WLODZIMIERZ ANDRZEJ, biologist, geographer, librarian; b. Kozmin, Poland, Mar. 10, 1938; s. Andrzej and Irena (Borowska) G.; m. Maria Malgorzata Grygiel, June 18, 1969; children: Dagmara, Filip. Degree, U. Mickiewicza, Poznan, Poland, 1968. Libr. Polish Acad. Sci., Poznan, 1968-75; dir. reading rm. U. Poly, Poznan, 1975-81; dir. main libr. U. Agr., Poznan, 1981—; cons. Green Libr., Poznan, 1990-92; mem. com. info. sci. Polish Acad. Sci., 1972—t. Contbr. to profl. publs. Roman Catholic. Home: Osiedle Przyjazni 11/91, Poznan 61685, Poland Office: Biblioteka Glowna AR, Ul Witosa 45, Poznan Poland

GOLBUS, MITCHELL S., geneticist; b. Chgo., Apr. 6, 1939. BS, Ill. Inst. Tech., 1959; MD, U. Chgo., 1963. Diplomate Am. Bd. Ob-Gyn. Rsch. fellow med. genetics and asst. rsch. geneticist U. Calif., San Francisco, 1971-73, clin. instr. dept. ob-gyn., 1972-73, asst. prof., 1973-77, assoc. prof. ob-gyn. and pediat., 1981—; mem. adv. com. genetics Calif. State Dept. Health, 1973—; mem. No. Calif. Tay-Sachs Disease Prevention Program, 1973—; clin. rsch. grant rev. com. March of Dimes, 1978—; NIH Task Force Predictors Hereditary Disease and Congential Defects, 1978-79; mem. med. adv. com. Nat. Genetics Found., 1981—; mem. sci. adv. com. Nat. Tay-Sachs and Allied Disease Assn., 1980—. Fellow Am. Coll. Obstetricians and Gynecologists; mem. AAAS, Inst. Medicine-NAS, Am. Soc. Human Genetics, Soc. Gynecol. Investigation. Office: UC-San Francisco School of Medicine 513 Parnassus Ave San Francisco CA 94143-0410*

GOLD, BARRY STEVEN, internist, educator; b. Balt., Feb. 25, 1947. BS, U. Md., 1969, postgrad., 1969-70, MD, 1974. Diplomate Am. Bd. Internal Medicine. Intern Md. Gen. Hosp., Balt., 1974-75, jr. asst. resident in medicine, 1975-76, sr. asst. resident in medicine, 1976-77, chief resident, 1977-78; instr. medicine Johns Hopkins U. Sch. Medicine, 1992-94, asst. prof. medicine, 1994—; pvt. in internal medicine and toxinology; cons. Nat. Aquarium, Balt. Zoo, Washington Zoo, Md. Poison Ctr., Nat. Capital Poison Ctr., Tenn. Poison Ctr., Office of the Inspector Gen., FBI, US Armed Forces; cons. med. dir. Md. Medicare, 1988-94; presenter in field. Contbr. articles to profl. jours. Recipient Best Article award Md. Med. Jour., 1990, Gov.'s citation, 1995. Fellow ACP; mem. Internat. Soc. Toxinology, Internat. Soc. Aquatic Medicine, Md. Herpetological Soc., Wilderness Medicine Soc., Med. and Chirurgical Faculty State of Md. (mem. peer rev. 1981-84, mem. pub. rels. com. 1984-87, mem. com. on drugs 1988-89, mem. com. on AIDS 1989-90, mem. third party liaison com. 1989—, chmn. carrier adv. com. liaison 1995—), Balt. City Med. Soc. Office: 122 Slade Ave Ste 201 Baltimore MD 21208

GOLD, BERNARD LEON, allergist; b. Dallas, Jan. 6, 1950; s. Allen Jay and Donnis Bolin (Fernandez) G.; m. Patricia; children: Benjamin, Courtney. BA, U. Mont., 1973; MD, Baylor U., Houston, 1977. Diplomate Am. Bd. Internal Medicine, Am. Bd. Allergy and Immunology. Resident internal medicine St. Joseph Hosp., Ann Arbor, Mich., 1981; resident allergy and immunology U. Mich., Ann Arbor, 1984; head allergy Toledo Clinic, 1984-90; clin. asst. prof. U. Mich., Ann Arbor, Mich., 1986—. Fellow Am. Coll. Allergy, Am. Acad. Allergy; mem. ACP, Mich. State Med. Soc., Sheldon Soc. Office: 4870 W Clark Rd Ste 203 Ypsilanti MI 48197-1104

GOLD, DANIEL HOWARD, ophthalmologist, educator; b. N.Y.C., Sept. 21, 1942; s. Isadore and Leona (Cotton) G.; m. Joann Aaron, Oct. 22, 1966 (div. Sept. 1985); m. Barbara Wood, June 19, 1988; children: David, Abigail, Michael. Student, U. Mich., 1959-66. Diplomate Am. Bd. Ophthalmology. Asst. chief dept. ophthalmology Walter Reed Army Med. Ctr., Washington, 1972-74; asst. prof. dept. ophthalmology Montefiore Hosp. Med. Ctr., Bronx, N.Y., 1974-76; asst. clin. prof. med. br. U. Tex., Galveston, 1977-85, assoc. clin. prof. med. br., 1986-91; physician, ophthalmologist Eye Clinic of Tex., Galveston, 1977—; clin. prof. ophthalmology med. br. U. Tex., Galveston, 1991—; mem. med. staff exec. com. St. Mary's Hosp., Galveston, 1989-90, 95-96, chmn. dept. surgery, 1995-96. Editor: (textbook) The Eye in Systemic Disease, 1990; sec. editor Duanes Clinical Ophthalmology, 1974—, Current Opinion in Ophthalmology, 1991—; contbr. articles to profl. jours. Maj. U.S. Army, 1972-74. Fellow Am. Acad. Ophthalmology (mem. self-assessment com. 1989-92, Honor award 1985), Royal Coll. Ophthalmologists Gt. Britain, N.Y. Acad. Medicine; mem. Macula Soc., Assn. for Rsch. in Vision and Ophthalmology, Pan Am. Assn. Ophthalmology, Galveston Physicians Svc. Assn. (bd. dirs. 1985—, pres. 1993—), Tex. Med. Assn. (coun. on pub. health 1995—). Jewish. Office: Eye Clinic Tex 2302 Avenue P Galveston TX 77550-7992

GOLD, JAY JOSEPH, retired internist, endocrinologist; b. N.Y.C., Feb. 17, 1923; s. Morris D. and Estelle S. (Spiegel) G.; m. Rhea Lane, June 11, 1950; children: Erica Sinsheimer, Leah Korth. MD, SUNY, N.Y.C., 1950. Diplomate Am. Bd. Internal Medicine. Intern Bklyn. Jewish Hosp., 1950-51, resident in medicine, 1951-52; resident in medicine Bronx (N.Y.) VA Hosp., 1954-55; fellow in endocrinology Columbia Presbyn. Med. Ctr., N.Y.C., 1952-54; dir. dept. human reprodn. Michael Reese Hosp., Chgo., 1955-64; chmn. sect. endocrinology St. Francis Hosp., Evanston, Ill., 1965-92; clin. prof. medicine U. Ill., Chgo., 1972-92, adj. prof. ob-gyn., 1972-92; lectr. Loyola Coll. Medicine, Chgo., 1972-92. Editor: Gynecologic Endocrinology, 1968, 4th edit., 1986. Sgt. U.S. Army, 1943-46; ETO. Fellow ACP, Am. Coll. Endocrinology; mem. Endocrine Soc., Am. Soc. Internal Medicine, Am. Assn. Clin. Endocrinology.

GOLD, JONATHAN W.M., internist, educator; b. N.Y.C., July 6, 1944; s. Abraham D. and Tanya L. Gold; m. Christy E. Joyce; children: Allison, Jennifer, Jeremy. BA, Columbia Coll., 1965; MD, Columbia U. Coll. Phys & Surg, 1971. Diplomate Am. Bd. Internal Medicine. From asst. to assoc. attending Mem. Sloan-Kettering Cancer Ctr., N.Y.C., 1978-90, from asst. to dir. spl. microbiology lab., 1978-90; assoc. prof. medicine Cornell U. Med. Coll., 1978-90; chief medicine Bronx Lebanon Hosp. Ctr., 1990—; prof. medicine Albert Einstein Coll. Medicine, 1990—. Linda Laubenstein award for HIV excellence N.Y. Dept. Health, 1993. Office: Bronx-Lebanon Hosp Ctr 1650 Grand Concourse New York NY 10457

GOLD, JOSEPH, medical researcher; b. Binghamton, N.Y., Jan. 17, 1930; s. Leon and Gertrude J. G.; m. Judith Barbara Taylor, June 12, 1955; children: Shannon Gabriel, Skye Raphael. AB, Cornell U., 1952; MD, SUNY Health Sci. Ctr., Syracuse, 1956. Fellow dept. pharmacology SUNY Health Sci. Ctr., Syracuse, 1961-62, rsch. asst. prof., 1962-64, asst. prof. pathology, 1964-65; dir. Syracuse Cancer Rsch. Inst., 1965—, trustee, 1965—. Author numerous articles on cancer research and therapy; contbr. chpts. to med. textbooks on ill effects of heat stress. Served with USAF, 1958-61. Recipient Presdl. citation for work in Mercury Astronaut Selection Program, 1960; USPHS postdoctoral rsch. fellow U. Calif. Sch. Medicine, 1956-58; named Disting. Grad. Binghamton Sch. Dist., 1994. Mem. Am. Assn. Cancer Rsch., Am. Assn. for Lab. Animal Sci., N.Y. Acad. Scis., Onondaga County Med. Soc., Med. Soc. State N.Y. Home: 127 Edgemont Dr Syracuse NY 13214-2010 Office: 600 E Genesee St Syracuse NY 13202-3111

GOLD, JOSEPH F., physician, health facility administrator; b. Phila., July 7, 1947; s. Saul J. and Rose (Rosenthal) G.; m. Ellen Susan Pievsky, Jan. 12, 1974; children: Brian Saul, Lauren Ivy. BA, Temple U., 1969; DO, Phila. Coll. Osteo. Med., 1974. Diplomate Am. Bd. Family Practice. Pvt. practice Phila., 1975—; clin. assoc. prof. Coll. Allied Health, Phila., 1978, Hahneman U., Phila., 1996; physician Olney Logan Med. Ctr., Phila., 1975—, med. dir., 1975-96; bd. dirs. Greater Del. Valley Ind. Practice Assn., Phila., 1994-95; dir. clin. trials and rsch. Therapeutic Cons., Phila., 1995-96, Joseph F. Gold D.O. and Assoc., Phila. Bd. dirs. Logan Bus. Assn., Phila., 1995. Mem. Am. Osteo. Medicine Assn., Pa. Osteo. Medicine Assn., Am. Coll. Osteo. Medicine Family Practice, Phila. County Osteo. Medicine, Pa. Osteo. Family Practice, Pa. State Osteo. Medicine Family Practice. Office: 4817-21 N Broad St Philadelphia PA 19141

GOLD, JUDITH HAMMERLING, psychiatrist; b. N.Y.C., June 24, 1941; d. James S. and Anne (Linder) Hammerling; m. Edgar Gold, June 27, 1965. M.D., Dalhousie U., 1965. Intern Victoria Gen. Hosp., Halifax, N.S., Can., 1964-65; resident Dalhousie U., Halifax, 1967-71; practice medicine specializing in psychiatry Halifax, 1971—; staff psychiatrist Dalhousie U. Student Health Clinic, 1971-73; vis. colleague U. Wales Med. Sch., 1973-75; asst. prof. dept. psychiatry Dalhousie U., Halifax, 1975-78, assoc. prof., 1978-80, part-time, 1980-87. Editor: Clinical Practice Series, 1987—, 5 books; contbr. articles to profl. jours. Bd. govs. Mt. St. Vincent U., 1981-87, chmn., 1986-87. Med. Research Council Can. fellow, 1973-75; Health and Welfare Bd. Can. grantee, 1976-78. Fellow Am. Psychiat. Assn., Am. Coll. Psychiatrists (1st v.p. 1990-91, pres.-elect 1991-92, pres. 1992-93); mem. Can. Psychiat. Assn. (pres. 1981-82), Royal Coll. Phys. Surgeons Can. (exec. mem. 1992-94, coun. 1991—), Order Can., Alpha Omega Alpha. Office: 5991 Spring Garden Rd Ste 375, Halifax, NS Canada B3H 1Y6

GOLD, LARRY ALAN, endocrinologist; b. Kansas City, Mo., Jan. 23, 1949; m. Susan E. Gold, June 9, 1974; children: Bennett, Zachary. BA, U. Kans., 1971, MD, 1974. Diplomate Am. Bd. Endocrinology & Metabolism. Intern, resident Jacksonville Hosp. Edn. Program, U. Fla., 1974-77; fellow U. Fla., Gainesville, 1977-79; pvt. practice Colorado Springs, 1979—. Office: 325 E Fontanero Colorado Springs CO 80907

GOLD, MARK STEPHEN, psychopharmacologist, physician; b. N.Y.C., May 6, 1949; s. Meyer M. and Helene (Levy) G.; m. Janice Finn, June 19, 1971; 4 children. BA, Washington U., 1967; MD, U. Fla., 1975. Neurobehavior fellow Yale U. Sch. Medicine, 1975-78; dir. research Fair Oaks Hosp., Summit, N.J., 1978-91; vis. prof. psychiatry and neuroscience U. Fla., 1991-92, prof. depts. neurosci., psychiatry, cmty. health, family medicine, 1992—; cons. substance abuse unit Yale U. Sch. Medicine, 1979-89; founder Nat. Cocaine Hotline 800-COCAINE, 1983; cons. Office Drug Abuse Policy White House, 1984-86; presdl. appointee White House Conf. for Drug Free Am., 1988, William Bennett Kitchen Cabinet, 1988-90; spl. cons. Office Nat. Drug Policy, 1995—; mem. adv. bd., Am. Coun. Drug Edn.; bd. dirs. P.R.I.D.E., Physicians for Prevention, DARE, Child Welfare League. Editor-in-Chief Facts About Tobacco, Alcohol and other Drugs; co-editor Internat. Jour. Psychiatry in Medicine, Advances in Substance and Alcohol Abuse, Jour. Substance Abuse Treatment, ASAM Prins. Addiction Medicine, Am. Jour. Drug and Alcohol; contbr. articles to profl. jours. and books; author: 800-Cocaine, 1984, Stop Drugs at Work, 1986, Wonder Drugs, 1987, The Good News About Depression, 1987, rev. edit., 1995, The Facts About Drugs and Alcohol, 1987, Marijuana, 1989, The Good News about Panic, Anxiety and Phobias, 1989, Alcohol, 1991, Dual Diagnosis in Substance Abuse, 1991, The Good News About Drugs and Alcohol, 1991, Cocaine, 1993, Pharmacological Therapies for Drug and Alcohol Addiction, 1995, Tobacco, 1995; patentee in field. Recipient Seymour F. Lustman award for research Yale U. Sch. Medicine, 1978, Founds Fund prize for research in psychiatry Am. Psychiat. Assn. Found., 1981, Presdl. award for Disting. Leadership in Psychiat. Research Nat. Assn. Pvt. Psychiat. Hosps., 1982, Silver Anvil award Am. Council Drug Edn., 1984, Nat. Fedn. Parents award, 1986; named one of Today's Most Valuable Persons, USA Today, 1986, one of People of Yr., 1987, one of Best Psychiatrists in Am., Good Housekeeping, 1995, one of Best Doctors in Am., 1993—; NIMH grantee. Fellow Am. Coll. Clin. Pharmacology; Fellow Am. Psychiat. Assn.; mem. AAAS, Am. Soc. Addiction Med., Soc. Neurosci., Internat. Soc. Psychoneuroendocrinology. Office: Brain Inst Depts Neurosci and Psychiatry PO Box 100244 Gainesville FL 32610-0244

GOLD, PAUL ERNEST, psychology educator, behavioral neuroscience educator; b. Detroit, Jan. 7, 1945; s. Hyman and Sylvia (Lerman) G.; children: Scott David Gold, Zachary Alexander Korol-Gold. BA, U. Mich., 1966; MS, U. N.C., 1968; PhD, 1971. NIH postdoctoral fellow, lectr. psychobiology U. Calif., Irvine, 1972-76; asst. prof. U. Va., Charlottesville, 1976-78, assoc. prof., 1978-81, prof., 1981—, dir. neurosci. grad. program, 1991-95. Editor: Psychobiology, Austin, Tex., 1990—; contbr. over 150 articles to sci. publs. Recipient James McKeen Cattell award, 1983, Sesquicentennial Assn. award, U. Va., 1983, 90; NIH fellow, 1967. Fellow APA, Am. Psychol. Soc. (mem. com. 1990-91, program com. 1991); mem. Soc. for Neurosci. com. on Animals in Rsch., NSF Adv. Panel for Behavioral and Computational Neuroscience, 1993—. Office: U Va Dept Psychology 102 Gilmer Hall Charlottesville VA 22903

GOLD, PHIL, physician, educator; b. Montreal, Sept. 17, 1936; m. Evelyn Katz; 3 children. BSc in Physiology with honors, McGill U., Montreal, 1957, MSc, M.D., 1961, PhD in Physiology, 1965; DSc (hon.), McMaster U., 1986. Licentiate Med. Council Can. Jr. rotating intern Montreal Gen. Hosp., 1961-62, jr. asst. resident in medicine, 1962-63, sr. resident in medicine, 1965-66, jr. asst. physician, asst. and assoc. physician, 1967-73, sr. physician, 1973—, physician-in-chief, 1980-95, dir. div. clin. immunology and allergy, 1977-80, dir. McGill U. Med. Clinic, 1980-95, also sr. investigator Research Ins.; faculty dept. physiology McGill U., 1964—, mem. faculty of medicine, 1965—, prof. medicine and clin. medicine, 1973—, chmn. dept. medicine and clin. medicine, 1985-90, prof. physiology, 1974—, prof. oncology, 1989—, mem. faculty of medicine exec. com. representing clin. depts., 1985—, D. G. Cameron prof. medicine (inaugural), 1987—; exec. dir. Clin. Rsch. Ctr. Mont. Gen. Hosp. and McGill U. Hosp. Ctr., 1995—; vis. scientist Pub. Health Research Inst. N.Y.C., 1967-68; Chester M. Jones Meml. lectr. Mass. Gen. Hosp., 1974; vis. prof. U. Caracas, Venezuela, 1974; Squires Club vis. prof. Wellesley Hosp., Toronto, 1983; Cecil H. and Ida Green vis. prof., 1984 autumn lectures U. Brit. Columbia; cons. in allergy and immunology Mt. Sinai Hosp., St. Agathe des Monts, Quebec, 1975—; hon. cons. dept. medicine Royal Victoria Hosp., Montreal; cons. dept. internal medicine Douglas Hosp. Ctr., Montreal; vice chmn. med. adv. com. Council of Physicians, Dentists and Pharmacists, 1985-90; mem. Conseil d'Adminstrn., Found. Quebecoise du Cancer, 1986-88; speaker at convocations and invited lectr. numerous univs. Mem. editorial bd. Clin. Immunology and Immunopathology, 1972—, Immunopharmacology, 1978—, Diagnostic Gynecology and Obstetrics, 1978-83, Oncodevelopmental Biology and Medicine, 1979—, Modern Medicine of Can., 1984-90, Jour. Internal Medicine, 1988—, Canadians for Health Rsch., 1989—, Current Therapeutic Rsch., 1992—, Nutrition Quar., 1992—; editorial cons. Jour. Chronic Diseases, 1981-84; mem. editorial adv. bd. Cancer Research, 1971-73, assoc. editor 1973-80; contbg. editor Practical Allergy and Immunology, 1991—; editl. bd. Can. Jour. Allergy & Clin. Immunology, 1996—; contbr. over 140 articles to med. jours. External referee Can. Red Cross Soc. Recipient Hiram Mills Gold medal, Mosby Scholarship Book award, Wood Gold medal, E.W.R. Steacie prize Nat. Research Council Can., 1973, Can. Silver Jubilee medal, 1977, Johann-Georg-Zemmerman prize for cancer research Medizinische Hochschule, Hannover, Fed. Republic Germany, 1978, Gold medal award of merit Grad. Soc. McGill U., 1979, Internat. award Gardner Found., Ernest C. Manning prize, F.N.G. Starr award Izzak Walton Killam Prize Can. Council, 1985, Tower of Hope award Israel Cancer Rsch. Fund, 1985, Sci. Achievement medal Govt. of Italy, 1990, Agora trophy Ambassador's Club, 1991, Internat. Soc.Oncodevelop. Biol. Medicine Internat. Abbott award, 1992, Commemorative medal 125th Anniversary of Can. Confedn., Govt. of Can., 1992; named Most Outstanding Can. Med. Personality of the past 25 years, MacLean's Mag., 1986; decorated companion Order of Can., 1986; Great Montrealer, 1986; Knight Comdr., Sovereign Order St. John Jerusalem, Knights of Malta, 1986; MacDonald scholar, J. Francis Williams scholar, Univ. scholar; L'Ordre nat. du Quebec. Master ACP; fellow Royal Coll. Physicians and Surgeons Can. (cert. internal medicine, medal 1965, chmn. examing bd., 1975-77, mem. research com. 1986-90), Royal Soc. Can., ACP ; mem. AAAS, Am. Acad. Allergy and Immunology, Am. Assn. Cancer Research, Am. Assn. Immunologists, Am. Fedn. Clin. Research, Am. Soc. Clin. Investigation, Assn. Am. Physicians, Am. Bd. Med. Lab. Immunology (mem. adv. panel 1978—), Assn. Medicale du Que., Can. Assn. Radiologists (hon.), Can. Fedn. Biologic Socs., Can. Oncology Soc. (founding mem., mem. sci. com. 1979—), Canllergy and Clin. Immunology (Ann. Rsch. award 1995), Can. Soc. Clin. Investigation (Disting. Svc. award 1992), Corp. Profl. des Medecins Que., Fedn. des Medecins Specialists Que., Montreal Physiol. Soc., N.Y. Acad. Scis., Reticuloendothelial Soc., Alzheimer Soc. Montreal (patron), Can. Soc. for Immunology (pres. 1975-77), Internat. Soc. for Oncodevel. Biology and Medicine (editorial bd. jour. 1979—, mem. constn. com. 1976—, pres. 9th ann. meeting 1981, Inaugural Outstanding Scientist award 1976), Can. Med. Assn. (F.N.G. Starr award), Med. Research Council Can. (chmn. panel 1972-77, chmn. grants com. 1981-83, council mem. 1986-92, exec. com. 1987-92, com. ethics and med. rsch. 1989-92, com. membership of coms. 1989—, chmn. Task Force on restructuring Med. Rsch. Coun./Pharm. Mfrs. of Can. Program 1995-96), Nat. Cancer Inst. Can. (mem. cancer grants panel B 1977-79, mem. research adv. com. 1984—, R.M. Taylor medal 1992), Med-Chi Soc. (pres. 1986-88), Sigma Xi, Alpha Omega Alpha, others. Office: Clin Rsch Ctr Montreal Gen Hosp, 1650 Cedar Ave, Montreal, PQ Canada H3G 1A4

GOLD, RICHARD HORACE, radiologist; b. N.Y.C., Nov. 20, 1935; s. Samuel Joseph and Edith (Vogel) G.; m. Gittelle Schneider, June 27, 1965; children: Lara, David. BA, NYU, 1956; MD, U. Louisville, 1960. Diplomate Am. Bd. Radiology. Intern Pa. Hosp., Phila., 1960-61; resident in radiology Yale-New Haven (Conn.) Hosp., 1963-66; fellow in skeletal radiology U. Calif., San Francisco, 1967-68, asst. prof. radiology, 1968-72; asst. prof. radiology UCLA, 1972-74, assoc. prof. radiology, 1974-78, prof. radiology, 1978—, chief div. gen. diagnostic radiology, 1986—, dir. radiology residency tng. program, 1991—, vice chair dept. radiol. scis., 1991—; exec. vice chair dept. radiol. scis., 1994—; cons. Wadsworth Vets. Hosp., Sepulveda V.A. Hosp., 1979-89. Author: Roentgen Appearance of Hand in Diffuse Disease, 1975, Clinical Anthrography, 2d edit., 1986, Breast Ultrasound, 1986, Breast Cancer Detection, 2d edit., 1987, MRI Atlas of the Musculoskeletal System, 1989, Film-Screen Mammography, 1992, Workbook for Quality Mammography, 1992; bd. adv. editors Clin. Orthopaedics and Related Rsch., 1978-94; bd. editors Investigative Radiology, 1983-90, Am. Jour. Roentgenology, 1989—; contbr. articles to profl. jours. Active Breast Task Force Am. Joint Com. on Cancer, 1979-90; chmn. breast cancer task force Calif. divsn. Am. Cancer Soc., 1984-87, mem. nat. task force breast cancer control, 1977-82, pres. L.A. Coastal Cities unit, 1991-92. Capt. USAF, 1961-63. Recipient Commr.'s Spl. Citation USPHS, 1981. Fellow Am. Coll. Radiology, Soc. of Breast Imaging; mem. Assn. Univ. Radiologists, Radiol. Soc. N.Am., Am. Roentgen Ray Soc., Internat. Skeletal Soc., Alpha Omega Alpha. Office: UCLA Sch Medicine Dept Radiol Scis Los Angeles CA 90024

GOLD, STEVEN NEAL, psychology educator; b. Jackson Heights, N.Y., Nov. 9, 1953; s. Leonard Carl and Shirley Lee (Bernstein) G.; m. Margaret Marie Angelici, Sept. 4, 1983; children: Andrea Lauren, Lylah Raquel, Adam Jacob. BA in Psychology, Washington U., St. Louis, 1975; MA in Psychology, Mich. State U., 1977, PhD in Psychology, 1981. Lic. psychologist, Fla.; cert. clin. hypnosis, Am. Soc. Clin. Hypnosis. Instr. Cen. Mich. U., Mt. Pleasant, 1980-81, asst. prof., 1981-82; asst. prof. Nova Southea. U., Ft. Lauderdale, Fla., 1982-86, assoc. prof., 1986—; pvt. practice psychology Plantation, Fla., 1983—; clin. supr. Cmty. Mental Health Clinic, Nova Southea. U., 1982-83, clin. dir., 1983-87, dir. sexual abuse survivors program, 1990—; cons. Elaine Gordon Treatment Ctr., Pembroke Pines, Fla., 1986-89. Bd. dirs. Ramat Shalom Synagogue, Plantation, 1985-86. NIMH fellow 1976, 77, 79; recipient grad. scholar award Mich State U., 1980. Mem. APA (divsn. psychotherapy, divsn. hypnosis, divsn. addictions), Fla. Psychol. Assn., Nat. Register Health Svc. Providers in Psychology, Am. Soc. Clin. Hypnosis, Internat. Soc. Study of Dissociation, Internat. Soc. Traumatic Stress Studies, South Fla. Soc. for Trauma-Based Disorders. Democrat. Jewish. Office: Nova Southea Univ 3301 College Ave Fort Lauderdale FL 33314-7721

GOLD, WILLIAM ELLIOTT, health care management consultant; b. Bklyn., Oct. 21, 1948; s. Theodore David and Debra (Fridovich) G.; m. Nili Rachel Scharf, June 1, 1972; children: Avitai, Doria Michelle. BA, SUNY, Stony Brook, 1970; MSS, Hebrew U. of Jerusalem, Israel, 1972; PhD, U. Minn., 1982. Rsch. asst. Hebrew U. of Jerusalem, 1971-72; cons. Dept. Health, Mpls., 1973-74; researcher Mt. Sinai Hosp., Mpls., 1973-74; hosp. adminstrn. instr. U. Minn., Mpls., 1974-75; coord., dir. Blue Cross/Blue Shield Greater N.Y. HMO, N.Y.C., 1975-85; pres. ANCHOR, Chgo., 1985-88; v.p. Rush-Presbyn. St. Luke's Med. Ctr., Chgo., 1985-88; pres. Gold Health Strategies, Inc., N.Y.C., 1988—; vice chmn. The HMO Group, 1987-88; steering com. U. Mo.-KC Nat. Ctr. for Managed Care Adminstrn., Kansas City, 1986—; chmn. N.Y. Bus. Group on Health Managed Care Task Force, N.Y.C., 1989—; asst. adj. prof. Columbia U., N.Y.C., 1989—. Founding editor Managing Employee Health Benefits. Fellowship Caldwell B. Esselstyn Found., 1991-92; mem. task force pub. health and managed care PEW Charitable Trust, 1995—; mem. task force improving cardiovascular health Am. Heart Assn., N.Y.C., 1995—. Home: 322 W 72nd St # 14B New York NY 10023-2676 Office: Gold Health Strategies Inc 250 Park Ave Ste 1300 New York NY 10177

GOLDANSKY, ALVIN EPHRAIM, physician; b. San Diego, Nov. 28, 1958; s. Armand and Eva Goldansky; m. Robin Jill Goldansky, Sept. 1, 1991; 1 child, Rebecca. MD, U. Nacional Autonoma de Mexico, Mexico City, 1984. Bd. cert. internal medicine. Intern, resident LaGuardia Hosp., Forest Hills, N.Y., 1985-88; with All Care Med. Group, Phoenix, 1988-90; staff physician Thomas Davis Med. Ctrs., Phoenix, 1990-91; ptnr., physician Ariz. Primary Care Physicians, Phoenix, 1991—. Mem. ACP. Office: Ariz Primary Care Physician 1728 W Glendale Ave #301 Phoenix AZ 85021

GOLDBARG, JEFFREY ROBBINS, psychiatrist; b. Brookline, Mass., Oct. 25, 1948; s. Julius Abraham Goldbarg and Shirley constance (Berlin) Goldbarg Kahn; m. Laurie Keller Hamlin, Jan. 4, 1948; children: Seth Hamlin, Mollie Robbins. AB, Harvard Coll., 1970; MD, Boston U., 1974. Diplomate Am. Bd. Psychiatry and Neurology. Fellow in child psychiatry McLean Hosp., Belmont, Mass., 1977-78; assoc. dir. psychiat. unit Framingham (Mass.) Union Hosp., 1978-81, vis. staff in psychiatry, 1978—, acting chief psychiatry, 1989; attending psychiatrist Boston State Hosp., 1975-83; cons. psychiatrist Framington Day Hosp., 1990—, Framingham State Coll., 1992—; program psychiatrist Concord Area Crisis Ctr., 1981-90; cons. Mass. Rehab. Commn., Natick, 1985—. Ruth Hunter Johnson award Boston U., 1974. Mem. Am. Psychiat. Assn., Mass. Med. Soc., Physicians for Social Responsibility. Democrat. Office: 14 Vernon St # 206 Framingham MA 01701-4783

GOLDBERG, ALAN MARVIN, toxicologist, educator; b. Bklyn., Nov. 20, 1939; s. William and Celia Ida (Rudman) G.; m. Helene Schoenbach, Aug. 14, 1960; children—Michael David, Naomi Jill. BS, Bklyn. Coll. Pharmacy, 1961; PhD in Pharmacology, U. Minn., 1966; DSc (hon.), L.I. U, 1995. Research asst. U. Wis., 1961-62; research asst. U. Minn., 1962-66; research assoc. Inst. Psychiat. Research Ind. U., 1966-67, asst. prof. dept. pharmacology, 1967-69; asst. prof. environ medicine Johns Hopkins U., Balt., 1969-71, assoc. prof., 1971-78, prof. dept. environ. health scis., 1978—, assoc. chmn. dept., 1978-80, acting dir. div. toxicology, 1979-80, dir. div. toxicology, 1980-82, dir. Ctr. Alternatives to Animal Testing, 1981—, assoc. dean rsch., 1984-94; assoc. dean corp. affairs Sch. Pub. Health, Balt., 1994—; adminstrv. head health edn. program Johns Hopkins U./Nat. Basketball Player Assn., 1990-95; prin. rsch. scientist Chesapeake Bay Inst., 1979-84; mem. health hazard evaluation team of chem. waste dumps State of Tenn.,

1980; mem. rev. panel EPA, 1980-82; mem. working group on harmonization of in vitro methods Orgn. Econ. and Cmty. Devel., 1995—; organizer 1st World Congress on Alternative and Animal Use in Life Scis., 1993. Mem. editorial bd. Jour. Am. Coll. Toxicology, assoc. editor In Vitro Toxicology; contbr. articles to profl. jours. Recipient award Ind. Neurol. Soc., 1967, Russell and Burch award Human Soc. of U.S., 1991; named Disting. Alumnus, L.I. Univ., 1992. Mem. AAAS, Am. Soc. Pharmacology and Exptl. Therapeutics, Soc. Neurosci. (pres. Balt. chpt. 1971-73), Am. Soc. Neurochemistry, Am. Epilepsy Soc., Assn. Univ. Tech. Mgrs., Internat. Soc. Neurochemistry, Soc. Toxicology, Internat. Study Group on Memory Disorders, Internat. Union Pharmacology, Office of Tech. Assessment Panel on Alternatives to Animal Use in Rsch. Testing and Edn. and Frontiers in Neuroscience, Nat. Acad. Sci., Inst. for Lab. Animal Resources. Home: 2231 Crest Rd Baltimore MD 21209-4227 Office: 111 Market Pl Ste 840 Baltimore MD 21202-6709

GOLDBERG, ALLAN SETH, podiatrist; b. Astoria, N.Y., Mar. 18, 1955; s. Samuel and Rita Lee (Stein) G.; m. Cindy Ilene Levy, Oct. 19, 1985; children: Samuel, Jaclyn. BS in Biology, Applied Math. and Stats., SUNY, Stony Brook, 1976; DPM cum laude, N.Y. Coll. Podiatric Medicine, 1981. Diplomate Am. Bd. Podiatric Surgery, Am. Bd. Quality Assurance and Utilization Review Physicians. Assoc. prof. grad. med. edn. N.Y. Coll. Podiatric Medicine, N.Y.C., 1993—, dir. podiatric surgical residencies, 1993—; coord. podiatric residency edn. N.Y. Coll. Podiatric Medicine, 1991—. Home: 10 Mitchell Ave Plainview NY 11803-3019

GOLDBERG, ALLEN I., physician, home health care executive; b. Bklyn., Feb. 27, 1943. AB, Columbia U., 1964; MD, SUNY Health Sci. Ctr., Bklyn., 1968; M Mgmt., Northwestern U., 1988; cert. in orgn. devel., Loyola U., Chgo., 1988. Diplomate Am. Bd. Pediatrics, Am. Bd. Anesthesiology, Am. Bd. Med. Mgmt. Pediatric resident Yale New Haven Hosp., 1968-70, U. Hosp. of Cleve., 1970-71; anesthesia resident Hosp. U. of Pa., Phila., 1973-75; resident in pediatric critical care Children's Hosp. of Phila., 1975, dir. pediatric intermediate ICU, 1975-78; dir. respiratory care Children's Meml. Hosp., Chgo., 1978-92; dir. pediatric home health Loyola U. Med. Ctr., Maywood, Ill., 1992—; exec. dir. Care for Life, Chgo., 1982-92. Contbr. articles to profl. publs. Mem. adv. bd., priority grants com., health/disability discrimination com. United Way of Chgo., 1982-92; bd. dirs. Gazette Internat. Networking Inst., St. Louis, 1992—. Maj. USAR, 1971-73. Fellow World Rehab. Fund Internat. Exch. of Experts and Info., 1983, WHO/USPHS, 1986; recipient Long Term award Gov. of State of Ill., 1991. Fellow Am. Coll. Physician Execs. (chair Soc. on Home Care Mgmt. 1992-94), Am. Coll. Chest Physicians (treas. 1994—), Am. Acad. Pediatrics (chair steering com. provisional sect. home health 1994—); mem. Am. Acad. Home Care Physicians (pres., bd. dirs. 1994—). Office: Loyola U Med Ctr Pediatric Home Health 2160 S 1st Ave Maywood IL 60153

GOLDBERG, BRUCE EDWARD, hypnotherapist; b. N.Y.C., Nov. 18, 1948; s. Samuel and Florence (Nussbaum) G. BA in Biology/Chemistry magna cum laude, So. Conn. State Coll., 1970; DDS, U. Md., 1974; MS in Counseling and Psychology, Loyola Coll., Balt., 1984. Dentist Balt., 1976-89, hynotherapist, 1976-89; hynotherapist L.A., 1989—; pres. L.A. Acad. Clin. Hypnosis, 1990—; cons. Westinghouse TV, CBS, NBC, ABC, 1985—. Author: Past Lives-Future Lives, 1988, The Search for Grace, 1994; cons., tech. advisor film The Search for Grace, 1994; contbr. articles to profl. jours. Acad. Gen. Dentistry fellow, 1982; recipient Sealah award Assn. for Parapsychology Healing and Rsch., 1987. Mem. ASCD, Am. Psychol. Soc., Acad. Psychosomatic Medicine, Assn. for Past Life Rsch. and Therapy (life). Home and Office: 4300 Natoma Ave Woodland Hills CA 91364-5625

GOLDBERG, BURTON DAVID, pathologist, researcher, educator; b. Milw., Jan. 6, 1927; s. Esrael and Martha Goldberg; m. Geraldine Anne Yencha, Dec. 15, 1984. BS, Northwestern U., 1948, MD, 1950. Internship Cin. Gen. Hosp., 1951-52; residency in pathology Mallory Inst. Boston City Hosp., 1952-55; rsch. fellow in biochemistry MIT, Cambridge, 1955-57; asst. prof. pathology NYU Med. Sch., 1957-59, assoc. prof. pathology, 1959-71, prof. pathology, 1971-84; prof., chmn. dept. pathology U. Wis. Med. Sch., Madison, 1985-93, prof. emeritus, 1993—; vis. scientist Inst. Pasteur, Paris, 1993-94. Contbr. articles to profl. jours.; contbr. chpt. to Connective Tissue in Histology, 1988. With USN, 1944-45. NIH grantee, 1959—; recipient Career Devel. award USPHS, 1960-70. Mem. Am. Soc. Experimental Pathology, Am. Soc. Biol. Chemistry and Molecular Biology, Am. Soc. Cell Biology.

GOLDBERG, CARL, psychotherapist, writer; b. N.Y.C., Jan. 21, 1938; s. Samuel and Mollie (Hecht) G. BA in Philosophy, Am. Internat. Coll., 1960; MA in Philosophy, U. Wyo., 1961; PhD, U. Okla., 1966; cert. in analytic psychotherapy, Washington Sch. Psychiatry, 1970. Chief psychology St. Elizabeths Hosp., Washington, 1967-71; dir. Cmty. Mental Health Ctr., Prince Georges County, Md., 1971-74; assoc. clin. prof. dept. Psychiatry George Washington U. Med. Sch., Washington, 1974-81; dir. group Psychotherapy program for psychiatric residents Mt. Sinai Hosp. Svcs., Elmhurst, N.Y., 1981-85; assoc. clinical prof. dept. Psychiatry Albert Einstein Coll. Medicine, N.Y.C., 1981-94; psychotherapist pvt. practice, N.Y.C., 1980-95; coord. group Psychotherapy Tng. Program St. John's U., N.Y.C., 1988-91; adj. assoc. prof. psychology St. John's U., 1988-91, NYU, 1988-94; clin. assoc. CUNY, Psychol. Ctr., 1982; rsch. assoc. Psychohistory Forum, 1986; bd. advisors, vis. faculty Change Inst. Human Growth, Montreal, 1978—, N.Y. City for Psychodrama Tng., 1976—. Author, co-editor 11 books; editor Jour. Adult Devel.; editor-for-the-Americas: Internat. Jour. Psychotherapy; contbr. over 150 articles to profl. jours. Home and Office: 305 E 24th St Lobby C New York NY 10010-4011

GOLDBERG, DANIEL BERNEY, eye surgeon; b. Newark, Oct. 18, 1948; s. Bernard R. and Ruth V. (Berney) G.; m. Catherine A. Connelly, Sept. 12, 1976; children: Adam, Jeffrey. BA, U. Calif., Berkeley, 1970; MD, SUNY, Bklyn., 1974. Intern George Washington U. Hosp., Washington, 1974-75; resident SUNY Downstate Med. Ctr., Bklyn., 1975-78; surgeon Atlantic Eye Physicians, Long Branch, N.J., 1979—; chmn. N.J. Eye Care, 1996—; pres., bd. chmn. N.J. Acad. Ophthalmology, 1988; dir. ophthalmology Monmouth Med. Ctr., Long Branch, 1984-93. Contbr. articles to profl. jours. Fellow Am. Acad. Ophthalmology (councillor 1990-95), Am. Coll. Eye Surgeons; mem. Am. Soc. Cataract & Refractive Surgery, Soc. Surgeons N.J., Internat. Soc. Refractive Surgery, Castroviejo Cornea Soc. Jewish. Office: Atlantic Eye Physicians 279 3d Ave Long Beach NJ 07740

GOLDBERG, EDWIN, rehabilitation specialist; b. Bklyn., 1937; s. Mary and Daniel Goldberg; m. June Light, June 21, 1972; children: Paul, Joseph, Robert. student Bklyn. Coll., 1955-56; D of Chiropractic, Columbia Inst. Chiropractic, 1960, diploma X-ray, 1960; postgrad. Columbia U., Am. Inst. Psychoanalysis, C.G. Jung Found., N.Y.C., 1972-73, NYU, 1973-74, Karen Horney Clinic Moreno Inst. Psychodrama, N.Y. Inst. Behavior Therapy; cert. of study Alfred Adler Inst., Fordham U., 1970; M.A. in Edn., Hebrew Union Coll., 1971; cert. in crisis mgmt., Cornell U., 1972, profl. diploma rehab. mgmt., 1973; diploma Sch. of Hygiene, Sussex Tng. Coll., Eng., 1976; cert. assessment in aging, U. Pa., 1987. Cert. med. rehab. coord., rehab. therapist, rehab. counselor, master therapeutic recreation specialist, Nat. Bd. of Cert. Counselor; registered recreation adminstr., N.J.; cert. mobility instr., rehab. tchr., N.Y.; nat. cert. profl. rehab. tchr. of the blind AER.; cert. Rehab. dir. OVR accredited facilities, Staff coagulation lab. Issac Albert Rsch. Inst., Bklyn., N.Y, 1957-60; tech. eye bank and clin. Lab. Bklyn. Eye & Ear Hosp., 1958-59, exec. Greater N.Y. couns. Boy Scouts Am., 1960-63; supr. Charles Pfizer & Co., N.Y.C., 1963-64; assoc. dir. Western Mediterranean ops. USO, Nice, France, 1964-65; coord. rehab. skills Jewish Guild Blind, N.Y.C., 1965-68, asst. dir., 1968-77; dir. rehab. svcs., sect. chief Trenton (N.J.) Psychiat. Hosp., 1977-78; mobility cons., Elm & Maple Halls, Ancora Hosp., 1977-82; dir. Work Adjustment Ctr., Jewish Employment and Vocat. Svc., Phila., 1979-80; dir. S.I. (N.Y.) Aid for Retarded Children Rehab. Ctr., 1980-82; Rehab. con. Aetna private law firm, Phila., 1980-83, sr. rehab. counselor/acting dir. Vocat. Rehab. dept. Ancora Hosp., Hammonton, N.J., 1982-87, rehab. con. Dominican Coll. of Blauvelt; habilitation plan coord. State of N.J. Div. Devel. Disabilities, Hammonton, 1988-91, North Princeton Devel. Ctr., New Lisbon Devel. Ctr., 1991-93; vocat. rehab. counselor N.J. State Commn. for the Blind, 1992—; rehab. cons. Beth Israel Hosp., N.Y.C., Goldwater Meml. Hosp., N.Y.C., Montefiore Med. Ctr., Bronx, N.Y., Harlem Med. Ctr., Bronx, Kingsbrook Jewish Med. Ctr., Bklyn., Jewish Home and Hosp. for Aged, N.Y.C., Inst. Rehab. Medicine, NYU, Hillside Med. Ctr., Bklyn. Devel. Ctr., Manhattan (N.Y.) Psychiat. Hosp., Keener Unit of Gov. Hosp., Zeman Ctr. for Instrn., N.Y.C., Albert Einstein Coll. Medicine, Bronx, Downstate Med. Ctr., Bklyn., Manhattanville Coll., Westchester, N.Y., L.I. U., Bklyn., State of Israel Dept. of Def. and Ministry of Health, Yonker (N.Y.) Home for the Aged Blind, Trenton State Coll., Bank Street Coll. of Edn., Staten Island C.C., Zeman Ctr. for Instrn., N.Y.C. Kingsbrook C.C.; mobility specialist for severely disabled blind State of N.Y., 1968—; coord. corrective therapy, internship program VA-Hunter Coll., 1971-77; adj. asst. prof. adapted phys. edn. Hunter Coll., 1970-77; rehab. tng. specialist multiple disabled blind in N.Y. area, 1970-77; instr. group rels. ongoing workshops; lectr. in field, 1970—; legis. rep. N.Y. State Fedn. Workers for Blind, 1973-76, program chmn., 1974; cons. legis. U.S. Senate and Congl. Subcoms., 1972-77; lectr. rehab. skills tng. of vision impaired Geriatrics Ctr. for Instrn., 1968-77; mem. Nat. Eagle Scout Assn. Boy Scouts Am. Recipient Dr. Frank E. Dean Meml. award for outstanding contbns. to sci. edn., 1976, Thomas E. Watson Silver citation Citizenship in Action medal SAR. Fellow N.Y. Acad. Scis., Royal Soc. Promotion Health, N.Y. Hist. Soc., Am. Soc. Tng. and Devel.; mem. Am. Orthopsychiatric Assn. Assn. for Applied Psychoanalysis, Royal Soc. Medicine (affiliate mem.), Assn. for Edn. and of the Visually Handicapped and Blind, Am. Congress Rehab. Medicine, Royal Soc. Health, Royal Inst. Pub.Health and Hygiene, Am. Assn. Rehab. Therapy, Am. Anthrop. Assn., John Burroughs Meml. Assn. (life mem.). Author: Mobility Training Manual for Teachers of Visually Impaired Children, 9; Isolation From the Human Scene: The Meaning and Direction of Loneness, 1972, Adapted and Corrective Physical Education Curriculum Handicapped, 1972, Rehabilitation Assessment in Psychiatric Faciliitities, 1984, Overcoming Feelings of Inferiority: The Role of Mobility Training for the Blind An Adlerian Viewpoint, 1986. Office: 11 Royal Oak Rd Trenton NJ 08648-3234

GOLDBERG, GERALD N., dermatologist; b. Washington, May 21, 1951; s. Monroe Bernard and Gertrude (Edelson) G. m. Barbara Segal, May 7, 1978; children: Matthew, Julia. BA, Princeton U., 1973; MD, SUNY, 1978. Diplomate Am. Bd. Pediatrics, Am. Bd. Dermatology. Resident in dermatology, pediatrics U. Ariz., Tucson, 1978-84; pvt. practice dermatology Tucson, 1984—; assoc. clin. prof. neonatology and pediatrics U. Ariz., Tucson, 1995—. Editl. bd. Pediat. Dermatology Jour., 1988—; profl. adv. bd. Sturge-Weber Found., 1991—. Fellow Am. Soc. Laser Medicine & Surgery, Am. Soc. Dermatol. Surgery, Am. Acad. Dermatology, Am. Acad. Pediatrics; mem. Sonoran Dermatology Soc. (pres. 1991-92, sec. 1990-91), Soc. Pediat. Dermatology, Tucson Dermatol. Soc. (pres. 1990-92), Pacific Dermatol. Assn., Pima County Med. Soc. (bd. dirs. 1989-90), Am. Acad. Dermatology, Ariz. Pediat. Soc., Southwestern Dermatol. Assn., Princeton Alumni Assn. Tucson (pres. 1985-89), Dermatol. Therapy Assn., Alpha Omege Alpha. Democrat. Jewish. Office: 2260 N Rosemont Ste 100 Tucson AZ 85712

GOLDBERG, HAROLD HOWARD, psychologist, educator; b. N.Y.C., Apr. 30, 1924; s. Julius and Fannie (Somers) G.; m. Roslyn Jacobowitz, June 26, 1948; children: Barbara Balsam, Susan Fitcher, Lisa Shirvan. BA, NYU, 1948, MA, 1949; PhD, AMW U., Tulsa, 1970. Cert. psychologist, sch. psychologist, sch. adminstr., therapist, psychol. diagnostician; approved fellow in marital and family therapy. Psychotherapist in pvt. practice N.Y.C., 1949—; chief psychologist Queens-Island Reading Ctrs., N.Y.C., 1959-62; sch. adminstr. League Sch./Rsch. Ctr. for Seriously Emotionally Disturbed, Bklyn., 1967-78; acting dir. Community Guidance Svc., N.Y.C., 1977-78; acting dir. Am. Inst. for Psychotherapy and Psychoanalysis, N.Y.C., 1977-78, mem. faculty, 1974-78; mem. faculty Greenwich Inst. for Psychotherapy and Psychoanalysis, N.Y.C., 1978—; supr. of psychotherapists 5th Ave. Ctr. for Psychotherapy, Nat. Inst. for the Psychotherapies. Founder, editor Jour. Clin. Issues in Psychology, 1969-78, Profl. Digest of N.Y. Soc. Clin. Psychology, 1965-69, News and Notes, 1963-65; editor Newsletter for the N.Y. Soc. Clin. Psychologists, 1965-69. With USAF, 1942-45. Mem. APA, N.Y. Soc. Clin. Psychologists (pres. 1972-73), N.Y. Psychol. Assn., N.Y. Acad. Scis., Am. Assn. Marriage and Family Therapy, Psi Chi, Phi Delta Kappa, Kappa Delta Pi Office: 105 E 63rd St Apt 3A New York NY 10021-7328

GOLDBERG, HERB, psychologist, educator; b. Berlin, Germany, July 14, 1937; came to U.S., 1941; s. Jacob and Ella (Nagler) G.; 1 child, Amy Elisabeth. BA cum laude, CUNY, 1958; PhD, Adelphi U., 1963. Lic. psychologist, Calif. Pvt. practice, L.A., 1965—; prof. Calif. State U., L.A. Author: Creative Aggression, 1972, The Hazards of Being Male, 1976, Money Madness, 1978, The New Male, 1979, The Inner Male, 1986, The New Male/Female Relationship, 1982, What Men Really Want, 1991. Mem. APA, Phi Beta Kappa. Office: 1100 Glendon Ave Ste 939 Los Angeles CA 90024-3513

GOLDBERG, HERBERT, podiatrist; b. Bklyn., Feb. 14, 1930; s. Benjamin and Betty G.; BA, Bklyn. Coll., 1955; grad. U. Buffalo, 1956; D in Podiatric Medicine, Temple U., 1960; m. Renee Silverstein, Aug. 30, 1959; children: Robin Jennifer, Jacqueline. Phys. therapist Rolling Hill Hosp., Phila., 1957-60; chief therapist Rochester (N.Y.) Rehab. Ctr., 1961-62; phys. therapist Hamot Hosp., Erie, Pa., 1962; chief phys. therapist Erie County (Pa.) Hosp., 1967-74; chief phys. therapist Twinbrook Nursing Home, Erie, Pa., 1977-82; dir. rehab. svcs. Twinbrook Med. Ctr., 1982-83; pvt. practice podiatric medicine, Erie, Pa., 1961—; vis. podiatrist Erie VA Hosp., 1969—, Mercy Ctr. on Aging, 1975—, Christian Health Ctr., 1982—, St. Vincent Health Ctr., 1977—; instr. gen. biology, physiology Mercyhurst Coll., 1964-68; instr. physiology, microbiology Villa Maria Coll., 1967-71; instr. phys. edn. Mercyhurst Coll., 1967-70. Bd. dirs. Erie Civic Ballet; pres. men's club Temple Anshe Hesro, 1987-88, pres. bd. govs., 1990-92. With AUS, 1953-55. Fellow Acad. Ambulatory Foot Surgery; mem. APHA, Am. Podiatry Assn., Am. Phys. Therapy Assn., Soc. Orthop. Medicine, Erie County Podiatry Assn. (pres. 1981-82). Jewish (mem. cmty. coun.). Author: Fanny Crinkelmier Girl Sugar Cookie. Home: 2047 Berkshire Ln Erie PA 16509-1762 Office: 1561 W 38th St Erie PA 16508-2348

GOLDBERG, IRVING HYMAN, molecular pharmacology and biochemistry educator; b. Hartford, Conn., Sept. 2, 1926; s. Morris Wolfe and Rose (Krechevsky) G.; m. Margaret Field Ziskin, Apr. 15, 1956; children: Daniel Eliot, Nancy Elizabeth. BS, Trinity Coll., 1949; MD, Yale U., 1953; PhD, Rockefeller U., 1960; AM (hon.), Harvard U., 1964. Intern Columbia-Presbyn. Med. Ctr., N.Y.C., 1953-54; asst. resident, chief resident, instr. medicine Columbia-Presbyn. Med. Ctr. (Coll. Phys. and Surgs.), 1954-57; asst. prof. medicine, biochemistry U. Chgo., 1960-64, assoc. prof., 1964; assoc. prof. medicine Med. Sch. Harvard, 1964-68; prof. medicine Med. Sch. Harvard U., 1968—, chmn. div. med. scis. Faculty Arts and Scis. 1968-70, Gustavus Adolphus Pfeiffer prof. pharmacology, 1972-83, chmn. dept. pharm., 1972-86, Otto Krayer prof. pharmacology, 1983-86, Otto Krayer prof. biol. chemistry and molecular pharmacology, 1986—; chief endocrinology-metabolism unit Beth Israel Hosp., 1964-68, physician, 1964-72, mem. bd. consultation in medicine, 1972—; cons. in pharmacology Dana-Farber Cancer Inst., Boston, 1980-87; mem. rev. panel internat. program Howard Hughes Med. Inst., 1994; cons. in clin. pharmacology Children's Hosp. Med. Ctr., Boston, 1972-91; mem. rsch. com. Med. Found., Boston, 1968-77; mem. exptl. therapeutics study sect. NIH, 1974-77; mem. com. proposed legis. to restructure FDA Assembly Life Scis., NAS-NRC, Inst. Medicine, 1976; mem. sci. adv. com. Damon Runyon-Walter Winchell Cancer Fund, 1982-86; mem. life scis. panel NRC, 1992-93. Mem. editorial bd. Endocrinology, 1964-68, Antimicrobial Agents and Chemotherapy, 1974-88; hon. editorial adv. bd. Jour. Biochem. Pharmacology, 1973-84; mem. editorial adv. bd. Biochemistry, 1986—. Rev. panel mem. Internat. Program Howard Hughes Med. Inst., 1994. Served with USNR, 1945-46. Recipient Faculty Research award Am. Cancer Soc., 1960-71; Guggenheim fellow dept. genetics Oxford (Eng.) U., 1970-71; sr. fellow Trinity Coll., 1974-76. Mem. Inst. Medicine NAS, Am. Soc. Biochemistry and Molecular Biology, Am. Soc. Clin. Investigation, Endocrine Soc., Am. Acad. Arts and Scis., Assn. of Am. Physicians, Am. Chem. Soc., Am. Soc. Pharmacology and Therapeutics (Otto Krayer award 1994), Am. Soc. Microbiology, Brit. Pharm. Soc., Phi Beta Kappa, Sigma Xi, Alpha Omega Alpha. Home: 987 Memorial Dr Apt 472 Cambridge MA 02138-5737 Office: Harvard U Med Sch 25 Shattuck St Boston MA 02115-6027

GOLDBERG, JANE G., psychoanalyst; b. New Orleans, May 31, 1946; d. Meyer and Madeleine Malvina (Levy) Goldberg; children: Molly Malvina. BA, Washington U., 1968; postgrad., Pratt Inst., 1969-72; MA, New Sch. for Social Rsch., 1971; PhD, CUNY, 1978. Lic. psychologist, N.Y.; cert. psychoanalyst N.Y., psychoanalytic psychotherapist, N.Y. Pvt. practice psychotherapy and psychoanalysis N.Y., N.J., 1973—, pvt. practice supervision psychotherapy and psychoanalysis, 1980—; staff psychotherapist art therapy program Hillside Hosp., Queens, N.Y., 1970-72, Advanced Ctr. for Psychotherapy, Jamaica, N.Y., 1974-81; rsch. assoc. dept. psychology New Sch. for Social Rsch. Grad. Faculty, N.Y.C., 1971-72, dept. med. oncology Kingsbrook Jewish Med. Ctr., Bklyn., 1979-80; faculty psychology dept. CUNY, N.Y.C., 1972-76; faculty Fifth Ave. Ctr. for Counseling and Psychotherapy, N.Y.C., 1982-84, Ctr. for Modern Psychoanalytic Studies, N.Y.C., 1984—; mem. faculty Treatment and Referral Svc. N.Y.C., 1984—, Psychoanalytic ctr. N.J., Morristown, 1986—, Boston Ctr. Modern Psychoanalytic Studies, 1986—; lectr. in field. Author: Psychotherapeutic Treatment of Cancer Patients, 1982, Deceits of the Mind (and their effects on the body), 1991, The Dark Side of Love: the positive role of our negative emotions, 1993; mng. editor: Modern Psychoanalysis; column writer: "News and Notes" in Modern Psychoanalysis; TV talk show co-host: "Schmoozing, " N.Y.C.; numerous mag. and newspapers interviews; numerous TV and radio appearances; contbr. articles to profl. jours. Asst. to exec. dir. Found. for the Advancement of Cancer Therapies; dir. La Casa de Vida Natural, Rio Grande, P.R., 1987—, La Casa Day Spa, N.Y.C., 1993—. Home: 41 E 20th St New York NY 10003-1324

GOLDBERG, JOEL SAMUEL, osteopathic family physician, educator; b. Phila., Apr. 18, 1953; s. Louis Benjamin and Marion Tzirlion Goldberg; m. Mickey Ann Zitarelli; children: Daniel, Kasey. BA in English and Biology, Temple U., 1975; DO, Phila. Coll. Osteo. Medicine, 1979. Diplomate Am. Osteo. Bd. Family Medicine. Intern Tri-County Hosp., Delaware County, Pa., 1979-80; pvt. practice, Boothwyn, Pa., 1980—; asst. prof. medicine Med. Coll. Pa., Phila., Hahnemann U., Phila.; series editor Sage Publs., Calif., 1994—. Author: What Your Doctor Should Do for You, 1996. Mem. Am. Osteo. Assn., Pa. Osteo. Med. Assn., Pa. Osteo. Gen. Practice Soc., Profl. Assn. Diving Instrs. Office: 4015 Chichester Ave Boothwyn PA 19061

GOLDBERG, LESLIE PHILIP, ophthalmologist; b. Tampa, Fla., Mar. 22, 1945; s. Oscar and Irma Ruth (Rosner) G.; m. Zehava Kupperman, Jan. 24, 1970; children: Shelley, Michael. BA, Cornell U., 1966; MD, The Chgo. Med. Sch., 1970. Diplomate Am. Bd. Ophthalmology. Intern in surgery Columbia-Presbyterian Med. Ctr., N.Y.C., 1970-71; resident, chief resident in ophthalmology NYU Med. Ctr., N.Y.C., 1973-76; pvt. practice, ophthalmologist L.I. Eye Surgeons, P.C., Manhasset, N.Y., 1976—; chief of ophthalmology, St. Francis Hosp., Roslyn, N.Y., 1993—. Mem. planning bd. Inc. Village of Roslyn, 1995—. Capt. U.S. Army, 1971-73. Recipient achievement award Upjohn Pharm. Col., 1970. Fellow Am. Acad. Ophthalmology, Am. Coll. Surgeons; mem. Med. Soc. State of N.Y., Nassau County Med. Soc., N.Y. State Ophthalmol. Soc., L.I. Opthalmol. Soc., Alpha Omega Alpha. Office: LI Eye Surgeons PC 2110 Northern Blvd Manhasset NY 11030

GOLDBERG, LINN, physician; b. Portland, Oreg., June 25, 1947; s. Herman and Anita (Mazurosky) G.; m. Marsha Lynn Serling, Feb. 18, 1979; children: Gabriel, Andrew, Aaron, Michael, Alex. BS, U. Oreg., 1970; MD, George Washington U., 1975. Chmn. ambulatory care com. Oreg. Health Sci. U., Portland, 1985-86, dir. human performance lab, 1983—, dir. gen. med. clinics, 1989-93, sec. faculty, 1988—, chief sect. health promotion and sports medicine, 1994—; spl. cons. Inspector Gen. U.S., Dept. Health and Human Svcs., 1990; tech. panel mem. WHO, 1994; crew chief U.S. Olympic Com., 1995—. Co-author/co-editor: Exercise for Prevention and Treatment of Illness, 1994; contbr. articles to profl. jours.; med. reviewer Chest, Adolescent Health Care, Archives of Internal Medicine. Grantee Biomed. Rsch., 1980, 81, Tektronix Found., 1982, Nordictrack and Pro Form, Inc., 1985, Fitness Master Inc., 1985, Amoco Fabrics, Inc., 1985, Bally Fitness Products, 1985, Schering-Plough, 1986, 87, 89, Collin's Found., 1988, Hoechst-Roussel Pharms., Inc., 1991, Alzheimer Disease Ctr. Oreg., 1993, NIH, 1993—, Merck Sharp and Dohme, Inc., 1993, Med. Rsch. Found. of Oreg., 1995. Fellow Am. Coll. Sports Medicine, Alpha Omega Alpha. Jewish. Office: Oreg Health Scis Univ 3181 SW Sam Jackson Park Rd Portland OR 97201

GOLDBERG, MARCIA B., medical educator; b. Boston, July 29, 1957. AB in Biology summa cum laude, Harvard U., 1979, MD, 1984. Diplomate Am. Bd. Internal Medicine, Am. Bd. Infectious Diseases. Intern in primary care internal medicine Mass. Gen. Hosp., Boston, 1984-85, jr. and sr. resident in primary care internal medicine, 1985-87, clin. and rsch. fellow in medicine, 1987-90; rsch. fellow in medicine Harvard Med. Sch., Boston, 1987-90; rsch. fellow Unite de Pathogenie Microbienne Moleculaire, Inst. Pasteur, Paris, 1991-93; asst. prof. Dept. Microbiology and Immunology, Dept. Medicine divsn. Infectious Diseases Albert Einstein Coll. of Medicine, Bronx, N.Y., 1993—; mem. joint med./nursing care com. Mass. Gen. Hosp., 1986-87, benefit com. Boston Health Care for the Homeless, 1988, admissions com. Med. Scientist Tng. Program, Albert Einstein Coll. of Medicine, 1993—, assoc. dir., 1995—, mem. steering com. Med. Student Fellowship, Am. Heart Assn., Albert Einstein Coll. of Medicine, 1994—, rsch. residency com. Dept. of Medicine, 1994—, adv. com. Hybridoma/Media Facility, 1994—, divsn. rsch., 1996—. Contbr. articles and revs. to profl. jours. Hon. Nat. scholar Radcliffe Coll., 1975; Inst. Nat. de la Sante et de la Recherche Med. fellow, 1991; Moseley Traveling fellow Harvard Med. Sch., 1991-92; Fulbright scholar, 1991-92; Pew scholar, 1994—; recipient Rsch. award Fundaciion para la Edn. Superior, 1981, Proctor-Wellington Fund award, 1987, Stuart Pharms. Travel award Nat. Found. Infectious Diseases, 1990, Young Investigator award Maxwell Finland, 1991, Intersci. Conf. on Antimicrobial Agents and Chemotherapy, 1991, Established Investigator award Am. Heart Assn., 1996. Mem. Am. Soc. Microbiology, Infectious Diseases Soc. Am., Phi Beta Kappa. Office: Albert Einstein Coll of Medicine 1300 Morris Park Ave Bronx NY 10461

GOLDBERG, MARK ARTHUR, neurologist; b. N.Y.C., Sept. 4, 1934; s. Jacob and Bertha (Grushlawska) G.; 1 child, Jonathan. BS, Columbia U., 1955; PhD, U. Chgo., 1959, MD, 1962. Resident neurology N.Y. Neurol. Inst., N.Y.C., 1963-66; asst. prof. neurology Columbia U. Coll. Phys. and Surgs., N.Y.C., 1968-71; assoc. prof. neurology and pharmacology UCLA, 1971-77, prof. neurology and pharmacology, 1977—; chair dept. neurology Harbor UCLA Med. Ctr., Torrance, 1977—. Contbr. articles to profl. jours., chpts. to books. Capt. U.S. Army, 1966-68. Fellow Am. Neurol. Assn., Am. Acad. Neurology; Am. Soc. Neurochemistry, Soc. Neurosci., Assn. Univ. Profs. Neurology. Office: Harbor UCLA Med Ctr PO Box 492 Torrance CA 90508-0492

GOLDBERG, MARTIN, physician, educator; b. Phila., Sept. 15, 1930; s. Samuel and Esther (Shreibman) G.; m. Lynn Taksey, June 17, 1951 (dec. Aug. 31 1976); children: Meryl I., Karen L., Dara S.; m. Marion Lindblad, May 26, 1978; 1 child, David S. BA, Temple U., 1951, MD, 1955; MA (hon.), U. Pa., 1971. Diplomate: Am. Bd. Internal Medicine (chmn. nephrology com. 1976-79, bd. govs. 1976-79), Nat. Bd. Med. Examiners. Intern Phila. Gen. Hosp., 1955-56, resident, 1957-59, sr. attending physician, 1970-76; resident Cleve. Clinic, 1956-57; fellow nephrology Hosp. U. Pa., Phila., 1959-61; sr. attending physician Hosp. U. Pa., 1962-79; mem. faculty U. Pa. Sch. Medicine, 1960-79, prof. medicine, 1970-79, chief renal electrolyte sect., 1966-79, acting chmn. dept. medicine, 1975-76; sr. attending physician Phila. VA Hosp., 1968-79; Gordon and Helen Hughes Taylor prof. medicine U. Cin., 1979-86; chmn. internal medicine U. Cin. Coll. Med. and Hosp., 1979-86; prof. medicine Temple U. Sch. Medicine, Phila., 1986—, dean, vice pres., 1986-89; chmn. sci. adv. com. Gen. Clin. Rsch. Ctr. Temple U. Hosp., 1993—; mem. sci. adv. bd. Nat. Kidney Found., 1970-76; chmn. kidney council Am. Heart Assn., 1973-74; study cons. NIH, 1968-72, 82-85; bd. mgrs. St. Christopher's Hosp. Children, 1986-89. Mem. editl. com. Jour. Clin. Investigation, 1969-70, Kidney Internat., 1972-74, Jour. Mineral and Electrolyte Metabolism, 1977-91; mem. editl. bd. Am. Jour. Hypertension, 1990—; physician-editor Nephrology MKSAP Am. Coll. Physicians, 1991-94; assoc. editor MKSAP 11 ACP, 1996—. Recipient Alumni prize Temple U. Sch. Medicine, 1955, Lindback award for distinguished teaching U. Pa., 1972; Disting. Med. Scientist of Yr. award Med. Alumni Temple U. Sch. Medicine, 1985; Research Career Devel. award NIH, 1963-70; research grantee NIH, 1962-89; research grantee John Hartford Found., 1970-73. Fellow ACP (nat. sci. program com. 1976-81), Am. Coll. Clin. Pharmacology, Royal Soc. Medicine; mem. Assn. Am. Med. Colls. (coun. of deans 1986-89), Assn. Am. Physicians, Am. Soc. Clin. Investigation, Am. Physiol. Soc., Am. Fedn. Clin. Rsch. (chmn. ea. sect. 1967), Am. Soc. Nephrology (sec.-treas. 1975-78), Interurban Clin. Club, Internat. Soc. Nephrology (coun. 1975-84), Am. Med. Informatics Assn., Coll. Physicians Phila., Physicians for Social Responsibility (adv. bd. Phila. chpt.), Alpha Omega Alpha. Office: Temple U Health Scis Ctr Nephrology Parkinson Pavilion Philadelphia PA 19140

GOLDBERG, MARVIN ELEAZER, radiologist; b. Mpls., Nov. 30, 1926; s. Max Wilbert and Frances Lillian (Halpern) G. BA magna cum laude, U. Minn., 1949, BS, 1950, MB, 1952, MD, 1953. Diplomate Am. Bd. Radiology, Am. Bd. Nuclear Medicine. Radiologist Mt. Sinai Hosp., Mpls., 1957-71; assoc. prof. radiology U. Minn., Mpls., 1971—; chief of staff U. Minn. Hosp., 1994—. Contbr. articles to profl. jours. Served with USN, 1945-46. Fellow Am. Coll. Radiology; mem. Minn. Radiol. Soc. (pres. 1980-81), Radiol. Soc. N.Am., Am. Roentgen Ray Soc., Assn. Univ. Radiologists, Soc. Uroradiology, Soc. Nuclear Medicine, Sigma Xi. Home: 5049 Abbott Ave S Minneapolis MN 55410-2142 Office: U Hosp Dept Radiology Minneapolis MN 55455

GOLDBERG, MELVIN JULIUS, physiatrist; b. Lakewood, N.J., June 18, 1935; s. Nathan and Regina (Vormund) G.; m. Sharon Ruth Judlowe, Nov. 25, 1957 (div. June 1973); children: Sandra Lynn, Joanne Louise, Lisa Ellen; m. Linda Gene Zagalia, Aug. 19, 1973; 1 child, Mark Erik. MD, SUNY Bklyn., 1960; MS, U. Minn., 1967. Diplomate Am. Bd. Phys. Medicine and Rehab., Nat. Bd. Med. Examiners. Physiatrist-in-chief Bklyn.-Cumberland Med. Ctr., 1966-69; chmn. dept. rehab. medicine St. Joseph's Hosp., Paterson, N.J., 1969-77; dir. rehab. medicine Daus. Miriam Ctr. for Aged, Clifton, N.J., 1977-89; pvt. practice Clifton, 1990—; profl. adv. com. mem. Bergen Cmty. Health Care, Westwood, N.J., 1986—; med. adv. com. mem. Blue Cross-Blue Shield N.J., Newark, 1990—. Patentee in field. Jewish. Home: 305 Park St Upper Montclair NJ 07043-2210 Office: 970 Clifton Ave Clifton NJ 07013-2789

GOLDBERG, MORRIS, internist; b. N.Y.C., Jan. 23, 1928; s. Saul and Lena (Schanberg) G.; BS in Chemistry cum laude, Poly. Inst. Bklyn., 1951; MD, SUNY, Bklyn., 1956; m. Elaine Shaw, June 24, 1956; children: Alan Neil, Seth David, Nancy Beth. Intern, Jewish Hosp. Bklyn., 1956-57, resident, 1957-58, 61-62, renal fellow, 1958-59; practice medicine, specializing in internal medicine, N.Y.C., 1962-71, Phoenix, 1971—; instr. to asst. clin. prof. internal medicine State U. N.Y. Coll. Medicine, Bklyn., 1962-71; clin. investigator, metabolic research unit Jewish Hosp. Bklyn., 1962-71; cons. in field; mem. staff Phoenix Bapt., Maryvale Samaritan, Good Samaritan, St. Joseph's Hosp., Vets. Affairs Med. Ctr., Phoenix. Served to capt. M.C., U.S. Army, 1959-61. Diplomate Am. Bd. Internal Medicine. Fellow ACP; mem. AMA, Am. Soc. Internal Medicine, Am. Coll. Nuclear Physicians (charter mem.), Am. Soc. Nephrology, Am. Soc. Hypertension (charter mem.), Ariz. Med. Assn., 38th Parallel Med. Soc. S. Korea, Ariz., Maricopa County Med. Assn., Sigma Xi, Phi Lambda Upsilon, Alpha Omega Alpha. Contb articles to med. jours. Home: 24 E Wagon Wheel Dr Phoenix AZ 85020-4063

GOLDBERG, MORTON EDWARD, pharmacologist; b. Phila., July 11, 1932; s. Herman and Ethel (Shill) G.; m. Janet Louise Werlin, Aug. 15, 1954; children—Shellie, Ellen, David. B.S., Phila. Coll. Pharmacy and Sci., 1954, M.S. in Pharmacology, 1955, DSc in Pharmacology, 1958. Sr. pharmacologist Abbott Labs., North Chicago, Ill., 1958-60; asst. dir. pharmacology Union Carbide Corp., Tuxedo, N.Y., 1960-69; dir. pharmacodynamics Warner Lambert Research Inst., Morris Plains, N.J., 1969-73; dir. pharmacology Squibb Inst. Med. Research, Princeton, N.J., 1973-77; v.p. biomed. research Stuart Pharms. div. ICI Americas, Wilmington, Del., 1977-84; v.p. rsch., devel., and regulatory affairs ICI Pharm. Group divsn. ICI Ams. (now Zeneca Pharm.), Wilmington, Del., 1984-92; clin. prof. pharmacology and exptl. therapeutics Dept. Pharmacology U. Pa. Sch. Medicine, Phila., 1992—; vis. prof. toxicology Phila. Coll. Pharmacy and Sci.; vis. prof. Med. Coll. Pa., Phila., Hahnemann U., Phila.; cons. to pharm. industry in drug discovery and devel., 1992—; mem. Extramural Sci. Adv. Bd., NIDA, 1993—. Editor-in-chief: series Pharmacological and Biochemical Properties of Drug Substances; contbr. articles to profl. jours. Asst. scoutmaster Boy Scouts Am., Glen Rock, N.J., 1968-72. NIH grantee, 1961-64. Fellow Acad. Pharm. Sci., AAAS, N.Y. Acad. Sci.; mem. Am. Soc. Pharmacology and Exptl. Therapeutics, Behavioral Pharmacology Soc., Internat. Soc. Biochem. Pharmacology, Soc. Toxicology (charter), Sigma Xi, Rho Chi. Home: 715 Severn Rd Wilmington DE 19803-1725

GOLDBERG, MORTON FALK, ophthalmologist, educator; b. Lawrence, Mass., June 8, 1937; s. Maurice and Helen Janet (Falk) G.; m. Myrna Davidov, Apr. 6, 1968; children—Matthew Falk, Michael Falk. A.B. magna cum laude, Harvard U., 1958, M.D. cum laude, 1962; Doctoris Honoris Causa, U. Coimbra, Portugal, 1995. Diplomate Am. Bd. Ophthalmology. Intern Peter Bent Brigham Hosp., Boston, 1962-63; resident Wilmer Inst. John Hopkins Hosp., Balt., 1963-67, head dept., dir. Wilmer Inst., 1989—; prof. and head ophthalmology Eye and Ear Infirmary U. Ill. Hosp., Chgo., 1970-89. Author: (with D. Paton) Injuries of the Eye, the Lids and the Orbit: Diagnosis and Management, 1968, Management of Ocular Injuries, 1976; editor: Genetic and Metabolic Eye Disease, 1974, (with G.A. Peyman and D.R. Sanders) Principles and Practice of Ophthalmology (3 vols.), 1980; editor-in-chief Archives of Ophthalmology, Chgo., 1984-94; contbr. articles to profl. jours. Lt. comdr. USPHS, 1967-69. Recipient award for outstanding contbns. in the field of vision research Alcon Research Inst., 1987, Univ. Scholar award U. Ill.-Chgo., 1986. Fellow Royal Australian Coll. Ophthalmologists (hon.), Am. Acad. Ophthalmology (sr. honor award 1985); mem. Am. Ophthal. Soc., Chgo. Ophthal. Soc. (pres. 1985-86), Assn. Rsch. in Vision and Ophthalmology (trustee 1985-90, pres. 1989-90), Assn. Univ. Profs. Ophthalmology (trustee 1985-91, pres. 1990-91), Macula Soc. (pres. 1980-82). Home: 3607 Anton Farms Rd Baltimore MD 21208-1705 Office: Johns Hopkins Med Insts Wilmer Eye Inst 600 N Wolfe St Baltimore MD 21205-2104

GOLDBERG, NEIL S., dermatologist; b. N.Y.C., June 16, 1958; m. Debra Karen Funt, Jan. 26, 1991; two children. BS, Northwestern U., 1978, MD, 1982. Diplomate Am. Bd. Dermatology. Assoc. prof. dermatology N.Y. Med. Coll., Valhalla, N.Y., 1986-93; pvt. practice dermatology White Plains, Bronxville, N.Y., 1994—; mem. data and safety com. Lyne Vaccine Study Connaught Labs., 1994—; mem. edtl. bd. Skin and Allergy News, 1994—. Contbr. over 40 articles to profl., peer-reviewed jours. Fellow Am. Acad. Dermatology. Office: 77 Pondfield Rd Bronxville NY 10708 Other: 222 Westchestr Ave White Plains NY 10604

GOLDBERG, PAUL BERNARD, gastroenterologist, clinical researcher; b. Bklyn., Apr. 11, 1950; s. Samuel and Eva (Turkenitz) G.; m. Harriet Ruth Ferrer, July 8, 1973 (div. 1987); children: Deborah Lynn, Susan Michelle; m. Mary Alice Denaro, June 23, 1990; 1 child, Laura Alicia. BA in Chemistry summa cum laude, Cornell U., 1967-71, MD, 1971-75. Diplomate Am. Bd. Internal Medicine, Am. Bd. Gastroenterology. Intern in medicine Hosp. of U. of Pa., Phila., 1975-76, resident in medicine, 1976-78, fellow in gastroenterology, 1978-80, fellow in nutritional support svc., 1979-80; med. coord. and founder nutritional support svc. Lakeland (Fla.) Gen. Hosp., 1980-81; attending physician Halifax Med. Ctr., 1980—, Ormond Meml. Hosp., 1980—, Humana Hosp., 1980—, Fish Meml. Hosp., New Smyrna Beach, Fla., 1989—, Peninsula Med. Ctr., 1989-94; pres. Sunshine Health Care Plan, Inc., 1983-86, v.p., 1986-87; chief staff Humana Hosp., Daytona Beach, 1986-88, trustee, 1986-89, mem. exec. comj., 1984-91; mem. rev. bd. Coastal Instnl. Rev., 1990-93, chmn. rev. bd., 1993—; expert reviewer Fla. Dept. Profl. Regulation, 1990—; pres. med. staff Halifax Hosp., 1996-97; clin. asst. prof. medicine dept. family medicine U. South Fla. Rschr. and author in field. Physician adv. Daytona chpt. Crohn's and Colitis Found., 1991-95. Recipient Nat. award Ford Future Scientists of Am., 1967, Westinghouse Sci. Talent Search finalist, 1967. Fellow ACP, Am. Coll. Gastroenterology; mem. Am. Gastroent. Soc., Am. Soc. Gastrointestinal Endoscopy, Am. Soc. for Parenteral and Enteral Nutrition (pres. Fla. chpt. 1991-92), Volusia County Med. Soc. (exec. com. 1991-94, co-chmn. mini internship program 1992-94), Fla. Gastrointestinal Soc., Fla. med. Assn. (alt. del. to ho. of dels. 1990-95), Fla. Assn. Nutritional Support (1st pres.), Rotary, Phi Beta Kappa, Alpha Omega Alpha. Office: Gastrointestinal Assocs 201 N Clyde Morris Blvd Ste 100 Daytona Beach FL 32114-2734

GOLDBERG, RICHARD JEROME, psychiatrist; b. Brookline, Mass., Mar. 14, 1949; s. Ralph and Rosalind C. (Cubell) G.; children: Emily Dara, Jenna Suzanne; m. Sandra Livingston. AB, Cornell U., 1970; MD, SUNY, Buffalo, 1974. Diplomate Am. Bd. Psychiatry and Neurology. Intern Albert Einstein Med. Ctr., Phila., 1974-75; resident in psychiatry Yale U., 1975-78; psychiatrist-in-chief R.I. Hosp., Womens and Infants Hosp., Providence, 1986—; prof. psychiatry and human behavior; prof. dept. medicine, 1991. Fellow Am. Psychiat. Assn.; mem. Am. Assn. Gen. Hosp. Psychiatry (pres.). Office: RI Hosp Dept Psychiatry Providence RI 02903

GOLDBERG, ROBERT ALAN, ophthalmology educator; b. L.A., Mar. 25, 1957; m. Jan Takasugi; children: Kevin, Gina. BA in Psychology with distinction, Stanford U., 1979; MD, UCLA, 1983. Diplomate Am. Bd. Ophthalmology. Resident in internal medicine St. Mary Med. Ctr., Long Beach, Calif., 1983-84; resident in ophthalmology Jules Stein Eye Inst., UCLA Sch. Medicine, 1984-87, fellow in ophthalmic plastic and reconstructive surgery, 1987-88, fellow in orbital oncology, 1988-89, vis. asst. prof., 1988, asst. prof., 1989-94, assoc. prof., 1994—, chief orbital and ophthalmic plastic surgery divsn., 1990—, dir. Orbital Disease Ctr., 1993—; attending physician Wadsworth VA Hosp., L.A., 1988—, Sepulveda VA Hosp., L.A., 1988—, Olive View-UCLA Med. Ctr., 1989—; presenter, vis. lectr. in field at numerous med. ctrs., univ., congresses, meetings in field. Contbr. over 50 articles and abstracts to med. jours., chpts. to books. Grantee Karl Kirchgessner Found. Ophthalmology Endowment Fund, 1989, UCLA, 1991, 93, 94, 95, IOLAB Corp., 1993, also others. Fellow Am. Soc. Ophthalmic Plastic and Reconstructive Surgery (edn. com. 1993-94, program chmn. 1994-95, exec. com. 1994—, pub. rels. and promotions com. 1995—, Lester T. Jones Surg. Anatomy award 1995), Am. Acad. Ophthalmology (Physician's honor award 1994); mem. AMA (Physician's Recognition award 1994), Rsch. To Prevent Blindness (ophthal. assoc., grantee 1992), Assn. for Rsch. in Vision and Ophthalmology, Pacific Coast Oto-Ophthal. Soc., Calif. Med. Assn., L.A. Med. Assn., L.A. Soc. Ophthalmology, Bay Surg. Soc., Phi Beta Kappa. Office: UCLA Sch Medicine Jules Stein Eye Inst 100 Stein Plz Los Angeles CA 90095-7006

GOLDBERG, ROBERT LEWIS, preventive and occupational medicine physician; b. Phila., Aug. 13, 1953. MD, Jefferson Med. Coll., 1976. Diplomate Am. Bd. Preventive Medicine. Resident in family medicine Scenic Gen. Hosp., Modesto, Calif., 1976-77; intensive resident occupl. medicine U. Calif., San Francisco, 1987-88; pres., med. dir. Valley Occupl. Med. Group, Modesto, 1978—. Fellow Am. Coll. Occupl. Medicine; mem. Am. Bd. Preventive Medicine (trustee 1995—), Am. Coll. Occupl. and Environ. Medicine (bd. dirs.). Office: Valley Occupl Medical Group 1524 McHenry Ave Ste 520 Modesto CA 95350

GOLDBERG, STANLEY JULIAN, pediatric cardiologist; b. Louisville, Oct. 17, 1934; s. Joseph Emanuel and Sara (Kaplan) G.; m. Elaine Goldberg, June 21, 1959; children: Susan, Steven Mark. AB, Ind. U., 1956; MD, Ind. U., Indpls., 1959. Diplomate in pediatrics and pediatric cardiology Am. Bd. Pediatrics. Intern L.A. County Hosp., 1959-60; resident in pediatrics Western Resume U. Hosp., 1960-62; fellow in pediatric cardiology UCLA, 1962-64; from assoc. prof. to prof. pediatric cardiology U. Ariz., Tucson, 1970—; from asst. prof. to assoc. prof. UCLA, 1964-70. Author: Peditaric and Adolescent Echocardiography, 1975, 2d edit., 1980, Doppler Echocardiography, 1985, 2d edit., 1988. Office: U Ariz 1501 N Campbell Tucson AZ 85724-5073

GOLDBERGER, DAVID, ophthalmologist; b. Bronx, Mar. 6, 1948; s. Sam and Sarlota (Jakobowits) G.; m. Arlene Sharon Levy, Feb. 20, 1977; children: Seth, Sasha, Elizabeth. BS, CCNY, 1969; MD, NYU, 1973. Diplomate Am. Bd. Ophthalmology. Intern Lenox Hill Hosp., 1973-74; resident L.I. Jewish Hosp., 1974-77; ophthalmologist pvt. practice, Hallandale, Fla., 1977—, Pembroke Pines, Fla., 1985—. Office: 2221 N University Dr B Pembroke Pines FL 33024

GOLDBERGER, LEO, psychologist, educator; b. Vukovar, Yugoslavia, June 28, 1930; came to U.S. 1952, naturalized 1959; s. Eugene and Helen (Berkovitz) G.; m. Nancy R. Rule, Aug. 19, 1970; 1 child, Jessica. B.A., McGill U., 1951; Ph.D., NYU, 1958; Diploma, N.Y. Psychoanalytical Inst., 1967. Research psychologist Cornell U. Med. Coll., N.Y.C., 1955-56; prof., dir. Research Ctr. Mental Health, NYU, N.Y.C., 1969—; cons. in field . Editor in chief Psychoanalysis and Contemporary Thought, 1970—. Editor: (with S. Breznitz) Handbook of Stress, 1982, 2d edit., 1993; (with others) LSD: Personality and Experience, 1972; editor: The Rescue of the Danish Jews, 1987. Contbr. articles to profl. jours. NIMH research career devel. awardee, 1956-58; U.S. Air Force grantee, 1958-61; NIMH grantee, 1963-77; recipient Knight's Cross by Queen Margrethe II of Denmark, 1993. Fellow Am. Psychol. Assn.; mem. Am. Psychoanalytic Assn., Inetrnat. Psychoanalytic Assn. Office: NYU Dept Psychology 6 Washington Pl New York NY 10003-6634

GOLDBERGER, NEAL MICHAEL, anesthesiologist; b. Schenectady, N.Y., Jan. 7, 1957; s. Alfred Lewis and Helen Sylvia (Cohen) G.; m. Lee Ann Soowal, Sept. 20, 1987; 1 child, Tess Lillian. BA magna cum laude, U. Pa., 1978; MD, Tufts U., 1982. Diplomate Am. Bd. Anesthesiology, with cert. in pain mgmt. Resident in anesthesia Letterman Army Med. Ctr., San Francisco, 1982-86; chief of anesthesia Blanchfield Army Hosp., Ft. Campbell, Ky., 1986-90; anesthesiologist Hartford (Conn.) Anesthesiology Assocs., 1990—; anesthesiologist, pain specialist Hartford Hosp., 1990—; med. dir. Pain Therapy Cons., Farmington, Conn., 1992—; clin. fellow pain U. Cin., 1985; clin. fellow pain Vanderbilt U., Nashville, 1988-89, asst. clin. prof. anesthesia, 1989-90; instr. anesthesia U. Conn., Hartford, 1995—. Contbg. author: Contemporary Issues in Chronic Pain Management, 1991. Lt. col. USAR, 1978—. Fellow Am. Coll. Pain Medicine; mem. Am. Soc. Anesthesiologists. Office: Hartford Anesthesiology Assocs 50 Columbus Blvd Hartford CT 06106

GOLDBLATT, STEVEN BRYCE, cardiologst; b. Long Branch, N.J., Feb. 26, 1959; s. Seymour and Sheila Golodblatt; m. Patricia Coughlin, May 6, 1990; 1 child, Ian Coughlin. BA in Biology and Psychology, SUNY, Buffalo, 1982; MD, SUNY, Syracuse, 1986. Diplomate Am. Bd. Internal Medicine, Am. Bd. Cardiology. Intern, then resident in internal medicine Hartford (Conn.) Hosp., 1986-89, fellow in cardiology, 1990-93; pvt. practice, Hartford, 1993—. Fellow Am. Coll. Cardiology. Office: Hartford Cardiology Group 100 Retreat Ave Ste 402 Hartford CT 06106

GOLDBLUM, CARL MARTIN, surgeon; b. N.Y.C., July 14, 1942; arrived in Israel, 1975.; s. Kenneth Bernard and Adele Judith (Brochin) G.; m. Anita Steiner, July 3, 1966 (div. Nov. 1984); children: Rishona, Hillel, Nataniel; m. Krystyna Nawadov, June 10, 1985; children: Kim, Korain. BA in Biology, U. Pa., 1963; MD, Albany Med. Coll., 1968. Diplomate Am. Bd. Surgery, Nat. Bd. Med. Examiners. Sr. surgeon Barzilai Med. Ctr. Hosp., Ashkelon, Israel, 1975-86, asst. chief dept. surgery, 1986-88, sr. asst. chief dept. surgery, 1989—; surgeon Macabi Health Maintenance Orgn., Ashkelon, Kiryat Gat, Israel, 1989—; cons. surgeon Taegu (Korea) Presbyn. Hosp., 1973-75. Active Congregation Netzach Yisrael, Ashkelon, 1975—, Assn. Americans and Canadians in Israel, 1976—, Yated-Children with Down Syndrome, Israel, 1987—. Major USMC, 1973-75, med. corps Israel Def. Forces, 1975-93. Mem. Israel Surg. Soc., Israel Soc. Colon and Rectal Surgeons, Israel Trauma Soc., Israel Med. Assn., Alpha Omega Alpha (fellow Theta chpt. 1968—). Home: Rechov Zvi Segal 104, 78487 Barnea Ashkelon Israel Office: Barzilai Med Ctr Hosp, Dept Surgery, Ashkelon Israel

GOLDE, DAVID WILLIAM, physician, educator; b. N.Y.C., Oct. 23, 1940. BS in Chemistry, Fairleigh Dickinson U., 1962; MD, McGill U., 1966. Diplomate: Am Bd. Internal Medicine, Am. Bd. Med. Oncology, Nat. Bd. Med. Examiners. Asst. research chemist Gen. Foods Corp., 1962; intern. U. Calif. Hosps., San Francisco, 1966-67, resident in medicine, 1970-72, fellow Cancer Research Inst., 1971-72; staff cons. continuing edn. and tng. br. div. regional med. program (NIH), 1967-68, resident in clin. pathology, 1968-70; hematology fellow NIH, 1969-70; instr. medicine U. Calif., San Francisco, 1972-73, asst. prof., 1973-74; asst. prof. medicine UCLA, 1974-75, assoc. prof., 1975-79, prof., 1979-91, chief div. hematology-oncology, 1981-91, prof. emeritus, 1991—, co-dir. Clin. Rsch. Ctr., 1974-87, dir., 1987-91, dir. AIDS Ctr., 1986-90; Enid A. Haupt prof. hematologic oncology Meml. Sloan-Kettering Cancer Ctr., N.Y.C., 1991—; attending physician Sloan-Kettering Cancer Ctr., N.Y.C., 1991—, head divsn. hematologic oncology, 1991-96; mem. Sloan-Kettering Inst., 1991—; prof. medicine Cornell U. Med. Coll., N.Y.C., 1991—; prof. molecular pharmacology and therapeutics Cornell U. Grad. Sch. Med. Scis., N.Y.C., 1992—; physician-in-chief Meml. Hosp., 1996—. Mem. editorial bd. Blood, 1978-81, Peptides, 1979-83, Leukemia, 1986—, Scand. Jour. Haematology (now European Jour. Haematology), 1986-93; editor Blood Revs., 1986-93; assoc. editor Cancer Rsch., 1989—; contbr. numerous articles to profl. jours. With USPHS, 1967-70. Fellow ACP; mem. AAAS, Am. Assn. Cancer Research, Am. Fedn. Clin. Research, Am. Soc. Clin. Investigation, Am. Soc. Clin. Oncology, Am. Soc. Hematology, Assn. Am. Physicians, Endocrine Soc., Internat. Soc. Exptl. Hematology (councillor 1995—), Soc. Biological Therapy, Internat. Assn. for Comparative Rsch. on Leukemia, Soc. Exptl. Biology and Medicine, Western Soc. Clin. Investigation (pres. 1989-90), Western Soc. Clin. Rsch., Alpha Omega Alpha. Office: Meml Sloan-Kettering Ctr 1275 York Ave New York NY 10021-6007

GOLDEN, ALFRED, pathologist; b. N.Y.C., Aug. 4, 1908; s. Bernard and Rheba (Dryer) G.; m. Libby Siegel, Sept. 8, 1955; children—David Alfred, Frederick Leonard. B.S., U. Wis., 1930, M.S., 1932; M.D., Washington U., St. Louis, 1938. Diplomate Am. Bd. Pathology. Assoc. prof. pathology U. Tenn., Memphis, 1946-48, U. Buffalo, 1948-55; dir. labs. Jennings Meml. Hosp. and Blain Meml. Hosp., Detroit, 1955-72, St. Vincent Med. Ctr., Toledo, Ohio, 1972-77; cons. pathologist Takoma Park Gen. Hosp., Md., 1942-46; cons. to hosps. and med. ctrs., Detroit, 1955-72. Contbr. articles to profl. publs. Bd. dirs., pres. Physicians for Social Responsibility, Phoenix, 1981—. Served to lt. col. USMC, 1941-46. Fellow Am. Coll. Pathologists, ACP, Am. Soc. Clin. Pathologists; mem. Am. Cancer Soc. (v.p., bd. dirs. Ariz. div. 1984—), Scottsdale Ctr. for Arts. Club: Mens League (Scottsdale, Ariz.) (bd. dirs. 1982—). Home: 7527 N Del Norte Dr Scottsdale AZ 85258-3564

GOLDEN, CHARLES JOSH, neuropsychologist, consultant; b. L.A., Nov. 8, 1949; s. Joseph Arnold and Jennie (Elhai) G.; m. Heather Phillips, Oct. 26, 1986; children: Zarabeth, Leila, Chloe. BA, Pomona Coll., 1971; PhD, U. Hawaii, 1975. Diplomate Clin. Psychology and Neuropsychology. Asst. prof. U. S.D., Vermillion, 1975-78; assoc. prof. Med. Ctr. U. Nebr., Omaha, 1979-83, prof. Med. Ctr., 1983-87; prof. Drexel U., Phila., 1987-90; dir. neuropsychology, dir. program ops. Schirm Assocs., Milford, Pa., 1990-93; dir. neuropsychology Nova Care Chesapeake Rehab. Hosp., 1993-94; prof. psychology Nova Southeastern U., Fort Lauderdale, Fla., 1994—. Author: Diagnosis and Rehabilitation in Clinical Neuropsychology, 1979, 2d edit., 1981, Clinical Interpretation of Object Tests, 1981, 2d edit., 1989, Luria-Nebraska Neuropsychology, 1981, 2d edit., 1985; editor Internat. Jour. Clin. Neuropsychology, 1981—. Fellow APA (div. bd. dirs. 1978-81), Nat. Acad. Neuropsychologists (pres. 1980-82). Home: 2862 NE 35th Ct Lghthse Point FL 33064-8574 Office: 3301 College Ave Fort Lauderdale FL 33314

GOLDEN, ELOISE ELIZABETH, community health nurse; b. Hope, Ind., Nov. 20, 1938; d. John M. and Hazel E. (Gosch) Holder; m. Don Golden, Aug. 2, 1959; children: David, Susanne. Diploma, Ball State U., 1959. RN. Office nurse Columbus, Ind.; staff nurse Pub. Health Dept. Bartholomew County, Columbus; parish nurse, clinicare staff nurse, housecall coord. Bartholomew County Hosp., Columbus, intake coord. Hospice, 1991—. Lutheran. Home: 11635 E 600 N Hope IN 47246

GOLDEN, KIMBERLY KAY, critical care, flight nurse; b. Munich, July 31, 1961; came to U.S., 1961; d. Henry Davis and Mary Walker G. AA, Hinds Jr. Coll., Raymond, Miss., 1980, ASN, 1984; BSN, U. Miss., Jackson, 1987, AS in EMT-Paramedic, 1990. Cert. ACLS instr., PALS provider and instr.; emergency nurse, crit. care RN; cert. paramedic, Miss., Tenn. Staff nurse neuro ICU U. Miss. Med. Ctr., 1984-85, staff nurse surg. ICU, 1985-87; staff nurse emergency rm. Rankin Gen. Hosp., Brandon, Miss., 1987-88; flight nurse Lifestar Helicopter Flight Svc., 1988-91; staff nurse emergency rm., ICU Nightingale Nursing, Jackson, 1988-91, Riveroaks Hosp., Jackson, 1990-91; staff RN emergency rm., Aerovesta flight Midland Meml. Hosp., Tex., 1991-93; flight nurse Hosp. Wing BTLS, Memphis, Tenn., 1993—; examiner Nat. Registry EMT-P; advanced trauma life support station instr.; affiliate faculty paramedic program U. Miss. Faculty scholar Hinds Jr. Coll., 1983. Mem. AACN, Nat. Flight Assn., Emergency Nurses Assn. Baptist. Office: PO Box 140466 Austin TX 78714-0466

GOLDEN, MICHAEL ARTHUR, vascular surgeon; b. Phila., Dec. 21, 1955; s. Mano Robert and Sue (Aronsohn) G.; m. Susan Andrea Jacobson, Sept. 29, 1985; children: Elizabeth, Robert. BA, Amherst Coll., 1977; MD, U. Penn. Sch. of Med., 1981. Diplomate Am. Bd. Surgery, Am. Bd. Vascular Surgery. Intern Brigham and Womens Hosp., Boston, 1981-82, resident in gen. surgery, 1981-87; fellow in gen. vascular surgery Brigham and Womens Hosp., 1989-90; fellow in resh. U. Wash., Seattle, Wash., 1987-89; asst. prof. U. Pa. Sch. of Med., Phila., 1990—; staff vascular surgeon Hosp. U. of Pa., Phila., 1990—; Dir. Vascular Fellowship Program, Hosp. U. of Pa., Phila., 1994—, Co-dir. Vascular Noninvasive Lab., VA Med. Ctr., 1990—, Editorial Bd. Vascular Surgery, Glen Cove, N.Y., 1995—, resh. scientist, Hosp. U. of Pa., 1990—. Recipient of grant Am. Heart Assoc., resh. grant, VA, 1991-93. Fellow ACS; mem. Internat. Soc. Cardiovasc. Surgery (Lifeline Found. Rsch. award 1995), Internat. Soc. for Applied Cardiovasc. Biology (Young Investigator award1989), Assn. for Acad. Surgery, Eastern Vascular Soc., Am. Soc. for investigative Pathology. Office: Hosp of Univ of Pa Silverstein Bldg. 4th Flr. 3400 Spruce St Philadelphia PA 19104

GOLDEN, REYNOLD STEPHEN, family practice physician, geriatrician; b. Herkimer, N.Y., Jan. 11, 1937; s. Harold Theodore and Ethel Anne (Myers) G.; m. Gale Holtz, Nov. 26, 1959 (div. May 1978); children: Nathan Myers, Jennifer Lynn (dec.), Laura Beth (Lieba); m. Ellen Jean Moore, Sept. 9, 1978; children: Melissa Nan, Benjamin Harold. AB cum laude, Harvard Coll., 1958; MD, SUNY, Syracuse, 1962. Diplomate Am. Bd. Family Practice, Am. Bd. Internal Medicine. Intern Lankenau Hosp., Phila., 1962-63; resident in internal medicine SUNY, Syracuse, 1963-66; pvt. practice Utica, N.Y., 1966-78; dir. family practice residency St. Elizabeth Hosp., Utica, 1978-92, St. Francis Hosp., Poughkeepsie, N.Y., 1992-95; clin. assoc. prof. dept. family medicine SUNY, Syracuse, 1991—; chief of geriatrics Rochester Park Med. Group, 1995—; med. dir. long-term care Park Ridge Health Sys., Rochester, 1995—; cons. residency assistance program, Kansas City, Mo., 1988—; charter mem. N.Y. State Coun. on Grad. Med. Edn., N.Y.C., 1987-89. Editor N.Y. Family Physician, 1987-92. Mem. N.Y. State Acad. Family Physicians (chmn. bd. dirs. 1988-89, pres. 1992-93, Presdl. Citation 1985, 86, 88), Cen. N.Y. Acad. Medicine (pres. 1977-79, Golden Torch award 1989). Jewish. Office: 500 Island Cottage Rd Rochester NY 14612

GOLDEN, ROBERT NEAL, psychiatrist, researcher; b. Phila., Aug. 27, 1953; s. Maxwell Solomon and Rosalie (Shragowitz) G.; m. Shannon Celeste Kenney, May 27, 1979; children: Troy, Blair, Sean. BA, Yale U., 1975; MD, Boston U., 1979. Diplomate Am. Bd. Psychiatry and Neurology. Resident in psychiatry U. N.C., Chapel Hill, 1979-83, chief resident, 1982-83, asst. prof. psychiatry, 1985-89, assoc. prof. psychiatry, 1989-94; prof., chair U. N.C., Chapel Hill, Md., 1994—; assoc. dir. Gen. Clin. Rsch. Ctr. U. N.C., 1990-95, Mental Health Clin. Rsch. Ctr. U. N.C., 1989-94. Contbr. articles to profl. jours. Ginsburg fellow Group Advancement Psychiatry, 1981-82, Laughlin fellow Am. Coll. Psychiatry, 1983. Mem. AAAS, Am. Psychiat. Assn., Soc. Biol. Psychiatry, Internat. Soc. Psychoneuroendocrinology. Office: U NC Sch Medicine Dept Psychiatry Chapel Hill NC 27599

GOLDEN, RONALD AARON, physician, nephrologist; b. Kew Gardens, N.Y., Apr. 5, 1943; s. Max and Sally (Hoffman) G.; m. Ruthe Susan Feigenbaum, Mar. 11, 1967; children: Meredith Lynn, Lauren Hillary, Jessica Amy. BS, Hobart Coll., 1963; MD, NYU, 1967. Diplomate Am. Bd. Internal Medicine, Am. Bd. Nephrology. Attending nephrologist N.Y. Hosp. Med. Ctr. of Queens, 1974—, Montefiore Med. Ctr., Bronx, N.Y., 1974—; cons. Misericordia Hosp. Pelham Bos Divsn., St. Barnabas Hosp., La Guardia Hosp., 1975—. Lt. comdr. USN, 1972-73. Mem. Am. Soc. Nephrology, Internat. Soc. Nephrology, Renal Physicians Assn. Jewish.

Office: Nephrology Assoc PC 1874 Pelham Pky S Bronx NY 10461-3733 also: NY Hosp Med Ctr Queens 56-45 Main St Flushing NY 11355

GOLDEN, SUSAN ALBEA, medical technologist; b. Anniston, Ala., July 15, 1959; d. Albert P. and Helen Louise (King) Albea; m. Philip Eugene Golden, Dec. 25, 1986. BS in Biology, Jacksonville State U., 1986, MS in Biology, 1995. Cert. med. technologist. Rsch. asst. U. Ala., Birmingham, 1986-89; med. technologist St. Clair Regl. Hosp., Pell City, Ala., 1989—. Mem. PETA, World Wildlife Fund, Doris Day Animal League, Humane Soc. of U.S., Environ. Def. Fund. Home: 1805 Truss Ferry Rd Pell City AL 35125 Office: St Clair Regl Hosp 2805 Hospital Dr Pell City AL 35125

GOLDEN, WILLIAM EDWARD, physician; b. Brooklyn, N.Y., Dec. 26, 1953; s. Morton M. and Margaret (Polusky) G.; m. Kimberly Ann Johnson, Feb. 27, 1982; children: Emily Jane, Abigail Anne. AB, Brown U., 1975; Baylor Coll. of Med., 1978; attended, Wharton Business Sch., 1982. Resident Presbyterian-St. Luke's Med. Ctr., Chicago, Il., 1978-79 1980-82, chief resident, 1982; Morris Fishbeen fellow, 1979-80; RWJ clin. scholar U. Pa., Philadelphia, Pa., 1982; asst. prof. U. Arkansas for med. sci., Little Rock, Ar., 1984-90, assoc. prof., 1990—; dir. gen. internal med. U. Ark.for Med. Scis., Little Rock, Ark., 1984—; prin. clin. coord. Ark. Found. for Med. Care, 1992—; trustee Am. Soc. Internat. Med., Washington, 1986-95, pres., 1995-96; mem. Am. Med. Review Rsch. Ctr., Washington, 1990—, chair, 1995—; mem. Am. Med. Assn. coun. on med. edn., Chgo., 1989—. Fellow ACP; mem. AMA (accreditation coun. continuing med. edn. 1990-92, liaison com. for med. edn. 1992—), Am. Assn. Med. Colls., Am. Soc. Internal Medicine, Soc. of Gen. Internal Medicine. Office: U. Arkansas for Med Sci 4301 W Markham St # 641 Little Rock AR 72205-7101

GOLDENBERG, DON LEE, rheumatologist, medical educator; b. Milw., Feb. 9, 1944; s. Charles and Marion (Werba) G.; m. Patty Konheim, July 4, 1965; children: Wendy Goldenberg Hagen, Julie. BS, U. Wis., 1965, MD, 1969. Diplomate Am. Bd. Internal Medicine, Am. Bd. Rheumatology. Intern Albert Einstein Coll. Medicine, Bronx, N.Y., 1969-70; resident Montefiore Hosp. and Med. Ctr., Bronx, 1970-72; clin. and rsch. fellow in rheumatology Boston U. Sch. Medicine, 1972-73, asst. prof. medicine, 1975-79, clin. program dir. arthritis sect., 1979-88, assoc. prof. medicine, 1979-87, prof. medicine, 1988; prof. medicine Tufts U. Sch. Medicine, 1989—; chief rheumatology Madigan Army Med. Ctr., Tacoma, 1973-75; asst. vis. physician Boston City Hosp., 1975-79, chmn. med. records com., 1976-79, physician-in-charge Arthritis Clinic, 1977-82, assoc. dir. dept. medicine, 1977-86, dir. internship selection com. dept. medicine, 1977-86, chmn. affirmative action com., 1978-80, assoc. vis. physician, 1979-87; chief rheumatology, dir. arthritis fibromaylgia ctr. Newton-Wellesley (Mass.) Hosp., 1988—, chair clin. rsch. com., 1991—. Mem. editl. bd. Arthritis and Rheumatism, 1988-92, assoc. editor, 1990-95; mem. editl. bd. Jour. Intensive Care Medicine, 1985—, Jour. Musculoskeletal Pain, 1992—; contbr. over 150 articles to profl. jours., chpts. to books. Mem. profl. edn. com. Arthritis Found., 1980-84. Fellow ACP; mem. Am. Coll. Rheumatology (chmn. undergrad. edn. subcom. 1978-86, chmn. edn. devel. com. 1986-88), Mass. Med. Soc., N.E. Rheumatism Assn., New Eng. Rheumatism Soc. (pres. 1986-87). Office: Arthritis-Fibromyalgia Ctr 2000 Washington St Ste 304 Newton MA 02162

GOLDENBERG, GEORGE, retired pharmaceutical company executive; b. N.Y.C., Mar. 12, 1929; s. Gersh and Rose (Kolpacci) G.; m. Arlene Sandra Yudell, May 22, 1955; children: Steven Alan, Heidi Michele Goldenberg Handelsman, Jeffrey Evan Student, Blkyn. Coll., 1946-47; BS, Bklyn. Coll. Pharmacy of L.I. U., 1951. Pharmacist Dolcorts Pharmacy, N.Y.C., 1951-56; export mgr. Chem. Specialties Co., Inc., N.Y.C., 1956-58; sales mgr. Syntex Chem. Co., Inc., N.Y.C., 1958-60; asst. to pres. Syntex Labs., Inc., N.Y.C., 1960-61; gen. sales mgr. Panray-Parlam Corp., Englewood, N.J., 1961-63; v.p. Ormont Drug & Chem. Co., Inc., Englewood, 1963-64, exec. v.p., dir., 1964-66, pres., dir., 1966-81; sec., dir. Goldleaf Pharmacal Co., Inc., Englewood, N.J., 1966-81; pres., dir. Moleculon, Inc., 1982-88; pres., chief exec. officer, dir. Argus Pharmaceuticals Inc., The Woodlands, Tex., 1988-92; bd. dirs. Fed. Pharmacal Co., Ft. Lauderdale, Fla., Bedford Acme Surg. Co., Inc., Bklyn., Lawton Labs., Inc., Englewood, Ormont Diagnostics Ltd., London. Trustee L.I. U., Bklyn. Coll. Pharmacy. Mem. Bklyn. Coll. Pharmacy Alumni Assn. (pres.), Fedn. Alumni Assns. L.I. U. (pres.), Am. Pharm. Assn., Englewood Jr. C. of C., Young Pres. Orgn., Am. Mgmt. Assn., Drug and Allied Trades Assn., Delta Sigma Theta. Club: B'nai B'rith, The Polo Club of Boca Raton. Home: 16730 Colchester Ct Delray Beach FL 33484-6946

GOLDENBERG, KIM, university dean, internist. BS, SUNY, Stonybrook, 1968; MS, Polytech. Inst. N.Y., 1972; MD, Albany (N.Y.) Med. Coll., 1979. Dir. gen. internal medicine Wright State U., Dayton, Ohio, 1983-89; assoc. dean for students and currculum Sch. Medicine Wright State U., Youngstown, Ohio, 1989-90; dean Sch. Medicine Wright State U., Dayton, Ohio, 1990—; assoc. dean for students and curriculum Wright State U. Sch. Medicine, Dayton, Ohio, 1989-90, dean, 1990—. Office: Wright State U Sch Medicine PO Box 927 Dayton OH 45401-0927

GOLDENBERG, MARC R., cardiothoracic surgeon; b. Cin., Feb. 5, 1947; m. Nancy Jean Jacobs, June 25, 1972; children: Jack, Alice. BA, Washington U., St. Louis, 1969; MD, Jefferson Med. Coll., 1973. Diplomate Am. Bd. Surgery, Am Bd. Thoracic Surgery. Attending surgeon Grad. Hosp., Phila., 1983—; pvt. practice Phila. Mem. ACS, Soc. Thoracic Surgeons. Office: Louis F Plzak Jr MD One Graduate Plz Philadelphia PA 19146*

GOLDENBERG, MARVIN MANUS, pharmacologist, pharmaceutical developer; b. N.Y.C., July 7, 1935; s. Jacob and Sarah Goldenberg; m. Esther K. Gelman, Sept. 8, 1957; children: Sol Jeffrey, Lisa Shari. BS, Bklyn. Coll. Pharmacy, 1957; MS, Temple U., 1959; PhD, Med. Coll. Pa., 1965. Lic. pharmacist, N.Y., Pa. Group leader Norwich-Eaton Pharms., Norwich, N.Y., 1965-80; dir. immunopharmacology rsch. Merck Sharp & Dohme, Rahway, N.J., 1980-85, asst. dir. clin. rsch., 1985-88; dir. ophthalmic R&D Am. Cyanamid, Pearl River, N.Y., 1988-89, dir. ophthalmic rsch., 1989-91; v.p. pharm. product devel. and mfg. Reed and Carnrick div. Block Drug Co., Jersey City, N.J., 1991-92; v.p. pharmacology & clin. design, 1992-93; v.p. pharmacology clin. design, pres., asst. dir. drugs/IRB Mt. Sinai Med. Ctr., N.Y.C., 1994—; grant reviewer NIH and DRG, Bethesda, Md., 1978-95, fellowship reviewer, 1984-89. Author: The Role of Arachidonic Acid Oxygenation Products, 1984, Gastric Cytoprotection with Prostaglandins, 1985, Critical Review of Losartan, 1995, Analysis of the Asthma Drug Zileuteon, 1996; contbr. numerous articles to profl. jours.; inventor on numerous patents. Pres. Temple, Norwich, N.Y., 1972. Fellow Am. Soc. for Pharmacology, Am. Gastroent. Assn., Inflammation Rsch. Assn., Soc. of Clin. Pharmacology; mem. Am. Assn. Pharm. Scientists, N.Y. Soc. Health Care Specialists, Masons (pres. Norwich, N.Y. 1975). Office: Mt Sinai Med Ctr One Gustave L. Levy Pl New York NY 10029 also: 721 Shackamaxon Dr Westfield NJ 07090-3407

GOLDENBERG, SAMUEL, optometrist, school administrator; b. N.Y.C., Dec. 6, 1920; s. Marcus and Anna (Kantrowitz) G.; m. Renee Weiss, Mar. 30, 1950; 1 child, Ilene. OD, So. Coll. Optometry, Memphis, 1942; BA, Drew U., 1944; MA, Seton Hall U., 1955; PhD, NYU, 1967. Cert. optometrist, N.J.; cert. tchr., ednl. adminstr., sch. prin., N.J. Optometrist Convent Station, N.J., 1943—; tchr. Rockaway Twp. (N.J.) Pub. Schs., 1951-62; tchr. Morris Twp. (N.J.) Pub. Schs., 1962-68, prin., 1968-71, asst. supt., 1971-72; prin. Morristown (N.J.) Pub. Schs., 1972-78, sch. adminstr., 1978—. Cpl. USAF, 1944-45. Recipient citation USAF, 1945. Mem. N.J. Prins and Suprs. Assn., Morris Sch. Dist. Adminstrs. Assn., N.J. Adminstrs. Assn. Home: 325 Madison Ave Convent Station NJ 07961 Office: Morris Sch Dist 50 Early St Morristown NJ 07960

GOLDENTHAL, NATHAN DAVID, physician; b. Toronto, Can., Sept. 13, 1951; m. Elaine Zaifman, May 26, 1977. MD, U. Toronto, 1975; MPH, U. N.C., 1990. Diplomate Am. Bd. Forensic Examiners, Am. Bd. Forensic Medicine, Am. Bd. Preventive Medicine. Med. dir. Peoria (Ariz.) Med. Clinic, 1977-85; pvt. cons. Peoria, 1985-89; med. developer U. N.C., Chapel Hill, 1989-90; chief profl. svcs. USAF Logistics Command, Dayton, Ohio, 1990-92; dir. Ariz. Inst. Occupl. Safety and Health, Phoenix, 1992—; site physician TRW-Air Bag Safety, Mesa, Ariz., 1995—. Author: Understanding the American with Disabilities, 1993; manuscript reviewer Am. Indsl. Hygiene Jour., 1994-95; contbr. articles to profl. jours. Med. dir. Lyons Aquatic Rehab. Program, Phoenix, 1994-95; mem. tech. com. State Govern ACERP Project, Phoenix, 1994-95; chmn. occupl. health coun. Dept. Def., Dayton, Ohio, 1991-92, chmn. dept. strategic planning, 1991-92. Recipient Nat. Med. fellowship U. N.C., 1989, Pub. Health traineeship U. N.C., 1989. Fellow Am. Coll. Preventive Medicine; mem. Am. Coll. Occupl. Environ. Medicine, Maricopa County Med. Soc. Office: Ariz Inst Occupl Safety and Health 4105 N 20th St Ste 205 Phoenix AZ 85016

GOLDFARB, ALLEN L., cardiologist; b. Buffalo, Mar. 28, 1926; s. Samuel and Esther (Morrison) G.; m. Jo Anne Setel, June 26, 1949; children: Sandra, Donna, Carl. MD, U. Buffalo (now SUNY), 1951. Diplomate Am. Bd. Internal medicine. Private practice Buffalo, 1955-71; dir. coronary care unit Millard Fillmore Hosp., Buffalo, 1971-94, dir. noninvasive cardiac lab., 1994—. With U.S. Army, 1944-46, Japan. Mem. Buffalo Launch Club. Republican. Home: 41 Chatham Ave Buffalo NY 14216 Office: Millard Fillmore Hosp 3 Gates Cir Buffalo NY 14209

GOLDFARB, JOEL PETER, internist, gastroenterologist; b. Fitchburg, Mass., Jan. 17, 1949; s. Abraham and Eunice (Caplan) G.; m. Elizabeth Weinshel, Dec. 5, 1954. BA, Yale U., 1971; MD, NYU, 1975. Diplomate Am. Bd. Internal Medicine, Am. Bd. Gastroenterology. Resident NYU Bellevue, N.Y.C., 1975-78; fellow (liver) Yale, New Haven, Conn., 1978-79; fellow (G.I.) Columbia, N.Y.C., 1979-81; asst. prof. medicine Yeshiva U., Bronx, N.Y., 1981-84; ptnr. D. Penn MD, J. Patrowitz MD, J. Goldfarb MD, PA., Fort Lee, N.J., 1984—. Named one of Best Doctors of N.J., N.J. Monthly Mag. Fellow Am. Coll. Physicians, Am. Coll. Gastroenterology. Home: 2621 Palisade Ave Apt 5B Bronx NY 10463-6108 Office: 1600 Parker Ave Fort Lee NJ 07024

GOLDFARB, MARK STEWART, ophthalmologist; b. N.Y.C., Jan. 25, 1946; s. William Sidney and Ruth May (Green) G.; m. Margaret Sue Ravits, Oct. 5, 1975; children: Julia, Sharon, Lauren. BA, NYU, 1966, MD, 1970. Diplomate Nat. Bd. Med. Examiners, Am. Bd. Ophthalmology. Intern in surgery Bellevue Hosp. Ctr., N.Y.C., 1970-71; resident in ophthalmology Mt. Sinai Hosp., N.Y.C., 1973-75, chief resident dept. opthalmology, 1975-76, asst. dept. opthalmology, 1976—, clin. instr. dept. ophthalmology, 1973-76, attending ophthalmologist, 1976—; attending ophthalmologist Holy Name Hosp., Teaneck, N.J., 1973-76, Hackensack (N.J.) U. Med. Ctr., 1976—; cons., attending ophthalmologist Bergen Pines County Hosp., Paramus, N.J., 1977—; pvt. practice Mark S. Goldfarb MD, FACS, PA, Hackensack-River Edge, N.J., 1976—; cons. Inst. for Child Devel., Hackensack U. Med. Ctr., 1976-95. Contbr. articles to profl. jours. Pres. Congregation Beth Tefillah, Paramus, 1991-93, bd. dirs., 1989—; physicians cabinet com. United Jewish Appeal of Bergen County, River Edge, N.J., 1980—. Lt. comdr. USPHS, 1971-73. Recipient Paramus honoree United Jewish Cmty., River Edge, 1987, Physician award Friends of Lubavitch, Teaneck, 1988, Ann. Dinner honoree Congregation Beth Tefillah, 1994. Fellow Am. Acad. Ophthalmology, Am. Coll. Surgeons; mem. AMA, Commd. Officers Assn. of USPHS, Assn. for Rsch. in Vision and Ophthalmology, Am. Assn. for Ophthalmology, Bergen County Med. Soc. (del./alt.), N.J. Acad. Ophthalmology, N.J. Med. Soc., Am. Soc. Cataract and Refractive Surgery, Contact Lens Assn. of Ophthalmologists, Internat. Glaucoma Congress, Am. Soc. Contemporary Ophthalmology, Mt. Sinai Ophthalmology Alumni Soc. (sec., founder), N.Y. Soc. Clin. Ophthalmology. Jewish. Office: Mark S Goldfarb MD FACS 130 Kinderkamack Rd Ste 205 River Edge NJ 07661-1932

GOLDFARB, ROBERT PAUL, neurological surgeon; b. St. Paul, Minn., July 17, 1936; s. Jack and Frances S. (Singer) G.; m. Lesley G. Zatz, Aug. 11, 1963; children: Jill, Pam. BA, U. Ariz., 1958; MD, Tulane U., 1962. Diplomate Am. Bd. Neurol. Surgery. Intern Michael Reese Hosp., Chgo., 1962-63; resident gen. surgery Presbyn. St. Luke's Hosp., Chgo., 1963-64; resident neurol. surgery U. Ill. Rsch. Hosp., Chgo., 1963-67; pres. med. staff Crippled Children's Svcs. So. Ariz., Tucson, 1973-75, Tucson Med. Ctr., 1978-80; neurol. surgeon Western Neurosurgery, Ltd., Tucson, 1980—; cons. U. Ariz. Athletics, Tucson, 1980—. Maj. USAFR, 1962-70. Fellow Am. Coll. Surgeons; mem. Am. Assn. Neurol. Surgeons, Congress Neurol. Surgeons, Am. Coll. Physician Execs. Office: Western Neurosurgery Ltd 2100 N Rosemont Blvd #110 Tucson AZ 85712

GOLDFARB, STANLEY, internist, educator; b. N.Y.C., Dec. 18, 1943; s. Robert Melvin and Mary Ann (Siegel) G.; m. Rayna Lynne Block, Aug. 30, 1970; children: Rachael, Michael. AB, Princeton U., 1965; MD, U. Rochester, 1969; MS, U. Pa., 1986. Intern Hosp. U. Pa., Phila., 1969-70, resident, 1970-73; asst. prof. U. Pa., Phila., 1974-84, assoc. prof., 1984-88, prof. medicine, 1988—; mem. nephrology bd. Am. Bd. Internal Medicine, Phila., 1988—. Editor: Hormones, Autocoids and Kidney, 1991. Bd. dirs, bd. regents ACP; bd. dirs. Nat. Kidney Found. Pa., Phila, 1988-90. NIH grantee, Washington, 1984-88; recipient Vol. award Nat. Kidney Found., N.Y.C., 1990. Mem. Am. Soc. Clin. Investigation. Home: 801 Murfield Rd Bryn Mawr PA 19010-1940 Office: Graduate Health System 22 & Chestnut Sts Philadelphia PA 19103

GOLDFINGER, STEPHEN MARK, psychiatrist; b. Bklyn., May 15, 1951; s. Bernard and Muriel (Scharfman) Goldfinger. AB, Harvard Coll., 1972; MD, Yale Med. Sch., 1976. Diplomate Am. Bd. Psychiatry and Neurology. Intern, resident Mt. Zion Hosp., U. Calif., San Francisco, 1975-79; dir. psychiat. emergency svcs. Dept. Psychiatry San Francisco Gen. Hosp., 1979-82, dir. outpatient svcs., 1982-85, dir. inpatient svcs., 1985-88; asst. prof. psychiatry U. Calif., San Francisco, 1980-88, assoc. prof., 1988; assoc. clin. dir. Mass. Mental Health Ctr., Boston, 1988-91, acting clin. dir., 1991-95; asst. prof. psychiatry Harvard Med. Sch., Boston, 1988—; sr. psychiatrist Mass. Dept. of Mental Health, 1994—; bd. dirs. Am. Assn. Community Psychiatrists, 1988—; cons. in field; prin. investigator NIMH Grant, Ind. Living vs. Evolving Consumer Households for the Homeless Mentally Ill; program com. Hosp. and Community Psychiatry Inst., 1991—; examiner Am. Bd. Psychiatry and Neurology, 1991—. Editor: Psychiatric Emergency Services at the Crossroads, 1988, Annual Review of Psychiatry, 1990, 1991, Psychiatric Aspects of AIDS and HIV Infections, 1990; contbr. numerous articles to profl. jours. Mem. San Francisco Mayors Task Force on Homeless, 1985-88; bd. dirs. Episcopal Sanctuary, San Francisco, 1985-86; mem. Am. Psychiat. Assn. Task Force on Homeless, Washington, 1983-84, 1989-92. Recipient NIMH Grant, 1990-96. Mem. Am. Psychiat. Assn. (chair com. on chronically mentally ill 1989-93, chair com. on homelessness 1993—, co-chair program com. 1988-90), Am. Assn. Gen. Hosp Psychiatrists (chair program com. 1984-88), Hosp. and Cmty. Psychiatry Inst. (program com. 1991-96), Group Advancement Psychiatry, Am. Assn. Cmty. Psychiatrists (bd. dirs.), Am. Assn. Emergency Psychiatrists (bd. dirs.), Am. Bd. Psychiatry and Neurology (examiner). Office: Mass Mental Health Ctr 74 Fenwood Rd Boston MA 02115-6113

GOLDFINGER, TEDD M., physician; b. Bklyn., May 24, 1956; children: Adam, Ryan. BA cum laude, CUNY, 1977; DO, Coll. Osteo. Medicine & Surg., Des Moines, 1980. Diplomate Am. Bd. Internal Medicine, Am. Bd. Cardiovasc. Disease. Cardiologist, med. officer USPHS, Sells, Ariz., 1983-84; cardiologist Canyon Cardiology, Tucson, 1986-90, Desert Cardiology of Tucson, Tucson, 1990—. Fellow Am. Coll. Cardiology, Am. Coll. Chest Physicians, Am. Coll. Cardiovasc. Interventionists; mem. AMA (Physician's Recognition award 1983-86), ACP, Pima County Med. Soc., Sigma Sigma Phi. Office: Desert Cardiology of Tucson 1925 W Orange Grove Rd 201 Tucson AZ 85704

GOLDFRANK, LEWIS ROBERT, physician; b. N.Y.C., Sept. 8, 1941; s. Herbert John and Helen (Colodny) G.; m. Susan M. Harrington, Aug. 29, 1964; children: Michelle, Andrew, Jennifer, Rebecca. BA, Clark U., 1963; MD, U. Brussels, Belgium, 1970. Resident Montefiore Hosp., Bronx, N.Y., 1971-73; dir. emergency medicine Morrisania Hosp., Bronx, 1973-76, North Cen. Bronx Hosp., 1976-79, Montefiore Hosp., 1976-79, Bellevue Hosp., Manhattan, N.Y., 1979—, NYU Med. Ctr., Manhattan, 1979—; dir. N.Y. City Poison Ctr., Manhattan, 1979—; bd. dirs. Soc. Acad. Emergency Medicine, 1990—. Author, editor: Goldfrank's Toxicologic Emergencies, 1978, 5th edit., 1994, Emergency Doctor, 1987, Diagnostic Testing in the Emergency Department, 1984. Recipient Am. Med. Writer's Assn. Hon. Mention, 1988, Hal Jayne Acad. Excellence award Soc. Acad. Emergency Medicine, 1990. Fellow Am. Coll. Emergency Physician, Am. Acad. Clin. Toxicology, Am. Coll. Physicians; mem. Am. Bd. Med. Toxicology (dir., chmn. 1985—). Home: 55 Grace Ln Ossining NY 10562-2129 Office: Bellevue Hosp Ctr First Ave # 27th St New York NY 10016

GOLDFRIED, ANITA POWERS, social worker, psychotherapist; b. N.Y.C., Feb. 11, 1940; m. Marvin R. Goldfried; children: Daniel, Michael. BS, CCNY, 1960, MS, 1962; MSW, SUNY, Stony Brook, 1980. Diplomate in clin. social work. Staff psychologist Jewish Vocat. Svc., Boston, 1962-64; rsch. assoc. SUNY, Stony Brook, 1967-69, 73-76; psychiat. social worker North Richmond Community Mental Health Ctr., S.I., N.Y., 1980-84; pvt. practice in psychotherapy N.Y.C., 1983—. Contbr. chpt. to book. Mem. NASW, Assn. Advancement Behavior Therapy, Behavior Therapy Soc. N.Y., Acad. Cert. Social Workers, Nat. Register Clin. Social Workers. Office: 127 E 69th St New York NY 10021-5017

GOLDHABER, PAUL, dental educator; b. N.Y.C., Mar. 16, 1924; married, 1949; 2 children. DDS, NYU, 1948; BS, CCNY, 1954; MA (hon.), Harvard U., 1962. Diplomate Am. Bd. Periodontics. Asst. ophthalmology rsch. Harvard Med. Sch., 1948-50; asst. dentist Sch. Dental and Oral Surgery Columbia U., 1950; rsch. fellow dental medicine Harvard Sch. Dental Medicine, 1954-55, rsch. assoc. oral pathology, 1955-56, assoc., 1956-59, from asst. prof. to assoc. prof., 1959-66, dir. postdoctoral studies, 1962-68, dean, 1968-90, prof. periodontics, 1966—, emeritus dean, 1990—; vis. rsch. fellow Sloan-Kettering Inst. Cancer Rsch., 1954-55, rsch. fellow, 1955-56, USPHS sr. rsch. fellow, 1956-61; chmn. dental study sect. NIH, 1968-71. Mem. Am. Assn. Dental Rsch. (pres. 1973-74), Inst. of Medicine, Internat. Assn. for Dental Rsch. (pres. 1985-86). Office: Harvard U Sch Dental Medicine 188 Longwood Ave Boston MA 02115-5819*

GOLDHAMER, DAVID J., medical educator, researcher. BS in Biology, Purdue U., 1979; PhD in Devel. Biology, Ohio State U., 1988; postgrad., Marine Biol. Lab., Woods Hole, Mass., 1984. Rsch. assoc. lab. renewable resources engring. Purdue U., 1979-82; grad. tchg. asst. Ohio State U., 1982-87; asst. instr. embryology Marine Biol. Lab., Woods Hole, Mass., 1985; postdoctoral fellow U. Va., 1988-91; rsch. assoc. Inst. for Cancer Rsch. Fox Chase Cancer Ctr., 1991-92; asst. prof. dept. cell and devel. biology U. Pa. Sch. Medicine, 1993—. Contbr. articles to profl. jours.; reviewer: Biochimica and Biophysica Acta, Devel., Devel. Biology, Differentiation, DNA and Cell Biology, Molecular and Cellular Biology, Trends in Cardiovasc. Rsch.; lectr. in field. Recipient Grad. Student Alumni Rsch. award, 1987, Established Investigatorship award Am. Heart Assn., 1996—; NIH Tng. grantee, 1984, Sigma Xi grantee, 1986; Presdl. fellowship Ohio State U., 1987-88, MDA Postdoctoral fellowship, 1988-89, MDA Jere Thompson Neuromuscular Rsch. fellowship, 1989-91. Mem. AAAS, Soc. for Devel. Biology, John Morgan Soc., Pa. Muscle Inst. (co-organizer seminar series on muscle devel. 1994, co-organizer ann. retreat 1995). Office: U Pa Sch Medicine 720 Blockley Hall 423 Guardian Philadelphia PA 19104*

GOLDIN, GURSTON DAVID, psychiatrist; b. N.Y.C., Mar. 18, 1930; s. Harry and Anna Edith (Eskolsky) G.; m. Marjorie Beckhardt, Mar. 17, 1968; children: Davidson Gurston, Nicholas Stoloff. AB, Columbia Coll., 1951; MD, Columbia U., 1955, MS, 1963. Diplomate Am. Bd. Psychiatry and Neurology. Intern in medicine Johns Hopkins Hosp., Balt., 1955-56; assoc. clin. ctr. NIH, Bethesda, Md., 1956-58; asst. resident in psychiatry Presbyn. Hosp. and N.Y. State Psychiat. Inst., N.Y.C., 1958-60, resident in psychiatry, 1960-61; lectr. in econs. Columbia U., N.Y.C., 1960-61, assoc. in clin. psychiatry, 1966—; assoc. psychiatrist Presby. Hosp., N.Y.C., 1966—, N.Y. State Psychiat. Inst., N.Y.C., 1966—; cons. in psychiatry Rockefeller U. Hosp., 1991—; lectr. in psychiatry Cornell U. Med. Coll., 1991—. Trustee SUNY, Albany, 1985-90, City U. Constrn. Fund, N.Y.C., 1979—, bd. dirs. rsch. found., Albany, 1986-90. Mem. Am. Psychiat. Assn., N.Y. Acad. Medicine; mem. Assn. for Rsch. in Nervous and Mental Disease, Phi Beta Kappa. Office: 166 E 63rd St New York NY 10021-7636

GOLDIN, MARSHALL D., cardiovascular surgeon; b. Chgo., Jan. 15, 1939; s. Aaron and Helen G.; m. Joann Goldin; children: Michael, Steven, Adam. BA, U. Ill., 1959; MD, U. Ill., Chgo., 1963, MS, 1966. Dir. SICU Rush-Presbyn.-St. Luke's Med. Ctr., Chgo., 1968—, sr. attending surgeon, 1984—; courtesy staff Rush-N. Shore Med. Ctr., Skokie, Ill., 1989—; consulting staff Elmhurst (Ill.) Meml. Hosp., 1989—, Holy Family Med. Ctr., Des Plaines, Ill., 1995—; assoc. prof. of surgery Rush Med. Coll., Chgo., 1985—. Bd. dirs. Spertus Coll. Judaica, Chgo. Mem. ACS, Chgo. Surg. Soc. (sec. 1990-94), Rush Surg. Soc. (v.p. 1989-90, pres. 1990-91). Office: Cardiovasc Surg Assocs 1725 W Harrison # 1156 Chicago IL 60612

GOLDING, ANTHONY MARK BARRINGTON, public health physician, consultant; b. London, Aug. 21, 1928; s. Mark and Marian Rosalie (Benjamin) G.; m. Olwen Valery Bridgeman, Aug. 29, 1962; children: Rosemary, Richard, Catherine, Charlotte. BA with honors, Cambridge (Eng.) U., 1948, MB BChir, 1952, MA, 1954. Prin. asst. sr. med. officer N.W. Met. Regional Hosp. Bd., London, 1960-68; med. officer Dept. Health & Social Security, London, 1968-72; prin. asst. sr. med. officer S.E. Met. Regional Hosp. Bd., Croydon, Eng., 1972-74; dist. comty. physician King's Health Dist., London, 1974-82; dist. med. officer Camberwell Health Authority, London, 1982-86, sr. cons. in comty. medicine, 1986-88; cons. in pub. health medicine Redbridge and Waltham Forest Health Authority, London, 1989-96, ret., 1996; hon. sr. lectr. King's Coll. Hosp. Med. Sch., London, 1977—. Sr. editor: Water and Public Health, 1994; editor: Health and Hygiene, 1988—; contbr. articles to profl. jours. Capt. Royal Army M.C., 1954-56. Fellow Faculty Pub. Health Medicine U.K., Royal Inst. Pub. Health and Hygiene (mem. coun. 1995—), Royal Soc. Medicine (coun. mem. 1995—, v.p. sect. pub. health and epidemiology); mem. Royal Coll. Ophthalmologists. Home: 12 Clifton Hill, London NW8 OQG, England

GOLDING, LAWRENCE ARTHUR, physiology educator; b. Capetown, South Africa, May 8, 1926; came to U.S. 1946; s. Reginald Gerald and Maizie (Mitchell) G.; m. Carmen Golding, Aug. 9, 1952; children: Scott Mitchell, Neal Lawrence, Kirk Louis. BS, U. Ill., 1950, MS, 1953, PhD, 1958. Asst. prof. U. Idaho, Moscow, 1953-56; asst. prof. U. Ill., Champaign, 1956-58; prof. physiology exercise Kent State U., Ohio, 1958-76; prof. U. Nev., Las Vegas, 1976—; cons. Nat. YMCA, Chgo., 1958—, Cleve. Indians, 1960-66, Akron Civil Service Commn., 1970-76. Author: Scientific Foundations of Physical Fitness, Y's Way to Physical Fitness, 1967. Contbr. articles to profl. jours. Grantee: NIH, 1960-65, NSF, 1960-62, Portage County Heart Assn., 1964-76; Barrick fellow, 1983. Fellow Am. Coll. Sports Medicine (Healthy Am. award, 1992, exec. dir. southwest region chpt.), AAHPER; mem. Am. Coll. Sports Medicine (bd. trustees, editor-in-chief Health and Fitness Jour.), Acad. Sci., Sigma Xi, Phi Epsilon Kappa. Republican. Congregationalist. Home: 3258 Redwood St Las Vegas NV 89102-6508 Office: U Nev Las Vegas Exercise Physiology Lab Las Vegas NV 89154-3016

GOLDMAN, ALLAN LARRY, physician, consultant, educator; b. Mpls., June 3, 1943; s. Oscar Goldman and Ruth (Goldman) Gulinson; m. Barbara Elaine Francisco, Aug. 17, 1969; children: Lisa, Carrie, Jennifer, Lindsey. BSBA, U. Minn., 1964, MD, 1968. Diplomate Am. Bd. Internal Medicine. Prof., chmn. dept. internal medicine U. South Fla., Tampa, 1974—; pres. faculty U. South Fla. Coll. Medicine, 1990-91. Contbr. articles to profl. jours. Mem. Am. Lung Assn.; bd. dirs. Fla. Lung Assn., 1976-91. Maj. U.S. Army, 1969-74. Fellow ACP, Am. Coll. Chest Physicians; mem. Va. Pulmonary Physicians Assn. (pres. 1978-79). Jewish. Home: 4915 Lyford Cay Rd Tampa FL 33629-4828 Office: VA Hosp 13000 Bruce B Downs Blvd Tampa FL 33612-4745

GOLDMAN, BERT ARTHUR, psychologist, educator; b. N.Y.C., Apr. 4, 1929; children: Lisa, Linda. B.A., U. Md., 1951; M.Ed., U. N.C., 1956; Ed.D., U. Va., 1960. Mem. faculty U. N.C., Greensboro, 1965—, prof. ednl. psychology, 1971-85, dean acad. advising, 1970-85, prof. higher ednl. adminstrn., 1985—, acting chair dept. ednl. adminstrn., higher edn. and ednl. rsch., 1987-88, dept. coord., 1991-92. Served with U.S. Army, 1951-53. Mem. APA, Am. Coun. Measurement Edn., N.C. Assn. for Rsch. in Edn., Am. Ednl. Rsch. Assn. Office: U NC Psychology Dept Greensboro NC 27412

GOLDMAN, EMANUEL, microbiology and molecular genetics educator; b. N.Y.C., Feb. 19, 1945; s. Yehuda and Anne (Slochower) G.; M. Joan Wendy

Millner, May 29, 1966 (div. 1975); m. Jill Katherine Brannis, Mar. 14, 1986 (div. 1992). BA cum laude, Brandeis U., 1966; PhD in Biochemistry, MIT, 1972. Fellow in viral oncology Pub. Health Research Inst., N.Y.C., 1972-73; research fellow in pathology Harvard U. Med. Sch., Boston, 1973-75; assoc. in med. microbiology U. Calif., Irvine, 1975-77, asst. research microbiologist, 1977-79; asst. prof. microbiology N.J. Med. Sch., Newark, 1979-83, assoc. prof. microbiology, 1983-93; prof. microbiology, 1993—; cons. in pathology Harvard Med. Sch., 1976; coord. N.Y. Area Rsch. Club Columbia U., 1982-85; piano player cocktail lounges, restaurants. Author film critiques New U., Irvine, 1975-79; asst. editor, author film critiques, Boston, Phoenix, 1969-70; assoc. editor, author Boston Rev. of Arts, 1970-72; author sci. research papers. Active ACLU, Sierra Club, NOW. Damon Runyon fellow, 1973-75; Lievre sr. fellow, Calif. div. Am. Cancer Soc., 1977-79; research career devel. awardee Nat. Cancer Inst., NIH, 1983-88; recipient Faculty Exceptional Merit awards, U. Medicine and Dentistry N.J., 1980, 82. Mem. Am. Soc. Biochemistry and Molecular Biology, Am. Soc. for Microbiology, N.Y./N.J. Molecular Biology Club (officer, coord. 1985—), N.Am. Vegetarian Soc. Democrat. Jewish. Home: 19 Garrison Ave Jersey City NJ 07306-5617 Office: Dept Microbiology NJ Med Sch Newark NJ 07103

GOLDMAN, GEORGE DAVID, psychologist, psychoanalyst; b. N.Y.C., Jan. 8, 1923; s. Irving Israel and Hattie Anna (Bennett) G.; m. Belle Hans, Sept. 11, 1948; children: Ira Stephen, Carol Marcia Goldman Reife, Deborah Sue Goldman Cohen. BS in Social Sci., CCNY, 1943; MA, NYU, 1946, PhD, 1950; cert. in psychoanalysis, William A. White Inst., N.Y.C., 1958. Diplomate Am. Bd. Profl. Psychology. Fellow CCNY, 1946-47, instr. psychology, 1947-53; instr. psychology NYU, 1948-51; pvt. practice psychology N.Y.C., N.Y., 1952-95; pvt. practice Jericho, N.Y., 1952—; clin. psychologist Bronx VA Hosp., Montrose VA Hosp., 1947-52; staff psychotherapist Low Cost Psychoanalytic Svc. William Alanson White Inst., N.Y.C., 1952-58; clin. prof., supr., dir. clin. svcs. Postdoctoral Psychotherapy Ctr., Derner Inst., Adelphi U., Garden City, N.Y., 1958-94; supr. psychotherapy grad. div. Ferkauf Sch., Yeshiva U., Bronx, 1976-80; cons. to supt. Manhasset (N.Y.) Pub. Schs., 1956-61; cons. psychotherapy VA, N.Y. area, 1959-79; mem. arbitration panel on marital conflicts Am. Arbitration Assn., 1968—. Co-editor: (with D.S. Milman) Modern Woman: Her Psychology and Sexuality, 1969, Psychoanalytic Contributions to Community Psychology, 1970, Innovations in Psychotherapy, 1971, The Neurosis of Our Time: Acting Out, 1973, Group Process Today, 1974, Man and Woman in Transition, 1978, Psychoanalytic Perspectives on Aggression, 1978, Modern Man: The Psychology and Sexuality of the Contemporary Male, 1979, Parameters in Psychoanalytic Psychotherapy, 1979, Therapists at Work: A Demonstration of Theory and Technique, 1979, Addiction—Theory and Treatment, 1980, Techniques of Working with Resistance, 1987; (with G. Stricker) Practical Problems of a Private Psychotherapy Practice, 1972, 2d edit., 1981; (with L. Saretsky) Integrating Ego Psychology and Object Relations Theory: Psychoanalytic Perspectives on Psychopathology, 1979; contbr. articles to profl. jours. Mem. profl. adv. bd. Nassau County chpt. Parents without Ptnrs., 1970—; pres. psychology div., bd. dirs. Am. Friends of Hebrew U. of Jerusalem, N.Y.C., 1975—. With U.S. Army, 1943-45. Decorated Bronze Star, Purple Heart with oak leaf cluster; named Disting. Practitioner in Psychology, Nat. Acads. of Practice, 1983; recipient Outstanding Contbn. to Psychology award CCNY, 1989. Fellow APA (divsn. psychologists in ind. practice, pres. 1987, psychotherapy, clinic psych., mem. divsn. psychoanalysis, pres. 1982, Disting. Contbn. award 1988, Disting. Psychologist award Divsn. 42 1989, Divsn. 39 award 1990), Am. Group Psychotherapy Assn.; mem. N.Y. State Psychol. Assn. (past bd. dirs. clin. div.), Nassau County Psychol. Assn. (past bd. dirs.), N.Y. Soc. Clin. Psychologists (pres. 1979), Am. Acad. Psychotherapists (past bd. dirs. and sec.). Democrat. Jewish. Office: 305 E 86th St # 22a-w New York NY 10028-4702

GOLDMAN, GEORGE J., cardiologist; b. Bronx, N.Y., Dec. 4, 1951; s. David and Joan Frances (Matus) G.; m. Louise Beth Shapiro, Aug. 12, 1973. BS in Biology, SUNY, Stony Brook, 1972; MD, SUNY, Bklyn., 1976. Diplomate Am. Bd. Internal Medicine. Intern internal medicine L.I. Jewish Hosp., New Hyde Park, N.Y., 1976-77, resident, 1977-79, chief resident medicine, 1981-82; fellow cardiology Mount Sinai Hosp., N.Y.C., 1979-81; pvt. practice Cmty. Cardiology, Manhasset, N.Y., 1982—. Fellow Am. Coll. Cardiology. Office: Cmty Cardiology 800 Community Dr Manhasset NY 11030

GOLDMAN, HARVEY S., therapist, rabbi; b. Malden, Mass., Jan. 15, 1935; s. Samuel A. and Mildred M. (WWallach) G.; m. Seena Chandler, Aug. 31, 1958 (div. Mar. 1980); children: Joel, Steven, Karen; m. Judith Zimmerman, Sept. 6, 1981; children: Harlan, Darren, Jordan. BA, Boston U., 1961; MA in Hebrew Lit., Hebrew Union Coll., Cin., 1966; D Ministry, Rochester-Colgate U., 1975; DD (hon.), Hebrew Union Coll., N.Y.C., 1991. Rabbi, 1966. Asst. rabbi Main Line Reform Temple, Wynnewood, Pa., 1966-69; rabbi Temple Sinai, Rochester, N.Y., 1969-78; sr. rabbi Temple Israel, Columbus, Ohio, 1978-85, Sharey Tefilo-Israel, South Orange, N.J., 1985—; mem. exec. com. Nat. Jewish Community Rels. Com., N.Y.C., 1969-79. Speechwriter White House, Washington, 1981; bd. dirs. Jewish Community Rels. Com., Rochester and Columbus, 1968-73, Planned Parenthood, Columbus, 1978-85. With USN, 1953-57. Mem. Cen. Conf. Am. Rabbis, Am. Assn. Marriage and Family Therapists (clin.), Am. Assn. Sex Educators, Am. Assn. Hypnotherapists, Counselors and Therapists (chmn. Ohio sect. 1984-85). Home: 450 N Ridgewood Rd South Orange NJ 07079-1624 Office: Sharey Tefilo-Israel 432 Scotland Rd South Orange NJ 07079-3008

GOLDMAN, IRA STEVEN, gastroenterologist; b. Bronx, N.Y., May 19, 1951; s. George David and Belle (Hans) G.; m. Niki Ellen Kantrowitz, Jan. 20, 1980; children: Zachary, Joshua. BA, U. Rochester, 1973; student, Oxford U., 1972; MD, Columbia U., 1977. Diplomate Am. Bd. Internal Medicine, Subspecialty Gastroenterology. Internal medicine intern Columbia Presbyn. Med. Ctr., N.Y.C., 1977-78, resident in internal medicine, 1978-80; fellow in gastroenterology and liver diseases Sch. Medicine U. Calif., San Francisco, 1980-83; instr. in anatomy Columbia U., N.Y.C., 1978; asst. prof. medicine U. Calif., San Francisco, 1983-85; asst. prof. medicine med. coll. Cornell U., N.Y.C., 1985-91; assoc. prof. clin. medicine med. coll. Cornell U., 1991-96; attending physician North Shore Univ. Hosp., Manhasset, N.Y., 1985—; assoc. prof. clin. coll. medicine NYU Sch. Medicine, 1996—; mem. physicians adv. bd. Am. Liver Found., Greater N.Y. chpt., 1985—; mem. sci. adv. commn. L.I. chpt. Nat. Found. for Ileitis and Colitis, 1985-91; vice chair clin. practice sec. Am. Gastroent. Assn., 1995—. Reviewer jours. Gastroenterology; contbr. articles, book chapts., case reports, and abstracts to profl. jours., sci. meetings. Recipient Am. Liver Found. Rsch. fellowship award, 1982, Nat. Insts. Health, Clin. Investigator award, 1983. Fellow ACP, Am. Coll. Gastroenterology; mem. Am Fedn. for Clin. Rsch., Am. Assn. for Study of Liver Diseases, Med. Soc. State of N.Y., Nassau County Med. Soc., Nassau County. Acad. Medicine, N.Y. Soc. for Gastrointestinal Endoscopy (pres. 1996—), Alpha Omega Alpha. Office: North Shore Univ Hosp 300 Community Dr Manhasset NY 11030-3801

GOLDMAN, JACK LESLIE, health professions educator; b. Chgo., Nov. 20, 1935; s. Mandel and Katherine (Kaplan) G. BA, BS, U. Chgo., 1958; MS, Loyola U., 1963, PhD, 1966. Lectr. chemistry Mundelein Coll., Chgo., 1963-65; head phys. chemistry Velsico Corp., Chgo., 1966-67; head natural scis. Shimer Coll., Mt. Carroll, Ill., 1967-71; lectr. chemistry Loyola U., Chgo., 1972-82; lectr. natural scis. Roosevelt U., Chgo., 1980-83; lectr. math. Loyola U., Chgo., 1982-87, dir. health professions, 1987-95; cons. Cardinal Newman Coll., Detroit, 1975-76. Fellow Am. Inst. Chemists. Mem. AAAS, Park Ridge Ctr., Hastings Inst., Nat. Assn. Advisors to the Health Professions. Jewish.

GOLDMAN, JANICE GOLDIN, psychologist, educator; b. Phila., Feb. 15, 1938; d. Samuel and Dorothea (Berenson) Goldin; m. Arthur S. Goldman, Aug. 31, 1958; children: Jill Ann Goldman-Callahan, Joshua N., Jennifer S. BA, U. Pa., 1960, MA, 1962; MS, Hahnemann Med. Coll., 1972, D in Psychology, 1975. Lic. psychologist, Pa. Chief psychologist Charles Peberdy Child Psychiatry Ctr. Hahnemann U., Phila., 1975-87, from clin. asst. to assoc. prof., 1985-87; pvt. practice Jenkintown, Pa., 1977—; cons. Haverford (Pa.) State Hosp., 1982, Assn. for Mental Health Affiliates with Israel, 1984, 86; mem. profl. adv. bd. Pub. Radio Sta WHYY, Phila., 1984-86; workshop leader Women's Ctr. of Montgomery County, Jenkintown, 1982—. Contbr. articles to profl. jours. Board dirs. Assn. for Mental Health Affiliate with Israel, nationwide, 1984-88, Or Hadash Synogogue, Wyncote, Pa., 1989. Mem. APA, Am. Family Therapy Acad., Nat. Register Health Svc. Providers, Phila. Soc. Clin. Psychology (sec. 1977-79), Am. Amnesty Internat., Internat. Soc. for Study Dissociation, Greater Phila. Soc. Clin. Hypnosis, Am. Soc. Clin. Hypnosis, Phi Beta Kappa. Democrat. Office: The Plaza at Foxcroft 1250 Greenwood Ave Jenkintown PA 19046-2901

GOLDMAN, JERI JOAN, psychologist; b. Oklahoma City, Apr. 11, 1934; d. Clarence William and Opal Louise (Leach) Richards; div.; children: Susan, Lisa, Eric. BA, Trinity U., 1955; MA, So. Meth. U., 1956; PhD, Stanford U., 1961; MEd, Temple U., 1982. Cert. sch. psychologist, sch. adminstrn. Chief psychologist, asst. dir. West River Mental Health Ctr., Rapid City, S.D., 1961-65; chief psychologist Woods Schs. and Residential Treatment Ctr., Langhorne, Pa., 1965-66, 74-89, health and clin. services adminstr., 1985-87, dir. clin. services, 1987-88; dir. Devel. Evaluation Ctr., Langhorne, 1971-72; supr. spl. edn. Camden (N.J.) City Pub. Schs., 1989—; cons. schs., clinics in Pa., N.J., 1966-71. Contbr. numerous articles to profl. jours. and books. Trustee Ea. State Sch. and Hosp., Trevose, Pa. Fellow Am. Orthopsychiat. Assn. (life), Pa. Psychol. Assn.; mem. APA, Am. Assn. Mental Retardation, N.J. Psychol. Assn., Pa. Tourette Syndrome Assn., Nat. Assn. for Perinatal Addiction Rsch. and Edn. Office: Bd Edn Front & Cooper Sts Camden NJ 08102

GOLDMAN, JOHN MICHAEL, physician, consultant hematologist, educator; b. London, Nov. 30, 1938; s. Carl Heinz and Bertha (Brandt) G. BM BCh, Oxford U., 1963, DM, 1981. Dir. LRF Centre for Adult Leukaemia Royal Postgrad. Med. Sch., London, 1989—, chmn. dept. haematology, 1994—; med. dir. Anthony Nolan Rsch. Centre, London, 1989—. Editor Bone Marrow Transplantation, 1985—. Mem. Royal Coll. Physicians, European Group for Bone Marrow Transplantation (pres. 1990-94). Office: Royal Postgrad Med Sch, Du Cane Rd, London W12 0NN, England

GOLDMAN, LEE, physician, educator, researcher; b. Phila., Jan. 6, 1948; s. Marvin and Kathryn (Schwartz) G.; m. Jill Steinhardt, Mar. 21, 1971; children: Jeff, Daniel, Robyn Sue. BA, Yale U., 1969, MD, 1973, MPH, 1973. Diplomate Am. Bd. Internal Medicine, Am. Bd. Cardiovascular Disease. Intern U. Calif.-San Francisco, 1973-74, resident in med., 1974-75, Mass. Gen. Hosp., Boston, 1975-76; fellow in cardiology Yale-New Haven Hosp., 1976-78; asst. prof. medicine Harvard Med. Sch., 1978-83, assoc. prof., 1983-89, prof., 1989-95; asst. physician-in-chief dept. med. Brigham and Women's Hosp., Boston, 1983-87, vice chmn., 1987-93; dir. div. clin. epidemiology dept. medicine Brigham and Women's and Beth Israel Hosps., 1987-93, chief med. officer, 1993-95; mem. operating com. Ptnrs. Health Care Inc., 1993-95; chair dept. medicine, assoc. dean clin. affairs U. Calif., San Francisco, 1995—; bd. dirs. Inst. Medicine, 1995—, Am. Bd. Internal Medicine, 1996—. Contbr. numerous articles to profl. jours.; assoc. editor New England Jour. Medicine, 1989-95. Bd. dirs. Temple Shir Tikva, Wayland, Mass., 1982-84, v.p. 1985-86, pres. 1986-88. ACP teaching and research scholar, 1980-83; Henry J. Kaiser Family Found. scholar, 1982-87. Fellow ACP and Am. Coll. Cardiology; mem. Am. Soc. Clin. Investigation, Soc. Gen. Medicine (sec.-treas. 1986-88, pres. 1990—), Assn. Am. Physicians (recorder 1993—). Office: U Calif Dept of Medicine 505 Parnassus Ave San Francisco CA 94143

GOLDMAN, LISA EACHUS, health facility administrator; b. Waltham, Mass., June 24, 1955; d. George Bloomfield and Genivive (Foti) Gallub; m. Edward Elliot Goldman, July 1, 1984; children: Melissa Ann, Audrey Carol. BS, Barry U., 1983, MBA, MPA, 1994. Tchr. Dade County and Miami (Fla.) Tech. Inst., 1982-84; v.p. Point Adult Communities, North Miami Beach, Fla., 1984-92; CEO, owner Fla. Behavioral Network, Miami, 1993—; pres. Statewide Mgmt. & Fin. Svcs. Corp., Miami, 1993—; exec. v.p. Assocs. in Geriatric Psychology, Inc., Pembroke Pines, 1992—; ptnr. Goldsel Inc., Fort Lauderdale, Fla., 1990-92; real estate investor, Miami, 1976-88; instr. acctg. Barry U., 1993. Co-author: Bi-Lingual Resource Jour., 1990, 91. Active Miami Shores Performing Theater; mem. bd. overseers U. Miami. Mem. Alzheimer's Assn. (v.p. 1993), Fla. State Coun. on Alzheimer's Disease, Nat. Long Term Care Com. (bd. dirs. Dade County chpt. 1991), Nat. Coun. Jewish Women (v.p. 1989-91), S.O.A.R.I.N.G. (chpt. pres.), Infants in Need Inc. Home: 7120 W Cypresshead Dr Parkland FL 33067 Office: Fla Behavioral Network 1001 Ives Dairy Rd Ste 206 Miami FL 33179

GOLDMAN, MARTYN ALAN, orthopedic surgeon; b. Chgo., Sept. 5, 1930; s. Charles C. and Helen E. (Ravid) G.; m. Toni E. Gladstein; children: Kim, Bart, Jamie. BS, Northwestern U., 1950, MS, 1953, MD, 1954. Diplomate Am. Bd. Med. Examiners, Am. Bd. Orthopaedic Surgery. Intern Chgo. Wesley Meml. Hosp., 1954-55; capt. U.S. Army med. corps, Fort Carson, Colorado Springs, Colo., 1955-57; resident, gen. surgery Chgo. Wesley Meml., 1957-58, resident, orthopedic surgery, 1958-60; resident, orthopaedic surgery Kosain Crippled Children's Hosp., Louisville, Ky., 1960-61; pvt. practice Louisville Orthopaedic Inst. PSC, Louisville, 1961—; clinical asst. prof. U. Louisville Sch. of Med., 1975—; pres., med. staff Children's Hosp. Kosain, Louisville, 1966-67, Jewish Hosp., Louisville, 1970-71. Bd. dirs. Jewish Community Fedn. of Louisville, 1970—, v.p., 1983-87; trustee Jewish Hosp., Louisville, 1981-87. Fellow Am. Acad. Orthopaedic Surgeons (bd. councilors, 1976-82), Am. Coll. Surgeons (Ky. councilor 1980); mem. AMA, Ky. Med. Soc., Jefferson County Med. Soc., Mid-Am. Orthopaedic Assn. (bd. dirs. 1983-85), Ky. Orthopaedic Assn. (pres. 1977-78, exec. com. 1978-82), Louisville Orthopaedic Soc. (pres. 1973-74), Standard Club. Republican. Jewish. Office: Louisville Orthopaedic Inst 250 E Liberty St Louisville KY 40202-1530

GOLDMAN, RALPH FREDERICK, research physiologist, educator; b. Boston, Mar. 3, 1928; s. Harry and May (Field) G.; m. Joan R. Krinsky, May 27, 1957; children: Harry, Ellen. BS in Chemistry, U. Denver, 1949; MA in Physiology, Boston U., 1951, PhD in Physiology, 1954; MS in Engring., Northeastern U., Boston, 1962. Rsch. physiologist Natick (Mass.) Labs., U.S. Army, 1955-61; dir. div. environ. medicine U.S. Army Rsch. Inst., Natick, 1961-82; prin. cons. Dept. of Army for Environ. Physiology, Natick, 1971-82; chief scientist Multi-Tech Corp., Natick, 1982-88; chief scientist, R&D, clothing and human comfort Comfort Tech., Inc., Natick, 1989—; sr. cons. tech. and product devel. Arthur D. Little, Inc., Cambridge, Mass., 1993—; adj. prof. Boston U., 1970—, N.C. State U., 1989—; lectr. MIT, Cambridge, 1974—; vis. scientist Peoples Rep. of China, 1981—; vis. scholar lectr. Springfield (Mass.) Coll., 1977, Ohio State U., 1977, 88; chmn. rsch. group biomed. effects of clothing, NATO, 1981-86. Author 2 books; contbr. over 500 articles, abstracts and tech. reports to profl. pubs., 15 chpts. to books. Scoutmaster Boy Scouts Am., Natick-Framingham, (Mass.), 1956-90; mem. town meeting Town of Framingham, 1983-88. Recipient Meritorious Civilian Svc. award U.S. Army R&D Command, 1963, Exceptional Civilian Svc. award Sec. of Army, 1976, Sr. Exec. Svc. award U.S. Civil Svc., 1979, Silver Beaver award Boy Scouts Am., 1981. Fellow ASHRAE (bd. dirs. 1982-85, assoc. editor Internat. Jour. HVAC&R Rsch., Disting. Fellow award 1992), Am. Coll. Sports Medicine (editl. bd. 1979-85), Ergonomics Soc. (hon.); mem. IEEE (AEMB coun. 1978-84), ASTM, Am. Physiol. Soc. (editl. bd. 1972-78), Assn. Mil. Surgeons U.S., Framingham Amateur Radio Assn. (treas. 1970-84), Cape Cod Yacht Club (Falmouth, Mass.), Pelican Isle Yacht Club (Naples, Fla.). Jewish. Office: Arthur D Little Inc 1 Acorn Park Cambridge MA 02140-2301 also: Comfort Tech PO Box 847 Framingham MA 01701-3761

GOLDMAN, ROBERT DAVID, cell biologist, educator; b. Port Chester, N.Y., July 23, 1939; married; two children. B.A., U. Vt., 1961, M.S., 1963; Ph.D. in Biology, Princeton U., 1967. With Royal Postgrad. Med. Sch., London, 1967-69; with Med. Research Council Great Britain, Glasgow, Scotland, 1967-69; asst. prof. biology Case Western Res. U., 1969-74; prof. biology Mellon Inst. Sci., Carnegie-Mellon U., 1974-81; prof., chmn. dept. cell biology and anatomy Northwestern U. Med. Sch., Chgo., 1981-89, prof., chmn. dept. cell, molecular and structural biology, 1989—. Office: Northwestern U Med Sch 303 E Chicago Ave Chicago IL 60611-3008

GOLDMAN, STANFORD MILTON, medical educator; b. Salt Lake City, Nov. 28, 1940; s. Osher and Mirian (Soloman) G.; m. Harriet Kaplow, Apr. 2, 1965; children: Etan, Nava. BA, Yeshiva U., 1961; MD, Einstein Coll. Medicine, 1965. Intern Jefferson U. Sch. Medicine, Phila., 1965-66; resident Einstein Coll. Medicine, Bronx, 1966-69; chmn. dept. radiology USPHS Phoenix Indian Med. Ctr., 1969-71; asst. prof. radiology Einstein Coll. Medicine, Bronx, 1971-72; instr. radiology Johns Hopkins U. Sch. Medicine, Balt., 1972-74, asst. prof. radiology, 1974-79; asst. prof. U. Md., Balt., 1975-79, assoc. prof., 1978-81; assoc. prof. Johns Hopkins U., 1979-86; clin. prof. Uniformed Svcs. U., Bethesda, Md., 1981-94; prof. radiology Johns Hopkins U., 1986-94, prof. urology, 1988-93; prof., chmn. radiology U. Tex. Med. Sch., Houston, 1993—; adj. prof. Baylor Coll. Medicine, Houston, 1994—; med. dir. radiology Houston C.C., 1994; prof. radiology M.D. Anderson Cancer Ctr., Houston, 1995. Editor: Computed Tomography of Kidneys & Adrenals, 1983, CT & MRI of the Genitourinary Tract, 1990, Tc E Rm Del Trattos Genito-Urinario, 1994. Mem. Radiation Control Adv. Bd., Md., 1989-93. Lt. comdr. USPHS, 1969-71. Mem. AMA, Am. Assn. for History Medicine, Am. Coll. Radiology, Am. Roentgen Ray Soc., Am. Soc. Emergency Medicine, Am. Urological Assn., Radiological Soc. N.Am., Tex. Med. Soc., Tex. Med. Found., Tex. Radiological Soc., Houston Med. Soc., Houston Radiological Soc., European Soc. Iroradiologists, Assn. Univ. Radiologists, Johns Hopkins Med. and Surg. Assn., Soc. Uroradiology, Soc. Nuclear Medicine, GynecoRadiology Soc., Soc. of Chmn.of Acad. Radiology Depts., U. Md. Alumni Assn. (assoc.), Albert Einstein Disting. Alumni Assn. award, 1996. Jewish. Office: U Tex Med Sch Dept Radiology 6431 Fannin St Ste 2-132 Houston TX 77030

GOLDNER, JONATHAN ANDREW, physician; b. Freeport, N.Y., July 8, 1957; s. Malvin Abner and Lillian Florence (Stone) G.; m. Lisa Cohen, Apr. 20, 1985; children: Breanna, Hayley. BA, Lehigh U., 1979; DO, Chgo. Coll. Osteopathic, Medicine,, 1983. Diplomate Am. Bd. Internal Medicine; subspecialties in critical care and geriatric medicine. Intern U. Medicine and Dentistry of N.J., Stratford, 1983-84; resident in internal medicine Lehigh Valley Hosp. Ctr., Allentown, Pa., 1984-87; attending physician, dept. medicine Pocono Med. Ctr., East Stroudsburg, Pa., 1987—; ptnr., 1989—; dir. crit. care Pocono Med. Ctr., 1991—, chmn. orgn. donor coun., 1994—, sec. med. staff, 1990-92. Fellow Am. Coll. Chest Physicians; mem. Soc. Crit. Care Medicine, Am. Coll. Physicians, AMA, Pa. Med. Soc., Sigma Sigma Phi. Office: Pocono Internal Medicine Specialists Ltd 175 E Brown St East Stroudsburg PA 18301

GOLDNEY, ROBERT DONALD, psychiatrist, educator; b. Adelaide, Australia, Dec. 2, 1943; s. Murray Rufus and Nance (Panton) G.; m. Helen Christine Parsons, May 13, 1967; children—Katherine Ann, Jane Louise, Timothy Robert. M.B.B.S., Adelaide U., 1967, M.D., 1979. Intern Launceston Hosp. (Tasmania), 1968; resident Repatriation Hosp., South Australia, 1969; resident Glenside Hosp. (South Australia), 1970-72, psychiatrist, 1973-74, dir. Dibden research unit, 1981-85; sr. lectr. U. Adelaide (South Australia), 1974-81; clin. assoc. prof. Flinders U. (South Australia), 1981—; sr. vis. cons. Royal Adelaide Hosp., 1981-91, Clin prof. U. Adelaide, 1992-96, prof. U Adelaide, 1996—. Contbr. articles on suicidal behavior and psychiat. edn. to profl. jours. Fellow Royal Australian and N.Z. Coll. Psychiatrists, Royal Coll. Psychiatrists. Office: The Adelaide Clin, Park Tce, Gilberton 5081, Australia

GOLDRICH, STANLEY GILBERT, optometrist; b. N.Y.C., Sept. 22, 1937; s. Joseph and Doris (Stelzner) G. BA, Queens Coll., 1959, MA, 1965; PhD, CUNY, 1966; OD, Mass. Coll. Optometry, 1974. Lic. optometrist, N.Y., Calif. Rsch. assoc. U. Wis. Primate Ctr., Madison, 1965-67; asst. prof. Ohio State U., Columbus, 1967-72; assoc. clin. prof. SUNY Coll. Optometry, N.Y.C., 1974—; cons. U. Optometry Assocs., N.Y.C. Contbr. articles to profl. jours.; inventor in field. With USAR, 1960-65. NSF grantee, 1967. Fellow Am. Acad. Optometry; mem. Am. Psychol. Assn., Am. Optometric Assn., N.Y. State Optometric Assn. Jewish. Home: 150 Lexington Ave New York NY 10016 Office: SUNY 100 E 24 St New York NY 10010

GOLDSCHMIDT, KARL, psychotherapist; b. Nuremberg, Bavaria, Fed. Rep. of Germany, May 29, 1923; came to U.S., 1933; s. Siegfried and Gertrude (Loewensohn) G.; m. Lori Finclaire; children: Wendy, Kim. BEE, Columbia U., 1948, MEE, 1956; MSW, Fordham U., 1981. LCSW, N.J. Mem. tech. staff Bell Telephone Labs., N.Y., N.J., 1948-79; sch. social worker Long Branch (N.J.) Schs., 1981-82; psychotherapist The Consultation Ctr., Freehold, N.J., 1982-83, Family & Community Svcs., Red Bank, N.J., 1983-89; pvt. practice and workshop facilitator Tinton Falls, N.J., 1985—; mgmt. cons. Bus. Effectiveness Cons., Tinton Falls, 1985—. Designer 15 workshops including Self-Therapy, Stress Mgmt., Time Mgmt., Getting Well Again, 1981—; inventor in telephony field, 1950-70. Tchr., recreation leader Monmouth Folk Dancers, Red Bank, 1961—. With U.S. Army, 1943-46. Pulitzer scholar Columbia U., 1941. Mem. IEEE, NASW, Acad. Cert. Social Workers. Office: 296 Riveredge Rd Tinton Falls NJ 07724-2753

GOLDSCHMIDT, MILLICENT EDNA, microbiology educator; b. Erie, Pa., June 11, 1926; d. Isaac Jerry and Mary Tilly (Samuel) Cohen; m. Eugene P. Goldschmidt, Apr. 10, 1949 (dec. 1980); children: Richard, Carol Goldschmidt Warley. BA, Case-Western Res. U., 1947; MA, Purdue U., 1950, PhD, 1952. Instr. chemistry Hood Coll., Frederick, Md., 1958-60; asst. prof. medicine U. Md./U.S. Army Med. Unit, Frederick, 1960-61; NIH postdoctoral fellow U. Tex., Austin, 1961-63; rsch. instr. Baylor Med. Sch., Houston, 1963-67; assoc. microbiologist, acting chief microbiology sect. U. Tex.-M.D. Anderson Cancer Ctr., Houston, 1967-71; assoc. prof. U. Tex. Health Sci. Ctr., Houston, 1971-73, assoc. prof. clin. microbiology Med. Sch., 1973-76, NIH postdoctoral fellow dental br., 1976-78, assoc. prof. dental br., 1979-95; prof., 1995—; dir. grad. program in microbiology U. Tex. Health Sci. Ctr., 1981-89; coord. Baylor Protocol to Help Plan Lunar Receiving Labs. at NASA, 1966-67; vis. prof. summer course, Kans. State U., 1981—; mem. evaluation panel in biomed. scis. NSF grad. fellowship program, Washington, 1989-92, USDA panel mem. small bus. innovative rsch. grants in food sci. and nutrition, Washington, 1994—. Author monographs, rsch. papers and abstracts; assoc. editor Jour. Rapid Methods and Automation in Microbiolgy. Mem. sci. rev. bd. Sci. and Engring. Fair Houston, 1975—; host family Inst. Internat. Edn., Houston, 1975—; mem. adult edn. com. Temple Beth Israel, Houston, 1984—; treas. Houston Gt. Books Coun., 1988—. Recipient Tex. Woman's Achievement in Sci. award Woman's Hosp. System Tex., 1986. Fellow Am. Acad. Microbiology (bd. govs. 1985-87); mem. Am. Soc. Microbiology (pres. Tex. br. 1981-82, nat. coun. policy com. 1986-89, found. lectr. 1988-89, vis. scientist minority students sci. careers support program 1986—, Disting. Svc. award Tex. br. 1980), Assn. for Women in Sci. (chpt. pres. 1985-86, Outstanding Woman in Sci. Gulf Coast chpt. 1985-88), Houston Assn. Med. Microbiologists (pres. 1982-84), Internat. Assn. Dental Rsch., Sigma Xi (chpt. pres. 1985-86, nat. dir.-at-large 1991—, nat. exec. bd. 1991-94, 96—). Home: 3611 Cloverdale St Houston TX 77025-4103 Office: U Tex Health Sci Ctr 6516 John Freeman Blvd Houston TX 77030-3402

GOLDSCHMIDT, PASCAL JOSEPH, medical educator, cardiologist; b. Brussels, Belgium, Apr. 12, 1954; m. Emily Ann Boches. BS, Univ. Libre de Brussels, 1976, MD, 1980. Lic. physician Md., Belgium. Intern and resident in medicine/cardiology Erasme Acad. Hosp./U. Libre de Brussels, 1980-83; rsch. fellow dept. immunology and microbiology Med. U. S.C., Charleston, 1983-86; resident in medicine Union Meml. Hosp., Balt., 1986-88; clin. and rsch. fellow cardiology/cell biology/anatomy Johns Hopkins U., Balt., 1988-91, assoc. prof. dept. medicine/cardiology divsn., 1991—; dir. Bernard Lab. of Vascular Biology, Balt., 1991—; attending CCU Johns Hopkins Hosp., Balt., 1991—, co-dir. Thrombosis Ctr., 1994—; co-dir. Henry Ciccarone Ctr. for Prevention Heart Disease, Balt., 1991—; lectr. in field. Contbr. numerous articles and abstracts to profl. jours., chpts. to books; reviewer New Eng. Jour. Medicine, Annals of Internal Medicine, Biochemistry, Blood, Cell, Cell Adhesion and Comm., Circulation Rsch., Jour. Cell Biology, Molecular Biology of the Cell, Am. Heart Assn., NIH. Recipient NATO Sci. award, 1983, 84; grantee Clinician Scientist Award, 1991-93, Syntex Scholars Program, 1992-95, Am. Heart Assn., 1992-94, 95—, NIH, 1992-96, 94-96, 95—; Am. Heart Assn. fellow, 1990, Med. U. S.C., 1984, 85. Mem. AAAS, Am. Heart Assn. Home: 2720 Quarry Heights Way Baltimore MD 21209 Office: Johns Hopkins Hosp 1023 Ross Rsch Bldg 720 Rutland Ave Baltimore MD 21287

GOLDSCHMIDT, PETER GRAHAM, physician executive, business development consultant; b. Cardiff, Wales, Feb. 18, 1945; came to U.S., 1970; s. Heinz Joachim Siefried and Marjorie (Sweet) G. DMS, U. Westminster, 1968; MB, BS, U. London, 1970; MPH, Johns Hopkins U., 1971, DPH, 1980. Rsch. assoc. Johns Hopkins U. Sch. Hygiene and Pub.

Health, Balt., 1972-75; v.p., dir. Policy Rsch. Inc., Balt., 1974-81; dir. health svcs. R&D svc. VA, Washington, 1981-86; v.p., dir. Quality Standards in Medicine, Inc., Boston, 1986-90; pres. World Devel. Group, Inc., Bethesda, Md., 1986—; bd. dirs. Quality Standards in Medicine, Inc., Boston; pres. Health Improvement Inst., Bethesda, 1991—, Med. Care Mgmt. Corp., Bethesda, 1992—. Author: Quality Management in Health Care, 1995; contbr. numerous articles to profl. jours. Bd. dirs. Policy Rsch. Inst., Balt., 1978-87. Recipient various grants. Mem. AMA, APHA, Balt.-Washington Venture Group. Office: Med Care Mgmt Corp 4340 East West Hwy Ste 105 Bethesda MD 20814-4411

GOLDSMITH, ETHEL FRANK, medical social worker; b. Chgo., May 31, 1919; d. Theodore and Rose (Falk) Frank; m. Julian Royce Goldsmith, Sept. 4, 1940; children: Richard, Susan, John. BA, U. Chgo., 1940. Lic. social worker, Ill. Liaison worker psychiat. consultation service U. Chgo. Hosp., 1964-68; med. social worker Wyler Children's Hosp., Chgo., 1968—. Treas. U. Chgo. Service League, 1958-62, chmn. camp Brueckner Farr Aux., 1966-72; pres. Bobs Roberts Hosp. Service Commn., 1962; bd. dirs. Richardson Wildlife Sanctary, 1988—; mem. Field Mus. Women's Bd., 1966—; bd. dirs. Hyde Park Art Ctr., 1964-82, Chgo. Commons Assn., 1967-77, Alumni Assn. Sch. Social Service Adminstrn., 1976-80, Self Help Home for Aged, 1985—. Recipient Alumni Citation Pub. Service, U. Chgo., 1972. Mem. Phi Beta Kappa. Home: 5631 S Blackstone Ave Chicago IL 60637-1827 Office: Wyler Hosp Dept Social Svc 5841 S Maryland Ave Chicago IL 60637-1463

GOLDSMITH, GARY NORMAN, psychiatrist, psychoanalyst; b. N.Y.C., Oct. 30, 1948; s. Walter J. and Mildred (Cohen) G. BA, Brandeis U., Waltham, Mass., 1969; MD, Georgetown U., 1973. Intern Evanston (Ill.) Hosp., 1973-74; clin. fellow in psychiatry Med. Sch. Harvard U., Boston, 1974-77; resident in psychiatry Mass. Mental Health Ctr., Boston, 1974-77; pvt. practice psychiatry Brookline, Mass., 1977—; faculty Psychoanalytic Inst. New Eng., Needham, Mass., 1988—; mem. faculty, supervising analyst Mass. Inst. for Psychoanalysis, 1994—; cons. in psychiatr. R.I. Inst. Mental Health, Cranston, 1977-78; staff psychiatrist VA Med. Ctr., Brockton, mass., 1978-82; med. dir. Brockton Area Multi-Svcs., Inc., 1982-84; staff psychiatrist Tufts-New Eng. Med. Ctr., 1984-86; assoc. in psychiatry Beth Israel Hosp., Boston, dir. Russian lang. psychiat. svcs., 1994— ; clin. instr. psychiatry Harvard U., 1977-82, 89—. Mem. Am. Psychiat. Assn., Am. Psychoanalytic Assn. Office: 1419 Beacon St Brookline MA 02146-4808

GOLDSMITH, HARRY SAWYER, surgeon, educator; b. Newton, Mass., Sept. 30, 1929; s. Leo and Dorothy Amy (Appleton) G.; m. Linda Perry, Dec. 8, 1961; children: John, Robert, Lynne. A.B., Dartmouth, 1952; M.D., Boston U., 1956; hon. degree, Shanghai Second Med. U., People's Republic of China, 1988; Xuzhou (China) Med. Coll., 1995. Intern Boston City Hosp., 1956-57, resident in surgery, 1957-61; resident in surgery Meml. Sloan Kettering Inst., N.Y.C., 1963-65; chief gastric and mixed tumor service Meml. Sloan Kettering Inst., 1965-70; practice medicine specializing in surgery Phila., 1970-77; staff Univ. Hosp., Boston; Samuel D. Gross prof. surgery, chmn. dept. Jefferson Med. Coll., Phila., 1970-77, disting. prof. surgery, 1977—; prof. surgery Dartmouth Coll. Med. Sch., Hanover, N.H., 1977-83; prof. surgery, adj. prof. neurosurgery Boston U. Sch. Medicine, 1983-95; surgeon-in-chief Jefferson U. Hosp., 1970-77. Editor-in-chief: Goldsmith's Practice of Surgery, 1976-89; editor: The Omentum: Research and Clinical Applications, 1990; contbr. articles to profl. jours. Served as capt. U.S. Army, 1961-63. Mem. A.C.S., Soc. Vascular Surgery, British Assn. Surg. Oncology, Soc. for Surgery of Alimentary Tract, Soc. Internat. de Chirugie, New Eng. Surg. Soc. Address: PO Box 11017 South Lake Tahoe CA 96155

GOLDSMITH, J(OSEPH) PATRICK, psychologist; b. Lancaster, S.C., July 18, 1944; s. Brooks Pope and Margaret (Ussery) G.; m. Jean Horton; 1 child, Brook. BA in Psychology, Presbyn. U., 1966; MEd, U. Ga., 1967; EdD, Auburn U., 1976. Lic. psychologist, S.C. Vocat. rehab. counselor State Ga., Athens, 1970-71; grad. teaching asst. Auburn (Ala.) U., 1971-74; sales rep. Xerox Corp., Cola, S.C., 1974-76, Pfizer Corp., Springfield, Va., 1976-77; psychologist Catawba Ctr. for Growth and Devel., Lancaster, S.C., 1976-78; program dir. Community Living Svc. Western Carolina Ctr. and Broughton Hosp., Morganton, N.C., 1977-78; psychologist Psychol. Assocs., Lancaster, 1978—; cons. alcohol and drug abuse Elliott White Springs Meml. Hosp., Lancaster, 1978—; cons. staff psychologist Rebound, Lancaster, Piedmont Med. Ctr., Rock Hill, S.C.; psychologist Dept. Juvenile Placement and Aftercare, Dept. Social Svcs.; sec. Lancaster County Child Abuse Com.; mem. Multidisciplinary Steering Com. for Child Abuse; bd. dirs., treas. Catawba Ctr. for Growth and Devel.; bd. dirs. Lancaster County Commn. on Alcohol and Drug Abuse; chmn. Lancaster and Rock Hill Vocat. Rehab. Workshops. Author: (pamphlet) Loving Yourself: The Psychology of Self-Esteem. Capt. U.S. Army, 1968-70. Mem. Am. Assn. Marriage and Family Therapists (clin.). Baptist. Home: 703 W Barr St Lancaster SC 29720-1953 Office: Psychol Assocs PO Box 669 Lancaster SC 29721-0669

GOLDSMITH, LOWELL ALAN, medical educator; b. Bklyn., Mar. 29, 1938; s. Isidore Alexander and Ida (Kaplan) G.; m. Carol Amreich, June 11, 1960; children: Meredith, Eileen. AB, Columbia Coll., 1959; MD, SUNY, Bklyn., 1963. Diplomate Am. Bd. Dermatology. Intern, then resident in medicine UCLA Med. Ctr., 1963-65; resident in dermatology Harvard Med. Sch., Boston, 1967-69; asst. prof. dermatology Harvard U. Med. Sch., Boston, 1970-73; asst. in dermatology Mass. Gen. Hosp., Boston, 1970-71, asst. dermatologist, 1971-73; assoc. prof. medicine Duke U. Med. Ctr., Durham, N.C., 1973-78, prof., 1978-81; James H. Sterner prof. dermatology Sch. Medicine and Dentistry, U. Rochester, N.Y., 1981—, chief dermatology unit, 1981-87, acting chmn. dept. medicine, 1985-87, chmn. dept. dermatology, 1987—; dean Sch. Medicine and Dentistry U. Rochester, N.Y.; mem. dermatology adv. com. FDA, 1983-87; chmn. Gordon Rsch. Cong. on Epithelial Differentiation and Keratiniazation, 1987, AAD-CDC Conf. on skin cancer prevention and edn., Washington, 1995; mem. gen. medicine A study sect. USPHS, NIH, 1988-92, chmn., 1990-92; mem. coun. NIAMS, NIH, 1996—; chmn. med. adv. bd. Nat. Alcopecia Areata Found., 1981-87, 90—, bd. dirs.; bd. dirs. Monroe Cmty. Hosp., Rochester, Ctr. for Alternatives in Animal Testing, Balt.; chmn. NIH Consensus Conf. on Diagnosis and Treatment of Early Melanoma, Bethesda, 1992. Author, editor: Biochemistry and Physiology of the Skin, 1983, 2d edit., 1991; Physiology, Biochemistry and Molecular Biology of the Skin, 1991; mem. editorial bd. Archives Dermatology, 1981-92, Clinics in Dermatology, 1982—, Jour. Investigative Dermatology, 1987—, Seminars in Dermatology, 1991—, Jour. Dermatological Sci., 1994—; also numerous articles. With USPHS, 1965-67. Recipient Rsch. Career Devel. award USPHS, 1975-80; Macy Found. fellow, 1978-79. Mem. Assn. Am. Physicians, Am. Soc. Clin. Investigation, Am. Acad. Dermatology (bd. dirs.), Soc. Investigative Dermatology (bd. dirs., pres. 1994-95), Nat. Ichthyosis Found. (chmn. adv. bd. 1981-85), Assn. Profs. Dermatology (bd. dirs. 1984-87, pres. 1992-94), Am. Bd. Dermatology (bd. dirs.), N.Y. State Soc. Dermatology (pres. 1985-89), Buffalo-Rochester Dermatology Soc. (pres. 1987), Rochester Dermatology Soc., Rochester Acad. Medicine, Polish Dermatol. Assn. (hon.), Alpha Omega Alpha. Office: U Rochester Sch Med Dept Dermatology PO Box 697/601 Elmwood Ave Rochester NY 14642-0001

GOLDSMITH, MICHAEL ALLEN, oncologist, educator; b. Bronx, N.Y., Jan. 28, 1946; s. Walter and Bertha (Tannenberg) G.; m. Judith Harriet Plaut, June 6, 1971; children: Sharon, Esther, Eva, Steven. BA, Yeshiva U., 1967; MD, Albert Einstein Coll. Medicine, 1971. Diplomate Am. Bd. Internal Medicine. Intern Bronx Mcpl. Hosp. Ctr., 1971-72; staff assoc. Nat. Cancer Inst., Bethesda, Md., 1972-74; resident in medicine Mt. Sinai Hosp., N.Y.C., 1974-75, fellow in neoplastic diseases, 1975-77, asst. clin. prof. medicine and neoplastic diseases, 1977—; attending physician Oncology Consultants, P.C., N.Y.C., 1977—; reviewer Jour. AMA, 1988-90, New Eng. Jour. Medicine, 1995—. Contbr. articles to med. jours. Vice-pres. Congregation Orach Chaim, N.Y.C., 1978-83. Lt. comdr. USPHS, 1972-74. Fellow ACP; mem. Am. Soc. Clin. Oncology, Am. Assn. Cancer Rsch. Office: Oncology Cons PC 1045 5th Ave New York NY 10028-0138

GOLDSMITH, NANCY CARROL, business and health services management educator; b. Conemaugh, Pa., May 11, 1940; d. John and Mary (Appley) Stinich; m. Sidney Goldsmith, Apr. 2, 1966. RN, Temple U., 1961; Assoc. summa cum laude, C.C. Phila., 1984; BS in Health Care Mgmt. summa cum laude, Phila. Coll. Textiles and Sci., 1986; MA in Health Care Adminstrn. summa cum laude, Antioch U., Yellow Springs, Ohio, 1988; PhD in Health Svcs. and Hosp. Adminstrn. summa cum laude, Southwest U., New Orleans, 1990. Nurse, head nurse to med. surg. supr. Temple U. Hosp., Phila., 1961-67; nursing rsch. assoc. Smith Klein & French, Inc. and Ames Med. Co., Phila. and Elkhart, Ind., 1967-69; sr. nursing rsch. assoc. NIH, Washington, 1969-75; adminstrv. supr. nursing svcs. Rolling Hill Hosp. and Diagnostic Ctr., Elkins Park, Pa., 1975-87, lectr. legal aspects nursing, 1980-90, dir. cost containment strategies, 1987-89, lectr. in health svcs. mgmt., 1989—, asst. dir. nursing svcs. 1988-89, nursing svcs. dir., 1989-90; prof. health svcs. adminstrn. and svcs. Phila. Coll. Textiles and Scis., 1991—, prof. bus. mgmt., 1992—; mem. adv. bd. health and wellness programs Phila. Coll. Textiles and Sci., 1993—; prof. managed care in health svcs. adminstrn. Ea. Coll., St. Davids, Pa., 1996—; lectr. Sr. Edn. League, 1992—; lectr. healthcare fin. and health svcs. adminstrn. Pa. State U., 1994; lectr. health svcs. reform C.C. Phila., 1993—, Free Libr. Phila., 1994—; instr. med./surg. nursing Sch. Nursing, Temple U., 1964-67, chmn. ann. fundraising, 1978-86. Author 2 books. Inventor use of dextrostix in hypoglycemic range, 1972 (Rsch. award 1974); co-patentee multipurpose biopsy needle, 1972; mem. editorial bd. Coll. Textiles Newletter, 1993—. Recipient Mayor's Liberty Bell award City of Phila., 1978, Legion of Honor award Chapel of Four Chaplains, 1981, Capitol award Nat. Leadership Coun., 1991, Excellence in Teaching Highest award Pa. Coll. Textiles and Sci., 1993; named to Hall of Fame, Internat. Profl. and Bus. Women's Assn., 1994. Mem. Am. Hosp. Assn., Am. Mgmt. Assn., Temple U. Nurse's Alumni Assn. (bd. dirs., v.p. 1991-92, pres. 1993-94, dir. continuing edn com. 1986—), Temple U. Gen. Alumni Assn. (bd. dirs. 1980-88, 93—, Disting. Svc. award 1984), Downtown Club Temple U., Phi Beta Kappa, Phi Theta Kappa (pres. Delta of Pa. chpt. 1991-94, Honors Hall of Fame 1991). Jewish. Office: Phila Coll Textiles & Sci School House Ln Henry Ave Philadelphia PA 19144

GOLDSMITH, SIDNEY, physician, scientist, inventor; b. N.Y.C., Dec. 21, 1930; s. Max and Annie (Schneider) G.; m. Nancy Carrol Stinich, Apr. 2, 1966. B.Sc. cum laude, CCNY, 1950; M.Sc., U. Geneva, Switzerland, 1952, M.D., 1956. Diplomate: Am. Bd. Internal Medicine. Intern Hosp. for Joint Diseases, N.Y.C., 1957-58; resident internal medicine Bronx VA Hosp. and Columbia-Presbyn. Hosp., N.Y.C., 1958-61; fellow gastroenterology Temple U., 1961-62, instr. medicine, 1962-64, assoc. prof., 1964; research assoc. Fels Research Inst., Temple U. Hosp., Phila., 1962-65; practice medicine specializing in internal medicine and gastroenterology Phila., 1963—; prof. medicine, chmn. dept. St. George's U. Sch. Medicine, Grenada, W.I., 1981—; cons. Hahnemann Med. Coll. and Hosp., Phila.; cons. medicine Merck & Co., Rahway, N.J.; chief cons. internal medicine City of Phila. Police and Fireman's Med. Clinic; chief med. cons. Quick Test Inc., Phila.; cons. gastroenterology Oxford Hosp.; med. cons., advisor Lyndon B. Johnson, 1967-69, med. cons., advisor Richard M. Nixon, 1969-74. Book reviewer: Am. Jour. Med. Scis. Served as capt. M.C. AUS, 1959-64. Recipient prize in immunology Pasteur Inst., Paris, France, 1956, meritorious achievement award Inventors Mfrs. Exchange, 1969; Author's certificate in medicine and sci. Govt. USSR; Legion of Honor award Chapel of Four Chaplains, 1978. Fellow A.C.P.; mem. Am. Gastroenterol. Assn., Phila. Gastrointestinal Research Forum, N.Y. Acad. Scis., French Nat. Acad. Medicine, Internat. Platform Assn., AAAS, Assn. Advancement Med. Instrumentation. Home and Office: 6912 Loretto Ave Philadelphia PA 19111-4515

GOLDSMITH, STANLEY JOSEPH, nuclear medicine physician, educator; b. Bklyn., Aug. 17, 1937; s. Jack and Mae (Greenzweig) G.; m. Miriam Schulman, June 6, 1959; children: Ira, Arthur, Beth, Mark. BA, Columbia U., 1958; MD, SUNY-Downstate Med. Ctr., 1962. Diplomate: Am. Bd. Internal Medicine (endocrinology and metabolism), Am. Bd. Nuclear Medicine (bd. dirs. 1990-96, treas. 1995-96). Intern SUNY-Kings County Med. Center, Bklyn., 1962-63, resident, 1965-66, chief resident, 1966-67; fellow in endocrinology Mt. Sinai Hosp., N.Y.C., 1967-68, dir. physics nuclear medicine, 1973-92; Clin. Dir. Nuclear Medicine, Meml. Sloan Kettering Cancer Ctr., N.Y.C., 1992-95; dir. nuclear medicine N.Y. Hosp.-Cornell Med. Ctr., 1995—; rsch. assoc. radioisotope svc. Bronx (N.Y.) VA Hosp., 1968-69; dir. nuclear medicine, asst. dir. endocrine dept. Nassau County Med. Ctr., East Meadow, N.Y., 1969-73; asst. prof. medicine radiology SUNY-Stony Brook Health Sci. Ctr., 1971-73, asst. prof. medicine Mt. Sinai Sch. Medicine, 1973-76, assoc. prof., 1976-84, prof. clin. medicine, 1985-91, prof. radiology and medicine, 1991-92, Cornell U. Med. Coll., 1993—, prof. radiology, medicine; bd. dirs. Capintec, Inc., Ramsey, N.J.; rsch. collaborator Brookhaven Nat. Labs., Upton, N.Y., 1971-75; cons. nuclear medicine; cons. dept. health State of N.Y., 1973-77, Health Svcs. Adminstrn., N.Y.C., 1976; mem. radiopharm. adv. com. FDA, 1987-90, low level radioactive waste diposal site commn., N.Y., 1987-95. Assoc. editor Newline 1984-93, Jour. Nuclear Medicine, editor-in-chief, 1993—; mem. editorial bds. Am. Jour. Cardiology, 1978-82, European Jour. Nuclear Medicine, 1993—; reviewer: Israeli Jour. Med. Scis., 1979, Jour. AMA, 1983-92, Jour. Am. Coll. Cardiology, 1984-94, Jour. Nuclear Medicine, 1989-93. Capt. U.S. Army, 1963-65. Fellow Am. Coll. Cardiology, ACP, Am. Coll. Nuclear Physicians (chmn. nuclear med. tech. affairs, chmn. Washington oversight com.), N.Y. Acad. Medicine; mem. AAAS, Am. Fedn. Clin. Rsch., Am. Coll. Radiology, Endocrine Soc., N.Y. Acad. Scis., Radiol. Soc. N.Am., Soc. Nuclear Medicine (trustee 1982-84, pres.-elect 1984-85, pres. 1985-86, chmn. govt. rels. com. 1991-93, sec. Greater N.Y. chpt. 1975-78, pres. 1979-80, chmn. govt. rels. com. 1991-93). Home: 72 Ivy Way Port Washington NY 11050-3817 Office: NY Hosp Cornell Med Ctr 525 E 68th St New York NY 10021

GOLDSTEIN, ALLAN LEONARD, biochemist, educator; b. Bronx, N.Y., Nov. 8, 1937; s. Morris and Miriam (Siegel) G.; m. Linda Jo Tish, Dec. 23, 1975; children: Jennifer Joy, Dawn Eden, Adam Lee. BS, Wagner Coll., 1959; MS, Rutgers U., 1961, PhD, 1964. Teaching asst. Rutgers U., New Brunswick, N.J., 1959-61; asst. instr. biology, 1961-63, instr. physiology, 1963-64; research fellow Albert Einstein Coll. Medicine, 1964-66, instr. biochemistry, 1966-67, asst. prof., 1967-71, asso. prof., 1971-72; prof., dir. div. biochemistry U. Tex. Med. Br., Galveston, 1972-78; acting dir. multidisciplinary research program in mental health U. Tex. Med. Br., 1973-78; prof., chmn. dept. biochemistry and molecular biology George Washington U. Sch. Medicine, Washington, 1978—, pres., sci. dir. Inst. for Advanced Studies in Immunology and Aging,, 1985-95; chmn. bd. Alpha 1 Biomeds., 1982—; cons. Syntex Rsch., 1972-74, Hoffmann-LaRoche, 1974-82; spl. cons. bd. sci. counselors Nat. Inst. Allergy and Infectious Diseases, 1975; mem. med. rsch. svc. rev. bd. in oncology VA, 1977-80; cons. mem. decisive network com. Biol. Response Modifiers program Div. Cancer Treatment, Nat. Cancer Inst., 1982-84; mem. sci. adv. com. to pres. Papanicolaou Cancer Rsch. Inst. Miami, Inc., 1981-84; mem. AIDS task force adv. com. Nat. Cancer Inst., 1983-84; mem. sci. bd. Alliance for Aging Rsch., 1986—. Discoverer (with Abraham White) Thymosins, hormones of thymus gland and HGP-30 a "core" based p17 AIDS Vaccine currently undergoing Phase I human testing. Decorated Chevalier des Palmes Academiques (France), 1993; recipient Career Scientist award N.Y.C. Health Rsch. Coun., 1967, Alumni Achievement award Wagner Coll., 1974, Gordon Wilson medal Am. Clin. and Climatol Soc., 1976, Disting. Faculty Rsch. award U. Tex. Sch. Biomed. Scis., 1976, Van Dyke award in pharmacology Columbia Coll. Physicians and Surgeons, 1984; vis. prof. award Burroughs Wellcome Found., FASEB, 1986, Fernandez-Cruz award, 1989, Martin Rubin award Am. Coll. Advancement in Medicine, 1990, Michele Fodera Internat. prize for Biomed. Rsch., 1990. Mem. AAAS, Endocrine Soc., Am. Soc. Biol. Chemists and Molecular Biologists, Am. Assn. Immunologists, Internat. Soc. Immunopharmacology (coun. mem. 1985-94), Assn. Med. Sch. Chm. of Depts. Biochemistry, AAUP, Acad. Medicine of Washington, Toastmasters Internat. (pres. N.Y. chpt. 1971), Sigma Xi. Home: 6407 Bradley Blvd Bethesda MD 20817-3245 Office: George Washington U Med Ctr Dept Biochemistry/Molecular Biology 2300 I St NW Washington DC 20037-2337

GOLDSTEIN, AVRAM, pharmacology educator; b. N.Y.C., July 3, 1919; s. Israel and Bertha (Markowitz) G.; m. Dora Benedict, Aug. 29, 1947; children—Margaret, Daniel, Joshua, Michael. A.B., Harvard, 1940, M.D., 1943. Intern Mt. Sinai Hosp., N.Y.C., 1944; successively instr., assoc., asst. prof. pharmacology Harvard U., 1947-55; prof. dept. pharmacology Stanford U., Palo Alto, Calif., 1955-89, exec. head dept., 1955-70, prof. emeritus, 1989—; dir. Addiction Research Found., Palo Alto, Calif., 1973-87. Author: Biostatistics, Principles of Drug Action, 1965, ADDICTION: From Biology to Drug Policy, 1994. Served from 1st lt. to capt., M.C. AUS, 1944-46. Mem. AAAS, NAS and Inst. Medicine, Am. Acad. Arts and Scis., Am. Soc. Pharmacology and Exptl. Therapeutics, Am. Soc. Biol. Chemists. Home: 735 Dolores St Palo Alto CA 94305-8427

GOLDSTEIN, BERNARD DAVID, physician, educator; b. Bronx, N.Y., Feb. 28, 1939; s. Leon Louis and Emily (Bergen) G.; children: Lara, Ross. B.S., U. Wis., 1958; M.D., NYU, 1962. Diplomate Am. Bd. Toxicology, Am. Bd. Internal Medicine, Am. Bd. Hematology. Intern, asst. resident, resident 3d and 4th (NYU) med. divs. Bellevue Hosp., N.Y.C., 1962-65; NIH postdoctoral rsch. fellow NYU Med. Ctr., N.Y.C., 1965-66; instr. in medicine Sch. Medicine, NYU, 1968-70, asst. prof. depts. environ. medicine and medicine, 1970-75, assoc. prof., 1975-80; attending physician Bellevue and Univ. Hosps., N.Y.C., 1968-80; prof., chmn. dept. environ. and community medicine U. Medicine and Dentistry, N.J.-Robert Wood Johnson Med. Sch., Piscataway, 1980—, dir. grad. program in pub. health, 1982-89, dir. environmental and occupational health scis. inst., 1985—; asst. adminstr. for research and devel. EPA, Washington, 1983-85; dir. Nat. Inst. Environ. Health Scis. Ctr. of Excellence, 1988-94; chmn. clean air sci. adv. com. EPA, 1982-83; mem. toxicology study sect. NIH, 1980-84, chmn., 1982-84; mem. bd. sci. dirs. Risk Sci. Inst., 1986—; chmn. com. molecular markers NAS, 1986-89, on risk assessment methodology, 1990—, on role of physician in occupational an environ. medicine Inst. Medicine, 1986—, on enhancing role of primary care practitioners in environ. and occupational health Inst. Medicine, 1989; chmn. ad hoc com. on dioxin, EPA, 1988-89; vice chmn. sci. group on methodology for sci. evaluation chems., 1989—; chmn. mem. working group on Air Quality Guidelines for Major Urban Air Pollutants, 1985; mem. health rev. com. Health Effects Inst., 1987—; mem. nat. adv. environ. health effects coun. NIH, 1987-91; bd. dirs. Lovelace Inst., Internat. Life Sci. Inst. Contbr. articles to profl. jours., chpts. to books. Fellow ACP, Am. Coll. Preventive Medicine; mem. NAS Inst. Medicine, WHO Commn. Health and Environment, Am. Soc. Clin. Investigation. Home: 835 Hoes Ln Piscataway NJ 08854 Office: Rutgers University UMDNJ Enviro & Occupational Health Scis Inst Piscataway NJ 08855-1179

GOLDSTEIN, CHARLES MEYER, dental educator; b. Providence, Apr. 21, 1921; s. Sigmund Alexander and Beatrice Goldstein; m. Shirley Eleanor Spector, Apr. 28, 1943; children: Jeffrey, Jonathan, Judith, Joel. BS, DDS, U. Calif., San Francisco, 1944; MPH, UCLA, 1967. Pvt. practice, Santa Monica, Calif., 1946-71, West Los Angeles, Calif., 1971-83; dir. mobile clinic sch. dentistry U. So. Calif., L.A., 1970-81, prof., chmn. dept. practice dynamics, 1981-87, clin. prof. pub. health and community dentistry, sect. chmn., 1989—; mem. adv. com. dental sect. Calif. Dept. Health, 1979-82; founder Tel Aviv U. Dental Sch., 1981, Hebrew U. Dental Sch., Jerusalem, 1976; mem. adv. bd. Clinica Oscar Romero, L.A., 1988—; sponsor mobile clinic to El Salvador, Monsenor Oscar Romero C.Am. Refugee Com., Santa Cruz, Calif., 1990—; hon. prof. U. Autonoma Guadalajara, Mex., 1975. Author: Ethics in Dentistry, 1989; co-author: Ethics in Dentistry; contbr. articles to dental jours., chpt. to Geriatric Dentistry, 1991. Dental cons. United Farm Workers, Calif., 1965-67; cons. dental program Synanon, Calif., 1961-87; cons. fluoride rinse bill Calif. Dept. Edn., 1981-83. Lt. USN, 1944-46, PTO. Recipient humanitarian award Latin Am. Dental Soc., 1974, recognition award ADA, 1989, presdl. commendation award for meritorious svc. U. S.C. Dental Sch. Alumni, 1994; named Citizen of Week, Sta. KNX, 1993. Fellow Am. Soc. Geriatric Dentistry, Acad. Dentistry Internat., Am. Coll. Dentists, Internat. Coll. Dentists; mem. Am. Soc. Dentistry for Children (pres. So. Calif. sect. 1983-84, Disting. Svc. award 1974), Pierre Fauchard Acad. Democrat. Jewish. Home: 3485 Mandeville Canyon Rd Los Angeles CA 90049-1019 Office: U So Calif Sch Dentistry 925 W 34th St Los Angeles CA 90089-0641

GOLDSTEIN, DAVID ARTHUR, biophysicist, educator; b. Rochester, N.Y., Nov. 8, 1934; s. Jacob David and Elizabeth Maude (Brown) G.; m. Marie Elaine Nardone, May 25, 1969; 1 child, David James. AB in Physics, Harvard U., 1956, MD, 1960. Rsch. fellow biophysical lab. Harvard Med. Sch., Cambridge, Mass., 1960-62; rsch. assoc. biophys. lab. biophysical lab. Harvard Med. Sch., Cambridge, 1964-65; asst. prof. radiation biology and biophysics Rochester Med. Coll., 1965-68, assoc. prof. biophysics, 1968—, assoc. prof. biomath., 1969-74, assoc. prof. med. informatics, 1988—; dir. Med. Ctr. Computing, U. Rochester Med. Sch., 1975-77, assoc. chmn. dept. radiation biology and biophysics, 1980-85, dir. divsn. med. informatics, 1988—; cons. mathematician NIMH, Bethesda, Md., 1963-64. Contbr. articles to profl. jours. Treas. Stormers Soccer Club, Rochester, 1983-93; bd. dirs. Monroe County Girls Soccer League, Rochester, 1988-93. Surgeon, USPHS, 1963-64. Grantee AEC, NIH, NSF, ERDA, DOE, 1965—. Mem. AAAS, Biophys. Soc., Am. Med. Informatics Assn. (mem. edn. working group), Nat. Edn. Med. Sch. Consortium, Assn. Computing Machinery, N.Y. Acad. Scis., Harvey Soc. Home: 75 Deer Creek Rd Pittsford NY 14534-4147 Office: U Rochester Dept Biophysics Med Ctr Box BPHYS Rochester NY 14642

GOLDSTEIN, GARRY ARNOLD, internist, occupational medicine physician; b. Norfolk, Va., Jan. 4, 1931; s. Sam Ralph and Sarah (Kaminsky) G.; m. Carol Michael Hayes, June 26, 1958; children: Beth Allison Goldstein Oliphant, Brad L., Steven R. BA, Duke U., 1952; MD, U. Va., 1959; MPH, Med. Coll. Wis., 1995. Med. intern U. Ala., 1959-60, asst. resident in medicine, 1960-61; rsch. fellow in medicine Beth Israel Hosp., Harvard Med. Sch., Boston, 1961-62, chief resident in medicine, 1963-64; postdoctoral fellow in biochemistry MIT, Cambridge, 1962-63; pvt. practice, 1964-89; med. dir. Holmes Transp. Co. of New Eng., 1980-85; regional med. examiner UPS, 1980-85; med. dir. C.P.C. Gen. Motors, Framingham, Mass., 1985-89; med. dir. N. Am. Ops. Gen. Motors, Wilmington, Del., 1989—. Contbr. articles to profl. jours. Past dir. Algonquin Coun. Boy Scouts of Am., Framingham Country Club; corporator Framingham Union Hosp. With U.S. Army, 1952-54; sr. asst. surgeon USPHS, 1959—. Recipient Cert. of Merit, ARC, 1954. Mem. Am. Coll. Occupational Medicine, Del. Coll. Occupational Medicine, Am. Diabetes Assn., Am. Heart Assn., Mass. Med. Soc., Del. Med. Soc., New Castle County Med. Soc., Del. Acad. Medicine, Radley Run Country Club, Beta Beta Beta, Jewish. Jewish. Office: Gen Motors/N Am Ops Boxwood & Centerville Rds Wilmington DE 19806

GOLDSTEIN, HARRIS SIDNEY, psychiatrist; b. Chgo., Mar. 6, 1934; s. Herman Bendorf and Lillian (Sain) G.; m. Brigitte Maria Wolbert, Dec. 6, 1961; children: Marcel, Michael, Nicole, Sharon. BS, U. Ill., Urbana, 1955; MD, U. Ill., Chgo., 1959; MLA, Johns Hopkins U., 1966; DSc, SUNY, Bklyn., 1971. Cert. psychiatry, child psychiatry. Intern Cook County Hosp., Chgo., 1959-60; resident in psychiatry Sheppard-Pratt Hosp., Towson, Md., 1963-66; rsch. fellow SUNY, Downstate Med. Ctr., Bklyn., 1966-68, asst. prof., 1968-73, assoc. prof., 1973-75; prof. Robert Wood Johnson Med. Sch. U. Medicine and Dentistry N.J., Piscataway, 1975—; dir. tng. child and adolescent psychiatry, 1993-95. Contbr. articles to profl. jours. Capt. U.S. Army, 1960-62. Mem. Am. Psychiat. Assn., Am. Psychosomatic Soc., Am. Acad. Child and Adolescent Psychiatry, Phi Beta Kappa. Jewish. Home: 102 Lincoln Ave Highland Park NJ 08904-1852 Office: Robert Wood Johnson Med Sch 102 Lincoln Ave Highland Park NJ 08904-1852

GOLDSTEIN, HARRY HAROLD, retired dentist; b. N.Y.C., June 19, 1922; s. Michael and Alice (Nochimov) G.; m. Mimi M. Kenzer, Dec. 8, 1945; children: Carol Lynn, Myra P. Goldstein Hersh. BS, NYU, 1943, DDS, 1945, postgrad., 1947-51. Pvt. practice N.Y.C., Hartsdale, N.Y., 1947-88; chief dentistry Hebrew Hosp., Bronx, N.Y., 1949-74; orthodontist Sydenham Hosp., N.Y.C., 1951-62; sec. med. bd. Hebrew Hosp., Bronx, 1954-58. Mem. panel Jewish Child Care Assn., N.Y.C., 1952-62; founder, gen. chmn. Sigma Epsilon Delta Cleft Palate Ctr., Haifa, Israel, 1966-75; chmn. Golf Day South Palm Beach Jewish Fedn.-Boca Woods Country Club, 1993; toastmaster Bonds for Israel, Westchester, N.y., 1972-76. Lt. USN, 1945-47. Fellow Internat. Acad. Dentists; mem. ADA (ret. life), Am. Soc. Ret. Dentists (asst. exec. dir. 1990), Boca Woods Country Club (gov. 1989-92), Jewish War Vets., B'nai Brith, Edward Goldberger Lodge (pres. 1950-52), Sigma Epsilon Delta (Man. of Yr. 1968). Democrat. Home: 11235 Boca Woods Ln Boca Raton FL 33428-1840

GOLDSTEIN, JACK, health science executive, microbiologist; b. N.Y.C., June 7, 1947; s. Arnold L. and Rachel (Vogel) G.; m. Laurie Ann Sacks, Aug. 28, 1969; 1 child, Justin T. BA, Rider Coll., Trenton, N.J., 1969; MS, St. John's U., Jamaica, N.Y., 1974, PhD, 1976. Diplomate Am. Bd. Med.

Microbiology. Asst. dir. microbiology Queens Hosp. Ctr., Jamaica, 1976-81; dir. diagnostic labs. API div. Sherwood Med. Co., Plainview, N.Y., 1981-83; v.p. research and devel. MicroScan div. Baxter Travenol, Sacramento, 1983-86; group v.p. Ortho Diagnostic Systems Inc. div. Johnson & Johnson Co., Raritan, N.J., 1986-88; group v.p., gen. mgr. infectious disease bus. Ortho Diagnostic Systems, Inc. div. Johnson & Johnson Co., Raritan, N.J., 1988-92; exec. v.p. worldwide Ortho Diagnostic Sys. Inc. divsn. Johnson & Johnson Co., Raritan, N.J., 1992-93, pres., 1993—; mem. exam. com. Am. Bd. Med. Microbiology, Washington, 1984-91. Mem. editl. bd. Jour. Clin. Microbiology, Wasington, 1983-91; contbr. articles to profl. jours. Mem. Am. Soc. Microbiology, Am. Soc. Clin. Chemistry, Beta Beta Beta. Office: Ortho Diagnostic Systems Inc 1001 Us Highway 202 Raritan NJ 08869-1424

GOLDSTEIN, JAY CARL, podiatrist; b. Cleve., Sept. 10, 1948; s. Morton and Glady (Klein) G.; m. Marleen London, Aug. 1, 1971; children: Sarah Rose, Kerry Samuel. BS in Biomed. Engring., BS in Med. Scis., Case Western Res. U., 1970, MS in Biology, 1972, DPM, 1976. Diplomate Am. Bd. Podiatric Surgery, Am. Bd. Podiatric Orthopedics; bd. cert. foot & ankle surgery, podiatric orthopedics, podiatric medicine. Chmn. podiatry divsn. Emanuel Hosp., Portland, Oreg., 1992—, Good Samaritan Hosp., Portland, 1992—; attending Legacy Podiatry Residency Program, Oreg. Contbr. articles to profl. jours. Bd. dirs. Am. Diabetes Assn., Oreg., 1981-87; founder, dir. Rock Creek (Oreg.) Half Marathon, 1981-87; vol. podiatrist Wallace Med. Concern, Portland. Mem. Am. Podiatric Med. Assn. (Recognition award 1984), Am. Bd. Podiatry Surgery, Am. Bd. Podiatric Orthopedics, Toastmasters. Republican. Jewish. Office: 2250 NW Flanders # 101 Portland OR 97210

GOLDSTEIN, JEFFREY HASKELL, psychology educator; b. Norwalk, Conn., Aug. 11, 1942; s. Robert and Sylvia (Schwartz) G. BA, U. Conn., 1964; MS, Boston U., 1966; PhD, Ohio State U., 1969. Prof. psychology Temple U., Phila., 1973-91; vis. prof. Inst. of Edn. U. London, 1987-89, U. Utrecht (The Netherlands), 1990—; cons. British Toy and Hobby Assn., London, 1987—, Toy Mfrs. Europe, 1990—. Author: Aggression and Crimes of Violence, 1986; co-author: Psychology: An Introduction, 1990, Toys, Play & Child Development, 1994; editor: Sports, Games and Play, 1989; editor jour. Current Psychology, 1988-89. Fellow APA, Am. Psychol. Soc., Internat. Soc. for Rsch. on Aggression (Idiodynamics award); mem. Nat. Toy Coun. (Eng.), European Assn. for Exptl. Social Psychology. Office: Social & Orgnl Psychology, Univ Utrecht, 3564 CS Utrecht The Netherlands

GOLDSTEIN, JOSEPH LEONARD, physician, medical educator, molecular genetics scientist; b. Sumter, SC, Apr. 18, 1940; s. Isadore E. and Fannie A. Goldstein. BS, Washington and Lee U., Lexington, Va., 1962; MD, U. Tex., Dallas, 1966; DSc (hon.), U. Chgo., 1982, Rensselaer Poly. Inst., 1982, Washington and Lee U., 1986, U. Paris, 1988, U. Buenos Aires, 1990, So. Meth. U., 1993, U. Miami, 1996. Intern, then resident in medicine Mass. Gen. Hosp., Boston, 1966-68; clin. assoc. NIH, 1968-70; postdoctoral fellow U. Wash., Seattle, 1970-72; mem. faculty U. Tex. Southwestern Med. Ctr., Dallas, 1972—, Paul J. Thomas prof. medicine, chmn. dept. molecular genetics, 1977—, regental prof., 1985—; Harvey Soc. lectr., 1977; mem. sci. rev. bd. Howard Hughes Med. Inst., 1978-84, mem. med. adv. bd., 1985-90, chmn. med. adv. bd., 1995—; non-resident fellow Salk Inst., 1983-94; chmn. Albert Lasker Med. Rsch award jury, 1996—; mem. sci. adv. bd. Scripps Rsch. Inst., 1996—. Co-author: The Metabolic Basis of Inherited Disease, 5th edit., 1983; editorial bd. Jour. Biol. Chemistry, 1981-85, Cell, 1983—, Jour. Clin. Investigation, 1977-82, Ann. Rev. Genetics, 1980-85, Arteriosclerosis, 1981-87, Sci. 1985—. Mem. bd. trustees Rockefeller U., 1994—; mem. sci. adv. bd. Welch Found., 1986—; bd. dirs. Passano Found., 1985—. Recipient Heinrich-Wieland prize, 1974, Pfizer award in enzyme chemistry Am. Chem. Soc., 1976; Passano award Johns Hopkins U., 1978; Gairdner Found. award, 1981; award in biol. and med. scis. N.Y. Acad. Scis., 1981, Lita Annenberg Hazen award, 1982; Rsch. Achievement reward Am. Heart Assn., 1984; Louisa Gross Horwitz award, 1984; 3M Life Scis. award, 1984, Albert Lasker award in Basic Med. Rsch., 1985; Nobel Prize in Physiology or Medicine, 1985, Trustees' medal Mass. Gen. Hosp., 1986, U.S. Nat. medal of Sci., 1988. Mem. NAS (Lounsbery award 1979, coun. 1991—), ACP (award 1986), Assn. Am. Physicians, Am. Soc. Clin. Investigation (pres. 1985-86), Am. Soc. Human Genetics (William Allan award 1985), Amer. Acad. Arts and Scis., Am. Soc. Biol. Chemists, Am. Fedn. Clin. Research, Am. Philos. Soc., Inst. Medicine, Royal Soc. London (fgn. mem.), Phi Beta Kappa, Alpha Omega Alpha. Home: 3831 Turtle Creek Blvd Apt 22B Dallas TX 75219-4415 Office: U Tex Southwestern Med Ctr 5323 Harry Hines Blvd Dallas TX 75235-9046

GOLDSTEIN, LARRY BRUCE, neurologist, educator; b. N.Y.C., May 27, 1955; s. Daniel and Sharon (Kantrowitz) G.; children Sarah, Daniel. AB magna cum laude, Brandeis U., 1977; MD, Mt. Sinai Med. Sch., 1981. Intern Mt. Sinai Hosp., N.Y.C., 1981-82, resident in neurology, 1982-85, chief resident, 1985; fellow Duke U., Durham, N.C., 1985-86, assoc., 1986-88, asst. prof. medicine, 1989-95, assoc. prof., 1995—, asst. rsch. prof. Ctr. for Health Policy, 1989—. Fellow Am. Acad. Neurology (G. Milton Shy award 1979); mem. Nat. Stroke Assn., Internat. Behavioral Neurosci. Soc., Soc. for Neurosci., Am. Heart Assn. (fellow stroke coun.). Office: Duke Med Ctr Box 3651 Durham NC 27710

GOLDSTEIN, LEONARD BARRY, dentist, educator; b. Seaford, N.Y., Feb. 6, 1944; s. Jacob Martin and Adele (Pelzner) G.; m. Phyllis Lynn Kerwin, June 25, 1967; children: Marcie Ilene, Sherri Elysse. Student, Ind. U., 1961-63; DDS, Case Western Reserve U., 1967; Cert. in Orthodontics, Dewey Sch. Orthodontics, N.Y.C., 1969; PhD in Electro-Medicine, City U., Los Angeles, 1988. Diplomate Am. Acad. of Pain Mgmt. Gen. practice dentistry Smithtown, N.Y., 1969—; attending orthodontist Abe Stark Philanthropies Dental Clinic, Bklyn., 1970-77; guest prof. Dept. Phys. Edn. Queens Coll., N.Y., 1979—; guest lectr. Dept. Phys. Edn. Queensboro (N.Y.) Community Coll., 1980—; dir. dental services Good Samaritan Profl. Services, St. James, N.Y., 1979—, v.p. med. bd., 1979—; attending dental staff St. John's Episc. Hosp., 1980—, Community Hosp. Western Suffolk, 1980—; bd. dirs. L.I. Ctr. for Cranio-Facial Pain, Smithtown. Contbr. articles to profl. jours. Served to capt. Dental Corps, U.S. Army, 1967-69. Recipient fellowship in removeable prosthetics U.S. Army Dental Corps, 1967. Fellow Acad. Stress and Chronic Disease, Acad. Gen. Dentistry, Am. Endodontic Soc., Internat. Coll. Dentists; mem. Am. Equilibration Soc., Am. Coll. Sports Medicine, Internat. Acad. Preventive Medicine, Cranial Acad. of Am. Osteopathic Soc., Am. Orthodontic Soc., Internat. Soc. Orthodontists, Am. Dental Soc., Cronio-Mandibular Study Club of N.Y., L.I. Gnathological Study Club, Northeastern Gnathological Soc. Home: PO Box 217 178 Alexander Ave Nesconset NY 11767 Office: 50 Route 111 Smithtown NY 11787-3700

GOLDSTEIN, LOREN DAVID, dentist; b. Chgo., July 15, 1955; s. Harold and June Marlene Goldstein; m. Reneè Ann Boyd, Mar 20, 1982; children: Tayler Rè, Garrett William. BA, Drake U., 1977; certificate in Nuclear Medicine Tech., Hines VA Hosp., 1978; DDS, U. Ill., Chgo., 1982. Gen. practice dentistry Northbrook, Ill., 1982-83, Glencoe (Ill.) Dental Assocs., 1983—. Staff mem. Highland Park (Ill.) Hosp., 1985—. Mem. ADA, Acad. Gen. Dentistry, Am. Equilibration Soc., Chgo. Dental Soc. (mediation com. 1985—, chmn. peer rev. com. 1988, br. treas. 1991, br. v.p. 1994, chmn. peer rev. com. 1993, 94, 95, 96). Office: Glencoe Dental Assocs 630 Vernon Ave Ste D Glencoe IL 60022-1684

GOLDSTEIN, MARTIN BARNET, osteopathic physician, psychiatrist; b. N.Y.C., Jan. 9, 1933; s. Samuel Eli and Bessie Leah (Kurman) G.; m. Nov. 23, 1963. BS in Pharmacy, L.I. U., 1955; DO, Chgo. Coll. Osteo. Medicine, 1959. Diplomate Am. Osteo. Bd. Neuropsychiatry, Am. Bd. Sexology. Intern Met. Hosp., Phila., 1959-60; pvt. practice Phila., 1960—; pres., chief exec. officer Neuro-Rsch. Inc., Phila., 1978-84, Lafayette Psychiat. Assocs., Whitemarsh, Pa., 1981-84; chmn. bd. dirs. Equibank Del., Wilmington, 1987-89; bd. dirs. Equimark, Pitts., 1985-89. Author: The Judgement of J.D., 1994; editor Jour. Med. Aspects Human Secuality, 1986-90; contbr. over 100 articles to med. jours. Mem. Penn Valley (Pa.) Civic Assn., 1966—. Fellow Am. Coll. Neuropsychiatrists, Am. Acad. Clin. Sexologists; mem. Am. Osteo. Assn. (editorial referee Jour. 1966—), Am. Psychiat. Assn., Pa. Osteo. Med. Asssn., Phila. Osteo. Med. Assn., Philadelphia County Osteo. Soc. Republican. Jewish. Office: 2400 Chestnut St Apt 2506 Philadelphia PA 19103-4323

GOLDSTEIN, MARVIN NORMAN, physician; b. Balt., Aug. 10, 1940; s. Manuel Quezon and Sylvia (Wagenheim) G.; m. Athene Schiffmann, July 1, 1962; children: Joshua, Claire. AB summa cum laude, Western Md. Coll., 1960; MD, U. Md., 1964. Diplomate Am. Bd. Psychiatry and Neurology. Intern in internal medicine U. Chgo. Hosp., 1964-65; resident in neurology Strong Meml. Hosp., U. Rochester, N.Y., 1965-68; chief resident in neurology Strong Meml. Hosp., U. Rochester, 1967-68; asst. attending neurologist, instr. U. Md. Hosp., Balt., 1968-69, Johns Hopkins Hosp., Balt., 1969-70; asst. prof. neurology and anatomy U. Rochester Sch. Medicine and Dentistry, 1970-74, clin. asst. prof. neurology and anatomy, 1974-78, clin. assoc. prof. neurology and anatomy, 1978—; sr. attending neurology The Genesee Hosp., Rochester, 1978—, dir. neurology unit, 1996—; instr. in neurology and anatomy U. Rochester Sch. Medicine and Dentistry, 1965-68, Sch. Medicine, Georgetown U., Washington, 1968-70; staff neurologist U.S. Naval Hosp., Bethesda, 1968-70; med. staff exec. com. The Genesee Hosp., Rochester, 1989-90. Contbr. articles to profl. jours. Bd. dirs. Rochester Area Multiple Sclerosis, Rochester, 1972-78: adult edn. com. Temple Beth El, Rochester, 1985-90. Lt. comdr. USNR, 1968-70. Grantee NIH, 1972-74. Fellow Am. Acad. Neurology, Royal Soc. Medicine; mem. Am. Epilepsy Soc., Am. Acad. Clin. Neurophysiology, Sigma Xi. Home: 20 Varinna Dr Rochester NY 14618-1508 Office: 222 Alexander St Rochester NY 14607-4005

GOLDSTEIN, MARY KANE, physician; b. N.Y.C., Oct. 24, 1950; d. Edwin Patrick and Mary Kane; m. Yonkel Noah Goldstein, June 24, 1979; children: Keira, Gavi. Philosophy degree, Columbia U., 1973, MD, 1977; MS in Health Svcs. Rsch., Stanford U., 1994. Resident Duke U. Med. Ctr., Durham, N.C., 1977-80; asst. prof. medicine U. Calif., San Francisco, 1980-84; staff physician Cowell Student Health Ctr. U. Calif., Santa Cruz, 1984-85, clin. instr. dept. family and cmty. preventive medicine, 1984-85; staff physician Mid-Peninsula Health Svc., Palo Alto, Calif., 1986-88; dir. grad. med. edn. divsn. gerontol. Stanford (Calif.) U., 1986-93, Agy. for Health Care Policy Rsch. fellow Sch. Medicine, 1991-94; sect. chief for gen. internal medicine Palo Alto (Calif) VA Med. Ctr., 1994-96; editor Computer Ctr. Pubs., N.Y.C., 1971-72; computer programmer Columbia U., N.Y.C., 1972-73; faculty assoc. Stanford Sch. Medicine, 1992; chair ethic com. U. Calif./Natividad Med. Com., San Francisco, 1984. Author chpt. to book; contbr. articles to profl. jours. Recipient Rsch. award Far West HSR & D, 1990, Expanding Rsch. award Charles H. Dana Found., 1990, Cost Implications award Hartford Found. Geriatric Ctr., 1991, Preference Assessment in Geriatrics award Palo Alto Inst. for Rsch. and Edn., 1992. Fellow Am. Geriatrics Soc. (bd. dirs. 1996—); mem. Am. Bd. Family Practice (bd. dirs. 1993—), Am. Fedn. Clin. Rsch., Geriatric Test Com. Office: Palo Alto VA Med Ctr 182B MPD 3801 Miranda Ave Palo Alto CA 94304-1207

GOLDSTEIN, MICHAEL L., neurologist; b. Chgo., June 14, 1945; s. Charles and Dorothy (Mack) G.; m. Barbara Joan Raplan, June 18, 1967; children: Rachel, Elizabeth, Adam. AB, Princeton, 1966; MD, U. of Chgo., 1970. Intern Stanford U., 1970-71; resident in neurology Beth Israel Hosp., Boston, 1971-74; fellow in neurology Harvard U. Med. Sch., 1971-74; chief resident in neurology Children's Hosp., Boston, 1973-74; with Western Neurol. Assoc., Salt Lake City; cons. Soc. Sec., Balt., 1990-91; bd. dirs., edn. comm. chmn. Rowland Hall, Stimasks Sch., Salt Lake City, 1986-92; examiner Am. Bd. Psychology and Neurology, M pls., 1987—; clin. assoc. prof. U. Utah Med. Sch., Salt Lake City, 1977—. Co-author: Managing Attention Disorders, 1990, Parent's Guide to ADD, 1993; co-producer: Educating Inattentive Children, 1992, It's Just Attention Disorder, 1993. Pres. synagogue, Salt Lake City, 1985-86. Fellow Am. Acad. Pediat., Am. Acad. Neurology (chair practice com, 1995—). Office: Western Neurol Assn 1151 E 3900 S Salt Lake City UT 84124

GOLDSTEIN, MILTON HOUSEMAN, rehabilitation facility administrator; b. Bklyn., Jan. 10, 1937; s. Benjamin and Gertrude (Houseman) G.; m. Ella Stickle Goldstein, Sept. 18, 1961; children: Cindy Goldstein Getty, Alan Goldstein. BS, NYU, 1959. Vocat. trainer United Cerebral Palsy Assn., Roosevelt, L.I., N.Y., 1959-61; workshop supr. Internat. Ctr. for Disabled, N.Y.C., 1961-63; exec. dir. Gateway Industries Inc., Kingston, N.Y., 1963-65, The Workshop Inc., Menands, N.Y., 1965-82; pres. MGA Assocs., Albany, N.Y., 1982-85; exec. dir. Challenge Industries Inc., Ithaca, N.Y., 1985—; mem. adv. bd. N.Y. State Sch. Indsl. and Labor Rels., Cornell U., Ithaca, 1987—; v.p. Finger Lakes Indsl. Ctr., Ithaca, 1988-90; bd. dirs. N.Y. State Assn. Rehab. Facilities, Albany, 1986-89. Trustee Tompkins County Pub. Libr., 1993—, chairperson, 1994-96; bd. dirs. WCNY Pub. Broadcasting, 1995—. With U.S. Army N.G., 1957-63. Mem. Tompkins County Mental Health Assn. (pres. 1990-91), Tompkins County C. of C. (bd. dirs. 1988-95, v.p. 1990-91, chmn. bd. 1992), Rotary. Home: 29 Hunter Ln Ithaca NY 14850-9662 Office: Challenge Industries Inc 402 E State St Ithaca NY 14850-4410

GOLDSTEIN, NAOMI, psychiatrist; b. N.Y.C., Apr. 24, 1932; d. Eli and Caroline (Kleppner) G.; m. Franklin Feldman, June 3, 1956; children: Sarah, Eve, Jacob. AB, Vassar Coll., 1952; MD, N.Y. Med. Coll., 1956. Diplomate in psychiatry Am. Bd. Psychiatry and Neurology. Pvt. practice N.Y.C., 1960—; staff psychiatrist Criminal Ct. Psychiat. Clinic, 1961-68; psychiat. adminstr. N.Y.C. Probation Methadone Clinic, Bernstein Inst., 1970-72; dir. Supreme and Criminal Ct. Psychiat. Clinics, 1968-72; staff psychiatrist Liaison Svc. Bellevue Hosp., 1972-74; chief psychiatry Met. Correction Ctr. Fed. Bur. Prisons, N.Y.C., 1974-78; attending psychiatrist Bellevue Hosp., 1978-90; clin. prof. psychiatry NYU Med. Sch., N.Y.C., 1990—; pres. Am. Bd. Forensic Psychiatry, Balt., 1988-89; mem. N.Y. State Bd. Profl. Med. Conduct, Albany, 1978—, chmn., 1982-84; lectr. law Columbia U., N.Y.C., 1988; bd. advisors Fed. Correctional Instn., Otisville, N.Y., 1980-85. Contbr. articles to profl. jours. Fellow Am. Psychiat. Assn. (life, trustee-at-large 1982-85, pres. N.Y. County dist. br. 1985-86), N.Y. Acad. Medicine (chmn. psychiatry sect. 1993-94)m, Am. Acad. Psychiatry and the Law, Assn. Women Psychiatrists, Am. Med. Women's Assn., AMA, Acad. Hon. Soc. N.Y. Med. Coll., Phi Beta Kappa. Jewish. Office: 16 E 79th St New York NY 10021-0150

GOLDSTEIN, NEIL HOWARD, physician; b. Yonkers, N.Y., Mar. 27, 1952; s. A. Leonard and Jean (Simon) G. BA with honors in biology, Brandeis U., 1974; MD, U. Mass., 1979. Diplomate Am. Bd. Internal Medicine, Am. Bd. Infectious Disease. Intern in internal medicine George Washington U. Hosp., Washington, 1979-80, resident in internal medicine, 1980-82, fellow in infectious disease, 1982-84; cons. infectious disease Chester County Hosp., West Chester, Pa., 1984-89; mem. rsch. staff Wilmington Med. Ctr., 1988—; dir. infectious disease Sterling Winthrop Inc., Malvern, Pa., 1990-93; sr. dir. clin. rsch. Sanofi Winthrop, Inc., Malvern, Pa., 1994—. Contbr. articles to profl. jours. Fellow Coll. of Physicians of Phila.; mem. AMA, ACP, Am. Soc. Microbiology, Am. Soc. Internal Medicine, AMA. Office: Sanofi WInthrop Inc 9 Great Valley Pkwy PO Box 3026 Malvern PA 19355

GOLDSTEIN, SIR NORMAN, dermatologist; b. Bklyn. July 14, 1934; s. Joseph H. and Bertha (Docteroff) G.; B.A., Columbia Coll., 1955; M.D., SUNY, 1959; m. Ramsay, Feb. 14, 1980; children: Richard, Heidi. Intern, Maimonides Hosp., N.Y.C., 1959-60; resident Skin and Cancer Hosp., 1960-61, Bellevue Hosp., 1961-62, NYU. Postgrad. Center, 1962-63 (all N.Y.C.); ptnr. Honolulu Med. Group, 1967-72; practice medicine specializing in dermatology, Honolulu, 1972—; clin. prof. dermatology U. Hawaii Sch. Medicine, 1973—; bd. dirs. Pacific Laser. Bd. dirs. Skin Cancer Found., 1979—; trustee Dermatol. Found., 1979-82, Hist. Hawaii Found., 1981-87; pres. Hawaii Theater Ctr., 1985-89, Hawaii Med. Libr., 1987; mem. Oahu Heritage Council, 1986-94. Served with U.S. Army, 1960-67. Recipient Henry Silver award Dermatol. Soc. Greater N.Y., 1963; Husik award NYU, 1963; Spl. award Acad. Dermatologia Hawaiiana, 1971, Outstanding Scientific Exhibit award Calif. Med. Assn., 1979, Special award for Exhibit Am. Urologic Assn., 1980, Svc. to Hawaii's Youth award Adult Friends for Youth, 1991, Nat. Cosmetic Tattoo Assn. award, 1993, Cmty. Svc. award Am. Acad. Dermatology, 1993; named Physician of Yr., Hawaii Med. Assn., 1993. Fellow ACP, Am. Acad. Dermatology (Silver award 1972), Am. Soc. Lasers Medicine & Surgery, Royal Soc. Medicine; mem. Internat. Soc. Tropical Dermatologists (Hist. and Culture award), Soc. Investigative Dermatologists, AAAS, Am. Soc. Photobiology, Internat. Soc. Cryosurgery, Am. Soc. Micropigmentation Surgery, Small Bus. Council Am. (bus. adv. council), Pacific and Asian Affairs Council, Navy League, Assn. Hawaii Artists, Nat. Stereoscopic Soc., Biol. Photog. Assn., Friends of Photography, Health Sci. Communication Assn., Internat. Pigment Cell Soc., Am. Med. Writers Assn., Physicians Exchange of Hawaii (bd. dirs.), Am. Coll. Cryosurgery, Internat. Soc. Dermatol. Surgery, Am. Soc. Preventive Oncology, Soc. for Computer Medicine, Am. Assn. for Med. Systems and Info., computer Security Inst., Japan Am. Soc. Hawaii (bd. dirs.), Pacific Telecom Council, Hawaii State Med. Assn. (mem. public affairs com.), Hawaii Dermatol. Soc. (sec.-pres.), Hawaii Public Health Assn., Pacific Dermatol. Assn., Pacific Health Research Inst., Honolulu County Med. Soc. (gov.), Nat. Wildlife Fedn., C. of C., Preservation Action, Am. Coll. Sports Medicine, Rotary, Ancient Gaelic Nobilitary Soc. (named Knight of the Niadh Nask, 1995), Outrigger Canoe Club, Plaza Club (pres. bd. dirs. 1990-92), Chancellor's Club, Oahu Country Club. Editor: Hawaii Med. Jour.; contbr. articles to profl. jours. Office: Tan Sing Bldg 1128 Smith St Honolulu HI 96817-5139

GOLDSTEIN, PAUL H(ENRY), ophthalmologist, educator; b. Chgo., May 20, 1936; s. Alex and Leah (Swabsky) G.; m. Marilyn Gail Holtzman, Sept. 4, 1960; children: Todd, Jordan, Karen, Ross. BS, U. Ill., 1956; MD, U. Ill., Chgo., 1960. Diplomate Am. Bd. Ophthalmology. With basic and clin. sci. ophthalmology Harvard Med. Sch., 1961-62; intern Cook County Hosp., Chgo., 1960-61, resident, 1962-64; pvt. practice Milw., 1965—; asst. clin. prof. Med. Coll. of Wis., Milw., 1965—; chief of ophthalmology Sinai-Samaritan Med. Ctr., Milw., 1989—. Mem. Milw. Ophthal. Soc. (pres. 1973), Alpha Omega Alpha. Office: Eye Physicians Assn 2901 W Kinnickinnic River Pky Milwaukee WI 53215-3660

GOLDSTEIN, ROBERT LEE, health facility administrator; b. N.Y.C., Feb. 15, 1951; s. Harry and Ethel (Shapiro) G.; m. Diane Hope Silverman, Jan. 5, 1974; children: Beth Renee, Adam Jay. Student, Syracuse (N.Y.) U., 1969-71; BS, SUNY, Stony Brook, 1973; M in Health Adminstrn., Duke U., 1975. Adminstrv. resident Ochsner Clinic, New Orleans, 1975-76, asst. adminstr., 1984-88, assoc. adminstr., 1988-90; asst. clinic mgr. Med. Ctr. Clinic, Pensacola, Fla., 1976-84; chief adminstrv. officer Browne-McHardy Clinic, New Orleans, 1990—; adj. prof. dept. health svcs. adminstrn. U. Ala., Birmingham, 1990—. Fellow Am. Coll. Med. Practice Execs. (bd. dirs. 1990-95, sec.-treas. 1992-93, pres. 1993-94); mem. Med. Group Mgmt. Assn. (bd. dirs. 1990-92, v.p. So. chpt. 1989, 1st v.p. 1989-90, pres. 1991-92), Am. Group Practice Assn. (editl. adv. com. 1993—). Home: 4013 Rivage Ct Metairie LA 70002-1345 Office: Browne-McHardy Clinic 4315 Houma Blvd Metairie LA 70006-2981

GOLDSTEIN, ROBERT MICHAEL, transplant surgeon; b. Elizabethton, Tenn., Mar. 21, 1953; s. Buford Jack and Mary Jane Goldstein; m. Amanda Elizabeth Goldstein, May 16, 1992. BA, U. Tenn., 1975; MD, U. Tenn., Memphis, 1981. Diplomate Am. Bd. Gen. Surgery., Am. Bd. Surg. Care. Pediatric intern Ohio State U., Columbus, 1981-82; surgery resident W.Va. U., Morgantown, 1982-84, 85-87; rsch. fellow Johns Hopkins, Balt., 1984-85; transplant fellow U. Pitts., Pa., 1987-88; transplant fellow Baylor U. Med. Ctr., Dallas, 1987-88, asst. dir. transplant svcs., 1988—, dir. transplant intensive care, 1990—. Fellow ACS; mem. Am. Bd. Surg. Critical Care. Office: Baylor Univ Dept Transplantation Dallas TX 75246

GOLDSTEIN, ROBERT STANLEY, orthopedic surgeon, educator; b. Bklyn., Nov. 14, 1936; s. Herman Joseph Goldstein and Eva Malkin; m. Barbara Ellen Kantin, Mar. 28, 1941; children: Sara Beth, Helaine Jill, Laura Emily, Allison Lisa. BA, Johns Hopkins U., 1958; MD, N.Y. Med. Coll., 1962. Diplomate Am. Bd. Orthopedic Surgery. Intern Nassau County Med. Ctr., East Meadow, N.Y., 1962-63; resident in orthopedic surgery N.Y. Med. Coll., N.Y.C., 1965-69; pvt. practice N.Y.C., 1969—; asst. prof. orthopedic surgery N.Y. Med. Coll., Valhalla; attending orthopedic surgery Hosp for Joint Diseases, N.Y.C.; clin. asst. prof. orthopedic surgery NYU Med. Ctr., 1995-96. Trustee Village of Gt. Neck Estates (N.Y.), 1983-91, police commr., 1983-91. Capt. M.C., U.S. Army, 1963-65. Fellow ACS, Internat. Coll. Surgeons; mem. Arthroscopy Assn. N.Am., Internat. Arthroscopy Assn. Jewish. Home: 96 Ash Dr Great Neck NY 11021-1926 Office: 1245 Madison Ave New York NY 10128-0554

GOLDSTEIN, ROBERTA, social worker; b. Bklyn., Sept. 13, 1950; d. Sol and Martha (Novick) Zeile; m. Alvan Eugene Goldstein, May 28, 1972; 1 child, Alanna. Student, Queensborough Community Coll., Bayside, N.Y., 1968-70, Downstate Med. Coll., Bklyn., 1970-71; BA, Queens Coll., Flushing, N.Y., 1973; MSW, Hunter Sch. Social Work, N.Y.C., 1979. Social worker Beth Israel Med. Ctr., N.Y.C., 1973-79, St. Vincents Med. Ctr., Jacksonville, Fla., 1979-81, Miami (Fla.) VA Med. Ctr., 1981-83; adminstrv. coord. EX-POW program Miami (Fla.) VA, 1983-86; social worker Oakland Park (Fla.) VA Out-Patient Clinic, 1986—; cons. Am. Ex-POWs, Broward County, Fla., 1986—. Coord. Ramat Shalom Soviet Resettlement Program, Plantation, Fla., 1991; mem. steering com. Can Surmount program Am. Cancer Soc., Ft. Lauderdale, Fla., 1990, mem. svc. and rehab. com., 1990, mem. steering com. resource dir., 1990; bd. dirs. Jewish Family Svc., 1996—, Ramat Shalom Synagogue, 1996—. Recipient cert. of appreciation Am. Legion, 1990. Mem. NASW, Acad. Cert. Social Workers. Democrat. Jewish. Home: 2420 NW 110th Ter Sunrise Fla Fort Lauderdale FL 33322-2549 Office: VA Out-Patient Clinic 5599 N Dixie Hwy Fort Lauderdale FL 33334-3406

GOLDSTEIN, RONALD ERWIN, dentist, author, educator, consultant, lecturer; b. Atlanta, Nov. 1, 1933; s. Irving and Helen (Mendel) G.; m. Judith Salzberg; children: Cary, Cathy, Richard, Kenneth. Student, U. Mich., 1951-53; DDS, Emory U., 1957. Clin. prof. restorative dentistry Sch. Dentistry, Med. Coll. Ga., Augusta, 1983—; with Goldstein, Goldstein & Garber DDS, Atlanta; vol. in charge of cosmetic dentistry Ben Massell Dental Clinic, Atlanta, 1967-80; spl. lectr. periodontology Sch. Dentostry, Emory U., 1972-79, spl. lectr. in esthetic dentistry, 1980-93, faculty continuing edn. Sch. Dentistry, U. Pitts., 1972-75; assoc. clin. prof. continuing edn. Boston U. Henry M. Goldman Sch. Dental Medicine, 1980-90, adj. clin. prof. prosthodontics, 1990—; vis. prof. oral/maxillofacial imaging and continuing edn. U. So. Calif. Sch. Dentistry, L.A., 1993—; adj. prof. restorative dentistry U. Tex., San Antonio, 1993—; cons. PM Mag., 1979-82; producer dental hygiene programs Sta WGST, Atlanta, 1982. Author: Esthetics in Dentistry, 1976, Change Your Smile, 1984; co-author: Bleaching Teeth, 1987, Porcelain Laminate Veneers, 1988, Porcelain and Composite Inlays and Onlays, 1994, Complete Dental Bleaching, 1995; contbg. editor: The Wonderful World of Modern Dentistry, 1972; co-editor-in-chief Jour. of Esthetic Dentistry, 1993—; mem. editl. bd. Current Opinion in Dentistry, 1972; contbr. articles to profl. jours. Founder Atlanta Health Coun., 1962, pres. 1966-69; nat. chmn. program on mental health and mental retardation U.S. Jaycees, 1963; membership com. Ahavath Achim Synagogue, 1964; v.p. Ga. Assn. for Mental Health, 1964-66; past chmn. Gov.'s Com. on Employment of the Emotionally Restored; bd. dirs. Atlanta Lodge B'nai B'rith, 1961-62, trustee Gate City Lodge, 1970; bd. dirs. Family Counseling Svc. Soc., 1963-69, Met. Atlanta Mental Health Assn., 1964-67, Met. Atlanta Community Chest, 1964-68, Atlanta USO-JWB, 1966-68, Jewish Children's Svcs., 1969—; bd. advisors Anti-Defamation League, 1970; sci. advisor Princeton Dental Resource Ctr., 1991-95, Ctr. for Dental Info., 1995-96. Recipient John Muir Med. Film Festival award 1982, Outstanding Contbn. to Cosmetic Dentistry award Am. Acad. Cosmetic Dentistry, 1992; named Citizen of the Week, Sta. WPLO, 1963, Outstanding Young Man of the Yr. award Atlanta Jr. C. of C., 1962, Top Four Lectrs. Dentist Mag. #1 Esthetic Dentistry, 1989; featured practice in Dentistry Today, Dec. 1991, Jan. 1994. Fellow Am. Coll. Dentists, Internat. Coll. Dentists; hon. fellow Ga. Dental Assn. (chmn. fluoridation com. 1964-65); mem. ADA, Am. Acad. Cranio-Mandibular Disorders, Am. Acad. Periodontology, Am. Acad. Fixed Prosthodontics, No. Dist. Dental Soc. (founder, 1st chmn. emergency dental svc. 1959), 5th Dist. Dental Soc. Pub. Health Com. (past pres., editor Preview-Rev. 1966-67), Internat. Acad. Gnathology, Am. Acad. History of Dentistry, Am. Jewish Com., Emory U. Alumni Assoc., Atlanta Jr. C. of C. (v.p. 1963), Ga. Heart Assn. (chmn. dental div. 1971), Am. Acad. Esthetic Dentistry (co-founder, pres. 1975-78, Top Four Lectrs. by Dentist Mag., #1 Esthetic Dentistry 1989), Nat. Acads. Practice (disting. practitioner), Alpha Omega (past pres. local, internat. chpts.), Omega Kappa Upsilon (hon.).

Office: Goldstein Goldstein Garber Ste 200 1218 W Paces Ferry Rd NW Atlanta GA 30327-2308

GOLDSTEIN, SIDNEY, pharmaceutical scientist; b. Phila., Mar. 27, 1932; s. Israel and Gertrude (Stein) G.; m. Janice Levy, June 19, 1955; children: Rhonda, David, Nina. BSc in Pharmacy, Phila. Coll. Pharmacy & Sci., 1954, MSc in Pharmacy, 1955, DSc in Pharmacy, 1958. Cardiovascular unit head Eaton Labs, Norwich, N.Y., 1958-59; anti-inflammatory unit head Lederle Labs, Pearl River, N.Y., 1959-61; with Merrell Dow Rsch. Inst., Cin., 1961-93; v.p. global pharm. and analytical scis. Marion Merrell Dow Inc., Kansas City, Mo., 1991-93; v.p. sci. and tech. Duramed Pharm., Inc., Cin., 1994—; adj. assoc. prof. U. Cin. Coll. Pharmacy, 1984—; lectr. pharmacology Phila. Coll. Pharmacy, 1967-70. Contbr. articles to profl. jours. Bd. trustees Glen Manor Home for Aged, Cin., 1983-89. Recipient Award for Nicoderm, R&D Mag., 1992. Mem. Am. Assn. Pharm. Scientists, Am. Soc. Clin. Pharmacology and Therapeutics, Soc. Exptl. Biology and Medicine, Am. Soc. Pharmacology and Exptl. Therapeutics, B'nai B'rith (chpt. v.p. 1978). Home: 1125 Fort View Pl Cincinnati OH 45202-1713 Office: Duramed Pharmaceuticals 5040 Duramed Dr Cincinnati OH 45213-2520

GOLDSTEIN, STEVEN EDWARD, psychologist; b. Bronx, N.Y., Nov. 25, 1948; s. Maurice and Matilda (Weiss) G.; BS in Psychology, CCNY, 1970, MS in Sch. Psychology, 1971; EdD in Sch. Psychology, U. No. Colo., 1977. Tchr., N.Y.C. Public Schs., 1970-71, 72-73, tchr., counselor, 1974; extern in sch. psychology N. Shore Child Guidance, 1972; sch. psychologist Denver Pub. Schs., 1975; asst. prof. psychology Northeastern Okla. State U., Tahlequah, 1976-78; coord. inpatient, emergency svcs. Winnemucca (Nev.) Mental Health Center, 1978-80; dir. Desert Devel. Ctr., Las Vegas, Nev., 1980-82; sr. psychologist Las Vegas Mental Health Ctr., 1982-92; pvt. practice psychology, Las Vegas, 1983—; sr. psychologist Desert Regional Ctr., 1992—; participant NSF seminar on biofeedback, 1977. Sec. grad. coun. CUNY, 1971; pres. grad. coun. in edn. CCNY, 1971. Lic. psychologist, Nev.; cert. sch. psychologist, N.Y., Calif. Mem. APA (Nev. coord. office of profl. practice 1987-88), Biofeedback Soc. Nev. (membership dir. 1982-90), Nev. Soc. Tng. and Devel. (dir. 1982-83), So. Nev. Soc. Cert. Psychologists (pres. 1984-86). Presenter papers to profl. confs. Office: 1391 S Jones Blvd Las Vegas NV 89102-1206 also: 3180 W Sahara Ave Ste C-25 Las Vegas NV 89102-6005

GOLDSTEIN, STEVEN HOWARD, podiatrist; b. Bklyn., Nov. 23, 1954; s. Arthur and Miriam Rosalyn (Gilden) G.; m. Susan Kobetz, June 15, 1980; children: Elyssa, Stacey. AAS in Med. Tech., SUNY, Farmingdale, 1974; BA, SUNY, Buffalo, 1976; D Podiatric Medicine, Ohio Coll. Podiatric Medicine, 1980. Resident in surgery Brent Gen. Hosp., Detroit, 1980-81; pvt. practice, Livingston, N.J., 1981—; asst. dir. residency edn. Roseland (N.J.) Surg. Ctr., 1994—; mem. antibiotic rev. com. Chilton Meml. Hosp., Pompton Plains, N.J., 1994—. Mem. Am. Diabetes Assn., Am. Coll. Sports Medicine, Am. Running and Fitness Assn. Office: Family Footcare Livingston 349 E Northfield Rd Livingston NJ 07039

GOLDSTEIN, STUART FREDERICK, biologist; b. Beloit, Wis., Sept. 11, 1939; s. Simon H. and Mitzi (Laden) G.; m. E. Mary Martini, Nov. 25, 1978; children: Sarah, Laura. PhD, Calif. Inst. Tech., 1968. Asst. prof. U. Minn., St. Paul, 1971-76, assoc. prof., 1977—. Mem. AAAS, Am. Assn. for Cell Biology, Sigma Xi. Home: 358 Roslyn Pl Minneapolis MN 55419-2547 Office: Univ of Minn 250 Biol Scis Ctr Saint Paul MN 55108

GOLDSTRICH, JOE DANIEL, physician; b. Dallas, May 13, 1938. BS, Southern Meth. Univ., 1959; MD, Univ. Tex., 1964. Diplomate Am. Bd. Internal Medicine, Am. Bd. Cardiovascular Disease. Internship Dallas Vets. Adminstrn. Hosp., 1964-65; jr. asst. resident internal medicine U. N.C. Meml. Hosp., Chapel Hill, 1967-68, sr. asst. resident internal medicine, 1968-69; cardiology fellow Dallas Vets. Adminstrn. Hosp., 1969-70; nat. dir. edn. and cmty. programs Am. Heart Assn., Dallas, 1975-77; chief cardiologist Pritikin Longevity Ctr., Santa Barbara, Calif., 1977-78; medical dir. Pritikin Longevity Ctr., Santa Monica, Calif., 1982; pvt. practice Santa Monica, Calif., 1983—; clinical asst. prof. medicine Southwestern Medical Sch. Univ. Tex. Health Sci. Ctr., Dallas; sr. attending medicine Parkland Meml. Hosp., Dallas; adj. prof. clinical ecology North Tex. State Univ., Denton; cons. to preventive cardiology program, UT Health Sci. Ctr., Dallas. Author: The Best Chance Diet, 1982, The One Day At A Time Diet, 1990, Healthy Heart Longer Life, 1996; contbr. articles to profl. jours. Bd. dirs. Dallas City Council's Drug Abuse Coun., Dallas Free Clinic, Dallas Coun. On Alcoholism, Dallas Cardiac Inst., Dallas Diabetes Assn., Inc., Am. Heart Assn. With U.S. Army 1965-67. Fellow Am. Coll. Cardiology. Office: 17480 Dallas Pkwy Ste 220 Dallas TX 75287-7304

GOLDSZER, ROBERT CHARLES, physician, educator; b. Pitts., May 23, 1950; s. Louis and Beatrice (Feldman) G.; m. Madalyn L. Mann, Mar. 29, 1981; children—Jennifer Rachel, Sarah Daniell. B.A., U. Wis., 1972; M.D., Hahnemann U., 1976. Resident in internal medicine Hahnemann U., Phila., 1976-79, chief med. resident, 1978-79; fellow in medicine Harvard U. Med. Sch., Boston, 1979-82, instr. medicine, 1982-87; research fellow Brigham and Women's Hosp., Boston, 1979-82, staff, 1982—; asst. prof. medicine Harvard Med. Sch., 1987—; clin. research fellow in medicine Peter Bent Brigham Hosp., Boston, 1979-80. Contbr. articles to profl. jours. Named Resident of the Year, Hahnemann U., 1979; Eastern Pa. Am. Coll. Physicians Assocs. award, 1980; Milton Fund fellow, 1982; ACP fellow, 1984. Mem.Internat. Soc. Nephrology, ACP, Norfolk County Med. Soc., Mass. Med. Soc., Am. Soc. Internal Medicine, Am. Soc. Nephrology. Jewish. Avocations: marathon running, sailing. Office: Brighams Women's Hosp 45 Francis St Boston MA 02115-6105

GOLDWATER, WILLIAM HENRY, research consultant, research program manager; b. Plattsburgh, N.Y., Apr. 4, 1921; s. Alex and Lillian Dorothy (Berg) G.; m. Marilyn Rubin, Aug. 8, 1948; children: Charles A., Diane L. AB, Columbia U., 1941, PhD, 1947. Rsch. chemist Mt. Sinai Hosp., N.Y.C., 1947-48; asst. prof. Tulane U. Med. Sch., New Orleans, 1948-51; radiol. biologist Naval Radiol. Def. Lab., San Francisco, 1952-59; exec. sec. div. Rsch. Grants NIH, Bethesda, Md., 1959-62; chief spl. projects br. Nat. Heart Inst., Bethesda, Md., 1962-69; assoc. dir. extramural programs Inst. Environ. Health Scis., Research Triangle Park, 1969-70; spl. asst., extramural programs policy officer NIH Office Extramural Rsch. and Tng., Bethesda, Md., 1970-84; dir. extramural programs mgmt. office NIH Office Extramural Rsch., Bethesda, Md., 1984-93; mem. R & D and grants study groups Commn. Govt. Procurement, Washington, 1971-72. Mem. editl. bd. Grants Mag., 1981-93. Mem. temple and brotherhood bds. Temple Sinai, Washington, 1963-69; pres. Mid-Bethesda Civic Assn., 1973-74; bd. dirs. Jewish Cmty. Ctr., Rockville, Md., 1981-87, Jewish Cmty. Coun., Rockville, 1989—, Jewish Coun. Aging, Rockville, 1981—, pres., 1986-88; bd. dirs. United Jewish Appeal Fedn., Rockville, 1984-95, chmn. pub. social policy com., 1989-91, human svcs. and group work divsns., 1982—. Recipient Superior Svc. award USPHS, 1989, Dir.'s award NIH, 1978. Fellow AAAS, Am. Heart Assn. Coun. Epidemiology; mem. Am. Chem. Soc., N.Y. Acad. Scis., Nat. Grants Mgmt. Assn. (sec. 1984-85), Soc. Rsch. Adminstrs. (mem. editl. bd. 1989-93), NIH Alumni Assn. (bd. dirs. 1995—). Democrat. Jewish. Home and Office: 5508 Durbin Rd Bethesda MD 20814-1012

GOLEMBA, MICHAEL EDWARD, psychologist; b. Providence, Apr. 29, 1940; s. Frank William and Alyce (Hertz) G. BA, Brown U., 1961; MA, Temple U., 1963; PhD, SUNY, Albany, 1973. Lic. clin. psychologist, Va. Psychology intern VA Hosp., Albany, N.Y., 1965; dir. psychology Ladd Sch., Exeter, R.I., 1963-64, Seaside Regional Ctr., Waterford, Conn., 1966-72, Bayberry Psychiat. Hosp., Hampton, Va., 1973-80; pvt. practice Hampton, 1980—; med. staff Peninsula Ctr. for Behavioral Health, Hampton, 1980—, Charter Colonial Inst., Newport News, Va., 1984-91, Sentara Hampton Gen. Hosp., 1981-94; instr. psychiatry Ea. Va. Med. Sch., Norfolk, 1975-81. Chmn. Mayor's Com. on Handicapped, Hampton, 1982-84, Gov.'s Com. on Handicapped, New London, Conn., 1968. Recipient Doctoral fellowship SUNY-Albany, 1964-66. Mem. APA, Va. Acad. Clin. Psychology, Va. Psychol. Assn., Masons, Scottish Rite, Shriners, Touro Fraternal Assn. Republican. Jewish. Home: 2218 Crescent Dr Hampton VA 23661-3228 Office: 2115 Executive Dr Ste 6A Hampton VA 23666-2452

GOLITZ, LOREN EUGENE, dermatologist, pathologist, clinical administrator, educator; b. Pleasant Hill, Mo., Apr. 7, 1941; s. Ross Winston and Helen Francis (Schupp) G.; MD, U. Mo., Columbia, 1966; m. Deborah Burd Frazier, June 18, 1966; children: Carrie Campbell, Matthew Ross. Intern, USPHS Hosp., San Francisco, 1966-67, med. resident, 1967-69; resident in dermatology USPHS Hosp., Staten Island, N.Y., 1969-71; dep. chief dermatology, 1972-73; vis. fellow dermatology Columbia-Presbyn. Med. Ctr., N.Y.C., 1971-72; asst. in dermatology Coll. Physicians Surgeons, Columbia, N.Y.C., 1972-73; vice-chmn. Residency Rev. Com. for Dermatology, 1983-85. Earl D. Osborne fellow dermal. pathology Armed Forces Inst. Pathology, Washington, 1973-74; assoc. prof. dermatology, pathology Med. Sch. U. Colo., Denver, 1974-88; prof., 88—; chief dermatology Denver Gen. Hosp., 1974—; med. dir. Ambulatory Care Ctr., Denver Gen. Hosp., 1991—. Diplomate Am. Bd. Dermatology, Nat. Bd. Med. Examiners. Fellow Royal Soc. Medicine; mem. Am. Soc. Dermatopathology (sec., treas. 1985-89, pres.-elect 1989, pres. 1990), Am. Acad. Dermatology (chmn. coun. on clin. and lab. svcs., coun. sci. assembly 1987-91, bd. dirs. 1987-91, chmn. 1991), Soc. Pediatric Dermatology (pres. 1981), Soc. Investigative Dermatology, Pacific Dermatol. Assn. (exec. com. 1979-89, sec.-treas. 1984-87, pres. 1988), Noah Worcester Dermatol. Soc. (publs. com. 1980, membership com. 1989-90), Colo. Dermatol. Soc. (pres. 1978), Am. Bd. Dermatology Inc. (chmn. part II test com. 1989—, exec. com. 1993—, v.p. 1994, pres.-elect 1995, pres. 1996), Colo. Med. Soc., Denver Med. Soc., AMA (residency rev. com. for dermatology 1982-89, dermatopathology test com. 1979-85), Denver Soc. Dermatopathology, Am. Dermatol. Assn. Editorial bd. Jour. Cutaneous Pathology, Jour. Am. Acad. Dermatology, Advances in Dermatology (editorial bd. Current Opinion in Dermatology), Women's Dermatologic Soc., So. Med. Assn., Internat. Soc. Pediatric Dermatology, Am. Contact Dermatitis Soc., Am. Soc. Dermatologic Surgery, Physicians Who Care, Am. Bd. Med. Specialties (del.), N.Y. Acad. Scis., AAAS, Brit. Assn. Dermatologists (hon.), Brazilian Soc. Dermatology (hon.), U. Mo. Med. Alumni Orgn. (bd.govs. 1993—); contbr. articles to med. jours. Home: 11466 E Arkansas Ave Aurora CO 80012-4106 Office: Denver Gen Hosp Dept Dermatology 777 Bannock St # 0146 Denver CO 80204-4507

GOLLAND, JEFFREY H., psychologist, psychoanalyst, educator; b. Bklyn., Apr. 28, 1941; s. Gerald Edward and Rose Alice (Finkelstein) G.; m. Patricia Elaine Yeager, July 14, 1969 (div. July 1991); children: David Hamilton, Richard Morris; m. Marcia Bergson, June 27, 1993. A.B. cum laude, Brandeis U., 1961; A.M., NYU, 1962, Ph.D., 1966; cert. in psychoanalysis, N.Y. Freudian Soc., Inc., 1973. Lic. psychologist, N.Y. From psychologist to chief psychology Brooke Gen. Hosp., San Antonio, 1966-68; psychologist-in-charge out patient clinic Bellevue Psychiat. Hosp., N.Y.C., 1968-70; instr. psychiatry NYU Med. Ctr., 1968-70; asst. prof. edn. Baruch Coll. CUNY, 1970-75, chmn. dept., 1974-79, assoc. prof., 1975—; solo practice psychoanalysis and psychology, N.Y.C., 1968—; field supr. psychotherapy Rutgers Grad. Sch. Psychology, Piscataway, N.J., 1975-85; with faculty Am. Inst. for Psychoanalysis and Psychotherapy, N.Y.C., 1976-84, N.Y. Freudian Soc., 1984—. Author book chpts. and revs. Contbr. articles to profl. jours. Trustee Brandeis U., Waltham, Mass., 1985-89, The Village Temple, N.Y.C., 1984-92; pres. emeritus 145 Fourth Ave. Tenants Assn., N.Y.C., 1977—. Served to capt. U.S. Army Res., 1966-68. Recipient Founders Day award NYU, 1967. Mem. Am. Psychol. Assn. (pres. sect. 1, divsn. 39 1995), N.Y. Freudian Soc. (treas. 1984-90), Brandeis U. Alumni Assn. (bd. dirs. 1976-91, pres. 1985-89), Phi Delta Kappa. Democrat. Jewish. Avocations: tennis, running, skiing. Home: 145 4th Ave New York NY 10003-4906 Office: CUNY Baruch Coll Box G-1631 17 Lexington Ave New York NY 10010-5526

GOLLIN, SUSANNE MERLE, cytogeneticist, cell biologist; b. Chgo., Sept. 22, 1953; d. Harvey A. and Pearl (Reiffel) G.; m. Lazar M. Palnick; 1 child, Jacob Hillel Palnick, Oct., 1991. BA in Biology, Northwestern U., 1974, MS, 1975, PhD, 1980. Diplomate Am. Bd. Med. Genetics, Clin. Cytogenetics. Postdoctoral fellow U. Rochester Med. Ctr. (N.Y.), 1979-81; rsch assoc. in cell biology Baylor Coll. of Medicine, Houston, 1981-83, rsch. assoc. in genetics, 1983-84; asst. prof. dept. pathology and pediatrics U. Ark. Med. Scis., 1984-87; dir. cytogenetics lab. Ark. Children's Hosp., 1984-87; assoc. mem. Pitts. Cancer Inst., 1987-95, mem., 1995—; asst. prof. human genetics U. Pitts., 1987-95, dir. clin. cytogenetics lab., 1988—, assoc. prof. human genetics, 1995—; mem. pediatric oncology group., mem. exec. com. Ark. Genetics Program, 1984-87; mem. organizing com. Am. Cytogenetics Conf., 1990—; mem. Allegheny County Bd. Health, 1992—, clin. lab. improvement adv. com. Ctrs. Disease Control and Prevention, HHS, 1994—; vis. sci. Deutsches Krebsforschungszentrum, Heidelberg, Germany, 1995. Contbr. articles to profl. jours. Mem. deans' adv. com. Pa. Sch. Excellence for Healthcare Profls., 1991-95; mem. faculty senate exec. com. U. Pitts. Grad Sch. Pub. Health, 1992—, pub. health affirmative action com., 1992-94, v.p. faculty senate, 1994-95; vol. Lighthouse for the Blind, Houston, 1983; chmn. med. ethics and civil liberties com. ACLU, Pitts., 1989-91; alt. del. Dem. Nat. Conv., 1992. Fellow Am. Coll. Med. Genetics (founder); mem. AAAS, Am. Assn. Cancer Rsch., Women in Cancer Rsch., Am. Soc. Human Genetics, Am. Soc. Cell Biology, Soc. Analytical Cytology, Pitts. Cancer Inst., Southwest Oncology Group (core com. cytogenetics), Pitts. Cytogenetics Club (founder, coord. 1989-95), Sigma Xi. Avocations: gardening, photography, pulled thread embroidery. Office: U Pitts Dept Human Genetics 130 Desoto St Pittsburgh PA 15213-2535

GOLLIS, ELAINE SANDRA, nurse, administrator; b. Fall River, Mass., Mar. 30, 1938; d. Harold and Esther (Packer) G.; m. Pasquale Margiotta, May 16, 1968 (div. Oct. 1986); children: Ellen, Mark. Nurse, Worcester City Hosp., 1959; BS, Post Coll., 1989; MS, Hartford Grad. Ctr., 1992. RN, Conn.; cert. nurse adminstr. Dir. nursing Hebrew Home and Hosp., Hartford, Conn., 1963-68, Jewish Home for Aged, San Francisco, 1968; clin. supr. Hebrew Home and Hosp., Hartford, 1971-81, coord. patient care, 1981-82, clinic coord. ambulatory care, 1982-84, ombudsman, 1984, acting dir. nursing, 1984-85, asst. dir. nursing, 1985-95, assoc. dir. nursing svcs., 1995—; clin. assoc. dept. behavioral sci. Sch. Dental Med. U. Conn., Farmington, 1986—. Mem. ANA (cert. nurse adminstr.), Conn. League for Nursing, Conn. Hosp. Assn., Conn. Assn. Not-For-Profit Providers For the Aging (dir. nurses coun.). Jewish. Office: Hebrew Home and Hosp 1 Abrahms Blvd West Hartford CT 06117-1508

GOLOMB, CLAIRE, psychology educator; b. Frankfurt am Main, Germany, Jan. 30, 1928; came to U.S., 1958; d. Chaskel and Fanny (Monderer) Schimmel; m. Dan S. Golomb, Feb. 24, 1954; children: Mayana, Anath. BA, Hebrew U., Jerusalem, 1954; MA, New Sch. for Social Rsch., 1959; PhD, Brandeis U., 1969. Instr. psychology Wellesley (Mass.) Coll., 1969-70; asst. prof. Brandeis U., Waltham, Mass., 1971-74; assoc. prof. psychology U. Mass., Boston, 1974-77, prof., 1977—. Author: Young Children's Sculpture and Drawing, 1974, The Child's Creation of a Pictorial World, 1992; editor: The Development of Artistically Gifted Children: Selected Case Studies, 1995. Fellow APA; mem. Jean Piaget Soc. Office: U Mass Harbor Campus Boston MA 02125

GOLOMB, FREDERICK MARTIN, surgeon, educator; b. N.Y.C., Dec. 18, 1924; s. Jacob J. and Hannah (Loewy) G.; m. Joan E. Schneider, Nov. 28, 1954; children: James Bradley, Susan Lynn. B.S., Yale U., 1945; M.D., U. Rochester, 1947. Diplomate: Am. Bd. Surgery. Intern Johns Hopkins Hosp., 1949-50; resident NYU Hosp., 1950-56; pvt. practice specializing in surgery N.Y.C.; mem. staff NYU Med. Center, 1950—, dir. chemoimmunotherapy divsn. tumor svc. dept. surgery, 1967—; attending surgeon Tisch Hosp., Beth Israel North Hosp.; cons. in gen surgery Manhattan VA Hosp.; cons. surgeon Cabrini Health Care Center; vis. surgeon Bellevue Hosp.; mem. faculty NYU Sch. Medicine, 1956—, prof., clin. surgery, 1977—; cons. N.Y.C. div. Am. Cancer Soc., 1968—; mem. clin. trials rev. com. Nat. Cancer Inst., 1976-79; chmn. melanoma com. Eastern Coop. Oncology Group, 1978-80; prin. investigator Central Oncology Group, 1969-77, exec. com., 1976-77; mem. met. med. com. Chemotherapy Found.; co-prin. investigator Ea. Coop. Oncology Group NYU, 1978-95. Editorial adv. bd., contbg. editor Oncology News; contbr. articles to profl. jours. Served with M.C. AUS, 1953-54, Korea. Fellow ACS; mem. AMA, Soc. Head and Neck Surgeons, Soc. Surgery Alimentary Tract, Am. Assn. Cancer Rsch., Am. Soc. Clin. Oncology, N.Y. Cancer Soc. (pres. 1974-75), N.Y. Surg. Soc., N.Y. State Med. Soc., N.Y. County Med. Soc., Soc. Surg. Oncology, George Hoyt Whipple Soc., Brit. Assn. Surg. Oncology (editl. adv. panel 1980-85), Pan Am. Med. Soc., Am. Alpine Club, Explorers Club, Sigma Xi. Office: NYU Sch Medicine 530 1st Ave New York NY 10016-6402

GOLOMB, HARVEY MORRIS, oncologist, educator; b. Pitts., Feb. 13, 1943; s. Russell Austin and Dorothy (Simon) G.; m. Lynne Rooth, Dec. 28, 1965; children: Adam, Sara. BA, U. Chgo., 1964; MD, U. Pitts., 1968. Diplomate Am. Bd. Internal Medicine, Am. Bd. Med. Oncology. Intern Boston City Hosp., 1968-69; resident Johns Hopkins U., Balt., 1971-72; fellow U. Chgo., 1973-75, asst. prof. dept. medicine, 1975-79, assoc. prof., 1979-83, prof., 1983—, chief sect. hematology/oncology, 1981—; chmn. subspecialty bd. med. oncology Am. Bd. Internal Medicine, 1991-95. Contbr. over 300 articles, papers to profl. publs.; co-editor: Lung Cancer, 1988. Capt. U.S. Army, 1971-73. Mem. Am. Soc. Hematology (bd. dirs. 1987-91), Am. Soc. Oncology (pres. elect 1989-90, pres. 1990-91). Office: U Chgo MC 2115 5841 S Maryland Ave Chicago IL 60637-1463

GOLSTON, JOAN CAROL, psychotherapist; b. Vancouver, B.C., Can., Aug. 10, 1947; came to U.S., 1958; d. Stefan and Lydia Barbara (Fruchs) G. Student, Reed Coll.; BA, U. Wash., 1977, MSW, 1979. Cert. social worker; bd. cert. diplomate in clin. social work ABECSW. Clin. supr. Crisis Clinic, Seattle, 1975-77; psychiatric social worker Valley Gen. Hosp., Renton, Wash., 1979-82; psychotherapist pvt. practice, Seattle, 1981—; sch. counselor Northwest Sch., Seattle, Seattle Acad.; clin. cons. outpatient dept. Valley Cities Cmty. Mental Health, Renton, 1991, Seattle Counseling Svcs., 1991-96, emergency svcs., 1975-89; cons., trainer and presenter in field. Contbr. articles to profl. jours. Bd. dirs. Open Door Clinic, Seattle, 1975-76, Northwest Family Tng. Inst., Seattle, v.p., 1990, pres., 1991, mem. exec. com., 1988-91; mem. adv. bd. Ctr. Prevention of Sexual and Domestic Violence, 1993—, AIDS Risk Reduction Project Sch. Social Work U. Wash., 1988-93. Nat. Merit scholar, 1964. Mem. NASW (diplomate), Wash. State chpt. NASW (mem. com. on ethics 1992—), Internat. Soc. Study of Dissociation, Internat. Soc. Trauma Stress Studies, Acad. Cert. Social Workers. Office: 726 Broadway Ste 303 Seattle WA 98122-4337

GOLTZMAN, DAVID, endocrinologist, educator, researcher; b. Montreal, Que., Can., Sept. 22, 1944; s. Jack and Lily (Roth) G.; m. Naomi Lyon, Dec. 29, 1968; children: Jonathan, Rebecca, Daniel. BSc, McGill U., 1966, MD, 1968. Diplomate Am. Bd. Internal Medicine, Am. Bd. Endocrinology and Metabolism. Med. intern Royal Victoria Hosp., Montreal, 1968-69; med. resident Columbia U. Coll. Physicians and Surgeons, N.Y.C., 1969-71; clin. and rsch. fellow in endocrinology Mass. Gen. Hosp., Boston, 1971-75; instr. medicine Harvard Med. Sch., Boston, 1974-75; asst. prof. medicine McGill U., Montreal, 1976-78, assoc. prof., 1978-83, prof., 1983—, chmn. physiology, 1988-93, dir. calcium rsch. lab., 1981—, hosmer prof. physiology, 1992-93, Massabki prof. medicine, 1994—; chmn. medicine, 1994—; sr. physician dept. medicine Royal Victoria Hosp., 1987-94, physician-in-chief, 1994—; chmn. exptl. medicine com. Med. Rsch. Coun. Can., Ottawa, Ont., 1984-88; mem. gen. medicine B study sect., NIH, Bethesda, Md., 1987-91; active Exec. Med. Rsch. Coun. Can., 1993—. Author: (with others) Metabolic Basis of Endocrinology, 1979, Pediatric Endocrinology, 1989, Principles and Practice of Endocrinology and Metabolism, 1990; editl. bd. Endocrinology Jour., 1985-90, Jour. Bone Mineral rsch., 1985-90, Bone and Mineral, 1991-94, Osteoporosis Internat., 1991-94, Assoc. Edn. Bone, 1989-94; assoc. editor: Jur. Bone Mineral research, 1995—; contbr. numerous articles to profl. jours. Recipient Chercheur Boursier award Que. Med. Rsch. Coun., 1980-83, Scientist award Med. Rsch. Coun. Can., 1983-88, Andre Lichtwitz prize Nat. Inst. for Med. Rsch., France, 1987. Fellow Royal Coll. Physicians and Surgeons, Royal Soc. Canada; mem. Can. Soc. Endocrinology and Metabolism (pres. 1990-92), Am. Soc. for Bone and Mineral Rsch. (chmn. program com. 1989-90), Am. Assn. Physicians, Endocrine Soc. (program com. 1989-91), Can. Soc. Clin. Investigation (councillor 1986-89) Am. Soc. Clin. Investigation. Office: Royal Victoria Hosp, 687 Pine Ave W, Montreal, PQ Canada H3A 1A1

GOLUB, JAMES ROBERT, internist, allergist; b. N.Y.C., July 1, 1928; s. Jacob Joshua and Helene (Dankner) G.; m. Shirley Rene Panzer (div.); children: Jennifer Loren, Melissa Jane; m. Anne DeMarinis, Mar. 8, 1981. BS, Yale U., 1949; MD, Columbia U., 1953. Diplomate, Am. Bd. Internal Medicine, Am. Bd. Allergy, Am. Bd. Allergy and Immunology. Intern Bellevue Hosp., N.Y.C., 1953-54, resident, 1957-58; fellow Presbyn. Hosp., N.Y.C., 1956-57; resident Mt. Sinai Hosp., N.Y.C., 1958-59; pvt. practice medicine specializing in allergy, immunology New Rochelle, N.Y., 1959—; attending physician, chief sect. on allergy New Rochelle Hosp. Med. Ctr., 1964—, chief allergy sect. divsn. medicine Westchester County Med. Ctr., 1971-92, attending physician, 1971—; clin. assoc. prof. medicine N.Y. Med. Coll., Valhalla, 1981-86. Contbr. to sci. and med. publs. Fellow Am. Acad. Allergy, Am. Coll. Allergy. Office: 150 Lockwood Ave New Rochelle NY 10801-4916

GOLUB, SHARON BRAMSON, psychologist, educator; b. N.Y.C., Mar. 25, 1937; m. Leon M. Golub, June 1, 1958; children: Lawrence E., David B. Diploma, Mt. Sinai Hosp. Sch. Nursing, 1957; BS, Columbia U., 1959, MA, 1966; PhD, Fordham U., 1974. Head nurse Mt. Sinai Hosp., N.Y.C., 1957-59; contbg. editor RN Mag., Oradell, N.J., 1967-74; asst. prof. psychology Coll. New Rochelle, N.Y., 1974-79, assoc. prof., 1979-86, prof., 1986—, dir. women's studies, 1978-79, chmn. dept. psychology, 1979-82; pvt. practice individual and group psychotherapy Harrison, N.Y., 1976—; adj. prof. psychiatry N.Y. Med. Coll., Valhalla, 1980-94. Editor: Menarche, 1983 (Assn. Women in Psychology Disting. Pub. award 1984, Book of Yr. award Am. Jour. Nursing 1984), Lifting the Curse of Menstruation, 1983, Health Care of the Female Adolescent, 1984, Health Needs of Women as They Age, 1984, PERIODS from Menarche to Menopause, 1992; (with Rita Jackaway Freedman) Psychology of Women: Resources for a Core Curriculum, 1987; editor Women and Health, 1982-86, mem. editorial bd., 1986—; mem. editorial bd. Psychology of Women Quar., 1989—. Grantee Nat. Libr. Medicine, 1983-84; NIH rsch. fellow, 1971-74. Fellow Am. Psychol. Assn. (chmn. task force on teaching psychology of women 1980-83), Am. Psychol. Soc., Am. Assn. Applied and Preventive Psychology; mem. Soc. for Menstrual Cycle Rsch. (pres. 1981-83, bd. dirs. 1981-93), Assn. Women in Psychology, Phi Beta Kappa, Sigma Xi, Psi Chi. Office: Coll New Rochelle Dept Psychology New Rochelle NY 10805

GOLUB, SHELDON, physician; b. N.Y.C., June 1, 1937; s. Louis and Rose Golub; married; children: Justin, Nathaniel, Beryn. AB, Columbia U., N.Y.C., 1959; MD, SUNY, 1963. Intern L.I. Jewish-Hillside Hosp., New Hyde Park, N.Y., 1963-64; resident Mass. Mental Health Ctr., Boston, 1966-69; teaching fellow Med. Sch. Harvard U., Boston, 1966-69; fellow Albert Einstein Coll. Medicine, Bronx, N.Y., 1969-71; pvt. practice Great Neck, N.Y., 1971—; psychiat. dir. North Shore Child & Family Guidance Ctr., Roslyn Heights, N.Y., 1974—; mem. N.Y. Coun. on Child Psychiatry. Contbr. articles to profl. jours. Capt. USAF, 1964-66, Vietnam. Decorated Bronze Star, Air medal. Fellow Am. Psychiat. Assn., Nassau Acad. Medicine; mem. Am. Acad. Child Psychiatry, Soc. Adolescent Psychiatry. Office: 11 Nassau Dr Great Neck NY 11021-2157

GOLUBSKI, JOSEPH FRANK, pathologist, physician; b. Cleve., Apr. 30, 1953; s. Joseph John and Rita Dolores (Krysinski) G.; m. Wanda Beth Kalencki, Nov. 11, 1983; children: Anne Elise, Joseph Edward. BA, Ohio Wesleyan U., 1975; MS, Cleve. State U., 1976; DO, U. Health Scis., Kansas City, Mo., 1980. Diplomate Am. Bd. Pathology; cert. med. rev. officer, Am. Assn. of Med. Rev. Officers. Intern Brentwood Hosp., Warrensville Heights, Ohio, 1980-81, chmn. pathology dept., 1987-88; resident in pathology Naval Regional Med. Ctr., Portsmouth, Va., 1981-85, mem. staff, head of autopsy svc. and clin. chem., 1985-87; assoc. pathologist Sheboygan (Wisc.) Meml. Med. Ctr., 1988—; cons. pathology Naval Hosp. Guantanamo Bay, Cuba, 1985-87; asst. clin. prof. pathology Ea. Va. Med. Sch., Norfolk, 1985-87. Comdr. USNR-IRR (Ind. Ready Res.), 1990—. Hall undergrad. fellow in chem. Ohio Wesleyan U, 1974. Fellow Am. Coll. Pathologists, Am. Soc. Clin. Pathologists; mem. AMA, Am. Osteo. Assn., Wis. Med. Assn., Sheboygan County Med. Soc. (sec.-treas. 1992—), Farmer's and Sportsman's Conservation Club (bd. dirs. 1990), Sheboygan Falls Conservation Club, Sheboygan Yacht Club. Home: 2232 N 7th St Sheboygan WI 53083-4923 Office: Sheboygan Meml Med Ctr 2629 N 7th St Sheboygan WI 53083-4932

GOLUSIN, MILLARD R., obstetrician and gynecologist; b. Detroit, Feb. 14, 1947; s. Raddie and Joan (Lalich) G.; m. Yvonne Marie Cronovich, Sept.

29, 1974; children: Milan, Marko, Matthew. BS with honors, Wayne State U., 1968, MS, 1970, MD, 1975. Diplomate Am. Bd. Obstetrics and Gynecology. Intern, then resident William Beaumont Hosp., Royal Oak, Mich., 1975-78; practice medicine specializing in obstetrics and gynecology Village Gynecologic and Obstetric Assocs., P.C., Southfield and Troy, Mich., 1978-92; pvt. solo practice specializing in obstetrics and gynecology Troy, Mich., 1992—; mem. quality assurance com. William Beaumont Hosp., Royal Oak, Mich., 1979—, mem. gynecol. quality assurance com., 1993—; charter mem., pres. Preferred Ob-Gyn. Mgmt. Group L.L.C. Trustee United Beaumont Physicians Group, 1993—. Served with U.S. Army, 1969-71. Fellow ACOG; mem. Am. Soc. Reproductive Medicine, Mich. State Med. Soc., Am. Inst. Ultrasound Medicine, Serbian Singing Soc., Ravanica (musical dir. 1967—, pres. 1981-82). Republican. Serbian Eastern Orthodox. Office: 1050 Wilshire Dr Ste 100 Troy MI 48084-1526

GOMEZ, EDWARD CASIMIRO, physician, educator; b. Key West, Fla., Nov. 30, 1938; s. Edward C. and Francisca (Pijuan) G.; m. Barbara Jeanne Wilson, 1960 (div. 1979); 1 child, Marielle Elise; m. Ellen Elizabeth Mack, 1980. AB in Biol. Scis., Johns Hopkins U., 1960; MD, U. Miami, 1965, PhD, 1971. Diplomate Am. Bd. Dermatology; bds. cert. spl. competence in dermopathology. Pediatric intern U. Miami, Fla., 1966-67, resident in dermatology, 1969-72; research coordinator Dept. Dermatology Mt. Sinai Med. Ctr., Miami Beach, Fla., 1972-75, dermatopathology fellow, 1976-77; assoc. prof. dermatology NYU, 1977-80; prof. dermatology Sch. Medicine U. Calif., Davis, 1980-91, prof. emeritus, 1991—, assoc. dean for affiliate programs, 1983-86, assoc. dean for clin. affairs, 1987-90; regional chief of staff VA Western Region, San Francisco, 1991-93; assoc. chief staff No. Calif. Sys. Clinics, Pleasant Hill, 1993—; asst. chief to chief dermatology sect. VA Med. Ctr., N.Y.C., 1977-80; assoc. chief to chief of staff, VA Med. Ctr., Martinez, Calif., 1983-86; mem. VA Dermatology Field Adv. Group, Washington, 1978-80, task force on Chloracne, 1979-84; cons. U.S. Army Med. Research and Devel. Command, Frederick, Md., 1979-80, Johnson and Johnson Corp., New Brunswick, N.J., 1979-80; expert witness FDA, Washington, 1978; Gov.'s appointee Med. Quality Rev. Com., Alameda and Contra Costa counties, Calif., 1984-87. Editor 1 book; contbr. articles to profl. jours. Served to lt. comdr., USNR, 1967-69. Fellow Soc. Investigative Dermatology, Am. Acad. Dermatology; mem. Am. Fedn. Clin. Research, Am. Soc. Dermatopathology, Am. Coll. Physician Execs., Alpha Omega Alpha, Phi Kappa Psi. Republican. Office: No Calif Sys Clinics 2300 Contra Costa Blvd Pleasant Hill CA 94523

GOMEZ, ROSE, psychiatrist; b. Havana, Cuba, Jan. 9, 1946; d. Jose Manuel and Maria (Rivera) G. Student, U. Ill., Chgo., 1972-74; MD, Loyola U., Maywood, Ill., 1977. Diplomate Am. Bd. Psychiatry and Neurology; bd. cert. addiction medicine. Intern Loyola, Maywood, Ill., 1978; resident in psychiatry Northwestern U., Chgo., 1981; practice medicine specializing in psychiatry Chgo., 1981—; assoc. prof. psychiatry Northwestern U. Med. Sch., 1981—; med. dir. Little Co. Mary Hosp. Chem. Dependency Program, Evergreen Park, Ill., 1982-86; med. dir. Palos Community Hosp. Chem. Dependency Program, Palos Hills, Ill., 1984-93, chmn. dept. psychiatry, 1985-93, med. dir. psychiatric unit, 1985-93. James scholar U. Ill., 1973. Fellow APA; mem. Am. Soc. Addiction Medicine (cert. addictionologist), Ill. Psychiat. Soc. (chmn. com. on women 1985-86). Roman Catholic. Home: 132 E Delaware Pl Apt 4906 Chicago IL 60611-1442 Office: Ste 1900 676 N St Clair Chicago IL 60611 Office: 4700 W 95th St Suite 308 Oaklawn IL 60453

GOMEZ, ROY CLEMENT, pediatrician; b. Rengam, Kuala Lumpur, Malaysia, May 8, 1943; came to U.S., 1976; s. Alphons G. and Elizabeth Bella (Fernandez) G.; m. Prescilla Eileen Miranda, May 25, 1970; children: Mary Shereen, Derek Rabourn. BS, Kerala U., India, 1965, diploma in child health, 1972; AB in Pediatrics, N.Y. Med. Coll., 1981. Diplomate Am. Bd. Pediatrics. Chief of pediatrics Mattie Williams Hosp., Richlands, Va., 1979-85; pvt. practice Richlands Community Med. Ctr., Cedar Bluff, Va., 1985—. Fellow Am. Acad. Pediatrics, Am. Acad. Family Practice, Am. Assn. Allergy and Immunolgy; mem. AMA, Va. Med. Soc., Tazewell County Med. Soc. Roman Catholic. Home: 537 Linwood Dr Richlands VA 24641-2610 Office: Richlands Community Med Ctr Rte 460 Cedar Bluff VA 24609

GOMEZ FARIAS, MARLO A., nephrologist; b. Mexico City, Mex., Sept. 3, 1960; came to U.S., 1985; s. Armando Carlos and Dolores (Molina) G.F.; m. Debbie Beth Beallo, Sept. 18, 1985; children: Benjamin Rosen, Hannah Rose. MD, La Salle U., Mexico City, Mex., 1984; MPH, Emory Univ., 1987. Diplomate Am. Bd. Internal Medicine. Transitional intern United Hosp., Newark, N.J., 1987-88; internal medicine resident Emory Univ., Atlanta, 1988-91, Lyndhurst Nephrology fellow, 1991-93; assoc. Physicians Specialty Group, Boca Raton, Fla., 1993-95; mem. dialysis com., Boca Raton Cmty. Hosp., 1994-95. Contbr. articles to Kidney Internat., Am. Jour. Kidney Disease, Am. Jour. Disease in Children. Mem. ACP. Democrat. Jewish. Office: Physician Specialty Group 600 S Duqe Hwy Boca Raton FL 33432

GÓMEZ-JIMÉNEZ, CARLOS, biology educator; b. Mayagüez, P.R., Sept. 1, 1964; s. Carlos Gómez and Emma Jiménez. BS in Biology, U. P.R., Mayagüez, 1986, MS in Microbiology and Genetics, 1991; postgrad., Alliance Theol. Sem., P.R. Tchr. asst. U. P.R., Mayagüez, 1986-88, 91, biochemistry lab. technician, 1988; quality assurance analyst Microbiology and Cell Culture Lab. Ortho Biologics, Inc., Manatí, P.R., 1989-90; prof. U. P.R., Aguadilla, 1992—; cons., advisor Academia Investigación Científica Maestros Estudiantes Talentosos-Inter Am. U., San Germán, P.R., 1992—, Young Scholars Program-NFS-Inter Am. U., San Germán, 1992—; cons. drug, alcohol, violence & HIV/AIDS Prevention programs U. P.R., Aguadilla, 1992—, coord. honor program, 1996—. Editor (newsletters) The Probe-Caribbean Soc. Biotech., Inc., 1994—, Biosfera-U. P.R.-Aguadilla, 1994—; contbr. articles to profl. jours. Co-founder Primera Iglesia Bautista de Leguísamo, Mayagüez, 1977—; first tenor Mayagüez Choir, 1994—. Mem. AAAS, Caribbean Soc. Biotechnology (bd. dirs. 1994—), P.R. Soc. Microbiologists, P.R. Sci. Tchr. Assn., Biostudy I (hon., counselor), Bapt. Student Union (hon.), Beta Beta Beta (hon., Zeta Alpha chpt.). Baptist. Home: PO Box 1595 Mayagüez PR 00681-1595 Office: U PR Aguadilla-Dept Nat Scis PO Box 250160 Aguadilla PR 00604-0160

GOMOLL, ALLEN WARREN, cardiovascular pharmacologist; b. Chgo., July 10, 1933; s. Herbert Fredrick and Sara Evelyn (Cowan) G.; m. Elaine L. Kirkpatrick, Sept. 17, 1955; children: Gary A., Lisa E. BS in Pharmacy, U. Ill., Chgo., 1955, MS, 1958, PhD, 1961. Instr. U. Ill. Coll. Medicine, Chgo., 1960-61, asst. prof., 1961-66; group leader Mead Johnson, Evansville, Ind., 1966-70, sect. leader, mgr., 1970-81; prin. rsch. scientist Bristol-Myers, Evansville, 1981-84; rsch. fellow Bristol-Myers, Wallingford, Conn., 1984-90; sr. rsch. fellow Bristol-Myers Squibb, Princeton, N.J., 1990—. Reviewer Life Scis., 1973—, Jour. Med. Chemistry, 1975—, Circulation, 1989—; contbr. sci. articles to profl. jours. Fellow Am. Coll. Cardiology, Am. Heart Assn. Coun. Circulation and Basic Sci. Coun.; mem. Am. Soc. Pharmacology & Exptl. Therapy, Internat. Soc. Heart Rsch., Sigma Xi. Office: Bristol-Myers Squibb PRI PO Box 4000 Princeton NJ 08543-4000

GONG, ALICE KIM, neonatologist, educator, researcher; b. Canton, People's Republic China, Sept. 28, 1954; came to U.S., 1963; d. Kwing Sheung and Grace (Tong) G.; m. Richard John Gong, 1982; children: Karis Anne, Kathleen Rose, Paul Michael. BS, Miss. Coll., 1976; MD, U. Miss., 1980. Diplomate, bd. cert. in pediatrics; sub-bd. cert. in neonatal-perinatal medicine. Resident U. Tex., Galveston, 1980-82; resident SUNY, Buffalo, 1982-83, fellow neonatology, 1983-85; asst. clin. prof. U. Tex. Health Sci. Ctr., San Antonio, 1985-86, asst. prof., 1986-94; assoc. prof., 1994—; dir. nurseries Bapt. Meml. Hosp. System, San Antonio, 1988—; cons. Bur. Chronically Ill and Disabled Children, Austin, 1989—; regional instr. Neonatal Resuscitation Course, San Antonio, 1989—. Contbr. articles to profl. jours. Physician cons. and instr. Safe Sitter, San Antonio, 1989—. Grantee March of Dimes, San Antonio, 1987. Mem. Am. Acad. Pediatrics, Southern Soc. Pediatric Rsch., Tex. Perinatal Assn., Women's Faculty Assn., Tex. Pediat. Soc., San Antonio Pediat. Soc. Baptist. Office: U Tex Health Sci Ctr Dept Pediatrics 7703 Floyd Curl Dr San Antonio TX 78284-6200

GONICK, HARVEY CRAIG, nephrologist, educator; b. Winnipeg, Man., Can., Apr. 10, 1930; s. Joseph Wolfe and Rose (Chernick) G.; m. Gloria Granz, Dec. 16, 1967; children: Stephan, Teri. BS in Chemistry, UCLA, 1951; MD, U. Calif., San Francisco, 1955. Diplomate Am. Bd. Internal Medicine, Am. Bd. Nephrology. Intern Peter Bent Brigham Hosp., 1955-56; fellow in nephrology Mass. Meml. Hosp., 1956-57; fellow in nephrology, resident in internal medicine Wadsworth VA Hosp., Los Angeles, 1959-61, clin. investigator, 1961-64, chief metabolic balance unit, 1964-67; instr. medicine Sch. Medicine, UCLA, 1961-64, asst. prof., 1964-69, assoc. prof., 1969-72, adj. assoc. prof., 1972-76, adj. prof., 1976—, assoc. chief div. nephrology, 1965-72, co-dir. Bone and Stone Clinic,, 1972-76, coordinator postgrad. nephrology edn., 1975-78; mem. staff St. John's Hosp., Santa Monica, Calif.; mem. staff Century City Hosp., L.A., med. dir. dialysis unit, 1972-79, chief medicine, 1978-79; mem. staff Cedars-Sinai Med. Ctr., L.A., dir. trace element lab., 1979-96, clin. chief nephrology, 1983-85, coord. renal tng., dir. hypertension rsch., 1996—; practice medicine specializing in nephrology Los Angeles, 1972-94; co-founder, med. dir. Berkeley East Dialysis Unit, Santa Monica, 1971-75; co-founder, cons. Kidney Dialysis Care Units Inc., Lynwood, Calif., 1971-78; co-dir. Osteoporosis Prevention and Treatment Ctr., Santa Monica, 1987-93; mem. numerous adv. coms. to state and fed. agys., 1969-83. Contbr. articles to profl. jours.; editor: Current Nephrology, 1977—. Served to capt. M.C., USAF, 1957-59. Fellow Charles Nelson Fund, Kaiser Found., NIH; recipient Oliver P. Douglas Meml. award Los Angeles County Heart Assn., 1959, Vis. Scientist award Deutscher Academischer Austauschendienst, 1978. Fellow ACP; mem. AMA, AAAS, Internat. Soc. Nephrology (organizing com. internat. cong. 1984), Am. Soc. Nephrology, European Dialysis and Transplant Assn., Soc. Exptl. Biology and Medicine, Calif. Med. Assn., Los Angeles County Med. Assn., Nat. Kidney Found. (active ann. conf. 1963-65, sec. nat. med. adv. coun. 1969-70, regional rep. and legis. com. nat. med. adv. coun. 1970-73, grantee 1963), So. Calif. Kidney Found. (chmn. sci. adv. coun. 1968-70, co-chmn. legis. com. 1970-73, bd. dirs. 1974-83, honoree 1979), Am. Soc. Bone and Mineral Rsch., Am. Coll. Toxicology, Soc. Toxicology, Am. Heart Assn. (renal sect. of coun. on circulation), Am. Fedn. Clin. Rsch., Western Soc. Clin. Rsch., Western Assn. Physicians, Phi Beta Kappa, Sigma Xi, Alpha Omega Alpha, Phi Eta Sigma, Alpha Mu Gamma, Phi Lambda Upsilon. Office: Cedars-Sinai Med Ctr 8700 Beverly Blvd Los Angeles CA 90048

GONNERING, RUSSELL STEPHEN, ophthalmic plastic surgeon; b. Milw., Nov. 21, 1949; s. Russell Richard and Virginia Mary (Mlinar) G.; m. Sandra Lynne Brubaker, Aug. 6, 1971; children: Julie Kathleen, Stephen Russell, Scott Duncan. Student, U. Vienna, Austria, 1969-70; AB in History cum laude, Boston Coll., 1971; MD, Med. Coll. Wis., 1975. Diplomate Am. Bd. Ophthalmology; lic. physician, Wis. Intern St. Luke's Hosp., Milw., 1975-76; fellow in ophthalmic plastic and reconstructive surgery U. Wis., Madison, 1980-81, asst. clin. prof. dept. ophthalmology, 1981-92, assoc. clin. prof. dept. ophthalmology, 1992-96, clin. prof. dept. ophthalmology, 1996—; resident in ophthalmology Med. Coll. Wis., Milw., 1977-80, asst. clin. prof. dept. ophthalmology, 1985—; ophthalmologist Children's Hosp. Wis., Milw., St. Joseph's Hosp., Milw.; ophthalmologist St. Luke's Hosp., Milw., chief ophthalmologist, 1983-92; pvt. practice Ophthalmic Plastic & Reconstructive Surgery, 1981—; rsch. assoc. in corneal physiology Med. Coll. Wis., 1976-77; rsch. advisor to fellowship in ophthalmic plastic and reconstructive surgery U. Wis., Madison, 1983—. Author: (with others) Infections of the Eye and Ocular Adnexa, 1986, Oculoplastic, Orbital and Reconstructive Surgery, 1988, Oculoplastic and Orbital Emergencies, 1990; sect. editor: Principles and Practice of Ophthalmic Plastic and Reconstructive Surgery, 1995; contbr. numerous articles to profl. jours.; presenter in field. Fellow ACS, Am. Acad. Ophthalmology (basic and clin. sci. course com. 1986-92, chmn. 1988-92, Honor Award 1990, Ruedemann lectr. 1994), Am. Soc. Ophthalmic Plastic and Reconstructive Surgery (editl. bd. 1987—, edn. com. 1988—, vice chmn. edn. com. 1995—, Marvin H. Quickert award 1982, Rsch. award 1982); mem. AMA, Internat. Soc. for Orbital Disorders, European Soc. Ophthalmic Plastic and Reconstructive Surgery, Internat. Dacryology Soc., Assn. for Rsch. in Vision and Ophthalmology, Med. Soc. Wis., Milw. County Med. Soc. (del. to state med. soc. 1987-90, bd. dirs. 1989-94, Dirs. citation 1994), Milw. Acad. Medicine, Milw. Ophthalmol. Soc. (treas. 1989-90, sec. 1990-91, v.p. 1991-92, pres. 1992-93), Am. Soc. Ocularists (med. adv. bd. 1987—), Nat. Soc. to Prevent Blindness (med. adv. bd. Wis. chpt. 1987-88). Office: Oculoplastic & Orbital Cons 2600 N Mayfair Rd Ste 950 Milwaukee WI 53226-1307

GONSALVES, MARIANNE ETHEL, oncological nurse, consultant, nurse epidemeologist; b. Santa Monica, Calif., Jan. 10, 1954; d. Henry Charles and Theodora (Axenty) Griswold. BSN, Calif. State U., Long Beach, 1978, nurse practitioner cert., 1983, postgrad. RN, Calif., oncology cert. nurse. Radiation therapy asst. South Bay Hosp., Redondo Beach, Calif., 1973, radiation therapy rsch. asst., 1973; relief charge nurse, staff nurse Kimberly Nurses Registry, Long Beach, Calif., 1977-79, La Jolla (Calif.) Nurses Registry, 1977-79; head nurse oncology Mission Cmty. Hosp., Mission Viejo, Calif., 1980; clin. oncology nurse Med. Oncology Office, Rajendra G. Desai, M.D., Fountain Valley, Calif., 1980-82; clin. instr. dept. nursing Calif. State U., Long Beach, 1982-83; home health nurse Vis. Nurses Assn. of Orange County, Calif., 1982-84; adult nurse practitioner oncology John S. Link, M.D., Med. Oncology, Long Beach, Calif., 1984-87; home parental therapy nurse Oncology Care, Long Beach, 1985-87; adminstr., nurse mgr. cancer ctr., Irvine Med. Ctr. U. Calif., Orange, Calif., 1987-89; ednl. cons. nursing rsch. and edn. U. Calif., San Diego, 1989-90; lectr. adult geriatric oncology nurse practitioner program Calif. State U., Long Beach, 1990-91; nurse epidemiologist cancer rsch. U. So. Calif., L.A., 1985-95; dir. cancer program We. Med. Ctr., Santa Ana, Calif., 1992-94; adult nurse practitioner oncology Pacific Coast Oncology/Hematology, Fountain Valley, Calif., 1995—; lectr., cons. in field. Mem. med. adv. bd. Telesis Home Care, Inc., 1992—; mem. Women's Information Network, Newport Beach, 1992-94; mem. clin. svcs. com. AIDS Svc. Found., 1988-90. Mem. Am. Hosp. Assn., Am. Cancer Soc., Oncology Nursing Soc., Calif. Coalition Nurse Practitioners, We. Med. Specialties, Vis. Nurses Assn., Sigma Theta Tau. Republican.

GONSALVES, PATRICIA E., surgical nurse; b. N.Y.C., Oct. 28, 1943; d. John A. Gonsalves and Julia Rivera Brosa. Diploma in practical nursing, Caledonian Hosp., Bklyn., 1963; student, Cornell Med. Ctr., 1965-66, L.I. U., 1971, SUNY, L.I., 1988. Lic. practical nurse; cert. surg. technologist, preceptor, oper. rm., med. photographer. Lic. practical nurse Luth. Med. Ctr., Bklyn.; assoc. primary nurse, lic. practical nurse Maimonides Med. Ctr., Bklyn., LPN, surg. technologist, oper. rm. vascular surg. specialist. Contbr. articles to profl. jours. Guild del. Local 1199, Freedom of Health Choice, polit. Dem. endorser. Mem. NAACOG (Outstanding Leadership Recognition award), Nat. Assn. Practical Nurse Edn. and Svc., Nat. Surg. Asst. Assn., Soc. Peripheral Vascular Nursing, Assn. Surg. Technologists (pres. chpt. Metro 47 1994-96, nat. bd. dirs. 1993-94, apptd. mem. exam. rev. com. Outstanding Leadership Hon. Mention Recognition award Med. Photographer award 1992), Nat. Ctr. Homeopathy, Found. for Advancement of Innovative Medicine. Home: 814 57th St Apt 2A Brooklyn NY 11220-3631

GONSHAK, ISABELLE LEE, nurse; b. Newark, Apr. 4, 1932; d. Robert John and Clara Kate (Cooperman) McClelland; m. David M. Gonshak, Aug. 8, 1953; children: Evan J., Brett A., Kathryn Susan. RN, N.J. Nurse Newark City Hosp., 1953. Tchr. Ideal Sch. for Nurse's Aides, Miami, Fla., 1972-74; vocal soloist numerous TV and social affairs. Bd. dirs. Miami Beach Symphony, 1971—, pres. 1978-79; bd. dirs. South Fla. Symphony; mem. Opera Guild Soc. Ft. Lauderdale (life); active Statue of Liberty Refinishing Com. Mem. Greater Miami Opera Assn., Hadassah (life). Jewish. Home: 1700 SW 72nd Ave Plantation FL 33317-5037

GONTIER, JEAN ROGER, internist, physiology educator, consultant; b. Lens, France, Mar. 8, 1927; s. Paul Maurice and Marie Jeanne (Tricoche) G.; m. Sylviane Prevost, Dec. 8, 1968; children: Sylviane, Yannick, Jean-Yves, Yann. AB magna cum laude, Coll. d'Etampes, France, 1945; MS magna cum laude, Coll. Scis., Paris, 1947; MD summa cum laude, Sch. Medicine, Paris, 1965. Prof., chair dept. physiology UGSEL, Paris, 1957-62; instr. in medicine Sch. Medicine, Paris, 1960-65; intern Hop Cochin, Paris, 1965; resident Hop Bicetre, Paris, 1966; dir. physiology Sch. Medicine, Reims, 1966-68; prof. physiology U. Montreal, 1970-78; cons. in internal medicine Paris, 1979—; cons. in physiology Bicetre U. Hosp., Paris, 1967-68; cons. editor various pubs., N.Y.C., 1975-78, Paris, 1969-73, Montreal, 1986-89; rsch. in diving physiology in man. Author: (textbooks) Hormones, Nervous System and Digestion, 1968, Respiration, 1971, 77, Digestion, 1969, 82, Textbook of Medical Physiology, 1980, Human Physiology, 1989. Recipient Silver medal Sch. Medicine, Paris, 1965. Mem. AAAS, Am. Physiol. Soc. (teaching physiology/respiration/history sects.), Can. Physiol. Soc., N.Y. Acad. Scis., French Physiol. Soc., Cercle de l'Etrier Club, La Baule Country Club. Roman Catholic. Home and Office: 133 Rue Michel Ange, F75016 Paris France

GONWA, THOMAS ARTHUR, nephrologist, transplant physician; b. Chgo., Sept. 2, 1949; s. George Joseph and Darline (Sears) G.; m. Mary Alice Westrick, Sept. 28, 1974; children: Claire, Charlotte. BS, St. Joseph's Coll., 1971; MD, U. Ill., 1975. Diplomate Am. Bd. Internal Medicine, Nephrology, Critical Care Medicine. Resident Bowman Gray, Winston-Salem, N.C., 1975-78, renal fellow, 1978-80; postdoctoral rsch. fellow U. Calif., San Francisco, 1980-82, instr., 1982-83; asst. prof. U. Iowa, Iowa City, 1983-86; staff physician Dallas Nephrology, 1986—; assoc. dir. transplant Baylor U. Med. Ctr., Dallas, 1987—; clin. assoc. prof. medicine Southwestern Med. Sch., 1993—. Assoc. editor Jour. Immunology, 1985-86; contbr. more than 100 articles to profl. jours. Recipient rsch. award VA, 1984. Fellow ACP; mem. Am. Soc. Transplant Physicians (sec., treas. 1990-93, pres.-elect 1993-94, pres. 1994-95, Upjohn award 1983), Am. Soc. Nephrology, Am. Assn. Immunologists, Transplantation Soc. Office: Dallas Nephrology 3601 Swiss Ave Dallas TX 75204

GONZALES, GUILLERMO, JR., urologist; b. The Philippines, Jan. 9, 1945; came to U.S., 1974; s. Guillermo Sr. and Irene (Petalver) G.; m. Ofelia Gonzales; children: Gemma, Guillermo Ian. MD, U. Santo Tomas, 1969. Resident Grant Hosp., Chgo., 1978, Mt. Sinai Hosp., Chgo., 1980, 83; chmn. dept. surgery, urology Norwegian Am. Hosp., Chgo., 1990—; chmn. Century PHO, Chgo., 1994—. Mem. AMA, Am. Assn. Clin. Urologists. Home: 4326 Hatch Ln Lisle IL 60532 Office: Physician Specialty Ctr 1044 N Francisco Ave Chicago IL 60622

GONZALES, THERESA I., health care facility administrator; b. New Haven, Mar. 30, 1957; d. Francis Louis and Ethel Mae (Onofrio) Imperato. BA, Ohio Dominion Coll., 1979; MS, U. New Haven, 1982, MBA, 1985, DSc, 1995. Dir. ops. Ocean Med. Svc., New London, Conn., 1979-90; adminstr. Aid & Assistance, New London, 1986-90; prof. Sacred Heart U., Fairfield, Conn., 1991—; cons. in field, 1991—; vis. team mem. New Eng. Assn. Schs. & Colls., Mass., 1993—; v.p. New England Med. Equipment Dealers, Avon, Mass., 1988-94, pres., Conn., 1986-88. Mem. Am. Mgmt. Assn., Acad. Mgmt. Home: PO Box 43 Voluntown CT 06384 Office: Sacred Heart U 5151 Park Ave Fairfield CT 06432

GONZALEZ, HECTOR HUGO, nurse, educator, consultant; b. Roma, Tex., Mar. 9, 1937; s. Amadeo Lorenzo and Carlota (Trevino) G. BS in Nursing, Incarnate Word Coll., 1963; MS in Nursing, Cath. U. Am., 1966; PhD in Edn., U. Tex., Austin, 1974. RN, Tex. Staff nurse Santa Rosa Med. Ctr., San Antonio, 1962-65; asst. dir. nursing div. Incarnate Word Coll., San Antonio, 1968-72; prof., chmn. dept. nursing San Antonio Coll., 1972-92, dir. Ctr. for Assoc. Degree Edn. Rsch. and Svc., 1987-92, prof., chmn. emeritus, 1993—; cons. NIMH, 1973, FDA, 1968-93, numerous ednl. instns. and hosps. in U.S., Mex., P.R., Kuwait; mem. Nat. Adv. Coun. on Alcohol and Alcohol Abuse of Alcohol, 1976-80; mem. nat. adv. coun. nurses edn. and practice NNS, 992—; mem. panel on nursing practice U.S. Pharmacopeia. Contbr. articles to profl. jours.; peer reviewer Nursing Outlook, 1983, Advancing Clinical Care. Mem. legis. affairs adv. com. State Senator Glen Kothman, San Antonio, 1983; bd. dirs. Family Svcs. Assn. San Antonio; mem. multidisciplinary academic external com. U. Autonoma de Nuevo Leon, Mex., 1986-88. Capt. nurse corps U.S. Army, 1966-68. Recipient cert. of appreciation Citizens of Bexar County, San Antonio, 1970, Nat. Student Nurses Assn., 1977; grantee ACS/NAHN, 1993-96. Mem. Nat. Assn. Hispanic Nurses (pres. 1982-84, bd. dirs. 1995—), Nat. League for Nursing (bd. dirs. 1973-81). Democrat. Roman Catholic. Home: 114 Magnolia Dr San Antonio TX 78212-3115

GONZALEZ, JAMES RAYMOND, hospital administrator; b. N.Y.C., Sept. 8, 1953; s. Raymond and Ana (Delfaus) G. BS in Psychology, Northeastern U., Boston, 1976; M.Pub. Health, Yale U., 1978. Lic. nursing home adminstr., N.J. Adminstrv. resident Kings Park (N.Y.) Psychiatric Ctr., 1977; asst. dir. clin. svc. Bellevue Hosp. Ctr., N.Y.C., 1978-79; asst. adminstr. U. Hosp.-SUNY, Stony Brook, 1979-82, NYU Med. Ctr.-Rusk Inst., N.Y.C., 1982-83; v.p. profl. svcs. Bayshore Community Hosp., Holmdel, N.J., 1983-89; v.p. ops. Christ Hosp., Jersey City, 1989-95; exec. v.p., coo East Orange (N.J.) Gen. Hosp., 1995—. Bd. dirs. Pleasant Valley Adult Day Ctr., Holmdel, N.J., 1987—. Mem. N.J. Soc. Nursing Home Adminstrs., N.J. Healthcare Execs. Assn. Episcopalian. Home: 50 Howard Pl Nutley NJ 07110-3638 Office: East Orange Gen Hosp 300 Central Ave East Orange NJ 07019

GONZALEZ, JORGE ANTONIO, neurologist; b. Havana, Cuba, Apr. 18, 1956; came to U.S., 1961; s. Antonio Jesus and Rosario Eugenia (Diaz) G.; m. Maria Angelina Salvat; children: Carolina, Jorge, Victoria. BS in Biochemistry, Fairleigh Dickinson U., 1978; MD, U. Navarra, Pamplona, Spain, 1985. Neurology resident Hahnemann U. Hosp., Phila., 1992; fellow in neurorehabil. U. Miami, 1992-93, clin. instr. neurology, 1993, asst. prof. neurology, 1993-95; co-med. dir. N.W. Okla. Rehab. Hosp., Tulsa, 1995—. Recipient award Muscular Dystrophy Assn. of Miami, 1993. Mem. AMA, Am. Acad. Neurorehab., Am. Acad. Neurology. Office: 3219 S 79th East Ave Tulsa OK 74145

GONZALEZ, MICHAEL JOHN, nutrition educator, nutriologist; b. N.Y.C., July 5, 1962; s. R. Miguel and Daisy (Guzman) G.; m. Enid J. Bauza, Mar. 28, 1987; children: Michael John Jr., Michael Joseph. BS in Biology, Cath. U., 1983; MS in Cell Biology, Nova Coll., 1985; MNS in Nutrition and Biochemistry, U. P.R., 1986; NMD in Nutrition, John F Kennedy, 1988; DSc in Health Sci, Lafayette U., 1989; PhD in Tumor Biology, Mich. State U., 1993; postgrad. in geriatrics, U. P.R., 1993-95. Rsch. asst. dept. chemistry Cath. U., Ponce, P.R., 1982-83; lab. instr. dept. biology U. P.R., Mayaguez, 1983-85; rsch. asst. dept. biochemistry U. P.R., Rio Piedras, 1985-86; mem. dept. biology faculty Cath. U., Ponce, 1986-87; rsch. asst. dept. human nutrition Mich. State U., East Lansing, 1987-90, sci. instr. dept. Upward Bound, 1990-91, lab. instr., rsch. asst. dept. food sci. and pharmacology, 1991-93; asst. prof. U. P.R. Med. Sci., San Juan, 1993-96, assoc. prof., 1996—; mem. faculty Sch. Pub. Health U. P.R. Med. Scis., 1989-93. Reviewer, contbr. articles to profl. jours. Fellow Am. Nutritional Med. Assn. (v.p. 1991—); mem. Am. Inst. Nutrition, Am. Assn. Cancer Rsch., Soc. for Exptl. Biology, N.Y. Acad. Sci., Am. Assn. Police, United Farmers. Democrat. Roman Catholic. Office: Univ PR Med Sci Sch of Pub Health B-456 GPO Box 365067 San Juan PR 00936

GONZALEZ, SISTER PAULA, futurist, educator, environmentalist; b. Albuquerque, Oct. 25, 1932; d. Hilario Chavez and Emilia Anna (Sanchez) G. BA, Coll. Mt. St. Joseph, Cin., 1952; MS, Cath. U. Am., 1962, PhD, 1966. Joined Sisters of Charity of Cin., Roman Cath. Ch., 1954. Instr. sci. Regina Sch. Nursing, Albuquerque, 1952-54; tchr. biology Seton High Sch., Cin., 1955-60; assoc. prof. biology Coll. Mt. St. Joseph, 1965-70, prof., 1970—; freelance futurist, educator, environmentalist, lectr., condr. workshops, cons.; founder, pres. EarthConnection, 1992—. Asst. editor Nursing Mgmt. Jour., 1985—. Fellow USPHS, 1961-65. Mem. Alt. Energy Assn. (pres. 1988-90), Union Concerned Scientists, Inst. Noetic Scis. Office: EarthConnection 370 Neeb Rd Cincinnati OH 45233-5101

GONZALEZ, RAQUEL MARIA, pharmacist; b. Veguitas, Oriente, Cuba, June 1, 1952; d. Ernesto Esteban and Evora Cristina (Ramirez) G. BS in Biology, Ga. Coll., 1974; BS in Pharmacy, Mercer U., 1977. Registered pharmacist, Ga., Fla., Tenn.; registered pharmacist cons., Fla. Staff pharmacist Cobb Gen. Hosp., Austell, Ga., 1978; staff pharmacist VA Hosp., Nashville, 1978-79, Decatur, Ga., 1979-81; staff pharmacist Lewisburg (Tenn.) Community Hosp., 1981-89; pharmacist Pharmacy Staffing Svcs. Inc., Brentwood, Tenn., 1989—; chief pharmacist Super D Drug Store # 50, Fayetteville, Tenn., 1989-93; chief of pharmacy Fred's Discount Pharmacy, Lewisburg, Tenn., 1993—; relief pharmacist Farmer's Market Pharmacy (Kroger), Nashville, 1989—. Mem. Ducks Unltd. Republican. Roman Catholic. Club: Atlanta Ski. Home: RR 1 Box 35 Belfast TN 37019-9801 Office: Pharmacy Staffing Svcs Inc 1413 Bowman Ln Brentwood TN 37027-6922 Office: Fred's Discount Pharmacy 1800 Mooresville Hwy Lewisburg TN 37091-2010

GONZALEZ, RICARDO, urologist; b. Buenos Aires, June 26, 1943; s. Salvador Maria and Clyde Alcira (Prevettoni) G.; m. Maria Graciela Estevez, Dec. 16, 1968; div.; children: Diego Andres, Carlos Ricardo. B, Coll. Nacional San Isidro, Buenos Aires, 1959; MD, U. Buenos Aires, 1965. Diplomate Am. Bd. Urology. Resident in surgery Hosp. Militar Cen., Buenos Aires, 1966-68; intern in surgery U. Minn., 1969-70, resident (med. fellow) in urologic surgery, 1970-74; instr. urology U. Minn., Mpls., 1974-76, asst. prof. urology, 1976-78, assoc. prof. urology, 1978-85, prof. urology, 1985-94, prof. pediat., 1993-94; chief, pediat. urology Children's Hosp. of Mich., Detroit, 1995—; prof. urology Wayne State U., Detroit, 1994—; pres. Pediatric Urology P.C., Detroit, 1995—; vis. prof. Harvard U., Cambridge, Mass., 1994, Johns Hopkins U., Balt., 1995, U. Washington, Seattle, 1995, U. Calif., San Francisco, 1996. Contbr. 140 articles to profl. jours., 50 chpts. to books; author 40 invited papers and editls.; editor 2 books; internat. presenter in field (surg. demonstration). Am. Acad. Pediat. fellow, 1981, Nat. Kidney Found. rsch. fellow 1974-76; co-prin. investigator USPHS cancer grant 1976-78. Fellow Am. Acad. Pediat. (mem. exec. sect. on urology com. 1995-96); mem. Am. Urologic Assn., Mex. Coll. Urology (hon.), Venezuelan Soc. for Spina Bifida, Argentine Confedn. Urology, Societé Internat. d'Urologie, Ibero-Am. Soc. Pediat. Urology (pres. 1995—). Office: Pediatric Urology PC 3901 Beaubien Blvd Detroit MI 48201

GONZALEZ-BARRETO, ANDRES, physician, neurologist; b. Ciego de Avila, Cuba, Sept. 22, 1959; came to U.S., 1969; s. Andres Eusebio and Carmen (Bareto) G.; m. Linda Rose Peters, Dec. 15, 1989; 1 child, Andrew Jordan. MD, U. Ctrl. del Este, Dominical Republic, 1983. Diplomate Am. Bd. Internal Medicine; diplomate in neurology and clin. neurophysiology Am. Bd. Psychiatry and Neurology. Assst. clin. instr. SUNY Health Sci. Ctr., Bklyn., 1985-90; clin. instr. Robert Wood Johnson U. Hosp., New Brunswick, N.J., 1990-91; attending in neurology Md. Neurol. Ctr., 1991-92; asst. attending in neurology Queens Hosp. Ctr., Jamaica, N.Y., 1992—. Fellow Am. Assn. Electrodiagnostic Medicine; mem. AMA, ACP, Am. Acad. Neurology. Republican. Roman Catholic. Office: Queens Hosp Ctr 82-68 164th St Jamaica NY 11432

GONZALEZ DE RIVERA, JOSE LUIS, psychiatrist, psychoanalyst, educator; b. Bilbao, Spain, Nov. 12, 1944; s. Francisco and Ana Maria (Revuelta) Gonzalez de R.; children: Laura, Lydia, Jose Luis, Javier; m. Ana Luisa Monterrey; children: Leonor, Justo. BSc, Santiago Apostol, Bilbao, 1961; MD, U. Navarra, Pamplona, Spain, 1969; DSc, U. Pais Vasco, Bilbao, 1976. Lic. Med. Council Can., 1973. Intern in psychiatry Laval U. Med. Ctr., Que., Can., 1970-71; resident McGill U. diploma course in psychiatry Montreal (Que.) Gen. Hosp., 1971-73; asst. chief resident, teaching fellow Douglas Hosp., Montreal, 1973, Montreal Children's Hosp., 1974, Royal Victoria Hosp. and Montreal Neurol. Inst., 1974-75; clin. instr. McGill U., Montreal, Can., 1975-76; asst. clin. prof. Autonomous U., Madrid, 1976-81; prof., acting chmn. dept. psychiatry U. La. Laguna, Tenerife, Spain, 1980-84; prof. psychiatry McMaster U., Hamilton, Ont., Can., 1984-86; chief psychiatry Hamilton Civic Hosps., 1984-86; assoc. dean Med. Sch. U. La Laguna, Tenerife, Spain, 1987-92, prof., chmn. dept. psychiatry, 1986-95; dir. dept. psychiatry U. Canary, Tenerife, 1986-95; chief dept. psychiatry Fundacion Jimenez Diaz, Madrid, 1995—; prof. psychiatry Madrid Autonomous U., 1995—; pres. bd., chmn. European Sch. Psychotherapy, 1989—. Editor Handbook of Psychiatry, 1980; editor-in-chief PSIQUIS, Revista de Psiquiatria, 1977—; author monograph; contbr. numerous sci. papers and chpts. to profl. publs. 2d lt. Spanish Cavalry, 1967-69. Fellow Royal Coll. Physicians Can. (cert.), Royal Soc. Medicine (Eng.), Royal Acad. Medicine Canary, Am. Acad. Psychoanalysis (cert.), Internat. Coll. Psychosomatic Medicine; mem. Am. Psychiat. Assn. (corr.), Spanish Soc. Psychiatry (exec. com. 1994—), Canarian Soc. Psychiatry (founding, pres. 1987), Spanish Soc. for Autogenic Psychotherapy (pres. 1987—), Ateneo Club, Aero Club. Home: Avenida Filipinas 52, 28003 Madrid Spain Office: Fundacion Jimenez Diaz, Avenide Reyes Cetolices 2, 28040 Madrid Spain

GONZALEZ DE VEGA, CARLOS, sports physician; b. Granada, Andalucia, Spain, Apr. 1, 1955; s. Norberto Gonzalez De Vega and Teresa San Roman; m. Marta Buenaventura, July 21, 1980; children: David, Andrea. MD, U. Granada, 1979; degree in internal medicine, Toronto, Onc., Can., 1981, Madrid, 1984. Cert. sports physician, Spain. Cons. internal medicine F.J.D. Hosp., Madrid, 1985; rschr. R. C. Hosp., Madrid, 1986-87; med. dir. Sports Ctr., Madrid, 1987-88, 89, Clinica C. Ferrer, Madrid, 1990—, S. Medicine Ctr. Zulaica, Madrid, 1995—; med. dir. Spanish Triathlon Fedn., Madrid, 1987-92; mem. med. com. European Triathlon Union, 1990-92; chmn. med. com. Internat. Triathlon Union, 1991-92. Co-author: Triathlete in Training, 1995, Exercise and Health, 1996. Officer Spanish Infantry, 1978-79. Fellow Sports Medicine Spanish Assn.; mem. Am. Coll. Sports Medicine. Home: Luchana 4, 28010 Madrid Spain Office: Centro Zulaica, Fernando El Catolico 12, 28015 Madrid Spain

GONZALEZ-FAJARDO, JOSE ANTONIO, surgeon, educator; b. Malaga, Spain, May 14, 1961; s. Antonio and Josefa (Fajardo) Gonzalez; m. Beatriz Aguirre, Oct. 19, 1991; 1 child, Jose A. MD, Med. Sch., Malaga, 1985; splty. in angiology and vascular surgery, Univ. Hosp., Valladolid, Spain, 1991; PhD, Valladolid U., 1992. Diplomate Bd. Angiology and Vascular Surgery. Resident U. Hosp., Valladolid, 1987-91; vascular surgeon Univ. Hosp., Valladolid, 1992—; rsch. fellow Wayne State U., Detroit, 1992; assoc. prof. surgery U. Valladolid, 1994—. Lt. Spanish Mil., 1985-87. Recipient prize Internat. Union Angiology, 1995. Mem. Soc. Vascular Sugery (Martorell award 1994), Coll. Vascular Surgeons Spanish Lang. (Edwin Beven award 1995), Acad. Medicine Valladolid, N.Y. Acad. Scis., Instnl. Rsch. and Ethical Com. Roman Catholic. Office: Hosp Universitario, Divsn Vascular Surgery, 47011 Valladolid Spain

GONZALEZ-SCARANO, FRANCISCO ANTONIO, neurologist; b. Ponce, P.R., Mar. 23, 1950; s. Francisco and Genoveva (Scarano) Gonzalez-Hernandez; m. Barbara Jean Turner, June 23, 1979; children: Genevieve Carre, Stephanie Katharine, Lisa Frances. BA, Yale U., 1971; MD, Northwestern U., Chgo., 1975; MA, U. Pa., Phila., 1988. Diplomate Am. Bd. Neurology. Intern Hosp. U. Pa., 1975-76, neurology resident, 1976-79; fellow U. Pa., 1979-82, NIMR, London, 1981-82; asst. prof. depts. neurology and microbiology U. Pa., Phila., 1982-88, assoc. prof., 1988-94, prof., 1994—; chair bd. sci. counselors Nat. Inst. Neurol. Diseases and Stroke, Bethesda, Md., 1991—. Assoc. editor Viral Pathogenesis, 1997; assoc. editor Jour. Neurovirology, 1995—; contbr. over 100 articles to profl. jours. Harry Weaver scholar Multiple Sclerosis Soc., N.Y.C., 1982-87. Mem. Am. Neurol. Assn., Am. Acad. Neurology (mem. sci. issues com. 1985-89, profl. and pub. issues com. 1987-93), Am. Soc. Clin. Investigation, John Morgan Soc., Penn Club. Presbyterian. Office: U Pa Dept Neurology CRB 415 Curie Blvd Philadelphia PA 19104-6146

GONZALEZ-SUAREZ, CARLOS PEDRO, psychiatrist; b. Santa Clara, Las Villas, Cuba, June 29, 1954; came to U.S., 1962; s. Armando P. Gonzalez and Hilda E. Suarez; m. Lydia Masud, May 15, 1981; 1 child, Daniel F. BS, Northwestern U., 1976; MD, Northwestern U., Chgo., 1978. Diplomate Am. Bd. Psychiatry and Neurology. Staff psychiatrist Grant Ctr. Hosp., Miami, Fla., 1982-86, dir. young adult program, 1984-86; pvt. practice Miami, 1986—. Recipient A. A. Goldsmith award Northwestern Meml. Hosp., 1979. Mem. Am. Psychiat. Assn., Dade County Med. Assn., Amnesty Internat., Internat. Palm Soc. Office: 1500 San Remo Ave # 205 Coral Gables FL 33146

GOOCH, CAROL ANN, psychotherapist consultant; b. Meridian, Miss., Apr. 17, 1950; d. James Tackett and Chris M. Page; (div.); 1 child, Aaron Patrick Gooch. BS, Fla. State U., 1972, DS, 1975; MS, Troy State U., 1974. Lic. profl. counselor, Tex.; lic. chem. dependency counselor, Tex.; lic. marriage and family therapist, Tex.; cert. chem. dependency specialist, Tex.; cert. compulsive gambling counselor, Tex. Tchr. Okaloosa Sch. Dist., Fort Walton, Fla., 1972-77; counselor USAF, Osan AFB, Korca, 1977-79; sch. counselor Tomball (Tex.) Sch. Dist., 1983-90; cons. Montgomery (Tex.) Sch. Dist., 1992—; psychotherapist pvt. practice, Houston, 1990—; cons. school systems, Houston, 1990—; coord. sr. program Forest Springs Hosp., Houston, 1993—, Cypress Creek Hosp., 1994—. Vol. cons. PTO, Woodlands, Tex., 1990. Recipient fellowship Fla. State U., Tallahassee, 1973, Nat. Disting. Svc. award Ex Coun. U.S. Pubs., N.J., 1989; named Outstanding High Sch. Counselor, Tomball Ind. Sch. Dist., 1989. Mem. ACA, ASCD, Tex. Sch. Counselors Assn., Am. Mental Health Counselors Assn., Tex. Mental Health Counselors Assn., Am. Bus. Women's Assn., Fla. State U. Alumni Assn., Kappa Delta Pi. Home and Office: Carol A Gooch MS LPC PO Box 1308 Montgomery TX 77356

GOOD, JANET LOIS, occupational health nurse; b. Coudersport, Pa., Mar. 18, 1938; d. Warren Worth and Jeannette (Britton) Ohlman; m. Robert Jack Good, Feb. 14, 1960; children: Diana Ivy, Robert Warren. Diploma in nursing, Pa. Hosp., 1958; cert. in alcohol studies, U. N.D., 1970; cert. in nurse practition, U. Colo., 1973; BS in Health Care Adminstrn., St. Joseph Coll., 1987. Cert. occupational health nurse, cert. instr. CPR, cert. audiometry, spirometry. Staff and recovery room nurse Children's Hosp., Phila., 1958-60; supr. male div. Pennhurst State Sch. for Mentally Retarded, Spring City, Pa., 1961-65; office nurse Pediatric Clinic, Denver, 1966-69; nurse practitioner mgr. Mountain Bell, Denver, 1969-82; adminstrv. nurse Atlantic Richfield Co., Denver, 1982-94; mgr. faculty/staff health svcs. U. Colo. Wardenberg Student Health Ctr., Boulder, Colo., 1994—; presenter health care topics 1978—; U. Colo. Nightingale Awards com. 1992—; Cardiovascular Disease Bi-annual Conf. Planning com., 1990—. Rep. com. woman Adams County, Northglenn, Colo., 1980; del. Rep. State Conv., Denver, 1980; counselor merit badges Boy Scouts Am. Northglenn, 1984-85. Mem. Am. Nurses Assn. (cert.), Am. Nurses Assn. Primary Coun. Nurse Practitioners, Am. Assn. Occupational Health Nurses (bd. dirs. 1983-87, sec. 1987-91), Colo. Assn. Occupational Health Nurses (corr. sec. 1975-76, pres.-elect 1977-78, pres. 1978-79, named Occupational Health Nurse of Yr. 1979, Schering Occupational Health Nurse 1985), Denver Assn. Occupational Health Nurses. Lodge: Order Eastern Star. Office: Univ Colorado at Boulder Campus Box 119 Boulder CO 80309-0119

GOOD, JOHN LEON, III, health care executive; b. Melrose, Mass., May 12, 1943; s. John Leon Jr. and Pearl McLean (Phelps) G.; m. Susan Ruth Butterfield, Apr. 9, 1967; children: Travis James, Bonnie Elizabeth. Student, Bentley Coll., 1960-62; BS, Gordon Coll., 1966; MRE, Gordon Conwell Theol. Sem., 1970; MBA, New Hampshire Coll., 1980. Dir. pub. relations Gordon Coll., Wenham, Mass., 1964-67; dir. coll. and alumni relations, asst. to v.p. Gordon Coll., Wenham, 1970-78; dir. devel. Lexington (Mass.) Christian Acad., 1967-70; dir. community relations and devel. Beverly (Mass.) Hosp., 1978-84, v.p., 1984—; pres. North Shore Emergency Med. Svc., Inc., Lynn, Mass., 1986-89; trustee Beverly Nat. Bank, 1987—. Contbr. articles to profl. jours. and publs. Chmn. exec. commn. Am. Heart Assn., 1987; sec., clk. North Shore Cmty. Arts Found., Beverly, 1982—, bd. dirs., 1982—; vol. Essex Fire Dept., 1970—, lt., 1986-87; mem. Essex Rep. Town Com., 1972-82, 84-85, chmn., 1974-80; mem. Beverly Cmty. Coun., 1979—, Beverly Cable TV Program Commn., 1981-85; bd. dirs. Beverly Sch. for the Deaf, 1980—, Greater Beverly Red Cross, 1981-89; bd. dirs. Am. Cancer Soc., 1979-80, v.p., 1980. Fellow Nat. Assn. for Hosp. Devel.; mem. New Eng. Assn. for Hosp. Devel. (pres. 1988-90, spl. presdl. citation 1986), Mass. Soc. for Fund Raising Execs., Nat. Soc. for Fund Raising Execs., Am. Coll. of Healthcare Execs., Am. Coll. Healthcare Mktg., Acad. for Health Svc. Mktg., Rotary (pres. 1986-87), North Shore Press Club, B'nai B'rith (Man of Yr. 1982). Republican. Baptist. Home: 85 Martin St Essex MA 01929-1218 Office: Beverly Hosp 85 Herrick St Beverly MA 01915-1776

GOOD, LARRY IRWIN, physician, consultant; b. N.Y.C., Feb. 8, 1948; s. Samuel and Lillie (Sternlight) G.; m. Judy Chafetz, Aug. 16, 1969; children: Adam Eric, Lauren Elyse, Bryan Scott, Allison Jill. BA, Colgate U., 1969; MD, Med. U. of S.C., 1973. Diplomate Am. Bd. Internal Medicine, Am. Bd. Gastroenterology. Intern in medicine Teaching Hosp. Med. U. of S.C., 1973-74, resident in medicine Teaching Hosp., 1974-75, chief resident in medicine Teaching Hosp., 1975-76; fellow in gastroenterology U. Pa., 1976-78; with Hempstead (N.Y.) Gen. Hosp., 1978—, Nassau County Med. Ctr., East Meadow, N.Y., 1978—; with South Nassau Communities Hosp., Oceanside, N.Y., 1978—, chief div. gastroenterology dept. medicine, 1989; asst. prof. Sch. of Medicine, SUNY, Stony Brook, 1978; mem. health adv. bd. Hofstra Health Dome Uniondale, N.Y., 1983; with Lydia E. Hall Hosp., Freeport, N.Y., 1978-86, Mercy Hosp., Rockville Centre, N.Y., 1978-80. Contbr. articles to Am. Jour. Gastroenterology, The Papilla Vateri and its Diseases, Med. Times, New Eng. Jour. Medicine., Gastroenterology, Alpha Omega Alpha. Trustee, dir. Little Village Sch. & House, Garden City, N.Y., 1985—. Recipient Rsch. Svc. award NIH, 1977. Fellow Am. Coll. Gastroenterology; mem. AMA, ACP, L.I. Gastroenterologic Assn., Am. Gastroenterologic Assn. Jewish. Office: 999 Franklin Ave Garden City NY 11530

GOOD, MARK CAMERON, social worker; b. San Diego, June 3, 1946; s. Robert C. and Genevra (Bennett) G.; m. Susan Lyons Forve, Dec. 29, 1971; children: Joshua, Monique, Rebekah. BA in Math., Cornell U., 1968; MA in Religion and Counseling, Covenant Theol. Sem., St. Louis, 1977; PhD in Social Wk., U. Md., 1988. Cert. social worker, Md. Asst. prof. counseling Chesapeake Theol. Sem., Linthicum Heights, Md., 1987—; instr. U. Md., Balt., 1990—; cert. profl. counselor Arnold, Md., 1980—; staff cons. Birthright of Annapolis, 1981-82, Palmer Family, Inc., Prince Frederick, Md., 1980-82; conductor workshops in field. Pres. Anne Arundel County Children's Coun., Annapolis, 1984-85. With U.S. Army, 1968-71. Mem. Am. Assn. for Marriage and Family Therapy, Am. Assn. Christian Counselors. Reformed Presbyterian. Office: 1507 Ritchie Hwy Ste 104 Arnold MD 21012-2743

GOOD, MICHAEL IAN, psychiatrist, educator; b. New Ulm, Minn., May 23, 1944; s. Rudolph I. and Raleigh (Aaronson) G.; m. Bambi Zimmerman. BA summa cum laude, U. Minn., 1966; MD, Harvard U., 1970; grad., Psychoanlytic Inst. New Eng. East, 1990. Diplomate Am. Bd. Psychiatry and Neurology. Resident in psychiatry Mass. Mental Health Ctr., Boston, 1971-74, fellow in child psychiatry, 1974-76; resident in psychiatry Peter Bent Brigham Hosp., Boston, 1973-74; dir. child psychiatry West-Ros-Park Mental Health Ctr., Boston, 1976-91; mem. sr. psychiat. staff Medfield (Mass.) State Hosp., 1991-92, Westborough (Mass.) State Hosp., 1992—; clin. instr. psychiatry Harvard U. Med. Sch., Boston, 1976-81, asst. clin. prof., 1981—; candidate in child psychoanalysis Boston Psychoanalytic Inst., Psychoanalytic Inst. New Eng., 1991—; mem. faculty Psychoanalytic Inst. New Eng., East, 1994—. Contbr. articles to profl. jours. Fellow Am. Psychiat. Assn.; mem. Am. Acad. Child Psychiatry, Am. Psychoanalytic Assn., Am. Orthopsychiat. Assn., Mass. Psychiat. Soc., New Eng. Coun. Child and Adolescent Psychiatry. Home and Office: 74 Craftsland Rd Chestnut Hill MA 02167-2632

GOOD, REBECCA MAE WERTMAN, learning and behavior disorder counselor, grief and loss counselor, hospice nurse; b. Barberton, Ohio, May 13, 1943; d. Frederick Daniel Wertman and Freda Beam Wertman Lombardi; m. William Robert Good Jr., Aug. 15, 1964; children: William Robert III, John Joseph, Matthew Stephan. RN diploma, Akron Gen. Med. Ctr., Ohio, 1964; BS in Psychology, Ramapo Coll., Mahwah, N.J., 1986; MA in Counseling, NYU, 1990. RN, N.Y.; nat. cert. counselor. Staff nurse Green Cross Gen. Hosp., Cuyahoga Falls, Ohio, 1965-68; staff nurse, relief supr., psychiat. nurse F.D.R. VA Hosp., Montrose, N.Y., 1971-72; geriatric staff and charge nurse Westledge Extended Care Facility, Peekskill, N.Y., 1972-77; infirmary and ICF nurse St. Dominics Home, Orangeburg, N.Y., 1981-83; allergy and immunology nurse Dr. Andre Codispoti, Suffern, N.Y., 1979-89; rsch. asst. counselor NYU, N.Y.C., 1989-90; Rockland advocate Student Advocacy Inc., White Plains, N.Y., 1989-90; exec. dir. Rockland County Assn. for Learning Disabled, Orangeburg, 1990-91; life skills counselor Bd. Coop. Edn., West Nyack, N.Y., 1991-93; learning and behavior disorders counselor, Suffern, 1991-93, Salt Lake City, 1994—; hospice nurse United Hospice Rockland, 1991-93; assessment and referral counselor/case mgr. CPC Olympus View Hosp., Salt Lake City, 1994—; practitioner, tchr. Therapeutic Touch, 1990—. Co-chmn. Rockland County Coordinating Coun. for Devel. Disabled Offenders, New City, N.Y., 1990-93; bd. visitors Rockland Children's Psychiat. Ctr., Orangeburg, 1991-93, sec., 1992; mem. U.S. Congressman Benjamin Gilman's Handicapped Adv. Com., Rockland County, 1985-94; pres. Ramapo Ctrl. Sch. Dist. Spl. Edn. PTA, 1982-86. Ramapo Coll. of N.J. Pres.'s scholar, 1986. Mem. ACA, Utah Counselors Assn., Children and Adults with Attention Deficit Disorders (coord. Rockland chpt. 1992-93), Hospice Nurses Assn., Nurse Healers Profl. Assn., Utah Networker Nurse Healers Profl. Assn. Episcopalian. Office: 7730 S Quicksilver Dr Salt Lake City UT 84121-5500

GOOD, ROBERT ALAN, physician, educator; b. Crosby, Minn., May 21, 1922; s. Roy Homer and Ethel Gay (Whitcomb) G.; m. Noorbibi K. Day, 1986; children from previous marriage: Robert Michael, Mark Thomas, Alan Maclyn, Margaret Eugenia, Mary Elizabeth. BA, U. Minn., 1944, MB, 1946, PhD, 1947, MD, 1947, DSc (hon.), 1989; MD (hon.), U. Uppsala, Sweden, 1966; DSc (hon.), N.Y. Med. Coll., 1973, Med. Coll. Ohio, 1973, Coll. Medicine and Dentistry N.J., 1974, Hahnemann Med. Coll., 1974, U. Chgo., 1974, St. John's U., 1977, U. Health Scis., Chgo. Med. Sch., 1978, Miami Children's Hosp., 1986, Med. Sch., U. Minn., 1989, U. Rome, Rome. Teaching asst. dept. anatomy U. Minn., Mpls., 1944-45; instr. pediatrics U. Minn. (Med. Sch.), 1950-51, asst. prof., 1951-53, asso. prof., 1953-54, Am. Legion Meml. research prof. pediatrics, 1954-73, prof. microbiology, 1962-72, Regents prof. pediatrics and microbiology, 1969-73, prof., head dept. pathology, 1970-72; intern U. Minn. Hosps., 1947, asst. resident pediatrics, 1948-49; pres., dir. Sloan-Kettering Inst. for Cancer Research, 1973-80, mem., 1973-81; prof. pathology Sloan-Kettering div. Grad. Sch. Med. Scis. Cornell U., 1973-81, dir., 1973-80; adj. prof., vis. physician Rockefeller U., 1973-81; prof. medicine, pediatrics and pathology Cornell U. Med. Coll., 1973-81; dir. research Meml. Sloan-Kettering Cancer Ctr., v.p., 1980-81; dir. research Meml. Hosp. for Cancer and Allied Diseases, 1973-80, also attending physician depts. medicine and pediatrics; attending pediatrician N.Y. Hosp., 1973-81; mem., head cancer research program Okla. Med. Research Found., 1982-85; prof. pediatrics, research prof. medicine, Okla. Med. Rsch. Found. prof. microbiology and immunology U. Okla. Health Scis. Ctr., 1982-85; attending physician, head div. immunology Okla. Children's Meml. Hosp., 1982-85; attending physician in internal medicine Okla. Meml. Hosp., 1983-85; physician-in-chief All Children's Hosp., St. Petersburg, Fla., 1985—; prof., chmn. dept. pediatrics U. South Fla., St. Petersburg, 1985-91, prof. depts. pediatrics, microbiology, immunology and medicine, 1985—, head allergy and clinical immunology, dept. pediatrics, 1985—, disting. grad. rsch. prof., 1989—; vis. investigator Rockefeller Inst. for Med. Rsch., N.Y.C., 1949-50, asst. physician to Hosp., 1949-50; attending pediatrician Hennepin County Gen. Hosp., 1950-73, cons., 1960-73; mem. Unitarian Svc. Commn. Med. Exch. Team to France, Germany, Switzerland and Czechoslovakia, 1958; cons. VA Hosp., Mpls., 1959-60; cons., sci. adviser Nat. Jewish Hosp., Denver, Children's Asthma Rsch. Inst. and Hosp., Denver, 1964-69; mem. study sects. USPHS, 1952-69; mem. expert adv. panel on immunology WHO, 1967—; cons. Merck & Co., N.J., 1968-72, Nat. Cancer Inst., 1973-74; mem. ad hoc com. Pres.'s Sci. Adv. Coun. on Biol. and Med. Sci., 1970, Pres.'s Cancer Panel, 1972; mem. Lyndon B. Johnson Found. awards com., 1972; mem. adv. com. Bone Marrow Transplant Registry, 1973—; chmn. Internat. Bone Marrow Registry, 1977-79; bd. dirs. Nat. Marrow Donor Program, 1987-94; fgn. adv. Acad. Med. Scis., People's Republic of China, 1980—; chmn. Fla. Gov.'s Task Force on AIDS, 1985-87, mem., 1988-94. Author, editor numerous books; contbr. many articles to profl. jours. Mem. adv. council Childrens Hosp. Research Found., Cin., 1954-58; bd. dirs. Allergy Found. Am., 1973; bd. sci. advisers Jane Coffin Childs Meml. Fund Med. Research, 1972-74, Merck Inst. Therapeutic Research, 1972-76; trustee Eleanor Naylor Dana Charitable Trust, 1982—. Recipient Borden Undergrad. Research award U. Minn. Med. Sch., 1946, E. Mead Johnson First award, 1955, Theobald Smith award, 1955, Parke-Davis 6th Ann. award, 1962, Rectors medal U. Helsinki, 1963-64, Pemberton Lectureship award, 1966, Gordon Wilson Gold medal, 1967, R.E. Dyer Lectureship award, 1967, Clemens Von Pirquet Gold medal 9th Ann. Forum on Allergy, 1968, Presidents medal U. Padua, Italy, 1968, Robert A. Cooke Gold medal Am. Acad. Allergy, 1968, John t Meml. award Dalhousie U., 1969, Borden award Assn. Am. Med. Colls., 1970, Howard Taylor Ricketts award U. Chgo., 1970, Gairdner Found. award, 1970, City of Hope award, 1970, Am. Acad. Achievement golden plate award, 1970, Albert Lasker award for clin. and med. research, 1970, ACP award, 1972, Am. Coll. Chest Physicians award, 1974, Lila Gruber award Am. Acad. Dermatology, 1974, award in cancer immunology Cancer Research Inst. N.Y., 1975, Outstanding Achievement award U. Minn., 1978, award Am. Dermatological Soc. Allergy and Immunology, 1978, 1st Sarasota Med. award, 1979, sect. on mil. pediatrics award Am. Acad. Pediatrics, 1980, recipient Univ. medal Hacettepe U., Ankara, Turkey, 1982, Pres.' medal U. Lyon, France, 1986, Merieux Found. award Internat. Soc. Preventive Oncology, 1987, Claude Bernard prize World Med. Communications, Inc., 1987, Disting. Med. Sci. of Fla. award Fla. Soc. Pathologists, 1989, Gold-Headed Cane award Dept. Pediatrics U. Minn., 1990, Askounces-Ashford Disting. Scholar award, USF, 1990, Excellence award Ronald McDonald Children's Charities, 1991, Councill C. Rudolph award, All Children's Hosp., 1991, Merit award for outstanding and superior res., Dept. Health and Human Services, Md., 1992, Lifetime Achievement award Immune Deficiency Found., Md., 1992, Asthma and Allergy Found. Am. award 1993, Univ. Rsch. medallion award Disting. Rsch. Prof. U. South Fla., 1993, Immune Deficiency Found. award, 1993, Internat. Nutritional Immunology Group award, 1993, Paul Harris Fellow award Rotary Found. of Rotary Internat., 1994, numerous others; named one of top physicians in U.S., The Best Doctors in Am., 1992, 94-95; Endowment chair named in honor Children's Hosp. and U. South Fla., 1994; Fellow Nat. Found. for Infantile Paralysis, 1947, Helen Hay Whitney Found. fellow, 1948-50; Markle Found. scholar, 1950-55. Fellow AAAS, Am. Coll. Physicians (award 1993), Royal Soc. Medicine, Acad. Multidisciplinary Research, N.Y. Acad. Sci., Am. Acad. Arts and Scis., Am. Coll. of Allergy and Immunology (hon., John P. McGovern Lectureship award 1993, Schering Jaros Lecture award 1993), Am. Acad. Pediat. (1st hon. fellow sect. on allergy and immunology), The Philippine Pediat. Soc. (hon.); mem. NAS, Am. Soc. Transplant Surgeons (hon.), Am. Assn. History of Medicine, Am. Fedn. Clin. Research, Am. Assn. Anatomists, Am. Assn. Immunologists (past pres.), AAUP, Am. Pediatric Soc. (John Howland award 1987), Mpls. Pediatric Soc., Northwestern Pediatric Soc., Am. Rheumatism Assn., Am. Soc. Clin. Investigation (past pres.), Am. Soc. Exptl. Pathology (past pres.), Am. Soc. Microbiology, Assn. Am. Physicians, Central Soc. Clin. Research (past pres.), Harvey Soc., Infectious Disease Soc. Am. (Squibb award 1968), Internat. Soc. Nephrology, Internat. Acad. Pathology, Internat. Soc. for Transplantation Biology, Minn. State Med. Assn., NAS Inst. Medicine (charter), Reticuloendothelial Soc. (past pres.), Soc. for Exptl. Biology and Medicine (past pres.), Soc. for Pediatric Research, Am. Clin. and Climatol. Assn. (Gordon Wilson Gold medal 1967), Detroit Surg. Assn. (McGraw medal 1969), Internat. Soc. Blood, Transfusion, Practitioners' Soc., Am. Assn. Pathologists, Internat. Soc. Exptl. Hematology (award in pioneering leadership and accomplishments 1994), Transplant Soc., Western Assn. Immunologists, Internat. Soc. Immunopharmacology (founding mem.), Am. Soc. Transplant Surgeons, Pioneer, Internat. Bone Marrow Transplant Registry (charter), Phi Beta Kappa, Sigma Xi, Alpha Omega Alpha. Office: All Children's Hosp 801 6th St S Saint Petersburg FL 33701-4816

GOODE, ANTHONY WILLIAM, surgeon, educator; b. Newcastle, Eng., Aug. 3, 1944; s. William Henry and Eileen Veronica (Brannan) G.; m. Patricia Josephine Flynn, Sept. 26, 1987. MB BS, U. Newcastle upon Tyne, 1968, MD, 1978. Clin. asst. Newcastle Hosp. Group, 1968-76, U. London Teaching Hosps., 1976—; prof. endocrine and metabolic surgery U. London; cons. surgeon The Royal London Hosp. and St. Bartholomew's Hosp., London. Editor in chief Medicine Science and the Law. Fellow Royal Coll. Surgeons (Eng.)., Royal Soc. Medicine; mem. Brit. Acad. Forensic Scis. (asst. sec.-gen. 1982-87), Brit. Assn. Endocrine Surgeons (hon. sec. 1983—), Internat. Soc. Surgery, N.Y. Acad. Scis. Office: Royal London Hosp Surg Unit, Whitechapel, London E1 1BB, England

GOODE, JENNIFER POWELL, nurse; b. Sheffield, Ala., June 9, 1968; d. Gary Wayne and Sherron Dianne (Retherford) P.; m. Charles Wade Goode, Dec. 12, 1992. ADN, Northwest C.C., Phil Campbell, Ala., 1994; BS in Biology, U. North Ala., 1996. RN, Ala. Human resources clk. Eliza Coffee Meml. Hosp., Florence, Ala., 1991-92, labor and delivery technician, 1992-94; resident asst. Muscle Shoals (Ala.) Nursing Home, 1994, RN, 1994; RN and office supervisor Dr. John P. Hagler, Russellville, Ala., 1995; RN, instr. prenatal/postnatal classes BOJ Mgmt. Svcs./Eliza Coffee Meml. Hosp./Ob-Gyn Clinic, Florence, 1995—. Mem. Americans with Disabilities Assn. (com. mem. 1992), Ala. Nurses Assn. Democrat. Baptist.

GOODE, PAUL, educational consultant, psychologist; b. Bklyn., Nov. 14, 1937; s. Arthur and Bertha (Rose) G.; m. Judith Granich, June 22, 1960; children: Lawrence J., Andrew P., Joshua S. BA in Psychology, Bklyn. Coll., 1959; MA in Sch. Psychology (rsch. asst.), Syracuse U., 1962; EdD in Sch. Psychology (doctoral fellow 1967-68), Temple U., 1972. Unemployment ins. claims examiner N.Y. State Employment Service, Cortland, 1961-62; sch. psychologist Steuben County Bd. Coop. Ednl. Services, Bath, N.Y., 1962-66,

Camden (N.J.) Bd. Edn., 1966-67; sch. psychologist Delaware County Bd. Sch. Dirs., Media, Pa., 1967-68, intern psychologist, 1968-69 ; sch. psychologist specialist Phila. Non-Public Elem. Schs., 1969-70; assos. dir. clin. ednl. services project King of Prussia (Pa.) Intermediate Unit # 23, 1970-73; coordinator suburban unit Nat. Regional Resource Center of Pa., King of Prussia, 1971-74, asso. dir., 1974-75; dir. Pa. Area Learning Resources Center, Doylestown, 1975-77; dir. IEP devel. program Bucks County (Pa.) Intermediate Unit # 22, Doylestown, 1977-79, coordinator fed. programs in spl. edn., 1979-81; acting dir. spl. edn., 1980-81; asst. exec. dir. and dir. spl. edn., 1981-93; mem. adj. faculty Temple U., Phila., 1988—; pvt. practice Melrose Park, Pa., 1993—; vis. prof. Universidad de Antioquia (Colombia), 1964-65; part-time instr. Corning (N.Y.) Community Coll., 1965-66, Cabrini Coll., Radnor, Pa., 1972; instr. diagnosis of ednl. disabilities Pa. State U., Ogontz, 1972-84. Treas., Cub Scout pack 190, 1970-80; mgr. Old York Rd. Little League, 1970-80. Recipient Alumni award Temple U., 1980. Fellow Pa. Psychol. Assn. (editor divsn. newsletter 1975-77, pres. sch. psychology divsn. 1978-79, pres. 1981-82); mem. APA (divsn. 16), Coun. Exceptional Children, Coun. Orgn. Edn. (pres. 1989-90), Pa. Assn. Sch. Adminstrs., Pa. Assn. Pupil Personnel Adminstrs., Phi Delta Kappa. Asso. editor Archives, newsletter NRRC/P, 1970-72. Home and Office: 7610 Montgomery Ave Elkins Park PA 19027-2901

GOODE, STEPHEN MARK, healthcare administrator, educator; b. Ft. Worth, Aug. 10, 1956; s. Loren Grant and Genetta Mae (Cullers) G.; m. Sheri Denise Reagan, June 29, 1979; children: Holly, Lisa, Mark. BS in Biology, U. Tex., Arlington, 1978; MS in Health Care Adminstrn., Tex. Woman's U., Dallas, 1984. Adminstr. Crane (Tex.) Meml. Hosp., 1991-93, Plains Meml. Hosp., Dimmitt, Tex., 1993—; CEO Castro County Hosp. Dist., Dimmitt, 1993—; cons. Kent County Nursing Home, Jayton, Tex., 1993; prof. Wayland Bapt. U., Amarillo, Tex., 1994—. Author: Information Manual of Business Subjects for Nursing Management, 1984; contbr. articles to profl. jours. Bd. dirs. local chpt. Am. Cancer Soc., Dimmitt, 1995—, Sr. Citizens Ctr., El Dorado, Tex., 1989-91, Coke County EMS, Robert Lee, Tex., 1985. Mem. Am. Coll. Healthcare Execs. (diplomate), Lions Club (sec. 1989-91, v.p. 1991-93). Office: Castro County Hosp Dist 310 W Halsell Dimmitt TX 79027

GOODENBERGER, DANIEL MARVIN, medical educator; b. McCook, Nebr., Apr. 24, 1948; s. Marvin Eugene and Mary Ellen (Marshall) G.; m. Janet Ann King, July 30, 1979; children: James Michael, Katherine Elizabeth. BS, U. Nebr., 1970; MD, Duke U., 1974. Diplomat Am. Bd. Internal Medicine, Am. Bd. Emergency Medicine, Am. Bd. Pulmonary Disease, Am. Bd. Critical Care Medicine. Intern Peter Bent Brigham Hosp., Boston, 1974-75, resident in internal medicine, 1975-76; clin. assoc. Nat. Cancer Inst., Boston, 1976-78; fellow pulmonary and criticial care medicine Boston U. Med. Ctr., St. Louis, 1985-88; assoc. dir. emergency dept. Arlington (Va.) Hosp., St. Louis, 1979-82; edn. dir. emergency dept. Georgetown U. Hosp., Washington, 1982-85; dir. emergency svcs. U. Hosp., Boston, 1986-87; dir. pulmonary and critical care fellowship Washington U. Med. Schs., St. Louis, 1989-93; dir. pulmonary cons. svcs. Barnes Hosp., St. Louis, 1990-93, dir. internal medicine residency program, 1992—; assoc. prof. medicine Washington U., St. Louis, 1995—. Lt. comdr. USPHS, 1973-78. Winthrop Breon and Am. Coll. Chest Physicians scholar, 1987. Fellow Am. Coll. Physicians, Am. Coll. Chest Physicians; mem. AMA, Am. Thoracic Soc., Assn. Program Dirs. Internal Medicine (nominating and publs. com. 1991—), Phi Beta Kappa, Alpha Omega Alpha. Methodist. Home: 441 Oakley Dr Clayton MO 63105 Office: Washington U Sch Medicine Box 8121 660 S Euclid Saint Louis MO 63110

GOODES, MELVIN RUSSELL, manufacturing company executive; b. Hamilton, Ont., Can., Apr. 11, 1935; s. Cedric Percy and Mary Melba (Lewis) G.; m. Arlene Marie Bourne, Feb. 23, 1963; children: Melanie, Michelle, David. B in Commerce, Queen's U., Kingston, Ont., Can., 1957; MBA, U. Chgo., 1960. Rsch. assoc. Can. Econ. Rsch. Assocs., Toronto, Ont., 1957-58; market planning coord. Ford Motor Co. Can., Oakville, Ont., 1960-64; asst. to v.p. O'Keefe Breweries, Toronto, 1964-65; mgr. new product devel. Adams Brands div. Warner-Lambert Can., Scarborough, Ont., 1965-68; area mgr. Warner-Lambert Internat., Toronto, 1968-69; regional dir. confectionary ops. Warner-Lambert Europe, Brussels, 1969-70; pres. Warner-Lambert Mex., 1970-76; pres. Pan-Am. zone Warner-Lambert Internat., Morris Plains, N.J., 1976-77, pres. Pan-Am. and Asian zone, 1977-79; pres. consumer products div. Warner-Lambert Co., Morris Plains, N.J., 1979-81, sr. v.p., pres. consumer products group, 1981-83, exec. v.p., pres. U.S. ops., 1984-85, pres., COO, 1985-91, chmn., CEO, 1991—, also bd. dirs.; bd. dirs. Ameritech Corp., Chem. Banking Corp., Chem. Bank, Unisys; mem. exec. adv. coun. Nat. Ctr. Ind. Retail Pharmacy, 1984-85. Bd. dirs. Coun. on Family Health, N.Y.C., 1981-86, Advt. Edn. Found., N.Y.C., 1989-91; mem. fin. com. Nat. Coun. on Econ. Edn., 1984—, mem. exec. com., 1986—; mem. Internat. Exec. Svc. Corps., 1989—; mem. adv. coun. Sch. of Bus. Queen's U., Kingston, Ont., Can., 1980-84; trustee Drew U., Madison, N.J., 1985-88, Queen's U., 1988—. Fellow Ford Found., 1958, Sears, Roebuck Found., 1959. Mem. Nat. Wholesale Druggists Assn. (assoc. adv. com.), Nat. Assn. Retail Druggists (exec. adv. coun. 1983-85), Pharm. Mfrs. Assn. (bd. dirs. 1989-91), Proprietary Assn. (v.p. 1983-88, bd. dirs., exec. com. 1981-88), Nat. Alliance Bus. (bd. dirs. 1984-86), Plainfield Country Club (N.J.), Pine Valley Golf Club (N.J.). Unitarian. Office: Warner-Lambert Co 201 Tabor Rd Morris Plains NJ 07950-2614*

GOODEY, ILA MARIE, psychologist; b. Logan, Utah, Feb. 1, 1948; d. Vernal P. and Leona Marie (Williams) Goodey. BA with honors in English and Sociology, U. Utah, 1976; Grad. Cert. Criminology, U. Utah, 1976, MS in Counseling Psychology, 1984, PhD in Psychology, 1985. Speech writer for dean of students U. Utah, Salt Lake City, 1980-85, psychologist Univ. Counseling Ctr., 1984—; cons. Dept. Social Services, State of Utah, Salt Lake City, 1983—; pvt. practice psychology Consult West, Salt Lake City, 1985-86; pub. relations coordinator Univ. Counseling Ctr., 1985—; cons. Aids Project, U. Utah, 1985—; pvt. practice psychology, Inscapes Inst., Salt Lake City, 1987-88; writer civic news Salt Lake City Corp., 1980—; mem. Senator Orrin Hatch's Adv. Com. on Disability Oriented Legis., 1989—. Author book: Love for All Seasons, 1971, Poemspun, 1994, Echoes, 1995, Rapture, 1996; play: Validation, 1979; musical drama: One Step, 1984. Contbr. articles to profl. jours. Chmn. policy bd. Dept. State Social Service, Salt Lake City, 1986—; campaign writer Utah Dem. Party, 1985; appointed to Utah State Legis. Task Force on svcs. for people with disabilities, 1990; chmn. bd. Utah Assistive Tech. Program, 1990—. Recipient Creative Achievement award Utah Poetry Soc., 1974, English SAC, U. Utah, 1978, Leadership award YWCA, 1989, Nat. Golden Rule award J.C. Penny, Washington, 1989, 90, Volunteerism award State of Utah, 1990; Ila Marie Goodey award named in honor. Mem. AAUW, Am. Psychol. Assn., Utah Psychol. Assn., Internat. Platform Assn., Mortar Board, Am. Soc. Clin. Hypnosis, Utah Soc. Clin. Hypnosis, Soc. Psychol. Study Social Issues, League of Women Voters, Phi Beta Kappa, Phi Kappa Phi, Alpha Lambda Delta. Mormon. Clubs: Mormon Theol. Symposium, Utah Poetry Assn. Avocations: theatrical activities, creative writing, travel, political activities. Office: U Utah Counseling Ctr 2450 SSB Salt Lake City UT 84112

GOODHEART, CLYDE RAYMOND, virologist, scientific laboratory executive; b. Erie, Pa., June 9, 1931; s. Edmund James and Helen (Husted) G.; m. Barbara Jean Peterson, Dec. 26, 1953; children—Kenneth James, Karen Jean, Diane Louise. B.S., Northwestern U., 1953, M.S., 1957, M.D., 1957, MM, 1987. Research fellow Cal. Inst. Tech., 1958-61; asst. prof. pediatrics, then assoc. prof. Children's Hosp., Los Angeles, 1961-65; assoc. mem., then mem. Inst. Biomed. Research, Edn. and Research Found., AMA, 1965-70; sr. microbiologist Rush-Presbyn.-St. Luke's Med. Center, Chgo., 1970-71; prof. microbiology Rush Med. Coll., 1971-80; pres. BioLabs, Inc., Lincolnshire, Ill., 1971—; tchr. microbiology UCLA, 1961-64; bd. dirs. Fibrogenex Inc. Author: An Introduction to Virology, 1969; co-author: Fundamentals of Microbiology, 1974; Contbr. papers in field. Mem. Am. Soc. for Microbiology, Ill. Soc. for Microbiology (pres. 1974), AAAS, Tissue Culture Assn., Phi Beta Kappa, Sigma Xi, Phi Rho Sigma. Home and Office: 15 Sheffield Ct Lincolnshire IL 60069-3161

GOODHUE, PETER AMES, obstetrician and gynecologist, educator; b. Ft. Fairfield, Maine, Feb. 26, 1931; s. Lawrence and Zylpha (Ames) G.; m. Edith Ann Helfenstein, June 21, 1958; children: Lisa Grace, Scott Ames. BA, Amherst Coll., 1954; MD, U. Vt. 1958. Diplomate Am. Bd. Ob-Gyn. Intern Bellevue Hosp., N.Y.C., 1958-59; resident Yale-New Haven Med. Center, 1959-62; practice medicine specializing in ob-gyn, Stamford, Conn., 1964—; assoc. clin. prof. ob-gyn N.Y. Med. Coll. Contbr. articles to profl. jours. Served to capt. USAF, 1962-64. Recipient Carbee prize, U. Vt., 1958. Fellow ACS, Am. Fertility Soc., Am. Coll. Obstetricians and Gynecologists (chmn. Conn. sect. 1976-76, pres. Conn. sect. 1973-76), Am. Soc. For Colposcopy and Cervical Pathology, Am. Assn. Of Gynecologic Laproscopists; mem. Conn. Med. Soc., Conn. Soc. Am. Bd. Obstetricians and Gynecologists (pres. 1973-76), Fairfield County Med. Soc., Fairfield County Gynecol. and Obstet. Soc., Stamford Med. Soc. (pres. 1989-90). Republican. Episcopalian. Office: Stamford Gynecology PC 70 Mill River St Stamford CT 06902-3725

GOODHUE, WILLIAM WALTER, JR., pathologist, army officer; b. St. Louis, Feb. 5, 1945; s. William W. and Rose Marie (Vahousek) G.; B.S. cum laude with honors, Georgetown U., 1966; M.D., Cornell U., 1970. Diplomate Am. Bd. Pathology. Intern anat. pathology N.Y. Hosp.-Cornell Med. Center, N.Y.C., 1970-71, resident anat. pathology, 1971-74; chief resident pediatric anat. pathology Columbia-Presbyn. Med. Center, N.Y.C., 1974-75; resident clin. pathology Tripler Army Med. Center, Honolulu, 1976-78, chief resident, 1978; practice medicine specializing in pathology, 1975—; instr. pathology U. Hawaii Sch. Medicine, Honolulu, 1975-76; chief dept. pathology U.S. Army Hosp., Ft. Campbell, Ky., 1978-80; chief dept. pathology, med. dir. Sch. Med. Tech., dir. pathology residency tng. Gorgas Army Hosp., C.Z. and assoc. prof. med. tech. Panama Canal Coll., 1980-82; resident officer U.S. Army Command and Gen. Staff Coll., Ft. Leavenworth, Kans., 1982-83, div. surgeon 2d Inf. Div., 1983-84; dep. comdr. clin. services, chief dept. primary care and community medicine, staff pathologist, acting comdr. Bayne-Jones Army Hosp., Ft. Polk, La., 1984-85; chief dept. pathology and area lab. services, dir. pathology residency tng. Dwight David Eisenhower Army Med. Ctr., Ft. Gordon, Ga., 1985-94; clin. assoc. prof. pathology Med. Coll. Ga., Augusta, 1986-94; chief pathology grad. med. edn. Tripler Army Med. Ctr., Honolulu, 1994—; cons. in pathology Eisenhower health service region to comdg. gen.; cons. ARC, 1978-80; rep. Alt. Army Med. Dept. to Coll. of Am. Pathologists House of Del., Am. Soc. Clin. Pathologist Adv. Coun., 1990—; mem. profl. adv. bd. Med. Lab Observer, 1993-95; Army councillor-at-large Armed Forces Med. Lab. Scientists, 1993—. Served to col., M.C., U.S. Army, 1975—. USPHS research fellow, 1971-74; decorated Order Mil. Med. Merit. Fellow Am. Soc. Clin. Pathologists, Internat. Acad. Pathology, Coll. Am. Pathologists (lab. accreditation insp. inspection and accreditation program 1988—), Am. Soc. Abdominal Surgeons; mem. Soc. for Pediatric Pathology, Med. Assn. Isthmian C.Z. (v.p. 1980-81), Assn. Mil. Surgeons U.S., Am. Assn. Blood Banks, Nashville Pathology Soc., Hawaii Soc. Pathologists, AAAS, N.Y. Acad. Scis., Soc. Armed Forces Med. Lab. Scientists, Assn. Practitioners in Infection Control, Clin. Lab. Mgrs. Assn. (bd. dirs. 1989-92), Central Savannah River Area Assn. Med. Lab. Personnel, Assn. U.S. Army, AMA (Physician's Recognition award 1976, 78, 80, 82, 86, 89, 92, 95), Alliance Francaise, Sigma Xi, Phi Beta Kappa. Republican. Roman Catholic. Clubs: Cornell of N.Y.; Kauai Yacht. Contbr. articles on pathology to profl. jours.; research in clin. pathology. Home: 45-049 Ka-Hanahou Pl Kaneohe HI 96744-3014 Office: TAMC DPALS Honolulu HI 96859-5000

GOODIN, JULIA C., medical investigator, state official, educator; b. Columbia, Ky., Mar. 10, 1957; d. Vitus Jack and Geneva (Burton) G. BS, Western Ky. U., 1979; MD, U. Ky., 1983. Diplomate Am. Bd. Clin. and Anatomic Pathology, Am. Bd. Forensic Pathology. Intern Vanderbilt U. Med. Ctr., Nashville, 1983, resident in anatomic and clin. pathology, 1984-87; fellow in forensic pathology Med. Examiner's Office, Balt., 1987-88; asst. med. examiner Office of Chief Med. Examiner, Balt., 1988-90; dep. chief med. examiner State of Tenn., 1990-94; asst. med. examiner Nashville, 1990-93, chief med. examiner, 1993-94; asst. med. investigator State of N.Mex., Albuquerque, 1994-96; asst. prof. U. N.Mex., Albuquerque, 1994-96; clin. assoc. prof. U. of South Ala. Sch. Medicine, 1996—; asst. med. examiner State of Ala., 1996—; state med. examiner Ala. Dept. Forensic Scis., Mobile, 1996—; clin. prof. U. Md. Med. Sch., Balt., 1988-90, Vanderbilt U. Med. Ctr., 1990-94. Comdr. USNR, 1985—. Mem. Am. Acad. Forensic Sci., Assn. Mil. Surgeons of U.S., AMA. Home: 352 McDonald Ave Mobile AL 36604 Office: Mobile Med Examiner 2451 Fillingim St Mobile AL 36617

GOODKIN, DONALD ELIOT, neurologist; b. Brookline, Mass., July 9, 1946. BS, Duke U., 1968; MD, U. Miami, 1972. Diplomate Am. Bd. Psychiatry and Neurology, Electrodiagnostic Medicine, Nat. Bd. Med. Examiners; lic. Calif. Intern, resident U. Vt. Coll. Medicine, 1972-76, asst. prof. neurology, 1976-83; assoc. prof. neurology U. N.D. Sch. Medicine, 1983-88; fellow, clin. assoc., staff neurologist Cleve. Clin. Found., 1988-93; assoc. prof. neurolgist U. Calif. San Francisco, 1993—; attending physician U. Calif. San Francisco Hosps. and Clinics, 1993—, Mount Zion Hosp., 1993—; lectr. in field. Co-editor: Advances in Treatment of Multiple Sclerosis: Trial Design, Results and Future Perspectives, 1996; assoc. editor The Online Jour. Current Clin. Trials, 1991—; mem. editl. bd. Neurology Chronicle, 1993—; reviewer several jours.; contbr. chpts. in books and articles to profl. jours. Bd. dirs. Nat. Multiple Sclerosis Soc. No. Calif. chpt., prof. adv. com., 1994—. Grantee Nat. Insts. Neurol. Diseases and Stroke, 1987, Nat. Multiple Sclerosis Soc., 1983-96. Fellow Am. Assn. Electrodiagnostic Medicine; mem. AMA (Certificate of Appreciation 1991), Am. Assn. Electromyography and Electrodiagnosis, Am. Acad. Neurology, Am. Soc. Neurorehab. (cert.), Am. Neurol. Assn. Office: Univ Calif San Francisco Mount Zion Med Ctr 1600 Divisadero St San Francisco CA 94115

GOODMAN, ALVIN IRWIN, internist, nephrologist, educator; b. N.Y.C., July 12, 1929; s. Morris and Fanny (Rifkin) G.; m. Suzanna Elizabeth Gebhard; children: Nadine, Derek, Danielle, Leslie, Reva. BA, NYU, 1949; MD, U. Geneva, 1955. Diplomate Am. Bd. Internal Medicine, Am. Bd. Nephrology. Intern Jewish Hosp. Bklyn., 1956, resident in medicine, 1957-58; fellow in medicine Yale U. Sch. Medicine, New Haven, 1960-62, resident in medicine, 1962-63; dir. nephrology and renal ctr. Westchester County Med. Ctr., Valhalla, N.Y., 1963—; prof. medicine, dir. nephrology N.Y. Med. Coll., Valhalla, 1976—; cons. nephrologist Bird S. Coler Hosp., N.Y.C.; dir. endstage renal disease program Bur. Quality Assurance, USPHS, Rockville, Md., 1974-75. Contbr. numerous articles to medl jours. Capt. M.C., U.S. Army, 1958-60. Recipient President's award Nat. Kidney Found., 1977, Cardinal Cook award N.Y. Med. Coll., 1986. Fellow ACP; mem. Am. Soc. Nephrology, Internat. Soc. Nephrology, Am. Soc. Transplant Physicians, N.Y. Soc. Nephrology (pres. 1980-81), Beta Lambda Sigma. Office: Westchester County Med Ctr Ny Med College Valhalla NY 10595

GOODMAN, DAVID BARRY POLIAKOFF, physician, educator; b. Lynn, Mass., June 1, 1942; s. Nathan and Eva (Poliakoff) G.; children—Derek, Alex. A.B., Harvard Coll., 1964; M.D., U. Pa., 1968, Ph.D., 1972. Intern dept. pathology U. Pa. Hosp., Phila., 1971-72; assoc. pediatrics and biochemistry U. Pa. Sch. Medicine, Phila., 1972-73, research asst. prof., 1973-76, assoc. prof., 1980-82, prof. pathology and lab. medicine, 1982—, dir. div. lab. medicine, 1980-83; dir. endocrinology-oncology lab., 1984—; asst. prof. internal medicine Yale U. Med. Sch., New Haven, 1976-79, assoc. prof., 1979-80; cons. NSF, VA, Ctr. Oral Health Research, U. Pa. Contbr. numerous articles to profl. jours.; mng. editor: Metabolic Bone Disease and Related Rsch., 1981-90; editor Hormonal Regulation Epithelial Transport Ions and Water, 1981, Technology Impact: Potential Directions for Laboratory Medicine, 1984. Recipient Achievement award Upjohn Co., 1968; Roland Jackson scholar, 1964-68; Pa. Plan scholar, 1968-72. Fellow N.Y. Acad. Scis. (Lamport award 1981); mem. Acad. Clin. Lab. Physicians and Scientists, AAAS, Am. Assn. Pathologists, Am. Fedn. Clin. Research, Am. Heart Assn., Am. Physiol. Soc., Am. Soc. Bone and Mineral Research, Soc. Devel. Biology, Soc. Neurosci. Home: 1201 Grenox Rd Wynnewood PA 19096-2218 Office: U Pa Hosp Dept Path & Lab Med 3400 Spruce St Philadelphia PA 19104

GOODMAN, EDMUND NATHAN, surgeon, pain management consultant; b. N.Y.C., July 14, 1908; s. Benjamin Harry and Sophia (Schweisheimer) G.; m. Marian Powers, Mar. 9, 1950; children—Wendy, Tonne, Edmund Jr., Stacy. B.S., CCNY, 1928; M.D., Columbia U., 1933, MED. D.Sc., 1942; postgrad. Cambridge U., 1935-36. Intern in surgery Columbia-Presbyterian Hosp., N.Y.C., 1936-38, asst. resident, then resident in surgery, 1938-41, instr. in surgery, 1941, asst. clin. prof. surgery, 1950-65, assoc. clin. prof., 1965-81; attending surgeon Mt. Sinai Hosp., N.Y.C., 1947-49; practice medicine specializing in surgery, Roslyn, N.Y., 1982—. Served as lt. comndr. U.S. Navy, 1941-46. Mem. N.Y. Surgical Soc., N.Y. Acad. Med., Am. Coll. Surgeons, Am. Bd. Surgery. Home: 35 Sterling Ln Sands Point NY 11050 Office: 1405 Old Northern Blvd Roslyn NY 11576-2146

GOODMAN, GWENDOLYN ANN, nursing educator; b. Davenport, Iowa, Aug. 7, 1955; d. Merle Erwin and Loraine Etta (Mahannah) Langfeldt; m. Mark Nathan Goodman, Oct. 24, 1982; children: Zachary Aaron, Alexander Daniel. BS in Nursing, Ariz. State U., 1977. RN, Ariz. Staff nurse surg. fl. and intensive care unit St. Luke's Hosp. and Med. Ctr., Phoenix, 1977-81; staff nurse intensive care unit Yavapai Regional Med. Ctr., Prescott, Ariz., 1981-82; instr. nursing Yavapai Coll., Prescott, 1982-88, cons., 1986; part-time staff nurse Ariz. Poison Control Ctr., Phoenix, 1980-81; mem. profl. adv. com. Home Health Agy. Yavapai Regional Med. Ctr., 1988-93. Mem. Sigma Theta Tau. Democrat. Home: PO Box 450 Prescott AZ 86302-0450

GOODMAN, HUBERT THORMAN, psychiatrist, consultant; b. Oklahoma City, Mar. 5, 1933; s. Hubert Thorman and Belle (Wilkonson) G.; m. Doris Aline Knight, Feb. 1, 1957 (div. 1975); children: Mark, Martha Harris, Mary, Carmen Lugo, Valerie Freeman; m. Paulette Sue Freeman, Oct. 28, 1988. MD, Ind. U., 1957. Diplomate Am. Bd. Forensic Examiner, Am. Bd. Forensic Medicine; sr. disability analyst, diplomate Am. Bd. Disability Analysts. Intern Riverside Hosp., Toledo, 1957-58; resident in pub. health Miss. Dept. Health, Jackson, 1958-60; resident in psychiatry Cen. Ohio Psychiat. Hosp., Columbus, 1960-63; Ctrl. Ohio Psychiat. Hosp.; officer Pub. Health Svc., Jackson, 1958-60; pvt. practice Columbus, 1964—; clin. asst. prof. psychiatry Ohio State U., 1972-91; cons. Dept. Mental Health, 1990-95, Peer Rev. Sys. Ohio, 1990—. Contbr. articles to profl. jours. Capt. USPHS, 1958-60. Recipient Felix Underwood award Miss. Med. Assoc., 1963. Mem. AMA, Am. Psychiat. Assn., Ctrl. Ohio Med. Assn., Ohio State Med. Assn., Ctr. Ohio Psychiat. Assn. Home: 4770 Dierker Rd Columbus OH 43220-2985 Office: 4700 Reed Rd Columbus OH 43220-3074

GOODMAN, JULIE, nurse midwife; b. Dec. 14, 1937; m. Michael B. Goodman; children: Julia, Christopher, Jennifer. BAin Nursing, Coll. St. Catherine, 1960; MSN, U. Minn., 1975, PhDin Adult Edn., 1990. RN, Minn.; CNM. Staff nurse St. Joseph's Hosp., St. Paul, 1960-61; pub. health nurse Family Nursing Svc., St. Paul, 1961-63; instr. nursing U. S.D., Vermillion, 1963-66, Saint Mary's Sch. Nursing, Rochester, Minn., 1966-68, Rochester (Minn.) C. C., 1960-83; nurse practitioner Planned Parenthood, Rochester, Minn., 1978-81; dir. nursing cont. edn. Rochester (Minn.) C. C., 1983-88, dir. nursing, 1989—, assoc. dean acad. affairs, 1994—; adv. bd. Family Consultation Svc., Rochester, Minn., 1983-86. Author, editor: Child and Family, 1982, 2nd edit. 1987; contbr. articles to profl. jours. Mem. Am. Nurses Assn. (nat. del.), Nat. League Nursing, Minn. Orgn. Assoc. Degree Nursing (co-pres. 1994—), Minn. Nurses Assn. (chair nursing edn. com. 1982-87, 87-89, bd. dirs. 6th dist.), Great Plains Perinatal Assn., Sigma Theta Tau. Office: Rochester Comm Coll 851 30th Ave SE Rochester MN 55904

GOODMAN, LILLIAN RACHEL, dean, nursing educator; b. Hanover, N.H.; d. Benjamin and Anna (Tapper) Goodman; R.N., Peter Bent Brigham Hosp. Sch. Nursing, 1947; B.S. in Nursing, Boston U., 1950, M.S., 1954, Ed.D., 1969; ScD (hon.), U. Mass., Worcester, 1991. Dir. nurses Boston State Hosp., 1955-63; asst. chief supr. psychiat. nursing Mass. Dept. Mental Health, Boston, 1963-69; prof., acting dean U. Mass. Sch. Nursing, Amherst, 1970-73; prof. chmn. dept. nursing, Worcester (Mass.) State Coll., 1973-91; dean, prof. U. Mass. Grad. Sch. Nursing, Worcester, 1991—; assoc. clin. prof. Boston U. Sch. Nursing, 1957-69; cons. VA Hosp., Brockton, Mass., 1960-67. Mem. editorial bd. Nursing and Health Care, 1983-87. Mem. Am. Nurses Assn., Mass. Nurses Assn. (leadership award 1979), Nat. League for Nursing, Vis. Nurses Assn. of Worcester (pres. 1982-85, v.p. 1979-82), Sigma Theta Tau. Co-author: The Schizophrenic's Mother, 1963; mem. editorial bd. Perspectives in Psychiat. Care, 1961-76. Office: U Mass Worcester Grad Sch Nursing 55 Lake Ave N Worcester MA 01655-0002

GOODMAN, LOUIS SANFORD, pharmacologist; b. Portland, Oreg., Aug. 27, 1906; married, 1933; 2 children. BA, Reed Coll., 1928; MD, MA, U. Oreg., 1932; DSc (hon.), U. Man., 1965, U. Utah, 1969, Med. Coll. Wis., 1973. Asst. psychologist Reed Coll., 1927-29; asst. neurologist, pharmacologist Sch. Medicine U. Oreg., 1929-32; house officer medicine Johns Hopkins Hosp., 1932-33; Nat. Rsch. Coun. fellow Sch. Medicine Yale U., 1934, instr. pharmacology and toxicology, 1935-37, asst. prof., 1937-43; prof. pharmacology and physiology, chmn. dept. Coll. Med. U. Vt., 1943-44; prof. pharmacology, chmn. dept. Coll. Medicine U. Utah, Salt Lake City, 1944-72, disting. prof. pharmacology Coll. Medicine, 1972—; mem. pharmacol. study sect. USPHS, 1948-52, pharmacol. and exptl. therapeutics study sect., 1954; mem. med. bd. Myasthenia Gravis Found., 1953-58; mem. Nat. Adv. Neurol. Disorder and Blindness Coun., 1954-58; mem. pharmacol. test com. Nat. Bd. Med. Exam, 1955-59; chmn. pharmacol. tng. com. NIH, 1958-61; mem. adv. com. psychopharmacol. svc. ctr. NIMH, 1958-62. Editor-in-chief Pharmacol. Rev., 1949-53. Fellow Am. Coll. Neuropsychopharmacology, N.Y. Acad. Sci.; mem. AAAS, NAS, Am. Soc. Pharmacol. and Exptl. Therapeutics (pres. 1959-60). Office: U Utah Coll Medicine Dept Pharmacology Salt Lake City UT 84132*

GOODMAN, MADELEINE JOYCE, dean, human geneticist, educator; b. N.Y.C., Sept. 11, 1945; d. Joseph and Pauline Ida (Applebaum) Schwarzbach; m. Lenn Evan Goodman, Aug. 29, 1965; children: Allegra, Paula. BA, Barnard Coll., 1967; Diploma in Human Biology, Oxford U., 1968; PhD, U. Hawaii, 1973. Asst. prof. U. Hawaii, Honolulu, 1974-79, assoc. prof. 1979-85, prof. 1985-94, dir. women's studies, 1978-85, asst. v.p. Acad. Affairs, 1986-94, interim sr. v.p. Acad. Affairs, 1992-93; dean Coll. Arts & Scis., Vanderbilt U., Nashville, 1994—, prof. biology 1994—; pres. Pacific Health Research Inst., Honolulu, 1982-86. Author: Sex Differences in the Life Cycle, 1983, The Sexes in the Human Population, 1984 (textbooks). Contbr. articles to profl. jours. Officer Disciplinary Council Hawaii State Supreme Ct., Honolulu, 1983-94. Grantee NSF, 1981-84, Am. Cancer Soc., 1982-83, Pub. Health Svc., 1987-94. Mem. AAAS, Hawaii Assn. Women in Sci. (pres. 1981-83), Human Biology Council, Sigma Xi (nat. lectr. 1987-89, pres. Hawaii chpt., mem. nat. bd. dirs., chair. nat. nominating com.). Office: Vanderbilt U Office of Dean 301 Kirkland Hall Nashville TN 37240

GOODMAN, MICHAEL HOWARD, pediatrician; b. Phila., Apr. 25, 1960; s. Norman Robert and Arlene Marilyn (Marshall) G.; m. Michele Berlinerbleu, June 22, 1986; 1 child, Marc Philip. BS, Lebanon Valley Coll., 1982; MD, Ross Univ., 1986. Diplomate Am. Bd. Pediatrics, Am. Bd. Psychiatry & Neurology, Am. Bd. Clin. Neurology. Asst. clin. instr. SUNY, Bklyn., 1989-92; asst. prof. clin. pediatrics Univ. Medicine and Dentistry N.J., Camden, 1994-96; dir. evoked potentials lab. A.I. duPont Inst. Contbr. chpt. to book. Fellow Am. Acad. Pediatrics; mem. Am. Acad. Neurology, Am. Epilepsy Soc., Am. Electroencephelographic Soc., Child Neurology Soc., Phila. Neurol. Soc. Office: AI Dupont Inst 1600 Rockland Rd Wilmington DE 19899

GOODMAN, MORRIS, anatomy educator; b. Milw., Jan. 12, 1925; s. Benjamin and Sara (Bratt) G.; m. Selma Kessler, Apr. 5, 1946; children: Louise, Julia, David. BS, U. Wis., 1948, MS, 1949, PhD, 1951. Rsch. assoc. U. Ill. Coll. Medicine, Chgo., 1952-54, Detroit Inst. Cancer Rsch., 1954-58; sr. investigator immunology Lafayette Clinic, 1958-65; rsch. assoc. prof. Wayne State U., Detroit, 1960-66, prof. dept. anatomy, 1966—; dir. rsch. Plymouth (Mich.) State Home, 1966-72; mem. adv. panel for systematic biology, div. biol. and med. scis. NSF, 1969-72; Disting. vis. scholar Christ's Coll., Cambridge U., Eng., 1984; von Hofsten Meml. lectr. U. Uppsala, Sweden, 1987. Editor: Molecular Anthropology, 1976, Macromolecular Sequences in Systematic and Evolutionary Biology, 1982; co-editor: Jour. Human Evolution, 1971-77, editor, 1972; mem. editorial bd. Human Biology, 1974, Advances in Primatology, 1975, Jour. Molecular Evolution, 1975, Molecular Biology and Evolution, 1983; editor in chief Jour. Molecular Phylogenetics and Evolution, 1991; contbr. articles to profl. jours. Mem. rsch. com. Mich. Assn. for Retarded Citizens, 1981—; bd. dirs. Voice of Reason, 1982—. With USAF, 1943-45; ETO. Recipient Disting. Grad. Faculty award Wayne State U., 1986, Gershenson Disting. Faculty Fellow award, 1986, Sigma Xi Faculty Rsch. award, 1989-90 Lawrence M. Weiner award Wayne State U. Sch. Medicine Alumni Assn., 1995; grantee NSF,

NIH; pres. Wayne State U. Acad. of Scholars, 1991. Fellow Am. Acad. Arts & Scis.; mem. Soc. Systematic Zoology, Am. Assn. Anatomists, Soc. for Study Evolution, Genetics Soc. Am., Am. Naturalist Soc. Home: 24211 Oneida St Oak Park MI 48237-1749 Office: Wayne State U Sch Medicine 540 E Canfield St Detroit MI 48201-1928

GOODMAN, MYRNA MARCIA, school nurse; b. Bklyn., Mar. 5, 1936; d. Louis and Anna R. (Bernowitz) Sheinberg; m. Stanley M. Goodman, June 30, 1957; children: Farrell Jay, Blayne Barrie, Devin Josh, Danica Janine. Diploma, L.I. Coll. Hosp., Bklyn., 1956; B in Elected Studies, Thomas More Coll., 1980; postgrad., Xavier U., 1984-86. Cert. sch. nurse, Ohio. Sch. nurse, supr. health and wellness svcs. L.I. Coll. Hosp., 1956-58; nurse, office mgr. Pediatric Assocs. of Fairfield (Ohio), Inc., 1962-72; nurse Fairfield City Sch. Dist., 1972-89, dir. health svcs., 1989-92, supr. health and wellness svcs., 1992—, sch. nurse Kindergarten Ctr., 1995; sch. nurse Kindergarten Ctr.; sec. Fairfield City Safety Coun., 1987-90; mem. Intervention Team for At-Risk Students, 1987-90, 95-96, Del. to Study Sch. Health, Australia, 1989; keynote spkr. Ohio Comprehensive Sch. Health Conf., 1991; conf. spkr. Ohio Assn. Health, Phys. Edn., Recreation and Dance, 1990, Nat. Sch. Bds. Assn., 1993. Mem. adv. coun. on drug free schs. and cmty. Butler County Mental Health Assn., 1988; chmn. sch. site com. Am. Heart Assn., 1981, coord. heart-at-work program; chmn. employee wellness com., spkr. del. assembly Ohio affiliate, 1992, pres., 1995, co-pres. Hamilton-Fairfield div., 1995, mem. adv. com. for county practical nurse program, 1994-95; pres. Fairfield Tempo Club, 1976; com. mem. Fairfield Sister City Program; mem. Modern Music Masters, 1976; mem. adv. coun. Daytime Ctr. for Girls; bd. dirs. Greater Hamilton Safety Coun., 1988; mem. adv. com. Fairfield Pub. Presch.; chmn. adv. com. Fairfield Schs. Food Svc. Recipient Outstanding Svc. award Fairfield Cen. Sch., 1974, 77, 78, 89, Letters of Recognition for Outstanding Svc. to Fairfield Sch. Dist. Supt., 1980, 86, 89, 90, March of Dimes, Am. Lung Assn., 1980, Am. Heart Assn., 1988, 89, 90, Hall of Fame award Am. Heart Assn., 1992, co-recipient Cert. of Appreciation, Am. Heart Assn. Sch. Site Task Force, 1992. Mem. NEA, ASCD, Ohio Edn. Assn., Ohio Assn. Sch. Nurses (conf. speaker 1993), S.W. Ohio Sch. Nurses Assn. (sec. 1987-90), Am. Sch. Health Assn., Nat. Assn. Sch. Nurses, Parents and Tchrs. for Children, Ohio Assn. Secondary Sch. Adminstrs., Nat. Assn. Secondary Sch. Adminstrs. Home: 5180 Suwannee Dr Fairfield OH 45014-2482 Office: Fairfield City Sch Dist 211 Donald Dr Fairfield OH 45014-3006

GOODMAN, ROBIN FERN, therapist, psychologist, educator; b. Hartford, Conn., Dec. 3, 1955; d. Morris and Sarah Frances (Buchman) G. BA magna cum laude, Smith Coll., 1977; MA in Art Therapy, NYU, 1979; PhD in Clin. Psychology, Adelphi U., 1989. Rsch. asst. Smith Coll., 1976-77; tchg. asst. Adelphi U., 1986-88; art therapist Edwin Gould Svcs., Bronx, N.Y., 1979-80, Bronx (N.Y.) Children's Psychiat. Hosp., 1979-82; child life specialist Mt. Sinai Hosp., N.Y.C., 1982-85; psychology clk. Interfaith Hosp., Bklyn., 1985-86; cons. Sheltering Arms, N.Y.C., 1987; instr. Assn. per la Prerzione e lo Studio del Disagio Esisterziale, Torino, Italy, 1988; intern Bellevue Hosp., N.Y.C., 1988-89; psychologist NYU Med. Ctr., N.Y.C., 1989-94, sr. psychologist, 1994—; adj. assoc. prof. NYU, 1985-94; adj. faculty Vt. Coll., 1985-90, lectr., 1991—; vis. isntr. A.D.E.G., Torino, Italy, 1988; acting dir. grad. art therapy program NYU, 1990. Exhibited graphics in group shows, 1974-79; published in field; mem. editorial bd. Am. Jour. Art Therapy, 1994—. Recipient rsch. prize Adelphi U., 1990. Mem. Am. Art Therapy Assn. (membership comn. 1981-85, pres.-elect 1989-91, pres. 1991-93), N.Y. Art Therapy Assn. (bd. dirs., membership chmn. 1978-80, chmn. govt. affairs 1979-83), Phi Beta Kappa, Psi Chi.

GOODMAN, STANLEY ERWIN, surgeon; b. Norwalk, Conn., May 4, 1926; s. Robert M. and Francine (Cotler) G.; BS, Trinity Coll., Hartford, 1947; MA, U. Pa., 1949; MD, Cornell U., 1953; m. Alice Marie Vanderbecq, June 20, 1962; m. 2d, Francine Joan. Intern, Strong Meml. Hosp., Rochester, N.Y., 1953-54; asst. resident surgery Mt. Sinai Hosp., N.Y.C., 1954-55; asst. resident surgery Kings County Hosp., Bklyn., 1955-58, chief resident surgery, 1958-59, attending surgeon vascular service and breast tumor bd., 1959—; research asst. State U. N.Y. Med. Sch., Bklyn., 1956-57; gen. surgery practice, Norwalk, 1959-88; sr. attending surg. staff Norwalk Hosp., former chief sect. neoplastic diseases; asst. instr. SUNY Med. Sch., 1956-57, instr. clin. surgery, 1959-87; bd. regional advisors People's Bank Bridgeport, Conn. Bd. dirs. So. Fairfield County unit Am. Cancer Soc.; bd. regional advs. Norwalk Tech. Coll.; bd. dirs. Greater Norwalk Community Council. Served with USNR, 1944-46, Diplomate Am. Bd. Surgery. Fellow ACS; mem. AAAS, Royal Soc. Health, Pan Am. Med. Assn., Norwalk Med. Soc. (past pres.), N.Y. Acad. Medicine, Am. Heart Assn. Home: 40 Pequot Trl Westport CT 06880-2931

GOODMAN, STUART B., medical educator; b. Toronto, May 15, 1951; married. BS, U. Toronto, 1974, MD, 1978; MS, Inst. Med. Sci./U. Toronto, 1982. Diplomate Am. Bd. Orthopaedic Surgery. Intern Toronto Gen. Hosp., 1978-79; resident orthopaedic surgery U. Toronto, 1979-84; rsch. fellow Hosp. for Sick Children, Toronto, 1979-80; orthopaedic arthritis and trauma fellow Wellesley Hosp./Sunnybrook Med. Ctr., Toronto, 1984-85; acting asst. prof., attending orthopaedic surgeon Stanford U. and Med. Ctr., 1985, asst. prof., attending orthopaedic surgeon, 1985-92; chief of orthopaedic trauma, asst. dir. surg. arthritist Stanford U. Med. Ctr., 1986-90, assoc. faculty - biomechan. engrng. program, 1990—, assoc. prof. with tenure, dept. function restoration, 1992—; head Divns. of Orthopedic Surgery Stanford U. Sch. Medicine, 1994—; vis. prof./lectr. numerous orgns. including Harrington Arthritis Rsch. Symposium, Scottsdale, Ariz., 1990, U. Lund, Sweden, 1991, Fifth Internat. Con. on Surface Technologies, Birmingham, U.K., 1992, U. Gothenberg, Sweden, 1991, Ctr. for Implant Surgery/Bnai Zion Med. Ctr. and Technion U., Haifa, Israel, 1992, Internat. Knee Course, Zell am See, Austria, 1993, others. Editl. bd. Orthopaedic Capsule and Comment, 1990-92, Jour. of Arthroplasty, The Joint Letter; reviewer jours. in field; contbr. articles to profl. jours. and pubs. Fellow Am. Coll. Surgeons, Am. Acad. Orthopaedic Surgeons; mem. Royal Coll. Physicians and Surgeons of Can., Can. Orthopaedic assn., Ont. Med. Assn., Can. Med. Assn., Calif. Orthopaedic Assn., Santa Clara Orthopaedic Assn., Calif. Med. Assn., Santa Clara Med. Assn. Office: Stanford Med Ctr Divsn Ortho Surg Sch of Medicine R-144 Stanford CA 94305-5341*

GOODMAN, TERRY CARL, health facility administrator; b. Syracuse, N.Y., Oct. 23, 1946; s. Harold and Zelda (Sack) G.; m. Barbara Steinman, Oct. 14, 1984; children: Lisa, Kara. BS, Syracuse U., 1970, MBA, 1974. Supr. ctrl. svc. Cmty. Gen. Hosp., Syracuse, 1971-76; exec. dir., CEO Jewish Home of Ctrl. N.Y., Syracuse, 1976-83; adminstr., CEO Swanholm Nursing & Rehab. Ctr., St. Petersburg, Fla., 1983-86; assoc. exec. dir., COO Miami (Fla.) Jewish Home & Hosp., 1986—, CEO, 1996—; chmn. Fla. Bd. Nursing Home Adminstrs., Tallahassee. Mem. Am. Coll. Nursing Home Adminstrs., Am. Coll. Health Care Adminstrs., Fla. Health Care Assn., Fla. Assn. Homes for the Aged. Home: 10786 SW 74th Ave Miami FL 33156 Office: Miami Jewish Home & Hosp 5200 NE Second Ave Miami FL 33156

GOODMAN, VALERIE DAWSON, psychiatric social worker; b. Bluefield, W.Va., Feb. 2, 1948; d. Francis Carl and Lesly (Collett) Dawson; m. David William Goodman, June 9, 1985; 1 child, Amanda Lynn. BS, W.Va. U., 1970, MS, 1972; MSW, U. Md., 1980. Lic. clin. social worker, Md. Social worker Md. Children's Aide Family Svcs. Soc., Balt., 1972-78; social worker III Montgomery County Dept. Social Svcs., Rockville, Md., 1980-81; clin. social worker Johns Hopkins Hosp., Balt., 1981-83; pvt. practice Suburban Psychiat. Assoc. Hopkins at Greenspring Station, Balt., 1986—; supr. Johns Hopkins Hosp., 1983-86, chair Brogden com., 1984-85, spl. events com. depression and related affective disorders dept. psychiatry, 1994; spkr. in field. Parent vol. Park Sch. Mem. Kappa Delta. Home: 54 Bellchase Ct Pikesville MD 21208-1300 Office: Suburban Psychiat Svc Md Adult Ctr ADD Johns Hopkins at Greenspring Sta Falls Concourse Falls Rd Ste 306 Lutherville MD 21093

GOODMAN, WARREN H., psychiatrist; b. N.Y.C., Nov. 10, 1935; m. Beverly Hallquist, Nov. 27, 1970; 3 children. BA, Columbia Coll., 1955; MD, SUNY, N.Y.C., 1959, cert. in psychoanalysis, 1976. Diplomate Am. Bd. Psychiatry and Neurology; cert. in psychiatry. Intern Montefiore Hosp., N.Y.C., 1959-60; resident in psychiatry Bellevue Hosp., N.Y.C., 1960-61, Hillside Hosp., Queens, N.Y., 1961-53; clin. asst. prof. Cornell U. Med. Coll., N.Y.C., 1977—; clin. asst. prof. psychiatry AECOM Albert Einstein Coll. Medicine, N.Y.C., 1988—; clin. asst. prof. psychiatry NYU Coll. Medicine, 1980—; attending psychiatrist L.I. Jewish Med. Ctr., Dept. Psychiatry, Queens, N.Y., 1965—, North Shore U. Hosp., Manhasset, N.Y., 1977—. Author book revs. Psychoanalutic Quar., 1980—. Comdr. USPHS, 1967-69. Fellow Am. Psychiat. Assn., Nassau Acad. Medicine; mem. AMA, Am. Psychoanalytic Assn., Nassau Psychiat. Assn. (pres. 1983-84), L.I. Psychoanalytic Assn., Psychoanalytic Assn. of N.Y. Home and Office: 3 Weigt Ct Great Neck NY 11021-1618

GOODNICK, PAUL JOEL, psychiatrist; b Phila., Sept. 29, 1950. BA magna cum laude, U. Pa.; MD with honors, SUNY Downstate Med. Ctr., Bklyn. Diplomate Am. Bd. Psychiatry and Neurology. Resident Washington U., St. Louis, Mo., Columbia U., N.Y.C.; fellow Mt. Sinai Hosp., N.Y.C.; asst. prof. psychiatry Wayne State U., Detroit, 1980-81, U. Chgo., 1981-84, Columbia U., N.Y.C., 1984-87; asst. prof. psychiatry U. Miami, Fla., 1987-89, clin. assoc. prof. psychiatry, 1989-90, assoc. prof., 1990-93, prof., 1993—, dir. mood disorders program, dept. psychiatry, 1989—; dir. outpatient svcs. and affective disorders program Fair Oaks Hosp., Boca/Delray, Fla., 1987-90; cons. APA, 1991. Assoc. editor jour. Lithium, 1989—; editor: Chronic Fatigue and Related Immune Deficiency Syndromes, 1992, Predictors of Response in Mood Disorders, 1994, Mania, 1996. Mem. nat. adv. bd. Jerusalem Health Ctr. Recipient Clin. Excellence award N.Y. Alliance for Mentally Ill, 1987. Fellow Am. Psychopathological Assn., Am. Psychiat. Assn.; mem. Soc. Biol. Psychiatry, N.Y. Acad. Sci., AAAS, Am. Acad. Clin. Psychiatry, KP. Office: U Miami Dept Psychiatry 1400 NW 10th Ave Ste 304 Miami FL 33136-1000

GOODNUFF, JEFFREY LYNN, ophthalmologist; b. Detroit, June 2, 1941; s. Earl and Catherine (Finney) G.; m. Margie Lucile Williams, Aug. 26, 1967; 1 child, David. BS in Engring., Mich. State U., 1962, MS in Engring., 1963, PhD in Engring., 1967, MD, 1979. Diplomate Am. Bd. Ophthalmology. Asst. prof. Mich. State U., East Lansing, 1966-68; sr. rsch. engr. autonetics divsn. Rockwell Internat., Anaheim, Calif., 1968-75; chief resident Beaumont Hosp., Royal Oak, Mich., 1982; pvt. practice ophthalmologist St. Paul, 1983—; cons. in vision stds. Unisys Corp., St. Paul, 1985-87, State of Minn., St. Paul, 1995. Troop advancement chmn. Boy Scouts Am., Edina, Minn., 1983-93. Fellow ACS; mem. AMA, Minn. Med. Assn., Minn. Acad. Ophthalmology, St. Paul Ophthalmology Soc. (pres. 1985), Ramsey County Med. Soc., Phi Kappa Phi, Tau Beta Pi, Eta Kappa Nu. Office: 1076 N 7th St Saint Paul MN 55102

GOODPASTURE, JESSIE CARROL, research executive; b. Oak Park, Ill., Nov. 27, 1952; d. James Slocum and Elizabeth Virginia (Goddard) G. BA, So. Ill. U., 1973, MS, 1975; PhD, U. Ill., Chgo., 1979. Rsch. asst. U. Ill. Med. Ctr., Chgo., 1976-80; asst. prof. Sch. Medicine U. Essen, Germany, 1980-81; staff rschr. I Syntex Rsch., Palo Alto, Calif., 1981-83, staff rschr. II, 1983-89, clin. program dir., 1989-92; leader Drug Devel. Optimization Program, 1992-93, sr. clin. program dir., 1992-94, dir. clin. rsch., 1994-95; dir. ops. BRI Internat., Inc., South San Francisco, Calif., 1996, exec. dir. West coast, 1996—; cons. NuCapital Access Group, Oakland, Calif., 1993—, Brooks Comms., Belmont, Calif., 1993—; mem. fellowships award panel AAUW, Washington, 1988—. Author: (with others) Reversal of Sterilization, 1978, IUD Technology, 1982, Long Acting Contraceptive Delivery Systems, 1984, Male Contraception: Advances and Future Prospects, 1986, Advances in the Study of GnRH Analogues, 1992; contbr. articles to profl. jours. Scholar So. Ill. U., 1971-73, U. Ill., 1975-79. Mem. Internat. Soc. Andrology, Am. Soc. Andrology, Am. Fertility Soc., Endocrine Soc. Home: 12 Antique Forest Ln Belmont CA 94002-2308

GOODRICH, ISAAC, neurosurgeon, educator; b. Milledgeville, Ga., Sept. 19, 1939; s. Ellis and Frieda (Bergman) G.; m. Dianne L. Brittain, Aug. 28, 1965; children: Mindy Ann, Scott David, Jennifer Gale. AA, Ga. Mil. Coll., 1959; BS, U. Ga., 1961; MD, Med. Coll. Ga., 1964. Cert. Am. Bd. Neurol. Surgery. Intern, Columbia-Presbyn. Med. Center, N.Y.C., 1964-65, resident in neurosurgery, Yale-New Haven Med. Center, 1967-71; practice medicine specializing in neurosurgery, New Haven, 1971—; instr. neurosurgery, Yale U. Med. Sch., 1970-71, asst. clin. prof., 1978-86; assoc. clin. prof., 1986—; attending neurosurgeon Yale-New Haven Hosp., 1973—, Hosp. St. Raphael, 1971—; mem. courtesy staff Milford Hosp., 1986—; cons. staff Vets. Meml. Med. Ctr., 1986—, VA Hosp., West Haven, 1990—, Griffin Hosp., 1992—; attn. staff St. Mary's Hosp., 1995—. Served as capt., U.S. Army, 1965-67. Decorated Bronze Star, Air Medal; recipient Disting. Alumni award Ga. Mil. Coll., 1980. Fellow ACS, Internat. Coll. Surgeons, Royal Soc. Medicine; mem. AMA (Physicians Recognition award for Continuing Med. Edn. 1969, 72, 75, 78, 81, 85, 88, 91, 94), Congress of Neurol. Surgeons, New Eng. Neurosurg. Soc., Pan Pacific Surg. Assn., Am. Assn. Neurol. Surgeons, Conn. State Neurol. Soc., Conn. State Med. Soc., New Haven City, New Haven County med. assns., AAAS, N.Y. Acad. Scis. Jewish. Designated hon. citizen, Boys Town, Nebr., 1971; contbr. articles, papers to med. publs., meetings. Home: 264 Rimmon Rd Woodbridge CT 06525-1847 Office: 60 Temple St New Haven CT 06510-2716

GOODRICH, JAMES TAIT, neuroscientist, pediatric neurosurgeon; b. Portland, Ore., Apr. 16, 1946; s. Richard and Gail (Josselyn) G.; m. Judy Loudin, Dec. 27, 1970. Student, Golden West Coll., 1971-72; A.A., Orange Coast Coll., 1972; B.S. cum laude, U. Calif.-Irvine, 1974; M.Phil., Columbia U., 1979, Ph.D., 1970 M.D., 1980; Diplomate Am. Bd. Neurological Surgery. Neuroscientist, pediatric neurosurgeon N.Y. Neurol. Inst., N.Y.C., 1981-86; dir. div. pediatric neurosurgery Albert Einstein Coll. Medicine, N.Y.C., 1986—, assoc. prof. neurological surgery, pediatrics, plastics and reconstructive surgery, 1992—. Contbr. articles to profl. jours. Recipient Roche Labs. award in neuroscis., 1978, Mead-Johnson award, 1978, Bronze medal Alumni Assn. Coll. Physicians and Surgeons, 1980, Sandoz award for outstanding research, 1980; Willamette Industries scholar; NIH grantee. Fellow Royal Soc. Medicine (London); mem. Internat. Soc. Pediatric Neurosurgeons, Worshipful Soc. Apothecaries (London), N.Y. Acad. Medicine (Melicow award 1980), Am. Assn. History of Medicine (Sir William Osler medal 1977-78), AMA, Brit. Brain Research Assn., European Brain Research Assn., Friends of Columbia U. Libraries, Friends of Osler Library of McGill U., N.Y. Acad. Scis., Am. Assn. Neurol. Surgeons, Am. Assn. Neurological Surgery (chmn. sect. on history of neurological surgery), Congress Neurol. Surgeons, Med. History Soc. N.J., ISIS History of Sci. Soc., Soc. for Bibliography of Natural History (London), Columbia Presbyn. Med. Soc., U. Calif. Alumni Assn., Soc. Ancient Medicine, AAAS, Am. Osler Soc., Les Amis du Vin, South Coast Wine Explorers Club (past chmn.), Friends of Bacchus Wine Club (past chmn.), Dionysius Council of Presbyn. Hosp. of N.Y.C., Sigma Xi, Alpha Gamma Sigma. Research on neuronal regeneration, brain reconstruction and craniofacial reconstruction. Home: 125 Tweed Blvd Grandview NY 10960 Office: Albert Einstein Coll Medicine Montefiore Med Ctr Div Pediatric Neurosurgery New York NY 10457

GOODRICH, SAMUEL MELVIN, obstetrician, gynecologist; b. Milledgeville, Ga., May 4, 1936; s. Ellis and Frieda (Bergman) G.; m. Ellen Schneider, Mar. 31, 1971; children: Jason Alexander, Harriet Schneider, Ashley Ann, Rachel Leigh. BS, U. Ga., 1957; MD, Med. Coll. of Ga., Augusta, 1961. Diplomate of Am. Bd. Ob-Gyn. Asst. prof. ob-gyn Med. Coll. of Ga., 1968-69; pvt. practice ob-gyn Milledgeville Ob-Gyn, 1969—; asst. clin. prof. Med. Coll. of Ga., 1969—; bd. dirs. First Nat. Bank Baldwin County, Milledgeville. Maj. U.S. Army Med. Corps, 1966-68. Mem. Ga. State Ob-Gyn Soc. (pres. 1978-79, chmn. sect. 1985-88), South Atlantic Assn. Ob-Gyn (v.p. 1992-94, pres. 1994-95), So. Med. Assn. (sec. gynecol. sect. 1989—, sect. chmn. 1996), Med. Coll. Ga. Medicine Alumni (pres.-elect 1990-91, pres. 1991-92). Home and Office: Milledgeville Ob-Gyn Assocs 750 N Cobb St Milledgeville GA 31061-2390

GOODRIDGE, ALAN GARDNER, research biochemist, educator; b. Peabody, Mass., Apr. 2, 1937; s. Lester Elmer and Gertrude Edith (Gardner) G.; m. R. Ann Funderburk, Aug. 19, 1960; children—Alan Gardner, Jr., Bryant C. B.S. in Biology, Tufts U., 1958; M.S. in Zoology, U. Mich., 1963, Ph.D. in Zoology, 1964. Rsch. fellow dept. biochemistry Harvard Med. Sch., Boston, 1964-66; asst. prof. physiology U. Kans. Med. Ctr., Kansas City, 1966-68; assoc. prof. Banting and Best dept. med. rsch. U. Toronto, Ont., Can., 1968-76; prof. Banting and Best dept. med. rsch. U. Toronto, 1976-77; prof. pharmacology and biochemistry Case Western Res. U., Cleve., 1977-87; prof., head dept. biochemistry U. Iowa, 1987-96; prof. biochemistry, dean coll. biol. scis. Ohio State U., 1996—. Assoc. editor Jour. Biol. Chemistry, 1990—, Ann. Rev. of Biochemistry, 1994—, Jour. Lipid Rsch., 1995—; contbr. numerous articles to profl. jours. Served with USN, 1958-61. Grantee Med. Rsch. Coun. Can., 1968-77, NIH, 1966-68, 77—; Josiah Macy Jr. faculty scholar, 1975-76, USDA, 1986-90, 93—. Mem. AAAS, Am. Soc. Biochemistry and Molecular Biology, Thyroid Assn., Assn. Med. and Grad. Sch. Depts. Biochemistry (treas. 1990-92, pres.-elect 1993, pres. 1994). Home: 844 W Orange Rd Powell OH 43081 Office: Ohio State U Coll Biol Scis Columbus OH 43210-1293

GOODSON, BENNIE, physician assistant; b. Montgomery, Ala., Apr. 7, 1950; s. Raymond and Priscilla (Wallace) G.; m. Eunice Irvin, June 6, 1970; children: LeCheryl Y., Sharon L., Monica D. BS, Ala. State U., 1980; B in Med. Sci., Emory U., 1987. Cert. physician asst., Ala. Adj. prof. biology Troy State U., Montgomery, Ala., 1980-81; mental health technician State of Ala., Montgomery, 1981-85; physician asst. Surg. Clinic Inc., Opelika, Ala., 1987—. Named Outstanding Young Man of Am., 1988. Fellow Am. Acad. Physician Assts., Ala. Soc. Physician Assts. Republican. Home: 7144 Stamford Ct Montgomery AL 36117

GOODSON, SHANNON LORAYN, behavioral scientist, author; b. Beaumont, Tex., May 26, 1952; d. James Ernest and Lorayn (Miller) G. BS in Psychology, Lamar U., 1974, MS in Organizational Psychology, 1977. Co-founder, pres., CEO Behavioral Scis. Rsch. Press Inc., Dallas, 1979-92, pres., 1992—; presenter in field; guest on various radio talk shows. Co-author: (with G.W. Dudley) Earning What You're Worth?, 1992, Psychology of Call Reluctance, 1986; contbr. articles to profl. jours. and periodicals. Mem. SE Psychol. Assn. Office: Behavioral Scis Rsch Press 12803 Demetra Dr Ste 100 Dallas TX 75234-6101

GOODSTEIN, DANIEL BELA, oral and maxillofacial surgeon, consultant, educator; b. Bklyn., Oct. 27, 1937; s. Charles Benjamin and Florence Ann (Apfel) G.; B.A., U. Conn., 1959; D. Dental Medicine, Tufts U., 1963; postgrad. in oral surgery N.Y. U., 1964-65; m. Myra Goldberg, 1992; children: Kimberly Joy, Kara Hope, Lauren Faith, Marni Claire. Intern in oral and maxillofacial surgery Queens Hosp. Center, 1963-64, resident, 1965-66, attending oral and maxillofacial surgeon, 1968—, mem. med. bd.; practice dentistry, specializing in oral and maxillofacial surgery, Hempstead, N.Y., 1969-88; staff oral surgeon L.I. Jewish Hillside Med. Center, 1968—; assoc. prof. clin. oral and maxillofacial surgery Sch. Dental Medicine, SUNY-Stony Brook; adj. assoc. clin. prof. Mt. Sinai Sch. Medicine; exec. cons. Ind. Med. Exam. Co., Levittown, N.Y., 1988-95. Served with AUS, 1966-68. Decorated Army Commendation medal. Diplomate Am. Bd. Oral and Maxillofacial Surgery. Fellow Internat. Assn. Oral and Maxillofacial Surgeons; mem. ADA, Am., N.Y. State, Soc. Oral and Maxillofacial Surgeons, Am. Assn. Dental Schs., N.Y. State Dental Soc., Nassau County Dental Soc., Alpha Omega Alpha, Phi Epsilon Pi. Club: Masons. Contbr. articles to profl. jours. Research on effect of surg. correction of facial deformities on speech. Home: 21 Solar Ln Searingtown NY 11507

GOODSTONE, ERICA MAE, sex therapist, psychotherapist, health and physical education educator; b. N.Y.C., Apr. 16, 1946; d. Morris Goodstone and Muriel (Carnel) Goodstone Schaeffer. BA, Queens Coll., 1966; MA, N.Y. U., 1970, PhD, 1983. Lic. mental health counselor, marriage counselor, massage therapist; cert. clin. mental health counselor, sex therapist, family therapist, Rubenfeld synergist, registered polarity practitioner, oriental bodywork therapist; diplomate Am. Bd. Sexology, Am. Acad. Pain Mgmt. Primary tchr. Pub. Sch. 219, Queens, N.Y., 1966-67; exec. sec. Gotham Rec. Co., N.Y.C., 1967; tchr. 4th grade Pub. Sch. 106K, Bklyn., 1967-68; tchr. phys. edn., Women's tennis varsity coach, women's gymnastics varsity coach, Bayside H.S., Queens, 1969-74; prof. health and phys. edn. Fashion Inst. Tech., N.Y.C., 1974—; women's athletic dir., women's varsity tennis coach Fashion Inst. Tech., N.Y.C., 1974-82. adj. lectr. Kingsborough C.C., Bklyn., 1971-73, Manhattan C.C., 1983-85; pvt. practice sexual counseling, body psychotherapy. Mem. ACA, Soc. Sci. Rsch. Sex Therapy & Rsch., Sex. Edn. & Info. Counseling U.S., Nat. Assn. Rubenfeld Synergists, Polarity Therapy Assn., Am. Oriental Bodywork Therapy Assn., Am. Bd. Sexology, Assn. Humanistic Psychology, U.S. Assn. Body Psychotherapy, Am. Mental Health Counselors Assn., Am. Massage Therapy Assn., N.Y. State Soc. Med. Massage Therapists. Jewish. Contbr. articles to mags. Office: Fashion Inst Tech 227 W 27th St New York NY 10001-5902

GOODWIN, ANDREW WIRT, II, radiologist; b. Oil City, Pa., Feb. 4, 1932; s. Frank Bert and Florence Bickford (Green) G.; m. Anita Faye Adkins, May 27, 1987; children: Andrew, Victoria, Mary Elizabeth, Mark H., Martha J., Lisa R. BA, Colgate U., 1953; MD, U. Mich., 1957. Intern Mary Hitchcock Meml. Hosp., Hanover, N.H., 1957-58; resident in radiology Mayo Clinic, Rochester, Minn., 1958-62, resident, 1958-62; radiologist Associated Radiologists, Inc., Charleston, W.Va., 1961-86, Radiol. Assocs., Fairmont, W.Va., 1988—; pvt. practice, $D. Republican. Episcopalian. Home: 516 Shearwood Forest Dr Bridgeport WV 26330-1764 Office: Radiol Cons Assn 1000 Locust Ave Fairmont WV 26554-2409

GOODWIN, FREDERICK KING, psychiatrist; b. Cin., Apr. 21, 1936; s. Robert Clifford and Marion Cronin (Schmadel) G.; m. Rosemary Powers, Oct. 19, 1963; children: Kathleen Kelly, Frederick King, Daniel Clifford. B.S., Georgetown U., 1958; philosophy fellow, St. Louis U., 1958-59, M.D., 1963. Intern medicine and psychiatry SUNY, Syracuse, 1963-64; resident psychiatry U. N.C., Chapel Hill, 1964-65; commd. med. officer USPHS, 1965; clin. assoc. adult psychiatry br. NIMH, 1965-67; research fellow Lab. Biochemistry, Nat. Heart Inst., NIH, Bethesda, Md., 1967-68; chief sect. on psychiatry Lab. Clin. Sci., NIMH, Bethesda, 1970-77; chief clin. psychobiology br. Lab. Clin. Sci., NIMH, 1970-81, sci. dir., 1981-88; adminstr. Alcohol, Drug Abuse and Mental Health Adminstrn., Washington, 1988-92; pvt. practice medicine, specializing in psychiatry Bethesda, 1967—; dir. NIMH, Rockville, Md., 1992—; faculty George Washington U. Sch. Medicine, Washington Sch. Psychiatry, Uniformed U. Sch. Health Scis.; vis. prof. U. Calif., Irvine, U. Wis., Boston U., U. So. Calif., Duke U.; cons. AMA Council on Drugs; AIDS coordinator Alcohol, Drug Abuse and Mental Health Adminstrn., 1986—; participant pub. edn. programs on local and network television and radio. Author: (with K.R. Jamison) Manic-Depressive Illness, 1990 (Best Med. Book award 1990 Assn. Am. Pubsd.); editor in chief Psychiatry Research, 1979—; mem. editorial bd. Archives of Gen. Psychiatry, 1977—, Psychopharmacology, 1976-79; Contbr. articles to med. jours. Mem. adv. bd. Max Planck Inst., Munich, W. Ger. Recipient Psychopharmacology Research prize Am. Psychol. Assn., 1971, Internat. Anna Monica prize for research in depression, 1971, Taylor Manor award, 1976, Adminstrs. award HEW, 1977, Superior Service award USPHS, 1980, Strecker award, 1983, Sr. Exec. Service Presdl. Meritorious Rank award, 1982, Disting. Rank award, 1986, Disting. Exec. Service award Sr. Exec. Assn. Profl. Devel. League, 1986, Best Tchr. in Am. Psychiatry award CME Inc., 1989, Svc. to Sci. award Nat. Assn. for Biomed. Rsch., 1990, Pub. Svc. award. Fed. Am. Socs. for Exptl. BNiologhy, 1990, 1st recipient of Fawcett Humanitarian award NDMDA, 1990, McAlpin award NMHA, 1991; NIMH Spl. fellow, 1967-68. Fellow Am. Psychiat. Assn. (chmn. com. on protection of human subjects, task force on research tng., Hofheimer prize for research 1971, chmn. task force on future of psychiat. research), Am. Coll. Neuropsychopharmacology (chmn. com. on problems of public concern); mem. Inst. Medicine, Nat. Acad. Scis., AAAS, Am. Psychosomatic Soc., Soc. Biol. Psychiatry (A.E. Bennett award 1970), Am. Acad. Psychoanalysis, Soc. for Neuroscience, Psychiat. Research Soc., Washington Psychiat. Soc. (peer rev. com.). Club: Cosmos (Washington). Home: 5712 Warwick Pl Bethesda MD 20815-5502 Office: HHS NIMH 5600 Fishers Ln Rockville MD 20857-0001*

GOODWIN, JEAN MCCLUNG, psychiatrist; b. Pueblo, Colo., Mar. 28, 1946; d. Paul Stanley and Geraldine (Smart) McClung; m. James Simeon Goodwin, Aug. 8, 1970; children: Laura (dec.), Amanda Harding Goodwin, Robert Caleb, Paul Joshua, Elizabeth Cronin Goodwin. BA in Anthropology summa cum laude, Radcliffe Coll., 1967; MD, Harvard U., 1971; MPH, UCLA, 1972. Diplomate Am. Bd. Psychiatry and Neurology, Am. Bd. Forensic Psychiatry. Resident in psychiatry Georgetown U. Hosp., Washington, 1972-74; resident in psychiatry U. N.Mex. Sch. Medicine, 1974-76, asst. dir., dir. psychiat. residents tng., 1979-85; prof. Med. Coll. Wis., 1985-92, U. Tex. Med. Br., Galveston, 1992—; from inst. to assoc. prof. dept. psychiatry U. N.Mex. Sch. Medicine, 1976-85; cons. protective services Dept. Human Services, N.Mex., 1976-84; lectr. profl. groups. Author: Effects of High Altitude on Human Birth, 1969, Sexual Abuse: Incest Victims and Their Families, 1982, 2d edit., 1989, Rediscovering Childhood Trauma: Historical Casebook and Clinical Applications, 1993, Mischief and Mercy, 1993; mem. editl. bd. Jour. Traumatic Stress, 1985-93, Dissociation, 1988—; contbr. numerous articles on child abuse to profl. jours. Chmn. work group on child sexual abuse Surgeon Gen.'s Conference on Violence and Pub. Health, Leesburg, Va., 1985; mem. adv. bd. Nat. Resource Ctr. on Child Sexual Abuse, 1989-96. Recipient Saville Prize in Family Planning, UCLA Sch. Pub. Health, 1972, Esther Haar award Am. Acad. Psychoanalysis, 1990, Cornelia Wilbur award Internat. Soc. for Study of Dissociation, 1994; Nat. Cen. Child Abuse and Neglect grantee, 1979-82, Nat. Inst. Aging grantee, 1980-85. Fellow Internat. Soc. Study Dissociation (exec. com. 1991-96), Am. Psychiat. Assn. (dist. br. treas., sec. N.Mex. br. 1980-82, exhibits and programs subcoms. 1985-91); mem. Am. Profl. Soc. on Sexual Abuse in Children (bd. dirs. 1986-90), Am. Med. Women's Assn. (state dir. N.Mex. 1978-80). Democrat. Roman Catholic. Office: U Tex Med Br Dept Psychiatry and Behavioral Sci Galveston TX 77555

GOODWIN, JOEL FRANKLIN, SR., dentist; b. Shawnee, Okla., Sept. 9, 1924; s. Abb L. and Ethel Elizabeth (Broyles) G.; m. Betty Mashburn; children: Mary Carolyn, Joel Franklin Jr., John and Gene (twins). BS, Baylor U., 1951, DDS, 1952. Gen. practice dentistry Dallas, 1952—; instr. oral surgery Coll. Dentistry Baylor U., Dallas, 1952. Vice chmn. Dallas Mid-Winter Dental Clinic, 1961, gen. chmn., 1962; dental dir. United Fund, Dallas, 1966-67; sec. bd. trustees Baylor Coll. Dentistry, 1976-79, chmn. building com., 1971-77, trustee 1971-82; bd. dirs. War on Poverty, City of Dallas, 1966-67. Mem. Dallas County Dental Soc. (v.p. 1963-64, pres. 1966-67), Am. Coll. Dentists (Hon. degree 1968), Baylor U. Coll. Dentistry Alumni Assn. (v.p. 1985-86, sec., treas. 1954-85, pres. elect 1986-87, pres. 1987-88, trustee 1988-90, Disting. Svc. award 1969, Disting. Alumni award 1976), Dallas C. of C. (med. and dental coms. 1966-67). Baptist. Home: 6110 Sul Ross Ln Dallas TX 75214 Office: Baylor Doctors Bldg 3707 Gaston Ave Ste 716 Dallas TX 75246-1540

GOODWIN, MARK JAMES, cardiologist; b. Evergreen Park, Ill., Oct. 1, 1955; m. Maureen Goodwin; children: Christina, Lauren, Kevin, Shea. BA magna cum laude, Notre Dame U., 1977; MD, U. Ill., Chgo., 1981. Pvt. practice Midwest Heart Specialists, Naperville, Ill., 1986—; clin. asst. prof. medicine Loyola U., Maywood, Ill., 1989—. Fellow Am. Coll. Cardiology, Soc. for Cardiac Angiography, Am. Coll. Chest Physicians; mem. Am. Heart Assn., ACP, Am. Soc. Internal Medicine, Alpha Omega Alpha. Office: Midwest Heart Specialists 120 Spalding Dr Ste 206 Naperville IL 60540

GOODWIN, MARTIN BRUNE, radiologist; b. Vancouver, B.C., Can., Aug. 8, 1921; came to U.S., 1948; m. Cathy Dennison, Mar. 7, 1980; 1 child, Suzanne; stepchildren: Chuck Glikas, Dianna; 1 child from previous marriage, Nancijane Goodwin Hilling. BSA in Agriculture, U. B.C., 1943, postgrad., 1943-44; MD, CM, McGill U. Med. Sch., Montreal, Can., 1948. Diplomate Am. Bd. Med. Examiners, lic. Med. Coun. Can.; cert. diagnostic and therapeutic radiology Am. Bd. Radiology; cert. Am. Bd. Nuclear Medicine. Intern Scott & White Hosp., Temple, Tex., 1948-49; fellow radiology Scott & White Clinic, 1949-52, mem. staff, 1952-53; instr. U. Tex., Galveston, 1952-53; radiologist Plains Regional Med. Ctr., Clovis, N.Mex.; radiologist Plains Regional Med. Ctr., Portales, N.Mex., pres. med. staff; chief radiology De Baca Gen. Hosp., Ft. Sumner, N.Mex.; cons. Cannon AFB Hosp., Clovis; pvt. practice radiology Clovis, Portales, Ft. Sumner and Tucumcari, 1955—; adj. prof. health scis. Ea. N.Mex. U., 1976-77; adj. clin. prof. health scis. We. Mich. U., 1976-78. Apptd. N.Mex. Radiation Tech. Adv. Coun., N.Mex. Bd. Pub. Health; former chmn. N.Mex. Health and Social Svcs. Bd.; mem. Regional Health Planning Coun.; treas. Roosevelt County Rep. Ctrl. Com. Capt. U.S. Army M.C., 1953-55; Col. USAF M.C., 1975-79. Fellow AAAS, Am. Coll. Radiology, Am. Coll. Radiology (past councilor); mem. Am. Soc. Thoracic Radiologists (founder), Radiol. Soc. of N.Am. (past councillor), N.Mex. Med. Soc. (various coms., chmn. joint practice com., councillor bd. dirs.), N.Mex. Radiol. Soc. (past pres.), N.Mex. Thoracic Soc. (past pres.), N.Mex. Med. Review Assn. (bd. dirs. 1970-93), N.Mex. Med. Soc. Found. for Med. Care (bd. dirs. 1975—, former v.p., former treas.), County Med. Soc. (past pres., past v.p., past sec.), Clovis C. of C. (chmn. civic affairs com., bd. dirs.), Clovis Elks Lodge (past exalted ruler), Clovis Noonday Lions Club (past sec.). Republican. Presbyterian. Home: 505 E 18th St Portales NM 88130-9201 Office: Med Radiology Assocs 1001 Pile St Clovis NM 88101-5940

GOODWIN, MAURICE ROY, otolaryngologist, consultant; b. Bklyn., Nov. 28, 1911; s. Harris and Mary Goodwin; married, Sept. 21, 1933; children: Sheilah Helen, Lynne Ellen. BSc, NYU, 1928; MD, DDS, Vienna and Graz (Austria) U., 1931; postgrad., NYU, 1956-57. Diplomate Am. Bd. Otolaryngology. Cons. Our Lady of Mercy/Pelham Hosps., Bronx, 1961—; cons. in otolaryn. surgery Albert Einstein Coll. Hosp., Westchester Sq. Med. Ctr., Bronx, 1961—. Contbr. articles to profl. jours. Fellow ACS, Am. Acad. of Facial and Rconstructive Surgery, Am. Acad. of Otolaryn. and Head and Neck Surgery, Internat. Coll. Surgeons, Coll. Chest Physicians. Republican.

GOODWIN, PHILLIP HUGH, hospital administrator; b. Paragould, Ark., Sept. 10, 1940; s. Ray H. and Helen L. (Griffin) G.; m. Pamela J. Davis, June 24, 1962; children: Philip Grey, Julie Ann. BA in Bus. and Econs., Hendrix Coll., 1962; M in Hosp. Adminstrn., Washington U., St. Louis, 1968; LLD (hon.), U. Charleston, 1995. Bus. mgr. Stuttgart (Ark.) Meml. Hosp., 1962-64; asst. adminstr. Union Meml. Hosp., El Dorado, Ark., 1964-67; adminstrv. asst. to assoc. adminstr. Hillcrest Med. Ctr., Tulsa, 1968-77, v.p., adminstr., chief operating officer, 1977-82; exec. v.p. Charleston (W.Va.) Area Med. Ctr., 1982-87, pres., chief exec. officer, 1987—; adj. faculty Wash. U., St. Louis, W.Va. U., Med. Coll. Va., W.Va. Coll. Grad. Studies; bd. dirs. Auther B. Hodges Nursing Home, Charleston, One Valley Bank N.A., Charleston, One Valley BanCorp of W.Va.; frequent speaker ednl., profl. and bus. assns. Co-author: Time Management for Hospital Administrators; contbr. articles to profl. publs. Bd. dirs. Kanawha Hospice Inc., Charleston, 1987-89, W.Va. Bus. Roundtable, Wellness Coun. Am., Nat. Com. for Quality Health Care; vol. Mgmt. Assistance Program, Charleston, 1987-89, Nat. Inst. Chem. Studies, Charleston, 1988-91, Charleston Renisance Corp., Bus. and Industry Coun. of W.Va., Pvt. Industry Coun. of W.Va.; pres. Civitan Club, Tulsa, 1970. Fellow Am. Coll. healthcare Execs.; mem. W.Va. Hosp. Assn. (pres. 1987, 88), Am. Hosp. Assn. (ho. of dels. 1988—), Vol. Hosps. Am. (bd. dirs. 1978-82, bd. Wellness Coun. of Am. 1994), Charleston Ranaissance Soc., W.Va. C. of C., Charleston C. of C., Ducks Unltd., Berry Hill Country Club. Republican. Methodist. Office: Charleston Area Med Ctr PO Box 1547 Charleston WV 25326-1547

GOODWIN, R(OBIN) THAD, ophthalmologist; b. Bryan, Tex., Feb. 5, 1953; s. Robert Jennings and Mary Lee (Seitz) G. BS, William & Mary Coll., 1975; MD, U. N.C., 1979. Diplomate Am. Bd. Ophthalmology. Intern, resident U. Fla., Gainesville, 1979-83; pvt. practice opthalmology Ft. Myers, Fla., 1983—; adv. bd. mem. Visually Impaired Person Ctr., Ft. Myers, 1985—. Mem. Am. Acad. Ophthalmology, Fla. Med. Assn., Lee County Med. Soc. (chmn. grievance com. 1994—), Phi Beta Kappa, Alpha Omega Alpha. Republican. Office: Goodwin Eye Ctr 4755 Summerlin Rd #4 Fort Myers FL 33919

GOODWIN, SANDRA KIM SLUKA, nursing educator; b. Visalia, Calif., Sept. 14, 1959; d. Sherald Legor and Mary Ellen (Stromsodt) Sluka; m. Otis O'Neal Goodwin, Jr., Oct. 5, 1985. BSN, Calif. State U., Sacramento, 1982; instr. credential, U. Calif., Santa Cruz, 1988. RN, PHN. Operating rm. nurse Penrose Hosp., Colo. Springs, Colo., 1982-83; operating rm. nurse, infection control nurse, staff devel. nurse USAF, Castle AFB, Calif., 1983-86; clin. svcs. mgr. Merced (Calif.) Family Health Ctrs., Inc.; vocat. nursing instr. Merced (Calif.) Coll., 1987—, coord. student health svcs., 1995—; owner Lifeline Presentations, 1995—; seminar leader, speaker, health educator Merced, 1995. Literacy tutor Merced County Adult Literacy Ctr., 1995. 1st lt. USAF, 1983-86. Mem. Am. Seminar Leaders Assn., Calif. Vocat. Nurse Educators, Toastmasters Internat. Republican. Roman Catholic. Home: 3855 De Paul Ct Merced CA 95348 Office: Merced Coll 3600 M St Merced CA 95348

GOODWIN, SHARON, nurse, psychiatric consultant, therapist; b. N.Y.C., Oct. 19, 1944; d. Orland and Grace (Doonan) G. R.N., St. Louis City Hosp., 1965; Lic. chem. dependency coun. Psychiat. Assoc., Mo. Inst. Psychiatry, St. Louis, 1971. Staff nurse St. Louis City Hosp., 1965-66, head nurse isolation, 1966-67, head nurse psychiatry, 1966-68, community psychiatry developer, 1967-81; dir. nursing Fairground Nursing Home, St. Louis, 1970-71; asst. dir. med. program Community Placement Program, St. Louis, 1972-79; asst. dir., med. advisor Places for People, St. Louis, 1979-82; dir. outpatient alcoholism treatment program, St. Joseph Hosp., Houston, 1982-87, private practice Houston, 1987—; geriatric specialist chemical dependency counselor U. Houston, 1985-87; community psychiatry cons. Mo. Mental Health Div., St. Louis, 1979-82; community psychiatry trainer U. Mo. Social Work, St. Louis, 1981-82; bd. dirs., clin. advisor The Gathering Place Rehab Ctr.; founder, dir. The Recovery Collective; founder Women in New Growth Sobriety. Presenter Washington U. Social Services Dept., St. Louis, 1976-81. Mem. Internat. Assn. Psychosocial Rehab. Centers (presenter 1977), Tex. Assn. Drug & Alcohol Counselors (mem. chairperson, state rep.). Home: 5501 Valerie St Houston TX 77081-7303

GOODWIN, S(HEILA) DIANE, drug information scientist; b. Durham, N.C., Jan. 19, 1958; d. Leon Jackson and Mattie (Wilson) G. BS in Pharmacy, U. N.C., 1981; PharmD, Med. Coll. Va., 1986. Registered pharmacist, N.C., Va., Colo. Staff pharmacist Durham (N.C.) County Gen. Hosp., 1981-84; asst. prof. U. Fla. Coll. Pharmacy, Gainesville, 1988-89; clin. rsch. pharmacist Duke U. Med. Ctr., Ctr. AIDS Rsch., Durham, 1990-91; asst. prof. U. Colo., Sch. Pharmacy, Denver, 1991-94; drug info. sci. Burroughs Wellcome Co., Research Triangle Park, N.C., 1994-95; mgr. HIV/herpes program devel. Care Mgmt. divsn. Glaxo Wellcome, Inc., Research Triangle Park, 1995—; cons., reviewer, researcher, lectr. in field. Contbr. articles to profl. and sci. jours. Clin. pharmacy fellow Duke U. Med. Ctr., 1986-87, Millard Fillmore Hosp., 1987-88. Mem. Am. Coll. Clin. Pharmacy (chmn. pub. and profl. rels. com. 1991-92, Schering rsch. grantee 1990, chmn. pubs. com. 1996), Am. Soc. Health Sys. Pharmacists, Am. Soc. Microbiology, Soc. Infectious Diseases Pharmacists, Am. Pharm. Assn., Am. Soc. Clin. Pharmacology and Therapeutics, Kappa Epsilon, Rho Chi. Democrat. Baptist. Office: Glaxo Wellcome Inc 5 Moore Dr Research Triangle Park NC 27709

GOODWIN, SUSAN TEFS, healthcare organization official, nurse; b. Milw., Feb. 16, 1953; d. William Samuel and Joan Shirley (Rewolinski) Tefs; m. Joseph Marshall Goodwin, June 1, 1985. BSN, U. S.C., 1976; MS in Nursing Adminstrn., Andrews U., 1989. RN, Fla.; cert. healthcare risk mgr., Fla. Staff nurse Denver Children's Hosp., 1976-77, Brackenridge Hosp., Austin, Tex., 1977-80; staff nurse, coord. quality assurance Children's Hosp. of Kings Daus., Norfolk, Va., 1980-85; dir. quality and risk mgmt. Humana Hosp.-Sun Bay, St. Petersburg, Fla., 1985-90; market dir. quality mgmt. Humana, Inc., Tampa, Fla., 1990-92; regional dir. quality mgmt. Galen Healthcare, Mobile, Ala., 1992-94; corp. dir. quality mgmt. Columbia/HCA Healthcare Corp., Nashville, 1994—; mem. clin. faculty Joint Commn. on Accreditation of Healthcare Orgns., Oakbrook Terrace, Ill., 1994-96. Contbr. articles to profl. publs. Troop leader Gulfcoast coun. Girl Scouts U.S.A., 1986-90; sec., bd. dirs. Easter Seal Soc. S.W. Fla., Sarasota, 1988-90; chmn. coun. ministries 1st United Meth. Ch., Palmetto, Fla., 1988-95; mem. Jr. League Manatee County, Fla., 1989—. Mem. Am. Coll. Healthcare Execs. (assoc.), Am. Soc. for Quality Control, Nat. Assn. for Healthcare Quality, Sigma Theta Tau, Phi Kappa Phi. Republican. Home: 904 23d Ave W Palmetto FL 34221 Office: Columbia/HCA Healthcare Corp One Park Plz Nashville TN 37202

GOODWIN, WILLIAM JARRARD, otolaryngologist, educator; b. Niagara Falls, N.Y., Nov. 9, 1948; s. William Jarrard and Alice Louise (Becker) G.; m. Sharon Brooks Gould, Aug. 29, 1970; children: Melissa, Amanda, Courtney. BS, Rensselaer Poly. Inst., 1970; MD, Union U., 1972. Intern Case Western Res. U., Cleve., 1972-73; resident U. Miami/Jackson Meml. Hosp., 1973-77; fellow M.D. Anderson Hosp. and Tumor Inst., 1979-80; asst. prof. U. Miami, Fla., 1980-85, prof., chmn. dept. otolaryngology, 1989—; assoc. prof. Yale U., New Haven, Conn., 1985-89; dir. Sylvester Comprehensive Cancer Ctr. U. Miami Hosp. and Clinics, 1993—. Mem. editl. bd. Laryngoscope, Ear, Nose and Throat Jour.; contbr. articles to profl. jours. and chpts. to books. Vol. Am. Cancer Soc., Conn., 1985-89, Fla., 1990—; mem. Fla. Cancer Control Bd., 1992—. Major USAF, 1977-79. Faculty clin. fellow Am. Cancer Soc., 1981-84. Fellow Am. Acad. Otolaryngology-Head and Neck Surgery (Honor award 1986), ACS, Am. Soc. for Head and Neck Surgery, Soc. Head and Neck Surgeons. Office: U Miami Hosp Clinics Ste 4037 1475 NW 12th Ave Miami FL 33136-1002

GOOLD, FLORENCE WILSON, occupational therapist; b. Chgo., Aug. 26, 1912; d. Frank Elmer and Marie Louise (Walker) Wilson; m. Robert Charles Goold, Dec. 28, 1938; children: Frances Louise Goold Felty, Nancy Jean Gould Magurno, Elizabeth Jane Ill, Robert Charles, Jr. Student, U. Wis., 1934; BA, Boston Sch. Occupational Therapy, 1936. Occupational therapist Ypsilanti (Mich.) State Hosp., 1936-40, Michael Reese Hosp., Chgo., 1940-42, DuPage County Easter Seal Ctr., Villa Park, Ill., 1959-62; dir. occupational therapy Hinsdale (Ill.) Sanitarium and Hosp., 1962-71, Marianjoy Rehab. Hosp., Wheaton, Ill., 1971-73, Cen. DuPage Hosp., Winfield, Ill., 1972-73, Royal Oak Convalescent Home, Oak Park, Ill., 1973, Highland House Nursing Home, Downers Grove, Ill., 1973-75, St. Charles Med. Ctr., Aurora, Ill., 1975-78, Westmont (Ill.) Health Ctr., 1978-80, Americana Health Care Ctr., Naperville, Ill., 1981-84, Med. Pers. Pool, Chgo., 1985-89, Midwest Rehab. Svcs., Hinsdale, 1986-95. Pres. bd. dirs. DuPage County Easter Seal Ctr., Villa Park, 1942-59; bd. dirs. Community Adult Day Care, Downers Grove, 1985-95. Named Citizen of Yr., Downers Grove, 1987. Mem. PEO, Am. Occupational Therapy Assn., Ill. Occupational Therapy Assn. (past pres., Occupational Therapist of Yr. 1988), Phi Mu. Episcopalian. Home: 6582 Willowwood Ct Downers Grove IL 60516-3045 Office: Ill Occupational Therapy Assn 715 Lake St Ste 710 Oak Park IL 60301-1416

GOOLKASIAN, PAULA A., psychologist, educator; b. Methuen, Mass., Aug. 9, 1948; d. Paul K. and Sadie T. (Touma) G.; m. Francis C. Martin, July 29, 1978; 1 child, Christopher. BA, Emmanuel Coll., 1970; MS, Iowa State U., 1972, PhD, 1974. Asst. prof. U. N.C., Charlotte, 1974-79, assoc. prof., 1979-85, prof. psychology, 1985—, pres. faculty, 1989—; cons. in field. Contbr. articles to profl. jours. Nat. Def. Ednl. Act. fellow, 1971-74; grantee NSF, NIH, and numerous others. Mem. AAAS, APA, Psychonomics Soc., Ea. Psychol. Assn., Internat. Soc. Psychophysics, Soc. for Computers in Psychology (sec.-treas. 1989-91, pres. 1994), Sigma Xi, Phi Kappa Phi. Home: 7107 Preston Ct Charlotte NC 28215-3625 Office: U NC Dept Psychology Charlotte NC 28223

GOOREY, NANCY JANE, dentist; b. Davenport, Iowa, May 8, 1922; d. Edgar Ray and Glenna Mae (Williams) Miller; m. Douglas B. Miller, Sept. 12, 1939 (div. 1951); children: Victoria Lee, Nickola Ellen, Douglas George, Melahna Marie; m. Louis Joseph Roseberry Goorey, Feb. 22, 1980. Student, Wooster (Ohio) Coll., 1939-40; DDS, Ohio State U., 1955. Cert. in gen. anesthesiology. Mem. faculty coll. dentistry Ohio State U., Columbus, 1955-86, dir., chmn. div. dental hygiene coll. dentistry, 1969-86, asst. dean coll. dentistry, 1975-86, mem. grad. faculty colls. dentistry and medicine, 1980—, asst. dean, prof. emeritus colls. dentistry and medicine, 1986—; moderator, prodn. chmn. Lifesavers 40 Prodns., 1981—. Producer, video program Giving Your Mouth a Sporting Chance, 1990, video Operation TACTIC. Chmn. State Planning Com. for Health Edn. in Ohio, Columbus, 1976-77, 87-88, 95—; founder, chmn. Coun. on Health Info., Columbus, 1981-85, pres., 1985-86; trustee Caring Dentists Found., Mayor's Drug Edn. and Prevention Program, Columbus, 1980—; mem. edn. com. Franklin County Rep. com., exec. com., 1993—; mem. human svcs. com. The Columbus Found. Recipient Vol. of Yr. award Columbus Health Dept., 1988-89, Dental Hygiene award Ohio State U., 1988. Fellow Am. Coll. Dentists (pres.-elect 1989-90), Am. Soc. Dental Anesthesiology, Internat. Coll. Dentists; mem. ADA (nat. consumer advisor 1975-78), Am. Assn. Dental Schs. (v.p., pres. 1972-77), Ohio Dental Assn. (cons. 1979—, mem. subcoun. on dentists concerned for dentists 1994—, chmn. subcoun. chem. dependency, Ohio Disting. Dentist 1983), Columbus Dental Soc. (pres. bd. dirs. 1986-87, 89-91, chmn. coun. on constn. and bilaws on jud. affairs 1989—), Ohio State U. Starling Womens Club (pres. 1982-83), Ohio State U. Faculty and Profl. Womens Club (pres. 1971-72), The Found. of the Acad. of Medicine (v.p. 1993-94), Ohio State Med. Assn. Alliance (chmn. state com. legis. affairs 1993-94, chmn. state health promotions com. 1994-95, v.p. 1995—), Acad. of Medicine Aux. (pres. 1992—), Omicron Kappa Upsilon (chmn. Sports Dentistry com. 1995—), The Columbus Found. (human svcs. com.), Caring Dentists Found. (trustee). Republican. Episcopalian. Office: Ohio State U Coll Dentistry 305 W 12th Ave Columbus OH 43210-1249

GOOS, FREDERICK ERNEST, bereavement coordinator; b. Newport News, Va., Sept. 2, 1944; s. Frederick Harry and Janet Louise (Snook) G.; m. Maxine Elaine Simmons, June 27, 1981; children: Andrew Mac, Jennifer Louise. BA cum laude, U. Pa., 1966; MDiv, Luth. Sch. Theology, 1970; D in Ministry, Ea. Bapt. Theol. Sem., 1982; MA, Temple U., 1991, PhD, 1996. Cert. Phila. Marriage Coun.; lic. N.J. Bd. Marriage Counselor Examiners. Pastor Christ Evang. Luth. Ch., Oley, Pa., 1970-72; tchr. Chestnut Assembly of God, Vineland, N.J., 1972-75; pastor Pilgrim Congl. Ch., Vineland, 1975-80; chaplain coord. Newcomb Med. Ctr., Vineland, 1980-90; tchg. asst. Temple U., Phila., 1990-94; family therapist So. Jersey Hosp. Sys., Bridgeton, N.J., 1993-95; pvt. practice family therapy N.J., 1990—; bereavement coord. Cumberland County Hospice (name changed to Hospice Care of South Jersey), Vineland, 1995—; mem. ethics com. N.J. Hospice Orgn., Scotch Plains, 1995—. Bd. mem. Bridgeton Nazarene Ch., 1995—. Mem. Phi Beta Kappa. Home: 42 So State St Vineland NJ 08360 Office: Hospice Care of South Jersey 2848 So Delsea Dr Vineland NJ 08360

GOOSKENS, ROBERT HENRICUS JOHANNUS, pediatric neurologist; b. Eindhoven, Brabant, The Netherlands, Nov. 4, 1948; s. Theo M. and Anne Elisabeth (Gimbrère) G. MD, U. Utrecht, The Netherlands, 1975, PhD, 1988. Resident in neurology Univ. Hosp. Utrecht, 1975-81, resident in clin. neurophysiology, 1981-82; rsch. child neurologist Univ. Children's Hosp., Utrecht, 1982-84, cons. child neurologist, 1984—; cons. child neurologist Psychiat. Child Clinic, Vught, The Netherlands, 1984—. Contbr. articles to med. jours. Rsch. grantee Prevention Fund The Netherlands, 1987. Mem. Dutch Child Neurology Soc. (bd. dirs. 1990—), Dutch Spina Bifida Soc. (sec. 1990—), Internat. Child Neurology Assn., Internat. Soc. Rsch. into Hydrocephalus and Spina Bifida, Internat. Cerebral Palsy Soc., European Ultrasound Soc. Roman Catholic. Home: Prins Hendriklaan 35, 3583 EC Utrecht The Netherlands Office: U Childrens Hosp Child Neur, Heidelberglaan 100, 3584CX Utrecht The Netherlands

GOOTMAN, PHYLLIS MYRNA, physiology, biophysics, educator; b. N.Y.C., June 8, 1938; d. Albert and Ida (Krieger) Adler; m. Norman Gootman, June 1, 1958; children: Sharon Hillary, Craig Seth. BA cum laude, Barnard Coll., 1959; PhD, Yeshiva U., 1967. Rsch. assoc. dept. physiology and biophysics U. Wash., Seattle, 1963; instr. dept. physiology Albert Einstein Coll. Medicine, Bronx, N.Y., 1968-70, asst. prof., 1970-73; asst. prof. SUNY, Bklyn., 1973-75, assoc. prof., 1975-81, prof., 1981—; vis. asst. prof. dept. physiology Albert Einstein Coll. Medicine, Bronx, 1973-76, vis. prof. dept. Physiology and Biophysics, 1984-92; mem. clin. campus, 1989—. Contbr. articles to profl. jours.; mem. editl. bd. Jour. of Development Physiology, 1986-95. Recipient Hendel Family award Brandeis U., 1957; John Miles Davidson fellow in physiology Albert Einstein Coll. Medicine, 1973; recipient numerous grants. Fellow Royal Soc. Medicine; mem. AAAS, Soc. for Neuroscis., Biophys. Soc., Am. PHysiol. Soc., Am. Heart Assn., Am. Inst. Biol. Scis., Am. Autonomic Soc. (exec. bd.), Microcirculatory Soc., Soc. for Exptl. Biology and Medicine, Am. Assn. Lab Animal Sci., Internat. Soc. for Devel. of Neuroscis. Office: SUNY Health Sci Ctr Bklyn Dept Physiology Box 31 450 Clarkson Ave Brooklyn NY 11203-2098

GOPALAKRISHNAKONE, PONNAMPALAM, medical educator; b. Jaffna, Ceylon, Sept. 23, 1945; arrived in Singapore, 1982; s. Kana and Poniah (Pakiam) Ponnnampalam; m. Balaranee Balasingham, July 28, 1976; 2 children. MBBS, U. Ceylon, 1971; PhD, U. London, 1979. Physician Ministry of Health, Ceylon, 1971-73; demonstrator, anatomy U. Ceylon, 1973-74, lectr. anatomy, 1974-76; rsch. scholar U. London, 1976-79; sr. lectr. U. Ceylon, 1979-82; sr. lectr. Nat. U. Singapore, 1982-91, assoc. prof., 1991—; chmn. Venom & Toxin Rsch. Group, Singapore, 1986—; cons. Poison Info. Centre, Singapore, 1990—; founder pres. I.S.T. (Asia-Pacific), 1987-90; rsch. fellow Bio Sci. Centre, Singapore, 1995—. Mem. editl. bd. Toxicon, 1988—; author: A Field Guide to Dangerous Snakes, Snake Bites and Their Treatment; editor: Snakes of Medical Importance, 1990, Sea Snake Toxinology, 1994. Recipient Commonwealth Med. Scholarship, Eng., 1976-79, Brit. Coun. award, 1990, WHO fellowships. Fellow Acad. Medicine Singapore; mem. Internat. Soc. Toxinology (coun. mem. 1991—). Office: Nat U Singapore, Lower Kent Ridge Rd, 119260 Singapore Singapore

GOPPELT, JOHN WALTER, physician, psychiatrist; b. Saginaw, Mich., Jan. 20, 1924; s. Paul Gustave and Marion LeRoy (Payne) G.; m. Martha Keller Rowland, Mar. 31, 1956; 1 child, Edmund H. S.B., MIT, 1949; M.D., U. Pa., 1955. Diplomate Am. Bd. Psychiatry and Neurology. Rotating intern Bryn Mawr Hosp., Pa., 1955-56; resident in psychiatry Inst. of Pa. Hosp., Phila., 1956-59; practice medicine, specializing in psychiatry, Haverford, Pa., 1959—; from instr. to assoc. dept. psychiatry Sch. Medicine, U. Pa., Phila., 1960-74. Contbr. articles to profl. jours. Chmn. Drug and Alcohol Council of Delaware County, Media, Pa., 1979-83; committeeman Republican Party, Haverford Twp., Pa., 1980. Served with U.S. Army, 1943-46. Recipient Legion of Honor award Chapel of Four Chaplains. Mem. AMA, Am. Psychiat. Assn., N.Y. Acad. Scis., Math. Assn. Am., Sigma Xi. Avocation: mathematics. Address: 369 Exeter Rd Haverford PA 19041-1084

GORBY, WILLIAM GUY, anesthesiologist; b. Clarksburg, W.Va., Apr. 6, 1950; s. William Darrell and Sara Lucille (Harner) G.; m. Sharyn Louise Reitz; children: William Michael, Chad Robert, Brenna Lynn. BS, W.Va. U., 1972, MS, 1974; DO, W.Va. Sch. Osteo. Medicine, 1978; postgrad., Dickenson Sch. Law, Carlisle, Pa., 1995—. Diplomate Osteo. Bd. of Anesthesiology. Intern Met. Gen. Hosp., Pinellas Park, Fla., 1978-79; resident anesthesia Cuyahoga Falls (Ohio) Gen. Hosp., 1979-81; fellow pain mgmt. Cleve. Clinic Found., 1981-82; dir. pain mgmt. Geismger Med. Ctr., Danville, Pa., 1982-85; dir. anesthesia Washington County Hosp., Hagerstown, Md., 1985-92; assoc. prof. anesthesia W.Va. Sch. Osteo. Medicine, Lewisburg, 1992-93; part-time emergency rm. anesthesiologist Wetzel County Hosp., New Martinsville, W.Va., 1993—, War Meml. Hosp., Berkley Spring, W.Va., 1993—; assoc. prof. pulmonary medicine W.Va. Sch. Osteo. Medicine, 1982-90. Staff writer On the Trail mag.; contbr. articles to profl. jours. Mem. ABA (student mem.), Am. Coll. Osteo. Anesthesiology, Am. Osteo. Assn., Aircraft Owners and Pilots Assn. Home: 49 Brian Dr Carlisle PA 17013

GORDAN, DENNIS STUART, physiatrist, educator; b. N.Y.C., Sept. 24, 1945; s. Harold Bernard and Helen (Marberg) G.; m. Miriam Laufer, Sept. 5, 1971; children: Michael Noah, Rachel, Israel Moses. BS, Union Coll., Schenectady, 1967; MD, Union U., Albany, N.Y., 1971. Diplomate Am. Bd. Internal Medicine, Am. Bd. Phys. Medicine and Rehab., Am. Bd. Electrodiagnostic Medicine, Nat. Bd. Med. Examiners. Intern Albany Med. Ctr. Hosp., 1971-72, resident, 1972-73, 75-78; intern Albany med. Ctr. Hosp., 1971-72, resident internal medicine, 1972-73, 75-76, resident phys. med. and rehab., 1976-78; instr. rehab. medicine U. Wash. Med. Sch., Seattle, 1978-80; asst. prof. rehab. and internal medicine Tufts U. Sch. Medicine, Boston, 1980-89, clin. asst. prof. rehab. medicine, 1989—; med. dir. Weldon Ctr. for Rehab., Mercy Hosp., Springfield, Mass., 1989—; chief rehab. medicine svc. VA Med. Ctr., Boston, 1986-89; pres. We. Health Svcs., Inc., P.C., Springfield, 1989—; manuscript reviewer Archives Phys. Medicine and Rehab., Chgo. Contbg. author: The Practical Management of Spasticity in Children and Adults, 1990. Bd. dirs. Temple Beth El, Springfield, 1993—, Jewish Family Svcs., Springfield, 1995. Maj. M.C., USAF, 1973-75. Fellow Am. Acad. Phys. Medicine and Rehab., Am. Assn. Electrodiagnostic Medicine; mem. Assn. Acad. Physiatrists, New Eng. Soc. Phys. Medicine and Rehab. (pres. 1986), Mass. Med. Soc., Hampden Dist. Med. Soc. (co-editor Hampden Hippocrat 1995). Office: Weldon Ctr for Rehab 233 Carew St Springfield MA 01104

GORDAN, GILBERT SAUL, physician, educator; b. San Francisco, July 8, 1916; s. Gilbert Saul and Sadie (Joseph) G.; m. Cynthia Vaughan, Feb. 2, 1978. A.B., U. Calif., 1937, M.D., 1941, Ph.D., 1947. Intern U. Calif. Hosp., San Francisco, 1940-41; resident U. Calif. Hosp., 1941-42; mem. faculty U. Calif., San Francisco, 1946-85; prof. medicine U. Calif., 1962-85, prof. emeritus, 1985—; prof. medicine U. Calif., Davis, 1985-88; Lady Davis vis. prof. Hebrew U., Jerusalem, 1978; assoc. chief of staff for edn. VA Med.

Ctr., Martinez, Calif., 1985-88; cons. in field. Author: Endocrinology in Clinical Practice, 1953, The Parathyroids, 1971, Clinical Management of the Osteoporoses, 1976; editor: Yearbook of Endocrinology, 1951-63; contbr. numerous articles to profl. jours. Served with M.C. AUS, 1942-45. Decorated Bronze Star; recipient Disting. Achievement award Nat. Osteoporosis Found., 1992; Commonwealth fellow, 1947-48, 62-63; Guggenheim fellow, 1967-68. Fellow ACP, AAAS; mem. Assn. Am. Physicians, Am. Soc. Clin. Investigation, Endocrine Soc., Royal Soc. Medicine (hon.). Democrat. Jewish.

GORDEN, PHILLIP, federal agency administrator. Dir. Nat. Inst. Diabetes, Digestive and Kidney Diseases, HHS, Bethesda, Md. *

GORDINIER, RICHARD HENRY, physician; b. Denver, Jan. 16, 1932; s. Everett Wilbur and Verona Anna Blanche (Briar) G.; m. Margaret Rust, Oct. 14, 1990. BA, UCLA, 1957; MD, U. So. Calif., L.A., 1961; JD, So. Calif. Inst. Law, 1980. Intern Valley Med. Ctr., Fresno, Calif., 1961-62, resident in internal medicine, 1962-65; pvt. practice Santa Paula, Calif., 1961-73; dir. CCU/ICU Santa Paula Hosp., 1961-73; pvt. practice Ojai, Calif., 1973-87; dir. CCU/ICU Ojai Valley Hosp., 1973-87; asst. med. dir. Bristol Myers, Evansville, Ind., 1987-88; v.p. med. affairs, med. dir. Curative Tech., Stony Brook, N.Y., 1988-91; med. dir. St. Mary Med. Ctr., Long Beach, Calif., 1991-95, San Gabriel Valley Med. Group, Arcadia, Calif., 1995—; asst. clin. prof. medicine UCLA, 1965—; prof. legal medicine U. Evansville, 1972-78. Dir. Ventura County Heart Assn. With USN, 1950-54. Fellow ACP, Am. Coll. Legal Medicine. Home: 1561 S Oak Knoll Ave San Marino CA 91108 Office: 117 E Live Oak Arcadia CA 91006

GORDIS, ENOCH, science administrator, internist; b. N.Y.C., Feb. 21, 1931; s. Robert and Fannie (Jacobson) G. BA, Columbia U., 1950, MD, 1954. Fellow Dazian Found., N.Y.C., 1958-59; clin. fellow Mt. Sinai Hosp., N.Y.C., 1959, chief resident dept. medicine, 1960; assoc. prof. dept. medicine Mt. Sinai Sch. Medicine, N.Y.C., 1971-79, prof. medicine, 1979—; guest investigator Rockefeller U., N.Y.C., 1961-62, rsch. assoc., 1962-63, assoc. prof., 1965-71, adj. prof., 1971—; dir., mem. treatment prevention study sect. Nat. Inst. on Alcohol Abuse and Alcoholism, Rockville, Md., 1986—; extensive pub. appearances in U.S. and abroad on topics related to alcoholism and addiction. Author: (with others) Controversies in Clinical Care, 1981, Current Therapy in Gastroenterology and Liver Disease, 1986; manuscript reviewer Annals Int. Medicine, Butterworth Inc., Clin. Textbook of Addictive Disorders, European Jour. Clin. Investigation, Jour. Clin. Investigation, Jour. Lipid Rsch., Jour. Studies in Alcohol, Med. Letter, others; assoc. editor Alcoholism: Clin. and Exptl. Rsch., 1979—; mem. editorial bd. U. Medicine and Dentistry of N.J., N.J.Med. Sch.; contbr. articles, abstracts to profl. jours. Corr. Com. on Human Rights, 1988-89. Capt. M.C., U.S. Army, 1955-57. Fellow ACP; mem. Adv. Group on Fellowships in Alcohol and Drug Abuse, Am. Coll. Neuropsychopharmacology, Am. Fedn. for Clin. Rsch., Am. Gastroent. Assn., Am. Soc. Addiction Medicine, Am. Physiol. Soc., Inst. of Medicine of NAS (corr. com. human rights 1988-89), Rsch. Soc. on Alcoholism, Sigma Xi, Phi Beta Kappa. Office: Dept HHS NIH Nat Inst Alcohol Abuse Alcoholism 6000 Executive Blvd Bethesda MD 20892-7003

GORDIS, LEON, physician; b. N.Y.C., July 19, 1934; s. Robert and Fannie (Jacobson) G.; m. Hadassah Cohen, June 14, 1955; children: Daniel, Elihu, Jonathan. B.A., Columbia, 1954; B.H.L., Jewish Theol. Sem., 1954; M.D., SUNY, 1958; M.P.H., Johns Hopkins U., 1966, Dr.P.H., 1968. Intern, then resident in pediatrics Jewish Hosp., Bklyn., 1958-61; fellow in pediatrics Sch. Medicine Johns Hopkins U., 1962-66, instr. Sch. Medicine, 1966-68, assoc. prof. epidemiology, Sch. Hygiene and Pub. Health, 1971-73; asst. med. dir. ambulatory care Sinai Hosp., Balt., 1966-68; chief dept. community medicine Sinai Hosp., 1968-69; prof. epidemiology Johns Hopkins, 1973—, chmn. dept. epidemiology, 1975-93; prof. pediatrics, 1992—; assoc. dean admissions & Acad. affairs Johns Hopkins Sch. Medicine, 1993—; vis. prof. med. ecology Hebrew U., Jerusalem, 1969-71. Served with USPHS, 1961-65. Fellow Am. Acad. Pediatrics, AAAS; mem. Inst. Medicine, Nat. Acad. Sci., Soc. Epidemiologic Research (pres. 1979-80), Am. Epidemiol. Soc. (pres. 1983-84), Am. Pediatric Soc., Soc. Pediatric Research, Am. Public Health Assn., Am. Heart Assn., Assn. Tchrs. Preventive Medicine. Home: 105 Swanhill Ct Baltimore MD 21208-1608 Office: 615 N Wolfe St Baltimore MD 21205-2103

GORDON, ALAN GEORGE, gynecologist; b. Belfast, Ireland, Oct. 26, 1929; s. Ernest George and Ann (McFarland) G.; m. Mary Lilian Naylor, Aug. 20, 1963; children: Catherine, Claire, Patrick. Sr. cert., Meth. Coll., Belfast, 1947; MB, Queen's U., Belfast, 1953; F.R.C.S., Royal Coll. Surgeons, Edinburgh, 1962; F.R.C.O.G., Royal Coll. Obstet. Gynecol., London, 1974. Resident Belfast (Ireland) City Hosp., 1953-55; jr. specialist Royal Army Med. Corps., Hong Kong, 1955-58; asst. lectr. Queen's U., Belfast, Ireland, 1958-59; sr. house officer Royal Maternity Hosp., Belfast, Ireland, 1959-61, sr. tutor, 1961-64; lectr. Queen's U., Belfast, Ireland, 1964-65; cons. Princess Royal Hosp., Hull, Eng., 1965-92; hosp. recognition ctr., fellowship select ctr., ethics com., Royal Coll. OB/GYN, London; maternal death ctr., Dept. Health, London, 1983-92. Author: Gynaecological Endoscopy, 1988, Tubal Infertility, 1990, History of Laparoscopy, 1990, Safety in Hysterosurgery, 1991, Practical Laparoscopy, 1993, Practical Hysteroscopy, 1993. Capt. RAMC, 1955-58. Fellow Mercy Hosp., Melbourn, Australia, 1990. Fellow Eng. OB/GYN Soc; mem. Ulster OB/GYN Soc., European Soc. Hysteroscopy, British Soc. for Gynecol. Endoscopy (pres. 1990-92), Internat. Soc. Gynecol. Endoscopy, (pres. 1993-95), European Soc. Gynaecological Endoscopy (pres. 1992-94). Mem. Ch. of Eng. Home: 34 W Ella Way, Hull HU10 7LW, England Office: Hull and East Riding Hosp, Anlaby, Hull HU10 7AZ, England

GORDON, BENJAMIN DICHTER, medical executive, pediatrician; b. Bklyn., Mar. 4, 1927; s. Abraham S. and Selma F. (Dichter) G.; m. Ellen M. Nimaroff, June 10, 1951; children: Wendy, Marcy, Amanda. AB, Amherst Coll., 1947; MD, U. Md., 1951. Diplomate Am. Bd. of Pediatrics. Rotating intern Kings County Hosp., Bklyn., 1951-52, asst. resident in pediatrics, 1953-54; asst. resident in pediatrics Maimonides Hosp., Bklyn., 1952-53; research fellow Irvington House, Irvington-on-Hudson, N.Y., 1954-55; practice medicine specializing in pediatrics Stratford & Bridgeport, Conn., 1955-73; assoc. attendant, emergency dept. Bridgeport Hosp., 1973-78; asst. dir. emergency dept. Danbury (Conn.) Hosp., 1978-82; clin. dir. Union Carbide Corp., Danbury, 1982-87; med. dir. Chesebrough-Ponds, Inc., Trumbull, Conn., 1987-90; asst. prof. occupational medicine Yale U.; chmn. Rheumatic Fever com. Conn. State Heart Assn.; cons. to cosmetic industry and product-testing labs. Author: Practical Guide for New Parents, 1970; contbr. articles to profl. jours. Served with USNR, 1945-46. Fellow Am. Acad. Pediats., Am. Coll. Occupational and Environ. Medicine, Am. Acad. Dermatology (spl. affiliate); mem. Conn. State Med. Soc. (past chmn. comty. pub. health), Fairfield County Med. Soc. (past chmn. pub. health com.), Occupational Med. Assn. Conn. (pres. 1987-88), Williams Club (N.Y.C.). Jewish. Home: 14 Hillsea Rd Yarmouthport MA 02675

GORDON, BETTY L., health services administrator; b. Sayre, Pa., Apr. 4, 1947; d. Manley and Helen (Featherman) Rockman; m. Alan F. Gordon, Dec. 29, 1972. BSN, Russell Sage Coll., 1964; postgrad., Boston U., 1973-74; MPH in Health Svcs. Adminstrn., John Hopkins U., 1981. RN, Mass., N.Y. Gen. staff nurse Robert Packer Hosp., Sayre, Pa., 1968; staff nurse, team leader Vis. Nurse Assn. Allegheny County, Pa., 1968-71; nurse pub. health Vis. Nurse Assn. Boston, 1971; staff continuing care coord. Faulkner Hosp., Jamaica Plain, Mass., 1972-74; nurse pub. health, home health coord. Arlington County Dept. Human Resources, Va., 1974-78; dir. patient care svcs. Hospice Met. Denver, 1978-80; project site dir. long term care channeling demonstration City Balt., 1981-83; sr. v.p. clin. svcs. Kimberly Quality Care, Boston, 1983-94; assoc. v.p. Simione Ctrl., Inc., Framingham, Mass., 1994—. Home: 151 Coolidge Ave Apt 713 Watertown MA 02172-2867 Office: 550 Cochituate Rd Framingham MA 01701-4600

GORDON, CRAIG JEFFREY, oncologist, educator; b. Detroit, Feb. 10, 1953; s. Maury Allen and Shirley Phoebe (Jacoby) G.; m. Susan Ann Blase, Aug. 3, 1980; children: Sari, Scott, Brittany. BS, Oakland U., 1978; DO, U. Osteopathic Medicine and, Health Scis./Des Moines, 1983. Diplomate Am. Bd. Internal Medicine, Am. Bd. Med. Oncology. Intern-chief Botsford Gen. Hosp., Farmington Hills, Mich., 1983-84, resident, 1984-87; fellow in hematology and oncology Wayne State Univ. (affiliated Hosp.'s Prog.), Detroit, 1987-90, fellow-chief, 1989-90; clin. asst. prof. dept. medicine Wayne State U., Detroit, 1990—; dir. divsn. hematology and oncology Botsford Hosp., Livonia, Mich., 1992—; med. dir. Angela Hospice, 1993—; mem. extrarenal transplantation com. Mich. Dept. Pub. Health; physician advisor Gilda's Club Mich. Contbr. articles to profl. jours. Named Intern of the Yr. Botsford Hosp. Staff, 1984, Resident of the Yr., 1985-87; clin. fellow Am. Cancer Soc., 1987-90. Fellow Am. Coll. Osteo. Internists; mem. AAAS, Am. Osteo. Assn., Assn. Adminstrs. and Cancer Execs., Mich. Assn. Osteo. Physicians and Surgeons, Assn. Cancer Execs., So. Med. Assn., S.W. Oncology Group, Am. Soc. Clin. Oncologists, Oakland County Osteo Assn. Office: Botsford Gen Hosp Ste 300 28595 Orchard Lake Rd Farmington Hills MI 48334

GORDON, DAVID HUGH, physician; b. Phila., June 30, 1945; s. Meyer Michael and Sylvia Sonja (Robinson) G.; m. Jayne Eisenberg; children: Megan, Michael. BS in Biology, Trinity Coll., Hartford, Conn., 1967; MD, Case Western Res. U., 1971. Cert. internal medicine, oncology, hematology Am. Bd. Internal Medicine. Intern Hartford (Conn.) Hosp., 1971-72, resident, 1972-73; resident U. Minn. Hosps., Mpls., 1973-74; hematology fellow U. Rochester (N.Y.) Med. Ctr., 1974-75, med. oncology fellow, 1975-77; physician S.W. Oncology Assocs., 1977-79, San Antonio Tumor and Blood Clinic, P.A., 1979—; instr. medicine U. Minn., 1973-74, inst., trainee dept. medicine hematology unit, 1974-75, instr. and trainee in oncology in medicine, 1975-77; attending physician Monroe Cmty. Hosp., Rochester, 1975-77; clin. instr. dept. medicine U. Tex., San Antonio, 1977-80, clin. asst. prof., 1980-83, clin. assoc. prof., 1983—; assoc. bd. trustees Bapt. Meml. Hosp. Sys., 1988-90, chief of staff, 1988, pres. med. exec. bd., 1989, dir. cancer update annual cancer conf., 1990—; mem. carrier adv. com. Medicare, State of Tex., 1993-98; bd. dirs. Am. Cancer Soc., San Antonio Metro Unit, 1991—. Contbr. articles to profl. jours. Mem. Am. Soc. Clin. Oncology, Am. Soc. Hematology (com. on practice 1989-96), Tex. Med. Assn., Bexar County Med. Soc. (alt. del. to Tex. Med. Assn. 1988-89, bd. mediations 1989-91, chmn. 1991, bd. dirs. 1992-94, v.p. 1995), Phi Delta Epsilon. Home: 35 Devon Wood San Antonio TX 78257 Office: San Antonio Tumor & Blood Clinic 8527 Village Dr #101 San Antonio TX 78217

GORDON, ELLA DEAN, women's health nurse; b. Chgo., Jan. 19, 1947; d. Ed and Mozelle (Jordan) Hall; m. Starling Alexander Gordon, Aug. 2, 1969; children: Gerald Alexander, Dana Rolean. Diploma, Grady Meml. Hosp., 1968; student, Ga. State U., 1969-75; BSN, Med. Coll. Ga., 1976; M in Health Sci., Armstrong State Coll., 1983. RN, Ga., Tex. Charge nurse pediatrics evenings Grady Meml. Hosp., Atlanta, 1968-71; staff nurse pediatrics Dr.'s Meml. Hosp., Atlanta, 1971; charge nurse Pediatricians Office, Decatur, Ga., 1971-72; staff nurse VA Hosp., Atlanta, 1972-76; nurse primary care med. ICU VA Hosp., San Antonio, 1983; charge nurse, army nurse corps Eisenhower Army Med. Ctr., Ft. Gordon, Ga., 1976-79; staff nurse obstet. Noble Army Hosp., Ft. McClellan, Ala., 1984; instr. clin. nursing Jacksonville (Ala.) State Coll. Nursing, 1984-85; clin. nurse obstet. Gorgas Army Hosp., Republic of Panama, 1987-89; charge nurse oncology days Eisenhower Army Med. Ctr., Ft. Gordon, Ga., 1989-90; charge nurse obstet. Brooke Army Med. Ctr., Ft. Sam Houston, Tex., 1990-95; mem. labor & delivery Wilford Hall Air Force Med. Ctr., Lackland AFB, Tex., 1996—; cons. health edn. ETOWAH County Clinics, Gadsden, Ala, 1985; health educator Cardiovascular Coun. of Savannah, Ga., 1983, Parent/Child Devel. Svcs., Savannah, 1982. Contbr. articles to profl. jours. Instr. ARC, Ft. McClellan, 1985-86, chmn., vols., 1986-87. Capt. U.S. Army, 1976-79; col. USAR, 1991. Named One of Outstanding Young Women in Am., 1979, 83. Mem. Assn. Mil. Surgeons, Assn. of Women's Health, Obstets. and Neonatal Nurses, Res. Officer Assn., Officers Wives Club (publicity chmn. 1982-83), Sigma Theta Tau. Democrat. Home: 12810 El Marro St San Antonio TX 78233-5832 Office: Wilford Hall AF Med Ctr Lackland A F B TX 78236

GORDON, FRANK JEFFREY, medical educator; b. Washington, Dec. 5, 1948; married; 2 children. Attended, Case Western Reserve U., 1966-69; BS in Biology, N.Mex. State U., 1972, MA in Psychology, 1974; PhD in Biopsychology, U. Iowa, 1980. Interdisciplinary rsch. fellow U. Iowa, Iowa City, 1978-80, postdoctoral rsch. fellow Dept. Internal Medicine, 1980-81, rsch. scientist, 1981-82; asst. prof. Dept. Pharmacology Emory U. Sch. Medicine, Atlanta, 1982-88, assoc. prof., 1988—; spkr. in field. Editl. bd. Am. Jour. Physiology, 1989-93. Mem. com. on risk factors Iowa Heart Assn., 1982. USPHS pre-doctoral fellow, 1978-80, post-doctoral fellow, 1980-82; rsch. starter grantee Pharm. Mfgs. Assn. Found., 1983-85. Fellow Coun. High Blood Pressure Rsch.; mem. Am. Physiol. Soc., Am. Soc. Pharmacology and Exptl. Therapeutics, Am. Heart Assn. (rsch. investigatorship Ga. affiliate 1987-88, AHA established investigator 1989-94), Soc. Neurosci., Sigma Xi. Office: Dept Pharmacology Rm 5011 Rollins Rsch Ctr Atlanta GA 30322

GORDON, GARY VICTOR, rheumatologist, educator; b. Worcester, Mass., Jan. 29, 1947; s. Haskell Robert and Ina Evelyn (Rose) G.; m. Nancy Jane Bregstein, Mar. 21, 1987; children: Benjamin, Deborah, Jeffrey, Daniel. BA cum laude, Brown U., 1969; MD, Yale U., 1973. Diplomate Am. Bd. Internal Medicine, Rheumatology; lic. MD, Pa. Intern U. Mich. Med. Ctr., Ann Arbor, 1973-74; resident Waterbury (Conn.) Hosp., 1974-76; fellow U. Pa., Phila., 1976-78; chief rheumatology sect. Grad. Hosp., Phila., 1978-82; rheumatologist Lankenau Hosp., Wynnewood, Pa., 1982—; clin. assoc. prof. Thomas Jefferson U., Phila., 1985—. Contbr. articles to profl. jours. Fellow ACP, Am. Coll. Medicine, Am. Coll. Rheumatology; mem. Ea. Pa. Arthritis Found. (chmn. pub. edn. com.), Phila. Rheumatism Soc. Office: Lankenau Hosp 320 Lankenau Med Bldg 100 Lancaster Ave Wynnewood PA 19096

GORDON, HORACE EARL, surgeon, educator; b. Arbuckle, Calif., July 21, 1924; s. Horace Curby and Matilda (Richter) G. AB, U. Calif., Berkeley, 1944; MD, U. Calif., San Francisco, 1947. Diplomate Am. Bd. Surgery. Intern San Francisco Gen. Hosp., 1947-48; resident Highland-Alameda County Hosp., Oakland, Calif., 1950, V.A. West L.A. Med. Ctr., 1954-58; asst. chief surg. svc. VA West L.A. Med. Ctr., 1960-63, chief surg. svc., 1963-77, chief of staff, 1977-92, cons. gen. surgery, 1992—; assoc. prof., vice chair dept. surgery UCLA Sch. Medicine, 1970-77, prof. surgery, asst. dean, 1977-92, prof. surgery, emeritus, 1992—; consulting staff St. John's Hosp., Santa Monica, Calif., 1966—. Author: (chpt.) Vascular Access Surgery, 1st, 2nd and 3d edits., 1995; co-author: (chpt.) Cancer Treatment, 1st, 2nd, 3rd, and 4th edits., 1995; contbr. articles to profl. jours. Pres. coastal cities unit Am. Cancer Soc., L.A., 1982-83, bd. dirs., 1974—. Lt. USN Med. Corps, 1943-46, 50-53, Korea. Recipient Rsch. grant USPHS, 1962-64. Fellow Am. Coll. Surgeons (gov. 1979-82); mem. L.A. Surg. Soc. (pres. 1973-74), Assn. VA Surgeons (president 1974-75), Bay Surg. Soc. (pres. 1969-70), Western Surg. Assn., Pacific Coast Surg. Assn., Soc. for Surgery of Alimentary Tract. Home: 3754 Scadlock Ln Sherman Oaks CA 91403 Office: UCLA Sch Medicine Divsn Gen Surgery 10833 Le Conte Ave Los Angeles CA 90024

GORDON, IRVING MARTIN, osteopathic physician; b. Canton, Ohio, Aug. 10, 1926; s. Harry and Sarah (Axelrod) G.; m. Roberta Levine, Feb. 12, 1956; children: Ellen, Nina, Bruce, Roger. BA, Case Western Res. U., 1949; BS, Kent State U., 1950; DO, Chgo. Coll. Osteo. Medicine, 1954. Lic. osteo. physician, Ohio, S.C.; cert. in family practice Am. Bd. Family Practitioners in Osteo. Medicine and Surgery. Intern, Detroit Osteo. Hosp., 1954-55; locum tenens, Fort Lee, N.J., 1955-56; gen. practice osteo. medicine, Massillon, Ohio, 1957-63, Gordon & Sharkis, 1963-70, Gordon, Sharkis & Larusso, Inc., 1970-71; pres. Perry Family Practice Ctr., Inc., 4 physician group; gen. practice family medicine Perry Family Practice Ctr., Inc., Massillon, 1972—; clin. asst. prof. family practice Ohio U. Coll. Osteo. Medicine, 1977—; lectr. Chgo. Coll. Osteo. Medicine, 1980, 81; lectr. Howard U. Hosp., Washington, and Grandview Hosp., Dayton, Ohio, Ohio U. Coll. Osteo. Medicine, 1984, Des Moines Gen Hosp., 1984, Botsford Hosp., Farmington, Mich., 1985. Trustee Wooster Eight County Health Systems Agy. (Ohio), 1975-81; mem. pres.'s adv. bd. Stark Tech. Coll., Canton, 1980—, trustee, 1983—, found. trustee, 1982, bd. dirs., pres. bd. trustees, 1992-94; mem. annual fund-raising com. United Jewish Appeal, 1970—, fin. com. Temple Israel, 1979—; founding mem., trustee Doctors Hosp. Stark County (Ohio), 1963—, chief of staff, 1969, 70, mem. fin. com., chmn. community affairs com., mem. steering com. 25th-anniversary gala 1988-91, post-grad. edn. com., 1992—; emeritus mem. bd. trustees Drs. Hosp. Served to cpl. USAF, 1945-46. Fellow Am. Coll. Family Practice; mem. AMA, Am. Osteo. Assn., Ohio Osteo. Assn., Akron-Canton Acad. Osteo. Medicine and Surgery (pres. 1974-75), Ohio Soc. Am. Coll. Gen. Practitioners Osteo. Medicine and Surgery (pres. 1981-82), Stark County Med. Soc., Ohio Med. Assn. Clubs: Canton, Glenmoor Country (fin. com. 1991—), Nat. Amateur Radio Relay League, Med. Amateur Radio Council (founding mem.), Canton. Lodges: Masons, Shriners. Office: 4125 Lincoln Way E Canton OH 44646

GORDON, JAMES SAMUEL, psychiatrist; b. N.Y.C., Oct. 12, 1941; s. Jules David and Cynthia (Hymanson) G. AB, Harvard U., 1962, MD, 1967. Diplomate Am. Bd. Psychiatry and Neurology. Research psychiatrist NIMH, Rockville, Md., 1971-82, cons. alternative forms of svc., 1974-82, dir. spl. study Pres.'s Commn. Mental Health, 1977-78; chief adolescent svcs. St. Elizabeth's Hosp., Washington, 1980-82; clin. prof. Georgetown U. Med. Sch., Washington, 1980—; chair program adv. coun. Office of Alternative Medicine NIH, 1994—. Author: The Golden Guru, 1987, Holistic Medicine, 1988, Transforming Medicine, 1996, Manifesto for a New Medicine, 1996; editor: Health for the Whole Person (Med. Self Care Book award 1980), Mind, Body and Health: Towards and Integral Medicine, 1984. Commdr. USPHS, 1971-82. Recipient award Ford Found., 1982. Fellow Am. Assn. Social Psychiatry; mem. Am. Psychiat. Assn., Am. Holistic Med. Assn. (founding mem. 1980, trustee 1980-86), Am. Assn. Med. Acupuncture (founding mem. 1987), Physicians for Social Responsibility (exec. com. 1984-86). Office: 5225 Connecticut Ave NW Washington DC 20015-1845

GORDON, JOEL CHARLES, healthcare association officer; b. Crofton, Ky., Jan. 5, 1929; s. George B. and Tillie (Klyman) G.; m. Bernice Weingart; children: Sherrie Eisenman, Robert, Frank, Gai Jacobs. BS in Commerce, U. Ky., 1951. V.p. Cain Sloan Co., Nashville, 1956-69; pres. Gen. Care Corp., Nashville, 1970-80; chmn. Surg. Care Aff. Inc., Nashville, 1982-96; bd. dirs. Sun Trust Bank, Nashville, Genesco, Inc., Healthwise of Am., HealthSouth Inc., D.C. Bd. dirs. Leadership Nashville, 1988-89; pres. Jewish Community Ctr., Nashville, 1977-79; chmn. Tenn. Performing Ctr., Nashville, 1988-89; bd. dirs. Cheekwood-Tenn. Fine Arts Ctr., Nashville, 983-85; mem. exec. com., Med. Ctr. bd. dirs. Vanderbilt U. Lt. USAF, 1951-53. Home: 6408 E Valley Ct Nashville TN 37205-3533

GORDON, JOHN CHARLES, orthopaedic surgeon; b. Fresno, Calif., July 20, 1942; s. Charles Walter and Agnes Elizabeth (Leffler) G. AB, Holy Cross Coll., 1964; MD, George Washington U., 1968. Diplomate Am. Bd. Orthopaedic Surgery. Intern, resident Washington Hosp. Ctr., 1968-70; resident orthop. Union Meml. Hosp., Johns Hopkins U., Balt., 1972-75; pvt. practice Balt., 1975—. Office: 617 Stemmers Run Rd Ste H Baltimore MD 21221

GORDON, JOHN LAURIE, research scientist, science foundation director; b. Dumfries, Scotland, July 28, 1944; s. James Hilston and Catherine Isabel (Halliday) G.; m. Sandra Elizabeth MacGregor, Oct. 28, 1965 (div. 1989); children: Jacqueline, Catriona; m. Diana Madeleine Hawkins, Apr. 28, 1990. BS, Glasgow (Scotland) U., 1966; PhD, Cambridge (Eng.) U., 1971, DSc, 1987. Pharmacologist Beecham Labs., 1966-71; sr. asst. in rsch. Cambridge U., 1972-76; prin. sci. officer ARC Inst., Babraham, 1976-83; head vascular biology MRC Rsch. Ctr., Harrow, 1983-87; dir. rsch. Brit. Biotech., Oxford, 1987-94; chief exec. Neures Ltd., Oxford, 1994-96; assoc. lectr. Cambridge U., 1977-83; exec. dir. Brit. Biotech., 1988-96; mem. adv. bd. Oxford Glycoscis., 1995—; chmn. Quercus Ltd., 1996—. Editor: (series of books) Platelets in Biology and Pathology, 1976-1987; contbr. articles to profl. jours. Fellow Corpus Christi Coll., Cambridge, 1974-86. Mem. Pharm. Soc., Royal Coll. Pathologists. Office: Quercus Mgmt Ltd, Bishop Oak Boars Hill, Oxford OXI 5JF, England

GORDON, JONATHAN DAVID, psychologist; b. Watertown, N.Y., Nov. 5, 1949; s. Morton Lawrence and Anna (Lesser) G.; m. Doris Susan Perkel, Jan. 16, 1972 (div.); 1 child, Pamela Michelle; m. Janet S. Levick, Nov. 25, 1984; children: Lisa Danielle, Sharon Rachelle, Jaclyn Gabrielle. BA, Fairleigh Dickinson U., 1971, MA, 1973; PhD, Hofstra U., 1976. Diplomate Am. Bd. Med. Psychotherapists, Internat. Acad. Behavioral Medicine, Am. Acad. Pain Mgmt., Nat. Registry Neurofeedback Providers. Team supr., psychologist dept. ambulatory care Mt. Sinai Med. Ctr., N.Y.C., 1976-80; pvt. practice clin. psychology, Teaneck, N.J., 1978—; chief psychologist, coord. profl. services Holley Child Care and Devel. Ctr. Youth Consultation Svc., Hackensack, N.J., 1980-85; staff psychologist div. psychol. svcs. Fairleigh Dickinson U., Hackensack, 1982-85, acting dir., 1989; dir. adult outpatient psychiatry Jersey City Med. Ctr., 1985-87; dir. Bergen Biofeedback and Psychotherapy Ctr., Teaneck, 1986—; sch. cons. Leonia (N.J.) High Sch., 1987-88. Mem. Am. Psychol. Assn., N.J. Psychol. Assn., N.Y. State Psychol. Assn., Bergen County Assn. Lic. Psychologists, Assn. for Applied Psychophysiology and Biofeedback, Biofeedback Cert. Inst. Am. (cert.), Perineometer Rsch. Inst. (cert.). Office: 757 Teaneck Rd Teaneck NJ 07666-4241

GORDON, KENNETH HICKOK, psychiatrist; b. Altoona, Pa., Dec. 18, 1924; s. Kenneth Hickok Sr. and Ines Frae (McClellan) G.; m. Janice Taylor, June 16, 1951; children: Deirdre, Pamela, Sheila. MD, Temple U., 1948, MS in Psychiatry, 1956. From instr. to assoc. prof. Temple U., Phila., 1954-61, from asst. to assoc. prof., 1961-66, prof., adj. prof., 1966—; assoc. dept. psychiatry Lankenau Hosp., Phila., 1971—; clin. prof. psychiatry and human behavior Jefferson Med. Coll., Phila., 1979—; attending physician Jefferson U. Hosp., Phila., 1979—; chmn. Advs. for Children of Pa., Phila., 1979-82; bd. dirs. Emily Bacon Child Psychiatry Clinic, Phila. Contbr. articles to profl. jours.; producer video tape Comprehensive Treatment of Spinal Cord Injuries, 1982. Co-founder Main Line Mental Health and Mental Retardation Ctr., Phila., 1966; pres. World Federalists Assn., Phila., 1971-87, Citizens for Valley Forge, Pa., 1975-78; chmn. Valley Forge Land Use Task Force, 1974-77. Fellow Am. Psychiat. Assn. (life), Phila. Coll. Physicians, Am. Acad. Child and Adolescent Psychiatry; mem. AMA, Am. Soc. for Adolescent Psychiatry, Spinal Injury Assn., Regional Coun. Child Psychiatry (pres. 1977-79, 91-93), Franklin Inn Club, Alpha Omega Alpha.

GORDON, LEONARD VICTOR, psychologist, educator emeritus; b. Montreal, Que., Aug. 15, 1917; came to U.S., 1936, naturalized, 1938; s. Peter Z. and Bessie Victoria (Kirsch) G.; m. Katharine Ann Burton, Nov. 30, 1946; children: John Christopher (dec.), Jeffrey Burton. Instr. Ohio State U., Columbus, 1947-49, research assoc., 1949-50; assoc. dir. Office Research Services Boston U., 1950-51; vis. asst. prof. U. N.Mex., Albuquerque, 1951-52; div. dir. Naval Personnel Research Activity, San Diego, 1952-62; lab chief U.S. Army Personnel Research Office, Washington, 1962-66; prof. ednl. psychology and stats. SUNY-Albany, 1966-87, prof. emeritus, 1987—; pres. Intertest, Guilderland, N.Y, 1985—; Disting. vis. prof. Wilford Hall U.S. Air Force Med. Ctr., Lackland AFB, Tex., 1977-79. Author: (with Ross L. Mooney) Mooney Problem Check Lists, 1950, Gordon Personal Profile, 1953, (rev. edit. 1993), 1978, Gordon Personal Inventory, 1956, (rev. edit. 1993), 1978, Global edit., 1992, Survey of Interpersonal Values, 1960, (rev. edit.), 1976, Gordon Occupational Check List, 1963, (rev. edit.), 1981, Work Environment Preference Schedule, 1973, Measurement of Interpersonal Values, 1975, (with Akio Kikuchi) Social Psychology of Values, 1975, (rev. edit. with Akio Kikuchi), 1981, Survey of Personal Values, 1967, (rev. edit.), 1984, School Environment Preference Survey, 1978; contbr. articles to profl. jours. Rsch. coord. Peace Corps, Washington, 1964-65. With USAAC, 1941-44. Univ. Exchange scholar SUNY, 1969-71. Fellow Am. Psychol. Assn., AAAS; mem. Internat. Assn. Applied Psychology, Am. Ednl. Research Assn., Nat. Council Measurement in Edn., Author's Guild. Home: 385 Highland Dr Schenectady NY 12303-5727 Office: Intertest PO Box 27 Guilderland NY 12084-0669

GORDON, LINNEA HAMMERSTEN, health care services consultant; b. Boston, June 21, 1945; d. Vincent Nils and Shirley Hammersten; m. Robert L. Gordon, June 3, 1978. AA, Colby Sawyer Coll., 1965; BSN, Cornell U., 1968; MS, Boston Coll., 1980. RN, Mass. Nursing mgr. Payne Whitney Psychiatric Clinic, N.Y. Hosp., N.Y.C., 1968-71; evening charge nurse Chetwynde Nursing Home, West Newton, Mass., 1971; staff nurse Monroe (Mich.) County Health Dept., 1973-74; from cmty. health nurse to supr. Blue Cross Coord. Home Care/VNA of Upper Cape Cod, Falmouth, Mass., 1974-79; exec. dir. Health Resource Ctr., West Barnstable, Mass., 1981-88; nursing instr. Cape Cod Community Coll., 1983-86, 88; nursing mgmt., mktg. rep. Alternative Care, 1988-89; adminstr. All Cape Health Care, 1991-

93; sr. dir. clin. svcs. Colonial Care Cert., Falmouth, 1991-93; home health care cons. in field, 1993—; home care surveyor Joint Commn. Accreditation Healthcare Orgns., 1996. Author: Alzheimer's Disease: A Family Care Guide, 1987. Named Woman of Yr., Bus. and Profl. Women's Club of Cape Cod, 1983. Mem. Mass. Nurses Assn.,Image of Profl. Nursing award, 1986, Achievement award for Outstanding Svc. 1985), Sigma Theta Tau.

GORDON, LORI HEYMAN, marriage and family therapist; b. S.I., N.Y., Jan. 31, 1929; d. Julius and Bertha (Hahn) Heyman; m. Morris Gordon, Sept. 5, 1982; children: Beth, Jon, David, Seth. BA, Cornell U., 1950; MSW, Cath. U. Am., 1963; PhD, Summit U. La., 1993. Lic. clin. social worker, accredited supr., Va. Founder, dir. Family Rels. Inst., Falls Church, Va., 1969; condr. psychoednl. tng. seminars nat. and internat. PAIRS (Practical Application Intimate Relationship Skills), Falls Church; instr. family therapy Am. U. Grad. Sch. Counesling Edn., Washington; field supr. Cath. U. Am. Sch. Social Work, Washington; frequent presenter profls. cons., including Am. Assn. Marriage and Family Therapy Conf., 1988, 89, 90, 91, Va. Assn. Marriage and Family Therapy Conf., 1989, ABA Family Law divsn. ptnrs. program, 1994; founder Ctr. for Separation and Divorce Mediation, 1980; founder, dir. PAIRS Ltd., 1984, PAIRS Inst., 1990; exec. dir. PAIRS Found., Ltd., 1991, dir. tng., 1995. Author: Love Knots - How To Untangle Daily Frustrations, 1990, Passage to Intimacy, 1993, Book of Untangling Love Knots, 1996; contbr. articles to profl. jours. and mags. Mem. Am. Assn. Marriage and Family Therpists, Acad. Cert. Social Workers, Acad. Family Therpists, Inst. Noetic Scis. Home: 1056 Creekford Dr Fort Lauderdale FL 33326-2836 Office: PAIRS Inst 3705 S George Mason Dr Falls Church VA 22041-3759

GORDON, LOUIS EDWARD, healthcare consultant; b. Jackson, Mich., Dec. 18, 1933; s. George Edward and Anna A. (Hansmann) G.; m. Shirley Winifred Bishop, Nov. 14, 1954; children: Jan Alyce, Jill Annette, Traci Lynn. BA, Andrews U., 1953; MA, Mich. State U., 1957. Adminstr. Battle Creek (Mich.) Sanitarium, 1961-67; dir. Liberian Nat. Med. Ctr. Project, Liberia, 1967-72; dir. Kino Community Hosp., also dept. hosps. and nursing homes, Pima County, Tucson, 1972-78; adminstr. Bannock Regional Med. Ctr., Pocatello, Idaho, 1978-83; pres. Tucson Hosp. Med. Edn. Program, 1975-76; exec. v.p. Shawnee Mission Med. Ctr., Kans., 1983-85, pres. Western Mo. Med. Ctr., 1985-89; dir. Royal commn. Med. Ctr., Saudi Arabia, 1989-92; pres. Nev. Regional Med. Ctr., 1992-95; cons. Health Care Orgn. and Devel., 1995—; mem. faculty Idaho State U., Pocatello, Cen. Mo. State U. Bd. dirs., v.p. Mountain States Shared Service Corp., 1978-83; chmn. Cen. Mo. Health Resources Inst.; city commr. City of Battle Creek; pres., founder, Idaho Health Services Consortium, 1978-83; pres. South Ariz. Hosp. Council, 1976. Served with U.S. Army, 1952-54. Decorated Govt. of Liberia, 1973; recipient Unity for Service award Nat. Exchange Club, 1967, Meritorious Honor award U.S. Dept. State. Fellow APHA (life); mem. Am. Coll. Hosp. Adminstrs. (life), Am. Hosp. Assn. (life), Idaho Hosp. Assn. (dir. 1978-83), Idaho Hosp. Research and Edn. Found. (pres.). Lodges: Rotary, Masons, Shriners. Home and Office: 15113 Dearborn St Overland Park KS 66223-3210

GORDON, MARC STEWART, pharmacist, scientist; b. Cleve., June 13, 1958; s. Eugene and Eileen (Israel) G.; m. Diane Southwell, Aug. 11, 1985; children: Evan, Emma. BS in Pharmacy, U. Mich., 1982. Registered pharmacist, Calif. Staff rschr. II, mgr. Syntex Rsch., Palo Alto, Calif., 1982-95; sr. scientist Inhale Therapeutic Systems, Palo Alto, Calif., 1995—. Contbr. numerous articles to profl. jours. Mem. Am. Assn. Pharm. Scientists, Am. Pharm. Assn., No. Calif. Pharm. Discussion Group, Rho Chi. Home: 1474 Samedra St Sunnyvale CA 94087-4054 Office: Inhale Therapeutic Systems 1060 E Meadow Circle Palo Alto CA 94303

GORDON, MARTIN NEIL, pulmonologist; b. Syracuse, N.Y., July 10, 1947; s. Isadore and Esther M. G.; m. Marie A., June 27, 1975; children: Carrie, Jessica, Justin. BS, Syracuse U., 1969; MD, Mt. Sinai Sch. Medicine, 1973. Intern in internal medicine Mt. Sinai Hosp., N.Y.C., 1973-74; resident in internal medicine Mt. Sinai Hosp., 1974-76; chief med. resident Cedars-Sinai Med. Ctr., L.A., 1976-77; fellow in pulmonary medicine Cedars-Sinai Med. Ctr., 1977-79; asst. clin. prof. UCLA, 1977—; pvt. practice Beverly Hills, Calif., 1979—; dir. bronchoscopy svc. Cedars-Sinai Med. Ctr., 1980-82; dir. med. edn. Midway Med. Ctr., L.A., 1984—, chief of staff, 1989-91. Office: 9001 Wilshire Blvd #307 Beverly Hills CA 90211

GORDON, MARVIN JAY, physician; b. Balt., Jan. 11, 1946; s. Joseph Nathan and Sarah Henrietta (Seidel) G.; m. Linda Susan Merican, Dec. 23, 1968 (div. Oct. 1984); m. Myra Eleanor Sklar, Jan. 27, 1985; children: David, Joseph, Allison, Lisa. BS, U. Md., College Park, 1965; MD, U. Md., Balt., 1969. Diplomate Am. Bd. Internal Medicine, Am. Bd. Gastroenterology, Am. Bd. Quality Assurance and Utilization. Resident in internal medicine U. Md., Balt., 1969-72, Gastroenterology fellowship, 1972-74; pvt. practice Laguna Beach, Calif., 1976—. Contbr. articles to profl. jours. Pres. Temple Beth El, Laguna Niguel, Calif., 1984-85. Major USAF, 1974-76. Fellow Am. Coll. Gastroenterology; mem. Am. Gastroenterol. Assn. Home and Office: 31852 S Coast Hwy Ste 300 Laguna Beach CA 92677-3288

GORDON, MAXWELL, pharmaceutical company executive; b. Kamenka, Ukraine, Feb. 13, 1921; came to U.S., 1923; s. Abraham and Sarah Gordon; m. Ethel Mayer, June 5, 1949 (dec. Sept. 1980); m. Barbara Ullman, Apr. 10, 1983; children: Alan Michael, Sandra Lynn, Anthony Ullman, Claudia Marie Ullman. B.S., Phila. Coll. Pharmacy and Sci., 1941; M.A., U. Pa., 1946, Ph.D., 1948; D.I.C., Imperial Coll. Sci., London, 1953. Rsch. fellow NIH, Zurich, Switzerland, 1948-49; fellow AEC U. Calif., Berkeley, 1949-50; exchange fellow Am. Cancer Soc. Imperial Coll., London, 1950-51; Research assoc. Squibb Inst. for Med. Research, New Brunswick, N.J., 1951-55; assoc. dir. research Smith Kline & French Labs., Phila., 1955-70; sr. v.p. sci. and tech. group Bristol-Myers Co., N.Y.C., 1970-87; chmn. bd., CEO Lenti-Chemico Pharm. Lab., Inc. subs. Ajinomoto Co., Inc., Tokyo, 1988-93; pres., CEO Ajinomoto Pharmaceuticals, USA, Inc., Teaneck, N.J., 1993—; mem. com. on chem. documentation NRC, 1960-66; assoc. com. on problems of drug dependence NAS/NRC, 1960-64. Author: Handbook of Toxicology-Tranquilizers, 1959; editor: Psychopharmacological Agents, 1960, Bristol-Myers Symposium Series in Cancer Research, vols. 1-8, 1977-85. Fellow NIH, AEC. Fellow AAAS; mem. Am. Chem. Soc., Chem. Soc. London, Austrian Chem. Soc., Swiss Chem. Soc., Chem. Soc. Japan. Office: Ajinomoto Co Inc Glenpointe Ctr W Teaneck NJ 07666

GORDON, MICHAEL DUANE, optometrist; b. Coffeyville, Kans., Apr. 14, 1949; s. Otho Wayne and Wilma Lea (Hodges) G.; B.S. cum laude, U. Houston, 1973, O.D. magna cum laude, 1973; m. Vicki Jo Baker, May 31, 1969; children—Kimberly Michelle, Ryan Michael, Nicole Tasha. Pvt. practice optometry, sports vision specialist, Wichita, Kans., 1973—, Derby, Kans., 1977—; optometric cons. VA Hosp., Wichita, 1975-84; v.p. Rota Systems, Inc., Derby, 1978-81, pres., 1981—; cons. Winfield State Mental Hosp., 1980-85; FDA clin. investigator for Cooper Labs., 1981—, for Baush & Lomb Soflens, 1981—, for Ciba-Geigy, 1990—; pres. Sports Vision USA, 1991—; pres. Eyes Inc., 1994—; dir. Bank 4 Derby. Mem. Coll. Optometrists in Vision Devel., Am. Optometric Assn., Optometric Extension Program Found., Inc., Kans. Optometric Assn., Wichita Optometric Soc., Derby C. of C. Republican. Co-inventor, patentee motorized revolving visual exam. center; inventor soft contact lens measuring device; co-inventor Rota module. Home: 10225 E 71st St S Derby KS 67037-9179 Office: 8100 E 22nd St N Bldg 1600 Wichita KS 67226-2301 also: 234 Greenway St Derby KS 67037 also: 110 N Washington Wellington KS 67152

GORDON, MICHAEL HERBERT, rheumatologist; b. N.Y.C., Oct. 4, 1941; s. Robert J. and Charlotte J. (Goldstein) G.; m. Beth W. Aisley, June 19, 1966; children—Jill, Stephanie, Craig. B.A., Boston U., 1963; M.D., Chgo. Med. Sch., 1967. Diplomate Am. Bd. Internal Medicine, Am. Bd. Rheumatology. Intern, Cedars-Sinai Hosp., 1967-68; resident Jackson Meml., Miami, 1968-69, 71-72; fellow Albert Einstein No., Phila., 1972-74; practice medicine specializing in rheumatology, Ft. Lauderdale, Fla., 1974—. Served to capt. USAF, 1969-71. Mem. Am. Rheumatism Assn., ACP, AMA, Fla. Med. Assn., Fla. Rheumatology Soc., Broward County Med. Soc. Jewish. Office: 2001 NE 48th Ct Fort Lauderdale FL 33308-4512

GORDON, MILDRED HARRIET GROSS, hospital executive; b. Phila., Mar. 13, 1934; d. Nathan and Kate (Segal) Gross; m. Ivan H. Gordon, June 13, 1954; 1 dau., Radene Lara. Student U. Pa., 1952-56; B.S., Kutztown State U. Pa., 1960; M.S. (Falk Found. fellow), Med. Coll. Pa., 1970, Ph.D. in Psychiatry (fellow), 1972. Tchr. sci. public schs., 1961-66; with Family Guidance Center, 1966-70; dir. dept. psychiatry Mental Health Treatment Center, Reading Hosp., West Reading, 1972—; cons. Ctr. for Mental Health-Reading Hosp. and Med. Ctr.; clin. instr. dept. psychiatry Med. Coll. Pa., Phila., 1972-78; clin. asst. prof. dept. psychiatry Temple U. Med. Sch.; pvt. practice DGR, Mgmt., Inc., Wyomissing, Pa.; mem. Pa. Gov.'s Council on Drug and Alcohol Abuse, 1972-78. Bd. dirs. Confront, 1971-73, Council on Chem. Abuse, 1971-73. Mem. Am. Psychol. Assn. Home: 1850 Oak Ln Reading PA 19604-1641 Office: Reading Hosp K Bldg Reading PA 19603 also: 560 Van Reed Rd Wyomissing PA 19610-1799

GORDON, MORRIS AARON, medical mycologist, microbiologist; b. Waterbury, Conn., Apr. 3, 1920; s. Samuel and Anna (Rubinstein) G.; m. Ruth Kathryn McKee, May 22, 1945 (div. 1970); children: Barbara Jean, David Spencer, Sarah Elizabeth. BS, City Coll. N.Y., N.Y.C., 1940; MS, U. Chgo., 1942; PhD, Duke U., 1949. Diplomate Am. Bd. Microbiology; cert. lab. dir., N.Y. Lab. officer Regional Hosp., U.S. Army, Camp Blanding, Fla., 1945-46; mycologist Communicable Disease Ctr., Atlanta, 1949-54; biol. warfare specialist Chem. Corps Training Command, Fort McClellan, Ala., 1954-55; assoc. prof. microbiology Med. Coll. S.C., Charleston, 1955-59; sr. to prin. rsch. scientist, dir. mycology labs. N.Y. State Dept. Health, Albany, 1959-87, dir. clin. microbiology & mycology labs., 1983-87, dir. emeritus clin. microbiology and mycology labs., 1987—; study sect. NIH, Washington, 1971-75; adv. com. Brown-Hazen Awards, N.Y.C., 1974-78; cons. VA Hosp., Albany, 1959-96; rsch. prof. Albany Med. Coll., 1975-90. Author: Laboratory Identification of Pathogenic Fungi, 1970; founder/editor Bull. Med. Mycol. Soc. Ams., 1976-94; contbr. articles to profl. jours. Lt. comdr. USPHS, 1949-54. Recipient various rsch. grants NIH, teaching fellowship Duke U., 1947-49; Fulbright professor, 1978, Inter-Am. fellow La. State U., 1959. Mem. Med. Mycol. Soc. Ams. (pres. 1978-79, Benham award 1988), Internat. Soc. Human and Animal Mycology (v.p. 1982-85, Georg award 1991), Am. Soc. Microbiology (pres. mycology sect.), Phi Beta Kappa, Sigma Xi (pres. Albany chpt. 1972). Address: 501 Penncross Dr Raleigh NC 27610

GORDON, MYRON, psychologist; b. Bklyn., Apr. 12, 1920; s. Samuel E. and Bella (Horowitz) Goldfarb; B.S.S., CCNY, 1941, M.S., cert. in clin. psychology, 1942; fellow Rochester (N.Y.) Guidance Center, 1942-43; Ph.D., N.Y.U., 1952; m. Jetta Hendel, Nov. 10, 1949; children—Tamar, Eve. Cert. group psychotherapist. Staff psychologist Kings County Hosp., Bklyn., 1947-48; staff psychologist Queens Coll. Ednl. Clinic, 1949-53, psychologist Queens Speech and Hearing Center, 1953-54; cons. psychologist Children's Day and Night Shelter, N.Y.C., 1953-59; asso. prof. student personnel Queens Coll., 1961-83; practice in individual and group psychotherapy, 1952—; co-chmn. Queens County Mental Health Soc., 1969-76. Served with USAAF, 1943-45, AUS, 1945-46. Mem. Am. Psychol. Assn., Am. Group Psychotherapy Assn., N.Y. Soc. Clin. Psychologists (exec. bd. 1957-60), Queens Psychologists in Psychotherapeutic Practice (pres. 1957-58). Author: Theme-Centered Interaction: An Original Focus on Counseling and Education, 1971; Making Meetings More Productive, 1981. Editor Teaching-Learning Jour., 1974-76. Home: 41 Slocum Cres Flushing NY 11375-5236 Office: 11406 Queens Blvd Forest Hills NY 11375-7001

GORDON, NEIL SIMSON, retired pediatric neurologist; b. Edinburgh, Scotland, May 28, 1918; s. Ronald Grey and Agnes Theodora (Henderson) G.; m. Valerie Margaret Gray; children: Ann Cecily, Keith Gray. MB BChir, Edinburgh U., 1940, MD, 1943. House physician Royal Infirmary, Edinburgh, 1940-41, registrar, 1946-48; house physician, registrar Nat. Hosp. for Nervous Diseases, London, 1950-55; sr. registrar St. Mary's Hosp., London, 1955-58; cons. pediat. neurologist Nat. Health Svc., Manchester Children's Hosp., 1958-83; vis. lectr. U. Calif., San Francisco, 1952. Author, editor: Pediatric Neurology for the Clinician, 1976, Neurological Problems in Childhood, 1993; editor: (with others) Helping Clumsy Children, 1980, Neurologically Handicapped Children, 1986, Neurologically Sick Children, 1986; contbr. papers in field of epilepsy and learning disorders to profl. jours. Squadron leader R.A.F., 1941-46. Priorsfield fellow Sch. of Edn., Birmingham, 1974, Hackett fellow Auckland (New Zealand) Hosp. Bd., 1970. Fellow Royal Coll. Physicians Edinburgh, Royal Coll. Physicians London, Coll. Speech and Lang. Therapists; mem. Internat. Child Neurol. Assn. (bd. dirs. 1986-90), European Fedn. Child Neurology Soc. (pres. 1978-81), Brit. Pediat. Neurology Assn. (chmn. 1975-81). Anglican. Home: Huntlywood 3 Styal Rd, Wilmslow SK9 4AE, England

GORDON, ROBERT ALLEN, ophthalmologist, researcher; b. New Orleans, Apr. 4, 1944; s. Thomas Whitney and Christine (Montgomery) G. Jr.; m. Connie Marshall, Aug. 3, 1968; children: Melanie, Bradley, Travis. BS, Tulane U., 1965, MD, 1969. Diplomate Am. Bd. Ophthalmology. Chief resident ophthalmology Tulane U., New Orleans, 1972-73; chief of ophthalmology USN Regional Hosp., New London, Conn., 1973-75; fellow, ophthalmology and strabismus U. Ind., Indpls., 1976; asst. prof. ophthalmology Tulane U., 1975-78, acting chmn. ophthalmology, 1977-78, assoc. prof. ophthalmology, 1978—, assoc. prof. pediat., 1980—, vice chmn., 1989—; chief pediatric ophthalmology and strabimus svc. Tulane Med. Ctr., Charity Hosp., New Orleans, 1976—; cons. Acadiana Regional Ophthalmology Ctr., Lafayette, La., 1982—; attending staff Pediatric Ophthalmology and Strabismus Cinic, Eye, Ear and Nose Hosp., New Orleans, 1976—; dir. La. Handicapped Children Eye Clinics, New Orleans and Greensberg; vis. faculty Orbis Internat., 1988-92; cons. pediatric ophthalmology Tex. Tech. U./U. Health Sci. Ctr., 1989-94, M&S Techs., Inc., Darien, Ill., 1992—; mem. intraocular lens. adv. com. FDA, 1994-96; cons. Audubon Zoo Inst., New Orleans. Reviewer (audiotape) Practival Revs. in Ophthalmology, 1985—; manuscript referee Am. Jour. Ophthalmology, Archives of Ophthalmology, Am. Jour. Diseases of Children, Jour, Pediatric Ophthalmology and Strabismus, Ophthalmology; contbr. numerous articles to profl. jours.; designer pediatric visual device SmartSystem, 1991. Lt. cmdr. USN, 1973-75. Fellow Am. Acad. Ophthalmology (Honor award 1994); mem. AMA, Am. Assn. Pediatric Ophthalmology and Strabismus, Assn. Rsch. to Prevent Blindness, La. State Med. Soc., Orleans Parish Med. Soc., New Orleans Acad. Ophthalmology, Greater New Orleans Pediatric Soc., Theobald Ocular Pathology Soc., Tulane Eye Alumni Assn., Ind. U. Pediat. Ophthalmology Fellows Assn., Tulane Med. Alumni Assn., New Orleans Mus. Art, Friends of Charity, Friends of the Audubon Zoo, WYES Ednl. TV, Metairie (La.) Beach Club. Office: Tulane Univ Dept Ophthalmol 1430 Tulane Ave SL69 New Orleans LA 70112

GORDON, ROBERT DANA, transplant surgeon; b. N.Y.C., Jan. 25, 1945; s. Gerson George and Muriel Ruth (Danish) G.; m. Linda Susan Svirsky, July 9, 1970; children: David Charles, Daniel Lawrence. BA, Amherst Coll., 1966; MD, Cornell U., 1971. Diplomate Am. Bd. Surgery. Intern in surgery Mass. Gen. Hosp., Boston, 1971-72, resident in surgery, 1972-74, 77-78; vis. scientist transplantation biology unit Clin. Rsch. Ctr., Harrow, U.K., 1974-76; rsch. fellow Mass. Gen. Hosp./Harvard Med. Sch., Boston, 1974-76; clin. fellow Harvard Med. Sch., Boston, 1977-78; asst. prof. surgery U. Colo., Denver, 1979-83; asst. prof. surgery U. Pitts., 1983-88, assoc. prof. surgery, 1988-92; prof. surgery, chief liver transplant svc. Emory Univ., Sch. Medicine, Atlanta, 1992—; attending surgeon Egleston Children's Hosp., Atlanta, 1992—; attending surgeon, co-dir. organ transplant svcs., Emory U. Hosp., Atlanta, 1992—; chmn. fgn. rels. com. United Network Organ Sharing, Richmond, Va., 1987-90. Bd. dirs. Pitts. chpt. ARC; corp. trustee The Jackson Lab., Bar Harbor, Maine, 1994—. Fellow ACS; mem. Internat. Soc. Cardiovascular Surgery, Ctrl. Surg. Assn., Soc. Univ. Surgeons, Am. Soc. Transplant Surgeons, Transplantation Soc., Internat. Liver Transplantation Soc., Am. Assn. for Study Liver Diseases, Pan Am. Med. Assn. (pres. sect. organ transplantation 1992-94), Ga. Surg. Soc., Pa. Soc. Biomed. Rsch. (bd. dirs. 1991-92). Office: Emory U Hosp 1364 Clifton Rd NE Atlanta GA 30322-1059

GORDON, SCOTT ROBERT, hospital administrator, consultant; b. Kenosha, Wis., July 25, 1948; s. Robert Lee and Bobbye Louise (Chevallier) G.; m. Barbara Needham, May 17, 1977 (div. Mar. 1980); m. Carolyn Layman, Nov. 24, 1985; 1 child, Joseph Robert. BA in Psychology and Philosophy, Calif. Luth. Coll., Thousand Oaks, 1970; MA in Psychology, La. State U., 1972; MSW in Program Mgmt., U. Ark., Little Rock, 1977. Diplomate Am. Acad. Cert. Social Workers; lic. cert. social worker, Ark. Assoc. psychologist Shreveport Mental Health Ctr., 1971-73; pvt. practice psychology Shreveport, 1973-76; casework supr. Rutherford House, Shreveport, 1977-79; program dir. Youth Home, Inc., Little Rock, 1979-81; commr. Div. Youth Svcs., State of Ark., Little Rock, 1981-86; program dir. Ark. Children's Hosp., Little Rock, 1986-87, assoc. adminstr., 1987-89, dir. legal affairs and affiliations, 1989-93, dir. bus. devel., 1993—; mem. Ark. Social Work Licensing Bd., vice chmn., 1990-92; participant, cons. Internat. Study Program, Fed. Republic of Germany, 1986; cons., owner Creative Comms. Cons., Little Rock, 1979—; lectr. social work U. Ark., Little Rock, 1991—; bd. dirs. Children's Healthcare Sys., Inc., 1994—. Editor: (handbook for teenagers) You Have the Right If You Know It, 1984, Arkansas Criminal Manual, 1985; co-author: Basic Management for Children and Adolescents, Treatment Planning, Goals and Objectives, 1987. Delegation leader-juvenile justice People to People, Gt. Britain, Sweden, USSR, West Germany, 1982, Japan, Peoples Republic of China, Hong Kong, Republic of China, 1984; bkd. dirs. Greater Little Rock Optimist Club, 1985; trustee Home Instrn. Program for Pre-sch. Youngsters, U.S.A., N.Y.C., 1990—. Mem. Am. Soc. Healthcare Risk Mgmt. Episcopalian. Home: 306 Midland St Little Rock AR 72205-4206 Office: Ark Children's Hosp 800 Marshall St Little Rock AR 72202-3510

GORDON, SUSAN JOAN, physician, educator; b. Atlantic City, Aug. 14, 1942. Student Goucher Coll., 1959-62; M.D., Jefferson Med. Coll., 1966. Diplomate Am. Bd. Internal Medicine, Am. Bd. Gastroenterology. Intern in medicine Hahnemann Med. Coll. and Hosp., Phila., 1966-67; resident in medicine Jefferson Med. Coll. Hosp., 1967-69; instr. Thomas Jefferson U. Phila., 1971-73, asst. prof., 1973-78, assoc. prof., 1978-87, clin. prof. medicine, 1987—; jr. coordinator medicine Jefferson Med. Coll., Phila., 1971-82. Contbr. articles to profl. jours. Mem. Am. Gastroenterol. Assn. (mem. biliary sect., abstract reviewer, chairperson clin. biliary sect.), Am. Assn. Study Liver Disease, Pa. Med. Soc., Phila. Gastrointestinal Rsch. Forum, Sigma Xi. Office: Jefferson Med Coll 480 Main Bldg 132 S 10th St Philadelphia PA 19107-5244

GORDONSON, LEWIS CHESTER, ophthalmologist; b. Bronx, N.Y., Feb. 12, 1932; s. Samuel and Bertha Gordonson; m. Rita Gordonson, June 27, 1954; children: Steven, Sara, Rena. BSc in Optometry, Ohio State U., 1954; postgrad., CCNY, 1956-57, NYU, 1958-59; MD, SUNY, 1963. Diplomate Am. Bd. Ophthalmology. Clin. asst., instr. ophthalmology Cornell U. Med. Ctr., 1971-78, clin. asst., prof. ophthalmology, 1982—; assoc. attending St. Francis Hosp., Roslyn, N.Y., 1974—; attending North Shore Hosp., Manhasset, N.Y., 1971—; asst. attending L.I. Jewish, New Hyde Park, N.Y., 1968—; active staff Little Neck (N.Y.) Hosp., 1968—. 1st lt. Med. Svc. Corp., 1955-57. Fellow ACS, Am. Acad. of Ophthalmology, Nassau Acad. of Medicine; mem. Nassau County Acad. of Medicine, L.I. Ophthalogical Soc. (pres., chmn. 1967—). Jewish. Office: Lewis C Gordonson 200 Lake Ville Rd Great Neck NY 11020

GORE, DONALD RAY, orthopedic surgeon; b. Michigan City, Ind., Mar. 13, 1936; s. Clarence Bernard and Susan Leone (Fuller) G.; m. Jacqueline Marie Kraabel, Aug. 25, 1956; children: Donald, Daniel, Jennifer, Elizabeth. BS, U. Ill., 1958, MD, 1960; MS, Marquette U., 1967. Cert. Am. Bd. Orthopaedic Surgery. Intern Milw. County Gen Hosp., 1960-61; resident gen. surgery Marquette U. Sch. Medicine, Milw., 1961-64, resident orthopaedic surgery, 1964-67; fellow Biomechanics Lab U. Calif., San Francisco, 1967-68; practice medicine specializing in orthopaedic surgery Sheboygan (Wis.) Orthopaedic Assocs., S.C., 1968—; clin. prof. dept. orthopaedic surgery Med. Coll. Wis., Milw., 1980—; staff St. Nicholas Hosp., Sheboygan, Sheboygan Meml. Hosp.; cons. surgery Wood (Wis.) VA Hosp., 1970—; asst. instr. dept. surgery Med. Coll. Wis., 1964-68, clin. instr. dept. surgery, 1969-72, asst. clin. prof., 1972-73, assoc. clin. prof., 1973-80; research assoc. VA Med. Ctr., Milw., 1970—, co-investigator kinesiology research lab., 1970-84. Mem. bd. editors Jour. Orthopaedic Surg. Techniques, 1985—; contbr. articles to profl. jours. Served to capt. USAF, 1962-63. Fellow Am. Acad. Orthopaedic Surgeons (bd. councilors 1985—); mem. AMA, Mid-Am. Orthopaedic Soc., Clin. Orthopaedic Soc., Wis. Orthopaedic Soc. (pres. 1982-84), Milw. Orthopaedic Soc., Wis. Arthritis Found. (bd. dirs. 1974-82), Sierra Cascade Trauma Soc., Cervical Spine Research Socs. Republican. Lutheran. Home: 2528 N 3rd St Sheboygan WI 53083-5007 Office: Sheboygan Orthopaedic Assocs SC 2920 Superior Ave Sheboygan WI 53081-1944

GORE, LISA ELLEN, orthopedics nurse; b. Columbia, Mo., Aug. 17, 1965; d. Lee and Louise G.; (div.); 1 child, Taylor Laurenne Shaw. AAS, Hannibal (Mo.) LaGrange Coll., 1988, ASN, 1992; BSN, Mo. U., 1995. RN, Mo. Mem. nursing staff Columbia (Mo.) Regional Hosp., 1992-93; staff nurse Univ. Hosps. and Clinics, Columbia, 1993-94, clin. supr., 1994—. 2d lt. USAR, 1993—, 1st lt. USAR, 1996. Office: Univ Hosps and Clinics 1 Hosp Dr Columbia MO 65201

GORELICK, KENNETH PAUL, psychiatrist; b. Paterson, N.J., Apr. 16, 1942; s. Irving and Sylvia (Glassman) G. BA, Rutgers U., 1962; MD, Harvard U., 1967. Diplomate Am. Bd. Psychiatry and Neurology. Intern Mt. Zion Hosp. and Med. Ctr., San Francisco, 1967-68; resident in psychiatry Mass. Mental Health Ctr., Boston, 1968-71; asst. surgeon USPHS, St. Elizabeth's Hosp., Washington, 1971-73; tng. officer, psychiatry St. Elizabeth's Hosp., Washington, 1973-79, chief continuing med. edn., 1979-87; chief continuing med. edn. D.C. Commn. on Mental Health Svcs., Washington, 1987—; assoc. clin. prof. psychiatry, behavioral sci. George Washington U., Washington, 1987—. Contbg. editor Jour. Poetry Therapy, 1987—; mem. editorial bd. Jour. Arts in Psychotherapy, 1987—. Fellow Am. Psychiat. Assn.; mem. Washington Psychiat. Soc. (coun. mem. D.C. chpt. 1985-86), Nat. Assn. for Poetry Therapy (pres. 1987-89, 89-91). Home: 2625 Woodley Pl NW Washington DC 20008-1525 Office: DC Commn Mental Health Svcs Ste 1200 2700 Martin Luther King Jr Ave SE Washington DC 20032-2698

GORELIK, ASHER RAPHAEL, psychiatrist; b. Bklyn., Aug. 24, 1957; s. Harvey Benedict and Lillian (Masnikoff) G.; m. Barbara Gail Stephenson, Mar. 15, 1980; stepchildren: Brooke, Abigail. BA cum laude, Cornell U., Ithaca, N.Y., 1978; MD, U. South Fla., 1981. Diplomate Am. Bd. Psychiatry and Neurology in psychiatry and geriatric psychiatry, Nat. Bd. Examiners. Intern U. South Fla., Tampa, 1981-82, resident in psychiatry, 1981-85; pvt. practice Anniston, Ala., 1985-87; chief of psychiatry N.E. Ala. Med. Ctr., Anniston, 1985-87; clin. dir. Resource Ctr. Medfield Ctr., Largo, Fla., 1987-89; pvt. practice Clearwater, Fla., 1987—; adult svc. chief Medfield Hosp., Largo, Fla., 1989-90; med. dir. adult and geriatric psychiatry Morton Plant Hosp., Clearwater, 1991-92, chair dept. psychiatry, 1994-96; med. dir. Morton Plant Mease Psychiatry Ctr., 1995-96. Recipient Chmn.'s award dept. psychiatry U. South Fla., 1985. Mem. AMA, Am. Psychiat. Assn., Pinellas County Psychiat. Soc. (sec.-treas. 1989, pres.-elect 1990, pres. 1991), Fla. Psychiat. Soc. Democrat. Office: 2454 N Mcmullen Booth Rd Clearwater FL 34619-1340

GORFINE, STEPHEN RICHARD, colorectal surgeon; b. Brookline, Mass., Dec. 21, 1949; s. Morris and Esther Fera (Pasarevsky) G.; m. Laurie Ann Schwarz, Mar. 1, 1986; children: Jennifer Leigh, Amanda Rachel. BA, Cornell U., 1971; Candidate Sci. Med., U. Libre de Brussels, Belgium, 1974; Dr.med., U. Mass., 1978. Diplomate Am. Bd. Internal Medicine, Am. Bd. Surgery, Am. Bd. Colon and Rectal Surgery. Intern in internal medicine then resident Mt. Sinai Hosp., N.Y.C., 1978-81; resident surgery Mt. Sinai Hosp., 1981-85; resident colorectal surgery Ferguson Hosp., Grand Rapids, Mich., 1986-87; clin. asst. surgeon Mt. Sinai Hosp., 1987-89, asst. attending surgeon, 1990-96, assoc. attending surgeon, 1996—; asst. clin. prof. Mt. Sinai Sch. Medicine, Grand Rapids, Mich., 1990—; ptnr. Kreel, Gelernt, Bauer, Gorfine, Harris, N.Y.C., 1988—. Fellow ACS, ACP, Am. Soc. Colon and Rectal Surgeons; mem. AMA, Soc. for Surgery of Alimentary Tract. Office: Kreel Gelernt et al 25 E 69th St New York NY 10021-4925

GORIN, LEONARD JOSEPH, dentist; b. N.Y.C., Dec. 16, 1917; s. Louis and Anna (Hottenstien) G.; B.A., NYU, 1939, D.D.S., 1943; cert. Tokyo Dental Coll., 1983, Med. Dental Coll., Peoples Republic China, 1983. Clin. dir. dental service N.Y.C. Fire Dept., 1952-76; attending dentist Mt. Sinai Hosp., N.Y.C., 1965-76; chief dental research Cabrini Health Care Center, N.Y.C., 1970-76; research fellow N.Y.U. Coll. Dentistry, 1974-76; pvt.

dental practice, N.Y.C., 1947—; lectr., clinician micro bio quantum physics of human tissue. Democratic county committeeman, 1960's. Served with USPHS, 1944-47. Recipient commendation sci. contbrn. Faculte de Medicine de Paris, 1969. Knight of Malta. Fellow Royal Soc. Medicine, Royal Soc. Health, Acad. Gen. Dentistry, Collegium Internat. Oris Implantatorum, Internat. Coll. Dentists; mem. ADA, Assn. Mil. Surgeons, Am. Acad. Implant Dentistry (commendation), Am. Assn. Hosp. Dentists, Northeastern Soc. Periodontists, Phila. Soc. Periodontology, N. Am., Internat. assns. dental research, Spanish Soc. Stomatology (v.p.), Italian Group for Implant Study, Am. Soc. Microbiology. Contbr. articles to profl. jours. Achievements include development of a system of microscopal spatial documentation based on Einstein's theories of relativity and the fourth dimension.

GORLIN, ROBERT JAMES, medical educator; b. Hudson, N.Y., Jan. 11, 1923; s. James Alter and Gladys Gretchen (Hallenbeck) G.; m. Marilyn Alpern, Aug. 24, 1952; children: Cathy, Jed. AB, Columbia U., 1943, postgrad., 1947-50; DDS, Washington U., St. Louis, 1947; MS, State U. Iowa, 1956; DSc (hon.), U. Athens, Greece, 1982, U. Thesallonike, Greece, 1993. Oral pathologist VA Hosp., Bronx, N.Y., 1950-51; instr. dentistry Columbia U., N.Y.C., 1950-51; dental dir., pathologist Op. Blue Jay, Thule, Greenland, 1951-52; mem. exec. faculty, chmn. oral pathology and genetics Sch. Dentistry U. Minn., Mpls., 1956-90, assoc. prof. div. oral pathology Sch. Dentistry, 1956-58, prof. Sch. Dentistry, 1958-93, prof. pathology and dermatology Sch. Medicine, Sch. Dentistry, 1971-93; prof. pediatrics, ob-gyn, otolaryngology Sch. Medicine U. Minn., 1973-93; Regents' prof. oral pathology U. Minn., Mpls., 1978-93; Fulbright exch. prof., Guggenheim fellow Royal Dental Coll., Copenhagen, 1961; 1st Lingamfelter lectr. dermatology U. Va., 1971; 1st Boyle lectr. Case Western Res. U. Med. Ctr., Cleve., 1972; vis. prof. UCLA-Harbor Gen. Hosp., 1972; asst. chief dental service Glenwood Hills Med. Ctr., 1959-61, chief, 1962-64, cons., 1969-73; cons. pediatrics and oral pathology U. Minn. Hosps., 1956—; cons. oral pathology Mpls. VA Hosp., 1958—, Mt. Sinai Hosp., Mpls., 1958-91; cons. pediatrics Hennepin County Gen. Hosp., St. Paul's Children's Hosp., Ramsey County Gen. Hosp., Mpls. Children's Hosp., Gillette State Hosp. Crippled Children; mem. Minn. Adv. Com. Human Genetics, 1959-73; Minn. mem. U.S. Congl. Liaison Com. for Dentistry, 1963-80 ; mem. Ctr. Histologic Nomenclature and Classification of Odontogenic Tumors and Allied Lesions, WHO, 1966-80 ; mem. adv. com. periodontal disease and soft tissue study NIH, 1967-78 , mem. dental sect., 1970-73; mem. adv. com. Nat. Found. Clin. Rsch., 1974—; vis. prof. Tel Aviv U., 1980, Sch. Dentistry, Jerusalem, Israel, 1981; 2nd Edward Sheridan lectr., Dublin, Ireland, 1989; Windermere lectr. Brit. Paediatric Assn., 1990; founder, bd. dirs. Found. for Developmental and Medical Genetics, 1994. Author: (with J. Pindborg and M. Cohen) Syndromes of the Head and Neck, 1964, 76, 90, (with R. Goodman) The Face in Genetic Disorders, 1970, 77, The Malformed Infant and Child, 1983, (with B. Konigsmark) Genetic and Metabolic Disorders, 1977, Hereditary Hearing Loss and Its Syndromes, 1995; co-contbr.: Computer Assisted Diagnosis in Pediatrics, 2d edit., 1971; editor: (with H. Goldman) Thoma's Oral Pathology, 1970, Chromosomes and Human Cancer (J. Cervenka and B. Koulischer), 1972; editorial cons. Jour. Dental Rsch., Geriatrics, Archives of Oral Biology, Jour. Pediats., Pediats., Am. Jour. Diseases of Children, Syndrome Identification, Radiology; editor oral pathology Oral Surgery, Oral Medicine, Oral Pathology, Clin. Pediats.; assoc. editor Am. Jour. Human Genetics, 1970-73, Jour. Oral Pathology, 1972-83, Jour. Maxillofacial Surgery, 1973—, Cleft Palate Jour., 1976—, Clin. Pediats., 1985—; mem. bd. Excerpta Medica, 1976-80, Jour. Craniofacial Genetic Devel. Biology, 1980—, Jour. Clin. Dysmorphology, 1982-86, Gerodontics, 1984-86, Birth Defects Ency., 1986—, Dysmorphology Clin. Genetics, 1987—; cons. editor Stedman's Med. Dictionary, 1959—; contbr. numerous articles to profl. jours. Bd. dirs. Minn. div. Am. Cancer Soc., 1959-60, mem. nat. clin. fellowship com., 1962-65. With U.S. Army, 1943-44; lt. USNR, 1953-55. Columbia U. fellow, 1947-48, NIH fellow 1948-49, Nat. Insts. Dental Rsch. fellow, 1949-50; recipient Fredrick Birnberg Rsch. award Columbia U., 1987, Lifetime Achievement award March of Dimes, 1989, Am. Cleft Palate Assn. award, 1993, Spinoza chair U. Amsterdam, 1995, Norton Ross prize ADA, 1995. Fellow Am. Acad. Oral Pathology (v.p. 1957-58, 64-65, sec. 1958-64, pres. 1966-67, award 1993), Am. Bd. Oral Pathology, Am. Bd. Med. Genetics, Royal Soc. Surgeons of Ireland, Royal Soc. Surgeons of Eng.; mem. ADA (cons. coun. dental edn.nternat. Assn. Dental Rsch. (sec. Minn. div. 1958-59, pres. 1959-60), Minn. Soc. Pathologists, Am. Soc. Human Genetics, Am. Acad. Oral Pathology (pres. 1966-67, 75-76, diplomate, bd. dir. 1970-76, v.p. 1974-75), Royal Soc. Medicine London (Burrough Welcome fellow 1991, R. Abercrombie award Med. Genetics 1994), Internat. Acad. Oral Pathology (assoc.), Skeletal Dysplasia Soc. (hon.), Internat. Skeletal Soc., Internat. Soc. Craniofacial Biology (bd. dir. 1966-67, v.p. 1967-68, pres. 1969-70), Hollywood Acad. Medicine (hon.), Sigma Xi, Omicron Kappa Upsilon. Office: U Minn 16-206 Health Sci Unit A Minneapolis MN 55455

GORMAN, KAREN MACHMER, optometric physician; b. Poughkeepsie, N.Y., June 4, 1955; d. James Andrew and Joan (Benton) Machmer; m. D.L. McCartney III, Aug. 16, 1976 (div. June 1982); m. N. David Gorman, Oct. 16, 1985; 1 stepchild, Danette Y. Gorman. BS in Optometry, U. Houston, 1976, OD, 1978; therapeutic pharm. lic., U. Mo., St. Louis, 1993. Diplomate Nat. Bd. Examiners Optometry; lic. optometrist, Colo., Mo., Tex. Pvt. practice Dallas, 1978-83, 1984-85, Hurst, Tex., 1984-85, St. Joseph, Mo., 1986—; charter mem. optometric adv. panel Pearle, Inc., 1991-93; lectr. on eyecare to community groups; free-lance journalist St. Joseph News-Press, Benson (N.C.) Rev. Contbr. poetry to lit. jours. including Nat. Libr. of Poetry and Typo mag., articles to profl. jours. including St. Joseph News Press and Benson (N.C.) Review; lead actress (play) None Come Back Innocent, Robidoux Resident Theatre, St. Joseph, 1990, Hay Fever, 1991, The Best Man, 1992, Wedded But No Wife, 1993, Mousetrap, 1993, Diary of Anne Frank, 1994, Death and the Maiden, 1995, Veronica's Room, 1996. Vol. Dallas Humane Soc., 1981, YWCA Women's Abuse Shelter; patron Robidoux Resident Theatre, St. Joseph, 1988-92, Ice House Theatre, St. Joseph, Kemper Albrecht Art Mus., St. Joseph, St. Joseph Animal Shelter; sponsor, coach, cheerleader and drill team Mo. Western State Coll., St. Joseph, 1985-86; legis. corr. Humane Soc. U.S., 1990-92; mem. Nat. Soc. Newspaper Columnists. Recipient Optometric Recognition awards Pearle, Inc., 1986-90; U. Houston scholar, 1972-76. Mem. U. Houston Alumni Assn., CWENS, Nat. Assn. Newspaper Columnists, St. Joseph Lit. Guild, Tau Sigma.

GORMAN, PATRICK DANIEL, cardiologist; b. Santa Ana, Calif., June 29, 1957; s. Herbert Russell and Mary Elizabeth (Denton) G.; m. Tracy Jeanette Williams, Dec. 9, 1989. BS in Biology/Physics, Pacific Luth. U., 1981; MD, U. Health Svcs., Bethesda, Md., 1985. Diplomate Am. Bd. Internal Medicine. Enlisted U.S. Army, 1981, advanced through grades, 1988—; dir. cardiac lab. Walter Reed Army Med. Ctr., Washington, 1988—. Fellow Am. Coll. Cardiologists; mem. ACP. Home: 8328 Quill Point Dr Bowie MD 20720 Office: Walter Reed Army Med Ctr Georgia Ave Washington DC 20307

GORMAN, STEVEN, health insurance executive; b. L.A., Sept. 9, 1945; m. Sherry Moncrieff, Aug. 3, 1985; 1 child, Brian. Pres., ceo Alt. Health Ins. Svcs., Inc., Thousand Oaks, Calif., 1985—; pres., ceo Alliance for Alternatives in Healthcare, Inc., Thousand Oaks, 1990—. Office: The Alt Health Group PO Box 6279 Thousand Oaks CA 91359

GORMLEY, DANIEL EUGENE, dermatologist, educator; b. Oakland, Calif., Nov. 20, 1935; s. David Eugene and Dorothy Elizabeth (McGuire) G.; children: Brendan Daniel, Christopher Patrick. BS, St. Mary's Coll., 1958, U. Calif., Berkeley, 1959; MD, U. Calif., San Francisco, 1963. Diplomate, Am. Bd. Dermatology. Rotating intern SUNY, Syracuse, 1963-64, resident in radiology, 1964-65; asst. resident in medicine U. Utah Hosp., Salt Lake City, 1965-67; resident in dermatology Washington U. Med. Ctr., St. Louis, 1967-70; pvt. practice Glendora, Calif., 1970—; asst. clin. prof. Ctr. Health Scis., UCLA, 1978—; mem. staff Foothill Presbyn. Hosp., San Dimas Cmty. Hosp., Glendora Cmty. Hosp., UCLA Ctr. Health Scis., Pomona Valley Med. Ctr., Inter Cmty. Med. Ctr. Patentee biol. surface contour measurement device; contbr. articles to med. publs. Fellow Am. Acad. Dermatology, Pacific Dermatologic Assn., Met. Dermatol. Soc., Am. Soc. Dermatologic Surgery (bd. dirs. 1973-76, v.p. 1980), Soc. Investigative Dermatology; mem. Calif. Med. Assn., Internat. Soc. Bioengring. and Skin, Pacific Dermatologic Soc., L.A. Met. Dermatologic Soc. Republican. Office: 412 W Carroll Ave Ste 207 Glendora CA 91741-4240

GORMLEY, FRANICS XAVIER, JR., social worker; b. Boston, Apr. 27, 1953; s. Francis Xavier and Catherine Caroline (Ireland) G. Student, Massasoit Community Coll., 1973; BA in Psychology, U. Mass., Boston, 1981; MSW, U. Wash., 1984. Lic. social worker, Hawaii. Coordinator Gerontology Career Program Elder Fest, Chico, Calif., 1981; mgr. Arnold's Restaurant, Cardiff, Wales, 1981-82; med. social worker Harborview Med. Ctr., Seattle, 1983-84; psychotherapist Seattle Counseling Svc., 1982-38; clin. social worker Pain Ctr. Swedish Hosp., Seattle, 1984-88, Valley Med. Ctr., Renton, Wash., 1987-88; clin. social worker AIDS program, virology clinic Univ. Hosp., Seattle, 1988-94; mgr. clin. ops. dept. social work The Queen's Med. Ctr., Honolulu, 1994—; speaker U. Wash Sch. Social Work Graduation Class, 1984, Social Sensitivity in Health Care U. Wash., 1985—; coord. Coping with AIDS Swedish Hosp. Tumor Inst., 1985; participant Coun. of Internat. Fellowship Italia, Placement Servizi Socio-Sanitari AIDS-Roma, 1991; guest speaker Sta. KIRO-TV, Seattle, 1985, Sta. KPLZ, Seattle, 1985; presentor psychosocial aspects HIV/AIDS Northwest AIDS Edn. & Tng. Ctr. Program, U. Wash. Med. Ctr., 1992, clin. mgmt. of patient with HIV/AIDS El Rio Health Ctr., Pima Colo. Pub. Health Dept., 1992, Queen's Cancer Inst. Symposium, 1996; cons. Assn. Workers Resources, Seattle, 1985—; practicum instr. U. Wash. Seattle Sch. Social Work, 1989—; preceptor, intern Residency Tng. Project Sch. of Medicine/Health Scis., Univ. Wash; HIV/AIDS planning coun. Seattle/King County Pub. Health Dept., 1993; com. for the 25th health scis. open house U. Wash. Editor abstract form Comprehensive Multi-Disciplinary Documentation, Western U.S.A. Pain Soc., 1986; contbr. articles to profl. jours. Mem. Seattle Aids Network, 1985—. Mem. NASW (mem. bd. Wash. state chpt. 1988-90), Acad. Cert. Social Workers, Occupational Social Work Orgn. of NASW, Coun. Internat. Fellowship, U. Wash. Alumni Assn., U. Mass. Alumni Assn., Green Key Soc. Democrat. Office: The Queen's Med Ctr Social Work Dept 1301 Punchbowl St Honolulu HI 96813-2413

GORNEY, MARILYN ANN, physician; b. Orange, N.J., Sept. 15, 1966; d. Henry Stanley and Katherine Joan (Jantelle) G.; m. James Joseph Daley, May 20, 1995. BA magna cum laude, Lehigh U., 1988; DO, U. Med. & Dentistry of N.J., 1993. Diplomate Nat. Bd. Osteo. Med. Examiners; lic. physician, N.J. Academic adminstr. Montclair State Coll., Upper Montclair, N.J., 1988-89; intern Kennedy Meml. Hosp., Stratford, N.J., 1993-94; resident Robert Wood Johnson Med. Sch., Piscataway, N.J., 1994-95; clinic physician Planned Parenthood of Greater No. N.J., Inc., Flemington, 1996—; pub. health resident N.J. Dept. of Health, Trenton, 1995—, adv. com., 1995—. Mem. AMA, Am. Osteo. Assn., N.J. Assn. Osteo. Physicians and Surgeons, Assn. Preventive Medicine Residents (rep. 1996). Office: NJ Dept of Health Divsn Epidemiology 3635 Quakerbridge Rd Trenton NJ 08625-0369

GORNEY, MARY JANE, nurse; b. Bay, Mich., May 19, 1939; d. Paul Arthur and Pearl Amelia (Stevenson) McCure; m. Thomas Joseph Gorney, June 16, 1956; children: Thomas Joseph Jr., Kenneth Paul. Degree in nursing arts, psychology, Delta Coll., 1974. RN, Mich.; cert. tchr. Mich. Office mgr. Auburn (Mich.) Clinic P.C., 1963-74; staff nurse Mercy Hosp., Bay, 1975; patient care coord. Bay Med. Ctr., 1977-78, staff nurse, 1979—; instr. Bay Arenac Skill Ctr., 1981—. Min. Wine & Bread and Min. of the Word, St. Hyacinths Parish., Bay, 1988—. Mem. ANA, Am. Assn. Neurosci. Nurses (cert. oncology antineoplastic nurse). Democrat. Home: 2809 Fitzhugh St Bay City MI 48708-8678

GORNEY, RODERIC, psychiatry educator; b. Grand Rapids, Mich., Aug. 13, 1924; s. Abraham Jacob Gorney and Edelaine (Roden) Harburg; m. Carol Ann Sobel, Apr. 13, 1986. BS, Stanford U., 1948, MD, 1949; PhD in Psychoanalysis, So. Calif. Psychoanalytic Inst., 1977. Diplomate Am. Bd. Psychiatry and Neurology. Pvt. practice psychiatry San Francisco, 1952-62; asst. prof. UCLA, 1962-71, assoc. prof., 1971-73, prof. psychiatry, 1980—, dir. psychosocial adaptation and the future program, 1971—; faculty So. Calif. Psychoanalytic Inst. Author: The Human Agenda, 1972. Served with USAF, 1943-46. Fellow AAAS, Acad. Psychoanalysis, Am. Psychiatric Assn. (essay prize 1971), Group for Advancement of Psychiatry. Office: UCLA Neuropsychiatric Inst 760 Westwood Plz Los Angeles CA 90024-8300

GORODISCHER, RAFAEL, pediatrician; b. Santiago, Chile, Apr. 26, 1939; arrived in Israel, 1969; s. Nathan and Berta (Rapaport) G.; m. Michal Skolnick, June 3, 1979; children: Anat, Yonathan, Na'ama. MD, U. Chile, Santiago, 1964. Intern U. Chile, 1963; resident Children's Hosp. Buffalo, 1964-66; fellow in pediatric pharmacology SUNY, Buffalo, 1966-69; dir. pediatric svc. A Soroka Med. Ctr., Beer-Sheva, Israel, 1979—; chmn. dept. pediatrics Soroka Med. Ctr., Beer-Sheva, 1984-91; prof. pediatrics Ben-Gurion U., Beer-Sheva, 1989—, Milada Ayrton prof. pediat., 1989; vis. scientist FDA, Washington, 1985-86; mem. exam. com. Israel Pediat. Bd., 1990-92; expert Internat. Pediat. Assn., 1990-95; vis. prof. Hosp. for Sick Children, U. Toronto, Ont., Can., 1992-93. Contbr. chpts. to books. Capt. Israel Def. Force Res. Fellow United Health Found., N.Y., 1968. Mem. AAAS, European Soc. Pediat. Rsch., Soc. for Pediat. Rsch., Israel Pediat. Assn. (exe. com. 1991-95), European Soc. for Devel. Pharmacology, N.Y. Acad. Scis. Home: 21 Hardoof St, 84965 Omer Israel Office: Soroka Med Ctr, PO Box 151, 84101 Beersheva Israel

GORRA, MARILYN NOVAL, public health professional; b. Liloan, Cebu, The Philippines, Oct. 14, 1948; d. Marcela Cabatingan Noval; m. Rudy De Castro Gorra, Feb. 15, 1976; 1 child, Kristina. BS in Hygiene, U. The Philippines, Quezon City, 1969, MPH, 1974, DPA, 1994. Credit asst. Marsman and Co., Cebu, The Philippines, 1971-73; scientist II health physics dept. AEC, Quezon City, The Philippines, 1974; social svcs. specialist Nat. Econ. and Devel. Authority, Manila, 1974-85; evaluation cons. USAID Econ. Devel. Found., Manila, 1985; planning cons. UNICEF Negros (The Philippines) Project, 1986; exec. dir. Intercare Rsch. Found., Manila, 1987-89; mng. dir. Health, Edn. and Welfare Specialists, Inc., Manila, 1989—; social planning cons. UN Ctr. for Regional Devel., Nagoya, Japan, 1985-86; free-lance cons. Asian Devel. Bank, Manila, 1987, 89; cons. Dept. Health, Manila, 1988—; bd. dirs. San Antonio HMO, Binan, Laguna, The Philippines, Shipfinders Philippines, Inc., Makati. Contbr. articles to profl. jours. Organizer San Antonio HMO, Binan, 1987-88, UP HMO, Quezon City, 1987-88, bd. dirs., 1989—. Rsch. grantee UN Population Fund, U. of The Philippines Population Inst., Manila, 1990. Nat. Sci. Devel. Bd. scholar, 1973-74, Bailon Dela Rama Endowment scholar, 1967-69, U. The Philippines scholar, 1964-67; fellow Econ. Devel. Inst. World Bank, 1979, U.S. Agy. for Internat. Devel., 1976. Mem. U.P. Coll. Pub. Health Alumni Assn., Philippines Assn. Tech. Asst. Participants, Philippines Assn. Nutrition, Health Rsch. Network, Philippines Population Assn. Home: 11 Lipton 1 St, Filinvest II-G, Quezon City Metro Manila, The Philippines Office: Health Edn & Welfare Specialists, Horizon Condominium #801, Meralco Ave Ortigas Ctr, Pasig Metro Manila 1605, The Philippines

GORROD, JOHN WILLIAM, biopharmacy research educator; b. London, Oct. 11, 1931; s. Ernest Lionel and Carrie Rebecca (Richardson) G.; m. Doreen Mary Collins, Apr. 3, 1954; children: Julia Caroline, Simon Jonathon William, Nicholas Ernest Freeman. Diploma, Chelsea Coll., London, 1961; PhD, London U., 1979, DSc, 1982. Tech. officer Chester Beatty Rsch. Inst., London, 1955-65; rsch. fellow biochemistry U. Bari, Italy, 1964; rsch. fellow Royal Commn. Exhibition of 1851, 1965-67; lectr. biopharmacy Chelsea Coll., London, 1968-80, reader biopharmacy, 1980-84; prof., head Dept. of Pharmacy King's Coll., London, 1984-90, head div. Health Scis. Faculty of Life Sci., 1988-89, rsch. prof., 1990—, elected fellow, 1996—; dir. Drug Control and Tchg. Ctr., Sports Coun., 1985-91; vis. prof. U. Bologna, U. Bari, U. Kebangan, Malaysia; Can. MRC vis. prof. U. Man., U. Sask., 1988; vis. prof. Chinese Acad. of Preventive Medicine, 1991. Author: (with others) Metabolism of Xenobiotics, 1988, Molecular Aspects of Human Disease, vol. 2, 1989, Biological Oxidation Systems, vol. 1, 1990, Biological Oxidation of Nitrogen in Drug Molecules, 1990, Molecular Basis of Neurological Disorders and Their Treatment, 1990, Nicotine and Related Alkaloids, 1993; contbr. articles to profl. jours.; editl. bd. Xenobiotics, European Jour. Metabolism and Pharmokinetics, Toxicology Letters, Ann. Cancer Rsch. Recipient Gold medal of Comenius, U. Bratislava, 1991. Fellow Pan-Hellenic Assn. Pharmacists (hon.), Turkish Pharm. Soc. (hon.), Royal Coll. Pathologists, Royal Soc. Chemistry; mem. Internat. Soc. Study Xenobiotics (founder, mem. coun., chmn. membership affairs com.), Pharm. Soc. Gt. Britain (hon., mem. edn. com.), German Pharm. Soc. (corr.), Assocs. for Rsch. in Substances of Enjoyment, Assocs. for Rsch. on Indoor Air, Indoor Air Internat. (mem. coun.), Air Transport Users Assn., Athenaeum Club, Hillingdon Athletic Club. Home: Kingsmead 13, Park Ln, Hayes Hayes UB4 8AA, England Office: King's Coll U London, Chelsea Campus Manresa Rd, London SW3 6LX, England

GORRY, G. ANTHONY, medical educator. BSE, Yale U., 1962; MS, U. Calif., Berkeley, 1962; PhD in Computer Sci., MIT, 1967. From asst. prof. to assoc. prof. Sloan Sch. Mgmt., 1967-73, assoc. prof. computer sci., 1973-75; from assoc. prof. cmty. medicine to prof. health mgmt. Baylor Coll. Medicine, Houston, 1975-85, prof. divsn. neurosci., v.p. info. tech., 1986—; assoc. faculty Oper. Rsch. Ctr., MIT, 1971-75; lectr. dept. med. Tufts U. Sch. Med., 1971-75; adj. assoc. prof. math. sci. Rice U., 1975-78, adj. prof. dept. computer sci., 1985—; adj. prof. bus. and econ. Tex. Womens U., 1978-79; com. mem. Nat. Libr. Med., 1984-88; dir. W.M. Keck ctr. computer biology Baylor Coll. Med. and Rice U.; dir. evaluation rsch. group Nat. Heart and Blood Vessel Rsch. and Demonstration Ctr., 1975-82, dir. health mgmt. rsch., 1978-80; adj. prof. neurosci. and cmty. medicine Baylor Coll. Med. Fellow Am. Coll. Med. Informatics; mem. Inst. Med.-Nat. Acad. Sci. Office: Baylor Coll of Medicine Dept Of Neuroscience Houston TX 77030 Office: Rice University PO Box 1892 6100 South Main Houston TX 77251*

GORSKI CROISSANT, KATHLEEN, occupational therapist; b. Cleve., July 27, 1958; d. Michael Robert and Marian Frances (Doubrava) G.; m. Ronald B. Croissant, Apr. 1993; children: Deandra Croissant, Kevin Croissant. AAS, Cuyahoga Community Coll., Cleve., 1981; BS, Ea. Mich. U., 1983. Reg. occupational therapist; cert. aerobics instr., personal trainer. Activity dir. Dover Nursing Home, Westlake, Ohio, 1981-82; staff therapist U. Hosps. of Cleve., 1984-86, sr. therapist, 1986-87, clin. specialist, 1989-90, clin. mgr., 1990-95; pres. Kathleen Gorski Rehab., Westlake, Ohio, 1989—, Fairview Health Sys., Cleveland, 1995—; occupational therapist UPS, Cleve., 1987-89. Named Outstanding Clinician, Cleve. Dist. O.T. Assn., 1988; recipient Humanitarian award Ea. Mich. U., 1983. Mem. Cleve. Dist. Occupational Therapists Assn., Ohio Occupational Therapists Assn., Am. Occupational Therapists Assn. Republican. Roman Catholic. Office: Fairview Health Sys 18101 Lorain Ave Cleveland OH 44111

GORTATOWSKI, MELVIN JEROME, retired chemist; b. Chgo., Oct. 30, 1925; s. Walter Harry and Anna Martha (Santowski) G. BS, U. Ill., 1950, PhD, 1955; MS, Wash. State U., 1952. Research instr. biochemistry U. Utah, Salt Lake City, 1955-58, research assoc. psychiatry, 1958-59, research instr. biochemistry, chemist VA Hosp., 1959-65; assoc. investigator, asst. rsch. prof. pediatrics, biochemistry U. So. Calif. Children's Hosp., Los Angeles, 1965-71; dir. bur. clin. chemistry Utah State Health Lab., Salt Lake City, 1971-87, safety officer, 1980-87. Contbr. articles to jours. Served with U.S. Army, 1944-46. Eastman Kodak fellow U. Ill., 1954. Mem. Am. Chem. Soc., Mineral Collectors Utah, Utah Numismatic Soc. (bd. dirs. 1976-77), Sigma Xi, Phi Lambda Upsilon. Roman Catholic. Home: 4045 Foubert Ave Salt Lake City UT 84124-3410

GORTNER, SUSAN REICHERT, nursing educator; b. San Francisco, Dec. 23, 1932; d. Frederick Leet and Erida Louise (Leuschner) R.; m. Willis Alway Gortner, Aug. 25, 1960 (dec. Sept. 1993); children: Catherine Willis, Frederick Aiken. AB, Stanford U., 1953; M Nursing, Western Res. U., 1957; PhD, U. Calif., Berkeley, 1964; postgrad., Stanford U., 1983. Staff nurse, instr., supr. Johns Hopkins Hosp. Sch. Nursing, Balt., 1957-58; instr. to asst. prof. Sch. Nursing U. Hawaii, Honolulu, 1958-64; staff scientist, rsch. adminstr. div. nursing USPHS, Bethesda, Md., 1966-78; assoc. dean rsch. Sch. Nursing U. Calif., San Francisco, 1978-86, acting chmn. dept. family health, 1982, prof. dept. family health care nursing, 1978-94; prof. emerita, 1994—; fellow, assoc. mem. faculty Inst. Health Policy U. Calif., San Francisco, 1979-94, mem. affiliated faculty Inst. for Aging and Health, 1981-94, adj. prof. internal medicine dept. gen. medicine, 1989-94, dir. cardiac recovery lab. Sch. Nursing, 1987-95, spl. asst. to dean, 1993-94; Fulbright lectr., rsch. scholar Norwegian Fulbright Commn., Oslo, 1988. Contbr. articles, papers to profl. publs., chpts. to books. Health advisor N. Fork Assn., Soda Springs, Calif., 1981—. Disting. scholar Nat. Ctr. Nursing Rsch., 1990; named Disting. Alumna Frances Payne Bolton Sch. Nursing, 1983. Fellow Am. Acad. Nursing; mem. ANA (chair exec. com., coun. nurse rsch. com. 1976-80, cabinet on nursing rsch. 1984-86), Am. Heart Assn. (coun. cardiovascular nursing exec. com. 1987-91, coun. epidemiology 1989—, Katharine A. Lembright award 1991, fellow in cardiovascular nursing coun. 1992), Sigma Theta Tau (Alpha Eta chpt., Margretta M. Styles award 1990). Home: PO Box 1056 Soda Springs CA 95728-1056 Office: U Calif 4th And Parnassus # N411Y San Francisco CA 94143

GOSCHE, JOHN ROBERT, medical educator; b. Shelby, Ohio, May 4, 1959; s. Firmin Albert and Margaret Loretta (Wechter) G.; m. Susan Lynn Marshall, June 27, 1994; children: Beau, Kelsey. BA in Biology, BA in Chemistry, U. South Fla., 1981; MD, U. South Fla., 1985; PhD in Physiology, U. Louisville, 1992. Diplomate Am. Bd. Surgery. Intern dept. surgery U. Louisville, Ky., 1985-86; resident surgery U. Louisville, 1986-88, 90-92; fellow pediat. surgery Columbus (Ohio) Children's Hosp., 1992-94; asst. prof. Yale U. Sch. Medicine, New Haven, 1994—. Contbr. articles to profl. jours. Recipient Annual Essay award for best basic sci. paper Assn. VA Surgeons, 1990. Fellow ACS (assoc.); mem. Assn. for Acad. Surgery. Office: Yale Univ Sch Medicine Dept Surgery 333 Cedar St FMB 132 New Haven CT 06520

GOSIN, ROBERT FABIAN, dentist; b. Buffalo, Aug. 18, 1955; s. Robert Fabian and Doloros (Boute) G.; m. Cathy Sue Willy, Dec. 16, 1994; children: Stacy, Jason. BS, Creighton U., 1980, DDS, 1985. Developer Calif. Benefits Dental Plan, Huntington Beach, 1991, CEO, 1992—. Mem. Calif. Assn. Dental HMOs. Office: Calif Benefits Dental Plan 4911 Warner Ave # 203 Huntington Beach CA 92649

GOSS, ANNA J., nursing home administrator; b. N.Y.C., July 28, 1929; d. Saverio and Rose (Sacco) Marcantonio; m. Frank X. Goss, May 16, 1953; children: Eileen Goss Whelley, James, Peggy Goss Limmer, Mary Myles, Kathleen, Sheila, Kevin. RN, Mt. Vernon Hosp. Sch. of, Nursing, N.Y., 1951; BS in Health Svcs. Adminstrn., Empire State Coll., 1985. RN; cert. nursing home administrator. Relief charge nurse Glens Falls (N.Y.) Hosp., 1967-72; head nurse Ft. Hudson Nursing Home, Ft. Edward, N.Y., 1972-73, day supr., in-svc. dir., 1973-76, asst. dir. nursing, infection control, 1976-78, dir. nursing, 1978-85; dir. nursing Geneva (N.Y.) Hosp. Nursing Home, 1985-87, adminstr., 1987-90; sr. adminstr. Huntington Nursing Home, Waterloo, N.Y., 1990-93; v.p., long term care Huntington and Geneva Nursing Home, Waterloo and Geneva, 1993-95; surveyor and faculty, Joint Commn. on Accrediation Health Care Orgns., Oak Brook Terrace, Ill., 1995—; cons. in field. Mem. Am. Coll. Health Care Adminstrs., N.Y. Assn. Long-Term Care Adminstrs. Roman Catholic. Home: 1 Main St Hudson Falls NY 12839 Office: JCAHO 1 Renaissance Blvd Oakbrook Terrace IL 60181

GOSS, DAVID ARTHUR, optometry educator, researcher; b. Joliet, Ill., July 22, 1948; s. Arthur L. and Virginia A. Goss; m. Dawn A. Goss. BA in Biology, Ill. Wesleyan U., 1970; BS in Optometry, Pacific U., Forest Grove, Oreg., 1972, OD, 1974; PhD in Physiol. Optics, Ind. U., 1980. Optometrist Drs. Lande & Crouch, Storm Lake, Iowa, 1974-75; assoc. instr. optometry Ind. U., Bloomington, 1976-79, rsch. assoc., 1979-80; asst. prof. optometry Northeastern State U., Tahlequah, Okla., 1980-85, assoc. prof., 1985-89, prof., 1989-92; prof. Ind. Univ., Bloomington, 1992—; mem. working group on myopia prevalence and progression NRC, 1984-87. Author: Ocular Accommodation Convergence and Fixation Disparity, 1986, 2d edit., 1995; editor: Eye and Vision Conditions in the American Indian, 1990; contbr. articles to profl. jours. Grantee, Am. Optometric Found., 1985-87, Nat. Eye Inst., 1987-88, Okla. Ctr. for Advancement Sci. and Tech., 1989-91, faculty of yr. rsch. and scholarly activity Northeastern State U., Tahlequah, Okla., 1990-91. Fellow Am. Acad. Optometry; mem. Am. Optometric Assn. (mem. rev. bd. jour. 1988-94, rev. panel, clin. Practice Guideline on Comprehensive Adult Eye Examination, 1993-94, cons. editor jour. 1994—), Assn. Optometric Educators (pres. 1988-90), Optometric Hist. Soc. (newsletter editor 1996—), Optical Soc. Am., Assn. for Rsch. in Vision and Ophthalmology, Sigma Xi. Office: Sch of Optometry Indiana Univ Bloomington IN 47405

GOSS, JEROME ELDON, cardiologist; b. Dodge City, Kans., Nov. 30, 1935; s. Horton Maurice and Mary Alice (Mountain) G.; m. Lorraine Ann Sanchez, Apr. 20, 1986. BA, U. Kans., 1957; MD, Northwestern U., 1961. Diplomate Am. Bd. Internal Medicine, Am. Bd. Cardiology (fellow, bd. govs. 1981-84). Intern Met. Gen. Hosp., Cleve., 1961-62; resident Northwestern U. Med. Ctr., Chgo., 1962-64; fellow in cardiology U. Colo., Denver, 1964-66; asst. prof. medicine U. N.Mex., Albuquerque, 1968-70; practice medicine specializing in cardiology N.Mex. Heart Clinic, 1970—; mem. bd. alumni counsellors Northwestern U. Med. Sch., 1977-89, mem. nat. alumni bd., 1991—; chief dept. medicine Presbyn. Hosp., Albuquerque, 1978-80, mem. exec. com., 1980-82, dir. cardiac diagnostic svcs., 1970—. Contbr. articles to profl. jours. Bd. dirs. Presbyn. Heart Inst., Ballet West N.Mex., N.Mex. Symphony Orch.; pres. Albuquerque Mus. Found. Lt. comdr. USN, 1966-68. Nat. Heart Inst. research fellow, 1965-66; named one of Outstanding Young Men Am., Jaycees, 1970; recipient Alumni Service award Northwestern U. Med. Sch., 1986. Fellow ACP, ACC, Coun. Clin. Cardiology of Am. Heart Assn., Soc. Cardiac Angiography; mem. Albuquerque-Bernalillo County Med. Soc. (sec. 1972, treas. 1975, v.p. 1980), Alpha Omega Alpha. Republican. Methodist. Office: NMex Heart Clinic 1001 Coal Ave SE Albuquerque NM 87106-5205

GOSS, JOSEPH B., psychopharmacologist; b. Bklyn., June 1, 1956; s. Bernard David and Catherine (Marino) G.; m. Linda M. Goss, Dec. 28, 1979; children: Catherine, Jessica, Joseph S. B in Pharmacology, St. John's U., 1982; PhD in Psychology, LaSalle U., 1994. Diplomate Am. Bd. Psychopharmacology and Psychotherapy. Prof. Union U., Albany, 1985—; dir. pharmacy O'Connor Hosp., Delhi, N.Y., 1985; v.p. for pharmacy svcs. Advanced Med. Cons., N.Y.C., 1987-93; psychiatric pharmacotherapeutics Stratton VA Med. Ctr., Albany, 1993—; regional dir. Med. Pharmacology Rsch. Unit, Albany, 1993—; med. dir. A.E.C.H.O., Malta, N.Y., 1994—; chair mental health N.Y. State Coun. of Hosp. Pharm., Albany, 1995—; mem. regonal IRB Albany Med. Coll., 1993, others. Author: Hydroponic Workbook, 1985; adv. bd. mags., 1987-94.

GOSS, THOMAS PIXTON, orthopaedic surgeon; b. Boston, Mar. 1, 1947; s. William Oscar and Catherine Jeanette (Van Dyke) G.; m. Joan Mary Maughan, May 19, 1979; children: Thomas William, Christine Anne, John Michael. AB, Dartmouth Coll., 1968; BMS, Dartmouth Med. Sch., 1969; MD, Harvard U., 1971. Diplomate Am. Bd. Orthop. Surgery. Surgical intern and resident Roosevelt Hosp., N.Y.C., 1971-73; orthop. resident Columbia-Presbyn. Hosp., N.Y.C., 1973-76, orthop. fellow, 1976-77; med. officer USN Regional Med. Ctr., Portsmouth, Va., 1977-79; attending orthop. surgeon U. Mass. Med. Ctr., Worcester, 1979—; chief shoulder svc. dept. orthop. surgery, U. Mass. Med. Ctr., Worcester, 1979—; asst. prof. orthop. surgery, U. Mass. Med. Sch., Worcester, 1979-84, assoc. prof., 1984-89, prof., 1990—; vis. prof. Ohio State U., 1996; cons. reviewer Jour. Bone and Joint Surgery, Jour. Shoulder and Elbow Surgery; presenter numerous local and regional presentations to gen. public, students, sci groups and some nat. and internat. profl. socs. Contbr. articles to profl. jours. Lt. cmmdr. USN, 1977-79. Fellow Am. Acad. Orthop. Surgeons; mem. Am. Shoulder and Elbow Surgeons, Orthop. Trauma Assn., New Eng. Orthop. Soc. (treas. 1995—). Roman Catholic. Office: U Mass Med Ctr Dept Orthop Surgery 55 Lake Ave N Worcester MA 01655

GOSSELIN, BENOIT JEAN, otolaryngologist, head and neck surgeon; b. Quebec City, Can., Oct. 24, 1962. BSc, U. Ottawa, 1983, BSc with honors, 1984, MD, 1988. Diplomate Am. Bd. Otolaryngology. Resident in otolaryngology U. Ottawa, 1989-93; fellow head and neck surgery U. Toronto, 1993-94; fellow in microvascular and facial plastic surgery Mercy Hosp. Pitts., 1994-95; asst. prof. surgery Dartmouth Coll., Hanover, N.H., 1995—; staff otolaryngology sect. Dartmouth-Hitchcock Med. Ctr., Lebanon, N.H., 1995—. Fellow Royal Coll. Surgeons (Can.); mem. AMA, Am. Acad. Otolaryngology, Head and Neck Surgery, Am. Acad. Facial Plastics and Reconstructive Surgery, Can. Soc. Otolaryngology, Head and Neck Surgery, Can. Med. Assn. Office: Dartmouth-Hitchcock Med Ctr Sect Otolaryngology One Medical Ctr Dr Lebanon NH 03755

GOSSER, JON WALTER, educator; b. Seattle, May 15, 1941; s. Lawrence and Ellinore (Jones) G.; B.S. cum laude, U. Wash., 1962, M.S., 1964, postgrad., 1964-65; postgrad. U. Kans., 1965-67. Reader in stats. U. Wash., Seattle, fellow research asst. in psychology, 1962-63, USPHS predoctoral research fellow NIMH, 1963-65; predoctoral trainee in ednl. research Bur. Child Research, U. Kans., Kansas City, 1965-66; tchr. psychology, logic and marriage and family relations Kansas City (Kans.) Community Jr. Coll., 1966-67; instr. psychology Delta Coll., University Center, Mich., 1967-69, asst. prof., 1970-75, asso. prof., 1975—, dir. Mid-Mich. Psychologist, Inc., 1973-76, 79—, treas., 1978—; pres. Nat. Ednl. Network, Inc., 1984—, bd. dirs. 1982—. Mem. Data Processing Mgmt. Assn. (dir. 1971-73; individual performance award 1981), Am. Psychol. Assn., AAAS, AAUP (corr. sec. Delta chpt. 1969), Am. Ednl. Research Assn., Assn. Behavior Analysis, Mich. Acad. Sci., Arts and Letters, Internat. Soc. for Individual Instrn., Sigma Xi. Author: (with Harbans Lal) Research on Teaching Pharmacy: The Role of Student Ratings, 1968; A Computerized Method of Longitudinal Evaluation of Student Performance, 1969; Computerized Test Library, 1974; Longitudinal Evaluation and Improvement of Teaching: An Empirical Approach Based on Analysis of Student Behaviors, 1975; (with Packwood and Walters) The Effect of Repeated Testing on Long Term Retention and Generalization in a General Psychology Course, 1979. Home and Office: 3200 Noeske St Midland MI 48640-3349

GOSSLEE, MARY JUNE, chiropractor; b. Seattle, Jan. 3, 1957; d. Norman Arthur G. and Carol Mae (Tozier) Eller. BS, SUNY, 1988; D of Chiropractic, Logan Coll. Chiropractic, 1991. EMT Shepard Ambulance, Seattle, 1983-85; paramedic Abbott Ambulance, St. Louis, 1985-90; teaching asst. Logan Coll. Chiropractic, St. Louis, 1990-91; assoc. Woodway Chiropractic, Lynnwood, Wash., 1993; chiropractor Family Health Ctr., Bellevue, Wash., 1993—; bd. dirs. Successful Women's Network, Bellevue,; founding dir. Discovery Inst. for Healing Arts, Issaquah, Wash., 1995; speaker in field. Recipient Alumni Rsch. award Logan Coll. Alumni Assn., 1991. Mem. Am. Chiropractic Assn., Women Entrepreneur's Network (v.p. 1993-94), Women Bus. Owners (bd. dirs. 1996), Emerald City Bus. Network, Bus. Network Internat., Chi Rho Sigma. Office: Family Health Ctr 10230 NE 10th St Bellevue WA 98004

GOSSLING, HARRY ROBERT, orthopaedic surgeon, educator; b. Phila., July 20, 1922. MD, Temple U., 1947; MSc in Orthopaedic Surgery, U. Tenn. Intern Hartford Hosp., 1947-48, res. gen. surgery, 1948-49, sr. attending, dir. dept. orthopaedic surgery, 1965-76; orthopaedic surgeon Campbell Clinic, Memphis, 1950-51, 53-55; chief div. orthopaedics Conn. Health Ctr., Farmington, 1975-84; prof. orthopaedic surgery U. Conn. Sch. Medicine, Farmington, 1975—; chmn. dept. orthopaedic surgery U. Conn. Sch. Orthopaedics, 1975-90, Gray Gossling prof. orthopaedic surgery, 1990-92, prof. emeritus, 1992—; assoc. orthop. surgery, corporator Conn. Children's Med. Ctr.; corporator Hartford Sem., 1983—; chmn. parent co. Hosp. for Spl. Care (formerly New Britain Meml. Hosp.), 1992-96, bd. dirs., 1996—; bd. dirs. Fidelco Guide Found.; cons. orthop. surgery Manchester Meml. Hosp., Mt. Sinai Hosp., Hartford, Conn. Editor-in-Chief Complications in Orthopaedic Surgery, 1986—. Capt. U.S. Army, 1951-53. Fellow AMA, ACS, ASOS, La Soc. Internationale Re Chirurgie Orthopedique et de Traumatologie; mem. Am. Orthopaedic Assn. (v.p. 1987-88), Orthopaedic Rsch. Soc., Ea. Orthopaedic Assn. (pres. 1987), Am. Acad. Orthopaedic Surgeons. Office: U Conn Sch Medicine Dept Orthopaedic Surgery 10 Talcott Notch Rd Farmington CT 06034-4037

GOSSLING, JENNIFER, microbiologist; b. Welwyn Garden City, England, July 25, 1934; came to U.S., 1962; d. Richard S. and Millicent E. (Hodson) Sayers; m. William Frank Gossling, Nov. 3, 1956. BA, Cambridge (Eng.) U., 1955; PhD, W.Va. U., 1973. Asst., instr. U. Manchester, Eng., 1966-69, W.Va. U. Med. Ctr., Morgantown, 1969-73, Med. Col.. Ohio, Toledo, 1975; postdoctoral scholar Dental Rsch. Inst., U. Mich., Ann Arbor, 1978-79; mem. staff Indiana (Pa.) Hosp., 1979-80; med. technologist Jewish Hosp. of St. Louis, 1980—; asst. prof. Sch. of Dental Medicine, Washington U., St. Louis, 1981-91, St. Louis Coll. Pharmacy, 1993-95; Contbr. to Bergey's Manual of Systematic Bacteriology, Vol. 3, 1989.

GOTCHER, JACK EVERETT, JR., oral and maxillofacial surgeon; b. Wichita Falls, Tex., May 11, 1949; s. Jack Everett Sr. and Josephine Caroline (Kruh) G.; m. Kathyanne Mary King, Dec. 30, 1972; children: Elizabeth Gayle, Jeffrey Everett. BS in Chemistry and Biology, Midwestern U., 1971; DMD magna cum laude, Harvard U., 1975; PhD, U. Utah, 1979. Diplomate Am. Bd. Oral and Maxillofacial Surgery, 1984. Resident in oral and maxillofacial Surgery U. Tenn., Knoxville, 1982; asst. prof. Emory State U., Atlanta, 1982-83; assoc. prof. U. Tenn., Knoxville, 1983—; cons. Proctor and Gamble Co., Cin., 1977, VA Hosp., Atlanta, 1982-83, The Upjohn Co., Kalamazoo, Mich., 1984-88, Am. Assn. Oral and Maxillofacial Surgery, Chgo., 1986—. Contbr. articles profl. jours. Chmn. profl. edn. com. Am. Cancer Soc., Knoxville, 1988—. Recipient Am. Inst. Chemists award, 1971; NIH fellow, 1975-78, Am. Cancer Soc. fellow, 1978-79. Fellow Am. Assn. Oral and Maxillofacial Surgeons (del. 1988—); mem. ADA, Tenn. Dental Assn. (del. 1989—), Am. Cleft Palate-Craniofacial Assn. Presbyterian. Home: 1409 Kensington Dr Knoxville TN 37922-6039 Office: U Tenn Med Ctr PO Box I 1928 Alcoa Hwy Knoxville TN 37920-1502

GOTH, ROBERT WILLIAM, plant pathologist; b. Phillips, Wis., May 10, 1927; s. William Edward and Rose (Dolezalek) G.; m. Joyce Marie Nelson, Dec. 29, 1954; children: Valerie, Robert W. Jr., Stephen. BS, U. Wis., Superior, 1954; MS, U. Minn., 1958, PhD, 1961; postgrad., U. Calif., Davis, 1965-66. Rsch. plant pathologist vegetable lab. Agrl. Rsch. Svc. USDA, Beltsville, Md., 1961—. Author: (with others) Fungal Wilts of Plants, 1981. Sgt. U.S. Army, 1945-52. Recipient Researcher of Yr. award Nat. Potato Coun., 1994; grad. scholar Tozer Found., 1959. Mem. Am. Phytopathol. Soc. (sec. treas. Potomac divsn. 1981-84, v.p. 1984-85, pres. 1985-86), Potato Assn. Am. (hon. life,pres. pathology sect. 1983), Sigma Xi, Gamma Alpha. Office: USDA Barc-W Bldg 010 A Rm 226 Beltsville MD 20705

GOTKIN, ROBERT HAROLD, physician; b. Washington, Oct. 12, 1954; s. William and Adela Francis (Rumshin) G.; m. Deborah Susan Sarnoff, May 28, 1983; 1 child, William Ross. BS, U. Md., 1976; MD, Howard U., 1980. Diplomate Am. Bd. Plastic Surgery. Intern in internal medicine Washington Hops. Ctr., 1980-81; resident in gen. surgery Stony Brook (N.Y.) Univ. Hosp., 1981-85; fellow in burn care Stony Brook (N.Y.) U. Hosp., 1985-86; resident in plastic surgery Georgetown U. Hosp., Washington, 1986-88; pvt. practice in plastic surgery Greenvale, N.Y., 1988—. Contbr. articles to profl. jours. Fellow Am. Coll. Surgeons; mem. Am. Soc. Aesthetic Plastic Surgery, Am. Soc. Plastic and Reconstructive Surgeons, Am. Burn Assn., Nassau Surg. Soc., Plastic Surgery Edn. Found. Office: Cosmetique Dermatology Laser and Plastic Surgery 31 Northern Blvd Greenvale NY 11548

GOTLIEB, JAQUELIN SMITH, pediatrician; b. Washington, Oct. 20, 1946; d. Turner Taliaferro and Lois Barbara (Fisk) Smith; m. Edward Marvin Gotlieb, June 25, 1970; children: Sarah Ruth, Aaron Franklin, David Jacob. BS in Zoology, Duke U., 1968; MD, Med. Coll. Va., 1972. Diplomate Am. Bd. Pediat. Rotating intern Med. Coll. Va. Hosps.-Va. Commonwealth U., Richmond, 1972-73, resident in pediat., 1973-74; pvt. practice Richmond, 1974-75, Stone Mountain, Ga., 1976-86, 87—; resident in pediat. U. Colo., Denver, 1975-76; med. dir., cons. CIGNA Healthplan Ga., Atlanta, 1986-87; sch. physician Richmond City Schs., 1974-75. Bd. dirs. Ga. Health Found., Atlanta, 1985-95, vice chmn., 1995—. Fellow Am. Acad. Pediat. (Ga. chpt. bd. dirs. 1996—); mem. Med. Assn. Ga., Ga. Perinatal Assn. (bd. dirs. 1994—), DeKalb Med. Soc. (chmn. com. 1976). Office: Pediatric Ctr 5405 Memorial Dr Ste D Stone Mountain GA 30083-3258

GOTLIN, ROBERT S., physician; b. N.Y.C., June 2, 1958; s. Max and Belle (Spanower) G.; m. Marcia E. Simon, June 14, 1959; children: Matthew, Adam, Samantha. BS, SUNY, Stony Brook, 1979, Nat. Coll. Chiropractic, 1981; D Chiropractic, Nat. Coll. Chiropractic, 1982; DO, Southeastern Univ. of Health, Scis., N. Miami Beach, Fla., 1987. Cert. Am. Bd. Phys. Medicine/Rehabilitation, Am. Osteo. Bd. Phys. Medicine/Rehab. Intern Brookdale Hosp. Med. Ctr., Bklyn., 1982-88; resident phys. medicine/rehab. Mt. Sinai Med. Ctr., N.Y.C., 1988-91; physician-in-charge, orthopaedic sports and spine sect. Beth Israel Med. Ctr. North, N.Y.C., 1991—, asst. chmn., dept. phys. medicine/rehab., 1994—; program chmn. N.Y. Soc. of Phys. Medicine/Rehab., N.Y.C., 1991-95. Contbg. author: Sports Medicine, Primary Care and Rehabilitation, 1996, Dr. Scott's Knee Book, 1996; contbr. articles to profl. jours. Mem. Physiatric Assn. of Sports, Spine and Occupational Rehab. (co-chmn. 1995—), Am. Coll. Sprots Medicine. Office: Beth Israel Med Ctr 170 E End Ave New York NY 10128

GOTO, SATARO, biochemistry educator, researcher; b. Tokyo, May 2, 1941; s. Masakatsu and Yoshie (Suzuki) G.; m. Mariko Sato, Apr. 20, 1971; children: Maki, Kensuke, Miki. Bachelor's degree, U. Tokyo, 1965, Master's degree, 1967, PhD, 1970. Nat. lic. pharmacist, Japan. Rsch. assoc. U. Tokyo, 1970-79; postdoctoral fellow Karolinska Inst., Stockholm, 1971-73, Pasteur Inst., Paris, 1974-75; assoc. prof. U. Tokyo, 1979; prof. Toho U., Chiba, Japan, 1979—; vis. rschr. Tokyo Met. Inst. Gerontology, Tokyo, 1988-95; part-time lectr. faculty medicine U. Tokyo, 1992—; bd. trustees Toho U., Chiba, 1982-88, 94—; reviewer Human Frontier Sci. Program, Strasburg, France, 1989—. Author: Oxidative Stress and Aging, 1995 (grantee Japan Found. Aging and Health 1994); mem. editl. bd.: (jour.) Archives of Gerontology and Geriatrics; contbr. articles to profl. jours. Internat. Agy. for Rsch. on Cancer fellow WHO, 1971-73, European Molecular Biology Orgn. fellow, 1974-75. Mem. Internat. Assn. Gerontology (chmn. biol. sect. Asia/Oceania region 1993—), Sci. Coun. Japan (mem. liaison com. cancer rsch. and aging sci. 1994—), Japan Soc. Biomed. Gerontology (coun. mem.). Home: Yonbancho 8-3-701, Chiyodaku Tokyo 102, Japan Office: Toho U Sch Pharm Scis, Miyama 2-2-1, Funabashi Chiba 274, Japan

GOTSCHLICH, EMIL CLAUS, physician, educator; b. Bangkok, Thailand, Jan. 17, 1935; came to U.S., 1950, naturalized, 1955; s. Emil Clemens and Magdalene (Holst) G.; m. Kathleen-Anne Haines, May 24, 1975; children: Emil Christopher, Hilda Christina, Emil Chandler, Emily Claire. BA, NYU, 1955, MD, 1959. Intern Bellevue Hosp., N.Y.C., 1959-60; mem. faculty Rockefeller U., N.Y.C., 1960—, prof. microbiology, 1978—, sr. physician, 1978—. Capt. M.C., U.S. Army, 1966-68. Decorated Army Commendation medal; recipient Squibb award Am. Soc. Infectious Disease, 1974; Lasker award Albert and Mary Lasker Found., 1978. Mem. NAS, Am. Assn. Immunologists, Assn. Am. Physicians, Am. Soc. for Clin. Investigation, Peripatetic Club, Sigma Xi, Alpha Omega Alpha. Office: Rockefeller U Dept Immunology 1230 York Ave New York NY 10021-6307*

GOTSHALL, MARK EDWARD, employee assistance executive; b. Cin., Dec. 4, 1960; s. Raymond E. and Delores M. A. (Kuehm) G. AA, William Rainey Harper Coll., Palatine, Ill., 1981; BS, Carroll Coll., Waukesha, Wis., 1984; MA, Ctrl. Mich. U., 1992. Cert. chem. dependency counselor; lic. profl. counselor, Mich.; registered social worker. Child care worker St. Rose Residence, Milw., 1984; group home counselor DePaul Rehab. Hosp., Milw., 1984; counselor Mercy Health Ctr., Dubuque, Iowa, 1984-88; family counselor extended care program St. Luke's Hosp., Cleve., 1988-89; clin. supr. Bay Haven Chem. Dependency Programs, Bay City, Mich., 1990-91, integrated care mgr., 1991-93; employee assistance counselor Health Mgmt. Sys. Am., East Pointe, Mich., 1994-95; regional supr. G.A.P., 1995—. Mem. Nat. Assn. Alcoholism and Drug Abuse Counselors. Methodist. Home: 3427 Canal Ave SW Apt 8 Grandville MI 49418-1555

GOTTA, ALEXANDER WALTER, anesthesiologist, educator; b. Bklyn., Apr. 10, 1935; s. A. Walter and Helen C. (Bruskewic) G.; m. Colleen A. Sullivan, July 17, 1965; 1 child, Nancy C. B.S. summa cum laude, St. John's U., 1956; M.D., NYU, 1960. Diplomate Am. Bd. Anesthesiology, Am. Bd. Med. Examiners. Intern, U. Chgo., 1960-61; resident Boston City Hosp., 1961-62, N.Y. Hosp.-Cornell U., 1962-64; instr. anesthesiology Cornell U., 1964-66, asst. prof., 1978-79; dir. anesthesia St. Mary's Hosp., Bklyn., 1968-78; asst. prof. SUNY-Bklyn., 1968-78, assoc. prof., 1978-85, prof., 1985—; dir. anesthesia L.I. Coll. Hosp., Bklyn., 1983-90; dir. anesthesia Kings County Hosp. Ctr., 1990—; speaker in field. Contbr. articles to profl. jours. Served to capt. U.S. Army, 1966-68, Vietnam. Fellow N.Y. Acad. Medicine (chmn. anesthesia sect. 1990), Am. Coll. Anesthesiologists, Am. Soc. Anesthesiologists (ho. of del. 1986—, chmn. refresher course com. 1995); mem. N.Y. Soc. Anesthesiologists (bd. dirs. 1983—, chmn. sci. program com. 1991-93, chmn. PGA 1994-96, v.p. 1994, pres.-elect 1995, pres. 1996), N.Y. Soc. Critical Care Medicine (pres. 1985), Assn. Univ. Anesthesiologists, Acad. Anesthesia. Republican. Roman Catholic. Avocation: history. Home: 29 Ascot Ridge Rd Great Neck NY 11021-2912 Office: Kings County Hosp Ctr 451 Clarkson Ave Brooklyn NY 11203-2054

GOTTESMAN, JAMES EDWARD, urologist; b. Detroit, May 1, 1945; s. Harvey Robert and Adele (Wilensky) G.; m. Gloria L. Brown, Aug. 14, 1966; children: Gregory, Daniel, Timothy. BS, U. Calif., San Francisco, 1967, MD, 1970. Intern. U. Calif., San Francisco, 1970-71, resident, 1971-72; resident U. Calif., L.A., 1972-76; asst. prof., Rush Med. Sch., Chgo., 1976-78; clin. asst. prof. U. Wash., Seattle, 1978-93, clin. prof. urology, 1993—; presenter in field. Contbr. articles to profl. jours.; patentee in field. Mem. AMA, Am. Urol. Assn., Northwest Urol. Soc., Southwest Oncology Group (urologic com. 1978—), Washington State Med. Assn., Washington State Urol. Soc., King County Med. Soc., Seattle Urol. Assn., Soc. Genitourinary Oncologists, Alpha Omega Alpha.

GOTTESMAN, RIVA REGINA, medical records director; b. N.Y.C., Dec. 29, 1969; d. Philip and Melinda (Gross) G. BA, Hunter Coll., 1990. Dir. med. records Wayne Nursing Home, Bronx, N.Y., 1991-95, Holliswood Care Ctr., Queens, N.Y., 1995—. Mem. Am. Health Info. Mgmt. Assn. (accredited record technician). Democrat. Jewish. Home: 200 Bennett Ave New York NY 10040 Office: Holliswood Care Ctr 195-44 Woodhull Ave Hollis NY 11423

GOTTFREDSON, DENISE CLAIRE, sociologist; b. Providence, Dec. 29, 1952; d. Albert Eugene and Marjorie Claire (Wyman) Ruff; m. John Alden Daiger Jr., June 9, 1973 (div. Dec. 1979); m. Gary Don Gottfredson, Dec. 31, 1979; 1 child, Nisha Claire. BA in Psychology, Fairleigh Dickinson U., 1974; PhD in Social Rels., Johns Hopkins U., 1980. Rsch. asst. Johns Hopkins U., Balt., 1974-78, rsch. assoc., 1978-80, assoc. rsch. scientist, 1980-86, rsch. scientist, 1986; asst. prof. U. Md., College Park, 1986-91, assoc. prof., 1991-95, prof., 1995—; v.p. Gottfredson Assocs., Ellicott City, Md., 1993—. Author: Victimization in Schools, 1985; contbr. articles to profl. jours. Grantee U. Mich., 1989-90, Md. Dept. Juvenile Svcs., 1992-94, Md. Gov.'s Drug and Alcohol Abuse Commn., 1990-96, Ctr. for Substance Abuse Prevention, 1991-96. Mem. Am. Sociol. Assn., Am. Ednl. Rsch. Assn., Am. Soc. Criminology. Home: 11444 Old Frederick Rd Marriottsville MD 21104 Office: U Md Lefrak Hall Rm 2220H College Park MD 20742

GOTTFRIED, EUGENE LESLIE, physician, educator; b. Passaic, N.J., Feb. 26, 1929; s. David Robert and Rose (Chill) G.; m. Phyllis Doris Swain, Aug. 16, 1957. AB, Columbia U., 1950, MD, 1954. Cert. Nat. Bd. Med. Examiners, Am. Bd. Internal Medicine. Intern Presbyn. Hosp., N.Y.C., 1954-55, asst. resident in medicine, 1957-58; resident Bronx (N.Y.) Mcpl. Hosp. Ctr., 1958-59, fellow in medicine, 1959-60; asst. instr. medicine Albert Einstein Coll. Medicine Yeshiva U., N.Y.C., 1959-60, instr., 1960-61, assoc., 1961-65, asst. prof., 1965-69; assoc. prof. medicine Cornell U. Med. Coll., N.Y.C., 1969-81, assoc. prof. pathology, 1975-81; clin. prof. dept. lab. medicine U. Calif., San Francisco, 1991-93, prof., 1993—, vice chmn. dept. lab. medicine, 1981—; hosp. appointments include asst. vis. physician Bronx Mcpl. Hosp. Ctr., 1960-66, assoc. attending physician, 1966-69; assoc. attending physician N.Y. Hosp., N.Y.C., 1969-81, assoc. attending pathologist, 1975-81, dir. lab. clin. hematology, 1969-81; chief lab. medicine San Francisco Gen. Hosp. Med. Ctr., 1981—, dir. clin. labs., 1981—. Assoc. editor Jour. Lipid Research, 1971-72, 75-77; mem. editorial bd. Jour. Lipid Research, 1972-77. Lt. comdr. USNR, 1955-57. Recipient Career Scientist award Health Research Council City of N.Y., 1964-72. Fellow ACP, Am. Soc. Hematology, Internat. Soc. Hematology, Acad. Clin. Lab. Physicians and Scientists; mem. AAAS, Nat. Com. for Clin. Lab. Stds., Phi Beta Kappa, Alpha Omega Alpha. Office: San Francisco Gen Hosp Clin Labs 1001 Potrero Ave San Francisco CA 94110-3518

GOTTHOLD, WILLIAM EUGENE, surgeon; b. Long Beach, Calif., Sept. 20, 1942. MD, Tulane U., 1969. Cert. emergency medicine. Intern Letterman Army Med. Ctr., San Francisco, 1969-70, resident gen. surgery, 1970-72; mem. staff Ctrl. Wash. Hosp., Wenatchee, 1978—. Mem. AMA, Am. Coll. Emergency Physicians, Wash. State Med. Assn., Am. Bd. Emergency Medicine (dir.). Office: Ctrl Wash Hosp 1300 Fuller St Wenatchee WA 98801

GOTTLIEB, A(BRAHAM) ARTHUR, medical educator; b. Dec. 14, 1937; m. Marise S. Gottlieb, 1958; children: Mindy, Joanne. AB summa cum laude, Columbia Coll., 1957; MD, NYU, 1961. Med. house officer Peter Bent Brigham Hosp., Boston, 1961-62, asst. resident, 1962-63; rsch. fellow in chemistry, tutor in chemistry Harvard U., Peter Bent Brigham Hosp., Boston, 1965-67; assoc. in medicine Harvard U., Peter Bent Brigham Hosp., 1968; asst. prof. medicine Harvard Med. Sch., 1969; assoc. prof. microbiology Inst. Microbiology, Rutgers U., New Brunswick, N.J., 1969-72, prof. microbiology, 1972-75; prof., chmn. microbiology and immunology Tulane U. Sch. Medicine, New Orleans, 1975—, prof. medicine, 1975—; pres., sci. dir. IMREG, Inc., New Orleans; cons. in field; vis. prof. Walter and Eliza Hall Inst. Med. Rsch., Melbourne, Australia, 1979, Wakayama Med. Coll. and Gunma Med. Coll., Japan, 1980; vis. prof. medicine and pharmacology Shanghai Med. U., People's Republic of China, 1991-92. Mem. editorial adv. bd. several profl. publs. Mem. sci. adv. bd. Cancer Assn. Greater New Orleans, 1979-84; mem. tech. rev. bd. U. New Orleans, 1984-90. Recipient Frances Stone Bunrs award Am. Cancer Soc., 1968, Rsch. Career Devel. award Nat. Inst. Gen. Med. Scis., 1968-69; Mary Inst. Med. Edn. felow Harvard U., 1995-96. Fellow ACP, Am. Assn. Cancer Rsch., Am. Assn. Immunologists, Am. Chem. Soc., Am. Soc. Biol. Chemists, Am. Soc. Cell Biology, Am. Soc. Clin. Investigation, Am. Soc. Microbiology, Am. Acad. Microbiology, Internat. Assn. Comparative Rsch. on Leukemia and Related Diseases, N.Y. Acad. Scis., Reticulendothelial Soc. (chmn. pubs. com.), Assn. Med. Sch. Microbiology (chmn.), AAAS, Phi Beta Kappa, Sigma Xi, Alpha Omega Alpha. Office: Tulane Med Sch 1430 Tulane Ave New Orleans LA 70112-2699

GOTTLIEB, FRED, ophthalmologist; b. Siegburg, Germany, Sept. 21, 1929; came to the U.S., 1940; s. Leo and Johanna (Rosenberg) G.; m. Lora Hirschberger, Sept. 7, 1952; children: Daniel, Michael. BA in Arts and Sci., NYU, 1951; MD, State U. Leiden, Holland, 1956. Intern Bklyn. Jewish Hosp., 1957; resident ophthalmology Kings County Hosp., Bklyn., 1958, Bklyn. Eye & Ear Hosp., 1959-60; fellow Mass. Eye & Ear Infirmary, Boston, 1961-62; dir. retina svc. Bklyn. Eye & Ear Hosp., 1962-75; dir. retina svc. Brookdale Hosp., Bklyn., 1975—, chmn. dept. ophthalmology, 1983-88; lectr. in ophthalmology Brookdale Hosp., Bklyn., 1975—; assoc. attending ophthalmologist N.Y. Eye & Ear Infirmary, N.Y.C., 1982—. Contbr. articles to profl. jours. Fellow Am. Acad. Ophthalmology, Retina Soc. Jewish. Office: Met Retina Assocs 2035 Ralph Ave Brooklyn NY 11234

GOTTLIEB, GILBERT, psychobiologist, educator; b. Bklyn., Oct. 22, 1929; s. Leo and Sylvia Sherman; m. Nora Lee Willis, Feb. 28, 1961; children: Jonathan Brian, David Herschel, Aaron Lee, Marc Sherman. A.B., U. Miami, Fla., 1955, M.S., 1956; Ph.D., Duke U., 1960. Clin. psychologist Dorothea Dix Hosp., Raleigh, N.C., 1959-61; research scientist N.C. Div. Mental Health, Raleigh, 1961-82; head psychology dept. U. N.C.-Greensboro, 1982-86, Excellence Found. prof., 1982-95; Guest Czechoslovak Acad. Scis., 1967, USSR Acad. Scis., 1989; advisor German NSF, 1977; U.S. del. Internat. Ethological Congress com., 1977-83; faculty Carolina Consortium human devel. U. N.C., Chapel Hill, 1988—, exec. com. NIMH ctr. for devel. sci., U. N.C., 1993—, rsch. prof. psychology dept., Chapel Hill, 1995—; vis. lectr. Inst. Child Devel. U. Minn., 1975; vis. scholar Ctr. Interdisciplinary Rsch. U. Bielefeld, Germany, 1977; disting. vis. prof. psychology dept. U. Colo., Boulder, 1985; vis. fellow The Neuroscis. Inst., San Diego, 1996. Author: Development of Species Identification in Birds, 1971, Individual Development and Evolution: The Genesis of Novel Behavior, 1992 Prenatal Roots of Instinctive Behavior: A Theoretical and Experimental Exposition of Probabilistic Epigenesis, 1996; editor: Behavioral Embryology, 1973, Aspects of Neurogenesis, 1974, Neural and Behavioral Specificity, 1976, Early Influences, 1978, Measurement of Audition and Vision in the First Year of Postnatal Life, 1985. assoc. editor Jour. Comparative and Physiol. Psychology, 1974-80; editorial cons. various sci. jours. and pub. houses. NSF grantee, 1963, 85-88; Nat. Inst. Child Health grantee, 1963-85; NIMH grantee, 1989—. Mem. Internat. Soc. Devel. Psychobiology (pres. 1986-87),

Internat. Conf. Infant Studies. Home: 4908 Forestville Rd Raleigh NC 27604-9782 Office: U NC Ctr Devel Sci Chapel Hill NC 27599-8115

GOTTLIEB, H. DAVID, podiatrist; b. Washington, Mar. 2, 1956; s. Julius J. and Charlotte G.; m. Wendy Ilene Weisbard, June 17, 1979; children: Jason, Cheryl. BA, Cornell U., 1978; DPM, Pa. Coll. Podiatric Medicine, 1982. Diplomate Nat. Bd. Podiatry Examiners, Am. Acad. Pain Mgmt., Am. Coun. Cert. Podiatric Physicians and Surgeons, Am. Bd. Podiatric Orthopedics and Primary Podiatric Medicine. Podiatrist Dr. Julius J. Gottlieb, P.C., Washington, 1982-91; prin. H. David Gottlieb, DPM, P.C., Washington, 1991—. Author (book chpt.) Laser Surgery of the Foot, 1988. Mem. Chevy Chase (D.C.) Citizens Assn., 1982—; den master Cub Scouts Am., Gaithersburg, Md., 1991-93; pres. Young Couples Club Gaithersburg Hebrew Congregation, 1982-85. Fellow Acad. Ambulatory Foot Surgery, Am. Coll. Foot and Ankle Orthopedics and Medicine; mem. Am. Podiatric Med. Assn., Am. Assn. Podriatric Physicians and Surgeons, Am. Running and Fitness Assn. Office: 3900 Mckinley St NW Washington DC 20015-2943

GOTTLIEB, JULIUS JUDAH, podiatrist; b. Jersey City, May 27, 1919; s. Joseph Uziel and Gussie (Farber) G.; m. Charlotte Papernik, Oct. 18, 1942; children: Sheldon, Cynthia, Lorinda, David, Jonathan. Student, NYU, 1938-39, Ill. Coll. Podiatric Medicine, 1940-42; DPM, Ohio Coll. Podiatric Medicine, 1943. Diplomate Am. Podiatric Med. Specialties Bd. Pvt. practice podiatric medicine Washington, 1943-92; pres. Chevy Chase Profl. Cons., 1993-96; past cons. Army Footwear Clinic. Co-inventor fiberglass foot prosthetics and plastic shoe lasts. Podiatry dir. Greater Washington Hebrew Home for the Aged, 1963; pres. Franklin Knolls Citizens Assn., 1963, Ridgefield Citizens Inc., 1994-96; chmn. com. Nat. Capital Area coun. Boy Scouts Am., 1969-73. Recipient Shofar award Boy Scouts Am. Fellow Acad. Ambulatory Foot Surgeons (region 8 sci. chmn. 1987-88); mem. Am. Podiatric Med. Assn. (life), Am. Pub. Health Assn., Am. Podiatric Circulatory Soc., Am. Bd. Foot Surgeons (founding diplomate), D.C. Podiatric Med. Soc. (past pres.), Am. Assn. Foot Specialists (past pres., Foot Specialist of the Yr. 1973), Am. Assn. Individual Investors, Internat. Platform Assn., Am. Physicians Fellowship Inc. for Medicine in Israel, Columbia Heights Bus. Men's Assn. (past pres., Man of Yr. 1964), Parents Assn. U. Md. (co v.p. parents fund 1980-81, co-recipient Outstanding Svc. Award), Chevy Chase Citizens Assn., B'nai B'rith. Republican. Jewish. Home and Office: 15812 Ancient Oak Dr Darnestown MD 20878-2110

GOTTLIEB, LEONARD SOLOMON, pathology educator; b. Boston, May 26, 1927; s. Julius and Jeanette (Miller) G.; m. Dorothy Helen Apt, Mar. 23, 1952; children: Julie Ann, William Apt, Andrew Richard. AB cum laude, Bowdoin Coll., 1946; MD, Tufts U., 1950; MPH, Harvard U., 1969. Diplomate Am. Bd. Anatomic Pathology. Intern, resident Mallory Inst. Pathology, Boston City Hosp., 1950-55; asst. chief pathology U.S. Naval Hosp., Chelsea, Mass., 1955-57; assoc. pathologist Mallory Inst. Pathology, Boston, 1957-66, assoc. dir., 1966-72, dir., 1972—; chief pathology dept. Boston U. Med. Ctr. Hosp., 1973—; prof. pathology & lab. medicine Sch. Medicine Boston U., 1970—, chmn. dept., 1980—; dir. Mallory Inst. Pathology Found., 1980—; pathologist-in-chief divsn. pathology Boston City Hosp., 1994—; lectr. Harvard med. Sch., 1963—; dir. student faculty exch. program Boston U. and Hebrew U., Hadassah Med. Sch., 1988—. Gen. editor Biopsy Pathology Series, Chapman and Hall, 1981-93; mem. editorial bd. Am. Jour. Surg. Pathology; author/co-author more than 100 articles on exptl. and human gastrointestinal and liver diseases. Assoc. mem. bd. govs. Hebrew U. Jerusalem, 1991-95, mem. bd. govs., 1995—; pres. New Eng. region Am. Friends of Hebrew U., 1989—, coun. trustees, 1992—, founder, 1991—; mem. sci. adv. bd. Boston chpt. Israel Cancer Rsch. Fund, 1991-92; mem. Greater Boston chpt. State of Israel Bonds Cabinet, 1991—; pres. Am. Physicians Fellowship for Medicine in Israel, 1990-93; class sec. 1977 Program for Health Sys. Mgmt., Harvard Bus. Sch., 1995—. Lt. M.C. USNR, 1955-57, lt. comdr. M.C. USNR, 1960-63. Recipient Stanley L. Robbins award for excellence in teaching, 1986, Jerusalem City of Peace award Boston chpt. State of Israel Bonds, 1992, Disting. Bowdoin Educator award, 1995; named hon. mem. faculty medicine Hebrew U., 1987; James Bowdoin scholar, 1945, Bingham scholar, 1944-50. Mem. Am. Assn. Pathologists, Am. Assn. for Study of Liver Disease, U.S.-Can. Acad. Pathology, Am. Soc. for Cell Biology, Am. Gastroent. Assn., Am. Coll. Physician Execs., New Eng. Soc. Pathologists (pres. 1968-69), Am. Soc. Clin. Pathologists, Am. Soc. for Investigative Pathology, Coll. Am. Pathologists, Alpha Omega Alpha (faculty mem.). Office: Boston U Sch Medicine Dept Path and Lab Medicine 80 E Concord St Boston MA 02118-2307

GOTTLIEB, RONALD SAUL, cardiologist; b. Phila., Jan. 13, 1940; m. Gloria Gottlieb, 1962; children: Mark, Neil. BA, Franklin and Marshall Coll., 1961; MD, U. Pa., 1965. Diplomate Am. Bd. Internal Medicine with subspecialty in cardiovasc. disease; lic. physician, Pa. Intern in medicine Thomas Jefferson U. Hosp., Phila., 1965-66, resident in medicine, 1966-67, fellow in cardiology, 1971-73; resident in neurology Hosp. of U. Pa., Phila., 1967-68, resident in medicine, 1970-71; pvt. practice Graduate Cardiology Cons., Inc., Phila., 1973—; instr. medicine Thomas Jefferson U. Hosp., 1973-75, asst. prof., 1975-79, assoc. prof., 1979-87, adj. assoc. prof., 1987—, assoc. dir. cardiac catheterization lab., 1977-80; clin. assoc. prof. medicine in assoc. faculty Sch. Medicine, U. Pa., 1981—; dir. interventional cardiology The Grad. Hosp., 1989—; physician adv. bd. Advanced Cardiovascular Sys., Inc., Devices for Vascular Intervention, Inc.; lectr. in field. Contbr. numerous articles and abstracts to profl. jours. With U.S. Army, 1968-71. Fellow ACP, Am. Coll. Cardiology, The Soc. for Cardiac Angiography and Interventions, Phila. Coll. Physicians; mem. AMA, Am. Heart Assn. (fellow on clin. coun.), Pa. Med. Soc., Phila. County Med. Soc., Phila. Acad. Cardiology, Southeastern Pa. Heart Assn., Soc. Interventional Cardiologists (tri-state area governing body). Office: Graduate Cardiology Cons One Graduate Pla #101 18th and Lombard Sts Philadelphia PA 19146

GOTTLIEB, SHELDON FRED, biologist, educator; b. Bronx, N.Y., Dec. 22, 1932; s. Elias and Dorothy (Gerstenfeld) G.; m. Eda Judith Robin Held, Aug. 25, 1956; children: Stephen Eric, Pamela Lynn, Glenn Ira, William Scott. B.A., Bklyn. Coll., 1953; M.S., U. Mass., 1956; Ph.D. (teaching fellow), U. Tex. Med. Br., 1959. Research physiologist Linde div. Union Carbide Corp., Tonawanda, N.Y., 1959-64; asst. prof. physiology and anesthesiology Jefferson Med. Coll., Phila., 1964-68; prof. biol. scis. Ind. U.-Purdue U., Fort Wayne, Ind., 1968-80; prof. biol. scis. U. South Ala., Mobile, 1980—, dean grad sch., dir. rsch., 1980-85, adj. prof. physiology Coll. Medicine, 1990—; dir. rsch. Jo Ellen Smith Baromed. Rsch. Inst., 1985—; courtesy prof. physiology Sch. Medicine, La. State U., also courtesy prof. dept. medicine; cons. Edn. Devel. Ctr., Inc., 1976-80, hyperbaric unit, Brooks AFB, San Antonio, 1975-80, Gorsuch Scarisbrick publs., 1978-80; mem. Coun. Grad. Deans, Ala. Commn. Higher Edn., 1980-85, exec. bd., 1981-85; guest speaker various radio and TV programs, 1969—; guest lectr. various civic, ednl., religious and profl. orgns., 1968—. Contbr. articles to sci. jours. Chmn. com. troop 491 Boy Scouts Am., 1969-70; judge Sci. Fair, Fort Wayne Community Schs., 1969-75, 77-79; mem. Ind. State Bd. advs., Anti-Defamation League B'nai B'rith, 1968-80, Jewish Community Relations Council Fort Wayne, 1969-80; pres. B'nai Jacob Synagogue, 1972, Tamarack Homeowners Assn., 1970-71; mem. Coalition for Environment, Fort Wayne, 1970-80, pres., 1970-71; mem. NE area adv. council No. Ind. Health Systems Agy., 1976-80; bd. dirs. Miss.-Ala. Sea Grant Consortium, 1980-85, vice chmn., 1981-82, chmn., 1982-83; co-chmn. Mobile Anti-Defamation League com. of Beth Zur lodge B'nai B'rith, 1981-82, v.p., 1982-83, pres. 1983-87; bd. dirs. Mobile chpt. Nat. Multiple Sclerosis Soc., 1986—, Ala. NCCJ, 1985-90, Ala. Gov.'s Holocaust Adv. council, 1985—; bd. dirs. Crack Attack, Mobile, 1986-88. Served with U.S. Army, 1954-56. Eli Lilly Found. grantee, 1968; NIH grantee, 1968; Hoffman La Roche grantee, 1977. Mem. Am. Inst. Biol. Scis., Am. Physiol. Soc., Am. Soc. Microbiology, Soc. Gen. Physiologists, Fedn. Am. Socs. for Explt. Biology (nat. corr. 1976-80), Undersea and Hyperberic Med. Soc. (pres. Gulf Coast chpt. 1984-85), AAAS, Aerospace Med. Assn., N.Y. Acad. Scis., Nat. Assn. Scholars, Am. Heart Assn. (dir. Allen County br. 1969-80, pres. N.E. Ind. chpt. 1971-79, pres. 1974, dir. Ind. affiliate 1974-80, dir. Mobile County 1980-88), Divers Alert Network (co-dir. Gulf region 1987—), Sigma Xi (pres. elect chpt. 1983-84, pres. 1984-86). Home: 2532 Tahoe Dr Mobile AL 36695-3669 Office: U South Ala 27 LSCB Mobile AL 36688

GOTTLIEB, SIDNEY ALAN, optometrist; b. Pitts.; s. Walter Coleman and Jennie (Moskovitz) G.; m. Kathie Sue Block, Apr. 30, 1989; 1 child, Jamie Lauren. BSA, U. Ga., 1981; BS, Pa. Coll. of Optometry, 1982, OD, 1985. Lic. optometrist. Optometrist Gottlieb Vision Group, Stone Mountain, Ga., 1985-88, Opticare Assocs., Marietta, Ga., 1988, Stephen E. Schock and Assocs., Norcross, Ga., 1988-94; pvt. practice Woodstock, Ga., 1994—; vision cons. Ga. Ctr. for Multi-handicapped, Atlanta, 1986-88, Peachtree Reentry Program for the Head Injured, Lawrenceville, Ga., 1986-88, Shephard Spinal Ctr., Atlanta, 1988-94, DeKalb Med. Ctr., Decatur, Ga., 1991—. Mem. Am. Optometric Assn., Ga. Optometric Assn., So. Coun. of Optometry, Brain Injury Assn., Ga. Assn. for Children with Learning Disabilities, Young Couples Club (v.p. 1989-90). Democrat. Jewish. Office: Lenscrafters 210 Gatsby Pl Alpharetta GA 30202-6160

GOTTO, ANTONIO MARION, JR., internist, educator; b. Nashville, Tenn., Oct. 10, 1935; s. Antonio M. and Reather (Gray) G.; m. Anita Louise Safford, July 21, 1959; children: Jennifer, Gillian, Teresa. B.A. magna cum laude, Vanderbilt U., 1957, M.D., 1965; D. Phil., Oxford (Eng.) U., 1961; LL.D. (hon.), Abilene Christian U., 1979; M.D. (hon.), U. Bologna, 1982. Diplomate Am. Bd. Internal Medicine. Intern Mass. Gen. Hosp., Boston, 1965-66, resident, 1966-67; practice medicine specializing in internal medicine, 1967—; head molecular disease br. Nat. Heart and Lung Inst. NIH, Bethesda, Md., 1969-71; dir. and prin. investigator Lipid Research Clinic, Houston, 1971-77; prof. medicine, chief dir., arteriosclerosis and lipoprotein rsch. Baylor Coll. Medicine, Houston, 1971—; dir., prin. investigator specialized center rsch in arteriosclerosis Nat. Heart, Lung and Blood Inst., 1971—; dir., prin. investigator Spl. Ctr. Rsch. Arteriosclerosis Nat. Heart, Lung, and Blood Inst., 1971—; J.S. Abercrombie prof. Baylor Coll. Medicine, 1976—, Disting. Service prof., 1985—; sci. dir. Meth. Hosp. and Baylor Nat. Research and Demonstration Center, 1974-83, 87-90; Bob and Vivian Smith prof. and chmn. dept. medicine Baylor Coll. Medicine, 1977—; chief internal medicine svcs. The Meth. Hosp., 1977—; hon. guest lectr. various med. socs., schs. and hosps., 1972—; mem. nat. diabetes adv. bd. HEW (now HHS), 1977-84; mem. steering com. Italian-Am. com. on cardiovascular disease NIH, 1978—; mem. adv. council Nat. Heart, Lung and Blood Inst., 1987-91; hon. prof. U. Buenos Aires, 1985. Author: (with Michael E. DeBakey), The Living Heart, 1977, The Living Heart Diet, 1984, The New Living Heart Diet, 1996; contbr. articles on biochem and cardiovascular rsch. to profl. publs.; mem. editorial bd. Jour. Biol. Chemistry, 1976-81, Advanced in Lipid Rsch., 1973-78, Am. Heart Jour., 1981—, Arteriosclerosis, 1981-89, Circulation Rsch., 1974-79, Cardiovascular Rsch. Ctr. Bull., 1972—; co-editor Atherosclerosis Rev. Series, 1976-92, Jour. Cardiovascular Risk, 1994—. Mem. sci. adv. bd. Fondation Cardiologique Princesse Liliane, Brussels, Belgium, 1976—, Lorenzini Found., Milan, Italy, Fritz Thyssen Found., Cologne, Germany; mem. Mission of Houston Econ. Devel. Council, 1985. Served with USPHS, 1967-69; walkathon chmn. Juvenile Diabetes Found., 1986. Decorated knight Order of Merit (Italy); Order of the Lion (Finland); recipient Albert Weinstein award, 1965, Laurea ad Honorem, U. Bologna, Seal Harris award So. Med. assn., 1995; John A. Hartford Found. grantee, 1971-75; named hon. cons. Adm. Bristol Hosp., Istanbul, Turkey, Houston Internat. Exec. Yr., 1987. Fellow Am. Coll. Cardiology; mem. Inst. Medicine of NAS, Am. Soc. Clin. Investigation (v.p. 1980-81), So. Soc. Clin. Investigation, Internat. Soc. of Atherosclerosis (Achievement award 1982, pres. 1985—), Am. Assn. Physicians, Am. Soc. Biol. Chemists, Am. Diabetes Assn., Am. Heart Assn. (pres. 1983-84, past pres. 1984-86, Paul Ledbetter award for Disting. Service, Paul Dudley White award for Outstanding Contbns., Gold Heart award 1989), Am. Bd. Internal Medicine, Am. Assn. of Rhodes Scholars, Am. Longevity Assn., Alpha Omega Alpha. Mem. Ch. of Christ. Club: River Oaks Country. Home: 3439 Piping Rock Ln Houston TX 77027-4112 Office: Baylor Coll Medicine Meth Hosp 6550 Fannin MS 1423 Houston TX 77030-2707

GOTTSCHALK, CARL WILLIAM, physician, educator; b. Salem, Va., Apr. 28, 1922; s. Carl and Lula (Helbig) G.; m. Helen Marie Scott, Nov. 22, 1947 (dec. June 1988); children: Carl S., Walter P., Karen E.; m. Susan K. Fellner, May 25, 1996. BS, Roanoke Coll., 1942, ScD, 1966; MD, U. Va., 1945; Docteur honoris causa, University of Mons-Hainout, Belgium, 1992. Intern, asst. resident, resident in medicine Mass. Gen. Hosp., Boston, 1945-52; research fellow physiology Harvard U., 1948-50; fellow U. N.C. Med. Sch., Chapel Hill, 1952-53; faculty U. N.C. Med. Sch., 1953-92, Kenan prof. medicine and physiology, 1969-92, disting. rsch. prof. medicine and physiology, 1992—; established investigator Am. Heart Assn., 1957-61, career investigator, 1961-92; Bowditch lectr., 1960, Harvey lectr., 1962; Mem. physiology study sect. NIH, 1961-65; mem. research career award com. Nat. Inst. Gen. Med. Scis., 1965-69, mem. physiology tng. com., 1970-73, mem. med. scientist tng. com., 1973; chmn. com. chronic kidney disease Bur. Budget, 1966-67; adv. com. biol. and med. scis. NSF, 1967-69, vice chmn., 1968, chmn., 1969; mem. Nat. Adv. Gen. Med. Scis. Council, 1977-80, Nat. Arthritis, Diabetes and Digestive and Kidney Diseases Adv. Council, 1982-86; lectr. The Dr. Richard Bright Soc., 1995. Author books and papers on physiology of kidney. Mem. adv. com. Burroughs Wellcome Fund for Clin. Pharmacology, 1980-93, Student Sci. Enrichment Adv. Com., 1996—; pres. Children's Theatre N.C., 1967-68. Served to capt. M.C., AUS, 1946-48. Recipient N.C. award, 1967, Modern Medicine Distinguished Achievement award, 1966, Horsley Meml. prize U. Va., 1956, Homer W. Smith award N.Y. Heart Assn., 1970, David Hume award Nat. Kidney Found., 1976, O. Max Gardner award U. N.C., 1978; Gottschalk lectr. in basic scis. named in his honor N.c. Med. Sch., 1992. Mem. ACP, NAS, AAUP (coun. 1970-73), Assn. Am. Physicians, Am. Physiol. Soc. (Robert W. Berliner award 1993, Carl W. Gottschalk Disting. Lectureship of Renal Physiology sect. established 1993), Am. Soc. Clin. Investigation, Am. Clin. and Climatol. Assn., Soc. Exptl. Biology and Medicine, Inst. Medicine of NAS, Internat. Soc. Nephrology (hon. mem., A.N. Richards award 1990), Am. Soc. Nephrology (coun. 1971-77, pres. 1975-76), Am. Acad. Arts and Scis., Phi Beta Kappa, Sigma Xi, Alpha Omega Alpha. Home: 1300 Mason Farm Rd Chapel Hill NC 27514-4604

GOTTSCHALK, LOUIS AUGUST, neuropsychiatrist, psychoanalyst; b. St. Louis, Aug. 26, 1916; s. Max W. and Kelmie (Mutrux) G.; m. Helen Reller, July 24, 1944; children: Guy H., Claire A., Louise H., Susan E. AB, Washington U., St. Louis, 1940, MD, 1943; PhD, So. Calif. Psychiat. Inst., 1977. Asst. in neuropsychiatry Sch. Medicine Washington U., 1944-46; commd. asst. surgeon USPHS, 1946, advanced through grades to med. dir., 1979; instr. psychiatry S.W. Med. Coll., Dallas, 1947-48; rsch. psychiatrist NIMH, Bethesda, Md., 1950-53; coord. rsch., rsch. prof. psychiatry Coll. Medicine U. Cin., 1953-67; attending psychiatrist Cin. Gen. Hosp., 1953-67; mem. faculty Inst. Psychoanalysis, Chgo., 1957-67, So. Calif. Psychiat. Inst., L.A., 1970—; prof. psychiatry, social sci. and social ecology dept. psychiatry and human behavior Coll. Medicine U. Calif., Irvine, 1967—, chmn. dept., 1967-78, program dir. psychiat. residency tng., 1967-78; sci. co-dir. Nat. Ctr. Alcoholism Rsch. Ctr. U. Calif.-Irvine Med. Ctr., 1978-84; dir. cons. and liaison program U. Calif.-Irvine Med. Ctr., 1978-87; chmn. rsch. com. Hamilton County (Ohio) Diagnostic Ctr., 1958-67; mem. clin. psychopharmacology study sect. NIMH, 1968-71; mem. rsch. rev. com. Nat. Inst. Drug Abuse, 1973-77, Mental Health Study Ctr., 1978-84. Author: (with G.C. Gleser) The Measurement of Psychological States through the Content Analysis of Verbal Behavior, 1969, How to Understand and Analyze Your Own Dreams, 1975, Greek edit., 1978, Spanish edit., 1981, 3rd. rev. edit., 1994; editor: Comparative Psycholinguistic Analysis of Two Psychotherapeutic Interviews, 1961, (with A.H. Auerbach) Methods of Research in Psychotherapy, 1966, (with S. Merlis) Pharmacokinetics of Psychoactive Drugs: Blood Levels and Clinical Responses, 1976, Pharmacokinetics of Psychoactive Drugs: Further Studies, 1979, The Content Analysis of Verbal Behavior: Further Studies, 1979, (with F.L. McGuire and others) Drug Abuse Deaths in Nine Cities: A Survey Report, 1980; (with R. Cravey) Toxicological and Pathological Studies on Psychoactive Drug-Involved Deaths, 1980; (with Winget, Gleser and Lolas) Analisis de la Conducta Verbal, 1984; The Tree of Knowledge, 1985), (with F. Lolas and L.L. Viney) The Content Analysis of Verbal Behavior: Significance in Clinical Medicine and Psychiatry, 1986, (with Lolas) Estudios Sobre Analisis del Comportamiento Verbal, 1987, How to do Self-Analysis and Other Self-Psychotherapies, 1989, (with R. Bechtel) Computerized Content Analysis of Natural Language or Verbal Texts, 1993, The Content Analysis of Verbal Behavior: New Findings and Clinical Applications, 1995; editl. bd. Psychosomatic Medicine, 1960-70, Psychiatry, 1967—, Am. Jour. Psychotherapy, 1975—, Methods and Findings in Exptl. and Clin. Pharmacology, 1978—, others; contbr. numerous articles to tech. lit. Rockefeller fellow Bellagio Study Ctr., Italy, 1985; recipient Hofheimer Rsch. award, 1955, Franz Alexander Essay prize So. Calif. Psychoanalytic Inst., L.A., 1973, Disting. Rsch. award U. Calif.-Irvine Alumni Assn., 1974; named Disting. Practitioner, Nat. Acad. Med. Practice, 1984, NIMH Rsch. Career award, 1960-67, Am. Psychiat. Assn. Found. rsch. prize, 1978, Aldrich Disting. Univ. Svc. award, 1992, U. Calif., Irvine, 1996. Fellow AAAS, Am. Coll. Neuropsychopharmacology (mem. pubs. bd. 1995—), Am. Coll. Psychiatrists; mem. AMA, Assn. for Rsch. of Nervous and Mental Diseases, Am. Psychosomatic Soc., Cin. Soc. Neurology and Psychiatry (past pres.), Am. Psychoanalytic Assn., Orange County Med. Assn., So. Calif. Psychiat. Soc., Am. Assn. Child Psychoanalysts, So. Calif. Psychoanalytic Soc., Cosmos Club, Balboa Bay Club, Phi Beta Kappa, Sigma Xi, Alpha Omega Alpha, Omicron Delta Kappa. Home: 4607 Perham Rd Corona Del Mar CA 92625-3124 Office: U Calif Coll Medicine Dept Psychiatry & Human Behavior Irvine CA 92717

GOTTSCHALK, WERNER MAX, geneticist, educator; b. Marienberg, Germany, May 15, 1920; s. Max and Elsa (Neubauer) G.; m. Anna Marie Schneider, Apr. 3, 1950; children: Roswitha, Dagmar, Barbara. Dr.rer.nat., U. Bonn, Fed. Republic Germany, 1950. Rsch. asst. U. Freiburg, U. Giessen, U. Göttingen, Fed. Republic Germany, 1950-56; head div. genetics U. Bonn, 1956-64, prof. genetics, 1960—, dir. Inst. Genetics, 1965-85, dir. emeritus, 1985—; cons. UN, Mex., 1964, India, 1971, Poland, 1981; mem. internat. expedition South Am., 1957-58; mem. mutation adv. group UN, 1964—; permanent collaborator Progress in Botany; mem. editorial, adv. bd. various internat. jours. Author: Influence of Mutant Genes on Morphology and Function of Plant Organs, 1964, Significance of Gene Mutations in Plant Evolution, 1971, Mutations, Mechanisms of Evolution, 1974, Significance of Polyploidy in Plant Evolution, 1976, General Genetics, 1978, 4th edit., 1994, Japanese edit., 1982, Spanish edit., 1984, Induced Mutations in Plant Breeding, 1983; editor: Seed Proteins: Biochemistry, Genetics, Nutritive Value, 1983; contbr. over 300 articles to profl. jours. 1st lt. armed forces, 1939-45. Mem. German Botanical Soc., German Genetics Soc., German Soc. Applied Botany, European Soc. Nuclear Methods in Agr. Office: Inst Genetics, U Bonn, C 53115 Bonn Germany

GOTZOYANNIS, STAVROS ELEUTHERIOS, cardiologist; b. Piraeus, Greece, June 18, 1933; s. Eleutherios G. and Irene Stavros (Nikitaki) G.; M.D. (Greek Govt. scholar), U. Salonica, 1957; Doctorate, U. Athens, 1968; m. Ourania Cavoulacou, Nov. 20, 1969. Intern, 401 Army Gen. Hosp., Athens, 1957-58; resident in internal medicine Army Pansion Share Hosp., Athens, 1960-63; fellow in cardiology Hellenic Red Cross Hosp., Athens, 1964-65; commd. 2d lt. M.C., Greek Army, 1957, advanced through grades to brig. gen., 1984; dir. internal medicine 403 Army Gen. Hosp., Kozani, 1963-64; research asso., div. cardiology Phila. Gen. Hosp., 1970-71; asst. attending physician Georgetown U. Hosp., Washington, 1971-72; asso. CCU, 401 Army Gen. Hosp., Athens, 1972-75, dir. cardiac catheterization lab., 1975-76; dir. cardiology dept. 409 Army Gen. Hosp., Patras, 1976-78; cardiology cons. to chief Hellenic Nat. Def. Gen. Staff, 1978-80; mem. staff cardiology dept. Army Pansion Share Hosp., Athens, 1980-81; dir. div. cardiology dept. 401st Army Gen. Hosp., Athens, 1981-83; cons. cardiology Hellenic Red Cross Hosp., Athens, 1965-69; instr. Army Nursing Sch., Athens, 1976. Fellow Fedn. Internat. Sport Medicine, Am. Coll. Cardiology; mem. Athens Med. Assn., Hellenic Cardiologic Soc., Greek Assn. Sports. Greek Orthodox. Contbr. papers, abstracts to med. books, jours. Home: 3 Evrou St, GR 115 28 Athens Greece

GOUDY, JOSEPHINE GRAY, social services administrator; b. Des Moines, Nov. 30, 1925; d. Gerald William and Myrtle Maria (Brooks) Gray; BA, State U. Iowa, 1953, MSW, 1966; m. John Winston Goudy, June 5, 1948; children: Tracy Jean, Paula Rae. Clin. social worker, Iowa, Ill.; Diplomate in Clin. Social Work. Child welfare supr. Iowa Dept. Social Svcs., 1960-68; psychiat. social worker Community Mental Health Ctr. Scott County (Iowa), 1966-71; social work instr. Palmer Jr. Coll., Davenport, Iowa, 1967-70; psychiat. social worker, chief social svcs. Jacksonville (Ill.) State Mental Hosp., 1971-74; coord. community mental health outpatient services McFarland Mental Health Ctr., Springfield, Ill., 1974; exec. dir. Macoupin County Mental Health Ctr., Carlinville, Ill., 1974—; chmn. Human Svcs. Edn. Coun., Springfield, 1979-81; bd. mem. Alzheimer's Disease and Related Disorders Assn., Springfield Ill. Area Chpt., past exec. Davenport Community Welfare Coun.; adj. prof. dept. psychiatry So. Ill. U., Carbondale. Mem. Nat. Assn. Social Workers (Social Worker of Yr. Central Ill. area 1983), Acad. Cert. Social Workers, AAUW (br. pres. 1964-66, mem. state bar 1966-68, br. grantee 1975), Internat. Fedn. U. Women, U. Iowa Alumni Assn., Bus. and Profl. Women (Woman of Yr. 1983), Delta Kappa Gamma, Kappa Delta Pi. Republican. Methodist. Club: Carlinville Women's (pres. 1975-77). Home: 364 W Tremont St Waverly IL 62692-1073 Office: 100 N Side Sq Carlinville IL 62626-1748

GOUGH, IAN RONALD, surgeon; b. Brisbane, Queensland, Australia, Apr. 12, 1947; s. Ruth Gough, Dec. 11, 1972; children: Jenny, Helen. MB, BS, U. Queensland, Australia, 1970, MD, 1994. Cert. specialist gen. surgeon. Resident med. officer Princess Alexandra Hosp., Brisbane, Australia, 1971-72; surg. registrar NHS Hosps., 1973-75; lectr., sr. lectr. surgery U. Queensland, Brisbane, 1976-84, assoc. prof. surgery, 1984-91, clin. prof. surgery, 1991—; sr. cons. surgeon Royal Brisbane Hosp., 1991—; dep. dean U. Queensland Med. Sch., Brisbane, 1984-87; vis. prof. various univs., U.S.A., Sweden, Australia, 1984—. Mem. editl. bd. Australian and New Zealand Jour. Surgery, Current Surgery. Recipient travel grants, rsch. grants, 1971—. Fellow ACS, Royal Coll. Surgeons Edinburgh, Royal Australasian Coll. Surgeons (chmn.bd. gen. surgery 1988—, chmn. sect. endocrine surgery 1993—); mem. Royal Coll. Physicians U.K., Internat. Assn. Endocrine Surgeons, Societe Internat. de Chirurge. Office: Wesley Med Ctr, 40 Chasely St, Auchenflower 4066, Australia

GOULD, HARRY J., III, neurology educator; b. Columbus, Ohio, Mar. 1, 1947; s. Harry J. Jr. and Madeline (Folger) G.; m. Anne Marie Thompson, Jan. 30, 1971; children: Trevor Nicholas, Laura Nicole. BS, SUNY, Stony Brook, 1969; PhD, Brown U., 1974; MD, La. State U., 1990. Asst. prof. Med. Sch. U. Cin., 1974-80; asst. prof. Med. Sch., La. State U., New Orleans, 1980-86, assoc. prof., 1986, resident in neurology, 1990-94; asst. prof. med. sch. La. State U., New Orleans, 1994—, dir. Multidisciplinary Pain Ctr. Contbr. articles to profl. jours. With USAR, 1970-76. NSF grantee, 1986-89. Mem. AMA, Internat. Assn. for the Study Pain, Soc. for Neurosci., Am. Assn. Anatomists, Am. Acad. Neurology, Cajal Club. Republican. Methodist. Home: 104 Paradise Pt Slidell LA 70461-3225 Office: La State U Med Ctr Dept of Neurology 1542 Tulane Ave New Orleans LA 70112-2825

GOULD, KENNETH LANCE, physician, educator; b. Wilsonville, Ala., Oct. 28, 1938; s. Kenneth Newton and Elizabeth May (Barrett) G.; m. Helene Freiin von Eckardstein, Sept. 28, 1970; 1 son, Stefan Anton. B.A. in Physics, Oberlin Coll., 1960; M.D., Western Res. U., 1964. Intern U. Wash. Hosps., Seattle, 1964-65, resident, 1965-67; instr. medicine U. Wash., Seattle, 1970-72, asst. prof., 1972-76, assoc. prof., 1976-79; prof. dept. internal medicine and cardiology U. Tex., Houston, 1979—, dir. div. cardiology, 1979-85, vice chmn. clin. affairs dept. medicine, 1980-84, dir. Positron Diagnostic and Research Ctr., 1979-87. Mem. editorial bds. Circulation, 1988-92, Circulation Res., 1982-87, Jour. Am. Coll. Cardiology, 1982-88, Am. Jour. Cardiology, 1978-86; assoc. editor Circulation, 1993—; contbr. articles to profl. jours. Recipient George von Hevesy prize, 1978, ACC Young Investigators award, 1983. Fellow Am. Coll. Cardiology (trustee 1984-89), Am. Heart Assn. (chmn. coun. on circulation, Brown Meml. lectr. 1990); mem. Am. Soc. Clin. Investigation, Soc. Nuclear Medicine, N.Am. Soc. Cardiac Radiology, Am. Physiologic Soc., Assn. Am. Physicians, Assn. Univ. Cardiologists, NIH diagnostic radiol. study sect., Houston Cardiol. Soc. (pres. 1983). Democrat. Office: PO Box 20708 Houston TX 77225-0708

GOULD, SAMUEL HALPERT, pediatrics educator; b. Balt., June 14, 1922; s. Herman and Theresa Gould; m. June Linda Walter, June 17, 1952; children: Hallie, Phyllis, Cynthia, Nancy. MD, State U. Iowa, 1951. Diplomate Am. Bd. Pediat. Intern Balt. City Hosp., 1951-52, Johns Hopkins Hosp., Balt., 1952-53; resident U. Iowa Hosps., Iowa City, 1953-54; pvt. practice, Benton Harbor, Mich., 1957-86; assoc. prof. pediat. U. Chgo., 1986—, chief sect. gen. pediat., 1993—. Mem. Alpha Omega Alpha. Home:

1555 N Astor St Chicago IL 60610-1673 Office: U of Chgo Pritzker Sch of Medicine 5841 S Maryland Ave MC 1057 Chicago IL 60637-1463

GOULD, SUSAN EILEEN, social worker; b. New Brunswick, N.J., Sept. 2, 1959; d. Samuel and Marion (Louis) Naar; m. Brian Jay Gould, Apr. 10, 1983; children: Leah, Lauren. BA in Sociology, U. Hartford, 1981; BSW, St. Joseph's Coll., West Hartford, Conn., 1981; MSW, Rutgers U., 1982. Caseworker Big Bros./Big Sisters, Houston, 1982; social worker Millhill Child & Family Devel. Ctr., Trenton, N.J., 1983, Cath. Welfare Bur., Trenton, 1983-86, Richard Hall Community Mental Health Ctr., Bridgewater, N.J., 1986-87, Family Svc. Assn. Middlesex County, Old Bridge, N.J., 1987-88, CPC Mental Health Svcs., Morganville, N.J., 1989-90, Princeton (N.J.) YWCA-Interim Homes, 1990-92; with HIP/Rutgers Health Plan, 1992-94, Corner House, Princeton, N.J., 1994-96; social worker BEI, Plainsboro, N.J., 1996—. Mem. NASW, Nat. Foun. Ileitis and Colitis. Home: 7 Mifflin Ct Plainsboro NJ 08536-2331 Office: BEI Ste 501 660 Plainsboro Rd Plainsboro NJ 08536

GOULET, JAMES ALAN, orthopedic surgeon, physician; b. Manchester, Conn., Apr. 3, 1982; s. Alfred Walter and Stella Helen (Linkovich) G.; m. Lisa Sue Mazer, Apr. 3, 1982; children: Rachel, Julia. MD, Cornell U., 1961; MA, Middlebury Coll., 1977. Instr. U. Calif., Davis, 1986-87; orthopedic surgery instr. U. Mich., Ann Arbor, 1987-89, asst. prof. orthopedic surgery, 1989-94, assoc. prof. orthopedic surgery, 1994—; cons. reviewer Jour. Bone and Joint Surgery, 1992—, Clin. Orthopedics & Related Rsch., 1993—, Jour. Am. Acad. Orthopedic Surgeons, 1994—. Fellow Am. Acad. Orthopedic Surgeons; mem. Orthopedic Trauma Assn. (membership chmn. 1994—), Mich. Orthopedic Soc. (v.p. 1995—). Home: 3451 Yellowstone Dr Ann Arbor MI 48105 Office: U Mich Orthopedic Surgery 1500 E Medical Center Dr Ann Arbor MI 48109-0328

GOURAS, PETER, ophthalmology educator; b. N.Y.C., Apr. 15, 1930; s. Demetrius and Julia (Crowley) G.; m. Ute Keppler, Aug. 29, 1959; children: Eckhart, Gunnar, Roswitha. AB, Johns Hopkins U., 1951, JD, 1955. Intern in surgery Johns Hopkins Hosp., Balt., 1955-56; research scientist NIH, Bethesda, Md., 1956-58, staff scientist, 1960-68, chief neurophysiology sect. ophthal. br., 1968-70; fellow Cambridge (Eng.) U., 1958-59; chief neurophysiology sect. Nat. Eye Inst., Bethesda, 1971-78; assoc. prof. dept. ophthalmology Columbia U., N.Y.C., 1978-81, prof. dept. ophthalmology, 1981—; Humboldt prof., Freiburg, Fed. Republic Germany, 1974-75; prof. ophthamology U. P.R., San Juan, 1979; dir. retinitis pigmentosa ctr. Columbia Presbyn. Med. Ctr., N.Y.C., 1979—; mem. sci. adv. bd. N.Y. Eye Bank, N.Y.C. Author: Neurocircuitry of the Retina, 1985, The Perception of Colour, 1991; co-author: (with S. Federman) The Retina and Vitreous, 1993; mem. editorial bd. Clin. Vision Scis. Chmn. vonSallmann Prize com., N.Y.C., 1980—; bd. dirs. Wave Hill. Served to med. dir. USPHS, 1956-78. Recipient Professorship award Research to Prevent Blindness, 1978-83, Sr. Sci. Investigator award, 1990, Alcon Rsch. Inst. award, 1990. Home: 5225 Sycamore Ave Bronx NY 10471-2835 Office: Columbia U Dept of Ophthalmology 630 W 168th St New York NY 10032-3702

GOURLEY, DESMOND ROBERT HUGH, pharmacologist, educator; b. Thunder Bay, Can., Nov. 2, 1922; s. Hugh and Ida (Wilson) G.; m. Marjorie Edith Curl, Sept. 6, 1946; children—Robin C., David W., Alan W.H., Bruce D., Donald R. B.A., U. Toronto, 1945, Ph.D., 1949; postgrad., U. Freiburg, 1968-69. Demonstrator in zoology U. Toronto, 1945-49; research asst. U. Va., Charlottesville, 1949-51; asst. prof. U. Va., 1951-53, asso. prof., 1953-62, prof. pharmacology, 1962-73, acting chmn. dept. pharmacology, 1965, chmn., 1967-68, adj. instr. Sch. Continuing Edn., 1970-91, mem. Senate, 1966-73; prof., chmn. pharmacology Eastern Va. Med. Sch., Norfolk, 1973-86, prof. emeritus, 1991—; adj. prof. dept. chem. scis. Old Dominion U., Norfolk, 1975-86; mem. U.S. Pharmacopeial Conv., 1960, 80. Author: Interactions of Drugs with Cells, 1971, Problems in Pharmacology, 4th edit, 1981; Contbr. articles to profl. jours. Fellow A. Von Humboldt Found., Germany, 1968. Mem. Am. Physiol. Soc. (emeritus), Am. Soc. Pharmacology and Exptl. Therapeutics (emeritus), Pharmacology Soc. Can. (emeritus), Soc. for Exptl. Biology and Medicine (emeritus). Home: 255 College Cross Wintergreen Resort Roseland VA 22967

GOURLEY, MARK FLANDERS, physician; b. Grand Forks, N.D., Aug. 26, 1958; s. Harry Lee and Phyllis Niomi Gourley; children: Jamie Lynne, Lindsey Anne. BS in Bacteriology, N.D. State U., 1981; BS in Medicine, U. N.D., 1983; MD, Tulane U., 1985. Diplomate Am. Bd. Internal Medicine, Am. Bd. Rheumatology. Intern, resident U. Wis. Hosp. and Clinic, Madison, 1985-88; sr. staff fellow NIAMS/NIH, Bethesda, Md., 1988-95; attending rheumatologist Washington Hosp. Ctr., 1996—. Arthritis Found. fellow, 1990-93. Mem. ACP, Am. Coll. Rheumatology. Office: Washington Hosp Ctr Sect of Rheumatology Rm 2A-38H 110 Irving St NW Washington DC 20010

GOURLEY, TERRY LEE, physician assistant, paramedic; b. Salina, Kans., Mar. 20, 1950; s. Dee Duane and Mary Ann (Sowens) G.; m. Jackie Lu McGlaufflin, Apr. 17, 1961; 1 child, Samantha Danielle. BS in Physicians' Assistance, Wichita State U., 1994. Parts, svc. mgr. Gourley Motor Ford, Lincoln, Kans., 1971-85; EMS dir. Lincoln County Ambulance, 1985-87; paramedic Salina (Kans.) Fire Dept., 1987-92; physician asst. Sharps Meml. Clinic, Osborne, Kans., 1994. With U.S. Marines, 1968-70, Vietnam. Mem. Nazarene Ch. Home: 231 W New Hampshire Osborne KS 67473 Office: Sharpe Meml Clinic 218 S 5th Osborne KS 67473

GOUTI, SAMMY YASIN, psychology educator, psychotherapist; b. Gaza, Jordan, June 19, 1963; came to the U.S., 1981, naturalized, 1994; s. Yasin Ahmed and Helala Yossef (Abomarie) G.; 1 child, Chelsey Ann. AS, San Jacinto Coll., Pasadena, Tex., 1984; BS, U. Houston-Clear Lake, 1987, MA, 1989, postgrad., 1993-95; Cert. Massage Therapy, Phoenix Sch. Massage, Houston, 1992; student, TVI Actors Studios, Hollywood, Calif., 1995; cert. in acting, The Mayo Hill Sch., 1994; postgrad., Sam Houston State U., 1995. Lic. profl. counselor-intern. Asst. tchr. presch. U. Houston Human Lab. Sch., 1986-87; social sci. instr. George I. Sanchez High Sch., Houston, 1989-90; psychotherapist Life Resource-A Mental Health Ctr., Beaumont, Tex., 1990-91; psychology instr. Lamar U., Orange, Tex., 1991; assoc. clin. psychologist Tex. Dept. Mental Health and Mental Retardation, Beaumont, 1991-92; counseling program Sam Houston State U., 1995; massage therapist The Houstonian Health Club, 1993-95; prof. U. Houston-Downtown, 1992—; founder The Ctr. for stress Release, Houston, 1992, The SHUMS World Magic Ctr., Houston, 1992; adj. prof. Kingwood Coll., 1996—. Trade Mark (TM) Super Human Universal Monkeys, 1993; appeared in 2 music videos, 1995; featured in 2 Hollywood motion pictures, 1996. Recipient Editor's Choice award Nat. Libr. Poetry, 1993, 94, 95; U. Houston scholar, 1986-87, 88-89. Mem. ACA, Am. Film Inst., Internat. Soc. Poets (life), Assn. for Humanistic Psychology, Inst. Noetic Scis., Nat. Guild Hypnotists, Assn. for Body and Massage Profls., Golden Key, Psi Chi, Alpha Epsilon Delta. Office: U Houston Downtown Dept Social Scis 1 Main St Houston TX 77002-1001

GOVAN, GLADYS VERNITA MOSLEY, retired critical care and medical/surgical nurse; b. Tyler, Tex., July 24, 1918; d. Stacy Thomas and Lucy Victoria (Whitmill) Mosley; m. Osby David Govan, July 20, 1938; children Orbrenett K. (Govan) Carter, Diana Lynn (Govan) Mosley. Student, East Los Angeles Coll., Montebello, Calif., 1951; lic. vocat. nurse, Calif. Hosp. Med. Ctr., L.A., 1953; cert., Western States IV Assn., L.A., 1978. Lic. vocat. nurse, Calif.; cert. in EKG. Intravenous therapist Calif. Hosp. Med. Ctr., cardiac monitor, nurse; ret. Past pres. PTA, also hon. mem., 1963—; charter mem. Nat. Rep. Presdl. Task Force.

GOWANS, JAMES LEARMONTH, science administrator, immunologist; b. Sheffield, Eng., May 7, 1924; s. John Gowans and Selma Ljung; m. Moyra Leatham, July 28, 1956; children: William, Jenny, Lucy. MB, BS, U. London, 1947; MA, DPhil, Oxford U., 1953; ScD (hon.), Yale U., 1966; DSc (hon.), U. Chgo., 1971, U. Birmingham, Eng., 1978, U. Rochester, 1987; MD (hon.), U. Edinburgh, Scotland, 1979; DM (hon.), U. Southampton, Eng., 1987; LLD, U. Glasgow, Scotland, 1988. Rsch. prof. sch. pathology Oxford U., Eng., 1962-77, dir. med. rsch. coun. cellular immunology unit, 1963-77; sec. (chief exec.) U.K. Med. Rsch. Coun., 1977-87; cons. WHO Global Program on AIDS, Geneva, Switzerland, 1987-88; mem. rsch. programs adv. com. Nat. Multiple Sclerosis Soc., N.Y.C., 1988-90; sec.-gen. Human Frontier Scis. Program, Strasbourg, France, 1989-93; chmn. European Med. Rsch. Coun., 1985-87; mem. governing coun. Internat. Agy. for Rsch. on Cancer, Lyon, France, 1980-87; mem. awards assembly GM Cancer Rsch. Found., N.Y.C., 1988-92; dir. European Iniatives for Communicators of Sci., Munich, Germany, 1995—. Contbr. articles on cellular immunology to profl. jours. Recipient Gairdner Found. award, 1968, Paul Ehrlich prize, 1974, Feldberg award, 1979, Wolf prize in medicine, 1980, Medawar prize, 1990. Fellow Royal Soc. (Royal Medal 1976); mem. NAS (fgn. assoc.), Am. Assn. Immunologists (hon.), Am. Assn. Anatomists (hon.). Home: 75 Cumnor Hill, Oxford OX2 9HX, United Kingdom

GOWDA, CHANNE D., medical educator; b. Mandya, Karnataka, India, Mar. 9, 1953; came to U.S., 1989; s. Dase and Kadamma Gowda; m. Malathi C. Gowda, June 8, 1984; children: Nikhil C., Nischitha C. BSc, Mysore (Karnataka, India) U., 1974, MSc, 1976; PhD, Bangalore (India) U., 1988. Asst. prof. Bharati Coll., Mandya, Karnataka, India, 1976-88, assoc. prof., 1988-89, prof., 1994—; postdoctoral fellow U. Ala., Birmingham, 1989-90, rsch. asst. prof., 1992-94, vis. prof., 1995—; sr. peptide chemist Bioelastic Rsch. Ltd., Birmingham, 1990-92, cons. scientist, 1989-90, 92—. FIP fellow Univ. Grand Commn., New Delhi, India, 1980; NIH Drug Delivery grantee, 1993. Home: 8470 Emerald Lake Dr W Pinson AL 35126 Office: Univ of Alabama Lab of Molecular Biophysics Birmingham AL 35294

GOWDY, MIRIAM BETTS, nutritionist; b. Nelsonville, Ohio, Jan. 9, 1928; d. Charles Donald and Lillian Mary (Linscott) B.; m. Robert Averill Gowdy, Oct. 12, 1950 (div. 1977); children: Carol Jo, Robert Jr., Bruce. BA in Home Econs., Ohio Wesleyan U., 1949; student, Duke U., 1949-50, Calif. State U., L.A., 1975-76. Registered dietitian. Dietitian L.A., 1977-91; cons. Nat.-in-Home Health, Van Nuys, Calif., 1984-87; clin. dietitian Lake Mead Hosp., 1991-94; pvt. practice cons. nutritionist Las Vegas, Nev., 1994—; contracting dietitian Pulse Health Svcs., Las Vegas, 1995—; contract dietitian Pulse Health Svcs., 1995—. Mem. Am. Diabetes Assn. (con. San Fernando Valley unit 1976-80, bd. dirs. N.W. chpt. 1977-82), Nev. Dietetic Assn. (nominating com. 1995—), So. Nev. Dietetic Assn. (mem. chmn. 1991-92, pres. 1993-94), Cons. Nutritionists (chmn.-elect So. Calif. chpt. 1979-81), Calif. Dietetic Assn. (chmn. diabetes care practice 1979-81), Am. Heart Assn. (mem. governing bd. N.W. chpt. 1988-89), Sierra Club, Nat. Audubon Soc. Republican. Methodist. Home and Office: 9713 White Cloud Dr Las Vegas NV 89134-7840

GOYAN, JERE EDWIN, university dean, former government official; b. Oakland, Calif., Aug. 3, 1930; s. Gerald H. and Lucille (Johnson) G.; m. Patricia B. Mesirow, Aug. 24, 1952 (divorced); children: Pamela, Terrence H., Andrea. B.S., U. Calif. Sch. Pharmacy, 1952, Ph.D., 1957. Asst. prof. pharmacy U. Mich., 1956-61, assoc. prof., 1961-63; assoc. prof. pharmacy and pharm. chemistry U. Calif. at San Francisco, 1963-65, prof., 1965-79, 81—; assoc. dean Sch. Pharmacy, 1966-67, dean, 1967-79, 81—; commr. FDA, 1979-81. Fellow AAAS; mem. Inst. Medicine of NAS, N.Y. Acad. Scis., Am. Pharm. Assn., Acad. Pharm. Scis., Am. Assn. Pharm. Scientists (pres. 1990), Calif. Pharm. Assn., Am. Assn. Colls. Pharmacy (pres. 1978-79), Sigma Xi, Rho Chi, Phi Lambda Upsilon. Office: U Calif Sch Pharmacy San Francisco CA 94143*

GOYER, ROBERT ANDREW, pathology educator; b. Hartford, Conn., June 2, 1927; s. Andrew R. and Cecelia P. (Castonquay) G.; m. Mary Ellen Wilke, Feb. 4, 1955; children—Barbara, John, Peter, Ellen. B.S., Holy Cross Coll., 1950; M.D., St. Louis U., 1955. Diplomate: Am. Bd. Pathology. Intern St. Francis Hosp., Hartford, 1955-56; resident in pathology St. Louis U. Hosps., 1956-60; practice medicine specializing in pathology St. Louis, 1956-65; instr. pathology St. Louis U., 1960-62, asst. prof., 1962-65; asst. prof. Sch. Medicine, U. N.C., Chapel Hill, 1965-68; assoc. prof. Sch. Medicine, U. N.C., 1968-71, prof. pathology, 1971-74, adj. prof. pathology, 1979-87; clin. pathologist Cardinal Glennon Meml. Hosp. for Children, St. Louis, 1961-62; dir. labs. Cardinal Glennon Meml. Hosp. for Children, 1962-64; staff pathologist N.C. Meml. Hosp., Chapel Hill, 1965-74; chief pathology U. Hosp., London, Ont., Can., 1974-79; prof. pathology Health Scis. Centre, U. Western Ont., Can., 1974-79, 87-92; prof. emeritus Health Scis. Centre, U. Western Ont., 1992—; dept. dir. Nat. Inst. Environ. Health Scis., Research Triangle Park, N.C., 1979-87; pvt. cons. health effects, toxic metals Chapel Hill, N.C., 1992—. Contbr. articles to profl. jours.; mem. editorial bd. Yearbook Pathology, 1979-88, AMA Archives of Pathology, 1973-82. Served with USN, 1945-47. Nat. Found. fellow, 1959-60. Mem. Coll. Am. Pathology, Am. Assn. Pathologists, Internat. Acad. Pathology, Soc. Exptl. Biology and Medicine. Roman Catholic. Office: 6405 Huntingridge Rd Chapel Hill NC 27514-8614

GOYINGS, BETTY FARABOW, mental health administrator, therapist; b. Fuquay, N.C., Aug. 16, 1929; d. Sidney S. and Annie (Jones) Farabow; m. Ezra Goyings Jr., Dec., 1956 (dec. 1975); children: Karen, Katherine, Leigh, Jonathan. BS in Sociology, Queens Coll., 1952; MSW, Coll. of William & Mary, 1954. Lic. social worker, Fla. Clin. social worker Meml. Guidance Clinic, Richmond, Va., 1954-55; office mgr. Winter Park, Fla., 1958-63; clin. social worker Fla. State Bur. of Alcoholism, Orlando, 1963-68, Orlando Regional Med. Ctr., 1968-75; pvt. practice Winter Park, 1975-78; exec. dir. N.E. Orange Community Mental Health Clinic, Winter Park, 1978-83; dir. personal svcs. Mental Health Svcs., Orange County, Fla., 1983-85; pvt. practice Fla. Psychiat. Cons., Longwood, 1985-86; clin. dir. Tri-County Community Mental Health Clinic, St. Augustine, Fla., 1986-87, New Horizons Mental Health Ctr., Ft. Pierce, Fla., 1987—; pvt. practice, 1991—. Office: New Horizons Treasure Coast Inc Community Mental Health Ctr 800 Ave H Fort Pierce FL 34950-3163

GOZENPUT, MIKHAIL, physician assistant; b. Bobruysk, USSR, Nov. 5, 1953; came to U.S., 1989; s. Semen and Maya (Gayster) G.; m. Margarita Tseyflin, Sept. 1, 1979; children: Yeugeny, Ernest. MD, Pediatric Med. Sch., Leningrad, USSR, 1977; Physician Asst., Cornell U., 1992. Cert. physician asst. Attending Ear, Nose and Throat Emergency Hosp., Belarus, USSR, 1977-89; physician asst. Maimonides Med. Ctr., N.Y.C., 1992—, Kings Brook Jewish Med. Ctr., N.Y.C., 1992—. Mem. Am. Assn. Physician Assts. Republican. Home: 1303 Jerome Pl Fair Lawn NJ 07410

GRABARZ, DONALD FRANCIS, pharmacist; b. Jersey City, Sept. 18, 1941; s. Joseph and Frances (Zotynia) G.; m. Joan Isoldi, Aug. 13, 1966; children: Christine, Robert, Danielle. BPharm, St. Johns U., N.Y.C., 1964. Lic. pharmacist, N.Y., Vt. Dir. qualtiy control and assurance Johnson and Johnson Co., New Brunswick, N.J., 1965-72; dir. quality assurance and regulatory affairs Bard Parker div. Becton Dickinson, Franklin Lakes, N.J., 1972-76; asst. corp. dir. regulatory affairs Becton Dickinson, 1976-80; corp. dir. regulatory affairs C.R. Bard Inc., Murray Hill, N.J., 1980-85; v.p. regulatory affairs, qualtiy assurance Symbion Inc., Salt Lake City, 1985-86; cons., pres. DFG & Assocs., Inc., Salt Lake City, 1986—; mng. dir. Internat. Regulatory Consultants, L.C., Salt Lake City, Boston, also U.K., 1987—; adj. prof. Salt Lake C. C., 1993—; lectr. Inst. for Applied Tech., Inst. Internat. Rsch., Ernst & Young, Salt Lake C.C. Co-author, technical advisor, editor Inspection and Recall Film; co-author: Science, Technology, and Regulation in a Competetive Environment, 1990; contbr. articles to profl. jours. Bd. dirs. v.p., asst. treas. Am. Lung Assn., N.J., 1972-75; chmn. Drug Edn., DuPage County, Ill., 1968. Mem. Health Industry Mfg. Assn. (chmn. Legal and Regulatory commn. 1983), Regulatory Affairs Profl. Soc. (lectr.), Am. Soc. Quality Control, Am. Mfr. Med. Instrumentation Assn., Am. Pharm. Assn., Food and Drug Law Inst., Cottonwood Country Club (bd. dirs., treas. 1995—, v.p. 1996—). Office: Internat Regulatory Cons, LC PO Box 17801 Salt Lake City UT 84117-0801

GRABEK, JAMES ROBERT, medical company executive; b. Chgo., Aug. 30, 1945; s. Joseph Richard and Dorothy (Luecht) G.; m. Penelope Jean Chipain, Aug. 20, 1967; children: Justin Ryan, Seth Alexander, Christopher Joseph, Nicholas James. BS, Northern Ill. U., 1968, MS, 1969. Sales supr. Convertors Am., Mpls., 1972-74; region sales mgr. New Dimensions in Medicine, Atlanta, 1974-78; midwest regional ops. mgr. Am. Mgmt Services, Denver, 1978-79; regional sales dir. U.S. Surgical Corp., Mpls.; dir. world sales St. Jude Med., Inc., St., 1980-82; pres. Horizon Industries, Inc., 1982-83; pres., chief exec. officer GV Med., Inc., Mpls., 1983-91; founder, chmn., CEO Comedicus Inc., Columbia Heights, Minn., 1992—; staff Faculty Entrepreneurship Ctr., Grad. Sch. Bus., U. St. Thomas, St. Paul, 1991—. Founder Laser Enhanced System, 1983. Council mem. City Orono 1983-86, mayor City Orono 1987—. Mem. Am. Electronics Assn. Home: 3050 Jamestown Rd Long Lake MN 55356-9599 Office: Comedicus Inc Ste 610 3989 Central Ave NE Columbia Heights MN 55421

GRABER, CAROLINE RIGSBY, health facility coordinator; b. Ashland, Ky., Sept. 23, 1942; d. Fred Everett and Mary Midlred (White) Rigsby; m. Glenn Campbell Graber, Aug. 1, 1964; children: Janna Campbell, Rosalie Caroline. AB, Transylvania U., 1964; MS, U. Mich., Ann Arbor, 1966; BSN, U. Tenn., 1979. RN, Tenn.; cert. infection control nurse. Rsch. asst. U. Mich., Ann Arbor, 1966-68, U. Tenn., Knoxville, 1970-74; homebound tchr. Knoxville Schs., 1974-79; dir. infection control East Tenn. Children's Hosp., Knoxville, 1979—. Mem. Assn. Practitioners Infection Control (sec. 1989-90, bd. dirs. 1991, pres.-elect 1995-96), Daus. Am. Colonists (sec. 1991—). Democrat. Episcopalian. Office: East Tenn Children s Hosp PO Box 15010 Knoxville TN 37901-5010

GRABER, DORIS APPEL, political scientist, editor, author; b. St. Louis, Nov. 11, 1923; d. Ernest and Martha (Insel) Appel; m. Thomas M. Graber, June 15, 1941; children: Lee Winston, Thomas Woodrow, Jack Douglas, Jim Murray, Susan Doris. AB, Washington U., St. Louis, 1941, MA, 1942; PhD, Columbia U., 1947. Feature writer St. Louis County Observer, Univ. City Tribune, St. Louis, 1939-41; civilian dir. U.S. Army Ednl. Reconditioning Program, Camp Maxey, Tex., 1943-45; editor legal mags. Commerce Clearing House, Chgo., 1945-46; lectr. polit. sci. Northwestern U., 1948-49; lectr. polit. sci. U. Chgo., 1950-51, rsch. assoc. Ctr. for Study Am. Fgn. and Mil. Policy, 1952-71; lectr. polit. sci. North Park Coll., 1952; mem. faculty U. Ill., Chgo., 1964—, assoc. prof. polit. sci., 1964-69, prof., 1970—; editor textbooks Harper & Row, Evanston, 1956-63. Author: The Development of the Law of Belligerent Occupation, 1949, 68, Crisis Diplomacy: A History of U.S. Intervention Policies and Practices, 1959, Public Opinion, The President and Foreign Policy, 1968, Verbal Behavior and Politics, 1976, Mass Media and American Politics, 1980, 84, 89, 93, 96, Crime News and the Public, 1980, (with others) Media Agenda Setting in a Presidential Election, 1981, Processing the News: How People Tame the Information Tide, 1984, 88, 94, Public Sector Communication: How Organizations Manage Information, 1992; editor, contbr. The President and the Public, 1982; editor: Media Power in Politics, 1984, 90, 94, Political Comm., 1992—; contbr. articles to profl. jours. Mem. LWV, Am. Assn. Pub. Opinion Rsch., Midwest Assn. Pub. Opinion Rsch. (program chmn. 1978-79, pres. 1980-81), Midwest Polit. Sci. Assn. (past pres.), Am. Polit. Sci. Assn. (coun. 1978-79, v.p. 1980-81, program chmn. 1984, 89-90, chmn. polit. comm. sect. 1989-91, chmn. editl. bd. P.S. 1992-94), Internat. Polit. Sci. Assn., Internat. Commn. Assn. (divsn. program chmn. 1978-80, divsn. chmn. 1980-82), Assn. Edn. for Journalism, Acad. Polit. Sci., Am. Acad. Polit. and Social Sci., Internat. Soc. Polit. Psychology (coun. 1992-93, co-program chmn. 1993-94, pres. 1995-96), Phi Beta Kappa (pres. Iota of Ill. chpt. 1991-92), Pi Sigma Alpha, Pi Alpha Alpha. Home: 2895 Sheridan Pl Evanston IL 60201-1725 Office: U Ill 1007 W Harrison St Chicago IL 60607-7135

GRABER, EDWARD ALEX, obstetrician, gynecologist, educator; b. Chgo., July 24, 1914; s. Irving D. and Grace (Davis) G.; m. Sylvia H. Hess, Nov. 24, 1938; 1 son, Fredric Jay. MD, Emory U., 1936. Diplomate: Am. Bd. Gyn. Assoc. dir. ob-gyn Lenox Hill Hosp., N.Y.C., 1972-75; prof. ob-gyn Med. Sch. Cornell U., N.Y.C., 1975—, emeritus Med. Sch., 1988; hon. attending physician N.Y. Hosp.-Cornell Med. Ctr., N.Y.C., 1971—. Author: Gynecologic Endocrinology, 1961, (with Barber) Are The Pills Safe?, Obstetric and Gynecology Procedures, 1969, Gynecological Oncology, 1970, Surgical Disease in Pregnancy, 1974, (with G. Schaefer) Complications of Gynecological Surgery, 1982; contbr. articles to profl. jours. Fellow Am. Coll. Ob-Gyn, ACS, N.Y. Acad. Medicine (pres. ob-gyn sect. 1971-72), N.Y. Gynecol. Soc. (pres. 1972-73); mem. AMA. Home: 130 E 75th St New York NY 10021-3277

GRABHORN, JUANITA JONES, dietitian; b. Vinegar Bend, Ala., Mar. 6, 1944; d. Johnnie abd Sarah Jane (Walley) Jones; m. Larry Lee Grabhorn, Jan. 25, 1975; 1 child, Kenneth John. BS, U. So. Miss., 1962-66; MS, U. Ala., 1975. REgistered lic. dietitian, Tex. Commd. 2d lt. US. Army, 1965, advanced through grades to lt. col., 1980; staff dietitian Brooke Army Med. Ctr., Ft. Sam Houston, Tex., 1967-69; asst chief food service div. Madigan Army Med. Ctr., Tacoma, 1969-71; C food service div. Lyster Army Hosp., Ft. Rucker, Ala., 1971-74; chief food service div. Darnall Army Hosp., Ft. Hood, Tex., 1975-78; asst. chief food service div. Womack Army Hosp., Ft. Bragg, N.C., 1978-81; chief nutrition care div. Reynolds Army Hosp., Ft. Sill, Okla., 1981-85; chief production and service br. Brooke Army Med. Ctr., 1985-86; spl. studies officer Acad. Health Scis. Army Med. Specialist Corps, Ft. Sam Houston, 1986-87; dir. food and beverages Army Residence Community, San Antonio, 1987—. Fellow Am. Dietetic Assn. Democrat. Methodist. Home: 8607 Autumn Sunset San Antonio TX 78239-2616

GRABINSKI, C. JOANNE, gerontologist, educator; b. Bend, Oreg., Dec. 8, 1941; d. Jack George and Helen Margaret (Thomsen) Huffman; m. Roger Neil Grabinski, Aug. 13, 1966; 1 child, Lawrence Neil. BS, MS in Home Econ. Edn., Oreg. State U., 1963, 68; MA in Ednl. Adminstrn./Cmty. Leadership, Ctrl. Mich. U., 1976, MA in Family Rels., 1980; postgrad., Mich. State U., 1982-87. Dept. chair, tchr. home econs. Oakridge (Oreg.) Jr./Sr. High Sch., 1963-67, Briggs Jr. High Sch., Springfield, Oreg., 1967-68; prof. home econs. Lane C.C., Eugene, Oreg., 1968-69; residence hall dir., assoc. dir. Western Mich. U., Kalamazoo, 1970-72; dir., spl. interest coord. Mt. Pleasant (Mich.) Pub. Schs., 1976-77; money mgmt. counselor Coop. Ext. Svc./DSS, Mt. Pleasant, 1977-78; asst. prof. ednl. adminstrn./community leadership Ctrl. Mich. U., Mt. Pleasant, 1976, 77, asst. prof. home econs., 1980-86, dir./asst. prof. interdisciplinary gerontology program, 1984-91; pres., cons. cjgGERONTOLOGY, Mt. Pleasant, 1991—; project dir. Region 7 Alzheimer's Disease and Related Conditions Caregiver Edn. Project, Mich. Dept. Mental Health, Ctrl. Mich. U., 1986-91; adj. prof. gerontology, lectr. Western Mich. U., Kalamazoo, 1992-94; continuing edn. rep., lectr. gerontology Ea. Mich. U., 1992-96, continuing edn. coord.-gerontology Ea. Mich. U., 1996—; Ea. Mich. U. Elderwise liaison, 1995-96; ctr. coord. Ea. Mich. U. at NMC U., 1996—. Mem. editl. bd. AGHE Exch., 1988-91, asst. editor, 1988-91; contbr. articles to profl. jours. Bd. dirs. Hospice of Cen. Mich., Mt. Pleasant, 1986-89, Cen. Mich. U. Dames, 1974-78, pres., 1976-77; bd. dirs. Mt. Pleasant Welcome Wagon Newcomers Club, 1972-76, pres., 1974-75; team mem. Bldg. Ties, Isabella County, Mich., 1983-84. Marie Dye Grad. fellow Mich. Home Econ. Assn., 1983; named Outstanding Faculty Mem., Ctrl. Mich. U. Mortar Bd. Mem. Am. Soc. on Aging, Gerontol. Soc. Am., Nat. Coun. on Aging, Mich. Coun. on Family Rels. (bd. dirs. 1984-87), Nat. Coun. Family Rels., Assn. Gerontology Higher Edn. (instnl. rep.), Kappa Omicron Nu, Omicron Nu, Kappa Omicron Phi, Phi Delta Kappa. Democrat. Lutheran. Home: 310 Apricot Ln Mount Pleasant MI 48858-6156 Office: cjgGERONTOLOGY PO Box 868 Mount Pleasant MI 48804-0868

GRABLE, HARVEY ROBERT, medical consultant; b. N.Y.C., May 3, 1937; s. Harry and Sylvia Grable. BA, Dartmouth U., 1958; MD, U. Ark., 1964; JD, N.Y. Law Sch., 1983; MS, NYU, 1986. Diplomate Am. Bd. Orthop. Surgeons, Am. Bd. Quality Assurance and Utilization Rev., Am. Bd. Legal Medicine. Pvt. practice cons. N.Y.C., 1972—; assoc. prof. N.Y. Med. Coll., N.Y.C., 1988-96. Maj. USAF, 1970-72. Republican. Office: 60 Plaza St Brooklyn NY 11238

GRABLE, MICHAEL S., physician; b. Flint, Mich., June 22, 1955; s. Buford C. and Donna J. (Russell) G.; m. Rosemary Jonasz, Sept. 5, 1981; children: Stephen, Ashley. BS, U. Mich., 1977, MD, 1981. Diplomate Am. Bd. Urology. Urology residency U. Fla., Gainesville, 1986; physician Volusia Urology, Deland, Fla., 1986—; commn. West Volusia Hosp. Authority, Deland, Fla., 1992—; clinical assoc. prof. urology Univ. Fla., Gainesville, 1981—. Office: Volusia Urology 685 Peachwood Dr Deland FL 32720

GRABOWSKI, ELIZABETH, healthcare administrator; b. Laskowiec, Poland, July 24, 1940; came to U.S., 1948.; d. Stanley and Marianna (Tatko) Backiel; m. John A. Grabowski; children: Elizabeth C. Taylor, Julia M. Smith, John A., Emilia A. AAD in Nursing, Memphis State U., 1975; BSN, Elmhurst Coll., 1981; MSN, U. Louisville, 1988. Clin. dir., owner Diabetes Resource Ctr., Louisville, 1989—; diabetes nurse clinician edn. dept.

Humana Hosp. Audubon, Louisville, 1983-84; mem. adj. faculty U. La. Sch. Nursing, Spalding Univ. Grad. Sch. Nursing, 1994—. Abstracts editor Diabetes Educator Jour., 1986—; contbr. articles to profl. jours. Chmn. adv. bd. Oldham County affiliate ARC, 1989-92, chmn. tech. adv. com. for nursing svcs. Medicaid programs, Ky., 1987-91, chmn. Ky. Nurse Recognition Banquet com., 1987-91. Recipient Hoechst-Roussel Pharms. award for clin. excellence, academic scholarship Kiwanis Internat., Clairol Found., others. Fellow ANA (Med.-Surg. Nurse of Yr. 1990); mem Ky. Nurses Assn. (state and dist. 1), Am. Assn. Diabetes Educators, Greater Louisville Assn. Diabetes Educators, Sigma Theta Tau, others. Home: 4010 Dana Rd Crestwood KY 40014-9224 Office: Diabetes Resource Ctr Inc 1001 Dupont Sq North Louisville KY 40207-4715

GRABOWSKI, SANDRA REYNOLDS, biology educator, writer; b. Chgo., Mar. 3, 1943; d. Glenn Edward and Helen (McDaniel) Reynolds; m. Zbigniew W. Grabowski, Jan. 23, 1965. BS, Purdue U., 1965, PhD, 1973. Postdoctoral rsch. assoc. Purdue U., West Lafayette, Ind., 1973-76, instr., 1977—. Co-author: (with G.J. Tortora) Principles of Anatomy and Physiology, 1996. NDEA/NIH fellow Purdue U., 1972. Mem. Nat. Assn. Biology Tchrs., Assn. for Women in Sci., Assn. Biology Lab Educators, Nat. Sci. Tchrs. Assn., Soc. for Coll. Sci. Tchrs., Human Anatomy and Physiology Soc. (editor 1990-92, pres.-elect 1992-93, pres. 1993-94), Phi Kappa Phi. Office: Purdue U Lilly Hall Life Scis Dept Biol Scis West Lafayette IN 47907-1392

GRACE, MARCELLUS, pharmacy educator, university dean; b. Selma, Ala., Oct. 17, 1947; s. Capp and Mary (Davis) G.; m. Laura Dunn, Sept. 8, 1973; children: K'Chebe M., Syreeta L., Marcellus Jr. BS in Pharmacy, Xavier U. La., 1971; MS in Hosp. Pharmacy, U. Minn., 1975, PhD in Pharmacy Adminstrn., 1976. Registered pharmacist, La., Ohio, Calif., Minn., D.C. Hosp. pharmacy resident USPHS Hosp., Balt., 1971-72; staff pharmacist USPHS Hosp., Boston, 1972-73, Thrifty Drug Stores, L.A., 1973; asst. dir. pharmacy Bethesda Hosps., Cin., 1975; dir. pharmacy svcs. Tulane U. Med. Ctr., New Orleans, 1976-77; assoc. prof., asst. dean Howard U., Washington, 1979-82; asst. prof. clin. pharmacy Xavier U. La., New Orleans, 1976-78, prof. pharmacy adminstrn., dean, 1983—; mem. adv. coun. Nat. Heart Lung and Blood Inst., NIH, Bethesda, 1990-93; mem. Walgreens Pharmacy adv. coun., 1993—; chair pharmacy panel Peer Health Professionscomm., 1991-92; bd. dirs. New Orleans Regional Med. Complex, 1993—, Ernest N. Morial Asthma and Respiratory Disease Ctr., 1995—, La. Cancer and Lung Trust Fund, 1995—, Alton Ochsner Med. Found., 1996—. Contbr. articles and abstracts to profl. jours. Recipient cert. appreciation Nat. Assn. Bds. Pharmacy, 1983. Mem. Am. Assn. Colls. Pharmacy (bd. dirs. 1992-94), N.Y. Acad. Scis., Assn., Rho Chi. Democrat. Baptist. Office: Xavier U La Coll Pharmacy 7325 Palmetto St New Orleans LA 70125-1056

GRACE, THOMAS LEE, healthcare administrator, nurse; b. Huntingdon, Pa., Mar. 29, 1955; s. Robert Leroy and Mary Elizabeth (Isenberg) G.; m. Renee Lee Ramsey, Oct. 20, 1979; children: Elliott, Amanda. ASN, Robert Morris Coll., 1978; diploma in nursing, Sewickley (Pa.) Valley Hosp., 1979; BSN, LaRoche Coll., 1984; M in Pub. Mgmt., Carnegie Mellon U., 1985. RN, Pa. Staff nurse ortho dept. McKeesport (Pa.) Hosp., 1979-80; staff nurse emergency rm. Allegheny Gen. Hosp., Pitts., 1980-81; flight nurse Life-Flight-Allegheny Gen. Hosp., Pitts., 1981-85; chief flight nurse Aries-Fairfax Hosp., Falls Church, Va., 1985-86; coord. emergency svcs. Fairfax Hosp., Falls Church, 1986-87; flight program dir. Pennstar U. Pa. Med. Ctr., Phila., 1987-91; asst. adminstr. Hosp. of U. Pa., Phila., 1991-96; dir. safety mgmt. U. Pa. Health Sys., 1996—. Inventor crico ventilation device; contbr. articles to profl. jours. Citizen rep. Upper Merion Twp. (Pa.) Emergency Svc. Bd., 1994—; mem. Huntingdon Vol. Fire Dept., 1972—, Valley Ambulance Authority, Corapolis, Pa., 1977-79; bd. dirs., citizen rep. Lafayette Ambulance Svc., King of Prussia, Pa.; del. Ctrl. Dist. Fireman's Assn., Tyrone, Pa., 1983—; scoutmaster Sewickley Math. Ch. troop Boy Scouts Am., 1978-79. With U.S. Army, 1973-76. Mem. ENA, Nat. Flight Nurses Assn. (past pres.), Am. Mgmt. Assn., Am. Phys. Plant Adminstrs., Am. Soc. Hosp. Engrs., Am. Legion. Democrat. Home: 594 Forest Rd Wayne PA 19087-2322

GRACY, ROBERT, science educator. Assoc. dean rsch. and bio tech U. North Tex. Health Sci. Ctr., Ft. Worth. Recipient Wilford I. Doherty award Am. Chem. Soc., 1995. Office: U North Tex Health Sci Ctr 3500 Camp Bowie Blvd Fort Worth TX 76107

GRADITOR, WARREN BYRON, clinical psychologist; b. Pitts., Nov. 14, 1949; s. Milton Harry and Doris (Linda) G.; m. Linda Gail Karafin, June 18, 1977; 1 child, Sara Elizabeth. BA, The Am. U., 1971; MS, Nova U., 1974, PhD, 1979. Lic. psychologist, Fla. Clin. intern Eastern Pa. Psychiat. Inst., Phila., 1977-79; adj. prof. Nova U., Ft. Lauderdale, Fla., 1979-80; clin. psychologist, pvt. practice Broward Psychol. Group, Hollywood, Fla., 1979—. Author: Selection and Training of Foster Parents As Paraprofessionals, 1976. Bd. dirs. Jewish Family Svcs., Hollywood, 1981-82. Mem. APA, Am. Orthopsychiatric Assn., Fla. Psychol. Assn., Nat. Register Health Svc. Providers in Psychology. Office: Broward Psychol Group 4400 Sheridan St Hollywood FL 33021-3514

GRADY, JENNIFER ERIN, emergency room staff nurse, military officer; b. Bristol, Conn., Oct. 1, 1970; d. Peter Michael and Mary Grace (Morrison) G. BSN, Villanova U., 1993. RN, Calif. Commd. lt. (j.g.) USN, 1993; staff nurse, pediat. Naval Med. Ctr., San Diego, 1993-94, staff nurse, emergency room, 1994—. Office: USN Naval Med Ctr San Diego Box 149 San Diego CA 92134-5000

GRADY, JOHN M., health facility administrator; b. Chgo., Sept. 4, 1958; s. John Joseph and Geraldine Francis (Poliask) G.; m. Vera D. Dam, May 29, 1982; children: Kevin, Sean. BS in Microbiology, U. Ill., 1980; MHA, U. Iowa, 1982. Adminstrv. pres. Mpls. Va Med. Ctr., 1982-83; asst. dir. bldg. sys. Albany VA Med. Ctr., 1983-84, staff asst. to dir., 1984-85; staff asst. to CEO Miami (Fla.) VA Med. Ctr., 1985-86; assoc. to chief of staff West Haven (Conn.) VA Med. Ctr., 1986-89; staff asst. region 5 VA Ctrl. Office, Washington, 1989-90, staff asst. constrn., 1990-91; asst. dir. Balt. VA Med. Ctr., 1991-92; chief operating officer FDR Va. Hosp., Montrose, N.Y., 1992—. Bd. dirs. Reformed Ch. Cortlandtown, Montrose, 1995-96; dir. midnight run Presbyn. Ch. Dobbs Ferry (N.Y.), 1995-66. Mem. ACHE (assoc.), NORNET, GYNHA. Office: FDR VA Hosp PO Box 100 Montrose NY 10548

GRAESSLE, WILLIAM RUDOLF, physician, educator; b. Point Pleasant, N.J., Jan. 29, 1964; s. Frederick William and Marilyn Ann (Meyer) G.; m. Tracy Lynn Roscoe; 1 child, Rebecca Lynn. BS, Trenton State Coll., 1986; MD, UMDNJ, 1991. Intern Univ. Hosp., Newark, 1991-92; resident St. Christopher's Hosp., Phila., 1992-94; clin. instr. Cooper Hosp., Camden, N.J., 1994-95; asst. prof. Med. Coll. Pa., Phila., 1996—. Fellow Am. Acad. Pediats.; mem. Phila. Pediat. Soc. Home: 30 Tall Timber Ln Burlington NJ 08016 Office: Med Coll Pa 3300 Henry Ave Philadelphia PA 19129

GRAF, BEN KIM, surgeon; b. Plymouth, Wis., Sept. 21, 1955; s. Carl G. and Nancy L. (Lutzke) G.; m. Nediljka A. Graf; two children. BA, U. Wis., 1978, MD, 1979. Resident in orthopedics U. Wis., Madison, 1979-84, assoc. prof., 1985—. Contbr. articles to profl. jours. and chpts. to books. Grantee Whittaker Found., 1992. Office: U Hosp Rm G5/322 600 Highland Ave Madison WI 53792

GRAF, JEFFREY HOWARD, cardiologist; b. N.Y.C., Apr. 6, 1955; s. Rudolf F. and Bettina L. (Knisbacher) G.; m. Roberta Ruth Rubin, June 26, 1982; children: Allison, Daniel, Russell. BA magna cum laude, NYU, 1976, MD, 1980. Diplomate Am. Bd. Cardiology, Am. Bd. Internal Medicine. Cardiology fellow Mt. Sinai Med. Ctr., N.Y.C., 1983-86; cardiologist educator Mt. Sinai Sch. Medicine, Beth Israel Med. Ctr., N.Y.C., 1986—; cons., 1986—. Fellow Am. Coll. Cardiology; mem. Phi Beta Kappa, Alpha Omega Alpha. Office: 1111 Park Ave New York NY 10128-1234

GRAFF, HAROLD, psychiatrist, psychoanalyst, hospital administrator; b. Phila., Apr. 11, 1932; s. Joseph and Blanche (Katz) G.; children from previous marriage: David, Caron; m. Diane Goldblum; 1 child, Robert. BA, U. Pa., 1954, MD, 1958. Intern Phila. Gen. Hosp., 1958-59; resident Inst. Pa. Hosp., Phila., 1959-62; postdoctoral fellow Inst. Neurol. Sci., U. Pa., 1959-62; psychoanalytic trainee Inst. of Phila. Assn. for Psychoanalysis, Bala Cynwyd, Pa., 1962-67; research scientist, dept clin. sci. Eastern Pa. Psychiat. Inst., Phila., 1963-74; dir. div. psychoanalytic studies, dept. clin. research and tng. Eastern Pa. Psychiat. Inst., 1974-79; dir. adolescent psychiatry Pa. Dept. Pub. Welfare, 1977-79; chmn. research and publs. com. Inst. of the Pa. Hosp., Phila., 1968-78; chmn. psychoanalytic research group, 1968-78; clin. prof. psychiatry Thomas Jefferson U., 1977-89, lectr., 1990-91; clin. assoc. prof. psychiatry Health Scis. Center Temple U., 1974-77; research asst. prof. psychiatry Hahnemann Med. Coll., Phila., 1963-70; assoc. prof. Hahnemann Med. Coll., 1970-74; vis. prof., psychiat. cons. Inst. for Human Resource Devel., 1974-76; adj. assoc. prof. psychiatry Widener U., Chester, Pa., 1989—; pres., research dir. Psychiat. Services, Inc., Wynnewood, Pa., 1969-81; dir., chief of psychiatry St. Francis Hosp., 1980-88; clin. dir. adolescent psychiatry Rockford Ctr., Newark, Del., 1988-92, bd. trustees, 1989-92, med. staff pres., 1996; pres. Psychiatry Mgmt. of Del., 1991-94, Mental Health Resources Inc., 1992-93; dir. med. svcs. Prudential Psych Mgmt., 1996—; dir. med. svc. PruPsych Prudential Ins. Co. Am., Horsham, Pa., 1996—; mem. staff Wilminton Med. Ctr., Rockford Ctr.; spl. cons. Spl. Action Office for Drug Abuse Prevention, Washington, 1973-74; cons. psychiatry Republic of Panama, 1980. Contbr. articles to profl. jours. Pres. Regional Coun. of Child and Adolescent Psychiatry, 1992. Fellow Am. Psychiat. Assn. (life), Pa. Psychiat. Assn., Phila. Coll. Physicians; mem. AAAS, Am. Soc. Adolescent Psychiatry (chmn. Eastern States liason com. 1977-78, cluster chmn. internal affairs 1979-81), Am. Psychoanalytic Assn., Internat. Psychoanalytic Assn., Phila. Psychoanalytic Assn., Del. Psychiat. Soc. (counsellor 1981-83, treas. 1983, sec. 1985-86, pres. 1987-88, chmn. ethics com. 1990-93), Del. Assn. Child and Adolescent Psychiatry (pres. 1984-86), Dirs. of Psychiatry in Del. (chmn. 1982-87) Regional Coun. Child and Adolescent Psychiatry (pres. 1993), Del. Med. Assn., New Castle County Med. Assn., Phila. Soc. Adolescent Psychiatry (pres. 1978-79), Med. Club Phila., Phila. Coll. Physicians, Mensa, Phi Beta Kappa. Office: Prudential Health Care Omega Profl Ctr PO Box 911 Horsham PA 19044-0911

GRAFF, MARC DAVID, psychiatrist, educator; b. Chgo., Nov. 5, 1948; s. Norman and Phyllis Lenore (Firestone) G.; m. Laura Lee Kunstler, Sept. 24, 1972; children: Rebecca Sara, Benjamin Louis. Student, Coll. of San Mateo, 1965-67; BA in Zoology with honors, U. Calif., Berkeley, 1970; postgrad., U. Wis., 1971; MD, U. Chgo., 1974. Diplomate Am. Bd. Psychiatry and Neurology. Intern U. Rochester (N.Y.), 1974-75, resident in psychiatry, 1975-78; asst. prof. psychiatry U. Pitts., 1978-80; grad. fellow Rand Grad. Sch., Santa Monica, Calif., 1980; cons. Rand Corp., Santa Monica, 1981; HMO practice Inglewood, Calif., 1981-83; pvt. practice Van Nuys, Calif., 1983—; asst. chief dept. psychiatry So. Calif. Permanente Med. Group, Panorama City, 1991-95; asst. clin. prof. Neuropsychiat. Inst. UCLA, 1983—. Mem. profl. adv. bd. peer counseling orgn. Mishpachah Sh'lemah Temple Ahavat Shalom, Northridge, Calif., 1987-90. Fellow Am. Psychiat. Assn.; mem. AAAS, Soc. Calif. Psychiat. Soc. (co-chmn. pub. info. com. 1986-88, chmn. 1993-96, rep. coun. 1990-93, sec. 1993-94, pres.-elect 1995-96, pres. 1996—), Assn. for Pub. Policy Analysis, Clarif. Turtle and Tortcise Club (pres. San Fernando Valley chpt. 1983-92, exec. bd. treas. 1987-88, v.p. 1988-89, 92-94, pres. and chmn. bd. 1989-92, 94—), Desert Tortoise Coun. (bd. dirs. 1990—, co-chair 1992-94). Democrat. Home: 17259 Ballinger St Northridge CA 91325-1929 Office: So Calif Permanente Med Group 13746 Victory Blvd Van Nuys CA 91401

GRAFF, STEVEN MARTIN, psychologist; b. Topeka, Kans., Mar. 9, 1953; s. Norman and Phyllis (Firestone) G.; m. Kimberly Susan Honig, May 6, 1984; children: Shoshana, Daniel. BA, Pomona Coll., 1975; MS, U. So. Calif., 1983, PhD, 1988. Lic. psychologist, Calif. Rsch. asst. Carnegie Inst., Stanford, Calif., 1976-81; counselor intern South Bay Human Svcs. Ctr., Torrance, Calif., 1982-87; psychologist intern L.A. County Sheriff Dept., 1984-86; postdoctoral fellow in psychology Devereux Found., Santa Barbara, Calif., 1988-89, psychologist, 1990-92, sr. clin. case mgr., 1992-94, clin. psychologist II, 1994-95; staff psychologist Tricounties Regional Ctr., Oxnard, Calif., 1995—; mem. adv. bd. Ventura County (Calif.) Dept. Mental Health, 1991—, Santa Clara County Dept. Mental Health, Palo Alto, Calif., 1979-81. Editor jour. Devereux Independence, 1994, 95; contbr. sci. papers to profl. publs. Mem. APA (reviewer of self-help books 1995), Calif. Psychol. Assn., Santa Barbara Psychol. Assn., Ventura County Astron. Soc., Phi Delta Kappa. Office: 28 W Arrellaga St Santa Barbara CA 93101

GRAHAM, ANNA REGINA, pathologist, educator; b. Phila., Nov. 1, 1947; d. Eugene Nelson and Anna Beatrice (McGovern) Chadwick; m. Larry L. Graham, June 29, 1973; 1 child, Jason. BS in Chemistry, Ariz. State U., 1969, BS in Zoology, 1970; MD, U. Ariz., 1974. Diplomate Am. Bd. Pathology. With Coll. Medicine U. Ariz., Tucson, 1974—, asst. prof. pathology, 1978-84, assoc. prof. pathology, 1984-90, prof. Pathology, 1990—. Fellow Am. Soc. Clin. Pathologists (bd. dirs. Chgo. chpt. 1993—, sec. 1995—), Internat. Acad. Pathology, Internat. Acad. Telemedicine, Coll. Am. Pathologists; mem. AMA (alt. del. Chgo. chpt. 1992—), Ariz. Soc. Pathologists (pres. Phoenix chpt. 1989-91), Ariz. Med. Assn. (treas. Phoenix chpt. 1995—). Republican. Baptist. Office: Ariz Health Scis Ctr Dept Pathology Tucson AZ 85724

GRAHAM, BARBARA JEAN MCKAY, health economist; b. Edinburgh, Scotland, Mar. 12, 1959; d. William Donald Graham and Jean McKay Reid. BSc with honors, U. London, 1982; MPhil with distinction, U. St. Andrews, Scotland, 1991. Sr. technician Med. Rsch. Coun., Johannesburg, South Africa, 1983-85; rsch. officer Med. Rsch. Coun., Edinburgh, 1986-90; tutor U. St. Andrews, Scotland, 1990-91; sr. info. analyst Lothian Health, Edinburgh, 1991-94; rsch. fellow U. Edinburgh, 1994—; dir. pharmoecons. unit dept. pharmacy U. Witwatersand Med. Sch., Johannesburg, South Africa, 1996—; health economist in orthopedics Scottish Needs Assessment Programme, 1995-96; mem. Health Econs. Methods Group of Cochrane Collaboration, 1994—; reviewer Adis Pubs., 1995—, Office Health Econs., London, 1995—. Sub.-lt. Royal Naval Res., 1989-91. Nuffield Provincial Hosps. Trust rsch. fellow, 1994-96. Mem. Health Econs. Group, Health Econs. Group Scotland (steering com. 1994-96), Internat. Health Econs. Assn. Conservative. Episcopalian. Home: 13, Crozier St, Johannesburg 2190 Gauteng South Africa Office: U Edinburgh, Sch Pub Health Sci, Teviot Pl, Edinburgh EH8 9AG, Scotland

GRAHAM, CHARLES, psychologist; b. Atlantic City, N.J., Nov. 21, 1937; s. Charles Leroy and Margery (Kaplan) G.; m. Sally Jones, Dec. 8, 1962 (div. Apr. 1974); children: Ronna, Christopher, Glen. BS, U. Md., 1966; MS, Pa. State U., 1968, PhD, 1970. Rsch. assoc. Inst. Pa. Hosp., Phila., 1970-74; instr., lectr. U. Pa. Dept. Psychiatry, Phila., 1970-74; sr. psychologist Midwest Rsch. Inst., Kansas City, 1974-78; prin. psychologist Midwest Rsch. Inst., 1979-94, sr. advisor for life scis., 1994—; mgr. Bioelectromagnetics Rsch. Program. With U.S. Army, 1960-62. NIH grantee, 1975—. Mem. Am. Psychol. Assn., Soc. Psychophysiol. Rsch., Claude Bernard Soc., Sigma Xi. Office: Midwest Rsch Inst 425 Volker Blvd Kansas City MO 64110-2241

GRAHAM, DAVID GREGORY, preventive medicine physician, psychiatrist; b. Nov. 17, 1949; s. Thomas and Catherine G.; m. Katherine A. Graham; children: Brigitte, John. BA magna cum laude, Walsh U., 1971; MD, U. Puerto Rico, 1980; MPH, Columbia U., 1985. Diplomate Am. Bd. Preventive Medicine, Am. Bd. Clin. Psychiatry. Intern, then resident in psychiatry SUNY, Stony Brook, 1980-84, resident in preventive medicine, 1984-86, asst. prof. preventive medicine, 1985—; attending physician VA Med. Ctr., Northport, N.Y., 1985—; chief, Bur. Preventive Svcs. Suffolk County (N.Y.) Dept. Health Svcs., 1986—. Author: Medieval Minds, 1985, Profiles in Protest, 1987, Statistics, 1987, Mental Status Manual, 1989. Fellow Am. Coll. Preventive Medicine; mem. APHA, Am. Psychiatric Assn., Am. Assn. Pub. Health Physicians, Alumni Assn. Columbia U. Office: County Dept Health Svcs 225 Rabro Dr E Hauppauge NY 11788

GRAHAM, DAVID LAWRENCE, surgeon; b. Independence, Mo., June 8, 1944; s. David J. and Dorothy B. (Boone) G.; m. Lee Ann Kistler, Feb. 3, 1992; 1 child, David A. BS, Ctrl. Mo. State U. 1980; DO, U. Health Scis., Kansas City, Mo., 1987. Cert. EMT; cert. Type I paramedic, Mo. Assoc. prof. biology J.C. C.C., Overland Park, Kans., 1990-91; adminstr. Blue Valley Med. Group, Overland Park, Kans., 1991-92; dir. continuing edn. Blue Valley Med. Group, Overland Park, 1993-95; family practice resident Dallas Meml. Hosp., 1992-93; adminstr. Healthcare Clinics, Dallas, 1995—. Author: (interactive video program) Fast Track Self Help for Post-Traumatic Stress Disorder, 1995; author (computer program) Automated Progress Notes, 1994. Nat. chmn. Vietnow Nat. Hdqrs., Rockford, Ill., 1992—; pres. Vietnow, Kansas City. With U.S. Army, 1981-91. Mem. Am. Osteo. Assn., Tex. Osteo. Med. Assn., Mo. Assn. Osteo. Physicians and Surgeons. Republican. Latter Day Saints.

GRAHAM, DAVID RICHARD, orthopedic surgeon; b. Detroit, May 15, 1940; s. Lewis J. and Elberta Y. (Frees) G.; m. Dorothy T. Young, June 11, 1966; children: Rebecca, Jeffrey. BA cum laude, Harvard U., 1962; MD, U. Rochester, 1966. Diplomate Am. Bd. Orthop. Surgery. Intern Highland Hosp., Rochester, N.Y., 1966-67, resident in surgery, 1967-68; resident in orthopaedic surgery Henry Ford Hosp., Detroit, 1970-72; orthopaedic surgeon Elmira (N.Y.) Orthopaedic Assocs., P.C., 1972-96; pres. Elmira (N.Y.) Orthop. Assocs., P.C., 1992—; pres. Arnot Ogden Med. Staff, Elmira, 1990; clin. assoc. Sch. Medicine & Dentistry U. Rochester, 1992-96. Lt. cmmdr. U.S. Navy, 1968-70. Fellow Am. Coll. Surgeons, Am. Acad. Orthop. Surgeons; mem. AMA, Med. Soc. State N.Y., Ea. Orthop. Assn., Am. Coll. Sports Medicine, Chemung County Med. Soc. (pres. 1993-94), Elmira Torch Club (pres. 1990). Republican. Presbyterian. Home: 690 W Clinton St Elmira NY 14905 Office: Elmira Orthop Assocs 722 W Water St Elmira NY 14905

GRAHAM, FRANCES KEESLER (MRS. DAVID TREDWAY GRAHAM), psychologist, educator; b. Canastota, N.Y., Aug. 1, 1918; d. Clyde C. and Norma (Van Surdam) Keesler; m. David Tredway Graham, June 14, 1941; children: Norma, Andrew, Mary. BA, Pa. State U., 1938; PhD, Yale U., 1942; DSc (hon.), U. Wis., 1996. Acting dir. St. Louis Psychiat. Clinic, 1942-44; instr. Barnard Coll., 1948-51; research assoc. Sch. Medicine, Washington U., St. Louis, 1942-48, 53-57, U. Wis., Madison, 1957-64; asso. prof. pediatrics and psychology U. Wis., 1964-68, prof., 1968-86, Hilldale research prof., 1980-86; prof. U. Del., Newark, 1986-89, prof. emerita, 1989—; Disting. faculty lectr., U. Del., Newark, 1989; cons. Nat. Inst. Neurol. Diseases and Blindness perinatal research br.; mem. exptl. psychology research review com. NIMH, 1970-74, NRC, 1971-74; mem. bd. sci. counselors NIMH, 1977-81, chmn., 1979-81; mem. Pres.'s Commn. for Study of Ethical Problems in Medicine and Biomed. and Behavioral Research, 1980-82. Mem. editorial bd. Jour. Exptl. Child Psychology, 1964-67, Child Devel., 1966-68, Jour. Exptl. Psychology, 1968-73, Psychophysiology, 1968-73; contbr. articles to profl. jours. Recipient Rsch. Scientist award NIMH, 1964-89, Disting. Alumna award Pa. State U., 1983, Wilbur L. Cross medal Yale U., 1992, Gold medal Am. Psychol. Found., 1995. Fellow AAAS (chmn. sect. psychology 1979, mem. nominations com. 1992-95), APA (coun. 1975-77, pres. div. physiol. and comparative psychology 1978-79, G. Stanley Hall award 1982, Disting. Scientist award 1990); mem. NAS, Am. Psychol. Soc. (William James fellow 1990), Soc. Rsch. Child Devel. (council 1965-71, pres. 1975-77, Disting. Sci. Contbns. award 1991), Soc. Psychophysiol. Rsch. (dir. 1968-71, 72-75, pres. 1973-74, Disting. Contbns. award 1981), Soc. Exptl. Psychologists, Soc. Neurosci., Fedn. Behavioral Psychol. and Cognitive Scis. (exec. com. 1991-94), Psychonomic Soc., Acoustical Soc. Am., Internat. Soc. Devel. Psychobiology, Phi Beta Kappa, Sigma Xi. Home: 311 Dove Dr Newark DE 19713-1211

GRAHAM, JAMES HERBERT, dermatologist; b. Calexico, Calif., Apr. 25, 1921; s. August K. and Esther (Choudoin) G.; m. Anna Kathryn Luiken, June 30, 1950 (dec. May 1987); children: James Herbert, John A., Angela Joann; m. Gloria Boyd Flippin, July 29, 1989. Student, Brawley Jr. Coll., 1941-42; AB, Emory U., 1945; MD, Med. Coll. Ala., 1949. Diplomate: Am. Bd. Dermatology (dir. 1977-87, v.p. 1985-86, pres. 1986-87, Disting. Service medal 1987); diplomate in dermatopathology Am. Bd. Dermatology and Am. Bd. Pathology. Intern Jefferson-Hillman Hosp., Birmingham, Ala., 1949-50; resident in dermatology VA Center and UCLA Med. Center, 1953-56; clin. asst. instr. in medicine UCLA, 1954-56; Osborne fellow and NRC fellow in dermal pathology Armed Forces Inst. Pathology, Washington, 1956-58; vis. scientist Armed Forces Inst. Pathology, 1958-69, chmn. dept. dermatopathology, 1980-88; registrar Registry of Dermatopathology, Armed Forces Inst. Pathology, 1980-88, also program dir. dermatopathology, 1979-88; program dir. dermatopathology Walter Reed Army Med. Center, Washington, 1979-88; asst. prof. dermatology and pathology Temple U., 1958-61, assoc. prof., 1961-65, prof. dermatology, 1965-69, assoc. prof. pathology, 1965-67, prof. pathology, 1967-69; prof. medicine, chief div. dermatology, prof. pathology, dir. sect. dermal pathology and histochemistry U. Calif., Irvine, 1969-78; chief dermatology U. Calif. Med. Ctr., Irvine, 1977-78; prof. emeritus Coll. Medicine, U. Calif., 1978—; head sect. dermatology Orange County (Calif.) Med. Center, 1969-73; cons. dermatology VA Hosp., Long Beach, Calif., 1969-73; chief dermatology sect. VA Hosp., 1973-78, acting chief med. service, 1976; cons. dermatology, dermal pathology Regional Naval Med. Center, San Diego, 1969-82, Long Beach, 1969-78, Camp Pendleton, Calif., 1972-78; cons. dermatology, dermal pathology Meml. Hosp. Med. Center, Long Beach, 1972-86, Fairview State Hosp., Costa Mesa, Calif., 1969-78; cons. for career devel. for rev. clin. investigator applications VA Central Office, Washington, 1973-78; Disting. Eminent physician VA physician and dentist-in-residence program, 1980-88; mem. organizational com. Am. Registry Pathology, Armed Forces Inst. Pathology, Washington, 1976-77; mem. exec. com. Am. Registry Pathology, Armed Forces Inst. Pathology, 1977-78; prof. dermatology, clin. prof. pathology Uniformed Services U. of Health Scis., Bethesda, Md., 1979-88, prof. emeritus, 1989—; program dir. dermatopathology Naval Hosp. and Scripps Clin. and Rsch. Found., San Diego, 1991-94; head divsn. dermatopathology, dept. pathology Scripps Clinic and Rsch. Found., LaJolla, Calif., 1988-94, ret., 1994. Sr. author: Dermal Pathology, 1972; contbr. articles to profl. publs. Served with M.C. USNR, 1949-53. Named Disting. Alumnus, Med. Coll. Ala., 1994. Mem. AMA and Accreditation Coun. for Grad. Med. Edn. (residency rev. subcom. for dermatology 1974-87, residency rev. com. for dermatology 1977-87, chmn. 1984-87, cert. of merit 1960), Soc. Investigative Dermatology, U.S. and Can. Acad. Pathology, Am. Soc. Investigative Pathology (emeritus mem. 1995), Am. Dermatol. Assn. (essay award 1958, v.p. 1986-87), Am. Soc. Dermatopathology (pres. 1975-76, Founder's award 1990, rep. to bd. of mem. Am. Registry Pathology 1988-92), Dermatopathology Club (pres. 1980-81), Assn. Mil. Dermatologists, Am. Acad. Dermatology (life, dir. 1974-77, 82, v.p. 1980-81, rep. to bd. mems. Am. Registry Pathology 1977-78), N.Am. Clin. Dermatologic Soc. (hon.), 1973, Pa. Acad. Dermatology, Pacific Dermatol. Assn. (dir. 1972-75, hon. mem. 1981), Dermatology Found., Leader's Soc. Washington Dermatol. Soc. (spl. hon.), Phila. Dermatol. Soc. (pres. 1967-68, hon mem. 1994), San Diego Dermatol. Soc., Cutaneous Therapy Soc., Alpha Omega Alpha, Cosmos Club (Washington).

GRAHAM, JAMES MILLER, physiology researcher; b. St. Louis, Oct. 16, 1945; s. Alvin Rudd and Edrie (Miller) G.; m. Linda Kay Edwards, May 3, 1969; children: Michael Edwards, Melissa Edwards. MA, U. Mich., 1968, PhD, 1979. Postdoctoral scholar environ. engring. U. Mich., Ann Arbor, 1979-80; lectr. zoology U. Wis., Madison, 1981-82, rsch. assoc. physiology, 1983-88, lectr. botany, 1987-88, physiology researcher, 1988—; reviewer Phycological Soc. Am., Jour. Great Lakes Rsch., Microbial Ecology. Contbr. chpt. to Periphyton of Freshwater Ecosystems, 1983; contbr. articles to profl. jours. With U.S. Army, 1969-72. Mem. Am. Soc. Limnology and Oceanography, Am. Inst. Biol. Scis., Phycological Soc. Am., Soc. Protozoologists, Phi Beta Kappa, Sigma Xi. Office: U Wis Dept Physiology 1300 University Ave Madison WI 53706-1510

GRAHAM, JOHN BORDEN, pathologist, writer, educator; b. Goldsboro, N.C., Jan. 26, 1918; s. Ernest Heap and Mary (Borden) G.; m. Ruby Barrett, Mar. 23, 1943; children: Charles Barrett, Virginia Borden, Thomas Wentworth. B.S., Davidson Coll., 1938, D.Sc. (hon.), 1984; M.D., Cornell U., 1942. Asst. Cornell U., 1943-44; mem. faculty U. N.C., Chapel Hill, 1946—; Alumni Disting. prof. pathology U. N.C., 1966—, chmn. genetics curriculum, 1963-85, assoc. dean medicine for basic scis., 1968-70, coordinator interdisciplinary grad. programs in biology, 1968—, dir. hemostasis program, 1974-87; vis. prof. haematology St. Thomas's Hosp. Med. Sch., London, 1972; vis. prof. Teikyo U. Med. Sch., Tokyo, 1976; mem. selection com. NIH research career awards, 1959-62; genetics tng. com. USPHS, 1962-66, chmn., 1967-71; mem. genetic basis of disease com. Nat. Inst. Gen. Med. Scis., 1977-80; mem. pathology test com. Nat. Bd. Med. Examiners, 1963-67; mem. research adv. com. U. Colo. Inst. Behavioral Genetics, 1967-71; mem. Internat. Com. Haemostasis and Thrombosis, 1963-67; chmn. bd. U. N.C.

Population Program, 1964-67; sec. policy bd. Carolina Population Center, 1972-78; cons. Environ. Health Center, USPHS, WHO, Bolt, Beranek & Newman, Inc.; mem. med. and sci. adv. council Nat. Hemophilia Found., 1972-76; hon. cons. in genetics Margaret Pyke Centre, London, 1972—. Author: (autobiography) Sand in the Gears, 1992, How It Was, 1896-1973, 1996; mem. editl. bd. N.C. Med. Jour., 1949-66, Am. Jour. Human Genetics, 1958-61, Soc. Exptl. Biology and Medicine, 1959-62, Human Genetics Abstracts, 1962-72, Haemostasis, 1975-80, Christian Scholar, 1958-60. Recipient O. Max Gardner award U. N.C., 1968, Disting. Svc. award U. N.C. Med. Sch., 1992; Markle scholar in med. sci., 1949-54. Mem. AMA, AAAS, Elisha Mitchell Sci. Soc. (pres. 1963), AAUP, Soc. Exptl. Biology and Medicine, Am. Soc. Exptl. Pathology, Assn. Univ. Pathologists, Am. Assn. Pathologists and Bacteriologists, Am. Soc. Human Genetics (sec. 1964-67, pres. 1972), Genetics Soc. Am., Internat. Soc. Hematology, Am. Inst. Biol. Sci., Royal Soc. Medicine (London), Med. Soc. N.C., Mayflower Soc., Sigma Xi. Democrat. Presbyterian. Home: 108 Glendale Dr Chapel Hill NC 27514-5910

GRAHAM, JOHN MATHEWSON, pediatrician, medical geneticist; b. Wilmington, Del., Mar. 8, 1947; s. John M. Sr. and Dorothy (Channell) G.; m. Elizabeth Spear, July 4, 1977; chldren: Zack, George; 1 child from previous marriage, John M. III. BA in Natural and Behavioral Scis., Johns Hopkins U., 1969, ScD in Pub. Health Adminstrn., 1981; MD, Med. U. S.C., 1975. Diplomate Am. Bd. Med. Genetics, Am. Bd. Pediatrics. Med. dir. genetics svcs. Pub. Health Svcs., Concord, N.H., 1981-88; asst. prof., assoc. prof. maternal and child health Dartmouth Med. Sch., Hanover, N.H., 1981-88, dir. clin. genetics and dysmorphology program, 1981-88; assoc. prof. pediatrics UCLA Sch. Medicine, 1988-90, prof., 1990—; mem. staff Cedars-Sinai Med. Ctr., L.A., 1988—, dir. clin. genetics and dysmorphology, 1988—, dir. craniofacial program, 1990—; dir. fetal dysmorphology and pathology program Cedars-Sinai Med. Ctr., 1991—, co-dir. CSMC med. genetics tng. program, 1991—. Contbr. some 40 chpts. to books, 200 articles to profl. jours. Recipient numerous awards and grants. Fellow Am. Coll. Med. Genetics (founding); mem. AMA, Am. Soc. Human Genetics, European Soc. Human Genetics, Am. Acad. Pediatrics, Soc. Pediatric Rsch., Am. Pediatric Soc., We. Soc. for Pediatric Rsch., European Soc. for Pediatric Rsch., Soc. for Behavioral Pediatrics, Behavioral Genetics Assn., Teratology Soc., West Coast Teratology Soc., Am. Cleft Palate-Craniofacial Assn., Soc. Craniofacial Genetics, Alpha Omega Alpha, Delta Omega. Office: Cedars-Sinai Med Ctr # 1001 444 S San Vicente Blvd Los Angeles CA 90048

GRAHAM, JOYCE VADA, pediatrics nursing supervisor; b. Atkinson, Nebr., June 25, 1927; d. Willard and Lula Mae (Drohman) Hoffman; m. Raymond F. Wilson, Jan. 23, 1945; children: Raymond Jr., Barbara, Vickie, James, Jack; m. Kirk Graham, Aug. 31, 1972. Student, Casper (Wyo.) Coll., 1969; Assoc. Diploma Nursing, So. State U. Ark., 1973. Staff nurse Med. Pk. Hosp., Hope, Ark., pediat. nursing supr., ob mothers supr., head nurse, 1989, ret., 1989. Mem. ANA. Home: 2102 Roselle St Hope AR 71801-9220

GRAHAM, KENNETH ROBERT, psychologist, educator; b. Phila., June 5, 1943; s. Edgar and Margit (Leafgreen) Graham; m. Michele Carolyn Monroe, Aug. 10, 1968; children: Mark Andrew, Richard Alan. BA, U. Pa., 1964; PhD, Stanford U., 1969. Lic. psychologist, Pa. Asst. prof. Muhlenberg Coll., Allentown, 1970-77, assoc. prof., 1977-84, prof., 1984—, head psychology dept., 1984-93; rsch. psychologist Unit for Exptl. Psychiatry Inst. of Pa. Hosp., Phila., 1969-70; adjunct asst. prof. U. Pa., Phila., 1969-70; cons. smoking cessation various hosps., 1985—. Author: (text) Psychological Research, 1977; contbr. over 30 articles to profl. and sci. jours. Bd. dirs., pres. Lehigh Valley Child Care, Allentown, 1979-85; advisor Pathways (Conf. of Chs.), Allentown, 1989—, N.E. Pa. Synod Luth. Ch. in Am., Wescosville, Pa., 1989-93. Mem. APA (pres. divsn. psychol. hypnosis 1980-81), Am. Soc. Clin. Hypnosis (asst. editor Jour. Clin. Hypnosis 1974—), European Soc. Hypnosis in Psychotherapy and Psychosomatic Medicine, Kiwanis (pres. Allentown chpt. 1991-92, lt. gov. Pa. dist. 1994-95). Democrat. Office: Muhlenberg Coll Psychology Dept Allentown PA 18104

GRAHAM, MARTIN LAREN, radiologist; b. Hutchinson, Kans., Mar. 5, 1942; s. George F. (Bill) and Hazel Pauline (Pittman) G.; m. Karen Mae Holben, Aug. 19, 1967; children: Sarah Jane, John Martin, Michael George. BA, UCLA, 1965; MD, U. Calif., San Francisco, 1969. Diplomate Am. Bd. Radiology. Intern U. So. Calif., L.A. County Med. Ctr., 1969-70; resident in radiology U. Mich. Med. Ctr., Ann Arbor, 1972-75; radiologist Dignostic Imaging N.W., Tacoma, 1975—. Lt. U.S. Navy, 1970-72. Mem. Am. Coll. Radiology, Wash. State Radiol. Soc., Pacific NW Radiologic Soc., Pierce County and Wash. State Med. Socs., Radiol. Soc. N.Am. Presbyterian. Office: 7424 Bridgeport Way W Ste 103 Tacoma WA 98467-2543

GRAHAM, PATRICK VINCENT, plastic surgeon; b. Toronto, Can., June 16, 1947; s. Robert Patrick and Naureen Mary (Doherty) G.; m. Phyllis C. Lofaso, Oct. 8, 1982; children: Darryl, Jeffrey, Douglas. BA, Marquette U., 1969; MD, N.Y. Med. Coll., 1977. Pvt. practice Delray Beach, Fla., 1983—. Fellow ACS; mem. Am. Soc. Plastic Reconstructive Surgery, Am. Soc. Aesthetic Surgeons, Fla. Soc. Plastic Surgeons, Palm Beach Soc. Plastic Surgeons, S.E. Soc. Plastic Surgeons, Fla. Med. Soc. Office: 5258 Linton Blvd # 205 Delray Beach FL 33484

GRAHAM, ROBERT, medical association executive; b. Pueblo, Colo., Feb. 15, 1943; married. AB, Earlham Coll., 1965; MD, U. Kans., 1970. Asst. adminstr. agy. goals Health Svc. & Mental Health Admn. Dept. Health Edn. & Welfare, Washington, 1970-73; asst. dir. divsn. edn. Am. Acad. Family Physicians, Kansas City, Mo., 1973-76; dep. dir. Bur. Health Manpower, Health Resources Adminstrn. Dept. Health Edn. & Welfare, 1976-78, dep. adminstr., 1978-79; profl. staff mem. subcom. health & sci. rsch. Comty. Labor & Human Resources, U.S. Senate, 1979-80; acting adminstr. health resources adminstrn. Dept. Health & Human Svc., 1981-82, adminstr., 1982-85; exec. v.p. Am. Acad. Family Physicians, Kansas City, Mo., 1985—; resident family practice Bapt. Meml. Hosp., 1974-75; staff Prog. Health Mgmt., Baylor Coll. Medicine, 1976; exec. sec. Grad. Med. Edn. Nat. Adv. Com., 1978-79; bd. dirs. Alliance for Health Referendum, 1994—, Sun Valley Forum Nat. Health. Mem. AMA, Inst. Medicine-NAS, Assn. Am. Med. Colls., Am. Acad. Family Physicians, Am. Acad. Med. Dirs., Am. Assn. Med. Soc. Execs., Am. Soc. Assn. Execs. Office: Am Acad Family Physicians 8880 Ward Pkwy Kansas City MO 64114

GRAHAM, RONALD EUGENE, physician; b. Tulsa, Nov. 24, 1955; s. Raymond Willard and Leona Vaudell (West) G.; m. Pamela Louise French, Sept. 7, 1985; 1 child, Melanie Lynn. Student, U. Okla., 1974-78; DO, Okla. State U., 1981. Intern Lakeview Osteo. Hosp., Milw., 1981-82; commd. 2d lt. U.S. Army, 1982, advanced through grades to maj.; med. officer U.S. Army, Ft. Polk, La., 1982-84; resident physician U.S. Army, Ft. Hood, Tex., 1984-86; chief emergency care U.S. Army, Ft. Benning, Ga., 1986-89; resigned U.S. Army, 1989; asst. dir. emergency rm. Phenix Med. Park Hosp., Phenix City, Ala., 1989-90; emergency rm. physician Spalding Regional Hosp., Griffin, Ga., 1990-91, Pinnacle Emergency Cons., Newnan, Ga., 1991-92, West Ga. Med. Ctr., LaGrange, 1992-95; med. dir. emergency svcs. Jackson County Hosp., Scottsboro, Ala., 1995—. Benefactor, planner West Cemetary Assn., Chouteau, Okla., 1991; med. vol. The Ga. Games, Atlanta, 1991—. Fellow Am. Coll. Emergency Physicians; mem. Am. Osteo. Assn., Nat. Assn. Watch and Clock Collectors. Home: 2104 Pell St Scottsboro AL 35768 Office: Jackson County Hosp Woods Cove Rd Scottsboro AL 35768

GRAHAM, (LLOYD) SAXON, epidemiology educator; b. Buffalo, Jan. 14, 1922; s. Lloyd S. and Kathryn (Graser) G.; m. Caroline Lee Morgan, June 19, 1948; children: Robin Porter, Saxon Parker, Morgan Graser. BA, Amherst Coll., 1943; MA, Yale U., 1949, PhD, 1951; DSc (hon.), SUNY, Buffalo, 1996. Asst. prof. Chatham Coll., Pitts., 1951-53; asst. prof. biostats. U. Pitts., 1953-56; from asst. prof. to prof. epidemiology dept. sociology and dept. social and preventive medicine SUNY, Buffalo, 1957—, chmn. dept. social and preventive medicine, 1981-91, prof. emeritus, 1992—; assoc. to prin. cancer rsch. scientist Roswell Pk. Cancer Inst., Buffalo, 1956-65, prof. SUNY div., 1967—; mem. epidemiology and disease control sect. NIH, Bethesda, Md., 1966-70; cons. WHO, Switzerland, 1965-66; dir. demographic studies, Kabul, Afghanistan, 1970-74; chmn. adv. com. to study long-term effects of plutonium Los Alamos (N.Mex.) Nat. Lab., 1976-86; mem. coun. advisors divsn. cancer rsch., resources and ctrs. Nat. Cancer Inst., Bethesda, 1973-77, mem. bd. sci. councillor divsn. cancer prevention and control, 1982-86; mem. sci. coun. Internat. Agy. Rsch. on Cancer, Lyon, France, 1986-90. Author: American Culture, 1957; contbr. numerous articles to profl. jours. Spl. agt. Counter Intelligence Corps, U.S. Army, 1943-46, PTO. Nat. Cancer Inst. grantee, 1969—. Fellow Am. Coll. Epidemiology, Am. Pub. Health Assn., Am. Sociologic Assn.; mem. Soc. Epidemiologic Rsch. (pres. 1987-88), Am. Epidemiol. Soc., Planned Parenthood, Nat. Abortion Rights League, Orchard Pk. Country Club, Concord Ski Club (Ellicottville, N.Y.), Scriptores (Buffalo). Republican. Home: 32 Stonehenge Rd Orchard Park NY 14127-2847 Office: SUNY/Dept Social & Preventive Medicine 270 Farber Hall Buffalo NY 14214-2648

GRAHAM, THOMAS HILD, neurologist; b. Abington, Pa., Nov. 6, 1953; s. John Harry and Mary Louise (Hild) G.; m. Susan Mae Houpt, Dec. 27, 1975; children: Lauren, Nathaniel, Jeremy. BS in Biology, Ursinus Coll., 1975; MD, Pa. State U., 1978. Bd. cert. electrodiagnostic medicine Am. Bd. Electrodiagnostic Medicine; bd. cert. neurology Am. Bd. Psychiatry and Neurology. Intern medicine Hosp. of the U. Pa., Phila., 1978-79, resident neurology, 1979-82, fellow neurology, 1982-83; neurologist Neurology Cons., Bryn Mawr, Pa., 1983-89; ptnr., neurologist Neurology Cons., Bryn Mawr, 1989—; chief divsn. neurology Bryn Mawr (Pa.) Hosp., 1994—; attending neurologist Phoenixville (Pa.) Hosp., 1982—, Bryn Mawr (Pa.) Hosp., 1983—, Paoli (Pa.) Meml. Hosp., 1983—; clin. asst. prof. neurology U. Pa. Med. Coll., Phila., 1983—; courtesy staff Chester County Hosp., West Chester, Pa., 1995—. Contbg. editor Internal Medicine Bulletin, 1992-94. Trustee bd. dirs. The Crossroads Sch., Paoli, 1994—. Recipient Nat. Rsch. Svc. award Pub. Health Svc., 1982. Fellow Am. Acad. Neurology, Stroke Coun.-Am. Heart Assn.; mem. AMA, Pa. Med. Soc., Chester County Med. Soc., Phila. Neurol. Soc. Office: Neurology Cons Bryn Mawr Bldg S Ste 106 875 County Line Rd Bryn Mawr PA 19010

GRAHAM, THOMAS PEGRAM, JR., pediatric cardiologist; b. Charlotte, N.C., Mar. 1, 1937; s. Thomas P. and Margaret (Martin) G.; m. Carol Ann Noggle, June 1, 1960; children: Bethany, Brent, Brooke. A.B., Duke U., 1959, M.D., 1963. Diplomate Am. Bd. Pediatrics. Resident in pediatrics Children's Hosp., Boston, 1963-65; research assoc. Nat. Heart Inst., Bethesda, Md., 1965-67; fellow in pediatric cardilolgy Duke U., Durham, N.C., 1967-69, asst. prof. pediatrics, 1969-71; dir. pediatric cardiology, prof. pediatrics Vanderbilt U., Nashville, 1971—. Contbr. articles to profl. jours. Fellow Am. Acad. Pediatrics (exec. com. 1972-74), Am. Coll. Cardiology (chmn. pediatric cardiology subcom. 1979-86), Am. Heart Assn. (chmn. council on cardiovascular disease in the young 1981-83). Presbyterian. Office: Vanderbilt U West End Ave Nashville TN 37232 also: 21st S At Garland Ave S Nashville TN 37232

GRAHAM, VICTORIA, speech pathologist; b. Scranton, Pa., Oct. 9, 1942; d. Domenick and Anna (Cardoni) Sellano; m. Dean M. Graham, Apr. 14, 1973. MS in Edn., SUC Oneoneta, 1976; MS, Coll. St. Rose, 1981; PhD, Columbia Pacific U., 1984. Cert. clin. competence, ASHA; lic. speech pathologist, N.Y.; elem. edn. profl. N.Y. Dir., chief exec. officer Victoria Graham Assocs., Inc., Stamford, N.Y., 1985-94; allied health staff A.O. Fox Meml. Hosp. and Nursing Home, 1986-94, Oneonta Nursing Home, 1987-94, Pub. Health Nursing Delaware County, 1989-94, Delaware County Home and Infirmary,, 1986-94, Community Skilled Nursing Facility, 1981-94, Catskill Area Hospice, 1988-94, At Home Care, Inc., 1988-94; adj. faculty Coll. of St. Rose, Albany, N.Y.; treas., bd. dir. Robinson Terr. Nursing Home; bd. dirs. A.O. Fox Meml. Hosp. and Nursing Home. Recipient Cmty. Svc. award Beta Omicron chpt. Delta Kappa Gamma Soc., 1985. Mem. Am. Speech, Lang. and Hearing Assn. (award for continuing edn.), N.Y. State Speech, Lang. and Hearing Assn. Home: PO Box 129 Stamford NY 12167-1049

GRAHAM, WALTER RALEIGH, JR., dermatologist; b. Charlotte, N.C., Feb. 16, 1944; s. Walter Raleigh and Rachel (Jones) G.; m. Cynthia Jean Armstrong, May 23, 1970. BA, U. N.C., 1966; MD, U. Pa., 1970. Diplomate Am. Bd. Dermatology. Intern Pa. Hosp., Phila., 1970-71; med. officer USPHS, Eagle Butte, S.D., 1971-73; resident Hosp. U. Pa., Phila., 1973-76; pvt. practice Charlotte, 1976-87, First Coast Med. Group, Jacksonville, Fla., 1987—. USPHS, 1971-73. Morehead scholar, 1962. Fellow Am. Acad. Dermatology; mem. AMA, Jacksonville Dermatol. Soc., Phi Beta Kappa. Republican. Home: 6804 Linford Ln Jacksonville FL 32217-2661 Office: First Coast Med Group 2005 Riverside Ave Jacksonville FL 32204-4441

GRAHAM, WILLIAM B., pharmaceutical company executive; b. Chgo., July 14, 1911; s. William and Elizabeth (Burden) G.; m. Edna Kanaley, June 15, 1940 (dec.); children: William J., Elizabeth Anne, Margaret, Robert B.; m. Catherine Van Duzer, July 23, 1984. SB cum laude, U. Chgo., 1932, JD cum laude, 1936; LLD, Carthage Coll., 1974, Lake Forest Coll., 1983; LLD (hon.), U. Ill., 1988; LHD, St. Xavier Coll. and Nat. Coll. Edn., 1983. Bar: Ill. 1936. Patent lawyer Dyrenforth, Lee, Chritton & Wiles, 1936-40; mem. Dawson & Ooms, 1940-45; v.p., mgr. Baxter Internat., Inc., Deerfield, Ill., 1945-53, pres., 1953-71; CEO Baxter Internat., Inc., Deerfield, 1960-80; chmn. bd. Baxter Internat., Inc., Deerfield, Ill., 1980-85, sr. chmn., 1989-95, chmn. emeritus, 1995—; prof., chair Weizmann Inst. Sci., Rehoboth, Israel, 1978; lectr. U. Chgo., 1981-82. Chmn. bd. dirs. Lyric Opera Chgo.; bd. dirs. Big Shoulders, Wendy Will Care Fedn., Chgo. Hort. Soc.; trustee Orchestral Assn., U. Chgo., Evanston (Ill.) Hosp.; past pres. Cmty. Fund of Chgo. Recipient V.I.P. award Lewis Found., 1963, Disting. Citizen award Ill. St. Andrew Soc., 1974, Decision Maker of Yr. award Am. Statis. Assn., 1974, Marketer of Yr. award AMA, 1976, Found. award Kidney Found., 1981, Chicagoan of Yr. award Chgo. Boys Club, 1981, Bus. Statesman of Yr. award Harvard Bus. Sch. Club Chgo., 1983, Achievement award Med. Tech. Svcs., 1983, Disting. Fellows award Internat. Ctr. for Artificial Organs and Transplantations, 1982, Chgo. Civic award DePaul U., 1986, Internat. Visitors Golden Medallion award U. Ill., 1988, Chgo. medal U. Chgo., 1992, Laureate award Lincoln Acad. Ill., 1992, Lyric Opera Carol Fox award, 1992, Good Scout award N.E. Coun. Boy Scouts Am., 1993, Making History award Chgo. Hist. Soc., 1996; recognized for pioneering work Health Industry Mfrs. Assn., 1981; inducted Jr. Achievement Chgo. Bus. Hall of Fame, 1986, Modern Healthcare Hall of Fame, 1994. Mem. Am. Pharm. Mfrs. Assn. (past pres.), Ill. Mfrs. Assn. (past pres.), Pharm. Mfrs. Assn. (past chmn., award for spl. distinction leadership 1981), Chgo. Club (past pres.), Commonwealth Club, Comml. Club, Indian Hill Club, Casino Club, Old Elm Club, Seminole Club, Everglades Club, Bath and Tennis Club, Links Club, Phi Beta Kappa, Sigma Xi, Phi Delta Phi. Home: 40 Devonshire Ln Kenilworth IL 60043-1205 Office: Baxter Internat Inc 1 Baxter Pky Deerfield IL 60015-4625

GRAHAM, WILLIAM PATTON, III, plastic surgeon, educator; b. Plainfield, N.J., Apr. 30, 1934; s. William Patton and Mary Alice (Bucher) G.; m. Susan Ames Fox, Nov. 27, 1968; children: Susan Patton, Elizabeth Ames. AB, Princeton U., 1955; MD, U. Pa., 1959. Diplomate Am. Bd. Surgery (cert. in hand surgery 1989), Am. Bd. Plastic Surgery (chmn. 1985-86). Intern U. Colo. Med. Ctr., Denver, 1959-60; resident in surgery VA Hosp., Denver, 1960-61, U. Calif., San Francisco, 1961-64; chief resident in surgery U. Calif., 1964-65; resident and instr. plastic surgery U. Pa., Phila., 1965-67; asst. prof. surgery U. Pa., 1967-70; assoc. prof. surgery Pa. State U., Hershey, 1971-74; prof. surgery Pa. State U., 1974-85, chmn. divsn. plastic surgery, 1971-85, 1996—, clin. prof. surgery, 1985-96; prof. surgery U. Colo., 1994—; chmn. Plastic Surgery Research Council, Hershey, 1979-80. Co-author: The Hand-Surgical and Non-Surgical Management, 1977, Practical Points in Plastic Surgery, 1980. Trustee Harrisburg Acad., 1980-85. Maj. USAR, 1960-73. USPHS research grantee, 1974-76; advanced clin. fellow Am. Cancer Soc. Phila., 1969-70. Fellow ACS; mem. Am. Surg. Assn., Am. Assn. Plastic Surgeons (trustee 1983-86, 91-94), Am. Soc. Surgery of Hand (mem. coun. 1989-92), Soc. Head and Neck Surgeons, Am. Soc. Aesthetic Plastic Surgery (pres. 1992-93), Northeastern Soc. Plastic Surgeons (pres. 1988-89, Newport R.I.), Robert H. Ivy Soc. (pres. Hershey 1974-75), Sigma Xi (full), Alpha Omega Alpha, Nu Sigma Nu, Tower Club (Princeton, N.J.). Republican. Office: Aesthetic & Reconst Surgery 816 Belvedere St Carlisle PA 17013-4001

GRAINGER, CARON, public health medicine consultant; b. Coventry, West Midlands, England, Oct. 28, 1965; d. Robert and Ruth (Eastwood) G. MB ChB, U. Leeds, England, 1988. Registrar, sr. registrar pub. health medicine West Midlands RHA, England, 1991-95; cons. in pub. health medicine, NHS exec. West Midlands RMA, England, 1995—; hon. sr. clin. lectr. U. Birmingham, 1992—. Author: (book) Stress Survival Guide, 1994; contbr. articles to profl. jours. Pres. Birmingham (England) Jr. C. of C., 1994; mem. Lunar Soc., Birmingham, 1996. Mem. British Med. Assn., Faculty Pub. Health Medicine. Office: NHS Exec, 146 Hagley Rd, Edgbaston B169PA Birmingham B169PA, England

GRAMDORF, MARILYN CAROL, nurse, accessory specialist; b. Watertown, Wis., Jan. 12, 1948; d. Harry Herman Joseph and Ruth Gertrude (Roth) G. Diploma in nursing Bellin Sch. Nursing, Green Bay, Wis., 1969; BS, U. Wis.-Madison, 1981. Lic. nurse, Wis. Head nurse Bethesda Lutheran Home, Watertown, 1969-73, Lake Shore Manor, Madison, 1973-76; nurse II, U. Wis. Hosp. and Clinic, Madison, 1976—; accessory specialist Home Interiors and Gifts, Madison, 1981-90; owner Mari Dolls, 1991—; sales person Tandy Leather Co., Madison, 1984-86; union rep. United Profls. for Quality Health Care, Madison, 1980-82, lobbyist, 1980-90; chart auditor Clin. Sci. Ctr., Madison, 1985—; mem. com. to revise orientation manual for inpatient unit, U. Hosp., Madison, mem. quality assurance coms., 1987-89, mem unit primary nursing com., 1989—, mem. products com., 1989-91, surg. div. nursing rsch. com., 1992—; speaker, com. mem. Spl. Concerns of Elderly, Pre-Operative Teaching Conf., 1985. Author: (with others) teaching booklet If You're Having Surgery, 1984. Mem. Wis. Alumni Assn., Old Stage Dance Club, Milw. Club. Avocations: leather crafting, reading, writing, gardening, music. Office: Clin Sci Ctr D4-6 600 Highland Madison WI 53704 Also: 4810 School Rd Madison WI 53704-1348

GRAMMER, FRANK CLIFTON, oral surgeon, researcher; b. El Dorado, Ark., Aug. 12, 1943; s. Norman Alexander and Lillie Mae (Martin) G.; m. Ann Marie Beller, Feb. 8, 1964 (div. Feb. 1980); children: William Cody, Tamara Ann; m. Sandra Lanier Boyd, July 5, 1980; 1 child, Jeremy Boyd. BS, Washington U., St. Louis, 1966, DDS summa cum laude, 1968; MSD, U. Minn., 1972, PhD, 1973. Diplomate Am. Bd. Oral and Maxillofacial Surgery. Research fellow U. Minn., Mpls., 1968-73; practice dentistry specializing in oral surgery, Fayetteville, Ark., 1973—; cons. Cambridge Hosp., Minn., 1972-73; instr. U. Ark., Fayetteville, 1978-79; asst. prof. U. Tenn., Memphis, 1979-80; mem. adv. com. Am. Bd. Oral and Maxillofacial Surgery, Chgo., 1979-85; bd. govs. Antaeus Research Inst., Fayetteville, 1979-85. Editor Arkansas Dentistry, 1992—; contbr. articles to profl. jours. Recipient Research award Am. Soc. Oral Surgeons, 1973. Fellow Am. Coll. Oral and Maxillofacial Surgeons, Am. Dental Soc. of Anesthesiologists, Internat. Coll. Dentists, Am. Coll. Dentists; mem. Ark. Soc. Oral and Maxillofacial Surgeons (pres. 1982-84), Ark. State Dental Assn. (v.p. 1988-89, pres. 1990-91), N.W. Dist. Dental Soc. (pres. 1983-84). Republican. Presbyterian. Club: Fayetteville Country (pres. 1980-81, 94—). Avocations: golf, tennis, hunting. Home: 359 Fairway Ln Fayetteville AR 72701-7159 Office: PO Box 1807 Fayetteville AR 72702-1807

GRAMS, ARMIN EDWIN, retired psychologist and educator; b. Chgo., Oct. 20, 1924; s. Adolf and Anna Carolina (Mueller) G.; m. Norma Mueller, Aug. 23, 1947 (dec.); children: Paul Mueller, Elisabeth Grams Haxby, James Carlton, John Frederick. BS, Concordia Coll., 1945; MA, DePaul U., 1947; PhD, Northwestern U., 1952. Tchr., prin. various elem. schs., Chgo., 1945-49; instr. dept. edn. and psychology DePaul Univ., Chgo., 1949-52, asst. prof. dept. edn. and psychology, 1952-55; assoc. prof. dept. psychology LaCrosse (Wis.) State Coll., 1955-57; assoc. prof., Inst. Child Devel. Univ. Minn., Mpls., 1957-62; prof. The Merrill Palmer Inst. of Human Devel. and Family Life, Detroit, 1962-71; prof. dept. human devel. Univ. Vt., Burlington, 1971-90; co-dir. Ctr. for Study of Aging U. Vt., Burlington, 1995—; prof. emeritus Univ. Vt., Burlington, 1990—; psychologist Dyslexia Meml. Inst., Chgo., 1950-55; bd. dirs. Search Inst., Mpls., 1958-86, chair, 1972-79, guest prof. Eberhard-Karls-U., Tübingen, Germany, 1967-68; human devel. cons. Gen. Learning Corp., Chgo., 1984-90; co-dir. Ctr. for the Study of Aging, U. Vt., 1995—. Author: Children and Their Parents, 1963, Facilitating Learning and Individual Development, 1966, Changes in Family Life, 1968, Sex Education: A Guide for Teachers and Parents, 2d edit., 1970; co-editor: Promoting Successful and Productive Aging, 1995; contbr. more than 50 articles to profl. jours. Mem. Gov.'s adv. coun. Vt. Office on Aging, Waterbury, 1977-80; Vt. del. Nat. Rural Aging Strategy Conf., Des Moines, 1979; Vt. state coord. White House COnf. on Families, Washington, 1979-81; del. White House Conf. on Aging, 1995. Mem. APA, GSA, Nat. Coun. on the Aging, Inc. (bd. dirs. 1988-90), Assn. for Gerontology in Higher Edn. (exec. com. 1987-94, pres. 1992-93). Home: 134 Spear St S Burlington VT 05403-6146 Office: U Vt Ctr Study of Aging 322 S Prospect St Burlington VT 05401

GRANACHER, ROBERT PHILLIP, JR., psychiatrist; b. Peoria, Ill., July 29, 1941; s. Robert Phillip and Mildred Eileen (Spires) G.; B.A., U. Louisville, 1969; M.D., U. Ky., 1972; m. Mary Linda Farmer, July 6, 1968; 1 son, Phillip Garner. Resident, chief resident psychiatry, U. Ky. Med. Sch., Lexington, 1972-74; fellow Harvard Med. Sch./Mass. Gen. Hosp., Boston, 1974-75; asst. prof. psychiatry U. Ky. Med. Sch., Lexington, 1975-77, asso. clin. prof. psychiatry, 1977-82, clin. prof., 1982—; practice medicine, specializing in gen., forensic and neuro-psychiatry, Lexington, 1978—; med. dir. Sleep Disorders Ctr., St. Joseph Hosp., Lexington, 1983—; nat. cons. in forensic psychiatry; cons. in psychopharmacology U.S. Dept. Justice, Washington, 1977-92. Served with U.S. Army, 1961-62. Diplomate Am. Bd. Psychiatry and Neurology, Am. Bd. Forensic Psychiatry; accredited clin. polysomnographer. Mem. Am. Acad. Psychiatry and the Law, Am. Psychiat. Assn., Am. Soc. Clin. Psychopharmacology, AAAS. Author: (with A. Mason) Clinical Handbook of Antipsychotic Drug Therapy, 1980; contbr. articles to profl. jours. Office: St Joseph Office Park 1401 Harrodsburg Rd Lexington KY 40504

GRANADOS, CANDACE MICHELE, physical therapist; b. Albuquerque, Nov. 5, 1958; d. Lewis Ray and Pristina (Chavez) G. BS in Phys. Therapy, U. N.Mex., 1981. Chief phys. therapist CHI, Albuquerque, 1981; adminstr. Sports Phys. Therapy & Rehab., Albuquerque, 1982-83; v.p. N.Mex. Phys. Therapist Inc., Albuquerque, 1983-88; v.p. Northeastern NMPT Inc.; mem. admissions com. U. N.Mex. Dept. Phys. Therapy, 1982-88, mem. clin. edn. staff, 1982—; com. Bernallilo County Sports Medicine Com., 1986-88; pvt. practice as physical therapist, 1988—; owner Granados Phys. therapy Svcs.; bd. dirs. N.Mex. Phys. Therapist Inc., Northeastern N.Mex. Phys. Therapist Inc. Mem. NAFE, C. of C., Am. Phys. Therapy Assn., N.Mex. Phys. Therapy Assn., Albuquerque Medicine/Bus. Coalition, Am. Coll. Sports Medicine. Democrat. Roman Catholic. Avocations: water skiing, jogging, weight training, racquetball. Office: 4 Zia Trl Corrales NM 87048-9694

GRANADOS, PERO MIGUEL ANGEL, surgeon; b. Caballero, Paraguay, Feb. 22, 1938; came to the U.S., 1965; s. Rafael and Amalia (Angeloni) G.; m. Alicia Pallarolas, Feb. 6, 1965; 3 children. BS, Col. Benjamin Aceval U., 1956; MD, U. Nac. de Asuncion, 1962. Intern Detroit Meml. Hosp., 1965-66; resident in surgery W. Beaumont Hosp., Royal Oak, Mich., 1966-70; staff surgeon Met. Hosp., Detroit, 1970-71, Annapolis Hosp., Wayne, Mich., 1971-80, U. Hosp. U. Nac. Asuncion, Paraguay, 1981-83; prof. surgery U. Nac. Asuncion, 1984—; mem. organizing coms. 7 profl. confs. in surgery and gastroenterology, 1982-95. Contbr. articles to profl. jours. and chpts. to books. Sgt. Paraguayan Army, 1955-58. Fellow ACS; mem. Soc. Paraguay de ci Rugia, Soc. Paraguay de Gastroenterologia. Roman Catholic. Office: Mcal Estigarribia Brasil 1070, Asuncion Paraguay

GRANATIR, WILLIAM LOUIS, psychiatrist; b. Phila., Apr. 1, 1916; s. Jacon and Anna (Stein) G.; m. Mildred Silver, July 4, 1941; children: John Robert, Joseph Paul, Thomas Alan, Charles Elliot. BA, U. Pa., 1936; MD, Hahnemann Med. Coll., Phila., 1941. Diplomate Am. Bd. Psychiatry and Neurology. Intern Mt. Sinai Hosp., Phila., 1941-42; resident St. Elizabeth's Hosp., Washington, 1946-48, psychiatrist, 1946-48; dir. Washington Inst. Mental Hygiene, 1948-50; pvt. practice Washington, 1950-93; supervising tng. analyst Washington Psychoanalytic inst., 1965-78, supervising analyst, 1982—; clin. prof. Med. Sch. George Washington U., 1979-93, ret., 1993. Flight surgeon U.S. Army Air Corps, 1942-46. Fellow Am. Psychiat. Assn.; mem. Am. Psychoanalytic Assn. (life), Washington Psychoanalytic Soc. (life, pres. 1973-75).

GRANATO, JEROME ERNEST, cardiologist; b. Bronx, N.Y., Aug. 9, 1953; s. Michael and Filomena (Feo) G.; m. Judith Wartko, Jan. 4, 1987; 1 child, Matthew Ernest. BS in Engring., Stevens Inst. Tech., Hoboken, N.J., 1974; MD, Johns Hopkins U., 1979. Diplomate Am. Bd. Internal Medicine,

Am. Bd. Cardiology. Asst. prof. U. Pitts., 1985-87; sr. attending physician Allegheny Gen. Hosp., Pitts., 1987—; dir. coronary care unit Presbyn. Univ. Hosp., 1986-87; dir. cardiac fellowship tng. Allegheny Gen. Hosp., 1988-94; asst. prof. Med. Coll. Pa., Pitts., 1988—; cons. in field, 1985—. Fellow Am. Coll. Cardiology, Am. Heart Assn.; mem. Pa. Med. Soc., Allegheny County Med. Soc. Office: Pitts Cardiology Assocs Ste 2210 One Mellon Bank Ctr Pittsburgh PA 15219

GRANET, KENNETH M., internist; b. Manhasset, N.Y., Mar. 22, 1957; s. Irving and Arlene Granet; m. Wendy Granet. BA summa cum laude, Hofstra U., Hempstead, N.Y., 1979; MD, SUNY-Downstate Med. Ctr., Bklyn., 1984. Diplomate Am. Bd. Internal Medicine. Intern/resident in medicine North Shore Univ. Hosp., Manhasset, 1984-87, Meml. Sloan Kittering Cancer Ctr., N.Y.C., 1984-87; pvt. practice L.I., N.Y., 1987-93, Eatontown, N.J., 1993—; asst. program dir. dept. medicine Monmouth Med. Ctr., Long Branch, N.J., 1993—; clin. asst. prof. medicine Hahnemann U. Sch. Medicine, Phila., 1993—; med. dir. Cerebral Palsy, Monmouth, 1993—; lectr. in field. Contbr. articles to profl. jours. Organizer/founder 5 mile Spring Health Run, North Shore Univ. Hosp., 1987-92. Recipient Dean's Spl. award for excellence in clin. teaching Hahnemann U. Sch. Medicine, 1995; named Attending of the Yr., Dept. Medicine, Monmouth Med. Ctr., 1993-94. Fellow ACP (preceptor/mentor program); mem. N.J. Med. Soc., Monmouth County Med. Soc. (exec. com. 1994—), Phi Beta Kappa. Office: Victoria Plz 615 Hope Rd Eatontown NJ 07724

GRANET, ROGER B., psychiatrist; b. Newark, May 6, 1947; s. A. Lester and Lois E. (Ligham) G.; m. Valerie Joyce Waters, Dec. 20, 1970; children: Courtney, Jamie. BA, NYU, 1970; MD (NIH fellow), U. Medicine and Dentistry N.J., 1974. Diplomate Nat. Bd. Med. Examiners, Am. Bd. Psychiatry and Neurology (examiner 1981—). Resident in psychiatry N.Y. Hosp.-Cornell U. Med. Center, 1974-77, cons. in psychiatry dept. neurology, 1980—, also attending staff; 1st alt. Falk residency fellow Am. Psychiat. Assn., 1976-77; asst. unit chief Payne Whitney Psychiat. Clinic, 1976-77; cons. psychiatry Marymount Coll., 1976-77; fellow dept. psychiatry Cornell U. Med. Coll., 1975-77; practice medicine specializing in psychomatics and psychopharmocology psychiatry, Morristown, N.J., 1977—; med. dir. Ctr. Behavioral Oncology, Morristown, 1993—; mem. resident selection com. Payne Whitney Clinic Cornell Med. Coll., 1987—; mem. adv. bd. Internat. Physician Commn. for the Protection of Prisoners; mem. adv. bd. Psychoanalytic Ctr. of N.J., 1987—; cons. staff Morristown Meml. Hosp., 1985-90, dir. cons. liaison psychiatry, 1985—, attending physician, 1990—; cons. Oncology divsn., 1992—; asst. clin. prof. psychiatry Rutgers U., 1977-79; clin. instr. psychiatry Cornell U. Med. Coll., 1978-81, clin. asst. prof., 1981-88, assoc. prof., 1989—; lectr. psychiatry Columbia U.; adj. consulting psychiatrist dept. neurology Meml. Sloan Kettering Cancer Ctr., 1993—. Recipient residents rsch. award N.Y. Dist. Br., 1978; named Clin. Tchr. of Yr., Payne Whitney Psychiat. Clinic, Cornell U., 1985, 88, 92. Fellow Am. Assn. Social Psychiatry, Am. Psychiat. Assn., Acad. Medicine N.J., Am. Physicians For Medicine in Israel; mem. AMA (Physician's Recognition award 1980—), AAAS, Am. Psychiat. Assn. (Marie Eldredge Award bd.), N.J. Med. Soc., Morris County Med. Soc., Tri-County Psychiat. Assn., N.Y. Psychiat. Assn., Am. Acad. Psychiatrists in Alcoholism/Addictions (founding mem. 1985), Am. Soc. Psychiat. Oncology (founding mem. 1988, edn. and clin. care com. 1989—), Acad. Psychosomatic Medicine, Am. Soc. Psychopharmacology. Author: The World's A Small Town, 1993, Is It Alzheimer's ?: What To Do When A Loved One Can't Remember What They Should Do, 1996, Museum of Dreams, 1996, contbr. articles to profl. jours., also textbooks; contbr. poetry to N.Y. Times, literary jours.; reviewer profl. jours. Office: 261 James St Ste 2E Morristown NJ 07960-6348

GRANGAARD, DANIEL ROBERT, psychologist; b. Fond du Lac, Wis., Jan. 7, 1950; s. Lawrence Robert and Dorothy Ruth (Giove) G.; m. Becky Anne Byas, June 16, 1979; children: Dawn Michelle, Scott Robert. BA, Baylor U., 1972, MS, 1974, EdD, 1976. Lic. psychologist; cert. sch. psychologist. Teaching fellow Baylor U., Waco, Tex., 1974-76; assoc. sch. psychologist Edn. Svc. Ctr. Region XII, Waco, 1976-77; sch. psychologist Austin (Tex.) Ind. Sch. Dist., 1977-85; psychologist in pvt. practice Austin, 1985-89; dir. testing, internship tng. Minirth-Meier Tunnell & Wilson Clinic, Austin, 1989-94; pvt. practice, psychologist Austin, 1994—; psychologist Genesis unit Shoal Creek Hosp., Austin, 1987-92, 94-95; cons. psychologist Charter Hosp., Austin, 1984-94, United Cerebral Palsy Austin, 1992—, Genesis Behavioral Health Clinic, Austin, 1994-95, Austin Child Guidance Ctr., 1995—; instr. psychology Austin C.C., 1995—. Contbr. chpts. to books, articles to profl. jours. Westcreek rep. Austin Neighborhood Coun., 1980; coach YMCA Little League Baseball; dir. counseling First Evangel. Free Ch., Austin, 1994-95, elder, 1993—. Mem. Am. Psychol. Assn., Tex. Psychol. Assn., Capital Area Psychol. Assn. Republican. Mem. Evangelical Free Ch. Office: Bldg 5 Ste A 200 1000 Westbank Dr Austin TX 78746-6687

GRANGER, WESLEY MILES, medical educator; b. Tampa, Fla., Jan. 12, 1951; s. Reeves C. and Mary Jane (Parker) G.; m. Elizabeth Dianne Dunaway, June 14, 1975; children: Darah Elizabeth, John Wesley. BA, U. S. Fla., 1972; A. Deg. by Examination, U. Chgo. Hosps. and Clinics, 1972; PhD in Physiology, Med. Coll. Ga., 1983. Registered respiratory therapist; cert. respiratory therapy technician; lic. registered respiratory therapist, La. Trainee to CRTT and registry eligible therapist Univ. Community Hosp., Tampa, 1970-74; part-time staff therapist Ga. Bapt. Med. Ctr., Atlanta, 1974-76; staff therapist Emory U. Hosp., Atlanta, 1976-77; shift supr., insvc. instr. Aiken (S.C.) Community Hosp., 1977-79; grad. teaching asst. Med. Coll. Ga., 1979-81; part-time staff therapist Doctors Hosp. of Augusta (Ga.), 1979-83; instr. respiratory therapy program Univ. Ala., Birmingham, 1983-84; asst. prof. cardiopulmonary sci. La. State U. Med. Ctr., 1984-89, assoc. prof., 1989-96; respiratory therapy program dir., assoc. prof. U. Ala., Birmingham, 1996—; lectr. in field; conductor seminars in field. Contbr. articles to profl. jours. Mem. ASCD, Math. Assn. Am., Am. Assn. Respiratory Care, La. Soc. Respiratory Care, Soc. for Computer Simulation. Office: U Ala Sch Health Related Professions Respiratory Therapy Program 1714 9th Ave S Birmingham AL 35294

GRANT, SISTER BARBARA LEE, nun, religions community leader; b. Jackson, Miss., Aug. 13, 1946; d. Robert Emmett and Patricia (Horan) G. BSN, Marillac Coll., 1970; M of Health Adminstrn., Washington U., St. Louis, 1980. Joined Sisters of Mercy, St. Louis, 1964. Staff nurse St. John's Mercy Med. Ctr., St. Louis, 1970-74; adminstrv. asst. St. Edward Mercy Med. Ctr., Ft. Smith, Ark., 1974-78; resident Mercy Health Svcs., Farmington Hills, Mich., 1980-81; asst. adminstr. Mercy Hosp., New Orleans, 1981-85, COO, 1985-87, CEO, 1987-94; exec. v.p. Mercy & Bapt. Med. Ctr., New Orleans, 1993-95; sabbatical, 1995-96; leadership team Sisters of Mercy, St. Louis, 1996—. Trustee Mercy Regional Med. Ctr., Laredo, Tex., 1984-90, Mercy Med. Group S.W. Mo., Rolla, 1992-94; bd. dirs. St. Thomas Health Svcs., New Orleans, 1989-92; chairperson Met. Hosp. Coun., New Orleans, 1991; mem. exec. com. Met. Area Com., 1991-95; trustee St. John's Regional Health System, 1994-95. Mem. La. Cath. Health Assn. (pres. 1989-90). Home and Office: 2039 N Geyer Rd Saint Louis MO 63131

GRANT, BRADLEY CAMERON, physician; b. Olean, N.Y., Sept. 10, 1954; s. Murray and Trudy (Shein) G.; m. Kristine Grant, May 7, 1988. Student, La. State U., 1972-73, U. Md., 1973-75, Colo. Coll., 1974, Towson State U., Balt., 1975; BA in Biology, Western Md. Coll., Westminster, 1976; DO, Coll. Osteo. Medicine & Surgery, Des Moines, 1979; postgrad., Western State Coll. U., Fullerton, Calif., 1984—; MSEd, U. So. Calif., 1987; postgrad., U. LaVerne, 1991—. Diplomate Am. Bd. Family Practice, Am. Bd. Med. Mgmt., Am. Acad. Pain Mgmt. Intern U.S. Pub. Health Services Hosp., Staten Island, N.Y., 1979-80, Rocky Mountain Hosp., Denver, 1980; mem. staff Community Health Ctr., Garden Grove, Calif., Circle City Hosp., Corona, Calif.; practice medicine specializing in osteo. medicine Lake Elsinore, Calif., 1981—; team physician Elsinore High Sch., 1981—; asst. med. dir. U. So. Calif., 1984; sports med. dir. Grant Med. Group, Corona, 1987; guest physician U.S. Olympic Tng. Ctr., Colorado Springs, Colo., 1990, resident physician, 1990; staff emergency rm. physician L.A. Drs.' Hosp., 1990-91, El Monte Hosp., 1991; expedition leader, med. lectr. Adventure Med. Seminars, Burlington, Vt., 1991; bd. dirs. Inland Med. Group, Inc., chmn. quality assuranceand utilization rev. bd.; mem. infection control pharmacy and therapeutics com. Inland Valley Med. Ctr., 1991-92; lectr. in field. Contbr. numerous articles to profl. jours. Mem. AAAS, Am. Osteo. Assn., Osteo. Physicians & Surgeons Calif. (chmn. pub. rels. com. 1991-92, membership chmn. 1991-92, bd. dirs. 1991—, long-range planning com. 1991-92), United Am. Acad. Osteopathy, Am. Coll. Sports Medicine (co-chmn. internat. med. dept. of Pacific), Am. Coll. Emergency Medicine, Am. Coll. Osteo. Emergency Physicians, Am. Med. Soc. Alcohol and Drug Dependence, Am. Osteo. Soc. Alcohol and Drug Dependence, Am. Quality Assurance and Utilization Rev. Soc., Am. Med. Soc. Preventative Medicine, Am. Osteo. Wilderness Med. Assn., Calif. Med. Assn., Riverside County Med. Soc., Riverside County Osteo. Med. Soc. (founder, conv. chmn. 1992, pres. exec. officers and bd. liaison 1991), Am. Coll. Gen. Practitioners Osteo. Medicine Surgery Calif (pres. 1984-86), Osteo. Alumni Assn., Orange County Osteo. Med. Soc., San Bernardino Osteo. Med. Soc., San Diego Osteo. Med. Soc., Denver Med. Soc., Colo. Osteo. Med. Soc. (editor newsletter 1985-87, pub. rels dir. 1985), Am. Med. Jogger Assn., Am. Soc. Preventative Medicine Health, Am. Soc. Sports Medicine, Am. Med. Assn. Substance Abuse and Chem. Dependency, Union Am. Physicians and Denstists, Sigma Sigma Phi. Home: 25214 Parkcrest Dr Murrieta CA 92562-5950 Office: 17037 Lakeshore Dr Lake Elsinore CA 92530-4903

GRANT, CLIVE STANNARD, physician, surgeon; b. Denver, May 23, 1949; m. Karen Luree, June 1971; children: Kelly, Elise, Stephanie, Justin. BA, U. No. Colo., 1971; MD, U. Colo., Denver, 1975. Diplomate Am. Bd. Surgery. Fellow in surgery Mayo Clinic, Rochester, Minn., 1975-80; instr. surgery Mayo Med. Sch., Rochester, 1980-83, asst. prof., 1983-88, assoc. prof., 1988-94, prof., 1994—; cons. in surgery Mayo Clinic, 1980—. Author: The Manual of Endocrine Surgery, 1984; mem. editorial bd. Acta Chirurgica Austriaca, Vienna, 1991—. Fellow ACS; mem. Am. Assn. Endocrine Surgeons (program com. 1989-92, bylaws com. 1991-92, edn. and rsch. com. 1995—, exec. coun. 1992), Priestley Soc. (exec. coun. 1994—), Ctrl. Surg. Assn., We. Surg. Assn., Soc. Surgery Alimentary Tract, Minn. surg. Soc. (program dir. 1984-86). Office: Mayo Clinic 200 1st St SW Rochester MN 55905

GRANT, DAVID JAMES WILLIAM, pharmacy educator; b. Walsall, Eng., Mar. 26, 1937; came to U.S., 1988; s. James and Attie Hilda May (Stringer) G. BA in Chemistry with 1st class honors, Oxford U., Eng., 1961, MA, DPhil in Phys. Chemistry, 1963, DSc in Phys. Sci., 1990. Lectr. in chemistry U. Coll. of Sierra Leone, Freetown, 1963-65; lectr. then sr. lectr. in pharm. chemistry U. Nottingham, Eng., 1965-81; prof. phys. pharmacy Sch. Pharmacy, U. Toronto, Ont., Can., 1981-88, assoc. dean grad. studies and research, 1984-87; endowed prof. pharmaceutics Coll. Pharmacy, U. Minn., Mpls., 1988—; mem. grants com. for pharm. sci. Med. Rsch. Coun. Can., Ottawa, 1983-87; mem. com. on health rsch. Ont. Univs., Toronto, 1985-87; vis. prof. Med. Rsch. Coun. Can.; mem. adv. panel of phys. test methods and functionality for U.S. Pharmacopeia, 1991—; cons. to numerous chem. and pharm. cos. Co-author: Physical Chemistry for Students Pharmacy and Biology, 1977, Solubility Behavior of Organic Compounds, 1990; mem. editl. bd. Jour. Pharm. Scis., 1990-93, assoc. editor, 1994—; mem. editl. adv. bd. Pharm. Devel. and Tech., 1995—; contbr. over 100 articles to sci. jours. Served to lt. Brit. Army, 1955-57. Recipient Research award Leverhulme Found., U.K., 1969; grantee research councils and indsl. cos., U.K., Can., U.S. Fellow Royal Soc. Chemistry, Am. Assn. Pharm. Scientists (sustaining charter mem. 1986—); mem. Am. Inst. Chem. Engrs., Am. Pharm. Assn., Am. Chem. Soc., Am. Assn. Coll. Pharmacy. Office: U Minn Weaver-Densford Hall 308 Harvard St SE Minneapolis MN 55455-0343

GRANT, EDWARD VINCENT, hospital consultant; b. Jersey City, May 20, 1918; s. John Joseph and Honoriah (Cody) G.; student parochial schs.; m. Helen Joan Grabowski, Apr. 19, 1942; children—Edward, Richard, Robert, Martin, John, Mary Ellen. Barker, Worlds Fair N.Y., 1939; with Lenox Hill Hosp., N.Y.C., 1939-42, 45-55; adminstr. Hunterdon Med. Center, Flemington, N.J., 1955-67; exec. dir. N.Y. Infirmary, N.Y.C., 1967-79; exec. v.p., chief exec. officer N.Y. Infirmary-Beekman Downtown Hosp., from 1979; now hosp. cons.; lectr. Columbia Sch. Public Health and Adminstrv. Medicine, 1958; dir. Hosp. Bur. N.Y.C., 1950-68; preceptor dept. epidemiology and public health Yale U., 1960-65; med. coordinator Hunterdon County (N.J.) CD, 1957-67; preceptor hosp. adminstrn. program Wagner Coll., N.Y.C., 1970-72; guest lectr. Northwood Inst., Midland, Mich. Mem. planning bd. Town of Clinton, 1962-67; chmn. Clinton Citizens Com., 1965-67. Trustee George K. Large Found., Flemington, St. John's Roman Cath. Ch., music minister, 1986—; charter mem. Rep. Presdl. task force, 1990. Served from 2d lt. to maj. AUS, 1942-45. Mem. Am. Coll. Hosp. Adminstrs. Assn., Am. Hosp. Assn. (com. home and ambulatory care 1963-66), N.J. Hosp. Assn. (trustee), Council Hosp. Adminstrs., N.J. Hosp. Adminstrs. Soc., Adminstr. Conf. Group, Adminstrs. Club. Mem. adv. bd. Health Instns. Purchasing Mag. Home and Office: 1869 Sea Oats Dr Atlantic Beach FL 32233

GRANT, JAMES DENEALE, health care company executive; b. Washington, July 9, 1932; s. Deneale and Frances (Hoskins) G.; m. Bonnie Carol Johnson, June 14, 1955; children: Glenn James, Bruce William, Scott Stockman. B.S., William and Mary Coll., 1954; M.B.A., Wharton Sch. U. Pa., 1956; postgrad. (Pub. Affairs fellow), Stanford U., 1963-64. Mem. staff AEC, Washington, 1956-64; v.p. Nat. Inst. Pub. Affairs, Washington, 1964-69; dep. dir. White House Conf. Food, Nutrition and Health, 1969-70; dep. commr. FDA, Washington, 1970-72; asst. to chmn. CPC Internat. Inc., Englewood Cliffs, N.J., 1972-73, v.p., 1973-86; chmn., chief exec. officer T Cell Scis., Inc., 1986-92, chmn., 1992—; bd. dirs. Targeted Genetics Corp., Internat. Biotech. Trust, U.K., Biocompatibles, Ltd., U.K., Biocompatibles, Inc. (U.S.A.); cons. U.S. Bur. Budget, 1965-69, U.S. Civil Svc. Commn. (Office Pers. Mgmt.), 1965-69; mem., vice chmn., sec. adv. com. HHS, FDA, 1990-91. Chmn. Bergen County United Fund, 1974-75; trustee Nutrition Found., 1973-78; chmn. adv. group to sec. gen. UN Conf. on Sci. and Tech. for Devel., 1979. Recipient U.S. Govt. Career Edn. award, 1963. Mem. AAAS, Am. Chem. Soc., Omicron Delta Kappa. Presbyterian. Club: Univ. (N.Y.C.). Home: 860 5th Ave New York NY 10021-5856

GRANT, J(OHN) ANDREW, JR., medical educator, allergist; b. Tallahassee, Jan. 2, 1941; s. John Andrew and Herschel Elizabeth Grant; m. Eleanor Cunkle, Dec. 29, 1962; children: Julian Andrew, Brian Arthur, Dean Evan. BA cum laude, Harvard U., 1962; MD, Duke U., 1966. Diplomate Am. Bd. Internal Medicine, Am. Bd. Allergy and Immunology, Am. Bd. Lab. Immunology. Med. resident Cornell U., N.Y. Hosp., N.Y.C., 1966-68; clin. assoc. NIH, Bethesda, Md., 1968-71; fellow Johns Hopkins Univ., Balt., 1971-73; prof., vice chmn. U. Tex. Med. Br., Galveston, 1973—; bd. dirs. Am. Bd. Allergy and Immunology, 1993—; cons. and lectr. in field. Contbr. articles to profl. jours. Elder First Presbyn. Ch., Galveston. Lt. comdr. UPHS, 1968-71. Recipient Cub Scout Leader award Boy Scouts Am., 1983. Fellow ACP, Am. Acad. Allergy and Immunology (Spl. Recognition award 1994); mem. Tex. Allergy Soc. (pres. 1992—), Rotary (Youth Leadership award 1993). Democrat. Office: U Tex Med Br Clin Scis # 409/R-G62 Galveston TX 77555-0762

GRANT, JOHN L., neurosurgeon; b. Ann Arbor, Mich., Aug. 6, 1946; s. Leland P. and Virginia M. (Wylie) G.; m. Alice Jennette Cook, Aug. 26, 1978; children: Leland B., Austin M., Clayton K. Student, John Carroll U., 1970; MD, Ohio State U., 1975. Diplomate Am. Coll. Surgeons. Intern Shands Tchg. Hosp., Gainesville, Fla., 1975-76, resident to chief resident, 1976-81; neurosurgeon ptnr. Matuk & Grant, inc., Rockledge, Fla., 1981-86; neurosurgeon, pres. Portsmouth, Va., 1986—; prof. dept. neurosurgery, EVMS, Norfolk Va., 1990—. Author rsch. publs. in field. Recipient Physician Recognition award Mayfield Neurol. Inst. of Cin., 1986. Mem. Congress of Neurol. Surgery (Physician Recognition award 1985), Am. Assn. Neurol. Surgeons, Neurol. Soc. of Va., So. Neurosurg. Soc., Va. Med. Soc., Portsmouth Acad. Medicine. Roman Catholic. Office: Ste 2-E 3640 High St Portsmouth VA 23707

GRANT, KATHRYN ANN, nurse; b. Tooele, Utah, Feb. 11, 1946; d. Thomas Michael and Leone Kathryn (Olson) Keegan; m. Wayne A. Grant, III, Nov. 17, 1973 (div. 1986). RN diploma, Luth. Deaconess Hosp. Sch. Nursing, 1969; BA, Park Coll., 1978; MA, Webster U., 1982. Cert. psychiat. and mental health nurse, ANA. Tchr. asst. Black Hills State Coll., Spearfish, S.D., 1964-65; nurse aide Lutheran Deaconess Hosp., Mpls., Minn., 1966-69; office mgr., peer counselor Washington D.C. Rape Crisis Ctr., 1974-76; registered nurse USAF and Air N.G., U.S. and Japan, 1970-76; direct sales rep., group sales leader Avon Products, Inc., Fairview Heights, Ill., 1976-84; chiropractic asst. Faulkner Chiropractic Clinic, Fairview Heights, 1983-86; office mgr., chiropractic asst. Dr. Swiller's Chiropractic Office, Hartford, Conn., 1986; asst. head nurse psychiatry VA Med. Ctr., Newington, Conn., 1986-89; asst. nurse mgr. inpatient psychiatry New Britain (Conn.) Gen. Hosp., 1989-91; pvt. practice holistic health The Natural Choice Wellness Ctr., Newington, 1991—; staff nurse V.A. Med. Ctr., West Haven, Conn., 1992—. Author, Poems, "Thoughts", 1987. Sec. parish planning coun. Faith Luth. Ch., Fairview Heights, 1982-84; vol. nurse USAF Med. Ctr., Washington, 1975-76. Recipient Legion of Honor award Chapel of Four Chaplains, Valley Forge, Pa., 1987. Mem. NAFE, Touch for Health Found. (instr. 1984—), Parker Chiropractic Rsch. Found., Am. Holistic Nurses Assn. (cert.), Nurse Healers Profl. Assocs., Sigma Kappa.

GRANT, RICHARD EARL, medical and legal consultant; b. Spokane, Wash., Aug. 27, 1935; s. Conrad Morrison and Sylva Celeste (Sims) G.; m. Susan Kimberly Hawkins, Mar. 17, 1979; children: Paaqua A., Camber Do'otsie O. BSc cum laude, U. Wash., 1961; MEd, Whitworth Coll., 1974; PhD, Wash. State U., 1980. Cert. ins. rehab. specialist; cert. case mgr. Supr. nursing Providence Hosp., Seattle, 1970-72; asst. prof. nursing Wash. State U., Spokane, 1972-78; dir. nursing Winslow (Ariz.) Meml. Hosp., 1978-79; adminstr. psychiat. nursing Ariz. State Hosp., Phoenix, 1979-80; asst. prof. Ariz. State U., Tempe, 1980-83; assoc. prof. Linfield Coll., Portland, Oreg., 1983-86, Intercollegiate Ctr. for Nursing Edn., Spokane, 1986-88; sr. med. care coord. Fortis Corp., Spokane, 1988-92; med. svcs. cons. CorVel Corp., Spokane, 1992-94; owner Richard Grant & Assoc., Spokane, 1995—; cons. Ariz. State Hosp., 1980-82, Pres.'s Commn., Washinton, 1981-83, U. No. Colo., Greely, 1985-86; area med. svcs. cons., 1992—. Author: The God-Man-God Book, 1976, Publications of the Membership (Conaa), 1983, 3d rev. edit., 1985, 4th rev. edit., 1988, Predetermined Careplan Handbook-Nursing, 1988; contbr. articles to profl. jours. Judge Student Space Shuttle Project, Portland, 1983, N.W. Sci. Expo, Portland, 1983. With U.S. Army, 1953-56. Grantee NIMH, U. Wash., 1961; named one of top Hopi Scholars, Hopi Tribe, Second Mesa, Ariz., 1981. Mem. AAAS, Nat. League for Nursing, Wash. League for Nursing (v.p. 1988-90), Coun. on Nursing and Anthropology (editor 1982-90), N.Y. Acad. Scis., Case Mgmt. Soc. Am., Sigma Theta Tau.

GRANT, RONALD ALFRED, psychiatrist, psychoanalyst, pastoral counselor; b. Providence, May 28, 1938; s. Alfred Edward and Althea G.; children: Andrew Edward, Kathryn Caroline. AB, Tufts U., 1959; BD, Andover Newton Theol. Sem., 1963, STM, 1964, D in Ministry, 1972; MD, Boston U., 1969. Cert. psychoanalysis, med. psychotherapy. Intern Mary Imogene Bassett Hosp. affiliate Columbia U. Med. Ctr., Cooperstown, N.Y., 1969-70, resident, 1970-71; resident N.Y. State Psychiatric Inst. and Columbia Med. Ctr., N.Y.C., 1971-73; pvt. practice pastoral counselor, 1972—; pvt. practice psychiatry, Weston, Greenwich, Conn., 1973—, pvt. practice psychoanalysis,, 1981—; mem. faculty, tng. and supervisory analyst C.G. Jung Inst. N.Y., 1981, med. dir., 1983-87; psychiat. cons. Montessori Sch. Wilton, Conn., 1987—; staff psychiatrist, supr. Temenos Inst., Westport, Conn., 1987—; mem. adj. faculty Andover Newton Theol. Sem., 1991—. Mem. editorial bd. Human Devel. Jour., 1986-94. Named one of Outstanding Young Men in Am., 1970. Mem. AMA, Am. Psychiat. Assn., Am. Inst. Homeopathy, N.Y. Assn. Analytical Psychology, Internat. Assn. Analytical Psychology. Office: 45 E Putnam Ave Greenwich CT 06830-5606

GRANT, VERNE EDWIN, biology educator; b. San Francisco, Oct. 17, 1917; s. Edwin and Bessie (Swallow) G.; m. Alva Day, June 12, 1946 (div. Aug. 1959); children: Joyce Grant Mixon, Brian, Brenda Grant Aley; m. Karen Alt, Nov. 3, 1960. AB, U. Calif., Berkeley, 1940, PhD, 1949. Teaching asst. botany U. Calif., Berkeley, 1946-49; NRC fellow Carnegie Inst., Stanford, Calif., 1949-50; geneticist Rancho Santa Ana Bot. Garden, Claremont, Calif., 1950-67; asst. prof. Claremont Grad. Sch., 1951-53, assoc. prof., 1953-57, prof., 1957-67; prof. biology Inst. Life Sci., Tex. A&M U., College Station, 1967-68; prof., dir. Boyce Thompson Southwestern Arboretum U. Ariz., Superior, 1968-70; prof. botany U. Tex., Austin, 1970-87, prof. emeritus, 1987—. Author: Natural History of the Phlox Family, 1959, The Origin of Adaptations, 1963, The Architecture of the Germplasm, 1964, (with Karen Grant) Flower Pollination in the Phlox Family, 1965, (with Karen Grant) Hummingbirds and Their Flowers, 1968, Plant Speciation, 1971, 2d edit., 1981, Genetics of Flowering Plants, 1975, Organismic Evolution, 1977, The Evolutionary Process, 1985, 2d edit., 1991; mem. editorial bd. Ency. Americana, 1955-64, Brittonia, 1957-62, Evolution, 1960-62, Am. Naturalist, 1964-67, Biologisches Zentralblatt, 1974—; contbr. numerous articles to profl. jours. Recipient Sci. award Phi Beta Kappa, 1964. Fellow Am. Acad. Arts and Scis.; mem. NAS, Am. Soc. Naturalists, Soc. for Study of Evolution (pres. 1968), Bot. Soc. Am. (cert. of merit 1971), Internat. Soc. Plant Taxonomists, Am. Soc. Plant Taxonomists, Genetics Soc. Am. Home: 2811 W Fresco Dr Austin TX 78731-5028 Office: U Tex Dept Botany Austin TX 78712

GRANT, VICKI CAIN, health and social policy research administrator; b. Hartsville, S.C., Feb. 22, 1954; d. Richard Calhoun and Dorothy Ann (Cain) G. BA, Winthrop Coll., 1974; MSW, U. S.C., 1979; PhD, Brandeis U., 1992. Project developer S.C. Commn. on Alcohol and Drug Abuse, Columbia, 1974-77; staff devel. and tng. coord. S.C. Dept. Social Svcs., Columbia, 1979-81; dep. dir. div. health and human svcs. S.C. Gov.'s Office, Columbia, 1981-85, cons., 1985-86; rsch. dir. Sarah Shuptrine and Assocs., Columbia, 1987—, So. Inst. on Children and Families, Columbia, 1992—. Pew fellow Heller Grad. Sch. Brandeis U., 1985-87. Democrat. Methodist. Office: Sarah Shuptrine and Assocs 620 Sims Ave Columbia SC 29205-2411

GRASMANN, EDWIN JOHN, physician; b. Bklyn., Apr. 16, 1955; s. Edwin John and Helen Mabel (Tower) G.; m. Joan Elizabeth Mayberger, Feb. 14, 1993; children: Katie, Peter, Matthew. BS, SUNY, 1980; DO, N.Y. Coll. Osteo. Medicine, 1985. Diplomate Am. Bd. Family Practice. Resident U. Med. Ctr., Stony Brook, N.Y., 1985-88; physician pvt. practice, St. Sinai, N.Y., 1988—. Mem. AMA, Am. Acad. Family Physicians, N.Y. State Med. Soc., Suffolk County Med. Soc. Office: 5505 Mesconset Hwy Mount Sinai NY 11766

GRASS, ELLEN ROBINSON, medical products company executive; b. Taunton, Mass., Mar. 29, 1914; d. Francis J. and Laura (Waldron) Robinson; m. Albert M. Grass, June 28, 1936; children: Robert W., Henry J. AB in Biology, Radcliffe Coll., 1935, MA, 1936; LLD (hon.), Regis Coll., 1973; ScD (hon.), St. Louis U., 1990. Sales mgr., treas. Grass Instrument Co., Quincy, Mass., 1935-92, pres., 1992-94; pres. Grass Found., 1967—. Pres. Am. Epilepsy Fedn., 1959-60, Internat. Bur. Epilepsy, 1966-78; mem. adv. coun. Nat. Inst. Neurol. Disease and Stroke, 1969-73; mem. Mass. Devel. Disabilities Coun., 1971; mem. vis. com. bd. overseers Grad. Sch. Arts and Scis., Harvard, 1970-76, Nat. Commn. Multiple Sclerosis, 1973-74; trustee Regis Coll., Weston, Mass., 1974-86, 88-92, Marine Biol. Lab., 1984-93; dir. Epilepsy Found. Am., 1968—. Mem. Am. Soc. EEG Tech., Am. EEG Soc., Assn. Advancement Med. Instrumentation, Phi Beta Kappa. Home: 77 Reservoir Rd Quincy MA 02170-3610

GRASS, GEORGE MITCHELL, IV, pharmaceutical executive; b. Bryn Mawr, Pa., Dec. 31, 1957; s. George Mitchell III and Irma Lucy (Schaffer) G. PharmD, U. Nebr., Omaha, 1980; PhD, U. Wis., 1985. Lic. pharmacist. Staff rschr. Syntex Rsch., Palo Alto, Calif., 1985-91; pres. Precision Instrument Design, Tahoe City, Calif., 1987—; cons. Costar Corp., Cambridge, Mass., 1990—, various pharm. cos., 1991—; co-founder Raptor Graphics, Snohomish, Wash. Contbr. numerous articles to profl. jours. Recipient Ebert prize Jour. Pharm. Sci., 1989. Mem. AAAS, Am. Assn. Pharm. Scientists, Sigma Xi.

GRATTAROLA, MASSIMO ITALO, bioengineering educator; b. Genoa, Italy, Jan. 27, 1950; s. Luciano and Vittoria (Picenni) G.; m. Brunella Tedesco, Mar. 5, 1977; 1 child, Maddalena. Maturità Scientifica, Liceo Cannizzaro, Roma, Italy, 1968; Laurea in Physics, Genoa U., Italy, 1975. Vis. scientist Temple U., Phila., 1977; asst. prof. Genoa (Italy) U., 1978-84, assoc. prof., 1985—. Contbr. articles to profl. jours. Mem. IFMBE, Biophys. Soc., N.Y. Acad. Scis.

GRATZ, PAULINE, former nursing science educator; b. N.Y.C., Mar. 30, 1924; d. John and Rose (Berman) G.; m. Sidney Aaronson, July 25, 1959. B.A., Hunter Coll., 1945; M.A., Columbia U., 1948, Ed.D., 1961. Jr.

bacteriologist Queens Gen. Hosp., 1945-47; research technician Jewish Hosp. Bklyn., 1947-48; instr. biology and phys. sci. Bayonne (N.J.) Hosp. Sch. Nursing, 1948-51; sci. coordinator N.Y. Med. Coll. Sch. Nursing, 1951-56, New Rochelle (N.Y.) Hosp. Sch. Nursing, 1956-61; instr. nursing edn. Columbia U., 1961-62, asst. prof. natural scis. and nursing edn., 1963-65, asst. prof. natural scis., 1965-67, assoc. prof., 1967-69; prof. human ecology Duke U., Durham, N.C., 1969-85; prof. emeritus Duke U., 1985—; vis. prof. physiology N.C. Health Manpower Project, summer 1973; cons. in field. Author: Integrated Science, 1966, (with others) Human Physiology, 1987, Experiments in Physiology, 1987, Teachers Edition in Human Physiology, 1987; contbg. author chpts. to books. NSF fellow, 1965; Shell fellow, 1969. Fellow AAAS; mem. Kappa Delta Pi, Pi Lambda Theta, Iota Sigma Pi, Sigma Theta Tau (hon.). Home: 42 Willow Oak Ct Durham NC 27705-5646

GRAUBARD, KATHERINE, neuroscience educator; b. Charlotte, N.C., Feb. 10, 1943; d. Seymour John and Blanche (Kazon) G.; m. William Howard Calvin, Sept. 1, 1966. AB with distinction, Smith Coll., 1964; PhD, U. Wash., 1973. Rsch. assoc. U. Wash., Seattle, 1974, 78-88, postdoctoral fellow, 1976-77, sr. rsch. assoc., 1989-91, rsch. assoc. prof., 1991—; postdoctoral fellow U. Calif., San Diego, 1975, Hebrew U., Jerusalem, 1978; mem. ad hoc panel, NIH Physiology Study Sect., Bethesda, Md., 1983; mem. editorial bd. Jour. Neurobiology, 1981-86, Jour. Electrophysiological Techniques, 1986-87. Contbr. articles to profl. jours.; editor: (issue) Seminars in the Neurosciences, 1991; author: (book chpts.), 1979, 87. Dem. precinct committeeman, Seattle, 1968—; del. King County and State Dem. convs. Recipient rsch. grants from NIH, 1979—, NSF, 1985-88. Mem. Soc. for Neuroscience, Biophysical Soc., Soc. Gen. Physiologists, Marine Biol. Labs., Assn. of Women in Sci., Women in Neuroscience, Phi Beta Kappa, Sigma Xi. Office: U Wash Dept Zoology Box 351800 Seattle WA 98195-1800

GRAUER, THEODORA, nursing educator; b. N.Y.C., May 3, 1936; d. Jerome and Etta (Skolnick) Trichter; m. Seymour David Grauer, Dec. 13, 1964; children: Edward, Michael, Robert. Diploma, Bellevue Hosp. Sch. Nursing, 1959; BS, CUNY-Hunter Coll., 1963; MS, Adelphi U., 1978, PhD, 1988. Cert. childbirth preparation, 1972. Staff nurse Bellevue Hosp. Med. Ctr., 1959-61, clin. instr., 1961-66; educator, childbirth East Nassau Med. Group Ctrs., 1972-85; program dir. Ctr. Parents and Children, Glen Cove Cmty. Hosp., 1980-81; instr. Sch. Nursing Adelphi U., 1978-82; asst. prof. dept. nursing L.I. U., 1982-89, assoc. prof., chairperson dept. nursing, 1989-96, prof., chair dept. nursing, 1996—; adj. asst. prof. Sch. Nursing Adelphi U., 1988, SUNY, 1987-88. Contbr. articles to profl. jours. C.W. Post Rsch. grantee, 1986-87. Mem. ANA, NAACOG, APHA, Am. Soc. Psychoprophylaxis Obstetrics, N.Y. State Nurses Assn., Sigma Xi, Sigma Theta Tau (rsch. grantee 1987). Home: 20 Deer Path Ln Syosset NY 11791-6115

GRAVEN, STANLEY NORMAN, pediatrician, educator; b. Greene, Iowa, May 20, 1932; s. Henry Norman and Helen T. (Davis) G.; m. Mavis Nadine Johnson, Aug. 21, 1954; children: Nadine E., Michael A., Kendall E., Douglas B. Student, St. Olaf Coll., 1951-52; BS, Wartburg Coll., 1955; MD, U. Iowa, 1956; postgrad., U. Wis., 1964-66. Diplomate Am. Bd. Pediatrics, Am. Bd. Neonatal-Perinatal Medicine. Chief pediatrics USAF, Spokane, Wash., 1960-62; dir. nurseries USAF, San Antonio, 1962-64; asst. prof. dept. pediatrics U. Wis., Madison, 1966-69, assoc. prof. dept. pediatrics, 1969-72, prof. dept. pediatrics, 1972-76; prof. dept. pediatrics U. S.D., Sioux Falls, 1976-80, U. Mo., Columbia, 1980-84; prof. Coll. of Pub. Health, U. So. Fla., Tampa, 1984-86; prof., chmn. U. So. Fla., Tampa, 1986-93, dir. divsn. child devel., prof. dept. pediatrics, 1993—; chmn. Neonatal-Perinatal Medicine Bd., 1974-76; project dir. Egyptian Newborn Care Program, Cairo, 1978-85; sr. program cons. Robert Wood Johnson Found., Princeton, N.J., 1978-85. Contbr. articles to profl. jours. Capt. USAF, 1956-64. Recipient Borden Undergrad. Rsch. award U. Iowa, 1956, Stanley Graven award Nat. Perinatal Assn., 1988; named John & Mary Markle scholar, 1968. Fellow Am. Acad. Pediatrics; mem. Am. Pub. Health Assn. (gov.'s coun. 1986-90), Soc. Pediatric Rsch., Am. Pediatric Soc., Fla. Perinatal Assn., Nat. Perinatal Assn., Fla. Pediatric Soc., Fla. Med. Assn. Democrat. Lutheran. Home: 14930 Lake Forest Dr Lutz FL 33549-3268

GRAVENSTEIN, JOACHIM STEFAN, anesthesiologist, educator; b. Berlin, Germany, Jan. 25, 1925; came to U.S., 1952, naturalized, 1959; m. Alix Trutschler, Aug. 27, 1949; children—Nikolaus, Alix, Frederike, Stefan, Ruprecht, Dietrich, Constanze, Katharina. MD, U. Bonn, Germany, 1951, Harvard, 1958; MD (hon.), U. Graz, Austria, 1988. Resident and staff appointments anesthesia Mass. Gen. Hosp., 1952-58; fellow, tchr. Harvard Med. Sch., 1952-58; chief anesthesiology Coll. Medicine, U. Fla., 1958-69; prof. anesthesiology, chmn. dept. Case Western Res. Med. Sch., 1969-79; grad. research prof. Coll. Medicine, U. Fla., Gainesville, 1979—. Mem. Am. Soc. Anesthesiology. Home: 7424 NW 18th Ave Gainesville FL 32605-3132 Office: U Fla Coll Medicine Gainesville FL 32610

GRAVES, MAUREEN ANN, counselor; b. Sioux City, Iowa, July 10, 1946; d. Jack Milford and Elizabeth Mildred (St. George) Dryden; m. Thomas Darrel Graves, Oct. 9, 1965; children: Michael James, Lorrie Michelle. G-rad., Gestalt Inst. Iowa, 1980. Cert. drug and alcohol counselor, Nebr.; cert. profl. asst., U. S.D.; cert. hypnotherapist. Counselor Siouxland Coun. on Alcoholism and Drug Abuse, Sioux City, 1979-81; counselor, co-founder New Hope Alcohol and Addiction Ctr., South Sioux City, Nebr., 1981—; cons. St. Luke Hosp. Addiction Ctr., Sioux City, 1987—; trainer Va. Satir-Internat. Tng. Inst., Crested Butte, Colo., 1988-89. Vol. co-facilitator Siouxland Coun. on Alcoholism and Drug Abuse, Sioux City, 1976-79; mem. exec. team couple World Wide Marriage Encounter, N.E. Nebr., 1979-82; trainer Va. Satir-Internat. Tng. Inst., Crested Butte, Colo., 1992; co-leader Satir Family Camp, San Jose, 1992, 93, 94, 95, 96; mem. Avanta Governing Coun., 1994-96. Mem. Avanta Network, Am. Mental Health Counselors Assn., Moscow Inst. for Profl. Devel. of Psychologists and Social Workers (founding), AACD. Roman Catholic. Home: 424 W 16th St South Sioux City NE 68776-2233 Office: New Hope Alcoholism & Addiction Ctr Inc PO Box 35 South Sioux City NE 68776

GRAVES, MAXINE, medical and surgical nurse; b. Mobile, Ala., July 16, 1941; d. Leon Sr. and Mary E. (McDaniel-Lane) Grove; m. Perry R. Graves. Oct. 29, 1966; children: Dennis, Anita Graves Ricks. AD, Delaware County Community Coll, Media, Pa., 1972; BSN, Gwynedd Mercy Coll., Gwynedd Valley, Pa., 1983. Tchrs. aide Chester (Pa.)-Upland Sch. Dist.; simulation lab. instr. Delaware County Community Coll.; ambulatory care staff nurse Crozer-Chester Med. Ctr.; nurse mgr. Crozer Internal Medicine Assocs. Editor newsletter Sleuth, 1989. Mem. ANA, Pa. Nurses Assn. (past. chmn. membership com.).

GRAVES, ROY WILLIAM, emergency physician; b. Schenectady, N.Y., Aug. 3, 1952; s. William L.O. and Muriel Isobel (McCannell) G.; m. Judith Ann Reid, June 24, 1983; 1 child, Ryan Malcolm. BS in Biology, U. Wash., 1974, MD, 1978. Diplomate Am. Bd. Emergency Medicine. Attending physician Valley Med. Ctr., Renton, Wash., 1983-84, Group Health Coop., Seattle, 1984-85; asst. prof. emergency medicine East Carolina U., Greenville, N.C., 1985-86; attending physician Highline Hosp., Seattle, 1986-88, Group Health Coop., Seattle, 1988—. Contbr. articles to profl. jours. Team physician Seattle-King County Disaster Team, 1987—, Nat. Ski Patrol, Crystal Mountain, Wash., 1988-94. Fellow Am. Coll. Emergency Medicine. Office: Group Health Coop 200 15th Ave E Seattle WA 98112

GRAVITZ, MELVIN A., clinical psychologist; b. Balt., Dec. 8, 1927. BA, George Washington U., 1950, MA, 1951; PhD, Adelphi U., 1955. Diplomate Am. Bd. Profl. Psychology (pres. 1980-81), Am. Bd. Psychol. Hypnosis (pres. 1975-78), Am Bd. Forensic Psychology. Intern clin. psychology Springfield State Hosp., Sykesville, Md., 1953-54; clin. psychologist County Health Dept., Tampa, Fla., 1955-57; chief clin. psychologist Dept. Pub. Health D.C., 1957-64; pvt. practice Washington, 1964—; clin. prof. psychiatry George Washington U., Washington, 1966—. Contbr. numerous chpts. to books and articles to profl. jours. Named Disting. Practitioner Nat. Acad. Practice, 1982. Fellow Am. Soc. Clin. Hypnosis (pres. 1978-79), APA (coun. rep. 1988-91, pres. divsn. hypnosis). Office: Ste 105 1325 18th St NW Washington DC 20036

GRAY, BARBARA BRONSON, nurse, writer; b. Van Nuys, Calif., June 3, 1955; d. Gerald M. and Jane Marie (Strauss) Bronson; m. Thomas Stephen Gray, Aug. 27, 1977; children: Jonathan Thomas, Katherine Marie. BS, UCLA, 1977, M in Nursing, 1981. RN, Calif. Staff nurse Valley Presbyn. Hosp., Van Nuys, Calif., 1977-80; asst. adminstr. Calif. Med. Ctr., L.A., Calif., 1981-84; freelance writer Agoura, 1984—; exec. dir. Nurseweek, 1995—; cons. St. John's Hosp. and Health Ctr., Santa Monica, Calif., 1986-90, Los Robles Regional Med. Ctr., Thousand Oaks, Calif., 1993—; lectr. UCLA Sch. Nursing, 1991—. Author: 120 Years of Medicine in Los Angeles County, 1991; contbr. articles to jours., mags. and newspapers; syndicated by L.A. Times Syndicate. Recipient Outstanding Achievement award Perinatal Network, Santa Clara County, Calif., 1994; named Writer of Yr., Nurseweek, 1991; Kellogg fellow, 1979-81. Mem. Nat. Assn. Sci. Writers, Sigma Theta Tau (Cert. of Appreciation 1994, Internat. Media award 1995). Republican. Episcopalian. Home: 4909 Cardinal Way Agoura CA 91301-4762

GRAY, GREGORY EDWARD, physician, administrator, educator; b. L.A., Sept. 27, 1954; s. Bruce Everett Gray and Louise (Dillon) Young; m. Lorraine Kulhanek, Feb. 19, 1977; 1 child, Thomas Edward. BS, U. Calif., Davis, 1975, MS, 1976; PhD, U. So. Calif., L.A., 1980, MD, 1983. Diplomate Am. Bd. Psychiatry and Neurology. Nutritionist Cancer Ctr. U. So. Calif., L.A., 1977-79; postgrad. physician L.A. County/U. So. Calif., 1983-87; asst. prof. dept. psychiatry Sch. Medicine, U. So. Calif., 1987-91, assoc. prof., 1991—, chmn. dept. psychiatry, 1993—; CEO U. So. Calif. Psychiatry and Psychology Assocs., Inc., 1993—; chief of psychiatry L.A. County-U. So. Calif. Med. Ctr.; chief psychiatry U. So. Calif./Norris Cancer Hosp., 1994—; dir. inpatient psychiatry L.A. County-U. So. Calif. Psychiat. Hosp., 1991-93; dir. Pacific Geriatric Edn. Ctr., L.A., 1989-92. Contbr. articles to profl. jours. U. Calif. fellow, 1975-76. Mem. AMA, APHA, Am. Coll. Physician Execs., Acad. Orgnl. and Occupl. Psychiatrists, Assn. Acad. Psychiatrists, Assn. for Health Svcs. Rsch., Alpha Omega Alpha. Office: U So Calif Dept Psychiatry Ste 600 1510 San Pablo St Los Angeles CA 90033

GRAY, JEANNE HULL, marriage and family therapist; b. Watervliet, N.Y., Aug. 9, 1946; d. Raymond Joseph and Jeanne Therese (Cahill) Hull; m. Donald Peter Gray, Nov. 24, 1979; 1 child, Jessica. B in Urban Studies/Sociology, Marymount, Manhattan Coll., N.Y.C.; M in Pastoral Ministry, Fairfield (Conn.) U.; M in Family Therapy, So. Conn. State U., New Haven, 1986. Cert. marriage and family therapist, Conn.; lic. drug and alcohol counselor. Counselor Rikers Island Prison, N.Y.C., 1971-72; youth dir. St. Mary's Parish, Oneonta, N.Y., 1972-75; counselor Bridgeport (Conn.) Correctional Ctr., 1975-77; high sch. guidance counselor Cen. Cath. High Sch., Norwalk, Conn., 1977-79, Stamford (Conn.) Cath. High Sch., 1979-81; counselor Bridgeport Network Programs, 1983-84; intern family therapy APT Found., Daytop, Newtown, Conn., 1984-85, family therapist, 1985-87; pvt. practice family therapy Woodbury, Conn., 1987—; supr. Bristol Hosp. Family Therapy Tng. Inst., 1991-93; adj. tchr. Fairfield U., 1989—. Mem. Am. Assn. Marriage and Family Therapists, World Fedn. Mental Health, Ind. Mental Health Profls. Network, Am. Assn. Counseling and Devel., Pierrs Cons., Conn. Fedn. Alcoholism and Drug Abuse Counselors, Conn. Assn. Marriage and Family Therapists. Democrat. Roman Catholic. Home: 1 Shagbark Ln Woodbury CT 06798-3206 Office: Family Therapy & Wellness 127 Main St N # 253 Woodbury CT 06798-2915

GRAY, LAMAN A., JR., thoracic surgeon, educator; b. Louisville, May 28, 1940; m. Julie Gray; children: Juliet, Alice, Virginia. B.A. with distinction in Chemistry, Wesleyan U., Middletown, Conn., 1963; M.D., Johns Hopkins U., 1967. Diplomate Am. Bd. Surgery, Am. Bd. Thoracic Surgery. Intern U. Mich. Hosp., Ann Arbor, 1967-68; resident in gen. surgery, 1968-72, resident in thoracic and cardiovascular surgery, 1972-74; practice medicine specializing in thoracic and cardiovascular surgery, Louisville, 1974—; asst. prof. surgery, div. thoracic and cardiovascular surgery U. Louisville, 1974-78, assoc. prof., 1978-84, prof., 1984—, dir. thoracic and cardiovascular surgery, 1976—; mem. staff Univ. Hosp., Norton's Children's Hosp., Ky. Bapt. Hosps., Meth. Hosp., Jewish Hosp., VA Hosp., Suburban Hosp.; presenter at profl. confs. Pioneer in heart transplant and use of ventricular assist devices in Ky. Contbr. numerous articles, abstracts to profl. publs., chpts. to books. Grantee Humana Inc., 1984-87. Mem. Am. Assn. Thoracic Surgery, Am. Coll. Cardiology (gov. Ky. chpt. 1992-95), Am. Coll. Chest Physicians (com. on cardiovascular surgery, pres. Ky. chpt. 1978-79), ACS, Am. Thoracic Soc., Am. Soc. Artificial Internal Organs, Innominate Soc. Med. History, Jefferson County Med. Soc., John Alexander Soc. (exec. com.), Ky. Surg. Soc., Ky. Thoracic Soc., Louisville Heart Assn. (pres. 1983-85), Louisville Medico-Chirurgical Soc., Louisville Surg. Soc., Med. Forum (v.p. 1976-77), Societe Internationale de Chirurgie, Soc. Thoracic Surgeons, So. Surg. Assn., So. Thoracic Surg. Assn. (exec. council 1983-84, chmn. membership com. 1983-84), Ky. Heart Assn. (research rev. com. 1975-79), Sigma Xi. Office: U Louisville Dept Surgery Louisville KY 40292

GRAY, LAWRENCE NEAL, plastic surgeon; b. Chgo., May 28, 1953; s. Samuel Howard and Gloria (Crohn) G.; m. Ruth Soper, Aug. 31, 1980; children: Evan, Whitney, Andrew. BA, Washington U., St. Louis, 1975; MD, Ind. U., Indpls., 1979. Diplomate Am. Bd. Plastic Surgery, with specialization in surgery of the hand. Resident in gen. surgery Boston U., 1979-82; resident in plastic surgery Loyola U., Maywood, Ill., 1982-85; plastic surgeon Atlantic Plastic Surgery Assocs., Portsmouth, N.H., 1985—. Mem. AMA, Am. Soc. Plastic and Reconstructive Surgeons, Am. Assn. Hand Surgeons, Am. Soc. for Aesthetic Plastic Surgery,. Jewish. Office: Atlantic Plastic Surgery Assocs 330 Borthwick Ave Portsmouth NH 03801-4174

GRAY, MICHAEL WILLIAM, osteopathic, general and aesthetic plastic and barratric surgeon; b. N.Y.C., Sept. 5, 1962; s. Alfred Eugene and Sheila Joyce (Roter) G.; m. Rena Suzanne Kaplan, Aug. 17, 1991; 1 child, Ariana Amanda. BS cum laude, U. Miami, 1984; DO, S.E. Coll. Osteo. Medicine, North Miami Beach, Fla., 1988. Cert. ACLS, advanced trauma life support, advanced laporoscopic techniques, Rush-Presbyn. St. Lukes Hosp. Intern Brookdale Hosp. Med. Ctr., Bklyn., 1988-89; resident in gen. surgery Midwestern U.-Chgo. Osteo. Med. Ctrs., 1989-93, chief surg. resident, 1992-93, fellowship in aesthetic plastic surgery, 1993-94; fellowship in aesthetic plastic surgery Northwestern U. Sch. Dentistry, Chgo., 1993-94; lectr. in field. Contbr. articles to profl. jours. Presdl. scholar, 1980-84. Mem. Am. Osteo. Assn., Am. Coll. Osteo. Surgeons, Am. Soc. Geriat. Surgeons, Alpha Lambda Delta, Phi Eta Sigma, Tri Beta, Golden Key, Nat. Honor Soc. Home: 2726 Maitland Dr Ann Arbor MI 48105 Office: PO Box 454 Frank Lloyd Dr Ann Arbor MI 48105

GRAY, PHILIP HOWARD, retired psychologist, educator; b. Cape Rosier, Maine, July 4, 1926; s. Asa and Bernice (Lawrence) G.; m. Iris McKinney, Dec. 31, 1954; children: Cindelyn Gray Eberts, Howard. M.A., U. Chgo., 1958; Ph.D., U. Wash., 1960. Asst. prof. dept. psychology Mont. State U., Bozeman, 1960-65; assoc. prof. Mont. State U., 1965-75, prof., 1975-92; ret., 1992; vis. prof. U. Man., Winnipeg, Can., 1968-70, U. N.H., 1965, U. Mont., 1967, 74, Tufts U., 1968, U. Conn., 1971; pres. Mont. Psychol. Assn., 1968-70 (helped write Mont. licensing law for psychologists); chmn. Mont. Bd. Psychologist Examiners, 1972-74; spkr. sci. and geneal. meetings on ancestry of U.S. presidents; presenter, instr. grad. course on serial killers and the psychopathology of murder. Organizer folk art exhbns. Mont. and Maine, 1972-79; author: The Comparative Analysis of Behavior, 1966, (with F.L. Ruch and N. Warren) Working with Psychology, 1963, A Directory of Eskimo Artists in Sculpture and Prints, 1974, The Science That Lost Its Mind, 1985, Penobscot Pioneers vol. 1, 1992, vol. 2, 1992, vol. 3, 1993, vol. 4, 1994, vol. 5, 1995, vol. 6, 1996; contbr. numerous articles on behavior to psychol. jours.; contbr. poetry to lit. jours. With U.S. Army, 1944-46. Recipient Am. and Can. research grants. Fellow AAAS, APA, Am. Psychol. Soc., Internat. Soc. Rsch. on Aggression; mem. NRA (life), SAR (v.p. Sourdough chpt. 1990, pres. 1991-96, trustee 1989, v.p. Mont. state soc. 1996—), Nat. Geneal. Soc., New Eng. Hist. Geneal. Soc., Gallatin County Geneal. Soc. (charter, pres. 1991-93), Deer Isle-Stonington Hist. Soc., Internat. Soc. Human Ethology, Descs. Illegitimate Sons and Daus. of Kings of Britain, Piscataque Pioneers, Order Desc. Colonial Physicians and Chirugiens, Flagon and Trencher, Order of the Crown of Charlemagne. Republican. Home: 1207 S Black Ave Bozeman MT 59715-5633

GRAY, RAYMOND GEORGE, clinical biochemist; b. Kingston-Upon-Hull, Yorkshire, Eng., Sept. 12, 1948; s. Frederick Harold and Eileen Edna (Johnson) G.; m. Anne Bernadette Higgins, Oct. 1, 1988. BSc, U. Hull, Eng., 1970; MSc, U. Newcastle, Eng., 1971; PhD, U. Sheffield, Eng., 1976. Rsch. asst. U. Sheffield, 1976-84; clin. biochemist Birmingham (Eng.) Childrens Hosp., 1984—. Author: Fetal and Neonatal Neurology and Neurosurgery, 1995; contbr. articles to profl. jours. Mem. Soc. for the Study of Inborn Errors of Metabolism, Assn. Clin. Biochemists, Brit. Soc. for Human Genetics. Office: Childrens Hosp Dept Clin Chemistry, Ladywood Middleway, Birmingham B16 8ET, England

GRAY, SHEILA HAFTER, psychiatrist, psychoanalyst; b. N.Y.C., Oct. 19, 1930; m. Oscar Shalom Gray, Apr. 8, 1967. MD, Harvard U., 1958. cert. Washington Psychoanalytic Inst., 1969. Intern St. Elizabeths Hosp., Washington, 1958-59; resident McLean Hosp., Belmont, Mass., 1959-61; clin. and rsch. fellow Mass. Gen. Hosp., Boston, Mass., 1961-62; staff psychiatrist Chestnut Lodge, Inc., Rockville, Md., 1962-64; practice medicine, specializing in psychiatry and psychoanalysis Washington, 1964—; clin. asst. prof. psychiatry U. Md. Sch. Medicine, Balt., 1968-75, clin. assoc. prof., 1975-83, clin. prof., 1983—; instr. Washington Psychoanalytic Inst., 1971-75, tchg. analyst, 1975-96; tchg. analyst Balt.-Washington Inst. for Psychoanalysis, 1996—; mem. staff U. Md. Hosp., Balt.; physician mem. Commn. on Mental Health, Superior Ct. of D.C., 1972—; bd. govs. Nat. Capital Reciprocal Ins. Co., 1981—; treas. NCRIC Physicians Orgn., 1994—; cons. Walter Reed Army Med. Ctr., Washington, 1983—. Mem. Mayor's Adv. Com. on Mental Health Svcs. Reorgn., Washington, 1984; mem. adv. panel for Mayor's Environ. Design Awards Program, 1988-89; mem. exec. com. D.C. Fedn. Civic Assns., 1984—, asst. rec. sec., 1985, rec. sec., 1986-88, 2d v.p., 1989-90, pres., 1991-92, del.-at-large, 1993—; v.p. programs Women's Equity Action League Met. D.C., 1986; commr. D.C. Adv. Neighborhood Commn., 1986-88; mem. Met. Washington Coun. of Govt.'s Partnership for Regional Excellence, 1992—. Fellow Am. Psychiat. Assn. (chair com. quality assurance and improvement, Coun. on Econ. Affairs, 1996—); mem. Am. Psychoanalytic Assn. (diplomate Bd. Profl. Stds.), Am. Acad. Psychoanalysis (trustee 1996—), Washington Psychiatric Soc. (councillor 1981-83), Med. Soc. D.C. (exec. bd. 1982, ho. dels. 1992—), Washington Psychoanalytic Soc. (chmn. bd. dirs. psychoanalytic clinic and councillor ex officio 1987-90), Palisades Citizens Assn. (bd. dirs. 1980—, treas. 1983-84, pres. 1984-86). Office: PO Box 40612 Palisades Sta Washington DC 20016

GRAY, WILLIAM, psychiatrist; b. Omaha, May 31, 1917; s. William and Nettie (Ellenbogen) G.; m. Lucille Pearl Radlo, Mar. 19, 1944; children: Carolyn A., Edward S., Nicholas. Student, Creighton U., 1934-37; BS in Medicine, U. Nebr., 1940, MD, 1941. Diplomate Am. Bd. Psychiatry and Neurology. Intern Michael Reese Hosp., Chgo., 1941-42, resident, 1942-43; resident in medicine Beth Israel Hosp., Boston, 1943-44, Sch. Military Neuropsychiatry Mason Gen. Hosp., Brentwood, N.Y., 1944-45; resident in psychiatry Worcester State Hosp., Cushing VA Hosp., Boston U. Med. Ctr., Boston VA Outpatient Mental Hygiene Clinic, 1947-48; staff psychiatrist West Roxbury VA Hosp., Mass., 1949; resident in psychiatry Beth Israel Hosp., Boston, 1950, visiting psychiatrist, 1951-56; staff psychiatrist VA Outpatient Clinic, Boston, 1956-65; chief psychiatrist VA Mental Hygiene Clinic, Worcester, Mass., 1965-71, Springfield, Mass., 1968-74; vis. psychiatrist outpatient clinic Mass. Gen. Hosp., Boston, 1965-68; dir. Malden (Mass.) Ct. Clinic, Mass. Dept. Mental Health, 1969-83; cons. in psychiatry Mission of the Immaculate Virgin, S.I., N.Y., 1978-79; pvt. practice of psychiatry Boston and Newton, Mass., 1951—; cons. in field. Editor: Gen. Systems Theory and Psychiatry, 1969, Unity Through Diversity, 1973, General Systems Theory and the Psychological Sciences, 1982; cons. editor: Man-Environment Systems, 1986—; contbr. numerous articles to profl. jours. Capt. U.S. Army, 1944-46. Recipient Award of Distinction Assn. for the Profl. Treatment of Offenders, 1979. Fellow Am. Psychiat. Assn. (life); mem. AAAS, Assn. for Study Man and Environ. Rels., Mass. Med. Soc., Am. Assn. for Social Psychiatry, World Assn. for Social Psychiatry. Home and Office: 58 Pine Crest Rd Newton MA 02159-2118

GRAY, W(ILLIAM) MICHAEL, biology educator; b. Salt Lake City, Apr. 8, 1950; s. Thomas Leland and Shirley Lois (Hoffman) G.; m. Carol Ann Cleaver, June 4, 1971; children: Heidi, Jennifer, William, Colin, Melissa. BS, Bob Jones U., Greenville, S.C., 1971; MS, Clemson U., 1974, PhD, 1978. Chmn. sci. dept. Lynchburg (Va.) Christian Acad., 1971-72; grad. teaching asst. Clemson (S.C.) U., 1972-77; chmn. biology dept. Pensacola (Fla.) Christian Coll., 1978-81; prof. biology Bob Jones U., Greenville, S.C., 1981—, chmn. sci. edn. dept., 1985-90; textbook cons. A Beka Book Publs., Pensacola, 1978-81; editl. cons. in cell and molecular biology Garland Pub., N.Y.C., 1994—; microbiology cons. to pharm. mfg. cos., Greenville, S.C. and Bohemia, N.Y., 1984-89; mem. agrl. biotech. policy adv. com., Clemson U., 1987; spkr. ednl. workshops, 1988—; mem. com. on nat. tchr. exams. S.C. Dept. Edn., 1987, mem. sci. curriculum com., 1991-95, 1st S.C. Curriculum Congress; presenter various sci. meetings on methods in anaerobic microbiology, 1973-79. Sci. fair judge Am. Assn. Christian Schs., 1985—, local pub. high schs. and Upper S.C. regional competition, 1986, 87, 89; mem. corp. spelling bee team Greenville Literacy Assn., 1990; tchr. adult Sunday sch. Faith Bapt. Ch., Taylors, S.C., 1990—. Mem. Am. Soc. Microbiology (scientist educator teams 1992-95). Home: 120 Twinbrook Dr Greenville SC 29607-1214 Office: Bob Jones U 1700 Wade Hampton Blvd Greenville SC 29614-1000

GRAYBIEL, ASHTON, physician, researcher, administrator; b. Boston, July 16, 1938; s. Ashton Graybiel and Moira (Barkley) Martin. AB, Harvard U., 1961; BS, U. N.D., 1963; MD, Wake Forest U., 1965. Commd. ensign USN, 1964, advanced through grades to comdr., 1972, resigned, 1974; intern Bethesda (Md.) Naval Hosp., 1966-67, resident in internal medicine, 1968-71, resident in rheumatology, 1970-71; ptnr. Rheumatology Assocs., Pensacola, Fla., 1974—; med. dir. Rheumatology Assocs. Lab., Pensacola, 1974-91; asst. prof. rheumatology La. State U. Sch. Medicine, New Orleans, 1974-86. Fellow Am. Rheumatism Assn. (founding); mem. ACP. Office: 2441 N 9th Ave Pensacola FL 32503-3911

GRAY-NIX, ELIZABETH WHITWELL, occupational therapist; b. Milton, Mass., Apr. 9, 1956; d. Roland and Susan (Brooks) Gray; m. Ronald Harding Nix; 1 child, Roger Harrison Nix. BS, Utica Coll. of Syracuse U., N.Y., 1978. Reg. occupational therapist. Staff occupational therapist Walter E. Fernald State Sch., Waltham, Mass., 1978-82; head occupational therapist Walter E. Fernald State Sch., 1982-84, clin. supr., 1984—. Trustee Mass. Jaycees Charitable Trust, Mansfield, 1983-91; dir.-at-large South End Hist. Soc., Boston, 1983-85, fundraising dir., 1985-87; alumni rep. Beaver country Day Sch., Brookline, 1974—, alumni sec., 1988-94. 0ecipient Baystater award #060, Mass. Jaycees, 1984, Armbruster Keyman award, 1981, Award of Merit, Maddak, Inc., 1991, 96, Jaycee Internat. Senatorship award, 1992. Mem. Mass. Occupational Therapists Assn., State Employed Occupational Therapists Assn. (union rep.), Am. Occupational Therapists Assn., World Fedn. Occupational Therapists, Jaycees Internat. (Mass. sec., pres. Riverside chpt. 1983, mem. coun. Newton chpt. 1979-82, state sec. 1994-95), Boston Ctr. for Arts (mem. coun. 1979-84). Home: 90 Pelham Island Rd Sudbury MA 01776-3132 Office: Walter E Fernald Devel Ctr 200 Trapelo Rd Waltham MA 02154-6332

GRAYSON, HENRY, psychoanalyst; b. Atmore, Ala., Oct. 25, 1935; s. Henry T. and Ethel (Sageser) G.; m. Elizabeth Cauthen, Apr. 1, 1959; children: Pegine, Douglas; m. Pamela Pirnie, May 30, 1987; 1 child, Christopher. AB, Asbury Coll., 1957; BD, Emory U., 1960; STM, Boston U., 1963, PhD, 1967, postdoctoral cert., psychoanalysis and psychotherapy Postgrad. Ctr. for Mental Health, N.Y.C., 1971. Diplomate Am. Bd. Profl. Psychology, Am. Bd. Psychotherapy; lic. psychologist, N.Y. Instr. dept. psychology Mt. Ida Jr. Coll., Newton, Mass., 1963-67; from asst. to assoc. prof. CUNY, Bklyn., 1967-78; sole practice psychology, N.Y.C., 1967—; founder, exec. dir. Nat. Inst. Psychotherapies, N.Y.C., 1970-82, chmn. bd., 1970—; dir. Counseling & Family Therapy Assocs., Mahopac and Croton-on-Hudson, N.Y. 1981—; bd. dirs. Ctr. Marital and Family Therapy, N.Y.C., 1981-94; founder, dir., Am. Eating Disorders Ctr., N.Y.C., 1983—; pres. F.A.T. Seminars, N.Y.C., 1982-87. Author: Three Psychotherapies, 1975; author, editor: Short-term Approaches to the Psychotherapies, 1979, Changing Approaches to the Psychotherapies, 1978. Fellow Am. Group Psychotherapy Assn.; mem. Assn. Humanistic Psychology, Am. Anorexia & Bulimia Assn., Ea. Group Psychotherapy Soc. (treas. 1978-79), Am. Psychol.

Assn., Am. Acad. Psychotherapists, N.Y. State Psychol. Assn., Conn. Psychol. Assn. Office: 330 W 58th St New York NY 10019-1827 also: 3 Mystic Ln Westport CT 06880

GRAYSTON, J. THOMAS, medical and public health educator; b. Wichita, Kans., Sept. 6, 1924; s. Jesse T. and Luzia B. (Thomas) G.; children: Susan, Jesse, David; m. M. Nan Bryant, June 7, 1980. Student, Carleton Coll., 1942-43; B.S., U. Chgo., 1947, M.D., 1948, M.S., 1952. Diplomate: Am. Bd. Internal Medicine, Am. Bd. Preventive Medicine. Intern Albany (N.Y.) Med. Sch., 1948-49; Seymour Coman fellow preventive medicine U. Chgo., 1949-50, asst. resident medicine, 1950-51; epidemiologist epidemic intelligence service USPHS, U. Kans. Med. Center, 1951-53; chief resident medicine U. Chgo., 1953-54, instr. medicine, 1953-55; fellow Nat. Found. Infantile Paralysis, 1954-56; asst. prof. medicine U. Chgo., 1955-60, asso. prof., 1960; chief div. microbiology and epidemiology U.S. Naval Med. Research Unit 2, Taipei, Taiwan, 1957-60; cons. U.S. Naval Med. Research Unit 2, 1960-79; prof. preventive medicine, chmn. dept. Sch. Medicine, U. Wash., 1960-70, founding dean Sch. Pub. Health and Community Medicine, 1970-71, v.p. for health scis., 1971-83, prof. dept. epidemiology, 1970—, adj. prof. pathobiology, 1982—; mem. exec. com. Regional Primate Research Center, 1964-70, research affiliate, 1967-70; attending physician medicine Univ. Hosp., Seattle, 1960-70; asso. mem. commn. acute respiratory diseases Armed Forces Epidemiol. Bd., 1962-65, mem., 1965-73; mem. research and engrng. adv. panel biology and medicine Dept. Def., 1963-67; sci. group trachoma research WHO, 1963; virology and rickettsiology study sect. NIH, 1963-67; mem. internat. centers com. Nat. Inst. Allergy and Infectious Diseases, 1967-71; mem. expert adv. panel on Trachoma, WHO, 1970-88; chmn. exec. com., mem. nat. adv. council on health professions edn. NIH, 1972-75. Contbr. numerous articles to profl. jours. Fellow Am. Coll. Preventive Medicine (v.p. gen. preventive medicine 1970-71, regent 1971-74), Am. Pub. Health Assn. (governing bd. 1978-80); mem. Am. Assn. Immunologists, Am. Assn. Physicians, Am. Epidemiol. Soc. (pres. 1982-83), Am. Fedn. Clin. Research, Am. soc. Microbiology, Am. Soc. Clin. Investigation, Am. Soc. Tropical Medicine and Hygiene, Assn. Acad. Health Centers (dir. 1975-80, pres. 1978-79), Assn. Tchrs. Preventive Medicine, Infectious Diseases Soc., Internat. Epidemiol. Assn., Soc. Exptl. Biology and Medicine, Inst. Medicine of Nat. Acad. Scis., Western Assn. Physicians, Western Soc. Clin. Rsch. Office: U Washington Dept Epidemiology Box 357236 Seattle WA 98195

GRAZIANI, JEANNE PATRICIA, health facility administrator; b. Cooperstown, N.Y., Jan. 7, 1957; d. Jospeh Patrick and Catherine Lucey (Kelly) Killian; children from previous marriage, Jessica Patricia Johnson, Christina Catherine Johnson; m. Anthony E. Graziani, Sept. 5, 1992. AS, SUNY, Farmingdale, 1982; BS, SUNY, Stony Brook, 1984. Registered respiratory therapist; cert. profl. healthcare quality. Clinician IV, neonatal and pediatric specialist Univ. Hosp., Stony Brook, 1984-87; supervising pulmonary function technologist Syosset (N.Y.) Community Hosp., 1987-95; mgr. credentialing, adminstr. clin. performance improvement Queens-L.I. Med. Group, P.C., Uniondale, N.Y., 1995—; mem. Nat. Bd. Respiratory Care. Mem. Am. Heart Assn., Am. Lung Assn., Happauge, N.Y., 1987—. Recipient honors award, cert. appreciation McMahon Svcs. for Children, N.Y.C., 1991. Mem. NAFE, Nat. Parks and Conservation Assn., Nat. Assn. Healthcare Quality. Republican. Mem. Christian Ch. Office: Queens L I Med Group P C West Tower 12th Fl 106 EAB Plz Uniondale NY 11556

GRAZIANI, LEONARD JOSEPH, pediatric neurologist, researcher; b. Phila., Nov. 17, 1929; s. Annibale and Norina (Ditomasi) G.; m. Amelia Honeyford, June 29, 1956; children: Paul, Amy, Virginia, David. BA, LaSalle Coll., Phila., 1951; MD, Jefferson Med. Coll., Phila., 1955. Diplomate Am. Bd. Pediatrics, Am. Bd. Psychiatry and Neurology. Intern Valley Forge Army Hosp., Pa., 1956; resident Brooke Army Hosp., San Antonio, 1959; chief pediatric svc. Ireland Army Hosp., Ft. Knox, Ky., 1960-61; neurology fellow Bronx Mcpl. Hosp. Ctr., N.Y., 1961-64; interdisciplinary fellow Albert Einstein Coll. Medicine, Bronx, N.Y., 1964-66, asst. prof. pediatrics and neurology, 1964-68; career scientist Health Rsch. Coun., N.Y.C., 1967-68; attending pediatrician, neurologist Thomas Jefferson U. Hosp., Phila., 1968—; chief div. pediatric neurology dept. pediatrics Jefferson Med. Coll., Thomas Jefferson U., Phila., 1974—, vice chair dept. pediatrics, 1988—, prof. pediatrics, neurology, 1968—; cons. neurologist The Woods Schs., Langhorne, Pa., 1968—, Children's Rehab. Hosp., Phila.; cons. pediatrician Wills Eye Hosp., Phila.; staff cons. Wilmington (Del.) Med. Ctr.; staff E.I. duPont Inst., Wilmington, 1984—. Contbr. articles to profl. jours. Capt. U.S. Army, 1955-61. Fellow Am. Acad. Neurology, Am. Acad. Pediatrics; mem. Am. Pediatric Soc., Soc. Pediatric Rsch., Child Neurology Soc., Alpha Omega Alpha, Sigma Xi. Office: Jefferson Med Coll 1025 Walnut St Philadelphia PA 19107-5001

GREACEN, SHARON HOPE O'NEAL, microbiologist, medical technologist; b. Omaha, Nov. 21, 1942; d. Donald Merideth and Eleanor Doris (Palasek) S.; m. Jerry Lynn O'Neal, Aug. 3, 1963 (div. Mar. 1975); m. Thomas Edmund Greacen III, Sept. 2, 1988; children: Tamara Cherie O'Neal, Bryan Segard O'Neal, Christopher Edmund Greacen, Abigal Greacen. Music, pharmacy, U. Nebr., Lincoln, 1963; MS in Microbiology, ID State, Pocatello, 1966, MS in Med. Tec., 1967, grad. sch., 1972. Med. Technologist. Med. technologist Med. Coll. Hosp., Charleston, S.C., 1968-69; dir. regional lab. ID State Pub. Health, Pocatello, ID, 1969-75; supr. adminstrv. med. tech./microbiologist Physicians Med. Labs., Portland, Oreg., 1975-76; microbiology supr. Internat. Clinic labs., Memphis, 1976-78; adm. med. tech./microbiology U. Tenn. Med. Coll., Memphis, 1978-80; supr. med. tech. Grady Meml. Hosp., Atlanta, 1980-82; microbiology supr. Med. Tech. U.S. Pub. Health Svc., Tuba City, Ariz., 1982-88; occupational safety and health mgr. USPHS Indian Health Svc., Tuba City, Ariz., 1988-90; lab. mgr. U.S. Pub. Health Svc., Dulce, N.Mex., 1990—; community coll. instructor, Yavapi Community Coll., Prescott, Ariz., 1984-85, Navajo Community Coll. Tsaile, Ariz., 1986-88; microbiology cons. Navajo Area Pub. Health Svc., Window Rock, Ariz., 1986-88; expert witness, Micro State of ID, Pocatello, ID, 1973-75; music tchr., Environ. Ind. 1960-66. Author: Swimming Pool Operators, Public Health, Food Handlers, GC. Mem. Young Rep., Long Beach, Calif., 1960. Recipient Performance Awards, Med. Coll. Hosp., Memphis, 1978; Womens Mgmt. Training Initiative, U.S. Dept. of Health and Welfare, Washington, 1988-89. Mem. Nat. Assn. of Female Execs., nat. Assn. of Univ. Women, Am. Soc. of Microbiologists, Am. Soc. of Med. Techs. Sec. Republican. Lutheran. Home: PO Box 997 Dulce NM 87528-0997 Office: US Pub Health Svc Dulce Health Ctr Dulce NM 87528

GREATBATCH, WILSON, biomedical engineer; b. Buffalo, Sept. 6, 1919; married; 5 children. BEE, Cornell U., 1950; MSEE, U. Buffalo, 1957; ScD (hon.), Houghton Coll., 1971, SUNY, Buffalo, 1984, Clarkson U., 1987, Roberts Wesleyan Coll., 1988. Project engr. Cornell Aeronaut Lab. Inc., 1950-52; asst. prof. elec. engring. U. Buffalo, 1952-57; mgr. electronics div. Taber Instrument Corp., 1957-60; v.p. Mennen Greatbatch Electronics Inc., 1962-78; adj. prof. elec. engring. SUNY, Buffalo, 1981—; adj. prof. engring. Cornell U., Ithaca, N.Y., 1989—; adj. prof. physical scis. Houghton (N.Y.) Coll., 1978—. Contbr. over 100 articles to sci. jours; holder over 150 U.S. and fgn. patents. Recipient Holley medal ASME, 1986, Chancellor Morton medal U. Buffalo, 1990, disting. svc. award NSPE, 1984, Pacemaker award Prince Rainier of Monaco, 1988, Nat. Medal of Tech. Pres. Bush, 1990, Vladimir Karapetoff award Eta Kappa Nu, 1992, Washington award Western Engrng. Soc., Chgo., 1995; named to Am. Inventors Hall of Fame, 1986, U.s. Space Tech. Hall of Fame, 1993; Paul Harris fellow Rotary Internat., 1993. Fellow AAAS, IEEE, Am. Coll. Cardiology, Royal Soc. Health, Am. Soc. Angiology, Am. Inst. Med. and Biol. Engrng. (founder), N.Y. Acad. Scis.; mem. NAE, Am. Soc. Mech. Engring., Assn. Advancement Med. Instrumentation (Laufman award 1982), Sigma Xi. Office: Greatbatch Gen Aid Ltd 10871 Main St Clarence NY 14031-1724

GREATHOUSE, JOANNE S., radiographer; b. Canton, Ill., Feb. 9; d. Martin R. and Mary L. (Abbadusky) Ludwig; m. George D. Greathouse, June 5, 1971. BA in English, Carthage Coll., Kenosha, Wis., 1971; Radiography Diploma, Meth. Hosp., Peoria, Ill., 1973; MEd in Adult Edn., Va. Commonwealth U., 1978; CAGS, Va. Poly. Inst. and State U., 1982; EdS in Higher Edn. Adminstrn., Coll. William and Mary, 1989. Registered radiologic technologist. Clin. instr./radiographer Meth. Hosp. Ctrl. Ill., Peoria, 1973-74; radiographer Med. Coll. Va. Hosps., Richmond, 1974-75, nuclear medicine technologist, 1975-76, assoc. prof./dept. chair, 1976—; cons. Pa. Dept. Edn., 1988, Fla. Dept. Edn., 1990; mem. med. adv. bd. EDUMED Corp., Lakeville, Minn., 1995—; accreditation site visitor/team chair Joint Rev. Com. on Edn. in Radiologic Tech., Chgo., 1976—. Contbr. articles to profl. jours.; chair editl. rev. bd. Radiologic Tech., 1995—. Vol. Am. Heart Assn. Named to Outstanding Young Women of Am., 1978-83. Fellow Am. Soc. Radiologic Technologists; mem. Va. Soc. Radiologic Technologists (life, pres., bd. dirs., chmn. Geisberger Lectr. 1986, Ailsworth award 1987), Assn. Educators in Radiol. Scis., Capital Dist. Soc., Radiologic Technologists (pres.), Am. Legion Aux., Alpha Mu Gamma, Sigma Lambda, Sigma Tau Delta, Phi Kappa Phi, Kappa Delta Pi. Lutheran. Office: Virginia Commonwealth Univ Dept Radiation Scis Box 980495 Richmond VA 23248-0495

GREATHOUSE, RICHARD FRANCIS, pediatrician; b. Wilmore, Ky., July 28, 1923; s. Robert Edward and Gladys (Millard) G.; m. Martha, Apr. 5, 1945 (div. 1995); children: Richard Lee, Stephen Patrick, Kathryn Ann (dec.), Carolyn June. BS, U. Ky, 1947; MD, U. Louisville, 1951. Diplomate Am. Bd. Pediatrics. Clin. prof. pediatrics Sch. Medicine U. Louisville, Louisville, 1955—; coroner Jefferson County, Louisville, 1974-96; cons. Dept. Human Resources, Frankfort, Ky., 1971-92, Jefferson County Dept. Human Resources, Louisville, 1987-92. Author: (with others) Post Hospital Management of Diabetes, 1963. Bd. dirs. March of Dimes, Louisville, 1970-80, Suicide Prevention, Louisville, 1983-86. Capt. USNR, 1943-85, ret. Fellow Am. Acad. Pediatrics (vice chmn. Ky. chpt. 1962-70); mem. Internat. Assn. Coroners and Med. Examiners (pres. 1980), Ky. Med. Assn. (speaker ho. of dels. 1968-78, Svc. award 1978), Jefferson County Med. Soc. (del. to Ky. Med. Assn. 1968-78), Am. Acad. Forensic Scis., Big Springs Country Club, Masons (sr. warden 1947-48). Democrat. Home and Office: 3806 Taylorsville Rd Louisville KY 40220-1304

GREAVES, IAN ALEXANDER, occupational physician; b. Darwin, Australia, June 1, 1947; came to U.S., 1981; s. George A. and Norma J. (Blair) G.; m. Alison Mary Street, Nov. 23, 1972 (div. 1985); m. Melana Dee Catlett, June 19, 1987. BSc in Medicine, Monash U., 1969, MB BS, 1971. Med. resident Alfred Hosp., Melbourne, Australia, 1972-75; med. registrar Prince Henry Hosp., Sydney, Australia, 1976-77; rsch. fellow U NSW, Sydney, 1978-80; vis. fellow Harvard Sch. Pub. Health, Boston, 1981-83, asst. prof., then assoc. prof., 1983-89; assoc. prof., div. head environ. and occupational health U. Minn. Sch. Pub. Health, Mpls., 1989—; mem. com. on toxicology Nat. Acad. Sci., Washington, 1989-95; dir. Midwest Ctr. Occupational Health and Safety, Mpls., 1990—, Minn. Ctr. Rsch. in Agrl. Safety and Health, Mpls., 1991—. Contbr. articles to profl. publs. Recipient Outstanding Svc. award Am. Lung Assn. Mass., 1989. Fellow AAAS; mem. Assn. Univ Programs in Occupational Health and Safety (pres. 1990-95). Office: U Minn Box 807 420 Delaware St SE Minneapolis MN 55455-0374

GREBLER, ARNOLD M., urologist; b. Newark, June 2, 1945; m. Jill Grebler; children: Hallie, Marisa. BA, Rutgers U., 1967, MS, 1968; MD, U. Bologna, 1974. Pvt. practice Long Branch, N.J., 1979-83, 1984—. Fellow ACS, Acad. Medicine N.J., Am. Soc. for Laser Medicine and Surgery; mem. Urol. Soc. N.J. (v.p. 1995-96). Office: Shore Urology PA 279 3d Ave Long Branch NJ 07740

GRECCO, PATRICK RONALD, psychologist; b. Bronx, Jan. 14, 1949; s. Nicholas Peter and Rose (DiLorenzo) G.; children: Elizabeth, Nicholas, Emily. BA, NYU, 1970; MA, Columbia U., 1976, MEd, 1977; PhD, Calif. Sch. Profl. Psychology, 1980. Lic. psychologist, N.Y., Pa. Vol. U.S. Peace Corps, Niger, West Africa, 1970-71; caseworker Mission of the Immaculate Virgin, S.I., N.Y., 1971-74; with N.Y. State Dept. Social Svcs., N.Y.C., 1974-75; mental health technician St. Vincents Med. Ctr. of S.I., 1976-77; vocat. rehab. counselor N.Y.State Dept. Edn., S.I., 1977-80; lectr., counselor Chestnut Hill Coll., Phila., 1985-86; clin. cons. U. Pa., Ctr. for Cognitive Therapy, Phila., 1985-88; psychologist Charles Drew Community Mental Health Ctr., Phila., 1986-87, N.Y. Foundling Hosp., S.I., 1987—; counselor Fresno City Coll., 1983-84; doctoral intern Merced County Cmty. Mental Health Ctr., 1982-83, The Bridge, Merced, 1981-83; postdoctoral fellow Med. Sch. U. Pa., 1984-85; cons. Svc. Cognitive Therapy Ctr. N.Y., 1992-94; behavior specialist Penn Found., Sellersville, Pa., 1993-95. Fellow Am. Psychol. Assn.; mem. Allied Assn. in Mental Health (pres. 1995—), Pa. Psychol. Assn. Office: One Chesney Ln Erdenheim PA 19038-7801

GRECO, JOSEPH M., physician; b. Tyler, Tex., Apr. 2, 1945; s. Pasquale A. and Dorothy (Davies) G.; m. Cheryl Zupon, Aug. 4, 1979; children: Jessica, Rebecca, Alexander, J. Brady. BA, Yankton Coll., 1968; MD, SUNY, Buffalo, 1973. Diplomate Am. Bd. Urology. Resident Millard Fillmore Hosps., Buffalo, 1970-71, staff urologist, 1979; resident Johns Hopkins Hosp., Balt., 1973-75, fellow nat. prostatic cancer project Am. Cancer Soc., 1976-77; clin. asst. prof. SUNY, Buffalo, 1979; pvt. practice Amherst Urology, P.C., Buffalo, 1977-79; active staff Sister's Hosp.; courtesy staff Buffalo Gen. Hosp., Children's Hosp. Buffalo, Kenmore Mercy Hosp., Roswell Park Cancer Inst., St. Joseph Hosp., W. Seneca Devel. Ctr. Office: Amherst Urology PC Windsong Med Park 55 Spindrift Dr Ste 240 Buffalo NY 14221 also: Gates Circle Med Bldg 50 Gates Cir Buffalo NY 14209 also: Amherst Urology PC 6000 Brocton Dr Ste 102 Lockport NY 14094

GRECO, RALPH STEVEN, surgeon, researcher, medical educator; b. N.Y.C., May 25, 1942; s. Charles Mario and Lydia Antoinette (Barone) G.; m. Irene Leonor Wapnir, Feb. 23, 1991; children: Justin Michael, Eric Matthew, Ilana Rose. BS, Fordham U., 1964; MD, Yale U., 1968. Instr. Yale U., New Haven, 1972-73; asst. prof. Rutgers Med. Sch., Piscataway, N.J., 1975-79; assoc. prof. Med. Sch. Rutgers U., Piscataway, N.J., 1979-83; chief of gen. surgery Robert Wood Johnson Med. Sch. U. Medicine & Dentistry of N.J., New Brunswick, 1982—, prof. Robert Wood Johnson Med. Sch., 1983—; vice chmn. Dept. of Surgery, 1993; cons. Nat. Heart, Lung and Blood Inst.-NSF, Bethesda, Md., 1981. Contbr. articles to profl. jours. Maj. U.S. Army, 1973-75. NHLBI grantee, 1980-84. Fellow Am. Surg. Assn.; mem. Soc. Univ. Surgeons. Home: 2 Quail Run Warren NJ 07059-7134 Office: U Medicine & Dentistry NJ Robert Wood Johnson Med Sch 1 Robert Wood Johnson Pl # 19cn New Brunswick NJ 08901-1928

GREDEN, JOHN FRANCIS, psychiatrist, educator; b. Winona, Minn., July 24, 1942; m. Renee Mary Kalmes; children: Daniel John, Sarah Renee, Leigh Raymond. BS, U. Minn., 1965, MD, 1967. Diplomate Am. Bd. Psychiatry and Neurology. Assoc. dir. psychiat. research Walter Reed Army Med. Ctr., Washington, 1972-74; asst. prof. Dept. Psychiatry U. Mich., Ann Arbor, 1974-77, assoc. prof., 1977-81, dir. clin. studies unit for affective disorders, 1980-85, prof., 1981—, chmn., research scientist, 1985—. Contbr. 188 articles to profl. jours., 28 chpts. to books. Served to maj. U.S. Army, 1969-74. Recipient A.E. Bennett research award Cen. Neuropsychiat. Found., 1974, Ralph Patterson Meml. award Ohio State U., 1980, Nolan D.C. Lewis Vis. Scholar award Carrier Found., 1982. Fellow Am. Psychiat. Assn.; mem. AAAS, Soc. Biol. Psychiatry (past pres.), Am. Coll. Neuropsychopharmacology, Psychiat. Rsch. Soc. (past pres.). Office: U Mich Med Ctr Dept Psychiatry 1500 E Medical Ctr Dr Ann Arbor MI 48109-0704*

GREELEY, JAMES MICHAEL, surgeon; b. Providence, Sept. 15, 1937; s. Joseph Edward and Isabel (Gibbons) G.; m. Jacquelin Kierstead, June 21, 1958; children: David Michael, Pamela Holly. MD, Med. U. S.C., 1974. Diplomate Am. Bd. Surgery. Commd. capt. USAF, 1978—, advanced through grades to col., 1993; commdr. ops. squadron USAF, Bilcxi, Miss.; intern, resident Richland Meml. Hosp., 1974-79. Mem. ACS, NBME, SBGES, AHA. Office: 81st Med Group Keesler AFB MS 31098-1149

GREEN, ARTHUR CHRISTOPHER HAUGHTON, pediatrician; b. Belfast, Northern Ireland, Feb. 23, 1943; arrived in Australia, 1973; s. Ronald Frank and Margaret (McBride) G.; m. Hilary Boal, Mar. 10, 1973; children: James, Timothy. B in Medicine and Surgery, Queens U., Belfast, 1968. Tng. pediatrician, 1968-76; cons. pediatrician, lectr. in child health Queens U., 1976-79; head child devel. unit Childrens Hosp. of Sydney, Australia, 1979—. Author: Toddler Taming, 1984, 86, 90, Babies, 1988, Understanding ADD, 1994. Fellow Coll. Physicians Ireland, Royal Coll. Physicians Australia; mem. Coll. Physicians U.K. Office: The Childrens Hosp Sydney, Child Devel Unit, Westmead Sydney 2145, Australia

GREEN, BARBARA STRAWN, psychotherapist; b. Cleve., May 31, 1938; d. Charles Everard and Dorothy Haring (Strawn) G. BA, Pa. State U., 1960; MS, Columbia U., 1962; postgrad. in psychotherapy and psychoanalysis, Postgrad. Ctr. for Mental Health, N.Y.C., 1975. Cert. social worker, N.Y.; lic. social worker, Pa.; cert. Rutgers Summer Sch. Alcoholism Studies, 1982. Social worker VA, N.Y.C., 1962-66; sr. psychiat. social worker in child psychiat. Downstate Med. Ctr., Bklyn., 1966-71; staff therapist Inst. for Contemporary Psychotherapy, N.Y.C., 1971-73; social worker Lower East Side Service Ctr., N.Y.C., 1975-77; intake coordinator alcoholism program Postgrad. Ctr. for Mental Health, N.Y.C., 1981-82; program coordinator Bowery Residents Com., N.Y.C., 1984-86; pvt. practice psychotherapy N.Y.C., 1973—, Dingmans Ferry, Pa., 1994—; sec. alcoholism com. N.Y.C. chpt. NASW, 1987-89. Author: Jogging the Mind, 1995. Participant N.Y.C. Marathon, 1991, 92. Mem. Social Workers Helping Social Workers (chmn. 1982-84).

GREEN, BART N., chiropractor; b. Whittier, Calif., Jan. 12, 1968; s. Larry G. and Lyndell R. (Welch) G.; m. Claire D. Johnson, July 31, 1993. AA, AS, Mt. San Antonio Coll., 1989; D of Chiropractic, L.A. Coll. Chiropractic, 1992. Diplomate Am. Chiropractic Bd. of Sports Physicians. Chiropractic pvt. practice, Whittier, Calif., 1994—; instr. L.A. Coll. Chiropractic, Whittier, Calif., 1993-95, asst. prof., 1995—. Contbr. articles to profl. jours. Team dr. Chevrolet/L.A. Sheriff's Cycling, So. Calif., 1995-96. Mem. Assn. History of Chiropractic (bd. dirs. 1995—). Office: LA Coll Chiropractic 16200 E Amber Valley Dr Whittier CA 90609

GREEN, BETH INGBER, intuitive practitioner, counselor, musician, composer; b. N.Y.C., Feb. 28, 1945; d. Frank and Lillian Ingber; m. John Ingber Green, 1995. BA, Bklyn. Coll., 1970; MA, UCLA, 1978. Cert. in intuitive consulting, counseling, tchg. and learning, body and kinetic intervention. Spiritual dir. and founder The Stream, L.A., 1980-86; ptnr., co-founder The Healing Partnership, L.A. and Ramona, 1986-90; spiritual dir. and founder The Triple Eye Found., Escondido, Calif., 1990-93; intuitive practitioner, counselor, cons. and tchr. Ramona, 1980—; owner Let's Talk, Ramona, Calif.; spiritual activist, co-founder Rising Mountains Setting Suns, Ramona, 1993-95; co-founder Spiritual Activist Movement, L.A. and Ramona, 1993-95; owner Treehouse Music. Author: The Autobiography of Mary Magdalene, 1988; spoken tapes include: The Healing of God, The Alienation of Love, Spirituality: The Last Block to Freedom, Beyond the Mystery, Sasa in the Clouds; videotapes include Breaking the "I" Barrier, 19. West Coast coord. Wages for Housework Campaign, L.A., 1974-78; co-founder The Looseleaf Directory: Linking Bodies, Minds and Spirits in the Healing Arts, 1994-95.

GREEN, BEVERLY JEAN, nurse; b. Ithaca, N.Y., Aug. 6, 1955; d. Arthur W. Sr. and Edna M. (Pearson) G. Diploma, Arnot-Ogden Sch. Nursing, 1977. RN, S.C.; cert. ACLS, CEN, trauma nursing care course, pediatric advanced life support. Staff RN Arnot Ogden Meml. Hosp., Elmira, N.Y., 1977-88; staff nurse Loris (S.C.) Comty. Hosp., 1988-94; staff RN, supr. Columbia-Brunswick Hosp., Supply, N.C., 1988—. Mem. Emergency Nurses Assn. Home: 2140 Adams Cir Little River SC 29566-9111

GREEN, CHRISTINA BERRY, optometrist; b. Athens, Greece, Aug. 7, 1964; came to U.S., 1981; d. Richard Erwin and Sophie Sirpoui (Vozikian) Berry; m. Richard Brandt Green, May 19, 1990; children: Collin, Alexandra. BA in Biology, Rollins Coll., Winter Park, Fla., 1985; OD, U. Houston, 1990. Lic. optometrist Fla., Colo. Resident Medivision, Miami, Fla., 1990-91; optometrist Visionworks, Miami, 1991-93; optometrist/techr. Southeastern Coll., Miami, 1992-93, Optical Masters, Denver, 1993—. Mem. Kappa Alpha Theta. Home: 11245 E Parker Rd Parker CO 80134

GREEN, DAVID ROBERT JOHN, development scientist, researcher; b. Romford, Essex, Eng., Mar. 24, 1959; s. Robert Douglas and Doreen Joan (Rand) G.; m. Elisabeth Caton Pollard, Oct. 1, 1988; children: Luke Samuel Matthew, Daniel Thomas. BSc, Salford (Eng.) U., 1981; PhD, Liverpool (Eng.) U., 1985. Rsch. technician Shell Rsch. Ltd., Sittingbourne, Eng., 1979-80; rsch. assoc. Liverpool U., 1984-87; scientist oral care rsch. Colgate Palmolive, Manchester, Eng., 1987-88; devel. scientist Pearce Labs., Leeds, Eng., 1988-89; sect. leader oral care rsch. Smithkline Beecham Consumer B, Weybridge, Eng., 1989-92; team leader formulation devel. Zyma Healthcare, Somercotes, Eng., 1993—. Contbr. sci. articles to profl. jours.; patentee in field. Gov. Wirksworth (Eng.) Cofe Primary Sch., 1995—. Mem. Royal Soc. Chemistry, Internat. Assn. Dental Rsch., Royal Pharm. Soc. Gt. Britain (pharms. scis. group). Mem. Labor Party. Home: 47 Yokecliffe Dr, Wirksworth DE4 4EX, England Office: Zyma Healthcare, Wimsey Way, Somercotes DE55 4PT, England

GREEN, DAVID THOMAS, retired surgical company research and development executive, inventor; b. Biggleswade, Eng., Aug. 5, 1925; came to U.S., 1961; s. George and Elizabeth (Course) G.; m. Jeanne Mary Todd, June 30, 1951; children: Lawrence, Lynn, Peter. Cert., Luton Inst. Tech., Eng., 1945. Engr. apprentice Weatherly Oil Gear, Biggleswade, 1941-45, design engr., 1948-52; group leader spl. purpose machines Orenda Aircraft Group, Malton, Ont., Can., 1952-61; mgr. design automotive emission controls Am. Machine and Foundry, L.A., 1961-65; sr. v.p. R&D U.S. Surg. Corp., Norwalk, Conn., 1966-94. Holder 129 patents in surg. stapling and clip devices. Sgt. Brit. Army, 1945-48. Recipient Inventor of Yr. award N.Y. Patent, Trademark and Copyright Law Assn., Inc., 1991.

GREEN, EDWARD CROCKER, international health organization consultant; b. Washington, Nov. 29, 1944; s. Marshall and Lispenard Seabury (Crocker) G.; m. K. Shannon McCaffray, Sept. 22, 1967 (div. 1977); 1 child, Timothy A.; m. M. Sue McLaughlin, Apr. 24, 1990. BA, George Washington U., 1967; MA, Northwestern U., 1968; PhD, Cath. U. Am., 1974; postdoctoral, Vanderbilt U., 1978-79. Asst. prof. W.Va. U., Morgantown, 1976-78; devel. cons. various orgns., Washington, 1979—; mgr. internat. programs John Short & Assocs., Columbia, Md., 1986-88; mgr. and researcher The Futures Group, Washington, 1988-89; social scientist Acad. for Ednl. Devel., Swaziland, 1981-84; personal svcs. contractor U.S. AID, Swaziland, 1984-85; advisor Mozambique Govt., 1994-95. Author: Planning Psychiatric Services for Southern Africa, 1979, Practicing Development Anthropology, 1986, AIDS and STDs in Africa, 1994, Healers and the African State, 1996; contbr. 95 articles to profl. jours. Recipient Mozambique govt. award for health rsch., 1992, Praxis award Washington Assn. Profl. Anthropologists, 1982, 83; NIMH postdoctoral fellow, 1978-79; rsch. grantee Sigma Xi, 1971. Mem. Am. Anthrop. Assn., Soc. Applied Anthropology; mem. N.Y. Acad. Scis., Soc. Med. Anthropology, Nat. Coun. Internat. Health, World Population Soc. (bd. dirs.), Global Initiative for Traditional Sys. of Health (co-chair com.), Sigma Xi. Home and Office: 2807 38th St NW Washington DC 20007

GREEN, ELBERT P., university official; b. Laneview, Va., June 9, 1935; s. James H. and Levallia C. (DeLeaver) G.; m. Mary M. Green, July 6, 1961; children: Mark B., Marsha B. BS, Va. State Coll., 1957; BD, Felix Adler Meml. U., Chapel Hill, N.C., 1969; MS in Edn., Troy State U., Montgomery, Ala., 1988; MBph, Am. Bible Sch., Kansas City, Kans., 1968; PhD, S.W. U., New Orleans, 1991. Cert. tchr., Ala., cert. hypnotherapist; ordained minister. 2d lt. U.S. Army, 1958, advanced through grades to maj.; ret., 1979; dir. jr. ROTC, Indianola (Miss.) City Schs., Macon County (Ala.) Schs.; dir. residence hall Tuskegee (Ala.) U. Author: Poetry Is Soul, 1988, Poetry Is Gold, 1982, The Light of the World Is Poetry, 1995; contbr. articles to newspapers. Mem. Internat. Soc. of Poets, Profl. Educators Orgn., Am. Legion, Lions Internat., Scabbard and Blade, Phi Beta Sigma, Phi Delta Kappa, Gamma Beta Phi. Home: 2910 W Martin L King Hwy Tuskegee AL 36083-3030

GREEN, GEORGE CAMERON, orthopedic surgeon; b. Sonoma, Calif., Aug. 1, 1945; s. Strother S. and Agnes Cameron (Murrey) G.; m. Cathy Stewart, Apr. 21, 1990. BS in Engring., Tulane U., 1967, MS in Engring., 1969, PhD, 1977, MD, 1981. Diplomate Am. Bd. Orthopaedic Surgery. Intern Charity Hosp., New Orleans, 1982; resident Tulane Med. Sch., 1986; fellow in joint replacement Christ Hosp., Cin., 1991; pvt. practice Hendersonville (N.C.) Orthopaedics, 1991-93, Tidewater Orthopaedics, Hampton, Va., 1993-94, Rapahannock Orthopaedics, Kilmarnock, Va., 1994—. Comdr. USN, 1988-90. Fellow Am. Acad. Orthopaedic Surgeons; mem. So. Orthopaedic Assn., Va. Orthopaedics Soc., No. Neck Med. Soc., Am. Med. Soc. Home: PO Box 582 Irvington VA 22480 Office: Rappahannock Orthopaedics PO Box 609 Kilmarnock VA 22482

GREEN, HAROLD DANIEL, dentist; b. Scranton, Pa., Feb. 4, 1934; s. Harold Charles and Viola Mildred (Brown) G.; m. Cornelia Ann Ellis, Aug. 1, 1959; children: Scott Alan, Mary Ann. BA, Beloit Coll. (Wis.), 1956; DDS, Northwestern U., 1960. Gen. practice dentistry, Beloit, Wis., 1964—; dir. Beloit Savs. Bank, chmn. trust com., 1989—; mem loan com. Blackhawk State Bank, mem. fin. com., 1993. Contbr. articles to profl. jours. Active Wis. div. Am. Cancer Soc., 1964-75; 1st pres., co-organizer Citizen's Council Against Crime, Beloit; past officer, chmn. membership Beloit YMCA; pres. Beloit Brewers, chmn. bd., 1988-91, class A midwest league affiliate of Milw. Brewers baseball team, 1986-87; chmn. Student Achievers Program, Wis., No. Ill.; mem. adv. bd. Salvation Army; chmn. Beloiters for Coun.-Mgr., 1989; stateline chmn. Student Achiever Program, 1988, 93; bd. dirs. Greater Beloit Found., 1989—; chmn. nominating com. Greater Beloit Community Trust, Inc., 1991,93; chmn. adminstrv. bd., chmn. Council of Ministries, First United Methodist Ch., Beloit, pastor parish rels., 1995—; chmn. ann. dinner, bd. dirs., nominating com., fundraising, pub. speakers Beloit Crime Stoppers, 1993—, chmn., 1995-96; chmn. facilities study com. Sch. Dist. Beloit, 1991—; chmn. Eagle Scout bd. rev. Sinnisippi coun. Boy Scouts Am., 1995-96. Recipient award for creativity in dentistry Johnson & Johnson Co., 1970; 3 citations for Community Service United Givers Fund, 1970-75; Disting. Sevice citation Greater Beloit Assn. Commerce. Fellow Acad. Gen. Dentistry, Internat. Coll. Dentists. (Wis. editor), Am. Acad. Dental Practice Adminstrn. (past chmn. profl. liaison; mem. ADA (chmn. council on dental practice 1982-84), Wis. Dental Assn. (pres. 1979-80, trustee 1968-74), Wis. Dental Assn. Found., Rock County Dental Soc. (pres. 1976), Wis. Council of Professions (bd. dirs. 1974-80, pres. 1973-75), Chgo. Dental Soc., Greater Milw. Dental Assn., Fedn. Dentaire Internationale, Pierre Fauchard Acad., Am. Acad. History of Dentistry, Lions (beloit programs, 1993—, past pres.)Delta Sigma Delta. Avocations: cycling, golf, basketball, running, fishing. Home: 2207 Collingswood Dr Beloit WI 53511-2332 Office: 419 Pleasant St Beloit WI 53511-6249

GREEN, HENRY LEONARD, physician; b. Detroit, Apr. 9, 1931; s. Albert and Fanya (Newman) G.; m. Loretta Laurie Teplitz; children: Toby, Jennifer, Cheryl, Joseph. BA with distinction, U. Mich., 1951, MD, 1955. Cert. Am. Bd. Internal Medicine in internal medicine and cardiology. Intern Detroit Receiving Hosp., 1955-56; resident internal medicine Henry Ford Hosp., Detroit, 1956-59, resident cardiology, 1959-61; pvt. practice Southfield, Mich., 1963—; dir. cardiac care unit surveillance project, 1969-74; attending physician Sinai Hosp. of Detroit, 1963—, Providence Hosp., Southfield, 1963—; clin. assoc. prof. Wayne State U. Sch. Medicine, Detroit; attending physician William Beaumont Hosp., 1995; dir. pacemaker clinic Providence Hosp.; mem. adv. and exec. coms. Inter-Soc. Commn. for Heart Disease Resources, N.Y.C., 1968-84. Author various med. software programs; contbr. articles to med. jours.; author various oral presentations nat. and local med. meetings. Lt. comdr. USN, 1961-63. Recipient Grand award Mich. Hosp. Assn., Detroit, 1973. Fellow ACP, Am. Coll. Cardiology, Am. Heart Assn., Mich. Heart Assn. (assoc. Coun. on Clin. Cardiology); mem. Phi Beta Kappa, Alpha Omega Alpha. Office: 22250 Providence Dr Ste 600 Southfield MI 48075-6214

GREEN, JACK PETER, pharmacology educator, medical scientist; b. N.Y.C., Oct. 4, 1925; s. Maurice and Tillie (Herman) G.; m. Arlyne Genevieve Frank, Oct. 25, 1958. B.S., Pa. State U., 1947, M.S., 1949; Ph.D., Yale, 1951, M.D., 1957; postgrad., Poly. Inst., Copenhagen, 1953-55, Inst. de Biologie Physico-Chimique, Paris, 1964-65. Vis. scientist Poly. Inst., Copenhagen, 1953-55, Inst. de Biologie Physico-Chimique, Paris, 1964-65; asst. prof. Yale, 1957-61, asso. prof., 1961-66; asso. prof. Cornell U. Med. Coll., 1966-68; prof., chmn. dept. pharmacology Mt. Sinai Sch. Medicine, 1968—; Mem. research grant rev. com. USPHS; mem. N.Y.C. Health Research Council, Dysautonomia Found., Irma T. Hirsch Trust. Contbr. articles profl. jours.; Mem. editorial bds. profl. jours. Recipient Claude Bernard Vis. Professorship U. Montreal, 1966. Mem. N.Y. Acad. Sci., Am. Chem. Soc., Am. Soc. Biol. Chemists, Soc. Drug Research, N.Y. Acad. Medicine, Harvey Soc., A.A.A.S., Am. Soc. Pharmacology and Exptl. Therapeutics, Internat. Soc. Quantum Biology, Am. Coll. Neuropsychopharmacology, Am. Soc. Neurochemistry, Soc. for Neurosci., Sigma Xi, Alpha Omega Alpha, Phi Lambda Upsilon, Gamma Sigma Delta. Home: 1212 Fifth Ave New York NY 10029-5210 Office: Mt Sinai Sch Medicine Dept Pharmacology Fifth Ave at 100th St New York NY 10029

GREEN, JAMES BUTLER, JR., general surgeon; b. Memphis, Sept. 13, 1937; s. James Butler Sr. and Villa Mae (Carmack) G.; m. Mary Elizabeth Brown, June 16, 1961; children: Elizabeth Green Blaylock, Susan Green Thompson, Mary Green Moore, Jennifer Green Spink. Student, U. Memphis, 1955-58; MD, U. Tenn., 1961. Diplomate Am. Bd. Surgery. Intern Meth. Hosp., Memphis, 1961-62; resident in pathology Meth. VA Hosp., Memphis, 1962-63, gen. surgery resident, 1963-67; pediatric surgery rotation Lebonheur Children's Hosp., Memphis, 1964, 65; gynecology rotation Meth. Hosp., Memphis, 1965; surgeon USS Coral Sea (CVA 43), 1967-68, U.S. Naval Hosp., Millington, Tenn., 1968, 69; surgery staff Meth. Hosp., Memphis, 1969—; cons. staff St. Francis Hosp., Memphis, 1975—; cons. Memphis VA Hosp., U.S. Naval Hosp., Millington, 1969—; v.p. Meth. North Hosp., Memphis, 1976, sec. 1984-86, dep. chief of staff 1984-86. Lt. comdr. USNS, 1967-69. Fellow ACS, SE Surg. Conf., Memphis Surg. Soc. (sec.-treas., pres.); mem. Pan Pacific Surg. Assn., Soc. Laparoendoscopic Surgeons. Methodist. Home: 6040 River Oaks Rd Memphis TN 38120 Office: #202 3980 New Covington Pike Memphis TN 38128

GREEN, JANICE STRICKLAND, emergency services nurse; b. Norfolk, Va., Nov. 13, 1939; d. William H. and Naomi Strickland; m. Benny H. Green, 1962. Diploma in nursing, DePaul Hosp., 1960; BSPA in Healthcare Admin., St. Joseph's Coll., 1981. Staff nurse Cabbarus Meml. Hosp., Concord, N.C.; staff nurse DePaul Hosp., Norfolk, Va., head nurse; dir. emergency svcs. DePaul Med. Ctr.; adminstr., govt. svcs. dir. PHP Healthcare Corp. Mem. ACHE, HCAT, AAACN. Home: 5537 Cape Henry Ave Norfolk VA 23513-2412

GREEN, JEFFREY EMANUEL, physician; b. Phila., Nov. 20, 1954; s. Norman Maurice and Hadassa (Alperstein) G. AB, Princeton U., 1976; postgrad., U. Munich, 1977; MD, McGill U., Que., Can., 1981. Diplomate Am. Acad. Pediatrics, Nat. Bd. Med. Examiners, Can. Med. Coun., Am. Bd. Med. Genetics. Intern Children's Hosp. of Phila., 1981-82, resident, 1982-84; med. staff fellow NIH, Bethesda, Md., 1984-86; biotech. fellow Nat Cancer Inst., Bethesda, 1986-90; sr. investigator Nat. Cancer Inst., Bethesda, 1990—; commd. officer USPHS USPHS, 1990; cons. Children's Hosp. Nat. Med. Ctr., Washington, 1987—. Contbr. articles to profl. jours. Fellow Am. Soc. Human Genetics; mem. Am. Coll. Med. Genetics, Soc. Pediat. Rsch. Office: FCDRC-NIH 469/237 Frederick MD 21702

GREEN, JEFFREY HARRIS, psychiatrist; b. Phila., July 8, 1956. BS summa cum laude, Muhlenberg Coll., 1978; MD, U. Chgo., 1982. Diplomate, Am. Bd. Psychiatry and Neurology. Intern Pa. Hosp., Phila., 1982-83; resident in psychiatry Inst. Pa. Hosp., Phila., 1983-86; pvt. practice Princeton, N.J., 1986—; asst. instr. U. Pa., Phila., 1083-86; clin. asst. prof. dept. psychiatry U. Medicine Dentistry N.J., Piscataway, 1986—; cons. Family Svc. Assocs. Trenton/Hopewell Valley, 1989-93, The Corner House, 1990—. Mem. Am. Psychiat. Assn. (sec.-treas. N.J. chpt. 1988-89, v.p. cen. N.J. chpt. 1989-90, pres. 1990-91, coun. rep. 1991-92), Phi Beta Kappa, Omicron Delta Kappa, Tau Kappa Epsilon. Office: 170 Cold Soil Rd Princeton NJ 08540-4202

GREEN, JEROME GEORGE, federal government official; b. Bklyn., June 20, 1929; s. Samuel N. and Esther (Deiber) G.; m. Marie Charlotte Roder, Aug. 2, 1952; children—Karen Ann, Paul Jonathan. B.S. magna cum laude, Bklyn. Coll., 1950; M.D., Albany Med. Coll., 1954. Intern Albany (N.Y.) Hosp., 1954-55; mem. staff br. grants and tng. Nat. Heart Inst., NIH, Bethesda, Md., 1955-57; asso. dir. extramural research and tng. Nat. Heart Inst., NIH, 1965-72; resident USPHS Hosp., San Francisco, 1957-59; spl. fellow in cardiopulmonary research Cardiovascular Research Inst., U. Calif., San Francisco, 1959-60; research div. Cleve. Clinic, 1960-65; dir. div. extramural affairs Nat. Heart, Lung and Blood Inst., 1972-85; dir. div. research grants NIH, Bethesda, 1986-95; asst. surgeon gen. USPHS, 1988-95. Fellow Am. Coll. Cardiology, Am. Heart Assn.; mem. Phi Beta Kappa, Alpha Omega Alpha. Home: 8304 Loring Dr Bethesda MD 20817-3150

GREEN, JONATHAN RICHARD CORTIS, physician assistant; b. New London, Conn., Oct. 30, 1948; s. Richard Cortis and Helen Marie (Chelland) G.; m. Ellen Kay Wilson, Feb. 20, 1988; children: Victoria Elian, Dylan Lawford. BA, U. Calif., 1970; MPH, Okla. Univ. Health Ctr., 1993. Asst. chief malaria ctrl. zones Peace Corps, Kanchanaburi, Thailand, 1973-75; enlisted U.S. Army, 1970—; ambulance driver 560th Med. Co., Pyong Taek, Korea, 1977-78; co. aid 19th Engrs., Ft. Knox, Ky., 1978-80; evacuation sect. sgt. 5/33 Armor, Ft. Knox, 1978-80; battalion surgeon 15th Engrs., Ft. Lewis, Wash., 1983-84, 5th Support Battalion 9th Infantry Div., Ft. Lewis, 1984-86, 1/68 Armor, Wildflecken, Germany, 1986-89; physician asst. Reynolds Army Cmty. Hosp., Fort Sill, Okla., 1989-91; asst. chief preventive medicine Winn Army Cmty. Hosp., Ft. Steward, Ga., 1993—. Fellow Am. Acad. Physician Assts.; mem. Am. Pub. Health Assn., Assn. Mil. Surgeons U.S., Soc. Army Physician Assts., Am. Acad. Physician Assts. in Occupational Medicine (columnist newsletter 1995—), Nat. Peace Corps. Assn. Methodist. Home: 126 Blue Wing Dr Richmond Hill GA 31324 Office: USA MEDDAC Attn: MCUB-PMS-OH Fort Stewart GA 31314

GREEN, KARL WALTER, orthopedic surgeon; b. N.Y.C., Aug. 14, 1940; children: Kevin, Michelle, Bradley. BS cum laude, SUNY, Bklyn., 1966, MD cum laude, 1966. Diplomate Am. Bd. Orthopaedic Surgery, Nat. Bd. Med. Examiners. Intern, resident L.I. Jewish Med. Ctr., New Hyde Park, N.Y., 1966-68; resident in gen. surgery and orthopaedics St. Joseph Hosp., Paterson, N.J., 1968-71; pvt. practice Homestead, Fla., 1973—. Col. M.C., USAF, 1971-73. Fellow Am. Acad. Orthopaedic Surgeons; mem. Fla. Med. Assn., Dade County Med. Soc. Republican. Jewish. Office: South Dade Orthopaedic Asso 9299 SW 152d St Ste 103 Miami FL 33157

GREEN, LARRY ALTON, physician, educator; b. Ardmore, Okla., Mar. 27, 1948; s. Thomas Alton and Mary Lou (Gaunt) G.; m. Margaret Joyce Ball, Mar. 27, 1971; children: Nathaniel, Katherine. BA, U. Okla., 1969; MD, Baylor Coll. Medicine, Houston, 1973. Diplomate Am. Bd. Family Practice. Intern then resident U. Rochester, Highland Hosp., N.Y., 1973-76; asst. prof. U. Colo., Denver, 1977-82, assoc. prof., 1982-85, prof., chmn. dept., 1985—, Woodward-Chisholm chair, 1989—; vis. prof. various univs., U.S., New Zealand, U.K., Republic of South Africa, 1982—; dir. residency Mercy Med. Ctr., Denver, 1980-85; found. pres. Ambulatory Sentinel Practice Network, Denver. Contbr. articles to profl. jours. Elder Presbyn. Ch., Denver, With USPHS, 1976-77. Grantee USPHS, 1978—, Kellogg Found., 1982-87. Mem. Assn. Depts. Family Medicine (pres. 1987-89), N.Am. Primary Care Rsch. Group (bd. dirs. 1989-93), Am. Acad. Family Physicians, Soc. Tchrs. Family Medicine, Inst. Medicine. Office: U Colo Health Scis Ctr Dept of Family Medicine 1180 Clermont St Denver CO 80220-6216

GREEN, LAWRENCE, neurologist, educator; b. Atlantic City, N.J., Oct. 23, 1938; s. Martin and Lillian (Spector) G.; m. Ann Buchberg, Aug. 21, 1970; 1 child, Louis Aaron; stepson, Jonathan Rapkin. BS in Chemistry cum laude, Dickinson Coll., 1960; MD, Jefferson Med. Coll., 1964. Diplomate Am. Bd. Psychiatry and Neurology, Am. Bd. Clin. Neurophysiology; cert. in neurology with added qualifications in clin. neurophysiology. Intern Lankenau Hosp., Phila., 1964-65; resident in neurology Jefferson Med. Coll. Hosp., Phila., 1965-68; fellow in clin. neurophysiology Boston Va. Hosp., 1970-71; attending neurologist Phila. Gen. Hosp., 1971-72; chief, div. neurology and clin. neurophysiology Crozer-Chester (Pa.) Med. Ctr., 1971—, med. dir., Sch. of EEG Tech., 1974—; chief EEG Lab. Hahnemann U. Hosp., Phila., 1972-78, 87-91, electroencephalographer, 1978-87; asst. prof. neurology to clin. prof. neurology Hahnemann Univ., Phila., 1971—; instr. in neurology Boston U. Sch. Medicine, 1970-71; adj. prof. bioengring. Widener Coll., Chester, Pa., 1975-77; cons. in neurology and EEG Taylor Hosp., Ridley Pk., Pa., 1971—, St. Agnes Med. Ctr., Phila., 1971—, Hahnemann U. Hosp., 1972—; assoc. examiner Am. Bd. Clin. Neurophysiology, Am. Bd. Registered EEG Tech. Contbr. articles to Neurology, Experientia, Electroencephalography and Clin. Neurophysiology, Low Back Pain, Annals of Neurology. Lt. comdr. USNR, 1968-70. Fellow Am. EEG Soc. (coun., lab. accreditation bd., rep. 1988-92, cons. to com. on allied helath accreditation 1988-94, commr. to com. for accreditation allied health edn. programs 1994—, program com. 1991); mem. AMA, ACP, Am. Acad. Neurology (clin. practice expert panel 10, misc. internal medicine 1995—, rep.), Am. Epilepsy Soc., Am. Assn. EMG & ED, Pa. Med. Soc., Alpers Soc. for Clin. Neurology (past pres., sec., treas.), Alpha Omega Alpha. Office: Clin Neurophysiology Lab Crozer Chester Med Ctr Med Ctr Blvd Upland PA 19013

GREEN, LENNIS HARRIS, psychologist; b. Indpls., July 14, 1940; d. William James and Anna Jane (McLane) Harris. BS, Ohio State U., 1962, MA, 1966, PhD, 1971. Lic. psychologist, Ohio. Program dir. Lattie Lazarus Counseling Ctr., Columbus, 1971-72; pvt. practice psychology Columbus, Ohio, 1968—; bd. dirs. North Area Mental Health, Inc., Columbus, 1980-85, clin. cons., 1985—; clin. cons. Midwest Career Ctr., Columbus, 1985-90, Worthington Counseling Ctr., Columbus, 1986-87; prin. rsch. investigator Proctor Fund, Honolulu, 1984. Contbr. articles to mags. Del. Nigerian Consultation, Episc. Ch., Geneva, Switzerland, 1983; bd. dirs. Transcultural Family Inst., Columbus, 1983-84. Behavioral and Sci. Inst. fellow, U. Hawaii, Honolulu, 1985. Mem. Internat. Council Psychologists, Internat. Assn. Crosscultural Psychology, Am. Psychol. Assn., Am. Anthropology Assn. Home and Office: 1899 Greenglen Ct Columbus OH 43229-2015

GREEN, LEON MORTON, psychiatrist; b. Berkeley, Calif., July 3, 1949; s. Morton and Elizabeth Ann (Griffith) G.; m. Gwendolyn Gail Ditmars, June 5, 1971 (div. Sept. 1975); m. Mary Ann Donahue, May 3, 1980; stepchildren: Jill Robin Swartz, Meghan Marie Swartz. BA, U. Kans., Lawrence, 1971; cert., Leningrad State U., USSR, 1972; BSM, U. S.D., 1974; MD, George Washington U., 1976. Diplomate Am. Bd. Med. Examiners. Intern C.S. Wilson Meml. Hosp., Johnson City, N.Y., 1976-77; resident Shephard Eno Pratt Hosp., Towson, Md., 1977-79, fellow, 1979-80; psychiatrist Associated Psychiatric Svcs., Newark, Del., 1980-81; pvt. practice Wilmington, Del., 1981—. Adv. bd. Mental Health Assn. in Del., Wilmington, 1988-90; hon. bd. mem., 1983-88. Mem. AMA, Am. Psychiat. Assn., Psychiat. Soc. Del. (sec. 1983-85, pres. 1986-87), Com. for Sci. Investigation Claims of Paranormal. Democrat. Office: 1 Middleton Dr Ste 150 Wilmington DE 19808-4320

GREEN, LINDA GAIL, international healthcare and management consultant; b. Kalamazoo, Nov. 29, 1951; d. Jesse Floyd and Mattie Dean (Fulcher) G. BS in Nursing, Fla. State U., Tallahassee, 1974; postgrad., Nova U., Ft. Lauderdale, Fla. Staff nurse med./surg. unit St. Mary's Hosp., West Palm Beach, Fla., 1974, staff nurse coronary care, 1974-75, relief charge nurse ICU, 1975-76, asst. nursing care coord. post anesthesia recovery rm., 1976-78, insvc. instr., 1978-81, asst. dir. staff devel. and edn., 1981-83; dir. insvc. H.H. Raulerson Hosp., Okeechobee, Fla., 1983-84; adminstr. Med. Personnel Pool, Palm Beach, Fla., 1984-90; regional exec. healthcare divsn. Interim Svcs., Inc. (formerly Pers. Pool of Am.), Ft. Lauderdale, 1990-93; pres. L.G.I. Consulting/Cmty. Health Educator, West Palm Beach, 1993—; Spkr. in field. Author: Sexual Harassment in Home Healthcare, 1993; pub. Everything the Doctor Ordered. Past bd. dirs. Vinceremos Therapeutic Riding Ctr., Inc. for Physically and Mentally Challenged, 1990-95. Mem. ANA, AHA (heart walk industry leader 1994, 95), Fla. Nurses Assn., Palm Beach County Health Educators (past sec.), Palm Beach County Patient Educators (pres. 1989, Leadership and Spirit awards 1989), Royal Palm Beach Bus. Assn., Palms West C. of C. (v.p. 1987-88, Dedicated and Outstanding Svc. award 1989, Cert. of Appreciation 1986, 87), Zonta Internat. (pres. 1994-95, past v.p. Palms West chpt., del. to internat. conf., Hong Kong, 1992), Exec. Women of Palm Beaches. Office: PO Box 15301 West Palm Beach FL 33416-5301

GREEN, MARK RONALD, internist; b. Norwalk, Conn., 1945. MD, Harvard U., 1970. Cert. internal medicine, oncology. Intern Beth Israel Hosp., Boston, 1970-71, resident, 1971-72; resident Stanford U. Hosp., 1974-75, fellow in oncology, 1975-76; fellow in oncology Nat. Cancer Inst., Bethesda/Balt., 1972-74; prof. medicine U. Calif. Sch. Medicine, San Diego, 1974-96; dir. Hollings Cancer Ctr./Med. U. S.C., Charleston, 1996—. Mem. ACP, Am. Soc. Clin. Oncology. Office: #8421 U Calif Med Ctr San Diego CA 92103

GREEN, MARY ELOISE, nutrition and food management educator; b. East Liberty, Ohio, June 10, 1903; d. Milton M. and Sylvia M. (Creviston) G. BS, Ohio State U., 1928, MS, 1933; PhD, Iowa State U., 1949. Elem. tchr. Perry Twp. Sch., East Liberty, 1923-26; high sch. tchr. Monroe Twp. Sch., West Liberty, Ohio, 1928-37, Brown Twp. Sch., Kilbourne, Ohio, 1937-39; instr. Ohio Wesleyan U., Del., 1937-39; from instr. to prof. Ohio State U., Columbus, 1939-72, prof. emeritus, 1972—. Fellow AAAS; mem. Am. Dietetic Assn., Am. Assn. Family and Consumer Scis., Inst. of Food Technologists, Pi Lambda Theta, Sigma Delta Epsilon, Iota Sigma Pi, Kappa Omicron Nu, Am. Assn. Univ. Women, Order of Eastern Star. United Methodist. Home: 116 W Como Ave Columbus OH 43202-1028

GREEN, MAURICE, molecular biologist, virologist, educator; b. N.Y.C., May 5, 1926; s. David and Bessie (Lipschitz) G.; m. Marilyn Glick, Aug. 20, 1950; children—Michael Richard, Wendy Allison Green Lee, Eric Douglas. B.S. in Chemistry, U. Mich., 1949; M.S. in Biochemistry and Chemistry, U. Wis.-Madison, 1952, Ph.D. in Biochemistry and Chemistry, 1954. Instr. biochemistry U. Pa. Med. Sch., Phila., 1955-56; asst. prof. St. Louis U. Health Scis. Ctr., 1956-60, assoc. prof., 1960-63, prof. microbiology, 1963-77; prof., chmn. Inst. for Molecular Virology, 1964—. Office: St Louis U Health Sci Ctr Inst for Molecular Virology 3681 Park Ave Saint Louis MO 63110-2511

GREEN, MAURICE RICHARD, neuropsychiatrist; b. Chgo., Oct. 28, 1922; divorced; children: Melissa, Suzanne, Constance. BS, Northwestern U., 1942; BM, Northwestern U. Med. Sch., 1945, MD, 1946; cert. in Psychoanalytic Tng., William Alanson White Inst., N.Y.C., 1954. Diplomate Am. Bd. Psychiatry and Neurology. Intern Passavant Hosp., Chgo., 1945-46; resident in psychiatry Bronx (N.Y.) VA Hosp., 1948-51; cons. psychiatrist Brookwood Hall, East Islip, L.I., N.Y., 1955-58; staff psychiatrist Psychiatric Clinic Ct. Spl. Sessions, 1956-60; cons. psychiatrist Bleuler Psychotherapy Ctr., Queens, N.Y., 1956-68; research psychiatrist, mem. psychiat. epidemiology sect. William Alanson White Inst., N.Y.C., 1968-72; attending geriatric psychiatrist Albert Einstein Med. Sch., 1974-76; attending child and adolescent psychiatry Harlem Hosp. of Columbia Presbyn. Med. Ctr., N.Y.C., 1974-75; med. dir. geriatric and family psychiatry Lincoln Hosp., 1974-76; chief psychiatrist Family Ct. Services div. South Beach Psychiat. Ctr., S.I., N.Y., 1976-80; sr. attending psychiatrist Columbia-Presbyn. at St. Luke's-Roosevelt Hosp., N.Y.C., 1978—; cons. psychiatrist Liaison-Consultation Service NYU Med. Ctr., N.Y.C., 1985-86; psychiatrist spl. evaluation and treatment unit Rockland Psychiat. Ctr., 1985-87; mem. faculty William Alanson White Inst., N.Y.C., 1957—; cons. Goddard Coll., 1961-68; assoc. attending psychiatrist Bellevue Hosp., 1962-85, presently attending physician; supervisory and tng. analyst William Alanson White Inst., 1962—; clin. prof. psychiatry NYU Med. Sch., 1964—; mem. med. bd. Roosevelt Hosp., 1965-76; prin. investigator Diamox-Thiamine Research Unit Nathan S. Kline Research Inst., 1987; project dir. Brain Chemistry of Schizophrenia at Nathan Kline Inst., 1988-93; med. dir. Neurologic Systems, Inc., 1987; presidium Inst. for Brain Function Research, Inc., 1987; mem. Treatment Innovations Task Force-Soc. for Traumatic Stress Studies, 1987. Author: Interpersonal Psychoanalysis: Selected Papers of Clara Thompson, 1971, Psicoanalisi interpersonale, 1972, L'Experiencze Prelogica, 1972, Violence and the Family, 1980; (with Edward S. Tauber) Prelogical Experience, 1959; assoc. editor Contemporary Psychoanalysis jour., 1968—; contbr. articles to profl. jours. Project dir. Nathan Kline Rsch. Inst., 1988—. Fellow Am. Psychiat. Assn. (com. on aging N.Y. Dist. br.), Am. Orthopsychiat. Assn. (publs. com. Anniversary Vol. 1968-71), Am. Acad. of Child and Adolescent Psychiatry (com. on hospitalization of children, nat. legis. network 1982-86), N.Y. Acad. Medicine; mem. AMA, N.Y. Coun. on Child Psychiatry, Am. Soc. Psychoanalytic Physicians, N.Y. Soc. Clin. Psychiatry, William Alanson White Psychoanalytic Soc., Physicians for Social Responsibility, Nat. Assn. Patients Rights and Advocacy, Soc. Biol. Psychiatry, World Assn. for Psychosocial Rehab. (v.p. USA br.), Internat. Soc. of Psychoneuroendocrinology, Am. Assn. for Geriatric Psychiatry. Home and Office: 275 Central Park W Apt 15 D New York NY 10024-3058

GREEN, MICHAEL JEFFREY, psychologist, consultant, mediator; b. Boston, July 9, 1942; s. Bernard and Ruth (Paretsky) G.; BS in BA, Babson Coll., 1964; JD, Boston U., 1967, MEd, Boston Coll., 1970. Asst. athletic dir. Babson Coll., Babson Park, Mass., 1966-68; dir. student activities Bryant & Stratton Jr. Coll., Boston, 1968-69; dir. West Campus Boston U., 1969-72; clin. dir. Brockton Area Drug Program, Mass., 1973-74; psychologist and administrator Brockton Multi Service, 1974-78; dir., psychologist Family Counseling Assocs., Taunton, Mass., 1978-93; dir. youth programs Vol. of Am., Boston, 1993-94, dir. of ops., 1994—; bd. dir. Mass. Council Family Mediation, Boston, 1984-90; cons. Bridgewater Schs., Mass., 1984-89, Bristol-Plymouth Voke, 1985-94; Vols. Am. 1991-93; clin. dir. The Road Back, 1989-90, dir., 1990—. Mem. Zoning Bd. Appeals, Middleboro, 1983-89, town mgr. selection com., Middleboro, 1985; exec. dir. New England Interncollegiate Soccer League, Boston, 1967-72; water safety instr. trainer ARC, Boston, 1966—; pres. Friends of Middleboro Pub. Libr., 1985-87, 88-90, v.p. 1990-93, bd. dirs., 1987-92; bd. dirs. Cmty. Choice, 1995—. Mem. Mass. Bar Assn. (teaching faculty 1986), Nat. Assn. Group Psychotherapy, N.E. Group Psychotherapy Assn. Democrat. Jewish. Avocations: gardening, reading, writing profl. articles, listening to music. Home and Office: 185 Quincy Shore Dr A73 North Quincy MA 02171-2954

GREEN, MORRIS, physician, educator; b. Indpls., May 27, 1922; s. Coleman and Rebecca (Oleinick) G.; m. Janice Barber Gorton, Mar. 11, 1955; children: David Schuster, Alan Coleman, Carolyn Ann, Susan Elaine, Marcia Ruth, Sylvia Rebecca. A.B., Ind. U., 1942, M.D., 1944. Intern Ind. U. Med. Center, 1945; resident pediatrics U. Ill. Research and Ednl. Hosps., 1947-49; instr. pediatrics U. Ill. Coll. Medicine, 1949-52; asst. prof. Yale Sch. Medicine, 1952-57; faculty Ind. U. Sch. Medicine, Indpls., 1957—, Perry W. Lesh prof. pediatrics, 1963—; chmn. dept. pediatrics, physician-in-chief James Whitcomb Riley Hosp. for Children, Indpls., 1967-88; commr. health State of Ind., 1990-91. Author: Pediatric Diagnosis, 5th edit., 1992; co-editor: Ambulatory Pediatrics, 1968, 2d edit., 1977, 3d edit., 1983, 4th edit., 1990; mem. editorial bd. Pediatrics in Rev., Contemporary Pediatrics, Current Problems in Pediatrics, Jour. Devel. and Behavioral Pediatrics, Social Work in Health Care; nat. adviser Children Today. Served to capt. M.C. AUS, 1945-47. Recipient George Armstrong award in ambulatory pediats., 1971, C. Anderson Aldrich award in child devel., 1982, Irving S. Cutter award Phi Rho Sigma, 1984, Ross award for pediat. edn., 1985, Simon Wile award Am. Acad. Child and Adolescent Psychiatry, 1990, Joseph W. St. Geme award Fedn. Pediat. Orgns., 1992, Disting. Career award Ambulatory Pediat. Assn., 1996. Mem. AMA (Abraham Jacobi award 1990), Am. Pediatric Soc., Soc. Pediatric Research, Am. Fedn. Clin. Research, Am. Acad. Pediatrics (Abraham Jacobi award 1990), Am. Orthopsychiat. Assn., Inst. Medicine, Soc. Research Child Devel., Phi Beta Kappa, Sigma Xi, Alpha Omega Alpha. Home: 1840 Brewster Rd Indianapolis IN 46260-1561 Office: 702 Barnhill Dr Indianapolis IN 46202-5128

GREEN, RICHARD, psychiatrist, lawyer, educator; b. Bklyn., June 6, 1936; s. Leo Harry and Rose (Ingber) G.; m. Melissa Hines; 1 child, Adam Hines-Green. AB, Syracuse U., 1957; MD, Johns Hopkins U., 1961; JD, Yale U., 1987. Diplomate Am. Bd. Psychiatry and Neurology; bar: Calif. 1987, D.C. 1989. Intern Kings County Hosp., Bklyn., 1962-64; resident in psychiatry UCLA Neuropsychiat. Inst., 1962-64, Nat. Inst. Mental Health, Bethesda, Md., 1965-66; asst. prof., assoc. prof., then prof. dept. psychiatry UCLA, 1968-74; prof. psychiatry and psychology SUNY, Stony Brook, 1974-85; prof. psychiatry UCLA, 1986-94, prof. law, 1988-90, prof. emeritus psychiatry, 1994—; mem. faculty of law Cambridge U., 1994—; part-time faculty mem. law sch. UCLA, 1991-92; cons. psychiatrist Gender Identity Clinic Charing Cross Hosp., London; vis. fellow, sr. rsch. fellow Inst. Criminology, Cambridge U., 1994—. Author: Sexual Identity Conflict in Children and Adults, 1974, Impotence, 1981, The Sissy Boy Syndrome and the Development of Homosexuality, 1987, Sexual Science and the Law, 1992; co-editor: Transsexualism and Sex Reassignment, 1969; editor: Human Sexuality: A Health Practitioner's Text, 1975, 2d edit., 1979; editor Jour. Archives of Sexual Behavior, 1971—. Vol. atty., ACLU, LA. Vis. scholar U. Cambridge, Eng., 1980-81, Fulbright scholar King's Coll., London, and Univ. Cambridge, 1992; fellow Ctr. Advanced Study in Behavioral Scis., Stanford, Calif., 1982-83. Fellow Soc. Sci. Study of Sex (pres. 1974-77), Internat. Acad. Sex Rsch. (founding pres. 1973); mem. Calif. Bar Assn., D.C. Bar Assn., Royal Coll. Psychiatrists. Office: Charing Cross Hosp, Gender Identity Clinic Dept Psychiatry, London W6 8RF, England

GREEN, ROBERT EDWARD, neurosurgeon, writer; b. N.Y.C., Mar. 30, 1921; s. Bud and Anna Marie (vonHinken) Green; m. Beverly Jane Horn, Oct., 1945; children: James Kimball, Gwynneth Marie, Thomas Carter, Cathlin Louise. BA, Columbia U., 1941; MD, Cornell U., 1944. Diplomate Am. Bd. Neurol. Surgery. Intern U. Chgo. Clinics, 1944-45, resident, 1945-46; resident in neurosurgery Johns Hopkins Hosp., Balt., 1948-51, instr. neurosurgery, 1950-51; attending neurosurgeon St. Barnabas Med. Ctr., Newark, 1951-64, Hosp. Ctr. at Orange, N.J., 1951-92; chief div. neurosurgery St. Barnabas Med. Ctr., Livingston, N.J., 1964-92; trustee Med. Ctr. at Livingston, Newark, N.J., 1981-90, dir. neurosurgical edn. and resident tng., 1989-92; chief div. neurosurgery Hosp. Ctr. at Orange, N.J., 1959-92; practice now ltd. to consultations and forensic medicine; cons. Hosp. Ctr. at Orange, St. Barnabas Med. Ctr. Author, mem. editorial bd: A History of Neurological Surgery, 1951; writer, narrator tape recording Forever Green -50 Years of Songs by Buddy Green, 1983; contbr. med. articles to publs. Capt. M.C., U.S. Army, 1946-47, ETO. Fellow ACS, Internat. Coll. Surgeons; mem. Am. Assn. Neurol. Surgeons, Congress Neurol. Surgeons, N.J. Neurol. Soc. (pres. 1961-62, peer rev. com. 1983—), Chaine des Rotisseurs (Regional Bailli, N.E. 1979-81), Chaine des Rotisseurs (Chambellan 1982-86, hon. 1986—, asst. regional Bailli, N.E., 1988-90, regional Bailli, N.E, 1990—, bd. dirs., Ordre Mondial de Gourmets Degostateurs Consul Regional N.E. 1991—). Republican. Congregationalist.

GREEN, ROBERT LEONARD, hospital management company executive; b. Los Angeles, Mar. 20, 1931; s. Leonard H. and Helene (Rains) G.; m. Susan Wolf, June 9, 1957; children—Wendy, Julie. B.A., Stanford U., 1952, LL.B., 1956. C.P.A., Calif. Acct. John F. Grieder, San Francisco, 1957-59; assoc. Heller, Ehrman, White & McAuliffe, San Francisco, 1959-61; pres. Sutter Capital Co., San Francisco, 1961-69; chmn. bd. Community Psychiat. Ctrs., San Francisco, 1969-89; chmn. bd. VIVRA, 1989-94, pres., 1989-92; chmn. Edn. Ptnrs., San Francisco, 1994—. Trustee Sta. KQED-Pub. TV, San Francisco, 1981-91, Mus. Modern Art, 1984-89, Mt. Zion Hosp., 1985-86. 1st lt. U.S. Army, 1954-56. Office: 2601 Mariposa St San Francisco CA 94110

GREEN, S. EMILIE, clinical social worker; b. Brookline, Mass., July 29, 1948. BA, Barnard Coll., 1970; MSW, Boston U., 1978. Lic. ind. clin. social worker, Mass.; bd. cert. diplomate clin. social work. Social worker Judge Baker Guidance Clinic, Boston, 1977-78; sch. social worker Lincoln Pub. Schs., Lincoln, 1978-80; pvt. practice Needham, Mass., 1980—; sch. social worker Needham Pub. Schs., 1980—; exec. co-dir. Families By Choice, Needham, 1988-92. Mem. Acad. Cert. Social Workers (sch. social work specialist). Home: 1153 Beacon St Brookline MA 02146-5509 Office: Needham Pub Schs 1330 Highland Ave Needham MA 02192-2613

GREEN, STEPHEN HOWELL, surgeon; b. Bronx, N.Y., July 24, 1940; s. Louis and Jeanette Roslyn (Grabiner) G.; m. Lorraine Carrol Hollander, Dec. 15, 1968; children: Dawn Syndi, Darin Scott. BA in Chemistry, Brooklyn Coll., 1962; MD, NYU, 1966. Diplomate Am. Bd. Surgery. Intern Bronx (N.Y.) Muni. Hosp., 1966-67, resident, 1967-72; fellow in breast cancer Am. Cancer Soc., Bronx, 1969-70; pvt. practice, Patchogue, N.Y., 1975—. Contbr. articles to med. jours. Vice pres. Temple Shalom, Sayville, N.Y., 1994—. Lt. col. M.C., USAF, 1972-75. Fellow ACS; mem. Am. Soc. Colon and Rectal Surgeons, Pan Pacific Surg. Soc., Am. Soc. Abdominal Surgeons, N.Y. State Soc. Surgeons, Med. Soc. State N.Y., Suffolk County Med. Soc., Suffolk Acad. Medicine. Office: 285 Sills Rd Ste 2A Patchogue NY 11772

GREEN, STUART ALAN, orthopedic surgeon; b. N.Y.C., Oct. 3, 1942; s. Leo Arthur and Mary Gertrude (Cohen) G.; m. Adrienne Joyce Jakobsons, June 21, 1964; children: Andrew, Hillary. AB in Psychology, Lafayette Coll., Easton, Pa., 1963; MD, N.Y. Med. Coll., 1967. Ptnr. Greater Long Beach (Calif.) Orthop. Group, 1973—; asst. prof. orthop. surgery U. So. Calif., L.A., 1980-87; prof. orthop. surgery U. Calif., Irvine, 1987—. Author: Complications of External Fixation, 1981; co-author: External Fixation and Functional Bracing, 1989; inventor Rancho cubes, GSH nail. Office: Greater Long Beach Orthop 3801 Katella Ave Los Alamitos CA 90720

GREEN, WAYNE HUGO, psychiatrist, psychoanalyst; b. Schenectady, N.Y., July 23, 1941; s. Albert George and Mildred (Hugo) G.; AB, U. Chgo., 1963; MD, NYU, 1967; cert. in Psychoanalysis, William Alanson White Inst. Psychiatry, Psychoanalysis and Psychology, 1977. Intern, Lenox Hill Hosp., N.Y.C., 1967-68; resident in psychiatry N.Y. U.-Bellevue Med. Ctr., 1970-72, fellow in child psychiatry, 1972-74; asst. dir. Children's Mental Hygiene Clinic, Bellevue Psychiat. Hosp., N.Y.C., 1974-77; unit chief Children's Psychiat. In-patient Service, Bellevue Hosp., N.Y.C., 1978-86; unit chief child and adolescent outpatient clinic, 1986—, asst. clin. prof. psychiatry N.Y. U., 1977-79, asst. prof. psychiatry, 1979-85, assoc. prof. clin. psychiatry, 1985—; asst. attending dept. psychiatry N.Y. U. Med. Ctr., Univ. Hosp., N.Y.C., 1974—; asst. attending psychiatrist Bellevue Hosp. Ctr., N.Y.C., 1974—; dir. tng. & edn. NYU Residency in Child and Adolescent Psychiatry, 1995—. Served with USPHS, 1968-70. Diplomate Am. Bd. Psychiatry and Neurology. Fellow Am. Acad. Child Psychiatry, N.Y. Council Child Psychiatry. Author: (book) Child and Adolescent Clinical Psychopharmacology, 2d edit., 1995; contbr. articles in field to profl. jours. Office: 110 Bleecker St New York NY 10012-2105 Office: Bellevue Hosp-A244 Child & Adolescent Psychiatric Clinic 27th St & 1st Ave New York NY 10016

GREEN, WILLIAM EDWARD, medical administrator, emergency coordinator; b. Rockville Ctr., N.Y., June 14, 1943; s. Edmund Francis and Mary Margaret (Strupel) G.; m. Martha Ann Sweeney, Sept. 21, 1968; children: William Edward Jr., John Patrick. AAS in Bus. Adminstrn., Nassau Community Coll., 1965; BS in Econs. and Bus., Hofstra U., 1967; M Profl. Studies in Health Care Adminstrn, L.I. U., 1979. Adminstrv. asst. VA Med. Ctr., Northport, N.Y., 1974-76; asst. med. adminstr. VA Extended Care Ctr., St. Albans, N.Y., 1976-77, VA Med. Ctr., Bklyn., 1977-80; pub. health advisor USPHS, N.Y.C., 1980-81; chief med. adminstrn. office VA Outpatient Clinic, Bklyn., 1981-83; asst. med. adminstr. VA Med. Ctr., Bronx, 1983-86, program mgmt. officer, 1986; patient adminstr. Hqrs NYARNG, Latham, N.Y., 1987-91; exec. officer 244th Med. Group NYARNG, 1991-93; pub. health advisor emergency preparedness USPHS Region II, N.Y.C., 1994—. Lt. col. Army Med. Svc. Corps., 1968-93. Fellow Am. Acad. of Med. Adminstrs. (diplomate); mem. Alliance of ARNG Health Care Profls. (charter), Am. Acad. Med. Adminstrs. (state dir. 1984-89, regional dir. 1989-91, exec. coun.), Assn. Mil. Surgeons U.S. (pres. N.Y. chpt. 1987, v.p. 1986), DAV (life), Res. Officers Assn., Civil War Roundtable (mem. excelsior chpt.), Gold Key, Upsilon Gamma Alpha. Republican. Roman Catholic. Home: 365 Smith St Freeport NY 11520-3228 Office: USPHS Region II 26 Federal Plz Rm 3337 New York NY 10278-0004

GREEN, WILLIAM F., mental health rehabilitation services professional; b. Phila., June 22, 1948; s. Frank and Anna (Jenkins) G.; m. Denise Green, Feb. 9, 1986; 1 child, Stephanie. BS, St. Joseph's U., 1970; MS, Boston U., 1986. Cert. rehab. counselor, N.J., mental health screener. Vocat. adjustments svcs. asst. dir. Phila. State Hosp., 1970-87; rehab. svcs. dir. Transitional Residence Independence Svc. Inc., Stratford, N.J., 1987-90; dir. acute care svcs. Steininger Ctr., Cherry Hill, N.J., 1990—. Recipient long term grant for rehab. of the mentally ill. Mem. Nat. Alliance for the Mentally Ill, Internat. Assn. of Psychosocial Rehab. Svcs., Am. Assn. for Counseling and Devel., Am. Rehab. Counseling Assn., Am. Mental Health Counselors Assn. Home: 3000 Rawle St Philadelphia PA 19149-2507 Office: 19 E Ormond Ave Cherry Hill NJ 08034-2053

GREENBAUM, CHARLES HIRSCH, retired dermatologist; b. Phila., Feb. 22, 1925; s. Sigmund Samuel and Rae Shirley (Refowich) G.; m. Julia Heimowitz, July 3, 1955; children: Steven Samuel, Lynne Carol, Robert David. AB, U. Pa., 1948; MD, Jefferson Med. Coll., 1954. Intern, Phila. Gen. Hosp., 1954-55; resident U. Pa. Grad. Sch. Medicine, 1955-56, Pa. Hosp., 1956-57, Hosp. U. Pa., 1957-58; practice medicine specializing in dermatology, Phila., 1958-95; instr. dermatology Jefferson Med. Coll., Phila., 1958-72, clin. assoc. prof., 1972-81, clin. prof., 1981-95, hon. prof. dermatology, 1995—; attending physician, chief dermatology Holy Redeemer Hosp., Meadowbrook, Pa., 1958-95, emeritus staff, 1995—; instr. dermatology U. Pa. Grad. Sch. Medicine, 1958-70; med. advisor Pa. Blue Cross, 1973—. Contbr. articles in field to profl. jours. Bd. trustees Dermatology Found.; bd. dirs. Holy Redeemer Hosp. Served with USMC, 1943-46. Diplomate Am. Bd. Dermatology. Fellow Am. Acad. Dermatology, ACP; mem. Am. Dermatol. Assn., Soc. Investigative Dermatology, Am. Acad. Dermatology (chmn. adv. bd. council 1977, chmn. com. eval. 1979-82, chmn. audit com. 1991-93), AMA (mem. sect. on dermatology 1978), Pa. Acad. Dermatology (pres. 1976-77), Phila. Dermatol. Soc. (pres. 1976-77), Coll. Physicians Phila., Solomon Solis-Cohen Med. Lit. Soc. (pres. 1978), Pa., Phila. County (pres. N. br. 1976, dir. 1977) med. socs. Home: 1420 Lewis Rd Rydal PA 19046-1412

GREENBAUM, LARRY MARC, physician; b. N.Y.C., Feb. 26, 1958; s. Arthur and Roslyn Greenbaum. MD, SUNY, Bklyn., 1984. Diplomate in internal medicine and rheumatology Am. Bd. Internal Medicine. Intern, resident in internal medicine Winthrop U. Hosp., Mineola, N.Y., 1984-87; fellow rheumatology U. Cin., Cin., 1987-89; physician Med. Specialists, Inc., Zanesville, Ohio, 1989-93, Ind. Internal Medicine Cons., Indpls., 1993—. Office: Ind Internal Medicine Cons Ste W 110 N 17th Ave Ste 301 Beech Groves IN 46107

GREENBAUM, MITCHELL A., podiatrist; b. Plainview, N.Y., Feb. 9, 1963; s. William and Linda Ruth (Troum) G.; m. Carrie Ellen Peshkin, Aug. 31, 1995. BA in Biology, SUNY, Binghamton, 1985; DPM, N.Y. Coll. Podiatric Medicine, 1989. Diplomate Am. Bd. Podiatric Surgery. Podiatrist Family Footcare, Williston Park, N.Y. Fellow Am. Coll. Foot and Ankle Surgeons, Am. Coll. Foot Orthopedists; mem. Am. Podiatric Med. Assn. (mem. chmn. 1993—), Met. Athletic Congress, Am. Diabetes Assn. Office: 525 Woodbury Rd Plainview NY 11803

GREENBERG, E. ROBERT, medical research administrator; b. Birmingham, Ala., Mar. 14, 1944. BA, Case Western Res. U., 1966, MD, 1969; postgrad., U. Liverpool Sch. Trop. Med., 1968. Diplomate Am. Bd. Internal Medicine, Nat. Bd. Med. Examiners; lic. physician Vt., N.H. Rotating intern Mary Imogene Bassett Hosp., Cooperstown, N.Y., 1969-70; med. resident Dartmouth Affiliated Hosps., Hanover, N.H., 1972-74, chief med. resident, instr. medicine, 1974-75; asst. prof. to assoc. prof. comty./ family med., clin. med. Dartmouth Med. Sch., Hanover, 1975-88, prof. comty./family med., clin. med., 1988—, James J. Carroll prof., 1995—; Milbank epidemiology fellow dept. comty. medicine and gen. practice Oxford (Eng.) U., 1983-84; vis. scientist U. Calif. Sch. Medicine, San Diego, 1993-94; attending physician Mary Hitchcock Meml. Hosp., Hanover, 1977—; dir. epidemiology program Norris Cotton Cancer Ctr., Hanover, 1980—, dir., 1994—; mem. ad hoc study sects. and adv. coms. NIH, 1983—; bd. sci. counselors divsn. cancer prevention and control Nat. Cancer Inst., 1991—. Mem. editl. bd.: Stats. in Medicine, 1981-91, Jour. Nat. Cancer Inst., 1987-92, Cancer Epidemiology, Biomarkers and Prevention, 1991—; reviewer: New Eng. Jour. Medicine, Am. Jour. Epidemiology, Jour. AMA, others; contbr. numerous book chpts., articles, and abstracts to profl. publs. Recipient Article of Yr. award Assn. for Health Svcs. Rsch, also numerous rsch. grants. Mem. Am. Soc. Preventive Oncology (bd. dirs. 1990—), Phi Beta Kappa. Office: Dartmouth-Hitchcock Med Ctr One Medical Center Dr Lebanon NH 03756

GREENBERG, GEORGE, psychologist, consultant; b. N.Y.C., Jan. 24, 1935; s. David and Mary (Mittleman) G.; m. Amalia Nellie Wiesel, Oct. 12, 1954 (div. Apr. 1975); children: Jeffery, Leon; m. Deborah Zeigler, Dec. 30, 1988. BA, CUNY, 1955; PhD, Duke U., 1960. Lic. psychologist, N.Y., N.J. Clin. trainee, intern Butner (N.C.) State Hosp., Duke Hosp., Durham VA Hosp., 1956-59; rsch. assoc. Duke U., Durham, N.C., 1959-60; rsch. psychologist Mitre Corp., Boston, 1960-62; sr. specialist, supr. ITT, Paramus, N.J., 1962-64; asst. prof. psychology Fairleigh Dickinson U., Teaneck, N.J., 1964-67; psychotherapist Mental Health Cons. Ctr. of Bergen County, Teaneck, 1964-67; pvt. practice N.Y. and N.J., 1967—; mem. staff N.Y. Hosp.; mem. faculty med. sch. Cornell U., 1975—. Contbr. articles to profl. jours. Mem. APA, Soc. for Indsl. and Organizational Psychology, Am. Acad. Psychotherapists, N.Y. Soc. Clin. Psychologists, Am. Soc. Clin. Hypnosis, Assn. for the Advancement of Behavior Therapy, Soc. for the Exploration of Psychotherapy Integration, Bergen County Assn. Lic. Psychologists. Office: 167 Pinewood Pl Teaneck NJ 07666-4922

GREENBERG, GEORGE STANLEY, psychotherapist; b. Balt., Apr. 20, 1942; s. Herbert Herman and Frances (Kolodner) G.; m. Karen Jacobson, June 23, 1966. BA, Franklin & Marshall, 1964; M in Social Work, Ohio State U., 1971; D in Social Work, Tulane U., 1974. Diplomate Am. Bd. Examiners Clin. Social Work. Founder, dir. Family Therapy Inst., New Orleans, 1971—; rsch. fellow Mental Rsch. Inst., Palo Alto, Calif., 1972-73; rsch. assoc. Mental Rsch. Inst., Palo Alto, 1973-81; asst. prof. social work U. Houston, 1975-77; asst. prof. psychiatry La. State U. Med. Sch., New Orleans, 1978-80, clin. asst. prof. psychiatry, 1980-91, clin. assoc. prof. psychiatry, 1991—; spl. lectr. Tulane U., New Orleans, 1977—; dir. strategic interactional psychotherapies Davis program River Oaks Hosp., New Orleans, 1983-90, pres. allied health svcs. staff, 1989—; dir. employee assistance program Coca Cola Bottling Co., New Orleans, 1980-85, Oreck Corp., New Orleans, 1990—; bd. dirs. F.I.R.S.T. Children's Hosp., New Orleans, 1991; edn. dept. mem. Family Process, 1979-83; ednl. bd. mem. Zest Schrift for Systemische Therapie, 1983—. Contbr. chpts. in books and articles to profl. jours. Grantee NIMH, 1971-73; postgrad. fellow Tulane U. Med. Sch., 1975. Mem. Nat. Soc. Clin. Social Work, Am. Soc. Clin. Hypnosis (cert. cons.), Assn. Clin. Social Work Vendorship, Assn. Advancement Behavior Therapy, La. Group Psychotherapy Assn. (cert. group psychotherapist), Am. Group Psychotherapy Assn., La. Soc. Clin. Social Work. Home: 1116 Jena St New Orleans LA 70115-2816

GREENBERG, HARRY BERTRAND, geriatrician; b. Milw., Jan. 5, 1920; s. Harry and Josie (Krauss) G.; m. JoAnn Flom, 1952; children: Jane Susan, Albert Gordon, John Flom. BS, Tulane U., 1940, MD, 1943. Diplomate Am. Bd. Internal Medicine. Intern Touro Infirmary, New Orleans, 1943-44; resident Charity Hosp. La., New Orleans, 1946-49; clinician Health Dept. City of New Orleans, 1949-90; mem. clin. faculty Sch. Medicine, Tulane U., New Orleans, 1949—; pvt. practice New Orleans, 1949—; clin. prof. emeritus Tulane U., New Orleans, 1990—; cons. Med. Ctr. La., Tulane U. Med. Ctr., Touro Infirmary, St. Charles Gen. Hosp.; assoc. med. staff Tulane U. Med. Ctr. Clin. and Hosp. Contbr. numerous articles to profl. jours. With U.S. Army, 1944-46 (Bronze Star). Fellow ACP, Am. Coll. Chest Physicians (emeritus); mem. AMA, La. State Med. Soc., Orleans Parish Med. Soc., VFW, U.S. Am. Legion, Fifty Yr. Club of Am. Medicine. Jewish. Office: 3707 Octavia St New Orleans LA 70125-4315

GREENBERG, HARVEY ROY, psychiatrist; b. Phila., June 27, 1935; s. Murry Harry and Dora (Cohen) G.; m. Sharon Messitte; children: Matthew, Paul, Nicholas. AB, Columbia Coll., N.Y.C., 1955; MD, Cornell U., 1959; psychoanalysis degree, N.Y. Med. Coll., 1970. Diplomate Am. Bd. Psychiatry and Neurology. Internship N.Y. Hosp. Cornell U. Med. Ctr., N.Y.C., 1959-60; resident in psychiatry NYU/Bellevue Med. Ctr., 1960-63; Pvt. practice psychiatry and psychoanalysis N.Y.C., 1965—; supervising psychiatrist, lectr. adolescent psychiatry Bronx Children's Psychiat. Ctr., Bronx, N.Y., 1975-96; clin. prof. psychiatry Albert Einstein Med. Coll., Bronx, 1981—; faculty L.I. Inst. Psychoanalysis, L.I., N.Y., 1986—; residency Bellevue Psychiat. Hosp., NYU Med. Ctr., N.Y.C., 1963-65. Author: Emotional Illness in the Family, 1989, Screen Memories: Hollywood Cinema on the Psychoanalytic Couch, 1993; contbr. articles to profl. jours. Capt. U.S. Army, 1963-65. Fellow Am. Psychiat. Assn. (film com. 1977—), Am. Acad. Psychoanalysis; mem. Am. Soc. Adolescent Psychiatry, N.Y. Med. Soc. Home and Office: 320 W 86th St New York NY 10024-3139

GREENBERG, IRA ARTHUR, psychologist; b. Bklyn., June 26, 1924; s. Philip and Minnie (S.) G.; m. Martha Estella Cantrell, 1949 (div. 1950); m. Judith Linda Burgard-Rials, 1952 (div. 1954); m. Monita Ruth Niborod, 1961 (div. 1965). BA in Journalism, U. Okla., 1949; MA in English, U. So. Calif., 1962; MS in Counseling, Calif. State U. L.A., 1963; PhD in Psychology, Claremont (Calif.) Grad Sch., 1967; Grad. Marine Corps Inst.'s Command and Staff Coll., 1992. Editor, Ft. Riley (Kans.) Guidon, 1950-51; copy editor, reporter Columbus (Ga.) Enquirer, 1951-55; reporter Louisville Courier-Jour., 1955-56, L.A. Times, 1956-62; free-lance writer, L.A., Montclair, Camarillo, Calif., 1960-69, 76—; counselor Claremont Coll. Psychol. Clinic and Counseling Ctr., 1964-65; lectr. psychology Chapman Coll., Orange, Calif., 1965-66; psychologist Camarillo State Hosp., 1967-69, supervising psychologist, 1969-73, part-time clin. psychologist, 1973-93; part-time asst. prof. edn. San Fernando Valley State Coll., Northridge, Calif., 1967-69, lectr. psychodrama, social welfare U. Calif. Extension Div., Santa Barbara, 1968-69; vis. prof. edn. U. Nev., Reno, 1977—; vol. psychologist Free Clinic, L.A., 1968-70; staff dir. Calif. Inst. Psychodrama, 1969-71; tng. cons. Topanga Ctr. for Human Devel., 1970-75, bd. dirs., 1971-74, faculty Calif. Sch. Profl. Psychology, 1970-80; founder, exec. dir. Behavioral Studies Inst., mgmt. cons., L.A., 1970—; pvt. practice cons. in psychology, psychodrama, hypnosis, 1970—; founder, exec. dir. Psychodrama Ctr. for L.A., Inc., 1971—, Group Hypnosis Ctr., L.A., 1976—; producer, host TV talk show Crime and Pub. Safety, Century Cable, Channel 3, 1983—. Vol. humane officer State of Calif., 1979-89; res. officer L.A. Police Dept., 1980-86; bd. dirs. Humane Educators Coun., 1982-86. With AUS 11th engrng. combat bn., XXI Corps, Seventh Army, ETO, 1943-46; USAR, 1950-51; capt. Calif. State Mil. Res., 1986-93, maj. 1993—. Fellow Am. Soc. Clin. Hypnosis, Am. Soc. Group Psychotherapy and Psychodrama; mem. Am. Psychol. Assn., Calif. Psychol. Assn., L.A. County Psychol. Assn., So. Calif. Soc. Clin. Hypnosis (pres. 1977-78), Group Psychotherapy Assn. So. Calif. (pres. 1987-88), So. Calif. Psychotherapy Affiliation (dir. 1976-85), Assn. Psychical Rsch., Assn. Rsch. and Enlightenment. Peace Officers Assn., L.A. County Acad. TV Arts and Scis., Nat. Acad. Cable Programming, Am. Film Inst., Fraternal Order of UDT/SEAL, Navy Amphibious Scouts and Raiders Assn., 11th Engr. Combat Battalion Assn., 78th Infantry Divsn. Assn., VFW, Am. Legion, Jewish War Vets., State Def. Forces Assn. Am., State Def. Forces Assn. Calif., Mensa, Am. Zionist Fedn., NRA, Calif. Rifle and Pistol Assn., SW Pistol League, Animal Protection Inst. Am., L.A. SPCA, Sigma Delta Chi. Clubs: Sierra, Greater L.A. Press; B'nai B'rith; Beverly Hills Gun. Author: Psychodrama and Audience Attitude Change, 1968. Editor, author: Psychodrama: Theory and Therapy, 1974; Group Hypnotherapy and Hypnodrama, 1977. Office: BSI & Group Hypnosis Ctr 8939 S Sepulveda Blvd 318 Los Angeles CA 90045-3605

GREENBERG, JERROLD SELIG, health education educator; b. N.Y.C., Jan. 19, 1942; s. David and Bess G.; m. Karen Lider, Aug. 29, 1970; children: Todd, Keri. B.S., CCNY, 1964, M.S., 1965; Ed.D., Syracuse U., 1969. Tchr. N.Y.C. and Syracuse Pub. Sch. Dists., 1964-67; instr. Syracuse U., 1968-69; asst. prof. Boston U., 1969-71; prof. health edn. SUNY, Buffalo, 1971-79, U. Md., 1979—. Author: Student Centered Health Instruction: A Humanistic Approach, 1978, Health Through Discovery, 1980, 83, 86, 89, Sexuality Education: Theory and Practice, 1981, 88, 94, Comprehensive Stress Management, 1983, 87, 90, 93, 96, Sexuality: Insights and Issues, 1986, 89, 93, Physical Fitness: A Wellness Approach, 1986, 89, Stress and Sexuality, 1987, Health Education: Learner-Centered Instructional Strategies, 1989, 95, Coping with Stress: A Personal Guide, 1990, The College Student's Health Self-Care Diary, 1991, Exploring Health, 1992, Your Personal Stress Profile and Activity Workbook, 1992, 96, The Health Education Ethics Book, 1992, The Caregiver's Guide, 1992, Holt Health, 1994, Physical Fitness and Wellness, 1995; assoc. editor Jour. of Sch. Health, 1978-80, Jour. Health Edn., 1991-94; contbg. editor Health Education, 1974-76; exec. prodr. stress mgmt. videotapes and synchronized audiotapes/slides, 1985; author: (computer software program) Stress Management: Taking Control of Your Life, 1990; contbr. articles to profl. jours.; presentations, workshops on stress mgmt. for businesses and profl. groups. Served with U.S. Army, 1967. Grantee Western N.Y. chpt. Am. Heart Assn., 1977-78; Research Found. of SUNY, 1979-80, Met. Life Found., 1985-86. Fellow Am. Sch. Health Assn. (Disting. Svc. award); mem. AAHPERD (Alliance scholar), APHA, Assn. Advancement Health Edn. (presdl. citation, Profl. Svc. to Health Edn. award, Scholar award), Soc. Pub. Health Edn., Eta Sigma Gamma. Jewish. Home: 9412 Reach Rd Rockville MD 20854-2852 Office: U Md College Park MD 20742

GREENBERG, JONATHAN, neurosurgeon; b. Fall River, Mass., Nov. 6, 1950; s. Paul and Thelma Faith (Bernstein) G.; children: Ilana, Nathaniel, Danielle; m. Myriam Garzon, May 5, 1991. BA, Columbia U., 1971, MD, 1977, JD, 1977. Diplomate Am. Bd. Neurological Surgery. Intern Johns Hopkins Hosp., Balt., 1977-78, resident in gen. surgery, 1978-79; resident in neurosurgery Med. Ctr. NYU, N.Y.C., 1979-84; attending neurosurgeon Md. Inst. Emergency Med. Svcs. System, Balt., 1985-87; clin. instr., asst. prof. U. Md. Sch. Medicine, Balt., 1985-87; asst. prof. U. Miami (Fla.) Sch. Medicine, 1987-93; chief neurtrauma svcs. Jackson Meml. Hosp., Miami, 1987-92, med. co-dir. neurosurg. ICU, 1987-92; mem. surg. teaching faculty Orlando Regional Healthcare System, 1993, acting chmn. dept. neurol. surgery, 1996. Editor: Handbook of Head and Spine Trauma, 1993; contbr. chpts. to books, article to profl. publ. Mem. Dade County Trauma Adv. Com., Miami, 1989-93. Mem. Am. Coll. Surgeons, Congress Neurol. Surgeons, Soc. Critical Care Medicine, Soc. Neurosurg. Anesthesia and Critical Care, Am. Assn. Neurol. Surgeons. Republican. Jewish.

GREENBERG, LARRIE WARREN, pediatrician; b. Toledo, July 15, 1940; s. Leonard and Lillian (Webne) G.; m. Joyce Godofsky; children: Abby, Jeffrey. BS, U. Toledo, 1961; MD, Ohio State U., 1965. Intern Buffalo (N.Y.) Children's Hosp., 1965-66; resident Columbus (Ohio) Children's Hosp., 1966-68, chief resident, 1968-69; chief pediat. Kimbrough Army Hosp., Ft. Meade, Md., 1969-71, Alyn Orthop. Hosp., Jerusalem, 1971-72; asst. prof. Johns Hopkins U., Balt., 1972-73; dir. pediat. edn. Holy Cross Hosp., Silver Spring, Md., 1974-78; dir. med. edn. Children's Hosp. Nat. Med. Ctr., Washington, 1978—, pres. med. staff, 1988-90. Contbr. chpts. to med. texts; contbr. articles to med. jours. Bd. dirs. United Jewish Appeal Greater Washington, 1974-96. Maj. U.S. Army, 1969-71. Recipient Gold T award U. Toledo Alumni Assn., 1995, Ray Helter award for Outstanding Rsch. in Med. Edn., APA, 1996. Fellow Am. Acad. Pediat.; mem. Am. Pediat. Soc., Assn. Am. Med. Colls. (rsch. med. edn. com. 1990—, chmn. N.E. group on ednl. affairs 1993), Ambulatory Pediat. Assn. (bd. dirs. 1988-91), Am. Ednl. Rsch. Assn., Coun. on Med. Student Edn. in Pediat. (pres. 1994-96). Office: Childrens Hosp Nat Med Ctr 3800 Reservoir Rd NW Bldg 2phc Washington DC 20007-2196

GREENBERG, LEONARD DAVID, clinical psychologist; b. Atlanta, Aug. 23, 1947; s. Irving Lawrence and Regina (Gabler) G. BA, Duke U., 1969; MA, Ga. State U., 1974; PhD, Case Western Res. U., 1981. Staff psychologist Ctr. Mental Health, Waltham, Mass., 1980-90; dir. family therapy Trinity Mental Health, Framingham, Mass., 1986-87; dir. tng. mental health unit Marlboro (Mass.) Hosp., 1987-88, cons., 1988-90; pvt. practice Lexington, Mass., 1985—; mem. tng. faculty Atlanticare Med. Ctr., Lynn, Mass., 1988—; faculty Family Inst. of Washington, Boston campus, 1990—; cons. Beavabrook Guidance Ctr., Waltham, 1984-88, Options Day Treatment, Watertown, Mass., 1985-90, York County Counseling, Saco, Maine, 1986-88, DSS S.E. Mass. region, 1992-95. Mem. APA, Soc. Family Theraphy and Rsch. Home: 106 Wildwood Ave Arlington MA 02174-6224 Office: 76 Bedford St Lexington MA 02173-4440

GREENBERG, MICHAEL RICHARD, urban studies and community health educator; b. N.Y.C., Aug. 22, 1943; s. Sidney Saul and Mildred (Saletra) G.; m. Gwendolyn Barker, Jan. 19, 1978; children: Seana Deal, Heather Suggs, Joshua Suggs, Alexandra Greenberg. BA, CUNY, 1965; MA, Columbia U., 1966, PhD, 1969. Asst. prof. Columbia U., N.Y.C., 1969-71; assoc. prof. Rutgers U., New Brunswick, N.J., 1971-73, prof., 1973-78, disting. prof., 1978-82, prof. urban studies and community health, 1982—; dir. pub. policy Hazardous Substure Mgmt. and Rsch. Ctr., Newark, 1984—; co-dir. pub. health N.J. Grad. Progam in Pub. Health, New Brunswick, 1983—; dir. policy Environ. Occupational Health Sci. Inst., New Brunswick, 1985—. Author: Urbanization and Cancer Mortality, 1983, Public Health and the Environment, 1988, Environmental Risk and the Press, 1989 (award 1988), Environmental Reporter's Handbook (award 1989), Environmentally Devastated Neighborhoods, 1996. Recipient Spl. Merit award EPA, 1977. Mem. APHA, Soc. for Epidemiol. Rsch., Assn. of Am. Geographers, Soc. for Risk Analysis. Home: 228 Lawrence Ave Highland Park NJ 08904-1838 Office: Rutgers U Dept Urban Studies 33 Livingston Ave Ste 100 New Brunswick NJ 08901-1958

GREENBERG, ROBERT MILTON, retired psychiatrist; b. Silver Spring, Md., Oct. 24, 1916; s. Joseph and Rae (Levin) G.; m. Johanna Falletti, July 30, 1942 (dec. 1970); children: Roberta Rae, Harold Ellis; m. Jean Mildred Halpern, June 18, 1972; children: Susan, Elaine, Jill. AB, George Washington U., 1937, MD, 1941. Diplomate Am. Bd. Psychiatry and Neurology, Nat. Bd. Med. Examiners. Intern Sibley Meml. Hosp., Washington, 1941-

42; resident, staff physician VA Hosp., Coatesville, Pa., 1946-51; pvt. practice psychiatry Chevy Chase, Md., 1951-93; faculty to assoc. clin. prof. psychiatry George Washington U., 1951-87; chief psychiatric cons. Hebrew Home of Greater Washington, 1951-81. Contbr. articles to medico-legal jour. Trauma. Lt. comdr. USNR, 1942-46. Fellow Am. Soc. Psychoanalytic Physicians (pres. 1968-69), Am. Psychiat. Assn. (life); mem. AMA, Wash. Psychiat. Soc., Am. Coll. Psychiatrists (emeritus), Jewish War Vets. (founder and trustee Silver Spring chpt.). Democrat. Jewish. Home: 5600 Wisconsin Ave Apt 405 Chevy Chase MD 20815-4409

GREENBERG, ROGER PAUL, psychologist, educator; b. Jamaica, N.Y., July 2, 1941; s. Matthew Robert and Bertha Sylvia G.; B.A., Bklyn. Coll. CUNY, 1963; M.S. (USPHS fellow), Syracuse U., 1966, Ph.D. (USPHS fellow), 1968; m. Vivian Vicki Miller, Aug. 30, 1964; 1 son, Michael. Intern in clin. psychology Syracuse (N.Y.) VA Hosp., 1966-67; asst. prof. psychiatry SUNY Upstate Med. Center, Syracuse, 1968-72, assoc. prof., 1972-78, prof., dir. psychology internship tng., 1978—. Lic. psychologist, N.Y. Mem. Am. Psychol. Assn. (accreditation site visitor). N.Y. State Psychol. Assn., Central N.Y. Psychol. Assn. Author: (with Seymour Fisher) The Scientific Credibility of Freud's Theories and Therapy, 1977 (Library Jour.'s One of Ten Best Books in Psychology 1977); contbr. numerous articles to internat. profl. jours.; manuscript referee for profl. jours. Office: 750 E Adams St Syracuse NY 13210-2306

GREENBERG, ROSS HILLARD, physician, geriatric psychiatrist, educator; b. Phila., Nov. 25, 1961; s. Gordon Greenberg and Marilyn June (Eckman) Goldstein; m. Marjorie Ann Meiman, June 7, 1987 (div. 1988); m. Judith Ellen Cook, Jan. 11, 1992. BA with highest distinction in History, Rutgers Coll., 1983; DO, Phila. Coll. Osteo. Medicine, 1987. Diplomate Am. Bd. Psychiatry and Neurology with added qualifications in geriatric psychiatry. Comd. 2d lt. U.S. Army, 1987, advanced through grades to maj.; intern Tripler Army Med. Ctr. U.S. Army, Honolulu, 1987-88, resident in psychiatry Tripler Army Med. Ctr., 1988-91; chief divsn. mental health U.S. Army, Ft. Polk, La., 1991-92, chief divsn. mental health 2d Armored Divsn., 1992-93; chief divsn. mental health 2d Armored Divsn. U.S. Army, Ft. Stewart, Ga., 1993-94, chief outpatient psychiatry, 1994-95; asst. prof. psychiatry U. Medicine and Dentistry N.J., Stratford, 1995—, geriat. psychiatrist, 1995—. Decorated Army Commendation medal; Recipient Bausch and Lomb Hon. Sci. award, 1979; Big Bros. Am. scholar, 1979. Mem. Am. Osteo. Assn., Am. Psychiat. Assn., AMA, N.J. Assn. Osteo. Physicians and Surgeons, Am. Legion. Democrat. Jewish. Office: U Med & Dentistry NJ Ctr for Aging 42 E Laural Rd Ste 3200 Stratford NJ 08084

GREENBERG, SAUL NORMAN, retired orthodontist, educator; b. Bklyn., June 20, 1923; s. Paul and Rebecca (Kaplan) G.; m. Joan Ratner (dec.); children: Stephen, Andrew, David; m. Sheila Pollack, Apr. 8, 1984. BA, Bklyn. Coll., 1943; DDS, NYU, 1947; Cert. in Orthodontics, Columbia U., 1955. Diplomate Am. Bd. Orthodontists. Chmn. orthodontics Inst. for Grad. Dentists, N.Y.C., 1975-80; chief orthodontics dept. Flushing (N.Y.) Hosp., 1980—; prof. orthodontist NYU Coll. Dentistry, 1987-95; ret., 1995. Author: So You Want To Be A Dentist, 1964; contbr. articles to profl. jours. 1st lt. U.S. Army, 1951-53. Fellow Am. Coll. Dentists; mem. Am. Assn. Orthodontists, ADA, Omicron Kappa Upsilon. Home: 50 Hillpark Ave Great Neck NY 11021-3757

GREENBERG, SHELDON BURT, plastic and reconstructive surgeon; b. Bklyn., July 8, 1948; s. Morris and Lillian (Liss) G.; m. Andrea R. Levy, Feb. 10, 1991. BS, Muhlenberg Coll., 1970; MD, Chgo. Med. Sch., 1974. Diplomate Am. Bd. Otolaryngology, Plastic Surgery. Resident in surgery Lenox Hill Hosp., N.Y.C., 1974-75; resident in otolaryngology Met. Hosp., Manhattan Eye and Ear Hosp., N.Y.C., 1978; resident in plastic surgery Akron (Ohio) City Hosp., 1978-80, fellow in hand surgery, 1980; pvt. practice, Norwalk, Conn., 1981—. Fellow Am. Coll. Surgeons, Am. Soc. Plastic and Reconstructive Surgeons; mem. Conn. Med. Soc., Fairfield County Med. Soc., Fairfield Men's Club. Republican. Jewish. Office: 40 Cross St Norwalk CT 06851-4647

GREENBERG, STEPHEN ROBERT, retired pathology educator; b. Omaha, May 5, 1927; s. Nathan Henry and Ruth (Levey) G.; m. Constance Bettine, June 4, 1952; children: Andrew Eugene, Nathan Henry. BS, St. Louis U., 1951, MS, 1952, PhD in Pathology, 1954. Asst. in pathology Clarkson Hosp., Omaha, 1954-55; instr. pathology Chgo. Med. Sch., 1955-57, assoc. in pathology, 1957-62, asst. prof., 1962-69, assoc. prof. pathology, 1969-93; lectr. Cook County Grad. Sch. Medicine, Chgo., 1973—. Contbr. over 150 articles to profl. jours. Forensic Scis. Found. grantee, 1988-91. Fellow Inst. of Medicine of Chgo.; mem. Am. Soc. Clin. Pathologists, Am. Acad. Forensic Scis., Am. Assn. Clin. Anatomists, Internat. Acad. Pathology, Masons (33 deg.). Republican. Hebrew.

GREENBERG, WILIAM RONALD, neurologist; b. Miami Beach, Fla., Feb. 19, 1953; s. Joseph H.M. and Anna (Katz) G.; m. Abbe B. Kleinberg, Nov. 22 (div. Mar. 1988); children: Erica, Adam; m. Nancy Schick, Apr. 14, 1991. BA, Yeshiva U., 1974; MD, U. Miami, Fla., 1978. Intern Michael Reese Hosp. and Med. Ctr., Chgo., 1978-79; resident U. Pitts., 1979-82; pvt. practice St. Petersburg, Fla., 1992—; mem. staff Palms of Pasadena Hosp., St. Petersburg Gen. Northside. Co-chair Maimonides divsn. Jewish Fedn., Pinellas County, 1995—; bd. dirs. Pinellas County Jewish Day Sch., 1991-94. Mem. Am. Acad. Neurology, Pinellas County Med. Soc. Office: Ste 4W 5425 Park St N Saint Petersburg FL 33709-7042

GREENBERG, WILLIAM MICHAEL, psychiatrist; b. Bklyn., Oct. 19, 1946; s. Benjamin Greenberg and Marilyn (Berger) Hamberg; m. Wendy Faith Megerman, June 14, 1992. BA, Queens Coll., 1968; postgrad., U. Medicine & Dentistry N.J., 1974-76; MD, Albert Einstein Coll. Medicine, 1978. Diplomate Am. Bd. Psychiatry and Neurology. Computer programmer Western Electric Co., N.Y.C., 1970-73; rsch. asst. Bklyn. Jewish Hosp., 1973-74; resident in psychiatry Bronx (N.Y.) Mcpl. Hosp. Ctr., 1978-83, house staff pres., 1981-82; acting med. dir. Met. Ctr. for Mental Health, N.Y.C., 1983; staff psychiatrist Bronx Psychiat. Ctr., 1983-84; dir. psychiatry clinic North Cen. Bronx Hosp., 1984-88; psychiatrist, cons. Montefiore Mental Health Svcs. at Rikers Island, East Elmhurst, N.Y., 1985-86; pvt. practice Bronx, 1985-88; chief psychiatrist, attending staff mem. Bergen Pines County Hosp., Paramus, N.J., 1988—, dir. of psychiat. rsch., 1993—; asst. clin. prof. Albert Einstein Coll. Medicine, Bronx, 1988-90; vis. asst. prof. Med. Coll. Pa., 1990-94; adj. asst. prof. Med. Coll. Pa. and Hahnemann U., 1994—; chmn. Bergen Pines Instnl. Rev. Bd., 1996—; prin. investigator for clin. drug trials. Asst. editor Community Psychiatrist, 1985-89; mem. editorial bd. Einstein Quar. Jour. Biology and Medicine, 1987—; contbr. articles to profl. jours.; reviewer profl. jours., books. Union rep. Com. Interns and Residents, N.Y.C., 1979-81; speaker's bur. Physicians for Social Responsibility, N.Y.C., 1982-84, Bergen Pines County Hosp., 1988—. Rock Sleyster Meml. scholar AMA, 1977; recipient Bergen Pines Psychiatry Residency Teaching award, 1991. Mem. AAAS, APHA, Am. Psychiat. Assn., Am. Assn. Community Psychiatrists, Assn. for Advancement of Philosophy and Psychiatry. Office: Bergen Pines County Hosp Div Psychiatry Paramus NJ 07652

GREENBERGER, NORTON JERALD, physician; b. Cleve., Sept. 13, 1933; s. Sam and Lillian (Frank) G.; m. Joan Narcus, Aug. 10, 1964; children: Sharon, Rachel, Wendy. A.B., Yale U., 1955; M.D., Western Res. U., 1959. Diplomate: Am. Bd. Internal Medicine (sec.-treas. 1980-82). Intern Univ. Hosps., Cleve., 1959-60, resident internal medicine, 1960-62; USPHS fellow in gastroenterology Harvard U., 1962-65, Mass. Gen. Hosp., Boston, 1962-65; with Ohio State U., Columbus, 1965-72, dir. div. gastroenterology, 1967-72, prof., 1971-72; prof., chmn. dept. medicine U. Kans., Kansas City, 1972—; mem. Nat. Bd. Med. Examiners, 1971-75; mem. gen. medicine study sect. A, NIH, 1973-76. Author: Gastrointestinal Disorders: A Pathophysiologic Approach, 1976, 4th rev. edit., 1989, Medical Book of Lists, 4th rev. edit., 1994, History Taking and Physical Examination: Essentials and Clinical Correlates, 1992; co-editor gastroent. sect. Yearkbook of Medicine, 1969—; editor Yearbook of Digestive Diseases, 1984—; contbr. articles to med. jours. Recipient Outstanding Teaching award House Staff Dept. Medicine Ohio State U., 1970-71, Outstanding Teaching award Kans. U. Med. Sch. Class of 1978, Outstanding Med. Educator, 1984, 85, 90, 91. Fellow ACP (editorial com. gastorenterology sect. 1975-77, regent 1984-92, chmn. bd. regents 1988-89, pres. 1990-91); mem. Am. Fedn. Clin. Rsch. (pres. Midwestern sect. 1973-74), Ctrl. Soc. Clin. Rsch. (councillor 1975, pres. 1979-80), N.Y. Acad. Scis., Midwestern Gut Club, Am. Gastroent. Assn. (pres.-elect 1983-84, pres. 1984-85, Disting. Educator award 1995), Am. Soc. Clin. Investigation, Am. Soc. Pharmacology and Exptl. Therapeutics, Assn. Am. Physicians, Assn. Profs. Medicine (pres. 1986-87), Phi Beta Kappa, Sigma Xi, Alpha Omega Alpha. Home: 2611 W 70th Ter Shawnee Mission KS 66208-2745 Office: U Kans Med Ctr 3901 Rainbow Blvd Kansas City KS 66160-0001

GREENBURG, A. GERSON, surgeon, medical educator; b. Chgo., Mar. 23, 1939; s. Benjamin J. and Marcella (Katz) G.; m. Reva Pollack, Dec. 15, 1962; children: Beth Greenburg-Hughes, Joan P., Lara. BS, U. Chgo., 1959, MD, 1963; PhD, Northwestern U., 1972; MA (hon.), Brown U., 1987. Intern surgery U. Chgo., 1963-64, surg. resident, 1964-65, 67-70; sr. resident surgery U. Ill., Chgo., 1970-71, asst. prof. surgery, 1972-73; prof. surgery U. Calif., San Diego, 1973-86, Brown U., Providence, 1986—; surgeon-in-chief The Miriam Hosp., Providence, 1986—; chair surgery test com. Nat. Bd. Med. Examiners, Phila., 1988-94; chair U.S. Med. Licensing Exam. Step 2, Phila., 1990-95; med. dir. Hemosol, Inc., Toronto, 1994—. Fellow Am. Coll. Surgeons (chair pre-post operative com. 1990-94); mem. Am. Surg. Assn., Am. Assn. Surgery of Trauma, Soc. U. Surgeons, Shock Soc. Office: The Miriam Hosp 164 Summit Ave Providence RI 02906

GREENBURG, SHARON LOUISE, psychologist; b. Chgo., Aug. 29, 1941; d. Irving and Ethel (Vinitzky) Rosenholtz; m. Joel H. Greenburg, Apr. 11, 1963; children: Douglas Neil, Jayne Ellen. BS, Northwestern U., 1963; MEd, Loyola U. Chgo., 1978, PhD, 1981. Pvt. practice psychologist Chgo., 1981—, Arlington Heights, Ill., 1987—; adj. prof. Loyola U., Chgo., 1981-86; cons. Cyborg Corp., Chgo., 1986—, Premark Corp., Deerfield, Ill., 1986—. Author: (with others) Casebook of Multimodal Therapy; contbr. articles to profl. jours. Bd. dirs. Chgo. chpt. Am. Jewish Com. Mem. Am. Psychol. Assn. (div. 42 psychologists in ind. practice), Ill. Psychol. Assn. Office: 875 N Dearborn St Ste 404 Chicago IL 60610-3386

GREENE, ALBERT LAWRENCE, hospital administrator; b. N.Y.C., Dec. 10, 1949; s. Leonard and Anne (Birnbaum) G.; m. Jo Linda Anderson, Sept. 3, 1972; children: Stacy, Jeremy. BA, Ithaca Coll., 1971; MHA, U. Mich., 1973. Adminstrv. asst. Harper Hosp., Detroit, 1973-74, asst. adminstr., 1974-77, assoc. adminstr., 1977-80; adminstr. Grace Hosp., Detroit, 1980-84, Harper Hosp., Detroit, 1984-87; pres., chief exec. officer Sinai Samaritan Med. Ctr., Milw., 1988-90, Alta Bates Med. Ctr., Berkeley, Calif., 1990—; bd. dirs. Acuson Corp., Calif. Assn. Hosps. and Health Sys., Hosp. Coun. No. and Ctrl. Calif. Trustee Huron Valley Hosp., Milford, Mich., 1984-87. Mem. Am. Coll. Healthcare Execs., Young Pres. Orgn., Rotary, Blackhawk Country Club, Lakeview Club. Home: 3819 Cottonwood Dr Danville CA 94506-6007 Office: Alta Bates Med Ctr 2450 Ashby Ave Berkeley CA 94705-2067

GREENE, BARNETT ALAN, anesthesiologist; b. N.Y.C., July 30, 1907; s. Harris and Sarah (Frischman) G.; m. Lee Adelman, Dec. 24, 1932; children: Stuart A., William H. BSc cum laude, CCNY, 1929; MD cum laude, NYU, 1934. Diplomate Am. Bd. Anesthesiology. Intern, house officer Lincoln City Hosp., Bronx, N.Y., 1934-36, resident in anesthesiology, 1936-39; anesthesiologist Bklyn. Cancer Inst., Dept. Hosps. of N.Y.C., 1939-47; dir. dept. anesthesiology Prospect Heights Hosp., Bklyn., 1939-46, Unity Hosp., Bklyn., 1940-75, Bklyn. Hebrew Home and Hosp. for Aged, 1939-75, Adelphi Hosp., Bklyn., 1939-74, Bklyn. Women's Hosp., 1946-75, Cumberland Hosp. of Dept. of Hosps. City of N.Y., 1955-70, Luth. Hosp., Bklyn., 1963-78; pres. Greene, Berkowitz and Goffen, Physicians, P.C., 1971-81, Barnett A. Greene, M.D. P.C., 1978-92; Greene Family Svcs. Corp., 1992—; clin. assoc. prof. anesthesiology SUNY Downstate Med. Ctr., 1958-75; clin. practice examiner Am. Bd. Anesthesiology, 1946-52; vis. anesthesiologist Kings County Hosp., 1951-55, acting dir. dept. anesthesiology, 1951-55; attending anesthesiologist Bklyn.-Cumberland Hosp. Med. Ctr., 1970-75, emeritus, 1975—; chmn. bd. trustees Bklyn. Women's Hosp. Clinic, 1975-78; mem. malpractice mediation panel Kings County Supreme Ct., 1978-90. Contbr. articles to profl. publs. Maj. Med. Corps, U.S. Army, 1943-46. Decorated Bronze Star. Fellow Am. Anesthesiologists, N.Y. Acad. Medicine; mem. AMA, N.Y. State Med. Soc. (mem. com. on peer rev. 1981, com. on operating rm. safety 181-83), Kings County Med. Soc. (McAteer prize 1940, mem. continuing edn. com. 1977-80), Phi Beta Kappa, Alpha Omega Alpha. Jewish.

GREENE, BEVERLY ANN, clinical psychologist; b. Orange, N.J., Aug. 14, 1950; d. Samuel and Thelma G. BA, NYU, 1973; postgrad. Marquette U., 1973-74; MA, Adelphi U., 1977, PhD, 1983. Lic. psychologist, N.Y., N.J. Fellow in psychology Mental Retardation Inst., N.Y. Med. Coll., Valhalla, N.Y., 1974-76; psychol. cons. Williamsburg Child Devel. Ctr., Bklyn., 1976-78; psychology intern East Orange VA Med. Ctr., 1978-79; rsch. asst. dept. neurosci. N.J. Coll. Medicine and Dentistry, Vet.'s Hosp., 1979-80; psychology trainee, Children's Partial Hospitalization Unit, Brookdale Hosp. and Med. Ctr., 1980; cert. sch. psychologist N.Y.C. Bd. Edn., 1980-82, staff psychologist, 1982-84; sr. psychologist, dir. inpatient child and adolescent psychol. svcs. King's County Psychiat. Hosp., 1984-89; supervising psychologist Community Mental Health Ctr., U. Medicine and Dentistry N.J., Newark, 1989-91; clin. instr. in psychiatry Downstate Med. Sch., 1982-85, clin. asst. prof., 1985-89, acting dir. Children's Inpatient Unit, 1985-86; clin.asst. prof. dept. psychiatry U. Medicine and Dentistry of N.J., Newark, 1989-91; assoc. clin. prof. dept. psychology St. Johns U., N.Y., 1991-93, assoc. prof. dept. psychology, 1993-95, prof., 1995—. Contbr. articles to profl. jours.; co-author books. Recipient Disting. Humanitarian award Am. Assn. Applied & Preventive Psychology, 1994; Martin Luther King scholar, 1968-72, NIMH fellow, 1976-77. Fellow APA (soc. for the psychol. study of ethnic minority issues, co-chair continuing edn. Women's div. 1991-93, diversity in clin. psychology task force, fellow clin. psychology, psychotherapy, psychology of women, lesbian and gay issues and ethnic minority issues divsn., co-editor divsn. 44 ann. pub., Dist. Profl. Contbns. to Ethnic Minority Issues award divsn. 44, 1992, Soc. for the Psychol. Study Lesbian and Gay Issues, Psychotherapy with Women Rsch. award 1995, Outstanding Achievement award Com. Lesbian and Gay Concerns 1996), Am. Orthopsychiat. Assn.; mem. Internat. Neuropsychol. Soc., Nat. Assn. Black Psychologists, N.Y. Assn. Black Psychologists, Nat. Assn. Women in Psychology (Women of Color Psychologies Publ. award, 1991, 95, Disting. Publ. award 1995), N.Y. Assn. Women in Psychology, N.Y. Coalition of Hosp. and Instnl. Psychologists.

GREENE, DONALD RICHARD, dermatologist, educator; b. Buffalo, Aug. 20, 1947; s. Norman Sanborn and Helen Jean (Second) Powers; m. JoAnne D'Amico, Mar. 5, 1982; children: Patrick Ryan, Claire Elizabeth. B.A., SUNY, Buffalo, 1970, M.D., 1974. Diplomate Am. Bd. Dermatology. Intern Buffalo Gen. Hosp., 1974-75; resident Hosp. of U. Pa., Phila., 1975-76; resident Yale-New Haven Hosp., 1976-79, chief resident, 1978-79; clin. instr. Yale U. Sch. Medicine, New Haven, 1979-82, clin. asst. prof., 1982—; attending physician Yale-New Haven Hosp., Hosp. St. Raphael, 1979—; med. bd. Branford (Conn.) Health Care Ctr., 1983—. Recipient Physiology award SUNY-Buffalo, 1971; Am. Cancer Soc. grantee, 1972. Fellow Am. Acad. Dermatology; mem. AMA, Conn. State Med. Soc. (pres. dermatology sect. 1984-85), New Haven County Med. Assn., New Haven City Med. Assn., New England Dermatologic Soc., Assn. of Attendings at Yale U. Sch. Medicine, Rotary, Yale Club New Haven, Penn Club N.Y., Madison Winter Club, Mory's Assn. Episcopalian.

GREENE, ERNEST RINALDO, JR., anesthesiologist, chemical engineer; b. Mobile, Ala., Jan. 26, 1941; s. Ernest Rinaldo and Dorris Rolinha (Lassiter) G.; m. Lois Ellen Laura Zullig, Sept. 23, 1967; children: Laura Rolinha, Ernest Rinaldo III, Ellen Victoria, Max McKeen. BA, Rice U., 1962, BS, 1963; MA, Princeton U., 1966, PhD, 1968; MD, Washington U., St. Louis, 1981. Diplomate Am. Bd. Anesthesiology; diplomate, Nat. Bd. Med. Examiners; registered profl. engr., Ala. Tenured asst. prof. engrng. U. Ala., Birmingham, 1970-84, asst. prof. anesthesiology, 1986-88; chief anesthesiology Cooper Green Hosp., Birmingham, 1986-90, VA Med. Ctr., Birmingham, 1987-90; assoc. prof. anesthesiology U. Ala., Birmingham, 1988-90; chief anesthesiology Vaughan Regional Med. Ctr., Selma, Ala., 1990-92; adjunct assoc. prof. biomed. engrng. U. Ala., Birmingham, 1990—; founder, CEO Hivex, Inc.; with Anes Care, Phenix City, Ala., 1994—; reviewer (bioengring.) NSF, Washington, 1981-90; guest reviewer Anesthesiology (jour.), Phila., 1988-90. Author: Homogenous Enzyme Kinetics, 1984, Immobilized Enzyme Kinetics, 1984; (with others) New Anesthetic Agents, Devices and Monitoring Techniques, 1984, Pain Management of AIDS Patients, 1991. Mem. AIChE, Am. Soc. Anesthesiologists, Internat. Anesthesia Rsch. Soc., SAR, S.R., Soc. Colonial Wars, Gen. Soc. of War of 1812, Sigma Xi (assoc.), Tau Beta Pi, Phi Lambda Upsilon, Sigma Tau. Republican. Methodist. Office: PO Box 950 Phenix City AL 36868-0950

GREENE, JAMES ALLEN, physician, real estate developer; b. Sneedville, Tenn., Mar. 15, 1939; s. A. Kyle and Argelene (Surgenor) G.; m. Rebecca Rita O'Connor, Sept. 18, 1970; children: John Robert, Rebecca Allen. MD, U. Tenn.-Memphis, 1963. Diplomate Am. Bd. Family Practice. Intern, U. Tenn., Knoxville, 1963-64; assoc. dir. Oak Ridge Mental Health Clinic, 1969-70; assoc. Psychiatry Assocs., Birmingham, Ala., 1970-79; chief geriatrics James Healy Hosp., Tampa, Fla., 1980-81; med. dir. Gerontology Ctr., Knoxville, 1981-86, med. dir. Sr. Health Ctr. Park West/Hosp. Corp. Am. Med. Ctrs., Knoxville, 1986—; pres., CEO Geriat. Med. Care, Inc., 1992—; pres. Health and Creative Aging Clinic, Knoxville, 1980—, Health and Creative Aging Devel. Corp.; med. dir. East Tenn. Bapt. Hosp. Gerontology Ctr., Knoxville, 1982-83; asst. med. dir. Pain Ctr., Knoxville, 1983-84; cons. med. dir. Nat. Health Corp., 1984-87; clin. assoc. psychiatry U. Tenn.; clin. prof. family practice East Tenn. State U. Coll. Medicine. Columnist: Successful Aging, Knoxville Jour., 1982-83, Geriatric Medicine, Tenn. Med. Jour., 1983—; author: Eight Day Week, 1976; contbr. articles to profl. jours. Bd. dirs. Council on Aging, Knoxville, 1983, Alzheimer's Support Group, Knoxville, 1983-84; Ptnrs. Health Care, Nashville. Served to capt. USAF, 1968-69. Fellow Am. Psychiat. Assn., So. Psychiat. Assn.; mem. Tenn. Med. Assn. (chmn. geriatric and long term care 1982-88). Recipient Distng. Svc. award Tenn. Hosp. Assn., 1988; Clin. of Yr. Am. Geriatrics Soc., 1989. Methodist. Club: LeConte (Knoxville). Home: 4047 Alta Vista Way Knoxville TN 37919-6602 Office: 1900 Winston Rd Knoxville TN 37919

GREENE, JODY LEE, medical association administrator; b. Kennesaw, Ga., June 5, 1963; s. Everette Greene and Pat Ann (Byrd) Hayes. BBA in Mktg., Ga. So. U., 1985. Cert. Ins. Claims Adjuster, S.C. Claims adjuster Liberty Mutual Ins., Columbia, S.C., 1985-88; claims supr. Liberty Mutual Ins., Columbia, 1988-90; mktg. mgr. Rebound, Inc., Columbia, 1990-91, regional managed care rep., 1991-92, mgr. regional managed care, 1992-94; dir. managed care mktg. FMD, Winter Pk., Fla., 1994-96; gen. mgr. Med. Practice Solutions, Winter Pk., 1995-96; cons. CPC Hosps., Atlanta, 1994; mem. adv. bds. S.C. Case Mgmt. Assn., Columbia, 1993-94. Mem. S.C. C. of C., S.C. Case Mgmt. Assn. (pres. 1993-94). Home: 1219 Summerville Ave Columbia SC 29201 Office: Med Practice Solutions 1201 Louisiana Ave Winter Park FL 32789

GREENE, JOHN CLIFFORD, dentist, former university dean; b. Ashland, Ky., July 19, 1926; s. G. Norman and Ella R. G.; m. Gwen Rustin, Nov. 17, 1957; children: Alan, Lisa, Laura. A.A., Ashland Jr. Coll., 1947; student, Marshall Coll., 1948; D.M.D., U. Louisville, 1952, Sc.D. (hon.), 1980; M.P.H., U. Calif., Berkeley, 1961; Sc.D. (hon.), U. Ky., 1972, Boston U., 1975. Diplomate: Am. Bd. Dental Public Health (pres.). Intern USPHS Hosp., Chgo., 1952-53; staff USPHS Hosp., San Francisco, 1953-54; asst. regional dental cons. Region IX, San Francisco, 1954-56; asst. to chief dental officer USPHS, Washington, 1958-60; chief epidemiology program Dental Health Center, 1961-66; dep. dir. Div. Dental Health, 1966-70, acting dir., 1970, dir., 1970-73; acting dir. Bur. Health Resources Devel., 1973-74, dir., 1974-75; chief dental officer USPHS, 1974-81, dep. surgeon gen., 1978-81; with Epidemic Intelligence Service, Communicable Disease Center, Altanta and Kansas City, Mo., 1956-57; epidemiology and biometry br. Nat. Inst. Dental Research, NIH, Bethesda, Md., 1957-58; prof. and dean sch. dentistry U. Calif., San Francisco, 1981-94; prof. and dean emeritus, 1994—; spl. cons. WHO, India, 1957; faculty Calif., U. Mich., U. Pa.; cons. Am. Dental Assn. Council, Nat. Health Professions Placement Network. Contbr. writings to profl. publs. Served with USN, 1945-46. Recipient citation Sch. Grad. Dentistry Boston U., 1971, citation U. of the Pacific, 1977, Meritorious and Disting. Service awards HEW, 1972, 75, Outstanding Alumnus award U. Louisville, 1980, award of merit FDI, 1978; Alumnus of Yr. award U. Calif. Sch. Pub. Health, Berkeley, 1984. Fellow Internat. Coll. Dentists, Am. Coll. Dentists; mem. ADA, Calif. Dental Assn., San Francisco Dental Soc., Internat. Assn. Dental Research (pres.), Am. Assn. Dental Rsch. (pres.), Am. Assn. Pub. Health Dentists, Am. Acad. Periodontology, Am. Assn. Dental Schs. (v.p., chair coun. of deans.), Inst. of Medicine of Nat. Acad. Sci. (gov. coun.), Federation Dentaire Internationale (chmn. commn. on public dental health, mem. WHO panel of experts on dental health), U.S. Preventive Svcs., Omicron Kappa Upsilon, Delta Omega. Home: 103 Peacock Dr San Rafael CA 94901-1551 Office: U Calif Sch Dentistry 513 Parnassus Ave Rm 630S San Francisco CA 94122-2722

GREENE, LAURENCE WHITRIDGE, JR., surgical educator; b. Denver, Jan. 18, 1924; s. Laurence Whitridge Sr. and Freda (Schmitt) G.; m. Frances Steger, Sept. 16, 1950 (dec. Dec. 1977); children: Charlotte Greene Kerr, Mary Whitridge Greene, Laurence Whitridge III; m. Nancy Kay Bennett, Dec. 7, 1984. BA, Colo. Coll., 1945; MD, U. Colo., 1947; postgrad., U. Chgo., 1948-50. Diplomate Am. Bd. of Surgery. Intern St. Lukes Hosp., Denver, 1947-48; sr. intern in ob./gyn. U. Chgo. Lying-In Hosp., 1948-49; surg. resident U. Cin. Gen. Hosp., 1952-55, sr. surg. resident, 1955-57, chief surgery resident, 1957-58; clin. surgery asst. Sch. of Medicine U. Colo., Denver, 1958-61, clin. instr. Sch. of Medicine, 1961-67, asst. clin. prof. Sch. of Medicine, 1967-75, assoc. clin. prof. Sch. of Medicine, 1975-87, clin. prof. Sch. of Medicine, 1987—; adj. prof. zoology and physiology U. Wyo., Laramie, 1970-80; mem. staff Ivinson Meml. Hosp., Laramie, 1958—; chmn. Wyo chpt. Com. on Trauma, 1973-89; tchr., mem. adv. staff U. Colo. Med. Sch., Denver, 1958-83; mem. advisor, surgeon U. Wyo. Athletics, Laramie, 1975-80, Wyo. Hwy. Patrol, 1950—. Contbr. numerous articles to profl. jours. Lt. M.C. (s.g.) USN, 1950-52, Korea. Fellow ACS; mem. Am. Assn. for Surgery of Trauma, Southwestern Surgery Congress, Western Surg. Assn., Mont Reed Soc., Masons, Shriners, Sigma Xi. Republican. Episcopalian.

GREENE, MURRAY A., cardiologist; b. Bklyn., May 20, 1927; s. Max and Beatrice (Kolomer) G.; m. Eileen Smolkin, Dec. 19, 1953; children: Barry T., Larry B. AB, NYU, 1948; MD, Columbia U., 1952. Diplomate Am. Bd. Internal Medicine. Intern Maimonides Hosp., Bklyn., 1952-53; asst. resident in medicine Maimonides Hosp., 1953-54; research fellow cardiopulmonary lab. Maimonides Hosp. and SUNY Downstate Med. Ctr., 1954-55, 56-57; resident in medicine Montefiore Hosp., N.Y.C., 1955-56; chief div. cardiovascular diseases, dir. intensive care unit and cardiopulmonary lab. Bronx-Lebanon Hosp., N.Y.C., 1957-71, attending physician dept. medicine, 1957—; asst. clin. prof. medicine Albert Einstein Coll. Medicine, N.Y.C., 1972—. Contbr. numerous articles to med. jours. Served with U.S. Army, 1945-47. Fellow ACP, Am. Coll. Chest Physicians, Am. Fedn. Clin. Research; mem. AMA, Am. Physicians Fellowship Assn., N.Y. Acad. Scis., Am. Heart Assn., N.Y. Heart Assn., Am. Soc. Internal Medicine, N.Y. Soc. Internal Medicine, Med. Soc. State N.Y., Phi Beta Kappa. Home: 103 Tewksbury Rd Scarsdale NY 10583-6023

GREENE, ROBERT JAY, surgeon, oncologist; b. Phila., Jan. 17, 1930; s. Samuel Robert and Kathryn (Purisch) G.; m. Edith Morse, Dec. 27, 1952 (div. 1961); children: Steven, Linda, Karen; m. Barbara Lee Bassin, May 21, 1962; 1 child, David. AB, U. Pa., 1950; MD, Harvard U., 1954. Diplomate Am. Bd. Surgeons. Intern Univ. Hosps. Cleve., 1954-55, resident in gen. surgery, 1955-56; resident in gen. surgery Beth Israel Hosp., Boston, 1958-62; sr. surgeon St. Luke's Hosp., New Bedford, Mass., 1962—. Capt. U.S. Army, 1956-58. Fellow ACS; mem. Am. Soc. Clin. Oncology, Mass. Med. Soc. Democrat. Jewish. Home and Office: New Bedford Surg Assocs Inc 49 Hawthorn St New Bedford MA 02740-3419

GREENFELD, NORMAN, psychology educator; b. Bklyn., May 9, 1925; s. Joseph and Ettie (Schultz) G.; m. Elinor Freedman, Aug. 26, 1956; 1 child, Jennifer. BA, Utica Coll., 1951; MA, Syracuse U., 1953; MS, U. Mass., 1955, PhD, 1957. Faculty SUNY, Albany, 1956-95, prof. psychology, 1967-95, prof. emeritus, 1995-96, ret., 1995. Contbr. articles to profl. jours. Served with U.S. Army, 1943-44. Mem. Sigma Xi, Phi Kappa Phi, Pi Delta Epsilon. Jewish. Home: 51 Northgate Dr Albany NY 12203-5130

GREENFIELD, GEORGE B., radiologist; b. N.Y.C., May 4, 1928; s. Jacob and Rose (Wolf) G.; m. Barbara Anne O'Driscoll, Mar. 3, 1956; children: Edward James, Sheelagh Anne. B.A., NYU, 1949; M.D., State U. Utrecht, Netherlands, 1956. Diplomate: Am. Bd. Radiology, Am. Bd. Nuclear Medicine. Intern Bridgeport (Conn.) Hosp., 1956-57; resident radiology Presbyn.-St. Lukes Hosp., Chgo., 1957-60; practice medicine, specializing in radiology Chgo., 1960—; radiologist Cook County Hosp., 1961-66, asst. dir. diagnostic radiology, 1966-69; assoc. prof. radiology U. Ill., 1966-69; prof., chmn. dept. radiology Chgo. Med. Sch., 1969-74; prof., chmn. dept. radiology Mt. Sinai Hosp. Med. Center, 1969-89, pres. med. staff, 1983-85; prof. diagnostic radiology Rush Med. Coll., 1975-87; prof. radiology Cook County Grad. Sch. Medicine.; prof. radiology Chgo. Med. Sch., 1987-89, vice chmn. dept. radiology, 1988-89; prof. radiology U. S.Fla., Tampa, 1989—; attending radiologist H. Lee Moffitt Cancer Ctr. and Rsch. Inst., Tampa; cons. radiologist Shriner's Hosp. for Crippled Children, Tampa, 1989. Author: Radiology of Bone Diseases, 5th edit., 1990; sr. author: A Manual of Radiographic Positioning, 1973, Computers in Radiology, 1985, Imaging of Bone Tumors, 1995; contbr. articles to profl. jours. Trustee Mt. Sinai Hosp., 1986-89. Served with U.S. Army, 1951. Fellow Am. Coll. Radiology; mem. AMA, Chgo. Med. Soc., Chgo. Roentgen Soc., Am. Roentgen Ray Soc., Radiol. Soc. N.Am., Inst. Medicine Chgo., Assn. Univ. Radiologists, AAAS, Internat. Skeletal Soc. Office: Moffitt Cancer Ctr & Rsch Inst 12901 N 30th St Box 17 Tampa FL 33612

GREENFIELD, JOSEPH CHOLMONDELEY, JR., physician, educator; b. Atlanta, July 20, 1931; s. Joseph Cholmondeley and Agnes (Game) G.; m. Mary Ruth Fordham, Aug. 13, 1955; children—Mary Agnes, Ruth Ann, Susan Lee. A.B. in History, Emory U., 1954, M.D., 1956. Intern, resident in medicine Duke Med. Center, Durham, N.C., 1956-59; asst. prof. medicine Duke Med. Center, 1962-65, assoc. prof. medicine, 1965-70, prof. medicine, 1970—, James B. Duke disting. prof., 1981—; clin. assoc. NIH, USPHS, 1959-62, mem. cardiovascular and pulmonary study sect., 1974-78, chmn. sect., 1975-78, cardiovascular rev. com., 1980-84, chmn. cardiovascular rev. com., 1983-84; mem. staff Duke Med. Center, 1962—, chief cardiovascular div., 1981-89, chmn. dept. medicine, 1983-95; mem. staff VA, Durham, N.C., 1962—. Contbr. numerous articles profl. jours. Fellow ACP, Am. Coll. Cardiology (disting. sci.l award 1985); mem. Am. Heart Assn. (fellow coun. clin. cardiology), Am. Soc. Clin. Investigation, Am. Physiol. Soc., Assn. Am. Physicians, Inst. Medicine, Sons Confederate Vets., Phi Beta Kappa, Alpha Omega Alpha, Kappa Alpha. Methodist. Home: 1212 Virginia Ave Durham NC 27705-3264 Office: Duke U Med Ctr PO Box 3246 Durham NC 27715-3246

GREENFIELD, LAZAR JOHN, surgeon, educator; b. Houston, Dec. 14, 1934; s. Robert G. and Betty B. (Greenfield) Heath; m. Sharon Dee Bishkin, Aug. 29, 1956; children: John, Julie, Jeff. Student, Rice U., 1951-54; M.D., Baylor U., 1958. Diplomate: Am. Bd. Surgery (dir. 1976-82), Am. Bd. Thoracic Surgery, cert. gen. vascular surgery, 1991. Intern Johns Hopkins Hosp., Balt., 1958-59; resident Johns Hopkins Hosp., 1961-66; chief surgery VA Hosp., Oklahoma City, 1966-74; prof. dept. surgery U. Okla. Med. Center, 1971-74; Stuart McGuire prof., chmn. dept. surgery Med. Coll. Va., Richmond, 1974-87; F.A. coller prof., chmn. dept of surgery U. Mich., 1987—; mem. surgery A study sect. NIH. Author: Surgery in the Aged, 1975; editor-in-chief Surgery, Scientific Principles and Practice, 1993; editor Complications in Surgery and Trauma, 1983, 2d edit., 1990; contbr. to profl. publs. Served with USPHS, 1959-61. Thomas R. Franklin scholar, 1952; John and Mary Markle scholar in med. sci., 1968-73. Mem. Inst. of Medicine of NAS, Am. Surg. Assn., Am. Assn. Thoracic Surgery, Assn. Acad. Surgery, Soc. Univ. Surgeons, Phi Delta Epsilon. Home: 505 E Huron St Ann Arbor MI 48104-1573 Office: U Mich Med Sch 2101 Taubman Ctr Ann Arbor MI 48109-0346

GREENFIELD, ROBERT THOMAS, JR., physician; b. Washington, July 8, 1933; s. Robert Thomas and Auis Aileen (Gadson) G.; m. Wilma Sue Robertson, Sept. 25, 1953; children: Kimberly, Karyn, Robert III, Richard, Brian, Ashley. BS, Howard U., 1954, MD, 1958. Diplomate Am. Bd. Ob/Gyn. Intern Madigan Gen. Hosp., Tacoma, 1958-59; resident Freedmen's Hosp., Washington, 1963-67, pres. ob-gyn., 1963-67; pvt. practice Washington, 1968—; instr. ob/gyn. Howard U., Washington, 1967—, Georgetown U., Washington, 1980—; mem. State Health Coord. Com., Washington, 1976-80; pres. med. staff Columbia Hosp. for Women, Washington, 1984-86. Capt. M.C., U.S. Army, 1958-63. Fellow Am. Coll. Ob/Gyn. (chmn. D.C. sect. 1978-80), Am. Coll. Surgeons; mem. NCCAP (life), Washington Med. Soc., Internat. Coll. Surgeons, Urban League, Alpha Omega Alpha. Democrat. Roman Catholic. Office: Drs Clark & Greenfield Chartered 525 School St SW Washington DC 20024

GREENFIELD, RONALD ALAN, physician, educator; b. McKeesport, Pa., Dec. 13, 1951; s. Seymour and Elaine Greenfield; m. Tawana Elane, Dec. 19, 1993. BS, Ohio State U., 1972; MD, SUNY, Syracuse, 1977; MS in Biostatistics, U. Okla., 1994. Diplomate Am. Bd. Internal Medicine and Infectious Diseases. Intern and resident U. Wis. Hosps., Madison, 1977-80; prof. Health Scis. Ctr. U. Okla., Oklahoma City, 1994—. Contbr. articles to profl. jours. Fellow ACP, Infectious Diseases Soc. Am.; mem. Am. Soc. Microbiology, Am. Fedn. Clin. Rsch., Cen. Soc. Clin. Rsch., Internat. Soc. Human and Animal Mycology, Med. Mycologic Soc. Ams. Democrat. Jewish. Home: 1101 Coffey Cir Edmond OK 73013-6133 Office: U Okla Health Scis Ctr 921 NE 13th St Oklahoma City OK 73104-5007

GREENFIELD, VAL SHEA, ophthalmologist; b. N.Y.C., Apr. 20, 1932; s. Frank Lynne and Helen (Meyers) G. Student, Brown U., 1948-49, 50-51, St. John's U., 1949; BA cum laude, Bklyn. Coll., 1952; MD, Yale U., 1956. Diplomate Am. Bd. Ophthalmology; lic. physician, pa., N.Y., N.J. Intern Walter Reed Army Hosp., Washington, 1956-57; asst. chief U.S. Army Dispensary, Phila., 1957-59, chief, 1959-60; postgrad. preceptorship in ophthal. under co-chief ophthal. Presbyn.-U. Pa. Med. Ctr., Phila., 1963-66; practice medicine specializing in obstetrics Phila., Riverside, N.J., 1960-63; practice medicine specializing in ophthalmology Phila., 1966—; assoc. dir., lectr. in neuro-ophthalmology Hahnemann U., Phila., 1978—, from asst. prof. to assoc. prof. ophthalmology Sch. Medicine, 1977-88; assoc. clin. prof. Robert Wood Johnson Med. Sch.-N.J. U. Medicine and Dentistry, 1988—; attending surgeon in ophthalmology Frankford and Rolling Hills Hosps., Phila., 1970—; lectr. Bibl. topics U.S., Israel, Europe, New Zealand, USSR; guest speaker TV stas. and clubs. Contbr. articles to profl. jours., chpts. to textbooks. Mem. bd. deacons Cmty. Ch., Mt. Laurel Chapel and Fellowship, 1970—; bd. dirs. Hebrew Christian Outrach of Ch. of Our Lord Jesus Christ, 1958—. Served to capt. M.C., U.S. Army, 1955-60. Inducted into Chapel of 4 Chaplains, Temple U., 1981; inducted Hon. Brave Cherokee Indians by Chief Rising Sun, Chief and High Priest of N.Am. and S.Am. Indian Tribes and Couns., 1947; recipient AMA Physicians Recognition award in med. edn., tri-annually, 1974—. Fellow ACS, Phila. Coll. Physicians; mem. AMA, Pa. Med. Soc., Phila. County Med. Soc., Am. Acad. Ophthalmology, N.Y. State Ophthal. Soc., Pa. Acad. Ophthalmology, Pan-Am. Soc. Ophthalmology, Soc. Contemporary Ophthalmology, Christian Med. Soc., Am. Soc. Cataract and Refracture Surgery, Internat. Platform Soc., Am. Judeo-Christian Fellowship, Alpha Kappa Kappa. Home: 623 S Church St Mount Laurel NJ 08054 also Office: David B Soll MD Eye Assocs 5001 Frankford Ave Philadelphia PA 19124

GREENGOLD, JULIAN B., physician; b. Paterson, N.J., Dec. 18, 1948; s. Benjamin P. and Marian Greengold; m. Elizabeth Ann Palkes, Aug. 13, 1972; children: Alexander, Laura, Dana. AB, Rutgers U., 1969; MD, St. Louis U., 1973. Diplomate Am. Bd. Family Practice. Rotating intern Waterbury (Conn.) Hosp.-Yale U., 1973-74; pvt. practice Naugatuck, Conn., 1974-82, Clearwater, Fla., 1982-92; family practice physician Morton Plant Primary Care, Clearwater, Fla., 1993—, chmn. adv. bd., 1994—; dir. med. edn. Morton Plant Hosp., Clearwater, 1993—, pres. med. staff, 1991. Fellow Am. Acad. Family Physicians; mem. Fla. Med. Assn., Pinellas County Med. Soc., Clearwater Yacht Club, Clearwater Optimist Club (pres. 1987-88). Office: 1106 Druid Rd 3 # 101 Clearwater FL 34616

GREENHAWT, MICHAEL H., oncologist, hematologist; b. Atlantic City, N.J., May 13, 1948; s. Edwin and Helen (Apfelbaum) G.; m. Susan Frances Beckstrom, Feb. 12, 1977 (div. Sept. 1991); children: Rachel, Lauren. MD, Jefferson Med. Coll., Phila., 1973. Diplomate Am. Bd. Internal Medicine (subspecialty med. oncology). Intern then resident U. Miami (Fla.) Hosps., 1973-76; fellow in med. oncology Jackson Meml. Hosp., Miami, 1976-78; pvt. practice Aventura, Fla., 1978—. Mem. ACP, Am. Soc. Clin. Oncology, Fla. Soc. Clin Oncology, Fla. Med. Assn., So. Med. Assn., So. Assn. Oncology. Office: 2925 Aventura Blvd # 207 Aventura FL 33180

GREENLAND, PHILIP, cardiologist, educator; b. Cin., Oct. 11, 1948; s. Max and Dorothy (Korros) G.; m. Aviva Wolff, Dec. 24, 1972; children: Micah, Shira, Talia, Aliza. BA, Williams Coll., 1970; MD, U. Rochester, 1974. Diplomat Am. Bd. Internal Medicine. Intern, then resident in medicine U. Rochester, N.Y., 1974-78, asst. prof. medicine, 1980-86, assoc. prof. medicine, 1986-91; fellow in cardiology U. Minn., Mpls., 1978-80; prof., chair dept. prevention medicine Northwestern U., Chgo., 1991—, Harry W. Dingman prof. cardiology Med. Sch., 1991—; advisor Atherosclerosis, Hypertension, Lipid, Metabolism Adv. Coun., Nat. Heart, Lung, Blood Inst., Bethesda, Md., 1990-93. Mem. Chgo.'s mayor's task force on women's health, 1993; mem. rsch. com. Coun. on Jewish Elderly, Chgo., 1995—. Fellow ACP (tchg. and rsch. scholar 1983-86), Am. Heart Assn., (coun. on epidemiology and prevention, mem. exec. com., mem. com. pub. policy 1994—, bd. govs. 1993—), Am. Coll. Cardiology (prevention com.) mem. Phi Beta Kappa, Alpha Omega Alpha. Office: Northwestern U Med Sch 680 N Lake Shore Dr Ste 1102 Chicago IL 60611

GREENLEAF, WAYNE ALLAN, psychologist; b. Lake Charles, La., Sept. 20, 1942; s. A.J. and Irene (Butaud) G.; m. Andrée Lane Hunter, July 7, 1975; children: A. Graham, Jaimée, Jason. BA, La. Coll., 1964; MA, La. State U., 1967, PhD, 1972; MBA, Tulane U., 1992. Lic. psychologist, La. Psychol. asst. Cen. La. State Hosp., Pineville, 1969-72, clin. psychologist, 1972-74, dir. adolescent svcs., 1974-77; dir. pupil appraisal svcs. La. State Dept. Edn., Baton Rouge, 1977-81; exec. dir. spl. edn. programs Office of Spl. Edn., Baton Rouge, 1981-82; regional adminstr. mentally retarded and devel. disabled Met. Devel. Ctr., Belle Chasse, La., 1982-88; psychologist New Orleans Adolescent Hosp., 1988-89; clin. assoc. Ctr. for Individual and Family Therapy, Gretna, La., 1988-91; adminstr. mental health svcs. Charity Hosp. of La. at New Orleans, 1989; assoc. prof. clin. psychiatry dept. La. State U. Med. Ctr., New Orleans, 1989—; instr. psychology La. Coll., Pineville, 1967-68, asst. prof., 1969-77; cons. psychologist La. Tng. Inst., Ball, 1968-77, Family Counseling Agy., Shreveport, La., 1973-74; bd. dirs., program cons. Renaissance Home for Adjudicated Youth, Alexandria, La., 1974-77; coord. Adam A. Mgmt. Office, New Orleans, 1989; mem. La. State Bd. Examiners in Psychology, 1979-82, chmn., 1981-82; presenter in field. Contbr. articles to profl. publs. Past bd. dirs Bd. Advisors for Community Receiving Home, Inc.; past bd. dirs., v.p. People for People. Mem. APA, La. Psychol. Assn. (pres. 1975-76), Coun. for Exceptional Children, Am. Assn. Mental Retardation, La. Assn. for Mental Health. Home: 408 Avenue A Belle Chasse LA 70037-2305

GREENLEE, JOHN EDWARD, neurologist; b. Mercedes, Tex., Sept. 24, 1940; s. Walden Gillespie and Nelle (Whitehead) G.; m. Anabel Wyatt Williams, Aug. 14, 1965; children: Harriet Washington, John Wyatt, Margaret Gillespie. BA, Hamilton Coll., 1962; postgrad., Free U. Berlin, 1962-63, Columbia U., 1963-64; MD, U. Rochester, 1969. Intern medicine U. Va. Hosp., Charlottesville, 1969-70, resident medicine, 1970-71, resident neurology, 1971-73, chief resident, 1973-74; fellow neurology Johns Hopkins Hosp., Balt., 1974-76; from. asst. prof. to assoc. prof. neurology U. Va., Charlottesville, 1976-86; prof., vice chair neurology U. Utah, Salt Lake City, 1986—; chief neurology svc. VA Med. Ctr., Salt Lake City, 1986—; mem. adv. bd. Blue Ridge chpt. Nat. MS Soc., Charlottesville, 1977-86; mem. exptl. virology study sect. NIH, Bethesda, Md., 1984-86; mem. neurology adv. group VA Ctrl. Office, Washington, 1987—. Contbr. articles to profl. jours. Bd. dirs. Utah Scottish Assn., Salt Lake City, 1990-93, Ulster Project, Salt Lake City, 1993—. Recipient Dankstipendium Deutschen Adakamischen Austauschidienests, 1962-63, Tchr.-Investigator award NIH, 1978-83. Fellow Am. Acad. Neurology; mem. Am. Assn. Neuropathology, Am. Neurol. Assn., Soc. Exptl. Neuropathology (bd. dirs. 1996). Office: VA Med Ctr 500 Fotthill Dr Salt Lake City UT 84148

GREENLEES, THOMAS WILLIAM, surgeon; b. N.Y.C., Aug. 2, 1926; s. William and Theresa (Kensler) G.; m. Taeko Atsumi, June 21, 1960; children: Christine, Lisa. BA, Cornell U., 1945; MD, N.Y. Med. Coll., 1949; MPH, Harvard U., 1983. Diplomate Am. Bd. Surgery. Intern Flower Fifth Ave Hosp., N.Y.C., 1949-50; resident Met. Hosp., N.Y.C., 1950-51, 53-56; med. dir. Textron Corp., Wilmington, Mass. 1985—; attending physician, acting dir. occupl. health program Boston (Mass.) U. Med. Ctr./Univ. Hosp., 1994. Bd. dir. Mohawk Valley Econ. Devel. Dist., N.Y. State, 1970—, SUNY Found., Cobleskill, N.Y., 1986—. Lt. comdr. USNR, 1956-59, Japan. Fellow ACS, Am. Coll. Occupl. and Environ. Medicine; mem. AMA, New Eng. Occupational Med. Assn. (pres. 1990). Methodist. Home: PO Box 910 Cobleskill NY 12043-0910

GREENLICK, MERWYN RONALD, health services researcher; b. Detroit, Mar. 12, 1935; s. Emanuel and Fay (Ettinger) G.; m. Harriet Cohen, Aug. 19, 1956; children—Phyllis, Michael, Vicki. B.S., Wayne State U., 1957; M.S., U. Mich., 1961, Ph.D., 1967. Pharmacist Detroit, 1957-60; spl. instr., instr. pharmacy adminstrn. Coll. Pharmacy Wayne State U., 1958-62; dir. of research n.w. region Kaiser-Permanente, Portland, 1964-95; v.p. (research) Kaiser Found. Hosps., 1981-95; sr. fellow Ctr. for Advanced Study in the Behavioral Scis., Stanford, Calif., 1995-96; adj. prof. sociology and social work Portland State U., 1965—; clin. prof. preventive medicine and pub. health Oreg. Health Scis. U., 1971-89, prof., acting chair preventive medicine and pub. health, 1990-93, prof., chair preventive medicine and pub. health, 1993—; mem. Gov.'s Commn. on Health Care, 1988; cons. Gov.'s Health Manpower Coun. Bd. dirs. Washington County Community Action Orgn., 1966-70; pres. Jewish Edn. Assn., Portland, 1976-78; bd. dirs. Jewish Fedn., 1975-79. USPHS trainee, 1962-63, 63-64. Fellow Am. Pub. Health Assn.; mem. AAAS, NAS, Inst. Medicine, Assn. Health Svcs. Rsch., Am. Statis. Assn. Jewish. Home: 712 NW Spring Ave Portland OR 97229-6913 Office: Oreg Health Svcs U CB 669 3181 SW Sam Jackson Park Rd Portland OR 97201

GREEN-MACK, T. LYNETTE, physiatrist; b. July 27, 1952; m. Richard K. Mack. BA, Wittenberg U., 1974; MD, Ohio State U., 1980. Bd. cert. phys. medicine and rehab. Resident phys. medicine and rehab. Riverside Meth. Hosp., Columbus, Ohio, 1980-81; resident Ohio State U., Columbus, 1981-83, clin. instr. phys. medicine and rehab., 1980-83; asst. prof. phys. medicine and rehab. Ea. Va. Med. Sch., 1983; med. dir. Sentara Hampton Gen. Hosp., 1984-86, Sentara Norfolk Gen., 1985-87; residency dir. phys. medicine and rehab. Ea. Va. Med. Sch., 1988-89; pvt. practice phys. medicine and rehab. Ind. Ctr. for Rehab. Medicine, 1989-92, The Spine Inst., 1993—; first aid physician Jehovah's Witnesses Assembly Hall, London, Ohio, 1979-83; med. cons. Jehovah's Christian Witnesses, Bklyn., 1979—, Social Security Disability Determination, State Agy. Office, Columbus, 1981-83; active staff St. Vincent's Hosp., 1989—; courtesy staff Meth. Hosp. Ind., 1989—, Winona Hosp., 1989—, Cmty. South, 1992—; provisional staff St. Francis Hosp., 1992—. Mem. AMA, Am. Acad. Phys. Medicine and Rehab., Assn. Acad. Physiatrists, Am. Assn. Electromyographers and Electrodiagnosis (assoc.), Ind. State Phys. Medicine and Rehab., Ind. State Med. Assn., Am. Spinal Injury Assn., Nat. Med. Assn., Aisculapian Med. Soc., Marion County Med. Soc. Office: The Spine Inst Ste 200 13431 Old Meridian St Carmel IN 46032

GREENMAN, DAVID LEWIS, research physiologist, toxicologist; b. Williamston, Mich., Jan. 19, 1934; s. Asa J. and Lucy B. (Hoover) G.; m. Jessie E. Blackman, Aug. 10, 1956; children: Karen, Martha. BA, Asbury Coll., 1956; MS, Purdue U., 1959, PhD, 1962. Asst. prof., rsch. assoc. Johns Hopkins U., Balt., 1964-70; pharmacologist FDA, Washington, 1970, EPA, Washington, 1970-72; rsch. pharmacologist Nat. Ctr. for Toxicol. Rsch., FDA, Jefferson, Ark., 1972-76, rsch. physiologist, 1976-94; chmn. precautionary labelling com. Assn. Am. Pest Control Operators, Washington, 1971-72; mem. adv. bd. Handbook Endocrinology, CRC Press, Inc., Boca Raton, Fla., 1981; FDA cons. Nigerian FDA, Lagos, 1982; chmn. Institutional Animal Care and Use Com., 1990-92. Contbr. articles to Steroids, Endocrinology, Lab. Animal Sci., Jour. Nat. Cancer Inst., Jour. Toxicological Environ. Health. Chmn. Old York Community Coun., Balt., 1967-68; del. NE Community Orgn., Balt., 1969-70. Recipient Spl. Svc. award FDA, 1988; fellow NSF, 1959-62, Nat. Cancer Inst., 1963-64; rsch. grantee NIH, 1965-70. Baptist.

GREENMAN, MAXWELL, ophthalmologist; b. N.Y.C.. MD, NYU, 1967. Diplomate Am. Bd. Ophthalmology. Ophthalmologist in pvt. practice Charlotte, N.C . Maj. U.S. Army, 1971-73. Office: Carolina Eye Assocs 2200 E 7th St Charlotte NC 28204

GREENOUGH, WILLIAM BATES, III, medical educator; b. Providence, Jan. 3, 1932; s. William Bates Jr. and Dorothy Garrison (Rand) G.; m. Jane Cheney Woodruff, Aug. 14, 1954 (dec. 1964); children: William Beckley, Kate, Thomas Clark, Elisabeth Bates; m. Quaneta Ahmed, 1965; 1 child, Zarin Farah Naz. BA magna cum laude, Amherst Coll., 1953; MD cum laude, Harvard U., 1957. Intern, asst. resident Columbia U. Coll. Physicians and Surgeons, N.Y.C., 1952-59; sr. rsch. fellow Mary Imogene Bassett Hosp., Cooperstown, N.Y., 1959-61; sr. resident Peter Bent Brigham Hosp., Boston, 1961-62; staff assoc. Nat. Heart Inst. Cholera Rsch. Lab., Dhaka, Bangladesh, 1962-65; chief infectious diseases div. Johns Hopkins U. Sch. Medicine, Balt., 1970-76, dir. Robert Wood Johnson Clin. Scholars Program, 1974-77, prof. medicine, 1983—, prof. internat. health sch. pub. health, 1985—; dir. Internat. Ctr. for Diarrhoeal Disease Rsch., Dhaka, Bangladesh, 1979-85; mem. geriatric medicine div. Johns Hopkins U., 1985—; cons. infectious diseases Perry Point VA Hosp., 1972-77, Internat. Rescue Com., N.Y.C., 1971-72; mem. bacteriology and mycology study sect. NIH, 1972-76, chmn., 1974-76; mem. ad hoc study group on enteric disease Walter Reed Army Inst. Rsch., 1975-77; pres. Bangladesh Info. Ctr., Washington, 1971-84; mem. adv. coun. Bangladesh Found., Chgo., 1972; active Md. Gov.'s Commn. on Phys. Fitness and Marathon Commn., 1971-77; pres., chmn. bd., trustee Internat. Child Health Found., Columbia, Md., 1985-95. Editor Infection and Immunity, 1975-78, Topics in Infectious Disease, 1976—, Jour. Diarrhoeal Disease Rsch., 1983-85, 93—; author monographs; contbr. articles and revs. to med. jours., chpts. to books; patentee in field. Sr. surgeon USPHS, 1962-67. Recipient Internat. Prize in Medicine, King Faisal Found., 1984; Maurice Pate prize UNICEF, 1984, recognized for svc. to children, 1983. Fellow AAAS, ACP; mem. Assn. Am. Physicians, Am. Soc. for Clin. Investigation, Infectious Diseases Soc. Am., Am. Geriatric Soc., Bangladesh Assn. for Advancement Scis., Am. Fedn. Clin. Rsch., Am. Soc. Microbiology, Internat. Epidemiol. Assn., Bangladesh Med. Soc. Islam. Home: 1300 Hollins Ln Baltimore MD 21209-2237 Office: Johns Hopkins Geriatrics Ctr. 5505 Hopkins Bayview Cir Baltimore MD 21224-6821

GREENSPAN, DANIEL S., molecular biologist; b. Jersey City, Aug. 31, 1951; s. Aaron and Doris (Greenspan) G. BA, NYU, 1974, MS, 1978, PhD, 1981. Postdoctoral fellow dept. human genetics Yale U., New Haven, 1981-84, rsch. scientist, mem. faculty, 1984-86; asst. prof. pathology & lab. medicine U. Wis., Madison, 1986-92, assoc. prof., 1992—. Contbr. articles to profl. jours. Arthritis Found. fellow, 1984-87; prin. investigator NIH. Mem. Am. Soc. Biochemistry and Molecular Biology, N.Y. Acad. Scis., Am. Soc. Microbiology, Am. Soc. Human Genetics, Sigma Xi. Jewish. Avocations: sailing, scuba diving. Office: U Wis Dept Pathology 470 N Charter St Madison WI 53706-1509

GREENSPAN, DAVID ARNOLD, ophthalmologist, educator; b. Newark, May 30, 1940; s. Martin J. and Rose (Mager) G.; m. Jan Sharyn Richie, Dec. 3, 1967. BA, U. Tex., 1961, MD, 1963. Diplomate Am. Bd. Ophthalmology. Intern Hermann Hosp., Houston, 1963-64; resident U. Tex. Med. Br., Galveston, 1964-67; pvt. practice, Pasadena, Tex., 1969—; cons. U.S. Army, Ft. Hood, Tex., 1969—; asst. clin. prof. U. Tex. Health Sci. Ctr., Houston, 1970—, U. Tex., Galveston, 1970—; pres. Houston Ophthal. Soc., 1987-88. Bd. dirs. Pasadena C. of C., 1970-71; pres. S.E. Harris County Med. Soc., Pasadena, 1991; exec. bd. Harris County Med. Soc., Houston, 1991; med. dir. Tex. Soc. Prevent Blindness, Houston, 1991-92, pres., 1983-84. Maj. U.S. Army, 1967-69. Fellow Am. Acad. Ophthalmology; mem. AMA, Tex. Ophthal. Soc., Am. Soc. Cataract and Refractive Surgery, Rotary Club, Chaine des Rotisseurs (vice conseiller gastronomique), Internat. Wine and Food Soc., Les Amis de Escoffier, L'ordre Mondial des Gourmet Degustateurs. Home: 411 Menking Ct Houston TX 77024-6807 Office: Pasadena Eye Assocs 901 Curtis Ave Ste 18 Pasadena TX 77502-2436

GREENSPAN, JOHN S., dentistry educator, educator and administrator; b. London, Jan. 7, 1938; came to U.S., 1976; s. Nathan and Jessie (Dion) G.; m. Deborah, Dec. 1962; children: Nicholas J., Louise C. BSC in Anatomy with 1st class honors, U. London, 1959, B in Dental Surgery, 1962, PhD in Exptl. Pathology, 1967; ScD (hon.), Georgetown U., 1990. Licentiate in dental surgery Royal Coll. of Surgeons of Eng. Asst. house surgeon in conservation and periodontology Royal Dental Hosp. London, 1962; asst. lectr. oral pathology Sch. of Dental Surgery Royal Dental Hosp. of London, U. London, 1963-65, lectr. oral pathology Sch. of Dental Surgery, 1965-68, sr. lectr. oral pathology Sch. of Dental Surgery, 1968-75; prof. oral biology and oral pathology Sch. of Dentisty, U. Calif., San Francisco, 1976—, vice chmn. dept. oral medicine and hosp. dentistry, 1977-82, chmn. div. oral biology, 1981-89, coord. basic scis. Sch. of Dentistry, 1982—; chmn. dept. stomatology U. Calif., San Francisco, 1989—; cons. oral pathology St. John's Hosp. and Inst. of Dermatology, London, 1973-76; cons. dental surgeon St. George's Hosp., 1972-76; prof. dept. pathology Sch. Medicine U. Calif., San Francisco, 1976—; dir. U. Calif. AIDS Specimen Bank, San Francisco, 1982—, U. Calif. Oral AIDS Ctr., San Francisco, 1987—; asso. dir. dental clin. epidemiology program U. Calif., San Francisco, 1987—; dir. U. Calif. AIDS Clin. Rsch. Ctr., San Francisco, 1992—; presenter, lectr. Author: (with others) Opportunistic Infections in Patients with the Acquired Immunodeficiency Syndrome, 1989, Contemporary Periodontics, 1989, Gastroenterology Clinics of North America, 1988, Perspectives on Oral Manifestations of AIDS, 1988, AIDS: Pathogenesis and Treatment, 1988, others; contbr. articles to profl. jours.; editorial cons. Achives of Oral Biology, 1968—, Jour. of Calif. Dental Assn., 1980—; editoral adv. bd. Jour. of Dental Rsch., 1977—; editorial bd. AIDS Alert, 1987-89. Rsch. grantee NIH-Nat. Inst. Dental Rsch., 1978-82, 86-92, U. Calif. Task Force on AIDS, 1983—, rsch. com. Royal Dental Hosp., London, 1964-76, Med. Rsch. Coun. of U.K., 1974-77, chmn. U. Calif. San Francisco Acad. Senate, 1983-85; Nuffield dental scholar, 1958-59; fellow Am. Coll. Dentists, 1982—, AAAS, 1985—; recipient Seymour J. Kreshover Lecture award Nat. Inst. Dental Rsch., NIH, 1989, Rsch. in Oral Biology award Internat. Assn. Dental Rsch., 1992. Mem. ADA, AAAS, Am. Assn. Dental Rsch. (pres. 1988-89), Inst. Medicine of Nat. Acad. Scis., Internat. Assn. Dental Rsch. (pres. 1996), Royal Soc. Medicine (U.K.), Pathological Soc. (U.K.), Oral Pathology Soc. (U.K.), Royal Coll. Pathologists (U.K.), Am. Acad. Oral Pathology, Bay Area Tchrs. Oral Pathology, Internat. Assn. Oral Pathologists, San Francisco Dental Soc., Calif. Dental Assn., Calif. Soc. Oral Pathologists Histochem. Soc., Am. Assn. Pathologists. Office: U Calif Dept Stomatology Box 0422 Sch Dentistry San Francisco CA 94143

GREENSPAN, LINDA IRENE, physician; b. N.Y.C., Feb. 20, 1950; d. Arpad and Olga (Weiss) Fried; m. Jay Greenspan, June 15, 1969; children: Paul, Mark, Brian, Rachel. AS, Queensboro Cmty. Coll., 1970; BS, Fairleigh Dickenson U., 1986; DO, U. Osteo. Medicine, 1990. Lab. technician Wycoff Heights Med. Ctr., Bklyn., 1970-72, lab. technologist, 1972-74; intern Union Hosp., 1990-91, resident, 1991-93; staff physician Primary Care Physicians, Rockaway, N.J., 1993-94, Physician Group Practice Assn., Clifton, N.J., 1995—. Mem. Rep. county com. Rep. Party, Parsippany, N.J., 1979-82. Mem. Am. Osteo. Assn., Am. Coll. Osteo. Family Physicians, N.J. Osteo. Assn. for Physicians and Surgeons, Morris County Osteo. Soc. Jewish. Office: Blue Cross Blue Shield Health Ctr 1135 Broad St Clifton NJ 07013

GREENSPAN, NEIL SANFORD, immunological researcher; b. Chgo., Nov. 15, 1953; s. Irving and Francine Rose (Greenberg) G.; m. Judith Ann Keene, June 22, 1980; children: Aaron Jacob, Simon Keene. AB in Biochem. Scis., Harvard U., 1975; MD, U. Pa., 1981, PhD in Immunology, 1981. Resident in lab. medicine Barnes Hosp./Washington Univ., St. Louis, 1981-86; postdoctoral fellow Washington U., St. Louis, 1982-85; asst. prof. of pathology Case Western Res. U., Cleve., 1986-93, assoc. prof. pathology, 1993—; dir. clin. histocompat. lab. U. Hosps. of Cleve., 1986—; tech. staff expert Teltech, Inc., Mpls., 1991—. Contbr. articles to profl. jours. Blood donor ARC, Cleve., 1987—. Rsch. grantee NIH, 1989-95. Mem. AAAS, Am. Assn. of Immunologists, Am. Soc. for Investigative Pathology, Clin. Immunology Soc. Jewish. Office: Case Western Res Univ Biomed Rsch Bldg Rm 927 10900 Euclid Ave Cleveland OH 44106-4943

GREENSPAN, STANLEY IRA, psychiatrist; b. N.Y.C., June 1, 1941; m. Nancy Thorndike; children: Elizabeth, Jake, Sarah. BA cum laude, Harvard U., 1962; MD, Yale U., 1966. Intern SUNY Upstate Med. Ctr., Syracuse, 1966; resident in psychiatry Psychiat. Inst., Columbia Presbyn. Med. Ctr., N.Y.C., 1967; fellowship in adolescent and child psychiatry Hillcrest Children's Ctr., Children's Hosp. Nat. Med. Ctr., 1969; cons. to student health George Washington U., 1969; clin. practice child/adult psychiatry and psychoanalysis, 1970—; clin. prof. psychiatry, behavioral sci. and pediatrics George Washington U. Med. Sch., 1982—; rsch. psychiatrist Lab. Psychology, NIMH, 1970, Mental Health Study Ctr., NIMH, 1972-74, asst. chief, 1974, acting chief, 1974-75, chief, 1975-82; dir. Clin. INfant Devel. Program, NIMH, 1975-82; chief Clin. Infant Devel. Rsch. Unit, Lab. Psychology and Psychopathology, IRP, NIMH, 1982-84; chief Clin. Infant/Child Devel. Rsch. Ctr., DMCH, HRSA and NIMH, 1984-86; founder Nat. Ctr. for Clin. Infant Programs, pres. 1975-84, chmn. diagnostic classification com.; others. Editorial bd.: Jour. Am. Psychoanalytic Assn., Jour. Preventive Psychiatry, Jour. Psychoanalytic Inquiry, Infant Mental Health Jour., Jour. Psychotherapy Practice and Rsch.; author, editor of monographs and books; contbr. chpts. to books and articles to profl. jours. Past mem. Surgeon Gen.' Task Force on Infant Mortality; past regional v.p. World Assn. for Infant Psychiatry and Allied Disciplines. Recipient Edward A. Strecker award for outstanding contbrs. to Am. psychiatry, Pub. Health Svc. Spl. Recognition award, Heintz Hartman prize for contbrs. to psychoanalysis. Fellow Am. Psychiat. Assn. (Ittleson prize for outstanding contbrns. to child psychiatry rsch.); mem. Am. Psychoanalytic Assn. (chmn. com. on program liaison, cert. in adult, child and adolscent psychoanalysis 1979), Am. Coll. Psychiatry, Am. Coll. Psychoanalysis. Office: 7201 Glenbrook Rd Bethesda MD 20814-1242

GREENSPAN-MARGOLIS, JUNE E., psychiatrist; b. N.Y.C., June 28, 1934; d. Benjamin Robert and Theresa (Cooperstein) Edelman; divorced; 1 child, Alisa Greenspan; m. Gerald J. Margolis. AB, Bryn Mawr Coll., 1955; MD, Med. Coll. Pa., 1959; grad., Inst Phila Assn Psychoanalysis, Bala Cynwyd, 1975. Intern Albert Einstein Med. Ctr., Phila., 1959-60; pvt. practice medicine specializing in pediatrics Cinnaminson, N.J., 1961-67; psychiat. resident Hahnemann Med. Coll., Phila., 1967-71; practice medicine specializing in adult and child psychiatry, psychoanalysis Jenkintown, Pa., 1971—; instr. U. Pa. Sch. Medicine, Phila., 1975-77, clin. assoc. 1977-81, clin. asst. prof. 1981-85, clin. assoc. prof. 1986—; tng. and supervisory analyst Inst. of the Phila. Assn. Psychoanalysis, Bala Cynwyd, Pa., 1986—. Fellow Am. Coll. Psychoanalysts; mem. AMA, Am. Psychiat. Assn., Am. Psychoanalytic Assn. (cert. adult and child psychoanalysis), Am. Acad. Child Psychiatry, Ctr. for Advanced Psychoanalytic Studies (Princeton). Office: Benson East Suite 223-C 100 Old York Rd Jenkintown PA 19046

GREENSTEIN, JEFFREY IAN, neurologist; b. Durban, South Africa, July 27, 1947; s. Joseph and Miriam (Shamos) G.; m. Goldie Queenie Brown. MD, U. Cape Town, S. Africa, 1971. Diplomate Am. Bd. Neurology and Psychiatry. Asst. to assoc. prof. neurology Temple U. Sch. Med., Phila., 1983-89, prof. and chmn. neurology, 1989—. Mem. AAAS, Am. Acad. Neurology, N.Y. Acad. Sci., Nat. Multiple Sclerosis Soc. (chmn. profl. adv. com. Phila. 1992-95). Office: Temple Univ Sch Medicine 3401 N Broad 85 Philadelphia PA 19140

GREENSTONE, JAMES LYNN, psychotherapist, police psychologist, mediator, consultant, author, educator; b. Dallas, Mar. 30, 1943; s. Carl Bunk and Fifi (Horn) G.; children: Cynthia Beth, Pamela Celeste, David Carl. BA in Psychology, U. Okla., 1965; MS in Clin. Psychology, North Tex. State U., 1966, EdD in Edn. and Psychology, 1974; JD, Northwestern Calif. U., 1991. Lic. marriage and family therapist, profl. counselor. Psychologist Beverly Hills Hosp., Dallas, 1966-67; therapist Family Guidance Service, Dallas, 1967-68; instr. Dallas County Community Coll. Dist., 1967-72, 78-79, 87-89; asst. prof. Tex. Women's U., 1979; assoc. prof. psychology and criminal justice Tarrant County Jr. Coll., 1987-89; tng. faculty Am. Acad. Crisis Interveners, Louisville, 1972-78; tng. dir. Southwestern Acad. Crisis Interveners, Dallas, 1977—; police instr. Dallas Sheriff's Acad., 1979-86; hostage negotiator and trainer Lancaster Police Dept., Tex., 1986-92; pvt. practice psychotherapy, 1966-96; dir. psychol. svcs. unit Ft. Worth Police Dept., 1992—; cons. Dallas County Jails, 1979-82, 89-90; dir. res. tng. Dallas Sheriff's Res., 1983-84; panel arbitrators Am. Arbitration Assn.; adj. prof. psychology Columbia Coll., Northwood Inst., 1987-89; adj. faculty dispute mediation North Tex. State U., 1987-88; instr. hostage negotiations North Cen. Tex. Council Govts. Regional Police Acad., 1987—; assoc. prof. psychology, criminal justice; adj. prof. law Tex. Wesleyan U. Sch. Law, 1991—; dir. psychol. svcs. unit Ft. Worth Police Dept. Author: Crisis Intervener's Handbook, Vol. 1, 1980; Crisis Intervener's Handbook, Vol. II, 1982; Hotline: Crisis Intervention Directory, 1981; Crisis Management: Handbook for Interveners, 1983; Winning Through Accommodation: Handbook for Mediators, 1984, Elements of Crisis Intervention, 1993; cassette tapes: Crisis Management and Intervener Survival, 1981; Stress Reduction: Personal Energy Management, 1982; Training the Trainer, 1983; contbr. chpts. to books, articles to profl. jours.; sr. editor: Crisis Intervener's Newsletter; editor-in-chief Emotional First Aid: A Jour. of Crisis Intervention, The Jour. of Crisis Negotiations, 1994-96; and others. Trustee Southeastern U., New Orleans; bd. dirs. Jewish Community Ctr., Jewish Family Service, Temple Shalom, Congregation Shearith Israel, 1975-80; active Dallas Sheriff's Res., 1978-86; v.p. Jewish Nat. Fund Dallas; adv. bd. Parents Without Ptnrs.; founder Carl B. Greenstone Meml. Library; past dir. Carrollton Rotary Club, Nat. Jewish Com., Scouting, Circle 10 Council Boy Scouts Am. With USNR, 1961-65, USMCR, 1965-67, USAR, 1967-69. Recipient Disting. Service award Southeastern Acad. Crisis Interveners, 1981; Disting. Service award Res. Law Officers Assn. Am., 1982. Mem. Am. Assn. Marriage and Family Therapy, Soc. Profls. in Dispute Resolution, Acad. Family Mediators, Am. Bd. Examiners in Crisis Intervention (diplomate), Am. Acad. Crisis Intervention, Southwestern Acad. Crisis Interveners, Acad. Criminal Justice Scis., Am. Acad. Psychotherapists, Am. Assn. Profl. Hypnotherapists, Assn. Mil. Surgeons U.S., Soc. of Police and Crim. Psychology (diplomate in police psychology), Dallas Assn. Marriage and Family Therapists. Democrat. Lodges: Masons, Scottish Rite. Office: PO Box 670292 Dallas TX 75367-0292

GREENWALD, MARC L., colon and rectal surgeon; b. N.Y.C., Feb. 28, 1959; s. Richard M. and Joyce S. (Lehrer) G.; m. Yvette Olstein, Mar. 21, 1991; children: Samuel, Julia. BA with distinction, Cornell U., 1981; MD, Albert Einstein Coll. Med., 1985. Diplomate Am. Bd. Surgery, Am. Bd. Colon and Rectal Surgery. Intern, resident Montefiore Med. Ctr., Albert Einstein Coll. Medicine, 1985-90; fellow in colon and rectal surgery St. Francis Hosp., U. Conn., 1990-91; colon and rectal surgeon North Shore Surgical Specialists, Great Neck, N.Y., 1991—; attending surgeon North Shore U. Hosp., Manhasset, N.Y., 1991—, Long Island Jewish Hosp., New Hyde Park, N.Y., 1993—, Winthrop U. Hosp., Mineola, N.Y., 1992—; clin. instr. surgery Cornell U., N.Y.C., 1993—. Contbr. chpts. to books: Problems in General Surgery, 1992, (textbook)ú Fundamentals of Anorectal Surgery, 1992. Fellow ACS, N.Y. Soc. Colon and Rectal Surgeons; mem. AMA, Am. Soc. Colon and Rectal Surgeons, Soc. Am. Gastrointestinal Endoscopic Surgeons, Phi Beta Kappa. Office: North Shore Surg Specialist 310 East Shore Rd Great Neck NY 11023

GREENWALD, PETER, physician, government medical research director; b. Newburgh, N.Y., Nov. 7, 1936; s. Louis and Pearl (Reingold) G.; m. Harriet Reif, Sept. 6, 1968; children—Rebecca, Laura, Daniel. BA, Colgate U., 1957; MD, SUNY Coll. Medicine, 1961; MPH, Harvard U., 1967, DrPH, 1974. Intern Los Angeles County Hosp., 1961-62; resident in internal medicine Boston City Hosp., 1964-66; asst. in medicine Peter Bent Brigham Hosp., 1967-68; mem. epidemiology and disease control study sect. NIH, 1974-78; mem. N.Y. State Gov.'s Breast Task Force, 1976-78; with N.Y. State Dept. Health, Albany, 1968-81; dir. N.Y. State Dept. Health, 1976-86, dir. epidemiology, 1976-81; prof. medicine Albany Med. Coll., 1976-81; attending physician Albany Med. Ctr. Hosp., 1968-81; adj. prof. biomed. engring. Rensselaer Poly. Inst., Troy, N.Y., 1976-81; assoc. scientist Sloan-Kettering Inst. for Cancer Research, N.Y.C., 1977-81; dir. Div. Cancer Prevention and Control, Nat. Cancer Inst., NIH, 1981—; mem. VA Merit Rev. Bd. Med. Oncology, Washington, 1972-74. Editor-in-chief Jour. Nat. Cancer Inst., NIH, 1981-87; contbr. articles to profl. jours. Rear adm. USPHS, 1962-64, 81—. Recipient Disting. Svc. award N.Y. State Dept. Health, 1975; Redway medal and award for med. writing N.Y. State Jour. Medicine, 1977, N.Y. State Gov.'s Citation for pub. health achievement, 1981, PHS commendation 1983, 88, Disting. Svc. medal, 1993, Dir.'s award NIH, 1994. Fellow ACP, Am. Coll. Preventive Medicine, APHA (epidemiology sect. chmn. 1981); mem. Am. Assn. Cancer Rsch., Am. Soc. Clin. Oncology, Am. Coll. Epidemiology (bd. dirs. 1981-82), AMA, Am. Soc. Preventive Oncology, Am. Inst. Nutrition, Internat. Cancer Registry Assn., Internat. Epidemiology Soc., Nat. Acad. Scis. (food and nutrition bd. 1982-88).

GREENWALT, MARY SUSAN, counselor; b. St. Louis, Dec. 26, 1946; d. LeGrand West and Susan Frances (Frier) Wheeler; m. Allen Duane Greenwalt, Apr. 11, 1992; stepchildren: Scott Harrison, Emily Megan. BS, So. Ill. U., 1968, MS, 1972; MBA, St. Louis U., 1982. Tchr. Lindbergh Sch. Dist., St. Louis, 1968-79, counselor, 1979—. Stage mgr. V-P Fair, St. Louis, 1984-93; vol. St. Louis Nursery Found. Book Fair, 1985-93. Recipient Tuition grant for women MBA students IBM, 1977. Mem. NEA, Mo. Edn. Assn., Lindbergh Edn. Assn. (pres. 1982-83), Am. Counseling Assn., Mo. Sch. Counselors Assn., St. Louis Suburban Sch. Counselors Assn. (Elem. Counselor of Yr. 1993), Jr. League St. Louis, Alpha Gamma Delta (St. Louis Alumnae Club). Republican. Methodist. Home: 14 Girard Dr Saint Louis MO 63119-4802 Office: Crestwood Elem Sch 1020 S Sappington Rd Saint Louis MO 63126-1005

GREENWALT, TIBOR JACK, physician, educator; b. Budapest, Hungary, Jan. 23, 1914; came to U.S., 1920, naturalized, 1943; s. Bela and Irene (Foldes) G.; m. Shirley Johnson, Aug. 6, 1960 (dec. Sept. 1970); 1 child, Peter H.; m. Pia Glas, Feb. 27, 1971. B.A. summa cum laude, NYU, 1937, M.D., 1937. Diplomate Am. Bd. Internal Medicine. Intern pathology and bacteriology Mt. Sinai Hosp., N.Y.C., 1937-38; rotating intern Kings County Hosp., Bklyn., 1938-40; resident medicine Montefiore Hosp., N.Y.C., 1940-41; research asso. New Eng. Med. Center, Boston, 1941-42; med. dir. Milw. Blood Center, 1947-66; faculty medicine Marquette U. Sch. Medicine, 1948-66, prof. medicine, 1963-66; cons. hematology VA Hosp., Wood, Wis., 1946-66, Milw. County Gen. Hosp., 1948-66; dir. blood program ARC, 1967-78, sr. sci. adviser blood program, 1978-79; clin. prof. medicine George Washington U. Sch. Medicine, 1967-79; prof. medicine U. Cin. Med. Center, 1979-84, prof. emeritus medicine and pathology, 1984—; dir. Hoxworth Blood Center, 1979-87, dir. research, 1987—; chmn. com. blood and transfusion problems NAS-NRC, 1963-66; mem. hematology study sect. NIH, 1960-63, chmn., 1970-72; vis. prof., speaker throughout, U.S., 1960—; mem. Med. Rsch. Srv. Merit Rev. Bd. for Hematology, VA, 1981-83; mem. blood diseases and resources adv. com. Nat. Heart, Lung and Blood Inst., 1983-87, adv. coun. 1986-90, coordinating com., Nat. Blood Resources Edn. Program, adv. com. Office of Prevention Edn. and Control, 1987-91.—. Author: (with others) Hemolytic Syndromes, 1942, (with Shirley Greenwalt) Coagulation and Transfusion in Clinical Medicine, 1965; editor: (with Graham A. Jamieson) The Red Cell Membrane, 1969, Formation and Destruction of Blood Cells, 1970, Glycoproteins of Plasma and Membranes, 1971, The Human Red Cell in Vitro, 1974, Transmissible Disease and Blood Transfusion, 1974, Trace Proteins of Plasma, 1976, The Granulocyte, 1977, Blood Substitutes and Plasma Expanders, 1978, The Blood Platelet in Transfusion Therapy, 1978, Methods in Hematology: Blood Transfusion, 1988; editor, contbr. Immunogenetics, 1967; editor-in-chief Transfusion, 1960-66, assoc. editor, 1966-86; editorial bd. Gen. Principles of Blood Transfusion, 1962-83, Vox Sanguinis, 1956-76, Haematologia, 1968-90, Blood, 1979-84; contbr. articles to profl. lit. Served to maj. M.C., AUS, 1942-46. Recipient Gold medal Caduceus Soc., NYU, 1933, Jr. Achievement award for outstanding contbn. sci., 1958, 1st Charles R. Drew award ARC, Washington, 1981, Disting. Citizen's award Allied Vets. Coun., 1963, award pioneer blood group rsch. Ctr. for Immunology, SUNY, Buffalo, 1976, Witebsky lectureship, 1994. Fellow AAAS, N.Y. Acad. Scis.; mem. NAS, Inst. Medicine (sr.), Am. Assn. Blood Banks (v.p. 1959-60, med. dir. central file rare donors 1960-66, John Elliot award 1966, Grove-Rasmussen award 1988, Bernard Fantus medal 1993), Internat. Soc. Hematology, ACP, Internat. Soc. Blood Transfusion (pres. 1966-72, historian 1975-96), Am. Soc. Clin. Pathologists, Central Soc. Clin. Research, Ohio Sci. Roundtable, Am. Soc. Hematology (treas. 1963-67), Am. Assn. Immunologists, Soc. Exptl. Biology and Medicine, Am. Soc. Human Genetics, Sigma Xi, Alpha Omega Alpha. Club: Cosmos. Home: 328 Compton Hills Dr Cincinnati OH 45215-4118 Office: Hoxworth Blood Ctr 3130 Highland Ave Cincinnati OH 45267-0055

GREENWELL, ARNOLD, biologist; b. Tokyo, Mar. 3, 1956; came to U.S., 1958; s. Charles Warren Greenwell and Miyoko (Takahashi) Wallace. AS cum laude, Lees-McRae Coll., 1976; BA, U. N.C., 1979. Research technician dept. zoology U. N.C., Chapel Hill, 1977-79; research technician Howard Hughes Med. Inst., Durham, N.C., 1979-80; biol. lab. technician Nat. Inst. Environ. Health Scis., Research Triangle Park, N.C., 1980-84, research biologist, 1984—; pvt. pilot, 1982—; free-lance photographer, 1977—. Contbr. articles to profl. jours. Mem. Aircraft Owners and Pilots Assn., Exptl. Aircraft Assn., Chapel Hill Flying Club, Nat. Inst. Environ. Health Scis. Camera Club (v.p. 1981-83, sec. 1987—), Phi Theta Kappa. Republican. Home: 305 Barclay Rd Chapel Hill NC 27516-1408 Office: Nat Inst Environ Health Scis PO Box 12233 Durham NC 27709-2233

GREENWOOD, JANET KAE DALY, psychologist, educational administrator; b. Goldsboro, N.C., Dec. 9, 1943; d. Fulton Benton and Kelminy Ethel Esther (Ball) Daly; 1 child, Gerald Thompson. AA, Peace Coll., 1963; BS in English and Psychology, East Carolina U., 1965, MEd in Counseling, 1967; postgrad., N.C. State U., 1967-69, U. London, 1969; PhD in Counseling and Higher Ednl. Adminstrn., Fla. State U., 1972. Tchr. English Kinston (N.C.) City Schs., 1965-66, Goldsboro City Schs., 1966-67; counselor and psychometrist primary and secondary schs. County of Wake, N.C., 1967-69; coord. Am. Inst. for Fgn. Study, 1969; supr. student tours in Eng., France, Switzerland, Italy, and Capri, 1969; counselor Fla. State U., Tallahassee, 1969-72; asst. dir. counseling Rutgers U., New Brunswick, N.J., 1972-73; cons. to v.p. for student svcs. Rutgers U., New Brunswick, 1973-74, lectr. in counseling psychology, 1972-74; coord. and assoc. prof. counselor edn. U. Cin., 1974-77, adviser to grad. students, 1974-77, vice provost student affairs, 1977-81; cons. guidance South Plainfield Pub. Schs., 1973-76; adviser Parents Without Ptnrs., 1976; pres. Longwood Coll., Farmville, Va., 1981-87, U. Bridgeport, Conn., 1987-92; cons., ptnr. Heidrick & Struggles, Washington D.C., 1992—, bd. dirs. The Hydraulic Co., Gov.'s Partnership to Prevent Substance Abuse in the Workforce, audit com. and cmty., govt. rels. com. Contbr. articles to profl. jours. Mem. Gov.'s Ad Hoc Edn. Com. on Tchr. Edn. and Counselor Edn., State of Ohio, 1975; mem. state planning commn. Nat. Identification of Women Project; chair Twin Rivers Tenants Rights Assn., 1972-74; bd. dirs. Bridgeport Hosp., Bridgeport Bus. Coun.; mem. adv. com. Bridgeport Pub. Edn. Fund; bd. dirs. Conn. Ballet Theatre, chair South End streeting com; mem. mgmt. adv. com. City of Bridgeport; mem. adv. com. United Way Tri-State; chair South End Partnership Com; mem. The Schiavone Steering Com./Downtown Bridgeport Project, YWCA Bd., Champion/United Way, United Way Community Human Svcs. Planning Coun., Bridgeport Symphony Bd., Bridgeport Opera Bd., Bridgeport Area Coll./Univ. Consortium, Conn. Conf. Ind. Colls., The Newcomen Soc. of U.S., The United Way Ea. Fairfield County; mem. adv. bd. Sacred Heart/St. Anthony Sch., Roosevelt Sch; mem. ct. com. Regional Plan Assn. Fairfield 2000; bd. dirs. Conn. Ballet Theatre; chair The Bridgeport Regional Bus. Coun. Brass Ring Task Force on Leadership; bd. govs. Fairfield County Study; mem. hon. bd. dirs. Conn. Earth Day 20, Inc.; chair L.I. Sound Western Regional Coun.; mem. L.I. Sound Assembly; mem. membership com., campus partnership subcom. Drugs Don't Work program, 1989—. Recipient Spl. award Black Arts Festival, Meritorious Svc. award Am. Assn. State Colls. and Univs. Mem. AAUP, Am. Coll. Pers. Assn. (editor and chair media bd. 1975—), Am. Pers. and Guidance Assn., Cin. Pers. and Guidance Assn., Ohio Psychol. Assn., Cin. Psychol. Assn., Organizational Behavior Assn., Am. Sch. Counselors Assn., Ohio Sch. Counselors Assn., Assn. for Women Faculty, Ohio Counselor Edn. and Supervision Assn., Kappa Delta Pi.

GREENWOOD, JOHN, doctor of optometry; b. Altenburg, Germany, Dec. 2, 1922; s. Abraham Adolf Daniel and Bettina B.B. (Alt) G.; m. Elsie Brownwald, Sept. 2, 1951; children: Deborah J., Judith E., Lucy R. OD, Ill. Coll. of Optometry, 1952; MS in Forensic Sci., George Washington U., 1975. Bd. cert. optometrist, Md., Ariz.; cert. in diagnostic pharm. drugs. Optometrist Dr. John Greenwood, Washington, 1952-85, Optometric Assn., Chevy Chase, Md., 1985-87; staff optometrist Kaiser Permanente Med. Ctr., Kensington, Md., 1988—; pres. Optometric Soc. of D.C., 1961-62, Internat. Assn. Bds. of Examiners in Optometry, Washington, 1975-76; mem. peer rev. Medicaid, Pub. Health Dept., Washington, 1975-77. Editor Grand Lodge Procs., 1969-73; contbr. articles to profl. jours. V.p. Citizens Assn., Arlington, Va., 1953-54; lectr. hwy. safety Met. Police Dept., Washington, 1961-73; mem. Hackers Lic. Appeals Bd., Washington, 1969-74, Citizens Traffic Bd., Washington, 1969-79; pres. exec. chpt. City of Hope Nat. Med. Rsch. Ctr., Washington, 1978. Named Optometrist-of-Yr., Optometric Soc. D.C., 1968, 70; recipient Disting. Svc. award Govt. D.C., 1969, fellowship Superior Profl. Stature, APHA, 1970, Grand Lodge Disting. Svc. medal Grand Lodge FAAM, 1990; 33rd degree Supreme Coun. Scottish Rite, So. Jurisdiction, 1991. Fellow Am. Acad. Optometry, Nat. Eye Rsch. Found. (Named for Outstanding Contbn. to Eye Care 1970), Rotary Internat.; m. Allied Masonic (sovereign master 1994-95), Grand Royal Arch of D.C. (grand master 2nd veil, high priest 1994-95), Masonic and Eastern Star Home (grand lodge rep. 1992-96), Scottish Rite D.C. (lt. uniformed unit 1979—), Pythagoras Lodge of Rsch. (sr. master 1967).

GREER, DAVID S., university dean, physician, educator; b. Bklyn., Oct. 12, 1925; s. Jacob and Mary (Zaslawsky) G.; m. Marion Clarich, June 25, 1950; children—Jeffrey, Linda. B.S., U. Notre Dame, 1948; M.D., U. Chgo., 1953; M.A. (hon.), Brown U., 1975; L.H.D. (hon.), Southeastern Mass. U., 1981. Diplomate: Am. Bd. Internal Medicine. Intern Yale-New Haven Med. Center, 1953-54; resident in medicine U. Chgo. Clinics, 1954-57; instr. endocrinology and medicine U. Chgo., 1957; practice medicine specializing in internal medicine Fall River, Mass., 1957-74; chief staff dept. medicine Fall River Gen. Hosp., 1959-62; med. dir. Earle E. Hussey Hosp., Fall River, 1962-75; chief staff dept. medicine Truesdale Clinic and Truesdale Hosp., Fall River, 1971-74; pres. med. staff Truesdale Clinic and Truesdale Hosp., 1968-70; sr. clin. instr. medicine Tufts U. Coll. Medicine, 1969-71, asst. clin. prof., 1971-78; clin. asso. prof. community health Brown U., 1973-75, dir. family practice residency program, 1975-78, prof. community health, 1975—, asso. dean medicine, 1974-81, dean medicine, 1982-92, chmn. sect. community health, 1978-81; mem. Gov.'s Task Force on Quality of Care, Medicaid Program, Commonwealth of Mass., 1969-70; del. White House Conf. Aging, 1971, 81; Pres. Ind. Living Authority, State of R.I., 1975-81; mem. exec. com. Cancer Control Bd. R.I., 1975-80; mem. R.I. Gov.'s Task Force for Inst. of Mental Health, 1976—; bd. dirs. Health Planning Council, Inc., Providence, 1976-78; chmn. com. on aging Jewish Fedn. R.I., 1978-80; chmn. Gov.'s Commn. on Provision of Comprehensive Mental Health Services in R.I., 1980-81; trustee Southeastern Mass. U., 1970-81, chmn., 1973-74; chmn. Providence Mayor's Sr. Citizens Task Force, 1975; bd. dirs. Assn. Home Health Agys. R.I., 1975—; founding dir. Internat. Physicians for Prevention of Nuclear War, Inc., 1980—; vis. prof. dept medicine Georgetown U., 1992-93; scholar-in-residence Assn. Am. Med. Colls., 1992-93. Contbr. articles to profl. jours. Fellow in health Kellogg Found. Internat., 1986-89; vis. fellow Green Coll. Oxford U., 1985; recipient Outstanding service award Mass. Easter Seal Soc., 1970; Outstanding Citizens award Jewish War Vets. Aux., 1973; Disting. Service award U. Chgo. Med. Alumni Assn.; Cutting Found. medal Andover Newton Theol. Sem., 1976; Professor of the Yr., Brown U., 1992. Master ACP; mem. Inst. Medicine, Gerontol. Soc., Am. Congress Rehab. Medicine, Internat. Soc. Rehab. Medicine, R.I. Med. Soc. Jewish. Office: Brown U Box G Providence RI 02912

GREER, DONALD MERRILL, plastic surgeon; b. Chgo., Nov. 14, 1936; s. Donald M. and Mary Elizabeth (Adams) G.; m. Anne Lindsay, June 11, 1966 (div. 1979); children: Donald, William; m. Jane Deely Carr, July 17, 1981; 1 child, Steven. BSc, U. Chgo., 1958; MD, U. Cin., 1962. Diplomate Am. Bd. Plastic Surgery. Resident in surgery U. Chgo., 1962-66, 68-70; resident in plastic surgery U. Mich., Ann Arbor, 1970-72; asst. prof. U. Fla., Gainesville, 1972-75; assoc. prof. U. Tex., San Antonio, 1975-87; pvt. practice Casper, Wyo., 1987—. Lt. comdr., USNR, 1966-68. Fellow ACS; mem. Am. Burn Assn., Am. Soc. Plastic and Reconstructive Surgeons, Am. Cleft Palate Assn. Office: 1300 E A St Casper WY 82601-2260

GREER, JONATHAN M., rheumatologist; b. Agana, Guam, Jan. 12, 1957; s. Melvin and Arline (Ebert) G.; m. Tammy Dee Suggs, May 4, 1996. BA, Oberlin Coll., 1979; MD, U. Fla., 1983. Assoc. physician Med. Ctr. Clin., Pensacola, Fla., 1988—; clin. instr. Navy Hosp. Family Practice, Pensacola, Fla., 1990—, Eglin Air Force Family Practice, Ft. Walton Beach, Fla., 1995—. Fellow Am. Coll. Physicians, Am. Coll. Rheumatology. Office: Med Ctr Clin PA 8333 N Davis Hwy Pensacola FL 32514-6048

GREER, KENNETH E., dermatologist; b. Marion, Va., 1941. MD, U. Va., 1967. Intern Strong Meml. Hosp., Rochester, N.Y., 1967-68, resident, 1968-69; resident U. Va., Charlottesville, 1971-74, mem. med. staff; prof. dermatology U. Va. Sch. Medicine, Charlottesville. Mem. AMA, Am. Dermatology Assn., NWDS, Va. Dermatology Soc. Office: U Va Hosp Dept Dermatology Primary Care Ctr Bldg Charlottesville VA 22908*

GREER, MACK VARNEDOE, physician; b. Valdosta, Ga., July 29, 1927; s. Lloyd Barton and Julie Winn (Varnedoe) G.; A.B., Emory U., 1951; postgrad. Valdosta State U., 1955-56; M.D., Med. Coll. Ga., 1960; m. Betty Dame English, Dec. 27, 1951; children: Betty June, Mack Varnedoe. Adjuster, Crawford & Co., ins. adjusters, Atlanta, 1951-52; high sch. math. and sci. tchr., football coach Clinch County (Ga.) and Waycross (Ga.) High Sch., 1952-55; rotating intern Bapt. Meml. Hosp., Jacksonville, Fla., 1960-61; gen. practice medicine and surgery, Homerville, Ga., 1961-72; mem. staff South Ga. Med. Center, chief staff, 1980; Coll. athletic physician; coll. physician, also assoc. prof. biology Valdosta State U., 1972-95; now emeritus prof. Former bd. dirs. Valdosta (Ga.) Girls Club. Served with USMCR, World War II, Korea; ret. capt. M.C., USNR. Diplomate Am. Bd. Family Practice. Mem. AMA, Ga. med. assns., S.Ga. Med. Soc., Am. Coll. Emergency Physicians, Pi Kappa Alpha, Alpha Kappa Kappa. Presbyterian. Club: Valdosta (Ga.) Touchdown, Valdosta Country. Home: 912 S Lakeshore Dr Valdosta GA 31602

GREER, MELVIN, medical educator; b. N.Y.C., Oct. 14, 1929; s. Aaron and Ceil (Cohen) Jefkel; m. Arline Ebert, Dec. 16, 1951; children: Jonathan, Richard, Alison, David. B.A. magna cum laude, NYU, 1950, M.D., 1954. Intern, resident Bellevue Hosp., N.Y.C., 1954-56; fellow N.Y. Neurol. Inst., Columbia, 1958-61; prof., chmn. dept. neurology U. Fla. Coll. Medicine, Gainesville, 1963—; cons. NIH, 1971—, Fla. Div. Corrections, 1971—; lectr., cons. Navy Dept.; chmn. med. adv. com. Community Clinic, Gainesville, 1971-73; endowed professorship neurology U. Fla. Coll. Medicine, Gainesville, 1991—. Author: Mass Spectrometry of Biologically Important Aromatic Acids, 1969, Differential Diagnosis of Neurological Diseases, 1977; also articles.; Editorial bd.: Neurology, Geriatics, 1968—. Served to lt. comdr. USNR, 1956-58. Recipient Medallion award Columbia U., 1968, Hippocratic award U. Fla., 1970, Outstanding Clin. Tchr. award, 1975, 79; NIH grantee, 1962-71. Fellow Am. Acad. Neurology (councillor, sec.-treas. 1977-81, pres.-elect 1983-85, pres. 1985-87), Am. Acad. Pediatrics; mem. Am. Neurol. Assn. (councillor), Soc. Pediatric Research, Am. Pediatric Soc., Phi Beta Kappa, Alpha Omega Alpha. Home: 2058 NW 14th Ave Gainesville FL 32605-5245

GREER, MONTE ARNOLD, physician, educator; b. Portland, Oreg., Oct. 26, 1922; s. William Wallace and Rose (Rasmussen) G.; m. Peggy Johnson, Dec. 31, 1943; children: Susan Elizabeth, Richard Arnold. Student, Oreg. State U., 1940-43; AB, Stanford U., 1944, MD, 1947. Intern San Francisco Gen. Hosp., 1946-47; rsch. fellow endocrinology New England Med. Ctr., Boston, 1947-49; resident internal medicine Mass. Meml. Hosp., Boston, 1949-50; rsch. assoc. in endocrinology New England Med. Ctr. Hosp., 1950-51; sr. investigator, sr. asst. surgeon USPHS, Nat. Cancer Inst., NIH, Bethesda, Md., 1951-55; chief radioisotope unit D.C. Gen. Hosp., Washington, 1951-55; clin. asst. prof. medicine UCLA, 1955-56; chief radioisotope svc. VA Hosp., Long Beach, Calif., 1955-56; head div. endocrinology Oreg. Health Scis. U. (formerly U. Oreg. Med. Sch.), Portland, 1956-80, assoc. prof., 1956-62, prof. medicine, 1962—, prof. physiology, 1992—, head divsn. endocrinology, metabolism and clin. nutrition, 1980-84, head sect. endocrinology, 1984-90. Author: (with H. Studer) The Regulation of Thyroid Function in Iodine Deficiency, 1968, (with P. Langer) Antithyroid Drugs and Naturally Occurring Goitrogens, 1977; editor: The Thyroid Gland, 1990, (with D.H. Solomon) The Thyroid, 1974; mem. editorial bd. Endocrinology, 1960-72, Neuroendocrinology, 1965-76, Endocrine Regulations, 1971—; contbr. articles to profl. jours. Mem. Thyroid Task Force NIH Com. for Evaluation of Endocrinology and Metabolic Diseases, 1977-80, Endocrinology Study Sect., NIH, 1977-80. Pharmacol. and Endocrinology fellowship study sect. NIH, 1968-72; recipient Oppenheimer award Endocrine Soc., 1958, Rsch. Career award NIH, 1962-81, Discovery award Med. Rsch. Found. Oreg., 1985, DeMolay Legion of Honor award, 1988. Mem. AAAS, Am. Fedn. for Clin. Rsch. (chmn. Western sect. 1958-59), Western Soc. for Clin. Rsch. (v.p. 1963-64, pres. 1967-68), Endocrine Soc. (mem. council 1965-68, v.p. 1976-77), Am. Thyroid Assn. (v.p., dir. 1974-77, pres. 1980, Disting. Service award 1985), Am. Soc. Clin. Investigation, Soc. Exptl. Biology and Medicine, Western Assn. Physicians (sec.-treas. 1974-77), Assn. Am. Physicians, Internat. Brain Rsch. Orgn., Internat. Soc. Neuroendocrinology, European Thyroid Assn., Japan Endocrine Soc. (hon.), Czechoslovak Endocrine Soc. (hon.), Rotary, Sigma Chi. Office: Oreg Health Scis U Portland OR 97201

GREFF, LINDA JOY, ophthalmologist, educator; b. Cin., July 16, 1959; d. Irwin and Evelyn (Mayerson) G. BS, U. Mich., 1981; MD, Ohio State U., 1985. Diplomate Am. Bd. Ophthalmology. Resident in Ophthalmology Ohio State U., 1986-89; fellowship in glaucoma Harvard U. Med. Sch., 1990-91; clin. fellow Mass. Eye & Ear Infirmary, Boston, 1990-91; staff physician Cin. Eye Inst., 1991—; attending physician Jewish Hosp., Cin., 1991—, Children's Hosp., Cin., 1991—, Bethesda Hosp., Cin., 1991—; vol. asst. prof. U. Cin., 1993—; bd. dirs. Cin. Soc. Ophthalmology, 1996-97; adv. bd. So. Ohio Coll., Cin., 1992-95; co-dir. Midwest Glaucoma Soc., Cin., 1994; course dir. for ophthalmology update Bethesda Hosp., 1993. Co-author: (book chpt.) Principles & Practice of Ophthalmology, 1994; contbr. articles to profl. jours. Participant Women's Conf. Circle, White House, 1996. Fellow Am. Acad. Ophthalmology, Internat. Coll. Surgeons; mem. AMA, Ohio State Med. Assn., Assn. Women Surgeons, Chandler-Grant Soc. Office: Cin Eye Inst 10494 Montgomery Rd Cincinnati OH 45242-4420

GREGER, JANET LEE, health, nutrition author, educator; b. Joliet, Ill., Feb. 18, 1948; d. Harold Michael and Marjorie Marie (Smith) G. BS, U. Ill., 1970; MS, Cornell U., 1971, PhD, 1973. Asst. prof. Purdue U., Lafayette, Ind., 1973-78; asst. prof., assoc. prof. U. Wis., Madison, 1978-83, prof., 1983—; adminstrv. intern U. Wis. Sys., 1989; assoc. dean grad. sch. U. Wis., 1990-96, med. sch., 1996—; mem. study sect. NIH, 1984-89; mem. Am. Assn. Accreditation Lab. and Animal Care Bd., 1992—, Coun. on Govt. Rels. Bd. Mgmt., 1993—. Author: Nutrition for Living, 1985, 88, 91, 93; contbr. articles to profl. jours. AAAS Congl. Sci. fellow, 1984-85. Mem. Am. Inst. Nutrition, Am. Soc. Clin. Nutrition, Inst. Food Tech., Am. Assn. for Accreditation of Lab. Animal Care (bd. dirs. 1992—), Sigma Xi. Office: U Wis 1415 Linden Dr Madison WI 53706-1527

GREGG, DONALD B., education counselor. BA, Montclair State Coll., 1951, MA, 1956; EdD, Lehigh U., 1967. Cert. tchr., counselor, N.J. Tchr. pub. schs. Hasbrouck Heights, N.J., 1951-52, 54-56; dir. guidance Livingston, N.J., 1956-60; mem. faculty dept. counseling, human svcs. and guidance Montclair State U., Upper Montclair, N.J., 1961-92. Mem. ACA, NEA, Assn. Specialists in Group Work, N.J. Profl. Counselors and Suprs., N.J. Assn. Alcoholism Counselors.

GREGG, JOHN BAILEY, surgery educator, researcher; b. Sioux Falls, S.D., June 5, 1922; s. John B. and Anna Elida (Bailey) G.; m. Pauline Benfer Snyder, June 29, 1946: children: Michele Lee, John Benfer, Stewart David, Rebecca Jo Anderson. BA, Iowa U., 1943, MD, 1946; DSc (hon.), U. S.D., 1989. Diplomate Am. Bd. Otolaryngology. Asst. prof. otolaryngology U. Iowa Hosps., Iowa City, 1959-60; prof. anthropology U. Tenn., Knoxville, 1972—; chmn. div. otolaryngology Sch. of Medicine U. S.D., Sioux Falls, 1968-72, vis. prof. Sch. of Medicine, 1972-75, dir. specialties of surgery Sch. Medicine, 1972-88; cons. VA Hosps, Iowa City and Sioux Falls, 1946-79, USPHS Indian Hosps., Rosebud, Pine Ridge and Wagner, S.D., 1956-75, U. S.D. Speech & Hearing Clinic, Vermillion, 1960—; dir. med. svcs. S.D. Dept. Health, 1982-84, dir. Div. Pub. Health, 1983-84. Author: Dry Bones, 1987, 2d rev. edit., 1989; author: (with others) Benigh Diseases of the Esophagus, 1982; contbr. over 200 articles to profl. jours. Speaker Ho. of Dels., S.D. State Med. Assn., Sioux Falls, 1973-75. Lt. (j.g.) USNR, 1942-49. Mem. Sioux Falls Elks, Sioux Falls Rotary. Republican. Episcopalian. Home: 2807 S Phillips Ave Sioux Falls SD 57105-4829

GREGG, LAWRENCE J., physician; b. Shawnee, Okla., July 29, 1944; s. L.J. and Annell (Criswell) G.; m. Lynda Antoinette Lawrence, May 15, 1985; children: Laura K., Kimberly B. Rogers, Lawrence James. BS, U. Okla., 1967, MD, 1970. Diplomate Am. Bd. Dermatology. Intern St. Francis Hosp., Wichita, 1970-71; resident in dermatology U. Okla., Oklahoma City, 1973-76; dermatologist Tulsa Dermatol. Clinic, 1976—; clin. prof. U. Okla., Tulsa. Capt., flight surgeon USAF, 1971-73. Fellow Am. Acad. Dermatology; mem. Dermatol. Surg. Soc., Okla. State Dermatol. Soc. (pres. 1981-82), Tulsa City Dermatol. Soc. (sec.). Office: Tulsa Dermatol Clinic PO Box 52588 2121 E 21st Tulsa OK 74152

GREGG, MICHAEL B., health science association administrator, epidemiologist; b. Paris, Jan. 6, 1930; married; three children. BA, Stanford U., 1952; MD, Western Reserve U. Sch. Medicine, 1956. Diplomate Am. Bd. Med. Examiners, Am. Bd. Preventive Medicine. Intern in internal medicine Presbyn. Hosp., N.Y.C., 1956-57, jr. asst. resident in internal medicine, 1957-58, sr. asst. resident in internal medicine, 1958-59; sr. asst. surgeon USPHS, NIH, Rocky Mountain Lab., 1959-61, surgeon, 1962; research assoc. div. infectious diseases U. Md. Sch. Medicine, 1962-63; research assoc. Inst. Internat. Medicine U. Md., 1963-64, asst. prof., 1964-66; acting assoc. dir. Pakistan Med. Research Ctr., Lahore, 1964, dir. dept. malariology, 1964, dir. dept. serology and immunology, 1964-65; chief epidemic intelligence service, epidemiology program Ctr. for Disease Control, 1966-68; dir. viral diseases div. Bur. Epidemiology, Ctrs. Disease Control, 1968-76, dep. dir., 1970-81; dep. dir. epidemiology program office Ctrs. for Disease Control, 1981-88, dir. epidemiology program office, 1988-89; pvt. practice specializing in epidemiology and disease control, 1989—; editor Ctrs. for Disease Control Morbidity and Mortality Weekly Report, 1967-88; cons. on poliomyelitis WHO, Geneva, 1969; cons. to govt. of Indonesia for WHO, 1969, 70, 72, 74, 78; internat. cons. to various countries for WHO, 1969-81; mem. com. on Viral Hepatitis div. Med. Scis., NRC, Washington, 1970-74; mem. Ctrs. for Disease Control Study Sect. Office Rsch. Grants, 1970-72; mem. Data Registry Com. Nat. Cystic Fibrosis Found., Atlanta, 1972-78; mem. U.S. Influenza Del. to the USSR, 1973. Fellow Am. Coll. Epidemiology; mem. AAAS, Am. Pub. Health Assn., Am. Epidemiol. Soc., Alpha Omega Alpha. Home and Office: RR 3 Box 363 Brattleboro VT 05301-8538

GREGG, ROBERT LEE, pharmacist; b. White River, S.D., Mar. 2, 1932; s. C.W. and Margaret (Maguire) G.; m. Julie D. Tyler, June 7, 1956; children: Allen, Mark, Susan. BS, S.D. State U., 1958. Registered pharmacist, S.D. Owner, mgr., pharmacist Kennebec (S.D.) Drug, 1958-79, Gregg Drug, Chamberlain, S.D., 1978—; mem. adv. coun. Coll. Pharmacy, S.D. State U., Brookings, 1985—; pres. S.D. Bd. Pharmacy, Pierre, 1992-93. Former sec. Indsl. Devel. Corp., Kennebec, S.D.; pres. Lake Francis Case Devel. Corp., Chamberlain, 1984-85. With Med. Svc. Corps, U.S. Army, 1953-55, Korea. Mem. S.D. Pharm. Assn. (pres. 1985-86, Bowl of Hygeia award 1992), Nat. Assn. Retail Druggists, Chamberlain C. of C., NRA (life), VFW (life, quartermaster Kennebec 1965-76, Outstanding Post Quartermaster award 1965), Am. Legion (life), Am. Quarter Horse Assn., S.D. Trail Riders (bd. dirs. 1986—), KC (4th degree). Republican. Roman Catholic. Home: PO Box 459 220 N Grace St Chamberlain SD 57325-1002 Office: PO Box 459 200 N Main St Chamberlain SD 57325-1326

GREGORATOS, GABRIEL, medical educator; b. Athens, Greece, Aug. 20, 1929; came to U.S., 1948.; s. Panos M. and Catherine (Monopoli) G.; m. Eva Gallay, Jan. 2, 1953; children: Katherine M., Barbara A., Nicholas S. AB, Hamilton Coll., 1950; MD, N.Y. Med. Coll., 1954. Intern St. Vincent's Hosp., N.Y.C., 1954-55; resident in internal medicine Tripler Army Med. Ctr., Honolulu, 1959-62; resident in cardiology Walter Reed Army Med. Ctr., Washington, 1962-64; commd. 1st lt. U.S. Army, 1956, advanced through grades to col., 1970; chief cardiology Letterman Army Med. Ctr., San Francisco, 1971-76; ret. U.S. Army, 1976; assoc. prof. to prof. of medicine U. Calif., San Diego, 1976-84; chief cardiology Pacific Presbyn. Med. Ctr., San Francisco, 1984-89; prof. medicine, dir. clin. cardiology U. Calif. Davis, Sacramento, 1989—; cons. FDA, Washington, 1973—, VA, San Francisco, 1986-89, Letterman Army Med. Ctr., 1985-92, NAval Hosp., San Diego, 1979-84; chair FDA adv. panel (circulatory system), 1992-93. Co-editor: Coronary Care, 1981; contbr. articles to profl. jours. Pres. San Francisco Heart Assn., 1988-89. Decorated Legion of Merit. Fellow ACP, Am. Coll. Cardiology (councillor Calif. chpt. 1989-92, pres. Calif chpt. 1994-95, gov. No. Calif. 1994—), Coun. of Clin. Cardiology, Am. Heart Assn. Democrat. Greek Orthodox. Office: U Calif Davis Med Ctr Ste 3500 4150 V St Sacramento CA 95817-5191

GREGORY, DANIEL KEVIN, pharmacist; b. New Orleans, Sept. 11, 1958; s. Conrad and Mildred (Knight) G.; m. Vicki Lynn Ivy, May 18, 1985; 1 child, Brandon Christopher. Student, La. State U., 1976-79; BS in Pharmacy, N.E. La. U., 1982; postgrad., La. State, 1982-84. Registered pharmacist. Pharmacist Our Lady of the Lake Regional Med. Ctr., Baton Rouge, 1982-84, pharmacist, night supr., 1985-92; cons. pharm. dir. Tau Ctr. Our Lady of the Lake Regional Med. Ctr., 1985-92; pharmacist Chem. Dependency Units of Baton Rouge, 1982-85; pharmacy supr. H.C.A. L.W. Blake Meml. Hosp., Bradenton, Fla., 1992-94; pharmacy asst. mgr. Walmart, Bradenton, 1994—; owner Darklite Graphics; artist-in-residence Eclipse Mag.; owner Oarkute Graphics. Mem. La. Arts and Artist's Guild, 1988-91. Finalist Illustrators of the Future competition, 4th quar., 1990, Hon. Mention, 1991. Mem. Fla. Soc. Hosp. Pharmacists Inc. (S.W. chpt.), Internat. Platform Assn., Suncoast Camera Club, Phi Delta Chi (v.p. 1980-81). Republican. Episcopalian. Home: 3108 48th Avenue Dr E Bradenton FL 34203-3928 Office: Wal Mart Pharmacy 815 44th Ave W Bradenton FL 34207

GREGORY, JOHN MICHAEL, urologist; b. Jax, Fla., Feb. 21, 1939; s. John Wellington and Anna Louise (Mahoney) G.; m. Helen Louise Theus, Aug. 12, 1961; children: Louise, Katherine, Michael Jr. BS, U. Ala., 1961; MD, Tulane U., 1964. Intern McCleod Infirmary, Florence, S.C., 1964-65; surg. asst. Byrne Inst., Columbia, S.C., 1965-66; fellow in urology Mayo Clinic, Rochester, Minn., 1968-72; pvt. practice Memphis Urology Group, 1972-78, Urology of Athens, Ga., 1978—. Capt. U.S. Army, 1966-68. Mem. Am. Assn. Clin. Urologists, Am. Urologic Assn., Ga. Urologic Assn. (pres.-elect 1996—), Athens County Club (pres. 1995-96), Athens City Club (pres. 1988-89), Cornerstone Soc. (co-chmn. membership com. 1992—). Republican. Episcopalian. Home: 634 Milledge Circle Athens GA 30606 Office: Urology of Athens 195 King Ave Athens GA 30606

GREGORY, LYNNE WATSON, oncology clinical nurse specialist; b. Atlanta, Dec. 4, 1946; d. Stephen Lawton and Louise (Baxter) Watson; m. Gerardo A. Gregory, July 10, 1976; children: Max, Alex, Sara. BSN with honors, Fla. State U., 1968; MN, Emory U., 1973; postgrad., U. Ga., 1983-88. RN, Tex.; cert. clin. nurse specialist, oncology cert. nurse. Evening charge nurse, emergency room Lakeland (Fla.) Gen. Hosp., 1968; staff nurse U.S. Army Hosp., various assignments, 1969-72, Emory U. Hosp., Atlanta, 1971-73; oncology nurse clinician Walter Reed Army Med. Ctr., Washington, 1974-77; instr. to asst. prof., Sch. of Nursing U. Tex. Health Sci. Center, San Antonio, 1977-80; asst. prof. dept. nursing Avila Coll., Kansas City, Mo., 1980-81; res. nurse USA Hosp., Ft. Ord, Calif., 1981-83; staff nurse to adminstrv. asst., staff dir. Hospice of the Monterey Peninsula, Carmel, Calif., 1981-83; res. nurse 382d. Field Hosp., Augusta, Ga., 1983-85; dir. St. Joseph Hospice St. Joseph Hosp., Augusta, Ga., 1985-88; nurse cons. N.Am. Health and Rehab. Svcs., Dallas, 1989-90; staff nurse, oncology Providence Meml. Hosp., El Paso, Tex., 1990-92, clin. nurse specialist, oncology svcs., 1992-94, clin. nurse specialist, continuing care divsn., 1994—. Presenter in field. Maj. Army Nurse Corps, 1969-76. Decorated Army Commendation medal with oak leaf cluster; recipient cert. of appreciation Bexar County unit Am. Cancer Soc. Mem. Am. Cancer Soc. (patient edn. com., screening com.), Oncology Nursing Soc. (treas. Rio Grande chpt.). Presbyterian. Home: 909 La Cabana Place El Paso TX 79912 Office: Providence Memorial Hosp 2001 N Oregon El Paso TX 79902

GREGORY, ROBERT SCOTT, pharmacist; b. Binghamton, N.Y., May 30, 1954; s. Floyd A. and Betty J. (Jenson) G.; m. Karen J. Shislo, Sept. 20, 1980. AA, Broome Community Coll., 1973; BS in Pharmacy, Mass. Coll. Pharmacy, 1977, MS in Pharmacy, 1983; MBA, U. Houston, 1992. Registered pharmacist, Washington, Md., N.H. Staff pharmacist Colonial Pharmacy, New London, N.H., 1977-78, Dartmouth-Hitchcock Med. Ctr., Hanover, N.H., 1978-80; pharmacy supr. Quincy (Mass.) City Hosp., 1980-83; pharmacy dir. Hosp. Corp. Am., Coronado Hosp., Pampa, Tex., 1983-86, Diagnostic Ctr. Hosp., Houston, 1986-93, Humana Group Health Plan, Washington, 1993-95, Chesapeake Health Plan, Balt., 1995—; cons. HCA Div. Support Network, Dallas and Fort Worth, Tex., 1986—. Mem. Am. Soc. Hosp. Pharmacists, Tex. Soc. Hosp. Pharmacists (bd. dirs. 1984-86), Panhandle Soc. Hosp. Pharmacists (pres. 1985-86, Pres.' award 1986), Houston-Galveston Soc. Hosp. Pharmacists, Acad. Managed Care Pharmacy, Rho Chi. Methodist. Office: Chesapeake Health Plan 814 Light St Baltimore MD 21230

GREIDER, BRADLEY W., ophthalmologist, surgeon; b. New Orleans, May 22, 1953. BA, U. Colo., 1975; MS, Stanford U., 1978, MD, 1980. Diplomate Am. Bd. Ophthalmology. Intern Harbor/UCLA Med. Ctr., Torrance, 1980-81; resident Jules Stein/UCLA Eye Inst., 1981-83; pvt. practice ophthalmology Vista, Calif., 1983—. Fellow ACS, Am. Acad. Ophthalmology. Office: 2067 W Vista Way Ste 120 Vista CA 92083

GREIDER, JACK LEELAND, surgeon; b. Decatur, Ill., July 13, 1947; divorced; 1 child. BS in biology, Boston Coll., 1969; MD, Medical Coll. Wis., 1974. Diplomate Am. Bd. Orthopedic Surgery, Nat. Bd. Medical Examiners. Clinical asst. prof. dept. orthopaedics Univ. Fla.; pres. Southeastern Hand Ctr., Jacksonville, Fla.; orthopaedic St. Luke's Hosp. Jacksonville, Bapt. Meml. Ctr., Meml. Medical Ctr., Jacksonville Surgery Ctr., Univ. Medical Ctr., St. Vincent's Hosp. Jacksonville, Meth. Hosp. Jacksonville; prog. chmn. Fla. Orthopaedic Soc., 1986, exec. com., 1987-90, mem. ambulatory surgery com. St. Luke's Hosp., 1992—. Contbr. numerous articles to profl. jours. Mem. AMA, Am. Acad. Orthopaedic Surgeons, Am. Soc. Surgery of the Hand, Am. Assn. Surgery of the Hand, Fla. Hand Soc., Duval County Medical Soc., Fla. Medical Assn., Northeast Fla. Orthopaedic Soc., Eastern Orthopaedic Soc., Fla. Orthopaedic Soc. Office: Southeastern Hand Ctr 6100 Kennerly Rd Jacksonville FL 32216

GREIF, GEOFFREY LEONARD, social work educator; b. Balt., Apr. 13, 1949; s. Leonard L. and Ann (Burgunder) G.; m. Maureen Lefton, Dec. 28, 1975; children: Jennifer, Alissa. BA, Ohio Wesleyan U., 1971; MSW, U. Pa., 1974; DSW, Columbia U., 1983. Lic. clin. social worker, Md. Social worker Camden (N.J.) Sch. System, 1974-76; psychiat. social worker Drenk Guidance Ctr., Burlington, N.J., 1976-79; tchr. Widener U., Chester, Pa., 1981-84; from asst. prof. to prof. U. Md., Balt., 1984—, assoc. dean, 1996—; cons., supr. Cmty. Counseling Ctr., Cockeysville, Md., 1985-90; cons. drug program Sinai Hosp., Balt., 1990—. Author: Single Fathers, 1985, (with others) Mothers Without Custody, 1988, The Daddy Track and the Single Father, 1990, When Parents Kidnap, 1993, Group Work with At-Risk Populations, Out of Touch: When Parents and Children Lose Contact After Divorce, also over 70 articles and book chpts. Bd. dirs. Parents Anonymous, Balt., 1985-92, Park Sch., Balt., 1987—. Young scholar Sch. Social Wk., 1989. Office: U Md Sch Social Work 525 W Redwood St Baltimore MD 21201-1777

GREIFINGER, ROBERT BERNARD, medical management consultant; b. Newark, May 18, 1945; s. William and Gertrude Frances (Fichman) G.; m. Maura Sima Bluestone, July 5, 1981; children: Rena Clare, Liza Beth. BA, U. Pa., 1967; MD, U. Md., 1971. Diplomate Am. Bd. Pediatrics. Intern Montefiore Med. Ctr., Bronx, N.Y., 1971-72, resident, 1974-76, asst. prof., 1976-77; med. dir. Community Health Plan-Suffolk, Hauppauge, N.Y., 1977-80; med. dir., v.p. Westchester Community Health Plan, White Plains, N.Y., 1980-85; dir. alternative delivery systems Montefiore Med. Ctr., Bronx, 1985-86; v.p. Health Care Systems, Montefiore Med. Ctr., Bronx, 1986-89; dep. commr., chief med. officer N.Y. State Dept. Correctional Svcs., 1989-95; med. mgmt. and prison health cons., 1995—; asst. prof. Albert Einstein Coll. Medicine, Bronx, 1976—; cons. Nat. Comm. Quality Assurance, Washington, 1982—. Contbr. articles on health and health care to profl. jours. Served to surgeon USPHS, 1974-76. Fellow ACPE. Democrat. Jewish. Home and Office: 32 Parkway Dr Dobbs Ferry NY 10522-3517

GREINER, JACK VOLKER, ophthalmologist, physician, surgeon, research scientist; b. Fountain Hill, Pa., Aug. 25, 1949; s. Harry Sandt and Vera Lilian G.; m. Cynthia Ann Mis., May 17, 1980; children: Ashley Lauren, Logan Nicholas Jack, Jordan Dean Jack. AA, Valley Forge Mil. Coll., 1969; BA, U. Vt., 1971; MS in Anatomy, Purdue U., 1974, PhD, U. Toledo, 1975; DO, Midwe. Univ., 1982. Rsch. fellow in ophthalmology Howe Lab. of Ophthalmology, Harvard U. Med. Sch. and Mass. Eye and Ear Infirmary, Boston, 1974-76; rsch. fellow in ophthalmology Harvard U. Med. Sch., Boston, 1975-78, instr. ophthalmology, 1988-90, clin. instr., 1991—; rsch. fellow in corneal and external diseases of eye Schepens Eye Rsch. Inst., Retina Found., 1976-78, clin. assoc. scientist, 1991—; rsch. assoc. in ophthalmology U. Ill. Eye and Ear Infirmary, Chgo., 1979-81, rsch. asst. prof. ophthalmology, 1981-83; med. intern Cook County Hosp., Chgo., 1982-83; resident in ophthalmology Georgetown U. Med. Ctr., 1983-86; adj. asst. scientist Eye Rsch. Inst., Retina Found., Boston, 1978; adj. asst. prof. ophthalmic pathology Midwe. Univ., 1979-82, asst. prof. dept. pathology, 1982-83, assoc. prof., 1983-87; co-dir. Eye Rsch. Lab., Chgo. Osteo. Hosp., 1980-87; clin. fellow in opthalmology Harvard Med. Sch./Mass. Eye and Ear Infirmary, 1986-88; mem. med. staff Beth Israel Hosp., Boston, Winchester Hosp., Lawrence Meml. Hosp., Medford, Melrose-Wakefield Hosp., New Eng. Meml. Hosp., Stoneham, Spaulding Rehab. Hosp., Boston. Patentee in field. Contbr. chpts. to books, over 100 articles to profl. publs. Served to capt. C.E. USAR, 1971-78. Fight For Sight grantee, 1980-82; Nat. Soc. to Prevent Blindness grantee, 1981—; NIH Nat. Eye Inst. grantee, 1982-85, 92—. Fellow Am. Acad. Osteopathic Surgeons (pres. 1995-96); mem. AMA, Mass. Soc. Eye Physicians and Surgeons, Am. Assn. Osteo. Specialists, Am. Assn. Osteo. Specialists (bd. cert. in surgery-ophthalmology), Nat. Soc. Prevent Blindness (bd. dirs. Prevent Blindness Mass.), Contact Lens Assn. Ophthalmologists, Assn. Rsch. in Vision and Ophthalmology, Mass. Med. Soc., Am. Acad. Ophthalmology, Sigma Xi, Phi Kappa Phi, Sigma Sigma Phi. Office: Harvard Med Sch 20 Staniford St Boston MA 02114-2508

GREINER, KENNETH DONALD, JR., nursing home company executive; b. Cushing, Okla., Aug. 19, 1938; s. Kenneth Donald Greiner and Billie Alene (Williams) Greiner/Kannady; m. Leitner Louise Jarrell, Sept. 2, 1961; children—Katherine Louise Pierce, Kenneth Donald III, Jennifer Lee, Cheryl Sue. B.S. in Econs., Okla. State U., 1960; M.B.A., Harvard U., 1962; B.S. in Health Care Adminstrn., Okla. Bapt. U., 1977. Adminstrv. asst. Doric Corp., Oklahoma City, 1962-64; asst. to treas. Skelly Oil Co., Tulsa, 1964-66; loan officer AID, Lahore, Karachi, Pakistan, 1966-69; ptnr. Resource Analysis & Mgmt. Group, Oklahoma City, 1969-74; v.p., dir. Texal Internat. Co., Oklahoma City, 1974-76; pres. Amity Care Corp., Oklahoma City, 1976—; asst. trustee in bankruptcy Four Seasons Nursing Ctrs. Am., Oklahoma City, 1972-73; bd. dirs., mem. exec. com. Will Rogers Bank, Oklahoma City, 1983-94; branch adv. dir. Oklahoma City Bank IV, 1994—; trustee in bankruptcy Gulf South Corp., Oklahoma City, 1974. Chmn. Cath. Social Ministries, Archdiocese of Oklahoma City, 1977-86; treas., bd. dirs. Neighborhood Services Orgn., Oklahoma City Met. Area, 1978-83; chmn. bd. New World Sch., Oklahoma City, 1973-74; mem. Putnam City Sch. Bd., 1988-93, pres. 1992-93; dir. Cowboy Golf, Inc., 1992—; trustee Hillcrest Hosp., Oklahoma City, 1989-93; mem. bd. govs. Okla. State U. Found., 1994. Mem. Okla. State U. CBA Assocs. (pres. 1993-94), Okla. Nursing Home Assn. (exec. bd. 1988-95, v.p. 1990-92), Nursing Home Assn. of Okla., Okla. State Bd. Nursing Homes (bd. dirs. 1988-92), Nat. Assn. Bds. of Examiners of Nursing Home Adminstrs. (pres. 1994-96), Phi Delta Theta Alumni (pres. Oklahoma City 1969-71). Republican. Roman Catholic. Clubs: Harvard Bus. School Alumni (pres. Oklahoma City 1970-71), Business Boosters (pres. 1985), Oklahoma City Dinner, Quail Creek Golf and Country, Ski Island Lake Inc. (pres. 1984-87). Home: 6224 W Commodore Ln Oklahoma City OK 73162-6813 Office: Amity Care Corp 4415 Highline Blvd Box 23017 Oklahoma City OK 73123

GREINER, PAUL THEODORE, internist; b. New Hyde Park, N.Y., June 13, 1942; s. Werner Hilmar and Elsie Rowena (Hausman) G.; m. Ellen Ann Hedberg, July 15, 1967; children: Abigail Elisa, Matthew Elliott. AB magna cum laude, Harvard U., 1963; MD, Harvard U., Boston, 1972. Diplomate Nat. Bd. Med. Examiners, Am. Bd. Internal Medicine. Pres. Physicians Group Practice, inc., Attleboro, Mass., 1975-95; med. co-dir. Mansfield (Mass.) Health Ctr., 1995—. Mem. ACP, Am. Soc. Internal Medicine, Mass. Med. Soc., Bristol North Med. Soc. Office: Mansfield Health Ctr 200 Copeland Dr Mansfield MA 02048

GREIVER, S(ANFORD) PHILIP, physician; b. Louisville, Sept. 19, 1930; s. Joseph and Sonia Greiver; m. Rosalind Hornstein, Aug. 20, 1961; children: Michael Evan, Jonathan Howard. BA, U. Louisville, 1951, MD, 1955. Diplomate Am. Bd. Internal Medicine, Am. Bd. Geriatric Medicine. Intern then resident in medicine Maimonides Hosp., N.Y.C., 1955-57; resident Barnes Hosp., St. Louis, 1959-60, Louisville Gen. Hosp., 1960-61; pvt. practice Louisville, 1961—; assoc. clin. prof. medicine U. Louisville, 1977—; med. dir. geriatric seminar Jewish Hosp., Louisville, 1965-91, med. advisor geriatric program, 1965-93. Mem. task force on aging Jewish Community Fedn., Louisville, 1991-93; chmn. careers in medicine com. Jefferson County Med. Soc., 1981-86. Capt. U.S. Army, 1957-59. Fellow Am. Coll. Physicians, Ky. Geratrics Soc. (pres. 1990-91); mem. Am. Geriatrics Soc., Ky. Med. Assn. (care of elderly com. 1987—), Louisville Soc. Internists (pres. 1987-88). Jewish. Office: 250 E Liberty St Ste 700 Louisville KY 40202-1537

GREIZERSTEIN, HEBE BEATRIZ, research scientist, educator; b. Buenos Aires, Argentina; came to U.S., 1961; d. Alberto Eduardo and Maria Belmonte; m. Walter Greizerstein, Oct. 5, 1960; children: Diana, Paul, Miriam. BA, U. Buenos Aires, 1957, PhD, 1960. Sr. rsch. scientist Rsch. Inst. on Alcoholism, Buffalo, N.Y., 1970-83; rsch. asst. prof. SUNY, Buffalo, 1970—; pres. EB Assoc. Labs., Williamsville, N.Y., 1984—; dir. analytical lab Toxicology Rsch. Ctr., Buffalo, 1987—. Office: EB Assocs Labs 90 Earhart Dr Ste 6 Williamsville NY 14221-7802

GREMILLION, CURTIS LIONEL, JR., psychologist, hospital administrator, musician; b. Slaughter, La., Feb. 26, 1924; s. Curtis Lionel and Beatrice (Watson) G.; m. Rosemary Duhon, Dec. 8, 1951; children: Suzanne Lynelle Gremillion (Rader), Curtis Lionel III, Monique Angele Gremillion Smith. BA in Psychology and Music, U. Southwestern La., 1948; postgrad. in psychology, La. State U., 1948-49, 53. Profl. musician, 1940-43, 46-53; staff psychologist East La. State Hosp., Jackson, 1949-83; dir. psychology and social svc. depts. East La. State Hosp., 1953- 57, asst. supt., 1957-62, adminstr., 1961, 62-64, supt., 1964-66, assoc. adminstr., 1966-81, patient advocate, 1981-83; cons. psychology, 1983—; clin. dir. Pace Ctr., Baton Rouge, 1983-88; notary pub., 1954—; dir. regional coun. Alcoholism and Drug Abuse, 1972-76; psychologist emeritus La. State Bd. Examiners of Psychologists; initiated numerous modern treatment programs for mentally ill, initiated clin. tng. for mental health pastorial counseling; established La. War Vets. Home. Author: History of The East Louisiana State Hospital; contbr. to publs. on New Orleans jazz. Bd. dirs. La. State Credit Union, 1962-68; chmn. East Feliciana Parish United Givers Fund, 1960; regional chmn. Am. Heart Assn., 1968-76, ARC, 1954-55, 62, Boy Scouts Am., 1964-69, Am. Cancer Soc., 1963-64; bd. dirs. So. Behavioral Rsch. Found., 1970-76. With USNR, 1943-46. Recipient Outstanding Leadership and Svc. award La. Dept. Hosps., 1966. Mem. La. Psychol. Assn. (charter), So. Sociol. Assn., La. Music Therapy Assn. (dir. 1966-74), Am. Legion, Internat. Platform Assn., Psi Chi, Sinfonia, Pi Gamma Mu, Kappa Delta Pi. Democrat. Baptist. Clubs: New Orleans Jazz, Lions. Address: PO Box 306 Slaughter LA 70777-0306

GRENDELL, JAMES HENRY, medical educator; b. Cleve., Dec. 7, 1949; married; 3 children. BS in Biology magna cum laude, John Carroll U., 1971; MD cum laude, Ohio State U., 1975. Diplomate Nat. Bd. Med. Examiners, Am. Bd. Internal Medicine with subspecialty in gastroenterology; lic. physician, N.Y. Intern in medicine Beth Israel Hosp., Boston, 1975-76, resident in medicine, 1976-78; fellow in gastroenterology U. Calif., San Francisco, 1978-81, asst. prof. medicine and physiology, 1981-88, assoc. prof., 1989-94; chief gastroenterology sect. San Francisco VA Med. Ctr., 1990-94; prof. medicine Cornell U., Ithaca, N.Y., 1994—; chief divsn. digestive diseases New York Hosp.-Cornell U. Med. Ctr., Ithaca, 1994—; lectr. in field. Contbr. numerous articles and abstracts to profl. jours., chpts. to books; assoc. editor Internat. Jour. Pancreatology, 1989—, Pancreas, 1993—; cons. editor Gastroenterology, 1982; ad hoc referee Sci. Jour. of Clin. Investigation, Annals of Internal Medicine, Gastroenterology, Am. Jour. Physiology, Digestive Diseases and Scis., Neuroendocrinology, Western Jour. Medicine, Fedn. Proc., Can. Jour. Physiology and Pharmacology, Endocrinology, Am. Jour. Gastroenterology, Jour. Lab. and Clin. Medicine. Rsch.

grantee Deutsche Forschungsgemeinschaft, 1983-85, 91-93, NIH, 1986-88, 87-88, Govt. Thailand, 1987-90, 88-89, 92-94. Mem. ACP (gastroenterology subcom. med. knowledge self-assessment program IX 1989-91), Am. Fedn. Clin. Rsch., Am. Gastroenterol. Assn. (com. on tng. and edn. 1990-94, chmn. tng. subcom. 1991-94, Fall postgrad. course assoc. dir. 1992, co-chair pancreative disorders sect. 1993-95, chair 1995—), Gastroenterology Rsch. Group, Am. Pancreatic Assn. (mem. governing coun. 1989-95, pres. 1993-94), Western Soc. for Clin. Investigation, Western Assn. Physicians, Internat. Assn. of Pancreatology, Alpha Omega Alpha, Landacre Soc. Office: 1300 York Ave New York NY 10021*

GRENFELL, RAYMOND FREDERIC, physician, researcher; b. West Bridgewater, Pa., Nov. 23, 1917; s. Elisha Raymond and Pearl (Bolland) G.; m. Maude Byrnes Chisholm, Aug. 19, 1944; children: Raymond Frederic, Milton Wilfred, James Byrnes, Robert Chisholm. B.S., U. Pitts., 1939, M.D., 1941. Intern Western Pa. Hosp., Pitts., 1941-42; practice medicine specializing in internal medicine, Jackson, 1946-79, practice medicine specializing in diagnosis and treatment of hypertension, 1979—; mem. staffs River Oaks East, St. Dominic-Jackson Meml. Hosp., Miss. Bapt. Hosp.; clin. instr. U. Miss. Med. Sch., Jackson, 1955-59, clin. asst. prof. medicine, 1959—, vis. teaching physician, 1977—, head hypertension clinic, 1956-79. Pres. Jackson Symphony Orch. Assn., 1961, Duling PTA, Jackson, 1963; deacon First Baptist Ch., Jackson, 1960—. Served to maj. U.S. Army, 1942-46. Recipient bronze medal Am. Heart Assn., 1963, silver medal, 1965. gov. Am. Coll. Angiology, 1979-86; Am. Coll. Chest Physicians; mem. Am. Soc. Clin. Pharmacology and Therapeutics (dir. 1968, v.p. 1976), Am. Fedn. Clin. Rsch., So. Med. Assn. (councilor 1968-73), Miss. Heart Assn. (pres. 1964-65), Am. Soc. Hypertension, Country Club, Univ. Club (gov. 1974-89). Republican. Home: 190 Ridge Dr Jackson MS 39216-4109 Office: 1151 N State Ste 601 Jackson MS 39202

GRESHAM, GLEN EDWARD, physician; b. Ft. Worth, Dec. 1, 1931; s. Perry Epler and Elsie Inez (Stanbrough) G.; m. Phyllis Elaine Kilmer, Nov. 9, 1957; children: Stephen Deane, David Epler, Elizabeth Anne Kilmer, Jennifer Gordon. B.A., Harvard Coll., 1953; M.D., Columbia U., 1958. Intern, then resident in internal medicine Univ. Hosps., Cleve., 1958-60, 62-64; asst. prof. preventive medicine Ohio State U., Columbus, 1964-69; asst. prof. medicine Yale U., New Haven, 1969-70; assoc. prof. rehab. medicine, medicine and cmty. medicine Tufts U., Boston, 1970-78; prof., chmn. dept. rehab. medicine SUNY, Buffalo, 1978—; med. dir. Erie County Med. Ctr., 1990-92. Served with USPHS, 1960-62. Nat. Found. fellow rehab., 1962-64; recipient Disting. Service award Mass. Council Orgns. Handicapped, 1972. Fellow ACP, Am. Coll. Rheumatology (emeritus); mem. Am. Congress Rehab. Medicine, Harvard Club (Boston), Saturn Club (Buffalo). Office: Erie County Med Ctr Dept Rehab Medicine 462 Grider St Buffalo NY 14215-3098

GRESS, DARYL RAY, neurologist; b. Albion, Nebr., Dec. 26, 1955; s. Gerald E. and Berniece B. (Keehn) G.; m. Carla DeLassus, May 21, 1983. BA, Washington U., St. Louis, 1978, MD, 1982. Resident in internal medicine Johns Hopkins Hosp., Balt., 1982-84; resident in neurology Mass. Gen. Hosp., Boston, 1984-87, fellow in neurocritical care, 1987-88, fellow in stroke, 1987-88, assoc. dir. stroke svc., 1988-94, dir. neurocritical care, 1991-94; dir. neurovascular svc. U. Calif., San Francisco, 1994—. Office: U Calif San Francisco Box 0114 San Francisco CA 94143-0114

GRESSER, MARK GEOFFREY, podiatrist; b. Flushing, N.Y., Feb. 28, 1958; s. Herbert David and Adele (Davidson) G. BS, BA, SUNY, Stony Brook, 1980; D of Podiatric Medicine, N.Y. Coll. Podiatric Medicine, 1984. Diplomate Am. Bd. Podiatric Orthopedics, Nat. Bd. Podiatry Examiners. Resident in podiatry Foot Clinics N.Y., N.Y.C., 1985; podiatrist North Country Podiatry, Miller Place, N.Y., 1986—, Ctr. Moriches, N.Y., 1988—; assoc. Am. Coll. Foot Surgeons, 1987—; radio announcer WUSB 90.1 FM, Stony Brook, N.Y.; freelance photographer; editor Long Island Blues Soc. Newsletter Backyard Blues; bd. dirs. Long Island Blues Soc. Acting chairperson Suffolk County Handicapped Adv. Bd., Hauppauge, N.Y., 1991—; adv. com. to bd. dirs. Suffolk Ind. Living Orgn. Mem. Am. Podiatric Med. Assn., Miller Pl.-Mt. Sinai C. of C. (v.p.), L.I. Blues Soc. (bd. dirs., editor newsletter). Democrat. Jewish. Home: 20 Bell Ave Blue Point NY 11715-1107 Office: N Country Podiatry 765-3 Route 25A Miller Place NY 11764

GREWE, JOHN MITCHELL, orthodontist, educator; b. Eau Claire, Wis., Feb. 6, 1938. BS, U. Minn., 1960, DDS, 1962, MSD in Oral Pathology, 1964, PhD in Anatomy, 1966, Cert. in Orthodontics, 1967. Pvt. practice dentistry Eau Claire, then Mpls., 1962-66; mem. dental staff U. Minn., 1967, VA Hosp. and Univ. Hosp., Iowa City, Iowa, 1968-69; practice orthodontics Univ. Md., 1969-77; pvt. practice orthodontics Towson, Md., 1977—; asst. prof., chmn. pediatric dental div. U. Minn., 1966-67, U. Iowa, Iowa City, 1967-69; assoc. prof. Coll. Dental Surgery, U. Md., Balt., 1969-75, prof., chmn. dept. orthodontics, 1969-78, part-time clin. prof., 1978-85; consulting orthodontist Johns Hopkins Hosp., Children's Hosp., Mercy Hosp.; cons. NIH, 1974, 76—, WHO, 1974-77, others. Contbr. articles to profl. jours.; assoc. editor Md. State Dental Jour. Fellow Internat. Coll. Dentists, Am. Coll. Dentists (chmn. Md. sect.); mem. AAAS, ADA, Internat. Assn. Dental Rsch., Am. Assn. Orthodontics, Mid-Atlantic Soc. Orthodontists (past pres), Md. Soc. Dentistry for Children (past pres.), Md. Soc. Orthodontics (past pres.), Fedn. Dentaire Internat., Sigma Xi.

GREYSON, CHARLES BRUCE, psychiatrist; b. Bklyn., Oct. 25, 1946; s. William Lawrence and Augusta Celia (DeBare) G.; m. Jane Alice Chapman, Mar. 23, 1968; children: Devon Lara, Eric Chapman. AB, Cornell U., 1968; MD, SUNY, Syracuse, 1973. Diplomate Nat. Bd. Med. Examiners, Am. Bd. Psychiatry and Neurology. Psychiat. resident U. Va., Charlottesville, 1973-76, asst. prof. psychiatry, 1976-78; asst. prof. psychiatry U. Mich., Ann Arbor, 1978-84; assoc. prof. psychiatry U. Conn., Farmington, 1984-93, prof. psychiatry, 1993-95; prof. psychiatry U. Va., Charlottesville, 1995—. Editor: The Near-Death Experience, 1984; editor Jour. Near-Death Studies, 1982—; contbr. sci. articles to profl. jours. Recipient William C. Menninger award Central Neuropsychiat. Assn., 1976. Fellow Am. Assn. Social Psychiatry; mem. Am. Psychiat. Assn., Am. Assn. Suicidology, Parapsychol. Assn., Internat. Assn. for Near-Death Studies (pres. 1982-83, dir. rsch. 1981—). Home: 2700 Gray Fox Trail Charlottesville VA 22901 Office: U Va Health Svcs Ctr Divsn Personality Studies Box 152 Charlottesville VA 22908

GREYSON, CLIFFORD RUSSELL, internist; b. N.Y.C., 1958. AB, Harvard Coll., 1980; MD, Stanford U., 1987. Cert. internal medicine and cardiovascular diseases. Resident in internal medicine Stanford U. Hosp., 1987-90, fellow in critical care, 1990-91; fellow in cardiovasc. disease U. Calif., San Francisco, 1991-95, faculty, cardiology divsn., 1995—. Elected to city coun. Town of Woodside, Calif., 1995. Recipient Clinician Scientist award Am. Heart Assn., 1995—. Mem. ACP. Office: San Francisco VA Med Ctr Cardiology 111C 4150 Clement St San Francisco CA 94121

GRIBBLE, T. JOHN, pediatrician, educator; b. Cardiff, Wales, Apr. 6, 1937; s. James W. and Doris (Riseley) G.; m. Geraldine Godek, Nov. 26, 1966; children: Joseph James, Julie Marie, Brian John. BS in Chemistry, U. of the South, 1959; MD, Stanford U., 1964. Cert. Am. Bd. Pediatrics, Am. Bd. Pediatric Hematology/Oncology. Intern in pediatrics Bellevue Hosp. Ctr., N.Y.C., 1964-65; resident Stanford U. Med. Ctr., 1965-66, research fellow in pediatric hematology, 1968, instr., 1968-69, chief resident in pediatrics, 1969, asst. prof. pediatrics, 1969-74, clin. assoc. prof., 1974-76; assoc. prof. U. N.Mex., Albuquerque, 1976—; dir. pediatric hematology/oncology U. N.Mex., 1976-87; dir. Ted R. Montoya Hemophilia Program, U. N.Mex., 1980—. Bd. dirs. Ronald McDonald House, Albuquerque, 1980-86; mem. State of N.Mex. AIDS Task Force, 1983-85; advisor to bd. dirs. Carrie Tingley Hosp., Albuquerque, 1982-86. Served with USPHS, 1966-68. Mem. Am. Acad. Pediat., Am. Soc. Hematology, Nat. Hemophilia Found., N.Mex. Pediat. Soc., Western Soc. Pediat. Rsch., World Fedn. Hemophilia, Hemophilia Rsch. Soc. (charter mem.), Alpha Omega Alpha, Sigma Pi Sigma, Phi Beta Kappa. Republican. Episcopalian. Office: U New Mexico Dept Pediatrics Albuquerque NM 87131

GRIBBON, ENDA MARTIN, medical researcher; b. Ballymoney, Northern Ireland, Jan. 2, 1967; s. Harry Alfonsus and Veronica Mary (Drain) G.; m. Helen Marie Igoe, June 24, 1994. BS with honors, U. Leeds, 1988, PhD in Microbial Physiology Biochemistry, 1991. Rsch. fellow Queen's U., Belfast, 1991-94; sect. leader Quadrant Healthcare, Cambridge, United Kingdom, 1994—. U.S. patentee Methods for Making Foamed Glass Matrices. Mem. Soc. for Gen. Microbiology, Biochem. Soc. Roman Catholic. Home: 18 Southmill Rd, Bishops Stortford CM23 3DP, England Office: Quadrant Healthcare, Maris Ln, Trumpington CB2 2SY, England

GRIDER, KATHY JILL, medical record professional; b. Painesville, Ohio, Apr. 30, 1954; d. Roy Emerson and Norma Jean (Whipple) Burkholder; m. Gary Snider, Sept. 1970 (div. 1980); children: Erin S., April Dawn; m. Stephen E. Prater, May 1981 (div. 1989); 1 child, Jonathan Evan; m. Dwight D. Grider, Oct. 1, 1989. BS in Med. Records Adminstrn., Ind. U., 1982; MBA, Ind. Wesleyan U., 1990. Registered records adminstr., Am. Health Info. Mgmt. Assn. Coding rev. supr. St. John's Med. Ctr., Anderson, Ind., 1982-84; dir. med. records New Castle (Ind.) State Hosp., 1984-85, Cmty. Hosp., Anderson, 1985-89; v.p., ptnr. Svc. Enterprises, Inc., Anderson, 1989-90; area mgr., COO Smart Corp., Pendleton, Ind., 1989-93; exec. adv. coun. Smart Corp., Torrance, Calif., 1991-92; pres. Dictation Svcs. Inc., 1993—; v.p., co-owner Midwest Med. Copy Svc., Inc., Pendleton, Ind., 1993—; with AMMCORP, Pendleton; instr. Ind. U., Indpls., 1991. Mem. Am. Med. Record Assn., Ind. Med. Record Assn. (mem. pub. rels. com. 1988-89, officer, exec. bd. 1988—, chmn. continuing edn. 1989-91, chmn. nominating and credentials com. 1980-90), Ind. Health Info. Mgmt. Assn. (v.p. 1993-94), Ctrl. Ind. Med. Record Assn. (officer, exec. bd. 1987-89). Democrat. Methodist. Office: AMMCORP Records Mgmt PO Box 308 PO Box 308 Pendleton IN 46064

GRIECO, MICHAEL BARRY, surgeon; b. Flushing, N.Y., Jan. 11, 1948; s. Michael Angelo and Ethel Marie (Kiss) G.; m. Elizabeth Lexine Wright, May 27, 1973 (div. Dec. 1994); m. Christine Mary Thornton, Aug. 12, 1995; children: Michael Christopher, Kristin Wright. AB, Hamilton Coll., 1970; MD, Albany Med. Coll., 1974. Resident in surgery North Shore Univ. Hosp., Manhasset, N.Y., 1975-79; fellow in surgery Lahey Clinic, Boston, 1979-80, Greater Balt. Med. Ctr., 1980-81; pvt. practice gen. surgery North Shore Univ. Hosp., Glen Cove, N.Y., 1981—; chief gen. surgery North Shore Univ. Hosp., 1988—, dir. dept. surgery, 1993—; adv. bd. Cancer Care, Inc., Woodbury, N.Y., 1995—. Bd. dirs. Boys and Girls Clubs, Glen Cove, 1991—, YMCA, 1981—, Cmty. Scholarship Fund, Inc., 1992—. Fellow Am. Coll. Surgeons, N.Y. Soc. Colon & Rectal Surgeons;; mem. Am. Soc. Colon & Rectal Surgeons, Nassau Surg. Soc., L.I. Gastroenterol. Soc. Roman Catholic. Home: 38 Westland Dr Glen Cove NY 11542 Office: 4 Medical Plz Glen Cove NY 11542

GRIER, ARNOLD MACFARLANE, retired surgeon; b. Musselburgh, Lothian, Scotland, Sept. 5, 1921; s. Arnold Thompson and Agnes Ingus (Milne) G.; m. Elisabeth Johanna Kluten, Sept. 27, 1962; children: Arnold Frederick, Geraldine Agnes, Hendrick Aitken. MB, ChB, U. Edinburgh, Scotland, 1955. Registrar ear, nose and throat dept. Royal Infirmary Edinburgh; cons. ear, nose and throat dept. Highland Health Bd., Inverness, Scotland, from 1962. Mem. local health coun. Capt. Royal Elec. and Mech. Engrs., 1943-45. Fellow Royal Coll. Surgeons (Edinburgh); mem. Scottish Assn. for Deaf (v.p.), Otorhinolarnynology Club. Home: Elmbank, 68 Culduthel Rd, Inverness IV2 4HI:, Scotland

GRIER, HARDY CANNON, emergency planner; b. Bristol, Va., May 17, 1950; s. Hardy Cannon G.; m. Marguerite Phyllis Edmands, Apr. 10, 1970. Student, Old Dominion U., 1968-71; BS in Psychology, U. Md., 1975; postgrad., Drexel U., 1984-85, Rutgers State U., 1985-86. Sr. rsch. asst. IBR-Bio Behavioral Labs., Washington, 1972-79; sr. rsch. asst. Coll. of Medicine Howard U., Washington, 1979-81; asst. investigator neuropsychology NIH, NIMH, Bethesda, Md., 1981-82; health physics cons., 1982—; emergency mgmt. cons. Mass., 1984—. Contbr. articles to profl. jours. VA Undergrad. scholar Old Dominion U., 1970. Mem. Am. Soc. Profl. Emergency Planners, Health Physics Soc. (plenary), Nat. Coord. Coun. on Emergency Mgmt., Internat. Sociol. Assn. (rsch. com. on disasters(, Am. Soc. Quality Control.

GRIES, LEONARD TODD, psychologist; b. Bklyn., July 13, 1945; s. Nathan and Lillian (Klein) G.; m. Susanne L. Simmons, Jan. 25, 1970; children: James, Adam, Matthew. BSc, Bklyn. Coll., 1967; MA, Hofstra U., Hempstead, N.Y., 1969, PhD, 1972. Lic. psychologist, N.Y. Psychology intern Psychol. Evaluation and Rsch. Ctr./Hofstra U., Hempstead, 1969-72; chief psychologist Bklyn. Developmental Svc., 1972-79; psychologist St. Christopher-Ottilie, Jamaica, N.Y., 1979—, dir. mental health svcs., 1983—; exec. dir. Inst. for Emotional Health, East Hills, N.Y., 1992—; adj. assoc. prof. Bklyn. Coll., 1979-80; psychotherapist Mid-Nassau Cmty. Guidance Ctr., Hicksville, N.Y., 1975-77; psychologist St. John's Episcopal Hosp., Bklyn., 1979-80; cons./lectr. Practising Law Inst., N.Y.C., 1989—, Little Flower Children's Svcs., Wading River, N.Y., 1990—, ABA Ctr. on Children and the Law, Washington, 1994, Task Force on Permanency Planning for Foster Children, Albany, N.Y., 1994, The Fresh Air Fund, N.Y.C., 1985, Green Chimneys Children's Svcs., Brewster, N.Y., 1995, Legal Aid Soc., N.Y.C., 1995, Wide Horizons for Children, Waltham, Mass., 1995. Author: Gregory of Zimbabwe, 1993; contbr. articles to profl. jours.; columnist The Roslyn News, 1986-89. Bd. dirs. Roslyn (N.Y.) Little League, 1986-89. Mem. APA, Nat. Register Health Svc. Providers in Psychology (charter mem., Platinum Cert. 1994), Com. of Psychologists of Voluntary Child Care Agencies, Bedford Athletic Club (founder, dir.), Psi Chi. Home: 33 South St East Hills NY 11577

GRIFFENHAGEN, GEORGE BERNARD, trade association executive; b. Portland, Oreg., June 9, 1924; s. Richard Bernard and Clara (Schoenian) G.; m. Joan Helen Houston, June 21, 1946; children: Gary Bernard, Gordon Wesley, Barbara Clare. BS in Pharmacy, U. So. Calif., 1949, MS, 1950; student, Fresno State Coll., 1946, U. London, 1948. Dir. research Nion Corp., Hollywood, Calif., 1950-52; curator div. med. scis. Smithsonian Instn., Washington, 1952-59; sec. sect. history of pharmacy Am. Pharm. Assn., Washington, 1952-59, pres. local chpt., 1958-59, assoc. exec. dir., 1959-89, hon. pres., 1990-91; trustee Am. Pharm. Assn. Found., Washington, 1989-94; editor Jour. Am. Pharm. Assn., Washington, 1960-76; sec.-gen. 4th Pan Am. Congress Pharmacy and Biochemistry, Washington, 1957; sec. organizing com. 31st Internat. Congress Pharm. Scis., Washington, 1971; sec.-gen. Internat. Congress History of Pharmacy, Washington, 1983, Japan-U.S. Congress of Pharm. Scis., Honolulu, 1987; v.p. Pan Am. Pharm. and Biochem. Fedn., 1963-82, 85-91, Pharmacy World Congress, Washington, 1991; U.S. del. Internat. Pharm. Fedn. Gen. Assemblies, London, 1955, Brussels, 1958, Copenhagen, 1960, Vienna, 1962, Amsterdam, 1964, Hamburg, 1968, Geneva, 1970, Lisbon, 1972, Rome, 1974, Warsaw, 1976, Cannes, 1978; U.S. del. FIP Coun., Bucharest, 1969, Dublin, 1975, Montreal, 1985, Helsinki, 1986, Amsterdam, 1987, Sydney, 1988, Munich, 1989, Istanbul, 1990, Lyon, 1992, Tokyo, 1993, Lisbon, 1994; congress coord., The Hague, 1977; U.S. del. Pan Am. Congress Pharmacy and Biochemistry Congresses, Mexico City, 1963, Buenos Aires, 1966, Caracas, 1969, Panama, 1972, Guatemala City, 1985, Santo Domingo, 1988, Buenos Aires, 1994; U.S. del. Internat. Congress History of Pharmacy, Budapest, Hungary, 1981, Fedn. Asian Pharm. Assns. Congress, Seoul, Korea, 1982; mem. Nat. Action Com. on Drug Edn., Office of Edn., 1970-71, Va. Gov.'s Coun. on Narcotic and Drug Abuse Control, 1970-72. Editor: Scalpel and Tongs, 1972-73; Contbr. articles to profl. jours. Mem. Fairfax County (Va.) Rep. Com., 1962-94; adminstrv. asst. to chmn. Va. State Rep. Com., 1969-71; life mem. Rep. Nat. Com., 1979—; founding pres. Nat. Coordinating Coun. on Drug Edn., 1968-69. Served with C.E. AUS, World War II, ETO. Recipient Pfizer Merit award U.S. CD Coun., 1964, U. So. Calif. Alumnus award, 1969; Hugo H. Schaefer award Am. Pharm. Assn., 1984; Disting. Svc. award Pharmacy Guild of Australia, 1988, Internat. Pharmacy Jour. Editor's prize, 1989, 95, Remington Honor medal Am. Pharm. Assn., 1991; named to Nat. Philatelic Writers Hall of Fame, 1990. Mem. Am. Inst. History of Pharmacy (pres. 1960-61, Edward Kremers award 1969, exec. sec. 1991—), Friends of Hist. Pharmacy (pres. 1957-58), Pharm. Wholesalers Assn. (Distinguished Service award 1971), Am. Topical Assn. (1st v.p. 1972-75, pres. 1976-79, pres. med. subjects unit 1969-72, Distinguished Topical Philatelist award 1970, Myrtle Watt Med. Philately Topicalist award 1980, editor Topical Time 1992—), Am. Philatelic Congress (Jere Hess Barr award 1969), Am. Philatelic Soc. (sec.-treas. Writers Unit 1982—, U.S. commr. to Internat. Exhbn. Thematic Philately, Basel, Switzerland 1983), Am. Revenue Assn. (named to Sterling Meml. Roll of Disting. Fiscalists 1979), Council Philatelic Orgns. (treas. 1983-91), Philatelic Lit. Assn., Academie Internationale d'Histoire de la Pharmacie (treas. 1971-81, 1989—), Pharm. Soc. Gt. Britain (hon.), Sigma Xi, Rho Chi, Phi Kappa Psi. Home: 2501 Drexel St Vienna VA 22180-6906 Office: Am Pharm Assn 2215 Constitution Ave NW Washington DC 20037-2975

GRIFFIN, ANNETTE L., critical care nurse, educator; b. Fall River, Mass., Oct. 21, 1959; d. Robert F. and Annette (Berard) Couture; m. Michael P. Griffin, Oct. 28, 1983; children: Brendan Patrick, Kate Elizabeth, Allison Ann, Trevor John. BSN, U. Mass., Dartmouth, 1981, MSN, 1990. Ops. mgr. HMO R.I., Providence, 1985-87; clin. coord. Charlton Meml. Hosp., Fall River, 1989-90; staff nurse CCU R.I. Hosp., Providence, 1987-90, clin. educator, 1990—. Mem. AACN, Sigma Theta Tau (Kappa Theta chpt., chpt. v.p. 1991-95, chairperson program com. 1991-95).

GRIFFIN, HERSCHEL EMMETT, retired epidemiology educator; b. Valley City, N.D., July 28, 1918; s. Herschel Raymond and Olive Buckley (Whalian) G.; m. Frances Helen Nye, June 6, 1943; children—Bruce Nye, Karen Lynn. A.A., Chaffey Jr. Coll., Ontario, Calif., 1937; B.A., Stanford U., 1939; M.D., U. Calif.-San Francisco, 1943. Diplomate Am. Bd. Preventive Medicine (sec., treas. 1978-79). Intern in surgery U. Calif. Hosp., 1944; resident surgery San Francisco Hosp., 1945; practice medicine Upland, Calif., 1947-50; became 1st lt., M.C. U.S. Army, 1943, advanced through grades to col., 1962; regtl. surgeon, div. preventive medicine officer Calif., comdg. officer med. br. Japan; div. surgeon Korea (40th Inf. Div.), 1950-52; comdg. officer (U.S. Army Hosp.), Sasebo, Japan, 1952-53; fellow in epidemiology Walter Reed Army Research and Grad. Sch., 1954-55; chief communicable disease br. Office Surgeon Gen., Dept. Army, 1955-58; theater epidemiologist U.S. Army, Europe; dep. for profl. services U.S. Army (9th Hosp. Center), Germany, 1959-62; asst. for profl. services Office Dep. Asst. Sec. Def., 1963-65; exec. officer Office Surgeon Gen., Dept. Army, 1965-66, chief preventive medicine div., 1966-69; ret., 1969; prof. epidemiology, dean Grad. Sch. Pub. Health, U. Pitts., 1969-80; prof. epidemiology Grad. Sch. Public Health, San Diego State U., 1980-87, prof. emeritus, 1987—; U.S. Army rep. Gorgas Meml. Inst., 1966-69, Leonard Wood Meml., 1966-69; cons. Walter Reed Army Inst. Research, 1972-77, WHO, 1972-77, chmn. expert com. on recommended requirements for schs. pub. health, 1972; del. Pa. Health Conf. Com., U. Health Center of Pitts., 1970-73, Pa. Health Council, 1972-74; sci. adviser U.S. EPA, 1973-87; pres. Pa. Health Council, 1973-74; cons. Uniformed Services U. of Health Scis., 1975-84; chmn. Pa. Health Conf. Com., 1973-74; chmn. com. on med. and biol. effects of environ. pollutants NRC/Nat. Acad. Scis., 1972-76; chmn. infectious disease adv. com. Nat. Inst. Allergy and Infectious Diseases, NIH, 1974-76; mem. Gov.'s Task Force on Health Edn. in Pa., 1974-76; mem. adv. com. Gov.'s Energy Council, 1974-79; bd. dirs. Pa. Health Research Inst., 1973-75; mem. Armed Forces Epidemiological Bd., 1973-84, pres., 1977-79, chmn. ad hoc study team on procurement standards, 1974-75; chmn. com. to study health effects of air pollution Allegheny County Bd. Health/Allegheny County Health Dept., 1974-76; mem. sci. adv. bd. and environ. health com. EPA, 1982-87, chmn. environ. health com., 1982-85, mem. exec. com., 1983-85, mem. drinking water com., 1985-87; mem. Gov's. Sci. Adv. Panel, 1987—. Contbr. articles to profl. jours. Decorated Legion of Merit, Bronze Star medal, Army Commendation medal; recipient Comdr.'s award for pub. service Dept. Army. Fellow ACP, Am. Pub. Health Assn.; mem. Assn. Schs. of Pub. Health (pres. 1971-73, exec. com. 1973-75), Internat. Health Soc. (pres.-elect 1985, pres. 1986-87), Soc. Med. Cons. to Armed Forces (chmn. preventive medicine com. 1970-73, pres. 1975-76). Home: 11274 Pabellon Ct San Diego CA 92124-2203

GRIFFIN, JAMES EARL, medical technologist; b. Montecello, Miss., Dec. 25, 1945; s. William James and Evelena (Eley) G.; m. Andrea Laverne Street; children: Lila, Michael. Student, Alcorn State U., Baylor U., 1975-76, DeKalls Coll., 1979-80, Mercer U., 1981-83. Cert. med. technologist. Staff sgt. U.S. Army, 1968-79; blood bank supr. U.S. Army, Fort Gordon, Ga., 1976-79; lab. generalist West Paces Ferry Hosp., Atlanta, 1979-81; office mgr. Blevedere Health Clinic, Decatur, Ga., 1981-90; lab. supr. Smith Kline Beecham Labs., Forth Worth, 1990-93; lab. mgr. Integrated, Atlanta, 1993—; lab. cons. Family Health Ctr., Covington, Ga., 1996—. Mem. Am. Med. Tech., Am. Legion, Ga. Med. Tech. Office: Integrated Med Lab 615 Peachtree St Ste 413 Atlanta GA 30308

GRIFFIN, JAMES FRANCIS, physician; b. N.Y.C., May 23, 1957; s. Gerald Patrick and Dorothy Margaret (Curran) G.; m. Lynn Marie Walters, June 1, 1991; children: Daniel Patrick, Clare Marie. BS, SUNY, Cortland, 1979; DC, Cleve. Chiropractic Coll., 1983; DO, U. Health Scis. Coll. of Osteo. Medicine, Kansas City, Mo., 1987. Diplomate Am. Bd. Internal Medicine. Rotating osteo. intern Union (N.Y.) Hosp., 1987-88; internal medicine resident Albany (N.Y.) Med. Ctr., 1988-91; staff physician Tanana Valley Clinic, Fairbanks, Alaska, 1991, Benedict Health Ctr., Ballston Spa, N.Y., 1991-94; anesthesia resident Albany (N.Y.) Med. Ctr. Hosp., 1994—; med. dirs. Benedict Health Ctr., 1993-94; vice-chmn. dept. medicine Saratoga Hosp., n.Y., 1993-94; adj. clin. asst. prof. N.Y. Coll. Osteo. Medicine, Old Westbury, 1993-94. Mem. Am. Soc. Anesthesiologists, N.Y. State Soc. Anesthesiologists, Soc. Crit. Care Medicine, Psi Sigma Alpha. Democrat. Roman Catholic. Office: Albany med Ctr 47 New Scotland Ave Albany NY 12203

GRIFFIN, JOHN HENRY, medical researcher; b. Seattle, June 26, 1943; s. John Henry and Lillian Louise (O'Connell) G.; m. Antonia Lastreto, 1965 (div. 1984); children—John, Deanna, Paul. B.S., U. Santa Clara, 1965; Ph.D., U. Calif., Davis, 1969. Teaching asst. U. Calif., 1967-69; research fellow Harvard Med. Sch., 1969-71; guest worker NIH, 1971-73; with staff Service de Biochimie Centre d'Etudes Nucleaires, Saclay, France, 1973-74; asst. dept immunopathology Scripps Clinic and Research Found., La Jolla, Calif., 1974-75, assoc. depts. immunopathology and molecular immunology, 1975-80, mem., prof. dept. molecular exptl. medicine, 1980-94, mem. Scripps Rsch. Inst., La Jolla, 1994—; peer rev. com. NIH, 1979—. Contbr. articles to profl. jours. Treas. San Diego Assn. Gifted Children, 1978-81; active Pub. Sch. Cluster Com., University City, S.D., 1984-85; mem. adv. com. High Sch. Community, University City, 1979-82, 86-88; . Recipient Research Career Devel. award NIH, 1976-81. RCA physics scholar 1961-64; fellow NIH, 1966-69, 72-73, Helen Hay Whitney Found. 1969-72. Mem. Am. Soc. Clin Investigators, Am. Soc. Hematology, Am. Chem. Soc., Am. Soc. Biochem. Molecular Biologists, Am. Assn. Pathologists, Am. Assn. Immunologists, Internat. Soc. Thrombosis and Hemostasis, Am. Heart Assn. (rsch. com.), Sigma Xi, Alpha Sigma Nu, Phi Kappa Phi. Current work: Basic and clinical research on regulation of hemostasis and thrombosis. Subspecialties: Biochemistry (medicine); Hematology.

GRIFFIN, LARRY PAUL, obstetrician, gynecologist, educator; b. Louisville, June 19, 1947; s. Elmer Paul and Emma Angella (Woehler) G.; children: Eric Paul, Craig Alan. BA, U. Louisville, 1969, MD, 1973. Diplomate Nat. Bd. of Med. Examiners, Am. Bd. Ob-gyn. (assoc. examiner 1991). Clk. Great Atlantic & Pacific Tea Co., Louisville, 1965-67; lab. asst. Celanese Coatings Co., Louisville, 1967-68; lab. tech. GE, Louisville, 1968-69; resident in ob-gyn. Louisville Gen. Hosp., 1973-76; fellow maternal/fetal medicine U. Louisville, 1976-77; ob-gyn., ptnr. Louisville Ob-Gyn. Assocs., 1977-90; asst. clin. prof. ob-gyn. U. Louisville, 1977—; assoc. clin. prof. Ind. U., 1989—; dir. ob-gyn. residency program St. Vincent Hosp., 1989-93; dir. Am. Coll. Ob-Gyn, Washington, 1993—; bd. dirs., chmn. Louisville mng. bd. PIE Mut. Ins. Co., 1989—; dir. Ctr. for MEd. Edn. and Health Policy Rsch., 1992-93. Mem. editorial bd. Jour. Gynecol. and Obstet. Nursing, 1982-86; contbr. articles to profl. jours. Bd. dirs. Ohio Valley chpt. March of Dimes, Louisville, 1979-89; task force mem. Jefferson County Drug Abuse Program, Louisville, 1986-89; chmn. Emergency Med. Svcs. Evaluation Task Force, 1986-87, State of Ky. Family Planning Task Force, 1988-92; mem. State of Ky. Health Svcs. Adv. Coun., 1988-92. Capt., MC, USNR, 1983—. Samuel McMurtry fellow U. Louisville Dept. Ob-Gyn., 1976; recipient William O. Johnson award Ob-Gyn. Soc., 1975. Fellow Am. Coll. Ob-Gyn. (chmn. Ky. sect., 1986-89, sec. dist. V 1989-93, dir. program svcs. 1993—); mem. Ky. Med. Assn. (trustee 1987-89), Jefferson County Med. Soc. (pres. 1986-87, chmn. bd. 1987-88), Louisville Ob-Gyn Soc. (chmn. 1986-87), Jefferson Club, Hurstbourne Club, Army Navy Club, Rotary, Capitol Hill Club. Republican. Office: 409 12th St SW Washington DC 20024-2125

GRIFFIN, SUZANNE MARIE, medical and surgical nurse; b. Scott City, Kans., Oct. 26, 1959; d. James Mick and Pia Lucy (Ruschetti) Tucker; m. Larry Dean Griffin I, June 9, 1990; children: Christopher Jared, Larry Dean II, LaTisha LeeAnne. Lic. Vocat. Nurse, Plainview Vocat. Nursing Sch., Tex., 1979; AAS, Garden City C.C., Kans., 1984. Cert. advanced cardiac life support, CPR instr. Staff nurse Hi-Plains Hosp. and E.O. Nichols Hosp., Hale Center and Plainview, Tex., 1979-83; house supr. Central Plains Regional Hosp., Plainview, 1983; med.-surg. supr. Cen. Plains Regional Hosp., Plainview, 1984-86; vocat. nurse instr. South Plains Coll., Plainview, 1986—; mem. allied health adv. bd. South Plains Coll. Mem. Tex. Assn. Vocat. Nurse Educators (past chpt. pres.).

GRIFFIN, THOMAS W., physician; b. Omaha, Feb. 16, 1945; s. Charles Ward and Nellie Forrest (Gaden) G.; m. Vickie Jo McCabe, Oct. 8, 1973; 1 child, Andrea Lynn. BS, U. Nebr., 1966, MD, 1970. Cert. Am. Coll. Radiology. Instr. U. Wash., Seattle, 1976-77, asst. prof., 1977-79, assoc. prof., 1979-83, prof., 1983—, chmn. dept. radiation oncology, 1979—; dirs. U. Wash. Cancer Ctr. Editor High LET Radiation Therapy, 1986; contbr. articles to profl. jours. Served to capt. U.S. Army, 1971-73. Mem. AAAS, Am. Soc. Therapeutic Radiology and Oncology, Am. Coll. Radiology, Am. Radium Soc., Soc. Chmn. Acad. Radiation Oncology Programs, Am. Coll. Radiation Oncology. Office: U Wash Box 356043 Dept Radiation Oncology 1959 NE Pacific St Seattle WA 98195-6043

GRIFFIN, TOMMY BREWER, dermatologist; b. Akron, Ohio, Jan. 1, 1936; s. Marcus Vann and Elizabeth (Brewer) G.; m. Freida Deaton, Mar. 28, 1964; children: Marcus Vann, Thomas Scott, Julia Elizabeth. BS, Davidson Coll., 1957; MD, U. Pa., 1961. Diplomate Am. Bd. Dermatology. Intern in internal medicine Grace New Haven (Conn.) Hosp., Yale U., 1961-62; resident N.C. Meml. Hosp., Chapel Hill, N.C., 1962-64, fellowship in dermatology, 1964-66; asst. prof. dermatology Sch. Medicine U. N.C., Chapel Hill, 1969-71; pres. Spartanburg (S.C.) Dermatology & Skin Surgery Clinic, P.C., 1971—; from asst. to assoc. clin. prof. medicine U. N.C. Sch. Medicine, 1971—; assoc. clin. prof. medicine Med. U. S.C., Charleston, 1971—. Contbr. articles to profl. jours. Bd. dirs. S.C. Polit. Action Com., Columbia, 1976; mem., chmn., bd. deacons Fernwood Bapt. Ch., Spartanburg, S.C., 1980-83. Maj. U.S. Army, 1966-69. Fellow Am. Soc. Dermatopathology; mem. AMA, Am. Acad. Dermatology, Piedmont Dermatol. Soc. S.C. (founder, pres. 1974-75, pres. 1984-85), Spartanburg County Med. Soc. (pres. 1975), Spartanburg Blood Bank (founder, bd. dirs. 1974-76), S.C. Dermatol. Assn. (pres. 1977-78), S.C. Med. Assn. (del. 1976-77). Republican. Office: Spartanburg Dermatology & Skin Surgery Clinic 2020 N Church Pl Spartanburg SC 29303-2706

GRIFFING, GEORGE THOMAS, medical educator, endocrinologist; b. Lawrence, Kans., Apr. 3, 1950; s. George W. and Roberta B. (Brown) G.; m. Bonnie Anne Brennen, June 14, 1985; children: Nathaniel, Samuel, Emily. Student, U. Utah, 1971; MD, Wayne State U., 1975. From instr. medicine to asst. prof. medicine Boston U. Med. Sch., 1980-87, mem. dept. physiology, assoc. prof. medicine, 1987-92; prof. medicine U. Mo., Columbia, 1992—; asst. vis. physician Boston City Hosp., 1981-92; dir. Cosmo Internat. Diabetes Ctr./U. Mo., Columbia, 1992—; dir. divsn. endocrinology/metabolism Sch. Medicine, U. Mo., Columbia, 1992—; vis. scientist dept. biochemistry Tufts U. Health Sci. Ctr., Boston,1986-92; mem. Problem Based Learning Task Force, Columbia, 1995—; chmn. admissions com. Sch. Medicine, U. Mo., 1994—; chmn. activities com. Mo. regional chpt. Am. Coll. Medicine, 1994—. Author: (jours.) Jour. Clin. Endocrine, New Eng. Jour. Medicine. Mem. Cosmopolitan Internat., Columbia, 1992. Named New Investigator, NIH, 1983-86, Phi Zeta hon. lectr. U. Mo. Vet. Sch., 1994. Fellow Coun. for High Blood Pressure, ACP (dir. sub-splty. update regional meeting 1994—); mem. Am. Fedn. Clin. Rsch., Endocrine Soc. Home: 2930 Ridley Wood Columbia MO 65203 Office: U Mo One Hospital Dr D110A Columbia MO 65212

GRIFFITH, BARBARA E., social worker, political activist; b. Bklyn., Feb. 17, 1943; d. Carl and Ruth (Cramer) Horowitz; m. Richard Michael Griffith, Feb. 12, 1942; children: Kim Griffith McFadden, David Wark. BSW, Ohio State U., 1965; postgrad., Adelphi U., 1965-66. Social worker Columbus Home for Mentally Disturbed Children, Columbus, Ohio, 1965; case worker Nassau County Social Svcs., L.I., N.Y., 1965-66, Red Bank (N.J.) Dept. Social Svcs., 1966-67, Dept. Social Svcs. Honolulu, 1967-69; asst. dir. nursery sch. Cleve., 1975-78; advt. mgr. mags. Toronto, Ont., Can., 1979-84; substitute tchr. West Windsor (N.J.) Plainsboro H.S., 1987-90; polit. activist Bus. & Profl. Women's Assn., N.J., 1989-93; owner R.M.G. Assocs., Inc., Princeton Junction, N.J., 1993—; v.p. mktg. and sales Thornhill Month Mag. Pub., 1985; real estate devel. cons., 1991—. Counselor for homeless people; active Clinton Presdl. Campaign, N.J.; dir. Hughes Congl. Campaign for U.S. Congress, 1992, N.J.; local town councilwoman, Can., 1982; participant Lobby Day, Washington, 1990-94. Mem. NOW, LWV (Princeton chpt. 1988—), N.J. Bus. & Profl. Women Assn. (chmn. N.J. legis. chpt. 1992-93), Women's Agenda (com. mem. N.J. law sect.). Home: 14 Zeloof Dr Lawrenceville NJ 08648-5409

GRIFFITH, BARTLEY P., cardiothoracic surgeon; b. Pitts., Jan. 27, 1949; m. denise Griffith; children: Bartley Jr., Cullen, David. BA in Biology, Bucknell U., 1970; MD, Jefferson med. Coll., 1974. Diplomate Am. Bd. Thoracic Surgery, Am. Bd. Surgery; lic. physician, Pa. Intern in surgery U. Pitts. Sch. Medicine/Health Ctr. Hosps., 1974-75, resident in gen. and cardiothoracic surgery, 1975-77, 78-79, rsch. fellow, 1977-78, chief resident in cardiothoracic surgery, 1979-81; asst. prof. surgery U. Pitts. Sch. Medicine, 1981-86, assoc. prof., 1986-88, Henry T. Bahnson prof. surgery, 1988—; staff cardiothoracic surgeon Presbyn. U. Hosp., Children's Hosp. of Pitts., St. Francis Gen. Hosp., Montefiore Univ. Hosp., Shadyside Hosp., Westmoreland Hosp., St. Margaret Meml. Hosp.; chmn. long range planning com. Family House, Inc., 1985—, exec. dir., 1986—; dir. U. Pitts. Surg. Rsch. Lab., 1986; mem. bd. dirs. Univ. Surg. Assocs., 1987—; dir. pulmonary transplant program U. Pitts., 1989-95, chief cardiothoracic divsn., 1990—, co-dir. Heart Inst., 1991—, co-dir. Comprehensive Lung Ctr., 1992—; bd. dirs. Health Rsch. and Svcs. Found., 1986-88; chmn., dir. traveling fellowship com. Evarts A. Graham Meml., 1990-91; co-dir. 3d Internat. Conf. on Circulatory Support Devices for Severe Cardiac Failure, Pitts., 1994; mem. NIH Surgery, Anesthesiology and Trauma Study Sect. Divsn. of rsch. grants, 1993-97. Fellow ACS; mem. AMA, Am. Surg. Assn., Soc. Clin. Surgery, Pa. Assn. Thoracic Surgery, Am. Assn. Thoracic Surgery, Soc. Univ. Surgeons, Soc. Thoracic Surgeons, Allegheny County Med. Soc., Pa. Med. Soc., Am. Soc. for Artificial Internal Organs, Assn. for Acad. Surgery, Transplantation Soc. Internat. Soc. for Heart Transplantation, Pitts. Acad. Medicine, Harbison Surg. Soc., Transplant Recipients Internat. Orgn. (hon. bd. dirs.), Thoracic Surgery Dirs. Assn. Home: 903 Notre Dame Pl Pittsburgh PA 15215 Office: Presbyn-U Hosp 200 Lothrop St Pittsburgh PA 15213-2546*

GRIFFITH, B(EZALEEL) HEROLD, physician, educator, plastic surgeon; b. N.Y.C., Aug. 24, 1925; s. Bezaleel Davies and Henrietta (Herold) G.; m. Jeanne B. Lethbridge, 1948; children: Susan, Tristan. BA, Johns Hopkins U., 1992; M.D., Yale U., 1948. Diplomate: Am. Bd. Plastic Surgery (dir. 1976-82, chmn. 1981-82). Intern Grace New Haven Community Hosp.-Yale U., 1948-49; resident in surgery VA Hosp., Newington, Conn., 1949-50; asst. resident in surgery 2d (Cornell) Surg. Div., Bellevue Hosp., N.Y.C., 1952-53; resident in plastic surgery VA Hosp., Bronx, 1953-55, U. Glasgow, Scotland, 1955, N.Y. Hosp. Cornell Med. Center, N.Y.C., 1956; rsch. fellow in plastic surgery Cornell U. Med. Coll., 1956-57; pvt. practice specializing in plastic surgery Chgo., 1957-96; attending plastic surgeon Northwestern Meml., Children's Meml., VA Lakeside hosps., Rehab. Inst. Chgo.; instr. surgery Northwestern U., 1957-59, assoc. in surgery, 1959-62, asst. prof. surgery, 1962-67, assoc. prof., 1967-71, prof., 1971-96, prof. emeritus, 1996, chief div. plastic surgery, 1970-91; chief plastic surgery Shriner's Hosp. for Crippled Children, Chgo., 1994-96; retired. Assoc. editor: Plastic and Reconstructive Surgery, 1972-78; contbr. articles to profl. jours. Lt. M.C., USNR, 1950-52. Fellow ACS, Am. Assn. Plastic Surgeons, Chgo. Surg. Soc., Royal Soc. Medicine; mem. AAAS, AMA, Am. Soc. Plastic and Reconstructive Surgeons (sec. 1972-74), Brit. Assn. Plastic Surgeons, Plastic Surgery Rsch. Coun. (chmn. 1969), Am. Cleft Palate Assn., N.Y. Acad. Scis., Ill., Chgo. Med. Socs., Midwestern Assn. Plastic Surgeons, Soc. Head and Neck Surgeons, Ill., Chgo. Hist. Socs., Civil War Round Table, Evanston Hist. Soc. (trustee 1974-78), Sigma Xi (pres. Northwestern U. 1986-87, 94-95). Club: Yale (Chgo.). Lodge: Masons.

GRIFFITH, BRIGITTE PIERRETTE, virologist, educator; b. Arcueil, France, Oct. 5, 1948; came to U.S., 1975; d. Nicolas and Marguerite Louise (Bettinger) Jung; m. Ezra Edward Griffith, Dec. 24, 1974; children: Veronique, Pierre. Dipl. pharmacy, U. Louis Pasteur, Strasbourg, France, 1971; PhD, U. Louis Pasteur, 1974. Postdoctoral fellow, rsch. assoc., asst. prof. Yale U. Sch. Medicine, New Haven, 1976-88, assoc. prof., 1988—; chief retrovirus diagnostic sect. VA Med. Ctr., West Haven, Conn., 1986-96, assoc. dir. Virology Reference Lab., 1996—; sci. reviewer NIH, Bethesda, Md., 1984, 85, 89, 93. Author: Virus et Grossesse, 1992; contbr. articles to profl. jours. Home: 6 Marlborough Rd North Haven CT 06473 Office: VA Conn Health Care Sys 950 Campbell Ave West Haven CT 06516

GRIFFITH, EZRA EDWARD HOLMAN, health facility administrator, educator; b. Barbados, W.I., Feb. 18, 1942; came to the U.S., 1956; s. Vincent Edward and Ermie (Morris) G.; m. Brigitte Jung; children: Veronique, Pierre. BA, Harvard U., 1963; MD, U. Strasbourg, France, 1973, diploma tropical medicine, 1973. Diplomate Am. Bd. Psychiatry and Neurology, Am. Bd. Forensic Psychiatry. Internship French and Polyclinic Health Ctr., N.Y., 1973-74; residency in psychiatry Albert Einstein Coll. of Medicine, Bronx, N.Y., 1974-77; asst. prof. psychiatry Sch. Medicine Yale U., New Haven, 1977-82, assoc. prof. psychiatry Sch. Medicine, 1982-91; prof. psychiatry Sch. Medicine, 1991—; lectr. dept. Afro-Am. studies Yale U., New Haven, 1979-84, assoc. prof. dept. Afro-Am. studies, 1986-91; prof. Afro-Am. studies, 1991—; assoc. dir. Conn. Mental Health Ctr., New Haven, 1986-89, acting dir., 1987-88, dir., 1989-96; dep. chmn. dept. psychiatry Sch. Medicine Yale U., New Haven, 1996—; cons. Pan Am. Health Orgn., Jamaica, W.I., 1983—, Antigua and St. Kitts, 1985—, Project HOPE Mental Health Program, Grenada, 1986-89, Comm. on Security and Cooperation in Europe, U.S. Congress; apptd. Conn. Psychiat. Security Rev. Bd., Hartford, 1988-94; external examiner dept. psychiatry, U. W.I., 1986, 95. Editor: Clinical Guidelines in Cross-Cultural Mental Health, 1988, Suicide and Ethnicity in the United States, 1989. Mem. Black Psychiatrists of Am. (pres. 1982-84), Am. Acad. Psychiatry and Law (v.p. 1993-94, pres. 1996—), Am. Psychiat. Assn. (mem. coun. psychiatry and law 1985-91), Conn. Psychiatry Soc. (mem. ethics com. 1983—, pres. 1991-92), Am. Orthopsychiat. Assn. (pres.-elect 1996—), Group for the Advancement of Psychiatry. Office: Conn Mental Health Ctr 34 Park St New Haven CT 06519-1109

GRIFFITH, JOHN FRANCIS, pediatrician, administrator, educator; b. Humboldt, Sask., Can., Feb. 14, 1934; came to U.S., 1963; s. J. Stuart and Grayce M. (Reid) G.; m. Shirley Shaw, Sept 2, 1961; children: Kathleen Ann, Karen Elizabeth, Kristine M., James Stuart. BA, U. Sask., 1956, MD, 1958. Diplomate Am. Bd. Pediatrics (chmn. bd. 1989—). Intern Montreal (Can.) Gen. Hosp., 1958-59, resident, 1959-60, gen. practice medicine, 1960-61; pediatric resident Montreal Children's Hosp., 1961-63, Case Western Res. U., Cleve., 1963-64, Mass. Gen. Hosp., Boston, 1964-67; research fellow neurology Harvard U. Med. Sch., Boston, 1964-66, research fellow neuropathology, 1966-67, teaching fellow neurology, 1967-69; research infectious diseases Children's Hosp. Med. Ctr., Boston, 1967-69; asst. prof. pediatrics Duke U. Med. Ctr., Durham, N.C., 1969-71, assoc. prof., 1971-76, assoc. prof. medicine, 1975-76; prof., chmn. dept. pediatrics U. Tenn., Memphis, 1976-86; prof. pediatrics and neurology, exec. v.p., dir. Med. Ctr., exec. dean Sch. of Medicine Georgetown U., Washington, 1986—; examiner, mem. written exam. com. Am. Bd. Pediatrics, Chapel Hill, N.C., 1979—, mem. task force on recert., 1979-80, bd. dirs., 1985—, exec. com. of bd. dirs., 1986, mem. time ltd. cert. planning com., 1985—, chair program dir. liaison com. and new directions com., 1985-86, chair research and rev. com. and chair guidelines for combined tng. program, 1987—, sec.-treas., 1986-87; mem. residency rev. com. Accreditation Council, Chgo., 1982—, chmn. evaluation com. on pediatric scientist tng. program, 1987—. Contbr. articles to profl. jours. Howard Hughes Found., 1971-74; Multiple Sclerosis grantee, 1969-71; Benjamen Miler Meml. grantee, 1971-74; FDA grantee, 1978-80. Mem. Assn. Am. Med. Colls. (com. on AIDS 1987—), Irish-Am. Pediatrics Soc., Soc. Pediatrics Rsch., Am. Pediatric Soc., AOA, Am. Acad. Pediatrics, Assn. Med. Sch. Pediatrics Dept. Chmn., Royal Coll. Physicians and Surgeons, Am. Bd. Pediatrics (chmn., bd. dirs. 1989-90), Sigma Chi. Office: Georgetown U Med Sch 3800 Reservoir Rd NW Washington DC 20007-2196

GRIFFITH, KAREN ANN, optometrist; b. Petaluma, Calif., Mar. 31, 1962. BS in Zoology, U. Calif., Davis, 1984; OD, U. Calif., Berkeley, 1988. Lic. optometrist, Calif. Pvt. practice, Petaluma, 1988—. Mem. Am. Optometric Assn., Calif. Optometric Assn., Redwood Empire Optometric Soc. (pres. 1995-96), Am. Diabetes Assn., AAUW (sec. 1995-96). Office: 135 Keller St Ste A Petaluma CA 94952

GRIFFITH, KEAN DONALD, surgeon; b. Joliet, Ill., Mar. 16, 1957; s. Richard Lee Griffith and Joyce Mae (DePriest) Phillips; m. Dawn Griffith, May 11, 1985; children: Alana, Allison, Amy, Grace, Adam, Rhys. BA, Knox Coll., 1979; MD, Rush Med. Coll., 1984. Diplomate Am. Bd. Surgery. Med. staff fellow in surg. oncology Nat. Ctr. Inst., Bethesda, Md., 1986-89; surgeon Surg. Svcs. of the Gt. Plains, Omaha, 1992—. Fellow Soc. Surg. Oncology, Southwestern Surg. Congress; mem. ACS (initiate), Am. Soc. Gen. Surgeons, Phi Beta Kappa, Alpha Omega Alpha. Baptist. Home: 4322 N 138th St Omaha NE 68164 Office: Surg Svcs of the Gt Plains 4242 Farnam Ste 270 Omaha NE 68131

GRIFFITH, KIRK M., psychologist; b. Atlanta, Aug. 16, 1956; s. Robert Winter and Mary Jane (Paine) G.; m. Susan P. Brown, Aug. 16, 1980; 1 child, Victoria Brown. BA, Stetson U., 1979; MA, U. South Fla., 1981, PhD, 1984. Lic. psychologist, Colo., Md. Clin. supr. Cleo Wallace Ctr., Broomfield, Colo., 1984-85; clin. dir. Griffith Ctr., Larkspur, Colo., 1985-89; clin. dir. child and family svcs. Green Spring Health Svcs., Columbia, Md., 1989-93, v.p. clin. svcs., 1993—; pvt. practice, Denver, 1986-89; cons. sch. psychologist Cherry Creek Schs., Englewood, Colo., 1987-89. Contbr. articles to profl. jours. Vol. cons. Mental Health Assn., Colo., Denver, 1989; Sunday sch. tchr. Montview Presbyn. Ch., Denver, 1989, Christ Meml. Presbyn. Ch., Columbia, 1990. Recipient Project Vol. award Mental Health Assn. Colo., 1989. Fellow Md. Psychol. Assn.; mem. APA, Colo. Psychol. Assn. (sec. 1986-88), Nat. Register Health Svc. Providers in Psychology. Office: Green Spring Health Svcs 5565 Sterrett Pl Ste 312 Columbia MD 21044-2614

GRIFFITH, LAWRENCE STACEY CAMERON, cardiologist; b. Washington, Sept. 16, 1937; s. Ernest Stacey and Margaret Dyckman (Davenport) G.; m. Anne Gorman Young, June 20, 1959; children: Lawrence, John, Melinda, Gordon. BA, Haverford Coll., 1959; MD with honors, U. Rochester, 1963. Diplomate Am. Bd. Internal Medicine, Am. Bd. Cardiovascular Disease. Intern in medicine and surgery Strong Meml. Hosp., Rochester, N.Y., 1963-64, asst. resident in surgery, 1964-65, asst. and assoc. resident in medicine, 1967-69; rsch. fellow in cardiology Johns Hopkins U., Balt., 1969-71, asst. prof. medicine Sch. Medicine, 1971-76, asst. prof. radiology, 1974-80, assoc. prof. medicine, 1976-88, prof. medicine, 1988—; cons. VA Coop. Study Surgery for Coronary Artery Disease, Program on Surg. Control of Hyperlipidemias, U. Minn. Contbr. numerous articles to profl. jours. Bd. dirs. Julia Dychman Andrus Meml., Inc., Yonkers, N.Y., 1971—, chmn., pres., 1976—; bd. dirs. John E. Andrus Meml. Home for Aged, Hastings-on-Hudson, N.Y., 1974—; bd. dirs. Surdna Found., N.Y.C., 1976—, v.p., 1988-94; chmn. adv. bd. Balt. Pastoral Counseling Svc. 1971-80. With USPHS, 1965-67. Fellow ACP, Coun. Clin. Cardiology of Am. Heart Assn., Am. Coll. Cardiology; mem. Alpha Omega Alpha. Democrat. Methodist. Home: 802 W Saint Georges Rd Baltimore MD 21210-1409 Office: Johns Hopkins Hosp Baltimore MD 21205

GRIFFITH, OWEN WENDELL, biochemistry educator; b. Oakland, Calif., June 19, 1946; s. Charles H. and Gladys C. (Farrar) G. BA, U. Calif., Berkeley, 1968; PhD, Rockefeller U., 1975. Asst. prof. Cornell U. Med. Coll., N.Y.C., 1978-81, assoc. prof., 1981-87, prof., 1987-92; prof., chmn. biochemistry Med. Coll. of Wis., Milw., 1992—; mem., chmn. med. biochemistry study sect. NIH, Bethesda, Md., 1988-92. Contbr. more than 130 articles to profl. jours. Grantee NIH. Mem. Am. Chem. Soc., Am. Soc. Biochemistry and Molecular Biology, Am. Soc. Pharmacology and Exptl. Therapeutics. Office: Med Coll Wis Dept Biochemistry 8701 W Watertown Plank Rd Milwaukee WI 53226-3548

GRIFFITH, ROBERT CHARLES, allergist, educator, planter; b. Shreveport, La., Jan. 9, 1939; s. Charles Parsons and Madelon (Jenkins) G.; m. Loretta Dean Secrist, July 15, 1969; children: Charles Randall, Cameron Stuart, Ann Marie. BS, Centenary Coll., 1961; MD, La. State U., 1965. Intern, Confederate Meml. Med. Ctr., Shreveport, 1965-66, resident in internal medicine, 1966-68; fellow in allergy and chest disease, instr. U. Va. Med. Sch. Hosp., Charlottesville, 1968-70; practice medicine specializing in allergies, Alexandria, La., 1970-72, The Allergy Clinic, Shreveport, 1972; pres. Griffith Allergy Clinic, Shreveport, 1973—; faculty internal medicine La. State U., 1972—; owner, planter Riverpoint Plantation, Caddo Parish, La. and Miller and Lafayette Counties, Ark. Bd. dirs. Caddo-Bossier Assn. Retarded Citizens, 1977-84, Access (fomerly Child Devel. Ctr.), Shreveport, 1979-85; mem. med. adv. com., spl. edn. adv. com. Caddo Parish Sch. Bd., 1977—; mem. commission on missions and social concerns First Methodist Ch., 1981-84, mem. adminstrv. bd., 1981-84; mem. med. panel for transfer Caddo Parish Sch. Bd., 1974-94; mem. adopt a flag program Confederate Meml. Mus. New Orleans; co-chair Loyola Fund Drive, 1994-95. Served to maj. M.C., U.S. Army, 1965-71. Recipient Physician of the Yr. award Shreveport-Bossier Med. Assts., 1984. Fellow Am. Coll. Asthma, Allergy and Immunology, Am. Coll. Chest Physicians (assoc.), Am. Thoracic Soc.; mem. AMA, SAR (chpt. surgeon 1994—), Am. Acad. Allergy, Asthma and Immunology, Jamestowne Soc., So. Med. Assn., La. Med. Soc., Shreveport Med. Soc. (allergy spokesman 1984—), La. Allergy Soc. (charter; past pres.), U. Va. Med. Alumni Assn. (life), Pace Soc. Am., La. State U. Med. Alumni Assn., Conferderate Soc. Am., Heritage Preservation Assn., So. League (charter, sustainer), So. League La. (bd. dirs.), Mil. Order Stars and Bars, Order of So. Cross, Pub. Solicitation Review Coun., Shreveport C. of C., Kappa Alpha, Methodist. Lodges: Masons (32 degree). Clubs: Shreveport Country, Petroleum of Shreveport, Shreveport, Ambs., Cotillion, Royal, Plantation, Jesters, Les Bon Temps., Demoiselle Club. Home: 7112 E Ridge Dr Shreveport LA 71106-4749 Office: 2751 Virginia Ave Shreveport LA 71103-3920

GRIGGS, HEIDI L., internist; b. South Bend, Ind., Mar. 28, 1966; d. Jack Frank and Donna Lynn (Neitzke) Griggs; m. Patrick Erwin Herzog, Sept. 3, 1995. BS, Andrews U., 1988; DO, Mich. State U., 1992. Intern Detroit Osteo. Hosp., Highland Park, Mich., 1992-93; resident in internal medicine St. Joseph Mercy Hosp., Ann Arbor, Mich., 1993-94; resident/chief resident Mich. State U.-KCMS, Kalamazoo, 1994—. Mem. ACP, Am. Osteo. Assn., Am. Soc. Internal Medicine, Mich. Assn. Osteo. Physicians. Seventh-Day Adventist. Home: 4401 Hemmingway Dr Kalamazoo MI 49009 Office: Mich State Univ-KCMS 1000 Oakland Dr Kalamazoo MI 49009

GRIGGS, LUCILLE S., school nurse; b. N.Y.C., Oct. 7, 1944; d. Leon and Natalie L. (Sarner) Gutman; m. Larry Ray Griggs, July 15, 1972; children: Tami Gayl, Larry Ray. Student, U. Tenn., Knoxville, 1963, Memphis State U., 1964, All Saints Episc. Hosp., Ft. Worth, 1971-72; BS, Tex. Christian U., 1975, BA, 1976. LVN, Tex.; LPN, Fla. Nurse All Saints Episc. Hosp., Ft.Worth, 1972-73, 76-77; pediatrics nurse Cape Canaveral Hosp., Cocoa Beach, Fla., 1978-80; head nurse podiatrist's office, Ft. Worth, 1980-85; sch. nurse Ft. Worth Pub. Sch., 1985-93, Flagler County Sch., Palm Coast, Fla., 1993—; nurse Palm Harbor Walk-In Clinic, Palm Coast, 1994—; mem. Flagler Health Adv. Com., Palm Coast, 1994—. Mem. Nat. Assn. Sch. Nurses, Fla. Assn. Nursing, Tex. Vocat. Nurses, Fla. Practical Nurses, Am. Heart Assn., Fla. Health Assn., Sch. Nurse Assn. Fla. Democrat. Jewish. Office: Flagler County Sch 4300 Belle Terre Blvd Palm Coast FL 32137

GRIGGS, ROBERT CHARLES, physician; b. Wilmington, Del., Jan. 8, 1939; s. Albert Bertin and Virginia (Robertson) G.; m. Rosalyne Hoggard, June 16, 1964; children—Jennifer, Heather. A.B., U. Del., 1960; M.D., U. Pa., 1964. Intern Case Western Reserve U., Cleve., 1964-65; resident Case Western Reserve U., 1965-66, Nat. Inst. Neurol. Disease and Blindness, Bethesda, Md., 1966-68; resident in medicine, neurology U. Rochester, N.Y., 1968-71; prof. neurology, medicine, pathology, pediatrics, co-dir. neuromuscular disease ctr. U. Rochester, 1972—, chmn. dept. neurology, 1986; practice medicine specializing in neurology Rochester, 1971—; hon. cons. Univ. Coll. Hosp., London, 1981-82. Author: Evaluation and Treatment of Myopathies; editor in chief Neurology, 1997—. Served to lt. comdr. USPHS, 1966-68. ACP Rsch. and Teaching grantee, 1971-74. Office: Strong Meml Hosp Dept Neurology 601 Elmwood Ave Rochester NY 14642-0001

GRIGGS, ROGER DALE, pharmaceutical company executive; b. Mishawaka, Ind., Oct. 22, 1949; s. William and Wanda Griggs; m. Katherine E. Neff; children: Jacob, Caleb, Abigail. BS, Ind. State U., 1973; MEd, Ind. U., 1979. Tchr., coach various high schs., LaGrange, Ind., 1973-82; sales rep. Lederle Labs., Valparaiso, Ind., 1982-84; dist. mgr. Lederle Labs., Birmingham, Ala., 1984-86; dir. instnl. sales Russ Pharms., Birmingham, 1986-90; founder, pres. Richwood Pharms., Florence, Ky., 1990—, also bd. dirs. Mem. adv. coun. coll. bus. adminstrn. No. Ky. U., Highland Heights, 1995—; active Richwood Presbyn. Ch., 1985—. Mem. Am. Mktg. Assn., Am. Pain Soc., Children with Attention Deficit Disorder, Nat. Pharm. Alliance, Adults with Attendtion Deficit Disorder. Office: Richwood Pharm Co Inc 7900 Tanners Gate # 200 Florence KY 41042

GRIGOR, WALLACE GLADSTONE, pediatrician; b. Sydney, NSW, Australia, Dec. 9, 1929; s. Bruce Gladstone and Edna Irene (Dean) G.; m. Mary Haworth Leslie, Mar. 30, 1957 (div. Dec. 1976); children: Anthony, Sally Ann, Judith; m. Catherine Georgeanna Jones. MS BS, Sydney U., 1952. Vis. med. officer Children's Hosp., Camperdown, NSW, 1960—, chief resident, 1967-70; v.p. bd. mgmt. Children's Hosp., Camperdown, 1983-88; chmn. Pharm. Benefits Adv. Com., Canberra, Australia, 1985-92. Chmn. Child Accident Prevention Found. of Australia, 1991-96. Recipient A.M. award Australian Govt., 1986. Fellow Royal Australian Coll. Physicians; mem. Australian Coll. Pediatrics (pres. 1989-91), Royal N.W. Inst. for Deaf and Blind Children (bd. dirs. 1981—). Home: 7 Killarney St, Mosman, New South Wales 2088, Australia Office: Wade House Cons Rms, Bridge Rd, Camperdown New South Wales 2050, Australia

GRIGSBY, J. ROBERT, optometrist; b. Florence, Ala., Oct. 6, 1964; s. James Kenneth and Kathryn Anne (Mason) G.; m. Bonnie Elizabeth Aiken, Dec. 7, 1991. BS, David Lipscomb U., 1987; OD, U. Ala., Birmingham, 1991. Bd. cert. optometry, N.C. Staff optometrist Optometric Eye Care Ctr., Salisbury, N.C., 1991-93; clin. dir. Optometric Eye Care Ctr., Salisbury, 1993—; mem. bd. dirs. The Laser Ctr., Winston-Salem, N.C., 1996—. Min. of music Northview Ch. of Christ, Statesville, N.C., 1994-96. Named Outstanding Young Men of Am., 1989, 91; recipient Gold Key award Gold Key Internat. Optometric Honor Soc., 1991. Mem. Am. Optometric Assn., N.C. Optometric Soc., Internat. Assn. On-Line Optometrist. Republican. Office: 2141 Statesville Blvd Salisbury NC 28147

GRIGSBY, PERRY WAYNE, physician; b. Cadiz, Ky., Aug. 11, 1952; s. Oscar McAtee and Irene (Freeman) G.; children: Allison, Amy, James, Thomas, Isabella, Barbara, David. BS in Zoology, U. Ky., 1974, MS in Physics, 1978, MD, 1982; MBA, Washington U., 1990. Intern, then resident Barnes Hosp., St. Louis, 1982-84; asst. chief resident Barnes Hosp., 1984-85, chief resident in radiology, 1985-86; prof. radiology Washington U./Barnes Hosp., 1986—; cons. in field to hosps. Contbr. articles to profl. jours. Vol. Girl Scouts U.S.A., St. Louis, 1984—, Am. Cancer Soc., St. Louis, 1983—. Recipient Am. Cancer Soc. Clin. Oncology award, 1987—; Am. Radium Soc. grantee, 1986, others. Mem. AMA (Physicians Recognition award 1985), Am. Assn. of Physicists in Medicine, Am. Coll. Radiology, Am. Soc. Clin. Oncology, Am. Soc. Therapeutic Radiology and Oncology. Home: 510 S Kingshighway Blvd Saint Louis MO 63110-1016 Office: Barnes Hosp 510 S Kingshighway Blvd Saint Louis MO 63110-1016

GRIMES, HUGH GAVIN, physician; b. Chgo., Aug. 19, 1929; s. Andrew Thomas and Anna (Gavin) G.; m. Rose Anne Leahy, Aug. 21, 1954; children—Hugh Gavin, Paula Anne, Daniel Joseph, Sarah Louise, Nancy Marie, Jennifer Diane. Student, Loyola U., 1947-50; B.S., U. Ill., 1952, M.D., 1954. Diplomate Am. Bd. Ob-Gyn. Intern St. Joseph Hosp., Chgo., 1954-55; resident in ob-gyn St. Joseph Hosp., 1955-58; practice medicine specializing in ob-gyn Chgo., 1960—; lectr., asst. clin. prof. Stritch Sch. Medicine, Loyola U., Chgo.; active staff St. Joseph Hosp., Chgo., also v.p. med. staff, 1977-78, pres. staff, 1979-80; asst. prof. clin. ob-gyn Northwestern U. Med. Sch., 1980—. Contbr. articles to profl. jours. Trustee Regina Dominican High Sch. Served to capt. M.C., AUS, 1958-60. Recipient nat. faculty award Am.

Bd. Ob-Gyn. Fellow Am. Coll. Ob-Gyn., Chgo. Gynecol. Soc.; mem. Am. Cancer Soc. (mem. profl. edn. com. Chgo. unit), Am. Soc. Reproductive Medicine, Cath. Physicians Guild, Assn. Am. Physicians and Surgeons, Am. Soc. Colposcopy and Colpomicroscopy, Am. Assn. Gynecologic Laparoscopists, Assn. Art Inst. Chgo., Assn. Field Mus., Assocs. Smithsonian Instn., Pi Kappa Epsilon. Office: 2800 N Sheridan Rd Ste 304 Chicago IL 60657-6156

GRIMES, ORVILLE FRANK, surgery educator; b. San Bernardino, Calif., Jan. 13, 1916; s. Nathan and Frances Marjorie (Aeillio) G.; m. June Levelle, June 14, 1941; children: Orville Frank Jr., Nancy L., Douglas N., Dianne Wilson. AB, U. Calif., Berkeley, 1937; MS, MD, Northwestern U., Chgo., 1942. Diplomate Am. Bd. Surgery, Am. Bd. Thoracic Surgery. Resident in surgery U. Calif., San Francisco, 1942-44, 46-49, mem. faculty, 1944-46, prof. surgery, 1949—, vice chmn. dept. surgery, 1955-61; cons. in surgery Calif. Med. Rev. Inc., San Jose, 1989-95. Contbr. over 150 articles to med. jours., chpts. to books. Maj. M.C., U.S. Army, 1944-46, ETO. Mem. ACS, Am. Surg. Assn., Pacific Coast Surg. Assn., Soc. Univ. Surgeons, Am. Assn. for Thoracic Surgery, San Francisco Surg. Soc. Republican. Episcopalian. Home: 12 Lagoon Pl San Rafael CA 94901 Office: U Calif 400 Parnassus Ave San Francisco CA 94143

GRIMLEY, CYNTHIA PATRIZI, rehabilitation consultant, special education educator; b. Sharon, Pa., Mar. 29, 1958; d. James Donald Sr. and Delores Virginia (Maykowski) Patrizi; m. Kevin Neil Grimley, Apr. 11, 1987; children: Ronald James, Jennifer Rose. BS, Youngstown (Ohio) State U., 1981; MS, Calif. State U., 1986. Lic. multiple subject tchr., spl. edn. and elem. tchr., severly handicapped edn. tchr., Ohio, Pa.; specialist credential, Calif.; cert. rehab. counselor, case mgr., human resources generalist. Residential program worker, supr., classroom tchr. Mercer County Assn. for the Retarded, Hermitage, Pa., 1980-82; tchr. spl. edn. Hermitage Sch. Dist., 1982-83; cons. property mgmt. Lorden Mgmt. Co., Covina, Calif., 1983-84; tchr. spl. edn. Fullerton (Calif.) Elem. Sch. Dist., 1984-87; vocat. rehab. cons. Profl. Rehab. Cons., Santa Ana, Calif., 1986-89, Pvt. Sector Rehab., Fullerton, 1989—i. Contbr. curriculum, articles in field. Coach Spl. Olympics, Fullerton, 1982-87; sec. So. Calif. Rehab. Exch., 1989, mem.-at-large, 1990, treas., 1991. Polish Art Club scholar, 1977. Fellow Am. Bd. Vocat. Experts, Am. Acad. Pain Mgmt., Am. Bd. Disability Analysts; mem. NEA, Nat. Assn. Rehab. Profls. in the Pvt. Sector, Calif. Assn. Rehab. Profls., Assn. Retarded Citizens. Democrat. Roman Catholic. Office: Pvt Sector Rehab 2555 E Chapman Ave Ste 300 Fullerton CA 92631-3618

GRIMLEY EVANS, JOHN, geriatric medical educator; b. Birmingham, Sept. 17, 1936; s. Harry Walter and Violet Prenter (Walker) Grimley Evans; m. Corinne Jane Cavender, Mar. 25, 1966; children: Edmund Thomas, Piers Siward, Freya Harriet. MA.MB, Cambridge U., Eng., 1958, MD, 1985. Rsch. asst. Clin. Med., Oxford U., Eng., 1963-64; vis. scientist U. Mich., Ann Arbor, 1966; rsch. fellow Dept. Medicine, Wellington, N.Z., 1966-70; lectr. U. London, 1970-71; clin. lectr. U. Newcastle, 1971-73, prof. medicine (geriatrics), 1973-85; prof. geriatric medicine U. Oxford, 1985—; cons. WHO, Geneva, 1983—; chmn. MRC Health Svc. Rsch. com. 1989-94. Contbr. articles to profl. jours.; editor various books. Fellow Royal Soc. Medicine, Royal Statis. Soc., Royal Coll. Physicians (2nd v.p. 1993-95); mem. Internat. Epidemiol. Assn., Am. Geriatric Soc. Office: Radcliffe Infirmary, Oxford England OX2 6ME

GRIMM, DONNA L., home care agency administrator; b. Crainesville, Pa., Dec. 7, 1943; d. Charles E. and Donna S. (Ball) Ebner; m. W. Wallace Grimm, Aug. 5, 1967; children: Rusty, Claudia, Tod J., Shelly. Diploma, Hamot Hosp. Sch. Nursing, Erie, Pa., 1964; BA in Psychology, Heidelberg Coll., Tiffin, Ohio, 1967. Staff nurse Hamot Hosp., 1964-65; sch. nurse Heidelberg Coll., 1965-67; nursing supr. Hayes Meml. Hosp., Fremont, Ohio, 1967-68; office nurse Bowling Green, Ohio, 1963-70; asst. dir. Bowling Area Sch. Practical Nursing, Bowling Green, 1970-72; vocat. instr. Ehove Joint Vocat. Sch., Milan, Ohio, 1972-74; nursing supr. Van Wert (Ohio) Area Vis. Nurses Assn., 1975-81, pres., CEO, 1981—; cons. home care agys. in Ohio; peer reviewer. Trustee Ohio Coun. Home Care, Columbus, 1979—, sec., 1995; pres. Ohio Coalitions of Vis. Nurses Assns., Akron, 1994; v.p. Preferred Alliance of Ohio, Columbus, 1995; vol. Am. Cancer Soc., March of Dimes, Am. Heart Assn., Hospice. Recipient Dorothy Royce award Ohio Coun. for Home Care, 1990; named Nurse of Hope, Am. Cancer Soc., 1989. Mem. Van Wert Area Vis. Nurses (trustee), Van Wert Rotary. Methodist. Office: Van Wert Area Vis Nurses Van Wert OH

GRIMM, JOHN ORVAL, orthopedic surgeon; b. Tokyo, June 22, 1951; came to U.S., 1952; s. James Orval Grimm and Kimie (Takano) Brinkerhoff; m. Patricia Maria Davis, June 20, 1981; children: John Thomas, Anna Camille, Adam Tobias. BS, U. Calif., Davis, 1974; MD, W.Va. U., 1980. Diplomate Am. Bd. Orthopedic Surgery. Rotating intern Ind. U. Med. Ctr., Indpls., 1981, orthopedic surgery resident, 1985; spine surgery fellowship So. Ill. U. Sch. of Medicine, Springfield, 1986; pediatric othopedic fellowship Miami Children Hosp., Miami, 1988; pvt. practice Med. Ctr. Clinic, Pensacola, Fla., 1986-88, Knoxville, Tenn., 1988-89, Tri-State Orthopedic Surgeons, Inc., Evansville, Ill., 1989—; shareholder The Ambulatory Care Ctr., Evansville, 1994—; ptnr. Tri-State Orthopedic Surgeons, Inc., Evansville, 1989—. Mem. AMA, Vanderburgh County Med. Soc., Ind. Orthopedic Soc., Ind. State Med. Assn., Am. Back Soc. Republican. Office: Tri-State Orthopedic Surgeons Inc 1101 Professional Blvd Evansville IN 47714

GRIMM, LARRY LEON, psychologist; b. Goshen, Ind., Aug. 16, 1950; s. Warren Arden and Elizabeth Ann (Rassi) G.; m. Ann Mae Nelson, July 16, 1977; 1 child, Kirsten Ann. BS in Elem. Edn., No. Ariz. U., 1975, MA in Early Childhood Edn., 1977, EdD in Ednl. Psychology, 1983. Lic. psychologist; cert. sch. psychologist, elem. tchr. Ariz., Nat. Tchr. elem. sch. Page (Ariz.) Unified Dist., 1975-76; grad. asst. Coll. Edn., No. Ariz. U., Flagstaff, 1976; tchr. elem. sch. Litchfield Sch. Dist., Litchfield Park, Ariz., 1976-80; grad. assoc. dept. ednl. psychology No. Ariz. U., Flagstaff, 1980-81; sch. psychologist intern Peoria (Ariz.) Unified Dist., 1981-82; adj. faculty Grand Canyon Coll., Phoenix, 1982; sch. psychologist Child Study Services, Prescott (Ariz.) Unified Sch. Dist., 1982-87; adj. assoc. prof. No. Ariz. U., Flagstaff, 1984—, vis. faculty, 1987-88; postdoctoral fellow in pediatric psychology Child Devel. Ctr. Georgetown U. Med. Ctr., Washington, 1988-89; pvt. practice, 1989—; cons. in field; presenter at convs. Contbr. articles to profl. jours. Chmn. project devel. com. Infant & Toddler Network, 1989-92; mem. family resource ctr. adv. bd. Yavapai Regional Med. Ctr., 1990—. Mem. Am. Psychol. Assn. (publs. com. div. 16), Ariz. Assn. Sch. Psychologists (bd. dirs. No. Ariz., regional dir. 1983-84, pres. 1986-87, newsletter editor, 1986-87, Pres.'s award 1985, 88, 89), Nat. Assn. Sch. Psychologists (Ariz. del. fiscal adv. com. 1987-88, Capitol Network 1988-89), Soc. Pediatric Psychologists, Christian Assn. Psychol. Studies. Republican.

GRINER, PAUL FRANCIS, physician; b. Phila., Jan. 1, 1933; s. John and Josepha (Snyder) G.; m. Miriam Millard; children: Laura, Paul Jr. BA, Harvard U., 1954; MD with honors, U. Rochester, 1959. Diplomate Am. Bd. Internal Medicine, Nat. Bd. Med. Examiners. Intern in medicine Mass. Gen. Hosp., Boston, 1959-60, asst. resident, 1960-61, sr. resident, 1963-64; chief resident in medicine Strong Meml. Hosp., Rochester, N.Y., 1964-65; fellow in pathology U. Rochester Sch. Medicine & Dentistry, 1956-57, instr. medicine, fellow in hematology, 1964-65, clin. instr., 1965-66, clin. sr. instr., 1966-67, asst. prof. medicine, 1967-69, assoc. prof., 1969-73, Samuel E. Durand prof. medicine, 1973—, head. gen. medicine unit, 1976-84, acting chmn. dept. medicine, 1977-79, chmn. dept. health svcs., 1985-94; gen. dir. Strong Meml. Hosp., 1984-94; v.p. dir. Assn. Am. Med. Colls., Washington, 1995—; dir. med. edn. Rochester Gen. Hosp., 1965-67, cons. 1969—; cons. Genesee Hosp., 1969—, Highland Hosp., 1969—; chmn., bd. dirs. Acad. Med. Ctr. Consortium, 1991-92. Contbr. numerous articles to profl. jours., chpts. to books. Mem. N.Y. Gov.'s Health Care Adv. Bd., 1990-94, Mayoral Commn. on Health and Hosps. Corp. of City of N.Y., 1991-92. Capt. USAF, 1961-63. Recipient Doran Stephens prize U. Rochester, 1959. Master ACP (mem. health and pub. policy com. 1981-84, 87-88, chmn. 1988-90; chmn bd. regents 1991-92, chmn. clin. efficacy assessment subcom. 1986-88, pres. 1993-94), Venezuelan Soc. Internal Medicine (hon.); mem. AAAS, Am. Clin. and Climatol. Assn., Am. Soc. Hematology, Internat. Soc. Tech. Assessment in Health Care, Soc. Med. Decision Making, So. Gen. Internal Medicine, Soc. Med. Adminstrs., Inst. Medicine Nat. Acad. Scis. (com. quality rev. and assurance in Medicare 1987-90, mem. bd. healthcare svcs. 1987—, mem. com. on future primary care 1994—), Sigma Xi, Alpha Omega Alpha. Office: Assn Am Med Colls 2450 N St NW Washington DC 20037*

GRINES, CINDY LEE, health facility administrator; b. Kalamazoo, May 17, 1955; children: Jessica, Derek. BS cum laude, Ohio State U., 1977, MD cum laude, 1980. Intern, resident Ohio State U. Hosps., Columbus, 1980-84; instr. internal medicine divsn. cardiology U. Mich., Ann Arbor, 1986-87; assoc. investigator rsch. dept. VA Med. Ctr., Ann Arbor, 1986-89, Lexington, Ky., 1986-89; asst. prof. medicine divsn. cardiology U. Ky., Lexington, 1987-90; dir. cardiac catheterization lab. William Beaumont Hosp., Royal Oak, Mich., 1990—; researcher in field. Contbr. articles to profl. jours. Cardiology fellow U. Mich. Hosp., 1984-87. Fellow Am. Coll. Cardiology; mem. Am. Heart Assn. (coun. clin. cardiology), Am. Coll. Angiology, Am. Coll. Physicians, Detroit Heart Club, Alpha Omega Alpha. Office: William Beaumont Hosp Divsn Cardiology 3601 W 13 Mile Rd Royal Oak MI 43073

GRINGAUZ, ALEX, chemistry educator, researcher, pharmacist, writer; b. Memel, Lithuania, May 18, 1934; came to U.S., 1947; s. Samuel and Marcia (Tanur) G.; m. Donna Jean Hengsteler, Aug. 29, 1959; children: Marshall, Daniel, Steven. BS in Pharmacy cum laude, Bklyn. Coll. of Pharmacy, 1956; MS, Purdue U., 1958, PhD, 1960. NIH postdoctoral fellow Purdue U., Lafayette, Ind., 1960-61; asst. prof. medicinal chemistry Bklyn. Coll. of Pharmacy, 1961-66, assoc. prof. medicinal chemistry, 1966-73; prof. medicinal chemistry Schwartz Coll. of Pharmacy L.I. U., Bklyn., 1973—; cons. Pioneer Chem. Co., Bklyn., 1970's. Author: Drugs—How They Act and Why, 1978, Introduction to Medicinal Chemistry; Drugs How They Act and Why, 1996; contbr. articles to Jour. Med. Chemistry, Jour. Pharm. Sci. and various profl. pharmacy pubs. Mem. Am. Chem. Soc., Am. Pharm. Assn., Sigma Xi. Jewish. Home: 1055 E Broadway Woodmere NY 11598-1336 Office: LI U Schwartz Coll Pharmacy 75 Dekalb Ave Brooklyn NY 11201-5497

GRIP, GORAN, anesthesiologist, author; b. Malmo, Sweden, Jan. 24, 1945; s. Stig and Birgit K.I. (Nordvall) G. MD, U. Lund, 1971, degree in anesthesiology, 1975. Jr. attending physician Hosp. Helsingborg, Sweden, 1975-80, Hosp. Skovde, Sweden, 1981-83; attending physician Hosp. Lidkoping, Sweden, 1983-88, Univ. Hosp. Uppsala, Sweden, 1988-96; author, 1996—; lectr. near-death experience U. Uppsala, 1988—, rsch. advisor, researcher; translator and workshop leader, author, 1996—. Author: Ethical Choices in Medical Practice, 1991, Everything Exists, Nothing Matters, 1994; editor Death is of Vital Importance: The Tape Recorded Lectures of Elisabeth Kübler-Ross, 1990; contbr. numerous articles to profl. jours.; translator numerous Am. books on the near-death experience, the past-life experience and related subjects into Swedish. Mem. Sci. and Med. Netowrk, Internat. Assn. Near-Death Studies (Scandinavian, U.S. and Eng. chpts.). Home and Office: Torbjornsgatan 10, S-75335 Uppsala Sweden

GRISHAM, JOE WHEELER, pathologist, educator; b. Smith County, Tenn., Dec. 5, 1931; s. William Wince and Grace (Allen) G.; m. Jean Evelyn Malone, July 2, 1955. B.A., Vanderbilt U., 1953, M.D., 1957. Intern Washington U.-Barnes Hosp., St. Louis, 1957-58; resident in pathology Washington U.-Barnes Hosp., 1958-60; mem. faculty Washington U., Med. Sch., 1960-73, prof. pathology and anatomy, 1969-73; assoc. pathologist Barnes Hosp., 1969-73; vis. instr. Makerere Med. Coll., Kampala, Uganda, 1961; prof. pathology, chmn. dept. U. N.C. Med. Sch., Chapel Hill, 1973—, Kenan prof., 1992—; also pathologist-in-chief U. N.C. Hosp., 1973—; mem. pathology study sect. A NIH, 1969-73, chmn., 1970-73, chmn. pathology study sect. B, 1979-83; bd. sci. counsellors Nat. Inst. Environ. Health Scis., 1974-78; mem. sci. advisory panel Chem. Industry Inst. Toxicology, 1977-88, chmn., 1980-88; adv. bd. Given Inst. Pathobiology, 1983-87. Contbr. articles to med. jours. Served to lt. comdr. USNR, 1961-63. John and Mary R. Markle scholar acad. medicine, 1964-69; fellow Life Ins. Med. Rsch. Fund, 1959-61, Am. Cancer Inst., 1958-59; Brindley prof. U. Tex. Med. Br., 1993; named Disting. Med. Alumnus Vanderbilt U., 1994. Mem. Am. Assn. Pathologists (pres. 1984-85), Am. Assn. Cancer Research, Fedn. Am. Soc. Exptl. Biology (pres., chmn. bd. 1984-85), Am. Assn. Study Liver Diseases, Am. Soc. Cell Biology, Univ. Assn. Research and Edn. in Pathology (v.p. 1985-86), Tissue Culture Assn., Internat. Acad. Pathology, Cell Kinetics Soc., AMA, AAAS. Home: 1703 Curtis Rd Chapel Hill NC 27514-7614 Office: Univ NC Med Sch Dept Pathology CB # 7525 Chapel Hill NC 27599

GRISHAM, RICHARD, health facility administrator; b. Ponca City, Okla., Sept. 4, 1945; s. Harold Edward and Billie Dean (Knight) G.; m. Carla Maxine Davis, Jan. 29, 1965; children: Richard William, Kristin Ann. BS in Pharmacy with honors, U. Okla., 1968; MS in Health Care Adminstrn., Washington U., St. Louis, 1973. Registered pharmacist, Okla., Mo. Aide Ctrl. State Mental Hosp., Norman, Okla., 1965-66; intern pharmacist Oklahoma City, 1966-68; mgr. Med-X Drug Co., Tulsa, 1969; chief pharmacist, dir. intravenous svcs., instr. pharmacology sch. nursing St. John's Hosp., Tulsa, 1969-71; relief pharmacist St. Joseph's Hosp., St. Louis, 1971-73; adminstrv. resident Barnes Hosp./Washington U. Med. Ctr., St. Louis, 1972-73; asst. dir. prof. svcs. Barnes Hosp., 1973-74, assoc. dir. profl. svcs., 1974-77, v.p., 1977-81; pres., CEO St. Anthony's Med. Ctr./St. Anthony's Hosp. St. Louis./St. Anthony's Med. Office Bldg., 1981—, also bd. dirs.; adj. prof. health care adminstrn. sch. medicine Washington U., St. Louis U. Med. Ctr., 1981—. Ist lt. med. svc. corps U.S. Army, 1968-69. Mem. Am. Coll. Hosp. Adminstrs., Cath. Health Assn. (alternative sponsorship com., Acad. for Cath. Healthcare Leadership, Hosp. Assn. Met. St. Louis (coun. on human resources), Rho Chi. Office: St Anthony's Med Ctr 10010 Kennerly Rd Saint Louis MO 63128-2106

GRISSOM, RAYMOND EARL, JR., toxicologist; b. Raleigh, N.C., Oct. 27, 1943; s. Raymond Earl and Edith (Ballance) G.; m. Lorraine Rankin, Aug. 11, 1974; children: Kelly Daniel, James Earl, Mary Elizabeth. 2 BS degrees with high honors, N.C. State U., 1976, PhD, 1982. Scientist N.C. Bd. Sci. and Tech., Raleigh, 1982-83; postdoctoral rsch. assoc. N.C. State U., Raleigh, 1983-87; toxicologist Environ Monitoring and Svcs., Inc., Chapel Hill, N.C., 1987-88; toxicologist Agy. for Toxic Substances and Disease Registry, Atlanta, 1988-90, sr. toxicologist, 1990—; cons. Becton Dickinson Rsch. Ctr., Research Triangle Park, N.C., 1986-87; speaker internat. symposiums, Eng., 1989, Malaysia, 1990, Can., 1993. Author book chpts., govt. documents; contbr. articles to profl. jours. Coach South Gwinnett League Basketball, Atlanta, 1990-96. Recipient citation for disting. svc. State of N.C., 1983, City of Atlanta, 1990-96. Mem. AAAS, Soc. Toxicology, Sigma Xi, Gamma Sigma Delta. Presbyterian. Home: 4959 Joy Ln SW Lilburn GA 30247-5119 Office: Agy Toxic Substances & Disease Registry 1600 Clifton Rd NE # E32 Atlanta GA 30329-4018

GRISWOLD, DAVID JAMES, therapist and physician's assistant; b. Morrisville, Vt., Aug. 6, 1940; s. Floyd Jerry and Gladys Nellie (Dowing) G.; m. Carol Ann Locke, Dec. 29, 1962; children: Gary Alan, Dana Scott. AS, Community Coll. of Vt., 1975. Lic. physician's asst., Vt. Psychiat. aide Vt. State Hosp., Waterbury, 1963-66, psychiat. technician, 1966-67, psychiat. charge, 1967-69, psychiat. ward coord., 1968-69, psychiat. team specialist, 1969-75; day hosp. therapist Washington County Mental Health, Montpelier, Vt., 1975-93, physician's asst., 1976—; asst. dir. Washington County Day Hosp., 1980-93. With U.S. Army, 1959-62. Methodist. Home: RR 2 Box 845 Waterbury VT 05676-9715 Office: 9 Heaton St Montpelier VT 05602-2489

GRISWOLD, GARRY MARTIN, optometrist; b. Cortland, N.Y., July 30, 1957; s. Hubert C. and Virginia F. (Martin) G.; m. Rebecca R. Gebert, Aug. 9, 1980; children: Sara, Jason, Christopher, Kyle. MusB, U Cin, 1979; OD, Ohio State U., 1993. Store mgr. sales Oakdale Music Ctrs., Rochester, N.Y., 1979-88; salesman Coyle Music Ctrs., Columbus, Ohio, 1989-93; optometrist Ada-Boise (Idaho) Vision Clinic, 1993—. Writer several mus. compositions. Umpire, bd. dirs. Little League Baseball, Boise, 1993—; choir dir. LDS Ch., 1984—. Recipient J. Harold Bailey Rsch. award Am. Optometric Found., Ohio State U. Coll. Optometry, 1993. Mem. Am. Optometric Assn. (contact lens sect.), Idaho Optometric Assn. Home: 4570 Patton Ave Boise ID 83704 Office: Ada-Boise Vision Clinic 1665 Hill Rd Boise ID 83702

GRISWOLD, KENT CARRIER, health care company executive; b. Bridgeton, N.J., Mar. 1, 1958; s. Lincoln Tracy and Jean Secord (Coghlan) G. AB, Harvard U., 1980; postgrad. in econs., U. Stockholm, 1984; MBA, U. Pa., 1985. Mgmt. assoc. Sun Co., Radnor, Pa., 1980-81; treasury analyst Phila., 1981-83; systems designer Spl. Care, Inc., Phila., 1984, gen. mgr., v.p., exec. dir., 1987-90, pres., 1990—, also bd. dirs.; rep. Pratt Group, Hong Kong, 1985-86; mgr. treasury Melbourne, Australia, 1986-87; pres. Fin. Health Svcs., Inc., 1989—; cons. trading A. Johnson & Co., Stockholm, 1984; cons. Mayne Ednl. Fund, Swannoanoa, N.C., 1987-91, trustee, 1991—. Creator: (bd. game) Mergers and Acquisitions, 1981. Mem. Savoy Co., Phila., 1981, 83, 88, 89, 90, 91, 92, 93, 94, 96. White House Fellowship finalist, 1992. Mem. Pa. Health Care Assn., Pvt. Care Assn., Am. Soc. on Aging, Young Entrepreneurs Orgn., Nuangola (pres.), Mensa, Rotary, Acad. Club, Fox Club. Republican. Presbyterian. Office: Spl Care Inc 707 Bethlehem Pike Erdenheim PA 19038-8101

GRISWOLD, PAUL MICHAEL, clinical psychologist, consultant; b. Milw., Sept. 26, 1945; s. Willard Matthew and Evelyn (Haerle) G.; m. AnnMari Gerardine La Valle, Aug. 2, 1969; children: Matthew Paul, Jennifer Jean. BA, Marquette U., 1967, MS, 1969; PhD, Kent State U., 1972. Sr. staff psychologist Wis. Div. Corrections, Milw., 1972-83; pvt. practice clin. and cons. psychology Menomonee Falls, Wis., 1973—; lectr. Mount Mary Coll., Milw., 1973-78; faculty Wis. Sch. of Profl. Psychology, Milw., 1981—; cons. Ethan Allen Sch. Wis. Div. Corrections, Wales, Wis., 1984—. Contbr. articles to profl. jours. Mem. Am. Psychol. Assn., Wis. Psychol. Assn., Milw. Area Psychol. Assn. Home: 1366 County Hwy J Hubertus WI 53033-9426 Office: Clin Psychology Assocs W156 N8327 Pilgrim Rd Menomonee Falls WI 53051-3776

GRITTS, GERALD LEE, home health nurse, AIDS care nurse, AIDS educator; b. Tulsa, Okla., May 14, 1956; s. Arlie Lee and Kathleen Joyce (Thomas) G. A in Health Sci., Greenville (S.C.) Tech. Coll., 1993. RN, Colo. With Preferred Mobile Nurses, Greeley, Colo., 1993-94; grad. RN Fair Acres Manor, Greeley, Colo., 1993-94; grad. RN Quality Home Healthcare Svcs., Greeley, Colo., 1994—, dir. nursing, 1996—; advisor/cons. HIV svcs. Quality Infusion Svcs., 1994—. Author: (pamphlets) Losing a Loved One to AIDS, 1994, When Your Partner Has AIDS, 1994; author, co-editor, co-producer: (videos) Tears, Smiles and Remembrances, 1993, Healthcare and AIDS: The PWA, Family, and Medical Professionals, 1996. Co-founder, advisor, media chairperson AIDS Pub. Edn. League, Ft. Collins, Colo., 1994-96; cons. HIV vols.; cons. student HIV svcs. Colo. State U., Ft. Collins, 1993—; vol. HIV patients No. Colo. AIDS Project, Ft. Collins, 1993—; vol. Parents, Friends of Lesbians and Gays, Denver, 1986—, Friends of the Names Project Quilt, 1994—. Recipient AIDS Health Educator award Straight, But Not Narrow Group, Ft. Collins, 1994, Profls. for AIDS Edn. award AIDS Pub. Edn. League, Ft. Collins, 1994, award of merit Wednesday Noon Moms Group for AIDS Care of Children, Adolescents and Adults, 1995. Mem. Assn. Nurses in AIDS Care, No. Colo. Aids Project (bd. dirs. 1995—, mem. speakers bur. 1994—), Grief and Loss Task Force of Weld County.

GRIZZELL, ROY AMES, biologist; b. Sweetwater, Tenn., Mar. 14, 1918; s. Roy Ames and Rena Bee (Williams) G.; m. Virginia Roe, Aug. 27, 1949; children: Linda, Diane. BSF, U. Ga., 1939; MF, U. Mich., 1947, PhD, 1951. Cert. fishery biologist. Biologist Ga. Game and Fish Commn., Atlanta, 1939-41, U.S. Fish and Wildlife Svc., Patuxent, Md., 1947-49; refuge mgr. U.S. Fish and Wildlife Svc., Golden Pond, Ky., 1953-55; biologist U.S. Soil Conservation Svc., Athens, Ga., 1955-60, Little Rock, 1960-77; cons. biologist Monticello, Ark., 1977—; adj. prof. U. Ark., Monticello, 1983-88; vis. prof. U. Okla., Norman, 1970, Miss. State U., Starkville, 1975, Tex. A&M, College Station, 1977, Ark. State U., 1977. Chmn. County Tax Equalization Bd., Monticello, 1987-92, County Hist. Mus., Monticello, 1985-90; mem. Pub. Facility Housing Bd., Monticello, 1987—. Named Man of Yr. Drew County C. of C., Monticello, 1988; recipient Home Town Spirit award Union Bank, Monticello, 1990. Fellow Soil-Water Conservation Soc.; mem. Wildlife Soc. (pres. Ark. chpt. 1975-76, Razorback chpt. 1965-67), Internat. Visitors Coun., Lions (pres. Monticello chpt. 1981-83, dist. gov. Ark. chpt. 1983-84, coun. chmn. 1984-85). Democrat. Presbyterian. Home: 138 Grizzell Ln Monticello AR 71655-9142

GROAH, LINDA KAY, nursing administrator and educator; b. Cedar Rapids, Iowa, Oct. 5, 1942; d. Joseph David and Irma Josephine (Zitek) Rozek; diploma St. Luke's Sch. Nursing, Cedar Rapids, 1963; student San Francisco City Coll., 1976-77; BA, St. Mary's Coll., Moraga, Calif., 1978; BS in Nursing, Calif. State U.; MS in Nursing, U. Calif.; m. Patrick Andrew Groah, Mar. 20, 1975; 1 child, Kimberly; stepchildren: Nadine, Maureen, Patrick, Marcus. Staff nurse to head nurse U. Iowa, 1963-67; clin. supr., dir. oper. and recovery room Michael Reese Hosp., Chgo., 1967-73; dir. oper. rooms Med. Ctr. Cen. Ga., Macon, 1973-74; dir. oper. and recovery rooms U. Calif. Hosps. and Clinics, San Francisco, 1974-90, asst. dir. hosps. and clinics, 1982-86; svc. dir. Kaiser Found. Hosp., San Francisco, 1990—; asst. clin. prof. U. Calif. Sch. Nursing, San Francisco, 1975—; cons. to oper. room suprs., to div. ednl. resources and programs Assn. Am. Med. Colls., 1976—; condr. seminars. Mem. Nat. League for Nurses, Am. Nurses Assn. (vice chmn. operating room conf. group 1974-76), Assn. Oper. Room Nurses (com. on nominations 1979-84, treas. 1981-83, 93-95, bd. dirs. 1991-93, pres.-elect 1995-96, pres. 1996—, bd. trustees 1995—, pres. found., 1992-95, Excellence award in Preoperative Nursing 1989), Ctr. for Study Dem. Instns. Author: Perioperative Nursing Practice, 1983, 3d edit., 1996; contbr. articles on operating room techniques to profl. jours. and textbooks; author, producer audio-visual presentations; author computer software. Home: 5 Mateo Dr Belvedere Tiburon CA 94920-1071 Office: 3020 Bridgeway Ste 399 Sausalito CA 94965-2839

GROB, GEORGE F., health science association administrator. M in Math., Georgetown U., 1969. Comptroller Office of Asst. Sec. Def.; ops. rsch. analyst Office of Asst. Sec. Navy for Fin. Mgmt.; dir. planning and policy coordination Office of Asst. Sec. Planning and Evaluation, USHHS, 1976-88; dep. insp. gen. evaluation and inspections USHHS, Washington, 1988—; chair Evaluation and Inspections Round Table adj. Pres.'s Coun. Integrity and Efficiency. Mem. Am. Evaluation Assn. (chair Evaluation Mgrs. and Suprs. Group). Home: 37823 Remington Dr Purcellville VA 22132 Office: USHHS Rm 5660 330 Independence Ave SW Washington DC 20201

GROB, GERALD N., historian, educator; b. N.Y.C., Apr. 25, 1931; s. Sidney and Sylvia G.; m. Lila Kronick, Dec. 25, 1954; children: Bradford S., Evan D., Seth A. B.S., CCNY, 1951; M.A., Columbia U., 1952; Ph.D., Northwestern U., 1958. Instr. history Clark U., Worcester, Mass., 1957-59; asst. prof. Clark U., 1959-61, assoc. prof., 1961-66, prof., 1966-69, chmn. dept. history, 1967-69; Henry E. Sigerist prof. of the history of medicine Rutgers U., New Brunswick, N.J., 1969—, chmn. dept., 1969-71, 73-74, 81-84; mem. fellowship adv. com. NEH, 1975-76; chmn. study sect. history of medicine NIH, 1975-77, 87-89, 93-97. Author: books including Ed Jarvis and the Medical World of 19th Century America, 1978, Workers and Utopia, 1961, The State and the Mentally Ill, 1966 (ann. prize Am. Assn. for State and Local History 1965), Mental Institutions in America, 1973, Mental Illness and America Society, 1875-1940, 1983, The Inner World of American Psychiatry, 1890-1940, 1985, From Asylum to Community, 1991, The Mad Among Us, 1994; contbr. articles to profl. jours. Elected to Inst. Medicine NAS. With C.E. U.S. Army, 1955-57. NIH grantee, 1960-65, 67-81, 84-92; NEH fellow, 1972-73, 89-90; Am. Council Learned Socs. fellow, 1976-77; Guggenheim fellow, 1980-81; fellow Davis Ctr., Princeton U., 1985-86. Mem. Am. Assn. for History of Medicine (coun. 1978-81, William H. Welch medal 1986, v.p. 1994-96, pres. 1996-98), Am. Antiquarian Soc., Orgn. Am. Historians. Jewish. Home: 821 Stare View Way Bridgewater NJ 08807-1824 Office: Rutgers U Inst Health Care Bldg 30 College Ave New Brunswick NJ 08901-1245

GROBOIS, BRIAN SAUL, physician; b. N.Y.C., July 12, 1957; s. Maurice and Judith Grobois; m. Susan Schnitzer, Dec. 16, 1989; children: Marshal Zohar, Julie Aviva. BA cum laude, U. Pa., 1978; MD, Sackler Sch. Medicine, Tel Aviv, Israel, 1983. Diplomate Am. Bd. Psychiatry and Neurology with qualifications in geriatric psychiatry and addiction psychiatry, Am. Bd. Adolescent Psychiatry. Psychiat. resident Albert Einstein Coll. Medicine/Montefiore Med. Ctr., Bronx, N.Y., 1983-87; session psychiatrist Our Lady of Mercy Med. Ctr., Bronx, N.Y., 1985-87; emergency rm.

psychiatrist North Ctrl. Bronx Hosp., 1985-87; vis. fellow Inst. Chronology/Sleep-Wake Disorders Ctr. N.Y. Hosp./Cornell Med. Ctr., White Plains, N.Y., 1986-87; fellow in pub. psychiatry N.Y. State Psychiatric Inst., Columbia Presbyn. Med. Ctr., N.Y.C., 1987-88; pvt. practice Montefiore Med. Ctr., Bronx, 1987-90; pvt. practice Queens, Bronx and Bklyn., 1987-90, N.Y.C., 1993—; visiting psychiatrist City of N.Y. Human Resources Adminstn., 1987-90; head emergency svcs. dept. psychiatry North Shore U. Hosp./Cornell U. Med. Coll., Manhasset, N.Y., 1990-92; chief div. acute psychiatry dept. vets. affairs FDR VA Hosp., Montrose, N.Y., 1992; chief community svcs. unit Mt. Sinai Med. Ctr., N.Y.C., 1992-93; clin. asst. prof. Mt. Sinai Sch. Medicine, N.Y.C., 1992—; assoc. chief psychiatry psychopharmacology & addiction svcs. Jewish Bd. Family and Children's Svcs., N.Y.C., 1993—; adj. asst. psychiatrist Inst. Chronobiology/Sleep-Wake Disorders Ctr. N.Y. Hosp.-Cornell Med. Ctr.-Westchester Divsn., 1986-87; neurology cons. North Ctrl. Bronx Hosp., 1986-87; psychiat. cons. New York County Health Svcs. Rev. Orgn., N.Y.C., 1985-90; chief divsn. acute psychiatry U.S. Dept. Vets. Affairs, Franklin Delano Roosevelt VA Hosp., Montrose, N.Y., 1992; rschr. in field. Mem. Am. Psychiat. Assn., Acad. Psychosomatic Medicine, Soc. for Liaison Psychiatry, Am. Acad. of Psychiatrists in Alcoholism and Addictions, Am. Assn. Geriatric Psychaitry, Am. Acad. Child and Adolescent Psychiatry, Am. Assn. Psychiat. Adminstrs., N.Y. Coun. on Child and Adolescent Psychiatry, Soc. for Sci. Study of Religion, Mesorah Soc., Alpha Epsilon Delta. Home: 26 Lovell Rd New Rochelle NY 10804-2115

GRODBERG, MARCUS GORDON, drug research consultant; b. Worcester, Mass., Jan. 27, 1923; s. Isaac and Rosalie (Hirsch) G.; m. Shirley Florence Merkle, Apr. 15, 1951; children: Joel David, Kim Gordon, Jeremy Daniel. AB, Clark U., Worcester, 1944; MS, U. Ill., 1948. Jr. research chemist Schenley Labs Inc., Lawrenceburg, Ind., 1944-47; research and devel. chemist Marine Products Co., Boston, 1948-50, Brewer and Co. Inc., Worcester, 1950-55; tech. dir. Gray Pharm. Co. Inc., Newton, Mass., 1955-58; dir. research and devel. Colgate Hoyt Labs., Canton, Mass., 1958-89; cons. Colgate, Sarasota, Fla., 1989—. Author: Fluorides; patentee in field. Asst. leader Cub Scouts, Newton, 1960-62, fund raiser United Fund, Newton, 1960-62. Mem. Internat. Assn. Dental Rsch., Fedn. Dentaire Internat., Am. Dental Assn., Nat. Osteoporosis Found. Jewish. Home: 4091 Hearthstone Dr Sarasota FL 34238-3201

GRODER, MARTIN GARY, psychiatrist; b. N.Y.C., Nov. 15, 1939; s. William Victor and Frances (Sturm) G.; m. Raquel Strauss, May 4, 1961 (div. Dec. 1984); children: Andrea Mia, Eric Bennett, Marc Alexander. BA, Columbia U., 1960, MD, 1964. Diplomate Am. Bd. Psychiatry and Neurology. Intern Maimonides Hosp., Bklyn., 1964-65; resident in psychiatry, Langley Porter Neuropsychiat. Inst. U. Calif., San Francisco, 1965-68; psychiatrist U.S. Bur. Prisons, 1968-72; warden-designate Fed. Corrections Inst., Butner, N.C., 1972-75; asst. clin. prof. Duke U., Durham, N.C., 1973—; practice medicine specializing in psychiatry Chapel Hill, N.C., 1975—; vis. prof. So. Ill. U., Carbondale, 1969-75. Author: Business Games, 1981. Served to lt. commdr. USPHS, 1968-70. Mem. Internat. Transactional Analysis Assn. (teaching mem.). Libertarian. Office: 104 S Estes Dr Ste 304 Chapel Hill NC 27514

GRODI, MICHAEL EDWARD, hospital administrator, respiratory therapist; b. Toledo, June 9, 1951; s. Leroy Edward and Laura Marie (Gibson) G.; m. Jacqueline Kay Schultz, May 12, 1973 (div. Apr. 1983); 1 child, Aaron; m. Yvette Marie Zimmerman, Apr. 14, 1984; 1 child, George. BS, U. Cin., 1975, MBA, 1986. Registered respiratory therapist. Respiratory therapist Deaconness Hosp., Cin., 1971-73, Children's Hosp. Med. Ctr., Cin., 1973, The Jewish Hosp., Cin., 1973-75; dir. respiratory therapy C.R. Holmes Hosp., Cin., 1975-78, asst. adminstr., 1978-85, sr. asst. adminstr., 1985-86; sr. asst. adminstr. U. Cin. Hosp., 1986-87, assoc. adminstr., 1987-93, adminstr., 1993—. Office: U Cin Hosp 234 Goodman St Cincinnati OH 45267-0701

GROEN, ELAINE SHARON, dietitian; b. Artesia, Calif., Feb. 28, 1944; d. Gradus Albert and Margaret (Toering) Vander Broek; m. Glenn Verlin Groen, Apr. 9, 1965 (div. 1975); 1 child, Melanie Marie. BA cum laude, Calif. State U., Long Beach, 1970. Registered dietitian. Intern in dietetics Loma Linda U. Med. Ctr., 1971; pvt. practice cons. dietitian Laguna Beach, Calif., 1971-72; dietitian, asst. food service mgr. South Coast Community Hosp., Laguna Beach, 1972-74; sales rep. Mead Johnson div. Bristol-Myers, Orange County, Calif., 1974-75; specialist nutrition sales Mead Johnson div. Bristol-Myers, So. Calif., 1975-77; sales trainer Mead Johnson div. Bristol-Myers, Evansville, Ind., 1977-79; regional cons. dietitian Mead Johnson div. Bristol-Myers, Western U.S.A., 1979-80; pvt. practice cons. nutritionist Walnut Creek, Calif., 1980—. Author: Healthy Cooking on the Run, 1983, 94, Fabulous Fiber Cookery, 1988; co-author newspaper column Successfully Slim, 1981-86, Nutri-Chat, 1982—; contbg. editor Contra Costa Woman mag., 1988-91. Recipient Crisco award, 1969. Mem. NAFE, AAUW (chmn. network women groups 1986-90), Am. Dietetic Assn., Calif. Dietetic Assn. (chmn. legis., info. and pub. policy, 3d party reimbursement task force cons. nutritionists 1984-86, nutrition svcs. payment sys. 1986-87, state expert on weight mgmt. 1993—), Bay Area Spkrs. Svc., Nat. Coun. Against Health Fraud, No. Calif. Tennis Assn. (nutritionist, sports sci. com. 1991—), Omicron Nu, Phi Kappa Phi. Democrat. Office: Relationship Counseling Ctr 33 Quail Ct Suite 201 Walnut Creek CA 94596

GROFF, DILLER BAER, surgeon; b. Washington, June 21, 1935; m. Katherine Painter; children: Giles, Pam, Paul. BA, Haverford Coll., 1957; MD, Duke U., 1961. Instr. in surgery George Washington U., Washington, 1962-67; asst. instr. surgery U. Pa., Phila., 1967-68; chief pediatric surgery Cath. Med. Ctr. Bklyn. and Queens Inc., Jamaica, N.Y., 1969-70; asst. prof. surgery N.J. Med. Sch., Newark, 1970-73, dir. divsn. pediatric surgery dept. surgery, 1970-78, assoc. prof. surgery, 1973, prof., 1973; prof., dir. divsn. pediatric surgery U. Louisville, 1978—; surgeon-in-chief Kosair Children's Hosp., Louisville, 1978—. Author: Handbook of Pediatric Surgical Emergencies, 1975, 81; contbr. chpts. to books. Recipient Continuing Edn. award AMA, 1982-85. Fellow ACS; mem. Am. Pediatric Surg. Assn. (chair membership 1980-83), Am. Trauma Soc., Southeastern Surg. Soc., Am. Acad. Pediatrics (surg. sect., chair publs. 1992-93), Rotary. Office: U Pediatric Surgery Assocs 233 E Gray St Ste 210 Louisville KY 40202

GROGAN, DENNIS PAUL, pediatric orthopaedic surgeon; b. Greenfield, Mass., Apr. 22, 1950; s. Paul George and Ruth Ann (Smith) G.; children: Jennifer, Kathryn, Lara, Sean. BS, Georgetown U., 1972, MD, 1976. Diplomate Am. Bd. Orthopaedic Surgeons. Assoc. med. dir. Carrie Tingley Hosp., Albuquerque, 1982-84; asst. chief of staff Shriners Hosp., Tampa, Fla., 1984-94, chief of staff, 1995—; assoc. prof.. U. South Fla., Tampa, 1988—. Author chpts. in books. Chmn. Georgetown U. Alumni Admissions Program, Tampa, 1990—. Fellow Am. Acad. Orthop. Surgeons; mem. Pediat. Orthop. Soc. N.Am., Scoliosis Rsch. Soc., Acad. Orthop. Soc., Am. Orthop. Foot and Ankle Soc., Hillsborough County Med. Assn. (exec. com. 1995—). Office: Shriners Hospital 12502 N Pine Dr Tampa FL 33612

GROGAN, JAMES TILLMAN, JR., dentist; b. Atlanta, Sept. 30, 1938; s. James Tillman and Allene (Baker) G.; m. Lynn Eldridge (dec. Oct. 1992), Mar. 23, 1963; children: James Tillman III, Dawn Michelle. BA, U. North Tex., 1961; DDS, Baylor U., Dallas, 1965; cert. in theology, Criswell Bible Inst., Dallas, 1974; cert. in orthodontics, So. Meth. U., 1981. Pvt. practice, Arlington, Tex., 1968-84, Dallas, 1984—. Capt. Dental Corps, U.S. Army, 1965-68. Fellow Acad. Gen. Dentistry, Acad. Dentistry Internat.; mem. ADA, Masons. Republican. Presbyterian. Home: 14781 Buckingham Ct Dallas TX 75240-7562 Office: Beedent Family Dental Ctr 4535 N Central Expy Dallas TX 75205-4211

GROGAN, WENDELL ARTHUR, neurologist, neurology educator; b. Columbia, Mo., Sept. 18, 1955; s. Clarence O. and C. Alice (West) G.; m. Sandra M. Shaner, June 17, 1978; children: Steven A., Byron C. BS in Med. Sci., Northwestern U., 1978, MD, 1980. Diplomate Am. Bd. Neurology; cert. in sleep disorders. Neurologist David Grant Med. Ctr., Travis AFB, Calif., 1984-87; neurologist, clin. instr. Jefferson Med. Coll., Phila., 1987-93; neurologist, clin. neurophysiologist Crozer Med. Ctr., Sleep Disorders Ctr., Upland, Pa., 1993—; dir. quality assurance Meth. Hosp., Phila., 1991-93. Asst. scoutmaster Boy Scouts of Am., Rose Valley, Pa., 1994—; deacon, moderator, Presbyn. Ch. U.S., 1993-96, elder, 1996—. Presbyterian. Office: Sleep Disorders ctr CCMC 1 Medical Ctr Blvd Upland PA 19103

GROLLI, FRANK THOMAS, retired pharmacist; b. Bklyn., July 25, 1933; s. Frank and Theresa D. G.; mem. Maria T. Cerbone, Mar. 30, 1974. BS in Pharmacy, Bklyn. Coll. Pharmacy, 1956. Registered pharmacist Ferro's Pharmacy, Bklyn., 1959-61; mgr., owner Associated Drugs, N.Y.C., 1961-66; mgr., pharmacist Frank's Pharmacy, Staten Island, 1966-76; asst. mgr., pharmacist Savon SuperX, Staten Island, 1976-84, asst. mgr., pharmacy supr., 1984-88, pharmacy coord., 1988-94; northeast region pharmacy coord. H.S.I., Rutherford, N.J., 1994; pharmacy supr. Revco D.S., Carteret, N.J., 1994-95, ret., 1995. Col. Med. Svc. Corps, 1961-86. Decorated Nat. Def. Svc. medal. Army Reserve Comp. Achievement medal, Meritorous Svc. medal. Mem. APHA, Pharm. Soc. of N.Y., N.Y.C. Pharm. Soc., Italian Pharm. Soc., Reserve Officers Assn., Assn. of Mil. Surgeons.

GROMAN, NEAL BENJAMIN, microbiology educator; b. Chisholm, Minn., May 21, 1921; s. Raphael Simon and Jenny Rebecca (Levine) G.; m. Elaine Ruth Spigle, Nov. 19, 1943; children: Jo Ann Tamarin, Nancy Sheffer, Richard, Ellen Groman Fair. BS, U. Chgo., 1947, PhD, 1950. Instr. U. Wash., Seattle, 1950-53, asst. prof., 1953-58, assoc. prof., 1958-63, prof. microbiology, 1963-89, prof. emeritus, 1989—, dir. office of biol. edn., 1971-75, acting chmn. dept. microbiology, 1981-82. Contbr. articles to profl. pubs. Served with AUS, 1942-46. John and Mary Markle Found. scholar, 1955-60; John Simon Guggenheim fellow, 1958-59; USPHS fellow, 1966-67. Fellow Am. Acad. Microbiology; mem. Am. Soc. Microbiology (chmn. virology sect. 1963-64), Acad. Am. Poets, Sigma Xi. Home: 4805 NE 40th St Seattle WA 98105-5216 Office: U Wash Dept Microbiology Seattle WA 98195

GROMKE, GEORGE DIETER, orthopedic surgeon; b. Chgo., Sept. 20, 1957; s. George B. and Gertrud Angela (Lischka) G.; m. JoAnne Virgilio, May 13, 1989; children: Megan, Mikaela, George. BS in Chemistry and Biochemistry, U. Ill., 1979; DO, Chgo. Coll. Osteopathy, 1985. Diplomate Nat. Bd. Oste. Medicine. Intern Grandview Hosp., Dayton, Ohio, 1985-86; resident Grandview Hosp., Dayton, 1987-91; reconstructive surgery fellow Tampa (Fla.) Gen. Hosp., 1991-92; pvt. practice in orthopedic surgery Grand Junction, Colo., 1992—; mem. planning com. spring clinics program St. Mary's Hosp., Grand Junction, 1994-95. Mem. Am. Osteo. Assn., Am. Osteo. Acad. of Orthopaedics, Colo. Soc. Osteo. Medicine, Mesa County Med. Soc., Sigma Sigma Phi. Roman Catholic. Office: Western Ortho & Sports Medicine 2020 N 12th St Grand Junction CO 81501

GRONBACH, ROBERT CHARLES, hospital system executive; b. Bklyn., May 18, 1928; s. Charles Herman and Martha (Lenzing) G.; m. Cynthia Kathleen Grant; 1 child, Garth Grant. BS, CCNY, 1951, MA, 1952. Personnel asst. IBM, N.Y.C., 1951-52; personnel rep. TWA, Queens, N.Y., 1955-58; personnel dir. Hartford (Conn.) Hosp., 1958-68, asst. hosp. dir. and dir. employee relations, 1969-81, v.p., employee relations, 1982-86; v.p. human resources Conn. Health Sys. and Hartford Hosp., 1987-93, 1994-96; adj. prof. and assoc. curriculum chmn. Hartford Grad. Ctr., 1976—; adj. lectr. U. Conn. Sch. Bus., Hartford, 1973-76. Contbr. articles to profl. jours. Bd. dirs., chmn. personnel com. Hartford YMCA, Immediate Med. Care Ctr., Inc., H.H. Real Estate Corp., H.H. Mgmt. Svcs. Corp. Mem. Conn. Hosp. Assn. (bd. dirs.), Am. Hosp. Assn., Am. Soc. Healthcare Human Resource Execs. (bd. dirs. 1965-67, pres. 1967), Med. Ctr. Employee Relations Assn. (pres. 1968-71). Home: 48 Stonepost Rd Glastonbury CT 06033-4139

GROND, STEFAN, anaesthesist; b. Cologne, Germany, Nov. 23, 1959; s. Adalbert and Sabine (Wehlack) G. MD, U. Cologne, 1985. Cert. anaestesist, 1990. Spl. tng. U. Cologne, Germany, 1985-90; rsch. fellow U. Cologne, 1990-94, anaestesist, 1995—. Author: Therapiekompendium Tumorschmerz, 1992. Recipient Forderpreis fur Schmerzforschung, 1993. Mem. Internat. Assn. for Study of Pain, European Acad. Anaesthesiology. Office: Klinik fur Anasthesiology, Joseph Stelzmann Str 9, 50924 Cologne Germany

GRONER, PAT NEFF, health care executive; b. Dallas, Dec. 21, 1920; s. Frank Shelby and Laura (Wyatt) G.; m. Louise Mary Rugg, May 5, 1944; children: Josephine Louise, Frank Shelby III. Student, East Tex. Bapt. U., LL.D. (hon.), 1975; A.B., Baylor U., 1941; LL.D. (hon.), U. West Fla., 1984. Airline pilot, 1946-47; asst. adminstr. Mary Fletcher Hosp., Burlington, Vt., 1947-48; adminstr. Barre (Vt.) City Hosp., 1948-50; chief exec. officer Baptist Hosp., Pensacola, Fla., 1950-80; pres. Bapt. Health Care, 1980-83, pres. emeritus, 1984—; pres. Hosp. Research and Devel. Inst., 1964-85; v.p., treas. Multihosp. Mut. Ins. Ltd., 1975-84; v.p., mem. exec. com. Vol. Hosps. of Am., 1977-84, sr. cons., 1984-88; mem. Fed. Hosp. Coun. HEW, 1972-76; mem. Coun. on Grad. Med. Edn. HHS, 1986-87. Exec. com. Blue Cross-Blue Shield Fla., 1952-81; mem. State Bd. Regents, 1987-93; mem., bd. dirs, numerous community svc. orgns.; bd. trustees Fla. TaxWatch, Inc., 1994—. With USMC, 1941-45. Recipient Good Govt. award Pensacola Jaycees, 1960, George Washington medal Freedom Found., 1961, Liberty Bell award Soc. Bar 1st Jud. Circuit Fla., 1970, award of merit Fla. Hosp. Assn., 1971, Disting. Service award Southeastern Hosp. Conf., 1972; named Citizen of Yr. Civitan, 1971-72, Disting. Alumnus award East Tex. Bapt. Univ., 1974, award for disting. community service United Way, 1980, Kiwanis Man of Year, 1980, Gold Medal award Am. Coll. Healthcare Execs., 1981, BIP Pioneer award Pensacola News-Jour. and Greater Pensacola C. of C. 1984. Fellow Am. Coll. Hosp. Adminstrs. (bd. regents 1966-70); mem. Am. Hosp. Assn. (trustee 1967-70, 82-85), Fla. Hosp. Assn. (pres. 1954-55), Southeastern Hosp. Conf. (pres. 1958-59). Club: Rotary (pres. 1966-67, Paul Harris fellow). Home: 2200 Banquos Trl Pensacola FL 32503-5804 Office: PO Box 17500 Pensacola FL 32522-7500

GRONSTEDT, GARY JOE, physician; b. Sedalia, Mo., Dec. 2, 1964; s. Joseph Francis and Alice Marie (Diefendorf) G. BA, U. Mo., 1987; DO, U. Health Scis., Kansas City, Mo., 1991. Intern Still Regional Med. Ctr., Jefferson City, Mo., 1992-93; resident physician Mental Health Inst., Cherokee, Iowa, 1993—. Mem. Am. Osteo. Assn., Am. Psychiat. Assn., Iowa Psychiat. Assn. Home: 900 65th St #71 Windsor Heights IA 50312

GROSE, CHARLES FREDERICK, pediatrician, infectious disease specialist; b. Faribault, Minn., Apr. 15, 1942; s. Frederick G. and Marie A. (Swelland) G. BA, Beloit Coll., 1963; MD, U. Chgo., 1967. Bd. cert. in pediatric infectious disease. Resident Albert Einstein Coll. Medicine, Bronx, N.Y., 1967-68, fellow, 1970-71; fellow U. Calif., San Francisco, 1975-76; asst. prof. Health Sci. Ctr. U. Tex., San Antonio, 1976-84; prof. pediatrics U. Iowa Hosp., Iowa City, 1985—; cons. NIH, Bethesda, Md., 1988—. Mem. editorial bd. Pediatric Infectious Disease Jour., 1991—, Virology Jour.; contbr. articles to profl. and sci. jours. Capt. U.S. Army Med. Corps., Vietnam, 1968-70. Grantee NIH, 1978—. Fellow Infectious Disease Soc. Am., Pediatric Infectious Disease Soc., Am. Acad. Pediatrics, Am. Soc. Virology. Office: U Iowa Hosp Pediatrics 200 Hawkins Dr Iowa City IA 52242-1009

GROSFELD, JAY LAZAR, pediatric surgeon, educator; b. N.Y.C., May 30, 1935; m. Margie Faulkner; children: Lisa, Denise, Janice, Jeffrey, Mark. A.B. cum laude, NYU, 1957, M.D., 1961. Diplomate: Am. Bd. Surgery (spl. qualification Pediatric Surgery). Intern in gen. surgery dept. surgery Bellevue and Univ Hosps. NYU, N.Y.C., 1961-62; resident in gen. surgery Bellevue and Univ. Hosps. NYU, N.Y.C., 1962-66; resident in pediatric surgery Ohio State U. Coll. Medicine, Children's Hosp., 1968-70 clin. instr. surgery NYU Sch. Medicine, N.Y.C., 1965-66, asst. prof. surgery and pediatrics, 1970-72; instr. surgery Ohio State U. Coll. Medicine, 1968-70; prof., dir. pediatric surgery Ind. U. Sch. Medicine, Indpls., 1972—, Lafayette F. Page prof., 1981—, chmn. Dept. Surgery, 1985—; surgeon-in-chief James Whitcomb Riley Hosp. Children. Author 4 textbooks, over 460 papers, reports, book chpts., articles for med. jours.; editor-in-chief Jour. Pediat. Surgery; editor Seminars in Pediat. Surgery. Served to capt. M.C. U.S. Army, 1966-68. Decorated Commendation medal; recipient numerous fellowships, grants, teaching awards. Fellow ACS (bd. govs. 1985-91), Am. Acad. Pediats. (exec. com. surg. sect. 1989-95, sec. surg. sect., chmn. surg. sect. 1994-95); mem. AMA, Assn. Acad. Surgery, N.Y. Cancer Soc., Am. Pediat. Surg. Assn. (bd. govs., pres.-elect, pres. 1994-95), Am. Surg. Assn., Soc. Univ. Surgeons, Marion County Med. Soc., Ind. State Med. Assn., Pediat. Surgery Biology Club, Am. Trauma Soc., Soc. Surgery Alimentary Tract, Ctrl. Surg. Assn. (sec. 1987—, pres.-elect 1988, pres. 1990), Brit. Assn. Pediat. Surgeons (exec. coun. 1990-93), Soc. Surg. Oncology, Western Surg. Assn., Internat. Soc. Surgery, Am. Bd. Surgery (bd. dirs. 1989—, vice chair 1995, chmn.-elect, chmn. 1996-97), World Fedn. Assn. of Pediat. Surgeons (v.p.), Am. Bd. Med. Specialities, Halsted Soc. (v.p. 1995-96, pres. 1996-97), Phi Beta Kappa./. Office: J W Riley Childrens Hosp 702 Barnhill Dr Indianapolis IN 46202-5128

GROSS, IAN, academic pediatrician, neonatologist; b. Pretoria, Republic of South Africa, Oct. 15, 1943; came to U.S., 1971; s. Kenneth and Gladys Bakst (Cooper) G.; m. Melanie Belman, Dec. 3, 1967; children: David Anthony, Adam Charles. BS, U. Witwatersrand, Johannesburg, Republic of South Africa, 1963, MBBCh, 1967. Diplomate Am. Bd. Pediatrics, Am. Bd. Neonatal-Perinatal Medicine. Rotating intern Johannesburg Gen. Hosp., 1968; pediatric resident U. Witwatersrand Hosps., Johannesburg, 1970-71, Children's Hosp. Harvard Med. Sch., Boston, 1971-72; postdoctoral fellow in pediatrics Harvard Med. Sch., Boston, 1972-73, Yale U., New Haven, Conn., 1973-74; asst. prof. Yale U. Sch. Medicine, New Haven, 1974-78, assoc. prof., 1978-85, prof., 1985—; dir. newborn spl. care unit Yale-New Haven Hosp., 1982—; mem. study sect. NIH, Bethesda, Md., 1981-85; mem. adv. bd. Mead Johnson Symposia, Evansville, Ind., 1985-94, Hood Found., Boston, 1988-94. Contbr. chpts. to books, numerous articles to profl. jours. Named Most Disting. Med. Grad. U. Witwatersrand, Johannesburg, 1967; James Hudson Brown fellow, Yale U., 1973; rsch. grantee NIH and Am. Heart Assn. Fellow Am. Acad. Pediatrics; mem. Soc. Pediatric Rsch., Am. Physiol. Soc., Am. Thoracic Soc., Am. Pediatric Soc. Office: Yale Sch Medicine 333 Cedar St New Haven CT 06510-3206

GROSS, JEROME, physician, biologist, educator; b. N.Y.C., Feb. 25, 1917; married 1947; 3 children. B.S., MIT, 1939; M.D., NYU, 1943. Rsch. fellow in medicine Harvard U. Med. Sch., 1948-50, rsch. assoc., 1950-54, assoc., 1954-57, asst. prof., 1957—, assoc. prof., to 1969, prof. medicine, 1969-87, prof. medicine emeritus, 1987; clin. and rsch. fellow Mass. Gen. Hosp., Boston, 1948-51, assoc. biologist, 1951-66, biologist, 1966—; acting assoc. dir. Cutaneous Biology Rsch. Ctr., Dept. Dermatology Mass. Gen. Hosp, 1989-91; sr. investigator cutaneous Biology Research Ctr. Dept. Dermatology Mass. Gen, Hisp., 1992—; rsch. assoc. MIT, 1946-55; mem. subcom. skeletal system NRC, 1955-62; mem. sci. adv. com. Helen Hay Whitney Found., 1956-91; established investigator Am. Heart Assn., 1956-61; mem. adv. panel molecular biology NSF, 1959-62; chmn. Bd. Sci. Counselors Nat. Inst. Dental Rsch., 1963-66; mem. molecular biology study sect. NIH, 1966-70, mem. breast cancer task force, 1975-78; bd. dirs. Med. Found., Inc., 1974-80. Adv. editor. Jour. Exptl. Medicine, 1963; cons. editor Devel. Biology, 1965. Trustee, mem. sic. adv. com. Helen Hay Whitney Found., 1985—; bd. dirs. sci. affairs com. W. Alton Jones Sci. Ctr., 1986—. Recipient CIBA award, 1959, Kappa Delta award Am. Acad. Orthopedic Surgery, 1965, Klemperer award N.Y. Acad. Medicine, 1988. Mem. Nat. Acad. Sci., Am. Acad. Arts and Sci., Am. Soc. Cell Biology, Am. Soc. Biol. Chemistry, Inst. Medicine, Histochem. Soc. (sec. 1956-60). Office: Mass Gen Hosp Rm 3032 Cutaneous Rschr Ctr 13th St # 149 Charlestown MA 02129-2000*

GROSS, JOE NEIL, social services administrator, social worker; b. Norman, Okla., Feb. 17, 1951; s. Virlus Leon and Annabell (Hull) G. BS, Okla. State U., 1973; MSW, U. Okla., 1975; EdD, U. Sarasota, 1986. Diplomate Am. Bd. Examiners in Clin. Social Work; cert. Nat. Bd. Cert. Counselors. Clin. social worker Childrens Guidance Ctr., Norman, 1973-74, VA Hosp., Oklahoma City, 1974-75; exec. dir., therapist Hominy (Okla.) Health Svcs., Inc., 1975—; cons. United Head Start Programs, Pawnee, Okla., 1984—; mem. Okla. Mental Health Planning and Coordination Bd., 1984-89. Author: Self-Image Development, 1986; weekly columnist Mental Health, 1980—. Bd. dirs. Okla. Health and Welfare Assn., Oklahoma City, 1980-84; mem. Osage County Coun. Social Agys., Pawhucka, Okla., 1990. MMemn. NASW (register clin. social workers), Acad. Cert. Social Workers, Assn. Mental Health Adminstrs. Home: 3745 E 46th St Tulsa OK 74135-1906 Office: Hominy Health Svcs Inc 3745 E 46th St Tulsa OK 74135-1906

GROSS, JOSEPH WALLACE, hospital administrator; b. Berwyn, Ill., June 15, 1945; married. B, Creighton U., 1968; M, U. Mo. Adminstrv. extern U. Hosp.-U. Nebr., Omaha, 1968; adminstrv. asst. Boone Hosp. Ctr., Columbia, Mo., 1971; exec. v.p. adminstrv. ops. Wausau (Wis.) Hosp. Ctr., 1971-78; pres. Luther Hosp., Eau Claire, Wis., 1978-86; pres., chief exec. officer St. Elizabeth Med. Ctr., Covington, Ky., 1986—. Mem. Ky. Hosp. Assn. (pres. 1990—). Office: St Elizabeth Med Ctr-North 401 E 20th St Covington KY 41014-1583*

GROSS, KENNETH BRUCE, physician, neurologist, educator; b. Bklyn., June 19, 1952; s. Edward I. and Irene (Kanelstein) G.; m. Laurie Ann Zeitlin, July 3, 1978; children: Jason, Amanda. BA, Colgate U., 1974; MD, SUNY, Stony Brook, 1980. Diplomate Am. Bd. Internal Medicine, Am. Bd. Neurology. Resident in internal medicine Montefiore Hosp., Bronx, N.Y., 1980-83; resident in neurology Albert Einstein Coll. Medicine/Montefiore Hosp., 1983-86; pvt. practice neurology Long Island and Queens, N.Y., 1986-95; dir. edn., lectr. Interactive Medicine Inst., Valley Stream, N.Y., 1995—; founder med. info. libr. Fusion Clin. Multimedia, Inc., 1995. Contbr. articles to profl. jours. Mem. Am. Acad. Neurology, Am. Soc. Internal Medicine, Am. Sleep Disorders Assn., Am. Assn. for Study of Headache, Am. Med. Writers Assn., Nat. Assn. Physician Broadcasters.

GROSS, LILLIAN, psychiatrist; b. N.Y.C., Aug. 18, 1932; d. Herman and Sarah (Widelitz) Gross. BA, Barnard Coll., 1953; postgrad. U. Lausanne (Switzerland), 1954-56; MD, Duke U., 1959. Diplomate Bd. Pediatrics, Am. Bd. Psychiatry and Neurology, Am. Bd. Child Psychiatry; m. Harold Ratner, Feb. 4, 1961; children: Sanford Miles, Marcia Ellen. Intern Kings County Hosp., Bklyn., 1959-60, resident, 1967-70, fellow in child psychiatry, 1969-70, psychiatrist devel. evaluation clinic, 1970-72; resident Jewish Hosp. Bklyn., 1960-62, fellow in pediatric psychiatry, 1962-63; physician in charge pediatric psychiat. clinic Greenpoint (N.Y.) Hosp., 1964-67; pvt. practice psychiatry, Great Neck, N.Y., 1970—; clin. instr. psychiatry Downstate Med. Ctr., Bklyn., 1970-74, clin. asst. prof., 1974—; lectr. in psychiatry Columbia U., 1974—; psychiat. cons. N.Y.C. Bd. Edn., 1972-75, Queens Children's Hosp., 1975—; mem. med. bd. Camp Sussex (N.J.), 1963—, Saras Ctr., Great Neck, N.Y., 1977—. Fellow Am. Acad. Pediatrics, Am. Acad. Psychiatry, Am. Acad. Child Psychiatry, Am. Soc. Clin. and Experiential Hypnosis, N.Y. Soc. Clinical Hypnosis (past pres.); mem. AMA, Am. Psychiat. Assn., Nassau Psychiat. Assn., Bklyn. Psychiat. Assn., Bklyn. Pediatric Soc. (sr. mem.), Nassau Pediatric Socs., Soc. Adolescent Psychiatry, N.Y. Coun. Child Psychiatry, Soc. Clin. and Exptl. Hypnosis, Am. Med. Women's Assn. (Nassau, pres. 1985-86, 95—), N.Y., Kings County med. socs., N.Y. Soc. Clin. Hypnosis (past pres.), Internat. Soc. for Study of Multiple Personality and Dissociation (founder, pres. L.I. component study group). Home and Office: 55 Blue Bird Dr Great Neck NY 11023-1001

GROSS, LUDWIK, physician; b. Cracow, Poland, Sept. 11, 1904; came to U.S., 1940, naturalized, 1943; s. Adolf and Augusta (Alexander) G.; m. Dorothy L. Nelson, Oct. 7, 1943; 1 dau., Augusta H. MD, Jagiellon U., Cracow, 1929; Prix Chevillon, Acad. Medicine, Paris, 1937; DSc with honors, Mt. Sinai Sch. Medicine, CUNY, 1983. Diplomate: Am. Bd. Internal Medicine. Intern and resident St. Lazar Gen. Hosp., Cracow, 1929-32; part time research exptl. cancer Pasteur Inst., Paris; postgrad. clin. tng. Salpetriere, U. Paris, 1932-39; cancer research Christ Hosp., Cin., 1941-43; chief cancer research VA Med Center, Bronx, 1946—; research prof. dept. medicine Mt. Sinai Sch. Medicine, N.Y.C., 1971-73, emeritus prof., 1973—; cons. Sloan Kettering Inst., Meml. Center, N.Y.C., 1955-57, assoc. scientist, 1957-60; Distinguished Leukemia lectr. U. So. Ala., 1976; 17th G.H.A. Clowes Meml. lectr., 1977. Author: Oncogenic Viruses, 1961, 3d edit., 1983; author numerous papers on cancer and leukemia in profl. jours. Served from capt. to maj. M.C. AUS, 1943-46. Decorated chevalier Legion of Honor France; recipient Robert R. De Villiers award for research on leukemia Leukemia Soc. N.Y., 1953, Walker prize Royal Coll. Surgeons Eng., 1962, Pasteur Silver medal Pasteur Inst., 1962, Lucy Wortham James award James Ewing Soc., 1962, WHO UN prize, 1962, The Bertner Found. award, 1963, Albert Einstein Centennial medal, 1965, Albion O. Bernstein award Med. Soc. N.Y. State, 1971, Spl. Virus Cancer Program award Nat. Cancer Inst., 1972, William S. Middleton award VA, 1973, Albert Lasker Basic Med.

Research award, 1974, Founders award Cancer Research Inst., 1975; prin. Paul Ehrlich-Ludwig Darmstaedter prize, 1978; Prix Griffuel Paris, 1978; Exceptional Service award VA, 1979; VA Disting. physician, 1977-81; Katherine Berken Judd award Meml. Sloan-Kettering Cancer Ctr., 1985; Alfred Jurzykowski Found. award, 1985. Fellow A.C.P., AAAS, Internat. Soc. of Hematology, N.Y. Acad. Scis.; mem. Am. Soc. Hematology, AMA, Nat. Acad. Scis., Am. Assn. Cancer Research (dir. 1973-76), Assn. Mil. Surgeons U.S., Soc. of Exptl. Biology and Medicine, Bronx County, N.Y. State med. socs. Office: VA Med Ctr 130 W Kingsbridge Rd Bronx NY 10468-3992

GROSS, MARY ELIZABETH, pharmacy manager, educator; b. Chgo., Nov. 20, 1957; d. Henry Thomas and Patricia (Kloska) G. BS in Pharmacy, Drake U., 1980; PharmD, U. Utah, 1982. Lic. pharmacist; cert. in gerontology. Resident in clin. pharmacy U. Utah, Salt Lake City, 1980-82; asst. prof. clin. pharmacy Sch. Pharmacy W.Va. U., Charleston, 1982-84, asst. prof. pharmacology Sch. Medicine, 1982-84; asst. prof. clin. pharmacy, clin. pharmacist Drake U. Coll. Pharmacy & Health Scis./Mercy Hosp. Med. Ctr., Des Moines, 1984-89, assoc. prof. clin. pharmacy, clin. pharmacist, 1989-93; mgr. pharmacy, assoc. prof. clin. pharmacy Mercy Hosp. and Drake U., Des Moines, 1993—; cons. pharmacist Madrid (Iowa) Home for the Aging, 1989-92; faculty assoc. W.Va. U. Gerontology Ctr., Morgantown, 1983; cons. pharmacist Iowa long-term care coordinating unit Case Mgmt. Project for the Frail Elderly, Crossroads of Iowa, 1991—. Author, editor monograph; contbr. articles to profl. jours. Mem. task force Dept. Elder Affairs, Des Moines, 1989—; mem. Health Older People Adv. Coun., Des Moines, 1985-86; chmn. Cancer Pain Relief Initiative, 1995—. Recipient State of Iowa Gov.'s Vol. award, 1991, Merck Clin. Pharmacy award U. Utah, 1982; grantee in field. Mem. Am. Assn. Colls. Pharamcy (profl. affairs com. 1992-93), Iowa Soc. Hosp. Pharmacists (chmn. nominations com. 1990-91, computer com. 1988-89, pres. 1989-90, key mem. 1990-94, Hosp. Pharmacist of Yr. award 1988), ASCP (edn. affairs coun. 1994-95, nat. LTC task force on pharmacy stds. 1996—), Am. Soc. Hosp. Pharmacists (commn. on therapeutics 1995—). Office: Mercy Hosp Med Ctr Pharmacy Dept Des Moines IA 50314

GROSS, PAUL, pathologist, educator; b. Berlin, June 8, 1902; s. Martin and Julia (Baumgarten) G.; m. Dorothy J. Mulac, Aug. 4, 1930; children: Julianne Gross Sauvageot, Paul James, Peter Martin, John Edwin. A.B., Western Res. U., 1924, M.D., 1927, M.A. (Crile research fellow pathology 1928-29), 1929. Intern St. Vincent's Charity Hosp., Cleve., 1927-28; resident pathology Cleve. City Hosp., 1929-31; pathologist St. Vincent's Charity Hosp., 1931-35; vol. asst. to Prof. Erdheim, Vienna, Austria, 1931-32; pathologist West Pa. Hosp., Pitts., 1935-44, St. Joseph's Hosp., Pitts., 1944-54; dir. research lab. Indsl. Health Found., Mellon Inst., also sr. fellow Inst., 1948-68, adv. fellow, 1968—; adj. prof. pathology indsl. diseases Grad. Sch. Pub. Health. U. Pitts., 1960-68; research prof. Grad. Sch. Pub. Health, U. Pitts., 1968-71, adj. prof., 1971-76; disting. research prof. pathology Med. U. S.C., 1971-76, adj. prof., 1976—. Author: (with T.F. Hatch) Pulmonary Deposition and Retention of Inhaled Aerosols, 1964, (with D.C. Braun) Toxic and Biomedical Effects of Fibers with Special Reference to Asbestos, Man-Made Vitreous Fibers and Organic Fibers, 1983; also numerous articles. Recipient Adolph G. Kammer merit in authorship award Indsl. Med. Assn., 1967. Fellow ACP; mem. Am. Coll. Chest Physicians, Indsl. Med. Assn., Coll. Am. Pathologists, Am. Thoracic Soc., Am. Indsl. Hygiene Assn. (hon.), Am. Assn. Pathologists and Bacteriologists, Internat. Acad. Pathology, Am. Soc. Clin. Pathologists, AMA, Am. Soc. Exptl. Pathology. Home: 28 Maui Cir Naples FL 33962-3724

GROSS, PETER ALAN, epidemiologist, researcher; b. Newark, Nov. 18, 1938; s. Meyer P. and Nathalie (Bass) Denburg) G.; m. Regina Teri Gittlin, May 30, 1964; children: Deborah Karen, Michael Philip, Daniel Brian. BA cum laude, Amherst Coll., 1960; MD, Yale U., 1964. Diplomate Am. Bd. Internal Medicine. Intern Yale-New Haven Hosp., 1964-65, jr. resident, 1965-66; sr. resident Peter Bent Brigham Hosp., Boston, 1968-69; research and edn. assoc. Va Hosp., West Haven, Conn., 1971-73, acting chief infectious disease sect., 1972-73; chief infectious disease sect. VA Hosp., West Haven, Conn., 1973-74, Hackensack (N.J.) U. Med. Ctr., 1974—; chmn. dept. medicine Hackensack (N.J.) Med. Ctr., 1980—, chmn. med. bd., 1986; prof. medicine N.J. Med. Sch., Newark, 1981—, vice chmn. dept. medicine, 1994—; assoc. clin. prof. medicine Columbia U. Coll. Physicians and Surgeons, N.Y.C., 1971-81, asst. clin. prof., 1974-77; asst. prof. medicine Yale U. Shc. Medicine, New Haven, 1971-74; ad hoc reviewer rsch. grants NIH, Nat. Inst. Allergy and Infectious Diseases; investigator Ctr. for Biologic Evaluation and Rsch. FDA, 1974—; mem. clin. indicators task force Joint Commn. on Accreditation of Healthcare Orgns., 1987-89. Author: Gram Strain Recognition, 1975, 2d edit., 1980, Managing Your Health, 1991; assoc. editor: Clinical Performance and Quality Health Care; mem. editorial bd. Jour. Clin. Microbiology, 1980—, Infection Control, 1980-90. Served to lt. comdr. USPHS, CDC, 1966-68. NIH fellow Yale U., 1969-71. Fellow Infectious Diseases Soc. Am. (clin. affairs com., chair practice guidelines com.); mem. AAAS, ACP (task force on adult immunization), Am. Acad. Microbiology, Am. Soc. Virology, Am. Soc. Microbiology, Soc. Healthcare Epidemiologists Am. (councillor 1986-88, v.p. 1992, pres.-elect 1993, pres. 1994), Assn. Profs. Medicine. Republican. Jewish. Office: Hackensack U Med Ctr Dept Infectious Disease Hackensack NJ 07601

GROSS, RAINER, pharmacologist, physiology educator; b. Mosbach, Germany, Jan. 22, 1943; s. Joseph and Pia Maria Barbara (Zeitler) G.; m. Christiane Koehler, June 16, 1976; children: Michael Andreas, Barbara Christina. Diploma in engring., Tech. U. Karlsruhe, Germany, 1966; Dr. med., U. Heidelberg, Germany, 1972; habilitatus, U. Heidelberg, Fed. Republic Germany, 1979. Research fellow U. Heidelberg, 1967-79, lectr. in physiology, 1979—; head cardiovascular pharmacology dept. Inst. Pharmacology, Bayer A.G., Wuppertal, Germany, 1981—. Bd. editors Archives Internat. Pharmacodynamie et Pharmacotherapie; contbr. articles to research jours. Mem. German Physiol. Soc., Deutsche Gesellschaft für Herz-U., Kreislaufforschung, Deutsche Gesellschaft für Arterioskleroseforschung, Medizinisch Naturwissenschaftliche Gesellschaft Wuppertal. Office: Bayer AG, Friedrich Ebert Str 217, D-42096 Wuppertal Germany

GROSS, RUTH TAUBENHAUS, physician; b. Bryan, Tex., June 24, 1920; d. Jacob and Esther (Hirshenson) Taubenhaus; m. Reuben H. Gross, Jr., Aug. 22, 1942; (div. June 1952); 1 son, Gary E. BA, Barnard Coll., 1941; MD, Columbi U., 1944. Intern, Charity Hosp., New Orleans, 1944; resident in pediatrics Tulane U., New Orleans, 1945, Columbia U., N.Y.C., 1946, 47; instr. Radcliffe Infirmary, Oxford, Eng., 1949-50; instr. pediatrics Stanford (Calif.) U., 1950-53, asst. prof., 1953-56, assoc. prof., 1956-60, prof., 1973-92, prof. emerita, 1992; acting exec. pediatrics, 1957-59, assoc. dean student affairs, 1973-75, dir. div. gen. and ambulatory pediatrics, 1975-85, dir. Stanford-Children's Ambulatory Care Ctr., 1980-85, nat. study dir. Infant Health and Devel. Program, 1983-92; assoc. prof. pediatrics, co-dir. div. human genetics Albert Einstein Coll. Medicine, Yeshiva U., N.Y.C., 1960-64, prof. pediatrics, 1964-66; clin. prof. pediatrics U. Calif. Med. Ctr., San Francisco, 1966-73; dir. dept. pediatrics Mt. Zion Hosp. and Med. Ctr., San Francisco, 1966-73. Commonwealth fellow human genetics Instituto de Genetica, Pavia, Italy, 1959-60. Mem. Inst. Medicine, NAS, Am. Fedn. Clin. Rsch., Am. Pediatric Soc., Soc. Pediatric Rsch., Am. Acad. Pediatrics, Ambulatory Pediatric Assn., Soc. Rsch. in Child Devel., Phi Beta Kappa, Alpha Omega Alpha, Sigma Xi. Contbr. articles to profl. jours.

GROSS, SAMSON RICHARD, geneticist, biochemist, educator; b. N.Y.C., July 27, 1926; s. Isidor and Ethel (Mermelestein) G.; m. Helen Hudi Steinmetz, Sept. 16, 1952; children—Deborah Ann, Michael Robert, Eva Elizabeth. B.A., NYU, 1949; A.M., Columbia, 1951, Ph.D. (USPHS fellow), 1953. Asst. prof. genetics Stanford U., 1956-57; asst. prof. genetics Rockefeller U., N.Y.C., 1957-60; assoc. prof. dept. microbiology and immunology Duke, Durham, N.C., 1960-65, prof. genetics and biochemistry, 1965-91, prof. emeritus genetics and biochemistry, 1991—; dir. div. genetics dept. biochemistry Duke, 1965-77, dir. univ. program in genetics, 1967-77; bd. dirs. Cold Spring Harbor Lab. Quantitative Biology, N.Y., 1967-72. USPHS Spl. fellow Weizmann Inst., 1969-70; Josiah Macy Found. fellow Hebrew U., 1977-78; John Simon Guggenheim fellow Hebrew U., 1985-86. Mem. Genetic Soc. Am., AAAS, Am. Soc. Microbiology, Am. Soc. Biol. Chemists, Phi Beta Kappa. Home: 2411 Prince St Durham NC 27707-1432

GROSS, STANLEY JAY, psychologist, consultant; b. Bklyn., Sept. 25, 1927; s. Albert S. and Selma G. (Krebs) G.; m. Carol Jacobs, Dec. 29, 1955 (div. Jan. 1975); children: Elizabeth, David, Jennifer; m. Julia L. McVay, Aug. 29, 1978. BBA, Baruch Coll., 1950; MA, Columbia U., 1953, EdD, 1959. Postdoctoral fellow U. Ill., Chgo., 1972-73; cen. treas. Baruch Coll., N.Y.C., 1953-55; social sci. instr. Orange County C.C., Middletown, N.Y., 1956-58; assoc. dean students SUNY Coll., Buffalo, 1958-61; dean students Rockford (Ill.) Coll., 1961-66; prof. counseling psychology Ind. State U., Terre Haute, 1966-88; clin. fellow Harvard Med. Sch., Boston, 1987; pvt. practice, Quincy, Mass., 1988—; instr. Columbia U. Tchrs. Coll., N.Y.C., 1955-56; cons. Addictions, Family and Recovery, Plymouth, Mass., 1987-92; lectr. Tufts U., Medford, Mass., 1991. Author: Of Foxes and Henhouses, Licensing and the Health Professions, 1984. With USN, 1945-46, U.S. Army, 1950-52. Mem. APA, Mass. Psychol. Assn., Avanta Network. Office: 110 W Squantum St Ste 17 Quincy MA 02171-2122

GROSS, STANLEY MERHL, chiropractor; b. Breese, Ill., June 27, 1953; s. Walter Frank and Priscilla Dean (Myers) G.; m. Katherine Ferlisi, June 27, 1993; children: Timothy, Carisa, Geno, Zachary, Jason. BS in Biomed., Washington U., St. Louis, 1982; PhD, Harvard U., 1983; BS in Biology, Logan Coll., Chesterfield, Mo., 1986, D Chiropractic, 1988. Diplomate Advanced Chiropractic Technique; cert. acupuncture Community Chiropractic Ctr. Pvt. practice, chief staff Community Chiropractic Ctr., O'Fallon, Mo., 1988—; instr., lectr. Logan Coll. Chiropractic, Chesterfield, Mo., 1988—. Author: Bio-Synergistic Integration, 1984. Dir. Ankylosing Spondytitis Assn., St. Louis, 1988—; alderman ward II, St. Paul, Mo., 1993—. Recipient Star Scholarship Logan Alumni Assn., Chesterfield, 1987. Mem. Acad. Advancement Sci., Am. Chiropractic Assn., Toastmasters Internat. (Most Able award 1992). Home and Office: 1002 Mueller Rd O'Fallon MO 63366

GROSS, STEPHEN MARK, pharmacist, academic dean; b. Bklyn., July 31, 1938; s. Arthur S. and Hazel F. (Marks) G.; m. Susan S. Farber, Nov. 5, 1961; 1 child, Julie S. B.S., Columbia U., 1960, M.A., 1969, Ed.D., 1975. Pharmacist/mgr. C.O. Bigelow Chemists Inc., N.Y.C., 1960-65, Bigelow-Americana Chemists Inc., N.Y.C., 1963-65; asst. to dean Coll. Pharm. Scis., Columbia U., 1965-68, asst. dean, 1968-71, asso. dean, 1971-72, acting dean, 1972-74, dean, 1974-76; dean grad. studies Arnold & Marie Schwartz Coll. Pharmacy and Health Scis. L.I. U., 1976-79; dean Sch. Bys. and Pub. Adminstrn., Bklyn. Ctr. L.I. U., 1983-84; dean grad. studies and research Conolly Coll. L.I.U., 1979-83, dean Faculties Pharmacy and Health Professions, 1984-88; dean Schwartz Coll. Pharmacy L.I. U., 1985—, dean Sch. of Health Professions, 1990—; dir. Arden House Confs. on Indsl. Pharmacy, 1966-79; v.p. Pond Assn., 1972, pres., 1976-78; mem. N.Y. State Bd. Pharmacy, 1991—; mem. health care quality improvement steering com. IPRO, 1995—. Mem. editorial bd.: U.S. Pharmacist, 1978-80, Am. Druggist, 1989-92; contbr. articles to profl. publs. Recipient numerous grants instnl. improvement. Mem. Am. Pharm. Assn., Am. Assn. Colls. Pharmacy (chmn. sect. continuing edn. 1979-80), Pharm. Soc. State N.Y., Nat. Assn. Retail Druggists, Am. Soc. Health-System Pharmacists, Soc. Am. Magicians (v.p. N.Y. Assembly 1981-83, pres. 1983-84). Home: 43 Knott Dr Glen Cove NY 11542-4116 Office: LI U 1 University Plz Brooklyn NY 11201-8423

GROSSBART, TED ALAN, clinical psychologist; b. Detroit, June 3, 1946; s. Samuel Alexander and Mary (Spilkin) G.; m. Rosely Traube, Feb. 9, 1974; children: Zachary, Matthew. AB, U. Mich., 1967; MA, Boston U., 1972, PhD, 1972. Diplomate Am. Bd. Med. Psychotherapists; lic. psychologist, Mass. Pvt. practice Boston, 1970—; instr. Harvard Med. Sch., Boston, 1973—; sr. assoc. clin. supr. Beth Israel Hosp., Boston, 1973-95; cons. Cancer Control Ctr. Boston U. Med. Sch., 1995. Author: Skin Deep: A Mind/Body Program for Healthy Skin, 1986, 3d edit., 1995. Bd. advisors Boston HELP. Mem. APA, Am. Bd. Med Psychotherapists (bd. advisors), Soc. for Clin. and Exptl. Hypnosis. Home: Goodwin's Landing Marblehead MA 01945 Office: 466 Commonwealth Ave Apt 201 Boston MA 02215-2710

GROSSBERG, GEORGE THOMAS, psychiatrist, educator; b. Hungary, Aug. 20, 1948; came to the U.S., 1957; s. Henry and Barbara (Rothman) G.; m. Darla Jean Brown, June 13, 1976; children: Jonathan, Anna-Leah, Aviva, Aliza Becky, Jeremy. BA, Yeshiva U., 1971; MD, St. Louis U., 1975. Diplomate Am. Bd. Psychiatry and Neurology. Chief resident in psychiatry St. Louis U., 1978-79, instr., 1979-81, asst. prof., 1982-86, assoc. prof., 1986-90, prof., 1990—, Samuel W. Fordyce prof. and chmn. dept. psychiatry, 1995; cons. on aging U.S. VA Hosps. Assn., Washington, 1990—. Contbr. articles to profl. jours. Adv. bd. St. Louis Alzheimers Assn., 1983—. Recipient Pub. Svc. award St. Louis Alzheimers Assn., 1989. Mem. Am. Assn. Geriatric Psychiatry (pres. 1989-90), Am. Psychiat. Assn. (cons. on aging 1990—, Falk fellow 1977-79), Am. Geriatric Soc., Gerontol. Soc. Am. Office: Saint Louis U Med Ctr 1221 S Grand Blvd Saint Louis MO 63104-1016

GROSSER, BERNARD IRVING, psychiatry educator; b. Boston, Apr. 19, 1929; s. John and Katherine (Russman) G.; children: Steven, Mark, Minda; m. Karen Grosser. BA, U. Mass., 1950; MS, U. Mich., 1953; MD, Case-Western Res. U., 1959. Diplomate Am. Bd. Psychiatry and Neurology. Intern U. Utah, 1959-60, resident in psychiatry, 1960-65; asst. prof. psychiatry U. Utah Sch. Medicine, Salt Lake City, 1967-71, assoc. prof., 1971-75, prof., 1975—, chmn. dept., 1978—; mem. pre-clin. and clin. psychopharm. rev. com. NIMH, Washington, 1974-79, 80-84, mem. sci. adv. bd., 1984-88; mem. merit rev. bd. VA, Washington, 1988-91; sr. sci. advisor Alcohol, Drug Abuse and Mental Health Adminstrn., Washington, 1987-88. Contbr. chpts. to books, articles to profl. jours. Capt. USAF, 1965-67. Grantee NIMH, 1959-84, FDA, 1985-88. Fellow Am. Psychiat. Assn. (life); mem. Internat. Soc. Psychoneuroendocrinology (treas. 1974-88), Utah Psychiat. Assn. (pres. 1995-96), Psychiat. Rsch. Soc. (pres. 1986-87), Am. Coll. Neuropsychopharmacology, Soc. Neurosci., N.Y. Acad. Scis. Republican. Jewish. Home: 511 Perrys Hollow Rd Salt Lake City UT 84103-4245 Office: U Utah Sch Medicine Dept Psychiatry 50 N Medical Dr Salt Lake City UT 84132

GROSSETT, DEBORAH LOU, psychologist, behavior analyst, consultant; b. Alma, Mich., Feb. 16, 1957; d. Charles M. and Margaret A. (Roethlisberger) G. BS, Alma Coll., 1979; MA, Western Mich. U., 1981, PhD, 1984. Lic. psychologist, Tex.; cert. in diagnostic evaluation, Tex.; registered behavior analyst, Tex. Grad. rsch. and teaching asst. Western Mich. U., Kalamazoo, 1979-84; asst. group home supr., community outreach Residential Opportunities, Kalamazoo, 1982-84; psychologist Richmond (Tex.) State Sch., 1984-87, Shapiro Devel. Ctr., Kankakee, Ill., 1987-88; clin. coord. Monroe Devel. Ctr., Rochester, N.Y., 1988; chief psychologist Denton (Tex.) State Sch., 1989-90; dir. psychol./behavioral svcs. Ctr. for the Retarded, Houston, 1990—; behavioral cons. Ctr. for Developmentally Disabled Adults, Kalamazoo, 1984, Goodman-Wade Enterprises, Houston, 1987; instr. psychology Houston Community Coll., 1985-86, U. Houston-Clear Lake, 1987, 92, 95. Contbr. chpt. to book, articles to profl. jours. Western Mich. U. fellow, 1984. Mem. Am. Psychol. Assn., Am. Assn. on Mental Retardation, Assn. for Behavior Analysis (chair Outreach Bd. 1989-91), Tex. Assn. for Behavior Analysis (bd. dirs. 1989-91). Democrat. Presbyterian. Home: 9750 Ravensworth Dr Houston TX 77031-3130 Office: Ctr for the Retarded Inc 3550 W Dallas St Houston TX 77019-1702

GROSSMAN, BURTON ALAN, psychologist; b. Cambridge, Mass., Apr. 23, 1940; s. Harold Isreal and Evelyn Grossman; children: Joel, Beth; m. Sara S. Brooks, Dec. 21, 1986; stepchildren: Laura, Ben. BS, Tufts U., 1961; MA, Mich. State, 1963, PhD, 1967. Registered psychologist, Ill. Project dir. Human Resources Ctr. U. Chgo., Chgo., 1967-73; sr. advisor mgmt. devel. Atlantic Richfield Co., L.A., 1973-74; cons. psychologist Elliott, Pfisterer & Chinetti, Chgo., 1974-78; mgr. Kearney Mgmt. Cons., Chgo., 1978-83; mgr. orgn. effectiveness Motorola, Inc., Plantation, Fla., 1983—. Mem. sch. bd. Congregation Beth Hillel, Wilmette, Ill., 1980; program com. Ill. Tng. Assn., Chgo., 1981; v.p. Assn. Orgnl. Psychologists, Chgo., 1981-83; bd. dirs. Wilmette Community Concert Assn., 1982. Faculty fellow Mich. State U., 1966. Mem. Am. Psychol. Assn., Broward County Mental Health Assn. (bd. dirs. 1990-92), Soc. Indsl. and Orgnl. Psychologists, Phi Kappa Phi. Office: Motorola Inc 8000 W Sunrise Blvd Fort Lauderdale FL 33322-4104

GROSSMAN, FRANCES KAPLAN, psychologist; b. Newport News, May 28, 1939; d. Rubin H. and Beatrice (Fischlowitz) Kaplan; m. Henry Grossman, July 26, 1970; children: Jennifer, Benjamin. BA, Oberlin (Ohio) Coll., 1961; MS, PhD, Yale U., 1965. Diplomate Am. Bd. Profl. Psychology. Asst. prof. Yale U., New Haven, 1965-69; asst. prof. Boston U., 1969-71, assoc. prof. psychology, 1971-82, prof. psychology, 1982—. Author: Brothers and Sisters of Retarded Children, 1971, Pregnancy, Birth and Parenthood, 1980. Trustee Oberlin Coll., 1990-92, pres. Alumni Assn., 1979-80. Recipient Cert. of Appreciation Oberlin Coll. Alumni Assn., 1983. Fellow APA (mem. ethics com. 1994—); mem. Mass. Psychol. Assn. (chair ethics com. 1989-91, Career Contbn. award 1991), Oberlin Coll. Alumni Assn., Sigma Xi, Phi Beta Kappa. Jewish. Office: Boston Univ Dept Psychology 64 Cummington St Boston MA 02215-2407

GROSSMAN, JEROME HARVEY, medical educator, administrator; b. Maplewood, N.J., Sept. 23, 1939; s. Abraham and Sally Grossman; m. Barbara Nan, June 9, 1968; children: Elizabeth, Katherine, Amelia. BS, MIT, 1961; MD, U. Pa., 1965. Fellow Mass. Gen. Hosp., Boston, 1966-69, assoc. dir. computer sci., 1969-72, dir. ambulatory care, 1974-79; asst. prof. Harvard Med. Sch., Boston, 1971-72, 74-79; pres. New Eng. Med. Ctr., Boston, 1979-84, chmn., CEO, 1984-95; chmn., CEO Health Quality LLC, Boston, 1996—; prof. Tufts U. Sch. Medicine, Boston, 1979—; program dir. Commonwealth Fund Acad. Health Ctr. Program, 1982-87; chmn. The Health Inst., 1988-95; scholar in residence Inst. of Medicine, 1996; dir. Med. Info. Tech. Inc., Westwood, Mass., Stryker Corp., Kalamazoo, Fed. Res. Bank, Boston, chmn., 1992—, Arthur D. Little Inc.; mem. nat. adv. com.; bd. dirs. Tufts Associated Health Maintenance Orgn., 1979-96. Mem. corp. devel. com. MIT, 1986—, trustee, 1990—; trustee Wellesley Coll., 1983—; mem. Bd. Edn., Commonwealth Mass., 1991-96, Jobs Coun., Commonwealth Mass., 1991—; chair Bd. Transition Sys., Inc., 1985-96. Lt. col. USAF, 1972-74. Mem. Inst. Medicine of NAS, Am. Fedn. Clin. Rsch., Assn. Am. Med. Colls. (adminstrv. bd. 1986-92, chmn. 1990-91), Acad. Med. Ctr. Consortium (chmn. 1992-95), Country Club, Somerset Club, Tavern Club, Cosmos Club, Mill Reef Club. Home: 72 Spooner Rd Chestnut Hill MA 02167-1820 Office: Health Quality LLC 500 Boylston St Ste 550 Boston MA 02116

GROSSMAN, JERROLD B., pharmaceutical executive; b. N.Y.C., Oct. 23, 1947. BA, Fairleigh Dickinson U., 1969, MBA, 1973; D of Profl. Studies in Bus. Mgmt., Pace U., 1989. Gen. mgr. Nomis Svc. Stores, Bklyn., 1969-72; fin. analyst Irving Trust Co., N.Y.C., 1972-74; sr. adminstr. Greater N.Y. blood program ARC, N.Y.C., 1974-79; dir. mktg., sales and biologics resources N.Y. Blood Ctr., 1979-85; v.p., dir. mktg. N.Am. Immuno-U.S., Inc., N.Y.C., 1985-90; pres. Genesis Bio-Pharm., Inc., Tenafly, N.J., 1990—; bd. dirs. Govan, Inc.; cons. Can. Red Cross, 1996. Author: Overview of Plasma Derivatives, 1984 (ency. sect.) Impact of Technology on the Plasma Derivative Industry, 1989, Blood and Plasma Industry, 1992. Bd. dirs. Temple Sinai Bergen County; mem. fin. com. Congressman Robert Torrialti, 1995-96. Sgt. N.Y. Nat. Guard, 1969-75. Mem. Am. Assn. Blood Banks.

GROSSMAN, KENNETH CEDRIC, health facility director; b. Chgo., Sept. 8, 1945; s. Walter Frederick and Frances (Kumskis) G.; m. Kathleen Cohan (div. 1980); children: Karina, Cynthia, Kristina, Kassandra; m. Jane Alta DeYoung, Oct. 14, 1983. Student, Ea. Mich. U., 1963-64, U. Nebr., 1966-71, U. Chgo., 1983-84; BA, Am. Inst. Hypnotherapy, 1989, PhD, 1990; CBA, U. Ill., Chgo., 1991. Cert. clin. hypnotherapist Nat. Bd. Hypnotherapy and Hypnotic Anesthesiology. Pres. Alpine Corp., Omaha, 1970-80; exec. dir. Am. Inst. Smoking Cessation, Hinsdale, Ill., 1980—. Served to sgt., USAF, 1962-66. Mem. Am. Assn. Counseling & Devel., Soc. of Group Behavioral Hypnotherapists (pres. 1990-91), Profl. Hypnotherapists, Specialists in Group Work, Nat. Speakers Assn., Profl. Speakers of Ill. Office: Am Inst Smoking Cessation PO Box 11 Hinsdale IL 60522-0011

GROSSMAN, LAWRENCE I., molecular biology educator; b. N.Y.C., Nov. 15, 1939; s. David Morris and Dora (Turkenich) G.; m. Andrea Auerbach (div.); m. Esta Paula Shaftel, Dec. 27, 1970; 1 child, Daniel Alan. BS, CCNY, 1961; PhD, Albert Einstein Coll. Medicine, Bronx, N.Y., 1970. Rsch. fellow in biology Calif. Inst. Tech., Pasadena, 1970-74; asst. prof. biochemistry Wayne State U., Detroit, 1974-78; asst. prof. biology U. Mich., Ann Arbor, 1978-85; sr. editor Sci. Mag., Washington, 1985-86; vis. scientist NIH, Bethesda, Md., 1985-86; assoc. prof. molecular biology and genetics Wayne State U. Sch. Medicine, Detroit, 1986-91, prof., 1991-94, assoc. chmn., 1992-94; prof., assoc. dir. Ctr. Molecular Medicine and Genetics, 1994—. Contbg. editor Sci. Mag., 1986-94; assoc. editor Applied and Theoretical Electrophoresis, 1989-93; consulting editor: McGraw Hill Encyclopedia of Science and Technology, 1989—; contbr. more than 75 papers and book chpts. on molecular biology. Rsch. grantee NSF, 1989-93, NIH, 1988-91, 93—, Muscular Dystrophy Assn., 1989-92, 94—. Mem. Internat. Electrophoresis Soc. (treas. 1989—), Am. Soc. for Biochemistry and Molecular Biology, Sigma Xi. Office: Wayne State U Sch Medicine 540 E Canfield St Detroit MI 48201-1928

GROSSMAN, LISA ROBBIN, clinical psychologist, lawyer; b. Chgo., Jan. 22, 1952; d. Samuel R. and Sarah (Kruger) G. BA with highest distinction and departmental honors in Psychology, Northwestern U., 1974, JD cum laude, 1979, PhD, 1982. Bar: Ill. 1981; registered psychologist, Ill. Jud. intern, U.S. Supreme Ct., Washington, 1975; pre-doctoral psychology intern Michael Reese Hosp. and Med. Center, Chgo., 1979-80; therapist Homes for Children, Chgo., 1980-83; psychologist Psychiat. Inst., Cir. Ct. Cook County, Chgo., 1981-87; pvt. practice, 1984—; invited participant workshop HHS, Rockville, Md., 1981. Contbr. articles to profl. jours. Mem. ABA, Am. Psychol. Assn. (com. on legal issues 1992-95, com. on profl. practice and stds. 1996—, state leadership organizing com. 1996—), Ill. Psychol. Assn. (pres. 1995-96), Chgo. Assn. for Psychoanalytic Psychologists (parliamentarian 1982), Ill. State Bar Assn., Chgo. Bar Assn., Soc. Personality Assessment, Mortar Bd., Phi Beta Kappa, Shi-Ai, Alpha Lambda Delta. Office: 500 N Michigan Ave Ste 1520 Chicago IL 60611-3703

GROSSMAN, MARC ROBERT, optometrist, acupuncturist; b. N.Y.C., Nov. 4, 1955; s. Irwin and Dorothy Grossman; m. Ellen Sandra Marshall, June 22, 1986. BA in Biology, SUNY, New Paltz, 1976; OD, SUNY, N.Y.C., 1980; Cert. in Learning Disabilities, SUNY, New Rochelle, 1986. Diplomate of acupuncture, Tri-State Inst. Chinese Medicine. Optometrist Rye, N.Y., 1980—; dir. Rye Learning Ctr., 1982—; adj. clin. instr. Optometric Ctr. N.Y., 1992—; med. vision cons. U.S. Mil. Acad. Performance Enhancement Ctr., West Point, N.Y., 1992—; ea. regional dir. Optometric Ext. Program, 1993—; mem. Coll. of Vision Devel., 1982—. Author: Magic Eye-A 3D Viewing Guide, 1995, Natural Vision Care, 1995. Mem. Am. Optometric Assn., Holistic Health Assn. (pres. 1986-94). Home: 111 Springtown Rd New Paltz NY 12561 Office: 20 Chestnut St Rye NY 10580

GROSSMAN, RICHARD S., physician; b. Alexandria, Va., Dec. 15, 1951; s. Isadore I. and Florence P. (Kaufman) G.; m. Kathleen E. Conrad, Dec. 28, 1974; 1 child, Conrad B. BA, Cornell U., 1973; MD summa cum laude, Harvard U., 1977. Diplomate Am. Bd. Internal Medicine. Resident in internal medicine Mass. Gen. Hosp., Boston, 1977-80; staff physician Bay Area Hosp., Coos Bay, Oreg., 1980—; mem. physician North Bend Med. Ctr., Coos Bay, 1980—. Bd. dirs. Bay Area Hosp., Coos Bay, 1995-96. Mem. AMA, Oreg. Med. Assn., Phi Beta Kappa, Alpha Omega Alpha. Office: North Bend Med Ctr 1900 Woodland Dr Coos Bay OR 97420

GROSSMAN, ROBERT GEORGE, physician, educator; b. N.Y.C., Jan. 24, 1933; s. Ferenc and Vivian (Isenberg) G.; m. Ellin Friedman, June 26, 1955; children—Amy, Kate, Ruth. B.A., Swarthmore Coll., 1953; M.D., Columbia U., 1957. Diplomate Am. Bd. Neurosurgery. Intern Strong Meml. Hosp., Rochester, N.Y., 1957-58; resident Presbyn. Hosp., Columbia U., N.Y.C., 1960-63; acad. practice medicine, specializing in neurol. surgery Houston, 1973—; instr., assoc. prof. neurol. surgery U. Tex. SW Med. Sch., 1963-68; assoc. prof., prof. neurol. surgery Albert Einstein Coll. Medicine, 1969-73; prof., chmn. div. neurol. surgery U. Tex. Med. Br., Galveston, 1973-80; prof., chmn. dept. neurol. surgery Baylor Coll. Medicine, 1980—; chief neurosurg. service Meth. Hosp., Houston, 1980—; chmn. neurology B study sect. USPHS, NIH, 1972-74; mem. bd. sci. counsellors Nat. Inst. Neurol. Diseases and Stroke, NIH, 1989-93; mem. nat. adv. coun. Nat. Inst. Neurol. Diseases and Stroke, NIH, 1993—. Author: (with W. D. Willis) Medical Neurobiology, 3d edit, 1981; chmn. editorial bd. Jour. Neurosurgery, 1987. Served with AUS, 1958-60. Mem. Am. Assn. Neurol.

Surgeons, ACS, Soc. Univ. Surgeons, Am. Bd. Neurol. Surgery (chmn. bd. 1989-90), Am. Acad. Neurol. Surgery (v.p.), Soc. Neurol. Surgeons (pres. 1995). Home: 1821 South Blvd Houston TX 77098-5421 Office: Tex Med Ctr 6565 Fannin St Houston TX 77030-2704

GROSSMAN, WILLIAM KING, psychiatrist; b. Danville, Pa., Oct. 22, 1945; s. Sydney Morris and Leona (Robins) G.; m. Joan Kalinosky, Nov. 25, 1972; children: David Aaron, Catherine Elise. BS, Pa. State U., 1966; MD, Jefferson Med. Coll., 1968. Diplomate Am. Psychgiatry and Neurology. Intern Jefferson Hosp., Phila., 1969-70; resident in psychiatry Inst. of Pa. Hosp., Phila., 1970-73; fellow in med. edn. Jefferson Med. Coll., Phila., 1973-74; chief psychiatry Wilkes-Barre (Pa.) VA Med. Ctr., 1974-87, chief staff, 1987—; dir. Sigmond Miller Rsch. Found., Harrisburg, Pa., 1973-88. Contbr. articles to med. jours. Office: VA Med Ctr East End Blvd Wilkes Barre PA 18711

GROSSNICKLE, NEVIN EDWIN, biology educator; b. Elgin, Ill., Mar. 3, 1950; s. Edwin Eugene and Victoria Fern (Dilling) G.; m. Jane Burton Luhman, Dec. 28, 1971 (div. Feb. 1994); 1 child, Amy Jane. BS in Natural Resources, U. Mich., 1972; MS in Zoology, U. Wis., Milw., 1974; PhD in Zoology, U. Wis., 1978. Rsch. asst. U. Wis., Milw., 1973-78; postdoctoral fellow Harbor Br. Instn., Ft. Pierce, Fla., 1978-79; asst. rsch. scientist U. Mich., Ann Arbor, 1979-82; asst. prof. biology Grand Canyon Coll., Phoenix, 1982-85, assoc. prof., biology, 1985-87, prof. biology, 1987-89; asst. prof. biology U Wis. Marathon Ctr., Wausau, 1989-93, assoc. prof. biology, 1993—; chair dept. biology U.. Wis. Ctrs., 1996—. Contbr. articles to Verhandlugen Internat. Vereinigen Limnology, Hydrobiologia, Limnology and Oceanography, Crustaceana. Chmn. North Ctrl. Regional Biology Olympics Com., Wausau, 1990-96. Recipient Faculty award Fulbright Scholar Program, U. Helsinki, Finland, 1988. Mem. Am. Soc. Limnology and Oceanography, Ecological Soc. Am., Internat. Assn. for Great Lakes Rsch., Soc. Internat. Limnology, Sigma Xi. Home: 2807 Teal Ave Wausau WI 54401-7392 Office: U Wis Marathon Ctr 518 S 7th Ave Wausau WI 54401-5362

GROSSNICKLE, WILLIAM FOSTER, psychology educator, program director; b. Nutley, N.J., Mar. 19, 1930; s. Foster Earl and Blanche (Dumas) G.; m. Betty Louise Depp, June 7, 1952 (dec. May 1994); children: C. Anne, Mark E. BA, Duke U., 1951; MA, George Washington U., 1958, PhD, 1965. Lic. psychologist, N.C. Employment interviewer Western Electric Co., Winston-Salem, N.C., 1954-58; mgr. corp. employment Blue Bell, Inc., Greensboro, N.C., 1958-62; part-time instr. George Washington U., Washington, 1963-65; asst. prof. psychology East Carolina U., Greenville, N.C., 1965-68, assoc. prof., 1968-70, prof., 1970—, prof., dir. grad. gen. program, 1983—; cons. to various profit and non-profit orgns. Contbr. numerous articles to profl. jours. Sgt. U.S. Army, 1952-54, Korea. Mem. APA, ASTD, Soc. Indsl. and Orgnl. Psychology, Am. Psychol. Soc., Acad. Mgmt., Sigma Xi, Psi Chi (Southea. v.p. 1970-76). Republican. Methodist. Home: 1105 Oakview Dr Greenville NC 27858-5228 Office: East Carolina U Dept Psychology Greenville NC 27858-4353

GROSSO, GINO, psychiatrist; b. Turin, Italy, Aug. 29, 1948; came to U.S., 1956; s. Nicholas Andrea and Mary (D'Amico) G.; m. Eileen Wood, Feb. 3, 1979; children: Amanda, Susannah. BA in Psychology cum laude, Syracuse U., 1971; MD, SUNY Health Scis. Ctr., Bklyn., 1975. Cert. adult psychiatry, forensic psychiatry, geriatric psychiatry, sleep disorders medicine; accredited clin. polysomnographer (physician sleep specialist). Resident in psychiatry Hosp. of U. Pa., Phila., 1976-79; fellow in forensic psychiatry Hosp. of U. Pa., 1978; pvt. clin. practice psychiatry and sleep disorder medicine Phila., 1980—; med. dir. Green Spring of Eastern Pa., 1994-96, assoc. med. dir., 1996—; attending psychiatrist Einstein Med. Ctr., Phila., 1979-85, dir. med. student teaching program, 1979-82; cons. Phila. Ct. Common Pleas, 1979-88; med. dir. Phila. Mental Health Clinic, 1979-87; fellow sleep medicine Med. Coll. Pa., Phila., 1985-87; med. dir. emergency psychiatry screening program Helene Fuld Med. Ctr., Trenton, 1988-92; dir. psychiat. peer rev. dept. TAO, Inc. (subs. Blue Cross-Blue Shield), 1992—. Mem. Am. Psychiat. Assn., Am. Sleep Disorders Assn., Am. Acad. Psychiatry and Law, Acad. Psychosomatic Medicine, Am. Geriatrics Soc., Am. Assn. for Geriatric Psychiatry, Assn. Medicine and Psychiatry, Am. Acad. Clin. Psychoanalysts.

GROSSO, MICHAEL ANTHONY, cardiothoracic surgeon, educator; b. Phila., Oct. 8, 1958; s. Michael Joseph and Lucy (Corrado) G.; m. Lisa Ramagli, Sept. 10, 1983; children: Ryan Michael, Jordan John. BS magna cum laude, Phila. Coll. Pharmacy/Sci., 1980; MD, U. Pa., Phila., 1984. Diplomate Am. Bd. Gen. Surgery, Am. Bd. Thoracic Surgery. Intern, resident, fellow U. Colo. Health Scis. Ctr., 1984-93; asst. prof. cardiothoracic surgery, head pulmonary surgery Cooper Hosp., U. Medicine & Dentistry N.J., Camden, 1993—. Contbr. articles to profl. jours., over 70 manuscripts and book chpts. Bd. dirs. Phila. Coll. Pharmacy Sci., 1992—. Maj. M.C. U.S. Army Res., 1990—. Recipient Nat. Rsch. award Alpha Omega Alpha, Ben Eiseman Surg. Rsch. award U. Colo, Gold Apple tchg. award. Assoc. fellow ACS; mem. Soc. Univ. Surgeons, Soc. Thoracic Surgeons, Assn. Acad. Surgery (program com. 1993—, nominating com., councilman, nat. rsch. fellow). Office: Cooper Hosp U Med Coll 3 Cooper Plz Ste 411 Camden NJ 08103

GROTH, KAREN E., nursing educator; b. Sept. 30, 1950. BSN, U. Wash., 1972, M in Physiol. Nursing, 1978; postgrad., Wash. State U., 1986-92. RN, Wash.; cert. med-surg. clin. specialist. Staff nurse med. and CCU Drs. Hosp., Seattle, 1972-73, head nurse med. telemetry, 1973-75; primary care nurse surg. ICU Evergreen Hosp., Kirkland, Wash., 1975-77; vis. nurse, coord. home health Group Health Coop. Home Health Svcs., Seattle, 1977-78; head nurse respiratory and med. unit Sacred Heart Med. Ctr., Spokane, Wash., 1978-80; staff nurse ICU Sacred Heart Med. Ctr., Spokane, 1990—; asst. prof. med-surg. nursing Intercollegiate Ctr. Nursing Edn., Spokane, 1980-81, 84-87, instr. med-surg. nursing, 1987-95; asst. prof. nursing Gonzaga U., Spokane, 1995—; asst. dir. staff devel. Hamad Gen. Hosp., Doha, ., Qatar, 1981-84; with Vis. Nurses Assn., Spokane, Wash., 1985-87; staff nurse ICU Valley Med. Ctr., Spokane, 1986-88, Sacred Heart Med Ctr, Spokane; bd. dirs. Group Health N.W. Eastern Wash. and No. Idaho, March of Dimes; rsch. on nutrition, cholesterol levels, bulimia. Contbr. articles to profl. jours. Den leader Boy Scouts Am., 1985-87, 92-93, cubmaster, 1992-93; vol. ARC, PTSA. Recipient Excellence in Tchg. award Internat. Coun. Nursing Educators, 1992. Mem. ANA, AACN, Am. Soc. Parenteral and Enteral Nutrition, Wash. State Nurses Assn. (nursing practice and edn. cabinet 1986), Am. Cancer Soc., March of Dimes, Sigma Theta Tau (pres. Delta Chi chpt. 1987-89, Excellence in Tchg. award 1994). Home: 14606 E Main Ave Spokane WA 99216-2099 Office: Gonzaga U E502 Boone Spokane WA 99202

GROTH, MICHAEL JOSEPH, oculoplastic surgeon; b. Phila., June 17, 1959; s. William Henry Jr. and Dorothy Ann (Tewksbury) G.; m. Ileana E. Zapatero, May 26, 1984; children: Michael, Gabriela, Caroline. BS in Chemistry, U. Fla., 1980; MD, U. Miami, 1984. Intern Mt. Sinai Med. Ctr., Miami, Fla., 1984-85; resident UCLA Jules Stein Eye Inst., L.A., 1985-88; plastic and reconstructive surgeon pvt. practice, Beverly Hills, Calif., 1989—; asst. clin. prof. UCLA Jules Stein Eye Inst., 1989—; clin. instr. Wodsworth VA Hosp., L.A., 1990—. Contbr. articles to profl. jours. Ophthalmic plastic surgery fellow UCLA Jules Stein Eye Inst., 1988-89. Mem. Am. Acad. Ophthalmology, Calif. Med. Assn., Calif. Assn. Ophthalmology, L.A. County Med. Assn., L.A. Soc. Ophthalmology. Office: 9675 Brighton Way Ste 410 Beverly Hills CA 90210

GROVE, JEFFREY SCOTT, family practice physician; b. Paxton, Ill., Sept. 21, 1964; s. Ronald Edwin and Delores Ann (Martensen) G.; m. Karen Beth Hanlon, June 17, 1989; 1 child, Garrett Jeffrey. BS in Biology, Fla. So. Coll., 1986; DO, Southeastern Coll. Osteo Med., North Miami Beach, Fla., 1990. Intern Suncoast Hosp., Largo, Fla., 1990-91, resident in family practice, 1991-93; pvt. practice Immediate MedCare and Family Doctor, Largo, 1993—; med. dir. Barrington Properties, Largo, 1994—, Oak Manor Nursing Ctr., Largo, 1993—; rep.-at-large exec. com. Suncoast Hosp., 1995—, chief adminstrv. resident, 1992-93, family practice teaching staff, geriatrics program dir., 1993—, faculty devel. com., 1994—, quality assurance/utilization rev. com., 1993—; bd. dirs. Suncoast Cmty. Care PHO, Largo, 1994—; clin. asst. prof. family medicine Nova Southeastern U. Coll. Osteo. Medicine, North Miami Beach, 1994—; clin. instr. Kirksville Coll. Osteo. Medicine, 1993—. Named to Outstanding Young Men of Am. Mem. Am. Osteo. Assn., Fla. Osteo. Med. Assn., Am. Coll. Osteo. Family Physicians, Nat. Eagle Scout Assn. (life), Scouting Res. Republican. Methodist. Home: 301 Osceola Rd Belleair FL 34616 Office: Immediate MedCare 360 N Clearwater-Largo Rd Largo FL 34640

GROVES, ANNE DUIGNAN, clinical social worker; b. Ephrata, Pa., Apr. 14, 1960; d. John Francis and Mary Jane (Donovan) Duignan. AA with honors, Harrisburg Area Community Coll, 1980; BS with honors, Pa. State U., 1982; MSW, Marywood Coll., 1987. Lic. social worker, Pa. Residential program supr. Pan Am Group Homes, Hershey, Pa., 1980-83; psychiat. asst. Philhaven Hosp., Mt. Gretna, Pa., 1981-85, caseworker, 1985-87, clin. social worker, 1987—. Vol. Women in Crisis, Hershey, 1980-82. Mem. NASW, Acad. Cert. Social Workers. Democrat. Roman Catholic. Home: 18 Shady Ln Annville PA 17003-9300 Office: Philhaven Hosp PO Box 550 Mount Gretna PA 17064-0550

GROVES, DONALD GEORGE, technical consultant; b. Syracuse, N.Y.; s. Perry Edward and Margarite H. (Grass) G.; m. Barbara Lee Matticks, Mar. 19, 1949. BSc, Syracuse U., 1939, MSc, 1949; PhD in Engring. Sci., Sussex (Eng.) U., 1976. Mech. designer Easy Washer Corp., Syracuse, Hudson Naval Arsenal, Detroit, 1941-43; systems engr. GE, Syracuse and Ft. Wayne, Ind., 1954-61; sr. staff scientist Nat. Acad. Sci., Washington, 1961-88; rsch. fellow Inst. Tech. and Strategic Rsch., Washington, 1988-89, Inst. Def. Analyses, Alexandria, Va., 1989-91; cons. Naval Rsch. Lab., Key West, Fla., 1991-92, Marcel Dekker Publ. Co., 1992; tech. cons. math. scis. and ocean scis. Key West, 1992-93; nat. judge Ford-Future Scientists Am., 1964; pres. Nat. Acad. Scis.-Nat. Acad. Engring Academies' Recreational Activities Assn., 1973. Author 3 books; mem. editl. bd. advisors to tech. jours. 1962-65; contbr. over 300 articles to profl. jours., chpts. to books. Pres. Washington Indsl. Baseball League, 1965-66, Md. Indsl. Baseball League, 1967; pres. Washington Athletic Club, 1969-70, bd. govs., 1967-75. Lt. comdr. USNR, 1943-70. Recipient Freedoms Found. Honor medal, 1970, 73, 74, 87, 89, 93, Admiral Dyer award Mil. Order World Wars, Washington, 1986, Alumni award Am. Grad. Sch. Internat. Mgmt., Phoenix, 1990; travel and maintenance grantee for ind. rsch. in Dominican Republic, U.S. Govt., 1950. Fellow Washington Acad. Sci.; mem. Syracuse C. of C. (chmn. econ. discussion groups 1959-60), Washington Ind. Writers. Republican. Roman Catholic. Home and Office: PO Box 5183 Sun City West AZ 85375-0183

GRUBB, ROBERT L., JR., neurosurgeon; b. Charlotte, N.C., May 9, 1940. MD, U. N.C., 1965. Intern Barnes Hosp., St. Louis, 1965-66, resident in gen. surgery, 1966-67, resident in neurosurgery, 1969-73; fellow NIH, Bethesda, Md., 1968-69; mem. staff Barnes-Jewish Hosp., St. Louis, Jewish Hosp., St. Louis, St. Louis Children's Hosp.; prof. neurosurgery Washington U., St. Louis. Fellow ACS; mem. Am. Acad. Neurol. Surgery, AANS, CNS, SNS. Office: Washington U. Sch Medicine Saint Louis MO 63110*

GRUEBEL, BARBARA JANE, internist, pulmonologist; b. Honolulu, May 12, 1950; d. Robert William and Elenor Jane (Perry) G.; BS, Stephen F. Austin State U., 1977; MD (Robert Wood Johnson Found. scholar Coll. Women's Club scholar), Baylor Coll. Medicine, 1974. Intern in internal medicine U. Rochester, 1974-75, resident in internal medicine, 1975-77; pulmonary fellow U. Mich., 1977-79; mem. med. staff Anthony L. Jordan Health Center, Rochester, N.Y., 1976-77, Univ. Health Service, Ann Arbor, Mich., 1978-79; med. dir. progressive respiratory care unit Meth. Med. Ctr., 1979-80; asst. prof. medicine U. Tex. Health Sci. Center, Dallas, 1979-80; cons. in pulmonary disease, Dallas, 1980-93; pvt. practice of pulmonary medicine, 1993—; clin. asst. prof. medicine U. Tex. Health Sci. Center, 1980—; nat. affiliate faculty Am. Heart Assn. Mem. TEXPAC. Recipient award for gen. excellence in pediatrics, 1974, Stanley W. Olson award for acad. excellence, 1974, John Richard Fox award, 1974, Stuart A. Wallace award in pathology, 1974; Welch Found. grantee, 1970; Am. Lung Assn. tng. fellow, 1977-79. Diplomate Nat. Bd. Med. Examiners. Fellow Am. Coll. Chest Physicians (named Young Pulmonary Physicians of Future 1979); mem. Am. Med. Women's Assn. (scholastic excellence award 1974), Am. Thoracic Soc., Am. Lung Assn., AMA, Am. Coll. Physicians, Dallas County Med. Soc., Tex. Med. Soc., Dallas Internist Assocs., Nat. Assn. Med. Dirs. Respiratory Care, Dallas Acad. Internal Medicine, Am. Cancer Soc., Dallas C. of C., Oak Cliff C. of C., Alpha Omega Alpha, Beta Beta Beta. Office: 221 W Colorado Blvd Ste 310 Dallas TX 75208-2310

GRUEBER, CYNTHIA MARIE, health services facility administrator; b. Saginaw, Mich., Jan. 23, 1957; d. Roy George and Arlene Louise (Kube) G. BSc. in Sociology, Mich. State U., 1979; M in Health Svc. Adminstrn., U. Mich., 1981. Rsch. asst. Mich. State U., East Lansing, 1978-79, U. Mich., Ann Arbor, 1979-80; adminstrv. extern Samaritan Health Ctr., Detroit, 1980, program asst., exec. asst., 1982-85, v.p. profl. & support svcs., 1985-87; v.p. profl. svcs. Mercy Hosps. and Health Svcs. of Detroit, 1987-90; assoc. dir. profl. svcs. Med. Coll. Va. Hosps., Richmond, 1990-91; dir. clin. programs Med. Coll. of Va. Hosps., Richmond, 1991-95; COO U. Ill. at Chgo. Med. Ctr., 1995—. Author/editor: Monograph On Health Care for the Uninsured, 1985; contbr. articles to profl. jours. Mem. Am. Coll. Health Care Execs. (nominee). Lutheran. Office: U Ill at Chgo Med Ctr 1740 W Taylor Ste 1400 Chicago IL 60612

GRUEN, ARNO, psychoanalyst; b. Berlin, May 26, 1923; s. James and Rose (Sygal) G; children: Margaret, Constance. BSS, CUNY, 1946; MA, NYU Grad. Sch. Arts and Sci., 1948, PhD, 1952. Diplomate Am. Bd. Profl. Psychology; cert. psychologist, N.Y., psychologist/psychotherapist, Switzerland. Intern Bellevue Psychiat. Hosp., N.Y.C., 1948, staff psychologist, 1949-52; instr. dept. psychiatry Downstate Med. Sch., N.Y.C., 1952-54; sr. psychologist and cons. dept. pub. health/preventive med. Cornell U. Med. Sch., 1954-58; rsch. assoc. dept. neurology, 1958-61; chief psychologist Northside Ctr. Child Devel., N.Y.C., 1956-60; cons. dept. psychiatry Maimonides Hosp. Ctr., N.Y.C., 1962-68; pvt. practice, psychoanalysis N.Y.C. and Switzerland, 1958—; vis. prof. psychology Rutgers U., Newark, 1964-79; mem. editorial bd. Psychoanalytic Rev., 1963-79. Author: Der Verrat am Selbst, 1986, Der Wahnsinn der Normalität: Realismus als Krankeit, 1987, The Betrayal of the Self, 1988, Der Frühe Abschied: Eine Deutung des Plötzlichen Kindstodes, 1988, Falsche Gotter: Ueber Liebe, Hass und die Schwierigkeit des Friedens, 1991; The Insanity of Normality: Realism as Sickness; Toward Understanding Human Destructiveness, 1992. With U.S. Army, 1943-46. Office: Rutistrasse 4, CH-8039 Zurich Switzerland

GRUEN, GERALD ELMER, psychologist, educator; b. Granite City, Ill., July 19, 1937; s. Elmer George and Velma Pearl G.; m. Karol Jane Selvidge, Mar. 20, 1960; children—Tami Jane, Christy Lynn. B.A., So. Ill. U., 1959; M.A., U. Ill., 1963, Ph.D., 1964. Postdoctoral fellow Heinz Werner Inst. of Developmental Psychology, Clark U. and Worcester (Mass.) State Hosp., 1964-66; asst. prof. dept. psychol. scis. Purdue U., West Lafayette, Ind., 1966-69; assoc. prof. Purdue U., 1969-74, prof., 1974—, head dept. psychol. scis. Author: (with T. Wachs) Early Experience and Human Development; contbr. chpt. to The Structuring of Experience, 1977; contbr. articles to profl. jours. Deacon Calvary Baptist Ch., West Lafayette. Recipient USPHS research awards, 1968-71, Nat. Research Service award NIMH, 1976-80, Research award Nat. Insts. Child Health and Human Devel., 1981-83. Fellow Am. Psychol. Assn., Am. Psychol. Soc. (charter mem.); mem. Midwestern Psychol. Assn., Soc. for Research in Child Devel., Sigma Xi. Home: 1001 Eton St West Lafayette IN 47906-1323 Office: Purdue U Psychology Dept West Lafayette IN 47907

GRUEN, PETER H., psychiatrist, educator; b. N.Y.C., June 6, 1939; s. Hans and Ilse (Marx) Wertheimer; B.A. in Psychology with honors, U. Calif. at Berkeley, 1961; M.D., U. Calif. at San Francisco, 1965; children: Arthur L., Kim J. Intern, Bronx Municipal Hosp. Center, 1965-66; resident in psychiatry Albert Einstein Coll. Medicine, Bronx, N.Y., 1969-72, chief resident, 1971-72; practice medicine specializing in psychiatry, N.Y.C., 1972—; asst. instr. psychiatry Albert Einstein Coll. Medicine, 1971-72, 1972-74, asst. prof. psychiatry, 1974-76; lectr. Psychiat. Inst. Columbia U. Coll. Physicians and Surgeons, 1976-77; head clin. rsch. unit dept. of psychiatry Bronx Mcpl. Hosp. Ctr., 1973-75, assoc. dir. psychobiol. rsch., 1975-76, dir. div. clin. psychopharmacology, 1977—; asst. prof. neurosci., assoc. prof. psychiatry Albert Einstein Coll. Medicine, 1978-87; clin. prof. psychiatry N.Y. Med. Coll., 1987-90, Sch. Medicine, NYU, 1990—; cons. attending psychiatrist Lenox Hill Hosp., N.Y.C., 1976—, Gracie Square Hosp., N.Y.C., 1975—; asst. attending psychiatrist Bronx Mcpl. Hosp. Ctr., 1972—, Presbyn. Hosp., N.Y.C., 1976-77; rsch. psychiatrist N.Y. State Psychiat. Inst., 1976-77. Maj. M.C., U.S. Army, 1966-69. Recipient Anne Monika Found. prize, 1975. Diplomate Am. Bd. Psychiatry and Neurology. Fellow Am. Psychiat. Assn.; mem. AAAS, Am. Psychosomatic Soc., Am. Psychopath. Assn., Alpha Omega Alpha. Contbr. articles to profl. jours. Home: 56 Sprain Valley Rd Scarsdale NY 10583-3106 Office: 18 E 77th St New York NY 10021-1722

GRUMBACH, MELVIN MALCOLM, physician, educator; b. N.Y.C., Dec. 21, 1925; s. Emanuel and Adele (Weil) G.; m. Madeleine F. Butt, Dec. 1, 1951; children: Ethan Malcolm, Kevin Lawrence, Anthony Havemeyer. Student, Columbia Coll., MD, 1948; DM (hon.), U. Geneva, 1991. Diplomate Am. Bd. Pediatrics, Am. Bd. Pediatric Endocrinology (com. mem. 1975-79). Resident in pediatrics Babies Hosp., Presbyn. Hosp., N.Y.C., 1949-51; vis. fellow Oak Ridge Inst. Nuclear Studies, 1952; postdoctoral fellow, asst. pediatrics Johns Hopkins Sch. Medicine, 1953-55; mem. faculty Columbia U. Coll. Physicians and Surgeons, N.Y.C., 1955-65; assoc. prof. pediatrics Columbia U. Coll. Physicians and Surgeons, 1961-65; asst. attending pediatrician to assoc. attending pediatrician, head pediatric endocrine div. and postdoctoral tng. program pediatric endocrinology Babies Hosp. and Vanderbilt Clin., Columbia-Presbyn. Med. Ctr., 1955-65; prof. pediatrics, chmn. dept. U. Calif. Sch. Medicine, San Francisco, 1966-86, Edward B. Shaw prof. pediatrics, 1983-94, Edward B. Shaw prof. emeritus pediatrics (active), 1994—, acting dir. Lab. Molecular Endocrinology, 1987-89; dir. pediatric svc. U. Calif. Hosps., 1966-86; vis. prof. Vanderbilt U., 1961, Emory U., 1962, U. Western Ont., 1962, U. N.C., 1963; Alpha Omega Alpha lectr. State U. N.Y. Downstate Med. Ctr., 1961, U. Calif. at San Francisco, 1966; univ. lectr. U. Zurich, 1971; Clausen vis. prof. U. Rochester, 1972; Richard E. Weitzman vis. prof. UCLA, 1981; Culpeper vis. prof. U. N.C., 1982; Frederick Moll lectr. U. Wash., 1979; Kenneth C. Haltalin vis. prof. U. Tex.-Dallas, 1983; Eley lectr. Harvard U. Med. Sch., Children's Med. Ctr., Boston, 1979; domestic lectr. Jour. Pediatrics Edn. Found., 1962, 79; Mali Dittman lectr. U. Chgo., 1980; Frederick M. Kenny lectr. Children's Hosp. Pitts., 1981; Winthrop award lectr. Am. Fertility Soc., 1981; Grover Powers lectr. Yale U., 1981; univ. lectr. Assembly of Profs., Coll. de France, Paris, 1979; Meredith Campbell lectr. Am. Urol. Assn., 1982; Prader lectr. Tel Aviv U. Med. Sch., 1982; Hopkins-Maryland lectr., 1983; Felton Bequests prof. Royal Childrens Hosp., Melbourne, 1983; Sandoz lectr. Can. Soc. Clin. Investigation, 1983; vis. prof. U. Minn., 1984, Royal Soc. Medicine, London, 1985, Joint Endocrine Societies of Great Britain, Oxford; John Lind lectr. Karolinska Inst., Stockholm, 1984; Bilderback lectr. Oreg. Health Scis. U., 1986; Mathew Steiner lectr. Northwestern U., Children's Meml. Hosp., 1989, Gurson lectr. U. Istanbul, 1991, Maranon Symposium lectr. Universidad Autonama de Madrid, Spain, 1991, Judson Van Wyk lectr. U. N.C., 1993, James Etteldorf lectr. La Bonheur Children's Hosp. U. Tenn., 1994; U.S. Plenary lect. X Asia Oceania Congress Endocrinology, Beijing, 1994 VIII Asia Oceania Congress of Endocrinology, Bangkok, 1986; Robert N. Ganz lectr. Mass. Gen. Hosp., 1996; cons. Letterman Gen. Hosp., 1966-94, Children's Hosp., San Francisco, U.S. Naval Hosp., Oakland, Calif., 1966-94, HEW, NIH, Nat. Bd. Med. Examiners, 1964-68; mem. human embryology and devel. study sect. NIH, 1962-66, endocrinology study sect., 1967-71; bd. sci. counselors Nat. Inst. Child Health and Human Devel., 1971-75; mem. gen. clin. rsch. ctrs. com., div. rsch. resources NIH, 1976-80; mem. com. for rev. NIH Clin. Ctr., 1984-85, nat. adv. coun. Nat. Inst. Child Health and Human Devel., NIH, 1991-96; mem. sci. adv. com., clin. rsch. adv. com. Nat. Found.-March of Dimes, 1969-94, chmn. clin. rsch. adv. com., 1974-82, Basil O'Connor starter scholar rsch. award comm., 1995—; mem. awards com. Lita Annenberg Hazen Award for Excellence in Clin. Rsch., 1981-86; mem. sci. adv. bd. Scripps Clinic and Rsch. Found., 1977-78; mem. sci. adv. bd. Princesse Marie Christine Found., Brussels, 1981—, U. Mich. Ctr. for Human Growth and Devel., 1982-89; mem. adv. bd. Nat. Pituitary Agy., 1965-69, NIH Evaluation of Endocrinology and Metabolic Diseases, 1977-79; mem. sci. adv. bd. U. Colo. Health Scis. Barbara Davis Ctr., 1986-93; Dean's Bof Vis., Mt. Sinai Sch. of Medicine, 1986-87; mem. sci. adv. bd. Hosp. for Sick Children, Toronto, 1984-88, Children's Hosp. of Los Angeles, 1987-92; sci. and med. adv. bd. Whittier Inst. Diabetes and Endocrinology, 1987-92; pres. bd. trustees Internat. Pediatric Rsch. Found., Inc., 1984-89; mem. sci. coun. Aid Pour la Recherche Medicale a l'enfance, Paris, 1981-89; del. to Chinese Acad. of Med. Scis., 1986; vis. prof. Peking Union Med. Coll. and Hosp., 1986; vis. prof. U. Hong Kong, 1986. Assoc. editor, mem. editorial bd. Jour. Clin. Endocrinology, 1957-70; adv. editor Jour. Pediatrics, 1966-73; editorial bd., 1973-79; assoc. editor Pediatric Rsch., 1970-84, Barnett Pediatrics, 14th-15th edits., Rudolph Pediatrics, 16th-20th edits., Current Topics in Experimental Endocrinology; mem. internat. editorial bd. pediatrics and pediatric surgery: Excerpta Medica, 1974—; editorial bd. Biology of Reproduction, 1968-70; editorial com. Endocrinologic Clinica Metabolismo, 1981—; editorial bd. Pediatrics in Rev., 1982-84, Jour. Endocrinol. Investigation, 1982-90, Endocrine Revs., 1984-88, Jour. Pediatric Endocrinology, 1984—, Trends in Endocrinology, 1989—, Monographs on Endocrinology, Springer-Verlag, 1975—, Clinical Pediatric Endocrinology (Jour. of the Japanese Soc. for Pediatric Endocrinology), 1992—; contbr. articles to med. and sci. books and jours. Served to capt. M.C. USAF, 1951-53. Postdoctoral fellow Nat. Found. Infantile Paralysis, 1953-55; recipient Joseph M. Smith prize Columbia U., 1962; Career Scientist award Health Research Coun. City N.Y., 1961-66; Silver medal Bicentennial Columbia Coll. Physicians and Surgeons, 1967, Gold medal, 1988; Clin. Endocrinology Trust medal (U.K.), 1985, Centennial Medallist award Babies Hosp., Columbia-Presbyn. Med. Ctr., 1987, Borden award, Am. Acad. Pediatrics, 1971, Robert H. Williams Disting. Leadership award, Endocrine Soc., 1980, Winthrop award, Am. Fertility Soc., 1981, Fred Conrad Koch award Endocrine Soc., 1992. Fellow Am. Acad. Arts & Scis., Am. Acad. Pediatrics, N.Y. Acad. Scis., AAAS; mem. NAS, Am. Pediatric Soc. (pres.-elect 1988-89, pres. 1989-90), Inst. Medicine of Nat. Acad. Scis. (com. on the Future of Pub. Health, 1985-87, com. to study AIDS rsch. program of NIH, 1989-91), Assn. Med. Sch. Pediatric Dept. Chairmen (exec. coun. 1967-72, pres. 1973-75, task force on Pediatric Scientist Tng. Program, 1984-91, chmn. selection com. 1986-91), Am. Soc. Clin. Investigation, Assn. Am. Physicians, Am. Soc. Human Genetics, Harvey Soc., Lawson Wilkins Pediatric Endocrine Soc. (pres. 1975-76), Western Soc. Pediatric Rsch. (pres. 1978-79), Soc. Pediatric Rsch., Teratology Soc., Endocrine Soc. (coun. 1968-71, 80-83, pres. elect 1980-81, pres. 1981-82, Internat. Endocrine Soc. (del. to central com. 1976-92; exec. com. 1984-92), Soc. Study Reprodn., European Soc. Pediatric Endocrinology (corr.), Société Française de Pediatrie (corr.), Internat. Neuroendocrinology Soc., Argentine Soc. Endocrinology and Metabolism (hon.), Can. Soc. Endocrinology and Metabolism (hon.), Japanese Soc. Pediatric Endocrinology (hon.), Western Assn. Physicians, Calif. Acad. Medicine, Western Soc. Clin. Rsch., Pacific Coast Fertility Soc. (hon.), Israeli Endocrine Soc. (hon.), Sigma Xi, Alpha Omega Alpha. Club: University (N.Y.C.). Office: U Calif Sch Medicine Dept Pediatrics San Francisco CA 94143-0434

GRUMET, GERALD WARREN, psychiatrist; b. N.Y.C., Oct. 10, 1937; s. Joseph J. and Julia May (Ross) G.; m. Madeleine Ruth Rotter, June 29, 1961; children: Amanda, Jason, Jessica. BA, Columbia Coll., 1959; MD, NYU, 1963. Cert. Nat. Bd. Med. Examiners, Am. Bd. Psychiatry and Neurology. Intern Phila. Gen. Hosp., 1963-64; resident psychiatry U. Rochester, Rochester, N.Y., 1964-67; Post-doctoral research fellow N.Y. State Psychiat. Inst., N.Y.C., 1967-68; clin. asst. prof. psychiatry U. Rochester, Rochester, N.Y., 1970—; dir. psychiat. emergency svcs. Rochester Gen. Hosp., 1971—. Contbr. articles in clin. psychiatry to profl. jours. N.Y. State Regents scholar, 1955. Mem. Am. Psychiat. Assn., Monroe County Med. Soc. Democrat. Jewish. Home: 73 Thackery Rd Rochester NY 14610-3358 Office: Rochester Gen Hosp 1425 Portland Ave Rochester NY 14621-3001

GRUNBERG, ROBERT LEON WILLY, nephrologist; b. Bucharest, Romania, July 23, 1940; came to U.S., 1972, naturalized, 1977; s. William A. and Isabelle L. (Rosen) G.; m. Donna M. Fishman, Oct. 19, 1975; children: Wendie I., Andrea B. MD, U. Orleans-Tours, France, 1969. Diplomate Am. Bd. Internal Medicine, Am. Bd. Nephrology. Intern, then resident in cardiology Vichy (France) Hosp., 1968-72; resident in internal medicine Albert Einstein Med. Ctr., Phila., 1972-74; fellow in nephrology-hypertension Hahnemann Univ. Hosp., Phila., 1974-76, sr. clin. instr. then asst. clin. prof. div. nephrology, 1976; pvt. practice medicine specializing in nephrology Allentown, Pa., 1976—; attending physician Allentown Hosp. (now Lehigh Valley Hosp.), St. Luke's Hosp., Bethlehem, Pa., Lehigh Valley Ctr. (now Lehigh Valley Hosp.), Allentown; attending charge divsn. nephrology Easton (Pa.) Hosp.; courtesy staff Hahnemann Univ. Hosp.; dir. Renal Dialysis Ctr. at Easton (Pa.) Hosp., 1989. Fellow ACP; mem. AMA (Physician's Recognition award 1975, 79, 82, 85, 88, 89-92, 92-95, 95-98), Pa. Med. Soc., Am. Soc. Nephrology, Am. Soc. Artificial Internal Organs, Internat. Soc. Hypertension, Internat. Soc. for Artificial Organs, Internat. Soc. Nephrology, Assn. for Advancement of Med. Instrumentation, Internat. Soc. for Peritoneal Dialysis, Nat. Kidney Found., N.Y. Acad. Scis. Office: 50 S 18th St Easton PA 18042-3912 also: 401 N 17th St Allentown PA 18104-5034

GRUNDER, FRED IRWIN, program administrator, industrial hygienist; b. Detroit, Aug. 17, 1940; s. Fritz and Mary Kathrine (Irwin) G.; m. Barbara Ann Ward, May 7, 1966; children: John Frederick, Robert William. BS in Engr. Physics, U. Mich., 1963, MS in Physics, 1967. Diplomte Am. Bd. Indsl. Hygiene. Rsch. assoc. U. Mich., Ann Arbor, 1960-69; chemist G.D. Clayton & Assocs., Southfield, Mich., 1969-72; lab. dir. Bethlehem (Pa.) Steel Corp., 1972-85; dir. indsl. hygiene Am. Med. Labs., Fairfax, Va., 1985-92; mgr. lab. accreditation programs Am. Indsl. Hygiene Assn., Fairfax, 1992—. Sect. editor: Methods for Biological Monitoring, 1988. Scoutmaster Boy Scouts Am., Bethlehem, 1972-84; pres. U. Mich. Club, Lehigh Valley, 1980-84; mem. toxic planning and oversight panel Chesapeake Rsch. Consortium, Solomons Island, Md., 1990-91, site visitor AIHA Lab., 1992. Mem. ASTM, Coun. Engring. and Sci. Soc. Execs., Am. Indsl. Hygiene Assn., Am. Chem. Soc., Am. Acad. Indsl. Hygiene. Democrat. Methodist. Office: Am Indsl Hygiene Assn 2700 Prosperity Ave Ste 250 Fairfax VA 22031-4320

GRUNDFAST, KENNETH MARTIN, otolaryngologist; b. Bklyn., Mar. 12, 1944; s. Theodore Harvey and Anne Gertrude (Goldberg) G.; m. Ruthanne Blatt Grundfast, May 26, 1974; children: Rena Brett, Dara Beth. BA, Johns Hopkins U., 1965; MD, SUNY, Syracuse, 1969. Clin. instr. dept. of community medicine Georgetown U. Sch. of Medicine, Washington, 1972-74; prof. depts. otolaryngology and pediat., 1996—; resident otolaryngology Boston U. Hosp., 1974-77; fellow in pediatric otolaryngology Childrens Hosp. of Pitts., 1977-78, staff otolaryngologist, 1978-79, asst. prof. of otolaryngology, 1978-79; prof. dept. otolaryngology, 1980-96; chmn. dept. otolaryngology Children's Nat. Med. Ctr., Washington, 1980-94, vice-chmn., 1994-96; prof. otolaryngology and pediatrics Georgetown U. Sch. Medicine, Washington, 1996—; lectr. in field. Author: (with others) Ear Infections in Your Child, 1987, Pediatric Otology/Neurotology, 1996; contbr. articles to profl. jours. Lt. comdr. USPHS, 1971-73. Fellow ACS, Am. Acad. Pediat.; mem. AMA (Humanitarian award 1973), Soc. for Ear, Nose and Throat Advancement in Children (bd. dirs. 1985, v.p. 1988, pres. 1989), Am. Bronchoesophagologic Soc., Montgomery-Prince George's County Pediatric Soc., Soc. of U. Otolaryngologists, Am. Neurotology Soc., Am. Soc. Pediatric Otolaryngology (pres. 1993-94), Am. Acad. Otolaryngology (v.p. 1994-96, Presdl. Citation award 1996). Office: Georgetown U Med Ctr Dept Otolaryngology 3800 Reservoir Rd NW Washington DC 20007

GRUSKIN, ALAN KEITH, physiatrist; b. Bklyn., Dec. 10, 1955; s. Max and Marcella (Bernhard) G.; m. Paulette Katz, July 4, 1979; 2 children. BS in Biology cum laude, Fairleigh Dickinson U., 1977; DO, N.Y. Inst. Tech., 1981. Diplomate Am. Bd. Ind. Med. Examiners, Am. Bd. Phys. Medicine and Rehab. Intern St. Joseph's Hosp., Flushing, N.Y., 1981-82; resident in rehab. medicine Columbia-Presbyn. Med. Ctr., N.Y.C., 1982-84, chief resident, vis. fellow, 1984-85; mem. staff Health South Sunrise (Fla.) Rehab. Hosp., 1985—, dir. pain mgmt. program, 1988-90, dir. indsl. medicine program, 1991-95, dir. outpatient dept., 1992-95; mem. staff Pinecrest Rehab. Hosp., Delray Beach, Fla., 1988—; mem. staff St. John's Rehab. Hosp., Ft. Lauderdale, Fla., 1985-90, dir. rehab. medicine, 1986-90; pvt. practice rehab. medicine, 1986—; mem. staff Fla. Med. Ctr., Laudedale Lakes, Fla., 1985—, dir. rehab. medicine, 1987—, dir. outpatient CORF, 1994—; clin. instr. The Southeastern Coll. Osteo. Medicine, 1987-94; mem. staff Boca Raton (Fla.) Cmty. Hosp., 1987—, dir. back rehab. program, 1989-91; mem. staff Univ. Hosp., Tamarac, Fla., 1994—, North Ridge Med. Ctr., Ft. Lauderdale, Fla., 1995—; dir. rehab. medicine Colonnade Med. Ctr., Lauderdale Lakes, 1992—; dir. phys. medicine and rehab. Boca Raton Rehab. Ctr., 1992—; dir. phys. medicine and rehab. svc. Palm-Court Nursing and Rehab. Ctr., Ft. Lauderdale, 1994—; clin. assoc. prof. neurology Nova Southeastern U., 1994—; presenter in field. Fellow Am. Acad. Phys. Medicine and Rehab., Am. Osteo. Coll. Rehab. Medicine, Assn. Spine, Sports and Occupl. Rehab.; mem. Phys. Medicine and Rehab. Assn. Fla., Am. Osteo. Assn., Fla. Osteo. Assn., N.Y. Osteo. Med. Soc., Phi Omega Epsilon. Office: 8100 N University Dr Ste 102 Fort Lauderdale FL 33321 also: Golf Med Inst 900 NW 13th St Ste 104 Boca Raton FL 33486

GRUSS, PETER, molecular biologist; b. Alsfeld, Germany, June 28, 1949; s. Heinrich and Ursula (Nowotka) G.; children: Daniel, Julia. Diploma, U. Darmstadt, Fed. Republic of Germany, 1973; PhD magna cum laude, U. Heidelberg, Fed. Republic of Germany, 1977. Postdoctoral fellow Inst. Virus Rsch., 1977-78; postdoctoral fellow Lab. Molecular Virology, NIH, Bethesda, Md., 1978-80, expert cons., 1980-81, vis. scientist, 1981-82; assoc prof. microbiology Heidelberg U., 1982-86; mem. directorate Ctr. for Molecular Biology U. Heidelberg, 1983-86; dir. molecular cell biology Max-Planck Inst., Gottingen, Fed. Republic of Germany, 1986—; hon. prof. Goettingen U., 1990—. Contbr. articles to profl. jours.; MOD editor a Jour. Developmental Biology. Recipient Robert Koch Career Devel. award Clausthal-Zellerfeld, 1983, Feldberg Prize, 1992, Leibniz prize, 1994, Louis Jeantet prize, 1995, Carus medal, 1995, others. Mem. Internat. Soc. Devel. Biology (pres. 1994), Max-Planck Soc., European Molecular Biology Orgn., Am. Soc. Differentiation, N.Y. Acad. Sci., Acad. Europaea, Leopoldina, Acad. Scis. Goettingen (Germany). Office: Max Planck Inst, Am Fassberg, 37077 Göttingen Germany

GRUSSMARK, STEPHEN MICHAEL, orthodontist; b. N.Y.C., Oct. 6, 1940; s. Harry Robert and Barbara Grussmark; m. Lori Ann Grussmark, Mar. 19, 1988; children: Harrison, Devon. AA, U. Fla.; DDS, U. Md.; MSD, Fairleigh Dickinson U. Pvt. practice orthodontics Miami, Fla., 1968—; asst. clin. prof. orthodontics Sch. Dentistry U. Fla., Gainesville, 1990—; rschr. Dade County Dental Rsch., Miami, 1968—; mem. staff Miami Children's Hosp., 1970—. Capt. USAF, 1964-66. Mem. ADA, So. Soc. Orthodontics, South Miami Dental Soc., Am. Assn. Orthodontics, East Coast Dist. Dental Soc., Fla. Cleft Palate Assn. (pres. 1980, So. Fla. Acad. Orthodontics (pres. 1987, Outstanding Mem. 1989), Alpha Omega. Home: 199 Cadra Ct Coral Gables FL 33143 Office: 7400 N Kendall Dr Miami FL 33156-7706

GRUYS, ROBERT IRVING, physician, surgeon; b. Silver Creek, Minn., Oct. 15, 1917; s. Herman and Dorothy (Vondergon) G.; m. Cornelia Mol, June 30, 1943 (div. 1976); children: Kathy, Robert, William, John. B in Medicine, U. Minn., 1946, MD, 1947. Gen. surgery resident Wayne County Gen. Hosp., Detroit, 1948-49, Mpls. VA Hosp., 1958-62; postgrad. Cook County Gen. Hosp., Chgo., 1957, 63, 64, Mayo Clinic, Rochester, Minn., 1949-58, U. Minn., 1958-68, 70-75; physician, surgeon Watkins Clinic, Wells, Minn., 1949-58, 63-67, 70-75, Ganado Presbyn. Hosp., Ariz., 1953-57, Southwest Clinic, Edina, Minn., 1967-68, Chiayi Christian Hosp., Taiwan, 1968-70, Estes Park Med. Clinic, Colo., 1975-79, St. Cloud VA Med. Ctr., 1979—; mem. staff Wells Community Hosp., 1951-75, Meth. Hosp., Mpls., 1967-68, Mt. Sinai Hosp., Mpls., 1967-68, North Meml. Hosp., Mpls., 1967-76, Fairview Southdale Hosp., Mpls., 1967-68, Met. Med. Ctr., Mpls., 1967-76, Elizabeth Knutson Meml. Hosp., Estes Park, Colo., 1975-79, Weld County Gen. Hosp., Greeley, Colo., 1976-79, St. Cloud VA Med. Ctr., 1979-94; prin. physician chem. dependence alcoholic unit, 1981-94. Mem. Am. Soc. Abdominal Surgeons, Internat. Coll. Surgeons, Christian Med. Soc., AMA, Physicians Serving Physicians in Minn., Stearns-Benton County Med. Soc., Internat. Doctors in Alcoholics Anonymous, Mission Aviation Fellowship, Pilots for Christ Internat., Alpha Omega Alpha. Lodge: Masons. Mem. Reformed Ch. Avocations: flying, country-western music. Home and Office: 2100 Pleasant Ave Saint Cloud MN 56303-0223

GRYNBAUM, BRUCE B., physician, medical facility administrator; b. Anapa, Russia, May 25, 1920; came to U.S., 1939; s. Maurycy and Gertrude (Wytrzyc) G.; m. Alice Anigstein, Sept. 3, 1943 (widowed 1977); children: Steven, Gail Ann; m. Joan Brandon Reid, Dec. 5, 1981. MD, Columbia U., 1943. Med. Diplomate. Dir. rehab. medicine N.Y.C. Dept. Hosp., 1950-70; dir. rehab. medicine svc. Beekman Downtown Hosp., N.Y.C., 1950-83; assoc. dir. rehab. medicine svc. Bellevue Hosp., N.Y.C., 1950-58, dir. rehab. medicine svc., 1958-87; prof. clin. rehab. medicine N.Y.U. Sch. Medicine, N.Y.C., 1968—; vice chmn. Dept. Rehab. Medicine, clin. dir. Rusk Inst. N.Y.U. Med. Ctr., 1983—; exec. com. Cen. Labor Rehab. Coun., N.Y.C., 1969—; bd. mem. N.Y. State Labor Community Svcs. Agy., 1986—; v.p. med. affairs World Rehab. Fund, 1989—. With U.S. Army, 1944-46. Recipient Silver Bicentennial medal Columbia U. Coll. Physicians and Surgeons, 1967, Disting. Clin. award Am. Acad. Phys. Medicine and Rehab., 1987, Howard A. Rusk award Aux. to Rusk Inst., 1990. Mem. Am. Acad. Phys. Medicine and Rehab., N.Y. Acad. Medicine, APHA, AMA, N.Y. Soc. Phys. Medicine and Rehab., Union League Club. Office: Rusk Inst Rehabilitation 400 E 34th St New York NY 10016-4901

GRZEBIENIAK, JOHN FRANCIS, psychologist; b. New Castle, Pa., Jan. 9, 1949; s. John and Helen (Mielcuszny) G.; married; children: Anna Helen, Sarah Mary, Andrew John. BA, Youngstown (Ohio) State U., 1970, MS in Edn., 1974; PhD, U. Pitts., 1982. Lic. psychologist, Ohio, Pa.; cert. chem. dependency counselor. Substance abuse counselor, mental health counselor Columbiana County Mental Health Counseling Ctr., 1974-82, intern in psychology, 1982-84; cons. psychologist Diagnostic and Evaluation Clinic, Youngstown, 1985—; staff psychologist Columbiana County Mental Health Ctr., 1984-95, sr. psychologist, 1995—; cons. psychologist Beaver (Pa.) Valley Psychol. Svcs., 1988-90; adj. prof. dept. psychology Kent (Ohio) State U., 1989—. Mem. APA. Roman Catholic. Office: Columbiana County Mental Health Ctr 40722 State Route 154 Lisbon OH 44432-8500

GRZESIAK, ROBERT CHARLES, therapist; b. Depew, N.Y., Feb. 2, 1948; s. Charles J. and Charlotte M. (Dzwigal) G.; m. Catherine L. Vella, Aug. 25, 1972; 1 child, Barry Robert. BA in Psychology cum laude, SUNY, Buffalo, 1971; D Clin. Hypnotherapy, Am. Inst. Hypnotherapy, Irvine, Calif., 1991; MA in Psychology, Newport U., 1993, postgrad, 1993—. Cert. hypnotherapist; registered hypnotherapist. Med. rehab. caseworker Erie County Dept. Health, Buffalo, 1971-73; supr. U.S. Dept. Commerce, Buffalo, 1973-74; foodsvc. sales mgr. Rath Packing Co., Dallas, 1974-84; food svc. sales mgr. Wilson Foods Co., Dallas, 1984—; pvt. practice therapist Arlington, Tex., 1991—. Republican. Roman Catholic. Home: 1005 Brook Hill Ct Arlington TX 76014-3353

GRZYBOWSKI, JACEK KAROL, biologist; b. Szrensk, Poland, June 4, 1939; s. Stanislaw and Honorata (Wrzesien) G.; m. Maria Rachubik, Mar. 7, 1964; children: Anna, Michal, Ewa. MS in Biology, U. Warsaw, 1971; PhD, Mil. Inst. Hygiene, 1976, docent, 1981, prof., 1995. Assoc. Mil. Inst. Hygiene and Epidemiology, Warsaw, 1971-76, asst. lectr., 1976-81, asst. prof., 1981-90, 92-95, prof., head dept. microbiology, 1995—; vis. scientist U. Calif. Med. Ctr., San Diego, 1990-92; scientific sec. com. immunology Polish Acad. Scis., Warsaw, 1980-89, mem. scientific coun. inst. biochemistry and biophysics, 1984-89; mem. scientific coun. Mil. Inst. Hygiene and Epidemiology, 1984—. Mem. editl. coun. Annals of Burns, 1995—. Mem. Polish Burn Assn. (bd. dirs. 1993—), Polish Soc. Microbiologists, Polish Soc. Immunology. Home: Zwierzyniecka 9/40, 00-719 Warsaw Poland Office: Mil Inst Hygiene and Epidemiology, Kozielska 4, 01-163 Warsaw Poland

GSCHWEND, PAUL, III, surgeon; b. Reading, Pa., Jan. 12, 1945; s. Paul and Jane Berenice (Treat) G.; m. Dorothy Louise Moore, Sept. 6, 1969; children: Katherine Hinchliffe, Jennifer Williams. BA, Hiram Coll., 1966; MD, U. Pa., 1970. Diplomate Am. Bd. Surgery. Intern Hosp. U. Pa., Phila., 1970-71; resident Grad. Hosp. U. Pa., Phila., 1974-77; gen. surgeon Lancaster, Pa., 1977—; chmn. dept. surgery St. Joseph Hosp., Lancaster, 1987-90, sect. chief gen. surgery, 1990—; pres. Pa. Regional Ind. Physicians Assocs., Lancaster, 1993—. Served to lt. cmdr. USNR, 1972-74. Fellow Am. Coll. Surgeons. Office: 822 Marietta Ave Lancaster PA 17603

GUARINO, ANTHONY MICHAEL, pharmacologist, educator, consultant, counselor; b. Framingham, Mass., Dec. 11, 1934; s. Alfred V. and Nellie L. (Beatrice) G.; m. Aida Iris Gerena, Nov. 9, 1957; children: Theresa, Elizabeth, Barbara, Cathy, Tom, Gregory, Paula, Phil, Richard, Paul. BS in Chemistry, Boston Coll., 1956; MS in Chemistry, U. R.I., 1963, PhD in Pharmacology and Toxicology, 1966; MA in Counseling, Liberty U., 1993. Lic. profl. counselor. Lt. comdr. USPHS, 1966, advanced through grades to capt., 1979; staff fellow pharmacology-toxicology rsch. assoc. program Nat. Heart Inst., NIH, Bethesda, Md., 1966-68; rsch. pharmacologist NCI Nat. Cancer Inst., NIH, Bethesda, Md., 1968-73, chief lab. toxicology, 1973-80; regulatory pharmacologist Ctr. for Drugs and Biologics-FDA, Md., 1980-84; lab. dir. seafood rsch. divsn. FDA, Dauphin Island, Ala., 1984-93; adj. prof. U. South Ala. Coll. Medicine, Mobile, 1984—, U. South Ala. Coll. Allied Health Professions, Mobile, 1996—; vice chmn. com. on animals as monitors in environ. hazards NAS. Contbg. author: Handbook of Experimental Pharmacology—Concepts in Biochemical Pharmacology, 1971, Handbook of Experimental Pharmacology, Antineoplastic and Immunosuppressive Agents, 1974, Methods in Cancer Research, 1979, Pesticides and Xenobiotics Metabolism in Aquatic Organisms, 1979, Pesticides and Xenobiotics Metabolism in Aquatic Organisms, 1979, Cisplatin—Current Status and New Developments, 1980, Modern Pharmacology, 1982; contbr. 106 articles to profl. jours. Mem. Am. Soc. Pharmacology and Exptl. Thearapeutics, Soc. Toxicology, Am. Chem. Soc., Am. Counseling Assn., Am. Assn. Christian Counselors. Roman Catholic. Home: 968 Westbury Dr Mobile AL 36609-3332 Office: U S Ala Coll Medicine Dept Pharmacology MSB 3130 Mobile AL 36688

GUARINO, MICHAEL J., medical educator; b. Phila., Dec. 30, 1953; s. Angelo A. and Clorinda (Fioravanti) G.; m. Patricia A. Tedesco, July 3, 1976; children: Andrew, Robert, Jeffrey, Suzanne. BS in Chemistry, St. Joseph's U., 1975; MD, Thomas Jefferson U., 1979. Diplomate Am. Bd. Internal Medicine, Am. Bd. Med. Oncology. Intern Med. Ctr. Del., 1979-80, residency in internal medicine, 1980-82; fellow, instr. in medicine Strong Meml. Hosp. U. Rochester (N.J.), 1982-84; sr. staff dept. medicine Med. Ctr. Del., Wilmington, 1984—; instr. medicine Thomas Jefferson U., Phila., 1984—; chmn. cancer com. Meml. Hosp. Salem (N.J.) County, 1985—; med. dir. Hospice Salem County, Salem, 1986—; dir. protocol office cancer ctr. Med. Ctr. Del., Wilmington, 1988—, mem. bone marrow transplant team, 1989—. Mem. AMA, Am. Soc. Internal Medicine, Am. Assn. Clin. Oncology. Democrat. Roman Catholic. Office: Med Oncology Cons 1941 Limestone Rd Wilmington DE 19808-5400

GUAY, ANDRÉ THEODORE, physician, researcher; b. Worcester, Mass., July 19, 1942; s. Theodore Alfred and Anna Estelle (Chabot) G.; m. Barbara Maria Madore, Aug. 14, 1965; children: Andrea, Danielle, Stephanie. BS in Biology, Boston Coll., 1964; MD, N.J. Coll. Medicine, Newark, 1968. Diplomate in internal medicine, endocrinology and metabolism Am. Bd. Internal Medicine. Fellow in endocrinology Mayo Clinic, Rochester, Minn., 1972-74; head endocrinology Naval Regional Med. Ctr., Portsmouth, Va., 1975-77; staff Lahey Clinic, Burlington, Mass., 1977—, head endocrinology, 1985-94; dir. Joslin-Lahey Diabetes Ctr., Lahey North, Peabody, Mass., 1994—; head Ctr. for Sexual Function, Lahey North, Peabody, 1994—; asst. prof. medicine Eastern Va. Coll. Medicine, Norfolk, 1975-77; asst. prof. medicine Harvard Med. Sch., Boston, 1985-96, assoc. prof., 1996—. Contbr. articles to profl. jours. Lt. comdr. M.C., USN, 1974-77. Fellow ACP, Am. Coll. Endocrinology; mem. The Endocrine Soc., Am. Soc. Andrology, Am. Soc. Clin. Endocrinologists. Home: One Wayside Ln Acton MA 01720 Office: Lahey-Hitchcock Clinic Lahey North One Essex Center Dr Peabody MA 01960

GUAZZO, EUGENE, family physician, educator; b. Orange, N.J., May 5, 1929; s. Eugene and Augustina (Pivano) G.; m. Shelby Smith Palmer, Oct. 1960; children: Eugene T., John Palmer, Dante E. 2d, Shelby Smith. BS in Edn., Auburn U., 1952, MS in Psychology, 1954; postgrad. in medicine, Upsala Coll., 1960-61; MD, Duke U., 1965. Diplomate Am. Bd. Family Practice, Nat. Bd. Med. Examiners; cert. lay reader, preacher Episcopal Ch., 1975. Resident in family practice Hunterdon Med. Ctr., Flemington, N.J., 1965-67; rsch. fellow in family medicine Harvard U., Boston, 1967-68; pvt. practice Mechanicsville, Md., 1968-73, Chaptico, Md., 1974—; asst. prof. family medicine U. Md. Sch. Medicine, Balt., 1974—; head newborn nursery St. Mary's Hosp., Leonardtown, Md., 1969-74, chief staff, 1977-78, bd. dirs., 1976-80; physician dir. Md. Infirmary, Chaptico, 1974—; mem. staff U. Md. Hosp., Balt. Contbr. articles to medl jours. and sports mags. Active Nat. Capital Area coun. Boy Scouts Am. Lt. USN, 1955-59. Holloway scholar, 1948; Mead Johnson scholar, 1966. Fellow Am. Acad. Family Physicians; mem. AMA (physician recognition award 1979, 81, 84, 87, 90, 93, 96), Mass. Med. Soc., Md. Med. Soc. (com. on med. ethics), St. Mary's County Med. Soc., Med. and Chirurg. Faculty Md., Trent Soc. History Medicine, Philos. Soc. Washington, U.S. Naval Inst., Am. Radio Relay League, Md. Assn. for Wildlife Conservation, Masters Foxhounds Assn. Am., Nat. Eagle Scout Assn., Army and Navy Club (Washington), St. Mary's River Yacht Club, Wicomico Beach Yacht Club, So. Md. Soc., Kappa Sigma, others. Republican. Home: Willow Glen Farm Maddox MD 20621 Office: U MD Infirmary Sch Medicine Chaptico MD 20621

GUBA, ALEXANDER MICHAEL, plastic surgeon; b. Chgo., Dec. 22, 1946; s. Alexander Michael Sr. and Laura G.; divorced; children: Katherine, Alexander M. III, Thomas. BA, Johns Hopkins U., 1968; MD, U. Ill., Chgo., 1972. Intern in surgery Johns Hopkins, 1972-73, resident in gen. surgery, 1973-74; resident in gen. surgery Walter Reed, 1974-77, rsch. fellow, 1977-79; resident in plastic surgery Johns Hopkins, 1979-81; plastic surgeon pvt. practice, Coral Gables, Fla., 1981-82, Johns Hopkins Sch. Medicine, Balt., 1982—. Maj. U.S. Army, 1974-79. Mem. Johns Hopkins Club. Office: 6565 N Charles St Ste 605 Baltimore MD 21204

GUBERMAN, RONALD MARK, podiatrist; b. Queens, N.Y., Dec. 13, 1960; s. Jack Solomon Guberman and Edith Lee (Stall) Grey; m. Denise Michele Reich, Aug. 16, 1986; 2 children: Ashley Nicole, Alec Tyler. BA, SUNY, Binghamton, 1983; D of Podiatric Medicine, N.Y. Coll. Podiatric Medicine, 1987. Resident Wyckoff Hts. Hosp., Bklyn., 1987-89, co-chief resident, 1988-89, site dir. podiatric residency program, 1989—, attending podiatric physician, 1989—; attending podiatric physician New Rochelle (N.Y.) Hosp., 1991—; pvt. practice Mamaroneck, Ridgewood, N.Y., 1989—. Author: (with others) Clinics in Podiatric Medicine, 1987, 89. Fellow Am. Coll. Foot Surgeons; mem. Am. Bd. Podiatric Surgery, N.Y. Acad. Scis., Am. Acad. Podiatric Sports Medicine. Office: 143 Mamaroneck Ave Mamaroneck NY 10543 Office: 6083 Myrtle Ave Ridgewood NY 11385-5908

GUBLER, DUANE J., research scientist, administrator; b. Santa Clara, Utah, June 4, 1939; s. June and Thelma (Whipple) G.; m. Bobbie J. Carroll, Mar. 1, 1958; children: Justin Chase, Stuart Jefferson. BS, Utah State U., 1963; MS, U. Hawaii, 1965; ScD, Johns Hopkins U., 1969; AS, So. Utah State U., 1962, DSc (hon.), 1988. Asst. prof. pathogiology Sch. Hygiene Johns Hopkins U., Balt. and Calcutta, 1969-71; assoc. prof. tropical medicine Sch. Medicine U. Hawaii, Honolulu, 1971-75; head virology dept. Naval Med. Rsch. Unit Number 2, Jakarta, Indonesia, 1975-78; assoc. prof. U. Ill., Urbana, 1978-79; rsch. microbiologist divsn. vector-borne viral diseases Ctrs. for Disease Control and Prevention, Fort Collins, Colo., 1980-81; dir. San Juan (P.R.) Labs. Ctrs. for Disease Control and Prevention, 1981-89; dir. divsn. vector-borne infectious diseases Ctrs. for Disease Control and Prevention, Ft. Collins, Colo., 1989—; cons. NRC, 1972, South Pacific Commn., 1972-76, WHO, Geneva, 1974—, AID, Washington, 1977—, Pan Am. Health Orgn., 1981—, Internat. Devel. Rsch. Ctr., Ottawa, Can., 1977—, Rockefeller Found., N.Y.C., 1987—, numerous nat. ministries of health, 1972—. Contbr. numerous articles to profl. jours. Lt. USN, 1975-77; capt. USPHS. Recipient Commendation medal, 1984, Outstanding Svc. medal, 1988, Meritorious Svc. medal, 1991, Outstanding Unit citation, 1995. Mem. AAAS, Am. Soc. Tropical Medicine (Charles Franklin Craig lectr. 1988), Am. Soc. Parasitologists, Am. Mosquito Control Assn., Entomol. Soc. Am. (highlights in med. entomology lecture 1979), Soc. Vector Ecologists, Infectious Disease Soc. Am., Rotary (Rotarian of Yr. San Juan chpt. 1986, Meritorious Svc. award Rotary Found., Evanston, Ill. 1990). Home: 717 Dartmouth Trl Fort Collins CO 80525-1522 Office: Ctrs for Disease Control and Prevention USPHS PO Box 2087 Fort Collins CO 80522-2087

GUDANEK, LOIS BASSOLINO, social worker; b. N.Y.C., Jan. 28, 1944; d. Frank and Anna (Scarlata) Bassolino; m. Richard Stanley Gudanek, Sept. 3, 1977. BA in Anthropology and Sociology, Queens Coll., 1973; postgrad., Hunter Coll., 1973-76, JRW Inst. Alcohol Studies, 1988-89; student Eating Disorders Inst., Rollins Coll., 1991; MSW, Fordham U., 1994. Cert. alcoholism counselor, social worker, HIV counselor, N.Y. Student intern Arms Acres, Carmel, N.Y., 1988-89; adult therapist Arms Acres, Carmel, 1989-91; vocat. counselor Westchester County Med. Ctr.-Alcoholism Treatment Svcs., Yonkers, 1991-94, Westchester County Med. Ctr.-WEST-PREP, Valhalla, N.Y., 1994-96; pvt. practice White Plains, N.Y., 1994—; social worker The Week-End Ctr., Mt. Kisco, N.Y., 1996—; lectr. JRW Inst. on Alcohol Studies, Yonkers, N.Y., 1991, St. Thomas Aquinas Coll., 1994; presenter in field. Mem. NASW, Internat. Assn. Eating Disorders Profls. (sec. tri-state region 1989-91, vice-chmn. 1991—, ednl. coord. 1992—), Nat. Assn. Alcoholism and Drug Abuse Counselors, N.Y. Fedn. Alcoholism and Chem. Dependency Counselors, N.Y. Womens Coalition on Chem. Dependency (treas. 1991-92, bd. dirs. 1994—), Adoptees' Liberty Movement Assn. Office: The Week-End Ctr 120 Kisco Ave Mount Kisco NY 10549 also: 200 Bloomingdale Rd Ste 1 White Plains NY 10605

GUDAS, LORRAINE JEAN, biochemist, molecular biologist, educator; b. Syracuse, N.Y., May 12, 1949; d. Albert Joseph and Eleanor (Bogden) G.; 1 child, Gregory Paul Wagner. BA, Smith Coll., 1970; PhD, Princeton U., 1975. Postdoctoral fellow U. Calif., San Francisco, 1975-80; mem. faculty Harvard Med. Sch., Boston, 1980—; prof., chmn dept. of pharmacology Cornell Med Coll, New York. Home: 431 E 85th St New York NY 10028-6301 Office: Dept of Pharmacologynst Cornell Medical College 1300 York Ave New York NY 10021*

GUDEON, ARTHUR, podiatrist; b. N.Y.C., Feb. 27, 1935; s. Samuel and Mina (Kaminsky) G.; m. Loretta Bachrach, June 16, 1957 (div. 1976); children: Karla, Marilyn, Adam; m. Susan Steinmetz, Apr. 8, 1979; 1 child, Andrea. BA, NYU, 1956; D Podiatric Medicine, N.Y. Coll. Podiatric Medicine, 1960. Diplomate Am. Bd. Podiatric Surgery, Am. Bd. Foot and Ankle Surgery. Pvt. practice podiatry Family Podiatry of Rego Park, N.Y., 1960—; sr. faculty, mem. residency selection com. St. Joseph's Hosp. Catholic Med. Ctr., N.Y.C., 1980—; clin. assoc. prof. surgery, external faculty N.Y. Coll. Podiatric Medicine, 1989—; dep. examiner N.Y. State Bd. Podiatry, 1981; podiatry chmn., mem. adv. coun. for occupational edn. N.Y.C. Bd. Edn., 1980—; cons. utilization and peer rev. coms. Vol. local health fairs, sch. programs, sports events, N.Y., 1965—. Fellow Am. Coll. Foot Surgeons (pres. N.Y. divsn. 1990-93), Am. Assn. Hosp. Podiatrists; mem. N.Y. State Podiatric Med. Assn. (chmn. sci. affairs com. Queens divsn. 1984—, chmn. N.Y. state sci. affairs com. 1986-90, Podiatrist of Yr. 1969, 74), Am. Soc. Podiatric Med. Assts. (hon., bd. dirs. 1983-87, Podiatrist of Yr. 1989), Am. Podiatric Med. Assn., Am. Podiatric Sports Medicine Acad. Democrat. Jewish. Office: Family Podiatry of Rego Pk 91-35 63rd Dr Rego Park NY 11374-3849

GUDJONSSON, BIRGIR, physician; b. Akureyri, Iceland, Nov. 8, 1938; s. Gudjon and Kristjana (Jakobsdottir) Vigfusson; m. Heidur Anna Vigfusdottir, Oct. 21, 1961; children: Asdis, Gunnar, Sigrun. MD, U. Iceland, 1965; postgrad. fellow Yale U., 1970-72. Diplomate internal medicine and gastroenterology; recert. in internal medicine. Intern, Stamford Hosp., Conn., 1966-67, resident, 1967-68; resident in medicine Yale New Haven Hosp., 1968-70; asst. prof. medicine Yale U. Med. Sch., 1972-73, 77-78, 82; practice medicine specializing in internal medicine and gastroenterology, Reykjavik, 1974—; cons. City Hosp., Reykjavik, 1974-77, Med. Clinic, 1974—. Author: (with H.M. Spiro) Controversies in Internal Medicine, 1980; contbr. articles to profl. jours., chpt. to sports medicine manual. Mem. Icelandic Athletic Fedn., 1981—. Fellow ACP, Royal Coll. Physicians London,, Royal Soc. Medicine; mem. Am. Gastroenterol. Assn., Brit. Soc. Gastroenterology, Brit. Assn. Sport and Medicine, Am. Coll. Sports-Medicine, World Assn. Hepato-Pancreato-Biliary Surgery, N.Y. Acad. Sci., Amateur Athletic Fedn. (mem. med. com.) Lutheran. Club: Reykjavik Athletic. Avocation: international judge in athletics and gymnastics. Home: Alftamyri 51, 108 Reykjavik Iceland Office: Medical Clinic, Alfheimum 74, 108 Reykjavik Iceland

GUEFT, BORIS, retired health facility administrator; b. Cannes, France, Nov. 10, 1916; came to U.S., 1917; s. Amshel and Nina (Oussoltseff) G.; m. Eula Mae Respess, June 25, 1943; children: Nina, Esther, Michael. AB, Columbia U., 1938; MD, NYU, 1941. Intern Sinai Hosp., Balt., 1941-42;

resident New Britain Gen. Hosp., 1942-43, fellow, 1946-47; resident, fellow Mt. Sinai Hosp., N.Y.C., 1947-50; lab. dir. Fairfield State Hosp., Newtown, Conn., 1950-55; dir. pathology VA Hosp., Cin., 1955-58; prof. pathology Albert Einstein Coll. Medicine, Bronx, N.Y., 1958-71; lab. dir. Union Hosp., Bronx, 1970-95; ret., 1995; prof. N.Y. Med. Coll., Valhalla, 1975—. Contbr. numerous articles to profl. jours. Capt. M.C., U.S. Army, 1943-46, ETO. Decorated Bronze Star. Fellow ACP, Am. Assn. Pathologists, Sigma Xi. Home: 25 Vanderbilt Rd Scarsdale NY 10583-7218

GUÉRITÉE, NICOLAS, endocrinologist; b. Bucharest, Romania, Dec. 29, 1920; s. Virgile-Georges and Marie-Antoinette (Gebhardt) G.; m. Gabriela Rizescu, Dec. 6, 1944 (div. 1954); 1 child, Jean-Claude; m. Lucienne Suzanne Taillebois, July 24, 1954; children: Catherine, Virginie. MD, U. Med. Sch., Bucharest, 1944, Faculté de Médecine, Paris, 1952. Pvt. practice medicine specializing in endocrinology Paris, 1957-85; cons. in endocrinology Hosp. of Nanterre, Paris, 1958-66, Endocrine Dept. Faculty of Medicine La Pitié-Salpétriére, Paris, 1960-85; head med. dept. French Sub. of Schering A.G. Berlin, Paris, 1949-58; head rsch. dept. Lab. Théramex SA, Monaco and Paris, 1958-75; bd. dirs. Laboratoire Théramex SA, 1975—; expert WHO, 1958; mem. French Nat. Com. of Qualification of the Endocrinologists, 1976-89; founder, exec. ann. Journees Francaises de'Endocrinologie Clinique, 1980—; pres. EEC Specialist Sect. of Endocrinology, 1989-94; mem. exec. com. European Bd. Endocrinology, 1994—. Founder, chief editor La Revue Francaise d'Endocrinologie Clinique, 1960—; inventor steroid compounds. Mem. French Nat. Union of Endocrinologists (founder, exec. pres. 1960-91), Societe Francaise d'Endocrinologie, Am. Soc. Bone and Mineral Rsch., Soc. for Study of Reprodn., Endocrine Soc. (Am.). Christian Orthodox.

GUERRANT, JOHN LIPPINCOTT, retired allergist, educator; b. Callaway, Va., Dec. 28, 1910; s. Samuel Saunders and Florence (Thomson) G.; m. Laura Elizabeth Bailey, Nov. 30, 1945; children: Laura Elizabeth Smith, Sallie Guerrant Herling. BS, Hampden Sydney Coll., 1933; MD, U. Va., 1937, MS, 1942. Lic. physician, Va. Resident physician Episcopal Hosp., Phila., 1938-40; fellow internal medicine U. Va. Hosp., Charlottesville, 1940-41, chief resident physician, 1941-42; instr. medicine to prof. medicine U. Va. Sch. Medicine, Charlottesville, 1946-80, emeritus prof. medicine, 1980-93; ret., 1993; dir. rev. orgn. Contbr. articles on lung disease and allergy to profl. jours. Maj. AUS, 1942-46. Named Endowed Chair, U. Va. Sch. Medicine, Charlottesville, 1985. Fellow ACP, Am. Acad. Allergy and Immunology (v.p.); mem. AMA, Am. Thoracic Soc., Va. Med. Soc. (pres.), Va. Lung Assn. (pres.), South East Allergy Assn. (pres.). Democrat. Presbyterian. Home: 108 Falcon Dr Charlottesville VA 22901-2013

GUERRERO, REUBEN CASTRO, medical oncologist, internist; b. Manila, Aug. 22, 1935; came to U.S., 1962, naturalized, 1978; s. Jacobo Tolentino and Francisca Claravall (Castro) G.; AA, U. Philippines, Manila, 1952, MD (Univ. scholar, 1955-56; United Drug Co. scholar, 1956-57), 1957; m. Celina V. Sison, June 18, 1962; children: Chiarina, Leonora, Anthony Paul. Intern, Philippine Gen. Hosp., Manila, 1956-57; mem. faculty Coll. of Medicine, U. Philippines, 1957-62; resident in medicine, Ch. Home and Hosp., Balt., 1962-64, chief resident, 1965-66; postdoctoral fellow in medicine Johns Hopkins Hosp., Balt., 1964-65, postdoctoral fellow in med. oncology, 1966-68; asst. prof. medicine, chief chemotherapy div. U. Philippines and Cancer Inst., 1968-73; med. oncologist, chmn. cancer com., chmn. dept. hematology-oncology Straub Clinic and Hosp., Honolulu, 1973—; clin. assoc. prof. John A. Burns Sch. Medicine, U. Hawaii; chmn. research Philippine Cancer Soc., 1969-73; pres. Hawaii-Pacific div. Am. Cancer Soc., 1989-90; CME coord. Aloha Med. Misson. Served with Philippine Army Res., 1957-58. Fellow ACP; mem. Am. Soc. Internal Medicine, Am. Soc. Clin. Oncology, Philippine Soc. Med. Oncology,Honolulu County Med. Soc., Hawaii Med. Assn. (cancer commn.), AMA, Am. Geriatric Soc., Aerospace Med. Assn., Honolulu Marathon Assn. Republican. Roman Catholic. Club: Honolulu. Contbr. articles to profl. jours. Home: 2159 Okoa St Honolulu HI 96821-2647 Office: Straub Clinic and Hosp 888 S King St Honolulu HI 96813-3009

GUERRIERO, DAVID JOHN, physician; b. Chgo., Oct. 2, 1963; s. E. John and Theresa (Cea) G.; m. Robin Lynn Taylor, Sept. 6, 1987; children: Alexandra Nichole, Grantly. BA, Taylor U., 1985; BS, Palmer U., 1990, DC, 1990. Diplomate Am. Acad. Pain Mgmt. Adj. prof. anatomy Valencia C.C., Orlando, Fla., 1991-93; chiropractor Fla. Chiropractic Medicine, Inc., Orlando; bd. dirs. Fla. Chiropractic Medicine, Inc. Contbr. articles to profl. jours. Fellow Am. Back Soc.; mem. Am. Chiropractic Assn., Fla. Chiropractic Assn., Nat. Assn. Chiropractic Medicine, Aircraft Owners and Pilots Assn., Exptl. Aircraft Assn., Profl. Assn. Diving Instrs. Office: Fla Chiropractic Medicine 4804 Edgewater Dr Orlando FL 32804

GÜERRISSI, JORGE ORLANDO, plastic surgeon, consultant; b. Viedma, Rio Negro, Argentina, Sept. 17, 1947; s. Antonio Guerrissi and Blanca Bancala; m. Maria Cristina Staffora, Nov. 3, 1973; children: Jorge, Sol, Sofia. BS, U. La Plata, Argentina, 1975. Resident in surgery Municipalidad Ciudad Buenos Aires, 1972, chief resident, 1976, instr. resident, 1978-85, fellow in plastic surgery, 1988; chief Dept. Plastic Surgery, Buenos Aires, 1990; cons. maxilofacial area sanatorio otamendi, Buenos Aires, 1989; univ. authorized docent U. Buenos Aires, 1995. Author: Craniomaxillofacial Trauma; contbr. chpts. to books and articles to profl. jours. Mem. Argentine Soc. Plastic Surgery, Argentine Soc. Pat. Cabeza y Cuello. Home and Office: Libertado 985, Quilmes Buenos Aires 1878, Argentina

GUESON, EMERITA TORRES, obstetrician, gynecologist; b. Angeles City, Philippines, Jan. 4, 1942; came to U.S., 1964; d. Lina (Torres) Gueson. AA, U. Sto. Tomas, Manila, Philippines, 1958, MD, 1963. Resident Phila. Gen. Hosp., 1966-71; attending physician Nazareth Hosp., Phila., 1973—, Holy Redeemer Hosp., Meadowbrook, Pa., 1983—; bd. dirs. Physicians Who Care; lectr. healthcare issues to consumer groups, Phila. Author: Doctors Under Fire, 1989, Scales of Justice: Exploring the Wilderness of Health Care and Society's Moral Conscience, 1992; pub. ThereseVision Publs.; also med. writer, screenplay writer, line dir., prodr. Fellow Am. Coll. of Ob.-Gyn., ACP; mem. Phila. County Med. Soc., Pa. Med. Soc., AMA, Pro-life Ob.-Gynecologists (charter). Office: 3336 Aldine St Philadelphia PA 19136 also: Holy Redeemer Med Ctr Med Bldg Ste 309 Meadowbrook PA 19046

GUESS, HARRY ADELBERT, epidemiologist; b. N.Y.C., Dec. 24, 1940; s. Harry Adelbert and Vista (Brabham) G.; m. Geraldine Graflund; children: Carol Ann, Alison Pauline. BS in Applied Math., Ga. Inst. Tech., 1964; MS in Ops. Rsch., PhD in Math., Stanford U., 1972; MD, U. Miami, 1979. Asst. prof. math. U. Rochester, N.Y., 1972-73; mem. tech. staff Bell Telephone Labs., Holmdel, N.J., 1973-75; rsch. mathematician Nat. Inst. Environ. Health Scis., Research Triangle Park, N.C., 1975-77; resident N.C. Meml. Hosp., Chapel Hill, 1979-82; from assoc. dir. to sr. dir. Merck Sharp & Dohme Rsch. Labs., Blue Bell, Pa., 1982-87, 88—, sr. dir. dept. epidemiology, 1988—; dir. epidemiology and post mktg. surveillance Glaxo Inc., Research Triangle Park, 1987-88; adj. prof. epidemiology and biostatistics U. N.C., Chapel Hill, 1991—; vis. scientist Mayo Clinic, Rochester, Minn., 1983—; vis. sr. rsch. assoc. European Inst. Oncology, 1995—; cons. Ctrs. Disease Control, 1990, FDA, 1990. Contbr. articles to profl. jours.; editorial adv. bd. Jour. Clin. Epidemiology, 1991—, Epidemiology, 1992—; reviewer for numerous jours. Lt. USN, 1964-69. Grantee NIH. Fellow Am. Acad. Pediat., Am. Coll. Preventive Medicine, Am. Coll. Epidemiology; mem. AMA, Drug Info. Assn. (pres. 1992), Soc. for Epidemiol. Rsch., Biometric Soc. Home: 104 Waterford Pl Chapel Hill NC 27514-6519 Office: U NC Sch Pub Health Dept Epidemiology McGavran-Greenberg Hall CB #7400 Chapel Hill NC 27599-7400

GUEST, RICHARD EUGENE, psychologist; b. LaJunta, Colo., Mar. 16, 1944; s. John William and Lorraine Alice (Smith) G.; m. Linda Jeanne Sand, June 5, 1966; children: Elise Michelle, Gregory Douglas. BS, Colo. State U., 1966, postgrad., 1966-67; MDiv, Iliff Sch. Theology, Denver, 1970; PhD, Northwestern U., Evanston, Ill., 1979. Lic. psychologist, Colo. Resident supr. Ft. Logan Mental Health Ctr., Denver, 1968-70; interim Protestant chaplain Denver Gen. Hosp., 1970; dir. Winnetka (Ill.) Youth Orgn., 1973-74; prin. chaplaincy rschr. McGaw Med. Ctr., Chgo., 1974-76; adminstr. dir. Des Moines Pastoral Counseling Ctr., 1976-79, co-dir., co-founder grief clinic, 1977-79; dir. Interfaith Ctr. for Edn. in Marriage and Family Living, Ft. Collins, Colo., 1979-81; EAP mgr. EAP Sys., Woburn, Mass., 1987-88; asst. prof. Colo. State U., Ft. Collins, 1988-90, faculty affiliate, 1990—; pvt. practice Ft. Collins, 1981—; dir. Ctr. Human Relationships, Ft. Collins, 1990—; psychol. cons. Iowa Conf. United Meth. Ch., Des Moines, 1977-79; cons. Iowa Children's Family Svcs., Des Moines, 1977-79; v.p., dir. tng. Transitions Mediation Svcs., Ft. Collins, 1982-86; allied health staff Poudre Valley Hosp., 1984-87 and Mountain Crest Hosp., Ft. Collins, 1990—; presenter workshops and presentations; psychologist New Beginnings, Ft. Collins, 1991-93. Co-author: Organization and Administration of Pastoral Counseling Centers, 1981; contbr. articles to profl. jours. Adv. coun. Resource Assistance Ctr. for Non-Profits, Ft. Collins, 1980-82; pres., bd. dirs. Crossroads Safehouse for Battered Women, Ft. Collins, 1981-84; psychol. advisor Hospice of Larimer County, Ft. Collins, 1984-86; co-founder, bd. dirs. Children and Family Ctr., Ft. Collins, 1994—. Named Outstanding Young Man of Sterling, Jaycees, 1972. Mem. APA, Am. Assn. for Marriage and Family Therapy (clin. mem.), Larimer County Mental Health Profls. Network, Ft. Collins Ind. Practice Assn., No. Colo. Mental Health Profls., Inc. (stds. com.), Beta Beta Beta, Alpha Kappa Delta. Office: Ctr Human Relationships 3000 S College Ave Ste 104 Fort Collins CO 80525-2558

GUGGENHEIMER, JAMES, dentist, educator; b. Belgrade, Yugoslavia, Mar. 4, 1936; came to U.S., 1938; s. Siegfried and Eta (Rubowitz) G.; m. Constance Fitzgerald, Mar. 27, 1969; children: Paul, Peter, Gregor. BS, CCNY, 1958; DDS, Columbia U., 1962. Diplomate Am. Bd. Oral Medicine. Intern VA Hosp., Albany, N.Y., 1962-63; resident oral surgery Strong Meml. Hosp., Rochester, N.Y., 1963-64; fellow oral medicine Phila. (Pa.) Gen. Hosp., 1964-66; asst. prof. Univ. Pitts (Pa.) Sch. Dental Medicine, 1966-70, assoc. prof., 1970-76, prof., 1976—; cons. staff Presbyn. Univ. Hosp., Pitts., 1968—, Montefiore Univ. Hosp., Pitts, 1968—; mem. Pitts. Cancer Inst., 1986—. Mem. tobacco control com. Am. Cancer Soc., Pitts., 1986; bd. dirs. Am. Chronic Pain Assn., Pitts., 1989. Mem. APHA, Am. Assn. Dental Rsch., Am. Acad. Oral Medicine, Omicron Kappa Upsilon. Home: 971 Wellesley Rd Pittsburgh PA 15206-1728 Office: Univ Pitts Sch Dental Med 3501 Terrace St Pittsburgh PA 15213-2523

GUGLIUZZA, KRISTENE KOONTZ, transplant and general surgery educator; b. Siloam Springs, Ark., May 2, 1956; d. Lloyd Lawson Koontz Jr. and Helen Ruth (Camfield) Smith; m. Joseph Thomas Gugliuzza III, Sept. 3, 1989. AS, Lake Land Coll., Mattoon, Ill., 1977; BS with honors, Ea. Ill. U., Charleston, 1978; MD, U. Ill., Rockford, 1982. Diplomate Am. Bd. Surgery. Intern dept. surgery Tulane U. Med. Sch. and Affiliated Hosps. New Orleans, 1982-83, resident, 1983-87, fellow divsn. transplantation, 1987-89, instr. surgery, rsch. assoc. in surgery and transplantation, 1989-90; asst. prof. U. Tex. Med. Br., Galveston, 1990—; spl. fellow in pancreas transplantation U. Minn., Mpls., 1989; courtesy staff St. Mary's Hosp., Galveston, 1991-96; recovery surgeon La. Organ Procurement Agy., New Orleans, 1989-90; presenter in field. Contbr. articles to med. jours. Fellow ACS; mem. AMA, Am. Diabetes Assn., Galveston County Med. Soc., Tex. Med. Assn., Cell Transplant Soc., Am. Med. Women's Assn., Assn. Women Surgeons, Singleton Surg. Soc., Assn. Acad. Surgery, Transplantation Soc., Tex. Transplant Soc., Tulane Surg. Soc., Southwestern Surg. Conf., N.Y. Acad. Scis., Am. Soc. Gen. Surgeons, Am. Soc. Transplant Physicians, Tex. Surg. Soc. Office: U Tex Med Br Dept Surgery 301 University Blvd Galveston TX 77555-0542

GUH, HSIAO Y., chemist, researcher; b. Taiwan, Nov. 28, 1950; came to U.S., 1973; m. Wendy M. Liu, June 7, 1979; children: Jessica, Emily. BS, Nat. Taiwan U., Taipei, 1973; MS, U. Mo., Kansas City, 1975; PhD, Mich. State U., 1981. Scientist Pfizer, Groton, Conn., 1981-87, project leader, 1987-93; rsch. mgr. R.W. Johnson Pharm. Rsch. Inst., Spring House, Pa., 1993—. Office: RW Johnson Pharm Rsch Inst Welsh and McKean Rds Spring House PA 19477

GUI, GERALD PENG HOCK, surgeon, tumor biologist; b. Kuala Lumpur, Malaysia, June 8, 1962; s. George Poh Chui and Lily Mee Foong (Chiew) G.; m. Corina Rosa Espinosa-Dorta, Sept. 8, 1992. MBBS, U. London, England, 1986, M Surgery, 1996. House officer posts in surgery and medicine London, Hertfordshire, 1986-87; anatomy demonstrator Royal Free Hosp., London, 1987-88; surg. sr. house officer St George's & Harefield, London, 1988-90; surg. registrar St. Bartholomews Hosp., London, 1991-93, rsch. fellow, 1993-94; lectr. & sr. registrar St. George's Hosp., London, 1994—; rsch. fellow Trustees of St. Bartholomews Hosp., London, 1993-94. Contbr. articles to profl. jours. Treas. U. London Life Saving Soc., 1982-85, pres. 1985-86. Recipient Suckling prize in neuroscience U. London, 1983, Surgeon in Tng. medal Royal Coll. Surgeons of Edinburgh, 1994, U. London Laurels, 1986, Rsch. awards S. Essex Med. Edn. Rsch. Trust, 1993-95. Fellow Royal Coll. Surgeons of Edinburgh, Royal Coll. Surgeons England; mem. British Oncological Assn., British Assn. Surg. Oncology, Surg. Rsch. Soc. (Travel award 1994). Home: 13 Jutland Close, N19 4EE London England Office: St Georges Hosp Med Sch, 1st Flr Jenner Wing Cranmer Terrace, SW17 ORE London England

GUICHETEAU, JOHN EDWARD, internist, respiratory therapy physician; b. Vineland, N.J., Apr. 26, 1947; m. Patricia White; children: Michael, Lauren, Robert. BS in Biology, St. Joseph U., Phila., 1969; MD, Creighton U., 1973. Diplomate Nat. Bd. Med. Examiners, Am. Bd. Internal Medicine, Am. Bd. Geriatric Medicine. Resident Wake Forest U., Winston-Salem, N.C., 1973-76; lt. USN/U.S. Health Corp., 1976-77; med. dir. Miners' Respiratory Clinic, Rock Springs, Wyo., 1978—; med. dir. respiratory therapy program Western Wyoming Coll., Rock Springs, 1978—; pvt. practice Rock Springs, 1984—; cons. Meml. Hosp. Sweetwater County, Rock Springs, 1977-84, chief of medicine, 1977-86, 91, dir. intensive care, 1980—, pres.-elect med. staff, 1984, pres. med. staff, 1985. Mem. affiliate faculty, course dir. CPR, ACLS Am. Heart Assn; med. dir. Am. Cancer Soc. Sweetwater County, 1983; med. co-dir. Wyo. State Respiratory Therapy Soc., 1981-90, 93—; mem. State Bd. Med. Examiners, 1989—, sec., 1993, v.p., 1994, pres., 1995; med. dir. Hospice of Sweetwater County, 1989—. Fellow ACP, Fedn. State Med. Bds.; mem. AMA, Wyo. State Med. Soc. (counselor 1977-86, regional chmn. PSRO 1977-78), Sweetwater County Med. Soc. (pres. 1987-89). Home: 2023 Carson Rock Springs WY 82901 Office: 430 Broadway Rock Springs WY 82901

GUIDANO, VITTORIO FILIPPO, psychiatrist, psychotherapist; b. Rome, Aug. 4, 1944; s. Federico Nicola and Angela (Zambrelli) G. BA in Liberal Arts, G.B. Vico Coll., Rome, 1963; MD, U. Rome, 1969. Residency in psychiatry, research asst. U. Pisa, Italy, 1969-72; research psychiatrist U. Rome, 1970-73, asst. prof. psycotherapy, 1974-85; founder, staff psychiatrist Ctr. for Cognitive Therapy, Rome, 1978—. Author: Cognitive Processes and Emotional Disorders, 1983, Complexity of the Self, 1987, The Self in Process, 1991. Mem. Assn. for Cognitive-Behavioral Therapies (founder, exec. bd. 1972—). Office: Ctr for Cognitive Therapy, Via Marcantonio Colonna 60, 00192 Rome Italy

GUILLAMA-ALVAREZ, NOEL JESUS, healthcare company executive; b. Havana, Cuba, Nov. 30, 1959; came to U.S., 1966; s. Jesus Mario Guillama and Rosa Maria Alvarez Guillama; m. Elayne Z. Cueto, July 6, 1985; 1 child, Jahziel Mikhail Guillama. Student, Palm Beach C.C., Lake Worth, Fla., 1978-80; BS in Bus. Adminstrn., Pacific We. U., L.A., 1992. Cert. bldg. contractor, Fla.; lic. real estate broker, mortgage broker, gen. ins. agt. Dir. programing Teleprompter Corp., West Palm Beach, Fla., 1976-79; pres., CEO JMG Holdings Inc, Palm Beach, Fla., 1980-90; v.p. ops. Quality Care Networks, Boca Raton, Fla., 1990-95; v.p. devel. Medpartners, Inc., Birmingham, 1995; pres., CEO Met. Health Networks, Boca Raton, 1995—; vice chair Palm Beach County Adv. Bd., West Palm Beach, 1990-92; co-founder, vice chair Lake Worth Cmty. Devel. Corp., 1990-92; co-founder, dir. Project Lake Worth, 1989-92. Writer weekly column Palm Beach Latino Newspaper, 1991-92. Recipient award Leukemia Soc. Am., 1979, Chin de Plata award Todo Mag., Miami, Fla., 1978. Mem. Am. Fin. Assn., Am. Coll. Healthcare Execs. (assoc.), Med. Group Practice Assn. Office: 5100 Town Center Cir Ste 560 Boca Raton FL 33486

GUILLEMIN, ROGER C. L., physiologist; b. Dijon, France, Jan. 11, 1924; came to U.S., 1953, naturalized, 1963; s. Raymond and Blanche (Rigollot) G.; m. Lucienne Jeanne Billard, Mar. 22, 1951; children: Chantal, Francois, Claire, Helene, Elizabeth, Cecile. B.A., U. Dijon, 1941, B.Sc., 1942; M.D., Faculty of Medicine, Lyons, France, 1949; Ph.D., U. Montreal, 1953; Ph.D. (hon.), U. Rochester, 1976, U. Chgo., 1977, Baylor Coll. Medicine, 1978, U. Ulm, Germany, 1978, U. Dijon, France, 1978, Free U. Brussels, 1979, U. Montreal, 1979, U. Man., Can, 1984, U. Turin, Italy, 1985, Kyung Hee U., Korea, 1986, U. Paris, Paris, 1986, U. Barcelona, Spain, 1988, U. Madrid, 1988, McGill U., Montreal, Can., 1988, U. Claude Bernard, Lyon, France, 1989. Intern, resident univs. hosps. Dijon, 1949-51; asso. dir., asst. prof. Inst. Exptl. Medicine and Surgery, U. Montreal, 1951-53; asso. dir. dept. exptl. endocrinology Coll. de France, Paris, 1960-63; asst. prof. physiology Baylor Coll. Medicine, 1953-57, assoc. prof., 1957-63, prof., dir. labs. neuroendocrinology, 1963-70, adj. prof., 1970—; resident fellow, chmn. labs. neuroendocrinology Salk Inst., La Jolla, Calif., 1970-89, adj. rsch. prof., 1989-94; Disting. Sci. prof. Whittier Inst., 1989—; med. and sci. dir., 1993-94; dir. Whittier Inst.; adj. prof. medicine U. Calif., San Diego, 1995—. Decorated chevalier Legion d'Honneur (France), 1974, officer, 1984; recipient Gairdner Internat. award, 1974; U.S. Nat. Medal of Sci., 1977; co-recipient Nobel prize for medicine, 1977; recipient Lasker Found. award, 1975; Dickson prize in medicine, 1976; Passano award sci., 1976; Schmitt medal neurosci., 1977; Barren Gold medal, 1979; Dale medal Soc. for Endocrinology U.K., 1980, Ellen Browning Scripps Soc. medal Scripps Meml. Hosps. Found., 1988. Fellow AAAS; mem. NAS, Am. Physiol. Soc., Am. Peptide Soc. (hon.), Assn. Am.Physicians, Endocrine Soc. (pres. 1986), Soc. Exptl. Biology and Medicine, Internat. Brain Rsch. Orgn., Internat. Soc. Rsch. Biology Reprodn., Soc. Neuro-scis., Am. Acad. Arts and Scis., French Acad. Scis. (fgn. assoc.), Academie Internationale de Medecine (fgn. assoc.), Swedish Soc. Med. Scis. (hon.), Academie des Scis. (fgn. assoc.), Academie Royale de Medecine de Belgique (corr. fgn.), Internat. Soc. Neurosci. (charter), Western Soc. Clin. Rsch., Can. Soc. Endocrinal Metabolism, (hon.), Club of Rome. Office: Whittier Inst 9894 Genesee Ave La Jolla CA 92037-1221

GUIMOND, ROBERT WILFRID, medical physiology educator, lawyer; b. Fall River, Mass., Sept. 4, 1938; s. Romeo A. and Jeannette (Boissoneault) G.; m. Elaine Brodie, July 13, 1963; children: Jefferson, Jameson. BA in History, U. R.I., 1961, PhD in Physiology, 1970; JD, New Eng. Sch. Law, 1978. Bar: Mass. 1978, U.S. Dist. Ct. Mass. 1980, U.S. Ct. Appeals (1st cir.) 1980, U.S. Supreme Ct. 1983. Asst. prof. zoology U. R.I., Kingston, 1970-71; prof. biology Boston State Coll., 1971-82; prof. biology U. Mass., Boston, 1982—; sole practice law, Boston and Fall River, 1978—. Mem. Conservation Law Found. Mem. Am. Physiol. Soc., ABA, Am. Soc. Law and Medicine, Am. Forestry Assn., Nature Conservancy. Democrat. Roman Catholic. Home: 307 Montgomery St Fall River MA 02720-4242 Office: U Mass Biology Dept 100 Morrissey Blvd Boston MA 02125

GUINAN, JOHN GRANGE, clinical psychologist; b. Bridgeport, Conn., Feb. 17, 1945; s. John Theodore and Mary (Heanue) G.; children: Alison Elisabeth, Paul Leslie, Justin Todd. AB, Coll. of Holy Cross, 1966; MA, Fordham U., 1968, PhD, 1974; cert. in psychoanalysis-psychotherapy, Westchester Ctr. for Study Psychoanalysis and Psychotherapy, White Plains, N.Y., 1979. Psychologist Putnam County Mental Health Ctr., Mahopac, N.Y., 1971-75, No. Westchester Guidance Clinic, Mt. Kisco, N.Y., 1975-84; dir. psychol. svcs. Wall St. Counseling Ctr., N.Y.C., 1983-86, dir., 1986—; cons. Harbor House, Bronx, N.Y., 1988-93. Democrat. Home: 8 Wolf Rd Croton On Hudson NY 10520-1922 Office: Wall Street Counseling Ctr 82 Wall St Ste 1105 New York NY 10005-3601

GUINANE, CAROLE SUSAN, health services administrator; b. Pueblo, Colo., Oct. 23, 1956; d. Frank John and Carole Beverly (Shosky) Ricotta; m. Thomas Edward Guinane, Dec. 11, 1976; children: Carissa Lynn, Jordon Elliott. AA, U. So. Colo., 1976, MBA, 1993; BSBA, U. Phoenix, 1988; student, U. Colo., 1990. RN, Colo. RN St. Mary Corwin Hosp., Pueblo, 1976-78; RN Parkview Episcopal Med. Ctr., Pueblo, 1978-81, nurse recruiter, mktg. rep., 1981-85, physician liaison, 1985-86, dir. edn./referral svcs., 1986-88, asst. v.p., 1988-91, v.p., 1991-94; cons. Quorum Health Resources, Brentwood, Tenn., 1994—; mem. Co-advancement ADN Orgn., Colo., 1987-89; nat. chair Rural Health Coop. Alliance, Kansas City, Mo., 1990-92; adv. mem. Healthcare Forum, San Francisco, 1990-93; industry chair Am. Heart Assn., Pueblo, 1992, 93. Co-author/dir.: (videos) Human Resource Mgmt., 1994, Clinical Pathways, 1994; author profl. publs. Bd. dirs. Chamber of Commerce Leadership, Pueblo, 1984, 88, Jr. League, Pueblo, 1982-87. Recipient Renatra Fusca award Odyssey of the Mind, Pueblo, 1992, 94, Clin. Mgmt. award MediQual, Boston, 1992, 93, others. Mem. Nat. Wildlife Fedn., Nat. Assn. for Healthcare Quality, Am. Soc. Quality Control, Sierra Club, Rotary, Sigma Theta Tau. Democrat. Roman Catholic. Office: Quorum Health Resources 105 Continental Pl Brentwood TN 37027

GUINN, JANET MARTIN, psychologist, consultant; b. Rapid City, S.D., Aug. 16, 1942; d. Verne Oliver and Carolyn Yetta (Clark) Martin; m. David Lee Guinn, Oct. 27, 1962 (div. June 1988); children: Cynthia Gail, Kevin Scott, Garrett Lee. BS in Psychology, U. Alaska, 1980, MS in Counseling Psychology, 1983; PhD in Clin. Psychology, Calif. Sch. Profl. Psychology, 1988. Lic. psychologist, Alaska, Nev. Pvt. practice Anchorage, 1988-93, Carson City and Reno, Nev., 1993—; clinician Behavior Medicine Cons., 1983-84; pvt. practice clinician, 1983-84; supr. Southcentral Counseling Ctr., Anchorage, 1984-85; cons. City/Borough of Juneau, Alaska, 1988; psychologist youth treatment program Alaska Psychiat. Inst., Anchorage, 1989-90; psychologist Nev. Mental Health Inst., Sparks, 1994—; cons. in field; cons. Alaska Small Bus. Coalition, Anchorage, 1990-92; reviewer Blors Corp. Contbr. articles to profl. jours. Active in politics. Mem. APA, Am. Coll. Forensic Examiners, Nev. Psychol. Assn., Internat. Neuropsychol. Soc., Rotary, Psi Chi. Republican. Office: 2470 Wrondel Way # 111 Reno NV 89502-3701

GUINOUARD, DONALD EDGAR, psychologist; b. Bozeman, Mont., Mar. 31, 1929; s. Edgar Arthur and Venabell (Ford) G.; m. Irene M. Egeler, Mar. 30, 1951; children: Grant M., Philip A., Donna I. BS, Mont. State U., Bozeman, 1954; MS, Mont. State U., 1955; EdD, Wash. State U., Pullman, 1960; postdoctoral, Stanford U., 1965; grad., Indsl. Coll. of the Armed Forces, 1964, Air War Coll., 1976. Lic. psychologist, Ariz., counselor, Wash., Mont.; cert. secondary tchr. and sch. adminstr., Wash., Mont. Advanced through grades to col. USAFR, 1946-84, ret., 1984; dir. counseling Consol. Sch. Dist., Pullman, Wash., 1955-60; assoc. prof. Mont. State U., Bozeman, 1960-66; field selection officer Peace Corps, U.S., S.Am., 1962-68; prof. counseling, counseling psychologist Ariz. State U., Tempe, 1966-90; prof. emeritus, 1990; co-owner Forensic Cons. Assocs., Tempe, 1970—; pvt. practice, 1990—; admissions liaison officer USAF Acad., Colo. Springs, 1967-84; assessment officer Fundamental Edn. Ctr. for the Devel. of the Latin American Community, Patzcuaro, Mex., 1963-64; expert witness on vocat. and psychol. disability for fed. and state cts. Contbr. articles to profl. jours. Mem. Ariz. Psychol. Assn., Am. Assn. Counseling & Devel., Reserve Officers Assn. Democrat. Methodist. Home and Office: 112 E Cairo Dr Tempe AZ 85282-3606

GUINSBURG, PHILIP FRIED, psychologist; b. N.Y.C., Sept. 13, 1946; s. Theodore and Elena (Fried) G.; m. Debrah Josias Guinsburg, June 15, 1968; children: Mark, Michael. BA, Columbia Coll., 1968; MA, U. N.D., 1970, PhD, 1973. Diplomate Am. Bd. Med. Psychotherapy. Clin. dir. Nashville Drug Treatment Ctr. Dede Wallace Ctr., 1973-78; pvt. practice Nashville, 1974—; asst. clin. prof. psychiatry Vanderbilt U., Nashville, 1987-93; cons. Crisis Intervention Ctr., 1974—; pres. Dreammakers, Inc., Nashville, 1989-91. Baseball coach Brentwood (Tenn.) Civitan Little League, 1982-92. Mem. APA, Am. Group Psychotherapy Assn., Am. Acad. Psychotherapists (chair continuing edn.), Tenn. Psychol. Assn., Nashville Area Psychol. Assn. Jewish. Home: 8121 Maryland Ln Brentwood TN 37027-7341 Office: 2313 21st Ave S Nashville TN 37212-4908

GULBRANDSEN, CHRISTIAN L., academic dean; b. Nov. 15, 1938. Dean U. Hawaii John A. Burns Sch. Medicine, Honolulu. Office: U Hawaii John A Burns Sch Medicine 1960 East-West Rd Honolulu HI 96822*

GULEVICH, STEVEN J., neurologist. BS, Stanford U., 1981; MD, Duke U., 1985. Diplomate Am. Bd. Psychiatry and Neurology, with spl. qualifications in Clin. Neurophysiology; diplomate Am. Bd. Electrodiagnostic Medicine, Nat. Bd. Med. Examiners. Med. intern U. Washington, Seattle, 1985-86, neurology resident, 1986-89; neurophysiology fellow U. Calif., San Diego, 1990-91, asst. clin. prof., 1991-92; assoc. dir. Ctr. Occupl. Neurology

& Neuromuscular Disease, 1992-94; pvt. practice, owner Colo. Neurol. Inst., Englewood, 1994—; rschr. HIV Neurobehavioral Rsch. Ctr., U. Calif., San Diego, 1990-92; assoc. dir. Electromyography Lab., La Jolla (Calif.) VA Med. Ctr., 1991-92; sr. investigator Reflex Sympathetic Dystrophy Clinic, Spalding Rehab. Ctr., Englewood, 1992—; regional investigator nat. randomized trial of acetyl-L-carnitine for diabetic neuropathy, 1993—; dir. Intrathecal Baclofen Program, Swedish Hosp. Med. Ctr., 1993-94; cons. neurologist Porter Meml. Hosp. Transplantation Program, 1993—; rural outreach neurologist, HealthONE Hosps., Sidney, Nebr., 1994—; mem. cumulative trauma disorders task force com., Divsn. Workers' Compensation, State of Colo.; chmn. subcom. neurophysiol. testing CTD; profl. rev. com. Arapahoe Med. Soc., 1995—; active staff Swedish Hosp. Med. Ctr., Englewood; cons. staff Porter Meml. Hosp., Denver, Craig Hosp., Englewood, Meml. Hosp., Sidney. Contbr. articles to profl. jours., chpts. to books. Presenter in field. Recipient Physician's Recognition award, AMA, 1994-97. Mem. AMA, Am. Acad. Neurology, Colo. Med. Soc., Arapahoe County Med. Soc. (del. state med. soc. 1993—). Office: 550 NE Hampden Ave # 100 Englewood CO 80110

GULICK, WALTER LAWRENCE, psychologist, former college president; b. Summit, N.J., July 4, 1927; s. Walter Lawrence and Carol (Dewey) G.; m. Winifred Bourn Frazee, Oct. 18, 1952; children—Hans, Tod, Kristina. A.B., Hamilton Coll., Clinton, N.Y., 1952; M.A. (Theta Delta Chi fellow), U. Del., 1955; M.A. (hon.), Dartmouth, 1968; Ph.D. (psychology scholar 1955-57), Princeton U., 1957; LHD (hon.), St. Lawrence U., 1989. Mem. faculty U. Del., 1957-65, prof. psychology, 1963-65, chmn. dept., 1964-65; prof. psychology Dartmouth, Hanover, N.H., 1965-74, chmn. dept., 1970-73, 74-75, Distinguished Class of 1925 prof., 1973-75; dean of coll. Hamilton Coll., 1975-79, prof. psychology, 1975-81, William R. Kenan prof., 1979-81; pres. St. Lawrence U., 1981-87, Gulick Assocs., 1987—; vis. prof. U. Vt., summer 1977; resident scholar U. Del., 1988—; cons. Presbyn. Hosp., Phila., 1961-63; editl. cons. Oxford U. Press, 1963—, McGraw-Hill Pub. Co., 1966-67, Harper & Row, 1971-73, Cambridge U. Press, 1979—. Author: Hearing: Physiology and Psychophysics, 1971, Human Stereopsis: Psychophysical Analysis, 1976, Hearing: Physiological Acoustics, Neural Coding and Psychoacoustics, 1989; contbr. to Encyclopedia of Human Behavior, 1994; contbr. articles to profl. jours. Mem. Hanover Sch. Bd., 1972-75, Dresden Bd. Sch. Dirs., 1972-75; Mem. grad. council Princeton U., 1972-75; mem. adv. council Nat. Inst. for Humanities, 1975—; mem. teaching evaluation project HEW. Served with AUS, 1946-48. Recipient nat. svc. award 1955, 81; Dale prize music Hamilton Coll., 1952, alumni achievement medal Hamilton Coll., 1995. Mem. N.Y. Acad. Scis., Ea. Psychol. Assn., Psychonomic Soc., Phi Beta Kappa, Omicron Delta Kappa, Sigma Xi (pres. Dartmouth chpt. 1967-68, Gold Medal Lifetime Achievement award 1995), Psi Chi (pres. U. Del. chpt. 1954-55). Home: 205 Winslow Rd Newark DE 19711-4531 Office: Gulick Assocs Inc PO Box 1036 Newark DE 19715-1036

GULKO, EDWARD, health care executive, consultant; b. Paterson, N.J., Nov. 22, 1950; s. Benjamin and Anita (Yankelevsky) G.; m. Judith Ilene Lee, May 29, 1977. BS in Indsl. Engring., N.J. Inst. Tech., 1972; MBA, Temple U., 1974. Cert. healthcare exec.; cert. med. practice exec. Health program analyst Morrisania Hosp., Bronx, N.Y., 1974-75; assoc. dir. Mission Health Ctr., San Francisco, 1976; supervising systems analyst Health and Hosp. Corp., N.Y.C., 1977-78; dep. exec. dir. Greenpoint Hosp., Bklyn., 1978-82; assoc. exec. dir. Woodhull Med. Ctr., Bklyn., 1982-84; adminstr. Montclair (N.J.) Med. Group, 1984-87; asst. adminstr. Summit Med. Group, Summit, N.J., 1987-91; adminstr. Wooster (Ohio) Clinic, Inc., 1991-96. Trustee Society Hill Townhouse Assn., 1986-90, v.p., 1987-88, pres., 1988-89; bd. dirs. Residential Support Svcs., 1993-96, v.p. 1993-96. Mem. Am. Coll. Healthcare Execs., Assn. Mil. Surgeons U.S. (exec. com. N.J. chpt. 1985-87, pres. 1987-90), Med. Group Mgmt. Assn. (nat. comm. com. 1993-95), Naval Res. Assn. (dist. v.p. 1987-91), Am. Acad. Med. Adminstrs., Naval Inst., Am. Coll. Med. Practice Execs. Democrat. Jewish. Home: 1547 Willoughby Dr Wooster OH 44691-2548 Office: Wooster Clinic 1740 Cleveland Rd Wooster OH 44691-2204

GULL, PAULA MAE, renal transplant coordinator, nephrology nurse, medical-sugical nurse; b. L.A., Mar. 7, 1955; d. Gerald Henry and Artemis (Cubillas) Balzer; m. Randell Jay Gull, July 10, 1976. AA, Cypress (Calif.) Coll., 1976; AS with high honors, Rancho Santiago Coll., Santa Ana, Calif., 1985; BSN with high honors, Calif. State U., 1993; MSN, Long Beach U., 1996. Cert. med. surg. nurse, nephrology nurse, nurse practitioner. Staff RN U. Calif. Irvine Med. Ctr., Orange, Calif., 1986-87, asst. nurse mgr., 1987-88, nurse mgr., 1988; med.-surg. nurse N000, 1990—; coord. renal transplant U. Calif.-Irvine Med. Ctr., Orange, 1992—. Mem. Am. Nephrology Nurses Assn., Phi Kappa Phi. Mormon. Home: 24974 Enchanted Way Moreno Valley CA 92557-6410

GULLANS, STEVEN ROLF, biomedical scientist; b. Troy, N.Y., Nov. 19, 1952; s. Rolf O. and Mary Lou (Clark) G.; m. Stenie Plater, Aug. 28, 1976; children: Emilie, Graham. BS, Union Coll., 1975; PhD, Duke U., 1982. Rsch. asst. U. Md. Chesapeake Biol. Lab., Solomons, 1976-77; postdoctoral fellow Yale Sch. Medicine, New Haven, Conn., 1982-85; rsch. assoc. Yale Sch. Medicine, New Haven, 1985; asst. prof. Harvard Med. Sch., Boston, 1982-91, assoc. prof., 1991—; assoc. physiologist Brigham & Women's Hosp., Boston, 1982-91, physiologist, 1992—. Named Established Investigator, Am. Heart Assn., 1992—. Mem. Fedn. Am. Socs. Exptl. Biology, Am. Soc. Nephrology, Soc. Gen. Physiologists, Nat. Kidney Found.

GULLEKSON, KRISTIN LEE, optometrist; b. Huntsville, Ala., Jan. 15, 1967; d. Keren Robert and Margaret Mary (Down) G. BS, Colo. State U., 1989; OD, So. Calif. Coll. Optometry, Fullerton, 1993. Lic. optometrist, Colo., Tex. Optometrist Abba Eye Care, Alamosa, Colo., 1993—. Recipient Nat. Merit scholarship, 1989, Watson Meml. scholarship IBM, 1989. Mem. Am. Optometric Assn., Colo. Optometric Assn., Coll. of Optometric Vision Devel., Alamosa Rotary Club. Roman Catholic. Office: Abba Eye Care 1322 Main St Alamosa CO 81101-2197

GULLICK, THOMAS H., healthcare consultant; b. Marshfield, Wis., July 16, 1949; s. Harold T. and Lenice M. (Swenson) G.; m. Susan Joan Fehrenbach, Nov. 25, 1972; 1 dau., Amy Sue. BS, U. Wis.-LaCrosse, 1971, MS, 1979; PhD, Marquette U., 1994. Pers. adminstr., county adminstr., clk. Juneau County, Mauston, Wis., 1976-80; asst. adminstr. St. Joseph's Hosp., Hillsboro, Wis., 1980-81; adminstr. VNA Home Care, Neenah, Wis., 1981—; VNA rep. Hospice of Neenah-Menasha. Blood chmn. ARC, Mauston, 1976-80; bd. dirs. Parkview Eldercare, Hillsboro, 1980—; loaned exec. United Way, Neenah, 1983. Recipient Meritorious Pub. Service award Am. Legion, 1977-78. Mem. Am. Coll. Health Care Adminstrs., Nat. Home Care Orgn., Wis. Home Care Orgn., U. Wis. Alumni Assn. Lodge: Rotary Internat. (dir. 1982-89, Rotarian of Yr. 1984). Home: 4409 W River Willows Ct Mequon WI 53092

GULLICKSON, KATHRYN E., optometrist; b. Danville, Pa., Aug. 26, 1966; d. Bruce C. and Suzanne (Parker) Artman; m. Darry M. Gullickson, Feb. 14, 1989. BA in Biology, U. Del., 1988; BS in Visual Sci., Pa. Coll. Optometry, Phila., 1992; OD, Pa. Coll. Optometry, 1993. Optometrist Pearle Express, Pitts., 1993-94, 95-96, Kandrot, Stout & Assocs., Pitts., 1994-95. Vol. Surrey Svcs. for Srs., Phila., 1983-93. Mem. Am. Optometric Assn., Pa. Optometric Assn. Office: Pearle Express 525 A&B Clairton Blvd Pittsburgh PA 15236

GULLINGSRUD, TIMOTHY MICHAEL, hospital administrator; b. Rapid City, S.D., Jan. 21, 1968; s. Terry Marlin and Marsha Claire (Natwick) G.; m. Wendy Elisabeth Bickford, Nov. 16, 1991; 1 child, Bryce Timothy. BA, Concordia Coll., Moorhead, Minn., 1990. Lic. nursing home adminstr., Mont. Adminstr. Liberty County Hosp. and Nursing Home, Chester, Mont., 1990-91, McKenzie County Meml. Hosp., Watford City, N.D., 1992—. Pres. McKenzie County Ambulance, Watford City, 1995—; v.p. Watford City Econ. Devel. Corp., 1995-96; trustee Watford City First Luth. Ch., 1995; bd. dirs. Drug-Free Schs. Adv. Coun., Watford, 1995. Mem. N.D. Hosp. Assn. (del. 1992—), Watford City Jaycees, Watford City Rotary (v.p. 1995-96), Badland's Shooting Club. Republican. Lutheran. Office: McKenzie Meml Hosp PO Box 548 508 N Main Watford City ND 58854

GULLUNG, WILLIAM HENRY, III, dermatologist; b. New Orleans, Nov. 3, 1951; s. William Henry Jr. and Elaine Teresa (Brinker) G.; m. Constance Fraser Larsen, Apr. 16, 1974; children: Lauren, Gregory, Jessica, Candace. BS, U. New Orleans, 1972; MD, La. State U., 1976. Intern John Sealy Hosp., Galveston, Tex., 1976-77; resident in dermatology Charity Hosp.-La. State U., 1977-80; pvt. practice Hattiesburg, Miss., 1980—. Office: Dermatology Clinic Hattiesburg 104 Asbury Circle Hattiesburg MN 39402

GULRAJANI, RAMESH MULCHAND, biomedical engineer, educator; b. Patna, Bihar, India, Dec. 12, 1944; arrived in Can., 1973; s. Mulchand T. and Saraswati Mirchandani G.; m. Lily Tikamdas Mani, Feb. 21, 1976; children: Nilima Ramesh, Rohan Ramesh. BEE, U. Bombay, 1964; MEE, Ill. Inst. Tech., 1965; MS in Physics, Syracuse U., 1972, DEng, 1973. Postdoctoral fellow dept. physiology U. Montreal, Can., 1973-75, rsch. assoc. dept. medicine, 1976-79, rsch. assoc. Inst. of Biomedical Engring., 1979-87, assoc. prof., 1987-90, prof., 1990—; vis. prof. dept. engring. sci. Auckland U., New Zealand, 1992-93; mem biomedical engring. grants com. Med. Rsch. Coun. of Can., Ottawa, 1988-91. Contbr. articles to profl. jours. and chpts. to books. Recipient Postdoctoral fellow Med. Rsch. Coun. of Can., 1973-75; rsch. scholarship Canadian Heart Found., 1978-81, sr. rsch. scholarship Fonds de la recherche en santé du Québec, 1986-89. Mem. IEEE, Biomed. Engring. Soc. Office: U Montreal Inst of BioMed Engring, PO Box 6128 Sta Ctr, Montreal, PQ Canada H3C 3J7

GUMPRIGHT, HERBERT LAWRENCE, JR., dentist; b. Newport, R.I., Apr. 23, 1946; s. Herbert Lawrence and Helen Marie (Broderick) G.; m. Cynthia Randolph Williams, June 16, 1972 (div. Apr. 1987); children: Broderick J., Tyler H. BS, U. R.I., 1968; DDS, NYU, 1972. Lic. dentist, Mass. Intern Waterbury (Conn.) Hosp. Affiliate Yale U. Sch. Medicine, 1972-73; assoc. Ronald J. Dowgiallo, DMD, Harwichport, Mass., 1973-78; pvt. practice Brewster, Mass., 1978—; prodr., host Your Dental Health, Cmty. Access TV, 1978-95. Fellow Acad. Gen. Dentistry; mem. Am. Dental Soc., Mass. Dental Soc., Cape Code Dist. Dental Soc. (treas. 1986-90, v.p. 1989, pub. rels. com. chmn. 1988-95), Pierre Fauchard Acad., Phi Sigma (Alpha Xi chpt.). Office: Box 1108 2452 Main St Brewster MA 02631

GUNBERG, EDWIN WOODROW, JR., counseling psychologist, consultant, researcher; b. Sioux Falls, S.D., Nov. 13, 1950; s. Edwin Woodrow and Eileen Marie Elizabeth (Youngdahl) G.; m. Elizabeth Ann Robbins, June 5, 1976; children: Edwin Christian, Emily Elizabeth. BA, Gustavus Adolphus Coll., St. Peter, Minn., 1972; MA, George Mason U., 1975; postgrad., Va. Poly. Inst. and State U., 1975-79; PhD, U. N.D., 1981. Asst. prof. counseling U. N.D., Grand Forks, 1981-82; dir. PSYCON, Sterling, Va., 1982—; pres. MARS Assessment Tech., Inc., Sterling, 1990—; exec. v.p. United Bus. Svcs., 1996—; cons. HumRRO Internat., Inc., Alexandria, Va., 1985-91; bd. dirs. Personality Assessment System Found., 1990—. Bd. dirs. Loudoun Symphony Assn., 1994—, pres. 1996—; mem. Rep. Senatorial Inner Circle, 1989, Loudoun County Rep. Com., 1992—. Mem. Am. Assn. for Marriage and Family Therapy (clin.), Am. Psychol. Soc., Confederte Air Force (col.), Aircraft Owner and Pilot Assn., Exptl. Aircraft Assn., Mooney Aircrft Pilots Assn. Lutheran. Home: 207 Winter Frost Ct Sterling VA 20165-5821

GUNDERMAN, J. RICHARD, neurologist; b. Buffalo, Mar. 22, 1939; s. John Frances and Mildred Ruth (Zastrow) G.; m. Ann W. Bacon, July 31, 1965; children: Rebecca Ann, J. Richard Jr. BS, Canisius Coll., 1960; MD, SUNY, Buffalo, 1965. Pvt. practice as child neurologist Tampa, Fla., 1974—; mem. adv. bd. Epilepsy Found. West Ctrl. Fla., Tampa, 1986—, CHADD, Tampa, 1995—; med. advisor United Cerebral Palsy, Tampa, 1981—; dir. neurosci. St. Joseph's Hosp., Tampa, 1988—. Capt. USAF, 1968-70. Mem. Am. Neurology Assn., CNS. Republican. Roman Catholic. Office: 5106 N Armenia Tampa FL 33603

GUNDERSON, CARL HARMON, neurologist, educator; b. South Bend, Ind., Nov. 6, 1933; s. Norris Elwood and Harriet Elizabeth (Harmon) G.; m. Anne Bruner, Sept. 7, 1957; children: Sarah, Carl, Katharine. BS, Notre Dame U., 1954; MS, MD, U. Chgo., 1958. Diplomate Am. Bd. Psychiatry and Neurology. Resident, fellow in neurology Yale U., New Haven, Conn., 1959-62; chief neurology svc. Womack Army Hosp., Ft. Bragg, N.C., 1962-64; chief psychiatry & neurology br. Med. Field Svc. Sch., Ft. Sam Houston, Tex., 1964-67; asst. chief neurology svc. Letterman Army Med. Ctr., Presidio of San Francisco, 1967-70; chief neurology svc. Brooke Army Med. Ctr., Ft. Sam Houston, 1970-80, Walter Reed Army Med. Ctr., Washington, 1980-96; chmn. dept. neurology Uniformed Svcs. U. Health Scis., Bethesda, Md., 1983—; cons. Surgeon Gen. Army, 1980-91. Author: Quick Reference to Clinical Neurology, 1982, Essentials of Clinical Neurology, 1990. Col. U.S. Army, 1962-96. Fellow Am. Acad. Neurology, Am. Heart Assn.; mem. AMA, Am. Neurologic Assn.

GUNDERSON, CLARK ALAN, orthopedic surgeon; b. Watertown, S.D., Aug. 27, 1948; s. Harvey Alfred and Eugenie (Tulson) G.; m. Robbie Gunderson; children: Ashley, Camille. Student, U. Minn., 1966-69; BS, U. S.D., 1971; MD, Baylor Coll. of Medicine, 1973. Diplomate Am. Bd. of Orthopaedic Surgery, 1979. Intern in gen. surgery Charity Hosp., New Orleans, 1973-74, resident in orthopedic surgery, 1974-78; chief of surgery Lake Charles (La.) Meml. Hosp., 1980-83, 90-91, sec., treas. med. staff, 1983-87, pres. med. staff, 1992-93, also trustee, 90-94; clin. assoc. prof. La. State U. Sch. of Medicine, New Orleans, 1987-90. Bd. dirs. Arthritic Found. La., 1987. Mem. AMA, ACS, Am. Acad. Orthopaedic Surgeons, La. Orthopaedic Assn. (pres. 1995-96), Calcasieau Parish Med. Soc., La. State Med. Soc., N.Am. Spine Assn., Mid Am. Orthopaedic Assn., Lake Charles Country Club (pres. 1987-89). Office: 2615 Enterprise Blvd Lake Charles LA 70601-7675

GUNDRY, JO ANN, mental health services professional; b. Minot, N.D., Apr. 11, 1945; d. James Edwin and Agnes Lucy (Gervais) G. BA, Mary Coll., 1971; MA, U. N.D., 1977, PhD, 1980. Lic. consulting psychologist. Tchr. St. Leo's Sch., Minot, 1966-67, 70-71, Colegio de las Hermanas Benedictinas, Bogota, Colombia, 1967-70, Little Flower Sch., Minot, 1971-75, St. Mary's Sch., Malta, Mont., 1975-76; elem. sch. counselor Grand Forks (N.D.) Pub. Schs., 1979-80, 81-82; mental health therapist Cath. Charities, Crookston, Minn., 1980-81, Counseling Assocs., Bemidji, Minn., 1983; psychologist, dir. outpatient svcs. program Hiawatha Valley Mental Health Ctr., Winona, Minn., 1983-90; pvt. practice, 1991—. Mem. APA, Minn. Psychol. Assn. Democrat. Roman Catholic. Office: PO Box 872 Winona MN 55987-0872

GUNN, ALBERT EDWARD, JR., internist, educator, lawyer, hospital and university administrator; b. Port Washington, N.Y., Oct. 31, 1933; s. Albert Edward and Esther Frances (Williams) G.; m. Joan Marie Jacoby; children: Albert Edward III, Emily Williams, Andrew Robert, Clare Margaret, Catherine Ann, Philip David. BS, Fordham Coll. 1955, LLB, 1958; MB, BCh, BAO, Nat. U. Ireland, Galway, 1967. Bar: N.Y. 1958, D.C. 1972. Owner, agent Albert E. Gunn Ins. Agy., Port Washington, N.Y., 1953-65; intern Montefiore Hosp., N.Y.C., 1967-68; med. resident Roosevelt Hosp., N.Y.C., 1968-70; USPHS trainee in neurology U. Rochester, 1970-72; asst. dir. govtl. relations AMA, Washington, 1972-74; med. dir. Geriatric Services Suffolk County (N.Y.), Hauppauge, 1974-75; med. dir. Rehab. Ctr., U. Tex./M.D. Anderson Cancer Ctr. 1975-88, chief rehab. sect., 1988-93, chief geriatrics sect., 1993—; asst. prof. medicine U. Tex. Med. Sch. at Houston, 1976-80, assoc. prof., 1980—, now also assoc. dean for admissions; med. dir. Region IV, Tex. Med. Found., 1986-93; del.-at-large White House Conf. on Handicapped Individuals, 1977; pres. Mus. Med. Sci., 1990; cons. Ctrs. for Disease Control, Legal Services Corp., Nat. Library of Medicine. Mem. nat. adv. health council HEW, 1974-75; mem. adv. com. Nat. Inst. Law Enforcement and Criminal Justice, Law Enforcement Assistance Adminstrn., U.S. Dept. Justice, 1974-76; mem. bd. regents Nat. Libr. of Medicine, NIH, 1983-87, chmn., 1986-87, chmn. lit. selection tech. adv. com., 1988-91; bd. dirs. Right to Life Advocates, 1977-78, Tex. Med. Ctr. Libr., 1990. With USAF, 1958-61. Diplomate Am. Bd. Internal Medicine. Fellow Am. Coll. Physicians; mem. Harris County (Tex.) Med. Soc. (exec. bd. 1986-90), Tex. Med. Assn. (trustee ins. trust), Royal Coll. Physicians (London) (licentiate), Royal Coll. Surgeons (Eng.), Houston Acad. Medicine (bd. dirs. 1986-90, pres. 1990), Houston Bar Assn., D.C. Bar, Nat. Fedn. Cath. Physicians Guilds (regional bd. dirs. 1992—), Sons. of Union Vets. of Civil War, Army and Navy Club, Cosmos Club. Roman Catholic. Co-author: Rehabilitation of the Cancer Patient, 1976, AIDS in Africa, 1988; editor, contbg. author: Cancer Rehabilitation, 1984; mem. editorial bd. Cancer Bull., 1977-90, Gerontology and Geriatrics Edn., Linacre Quar.; contbr. articles to profl. jours. Home: 2329 Watts St Houston TX 77030-1139 Office: U Tex M D Anderson Cancer Ctr 1515 Holcombe Blvd Houston TX 77030-4009

GUNN, ROBERT BURNS, physiology educator; b. Washington, July 12, 1939; s. Ross and Gladys J. (Rowley) G.; m. Sharon McClellan, Aug. 24, 1963; children: Lora, Heather, Molly, Ian. BS, U. Mich., 1961; MD, Harvard U., 1966. Spl. fellow U.S. Pub. Health Svc., 1969-71; rsch. assoc. dept. physiology and pharmacology Duke U. Med. Ctr., Durham, N.C., 1969-71, asst. prof. dept. physiology and pharmacology, 1971-75; assoc. prof. dept. pharmacol. and physiol. scis. Pritzer Sch. Medicine, U. Chgo., 1975-81; prof., chmn. dept. physiology Emory U. Sch. Med., Atlanta, 1981—; vis. researcher Inst. for Biophysics, U. Copenhagen, Denmark, 1971-72. Lt. commdr. USPHS, 1967-69. NATO fellow NSF, 1971. Mem. Biophysical Soc. (treas. 1987—, Kenneth S. Cole award 1987), Soc. Gen. Physiologists (treas. 1981-84, pres. 1989-90), Assn. Chmn. Depts. of Physiology (pres. 1989-90), Am. Physiol. Soc. (edn. com.). Methodist. Office: Emory U Sch Medicine Dept Physiology Atlanta GA 30322

GUNN, WALTER JOSEPH, psychologist, epidemiologist; b. Harrison, N.J., Dec. 9, 1935; s. Hugh Spofford and Dorothy (Feeley) G.; m. Bernice Kulick, Dec. 22, 1960; children: Suzanne, Sheryl Ann, Michelle, Joanne. BS in Engring., U.S. Merchant Marine Acad., 1959; MA in Psychology, U. Louisville, 1967, PhD in Psychology, 1969. Asst. project engr. Bendix Corp., Teterboro, N.J., 1960-63; elec. engr. Picatinny Arsenal, Dover, N.J., 1963-65, Army MEd. Rsch. Lab., Ft. Knox, Ky., 1965-67; sr. scientist George Washington U., Ft. Knox, 1967-69; asst. prof. U. Cin., 1969-70; rsch. assoc. Columbia U., Sch. Pub. Health, N.Y.C., 1970-71; asst. acad. dean U.S. Merchant Marine Acad., Kings Point, N.Y., 1971-73; head, psychoacoustics sect. NASA/Langley Rsch. Ctr., Hampton, Va., 1973-76; sr. rsch. psychologist Ctrs. Disease Control, Atlanta, 1976-92; ret., 1992; pres. Arlington Assocs. Inc., Datona Beach Shores, Fla., 1986—. Contbr. articles to profl. jours. Mission pilot Civil Air Patrol, 1989-90. Recipient Spl. Recognition award USPHS, 1987. Home: Ste 4505 4555 S Atlantic Ave Daytona Beach FL 32127

GUNNER, MURRAY, Jewish organization administrator; b. N.Y.C., Mar. 26, 1918; s. Abraham and Sadie (Schnee) G.; m. Pearl O. Katz, June 12, 1949; children: Marilyn Ruth, Janet Marie. BS, CCNY, 1938; MSW, Columbia U., 1946; cert., Hebrew U., 1971. Cert. social worker. Social worker, acting supr. N.Y.C. Dept. Welfare and Camp LaGuardia, 1940-45; adminstrv. asst. Coun. House, St. Louis, 1946-50; program dir. Jewish Community Ctr., Hartford, Conn., 1950-54; exec. dir. Jewish Community Ctr., Newburgh, N.Y., 1954-62, Bklyn., 1962-66, Yonkers, N.Y., 1966-83; cons. Jewish Community Ctr., Jewish Fedn., 1983-89; exec. dir. Jewish Coun. of Yonkers, 1989—; cons. Hudson River Mus., Elizabeth Seton Coll., 1989-89; co-chmn. commn. of synagogue rels. United Jewish Appeal Fedn., N.Y.C., 1980-81, co-chmn. Jewish Community Ctrs., 1981-82; co-chair adult edn. com. Greystone Jewish Ctr., Yonkers, 1980-82, bd. dirs., 1978-80. Contbr. author to various books. Mem. Charter Revision Commn., Yonkers, 1979, Mayor's Holocaust Commn. Yonkers, 1979, Mayor's Com. on Jewish Affairs, Yonkers, 1990—, Yonkers Crime Commn., 1975, Yonkers Mental Health Coun., 1978-83; bd. dirs. Yonkers United Way, 1981-83; mem. Mayor's Cmty. Rels. Com., Yonkers, 1992—; exec. com. Edn. 2000, Yonkers, 1992—; mem. State Senator (N.Y. State) Adv. Com., 1991—, Mentoring Com. for Youth at Risk, 1993—; bd. dirs. Cmty. Planning Agy., Yonkers, 1992—; task force City/County Youth Violence. Recipient Israel Cummings award Commn. on Synagogue Rels. Fedn., 1963, cert. of merit, 1992, Am. Com. on Italian Migration, 1992, cert. of recognition for outstanding svc. and contbns. Charles Gordon H.S., Yonkers, 1995, Yonkers Martin Luther King Commn. award, 1995, Cmty. Svc. award Mayor of City of Yonkers, 1995; Murray Gunner Day named in his honor City of Yonkers, 1983, County of Westchester, 1983. Mem. NASW (Gold Care mem.), Jewish Cmty. Ctrs. Assn., Rotary (chair pub. rels. com. 1988—, chair cmty. svcs., bd. dirs. 1993-94). Home: 10 Gateway Rd Yonkers NY 10703-1270 Office: Jewish Coun of Yonkers 584 N Broadway Yonkers NY 10701-1731

GUNNING, CAROLYN SUE, nursing educator; b. Ft. Smith, Ark., Dec. 16, 1943; d. Laurence George and Flora Irene (Garner) G. BS, Tex. Woman's U., 1965; MS, U. Colo., 1973; PhD, U. Tex.-Austin, 1981. Registered nurse, Tex. Clinician III, Bexar County Hosp., San Antonio, 1968-71; instr. U. Tex. Sch. Nursing, San Antonio, 1973-74, asst. prof., 1974-83, asst. to dean, 1977-79, assoc. prof., asst. dean undergrad. programs, 1983-84, assoc. dean, 1984-88; dean Sch. Nursing Marshall U., Huntington, W.Va., 1988-90; dean Coll. Nursing, Tex. Women's U., 1991—; accreditation site visitor Nat. League for Nursing, 1982-88 . Active Leadership San Antonio, 1978-79. Served to capt. Nurse Corps, U.S. Army, 1965-68; to lt. comdr. Army N.G., 1980-88. Decorated Army Commendation medal. Mem. ANA, Nat. League for Nursing, Sigma Theta Tau, Kappa Delta Pi. Contbr. articles to profl. jours.

GUNSALUS, ROBERT PHILIP, microbiologist, educator, molecular geneticist; b. Ithaca, N.Y., Aug. 24, 1947; s. Irwin and Merle G. BS, S.D. State U., 1970; MS, U. Ill., 1972, PhD, 1977. Postdoctoral fellow Stanford (Calif.) U., 1978-80; asst. prof. microbiology UCLA, 1981-87, assoc. prof., 1987, prof., 1992—; mem. Molecular Biology Inst. UCLA, Los Angeles, 1981—. Editor FEMS Microbiology Letters, Archives Microbiology; mem. editl. bd. Jour. Bacteriology, Molecular Microbiology, Biofactors. Chmn. Gordon Conf. on Methanogenesis, 1990. Mem. ASM (chair div. gen. microbiology 1992), AAAS, Am. Soc. Microbiology, Am. Chem. Soc., Am. Soc. Biochem. and Molecular Biologists. Office: Microbiology/Molecular Genetics Dept 1601 MSB UCLA Los Angeles CA 90095

GUNTER, LAURIE M., retired nurse educator. BS, Tenn A&I State U., 1948; MA, Fisk U., 1952; PhD in Human Devel., U. Chgo., 1959. Staff nurse George W. Hubbard Hosp., Nashville, 1943-44, 46-47, head nurse, 1945-46, supr., 1947-48; instr. Sch. Nursing, Meharry Med. Coll., Nashville, 1950-55, asst. prof., 1955-57, project dir. mental health tng., 1957-58, acting dean, 1957-58, dean, 1958-61; asst. prof. nursing UCLA, 1961-63, assoc. prof., 1963-65; prof. nursing Ind. U. Med. Ctr., Indpls., 1965-66; assoc. prof. U. Wash., Seattle, 1966-69, prof., 1969-71; head dept. nursing Pa. State U., 1971-75, prof., 1971-87, prof. emeritus, 1987. Contbr. articles to profl. jours. Mem. ANA, NAS, AAAS, APHA, AAUP, Gerontol. Soc. Home: 4008 47th Ave S Seattle WA 98118

GUNTHORPE, WAYNE WEST, psychologist, counselor; b. Larchmont, N.Y., Nov. 9, 1938; s. Earl Clifton and Francina Theodosia (West) G.; m. Carol Susan Tuch, Feb. 24, 1966; children: Kevin, Stacey, Dana. BS, Morgan State Coll., 1962; MEd, Rutgers U., 1973, DEd, 1977. Lic. sch. psychologist, N.J. Phys. edn. tchr. Mt. Vernon (N.Y.) Schs., 1965-69, kindergarten tchr., 1969-70; sch. psychologist Bethlehem (Pa.) Sch. Dist., 1973-74; cons. psychologist Grant Ave. Cmty. Ctr., Plainfield, N.J., 1986-91; sch. psychologist Piscataway (N.J.) Sch. Dist., 1974—. 1st lt. U.S. Army, 1962-64. Mem. APA, NEA, Assn. Black Psychologists, Piscataway Tchrs. Edn. Assn., Kappa Delta Pi, Phi Delta Kappa. Home: 50 Koenig Ln Freehold NJ 07728 Office: Piscataway Twp Sch Dist 1515 Stelton Rd Piscataway NJ 08854

GUPTA, KAILASH CHANDRA, molecular virology educator, researcher; b. Khargone, India, Sept. 6, 1943; came to U.S., 1975; s. Gokul Das and Gyarsi Bai Gupta; m. Ahilya Gupta, Apr. 30, 1968; children: Rajesh, Ram. MSc, Vikram U., Ujjain, India, 1966; PhD, Indian Inst. Sci., Bangalore, 1971. Asst. staff mem. St. Jude Children's Rsch. Hosp., Memphis, 1982-85; asst. prof. molecular virology Rush-Presbyn.-St. Luke's Med. Ctr., Chgo., 1985-89; assoc. prof. Rush-Presbyn.- St. Luke's Med. Ctr., Chgo., 1989-95, prof. immunology, microbiology and pharmacology, 1995—; Transfer of Tech. Through Expatriate Nats. (TOKTEN) cons. in biotech. Anna U., Madras, India, 1991; Japanese Soc. for Promotion in Sci. vis. fellow Hokkaido (Japan) U., 1992, Hiroshima (Japan) U., 1992. Contbr. articles to profl. jours. Rsch. grantee NSF, 1986-88, Am. Cancer Soc., 1987-94, Am. Heart Assn., 1989-95, NIH, 1989—. Mem. Am. Soc. Biochemistry and Molecular Biology, Am. Soc. Microbiology, Am. Soc. Virology, Protein Soc., Am. Assn. Cancer Rsch. Office: Rush-Presbyn-St Luke's Med Ctr 1653 W Congress Pky Chicago IL 60612-3833

GUPTA, KAUSHAL KUMAR, internist; b. Firozpur, Punjab, India, Nov. 9, 1949; came to U.S., 1975; s. Hardayal and Lilawati (Gupta) G.; m. Meena Anand, May 23, 1978; children: Ruchi, Ajay, Nishi. MBBS, MD, Christian Med. Coll., Ludhiana, India, 1975. Diplomate Am. Bd. Internal Medicine. Rotating intern Govt. Med. Coll. and Hosp., Jodhpur, India, 1974-75, Christian Med. Coll. and Hosp., Ludhiana, India, 1974-75; rsch. assoc. dept. pharmacology Baylor Coll. Medicine, Houston, 1975-76; resident in internal medicine St. John Hosp., Detroit, 1976-79; pvt. practice internal medicine Lansing, Mich., 1979-80, Houston, 1980—; mem. utilization rev. com. Parkway Hosp., Houston, 1994; quality assurance com. Houston N.W. Med. Ctr., 1989-92; chmn. ER/ICU com. Doctors Hosp.-Airline, Houston, 1992—. Contbr. articles to profl. jours. Mem. resource allocation and funding com. United Way, 1984; vol. physician Eastwood Health Clinic, Houston, 1985, 86; Congress key contact Am. Soc. Internal Medicine, 1993-94, ACP, 1994. Fellow ACP; mem. AMA, Tex. Med. Assn., Am. Soc. Internal Medicine, Am. Soc. Echocardiography, Mich. Med. Soc., Harris County Med. Soc., Indian Doctors Club of Houston (sec. 1988). Hindu. Home: 8015 Theisswood Rd Spring TX 77379-4637 Office: 11206 Airline Dr Houston TX 77037-1116

GUPTA, PRAMOD K., pharmaceutical scientist; b. Agra, India, Sept. 4, 1959; came to U.S., 1988; s. K.R. and S. Gupta; m. Kusum Gupta, Jan. 15, 1988; children: Shikha, Vishaal. B in Pharmacy, U. Sagar (India), 1983; PhD, U. Otago, Dunedin, New Zealand, 1987. Asst. prof. U. Otago, Dunedin, 1987-88; post-doctoral fellow U. Ky., Lexington, 1988-89; sr. scientist Abbott Labs., North Chicago, Ill., 1989—. Contbr. articles to profl. jours., also reviewer. Recipient Best Spkr. award Royal Soc. New Zealand, 1986. Mem. Am. Assn. Pharm. Scientists (gen. chair exec. com. midwest region 1994-95). Office: Abbott Labs 1400 Sheridan Rd North Chicago IL 60064

GUPTA, SUDHIR, immunologist, educator; b. Bijnor, India, Apr. 14, 1944; came to U.S., 1971; s. Tej S. and Jagdishwari Gupta; m. Abha, Jan. 28, 1980; children: Ankmalika Abha, Saurabh Sudhir. MD, King George's Med. Coll., Lucknow, India, 1966, PhD, 1970. Diplomate Am. Bd. Allergy and Immunology, Am. Bd. Diagnostic Lab. Immunology, Clin. Immunology Bd., Royal Coll. Physicians and Surgeons Can. Intern King George's Med. Coll., Lucknow, 1966, resident in medicine, 1967-70; teaching faculty fellow dept. medicine Tufts U. Med. Sch., Boston, 1971-72; vis. fellow in medicine Columbia U., N.Y.C., 1972-74; rsch. fellow Sloan-Kettering Inst. Cancer Rsch., N.Y.C., 1974-76, asst. prof., 1976-78, assoc. prof., 1978-82; instr. Cornell U., N.Y.C., 1976-77, asst. prof., 1977-79, assoc. prof., 1979-82; prof. medicine U. Calif., Irvine, 1982—, prof. microbiology and molecular genetics, 1984—, prof. pathology, 1986—, prof. neurology, 1988—, acting vice chair Dept. Medicine, 1994—; mem. adv. panel FDA, Washington, 1989—; sci. advisor Inst. Immunopathology, Kohn, Germany, 1990—; mem. allergy-immunology subcom. NIH, Bethesda, Md., 1985-89; vis. prof. Hematologic Rsch. Found., Roslyn, N.Y., 1992. Editor-in-chief Jour. Clin. Immunology, 1980—; editor: Immunology of Clinical and Experimental Diabetes, 1984, Mechanisms of Lymphocyte Activities and Immune Regulation I-V, 1985-94, New Concepts in Immunodeficiency Diseases, 1993. Pres. Nargis Dutt Meml. Found., So. Calif., 1990; vice-chair AIDS Task Force, Orange County (Calif.) Med. Assn., 1987—; mem. Indo-Am. Republican Club, Orange County, 1991—. Recipient Arthur Manzel Rsch. award R.A. Cooke Inst., N.Y.C., 1976, Outstanding Achievement award in med. scis. Nat. Fedn. Asian Indians in N.Am., 1986, Lifetime Achievement award Jeffrey Modell Found., N.Y.C., 1990, Disting. Scientists award Assn. Scientists Indian Origin in Am., 1994, Disting. Physician award Indian Med. Assn. Fellow ACP, Royal Coll. Physicians and Surgeons Can., Am. Soc. Medicine (London); mem. Am. Assn. Immunologists. Office: U Calif Dept Medicine C240 Med Sci I Irvine CA 92717

GUPTA, VENU GOPAL, psychology educator; b. Hoshiar Pur, Punjab, India, Apr. 3, 1934; came to U.S., 1966; s. Ram Dass and Ram Piari Aggarwal; m. Sunita Gupta, Nov. 29, 1961; children: Sunil, Sanjiv. BA with 1st class honors, Punjab U., 1953, MA 1st class 1st, 1955, MEd 1st class 1st, 1959; BEd, Delhi U., 1958; PhD, Ga. State U., 1974. Cert. counselor, Pa. Lectr. Colls. Punjab and Kurukshetra U. India, 1955-63; teaching and rsch. fellow U. Alta., Edmonton, Can., 1963-66; asst. prof. psychology U. Wis., Stevens Point, 1966-68; asst. prof. psychology and counseling Ea. Ky. U., 1968-72; teaching and rsch. fellow Ga. State U., 1972-74; prof. psychology Kutztown U. Pa., 1974—. Subject of interviews on radio and TV. Recipient Cert. of merit Dictionary Internat. Biography, 1970. Mem. AAAS, AACD, AAUP, Internat. Coun. Psychologists, Internat. Assn. Applied Psychology, Internat. Assn. for Cross-cultural Psychology, Internat. Coun. on Edn. for Teaching, Am. Psychol. Assn., Am. Ednl. Rsch. Assn., Am. Assn. for Counselor Edn. and Supervision, Am. Mental Health Counselors Assn., Phi Delta Kappa. Home: 744 Highland Ave Kutztown PA 19530-1306 Office: Kutztown U of Pa Dept Psychology Kutztown PA 19530

GURALNICK, WALTER, dental educator; b. Boston. BS, Mass. State Coll., 1937; DMD, Harvard U., 1941. Diplomate Am. Bd. Oral and Maxillofacial Surgeons. Prof. intern oral surgery Boston City Hosp., 1941-42; oral surgeon Beth Israel Hosp., Boston, 1947-82, Mt. Auburn Hosp., Cambridge, 1948-82, New Eng. Deaconess Hosp., Boston, 1950-82, Newton-Wellesley Hosp., 1950-82, New Eng. Bapt. Hosp., Boston, 1952-82; acting chief oral surgery svcs. Mass. Gen. Hosp., Boston, 1967-68, chief oral and maxillofacial surgery svcs., 1968-81, vis. oral and maxillofacial surgeon, 1981—; instr. dental medicine Sch. Dental Medicine Harvard U., 1954-55, instr. oral surgery, 1955-58, from asst. clin. prof. to clin. prof., chmn. dept., 1958-74, acting chmn. dept. dental medicine, 1966-67, chmn. dept. oral and maxillofacial surgery, 1974-81, from prof. to emeritus prof., 1981—. Contbr. more than 60 articles to profl. jours. Recipient award for Disting. Achievement in Oral and Maxillofacial Surgery, William J. Gies Found., 1987. Fellow Internat. Assn. Oral and Maxillofacial Surgeons, Am. Assn. Cancer Edn., Am. Assn. Dental Schs.; mem. Inst. Med.-NAS (sr.), ADA,. *

GUREVITCH, ARNOLD WILLIAM, dermatology educator; b. Los Angeles, Apr. 3, 1936; s. Leon and Freda Stella (Goldman) G.; m. Camille Abbott, June 12, 1960; children: Douglas Neal, Laura Judith. AB, Harvard U., 1958; MD, UCLA, 1962. Diplomate Am. Bd. Dermatology. Intern Los Angeles County Gen. Hosp., 1962-63; resident specializing in dermatology Los Angeles County Harbor Gen. Hosp., Torrance, Calif., 1963-66; practice medicine specializing in dermatology LA, 1966-67; staff physician Harbor-UCLA Med. Ctr., Torrance, 1969-73, acting chief dermatology, 1973-77, chief dermatology, 1977-96; asst. prof. dermatology UCLA Sch. Medicine, 1969-76, assoc. prof. to prof. dermatology, 1976-96; chief dermatology Los Angeles County-U. So. Calif. Med. Ctr., L.A., 1996—; prof. dermatology U. So. Calif. Sch. Medicine, 1996—; head task force on teaching Nat. Program for Dermatology, 1971-75; cons. USAF Clinic, Los Angeles, 1969—, U. So. Calif. div. med. research in edn., Los Angeles, 1975-76, GMENAC, Dept. Health Edn. and Welfare, 1979. Contbr. articles to profl. jours. Chmn. Community Sch., Los Angeles, 1975-76; pres. adv. council Bancroft Jr. High Sch., 1978-80, Fairfax High Sch., 1981-84. Fellow Am. Acad. Dermatology; mem. Soc. Investigative Dermatology, Pacific Dermatol. Assn. (sec.-treas. 1989-92, pres. 1992-93), L.A. Dermatol. Assn. (pres. 1978-79), Assn. Profs. Dermatology, L.A. Acad. Medicine (bd. govs. 1993—).

GURITZ, KAREN NOREEN, nurse, educator; b. Chgo., Apr. 16, 1950; d. Kenneth Edwin and Lucille Delores (Lee) G. BSN with honors, U. Fla., 1973; M of Nursing, U. Miss., Jackson, 1976. Cert. Lamaze childbirth educator. Charge nurse Johns Hopkins Hosp., Balt., 1973-74, L.W. Blake Hosp., Bradenton, Fla., 1974-75; instr. inservice obstetrics Orlando (Fla.) Regional Med. Ctr., 1976-77, ednl. coordinator, 1977-80, coordinator patient edn. obstetrics, 1980-86, specialist prenatal edn., 1986-91; prenatal edn. specialist State of Fla. (Orange, Osceola, and Seminole Counties), 1988—; ednl. specialist State of Fla., 1989—; edn. specialist Arnold Palmer Hosp for Women and Children, Orlando, 1991-94; instr. practical nursing Tech. Edn. Ctr. of Osceola, 1994-95, dir. health occupations, 1995—; adj. prof. U. Ctrl. Fla. Nursing Dept., 1986—. Mem. Fla. Network for Family and Patient Edn., Orlando, 1984-94. Mem. Internat. Childbirth Edn. Assn., Am. Soc. Psychoprophylaxis in Obestetrics (coord. 1982—), Coalition Fla. Childbirth Educators (bd. dirs. 1985-89, pres. bd. dirs. 1987-88). Republican. Lutheran. Office: Tech Edn Ctr of Osceola 501 Simspon Rd Kissimmee FL 34744

GURNEY, BRAD, podiatrist, osteopathic physician; b. Elizabeth, N.J., Oct. 25, 1956; s. Ira and Wilma (Namarovsky) G. BS, Rutgers U., 1978, MS, 1980; DPM, NY Coll. Podiatric Medicine, 1987; DO, UMDNJ Sch. Osteopathic Med., 1996. Dir. Lin Mar, Inc., Raritan, N.J., 1978-87; chief resident pediat. orthopedics NY Coll. Podiat. Medicine, N.Y.C., 1987-88; staff podiatrist Hosp. Care Ctr., Newark, 1988-96; chief podiat. svcs. The Heritage at Norwood, N.J., 1990-94; house officer Union (N.J.) Hosp., 1996—; pvt. practice podiat. medicine, Somerville, N.J., 1988—. Commr. Somerville Environ. Bd., 1993. Mem. Am. Acad. Family Physicians, Am. Coll. Osteopathic Family Physicians, Am. Osteopathic Assn., N.J. Assn. Osteopathic Physicians & Surgeons. Office: 32 Roosevelt Pl Somerville NJ 08876

GURR, HOWARD KEITH, psychologist; b. Queens, N.Y., May 29, 1951; s. Fred and Shirley (Izikler) G.; m. Robbin Schneider; 1 child, Danielle Jolie. B.A., York Coll., 1973; M.A., SUNY, New Paltz, 1974; M.A., Hofstra U., 1979, Ph.D., 1981. Psychometrician, L.I. Cons. Center, 1975-76; research psychometrician L.I. Jewish Hillside Med. Center, 1975-79; sch. psychologist Merrick-Bellmore Central High Sch. Dist.. Merrick, N.Y., 1979; sch. psychologist North Merrick Union Free Sch. Dist., Merrick, 1979-85, supervisory sch. psychologist Queens Coll., N.Y., 1981-85; sch. psychologist, Lynbrook, N.Y., 1985—; staff psychologist South Shore Child Guidance, Freeport, N.Y., 1982-83; pvt. practice psychology, L.I., N.Y., 1983—; adj. clin. supr. Yeshiva U., N.Y., 1988-90; faculty mem. Vocalis. L.I. Jewish/Hillside Hosp. research stipend grantee, 1974, 75. Mem. Am. Psychol. Assn., Eastern Psychol. Assn., Nassau County Psychol. Assn. (mem. exec. bd. 1990-93), Suffolk County Psychol. Assn., N.Y. State Psychol. Assn. Office: 2 Corwin Ct Huntington Station NY 11746-8314 also: 2631 Merrick Rd Ste 205 Bellmore NY 11710

GURRI, JOSEPH A., surgeon; b. Boston, Aug. 10, 1947; s. Joseph N. and Beba (Gonzalez-Plasencia) G.; m. Diana J. Beecroft; children: Kristen Elizabeth, Catherine Elena. BS, U. Miami, 1970, MD, 1975. Diplomate Am. Bd. Surgery. Surgery resident U. N.C. Hosp., 1975-80, fellow vascular surgery, 1980-81; attending surgeon Holmes Regional Med. Ctr., Melbourne, Fla., 1981—; pres. med. staff Holmes Regional Med. Ctr., Melbourne, 1988-89; Bd. dirs. Space Coast Quality Care, Melbourne. Fellow Am. Coll. Surgery; mem. Soc. Laparendoscopic Surgeons (adv. bd. 1990—), Ostomy Soc. (adv. bd.), Florida Surgical Soc.(bd. dirs. 1994—).

GURSKI, WALTER STEPHEN, podistrist; b. Newark, July 22, 1946; s. Walter Stephen and Alice Katherine (Bell) G.; m. Joekie van Bavel, Dec. 6, 1976; children: Stephen Walter, Nicole Joekie. BS in Biology, U. Charleston, 1970; D Podiatric Medicine, Ill. Coll. Podiatric Medicine, 1974. Podiatrist Danbury (Conn.) Podiatry Assocs., 1974—, Norwalk (Conn.) Podiatry Assocs., 1976—; CEO Podiatric Ind. Physicians Assn., Danbury, 1994—; lectr. in radiowave surgery in podiatry, 1990—; mgmt. cons., 1988—; podiatric cons. to med. product cos., 1989—. Contbr. articles to profl. publs. Chmn. bd. dirs. Mid Fairfield Coun. Campfire Girls, Danbury, 1982-84 mem. pres.'s club. Nat. Rep. Com. Mem. Am. Assn. Podiatric Physicians and Surgeons. Unitarian. Office: Norwalk Podiatry Assocs 9 Mott Ave Norwalk CT 06810

GURVITZ, MILTON SOLOMON, psychologist; b. Buffalo, Nov. 27, 1919; s. Isidor and Rebecca (Huravitz) G.; m. Sylvia Klein, June 20, 1948; children: Lynda Irene, Robert. B.S., SUNY, Buffalo, 1941; M.A., N.Y. U., 1948, Ph.D., 1950. Diplomate: Am. Bd. Profl. Psychology. Psychologist USPHS Hosp., Lewisburg, Pa., 1942-46, Center for Psychol. Services, N.Y.C., 1947-48; chief psychologist Hillside Hosp.-L.I. Jewish Med. Center, Glen Oaks, N.Y., 1949-55; clin. assoc. prof. Adelphi U., Garden City, N.Y., 1950-55; cons. psychologist Jewish Community Svcs. L.I., 1955-61; pvt. practice psychology Great Neck, N.Y., 1950-87; dir. Great Neck Consultation Center, 1960-85, dir. emeritus, 1986—; cons. Conn. Commn. on Alcoholism, 1947-53; clin. prof. postdoctoral program in psychoanalysis. chmn. child and adolescent faculty Adelphi U., 1968-87; pvt. practice psychology Sarasota, Fla., 1987; cons. psychologist Sarasota Child Protection Team, 1990, Jewish Family Svc. Sarasota, 1991—; active med. staff Sarasota Meml. Hosp., 1992; consulting psychologist Fla. State U.-Asolo Film Conservatory, 1993—. Author: Dynamics of Psychological Testing, 1950. Fellow Am. Psychol. Assn., Soc. Pers. Assessment; sr. mem. Nat. Psychol. Assn. for Psychoanalysis. Jewish. Home: 1111 N Gulfstream Ave Sarasota FL 34236-5563 Office: 5 Gulfstream Ave South Sarasota FL 34236-5719

GUSDON, JOHN PAUL, JR., obstetrics and gynecology educator, physician; b. Cleve., Feb. 13, 1931; s. John and Pauline (Malencek) G.; m. Marcelle Deiber, June 6, 1956 (dec. 1979); children: Marguerite, John Phillip, Veronique; m. R. Carolyn Gallager Aycock, July, 1989. BA, U. Va., 1952, MD, 1959. Diplomate Am. Bd. Ob-Gyn. Rotating intern U. Hosps. Cleve., 1959-60, resident, 1960-64; instr. ob-gyn. Sch. Medicine, Case Western Res. U., Cleve., 1964-66, asst. prof., 1967; asst. prof. ob-gyn. Bowman Gray Sch. Medicine, Wake Forest U., Winston-Salem, N.C., 1967-70, assoc. prof., 1970-74, prof., 1974-90, prof. emeritus, 1990—; staff IHS Hosps. Contbr. articles to sci. jours., chpts. to books. Lt. USN, 1952-55, Korea. Recipient John Horsley Meml. award U. Va., Charlottesville, 1968, Pres. award South Atlantic Assn. Ob-Gyn., 1973. Fellow ACOG (Pres. award 1970, 72), Am. Assn. Immunology; mem. Am. Soc. Immunology of Reproduction (founder, pres. 1981-84), Am. Gynecol. and Obstet. Soc. Republican. Roman Catholic.

GUSMORINO, PAUL, physician, educator; b. N.Y.C., Nov. 13, 1948; s. Paul and Josephine G.; m. Maria Antonietta Falvo D'Urso, July 31, 1972; children: Paul Alexander, Sabrina Greta. BS, SUNY, Stony Brook, 1969; MD, U. Rome, 1974. Cert. MD. Intern L.I. Coll. Hosp., Bklyn., 1975; resident in psychiatry Kings County Hosp.-Downstate Med. Ctr., Bklyn., 1976-78; fellow in child and adolescent psychiatry N.Y. Hosp.-Cornell Med. Ctr., White Plains, N.Y., 1978-80; med. dir. Orthopedic Arthritis Pain Ctr., N.Y.C., 1986—; asst. prof. Mt. Sinai Sch. of Med., N.Y.C., 1987—. Mem. Am. Pain Soc., Internat. Assn. Study of Pain, Am. Acad. of Pain Med., Eastern Pain Assn. Office: 301 E 17th St New York NY 10003-3804

GUSTAT, MATTHEW PETER, III, health care executive; b. Logansport, Ind., Oct. 27, 1938; s. Matthew Peter and Emily Amelia (Schmidt) G.; m. Nicole Marie Marraccini, Oct. 26, 1964 (dec. Feb. 1993); 1 child, Matthew Peter IV; m. Kathleen Claire Robison, Nov. 25, 1994. B.S. in Commerce, U. Ky., 1961; M.A. in Health Care Adminstrn., Central Mich. U., 1978. Commd. officer U.S. Army, 1961, advanced through grades to col.; healthcare adminstr. and logistician U.S. Army, Washington and Europe, 1961-76; project mgr. health automation, dir. Dept. Def., Bethesda, Md., 1977-84, ret., 1985; exec. v.p. Healthcare Concepts, Riverdale, Md., 1985-91; chmn. Mgmt. Assistance and Concepts Corp., Bethesda, Md., 1991—; cons., lectr. in field. Editor Materials & Fin. Strategy newsletter, 1985—. Contbr. articles to profl. jours. Mem. Republican Presdl. Task Force, 1982—; soccer coach Wheaton Boys and Girls Club, Md., 1979-83; v.p. Am. Nat. Standards Inst., 1980-82. Decorated Bronze Star, Commendation medal. Fellow Health Care Materials Mgmt. Soc. (disting. cert., v.p. 1978—, pres. 1986-87); mem. Am. Assn. Med. Systems and Informatics, Am. Mgmt. Assn., Am. Numis. Assn., Am. Legion. Methodist. Avocations: coins; stamps; golf; soccer. Home: 3200 Beret Ln Silver Spring MD 20906-3021 Office: Mgmt Assistance & Concepts Corp 203-A Calle Del Oaks Monterey CA 93940

GUSTIN, ANN WINIFRED, psychologist; b. Winchester, Mass., 1941; d. Bertram Pettingill and Ruth Lillian (Weller) G.; B.A. with honors in Psychology, U. Mass., 1963; M.S. (USPHS fellow), Syracuse U., 1966, Ph.D., 1969. Registered psychologist, Sask.; lic. psychologist, Ga.; Diplomate Am. Bd. Med. Psychotherapists. Research asst., psychology trainee U. Mass., Tufts U., Harvard U., Syracuse U., 1961-66; psychology intern VA, Canandaigua, N.Y., 1967-68; asst. prof. psychology U. Regina (Sask., Can.), 1969-74, assoc. prof. psychology, dir. counseling services, head clin. tng., 1974-78; pvt. practice psychology, Carrollton, Ga., 1978—, Atlanta, 1980—; staff tng. cons. Frobisher Bay Dept. Social Services, N.W. Territories, Can., 1979-80; cons. staff Tanner Hosp.; ancillary staff West Paces Ferry Hosp.; psychiat. cons. Social Security Adminstrn., Ga. Dept. Human Resources, 1980—. Membership chmn. Carroll County Mental Health Assn., 1979-81; mem. nat. mental health disaster response team ARC. Fellow Ga. Psychol Assn. (exec. divsn. lic. psychologists 1986-91, 92—, Nat. Red Cross disaster mental health team 1991—); mem. Am. Psychol. Assn., Can. Psychol. Assn., Sask. Psychol. Assn. (mem. exec. council 1971-72, registrar 1972-73), Nat. Assn. Disability Examiners, Ga. Assn. Disability Examiners. Office: 107 College St Carrollton GA 30117-3136 also: One Decatur Town Ctr 150 E Ponce De Leon Ave Ste 46 Decatur GA 30030-2553

GUTEKUNST, RICHARD RALPH, microbiology educator; b. Allentown, Pa., Jan. 20, 1926; s. George D. and Jennie L. (Alsop) G.; m. Anna Frances Fetterman, Dec. 27, 1946; children: Mary Jane Ellickson, Richard M., Jo Anne Loughery. B.S., Phila. Coll. Pharmacy and Sci., 1951; M.S., Cornell U., 1957, Ph.D., 1958. Commd. ensign U.S. Navy, advanced through grades to comdr., 1968; mem. faculty Hahnemann Med. Coll. and Hosp., Phila., 1968-80; prof. microbiology and immunology Hahnemann Med. Coll. and Hosp., 1974-80; dir. Clin. Micro Lab., 1968-75; dean Coll. Allied Health Professions, 1975-80, Coll. Health Related Professions; prof. dept. med. tech. and microbiology U. Fla., Gainesville, 1980-95; dean emeritus, 1995—. Vice pres. Lower Gwynedd (Pa.) Twp. Commrs., 1972-80; mem. coun. St. Peter's Luth. Ch., North Wales, Pa., 1972-77, pres., 1974-77; No. Ctrl. Fla. Regional Planning Coun., 1987-92; bd. dirs. Citizens' Crime Commn., Alachua County, 1984-88, vice-chmn., 1986-87; bd. dirs. United Way Alachua County, 1984-90, pres., 1988; bd. dirs. ARC of Alachua County, 1989-93; pres. Fla. Alliance of 100, Healthcare Manpower, 1988-90; mem. adv. bd. AIDS Inst., UF; mem. com. on pub. health FMA, 1986—, com. on allied health, 1991—, task force on nursing shortage, 1990—. Recipient Lindback award, 1975; Faculty Achievement award Coll. Allied Health Professions; Faculty Achievement award Hahnemann Med. Coll. and Hosp., Phila., 1980. Fellow Am. Acad. Microbiology, Am. Soc. for Allied Health Professions (pres.-elect 1981-82, pres. 1982-83); mem. AAAS, Assn. Practitioners Infection Control, Am. Soc. Microbiology, N.Y. Acad. Sci. Republican. Lutheran. Club: Masons. Home: 3942 NW 25th Cir Gainesville FL 32606-7435 Office: U Health Sci Ctr PO Box 100014 Gainesville FL 32610-0185

GUTENTAG, PATRICIA RICHMAND, social worker, family counselor, occupational therapist; b. Newark, Apr. 10, 1954; d. Joseph and Joan (Miller) Leflein; m. Herbert Norman Gutentag; children: Steven, Jesse. BS in Occupational Therapy, Tufts U., 1976; MSW, Boston Coll., 1979. Lic. family and marriage counselor, lic. clin. social worker, N.J.; diplomate Am. Bd. Examiners in Clin. Social Work; registered occupational therapist, N.J. Social worker Jewish Family Svc., Salem, Mass., 1979-82; pvt. practice family and marriage counselor Westfield and Red Bank, N.J., 1982—; cons. high stress, Westfield and Red Bank, 1982—. Fellow N.J. Soc. for Clin. Social Work; mem. NASW, Am. Occupational Therapists Assn., Registered Occupational Therapists Assn., Soc. for Advancement Family Therapy in N.J., Am. Anorexia-Bulimia Assn., Am. Assn. Marriage and Family Therapy. Office: 200 Maple Ave Red Bank NJ 07701-1732

GUTFREUND, DONALD E., internist, hematologist, oncologist; b. N.Y.C., June 10, 1938; s. James and Cora (Gross) G. BS, Union Coll., 1959; MD, NYU, 1963. Med. intern N.C. Meml. Hosp., Chapel Hill, 1963-64; med. resident Kings County Hosp., Bklyn., 1964-65, chief med. resident, 1965-66; clin. assoc. Nat. Cancer Inst., Balt. Cancer Rsch., 1966-68; fellow in hematology Mt. Sinai Hosp., N.Y.C., 1968-69, chief resident in hematology, 1969-70; clin. instr. in medicine Mt. Sinai Sch. Medicine, N.Y.C., 1968-70, assoc. in medicine, 1970-71; chief divsn. oncology St. Elizabeth Hosp., Elizabeth, N.J., 1976-79, attending in medicine, 1985—; pvt. practice internal medicine, hematology, oncology Elizabeth Med. Assocs., 1971—. Contbr. articles to profl. publs. Lt. comdr. USPHS, 1964-66. Mem. Am. Soc. Hematology, Phi Beta Kappa, Alpha Omega Alpha. Office: Elizabeth Med Assocs 469 Morris Ave Elizabeth NJ 07208

GUTGESELL, HOWARD PHILIP, physician; b. Wausau, Wis., June 6, 1942; s. Howard Philip and Myrtle E. (Sand) G.; m. Margaret Evans Kowitz, June 4, 1966; children: Heidi, Kirsten. BS, U. Wis., 1964, MS, 1966, MD, 1968. Intern Strong Meml. Hosp., Rochester, N.Y., 1968-69, resident, 1969-70; fellow in pediat. cardiology Baylor Coll. Medicine, Houston, 1972-75, asst. prof., 1975-78, assoc. prof., 1978-84; prof. U. Va., Charlottesville, 1984—. Fellow Am. Acad. Pediat., Am. Coll. Cardiology; mem. Am. Heart Assn. Office: Univ Va Med Ctr Pediatrics Box 386 Charlottesville VA 22908

GUTHOLM, DAVID DONALD, JR., emergency medical technician; b. Plainfield, N.J., Mar. 31, 1966; s. David Donald and Ilda Louise (LoCollo) G. Diploma in Food Svc., Brick (N.J.) Vo-Tech Sch., 1984, Diploma in Comml. Art, 1984; EMT, Ocean County Coll., Toms River, N.J., 1992. Cert. EMT, N.J. EMT Herbertsville First Aid Squad, Brick, 1992—, Clays Ambulance Svc., Farmingdale, N.J., 1992-96, Quality Ambulance Svc., Whiting, N.J., 1996—; engr. Herbertsville First Aid Squad, 1994, 95. Home: 208 Cleveland Ct Brick NJ 08724 Office: Herbertsville First Aid 208 Cleveland Ct Brick NJ 08724-1710

GUTHRIE, DIANA FERN, nursing educator; b. N.Y.C., May 7, 1934; d. Floyd George and A. May (Moler) Worthington; m. Richard Alan Guthrie, Aug. 18, 1957; children: Laura, Joyce, Tammy. AA, Graceland Coll., 1953; RN, Independence (Mo.) Sanitarium, 1956; BS in Nursing, U. Mo., 1957, MS in Pub. Health, 1969; EdS, Wichita State U., 1982; PhD, Walden U., 1985. RN, Mo., Kans.; lic. profl. counselor, Kans.; cert. in stress mgmt. edn.; cert.clin. hypnosis; lic. holistic nursing; cert. healing touch; advanced RN practitioner; registered marriage and family therapist. Instr. red cross U.S. Naval Sta., Sangley Point, Philippines, 1961-63; acting head nurse newborn nursery U. Mo., Columbia, 1963-64, birth defect nurse dept. pediatrics, 1964-65, nursing dir. clin. research ctr., 1965-67, research asst., 1967-73; asst. then assoc. prof. Sch. Medicine U. Kans., Wichita, 1974-85; prof. pediatrics and psychiatry Wichita State Sch. of Nursing, Wichita, 1982—; diabetes nurse specialist Sch. Medicine U. Kans., Wichita, 1973—; nurse cons. diabetes Mo. Regional Med. Program, Columbia, 1970-73; nat. advisor Human Diabetes Ctr. for Excellence, Lexington, Ky., 1982-90, Phoenix, 1983-92, Charlottesville, Ky., 1990-95; adj. prof. nursingU. Kans., Wichita, 1982—. Author: Nursing Management of Diabetes, 3d edit. 1991, The Diabetes Source Book, 1990, rev. edit., 1995; contbr. articles to profl. jours. Mem. health adv. bd. Mid-Am. All Indian Ctr., Wichita, 1978-80; bd. dirs. Wichita Urban Indian Health Clinic, 1980-82; trustee Graceland Coll., Lamoni, Iowa, 1996—. Recipient Explempary Recognition award Epsilon Gamma chpt. Sigma Theta Tau, 1996. Fellow Am. Acad. Nursing; mem. ANA, APHA, Am. Diabetes Assn. (affiliate bd. dirs. 1979-83, pres. Kans. affiliate 1980-81, 90-91, Outstanding Educator award 1979), Am. Assn. Diabetes Educators (cert., Disting. Svc. award 1984), Am. Assn. Med. Psychotherapists (profl. adv. bd. 1985—), Sigma Theta Tau (exemplar recognition award Epsilon chpt. 1996). Democrat. Mem. Reorganized LDS Ch.

GUTHRIE, HELEN A., nutrition educator, consultant; b. Sarnia, Ont., Can., Sept. 25, 1925; d. David and Helen (Sweet) Andrews; m. George Guthrie, June 4, 1949; children: Barbara, Jane, James. BA, U. Western Ont., 1946, DSc (hon.), 1982; MS, Mich. State U., 1948; PhD, U. Hawaii, 1968; DSc, U. Guelph, 1996. Registered dietitian, Pa. From instr. to prof. Pa. State U., University Park, 1949-73, chair dept., 1974-89, endowed prof. nutrition, 1989-91, prof. emerita, 1991—; v.p. Heinz Inst. Nutrition Scis., 1993—; nutrition cons. to industry, govt. and academia. Chmn. Bd. of Health, State College, Pa., 1977-82. Recipient Borden award Am. Home Econs. Assn., 1976, W.O. Atwater award USDA, 1989, Pacemaker award Pa. Nutrition Coun., 1994. Fellow Am. Inst. Nutrition (councillor 1982—, pres. 1987—, Elvehjhem award for pub. svc. 1989), Soc. Nutrition Edn. (pres. 1978-79, fellow, 1992), Internat. Life Sci. Inst.-Nutrition Found. (trustee 1979-92, v.p. nutrition 1986-89, editor Nutrition Today 1987—, Philippine Assn. Nutrition and Dietetics (hon.). Home: 1316 S Garner St State College PA 16801-6328 Office: Pa State U S-125 S Human Devel University Park PA 16802

GUTHRIE, JOHN ROBERT, physician, writer; b. Spartanburg, S.C., Mar. 8, 1942; s. Clarence L. and Rosa Jane (Thackston) G.; m. Natasha K. Guthrie, Sept. 18, 1993; 1 child, Alexi; children from previous marriage: Luke, Asia, Jason, Elizabeth. BS, Mercer U., 1969; MA, Duke U., 1971; DO, Chgo. Coll. Osteo. Medicine, 1979. Diplomate Am. Bd. Osteopathic Medicine and Surgery. Sci. and math. tchr. Mebane (N.C.) Med. Sch., 1969-71; instr. sci. N.C. Community Coll., 1971-75; intern Dr.'s Hosp., Atlanta, 1979-80; physician with family practice assoc. Spartanburg, S.C., 1980-82; med. dir. The Guthrie Clinic, PA, Spartanburg, 1982—; patient care com. Spartanburg Regional Med. Ctr., 1982-84; faculty student liaison com. Chgo.

Coll. Osteo. Medicine, 1978-79; med. cons. CBS-TV, Spartanburg, 1985-88; CEO, med. dir. The Agy. for Internat. Understanding. Author: The Dynamic Action Diet Fat Gram and Calorie Counter, 1993, The Dynamic Action Diet, 1994; contbr. articles to profl. jours., poetry and prose to various publs. Bd. dirs. Spartanburg Parents Who Care, 1984-85, Spartanburg Teen Ctr., 1984-85; v.p. S.C. Osteo. Med. Assn., 1980-81, 85, pres., 1986-87; 7th grade Royal Amb. group leader First Bapt. Ch., Spartanburg, 1985, childrens com., 1983-84. With USMC, 1961-65, comdr. M.C., USNR, 1982-88. Grantee NSF, 1971. Mem. Am. Soc. Bariatric Physicians, Spartanburg County Med. Assn., Acad. Am. Poets, Am. Physicians Poetry Assn., Carolina Country Club. Baptist. Office: The Guthrie Clinic PA 216 Beechwood Dr Spartanburg SC 29307

GUTHRIE, RANDOLPH HOBSON, JR., plastic surgeon, consultant; b. N.Y.C., Dec. 8, 1934; s. Randolph Hobson and Mabel Edith (Welton) G.; A.B., Princeton, 1957; M.D., Harvard, 1961; m. Beatrice Mills Holden, Mar. 20, 1965; children—Randolph Hobson III, Michael Phipps, Philip Holden. Intern N.Y. Hosp., N.Y.C., 1961-62, resident gen. surgery, 1962-63, resident plastic surgery 1969-71, chief resident, 1971, asst. chief plastic surgery, 1971-77 ; asst. attending surgeon, 1971-74, assoc. attending surgeon, 1974-89, attending surgeon, 1989—; resident gen. surgery St. Luke's Hosp., N.Y.C., 1963-66, chief resident, 1966; research fellow Sloan-Kettering Inst., N.Y.C., 1970-71; chief plastic and reconstructive surgery service Meml. Sloan-Kettering Cancer Center, 1971-77, attending surgeon, 1977-93, cons., 1994—; chief dept. plastic and reconstructive surgery N.Y. Downtown Hosp., 1979—; asst. prof. Cornell U. Med. Coll., 1971-74, assoc. prof., 1974-89, prof., 1989—. Pres., East River Med. Found., N.Y.C., 1970-80, Acacia Found., N.Y.C., 1980-94; alumni dir. St. Paul's Sch., Concord, N.H., 1979-83, form agt., 1983-87, term trustee, 1985-89, life trustee 1989-94. trustee Episcopal Sch., N.Y.C., 1976-84; bd. dirs. Am.-Italian Found. for Cancer Research, N.Y.C., 1985-94; bd. dirs., treas. Save Venice, Inc., 1985-89, pres., 1989—; trustee N.Y. Downtown Hosp., 1985-92. Served to maj. M.C., AUS, 1966-69. Mem. ACS, Plastic Surgery Research Council, Am. Geriatrics Soc., Am. Soc. Plastic and Reconstructive Surgeons, Pan Am. Med. Soc., N.Y. Soc. Plastic and Reconstructive Surgery, N.Y. Med. Soc., Med. Soc. County N.Y., Herbert Conway Soc. Clubs: Doubles, Knickerbocker (N.Y.C.). Author: The Truth About Breast Implants, 1994; co-author: Reconstruction and Esthetic Mammoplasty, 1989; contbr. articles to books and med. jours. Home and Office: 15 E 74th St New York NY 10021-2604

GUTIERREZ, PAMELA JEAN HOLBROOK, nurse, clinical perfusionist; b. Maryville, Mo., Jan. 13, 1956; d. John Peter and Doris Ladene (Allen) Curry; m. Mark Lee Gutierrez, Dec. 9, 1978. Student, U. Nebr., 1973-93, Nebr. Meth. Sch. Nursing, 1976; BSN, U. State N.Y., 1989; grad. Clin. Perfusionist, U. Nebr., 1992-94. RN, cert. perfusion scis. Charge nurse ICU St. Joseph's Hosp., Omaha, 1976-80, staff nurse emergency dept., 1980-81, flight nurse Life Flight, 1981-91, charge and staff nurse emergency dept., 1991-94; project nurse, rsch. asst. dept. surgery Creighton U., 1978-79; mem. PACU staff, nurse, clin. perfusionist Immanuel Med. Ctr., Omaha, 1994—; trauma nurse core course instr. emergency dept. Nurse's Assn., Neonatal Advanced Cardiac Life Support, 1990, Am. Heart Assn.; pediatric advanced life support instr.; advanced cardiac life support instr. Am. Heart Assn., 1985—; paramedic cert., pre-hosp. trauma life support instr. Nat. Assn. Emergency Med. Technicians and Paramedics, 1982. Contbr. articles to profl. jours. Mem. AACN, Nat. Flight Nurses Assn., Nat. Emergency Med. Svcs. Pilots Assn., Emergency Nurses Assn. Roman Catholic. Home: 4207 Woolworth Ave Omaha NE 68105-1752

GUTMAN, LUCY TONI, school social worker, educator, counselor; b. Phila., July 13, 1936; d. Milton R. and Clarissa (Silverman) G.; divorced; children: James, Laurie. BA, Wellesley Coll., 1958; MSW, Bryn Mawr Coll., 1963; MA in History, U. Ariz., 1978; MEd, Northwestern State U., 1991, MA in English, 1992; postgrad., U. So. Miss., 1992—. Cert. Acad. Cert. Social Workers, La. Bd. cert. social worker, sch. social work specialist, Nat. Bd. Cert. Counselor; diplomate in clin. social work; cert. secondary tchr., La. Social worker Phila. Gen. Hosp., 1963-65; sr. social worker Irving Schwartz Inst. Children and Youth, 1965-66; sr. psychiat. social worker Child Study Ctr. Phila., 1966-68; chief social worker Framingham (Mass.) Ct. Clinic Juvenile Offenders, 1968-72; cons. Nashua (N.H.) Community Coun., 1969-72; dir. clinic, supr. social work Tucson East Community Mental Health Ctr., 1972-74; coord. spl. adoptions program Cath. Social Svcs. So. Ariz., Tucson, 1974-75; social worker Met. Ministry, 1983; supr. social work Leesville (La.) Mental Health Clinic, 1984; sch. social worker Vernon Parish Sch. Bd., Leesville, 1984—; adj. instr. English, sociology, Am. and European history Northwestern State U., Ft. Polk, La., 1984—; part-time counselor River North Psychol. Svcs., Leesville, 1989-92; presenter ann. conf. NASW, 1987, 88, La. Sch. Social Workers Conf., 1986, 87, La. Spl. Edn. Conf., 1988, La. Conf. Tchrs. English, 1991, 94, So. Assn. women Historians, 1994. Contbr. articles to profl. jours. Nat. Soc. Colonial Dames scholar, 1978-79; fellow Pa. State, 1961-62, NIMH, 1962-63. Mem. NASW, AACD, MLA, LWV, Am. Coll. Pers. Assn., Acad. Cert. Social Workers (diplomate), Bus. and Profl. Women Assn., Am. Legion Aux., So. Hist. Assn., So. Assn. Women Historians, Gamma Beta Phi, Phi Alpha Theta. Home: 2004 Allison St Leesville LA 71446-5104 Office: Vernon Parish Sch Bd Leesville LA 71446

GUTMAN, ROBERT ALLAN, nephrologist; b. N.Y.C., Jan. 23, 1938; s. Arthur J. and Polly S. (Salomon) G.; m. Laura T., Apr. 2, 1963; children: Paula, Catherine. BS, U. Fla., 1958, MD, 1962. Intern U. Wash., Seattle, 1962-63, resident, 1963-64, 65-66, chief resident, 1968-69, asst. prof. medicine, 1969-71; asst. prof. medicine Duke U., Durham, N.C., 1971-75; assoc. prof. medicine Duke U., Durham, 1975-83, prof. medicine, 1983-84, cons. prof. medicine, 1984—; chief nephrology Durham VA Hosp., 1971-79; numerous bd. and com. positions Durham Regional Hosp., 1985—, pres. med. staff, 1996. Contbr. articles to profl. jours, chpts. to books. Seasonal bd., com. ruler N.C. & Southern Kidney Coun., Raleigh, 1973—, chmn. network, 1987. Lt. comdr. USN, 1966-68. Jewish. Office: Durham Nephrology Assocs 4016 Freedom Lake Dr Durham NC 27704

GUTOWICZ, MATTHEW FRANCIS, JR., radiologist; b. Camden, N.J., Feb. 23, 1945; s. Matthew F. and A. Patricia (Walczak) G.; m. Alice Mary Bell, June 27, 1977; 1 child, Melissa. BA, Temple U., 1968; DO, Phila. Coll. Osteo. Medicine, 1972. Diplomate Am. Bd. Radiology, Am. Bd. Nuclear Medicine. Intern Mercy Hosp., Denver, 1972-73; resident in diagnostic radiology Hosp. of U. Pa., Phila., 1973-76, fellow in nuclear medicine, 1976-77; chief dept. radiology and nuclear medicine Fisher Titus Med. Ctr., Norwalk, Ohio, 1977—; pres. Firelands Radiology, Inc., Norwalk, 1977—. Republican. Roman Catholic. Home: 23 Patrician Dr Norwalk OH 44857-2463

GUTSTEIN, DEBRA LEE, community health educator; b. Milw., Sept. 7, 1954; d. Cyril and Cecilia Gutstein. BS in Community Health Edn., Univ. Wis., 1979; BA in Nursing, St. Scholastic Sch. Nursing, 1981. Cert. first aid, adult CPR, community CPR, instr. trainer; RN, Ariz., Wis. Coord. home care Home Health Svcs., Inc., Milw., 1982-83; nursing supr. medicare/medicaid div. Upjohn Health Care Ctr., Milw., 1982-83; pub. health nurse Pub. Health Nursing, Milw., 1983-84; primary care nurse Camelback Hosp., 1985; mgr., coord., dir. Mesa Gen. Hosp. Pain Control Ctr., 1985-88; biofeedback therapist Desert Behavioral Health Assocs., Tempe, 1989-90; pub. info. office nurse specialist Maricopa County Dept. Health Svcs. Adminstrn., 1988-90; health svcs. adminstr. De Anza Co., 1990-95; pres. Futuristic Health, Inc., Phoenix, 1995—; teaching asst. physiol. psychology Univ. Wis., Milw.; instr. Am. Red Cross; presenter in field. Recipient 200 Notable Am. Women Honour award.

GUTTELING, EDWARD WILLIAM, orthopedic surgeon; married; one child. BS in Physics, U. Santa Clara, 1973; MS in Physics, San Diego State U., 1975; MS in Phys. Oceanography, U. Hawaii, 1981, MD, 1985. Diplomate Nat. Bd. Med. Examiners, Am. Acad. Orthopedic Surgery. Resident in surgery U. Medicine and Dentistry of N.J., Newark, 1985-87, resident in orthop. surgery, 1988-92; pvt. practice Hawaii Orthops., Inc., Hilo, 1992—; team physician varsity athletics U. Hawaii, Hilo; team physician Hilo Stars, Hawaii Winter League Profl. Baseball; chmn. surg. specialties com. Hilo Hosp. Contbr. articles to profl. jours. Office: Hawaii Orthops Inc PO Box 857 Hilo HI 96721

GUTTENPLAN, JOSEPH B., biochemistry researcher and educator; b. N.Y.C., May 16, 1943; s. Henry L. and Elizabeth (Phillips) G.; m. Hilde Krohn, Sept. 20, 1971; children: Nils, Alys. BS, Bklyn. Coll., 1965; MS, PhD, Brandeis U., 1970, MPH Columbia U., 1992. Postdoctoral fellow Max Plank Inst., Goettingen, W. Ger., 1969-71, U. Calif., Berkeley, 1971-73; research asst. prof. Mt. Sinai Sch. Medicine, N.Y.C., 1973-74; from asst. to assoc. prof. biochemistry NYU Dental Ctr., N.Y.C., 1974-87; full prof. biochemistry, 1987, coord. biochemistry/microbiology, 1991—, dir. rsch., 1993—; assoc. prof. environ. medicine NYU Med. Ctr., 1983—, acting chmn., 1987-88; cons. Mt. Sinai Med. Ctr., 1980-84; pvt. cons. Co-author: Biochemistry, 1995; contbr. articles to profl. jours. and chpt. to book. Mem. N.C.I. site visit tam Eppley Inst. Grantee NIH, 1976, 79, 83, 87. Fellow Am. Inst. Chemists (study sect. to rev. superfund grants); mem. Am. Assn. Cancer Research, Environ. Mutagen Soc., Am. Soc. Biol. Chemists. Home: 110 E Brookside Dr Larchmont NY 10538-1736

GUTTMANN, RONALD DAVID, medical educator, pharmaceutical and biotechnology consultant; b. Mpls., Aug. 16, 1936; s. George Neil and Florence (Schectman) G.; m. Dagmar Bruninghold, Jan. 11, 1964; children: Astrid, Gregory, Carla. BA, U. Minn., 1958, BS, 1959, MD, 1961. Instr. medicine Harvard U. Med. Sch., Boston, 1969-70; assoc. prof. medicine McGill U., Montreal, Que., Can., 1970-74, prof. medicine, 1975—, dir. ctr. clin. immunobiology and transplantation, 1988—; dir. transplant svc. Royal Victorial Hosp., Montreal, Que., Can., 1970-88; mem. McGill Cancer Ctr., Montreal, Que., Can., 1981-91; cons. WHO, Manila, 1982; chmn. med. adv. bd. Kidney Found., Can., 1982—; mem. sci. adv. bd. Nexia Biotechs. Inc., 1994, SangStat Med. Corp., 1994. Editor: Transplant, 1969, Immunology, 4th edit., 1981; mem. adv. bd. Current Topics in Transplantation, 1983, Renal Transplantation, 1986. Served to lt. USNR, 1962-64. Recipient Fraser associateship McGill U., 1974-83; Med. Rsch. Coun. grantee, 1971-96, Lifetime Achievement award Inst. Kidney Disease and Rsch. Ctr., 1996. Mem. Transplantation Soc. (v.p. 1981-83), Am. Soc. Transplant Physicians (pres. 1982-83, disting. achievement prize 1996), Am. Soc. Clin. Investigation (emeritus), Assn. Am. Physicians, Can. Inst. Acad. Medicine. Clubs: Univ. (Montreal); Hillside Tennis (Montreal). Home: 19 Aberdeen Ave, Montreal, PQ Canada H3Y 3A5 Office: McGill U Transplant Ctr, 687 av des Pins O, Montreal, PQ Canada H3A 1A1

GUY, MATTHEW JOEL, gastroenterologist; b. Bklyn., Aug. 23, 1945; s. Rubin and Gertrude (Feinberg) Guy; B.A. summa cum laude, Bklyn. Coll., 1966; M.D., Columbia U., 1970, Med.Sc.D., 1974; m. Barbara Mae Sachartof, Oct. 21, 1979; children—Reuven Maxwell, Judah Philip, Alan Louis, David Charles, Goldie Hannah-Cheryl. Intern, Maimonides Hosp., Bklyn., 1970-71, resident, 1971-72; resident St. Luke's Hosp., N.Y.C., 1972-73, Columbia-Presbyn. Med. Center, N.Y.C., 1973-74; practice medicine specializing in gastroenterology, Bklyn., 1974—; mem. staff Kings Hwy. Hosp., 1974—, dir. gastro-intestinal endoscopy, 1976—; mem. staff Maimonides Hosp., SUNY Downstate Med. Center (all Bklyn.); asst. prof. medicine SUNY Downstate Med Center. Trustee, mem. bd. edn. Yeshiva of Flatbush. Diplomate Am. Bd. Internal Medicine. Fellow Am. Coll. Gastroenterology, Am. Soc. Gastrointestinal Endoscopy; mem. ACP, AMA, Kings County Med. Soc., Phi Beta Kappa, Sigma Xi. Office: 2408 Gerritsen Ave Brooklyn NY 11229-5904

GUYER, CHARLES GRAYSON, II, clinical psychologist, educator; b. High Point, N.C., May 22, 1949; s. Charles Grayson Sr. and Mildred (Workman) G.; m. Ruth W. Guyer, June 28, 1986; children: Charles Grayson III, Jarvis Griffith. BA, Appalachian State U., 1972, MA, 1974; EdD, Coll. of William and Mary, 1978. Clin. psychology intern Human Resource Inst., Norfolk, Va., 1977-78; post-doctoral resident No. Wyo. Mental Health, Sheridan, Wyo., 1978-80; post-doctoral fellow U. N.C., Chapel Hill, 1980-81; dir. psychology dept. Holly Hill Hosp., Raleigh, N.C., 1980-81, Southeastern Mental Health, Wilmington, N.C., 1981-82; pvt. practice High Point, N.C., 1982-83, Associated Family Care, Greensboro, N.C., 1988—; clin. asst. prof. Duke U, Durham, N.C., 1980-81, U. N.C., Chapel Hill, 1988—; clin. prof. Webster U., St. Louis., 1983-88, U. N.C., Wilmington, 1981-83. Author: (with others) Hypnosis in Treatment of Behavior Disorders, 1991; editor The Relationship jour., 1984, assoc. editor, 1981; editor N.C. Newsletter of Clin. Hypnosis, 1991. Lt. USN, 1983-88. Fellow Am. Coll. Psychology, Acad. Family Psychology (sec. 1991-94), Am. Bd. Profl. Psychology, Am. Bd. Family Psychology (pres. 1992-94), Acad. Counseling in Psychology (pres. 1993-95); mem. APA, Am. Acad. Family Psychology (pres. 1995-96), Soc. Clin. and Exptl. Hypnosis, Am. Soc. Clin. Hypnosis, N.C. Soc. Clin. Hypnosis, N.C. Psychol. Assn. Methodist. Home: 6303 Westwind Dr Greensboro NC 27410-4975 Office: 409A Parkway Greensboro NC 27401-1616

GUYNN, ROBERT WILLIAM, psychiatrist, educator; b. Streator, Ill., Oct. 27, 1942; s. William Digby and Helen Louise (Dancey) G. BA, Mich. State U., 1963; MD, Johns Hopkins U., 1967. Diplomate Am. Bd. Psychiatry and Neurology. Clin. fellow Nat. Inst. of Mental Health, Washington, 1970-73; asst. prof. Dept. of Psychiatry and Behaviorial Scis. U. Tex., Houston, 1973-76, assoc. prof., 1976-83, vice-chmn., prof. psychiatry, 1983-87, interim chmn., 1987-89, chmn., 1989—; dir. U. Tex. Mental Scis. Inst., Houston, 1987—; exec. dir. Harris County Psychiat. Ctr., 1988—. Contbr. articles to profl. jours. and book chpts.; mem. editl. bd. Internat. Rev. Psychiatry, 1988-93, editor-in-chief, 1989-93. Bd. dirs. Vols. of Am., Houston, 1982-88, Harris County Mental Health Assn., Houston, 1992—. Full surgeon USPHS, 1970-73. Fellow Am. Psychiat. Assn.; mem. Am. Coll. Psychiatry, Am. Soc. Biol. Chemistry, Tex. Rsch. Soc. on Alcoholism (pres. 1985-87), Tex. Soc. of Am. Assn. Psychiat. Adminstrs. (treas. 1990-91, pres. 1992-93), Biochem. Soc., Rsch. Soc. on Alcoholism, Houston Psychiat. Soc. (v.p. 1989-90, pres. 1991-92), Harris County Med. Soc. (bd. ethics 1989-92). Office: U Tex Health Sci Ctr PO Box 20708 Houston TX 77225-0708

GUZE, PHYLLIS A., internist, educator, academic administrator. Grad., U. So. Calif. Sch. Medicine. Resident in internal medicine Harbor UCLA Med. Ctr., fellow; dean of edn. UCLA, 1991-95; chief of medicine West L.A. VA Med. Ctr. Contbr. numerous articles to profl. jours. Recipient Disting. Tchr. award in clin. scis. Assn. Am. Med. Colls., 1995. Mem. ACP, Am. Bd. of Internal Medicine (cert. com.), Assn. of Program Dirs. in Internal Medicine, Assn. of VA Chiefs of Medicine. Office: Chief Med Svc West LA VA Med Ctr U Calif Los Angeles CA 92101*

GUZE, SAMUEL BARRY, psychiatrist, educator, university official; b. N.Y.C., Oct. 18, 1923; s. Jacob and Jenny (Berry) G.; m. Joy Lawrence Campbell, June 7, 1946; children: Jonathan, Ann. Student, CCNY, 1939-41; MD, Washington U., 1945. Diplomate Am. Bd. Internal Medicine, Am. Bd. Psychiatry and Neurology. Mem. faculty Washington U. Sch. Medicine, St. Louis, 1951—, prof. psychiatry, assoc. prof. medicine, 1964—, asst. to dean, 1965-71, vice chancellor for med. affairs, 1971-89, asst. dir. Psychiatry Clinic, 1951-55, dir. Psychiatry Clinic, 1955-75, head dept. psychiatry, 1975-89, 93—, Spencer T. Olin prof., 1974—; pres. Washington U. Med. Center, 1971-89; mem. staff Barnes Hosp., St. Louis, 1951—, psychiatrist-in-chief, 1975-89, 93—; mem. psychiat. staff Renard Hosp., 1953—, psychiatrist-in-chief, 1975-89, 93—. Contbr. articles to profl. jours. Fellow ACP, Am. Psychiat. Assn., Royal Coll. Psychiatry, Am. Coll. Psychiatry; mem. AMA, Am. Fedn. for Clin. Rsch., Psychiat. Rsch. Soc., Am. Psychosomatic Soc., Assn. for Rsch. in Nervous and Mental Diseases, Am. Psychopathol. Soc., Soc. Biol. Psychiatry, Soc. Neurosci., Inst. of Medicine of NAS, Sigma Xi, Alpha Omega Alpha. Home: 17 Ridgemoor Dr Saint Louis MO 63105-3037 Office: 4940 Childrens Pl Saint Louis MO 63110-1002

GUZEK, JAN WOJCIECH, physiology educator; b. Lublin, Poland, Mar. 28, 1924; s. Józef and Maria (Pelczarska) G.; m. Barbara Moskalewska, Oct. 24, 1952 (dec. Nov. 10, 1980); children: Anna Maria, Maria Magdalena, Wojciech Józef. Grad. in medicine, Jagellonian U., Kraków, Poland, 1951; MD, U. Łódź, Poland, 1962; habilitation in human physiology, U. Łódz, Poland, 1968. Asst. lect. dept. gen. pathology, faculty of medicine U. Kraków, 1949-60; sr. lectr., reader, asst. prof. dept. physiology U. Łódź, 1960-74, vice dean Sch. Medicine, 1972, dep. dir. Inst. Physiology and Biochemistry, Sch. Medicine, 1973-74, prof.-in-ordinary, head dept. pathophysiology, 1974-94, prof. emeritus, part-time faculty mem., 1994—; mem. com. for physiol. scis. Polish Acad. Scis., 1984—, mem. com. for basic med. scis., 1987-93, com. for clin. pathophysiology, 1984-87, com. for cell pathophysiology, 1987-90. Editor, co-author textbooks in field, 1970, 80, 85, 90, 92; translator Hans Selye: The Stress of Life, Polish edit., 1960; contbr. articles to profl. publs. Mem. Internat. Parliament for Safety and Peace, Palermo, Italy, 1991—; mem. sci. coun. Ministry of Health, Warsaw, Poland, 1985-87. Rsch. fellow Free U., Brussels, 1963, U. Copenhagen, 1972, hon. rsch. fellow U. Coll. London, 1988; recipient Tchr. of Merit award State Coun. Poland, 1973, Chevalier of Polonia Restituta, State Coun. Poland, 1980, Sci. award Ministry of Health, Warsaw, 1987, 94, Hon. diploma, medal Charles U. Med. Faculty, 1994; named Knight Sovereign Mil. Templar Order, Jerusalem, 1991; selected World Intellectual, Internat. Biog. Ctr., 1993, Man of Yr., Am. Biog. Inst., 1994; nominated Internat. Cultural Diploma of Honor, Am. Biog. Inst., 1994. Mem. Polish Physiol. Soc. (hon.; pres. 1980-94), Polish Endocrinol. Soc., Internat. Soc. Neuroendocrinology, Internat. Brain Rsch. Orgn., European Neuroendocrine Soc., European Pineal Soc., Internat. Soc. Pathophysiology (chmn. ednl. commn., mem. coun. 1991—), Soc. Pathol. Physiology (corr.), Learned Soc. Lodz (pres. med. br. 1991—, mem. coun. 1994-96, v.p. 1996—), Gen. Sikorski's Inst. Polish History (London), Czech Med. Soc. J.E. Purkyne (hon.). Roman Catholic. Home: ul Narutowicza 120 m 2, 90-145 Łódź Poland Office: Sch Medicine Dept Pathophys, ul Narutowicza 60, 90-136 Łódź Poland

GUZMAN, RENATO FRANCISCO, surgeon; b. Manila, May 21, 1938; s. Jose Macuan and Adela (Francisco) G.; m. Iraida Emerita Reyes, June 19, 1963; children: Patrick, Carmela, Joseph, John, Christine. MD, U. Santo Tomas, Manila, 1962. Diplomate Am. Bd. Surgery. Intern St. Elizabeth Hosp., Youngstown, Ohio, 1963-64, resident, 1964-68, pvt. practice, 1982—. Recipient Recognition award So. Calif. Rural Hosp. Ctr., 1988; named Doctor of Yr. Hi Desert Med. Ctr., Joshua Tree, Calif., 1993. Fellow ACS, Internat. Coll. Surgeons. Office: 63532 29 Palms Hosp Joshua Tree CA 92252

GUZY, PETER MICHAEL, cardiologist, educator; b. Monongahela, Pa., Oct. 30, 1940. BS in Chemistry, U. Notre Dame, 1962; PhD in Biochemistry, U. Ky., 1970; MD, Med. Coll. of Ohio, 1973. Resident McMaster U., Hamilton, Ont., Can., 1973-75, U. Toronto, Ont., Can., 1975-76; fellow in cardiology UCLA Sch. Medicine, 1976-79; asst. prof. medicine UCLA div. Cardiology, 1979-83, assoc. prof. medicine, 1984-90, clin. prof. medicine, 1990—; dir. UCLA Pacemaker Clinic, 1980-95. Bd. dirs. Am. Heart Assn., 1984-87. Recipient Tchr. of Yr. award UCLA Dept. Medicine, 1981-82. Fellow Am. Coll. Cardiology, Royal Coll. Physicians, Surgeons of Can. Office: 100 UCLA Med Plz Ste 535 Los Angeles CA 90095-7053

GUZZETTA, PHILIP CONTE, JR., pediatric surgeon, educator; b. Great Lakes Naval Base, Ill., July 7, 1946; s. Philip Conte and Ann (Suchomel) G.; m. Cathleen Elizabeth Kah, Aug. 16, 1969; children: Angela Anne, Philip Conte III. BS in Biology, Marquette U., 1968; MD, Med. Coll. Wis., 1972. Diplomate Am. Bd. Surgery, Pediatric Surgery. Attending surgeon Children's Nat. Med. Ctr., Washington, 1981-92; chief clin. dept. surgery Children's Med. Ctr. Dallas, 1992—; from asst. prof. to prof. surgery George Washington U., Washington, 1981-92; prof. surgery U. Tex. Southwestern, Dallas, 1992—, chmn. pediatric surgery divsn., 1992—. Contbr. articles to profl. jours., chpt. in book. Maj. U.S. Army, 1977-79. Mem. ACS, Am. Pediatric Surg. Assn., Soc. Univ. Surgeons, Am. Soc. Transplant Surgeons, Am. Assn. Pediatrics, Parkland Surg. Soc. Office: Children's Med Ctr Dallas 1935 Motor St Dallas TX 75235

GWATHMEY, FRANK WINSTON, surgeon; b. Wilmington, N.C., Aug. 6, 1942; s. Richard Barbee and Louise De Rosset (Dick) G.; m. Marietta Clare Muller, Sept. 12, 1970; children: Frank Winston Jr., Clare Louise, William Richard. BA, U. Va., 1964; MD, U. N.C., 1968. Resident U. Va., Charlottesville, 1968-73; ptnr. Orthopedic Assocs. Va., Norfolk, 1976-82; pres. Norfolk Hand Surgery Ctr., 1982—; cons. in field; assoc. prof., orthopedics Med. Coll. Hampton Rds., Norfolk, 1976—. Contbr. articles to profl. jours. Head med. div. United Way, Norfolk, 1986. Maj. U.S. Army, 1973-75. Hand Surgery fellow, U. Minn., 1975, U. Va. Hosp., 1976. Mem. AMA, ACS (Va. chpt. bd. coun.), Am. Soc. Surgery of Hand, Am. Acad. Orthopedic Surgeons, Med. Soc. Va., Va. Orthopedic Soc., Norfolk Acad. Medicine (pres. 1985). Episcopalian.

GWATKIN, RALPH BUCHANAN LLOYD, biologist; b. Newport, Gwent, Wales, May 23, 1929; came to U.S., 1959; s. Ralph Lloyd and Ada Alexandra (Lennie) G.; m. Selma Lila Schatz, June 20, 1954; children: Sharon, Nadine, David. MA, U. Toronto (Can.), 1951; PhD, Rutgers U., 1954. Rsch. assoc. U. Toronto, 1956-61, Wistar Inst., Phila., 1956-61; asst. prof. vet. sch. U. Pa., Phila., 1962-66; from asst. dir. to dir. Merck Inst., Rahway, N.J., 1967-80; vis. prof. Dartmouth Coll., Hanover, N.H., 1980-81; prof. McMaster U. Med. Sch., Hamilton, Ont., Can., 1982-85; dir. Cleve. Clinic Found., 1986-89; pres. ReproGene, Beachwood, Ohio, 1990—; adj. prof. reproductive biology Case Western Res. U. Med. Sch.; founder, chair Gordon Conf. on Fertilization, Holderness, N.H., 1974; mem. reproductive biology study sect. NIH, Washington, 1980. Author: Fertilization Mechanisms, 1977; editor-in-chief: Molecular Reprodn. and Devel.; editor: Manipulation of Mammalian Development, 1986, Genes in Mammalian Reproduction, 1993; mem. editorial bd.: Developmental Biology: A Comprehensive Synthesis, 1982—; contbr. articles to profl. jours. Recipient Rsch. Career Devel. award NIH, 1964, Rubin award Am. Fertility Soc., 1967, Rsch. award Pacific Coast Fertility Soc., 1973; rsch. grantee NIH, NSF, MRC. Mem. Soc. Study Reproduction, Am. Soc. Cell Biology. Office: ReproGene 25460 Bryden Rd Cleveland OH 44122-4164

GYORY, ATTILA NICHOLAS, hospital specialist clinician; b. Budapest, Hungary, Mar. 19, 1933; arrived in Australia, 1951; s. Albert and Nora (Dingha) G.; m. Elizabeth Gizella Obrincsak, Mar. 30, 1959; children: Attila Eugene, Andrew Gerard, Peter Thomas. BS in Medicine, Sydney (N.S.W., Australia), 1959, B in Medicine and Surgery, 1962. Resident med. officer Canterbury (Australia) Hosp., 1962-64; family physician Sydney, 1967-68; resident med. officer Concord Hosp., Sydney, 1967-68; dir. rehab. medicine Concord Hosp., 1975—; med. registrar Royal Newcastle (Australia) Hosp., 1969-70, Rachel Forster/Royal Prince Alfred Hosp., Sydney, 1970-71; sr. rsch. registrar dept. rheumatology Guys Hosp., London, 1971-72; fellow Mayo Clinic, Rochester, Minn., 1972-74; vis. specialist Royal Prince Alfred Hosp., 1974-93. Fellow Am. Acad. Phys. Medicine and Rehab., Australian Coll. Rehab. Medicine (nat. pres. 1987-89, examiner, dep. chief censor 1980-92), Royal Australian Coll. Physicians (fellow Australian faculty rehab. medicine); mem. Royal Coll. Physicians (London). Office: Concord Hosp, Hospital Rd, Concord 2139, Australia

HAACK, DAVID WILFORD, biomedical consultant; b. Denver, Nov. 22, 1945; s. Robert Daniel and Jane Evangeline H.; m. Sharon Dee Sollars, June 19, 1987; children: Shelly, Stacey, Alexis. BS, Colo. State U., 1968, MS, 1971, PhD, 1974. Postdoctorate U. Mich., Ann Arbor, 1974-75, asst. prof. dept. anatomy, med. sch., 1975-80; research assoc. dept. physiology, med. ctr. U. Ariz., Tucson, 1980-83; new product devel., product specialist W.L. Gore & Assocs., Inc., Flagstaff, Ariz., 1983-86, coord. worldwide clin. trials, med. products divsn., 1986-88; founder, pres. Life Tech. Internat., Inc., Phoenix, 1988—; vascular specialist Dow Corning Wright Theratex Group, 1990-92; network liaison scientist Cardiovascular Astra Merck Inc., 1992—. Contbr. numerous articles to profl. jours.; speaker in field; patentee in field, 1986. Nat. Research Service award Nat. Inst. Health, 1974, 1980-83. Mem. AAAS, European Vascular Soc. Home and Office: 309 Horseshoe Ln Downingtown PA 19335-1609

HAAGA, DAVID ANDREW FOGEL, psychologist; b. Washington, July 25, 1961; s. Paul Galarneaux and Virginia Mary (Coughlan) H.; m. Candice Ann Fogel, June 7, 1987; children: Kevin Fogel and Megan Fogel. BA, Harvard U., 1983; MA, U. So. Calif., 1985, PhD, 1988. Lic. psychologist, Md., D.C. Rsch. asst. prof. psychology in psychiatry U. Pa., Phila., 1988-89; asst. prof. dept. psychology The Am. U., Washington, 1989-94. Contbr. articles to profl. jours. Named U. So. Calif. fellow, 1985-86; rsch. grantee NIH, 1985-86, 86-87, The Am. U., 1990, 94, Inst. for Rational-Emotive Therapy, 1995. Mem. Assn. for Advancement of Behavior Therapy. Democrat. Home: 5713 Stillwell Rd Rockville MD 20851-1933 Office: The American Univ Dept Psychology 4400 Massachusetts Ave NW Washington DC 20016-8062

HAAKENSON, PHILIP NIEL, pharmacist, educator; b. Hatton, N.D., Apr. 15, 1924; s. Martin Selmer and Theodora H.; m. Eldora Ida Robinson,

June 19, 1950; children: Mary Kim, Martin Niel. BS in Pharmacy, N.D. State U., 1950, MS in Pharmacy, 1965; PhD in Pharmacy Adminstrn., U. Wis., 1972. Owner Portland (N.D.) Drug, 1950-60, Hatton Drug, 1956-60; asst. prof. pharmacy adminstrn. N.D. State U., Fargo, 1961-65, assoc. prof., 1965-70, prof., 1970-87, prof. emeritus, 1987—, dean sch. of pharmacy, 1970-80; dir. Pharmacy Continuing Edn., 1982-87; vis. prof. Univ. Mont. Sch. Pharmacy, 1987-88, Univ. Man. (Can.), 1988-95. Editor Nodak Pharmacist, 1962-74, 1982-87. Mgmt. counselor Svc. Corps Ret. Execs. Assn. Served with USN, 1942-45. Mem. Am. Assn. colls. of Pharmacy, N.D. Pharm. Assn. (recipient Bowl of Hygiea 1979), Am. Pharm. Assn., Kappa Psi (named Outstanding Alumni 1974, Pharmacist of Yr. 1977), Sigma Xi. Republican. Lutheran. Lodges: Lions, Masons, Shriners. Home: 210 28th Ave N Fargo ND 58102-1624 Office: ND State U Sch of Pharmacy Fargo ND 58105 also: Svc Corps of Ret Execs Assn Box 3086 Rm 225 Main PO Bldg Fargo ND 58108-3086

HAAS, BRADLEY DEAN, pharmacy director, clinical pharmacist/consultant; b. Albion, Nebr., Nov. 24, 1957; s. Ernest Duane Jr. and Joy Lou (Fusselman) H. Student, Kearney State Coll., 1976-78; PharmD with distinction, U. Nebr., Omaha, 1981. Registered pharmacist, Nebr., Colo.; cert. hosp. pharmacy residency, basic life support instr. and provider, advanced cardiac life support instr. and provider. Resident hosp. pharmacy U. Nebr. Med. Ctr., Omaha, 1981-82; intensive care clin. pharmacist Mercy Med. Ctr., Denver, 1982-85; home care pharmacist Am. Abbey Homecare, Englewood, Colo., 1985; pharmacy dir. Charter Hosp. of Aurora, Colo., 1989-90; clin pharmacy coord. Porter Meml. Hosp., Denver, 1987-92; asst. dir. clin. pharmacy svcs. Luth. Med. Ctr., Wheat Ridge, Colo., 1992-94; dir. pharmacy Integrated Pharmacy Solutions, Inc./Pru Care Pharmacies, Denver, 1994—; cons. Porter Meml. Hosp. Chronic Pain Treatment Ctr., 1987-89, Charter Hosp., 1989-90; adj. asst. prof. pharmacy U. Colo., 1983—; mem. leadership adv. coun. sch. pharmacy U. Colo., 1987-89; mem. adv. bd. Instl. and Managed Healthcare, Ortho Biotech, Inc., 1992—; mem. State Colo./ Medicare D.U.R. Com., 1992—. Author, co-author in field. Vol. Colo. Hosp. Pharmacists Week, Poison Prevention Week, KUSA-TV Health Fair; lectr. Pathfinder's Youth Group- Careers Day; active Colo. Trust. Named Disting. Young Pharmacist of the Year Marion Labs., Colo., 1987, one of Outstanding Young Men of Am., 1987; recipient Acad. Scholarship U. Nebr. Med. Ctr, 1978-81, Excellence in Pharmacy Practice award U. Colo. Sch. Pharmacy, 1988; Marjorie Merwin Simmons Meml. scholar U. Nebr. Found. Fund., 1980; scholar VFW, 1978-81. Mem. Am. Soc. Hosp. Pharmacists (state chpt. grants program selection com. 1989, nominations com. 1990-91, ho. of dels. 1987, 90-92), Acad. Managed Care Pharmacy, Colo. Managed Care Pharmacy Dirs., Colo. Soc. Hosp. Pharmacists (presdl. officer 1987-89, chmn. numerous coms. and coms., Hosp. Pharmacy Practitioner Excellence award 1988, 89). Home: 10115 Granite Hill Dr Parker CO 80134 Office: Integrated Pharmacy Solutions PruCare Pharmacy 4643 S Ulster St Ste 1000 Denver CO 80237-2867

HAAS, CHARLES DAVID, dentist; b. N.Y.C., Jan. 3, 1941; s. Milton Harold and Elizabeth Esther (Newman) H.; m. Sheila Carole, July 26, 1964; Children: Andrew Scott, Gary Adam. AB, Boston U., 1962; DMD, Tufts U., 1966; postgrad., Monte Fiore Hosp., N.Y.C., 1966-67. Pvt. practice Miami Beach, Fla.; attending dentist Dade County Dental Rsch. Clinic, Jackson Meml. Hosp., Miami, Fla., 1985—; cons. migrant edn. project State of Mass., Boston, 1965-66. Author: Year Book of Dentistry, 1969; contbr. articles to profl. jours. Capt. U.S. Army, 1967-69. Fellow Royal Soc. Health; mem. Am. Assn. Forensic Dentists, Acad. Gen. Dentistry, ADA. Jewish. Home: 2220 NE 201st St Miami FL 33180-1834 Office: 1688 Meridian Ave Miami FL 33139-2705

HAAS, CHARLES NATHAN, environmental engineering educator; b. N.Y.C., Dec. 27, 1951; s. Louis and Gertrude (Abrams) H.; m. Victoria Soderholme, June 27, 1989. BS, Ill. Inst. Tech., Chgo., 1973, MS, 1974; PhD, U. Ill., 1978. Asst. prof. Rensselaer Poly. Inst., Troy, N.Y., 1978-81; ast. prof. Ill. Inst. Tech., Chgo., 1981-84, assoc. prof., 1984-87, prof., 1987-90; L.D. Betz prof. environ. engring. Drexel U., Phila., 1991—. Editor Jour. Water Environ. Rsch., 1991-96. Recipient Charles Ellet award Western Soc. Engrs., 1983, Octave Chanute medal, 1984. Mem. Am. Water Works Assn., Internat. Assn. Water Quality (pres. nat. com. 1994—), Water Environment Assn. Office: Drexel U 32d & Chestnut Sts Philadelphia PA 19104

HAAS, JOANNA FAITH, epidemiologist; b. N.Y.C., Jan. 27, 1947; arrived in France, 1994; d. David and Belle (Heller) H. BA in Med. Sci., Boston U., 1969, MD, 1969; MSc in Epidemiology, Columbia U., 1974. Diplomate Am. Bd. Internal Medicine, Am. Bd. Preventive Medicine. Intern Beth Israel Med. Ctr., N.Y.C., 1969-70; resident Montefiore Hosp., N.Y.C., 1970-71; postdoctoral scholar UCLA Sch. Pub. Health, 1973-74; asst. prof. Cornell U. Med. Coll., N.Y.C., 1974-80; scientist Acad. Sci., Berlin, 1980-85, Immuno, Vienna, Austria, 1985-87; med. project leader oncology Boehringer Ingelheim, Germany, 1987-89; head corp. drug safety Boehringer Ingelheim, Fed. Rep. of Germany, 1989-91; head epidemiology Boehringer Ingelheim, Germany, 1991-94; dir. worldwide corp. product safety Rhône-Poulenc Rorer, Antony, France, 1994—. Contbr. articles to profl. jours. Fellow ACP, Am. Coll. Preventive Medicine; mem. Am. Soc. for Clin. Pharmacology and Therapeutics. Office: Rhône-Poulenc-Rorer, 20 Ave Raymond Aron, 92165 Antony Cedex France

HAAS, MARK, pathologist; b. N.Y.C., Jan. 30, 1955; s. Alvin and Ruth (Heller) H. BA, Duke U., 1977, PhD, MD, 1982. Diplomate Am. Bd. Pathology. Assoc. rschr. dept. physiology Duke U., Durham, N.C., 1983; resident dept. pathology Yale-New Haven Hosp., 1983-85; postdoctoral fellow dept. physiology Sch. Medicine Yale U., New Haven, 1985-86; asst. prof. pathology Yale U., New Haven, 1986-89; asst. prof. pathology U. Chgo., 1989-93, assoc. prof., 1993—, dir. renal pathology, 1994—. Reviewer Am. Jour. Physiology, 1984—, mem. editorial bd., 1993—; reviewer Jour. Membrane Biology, 1985—, Kidney Internat., 1984—, Jour. Biol. Chemistry, 1987—, Jour. Clin. Investigation, 1990—, Sci., 1991—; contbr. articles to profl. jours. Recipient Established Investigator award, Am. Heart Assn., 1992—; rsch. grantee NIH, Am. Heart Assn., Cystic Fibrosis Found.; fellow John A. Hartford Found., 1986-89. Mem. Soc. Gen. Physiologists, Am. Physiol. Soc., Am. Soc. for Investigative Pathology, U.S. & Canadian Acad. of Pathology, Am. Soc. Nephrology, Alpha Omega Alpha (v.p., organizer symposium 1981-82), Sigma Xi. Office: U Chgo Dept Pathology 5841 S Maryland Ave MC6101 Chicago IL 60637-1463

HAASE, ASHLEY THOMSON, microbiology educator, researcher; b. Chgo., Dec. 8, 1939; s. Milton Conrad and Mary Elizabeth Minter (Thomson) H.; m. Ann DeLong, 1962; children: Elizabeth, Stephanie, Harris. BA, Lawrence Coll., 1961; MD, Columbia U., 1965. Intern Johns Hopkins Hosp., Balt., 1965-67; clin. assoc. Nat. Inst. Allergy and Infectious Disease, Bethesda, Md., 1967-70; vis. scientist Nat. Inst. Med. Rsch., London, 1970-71; chief infectious disease sect. VA Med. Ctr., San Francisco, 1971-84, med. investigator, 1978-83; prof. microbiology U. Minn., Mpls., 1984—, head dept., 1984—; mem. fellowship screening com. Am. Cancer Soc., San Francisco, 1978-81; mem. UNESCO Internat. Cell Rsch. Orgn., India, 1978; mem. nat. adv. coun. Nat. Inst. Allergy and Infectious Diseases, 1986-91, mem. task force onmicrobiology and infectious diseases, 1991, merit investigator, 1989, chair AIDS rsch. adv. com., 1993—, chmn. vaccine subcom.; Javits neurosci. investigator Nat. Inst. Neurol. and Communicative Disorders and Stroke, 1988-95; chmn. panel on AIDS, U.S.-Japan Coop. Med. Sci. Program, 1988-95; mem. OAR AIDS Rsch. Evaluation Working Group, 1995—; mem. adv. com. for career awards in biomed. scis. Burroughs-Wellcome Found., 1995. Editor: Microbial Pathogenesis, 1988-94; contbr. articles on neurovirology to profl. jours. Recipient Lucia R. Briggs Disting. Achievement award Lawrence Coll., 1990. Mem. Am. Soc. Microbiology, Assn. Am. Physicians, Am. Soc. Clin. Investigation, Am. Soc. Virology, Assn. Med. Schs. Microbiology Chmn., Infectious Diseases Soc. Am., Nat. Multiple Sclerosis Soc. (adv. com. 1978-84), Phi Beta Kappa, Alpha Omega Alpha. Democrat. Home: 14 Buffalo Rd Saint Paul MN 55127-2136 Office: U Minn Dept Microbiology 420 Delaware St SE Minneapolis MN 55455-0374

HAASE, KRIS ALLEN, podiatrist; b. Danville, Ind., June 10, 1963; s. Robert W. and Janice K. H.; m. Renee C., July 30, 1988; 1 child, Madison Rae. BS, Mich. State U., 1985; DPM, Dr. W.M. Scholl Coll., 1989. Diplomate Am. Bd. Podiatric Surgery. Assoc. Family Podiatry Ctrs., Milw., 1990-93; physician, owner North Oakland Foot and Ankle Ctr., Waterford, Mich., 1993—; instr. Greater Milw. Podiatric Surg. Residency Program, 1992-93; cons. in field. Mem. Am. Acad. Podiatric Sports Medicine. Office: 1255 N Oakland Blvd Waterford MI 48327

HAASLER, GEORGE B., cardiologist; b. Hamburg, Germany, Aug. 14, 1952; came to U.S., 1959; s. Doris Haasler; m. JoAnn Haasler; children: Erik, Christopher. BA in Math., SUNY, Buffalo, 1973; MD, Columbia U., 1977. Diplomate Am. Bd. Surgery, Thoracic Surgery, Laser Surgery. Intern gen. surgery Columbia U., N.Y.C., 1977-82, resident thoracic and cardiac surgery, 1982-85; asst. prof. cardiothoracic surgery Med. Coll. Wis., Milw., 1985-91, assoc. prof. cardiothoracic surgery, 1991—; chief cardiothoracic surg. sect. Zablocki Vets. Hosp., Milw., 1986-92; mem. thoracic surg. subcom. Radiation Therapy Oncology Group, Phila., 1988—; mem. exam. cons. com. Am. Bd. Thoracic Surgery, Evanston, Ill., 1996-97. Contbr. chpts. in med. textbooks and articles to profl. jours. Fellow ACS; mem. Internal Soc. for Heart and Lung Transplantation, Gen. Thoracic Surg. Club, Soc. Thoracic Surgeons, Tri-State Thoracic Soc. (gen. chmn.), Wis. Thoracic Soc., Pi Mu Epsilon. Office: Dept Cardiothoracic Surgery 9200 W Wisconsin Ave Milwaukee WI 53226

HABAL, MUTAZ BILLAH, plastic surgeon; b. Damascus, Syria, Apr. 27, 1938; s. Monier and Rabia (Rick) H.; m. Randa Habal, June 22, 1964; children: Rula, Bassam. MD, Am. U. Beirut, 1964; cert. and fellow, Coll. of Surgeons, Toronto, Can., 1972. Intern, resident U. Pa., Phila., 1964-65; resident, chief SUNY, Syracuse, 1965-69; resident Peter Bent & Children, Harvard U., Boston, 1969-71; fellow Harvard U., Boston, 1971-72; asst. prof. U. Ind., Indpls., 1972-74; assoc. prof. U. Fla., Gainesville, 1974-78; prof. and chmn. U. South Fla., Tampa, 1978-80, rsch. prof. and chmn., 1980—; clin. prof. U. Fla., Tampa, 1980—. Contbr. articles to profl. jours. Col. USAR, 1984—. Fellow ACS, Royal Coll. Surgeons, Internat. Coll. Surgeons, Am. Acad. Pediatric Surgeons, Country Med. Soc. (pres. 1995—). Republican. Moslem. Home: 6358 Maclaurin Dr Tampa FL 33647-1164 Office: Tampa Bay Craniofacial Ctr 801 W Martin Luther King Blvd Tampa FL 33603-3301

HABECK, DIETRICH A. E., medical educator; b. Stettin, Pomerania, Germany, Mar. 6, 1925; s. Paul Elisabeth (Brummund) H.; m. Marianne Horn, 1961; 3 children. MD, U. Münster, Germany, 1956. Prof. U. Münster, 1971, dean faculty of medicine, 1977-79, vice dean faculty of medicine, 1979-81, mng. dir. Inst. Med. Edn. and Student Affairs, 1986-93; chmn. German sect. Assn. Med. Edn. in Europe, 1980-94. Editor Medizinische Ausbildung, 1984—; contbr. articles to profl. jours.

HABENER, JOEL F., medical educator, researcher; b. June 29, 1937. AA in Chemistry, Santa Ana Coll., 1957; BS in Chemistry, U. Redlands, 1960; MD, UCLA, 1965. Diplomate Am. Bd. Internal Medicine. Med intern, asst. resident in medicine Johns Hopkins Hosp., Md., 1965-67; fellow in medicine Johns Hopkins U., Balt., 1965-67; rsch. assoc. lab. physiology Nat. Cancer Inst. NIH, Bethesda, Md., 1967-69; clin. and rsch. fellow endocrine unit Mass. Gen. Hosp., Boston, 1969-72, investigator Howard Hughes Med. Inst., 1976—, chief lab. molecular endocrinology, 1979—, dir. endocrine divsn., 1991—; vis. scientist dept. biology MIT, Cambridge, 1970-80; assoc. prof. medicine Harvard Med. Sch., Boston, 1975-88, prof. medicine, 1989—. Assoc. editor: Jour. Clin. Investigation, 1982-87; editor: Molecular Endocrinology, 1987-92, Jour. Neuroendocrinology, 1988-93, Jour. Biol. Chemistry, 1996—, Pathogenesis, 1996—; reviewing editor: Jour. Lab. and Clin. Medicine; contbr. artiles to profl. jours. Recipient Rsch. Career Devel. award USPH, 1972-76, Rsch. award Am. Diabetes Assn., 1995. Mem. Am. Soc. Clin. Investigation, Am. Soc. Biol. Chemists, Assn. Am. Physicians, Endocrine Soc. (Edwin A. Astwood lectr. award 1979), Alpha Omega Alpha. Office: Mass Gen Hosp Lab Molecular Endocrinology 50 Blossom St WEL 320 Boston MA 02114*

HABER, EDGAR, physician, educator; b. Berlin, Germany, Feb. 1, 1932; came to U.S., 1939, naturalized, 1944; s. Fred Siegfried and Dorothy Judith (Bernstein) H.; m. Carol Avery, Nov. 16, 1958; children: Justin, Graham, Eben. AB, Columbia U., 1952, MD, 1956; MA (hon.), Harvard U., 1968; MA, U. Oxford, 1991. Diplomate: Am. Bd. Internal Medicine. Intern in medicine Mass. Gen. Hosp., Boston, 1956-57; asst. resident in medicine Mass. Gen. Hosp., 1957-58, resident in medicine, 1961-62, asst. in medicine, 1963-64, asst. physician, 1965-68, physician, 1969—, chief cardiac unit, 1964-88; assoc. Lab. Cellular Physiology, Nat. Heart Inst., Bethesda, Md., 1958-61; hon. clin. asst. cardiac dept. St. George's Hosp., London, Eng., 1962-63; instr. medicine Harvard Med. Sch., Boston, 1963-64, assoc. in medicine, 1964-65, asst. prof., 1965-68, assoc. prof., 1968-71, prof., 1971-90, clin. prof., 1990-91, prof., 1991—; Elkan R. Blout prof., dir. div. biol. scis. Harvard Sch. Pub. Health, Boston, 1991—, dir. Ctr. for Prevention of Cardiovascular Disease, 1991—; pres. Squibb Inst. for Med. Research, Princeton, N.J., 1988-90, Bristol-Myers Squibb Pharm. Rsch. Inst., N.J., 1990-91; sr. physician Brigham & Women's Hosp., Boston, 1992—; fellow Lincoln Coll., Oxford, 1992—; mem. study sect. allergy and immunology NIH, 1965-68, vice chmn. panel on heart and blood vessel diseases, 1972-73, mem. arteriosclerosis task force, 1978; mem. task force on immunology and disease Nat. Inst. Allergy and Infectious Disease, 1972-73; mem. tissue and organ biology interdisciplinary cluster President's Biomed. Research Panel, 1975; mem. U.S. del. to U.S.-USSR Health Exchange, 1975; chmn. CIBA award com. Council for High Blood Pressure Research, 1980-81; vis prof. Stanford U., 1967, 78, 85, Emory U., 1971, U. Ala., 1971, 76, 86, Mayo Clinic, 1972, U. Calif., San Francisco, 1972, Los Angeles, 1987, Am. U., Beirut, Lebanon, 1972, Duke U., 1976, U. Miss., 1978, U. Tex., Dallas, 1982, Chinese Acad. Med. Scis., Beijing, 1982, Monash U., Melbourne, Australia, 1983, Royal Postgrad. Med. Sch., London, 1984, U. Queensland, Brisbane, Australia, 1985, Dartmouth Coll., 1986, SUNY, Syracuse, 1987; sr. physician Brigham Women's Hosp., Boston, 1992—; vis. scholar McGill U., Montreal, 1984; guest lectr. Biol. Soc. and Cardiol. Soc., Copenhagen, Denmark, 1971; WHO lectr., Santiago, Chile, 1973; Jennifer Jones Simon lectr. in med. scis. Calif. Inst. Tech., 1974; Alpha Omega Alpha lectr. La. State U., 1975; George C. Griffith sci. lectr., 1975; Centennial lectr. Meharry Med. Sch., 1976; John Kent Meml. lectr. Stanford U., 1978; Ives lectr. Soc. of Fellows, Scripps clinic and Research Found., 1979; Bunn Meml. lectr. Youngstown Hosp. Assn., N.E. Ohio Univs., 1979; John J. Sampson lectr. Mt. Zion Hosp. and Med. Center, San Francisco, 1979; 1st internat. lectr. Internat. Soc. and Fedn. of Cardiology, 1980; Pfizer lectr. Southwestern U., 1980, Clin. Research Inst., Montreal, Can., 1981, Plenary lectr. Japanese Soc. Hypertension, 1981, Berry Meml. lectr., Chandigarh, India, 1982; 1st George Pickering lectr. Brit. Hypertension Soc., 1983; 7th ann. Irvine Page lectr. Cleve. Clinic Found., 1984; Sommer Meml. lectr. U. Oreg., 1985; lectr. William Goldring Meml. NYU, 1985; lectr. R.T. Hall Lectureship of Cardiac Soc. Australia and New Zealand, 1986; lectr. Joseph A. Nicholson Lecture in Cardiology at Tufts U., 1987; lectr. James B. Herrick Lecture of Chgo. Heart Assn., 1987, 17th ann. Arvilla Berger lectr. N.Y. Cardiological Soc., 1990; bd. dirs. Ctr. for Prevention Cardiovascular Disease. Co-author: Digitalis, 1974, The Future of Antibodies in Human Diagnosis and Therapy, 1976; co-editor: The Practice of Cardiology, 1980; editor: Scientific American Molecular Cardiovascular Medicine, 1995; editor-in-chief: Hypertension, 1983-88; mem. editorial bd. Jour. Clin. Investigation, 1969-70, Immunochemistry, 1970-74, Jour. Immunology, 1971-73, Clin. Immunology and Immunopathology, 1971-89, new Eng. Jour. Medic79-81, Herz, 1980—, Circulation, 1978-81, Hybridoma, 1980—, Circulation Rsch., 1981-84, Jour. Hypertention, 1982-88. Trustee Boston Biomed. Research Inst., Inc. Served with USPHS, 1958-62. Named One of 10 Outstanding Young Men Boston Jr. C. of C., 1966; recipient medal of excellence Columbia U., 1976, Grand Sci. award Phi Lambda Kappa, 1984, Otsuka award for Outstanding Rsch., Internat. Soc. Heart Rsch., 1985, Rsch. Achievement award Am. Heart Assn., 1986, Dupont Specialty Diagnostic award Clin. Ligand Assay Soc., 1988, CIBA award for Hypertention Rsch , Am. Heart Assn., 1989, Joseph Mather Smith prize Coll. Physicians & Surgeons Columbia U., 1991. Fellow Am. Coll. Cardiology (Disting. Scientist award 1991), Am. Acad. Arts and Scis., AAAS; mem. Royal Soc. Medicine (London), Am. Soc. Biol. Chemists (membership com. 1971-73), Mass. Med. Soc., Am. Assn. Immunologists, Am. Soc. Clin. Investigation (nominating com. 1972, councillor 1975), Am. Fedn. Clin. Research, Brit. Soc. Immunology, Assn. Am. Physicians, Internat. Soc. Hypertension (Volhard Prize 1980), Am. Heart Assn. (fellow council on clin. cardiology, research com. 1970-76, v.p. for research 1973-74, pub. policy and govt. relations working group 1973-74, George E. Brown meml. lectr. 1973), Internat. Union Immunological Socs. (chmn. edn. com. 1971-73), New Eng. Cardiovascular Soc. (pres. 1978-79), Assn. Univ. Cardiologists (v.p. 1979-80, pres. 1980-81), Phi Beta Kappa, Alpha Omega Alpha. Club: Harvard (Boston). Home: PO Box 161 Salisbury NH 03268-0161 Office: Harvard Sch Pub Health 677 Huntington Ave Boston MA 02115-6028

HABER, MERYL HAROLD, physician, educator, author; b. Cleve., Dec. 28, 1934; s. Harry J. and Sadie P. Haber; m. Virginia J. Jackson, Oct. 1, 1959 (dec. June 1986); children: Michael, Jeffrey, Deborah; m. Jeanne Blank Miller, Nov. 25, 1989. B.S., Northwestern U., 1956, M.S., 1958, M.D., 1959. Diplomate Am. Bd. Pathology; cert. Anatomic and Clin. Pathology. Intern Los Angeles County Gen. Hosp., 1959-60; resident Chgo. Wesley Meml. Hosp., 1960-61; USPHS fellow in pathology Univ. Coll. Med. Sch., London, 1961-62; resident Passavant Meml. Hosp., Chgo., 1962-64; head anatomic pathology Passavant Meml. Hosp., 1964-66; instr. pathology Northwestern U. Med. Sch., 1963-66, prof. clin. pathology, 1981-85, univ. lectr. in pathology, 1985—; dir. labs. St. Francis Hosp., Honolulu, 1966-73; assoc. prof. pathology U. Hawaii, 1966-71, prof., 1971-73; prof. U. Nev., 1973-80, chmn. dept. pathology and lab. medicine, 1973-80; program dir. Sch. Med. Tech., 1973-80; med. dir. Consol. Labs., Rush-Presbyn.-St. Luke's Med. Ctr., 1989-91; prof. Rush Med. Coll., Chgo., 1980—, asst. dean, dir. continuing med. edn. Rush U., 1987-94, assoc. dean grad. med. edn. and continuing med. edn., 1994—, Borland prof. and chmn. dept. pathology, 1990—; exec. v.p. Am. Soc. Clin. Pathologists, Chgo., 1980-82; pres. Hawaii Soc. Pathologists, 1971. Author: Urine Casts: Their Microscopy and Clinical Significance, 1976, The Urinary Sediment, A Textbook Atlas, 1981, Medical Macrophotography: A Step-by-Step Guide, 1989, A Primer of Microscopic Urinalysis, 2d edit., 1991; editorial bd. Am. Jour. Clin. Pathology, 1976-82, The Pathologist, 1984-86; cover editor Lab. Medicine, 1978-82; reviewer Jour. AMA, 1989—. Pres. 1110 Lake Shore Dr. Homeowners Assn., 1985-89. USPHS fellow, 1958-64. Fellow Coll. Am. Pathologists, Internat. Acad. Pathology, Royal Coll. Medicine, Ill. Soc. Pathologists, Chgo. Pathology Soc., Soc. Med. Coll. Dirs. Continuing Med. Edn. (bd. dirs. 1995—, v.p. 1996—), Assn. Pathology Chmns., Clin. Lab. Mgrs. Assn. Office: 600 S Paulina St Chicago IL 60612-3832

HABER, PAUL, health psychologist, educator; b. Yonkers, N.Y., Jan. 30, 1936; s. Herbert Hubert and Sylvia Martha (Kliger) H.; m. Marsha Last, June 29, 1957 (dec. 1994); children: Kara Edin Haber Stevens, Robert Jacobs. BA in Psychology, St. Thomas U., Miami, Fla., 1978; MA in Counseling, Goddard Coll., Plainfield, Vt., 1979; PhD in Health Psychology, The Union Inst., Cin., 1981. Pres., dir. Stress Inst., Inc., Miami, 1978-94; pres. Stress Inst., Inc., Boulder, Colo., 1994—; co-founder, former v.p. and project dir. Child Assault Prevention Project of South Fla., Inc., Miami, 1984, cons., 1984—; faculty coord., co-creator child abuse and literacy graduate sch. curriculum Grad. Sch. Am., Mpls., 1994—; adj. prof. various ednl. instns., including St. Thomas U., U. Miami, Miami-Dade C.C., Union Inst., 1978-89. Writer, moderator 11-part TV series on child abuse, 1985-86; author: Health, Stress and Type A Behavior, 1984-86; co-author: The Stress Reduction Workbook, 1987, Protecting Your Child, 1988; creator The Stop Smoking Program, Refocusing, 1989. Active Fla. Com. for Prevention of Child Abuse, 1989—, Fla. Ctr. for Children and Youth, 1989—, Fla. Ctr. for Children and Youth, 1989—. Recipient Nat. Sony Innovator award, 1969. Fellow Am. Inst. Stress; mem. ACA, Am. Orthopsychiat. Assn., Am. Profl. Soc. on the Abuse of Children, Assn. Transpersonal Psychology, Assn. Psychol. Type, Inst. Noetic Sci., Phi Theta Kappa.

HABER, PIERRE CLAUDE, psychologist; b. Landau, Germany, June 8, 1931; s. Kurt S. and Hedwig (Kuhn) H.; came to U.S., 1943, naturalized, 1949; B.A., Bklyn. Coll., 1952; M.A., Duke U., 1953; Ph.D., U. Paris, 1956; Counselor, dir. adult edn. Central Sch. Dist. 2, Yorktown Heights, N.Y., 1956-59; psychologist Manpower Devel. Program, Bklyn., 1959-65; asst. prof. Queens Coll., 1965-70; exec. sec., exec. dir. Psychology Soc., N.Y.C., 1970—; cons. forensic psychologist N.Y. State, 1978—; assoc. prof. Jersey City State Coll., 1967-80. Bd. advisors Nat. Reference Inst. Mem. APA, Am., N.Y. State personnel and guidance assns., Psychology Soc., N.Y. Assn. Public Sch. Adult Educators (v.p. 1957-59), Pi Delta Phi. Republican. Jewish. Contbr. to Compton's Ency., also articles to profl. jours. Home and Office: 100 Beekman St New York NY 10038-1810

HABER, SANDRA K., speech-language pathologist; b. Newark, Aug. 19, 1940; d. Carl and Dora (Busch) Katcher; m. William Haber, May 15, 1960; children: Gary L., Lori L. BA, Newark State Coll., 1973; MA, Kean Coll., 1977. Lic. speech-lang. pathologist; cert. myofunctional therapist; cert. gen. elem. edn. tchr., learning disabilities tchr.-cons., adminstrv. supr., adminstrv. prin. Prin., dir., dialect coach Accent on Comm., Red Bank, N.J.; learning cons. spl. svcs. South Amboy (N.J.) Bd. Edn. Mem. Am. Speech-Lang.-Hearing Assn., N.J. Speech-Lang.-Hearing Assn., Myofunctional Therapy Assn. Am., Orton Dyslexia Soc., N.J. Assn. Learning Cons., N.J. Edn. Assn. Home: 525 Ocean Blvd West End NJ 07740

HABICHT, JEAN-PIERRE, public health researcher, educator, consultant; b. Geneva, Dec. 15, 1934; s. Max H. and Elizabeth (Peterson) Herzog; m. Pat Hinxman, Jan. 3, 1959 (div. Oct. 1990); children: Heidi, Christopher, Oliver. MD, U. Zurich, 1962, Dr. Med., 1964; MPH, Harvard U., 1968; PhD, MIT, 1969. Cert. in clin nutrition Am. Bd. Nutrition. Biochem. rsch. asst. Merck, Sharpe & Dohme, Rahway, N.J., 1958-59; pediatric intern Children's Hosp. Med. Ctr., Boston, 1965-66; med. officer WHO, Guatemala, 1969-74; prof. maternal and child health U. San Carlos, Guatemala, 1972-74; spl. asst. Nat. Ctr. for Health Stats., Washington, 1974-77; James Jamison prof. nutritional epidemiology Cornell U., Ithaca, N.Y., 1977—; cons. pub. health issues nat. and internat. govts., profl. agys., 1975—; mem. expert com. on nutrition WHO, Geneva, 1986-89, mem. com. on epidemiology and disease prevention, 1986-89; mem. epidemiology and disease control study sect. NIH, Washington, 1980-83; mem. food and nutrition bd. NAS, Washington, 1981-84, mem. com. evaluation of Women Infant and Child nutrition risk criteria, 1994-96, mem. com. internat. nutrition, 1994—; mem. adv. group coordinating subcom. on nutrition UN, 1983-89, chmn., 1986-87; mem. joint nutrition monitoring and evaluation com. HHS-USDA, 1982-86; chmn. expert com. phys. status: Use and Interpretation of Anthropometry, WHO, 1991-93. Contbr. articles to profl. publs., chpts. to books. Fellow Am. Coll. Epidemiology; mem. APHA, Am. Soc. Clin. Nutrition, Am. Inst. Nutrition (Kellogg Internat. prize 1994), Soc. for Epidemiologic Rsch., Internat. Epidemiol. Assn., Internat. Soc. Rsch. on Human Milk and Lactation (mem. exec. com. 1995-96), Sigma Xi, Gamma Sigma Delta, Delta Omega. Mem. Soc. of Friends. Office: Cornell U Div Nutritional Sci Savage Hall Ithaca NY 14853

HACHTEN, RICHARD ARTHUR, II, hospital administrator; b. L.A., Mar. 24, 1945; s. Richard A. and Dorothy Margaret (Shipley) H.; m. Jeanine Hachten, Dec. 12, 1970; children: Kristianne, Karin. BS in Econs., U. Calif.-Santa Barbara, 1967; MBA, UCLA, 1969. Mgmt. intern TRW Systems Group, Redondo Beach, Calif., 1969-72; adminstrv. asst. Methodist Hosp., Arcadia, Calif., 1972-73, asst. adminstr., 1973-74, assoc. adminstr., 1974-76, v.p. adminstrn., 1976-80, exec. v.p., adminstr., 1980-81, pres., adminstr., 1981-84; CEO Tri-City Hosp. Dist., Oceanside, Calif., 1984-91; pres. Bergan Mercy Health Sys., Omaha, 1991-95, Algent Health, Omaha, 1996—; instr. health care mgmt. Pasadena (Calif.) City Coll. Bd. dirs., pres. Hospice of Pasadena, Inc.; bd. dirs. ARC, Arcadia, Mercy Housing Midwest, Omaha. Mem. Am. Coll. Healthcare Execs., Hosp. Council San Diego and Imperial Counties (chmn., bd. dirs.), Nebr. Assn. Hosp. and Health Sys. (bd. dirs., chmn. dist. 1), Calif. Assn. Hosps. and Health Sys. (bd. dirs.), Beta Gamma Sigma. Republican. Methodist. Club: Rotary. Home: 2676 S 96th Cir Omaha NE 68124-1949 Office: Alegent Health 1010 N 96th St Ste 200 Omaha NE 68114

HACKER, NEVILLE FREDERICK, gynecological oncologist; b. Brisbane, Queensland, Australia, Jan. 16, 1944; s. Herbert Hacker and Olive Elsie Gillespie; m. Estelle Daphne Hawes, Feb. 22, 1944; children: Geoffrey Neville, Glaeme Anthony, Sharon Elizabeth. MB BS with honors, U. Queensland, 1967; MD, U. NSW, Australia, 1993. Intern Royal Brisbane (Australia) Hosp., 1968; resident med. officer Gympie Hosp., Australia, 19690-70; med. supr. Atherton Hosp., Australia, 1971-73; registrar in ob-gyn. Royal Women's Hosp., Brisbane, 1974-78; fellow in gynecologic oncology UCLA, L.A., 1978-80, asst. prof. dept. ob-gyn., 1981-86; dir. gynecologic oncology Royal Hosp. for Women, Sydney, Australia, 1987—;

cons. in gynecol. oncology St. Vincent's Hosp., Sydney, 1987—. Editor: Essentials of Obstetrics and Gynecology, 1985, 2nd edit., 1991, Practical Gynecologic Oncology, 1987, 2nd edit., 1992. Fellow ACS, ACOG, Royal Coll. Ob-Gyn., Royal Australian Coll. Ob-Gyn. (cert. gynecol. oncology); mem. Internat. Gynecol. Cancer Soc. (pres. 1995-96). Mem. Ch. of England. Office: Royal Hosp for Women, 188 Oxford St Paddington, Sydney New South Wales 2021, Australia

HACKETT, CAROL ANN HEDDEN, physician; b. Valdese, N.C., Dec. 18, 1939; d. Thomas Barnett and Zada Loray (Pope) Hedden; BA, Duke, 1961; MD, U. N.C., 1966; m. John Peter Hackett, July 27, 1968; children: John Hedden, Elizabeth Bentley, Susanne Rochet. Intern. Georgetown U. Hosp., Washington, 1966-67, resident, 1967-69; clinic physician DePaul Hosp., Norfolk, Va., 1969-71; chief spl. health services Arlington County Dept. Human Resources, Arlington, Va., 1971-72; gen. med. officer USPHS Hosp., Balt., 1974-75; pvt. practice family medicine, Seattle, 1975—; mem. staff, chmn. dept. family practice Overlake Hosp. Med. Ctr., 1985-86; clin. asst. prof. Sch. Medicine U. Wash. Bd. dirs. Mercer Island (Wash.) Preschool Assn., 1977-78; coordinator 13th and 20th Ann. Inter-profl. Women's Dinner, 1978, 86; trustee Northwest Chamber Orch., 1984-85. Mem. AAUW, Am. Acad. Family Practice, King County Acad. Family Practice (trustee 1993-96), King County Med. Soc. (chmn. com. TV violence), Wash. Acad. Family Practice, Wash. State Med. Soc., Va. Acad. Family Practice, DAR, Bellevue C. of C., NW Women Physicians (v.p. 1978), Seattle Symphony League, Eastside Women Physicians (founder, pres.), Sigma Kappa, Wash. Athletic Club, Columbia Tower, Seattle Yacht Club. Episcopalian. Home: 4304 E Mercer Way Mercer Island WA 98040-3826 Office: 1414 116th Ave NE Bellevue WA 98004-3801

HACKETT, EILEEN C., nursing educator; b. N.Y.C., Feb. 15, 1936; d. Louis and Josephine (Fullerton) Costello; m. Joseph F. Hackett, Apr. 30, 1971; children: Timothy, Kevin, Maureen, Joseph. RN, St. Vincent's Hosp., N.Y.C., 1956; BS, NYU, 1966, MA, 1970. Head nurse St. Vincent's Hosp., N.Y.C., clin. specialist, 1970; asst. prof. Brookdale Community Coll., Lincroft, N.J., 1983-91, asst. DON, 1996; assoc. prof. Coll. of Desert, Palm Desert, Calif., 1992—; mem. ednl. tech. com. Coll. of Desert, 1993—, chairperson task force on distance learning, 1996—. Recipient Founders Day award NYU, 1965. Mem. Nat. League for Nursing, Sigma Theta Tau. Home: 5 Camino Arroyo N Palm Desert CA 92260-0323

HACKETT, NORA ANN, patent agent; b. Abington, Pa., June 17, 1943; d. Frank and Kathryn Reed; m. Colin Edwin Hackett, Nov. 30, 1968; children: Catherine, Sarah, Rebecca. BS, Pa. State U., 1964; ScM, Brown U., 1967, PhD, 1969. Registered patent agt. U.S. Patent, Trademark and Copyright Office. Rsch. fellow biol. chemistry Harvard Med. Sch., Boston, 1968-69; rsch. fellow in medicine Miriam Hosp./Brown U., Providence, 1969-71; assoc. biologist Inhalation Toxicology Rsch. Inst., Albuquerque, 1975-79; ind. cons. Livermore, Calif., 1980-82; patent adviser office of pres. U. Calif., Berkeley, 1984-87; patent adviser Lawrence Livermore Nat. Lab., 1987-91; tech. liaison officer U. Calif., Davis, 1991—. Contbr. to refereed sci. jours., other publs. Mem. AAUW, Am. Physiol. Soc., Am. Thoracic Soc., Sigma Xi. Office: U Calif Office of Rsch Davis CA 95616-0808

HACKETT, WILLIAM EARLE, pathologist, consultant; b. Cork, Ireland, Apr. 26, 1921; arrived in Australia, 1958; s. James Reginald Hackett and Maud (Roxana) Belton; m. Eileen Carroll, 1946 (dec. 1988); children: Jane, Susan, John James. BA, Trinity Coll., Dublin, Ireland, 1942, MB, 1945, MD, 1949. Dir. Irish Nat. Blood Transfusion Svc., Dublin, 1949-53; reader in clin. pathology U. Dublin, 1954-57; med. rsch. fellow Inst. Med. Sci., Adelaide, Australia, 1958-62; dep. dir. Inst. Med. Sci., Australia, 1962-78; royal commr. non-med. use of drugs South Austrlian Govt., 1976-78; cons. pathologist, 1978—; vis. fellow Australian Nat. Univ., Canberra, 1982. Author: Blood, 1974, Organ Voluntaries, 1975, Lady Bones, 1984, Farts and Fevers, 1984, All Gustos, 1985. Chmn. trustees Art Gallery South Australia, Adelaide, 1970-78; vice chmn. Australian Broadcasting Commn., Sydney, 1973-76. Fellow Royal Coll. Pathologists Australasia, Royal Australasian Coll. Physicians. Office: PO Box 8, Edgecliff NSW 2027, Australia

HACKMAN, JOHN CLEMENT, neuropharmacology educator, neurophysiologist; b. Dayton, Ohio, May 16, 1947; s. Clem Frank and Martha Virginia (Schneble) H.; m. Susan Joan Pollard, June 3, 1968; children: Dawn, Jeffrey, Mark. BS, U. Miami, 1969, MS, 1976, PhD, 1979. Rsch. technologist VA Med. Ctr., Miami, Fla., 1975-78, rsch. physiologist, 1978—; rsch. asst. prof. Sch. Med. Neurology U. Miami, 1980-82, asst. prof., 1982-87, assoc. prof., 1988-95, prof., 1995—, asst. prof. Sch. Med. Pharmacology, 1991-96, assoc. prof., 1991-96, prof., 1996—; chief proctor Nat. Bd. Med. Examiners, Phila., 1987—. Contbr. chpts. to books, articles to profl. jours. Pres. Devonaire Villas Homeowners Assn., Miami, 1980-83; mem. boundary com. Dade County Pub. Schs., Miami, 1981-82; v.p. Devonaire PTA, Miami, 1981; treas. Devonaire Master Homeowners Assn., Miami, 1982-89; com. chair Pack 811 Boy Scouts Am., 1991-93, cubmaster, 1993-94, asst. scoutmaster, Troop 599, Miami, 1994—, com. chmn., 1995—. Decorated Army Commendation medal; Dept. Vets. Affairs grantee, 1994—. Mem. AAAS, Soc. for Neurosci., Am. Physiol. Soc., Am. Soc. for Pharmacology and Exptl. Therapeutics, N.Y. Acad. Sci., Southeastern Pharm. Soc. Home: 13611 SW 109th St Miami FL 33186-3309 Office: U Miami Sch Medicine 1600 NW 10th Ave Miami FL 33136-1015

HACKNEY, MARY ALICE, nurse; b. Middletown, Ohio, Mar. 7, 1955; d. Byron Allen and Joan Elaine (Meeker) H. AAS in Nursing, Miami U., 1975; BSN, U. Hawaii, 1991. CNOR. Staff nurse Shriners' Burn Inst., Cin., 1975-76, Cin. Gen. Hosp., 1976-77, Middletown (Ohio) Hosp., 1977-80; pub. health nurse Middletown Bureau Pub. Health Nursing, 1980-81; staff nurse Ambulatory Care Ctr., Centerville, Ohio, 1981-82, St. Francis Med. Ctr., Honolulu, 1982-84; mgr. Hawaiian Eye Surgictr., Wahaiwa, 1984-85; coord. operating rm. quality assurance and edn. St. Francis Med. Ctr., Honolulu, 1985-87; nurse mgr., patient care coord., surgery The Queen's Med. Ctr., Honolulu, 1987-88, staff nurse, 1988-91; clin. nurse III surgery Queen's Med. Ctr., Honolulu, 1991-96; clin. nurse III Kam 4 Cysto/KSCP, The Queen's Med. Ctr., Honolulu, 1996—; negotiator St. Francis Med. Ctr., 1983, 85, Queen's Med. Ctr., 1993. Mem. So. Poverty Law Ctr., 1992. Recipient Nat. Collegiate Nursing award, U.S. Achievement Acad., Lexington, Ky., 1990. Mem. NOW, ANA (mem. commn. on econ. and profl. security, 1995-96, mem. congress on nursing econs. 1995-96), Assn. Oper. Rm. Nurses (sec. Hawaii chpt. 1987-89, pres. 1989-91), Hawaii Nurses Assn. and Collective Bargaining Assn. (bd. dirs. 1991—, vice-chairperson 1994-95, chairperson 1995—, del. 1996, Hawaii rep. ANA Inst. Collective Bargaining 1992-96, vice chair 1994-95, chair 1995-96), Aquarian Found., Golden Key (charter), Sigma Theta Tau-Gamma Psi (scholar). Democrat. Buddhist. Home: 3071 Pualei Cir Apt 308 Honolulu HI 96815-4927

HACKNEY, PATRICIA ALENE, nurse-midwife, medical educator; b. Washington, Mar. 11, 1954; d. Richard Edmond and Peggy Alene Morrison; m. Thomas Preston Hackney III, June 16, 1973 (div. Apr. 1990); 1 child, Tristan Patrick. Diploma, St. Mary's Hosp. Sch. Nursing, Huntington, W.Va., 1978; BSN cum laude, Marshall U., 1992; cert. in nurse-midwifery, Frontier Sch. Midwifery, Hyden, Ky., 1995; MSN, Case Western Reserve U., 1996. RN, W.Va.; cert. Am. Coll. Nurse-Midwives. Staff nurse Cabell-Huntington Hosp., Huntington, W.Va., 1978, South Laguna (Calif.) Cmty. Hosp., 1978-80, Washington Hosp. Ctr., Washington, 1980-84, 86-87; staff nurse, mental health Guidance Clinic of the Middle Keys, Marathon, Fla., 1985-86, 88-90; staff nurse Cabell-Huntington Hosp., 1991-94; clin. staff, faculty Marshall U. Sch. Medicine, Huntington, 1995—; prenatal care coord. Valley Health Systems, Huntington, 1992-93. Advanced Practice scholar, W.Va. Bur. Pub. Health, 1993, Rural Health Initiative scholar, 1994. Mem. Am. Coll. Nurse-Midwives, Sigma Theta Tau (by-laws com. 1992-94). Office: Univ Physicians & Surgeons Univ ObGyn 1801 6th Ave Huntington WV 25703

HADDAD, FARES SAMI, orthopaedic surgeon; b. Beirut, Lebanon, Mar. 15, 1967; arrived in U.K., 1977; s. Sami Fares and Nina (Tamari) H. BSc with honors, U. London, 1987, MBBS, 1990. House officer Middlesex Hosp., Eng., 1990; sr. house officer U. Coll. Hosp., 1991, Royal Nat. Orthopaedic Hosp., 1992, St. Bartholomew's Hosp., 1973-94; registrar Royal Free Hosp., 1994; sr. registrar Royal Nat. Orthopaedic Hosp., London, 1996—. Contbr. articles to profl. jours. Recipient Lister medal Seddos Soc., 1995. Fellow Brit. Orthopaedic Assn. (assoc., Smith and Nephew prize 1996, Mukheresee prize 1995), Brit. Orthopaedic and Sports Trauma Assn., Royal Soc. Medicine, Royal Coll. Surgeons London, Royal Coll. Surgeons Edinburgh, Royal Coll. Surgeons Eng. Office: Great Ormond St Hosp, for Sick Children, London WC1 3JN, England

HADDAD, FUAD SAMI, neurosurgeon, researcher; b. Beirut, Lebanon, Mar. 31, 1924; s. Sami Ibrahim and Lamia (Morcos) H.; m. Aida Nassir, Nov. 10, 1956; children—George, Suhayl, Fadi, Nabih, Labib, Janane, M.D., Am. U., Beirut, 1948. Diplomate Am. Bd. Neurosurgery, Instr. physiology Am. U., Birut, 1948-50, insr. surgery, 1955, clin. asst. prof. neurosurgery, 1955-60, clin. assoc. prof. neurosurgery, 1960-74, clin. prof. neurosurgery, 1974—; mem. internat. adv. com. Cerebral Palsy Children, 1957-62; mem. nat. adv. com. on Cancer, 1964-72; mem. internat. adv. com. Scouting with Handicapped, 1966-70; mem. nat. adv. com. Physically Rehab., 1968-72; mem. Supreme Med. Council Lebanese Army, 1968-72. Fellow: Royal Coll Can. Surgeons, Am. Coll. Surgeons, Pan Pacific Surg. Assn., Pan Am. Med. Assn.; mem. Internat. Soc. Welfare of Physically Disabled (nat. sec. 1957-75), Lebanese Soc. Neurology Neurosurgery and Psychiatry, (past exec. sec.), Wold Fedn. Neurosurg. Socs. (hon. v.p. 1957-61), Middle East Neurosurgery Soc. (exec. sec. 1958—), World Fedn. Neurology (nat. sec. 1960-70), ACS (past gov. Lebanon 1977-80). Home: Madam Curie St, Beirut Lebanon Office: American U Med Center, Dept Neurosurgery, Beirut Lebanon

HADDAD, GABRIEL G., physician, pediatrics educator; b. Beirut, Nov. 20, 1947; came to U.S., 1974; s. George Gabriel and Ida (Bitar) H.; m. Karen Chmielski, June 14, 1975; children: Christopher, Diana Justin. BS in Biology and Chemistry, Am. Univ. Beirut, 1968, MD, 1972. Diplomate Am. Bd. Pediatrics. Fellow in pediatrics, pulmonary Columbia U., N.Y.C., 1975-78, asst. prof. pediatrics, 1978-84, assoc. prof. pediatrics, 1984-88, dir. sleep physiology lab., 1980-88; dir. sect. respiratory medicine Yale U. Sch. Medicine, New Haven, 1988—, prof. pediatrics, 1990—; mem. NIHD study sect. NIH, Md., 1982; mem. editorial bd. Jour. Applied Physiology, 1983-85, assoc. editor, 1989—; NIHLB site visitor NIH Program Project, Cleve., 1985; conf. chmn. NIHLB, 1987, NICHD, 1988, NIH subcom. chmn. Contbr. over 100 chpts. and articles and abstracts to profl. jours. and books. Recipient Edward Livingston Trudeau award Am. Lung Assn., 1979-82. Mem. AAAS, Am. Heart Assn. (established investigator 1985-90), Soc. for Pediatrics Rsch., Am. Physiol. Soc., Am. Thoracic Soc. (respiratory neurobiology & sleep sect.), Soc. for Neurosci. Home: 383 Schoolside Ln Guilford CT 06437-1854 Office: Yale U Sch Medicine 333 Cedar St Fitkin 506 New Haven CT 06510*

HADDAD, HESKEL MARSHALL, ophthalmologist; b. Baghdad, Iraq, Sept. 26, 1930; came to U.S., 1953, naturalized, 1962; s. Moshe M. and Masuda (Cohen) H.; m. Doris I. Fatzer, July 4, 1963; children: Ava Masuda, Andreas Moshe, Michael Albert. Student, Royal Coll. Medicine, Baghdad, 1945-50; M.D., Hebrew U., Jerusalem, 1953. Diplomate: Am. Bd. Pediatrics, Am. Bd. Ophthalmology. Intern Donolo Hosp., Jaffo-Tel Aviv, Israel, 1950-51; rotating intern Hadassah U. Hosp., Jerusalem, 1951-53; pediatric resident Children's Med. Center, Boston, 1953-56; fellow in pediatric endocrinology Johns Hopkins Hosp., Balt., 1956-58; fellow in clin. endocrine br. Nat. Inst. Arthritis and Metabolic Diseases, NIH, Bethesda, Md., 1958-59; pediatrician sect. clin. endocrinology NIH, 1959-60; asst. prof. pediatrics sch. medicine Howard U., Washington, 1959-60; resident, asst. dept. ophthalmology sch. medicine Washington U., St. Louis, 1960-64; leave of absence, 1962-63; fellow pediatric ophthalmology Inst. Visual Sci., San Francisco, 1962; research fellow Hôpital des Quinze-Vingts, Laboratoire de Physiologie de Vision, Ecole des Hautes Etudes, Paris, 1962-63; ophthalmologist Hôpital Beni Messous, Algiers, Algeria, 1964; asst. attending ophthalmic surgeon, also asst. prof. ophthalmology Mt. Sinai Hosp. and Sch. Medicine, N.Y.C., 1964-67; dir. dept. ophthalmology Beth Israel Med. Center, N.Y.C.; also assoc. prof. ophthalmology Mt. Sinai Sch. Medicine, 1967-71; clin. prof. ophthalmology N.Y. Med. Coll., 1971—. Author: Endocrine Exophthalmos, 1973, Metabolic Eye Diseases, 1974, Metabolic-Peditric Eye Diseases, 1979, Metabolic Ophthalmology: Diagnostic Techniques Vols. I and II, 1985, Jews of Arab and Islamic Countries: History, Problems and Solutions, 1984, (autobiography) Flight from Babylon, 1986; editor-in-chief: Metabolic Ophthalmology, 1976-79, Metabolic and Ophthalmology, 1976-79, Metabolic and Pediatric Ophthalmology, 1979-82, Metabolic, Pediatric and Systemic Ophthalmology, 1982—; contbr. numerous articles and revs. to profl. jours.; holder 7 U.S. patents. Pres. Am. Com. for Rescue and Resettlement of Iraqui Jews, World Orgn. Jews from Arab Countries, Parents' Assn. of Sch. of Performing Arts, 1980-83. Fellow ACS, Am. Inst. Chemists; mem. Am. Endocrine Soc., Am. Fedn. Clin. Research, Assn. Research Ophthalmology and Vision, AMA, New York County Med. Soc., AAAS, Am. Acad. Ophthalmology, N.Y. Acad. Medicine, N.Y. Acad. Scis., N.Y. Soc. Clin. Ophthalmology, Soc. Eye Surgeons, Société Française d' Ophthalmologie, German Ophthal. Soc., Internat. Soc. Metabolic Eye Disease (founder, sec.-treas. 1973—), World Soc. on Systemic Ophthalmology (founder, sec.-treas. 1982, chmn.), N.Y. County Med. Soc. (chmn. com. fgn. med. grads. 1985-90, del. N.Y. State Med. Soc. 1985-86). Office: 1125 Park Ave New York NY 10128-1243

HADDY, THERESA BREY, physician, educator, pediatric hematologist/oncologist; b. Wabasso, Minn., Feb. 27, 1924; d. Francis William and Elizabeth Katherine (Daub) Brey; m. Francis John Haddy, Sept. 21, 1946; children—Richard Ian, Carol Haddy Froelich, Alice Haddy Hellen. B.S., U. Minn., 1944, M.B., 1946, M.D., 1948. Diplomate Am. Bd. Pediatrics, Am. Bd. Pediatric Hematology/Oncology. Intern, Mpls. Gen. Hosp., Mpls., 1947-48; resident pediatrics U. Minn., Mpls., 1950-52; fellow hematology U. Okla., Oklahoma City, 1962-64; practice medicine specializing in gen. pediatrics, Des Plaines, Ill., 1954-61; asst. prof. U. Okla., Oklahoma City, 1964-66; chief child health Mich. Dept. Pub. Health, Lansing, 1966-69; assoc. prof. Mich. State U., East Lansing, 1969-76; expert blood diseases NIH, Bethesda, Md., 1977-79; assoc. prof. dept. pediatrics and child health Howard U., Washington, 1979-87, prof. 1987-89, prof. emeritus, 1989—; guest rschr. pediatric br. NIH, NCI, Bethesda, 1989—. Contbr. articles to med. and sci. jours. Mem. C&O Canal Assn., Washington. Mem. Am. Acad. Pediatrics, Am. Soc. Hematology, Am. Soc., Pediatric Hematology/Oncology, Washington Blood Club, NIH Alumni Assn. Episcopalian. Office: NIH NCI PB Bldg 10 Rm 13N240 Bethesda MD 20892

HADFIELD, WILLIAM ADRAIN, internist; b. Madison, Wis., May 8, 1923; s. William Adrian and Marie E. (Holz) H.; student Villanova U., 1940-43; m. Jean White, Dec. 29, 1945; children: Margaret, Marie, Marcia. MD, U. Pa., 1946. Intern, U. Pa. Hosp., Phila., 1946-47; resident in medicine VA Hosp., Boston, 1949-51; practice medicine specializing in internal medicine and geriatrics, Drexel Hill, Pa., 1953-89; mem. staff Delaware County Meml. Hosp., Drexel Hill, 1957—, dir. medicine, 1979-89, dir. quality assurance Keystone Health Systems, 1989—, pres. med. staff, 1978-80, trustee. Mem. Governing Bd. Health Systems Agy., Southeastern Pa., 1977-79. Served to capt. M.C., U.S. Army, 1947-49. Mem. ACP, AMA, Pa. Med. Soc. Republican. Roman Catholic. Office: Delaware County Meml Hosp Crozier-Keystone Health Syss 501 N Landsdowne Ave Drexel Hill PA 19026-4819

HADLEY, CAROLYN BETH, physician, educator; b. Dallas, Nov. 22, 1945; d. Charles Franklin and Sadie Beth (Humphreys) Hadley; m. Richard G. Suchan, Dec. 28, 1985; children: Richard C., Stephen G. BA with honors in Microbiology, U. Kans., 1968; MS in Clin. Microbiology, Columbia U. Coll. Physicians and Surgeons, 1974; MD, U. Pa., 1981. Diplomate Am. Coll. Med. Examiners., Am. Bd. Ob-Gyn. Maternal-Fetal Medicine. Lab technologist St. Joseph Mercy Hosp., Ann Arbor, Mich., 1968-70; sr. technologist, diagnostic microbiology svc. Columbia Presbyn. Med. Ctr., N.Y.C., 1970-73, sr. asst. supr., 1973-75; asst. microbiologist Hosp. of U. Pa., Phila., 1975-77, resident in ob-gyn., 1981-85, fellow in maternal fetal medicine, 1985-87; teaching asst. in microbiology U. Kans., 1968; teaching fellow microbiology U. Mich. Med. Sch., 1969; asst. prof. Med. Coll. Pa., 1987-91, assoc. prof., 1991-93, dir. obstetrics, 1992, asst. prof. anesthesiology, 1993. Recipient Undergrad. Rsch. award U. Kans., 1967; Phillip Williams prize in obstetrics, 1984; S. Leon Israel prize in obstetrics, 1985; Henrietta Ottinger/Huston MacFarlane scholar Med. Coll. Pa., 1978-93. Fellow Am. Coll. Ob-Gyn.; mem. AMA, Am. Soc. Microbiology (specialist in microbiology), Am. Soc. Clin. Pathologists (specialist microbiologist), Phila. Perinatal Soc., Soc. for Perinatal Obstetricians, DAR, U. Kans. Alumni Assn., Phila. Obstet. Soc., Phi Beta Kappa. Office: Med Coll Pa Dept Ob-Gyn 3300 Henry Ave Philadelphia PA 19129-1121

HADLEY, ROBERT GORDON, rehabilitation counselor educator, consultant; b. Portland, Oreg., Feb. 28, 1931; s. Howard E. Hadley and Carol (McElmurry) Hadley Bryans; m. Patricia Ann Stephan Meyer, Dec. 21, 1968; children: Vanita Spaulding, Stephanie Koza. BA, Reed Coll., 1953; MS, State U. Wash., 1955; PhD, UCLA, 1962. Cert. rehab. counselor. Psychology trainee U.S. VA, L.A., 1956-61, psychologist, 1961-65; asst. prof. Calif. State U., L.A., 1965-68, assoc. prof., 1968-73, prof., 1973-87, prof. emeritus, 1987—; ptnr. The Empowerment Group, Culver City, Calif., 1987—. Author: Professional Report Writing for Counselors, 1987, revised as Professional Counselor Reporting, 1992; co-author: Counseling Research and Program Evaluation, 1995. Mem. Direction 21 Com., Culver City, 1987-88; bd. dirs. Culver City Parks and Svc. Found., sec., 1996-97. Mem. ACA, APA, Phi Beta Kappa. Home: 11408 Diller Ave Culver City CA 90230-5376

HADLEY, WILLIAM MELVIN, college dean; b. San Antonio, June 4, 1942; s. Arthur Roosevelt and Audrey Merle (Barrett) H.; m. Dorothy J. Hadley, Jan. 21, 1967 (div. July 1989); children: Heather Marie, William Arthur; m. Jane F. Walsh, Oct. 13, 1990. BS in Pharmacy, Purdue U., West Lafayette, Ind., 1967, MS in Pharmacology, 1971, PhD in Toxicology, 1972. Registered pharmacist, Ind. Teaching and grad. asst. Purdue U., West Lafayette, 1967-72; asst. prof. U. N.Mex., Albuquerque, 1972-76, assoc. prof., 1976-82, prof., 1982—, asst. dean Coll. Pharmacy, 1984-86, acting dean Coll. Pharmacy, 1985, dean Coll. Pharmacy, 1986—; vis. scientist Lovelace Inhalation Toxicology Inst., Albuquerque, 1981, adj. scientist, 1991—; mem. adv. bd. Waste Edn. Rsch. Consortium, Las Cruces, N.Mex., 1989—; mem. NIH Proposal Rev. Panels, Bethesda, Md., 1983-84; mem. Gov.'s PCB Expert Adv. Panel, Santa Fe, 1985-86; toxicology cons. numerous law firms N.Mex.; mem. sci. adv. bd. Carlsbad Environ. Monitoring Ctr., 1992—; mem. sci. adv. com. S.W. Regional Spaceport, Las Cruces, 1992-94. Mem. steering com. United Fund, U.N.Mex., 1987, key person, 1988-94. NIH grantee, 1974-80, 83-87. Mem. AAAS, Am. Assn. Colls. of Pharmacy, Soc. Toxicology (pres. Rocky Mt. chpt. 1990-91), Western Pharmacology Soc., Southwestern Assn. Toxicologists. Office: U NMex Coll Pharmacy Albuquerque NM 87131

HAENECOUR, FRANZ, radiologist; b. Etterbeek-Brussels, Belgium, Sept. 5, 1927; s. Joseph and Wilhelmine (Duynstee) H.; m. Françoise Van Keerberghen, July 22, 1953; children: Bernard, Luc, Vincent, Véronique, Olivier. MD, U. Louvain, Belgium, 1953; Degree in Tropical Medicine, Antwerp, Belgium, 1953. Cert. radiology. Physician Mines (M.G.L.), Belgian Congo, 1953-60; radiological asst. St. John Clinic, Brussels, 1960-63; radiologist St. Vincent Clinic, Soignies, Belgium, 1964-92; adv. Radiological Union, 1980-90; v.p. Belgian Union of Physician Specialists, 1985-90; adv. Radiological Commn. of Ministry of Health, 1986. Recipient Paul Harris fellow, 1991. Mem. Rotary Soignies (pres. 1983-84). Home: Chemin De Nivelles 12, 7060 Soignies Belgium

HAENSLY, PATRICIA A., psychology educator; b. Kronenwetter, Wis., Dec. 4, 1928; d. Paul Frank and Valeria (Woyak) Banach; m. William E. Haensly, 1954; children: Paul, Robert, Thomas, James, John, David, Mary, Katherine. BS, Lawrence U., 1950; MS in Genetics, Iowa State U., 1953; PhD in Ednl. & Devel. Psychology, Tex. A&M U., 1982. Histo technique specialist dept. vet. pathology Iowa State U., Ames, 1958-63; asst. prof. dept. ednl. psychology Tex. A&M U., College Station, 1982—; instr. Blinn Jr. Coll., College Station; prin. Investigator Project Mustard Seed, U.S.D.O.E. Javits Grant, 1993-96; assoc. dir. programs Inst. for Gifted and Talented Tex. A&M U., College Station, dir. summer presch. program Minds Alive, 1987-95; prin. investigator project mustard seed U.S. Dept. Energy, 1993-96; adj. faculty mem. Western Wash. U., 1996—. Contbd. editor Roeper Rev., 1996—; contbr. articles to profl. publs., chpts. to books on mentoring creativity and giftedness; editl. rev. bd. Gifted Child Quar., 1996—. Recipient Outstanding Woman award AAUW, 1980, Govt. Rsch. Javits grante, 1993-96, Hon. Mention Hollingworth award Intertel Found., 1993. Mem. Tex. Assn. for Gifted and Talented (1st v.p. 1988, 89, editor news mag. 1988, 89), Nat. Assn. Gifted Children (co-chmn. rsch. and evaluation com. 1985-87, John Curtis Gowan Rsch. award 1981), World Coun. for Gifted and Talented Children, Inc., Southwestern Ednl. Rsch. Assn., Soc. for Rsch. in Child Devel., Coun. for Exceptional Children, Assn. for Childhood Edn. Internat., Am. Creativity Assn. (charter), Am. Psychol. Soc., Phi Kappa Phi. Home: 3384 Northgate Rd Bellingham WA

HAFER, MARILYN DURHAM, psychologist, consultant; b. Guthrie, Okla., Feb. 10, 1924; d. Walker Phillip and Elizabeth (Gooch) Durham; m. E.M. Hafer, July 4, 1943 (div. July 1955). BA in Psychology, Tex. Women's U., 1966; PhD in Psychology, Tex. Tech. U., 1971. Registered psychologist, Ill. Asst. prof. psychology Ill. Inst. Technology, Chgo., 1971-77; asst. prof. adminstrv. studies ctr. DePaul U., Chgo., 1977-78; psychologist U.S. Office Personnel Mgmt., Chgo., 1977-79; assoc. prof. rehab. inst. So. Ill. U., Carbondale, Ill., 1979-86; prof. emeritus So. Ill. U., Carbondale, 1986—; cons. in field, Commn. on Rehab. Counselor Cert., Chgo., 1981-83; tech. reviewer and panelist, U.S. Dept. Edn., Washington, 1985. Cons. editor Jour. Rehab. Adminstrn., 1981-88; mem. editorial bd. Rehab. Counseling Bulletin, 1983-89; contbr. articles to profl. jours. NSF fellow, 1966-70. Mem. Am. Psychol. Soc., Psi Chi. Home and Office: 14313 N Pennsylvania Ave B Oklahoma City OK 73134-6007

HAFFNER, ALDEN NORMAN, university official; b. Bklyn., Oct. 3, 1928; s. Irving and Irene (Gutfleisch) H. AB, Bklyn. Coll., 1948; OD, Pa. Coll. Optometry, 1952; MPA, NYU, 1960, PhD, 1964; DOS (hon.), Mass. Coll. Optometry, 1960; ScD (hon.), Pa. Coll. Optometry, 1973. Exec. dir. Optometric Center of N.Y., N.Y.C., 1957—; acting chief adminstrv. officer State Coll. Optometry, SUNY, N.Y.C., 1970-71; dean State Coll. Optometry, SUNY, 1971-76, pres., 1976-78; assoc. chancellor for health scis. SUNY, Albany, 1978-82, vice chancellor for research, grad. studies and profl. programs, 1982-87, pres. coll. optometry, 1987—; pub. svc. prof. health poligy Rockefeller Coll., SUNY-Albany, 1986; chmn. N.Y. State Com. on Health Personnel and Productivity, 1990—; cons. in field. Contbr. articles in field to profl. jours. Mem. adv. com. Commn. for Blind and Visually Handicapped, State Dept. Social Services, 1966-70; mem. bd. nat. study commn. on optometry Nat. Commn. on Accrediting, 1968-70; mem. health manpower planning com. Comprehensive Health Planning Agy., N.Y.C., 1969-73; project dir. Fed. Program of Identification, Counseling, Guidance and Recruitment of Minority Students in Profession of Optometry, 1968-74; mem. Mayor's Com. for Study of Aging, N.Y.C., 1958; chmn. bd. trustees Manhattan Health Plan, Inc., 1976-81. Served to 1st lt. M.C. U.S. Army, 1953-55. Recipient Albert Fitch Meml. award, 1962; Prof. Frederick A. Woll Meml. award, 1961; Distinguished Achievement award Alumni Assn., N.Y. U. Grad. Sch. Pub. Health Adminstrn., 1974. Fellow Am. Pub. Health Assn., AAAS, Am. Sch. Health Assn., Am., N.Y. Acad. Optometry; mem. N.Y. Acad. Scis., Group Health Assn. Am., Am. Pub. Welfare Assn., Am. Soc. Pub. Adminstrn., Nat. Rehab. Assn., Illuminating Engring. Soc., Am. Optometric Assn., N.Y. State Optometric Assn., Gerontol. Soc., Am. Assn. Univ. Adminstrs., Pub. Health Assn. City of N.Y. (dir. 1967—), Nat. Assn. Land Grant Colls. and State Univs. (com. health affairs 1981), Community Family Planning Coun., Am. Coun. on Edn., Assn. Cad. Health Ctrs., Hermann Biggs Soc., Beta Sigma Kappa (Gold Medal award 1974),. Home: 201 E 36th St New York NY 10016-3668 Office: SUNY Coll Optometry 100 E 24th St New York NY 10010-3610

HAFKENSCHIEL, JOSEPH HENRY, JR., cardiologist, educator; b. Youngstown, Ohio, Apr. 2, 1916; s. Joseph Henry and Anna Marie (Conroy) H.; m. Lucinda Buchanan Thomas, July 18, 1942 (dec. 1983); children: Joseph Henry III, Benjamin A. Thomas, Mark Conroy, John Proctor; m. Carol MacDonald Smith Rush, Jan. 25, 1985. AB, Swarthmore Coll., 1937; MD, Johns Hopkins U., 1941. Diplomate Am. Bd. Internal Medicine. Intern, U. Pa. Hosp., Phila., 1941-42, resident, 1948-49, fellow in cardiology, 1949; instr. pharmacology U. Pa. Sch. Medicine, Phila., 1946-47, instr. medicine, 1949-51, assoc. medicine, 1951-66; cardiovascular disease physician in pvt. practice, Phila., 1949-65, Palo Alto, Calif., 1969-78; med. dir. West Coast Office Sandoz Pharm., San Francisco, 1965-67; staff physician Cowell Student Health Svc. Stanford U., Calif., 1967-69, clin. instr. medicine, 1966-69, asst. to assoc. prof., 1969-84, emeritus clin. assoc. prof. medicine, 1984—;

staff physician Extended Care Service VA Med. Ctr., Palo Alto, 1978-84. Contbr. articles to profl. jours. Pres. Peninsula Meml. and Funeral Soc., Palo Alto, 1984. Served to maj. M.C., USAAF, 1942-46. Fellow Coll. Physicians Phila., ACP, Am. Heart Assn., Royal Soc. Medicine; mem. Air Force Assn., Am. Irish Hist. Soc., Am. Legion (post comdr. 1960-62), Sigma Xi. Republican. Roman Catholic. Clubs: San Francisco Golf; Merion Golf; Gulph Mills Golf, Ballybunion Golf (Ireland). Avocations: world travel, golf, gardening, art history. Home: 870 Lesley Rd Villanova PA 19085-1118

HAFLING, WILLIAM RUSSELL, psychologist; b. Animas City, Colo., Aug. 30, 1936; s. Owen Russell Haflinger and Mable Louella Roberts Murley; m. Marilyn Elizabeth Roelike, May 8, 1981. BSc in Econs., U. Minn., 1966; LLB, LaSalle U., Chgo., 1967; MA in Psychology, U. Minn., 1971, PhD, 1975. Lic. psychologist, Fla. Dir. rsch. Caribe Mackins Corp., Denver, 1959-65; editor sci. pubs. and rsch. chemist Archer Daniels Midland Corp., Bloomington, Minn., 1965-67; sr. sci. writer and psychiat. rsch. U. Minn., Mpls., 1967-78; adj. prof. psychology Family Practice Medicine U. So. Fla., St. Petersburg, 1978-82; pres., dir. Bay Area Psychol. Svcs., St. Petersburg, 1980—; chief cons. psychologist Women's Resource Ctr., Largo, Fla., 1983—. Author: The Jungle Guide; contbr. articles to profl. jours. Past pres., dir. ACLU, St. Petersburg, 1989. Recipient Patients' Svc. award, Am. Cancer Soc., 1983, Service award, Mental Health Assn., Pinellas, 1980, others. Mem. APA (cert. of profeciency in treatment of alcohol and other psychoactive substance use disorders, Health Psychology, Psychotherapy), Fla. Psychol. Assn., Pinellas Psychol. Assn., Internat. Soc. Behavioral Medicine, Internat. Congress of Psychology, Prescribing Psychologists' Register. Office: Bay Area Psychol Svcs 721 11th St N Saint Petersburg FL 33705-1320

HAFNER-EATON, CHRIS, health services researcher, educator; b. N.Y.C., Dec. 9, 1962; d. Peter Robert and Isabelle (Freda) Hafner; m. James Michael Eaton, Aug. 9, 1986; children: Kelsey James, Tristen Lee. BA, U. Calif., San Diego, 1986; MPH, UCLA, 1988, PhD in Health Svcs., 1992. Cert. health edn. specialist; internat. bd. cert. lactation cons. Cons. dental health policy UCLA Schl. Dentistry, 1989; grad. teachg asst. UCLA Sch. Pub. Health, 1987-92; health svcs. researcher UCLA, 1987-92; cons. health policy U.S. Dept. Health & Human Svcs., Washington, 1988—; analyst health policy The RAND/UCLA Ctr. Health Policy Study, Santa Monica & L.A., 1988-94; asst. prof. health care adminstrn. Oreg. State U. Dept. Pub. Health, Corvallis, 1992-95; pres. Health Improvement Svcs. Corp., 1994—; dir. rsch. rev. com. La Leche League Internat., 1996—; adj. faculty pub. health Linn-Benton Coll., 1995—; bd. dirs. Benton County Pub. Health Bd., Healthy Start Bd.; mem. Linn-Benton Breastfeeding Task Force, Samaritan Mother-Baby Dyad Team. Contbr. articles to profl. jours. Rsch. grantee numerous granting bodies, 1988-94. Mem. AAUW, NOW, La Leche League Internat. (area profl. liaison for Oreg.), AM. Pub. Health Assn. (med. care sect., women's caucus), Am. Assn. World Health, Oreg. Pub. Health Assn., Oreg. Health Care Assn., Assn. Health Svcs. Rsch., Soc. Pub. Health Edn., Physicians for Social Responsibility, UCLA Pub. Health Alumni Assn., Delta Omega. Home: 1807 NW Beca Ave Corvallis OR 97330-2636

HAGAN, CONNIE JUNE, college health nurse; b. Grove City, Pa., Apr. 15, 1954; d. Walter Glenn and Marthia Virginia (Kay) McFadden; m. William Neal Hagan, May 20, 1974; children: Eric William, Justin Glenn. ASN, Clarion State Coll., 1974; BSN cum laude, Slippery Rock U., 1989; postgrad., Clarion U./Slippery Rock. RN, Pa.; cert. in coll. health nursing. Staff nurse Grove City Hosp., 1974-80, United Cmty. Hosp., Grove City, 1980-86, Family Planning of Mercer Co., Grove City, 1987-88, Offices of Frederick R. Wilson DO, Slippery Rock, Pa., 1990-93; charge nurse Student Health Ctr., quality control nurse Slippery Rock U., 1993—. Bd. dirs. Homes for Brighter Futures, New Castle, Pa., 1994-95. Mem. Pa. Nurses Assn., Orgn. Coll. Health Svcs. Methodist. Office: Slippery Rock U Student Health Ctr Slippery Rock PA 16057

HAGAN, SHIRLEY SMITH, medical technologist, educator; b. Sherman, Tex., Apr. 20, 1936; d. J.B. and Frances Winnifred (Groce) Smith; diploma med. tech., Parkland Meml. Hosp., Dallas, 1961; B.S., Southeastern Okla. State U., 1977; M.S., Tex. Woman's U., 1981; m. George Phillip Hagan, Apr. 16, 1954; children—Philip Ray, Stephen Russell. Med. technologist hosps. in Tex., 1956-75; instr. med. lab. tech. Grayson County Coll., Denison, Tex., 1974—, program dir., 1985—. Mem. Am. Soc. Clin. Pathologists (assoc.), Am. Soc. Clin. Lab. Sci., Tex. Assn. Clin. Lab. Sci. Baptist. Home: PO Box 684 Sherman TX 75091-0684 Office: 6101 Grayson Dr Denison TX 75020-8238

HAGAR, MICHAEL GEORGE, optometrist; b. New Haven, Conn., July 18, 1956; s. Melvin Lawson Sr. and Thelma Mae (Ferritti) H. BS, So. Conn. State U., New Haven, 1981, MS in Analytical Chemistry, 1987; BS, Pa. Coll. Optometry, Phila., 1991, OD, 1994. Analytical chemist, 1982-89; pvt. practice Augusta, Maine, 1996—. Baptist. Office: 226 Western Ave Ste B Augusta ME 04330

HAGBERG, BENGT ARTHUR, pediatrics educator, child neurology consultant; b. Gothenburg, Sweden, Aug. 9, 1923; s. Eric and Gulli (Zachau) H.; m. Gudrun Wranne, Jan. 18, 1947; children: Gunilla, Barbro, Hans and Lars (twins), Kerstin. MD, Uppsala U., 1950. Resident in pediats. Uppsala, Sweden, 1950-53; resident in internal medicine Malmö, Sweden, 1954-56; asst. resident in neurology Gothenburg, Lund, Uppsala, Sweden, 1954-56; asst. prof. pediats. Uppsala, 1960-64; rschr. in pediat. neurology Swedish Med. Rsch. Coun., 1964-67; prof. pediat. neurology Uppsala U., 1967-71; prof. pediats. U. Gothenburg, 1971—, chmn. Instn. Pediats. II, 1971-90; adminstrv. head Childrens Hosp., Gothenburg, 1973-81, 84-87; prof. emeritus, cons. child neurologist East Hosp., Gothenburg, 1990—; head adminstrv. block for pediats., pediat. surgery, child psychiatry and child health City of Gothenburg, 1978-81; sci. advisor Swedish Social Coun., 1980s; participant expert commns. for small and less well known disorders and handicapped groups, 1990s. Contbr. numerous articles to profl. jours. Recipient Lennander award, 1974, Malte award, 1979, Guest Prof. award U. Dundee, 1985, Oskar Medins award, 1987, Folke Bernadotte award, 1988, Hower award Am. Child Neurol. Soc., 1993, Rosén von Rosenstein award, 1994, Cornelia de Lange award, 1994; named Ronnie Mac Keith lectr., 1980, Hon. BLF lectr., 1972, 83, Segawa Prize lectr., 1989, Guest Prof., U. Göttingen, 1991, 92, Per Dubb Price lectr., 1991. Mem. British Paediatric Neurology Assn. (hon.), Gesellschaft Neuropädiatrie (Germany). Home: Sågställaregatan 3, S-416 79 Gothenburg Sweden Office: East Hosp, Dept Pediatrics, S-416 85 Gothenburg Sweden

HAGE, STEPHEN JOHN, radiology administrator, consultant; b. Chgo., July 22, 1943; s. Steve and Irene (Lewandowski) H.; m. Constance Louise Simonis, June 10, 1967. AAS, YMCA C.C., Chgo., 1970. Registered radiol. tech. Staff tech. Highland Park (Ill.) Hosp., 1966-68; chief radiotherapy tech. VA Hines (Ill.) Hosp., 1968-70; chief radiology tech. Gottlieb Meml. Hosp., Melrose Park, Ill., 1970-71; radiology adminstr. S. Chgo. County Hosp., 1971-79; adminstrv. dir. radiology Cedars-Sinai Med. Ctr., L.A., 1979-93; CEO HumiPerfect Co., Chatsworth, Calif., 1994—; cons. Computer Sci. Corp., El Segundo, Calif., 1983—. Contbr. articles to profl. jours. Served with USMC, 1961-64. Recipient 1st pl. Essay award Ill. State Soc. Radiol. Technicians, 1966. Mem. Am. Hosp. Radiology Adminstrs. (charter), Am. Soc. Radiol. Technologists, AAAS, Phi Theta Kappa. Home and Office: HumiPerfect 22115 Halsted St Chatsworth CA 91311-4027

HAGEBAK, BEAUMONT ROGER, psychologist; b. Starbuck, Minn., June 17, 1936; s. C. Beaumont and Gertrude Elizabeth (Mork) H.; m. Lillian Kate Price, Dec. 27, 1957 (div. 1977); children: Beaumont William, Christen Daane, Haakon Price; m. Judith Eve Mertz, Feb. 2, 1978; 1 stepchild, Cory Randall Hula. BA, U. No. Iowa, 1960, MA, 1962; EdD, Ariz. State U., 1967. Lic. applied psychologist, Ga. Counselor Reinbeck (Iowa) Community Schs., 1961-63; assoc. prof., dir. psychology svcs. Mankato (Minn.) State U., 1964-69; dean student affairs Northland Coll., Ashland, Wis., 1969-72; dir. mental health ctr. West Health Dist., LaGrange, Ga., 1972-73; regional adminstr. Ga. Dept. Human Resources, LaGrange, 1973-77; cons. mental health USPHS, Atlanta, 1978-83, chief edn. sect., 1983-87, chief clin. mgr., 1987-90, dep. regional health adminstr., 1990—; mem. steering com. Ga. Network Human Svcs., Athens, 1983-85. Author: Getting Local Agencies to Cooperate, 1982, The Hagebak Book: Tracing Five Families, 1986; (with others) State and Local Government Administration, 1985. Bd. dirs. HUB Counseling Ctr., Atlanta, 1986, Metro Atlanta Coun. Alcohol and Drugs, 1987-90; chair membership coun. Unitarian Universalist Congregation Atlanta, 1989-90, bd. dirs., 1991. Sgt. U.S. Army, 1954-56. Recipient Joint Activity award Office of Assn. Sec. Health, Washington, 1991, Spl. Recognition award, 1991. Mem. Am. Soc. Pub. Adminstrn. (editor newsletter 1983-85), Am. Psychol. Assn., Ga. Psychol. Assn. Democrat. Home: 906 Heritage Pl Decatur GA 30033-4152 Office: USPHS Ste 1515 101 Marietta St Atlanta GA 30323-0001

HAGELE, MARY CATHERINE, clinical psychologist; b. St. Joseph, Mo., Jan. 3, 1942; d. Herbert Christian and Katherine Helen (Freund) H. BA, Maryville Coll., 1967; MRE, Seattle U., 1972; MA, Northwestern U., 1975; D Psychology, Chgo. Sch. Profl. Psychology 1989. Cert. addictions counselor. Mem. adult literacy staff Pruitt-Igoe Pub. Housing, St. Louis, 1965-66; Upward Bound staff Barat Coll., Lake Forest, Ill., 1966-67; tchr. Acad. of Sacred Heart, Cin., 1967-70; tchr., counselor Woodlands Acad., Lake Forest, 1970-81; psychotherapist Martha Washington Hosp., Chgo., 1989-91; pvt. practice clin. psychology Evanston, Ill., 1991—; mem. allied med. staff Hartgrove Hosp., Chgo., Rush Med. Ctr., Skokie, Ill. Mem. APA, Ill. Psychol. Assn., Chgo. Psychol. Assn., Jung Inst. Chgo., Mental Health Assn. Ill., Am. Assn. Marriage and Family Therapists, Northwestern Club Chgo. Democrat. Roman Catholic. Office: 708 Church St Ste 203 Evanston IL 60201-3840

HAGEN, EDNA MAE, retired medical nurse; b. Jasper, Ark., Nov. 30, 1932; d. Eugene and Dovie (Combs) Keef; m. Harry Hagen, Jan. 4, 1952; children: Catherine, Harry, Jr. ADN, Santa Barbara Coll., 1973. RN, Calif. Staff nurse Cottage Hosp., Santa Barbara, Calif., 1970-74; head nurse to pvt. physician L.A. Price, M.D., Inc., Santa Barbara, 1974-95; retired, 1995. Mem. U.S. Army Med. Corps, 1951-52. Mem. ANA, CNA.

HAGEN, JEFFREY AUGUST, thoracic surgeon; b. Milw., Oct. 1, 1959; s. Francis Dale and Darleen Marie (Day) H.; m. Mary Kathleen Slevin, June 16, 1984; children: Kaitlin Marie, Daniel August, Madison Margaret, Alexander Spalding. BS in Math., Creighton U., 1982, MD, 1986. Diplomate Am. Bd. Surgery, Am. Bd. Thoracic Surgery. Intern surgery Creighton U., Omaha, Nebr., 1986-87; resident surgery Creighton U., Omaha, 1987-91; esophageal surgery fellow U. So. Calif. Med. Ctr., L.A., 1991-92; thoracic surgery fellow Barnes Hosp. Washington U., St. Louis, 1992-94; asst. prof. surgery U. So. Calif., L.A., 1994—. Fellow Am. Coll. Surgeons, Soc. Thoracic Surgeons. Office: U So Calif Dept Surgery 1510 San Pablo St Ste 415 Los Angeles CA 90033

HAGEN, MICHAEL DALE, family physician educator; b. St. Louis, Nov. 11, 1949; s. Hubert Dale and Gwendel (Carden) H.; m. Barbara Carroll Keifer, Aug. 21, 1971; children: Laura Carrol, Sandra Ann. BS in Biology, Demson U., 1971; MD cum laude, U. Mo., Columbia, 1975. Cert. family practice bd. Pvt. practice Family Medicine Assocs., Aurora, Mo., 1978-81; asst. prof. dept. family practice U. Ky., Lexington, 1981-87, assoc. prof. dept. family practice, 1987-92, prof. dept. family practice, 1993—, interim chmn. dept. family practice, 1992-93, assoc. chmn. dept. family practice, 1993—; fellow Clin. Decision Making, New Eng. Med. Ctr., Boston, 1987-89; at-large dir. Am. Bd. Family Practice, Lexington, 1991-96, pres., 1995-96; residency rev. com. family practice Accreditation Coun. for Grad. Med. Edn., Chgo., 1994—. Author: Saunders Review Family Practice, 1992; contbr. articles to profl. jours. Mem. AMA, Am. Acad. Family Practice (clin. policies task force Kansas City chpt. 1994-95), Soc. for Med. Decision Making, Soc. for Tchrs. Family Medicine, Alpha Omega Alpha, Phi Kappa Phi, Omicron Delta Kappa. Presbyterian. Home: 2012 Blairmore Rd Lexington KY 40502 Office: Univ Ky Dept Family Practice 740 S Limestone Lexington KY 40536-0284

HAGEN, NICHOLAS STEWART, medical educator, consultant; b. Plentywood, Mont., Aug. 6, 1942; s. William Joseph and June Janette (Reuter) H.; m. Mary Louise Edvalson, July 26, 1969; children: Brian Geoffrey, Lisa Louise, Eric Christopher, Aaron Daniel, David Michael. BS in Chemistry, Ariz. State U., 1964; MBA in Internat. Bus., George Washington U., 1969; MD, U. Ariz., 1974. Lic. physician Ariz., Utah, Idaho.; diplomate Nat. Bd. Med. Examiners. Intern., resident Good Samaritan Hosp., Phoenix, 1974-75; pvt. practice Roy, Utah, 1975-77; dir. clin. rsch. Abbott Labs., North Chicago, Ill., 1977-84; v.p. med. affairs Rorer Group Inc., Ft. Washington, Pa., 1984-88; clin. prof. Ariz. State U., Tempe, 1988-90; pres. Southwestern Clin. Rsch., Tempe, 1987—, Travel Profl. Internat., Tempe, 1989—. Author: Valproic Acid: A Review of Pharmacologic Properties and Clinical Use in Pharmacologic and Biochemical Properties of Drug Substances, 1979; contbr. articles to med. jours.; patentee in field. Bishop Ch. Jesus Christ of Latter-day Saints, Gurnee, Ill., 1981-84; various positions with local couns. Boy Scouts Am., 1988—; active Rep. campaigns, Mesa, Ariz., 1988—. Lt. comdr. USCG, 1965-69. Joan Mueller-Etter scholar Ariz. State U., 1960, Phelps-Dodge scholar Ariz. State U., 1961; NASA fellow Brigham Young U., 1964. Mem. Am. Coll. Sports Medicine, Eagle Forum, Nat. Right-to-Life Assn., Utah Hist. Soc., Nat. Geneal. Soc., Bucks County Geneal. Soc., Sons of Norway, Soc. Descendants Emigrants from Numedal Norway, Blue Key, Archons, Kappa Sigma, Beta Beta Beta, Alpha Epsilon Delta, Phi Eta Sigma, Sophos. Republican. Mormon. Office: 2111 S Alma School Rd Ste 26 Mesa AZ 85210-4008

HAGER, MARY HASTINGS, nutritionist, educator, consultant; b. Upland, Calif., Mar. 27, 1948; d. Howard Benjamin and Miriam Agnes (Sahlmann) Hastings; m. Douglas Francis Hager, Jan. 4, 1982; children: Marghet Janet, Bettina Miriam. BS in Foods and Nutrition, U. Del., 1971; MS in Nutrition and Dietetics, U. Calif., Davis, 1973, PhD in Nutrition, 1978. Registered, lic. dietitian. Nutritionist U. Calif. Sch. Medicine, Davis, 1973-74; staff scientist Procter and Gamble Co., Cin., 1978-83, devel. staff, 1986-87; asst. prof. Coll. Mount St. Joseph, Cin., 1983-85, Tex. Christian U., Ft. Worth, 1987-89; vis. lectr. Rutgers U., New Brunswick, N.J., 1989-90; assoc. prof. Coll. St. Elizabeth, Morristown, N.J., 1991-96, prof., assoc. dean, 1996—; cons. IGA Grocers, Cin., 1984-85, Hoffman-LaRoche Corp., Nutley, N.J., 1989-90, Procter and Gamble Co., Cin., 1990—; dietetic internship site visitor. Contbr. articles and abstracts to profl. publs. Legis. network coord. N.J. Dietetic Assn., 1992—, pres.-elect, 1996-97; chmn. bd. dirs. Greater Cin. Nutrition Coun., 1985-86; mem. edn. task force Am. Heart Assn., Ft. Worth, 1988-89; pub. edn. com. Am. Cancer Soc., Ft. Worth, 1988-89; mem. Health Care Reform Adv. Bd., 11th Congl. Dist., 1993-94. Grad. fellow Procter and Gamble Co., 1975-78; Amy Rextrew scholar U. Del., 1970; grantee Tex. Christian U. Rsch. Fund, 1988. Fellow Am. Dietetic Assn.; mem. AAAS, Am. Inst. Nutrition (rsch. award 1978), Am. Soc. Enteral Parenteral Nutrition Soc. for Nutrition Edn., N.J. Nutrition Coun., Mortar Bd., Sigma Xi. Democrat. Episcopalian. Home: 9 Jay Dr Randolph NJ 07869-4102 Office: Coll of St Elizabeth Dept Foods and Nutrition Morristown NJ 07960

HAGER, PAULA MICHELE, critical care nurse; b. Palmerton, Pa., Sept. 29, 1957; d. Edward L. and Pauline A. (Macalush) H. Diploma, Hazleton (Pa.) State Gen. Hosp, 1978. CCRN, ACLS. Staff nurse, med./surgical Coaldale (Pa.) State Gen. Hosp., 1978-86, staff nurse ICU/CCU, 1986-92; staff nurse ICU/CCU Miners Meml. Med. Ctr., 1992—; instr. ACLS, CPR. Vol. Am. Heart Assn. Mem. Pa. Nurses Assn.

HAGERSON, LAWRENCE JOHN, healthcare consultant; b. Lakewood, Ohio, Dec. 30, 1931; s. John Lawrence and Ruth Evelyn (Watson) H.; m. Shirley Lorraine Carter, July 2, 1955; children: Nancy Lynn, Tracy Ann, Laura Jane. BS in Econs., U. Pa., 1954, postgrad. in Economics, 1957-59. Cons. John Price Jones Co., N.Y.C., 1960-62, U.S Agy. for Internat. Devel. Southeast Asia, 1970-74; asst. to chancellor U. Calif., Santa Barbara, 1962-63, U. Mo., Kansas City, 1967-70; cons. Asia Found., Singapore, Malaysia, 1964-67; exec. v.p. Mid. Am. Health Edn. Consortium, Kansas City, 1970-78; dir. bus. and devel. Inst. Logopedics, Wichita, Kans., 1978-88; dir. devel. The Conservancy, Naples, Fla., 1988-90. Mem., officer Kans. City Civic Orchestra Bd., 1976-78; bd. dirs. Greater Kans. City Urban Coalition, 1969-70. Served to lt. USN, 1954-56. Mem. Nat. Soc. Fund Raising Execs. (nat. bd. dirs. 1984-88). Republican. Presbyterian. Avocation: golf. Home: 4260 Hawaii Blvd Naples FL 33962-3730

HAGMEIER, CLARENCE HOWARD, anesthesiologist, retired; b. Pitts., Dec. 23, 1914; s. Clarence Howard and Bertha May (Rogers) H.; m. Hilda Marie Bronder, Oct. 30, 1942; children: Clarence, Roberta, Susan, David, Michael. BS with honor, U. Pitts., 1943, MD, 1950. Diplomate Am. Bd. Anesthesiology; Oreg. State Bd. Med. Examiners. Intern Good Samaritan Hosp., Portland, Oreg., 1950-51; resident Oreg. Med. Sch. and Hosp., 1951-53; pvt. practice Portland, 1953-87; ret., 1987. With USN, WWII. Fellow Am. Coll. Anesthesiologists, Internat. Coll. Surgeons, Theta Chi, Chi Rho Nu, Phi Rho Sigma. Republican. Home: 4907 SW Canterbury Ln Portland OR 97219

HAGNER, SAMUEL BENEDICT, retired psychiatrist; b. Phila., Nov. 1, 1925; s. George Wills Sr. and Evelyn (Benedict) H.; m. Elizabeth Jean Cunningham, July 22, 1950; children: Martha H. Leathe, David G., Thomas C. AB, Oberlin Coll., 1949; MD, Temple U., 1954; grad., Phila. Psychoanalytic Soc., 1969. Diplomate Am. Bd. Psychiatry and Neurology. Intern Germantown Hosp., Phila., 1954-55; resident in psychiatry Temple U., Phila., 1955-58, rsch. asst. Sch. Medicine, 1958-65, instr. Sch. Medicine, 1958-69; pvt. practice, Phila. and Dover, N.H., 1958-94; chief dept. psychiatry Wentworth-Douglass Hosp., Dover, 1982-83, cons., 1969-91; ret., 1994; examiner Social Security Disability Unit, Concord, N.H., 1978-94. Contbr. articles to profl. jours. Staff sgt. U.S. Army, 1944-46. Fellow Am. Psychiat. Assn. (life); mem. N.H. Psychiat. Soc. (continuing edn. com. 1972-76, peer rev. com. 1975-76, exec. coun. 1977-79), N.H. Med. Soc.

HAGOOD, M. FELTON, surgeon; b. Marietta, Ga., Oct. 18, 1941; s. Murl Miller and Mary Evelyn (Jones) H.; m. Martha Addie James, June 20, 1965; children: Gregory Felton, Robert Miller, Richard James. MD, Emory U., 1966. Diplomate Am. Bd. Surgery. Am. Bd. Colon & Rectal Surgery. Intern U. Va. Hosp., Charlottesville, 1966-67, surg. resident, 1967-68; med. officer Charleston Naval Hosp. U.S. Navy, 1968-70; resident gen. surgery Med. U. S.C., 1970-73; fellow colon & rectal surgery Ochsner Found. Hosp., New Orleans, 1973-74; pvt. practice-colon & rectal surgery Kennestone Hosp., Marietta, 1974—. past pres. Am. Cancer Soc., 1978. Lt. cmdr. USNR, 1968-70. Mem. Cobb County Med. Soc. (pres. 1993-94), Kiwanis Club, Phi Beta Kappa, Alpha Omega Alpha. Methodist. Home: 577 Keeler Woods Dr Marietta GA 30064-2043 Office: Surg Assocs of Marietta 790 Church St Ste 500 Marietta GA 30060-7290

HAGOOD, SUSAN STEWART HAHN, clinical dietitian; b. Balt., May 31, 1953; d. Paul Gilbert and Phyllis Jeanette (Mann) Hahn; m. Thomas Richard Hagood, Jr., Nov. 25, 1978; 1 child, Margaret Foster. BS, Western Ky. U., 1975; MS, Ga. State U., 1992. Registered and lic. dietitian. Dietetic trainee U. Hosp., Jacksonville, Fla., 1975-76; clin. dietitian VA Med. Ctr., Lake City, Fla., 1976-80; in-service and staff devel. dietitian VA Med. Ctr., Lake City, 1980-85; clin. specialist Clayton Gen. Hosp., Riverdale, Ga., 1985-88; grad. teaching asst. Ga. State U., 1991; ambulatory care dietitian VA Med. Ctr., Atlanta, 1992—. Pres. Lake City (Fla.) Hist. Preservation Bd., 1982-83; chmn. youth adv. com. Columbia County 4-H, Lake City, 1981-84; vol. instr. Tech. Assistance Health Resource Group, Lake City, 1982-84; co-chmn. Com. for Restoration Columbia County Hist. Mus., 1983-84; bd. dirs. Clayton County unit Am. Heart Assn., 1987-88; mem. Dekalb unit nutrition and cancer work group Am. Cancer Soc., 1993—; leader Avondale-Decatur svc. unit Girl Scouts U.S.A., 1993—. Mem. Am. Dietetic Assn., Atlanta Dist. Dietetic Assn., Atlanta English Speaking Union, DAR, Colonial Dames Am., Colonial Dames XVII Century, Phi Upsilon Omicron, Alpha Xi Delta. Republican. Presbyterian. Home: PO Box 982 Decatur GA 30031-0982 Office: VA Medical Ctr 1670 Clairmont Rd Decatur GA 30033

HAGOPIAN, GLORIA ANN, oncology nursing educator; b. Binghamton, N.Y., Oct. 10, 1938; d. Newman and Pearl Jeanette (Williams) H. BSN, U. Rochester, 1964, MSN, 1970, EdD, 1979. Staff nurse Binghamton (N.Y.) Gen. Hosp., 1959-62, instr. of nursing, 1964-68; instr. of nursing U. Rochester (N.Y.) Sch. of Nursing, 1970-73, asst. prof. nursing, 1973-77; asst. prof. nursing U. Pa., Phila., 1979-88, assoc. prof. of oncology nursing, 1988-93; assoc. prof. Coll. Nursing U. N.C., Charlotte, 1993—; assoc. project dir. Oncology Nursing, U. Pa., Phila., 1986-93. Co-author: (with others) Clinical Assessment: A Guide for Study, 1987, (with Hymovich) Chronic Illness in Children & Adults: A Psychosocial Approach, 1992; contbr. articles to profl. jours. Mem. ANA, N.C. Nurses Assn., Charlotte Area Chpt. Oncology Nursing Soc., Oncology Nursing Soc., Sigma Theta Tau. Home: 3220 Devon Croft Ln Charlotte NC 28269-9746 Office: U NC Coll Nursing Charlotte NC 28223

HAHIN, RICHARD, neurophysiologist; b. Buffalo, Nov. 23, 1946; s. Leo Paul and Nancy (Morabito) H. BSEE, Mich. State U., 1968; PhD in Physiology, U. Md., Balt., 1978. Elec. engr. Naval Ship Rsch. & Devel. Lab., Annapolis, Md., 1968-70; lab. scientist U. Md. Med. Sch., Balt., 1974-76; postdoctoral fellow SUNY, Stony Brook, 1978-80; assoc. U. Iowa, Iowa City, 1981-82, vis. asst. prof. biology, 1982-85; asst. prof. biology No. Ill. U., De Kalb, 1985-90, assoc. prof., 1991—; vis. scientist Australian Nat. U., Canberra, 1985, U. Md., Balt., 1985; cons. Harvard Med. Sch. Anesthesia Labs., Boston, 1989; mentor for students Ill. Math. & Sci. Acad., Aurora, 1989-93; delegation mem. Biophysicists in People's Rep. China, 1989. Contbr. articles to profl. jours. Muscular Dystrophy Assn. fellow, 1978; USPHS Jr. Faculty awardee, 1982; Dept. of Energy grantee, 1988; NSF grantee, 1985. Mem. Internat. Soc. Toxinology, Biophys. Soc., Soc. Gen. Physiologists, Soc. for Neurosci. Home: 4309 Susan Curve Cortland IL 60112 Office: No Ill U Biological Sciences Dept De Kalb IL 60115

HAHM, KI BAIK, gastroenterologist; b. Seoul, Korea, Mar. 3, 1959; s. Byung Han Hahm and Soon Ja Lee; m. Hye Won Choi, Feb. 25, 1984; 1 child, Yun Sum. MD, Yonsei U., Seoul, 1983, MS, 1986, PhD, 1992. Cert. Bd. Internal Medicine, Bd. Gastroenterology & Gastrointestinal Endoscopy. Chief 125 Med. Dispensary, Euijungbu, Korea, 1987-90; rsch. fellow Yonsei U., 1990-91, instr. medicine, 1992-94, asst. prof. medicine, 1994-96; cons. Korea Med. Ins. Corp., 1994—; rschr. Inst. Gastroenterology Sch. Medicine Yonsu U., 1992—, Inst. Med. Sci. Ajou U., 1995—, Inst. Cancer Rsch. Yonsei U., 1991—. Contbr. articles to profl. jours. Recipient Young Investigator award Internat. Soc. Gastroenterology, 1991, World Congress Gstroenterology, 1994. Mem. Korean Soc. Gastroentestinal Endoscopy (assoc.), Korean Soc. Free Radical Rsch., Korean Soc. Cancer. Office: Ajou U Sch Medicine, San 5 Wonchun-dong, Paldal-ku Suwon 442-749, Korea

HAHN, ELLIOT FRANK, pharmaceutical company executive; b. N.Y.C., June 28, 1944; s. Ludwig and Erna (Reisler) H.; m. Lillian R. Helfman, Aug. 11, 1968; children: Barry, David, Aviva. BS, CCNY, 1966; PhD, Cornell U., 1970. Vis. scientist Technion U., Haifa, Israel, 1971-72; investigator Inst. Steroid Rsch. Montefiore Hosp., N.Y.C., 1972-75; asst. prof. biochemistry Albert Einstein Coll. Medicine, N.Y.C., 1976-77; asst. prof. Rockefeller U., N.Y.C., 1977-83, assoc. prof., 1983-88; assoc. dir. rsch. and devel. IVAX Pharms., Miami, Fla., 1988-89; assoc. prof. biochemistry U. Miami (Fla.) Sch. Medicine, 1988—; v.p. rsch. Baker Cummins Pharms., Miami, 1989-92; v.p. sci. affairs IVAX Corp., Miami, 1992-93; pres. Andrx Corp., Ft. Lauderdale, Fla., 1993—; cons. Nova Pharms., Balt., 1983-86, Unigene Labs., Fairfield, N.J., 1984-88, Lark Labs., N.Y.C., 1982-86; prin. investigator NIH, 1987-90. Contbr. over 60 articles to profl. jours. mem. rsch. rev. com. Mental Health Ctr., Pomona, N.Y., 1977-83; cons. Rockland County Narcotic Task Force, New City, N.Y., 1977-85. N.Y. Heart Assn. fellow, 1982-87. Mem. AAAS, Am. Chem. Soc., N.Y. Acad. Scis., Am. Men and Women of Sci., Sigma Xi. Office: Andrx Corp 4001 SW 47th Ave # 201 Fort Lauderdale FL 33314-4030

HAHN, ROBERT GUSTAV, anesthesiology educator; b. Stockholm, Mar. 14, 1954; s. Gunnar Arvid and Elsa Karolina (Ekstrom) H.; m. Marie-Louise Anne Lindström, Sept. 14, 1991; children: Magdalena, Martina, Maria. Student, Dartmouth Coll., 1973-74; MD, Karolinska Inst., Stockholm, 1982, PhD, 1987. Intern Karolinska Inst., Stockholm, 1974-82; anesthetist Huddinge Hosp., Stockholm, 1982-86, cons. anesthesia, 1986-89, chief urol. and gynecol. anesthesia, 1989-93; assoc. prof. anesthesia Söder Hosp., Stockholm, 1993—; head dept., bd. Instn. of South Hosp., Stockholm, 1995—; mem. ednl. com. Karolinska Inst., Stockholm, 1995—. Contbr. articles and revs. to profl. jours. Sgt. Swedish Army, 1973, 78. Grantee Swedish Med. Rsch. Coun., Stockholm, 1993—. Mem. Swedish Anesthesiologists Assn., Nordic Assn. Anesthesiologists, Swedish Med. Assn. Home: Eklidsvägen 12, 14640 Tullinge, Stockholm Sweden Office: Söder Hosp, Dept Anesthesia, 11883 Stockholm Sweden

HAIGHT, DAVID HULEN, physician; b. Highland Park, Ill., Mar. 30, 1954; s. Thomas Hulen and Virginia Ellen (Olsson) H. AB in Biochemistry magna cum laude, Brown U., 1976; MD, Johns Hopkins U., 1980. Diplomate Am. Bd. Ophthalmology. Resident ophthalmology Manhattan Eye, Ear and Throat Hosp., N.Y.C., 1981-84, fellow in cornea dept., 1984-85, resident instr., ophthalmology, 1985-87, residency coord., 1989-91, chief Contact Lens Clinic I, 1986—, chief coord. investigator, 1991—, with laser rsch. study, 1991—; quality assurance com. Manhattan Eye, Ear and Throat Hosp., N.Y.C., 1987—, chmn. ophthalmology credentials com. 1993—; mem. adv. bd. N.Y. Eye Bank for Sight Restoration, N.Y.C., 1992—; skills transfer adv. com. Am. Acad. Ophthalmology, San Francisco, 1992—. Contbg. author: Corneal Surgery, 1986, 2nd edit., 1993. Fellow Am. Acad. Ophthalmology (honor award 1993); mem. Med. Soc. of State of N.Y., N.Y. State Ophthalmologic Soc., Internat. Soc. Refractive Surgery, Contact Lens Assn. of Ophthalmologists, Am. Soc. Cataract and Refractive Surgery, Phi Beta Kappa, Sigma Xi (assoc.). Office: 799 Park Ave New York NY 10021

HAIK, BARRETT GEORGE, ophthalmologist, educator; b. New Orleans, Sept. 8, 1951; s. George M. and Isabelle (Saloom) H.; m. Mary Bain, July 29, 1976; children: Barrett Christopher, Claire Marie. BS in Biology, Centenary Coll., 1972; MD, La. State U. Med. Ctr., 1976, MS in Anatomy. Diplomate Am. Bd. Ophthalmology. Intern Charity Hosp., New Orleans, 1977; resident in ophthalmology Edward S. Harkness Eye Inst.-Columbia U., N.Y.C.; vis. clin. fellow Columbia U., N.Y.C., 1977-80; asst. prof. Cornell U., N.Y.C., 1980-84, assoc. prof., 1984-86; asst. mem. clin. affiliated Meml. Sloan-Kettering Cancer Ctr., N.Y.C., 1984-86; prof. ophthalmology Tulane U. Med. Ctr., New Orleans, 1986-95; chmn. and Hamilton prof. U. Tenn. Dept. Ophthalmology, Memphis, 1995—; mem. Internat. Com. on Classification of Intraocular Retinoblastoma, 1994—. Named to Regent's Chair George M. Haik Sr. M.D., St. Giles Found. Prof. of Pediatric and Adult Ophthalmic Oncology, 1991. Fellow Am. Coll. of Surgeons, Am. Acad. Ophthalmology (Honor award 1988), N.Y. Acad. Medicine; mem. Am. Eye Study Club (pres. 1993-94), Am. Inst. Ultrasound in Medicine (chmn. ophthalmology sect. 1990-95), Memphis and Shelby County Med. Soc., Tenn. Acad. Ophthalmology. Office: U Tenn Dept Ophthalmology 956 Court Rm D228 Memphis TN 38163

HAIK, KENNETH GEORGE, ophthalmologist; b. New Orleans, Jan. 18, 1950; s. George Michel and Isabelle (Saloom) H.; children: K. Augutus, Edward Trippe. MD, Tulane U., 1975. Diplomate Am. Bd. Ophthalmology. Intern, resident Charity Hosp., New Orleans; pvt. practice New Orleans, 1978—; active staff Eye, Ear, Nose and Throat Hosp., Mercy-Bapt. Hosp., East Jefferson Gen. Hosp.; courtesy staff Kenner Regional Hosp., St. Charles Parish Hosp.; clin. instr. ophthalmology Tulane U., New Orleans, 1978-80, clin. asst. prof., 1980—; clin. asst. prof. La. State U., New Orleans, 1984—. Contbr. articles to profl. jours. Mem. So. Med. Assn., Am. Acad. Ophthalmology. Office: George M Haik Eye Clinic 1407 S Carrollton Ave New Orleans LA 70118-2809

HAIMOWITZ, DANIEL, physician; b. Phila., Aug. 25, 1960; s. Samuel Isaac amd Esthella (Halter) H.; m. Susan Jean Frick, Oct. 13, 1991. BS, Pa. State U., 1981; MD, Jefferson Med. Coll., 1983. Diplomate Am. Bd. Internal Medicine. Staff mem. Lower Bucks Hosp., Bristol, Pa., 1986—, St. Mary Med. Ctr., Langhorne, Pa., 1986—; med. dir. Attleboro Nursing & Rehab. Ctr., Langhorne, 1986—; staff physician Statesman Nursing Home, Levittown, Pa., 1986—, Langhorne Gardens Nursing Home, 1986—, Silver Lake Nursing Home, Bristol, 1986—, Crestview North Nursing Home, Langhorne, 1986-96, Leader of Yardley Nursing Home, 1986—; staff physician Millrun Personal Care, Bristol, 1986—, Yardley, 1995; adv. physician Arden Courts Assisted Living, Yardley, 1995—. Fellow Am. Coll. Physicians; mem. AMA, Am. Geriatric Soc., Am. Med. Dirs. Assn., Pa. Med. Soc., Delaware Valley Geriatrics Soc. Democrat. Jewish. Home and Office: 1 Gardenia Rd Levittown PA 19057

HAIMOWITZ, NATALIE READER, psychologist; b. N.Y.C., May 27, 1923; d. Philip Reader and Esther (Fetner) Reader Orel; m. Morris L. Haimowitz, Dec. 31, 1948; children: Carla, Myrna, Louise. BA in Psychology, Bklyn. Coll., 1944; MA in Clin. Psychology, Ohio State U., 1945; PhD in Human Devel., U. Chgo., 1948. Lectr. Bklyn. Coll., 1947-48; instr. U. Chgo., 1953-58; chief psychologist Women's and Children's Hosp., 1955-59; psychologist Milw. Psychiat. Svcs., 1960-64; clin. pvt. practice psychology, 1955—; co-dir. Haimowoods Inst., 1972—; trainer, supr. clin. practice psychology, 1968—; intern Ohio State U. Psychol. Clinic, 1944-45, mem. faculty dept. behavioral sci., U. Wis., 1978-79; extern Counseling Ctr., U. Chgo., 1946-47; postdoctoral trainee mental hygiene clinic U.S. VA, 1949-51; trainee Transactional Analysis Assn., 1967, teaching mem., 1971. Co-author: (with Morris Haimowitz) Human Development, 1960, revised edit., 1966, 73, (with Morris Haimowitz) Suffering Is Optional, 1976, (with others) Success in Psychotherapy, 1952; contbr. articles to profl. jours. Home and Office: 1101 Forest Ave Evanston IL 60202-1407

HAINES, FRANCIS XAVIER, psychiatrist; b. Binghamton, N.Y., Nov. 1, 1947. BS, U. Notre Dame, 1969; MD, Georgetown U., 1975. Cert. psychiatrist, R.I., Mass. Resident in psychiatry Brown U., Providence, 1975-78; staff psychiatrist Providence Ctr., 1978—; asst. prof. psychiatry Brown U., 1980—; pvt. practice Providence, R.I., 1985—; mem. staff Butler Hosp., Providence. Office: Family Assocs, Bldg B 35 S Angell St Providence RI 02906

HAINES, STEPHEN JOHN, neurological surgeon; b. Burlington, Vt., Sept. 4, 1949; s. Gerald Leon and Frances Mary (Whitcomb) H.; children: Christopher, Jeremy. AB, Dartmouth Coll., 1971; MD, U. Vermont, 1975. Diplomate Am. Bd. Neurological Surgery; diplomate Nat. Bd. Med. Examiners. Intern U. Minn., Mpls., 1975-76; neurol. surgery resident U. Pitts., 1976-81; asst. prof. neurosurgery U. Minn., Mpls., 1982-87, assoc. prof. neurosurgery and otolaryngology, 1987-93, prof. neurosurgery and otolaryngology and pediatrics, 1993—, head. div. pediatric neurosurgery, 1985—. Contbr. articles to profl. jour. Fellow ACS; mem. Am. Assn. Neurol. Surgeons (Van Wagenen fellow 1981), Congress Neurol. Surgeons (pres. 1996), Soc. Clin. Trials. Office: U Minn Dept Neurosurgery 420 Delaware St SE Minneapolis MN 55455-0374

HAINING, JEANE, psychologist; b. Camden, N.J., May 2, 1952; d. Lester Edward and Adina (Rahn) H. BA in Psychology, Calif. State U., 1975; MA in Sch. Psychology, Pepperdine U., 1979; MS in Recreation Therapy, Calif. State U., 1982; PhD in Psychology, Calif. Sch. Profl. Psychology, 1985. Lic. clin. psychologist 1987, lic. ednl. psychologist 1982. Crisis counselor Calif. State U., Northridge, 1973-74; recreation therapist fieldwork Camarillo (Calif.) State Hosp.-Adolescent/Children's Units, 1974—; Intern recreation therapist UCLA Neuropsychiatric Inst., L.A., 1975-76; substitute tchr./recreation therapist New Horizons Sch. for Mentally Retarded, Sepulveda, Calif., 1976-79; intern sch. psychologist Los Nietos (Calif.) Sch. Dist., 1977-79; sch. psychologist Rialto (Calif.) Unified Sch. Dist., 1979-82; clin. psychologist field work San Joaquin County Dept. Mental Health, Stockton, Calif., 1982-83; intern clinical psychologist Fuller Theol. Sem. Psychology Ctr., Pasadena, Calif., 1984-85; clin. psychologist U.S. Dept. Justice, Terminal Island, Calif., 1985-86; cmty. mental health psychologist L.A. County Dept. Mental Health, 1987-89; clin. psychologist Calif. Dept. Corrections, Parole Outpatient Clinic, L.A., 1990—, Mary Magdeline Project, Commerce, Calif., 1992—; mem. psychiat.-psychol. panel adult and juvenile Superior Ct., L.A., 1992—; mem. psychiat. panel U.S. Dist. Ct. (cen. dist.) Calif., L.A., 1989—; clin. psychologist O. Carl Simonton Cancer Ctr., Pacific Palisades, Calif., 1993—. Adv. bd. Camarillo (Calif.) State Hosp., 1994—; examiner Lic. Ednl. Psychologist Oral Examinations, Calif. Bd. Behavioral Sci. Examinations, Sacramento, 1985. Recipient award Outstanding Achievement Western Psychology Conf., Calif., 1974. Mem. Am. Psychol. Assn., Calif. Psychol. Assn., L.A. Psychol. Assn., Forensic Mental Health Assn. (con. planning com. 1993). Democrat. Lutheran. Office: 307 W 4th St Los Angeles CA 90013

HAINLINE, BRIAN, neurologist; b. Detroit, Dec. 23, 1955; s. Forrest Arthur Jr. and Nora Marie (Schrot) H.; m. Pascale Clauzet, Dec. 22, 1979; children: Clotilde, Arthur. BA, U. Notre Dame, 1978; MD, U. Chgo., 1982. Intern U. Chgo. Hosps. and Clinics, 1982-83; resident in neurology N.Y. Hosp., N.Y.C., 1983-86; attending neurologist North Shore U. Hosp., Manhasset, N.Y., 1986-91, program dir., acting co-chmn. dept. neurology, 1990-91; dir. sports and clin. neurology Hosp. for Joint Diseases, N.Y.C., 1991—, vice chmn. dept. neurology, 1994—, co-dir. The Pain Ctr., 1996—; instr. neurology Cornell U. Med. Coll., N.Y.C., 1986-87, asst. prof. neurology, 1987-91, NYU Sch. Medicine, 1991-95, clin. assoc. prof. of neurology, 1995—; med. rev. officer U.S. Tennis Assn., N.Y.C., 1991—; chief med. officer U.S. Open Tennis Championships, Flushing Meadows, N.Y., 1992—; mem. med. commn. Internat. Tennis Fedn., London, 1993—. Author: USTA Drug Education Handbook, 1992; co-author: Drugs and the Athlete, 1989; co-editor: Neurological Complications of Pregnancy, 1994; contbr. articles to profl. jours. and chpts. to books. Mem. Am. Acad. Neurology, Physicians for Social Responsibility, Am. Coll. Sports Medicine. Home: 122 Grosvenor St Flushing NY 11363-1007 Office: Hosp for Joint Diseases 301 E 17th St New York NY 10003-3804

HAITH, MARSHALL MYRON, psychology educator; b. Chilicothe, Mo., Apr. 23, 1937; s. Nathan and Frances (Rabicoff) H.; m. Sue Ann Schneider, June 8, 1962; children: Michael, Brian, Gary. BA, U. Mo., 1959; MA, UCLA, 1962, PhD, 1964. Predoctoral fellow UCLA, 1962-64; postdoctoral fellow Yale U., New Haven, 1964-66; asst. prof. Harvard U., Boston, 1966-72; prof. psychology U. Denver, 1972—. Author: Rules that Babies Look By, 1980, The Development of Future-Oriented Processes, 1994, Child Psychology: The Modern Science, 1995, Reason and Responsibility: The Passage Through Childhood, 1996. Recipient Research Scientist award NIMH; grantee NIH, 1985—, NIMH, 1972—; Guggenheim Found. fellow, 1978-79, fellowship Ctr. for Advanced Study in the Behavioral Scis., 1988-89. Fellow Am. Psychol. Assn., AAAS, Soc. Research in Child Devel., Internat. Soc. Study of Behavioral Devel. (editorial bd.). Home: 39 Viking Dr Englewood CO 80110-7003 Office: U Denver Psychology Dept Denver CO 80208

HAJCAK, FRANK, psychologist, cartoonist, writer, photographer, consultant; b. Pottsville, Pa., Nov. 3, 1940; s. Joseph Anthony and Celestine (Kassak) H.; m. Maria Komjati (div.); 1 child, Greg; m. Tricia Garwood, Sept. 28, 1985. BA, Rider Coll., 1967; MA, Temple U., 1969, PhD in Clin. Psychology, 1976; MA in Sch. Psychology, Millersville Coll., 1978. Lic. clin. psychologist; cert. sch. psychologist. Dir. psychol. and social services Don Guanella Sch., Springfield, Pa., 1971-76; pvt. practice clin. psychology West Chester, Pa., 1976—; instr. Immaculata (Pa.) Coll., 1976, Widener Coll., Chester, Pa., 1977; ednl. cons. Chester County Intermediate Unit, Coatesville, Pa., 1979-87; cons. Downingtown (Pa.) Com. on Child Abuse, 1986—; dir. Inst. for Study and Devel. Human Potential, West Chester, 1982—. Author: Expanding Creative Imagination, 1981, Hidden Bedroom Partners: Needs and Motives That Destroy Sexual Pleasure, 1987, French edit., 1990, Polish edit., 1994; co-author workbook Expanding Creative Imagination, 1983, Expanding Creative Imagination: Power Through Active Perception, 1993, Korean edit., 1995, (cartoon book) Great Moments in Olympic History: 5 Million B.C.-3002 A.D., 1993; contbr. articles and photographs to various publs.; poetry pub. in anthology Voice of Am. Cons. March of Dimes, Media, Pa., 1976; competitor Sunoco ultra team 1989 U.S. Open Volleyball Championships, Toledo. NIMH grantee, 1970. Mem. Pa. Psychol. Assn., Soc. for Sci. Study of Sex. Unitarian Universalist. Home and Office: 880 Downingtown Pike West Chester PA 19380-1935

HAKANSON, ERICK YNGVE, physician; b. Smaland, Sweden, Nov. 13, 1920; came to U.S., 1923; s. Theodor Erik and Amanda Charlotta Hakanson; m. Karin Maria Hellzen, Jan. 2, 1950; children: Sten Erik, Nina Maria, Lisa Hellzen, Karl Ivar. BS, U. Minn., 1942, BS in medicine, 1944, MD, 1945, MS, 1948. Postdoctoral fellow Nat. Cancer Industry, Bethesda, Md., 1949-50; fellow ob-gyn. U. Minn., 1950-53; dir. ob-gyn. dept. Anchor Hosp., St. Paul, 1954-64; head dept. ob-gyn. St. Paul Ramsey Hosp., 1964-89; prof. U. Minn., Mpls., 1979-89, prof. emeritus, 1989—. Nat. del. Democratic Conv., 1972. Lt. (j.g.) USNR, 1944-45, with USMC, 1945-46, lt. (s.g.) USNR, 1953-54. Postdoctoral fellow Nat. Cancer Inst., Bethesda, Md., 1949-50; various rsch. grants, 1966-86. Mem. Am. Coll. Ob-Gyn., Am. Uro Gynecology Soc., Am. Assn. Profs. of Ob-Gyn. Democrat. Home: 950 Lincoln Ave Saint Paul MN 55105 Office: St Paul Ramsey Med Ctr 646 Jackson Saint Paul MN 55105

HAKIM-ELAHI, ENAYAT, obstetrician, gynecologist, educator; b. Teheran, Iran, Nov. 23, 1934; came to U.S., 1959, naturalized, 1973; s. Mohamed-Ali and Masoomeh Rahimi; M.D., Med. Sch., Teheran, 1959; lic. physician, Maine, Conn., Vt., N.Y., N.H., Calif.; diplomate Am. Bd. Ob-Gyn. m. Renate Emsters, Nov. 15, 1967; 1 child, Cristina. Intern, Queens Hosp. Ctr., N.Y.C., 1960, resident in internal medicine, 1961, resident in ob-gyn, 1961-64, resident in radiotherapy of gynecologic cancer, Am. Cancer Soc. fellow Queens div., 1965; resident in gynecology Cancer Rsch. Inst., Columbia-Presbyn. Med. Ctr., N.Y.C., 1964-65; practice medicine specializing in ob-gyn, N.Y.C., 1968—; mem. staff N.Y. Hosp., N.Y.C.; med. dir. Margaret Sanger Ctr., N.Y.C., 1973—, Planned Parenthood of N.Y.C., 1977—, LaGuardia Hosp., Forest Hills, 1993-95; asst. prof. ob-gyn Cornell U. Med. Coll., N.Y.C., 1973—, assoc. prof., 1995—; dir. dept. of ob-gyn LaGuardia Hosp., 1990-95, med. dir., 1993-95; dir. dept of ob-gyn Harlem Hosp. Ctr., 1995—. Served with U.S. Army, 1965-67. Fellow ACS, Am. Coll. Obstetricians and Gynecologists, Internat. Coll. Surgeons, Am. Fertility Soc.; mem. Am. Soc. Gynecol. Laparoscopists, Am. Soc. Colposcopy and Cervical Neoplasia, Am. Pub. Health Assn., Am. Coll. Physician Execs., Assn. of Reproductive Health Profls., Royal Soc. Medicine (London), World Med. Assn., N.Y. State Med. Soc., Queens Gynecol. Soc. Contbr. articles to profl. jours.

HAKKARINEN, WILLIAM DAVID, family practitioner; b. Washington, Jan. 18, 1944; s. William and Vilma Helen (Pynnonen) H.; m. Bonnie Sue Schellinger, June 11, 1966 (div. June 1977); 1 child, Michael August; m. Marsha Dale Howes, Dec. 8, 1978; 1 child, Sirkka Elizabeth. BS in Zoology, U. Md., College Park, 1966; MD, U. Md., Balt., 1970. Diplomate Am. Bd. Family Practice. Intern family practice U. Md. Hosp., Balt., 1970-71; chief resident in family medicine M.S. Hershey (Pa.) Med. Ctr., 1972-73; med. dir. E.G. Frederick Health Ctr. Pa. State U., Millersburg, 1975-78; med. dir. Rural Health Corp. Northeastern Pa., Wilkes-Barre, 1978-82; program dir. Wyoming Valley Family Practice Residency, Kingston, Pa., 1982-89; chmn. dept. family practice Franklin Square Hosp. Ctr., Balt., 1989—; fellow in faculty devel. Mich. State U., East Lansing, 1985-86. Vol. B&O R.R. Mus., Balt., 1991—. Lt. comdr. M.C., USN, 1973-75. Fellow Am. Acad. Family Physicians (Mead Johnson award 1973); mem. AMA, Soc. Tchrs. Family Medicine, Md. Acad. Family Physicians (v.p. 1993-95). Office: Franklin Square Hosp Ctr 9000 Franklin Square Dr Baltimore MD 21237

HAKOLA, HANNU PANU AUKUSTI, psychiatry educator; b. Lapua, Finland, Feb. 22, 1932; s. Aukusti Jalmari and Toini Kyllikki (Tikkanen) H.; m. Maija-Leena Salo, Apr. 19, 1954; children: Jouni, Marja, Jorma, Jaakko. MD, U. Turku, Finland, 1956, MA, 1960, PhD, 1972. Diploma in health adminstrn. Nat. Bd. Health, Finland, 1979. Asst. physician Neuropsychiat. Clinic, Turku, 1956-60; chief psychiatrist Harjamäki Hosp., Siilinjärvi, Finland, 1960-69, Niuvanniemi Hosp., Kuopio, Finland, 1969-83; prof. forensic psychiatry U. Kuopio, Finland, 1983-95; med. dir. Harjamaki Hosp., Silinjarvi, 1969-95. Author: On Environmental Conditions of Criminal Psychopaths, 1959, Clinical Aspect of a New Hereditary Disease, 1972, Polycystic Lipomembranous Osteodysplasia with sclerosing Leukeoncephalopathy, 1990; editor: Symposium on Forensic Psychiatry, 1988; inventor Carbamazepine in Schizophrenia, 1982, Duraljan Superfamily, 1989; editorial bd. Med. Jour. Duodecim, 1975-81; contbr. over 250 articles to profl. jours. and chpts. to books. Bd. dirs. Kuopio U. Ctrl. Hosp., 1985-89, 93—. Decorated knight Finnish Order of White Rose; comdr. Finnish Order of Lion; Paulo Found. grantee, Helsinki, Finland, 1971, Aaltonen Found. grantee, Tampere, Finland, 1973; recipient Prize, Acta Psychiat. Scandinavia, 1972. Mem. Finnish Med. Assn. (de. com. 1964—, exec. bd. 1980-84), Med. Assn. North-Savo (hon.), Rotary (pres. Puijo club 1974-75, Paul Harris fellow 1982, Blue Stone fellow 1995). Home: Satamakatu 3 D 49, FIN-70100 Kuopio Finland Office: Niuvanniemi Hosp, FIN 70240 Kuopio Finland

HALASZ, GEORGE, psychiatrist, consultant; b. Budapest, Hungary, July 6, 1949; came to Australia, 1957; s. Laszlo and Alice (Klein) H. Intern Prince Henry's Hosp., Melbourne, Victoria, Australia, 1975-76; sr. house officer Brook Gen. Hosp., London, 1976; resident Beilinson Hosp., Petah Tikva, Tel Aviv, 1977; sr. house officer Middlesex Hosp., London, 1977; registrar King's Coll. Hosp., London, 1978-82; sr. registrar Maudsley, Bethlem Royal Hosp., London, 1982-84; cons. Austin Hosp., Melbourne, 1985-87, Monash Med. Ctr., Melbourne, 1987—; tutor Melbourne U., 1985—; hon. sr. lectr. Monash U., 1987-88; sr. lectr. 1988-93. Editorial bd. mem. Australian and New Zealand Jour. of Psychiatry, 1992—. Fellow Royal Australian and N.Z. Coll. Psychiatrists; mem. Royal Coll. Psychiatrists, Eng., Family Therapy Assn. Victoria, Assn. Psychoanalytic Psychotherapy (assoc.). Club: Lit. of Orlando (Fla.). Office: 30 Burke Rd East Med Stes, Melbourne Victoria 3145, Australia

HALBERSTADT, ROBERT BILHEIMER, optometrist; b. Stockertown, Pa., Feb. 11, 1918; s. Joseph Victor and Lillian (Bilheimer) H.; O.D., No. Ill. Coll. Optometry, 1939; m. Mary Margaret Gassner, Nov. 9, 1940; children: Mary Diane Seip, Victoria Milou Mackenzie. Optometrist, Nazareth, Pa., 1940—; cons. Optometry Whitehall-Coplay Sch. Dist., 1966-78, Pathway Sch., Norristown, Pa. 1966-67, Miller Clinic, Stroudsburg, Pa., 1971-74, Learning Center, Scranton (Pa.) Pub. Schs., 1971-72; staff optometrist, cons. Allentown State Hosp., 1967-68; extern Gesell Inst., New Haven, 1967-68. Active Lehigh Valley Assn. for Brain Damaged Child, 1965-68; 2d Assn. for Brain Damaged Children, 1966-68; program chmn. Lehigh Valley Assn. for Children with Learning Disabilities, 1969-74, bd. dirs., 1971-74, 1st v.p., 1973-74; mem. Council Exceptional Children; with Friendship House, Scranton, 1973-75; mem. pres.'s club Ill. Coll. Optometry, 1973—, Century Club, 1976-88; mem. nat. pilot project team on formation fo spl. edn. model Intermediate Sch. Unit 20 of Pa., 1980-81; mem. Nazareth Area Residents for Clean Air, 1991. With USNR, 1944-46. Mem. Optometric Extension Program (state dir. 1950-58, regional dir. 1958-84, life mem. Pioneer Fund 1987—), Pa. Optometric Assn. (treas. 1948-57). Address: 116 S Broad St Nazareth PA 18064-2118

HALE, ALBERT SPENCER, JR., radiologist; b. Salem, Va., Nov. 19, 1933; s. Albert Spencer and Julia Caldwell (Meyer) H.; m. Lorraine Helen Decker, June 7, 1958; children: David W., Sharon M., Stephen M., Michael A. BS, Bowman Gray Sch. Medicine, 1954; MD, Bowman Gray Sch. Medicine, Winston-Salem, N.C., 1958. Diplomate Am. Bd. Radiology., Am. Bd. Nuclear Medicine. Intern Grady Meml. Hosp., Atlanta, 1958-59; resident in radiology Bowman Gray Sch. Medicine, 1961-64; advanced through grades to col. USAF, 1959-89; chief profl. svcs. 517th Med. Group, Pease AFB, N.H., 1959-61; chief radiology svc. USAF Hosp. Carswell, Ft. Worth, 1964-67, USAF Hosp. Clark, Clark Air Base, The Philippines, 1967-69, USAF Acad. Hosp., Colo. Springs, Colo., 1969-74; chmn. dept. radiology Wilford Hall USAF Med. Ctr., Lackland AFB, Tex., 1974-89; chief radiology dept. Tex. Ctr. for Infectious Disease, San Antonio, 1990—. Fellow Am. Coll. Radiology; mem. Soc. Nuc. Medicine, Radiol. Soc. N.Am. Home: 5303 Chancellor St San Antonio TX 78229

HALE, BARBARA ANN, nursing administrator; b. Warren, Ind., Oct. 20, 1936; d. Dora Albert and Florence Helen (MacDonald) B.; m. Donald C. Hale, Sept. 14, 1957; children: Matthew Eric, Kimberly Ann. Diploma, Ft. Wayne Lutheran Sch. Nursin, 1954; BSN, Ind. U. Sch. Nursing, 1978, MSN, 1982. Cert. nurse administr., advanced. Staff nurse Lutheran Hosp., Ft. Wayne, Ind., 1957-60, Parkview Hosp., Ft. Wayne, 1960-62, Cookeville (Tenn.) Gen. Hosp., 1966-68; from staff nurse to v.p. ops./nursing Riverview Hosp., Noblesville, Ind., 1968—. Mem. ANA, Ind. Orgn. Nurse Execs. (lobbyist 1993, pres. 1994-95, sec./treas. 1988, legis. chmn. 1992), Ind. State Nurse Assn. (bd. dirs 1990-93), Sigma Theta Tau. Republican. Methodist. Office: Riverview Hosp 395 Westfield Rd Noblesville IN 46060

HALE, EDWARD HARNED, internist; b. Nashville, Sept. 15, 1923; s. William Jasper and Harriett Ewing (Hodgkins) H.; m. Barbara Benjamin Gandy Hale, Dec. 20, 1951 (div. Mar. 1970); children: Pamela, Deborah, Nancy, Barbara; m. Della Marie Ellis, July 26, 1975. BS, Tenn. State Coll., 1942; MD, Meharry Med. Coll., 1945; MS in Physiology, U. Ill., 1947. Diplomate Am. Bd. Internal Medicine. Instr. and rsch. assoc. dept. medicine Howard U., Washington, 1950-53; chief of medicine, acting dir. profl. svcs. VA Hosp., Pitts., 1955-58, cons./attending physc., 1958-62; pvt. practice pulmonary lab. West Penn Hosp., Pitts., 1958-92; staff physician VA Med. Ctr., Pitts., 1992—; clin. asst. prof. oral surgery U. Pitts. Dental Sch., 1994—; med. dir. West Penn Hosp. Home Care, 1967-85, exec. commr. and registrar, 1970-77; instr. physiology U. Ill., Chgo., 1946-47, instr. in medicine U. Pitts., 1957-63, Sch. Respiratory Therapy U. Ind., Pa., 1973-92; clin. asst. prof. oral surgery U. Pitts. Dental Sch., 1994—. Contbr. articles to numerous scientific publs. Bd. dirs. Lemington Nursing Home, Pitts., 1984-89, chmn. quality assurance, 1992—; bd. dirs. Villa de Marillac Nursing Home, Pitts., 1993—, West Peen Heart Assn., Pitts., 1967-72, Health Rsch. Svc. Found., Pitts., 1968-74. Capt. med. corps U.S. Army, 1953-55, Korea. Fellow Am. Coll. Physicians, mem. Am. Soc. Internal Medicine, Am. Thoracic Soc., Nat. Med. Assn. (past chmn. med. sect.), Sigma Pi Phi, Alpha Phi Alpha. Office: VA Med Ctr Med Svcs 7180 Highland Dr Pittsburgh PA 15206-1206

HALE, HARRY WILLIAM, surgeon, educator; b. N.Y.C., Feb. 3, 1917; s. Harry William and Caroline Bridgman (Noyes) H.; m. Mary Augustine Slusher, May 25, 1946; children: Nancy D., Harry W. III, Daniel L., Robert H., Alice M. BS in Biology, Rennselaer Poly Inst., 1938; MD, U. Rochester, 1943. Diplomate Am. Bd. Surgery. Intern in surgery Strong Meml. Hosp., Rochester, N.Y., 1943; resident in surgery E.J. Meyer Meml. Hosp., Buffalo, 1946-52; from instr. to prof. surgery SUNY, Buffalo, 1952-69; chmn. dept. surgery Maricopa Med. Ctr., Phoenix, 1969-86, attending surgeon, 1986-95; clin. prof. surgery U. Ariz., Tucson, 1979—; chmn. bd. dirs. Ariz. Emergency Med. Services, Phoenix, 1976-81. Contbr. chpts. to books and articles to profl. jours. Served to lt. commdr., USNR, 1944-46, 50-51. Fellow ACS (gov. 1963-69), Am. Assn. for Surgery of Trauma, Soc. Surgery of Alimentary Tract; mem. AMA, Cen. Surg. Assn., Western Surg. Assn., Southwestern Surg. Congress. Home: 3220 E Stanford Dr Paradise Valley AZ 85253-7525

HALE, MARY, nursing educator, emergency medicine nurse practitioner, occupational health nurse practitioner; b. Somerville, Mass., Nov. 26, 1946; d. John Lynn and Mary Josephine (Paro) H.; m. Laurence Gale, May 14, 1988. ADN magna cum laude, L.A. City Coll., 1981; BSN with highest honors, Calif. State U., L.A., 1982; MSN, U. Pa., 1984. RN, Calif., Pa.; cert. adult nurse practitioner. Crisis intervention counselor Do It Now Found., L.A., 1977-79; office nurse Neil Fond, MD, L.A., 1979-81; staff nurse UCLA Med. Ctr., 1981-83; primary nurse Staffbuilders, Phila., 1983-84; nurse student health emergency svcs. U. Pa., Phila., 1984; nurse practitioner Harbor UCLA Med. Ctr., Torrance, 1985, 94, L.A. Job Corps Ctr., 1985-87; occupational health specialist Northrop-Grumman, 1994—; clin. instr. Calif. State U., Long Beach, 1987—; assoc. prof., clin. preceptor UCLA Sch. Nursing, 1987—; clin. preceptor Mt. St. Mary's Coll., 1987—. Contbr. articles to profl. publs. Mem. ANA (commn. on nursing edn. 1981-82, cabinet on nursing edn. 1983), Internat. Coun. Nurses (planning com. 1979-81), Am. Acad. Nurse Practitioners, Am. Holistic Nurses Assn., Am. Assn. Occupational Health Nurses (local bd. dirs. 1995-96), Calif. Nurses Assn., Pa. Nurses Assn. (program dir., bd. dirs. dist. 1, 1984), Assn. County Midlevel Practitioners Nursing (founding), Sigma Theta Tau, Phi Kappa Phi.

HALEY, JOANNA KEYS, nursing administrator; b. Leonard, Tex., Apr. 7, 1957; d. Lewis and Irene (Ward) Keys; children: Lonnie Eugene, La Sandra Kay. Assoc. degree, Paris (Tex.) Jr. Coll., 1979; BSN, U. Tex., 1992. RN, cert. med. surgical nurse. Staff nurse Citizen Gen. Hosp., Greenville, Tex., 1978-79; charge nurse Oak Cliff Med. Surgical Hosp., Dallas, 1979-83; unit dir. Presbyn. Hosp. Greenville, 1984—; case mgr., project mgr., change agent, educator Presbyn. Hosp. Greenville, 1984—. Mem. Case Mgmt. Soc. Am., Soc. Gastroenterology Nurses, Tex. Hosp. Assn. Office: Presbyn Hosp Greenville Drawer 1059 4215 Joe Ramsey Blvd Greenville TX 75401

HALEY, PHILIP H., orthopaedic surgeon; b. St. Louis, Dec. 16, 1943; s. John Hardwick and Evelyn Virginia (Noell) H.; m. Susan Armel, Sept. 3, 1966; children: John, Ann Marie, Maureen. BS, U. Notre Dame, 1965; MD, Northwestern U., 1969. Diplomate Am. Bd. Orthopaedic Surgery. Orthopaedic surgeon USAMC, Ft. Hood, Tex., 1974-76, Anoka (Minn.) Orthopaedic Assocs., 1976-94, Orthopaedic Ptnrs., Anoka, 1995—. Maj. U.S. Army, 1974-76. Fellow Am. Acad. Orthopaedic Surgeons; mem. Internat. Coll. Surgeons, Am. Fracture Assn., Am. Bd. Ortopaedic Surgeons,

MidAm. Orthopaedic Soc., Minn. Orthopaedic Soc., Twin Cities Orthopaedic Soc., Minn. Med. Assn., Hennepin County Med. Soc. Roman Catholic. Office: Orthopaedic Ptnrs 3960 Coon Rapids Blvd #200 Coon Rapids MN 55433

HALEY, THOMAS JOHN, retired pharmacologist; b. Crosby, Minn., Nov. 4, 1913; s. Thomas Edward and Ida May (Young) H.; m. Edna Baker, June 1, 1944 (div. Sept. 1963); m. Jeanne Wall, Sept. 24, 1964; children: Kathyleen, Barbara. BS, U. So. Calif., 1938, MS, 1942; PhD, U. Fla., 1945. Lic. pharmacist, Calif., Nev. Grad. asst. instr. U. Fla., Gainesville, 1942-45; med. dir. E.S. Miller Labs Inc., L.A., 1945-47; chief pharmacology toxicologist Lab. Nuclear Medicine UCLA, 1947-66; prof. pharmacology U. Hawaii Med. Sch., Honolulu, 1966-69; leader pharmacology & toxicology Rsch. Triangle Inst., Research Triangle Park, N.C., 1969-71; adj. prof. pharmacology & toxicology U. N.C. Med. Sch., Chapel Hill, 1969-71; pharmacologist Food & Drug Adminstrn. Nat. Ctr. Toxicology Rsch., Pine Bluff, Ark., 1971-82; adj. prof. pharmacology U. Ark. Med. Ctr., Little Rock, 1971-82. Author: Clinical Toxicology, 1948, 1972, Respiratory Nervous System Ion Radiology, 1962, 1964, Manual of Toxicology, 1987. Sci. com. air pollution L.A. County, 1948-66. Mem. Inst. Strahlenhemat & Biol. (internat. mem.), L.A. C. of C. (clean air com. 1954-56), Oceanside City Coun. (hazard waste com. 1986-91). Democrat. Roman Catholic. Home: 774 Rivertree Dr Oceanside CA 92054-7456

HALFORD, SHARON LEE, legal studies administrator, victimologist, educator; b. Clifton, Colo., July 22, 1946; d. Robert Lee and Florence V. (Kubly) Eighmy; m. Allen A. Dreher, Jan. 29, 1967 (div. Jan. 1979); children: Heidi Ann, Gretchen Christine, Kirsten Beth; m. Donald Gary Halford, May 23, 1986. BS in Edn., U. Colo., 1969; postgrad., U. Denver, 1981-83; M in Criminal Justice, U. Colo., 1987. Legal asst. 1st Jud. Dist. Atty., Golden, Colo., 1979-81, legal rschr., 1981-83; victim witness coord. 18th Jud. Dist. Atty., Englewood, Colo., 1983-92; mem. faculty Aurora (Colo.) C.C. Criminal Justice Dept., 1989-95, chair Pub. Svc. Dept., 1995—; mem. faculty Colo. Faculty Adv. Coun., 1993—. Contbg. author, editor: Colorado Crime Victims Rights Contitutional Amendment Outreach Manual and Implementation Manual, 1992-93. Mem. Domestic Violence Task Force, Douglas County, Colo., 1985-92, Arapahoe County, Colo., 1985-94; trainer Rape Assistance and Awareness Program, Denver, 1985-91, MADD, 1990-92, Colo. Victim Witness Coord. Coalition, 1991; mem. 18th Judicial Dist. Child Advocacy Ctr. Com., 1990—, Gov.'s Victims' Compensation and Assistance Coord. Com., 1991-95, Colo. Victim Asst. and Law Enforcement Bd., 1991-95, Criminal Justice Educators Task Force, 1992—, chair, 1995—; mem. Colo. Corrections Consortium, 1992—, officer faculty senate, 1995—; mem. Colo. Crime Victim Rights Constl. Ammendment Com., 1990—; sec. Colo. Faculty Adv. Coun., 1993—; com. chair Colo. PACT Project, 1993-95. Fellow Nat. Orgn. for Victim Assistance, Nat. Victim Ctr.; mem. AAUW, Colo. Orgn. for Victim Assistance (pres.), S.W. Criminal Justice Educators Assn., Acad. Criminal Justice Scis., Am. Assn. Paralegal Educators, Nat. Fedn. Paralegal Assns., Rocky Mountain Paralegal Assn., Nat. Criminal Justice Assn., Internat. Platform Speakers Assn. Democrat. Methodist. Office: CC Aurora 16000 E Centretech Pky Aurora CO 80011-9057

HALIKAS, JAMES ANASTASIO, medical educator, psychiatrist; b. Bklyn., Nov. 26, 1941; s. Peter Simon and Olga Peter (Vavayianni) H.; BS (N.Y. State Regents scholar), Bklyn. Coll., 1962; MD, Duke U., 1966; m. Anna May Van Der Meulen, Aug. 20, 1967; children: Peter Christopher, Anna Catherine. Intern, Barnes Hosp., St. Louis, 1966-67; resident psychiatry Barnes/Renard hosps., Washington U. Sch. Medicine, St. Louis, 1967-70; rsch. fellow alcoholism and drug abuse Sch. Medicine, Washington U., St. Louis, 1969-70, instr. psychiatry, 1970-72, asst. prof., 1972-77, mem. com. on admissions, 1975-77; assoc. prof. psychiatry U. Louisville Sch. Medicine, 1978, dir. div. social and community psychiatry, 1978; assoc. prof. psychiatry Med. Coll. Wis., Milw., 1978-84, dir. div. alcoholism and chem. dependency, 1978-84, mem. human rsch. rev. com., 1981-84; prof. psychiatry, dir. psychiat. residency tng. U. Minn. Med. Sch., Mpls., 1984-90, mem. com. on the use of human subjects in rsch., 1985—, co-dir. chem. dependency treatment program U. Minn. Hosps. and Clinics, 1984-89, dir. 1989—, mem Coun. on Med. Edn., 1991—; asst. psychiatrist Barnes, Renard and Affiliated hosps., 1970-77; cons. Malcolm Bliss Mental Health Ctr., St. Louis, 1970-77; dir. psychiat. div. Webster Coll. Student Health Svc., Webster Groves, Mo., 1973-75; dir. Grace Hill Settlement House Psychiatry Clinic, St. Louis, 1973-77; clin. instr. dept. psychiatry Mo. Inst. Psychiatry, U. Mo., St. Louis, 1972-74; mem. profl. adv. com. Judevine Ctr. for Autistic Children, St. Louis, 1975-77; psychiat. rsch. cons. Reproductive Biology Rsch. Found., Masters and Johnson Inst., St. Louis, 1975-77. Mem. Mo. Gov.'s Adv. Council on Alcoholism and Drug Abuse, 1974-75; exec. com. Drug and Substance Abuse Council Met. St. Louis, 1973-77, pres., 1971-72; chmn. Children's Mental Health Svs. Council Met. St. Louis, 1973-74; host Sta. KMOX-TV weekly TV series Trips, 1971; adviser on drug abuse St. Louis County Juvenile Ct., 1970-72; mem. adv. bd. Drug Crisis Intervention Unit, St. Louis, 1971-77; mem. St. Louis Youth Ctr. profl. adv. com. Mo. Dept. Mental Health, 1977; adv. on drug abuse Drug Info. Ctr., St. Louis, 1970-74, Human Devel. Corp., St. Louis, 1970-73, Alliance for Regional Community Health, 1972-74; med. dir. for alcoholism svcs. Jefferson County Alcoholism and Drug Abuse Ctr. for Treatment and Rsch., Louisville, 1978; exec. and med. dir. River Region Mental Health-Mental Retardation Bd., Ky. Region VI Community Mental Health System, Louisville, 1978; bd. dir. Wis. Alcoholism and Drug Abuse Rsch. Inst., Milw., 1978-84; sr. Scientist U. Wis., Milw., 1978-84; attending psychiatrist, dir. med. edn. DePaul Rehab. Hosp., Milw., 1978-84; dir. rsch. and edn. in chem. dependency, sr. attending psychiatrist Milwaukee County Mental Health Complex, Milw., 1978-84, dir. psychiat. supervision div. long term care, 1983-84, dir. outpatient clinic, 1984, also chmn. or co-chmn. various coms.; sci. dir. DePaul Hosp. Found., Milw., 1978-84; assoc. psychiatrist U. Louisville Affiliated Hosps., 1978; attending psychiatrist Milw. Psychiat. Hosp., 1978-84, Columbia Hosp., Milw., 1980-84; attending psychiatrist U. Minn. Hosps. and Clinics, 1984—, Met. Med. Ctr., Mpls., 1985—; mem. planning com. Am. Med. Soc. on Alcoholism, 1977-78, mem. program com., 1983—, chmn. com. on med. edn., 1981—, mem. cert. com., 1985—, chmn. fellowship com., 1985—, Wis. state chmn., 1979-84; psychiat. cons. Social Security Disability Determination Svcs., 1984-87, Minn. Security Hosp., 1985-88, Moose Lake Regional Treatment Ctr., 1988—, Sandstone Fed. Correctional Inst., 1988-90; mem. Wis. Alcohol and Drug Abuse Adv. Com., HHS, 1981-84, St. Paul Mayor' Anti Drug Task Force, 1988-91; mem. Nat. Alcoholism Forum, 1978; co-chmn. clin. rsch. task force Nat. Drug Abuse Conf., Seattle, 1978; mem. Mental Health Assn. Louisville, 1978, Louisville Council on Alcoholism, 1978; cons. Midwestern Area Alcohol Edn. and Tng. Program, 1976-77. Bd. dirs. Mental Health Ast. Louis, 1973-77, chmn. St. Louis State Hosp. human research com., 1976-77; bd. dirs. Tellurian South Community, Inc., Madison, 1980—; mem. exec. council DePaul Rehab. Hosp., 1979-84; mem. med. appeals bd. Div. Motor Vehicles, State of Wis., 1980-84; mem. City of Mequon Bd. Appeals, 1980-84; mem. profl. adv. bd. Lactation Inst., L.A., 1981—; mem. dist. study and adv. council Moundsview Sch. Dist., 1987-88; also cons. Recipient NIMH Psychiatry Career Tchr. award in narcotics, drug abuse and alcoholism, 1972-75; diplomate Am. Bd. Psychiatry and Neurology, Nat. Bd. Med. Examiners. Mem. Am. Psychiat. Assn. (mem. Task Force on Substance Abuse Edn. in Psychiatry, 1985-87, task force postgrad. psychiatric edn. 1988—), Eastern Mo. Psychiat. Soc., Ky. Psychiat. Assn., Wis. Psychiat. Assn., Minn. Psychiat. Soc. (mem. com. on quality assurance and standards, 1987-89), Am. Psychopathol. Assn., Assn. for Med. Edn. and Rsch. in Substance Abuse, N.Y. Acad. Scis., AAAS, Ky. Med. Assn., Rsch. Soc. on Alcoholism, Assn. for Acad. Psychiatry, Am. Acad. Clin. Psychiatrists (bd. dirs. 1984-90, chmn. med. edn. com. 1984-90), Am. Assn. Dirs. of Psychiatric Residency Tng. (treas. 1987-89, chmn. liaison com. 1989-92), Soc. Biol. Psychiatry, Am. Acad. Psychiatrists in Alcoholism and Addictions (Midwest regional dir. 1990—), Am. Med. Assn., Am. Soc. Clin. Pharmacology and Therapeutics, Kappa Nu. Greek Orthodox. Contbr. numerous articles to profl. jours. Home: 22 Hill Farm Cir Saint Paul MN 55127-2007 Office: U Minn Dept Psychiatry PO Box 393 Minneapolis MN 55440-0393

HALL, BRIAN WILLIAM, physician assistant; b. Rhinebeck, N.Y., Mar. 18, 1958; s. William James and Janet Ruth (McGhee) H.; m. Lynn Anne Towers, Oct. 18, 1980; 1 child, Christopher Brian. AS in Biology, Dutchess C.C., Poughkeepsie, N.Y., 1978; BS in Biology, Siena Coll., 1980; BS in Health Scis., SUNY, Stony Brook, 1982, cert. physician asst. care, 1982. Registered physician asst., N.Y. Emergency rm. physician asst. Herkimer (N.Y.) Meml. Hosp., 1982-83; family practice physician asst. P.E. Rockwell MD, P.C., Canajoharie, N.Y., 1983-95, Bassett Healthcare, Canajoharie, N.Y., 1995—; med. cons. Canajoharie Fire Dept., 1991—. Bd. dirs. Canajoharie Youth Ctr., 1994—, Canajoharie Cmty. Chest, 1996—; pres. Canajoharie Little League, 1991-95, bd. dirs., 1995—. Fellow Am. Acad. Physician Assts., N.Y. State Soc. Physician Assts.; mem. Elks. Republican. Roman Catholic. Home: 35 Maple Ave Canajoharie NY 13317 Office: Bassett Healthcare 56 Montgomery St Canajoharie NY 13317

HALL, CHARLES P(OTTER), JR., educator consultant; b. Milw., July 7, 1932; s. Charles Potter Sr. and Myrtle P. (Pedersen) H.; m. Constance Nuzum, June 23, 1956; children: Peter C., Michael J., David E., Kristin E. BBA, U. Wis., 1954; PhD, U. Pa., 1961. CLU, CPCU. Spl. agt. Northwestern Mut. Life Ins. Co., Milw., 1955-58; asst. prof. U. Wash., Seattle, 1961-64; asst. dir. econ. rsch. AMA, Chgo., 1964-66; with Temple U., Phila., 1966—, assoc. dean, 1986-87, prof., dept. chair, 1986-75, 87-95; dir. Internat. MBA, Paris, 1995—; cons. Pa. Healthcare Cost Containment Coun., Harrisburg, 1987, Math. Policy Rsch., Inc., Princeton, N.J., 1988-89; bd. dirs. Delaware Valley Health Edn. Rsch. Found., Phila., 1983-89, community svcs., Vis. Nurse Assn. Ea. Montgomery Twp., Abington, Pa., 1985-91; bd. dirs. Penjerdel Employee Benefits Assn., 1988—, Ethix-Mid-Atlantic, 1990-94, Nat. Adv. Bd. Am. Assn. for Partial Hospitalization, 1989-93; v.p. Internat. Ins. Soc. Mem. editorial bd.: Hospital Risk Control, 1994—; contbr. articles to profl. jours. Elder Carmel Presbyn. Ch., Glenside, Pa., 1968-71, 82-87, trustee, 1974-80. Capt. USAFR, 1954-57. Fellow Am. Coll. Healthcare Execs. (regents adv. com. 1986-95); mem. Am. Risk and Ins. Assn. (pres. 1979-80), Am. Econ. Assn., Am. Pub. Health Assn., Am. Hosp. Assn., Internat. Ins. Soc. (v.p. 1991—), Internat. Health Econs. Assn. (sec. 1994-96), Nat. Assn. Health Svc. Execs. (adv. com. to Phila. chpt. 1991-95). Republican. Presbyterian. Home: 534 Custis Rd Glenside PA 19038-2012 Office: Temple U Sch Bus And Mgmt Philadelphia PA 19122

HALL, CHRISTINE MARIE, nursing consultant, geriatrics nurse; b. Morristown, N.J., Jan. 19, 1940; d. Thomas James and Helen Irene (Pedota) Montagna; children: Thomas Lee, Mark Edward. BSN, Tex. Woman's U., 1962. cert. IV therapist. Staff nurse med. - surg. unit, asst. dir. in-service tng. St. Paul Hosp., Dallas, 1962-64; instr., staff nurse ICU Parkland Hosp., Dallas, 1964-65; DON Silver Leaves Nursing Home, Garland, Tex., 1972-74; ombudsman Med. City Dallas Hosp., 1974-76; instr. health occupations Job Corps Ctr., McKinney, Tex., 1977-79; charge nurse Heritage Manor Nursing Home, Plano, 1979-88; asst. DON Christian Care Ctr., Mesquite, 1988-89, C. C. Young Long Term Care Facility, Dallas, 1989-90; supr. Collin County Home Care, Plano, 1990-91; pvt. practice Plano, 1995-96; wound care outreach educator Transitional Hosps. Corp., Arlington, Tex.; weekend supr. Carrollton (Tex.) Manor Nursing Home, 1990-91; legal nurse cons. So. Meth. U. Civil Clinic Program for the Elder Law Project. Contbr. articles to local newspapers and profl. jours. Mem. nursing advisory com. Collin C.C. Mem. ANA, Am. Assn. Legal Nurse Cons., Gerontol. Nurses Assn., Tex. Nurses Assn., Wound, Ostomy and Continence Nurses Soc., United Ostomy Assn., Sigma Theta Tau. Home: 1001 Ridge Field Plano TX 75075

HALL, COLIN DAVID, neurologist; b. Chester, Eng., May 11, 1941; came to U.S., 1969; s. David and Olive (Blanch) H.; m. Valerie Gordon, Sept. 22, 1961 (div. Dec. 28, 1989); children: Russell, Steven, Michael. MBChB, Aberdeen (Scotland) U., 1966. Diplomate Am. Bd. Electrodiagnostic Medicine, Am. Acad. Neurology. House officer Aberdeen Gen. Hosps., 1966-69; resident in neurology U. N.C., Chapel Hill, 1969-72, asst. prof. neurology and medicine, 1973-77, assoc. prof. neurology and medicine, 1977-82, prof. neurology and medicine, 1982—, also vice chair neurology, 1986—, interim chair neurology, 1995; rschr. in AIDS and neuromuscular disease U. N.C., Chapel Hill, 1992—. Mem. editl. bd. Jour. Neuro-AIDS, Jour. Neurovirology; ad hoc referee numerous jours.; ad hoc examiner Am. Bd. Neurol. Surgery; contbr. numerous articles to profl. jours. Mem. numerous NIH peer rev. coms. Fellow Am. Neurol. Assn.; mem. AMA, Am. Assn. Electrodiagnostic Medicine, Am. Assn. Electromyography and Electrodiagnosis, N.C. Med. Assn., N.C. Neurol. Assn., Orange-Durham County Med. Soc., N.C. Soc. Neuroscis. Office: Univ NC Dept Neurology Chapel Hill NC 27599

HALL, DONALD VINCENT, social worker; b. Ft. Dodge, Iowa, June 13, 1955; s. John William and Helen Evelyn (Swanson) H.; m. Marla Jo Adamson, May 28, 1977; children: Lucas William, Jessica Lauren. BSW, U. Iowa, 1977; MSW, U. Kans., 1979. Cert. clin. social worker; lic. social worker, Iowa; diplomate bd. clin. social work; qualified clin. social worker. Social worker Heartland Edn. Agy., Johnston, Iowa, 1979-91, facilitator conflict resolution and concensus decision making, cons. long range planning, presenter workshops, 1989—; pvt. practice clin. social worker, psychotherapist children, individuals, couples, families, groups Counseling and Assessment Svcs., P.C., 1991—; participant Des Moines Family Therapy Tng. Inst., 1991—. Bd. dirs. Johnston (Iowa) Community Sch., 1984-90, pres. bd., 1987-90. Presbyterian (ordained elder). Home: 6845 NW Beaver Dr Johnston IA 50131-1245 Office: Counseling and Assessment Svcs PC 2404 Forest Dr Des Moines IA 50312-5400

HALL, DOROTHY MARIE REYNOLDS, retired dental educator; b. Columbus, Ohio, Dec. 22, 1925; d. Thomas Franklin and Nellie May (Nail) R.; m. Grant Forrest Hall; children: Stacy L., Cynthia Kay Hall Henderson, Mark Kevin. Student Ohio State U., 1973-79, Sinclair C.C., 1976. Cert. Dental Asst. Dental asst., office mgr., dental offices in Westerville, Ohio, 1954-68, Columbus, Ohio, 1968-70; dental asst., staff supr., clinic instr. Good Samaritan Dental Clinic, Columbus, 1970; instr., staff supr., clinic instr. Ohio State U. Coll. Dentistry, 1970-72; instr. adult edn. Eastland Vocat. Center, Groveport, Ohio, 1969; instr. dental assisting Eastland Career Ctr., 1972-91; ret., 1991; examiner, mem., trustee Ohio Commn. on Dental Testing, Inc., 1979—, Commn. Ohio Dental Assts. Testing, Inc., 1977—, chief examiner, 1977-81, examiner, 1981—; mem. 12th grade competency examination reviewer com. Ohio Vocat. Edn. Rsch. Lab., 1993. Mem. Columbus Dental Assts. Soc. (pres. 1968-69, Dental Asst. of Yr. 1980), Ohio Dental Assts. Assn. (pres. 1978-79, 80-81), Am. Dental Assts. Assn. (cert., AQP dental asst., life mem.), Eastland Edn. Assn., Eastland Vocat. Assn. (pres. 1981-82), Ohio Vocat. Assn. (Dental Assisting Tchr. of Yr. award 1991), Nat. Ret. Tchrs. Assn. (life mem.), Ohio Vocat. Tchrs. Assn. (chairperson S.E. sect. 1986-91), Ohio Vocat. Asst. Tchrs. SE Region. Order Eastern Star, Iota Lambda Sigma. Mem. Reformed Ch. Am. Author: profl. publs.; developer, artist: A Manual of Lesson Plans for the Ohio Adult Dental Assistant Programs, 1981. Home: 4676 Big Walnut Rd Galena OH 43021-9528 Office: 4465 S Hamilton Rd Groveport OH 43125-9333

HALL, EDWIN PRESLEY, JR., psychologist; b. Montgomery, Ala., Nov. 10, 1941; s. Edwin Presley and Mildred (Guay) H.; m. Maureen McGeehan, June 25, 1988; children: Courtney, Morgan. BA, Am. U., 1962, MA, 1964; grad. prof. diploma, U. Ala., 1968, EdD, 1969. Asst. prof. Atlanta U., 1969-79; staff psychologist Douglas County Ga. Sheriff Dept., 1984-92. Mem. Am. Psychol. Assn., Ga. Psychol. Assn., Am. Soc. of Clin. Hypnosis, Kappa Delta Pi, Phi Delta Kappa. Methodist. Home: 5713 Roberts Dr Atlanta GA 30338-2735 Office: Atlanta Ctr Psychol Svcs Ste C 1864 Independence Sq Atlanta GA 30338-5150

HALL, ELLA TAYLOR, clinical school psychologist; b. Macon, Miss., Nov. 30, 1948; d. Essex and Mamie (Roland) Taylor; children: Banyikaai Monique (dec.), Motiqua Shante. BA, Fisk U., 1971, MA, 1973; PhD, George Peabody Coll., 1978. Mental health specialist behavioral sci. div. Meharry Med. Coll., Nashville, 1976-77; assoc. psychologist Bronx (N.Y.) Psychiat. Ctr., 1979; clin. psychologist Wiltwyck Residential Treatment Ctr., Ossining, N.Y., 1979-81; clin. cons. Abbott House, Irvington, N.Y., 1982-85; sch. psychologist Abbott Union Free Sch. Dist., 1985—; cons. psychologist Youth Theater Interactions, Inc., N.Y.; rschr in the field. Author: (poetry) Double Twister, Somebody, Clinging Tears, 1994, Maple Tree at Dawn, 1995, Down My Three Rows, 1995, Mama Sis, 1995, These Times, 1995, Ordinary, 1996, Young Wilted Flower; (art) In My Mind, 1994, Picking Cotton, 1995. Lay reader, acolyte Episcopal Ch. Mem. Yonkers schs. PTA; mem. Com. on Spl. Edn. NIMH tng. grantee, Kendall grantee; Crusade fellow. Mem. Schomburg Ctr. for Rsch., N.Y. State Psychol. Assn., Coun. Exceptional Children, N.Y. Bot. Soc., Delta Sigma Theta. Avocation: photography.

HALL, GARY, transplant coordinator; b. Melbourne, Victoria, Australia, Feb. 24, 1943; came to U.S., 1944; s. Scotty H. and Olive Melva (Axton) H.; m. Cheryl Diana, Feb. 12, 1972; children: Stephanie, Adam, Alexandra. Student, U. Ill., 1960-62; BS, Coll. William & Mary, 1965. Br. mgr., dist. supr. Prudential Mortgage Corp., Newport News, Va., 1965-66; br. mgr. Assocs. Fin. Svcs. Corp., Newport News, Va., 1966-69; br. mgr., exec. v.p. Wil-Var Enterprises, Inc., Norfolk, Va., 1969-77; dir. organ procurement U. Louisville, 1978-79; transplant coord. Mid-South Transplant Found., Memphis, 1979—. Contbr. articles to profl. jours. Mem. N.Am. Transplant Coords. Orgn. (Cert. merit 1985, 86, 87), Nat. Kidney Found. West Tenn. (Disting. Svc. award 1981, Pres. award 1984), Am. Liver Found., Southeastern Organ Procurement Found. (various coms.), United Network Organ Sharing. Republican. Methodist. Office: Mid-South Transplant Found 956 Court Ave Memphis TN 38163

HALL, HUGH DAVID, dentist, physician, educator; b. Henryetta, Okla., May 15, 1931; s. Hugh Colford and Mary Isabelle (Sadler) H.; m. Katherine Ayers Suydam, Feb. 20, 1960; children—Steven David, Andrew Durland, Brian Sadler. B.S., U. Okla., 1953; postgrad., U. Kansas City Sch. Dentistry, 1952-53; D.M.D., Harvard, 1957; M.D., U. Ala., 1977. Diplomate Am. Bd. Oral and Maxillofacial Surgery (adv. com. 1969-70, 81-86). Practice oral and maxillofacial surgery Birmingham, Ala., 1961-68, Nashville, 1968—; instr. oral surgery U. Ala. Sch. Dentistry, Birmingham, 1961-62; asst. prof. oral surgery, 1962-64, asso. prof. oral surgery, 1964, chmn. dept. oral surgery, 1965-68; prof., chmn. dept. oral surgery Vanderbilt U., Nashville, 1968—; vis. assoc. prof. physiology and biophysics U. Ala. Med. Ctr., Birmingham, 1970-92. Mem. editorial bd.: Jour. Oral Surgery, 1974-82; contbr. articles on salivary gland physiology, oral and maxillofacial surgery to tech. jours. Recipient Rsch. Career Devel. award Nat. Inst. Dental Rsch., 1962-64, Disting. Alumnus award Harvard Sch. Dental Medicine, 1980; USPHS Rsch. grantee, 1960-68. Fellow Internat. Assn. Oral and Maxillofacial Surgeons, AAUP; mem. Am. Dental Assn., Am. Assn. Oral and Maxillofacial Surgeons (Rsch. Recognition award 1991), Am. Soc. Maxillofacial Surgeons, Southeastern Soc. Oral and Maxillofacial Surgeons, Am. Physiol. Soc., AAAS, Internat. Assn. for Dental Rsch., Am. Soc. Temporomandibular Joint Surgeons (founder), Sigma Xi, Omicron Kappa Upsilon. Home: 3609 Knollwood Rd Nashville TN 37215-2012

HALL, JACK EDWARD, physician assistant; b. Mt. Sterling, Ill., Oct. 11, 1952; s. James Edward and Leota Lucille (Sorrells) H.; m. Jan Ann Teefey, July 8, 1972; children: Daniel, Matthew, Joshua. Grad., U.S. Army Pa. Sch., 1982; BS, Creighton U., 1991. Battalian surgeon U.S. Army, 1982-92; physician asst. Sidney (Nebr.) Med. Assocs., 1992—. Home: 1804 Keller Dr Sidney NE 69162 Office: Sidney Med Assocs 1625 Dorwart Dr Sidney NE 69162

HALL, JAMES BRYAN, gynecological oncologist; b. Dayton, Ohio, Nov. 24, 1946; s. Mitchell Z. and Moyne L. H.; m. Edith Miller, Mar. 22, 1975; children: James B. Jr., William B. AB, Taylor U., 1969; MD, Med. U. S.C., 1974. Diplomate Am. Bd. Ob-Gyn., Oncology. Rotating intern Miami Valley Hosp., Dayton, 1974-75; resident in ob-gyn. Wright State U.-Miami Valley Hosp., 1975-78, chief resident in ob-gyn., 1977-78; fellow in gynecologic oncology, asst. in gynecology Mass. Gen. Hosp., Boston, 1978-80; pvt. practice Charlotte, N.C., 1988-95; instr. ob-gyn. Harvard U., Boston, 1978-80; dir. gynecologic oncology, dept. ob-gyn. Carolinas Med. Ctr., 1980—, coord. med. student clerkship, 1982-87, acting dir. dept. ob-gyn., 1987-88, assoc. prof., 1986-88; asst. prof. U. N.C., Chapel Hill, 1980-86, assoc. prof., 1986-88, clin. prof., 1995—; spkr. at profl. confs. Contbr. numerous articles to med. jours. Fellow Am. Coll. Ob-Gyn.; mem. Soc.Gynecologic Oncology, Charlotte Gynecol. and Obstetrical Soc. (sec.-treas. 1984-86, v.p. 1986-87, pres. 1987-88), Am. Cancer Soc. (bd. dirs. Mecklenburg County chpt., chmn. profl. edn. com., exec. com.), AMA, N.C. Med. Soc., Assn. Profs. of Gynecologists and Obstetricians, James H. Nelson Jr. Oncology Soc. Republican. Evang. nondenominational. Office: Cancer Ctr Carolinas Med Ctr 100 Blythe Blvd Charlotte NC 28232

HALL, JAMES GRAYSON, family practice physician; b. Danbury, N.C., Oct. 29, 1929; s. John William and Sarah Blanche (Pepper) H.; m. Julia Draper Hunnicutt, Sept. 11, 1954; 1 child, James Grayson Jr. AB in Chemistry, U. N.C., 1951, MD, 1957. Pvt. practice Granite Quarry, N.C., 1961, Dobson, N.C., 1961—; med. dir. Hope Valley Med. Unit, Dobson, 1965—, Surry Rest Home, Dobson, 1970—, Dobson Med. Ctr., 1993—. Lt. USNR, 1958-63. Mem. NCMS, Am. Acad. Family Practitioners, N.C. Acad. Family Practitioners, S-Y Med. Soc., Masons, Shriners. Methodist. Home: 2629 Old Hwy 601 Mount Airy NC 27030 Office: 220 W Kapp St Dobson NC 27017

HALL, JAY, social psychologist; b. Houston, Oct. 18, 1932; s. Ernest James and Jamie (Clark) H.; m. Missy Hall; children: Kelly, Allison, Jeffrey. BA in Psychology, U. Tex., 1959, MA in Psychology, 1961, PhD in Psychology, 1963. Lectr. dept. psychology U. Tex., Austin, 1961-63, dir. S.W. Ctr. for Law and Behavioral Scis., 1964-66, assoc. prof. Grad. Sch. Bus., 1966-69; assoc. dir. Nat. Parole Insts., Austin, 1963-64; founder, chmn. bd. Teleometrics Internat., The Woodlands, Tex., 1969-93. Author: Ponderables: Essays on Managerial Choice-Past and Future, 1982, The Competence Connection: A Blueprint for Excellence, 1988, Models for Management: The Structure of Competence, 1988, The Executive Trap, 1992, Why Some Leaders are Better than Others, 1995; contbr. numerous articles and psychol. tests to profl. publs.; inventor Halford Grip sports/grip prosthesis. Trustee The Woodlands Med. Ctr., 1980-91, Community Life Found., 1985-88, The John Cooper Sch., The Woodlands, 1986-91; dir. Interfaith, The Woodlands, 1980-88. 1st lt. U.S. Army, 1955-58. Mem. Am. Psychol. Assn., AAAS, N.Y. Acad. Sci., Sigma Xi. Episcopalian.

HALL, JOHN EMMETT, orthopedic surgeon, educator; b. Wadena, Sask., Can., Apr. 23, 1925; came to U.S., 1971; s. Emmett Matthew and Isobel Mary (Parker) H.; m. Frances Norma Walsh, May 31, 1952; children—Maureen, Susan, Bruce, Peter, Martha, Thomas, David. B.A., U. Sask., 1948; M.D., C.M., McGill U., Montreal, 1952. Diplomate: Am. Bd. Orthopedic Surgery. Orthopedic surgeon Hosp. Sick Children, Toronto, 1958-71; chief orthopedic surgeon Hosp. Sick Children, 1966-71; asst. prof. U. Toronto Faculty Medicine, 1966-71; prof. orthopedic surgery Harvard U. Med. Sch., 1971—; clin. chief orthopedics Children's Hosp. Med. Center, Boston, 1971-81, sr. assoc. in orthopedic surgery, 1981-86; orthopedic surgeon-in-chief Boston Children's Hosp., 1986-94, sr. assoc. in orthopedic surgery, 1995—. Contbr. articles med. jours. Served with RCAF, 1942-46. Fellow A.C.S., Royal Coll. Surgeons Can.; mem. AMA, Can. Med. Assn., Am. Orthopedic Assn., Can. Orthopedic Assn., Acad. Orthopedic Surgeons, Scoliosis Research Soc. (pres. 1968-70), Pediatric Orthopedic Assn. (pres. 1978-80), Royal Can. Mil. Inst. Roman Catholic. Club: Harvard. Home: 36 Codman Rd Brookline MA 02146-7555 Office: 300 Longwood Ave Boston MA 02115-5724

HALL, JOHN FRY, psychologist, educator; b. Phila., Apr. 24, 1919; s. Harry R. and Alta (Herner) H.; m. Jean Midlam, May 14, 1943; 1 son, John. B.S., Ohio U., 1946; M.A., Ohio State U., 1947, Ph.D., 1949. Mem. faculty Pa. State U., University Park, 1949—; prof. psychology Pa. State U., 1958—; prof. emeritus, 1985—; Program dir. psychobiology NSF, Washington, 1966-67; vis. prof. U. Va., 1952, U. Wis., 1954, U. Calif. at Berkeley, 1962, U. Hawaii, 1968, Fla. State U., 1975-76. Author: Psychology of Motivation, 1961, Psychology of Learning, 1966, Readings in the Psychology of Learning, 1967, Verbal Learning and Retention, 1971, Classical Conditioning and Instrumental Learning, 1976, An Invitation to Learning and Memory, 1982, Learning and Memory, 1989; contbr. articles to profl. jours. Mem. Am. Psychol. Assn., Psychonomics Soc., A.A.A.S. Home: 334 Caloosa Palms Ct Sun City Center FL 33573-6938

HALL, JOHN RICHARD, surgery educator, researcher; b. Tucson, Mar. 21, 1952; s. John Owen and Evelyn Myra (Lowe) H.; m. Mary Cecelia Dean, Apr. 27, 1991; children: Corey Evelyn, Mary Elizabeth. BS in Chemistry with honors, Stanford U., 1974, BS in Biology, 1974; MD, U. Ariz., 1977. Diplomate Am. Bd. Surgery. Dir. trauma svc. Amarillo (Tex.) Critical Care Svc., 1985-86; asst. prof. surgery La. State U., Shreveport, 1986-87; dep. dir. pediatric trauma svc. Cook County Hosp. and U. Ill., Chgo., 1987-95; assoc. prof. surgery East Tenn. State U., Kingsport, 1996—; membership com. Ea. Assn. Surgery Trauma, 1993-94. Contbr. articles to profl. jours. Deacon

Presbyn. Ch., Chgo., 1995. Rsch. grantee U. Ill., 1988-94. Fellow Am. Coll. Surgeons; mem. Am. Assn. Surgery Trauma, Am. Trauma Soc., Am. Burn Soc., Western Trauma Assn., Ea. Trauma Assn. Office: Trauma Svc HVH 134 W Park Dr Kingsport TN 37660

HALL, JOHNNIE CAMERON, pathologist; b. Nashville, Nov. 30, 1958; s. Johnnie Claiborne and Mary Pauline (Roark) H. BS in Biochemistry, David Lipscomb Coll., 1980; MD, U. Tenn., 1984. Diplomate Nat. Bd. Med. Examiners, Am. Bd. Pathology. Intern U. Tenn., Memphis, 1984-85, resident in pathology, 1986-88; surg. pathology fellow U. Tenn./Bapt. Meml. Hosp., Memphis, 1988; pathologist Pathology Group of Midsouth (formerly Midsouth Path. Group), Memphis, 1989—; co-med. dir. Bapt. Regional Lab., Memphis, 1991-93; med. dir. Bapt. Regional Lab. Specialist Technologist Sch., Memphis, 1991-93; devel. coun. Freed-Hardeman U., 1993—; spkr. in field. Contbr. articles to profl. jours. Active Rep. Presdl. Task Force, Washington, 1990—, Nat. Taxpayers Union, Washington, 1990—. Fellow Coll. Am. Pathologists, Am. Soc. Clin. Pathologists; mem. AMA, Am. Soc. Microbiology, U.S. and Can. Acad. Pathologists, Tenn. Med. Assn., Memphis-Shelby County Med. Soc. (medicolegal com. mem.). Republican. Mem. Church of Christ. Home: 8375 Westfair Dr Germantown TN 38139-3259 Office: Midsouth Pathology Group 899 Madison Ave # 270 Ue Memphis TN 38103-3405

HALL, MARY NOMA, nursing educator; b. Sacramento, May 20, 1946; d. Donald J. and Noma Mary (Moore) Ratzlaff; m. Gordon S. Hall, Jan. 21, 1989; children: Wendy Corby, Nathan Daily. AA in Nursing, Sacramento City Coll., 1968; BSN, Calif. State U., Sacramento, 1976; MSN, U. Calif., San Francisco, 1980. Cert. clin. specialist in psychiat. nursing, cert. med.-surg. nurse Am. Nurses Credentialing Ctr. Staff nurse Woodland (Calif.) Meml. Hosp., Sutter Meml. Hosp., Sacramento; nurse educator Los Rios Community Coll. Dist., Sacramento. Home: 116 Glenville Cir Sacramento CA 95826-1714

HALL, PAMELA ELIZABETH, psychologist; b. Jacksonville, Fla., Sept. 10, 1957; d. Gary Curtiss and Ollie (Banko) H. BA, Rutgers U., 1979; MS in Edn., Pace U., 1981, PsyD in Psychology, 1984. Lic. psychologist, N.Y., N.J., Calif. Psychology extern St. Vincent's Med. Ctr., N.Y.C., 1981-82; intern in clin. psychology Elizabeth (N.J.) Gen. Med. Ctr., 1982-83, staff psychologist, 1983-85; staff psychologist J.F.K. Med. Ctr., Edison, N.J., 1985-87; pvt. practice Summit and Perth Amboy, N.J., 1985—; sr. supervising psychologist Muhlenberg Med. Ctr., Summit, N.J., 1987-90; rsch. affiliate/internat. lectr. NIMH field trials on assessment of dissociative disorders Yale U., New Haven, 1990—. Mem. Mayor's Com. on Substance Abuse, Perth Amboy, 1987. Named Henry Rutgers scholar, 1979. Mem. Am. Soc. Clin. Hypnosis, Internat. Soc. for Study of Dissociation (founder, pres. N.J. chpt. 1988—), Pace U. Alumni Assn., Rutgers U. Alumni Assn., Psi Chi. Home: PO Box 1820 Perth Amboy NJ 08862-1820

HALL, RICHARD C. WINTON, psychiatrist; b. N.Y.C., June 23, 1942; s. Frank and Dorothy (Brener) H.; m. Anne Klassen, Aug. 21, 1965; 1 child, Ryan C.W. BA, Johns Hopkins U., 1964; MD, U. Fla., 1968. Diplomate Am. Bd. Psychiatry and Neurology. Med. cons. NASA, 1975-76; ctr. dir. Brevard County Mental Health, 1974-76; psychiatric resident/fellow psychiatry and behavioral sci. Johns Hopkins U., Balt., 1969-72; examiner Am. Bd. Psychiatry and Neurology, 1977—; dir. clin. rsch. unit Tex. Rsch. Inst. Mental Sci., Houston, 1976-78; chief psychiatric cons./liaison svcs. and dir. resident tng. U. Tex. Med. Sch., Houston, 1978-80; chmn. dept. psychiatry Froedtert Meml. Luth. Hosp., Milw., 1980-82; dir. dept. psychiatry Milw. County Med. Ctr., 1980-82; chief staff VA Med. Ctr., Memphis, 1982-84; prof. psychiatry and medicine, assoc. dean U. Tenn., 1982-84; med. dir. psychiat. program Ctr. for Psychiatry, Fla. Hosp., Orlando, 1984-96; clin. prof. psychiatry U. Fla., Gainesville, 1984—; assoc. dean U. Tenn., 1982-84. Mem. editorial bd., reviewer numerous med. jours.; assoc. editor Psychosomatics; editor-in-chief Psychiat. Medicine, 1983-93; contbr. over 200 articles to profl. jours. Lt. comdr. USN, 1972-74. Mem. AAAS, AMA, Am. Acad. Psychiatry and the Law, Acad. Psychosomatic Medicine (pres. 1990), Am. Anorexia and Blumina Assn., Am. Coll. Physician Execs., Am. Psychiat. Assn., Am. Psychopathol. Assn., Am. Psychosomatic Soc., Assn. for Acad. Psychiatry, Assn. Mental Health Adminstrs., Fla. Med. Assn., Am. Coll. Psychiatrists, Fla. Psychiatry Soc., Internat. Health Soc., Orange County Med., So. Med. Assn. Office: Ste 210 100 East Sybelia Ave Maitland FL 32751

HALL, RICHARD CLAYTON, retired psychologist; b. Pitts., Apr. 29, 1931; s. Clayton LeClaire and Genevieve (Gorman) H.; m. Doris Margaret Bjorkland, Aug. 26, 1963; children: Karen, Janice, Dorothy. BS in Psychology with honors, Trinity Coll., 1952; MS, U. Pitts., 1959, PhD, 1963. Rsch. psychologist Polk (Pa.) Ctr., 1963-68, dir. behavior modification programs, 1968-75, chmn. subcom. human rights for behavior mgmt. procedures, 1987-89, staff psychologist, 1989-91; ind. researcher Key West, Fla., 1975-84, Polk, Pa., 1985-95; retired, 1995. Contbr. articles to profl. jours. With U.S. Army, 1953-55. NSF Coop. Grad. fellow, 1959. Mem. Sigma Xi, Pi Gamma Mu. Democrat. Presbyterian. Home: 101 Elm St Polk PA 16342

HALL, RICHARD WAIT, physician assistant; b. Jacksboro, Tex., Apr. 19, 1944; s. Elizabeth Grace (Risley) Hall; m. Bettie Lou Warren Mulhall, Sept. 18, 1964 (div. May 1985); 1 child, Stephanie Kae; m. Sherry Ann Jansohn, Apr. 22, 1989. BA in Chemistry, Tex. Christian U., 1970; BS, U. Tex. Med. Br., 1973; postgrad., St. Lucia Med. Sch., 1981-83. Cert. physician asst., Md., Fla. Physician asst. De Leon Clinic Assocs., 1973-80, Ft. Worth Fed. Correctional Inst., 1980-81, La Tuna Fed. Prison, 1982; engr. LTV Corp., 1983-84; physician asst. U.S. Coast Guard Air Sta., Clearwater, Fla., 1984—; physician asst. Neurology Assocs., 1980-81, Planned Parenthood of El Paso, 1982, Kaiser Permanente Health Care, Dallas, 1983-84, Oxon Hill Life and Health Ctr., 1984-87, MBLS Emergency Physicians, St. Petersburg, Fla., 1993—. Fellow Am. Acad. Physician Assts., Tex. Acad. Physician Assts. (charter); mem. Masons. Office: US Coast Guard Air Station Clearwater FL 34622

HALL, ROBERT JOSEPH, physician, medical educator; b. Buffalo, June 4, 1926; s. Joseph M. and Florence C. (Kirst) H.; m. Dorothy Nowak, Aug. 28, 1948; children: Thomas R., Kathleen A. Hall Noble, Mary J. Hall Stuart, Michael F., Steven E. Student, Canisius Coll., Buffalo, 1943-45; MD, U. Buffalo, 1948. Diplomate Am. Bd. Internal Medicine, Sub Bd. Cardiovascular Disease (mem. cardiovascular disease sect. 1969-75). Intern Mercy Hosp., Buffalo, 1948-49; commd. 1st lt. M.C. U.S. Army, 1948, advanced through grades to col., 1966; resident in internal medicine Walter Reed Gen. Hosp., Washington, 1949-52; resident in cardiovascular diseases Walter Reed Gen. Hosp., 1956-57; asst. cardiovascular research Walter Reed Army Inst. Research, 1957-58; service in Korea and Japan, 1952-55; chief cardiology service Brooke Gen. Hosp., Ft. Sam Houston, Tex., 1961-66, Walter Reed Gen. Hosp., 1966-69; ret., 1969; clin. assoc. prof. medicine Georgetown U. Med. Sch., 1967-69; clin. prof. medicine Baylor U. Coll. Medicine, Houston, 1969—, U. Tex. Med. Sch., Houston, 1977—; med. dir. Tex. Heart Inst., Houston, 1969-93; chmn. exec. com. profl. staff Tex. Heart Inst., 1969-93; dir. div. cardiology St. Luke's Episcopal Hosp., Houston, 1969-95; assoc. chief med. service St. Luke's Episcopal Hosp., 1970-83; dir. edn., cardiology Tex. Heart Inst. Tex. Heart Inst. and St. Luke's Episcopal Hosp., 1992—; cons. Tex. Children's, VA, Brooke Gen. hosps., M.D. Anderson Hosp. and Tumor Inst.; mem. cardiovascular study sect. NIH, 1958-61; mem. phys. evaluation team Gemini project NASA, 1958-61; mem. nat. adv. heart counseil Dept. Def., 1966-69; adv. council Mended Hearts, 1970-78. Contbr. numerous articles med. jours. Mem. President's Adv. Panel Heart Disease. Decorated Legion of Merit; recipient Disting. Alumnus award Canisius Coll., 1995. Fellow A.C.P., Am. Coll. Cardiology (gov. 1968-71-74, chmn. bd. govs. and trustee 1973-74); mem. Am. Heart Assn. (fellow council clin. cardiology; pres. Houston chpt. 1974-75, advisor corp. cabinet 1980-86), Assn. Mil. Surgeons U.S., Assn. Advancement Med. Instrumentation, Pan Am. Med. Assn. (chmn. sect. cardiovascular diseases 1978-81), Assn. Univ. Cardiologists, Tex. Med. Assn., Tex. Cardiology Club, Harris County Med. Soc., Houston Cardiology Soc. (chmn. 1976-77), Houston Soc. Internal Medicine, Alpha Omega Alpha, 1948—. Home: 5504 Sturbridge Dr Houston TX 77056-1623 Office: 6624 Fannin St Ste 2480 Houston TX 77030-2336

HALL, ROBERT P., social services administrator; b. Salisbury, Md., July 5, 1952; s. R. Paul and Elizabeth (Satterfield) H.; m. Conee Nelson, May 28, 1994. BA, U. Md., 1974; MDiv, Wesley Theol. Sem., 1977. Exec. dir. Delawareans United to Prevent Child Abuse, Wilmington; dir. devel. ARC, Wilmington; dir. planning Community Action of Greater Wilmington, Del. Contbr. articles to profl. jours. Winner Commr's. award, 1991. Mem. NASW, Am. Counseling Assn., Am. Mental Health Counselors Assn. (task force on childhood and adolescence).

HALL, STEPHANIE LYNN, surgical nurse; b. Canton, Ohio, Nov. 22, 1959; d. Charles Wilbur and Frances Dagmar (Steiner) H. BSN, Loretto Hts. Coll., Denver, 1983. Staff nurse, clin. nurse IV Swedish Med. Ctr., Englewood, Colo., 1983-94, operating rm. nurse, day surgery, 1994—. Mem. AAUW, Assn. Oper. Rm. Nurses. Home: 1410 S Youngfield Ct Lakewood CO 80228

HALL, THOMAS CHRISTOPHER, physician, educator; b. N.Y.C., Nov. 26, 1921; s. John Clarence and Theresa (McDonald) H.; m. Lorina Amanda Friesen, July 30, 1978; children: Christopher, Thomas, Seth, Amity, Bronwen, Nathan, Jinny, Nicholas. Student, Harvard U., 1944, MD magna cum laude, 1949. Diplomate Am. Bd. Internal Medicine, Am. Bd. Med. Oncology; lic. physician, Calif., N.Y., Mass., Hawaii, Wash., N.J. Intern Peter Bent Brigham Hosp., Boston, 1949-50; asst. resident Mass. Gen. Hosp., Boston, 1951-53; asst. in medicine Harvard Med. Sch., Boston, 1955, instr., 1957; dir. oncology Lemuel Shattuck Hosp., Boston, 1957-62; sr. research assoc. in biochemisty Brandeis U., Waltham, 1959, adj. assoc. prof. biochemistry, 1961; dir. Harvard Cancer Chemotherapy Unit Pondville Hosp., 1959-68; asst. physician Children's Hosp. Med. Ctr., 1961, research assoc. in pathology, 1961, sr. assoc. in medicine, 1963, asst. prof. medicine, 1965; co-chmn. eastern coop. oncology group NIH, 1961; sr. assoc. tumor therapy, physician-in-chief adult div. Children's Cancer Rsch. Found., 1961; chief clin. and biochemicalpharmacology Children's Cancer Research Found., 1964; assoc. in medicine, chief med. oncology Peter Bent Brigham Hosp., Boston, 1964; teaching assoc. Newton-Wellesley Hosp., 1967; physician Boston Hosp. for Women, 1967; dir. divsn. oncology, prof. medicine and pharmacology U. Rochester, N.Y., 1968-72; physician Strong Meml. Hosp., Rochester, 1968-72; assoc. dir. therapeutics, prof. medicine and biochemistry, physician-in-chief USC Cancer Hosp. and Research Ctr. U. So. Calif., Los Angeles, 1972-75; affiliate staff mem. Hosp. of Good Samaritan Med. Ctr., Los Angeles, 1973-75; dir. Cancer Control Agy. of B.C., Can., 1975-76; prof. faculty of medicine, depts. medicine and pharmacology U. B.C., Vancouver, 1975-77; scientist Pasadena Found. for Med. Research, Calif., 1977-78; clinician Tumor Clinic Med. Group, Inc., 1977-78; clin. prof. medicine U. Calif., Irvine, 1978-91; prof. medicine, pharmacology U. Hawaii, Honolulu, 1978; physician Queen's Med. Ctr., Honolulu, 1983; dir. cancer ctr. Programs in Cancer Control Edn. and Outreach U. Hawaii, Honolulu, 1978; v.p. clin. affairs Ctr. Molecular Medicine and Immunology, Newark, 1987-91; dir. adult oncology-hematology United Hosp. Med. Ctr., Newark, 1990-92; cons. oncology Long Beach VA Hosp., 1979; mem. staff, cons. oncology Queen's Med. Ctr., 1980; cons. St. Francis Hosp., Honolulu, 1980, Kuakini Med. Ctr., Honolulu, 1983; advisor cmty. cancer program St. Joseph Hosp., Bellingham, 1995; prin. investigator Cascadia Clin. Trials Prostate Cancer Prevention Trial, 1994. Contbr. articles to profl. jours. and numerous chpts. to books. NamedAm. Cancer Soc. prof., K.D. Allen prof., 6th Hubert Lectr., 2d Winfield Meml. prof. Mem. AAAS, AAUP, Am. Assn. for Cancer Edn., Am. Soc. Clin. Pharmacology and Chemotherapy, Endocrine Soc., Internat. Soc. Chemotherapy, Mass. Med. Soc., Soc. forCryobiology , Western Assn. Physicians, Western Assn. Gynecol. Oncology (hon.), Can. Oncologic Soc., USPHS Rsch. Soc. (hon.), Royal Coll. Physicians and Surgeons Can. (hon.), Sigma Xi, Alpha Omega Alpha. Office: Cons in Medicine 5335 Cordata Pky Bellingham WA 98226-8076 also: St Joseph Hosp Cancer Program 3217 Squalicum Pkwy Bellingham WA 98225

HALL, TIMOTHY C., biology educator, consultant; b. Darlington, Durham, Eng., Aug. 29, 1937; came to U.S., 1965; s. Gilbert Leslie and Dorothea Olive (Lindemann) H.; m. Sandra Severn, Aug. 20, 1960; children: Alexandra Vikki Anna, Liza Bryony, Peter Marcus Jeremy. BSc with honors, U. Nottingham, Eng., 1962, PhD in Plant Physiology, 1965. Louis W. and Maud Hill postdoctoral fellow dept. hort. sci. U. Minn., St. Paul, 1965-66; asst. prof. horticulture U. Wis., Madison, 1966-70, assoc. prof., 1970-75, prof., 1975-82, adj. prof. biophysics and genetics, 1982-84; dir. Agrigenetics Advanced Rsch. Div., Madison, 1980-84, Agrigenetics Rsch. Corp., Boulder, Colo., 1981-84; Disting. prof., head dept. biology Tex. A&M U., College Station, 1984-92, dir. Inst. Devel. and Molecular Biology, 1992—; sr. biotech. cons. Rhône-Poulenc Agrochimie, Lyon, France, 1985—; chair, organizer Gorden Conf. on Plant Molecular Biology, 1987; cons. plant biotech. Internat. Paper Co., Tuxedo Park, N.Y., 1987. Editor: (with J.W. Davies) Nucleic Acids in Plants, 2 vols., 1979, (with L. van Vloten-Doting and G.S.P. Groot) Molecular Form and Function of the Plant Genome, 1985; mem. editl. bd. Oxford Surveys Plant Molecular and Cell Biology, 1983—, Transgenic Rsch., 1991-95, Plant Jour., 1991—; contbr. numerous articles to profl. jours., book chpts.; patentee in field. Pilot Royal Air Force, 1956-58. Grantee NIH, NSF, USDA, NATO, Rhône-Poulenc Agrochimie, Internat. Paper Co., Tex. Advanced Tech. Program, Rockefeller Found. Fellow Indian Virol. Soc.; mem. AAAS, RNA Soc., Am. Assn. Cereal Chemists, Am. Soc. for Biochemistry and Molecular Biology, Am. Soc. for Microbiology, Am. Soc. Plant Physiologists (chair session on nucleic acids, genetics 1975, chair com. on recombinant DNA 1978-79), Am. Soc. for Virology, Am. Phytopathol. Soc., Soc. Gen. Microbiology, Fedn. Am. Socs. Exptl. Biology, Biochem. Soc., Internat. Soc. for Molecular-Plant Microbe Interactions, Internat. Soc. Plant Molecular Biology, Soc. for In Vitro Biology, RNA Soc., Squash Club Tex. A&M U., Sigma Xi. Office: Tex A&M U Inst Devel-Molecular Biol College Station TX 77843-3155

HALL, WANDA JEAN, mental health professional, consultant; b. Miami, Okla., July 3, 1943; d. Max Calvin Kinnaman and Dorothy D. (Peck) Fadler; m. James Marvin Hall, Apr. 10, 1964 (div. Feb. 1965); m. George Edward Hall, Mar. 21, 1973; children: Heather Renata, Samuel. AA, Stephens Coll., Columbia, Mo., 1963; BS, Kans. U., Pittsburg, 1965; MS, New Sch. for Social Rsch., N.Y.C., 1991. Asst. psychologist Parsons (Kans.) State Hosp., 1966-67; hosp. care investigator N.Y. Dept. Social Work, N.Y.C., 1968-70; social worker Drug Abuse Program, Amsterdam, The Netherlands, 1970-74; dir. Washington Park Co-op Presch., N.Y.C., 1974-75; project dir. Manhattan Devel. Ctr., N.Y.C., 1975-77; pvt. practice as human devel. specialist, N.Y.C., 1978-81; community rels. coord. Orange County Dept. Mental Health, Goshen, N.Y., 1981—; parenting cons. Teens Exploring Parenting, Inc., Middletown, N.Y., 1990-94; instr. Orange County C.C., Middletown, 1990—, Mt. St. Mary Coll., Newburgh, N.Y., 1993—. Producer, host radio talk show Conversation on Epilepsy, Radio Sta. WGNY, 1981; dir, narrator mental health skits Forum Players, 1980; producer, host 6 TV series Love from the 26, 000 Club, 1983. Bd. dirs. Orange County Coalition for Choice, Warwick, N.Y., 1981—, Orange County Task Force on Child Abuse/Neglect, 1984-89, Ct. Apptd. Spls. Assts., 1987-96, Bandwagon Cmty. Ctr., chairperson, 1990-95; mem. Planned Parenthood, Orange County, 1989—, Safe Homes, Orange County, 1987—, Middletown Coun. Cmty. Agys., 1980-96, Interagy. Coun. Child Sexual Abuse; co-founder Orange County Parenting Coalition., 1990—. Recipient DWI Alcohol Safety award N.Y. State Alcohol Bur., Albany, 1986, Cmty. Svc. award Youth Bur. Goshen, 1987, Zonta scholar award, 1989, Cmty. Svc. award Otisville (N.Y.) State Correction, 1989, Nat. Assn. Counties award Confident Parenting Program, 1993, Hospice Orange Vol. award, 1993, The Gilbert award, 1995, Human Rights award Orange County Human Rights Commn., 1995. Mem. NAACP. Methodist. Office: Orange County Dept Mental Health Drawer 471 Harriman Dr Goshen NY 10924

HALL, WILBUR DALLAS, JR., medical educator; b. Calhoun, Ga., June 22, 1938; s. Wilbur Dallas and Ruby (Koon) H.; m. Marguerite Holt, July 4, 1992; 1 child, Ashley. MD, Emory U., 1963. Diplomate Am. Bd. Internal Medicine and Nephrology. Chief med. resident Grady Meml. Hosp., 1966; prof. medicine, dir. div. hypertension Emory U., Atlanta, 1976—, program dir. Gen. Clin. Rsch. Ctr., 1988—. Author 3 books; contbr. chapters to books; also articles. Fellow Am. Coll. Physicians; mem. Ga. Heart Assn. (pres. 1984-85). Office: Emory Univ Sch of Medicine 69 Butler St SE Atlanta GA 30303-3033

HALL, ZACH WINTER, medical institute executive, researcher; b. Atlanta, Sept. 15, 1937; s. Dixon Winter and Marjorie Elizabeth (Owens) H.; m. Marion Nestle, Dec. 1973 (div. June 1985); m. Julie Ann Giacobassi, Nov. 9, 1987. BA, Yale U., 1958; PhD, Harvard U., 1966. Asst. prof., then assoc. prof. Harvard Med. Sch., Boston, 1968-76; prof. U. Calif., San Francisco, 1976-94; dir. Nat. Inst. Neurol. Disorders and Stroke, Bethesda, Md., 1994—; mem. Med. Adv. Bd., Chevy Chase, Md., 1995—, Howard Hughes Med. Inst.; Alexander Forbes lectr. Grass Found., 1994. Author, editor: Molecular Neurobiology, 1992; editor jour. Neuron, 1988-94. Mem. Am. Acad. Arts and Scis. Home: 6708 Fairfax Rd Chevy Chase MD 20815 Office: NIH Nat Inst Neuological Disorders & Stroke Bldg 31 8A52 Bethesda MD 20892

HALL ART, DIANE LOUISE, medical records administrator; b. Glendive, Mont., Jan. 18, 1948; m. G. Blake Hall, Dec. 21, 1985; children: David, Dean, Debbie, Dena. BA, Boise State U., 1992. Accredited records technician. Med. record dir. Walter Knox Meml. Hosp., Emmett, Idaho, 1992—; med. records cons. Weiser (Idaho) Meml. Hosp., 1995—; ednl. site Boise State U. med. records edn., 1992—; com. mem. Pro-West Ideal Med. Record, 1993. Mem. Am. Health Info. Mgmt. Assn. (nat. accreditation), Med. Transcription Assn. (Greater Boise area chpt.), Idaho Hosp. Assn., Idaho Health Info. Mgmt. Assn. (chmn. nominating com. 1992-93), Treasure Valley Health Info. Mgmt. Assn.. Home: 1330 Sunset Dr Emmett ID 83617 Office: Walter Knox Meml Hosp 1202 E Locust Emmett ID 83617

HALLBAUER, ANNA ELIZABETH, public health nurse, Lamaze educator; b. Herrin, Ill., Sept. 26, 1958; d. Alvin Edward and Olvetta Naomi (Burnett) Loeh; m. Michael Dean Loeh Hallbauer, Mar. 18, 1977 (div. Aug. 1994); children: Shawn L., Michelle D. AAS, Hutchinson (Kans.) C.C., 1987; BSN, Bethel Coll., North Newton, Kans., 1993. RN. Mem. nursing staff Carle Found. Hosp., Urbana, Ill., 1993, Meml. Hosp., Carbondale, Ill., 1993-94, Reno County Health Dept., Hutchinson, Kans., 1994-95. Mem. Sigma Theta Tau Internat., Beta Sigma Phi.

HALL-BOYER, KATHRYN L., emergency physician; b. Eureka, Calif., Feb. 7, 1956; d. William and Louise (Greenleaf) Hall; m. William F. Boyer, May 21, 1983; children: Garry, Craig, Kurtis. AB in Zoology, U. Calif., Davis, 1977; MD, Uniformed Svcs. U. Health Sci., Bethesda, Md., 1983. Diplomate Am. Bd. Emergency Medicine. Intern in internal medicine Naval Hosp., Bethesda, Md., 1983-84; head primary care Naval Hosp., Guatanamo Bay, Cuba, 1984-85; head emergency dept. Naval Hosp., Guatanamo Bay, 1985-86; resident in emergency medicine Naval Hosp., San Diego, Calif., 1986-88; head emergency dept. Naval Hosp., Camp Pendleton, Calif., 1988-89; attending physician and CQI dir. Naval Hosp. Emergency Dept., San Diego, 1989-93; staff emergency physician Newman (Ga.) Hosp., 1994-95; staff physician Ga. Bapt. Hosp. Urgent Care, Fayetteville, Ga., 1994-95; attending physician and asst. prof. Emory U. Divsn. Emergency Medicine, Atlanta, 1995—. Parent rep. Parent Profl. Adv. Coun. for Spl. Edn., Vista, Calif., 1990-93, Gifted Edn. Adv. Group, Vista, 1992-93. Lt. Commdr. US Navy, 1979-83. Fellow Am. Coll. Emergency Physicians; mem. AMA, Am. Med. Womens Assn., Am. Assn. of Women Emergency Physicians, Med. Assn. Ga., Physicians for a Violence Free Soc. Office: Emory U Divsn Emergency Medicine 69 Butler St SE Atlanta GA 30303

HALLE, MICHAEL ALAN, pediatrician. AB, Ohio U., 1961; MD, Howard U., 1965. Intern Maimonides Med. Ctr., Bklyn., 1965-66, resident, 1966-67; pediatrician Broward Gen. Med. Ctr., Ft. Lauderdale, Fla., 1971—, Plantation (Fla.) Gen. Hosp., 1971—, Fla. Med. Ctr., Laiderdale Lakes, 1973—, Fla. Med. Ctr. South, Plantation, 1996—. Contbr. articles to profl. jours. Maj. USMC, 1969-71. Pediatric svc. fellow Meadowbrook Hosp., East Meadow, N.Y., 1967-69. Mem. AMA, Fla. Med. Assn., Broward County Med. Assn., Phi Delta Epsilon, Phi Sigma Delta..

HALLENBORG, BRUCE P., psychiatrist; b. N.Y.C., Apr. 28, 1946; s. John and Henrietta (De La Guard) H.; m. Nyda Williams Brown, Oct. 29, 1988. MD, U. Pitts., 1973. Diplomate Am. Bd. Psychiatry and Neurology. Pvt. practice psychiatry Brown & Hallenborg, Atlanta, 1977—, pres., 1992—. Mem. Alpha Omega Alpha. Office: Brown & Hallenborg 2660 Peachtree Rd 9F Atlanta GA 30305

HALLER, LEE HIGDON, psychiatrist; b. Pitts., Aug. 19, 1947. BA in Psychology, U. Mich., 1968, MD, 1972. Diplomate Am. Bd. Psychiatry and Neurology, Psychiatry and Child and Adolescent Psychiatry, Forensic Psychiatry. Rotating intern Wayne County Gen. Hosp., Eloise, Mich., 1972-74; resident in gen. psychiatry Duke U. Med. Ctr., Durham, N.C., 1973-74; fellow child psychiatry Children's Psychiat. Hosp./U. Mich., Ann Arbor, 1975-77; pvt. practice Rockville, Md., 1979—; clin. asst. prof. psychiatry dept. psychiatry Georgetown U. Med. Ctr., Washington, 1979—, George Washington U. Med. Ctr., Washington, 1979—. Contbr. numerous articles to profl. jours. With U.S. Army, 1977-79. Mem. Am. Psychiat. Assn., Am. Acad. Psychiatry and the Law, Am. Soc. for Adolescent Psychiatry, Am. Acad. Child Psychiatry, Montgomery County Med. Soc., Phi Rho Sigma Med. Fraternity. Home and Office: 15225 Shady Grove Rd # 305 Rockville MD 20850-3234

HALLETT, MARK, physician, neurologist, health research institute administrator; b. Phila., Oct. 22, 1943; s. Joseph Woodrow and Estelle (Barg) H.; m. Judith E. Peller, June 26, 1966; children: Nicholas L., Victoria C. B.A. magna cum laude, Harvard U., 1965, M.D. cum laude, 1969. Diplomate Am. Bd. Psychiatry and Neurology. Resident in neurology Mass. Gen. Hosp., Boston, 1972-75; Moseley fellow Harvard U., London, 1975-76; lectr., assoc. prof. neurology Harvard U., Boston, 1976-84; head clin. neurophysiology lab. Brigham and Women's Hosp., Boston, 1976-84; clin. dir. Nat. Inst. Neurol. Disorders and Stroke, NIH, Bethesda, Md., 1984—. Author: (with others) Entrapment Neuropathies, 1990; editor: (with J. Jankovic) Therapy with Botulinum Toxin, 1994; contbr. numerous articles to profl. jours. Bd. dirs. Easter Seals Rsch. Found., Chgo., 1985-87; mem. med. adv. bd. Nat. Parkinson Found., Miami, 1985—, Dystonia Med. Rsch. Found., Chgo., 1989-93, Benign Essential Blepharospasm Rsch. Found., Beaumont, 1990—, Myoclonus Rsch. Found., Fort Lee, N.J., 1989—. Mem. Am. Assn. Electrodiagnostic Medicine, Am. Acad. Neurology, Am. Neurol. Assn., Am. Clin. Neurophysiology Soc., Soc. for Neurosci., Movement Disorder Soc., Phi Beta Kappa, Alpha Omega Alpha. Democrat. Jewish. Home: 5147 Westbard Ave Bethesda MD 20816-1413 Office: NINDS NIH Bldg 10 Rm 5N226 10 Center Dr MSC 1428 Bethesda MD 20892-1428

HALLIDAY, PENELOPE ANN, physician; b. Washington Court House, Ohio, Nov. 20, 1950; d. Charles F. and Marjorie V. Pensyl; m. John C. Halliday, Aug. 30, 1975; 1 child, Heather. BS, Bob Jones U., Greenville, S.C., 1973; MD, Ohio State U., 1979. Diplomate Am. Bd. Family Practice. Resident family practice Grant Med. Ctr., Columbus, Ohio, 1979-82; pvt. practice Washington Court House, 1986—; med. dir. Auburn Manor, Washington Court House; chief staff Fayette County Meml. Hosp., Washington Court House, 1995. Mem. Christian Med. and Dental Soc. Mem. Christian Ch. Home: 925 Glenn Ave Washington Court House OH 43160 Office: 403 E Market St Washington Court House OH 43160

HALLIDAY, WILLIAM ROSS, retired physician, speleologist, writer; b. Atlanta, May 9, 1926; s. William Ross and Jane (Wakefield) H.; m. Eleanore Hartvedt, July 2, 1951 (dec. 1983); children: Marcia Lynn, Patricia Anne, William Ross III; m. Louise Baird Kinnard, May 7, 1988. BA, Swarthmore Coll., 1946; MD, George Washington U., 1948. Diplomate Am. Bd. Vocat. Experts. Intern Huntington Meml. Hosp., Pasadena, Calif., 1948-49; resident King County Hosp., Seattle, Denver Children's Hosp., L.D.S. Hosp., Salt Lake City, 1950-57; pvt. practice Seattle, 1957-65; with Wash. State Dept. Labor and Industries, Olympia, 1965-76; med. dir. Wash. State Div. Vocat. Rehab., 1976-82; staff physician N.W. Occupational Health Ctr., Seattle, 1983-84; med. dir. N.W. Vocat. Rehab. Group, Seattle, 1984, Comprehensive Med. Rehab. Ctr., Brentwood, Tenn., 1984-87; dep. coroner, King County, Wash., 1964-66. Author: Adventure Is Underground, 1959, Depths of the Earth, 1966, 76, American Caves and Caving, 1974, 82; co-author: (with Robert Nymeyer) Carlsbad Cavern: The Early Years, 1991; editor Jour. Spelean History, 1968-73; contbr. articles to profl. jours. Mem. Gov.'s North Cascades Study Com., 1967-76; mem. North Cascades Conservation Coun., v.p., 1962-63; pres. Internat. Speleological Found., 1981-87; asst. dir. Internat. Glaciospeleological Survey, 1972-76. Served to lt. comdr.

USNR, 1949-50, 55-57. Recipient medal Geol. Soc. China; named Alumnus of Yr., George Sch., 1992. Fellow Am. Coll. Chest Physicians, Nat. Speleological Soc. (hon. mem. 1965, bd. govs. 1988-94), Explorers Club; mem. AMA, Hawaii Speleological Survey (chmn. 1989—), Internat. Symposia on Vulcanospeleology (1st, 3rd and 6th chmn.), Internat. Union Speleology Commn. on Volcanic Caves (chmn. 1990—), We. Speleological Survey (dir. 1957-83, dir. rsch. 1983—), Soc. Thoracic Surgeons, Wash. State Med. Assn., Tenn. State Med. Assn., King County Med. Soc., Am. Fedn. Clin. Rsch., Am. Spelean History Assn. (pres. 1968), Brit. Cave Rsch. Assn., Ukrainian Speleological Assn. (hon.), Nat. Trust (Scotland), Mountaineers Club (past trustee), Seattle Tennis Club.

HALLMAN, DEBRA JANIECE, pharmacist; b. Hanford, Calif., June 22, 1953; d. Keith Eugene and Patricia Marie (Falchi) Howe; m. John Alan Allen, July 24, 1976 (div. Dec. 1993); children: Sean Adrian, Tonya Danielle; m. Charles Addison Hallman, July 29, 1994; stepchildren: Charles Addison Jr., Brian Alan. Student, West Hills Jr. Coll., Coalinga, Calif., 1969-72; D of Pharmacy, U. of the Pacific, 1972-76. Registered pharmacist, Calif. Pharmacy clk. Svc. Pharmacy, Inc., Coalinga, 1972-73; hosp. pharmacy intern Dameron Hosp., Stockton, Calif., 1974-76; mgr. Kernville (Calif.) Rexall Drug, 1976-78; staff pharmacist Tulare (Calif.) County Gen. Hosp., 1978-80; founder full-time svc., designer floor plans, dir. pharmacy Corcoran (Calif.) Dist. Hosp., 1980-83; staff pharmacist Hillman Health Ctr.-Tulare County Health Svcs., Tulare, 1984-86; IV, staff pharmacist Pharmacy Corp. Am. (formerly Rush Pharmacy), Fresno, Calif., 1987-91; dir. pharmacy Homecare div. Nat. Med. Care, Inc., Fresno, 1991-93; IV rm. supr. St. Agnes Med. Ctr., Fresno, Calif., 1993—. Vol. Election Com. Tulare County, 1980, Petition Com. for the Prevention of Hosp. Closure, Tulare, 1980. Mem. Am. Soc. Health Sys. Pharmacists, Internat. Networking Assn., Lambda Kappa Sigma. Home: 5240 N Vernal Ave Fresno CA 93722-6105 Office: St Agnes Med Ctr Dept Pharmacy Fresno CA 93722-3943

HALLMAN, GRADY LAMAR, JR., surgeon; b. Tyler, Tex., Oct. 25, 1930; s. Grady Lamar and Mildred (Kennedy) H.; m. Martha Suit, June 7, 1953; children: Daniel S., David L., Charles H. BA, U. Tex., 1950; MD, Baylor U., 1954. Diplomate Am. Bd. Surgery, Am. Bd. Thoracic and Cardiovascular Surgery. Intern Chgo. Wesley Meml. Hosp., 1954-55; resident Baylor U. Coll. Medicine Hosps., 1955-56, 58-62, instr. dept. surgery, 1962-63, asst. prof., 1963-67, assoc. prof., 1967-69, clin. assoc. prof., 1969-71; pvt. practice medicine specializing in cardiovascular surgery Houston, 1962—; mem. staff St. Luke's Tex. Children's, Meth. hosps., 1970—; sr. cons. cardiovascular surgery Tex. Heart Inst., 1971—; clin. prof. surgery U. Tex. Med. Sch. at Houston, 1977—; cons. cardiovascular surgery Brooke Army Hosp., also; Lackland Air Force Hosp. Author: Surgical Treatment of Congenital Heart Disease, 1966, 3d edit., 1989; contbr. 300 articles to profl. jours. Served with M.C. AUS, 1956-58. Mem. ACS, Am. Coll. Chest Physicians, Soc. U. Surgeons, Am. Coll. Cardiology, Am. Assn. for Thoracic Surgery, Soc. Thoracic Surgeons, Internat. Cardiovascular Soc., Soc. Vascular Surgery, Southwestern Surg. Congress, Tex., Houston surg. soc., Royal Soc. Health, So. Surg. Assn., Am. Surg. Assn., So. Thoracic Surg. Assn., Internat. Soc. Surgery, Phi Beta Kappa, Alpha Omega Alpha. Home: 3443 Inwood Dr Houston TX 77019-3129 Office: Tex Heart Inst 1101 Bates Ave Houston TX 77030-2607

HALLOCK, GEOFFREY GADDIS, plastic surgeon; b. Washington, Mar. 29, 1947; s. Houghton Ross and Eleanor (Gaddis) H.; m. Patricia Ann Brown, Mar. 29, 1969; children: Laurel, Ross, Elizabeth, William. BS, MIT, 1969; MD, Jefferson Med. Sch., 1975. Diplomate Am. Bd. Surgery, Plastic Surgery, Hand Surgery. Pvt. practice Allentown, Bethlehem, Pa., 1982—; asst. chief divsn. plastic surgery Allentown Affiliated Hosps., 1986—; dir. Dorothy Rider Pool microsurgery lab. Lehigh Valley Hosp. Ctr., Allentown, 1985—; clin. assoc. prof. dept. surgery Temple U., Phila., 1988—. Mem. ACS, AMA, Am. Assn. Hand Surgery, Am. Assn. Plastic Surgeons, Am. Burn Assn., Am. Soc. Aesthetic Plastic Surgeons, Am. Soc. Plastic and Reconstructive Surgeons (sci. program com. 1991-92), Am. Soc. Reconstructive Microsurgery, Internat. Microsurg. Soc., Ea. Assn. Surgery of Trauma, Northeastern Soc. Plastic Surgeons (sci. program com. 1991-92), Robert H. Ivy Soc., Alpha Omega Alpha. Office: 1230 S Cedar Crest Blvd Allentown PA 18103

HALLOCK, JAMES ANTHONY, pediatrician, school dean; b. Paterson, N.J., Oct. 28, 1942; s. Anthony E. and Alice S. (Dahab) H.; m. Jeanne LaRossa, June 27, 1965; children: James A. Jr., Jeffrey D., Julie E. AB, Seton Hall U., 1963; MD, Georgetown U., 1967. Diplomate Am. Bd. Pediatrics. Resident in pediatrics Children's Hosp. of Phila., 1967-69; chief resident in pediatrics Hosp. of U. Pa., 1969-70; asst. prof. pediatrics U. South Fla., Tampa, 1972-75, assoc. prof., 1975-80, prof., 1980-88, assoc. dean, 1978-83, dep. dean, 1983-85; exec. dean U. South Fla., Tampa and St. Petersburg, 1985-88; prof. pediatrics, dean East Carolina U. Sch. Medicine, Greenville, N.C., 1988—, vice chancellor for health scis., 1990. Contbr. articles to profl. jours. Maj. USAF, 1970-72. Fellow Am. Acad. Pediatrics; mem. N.C. Med. Soc., N.C. Biomed. Rsch. (bd. dirs. 1989), Pitt County Med. Soc., Pitt/Greenville C. of C. (bd. dirs. 1989), Rotary (St. Petersburg and Greenville chpts.). Office: East Carolina U Office Vice Chancellor & Dean Sch Medicine Greenville NC 27858-4354

HALLORAN, WALTER H., cardiothoracic surgeon; b. Mpls., Dec. 9, 1957; m. Maura D. Kennedy, May 25, 1985; children: Kathryn, Brigid, John. BA magna cum laude, St. Johns U., 1980; MD, U. Minn., 1984; postgrad., U. Rochester, 1989, 91. Diplomate Am. Bd. Surgery, Am. Bd. Thoracic Surgery. Cardiovascular surgeon Meml. Hosp., South Bend, Ind., 1991—, St. Josephs Med. Ctr., South Bend, Ind., 1991—; dir. cardiovascular ICU Meml. Hosp., 1996—; cons. LaPorte (Ind.) Hosp., 1991—. Bd. dirs. South Bend Symphony Orch., 1993—, Am. Heart Assn., South Bend. Maj. USAR. Fellow ACS; mem. AMA, Soc. Thoracic Surgeons, Ind. State Med. Soc. Home: 17591 Fox Valley Ct Granger IN 46530 Office: Cardiothoracic Surgery South Bend 720 E Cedar St Ste 450 South Bend IN 46617

HALLPIKE, JEREMY FRANK, clinical neurologist; b. London, May 12, 1936; arrived in Australia, 1976; s. Charles Skinner and Barbara Lee (Anderson) H.; m. Jane Ainslie Page, Feb. 18, 1972. MB, BS, U. London, London, 1961; MD, U. London, 1971. House physician Guy's Hosp., London, 1961; sr. house officer Guy's Hosp., Hammersmith Hosp., Nat. Hosp., Brompton Hosp., London, 1962-63; resident med. officer Nat. Hosp., London, 1964-66; rsch. fellow dept. pathology Guy's Hosp., London, 1967-69; sr. registrar neurology dept. St. George's Hosp., London, 1970-71; lectr. Inst. Neurology, London, 1972; cons. neurologist Wessex Neurol. Ctr., Southampton, Eng., 1973-76; sr. vis. neurologist, clin. assoc. prof. Royal Adelaide Hosp., South Australia, 1976-94, emeritus neurologist, 1994—; mem. rsch. adv. bd. Nat. Multiple Sclerosis Soc. Australia, 1978-83, chmn., 1983-93; mem. exec. com. med. adv. bd. Internat. Fedn. Multiple Sclerosis Socs., 1989-94. Author: (with others) The Peripheral Nerve, 1972; editor: Multiple Sclerosis, Pathology Diagnosis and Managment, 1983; editor Current Opinion in Neurology and Neurosurgery jour., 1990-91: contbr. papers to profl. jours.; mem. editl. bd. Multiple Sclerosis, Clinical and Lab. Rsch. Fellow Royal Australasian Coll. Physicians, Royal Coll. Physicians London, Royal Soc. Medicine (neurology sect.); mem. Australian Assn. Neurologists, Assn. Brit. Neurologists, Brit. Neuropath. Soc., Australian Neurosci Soc., Brit. Med. Assn., Australian Med. Assn. Office: 12 O'Connell St, North Adelaide SA 5006, Australia

HALLWORTH, ROBERT EARL, anesthesiologist; b. Phila., Feb. 13, 1946; s. Robert Earl and Birdie Louise (Huppi) H.; m. Kathryn Celia Brown, Feb. 16, 1973; 1 child, Elizabeth Ann. BS in Pharmacy, Temple U., 1969; DO, Phila. Coll. Osteo. Medicine, 1979. Diplomate Nat. Bd. Med. Examiners, Am. Osteo. Bd. Anesthesiology, Am. Acad. Pain Mgmt. Staff pharmacists Albert Einstein Med. Ctr., Phila., 1973-75; intern Suburban Gen. Hosp., Norristown, Pa., 1979-80, anesthesia resident, 1980-82; anesthesia resident Met. Hosp., Phila., 1982-83; anesthesiologist Group Anesthesia Svcs., Norristown, 1983-87, Cmty. Anesthesia Assocs., Ltd., Lancaster, Pa., 1987—; program dir. anesthesia residency Cmty. Hosp. of Lancaster, 1989—; anesthesia rep. Medicare Carrier Adv. Com., Camp Hill, Pa., 1994—. With U.S. Army, 1971-72. Mem. Am. Osteo. Assn., Am. Soc. Regional Anesthesia, Am. Osteo. Coll. Anesthesiologists (examiner 1988—), Am. Soc. Anesthesiologists, Pa. Osteo. Med. Assn. (dist. 5 rep. 1993—), Lancaster Osteo. Med. Soc., Lancaster City and County Med. Soc., Sigma Sigma Phi. Home: 3230 Oakglen Ct Lancaster PA 17601 Office: Cmty Anesthesia Assocs Ltd 1100 E Orange St Lancaster PA 17604

HALMA, JOHN ROBERT, biology educator; b. Paterson, N.J., Nov. 8, 1935; s. John and Bertha (De Jong) H.; m. Linda Kim, Apr. 9, 1966; children: Thomas R., Kimberly. BS, Calvin Coll., Grand Rapids, Mich., 1957; MS, Syracuse (N.Y.) U., 1961; PhD, Lehigh U., 1974. Instr. Ea. Christian High Sch., North Haledon, N.J., 1957-60; asst. Syracuse U., 1960-62; instr., then prof. Cedar Crest Coll., Allentown, Pa., 1962—, v.p. acad. affairs, acting dean of faculty, 1991-92; acad. coord. Hawk Mountain Sanctuary Assn., Kempton, Pa., 1984-88; rschr. Pa. Power & Light Co., Allentown, 1977-78, 85-88; curator William F. Curtis Arboretum, Allentown, 1985-91, 94—; historian Pa. Acad. Sci., 1982-94. Author: (with others) The Poconos, 1988 (Conservation Communicator of Yr. award Pa. Wildlife Fedn., Harrisburg, Pa., 1988); tech. editor (with others): Aquatic Ecology, 1989; contbr. numerous research reports and articles to profl. jours., 1973—. Bd. dirs. Wildlands Conservancy, Emmaus, Pa., 1987-93; sec. Wescosville (Pa.) Fire Co., 1986-88. NSF fellow, 1959-62, 68; recipient Chataugua award NSF and AAAS, 1977, 79, 89, 95; with biology students 1st Place award Take Pride in Pa., Pa. Dept. Environ. Resources, 1989. Mem. Am. Inst. Biol. Scis., Ecol. Soc. Am. Republican. Presbyterian. Office: Cedar Crest Coll 100 College Dr Allentown PA 18104-6132

HALPER, JAROSLAVA, pathology educator; b. Prague, Czechoslovakia, Aug. 1, 1953; came to U.S., 1980; d. Karel and Susanne (Kulka) Tausinger; m. Edward Charles Halper, Aug. 19, 1979; children: Yehuda, Daniel, Aaron. Student, Charles U., Prague, 1972-76; MD, U. Toronto, 1980; PhD, U. Minn., Rochester, 1986. Diplomate Am. Bd. Pathology. Resident pathology Albert Einstein Coll. Medicine, Bronx, N.Y., 1980-81; postdoctoral fellow Mayo Clinic Found., Rochester, 1981-82, pathology resident, 1982-86; rsch. assoc. Vanderbilt U., Nashville, 1985-86; asst. prof. pathology U. Ga., Athens, 1986-91, assoc. prof., 1991—; clinician-investigator Mayo Clinic Found., 1984-86. NIH postdoctoral fellow Mayo Clinic Found., 1981-82; NIH rsch. grantee U. Ga., 1987-91, Am. Cancer Soc. grantee U. Ga., 1991-93; recipient Biotech award U. Ga., 1990. Mem. AAAS, Am. Soc. Cell Biology, Am. Soc. for Investigative Pathology, Internat. Acad. Pathology. Jewish. Home: 126 Henderson Ave Athens GA 30605-1035 Office: U GA Dept Pathology Athens GA 30602

HALPERIN, JEROME ARTHUR, pharmaceutical executive; b. Paterson, N.J., Feb. 21, 1937; s. Harry Nathan and Frieda (Niestat) H.; m. Barbara Anne Hott, Sept. 1, 1963; children: Alicia Jennifer Odom, Rachel Elizabeth Carr. BS, Rutgers U., 1958; MPH, Johns Hopkins U., 1962; MS, MIT, 1974; DSc (hon.), Mercer U., 1993, Mass. Coll. Pharm., 1995, Phila. Coll. Pharmacy and Sci., 1996. Commd. officer USPHS, 1958, advanced through grades to asst. surgeon gen. (rear adm.), 1983; staff pharmacist USPHS Hosps., Dept. HEW, Albuquerque and N.Y.C., 1958-61; radiol. health specialist Calif. Health Dept., Berkeley, 1962-65; agreement states coord. Bur. Radiol. Health, Rockville, Md., 1965-66; dir. indsl. radiation and air hygiene Kans. Dept. Health, Topeka, 1966-68; regional rep. Bur. Radiol. Health, Chgo., 1968-71; dir. Northeastern Radiol. Health Lab., FDA, HEW, Winchester, Mass., 1971-73; dep. assoc. dir. new drug evaluation Bur. Drugs, FDA, HEW, Rockville, Md., 1974-77, dep. dir., 1977-82; acting dir. Office of Drugs Nat. Ctr. for Drugs and Biologics FDA, Rockville, 1982-83; v.p. tech. CIBA Consumer Pharms., Edison, N.J., 1983-89; exec. dir. U.S. Pharmacopeial Conv., Inc., Rockville, Md., 1989-95, exec. v.p., CEO, 1995—; chmn. Conf. on Pharmacy 21st Century Va., 1984; cons. WHO, 1979—; trustee Am. Inst. History of Pharmacy, Food & Drug Law Inst., Am. Found. for Pharm. Edn. Contbr. articles to profl. jours. Mem. Bd. Health, Hoffman Estates, Ill., 1971; bd. dirs. Perspective Woods Citizen Assn., Olney, Md., 1977-80. Named Alumnus of Yr., Rutgers U Coll. of Pharmacy, 1981; recipient Outstanding Svc. award Federally Employed Women's Assn., 1983. Fellow AAAS, APHA, Am. Assn. of Pharm. Scientists; mem. Drug Info. Assn., Am. Pharm. Assn., Internat. Pharm. Fedn. (mem. bd. pharm. scis.). Jewish. Office: US Pharmacopeia 12601 Twinbrook Pky Rockville MD 20852-1717

HALPERIN, JOHN JACOB, neurology educator, researcher; b. Montreal, Que., Can., Jan. 25, 1950; came to U.S., 1967; s. David M. and Maizie (Pottel) H.; m. Toula Jaravinos, June 15, 1975; 1 child, Daniel Mark. SB in Physics, MIT, 1971; MD, Harvard U., 1975. Diplomate Am. Bd. Internal Medicine, Am. Bd. Psychiatry and Neurology, Am. Bd. Electrodiagnostic Medicine. Intern, resident in medicine U. Chgo., 1975-77; resident in neurology Mass. Gen. Hosp., Boston, 1977-80, fellow, 1980-83; asst. prof. SUNY, Stony Brook, 1983-89, assoc. prof., vice chmn. dept., 1989-91, acting chmn. dept., 1990-91; chmn. dept. North Shore U. Hosp., Manhasset, NY, 1992—; assoc. prof. Cornell U. Med. Coll., 1992-93, prof. 1993—. Contbr. numerous articles to med. jours., chpts. to books. Fellow Am. Acad. Neurology, Am. Assn. for Electrodiagnostic Medicine (edn. com. 1989-93, examiner 1991—, tng. com. 1995—); mem. Soc. for Neurosci., Am. Acad. Clin. Neurophysiology (exec. coun. 1993—), Am. Neurol. Assn. Office: North Shore U Hosp Dept Neurology Manhasset NY 11030

HALPERN, ABRAHAM LEON, psychiatrist; b. Warsaw, Poland, Feb. 2, 1925; came to U.S., 1957, naturalized, 1952; s. Rubin M. and Helen (Perelman) H.; m. Marilyn Lois Benjamin; children: Howard, Lon, Marnen, Heather Halpern Schneid, Mark, Emily Halpern Lewis, John. M.D., U. Toronto, Ont., Can., 1952. Diplomate Am. Psychiatry and Neurology with cert. in forensic psychiatry, Am. Bd. Forensic Psychiatry, Am. Bd. Addiction Medicine; cert. mental hosp. adminstr. Intern Toronto Western Hosp., 1952-53; resident Warren (Pa.) State Hosp., 1957-60, Ea. Pa. Psychiat. Inst., Phila., 1959; assoc. research scientist Mental Health Research Unit, Syracuse, N.Y., 1961-62; commr. mental health Onondaga County, 1962-67; practice medicine specializing in psychiatry Mamaroneck, N.Y., 1967—; dir. psychiatry United Hosp. Med. Ctr., Port Chester, 1967-91; attending psychiatrist Beth Israel Hosp., N.Y.C., 1968-73, Westchester County Med. Ctr., 1971—; cons. forensic psychiatry High Point Hosp., Port Chester, 1969-93; cons. St. Vincent's Hosp., Harrison, N.Y., 1973-93; clin. assoc. prof. psychiatry N.Y. Med. Coll., Valhalla, N.Y., 1973-80, clin. prof. psychiatry, 1980-94, prof. emeritus of psychiatry N.Y. Med. Coll., Valhalla, 1994—; cons. Eye (N.Y.) Hosp. Ctr., 1994—; attending psychiatrist Kirby Forensic Psychiat. Ctr., Ward's Island, N.Y., 1994-95; attending psychiatrist dept. alcohol/substance abuse treatment Yonkers (N.Y.) Gen. Hosp., 1995—; clin. dir. mental health svcs. Dept. Correctional Program, Westchester County, N.Y., 1996—; clin. asst. prof. SUNY, Syracuse, 1964-67; asst. clin. prof. Mt. Sinai Sch. Medicine, 1970-74; clin. assoc. prof. N.Y. Med. Coll., 1973-80, clin. prof. psychiatry, 1980-94, prof. emeritus, 1994—; clin. prof. forensic psychiatry, N.Y. Sch. Psychiatry, 1979-82; mem. med. adv. com. Vis. Nurse Assn., Syracuse, 1962-67; mem. N.Y. State Mental Hygiene Med. Rev. Bd., 1982-86; bd. govs. High Point Hosp., 1989-92 Assoc. editor Bull. Am. Acad. Psychiatry and the Law, 1982-88; mem. editorial bd. Psychiat. Jour. of U. Ottawa, 1979-91; mem. exec. editorial com. Psychiat. Quar., 1982-90, assoc. editor, 1990—. Chmn. Syracuse chpt. Com. to Abolish Capital Punishment, 1962-65; mem. profl. adv. com. N.Y. State Assn. for Mental Health, 1964-67; mem. N.Y. State Law Revision Adv. Com. on the Insanity Def., 1979-80; mem. Westchester County Community Mental Health Bd., 1976-78, chmn., 1977-78; mem. Westchester County Hosp. Bd., 1992—; bd. visitors Harlem Valley Psychiat. Center, 1978-82; mem. N.Y. State Correction Med. Rev. Bd., 1980-87, N.Y. State Mental Hygiene Med. Rev. Bd., 1982-85; bd. dirs. Westchester Council on Alcoholism, 1980-85. Served to surgeon lt. comdr. Royal Can. Navy, 1942-45, 53-57. Recipient Citizenship award N.Y. State Bar Assn., 1966, Liberty Bell award Onondaga County Bar Assn., 1966. Fellow ACP, Am. Acad. Forensic Scis., Am. Coll. Psychiatrists, Am. Psychiat. Assn. (com. psychiatry and law 1973-75, com. on abuse and misuse psychiatry and psychiatrists 1993—), Am. Assn. Psychoanalytic Physicians (dir. 1978-84), Am. Pub. Health Assn., Academia, Medicinae ad Psychiatriae Found. (charter); mem. AMA, N.Y. State Med. Soc. (com. on mental health, com. bioethical issues, com. on child abuse and domestic violence), Internat. Assn. Forensic Psychotherapy, Pan Am. Med. Assn. (mem. council sect. on psychiatry 1983-85), Westchester County Med. Soc., Westchester Psychiat. Soc. (pres. 1973-74), Soc. Med. Jurisprudence (trustee 1980-85), Internat. Acad. Law and Mental Health (pres. 1983-87), Am. Acad. Psychoanalysis (sci. assoc. 1987), Am. Acad. Psychiatry and Law (councilor 1978-81, pres. elect 1981-82, pres. 1982-83, Golden Apple award 1987), Accreditation Coun. on Fellowships in Forensic Psychiatry (pres. 1990-93), Internat. Coun. on Prison Med. Svcs. (v.p. 1991—). Home and Office: 720 The Pky Mamaroneck NY 10543-4227

HALPERN, ALAN S., clinical psychologist. Lic. psychologist, Pa., Mich. Psychology intern Beth Israel Med. Ctr., N.Y.C., 1966-67; staff psychologist Univ. Counseling Ctr., Colo. State U., Ft. Collins, 1970-71, Bergen Pines County Hosp., Paramus, N.J., 1972-75; clin. psychologist Mid-Hudson Psychiat. Ctr., New Hampton, N.Y., 1975-80; clin. supr. Genesee County Community Mental Health Svc., Flint, Mich., 1980-83; chief psychologist State Correctional Instn., Graterford, Pa., 1983-85; psychologist mgt. Allentown (Pa.) State Hosp., 1985—; pvt. practice, Whitehall, Pa., 1985—; mem. group practice Assocs. in Profl. Counseling, Allentown, 1988-90, Genessee Psychiat. Ctr., Flint, 1980-83; rsch. asst. Lemuel Shatluck Hosp., Harvard Med. Sch., Jamaica Plain, Mass., 1964. Lt. USN, 1967-70, Vietnam, 1968-69. Mem. APA, Phi Alpha Theta, Psi Chi. Home and Office: 1962 Pierce Dr Whitehall PA 18052-4002

HALPERN, BRUCE PETER, academic administrator; b. Newark, Aug. 18, 1933; s. Leo and Thelma (Rubin) H.; m. Pauline Touber Anklowitz, June 9, 1956; children: Michael Touber, Stacey Rachael. A.B., Rutgers U., 1955; M.Sc., Brown U., 1957, Ph.D., 1959. Asst. prof. physiology SUNY Health Sci. Ctr., Syracuse, N.Y., 1961-66; assoc. prof. psychology, neurobiology and behavior Cornell U., Ithaca, N.Y., 1966-73, prof., 1973-95, chmn. dept. psychology, 1974-90, 91-96, Susan Linn Sage prof. psychology, 1995—, prof. neurobiology and behavior, 1995—; mem. Adv. Panel Sensory Physiology and Perception NSF, 1976-79; mem. adv. com. Nat. Inst. Neurol. and Communicative Disorders and Stroke, NIH, 1978-79, 85-87, Internat. Commn. on Olfaction and Taste, Union of Physiol. Scis., 1986-94; Fogarty sr. internat. fellow, vis. prof. oral physiology Osaka U., 1982-83; chmn. Gordon Conf. on Chem. Senses: Taste and Smell, 1987-90; PHS-NIMH postdoctoral fellow physiology, rsch. assoc., lectr. psychology Cornell U., Ithaca, N.Y., 1959-61; vis. scientist Monell Chem. Senses Ctr., 1996—. Exec. editor Chem. Senses, 1984-88; contbr. articles to profl. jours. NIMH grantee, 1958-62; NIH grantee, 1963-72; NSF grantee, 1972-90. Mem. Am. Physiol. Soc., Assn. Chemoreception Scis. (exec. chair 1982-83). Office: Cornell U Uris Hall Ithaca NY 14853

HALPERN, JOSEPH ALAN, physician; b. Bklyn., Feb. 28, 1952; s. Lester A. and Adele Janet (Tax) H.; m. Cynthia Gould, Sept. 1, 1979; 1 child, Elyza. MD, N.Y. Med., Valhalla, 1978; AB, Bard Coll., Annandale on Hudson, N.Y., 1979. Diplomate ABEM, ABIM. Resident family practice SUNY, Buffalo, 1978-79; resident in medicine Norwalk (Conn.) Hosp., 1979-81, chief resident medicine, 1981-82; emergency physician Kent & Queen Anne Hosp., Chestertown, Md., 1982-83; attending emergency physician John Hopkins Hosp., Balt., 1986-87; emergency physician Anne Arundel Med. Ctr., Annapolis, Md., 1987—; attending physician Bayview Med. Ctr., Balt., 1992-94. Fellow Am. Coll. Emergency Physicians; mem. Am. Coll. Physicians, Med. Ctr. Md. Home: 2 Waters Rd Severna Park MD 21146 Office: Anne Arundel Med Ctr Franklin & Cathedral St Baltimore MD 21209

HALPERN, PEGGY LOUISE, social welfare researcher; b. Mpls., Sept. 12, 1942; d. Chester Calvin and Marian Rose (Nathanson) H. BA in Sociology, U. Minn., 1964; MSW, U. Pitts., 1966; PhD in Social Welfare, U. Md., 1981. Lic. ind. clin. social worker, D.C.; cert. ACSW; diplomate in clin. social work. Social worker Family and Children's Svcs., Mpls., 1967-71, Hennepin County Welfare Dept., Mpls., 1972-73; project mgr. Home Svcs. Assn., St. Paul, 1974-75; social worker Clin. Ctr., Bethesda, Md., 1976, Sachs Project, Balt., 1979; asst. prof. Sch. Social Work U. Hawaii, Honolulu, 1981-83; project mgr. Dept. of Health, Honolulu, 1983-84; sr. rsch. analyst Am. Pub. Welfare Assn., Washington, 1985-88; long term care program assoc. Nat. Assn. State Units on Aging, Washington, 1989-90; sr. rsch. assoc., project dir. CSR, Inc., Washington, 1990—; cons. Sociometrics, Inc., Hyattsville, Md., 1989. Mem. NASW, Coun. on Social Work Edn.

HALPERN, STEVEN LON, physician; b. Bklyn., Aug. 16, 1951; s. Emanuel and Dorothy (Leventhal) H.; m. Deborah Davidson, Dec. 23, 1979; children: Beverly, Dana. BA, U. Rochester, 1972; MD, U. Chgo., 1976. Diplomate Am. Bd. Pediatrics, Am. Bd. Pediatric Hematology-Oncology. Intern and resident in pediatrics St. Christopher's Hosp. for Children, Phila., 1976-79; fellow Children's Hosp. of Phila., 1979-82; assoc. dir. Valerie Fund Children's Ctr., Summit, N.J., 1982-87; dir. Valerie Fund Children's Ctr., Summit, 1988—. Fellow Am. Acad. of Pediatrics; mem. Am. Soc. of Oncology, Am. Soc. of Hematology, Am. Soc. of Pediatric Hematology. Office: Valerie Fund Children's Ctr Overlook Hospital Summit NJ 07901

HALSTED, CHARLES HOPKINSON, internist; b. Cambridge, Mass., Oct. 2, 1936; s. James Addison and Isabella (Hopkinson) H.; m. June 7, 1959, (div. 1986); children: John, Michael, Ellen; m. Ann Wyant, Dec. 20, 1986. BA, Stanford U., 1958; MD, U. Rochester, 1962; post grad., Cleve. Metro Gen. Hosp., 1966, John Hopkins U., 1970. Diplomate Am. Bd. Internal Medicine. Asst. prof. John Hopkins U., Balt., 1971-74; asst. prof. U. Calif., Davis, 1974-76, assoc. prof., 1976-80, prof., 1980—, div. clin. nutrition and metabolism, 1983—; dir. Clin. Nutrition Rsch. unit NIH, Davis, Calif., 1985—. Editor: Nutrition in Organ Failure, 1989; co-editor The Laboratory in Clinical Medicine, 1981; contbr. articles to profl. jours. Surgeon USPHS, 1966-68. Fellow Am. Coll. Physicians, mem. Am. Soc. Clin. Nutrition (pres. 1988-89), Am. Soc. Clin. Investigation, Am. Gastroenterological Assn., Am. Soc. for Study Liver Diseases, Western Assn. Physicians, Am. Bd. Nutrition (pres. 1990—), Calif. Acad. Medicine. Office: U Calif Sch Medicine Davis CA 95616

HALTER, JEFFREY B., internal medicine educator, geriatrician; b. Mpls., Aug. 25, 1945; s. Cyril Joel and Marcella (Medoff) H.; m. Ellen Laura Kuper, June 25, 1972; children: Alexander, Loren, Ethan, Amy. BA magna cum laude, U. Minn., 1966, BS, MD, 1969. Diplomate Am. Bd. Internal Medicine (test com. on geriatrics 1986-88), Am. Bd. Endocrinology and Metabolism. Intern, then resident in internal medicine Harbor Gen. Hosp., Torrance, Calif., 1969-71; resident U. Wash. Sch. Medicine, Seattle, 1973-74, fellow div. metabolism, endocrinology and gerontology, 1975-77, acting instr., asst. prof., then assoc. prof. dept. medicine, 1974-84; staff physician VA Med. Ctr., Seattle, 1974-75, assoc. dir. Geriatric Rsch., Edn. and Clin. Ctr., 1978-84; prof. internal medicine, chief div. geriatric medicine U. Mich. Med. Sch., Ann Arbor, 1984—, rsch. scientist, med. dir. Inst. Gerontology, 1984—, dir. Geriatrics Ctr., 1988—; chief geriatric sect. Ann Arbor VA Med. Ctr., 1984-92, dir. Geriatric Rsch., Edn. and Clin. Ctr., 1988—; participant, presenter numerous congresses, symposia, confs., workshops in field; vis. prof. numerous univs., including Karolinska Inst., Stockholm, 1983, U. Copenhagen, 1983, Johns Hopkins U., 1985, 91, U. So. Calif., 1985, Harvard Med. Sch., 1987, 89, UCLA, 1991, U. Chgo., 1991, U. Melbourne, 1991, U. Adelaide, 1991, McGill U., 1991, U. Md., 1994; cons. Nat. Inst. on Aging; numerous others. Mem. editl. bd. Jour. Clin. Endocrinology and Metabolism, 1984-88, Am. Jour. Physiology: Endocrinology and Metabolism, 1985-91, Diabetes, 1986-88, Yr. Book Endocrinology, 1986-91, Jour. Gerontology: Med. Scis., 1988-92; mem. editl. bd. Jour. Am. Geriatrics Soc., 1990-93, assoc. editor, 1993—; guest editor Supplement on Diabetes in Elderly, Diabetes Care, 1990; contbr. over 300 articles and abstracts to med. jours., chpts. to books. With USPHS, 1971-73. AMA Goldberger fellow U. Geneva Inst. Clin. Biochemistry, 1969; grantee VA, 1978—, Nat. Inst. on Aging, 1985—, Nat. Inst. Diabetes, Digestive and Kidney Diseases, John A. Hartford Found., 1988-94, Am. Fedn. for Aging Rsch., 1994-95, Univers Found., 1991-95. Fellow AAAS; mem. Am. Diabetes Assn. (chmn. com. on rsch. rev. 1989-90), Endocrine Soc., Am. Fedn. Clin. Rsch., Western Soc. Clin. Investigation, Am. Soc. Clin. Investigation, Gerontol. Soc. Am. (rsch., edn.-practice com. 1984-87, chmn. rsch. com. clin. medicine sect. 1986-87, chmn. clin. medicine sect., v.p. 1992-93), Am. Geriatrics Soc. (bd. dirs. 1990—, pub. policy com. 1993—, chmn. long range planning com. 1995—), Ctrl. Soc. Clin. Rsch. (chmn. endocrinology coun. 1993-94, chmn. geriatrics coun. 1995-96), Am. Physiol. Soc., Phi Beta Kappa, Alpha Omega Alpha. Office: U Mich Geriatrics Ctr 300 N Ingalls Rm NI 3A00 Ann Arbor MI 48109-0405

HALTERMAN, MARK WELLS, anesthesiologist; b. Tulsa, Okla., Sept. 7, 1959; s. Harry Wells and Norma Jean (Ray) H.; m. Clorinda Maria Robles, Aug. 29, 1992; 1 child, Alexander Wells. BS in Biology, Oral Roberts U., 1982; MS in Anatomy, U. Okla., 1984, MD, 1988. Mem. staff dept. anesthesia Boston U., 1990-93; emergency care staff physician New Eng. Bapt. Hosp., Boston, 1991-93; chief anesthesia Fisherman's Hosp., Marathon, Fla., 1993—. Contbr. articles to profl. jours. Instr. Cardiac Life Support Am.

Heart Assn., 1995. Mem. AMA, Am. Bd. Anesthesiology, Internat. Trauma Anesthesia, Fla. Physicians Assn., Mass. Med. Soc., Okla. State Med. Assn. Office: Marathon Anesthesia Assocs 5701 Overseas Hwy Ste 4 Marathon FL 33050

HALTERMAN, MARTHA LEE, social services administrator, counselor; b. Poole, Ky., Feb. 4, 1940; d. Byron Lee and Mary Helen (Reinhardt) Melton; m. John David Halterman Jr., Apr. 26, 1968; 1 child, Rebecca Marie. B in Psychology and Sociology, Henderson (Ky.) C.C., 1975, Brescia Coll., 1977; M in Psychology, U. Evansville, Ind., 1980; cert. in mgmt., U. So. Ind., 1990. Cert. clin. social worker, social worker, marriage and family therapist, intervention tng. I and II, Am. Mgmt. Assn., dir. Rainbow for All Children. Office cashier J. J. Newberry Co., Henderson, 1958-63; regional trainer, office cashier C.I.T. Fin. Corp., Henderson, 1965-74; intern Redbanks Nursing Home, Henderson, 1975; dir. counseling and family svcs. Cath. Charities Bur., 1978—; supr. family & children svcs. Cath. Charities Bur. Family Life Diocese of Evansville, 1985-94; counseling and family svcs. dir., 1994—; coord. family life Cath. Charities Bur. Family Life Diocese of Evansville, 1987-94, coord. total svcs., 1993-94. Diocesan rep. Ind. Pro-Life Task Force, Indpls., 1987-94; sec. Domestic Violence Task Force, Evansville, 1980-88; bd. dirs. v.p. Birthright, Evansville, 1983-94; mem. Green River Regional Mental Health and Mental Retardation Bd., Owensboro, Ky., 1990-94. Mem. Evansville Psychol. Assn., Am. Assn. Marriage and Family Therapy (clin.). Roman Catholic. Home: 117 N Bobolink Run Henderson KY 42420-4701 Office: Cath Charities 123 NW 4th St Rm 603 Evansville IN 47708-1717

HALTOM, CRISTEN EDDY, psychologist; b. Albion, N.Y., Oct. 22, 1948; d. Arthur Benedict and Susan (Cooper) Eddy; m. Maurice Haltom Jr., Apr. 5, 1980; children: Jhakeem, Ajemo, Rebecca. BA, Albion Coll., 1970; MS, Cornell U., 1974, PhD, 1978. Lic. psychologist, N.Y. Instr. Eisenhower Coll., Seneca Falls, N.Y., 1976, Elmira (N.Y.) Coll., 1976-77, Cornell U., Ithaca, N.Y., 1977-78; clin. psychology intern Benjamin Rush Ctr. Mental Health and Mental Retardation, Phila., 1978-79; assoc. psychologist Elmira Psychiat. Ctr., 1979-84; pvt. practice Ithaca, 1984—. Co-editor: Women and Problem Drinking, 1980; contbr. articles to profl. jours. Panelist Cable Channel 7 TV, Ithaca, 1988, arts & scis. career ctr. Cornell U., 1994. Mem. APA, Ctrl. N.Y. Psychol. Assn., World Fedn. Mental Health, Internat. Assn. Eating Disorders Profls., Christian Assn. Psychologists. Office: 215 N Geneva St Ithaca NY 14850-4135

HALUSKA, BONNIE FRATI, rehabilitation nurse; b. Taylor, Pa., Sept. 4, 1950; d. Emilio and Ann (Anselmi) Frati; m. John Andrew Haluska, May 20, 1972. RN, Mercy Hosp. Sch. Nursing, 1971. Cert. rehab. nurse. Charge nurse Mercy Hosp., Scranton, Pa., 1971-72; staff nurse Allied Svcs. Rehab. Hosp., Scranton, Pa., 1972-79, asst. dir. nursing, 1979-89, dir. nursing, 1989-95; coord. Spinal Cord Injury Ctr., 1988-95; exec. dir. programs and nursing Allied Svcs. Rehab. Hosp., Scranton, Pa., 1995—; mem. nursing community adv. bd. U. Scranton, 1992—. Recipient Florence Nightingale Recognition award Hosp. Assn. Pa., 1990, 91, 92, Pinnacle awards 1995 Innovation Recognition. Mem. Assn. Rehab. Nurses (bd. dirs. Montage chpt. 1992), Pa. Orgn. Nurse Execs., Alpha Sigma Lambda.

HALVER, JOHN EMIL, nutritional biochemist; b. Woodinville, Wash., Apr. 21, 1922; s. John Emil and Helen Henrietta (Hansen) H.; m. Jane Loren, July 21, 1944; children: John Emil, Nancylee Halver Hadley, Janet Ann Halver Fix, Peter Loren, Deborah Kay Halver Hanson. B.S., Wash. State U., 1944, M.S. in Organic Chemistry, 1948; Ph.D. in Med. Biochemistry, U. Wash., 1953. Plant chemist Asso. Frozen Foods, Kent, Wash., 1946-47; asst. chemist Purdue U., 1948-49; instr. U. Wash., Seattle, 1949-50; affiliate prof. U. Wash., 1960-75, prof. Sch. Fisheries, 1978-92, prof. emeritus, 1992—; condr. research on vitamin and amino acid requirements for fish; identified aflatoxin B1 as specific carcinogen for rainbow trout hematoma, identified vitamin C2 for fish; dir. Western Fish Nutrition Lab., U.S. Fish and Wildlife Service, Dept. Interior, Cook, Wash., 1950-75, sr. scientist, nutrition, Seattle, 1975-78; cons. FAO, UNDP, Internat. Union Nutrition Scientists, Nat. Fish Research Inst., Hungary, World Bank, Euroconsult, UNDP, IDRC; affiliate prof. U. Oreg. Med. Sch., 1965-69; vis. prof. Marine Sci. Inst., U. Tex., Port Arkansas; pres. Fisheries Devel. Technology, Inc., 1980-90, Halver Corp., 1978—. Served from pvt. to capt. U.S. Army, World War II; col. USAR. Decorated Purple Heart, Bronze Star with oak leaf cluster, Meritorious Service Conduct medal. Fellow Am. Inst. Fishery Research Biologists, Am. Inst. Nutrition; mem. Soc. Exptl. Biol. Medicine, Nat. Acad. Sci., Am. Sci. Affiliation, Am. Chem. Soc., Am. Fishery Soc., World Aquaculture Soc., Phi Lambda Upsilon, Pi Mu Epsilon, Alpha Chi Sigma. Methodist (lay leader 1965-70). Club: Rotary. Home: 16502 41st Ave NE Seattle WA 98155-5610 Office: U Wash Sch Fisheries HF-15 Seattle WA 98195

HALVERSON, PAUL BREKKE, rheumatologist, educator; b. Mpls., Feb. 22, 1947; s. Gene Wells and Elizabeth Mae (Dahlberg) H.; m. Gloria M. Halverson, May 31, 1969; children: Megan, Timothy. BA, Macalester Coll., 1969; MD, Med. Coll. Wis., 1973. Asst. to assoc. prof. Med. Coll. Wis., Milw., prof. Contbr. articles and revs. to profl. jours. and chpts. to books. Chair Wis. chpt. Arthritis Found., West Allis, 1996; mem. coun. of elders Elmbrook Ch., Brookfield, Wis., 1996. Named Vol. of Yr. Arthritis Found., 1995; recipient Robert Doucette Rsch. award Arthritis Found., 1987; named to Lupus Hall of Fame Lupus Soc. Wis., 1992. Fellow ACP; mem. Am. Coll. Rheumatology (counselor Midwest region 1994-96), Am. Soc. for Clin. Rsch., Milw. Acad. Medicine. Mem. Evangel. Ch. Office: Saint Josephs Hosp 5000 W Chambers St Milwaukee WI 53210

HALVERSON, PAUL KENNETH, healthcare executive; b. Downey, Calif., Mar. 21, 1959; s. Kenneth Gunnar and Doris M. (Laury) H.; m. Andrea Edwina Stenken, June 14, 1980; children: Melissa Nathalie, Kara Elizabeth. AA, Glendale Coll., 1980; BS, Ariz. State U., 1982, M of Health Svcs. Adminstrn., 1984; D Health Policy and Adminstrn., U. N.C., 1994. Various clin. positions John C. Lincoln Hosp., Phoenix, 1975-79; adminstr. Lincoln Inst. Surgery & Truama, Phoenix, 1979-84; adminstrv. resident Health Cen. System, Mpls., 1984; v.p. Mercy Med. Ctr., Coon Rapids, Minn., 1984-86; pres., chief exec. officer Cen. Mich. Community Hosp., Mt. Pleasant, Mich., 1986-92; asst. prof. dept. health policy and adminstrn. U. N.C., Chapel Hill, 1993—; sr. fellow Ctr. for Pub. Health Practice, 1994—, exec. liaison Office of Dean Sch. Pub. Health, 1995—; pres., CEO Health Faculty Cons., Inc., Chapel Hill, 1993—; sr. hosp. mgmt. specialist Rsch. Triangle Inst., Research Triangle Park, N.C., 1995—; adj. prof. Ctrl. Mich. U., Mt. Pleasant, 1986-92; pres., CEO Meridian Home Care, Inc., Mt. Pleasant, 1988-92. Chmn. bd dirs. Ctrl. Mich. Health Policy Coun., 1987-92; bd. dirs. United Way of Isabella County, Mt. Pleasant, 1987-92, Am. Heart Assn., Mt. Pleasant, 1988-92. Mem. Am. Hosp. Assn., Am. Mgmt. Assn., Med. Group Mgmt. Assn., Am. Coll. Healthcare Execs. (mem. regent's adv. coun. 1989—), Pres.'s Assn., Mich. Hosp. Assn. Republican. Office: U North Carolina CB #7400 1101 E McGavran Greenburg Bldg Chapel Hill NC 27599

HALVERSON, TIMOTHY GREENWOOD, biostatistician, zoologist; b. Oak Park, Ill., Oct. 22, 1953; s. Wendel Quelprud and Marian Lois (Phypers) H.; m. Jessica Phillips Dimuzio, Sept. 4, 1976. BA, U. Pa., 1975; PhD, U. Md., 1983. Biologist Nat. Pk. Svc., Washington, 1982-83; vis. asst. prof. Stockton State Coll., Pomona, N.J., 1983-84; adj. asst. prof. Dept. Biology St. Josephs U., Phila., 1984; field dir. Sch. for Field Studies Wildlife Program, Athi River, Kenya, 1985; program officer Wildlife Conservation Tng. Program Smithsonian Instn., Front Royal, Va., 1986-88; statistician, analyst SmithKline Beecham Pharm., Upper Merion, Pa., 1989-92, quality advisor, 1992-95; asst. dir. process improvement, 1995—; cons. Explore Mara Field Camp, Masai Mara Res., Kenya, 1985, Conservation and Rsch. Ctr., Nat. Zoo, Front Royal, Va., 1987-94, Elmwood Park Zoo, Norristown, Pa., 1993, City of Madison, Wis., 1992, other govtl. and pvt. orgns. Contbr. articles to profl. jours. Fellow Friends of the Nat. Zoo, 1987. Mem. AAAS, Am. Soc. Quality Control, Am. Inst. Biol. Scis., Biometrics Soc., Brit. Ecol. Soc., Soc. Conservation Biology. Office: SmithKline Beecham Pharm PO Box 1539 King of Prussia PA 19406-1539

HALVERSTADT, DONALD BRUCE, urologist, educator; b. Cleve., July 6, 1934; s. Lauren Oscar and Lillian Frances (Jones) H.; m. Margaret Ann Marcy, Aug. 4, 1956; children: Donna, Jeffrey, Amy. B.A. magna cum laude, Princeton U., 1956; M.D. cum laude, Harvard U., 1960. Diplomate Am. Bd. Urology. Intern, then resident in surgery Mass. Gen. Hosp., Boston, 1960-62, resident in urology, 1964-67; pvt. practice medicine specializing in urology Oklahoma City, 1967—; chief pediatric urology svc. Okla. Children's Meml. Hosp., Oklahoma City, 1967—, chief staff, 1974-79; clin. prof. urology and pediatrics U. Okla. Med. Sch., 1970—, vice chair dept. urology, 1982—; interim provost U. Okla. for Health Scis., Oklahoma City, 1979-80; spl. asst. to pres. for hosp. affairs Oklahoma U., 1980-84; CEO State of Okla. Teaching Hosps., 1980-83, also bd. dirs.; CEO State Regents for Higher Edn., 1988-93; mem. U. Okla. Bd. Regents, 1993—; founder, vice chmn., dir. Lincoln Nat. Bank, Oklahoma City. Contbr. articles to med. jours. Pres., chmn. bd. Okla. Ind. Phys. Svcs. Corp., 1986-96; trustee Columbia Presbyn. Hosp., 1990—, chmn., 1995-96. Fellow ACS; mem. AMA (physicians recognition award 1969, 72, 79, 82, 85, 91, 94, 96), Am. Urol. Assn., Am. Acad. Pediat., Soc. Pediatric Urology, Am. Soc. Nephrology, Soc. Univ. Urologists, So. Med. Assn., Okla. Med. Assn., Oklahoma County Med. Soc., Okla. State Regents for Higher Edn., Am. Coll. Physician Execs., Assn. Governing Bds. Colls. and Univs. (bd. dirs.). Presbyterian. Home: 2932 Lamp Post Ln Oklahoma City OK 73120-6105 Office: 711 Stanton L Young Blvd #707 Oklahoma City OK 73104-5023

HALWIG, J. MICHAEL, allergist; b. Denver, Apr. 15, 1954; s. John Philip and Hilda (Fuggis) H.; m. Nancy Diane Graupman, June 14, 1975; children: Courtney Elizabeth, J. Christopher. BA, Johns Hopkins U., 1975; MD, Northwestern U., Chgo., 1980. Diplomate Am. Bd. Allergy and Immunology, Am. Bd. Internal Medicine. Intern in internal medicine Northwestern U. Meml. Hosps., Chgo., 1980-81, resident in internal medicine, 1981-83; allergy fellowship Northwestern U. Med. Sch., Chgo., 1983-85; practice medicine specilizing in allergy, asthma, immunology Atlanta, 1985—; instr. Northwestern U. Med. Sch., Chgo., 1984-85, admissions amb., 1989—; clin. asst. prof. Emory U. Sch. Medicine, 1989—. Bd. dirs. Am. Lung Assn., Douglas County, Ga., 1994—, med. dir., 1994—, chmn. pediat. lung sects., 1994—, chmn. spkrs. bur., 1994—. Fellow Am. Coll. Allergy, Asthma and Immunology (allergy practice and practice guidelines com. 1992—), Am. Acad. Allergy, Asthma and Immunology; mem. AMA, Med. Asthma and Allergy Found. of Am. (founding mem. Ga. chpt., bd. dirs. 1994—, med. dir. 1994—, chmn. med. adv. com. 1995—), Med. Assn. Ga. (rep. Coun. on Legislation 1989—), Allergy, Asthma and Immunology Soc. Ga. (pres. 1993-95, v.p. 1991-93, program chmn. 1991-93, co-chmn. third party payors com. 1992—), So. Med. Assn., Cobb County Med. Assn., Douglas County Med. Soc., Joint Coun. on Allergy and Immunology, Am. Lung Assn. of Ga. (bd. dirs. 1996). Presbyterian. Office: Ste 404 1700 Hospital South Dr Austell GA 30001-8116

HAM, GARY MARTIN, psychologist; b. Lincoln, Nebr., Feb. 6, 1940; s. Wendell E. and Sally Bertha (Lind) H.; children: Jeffery M. BS in Psychology, Wash. State U., 1963, MS in Psychology, 1965; PsyD, Newport U., 1988. Lic. psychologist, Calif.; cert. tchr., Calif, counselor. Clin. psychologist Riverside (Calif.) County Dept. Mental Health, 1967—; tchr., cons., pub. speaker, researcher Riverside County Dept. Mental Health, 1967—; instr. U. Calif. Riverside, Chapman U. Clin. psychologist Riverside County, Critical Incidents Disaster Response Team, 1985—, ARC Disaster Team. 1st lt. USAF, 1964-67. Mem. APA, ASCD, Am. Mental Health Counselors Assn., Am. Critical Incident Stress Found., Calif. Psychol. Assn., Air Force Soc. Psychologists, Psi Chi, Sigma Phi Epsilon. Office: Riverside County Dept Mental Health 9990 County Farm Rd Riverside CA 92503-3518

HAMADA, JIN, biologist; b. Kyoto, Japan, Nov. 5, 1945; s. Minoru and Chikako (Honda) H.; m. Kaoru Yasutomi, Jan. 13, 1980; children: Miho, Haruna, Ran, Momoyo, Mume. BAgr, Kyoto U., 1968, MAgr, 1970, DAgr, 1979. Postdoctoral fellow dept. biology U. Pa., Phila., 1975-77; asst. prof. Toyama (Japan) Med. and Pharm. U., 1980—; lectr. Bukkyo U., Kyoto, 1978-80, Toyama U., 1981—, Toyama Gen. Nurse Sch., 1987-89. Author: Biology of Conjugales, 1990, 2d edit., 1991, Effects of Chemicals on Algae, 1990, Imported tRNA, 1976. Advisor Soc. for the Protection of Natural Environ. of Imizu, Toyama, 1987-93. Mem. Internat. Phycological Soc., Phycological Soc. Am., Japanese Soc. Phycology, Botanical Soc. Japan, Genetics Soc. Japan. Buddhism. Home: 9-44 Minamitaikoyama, Kosugimachi, Imizu-gun Toyama 939-03, Japan Office: Toyama Med and Pharm Univ, 2630 Sugitani, Toyama 930-01, Japan

HAMADA, RENEÉ MERELYN, psychologist; b. N.Y.C., June 2, 1948; d. Carl A. and Hilda (Reichman) H.; m. David A. Adler, Apr. 10, 1947; children: Michael, Edward, Eitan. BA, Queens Coll., 1970; MS in Edn., CCNY, 1971; MA, Tchrs. Coll., N.Y.C., 1983; PhD, Columbia U., 1986. Lic. psychologist, N.Y. Research asst. Office Edn. Research CCNY, N.Y.C., 1971-72; sch. psychologist Bethpage Pub. Schs., L.I., N.Y., 1972-75, Island Trees Pub. Schs., L.I., 1975-80, Hewlett-Woodmere Pub. Schs., L.I., 1984-86, Long Beach City Sch. Dist., L.I., 1986—; teaching asst. Tchrs. Coll., N.Y.C., 1981-82. NIMH fellow, 1980-82; recipient Ted Bernstein Meml. award N.Y. State Sch. Psychologists, 1986. Mem. APA, Nat. Assn. Sch. Psychologists, Nassau County Psychol. Assn., Phi Beta Kappa, Kappa Delta Pi. Democrat. Office: Long Beach City Sch Dist Dept psychologist Long Beach NY 11561

HAMADA, TAIZO, medical educator; b. Ube, Yamaguchi, Japan, June 3, 1944; s. Toshio and Matsuko Hamada; m. Hiroko Sakai, June 6, 1971; children: Ikuko, Naoko, Yukihiko. DDS, Osaka (Japan) U., 1969, PhD, 1973. From instr. to lectr. to assoc. prof. Hiroshima (Japan) U., 1973-81, prof., 1981—; hon. prof. Mahasaraswati U., Denpasar, Indonesia, 1990; prin. Dental Technicians Sch., Hiroshima, 1990-93. Author: Denture Plaque Control, 1983, Duplicate Denture, 1986, Denture Plaque, 1991, Denture Lining, 1991. Recipient Cert. of Merit, Indonesia Dental Assn., 1993. Mem. Japanese Dentistry for the Handicapped (pres. 1991), Japanese Prosthodontic Conf. (pres. 1996), Soc. Oral Physiology. Office: Hiroshima U, Kasumi 1-2-3, 734 Hiroshima Japan

HAMADANI, HOUSHANG GHARAGOZLOU, psychiatrist; b. Tehran, Iran, Oct. 14, 1936; s. Ali Gharagozlou and Malak (Moghadam) H.; m. Imelda Rodriguez, Aug. 15, 1966; children—Jasmine, Roya. B.S., Tehran U., 1958, M.D., 1962; diploma in Psychiatry, McGill U., Montreal, Que., Can., 1970. Rotating intern Deaconess Hosp., Buffalo, 1963-64; resident in psychiatry Binghamton State Hosp. (N.Y.) and Upstate Med. Ctr., Syracuse, N.Y., 1965-68, Queen Mary VA Hosp., Montreal, Que., Can., 1968-69; resident in child psychiatry Montreal Children's Hosp., 1969-70; assoc. prof. psychiatry Pahlavi U., Shiraz, Iran, 1970-72, chmn. dept., 1974-79; staff psychiatrist Allentown Hosp., 1979—; clin. dir. Hawaii State Hosp., Honolulu, 1972-74; practice medicine specializing in psychiatry, Allentown, Pa., 1980—; med. dir. MH/MR Clinic, Allentown, 1983-84; dir. children and adolescent unit Wyoming Valley Clinic, Wilkes-Barre, Pa., 1983-84, Mercy Hosp., 1988—; vis. prof. U. Pa., Phila., 1979-83. Contbr. articles to profl. jours.; fellow Am. Psychiatric Assn. Home: 4001 Lilac Rd Allentown PA 18103-9356 Office: Houshang G Hamadani M D 2895 Hamilton Blvd Allentown PA 18104-6172

HAMAS, ROBERT STEVEN, plastic surgeon; b. Cleve., Mar. 9, 1946; s. Steve and Matilda (Girman) H.; children: Wendy, Kevin, Reagan. BA, Coll. Wooster, Ohio, 1967; MD, Ohio State U., 1971. Diplomate Am. Bd. Plastic Surgery. Surg. intern Mt. Carmel Hosp., Columbus, Ohio, 1971-72; gen. surgery resident U. Tex. Med. Br., Galveston, 1972-73; hand surgery fellow U. N.Mex., Albuquerque, 1974, Grace Hosp., Detroit, 1974-75; resident in plastic surgery U. Pitts., 1977-79; pvt. practice Dallas, 1979—; faculty U. Tex. Southwestern Med. Ctr., Dallas, 1995—; instr. endoscopic surgery courses (various), 1993—. Contbr. articles to profl. jours.; prodr./writer: Endoscopic Plastic Surgery (videotape), 1995. Bd. dirs. Life Anew Adoption Agy., Paris, Tex., 1987-92. Maj. USAF, 1975-77. Fellow ACS; mem. Am. Soc. Plastic and Reconstructive Surgery, Lipoplasty Soc., Am. Assn. Accreditation Ambulatory Surgery Facilities (newsletter editor 1995—), Dallas Soc. Plastic Surgery (pres. 1989-91, sec.-treas. 1986-89). Office: 8345 Walnut Hill Ln #120 Dallas TX 75231

HAMBACHER, WILLIAM OTTO, pscyhologist; b. Bloomfield, N.J., May 13, 1925; s. William Hambacher and Katherine Louise (Winspur) Penberthy; m. Dorothy Jane Wright, June 30, 1950; children: David W., Michael J., Barbara L., Patricia L. BA, Upsala Coll., 1949; MA, U. Pa., 1952, PhD, 1956. Lic. psychologist, Pa.; cert. sch. psychologist, Pa.; cert. Nat. Sch. Psychology Cert. Bd.; diplomate Am. Bd. Vocat. Experts, Am. Bd. Profl. Disability Cons. Pvt. practice, psychology California, Pa., 1956—; prof. psychology, Calif. Univ. of Pa., 1968-88; rsch. psychologist Phila. Naval Base, 1955-56; chmn. psychology dept. Juniata Coll., Huntingdon, Pa., 1956-58, Augustana Coll., Rock Island, Ill., 1958-63; mgr. behavior sys. HRB-Singer, Inc., State College, Pa., 1963-67; project dir. Bur. Medicine USN, Bethesda, Md., 1967-68; cons. psychiat. hosps., various mental health ctrs., 1956—; forensic psychologist attys. and ct. sys., Pa., 1968—. Contbr. articles to profl. jours. Sgt. U.S. Army, 1943-46, ETO. Recipient grants Hagan Trust, Pitts., 1972, 73, 74, 76, Hosp. Improvement Prog./NIMH, Pitts., 1975-77. Fellow Am. Coll. Forensic Psychology, Profl. Acad. Custody Evaluators; mem. Masons. Methodist. Home: PO Box 466 California PA 15419-0466 Office: PO Box 466 California PA 15419-0466

HAMBLING, MILTON HERBERT, medical virologist consultant, lecturer; b. Southampton, Hampshire, Eng., Mar. 15, 1926; s. Herbert William Stanley and Kathleen Anna (Milton) H.; m. Diane Alderton, Mar. 29, 1952; children: Susan Gillian, Peter Timothy William. MB BS, St. Bartholomews Hosp. Med. Sch., London, 1951. M.R.C.S., England; L.R.C.P., London; Diplomate (obstetrics) R.C.O.G.; M.D., London; Diploma in Bacteriology, London. House surgeon, house physician Redhill County Hosp., Redhill, Surrey, Eng., 1951-52; sr. house officer in pathology Queen Elizabeth Hosp., Birmingham, Eng., 1955-56; registrar in pathology Radcliffe Infirmary, Oxford, Eng., 1956-57; grad. asst. in bacteriology Oxford (Eng.) U., 1957-58; asst. bacteriologist Pub. Health Lab. Svc., Colindale London, 1959-62, sr. bacteriologist, 1962-64; cons. virologist, dept. head Pub. Health Lab. Svc., Leeds, Eng., 1964—; ret., 1991; honorary cons. virologist The Yorkshire Regional Health Authority, West Yorkshire Police, The Yorkshire Clinic; sr. clin. lectr. Microbiology Dept., U. Leeds; mem. The Regional Working Party on AIDS, PHLS Working Group on AIDS, Leeds Standing AIDS Action Group. Contbr. numerous articles on virology to medical and profl. jours. Served to flight lt. with RAF, 1953-55. Recipient Grade A Merit award Distinction Award Com. Dept. of Health, London, 1987. Fellow The Royal Coll. of Pathologists; mem. British Med. Assn., Med. Defence Union, Yorkshire Bone Marrow Transplant Group. Mem. Ch. of England. Home: 2 Elmete Close, Leeds LS8 2LD, England

HAMBRICK, ERNESTINE, colon and rectal surgeon; b. Griffin, Ga., Mar. 31, 1941; d. Jack Daniel and Nannie (Harper) Hambrick Rubens. BS, U. Md., 1963; MD, U. Ill., 1967. Diplomate Am. Bd. Colon and Rectal Surgery, Am. Bd. Surgery. Intern surgery Cook County Hosp., Chgo., 1967-68, resident gen. surgery, 1968-72, fellow collon and rectal surgery, 1972-73, attending surgeon, 1973-74, part-time attending surgeon, 1974-80; pvt. practice colon and rectal surgery Chgo., 1974—; chief of surgery Michael Reese Hosp., Chgo., 1993-95. Contbr. articles to profl. jours. Trustee Rsch. & Edn. Found., Michael Reese Med. Staff, Chgo., 1994—. Mem. ACS, Am. Soc. Colon and Rectal Surgeons (v.p. 1992-93, trustee Rsch. Found. 1992—), Am. Coll. Gastroenterology. Office: 30 N Michigan Ave Ste 1118 Chicago IL 60602-3503

HAMBRICK, GEORGE WALTER, JR., dermatologist, educator; b. Charlottesville, Va., Dec. 4, 1922; s. George W. and Sallie Anna (McCallum) H. BS, Concord Coll., 1944; MD, U. Va., 1946. Intern Hosp. U. Iowa, 1946-47; asst. resident dermatology U. Va. Hosp., 1947-48; resident Columbia-Presbyn. Hosp., N.Y.C., 1950-51; fellow dermatology Duke Hosp., Durham, N.C., 1951-52; assoc. dermatology Duke Hosp., 1953; instr. Columbia, 1953-55, assoc., 1955-57, asst. prof., 1957-62; assoc. prof. U. Pa., 1962-66; assoc. prof. Johns Hopkins U., 1966-69, prof., 1969-76, dir. dermatology Johns Hopkins Med. Inst., 1967-76; prof. U. Cin., 1976-81, dir. dermatology, 1976-81; prof. Cornell U. Coll. Medicine, 1981-96; chief dermatology N.Y. Hosp., 1981-96; prof emeritus, 1996—. Served as capt., M.C. AUS, 1948-50. Fellow ACP, Royal Soc. Medicine, Australasian Coll. Dermatology; mem. AMA (del. 1981-90), Soc. Investigative Dermatology (pres. 1971-72, hon. mem.), Dermatology Found. (trustee, pres. 1974), Assn. Profs. Dermatology, Am. Dermatol. Assn., Am. Acad. Dermatology (dir. 1978), The Skin Disease Soc. (pres. 1988-92), Am. Skin Assn. (pres. 1992-93), Alpha Omega Alpha. Home: 500 A E 87th Apt 4A New York NY 10128 also: 3071 Stony Point Rd Charlottesville VA 22911

HAMBURG, JOSEPH, physician, educator; b. Phila., Sept. 9, 1922; s. Thomas and Gertrude (Shulitzky) H.; m. Minerva Glickman, July 10, 1949 (dec. June 6, 1983); children: Jay, Marianne, Bonnie; m. Estelle Guttman, Aug. 25, 1985. Student, Temple U., 1938-42; M.D., Hahnemann Med. Coll., 1951, Sc.D., 1979; LHD (hon.), Thomas Jefferson U., 1993. Diplomate: Am. Bd. Family Practice. Intern Stamford (Conn.) Hosp., 1951-52; pvt. practice medicine Stamford, 1952-63; asst. prof. Coll. Medicine U. Ky., Lexington, 1963-66; dean Coll. Allied Health Professions, 1966-84, prof. medicine, community medicine and allied health edn., 1971-91, dean and prof. emeritus, 1992—; cons. in field; pres. Ky. Peer Rev. Orgn., 1980; chmn. Nat. Coun. for Edn. Health Profls. in Health Promotion, 1986—. Gen. editor: Review of Allied Health Educations, Vols. 1-5, 1972-85. Served with U.S. Army, 1942-46. Mem. Am. Soc. Allied Health Professions (pres. 1972), AMA, Inst. Medicine, Ky. Med. Assn., Am. Acad. Family Practice, Ky. Acad. Family Practice. Home: 3212 S Ocean Blvd 608A Highland Beach FL 33487-2587 Office: U KY Coll Allied Health Professions Lexington KY 40506

HAMBURG, MARGARET ANN (PEGGY HAMBURG), city commissioner; b. Chgo., July 12, 1955; d. David Alan and Beatrix Ann (Mc Cleary) H.; m. Peter Fitzhugh Brown, May 23, 1992; children: Rachel Ann Hamburg Brown, Evan David Addison Brown. BA magna cum laude, Harvard/Radcliffe Coll., 1978; MD, Harvard, 1983. Diplomate Am. Bd. Internal Medicine, Nat. Bd. Med. Examiners. Intern, resident in internal medicine The N.Y. Hosp., Cornell Med. Coll., N.Y.C., 1983-86; spl. asst. to the dir., office of disease prevention and health promotion, office of the asst. sec. for health U.S. Dept. Health and Human Svcs., Washington, 1986-88; spl. asst. to the dir. Nat. Inst. Allergy and Infectious Diseases, NIH, Bethesda, Md., 1988-89, asst. dir., 1989-90; deputy commr. Family Health Svcs., N.Y.C. Dept. Health, N.Y.C., 1990-91; commr. of health N.Y.C. Dept. Health, N.Y.C., 1991—; guest investigator The Rockefeller U., N.Y.C., 1985-86; clin. instr. dept. medicine Georgetown U. Sch. Medicine, Washington, 1986-90; asst. prof. clin. pub. health Columbia U. Sch. Pub. Health, N.Y.C., 1991—; adj. asst. prof. medicine Cornell U. Med. Coll., N.Y.C., 1991—; scholar Pub. Health Leadership Inst. Ctr. for Disease Control U. Calif., 1992; bd. dirs. N.Y.C. Health Systems Agy., Med. and Health Rsch. Assn., Health Hosps. Corp, Nat. Coun. on Women's Health, Primary Care Devel. Corp.; steering com. women and aids NIH, 1991; bd. govs. Greater N.Y. Hosp. Assn., 1991—; mem. bd. sci. advisors. Nat. Pub. Radio, 1992—; com. mem. on substance abuse mental health issues in aides rsch., 1993—; advisory bd. mem. Medunsa Trust, Inc., Med. U. So. Africa, 1993—; mem. defense sci. bd. task force on Gulf War Syndrome U.S. Dept. Defense, 1993—; bd. mem. sci. counselors Nat. Ctr. Infectious Diseases, U.S. Ctrs. for Disease, 1994—. Editorial bd. mem. Jour. N.Y. Acad. Sci., 1992—, The Bull. of N.Y. Acad. Medicine, 1992—, Current Reviews in Pub. Health, 1993—; contbr. to numerous profl. jours. Vol. attending physician The Washington Free Clinic, Washington, 1988-90. Recipient commendation Pub. Health Svc., 1988, 90, Spl. Recognition award Pub. Health Svc., 1990, cert. of Honor The Women's Club of N.Y., 1993, N.Y. Rotary Club award, 1993, Robert F. Wagner Pub. Svc. award NYU, 1993. Fellow AAAS (med. scis. section com. 1989—); mem. ACP, APHA, Am. Med. Women's Assn., Coun. on Fgn. Rels., Health Care Exec. Forum, N.Y. Acad. Medicine, Pub. Health Assn. N.Y.C., Inst. Medicine, Soc. Social Biology, Women in Health Mgmt. Office: NYC Dept Health 125 Worth St New York NY 10013-4006

HAMBURG, PAUL, psychiatrist; b. Zurich, Switzerland, Nov. 9, 1945; came to U.S., 1950; s. Joseph and Anna (Gelberg) H.; m. Virginia Claire Morse, Aug. 31, 1968; children: Naomi, Sarah. BA, Harvard Coll., 1967; MD, Albert Einstein Coll. Medicine, 1972. Pvt. family practice North Bennington, Vt., 1973-83; resident in psychiatry Mass. Gen. Hosp., Boston, 1983-86, staff psychiatrist, 1986—; pvt. practice Brookline, Mass., 1986—; dir. Bennington Coll. Health Svc., 1974-78; asst. prof. of psychiatry Harvard Med. Sch., Boston, 1989—. Contbr. articles to profl. jours. Recipient Michael Rockefeller fellowship Harvard U., 1967. Mem. Am. Psychiat. Assn. (com. on religion and psychiatry 1986-89), Alpha Omega Alpha. Office: 9 Babcock St Brookline MA 02146-3003

HAMBURGER, MAX I., rheumatologist; b. Long Branch, N.J., June 26, 1947; s. Aaron and Dorothy Hamburger. BA, Rutgers U., 1969; MD, Albert Einstein Sch. Medicine, 1973. Intern, resident Bellevue Hosp., N.Y.C., 1973-76; clin. assoc. NIH, NIAID, Bethesda, Md., 1976-79; asst. prof. SUNY, Stony Brook, 1979—; ptnr. L.I. Rheumatology Assocs., Port Jefferson, N.Y., 1980—; cons. Baxter Travenol, Chgo., 1982-84, Imre Corp., Seattle, 1985-93; pres. Sports in Motion, Smithtown, N.Y., 1993—; med. dir. Arthritis Inst. St. Charles Hosp., Port Jefferson, 1993—. Chmn. med./scientific com. Arthritis Found., Melville, N.Y., 1988-90, sec. exec. coun., 1990—. Lt. comdr. USPHS, 1976-79. Fellow Am. Coll. Rheumatology, ACP; mem. L.I. Rheumatology Assn. (pres. 1981-89). Office: 7 Medical Dr Port Jefferson Station NY 11776

HAMBURGER, RICHARD JAMES, physician, educator; b. Phila., Feb. 2, 1937; s. W. Charles and Margaretha Gertrude (Schwab) H.; m. Mary Jane Murphy, Jan. 25, 1964; children: Ellen, Joan, Mary Lou, Richard, Maureen, James. BS, Villanova U., 1958; MD, Jefferson Med. Coll., 1962. Diplomate Am. Bd. Internal Medicine. Intern Jefferson Med. Coll., Phila., 1962-63; resident in medicine Jefferson Med. Coll., 1963-65, fellow in nephrology, 1965-66; practice medicine specializing in nephrology Indpls., 1968—; mem. staff Ind. U. Hosp., Wishard Mem. Hosp., VA Hosp.; asst. prof. Ind. U. Med. Sch., 1968-72, assoc. prof., 1972-77, prof., 1977—. Contbr. articles to profl. jours. Trustee Kidney Found. Ind., 1970-74, mem. med. adv. bd., 1969—. With AUS, 1966-68. Fellow ACP; mem. AMA, Ind. Soc. Internal Medicine (trustee 1975-77), North Ctrl. Dialysis and Transplant Soc. (bd. dirs. 1972-75, 78-81), Am. Soc. Nephrology, Internat. Soc. Nephrology, Am. Soc. Artificial Internal Organs, Am. Fedn. Clin. Rsch., Nat. Kidney Found. (bd. dirs. 1991-93), Am. Soc. Internal Medicine, Renal Physicians Assn. (bd. dirs. 1977-87, treas. 1981-87), Meridian Hills Country Club. Roman Catholic. Home: 1215 Chessington Rd Indianapolis IN 46260-1629 Office: Univ Hosp 550 University Blvd Rm 1115 Indianapolis IN 46202-5257

HAMBURGER, ROBERT N., pediatrics educator, consultant; b. N.Y.C., Jan. 26, 1923; s. Samuel B. and Harriet (Newfield) H.; m. Sonia Gross, Nov. 9, 1943; children: Hilary, Debre (dec.), Lisa. BA, U. N.C., 1947; MD, Yale U., 1951. Diplomate Am. Bd. Pediatrics, Am. Bd. Allergy and Immunology. Instr., asst. clin. prof. sch. medicine Yale U., New Haven, 1951-60; assoc. prof. biology U. Calif. San Diego, La Jolla, 1960-64, assoc. prof. pediatrics, 1964-67, prof., 1970-90, prof. emeritus, 1990—, asst. dean sch. medicine, 1964-70, lab. dir., 1970—, head fellows tng. program allergy and immunology divsn., 1970-90; cons. various cos., Calif., Sweden, Switzerland, 1986—; bd. dirs. La Jolla Diagnostics, Inc. Author 1 book; contbr. articles to profl. jours.; patentee allergy peptides, allergen detector. Vol. physician, educator Children of the Californias, Calif. and Baja California, Mex., 1993—. 1st lt. Air Corps, U.S. Army, 1943-45. Grantee NIH and USPHS, 1960-64, 64-84; Fulbright fellow, 1980, Disting. fellow Am. Coll. Allergy, Asthma, Immunology, 1986. Mem. U. Calif. San Diego Emeriti Assn. (pres. 1992-94). Office: U Calif San Diego Allergy Immunology Lab La Jolla CA 92093-0950

HAMBURGER, RONALD DANIEL, dermatologist; b. Boston, Jan. 19, 1943. BS, Colby Coll., 1964; MD, U. Lausanne, Switzerland, 1970. Fellow Am. Bd. Dermatology. Intern in internal medicine Boston, 1971; resident in pathology Beth Israel Hosp., Boston, 1972, Newton Wellesly Hosp., Boston, 973; resident in dermatology Boston City Hosp., 1974-76; pvt. practice in dermatology Melrose, Mass., 1976—. Mem. Am. Assn. Dermatologists, Mass. Med. Soc., Boston Dermatology Club. Office: 8 Porter St Melrose MA 02176

HAMBURG-EYLERS, MERRIE-ANNE, osteopath, anesthesiologist; b. Lakewood, Calif., Aug. 25, 1959; d. Harold Rudolf and Patricia Joyce (Dougherty) Hamburg; m. Hinrich Eylers, Mar. 24, 1991. BSN, Calif. State U., Fullerton, 1084; MS in Health Professions Edn., Coll. Osteo. Medicine Pacific, 1993, D Osteo. Medicine, 1993. RN, Calif., Ariz.; cert. ACLS, ACLS instr., pediatric advanced life support. Nurse NME-Lakewood (Calif.) Regional Med. Ctr., 1981-93, Charter Suburban Hosp., Paramount, Calif., 1983-86, Bozeman (Mont.) Deaconess Hosp., 1986-89; intern San Bernardino (Calif.) Med. Ctr., 1993-94; resident in anesthesiology, instr. Maricopa County Med. Ctr., Phoenix, 1994—; chart auditor for pvt. co., Long Beach, Calif., 1984-85. Mem. AMA, Am. Med. Women's Assn., Am. Soc. Anesthesiologists, Ariz. Med. Assn., Ariz. Soc. Anesthesiologists. Home: 2575 E Drake St Gilbert AZ 85234

HAMDY, RONALD CHARLES, geriatrician; b. Alexandria, Egypt, July 31, 1946; came to U.S., 1985; s. Charles and Mary Hamdy; m. Eleanor Gertrude Hamdy, Aug. 19, 1977; children: Conrad, Gerard, Ronan. MB, ChB with honours, U. Alexandria, 1968, DM, 1971. Rotating intern U. Alexandria, 1968-69; resident in internal medicine Al-Gomhouriya Gen. Hosp., Alexandria, 1969-70; resident registrar internal medicine U. Alexandria Main Teaching Hosp., 1970-72; sr. ho. officer geriatric and internal medicine Farnborough (Eng.) Hosp., Kent, 1972-73; registrar in geriatric medicine Bromley (Eng.) Group of Hosps., Kent, 1974; sr. registrar in geriatric medicine King's Coll. Group Hosps., London, 1975-77; consulting physician St. John's Hosp. Richmond (Eng.), Twickenham & Roehampton Health Authority, 1977-85; chmn. dept. clin. gerontology, ethics rsch. com. Richmond (Eng.), Twickenham & Roehampton Health Authority, Eng., 1981-85; prof. internal medicine, Cecile Cox Quillen prof. geriatric medicine, head divsn. gerontology East Tenn. State U., Mountain Home, 1985—, Cecile Cox Quillen prof. geriatric medicine, head divsn. gerontology, 1990—; chief geriatrics VA Med. Ctr., Mountain Home, 1985-88, assoc. chief of staff geriatric and extended care, 1988—; hon. sr. lectr. geriatric medicine St. George's Hosp. Med. Sch., U. London, 1981-85; planning team for elderly Wandsworth Health Care, 1982-85; med. dist. initiated peer rev. orgn. VA Hosps., Dist. 8, 1986-89; vis. prof. Health Care for Elderly, U. London, 1991-93; Burroughs Wellcome vis. prof. geriatric medicine Royal Soc. Medicine, 1994-95; co-chmn. pharmacy and therapeutics com. VA Med. Ctr., Johnson City, Tenn., chmn. adverse drug reaction com.; chmn. program com. Coll. Medicine Continuing Med. Edn., East Tenn. State U.; mem. Gov.'s task force on Alzheimer's Disease, Tenn., task force on edn., prevention and detection of osteoporosis; mem. advisor to pub. guardian 1st Tenn. Devel. Dist.; adv. bd. Colonial Hill Health Care Ctr., Johnson City, Golden J-55, Johnson City Med. Ctr. Hosp., Inc.; sr. health adv. com. 1st Tenn. Regional Health Office; adj. clin. prof. divsn. clin. nutrition and psychiatry East Tenn. State U. Author: Diuretic Therapy in the Older Patient, 1978, Paget's Disease in Bone, Assessment and Management, 1981, Geriatric Medicine: A Problem Oriented Approach, 1984; editor: (with J. Turnbull, M. Lancaster, L. Norman) Alzheimer's Disease: A Handbook for Caregivers, 1990, 2d edit., 1994; mem. editl. adv. bd. Revs. Clin. Gerontology, South Med. Jour., Geriatria; reviewer for med. jours.; contbr. chpts. to books, articles to profl. jours. Fellow ACP (com. geriatrics 1987-90, chmn. com. geriatrics MKSAP IX 1991-94), Royal Coll. Physicians; mem. Am. Geriatrics Soc. (membership com., reviewer jour., ann. meeting planning com. 1993), Gerontol. Soc. Am., Royal Coll. Surgeons, So. Med. Assn. (vice-chmn. coun. 1995-96, chmn. coun. 1996-97, editor geriatric medicine sect. Dial-Access program, from assoc. councilor to councilor state Tenn., chmn. adv. com. sci. activities, reviewer jour.), So. Assn. Geriatric Medicine (pres. 1990-92), Tenn. Med. Assn. (reviewer jour.), Tenn. Geriatrics Soc. (founding), Brit. Med. Assn., Brit. Geriatrics Soc., Bone and Mineral Soc., Alzheimer's Assn. (pres. bd. dirs. N.E. Tenn. chpt. 1990-91). Office: Ea Tenn State U Coll Medicine Box 70429 Johnson City TN 37614

HAMER, HAROLD ALEC, psychiatrist; b. Toronto, Ont., Can., Aug. 9, 1939; came to U.S., 1964; s. Joseph and Yetta (Goldkind) H.; m. Mona Zakaria, Aug. 31, 1986 (dec. 1986). MD, U. Toronto, Ont., 1963. Diplomate Am. Bd. Psychiatry and Neurology, Royal Coll. Physicians and Surgeons of Can. Intern Toronto (Can.) Gen. Hosp., 1963-64; resident in neurology Mt. Sinai Hosp., N.Y.C., 1965-66; resident in psychiatry Payne Whitney Clinic, N.Y. Hosp., N.Y.C., 1966-68; pvt. practice, N.Y.C., 1968—; mem. staff Gracie Square Hosp., N.Y.C., 1970—. Mem. Am. Psychiat. Assn. Office: 15 W 70th St New York NY 10023-4507

HAMERMAN, DAVID JAY, gerontologist, educator; b. N.Y.C., Apr. 20, 1925; s. Joseph and Bertha (Broder) H. MD, NYU, 1948. Diplomate Am. Bd. Internal Medicine. Intern Mt. Sinai Hosp., N.Y.C., 1948-49; resident in medicine Mt. Sinai Hosp., Montefiore, N.Y., 1949-51; chief resident in medicine Mt. Sinai Hosp., N.Y.C., 1951-52; dir. arthritis program Albert Einstein Coll. Medicine, N.Y.C., 1956-68, prof. medicine, 1968—; chmn. dept. medicine Montefiore Hosp. Albert Einstein Coll. Medicine, N.Y.C., 1968-79, head div. geriatrics, 1983-89, dir. Resnick Gerontology Ctr., 1990—. Author: Primer on Connective Tissue, 1968; editor: Osteoarthritis: Public Health Implications for an Aging Society, 1996; contbr. articles to profl. jours. Capt. U.S. Army, 1953-55. Markle Found. scholar, 1957-62; Sinsheimer Found. fellow, 1963-68, Fogarty Inst. Internat. fellow, 1980-81; recipient Geriatric Leadership Acad. award Nat. Inst. on Aging, 1986-92. Fellow ACP; mem. Am. Soc. for Clin. Investigation, Assn. Am. Physicians. Office: Montefiore Med Ctr 111 E 210th St Bronx NY 10467-2490

HAMILL, JAMES PAUL, hospital administrator; b. N.Y.C., May 28, 1944; married. B, Georgetown U., 1966; MHA, Ga. State U., 1973. Adminstrv. resident Mercy Hosp., Davenport, Iowa, 1972-73, asst. adminstr., 1973-74, v.p., 1974-77, acting pres., chief exec. officer, 1977, pres., 1977-83; pres. Misericordia Health Systems, Davenport, 1983-85; chief exec. officer Columbus-Cuneo-Cabrini Med. Ctr., Chgo., 1985-88; pres. Holy Cross Hosp., Silver Spring, Md., 1988—. Home: 7708 Hackamore Dr Potomac MD 20854-3821 Office: Holy Cross Hosp Silver Spring 1500 Forest Glen Rd Silver Spring MD 20910-1483*

HAMILTON, JOHN KENT, gastroenterologist, educator; b. Pauls Valley, Okla., Oct. 9, 1945; s. Jack Addison and Opal Lavern (Hammons) H.; m. Evelyn Rhodes Witte, July 5, 1969; children: Jack, Rhodes, David, Paul. BA in Chemistry, Baylor U., 1967; MD, U. Okla., Oklahoma City, 1971. Diplomate Am. Bd. Internal Medicine and Gastroenterology. Mem. staff Baylor U. Med. Ctr., Dallas, 1976—; clin. instr. U. Texas Southwestern Med. Sch., Dallas, 1978—; mem. medications com. Dallas County Med. Soc., Dallas, 1987—; bd. dirs. S.W. Physician Assocs., Dallas, 1987—. Author: Gastrointestinal Disease, 1988. Scoutmaster Boy Scouts Am., 1986-88. Recipient Best Tchr. award Gastroenterol. Svc., 1981. Mem. ACP, Am. Gastroenterology Soc., Am. Soc. for Gastrointestinal Endoscopy, Am. Soc. for Study of Liver Disease, Park City Club. Baptist. Office: Baylor U Med Ctr 3500 Gaston Ave Dallas TX 75246-2045

HAMILTON, KEVIN DUNCAN, chiropractor; b. Davenport, Iowa, Apr. 14, 1954; s. Robert Taylor and Liena Amelia (Pahnke) H. D Chiropractic cum laude, Palmer Coll. Chiropractic, Davenport, 1988. Diplomate Nat. Bd. Chiropractic. Assoc. dr. McMullen Chiropractic, Davenport, 1988-89; assoc. dr. Nelson Chiropractic, Tomah, Wis., 1989-90; assoc. dr./preceptor supr. LeRoux Chiropractic, Clinton, Iowa, 1990-91; ptnr. Davenport Chiropractic Group, 1991—; indsl. cons. Toro Mfg., Tomah, 1989-90, Sears Mfg., Davenport, 1991—; asst. spkr., Palmer Coll. Chiropractic, 1990—. Songwriter: (worship choruses), 1990—; recording artist sampler collected songs, 1990—; artist: (paintings), 1989. Spkr. in field. Mem. Davenport C. of C., 1995; supporter Crisis Prenancy Ctr., Davenport, 1988; fund raiser Marine Corps Toys for Tots, Davenport, 1985—; team leader (music) Cmty. Christian Fellowship, 1994—. Home: 208 Kirkwood Blvd Apt 3 Davenport IA 52803-4537 Office: Davenport Chiropractic 126 Kirkwood Blvd Davenport IA 52803

HAMILTON, LEONARD DERWENT, physician, molecular biologist; b. Manchester, Eng., May 7, 1921; came to U.S., 1949, naturalized, 1964; s. Jacob and Sara (Sandelson) H.; m. Ann Twynam Blake, July 20, 1945; children: Jane Derwent, Stephen David, Robin Michael. BA, Balliol Coll., Oxford U., Eng., 1943, BM, 1945, MA, 1946, DM, 1951; MA, Trinity Coll., Cambridge U., Eng., 1948, PhD, 1952. Diplomate Am. Bd. Pathology. USPHS research fellow U. Utah, 1949-50; mem. staff Sloan-Kettering Inst., N.Y.C., 1950-79, head isotope studies sect., 1957-64, assoc. scientist, 1965-79; mem. staff Meml. Hosp., N.Y.C., 1950-65; mem. faculty Sloan-Kettering div. Grad. Sch. Med. Scis. Cornell U., 1956-64; sr. scientist, head div. microbiology Med. Research Ctr. Brookhaven Nat. Lab., Upton, N.Y., 1964-76; head biomed. and environ. assessment div. Office. Environ. Policy Analysis, 1973-94; attending physician Hosp. Med. Research Ctr., 1964-85; dir. WHO Collaborating Ctr. for Assessment of Health and Environ. Effects of Energy Systems, 1983—, WHO focal point on health and environ. effects of energy systems and mem. expert adv. panel on environ. hazards, 1983—; prof. medicine Health Sci. Ctr., SUNY, Stony Brook, 1968—; adj. prof. biometry and epidemiology Med. U. S.C., Charleston, 1996—; cons. HEW, Ctr. Disease Control, Nat. Inst. Occupational Safety and Health, epidemiology study of Portsmouth Naval Shipyard, 1978-88; vis. fellow St. Catherine's Coll., Oxford U., 1972-73; mem. internat. panel experts on fossil fuel UN Environment Programme, 1978, panel on nuclear energy, 1978-79, panel on renewable sources and comparative assessment of different sources, 1980; mem. various coms. Nat. Acad. Sci.-NRC, Washington, 1975-80; mem. N.Y.C. Mayor's Tech. Adv. Com. on Radiation, 1963-77, N.Y.C. Commr. of Health Tech. Adv. Com. on Radiation, 1978—; mem. energy panel WHO Commn. on Health & Environment, 1990-91; mem. Interant. Expert Group 3, Comparative Environ. and Health Effects of Different Energy Systems for Electricity Generation, 1990-91; sr. expert Symposium on Electricity and the Environ., Helsinki, Finland, 1991; adj. prof. biometry & epidemiology Med. U. S.C., Charleston, 1996—. Editor: Gerrard Winstanley, Selections from His Works, 1944; Physical Factors and Modification of Radiation Injury, 1964; The Health and Environmental Effects of Electricity Generation—a Preliminary Report, 1974. Recipient Fed. Lab. Consortium award, 1990; Am. Cancer Soc. scholar, 1953-58; Commonwealth Fund grantee, 1955-62. Mem. AMA, Am. Assn. Cancer Rsch., Am. Soc. Clin. Investigation, Am. Soc. for Investigative Pathology, Soc. for Risk Analysis, Harvey Soc., Internat. Soc. Environ. Epidemiology, Cosmos Club (Washington). Home: Childs Ln Old Field Setauket NY 11733 Office: Brookhaven Nat Lab Environ Policy Analysis Upton NY 11973

HAMILTON, LINDA HELEN, clinical psychologist; b. N.Y.C., Dec. 2, 1952; d. Peter and Helen (Casey) Homek; m. Terrence White, Aug. 10, 1974 (div. 1983); m. William Garnett Hamilton, Dec. 29, 1984. BA summa cum laude, Fordham U., 1984; MA, Adelphi U., 1986, PhD, 1989. Lic. psychologist, N.Y. Dancer N.Y.C. Ballet, 1969-88; clin. psychologist Fair Oaks Hosp., Summit, N.J., 1989-90, Miller Inst. for Performing Artists, N.Y.C., 1989-95; pvt. practice N.Y.C., 1991—; rsch. assoc. Miller Inst. Performing Artists, N.Y.C., 1987-95; chair dance com. MedArt U.S.A., N.Y.C., 1990-92; cons. psychologist Sch. Am. Ballet, N.Y.C., 1991—, Women's Ctr. Health and Social Issues, St. Luke's-Roosevelt Hosp. Ctr., N.Y.C., 1996—; advice columnist Dance Mag., 1992—; co-leader Performing Arts Medicine Delegation to Russia and Ea. Europe, 1992; dir. eating disorders program Performing Arts Psychotherapy Ctr., N.Y.C., 1996—. Contbr. articles to profl. jours. and popular mags. Miller Inst. Performing Artists grantee, 1987. Mem. APA (Daniel E. Berlyne award 1993), Ea. Psychol. Assn., Soc. for Exploration Psychotherapy Integration. Office: 30 W 60th St New York NY 10023-7902

HAMILTON, MARGARET LAWRENCE, family psychologist; b. Pottstown, Pa., Oct. 12, 1948; d. Mansfield Wiggin and Margaret Lawrence (VanVechten) Williams; m. Jackson Douglas Hamilton, Dec. 19, 1971; children: Jake, Will. BA, Skidmore Coll., 1970; MA, Bryn Mawr Coll., 1974; PhD, Internat. Coll., 1983. Lic. marriage and family counselor, Calif., N.C.; lic. psychologist, Calif. Research assoc. Fels Inst., Phila., 1971-72, Bryn Mawr (Pa.) Child Study, 1972-74; psychotherapist Santa Monica, Calif., 1976-91; supervising therapist Arden, N.C., 1991—; dir. therapeutics svcs. Child Abuse Ctr., Asheville, N.C., 1994—; coord. disaster mental health Mountain Area Red Cross, 1995—; profl. staff Charter, Asheville, 1995—; debriefer trauma WNC/CISD, 1992—. Supr. Bel Aie (Calif.) Presbyn. Ch. Counselling Ctr., 1980-91; leader Santa Monica (Calif.) coun. Boy Scouts Am., 1984-91, pres. PTA, Santa Monica, 1988-90; moderator bd. deacons Bel Air PResbyn. Ch., 1987, elder, 1989-91; youth leader Calvary Epsicopal Ch., 1991—. Mem. APA, AAUW (study chmn. 1978-82), Internat. Transaction Analysis Assn., Calif. Psychol. Assn., Am. Assn. Marriage and Family Therapists (approved supr.), N.C. Psychol. Assn. Home: 101 Ledbetter Rd Arden NC 28704-9795

HAMILTON, MICHAEL A., medical educator; b. Nice, France, Sept. 26, 1935; children: Sebastian, Sunita. MusB, U. Rochester, 1955, MD, 1964; postgrad., Cath. U., 1957-59; MPH in Epidemiology, U. N.C., 1971. Pediatric intern U. Calif., San Francisco, 1964-65; U.S. Peace Corps vol. U. Nangrahar, Jalalabad, Afghanistan, 1965-67; med. resident U. Ky., Lexington, 1967-69; preventive medicine resident U. N.C., Chapel Hill, 1969-71; internist, adj. in medicine Lincoln Cmty. Health Ctr., Durham, 1971-75; dir. physician's asst. program Duke U., Durham, 1974-85; dir. diet and fitness ctr. Duke U. Med. Ctr., Durham, 1985—; cons. Nat. Bd. Med. Examiners, 1975, mem. recertifying examination com., mem. std. setting com., mem. test devel. com., chmn. patient mgmt. program test com. for physician asst. certifying exam.; cons. to Govt. of Guyana, 1983. CoOauthor: Reduction of Atherogenic Risk Factors on Short-Term Weight Reduction, 1987, Duke University Medical Center Book of Diet and Fitness, 1990; co-editor: Medicine and Pediatrics, 1988. Home: 1011 Ducian St Durham NC 27701 Office: 804 W Trinity Ave Durham NC 27701*

HAMILTON-CRAIG, IAN RAMSAY, cardiologist, medical author; b. Adelaide, Australia, Mar. 9, 1944; s. Douglas Clarence Ramsay and Phyllis Doreen (Hamilton-Knight) Craig; m. Marina Louisa Magasdi, June 7, 1968; 1 child, Christian Ramsay. MB, BS, U. Adelaide, 1968; PhD, McMaster U., Hamilton, Ont., Can., 1972. Rhodes scholar U. Adelaide, 1968; fellow Med. Rsch. Coun. Can., Hamilton, 1969-72; med. registrar Churchill Hosp., Oxford, Eng., 1972, Royal Melbourne Hosp., Victoria, Australia, 1973; sr. med. registrar Royal Adelaide Hosp., 1973; sr. lectr. Dept. Med., U. Adelaide, 1975-86; fellow in cardiology Alfred Hosp., Melbourne, 1982; sr. vis. cardiologist Repatriation Gen. Hosp., Australia, 1990-92; dir. Lipid Mgmt. Clin., Adelaide, 1986—; vis. scientist U. Göteborg, Sweden, 1978, U. Göttingen, Germany, 1980; cons. Health Sci. Ctr., San Antonio, 1979; med. dir. Family Heart Assn. Australia, 1990-92. Author: Cholesterol Control, 1987, Men's Health, 1990, Pupil Size in Syncope, 1987, Bypass, 1996; co-author: Valve Prostheses, 1989. Chmn. Australian Nutrition Found., Adelaide, 1988-91. Recipient Cairns Meml. Prize, Old Schllars Prize, Adelaide Boy's High Sch., 1961, Elder Prize, Sheridan Prize, Everard Scholarship, U. Adelaide;. Fellow Royal Australian Coll. Physicians, Australian Menopause Soc., Cardiac Soc. Australia, Am. Heart Assn., Australian Med. Assn., South Australian-Italian Med. Assn., Kooyonga Golf Club, Naval Mil. Club of South Australia. Anglican. Office: Lipid Management Clinic, 7 E Pallant St, North Adelaide 5006, Australia

HAMLIN, REGINA C., dermatologist; b. Chgo.; d. David D. and Olive M. Corn; m. Edwin M. Hamlin Jr. BA, U. Colo., 1965; postgrad., U. Tenn., 1966-67; MD, U. Calif., San Francisco, 1970. Diplomate Am. Bd. Dermatology. Intern San Francisco Gen. Hosp., 1970-71; resident in dermatology, instr.. U. Calif., San Francisco, 1971-74, chief resident in dermatology, 1974, clin. instr., 1974-81, asst. clin. prof. dermatology, 1981-86, assoc. clin. prof. dermatology, 1986—; mem. staff Kaiser Permanente, Hayward, Calif., 1975-76; staff dermatologist Valley Med. Ctr., Fresno, Calif., 1980; asst. chief medicine, chief dermatology VA Med. Ctr., Fresno, 1982—; staff physician dermatology Calif. State U., Fresno, 1987—; mem. staff Ctrl. Calif. Faculty Med. Group, 1982-93; pvt. practice Fresno, 1993—; mem. staff VA Med. Ctr., Valley Med. Ctr., Valley Children's Hosp.; lectr., spkr. in field; cons. com. on antibiotics in over the counter products FDA, 1971-74. Mem. Marjorie Mason Ctr. Com., 1982-83; mem. capital fund raising com. YMCA, 1982-83; vol. celebrity waiters Am. Lung Assn., 1986-87; vol. health screening day Fresno Health Dept., 1987, Fresno-Madera Med. Soc., 1988; vol. Female Vets. Group, 1988, 89, 90, 91, Women's Choices of Valley Med. Ctr. and Estee Lauder Inc. Gottschalks, 1988, Clovis Unified Sch., 1990, Fresno Names Project, 1990, Fresno Women's Network, 1990, Famkly Medicine Update, Fresno, 1992, Fresno County Jail, 1993, Calif. Soc. Internal Medicine, Monterey, Calif., 1993, March of Dimes, 1995, others; bd. dirs. Lupus Found. Am., Inc., 1988-92. Fellow Am. Acad. Dermatology; mem. Nat. Assn. VA Dermatologists, Fresno-Madera Med. Soc., Women's Dermatol. Soc., Fresno-Madera Women Physicians Assn. (exec. bd. 1983-87), Pacific Dermatol. Assn., San Francisco Dermatology Assn., Alumni Faculty Assn., U. Calif. Fresno Faculty Aux. Office: 7780 N Fresno St Ste 102 Fresno CA 93720

HAMLIN, ROBERT HENRY, public health educator, management consultant; b. Cambridge, Mass., Apr. 2, 1923; s. Howard E. and Margaret E. (Henry) H.; m. Beate Kraschewski, Dec. 16, 1960; 1 son, Andrew Werner. A.B. summa cum laude, Ohio State U., 1944; B.S.M., Northwestern Med. Sch., 1945, B.M., 1946, M.D. with honors, 1947; M.P.H. magna cum laude, Harvard, 1952, JD, 1953. Diplomate: Am. Bd. Preventive Medicine. Intern Johns Hopkins Hosp., Balt., 1946-47; cons. Mass. commn. reporting, preparing and promulgating legislation on pub. and mental health and pub. welfare, 1950-53; 1st asst. to commnr. pub. health Mass., 1952-53; asst. prof. legal medicine Harvard Law Sch., 1952-57; lectr. pub. health law and adminstrn. Harvard Sch. Pub. Health, 1952-57, asso. prof. pub. health adminstrn., 1959-62, Roger Irving Lee prof. pub. health, 1962-65, chmn. dept. pub. health practice, 1963-65; v.p. Booz, Allen and Hamilton (mgmt. cons.), 1965-67; ind. mgmt. cons., 1968; chmn. bd. MACRO Systems, Inc. (mgmt. cons.), Washington, 1969-80; clin. prof. dept. comprehensive medicine Coll. Medicine, U. South Fla., 1980-83; acting dir., prof. pub. health program Coll. Pub. Health, U. South Fla., 1983; pres. United Health Techs., Inc. (mgmt. cons.), 1981—; adj. prof. health adminstrn. Columbia U. Sch. Public Health and Adminstrv. Medicine, 1972-80; cons. Rockefeller Found., 1959-61; staff dir. spel. commn. Harvard health services, 1953-54; mem. U.S. Commn. for UNESCO, 1958-60; dir. pub. health, Brookline, Mass., 1953-57; cons. Hoover Commn. II, 1954-55; asst. to sec. health, edn. and welfare, 1957-59; vis. lectr. pub. health adminstrn. and law Harvard, 1957-59. Contbr. articles profl. publs. U.S. del. 10th session gen. conf. UNESCO, Paris, 1958, pub. health adminstrn. cons. to pvt. orgns., state and local govts. Served as apprentice seaman USN, 1943-46; lt. (j.g.) M.C. USNR, 1947-49. Fellow Am. Pub. Health Assn.; mem. Am. Pub. Welfare Assn., Am. Acad. Health Adminstrn. (dir. 1976-81), Mass. Med. Soc., Phi Beta Kappa, Phi Eta Sigma, Alpha Epsilon Delta, Alpha Omega Alpha, Delta Omega. Home: 13300 Indian Rocks Rd 1904 Largo FL 33774 Office: United Health Techs 13300 Indian Rocks Rd 1904 Largo FL 34644-2010

HAMM, RHONDA LYNETTE, psychiatrist; b. Bluefield, W.Va., May 12, 1962; d. Herbert Rolland and Norma Jean (Lilly) H. BA, Concord Coll., Athens, W.Va., 1984; MS, Radford (Va.) U., 1985; DO, W.Va. Sch. Osteo. Medicine, 1993. Counselor respite care New River Cmty. Svcs. Bd., Radford, 1985-86, infant devel. specialist Project STEP, 1986-87; clin. psychologist in pvt. practice Beckley/Bluefield, W.Va., 1987-89; intern Carson City (Mich.) Hosp., 1993-94; resident in psychiatry Mich. State U., East Lansing, 1995—; physician Delta Urgent Med. Care, Lansing, Mich., 1995—; physician emergency svcs. Cmty. Mental Health, Lansing, 1995—. Mem. AMA, Am. Osteo. Assn. (area 4 rep. 1996-97), Am. Coll. Neuropsychiatry, Mich. Psychiat. Soc. (bd. dirs. capital chpt. 1995—, pres. resident br. 1996-97), Alpha Omega Alpha. Home: 4934 Delray Dr Lansing MI 48910 Office: Michigan State Univ Dept Psychiatry West Fee Hall East Lansing MI 48824

HAMMACK, JULIE ELAINE, neurology educator, neuro-oncologist; b. Coffeyville, Kans., Apr. 29, 1960. BA, U. Colo., 1981; MD, U. B.C., Vancouver, Can., 1985. Diplomate Am. Bd. Psychiatry and Neurology, Am. Bd. Pain Medicine. Intern St. Michael's Hosp., Toronto, Ont., Can., 1985-86; fellow in neuro-oncology Meml. Sloan-Kettering Cancer Inst., N.Y.C., 1989-91, fellow in cancer pain, 1991; resident in neurology Mayo Clinic-Mayo Med. Sch., Rochester, Minn., 1986-89, asst. prof., 1992—. Mem. Am. Acad. Neurology, Am. Soc. Clin. Oncology, Assn. for Study Pain, Am. Pain Soc. Office: Mayo Clinic 200 1st St SW Rochester MN 55905

HAMMEL, ERNEST MARTIN, medical educator, academic administrator; b. Ashtabula, Ohio, May 2, 1939; s. Eugene Christian and Etna Maria (Costas) H.; m. Martha Lorene Hertzer, Dec. 16, 1961; children: Eric John, James Martin. BS, Heidelberg Coll., 1962; MPH, U. Mich., 1966, PhD, 1976. Program developer Mich. Assn. Regional Med. Programs, East Lansing, 1973-74, asst. dir. ops., 1975-76; exec. dir. OHEP Ctr. for Med. Edn., Southfield, Mich., 1976—; adj. faculty depts. cmty. and family medicine, Wayne State U. Sch. Medicine, Detroit, 1993—; adj. faculty, health svcs. adminstrn. Cen. Mich. U. Extended Degree Programs, Mt. Pleasant, 1980—; co-dir. SAVE100 Pharmacy Initiative of WSU-OHEP Consortium Quality, Cost-Effective Med. Care Program, 1995—. Trustee Kenny Mich. Rehab. Found., Rochester Hills, 1984-88; chmn. program consultation and continuing med. edn. devel. CME Accreditation Com. Mich. State Med. Soc., Lansing. Behavioral Sci. fellow U. Mich., 1969-70, Behavioral Sci. Rsch. fellow, 1971-72; grad. student Rsch. grantee Rackham Sch. Grad. Studies, U. Mich., 1972; Pub. Health Svc. trainee U. Mich., 1965-66, 70-71, 72-73; contract Nat. Ctr. for Health Svcs. R&D, 1973. Mem. Assn. Am. Med. Colls., Am. Pub. Health Assn., Assn. Health Svcs. Rsch., Assn. for Hosp.

Med. Edn., Assn. Tchrs. Preventive Medicine, Mich. Assn. for Med. Edn. (pres. 1995—), Mich. Pub. Health Assn. U. Mich. Alumni Assn., Heidelberg Fellows. Contbr. articles to profl. publs. Editor several med. care orgn. publs. Office: OHEP Ctr for Med Edn 21415 Civic Center Dr Ste 301 Southfield MI 48076-3954

HAMMEL, HAROLD THEODORE, physiology and biophysics educator, researcher; b. Huntington, Ind., May 8, 1921; s. Audry Harold and Ferne Jane (Wiles) H.; m. Dorothy King, Dec. 29, 1948; children: Nannette, Heidi. BS in Physics, Purdue U., 1943; MS in Physics, Cornell U., 1950, PhD in Zoology, 1953. Jr. physicist Los Alamos (N.Mex.) Lab., 1944-46, staff physicist, 1948-49; from instr. to asst. prof. U. Pa., Phila., 1953-61; assoc. prof., fellow John B. Pierce Lab. Yale U., New Haven, 1961-68; prof. Scripps Instn. of Oceanography U. Calif., San Diego, 1968-88, emeritus prof., 1988—; adj. prof. physiology and biophysics Ind. U., Bloomington, 1989—; fgn. sci. mem. Max Planck Inst. for Physiol. & Clin. Rsch., 1978—; U.S. sr. scientist Alexander von Humboldt Found., 1981. Author: (with Scholander) Osmosis and Tensile Solvent, 1976; contbr. over 200 articles to profl. jours. Fellow AAAS; mem. Am. Phys. Soc., Am. Physiol. Soc., Am. Soc. mammology, Norwegian Acad. Sci. & Letters. Democrat. Home: 1605 Ridgeway Dr Ellettsville IN 47429-9474 Office: Ind U Med Scis Program Bloomington IN 47405

HAMMER, EMANUEL FREDERICK, clinical psychologist, psychoanalyst; b. N.Y.C., Aug. 15, 1926; s. Isadore and Rebecca (Lieberman) H.; m. Lila Maralyn King, June 4, 1950; children: Diane Robin, Cary Marc. Student, Bklyn. Coll., 1944-45, 46-47; B.A. magna cum laude, Syracuse U., 1948; Ph.D., N.Y. U., 1951. Diplomate in clin. psychology Am. Bd. Profl. Psychology; cert. psychologist N.Y. Dir. intern tng. Lynchburg (Va.) State Colony, 1951-52; sr. research scientist N.Y. State Psychiat. Inst., 1952-55; dir. dept. psychology, Psychiat. Clinic N.Y.C. Criminal Cts., 1955-72; dir. Am. Projective Drawing Inst., N.Y.C., 1956—; chief psychologist Lincoln Inst. for Psychotherapy, N.Y.C., 1960-68; lectr. Bklyn. Coll., 1958-63, New Sch. for Social Research, 1972; adj. asso. prof. N.Y. U. Grad. Sch. Arts and Scis., 1966-76; psychiat. cons., therapist United Presbyn. Ch., 1966-80; prof. grad. art therapy dept. Pratt Inst., 1978-88; clin. prof. Postdoctoral Inst. Advanced Psychol. Studies, Adelphi U., 1980—. Author: The Clinical Application of Projective Drawings, 1958, Creativity, 1961, Use of Interpretation in Treatment, 1968, Antiachievement: Perspectives on School Drop-Outs, 1970, Creativity, Talent and Personality, 1984, Reaching the Affect: Style in the Psychodynamic Therapies, 1990, also 75 profl. papers. Served with USAF, 1945-46, PTO. Fellow Am. Psychol. Assn.; liaison fellow Am. Anthrop. Assn.; mem. Nat. Psychol. Assn. for Psychoanalysis (dir. admissions, sr. mem. and faculty), Soc. Personality Assessment (sec.), N.Y. Soc. Clin. Psychologists (pres. 1964-65). Home and Office: 381 W End Ave New York NY 10024-6158

HAMMER, ROBERT EUGENE, psychologist; b. Faribault, Minn., Aug. 7, 1931; s. Rolf Walter and Verona (Bakken) H.; m. M. Kitti Nations, Apr. 30, 1967 (div. Jan. 1988); children: Gregory Clay, Cynthia Beth; m. Bonnie Jo French, Nov. 12, 1988. BS in Counseling Psychology, U. Houston, 1959, MA, 1963; PhD in Spl. Edn. Adminstrn., U. Iowa, 1970. Lic. psychologist, Iowa; cert. health svc. provider in psychology. Tchr. educable mentally retarded Houston Ind. Sch. Dist., 1961-63; testing supr. U. Houston Counseling Ctr., 1963-65; child psychologist Mental Health Inst., Independence, Iowa, 1965-67, dir. adolescent treatment unit, 1969-74, dir. psychol. svcs., 1969-89, dir. adolescent treatment unit, 1989—; rsch. dir. Iowa Div. State Mental Health Resources; pvt. practice counseling and cons. psychologist, 1974—. Bd. dirs. Iowa Nursing Found.; vol. fireman; mem men's gospel quartet United Parish Ch. Served with USAF, 1950-53. Mem. Am. Psychol. Assn., Nat. Assn. Rural Mental Health, Am. Soc. Quality Control, State Mental Health Dirs. Assn., Iowa Psychol. Assn., Houston TKE Alumni Assn., SPEBSQSA, U.S. Chess Fedn., Evaluation Network, Am. Legion, Lions, Masons. Contbr. articles to profl. jours. Home: 120 2nd St S Coggon IA 52218-9616 Office: Mental Health Inst PO Box 111 Independence IA 50644-0111

HAMMER, WADE BURKE, oral and maxillofacial surgeon, educator; b. Lakeland, Fla., Apr. 21, 1932; s. Orval Seown and Lilly Pearl (Wade) H.; m. Betty Dean Webb, June 22, 1956; children: Robert Burke Hammer, Joanna Wade Hammer Dykes. A.A., U. Fla., 1956; D.D.S., Emory U., 1960. Diplomate Am. Bd. Oral and Maxillofacial Surgery. Pvt. practice dentistry Orange Park, Fla., 1960-61; resident in oral and maxillofacial surgery U. Pa. Grad. Sch. Medicine, Phila., 1961-62, Grady Meml. Hosp., Atlanta and Emory U., 1962-65; practice dentistry specializing in oral and maxillofacial surgery Atlanta, 1965-68; mem. staff Med. Coll. of Ga. Hosp., Augusta; asst. prof. oral and maxillofacial surgery Med. Coll. Ga., Augusta, 1968-71, assoc. prof., 1971-75, prof., 1975-93, prof. emeritus oral and maxillofacial surgery, 1993; staff VA Hosp. Complex, Augusta; cons. Ft. Gordon Army Med. Ctr., Univ. Hosp., Augusta. Contbr. articles to profl. jours. Chmn. exec. com. Gen. Faculty Orgn. Med. Coll. Ga., 1988. With USN, 1950-54, col. USAR, 1976-92, ret. Decorated Knight Hospitalar Order St. John of Jerusalem, Knight Sovereign Mil. Order of the Temple of Jerusalem. Fellow Am. Assn. Oral and Maxillofacial Surgeons, Am. Coll. Dentists, Am. Soc. Dental Anesthesiology; mem. ADA, Internat. Assn. Dental Rsch., Ga. Dental Assn., Ea. Dist. Dental Assn., Am. Assn. Dental Schs., Augusta Dental Soc., Ga. Soc. Oral and Maxillofacial Surgeons, Southeastern Soc. Oral and Maxillofacial Surgeons (pres. 1984-85), Res. Officers Assn. (Nat. Dental Surgeon 1990-92), Interallied Confedn. of Res. Officers (US. del. 1992—), Assn. Mil. Surgeons, Exptl. Aircraft Assn., Am. Legion, U.S. Sailing Assn., Boat-U.S., USCG Ret. Officers Assn., Omicron Kappa Upsilon (pres. Supreme chpt. 1980-81). Methodist. Office: Dept Vet Affairs Dental Svc Med Ctr 1 Freedom Way Augusta GA 30904-6258

HAMMERMAN, MARC RANDALL, nephrologist, educator; b. St. Louis, Sept. 29, 1947; s. Elmer and Lillian (Gaylor) H.; m. Nancy Tutt, Aug. 9, 1974; children: Seth, Megan. AB, Washington U., St. Louis, 1969, MD, 1972. Intern Barnes Hosp., St. Louis, 1972-73, resident, 1973-74; resident Mass. Gen. Hosp., Boston, 1976-77; instr. Washington U., St. Louis, 1977-78, asst. prof., 1979-84, assoc. prof., 1984-89, prof., 1989—, dir. renal div. Sch. Medicine, 1991—; mem. study sect. NIH, 1990-95; investigator Am. Heart Assn., 1984. Contbr. over 100 sci. articles, revs. to profl. publs., chpts. to books. Lt. comdr. USPHS, 1974-76. NIH grantee, 1980—. Mem. Am. Fedn. for Clin. Rsch., Am. Soc. Clin. Investigation, Assn. Am. Physicians. Office: Washington U Sch Medicine Renal Div Box 8126 660 S Euclid Ave Saint Louis MO 63110-1010

HAMMERSLEY, DONALD WOLTER, psychiatrist; b. Madison, Wis., May 10, 1925; s. Ralph Wolter and Mabel Della (Pierstorff) H.; m. Edith Marie Sasman, Nov. 12, 1949; children: Kathrine, Kim, Sue, Ron. Student, Harvard U., 1943-44; BA in Medicine, U. Nebr., Omaha, 1946; MD, U. Wis., 1948. Diplomate Am. Bd. Psychiatry and Neurology. Intern St. Luke's Hosp., Cleve., 1948-49; resident in psychiatry VA Hosp., Topeka, 1949-52, sect. chief, 1954-57; fellow Menninger Sch. Psychiatry, Topeka, 1949-52; chief profl. svcs. and profl. edn. VA Hosp., Topeka, 1957-61; chief profl. svcs. Am. Psychiat. Assn., Washington, 1961-71, dep. med. dir., 1971-88; pvt. practice, Bethesda, Md., 1988-95, ret., 1995. Editor Jour. Hosp. and Community Psychiatry, 1970-81; contbr. numerous articles on psychiatry, mental health, health, alcoholism, and human svcs. to med. jours. Trustee Menninger Found. Fellow Am. Psychiat. Assn. (life), Am. Coll. Psychiatrists, Am. Coll. Mental Health Adminstrn.; mem. Group for Advancement Psychiatry (com. on therapeutic care), Cosmos Club (Washington). Home and Office: 5925 Rossmore Dr Bethesda MD 20814-2231

HAMMERSTEAD, HERMAN EDWARD, surgeon; b. Huntington Park, Calif., Aug. 21, 1945; s. Herman Edward and Olga Louise (Neuman) H.; m. Penelope Marjy Fink, Sept. 18, 1983. BA in Psychology, USC, L.A., 1967; MD, U. Louisville, 1971. Cert. Am. Bd. Surgery, Am. Bd. Surgery-Surg. Critical Care. Pvt. practice physician San Diego, 1978—. Fellow ACS; mem. Grad. Soc. Surgeons. Office: 3405 Kenyon St #302 San Diego CA 92110

HAMMETT, BENJAMIN COWLES, psychologist; b. L.A., Nov. 18, 1931; s. Buell Hammett and Harriet (Cowles) Graham; m. Ruth Finstrom, June 18, 1957; children: Susan Hood, Sarah, Carol Bress, John. BS, Stanford U., 1957; PhD, U. N.C., 1969. Lic. psychologist, Calif. Staff psychologist Children's Psychiat. Ctr., Butner, N.C., 1965-67; sr. psychologist VA Treatment Ctr. for Children, Richmond, Va., 1968-71; asst. prof. child psychiatry Va. Commonwealth U., Richmond, 1968-71; instr. psychology Western Grad. Sch. Psychology, 1980—; pvt. practice clin. psychology Palo Alto, Calif., 1972-92; rsch. psychologist, 1992—; affiliate staff mem. O'Connor Hosp., San Jose, Calif., 1980-84; v.p. bd. dirs. Mental Health Rsch. Inst., Palo Alto, 1982-83, pres. bd. dirs., 1983-85, treas., 1990-92, mem. staff, 1992—, bd. dirs. emeritus, 1992—, rsch. affiliate, 1992-95, rsch. assoc., 1995—. Co-author chpts. two books. Scoutmaster Boy Scouts Am., 1952-54; 1st lt. Civil Air Patrol, 1969; vol. Peninsula Conservation Ctr., Palo Alto, 1983—, Calif. Acad. Scis., San Francisco, 1987—; treas. John B. Cary Sch. PTA, Richmond, Va., 1969-70; trustee Nat. Parks and Conservation Assn., 1995—. Named Eagle Scout, 1947; grantee NIMH, 1970. Mem. APA, Am. Psychol. Soc., Am. Group Psychotherapy Assn., Internat. Transactional Analysis Assn. (cert. clin. mem.), Assn. Applied Psychophysiology and Biofeedbck, Biofeedback Soc. Calif., Calif. Psychol. Assn., Assn. for the Advancement of Gestalt Therapy, El Tigre Club Stanford U. (sec. 1954). Democrat. Unitarian. Home: 301 Lowell Ave Palo Alto CA 94301-3812

HAMMOND, CHARLES BESSELLIEU, obstetrician, gynecologist, educator; b. Ft. Leavenworth, Kans., July 24, 1936; s. Claude G. and Alice (Sims) H.; m. Peggy A. Hammond, jUne 21, 1958; children: Sharon L., Charles B. BS, The Citadel, 1957, Duke U., 1961. Diplomate Am. Bd. Ob-Gyn. Intern in surgery Duke U., 1961-62, resident in ob-gyn, 1962-63, 66-69, fellow in reproductive endocrinology, 1963-64, asst. prof. dept. ob-gyn, 1969-73, asso. prof., 1973-78, prof., 1978-81, E.C. Hamblen prof., 1981—, chmn., 1980—. Contbr. in field. Served with USPHS, 1964-66. Mem. Am. Fertility Soc. (pres. 1985), Am. Coll. Ob.-Gyn., Assn. Profs. Obstetrics and Gynecology, Am. Gynecol. and Obstet. Soc. (pres. 1993-94), Soc. Gynecol. Investigation, N.C. Med. Soc., N.C. Soc. Obstetricians and Gynecologists (pres. 1985), Am. Gynecol. Club (pres. 1994). Presbyterian. Home: 2827 McDowell Rd Durham NC 27705-5604 Office: Duke U Med Ctr PO Box 3244 Durham NC 27715-3244

HAMMOND, C(LARKE) RANDOLPH, healthcare executive; b. Anniston, Ala., July 3, 1945; s. Clarke MacAlpin and Edna Odell (Webb) H.; m. Carolyn Jane Milam, Oct. 26, 1974; children: Chadwick, Kyle, Amanda. BS in BA, U. So. Miss., 1968; M.Health Adminstrn., U. Ala., Birmingham, 1978. CPA, Ark. Asst. adminstr., controller Helena (Ark.) Hosp., 1971-74; asst. adminstr. S. Highlands Hosp., Birmingham, 1974-77; adminstr. Brookwood Health Svcs., Rocky Mt., N.C., 1977-79; v.p. ops. Brookwood Health Svcs., Birmingham, 1979-81; pres., chief exec. officer Medlab, Birmingham, 1981-88; asst. v.p. Hoffman-LaRoche, Birmingham, 1988-90; sr. v.p.. Roche Biomed. Lab., Birmingham, 1988-90; v.p. Jemison Investment Co., Birmingham, 1990-92; chief exec. officer, pres. Textile Resource & Mktg., Dalton, Ga., 1990-92; COO, sr. v.p. ops. Diagnostic Health Corp., Birmingham, 1992-94; sr. v.p. ops. Healthsouth Corp., 1994-95; pres., COO Monitor MEDX, Inc., 1996—; bd. dirs. Med Occ, Birmingham, Ala., Kustem Threads, Birmingham, Puckett Labs., Hattiesburg, Miss., Touch & Know, Altanta. Pres. Diabetes Trust Fund, Birmingham, 1989, bd. dirs., 1984-89; chmn. deacons Valleydale Bapt. Ch., Birmingham, 1983, strategic planning com., 1983; chmn. bd. Liberty Recreation Ctr., Inc., Pensacola, 1989—. With USN, 1968-70. Mem. Am. Assn. Health Care Execs., Health Fin. Mgmt. Assn., U. Ala. Health Adminstrs. Alumni Soc. (pres. 1989), U. Ala. Alumni Assn. (bd. dirs. 1988-90), The Club, The Summit Club, N. River Yacht Club, Inverness Country Club, Greystone Country Club. Republican. Baptist. Home: 1011 Greymoor Rd Birmingham AL 35242-7210 Office: Monitor MEDX Inc Perimeter Park One S #315N Birmingham AL 35243

HAMMOND, ELIZABETH ATWATER, psychotherapist; b. New Haven, Sept. 22, 1921; d. Harry Hall and Martha Elizabeth (Russell) Atwater; m. Alden Wellington Hammond, June 6, 1942; children: John Alden, Martha Elizabeth, David Atwater, Stuart Oliver. BA in Child Study, Vassar Coll., 1943; MA in Marital and Family Counseling, Assumption Coll., 1979. Lic. marriage and family therapist; cert. social worker. Family therapist Auburn (Mass.) Family Inst.; psychiat. social worker Dept. of Mental Health, Worcester, Mass., Marlboro, N.J.; pvt. practice Family Focus, Sturbridge, Mass. Recipient Cert. of Recognition Worcester Area Community Mental Health Ctr., 1985. Mem. Am. Assn. for Marriage and Family Therapy (clin. mem.). Home: Finlay Rd Fiskdale MA 01518

HAMMOND, GEORGE DENMAN, physician, medical researcher, educator; b. Atlanta, Feb. 5, 1923; s. Percy W. and Elizabeth (Denman) H.; m. Florence Williams, Mar. 30, 1946; children: Lane Elizabeth Hammond Clark, Christopher Scott, Bruce Benedict, Kirk Denman. B.A., U. N.C.-Chapel Hill, 1944; M.D., U. Pa., 1948. Diplomate Am. Bd. Pediatrics. Intern Pa. Hosp., Phila., 1948-50; resident Children's Hosp., Phila., 1950, 52-53; research assoc. U. Calif. at San Francisco, 1954-55, instr. pediatrics, 1955-56, asst. prof., 1956-57; asst. prof. pediatrics Sch. Medicine U. So. Calif., Los Angeles, 1957-60, assoc. prof., 1960-64, prof., 1964—, founding dir. Comprehensive Cancer Ctr., 1971-81, founding dir. U. So. Calif. Kenneth Norris Cancer Hosp. and Research Inst., 1978-81, assoc. dean Sch. Medicine, 1981-85, assoc. v.p. health affairs, 1985—; pres., chief exec. officer Nat. Childhood Cancer Found., Arcadia, Calif., 1989—; assoc. hematologist Children's Hosp., L.A., 1957-60, head divsn. hematology-oncology, 1960-71; chmn. children's cancer study group Nat. Cancer Inst., 1968-92, mem. Cancer Rsch. Ctr. rev. com., 1972-74, presdl. appointee nat. cancer adv. bd., 1974-80; vis. investigator Inst. Genetica Medica, U. Turin, Italy, 1964-65; gov.'s appointee Cancer Adv. Coun., State of Calif.; prin. investigator, dir. nat. pediatric rsch. programs T.J. Martell Found., 1981—. Assoc. editor Cancer Jour.; mem. editorial bd. Am. Jour. Clin. Oncology, Internat. Jour. Oncology, Med. and Pediatric Oncology, Jour. Hematologic Oncology, Jour. Applied Physiology, Am. Jour. Physiology; contbr. articles to profl. jours. Mem. med. adv. bd. Nat. Leukemia Broadcast Coun.; vol. Am. Cancer Soc., bd. dirs. Calif. divsn., nat. dir.-at-larte, 1982-94, chmn. task force on children and cancer, chmn. med. and sci. coms., mem. exec. com., nat. officer dir., 1995—. Comdr. M.C. USNR, 1941-43, 50-52. Recipient Parker medal U. N.C., 1944, Patterson award U. N.C., 1944, Disting. Alumnus award U. N.C., 1974, Navy League award, 1979, Medal of Honor, Am. Cancer Soc., 1993, Jacob Ehrenzeller award Pa. Hosp., 1994; Giannini Found. fellow, 1954-56; Am. Cancer Soc. scholar, 1964-65. Fellow Am. Acad. Pediatrics; mem. Am., Western socs. pediatric research, Am. Assn. Cancer Edn., Internat. Union Against Cancer, Internat. Soc. Hematology, Am. Soc. Clin. Oncology, Am. Soc. Pediatric Hematology and Oncology (Disting. Career award 1992), Am. Fedn. Clin. Research, Am. Soc. Hematology, Am. Assn. Cancer Research, Assn. Am. Cancer Insts., Soc. Surg. Oncology (Lucy Wortham James award 1984), Am. Pediatric Soc., Soc. Exptl. Biology and Medicine, Société Internationale Oncologie Pediatrique. Home: 851 S El Molino Ave Pasadena CA 91106-4411 also: Nat Childhood Cancer Found 440 E Huntington Dr PO Box 600012 Arcadia CA 91066-6012

HAMMOND, HAROLD LOGAN, pathology educator, oral and maxillofacial pathologist; b. Hillsboro, Ill., Mar. 18, 1934; s. Harold Thomas and Lillian (Carlson) H.; m. Sharon Bunton, Aug. 1, 1954 (dec. 1974); 1 child, Connie; m. Pat J. Palmer, June 3, 1986. Student Millikin U., 1953-57, Roosevelt U., Chgo., 1957-58; DDS, Loyola U., Chgo., 1962; MS, U. Chgo., 1967. Diplomate Am. Bd. Oral and Maxillofacial Pathology. Intern, U. Chgo. Hosps., Chgo., 1962-63, resident, 1963-66, chief resident in oral pathology, 1966-67; asst. prof. oral pathology U. Iowa, Iowa City, 1967-72, assoc. prof., 1972-80, assoc. prof., dir. surg. oral pathology, 1980-83, prof., dir., 1983—; cons. pathologist Hosp. Gen. de Managua, Nicaragua, 1970-90, VA Hosp., Iowa City, 1977—. Cons. editor: Revista de la Asociation de Nicaragua, 1970-71, Revista de la Federacion Odontologica de Centroamerica y Panama, 1971-77. Contbr. articles to sci. jours. Recipient Mosby Pub. Co. Scholarship award, 1962. Fellow AAAS, Am. Acad. Oral and Maxillofacial Pathology; mem. Am. Men and Women of Sci., N.Y. Acad. Scis., AAUP, Internat. Assn. Oral Pathologists, Internat. Assn. Dental Rsch., Am. Dental Assn., Am. Assn. for Dental Rsch. Avocations: collecting antique clocks, collecting gambling paraphernalia, collecting toys. Home: 1732 Brown Deer Rd Coralville IA 52241-1157 Office: U Iowa Dental Sci Bldg Iowa City IA 52242-1001

HAMMOND, MARGARET C., physiatrist; b. 1953. MD, Med. Coll. Sic., 1979. Cert. in Phys. Med. Rehab. Mem. staff Seattle VA Hosp. Office: SEattle VA Hosp 1660 S Columbian Way # 128 Seattle WA 98108*

HAMMOND, S. KATHARINE, environmental health science researcher, educator; b. Phila., Feb. 6, 1949; d. Elton Foster and M. Katharine (Strong) H. BA, Oberlin Coll., 1971; PhD, Brandeis U., 1976; MS, Harvard U., 1981. Cert. indsl. hygienist. Instr. sci. Boston U., 1975-76; asst. prof. chemistry Wheaton Coll., Norton, Mass., 1976-80; postdoctoral tng. fellow Sch. Pub. Health Harvard U., Boston, 1980-81; research assoc. Sch. Pub. Health Harvard U., 1981-85, vis. lectr. indsl. hygiene, 1985—; asst. prof. family and community medicine and pharmacology U. Mass. Med. Sch., Worcester, 1985-89, assoc. prof., 1989-95, head environ. health divsn., 1993-95; assoc. prof. environ. health sci. divsn. Sch. Pub. Health U. Calif., Berkeley, 1994—, dir. indsnl. hygiene program, 1994—; cons. U.S. EPA Sci. Adv. Bd., 1990-94, Nat. Cancer Inst., U.S. EPA on passive smoking exposure, 1986-90, Occupl. Safety and Health Adminstrn., 1994—; mem. com. on health effects of incineration NRC/NAS, 1994—; mem. com. on health effects in Vietnam vets. of exposure to herbicides biennial update Inst. Medicine/NAS, 1995—; mem. adv. panel on acrylonitrite Nat. Cancer Inst. Editor: Bikelopedia, 1976; contbr. more than 60 articles to tech. publs., and 7 book chpts. Nat. bd. dirs. Am. Youth Hostels, 1971-75, pres. Greater Boston coun., 1973-76; cons. bicycle program Youth Enrichment Svcs., Boston, 1976-81. Recipient svc. award Am. Youth Hostels, 1984. Mem. AAAS, APHA, NAS (mem. com. on assessment exposure to herbicides among Vietnam Vets.), Am. Chem. Soc., Am. Indsl. Hygiene Assn. (v.p. occupl. epidemiology com. 1989-91, chair 1991-92), Am. Coun. Govt. Indsl. Hygienists (threshold limit value com. 1992—), Internat. Soc. for Exposure Analysis (councilor 1993—), Harriet Hardy Inst. (bd. dirs. 1988-94), Inst. Medicine. Office: U Calif Berkeley Sch Pub Health Berkeley CA 94720

HAMMOND, WILLIAM EDWARD, medical educator; b. Hendersonville, N.C., Jan. 9, 1935; m. Kay; children: William E. III, Michael. BSEE, Duke U., 1957, PhD, 1967, postgrad., 1967-68. Asst. prof. Duke U., Durham, N.C., 1968-71, chief med. info., 1971—, assoc. prof., 1971-80, prof., 1980—; chair Health Level Seven, Ann Arbor, Mich., 1996—; chair Computer Based Patient Record Inst., Chgo., 1996—; pres. Am. Coll. Med. Informatics, Bethesda, Md., 1994-96. Editor: Information Systems with Fading Boundaries, 1994; mem. editl. bd. Computers and Biomed. Rsch., 1985—, Clin. Info. Mgmt., 1996. Recipient Pres.'s award Am. Med. Info. Assn., Bethesda, 1993. Mem. Order of St. Patrick, Sigma Xi. Office: Duke U Med Ctr 2100 Erwin Rd Durham NC 27710

HAMMOND-KOMINSKY, CYNTHIA CECELIA, optometrist; b. Dearborn, Mich., Sept. 1, 1957; d. Andrew and Angeline (Laorno) Kominsky; m. Theodore Glen Hammond, Sept. 21, 1985. Student Oakland U., Rochester, Mich., 1976-77; OD magna cum laude, Ferris Coll. Optometry, 1981. Lic. optometrist, Mich.; cert. diagnostic and therapeutic pharm. agt. Intern, Optometric Inst. and Clinic of Detroit, 1980, Ferris State Coll., Big Rapids, Mich., 1980, Jackson Prison (Mich.), 1981; assoc. in pvt. practice, Warren, Mich., 1981-82; optometrist Pearle Vision Ctr., Sterling Heights, Mich., 1982-87, K-Mart Optical Ctr., Sterling Heights, 1982-87, Royal Optical, Sterling Heights, 1988—; provided eye care to nursing homes, Mt. Clemens, Mich. Inventer binocular low vision aid device. Avocations: music, sports, clogging, gardening, antique crystal. Home: 47626 Cheryl Ct Shelby Township MI 48315-4708 Office: Royal Optical Lakeside Mall 14300 Lakeside Cir Sterling Heights MI 48313-1326

HAMOSH, PAUL, physician; b. Subotica, Yugoslavia, Apr. 4, 1931; came to U.S., 1965, naturalized, 1977; s. Leo and Clara (Buchwald) H.; m. Margit Katz, Oct. 24, 1954; children—Ada, Leora, Tamar. M.D., Hebrew U., 1959. Intern Hebrew U.-Hadassah Hosp., 1959-60, resident, 1960-63; asst. prof. medicine George Washington U., Washington, 1970-72; asst. prof. physiology Georgetown U. Med. Sch., Washington, 1972-75, assoc. prof., 1975-85, assoc. prof. medicine, 1975-80, assoc. prof. pediatrics, 1980-85, prof. physiology, biophysics and pediatrics, 1985—. Contbr. articles to profl. jours. Fellow AAAS; mem. Am. Physiol. Soc., Am. Biophys. Soc. Democrat. Jewish. Avocations: photography. Office: Georgetown U 3900 Reservoir Rd NW Washington DC 20007-2187

HAMPL, GLORIA JANE, psychology educator; b. New Britain, Conn., Sept. 5, 1942; d. William Frank and Jane Mildred (Cerkanowicz) H. BS in Edn., Cen. Conn. State Coll., 1964, MS in Edn., 1966; postgrad., U. Hartford, 1970. Asst. instr. Cen. Conn. State U., New Britain, 1967-70, instr., 1970-84, asst. prof., 1984—, mem. com. on concerns of women. Mem. Am. Psychol. Assn., Conn. Psychol. Assn. Office: Cen Conn State U 1615 Stanley St New Britain CT 06053-2439

HAMPTON, JAMES WILBURN, hematologist, medical oncologist; b. Durant, Okla., Sept. 15, 1931; s. Hollis Eugene and Ouida (Mackey) H.; m. Carol McDonald, Feb. 22, 1958; children: Jaime, Clay, Diana, Neal. BA, U. Okla., 1952, MD, 1956. Intern U. Okla. Hosps., 1956-57; also resident; instr. to prof. U. Okla., Oklahoma City, 1959-77, clin. prof. medicine, 1977—, mem. admissions bd., 1965—, subcom., 1985-95, head hematology/oncology, 1972-77; head hematology rsch. Okla. Med. Rsch. Found., Oklahoma City, 1972-77; dir. cancer program and med. oncology Bapt. Med. Ctr., 1977-85, med. dir. Cancer Ctr. S.W., 1985-94, Troy and Dollie Smith Cancer Ctr., 1994—; AOR network oncologist, 1995—; cons. NIH, Biomed. and Nat. Cancer Inst.; vis. prof. Karolinska Inst., Stockholm; vis. scientist U. N.C., 1966-67; pres. Stewart Wolf Soc., 1990-92; founder Robert Montgomery Bird Soc., 1973—, pres., 1996. Contbr. over 100 articles to profl. jours. Chmn. network com. Cancer Prevention and Control for Am. Indians/Alaska Natives Nat. Cancer Inst., 1990—; mem. Intercultural Cancer Coun., 1996—; bd. dirs. Heritage Hills, Oklahoma City, 1972-90, initiator Hospice of Ctrl. Okla., 1982-89, Hospice of Okla. County, 1990—, Am. Cancer Soc., mem. at large, nat. bd. dirs., mem. com. task force on Cancer in the Socio-economically Disadvantaged, 1990—, chmn. divsn. svc. and rehab. com., 1988-91; chair Okla. Pain Initiative, 1996—; co-chmn. Save St. Paul's Episcopal Cathedral com., 1983, chmn. bishop's Okla. com. on Indian work, mem. province VII Indian com., alt. del. Diocesan conv. for Okla., 1991-95, mem. adv. com. Office Minority Health NIH, 1996—, others. NIH Career Devel. Award., 1966-76. Fellow ACP; mem. Am. Fedn. Clin. Rsch. (pres. midwest sect. 1970-71), Ctrl. Soc. Clin. Rsch. (assoc. editor Jour. Lab. and Clin. Medicine 1975-76), Okla. County Med. Soc. (editor bull. 1981—, bd. dirs. 1989-91), Internat. Soc. Thrombosis and Hemostasis, Assn. Am. Indian Physicians (pres. 1978-79, 88-89); Am. Physiol. Soc., Assn. Am. Pathologists, Am. Soc. Hematology, Am. Soc. Clin. Oncology, So. Soc. Clin. Investigation, Am. Psychosomatic Soc., English Speaking Union. Clubs: Oklahoma City Golf and Country, Blue Cord, Faculty House, Chaine des Rotisseurs. Home: 1414 N Hudson Ave Oklahoma City OK 73103-3721 Office: Troy and Dollie Smith Cancer Ctr Baptist Med Ctr 3300 NW Expressway St Oklahoma City OK 73112-4999

HAMRIC, PRISCILLA, medical technologist; b. Oct. 31, 1962; d. Billy A. and Ann R. Hamric; m. Edwin M. Koen, Jan. 20, 1995; children: David A. Boyce, Jacqueline G. Boyce. AAS in Med. Tech., Shelby State C.C., Memphis, 1990. Registered med. technologist. Microbiology tech. staff Bapt. Regional Lab., Memphis, 1990-92; chief technologist in spl. chemistry Bapt. Meml. Hosp., Oxford, Miss., 1992—. Methodist. Home: 201 Warren St Oxford MS 38655

HAMRICK, LEON COLUMBUS, surgeon, medical director; b. Ludville, Ga., Nov. 11, 1925; s. Harlie Monroe and Hattie Mae (Ballew) H.; m. Frances Marion Brannan, June 7, 1949; children: Martha, Leon Jr., Mary Nell, Catherine, Margaret Susan. BS, Emory U., 1949, MD, 1952; LLD (hon.), Birmingham So. Coll., 1993. Intern Columbus (Ga.) City Hosp., 1952-53; resident surgery Lloyd Noland Hosp., Fairfield, Ala., 1953-57; assoc. in surgery Lloyd Noland Hosp., Fairfield, 1957-72, med. dir., 1972—; pres. Lloyd Noland Found., Fairfield, 1972—; mem. city adv. bd. AM South Bank, Birmingham, 1974-94; founding dir. Mutual Assurance Soc. Ala., Birmingham, 1977—; clin. prof. surgery U. Ala. Sch. Medicine, Birmingham, 1983—; trustee Miles Coll., Fairfield, Ala., 1990—; bd. dirs. Health Maintenance Group Ala., Birmingham, 1977—. Mem. State Com. Pub. Health, Montgomery, Ala., 1972-81, chmn., 1975-81; mem. Ala. Bd. Med. Examiners, Montgomery, 1972-81, chmn., 1975-81; mem. State Bd. Censors, Med. Assn. State of Ala., Montgomery, 1972-81, chmn., 1975-81; mem. Ala. Med. Licensure Commn., Montgomery, 1981—, chmn., 1981-92; mem. Cert. of Need Rev. Bd., Montgomery, 1984-87; del. Gen. and Jurisdictional Confs. United Meth. Ch., 1984-96; dir. World Meth. Coun., 1985-96, Gen. Coun. on Ministries United Meth. Ch., 1988-96; mem. Jurisdictional Episcopy

Com. United Meth. Ch., 1988-96; chmn. Episcopacy com. North Ala. Conf. United Meth. Ch., 1992-96. With USN, 1943-46, ETO, PTO. Recipient Disting. Svc. award Ala. Hosp. Assn., Montgomery, 1986. Fellow ACS; mem. AMA, Med. Assn. State Ala. (Disting. Svc. award 1986), Jefferson County Med. Soc. Home: 3656 Rockhill Rd Birmingham AL 35223 Office: Lloyd Noland Hosp 701 Lloyd Noland Pkwy Fairfield AL 35064

HAN, JAOK, cardiologist, researcher, educator; b. Chinnampo, Korea, July 16, 1930; came to U.S., 1955, naturalized, 1970; s. Choon H. and Chung R. (Kim) H.; m. Yangsook Chun, Jan. 21, 1961; children: Sylvia, Julia, Andrew. M.D., Kyong-Puk Nat. U., Taegu, Korea, 1951; Ph.D., SUNY-Upstate Med. Ctr., 1962. Intern, Jersey City Med. Ctr., 1955-56; resident Mercy Hosp., Pitts., 1956-57; research assoc. Masonic Med. Research Lab., Utica, N.Y., 1961-66; fellow in cardiology U. Rochester Med. Ctr. (N.Y.), 1966-67; assoc. prof. medicine Albany Med. Coll. (N.Y.), 1968-73, attending cardiologist, 1968—, dir. electrocardiography, 1968—; prof. medicine Albany Med. Coll., 1973—; mem. research com. N.Y. State Heart Assn., 1968-73; mem. spl. project rev. coms. Nat. Heart and Lung Inst., 1972—, mem. cardiology adv. com., 1981—. Author: Cardiac Arrhythmias, 1972; mem. editorial bd. Jour. Electrocardiology, 1984—; contbr. numerous articles to med. jours. Fellow: Internat. Soc. Cardiology Found., 1960-61, Masonic Found. for Med. Research, 1961-63; NIH grantee, 1969—. Fellow Am. Heart Assn. (Council on Circulation; pres. northeastern N.Y. chpt. 1980-82; research com. 1976-79), Am. Coll. Cardiology; mem. Am. Physiol. Soc., Am. Fedn. Clin. Research, N.Y. Acad. Scis., Sigma Xi. Home: 29 Cobble Hl Albany NY 12211-1312 Office: Albany Med Coll Dept Medicine Albany NY 12208

HAN, JIAHUAI, medical researcher. BS in Biochemistry, Beijing U., 1982, MS in Protein Biochemistry, 1988; PhD in Molecular Biology, U. Brussels, 1990. Rsch. fellow Dept. Internal Medicine and Howard Hughes Med. Inst., U. Tex. Southwestern Med. Ctr., Dallas, 1987-92; rsch. assoc. Dept. Immunology, The Scripps Rsch. Inst., La Jolla, Calif., 1992-93, sr. rsch. assoc., 1993, asst. mem., 1993—. Contbr. articles to profl. jours. Recipient Established Investigator award Am. Heart Assn., 1995. Office: Scripps Rsch Inst 10550 N Torrey Pines Rd La Jolla CA 92037*

HANAK, MARCIA, nursing educator; b. Duluth, Minn., Mar. 27, 1948; d. Melvin and Mary (Pratt) Willson; m. Kenneth Rogers. BSN, U. Ariz., 1970; MA, NYU, 1983. CRRN, RN, Calif., N.Y., Colo. Staff and relief charge nurse med. spl. care and ICU Mass. Gen. Hosp., Boston, 1970-71, nurse clinician rehab. unit, 1973-74; staff nurse Orentreich Dermatology Clinic, N.Y.C., 1971-72; asst. head nurse Rusk Inst. NYU Med. Ctr., N.Y.C., 1972-73; team leader Vis. Nurse Svc., Tarrytown, N.Y., 1974-75; nurse coord. N.Y. Regional Spinal Cord Injury System, NYU Med. Ctr., N.Y.C., 1975-81; patient edn. coord., rehab. nurse specialist Rusk Inst. NYU Med. Ctr., N.Y.C., 1981-85; clin. coord. Mt. Sinai Med. Ctr., N.Y.C., 1986-88; assoc. Vocat. Econs., Inc., San Francisco and L.A., 1989—; pvt. practice rehab. cons., 1985—; cons., presenter in field. Author: Spinal Cord Injury: An Illustrated Guide for Healthcare Professionals, 1983, 2d edit. 1993, Patient Family Education: Teaching Programs on Chronic Disease and Disability, 1986, Rehabilitation Nursing for the Neurological Patient, 1992; author 2 profl. manuals, 2 patient handbooks; contbr. articles to profl. jours. and book chpts.; author nat. video program. Mem. Am. Assn. Spinal Cord Injury Nurses (bd. dirs. 1985-88, pres., 1986-87, Disting. Svc. award 1990), Assn. Rehab. Nurses.

HANAS, SVEN RAGNAR, pediatrician; b. Västeras, Sweden, July 3, 1951; s. Bertil Henrik and Ingrid Margareta (Wilson) H. MD, Uppsala (Sweden) U., 1977. Intern Uddevalla Hosp., Sweden, 1977-79, resident pediatrics, 1979-83; clin. fellow dept. pediatrics, sect. endocrinology U. Gothenburg (Sweden), 1984; cons. dept. pediatrician Uddevalla Hosp., Sweden, 1985—. Contbr. med. articles to profl. jours.; inventor indwelling catheter for insulin injections in diabetes treatment. Mem. Study Group Adolescent Medicine (treas. 1987-89), Study Group Childhood Diabetes, Internat. Soc. Pediatric and Adolescent Diabetes, European Assn. for Study Diabetes, Swedish Med. Assn., Swedish Pediatric Assn. Office: Uddevalla Hosp, Dept Pediatrics, S-451 80 Uddevalla Sweden

HANAWALT, PHILIP COURTLAND, biology educator, researcher; b. Akron, Ohio, Aug. 25, 1931; s. Joseph Donald and Lenore (Smith) H.; m. Joanna Thomas, Nov. 2, 1957 (div. Oct. 1977); children: David, Steven; m. Graciela Spivak, Sept. 10, 1978; children: Alex, Lisa. Student, Deep Springs Coll., 1949-50; BA, Oberlin Coll., 1954; MS, Yale U., 1955, PhD, 1959. Postdoctoral fellow U. Copenhagen, Denmark, 1958-60, Calif. Inst. Tech., Pasadena, 1960-61; rsch. biophysicist, lectr. Stanford U., Calif., 1961-65, assoc. prof., 1965-70, prof., 1970—, chmn. dept. biol. scis., 1982-89; mem. physiol. chemistry study sect. NIH, Bethesda, Md., 1966-70, chmn. pathology study sect., 1981-84; mem. sci. adv. com. Am. Cancer Soc., N.Y.C., 1972-76; chmn. 2d ad hoc senate com. on professoriate Stanford U., 1988-90; mem. NSF fellowship rev. panel, 1985; mem. carcinogen identification com. Calif. EPA, 1995—; mem. toxicology adv. com. Burroughs-Welcome Fund, 1995; mem. sci. adv. bd. Fogarty Internat. Ctr., NIH, 1995—; chmn. Gordon Conf. on Mutagenesis, 1996. Author: Molecular Photobiology, 1969; author, editor: DNA Repair: Techniques, 1983, 88, Molecular Basis of Life, 1968, Molecules to Living Cells, 1980; mng. editor DNA Repair Jour., 1982-93; assoc. editor Jour. Cancer Rsch., Molecular Carcinogenesis, Biotechniques; bd. rev. editors Sci.; contbr. more than 350 articles to profl. jours. Recipient Outstanding Investigator award Nat. Cancer Inst., 1987—, Excellence in Tchg. award No. Calif. Phi Beta Kappa, 1991, Environ. Mutagen Soc. Ann. Rsch. award, 1992, Peter and Helen Bing award for Disting. Tchg., 1992, Am. Soc. for Photobiology Rsch. award, 1996; Hans Falk lectr. Nat. Inst. Environ. Health Scis., 1990; Fogarty sr. rsch. fellow, 1993. Fellow AAAS, Am. Acad. Microbiology; mem. NAS, Am. Assn. Cancer Rsch. (bd. dirs. 1994-97), Genetics Soc., Biophys. Soc. (exec. bd. 1969-71), Am. Soc. Biochemistry and Molecular Biology, Environ. Mutagen Soc. (pres. 1993-94), Radiation Rsch. Soc. Home: 317 Shasta Dr Palo Alto CA 94306-4542 Office: Stanford U Herrin Biology Labs Stanford CA 94305-5020

HANBURY, RAYMOND FRANCIS, JR., psychologist, consultant; b. Jersey City, Mar. 28, 1945; s. Raymond Francis and Rose Ann (Doorley) H.; m. Patricia Ann Delaney, Mar. 9, 1974; children: Amy, Kim. BS, St. Peter's Coll., 1967; MA, Seton Hall U., 1969; PhD, NYU, 1980. Lic. psychologist, N.J.; diplomate, fellow Am. Bd. Med. Psychotherapists; diplomate Am. Bd. Vocat. Experts; cert. addictions specialist, rehab. counselor. Adj. asst. prof. dept. psychiatry Mt. Sinai Medicine, N.Y.C., 1980—; pvt. practice Manasquan, N.J., 1989; dir. clin. svcs. Mt. Sinai Med. Ctr., N.Y.C., 1970-90; dir. rehab. psychology dept. JFK Johnson Rehab. Inst., Edison, N.J., 1990—; adj. asst. prof. dept. phys. medicine and rehab., dept. psychiatry UMDNJ-Robert Wood Johnson Med. Sch.; adj. asst. prof. psychology Pace U., White Plains, N.Y., 1980-82; cons. Spring Lake Heights (N.J.) Police Dept., 1989—, VA Med. Ctr., Bronx, N.Y., 1978-79; crisis intervention specialist Mid-Bergen Cmty. Mental Health Ctr., Paramus, N.Y., 1980-89; state clin. dir. Critical Incident Stress Mgmt. Network N.J., 1990. Cons. editor Psychology Addictive Behaviors, 1987—; mem. edtl. bd. Jour. Addictive Diseases, 1990—; contbr. articles to profl. jours. Fellow Rehab. Svcs. Adminstrn., 1967-69; named Disting. Practitioner in Psychology, Nat. Academies of Practice, 1994. Mem. APA (pres. divsn. addictions 1994-95, pres. 1996), N.J. Psychol. Assn., N.J. Acad. Psychology, Soc. Psychologists in Addictive Behaviors (pres. 1989-91, newsletter editor 1989-94), Am. Acad. Health Care Providers in Addictive Disorders (internat. adv. bd. 1990—), Am. Congress Rehab. Medicine, Internat. Critical Incident Stress Found. Roman Catholic. Office: JFK Johnson Rehab Inst 65 James St Edison NJ 08820-3947

HANCE, ANTHONY JAMES, retired pharmacologist, educator; b. Bournemouth, Eng., Aug. 19, 1932; came to U.S., 1958; s. Walter Edwin and Jessie Irene (Finch) H.; m. Ruth Anne Martin, July 17, 1954; children: David, Peter, John. BSc, Birmingham U., 1953, PhD, 1956. Rsch.fellow in electrophysiology Birmingham U., Eng., 1957-58; rsch. pharmacologist UCLA, 1959-62; rsch. assoc. pharmacology Stanford U., Palo Alto, Calif., 1962-65, asst. prof., 1965-68; assoc. prof. U. Calif., Davis, 1968-94, ret. prof. emeritus, 1994. Contbr. articles to profl. jours. Mem. AAAS, Am. Soc. for Pharmacology and Exptl. Therapeutics, Biomed. Engring. Soc., Assn. for Computing Machinery. Home: 1103 Radcliffe Dr Davis CA 95616-0944 Office: U Calif Med Sch Dept Med Pharmacology & Toxicology Davis CA 95616-8654

HANCOCK, CLENRIC GUY, veterinary technician educator; b. Framingham, Mass., Oct. 14, 1948; s. Clenric Howard and Barbara Benet (Woodworth) H. DVM, Ohio State U., 1973 MEd, U. So. Fla., 1996. Lic. veterinarian, Ohio, Md., Fla. Veterinarian Belaire (Md.) Vet. Hosp., 1973-76, Animal Hosp. of Largo (Fla.), 1976-79, NW Vet. Clinic, St. Petersburg, Fla., 1986—; instr. St. Petersburg Jr. Coll., 1978-79; owner Belcher Animal Clinic, Clearwater, Fla., 1979-83; vet. tech. dir. St. Petersburg Jr. Coll., 1983—. Producer videotapes in field; contbr. chpts. to books. Mem. Leadership Pinellas, 1987-88; bd. dirs. Hospice Care, Inc., 1989—; program chmn. Vet. Tech. Distance Edn. Program, 1994—; bd. dirs. Hospice Inst., 1995. Mem. Am. Vet. Med. Assn., Fla. Vet. Med. Assn. (chmn. human-animal bond com. 1988—, Gold Star award 1984, 86, 90), Fla. Animal Health Found. (pres. 1991-95), Pinellas County Animal Found. (pres. 1987), Pinellas County Vet. Med. Soc. (pres., chmn. bd. dirs. 1989-90), Assn. Vet. Technician Educators (pres.-elect 1992-93, pres. 1993-95), Delta Soc. (pres. Fla. chpt. 1988-90). Office: St Petersburg Jr Coll PO Box 13489 Saint Petersburg FL 33733-3489

HANCOCK, MARY, nursing administrator; b. Socorro, N.Mex., Nov. 12, 1962; d. James C. and Opal A. (Williams) Whisenant; m. Reuben L. Hancock, Nov. 13, 1987; children: Samara, Christina. ADN, Ea. N.Mex. U., Roswell, 1984. RN, Tex. Staff nurse Ea. N.Mex. Med. Ctr., Roswell, 1984-85, St. Joseph's Hosp., Albuquerque, 1985-86; charge nurse U. N.Mex. Hosp., Albuquerque, 1986-87; emergency rm. nurse St. Anthony's Hosp., Amarillo, Tex., 1987-89; assoc. dir. profl. svcs. KOC Home Health, Amarillo, 1989-91; adminstr./DON Outreach Health Svcs., Amarillo, 1992—; case mgr. N.W. Tex. Cmty. Health Sys., Amarillo, 1995-96. Home health chair Home Health Coalition, Amarillo, 1993, 94, 95. Mem. Nat. Assn. Home Care, Tex. Assn. Home Care, Amarillo C. of C. Office: Outreach Health Svcs 724 S Polk #900 Amarillo TX 79101

HAND, DALE L., pharmacist; b. Boise, Idaho, Oct. 21, 1947; s. Robert Ray and Evelyn Mabel (McKenzie) H.; m. Gloria J. Lassen, Dec. 19, 1970; children: Travis D., Jason D. Student, Walla Walla Coll., 1965-66; B Pharmacy, Idaho State U., 1970; MS in Health Svcs. Adminstrn., Coll. St. Francis, Joliet, Ill., 1985. Intern Clinic Pharmacy, Pocatello, Idaho, 1968-70; pharmacognosy lab. tchng. asst. Idaho State U., 1969-70; hosp. pharmacy internship St. Luke's Hosp., Boise, 1970-71, clin. staff pharmacist, 1971-77; various to dir. pharmacy svcs. Porter Meml. Hosp., Denver, 1981-92, adminstrv. dir. dept. pharm. care, 1992—; pharmacy extern preceptor U. Colo., 1981—; cons. pharmacist McNamara Hosp. and Nursing Home, Fairplay, Colo., 1981-83; cons. Edn. Design, Inc., 1993—; lectr. in field; chmn. various hosp. coms. Contbr. articles to profl. jours. Bd. dirs. Arapahoe Sertoma, 1991—. Mem. Am. Soc. Health Sys. Pharmacists, Colo. Soc. Health Sys. Pharmacists. Seventh-Day Adventist. Home: 7269 W Chestnut Dr Littleton CO 80123-5699 Office: PorterCare Hosp 2525 S Downing St Denver CO 80210-5817

HAND, PAUL DESAUTELS, social work educator; b. New Bedford, Mass., May 31, 1931; s. Samuel Joseph and Lauretta (Desautels) H.; m. Gloria Elizabeth Zarrella, July 4, 1958; children: Mary E., Michele M., Annette M., Suzanne M., Paul D., Denise M., Joseph W. BA cum laude, Assumption Coll., Worcester, Mass., 1956; MSW, Boston U., 1959; MBA, Anna Maria Coll., Paxton, Mass., 1985. Caseworker ARC, Boston, 1957-58, Worcester (Mass.) Children's Friend Soc., 1959-72; faculty social work Anna Maria Coll., Paxton, 1965—; social wk. cons. Mill Hill Nursing Home, Worcester, 1976-93, Mass. Dept. Youth Svcs., Worcester, 1974-95, Notre Dame Long-Term Care Ctr., Worcester, 1985-94, Spring Valley Nursing Home, Worcester, 1988-95; clin. social worker Elmwood Counseling, Worcester, 1989—. Chmn. Worcester Human Rights Commn., 1985-88; chmn. human rights com. Mass. Dept. Mental Health, 1986-91; mem. affirmative action com. United Way, Worcester, 1986-90. Recipient Key of the City of Worcester, 1976, Appreciation award, City Mgr., Worcester, 1988. Mem. Nat. Assn. Social Workers, Coun. on Social Wk. Edn., Am Legion, Internat. Fedn. Mental Health, Delta Epsilon Sigma. Democrat. Roman Catholic. Home: 71 Morningside Rd Worcester MA 01602-2545 Office: Anna Maria College Paxton MA 01612-1198

HAND, ROGER, physician, educator; b. Bklyn., Sept. 25, 1938; s. Morton and Angela (Belvedere) H.; children: Christopher, Jessica. BS, NYU, 1959, MD, 1962. Intern, then resident in internal medicine NYU Med. Ctr., 1962-68; postdoctoral fellow, asst. prof. Rockefeller U., N.Y.C., 1968-73; clin. asst. prof. medicine Cornell U. Med. Coll., N.Y.C., 1970-73; asst. prof., then assoc. prof. medicine McGill U., Montreal, Que., Can., 1973-80; prof. medicine, dir. McGill Cancer Ctr., 1980-84; sr. physician Royal Victoria Hosp., Montreal, 1980-84; chmn. internal medicine Ill. Masonic Ctr., Chgo., 1984-88; prof. medicine U. Ill., Chgo., 1984—, chief sect. gen. internal medicine, 1988-95, prof. health policy and adminstrn. Sch. Pub Health, 1995—; prin. clin. coord. Ill. PRO, Chgo., 1996—. Contbr. articles to profl. jours. Brig. gen. USAR, 1963-71, 85—. Decorated Air medal, Meritorious Svc. medal, Army Commendation medal; med. rsch. grantee. Fellow ACP, Royal Coll. Physicians and Surgeons, Am. Coll. Med. Quality; mem. Am. Soc. Clin. Investigation, Am. Soc. Biol. Chemists, Am. Assn. Cancer Research, Am. Soc. Clin. Oncology, Infectious Disease Soc., Can. Soc. Clin. Investigation, Cen. Soc. Clin. Rsch., Am. Cancer Soc.(bd. dirs. Ill. div.). Office: U Ill Coll Medicine Dept Medicine 840 S Wood St Rm 787 Chicago IL 60612-7317

HANDEL, NEAL, plastic surgeon, researcher; b. L.A., Sept. 2, 1947; s. Max and Ruth H. BA, Columbia U., 1969; MD, Yale U., 1973. Diplomate Am. Bd. Plastic Surgery. Resident UCLA, 1975-76, Tulane U., New Orleans, 1976-78, U. Colo., Denver, 1978—; plastic and reconstructive surgeon The Breast Ctr., Van Nuys, Calif., 1982—, assoc. med. dir., 1982—; mem. adv. bd. Ctr. for Devel. Biology Calif. State U., Northridge, 1985—. Contbr. articles to profl. jours. Rsch. grantee Am. Soc. Aesthetic Plastic Surgery, 1991. Fellow ACS; mem. Am. Soc. Plastic and Reconstructive Surgery, Calif. Soc. Plastic and Reconstructive Surgeons. Office: The Breast Ctr 14624 Sherman Way Ste 506 Van Nuys CA 91405

HANDELMAN, WILLIAM ALAN, physician; b. Bronx, N.Y., Feb. 15, 1948; s. Herbert and Yetta (Aniess) H.; m. Leslie Ann Scott, May 17, 1981; children: Scott Alexander, Benjamin Isaac, Sarah Kim. AB, Columbia Coll., 1969; MD, SUNY, Bklyn., 1973. Diplomate Am. Bd. Internal Medicine, Am. Bd. Nephrology, Am. Bd. Med. Examiners. Resident Bronx (N.Y.) Mcpl. Hosp. Ctr., 1973-76; fellowship in nephrology U. Colo. Med. Ctr., Denver, 1976-79, asst. prof. med., 1979-80; pvt. practice Torrington, Conn., 1980—; co-dir. dialysis unit Charlotte Hungerford Hosp., Torrington, 1981—, chmn. dept. medicine, 1995—; clin. asst. prof. medicine U. Conn. Med. Ctr., Farmington, 1982—. Co-author: (book chpts.) Antimicrobial Therapy, 1980, Clinical Pharmacology and Therapeutics In Nursing, 1979, Textbook of Infectious Disease, 1982; editorial bd. Conn. Medicine Jour., New Haven, 1986—. Recipient advanced attainment in internal medicine, Am. Bd. Internal Medicine, Phila., 1988. Mem. ACP, Litchfield County Med. Soc. (exec. com. 1980—, pres. 1994-96), Conn. Med. Soc., Ind. Practice Assn. (bd. dirs. 1988—), Am. Soc. Internal Medicine, Renal Physicians Assn. Ind. Jewish. Home: 89 East St Morris CT 06763-1802 Office: 538 Litchfield St Ste 201 Torrington CT 06790-6667

HANDELSMAN, DAVID JOSHUA, endocrinologist, researcher; b. Melbourne, Victoria, Australia, Apr. 16, 1950; s. Salomon and Sulamit (Kagan) H.; m. Penelope Louise Hoskins, Aug. 8, 1986; children Timothy David, Nicholas, Elizabeth. MB, BSc, U. Melbourne, 1974; PhD, U. Sydney, NSW, Australia, 1984. Resident med. officer Royal Prince Alfred Hosp., Sydney, 1975-77, endocrinology registrar, 1978-79; rsch. fellow U. Sydney, 1980-83; overseas rsch. fellow Med. Rsch. Coun., U. Sydney, 1985-86, Wellcome sr. rsch. fellow, 1987—; rsch. fellow UCLA, 1984-85; dir. andrology unit Royal Prince Alfred Hosp., Sydney, 1985—, assoc. prof. reproductive endocrinology and andrology, 1989—. Contbr. articles to profl. jours. Fellow RACP; mem. Endocrine Soc., Am. Andrology Soc., Am. Fertility Soc., Internat. Soc. Neuroendocrinology, Australian Soc. Reproductive Biology, Endocrine Soc. Australia. Home: 18 N Arm Rd, Middle Cove, NSW Sydney 2068, Australia Office: U Sydney, Dept Medicine, NSW Sydney 2006, Australia

HANDELSMAN, RICHARD ERROL, physician; b. New York, Sept. 23, 1950; s. Irving Robert and Ronni (Kapchar) H.; m. Laura Marie Healy, June 20, 1976 (div. Apr. 1983); 1 child, Dawn; m. Margaret Cornell Vanderbilt, May 1, 1983; children: Kate, Jennifer, Gregory. BS, SUNY, 1972; DO, Coll. Osteopathic Medicine, 1976. Diplomate Am. Bd. Internal Medicine. Internship Detroit Bicountry Cmty. Hosp., 1976-77; pvt. practice Pomona, N.Y., 1980—; clinical instr. N.Y. Medical Coll., Valhalla, 1989—; physician South Orangetown Sch. Dist., 1983, 84; medical dir. Northern Met. Nursing Facility, 1988—; physician East Rampo Cen. Sch. Dist., 1990—; residency N.J. Medical Sch.-Martland Medical Ctr., Newark, 1977-78, Yale Affiliated Norwalk Hosp., Norwalk, N.J., 1978-80; police surgeon Ramapo Police Dept., 1991—; medical dir. Hillcrest Skilled Nursing Facility, 1992—; adv. bd. Vista PHOk Nyack Hosp., 1994-95, bd. dirs., 1995—, chmn. medical mgmt., 1995—; primary care physician Nyack Hosp., 1980—, editorial rsch. bd., chmn. utilization review, 1985-86, 87-88; preceptor Westchester County Medical Ctr., 1989—; sec./treas. Medical Dental Staff Nyack Hosp., 1991-92, acting medical dir. Northern Met. Health Related Facility, 1992. Vol. Am. Cancer Soc. examinations, 1981, 92, 93, 94. Recipient Physicians Recognition award, 1983-90. Fellow Am. Coll. Physicians; mem. Am. Acad. Sports Physicians, Nat. Alumni Assn., Rockland County Medical Soc., Am. Geriatric Assn., Am. Soc. Internal Medicine. Home: 13 Woodthrush Dr West Nyack NY 10994 Office: Assocs in Internal Medicine 7C Medical Park Dr Pomona NY 10970

HANDFORD, H. ALLEN, child psychiatrist; b. Des Moines, July 1, 1930; s. Harvey Eugene and Lenore (Allen) H.; AB, Harvard U., 1953; MD, State U. Iowa, 1957; m. Sandra Lee Betz, Sept. 3, 1955 (div.); children: Lee Allen, Christiana Lenore, Jennifer Miriam, Alice Faith; m. Laura Jane Diller, May 20, 1972 (div.). Intern, Broadlawns, Des Moines, 1957-58; fellow in psychiatry Pa. Hosp. Inst., 1958-60; fellow child psychiatry St. Christopher's Hosp., Phila., 1960-62; dir. rsch. unit autistic children Ea. State Sch. and Hosp., Phila., Pa., 1962-73; dir. children's unit Haverford (Pa.) State Hosp., 1973-74; dir. children and youth programs mental Pa. Dept. Pub. Welfare, 1976-79; clin. asst. prof. psychiatry and human behavior Jefferson Med. Coll., Phila., 1974-78; assoc. prof. psychiatry Coll. Medicine, Pa. State U., Hershey, 1978—, also dir. child psychiatry residency tng.; dir. psychiatry/psychology Univ. Hosp. Rehab. Ctr., 1979-84; dir. psychosocial program Hemophilia Ctr. Cen. Pa., 1979—; former mem. mental health com. Nat. Hemophilia Found. Contbr. articles to med. jours. Bd. dirs. Dauphin County Mental Health/Mental Retardation. Mem. AMA, Am. Psychiat. Assn., Am. Acad. Child and Adolescent Psychiatry, Pa. Med. Soc., Pa. Psychiat. Soc., Regional Coun. Child Psychiatry, Coll. Physicians Phila. Research on childhood autism, psychosocial aspects of hemophilia, childhood depression, child and parent reaction to Three Mile Island nuclear accident, sleep disorders of childhood. Home: 1232 Wood Rd Hummelstown PA 17036-9759 Office: Pa State U Hershey Med Ctr Div Child Psychiatry Dept Psychiatry Hershey PA 17033-0850

HANDLER, ENID IRENE, health care administrator, consultant; b. N.Y.C., Oct. 17, 1932; d. Solomon and Fran S. (Bernstein) Ostrov; m. Murry Raymond Handler, Nov. 22, 1952; children: Lowell S., Lillian Handler Koch, Evan Elliott. BS, Queens Coll., 1968; MS in Adminstrv. Medicine, Columbia U., 1973. Adminstrv. dir. Phelps Mental Health Ctr., North Tarrytown, N.Y., 1973-85; cons. to health care providers Cortland Manor, N.Y., 1986-92; mgmt. cons. Durham County (N.C.) Mental Health/Devel. Disabilities Svc., Chapel Hill, N.C., 1993-94; mem. bd. dirs. Orange County (N.C.) AIDS Svc. Agy., 1992-94, Inst. for Parapsychology, 1996—; presenter to profl. orgns. Contbr. articles and book revs. to profl. jours. Mem. adv. bd. Marymount Coll., North Tarrytown, 1983, Iona Coll., New Rochelle, N.Y., 1983; mem. adv. bd. Search for Change, Inc., White Plains, 1987-90; bd. dirs. Keon Sch., Montrose, N.Y., 1986-88; chair North Westchester County Mental Health Coun., 1974-80; pres. Westchester Assn. Vol. Agys., 1981-82; mem. Westchester County Community Svcs. Bd., 1980-86. NIH fellow Columbia U., N.Y.C., 1971-72. Fellow Am. Orthopsychiat. Assn.; mem. NAFE, Columbia U. Alumni Assn. Home and Office: Enid Handler Cons 9318 Laurel Springs Dr Chapel Hill NC 27516-5649

HANDLEY, KAREN MARIE, nurse administrator; b. Valparaiso, Ind., Apr. 9, 1960; d. Donald Edward and Ruth (Lenburg) Lyda; m. Vernon Lloyd, July 9, 1983; children: Timothy Lloyd, Karissa Marie. ADN, Purdue U., 1981; BS in Health Care Mgmt., Lindenwood Coll., 1996. RN, Ind., Mo. Staff RN NICU Porter Meml. Hosp., Valparaiso, 1981-85; staff RN nursery DePaul Health Ctr., Bridgeton, Mo., 1985-86; staff RN NICU Cardinal Glennon Childrens Hosp., St. Louis, 1986-87; utilization rev. coord. Sanus Health Plan, St. Louis, 1986-90; precertification supr. GenCare Sanus Health Plan, St. Louis, 1990-94; health rsch. analyst GenCare Health Systems, St. Louis, 1994-96, supr. health rsch., 1996—; childbirth instr. St. Joseph Health Ctr., St. Charles, Mo., 1988-94, CPR instr., 1985—, sibling class instr., 1988-93. Roman Catholic.

HANDMAN, HEIDI PEARL, neonatology fellow; b. Montreal, Ont., Can., Dec. 23, 1964; d. Frank Leon and Frima (Greenberg) H. BS, U. Fla., 1982; DO, Southeast Coll. Osteopathic, Miami, Fla., 1990. Diplomate Am. Bd. Pediatrics. Intern Botsford Hosp., Farmington Hills, Mich., 1990-91; resident in pediats. Shands Hosp., Gainesville, Fla., 1991-94; fellow in neonatology CHildren's Nat. Med. Ctr., Washington, 1994—. Mem. AMA, Am. Acad. Pediats., Am. Osteopathic Assn. Office: Childrens Nat Med Ctr 111 Michigan Ave NW Washington DC 20010

HANDY, CHRISTOPHER COLUMBUS, JR., physician assistant; b. Columbus, Ohio, June 17, 1941; s. Christopher Columbus Sr. and Cleora Monday (Pinkston) H.; m. LeVonia Teresa Sweeney (separated); children: Christina M., Clifton Joseph. BS in Medicine, U. Nebr., 1974. Cert. physician asst., N.C. Physician asst. Greater S.E. Cmty. Hosp., Washington, Dr. Jonathan McCone Med. Offices, Alexandria, Va. With USN, 1961-81. Office: Dr Jonathan McCone Office 8101 Hinson Farm Rd # 306 Alexandria VA 22306

HANEBRINK, EARL LEE, biology educator; b. Cape Girardeau, Mo., Mar. 24, 1924; s. Harry H. and Agusta (Fornkohl) H.; m. Vernalia Ann McCrady (dec.); children: Lisa Ann, Kay Lynn Hanebrink Noell. BS in Edn., S.E. Mo. State U., 1948; MS, U. Miss., 1955; EdD, Okla. State U., 1965. Cert. secondary tchr., Mo. Sci. and biology instr. Parma (Mo.) High Sch., 1948-52, Kennett (Mo.) High Sch., 1952-58; biology instr. Ark. State U., Jonesboro, 1958-60, asst. prof. biology, 1960-63, assoc. prof. biology, 1963-68, prof. biology, 1968—. Author: Flora of Southeast Missouri, 1958, Birds of Northeast Arkansas, 1980, Plankton, 1980. Cpl. U.S. Army, 1943-46, PTO. Environ. grantee U.S. Soil and Water Agy., U.S. Corp. Engrs., 1960—. Mem. Am. Pigeon Fanciers Coun. (pres. 1978), Ark. Aububon Soc. (pres. 1968), Ark. Acad. Sci., Nat. Audubon Soc., N.E. Ark. Audubon Soc. (pres. 1991—), Chgo. Herpetological Soc., Elks. Methodist. Office: Ark State U PO Box 67 State University AR 72467-0067

HANEY, DAVID GEORGE, ophthalmologist; b. Duluth, Minn., Jan. 22, 1931; s. Harry Harold and Ruth Elizabeth (Lucove) H.; m. Glenna A. Day; children: David, Graham, Jason, Grant, Lisa, Desmond, Margo, Andre. BA, U. Minn., 1953, BS, 1955, MD, 1957. Diplomate Am. Bd. Ophthalmology. Intern Wayne County Gen. Hosp., Eloise, Mich., 1957-58; resident Tulane U., 1958-61; asst. prof. ophthalmology Tulane U., La., 1962-64; chmn. divsn. ophthalmology U. Tex., Galveston, 1964-65; pvt. practice Glendora, Calif., 1965-88; chief ophthalmology Denver Gen. Hosp., 1988-90; pvt. practice Richmond, Ind., 1990-91, Eye Surgeons Assocs., Davenport, Iowa, 1991-93; missionary Lighthouse for Christ, Mombasa, Kenya, 1993-95; pvt. practice McAllen, Tex., 1995—. Contbr. revs. to profl. jours.; author numerous monographs in field. Troop leader Boy Scouts Am., Glendora, 1966-68. Fellow Am. Acad. Ophthalmology; mem. AMA, Am. Ophthalmology Assn., Tex. Med. Soc., Hidalgo-Starr County Med. Assn. Office: Internat Eye Care 301 Lindberg Ste B McAllen TX 78501

HANEY, JOHN FREDERICK BROWN, psychiatrist; b. Hempstead, N.Y., June 7, 1938; s. John Budd and Evelyn Mae (Brown) H.; m. Sara Jane Davidson, June 21, 1961 (div. 1985); m. Judith Lynn Frederick, Dec. 26, 1986; children: John, Jeffrey. BS in Chemistry, Yale U., 1959, MD, 1964. Lic. physician, Conn., 1965; diplomate Am. Bd. Psychiatry and Neurology. Intern in internal medicine U. Colo., Denver, 1964-65; resident in psychiatry Yale U. Sch. Medicine, New Haven, 1965-68; chief psychiatry US Naval

Submarine Base Hosp., Groton, Conn., 1968-70; psychiatrist U. Conn., Storrs, 1970-86; dir. staff growth and devel. Conn. Valley Hosp., Middletown, Conn., 1986-92; dir. treatment Conn. Valley Hosp., 1990-92; pvt. practice Mansfield Center, Conn., 1993—; attending psychiatrist Natchaug Hosp., 1993—; chmn. bd. dirs. Perception Programs, Inc., 1972—; cons. psychiatrist Youth Svc. Bur., Mansfield, 1972—; assoc. prof. U. Conn., Farmington, 1970—. Lt. comdr. USN, 1968-70, capt. Res. 1970-94. Fellow Am. Psychiatric Assn.; mem. AMA, Am. Group Psychotherapy Assn. Republican. Home: 341 Hanks Hill Rd Storrs Mansfield CT 06268-2349 Office: 354 Warrenville Rd Mansfield Center CT 06250-1130

HANEY, ROBERT JOSEPH, dentist; b. Chgo., May 16, 1946; s. Frank J. and Matilda Ann (Landolfi) H.; children: Brian, Kevin, Sean, Michael. Student, U. Ill., Champaign, 1964-66; DDS, U. Ill., Chgo., 1970. Instr. removabla prosthetics U. Ill. Coll. Dentistry, Chgo., 1970; pvt. practice Concord, N.H., 1972-93; with N.H. Bd. Dental Examiners, 1993—; dental coord. N.H. Tech. Inst., Concord, 1984-85, instr. dental hygiene dental dept., 1984-86. Capt. U.S. Army, 1970-72. Fellow Internat. Coll. Dentists (dep. regent N.H. chpt.), Am. Coll. Dentists, Pierre Fauchard Acad.; mem. Acad. Fixed Prosthodontics, Acad. Gen. Dentistry, N.H. Dental Soc. (pres.), Concord Dental Soc. (pres.), New Eng. Dental Soc., New Eng. Prosthodontic Soc. Office: 75 Clinton St Concord NH 03301-2310

HANF, CHARLES DAVID, surgeon; b. N.Y.C., Oct. 20, 1950; s. Nathan and Florence (Rothstein) H.; m. Arline Helen Reinking, Apr. 9, 1988; 1 child, Jennifer. SB, MIT, 1972; MD, Creighton U., 1977. Diplomate Am. Bd. Surgery and Critical Care. Resident surgery Creighton U., Omaha, 1977-82; pvt. practice surgery Omaha, 1982-85; fellow trauma and critical care Md. Inst. EMS Systems, Balt., 1985-86; pvt. practice surgery Long Beach, Calif., 1986-87; dir. surg. critical care Montefiore Med. Ctr., Bronx, N.Y., 1987—. Fellow ACS; mem. Soc. Critical Care Medicine, Assn. for Surg. Edn. Office: Montefiore Med Ctr 111 E 210th St Bronx NY 10467-2490

HANFLING, SUE CAROL (SUKI HANFLING), social worker; b. N.Y.C., Dec. 22, 1945; d. Seymour Leonard and Arline Jocelyn (Marcus) H.; 1 child, Michael Ian. BA magna cum laude, U. Rochester, 1968; BA, U. Chgo., 1969; MSW, Boston Coll., 1973. Dir. Walnut St. Ctr. for Retarded Adults, Somerville, Mass., 1970-71; social worker McLean Hosp. Adult Outpatient Clinic, Belmont, Mass., 1977—; pvt. practice Belmont, Mass., 1976—; founder, dir. Human Sexuality program McLean Hosp., Belmont, 1985—, co-founder, co-dir. McLean Inst. for Couples and Families, 1985—; cons. Watertown Multi-Svc., 1980-90; lectr. in field. Mem. Am. Assn. for Sex Educators, Am. Assn. Sex Therapists (cert.). Democrat. Jewish. Home: 4A Locust Ln Watertown MA 02172 Office: McLean Hosp Human Sexuality Program 115 Mill St Belmont MA 02178

HANFORD, PATRICK JOSEPH, osteopath; b. Kansas City, Mo., Nov. 26, 1952; s. Ralph Joseph and Margurette (Sorrell) H.; m. Sharon Lou Roach, Mar. 22, 1975; children: Ryan Joseph, Reese Taylor. BS, Angelo State U., 1976; DO, Tex. Coll. Osteo. Medicine, 1983. Diplomate Am. Bd. Quality Assurance, Am. Bd. Utilization Rev. Physicians, Am. Osteo. Bd. of Family Practice. Pvt. practice Lamesa, Tex., 1985-90; ptnr. Oakwood Family Practice, Lubbock, Tex., 1990—; assoc. prof. Tex. Coll. Osteo. Medicine, 1995—, Tex. Tech. Sch. Medicine; chief of staff Med. Arts Hosp., Lamesa, 1988, South Park Hosp., 1996; phycian cons. Tex. Med. Found., Lubbock, 1986—; chmn. med. Quality Com. Lab., Lubbock, 1991-95; med. dir. Oakwood Family Practice, Littlefield, Tex., 1991-92. Mem. Am. Heart Assn., Dawson County, Lamesa, 1985-90, pres., 1989-90. Fellow Am. Coll. Med. Quality; mem. Am. Coll. Osteo. Family Physicians (trustee 1993—), Tex. Med. Found. (mem. regional com. 1990—), Tex. Osteo. Med. Assn. (profl. edn. and adv. com. 1988—, sec.-treas. 1990-91), Am. Osteo. Assn., Am. Coll. Gen. Practitioners, Tex. Soc. Am. Coll. Family Practice (trustee 1993-96). Office: Oakwood Family Practice 4601 S Locp 289 Lubbock TX 79424-2208

HANFT, RUTH S. SAMUELS (MRS. HERBERT HANFT), health care consultant, educator, economist; b. N.Y.C., July 12, 1929; d. Max Joseph and Ethel (Schechter) Samuels; m. Herbert Hanft, June 17, 1951; children: Marjorie Jane, Jonathan Mark. BS, Cornell U., 1949; MA, Hunter Coll., 1963; PhD, George Washington U., 1989; ScD (hon.), U. Osteo. Med & Health Scis., 1993. Cons. Urban Med. Econs. Project, Hunter Coll., N.Y.C. and D.C. Dept. Health, 1962-63; health economist Office of Rsch. and Stats., Social Security Adminstrn., Washington, 1964-66; chief grants mgmt. health div. Office Econ. Opportunity, Washington, 1966-68; sr. health analyst Office of Asst. Sec. Planning and Evaluation HEW, Washington, 1968-71, spl. asst., asst. sec. health, 1971-72; dep. asst. sec. for health policy, rsch. and stats. Office of Asst. Sec. for Health HEW, 1977-79, dep. asst. sec. for health rsch., stats. and tech., 1979-81; health care cons., 1981-88; cons., rsch. prof. dept. health svcs. mgmt. and policy George Washington U., Washington, 1988-91, prof., 1991-95; cons., 1995—; vis. prof. Dartmouth Med. Sch., 1976—; sr. rsch. assoc. Inst. Medicine-NAS, Washington, 1972-76. Contbr. articles to profl. jours. Mem. Med. Assistance Svc. Bd. Commonwealth Va., 1984-89, Meharry Med. Coll. Bd. Trustees, 1989-94. Fellow Hastings Ctr.; mem. Inst. of Medicine, Nat. Acad. Sci. Jewish. Home: 3609 Cameron Mills Rd Alexandria VA 22305-1107

HANGER, LEANNA BLAIR, hospital administrator; b. Staunton, Va., Feb. 21, 1966; d. Blair Bowman and Jo Lee (Wood) H. BA, U. Richmond, 1988; M in Hosp. Adminstrn., Ga. State U., 1992, MBA, 1991. Diplomate Am. Coll. Healthcare Execs. Adminstrn. resident Presbyn. Hosp., Charlotte, N.C., 1991-92; v.p. ancillary svcs. Conway (S.C.) Hosp., 1992-95; adv. bd. Waccamaw Quality Coun., Myrtle Beach, S.C., 1994-95. Bd. dirs. Big. Bros./Big Sisters, Conway, 1994-95. Mem. Rotary. Methodist. Home: 3509 Lighthouse Way Myrtle Beach SC 29577 Office: Conway Hosp PO Box 829 Conway SC 29526

HANGER, PHILIP ANDREW, psychologist; b. Cherokee, Iowa, June 19, 1961; s. Herbert Lee and Suzanne Elizabeth (Klein) H.; m. Julie Ann Zillig Small, June, 1980 (div. Mar. 1987); children: Emily Elizabeth, Victoria Lynn; m. Maria Andujo, Dec. 22, 1990. BS, U. Iowa, 1984; MS, U. Fla., 1987, PhD, 1989. Lic. psychologist, Fla. Staff neuropsychologist St. John's Mercy Med. Ctr., St. Louis, 1990-91; dir. psychology Healthsouth Rehab. Hosp., Largo, Fla., 1991-92; clin. dir. brain injury Rehab. Inst. Sarasota, Fla., 1992-93; dir. psychol. svcs. Mediplex Rehab.-Bradenton, Fla., 1993-94; pvt. practice St. Petersburg, Fla., 1992—; instr. psychology Hillsborough C.C., Tampa, Fla., 1995—; mem. profl. adv. com., chpt. svcs. com., rsch. advocate Gulfcoast chpt. Nat. Multiple Sclerosis Soc., Tampa, 1992—. Recipient Catch the Spirit award Gulfcoast Multiple Sclerosis Soc., 1993. Mem. APA. Office: 405 Central Ave Ste 303 Saint Petersburg FL 33701

HANHILA, MATT O., JR., orthodontist; b. Kingman, Ariz., May 8, 1940; s. Matt Oscar and Merna (Ellis) H.; m. Jennifer Hanhila, June 28, 1963; children: Matt O. III, Hillary, Leeann Christa. BS in Edn., U. Ariz., 1962; DDS, U. So. Calif., L.A., 1966; MS, Loyola U., Chgo., 1970. Diplomate Am. Bd. Orthodontics. Pvt. practice Glendale, Ariz.; bd. examiner Ariz. Ortho Study Club, Phoenix, 1985—; peer rev. dental Ariz. Dental Soc., 1994—. Office: 5406 W Glenn Dr #2 Glendale AZ 85301-2628

HANIN, ISRAEL, pharmacologist, educator; b. Shanghai, China, Mar. 29, 1937; s. Leo and Rebecca (Lubarsky) H.; m. Leda Toni, June 12, 1960; children: Adam, Dahlia. BS, UCLA, 1962, MS, 1965, PhD in Pharmacology, 1968. Vis. scientist dept. toxicology Karolinska Inst., Stockholm, 1968; staff pharmacologist Lab. Preclin. Pharmacology, NIMH, Washington, 1969-73; from asst. prof. to assoc. prof. psychiatry and pharmacology U. Pitts. Sch. Medicine, 1973-81, prof., 1981-86; prof., chmn. Dept. Pharmacology and Exptl. Therapeutics, dir. Inst. Neurosci. and Aging, dir. MD/PhD program Loyola U. Chgo. Stritch Sch. Medicine, Maywood, Ill., 1986—; mem. rsch. grant rev. com. NIMH, 1979-82, Nat. Inst. Aging, 1987-92, NIH Res., 1991-95; mem. pharmacology test com. Nat. Bd. Med. Examiners, 1987-90; cons. UCB Pharm., Brussels, 1981—; mem. sci. adv. bd. Interneuron Pharms., Inc., Lexington, Mass., 1991—. Editor 13 books; contbr. articles to profl. jours. Served to 2d lt. Armored Corps, Israeli Army, 1955-58. NIMH, NIH, Nat. Inst. Aging grantee, 1965-92. Con. to UCB Pharms., Brussels, Belgium ,1981—; Mem. Neurosci. Soc. (pres. Pitts. chpt. 1982-83, pres. Chgo. chpt., 1990-91), Am. Chem. Soc., Am. Soc. Pharmacology and Exptl. Therapeutics (co-founder Great Lakes chpt. 1987, pres. 1990-92), Am. Soc. Neurochemistry, Am. Coll. Neuropsychopharmacology, Soc. Neurosci. Address: Loyola U Chgo Stritch Sch Medicine Dept Pharm Rm 3621 Bldg 102 Maywood IL 60153

HANISH, RICHARD USHER, clinical psychologist; b. N.Y.C., May 21, 1945; s. Martin Herman and Sima Esther (Chernin) H. BA, U. Wis., 1967; PhD, Ind. U., 1979. Lic. psychologist, Mass.; cert. sex therapist, cert. biofeedback psychologist, Nat. Register Health Service Providers in Psychology. Clin. dir. Youth Svcs., Inc., Braintree, Mass., 1972-75; pvt. practice clin. psychology, Hingham, Mass., 1982—; clin. cons. Mass. Bay Counseling, Boston, 1980-88, clin. cons. Mass. Respiratory Hosp., Braintree; clin. cons. South Shore Hosp., Braintree; bd. dir. behavioral medicine South Shore Counseling Assn., Inc., Hanover, Mass., 1975-82; USPHS fellow, 1968-69; recipient three Mass. Deliquency Prevention grants. Mem. Am. Psychol. Assn., Mass. Psychol. Assn., Am. Assn. Sex Educators, Counselors and Therapists (cert.), Assn. for Advancement of Behavior Therapy, Soc. Behavioral Medicine, Soc. Sci. Study of Sex, Biofeedback Soc. Mass. (cert.). Home: 214 Greenbrook Dr Stoughton MA 02072-4916 Office: 210 Whiting St Ste 5 Hingham MA 02043-3724

HANKES, LAWRENCE VALENTINE, clinical biochemical researcher; b. Chgo., Nov. 24, 1919; s. Michael John and Matilda Ann (Bachman) H.; m. Mary Catherine Hamm, Sept. 16, 1951; children—Lawrence Michael, Catherine Ann, Matthew William. A.B., De Pauw U., 1942; M.S., Mich. State U., 1943; Ph.D., U. Wis., 1949, 1950. Registered clin. lab. dir., N.Y. Instr. biochemistry Mich. State U., East Lansing, 1942-43; instr. biochemistry Northwestern U. Dental Sch., Chgo., 1943-44; indsl. research fellow U. Wis., Madison, 1947-49; head allergy group VA Hosp., Aspinwall, Pa., 1950; head clin. chemistry med. ctr. Brookhaven Nat. Lab., Upton, N.Y., 1951—, sr. scientist, 1968—; cons. and researcher in field. Contbr. articles to profl. jours. Served to comdr. U.S. Navy. Fellow Brit. Chem. Soc., Nat. Acad. Clin. Biochemists; mem. Am. Chem. Soc., Am. Soc. Biol. Chemists, Soc. Exptl. Biology & Medicine, Am. Assn. Clin. Chemists, Internat. Fedn. Clin. Chemists, Assn. Clin. Scientists, Alpha Chi Sigma, Sigma Xi, Phi Sigma. Club: Explorer's. Home: PO Box 1056 Setauket NY 11733-0804 Office: Brookhaven Nat Lab Med Research Ctr Upton NY 11973

HANKIN, ELAINE KRIEGER, psychologist, researcher; b. Scranton, Pa., Oct. 17, 1938; d. Maurice and Beatrice (Blumberg) Krieger; m. Abbe Hankin, Dec. 22, 1957; children: Susan Hankin-Birke, Elyse Rae Burton. BA, Temple U., 1979, MEd, 1980; PhD, Bryn Mawr Coll., 1984. Therapist Comac Youth Service Bur., Willow Grove, Pa., 1975-76; therapist, supr. interns Aldersgate Youth Service Bur., Willow Grove, 1975-84; staff psychologist, coord. diagnostic testing Buck's County Guidance Ctr., Doylestown, Pa., 1981-84; psychologist, ptnr., clin. dir. Abington (Pa.) Psychol. Assocs., 1984—; v.p., adminstr. dir. Corp. Devel. Systems, Abington, 1984—; mem. adj. staff Huntington Hosp., Willow Grove, Pa., 1986—, Eugenia Hosp., Ft. Washington, 1986—, Westmeade Ctr., 1990—, Friends Hosp., 1996. Mem. adv. bd. for Women and Minority Bus. President's scholar Temple U., 1979, Alumnae scholar Bryn Mawr Coll., 1982. Mem. AAUW, Am. Psychol. Assn., Nat. Coun. on Family Rels., World Fedn. for Mental Health, Pa. Psychol. Assn., Pa. Coun. on Family Rels., Pa. Soc. Behavioral Medicine and Biofeedback, Ea. Psychol. Assn., Phila. Soc. Clin. Psychologists (membership com.), Am. Soc. Clin. Hypnosis, Phila. Folk Song Soc., Phi Beta Kappa, Psi Chi. Home: 242 Ironwood Cir Breyer Woods Elkins Park PA 19027 Office: Abington Psychol Assocs Jenkins North Ct 668 Old York Rd Jenkintown PA 19046-2811

HANKINS, RALEIGH WALTER, microbiologist; b. Tokyo, July 18, 1958; s. Roland Raleigh and Maruko (Okawa) H.; m. Kazue Suzuki, Sept. 26, 1991. BA, Johns Hopkins U., 1980; MPhil, Yale U., 1983, PhD, 1985. Med. tchnician Health Scis. Rsch. Inst., Yokohama, Japan, 1980-81; postdoctoral assoc. Dept. Epidemiology and Pub. Health Yale U., New Haven, 1985-86; rsch. scientist Health Scis. Rsch. Inst. Third Diagnostic Divsn., Yokohama, 1986-89, chief scientist, 1989—, dep. dir., 1994—. Mem. AAAS, Am. Soc. Microbiology, Japan Molecular Biology Soc. Office: Health Scis Rsch Inst, 106 Godo-cho Hodogaya-ku, Yokohama Kanagawa 240, Japan

HANKOFF, LEON DUDLEY, psychiatrist; b. Balt., June 17, 1927; s. Benjamin and Ada (Filtzer) H.; m. Selma Ruth Mervis, Dec. 15, 1957; children: Eve, Sarah, Rachel, Rebecca. BS, U. Md., Balt., 1950, MD, 1952. Cert. in psychiatry Am. Bd. Psychiatry and Neurology. Intern Kings County Hosp., 1952-53; resident Kings County Hosp. Ctr., Bklyn., 1953-56; psychiatrist, sr. psychiatrist, clin. dir. Kings County Hosp. Ctr., 1956-65; dir. dept. psychiatry Queens Hosp. Ctr.-Hillside Hosp. Affiliation, N.Y., 1964-68; acting dir. Govt. Hosp.-Sha-ar Menashe, Israel, 1969-70; dir. dept. psychiatry Misericordia Hosp. Med. Ctr., N.Y., 1970-78; dir., chmn. Elizabeth Gen. Med. Ctr., Elizabeth, N.J., 1981—; clin. prof. U. Medicine and Dentistry N.J., N.J. Med. Sch., Newark, 1983—; adj. clin. prof. Cornell U. Med. Coll., N.Y.C., 1988—. Lt. USNR, 1956-58. Fellow Am. Psychiat. Assn. (life); mem. AMA. Jewish. Office: Elizabeth Gen Med Ctr 655 E Jersey St Elizabeth NJ 07206-1259

HANKS, CARL THOMAS, oral pathology educator, researcher; b. Cushing, Okla., Aug. 10, 1939; s. John Carl and Ruby Jewel (Bias) H.; m. Judith Melinda Sharp, Dec. 30, 1961; children: Stephanie Brett, John Conrad. BS, Phillips U., 1961; DDS, Washington U., St. Louis, 1964; PhD, SUNY, Buffalo, 1970. Diplomate Am. Bd. Pathology. Asst. prof. oral pathology SUNY, Buffalo, 1969-70; with Sch. of Dentistry U. Mich., Ann Arbor, 1970—, assoc. prof. Sch. of Medicine, 1978—, prof. oral pathology Sch. of Dentistry, 1979—. Contbr. articles to profl. jours. Fogarty Found. Internat. Fellow, 1976. Mem. Internat. Assn. for Dental Rsch. (pres. sect. 1989—), Am. Acad. Oral Pathology, Nat. Tissue Culture Assn., AAAS, Pulp Biology Group. Democrat. Home: 1276 Kuehnle Ct Ann Arbor MI 48103-2628 Office: U Mich 1011 E University Ave Ann Arbor MI 48109-1078

HANKS, GARY ARLIN, psychology educator; b. Salt Lake City, July 2, 1944; s. John D. and Erva (Wright) H.; m. Diana Twelves, 1968 (div. 1978); m. Suzanne Warnock Ostler, Dec. 20, 1984 (div. 1985); stepchildren: Shannon, Shawn, Ryan, Leslie. BS, U. Utah, 1968, MSW, 1972; clin. cert. dept. psychiatry Washingtonian, Harvard U., 1973; PhD in Psychology, Calif. U., L.A., 1977. Cert. social worker. Asst. prof. U. South Fla., Tampa, 1973-74; clinician LDS Ch. Social Svcs., L.A., 1975-77; chief psychiat. social worker William Beaumont Army Med. Ctr., El Paso, Tex., 1977-78; chmn. dept. psychology Internat. Relative Psychology Inst., Salt Lake City, 1984—; pres. Relative Analysis Assocs., Salt Lake City, 1994—, Mate Selection Internat., Salt Lake City, 1994—. Author: Maturity Analysis Test, 1985, Spirituality Analysis Test, 1986, Relative Psychology, 1991, Relative Religion, 1991, Relative Analysis, 1991, Relationship Maturity, 1994, Emotional Maturity Test Battery, 1994. Missionary LDS Ch., Fed. Republic Germany, 1963; polit. activist. Capt. U.S. Army, 1968-78. Rsch. grantee NIMH, 1973. Mem. Am. Fedn. Socs. Clin. Social Workers.

HANKS, GERALD E., oncologist; b. Ellensburg, Wash., Sept. 21, 1934; m. Barbara L. Fowble. BS cum laude, Wash. State Coll., 1955; MD cum laude, Washington U., St. Louis, 1959. Diplomate Am. Bd. Radiology. Intern in medicine Yale Univ. Svc./Grace-New Haven (Conn.) Hosp., 1959-60; fellow Divsn. Radiotherapy Stanford (Calif.) U., 1960-63, chief resident, Divsn. Radiotherapy, 1962-63; various faculty positions to prof. with tenure U. Pa. Sch. Medicine, Phila., 1985-92; chmn. dept. radiation oncology Fox Chase Cancer Ctr., 1985—; prof., chmn. dept. radiation oncology Med. Coll. of Pa., 1992—; various adminstrv. positions to vice-chmn. dept. radiation U. Pa., Phila., 1985-92, acting chmn. dept. radiation therapy, 1985-86, chmn. dept. radiation therapy, 1985—; cons. scientific adv. bd. dept. radiation oncology, U. Ariz., 1987; peer rev. cons. NIH; lectr. in field. Editorial bd.: Internat. Jour. of Radiation Oncology Biology Physics, Clin. Oncology: A Jour. of the Royal Coll. of Radiologists, Jour. of Surg. Oncology; contbr. numerous articles to profl. jours. and publs.; chpts. to books. With Med. Corp., USN Rev., 1959-63; active duty USN, 1963-65. Recipient C.V. Mosby Book award for scholastic excellence, 1959; recipient numerous grants in field including Radiation Therapy Oncology Group, 1981-86, 85-89, 89-92, 92-95, Patterns of Care Studies, 1980-85, 88-92, 92-93, 94-97, others. Fellow Am. Coll. Radiology (numerous offices and bds., gold medal 1996); mem. Am. Cancer Soc., Am. Soc. Clin. Oncology, AMA, Am. Radium Soc. (pres.-elect 1985, pres. 1986), Am. Soc. Therapeutic Radiology and Oncology (Gold medal 1994), Internat. Commn. on Radiation Units and Measurements, Internat. Congress of Radiation Oncology, InterSoc. Coun. for Radiation Oncology (pres. 1988-91), Joint Commn. on Accreditation of Health Care Orgns., Radiation Therapy Oncology Group, Nat. Coun. on Radiation Protection and Measurements Patterns of Care Study (prin. investigator 1988—), Calif. Radiation Therapy Assn. (pres. 1975-76), Calif. Radiologic Soc. (exec. com. 1976-83), No. Calif. Radiation Therapy Assn. (pres. 1974-75), others. Office: Fox Chase Cancer Ctr 7701 Burholme Ave Philadelphia PA 19111*

HANLEY, DAVID JEFFREY, plastic and hand surgeon; b. Eng., Aug. 25, 1940. Registrar Nat. Health Svc., Glasgow, Scotland, 1973-76; sr. registrar Nat. Health Svc., Stoke Mandeville, Eng., 1976-79; cons., pvt. practice Nat. Health Svc., Plymouth, Eng., 1979—; resident Gen. Hosp., Norfolk, Va., 1974. Fellow Royal Coll. Surgeons; mem. Brit. Assn. Plastic Surgeons, Brit. Soc. for Surgery of the Hand, Brit. Assn. Aesthetic Plastic Surgeons. Office: Nuffield Hosp, Derriford Rd, Plymouth PL6 8BG, England

HANLEY, JAMES RICHARD, III, pediatrician; b. Urbana, Ill., Nov. 28, 1957; s. James Richard and Priscilla Eva (Fournier) H.; m. Laura Elizabeth Fielding, Apr. 7, 1990 (div. June 1992); m. Denise Marie Mahoney, Mar. 17, 1995; children: Christopher, Nathaniel. BS in Chemistry, Auburn (Ala.) U., 1979; MD, Ea. Va. Med. Sch., Norfolk, 1988. Diplomate Am. Bd. Pediat.; lic. physician Fla., Va. Resident in pediats. U. Fla. Health Sci. Ctr., Jacksonville, 1988-91; pediat. emergency physician Emergency Physicians Inc., Jacksonville, 1991-94; pvt. practice Macclenny, Fla., 1991—; assoc. med. dir. Baker County EMS, Macclenny, 1991—; lectr. paramedic program Lake City (Fla.) C.C., 1992—. Mem. Civil Air Patrol; vol. physician homeless ctr. Jacksonville, Fla., 1992—. Lt. comdr. USN, 1979-83. Fellow Am. Acad. Pediat., Am. Acad. Family Physicians (assoc.); mem. Am. Coll. Emergency Physicians, Duval County Med. Soc. (we care com. 1994—), Fla. Med. Assn., No. Fla. Pediatric Soc. Office: MacClenny Pediatrics 28 W Macclenny Ave #5 Macclenny FL 32063

HANLEY, THOMAS PATRICK, obstetrician, gynecologist; b. St. Louis, Apr. 16, 1951; s. Thomas P. and Virginia Barbara (Lydon) H.; m. Patricia Ann McHargue, Dec. 27, 1975; children: Colleen, Thomas III, Timothy, Matthew. BA, St. Louis U., 1973, MD, 1977. Diplomate Am. Bd. Ob-gyn. Intern St. Louis U., 1977-78, resident, 1978-81; practice medicine specializing in ob-gyn St. Louis, 1981—; pres. med. staff St. Mary's Health Ctr., 1993; mem. staff Mo. Bapt. Hosp., Deaconess Hosp.; assoc. clin. prof. St. Louis U. Med. Sch., 1983—; mem. exec. com. St. Louis Med. Group, 1995—. Mem. AMA (Physicians Recognition award 1981—), Am. Coll. Ob-Gyn. (Physicians Excellence award 1986, 89, 92, 95), Gynecol. Laser Soc., St. Louis Gynecol. Soc. (pres. 1989-90), St. Louis Met. Med. Soc., West Borough Country Club. Republican. Roman Catholic. Office: 1035 Bellevue Ave Ste 208 Saint Louis MO 63117-1846

HANNA, DWIGHT CORWIN, surgeon; b. Port Allegany, Pa., Mar. 15, 1922; s. Dwight C. and Florence Christina (Finger) H.; m. Jane Ruth Atkinson, Sept. 23, 1944 (dec. Oct. 1994); children: Kathryn, Marilyn, Dwight, David; m. Mary Forbes Hawkins, Sept. 30, 1995. Student, Coll. of Wooster, 1940-42, Pa. State U., 1942-43; M.D., U. Pitts., 1946. Intern Western Pa. Hosp., 1946-47; resident Presbyn. and VA hosps., Pitts., 1949-54; practice medicine specializing in plastic surgery Pitts., 1954-87; assoc. staff Children's Hosp., Pitts., 1954-72; mem. attending staff Allegheny Gen. Hosp., Pitts., 1966-72; mem. staff U. Pitts. Med. Ctr., 1954-65; Western Pa. Hosp., Pitts., 1954—; pres. med. staff Western Pa. Hosp., 1975-78, chief of plastic and reconstructive surgery, 1971-87, med. dir., 1978-86; asst. prof. surgery U. Pitts. Sch. Medicine, 1954-68, prof. surgery, 1984—. Editor abstracts Jour. Plastic and Reconstructive Surgery, 1975-77, assoc. editor, 1985-95; assoc. editor Yearbook of Plastic and Reconstructive Surgery, 1975-80. Nat. pres. United Presbyn. Men, 1968; bd. dirs. Western Pa. Hosp., 1981-94; trustee Pitts. Theol. Sem., 1972-91, chmn., 1974-78; trustee Coll. Wooster, Ohio, 1972-78, 82-96, emeritus trustee, 1996—. Capt. U.S. Army, 1944-49. Recipient Gold Headed Cane award, Western Pa. Hosp., 1975. Fulbright scholar, Yugoslavia, 1983. Mem. ACS (bd. govs. 1978-84), Am. Soc. Plastic and Reconstructive Surgeons (ethics com. 1975-80), Am. Assn. Plastic Surgeons (trustee, pres. 1981-82), Am. Soc. Aesthetic Plastic Surgeons, Am. Cleft Palate Soc., Am. Burn Assn., Soc. Head and Neck Surgeons (treas. 1978-81), Pitts. Acad. Medicine (sec. 1969-72), Pa. Med. Soc., Allegheny County Med. Soc. (chmn. medicine and religion com. 1966-68, dir. 1977-80), AMA (mem. plastic and reconstructive residency rev. com. 1975-81, chmn. 1980-81), Pitts. Surg. Soc., Ohio Valley Plastic Surg. Soc. (pres. 1973-74), Interstate Plastic Surgery Soc., Northeast Plastic Surgery Soc. Republican. Presbyterian. Club: Oakmont Country.

HANNA, SUZANNE LOUISE, nurse; b. Mankato, Minn., Aug. 31, 1953; d. Frank Edward and Phyllis Ruth (Moeller) Wilkins; m. Thomas Ray Hanna, Sept. 15, 1973; children: Elizabeth Amy, Joseph Ryan, Thomas Wilkins. Diploma in nursing with highest honors, Iowa Western C.C., Council Bluffs, 1991. RN, Iowa; cert. provider ACLS, Am. Heart Assn. Exec. sec. First Nat. Bank, Mpls., 1971-72, Nat. Bank of Am., Salina, Kans., 1972; receptionist The Evening Sentinel, Shenandoah, Iowa, 1972-73; ins. sec. Wilson Ins. Agy., Shenandoah, 1973-79; med./surg. staff nurse Shenandoah Meml. Hosp., 1980-81; office nurse Dr. Floyd A. Jones, Shenandoah, 1983-95; clin. nurse Great Plains Physician Group, Omaha, Nebr., 1995—; emergency rm. nurse Shenandoah Meml. Hosp., 1992-95; bd. dirs. Ag-Pro Corp., Shenandoah; co-chairperson family life com., 1989-90. Alt. Rep. Page County Convs., 1988, 92; active ladies guild St. Mary Ch., Shenandoah, 1986—, mem. parish coun. bd., pres. parish coun., 1989-92, instr. religious edn., 1988-90, mem. choir, 1991—, organist, song leader, 1992—; bd. dirs. Shenandoah Music Assn., 1995—; mem. local Am. Legion Aux., 1994—. Mem. Beta Sigma Phi (pres. 1979-80). Roman Catholic. Home: 1302 Johnson Dr Shenandoah IA 51601-2606 Office: 300 Park Ave Shenandoah IA 51601-2351 also: 300 Pershing Ave Shenandoah IA 51601-2355

HANNAFIN, JO A., orthopaedic surgeon; b. Fall River, Mass., June 3, 1955; d. Arthur Calvert and Helen Cynthia (Walsh) H.; m. John Phillips Brisson, Nov. 6, 1982; children: Andrew Hannafin, Caitlin Phillips, Connor Anderson. ScB, Brown U., 1977; MS, PhD, MD, Albert Einstein Sch. Medicine, 1985. Bd. cert. orthopaedic surgery Am. Bd. Orthopaedic Surgery. Intern gen. surgery Montefiore Med. Ctr., Albert Einstein Coll. Medicine, Bronx, N.Y., 1985-86; resident orthopaedic surgery Montefiore Med. Ctr., Albert Einstein Coll. Medicine, Bronx, 1986-90; rsch. fellow lab. for comparative orthopaedic rsch. Hosp. for Spl. Surgery, N.Y.C., 1990-91, clin. fellow sports medicine and shoulder, 1991-92; asst. attending surgeon Hosp. for Spl. Surgery, N.Y. Hosp., N.Y.C., 1992—; instr. in surgery Cornell U. Med. Coll., N.Y.C., 1992—; assoc. dir. Lab. for Soft Tissue Rsch. Hosp. for Spl. Surgery, N.Y.C., 1992—; co-dir. Women Sports Medicine Ctr., Hosp. for Spl. Surgery, N.Y.C., 1993—; team physician U.S. Nat. Rowing Team, Indpls., 1994—; asst. team physician N.Y. Mets baseball; medicine and sci. com. N.Y. chpt. Arthritis Found., N.Y.C., 1994—. Contbr. chpts. to books and articles to profl. jours. Summer fellow Maine Heart Assn., 1976; Med. Scientist Tng. Program fellow NIH, 1979-85. Fellow Am. Acad. Orthopaedic Surgery; mem. AMA, N.Y. Med. Soc., Womens Med. Assn. N.Y., Ruth Jackson Orthopaedic Soc., Orthopaedic Rsch. Soc. (Young Investigator Recognition award 1993), U.S. Rowing Assn. (sports medicine and sci. com. 1993—), Alpha Omega Alpha, Sigma Xi. Lutheran. Office: Hosp for Spl Surgery 535 E 70th St New York NY 10021-4892

HANNALLAH, RAAFAT SAMY, anesthesiologist; b. Egypt, Sept. 17, 1944; m. Isis Hannallah; children: David, Michael. MB, BChir, Cairo U., 1966. Diplomate Am. Bd. Anesthesiology. Resident McGill U., Montreal, Que., Can., 1968-73; prof. anesthesiology and pediatrics Sch. Medicine George Washington U.; vice chmn. anesthesiology Children's Nat. Med. Ctr., Washington. Fellow Royal Coll. Physicians and Surgeons of Can. Office: Children's Nat Med Ctr 111 Michigan Ave NW Washington DC 20010-9999

HANNAN, DAVID THOMAS, family physician; b. Rochester, N.Y., May 4, 1951; s. Raymond G. and Rita P. Hannan; children: John, Luke, Erin, Mark, Matthew. BS, USAF Acad., Colo., 1973; MD, U. Colo., 1976; MPA, Golden Gate U., 1985. Diplomate Am. Bd. Family Practice. Commd. 2d lt. USAF, 1973, advanced through grades to maj., 1981; intern in family practice Tripler Army Med. Ctr., Honolulu, 1977, resident, 1977-79; chief family practice dept. Homestead USAF Hosp., Fla., 1980-82; dir. family practice intern tng. David Grant USAF Med. Ctr., Travis AFB, Calif., 1982-85; family physician, pres. Arcadia Family Practice, P.C., Newark, N.Y., 1985—; coroner Wayne County, N.Y., 1992—. Trustee Village of Newark, 1989—. Fellow Am. Acad. Family Physicians; mem. AMA (alt. del. 1995—), N.Y. State Acad. Family Physicians, Wayne County Med. Soc. (past pres.), Med. Soc. State N.Y. (councillor 1993—), Rotary. Office: Arcadia Family Practice PC 1202 Driving Park Ave Newark NY 14513

HANNERS, G(ARY) DALE, social worker; b. Leachville, Ark., Sept. 16, 1942. BS, Memphis State U., 1966; MS, Ark. State U., 1968; PhD, U. Memphis, 1995. Lic. psychol. examiner, Ark.; cert. sch. psychologist. Tchr. Memphis Pub. Schs., 1964-65; with personnel dept. Sears, Roebuck and Co., Memphis, 1965-66; supr. client svcs. Abilities Unltd., Jonesboro, 1966-70; rehab. counselor State of Ark., Jonesboro, 1970-74, psychol. examiner, 1979—; pvt. practice cons. human svcs., Ark., 1970-79; cons. Little People Am., Calif. Mem. Am. Psychol. Assn. (assoc.), Ark. Psychol. Assn., Ark. Sch. Psychol. Assn., Civitan (sec.-treas. Jonesboro chpt. 1967-70). Republican. Baptist. Home: PO Box 885 Jonesboro AR 72403-6100

HANNI, GERALDINE MARIE, therapist; b. Salt Lake City, Nov. 14, 1930; d. John Henry and Theresa Justine (Keirce) Gold; m. Kenneth J. Hanni, Mar. 14, 1951; children: Debra, Valerie, Kathleen, Cynthia, Kristine. BS, U. Utah, 1951, MSW, 1983. Lic. clin. social worker. Tchr. Hillside Jr. High Sch., Salt Lake City, 1970-73; intern Davis County Schs., Farmington, Utah, 1981-82, Westside Mental Health, Salt Lake City, 1982-83; group leader LDS Social Services, Salt Lake City, 1985; therapist ISAT, Salt Lake City, 1983-90, clin. dir., 1987-90; clin. instr. U. Utah, Salt Lake City, 1986-90; pvt. practice, 1990—; mem. bd. Salt Lake County Sexual Abuse Task Force, Salt Lake City; cons. LDS Social Services, Salt Lake City, 1984-86. Contbg. author: Abuse and Religion, Confronting Abuse—an LDS Perspective. Sect. dir. Mortar Bd. Honor Soc., western U.S., 1970; pres. Highland High PTA, Salt Lake City, 1980; chairperson Highland High Community Sch. Orgn., Salt Lake City, 1981. Mem. Nat. Assn. Social Workers (Utah chpt.). Democrat. Mormon.

HÄNNINEN, OSMO OTTO, physiology educator; b. Lahti, Finland, Apr. 30, 1939; s. Otto and Hilja Elisabet (Kauppi) H.; m. Auli Helena Karkiainen; children: Otto Olavi, Aino Helena. B degree in medicine, U. Helsinki, 1960; BSc in Biochemistry, U. Turku, Finland, 1962, MS in Biochemistry, 1962, MD, 1964, Dr.Med.Sci., 1966, Laudatur in genetics, 1967, PhD in Biochemistry, 1968. Cert. specialist in sports medicine Nat. Bd. Health. Rsch. asst., prof. K. Hartiala, Turku, 1962-64; asst. physiology U. Turku, 1964-65, laborator of physiology, 1966-67, docent of physiology, 1967—, assoc. prof. biochemistry, 1969-71; acting prof. planning office U. Kuopio, Finland, 1971-72, prof. physiology, chmn. dept., 1972—, rector, 1981-84, acting chmn. Lab. Animal Ctr., 1972-80; docent of physiology U. Joensuu, Finland, 1982—; sr. researcher Acad. Finland, 1980, rsch. prof., 1980-81, mem. com. on environ. rsch., 1980-82, mem. working group on ethics in rsch., 1980-81; mem. working com. on pharmacy edn. Ministry of Edn., 1976, vice chmn. working group on postgrad. edn., 1982-83; vice chmn. state com. U. Edn. in Eastern Finland, 1977-78; v.p. standing conf. on Univ. Problems, Coun. of Europe, 1987; mem. governing bd. Coun. Finnish Univ. Rectors, 1983-84; speaker in field. Author textbooks and monographs in field; assoc. editor News in Physiol. Scis., 1988-95; editor: In Vivo, 1987—, editor in chief Suomen Liikuntalääketiede, 1982—; mem. editorial bd. Exptl. and Clin. Gastroenterology, Pathophysiology, 1994—; contbr. articles to profl. jours. Named First Order Knight, Order of Finnish White Rose, 1979, Comdr. Order of Finnish Lion, 1988; recipient Kuopio prize, 1979, Medal of Merit, Def. Forces, Finland, 1987; grantee Acad. Finland, Ministry of Edn., Ministry of Agri- and Silviculture, Ministry of Commerce and Industry, Nat. Bd. Health, Fund for Occupational Safety, Juho Vainio Found., NIH, others. Mem. Nordic Physiol. Soc. (bd. dirs. 1985—), Internat. Coun. for Lab. Animal Sci. (mem. governing bd. 1983-88, chmn. constn. revision working group 1983-88, sec.-gen. 1988-95, editor-in-chief bull. 1988-95), Finnish Chemists' Soc., Finnish Med. Assn., Finnish Lab. Animal Scientists (pres. 1990-91), Finnish Pharmacol. Soc., Finnish Physiol. Soc. (pres. 1990—), Scandinavian Fedn. Lab. Animal Sci. (hon.), Internat. Soc. Pathophysiology (v.p. 1990—, pres.-elect 1994—), Internat. Union of Biol. Scis. (mem. exec. com. 1994—, mem. commn. bioindicators), Internat. Union of Physiological Scis. (mem. commn. of pathophysiology 1993—, mem. com. on ethical aspects of physiological scis. 1993—), Fedn. of European Physiological Socs. (mem. coun. 1992—). Office: U Kuopio Dept Physiology, PO Box 1627, SF-70211 Kuopio Finland

HANNON, VIVIAN NELL, home health nurse; b. Charleston, W.Va., Dec. 29, 1950; d. Harold Clinton Ramsey and Nora Tina Plumley Cooper; m. Jerry Roy Hannon, Feb. 10, 1968; children: Deborah, Mark, Brian, Kristina, Jessica. BSN, U. Ala. Huntsville, 1992. RN, Ala.; cert. EMT. Staff nurse, pediatrics Huntsville Hosp., 1992; staff nurse, home health Ala. Dept. Pub. Health, Guntersville, 1993—; mem. Ala. Nurse Practitioner Coun, Montgomery, 1994. Family history ctr. dir. Ch. of Jesus Christ of Latter Day Saints, Guntersville, 1988-94; rapid responder, sec. Grant (Ala.) Fire Dept., 1990-93. Mem. Ala. State Nurses Assn., Sigma Theta Tau, Omicron Delta Kappa, Phi Kappa Phi. Democrat. Home: 354 Cardesse Ln Grant AL 35747

HANOVER, KENNETH, health service administrator; b. Boston, Oct. 5, 1951; s. Alfred Stamford and Edith (Baron) H.; m. Sylvia Theresa Pazics, Oct. 25, 1975; children: Jonathan, Stephanie, Zachary, Caylen, Emily. BA, U. Mass., 1973; MPA, Cornell U., 1975. Staff assoc. Hosp. Assn. of Pa., Camp Hill, 1975-76, dir. quality assurance, 1976-78, v.p., 1979-84; asst. administr. Hosp. of U. Pa., Phila., 1978-79; sr. v.p. HealthLink, Portland, Oreg., 1984-89; pres. Bryn Mawr Rehab. Hosp., Main Line Health, Inc., Radnor, Pa., 1989-92; sr. v.p. adminstrn. Bryn Mawr & Lankenau Hosps., Main Line Health, Inc., Radnor, 1992-93, pres., 1993—; bd. dirs. The Chestnut Group, Inc., Wayne, Pa.; mem. med. adv. bd. Founders Bank, Bryn Mawr, 1995—. Author: Guide to Pennsylvania Regulations Affecting Hospitals, 1976, Guidelines for Release of Information in the Medical Record, 1978; contbr. articles to profl. jours. Bd. dirs. John Sharpe Found., Bryn Mawr, 1993—, Devon (Pa.) Horse Show and Country Fair, Inc., 1993—, Phila. Health Congress, 1993—, Surrey Svcs. for Srs., Berwyn, Pa., 1993—. Recipient 40 Under 40 award Phila. Bus. Jour., 1990, Bus. Excellence award Newcomen Soc., 1994. Mem. Am. Hosp. Assn. (ho. of dels. 1989-92), Am. Coll. Health Care Execs. (diplomate). Office: Bryn Mawr & Lankenau Hosps 130 S Bryn Mawr Ave Bryn Mawr PA 19010

HANOWELL, ERNEST GODDIN, physician; b. Newport News, Va., Jan. 31, 1920; a. George Frederick and Ruby Augustine (Goddin) H.; m. Para Jean Hall, June 10, 1945; children: Ernest D., Deborah J. Hanowell Orick, Leland H., Dee P. Hanowell Martinmaas, Robert G. Diplomate Am. Bd. Internal Medicine. Intern USPHS Hosp., Norfolk, Va., 1948-49; resident in internal medicine USPHS Hosp., Seattle, 1952-55; fellow cardiology New Eng. Ctr. Hosp., Boston, 1961-62; chief medicine USPHS Hosp., Ft. Worth, 1955-57; dept. chief medicine USPHS Hosp., Boston, 1957-59; chief medicine USPHS Hosp., Memphis, 1964-65, Monterey County Gen. Hosp., 1969-70; ret. med. dir., col. USPHS; mem. IM and Cardiology staff Kaiser Permanente Med. Group, Sacramento, 1971-87; writer Auburn, Calif., 1987--; clin. asst. Tufts Med. Sch., 1960-61; cons. chest disease Phila. Gen. Hosp., 1960-61; asst. prof. U. Md. Med. Sch., 1961-64; instr. U. Tenn. Med. Sch., 1964-65; asst. clin. prof. Sch. Medicine, U. Calif., Davis, 1973-81; mem. attending staff Cardiac Clinic Stanford U. Med. Sch. 1967-69. Mem. sch. bd. Salinas, Calif., 1968-69; bd. dirs. Am. Heart Assn., Tb and Health Assn. Served with AUS, 1943-46. Fellow ACP, Am. Coll. Chest Diseases; mem. AWA, Crocker Art Mus. Assn., Comstock Club (Sacramento), Phi Chi. Home and Office: 1158 Racquet Club Dr Auburn CA 95603-3042

HANRATTY, CARIN GALE, pediatric nurse practitioner; b. Dec. 31, 1953; d. Burton and Lillian Aleskowitz; m. Michael Patrick Hanratty, May 22, 1983; 1 child, Tyler James. BSN, Russell Sage Coll., 1975; postgrad., U. Calif., San Diego, 1980. Cert. CPR instr.; cert. NALS; cert. specialist ANA. PNP day surgery unit Children's Med. Ctr., Dallas, 1981-85; clin. mgr. pediatrics Trinity Med. Ctr., Carrollton, Tex., 1985-86; pediatric drug coord. perinatal intervention team for substance abusing women and babies Parkland Meml. Hosp., Dallas, 1990—. Guest talk show Morning Coffee, Sta. KPLX-FM, various TV programs. Rep. United Way, 1988—, blood donor chair Parkland Hosp., 1990—, chair March of Dimes, 1992—; bd. dirs., med. cons. KIDNET Found. Mem. ARC (profl., life), Nat. Assn. PNPs (v.p. Dallas chpt. 1982-83), Tex. Nurses Assn. Office: Parkland Meml Hosp PNP 5201 Harry Hines Blvd Dallas TX 75235-7708

HANS, MARK GUENTHER, orthodontist; b. Berea, Ohio, Sept. 3, 1953; s. Guenther and Ruth (Celke) H.; m. Susan Maikis, Sept. 1, 1979; children: Sarah, John Guenther, Thomas. BS in Chemistry, Yale U., 1975; DDS, Case Western Res. U., 1979, MS in Dentistry, 1981. Diplomate Am. Bd. Orthodontics. Clin. instr. dept. oral biology Case Western Res. U., 1981-84, clin. instr. dept. orthodontics, 1984-87, sr. clin. instr. dept. orthodontics, 1988, asst. clin. prof. dept. orthodontics, 1989, rsch. assoc. The Bolton-Brush growth study, 1989-91, asst. prof. deop. orthodontics, 1989-95, assoc. prof. dept. orthodontics, 1995—; cons. Am. Assn. of Orthodontists Ad Hoc Tech. Com., 1993-95. Editl. rev. bd. Am. Jour. of Orthodontics and Dentofacial Orthopedics, The Angle Orthodontist; contbr. articles to profl. jours. Grantee NIH, 1990-95, Am. Assn. of Orthodontists, 1991-92, 1993, Am. Assn. of Orthodontists Found. 1992, others. Fellow Am. Coll. Dentists; mem. AAAS, ADA, Am. Assn. of Orthodontists (orthodontic informatics oversight com. chmn. 1995—, workshop focus group recorder, 1992, chairpersons conf. focus group recorder 1993, bd. dirs. dental interactive simulations corp. 1994—, dental informatics task force 1994—, consortium on clin. info. systems 1994—), Great Lakes Soc. of Orthodontists (coun. on orthodontic edn. com. mem. 1993—), Ohio Assn. of Orthodontists, Cleve. Soc. of Orthodontists, Ohio Dental Assn., Cleve. Dental Soc., Edward H. Angle Soc. of Orthodontists (midwest component), Am. Cleft Palate-Craiofacial Assn., Am. Assn. of Dental Rsch. (craiofacial biology group), Internat. Assn. of Dental Rsch. (craniofacial biology group). Home: 191 Lee Rd Berea OH 44017 Office: Dentistry Case Western Res Dept Orthodontics 10900 Euclid Ave Cleveland OH 44106-4905

HANSEL, WILLIAM, biology educator; b. Vale Summit, Md., Sept. 16, 1918; s. John W. and Helen M. (Sperlein) H.; m. Milbrey Downey, Aug. 16, 1942; children: Barbara, Kay. MS, Cornell U., 1947, PhD, 1949. Asst. prof. Cornell U., Ithaca, N.Y., 1949-52, assoc. prof., 1952-61, prof., 1961-90, Liberty Hyde Bailey prof., 1983-90, chmn. physiology dept., 1978-83; Gordon D. Cain prof. La. State U., Baton Rouge, 1990—; scientific adv. Merck, Sharp and Dohme, Rahway, 1980-85, Smith, Kline, Beecham, Westchester, Pa., 1986-91. Author: Genetic Engineering of Animals, 1990; contbr. over 300 articles to profl. jours. Maj. U.S. Army, 1941-46, ETO. Fellow AAAS; mem. Soc. Study Reprodn. (pres. 1976), Am. Physiol. Soc., Endocrine Soc., Soc. Exptl. Biology and Medicine (treas. 1975), Gamma Sigma Delta, Sigma Xi, Phi Kappa Phi. Office: Pennington Biomed Rsch Ctr B-1047 Baton Rouge LA 70808

HANSELL, DAVID MATTHEW, consultant radiologist; b. London, Apr. 3, 1957; s. Peter and Jean (Nichol) H.; m. Mary-Anne Gadsden, July 18, 1981; children: Lydia May, Fiona Murray, Florence Cicely. Student, King's Coll., London, 1976-78; MB BS, Westminster Med. Sch., London 1981. Registrar, sr. registrar in radiology Westminster Hosp., London, 1984-88; cons. radiologist, hon. sr. lectr. Royal Brompton Nat. Heart and Lung Hosp., London, 1989—, clin. dir. imaging, 1993—. Author books and articles on imaging of diffuse lung disease; asst. editor Clin. Radiology, 1990—. King's Fund travelling scholar, London, 1988, Kodak Trust scholar Royal Coll. Radiology, 1989, Runcorn travelling fellow Westminster Med. Sch., 1989, du Boulay Rsch. Trust awardee Brit. Inst. Radiology, 1989. Fellow Royal Coll. Radiology; mem. Royal Coll. Physicians; mem. Assn. Chest Radiologists (sec. 1992-94), European Soc. Thoracic Imaging, Soc. Thoracic Radiology (U.S.), Brit. Thoracic Soc., Fleischner Soc. Anglican. Home: 76 Ellerby St, London SW6 6EZ, England Office: Royal Brompton Nat Heart and Lung Hosp, Sydney St, London SW3 6NP, England

HANSELL, RICHARD STANLEY, obstetrician, gynecologist, educator; b. Indpls., Nov. 18, 1950; s. Robert Mathey and Jewell (Martin) H.; m. Cathy C., Oct. 7, 1995; children: Elizabeth, Victoria. BA, DePauw U., 1972; MD, Ind. U., 1976. Cert. Am. Bd. Obstetrics and Gynecology. Practice medicine specializing in ob-gyn Cedarwood Med. Ctr., St. Joseph, Mich., 1980-86; assoc. prof. ob-gyn. Ind. U., Indpls., 1986-93, assoc. prof. ob-gyn, 1993—; instr. Western Mich. U., Kalamazoo, 1980-86; med. bd. Planned Parenthood, Benton Harbor, Mich., 1980-86; med. dir. Planned Parenthood of Ctrl. Ind., 1991-95. Mem. AMA, Am. Coll. Ob-Gyn, Assn. of Profs. of Gynecology and Obstetrics, Ind. State Med. Soc., Indpls. Med. Soc. Presbyterian. Lodge: Kiwanis. Office: Ind U Med Sch Dept Ob-Gyn 1001 W 10th St Indianapolis IN 46202-2859

HANSEN, ALAN EDWARD, mental health nurse; b. Hettinger, N.D., Jan. 12, 1953; s. Eugene and Evelyn (Tkachenko) H.; m. Rayleen Weisz, June 8, 1975; children: Derek, Brooke. BS in Nursing, Union Coll., Lincoln, Nebr., 1974; MHS, Whitworth Coll., Spokane, Wash., 1983. RN, Wash., Nebr. Psychiatric staff nurse State of Iowa Penal System, Oakdale, 1979-80, Sacred Heart Med. Ctr., Spokane, Wash., 1980-83; instr. Meth. Coll. Nursing, Omaha, Nebr., 1983-86; staff nurse Meth. Hosp., Omaha, 1986-90; chem. dependency nurse St. Francis Drug and Alcohol Treatment Ctr., Grand Island, Nebr., 1990-92, St. Francis Med. Ctr. Emergency Rm., Grand Island, Nebr., 1992—.

HANSEN, BARBARA CALEEN, physiology educator, scientist; b. Boston, Nov. 24, 1941; d. Reynold L. and Dorothy (Richardson) Caleen; m. Kenneth Dale Hansen, Oct. 8, 1976; 1 son, David Scott. B.S., UCLA, 1964, M.S., 1965; Ph.D., U. Wash., 1971. Asst. prof. then assoc. prof. U. Wash., Seattle, 1971-76; prof., assoc. dean U. Mich., Ann Arbor, 1977-82; assoc. v.p. acad. affairs and research, dean grad. sch. So. Ill. U., Carbondale, 1982-85, v.p. for grad. studies and research U. Md., Balt. and Baltimore County, 1985-90; prof. physiology, dir. obesity and diabetes rsch. ctr. U. Md., 1990—; mem. adv. com. to dir. NIH, Washington, 1979-83; mem. joint health policy com. Assn. Am. Univs., Nat. Assn. State Univs. and Land-Grant Colls., Am. Coun. on Edn., Washington, 1982-86; mem. nutrition study sect. NIH, 1979-83; mem. program com. Inst. Medicine-NAS, Washington, 1982-84; mem. Armed Forces Epidemiology Bd., 1991-95, Bd. Sci. Counselors, Nat. Toxicology Bd., NIEHS, NIH, 1992-94; mem. search com. Office of Rsch. Integrity, NIH, 1992-93. Contbr. articles to profl. jours.; editor: Controversies in Obesity, 1983; chpts. on physiology. Mem. adv. com. Am. Bur. Med. Advancement China, N.Y.C., 1982-85, Robert Wood Johnson Found., Princeton, N.J., 1982-91; mem. adv. bd. African-Am. Inst. 1987-91. U. Pa. Inst. Neuroscis. fellow, 1966-68; Arthur Patch McKinley scholar of Phi Beta Kappa, 1964. Mem. Am. Physiol. Soc., Inst. Medicine of NAS, Am. Inst. Nutrition, Am. Soc. for Clin. Nutrition (v.p., pres.-elect 1994-95, pres. 1995-96), Internat. Assn. for Study of Obesity (pres. 1986-90), N.Am. Assn. for Study of Obesity (pres. 1984-85, 86—), Nat. Assn. State Univs. and Land Grant Colls. (chaiperson coun. on rsch. policy and grad. edn. 1986-87), Phi Beta Kappa. Republican. Presbyterian. Office: U Md Sch Medicine Obesity and Diabetes Rsch Ctr 10 S Pine St MSTF6-00 Baltimore MD 21201-1192

HANSEN, DOLLY DORIS, anesthesiologist; b. Copenhagen, Oct. 24, 1935; came to U.S., 1971; d. Egun Edmund and Doris Christine (Hansen) H. MD, Copenhagen U., 1961. Intern Ctrl. Sygenset, Swendborg, Denmark, 1962-63; anesthesia resident Fredericks berg Hosp., Copenhagen, 1963-66; surgeon Mcpl. Hosp., Copenhagen, 1966-67; anesthesiology resident Univ. Hosp., Copenhagen, 1967, staff anesthesiologist, 1967-71; anesthesiology fellow Children's Hosp., Boston, 1971-72, staff anesthesiologist, 1972—; asst. prof. Harvard Med. Sch., Boston, 1980—. Contbr. articles to profl. jours., chpts. to books. Office: Children's Hosp Dept Anesthesia 300 Longwood Ave Boston MA 02195

HANSEN, DUANE ALAN, dentist, naval officer; b. St. Ansgar, Iowa, Jan. 15, 1933; s. Arthur and Marie Margarete (Denning) H.; m. Nancy Ann Cunningham, Apr. 20, 1968; children—Laurel Elizabeth, Leeann Marie. B.A., St. Olaf Coll., 1955; D.D.S., State U. Iowa, Iowa City, 1959; clin. fellow dental medicine Forsyth Dental Ctr. and Harvard Sch. Dental Medicine, Boston, 1961. Commd. lt. U.S. Navy, 1963; advanced through grades to comdr., 1969; clinic supr. 22d Dental Co., Camp Lejeune, N.C., 1971-74, head, br. dental clinic Naval Air Sta., Lakehurst, N.J., 1974-77, head dental dept. U.S.S. Gilmore, Sardinia, Italy, 1977-79, head dental annex The Basic Sch., Quantico, Va., 1979-84, dir. br. dental clinic Naval Surface Weapons Command, Dahlgren, Va., 1984-87, ret., 1987; contract dentist Marine Corps Base, Quantico, Va., 1987—. Mem. ADA, Acad. Gen. Dentistry. Republican. Presbyterian. Avocations: reading; traveling; bicycling; physical fitness.

HANSEN, FLORENCE MARIE CONGIOLOSI (MRS. JAMES S. HANSEN), social worker; b. Middletown, N.Y., Jan. 7, 1934; d. Joseph James and Florence (Harrigan) Congiolosi; m. James S. Hansen, June 16, 1959 (dec. Nov. 1989); 1 child, Florence M. BA, Coll. New Rochelle, 1955; MSW, Fla. State U., 1960; PhD, Union Inst., 1992. Caseworker, Orange County Dept. Pub. Welfare, N.Y., 1955-57, Cath. Welfare Bur., Miami, Fla., 1957-58; supr. Cath. Family Service, Spokane, Wash., 1960, Cuban Children's Program, Spokane, 1962-66; founder, dir. social service dept. Sacred Heart Med. Ctr., 1968-85, dir. Kidney Ctr., 1967-91. Asst. in program devel. St. Margaret's Hall, Spokane, 1961-62; trustee Family Counseling Svc. Spokane County, 1981—, also bd. dirs.; mem. budget allocation panel United Way, 1964-76, mem. planning com., 1968-77, mem. admissions com., 1969-70, chmn. projects com. 1972-73; mem. kidney disease adv. com. Wash.-Alaska Regional Med. Program, 1970-73. Mem. Spokane Quality of Life Commn., 1974-75; vol. Primary Health Care Nangoma Health Ctr., 1992—; cons. CARE Internat., Zambia, 1993-95. Recipient Ursula Laurus citation Coll. New Rochelle, 1990, Angela Merici medal, 1995. Mem. Nat. Assn. Social Workers (Wash. chpt. pres. 1972-74, Wash. State Social Worker of Yr. 1991, Nat. Social Worker of Yr. 1991), Acad. Cert. Social Workers (charter). Roman Catholic. Home: 5609 W Northwest Blvd Spokane WA 99205-2039 Office: Nangoma Health Ctr, Box 830022, Mumbwa Zambia

HANSEN, HOBART GARFIELD, psychiatrist, hospital superintendent; b. Hancock, N.Y., Aug. 10, 1923; s. Hobart Garfield and Dorothy (Nielsen) H.; m. Archer Ellis, Sept. 3, 1949; children—Christian Stowe, Margaret Ellis. A.B., Columbia, 1945, M.A., 1946; M.D., U. Va., 1957. Intern research psychology N.Y. State Psychiat. Inst. and Hosp., 1945-46; intern clin. psychology N.Y. State Dept. Mental Hygiene, 1946-47; clin. psychologist Elmira (N.Y.) Reception Center and Elmira Reformatory, 1947-51; chief psychologist Western State Hosp., Staunton, Va., 1951-53; med. intern U. Va. Hosp., 1957-58; staff physician Western State Hosp., 1958-60; resident psychiatry St. Elizabeth's Hosp., Washington, 1960-63; clin. dir. Western State Hosp., 1963-65, asst, supt., 1965-67, supt., 1967-77; med. dir. Massanutten Mental Health Center, 1977-86; psychiat. cons. Woodrow Wilson Rehab. Center, 1977-79; psychiatrist Rockbridge Mental Health Clinic, 1977-79, psychiat. cons., 1987-94; psychiat. cons. Valley Pastoral Counseling Ctr., 1987-88; clin. asst. prof. psychiatry U. Va. Sch. Medicine, 1965-91. Mem. Am. Psychiat. Assn., Neuropsy. Soc. Va. (pres. 1976-77). Home: 148 Fallon St Staunton VA 24401-2324

HANSEN, JAMES EDWARD, medical educator, researcher; b. Green Bay, Wis., Sept. 4, 1926; s. James Christian and Helen Dorothy (Terp) H.; m. Beverly May Kapke, June 5, 1948; children: Barbara Parry, Patricia Begley, Linda DeGroot, James H. Student, St. Norbert's Coll., 1942-43, U. Wis., 1943-44, Marquette U., 1944-45; MD, Johns Hopkins U., 1945-49. Diplomate Am. Bd. Internal Medicine. Intern, then resident Letterman Army Med. Ctr., San Francisco, 1949-53; commd. 1st lt. U.S. Army, 1949; advanced through grades to col. U.S. Army, Kans., Colo., London, Japan, France, and Jordan, 1975, physician, 1950-62; chief physiology div. U.S. Army Med. Rsch. and Nutrition Lab., Denver, 1962-65; sci. dir. U.S. Army Rsch. Inst. Environ. Medicine, Natick, Mass., 1965-71; chief clin. investigation svcs. Tripler Army Med. Ctr., Honolulu, 1971-75; assoc. prof. dept. medicine UCLA, Torrance, 1976-78, prof. dept. medicine, 1978-86; emeritus prof. dept. medicine UCLA, 1986—; instr., asst. prof. U. Colo., 1961-65; liaison mem. applied physiology study sect. NIH, 1965-71; cons. environ. medicine U.S. Army Surgeon Gen., Washington, 1965-73; lectr. environ. medicine Johns Hopkins U., Balt., 1966-71; clin. prof. physiology U. Hawaii, 1972-75. Co-author: Principles of Exercise Testing and Interpretation, 1986, 2d rev. edit., 1994; contbr. numerous articles to profl. jours. Chmn. congregation St. Matthew's Luth. Ch., Aurora, Colo., 1962-64, Gloria Dei Luth. Ch., Pearl City, Hawaii, 1972-74; sch. supt. Luth. Ch., Natick, 1967-69; elder, mission com. chmn. St. Peter's By the Sea Presbyn. Ch., Rancho Palos Verdes, Calif., 1992-95. Pulmonary fellow Fitzsimons Army Med. Ctr., 1960, UCLA Ctr. Health Scis., 1975-76; recipient Sustaining Membership award Assn. Mil. Surgeons, 1970, Calif. medal Am. Lung Assn., 1996. Fellow ACP, Am. Coll. Chest Physicians; mem. Am. Physiol. Soc., Am. Thoracic Soc. (sci. adv. bd. 1983—), Calif. Thoracic Soc. (pulmonary chmn. 1980-83, physiology com). Home: 1692 Morse Dr San Pedro CA 90732-4336 Office: Harbor-UCLA Med Ctr PO Box 24 1000 W Carson St Torrance CA 90509

HANSEN, JOHN T., anatomy educator; b. Sheboygan Falls, Wis., Oct. 10, 1947; s. Horace John and Elizabeth A. (Huibregtse) H.; m. Paula Ann Petty, Aug. 22, 1970; children: Amy Lynn, Sean Thomas. BA, Beloit Coll., 1970; MS, Creighton U., 1972; PhD in Anatomy, Tulane U., 1974. Asst. instr. Tulane U., New Orleans, 1974-75; instr. U. Tex. HSCSA, San Antonio, 1975-76, asst. prof., 1976-80, assoc. prof., 1980-85; assoc. prof. U. Rochester (N.Y.) Med. Sch., 1985-89, prof. of anatomy, 1989—, acting chmn. dept., 1991—; grant reviewer NIH, Bethesda, Md., NSF, Washington. Contbr. articles to profl. jours., chpts. to books. Vol. Habitat for Humanity, Rochester. Grantee NIH, Am. Heart Assn.; recipient Rsch. Career Devel. award NIH, 1980-85. Mem. AAAS, Am. Assn. Anatomists, Soc. for Neurosci., Clin. Anatomists. Office: U Rochester Med Ctr Dept Neurobiology & Anatomy 601 Elmwood Ave Box 603 Rochester NY 14642*

HANSEN, MARY CHRISTINA, nursing educator; b. Norfolk, Va., Mar. 8, 1948; d. Dale Francis and Mildred Irene (Thomas) Mincer; m. Roger V. Hansen; 1 child, Raymond. BSN, Creighton U., 1970; MSN, Tex. Woman's U., 1981; PhD, Iowa State U., 1993. RN, Iowa. Staff nurse Mercy Hosp., Des Moines, Iowa, 1970-72; instr. Mercy Sch. Nursing, Des Moines, 1972-86; asst. prof. div. nursing Grand View Coll., Des Moines, 1981-84; asst. prof. dept. nursing Drake U., Des Moines, 1986—; dir. Drake Ctr. Health Issues; cons. Des Moines, 1988—. Contbr.: Nurse Manager Problem Solver, 1994. Presdl. appointee Pres.'s Adv. Com. on Arts; mem. Senator Tom Harkin's Health Adv. Group, 1990—, Nat. Health Policy Coun., 1993—. Mem. Iowa League for Nursing (pres. 1991-93), Iowa Nurses Assn. (dist. pres. 1995—), Iowa Orgn. Nurse Execs., Tri-Coun. Iowa Nursing Orgns., Sigma Theta Tau. Home: 3212 Giles St West Des Moines IA 50265-3174 Office: Drake Univ Dept Nursing Olin Hall 427 Des Moines IA 50311

HANSEN, RANDALL GLENN, school psychologist, consultant; b. Fayetteville, N.C., Dec. 9, 1946; s. Glenn Sidney and Ramona Mary (Blocker) H.; m. Wanda Kay Moller (div. Dec. 1990); 1 child, Nicholas Glenn. BS in Secondary Edn., Black Hills State U., Spearfish, S.D., 1971; BA in Social Work, Chadron (Nebr.) State Coll., 1978; MEd in Counseling-Guidance-Pers. Svcs., S.D. State U., 1982; cert. sch. psychology licensing program, Moorhead (Minn.) State U., 1986; PhD in Clin. Sch. Psychology, Walden U., Mpls., 1991. Clin./sch. psychology nat. cert. counselor; cert. cognitive-behavioral therapist; lic. profl. counselor, S.D. Tchr., counselor Sky Ranch for Boys, Camp Crook, S.D., 1971-72; social worker I, S.D. Dept. Social Svcs., Rapid City, 1972-73; multi-county svc. area supr. S.D. Dept. Social Svcs., Mitchell and Sioux Falls, 1979-85; asst. mgr. Pioneer Market, North Platte, Nebr., 1973-74; county dir. Frontier County Div. Pub. Welfare, Curtis, Nebr., 1974-75; quality control reviewer Nebr. Dept. Pub. Welfare, Scottsbluff, 1975-77, asst. income maintenance rep., 1977-79; sch. psychologist Tracy (Minn.), Milroy, Balaton and Walnut Grove Schs., 1985-88, Palo Verde Unified Sch. Dist., Blythe, Calif., 1988—; pvt. practice Blythe Family Counseling Ctr., 1995—; sch. psychol. cons. Desert Ctr. Unified Sch. Dist., Eagle Mountain, Calif., 1988—; pub. speaker on learning disabilities and how mind processes info., 1986—. Author: (psychol. test) Children's Attention-Deficit Hyperactivity Inventory, 1991. Bd. dirs. Food Svcs. Ctr., Sioux Falls, 1980-85, Educators Interested in Spl. Edn., Marshall, Minn., 1985-88; counselor Crisis Line, Sioux Falls, 1981-85; softball coach Project Awareness, Sioux Falls, 1984. Named Vol. of Month, Crisis Line, 1984. Mem. ACA, NASP, Riverside Assn. Sch. Psychologists, Menninger Found., Doctorate Assn. N.Y. Educators. Democrat. Home: 8401 E Hobson Way Spc 34 Blythe CA 92225-2103 Office: Counseling Ctr 689 N Lovekin Blvd Blythe CA 92225-1136 also: Blythe Family Counseling Ct 149 W Hobsonway Blythe CA 92225

HANSEN, SIGVARD THEODORE, JR., orthopaedic surgeon, educator; b. Spokane, Wash., Nov. 30, 1935; s. Sigvard Theodore and Beverly Esther

(Means) H.; m. Mary Jane Weinmann, Aug. 20, 1960; children: Christopher Michael, Eric Theodore; m. Dalia Maria Nalis, Sept. 19, 1987. BA cum laude, Whitman Coll., 1957; MD, U. Wash., 1961. Diplomate Am. Bd. Orthopaedic Surgery. Intern, King County Hosp., Seattle, 1961-62; resident in surgery U. Wash., Seattle, 1965-69, asst. prof. orthopaedic surgery 1971-75, assoc. prof., 1975-79, prof., 1979—, chmn. dept., 1981-85; bd. overseers Whitman Coll., 1985—. Served with USN, 1962-65. NIH summer research fellow, 1957, 58; honoree, chair Sig T. Hansen Jr. Endowed Chair in Orthopaedic Traumatology Rsch. U. Wash. Mem. Am. Acad. Orthopaedic Surgery, Am. Orthopaedic Assn., Assn. Bone and Joint Surgeons, Western Orthopaedic Assn., Am. Orthopaedic Foot and Ankle Soc., AO-N. Am. Found. (pres. 1986-92), Assn. for Study Internal Fixation (bd. dirs. 1984—), M.E. Mueller Found. (bd. dirs. 1986—), Phi Beta Kappa. Editor, co-editor med. texts; contbr. articles to med. jours., chpts. to books. Home: 2563 Magnolia Blvd W Seattle WA 98199-3631 Office: 325 9th Ave Seattle WA 98104-2420

HANSEN, VALERIE ANN EMDIA, health science facility administrator; b. Mt. Pleasant, Iowa, Sept. 4, 1952; d. Harold Jr. and Mildred Annette (Mitchell) Emdia; m. Stephen Dale Hansen, Sept. 3, 1977; 1 child, Brittany Jean. BS in Zoology, Iowa State U., 1977. Lic. respiratory care practitioner; registered respiratory therapist. Respiratory staff technician Mary Greeley Meml. Hosp., Ames, Iowa, 1972-77; staff therapist Fairmont (Minn.) Community Hosp., 1977-80, dir. dept. respiratory care, 1980-82; assoc. vocat. prof. respiratory Amarillo (Tex.) Coll., 1984—; staff therapist High Plains Bapt. Hosp., Amarillo, 1986—. Mem. Am. Assn. for Respiratory Care (pres. Panandle dist. 1989-90, sec., N.W. region 1990-91, pres., 1992-93, sec. state 1993-94, past pres. N.W. region 1995-96), Tex. Soc. for Respiratory Care, Tex. Jr. Coll. Tchrs. Assn. Home: 8114 Marni Amarillo TX 79110-4766 Office: Amarillo Coll PO Box 447 Amarillo TX 79178-0001

HANSEN-FLASCHEN, JOHN HYMAN, medical educator, researcher; b. Hamilton, Ohio, June 25, 1950; s. Steward Samuel and Joyce (Davies) Flaschen; m. Susan Lauretta Hansen, Aug. 22, 1951; children: Lynn, Lauren. A.B., Brown U., 1972; M.D., NYU, 1976. Diplomate Am. Bd. Internal Medicine; cert. in pulmonary medicine, critical care medicine. Resident in medicine U. Pa., Phila., 1976-79, chief resident in medicine, 1980-81, pulmonary fellow, 1979-80, 81-82; asst. prof. medicine, 1982-87, attending physician, 1982—, dir. ednl. and tng. programs in pulmonary and critical care medicine, 1983-90, assoc. prof., 1988—, prof. medicine, 1996—, acting chief pulmonary and critical care sect., 1990—, dir. pulmonary and critical care div. Dept. of Medicine, dir. Comprehensive Lung Ctr., 1996—; chmn. ethics com. hosp. U. Pa. Mem. editorial bd. Clin. Pulmonary Medicine, Up to Date in Pulmonary and Critical Care Medicine; contbr. articles to profl. jours. Recipient spl. investigator award Am. Heart Assn., 1982-84; Measey Found. fellow, 1982-83. Fellow ACP, Am. Coll. Chest Physicians, Coll. Physicians of Phila.; mem. Am. Thoracic Soc. (chmn. postgrad. edn. com. 1995—), Soc. for Critical Care Medicine, Soc. for Bioethics Consultation, Laennec Soc. Phila. (pres. 1990-91), Drinker Soc. for Critical Care in Phila. (founder, 1st pres. 1988-90), Sigma Xi, Alpha Omega Alpha. Democrat. Home: 365 Penn Rd Wynnewood PA 19096-1401 Office: Hosp of U Pa 873 Mahoney Bldg 3400 Spruce St Philadelphia PA 19104

HANSON, JEANNE CAROL, health care administrator; b. New Haven, May 3, 1947; d. John Fletcher and Jeanne (Huttlinger) H. Diploma, Bryn Mawr (Pa.) Sch. Nursing, 1968; BS in Psychology, Eastern Coll., 1978; MBA in Health and Med. Service, Widener U., 1986. RN. Staff nurse pediatric unit Bryn Mawr (Pa.) Hosp., 1968-69; staff nurse psychiat. unit Haverford (Pa.) State Hosp., 1969-71, head nurse psychiat. admissions unit, 1971-73, instr. psychiat. nursing, 1973-80, dir. nursing edn. dept., 1980-87; asst. administr. Kendal-Crosslands, Kennett Square, Pa., 1987-91; exec. dir., administr. Friends Hall Nursing Home, 1991; exec. dir. Barclay Friends Corp., 1992—. Mem. Friends Com. on Aging, Religious Coun. West Chester; bd. dirs. Media (Pa.) Child Guidance and Cmty. Mental Health Ctr., 1st Nat. Bank Westchester, 1994—; bd. dirs., pres. Sr. Ctr. West Chester; v.p. YWCA of Greater Westchester. Mem. LWV, Widener Grad. Alumni Assn. (v.p. 1987-89). Republican. Mem. Soc. of Friends. Office: Barclay Friends 424 N Matlack St West Chester PA 19380

HANSON, R. SCOTT, internist; b. Northampton, Mass., Dec. 30, 1963; m. Meegan Kennedy, Oct. 14, 1989. BA in History, Yale U., 1985; MPH, MD, Tulane U., 1990. Lic. physician, R.I. Resident in primary care, internal medicine R.I. Hosp., Providence, 1994-96, chief resident internal medicine, 1996—; cons. diving medicine Divers' Alert Network, Durham, N.C., 1996—. Lt. USNR, 1987-94. Mem. AMA, Physicians for a Nat. Health Plan, Undersea Hyperbaric Med. Soc. Office: Rhode Island Hospital 593 Eddy St Providence RI 02903

HANSON, RICHARD WINFIELD, biochemist, educator; b. Oxford, N.Y., Nov. 10, 1935; s. John Vincent and Agatha Helen H.; m. Gloria M. Lucchesi, June 10, 1961; children: Paul, Benjamin, Daria. BS, Northeastern U., 1959; MS, Brown U., 1961, PhD, 1963. Asst. prof to prof. biochemistry Temple U. Sch. Medicine, Phila., 1965-78; prof., chmn. dept. biochemistry Case Western U. Sch. Medicine, Cleve., 1978—, Leonard and Jean Sheggs prof. biochemistry, 1993—; cons. USPHS, FDA. Assoc. editor Jour. Biol. Chemistry; contbr. articles to profl. jours. Served to capt. Med. Service Corps, U.S. Army, 1963-65. Mem. AAAS, Inst. Medicine NAS, Am. Soc. Biochemistry and Molecular Biology, Biochem. Soc., Am. Inst. Nutrition (Mead-Johnson award 1971, Kaiser Permanente award 1982, Maurice Saltzman award 1991, Osborne Mendel award 1995). Office: Case Western Res U Dept of Biochemistry 2119 Abington Rd Cleveland OH 44106-2333

HANSON, RONALD WINDELL, cardiologist, lawyer, physicist; b. Jeffersonville, Ind., Apr. 30, 1947; s. Erwin D. and Bernice (Windell) H. BS summa cum laude, Ariz. State U., 1968, MS, 1969, PhD in Physics, 1972; MD, U. Ala., 1977, JD, Birmingham Sch. Law, 1995. Diplomate Am. Bd. Internal Medicine, Am. Bd. Cardiovascular Diseases. Asst. prof. physics U. Ala., 1972-74; resident in internal medicine and cardiology Good Samaritan Hosp., Phoenix, 1977-82; practice medicine specializing in cardiology, Gadsden, Ala., 1982—; pvt. law practice, 1995—. Served to lt. col. CAP. Fellow Am. Coll. Cardiology, Am. Coll. Angiology, Soc. for Cardiac Angiography and Interventions; mem. ABA, Nat. Health Lawyers Assn., Ala. Bar Assn., Phi Eta Sigma, Phi Kappa Phi. Office: 300 Med Ctr Dr Ste 500 Gadsden AL 35903-1156

HANTGAN, GEORGE, social services administrator; b. N.Y.C., Mar. 29, 1916; s. Nathan and Eva (Dubraminsky) H.; m. Ida Hantgan, Nov. 27, 1949; children: Jeffrey Clyde, Roberta Elise, Richard Selden. BA, Bklyn. Coll., 1940; MPA, NYU, 1943; MSW, Columbia U., 1948. Exec. dir. United Jewish Fund, Jewish Community Ctr., 1950-81; endowment cons. United Jewish Community of Bergen County, 1950-81; exec. cons., endowment cons. United Jewish Fund of Englewood, 1981-83; pvt. practice United Jewish Fund, Jewish Community Coun., Englewood, N.J., 1983—. Recipient Medal United Jewish Appeal and Govt. Israel, Disting Svc. award Yeshiva U. Wurzweiler Sch. Social Work, Mayor LaGuardia award. Mem. Acad. of Cert. Social Workers, Nat. assn. of Social Workers (past state chmn.), Bergen County Health and Welfare Coun., assn. of Jewish Community Orgn. Profls. Home: 158 St Nicholas Ave Englewood NJ 07631-1639

HANTMAN, SARAH ANN, health professional; b. Wyandotte, Mich., Oct. 19, 1952; d. Paul Reginald and Betty Elaine (Wilson) Longfield; m. Barry Mark Hantman, Dec. 27, 1970; 1 child, Bryan Jonathan. BA in Journalism, Rider U., 1975. Bur. chief United Artists-Columbia CATV-NJ, Oakland, N.J., 1976-77; offset and sr. offset machine operator N.J. Dept. Labor, Trenton, 1980-88; tng. technician div. of AIDS prevention and control N.J. Dept. Health, Trenton, 1988-90, clearinghouse coord. div. of AIDS prevention and control, 1990-91, health profl. divsn. family health svc. WIC program, 1991-92, health profl., div. mgmt. and adminstrn., 1992—; co-owner Sabar Internat., West Trenton, N.J., 1984—. Community activist Grand Ave. Hist. Assn., West Trenton, 1989—. Recipient Letter and Plaque designating her house as hist. Ewing Twp. Hist. Commn. and Zoning Bd., West Trenton, 1989. Mem. NAFE, Nat. Trust and Hist. Preservation (preservation forum 1976—), Nat. Geog. Soc., The Wilderness Soc., Nat. Parks and Conservation Assn., Environ. Def. Fund, World Wildlife Fund. Presbyterian. Office: NJ Dept Health CN 350 John Fitch Plz Trenton NJ 08625-0360

HANTO, DOUGLAS WAYNE, surgeon; b. Great Falls, Mont., June 20, 1951; s. Norman Andrew and Marjorie (Gjertson) H.; m. Jill Jenkins, Dec. 28, 1974; children: Kristen, Lindsay, John. BA, St. Olaf Coll., Northfield, Minn., 1973; MD, U. Ariz., 1977; PhD, U. Minn., 1987. Diplomate Nat. Bd. Med. Examiners, Am. Bd. Surgery; lic. physician, Minn., Mo., Ill., Ark., Ohio. Intern then resident in gen. surgery U. Minn. Helath Scis. Ctr., Mpls., 1977-84, fellow, 1984-85; attending surgeon Barnes Hosp., St. Louis, 1985-91, Jewish Hosp. St. Louis, 1985-91, St. Louis Children's Hosp., 1985-91, U. Cin. Med. Ctr., 1991—, Children's Hosp. Med. Ctr., Cin., 1991—; cons. John Cochran VA Hosp., St. Louis, 1985-91, VA Hosp. Cin., 1991—; asst. prof. surgery Washington U., 1985-89, dir. tranplantation sect., 1988-90; assoc. prof. surgery, 1989-91; assoc. prof. surgery U. Cin., 1991—; lectr. in field. Contbr. numerous articles to profl. jours. Bd. trustees Cin. Hills Christian Acad., 1993—, mem. edn. com., 1993—. Smith, Kline and French fellow, 1986-88. Fellow ACS; mem. AAAS, Am. ASsn. Study Liver Diseases, Am. Assn. Immunologists, Am. Liver Found., Am. Soc. Transplant Physicians, Am. Soc. Transplant Surgeons; ohio Med. Assn., European Soc. Organ Transplantation, Ctrl. Surg. Assn., Internat. Hepato-Pancreato-Billary Assn., Internat. Liver Transplantation Soc., Internat. Assn. Rsch. Epstein-Barr Virus and Associated Diseases, Cin. Acad. Medicine, Cin. Grad. Surg. Soc., Assn. Academic Surgery, Christian Med. and Dental Soc., Cell Transplant Soc., Collegium Internat. Chirurgiae Digestivae, Soc. Leukocyte Biology, Soc. Univ. Surgeons, Surg. Infection Soc., Transplantation Soc., Blue Key Honor Soc., Phi Beta Kappa. Republican. Mem. Evangelical Free Ch. Office: U Cin Med Ctr 231 Bethesda Ave Cincinnati OH 45267-0558

HANUSCHAK, LEE NICHOLAS, physician; b. Warren, Ohio, Dec. 22, 1947; s. Michael and Clorinda (Rossi) H.; m. H. Dulcine Zdunski, Oct. 29, 1977; children: Gregor, Dulcinea. AB cum laude, Harvard Coll., 1969; MS, EES, Stanford U., 1971; MD, Case Western Reserve U., 1977. Stanford U., Palo Alto, Calif., 1969-73; NIH fellow, 1970-71; lectr. Med. Sch. Stanford U., Palo Alto, Calif., 1971-72; assoc. physician div. diabetes and metabolism Pa. Hosp., Phila., 1992—; pvt. practice in internal medicine and diabetes Phila., 1987—; clin. assoc. U. Pa. Sch. Medicine, 1980—; rsch. supr. Garfield Duncan Found., Phila., 1980-86; cons. internal medicine Wills Eye Hosp., Phila., 1981-91; founder, pres. Med. Decision-Making, Inc., Ardmore, Pa., 1986-88; med. dirs. Travelers Health Network, Phila., 1986-88; med. dir., founder Pa. Found., Phila., 1987—. Contbr. Diabetes Fact Book, 1981, Conn's Current Therapy, 1982; inventor computer program for adjustment of insulin doses. Recipient numerous corp. grants, 1980-86. Mem. ACP, Am. Diabetes Assn., Am. Soc. Internal Medicine, Harvard/Radcliffe Club of Phila. (schs. com.). Office: 829 Spruce St Philadelphia PA 19107-5752

HAPPEL, NANCY, marketing executive; b. Plant City, Fla., Feb. 26, 1954; d. Gus Joseph and Vera Ruth (Hermsmeier) H. AA in Dental Hygiene, Parkland Coll., 1976; BA, Ariz. State U., 1979; MBA, San Francisco State U., 1986. Program dir. Marin County Health Dept., San Rafael, Calif., 1982-85; cons. U.S. Pub. Health Svc., San Francisco, 1981-88; market analyst Merritt Peralta Med. Ctr., Oakland, Calif., 1987, program mgr., 1987-89, dir. mktg. and comty. rels., 1989—. Bd. dirs. St. Mary's Sr. Ctr., Oakland, 1988; mem. East Bay Jr. League, 1988. Mem. Am. Mktg. Assn., Am. Soc. Aging, No. Calif. Health Care Mktg. Assn., Pi Lambda Theta, Alpha Omega, Beta Gamma Sigma. Republican. Lutheran. Home: 1019 Circle Creek Ln Lafayette CA 94549-3203 Office: Summit Med Ctr 350 Hawthorne Ave Oakland CA 94609-3108

HAQ, ABID, physician; b. Nairobi, Kenya, Mar. 28, 1953; came to U.S. 1989; s. Mohamed Abdul and Sarwat Ara (Ghauri) H.; m. Ayesha Mansoor Ahmad; children: Amyr, Myra. MB, BCh, Ain Shams U., Cairo, 1984. Med. officer Coast Province Gen. Hosp., Mombasa, Kenya, 1984-86; sr. house officer Nat. Pub. Health Lab. Svcs., Nairobi, 1986-87; registrar U. Nairobi, Dept. Surgery, 1987-89; intern in internal medicine U. Calif. at Davis, VA Med. Ctr., Martinez, Calif, 1991-92; resident in internal medicine U. Calif. at San Francisco, Alameda County Med. Ctr., Oakland, Calif., 1992-94; staff physician urgent care dept. internal medicine Kaiser Permanente Med. Ctr., Santa Clarita, Calif., 1994—. Author: A Blow to Islam, 1978; contbr. articles to profl. jours. Exec. com. Kenya Scouts Coun., Nairobi, 1987-89. Mem. AMA, ACP, Royal Soc. Health. Muslim. Office: Kaiser Permanente Med Ctr 27107 Tourney Rd Santa Clarita CA 91355

HAQUE, MALIKA HAKIM, pediatrician; b. Madras, India; came to U.S., 1967; d. Syed Abdul and Rahimunisa (Hussain) Hakim; MBBS, Madras Med. Coll., 1967; m. C. Azeez Haque, Feb. 5, 1967; children: Kifizeba, Masarath Nashr, Asim Zayd. Diplomate Am. Bd. Pediatrics. Rotating intern Miriam Hosp., Brown U., Providence, 1967-68; resident in pediatrics Children's Hosp., N.J. Coll. Medicine, 1968-70; fellow in devel. disabilities Ohio State U., 1970-71; acting chief pediatrics Nisonger Ctr., 1973-74; staff pediatrician Children and Youth Project, Children's Hosp., Columbus, Ohio, also clin. asst. prof. pediatrics Ohio State U., 1974-80; clin. assoc. prof. pediatrics Ohio State U., 1981—, clin. assoc. prof. dept. internat. health Coll. Medicine, 1993—; pediatrician in charge cmty. Children's Hosp. Cmty. Helth Ctrs. Children's Hosp., Columbus, 1982—, dir. pediatric acad. assoc., Columbus Children's Hosp., Ohio State U., 1992—; cons. Central Ohio Head Start Program, 1974-79; med. cons. Bur. Rehab. and Devel. Disabilities for State of Ohio, 1990—. Contbr. articles to profl. jours. and newspapers. Charter mem. Rep. Presdl. Task Force, 1982—, Nat. Rep. Senatorial Com., 1985—, U.S. Senatorial Club; charter founder Ronald Reagan Rep. Ctr.; trustee Asian Am. Health Alliance Network, Columbus, 1994—. Recipient Physician Recognition award AMA, 1971-86, 88-91, 92—, Gold medals in surgery, radiology, pediatrics and ob/gyn; Presdl. medal of Merit, 1982. Fellow Am. Acad. Pediatrics; mem. Islamic Med. Assn., Am. Assn. of Physicians of Indian Orgin, Ambulatory Pediatric Assn., Cen. Ohio Pediatric Soc., Islamic Med. Assn. Muslim. Research on enuresis. Home: 5995 Forestview Dr Columbus OH 43213-2114 Office: 700 Childrens Dr Columbus OH 43205-2666

HARADON, DEBORAH LYNNE, social worker, consultant; b. Corning, N.Y., Jan. 6, 1950; d. Francis Raymond and Rita Anne (Sloan) H.; m. Paul Cardin Brooks, July 31, 1976; children: Erica, Chris, Colin. BSW, U. Dayton, Ohio, 1973; MSW, Temple U., 1989. Cert. social worker, N.Y. Counselor Steuben County Alcohol Abuse Program, Bath, N.Y., 1973-74; vocat. evaluator Steuben County Assn. for Retarded Citizens, Bath, 1976-79, dir. rehab., 1979-80; client coord. Pathways Day Treatment Program, Corning and Elmira, N.Y., 1980-85; case mgr. Chemung ARC Children's ICF, Elmira Heights, N.Y., 1985-89; social worker I Binghamton (N.Y.) Psychiat. Ctr., 1989-90; social worker behavioral sci. unit St. Joseph's Hosp., Elmira, 1990-91; social work cons. Chemung Co. ARC, Elmira, 1989-93; social worker Rehab. Programs Inc., Poughkeepsie, 1993-94; social workers mental health unit St. Francis Hosp., Poughkeepsie, 1994—; social worker svc. coordination and family counseling Early Intervention Program, Dutchess Co. Dept. Health, Poughkeepsie, 1994—. N.Y. State scholar Rutgers U., 1974. Mem. NASW (PACE trustee Hudson Valley Divsn.), NOW. Home: 220 Rogers St Ulster Park NY 12487-5015 Office: St Francis Hosp North Rd Poughkeepsie NY 12601

HARAMATI, AVIAD, physiology and biophysics educator, researcher; b. Jerusalem, Jan. 25, 1954; came to U.S., 1956; s. Amnon and Dinah Haramati; m. Claire Zeller, May 30, 1982; children: Talia, Ariel, Natan. BS, Bklyn. Coll., 1975; PhD, U. Cin., 1979. Postdoctoral fellow Mayo Clinic, Rochester, Minn., 1979-82, instr., 1981-82, asst. prof., 1982-85; asst. prof. Sch. Medicine Georgetown U., Washington, 1985-87, assoc. prof., 1987-92, prof., 1992—, dir. edn., 1995—; mem. rsch. com. Nat. Kidney Found., Washington, 1990—, chmn., 1992-94; mem. profl. adv. bd. NKF, 1993—. Contbr. numerous articles to profl. jours. Recipient Day Meml. Rsch. award Nat. Kidney Found., 1989, 90. Mem. Am. Physiol. Soc. (edn. com. 1993—), Kemp Mill Synagogue (v.p. 1991-96, pres. 1996—). Office: Georgetown U Sch Medicine 3900 Reservoir Rd NW Washington DC 20007-2187

HARARI, CARMI, clinical psychologist, psychoanalyst; b. N.Y.C., Dec. 4, 1920; s. Ezra and Dina (Katz) H.; m. Clara Soshen, June 19, 1942 (div.); children: Karen Tarnofsky, Michelle Kelly; m. Sarah Zaraleya Kurzweil, Dec. 31, 1979. BSS in Psychology, CCNY, 1946; MA in Clin. Psychology, NYU, 1947; EdD in Psychology of Family Life, Columbia U., 1968; cert. in psychoanalysis, 1978. Lic. psychologist, N.Y.; cert. psychologist, N.Y. State Dept. Mental Hygiene. Sch. psychologist N.Y.C., 1946-47; clin. psychologist VA Hosps. and Clinics, N.Y.C., 1947-50; lectr., asst. prof. NYU, Columbia U., CUNY, Met. Inst. Psychoanalytic Studies, N.Y.C., 1948-82; pvt. practice N.Y.C., 1950—; staff psychologist N.Y.C. Children's Ct., 1950-52, chief psychologist, 1953-57; dir. Community Consultation Svcs., N.Y.C., 1957-75; staff psychologist, 1957-70; exec. dir. Humanistic Psychology Ctr. of N.Y., N.Y.C., 1973—; dir. Interactions: Psychol. Svcs. for the Whole Family, New City, N.Y., 1990—; cons. various schs., N.Y.C., 1956-75, Ministry Social Welfare, Israel, 1961, Office Disability Determinations, N.Y. State Dept. Social Svcs., 1970—, others; adj. prof. various N.Y. colls.,1975-82; dir. internat. devel., mem. exec. bd. Assn. Humanistic Psychology, 1969-80; exec. sec. N.Y. Soc. Clin. Psychologists, 1967-69, pres. 1970-72; NGO rep. Internat. Coun. Psychologists, UNESCO, 1980—, bd. dirs. internat. liaison, 1988—; treas. Psychologists for Social Responsibility, Washington, 1982-88; rep. UNESCO, 1980-86. Author book chpts.; contbr. articles to profl. jours. and newsletters. Organizer, leader Group Psychotherapy Found., N.Y.C. Around the World Study Tour, 1966; chair adv. bd. Women's Ctrs. for Occupational Devel., N.Y.C., 1969-71; trustee Psychol. Svc. Ctr. N.Y., Soc. Clin. Psychologists, N.Y.C., 1969-72; organizer, leader internat. confs. humanistic psychology, Denmark, Eng., France, Iceland, Ger., India, Israel, Japan, Mex., Netherlands, Norway, Sweden, USSR, 1969-76; bd. dirs. Assn. for Humanistic Psychology, Humanistic Psychology Inst., San Francisco, 1970-76; adv. bd. Identity House, N.Y.C., 1972-73. With USAF, 1942-45. Recipient War Svc. scholarship, N.Y. State, 1952. Fellow APA (divsn. pres. humanistic psychology found. 1971-73, coun. rep. 1974-77, 78-81, 85-88, 91—, pres. proposed divsn. transpersonal psychology 1982-83, chmn. sub-com. on psychology of peace making, 1988-90, mem. com. on internat. rels. in psychology, divsn. social issues, clinical, ind. practice, group psychology and group psychotherapy); mem. Assn. Interam. Psychology Soc., Internat. Assn. for Cross Cultural Psychology, Internat. Assn. Applied Psychol (pres.-elect divsn. polit. psychology 1990), Phi Delta Kappa, Kappa Delta Pi. Home and Office: 10 Wyndham Ln New City NY 10956-4527 Office: 19 W 34th St New York NY 10001-3006

HARARY, KEITH, psychologist; b. N.Y.C., Feb. 9, 1953; s. Victor and Lillian (Mazur) H.; m. Darlene Moore, Oct. 22, 1985. BA in Psychology, Duke U., 1975; PhD, Union Inst., 1986. Crisis counselor Durham (N.C.) Mental Health Ctr., 1972-76; rsch. assoc. Psychical Rsch. Found., Durham, 1972-76; rsch. assoc. dept. psychiatry Maimonides Med. Ctr., Bklyn., 1976-79; dir. counseling Human Freedom Ctr., Berkeley, Calif., 1979; rsch. cons. SRI Internat., Menlo Park, Calif., 1980-82; design cons. Atari Corp., Sunnyvale, Calif., 1983-85; pres., rsch. dir. Inst. for Advanced Psychology, San Francisco, 1986—; freelance sci. journalist, 1988—; spl. projects editor Omni Internet, Inc., 1996—; invited lectr. Duke U., 1995; lectr. in field; adj. prof. Antioch U., San Francisco, 1985, 86; guest lectr. Lyceum Sch. for Gifted Children, 1985-89; vis. rschr. USSR Acad. Scis., 1983; rsch. cons. Am. Soc. for Psychical Rsch., 1971-72, Found. for Rsch. on Nature of Man, 1972, sci. applications Internat. Corp., 1991-93. Co-author: The Mind Race, 1984, 85, 30-Day Advanced Psychology Series, 1989-91, Who Do You Think You Are? Explore Your Many-Sided Self With the Berkeley Personality Profile, 1994, Who Do You Think You Are? Explore Your Many-Sided Self With the Berkeley Personality Profile, CD-ROM edit., 1996; featured monthly columnist in The Omni Mind Brain Lab in Omni Mag., 1995—; contbr. over 100 articles to profl. jours.; spl. projects editor Omni mag., 1996—. Mem. APA, Am. Psychol. Soc., Assn. for Media Psychology. Home and Office: 98 Main St # 637 Tiburon CA 94920

HARBAUGH, JOHN DAVID, insurance company consultant; b. Barberton, Ohio, Nov. 16, 1939; s. Richard David and Elsie May (Griffen) H.; m. Janet Louise Franks, Nov. 25, 1962; children: John David Jr., Jeffrey Daniel. BS in Pharmacy, Ohio No. U., 1961. Registered pharmacist, Ohio. Mgr. Phillip's Drug Store, Lodi, Ohio, 1961-62, 65-66; dir. pharm. svcs. Orient (Ohio) State Inst., 1966-74; adminstr. Frazier Health Ctr., Orient, 1974-78; CEO Morrow County Hosp., Mt. Gilead, Ohio, 1978-84, Wyandot Meml. Hosp., Upper Sandusky, Ohio, 1984-90; loss prevention coord., cons. Ohio Hosp. Ins. Co., Columbus, 1990—; mem. adv. bd. Tri-Rivers Joint Vocat. Sch., Marion, Ohio, 1978-89; vice chair hosp. adv. bd. Blue Cross of Ctrl. Ohio, Columbus, 1979-83; mem. small hosp. adv. com. Ohio Hosp. Ins. Co., 1987-90. Bd. dirs. Morrow County chpt. ARC, Mt. Gilead, 1978-84, 90—; v.p. dist. ops. Heart of Ohio coun. Boy Scouts Am., 1994—, mem. exec. bd. Harding Area coun., 1980—; mem. Morrow County Regional Planning Bd., Mt. Gilead, 1978-94; squadman, tng. officer Morrow County Emergency Med. Svc., 1988—. 1st lt. USAF, 1962-65. Recipient Silver Beaver award Boy Scouts Am., 1986, Dist. award of merit Boy Scouts Am., 1987, Clara Barton award ARC, 1989. Fellow Am. Acad. Med. Adminstrs. (diploma in healthcare adminstrn., Disting. Svc. award 1989), Am. Soc. Cons. Pharmacists (Spl. Recognition award 1993, 94); mem. Kiwanis (pres. Mt. Gilead club 1983-84, 93-94). Home: 188 N Main St Mount Gilead OH 43338 Office: Ohio Hosp Ins Co 155 E Broad St Columbus OH 43215

HARBERT, GUY MORLEY, JR., retired obstetrician, gynecologist; b. Fredericksburg, Va., Dec. 19, 1929; s. Guy Morley and Hannah (Turman) H.; m. Peggy Ann Simpson, Sept. 8, 1951; children—Lucille Hannah, Guy Morley, III, Michael Simpson. B.A., U. Va., 1952, M.D., 1956. Diplomate: Am. Bd. Ob-Gyn (maternal-fetal medicine). Intern Barnes Hosp., St. Louis, 1956-57; resident in ob-gyn U. Va. Hosp., 1959-63; med. faculty U. Va. Med. Sch., 1963—, prof. ob-gyn, 1976-95, prof. emeritus, 1995; mem. human embryology and devel. study sect. NIH, 1975-79. Author articles in profl. jours., chpts. in books. Served as officer M.C. USAF, 1957-59. Mem. Soc. Gynecol. Investigation (exec. council 1973-76), Perinatal Research Soc. (exec. council 1977-79), So. Perinatal Assn. (exec. council 1974-77), Am. Gynecol. Soc., Am. Assn. Obstetricians and Gynecologists, N.Y. Acad. Scis., Am. Coll. Obstetricians and Gynecologists, Assn. Profs. Ob-Gyn, S. Atlantic Assn. Obstetricians and Gynecologists, Sigma Xi. Presbyterian. Office: U Va Hosps Jefferson Park Ave Charlottesville VA 22908

HARBIN, BUFORD GOODWIN, pulmonary physician; b. Rome, Ga., Mar. 3, 1945; s. Bannester Lester and Jane (Goodwin) H.; m. Quinette Bass, May 28, 1975; children: Sara Bass, Benjamin Goodwin, Susan Turner. AB in Chemistry, Centre Coll., Danville, Ky., 1966; MD, Emory U., 1970. Diplomate Am. Bd. Internal Medicine; cert. in pulmonary diseases, critical care. Intership Med. Coll. Va., Richmond, Va., 1970-71; resident physician VA Hosp., Martinez, Calif., 1974-78; pulmonary physician Harbin Clinic, Rome, Ga., 1978—; sec., 1987-90; pres. med. staff Floyd Med. Ctr., Rome, 1986-88. Trustee Shorter Coll., Rome, 1981-86, 87-90. Fellow Am. Coll. Chest Physicians; mem. ACP, Am. Thoracic Soc., Kiwanis. Baptist. Home: 310 E 4th St Rome GA 30161-3202 Office: Harbin Clinic 1825 Martha Berry Blvd Rome GA 30165-1698

HARBIN, THOMAS SHELOR, JR., ophthalmologist; b. Annapolis, Md., May 31, 1945; s. Thomas Shelor and Margaret (Troutman) H.; m. Ellen Gregson, June 6, 1970; children: Katherine, Tommy. BA magna cum laude, Vanderbilt U., 1966; MD, Cornell U., N.Y.C., 1970; MBA, Ga. State U., 1991. Diplomate Am. Bd. Ophthalmology. Rotating intern U. Wash. Afiliated Hosps., Seattle, 1970-71; resident in ophthalmology Wilmer Inst., Johns Hopkins Hosp., Balt., 1971-74; fellow Glaucoma Ctr., Barnes Hosp., Washington U. Sch. Medicine, St. Louis, 1974-75; pvt. practice, Atlanta, 1976—; sr. v.p., dir. Prime Vision Health, Inc.; pres., CEO Accountable Eye Care, Inc.; clin. prof. Emory U., Atlanta, 1976—; chief ophthalmology staff Piedmont Hosp., Atlanta, 1984-94, vice chair, 1995—; mem. staff Grady Meml. Hosp.; bd. dirs. Ctr. for Visually Impaired, 1976-87, chmn., 1979-80; mem. med. adv. bd. Ga. Soc. to Prevent Blindness, 1977—,chmn. 1980, pres., 1987-89. Mem. editl. rev. bd. Rev. Ophthalmology, 1994—. Participant Leadership Ga., 1983; dir. med. campaign United Way, Ga., 1984. Fellow ACS; mem. AMA, Am. Acad. Ophthalmology (quality care com. 1989-94, state affairs com. 1991-94, trustee 1994—, chmn. young ophthalmologists com. 1994-95, chmn. membership adv. com. 1996—, exec. com. 1996—, mem. managed care advocacy com. 1994—, Honor award 1985), Med. Assn. Ga., Am. Glaucoma Soc. (founding), Ga. Soc. Ophthalmology (legis. com. 1977-85, chmn. 1978-91, pres. 1982-83), Atlanta Ophthal. Soc. (pres. 1982), Wilmer Residents Assn., Phi Beta Kappa. Home: 3888 Tuxedo Rd NW Atlanta GA 30342-4034 Office: Eye Cons Atlanta MD's PC 95 Collier Rd NW Ste 3000 Atlanta GA 30309-1710

HARBISON, DIANA, psychiatrist, medical director; b. Phila., July 29, 1951; d. Joseph F. and A. Patricia (McMullen) H.; m. Brett D. Carey, Sept. 24, 1988. BA, U. Pa., 1973, MD, 1986; MSS, Bryn Mawr Coll., 1978. Diplomate Am. Bd. Psychiatry and Neurology. Postdoctoral fellow Dept.

Psychiatry Yale U. Sch. Medicine, New Haven, 1990; unit chief Elmcrest Psychiat. Inst., Portland, Conn., 1990-92; pvt. practice Centerbrook, Conn., 1992—; med. dir. Psychotherapy Ctr. Essex Inc., Essex, 1994—; attending physician Yale Psychiat. Inst., New Haven, 1996—, Yale New Haven Hosp., 1996—, Hosp. St. Raphael, New Haven, 1995—. Mem. Child & Family Svcs. Southeastern Conn., New Haven, 1994—. Mem. Am. Psychiatry Assn., Am. Soc. Adolescent Psychiatry, Am. Soc. CLin. Psychopharmacology, New Haven Women's Med. Soc., Conn. Psychiat. Soc., Nat. Orgn. Women, ACLU. Office: Psychotherapy Ctr Essex Inc 28 Main St Essex CT 06426

HARCOURT, JOHN KENNETH, dentistry educator; b. Melbourne, Victoria, Australia, June 27, 1931; s. Kenneth K. and Marjorie R. (Gans) H. B. of Dental Sci., U. Melbourne, 1953, M. of Dental Sci., 1956, D. of Dental Sci., 1968. Cert. prosthodontics specialist, dentist. Staff dentist Dental Hosp. Melbourne, 1954; sr. demonstrator, tutor dental prosthetics Australian Coll. Dentistry, Melbourne, 1954-57, lect., 1957-63; sr. lectr. U. Melbourne, 1964-73, reader in dept. dental prosthetics, 1974-82, reader dept. restorative dentistry, 1983-90; assoc. prof., reader restorative dentistry Sch. Dental Sci., Melbourne, 1990—; hon. sr. clin. asst. Royal Dental Hosp. Melbourne, 1963-82, cons., 1983—; vis. assoc. prof. biol. materials Northwestern U. Dental Sch., Chgo., 1967-69, vis. prof., 1979-80; hon. reader dental materials U. Hong Kong. 1990-91; lectr. in field. Author: Dental Assistants' Manual, 3d edit., 1984; (with E. H. Greener and E. P. Lautenschleger) Materials Science in Dentistry, 1972; (with A. A. Grant) Dental Assistant's Manual, 2d edit., 1977; (with B. G. Radden) A History of the International Association for Dental Research in Australia and New Zealand 1960-1985, 1987; (with others) Guide to the Use of Dental Materials, 1989, 93, and others; contbr. articles to profl. jours. Sgt. Australian Army, 1952-53. Decorated medal Order of Australia. Fellow Royal Australasian Coll. Dental Surgeons (councillor 1982—, censor-in-chief 1988-93, v.p. 1993-94, pres. 1995-96); mem. Australian Dental Assn. (chmn. tariffs, instruments, materials and equipment com. 1976-82, vice chmn. edn.com. 1976-78, councillor for Victoria 1976-86, jour. editor 1985, Victorian new branch postgrad com. 1961-74, sec. 1966-67, chmn. 1973-74), Internat. Assn. Dental Rsch. (councilloer Australian and New Zealand divsn. 1974-76, sec.-treas. 1971-74, v.p. 1974, pres. 1975-76) Australian Soc. Prosthodontists (pres. 1994-96). Home: 24 Faircroft Ave, Glen Iris Victoria 3146, Australia Office: Sch Dental Sci, 711 Elizabeth St, Melbourne Victoria 3000, Australia

HARDAGE, PAGE TAYLOR, health care administrator; b. Richmond, Va., June 27, 1944; d. George Peterson and Gladys Odell (Gordon) Taylor; m. Thomas Brantley, July 6, 1968; 1 child, Taylor Brantley. AA, Va. Intermont Coll., Bristol, 1964; BS, Richmond Profl. Inst., 1966; MPA, Va. Commonwealth U., Richmond, 1982. Cert. tchr. Competent toastmaster, dir. play therapy svcs. Med. Coll. Va. Hosps., Va. Commonwealth U., Richmond, 1970-90; dir. Inst. Women's Issues, Va. Commonwealth U., U. Va., Richmond, 1986-91; adminstr. Childhood Lang. Ctr. at Richmond, Inc., 1991—; bd. dirs. Math. and Sci. Ctr. Found., Richmond, Emergency Med. Svcs. Adv. Bd., Richmond. Treas. Richmond Black Student Found., 1989-90, Leadership Metro Richmond Alumni Assn.; bd. dirs. Richmond YWCA, 1989-91; group chmn. United Way Greater Richmond, 1987; bd. dirs. Capital Area Health Adv. Coun.; commr. Mayors Commn. of Concerns of Women, City of Richmond. Mem. NAFE, ASPA, Adminstrv. Mgmt. Soc., Internat. Mgmt. Coun. (exec. com.), Va. Recreation and Park Soc. (bd. dirs.), Va. Assn. Fund Raising Execs., Rotary Club of Richmond. Unitarian. Office: Childhood Lang Ctr at Richmond Inc 4202 Hermitage Rd Richmond VA 23227-3755

HARDAWAY, ERNEST, II, oral and maxillofacial surgeon, public health official. BS, Howard U., 1957, DDS, 1966, cert. in oral and maxillofacial surgery, 1972; MPH, Johns Hopkins U., 1973. Intern, then chief resident oral and maxillofacial surgery Howard U. Med. Ctr., Washington, 1969-72; asst. prof., mem. attending staff Howard U. Coll. Medicine and Med. Ctr., Washington, 1974—; with Bur. Quality Assurance, HHS, Washington, 1974-77; various adminstrv. positions Bur. Med. Services and Health Services Adminstrn., USPHS, 1977-80; dep. commr., then commr. pub. health City of Washington, 1982-84; acting v.p. fin. and adminstrv. affairs Mile Sq. Health Ctr., Inc., 1984; asst. to regional health adminstr. Fed. Employee Occupational Health Program, 1985; dir. region 5, div. Fed. E Fed. Employee Occupational Health Program, Chgo., 1986—; mem. profl. staff Com. on Ways and Means, U.S. Ho. of Reps., 1972; spl. asst. to dir. Office Policy Planning and Evaluation, HEW, 1973; presenter at numerous profl. meetings. Contbr. articles to dental jours. Mem. D.C. Emergency Med. Care Adv. Com., D.C. Long-Term Planning Group, 1983, D.C. Health Coordinating Council, D.C. Commn. on Homelessness, 1984; mem. adv. bd. Rosemont Health Ctr., 1984; sec. D.C. Commn. on Licensure to Practice Healing Art, 1983; bd. dirs. United Black Fund, 1984, Potomac Valley Myastenia Gravis Found., 1984. Global Community Health fellow HEW, 1971, Louise C. Ball fellow, 1969; recipient Meritorious Service award USPHS, 1982, J.B. Johnson Nursing Ctr. award, 1983, Outstanding Service placque D.C. Village Choir, 1984, Disting. Service cert. Concerned Citizens for Alcohol Abuse, 1984, Whitman-Walker award for AIDS effort, 1984, Exceptional Accomplishment award Regional Health Adminstr., 1987. Fellow Am. Assn. Oral and Maxillofacial Surgeons (ho. of dels. 1977-80), Internat. Coll. Dentistry, Royal Soc. Health, Acad. Dentistry Internat., Am. Coll. Dentistry; mem. ADA (cons. council hosp. dental care 1976-77), D.C. Soc. Oral and Maxillofacial Surgeons (sec.-treas. 1979-81), Nat. Dental Assn. (Dentist of Yr. 1983, 1st ann. Disting. Service award 1984), Omicron Kappa Upsilon, Chi Delta Mu, Sigma Pi Phi. Home: 88 W Schiller St Apt 1204 Chicago IL 60610-2032 also: 88 W Schiller St Apt 1204 Chicago IL 60610-2032

HARDAWAY, ROBERT MORRIS, III, physician, educator, retired army officer; b. Camp John Hay, Philippines, Jan. 9, 1916; s. Robert Morris and Olive (Gray) H.; m. Lee H. Harkey, June 12, 1939; children—Robert Morris IV, Elizabeth J., Thomas G. II, Christopher L. A.B., U. Denver, 1936; postgrad., U. Colo. Med. Sch., 1935-37; M.D., Washington U., St. Louis, 1939. Diplomate Am. Bd. Surgery. Commd. 1st lt., M.C. U.S. Army, 1939, advanced through grades to brig. gen., 1970; ward officer, surg. service Fitzsimons Gen. Hosp., Denver, 1940-41, N. Sector Gen. Hosp., Hawaii, 1941-43; tchr. Med. Field Service Sch., Carlysle Barracks, Pa., 1943-45; surg. trainee Nichols Gen. Hosp., Louisville, 1945-46; resident surgery Madigan Gen. Hosp., Tacoma, 1946-47, Fitzsimons Gen. Hosp., 1949-50; chief surg. service 34th Gen. Hosp., Korea, 1947-49, Sta. Hosp., Ft. Belvoir, Va., 1950-54, 97th Gen. Hosp., Frankfurt, Germany, 1954-58, Martin Army Hosp., Ft. Benning, Ga., 1958-60; dir. div. surgery Walter Reed Army Inst. Research, Washington, 1960-67; comdg. officer 97th Gen. Hosp., Frankfurt, Germany, 1967-70; comdg. gen. William Beaumont Army Med. Ctr., El Paso, 1970-75; prof. surgery Tex. Tech U. Sch. Medicine, El Paso, 1976—; staff R.E. Thomason Gen. Hosp., El Paso, 1975—. Author: Syndromes of Disseminated Intravascular Coagulation, 1966, Clinical Management of Shock, Surgical and Medical, 1968, Capillary Perfusion in Health and Disease, 1981, Shock—the Reversible Stage of Dying, 1988, Treatment of Wounded in Vietnam, 1988, Blood Problems in Critical Care, 1989; contbr. articles on intravascular coagulation and hemorrhagic shock to jours. and books. Decorated Army Commendation medal with oak leaf cluster, Legion of Merit with oak leaf cluster, D.S.M.; recipient 2d prize for exhibit A.M.A., 1964; Silver award exhibit Am. Soc. Clin. Pathologists-Coll. Am. Pathologists, 1964; certificate of outstanding achievement U.S. Army Sci. Conf., 1964. Fellow ACS, Am. Coll. Angiology, Am. Assn. for Surgery Trauma, Microcirculation Assn.; mem. Assn. Mil. Surgeons U.S., AMA, Alpha Omega Alpha. Episcopalian. Office: Tex Tech U Sch Medicine 4800 Alberta Ave El Paso TX 79905-2709

HARDCASTLE, JACK DONALD, surgery educator; b. Apr. 3, 1933; s. Albert and Bertha (Ellison) H.; m. Rosemary Hay-Shunker, 1965; 2 children. BA, MA, Emmanuel Coll., Cambridge, Eng., 1954; MB BChir., MChir. with distinction, London Hosp., Cambridge, Eng., 1955. House physician surgery, resident accoucheur London Hosp., 1959-60; house surgeon to prof. Aird, Hammersmith Postgrad. Hosp., 1961-62; rsch. asst. London Hosp., 1962, lectr. surgery, 1963, registrar in surgery, 1964, registrar in surgery thoracic unit, 1965, sr. registrar in surgery, 1965; sr. registrar St. Mark's Hosp., London, 1968; sr. lectr. surgery London Hosp., 1968; prof. surgery U. Nottingham, Eng., 1970—; Sir Arthur Sims Commonwealth traveling prof. Royal Coll. Surgeons, 1985; Mayne vis. prof. U. Brisbane, 1987. Co-author: (with H.D. Ritchie) Isolated Organ Perfusion, 1973; contbr. articles to profl. jours. 20831095oyal Coll. Surgeons Eng. (mem. coun. 1995—, v.p. 1995—, dir. Raven Dept. Edn.), Royal Coll. Physicians (London, hon.), Royal Coll. Physicians and Surgeons (Glasgow). Home: Goverton Heights, Goverton Bleasby NG14 7FN, England

HARDEE, BILLIE CHARLENE, nurse; b. Williamson County, Tex., July 26, 1934; d. Robert Newton Gaines and Madge Leola (Fisher) Gaines Neal; student Huston-Tillotson Coll., Austin, 1952-58; L.V.N., Sid Peterson Sch. Vocat. Nurses, 1967; m. Raymond Julius Hardee, Aug. 20, 1958: children—Julius Earl, Todd Ray, Lateesha Charlene. With Sid Peterson Meml. Hosp., Kerrville, Tex., 1962-80, head nurse central service, 1970-80; activity therapist Kerrville State Hosp., 1985-86; tchr.'s aide Kerrville Ind. Sch. Dist., 1980-92, sch. nurse, 1992-94, instrnl. asst., 1994-95; coord., dir. Alternative Edn., 1995—; staff nurse Tex. Lions Camp, Kerrville, Tex., 1993, 94, 95. Bd. dirs. ARC; active Leadership Kerr County. Mem. Alpha Kappa Alpha. Methodist. Club: Home Demonstrators Civic. Home: 320 Pearl St Kerrville TX 78028-3259

HARDEN, JIMMIE LEIGH, nursing educator; b. Atlanta, Tex., Aug. 24, 1946; d. Earl Dewey and Elizabeth Delane (Field) H.; divorced; children: John, Joe, Malona. AA, Kilgore Coll., 1972; BS in Nursing, U. Tex., Tyler, 1978; MS, U. Tex., 1989; MS in Nursing, U. Tex., Arlington, 1980. RN, Tex. Nursing instr. Kilgore (Tex.) Coll., 1979-94; nursing supervisor Titus Regional Med. Ctr, Mt. Pleasant, 1995-96; staff nurse Gambro Healthcare, Longview, Tex., 1996—; part-time emergency room staff nurse various hosps., Tex.; nursing supr. Longview (Tex.) Regional Hosp., 1981-82, Summer Meadows Nursing Home, Longview, 1988-92; home health nurse East Tex. Vis. Nurses, Longview, 1988-89; office nurse Dr. Larry Smith, 1988, 90. Mem. Tex. Jr. Coll. Tchrs. Assn., Order Eastern Star, Tex. Faculty Assn., Internat. Platform Assn., Sigma Theta Tau. Home: 610 Holliday St Longview TX 75601-5712 Office: Gambro Healthcare N 4th St Longview TX 75605

HARDER, LLOYD, pharmacist; b. Linden, Tenn., Dec. 13, 1925; s. James Andrew and Victoria (Edwards) H.; m. Embree Prater, July 2, 1955; children: David Lloyd, Michael Andrew. BS in Pharmacy, U. Miss., 1952; PharmD, U. Tenn., 1983. Pharmacist Bunting's Drug Store, Bristol, Tenn., 1952-60, Harder's Drug, Bassett, Va., 1960-68; pharmacist, owner Ctr. Drug, Blacksburg, Va., 1968-74; pharmacist-in-charge, asst. mgr. Peoples Drug Store, Blacksburg, 1974-90; pharmacist CVS Pharmacy, 1990-91, Revco Drug # 460, 1991—. Served as sgt. U.S. Army, 1945-46. Mem. Miss. Pharmacists. Methodist. Lodges: Elks, Kiwanis. Home: 400 Franklin Dr Blacksburg VA 24060-3614

HARDESTY, ROBERT ALAN, plastic surgeon; b. St. Helena, Calif., Apr. 24, 1953; m. Marti F. Baum; children: Ashley, Bradford, Chelsea. BA, Loma Linda U., 1974, MD, 1978. Diplomate Am. Bd. Surgery, Am. Bd. Plastic Surgery. Resident in gen. surgery Loma Linda (Calif.) U. Med. Ctr., 1979-83, plastic surgeon, 1987—; resident in plastic surgery U. Pitts. Med. Ctr., 1984-86; fellow in craniofacial surgery Children's Hosp., Washington U., St. Louis, 1986-87; instr. dept. surgery, dept. emergency medicine Loma Linda U. Sch. Medicine, 1983-84; asst. prof. dept. surgery, divsn. plastic and reconstructive surgery Loma Linda U. Sch. of Medicine, 1987-90; assoc. prof. dept. pediatrics Loma Linda U. Sch. Medicine, 1995—; assoc. prof. dept. surgery, chief divsn. plastic and reconstructive surgery Loma Linda U. Sch. of Medicine, 1990—; prof. dept. surgery Loma Linda U. Sch. Medicine, 1995—; apptd. to various hosps. including Loma Linda Community Hosp., 1987—, Jerry L. Pettis VA Med. Ctr., Loma Linda, 1987—, Riverside (Calif.) Gen. Hosp., 1987—, San Bernardino (Calif.) County Med. Ctr., 1990—; instr. dept. surgery, divsn. plastic and reconstructive surgery Washington U. Sch. of Medicine, St. Louis, 1986-87; assoc. prof. dept. oral maxillofacial surgery Loma Linda U. Sch. of Dentistry, 1990—; mem. numerous coms. Loma Linda U., 1987—; chmn. various symposiums; lectr., rschr. in field. Guest editor: Clinics in Plastic Surgery, 1993; mem. internat. editorial adv. bd. Jour. Reconstructive Microsurgery, 1990-91, 91-92, 92-93; contbr. articles to profl. jours., chpts. to books. Recipient Clin. Resident Competition Second Prize award Robert H. Ivy Soc. Plastic and Reconstructive Surgeons, 1986, First prize Ohio Valley Soc. Plastic Surgery, 1986, Second prize Pitts. Acad. Medicine, 1986, Traveling Fellow award Royal Coll. Surgeons, 1991-92; Rsch. grantee Valley Lab, 1988, Plastic Surgery Ednl. Found., Am. Soc. Aesthetic Plastic Surgery, 1988, 93, Maxillofacial Surgeons Found., 1992; grantee Loma Linda U. Med. Ctr., 1989, NIH, 1989-92, Am. Cleft Palate-Craniofacial Assn., 1991, The Aesthetic Soc., 1992, Nat. Inst. Dental Rsch., 1992; Craniofacial Seed grantee Loma Linda U., 1992. Fellow ACS; mem. AMA, AAAS, Am. Acad. Pediatrics (plastic surgery sect.), Am. Assn. Clin. Anatomists, Am. Assn. Pediatric Plastic Surgeons, Am. Burn Assn., Am. Cleft Palate-Craniofacial Assn., Am. Soc. Maxillofacial Surgeons, Am. Soc. Plastic and Reconstructive Surgeons, Internat. Confedn. Plastic, Reconstructive and Aesthetic Surgery, Pan-Pacific Surg. Assn., Tri-County Surg. Soc., Calif. Med. Assn., Calif. Soc. Plastic Surgeons, San Bernardino County Med. Soc., Aesthetic Surgery Edn. and Rsch. Found., Adventist Internat. Med. Soc., Assn. Acad. Chairmen of Plastic Surgery, Lipoplasty Soc. N.Am., Loma Linda Med.- Dental Soc., Walter E. Macpherson Soc., Plastic Surgery Rsch. Coun., Wound Healing Soc., Alpha Omega Alpha. Home: 1515 W Cypress Ave Redlands CA 92373-5614 Office: Loma Linda U Med Ctr Divsn Plastic Surgery 11234 Anderson St Loma Linda CA 92354-2804

HARDESTY, STEVEN CONWAY, psychologist; b. Evansville, Ind., May 25, 1951; s. Jacob Conway and Margaret Virginia (Ridenour) H.; m. Janet Gail Gentry, Dec. 20, 1971 (div. July 1977); m. Cynthia Cameron Sprague, Aug. 28, 1983; children: Cameron Elizabeth, Michael Sprague. BA, So. Meth. U., 1973; PhD, U. Tex. Med. Ctr. at Dallas, 1990. Caseworker Dept. Human Resources, Dallas, 1974-78; prog. specialist Office of Human Devel., Dallas, 1978-80; ptnr. Hardesty and Samnson, Dallas, 1980-84; clin. dir. Suicide and Crisis Ctr., Dallas, 1986; exec. dir. Plano (Tex.) Child Guidance Clinic, 1986-91; staff psychologist Timberlawn North Dallas Ctr., 1991-95; cons. Pers. Decisions, Internat., Irving, Tex., 1995—; pvt. practice Alma Assocs., Irving, Tex., 1995—; mem. Coord. Coun. for Social Svcs., McKinney, Tex., 1986-91, Dallas Commn. on Children and Youth, Dallas, 1978-80; treas. Dallas Psychol. Assn., 1991—; bd. dirs. Mental Health Assn. Collin County, 1992—. Editor: (newsletter) Dallas Psychologist, 1990-91. Bd. dirs., treas. Home Health Svcs. of Dallas, Inc., 1978-81; staff Children and Youth Adv. Com./City Dallas, 1978-80. Recipient Belle May Brombey award So. Meth. U., Dallas, 1972, Experiment in Internat. Living Amb. grant, Japan, 1971. Mem. Dallas Psychol. Assn., Am. Psychol. Assn. Democrat. Home: 6704 Spokane Pl Plano TX 75023-1426 Office: Pers Decisions Internat Ste 1700 LB 142 600 Las Colinas Blvd Irving TX 75039

HARDIE, BRADFORD, III, ophthalmologist; b. El Paso, Tex., Oct. 30, 1920; s. Bradford Jr. and Mineta Jane (Henning) H.; m. Rebekah E. Hardie, Nov. 8, 1952; children: Rebekah, Barbara Leslie, Patricia, Sarah. BSEE, Tex. A&M U., 1942; MD, Johns Hopkins U., 1951. Diplomate Am. Bd. Ophthalmology. Pvt. practice, El Paso, 1954—. Capt. Signal Corps, U.S. Army, 1942-46, ETO. Decorated Bronze Star (2). Mem. Tex. Med. Assn. Home: 5963 Las Vegas Dr El Paso TX 79902 Office: 1501 Arizona Ave Ste 11-A El Paso TX 79902

HARDIN, CHARLES M., JR., association administrator; b. Cynthiana, Ky., Jan. 25, 1935; s. Charles M. Hardin Sr. and Jane (Box) Humphrey; m. Lavonne C. Barlow, Aug. 8, 1958; children: Darren, Lora. BS, Georgetown (Ky.) Coll., 1957; MPH, U. Okla., 1964. Tchr. sci. Williamstown (Ky.) Bd. Edn., 1957-58; exhibits mgr. Oak Ridge (Tenn.) Inst. Nuc. Studies, 1958-62; physicist Commonwealth of Ky., Frankfort, 1962-79; mem. tech. staff Ky. Legis. Rsch. Com., Frankfort, 1979-81; exec. dir. Conf. Radiation Control Program Dirs., Frankfort, 1981—; chmn. Tech. Electronic Product Radiation Safety Stds. Commn. FDA, Rockville, Md. Office: Conf Radiation Control Program Dirs 205 Capital Ave Frankfort KY 40601

HARDIN, CHRISTOPHER D., medical educator; b. Syracuse, N.Y., July 31, 1961. BS, Cornell U., 1983; MS in Physiology and Biophysics, U. Rochester, 1985; PhD, U. Cin., 1989. Sr. fellow Dept. Radiology U. Wash., 1989-91, rsch. asst. prof., 1991—; asst. prof. physiology U. Mo., Columbia, 1993—; tutor, mentor in field; spkr. in field. Contbr. articles to profl. jours. Albert J. Ryan fellow, 1986-89, tng. grant fellow U. Cin., 1985-86, univ. grad. fellow U. Rochester, 1983-85; recipient Kline-Eckstein Fund Travel award, 1986, 87, Grad. Student Assn. Travel award U. Cin., 1986, 87, 88, Jeffrey D. Doane Meml. award, 1987, Nat. Rsch. Svc. award, 1989-92. Mem. AAAS, Internat. Soc. Heart Rsch. (N.Am. sect), Am. Heart Assn. Sci. Coun. (basic sci.), Am. Physiol. Soc. (Proctor and Gamble Profl. Opportunity award 1988, Harold Lamport award Outstanding Young Invesitgator 1995), Biophysical Soc. (Samuel Talbot Travel award 1988). Home: 1210 Sunset Dr Columbia MO 65203 Office: Dept Physiology MA415 Med Scis Bldg Columbia MO 65212*

HARDIN, HILLIARD FRANCES, microbiologist; b. Columbia, S.C., Dec. 12, 1917; d. Lawrence Legare and Addria Eugenia (Chreitzberg) H. AB, Duke U., 1939, MA, 1949, PhD, 1953. Bacteriologist Bowman Gray Sch. of Medicine, Winston-Salem, N.C., 1941-42; instr. Med. Sch. Duke U., Durham, N.C., 1948-53; from instr. to asst. prof. Med. Sch. U. Ark., Little Rock, 1954-58; rsch. assoc. Sch. of Medicine Duke U., 1958-63; chief mycology tng. unit C.D.C., Atlanta, 1963-68; dir. microbiology dept. VA Hosp., Little Rock, 1968—. With USNR, 1942-45. Mem. N.Y. Acad. Scis., Med. Mycology Soc. Am., Am. Bus. Women's Assn. (v.p. 1986-87, pres. 1987-88, Top 10 of the Yr. 1988). Republican. Methodist. Home: 301 Kings Row Dr Apt 401 Little Rock AR 72207-4169

HARDIN, JEFFREY M., internist; b. Long Beach, Calif., Dec. 12, 1961; s. George Robert and Wilma Eileen (Pfund) H.; m. Susan Hope Goldner, Aug. 8, 1991 (div.). BA in Biology, Calif. State U., 1984; MD, Uniformed Svcs. U. Health Sci., 1988. Diplomate Nat. Bd. Med. Examiners, Am. Bd. Internal Medicine. Commd. ensign USN, 1984, advanced through grades to lt. comdr., 1994; intern in Transitional Program Naval Hosp., San Diego, 1988-89; gen. med. officer 1st Marine Divsn., Camp Pendleton, Calif., 1989-91; internal medicine resident Naval Hosp., Oakland, Calif., 1991-93, chief med. resident, 1993-94, staff internist, tng. dir. Internal Medicine Residency, 1994-95; head dept. internal medicine U.S. Navy Clinic, London, 1995—. Mem. ACP, AMA, Am. Soc. Internal Medicine, Undersea and Hyperbaric Medicine Soc., Naval and Mil. Club. Office: US Navy Med Clinic, 88 Blenhein Crescent, Ruislip HA4 7EG, England

HARDIN, JOHN CALVIN, JR., physician, surgeon; b. Smackover, Ark., Apr. 21, 1925; s. John Calvin and Sadie (Kendrick) H.; m. Lera Quay Carpenter, Dec. 26, 1949; 1 chlid, John Calvin III. DDS, Loyola U., New Orleans, 1946; MD, U. Tenn., Memphis, 1950. Diplomate Am. Bd. Surgery. Intern Confederate Meml. Med. Ctr., Shreveport, La., 1950-51, resident, 1951-52; resident USAF, Sewart AFB, Tenn., 1952-54, Confederate Meml. Med. Ctr.-Las. State U., Shreveport, 1954-56; pvt. practice surgery Shreveport, La., 1956-94; asst. prof. surgery La. State U. Med. Sch., Shreveport, 1994-95, clin. prof. surgery, 1995—. Capt. USAF, 1952-54. Home: 410 Briarwood Dr Shreveport LA 71106 Office: La State U Sch Medicine 1501 Kings Hwy Shreveport LA 71130

HARDIN, ROBERT A., cardiothoracic surgeon; b. Harrison County, Ky., Nov. 8, 1930; m. Jo Ann, Mar. 13, 1954; children: Tom, Jack, Bill, Katie. BA, Asbury Coll., 1952; MD, Vanderbilt U. Sch. Medicine, 1956. Diplomate Am. Bd. Thoracic Surgery. Surg. intern Ind. U. Med. Ctr., Indpls., 1956-57, surg. resident, 1957-58, 1960-64; pvt. practice Nashville, 1964-95; assoc. med. dir. Baptist Hosp., Nashville, 1995—. Capt. U.S. Army Med. Rsch. Lab., 1958-60. Office: Baptist Hosp 2000 Church St Nashville TN 37236

HARDING, CLIFFORD VINCENT, III, pathologist, cell biologist, immunologist; b. Arlington, Va., Jan. 31, 1957; s. Clifford Vincent Jr. and Drusilla (Van Hoesen) H.; m. Mina Kay Chung, 1983; children: Clifford Vincent IV, Andrew Richard. AB magna cum laude, Harvard U., 1979; MD, PhD in Cell Biology, Washington U., St. Louis, 1985. Diplomate Nat. Bd. Med. Examiners. Resident in pathology Washington U., 1985-89, chief resident, 1989-90, asst. prof., 1990-93; asst. prof. pathology Case Western Reserve U., Cleve., 1993-96, assoc. prof. pathology, 1996—. Mem. editl. bd. Advances in Anatomic Pathology; contbr. articles and abstracts to med. jours. Mem. AAAS, Am. Assn. Immunologists, Am. Soc. Cell Biology, Am. Assn. Pathologists, Am. Soc. Investigative Pathology, Phi Beta Kappa. Office: Case Western Res Univ Dept Pathology 2085 Adelbert Rd Cleveland OH 44106

HARDING, LINDA OTTO, nursing educator; b. Calicoon, N.Y., Apr. 30, 1944; d. Max Hermann and Leona (Kleb) Otto; m. Bruce Nelson Harding, June 4, 1966; children: Jonathan, Linette. Diploma, Robert Packer Hosp. Sch. of Nursing, Sayre, Pa., 1965; student, Phillips U., Enid, Okla., 1967-68. RN, N.Y., Pa.; cert. personal care home administr. Tb control nurse Madison County Dept. Health, Anderson, Ind., 1970-73; charge nurse Milford (Pa.) Valley Convalescent Home, 1974-83; office nurse Tri State Med. Assocs., Matamoras, Pa., 1983-91; coord. health care Twin Cedars Assisted Living Ctr., Shohola, Pa., 1990—. Founder Tri State Alzheimer's Support Group; dir. Share-Care Diabetes Support Group. Mem. ANA, Pa. Nurses Assn. (newsletter editor dist. 4, past treas., v.p.), Am. Assn. Diabetes Educators (cert.). Home: RR 2 Box 2530 Shohola PA 18458-9737

HARDING, MICHAEL BLAIN, cardiologist; b. Oct. 2, 1957; s. Donald H. and Ruby (Lamb) Bobicchio; m. Janet Marie Picklo, Jan. 3, 1981; children: Natalie, Lauren. BS in Chemistry, U. of the South, 1980; BS in Chem. Engring., Columbia U., 1980; MD, Vanderbilt U., 1985. Diplomate Am. Bd. Internal Medicine. Resident in internal medicine Vanderbilt U.; cardiology fellow Duke U.; interventional fellow Vancouver Gen. Hosp.; cardiologist N.Mex. Heart Inst., Albuquerque, 1992—. Wilkins scholar, U. of the South; recipient Organic Chemistry award. Fellow Am. Coll. Cardiology; mem. Soc. Cardiac Angiography and Interventions, Phi Lambda Upsilon. Office: NMex Heart Inst 1001 Coal Ave SE Albuquerque NM 87106

HARDISON, JOSEPH HAMMOND, JR., retired internist, educator; b. Raleigh, N.C., Apr. 25, 1932; s. Joseph Hammond and Katherine Clark (Smith) H.; m. Cynthia Ann Stoltze, Apr. 8, 1962; children—Joseph Hammond III, Sanborn Stoltze, Anna Katherine. Student Sewanee Mil. Acad., 1950, Duke U., 1950-52, M.D., 1956. Diplomate Am. Bd. Internal Medicine, 1964. Intern, resident Cornell Med. Ctr., N.Y. Med. Ctr., 1956-58; fellow in internal medicine Mayo Clinic, 1960-62, fellow in gastroenterology, 1962-64; practice internal medicine, Raleigh, N.C. (with Dr. Cynthia Hardison), 1964-68, (with Dr. Paar), 1968-71; sr. ptnr. Raleigh Internal Medicine Assocs. (name changed to Cardinal Health Care Assn.), 1971-91; asst. prof. medicine U. N.C., Chapel Hill, 1964-76, assoc. prof. medicine, 1976-91, retired. Mem. med. staff Rex, Wake Meml., Raleigh Community hosps.; chmn. dept. medicine Raleigh Community Hosp., 1978-79; dir. First Union Nat. Bank Raleigh, The Edwards and Broughton Co. Pres. Raleigh Heart Assn., 1967-68. Served to lt. commdr. M.C., USN, 1958-60. Recipient N.C. Heart Assn. Founders award. Mem. Wake County Med. Soc., N.C. Med. Soc., AMA, Am. Coll. Gastroenterology (bd. govs.), Raleigh Soc. Internal Medicine (pres. 1975-76). Democrat. Episcopalian. Clubs: Carolina Country, Capital City, Sphinx (Raleigh); Coral Bay Beach (Atlantic Beach, N.C.). Home: 1612 Oberlin Rd Raleigh NC 27608-2045

HARDWAY, JAMES EDWARD, vocational and rehabilitative specialist; b. Pueblo, Colo., Nov. 26, 1944; s. William Jeremiah and Margaret Ann (Rinker) H.; m. Mary Frances Walker, Sept. 9, 1967; children: Tina Marie, Catherine Ann, William James. BA, U. So. Colo., 1969; MS, U. Wis.-Stout, Menomonie, 1971; postgrad., U. Toledo, 1972—. Cert. vocat. evaluator, work adjustment specialist. Counselor Pueblo (Colo.) Diversified Industries, 1969-70; vocat. evaluator Penta County Vocat. Schs., Perrysburg, Ohio, 1971-82; dept. mgr. Magic City Enterprises, Cheyenne, Wyo., 1982-88; case mgr. Profl. Rehab. Mgmt., Cheyenne, 1989-91, regional mgr., 1992-94; pvt. practice vocational expert Cheyenne, 1994—; speaker State of Ohio Spl. Needs Conf., Ohio, 1972-80; cons. Wyo. State Tng. Sch., Lander, 1977. Pres. bd. dirs. Laramie County Community Action, Cheyenne; bd. dirs. Handicapped Employment Agy., Cheyenne, Wyo. Alzheimer's Assn. With U.S. Army, 1962-65. Fellow Am. Bd. Vocat. Experts; mem. Kiwanis (bd. dirs.). Home: 12309 White Eagle Rd Cheyenne WY 82009-9634

HARDWICK, CHARLES LEIGHTON, pharmaceutical company executive, state legislator; b. Somerset, Ky., Nov. 8, 1941; s. Joseph Fulton and Lucy Belle (Hall) H.; m. Patricia Ruth Johnson, Mar. 30, 1959 (div. July 1993); children: Virginia Lee, Charles Jr. BS, Fla. State U., 1962, MBA, 1964.

Sales supr. Continental Baking Co., Detroit, 1964-66; sales rep. Pfizer, Inc., N.Y.C., 1966-70, regional mgr., 1970-73, dir. mktg., 1973-77, dir. civic info., 1977—; v.p. state govt. rels. and external affairs Pfizer Pharmaceuticals, N.Y.C., 1977—; Rep. Assembly minority leader, Gen. Assembly State of N.J., 1985, speaker of assembly, 1986-89, N.J. Assembly minority leader emeritus, 1989-91; vice chmn. U.S. Trade Adv. Commn., Washington, 1983-85; mem. Presdl. Federalism Adv. Commn., Washington, 1981-83. Mem. Am. Legis. Exchange Council (bd. dirs. 1986—, named Legislator of Yr. 1986), Nat. Rep. Legislators Assn. (pres. 1982-84). Home: 25 E 83rd St New York NY 10028-0421

HARDY, JOEL ALLEN, microbiologist, educator; b. Los Angeles, Dec. 1, 1952; s. Allen Williams and Ina Carolyn (Cobia) H.; B.S., Weber State Coll., 1977; M.S., Idaho State U., 1979; m. Vicki Lynn Nickens, Dec. 20, 1974; children—Thomas Joel, Lucas Allen, Janna Marie, Jonica Anne. Chemist, Firestone Tire & Rubber Co., Salinas, Calif., 1980; instr. microbiology and chemistry Hartnell Coll., Salinas, 1980-82; microbiologist Internat. Shellfish Enterprises, Moss Landing, Calif., 1980-82; research specialist U. Utah Sch. Medicine, Salt Lake City, 1982-84, Gull Labs, Salt Lake City, 1984-89, Bio-Rad Labs., Hercules, Calif., 1989—. Idaho State U. research grantee, 1979. Mem. AAAS, Am. Soc. for Microbiology, Sigma Xi. Republican. Mormon. Home: 355 Woodhaven Dr Vacaville CA 95687-5955 Office: Bio-Rad Labs 5500 E 2nd St Benicia CA 94510

HARDY, MARK ADAM, surgeon, immunologist, educator; b. Lwow, Poland, Jan. 5, 1938; came to U.S., 1949, naturalized, 1956; s. Paul and Rose (Pomeranz) H.; m. Ruth C. Komisarow, Jan. 14, 1967; children—Peter, Arthur, Karen. A.B., Columbia U., 1958; M.D., Albert Einstein Coll. Medicine, 1962. Diplomate Am. Bd. Surgery. Asst. instr. surgery, intern, resident in surgery U. Rochester, N.Y., 1962-64; asst. prof. surgery Albert Einstein Coll. Medicine, 1971-75; fellow in transplantation Harvard Med. Sch., 1968-69; assoc. prof. Columbia U., N.Y.C., 1975-80, prof. surgery, 1980-90, Auchincloss prof. surgery, 1990—; dir. transplantation Albert Einstein Coll. Medicine, N.Y.C., 1971-75, Columbia Presbyn. Med. Ctr., N.Y.C., 1975—. Served to lt. comdr. USNR, 1964-70. NIH scholar. Mem. ACS, Soc. Univ. Surgeons, Am. Surg. Assn., Soc. Clin. Surgery, Internat. Soc. Cardiovasc. Surgery, Transplantation Soc., Am. Assn. Immunology, Am. Soc. for Transplant Surgery. Office: Presbyn Hosp Columbia-Presbyn Med Ctr New York NY 10032

HARDY, ROBERT CHARLES, neurosurgeon; b. Dallas, July 22, 1925; m. Ida Fae E. Hardy; children: Charles, Donald, Elissa (dec.), Brent, Melinda, Craig, Susan (dec.). BS, So. Meth. U., 1944; MD, Cornell U., 1948. Diplomate Am. Bd. Neurol. Surgeons, Nat. Bd. Med. Examiners; lic. physician, N.Y., Tex. Intern then resident Bellevue Hosp., N.Y.C., 1948-52, 55; resident U. Hosps., Iowa City, 1954-55; pvt. practice San Antonio, 1956—; assoc. clin. prof. neurosurgery U. Tex. health Sci. Ctr., San Antonio; cons. in field. Contbr. numerous articles to profl. jours. With U.S. Army, 1952-54. Mem. AMA, ACS (Cert. of Appreciation 1962, Physician's Recognition award), Am. Assn. Neurol. Surgeons, Tex. Med. Assn. (Cert. of Merit 1957), Tex. Assn. Neurol. Surgeons (pres. 1989-90), Bexar County Med. Soc., San Antonio Surg. Soc. (pres. 1985-86), Congress Neurol. Surgeons, So. Neurol. Soc., Soc. Univ. Neurosurgeons (pres. 1974-75), S.W. Found. Rsch. and Edn. (affiliate). Home: 200 Laburnum Dr San Antonio TX 78209 Office: 5430 Fredericksburg Rd #318 San Antonio TX 78229

HARDY, SALLY MARIA, retired biological sciences educator; b. San Juan, P.R., June 12, 1932; d. Obdulio Roberto Cordero and Maria Teresa (Judice) Perez; m. Anthony Michael Hardy, Apr. 22, 1962; children: Ricardo Antonio, Maria Isabel. BS, Midland Coll., Fremont, Nebr., 1952; MS, Fordham U., 1956, PhD, 1958. Tech. asst. Postgrad. Hosp., N.Y.C., 1952-54; tchr. Ursuline Acad., N.Y.C., 1957-58; asst. prof. Marymount Manhattan Coll., N.Y.C., 1957-62, 67-68, Queensborough Community Coll., CUNY, 1967-69; rsch. assoc. Am. Mus. Natural History, N.Y.C., 1967-73; assoc. prof. Bergen Community Coll., Bergen, N.J., 1969-70, Rutgers U., Piscataway, N.J., 1970-79; prof. biol. scis. La. State U., Shreveport, 1979-88; ret., 1988; mem. minority com. Grad. Record Exam. Bd., 1976-79; cons. Office Tech. Assessment, U.S. Ho. of Reps., 1985-87. Mem. editorial bd. Jour. Allied Health Professions, 1983-86; contbr. articles to profl. publs. Pres. Hispanic Youth Civic Assn., N.Y.C., 1954-57, PTA, Mendham, N.J., 1972-74; mem. Mendham Borough Bd. Edn., 1973-77, Mendham Borough Bd. Health, 1979; mem. Emerald Isle Vol. Rescue Squad, 1994, cons. program eval. and devel., 1994—. Recipient Faculty Merit award Rutgers U., 1978, Nuestro award Hispanic mag., 1978, award Assn. for Advancement Chicanos and Native Ams. in Sci., 1982. Mem. AAAS (chmn. Office Opportunities in Sci. 1979-85), N.Y. Acad. Scis., Assn. for Puerto Ricans in Sci. and Engring. (pres. 1981-84, bd. dirs. 1984-87), Sigma Xi, Pi Epsilon, Lambda Tau. Roman Catholic. Home: PO Box 4173 Emerald Isle NC 28594-4173

HARDY-LEE, MARTHA MARIA, mental health nurse; b. Montgomery, Ala., Apr. 18, 1936; d. Charlie Hardy and Delsie (King) Hardy; m. Dalton C. Lee, Feb. 1964. RN, St. Helena Sch. Nursing, Deer Park, Calif., 1959; BSN, Sonoma (Calif.) State U., 1973; MA, John F. Kennedy U., Orinda, Calif., 1983. Pub. health nurse, nurse practitioner Contra Costa County, Pittsburg, Calif.; charge nurse Brookside Hosp., San Pablo, Calif.; crisis intervention charge nurse Merrithaw Meml. Hosp., Martinez, Calif.; pvt. practice psychotherapist Benicia, Calif.; conductor workshops in field. Mem. Calif. Nurses Assn., Calif. Assn. Marriage Family and Child Therapists, Am. Assn. Christian Counselors, Nat. Coun. Negro Women, Mariners Internat. Tng. in Communication (charter).

HARE, HENRY PHILLIP, JR., psychiatrist; b. Paris, Tex., Apr. 4, 1925; s. Henry P. and Bertha (McIntosh) H.; children: Elizabeth Anne, John Keble. Student, Rice U., Houston, 1941-43; BA, U. Tex., Galveston, 1945, MD, 1947. Diplomate Am. Bd. Psychiatry and Neurology. Rotating intern U.S. Marine Hosp., Balt., 1947-48; fellow in psychiatry Menninger Sch., Topeka, 1951; staff to chief psychiatry USPHS Hosp., Ft. Worth, 1951-54; dir. psychotherapy Beverly Hills Clinic, Dallas, 1954-60; lectr. psychiatry Mansfield Coll., U. Oxford, Eng., 1960-61; assoc. to dir. Tulsa Psychiat. Found., 1961-63; pvt. practice Nix Med. Ctr., San Antonio, 1963—; clin. prof. psychiatry U. Tex. Health Sci. Ctr., San Antonio, 1965—; med. dir., chief profl. staff San Antonio State Hosp., 1989-93, forensic psychiatrist, 1993—; psychiat. examiner to Episcopal Bishop W. Tex., San Antonio, 1963—; psychiat. rep. to med. bd. Humana Met. Hosp., San Antonio, 1989-90. Contbr. articles to profl. jours. Mem. Bexar County Bd. Trustees for Mental Health and Mental Retardation, San Antonio, 1969-74; mem. distbns. com. San Antonio Area Found., 1975-78. Capt. USPHS, 1947—. Named Layman of Yr., Episcopal Diocese Dallas, 1959. Fellow Am. Psychiat. Assn. (life), So. Psychiat. Assn., Royal Soc. Health; mem. Bexar County Psychiat. Soc. (pres. 1967-68), Alcuin Club. Democrat. Home: 10314 Severn Rd San Antonio TX 78217-3945 Office: 1122 Nix Med Ctr San Antonio TX 78205

HARE, LEROY, JR., pharmaceutical company executive; b. Topeka, Nov. 1, 1955; s. LeRoy and Carol Darlene (Johnson) H.; m. Margaret Ann Burke, Dec. 30, 1982; children: Susan Audrey and Sarah Jean (twins). Student, Kans. State U., 1974-76; BBA, Washburn U., 1978. Book buyer Palmer News, Inc., Topeka, 1978-81; store mgr. Town Crier Book Store, Topeka, 1980-81; field sales rep. USV Labs., Topeka, 1981-84; field sales rep. Glaxo Inc, Topeka, 1985-90, field sales trainer, 1988-90, regional sales trainer, 1989-90, mem. profl. devel. program, 1989, managed care area account mgr., 1990-94; dist. sales mgr., 1994-95; co-founder Info Tec, LLC, DAPS, 1995-96; acct. mgr. Networks Plus, Prairie Village, Kans., 1996—; account mgr. Networks Plus, 1996—, dist. sales mgr., 1996—. Author sales tng. manual. Mem. adv. panel Marian Clinic, Topeka, 1989-94, Black Health Care Coalition, 1994-95.

HARE, SANDRA FLORENCE, internist, public health consultant; b. Phila., Oct. 23, 1952; d. John Dalrymple Hare and Hortense Cecelia (Daniels) Morris; divorced; 1 child, Meredith Tilse. BA, Clark U., 1974; postgrad. in medicine, Loyola U., Chgo., 1974-75; MPH, U. Ill., Chgo., 1978; MD, Chgo. Med. Sch., 1983. Diplomate Am. Bd. Internal Medicine, Nat. Bd. Med. Examiners. Tchr. chemistry and physics Wyoming Sem., Kingston, Pa., 1975-76; rsch. asst., assoc. U. Ill. Sch. Pub. Health, 1976-78, occupational medicine cons., 1983-84; preceptor Western Ala. Health Svcs., Eutaw, 1980; cons. Carnow, Conibear & Assocs., Chgo., 1983-84; resident in internal medicine Mercy Hosp. and Med. Ctr., Chgo., 1984-87; attending staff physician Nat. Health Svc. Corps Pub. Health Svc., Chgo., 1987-92; attending physician Cook County Hosp., Chgo., 1987-92; pvt. practice, North Suburban Clinic Ltd., Skokie, Ill., 1993—; clin. asst. in medicine U. Ill. Med. Ctr., Chgo., 1985-87. Chmn. Big Bro.-Big Sister Program, Worcester, Mass., 1972-74; bd. dirs. Sheridan Square Condominium Assn., Evanston, Ill., 1987-89. 1st lt. USPHS, 1978-79. AAUW scholar, 1970, Jonas Clark scholar, 1970-74, USPHS scholar, 1979-83. Mem. AMA (physician recognition award 1987), ACP, Ill. Med. Soc., Chgo. Med. Soc. Democrat. Unitarian. Office: 4801 Church St Skokie IL 60077-1362

HARELL, GEORGE S., radiologist; b. Vienna, Austria, Apr. 27, 1937; came to U.S., 1940; s. Isidore and Zinaida (Hilferding) Silbermann; m. Carol Deane Wright, Mar. 21, 1970, children: Mark, Ben. AB, Oberlin Coll., 1959; MD, Columbia U., 1963. Resident in radiology Med. Sch., Stanford (Calif.) U., 1967-71, asst. prof., 1971-78, assoc. prof., 1978-82; radiologist dept. radiology East Jefferson Gen. Hosp., Metairie, La., 1982-84, chmn. dept. radiology, 1984-94; clin. prof. radiology Tulane U., New Orleans, 1987—; project officer NIH, Washington, 1965-67. Author: (chpt.) The Oesophagus, 1986, 92. Lt. comdr. USPHS, 1963-65. James C. Picker Found. grantee, 1972-74, NIH grantee, 1977-80, 82-85, Am. Heart Assn. grantee, 1981-83. Mem. Soc. Computed Body Tomography/Magnetic Resonances, Soc. Gastrointestinal Radiologists, Phi Beta Kappa. Office: East Jefferson Gen Hosp 4200 Houma Blvd Metairie LA 70006-2970

HARGISS, JAMES LEONARD, ophthalmologist; b. Manhattan, Kans., June 15, 1921; s. Meade Thomas and Julia Baldwin (Wayland) H.; m. Helen Natalie Berglund, July 19, 1947; children: Phillip M., Craig T., D. Reid. BS, U. Wash., 1942; MD, St. Louis U., 1945; MSc in Medicine, U. Pa., 1952. Diplomate Nat. Bd. Med. Examiners, Am. Bd. Ophthalmology. Intern U.S. Naval Hosp., PSNS Bremerton, Washington, 1945-46; resident physician G.F. Geisinger Meml. Hosp. and Foss Clinic, Danville, Pa., 1949-51; practice medicine specializing in ophthalmic surgery Seattle, 1951-58; ophthalmic surgeon Eye Assocs. N.W., Seattle, 1958—, pres., 1962-91, CEO, 1985-91; asst. clin. prof. Sch. Medicine, U. Wash., 1995—. Contbr. chapter to book, 1987, articles to Ophthalmology, 1964-80. Dist. chmn. King County Rep. Cen. Com., 1962-70. Served as physician/surgeon with USNR, 1945-48. Recipient Citation of Merit Washington State Med. Assn., 1959, Cert. of Award Am. Acad. Ophthalmology and Otolaryngology, 1975; Wendell F. Hughes fellow, 1960. Fellow AMA (Cert. of award 1960), Am. Coll. Surgeons, Am. Acad. Ophthalmology (honor award), Am. Soc. Ophthalmic Plastic and Reconstructive Surgery (charter) (Lester T. Jones award 1979), De Bourg Soc. of St. Louis U., Lions (Lake City pres. 1960-61), Alpha Omega Alpha. Office: Eye Assocs NW 1101 Madison St # 600 Seattle WA 98104-1320

HARIMAN, ROBERT JACOBUS IWAN, internist, cardiologist, educator, researcher; b. Semarang, Indonesia, May 1, 1947; came to U.S., 1971, naturalized, 1977.; s. George and Inawati (Tan) H.; m. Listianingsih M.I. Onggosuwarno, O t. 24, 1977; children: Richard, Aileen. BA cum laude, U. Indonesia, Jakarta, 1968, MD cum laude, 1970. Diplomate Am. Bd. Internal Medicine, Am. Bd. Cardiovasc. Diseases, Am. Bd. Clin. Cardiac Electrophysiology. Rotating intern Gen. Hosp., Jakarta, 1968-70, L.I. Coll. Hosp., Bklyn., 1972; straight med. intern, then jr. resident in medicine Michael Reese Hosp., Chgo., 1973-74; sr. resident in medicine Mt. Sinai Hosp. program VA Hosp. (now VA Med. Ctr.), Bklyn., 1974-75, chief Non-Invasive Cardiac Lab., 1981-85, chief CCU and clin. cardiac electrophysiology, 1983-85, assoc. dir. cardiology svc., 1984-85; clin. fellow in cardiology U. Ky. Med. Ctr., Lexington, 1975-77; postdoctoral fellow dept. pharmacology Columbia U., N.Y.C., 1977-79, vis. rsch. assoc., 1979-85; dir. cardiac electrophysiology, assoc. prof. medicine U. Ill., Chgo., 1985-89; dir. cardiac electrophysiology Hines (Ill.) VA Hosp., 1989—; assoc. prof. medicine Loyola U., Maywood, Ill., 1989-93, prof., 1993—; asst. chief cardiolog USPHS, S.I., N.Y., 1979-88; reviewer Circulation Rsch., Circulation, Jour. Am. Coll. Cardiology, Am. Heart Jour., Am. Jour. Cardiology, Chest, 1979—. Contbr. numerous articles, abstracts and revs. to med. jours. Recipient tchg. award West Side VA Med. Ctr., Chgo., 1989; grantee Am. Cyanamid Co., 1982-83, VA, 1982-86, 92-99, Revlon Health Care, 1984-85, Eli Lilly Co., 1983-86, Nat. Heart, Lung and Blood Inst., 1985, Marion Labs., 1986-87, Chgo. Heart Assn., 1987-89, 90-92, Warner Lambert-Parke Davis, 1987-90, Ciba-Geigy, 1987-88, Du Pont de Nemours & Co. Inc., 1988-89, Boehringer Mannheim Pharms., 1987-90, 93, Wyeth Ayerst Rsch., 1990-92, Prizer Ctrl. Rsch., 1991, Sterling Rsch., 1991-92, Berlex Labs., Inc., 1991-92, Searle Pharm. Co., 1991-92, G.D. Searle and Co., 1994-95, also others. Fellow Am. Coll. Cardiology (young investigator award 1980), Ctrl. Soc. Clin. Rsch., N.Y. Heart Assn. (electrophysiology group). Office: Hines VA Hosp Cardiology Sect 111G Hines IL 60141

HARITON, JO ROSENBERG, psychiatric social worker, psychoanalyst; b. Albany, N.Y., June 12, 1948; d. Irving H. and Madeline P. Rosenberg; m. Frank J. Hariton; 2 children. B.A., Goucher Coll., Towson, Md., 1970; M.S., Columbia U., 1973; PhD, NYU, 1992; psychoanalysis cert. (fellow 1975-79), Postgrad. Center Mental Health, N.Y.C., 1979. With maternal and child health dept. Bronx (N.Y.) Mcpl. Hosp. Center, 1973-76, coordinator emergency services children dept. child psychiatry, 1976-79; field work instr. N.Y.U. Sch. Social Work, 1977-79; sr. psychiat. social worker div. child and adolescent psychiatry N.Y. Hosp.-Cornell Med. Center, Westchester div., White Plains, N.Y., 1979-82, social work coordinator, 1982—; faculty Cornell U. Med. Sch., 1982—pvt. practice psychoanalysis and psychotherapy, N.Y.C. Fellow N.Y. State Soc. Clin. Social Work Psychotherapists; mem. Nat. Assn. Social Workers, Acad. Cert. Social Workers, Am. Orthopsychiat. Assn., Am. Group Psychotherapy Assn. Contbr. articles on group therapy to profl. jours. Home: 1065 Dobbs Ferry Rd White Plains NY 10607-2212 Office: NY Hosp Dept Psychoanalyst White Plains NY 10605

HARKEN, ALDEN HOOD, surgeon, thoracic surgeon; b. Boston, 1941. MD, Case Western Reserve U., 1967. Diplomate Am. Bd. Surgeons, Am. Bd. Thoracic Surgeons. Intern Peter Bent Brigham Hosp., Boston, 1967-68, resident surgery, 1968-70, resident thoracic surgery, 1971-73; fellow cardio-vascular surgery Boston Children's Hosp., 1970-71; surgeon U. Colo. Hosp., Denver; prof., chmn. surgery dept. U. Colo. Sch. Medicine, Denver; part time pvt. practice surgery Denver. Mem. Am. Assn. Thoracic Surgeons, Soc. Univ. Surgeons, AATS. Office: U Colo Med Sch Dept Surg 4200 E 9th Ave Box C-305 Denver CO 80262-0001*

HARKER, CARLTON, healthcare executive; b. Le Mars, Iowa, Dec. 2, 1927; s. John Vincent and Eleanor (Carlton) H.; m. Rita Mary Satterlee, June 25, 1950; children: Carla Ann, Douglas James. BA, U. Iowa, 1950, MS, 1951. Enrolled actuary. Actuarial student Western & Southern, Cin., 1951-54, Mut. of Omaha, 1954-58; v.p., actuary Coastal States Life Ins. Co., Atlanta, 1958-65, Piedmont Life and successor cos., Atlanta, 1965-74; sr. v.p., actuary Booke & Co., Winston-Salem, N.C., 1974-82; pres., founder ACS Group, Winston-Salem, 1982—. Author (textbooks): Partial Termination of Pension Plans, 1980, Self-Funded Health Plans, 1980, Cost Containment of Health Care Plans, 1982; TPA Guide, 1986. Cpl. U.S. Army, 1946-48. Fellow Am. Acad. Actuaries, Soc. Actuaries, Life Office Mgmt. Assn. Office: ACS Actuarial Svcs Inc 8025 N Point Blvd Winston Salem NC 27106-3262

HARKINS, HERBERT PERRIN, otolaryngologist, educator; b. Scranton, Pa., Aug. 13, 1912; s. Percy Stoner and Myra (Perrin) H.; BS, Lafayette Coll., 1934; MD, Hahnemann Med. Coll., 1937; MSc, U. Pa., 1942; m. Anna Catherine Shepler, July 16, 1938; children: Herbert P., Sally Anne, Nancy Shepler. Lectr. otolaryngology Hahnemann Med. Coll., 1939-44, asso. prof., 1944-51, prof. head dept. otolaryngology, 1951; asst. prof. otolaryngology Grad. Sch. Medicine, U. Pa., 1951—; sr. staff otolaryngology Lankenau Hosp. Bd. Studies in Higher Edn. Trustee, Lafayette Coll. Served as comdr. U.S. Navy, 1945-48; Res. Diplomate Am. Bd. Otolaryngology. Fellow ACS, Am. Otorhinol. Soc. Plastic Surgery; mem. Am. Soc. Ophthalmic and Otolaryngologic Allergy (pres.), Am., Pa. acads. ophthalmology and otolaryngology, Coll. Physicians Phila., Phila. Laryngol. Soc., Phila County Med. Soc., AMA, Am. Laryngol., Rhinol. and Otol. Soc. Clubs: Union League, Phila. Country, Bachelors Barge. Contbr. numerous articles on ear, nose and throat to med. jours. Home: 701 Woodleave Rd Bryn Mawr PA 19010-1708

HARKNESS, DONALD RICHARD, hematologist, educator; b. Mitchell, S.D., Aug. 23, 1932; s. Kenneth McKenzie and Marguerite (Sherwood) H.; m. Mary Hideko Nishi, Aug. 22, 1954; children: Laurel Jean, Kenneth Bruce, Susan Marie, Jane Elizabeth. B.A. with highest honors in Zoology, U. Calif.-Berkeley, 1954; M.D. magna cum laude, Washington U., St. Louis, 1958. Med. intern Barnes Hosp.-Washington U., 1958-59, med. resident, 1959-60; research assoc. U.S. Pub. Health Service, NIH, 1960-64; asst. prof. med. faculty U. Miami, Fla., 1964-68, assoc. prof., 1968-73, prof., 1973-80; Love prof. medicine U. Wis., Madison, 1980—, chmn. dept., 1980-93, asst. dean for continuing med. edn. Med. Sch., 1996—; dir. Radiation Effects Rsch. Found., Hiroshima, 1993-95; mem. adv. com. on sickle cell disease NIH, Bethesda, Md., 1974-75; dir. Miami Comprehensive Sickle Cell Ctr., 1973-78; program specialist in hematology VA Central Office, Washington, 1974-77; chmn. bd. Univ. Health Care, Inc., 1983-91. Researcher in hematology; contbr. writing to profl. publs. John and Mary Markle Found. scholar in acad. medicine, 1966-71. Fellow ACP; mem. Am. Soc. Hematology (councilor 1978-81), Am. Soc. Clin. Investigation, Assn. Am. Physicians, Ctrl. Soc. for Clin. Rsch. (councilor 1986-88), Midwest Blood Club (councilor 1981-85), Nat. Blood Club (sec.-treas. 1976-77), So. Blood Club (pres. 1979-80), Alpha Omega Alpha. Republican. Presbyterian. Address: 110 Standish Ct Madison WI 53705 Office: H4 546 Clin Scis Ctr 600 Highland Ave Madison WI 53792

HARKONEN, WESLEY SCOTT, physician; b. Mpls., Dec. 17, 1951; s. Wesley Sulo and Frances (Fedor) H.; m. Barbara Jean Harkonen, Feb. 14, 1986; children: Kirsten, Alan. BA summa cum laude, U. Minn., 1973, MD, 1977. Resident internal medicine U. Minn., Mpls., 1977-81; fellow allergy and immunology U. Calif., San Francisco, 1983-85, fellow clin. pharmacology, 1984-85; project dir. Xoma Corp., Berkeley, Calif., 1983-87; rsch. assoc. Stanford U., 1987-88; assoc. med. dir. Becton Dickinson, Mountain View, Calif., 1988-89; v.p. med. affairs Calif. Biotechnology, Mountain View, Calif., 1989-91; v.p. med. and regulatory affairs Univax Biologics, Rockville, Md., 1991-95; sr. v.p. devel. and ops. Corrective Therapeutics, Palo Alto, Calif., 1995—. Author: Traveling Well, 1984; contbr. articles to profl. jours. J. Thomas Livermore Rsch. award, U. Minn., 1977. Mem. Am. Fedn. for Clin. Rsch. Office: Corrective Therapeutics 3400 W Bayshore Palo Alto CA 94303

HARLE, THOMAS STANLEY, radiologist; b. Detroit, Aug. 17, 1932; s. Edward John and Daisy O'Dell (Bacon) H.; m. Barbara Janette Chrestman, Oct. 15, 1960; children: Blair Thomas, Timothy John. Student, Mich. State U., 1950-53; BS, Northwestern U., 1954; MD, Northwestern U., Chgo., 1957. Diplomate Am. Bd. Radiology (trustee 1987—). Intern Passavant Meml. Hosp., Chgo., 1957-58; radiology resident Brooke Army Med. Ctr., San Antonio, 1958-61, asst. chief radiology, 1964-65; radiologist Ft. Detrick, Frederick, Md., 1961-62, Kelsey Seybold Clinic, Houston, 1965-66; chief of radiology Irwin Army Hosp., Ft. Riley, Kans., 1962-64; asst. prof., then assoc. prof. Baylor Coll. Medicine, Houston, 1966-69; assoc. prof. Duke U. Med. Ctr., Durham, N.C., 1969-71; prof. U. Tex. Med. Sch., Houston, 1975-78, 80-82, chmn. dept. radiology, 1975-78; prof. Mich. State U., East Lansing, 1978-80; prof. U. Tex. M.D. Anderson Cancer Ctr., Houston, 1982—, asst. v.p. acad. affairs, 1982-90, assoc. v.p. acad. affairs, 1990-94. Contbr. articles to profl. jours., chpts. to books. Maj. U.S. Army, 1958-65. Fellow Am. Coll. Radiology; mem. Assn. Univ. Radiologists (pres. 1983-84), Radiol. Soc. N.Am. (pres. 1993), European Assn. Radiologists (hon.), Faculty of Radiologists, Royal Coll. Surgeons in Ireland (hon.), Brit. Inst. Radiology (hon.). Republican. Baptist. Office: MD Anderson Cancer Ctr Dept Radiology 1515 Holcombe Blvd Houston TX 77030-4009

HARLESS, KEITH WESTON, internist, educator; b. Seattle, Apr. 12, 1946; s. Hubert R. and Eda Irene (Tasker) H.; m. Susan Jean Ettinger, Aug. 29, 1970; children: Wendy Eileen, Brian Richard. BS, Lewis and Clark Coll., 1968; MD, U. Oreg. Health Scis. Ctr., 1972. Diplomate Am. Bd. Internal Medicine, Pulmonary Disease, Critical Care Medicine. Intern Dartmouth-Mary Hitchcock Med. Ctr., Hanover, N.H., 1972-73; resident U. Oreg. Health Scis. Ctr., Portland, 1973-75, clin. assoc. prof., 1983—; pulmonary fellowship U. Oreg. Health Scis. Ctr. and Utah Med. Ctr., Salt Lake City, 1975-77; pvt. practice, Bend (Oreg.) Meml. Clinic, Bend, Oreg., 1977—; med. dir. critical care cluster St. Charles Med. Ctr. Contbr. articles to profl jours. Recipient Clean Air award Am. Lung Assn. Oreg., 1985, Dean's award Oreg. Health Scis. U., 1991, Oliver Nisbet award for tchg., 1991. Fellow ACP, Am. Coll. Chest Physicians; mem. AMA, Am. Thoracic Soc., North Pacific Soc. Internal Medicine, Soc. Critical Care Medicine, Alpha Omega Alpha. Office: Bend Meml Clinic 1501 NE Med Ctr Dr Bend OR 97701

HARLOW, EDWARD E., JR., oncologist. Recipient Alfred P. Sloan, Jr. medal GM Cancer Rsch. Found., 1995. Office: Mass Gen Hosp Cancer Ctr Lab Molecular Oncology Bldg 149 13th St Mailcode 1497330 Boston MA 02129*

HARLOW, STEPHEN RAY, consulting company executive; b. Waco, Tex., July 26, 1950; s. Raymond Francis and Mary Mozelle (Cotten) H.; m. Carolyn J. Snapka; children: Joy C., Jana T. BS in Microbiology, Baylor U., 1972; degree in health care adminstrn., Trinity U., 1981; BS in Med. Tech., Edison State Coll., 1983; MS in Human Rels. and Bus., Amber U., 1986. Lab. dir., asst. adminstr. East Town Hosp., Dallas, 1979-82; adminstr., lab. dir. Cigna Health Plan of Tex., Dallas, 1984-89; quality assurance/safety dir. Smith Kline Beechan Clin. Lab., Dallas, 1988-93; v.p., dir. med. design and engring. C-Power Cos., Rockwall, Tex., 1993-95; mng. dir., CEO Call-Tex. Svcs., Rockwall, 1982—; assoc. instr. microbiology, hematology, med. tech. El Centro C.C., Dallas, 1979-81; cons., mem. adv. bd. Smith Kline Beechan, Phila., 1989-92, Underwriters Lab., Northbrook, Ill., 1992—, Can. Stds. Assn., Toronto, 1992—, Automated Merchandising Health Industry Coun., Chgo., 1992—. Author: Biosafety in the Clinical Lab, 1991, Chemical Safety in the Clinical Lab, 1991; inventor SAFEVAC Blood Dropper System. Organizer Waco (Tex.) Sports Car Club, 1972, Rip Roaring Mesquite (Tex.) Balloon Open- Hot Air Balloon Festival, 1986. Mem. Clin. Lab. Mgrs. Assn., KC. Office: Call-Tex Svcs Box 1496 Rockwall TX 75087

HARLOWE, MICHAEL LOUIS, health services administrator; b. Louisville, Aug. 23, 1964; s. Stuart E. and Betty L. (Bundenthal) H. BA, Hanover Coll., 1986; MSW, U. Kans., 1988; MHA, Ind. U., 1993. ACSW; diplomate ACHE. Vice pres. profl. and support svcs. Good Samaritan Hosp., Vincennes, Ind. Bd. mem. Knox County United Fund, Vincennes, 1994—, United Way of Ind., Indpls., 1994—; chmn. Knox County Step Ahead-Health and Nutrition Coun., Vincennes, 1995—. Mem. Civitan Internat. (bd. mem., sec. 1993-95). Home: 1607 N 13th St Vincennes IN 47591 Office: Good Samaritan Hosp 520 S 7th St Vincennes IN 47591

HARŁOZIŃSKA, ANTONINA URSZULA, immunooncologist; b. Opoczno, Poland, May 7, 1939; d. Edward and Lucyna (Zaremba) Szczytowski; m. Jan Harłoziński, Dec. 26, 1960 (div. 1972); m. Janusz Jan Szmyrka, Oct. 23, 1976. MSc, U. Lódź, Poland, 1961; PhD, Inst. Immunology and Exptl. Therapy, Wrocław, Poland, 1969; DSc, U. Medicine, Wrocław, Poland, 1978. Asst. Inst. Immunology and Exptl. Therapy, Wrocław, 1962-73; asst. prof. U. Medicine, Wrocław, 1973-78, assoc. prof., 1978-88, prof. medicine, 1988—, head dept. tumor immunology, 1989—, vice dean med. faculty, 1984-90. Contbr. over 200 articles to profl. jours. including Jour. Nat. Cancer Inst., Am. Jour. Clin. Pathology, Blut, Anticancer Rsch., Exptl. Molecular Pathology, Acta Cytologica, European Jour. Surg. Oncology, Jour. Tumor Marker Oncology, Tumor Biology, Endocrine-Related Cancer, others. Recipient Sci. award Ministry of Health, Poland, 1976, 82, 89, 91, 93, Pres. of U. Medicine, 1979, 80, 82, 83, 85, 87, 88, 89, 90, 91. Mem. Polish Immunol. Soc., Polish Pathol. Soc., Polish Med. Soc., Polish Oncol. Soc., Wroctaw Sci. Soc., Polish Acad. Sci. (immunol. com. 1984—, tumor biology commn. cell pathophysiology com. 1984—), Am. Soc. Cell Biology, Internat. Soc. Oncodevelopmental Biology and Medicine. Office: Wrocław U Medicine Dept Tumor Immunology, Mikulicza-Radeckiego 7, 50-368 Wroclaw Poland

HARMATY, MYRON BOHDAN, emergency physician; b. Reichenberg, Czechoslovakia, Sept. 10, 1945; s. Paul and Maria (Tabaka) H.; m. Margarith Gerlinde, June 20, 1973; children: Marco, Nadija, Steve. BA in Biology, Seton Hall U., 1967; MD, Ludwig Maxmillian Univ., Munich, West Germany, 1973. Diplomate Am. Bd. Emergency Medicine, Am. Bd. Internal Medicine. Edn. physician Overlook Hosp.; internship Unite Hosp. Presbyterian, Newark, N.J., 1975; resident Overloor Hosp., Summit, N.Y., 1979-80; physician Somerser Med. Family Practices, Sommerville, N.Y., 1980-85, Chilton Meml. Hosp., Pompton Plains, N.J., 1985-87, St. Vincent Med. Ctr., Straten Island, N.Y., 1987-88; asst. dir. Cape Fear Valley Hosp., Fayetteville, N.C., 1988-89; physician Monmouth Med. Ctr., Long Branch, N.Y., 1990; asst. dir. Gaston Meml. Hosp., Gaston, N.C., 1990—; clin. instr. Family Practice Rutgers Med. Sch., Piscataway, N.Y., 1982. Republican. Roman Catholic. Office: Cleveland Meml Hosp PO Box 1747 201 Grove St Shelby NC 28053

HARMATZ, MORTON GERALD, psychology educator; b. N.Y.C., Mar. 25, 1939; s. Harry J. and Louise (Hershenfeld) H.; m. Lynne Deckered, Dec. 20, 1969 (div. 1982); 1 child, Mark D.; m. Robin Lynes, June 21, 1992. BA, Ohio State U., 1960; MS, U. Wash., 1962, PhD, 1963. Lic. Clin. psychologist, Mass. Asst. prof. U. Mass., Amherst, 1964-71; assoc. prof. U. Mass., 1971-77, full prof., 1977—; cons. Westfield (Mass.) Community Support Svcs., 1975—, Sprinfield (Mass.) Human Mental Health Assn., 1986—. Author: Abnormal Psychology, 1978, Human Sexuality, 1983; contbr. articles to publs. Fellow Am. Psychopathological Assn.; mem. Am. Psychol. Assn. Office: U Mass Psychology Dept Tobin Hall Amherst MA 01003

HARMEL, MEREL HILBER, anesthesiologist, educator; b. Cleve., May 19, 1917; s. Louis and Hermine (Greenbaum) H.; m. Armide Chilcoat, July 2, 1944 (dec. 1988); children: Nancy Armide, Ruth Courtney, Priscilla Gover, Mary Louise; m. Ernestine Friedl Levy, Dec. 27, 1990.. BA, Johns Hopkins U., 1938, MD, 1943. Diplomate Am. Bd. Anesthesiology. Fellow in anesthesiology NRC; anesthesiologist-in-chief Albany Med. Ctr., 1948-52; anesthesiologist-in-chief Kings County Med. Ctr., Bklyn., 1952-68, pres. med. bd., 1958-62, chmn. exec. com., 1964-65; cons. L.I. Jewish, St. Albans Naval, Maimonides, St. John's Episcopal, VA hosps., N.C. Eye and Ear Hosp., Durham; assoc. prof. anesthesiology (surgery) Albany Med. Coll., 1948-52; prof., chmn. dept. anesthesiology SUNY Downstate Med. Ctr., 1952-68, Pritzker Sch. Medicine, U. Chgo., 1968-71; prof. anesthesiology Duke Med. Ctr., Durham, N.C., 1971—, chmn. dept. anesthesiology ctr., 1971-83; prof. anesthesiology Duke Med. Center, 1983-87, prof. Emeritus, 1987—; vis. prof. dept. anesthesiology Sch. Medicine, Johns Hopkins U., 1985—. Contbr. articles to profl. jours. Commonwealth fellow Oxford U., 1961-62, hon. mem. Sr. Common Rm., Pembroke Coll., 1961; Merel Harmel vis. lectureship established Duke U. Med. Ctr., 1983. Fellow Am. Coll. Anesthesiology (bd. govs.), Royal Coll. Anaesthesia Faculty; mem. AMA, Am. Soc. Anesthesiologists (Living History Series), Assn. Univ. Anesthetists, Duke U. Med. Ctr. Founders Soc., Johns Hopkins U. Soc. Scholars, Japan Soc. Anesthesiologists (hon.), Assn. Anesthesiologists Français (hon.), Oxford Soc. Carolinas (hon. sec. 1990—). Office: Duke U Med Ctr Dept Anesthesiology PO Box 3094 Durham NC 27710

HARMER, CATHERINE MARY, psychologist, nun; b. Phila., Sept. 6, 1932; d. John Thomas and Frances Regina (Keogh) H. BA in Philosophy, Chestnut Hill Coll., 1957; MSLS, Cath. U. Am., 1962; MA in Psychology, Temple U., 1970, PhD in Psychology, 1973. Joined Med. Mission Sisters, Roman Cath. Ch., 1950. Libr. Med. Mission Sisters, Phila., 1957-62, instr., 1959-62; libr., instr. Med. Mission Sisters, Lipa City, 1963-65, Holy Family Hosp., Rawalpind, Pakistan, 1965-68; sector superior Med. Mission Sisters, Phila., 1976-82, renewal dir., 1988—; bd. dirs. Med. Mission Sisters, Phila., Rome, London, 1976-82; psychologist Mgmt. Design Inc., Cin., 1972-82; pvt. practice psychology Phila., 1982—; mem. program com., region III Leadership Conf. Women Religious, Phila., 1976-82; bd. dirs. Nat. Coun. Chs., N.Y.C., 1976-82, Fedn. Returned Missionaries Overseas, Detroit, 1990-95. Author: Books for Religious Sisters, 1964, Religious Life in the 21st Century, 1995; contbr. articles to profl. jours. NDEA Title IV fellow Temple U., Phila., 1971-73. Mem. LWV, APA, U.S. Cath. Mission Assn. (founding), Assn. Humanistic Psychology, Network, Assn. Psychol. Type, Delta Epsilon Sigma, Phi Beta Mu. Democrat. Home: 300 W Wellens St Philadelphia PA 19120-3333 Office: Med Mission Sisters 300 W Wellens St Philadelphia PA 19120

HARMON, DAVID EUGENE, optometrist, geneticist; b. Greeneville, Tenn., July 27, 1951; s. Carl Eugene and Kathryn Elizabeth (Colyer) H.; m. Kimberly Denise Brooks. BS, U. Tenn., 1973, MS, 1975; PhD, U. Ga., 1978; OD, New Eng. Coll. Optometry, 1989. Fellow U. Ga., Athens, 1978, U. Fla., Gainesville, 1979; vis. asst. prof. So. Ill. U., Carbondale, 1980-82; asst. prof. Clemson (S.C.) U., 1982-85, assoc. prof., 1985; internist VA Hosp., Boston, 1988, Children's Hosp., Boston, 1988-89, Dimock Community Health Ctr., Boston, 1989; eye specialist Morristown, Tenn., 1989—; geneticist Morristown, 1989—; genetic cons. Nigerian Govt., 1980—. Contbr. articles to profl. jours. Mem. Sunday sch. Trinity United Meth. Ch., Greeneville, 1954—; sch. rep. New Eng. Coll. Optometry, 1987. Recipient Breeder Al-Am. Dairy Animal award Am. Guernsey Cattle Club, 1973. Mem. Am. Optometric Assn., Am. Dairy Assn., Am. Soc. Animal Sci., Tenn. Optometric Assn., So. Coun. of Optometrists, Holstein Assn. Am., Sigma Xi, Alpha Zeta. Home and Office: 131 N Henry St Morristown TN 37814

HARMON, DAVID LYNN, psychiatrist; b. Harvey, Ill., May 16, 1958; s. Lawrence and Marlene Kay (O'Dell) H. BA, U. Mo., 1984; DO, U. Health Scis., 1989. Intern U. Kans. Med. Ctr., Kansas City, 1989-90; resident in adult psychiatry Kans. Med. Ctr., Kansas City, 1990-92, resident in child psychiatry, 1992-94; locum tenens physician, 1994-95; staff physician Valley Hosp., Owensboro, Ky., 1995—; clin. dir. child and adolescent svcs. Green River Regional Mental Health/Mental Retardation Bd., Owensboro, 1996—. With Kans. Army Nat. Guard, 1987-95. Mem. APA, AMA, Ky. Med. Assn., Am. Coll. Family Practitioners, Ky. Psychiat. Assn. (joint coord. com. ea. Ky. 1989-94). Home: 4125 Horseshoe Trce Owensboro KY 42303-4514

HARMON, JANE ELLEN, occupational therapist, writer; b. Muskegon, Mich.; d. Robert Junior and Edith (Boven) H. BS in Occupational Therapy, Western Mich. U., 1974; postgrad., Cleve., 1977. Registered occupational therapist; licensed occupational therapist, Tex.; cert. CPR/BCLS instr.-trainer. From vol. to staff therapist Hackley Hosp., Muskegon, 1972-75; head occupational therapy dept. Mercy Hosp., Muskegon, 1975-79; pvt. practice, 1976-79; with Mary Free Bed Hosp. & Rehab. Ctr., Grand Rapids, 1979; free-lance writer, 1979—; cons. Tri-City Health Ctr./Hosp., Dallas, 1993. Author: At Home with MS, 1996; contbg. writer Inside MS, 1996; contbr. articles to profl. jours.; contbg. editor, cons. Occupational Therapy Forum, 1993—. Active Arthritis Vol. Action Com., 1975-79; founder Vols. Against Multiple Sclerosis Mich. chpt. Nat. Multiple Sclerosis Soc., 1973 (recipient Individual Vol. of the Yr. award, 1994), co-chair Govtl. Rels. Com., mem. profl. adv. com. North Tex. chpt., mem. patient svc. com., MS Tex. CAN, 1996—; mem. HIV/AIDS Com. Bethel Ch., Dallas, 1992—, prayer chain coord., 1990-96, editor Bethel News, 1989-90; editor, cage bird cons. pet-facilitated therapy program Baylor Inst. for Rehab., Dallas, 1992-93; founder, dir. Project HAVEN Dallas Cage Bird Soc., 1991-93; vol. Dallas Ctr. for Ind. Living, 1990—; liaison Classis Pella Com. on Disability Concerns; founder, dir. Ecology Ministries, 1987—; rep. com. disability concerns Classis Pella, Christian Reformed Ch. N.Am., 1994—; mem. Nat. Svcs. Adv. Coun. Nat. Multiple Sclerosis Soc., 1996—; bd. dirs. Northeast Tex. chpt. Am. Parkinson Disease Assn., 1996—; mem. Greater Dallas/Ft. Worth chpt. Myasthenia Gravis Found., 1994—; mem. Dallas County CLASS adv. bd., 1996—; resource person MS & Degenerative Neurol. Diseases, 1991—. Mem. Tex. Occupational Therapy Assn., Environ. Health Assn. Dallas, Am. Occupational Therapy Assn., Write Shop Writer's Assn. Office: 14232 Marsh Ln Ste 320 Dallas TX 75234-3865

HARMON, JOHN WATSON, surgeon, educator; b. White Plains, N.Y., Apr. 22, 1943; m. Gail McGreevy; children: James Milton, Eve Page. BA, Harvard U., 1965; MD, Columbia U., 1969. Diplomate Am. Bd. Surgery (examiner 1990), Am. Bd. Surg. Critical Care. Intern, then resident in surgery Harvard surg. svc. Boston City Hosp. and New Eng. Deaconess Hosps., 1969-75; Harvard rsch. fellow in surg. gastroenterology Beth Israel Hosp., Boston, 1972; fellow in gastrointestinal and endocrine surgery Lahey Clinic, Boston, 1973; surg. investigator Walter Reed Army Inst. Rsch., Washington, 1975-85, dir. div. surgery, 1983-85; staff surgeon Walter Reed Med. Ctr., Washington, 1977-85; chief surgery VA Med. Ctr., Washington, 1985-96; prof. surgery Georgetown U., Washington, 1985-96, George Washington U., Washington, 1985-96; prof. surgery, vice chmn. dept. surgery Johns Hopkins Med. Sch., Balt., 1996—; chmn. sect. surg. scis. Hopkins Bayview Hosp., 1996—; asst. prof. Uniformed Svcs. U. Health Scis., Bethesda, Md., 1978-89, assoc. prof., 1979-85, prof., 1985; clin. prof. Howard U., Washington, 1985—; mem. surgery and bioengring. study sect. NIH, Army liaison, 1983-87, ad hoc mem., 1987, chmn. study section, 1991; ad hoc mem. surgery merit rev. bd. VA,1992, program specialist study sect., 1994-97; mem. panel VIII physics and medicine of wound ballistics and casualty care NATO, 1983-86; mem. task force on clin. rsch. in surgy Inst. Medicine, 1992. Contbr. over 200 articles to med. jours. Col. M.C., USAR, 1987—. Recipient ann. award for excellence in clin. rsch. in gastroenterology William Beaumont Soc., 1982, 1st prize for surg. rsch. fellow Washington Acad. Surgery, 1984. Mem. ACS, Shock Soc (program com. 1978-79), Soc. Univ. Surgeons (rep. to Am. Assn. Med. Colls. 1982-85), Assn. for Acad. Surgery (nominating com. 1982-84), Soc. for Surgery Alimentary Tract (membership com. 1984-87, pub. policy com. 1990—, nominating com. 1993-96), Assn. VA Surgeons (local arrangements chmn. 1986), Am. Fedn. for Clin. Rsch., Assn. Mil. Surgeons U.S., Collegium Internat. Chirurgiae Digestivae, Internat. Soc. Surgery, Am. Physiol. Soc., Pancreas Club, Am. Assn. Endocrine Surgeons, Assn. Program Dirs. in Surgery (assoc.), Am. Surg. Assn., Surg. Biology Club III, Chesapeake Vascular Soc., Cosmos Club (admissions com. 1994-97), Alpha Omega Alpha. Office: VA Med Ctr 50 Irving St NW Washington DC 20422-0001

HARMON, KEITH HANNA, pediatrician; b. Dallas, May 18, 1952; s. Fred Ingersoll and Marjorie Elfreda (Hanna) H.; m. Bonnie Gail Figer, July 10, 1976; children: Laura Dianne, Shannon Elise, Shelby Leigh. B Engring. Sci., U. Tex., 1974; MD, U. Tex., Dallas, 1978. Diplomate Am. Bd. Pediatrics. Intern then resident Children's Med. Ctr., Dallas, 1978-81; pvt. practice Arlington, Tex., 1981—; chmn. neonatal subcom. Arlington Meml. Hosp., 1984-86, vice-chmn. dept. pediat., 1988-90, chmn. pediat. peer rev., 1988-90, chmn. dept. pediat., 1990-92; bd. dirs. Physician Svcs. Orgn. of Arlington, 1992-96, Arlington Physician Group, 1995-96. Fellow Am. Acad. Pediatrics; mem. Mem. Arlington Pediatric Assn., Tex. Pediatric Assn., Tex. Med. Assn. Republican. Office: Arlington Physicians Group 950 N Davis Dr Ste 4 Arlington TX 76012-3247

HARMON BROWN, VALARIE JEAN, hospital laboratory director, information systems executive; b. Peoria, Ill., June 21, 1948; d. Donald Joseph and Frances Elizabeth (Classen) Harmon; m. James Roger Brown, Aug. 21, 1982 (dec. May 1994). BSMT, Northwestern U., Chgo., 1970. Med. tech. Evanston (Ill.) Hosp., 1970-71, chief tech., 1971-75; med. tech. II M.D. Anderson Hosp., Houston, 1975-76; dir. lab. Physicians Ref. Lab., Houston, 1978-81, Med. Ctr. Hosp., Conroe, Tex., 1981-91, Palo Pinto Gen. Hosp., Mineral Wells, Tex., 1993-94; sales mgr. Long Beach (Calif.) Meml. Med. Ctr., 1995-96; quality assurance/regulatory affairs mgr. Consol. Med. Labs., Lake Bluff, Ill., 1996—; lab. cons. Texaco Chem. Wellness Program, Conroe, 1989; health career sponsor Willis Ind. Sch. Dist., Tex., 1989, 90; mem. adv. bd. Med. Lab. Technician program Weatherford Coll., 1994. Coord. blood drive Gulf Coast Region Blood Ctr., 1986-91; sponsor colon cancer screening Montgomery County Health Fair, 1986; sponsor Camp Sunshine/Lions Club, 1988; sponsor cholesterol screening Med. Ctr. Hosp. Health Fair, 1989. Mem. NAFE, Am. Soc. Clin. Pathologists, Am. Soc. Med. Technologists, Clin. Lab. Mgmt. Assn. Republican. Roman Catholic. Home 1050 E Martingale Ln Round Lake Beach IL 60073 Office: Consol Med Labs Ste 1200 101 Waukegan Rd Lake Bluff IL 60044-1669

HARMS, DEAN MASON, ophthalmologist; b. Alden, Iowa, Oct. 25, 1942; s. Rudolph J. and Hyla A. (Severson) H.; m. Mary Jane Brinkman, June 11, 1966; children: Philip, Sarah, Mark. BS, Iowa State U., 1965; MD, U. Iowa, 1969. Resident Med. coll. Wis., Milw., 1975; ophthalmologist Iowa Eye Care Physicians, Ames, 1975—. Mem. AMA, Am. Acad. Ophthalmology, Iowa Med. Assn., Iowa Acad. Ophthalmology (pres. 1988-89), Story County Med. Assn. (pres. 1987-88). Office: Iowa Eye Care Physicians 1114 Duff Ave Ames IA 50010

HARMS, DEBORAH GAYLE, psychologist; b. Ft. Worth; d. Raymond O. Smith and Billie (Allen) Greenwade; m. Joel Randall Harms; children: J. Christopher, Ryan R., Catherine R. BA with honors with high distinction, Wayne State U., 1977; MA in Clin. Psychology, U. Detroit, 1979, PhD in Clin. Psychology, 1984. Lic. psychologist. Trainee in psychology Henry Ford Hosp., Troy, Mich., 1978-79; intern in psychology Detroit Psychiat. Inst., 1979-82; staff psychologist Eastwood Clinic, Harper Woods, Mich., 1983-86; pvt. practice Harms and Harms, PC, Birmingham, Mich., 1985—; staff psychologist Dominican Consultation Ctr., Detroit, 1986-89; sr. psychologist Oakland County Probate Ct., Pontiac, Mich., 1990. Teaching fellow U. Detroit, 1978-79. Mem. APA, Nat. Register Health Care Providers in Psychology, Mich. Psychol. Assn., Mich. Women Psychologists, Mensa, Phi Beta Kappa. Home: 21783 Corsaut Ln Beverly Hills MI 48025-2607 Office: Harms and Harms PC 199 W Brown St Birmingham MI 48009

HARNED, ROGER KENT, radiology educator; b. Madison, Wis., June 19, 1934; s. Lewis Boyer and Ermil Amelia (Caldwell) H.; m. Jacquelyn Sue Heal, Aug. 29, 1959; children: Roger Kent II, Jennifer Marie. BS, U. Wis., 1956; MD, U. Va., 1961. Am. Bd. Radiology. Intern Milw. County Gen. Hosp., 1961-62; resident in radiology Deaconess Hosp., Milw. Children's Hosps., 1964-67; instr. dept. radiology Sch. Medicine U. Va., Charlottesville, 1967-68; from asst. to assoc. prof. radiology Sch. Medicine U. Nebr., Omaha, 1969-79, prof. radiology, 1979-96, prof. emeritus, 1996—; cons. physician Omaha Vets. Hosp., 1969—; grad. faculty U. Nebr., Omaha, 1972—; peer rev. various med. jours. Contbr. articles on gastrointestinal radiology to profl. jours. Fellow Am. Coll. Radiology (emeritus, Armed Forces Inst. Pathology disting. scientist 1987-88); mem. Radiol. Soc. N.Am., Nebr. Radiol. Soc. (pres. 1982-83), Soc. Gastrointestinal Radiologists (pres. 1987-88). Presbyterian. Home: 12624 Martha St Omaha NE 68144-2626 Office: U Nebr Med Ctr Dept Radiology 600 S 42nd St Omaha NE 68105-1002

HARNER, LINDA JEANE, allied health educator; b. Alton, Ill., Mar. 22, 1952; d. LeRoy Homer and Jeane (Garrett) Campbell; children: Mary Jeane, Barbara Jo. BSN, St. Louis U., 1974, MS in Nursing of Children, 1976; EdD, So. Ill. U., 1993. RN, Ill., Mo. Staff nurse St. Louis Children's Hosp., 1973-75; faculty allied health Lewis and Clark C.C., Godfrey, Ill., 1976-87, coord. assoc. deg. nursing program, 1987—. Pres. Am. Lung Assn. of Ill., Springfield, 1994-95. Mem. Coun. of Deans and Dirs. of Assoc. Deg. Nursing Programs (chair 1990-92), Nat. League for Nursing, Order Ea. Star, Sigma Theta Tau, Kappa Delta Pi. Presbyterian. Home: 711 Riverview Dr Alton IL 62002-6025 Office: Lewis & Clark C C 5800 Godfrey Rd Godfrey IL 62035-2426

HARNER, STEPHEN GLEN, otolaryngologist; b. Winston-Salem, N.C., Aug. 21, 1940; s. Casper Glendon and Wanda Rae (Carmichael) H.; m. Carla June Kelly, Aug. 24, 1963; children: Kelly Ann, Jeffrey Glenn. AB, Washington U., St. Louis, 1962; MD, U. Mo., 1965. Cert. Bd. Otolaryngology, 1971. Commd. 2d lt. U.S. Army, 1964, advanced through grades to maj.; intern Brooke Army Hosp., San Antonio, 1965-66; resident in surgery Reynolds Army Hosp., Ft. Sill, Okla., 1966-67; resident in otolaryngology Fitzsimons Army Hosp., Denver, 1968-70; asst. chief otolaryngology Letterman Army Hosp., San Francisco, 1970-73; resigned U.S. Army, 1973; staff otolaryngologist Mayo Clinic, Rochester, Minn., 1973—; prof. otolaryngology Mayo Med. Sch., 1994—. Contbr. articles to profl. jours. Bd. dirs. Hiawatha Homes, Rochester, 1980—, sec., 1986-87, v.p., 1989, pres., 1990-92; mem. Gov.'s Coun. Devel. Disability, 1993-96. Named Tchr. of Yr., Mayo Fellow's Assn., 1979, 84, 86. Fellow ACS, Am. Acad. Otolaryngology, Am. Otologic Rhinologic & Laryngologic, Am. Otologic Soc.; mem. AMA, Minn. Med. Assn., Zumbro Valley Med. Assn., Soc. Univ. Otolaryngologists, Am. Neurotology Soc., Acoustic Neuroma Assn. (med. adv. bd.). Lutheran. Office: Mayo Clinic 200 1st St SW Rochester MN 55905-0001

HARPER, ALYCE LYNNE, microbiologist; b. Laconia, N.H. June 2, 1954; d. Nelson Lorie and Nyleen Marion (Cochrane) H. AS, SUNY, Albany, 1977, BS, 1983; BS, Franklin Pierce Coll., 1986. Cert. lab. technologist, med. technologist. Lab. trainee Concord (N.H.) Hosp., 1972-74; lab. technician Damon Med. Labs., Needham, Mass., 1974-75, Med. Assocs. Profl. Assn., Nashua, N.H., 1976-77; floating technician New Eng. Clin. Labs., Tilton, N.H., 1976-77; lab. scientist Profl. Assocs. of Sanford, Maine, 1977-80; med. lab. technician North Country Hosp., Newport, Vt., 1980-81; Baylor weekend lab. supr. Speare Meml. Hosp., Plymouth, N.H., 1981-84; tech. supr. clin. microbiology Pub. Health Labs. N.H. Divsn. Pub. Health Svcs., Concord, 1984—; cons. infection control com. N.H. Hosp., Concord, 1984-95. Editor newsletter N.H. Pub. Health Labs. Lab. Communicator, 1984-95. Vol. counselor Domestic Violence Rape Crisis Ctr., Boston, 1975; mem., vol. Capitol Ctr. for the Arts, Concord, 1995—, Nat. Abortion and Reproductive Rights Action League, Concord, 1987—. Mem. AAUW, Am. Soc. Clin. Lab. Scientists, Am. Med. Technologists (state sec. 1979-80), Am. Soc. Clin. Pathologists (assoc.), Order of Ea. Star. Office: NH Dept Health & Human Svcs Divsn Pub Health Svcs Lab 6 Hazen Dr Concord NH 03301

HARPER, CLIO ARMITAGE, III, ophthalmologist; b. Nashville, Sept. 8, 1961; s. Clio Armitage And Carole Yvonne (Schlich) H.; 1 child, Clio Armitage IV; m. Ruth A. Frye, Dec. 31, 1988; 1 child, Holly Catherine. BA, Vandebilt U., 1983; MD, U. Okla., 1988. Intern in internal medicine La. State U., New Orleans, 1988-89; resident in ophthalmology La. State U. Eye Ctr., New Orleans, 1989-92, chief resident, 1992-93; retina and vitreous fellow Casey Eye Inst. Oreg. Health Scis. U., Portland, 1993-95; rep. Physician's Roundtable, 1985-86, dean's adv. com. U. Okla., 1986-87, pres. Class of '88, 1986, 87, sec. treas. U. Okla.-Tulsa Med. Sch., 1986, rep. student exec. coun., 1986, coord. patient contact rotation, 1986, 87, "Rsch. Forum, 1987, 88; rep. residents' coun. La. State U. Eye Ctr., 1989-90, sec. residents; v.p. La. State U. dean's adv. coun., 1992-93. Contbr. articles to profl. jours. Recipient Glass-Nelson scholarship U. Okla., 1987. Fellow Am. Acad. Ophthalmology; mem. AMA, Oreg. Med. Assn., Oreg. Acad. Ophthalmology, Assn. for Rsch. in Vision and Ophthalmology.

HARPER, JAMES R., cardiologist; b. Kinston, N.C., Aug. 23, 1934; s. James H. and Emma Sloan (Robinson) H.; m. Ferrell Ann Curtis, Aug. 4, 1956; children: James R., Elizabeth Sloan. BA, U. N.C., 1956, MD, 1960. Diplomate Am. Bd. Internal Medicine. Intern, resident U. Fla., Gainesville, 1960-61; served in USPHS, Nashville, 1961-63; fellow in cardiology, resident U. N.C., Chapel Hill, 1964-65; fellow in cardiology Duke U., Durham, N.C., 1966-67; pvt. practice cardiology Chapel Hill, 1967-91; clin. prof. cardiology U. N.C., 1991—; bd. dirs. Nations Bank, Chapel Hill; med. dir. Orange Cardiovasc. Found., 1978-91. Fellow Am. Coll. Cardiology, Am. Coll. Physicians, Coun. Clin. Cardiology; mem. Phi Beta Kappa, Alpha Omega Alpha. Methodist. Office: U NC Divsn Cardiology CB#7075 Burnett-Womack Chapel Hill NC 27599-7075

HARPER, JEWEL BENTON, pharmacist; b. Springfield, Tenn., Nov. 14, 1925; s. William Henry and Violet Irene (Benton) H.; m. Josephine Cook, Feb. 12, 1953; children: Pamela Jewel, Karen Jo. BS, Austin Peay State U., 1948, BS, Samford U., 1950, Command and Gen. Staff Officer Course diploma U.S. Army Command and Gen. Staff Coll., 1968; cert. pharmacist, Tenn. Pharmacist Battlefield Pharmacy, Nashville, 1950-52, VA Hosp., Nashville, 1952-63, Lexington, Ky., 1963-67, Durham, N.C., 1967-76, Manchester, N.H., 1976-82, Vanderbilt U., Nashville, 1982-86, Nashville Meml. Hosp., 1986-91. Served to col. Med. Service Corps, USAR, 1944-85. Recipient Hosp. Adminstrn. Diploma, Acad. Health Scis., 1970, Nat. Security Mgmt. Diploma, Indsl. Coll. Armed Forces, 1973, Logistics Exec. Devel. Diploma U.S. Army Logistics Mgmt. Ctr., 1977. Mem. Assn. Mil. Surgeons U.S., Am. Pharm. Assn., Am. Soc. Hosp. Pharmacists, Res. Officers Assn. U.S. (pres. chpt. 1962-63, sec. 1970-73, dept. surgeon 1977-82), Assn. of U.S. Army, The Mil. Order of World Wars, The Retired Officers Assn., , Am. Legion, The Gideons Internat., Lambda Chi Alpha, Kappa Psi. Republican. Baptist. Avocations: country music, deep sea fishing, horticulture. Home and Office: 503 Cunniff Ct Goodlettsville TN 37072-3003

HARPER, LILAH MARIE, health science administrator, consultant; b. Tucson, Apr. 9, 1942; d. Riddley D. and Lilah M. (Earley) Jones; m. Kenneth W. Harper, July 7, 1961 (dec. Aug. 1986); children: Dennis W., Alan D., Kevin D., Brian L. BS in Nursing, U. Ariz., 1962, MA, 1974; postgrad., Harvard U. Sch. Pub. Health, 1978, Loma Linda U. RN. Nurse team leader St. Joseph's Hosp., Tucson, 1962-63; sch. nurse Tucson Pub. Sch., 1966, nursing inst., 1966-71; Dir. staff devel. and res. Tucson Med. Ctr., 1975-77, nursing adminstrn., 1977-79; dir. nursing svcs. El Cajon (Calif.) Valley Hosp., 1979-80; asst. adminstr. nursing svcs. Palomar Med. Ctr., Escondido, Calif., 1980-92; pres. Harper cons., 1992—; sr. cons. Anderson Continuing Edn., 1992—; lectr. nursing Pt. Loma Coll., San Diego, 1980-81; mem. Ariz. State Bd. Nursing, 1976-78. Bd. dirs. Boys Choir Soc., Tucson, 1976-79. Recipient TWIN award YWCA, 1987. Mem. Sigma Theta Tau, Pi Lambda Theta. Home: PO Box 2055 Valley Center CA 92082-2055

HARPER, MICHAEL JOHN KENNEDY, obstetrics and gynecology educator; b. London, Feb. 25, 1935; came to U.S., 1964; s. John Kennedy and Helen Malvina (Koeller) H.; m. Marian Wedd, July 23, 1960 (div. Feb. 1982); children: Charlotte G.K. Prather, Tristram J.K., Felicity W.K.; m. Ann Carlene Vandeventer, Feb. 16, 1985; 1 child, Helen H.K. BA in Agr., U. Cambridge, Eng., 1957, MA, 1961, PhD in Reproductive Physiology, 1962, ScD, 1979; post-grad. diploma, U. Reading, Eng., 1958; MBA, U. Tex., San Antonio, 1984. Tech. officer pharm. div. Imperial Chem. Industries Ltd., Cheshire, Eng., 1960-64, 65-66; vis. scientist Worcester Found. for Exptl. Biology, Shrewsbury, Mass., 1964-65; staff scientist Worcester Found. for Exptl. Biology, Shrewsbury, 1966-68, sr. scientist, 1968-72; med. officer Human Reproduction Sect. WHO, Geneva, 1972-75; assoc. prof. U. Tex. Health Sci. Ctr., San Antonio, 1975-81, prof. ob-gyn. and physiology, 1981-93; prof. ob-gyn. and cell biology Baylor Coll. Medicine, Houston, 1993-95; prof. ob-gyn Eastern Va. Med. Sch., Arlington, 1995—, dir. Consortium for Indsl. Collaboration in Contraceptive Rsch./ CONRAD Program, 1995—; lectr. Clark U., 1971; cons. NIH, Bethesda, Md., 1970—, WHO, Geneva, 1974-87, USAID, Arlington, Va., 1988—, Andrew W. Mellon Found., N.Y.C., 1991—; mem. com. on applications of biotechnology to contraceptive rsch. & devel. Inst. Medicine, 1994-95, also others. Author: Birth Control Technologies, 1983, paperback edit., 1985; contbr. numerous articles to profl. jours.; inventor alkene/alkanol derivatives (Tamoxifen), 1963, alkene devivatives, 1985. Recipient Woodman prize, U. of Cambridge, 1956, Agr. Food Products prize, U. Reading, Eng., 1958, Rsch. Career Devel. award, NIH, Bethesda, Md., 1968-72. Fellow Inst. of Biology (Eng.); mem. Soc. for Endocrinology (Eng.), Soc. for Study of Fertility (Eng.), Endocrine Soc., Am. Assn. of Anatomists, Soc. for Study of Reproduction, Soc. for Gynecologic Investigation, Am. Physiol. Soc. Office: Conrad Program E Va Medical Sch 1611 N Kent St Ste 806 Arlington VA 22209

HARPER, ROBERT ALLAN, consulting psychologist; b. Dayton, Ohio, Apr. 25, 1915; s. Earl Paull and Mary (Belden) H.; m. Flora Mie Bridges; children: Robert Belden, John Paull. Student, U. Dayton, 1934-36; B.A., Ohio State U., 1938, M.A., 1939, Ph.D., 1942. Instr. Kent State U., 1942-43; analyst War Manpower Commn., 1943; assoc. prof. Wagner Coll., 1943-45; psychiat. social worker U.S. Army, 1945-46; asst. prof. Ohio State U., 1946-50, dir. marriage counseling clinic, 1949-50; chmn. family life dept., dir. marriage counseling service Merrill-Palmer Inst., Detroit, 1950-53; pvt. practice psychotheraphy Washington. Author: (with John F. Cuber) Problems of American Society, 1948, Marriage, 1949, Psychoanalysis and Psychotherapy: 36 Systems, 1959, (with Albert Ellis) Creative Marriage, 1961, A Guide to Rational Living, 1961, 75, (with Walter R. Stokes) 45 Levels to Sexual Understanding and Enjoyment, 1971, The New Psychotherapies, 1975; Cons. editor: Jour. Sex Edn. and Therapy, Psychotherapy, Jour. Rational-Emotive Therapy, Jour. Contemporary Psychotherapy, Internat. Jour. Family Therapy. Fellow Am. Psychol. Assn. (pres. div. psychotherapy 1978-79, pres. div. cons. psychology 1980-81, pres. div. humanistic psychology 1983-84, exec. bd. div. ind. practice, coun. reps. 1978-84, 90-96), Am. Assn. Marriage Counselors (sec. 1954-58, pres. 1960-62), Nat. Coun. Family Rels. (dir. 1951-55), Am. Acad. Psychotherapists (pres. 1961-63), Am. Group Psychotheraphy Assn., Eastern Psychol. Assn., D.C. Psychol. Assn. (dir. 1982-85); mem. Am. Soc. Psychologists in Pvt. Practice (exec. com.), Soc. Sci. Study Sex, Interam. Soc. Psychologists, Am. Soc. Group Psychotherapy and Psychodrama, Internat. Council Psychologists (exec. bd. 1971-74), N.Y. Acad. Scis., Internat. Soc. Gen. Semantics, Inst. Rational Living (bd.), ACLU, Washington Soc. Clin. Psychologists (exec. com.), Nat. Acads. Practice (treas. 1982-88), Phi Beta Kappa. Club: Cosmos. Home: 4903 Potomac Ave NW Washington DC 20007-1541

HARPER, ROBERT GALE, psychology educator; b. Oakland, Calif., Jan. 1, 1944; s. Lawrence A. and Anna Virginia (McCune) H.; m. Doreen Kotik, Apr. 6, 1985. AB, U. Calif., Berkeley, 1966; PhD, U. Tex., 1971. Instr. pediatrics U. Md. Med. Sch., Balt., 1973-74; asst. prof. psychology U. Oreg. Med. Sch., Portland, 1974-79; assoc. prof. psychology (psychiatry) Baylor Coll. Medicine, Houston, 1979—. Author: Nonverbal Communication, 1978. 1st lt. U.S. Army, 1966-68. Office: Baylor Coll Med Psychiatry 1 Baylor Plz Houston TX 77030-3411

HARPER, SHIRLEY FAY, nutritionist, educator, consultant; b. Auburn, Ky., Apr. 23, 1943; d. Charles Henry and Annabelle (Gregory) Belcher; m. Robert Vance Harper, May 19, 1973; children: Glenda, Debra, Teresa, Suzanna, Cynthia. BS, Western Ky. U., 1966, MS, 1982. Cert. nutritionist and lic. dietitian, Ky. Dir. dietetics Logan County Hosp., Russellville, Ky., 1965-80; cons. Western State Hosp., Hopkinsville, Ky., 1983-84, instnl. dietetic adminstr., 1984-88; dietitian Rivendell Children's Psychiat. Hosp., Bowling Green, Ky., 1988-90; instr. nutrition Western Ky. U., Bowling Green, 1990-92; cons. Auburn (Ky.) Nursing Ctr., 1976-95, Belle Meade Home, Greenville, Ky., 1980—, Brookfield Manor, Hopkinsville, Ky., 1983—, Sparks Nursing Ctr., Central City, Ky., 1983—, Muhlenberg Cmty. Hosp., Greenville, 1989—, Russellville (Ky.) Health Care Manor, 1978-83, 92—, Westlake Cumberland Hosp., Columbia, Ky., 1993—, Franklin-Simpson Meml. Hosp., Franklin, Ky., 1993—; nutrition instr. Madisonville (Ky.) Cmty. Coll., 1995—. Mem. regional bd. dirs. ARC of Ky., Frankfort, 1990-96; vice chair ARC of Logan County, 1992-93, chmn., 1993-96; bd. dirs. Logan County ARC United Way, 1993—; co-chair adv. coun. devel. disabilities Lifeskills, 1992-93, adv. coun. Lifeskills Residential Living Group Home, 1993-96, human rights adv. coun., 1994-96; chair Let's Build our Future Campaign; nutrition del. Citizen Am. Program to USSR, 1990; adv. chair for vocat. edn., Russellville; mem. adv. coun. for home econs. and family living, We. Ky. U., 1990-93; bd. dirs. ARC of Logan County for United Way, 1993—. Recipient Outstanding Svc. award Am. Dietetic Assn. Found., 1993, Outstanding Svc. award Barren River Mental Health-Mental Retardation Bd., 1987, Svc. Appreciation award Logan-Russellville Assn. for Retarded Citizens, 1987, Internat. Woman of Yr. award for contribution to Nutrition and Humanity, Internat. Biographical Assn., 1993-94, World Lifetime Achievement award Am. Biographical Inst., 1995; inaugurated Lifetime Dep. Gov., Am. Biographical Rsch. Bd., 1995, Pres.'s award ARC of Logan County, 1996. Mem. Am. Dietetic Assn., Nat. Nutrition Network, Ky. Dietetic Assn. (pres. Western dist. 1976-77, Outstanding Dietitian award 1984), Bowling Green-Warren County Nutrition Coun., Nat. Ctr. for Nutrition and Dietetics (charter), Ky. Nutrition Coun., Logan County Home Economist Club (sec. 1994-95, v.p. 1995-96, pres. 1996-97), Internat. Biog. Assn., Internat. Platform Assn., Gerontol. Nutritionist, Oncology Nutrition, Diabetes Care and Edn., Dietitians in Nutrition Support, Dietitians in Gen. Clin. Practice, Cons. Dietitians in Health Care, Dietetic Educators of Practice Nutrition, Edn. of Health Profls., Nutrition Rsch. and Nutrition Edn. for Pub. Practice Groups, Phi Upsilon Omicron (pres. Beta Delta alumni chpt. 1994-96). Home and Office: 443 Hopkinsville Rd Russellville KY 42276-1286

HARPER, WILLIAM THOMAS, III, psychologist, educator; b. Newport News, Va., Sept. 10, 1956; s. William Thomas Jr. and Queen Vastie (Wilson) H. BS in Psychology, Va. State U., 1978, MEd in Counseling, 1980; cert. in teaching, Coll. William and Mary, 1987; postgrad., Old Dominion U., 1990—. Cert. tchr., Va. Edn. specialist, counselor U.S. Army, Arlington, Va., 1984-85; counselor Hampton (Va.) U., 1980-82, asst. supr. testing, dir. student support svcs., 1982-88; asst. to prin., home sch. coord. Hampton City Schs., 1988-89; dir. transition programs Norfolk (Va.) State U., 1989—; v.p. devel. AmChest Diversified Inc., Hampton, 1990—; crisis counselor Va. State U., Petersburg, 1978-80; counselor ManPower Tng. Svcs., Newport News, Va., 1980; rsch. assoc. Ea. Va. Med. Sch.-The Med. Coll. of Hampton Roads, Norfolk, Va.; rsch assoc. Health Promotions 1st Med. Group, USAF, Langley AFB, Hampton, Va.; exec. v.p. rsch. grants and devel. Lott Cary Hist. Found. Inc.; rsch. bd. advisors Am. Biog. Inst.; mental health technician, counselor Vets. Adminstrn. Med. Ctr., Hampton, Va.; tchr. Christopher Newport U. Excel Program. Spl. Olympic vol. Sarah Boswell Hudgins Regional Ctr., Hampton, 1983—; advisor Psi Chi Nat. Honor Soc., Hampton, 1986; v.p. rsch., grants and devel. Lott Cary Hist. Soc. Exec. Bd.; v.p. r&d The Lott Cary Hist. Found. Recipient Disting. Svc. award peer counselors Hampton U., 1982, U.S. Army Svc. award, 1985, Va. Coll. Pers. Assn. award, 1981, 85, Community Svc. award Kappa Alpha Psi, 1986, Edn. Achievement award, 1986, Va. State U. Alumni award, 1985, Historically Black Coll. Program Counselor Achievement award, 1985, Psi Chi Honor Soc. Achievement award, 1986, Leadership Devel. Tng. Achievement award Howard U., 1983, 85, 86, Hampton VA Med. Ctr. award, 1990, 91, Nat. Black Male Conf. Achievement award, 1990, 91, Black Am. Doctoral Rsch. award, 1991-92, Recognition awards Christopher Newport Coll., 1985-86, Boys Club of Greater Hampton Roads, 1987, 88, 89, 90, City of Alexandria Dept. Human Svcs., 1987, 88, Fraternal Order Police Hampton, Mayor of City of Newport News, 1990, 91, Bd. Govs. Coll. of William and Mary/Internat. Platform Assn., 1990, 4th Nat. Black Student Leadership Devel. 1990-91, Va. Alcohol Safety Action Program, 1990, 91, Commonwealth of Va. Ho. of Dels., 1991, others; Old Dominion U. grad. scholar, 1983, 85, Hampton U. Mobile Oil scholar, 1985. Mem. AACD, Nat. Assn. Black Psychologist, Nat. Assn. Alcoholism & Drug Abuse Counselors, Va. Assn. Alcoholism & Drug Abuse Counselors, Va. Assn. Adminstrs. in Higher Edn., Va. Assn. Black Psychologists (chmn. com.), Va. Assn. Black Psychologists, Peninsula Literacy Coun. (counselor), Internat. Platform Assn. (bd. govs. 1990), Kappa Alpha Psi. Democrat. Baptist. Home: 1042 44th St Newport News VA 23607-2313 Office: Norfolk State U 2401 Corprew Ave Norfolk VA 23504-3907

HARRELL, ALVIN C., law educator; b. 1948. BS, Oklahoma City U., 1967, JD, 1972, MBA, 1978; LLM, So. Meth. U., 1982. Prof. law Oklahome City U. Sch. Law, 1972—; pres., chmn. Home Savings & Loan Assn. Oklay., 1980—; exec. dir. Conf. on Consumer Fin. Law, 1993—; of counsel Pringle & Pringle, Oklahoma City; co-chair So. Meth. U. Banking Law Inst.. Editor Consumer Fin. Law Quar. Report, 1987—. Mem. ABA (sec. bus. law, chair task force on oil and gas financing UCC com. 1991—, chair subcom. on publs. consumer fin. svcs. com. 1992—, sec. fin. instns. and comml. law sect.), Okla. Bar Assn. (legis. review com.), Am. Coll. Comml. Fin. Lawyers. Office: Oklahoma City U Sch Law Oklahoma City OK 73106

HARRELL, CAROLYN HARDISON, nursing home administrator; b. Washington, N.C., Feb. 25, 1942; d. Dewey Jasper and Emma Blanche (Lilley) Hardison; RN, Petersburg (Va.) Gen. Hosp., 1963; B. Nursing, Pacific Western U., 1981, D. Sc. in Health care Adminstrn., 1982; m. Jerry W. Harrell, Apr. 18, 1979; children from previous marriage: Natalie Dawn, John Michael Cameron. Staff nurse Petersburg Gen. Hosp., 1963-66; staff nurse, supr., insvc. dir. Cen. State Hosp., Petersburg, 1963-73; owner, operator Cameron's Day Care Ctr., Colonial Heights, Va., 1973-74; dir. nurses Guarian Corp., Petersburg, 1974-76; adminstr. Am. Health Care Corp., Richmond, Va., 1976-77, Beverly Enterprises, Greenville, N.C., 1977-83, Pitt County Meml. Hosp., 1983-85, Britthaven, Inc., Kinston, N.C., 1985-86, regional dir. Britthaven, Inc., 1986-94, v.p. of operations, 1994—. Vocat. adv. com. Martin Community Coll., 1979. Recipient Citizenship award, 1960; named Employee of Month, Guardian Corp., 1974. Mem. Am. Coll. Nursing Home Adminstrs., Va. Health Care Facilities Assn., N.C. Health Care Facilities Assn. Republican. Club: Bus. and Profl. Women. Office: PO Box 6159 Kinston NC 28501-0159

HARRELL, JAMES ANDREW, SR., lay administrator, dentist; b. Elkin, N.C., July 14, 1922; s. Roy B. and Mattie Reid (Doughton) H.; m. Isabel Jane Gibbs, June 19, 1945; children: Jim Jr., Deborah, Gavin, Stephen. Student, U. N.C.; DDS, Med. Coll. Va., 1945. Pvt. practice Elkin, 1948—; bd. dirs. United Savings and Loan, N.C. Assn. of Professions; chmn., bd. dirs. Yadkin Valley Bank and Trust. Pres. United Fund, Elkin, 1960, YMCA, 1960; scoutmaster, Elkin; mayor of Elkin 3 terms, commr. 3 terms; mem. Tar Heel 100 adv. to bd. trustees U. N.C. at Chapel Hill, v.p., bd. dirs. Gen. Alumni Assn., pres., 1986-87; Final Selection Com. Morehead Scholars in Dentistry; mem. undergrad. Morehead Slection Com., Surry County; mem. U. N.C. Com. on Dentistry; bd. dirs. Dental Found. N.C., Inc., 1972—, N.C. Blue Cross Blue Shield, 1972-73; chmn. adminstrv. bd. and fin. com. United Meth. Ch., Elkin, served all lay positions and offices, ch. sch. tchr., 1954—, cert. lay speaker, lay leader North Wilkesboro dist.; chmn. conf. Laity W.N.C. Conf. Meth. Ch., 1984-86, conf. lay leader, 1986—, chmn. coun. on Laity, 1985—, del. gen. conf., 1988. Served with USN. Recipient Torch award Western N.C. Conf., Disting. Svc. award Dental Found. N.C. and U. N.C. Sch. Dentistry, 1977, fellowship Acad. Gen. Dentistry, 1977, John C. Brauer award Dental Alumni Assn. U. N.C., 1986, Disting Svc. medal Gen. Alumni Assn. U. N.C., 1989. Fellow Internat. Coll. Dentists, Acad. Dentistry Internat., Soc. John Wesley, Am. Coll. Dentists, Royal Soc. Health London; mem. ADA (Ho. of Dels. 14 yrs., credentials com., reference coms. 1983, chmn. 1984, 2d v.p. 1985-86), United Meth. Men (life), Am. Coll. Dentists (v.p. 1986-87, pres. 1989, regent-Regency III 1982—, chmn. Carolinas sect. 1980-81), Acad. Gen. Dentistry (Ho. of Dels., chmn. coun. constitution and bylaws 1978-79, pres. 1982-83), Am. Fund for Dental Health (state chmn. 1984-87, curriculum project Nat. Adv. Com. on Dental Quality Assurance, nat. adv. com. on program planning, 1982, trustee 1986-89), World Meth. Coun. Office: Disease Prevention & Health 200 IndependenceAve SW Washington DC 20201

HARRELL, JAMES EARL, SR., radiologist, educator; b. El Dorado, Ark., Dec. 25, 1931; s. Wilson M. and Edna Irene (Slater) H.; m. Betty Jacqueline (Rogers) Martin, Aug. 23, 1951 (div. 1977); children: James Earl, David Alan; m. Joan Marie Cordes, Oct. 20, 1977. B.A., Ouachita Baptist Coll., 1953, postgrad., 1956-57; M.D., U. Ark., 1962. Am. Bd. Radiology. Commd. 2d lt. U.S. Army, 1953, advanced through grades to lt. col., 1970; radiologist Walter Reed Gen. Hosp., 1963-71, Washington Hosp. Ctr., 1971-72; radiologist Methodist Hosp., Houston, 1972—, chief of radiology, 1976—; prof., chmn. dept. radiology Baylor Coll. Medicine, Houston, 1976—; physician-in-charge dept. radiology Harris County Hosp. Dist., Houston, 1976—; pres. Houston Radiology Associated, 1976—; chief of radiology Jasper (Tex.) Meml. Hosp., 1981-94, Lafayette (La.) Gen. Hosp., 1983-88; resigned U.S. Army, 1971. Served to maj. gen. USAR; dep. surgeon gen. for mobzn. and res. affairs USAR, 1983-86. Fellow Am. Coll. Radiology; mem. AMA, Harris County Med. Soc., Tex. Med. Assn. Republican. Office: Baylor Coll Medicine One Baylor Plz Houston TX 77030-3498

HARRELL, LINDY E., neurologist; b. Arlington, Va., Oct. 5, 1950; d. Leighton Earnest and Virginia Dick (Blackwell) Harrell; m. T. Steven Barlow, July 24, 1976. BA, U. Miami, Fla., 1971; MD, U. Miami, 1977; MS, U. Mass., 1973, PhD, 1974. Med. intern Duke U., Durham, N.C., 1977-78, resident in neurology, 1978-81, geriatric fellow, 1981-83; asst. prof. neurology U. Ala., Birmingham, 1983-87, assoc. prof., 1987-91, prof., 1991—, dir. Alzheimer's Disease Ctr., 1991—, dir. Memory Disorders clinic, 1984—, sr. scientist Ctr. for Aging, 1983—. Assoc. editor So. Med. Jour., 1990—; contbr. numerous articles to profl. jours. Bd. dirs. Alzheimers Ctrl. of Ala., Birmingham, 1992—. Recipient Busse Rsch. award Geriatric Assn., 1995; named Best Dr. in Am. Southeast region Woodward/White, Inc., 1995, 96; grantee VA, 1984—, Nat. Inst. Aging, 1991—. Mem. AMA, Am. Neurol. Assn., Am. Acad. Neurology, So. Med. Assn., Med. Assn. State of Ala. Office: Univ of Alabama Sparks Ctr 454 Birmingham AL 35294

HARRELL, ROBERT AUGUSTUS, III, internist, rheumatologist; b. Griffin, Ga., May 25, 1956; s. Robert A. Jr. and Dorothy (Whiteside) H.; m. Joanne Marie Jordan, May 8, 1982; children: Jordan, Catherine, Robert. BA, Johns Hopkins U., 1977, MD, 1980. Diplomate Am. Bd. Internal Medicine, Am. Bd. Rheumatology. Intern, then resident in internal medicine Duke U. Med. Ctr., Durham, N.C., 1980-83, fellow in rheumatology, 1983-85, cons. assoc., 1991—; pvt. practice, Durham, 1985—; owner Bonne Syrah Records, Durham, 1995—. Author: The Effective Scutboy, 1981, 83, 88; songwriter Heat Shock, 1996. Mem. Am. Soc. Internal Medicine, Johns Hopkins Med. and Surg. Soc. Office: 2609 N Duke St Ste 604 Durham NC 27704

HARRELL, WILLIAM EDWARD, JR., orthodontist; b. Columbus, Ga., Dec. 18, 1948; s. William Edward and Mimi (Milner) H.; m. Joyce Tatum Jackson, Dec. 21, 1974; children: Sara Tatum, William Edward III. BS, U. Ala., Tuscaloosa, 1971; DMD, U. Ala., Birmingham, 1975; cert. in orthodontics, U. Pa., 1977. Diplomate, Am. Bd. Orthodontists. Pvt. practice orthodontics/TMJ Alexander City, Ala., 1977—; orthodontic/TMJ instr. Normandie Study Group for Temporomandibular Joint Disfunction, Montgomery, Ala., 1981-86; lectr. temporomandibular joint disorders; chmn. NASA Project Lazar for State of Ala., 1990—; prin. investigator/researcher on three-dimensional x-ray and video imaging NIH. Mem. Ala. Assn. Orthodontists (sec.-treas. 1988-89, v.p. 1989-90, pres. 1990-91), Am. Assn. Orthodontists, So. Assn. Orthodontists (chmn. new mem. com. 1986-90, bd. dirs. 1995—), Coll. Diplomates Am. Bd. Orthodontists, Dental Soc. Ala. (v.p., then pres. 9th dist. 1986-88), Am. Bd. Orthodontists, Ala. Assn. Orthodontists, ADA, 9th Dist. Dental Assn. State of Ala., Am. Equilibration Soc., Farrar-Norgaard Radiol. Soc., Royal Soc. Medicine, Found. for Orthodontic Rsch. Methodist. Home: 379 Auburn Dr Alexander City AL 35010-2904 Office: 125 Allison Dr Alexander City AL 35010-2658

HARRIGAN, JOHN THOMAS, JR., physician, obstetrician-gynecologist; b. Perth Amboy, N.J., Apr. 20, 1929; s. John T. and Mary E. (Czapp) H.; m. Marlene Lulka, Apr. 14, 1961 (div.); children: John, Alisa, Edmund; m. Karen Teitjen, Aug. 23, 1992. Student, U. Va., 1946-49; M.D., George Washington U., 1953. Diplomate Am. Bd. Ob-Gyn. Intern Doctors Hosp., Washington, 1953-54; resident in ob-gyn Luth. Hosp., Balt., 1954-55, Providence Hosp., Washington, 1957-58, Free Hosp. for Women, Boston, 1958-59; practice medicine specializing in ob-gyn, sub specialist in maternal-fetal medicine Jersey City, 1960-65, Colonia, N.J., 1962-70, Madison Twp., N.J., 1965-70; asst. attending in ob-gyn Margaret Hague Hosp., Jersey City, 1960-65; attending physician in ob-gyn Rahway Hosp., N.J., 1962-70, South Amboy Hosp., N.J., 1965-73; sec. to med. staff South Amboy Hosp., 1970; attending in ob-gyn Martland Hosp. Unit, Newark, 1970-74; dir. dept. ob-gyn Monmouth Med. Ctr., Long Branch, N.J., 1974-76; dir. regional perinatal edn. program Monmouth Med. Ctr., 1975-78; dir. Monmouth Perinatal Ctr., Long Branch, 1975-78; sr. attending in ob-gyn St. Peter's Med. Ctr., 1978—; assoc. prof. ob-gyn Hahnemann Med. Coll., Phila., 1975-78; prof. dir. div. maternal-fetal medicine Rutgers Med. Sch., Piscataway, N.J., 1978—; prof. ob-gyn., dir. div. maternal-fetal medicine Rutgers Med. Sch., 1978-86, U. Medicine and Dentistry N.J., Robert Wood Med. Sch., 1986—; cons. in maternal-fetal medicine to physicians, Eastern N.J.; mem. maternal and infant care services com. N.J. Dept. Health, 1975—; dir. statewide premature delivery prevention project; med.-legal expert cons.; tech. adv. panel Healthstart program, N.J. Health Dept. Contbr. articles to med. jours.; reviewer med. jours. Mem. task force on biomed. causes and pub. rels. Gov.'s Coun. on Prevention Mental Retardation, N.J., task force on genetics and fetal defects, 1984—; mem. pub. affairs com. MOD Birth Defects Found.; pres. Perinatal Assn. N.J., 1991-93; mem. N.J. Commn. of Health and Parental and Child Health adv. Com., 1993—, vice chair, 1995—. Capt. M.C. U.S. Army, 1955-57. Fellow ACOG (vice chmn. N.J. sect. 1979-82, chmn. N.J. sect. 1982—, nat. adv. coun. 1982—, legis. rep., treas. dist. III 1986); mem. AMA, Med. Soc. N.J. (maternal infant care com. 1988—), Am. Inst. Ultrasound in Medicine (legis. com. 1994), Am. Fertility Soc., N.J. Perinatal Assn. (v.p. 1980-90, pres. 1990), N.J. Perinatal Tech. adv. Com. Baker channing Soc., N.J. Ob-gyn. Soc. (coun.), N.J. Maternal Fetal Medicine Soc. (pres. 1994-95). Democrat. Roman Catholic. Home: 301 Sussex Ave Spring Lake NJ 07762-1231 Office: Jersey Shore Med Ctr Perinatal Inst 1943 State Route 33 Neptune NJ 07753-4843

HARRIMAN, STEPHEN A., state public health commissioner; m. Priscilla Harriman. BA in Govt., Syracuse U.; MA, U. Conn. Exec. asst. to commr. of health State of Conn., Hartford, 1975-76; exec. dir. Conn. Med. Examining Bd., Hartford, 1976-78; dir. med. quality assurance divsn. Conn. Dept. Health, Hartford, 1978-82; chief bur. health systems regulation Conn. Dept. Pub. Health, Hartford, 1982-95; commr. Conn. Dept. Pub. Health, 1995—. Office: Conn Dept Pub Health Office of Commr 410 Capitol Ave, MS 13COM Hartford CT 01634*

HARRINGTON, ANNE WILSON, medical librarian; b. Phila., June 18, 1926; d. Edgar Myers and Jean Gould (DeHaven) Wilson; m. James Paul Harrington, June 11, 1948; children: Barbara Gould Harrington Murphy, Ian Edgar, Eric Bradley. BA, U. Pa., Phila., 1948; MS in Libr. Sci., Villanova U., 1977. Clk. Princeton U., 1948-51; CEO, ptnr. Teesdale Co., West Chester, Pa., 1954—; libr. asst. Franklin Inst., Phila., 1974-76; med. staff libr. The Chester County Hosp., West Chester, 1977—; mem., treas., chmn. sub-com. Consortium Health Info., Chester, 1977—. Trustee, sec., com. chmn. Wilmington (Del.) Friends Sch., 1963-72, 89; treas. com. on edn. Phila. Yearly Meeting Soc. Friends, 1980-91; mem., rep. Friends Coun. on Edn., Phila., 1991-96; overseer Quaker Info. Ctr., Phila., 1992-96; bd. mem., subcom. chmn. cmty. bd. Kendal Corp. CCRC, Kennett Square, Pa., 1973—. Mem. Med. Libr. Assn., Acad. Health Info. Profls. (sr.), Phila. Area Med. Library Assn., Lake Paupac Club (chmn. environ./ecol. com.), Friends Med. Soc. Democrat. Home: 1117 Talleyrand Rd West Chester PA 19382-7416 Office: Chester County Hosp West Chester PA 19380

HARRINGTON, DAVID SAMUEL, hospital biomedical services administrator; b. Kansas City, Mo., Apr. 10, 1947; s. Jes Rubert and Margie Ann (Samuel) H.; m. Linda Kay Burton, June 8, 1968; children: Kelly Lynn, Jes Burton. AAS in Biomed. Tech., Tex. State Tech., 1972, B of Tech. in Edn. in Biomed. Tech., 1972; MS in Indsl. Arts, Jackson State U., 1979. Biomed. equipment technician St. Mary Hosp., Port Arthur, Tex., 1973-74; field svc. engr. Gould, Inc., Houston, 1974-76; field svc. engr., owner Med. Equipment Sales & Svc., Clinton, Miss., 1976-85; instr. Hinds Community Coll., Raymond, Miss., 1985; dir. biomed. svcs. St. Dominic Hosp., Jackson, Miss., 1985-91; dir. biomed. engring./telecommunications Meth. Med. Ctr., Jackson, Miss., 1991—. Lay leader 1st United Meth. Ch., Clinton, 1990; coach Dixie Youth Baseball, Clinton, 1986-93; pres. Clinton Baseball/Softball Assn., 1992-93. Sgt. USAF, 1967-70, Vietnam. Recipient Citizenship award Am. Legion, 1965. Mem. Assn. for Advancement Med. Insts., Miss. Hosp. Assn./Hosp. Engrs. (past pres., bd. dirs. 1988—), Miss. Biomed. Assn. (pres.), Miss. Telecomms. Mgmt. Assn. (pres.), Kiwanis. Republican. Home: 101 Country Meadow Rd Clinton MS 39056-9770 Office: Meth Med Ctr 1850 Chadwick Dr Jackson MS 39204-3404

HARRINGTON, DONALD P., radiologist; b. St. Louis, Jan. 20, 1941; s. Paul and Louise (Anderson) H.; m. Mary Reilly, Nov. 26 1966; children: Anne, Katie. BS, U. of Ariz., 1962; MD, Marquette U. Sch. of Medicine, 1966. Diplomate Am. Bd. Radiology, Am. Bd. Nuclear Medicine. Intern Milw. County Gen. Hosp., 1966-67; resident in radiology Mpls. VA Hosp., 1967-70; fellow in cardiovascular radiology U. Minn., Mpls., 1970-71; staff radiologist and chief cardiovascular radiologist Mpls. VA Hosp., 1971-72; staff radiologist Johns Hopkins Hosp., Boston, 1972-79; cardiovascular and interventional radiologist Brigham and Women's Hosp., Boston, 1979-87, dir. cardiovascular and interventional radiology sect., 1987-91; cardiovascular and interventional radiologist U. of Calif. San Francisco Hosps. and Clinics, 1985-86, Ft. Miley VA Hosp., San Francisco, 1985-86; radiologist-in-chief U. Hosp. SUNY at Stony Brook, 1991—; instr. U. of Minn. Sch. Medicine, 1971-72; asst. prof. Johns Hopkins U. Sch. Medicine, 1972-79, assoc. prof., 1979; assoc. prof. Harvard Med. Sch., 1979-91; vis. assoc. prof. U. of Calif., San Francisco Sch. Medicine, 1985-86; prof. and chmn. Sch. of Medicine SUNY, Stony Brook, 1991—; lectr. various assn. meetings. Author: (with others) Pediatric Nuclear Medicine, 1974, Cardiac Diagnostic Procedures for the Clinician, 1982, Vascular and Interventional Radiology, 1983, Shackelford's Textbook on Surgery of the Alimentary Tract, 1983, The Guide to Cardiology, 1984, Non-Invasive Imaging Techniques in Cardiovascular Disease, 1985; contbg. editor Am. Jour. Roentgenology, 1978—, Cardiovascular Intervention Radiology, 1980—; contbr. articles to profl. jours. Fellow Coun. Cardiovascular Radiology Am. Heart Assn. (chmn. Nominating Com. 1986-88); mem. Soc. Nuclear Medicine, Johns Hopkins Med. Soc., Soc. Cardiovascular and Interventional Radiology (chmn. Rules Com. 1982-84), Inter-Am. Coll. Radiology, New Eng. Angiographic Soc. (pres. 1981-82), Rsch. Counc. Am. Heart Assn., A ssn. U. Radiologists, Soc. Thoracic Radiology, Long Island Radiological Soc., Suffolk County Med. Soc., Soc. of Chmn. of Acad. Radiology Depts. Office: SUNY Dept Radiology Sch Medicine Health Scis Ctr 4 092 Stony Brook NY 11794-8460

HARRINGTON, GEORGE EDWARD, JR., pharmacist; b. Tuscaloosa, Ala., Feb. 26, 1948; s. George Edward and Elizabeth (Reffler) H.; m. Dorothy Anne Boucher, Sept. 1, 1979; children: Rebecca Anne, George Edward III. BS in Pharmacy, Duquesne U., 1973. Pharmacist CVS Pharmacy, Woonsocket, R.I., 1973—. Mem. Md. Pharmacists Assn., Va. Pharm. Assn., Kiwanis. Democrat. Episcopalian. Home: 9593 Shannon Ln Manassas VA 20110 Office: CVS Pharmacy # 1801 9972 Liberia Ave Manassas VA 22110

HARRINGTON, JOHN NORRIS, ophthalmic plastic and reconstructive surgeon, educator; b. Dallas, Oct. 1, 1939; s. Marion Thomas and Ruth Evelyn (Norris) H.; m. Elizabeth Hunt, June 20, 1964; children: Thomas Wesley, Clinton Hunt. BA, Tex. A&M U., 196l, BS, 1964; MD, U. Tenn., Memphis, 1966. Diplomate Am. Bd. Ophthalmology. Intern Letterman Gen. Hosp., San Francisco, 1966-67; resident in ophthalmology Scott and White Clinic, Temple, Tex., 1970-73; fellow in ophthalmic plastic and reconstructive surgery U. Calif., San Francisco, 1973-74; plastic and reconstructive surgeon Tex. Ophthal. Plastic, Reconstructive & Orbital Surg. Assoc., Dallas, 1974—; clin. prof. ophthalmic plastic and reconstructive surgery U. Tex. Southwestern Med. Ctr., Dallas, 1974—; chief staff Mary Shiels Hosp., Dallas, 1986-88; active staff, dir. ophthalmic plastic and reconstructive surgery Baylor U. Med. Ctr., Dallas, active staff dept. oncology Baylor-Sammons Cancer Ctr. Mem. editorial bd. Ophthalmic Plastic and Reconstructive Surgery Jour.; contbr. chpts. to textbooks; contbr. articles to med. jours. Mem. Univ. Park Citizens League, Dallas, 1976-82; pres. Highland Park High Sch. Dads Club, Dallas, 1982-83; sec. bd. deacons Park Cities Bapt. Ch., Dallas, 198l. Maj. M.C., U.S. Army, 1966-70, Vietnam. Decorated Bronze Star. Fellow ACS, Am. Soc. Ophthalmic Plastic and Reconstructive Surgery (sec. 1991-93, v.p. 1994, pres.-elect 1995, pres. 1996, del. to AMA 1995—), Am. Acad. Ophthalmology (bd. counselors 1991-94, Honor award 1989); mem. AMA, Tex. Med. Assn., Dallas Acad. Ophthalmology (pres. 1986). Office: 2731 Lemmon Ave Ste 304 Dallas TX 75204-2831

HARRINGTON, JOHN TOLAN, medical educator, dean; b. Fall River, Mass., Dec. 30, 1936; s. John J. and Elizabeth C. (Tolan) H.; m. Gertrude Rose Hargraves, Aug. 27, 1960; children: Gertrude, Kathleen, Daniel, Ann, John, Mark, Timothy. BA magna cum laude, Coll. of the Holy Cross, 1958; MD cum laude, Yale U., 1962. Diplomate Am. Bd. Internal Medicine. Internship, residency N.C. Mem. Hosp., Chapel Hill, 1962-65; clin. and rsch. renal fellow Tufts-New Eng. Med. Ctr., Boston, 1965-68; intern, resident in internal medicine N.C. Meml. Hosp., Chapel Hill, 1962-65; clin. and rsch. fellow in nephrology Tufts-New Eng. Med. Ctr., Boston, 1965-68; nephrologist, dir. hemodialysis unit New Eng. Med. Ctr., Boston, 1971-81, chief gen. medicine divsn., 1981-86; chmn. dept. medicine Newton (Mass.)-Wellesley Hosp., 1986-94; dean academic affairs Tufts U. Sch. Medicine, Boston, 1994—, asst. prof. medicine, 1971-75, assoc. prof. medicine, 1975-79, prof. medicine, 1979—; dean ad interim Tufts U. Sch. Med., Boston, 1995—. Author: Acid-Base, 1982; editor (monthly jour. feature) Nephrology Forum in Kidney Internat., 1979—; contbr. articles to profl. jours. Pres. Hummocks Cmty. Orgn., Portsmouth, R.I., 1970-80, Nat. Kidney Found., Mass., 1988. Fellow ACP (gov. Mass. chpt. 1989-93), Royal Irish Coll. Physicians (hon.); mem. Internat. Soc. Nephrology, Am. Soc. Nephrology, Holy Name Soc. Democrat. Roman Catholic.

HARRINGTON, MARGUERITE ANN, academic program administrator; b. Phila., Mar. 31, 1949; d. S. Thomas F. and Marguerite Ann (Haggerty) H. Acad. diploma, Gwynedd-Mercy Acad., Pa., 1967; BA in English Lit., Immaculata Coll., Pa., 1971; MBA in Health Care Mgmt., Wharton Sch., Phila., 1976; MS in Social Adminstrn., London Sch. Econs., U. London, 1977. Field rep. Bur. Labor Stats., Phila., 1972-74; asst. sec. Hartford (Conn.) Ins. Group, 1979-86; asst. v.p. Lincoln Nat. Life Ins. Co., Ft. Wayne, Ind., 1986-88, 2nd v.p., 1988-90; v.p. planning Mercy Health Corp., Bala Cynwyd, Pa., 1991-95; dir. alumni affairs Wharton Sch. U. Pa., Phila., 1995—, 1995—. Mem. Health Care Aluni Assn. (bd. dirs. 1979—), Wharton Alumni Assn. (chmn., bd. dirs. exec. com. 1989-91).

HARRINGTON, MARION RAY, ophthalmologist; b. Dallas, Sept. 20, 1924; s. Silas Fredrick and Mary Katherine (Ray) H.; m. Nan Puckhober, Oct. 1, 1942; 1 child, Nan Katherine Kern. Student, U. Tex., 1942, M.D., 1947. Diplomate: Am. Bd. Ophthalmology. Intern St. Paul Hosp., Dallas, 1941-48; chief ophthalmology Portsmouth (Va.) Naval Hosp., 1950-52; practice medicine specializing in ophthalmology Dallas, 1952—; mem. faculty U. Tex., Southwestern Med. Sch., Dallas, 1952—; clin. prof. U. Tex., Southwestern Med. Sch., 1975—. Served with USN, 1947-48, 50-52. Fellow A.C.S., Internat. Coll. Surgeons; mem. Am., Tex. med. assns., Dallas

County, So. med. socs., Am. Acad. Ophthalmology and Otolarlyngology, Am. Assn., Am. Assn. Ophthalmology, Tex. Acad. Ophthalmology and Otolaryngology, Tex. Ophthalmologic Assn., Dallas Acad. Ophthalmologists, Royal Soc. Medicine, Internat. Lens Implant Soc., Contact Lens Soc. Episcopalian. Home: 3620 Overbrook Dr Dallas TX 75205-4327

HARRINGTON, MICHAEL BALLOU, health economist, systems engineer; b. Denver, Sept. 26, 1940; s. Theodore Charles Ballou and DeEtte June (Krastetter) H.; m. Mary Lynn Kijanka, Nov. 17, 1978; 1 child, Meredith Ballou. MS, U. Calif., Irvine, 1969, PhD (NDEA fellow), 1972. With Fgn. Service, Dept. State, 1972-74, Arthur Young & Co., 1975-78; sr. health economist/systems engr. GEOMET Technologies, Inc., Gaithersburg, Md., 1978-80; group leader The Mitre Corp., 1980-87, lead scientist, 1987—; adj. prof. Southeastern U., Washington, George Mason U., Fairfax, Va. Served with USMC, 1958-61. Mem. numerous profl. socs. Club: Potomac Valley Srs. Track. Avocation: writing. Contbr. articles to profl. jours.

HARRION, LOIS, nurse educator; b. Jackson, Miss.; m. Milton Harrion; 1 child, Karma. Diploma, Gilfoy Sch. Nursing, 1962; BA, U. Redlands, 1976; MS, U. LaVerne, 1980. RN; cert. community coll. instr., vocat. edn. credential. Instr. Simi Valley (Calif.) Adult Sch., 1983—, dir. vocat. nursing program, 1992—; item writer Nat. Coun. Licensure Examination Practical Nurse, 1993, 94. Author: Professional Issues in Practical/Vocational Nursing, 1992. Mem. Calif. Assn. Health Career Educators (past pres.), So. Calif. Vocat. Nurse Dirs., Calif. Vocat. Nurse Educators, Calif. Coun. Adult Edn., Ventura County Black Nurses Assn. (past v.p.).

HARRIS, ADRIAN LLEWELLYN, oncologist, educator; b. London, Oct. 8, 1950; s. Luke and Julia H. BS, MBChB, FRCP, U. Med. Sch., Liverpool, England, 1973; PhD, Corpus Christi Coll., Oxford, England, 1978. House physician Royal Liverpool Infirmary, 1973-74, house surgeon, 1974, sr. house officer, 1974-75; med. registrar, clin. scientist U. Dept. Clin. Pharm. Nuffield Dept. Medicine, Oxford, 1975-78; med. registrar Royal Free Hosp., 1978-79; sr. med. registrar Royal Marsden Hosp., London, 1979-81; prof. clin. oncology U. Newcastle, Newcastle upon Tyne, England, 1982-88; vis. rschr. Imperial Cancer Rsch. Fund, London, 1981-82; ICRF prof. clin. oncology, Oxford U. Contbr. articles to profl. jours. Office: ICRF Clin Oncology Dept, Churchill Hosp Headington, Oxford OX3 7LJ, England

HARRIS, BURTON H., surgeon; b. N.Y.C., Jan. 30, 1941; s. Mark and Nettie (Bilsky) H.; m. Marian Lichtiger, 1962 (div. 1973); children: David, Robert, Eileen; m. Kathleen Mary Donnelly, Nov. 28, 1973; 1 child, Mark. BA, Hobart Coll., 1961; MD, SUNY, N.Y.C., 1965. Intern, resident, and chief resident in surgery SUNY, 1965-71; chief resident in pediatric surgery Children's Hosp., Columbus, Ohio, 1971-73; prin. Drs. Wilkinson, Webb & Harris P.A., Jacksonville, Fla., 1973-81; dir. Kiwanis Pediat. Trauma Inst. New Eng. Med. Ctr., Boston, 1981-95, chief div. pediatric surgery, 1985-95, 1985-95; surgeon-in-chief Georgetown Children's Med. Ctr., Washington, 1995—; Orvar Swenson prof. pediatric surgery Tufts U. Sch. Medicine, Boston, 1981-95; prof. surgery & pediat. Sch. Medicine Georgetown U., 1995—. Editor: Progress in Pediatric Trauma, 1985, 87, 89, 92; assoc. editor Jour. Pediat. Surgery; contbr. articles to profl. jours. Med. advisor Profl. Golf Assn. Tour, Ponte Vedra, Fla., 1977—. Brig. gen. (OM) USAR, 1966—. Decorated Legion of Merit, D.S.M.; NIH fellow, 1961-64, Am. Cancer Soc. clin. fellow, 1971-73. Fellow ACS (chpt. pres. 1980-81, state com. chmn. 1989-95), Am. Coll. Emergency Physicians, Am. Cancer Soc., Am. Pediatric Surg. Assn., Am. Acad. Pediatrics, Soc. Pediatric Trauma (pres. 1989-91), Ea. Assn. for Surgery Trauma (pres. 1989-90), Am. Trauma Soc. (dir. 1986-92), Internat. Soc. Aeromed. Svcs. (pres. 1988-90), New Eng. Pediatric Surg. Soc. (pres. 1988-95), Wellesley (Mass.) Country Club, Tournament Players Club (Avenel, Md.). Republican.

HARRIS, CURTIS C., chemist. MD, U. Kans. Intern and resident in internal medicine and oncology; chief chemist Lab. Carcinogenesis Nat. Cancer Inst., NIH, Bethesda, Md., also head molecular genetics and carcinogenesis sect.; Deichmann lectr. VII Internat. Congress of Toxicology, 1995. Editor 10 books; exec. editor Carcinogenesis; contbr. over 250 articles and revs. to profl. jours. Mem. Chem. Industry Inst. Toxicology (mem. sci. adv. panel, chmn. 1989-94, Founder's award 1995). Office: NIH Nat Cancer Inst Lab Carcinogenis Rm 2C01 9000 Rockville Pike Bldg 37 Bethesda MD 20892-0001

HARRIS, DALE BENNER, psychologist, educator; b. Elkhart, Ind., June 28, 1914; s. Ward Manning and Lillian (Benner) H.; m. Elizabeth Saltmarsh, July 17, 1935; children—Ruthann E., James S., David B., Geoffrey M. A.B. with high distinction (Rector scholar), DePauw U., 1935; M.A., U. Minn., 1937, Ph.D., 1941. Ednl. dir. Minn. Tng. Sch. for Boys, 1936-38; staff Inst. Child Welfare U. Minn., 1939-59, prof., 1948-59, dir., 1954-59; prof. psychology Pa. State U., 1959-79, prof. emeritus, 1979—, chmn. dept. psychology, 1962-67; Fulbright vis. prof. Ochanomizu U., Tokyo, 1968-69. Author: Children's Drawings as Measures of Intellectual Maturity, 1963; co-author: Child Care and Training, 8th edit, 1958; Editor: The Concept of Development, 1957, Child Development Abstracts, 1964-71; editorial com.: Ann. Rev. of Psychology, 1956-62; Contbr. articles to profl. jours. Mem. Mpls. Citizens Com. on Pub. Edn., 1946-59, Gov.'s Adv. Com. on Children and Youth, 1950-55, on Exceptional Children, 1956-59; mem. bd. Children's Home Soc. Minn., 1954-59; mem. adv. com. young workers Bur. Labor Standards, Dept. Labor, 1955-59; mem. adv. com. Clearing House for Research Relating to Children, U.S. Children's Bur., 1962-68; mem. exec. bd. Joint Commn. Correctional Manpower and Tng., 1965-69; mem. task force Joint Commn. Mental Health Children, 1966-69; research adv. com. Commonwealth Mental Health Research Found.; Mem. bd. Pa. Mental Health Assn., 1970-76. Fellow Am. Psychol. Assn. (past pres. div. developmental psychology), A.A.A.S. (governing council 1962-72, v.p., sect. I chmn. 1972), Soc. for Research in Child Devel. (sec., mem. governing council 1957-61, cons. editor monographs); mem. Nat. Soc. Study Edn., AAUP, Am. Edn. Research Assn. (v.p. 1964), Phi Beta Kappa, Sigma Xi, Psi Chi, Phi Sigma, Phi Delta Kappa. Home: 1160 S Main St # 318 Middletown CT 06457

HARRIS, DAVID THOMAS, immunologist; b. Jonesboro, Ark., May 9, 1956; s. Marm Melton and Lucille Luretha (Buck) H.; m. Francoise Jacqueline Besencon, June 24, 1989; children: Alexandre M., Stefanie L. BS in Biology, Math. and Psychology, Wake Forest U., 1978, MS, 1980, PhD in Microbiology and Immunology, 1982. Fellow Ludwig Inst. Cancer Rsch., Lausanne, Switzerland, 1982-85; rsch. asst. prof. U. N.C., Chapel Hill, 1985-89; assoc. prof. U. Ariz., Tucson, 1989-96, prof., 1996—; cons. Teltech, Inc. Mpls., 1990—, Advanced Biosci. Resources, 1994—; bd. sci. advisors Cryo-Cell Internat., 1992—; bd. dirs. Ageria, Inc., Tuscon; dir. Cord Blood Stem Cell Bank, 1993—; sci. dir. Gene Therapy, 1994—; mem. Ariz. Cancer Ctr., Steele Meml. Children's Rsch. Ctr., Ariz. Arthritis Ctr. Program, sci. adv. bd. Cord Blood Registry, Inc., chief sci. div. Cord Blood Registry, Inc. Co-author chpts. to sci. books, articles to profls. jours.; reviewer sci. jours.; co-holder 3 scientific patents. Grantee local and fed. rsch. grants, 1988—. Mem. AAAS, Am. Assn. Immunologists, Reticuleondothelial Soc., Internat. Soc. Hematotherapy and Graft Engring., Internat. Soc. Devel. and Comparative Immunology, Scandanavian Soc. Immunology, Sigma Xi,. Democrat. Mem. Ch. of Christ. Office: U Ariz Dept Microbiology Bldg 90 Tucson AZ 85721

HARRIS, DON NAVARRO, biochemist, pharmacologist; b. N.Y.C., June 17, 1929; s. John Henry and Margaret Vivian (Berkley) H.; m. Regina Gwathney Brooks, July 29, 1954; children: Donna Michele Wolfe, John Craig, Scott Anthony. AB, Lincoln (Pa.) U., 1951; MS, Rutgers U., 1959, PhD, 1963. Sr. rsch. chemist Colgate Palmolive Rsch. Ctr., Piscataway, N.J., 1963-64; asst. rsch. specialist Rutgers U., New Brunswick, N.J., 1964-65; sr. rsch. scientist Squibb Inst. Med. Rsch., Princeton, N.J., 1965-84, rsch. fellow, 1984-89; rsch. fellow Bristol-Myers Squibb Pharm. Rsch. Inst., Princeton, 1989-93, cons. human resources, 1993—; cons. U.S. Army Sci. Bd., 1981-85. Mem. editorial bd. Jour. Enzyme Inhibition, 1985—; author/co-author more than 60 articles in profl. jours.; patentee in field. Recipient Black Achievers award Harlem YMCA, 1986, Minds in Motion award Sci. Skills Ctr., 1990, Success in Sci. award Rutgers U., 1991, Lincoln U. Alumni Achievement award, 1996, Charles R. Drew Med. award NAACP, 1996. Mem. Alpha Phi Alpha (pres. Theta Psi Lambda chpt. 1964-66, sec. 1988—), Sigma Pi Phi (sec. Mu Boule chpt. 1987—). Home: 26 Summerall Rd Somerset NJ 08873-2210 Office: Bristol Myers Squibb Pharm Rsch Inst PO Box 4000 Princeton NJ 08543-4000

HARRIS, DOUGLAS HERSHEL, research company executive; b. Indpls., Oct. 7, 1930; s. Douglas H. and Letha Mae (Baker) H.; BS, Iowa State U., 1952; MS (fellow), Purdue U., 1957, PhD, 1959; m. Cynthia Ann Brodeur, July 17, 1976; children by previous marriage: Kimberly Ann, Robin Lin. Project dir. Human Factors Research, Inc., L.A., 1958-62; group scientist Rockwell Internat. Corp., Los Angeles, 1962-69; lectr. U. So. Calif., 1962-72; pres. Anacapa Scis., Inc., Santa Barbara, Calif., 1969-87, chmn. bd., 1987—. Served with underwater demolition USNR, 1952-55; Korea. Fellow Human Factors Soc. (pres. 1983-84; Jack Kraft award 1975), Am. Psychol. Assn.; mem. Nat. Rsch. Coun. (com. human factors 1985-91, com. comml. aviation security 1995—). Republican. Author: Human Factors in Quality Assurance, 1969; Advanced (computer aided) Intelligence Analysis, 1986, Organizational Linkages, 1994; editorial bd. Human Factors Jour., 1968-87. Office: 2000 N Pantops Dr Charlottesville VA 22901-8646

HARRIS, EDWARD D., JR., physician; b. Phila., July 7, 1937; children: Ned, Tom, Chandler; m. Joan Z. Lonergan, 1993. A.B., Dartmouth Coll., 1958, grad. with honors, 1960; M.D. cum laude, Harvard U., 1962. Diplomate Am. Bd. Internal Medicine and Rheumatology (chmn. subsplty. bd. in rheumatology 1986-88). Intern Mass. Gen. Hosp., Boston, 1962-63, asst. resident, 1963-64, sr. resident, 1966-67, clin. research fellow arthritis unit, 1967-69, mem. staff arthritis unit, 1969-70; asst. prof. Dartmouth Med. Sch., Hanover, N.H., 1970-73, assoc. prof., 1973-77, prof., 1977-83, Eugene W. Leonard prof., 1979-83, chief connective tissue disease sect., 1970-83. mem. staff Mary Hitchcock Meml. Hosp., 1970-83; chief med. service Middlesex Gen. U. Hosp., New Brunswick, N.J., 1983—; instr. medicine Harvard U. Med. Sch., Boston, 1968-70, asst. prof., 1970; prof., chmn. medicine U. Medicine and Dentistry N.J.-Rutgers U. Med. Sch., New Brunswick 1983-88; Arthur L. Bloomfield prof. medicine Stanford U. Sch. Medicine, 1988-95, chmn. dept. medicine, 1988-95, George DeForest Barnett prof. medicine, 1995—; chief med. svc. Stanford U. Hosp., 1988-95. Fellow ACP. mem. Am. Rheumatism Assn. (numerous coms. 1967—, pres. 1985-86), New Eng. Rheumatism Assn. (pres. 1977-78), Assn. Profs. Medicine, Dartmouth Med. Alumni Coun., Harvard Med. Alumni Coun. Office: Stanford U Sch Medicine Ste 203 1000 Welch Rd Palo Alto CA 94304-1808*

HARRIS, EDWARD FREDERICK, orthodontics educator, physical anthropologist; b. San Jose, Calif., Oct. 2, 1947. s. Roy Hayward and Bonnie (Keeble) H.; m. Karen J. Morse, May 29, 1970 (div. July 1983); children: Jeremy T., Emily J. BA, San Jose State U., 1969; MA, Ariz. State U., 1972, PhD, 1977. Asst. prof. orthodontics U. Conn., Farmington, 1978-80; prof. orthodontics Coll. Dentistry, U. Tenn. Center for Health Scis., Memphis, 1980—. NIH fellow, 1973-80. Mem. Am. Assn. Phys. Anthropologists, Internat. Assn. Dental Research, Sigma Xi. Democrat. Methodist. Contbr. articles to profl. jours. Office: 875 Union Ave # 301S Memphis TN 38103-3513

HARRIS, ELIZABETH ABIGAIL, optometrist; b. Manchester, N.H., Nov. 27, 1967; d. Carl Dean and Martha Ellen (Partridge) Harris-Gaudes. BA in Biology, Clark U., 1989; OD, New Eng. Coll. Optometry, 1993. Lic. optometrist, Pa.; diplomate Nat. Bd. Examiners in Optometry. Pvt. practice, Allentown and Shillington, Pa., 1993—, Wyomissing, Pa., 1995—. Mem. Am. Optometric Assn., Pa. Optometric Assn., Beta Sigma Kappa. Home: 23 Telford Ave West Lawn PA 19609 Office: Office Dr Joseph Gackenbach 732 N 19th St Allentown PA 18104 also: Shillington Eye Assocs 453 E Lancaster Ave Shillington PA 19607

HARRIS, EMMA EARL, nursing home executive; b. Viper, Ky., Nov. 6, 1936; d. Andrew Jackson and Zola (Hall) S.; m. Ret Haney Marten Henis Harris, June 5, 1981; children: Debra, Joseph, Wynona, Robert Walsh. Grad. St. Joseph Sch. Practical Nursing. Staff nurse St. Joseph Hosp., Bangor, Maine, 1973-75; office nurse Dr. Eugene Brown, Bangor, 1975-77; dir. nurses Fairborn Nursing Home, Ohio, 1977-78; staff nurse Hillhaven Hospice, Tucson, 1979-80; asst. head nurse, 1980. Author: Thoughts on Life, 1988. Vol. Heart Assn., Bangor, 1965-70, Cancer Assn., Bangor, 1965-70. Mem. NAFE. Democrat. Avocations: theatre, opera. Home: 530 E Flores St Tucson AZ 85705-5723

HARRIS, IRA STEPHEN, secondary education educator, administrator; b. Bklyn., July 13, 1945; s. Simon and Vera (Vichness) H.; m. Arlene Cramer, Dec. 25, 1971; children: Elliot, David, Sara. BS, Fairleigh Dickinson U., 1968; MS, L.I. U., 1970, Profl. Diploma magna cum laude, 1978. Sci. educator 158Q Marie Curie High Sch., Bayside, N.Y., 1968-76; tchr. math., sci. and social studies, media specialist Campbell Jr. High Sch. 218Q, Flushing, N.Y., 1976-79, Beard Jr. High Sch. 189Q, Flushing, 1979-85; tech. specialist Carson Intermediate Sch. 237Q, Flushing, 1986—; asst. prin. Carson Intermediate Sch., Flushing, 1995—; judge sci. fair N.Y. Acad. Scis., N.Y.C., 1985—. Commodore Newbridge Boat Club, Bellmore, N.Y.; v.p., edn. chmn. Bellmore Jewish Ctr.; pres. East Bay Civic Assn., Bellmore. Mem. N.Y. Acad. Scis. Republican. Home: 2729 Claudia Ct Bellmore NY 11710-4740

HARRIS, JACQUELINE L., nursing educator, medical/surgical nurse; b. Viroqua, Wis., Sept. 28, 1960; d. Charles Henry and Sandra Alice (Mitchell) H. BSN, Harding U., 1983; MNSc, U. Ark Med. Scis., 1995. RN Ark., Tex., ONC. Staff nurse St. Vincent Infirmary, Little Rock, Ark., 1983-85, Seton Med. Ctr., Austin, Tex., 1985-91; instr. nursing Harding U., Searcy, Ark., 1991—; staff nurse St. Vincent Infirmary Med. Ctr., Little Rock, 1993—; sponsor Harding Student Nurses Assn., Searcy, 1992-93. Co-sponsor CARTsI Health Careers Summer Day Camp, Searcy, 1992; vol. White County Meml. Hosp. Health Fair, Searcy, 1993. Mem. Nat. Assn. Orthopaedic Nurses, Ark. Nursing Rsch. Consortium, Sigma Theta Tau (co-counselor Epsilon Omicron chpt. 1994—).

HARRIS, JAMES CAROL OVERTON, JR., psychiatrist, pediatrician; b. Birmingham, Ala., Nov. 6, 1940; s. James Carol and Mary Virginia (Respess) H. BS, Univ. Md., 1962; MD, George Washington U., 1966. Cert. Am. Bd. Pediatrics, Am. Bd. Psychiatry, Am. Bd. Child Psychiatry. With Peace Corps, Thailand, 1967-70; dir. developmental neuopsychiatry Johns Hopkins U., Balt., 1976; pres. med. staff Kennedy Krieger Inst., Johns Hopkins U., 1986-88; asst. prof. The Johns Hopkins Med. Insts., Balt., 1976-82, interim dir. div. of child psychiatry, 1978-82, dir. consultation/ liason svc., 1978-82, dir. edn. div. of child psychiatry, 1982-89, co-dir. autism clinic, 1983—, co-dir. sleep disorder clinic, 1983—, joint appointment dept. of mental hygiene, 1985—; adj. scientist Ctr. for Brain Evolution and Behavior, Poolesville, Md., 1978-84, assoc. prof. psychiatry, mental hygiene, pediatrics The Johns Hopkins Med. Inst., Balt., 1982—; adj. scientist Lab. Comparative Etiology, 1984-93. Author: Developmental Neuropsychiatry Fundamentals, 1995, Developmental Neuropsychiatry: Assessment, Diagnosis and Treatment, 1995; contbr. articles to profl. jours. Recipient: NIMH Trainee Award 1964-65, Foreign Fellowship, Assn. Am. Med. Colls. - Smith Kline & French, 1965, Pollen Award 1965-66. Fellow Am. Psychiat. Assn., Am. Acad. Child and Adolescent Psychiatry; mem. Md. Psychiat. Soc., Am. Assn. Dirs. of Psychiat. Residency Tng., Soc. for Neurosci., Am. Assn. Psychiatry and the Law, Soc. for the Study of Behavioral Phenotypes. Home: 200 Tuscany Rd Baltimore MD 21210-3010 Office: Johns Hopkins U Sch Medicine 600 N Wolfe St Baltimore MD 21205-2110

HARRIS, JAMES HERMAN, pathologist, neuropathologist, consultant, educator; b. Fayetteville, Ga., Oct. 19, 1942; s. Frank J. and Gladys N. (White) H.; m. Judy K. Hutchinson, Jan. 30, 1965; children: Jeffrey William, John Michael, James Herman. BS, Carson-Newman Coll., 1964; PhD, U. Tenn.-Memphis, 1969, MD, 1972. Diplomate Am. Bd. Pathology; sub.-cert. in anatomic pathology and neuropathology. Resident and fellow N.Y.U.-Bellevue Med. Ctr., N.Y.C., 1973-75; adj. asst. prof. pathology N.Y. U., N.Y.C., 1975-83; asst. prof. pathology and neurosci. Med. Coll. Ohio, Toledo, 1975-78, assoc. prof., 1978-82, dir. neuropathology and electron microscopy lab., 1975-82; cons. Toledo Hosp., 1979-82, assoc. pathologist/neuropathologist, dir. electron microscopy pathology lab., 1983-91, mem. courtesy staff, 1991—, mem. overview com., credentials com., appropriations subcom. medisgroup, interqual task force; chmn. clin. support services com., vice chmn. med. staff quality rev. com.; cons. neuropathologist Mercy Hosp., 1976-93, mem. courtesy staff, 1993—, U. Mich. dept. pathology, 1984-93; cons. med. malpractice in pathology and neuropathology; mem. AMA Physician Rsch. and Evaluation Panel; mem. ednl. and profl. affairs commn., exec. council Acad. Medicine; mem. children's cancer study group Ohio State U. satellite; chmn. tech. and issues subcom. of adv. com. Blue Cross, mem. task force on Cost Effectiveness N.W. Ohio; chmn. med. necessity appeals com. Blue Cross/Blue Shield; adv. bd. PIE Mut. Ins. Co. Chmn. steering com. Pack 198, Boy Scouts Am.; chmn. fin. com., dir. bldg. fund campaign First Baptist Ch., Perrysburg, Ohio; faculty chmn. Med. Coll. Ohio United Way Campaign; mem. adv. com. Multiple Sclerosis Soc. NW Ohio. Recipient Outstanding Tchr. award Med. Coll. Ohio, 1980; named to Outstanding Young Men Am., U.S. Jaycees, 1973; USPHS trainee, 1964-69, postdoctoral trainee, 1973-75; grantee Am. Cancer Soc., 1977-78, Warner Lambert Pharm. Co., 1978-79, Miniger Found., 1980, Toledo Hosp. Found., 1985, Promedica Health Care Found., 1986. Mem. Am. Profl. Practice Assn., Am. Pathology Found., Am. Soc. Law and Medicine, Coll. Am. Pathologists, Lucas County Acad. Medicine (bar acad. liaison com.), Ohio State Med. Assn. (fed. key contact), Med. Assn. Ga., Am. Assn. Neuropathologists (profl. affairs com., awards com., program com., constitution com.), Internat. Acad. Pathologists, Ohio Soc. Pathologists, Coll. Am. Pathologists, EM Soc. Am., Sigma Xi. Author med., sci. papers; reviewer Jour. Neuropathology and Exptl. Neurology. Republican. Avocations: tennis, real estate rehabilitation, bldg. developer, gardening, white water rafting. Home and Office: 9105 Nesbit Lakes Dr Alpharetta GA 30202-4028

HARRIS, JAN C., health care administrator; b. Ithaca, N.Y., Jan. 15, 1944; d. Frank and Shirley Ellen (Rickard) Caplan; m. Sonny G. Harris, Mar. 23, 1990; children: Josh, Greg, Irene, Mike, Ginger, Morgan, J.B. BSN, Cornell U., 1966; MA in Liberal Studies, Dartmouth Coll., 1974; MS in Healthcare Adminstrn., U. Colo., 1989. Coord. fed. programs, dir. instrn., tech. ctr. Northwest Arctic Sch. Dist., Kotzebue, Alaska, 1976-82; dir. planning and devel., interim pres., ops. exec. Maniilaq Assn., Kotzebue, 1985-93; adminstr. Maniilaq Health Ctr., Kotzebue, 1993—; cons. Walrus Works, Anchorage, 1982-85. Recipient Svc. award PHS/Indian Health Svc. Mem. Am. Coll. Healthcare Execs., Am. Soc. Quality Control, Healthcare Forum. Home: Box 62 Kotzebue AK 99752 Office: Maniilaq Health Ctr Box 43 Kotzebue AK 99752

HARRIS, JAY ROBERT, radiologist; b. Weehawken, N.J., June 29, 1944. MD, Stanford U. Sch. Medicine, 1970. Intern Jewish Hosp., St. Louis, 1970-71; resident in radiol. therapy Joint Ctr. Radiol. Therapy, Boston, 1973-76; fellow Harvard Med. Sch., Boston, 1976-77, prof. radiol. oncology. Mem. Am. Coll. Radiology, AMA, AAAS. Office: Joint Ctr Radiol Therapy 50 Binney St Boston MA 02115-6086*

HARRIS, JEFFREY SAUL, health facility administrator; b. Pitts., Mar. 13, 1949; s. Aaron Wexler and Janet Mary (Szerlip) Harris; m. Mary V. Anderson, Jan. 2, 1981; children: Sarah Ariel, Noah Aaron, Susannah Leia. BS in Molecular Biophysics/Biochemistry, Yale U., 1971; MD, U. N.Mex., 1975; MPH, U. Mich., 1982; MBA, Vanderbilt U., 1988. Diplomate Am. Bd. Preventive Medicine in Occupl. Medicine & Gen. Preventive Medicine & Pub. Health, Emergency Medicine, Medicine Quality, Ind. Med. Examination; lic. Md., Calif., Tenn., Alaska. Gen. med. officer USPHS, Juneau, Alaska, 1976-78; clin. dir. S.E. Alaska Native Health Corp, Juneau, 1978-79; asst. to commr. Tenn. Dept. Health and Environment, Nashville, 1980-83; dir. health care mgmt. Northern Telecom Inc., Nashville, 1983-88; pres. HDM, Inc., Nashville, 1988-90; med. dir. Aetna Health Plans of Tenn., Nashville, 1990-91; leader nat. practice, health strategy Alexander & Alexander Cons. Group, San Francisco, 1991-94; chief prevention, health and disability officer Indsl. Indemnity, San Francisco, 1994—; pres. Harris Assocs., Anchorage, Nashville, Mill Valley, Calif., 1979—. Author: Strategic Health Management, 1994; author, editor: Managing Employee Health Care Costs, 1992, Manual of Occupational Health and Safety, 1992, 96, Practice Guidelines, 1996, Occupational Medicine: Evaluation and Management of Common Health Problems and Disability in Workers; author, co-editor: Health Promotion in the Work Place, 1994; editl. bd. mem. Am. Journ. Health Promotion, 1985—, Occupl. Environment Med. Report, 1988; contbr. articles to profl. jours. Fellow Am. Acad. Family Practice, Am. Coll. Occupl. Environ. Medicine (dir., chair health care quality mgmt. com., practice guidelines com., Presdl. award 1996), Am. Coll. Preventive Medicine, Am. Coll. Med. Quality, Am. Bd. Ind. Med. Examiners. Home: 386 Richardson Way Mill Valley CA 94941 Office: Indsl Indemnity 255 California St San Francisco CA 94111

HARRIS, JEROME SYLVAN, pediatrician, pediatrics and biochemistry educator; b. N.Y.C., Feb. 27, 1909; s. Mark and Mary (Marcus) H.; m. Jacqueline Cato Hijmans, Oct. 23, 1958. A.B. summa cum laude, Dartmouth Coll., 1929; M.D. cum laude, Harvard U., 1933. Intern U. Chgo. Clinics, 1934; resident Boston Children's Hosp., 1935-36; mem. faculty Duke Sch. Medicine, Durham, N.C., 1937-79; J. Buren Sidbury prof. pediatrics, also prof. biochemistry Duke Sch. Medicine, 1950-79; chmn. dept. pediatrics Duke Med. Center, 1954-68; Cons. Nat. Bd. Med. Examiners, 1956-60; mem. human embryology and devel. study sect. NIH, 1959-63. Contbr. articles to profl. jours. Bd. dirs. Durham Child Guidance Clinic, 1950-54. Served to lt. col. M.C. AUS, 1942-46. Mem. Am. Soc. Clin. Investigation, Soc. Pediatric Research, Am. Acad. Pediatrics, Am. Pediatrics Soc., So. Soc. Pediatric Research, Phi Beta Kappa, Sigma Xi, Alpha Omega Alpha. Office: Duke Hospital Pediatrics Dept Durham NC 27710

HARRIS, JUDY ANN, rehabilitation nurse; b. Denver, Aug. 13, 1954; d. Michael and Marilyn Rose Buben; m. Donald Robert Harris, June 16, 1972; 1 child, Yvonne. BSN, U. Tex., Galveston, 1982; M in Rehab. Sci., Fla. State U., 1988. RN, Fla., Ga.; cert. registered rehab. nurse, case mgr., rehab. counselor. Staff nurse John Sealy Hosp., Galveston, Tex., 1982-83; staff nurse, supr. Tallahassee Meml. Regional Med. Ctr., 1983-88; rehab. cons. Grimsley Rehab. Assn., Tallahassee, 1988-92; dir. case mgmt., utilization rev.iew & risk mgmt. Healthsouth Rehab. Hosp. Tallahassee, 1992—. Reviewer jours. Mem. UR com. profl. adv. bd. Interim Healthcare, Tallahassee, 1993—; mem. commd. Fla. State Pain Mgmt., 1993—. Mem. Fla. Assn. Rehab. Nurses (legis. chair 1991-94, nominating chair 1991-94, pres. elect 1995—), Case Mgmt. Soc. Fla. (pres. Tallahassee chpt. 1994-96, state embership chair), Case Mgmt. Soc. Am. (sec. case mgmt. 1996), Tallahassee Assn. Rehab. Nurses (v.p. 1989-91, pres. 1992-93), Sigma Theta Tau. Home: 3196 Ferns Glen Dr Tallahassee FL 32308-2304 Office: Healthsouth Rehab Hosp Tallahassee 1675 Riggins Rd Tallahassee FL 32308-5315

HARRIS, KAREN, optometrist; b. Norwalk, Conn., Dec. 21, 1961; d. Donald Roy and Noreen Sheila (Levine) H.; m. Gary Sheids Benninghoff, Aug. 18, 1985; 1 child, Amanda Leigh. BS, U. Md., 1983; OD, Pa. Coll. Optometry, 1987. Optometrist Phila. Eye Glass Labs., Bensalem, Pa. Mem. Am. Optometric Assn. Republican. Jewish. Office: Phila Eye Glass Labs 1863 Street Rd Bensalem PA 18940

HARRIS, KERRY FRANCIS PATRICK, virologist; b. New Orleans, Aug. 6, 1941; s. Edward C-M. and Alice Claire (Noonan) H.; m. Lisa Jean Patricia Lambert, Mar. 7, 1987; 1 child, Lane Alan. BS, U. New Orleans, 1964; MS, Loyola U., 1968; PhD, Mich. State U., 1971. Instr., sci. New Orleans Sch. Bd., 1963-65; prof. Tex. A&M U., College Station, 1976—; dir. Virus-Vector Rsch. Lab. Tex. A&M U., 1993—; rsch. scientist in field. Editor: Aphids as Virus Vectors, 1977, Leafhopper Vectors and Plant Disease Agents, 1979, Vectors of Plant Pathogens, 1980, Plant Diseases and Vectors-Ecology and Epidemiology, 1981, Current Topics in Vector Research, 1981-84; editor-in-chief Advances in Disease Vector Research, 1987—; contbr. to profl. jours. Rsch. fellow NIH, 1965-68, 69-71, 73-75, NSF, 1968-69, Nat. Rsch. Coun. Can., 1971-73; Fulbright scholar, 1969-70, 72-73. Mem. Am. Phytopathological Soc., AAAS, Entomological Soc. Am., Internat. Soc. Plant Protection, Internat. Working Group Legume Viruses, Sigma Xi, Phi Sigma, Phi Kappa Phi. Home: 4109 Viceroy Dr Bryan TX 77802-6020 Office: Tex A&M U Dept Entomology College Station TX 77843-2475

HARRIS, LOUIS SELIG, pharmacologist, researcher; b. Boston, Mar. 27, 1927; s. Max Selig and Pearl (Oppochinski) H.; m. Ruth Irma Schaufus, Aug. 22, 1952; 1 child, Charles Allan. BA, Harvard U., 1954, MA, 1956, PhD, 1958. Sect. head, sr. rsch. biologist Sterling-Winthrop Rsch. Inst., Rensselaer, N.Y., 1958-66; lectr. in pharmacology Albany (N.Y.) Med. Coll., 1959-66; from assoc. prof. to prof. U. N.C., Chapel Hill, 1966-73; Harvey

Haag prof. Med. Coll. Va./Va. Commonwealth U., Richmond, 1972—, chmn. pharmacology, toxicology dept., 1972-92, assoc. v.p. health scis., 1996—; assoc. v.p. health sci. Med. Coll. Va./Va. Commonwealth U., 1996—; acting assoc. dir. Nat. Inst. on Drug Abuse, Rockville, Md., 1987-88; Sterling Drug vis. prof., 1983; mem. com. on problems of drug dependence NAS/NRC, 1973-77; mem. Com. on Problems of Drug Dependence, Inc., 1977-93, chmn., 1990-92; hon. prof. Beijing Med. U., People's Republic of China, 1990—. Editor: (monograph) NIDA Monographs, Proceedings, Committee on Problems of Drug Dependence, 1979—; author chpts. in books. Recipient Hartung Meml. award U. N.C., 1981, Univ. Excellence award Med. Coll. Va./Va. Commonwealth U., 1984, Outstanding Faculty award, 1984, Nathan B. Eddy award Com. on Problems of Drug Dependence, 1985, Abe Wikler award Nat. Inst. on Drug Abuse, 1991, Gov.'s award on Drug Abuse Rsch., 1992, Presdl. medallion Va. Commonwealth U., 1993. Fellow Am. Coll. Neuropsychopharmacology, Coll. Problems Drug Dependence; mem. AAAS, AAUP, Am. Soc. Pharmacology and Exptl. Therapeutics, Am. Chem. Soc., Am. Assn. for Med. Sch. Pharmacology, Am. Pain Soc. (charter 1977), Am. Pharm. Assn., Am. Soc. for Clin. Pharmacology and Therapeutics, Assn. Harvard Chemists, Elisha Mitchell Sci. Soc., Internat. Narcotic Enforcement Officers Assn., Soc. for Neurosci., Internat. Soc. Biochem. Pharmacology, Acad. of Scis., Internat. Soc. for Study of Pain, Collegium Internationale Neuro-Psychopharmacologicum, Va. Acad. Sci., Harvard Vlub Boston, Cosmos Club Washington. Home: 7830 Rockfalls Dr Richmond VA 23225-1049 Office: Va Commonwealth U PO Box 980027 Richmond VA 23201-0027

HARRIS, LOYD ERVIN, pharmacy educator; b. Ryan, Okla., Sept. 21, 1900; s. Howard Luther and Necie Emma (Culwel) H.; m. Cora Maurine Harris, June 19, 1923; children: Lorene Anne, Ronald David. BS in Pharmacy, U. Okla., 1922, MS in Chemistry, 1924; PhD in Pharm. Chemistry, U. Wis., 1926. Lectr. asst. chemistry U. Okla., Norman, 1921-22, asst. prof. pharmacy, 1922-25, prof. pharmacy, 1926-38, prof. chemistry, 1938-46; prof. pharmacy Ohio State U., Columbus, 1946-63, acting dean pharmacy, 1955-56; dean Coll. Pharmacy, prof. pharmacy U. Okla., Norman, 1963-70, dean emeritus, prof. emeritus, 1970—. Co-author: Inorganic Chemistry in Pharmacy, 1940. Mem. Grandview Heights Bd. Health, Columbus, 1953-63, pres., 1957-63; bd. dirs. Med. Rsch. Found., Oklahoma City, 1963-70. Col. U.S. Army, 1944-46, ETO. Mem. Okla. Pharm. Assn., Am. Pharm. Assn. (life), Lions (dist. sect. 1941-42), Sigma Xi, Phi Beta Kappa, Rho Chi, Phi Delta Chi, Lambda Chi Alpha, Gamma Alpha. Republican. Presbyterian. Home: 2514 S Pickard Ave Norman OK 73072-6920

HARRIS, MICHAEL, ophthalmologist; b. Newark, Aug. 1, 1944; s. David Edward and Elaine H. BS, Rutgers U., 1966; MD, SUNY, Syracuse, 1970. Diplomate Am. Acad. Ophthalmology. Resident Albert Einstein Coll. Medicine, Bronx, N.Y., 1976; assoc. clin. prof. Coll. Medicine and Dentistry, Newark, 1976—; assoc. prof. St. Barnabas Med. ctr., Livingston, N.J. Co-Author: Contacct Lens-Basic Fitting, 1990; contbr. articles to profl. jours. 1st lt. USN, 1973-76. Henry Rutgers scholar Rutgers U., 1965. Fellow Am. Acad. Ophthamology (Disting. Svc. award 1993); mem. Contact Lens Assn. Ophthalmologists, Med. Soc. N.J., Phi Beta Kappa. Office: 315 E Northfield Rd Livingston NJ 07039

HARRIS, MICHAEL ANTHONY, hematologist, oncologist, educator; b. Sioux Falls, S.D., Sept. 20, 1950; s. Michael Anthony and Cecilia Ann (Mutza) H.; m. Alice Ruth Platt, June 23, 1974; children: Rebecca Lynn, Daniel Charles. BA in Sociology, U. Mich., 1972; MD, Wayne State U., 1976. Diplomate Am. Bd. Internal Medicine, Am. Bd. Med. Oncology. Fellow in oncology Georgetown U. Hosp., Washington, 1980-82; pvt. practice, Mission Viejo, Calif., 1982—; staff hematologist and oncologist Mission Hosp. Regional Med. Ctr., Mission Viejo, 1982—, chief medicine, 1992-9, founder Found., 1994. Fellow ACP; mem. Calif. Med. Assn., Orange County Med. Assn. Office: Ste 344 27800 Medical Center Rd Mission Viejo CA 92691

HARRIS, MICHAEL GENE, optometrist, educator, lawyer; b. San Francisco, Sept. 20, 1942; s. Morry and Gertrude Alice (Epstein) H.; m. Dawn Block; children: Matthew Benjamin, Daniel Evan, Ashley Beth, Lindsay Meredith. BS, U. Calif., 1964, M. Optometry, 1965, D. Optometry, 1966, MS, 1968; JD, John F. Kennedy U., 1985. Bar: Calif., U.S. Dist. Ct. (no. dist.) Calif. Assoc. practice optometry, Oakland, Calif., 1965-66, San Francisco, 1966-68; instr., coord. contact lens clinic Ohio State U., 1968-69; asst. clin. prof. optometry U. Calif., Berkeley, 1969-73, dir. contact lens extended care clinic, 1969-83, chief contact lens clinic, 1983—, assoc. clin. prof., 1973-76, asst. chief contact lens svc., 1970-76, assoc. chief contact lens svc., 1976—, lectr., 1978-80, sr. lectr., 1980—, vice chmn. faculty Sch. Optometry, 1983-85, 95—, prof. clin. optometry, 1984-86; clin. prof. optometry, 1986—, dir. residency program, 1993—, asst. dean, 1994-95, assoc. dean, 1995—; John de Carle vis. prof. City U., London, 1984; vis. rsch. fellow U. New South Wales, Sydney, Australia, 1989; sr. vis. rsch. scholar U. Melbourne, Australia, 1989, 92; pvt. practice optometry, Oakland, Calif., 1973-76; mem. ophthalmic devices panel, med. device adv. com. FDA, 1990—; lectr., cons. in field; mem. regulation rev. com. Calif. State Bd. Optometry; cons. hypnosis Calif. Optometric Assn., Am. Optometric Assn.; cons. Nat. Bd. Examiners in Optometry, Soflens div. Bausch & Lomb, 1973—, Barnes-Hind Hydrocurve Soft Lenses, Inc., 1974-87, Pilkinton-Barnes Hind, 1987—, Contact Lens Rsch. Lab., 1976—, Wesley-Jessen Contact Lens Co., 1977—, Palo Alto VA, 1980—, Primarius Corp., Cooper Vision Optics Alcon, 1980—; co-founder Morton D. Sarver Rsch. Lab., 1986; Planning commr. Town of Moraga, Calif., 1986, vice-chmn., 1987-88, chmn. 1988-90; mem. Town Coun., Moraga, Calif., 1992—, , vice mayor, 1994—, Medi-Cal. Adv. Planning Comm., 1993—, chair, 1994—; founding mem. Young Adults div. Jewish Welfare Fedn., 1965—, chmn. 1967-68; commr. Sunday Football League, Contra Costa County, Calif., 1974-78. Charter Mem. Jewish Community Ctr. Contra Costa County; founding mem. Jewish Community Mus. San Francisco, 1984; Para-Rabbinic, Temple Isaiah, Lafayette, Calif., 1987, bd. dirs., 1990; life mem. Bay Area Coun. for Soviet Jews, 1976; bd. dirs. Jewish Community Rels. Coun. of Greater East Bay, 1979—, Campolindo Homeowners Assn., 1981—; pres. student coun. John F. Kennedy U. Sch. Law, 1984-85. Fellow U. Calif., 1971; Calif. Optometric Assn. Scholar 1965, George Schneider Meml. scholar, 1964. Fellow Am. Acad. Optometry (diplomate cornea and contact lens sect.; chmn. contact lens papers; mem. contact lens com. 1974—, vice chmn. contact lens sect. 1980-82, chmn. 1982-84, immediate past chmn. 84-86, chmn. jud. com. 1989—, chmn. by-laws com. 1989—), Assn. Schs. and Colls. Optometry (coun. on acad. affairs), AAAS, Prentice Soc.; mem. Assn. for Rsch. in Vision and Ophthalmology, Am. Optometric Assn. (proctor 1969—, cons. on hypnosis, mem. contact lens sect., mem. position papers com., com. on ophthalmic standards, subcom. on testing and certification), Calif. Optometric Assn., Assn. Optometric Contact Lens Educators, Am. Optometric Found., Mexican Soc. Contactology (hon.), Nat. Coun. on Contact Lens Compliance, Internat. Soc. Contact Lens Rsch., Calif. State Bd. Optometry (regulation rev. com.), Calif. Acad. Scis., U. Calif. Optometry Alumni Assn. (life), ABA, Assn. Trial Lawyers Am., Calif. Trial Lawyers Assn., Calif. Young Lawyers Assn., Contra Costa Bar Assn., Mus. Soc., JFK U. Sch. Law Alumni Assn., Benjamin Ide Wheeler Soc. U. Calif., Mensa. Democrat. Lodge: B'nai B'rith. Editor current comments sect. Am. Jour. Optometry, 1974-77; editor Eye Contact, 1984-86, assoc. editor The Video Jour. Clin. Optometry, 1988—, consulting editor Contact Lens Spectrum, 1988—; editor: Problems in Optometry, Special Contact Lens Procedures; Contact Lenses and Ocular Disease, 1990; contbr. chpts. to booes; contbr. articles to profl. pubs. Office: U Calif Sch Optometry Berkeley CA 94720

HARRIS, PATRICIA CAROL, business executive, consultant; b. Spokane, Wash., Aug. 30, 1943; d. Arthur Laverne and Hazel Kathryn (Wingegar) Fisk; m. Bernard J. Harris Jr., Sept. 14, 1962; children: Heather Kathryn, Holly Marie. BS in Bacteriology and Pub. Health, Wash. State U., 1965; MS in Clin. Microbiology and Immunology, U. Wash., 1977. Microbiologist San Francisco Health Dept., 1965-67, Seattle-King County Health Dept., 1967-68; chief microbiologist Gen. Hosp. of Everett, Wash., 1968-86; tech. specialist Baxter, Inc. Divsn. of Baxter, Issaquah, Wash., 1986-92, tech. mgr., 1992-95; dir. sales and mktg. Bartels, Inc. Divsn. of Dade, Issaquah, Wash., 1995-96; v.p. bus. devel. Bartels, Inc., Issaquah, Wash., 1996—; cons. clin. microbiologist, Everett, 1970-86; software devel. cons. CLINREL Micro Sys., Everett, 1983-86. Contbr. articles to profl. jours. Mem. Am. Soc. for Microbiology, Am. Soc. Clin. Pathologists, Clin. Lab. Mgrs. Assn. Home: 3617 255th SE # 27 Issaquah WA 98029 Office: Bartels Inc 2005 NW Sammamish Issaquah WA 98027

HARRIS, PATRICIA CROUSE, medical technologist; b. Sparta, N.C., Aug. 8, 1952; d. Herman Johnson and Beulah (Estep) Crouse; m. Marvin Edward Harris Jr., Dec. 26, 1974 (div. 1986); children: Jennifer Lynn, James Edward, Juliette Nicole. AS, Surry C.C., Dobson, N.C., 1992. Cert. med. technologist. Med. technologist Hugh Chatham Meml. Hosp., Elkin, N.C., 1988—; med. technologist Allephany Meml. Hosp., Sparta, 1981-89, 93—. Home: 1565 Spicer Mountain Rd Sparta NC 28675 Office: Hugh Chatham Meml Hosp Parkwood Dr Elkin NC 28622

HARRIS, ROBERT ALLISON, biochemistry educator; b. Boone, Iowa, Nov. 10, 1939; s. Arnold E. and Marie (Wilcox) H.; m. Karen Kaye Dutton, Dec. 27, 1960; children—Kelly, Chris, Heidi, Shawn. B.S., Iowa State U., 1962; Ph.D., Purdue U., 1965. Asst. research prof. U. Wis., 1968-69; assoc. prof. biochemistry Ind. U. Med. Sch., Indpls., 1970-75, prof., 1975-92, Showalter prof., 1992—, assoc. chmn. dept., 1983-88, chmn. dept., 1988—. Co-editor: Isolation, Characterization, and Use of Hepatocytes, 1983, Branched Chain Amino Acids Volume 166 of Methods in Enzymology, 1988; contbr. articles to profl. jours. Recipient Disting. Teaching award AMOCO, 1981, Young investigator award Ind. Diabetes Assn., 1977; Edward C. Moore award, 1985; Nat. Multiple Sclerosis Soc. fellow, 1966-68; established investigator Am. Heart Assn., 1969-74. Mem. Am. Soc. Biol. Chemists, Biochem. Soc., Am. Heart Assn., Am. Diabetic Assn., Am. Inst. Nutrition. Office: Dept Biochemistry Ind U Sch Medicine Indianapolis IN 46202-5122

HARRIS, ROGER CLARK, psychiatrist, consultant; b. Washington, Aug. 27, 1938; s. Lester Wilbur and Margaret Elizabeth (Gilligan) H.; m. Ann Marie Dorman, Sept. 22, 1962; children: Laura Colleen, Gregory Scott Henry. BS, U. Md., 1961; postgrad., U. Md., College Park, 1961-62; MD, U. Md. Sch. Medicine, Balt., 1964-68. Diplomate Am. Bd. Med. Examiners, Am. Bd. Psychiatry and Neurology. Intern Washington Hosp. Ctr., 1968-69; resident in psychiatry Med. Sch. U. Md., 1969-72; staff psychiatrist Portsmouth (Va.) Psychiat. Ctr., 1972-73, Larry H. Dizmang and Assoc., Annapolis, Md., 1973-74; pvt. practice Annapolis, 1974-75; prin. Roger C. Harris Group Practice of Psychiatry and Assocs., Annapolis, 1975—; pres. Chesapeake Comprehensive Counseling Ctrs., Inc., Washington and Balt., 1988—; co-founder Psychiatry Consultation Svc. of Baltimore City Police Dept., 1970-72; chief psychiatry svc. Anne Arundel Gen. Hosp., Annapolis, 1978-81; asst. clin. prof. psychiatry U. Md. Sch. Medicine, 1973—; acting dir. of outpatient clinic U. Md. Emergency Psychiat. Svcs., 1971-72, chief resident, 1971-72; primary founder Hosp. Inpatient Svcs., Anne Arundel Gen. Hosp. Mem. Disability Rev. Bd. for Anne Arundel County, 1985-87, Orgn. of Physicians for Social Responsiblity, 1985—. Recipient Cert. Appreciation Arundel Lodge, Inc., Annapolis, 1988, Mitchell Scholarship, Alpha Tau Omega Social Fraternity, College Park, Md., 1960. Mem. Chesapeake Bay Psychiat. Soc., Am. Psychiat. Assn., Md. Psychiat. Soc., Anne Arundel County Med. Soc., Am. Group Psychotherapy Assn., Orthopsychiat. Assn., Epping Forest Boat Club, Young Foresters Orgn., Alpha Tau Omega (sec. 1958-60). Democrat. Presbyterian. Home: 212 Eareckson Ln Stevensville MD 21666-3040 Office: Chesapeake Comprehensive Counseling Ctr 8 Willow St Annapolis MD 21401-3147

HARRIS, STEVEN THOMAS, endocrinologist, educator; b. Oakland, Calif., July 19, 1949. BA cum laude, Stanford U., 1970; MD, U. Calif., San Francisco, 1974. Diplomate Am. Bd. Internal Medicine, Am. Bd. Endocrinology and Metabolism. Intern San Francisco Gen. Hosp., 1974-75; resident U. Calif., San Francisco, 1975-77, chief resident, 1977-78, instr. in residence, medicine and anesthesiology, 1978-79, asst. clin. prof. medicine, 1983-89, assoc. clin. prof. medicine and radiology, 1989-95, clin. prof. medicine and radiology, 1995—; rsch. fellow Harvard Med. Sch., Boston, 1979-81, instr. in medicine, 1981-83; clin. and rsch. fellow in endocrinology Mass. Gen. Hosp., Boston, 1979-83. Contbr. articles to profl. jours., chpts. to books; presenter in field. Recipient Clin. Assoc. Physician award Gen. Clin. Rsch. Ctr., 1984-87. Fellow ACP; mem. Nat. Osteoporosis Found., Am. Soc. for Bone and Mineral Rsch., Paget's Disease Found., The Endocrine Soc., Am. Fedn. for Clin. Rsch., Osteogenesis Imperfecta Found., Gold-Headed Cane Soc., Phi Beta Kappa, Alpha Omega Alpha. Office: U Calif San Francisco 350 Parnassus Ave Ste 706 San Francisco CA 94117-3608

HARRIS, SUSANNA, immunologist, retired; b. Bklyn., May 11, 1919; d. Barnet and Rebecca (Goodman) Shapiro; m. T.N. Harris, Dec. 26, 1940; children: Joseph D., Elizabeth. BA, Bklyn. Coll., 1940; BS, Drexel U., 1942; PhD, U. Pa., 1948. Instr. bacteriology U. Pa. Sch. Medicine, Phila., 1948-51, asst. prof. pediatrics rsch., 1951-54, assoc. prof. immunology in pediatrics, 1954-82. Contbr. articles in profl. jours. Mem. Am. Acad. Microbiology, AM. Assn. Immunology, Sigma Xi. Home: Sutton Terrace # 502 50 Belmont Ave Bala Cynwyd PA 19004-2416 Office: Children's Hosp Abramson Rsch Bldg 34th Civic Ctr Blvd Philadelphia PA 19104

HARRIS, TIMOTHY JOHN ROY, biologist, researcher; b. London, May 11, 1950; s. Robert John Cecil and Annette (Brading) H.; m. Josephine Mary Foster, Sept. 7, 1974; children: Sarah Elizabeth, Frances Mary, Rebecca Jane, William Robert. BS in Biochemistry, Birmingham (Eng.) U., 1971, PhD, 1974. Scientist Animal Virus Rsch. Inst., Pirbright, Eng., 1974-81; postdoctoral fellow SUNY, Stony Brook, 1977-78; molecular biologist Celltech, Ltd., Slough, Eng., 1981-89; dir. biotech. Glaxo Group Rsch., Ltd, Greenford, Eng., 1989—; prof. biochemistry Birkbeck Coll. London U., 1987—. Contbr. over 60 rsch. papers and sci. articles to profl. publs. Fellow Inst. of Biology; mem. Biochem. Soc., Soc. Gen. Microbiology. Office: Glaxo Group Rsch Ltd, Greenford Rd, Greenford UB6 0HE, England

HARRIS, WILLIAM D., osteopath; b. Beaumont, Tex., June 23, 1953; s. William Houston and Kathryn Diane (Gerdes) H.; m. Cynthia Diane, Sept. 10, 1955; children: (twins) Geoffrey, Sean. BS, U. Iowa, 1976; DO, U. Health Scis., 1982. Instr. respiratory therapy U. Iowa Pediatric Pulmonary Lab., 1978-82; intern, resident in internal medicine St. Luke's Hosp., Kansas City, Mo., 1982-86; with Pub. Health Scholarship & Placement, Waterloo, Iowa, 1986-90; physician Rsch. Hosp., Overland Park (Kans.) Regional Hosp., 1990—; bd. dirs. So. Johnson County Fire & Ambulance Bd., Stilwell, 1994—. Asst. coach baseball Stilwell Elem. Sch., 1995, asst. coach soccer, 1995. Mem. AMA, AM. Coll. Physicians, Beta Beta Bata. Methodist. Office: Humana Healthcare 8550 Marshall Dr Lenexa KS 66215

HARRISES, ANTONIO EFTHEMIOS, biology educator; b. Manchester, N.H., Sept. 12, 1926; s. Efthemios John and Gramato (Kerageorge) H.; m. Mary Catherine Dennig, Aug., 1957; children: Anthony, Gregory, Stephen, Susan and Sally (twins). BA, St. Anselms' Coll., 1950; MS, U. N.H., 1952; PhD, U. Notre Dame, Ind., 1957. Prof. U. So. Miss., Hattiesburg, 1957-69, Salem (Mass.) State Coll., 1969—; dir. nuclear medicine tech. program Salem State Coll., 1981-91. Author: Monogenetic Trematoda. Cpl. USAAF, 1944-46, ETO. Am. Soc. Parasitologists, Helminthological Soc. Washington, Sigma Xi.

HARRIS-OFFUTT, ROSALYN MARIE, psychotherapist, counselor, nurse anesthetist, educator, author; b. Memphis; d. Roscoe Henry and Irene Elnora (Blake) Harris; 1 child, Christopher Joseph. R.N., St. Joseph Catholic Sch. Nursing, Flint, Mich., 1965; B.S. in Wholistic Health Scis., Columbia-Pacific U., 1984, postgrad., 1985—. RN; cert. registered nurse in anesthesia; nat. bd. cert. addiction counselor; cert. psychiat. nursing Kalamazoo State Hosp.; lic. profl. counselor, N.C.; cert. detoxification acupuncturist; Staff nurse anesthetist, clin. instr. Cleve. Clinic Found., 1981-82; pvt. practice psychiat. nursing and counseling; Assoc. Counselor in Human Services, Shaker Heights, Ohio, 1982-84; ind. contractor anesthesia Paul Scott & Assocs., Cleve., 1984, Via Triad Anesthesia Assocs., Thomasville, N.C., 1984-85; sec. Cons., Psychology and Counseling, P.A., pvt. practice psychiat. nursing and counseling, Greensboro, N.C., 1984-86, pvt. practice psychiat. nursing, counseling and psychotherapy UNA Psychol. Assocs., 1986—, staff cons. Charter Hills Psychiat. Hosp. in Addictive Disease, 1991—; nat. resource cons. Am. Assn. Nursing Anesthetists on Addictive Disease; cons. Ctr. for Substance Abuse Prevention, also adviser to assoc. and clin. med. dir. Ctr. Substance Abuse Prevention. Co-sponsor adolescent group Jack and Jills of Am., Inc., Bloomfield Hills, Mich., 1975; co-sponsor Youth of Unity Ctr., Cleveland Heights, Ohio, 1981-84; vol. chmn. hospitality Old Greensboro Preservation Soc., 1985; bd. dirs. Urban League, Pontiac, Mich., 1972; apptd. mem. gov's. coun. on alcohol and other drug abuse State of N.C., 1989—, gov's. coun. women's issues of addiction, 1991—; apptd. advisor to assoc. clin., med. dir. Ctr. for Substance Abuse Prevention, Dept. Health and Human Svcs. U.S., 1991—, nat. speakers bureau, 1991—, cons.; apptd. legis. com., mental health study commn. on child and adolescent substance abuse State of N.C., 1992—; lay speaking min. United Meth. Ch.; mem. Triad United Meth. Native Am. Ch. Mission . Columbia-Pacific U. scholar, 1983. Contbr. chpt. to book, also articles and columns in health field. Fellow Soc. Preventitive Nutritionists; mem. Am. Assn. Profl. Hypnotherapists (registered profl. hypnotherapists, adv. bd.), Am. Assn. Nurse Anesthetists (cert.), Nat. Alaska Native Am. Indian Nurses Assn., Assn. Med. Educators and Rsch. in Substance Abuse, Nat. Acupuncture Detoxification Assn., Am. Assn. Counseling and Devel., Assn. for Med. Edn. and Rsch. in Substance Abuse, Am. Assn. Clin. Hypnotists, Am. Assn. Wholistic Practitioners, Am. Nurse Hypnotherapy Assn. (state pres. 1992—), Am. Nurse Assn., Am. Holistic Nurses Assn. (charter mem.), Guilford Native Am. Assn., Negro Bus. and Profl. Women Inc. (v.p., parliamentarian 1961-83), Oakland County Council Black Nurses (v.p. 1970-74), Assn. Med. Educators (researcher substance abuse, ad hoc com. mem. cultural diversity 1994—), Zeta Phi Beta (Nu Xi Zeta chpt. 2d anti-basilevs 1992-93). Republican. Avocations: music, nature, reading, Egyptian history, metaphysics. Office: UNA Psychol Assocs 620 S Elm St Ste 371 Greensboro NC 27406-1371

HARRISON, BRYAN DESMOND, plant virologist, researcher, educator; b. Purley, Surrey, Eng., June 16, 1931; s. John William and Norah (Webster) H.; m. Elizabeth Ann Latham-Warde, Jan. 13, 1968; children: Peter, Robert, Claire. BSc, Reading U., England, 1952; PhD, London U., 1955; DAgr and Forestry (hon.), Helsinki (Finland) U., 1990. Rsch. trainee Rothamsted Exptl. Sta., Harpenden, Eng., 1952-54, sr. sci. officer, 1957-66; sci. officer Scottish Hort. Rsch. Inst., Dundee, Scotland, 1954-57; prin., sr. prin. then deputy chief sci. officer Scot. Crop (formerly Hort.) Rsch. Inst., Dundee, 1966-91; prof. Dundee U., 1991-96; vis. scientist Waite Agrl. Rsch. Inst., Adelaide, Australia, 1964; hon. prof. U. St. Andrews, Scotland, 1986—; Behrens lectr. U. Leeds, 1990. Co-author: (with Gibbs) Plant Virology: the Principles, 1976; contbr. over 150 articles to profl. jours. Recipient Comdr. Order of British Empire award H.M. Queen Elizabeth II, 1990. Fellow Royal Soc. London, Royal Soc. Edinburgh, Inst. Biology; mem. Assn. Applied Biologists (hon.), Soc. Gen. Microbiology (hon.), Phytopath. Soc. Japan (hon.). also: Scottish Crop Rsch Inst, Invergowrie, Dundee DD2-5DA, Scotland

HARRISON, DAWN SAUTTERS, charge nurse, flight nurse; b. Princeton, N.J., Aug. 1, 1967; d. Terry Glen and Carol Ann (Scharf) Sautters; m. Jonathan Warren Harrison, Aug. 6, 1994; 1 child, Macey Elizabeth. BSN, Radford U., 1989; student, East Tenn. State U., 1994—. RN, Tenn.; cert. Emergency Nurse Emergency Med. Technician, instr. emergency nursing pediat. course,; ACLS, pediat. ALS, neonatal ALS, BLS, Am. Heart Assn. Emergency room tech. Montgomery Regional Hosp., Blacksburg, Va., 1988-89; nurse externship program Montgomery Regional Hosp., Blacksburg, 1989, staff nurse emergency dept., 1989-90, 91, nurse mgr., 1990-91; staff nurse emergency dept. Radford (Va.) Cmty. Hosp., 1991-93, Pulaski (Va.) Cmty. Hosp., 1993; staff nurse emergency dept., flight nurse Johnson City (Tenn.) Med. Ctr. Hosp., 1993-95; med-flight nurse Bristol (Tenn.) Regional Med. Ctr., 1994-95; preceptor nurse externship program Montgomery Regional Hosp., Blacksburg, 1991, Johnson City Medical Ctr. Hosp., 1994—; spkr. BACCHUS group Radford U., 1993. Mem. Emergency Nurses Orgn., Nat. Flight Nurses Assn. Home: Rt 7 Box 3720 Elizabethton TN 37643

HARRISON, EMERSON EARL, urologic surgeon; b. Rocky Mount, N.C., Sept. 16, 1960; s. Charles Linburg and Lillie (Hedgepeth) H.; m. Cynthia Wright, Sept. 10, 1988; children: Emerson II, Christian. BS, Morehouse Coll., 1982; MD, East Carolina U., 1986. Diplomate Am. Bd. Urology. Urologist Atlanta Urol. Cons., 1992—. Bd. dirs. Butler St. YMCA, Atlanta, 1992—; cons. Am. Cancer Soc., 1994—. Fellow Am. Coll. Surgeons. Office: Atlanta Urol Cons 490 Peachtree St NE Atlanta GA 30308

HARRISON, JAMES WILBURN, gynecologist; b. Martin, Tenn., Mar. 23, 1918; s. Woodie and Georgia Harrison; m. Babs Wise Dudley, Jan. 29, 1948; children: James Wilburn Jr., James Michael, Babs Suzanne, Linda Denise. Student, U. Tenn., Martin, 1936-37, U. Tenn., Knoxville, 1937-38; MD, U. Tenn., Memphis, 1941; grad., U.S. Army Staff Coll., Ft. Leavenworth, Kans., 1972. Diplomate Am. Bd. Ob-gyn. Asst. resident Brooke Gen. Hosp., Ft. Sam Houston, Tex., 1947; chief surgery Saturn Hosp., Clark AFB, Philippines, 1948-49; resident, sr. resident Letterman Gen. Hosp., San Francisco, 1949-51; advanced through grades to col. U.S. Army, ret., 1954; chief staff St. Michael Hosp., Texarkana, Ark., Wadley Regional Med. Ctr., Texarkana, Tex., So. Clinic, Texarkana, Ark.; asst. clin. prof. ob.-gyn. U. Ark. Coll. Medicine, Little Rock. Chmn. Bowie County Child Welfare Bd.; mem. N.E. Tex. Mental Health Bd. Decorated Army Commendation medal, Legion of Merit. Fellow ACS (life), ICS (life), Am. Coll. Ob-gyn. (life), Assn. Mil. Surgeons U.S. (life), Tex. Soc. Ob-gyn. (life); mem. AMA (life), Tex. Med. Assn., Northridge Country Club (founding), Alumni Assn. U.S. Army Command and Gen. Staff Coll. Methodist. Home: 4009 Pecos St Texarkana TX 75503-2857

HARRISON, JOHN CRAIG, health facility administrator, psychologist; b. Bryn Mawr, Pa., Mar. 14, 1955; s. Richard Newell and Adele Doriet (Erickson) H. BA, Albright Coll., 1980; MA, West Chester U., 1986. Lic. psychologist, Pa. Therapist Community Counseling Svcs., Pottstown, Pa., 1980-83; clinical team leader Creative Health Svcs., Pottstown, Pa., 1983-89, outpatient therapist, 1988-89, student assistance coord., 1989, dir. partial hospitalization svcs., 1989-, dir. comm. residential program, 1989-; pvt. practice Collegeville Psychol. Ctr., Collegeville, Pa., 1989-. Mem. Pa. Psychol. Assn., Am. Assn. Partial Hospitals, Delaware Valley Partial Hospitals Assn., Psi Chi. Republican. Lutheran. Office: Creative Health Svcs Inc 361-365 High St Pottstown PA 19464

HARRISON, LOIS SMITH, hospital executive, educator; b. Frederick, Md., May 13, 1924; d. Richard Paul and Henrietta Foust (Menges) Smith; m. Richard Lee Harrison, June 23, 1951; children: Elizabeth Lee Boyce, Margaret Louise Wade, Richard Paul. BA, Hood Coll., 1945, MA, 1993; MA, Columbia U., 1946; LHD (hon.), Hood Coll., 1993. Counselor CCNY, 1945-46; founding adminstr., counselor, instr. psychology and sociology Hagerstown (Md.) Jr. Coll., 1946-51, registrar, 1946-51, 53-54, instr. psychology and orienta, 1954-56; registrar, instr. psychology, Balt. Jr. Coll., 1951-54; bus. mgr., acct. for pvt. med. practice Hagerstown, 1953—; trustee Washington County Hosp., Hagerstown, 1975—; chmn. bd. Washington County Hosp., 1986—; bd. dirs. Home Fed. Savs. Bank, Hagerstown, 1983—; speaker ednl. panels, convs. hosp. panels and seminars. Author: The Church Woman, 1960-65. Trustee Hood Coll., Frederick, 1972—, chmn. bd., 1979—; mem. Md. Gov.'s Commn. to Study Structure and Ednl. Devel. Commn., 1971-75; pres. Washington County Coun. Ch. Women, 1970-72; appointee Econ. Devel. Commn., County Impact Study Commn. Bd.; bd. dirs. Md. Hosp. Assn., Md. Chs. United, 1975—; chmn. bd. dirs. Md. Hosp. Edn. Inst., 1988—; pres. Ch. Consistory; chmn. Chesapeake Healthcare Forum, 1995—. Recipient Alumnae Achievement award Hood Coll., 1975, Washington County Woman of Yr. award, AAUW, 1984, Md. Woman of Yr. award, 1984, Md. Woman of Yr. award Francis Scott Key Commn. for Md.'s 350th Aniversary, 1984; named one of top 10 women Tri-State area, Herald-Mail Tri-State newspaper, 1990, Zonta Internat. Woman of Yr., 1994. Mem. Hagerstown C. of C. Republican. Home: 12835 Fountain Head Rd Hagerstown MD 21742-2748 Office: Washington Cty Hosp Off Chmn Bd Hagerstown MD 21740

HARRISON, LYNN HENRY, JR., cardiovascular surgeon; b. Oklahoma City, Jan. 8, 1944; s. Lynn Henry and Vera Alice (Pritchett) H.; m. Lura Ann Wright, June 21, 1969; children: Parker, Tyler. BA, Yale U., 1966; MD, U. Okla., 1970. Diplomate Am. Bd. Surgery, Am. Bd. Thoracic Surgery. Clin. assoc. surgery Nat. Heart and Lung Inst., Bethesda, Md., 1972-74; resident surgery Duke U., Durham, N.C., 1970-72, 74-78, teaching scholar surgery, 1978-79; asst. prof. surgery U. Okla. Sch. Medicine, Oklahoma City, 1979-84; clin. asst. prof. La. State U. Sch. Medicine, New Orleans, 1986-89, clin. assoc. prof., 1989; assoc. prof. surgery, chief sect. cardiovascular surgery, 1993—; ptnr. The O'Neill Surg. Group, New Orleans, 1984-91; pres. Crescent Surgical Assocs., Marrero, La., 1991-93.

Bd. dirs. Ballet Okla., Oklahoma City, 1983-85. Fellow ACS (counselor La. chpt. 1988—, pres. 1995); mem. Assn. Acad. Surgery, Soc. Thoracic Surgeons, Andrew G. Morrow Soc., David C. Sabiston Jr. Surg. Soc., Timberlane Country Club (bd. dirs.). Office: LSU Sch of Medicine Dept of Surgery 1542 Tulane Ave New Orleans LA 70112-2825

HARRISON, ROBERT W., telecommunications executive; b. Syracuse, N.Y., July 4, 1935; s. William Bradford and Marion Eloise (Fischer) H.; m. Lynda R. Whitney, June 20, 1965; 1 child, Heather. BA in Econs. and Bus., Alfred U., 1964. Gen. mgr. St. Mary's (W.Va.) Telephone Co., 1964-66; mgr. Cortland (N.Y.) Video Cable TV, 1966-73; tech. svcs. supr. SUNY, Cortland, 1973-86, telecommunications mgr., 1986—. Alderman City Common Coun., Cortland, 1989. Mem. Rotary. Office: SUNY PO Box 2000 Cortland NY 13045*

HARRIS-WARRICK, RONALD MORGAN, neurobiology and behavior educator; b. Berkeley, Calif., July 28, 1949; s. Morgan and Marjorie Ruth (Mason) H.; m. Rebecca Lamar, Apr. 5, 1975; children—Sheridan, Thomas. B.A. in Biol. Scis., Stanford U., 1970, Ph.D. in Genetics, 1976. Postdoctoral fellow NIH, Stanford U., Calif., 1976-78; Muscular Dystrophy Assn. postdoctoral fellow Harvard U., Boston, 1978-80; asst. prof. neurobiology Cornell U., Ithaca, N.Y., 1980-86; assoc. prof., 1986-92, prof., 1992—. Recipient Guggenheim fellow, 1986-87. Editor: Dynamic Biological Networks, 1992; contbr. articles to profl. jours. Mem. AAAS, Soc. for Neurosci., Internat. Soc. Neuroethology, Sierra Club, Audubon Soc., Phi Beta Kappa. Avocations: camping; skiing; mountaineering; music. Office: Cornell U Sect Neurobiology and Behavior Seeley Mudd Hall Ithaca NY 14853

HARRITOS, NANCY L(OUISE), family nurse practitioner; b. Attleboro, Mass., Oct. 5, 1960; d. Lawrence J. and Annette M. (Moreau) Gautreaux; m. James Harritos, Aug. 27, 1989. BSN, R.I. Coll., 1982; MSN, U. R.I., 1990. Cert. family nurse practitioner. Asst. head nurse Miriam Hosp., Providence, 1982-88; nurse practitioner R.I. Group Health Assn., Warwick, 1988-90, R.I. Hosp., Med. Primary Care Unit, 1990—; clin. nursing instr. R.I. Coll., 1990—. Vol., Traveler's Aid Med. Van. Mem. ANA, R.I. State Nursing Assn. Home: 40 Post Rd Warwick RI 02888-1608

HARROP, DANIEL SMITH, III, psychiatrist; b. Warwick, R.I., June 15, 1954; s. Daniel Smith and Dorothy Jane (Hickey) H. BA, Brown U., 1976, MD, 1979. Diplomate Am. Bd. Med. Examiners, Am. Bd. Psychiatry and Neurology, Am. Bd. Geriatrics. Resident in psychiatry Brown U., Providence, 1983; med. dir. East Bay Community Mental Health Ctr., Barrington, R.I., 1983-87; asst. unit chief Butler Hosp., Providence, 1988-89, chief gen. treatment unit, 1989-93; clin. asst. prof. psychiatry Brown U., Providence, 1985—; physician advisor Greenspring Mental Health Svcs., Patuxent, Md., 1991—; med. dir. United Behavioral Systems, Warwick, R.I., 1993-96; bd. dirs. Health Care Rev., Inc., Providence; cons. in field; chmn. utilization rev. Butler Hosp., Providence, 1983-95; pres. Roman Cath. Alumni of Brown U., 1982-83, 93-95. Pres. parish coun. St. Joseph's Ch., Providence, 1987-91, trustee, 1991—; bd. gov.'s Associated Alumni Brown U., Providence, 1988-92; pres. Assn. Class Officers Brown U., Providence, 1988-92. Mem. AMA, Am. Psychiat. Assn., R.I. Med. Soc., R.I. Psychiat. Soc. (pres. 1989-90), R.I. Group Psychotherapy Soc. (pres. 1989-91), Am. Group Psychotherapy (Assembly 1989—), Faculty Club of Brown U. (pres. 1994-95), Sci. Rsch. Soc. (Brown U. chpt.), Galilee Beach Club (Narragansett, R.I., pres. 1995—), Sigma Xi, Sigma Chi (grand coun. 1981—). Republican. Roman Catholic.

HARROW, RONNIE MERYLE, school psychologist; b. N.Y.C., June 13, 1949; d. Joseph and Ruth (Engle) Gross; m. Ronald Allan Harrow, May 30, 1969; children: Lindsay Sabrina, Dorian Blake. BS, CCNY, 1971; Edn. Specialist, U. Mich., 1978. Cert. sch. psychologist; limited lic. psychologist. Intern Hawthorn Ctr., Northville, Mich., 1973-74; sch. psychologist Livingston Ednl. Svc. Agy., Howell, Mich., 1974—; presenter in field. Co-pres. Livingston Intermediate Profl. Staff Assoc., Howell, 1995—. Mem. Mich. Assn. Sch. Psychologists, Phi Beta Kappa.

HARRYHILL, JOSEPH FRANCIS, urologist; b. Youngstown, Ohio, Sept. 6, 1960; m. Francine DiCioccio, June 29, 1991. BA in Chemistry, Case Western Res. U., 1982; MD cum laude, Ohio State U., 1986. Diplomate Am. Bd. Urology. Urology resident Temple U. Hosp., Phila., 1986-92; chief urology clinic Sheppard AFB (Tex.) Hosp., 1992-95; attending urologist Pa. Hosp., Phila., 1995—. Fellow ACS; mem. AMA, Am. Urol. Assn., Am. Soc. for Reproductive Medicine, Pa. Med. Soc., Phila. County Med. Soc., Phila. Urol. Soc., Christian Med. and Dental Soc. Office: Urol Ctr 299 S 8th St Philadelphia PA 19106

HARSHBARGER, DWIGHT, psychologist, management consultant; b. Huntington, W.Va., Feb. 1, 1938; s. George Kline Harshbarger ad Olivia (Stephens) Dailey; me. Emily Martin, June 18, 1960 (div. Oct. 1976); children: David Eric, Amy Beth; m. Rebecca Bukant, June 20, 1977 (div. Apr. 1990); m. Sandra Lane Craig, Sept. 1992; 1 child, Allison Craig. BA, W.Va. U., 1959, MA, 1961; PhD, U. N.D., 1969. Instr. Ventura (Calif.) Coll., 1964-65; assoc. prof. psychology Moorhead (Minn.) State Coll., 1965-67; rsch. assoc. U. N.D., 1967-69; prof. psychology W.Va. U., Morgantown, 1970-78; exec. dir. Fayette, Raleigh, Monroe, Summers Com. Mental Health Coun., Beckley, W.Va., 1977-80; cons. Rohrer, Hibler & Replogle, Chgo., 1980-81; v.p. human resources Sealy, Inc., Chgo., 1981-87; pvt. practice Chgo., 1987-88; sr. v.p. human resources Reebok Internat., Ltd., Stoughton, Mass., 1988-90; chmn. The Browns Group, Inc., Acton, Mass., 1990—; prin. Healthy Performance, LLC, Acton; bd. dirs. Cambridge (Mass.) Ctr. Behavioral Studies; mem. adv. bd. Coll. Arts and Scis. W.Va. U., 1983-92. Editor, contbr.: A Handbook of Service Human Organizations, 1973, Behavior Analysis and Systems Analysis, 1974; contbr. articles to profl. jours., chpts. to books. Bd. dirs. Jazz Inst. Chgo., 1983-88; mem. com. Harvard Sch., 1993—; trustee Cambridge (Mass.) Ctr. for Behavioral Studies. 1st lt. U.S. Army, 1962-64. Fellow Med. Sch. Harvard U., 1969-70. Fellow APA, Am. Psychol. Soc., Assn. for Applied and Preventive Psychology; mem. New Eng. Psychol. Assn., W.Va. Psychol. Assn. Episcopalian.

HARSHMAN, MORTON LEONARD, physician, business executive; b. Youngstown, Ohio, Apr. 21, 1932; s. Ben and Lilian (Malkoff) H.; m. Barbara Elmore, June 21, 1957; children—Beth, Melissa. B.S., Ohio State U., 1953, M.D., 1957. Charter diplomate Am. Bd. Family Practice. Intern Grant Hosp., Columbus, Ohio, 1957-58; practice medicine specializing in family practice Cin., 1960-92; v.p. med. staff Bethesda Hosp., 1974-75, pres., 1975-77; mem. staff Christ Hosp., Cin., Children's Hosp., Cin., Bethesda Hosp., Cin., Providence Hosp., Cin.; assoc. med. dir. Western-Southern Life Ins. Co., 1993—; pres. Pacific Isle Co.; pres., bd. dirs. Morton Harshman Inc., 880 Real Estate Co. Trustee Bethesda Hosp. and Deaconess Assn., 1972-79, Bethesda Hosp. Inc., 1991—, Cin. Chamber Orch., 1992—; v.p. bd. trustees Jewish Fedn. of Cin. With USNR, 1958-60. Fellow Am. Coll. Family Practice; mem. AMA, Ohio Med. Assn., Cin. Acad. Medicine, Am. Acad. Family Practice, Ohio Acad. Family Practice, Southwestern Ohio Acad. Family Practice, Ky. Col. Assn., Phi Beta Kappa, Alpha Epsilon Delta, Phi Delta Epsilon (Cin.). Home: 2121 Alpine Pl Apt 904 Cincinnati OH 45206-2691 Office: 400 Broadway St Cincinnati OH 45202-3312

HART, CECIL WILLIAM JOSEPH, otolaryngologist, head and neck surgeon; b. Bath, Avon, Eng., May 27, 1931; came to U.S., 1957.; s. William Theodore Hart and Paulina Olive (Adams) Gilmer; m. Brigid Frances Molloy, June 15, 1957 (dec. Nov. 1984); children: Geoffrey Arthur, Paula Mary, John Adams; m. Doris Crystel Katharina Alm, Mar. 14, 1987; children: Kristen-Linnea Alm, Erik Alm, Britt-Marie Alm. BA, Trinity Coll., Dublin, Ireland, 1952, MB, BCH, BAO, 1955, MA, 1958. Diplomate Am. Bd. Otolaryngology. Intern Dr. Steevens Hosp., Dublin, Ireland, 1956, Little Co. Mary Hosp., Evergreen Park, Ill., 1957; mem. staff Little Co. Mary Hosp., 1958-59; resident in otolaryngology U. Chgo. Hosp. and clinic, 1959-62; instr. U. Chgo. Med. Sch., 1962-64, asst. prof., 1964-65; practice medicine specializing in otolaryngology Chgo., 1958—; mem. staff Northwestern Meml. Hosp., 1972—, Rehab. Inst. Chgo., 1965—, Children's Meml. Hosp., 1972—, Little Co. of Mary Hosp., 1977-94, LaGrange (Ill.) Community Meml. Hosp., 1977-94; tchg. assoc. Cleft Palate Inst., 1968, dir. otolaryngology, 1969-92; asst. prof. dept. otolaryngology-head and neck surgery Northwestern U. Med. Sch., 1965-75, assoc. prof., 1975-92, prof., 1992—; lectr. dept. otorhinolaryngology Loyola U., 1972; med. adv. bd. So. Hearing and Speech Found., Nat. Inst. of Deafness and Other Communicative Disorders, 1989-95. Producer videos, movie; contbr. numerous articles to profl. jours. and mags.; also guest appearances various radio and TV talk shows. NIH fellow U. Chgo., 1962-63; NIH grantee, 1985-88. Fellow Am. Neurotology Soc. (pres. 1974-75, chmn. editorial review & publ. com. 1978-79, constn. and bylaws com. 1979—), Am. Acad. Otolaryngology-Head and Neck Surgery (chmn. subcom. on Equilibrium 1980-86, computer com. 1987-90), ACS, Inst. Medicine Chgo., Soc. for Ear Nose and Throat Advances in Children; mem. AMA, Brit. Med. Assn., Ill. State Med. Soc., Chgo. Med. Soc., Am. Cleft Palate Assn., Am. Council Otolaryngology, Am. Otological Soc., Chgo. Laryngological and Otological Soc. (v.p. 1975-76), Northwestern Clin. Faculty Med. Assn. (vice chmn. 1976-78, pres. 1979-81), Barany Soc., Royal Soc. Medicine, Irish Otolaryngological Soc., So. Hearing and Speech Found (med. adv. bd.), Chgo. Hearing and Balance Assn. (pres.), Sigma Xi. Roman Catholic. Office: 707 N Fairbanks Ct Chicago IL 60611-3042

HART, CHARLES ANTHONY, microbiology educator, researcher, physician; b. Stockton-on-Tees, Durham, Eng., Feb. 25, 1948; s. Edmund and Alice Edna (Griffin) H.; m. Jennifer Ann Bonnett, June 25, 1971; children: Caroline Joanne, Rachel Louise, Laura Jane. BSc, London U., 1969, B in Medicine and Surgery, 1972, PhD, 1978. Wellcome rsch. scholar Royal Free Hosp. Sch. of Medicine, London, 1974-76; registrar Liverpool (Eng.) Health Authority, 1977-78; MRC rsch. fellow U. Liverpool, 1978, lectr., 1979-82, sr. lectr., 1983-86, prof., 1986—; hon. cons. med. microbiology Roya-Liverpool Royal Liverpool Children's Hosp., 1983—; vis. prof. U. Santo Tomas, Manila, 1987—. Author: Colour Atlas of Pediatric Infectious Diseases, Handbook of Childhood Infections, Color Atlas of Medical Microbiology; editor: Jour. Med. Microbiology, Gut, Annals of Tropical Medicine, Jour. of Hosp. Infection. Fellow Royal Coll. Pathologists, Royal Soc. Tropical Medicine; mem. Liverpool Paediatric Club (pres. 1991-93). Office: U Liverpool, Dept Med Microbiology, PO Box 147, Liverpool L69 3BX, England

HART, DAVID, medical physicist; b. Darlington, Eng., Sept. 6, 1950; s. David Foster and Margaret (Huggins) H.; m. Doreen Carter, July 19, 1986. BSc in Physics, Univ. Coll., London, 1971; postgrad. diploma, U. Leeds, Eng., 1973; PhD, U. Edinburgh, Scotland, 1977. Postdoctoral rsch. fellow Imperial Coll., London, 1978-80; lectr., rschr. U. East Anglia, U.K., 1980-87; sr. sci. officer Nat. Radiol. Protection Bd., Eng., 1987—. Author: The Volta River Project, 1980, Nuclear Power in India, 1983; contbr. articles to profl. jours. Mem. Instn. Physics and Engring. in Medicine and Biology. Office: Nat Radiol Protection Bd, Chilton, Didcot Oxon OX11 0RQ, England

HART, DENNIS LEE, chiropractic physician; b. Inpendence, Mo., Nov. 13, 1951; s. Lee Otis and Margaret Corine (Snowden) H.; m. Pamela Sue, Mr. 13, 1976; children: Amber Michelle, Jennifer Marie. BA in Phys. Edn., Graceland Coll., 1973, BA in History, 1973; MA in Health, Phys. Edn. and Recreation, The Internat. Univ., 1975; Doctor of Chiropractic, Cleve. Choropractic Coll., 1989. Tchr. Kansas City Pub. Schs., 1973-75, dir., 1976-78; tchr. spl. edn. Grain Valley (Mo.) Pub. Schs., 1978-79; dir. Independence Stamp & Coin, 1979-84; tchr. St. Mary's Parochial, Independence, 1984-86; chiropractor I Love Chiropractic, Independence, 1989-92, Hart Family Chiropractic, Hickory, N.C., 1992—; tennis coach St. Mary's H.S., Independence, 1984-85; football coach Ctrl. Sr. H.S., Kansas City, 1973-75; soccer coach Blue Valley Activity Ctr., Independence, 1975-80; umpire A.S.A. and NSSA, INdependence, 1977. Mem. Good Govt. League, Independence, 1977. Fellow Acupuncture Soc of Am., Neurol. Soc. of Am., Pebble Creek Tennis Club, C. of C., Kiwanis. Mem. Reorganized Ch. LDS. Office: Hart Family Chiropractic 1960 Hwy 70 SE Ste 242 Hickory NC 28602

HART, DONALD AVERY, research executive; b. Lenoir, N.C., Aug. 17, 1936; s. Walter Avery and Bertha Mabel (Thompson) H.; m. Mary Jane Woods, Aug. 30, 1957; children: Donald Avery Jr., Marla Jean Hart Roberts. BS, N.C. State U., 1958, MS, 1970, EdD, 1975; MBA in Exec. Devel., Syracuse U., 1970. Mgmt. trainee, mgr. ops. Central Carolina Farmers Coop., Durham, N.C., 1958-62; divisional pers. mgr. Collins & Aikman Corp., Pa., 1962-66; mgr. adminstr. svcs. Corning Glass Works Biomed. Rsch. Labs., Raleigh, N.C., 1966-76; v.p. adminstrn., sec., treas., founding CFO adminstrv. Chem. Industry Inst. of Toxicology, Research Triangle Park, N.C., 1976-89; cons., bd. dirs. Knox Publs., N.C. Beacon; cons. Rsch. Parks, 1989-90, CCL, Research Triangle Park, 1987-89. Chmn. Rsch. Triangle Park Dirs. Club, 1988-89; exec. com. Rsch. Triangle Park Owners and Tenants, 1987-89. Mem. Adminstrv. Mgmt. Soc. (pres. 1982-83), Soc. Rsch. Adminstrs. Internat. (hon., pres. 1987-88), Soc. Human Resource Mgrs. (hon., pres. 1971-72), Masons, Rotary (pres., dir.). Democrat. Baptist. Home: 4808 Westminster Dr Raleigh NC 27604-6046

HART, EDWIN SIPLER, III, podiatrist; b. Phila., Nov. 26, 1957; s. Edwin Sipler Jr. and Alice Minerva (Wood) H.; m. Karen L. Esten, Feb. 1, 1991. BA, Temple U., 1979; D Podiatric Medicine, Pa. Coll. Podiatric Medicine, 1983. Diplomate Am. Bd. Podiatric Surgery, Am. Bd. Podiatric Orthopedics. Surgery resident Podiatry Hosp. Pitts., 1983-84; pvt. practice Bethlehem, Pa., 1985—; staff mem. Muhlenberg Hosp., Bethlehem, 1985—, Sacred Heart Hosp., Allentown, Pa., 1985—, St. Luke's Hosp., Bethlehem, 1995—. Advisor career exploration program Minsi Trail coun. Boy Scouts Am., Bethlehem, 1986, 87, 88; mem. Eagle Scouts. Fellow Am. Coll. Foot and Ankle Surgeons, Am. Coll. Foot and Ankle Orthopedics; mem. Am. Podiatric Med. Assn., Pa. Podiatric Med. Assn. (divsn. pres. 1988-89, 89-90), Masons (High Priest 1991, trustee Ezra Royal Arch chpt., Worshipful master Concordia lodge 1995, trustee Perm. Charity Fund). Republican Episcopalian. Office: 2305 Easton Ave Bethlehem PA 18017

HART, FONDA LEE, nurse; b. Ruston, La., Aug. 22, 1959; d. Barney Wright Hart and Mary Joan (Brumley) Wilson. BSN, Biola U., 1982. RN, Calif. Worldwide missionary, 1983-90; nurse per diem various orgns., 1990-92; infusion specialist CPS Advanced Infusion Sys., Mountain View, Calif., 1992-95; IV infusion specialist Bay Area IV Therapy, Sunnyvale, Calif., 1995—. Home: 561 Hyde Park Dr San Jose CA 95136

HART, JAMES HARLAN, retired emergency medicine physician; b. Hamilton County, Ill., Dec. 16, 1934; s. Gleason and Elizabeth Jane (Smith) H.; m. Sharon Lenore Darr, Sept. 20, 1937; m. 2d, Lora Rae Barnett, May 9, 1955; children: Shane, Kyle, Raelene. BS, Southwestern State U., Weatherford, Okla., 1963; MD, Okla. U., 1968. Intern, Mercy Hosp., Oklahoma City, 1968-69; resident in ob-gyn St. Anthony Hosp., Oklahoma City, 1969-72; practice medicine specializing in ob-gyn, Woodriver, Ill., 1972-77; practice medicine specializing in emergency medicine, Lincoln, Ill., 1977-80; emergency medicine physician St. Elizabeth Hosp., Danville, Ill., 1980-89; med. dir. emergency svc., 1980-89; emergency medicine physician, Danville, Ill., 1980-89; med. dir. urgent care clinic Community Hosp., Williamsport, Ind., 1989-92; dir. emergency med. dept., Williamsport Community Hosp., 1991; med. dir. emergency med. technicians program, 1989; clin. assoc. prof. U. Ill. Med. Sch., Urbana; ret. 1994. Served with U.S. Army, 1957-59. Mem. AMA, Am. Coll. Emergency Physicians, Ill. State Med. Soc., Ind. State Med. Soc., Warren County Ind. Med. Soc., Vermillion County Med. Soc. Republican. Home: RR 2 Williamsport IN 47993-9802

HART, JOSEPH BATCHELDER, urologist; b. L.A., Aug. 23, 1932; s. Edward Payson and Evelyn Elizabeth (Batchelder) H.; m. Maxine Widdowson, Oct. 17, 1954; children: Lisa, Stephen, Scott, Christopher. BA, Stanford Univ., 1953; MD, Yale Univ., 1956. Diplomate Am. Bd. Urology. Intern Letterman Army Hosp., San Francisco, 1956-57; resident Stanford Hosp., San Francisco, 1957-61; asst. prof. Univ. Calif., Irvine, 1966-78; pres. Orange County Urological Soc., 1980. Mem. Am. Urological Assn. (chmn. postgrad. edn. western sect. 1987-93), Am. Coll. Surgeons, Calif. Medical Assn. (chmn. adv. panel 1983-83, mem. scientific bd. 1987-90), Orange County Medical Assn., Orange County Urological Assn. Republican. Protestant. Office: Joseph B Hart MD 2011 Westcliff Dr Ste 4 Newport Beach CA 92660

HART, KAREN ANN, social services administrator; b. Olean, N.Y., July 11, 1943; d. John Eugene and Lillian Lila (Gardner) H. BSN, D'Youville Coll., Buffalo, 1965. RN, Ohio, N.Y., Calif. Staff nurse, head nurse, supr. Montefiore Med. Ctr., Bronx, N.Y., 1965-77; nurse recruiter L.A. New Hosp., 1978-79, Midway Hosp., L.A., 1979-80; dir. nurse recruitment Akron (Ohio) City Hosp., 1980-87; exec. dir. Nat. Assn. Health Care Recruitment, Akron, 1987—. Contbr. articles to profl. jours. Recipient Women in Comm. award Women Aware Program, 1986. Mem. Am. Soc. Assn. Execs., Nat. Assn. Health Care Recruitment (past officer, Disting. Mem. award 1986, 87), Northeastern Ohio Assn. Health Care Recruitment (past officer), Sigma Theta Tau. Democrat. Roman Catholic. Home and Office: 201 N Hawkins Ave Akron OH 44313

HART, KENNETH EINAR, psychology educator, researcher; b. Sudbury, Ont., Can.; s. Leo and Kaija Elizabeth (Hohter) H. BA, Laurentian U., Sudbury, Ont., 1978; MA, Lakehead U., Thunder Bay, Can., 1981; PhD, U. Houston, 1987. Teaching fellow U. Houston, 1982-86; rsch. asst. U. Tex. Med. Sch., Houston, 1985; postdoctoral fellow Uniformed Svcs. U., Bethesda, Md., 1986; dir. rsch. Hofstra U. Health Dome, Hempstead, N.Y., 1987; asst. prof. psychology Hofstra U., 1987-94; NIAAA rsch. scholar Ctr. for Alcohol Studies, Brown U., Providence, 1994-96; prof. psychology U. Wales, Swansea, 1996—. Cons. editor Jour. Applied Social Psychology, 1987, Psychol. Reports, 1988, Am. Jour. Cmty. Psychology, 1990, Health Psychology, 1991, Jour. Studies Alcohol, Jour. Psychosomatic Rsch., Jour. Soc. & Clin. Psychology, Jour. Soc. & Pers. Rels.; contbr. articles to profl. jours. Hofstra U. grantee, 1987, Lakehead U. scholar, 1980. Mem. APA, APS, Assn. for Advancement of Behavior Therapy, Western Psychol. Assn., Soc. for Behavioral Medicine, Soc. for Advancement of Social Psychology. Home: 6 Brynmill Terr, Swansea Wales SA2 0BA Office: U Wales, Swansea Wales SA2 8PP

HART, RICHARD TRAPNELL, engineer, educator; b. Wilmington, Del., Feb. 3, 1953; s. James Austin III and Anne White (Trapnell) H.; m. Silvia Sygulla, Dec. 28, 1979; children: Kathryn Trapnell, Julia Austin. BES, Ga. Inst. of Tech., 1975, MS, 1977; PhD, Case Western Res. U., 1983. Asst. prof. Tulane U., New Orleans, 1982-87, assoc. prof., 1987-95; prof., 1995—. Editor: Computer Simulations in Biomedicine, 1995; assoc. tech. editor Jour. BIomech. Engring.; reviewer Jour. of Biomechanics, Jour. of Biomech. Engring., Jour. of Orthopaedic Rsch., Pitts. Supercomputing Ctr., NSF, NIH; contbr. articles to profl. jours. and chpts. to books. NIH grantee, 1984-87, 91-95. Mem. ASME (assoc.), Am. Soc. Biomechanics, Orthopaedic Rsch. Soc. (local organizing chmn. 1990), Am. Acad. Mechanics, Alpha Eta Mu Beta, Tau Beta Pi, Sigma Xi. Office: Tulane U Dept Biomedical Engrin New Orleans LA 70118

HART, SEAN TIMOTHY, psychologist, social worker, consultant, psychotherapist; b. Poughkeepsie, N.Y., Feb. 23, 1953; s. Joseph Charles and Theresa Evelyn (Chester) H. BS, U. Scranton, Pa., 1975; MSW, Fordham U., 1977; D in Clin. Psychology, Chgo. Sch. of Profl. Psychology, 1989. Lic. social worker, clin. psychologist, Conn. Clin. social worker Dutchess County Mental Hygiene, Poughkeepsie, 1977-81; clin. social worker Med. Sch. Northwestern U., Chgo., 1983; resident in psychology Conn. Valley Hosp., Middletown, 1986-87; staff psychologist Brook Hollow Health Care Ctr., Wallingford, Conn., 1987-89; program dir. Hosp. of St. Raphael, New Haven, 1989-91; clin. dir. Guenster Rehab. Ctr., 1991—, Elmcrest Psychiat. Inst., 1992; prin. psychotherapist Chelsea Counseling Ctr., Wappings Falls, N.Y., 1978-81, Scranton Psychotherapy Group, New Haven, 1990—. Mem. APA, Am. Acad. Health Care Providers in Addictive Disorders, Soc. Personality Assessment. also: 34 Dale Rd Ste 212 Avon CT 06001

HART, WARD LAWRENCE, retired physician; b. San Francisco, Sept. 30, 1920; s. Frank Lawrence and Jessmyn Helen (Bernhard) H.; m. Frances Brunton, June 2, 1945; children—Sheron, Steven, Candace, Brad. A.B., Stanford U., 1941; M.D., St. Louis U., 1944. Diplomate Am. Bd. Internal Medicine. Intern St. Mary's Hosp., San Francisco, 1944-45, resident in internal medicine, 1947-50; chief resident Santa Clara (Calif.) County Hosp., 1949-50; practice medicine specializing in internal medicineSan Carlos, Calif., 1950-85; assoc. clin. prof. medicine Stanford U., 1974-86, prof. emeritus, 1986—; pres. Peninsula Med. Group, Inc., San Carlos, 1970-84; v.p. Peninsula Med. Lab., Menlo Park, Calif., 1980-87; chief of medicine Sequoia Hosp., 1979-83. Served to capt. M.C., U.S. Army, 1945-47, 1953, Korea. Fellow ACP; mem. Calif. Acad. Medicine, San Mateo County Med. Soc. (pres. 1964), Calif. Med. Soc., AMA, Calif. Soc. Internal Medicine, Am. Soc. Internal Medicine. Club: Sharon Heights Golf and Country (Menlo Park). Home: 460 Sandhill Cir Menlo Park CA 94025-7107

HARTEMANN, PHILIPPE GERALD, public health educator; b. Nancy, Lorraine, France, June 13, 1949; s. Pierre-Georges Hartemann and Suzanne Hartemann-Crozier; m. Denise-Marie Thomas, Sept. 3, 1971; children: Isabelle, Loic. MSc in Chemistry, U. Louis Pasteur, Strasbourg, France, 1970; PhD in Biochemistry, U. Nancy, France, 1974, MD, 1977. Rsch. asst. biochemistry Sch. of Medicine, Nancy, 1974-78, assoc. prof. hygiene, 1978-84, prof. pub. health, 1985—; chief of hosp. hygiene unit Centre-Hosp.-Univ., Nancy, 1984—; asst. dir., project officer W.H.O. Environ. Health Ctr., Nancy, 1992-93. Editor: Bottled Water, 1992. Asst. mayor Mcpl. Coun., They sous Vaudemont, France, 1986—. Office: Laboratoire D'Hygiene, 11 bis Rue G Peri, 54500 Vandoeuvre France

HARTFORD, CHARLES EDWARD, surgeon; b. Palmerton, Pa., June 8, 1932; s. Arthur William and Ruth Sarah (Sheaffer) H.; m. Kathryn Mary Delich, Sept. 5, 1953; children: Lois Ann Burkett, Jean Louise Boatman, John William Hartford. BS in Chemistry, Franklin & Marshall Coll., 1955; MD, Temple U., 1959. Diplomate Am. Bd. Surgery, Am. Bd. Surg. Critical Care. Dir. of burn unit U. Iowa Hosp., Iowa City, 1969-76; prof. surgery U. Iowa, 1976; dir. burn treatment ctr. Crozer Chester Med. Ctr., Chester, Pa., 1977-87; clin. prof. surgery U. Pa., Phila., 1986-88; dir. burn unit U. Colo. Health Sci., Denver, 1988—, prof. surgery, 1988—. Lt. USN, 1959-64. Fellow ACS, Am. Assn. for the Surgery of Trauma; mem. Am. Burn Assn. (sec. 1976-78, pres. 1991), Western Surg. Assn., Assn. of Program Dirs. in Surgery, Alpha Omega Alpha. Office: U Colo Health Sci Ctr Campus Box C298 4200 E 9th Ave Denver CO 80262

HARTIG, KAREN JOYCE, psychotherapist, social worker; b. N.Y.C., July 22, 1957; d. Thomas and Phyllis (Green) H.; m. Carlos Castrillo, June 10, 1990. BA, Queens Coll., 1979; MSW, Adelphi U., 1982. Cert. clin. social worker. Staff therapist South Bronx Mental Health Ctr., Bronx, N.Y., 1982-83, Coney Island Hosp., Bklyn., 1983-84; dir. Queens (N.Y.) Rape Counseling Ctr., 1985—; staff therapist New Hope Guild, Queens, 1987-88, Washington Square Inst., Manhattan, N.Y., 1988—, N.Y. Psychotherapy and Counseling Ctr., Bklyn., 1985-87; pvt. practice, 1985—. Contbr. articles in field to newspapers. Mem. Nat. Assn. Social Workers. Democrat. Office: Queens Rape Counseling Ctr 71-49 Loubet St Forest Hills NY 11375-6720

HARTLAGE, LAWRENCE CLIFTON, neuropsychologist, educator; b. Portsmouth, Ohio, May 11, 1934; s. Clifton Paul and Mary Louise (Pierron) H.; m. Patricia Louise Hughes, Jan. 21, 1967; 1 child, Mary Beth. B.S., Ohio State U., 1959; M.A., U. Louisville, 1962, Ph.D., 1968; postgrad., Ind. U. Med. Center, 1972. Dir. psychology Central State Hosp., Louisville, 1966-68; clin. dir. Asso. Psychol. Services, Louisville, 1968-70; head clin. psychology sect. pediatric neurology Ind. U. Med. Center, 1970-72; head neuropsychology sect., prof. neurology and pediatrics Med. Coll. Ga., Augusta, 1972-85; Marie Wilson Howell prof. U. Ark., 1985-86; dir. Augusta Neuropsychology Ctr., 1986—; cons. HEW, VA; vis. faculty Ind. and Ga. univs. Author: Mental Development Evaluation of the Pediatric Patient, 1973, Anthology of Theory, Practice and Research in Learning Disabilities, 1974, Neuropsychology of Individual Differences, 1985, Neuropsychological Evaluation Children and Adults, 1986, Essentials of Neuropsychological Assessment, 1987, Neuropsychological Evaluation of Head Injury, 1990, Preventable Brain Damage, 1992; co-editor: Clin. Neuropsychology. Served with AUS, 1956-58. Rehab. Service Adminstrn. research grantee, 1970-72, N.A.T.O. grantee, 1980, NIH grantee, 1980-82. Fellow Internat. Acad. Forensic Psychology, Am. Psychol. Assn. (pres. div. neuropsychology 1984-85), Nat. Acad. Neuropsychology (pres. 1978, 82-83); mem. Nat. Rehab. Tng. Inst. (pres. 1973-74), Nat. Rehab. Assn. (dir. 1972-73), Am. Soc. Human Genetics, Am. Bd. Profs. Neuropsychology (pres. 1984-85), Council for Exceptional Children, Sigma Xi. Home: 4227 Evans Rd Evans GA 30809

HARTLEY, JAMES MICHAELIS, aerospace systems, printing and hardwood products manufacturing executive; b. Indpls., Nov. 25, 1916; s. James Worth and Bertha S. (Beuke) H.; m. E. Lea Cosby, July 30, 1944; children: Michael D., Brent S. Student Jordan Conservatory of Music, 1934-35, Ind. U., Purdue U., Franklin Coll. With Arvin Industries, Inc., 1934-36; founder, pres. J. Hartley Co., Inc., Columbus, Ind., 1937—; founder, pres. Hartley Group, 1989—. Inventor of and patent on a prerotation system for transport-size aircraft landing gear. Pres. Columbus Little Theatre, 1947-48; founding dir. Columbus Arts Guild, 1960-64, v.p., 1965-66, dir., 1971-74; musical dir., cellist Guild String Quartet, 1963-73; active Indpls. Mus. of Art; founding dir. Columbus Pro Musica, 1969-74; dir. Regional Arts Study Commn., 1971-74; v.p. Ind. Coun. Rep. Workshops, 1965-69, pres., 1975-77; pres. Bartholomew County Rep. Workshop, 1966-67. Served with USAAF, 1942-46. Mem. AAAS, Am. Legion (life), NAM, Nat. Fedn. Ind. Bus., N.Y. Acad. Scis., Planetary Soc., Air Force Assn., Nat. Space Soc., U.S. C. of C., Phi Eta Sigma (honoris causa). Achievements include invention, patent prerotation system for transport-size aircraft landing gear. Office: J Hartley Co Inc 101 N National Rd Columbus IN 47201-7848

HARTLEY, JOHN H., physician; b. Atlanta, Nov. 27, 1934. BA, Emory U., 1956, MC, 1961. Diplomate Am. Bd. Plastic Surgery, Pan Am. Med. Assn. Surg. intern, resident Emory Hosp. and VA Hosp., Atlanta, 1962-63, asst. resident in surgery, 1962-63; sr. resident in surgery Piedmont Hosp., Atlanta, 1965-66; plastic surgery preceptorship Cronin and Brauer Clinic, Houston, 1966-68; assoc. with Drs. Hamm, Schatten, Hartley and Griffin, 1968-80, Drs. Hartley and Griffin, 1980-86, Dr. Hartley, 1986—; chief of surgery Met. Hosp. 1979-83, chief of staff, 1980, chief of plastic surgery, 1976-89; chief of plastic surgery West Paces Ferry Hosp., 1978, others; lectr., presenter in field. Contbr. articles to profl. jours. and publs. Bd. vis. Darlington Sch., 1984-90. Capt. USAF, 1963-65; col. USAF res., 1965—. Mem. Med. Assn. Atlanta, Med. Assn. Ga., AMA, Am. Soc. Plastic and Reconstructive Surgeons, Thoroughman Surg. Soc., McRae Surg. Soc., Ga. Soc. Plastic Surgeons (sec. 1974, v.p. 1975, pres. 1976), Am. Assn. Plastic Surgeons, Atlanta Clin. Soc., Am. Soc. Aesthetic Plastic Surgeons, So. Med. Assn. (various offices), Southeastern Soc. Plastic and Reconstructive Surgeons (various offices to pres. 1988), Am. Soc. Aesthetic Plastic Surgeons, Omicron Delta Kappa, Pi Delta Epsilon, others. Office: Bldg 8 4200 Northside Pkwy Atlanta GA 30327

HARTLEY, LOREN HOWARD, cardiologist, medical educator; b. Riverton, Kans.; s. Loren Roy and Genevie May (Ohler) H.; m. Marcia Anne Hartley, Mar. 1, 1959; children: Anne Elizabeth, Thomas Howard, John Matthew, Joseph Andrew. AA, Joplin (Mo.) Jr. Coll., 1954; student, Mo. U., 1955, MD, 1959. Diplomate Am. Bd. Internal Medicine; subsplty. bd. cert. in cardiovasc. diseases. Rotating intern Parkland Hosp., Dallas, 1959-60; resident in internal medicine U. Mo. Med. Ctr., Columbia, 1960-62, fellow in cardiology, 1962-63; fellow in cardiopulmonary diseases U. Colo. Med. Ctr., Denver, 1965-67; Spl. Nat. Insts. Health fellow (Sweden) Royal Gymnastic Inst., Stockholm, 1967-68; asst. in medicine Peter Bent Brigham Hosp., Boston, 1969-70; asst. in medicine Harvard Med. Svc., Boston City Hosp., 1969-71, assisting physician, 1971-74; assoc. physician Beth Israel Hosp., Boston City Hosp., 1974-89; asst. in medicine Mass. Gen. Hosp., Boston City Hosp., 1979-89; staff Brigham and Women's Hosp., Boston City Hosp., 1982—, dir. cardiac rehab., 1982—; clin. instr. medicine, Harvard Med. Sch., Boston, 1970-71, asst. prof. medicine, 1971-74, assoc. prof. medicine, 1974-78, assoc. prof. medicine Beth Israel Hosp., Harvard Med. Sch., 1978-79, assoc. prof. medicine Mass. Gen. Hosp., 1979-81, assoc. prof. medicine Brigham and Womens Hosp., Harvard Med. Sch., 1982—; pvt. practice internal medicine, Springfield, Mo., 1963-65; rsch. internist U.S. Army Res. Inst. Environ. Medicine, Natick, Mass., 1968-70, dir. physiology lab., 1970-71; core scientist New Engg. Regional Primate Rsch. Ctr., Southborough, Mass., 1977-85; cons. Nat. Heart, Lung and Blood Inst., 1982-85; mem. Am. Heart Assn. com. on exercise for developing nat. guidelines for exercise testing and cardiac rehab., 1989-95; pres. New Eng. chpt. Am. Coll. Sports Medicine, 1978; bd. dirs. Children's Hosp. Sports Medicine Found. Editl. bd. Am. Jour. Physiology, Jour. Cardiac Rehab., 1980-85; contbr. articles to profl. jours., chpts. to books, chpt. in Ency. of Sports Medicine, 1992. Pres. Greater Boston chpt. Amn. Heart Assn., 1983-85; bd. dirs. Mass. chpt. Am. Heart Assn., 1985; advisor Mass. Exec. Office of Elder Affairs, 1985; impartial examiner for Indsl. Accidents Bd., Mass., 1994—. Lt. col. AUS, 1968-71. Recipient rsch. grants NIH. Fellow ACP, Am. Coll. Cardiology, Am. Coll. Sports Medicine; mem. Am. Fedn. Clin. Rsch., Am. Physiology Soc. Episcopalian. Home: 22 Glezen Lane Wayland MA 01778 Office: Brigham and Women's Hosp Divsn Cardiology 75 Francis St Boston MA 02115

HARTLINE, DARRELL G., healthcare executive; b. Litchfield, Ill., Oct. 16, 1939; s. Robert Carl and Marguerite A. (Wells) H.; m. Jane A. Fesser, June 11, 1961; 1 child, Jeffrey Lynn. BS, So. Ill. U., 1962. Auditor Arthur Andersen & Co., Chgo., 1962-65; chief fin. officer Mercy Hosp., Davenport, Iowa, 1965-70, The Genesee Hosp., Rochester, N.Y., 1970-92, Quorum Health Resources, Inc., Nashville, 1992—; mem. various comns. N.Y. State Dept. Health, Albany, 1974-87; cons. N.Y. State Coun. on Health Care Financing, Albany, 1979-83, Health Mgmt. Svcs., Syracuse, N.Y., 1980-84, bd. dirs also. Bd. dirs., treas. Vis. Nurse Svcs., Rochester, N.Y., 1982-87, Rochester Dist. Heating Co-op, 1986-92, Vis. Nurse Found., Rochester, 1987-93; bd. dirs., chmn. Cmty. Care of Rochester, 1987-93; bd. dirs., treas. Piper Aviation Mus., 1995-96. With USAR, 1961. Mem. Hosp. Assn. N.Y. State (various coms.), Rochester Regional Hosp. Assn. (various coms.), Health Care Fin. Mgmt. Assn. (bd. dirs., past officer, William Fullmur award 1974, Robert H. Reeves award 1985, Frederick T. Muncie award 1992, Spl. Chpt. Recognition award 1992), Lock Haven Rotary Club. Lutheran. Home: 37 Cardinal Dr W Lock Haven PA 17745-9517 Office: Lock Haven Hosp 24 Cree Dr Lock Haven PA 17745-2639

HARTMAN, CHARLES HENRY, association executive, educator; b. Red Lion, Pa., Feb. 1, 1933; s. Earl Eugene and Jeannette (Kline) H.; m. Patricia A. Cooper, Aug. 3, 1956 (div. May 1974); children: Elizabeth Jean, Amy Joan; m. 2d Catherine M. Wheeler, June 7, 1975 (div. Aug. 1994); children: Eric Michael, Jennifer Leigh, David Wheeler, Scott Andrew. BS, Millersville U., 1954; MA, Mich. State U., 1958, EdD, 1962. Tchr. Hollidaysburg Pub. Schs., Pa., 1956-57; assoc. prof. Ill. State U., Normal, 1959-62; vis. lectr. edn. U. Wis., Madison, 1962-63, Milw., 1963-64; dir. edn. Automotive Safety Found./Hwy. Users Fedn., Washington, 1964-70; dep. adminstr. Nat. Hwy. Traffic Safety Adminstrn., U.S. Dept. Transp., Washington, 1970-73; pres. Motorcycle Safety Found., Irvine, Calif., 1973-84; also pres. Touchstone Mgmt. Svcs., Delta, Pa., 1984-88; pres. Strategic Mgmt. and Communications Group, Delta, 1991-93; exec. v.p. AAAHPERD, Reston, Va., 1988-90; exec. dir. Am. Coll. Health Assn., Balt., 1990—; lectr. bus. adminstrn. Capital Campus, Pa. State U., Middletown, 1987-88; dir. Nat. Safety Coun., Chgo., 1976-79, vice chmn. traffic conf., 1976-78; presdl. appointee Nat. Hwy. Safety Adv. Commn., Washington, 1977-80; gov.'s appointee Pa. Task Force on Alcohol and Hwy. Safety, 1981-82; vice chmn. Alliance for Traffic Safety, 1981-83, chmn. 1983-85; mem. policy commn. Hwy. Users Fedn.; cons. Nat. Assn. Women Hwy. Safety Leaders, Md. State Edn. Dept., 1969-70; bd. dirs. Lincoln Intermediate Unit #12, 1987-89, 91-93; speaker pub. meetings U.S. and abroad. Trustee Nat. Motorcycle Fund; pres. Howard County C. of C., Columbia, Md., 1985-87; sch. dir. Red Lion (Pa.) Area Schs., 1986—, also pres. sch. bd., 1988, 96, v.p., 1989-95. With AUS, 1954-56, ETO. Recipient Traffic Safety Educator of Yr. award Wis. Traffic Edn. Assn, 1972, Sec.'s award U.S. Dept. Transp., 1973; elected to Hall of Fame, Red Lion (Pa.) Area Sch. Dist., 1993. Fellow Am. Acad. Safety Edn. (pres. 1975-76); mem. NEA, Am. Soc. Assn. Execs. (vice-chmn. evaluation com. 1984-85, chmn. 1985-86), Soc. Automotive Engrs., Pres. Assn./Am. Mgmt. Assn., Am. Driver and Traffic Safety Edn. Assn., York 2000 Commn., Assn. for Advancement of Automotive Medicine, Pa. Sch. Bds. Assn., Phi Delta Kappa. Republican. Home: 122 E Mckinley Rd Delta PA 17314-9407 Office: Am Coll Health Assn PO Box 28937 Baltimore MD 21240-8937

HARTMAN, CHARLES RICHARD, health facility administrator; b. Kansas City, Mo., Oct. 1, 1937; s. Charles Sidney and Una C. (Hartman); m. Carolyn Joyce Hogan, Feb. 22, 1940; children: Heather, Holly, Brett. BA, U. Kans., 1962; MD, U. Kans., Kansas City, 1966. Cons. endocrinology Fitzsimons Army Hosp., Aurora, Colo., 1970-72; assoc. prof. medicine Kansas City VA, 1973-83; prof. medicine, COS Kansas City Sch. Medicine, 1973-89; v.p. med. affairs Washington Hosp. Ctr., 1989-92; v.p. med. and acad. affairs St. Vincent Med. Ctr., Toledo, 1992-95, Cmty. Med. Ctr., Scranton, Pa., 1995—. Contbr. articles to profl. jours. Maj. U.S. Army, 1970-72. Fellow Am. Coll. Physicians. Office: Cmty Med Ctr 1800 Mulberry St Scranton PA 18510

HARTMAN, DAVID ELLIOTT, psychologist; b. N.Y.C., Jan. 9, 1954; s. Harry Wilson and Marian Phyllis (Milchin) H.; m. Roberta Maller; children: Sarah Beth, Adam Maller. AB, Vassar Coll., 1975; MA, Princeton U., 1978; PhD, U. of Ill., Chgo., 1982. Diplomate Am. Bd. Profl. Neuropsychology; lic. psychologist, Ill. Intern Michael Reese Hosp.; asst. coordinator in emergency psychiatry Northwestern U. Hosp., Chgo., 1982; dir. psychology tng. Lincoln Park Clinic at Columbus Hosp., Chgo., 1982-92; dir. neuropsychology Rush Presbyn. St. Lukes Hosp. Isaac Ray Ctr., Rush Human Performance Lab., Chgo., 1992—; adj. asst. prof. psychology U. Ill. Med. Ctr., Chgo., 1984—. Author: Neuropsychological Toxicology, 1988, 2d edit., 1995; mem. editl. bd. Archives Clin. Neuropsychology, 1990-91, Neuropsychology Review; contbr. numerous articles to profl. jours. Fellow NIMH. Fellow Nat. Acad. Neuropsychology, Am. Coll. Profl. Neuropsychology; mem. APA, Ill. Psychol. Assn. (past clin. chmn.), Phi Beta Kappa. Office: Rush Presbyn St Lukes Hosp Isaac Ray Ctr Rm 021 1702 W Polk St Chicago IL 60612-4315

HARTMAN, GUY LESLIE, pediatrician; b. Big Flats, N.Y., Sept. 11, 1922; s. Fred Charles and Ruth Agnes (Andrews) H.; m. Shirley Fenn Baldwin, Dec. 28, 1943; children: Eric Vreeland, Fenn Elizabeth, Christina Louise, Peter Bain, Juliana Middaugh. BA in Zoology, Alfred U., 1943; MD, U. Buffalo, 1946. Diplomate Am. Bd. Pediatrics. Commd. med. officer USAF, 1943, advanced through grades to maj., 1950, ret., 1952; intern Med. Ctr., Jersey City, 1946-47; pediatrics resident Children's Hosp., L.A., 1957-59; pediatrician So. Calif. Permanente Med. Group, Fontana, 1952-87; med. cons. regional offices Diamond Bar, San Bernardino, 1990—; chmn. Cen. Valley Child Abuse Team, Fontana, 1975-87, San Bernardino County Child Abuse Council, 1986-87; bd. dirs., v.p. Calif. Consortium Child Abuse, 1981-86; pres. Southwestern Pediatric Soc. Los Angeles, 1984-85. Contbr. articles to profl. jours. and mags. Speaker civic orgns. nationally, and internationally. Recipient Citation Domestic Violence Task Force San Bernardino, 1984, Martha Lou Berkey award Inland Empire Child Abuse Task Force, 1985. Fellow Am. Acad. Pediatrics; mem. Southwestern Pediatric Soc. (chmn. 1984-85), Los Angeles Pediatric Soc., Hinterland Pediatric Soc., Internat. Soc. Prevention of Child Abuse and Neglect, Def. of Children, Collegium Aesculapium (bd. dirs., assoc. editor jour.). Republican. Mormon. Home: 2073 Harvard Oaks Cir Salt Lake City UT 84108-1983

HARTMAN, HENRY BOB, psychologist; b. Bronx, Nov. 9, 1951; s. Seymour Maurice and Esther (Seifer) H.; m. Susan Lynn Solomon, July 3, 1985; children: Jenna, Elana, Kayla. BA, NYU, 1973; MA, St. John's U., 1974; PhD, Hofstra U., 1979. Lic. psychologist, N.Y. Dep. dir., psychologist, asst. Psychiatry Svcs. Ctr., Inc., White Plains, N.Y., 1974-84; prin. Dr. Henry B. Hartman, White Plains, 1979—; psychologist St. Cabrini Nursing Home, Dobbs Ferry, N.Y., 1989—. Office: 12 Old Mamaroneck Rd White Plains NY 10605-2010

HARTMAN, HERBERT ARTHUR, JR., oncologist; b. Halstead, Kans., Aug. 8, 1947; s. Herbert Arthur and Margrete Laverne (Schroeder) H.; m. Cynthia Craig, Dec. 26, 1971; m. April Craig, Herbert Arthur III. BA in Chemistry, U. Kans., 1969, MD, 1973. Diplomate Am. Bd. Internal Medicine, Am. Bd. Med. Oncology. Resident internal medicine U. Nebr. Med. Ctr., Omaha, 1973-76, fellow in med. oncology, 1976-78; oncologist Radiologic Ctr. Inc., Omaha, 1978-79, Sole Proprietorship, Omaha, 1979-80, Oncology Assocs., Omaha, 1980—; chmn. dept. medicine Immanuel Med. Ctr., Omaha, 1988-90; clin. assoc. prof. internal medicine U. Nebr. Med. Sch., 1979—. Contbr. articles to med. jours. Pres. Nebr. Cancer Soc., 1991. Fellow Am. Coll. Physicians; mem. AMA, Am. Soc. Internal Medicine, Am. Soc. Clin. Oncology, Nebr. Med. Assn. (bd. dirs. 1989-95), Metro Omaha Med. Soc. (exec. com. 1987), N.Y. Acad. Scis., Mensa. Republican. Episcopalian. Home: 6211 Chicago St Omaha NE 68132-2727 Office: Oncology Assocs PC Meth Cancer Ctr 8303 Dodge St Ste 225 Omaha NE 68124-0639

HARTMAN, LAWRENCE PAUL, neurosurgeon; b. Pittsburgh, June 9, 1952; s. David Paul and Nancy Mary (Wyrough) H.; m. Jamie Catherine Holt, Sept. 13, 1975; children: Jason David, Byron Clement. BS, U. Fla., 1974; MD, U. South Fla., 1977. Diplomate Am. Bd. Neurol. Surgery. Intern Richland Meml. Hosp., Columbia, S.C., 1977-78; resident SUNY Health Sci. Ctr., Syracuse, 1981-86; neurosurgeon Brooke Army Med. Ctr., Ft. Sam Houston, 1986-89, Neurol. Inst. Ctrl. Ga., Macon, 1989—. Contbr. articles to profl. jours. Unit commr. Boy Scouts Am., Macon, 1989-95, dist. comdr., 1995-96. Lt. col. U.S. Army, 1974—. Mem. Am. Assn. Neurol. Surgeons (poster presenter 1988, oral presenter 1991), Congress Neurol. Surgeons, Ga. Neurosurg. Soc. (program chmn.), AMA, Med. Assn. Ga., Sports Car Club Am. (divsnl. med. adminstr. 1995—). Republican. Roman Catholic. Office: Neurol Inst Ctrl Ga 840 Pine St Ste 880 Macon GA 31201

HARTMAN, LENORE ANNE, physical therapist; b. Cleve., May 27, 1938; d. Howard Andrew and Emma Elizabeth (Beck) H. BS in Agriculture, Ohio State U., 1960, MS in Agriculture, 1963; postgrad., Kans. State U., 1963-67; cert. in phys. therapy, U. Kans., 1968. Staff phys. therapist R.J. Delano Sch. for the Handicapped, Kansas City, Mo., 1969-74; chief phys. therapist Children's Mercy Hosp., Kansas City, 1974-78; relief staff Mass Gen. Hosp., Boston, 1969-70; staff phys. therapist Menorah Med. Ctr., Kansas City, 1979-87; clin. instr. phys. therapy St. Louis U., 1974-78, U. Ky., 1974-78, U. Mo., Columbia, 1973-78, U. Kans. Med. Ctr., Kansas City, 1974-87; mem. med. adv. com. Hospice Care of Mid Am., Kansas City, 1984-87; staff phys. therapist S.W. Gen. Hosp., 1992—; phys. therapy cons. Rocky River Riding Therapeutic Riding Program, 1994—; chapel organist St. Luke's Hosp., Kansas City, 1978-87. Contbr. articles to profl. jours. Ohio del. Internat. Farm Youth Exch., Brazil, 1962. Mem. Internat. Farm Youth Exch. Assn. (life), Am. Phys. Therapy Assn. (del. to nat. 1975-76), Mo. Phys. Therapy Assn. (chmn. northwest dist. 1974-76), Am. Guild of Organists (chmn. profl. concerns com. Greater Kansas City chpt. 1983), Japan Am. Soc., Ohio State U. Alumni Assn. (life), Ohio Phys. Therapy Assn., Cleve. All-Breed Tng. Club, Western Res. Kennel Club, Pembroke Welsh Corgi Club of Western Res., Am. Morgan Horse Assn., N.Am. Riding Assn. for Handicapped, U.S. Dressage Fedn., North Ohio Dessage Assn., Omicron Delta Epsilon, Phi Delta Gamma. Office: Southwest Gen Health Ctr Dept Physical Therapy Middleburg Heights OH 44130

HARTMAN, ROBERT RAY, retired physician, medical consultant; b. Jacksonville, Ill., Feb. 17, 1914; s. Ray Adam and Blanche Margaret (Perry) H.; m. Beatrice Hayes, Feb. 20, 1937; children: Linda Skop, Suzanne Verticchio. AB, Ill. Coll., 1935; BM, Northwestern U., Chgo., 1940, MD, 1941; LLD (hon.), Ill. Coll., 1986. Intern St. Louis City Hosp., 1939-40, resident in ob-gyn, 1940-43; practice medicine specializing in ob-gyn Jacksonville, 1946-85; chief of staff Passavant Hosp., Jacksonville, Ill., 1955, 66; assoc. clin. prof. ob-gyn So. Ill. U., Springfield, 1976-87; cons. Ill. Dept. Pub. Aid, 1974-85, Ill. Dept. Pub. Health, Springfield, 1972-74, Ill. Maternal Welfare Com., 1954-84, chmn., 1964-74; chmn. Ill. Maternal Welfare Com., 1964-74; sec. bd. trustees Ill. Coll., Jacksonville, 1963-86. Contbr. articles to profl. jours. Mem. Jacksonville Planning Com., 1959-67, chmn., 1962-67; mem. Jacksonville Mayor's Flood Control Com., 1978-82; mem. Morgan County Bd. Health, Jacksonville, 1960-85, pres., 1968-80; mem. Ill. Com. To Rewrite and Revise Pub. Aid Code, Springfield, 1978-81; trustee emeritus Ill. Coll., Jacksonville, 1986—. Capt. U.S. Army, 1943-46. Recipient cert. of appreciation Morgan-Scott Med. Soc., 1979. Fellow ACOG; mem. ACS, AMA (alt. del. 1976-82), Internat. Coll. Surgeons, Ill. Ob-Gyn. Soc. (pres. 1965-66), Ill. Med. Soc. (trustee 1975-84m, v.p. 1977, chmn. bd. trustees 1978-80), Am. Assn. Med. Assistance (nat. physician adv. 1982-84), The Club (assoc.), Elks, Masons, Rotary (pres. 1951, Paul Harris fellow 1982). Republican. Mem. United Ch. of Christ. Home: 5B Justin Dr Jacksonville IL 62650-2757

HARTMAN, RUSSELL B., social worker; b. Pitts., May 17, 1957; s. George A. Hartman and Mary P. (Layfield) Cochrane. BSW, LaSalle Coll., 1979; MSW, Rutgers U., 1983. Lic. social worker, Pa.; ACSW. Social worker Children and Youth Svcs. of Delaware County, Chester, Pa., 1978-80, Hahnemann U. Hosp., Phila., 1980-83; asst. dir. Centro de Servicios Para Hispanos, Phila., 1983-86; assoc. clin. dir. Integra, Inc., Radnor, Pa., 1986-94; mgr. employee assistance program Main Line Health System, Bryn Mawr, Pa., 1994—; adj. instr. LaSalle U., Phila., 1991—; pvt. practice psychotherapy Ctr. for Psychol. Svcs., Elkins Park, Pa., 1995—. Mem. NASW, Employee Assistance Profl. Assn. (officer Del. Valley chpt. v.p. 1995—). Office: Main Line Health System 815 Old Lancaster Rd Bryn Mawr PA 19010

HARTMANN, LYDIA AVALLONE, speech-language pathologist; d. Alfonso A. and Margaret Avallone; m. Chris C. Hartmann, May 30, 1981. BA cum laude, Hofstra U., 1979, MA in Speech Pathology, 1980. Cert. clin. competence in speech lang. pathology; lic. speech pathologist, N.Y.; cert. tchr. speech hearing handicapped. Speech and lang. pathologist Rocky Point (N.Y.) Pub. Schs., 1980—, Speech Pathologists-Myofunctional Therapists, Stonybrook, N.Y., 1986-90. Mem. ASHA, The Myofunctional Therapy Assn. of Am., LISHA, Sigma Pi.

HARTMANN, RENE F., surgeon; b. Caracas, Venezuela, Mar. 10, 1948; came to U.S., 1971; s. Luis A. and Ligia M. (Ruiz) H.; m. Marialena Arregui; children: Enrique L., Gabrielle Marie. BS, Inst. Escuela, 1965; MD, U. Ctrl. Caracas, 1971. Resident Grant Hosp., Columbus, Ohio, 1981-91; asst. prof. clin. surgery, chief divsn. colon/rectal surgery U. Miami (Fla.), 1991—, assoc. prof. clin. surgery, 1996—; chief exec. Jackson Meml. Hosp., Miami, 1991—. Fellow Am. Coll. Surgeons, Am. Soc. Colon & Rectal Surgeons, Internat. Soc. Univ. Colon & Rectal Surgeons; mem. Soc. Clin. Pathology (assoc.), Soc. Clinicians Phile (hon.), Soc. Mex. Colon & Rectal Surgeons (hon.). Office: U Miami PO Box 016310 Miami FL 33124

HARTMANN, ROBERT CARL, retired physician, educator; b. Everett, Wash., July 23, 1919; s. Rudolf and Eugenie (Kaiser) H.; m. Margaretta O'Sullivan, Mar. 16, 1946 (div. Aug. 1975); children—Kathleen, Robert Carl, David, Richard, Margaret, Ellen; m. Joyce S. Anton, Sept. 4, 1977. A.B., Johns Hopkins U., 1941, M.D., 1944. Rotating intern Pa. Hosp., 1944-45, resident medicine, 1945-46; fellow medicine Johns Hopkins Sch. Medicine, 1948-49, 50-52, resident in medicine, 1949-50; faculty Vanderbilt U. Sch. Medicine, Nashville, 1952-74; prof. medicine Vanderbilt U. Sch. Medicine, 1963-74, dir. div. hematology, 1952-74; prof. medicine U. South Fla. Coll. Medicine, 1974-89, retired, chief sect. hematology/oncology, 1974-79, mem. staff div. hematology, 1979-89; part-time cons. J.A. Haley Vets. Hosp., 1989—; Cons. nat. nutrition survey USPHS; anemia and nutrition survey Inst. Nutrition for Central Am. and Panama, Guatemala, 1965-68; mem. hematology study sect., sub-com. platelet-glass-adhesion Internat. Commn. Haemostasis and Thrombosis, 1967-71; adv. com. blood disease and blood resources NIH, 1980-84. Mem. editorial staff Am. Jour. Hematology, 1985—; contbr. papers to profl. jours. Served with AUS, 1946-48. Mem. So. Soc. Clin. Research, Am. Soc. Clin. Investigation, Am. Soc. Clin. Oncology, Am., Internat. Socs. Hematology, Am. Fedn. Clin. Research, Am. Assn. Physicians, Johns Hopkins Alumni Assn. (pres. Tenn. chpt. 1967). Home: 3630 Little Rd Lutz FL 33549-4728 Office: JA Haley VA Hosp 13000 Bruce B Downs Blvd Tampa FL 33612-4745

HARTMANN, WILLIAM HERMAN, pathologist, educator; b. N.Y.C., Mar. 13, 1931; m. Loreen Moyer, Feb. 27, 1954; children: Daniel M., William Geoffrey, Lindsey M. Cather. BA, Syracuse U., 1951; M.D., SUNY, 1955. Diplomate: Am. Bd. Pathology (Anatomic Pathology, Clin. Pathology). Intern Detroit Receiving Hosp., 1955-56; resident Henry Ford Hosp., Detroit, 1956-58, Meml. Hosp. for Cancer and Allied Disease, N.Y.C., 1958-60; asst. prof. pathology Johns Hopkins U. Sch. of Medicine, Balt., 1962-66; assoc. prof. Johns Hopkins U. Sch. of Medicine, 1966-67; exchange prof. pathology Cayetano-Heredia Sch. Medicine, Lima, Peru, 1965; prof. pathology Vanderbilt U. Sch. Medicine, Nashville, 1971-87; chmn. dept. pathology Vanderbilt U. Sch. Medicine, 1973-87; chmn. pathology quality control program, breast cancer detection demonstration projects Nat. Cancer Inst.; med. dir. pathology Long Beach (Calif.) Meml. Med. Ctr., 1988-92; exec. v.p. Am. Bd. Pathology, 1993—; prof. pathology U. So. Fla., 1993—; mem. bd. trustees Am. Bd. Pathology, 1983-92. Contbr. articles to med. jours.; editor: Atlas of Tumor Pathology Series, 1976-87. Served with M.C. U.S. Army, 1960-62. Fellow Am. Soc. Clin. Pathologists, Coll. Am. Pathologists; mem. Internat. Acad. Pathology (pres. U.S.-Can. divsn. 1979-80), Am. Assn. Pathologists, Arthur Purdy Stout Soc. Surg. Pathologists (pres. 1984-86), Sociedad Latino Americana De Patologia. Office: Am Bd Pathology PO Box 25915 Tampa FL 33622-5915

HARTMANN-JOHNSEN, OLAF JOHAN, internist; b. Aalesund, Norway, Aug. 22, 1924; s. Odd and Helga Elisabeth (Hartmann) Johnsen; MB, BS, U. Queensland (Australia), 1956, MD, Oslo U., 1974; m. Mary Essil Archibald, 1956 (dissolved 1968); children: Sally, Helga Elisabeth; m. Mary Eldbjørg Hestad, May 23, 1969; children: Olaf Johan, Else Margrete. Physician, Royal Brisbane (Australia) Hosp., 1956-63, Oslo Univ. Hosp., 1964-65, Bundaberg Gen. Hosp., 1966, Hornsby Dist. Hosp., 1967-70, Upton Hosp., Slough, Eng., 1970, Blacktown Dist. Hosp., 1971-73, Ullevål Hosp., 1974-77, Vefsn Hosp., 1977-78, Kragerø Hosp., 1978-79; physician-in-chief St. Joseph's Hosp., Porsgrunn, 1979-82; cons. physician, chief med. officer Nesset County, 1982-91; govt. med. officer, 1982-91; tutor in medicine U. Oslo Med. Sch., 1975-77; communal med. officer Rauma County Aandalsnes, 1991-92; cons. in gen. practice and cmty. med., 1991—; staff physician Psychiatric Hosp., Hjelset, 1993—. Served with Royal Norwegian Air Force, 1942-47. Decorated King Haakon VII medal, Norwegian War Svc. medal, several British campaign medals. Mem. Norwegian Med. Assn., Coll. Norwegian Internists, N.Y. Acad. Scis. Conservative. Lutheran. Contbr. articles to med. jours. Home: Ranvik, 6460 Eidsvaag Norway Office: Psykiatrisk Storaudeling, Fylkesjukehuset 1 Molde, 6450 Hjelset Norway

HARTNELL, GEORGE G., radiologist; b. Oxford, Eng., July 19, 1952; came to U.S., 1991; s. Francis George and Margaret Eileen Hartnell. BSc in Anatomy, U. Bristol, 1973, MB ChB, 1976. Lic. Mass. Intern Can. Red Cross Meml. Hosp., Taplow, Bucks, Eng., 1976-77, St. Martin's Hosp., Bath, Avon, Eng., 1977; resident Can. Red Cross Meml. Hosp., Taplow, 1978-79; registrar Harefield (Eng.) Hosp., Middlesex, 1979-81, West Middlesex U. Hosp., Isleworth, Eng., 1981-83; resident radiology Hammersmith Hosp., London, 1983-85, sr. registrar, 1985-87; lectr., cons. U. Bristol, Eng., 1987-90; dir. cardiac radiology Deaconess Hosp., Boston, 1991—; assoc. prof. radiology Harvard Med. Sch., Boston, 1991—. Grantee Johns Hopkins Hosp. and Alexandria Hosp., 1985, Bristol and Weston Health Authority, 1989, 90, Cordis Ltd., 1989. Fellow Royal Coll. Radiologists, Cardiovascular and Interventional Soc. Europe, Am. Coll. Cardiology, Am. Heart Assn. (Coun. on Cardiovascular Radiology); mem. Royal Coll. Physicians of U.K., Soc. Cardiovascular and Interventional Radiology, N.Am. Soc. Cardiac Imaging, Assn. Univ. Radiologists, Brit. Inst. Radiology, Brit. Med. assn., Brit. Soc. Interventional Radiology, New Eng. Roentgen Ray Soc., New Eng. Soc. Cardiovascular and Interventional Radiology, Radiol. Soc. N.Am. Office: Deaconess Hosp Dept Radiol Scis 1 Deaconess Rd Boston MA 02215

HARTRAMPF, CARL ROERIG, JR., plastic and reconstructive surgeon; b. Atlanta, Aug. 5, 1932; s. Carl Roerig Sr. and Ethel Belle (Chambers) H.; m. Patricia Crawford, Aug. 24, 1951; children: Vallijeanne Hartrampf Arader, Carl R. III, Havalyn Ann. Hartrampf Hensley. Student, Emory U., 1951, U. Ga., 1952; MD, Med. Coll. Ga., Augusta, 1956. Diplomate Am. Bd. Surgery. Intern U. N.C./N.C. Meml. Hosp., 1956-57, resident in gen. surgery, 1957-61; resident in plastic surgery Washington U./Barnes Hosp., St. Louis, 1961-62; with St. Joseph's Hosp., Atlanta, 1963—, Northside Hosp., 1963—, Scottish Rite Children's Med. Ctr., 1963—; sec. Atlanta Plastic Surgery, P.A., 1968-94, with; clin. prof. in plastic surgery sch. medicine Emory U., Atlanta, 1984—; Diplomate Am. Bd. Surgery, Am. Bd. Plastic Surgery. Author: TAIF For Breast Recon, 1984, Hartrampf's Br. Recon c Living Tissue, 1990. Recipient ACS Medal of Honor, 1994. Fellow ACS; mem. AMA (Sci. Achievement award 1995), Am. Assn. Plastic Surgeons (James Barrett Brown award 1983), Am. Soc. Plastic and Reconstructive Surgeons (Presdl. award 1991), Am. Cancer Soc. (Disting. Svc. award 1995), Med. Assn. Ga. (Lamartine Hardman award 1984), Ga. Surg. Soc., Med. Assn. Atlanta, Southeastern Soc. Plastic and Reconstructive Surgeons (Excellence award 1985-90), Reconstructive Surgery Fedn. (bd. dirs. 1985—). Methodist. Office: Atlanta Plastic Surgery PA 975 Johnson Ferry Rd NE Ste 500 Atlanta GA 30342-1619

HARTSTEIN, GARY MARSHALL, anesthesiologist, educator; b. Staten Island, N.Y., May 17, 1955; arrived in Belgium, 1989; s. Alfred Bernard and Ingeborg Babette (Meyer) H.; m. Chantal Gilles, May 5, 1983; children:

Yannick, Chloë. BA in Neuroscis., U. Rochester, 1976; MD with highest distinction, U. Liege, Belgium, 1983, DSc with highest distinction, 1994. Diplomate Am. Bd. Anesthesiology. Resident in anesthesiology Albert Einstein Coll. Medicine, N.Y.C., 1983-85, chief resident anesthesiology, 1985-86, fellow in critical care medicine, 1986-87, instr. anesthesiology, 1987-89; specialist in residence U. Liege, 1989-93, asst. prof. anesthesiology, 1993—. Author: (with others) Pre-Anesthetic Assessment, vol. 1, 1988, vol. 2, 1989, Post-Anesthetic Assessment, 1990; contbr. numerous articles to profl. jours. Recipient Physicians Recognition award AMA, 1989. Mem. Am. Soc. Anesthesiologists, European Assn. Cardiothoracic Anesthesiologists, European Soc. Anesthesiology, Internat. Anesthesia Rsch. Soc., Belgian Soc. Anesthesiology and Intensive Care Medicine, Soc. Cardiovascular Anesthesiologists.

HARTSTEIN, HAROLD HERMAN, psychology educator, consultant; b. N.Y.C., Jan. 9, 1921; s. Samuel and Margaret Amanda (Wussow) H.; m. Marion Elizabeth Shea, Apr. 11, 1953; children: Marion Farnham Korzec, Margaret Ann. BGS, U. Nebr.-Omaha, 1971; MA, U. South Fla., 1972; EdD, Nova U., 1978. Enlisted U.S. Army, 1942, commd. 2d lt., 1948, advanced through grades to lt. col., 1967; served in ETO, 1944-45, Japan, 1949-50, Korea, 1950-51, W. Ger., 1955-57, Vietnam, 1960-61; with 3d Inf. Honor Guard, Washington, 1951-54; comdg. officer Signal Battalion, Korat, Thailand, 1967-68; gen. staff officer Hdqrs., U.S. Army Strategic Communications Command, Ft. Huachua, Ariz., 1968-70; ret., 1970; prof. psychology Hillsborough Community Coll., Tampa, Fla., 1973-91; ret. 1991; cons. textbook pubs. Decorated Legion of Merit, Bronze Star medal, Army Commendation medal. Mem. NEA, Ret. Officers Assn., Am. Assn. Ret. Persons, Am. Legion, Common Cause, U. Nebr. at Omaha Alumni Assn., U. South Fla. Alumni Assn., Nova U. Alumni Assn., Friends of Tampa Mus. Art. Democrat. Mem. United Ch. of Christ.

HARTSUCK, JAMES MALCOLM, surgeon; b. Cushing, Okla., Sept. 2, 1938; s. Joris Malcolm and Mary Winifred (Yarbrough) H.; m. Jean Ann Yarborough, June 17, 1962; children: Rebecca Ann, Mary Elizabeth, Katherine Jean. BS with spl. distinction, U. Okla., 1958; MD magna cum laude, Harvard U., 1962. Diplomate Am. Bd. General Surgery, Am. Bd. Thoracic and Cardiovascular Surgery. Intern, resident in surgery Peter Bent Brigham Hosp., Boston, 1962-68, chief resident, Arthur Cabot Tracy fellow, 1968, resident in thoracic surgery, 1968-70; asst. prof. dept. surgery U. Okla., Oklahoma City, 1970-74, asst. clin. prof., 1974—; pvt. clin. practice thoracic & cardiovascular surgery Oklahoma City, 1974—; chief thoracic surgery Mercy Hosp., Oklahoma City, 1990-93; bd. trustees Mercy Health Ctr., Oklahoma City, 1994—; credential com. Am. Coll. Surgeons, Oklahoma City, 1987-93. Maj. U.S. Army, 1966-72. Mem. AMA (dir. county assn. 1985-89), So. Thoracic Assn., S.W. Surg., Internat. Cardiovascular Soc. Republican. Episcopalian. Office: Cardiac Surgeons OKC 3433 NW 56th St Ste 660 Oklahoma City OK 73112

HARTUNG, ROLF, environmental toxicology educator, researcher, consultant; b. Bremen, Fed. Republic of Germany, Mar. 1, 1935; came to U.S., 1952, naturalized, 1958. B.S. in Wildlife Mgmt., U. Mich., 1960, M.W.M. in Wildlife Mgmt., 1962, Ph.D. in Wildlife Mgmt., 1964. Diplomate Am. Bd. Toxicology. Instr. in wildlife mgmt. U. Mich., Ann Arbor, 1963, lectr. in indsl. health, 1964, asst. prof. indsl. health, 1965-69, assoc. prof. environ. and indsl. health, 1969-73, prof. environ. toxicology, 1973—, chmn. toxicology program, 1974-80; com. or sub-com. mem. Nat. Acad. Scis., 1971-72, 79—, Mich. Dept. Natural Resources, 1977—; mem. Mich. Environ. Rev. Bd., 1982-86; mem. hazardous materials com. U.S. Congress Office Tech. Assessment, 1980-83; chmn. com. on environ. effects, transport and fate of sci. adv. bd. EPA, 1982-87, mem. exec. com. of sci. adv. bd., 1982-87. Editor, contbg. author: Environmental Mercury Contamination, 1972; assoc. editor Jour. Toxicology and Indsl. Health, 1984-87. Contbr. numerous chpts., articles to profl. publs. Recipient H. M. Wight award. U. Mich., 1963; NSF fellow, 1960-64. Mem. AAAS, Am. Indsl. Hygiene Assn., Mich. Indsl. Hygiene Assn., Soc. Environ. Toxicology and chemistry, Soc. Toxicology, Wildlife Disease Assn., Wildlife Soc., Sigma Xi, Phi Sigma, Phi Kappa Phi. Home: 3125 Fernwood St Ann Arbor MI 48108-1955 Office: U Mich Sch Pub Health Dept Environ Indsl Health Ann Arbor MI 48109

HARTWELL, LELAND HARRISON, geneticist, educator; b. Los Angeles, Oct. 30, 1939; s. Majorie (Taylor) H. BS, Calif. Inst. Tech., 1961; PhD, MIT, 1964. Postdoctoral fellow Salk Inst., 1964-65; asst. prof. U. Calif., Irvine, 1965-67, assoc. prof., 1967-68; assoc. prof. U. Washington, Seattle, 1968-73, prof., 1973—; rsch. prof. Am. Cancer Soc., 1990—. Recipient Eli Lilly award, 1973, GM Sloan award, 1991, Hoffman LaRoche Mattia award, 1991, Gairdner Found. Internat. award, 1992, Brandeis U. Rosenstiel award, 1993, Louisa Gross Horwitz prize Columbia U., 1995; Guggenheim fellow, 1983-84; Am. Bus. Cancer Rsch. grantee, 1983—; Am. Cancer Soc. scholar; laureate Passano Found., 1996. Mem. NAS, AAAS, Am. Soc. Microbiology, Am. Soc. Cell Biology, Genetics Soc. Am. (pres. 1990). Office: U Wash Dept Genetics SK-50 Seattle WA 98195

HARTWELL, RICHARD CONRAD, neurosurgeon; b. Jamaica, N.Y., Dec. 30, 1954; s. Harry and Stephanie (Maderic) H.; m. Sharon Marie Stremmel, Oct. 19, 1985; children: Catherine, Melissa, Suzanne. BA, Columbia U., 1974; PhD, U. Chgo., 1982, MD, 1982. Diplomate Am. Bd. Neurol. Surgeons. Surg. intern U. Pa., Phila., 1982-83, resident in neurosurgery, 1983-88, clin. assoc. neurosurgery, 1988—; attending neurosurgeon Cmty. Med. Ctr., Toms River, N.J., 1988—. Mem. Am. Assn. Neurol. Surgeons, Congress Neurol. Surgeons, Phi Beta Kappa. Office: Coastal NeuroSurgery 9 Hospital Dr Toms River NJ 08755

HARTWIG, JOHN E., federal official. BA, Rutgers U.; M Acctg. Scis., U. Ill. CPA, Ill. Auditor U.S. Gen. Acctg. Office, N.Y., 1972-79; spl. agt. Office Investigations HHS, N.Y., 1979-84; asst. regional inspector gen. investigations HHS, Phila., 1984-89, regional inspector gen., 1989; asst. inspector gen. criminal investigations Office of Investigations Criminal Investigations divsn. HHS, dep. inspector gen. Office of Investigations; lectr. in field. Office: HHS Office Inspector Gen Cohen Bldg 330 Independence Ave SW Rm 5459 Washington DC 20201*

HARTZ, RENEE SEMO, cardiothoracic surgeon; b. Bessemer Twp., Mich., Dec. 7, 1946; d. Rita Ann Semo; children: Tyler Joseph, Colin Wilson. BA, Western Mich. U., 1969; MD, Northwestern U., 1974. Diplomate Am. Bd. Surgery, Am. Bd. Thoracic Surgery. Intern pediatrics Children's Meml. Hosp., Chgo., 1974-75; intern gen. surgery Northwestern Meml. Hosp., Chgo., 1975-76, resident gen. surgery, 1976-79; chief resident cardiothoracic surgery Northwestern Meml. Hosp., 1979-81; instr. dept. surgery Northwestern U. Med. Sch., Chgo., 1978-81, assoc. in surgery, 1981-85; asst. prof. surgery med. sch. Northwestern U., Chgo., 1985-87, assoc. prof. surgery med. sch., 1987-92; prof. surgery, chief div. cardiothoracic surgery U. Ill. Hosp. & Clinics, Chgo., 1992—; apptd. to Northwestern Meml. Hosp., Chgo., Children's Meml. Hosp., Chgo., VA Lakeside Hosp., Chgo., Evanston (Ill.) Hosp., Columbus Hosp., Chgo.; laser researcher Northwestern U. Med. Sch., 1984—, U. of Ill. Hosp., West Suburban Hosp., Ill. Masonic Hosp. Contbr. articles to profl. jours.; contbr. chpts. to Perioperative Cardiac Dysfunction II, 1985, General Thoracic Surgery, 1989, New Technology in Vascular Surgery, 1988. Mem. Am. Coll. Chest Physicians, Am. Coll. Surgeons, Am. Heart Assn., Am. Women's Med. Assn., Assn. for Acad. Surgery, Chgo. Heart Assn., Chgo. Surg. Soc., Ill. Surg. Soc., Laser Inst. Am., Soc. Thoracic Surgeons, Soc. Univ. Surgeons, Am. Assn. Thoracic Surgeons, Sigma Xi. Office: U Ill Chgo 1740 W Taylor St # C 959 Chicago IL 60612-7232

HARTZELL, HARRISON CRISS, JR., biomedical research educator; b. Phila., Dec. 4, 1946; s. Harrison Criss and Jane Ann (Price) H.; m. Martha Ann Kroon, Feb. 1, 1969; children: Laura Brook, Robyn Elizabeth, Catherine Anne. BA magna cum laude, Lawrence U., 1968; PhD with distinction, Johns Hopkins U., 1973. Rsch. fellow in neurobiology Harvard Med. Sch., Boston, 1973-76; asst. prof. dept. anatomy Emory U. Sch. Medicine, Atlanta, 1976-81, assoc. prof. dept. anatomy and cell biology, 1981-85, prof. dept. anatomy and cell biology, 1985—, prof. dept. physiology, 1990—; vis. prof. U. Paris, Orsay, France, 1985-86, 87, 89; mem. physiology study sect. NIH, 1988-91; presenter in field. Mem. editl. bd. Am. Jour. Physiology, 1990—, Jour. Cardiac Electrophysiology, 1990—, Jour. Gen. Physiology, 1995—, Physiol. Revs., 1996—; contbr. chpts. to books and articles to profl. jours. including Jour. Gen. Physiology, Sci., Jour. Physiology, Nature, others. Named Rsch. fellow Muscular Dystrophy Assn., 1973-75; recipient NIH Rsch. Career Devel. award NIH, 1978-83, Albert E. Levy Faculty Rsch. award Sigma Xi, 1982, NIH Merit award Nat. Heart Lung & Blood Inst., 1988, James Clark Foye scholarship in chemistry Lawrence U. Mem. AAAS, Internat. Soc. for Heart Rsch., Am. Heart Assn., Biophysical Soc., Phi Sigma. Office: Emory Univ Sch Medicine Dept Anatomy Cell Biol Atlanta GA 30322

HARTZELL, IRENE JANOFSKY, psychologist; b. L.A. Vor-Diplom, U. Munich, 1961; BA, U. Calif., Berkeley, 1963, MA, 1965; PhD, U. Oreg., 1970. Lic. psychologist, Wash., Ariz. Psychologist Lake Washington Sch. Dist., Kirkland, Wash., 1971-72; staff psychologist VA Med. Ctr., Seattle, 1970-71, Long Beach, Calif., 1973-74; dir. parent edn. Children's Hosp., Orange, Calif., 1975-78; clin. psychologist Kaiser Permanente, Woodland Hills, Calif., 1979—; clin. instr. dept. pediatrics U. Calif. Irvine Coll. Medicine, 1975-78. Author: The Study Skills Advantage, 1986; contbr. articles to profl. jours. Intern Oreg. Legislature, 1974-75. U.S. Vocat. Rehab. Adminstrn. fellow U. Oreg., 1966-67, 69. Mem. APA, Pi Lambda Theta.

HARTZELL, MARYANN PATRICIA, podiatrist; b. Allentown, Pa., Nov. 25, 1964; d. Harry Albert and Audry Mary (Wolf) H.; m. Gregory Michael Sado, Aug. 12, 1989; 1 child, Alexis Elizabeth Sado. BS in Biochemistry/Mgmt., Chestnut Hill Coll., 1986; D Podiatric Medicine, Pa. Coll. Podiatric Medicine, 1991. Diplomate Am. Podiatric Med. Bd. Podiatric surg. resident Frankford Hosp., Phila., 1991-92, chief resident, pediatric surgery, 1992-93; pvt. practice Southampton, Pa., 1993—; tchr. Frankford Hosp., 1994—, diabetes educator/lectr., 1996. Recipient Edith Fitton Herrin scholarship Pa. Coll. of Podiatric Medicine, Phila., 1991. Mem. Am. Bd. Podiatric Medicine (assoc.), Am. Podiatric med. Assn., Pa. Podiatric med. Assn., Am. Assn. Women Podiatrists. Office: 643 Second St Pike Southampton PA 18966

HARTZEMA, ABRAHAM GIJSBERT, pharmacy educator, pharmacoepidemiologist; b. The Hague, The Netherlands, May 10, 1947; came to U.S., 1976; s. Gijsbert Egbertus and Johanna Jantine (Wolters) H.; m. Christine Monique Roth, July 23, 1983. PharmD, U. Utrecht, The Netherlands, 1976; MSPH, U. Washington, 1978; PhD, U. Minn. 1982. Asst. prof. U. N.C. Sch. Pharmacy, Chapel Hill, 1982-89, assoc. prof., 1989-91, prof., 1991—; prof. health policy adminstrn. U. N.C. Sch. Pub. Health, Chapel Hill, 1991—; dir. Ctr. for Pharm. Outcomes Rsch. U. N.C., Chapel Hill, 1994—. Author: Pharmaceutical Chartbook, 1995; editor: Pharmacoepidemiology: An Introduction, 1996; contbr. articles to profl. jours. Home: 6617 Turkey Farm Rd Chapel Hill NC 27514 Office: Univ North Carolina CB #7360 Chapel Hill NC 27599

HARTZLER, GEOFFREY OLIVER, retired cardiologist; b. Goshen, Ind., Nov. 6, 1946; s. Robert Willis and Emma Irene (Blosser) H.; m. Lois Anne Kauffman, June 1967 (div. May 1983); children: Abigail, Christine, Amanda; m. Dorothy Eloise Arnn, July 1985. BA, Goshen Coll., 1968; MD with honors, Ind. U., 1972. Diplomate Am. Bd. Internal Medicine, Bd. in Cardiovascular Disease. Intern in medicine Mayo Grad. Sch. Medicine, Rochester, Minn., 1972-73; fellow in medicine Mayo Grad. Sch. Medicine, Rochester, 1973-74, fellow in cardiology, 1974-76; assoc. cons. in internal medicine and cardiovascular disease Mayo Clinic, Rochester, 1976-77; instr. in medicine Mayo Med. Sch. and Grad. Sch Medicine, Rochester, 1976-79; cons. in cardiovascular disease and internal medicine Mayo Clinic and Mayo Found., Rochester, 1977-80; dir. invasive diagnostic electrophysiology Mayo Clinic, Rochester, Minn., 1979-80; cardiologist Cardiovascular Cons., Inc., Kansas City, Mo., 1980-93; clin. prof. medicine U. Mo., Kansas City, 1985-95; cons. cardiologist Mid-Am. Heart Inst., Kansas City, 1980-95; dir. advanced angioplasty fellowship program St. Luke's Hosp., Kansas City, 1985-92, med. dir. cardiovascular clin. rsch. ctr. Mid-Am. Heart Inst., 1993-95; cons. Advanced Cardiovascular Systems, Inc., Santa Clara, Calif., 1983-95; past mem. editl. or rev. bd. Am. Jour. Cardiology, Jour. Am. Coll. Cardiology, Cath. and CV Diagnosis, others; co-founder Ventritex, Inc., Sunnyvale, Calif., 1985-88, Triax Internat., Inc., Lenexa, Kans., 1989—; prin., bd. dirs. Kustom Signals, Inc., Lenexa, 1990—, LMP Steel & Wire Co., Maryville, Mo., 1992—, Lett Electronics, Inc., Topeka, 1995—. Contbr. numerous abstracts, articles to profl. jours., chpts. to books; made TV presentations to lay people on aspects of cardiology. Recipient KK Chen award, 1970, E.V. Allen scholarship, 1971, Osler award U. Miami, 1986, 1st Ann. Career Achievement award Cardiol. Rsch. Found., 1994. Fellow Am. Coll. Cardiology, Coun. on Clin. Cardiology of Am. Heart Assn., Soc. for Cardiac Angiography; mem. AMA, Mo. State Med. Assn., Kansas City Cardiovascular Roundtable, Jackson County Med. Assn., Am. Heart Assn. Office: 2600 Verona Rd Shawnee Mission KS 66208

HARTZOG, KENNETH DELTON, optometrist; b. Clio, Ala., June 12, 1948; s. Kenneth Dewell and Verlie Lee (Sutton) H.; m. Patricia Marie Lewis, Mar. 10, 1973; children; Heath Kendel, Stephanie Marie. BS in Chemistry, U. Ala., 1970; BS in Physiol. Optics, U. Ala., Brimingham, 1972, OD, 1975. Optometrist in pvt. practice Gadsden, Ala., 1975—; mem. adv. bd. Omega Eye Care Ctr., Birmingham, 1993—. Mem. Am. Optometric Assn., Ala. Optometric Assn. (zone rep. 1993—), N.E. Ala. Optometric Soc. (pres. 1993-95), Etowah Bapt. Assn. (bd. dirs. 1994-95), Gadsden C. of C., Gadsden Amateur Radio Club. Baptist. Home: 109 Clokey Dr Gadsden AL 35901 Office: 249 S 6th St Gadsden AL 35901

HARVAN, ROBIN ANN, health professions educator; b. Paterson, N.J., July 24, 1955; d. Robert L. and Victoria A. (Martin) Muccio; m. Christopher Harvan, Oct. 22, 1977. AAS cum laude, Felician Coll., Lodi, N.J., 1976; BS, Montclair (N.J.) State Coll., 1979; EdM, Rutgers U., 1983, EdD, 1989. Registered med. lab. technician. Med. lab. technician Holy Name Hosp., Teaneck, N.J., 1976; sr. lab. technician Warner-Lambert Co., Morris Plains, N.J., 1976-79; curriculum project coord. Rutgers U. Vocat.-Tech. Project, Piscataway, N.J., 1982; dental office mgr. J.C. Harvan, Manalapan, N.J., 1979-84; adj. instr. Montclair State Coll., 1984; grad. teaching asst. Rutgers U. Grad. Sch. Edn., New Brunswick, N.J., 1984-85, affiliate asst. prof., 1985-89; asst. prof. dept. interdisciplinary studies U. Medicine and Dentistry N.J., Newark, 1985-91, assoc. prof. clin. interdisciplinary studies, 1991-95; assoc. dir. grad. program in allied health edn. Rutgers U. Grad. Sch. Edn. & U. Medicine and Dentistry N.J., Newark, 1985-89, dir. grad. program in health professions edn., 1989-95, chair dept. interdisciplinary studies, 1992-95; dir. Office of Edn. U. Colo. Health Sci. Ctr., Denver, 1995—; chairperson com. on continuing edn. Sch. Health Related Professions U. Medicine and Dentistry of N.J., Newark, 1991-95; mem. faculty devel. Sch. Health Related Professions U. Medicine & Dentistry N.J., Newark, 1992-95; mem. univ.-wide adv. com. on continuing edn. U. Medicine and Dentistry N.J., Newark, 1992-95; dir. office edn. Health Scis. Ctr. U. Colo., Denver, 1995—, chair teaching com., chair bridge to future program, co-chair campus ctr. com. edn., 1995—; dir. Office Edn. U. Colo. Health Sci. Ctr., 1995—, chairperson tchg. com., 1995—; chairperson multicompetent practitioner task force U. Medicine and Dentistry N.J. Sch. Health-Related Professions, 1989-90, mem. task force on grad. edn., 1987—, mem. task force on grading policy, 1987-89; ednl. cons. N.J. Dental Sch., 1992-95; ednl. specialist Nat. Assn. Trade and Tech. Sch. Accreditation Team, 1984-95; cons. Dental Office Mgmt., 1980-95; graphic artist Program Brochure and Supplemental Materials Devel., 1984—. Contbr. articles to profl. jours., chpts. to books. Grantee N.J. Dept. Higher Edn., 1981-82, 86-88; recipient Excellence award Rutgers U. Alumni Assn., 1990. Mem. Assn. Schs. Allied Health Profns. (Outstanding Poster award 1992, state chpts. com. 1988-95, ethics com. 1994—, chair ethics com. 1995—), Am. Soc. Med. Tech., Assn. Moral Edn. (honorable mention award 1991), Soc. Health and Human Values, Am. Soc. Clin. Pathologists (assoc.), N.J. Soc. Allied Health Profns. (pres. 1987-89, 94-95, editor newsletter 1983-85, chair publs. com., pub. rels. com. 1984-86), Kappa Delta Pi, Omicron Tau Theta. Home: 3100 Pleasant View Dr Castle Rock CO 80104 Office: U Colo Health Scis Ctr/Office Edn Campus Box A075 Denver CO 80262

HARVEY, GLORIA-STROUD, physician assistant; b. Washington, D.C., Apr. 16; d. Ruth Elizabeth (Brown) Stroud; m. Jimmy Lawrence Harvey; children: Dana, Daman, Byron, Justin. BS, U. Md., 1968; physician asst. cert., Howard U., 1977. Physician asst. Weaver Clinic, Ahoskie, N.C., 1977-80, Western State Hosp., Staunton, Va., 1980-84, Walter Reed Army Med. Ctr., Washington, 1984-91, John Amsted Hosp., Butner, N.C., 1991—, U. N.C., Chapel Hill, 1991—; physician asst. Aroyga, Durham, N.C., 1992—. Bd. dirs. Unique Builders, Henderson N.C., 1994-95, Cultural Initiatives, 1995. Mem. Am. Bus. Women's Assn., N.C. State-Employed Physician Assts.' Assn. (chmn. 1994), Triangle Assn. for Physician Assts., N.C. Assn. for Physician Assts. Methodist. Home: 358266 Tar River Rd Oxford NC 27565

HARVEY, JOHN ADRIANCE, psychology and pharmacology educator, researcher, consultant; b. N.Y.C., Oct. 14, 1930; s. John Adriance Harvey and Paula Ann (Truhar) Oestreich; m. Rhoda S. Sadigur, Dec. 20, 1958; children—David Alexander, Andrew Martin, Michael Allen. A.B., U. Chgo., 1955, Ph.D., 1959. Research assoc. U. Chgo., 1959-61, asst. prof., 1961-67, assoc. prof., 1967-68; prof. psychology and pharmacology U. Iowa, Iowa City, 1968-88; prof. pharmacology and psychiatry, chief div. behavioral neurobiology Med. Coll. Pa. and Ea. Pa. Psychiat. Inst., Phila., 1988—; guest worker Maudsley Hosp., London, 1966-67; chmn. biopsychology rsch. rev. com. NIH, 1983-85; chmn. behavioral neurobiology rsch. rev. com. NIMH, 1986-90, mem. adv. panel; mem. extramural sci. adv. bd. Nat. Inst. on Drug Abuse, 1990—. Author: Behavioral Analysis of Drug Action, 1971; editor Jour. Pharmacology and Exptl. Therapeutics, 1990—; contbr. numerous articles to profl. jours. Recipient Research Devel. award NIMH, 1963-68, Research Scientist award, 1969-74. Fellow APA (pres. divsn. 28 1984-85), Am. Coll. Neuropsychopharmacology; mem. Am. Soc. for Pharmacology and Exptl. Therapeutics (editl. adv. bd.), Soc. for Neurosci. (fin. com.), Soc. for Neurochemistry, European Soc. for Neurochemistry, Pavlovian Soc., Soc. for Biol. Psychiatry, Beh. Pharmacol. Soc. (pres. 1996—). Home: 1 Druim Moir Ct Philadelphia PA 19118-4133 Office: MCP/EPPI Dept Pharmacology 3200 Henry Ave Philadelphia PA 19129-1137

HARVEY, JOHN COLLINS, physician, educator; b. Youngstown, Ohio, Sept. 11, 1923; s. J. Paul and Mary J. (Collins) H.; m. Adele Dillon, Nov. 26, 1949; children:Elizabeth V.R. (Mrs. Charles Yon), John Collins Jr., William Charles II, Amy L.R. (Mrs. L. F. Reese), Margaret J.B. Grad., Phillips Exeter Acad., 1941; BS, Yale U., 1944; MD, Johns Hopkins U., 1947, MLA, 1968; MAS, Johns Hopkins, 1974; MA, St. Mary's U., 1975, PhD in Theology, 1988; DSc (hon.), Barry U., 1992. Diplomate: Am. Bd. Internal Medicine. Successively house officer, asst. resident, resident Osler Med. Service, Johns Hopkins Hosp., 1947-53, physician, 1953-73; successively instr., asst. prof., asso. prof., prof. medicine Johns Hopkins, 1953-73; prof. medicine Georgetown U., Washington, 1973-89, prof. medicine emeritus, 1989—; sr. rsch. scholar Kennedy Inst. of Ethics, Georgetown U., Washington, 1989—, Ctr. for Clin. Bioethics, Georgetown Med. Ctr., 1993—; Vis. prof. medicine U. Ibadan, Nigeria, 1964; hon. assoc. prof. medicine Guy's Hosp., London, 1973. Co-editor: Catholic Perspectives on Medical Morals, Catholic Studies in Bioethics; Contbr. articles to profl. publs. Mem. various local, state and nat. govt. med. adv. coms.; trustee Washington Home for Incurables; mem. med. adv. com. Sacred Congregation for Causes of Saints, Holy See, Vatican City. Col. (ret.) M.C., USAR. A. Blaine Brower Traveling fellow ACP to Guy's Hosp. London, 1956; sr. scholar Kennedy Inst. Ethics, Georgetown U., 1973-89. Fellow ACP (master), APHA; mem. AAAS, AMA, Am. Clin. and Climatol. Assn., Biophys. Soc., Johns Hopkins Soc. Scholars, Peripatetic Club, Tudor and Stuart Club (Balt.), Yale Club (N.Y.C.), Chevy Chase Club, Cosmos Club, Knights of St. Gregory, Knights of Malta, Phi Beta Kappa, Sigma Xi, Alpha Omega Alpha. Republican. Roman Catholic. Home: 12610 Three Sisters Rd Potomac MD 20854-6359 Office: Georgetown U Med Ctr Bldg D Ctr Clin Bioethics Rm 234 4000 Reservoir Rd NW Washington DC 20007

HARVEY, W. HAYDEN, hematologist, medical oncologist; b. Shreveport, La., Feb. 12, 1949; s. Max Richard and Marion Lee (Polk) Campbell; m. M. Constance Mock, 1996; children: Merry Lee, Lexie Carl, Erica Dawn. BS, Ea. Tenn. State U., 1971; DO, Kirksville Coll. Osteo. Medicine, Kirksville, Mo., 1976. Diplomate Am. Osteo. Bd. Internal Medicine, Med. Oncology, Hematology. Intern Riverside Hosp. of Wichita (Kans.), 1976-77, resident in internal medicine, 1977-79; fellow jr. faculty Am. Cancer Soc.-M.D. Anderson Cancer Ctr., Houston, 1979-80; fellow in hematology and med. oncology Brooke Army Med. Ctr., San Antonio, 1980-82, dir. bone marrow transplant program, 1983-87; chief divsn. hematology and oncology Darnall Army Hosp., Ft. Hood, Tex., 1982-83; dir. bone marrow transplant lab., clin. rsch. U. Tex. Med. Br., Galveston, 1987-91; pvt. practice clin. rsch. Ft. Myers, Fla., 1991-93; clin. rschr. Hematology/Oncology Assocs. S.W. Fla., Naples, 1993—. Maj. M.C., U.S. Army, 1980-87. Recipient Army Svc. Ribbon, 1982, Army Commendation Medal, 1983, Meritorious Svc. medal, 1987, Def. Svc. Medal Desert Shield, 1990. Mem. AMA, AAAS, Internat. Soc. for Hematotherapy and Graft Engring., Am. Osteo. Assn., Am. Coll. Osteo. Internists, Assn. Mil. Osteo. Physicians and Surgeons, Assn. Mil. Surgeons U.S., S.W. Oncology Group, Am. Soc. Clin. Oncology, Pediat. Oncology Group, Am. Soc. Hematology, Am. Soc. for Blood and Marrow Transplantation, So. Med. Assn., So. Assn. for Oncology (founder), Fla. Soc. Clin. Oncology, Lee County Med. Soc., Collier County Med. Soc., Am. Cancer Soc. (chmn. lung cancer task force 1991-94, mem. exec. com. 1993-94), Leukemia Soc. Am. (mem. exec. com. 1994—). Office: Hematology/Oncology Assocs SW Fla 671 Goodlette Rd Ste 200 Naples FL 34102

HARVIS, LEE HOWARD, osteopath; b. Phila., July 24, 1963; s. Herbert Samuel and Janice (Cohn) H.; m. Cynthia Lou Cochran, Aug. 19, 1990; children: Mikinzi Cheyenne, Alek Keenan. BS in Aero. Engring., U. Mich., 1985; MA in Mgmt., Webster U., St. Louis, 1987; DO, Phila. Coll. Osteo. Medicine, 1996. With USAF, 1985-92. Decorated Air medal; recipient Sikorsky award Sikorsky Aircraft Corp., 1986-90. Mem. Am. Osteo. Ass., Am. Coll. Osteo. Family Physicians, Am. Acad. Family Physicians, Assn. Mil. Osteo. Physicians and Surgeons, Air Foce Assn., Aerospace Med. Assn.

HARWAY, MICHELE, psychology educator and researcher; b. Takoma Park, Md, Sept. 13, 1947; d. Maxwell and Georgette (Volcovici-Nadelar) H.; m. Bruce Eric Antman, Dec. 23, 1979; children: Sasha Antman, Alissa Antman. BS, Tufts U., 1969; MA, U. Maryland, 1971; PhD, U. Md., 1974. Asst. dean U. Calif., Irvine, 1974; rsch. psychologist Higher Edn. Rsch. Inst., UCLA, 1974-77; asst. rsch. prof. psychology U. So. Calif., L.A., 1978-81; assoc. prof. Calif. Grad. Inst., L.A.; prof., dir. rsch. Phillips Grad. Inst., Encino, Calif., 1987—; mem. rsch. faculty Fielding Inst., Calif., 1986—; cons. various orgns. including Hughes Aircraft, Met. Water Dist., U.S. Dept. State, others, 1978-87; mem. part-time faculty UCLA, Mt. St. Mary's Coll., Wright Inst., Calif. Sch. Profl. Psychology, Calif. State U., 1978-86. Editor: Handbook of Longitudinal Research, vol. 1 and vol. 2, 1984, Battering and Family Therapy: A Feminist Perspective, 1977, Sex Discrimination in Career Counseling and Education, 1977, Spouse Abuse: Assessing and Treating Battered Women, Batterers, and Their Children, 1994, Treating the Changing Family: Handling Normative and Unusual Events, 1996. Fellow APA. Home: PO Box 241865 Los Angeles CA 90024-9665

HARWICK, JEAN CRANDALL, ophthalmologist, educator; b. N.Y.C., Nov. 8, 1954; d. Robert Dean and Elaine Louise (Crandall) H.; m. Barry Eliot Hirsch, Sept. 25, 1982; children: David Crandall, Peter Crandall. BA, Goucher Coll., 1976; MD, Temple U., 1980. Bd. cert. Am. Bd. Ophthalmology. Resident, flexible intern Western Pa. Hosp., Pitts., 1980-81; resident ophthalmology Washington Hosp. Ctr., 1981-84; fellow cornea and external disease U. Pitts., 1984-85, clin. instr. ophthalmology, 1985—. Fellow Am. Acad. Ophthalmology; mem. AMA, Pa. Med. Soc., Pitts. Ophthalmology Soc., Cataract and Refractive Surg. Soc. Office: Med & Surg Eye Assoc Ste 200 2400 Ardmore Blvd Pittsburgh PA 15221

HARWOOD, ALICE, mental health nurse; b. Bklyn., Aug. 20, 1947; m. Paul W. Harwood, May 25, 1968; children: Paul Jr., Michael P. AAS, Suffolk Cmty. Coll., Brentwood, N.Y., 1993. RN, N.Y. Staff nurse SUNY Med. Ctr., Stony Brook, 1993-94, Kings Pk. (N.Y.) Psychiat. Ctr., 1994—. Mem. Oncology Nurses Assn. Home: 200 W Smoke Tree Rd Gilbert AZ 85233-6910

HARWOOD, CHRISTINE DIANE, nurse adminstrator; b. Berkeley, Calif., Mar. 2, 1953; d. Gerald Gene and Doris Mae (Fields) Emerson; m. Marcus Harwood, Sept. 12, 1989. ADN, Gavilan Coll., 1984; teaching cert., U. Calif., Santa Cruz, 1987; BA, St. Mary's Coll., Moriga, Calif., 1991. RN, Calif.; cert. emergency nurse's assoc., trauma nurse core curriculum. Staff nurse in med.-surg. Santa Teresa Hosp., San Jose, Calif., 1981-84, emergency staff nurse, 1984-89, charge nurse, emergency, 1989-90, asst. clin. coord. emergency dept./urgent care, 1990-94; clin. instr. med.-surg. nursing Gavilan Coll., 1988-95; dept. mgr. pediatrics Santa Teresa Cmty. Med. Ctr., San Jose, Calif., 1994—. Home: 5579 Makati Cir San Jose CA 95123-6234 Office: Santa Teresa Cmty Med Ctr 270 International Cir San Jose CA 95119-1130

HARWOOD, ROWAN HAROLD, physician; b. Barnet, Eng., Oct. 1, 1961; s. Harold Raymond and Veronica Florence (Reeves) H.; m. Jane Susan Laughton; children: Rosalind, Sebastian. BM, BCh, Cambridge U., Oxford, Eng., 1985, MA, 1986; MSc in Epidemiology, U. London, 1993; MD, U. Cambridge, 1996. Registrar U. Hosp. Nottingham, Eng., 1988-90, lectr., 1995—; lectr. London Hosp. Med. Coll., 1990-92; rsch. fellow Royal Free Hosp., London, 1992-95. Author: Manual of London Handicap Scale, 1995; contbr. articles to profl. jours. Mem. Royal Coll. Physicians U.K. Anglican. Office: Med Sch Dept Health Care of, Elderly B Floor, Queens Med Centre, Nottingham NG7 2UH, England

HARWOOD, VIRGINIA ANN, retired nursing educator; b. Lawrenceville, Ohio, Nov. 5, 1925; d. Warren Leslie and Ruth Ann (Wilson) H.; m. Kenneth Dale Juillerat, Dec. 21, 1946 (div. 1972); children: Rozanne Augsburger, Vicki Sue Terry, Carol Mann, Karen Juillerat. RN, City Hosp. Sch. Nursing, Springfield, Ohio, 1946; BSN, Ind. U., 1968; MS in Edn., Purdue U., 1973, PhD, 1982. Cert. psychiat./mental health nurse, ANA. Staff nurse various hosps., 1946-60; pub. health nursing supr. Whitley County Health Dept., Columbia City, Ind., 1960-65; nursing supr., coordinator staff devel. Ft. Wayne (Ind.) State Hosp., 1965-69; faculty sch. nursing Parkview Hosp., Ft. Wayne, 1969-74; faculty dept. nursing Ball State U., Muncie, Ind., 1974-77; dir. nursing program Thomas More Coll., Ft. Mitchell, Ky., 1977-79; faculty sch. nursing Purdue U., West Lafayette, Ind., 1979-80; dean sch. nursing Ashland (Ohio) Coll., 1980-83; retired, 1983-86; charge nurse admission psychiat. unit VA Med. Ctr., Marion, Ind., 1986-93, ret., 1994—. Active Rep. Nat. Com., 1978—, U.S. Senatorial Club, 1984—, Rep. Pres. Task Force, 1982—; mem. ch. coun. Grace Luth. Ch., Gas City, Ind., 1993—; bd. dirs. Luth. Ctr., Ball State U., Muncie, Ind. Mem. Am. Nurses Found., Mensa, Sigma Theta Tau. Home: 6611 Quail Ridge Ln Marion IN 46804

HASAN, ADNAN AHMAD, obstetrician, gynecologist, educator; b. Haifa, Israel, Apr. 12, 1946; s. Ibrahim Ahmad and Khadijeh Andel Korin (Ahmad) H.; m. Aman Adnan Sukhon; children: Leen, Reem, Maner. MBBCh, Cairo U., 1971. Diplomate Am. Bd. Ob-Gyn. Asst. prof. U. Jordan, Amman, 1980-85, assoc. prof., 1985-90, prof. ob/gyn., 1990—; cons., 1992—. Contbr. articles to profl. jours. Fellow Am. Coll. Ob/Gyn.; mem. Jordan Med. Assn., Jordan Soc. Obstetricians and Gynecologists. Home: Telal-Al-Ali PO Box 1549, Amman 11953, Jordan Office: Jordan Hosp, Amman Jordan

HASAN, MALIK M., health maintenance organization executive; b. 1938. Practicing neurologist Pueblo, Colo., 1967-91; co-founder, officer Pueblo Physicians, Inc. (merged with Qual-Med, Inc. 1986), 1983-86; founder, chmn. Qual-Med., Inc., Pueblo, 1985—; now also chmn. bd., CEO Health Systems Internat., Woodland Hills., Calif. Office: Health Systems Internat 21600 Oxnard St 17th Fl Woodland Hills CA 91367 also: Qual Med Inc 225 N Main St Pueblo CO 81003*

HASAN, SAIYID ZAFAR, social work educator, college dean; b. Allahabad, India, July 5, 1930; came to U.S., 1971, naturalized, 1979; s. Saiyid Akhtar and Alia (Khatoon) H.; m. Nuzhat Ara, Nov. 3, 1961; children: Shirin, Simin, Akbar, Jafar. BA with honors, U. Lucknow, India, 1948, MA, 1949, LLB, 1949, diploma in social service, 1950, MS in Social Work, 1955; D.Social Work, Columbia U., 1958. Cert. social worker, Ky. Rsch. asst. U. Lucknow, 1950-51, lectr. in social work, 1951-57, reader in social work, 1957-65, prof., head dept. social work, 1965-71; prof. social work U. Ky., Lexington, 1971—, dean Coll. Social Work, 1979—; mem. Coun. Social Work Edn., Washington, 1971—; mem. adv. council Multidisciplinary Ctr. on Gerontology and Human Devel., Lexington, 1981—. Author: Federal Grants and Public Assistance, 1963; Research in Sociology and Social Work, 1971; Mental Health Professionals Perceive Knowledge and Skill Needs, 1981—; Mental Health-Rural Aging Multidisciplinary Curriculums, 1982. Contbr. articles to profl. publs. Active civic and social orgns. India; pres. Tenant Svcs. and Assistance, Inc., Lexington, 1980-82; active United Way of Bluegrass, Lexington, 1983—. UN Social Welfare scholar, 1954-56. Mem. Indian Assn. Trained Social Workers, Council Social Work Edn., AAUP. Democrat. Islam. Home: 735 Brookhill Dr Lexington KY 40502-3312 Office: U Ky Coll Social Work Lexington KY 40506-0027

HASELTINE, FLORENCE PAT, research administrator, obstetrician, gynecologist; b. Phila., Aug. 17, 1942; d. William R. and Jean Adele Haseltine; m. Frederick Cahn, Mar. 12, 1964 (div. 1969); m. Alan Chodos, Apr. 18, 1970; children: Anna, Elizabeth. BA in Biophysics, U. Calif., Berkeley, 1964; PhD in Biophysics, MIT, 1964-69; MD, Albert Einstein Coll. of Medicine, 1972. Diplomate Am. Bd. Ob-Gyn, Am. Bd. Reproductive Endocrinology. Asst. prof. dept. ob-gyn. and pediatrics Yale U., New Haven, 1976-82, assoc. prof. dept. ob-gyn. and pediatrics, 1982-85; dir. Ctr. for Population Research, Nat. Inst. Child Health and Human Devel. NIH, Bethesda, Md., 1985—; founder Haseltine System, Inc., Products for the Disabled, 1995—. Co-author: Woman Doctor, 1976, Magnetic Resonance of the Reproductive System, 1987; co-editor 25 books on reproductive scis. Fellow Am. Coll. Ob-Gyn.; mem. AAAS (bd. dirs.), Inst. of Medicine, Am. Fertility Soc., Soc. Gynecol. Investigation, Soc. for Advancement Women's Health Rsch. (founder, bd. dirs.), Soc. Cell Biology. Office: NIH/NICHD Ctr Population Rsch 9000 Rockville Pike 6100/8B07 Executive Blvd Bethesda MD 20892

HASEMAN, JOSEPH KYD, biostatistician, researcher; b. Sheffield, Ala., July 20, 1943; s. Joseph Fish and Margaret Truella (Kyd) H.; m. Mary Janelle Hood, Nov. 25, 1972; children: David, Ashley. BS in Math. cum laude, Davidson Coll., 1965; PhD in Biostats., U. N.C., 1970. Rsch. math. statistician Nat. Inst. Environ. Health Scis., Research Triangle Park, N.C., 1970—; mem. working group Internat. Agy. for Rsch. on Cancer, 1986, 87. Assoc. editor Shorter Comm., Biometrics, 1979-84; bd. editors Environ. Health Perspectives, 1980—; mem. editorial bd. Fundamental and Applied Toxicology, 1986-92; contbr. articles to profl. jours. Pres. Tarheel Swimming Assn., Raleigh, N.C., 1990-91; officer Longbow coun. YMCA Indian Guides/Princesses, Raleigh, 1991. Recipient Dir.'s award NIH, 1983. Fellow Am. Statis. Assn.; mem. Biometric Soc., Soc. Toxicology, Genotoxicity and Environ. Mutagen Soc., Phi Beta Kappa. Democrat. Methodist. Home: 2408 Ferguson Rd Raleigh NC 27612-6904 Office: Nat Inst Environ Health Sci PO Box 12233 Research Triangle Park NC 27709

HASERODT, CHRISTOPHER NEIL, physician assistant; b. Chgo., Dec. 14, 1950; m. Kathleen Ann Ikkala, Sept. 16, 1972; children: Heidi, Molly. BS, Mercy Coll. Detroit, 1979. Physician asst. Iron County Clinic, Hurley, Wis., 1979-89, VA Med. Ctr., Iron Mountain, Mich., 1989—. Recipient Hands and Heart award Dept. Vet. Affairs, 1992. Mem. Physician Asst. Assn. (vet. affairs com., cert.). Office: VA Med Ctr West H St Iron Mountain MI 49801

HASHIMOTO, CHRISTINE L., physician; b. Chgo., June 29, 1947; d. Shigeru and Kiyo (Sato) H. BA, Oberlin Coll., 1968; MD, Med. Coll. of Pa., 1973. Clin. instr. internal medicine, emergency medicine Med. Coll. and Hosp. of Pa., Phila., 1976-77; asst. prof. medicine Health Service Ctr. U. Colo., Denver, 1977-80, clin. asst. prof. medicine, 1980-87; staff physician emergency dept. St. Joseph Hosp., Denver, 1980-83, Rose Med. Ctr., Denver, 1988-91, Luth. Med. Ctr., Wheatridge, Colo., 1991—. Mem. Colo. Med. Soc., Denver Med. Soc., Am. Coll. Emergency Physicians. Office: Luth Med Ctr 8300 W 38th Ave Wheat Ridge CO 80033-6005

HASHIMOTO, KEN, dermatology educator; b. Niigata City, Japan, June 19, 1931; came to U.S., 1956; m. Noriko Sakai, Oct. 3, 1961; children: Naomi, Martha, Eugene, Amy. MD, Niigata U., 1955. Cert. Am. Bd. Dermatology, 1968, Dermatopathology, 1972. Asst. prof. dermatology Tufts U. Sch. Medicine, Boston, 1965-68; assoc. prof. medicine, anatomy U. Tenn., Memphis, 1968-70; prof. medicine, assoc. prof. anatomy U. Tenn., 1970-77, dir., dermatopathology, prof., 1975-77; prof., dir. dermatology, prof. anatomy Wright State U., Dayton, Ohio, 1977-80; chief, dermatology sect., dir. elec. microscopy lab. VA Med. Ctr., Dayton, 1977-80; dermatologist in chief Detroit Med. Ctr., 1987—; prof., chmn. dermatology Wayne State U., Detroit, 1980—; mem. dermatol. drugs adv. com. FDA. Fulbright scholar, 1956-59; participant med. investigatorship career devel. program VA, 1969-77. Mem. Am. Soc. Dermatopathology (pres. 1986-87), Nat. Bd. Med. Examiners, Japanese Soc. Investigative Dermatology (hon.), Memphis Dermatological Soc. (pres. 1973-74), Soc. Investigative Dermatology (v.p. 1980-81, chmn. program com. 1985-86), Soc. Francaise de Dermatologie et de Syphilographie (corr. 1989), Japanese Assn. Dermatology (hon.). Home: 7000 Warren Rd Ann Arbor MI 48105-9722 Office: Wayne State U Sch Medicine Dept Dermatology 540 E Canfield St Detroit MI 48201-1928

HASHIMOTO, PAULO HITONARI, anatomy educator, physician; b. Amagasaki, Hyogo, Japan, Mar. 23, 1930; s. Sohei and Otei (Asakura) H.; m. Maria Elizabeth Yoshiko Inoue, May 5, 1960; children: Yoneichi, Kazuko, Hideko, Muneaki, Narutoshi. Intern, Osaka U., 1953-54; MD, Osaka (Japan) U., 1953, DMSc, 1960. Instr. Med. Sch. Osaka U., 1957-60, asst. prof., 1960-65, assoc. prof., 1965-74, prof. anatomy, 1974-93, hon. prof., 1993—; prof. Koshien U., Japan, 1993—; postdoc. fellow Harvard Med. Sch., Boston, 1963-65. Contbr. articles to profl. jours. Mem. AAAS, Am. Assn. Anatomists, Am. Soc. for Cell Biology, Internat. Brain Rsch. Orgn., N.Y. Acad. Scis., Japanese Assn. Anatomists (coun. 1974—), Japanese Soc. of Electron Microscopy (coun.), Japan Neurosci. Soc. (coun.), Japanese Soc. for Microcirculation (coun.). Roman Catholic. Office: Koshien U, 10-1 Momijigaoka Takarazuka, Hyogo 665, Japan

HASHIMOTO, SHIGEO, pathologist, educator; b. Kawaguchi, Saitama, Japan, Feb. 12, 1934; s. Jitsuzo and Ise (Shiba) H.; m. Reiko Yamaguchi, Apr. 29, 1961; 1 child, Shin. Student, Nihon U. Liberal Arts, Tokyo, 1954; MB, Nihon U. Sch. Medicine, Tokyo, 1959. Asst. dept. pathology Sch. Medicine Nihon U., 1960-66, instr., 1966-69, asst. prof., 1969-70; rsch. fellow in neuropathology N.Y. State Psychiat. Inst., N.Y.C., 1970-73; dir. clin. lab. Tokyo Met. Toshima Hosp., 1973-75; prof. Sch. Medicine Kinki U., Osaka, 1975—, dir. dept. pathology, 1975—; cons. Fujimoto Bio-Meds., Osaka, 1982—, Nihon Med. Clin. Exam Lab., Osaka, 1983—; med. examiner Osaka Med. Examiner Office, 1975—. Author: Neuropathology, 1978, Pathology of Brain Tumor, 1980; contbr. articles to profl. publs. Mem. Japanese Soc. Pathology, Japanese Soc. Neuropathology, Can. Assn. Neuropathologist, World Fedn. Neurology. Office: Kinki U Sch Medicine, 377-2 Ohnohigashi, Osakasayama, Osaka 589, Japan

HASKINS, KRISTEN ELIZABETH, psychologist; b. Cleve., Mar. 22, 1944; d. Lester Ray Haskins and Helen Pauline (Maiden) Ecsy. BA, Antioch Coll., 1967; MA, U. Dayton, 1975; PsyD, Wright State U., 1981. Lic. psychologist, Ohio; diplomate Bd. Cert. Forensic Examiners. Dir. Operation Big Sister, Springfield, Ohio, 1967-68; rsch. asst. Fels Rsch. Inst., Yellow Springs, Ohio, 1968-69; probation counselor Montgomery County Juvenile Ct., Dayton, Ohio, 1969-73, psychol. asst., 1973-74; clin. coord. Buckeye Boys Ranch, Inc., Grove City, Ohio, 1974-77, clin. dir., 1977-79; intern psychology Dayton Mental Health Ctr., 1979-80, Wayne A. Oliver, Ph.D., Columbus, Ohio, 1980-81; psychologist, asst. dir. Netcare Forensic Psychiatry Ctr., Columbus, 1981-93, asst. dir., 1987-92, dir., 1992-93; pvt. practice Grove City, 1988—; psychology cons. Ohio Rehab. Svcs. Commn. Bur. Disability Determination, 1993—, Ctrl. Ohio Psychiat. Hosp. Timothy B. Moritz Forensic Unit, 1994—. Jr. Women's Club scholar, 1962. Mem. APA, Am. Coll. Forensic Examiners, Ohio Psychol. Assn., Ctrl. Ohio Psychol. Assn. Home: 2627 Dartmoor Rd Grove City OH 43123-3336

HASLANGER, MARTIN FREDERICK, pharmaceutical company exxecutive, researcher; b. Dayton, Ohio, Mar. 27, 1947; s. John Frederick and M. Isabelle (McEowen) H.; m. Martha Louise Anderson, June 29, 1969; children: Andrea Louise, Jonathan Frederick. BS in Chemistry, Denison U., 1969; PhD in Chemistry, U. Mich., 1974. Postdoctoral fellow (with E.J. Corey) chemistry dept. Harvard U., Cambridge, Mass., 1974-76; rsch. investigator Squibb Inst. Med. Rsch., Princeton, N.J., 1976-80, sr. rsch. investigator, 1980-81, group leader, 1981-85; assoc. dir. Schering-Plough Rsch., Bloomfield, N.J., 1985-88, dir. chem. rsch., 1988-92; dir. chemistry, biochemistry pharm. Lilly Rsch. Labs., Indpls., 1992-94, dir. tech. core, 1994—; pres. Sphinx Pharms. div. Eli Lilly & Co., Indpls., 1994—. Contbr. articles to profl. jours., including Jour. Am. Chem. Soc., Jour. Organic Chemistry, Pharacologist, European Jour. Pharmacology, others. Mem. AAAS, Am. Chem. Soc., Am. Heart Assn., N.Y. Acad. Scis., Phi Lambda Upsilon. Home: 209 Sierra Dr Chapel Hill NC 27514

HASSAN, AMIN MOISES, neurologist; b. Managua, Nicaragua, June 19, 1946; s. Moises and Maria Elsa (Morales) H.; m. Yasmin Lovo, Dec. 9, 1973; children: Amin, Elsa Halima, Omar. MD, Nat. U., Managua, 1973. Intern Hosp. San Vicente, Leon, Nicaragua, 1972-73; resident Luis A. Somoza Hosp., 1974-77; resident in neurology Hosp. de Especialidades/Centro Medico La Raza, Mexico, 1977-80; chief resident Hosp. La Raza, Mexico City, 1980; neurologist Manolo Morales P. Hosp., Managua, 1980-82, dir. neurology dept., 1982—, EEG dept. dir., 1982—; prof. neurology Nat. U., Managua, 1982—; neurologist cons. Bapt. Hosp., Managua, 1982—. Mem. Assn. Ciencias Neurologias (treas. 1991-96). Mem. Movimiento de Accion Renovadora. Roman Catholic. Home: Apartado Postal A-6, Centro Comercial, Managua Nicaragua Office: Clinica Tiscapa SA, Planes de Altamira, Managua Nicaragua

HASSAN, OKAB T., educator. BA in Eng. Lit., Univ. Baghdad, Iraq, 1978; MEd, Tuskegee Univ.; MA in sch. adminstrn., Northeastern Ill. Univ. Sr. translator and editor Advertising Svcs. Group Co., Kuwait, 1978-81; fgn. language educator Mosque Found. Chgo., 1982-83, 89; teaching Eng. as fgn. language Kuwait Ministry of Edn., 1978-81; translator and editor Chgo. Bd. Edn., 1984-88; acting asst. prin. Anderson Cmty. Acad., 1991-92; bilingual facilitator Dists. 7, 8, 9, 10, 1992-95; bilingual/ESL coord., citywide Arabic bilingual programs coord. Region 5, 1995—; del. Chgo. Tchrs. Union, Tonti Sch., 1985-90; translator Euramerica, N.Y., Chgo; writer curriculum in math, reading dept. Curriculum, 1985; workshop presenter cultural awareness and sensitivity. Bd. mem. PTA, 1983-87; sec. gen. Arab Am. Ednl. Council, 1987-96; task force Chgo. Bd. Edn. Bilingual Edn., 1992, Chgo. Bd. Edn. Multicultural Edn., 1992; apptd. by mayor Cmty. Devel. Adv. Com. City Chgo; vol. reader and evaluator Chgo. Found. Edn; provider of svc. training Chgo. Police Acad. on dealing with Non-Eng. Speaking Adults. Home: 6531 S Rockwell St Chicago IL 60656*

HASSAN, STEVEN, psychotherapist; b. N.Y.C., May 29, 1954; s. Milton and Estelle (Gluckin) H. Student, Boston U., 1978; MEd, Cambridge Coll., 1985. Lic. counselor, Mass. Pvt. practice Mass.; founder EX-MOON Inc., 1979; past nat. coord. FOCUS; founder Hassan Ctr. for Freedom of Mind, 1996. Author: Combatting Cult Mind Control: The #1 Best-Selling Guide to Protection, Rescue and Recovery from Destructive Cults, 1988; guest various TV and radio programs, including 60 Minutes, Nightline, Oprah Winfrey Show, Sally Jessy Raphael, Larry King. Mem. ACA, Assn. for Humanistic Psychology. Home: PO Box 686 Newton MA 02258-0686

HASSMAN, ELISSA F., physician; b. Phila., Apr. 12, 1960; m. David J. Waldstein, June 2, 1960; 1 child, Sophia. BA, U. Pa., 1982; DO, Phila. Coll. Osteo. Medicine, 1986. Intern Kennedy Hosp., UMDNJ, Stratford, 1986-87; resident in ophthalmology Chgo. Osteo. Hosp., 1988-91; fellowship in cornea U. Ill. Eye Infirmary, Chgo., 1991-92; assoc. TriCounty Eye Physicians, Southampton, Pa., 1993-95, Wm. Brown, MD, PC, Newtown, Pa., 1995—. Co-chairperson Women's Divsn. Fedn. Allied Jewish Agys., Phila., 1995—. Fellow Am. Acad. Ophthalmology, Osteo. Coll. Ophthalmology; mem. Am. Osteo. Assn., Am. Soc. Refractive Surgery. Office: Commons West Ste 1-D 638 Newton-Yardley Rd Newton PA 18940

HAST, ROBERT, hematologist; b. Stockholm, Apr. 2, 1945; s. Nils and Brita Hast; m. Beatrice Krafft, June 14, 1969; children: Nils, Cecilia, Gustav. MD, Karolinska Inst., Stockholm, 1971, PhD, 1979. Asst. prof. medicine Karolinska Hosp., Stockholm, 1981-85, assoc. prof. medicine, 1985-87; assoc. prof. medicine Danderyd (Sweden) U. Hosp., 1987—; head div. hematology Danderyd Hosp., Stockholm, 1987—. Contbr. articles to profl. jours. Mem. Swedish Soc. Med. Sci., Swedish Soc. Hematology, Internat. Soc. Hematology. Office: Danderyd Hosp, S 182 88 Danderyd Sweden

HASTINGS, JOHN CLIFTON, III, cardiovascular and thoracic surgeon; b. Gainesville, Ga., May 23, 1958; s. John Clifton Jr. and Enid (McKinley) H.; m. Donna Gilstrap, July 10, 1982; children: John Clifton IV, William McKinley. BS in Chemistry, North Ga. Coll., Dahlonega, 1980; MD, Med. Coll. Ga., Augusta, 1984. Diplomate Am. Bd. Gen. Surgery, Am. Bd. Thoracic Surgery. Resident gen. surgery Charlotte (N.C.) Meml. Hosp., 1984-89; resident cardiothoracic surgery Carolinas Heart Inst., Charlotte, 1989-91; attending cardiothoracic surgeon Presbyn. and Mercy Hosps., Charlotte, 1991—. Contbr. articles to profl. jours. Bd. mem., pres.-elect Am. Heart Assn., Mecklenburg chpt., Charlotte, 1994—; deacon Providence Bapt. Ch., Charlotte, 1991—. Fellow ACS, Am. Coll. Chest Physicians, Am. Coll. Cardiology; mem. AMA, Quail Hollow Country Club. Baptist. Home: 7500 Baltusrol Ln Charlotte NC 28210 Office: Hawthorne Cardiovascular Surgeons 301 Hawthorne Ln Charlotte NC 28204

HATANAKA, MASAKAZU SHOICHI, virology educator; b. Osaka, Kansai, Japan, Mar. 23, 1933; s. Kazuo and Yasue (Sakai) H.; m. Kazuko Fujimoto, Apr. 10, 1963; children: Iwao, Takeshi, Melissa, Rachel, Brooke. MD, Kyoto (Japan) U., 1958, PhD, 1963. Diplomate. Rsch. assoc. Kyoto U., 1963-68; scientist Case Western Res. Med. Sch., Cleve., 1964-65, Salk Inst., San Diego, 1965-67, NIH, Bethesda, Md., 1967-70, Flow Labs., Rockville, Md., 1971-75; expert, sect. head Nat. Cancer Inst., Bethesda, 1975-80; prof. Kyoto U., 1980-95, dir. Inst. for Virus Rsch., 1991-95; dir. Shionogi Inst. Med. Sci., 1995—; rep. U.S.-Japan AIDS Com., Tokyo, 1990—; expert cons. NIH, Bethesda, 1975-80, Fogarty scholar-in-residence, 1995—; vis. prof. INSERM, Pasteur Inst., Paris, 1977. Editor: FEBS Letters, Amsterdam, 1991-95, Microbial Pathogenesis, London, 1991—, Vivus Genes, Dordrecht, 1987-95; contbr. articles to profl. jours. Mem. evaluation com. Ministry of Health and Welfare, Japan, 1990—, Ministry Fgn. Affairs, Japan, 1986-95, Agt. of Sci. and Tech., Japan, 1984. Grantee Mitsubishi Found., Tokyo, 1983, Yamada Sci. Found., Osaka, 1989, Uehara Meml. Found., Tokyo, 1989; Fogarty scholar-in-residence NIH, 1995—. Mem. Japanese Biochem. Soc. (bd. dirs.), Japanese Cancer Soc., Japanese Virus Soc., Japanese AIDS Soc. Home: 1405 Nakano-cho, 5-13-3 Miyakozima, Osaka 534, Japan

HATANO, SADASHI, molecular biology educator; b. Kobe, Japan, Apr. 12, 1929; s. Yoriaki and Kimiko Hatano; m. Kimie Hatano, May 27, 1958; children: Kazuko, Fumiko. BS, Osaka (Japan) U., 1954, MS, 1956, DSc, 1959. Rsch. assoc. Osaka U., 1959-60; rsch. assoc. Nagoya (Japan) U., 1961-71, assoc. prof., 1971-75, prof., 1975-93, prof. emeritus, 1993—. Editor: Cell Motility, 1979, 86, Molecular Biology of Physarum, 1986.

HATCH, EDWARD WILLIAM (TED HATCH), health care executive; b. Greenwich, Conn., Jan. 2, 1952; s. Denison Hurlbut and Louise (Bingham) H.; m. Jean Brummer, May 26, 1990. BA, Beloit Coll., 1974; MAHCA, George Washington U., 1978. Planning assoc. East Cen. Ill. Health Systems Agy., Champaign, 1978-81; mgr. planning & mktg. Evang. Health Systems, Oak Brook, Ill., 1981-82, coord. instl. planning & mktg., 1983-84; dir. mktg. Bethany Hosp., Chgo., 1985-86; v.p. planning Holy Family Hosp., Des Plaines, Ill., 1986-87; exec. dir. Behavioral Health Systems, Palos Heights, Ill., 1987-88, chief exec. officer, 1989-91; pres., CEO Behavioral Health Sys., Burr Ridge, Ill., 1991-94; phys. hosp. orgn. adminstr. Columbia Behavioral Health, Forest Park, Ill., 1996—. Contbr. articles to profl. jours. Mem. Am. Coll. Health Care Execs., Chgo. Health Execs. Forum (pres. 1989, sec. 1988, program chmn. 1987). Office: Behavioral Health Systems Ste 305 485 S Frontage Rd Burr Ridge IL 60521-7110

HATCH, FREDERICK TASKER, chemicals consultant; b. Boston, Aug. 27, 1924; s. Frederick Southard and Beatrice (Tasker) H.; m. Virginia Weeks, Mar. 3, 1946; children: Daniel F., Daphne A., Deborah J., Douglas E. BA, Dartmouth Coll., 1944; MD, Harvard U., 1948; PhD, MIT, 1960. Diplomate Nat. Bd. Med. Examiners. Intern Roosevelt Hosp., N.Y.C., 1948-49; rsch. fellow Columbia U., N.Y.C., 1949-52; established investigator Am. Heart Assn./Mass. Gen. Hosp., Boston, 1960-65; sr. scientist, sect. leader Lawrence Livermore (Calif.) Nat. Lab., 1965-80, asst. assoc. dir., 1980-87, cons., 1987—; mem. lipid metabolism adv. com. Nat. Heart, Lund and Blood Inst., Bethesda, Md., 1968-73. Assoc. editor Lipids Jour., 1964-73; author chpts. in books; contbr. numerous articles to profl. jours. Sec. Land Conservation Task Force, Meredith, N.H., 1989-90, chmn. Hwy. Task Force, 1994—. Capt. USAR, 1952-55. Fellow Am. Inst. Chemists; mem. Am. Chem. Soc., Am. Soc. Biochemistry and Molecular Biology, Environ. Mutagen Soc., Arteriosclerosis Coun. of Am. Heart Assn. (exec. com. 1971-73). Home and Office: 27 Pease Rd Meredith NH 03253-5506

HATCH, RICHARD, obstetrician, gynecologist; b. Stockton, Calif., Jan. 28, 1948; s. Elmer Webb and Tressa (Farr) H.; m. Leslie Yvonne Campbell; children: John Adams, Elizabeth Amanda, Abigail Sariah. BS cum laude, Brigham Young U., 1970; MD, U. Utah, 1974. Diplomate Am. Bd. Ob-gyn, Am. Bd. Reproductive Endocrinology. Resident in ob-gyn. U. Chgo., 1974-78, fellow in reproductive endocrinology, 1978-81, asst. prof. ob-gyn., 1981-85; pvt. practice medicine specializing in ob-gyn. and reproductive endocrinology Vernal, Utah, 1988-90; pvt. practice Augusta, Ga., 1990—. Contbr. articles to profl. jours. Fellow Am. Coll. Ob-Gyn; mem. Rotary, Phi Kappa Phi. Mem. LDS Ch. Office: 2047 Central Ave Augusta GA 30904-4178

HATCHER, CHARLES ROSS, JR., cardiothoracic surgeon, medical center executive; b. Bainbridge, Ga., June 28, 1930; s. Charles Ross and Vivian Elizabeth (Miller) H.; m. Phyllis Gregory Slappey, July 9, 1988; children by previous marriage: Marian Barnett Thorpe, Charles III. BS magna cum laude, U. Ga., 1950; MD cum laude, Med. Coll. Ga., 1954. Intern Johns Hopkins Hosp., Balt., 1954-55; resident in surgery Peter Bent Brigham Hosp., Boston, 1955-56; resident in surgery Johns Hopkins Hosp., 1958-62; prof. surgery, chief cardiothoracic surgery Emory U. Sch. Medicine, Atlanta, 1971-90, dir., chief exec. officer Emory Clinic, 1976-84; v.p. for Health Affairs, dir. Woodruff Health Scis. Ctr. of Emory U., 1984—; chmn., CEO Emory U. Sys. Health Care, 1995—; bd. dirs. Healthdyne Info. Enterprises, Life of the South Corp., Japan Am. Soc. Capt. U.S. Army, 1956-58. Mem. ACS, Am. Coll. Cardiology (bd. govs. 1976-80), Am. Coll. Chest Physicians (bd. regents 1977-81, bd. govs. 1974-77), Am. Surg. Assn., So. Surg. Assn., Am. Assn. Thoracic Surgery, Soc. Thoracic Surgeons (pres. 1986-87), Am. Cancer Soc., So. Thoracic Surg. Assn. (pres. 1984), Johns Hopkins Soc. Scholars, Capital City Club, Piedmont Driving Club, Buckhead Club, Bainbridge Country Club, Rotary (bd. dirs. Atlanta club 1976-80), Phi Beta Kappa, Sigma Xi, Alpha Omega Alpha. Methodist. Contbg. author profl. publs. Home: 1105 Lullwater Rd NE Atlanta GA 30307-1245 Office: Emory U Woodruff Health Scis Ctr 1440 Clifton Rd NE Atlanta GA 30307-1053

HATCHER, GORDON MERRELL, marriage and family therapist, mental health counselor; b. Sonora, Calif., Nov. 22, 1934; s. Gordon Andrew and Hazel Virginia (Kiser) Merrell Hatcher; m. Karen Janine Willowby; children: Merrell Hatcher, Jonathan Hatcher, Joe Stapp, Phillip Stapp, Tim Stapp. BA, Okla. Bapt. U., Shawnee, Okla., 1956; MRE, Ctrl. Bapt. Sem., Kansas City, Kans., 1957; MA, U. of the Pacific, Stockton, Calif., 1968; GS, New Orleans Bapt. Sem., 1968; PhD, Western Colo. U., Grand Junction, 1974; EdD, U. Ark., 1991. Lic. marriage and family therapist, mental health counselor, Fla.; lic. psychologist, vocat. counselor, Mo.; lic. prof. counselor, approved supr., Ark.; nat. cert. counselor; cert. clin. mental health counselor, nat. cert. career counselor, clin. cert. hypnotherapist; diplomate in logotherapy. Prof. psychology and sociology St. Gregory's, Shawnee, 1969-71, Oklahoma City S.W., 1969-71; dean student svcs. Crowder Coll., Neosho, Mo., 1971-84; grad. asst. instr. U. Ark., Fayetteville, 1984-89; prof. sociology Mo. Bapt. Coll., St. Louis, 1989-90; asst. prof. counseling edn. Henderson State U., Arkadelphia, Ark., 1990-92; adj. prof. Rollins Coll., Winter Park, Fla., 1993—; exec. dir. Church St. Counseling Ctr., Orlando, Fla., 1992—, The Turning Point, Orlando, 1995—. Contbr. articles on counseling to newspapers and bulls. Mem. ACA, Am. Assn. Marriage and Family Therapy, Fla. Assn. Marriage and Family Therapy (bd. dirs.), Ctrl. Fla. Assn. Marriage and Family Therapy (sec.), Internat. Assn. for Marriage and Family Counselors, Am. Counselor Educators and Suprs., Am. Mental Health Counseling Assn., Am. Assn. for Spiritual, Ethical and Religious Values in Counseling, Fla. Counseling Assn., Fla. Mental Health Counselors Assn., Am. Christian Counselors Assn. (charter mem.), others. Office: Church St Counseling Ctr 106 E Church St Orlando FL 32801 also: A Turning Point 545 Delaney Ave # 3B Orlando FL 32801

HATCHER, JEFFRY CLARK, family physician; b. Evansville, Ind., Aug. 14, 1955; s. Harley Hugh and Edna B. H.; m. Virginia Jean Todd, Jan. 5, 1980; children: Melissa, Virginia Suzanne. BA, Olivet Coll., 1978; MA, NE Mo. State U., 1980; DO, Mich. State U., 1989. Diplomate Am. Bd. Family Practice; cert. Am. Bd. Quality Assurance and Utilization Rev. Physician. Intern Pontiac (Mich.) Osteopathic Hosp., 1989-90; resident family practice Union Hosp., Terre Haute, Ind., 1990-92; family physician Hatcher Family Practice, Paris, Ill, 1992-94; staff physician Paris Cmty. Hosp., 1994—; faculty Ind. U. Sch. of Medicine, U. Ill. Sch. Medicine, Chgo./Peoria, Ind. State U. Sch. of Nursing. Chief of staff Senator Alan Cropsey, Lansing, Mich., 1982-84; exec. dir. for Mich. Reagan-Bush, 1984; pres. Edgar County Children's Home, 1994; elder First Christian Ch., Paris, Ill., 1984—; pres. Edgar County Bd. of Pub. Health, 1994—. Named Small Bus. of Yr. Paris C. of C., 1994. Fellow Ill. Inst. Pub. Health, Am. Acad. Family Practice; mem. Am. Acad. Pub. Health, Aesculapian Soc. (pres. 1994-95), Promise Keepers, Bass Anglers Sportsman Soc. Republican. Mem. Disciples of Christ. Office: Hatcher Family Practice 717 E Court St Paris IL 61944-2460

HATCHETT, JOHN GARNER, ophthalmologist; b. Chickasha, Okla., Dec. 2, 1939; s. Garner B. and Irene (Hensley) H.; m. Betty Rogers Bard, Dec. 21, 1971. MD, Okla. U., 1966. Diplomate Am. Bd. Ophthalmology. Intern U. Mo., Kansas City, Mo., 1966-67; resident U. Rochester (N.Y.) Sch. Medicine, 1969-72; pvt. practice El Paso, Tex., 1972—. Lt. USNR, 1967-69, Vietnam. Decorated Bronze Star. Fellow Am. Acad. Ophthalmology; mem. El Paso County Med. Soc., Tex. Med. Assn., Tex. Ophthal. Assn. Republican. Methodist. Office: John G Hatchett MD 6955 N Mesa St Ste 112 El Paso TX 79912-4424

HATFIELD, ELAINE CATHERINE, psychology educator; b. Detroit, Oct. 22, 1937; d. Charles E. and Eileen (Kalahar) H.; m. Richard L. Rapson, June 15, 1982. BA, U. Mich., 1959; PhD, Stanford U., 1963. Asst. prof. U. Minn., Mpls., 1963-64, assoc. prof., 1964-66; asso. prof. U. Rochester, 1966-68, U. Wis., Madison, 1968-69; prof. U. Wis., 1969-81; now prof. U. Hawaii, Honolulu; chmn. dept. psychology U. Hawaii, 1981-83. Author: Equity: Theory and Research, 1978, Human Sexual Behavior, 1985, Mirror, Mirror: The Importance of Looks in Everyday Life, 1986, Psychology of Emotions, 1991, Love, Sex and Intimacy, 1993, Emotional Contagion, 1994, Love and Sex: Cross-cultural Perspectives, 1996; contbr. articles to profl. jours. Recipient Disting. Scientist award Soc. for Sci. Study of Sex, 1994, Soc. Exptl. Social Psychology, 1993. Fellow APA. Home: 3334 Anoai Pl Honolulu HI 96822-1418 Office: U Hawaii 2430 Campus Rd Honolulu HI 96822-2216

HATFIELD, WENDELL BENTON, physician; b. Wichita, Kans., Sept. 21, 1931; s. Harold Benton and Ruth Wilhelmina (Schmidt) H.; m. Charlotte Behre, Sept. 1, 1954; children: Christopher, Catherine, Dana Wendell, Susan. BA, Columbia Coll., 1953; MD, Columbia U., 1956. Diplomate Am. Bd. Internal Medicine. Intern Presbyn. Hosp., N.Y.C., 1956-57, asst. resident in medicine, 1957-59, fellow in rheumatology, 1959-60, chief resident in medicine, 1960-61; instr. in medicine Columbia U., N.Y.C., 1963-65, assoc. in medicine, 1966-69; assoc. clin. prof. of medicine U. Colo., Denver, 1978-89, clin. prof. of medicine, 1990—; asst. prof. clin. medicine Columbia U., Englewood, Colo., 1970-74; practice of rheumatology Colorado Arthritis Ctr., Englewood, Colo., 1977—; acting dir. Divsn. of Rheumatology, Columbia U./Presbyn. Hosp., N.Y.C., 1975-77; chmn. dept. medicine, Swedish Med. Ctr., Porter Hosp., Denver, 1982-86. Contbr. articles to profl. jours. Bd. dirs. Swedish Med. Ctr. Found., Englewood, Colo., 1987-93, v.p., 1993-94. Capt. U.S. Army, 1961-63, PTO. Recipient Harvard Book award Harvard Club of Colo., 1948, Woodbury medal Woodbury B., 1949, Van Amringe medal Columbia Coll., 1952. Fellow Am. Coll. Rheumatology; mem. Rocky Mountain Rheumatism Soc. (pres. 1987-88), Rocky Mountain Metabolic Bone Soc., Am. Soc. for Clin. Densitometry, Colo. Med. Soc., Arapahoe County Med. Soc. Home: 7585 S Prince St Littleton CO 80120 Office: Colorado Arthritis Ctr 701 E Hampden Ave Englewood CO 80110

HATHAWAY, DAVID ROGER, physician, medical educator, scientist; b. Lafayette, Ind., Jan. 8, 1948; s. Ralph Roger Hathaway and Marjorie Alice Friend; m. Elaine Mary Green, Aug. 3, 1974; children: Julia E., Alison S. AB, Ind. U., 1970, MD, 1975. Diplomate Am. Bd. Internal Medicine, Cardiovascular Diseases. Clin. asst. NHLBI/NIH, Bethesda, Md., 1977-79; intern Ind. U. Med. Ctr., Indpls., 1975-76, resident, 1976-77, chief resident, 1979-80, from asst. prof. to assoc. prof., 1980-86, prof., 1986-95, chief cardiovascular divsn., 1990-95, dir. Krannert Inst. Cardiology, 1990-95; exec. dir. cardiovasc. rsch. Bristol-Myers Squibb Pharm. Rsch. Inst., Princeton, N.J., 1995—. Lt. comdr. USPHS, 1977-79. Fellow Am. Coll. Cardiology; mem. Am. Fedn. for Clin. Rsch. (pres. 1987-88), Am. Soc. for Clin. Investigation, Assn. Am. Physicians (sec. 1991—), Assn. Univ. Cardiologists, Phi Beta Kappa, Alpha Omega Alpha. Office: Bristol-Myers Squibb Pharm Rsch Inst PO Box 4000 Princeton NJ 08543-4000

HATLESTAD, STEVEN P., healthcare marketing company executive; b. Ames, Iowa, July 1, 1953; s. Edwin Samuel and Jeanette A. (Pluemer) H.; m. Deborah L. LaBadie, Sept. 17, 1978; children: Cari, Jenna. BS, U. Md., 1976. Adminstr. Manor Care, Silver Spring, Md., Mid-Am. Long Term Care, Harrisonville, Mo.; adminstr., regional mgr. Americare Corp., Columbus, Ohio, Horizon Health Care, Kansas City, Mo.; regional mgr. Am. Health Corp., Conshohocken, Pa.; v.p. midwest ops. New Health Mktg., Inc., Bala Cynwyd, Pa. Bd. dirs. Tracy Siemian Found., Kansas City; pres. Green Springs Elem. Sch. PTO, Olathe, Kans. Fellow Am. Coll. Healthcare Adminstrs.; mem. Mo. Health Care Assn. (bd. dirs., pres. dist. 1). Home and Office: 15738 W 150th St Olathe KS 66062 Office: New Health Mktg Inc 401 City Ave Ste 310 Bala Cynwyd PA 19000

HATTERVIG, ROBIN LYNN, dentist; b. Desmet, S.D., Apr. 4, 1958; s. Gene Willis and Harriet Ione (Larson) H.; m. Mirinda Marie Noonan, May 7, 1988; children: Erik Hunter, Auden Archer. BS, U. S.D., 1980; DDS, U. Nebr., 1984. Pvt. practice dentistry Howard, S.D., 1984—. Bd. dirs. East River Healthcare, 1991—, pres., 1992-94; trustee Bethany Luth. Ch., 1988-93, v.p., 1995—. Fellow Acad. Gen. Dentistry (pres. S.D. chpt. 1996—); mem. ADA, Am. Soc. Dentistry for Children, S.D. Dental Assn., S.D. Dental Found., Pierre Fauchard Acad., Howard Cmty. Club, Howard Svc. Club, Phi Beta Kappa, Omicron Kappa Upsilon. Republican. Lutheran. Home: 302 E Howard Ave Howard SD 57349-9021 Office: 112 N Main St Box W Howard SD 57349

HATTERY, ROBERT R., radiologist, educator; b. Phoenix, Dec. 15, 1939; s. Robert Ralph and Goldie M. (Secor) H.; m. D. Diane Sittler, June 18, 1961; children: Angela, Michael. B.A., Ind. U., 1961, M.D., 1964; cert. in diagnostic radiology, Mayo Grad. Sch. Medicine, 1970. Diplomate: Am. Bd. Radiology. Intern Parkland Meml. Hosp.-Southwestern Med. Sch., Dallas, 1964-65; fellow Mayo Clinic, Rochester, Minn., 1967-70, cons., 1970-81, chmn. dept. diagnostic radiology, 1981-86; instr. radiology Mayo Med. Sch., 1973-75, asst. prof. radiology, 1975-78, assoc. prof. radiology, 1978-82, prof. radiology, 1982—; chair Mayo Group Practice Bd., 1991-93; chmn. bd. govs Mayo Clinic, Rochester, 1994—. Author numerous jour. articles and abstracts, book chpts. Served to capt. USAF, 1965-67, Willford Hall Hosp., San Antonio. Fellow Am. Coll. Radiology; mem. Radiol. Soc. N.Am., Am. Roentgen Ray Soc., Soc. Computed Body Tomography (pres. 1982-83), Soc. Genitourinary Radiography (pres. 1986-88). Office: Mayo Clinic 200 1st St SW Rochester MN 55905-0001

HATTNER, ROBERT STEPHEN, medical educator; b. Detroit, Jan. 9, 1940; s. John Jay and Linnaea Mercedes (Johnson) H.; m. Leslie Sandra Day, Dec. 23, 1995; children: Sabra, Marika, Kari. BS, Wayne State U., 1961, MD, 1965; postgrad., U. Calif., Berkeley, 1971-72. Med. intern., asst. in medicine Stanford (Calif.) U. Sch. Medicine, 1965-66; rsch. assoc. USPHS, San Francisco, 1966-68; rsch. fellow in nutrition Harvard Sch. Pub. Health, Boston, 1968-70; asst. in medicine Peter Bent Brigham Hosp., Boston, 1968-70; asst. resident in medicine U. Calif., San Francisco, 1970-71; trainee nuclear medicine U. Calif., Berkeley, 1971-72; resident nuclear medicine U. Calif., San Francisco, 1972-73, asst. prof. radiology, 1973-76, assoc. prof. radiology, 1976—, chief nuclear medicine, vice chmn., 1978-88; mem. nuclear med. adv. com. Calif. Med. Assn., Sacramento, 1978-90; cons. nuclear medicine study panel VA, Washington, 1980—; cons. diagnostic therapy tech. assessment ref. panel AMa, Chgo., 1990; editl. reviewer various jours., 1974—. Contbr. chpts. to books and articles to profl. jours.; patentee in field. Lt. comdr. USPHS, 1966-68. NIH Spl. fellow, Harvard Sch. Pub. Health, 1967-68. Mem. Soc. Nuclear Medicine, Radiol. Soc. N.Am., Assn. Univ. Radiologists, Am. Coll. Nuclear Physicians (charter). Home: 67B Lovell Ave Mill Valley CA 94941 Office: Nucl Med L 340 Univ Calif San Francisco San Francisco CA 94143-0252

HAU, TONI, surgeon, researcher; b. Cologne, Germany, Dec. 23, 1941; s. Heinrich Georg and Anna Maria (Hermann) H.; m. LeeNora Hau, Apr. 17, 1971; children: Angela Maria, Michael Anton. MD, U. Cologne, Fed. Republic of Germany, 1965; PhD, U. Minn., 1978. Diplomate Am. Bd. Surgery, cert. Ärztekammer Nordrhein. Internship Deaconess Hosp., Milw., 1970-71; residency Kanton Hosp., Basle, Switzerland, 1971-73, U. Minn. Hosp., Mpls., 1973-78; asst. prof. U. Ill., Chgo., 1978-81; assoc. prof. Case Western Reserve U., Cleve., 1981-85; chief of surgery St. Willehad Hosp., Wilhelmshaven, Fed. Republic Germany, 1985-89; prof. surgery Medizinische Hochschule, Hannover, Fed. Republic Germany, 1986—; chief of surgery Nordwestkrankenhaus Sanderbusch, Sande, Fed. Republic Germany, 1989—. Editor: Renal Transplantation, 1987, Update in Antibiotic Prophylaxis in Surgery, 1990; contbr. papers and articles to profl. jours. Recipient Nat. Rsch. Svc. award NIH, 1976, Resident's Rsch. award Assn. Acad. Surgery, 1976. Mem. Am. Coll. Surgeons (German chpt. treas. 1988—), Am. Soc. Transplant Surgeons (corr. mem.), Surg. Infection Soc. Europe (recorder 1987-89, sec. 1988-94, pres. 1996—), Deutsche Ges. für Chirurgie, Soc. Internat. de Chirurgie (scientific program com. 1987-89). Home: Beim Langen Rick 14, Niedersachsen, 26441 Jever Germany Office: Nordwestkrankenhaus Sanderbusch, Hauptstr 1, 26452 Sande Germany

HAUBER, FREDERICK AUGUST, ophthalmologist; b. Pitts., July 3, 1948; s. Michael H. and Cecilia (Azinger) H.; m. Cathy Lu Rosellini, Aug. 3, 1981; children: Elizabeth Alexandra, Natalia Fredericka. BS in Microbiology cum laude, U. Pitts., 1970; MD, U. Tenn., 1974. Intern U. South Fla., Tampa, 1975, resident in ophthalmology, 1982; pvt. practice Pasco Eye Inst., New Port Richey, Fla., 1983—; asst. clin. prof. U. South Fla., Tampa, 1984—; rechr., spkr. in field, 1990—; cons. Optimed, Inc. Contbr. articles to profl. jours. Advisor health care cost containment com., Tarpon Springs, Fla., 1988; founder Pasco County Diabetes Assn.; mem. bd. counsellors U. Tampa. Fellow ACS, Am. Acad. Ophthalmology; mem. Southeastern U.S. Debate Soc. Office: Pasco Eye Inst 5347 Main St New Port Richey FL 34652-2506

HAUDENSCHILD, CHRISTIAN CHARLES, pathologist, educator; b. St. Gallen, Switzerland, May 3, 1939; came to U.S., 1972; s. Charles Haudenschild. MD, U. Basel, 1968. Diplomate Am. Bd. Pathology. Rsch. fellow, assoc. F. Hoffman-LaRoche Exptl. Medicine, Basel, Switzerland, 1968-72; rsch. assoc. Children's Hosp. Med. Ctr., Boston, 1973-74; rsch. assoc. in surgery and pathology Harvard U. Med. Sch., Boston, 1974-76, clin. instr. pathology, 1976-80; resident in pathology Boston City Hosp., 1974-76; asst. prof. pathology Boston U. Sch. Medicine, 1976-79; assoc. pathologist Mallory Inst. Pathology, Boston, 1977-92; assoc. prof. Boston U. Sch. Medicine, 1977-92, prof., 1982-92; assoc. vis. physician Boston City Hosp., 1977-92; adj. prof. pathology Boston U. Sch. Medicine, 1992—, Georgetown U., Washington, 1992—; rsch. prof. pathology George Washington U. Sch. Medicine, Washington, 1992-95, rsch. prof. pathology and medicine, 1995—; cons. pathologist Boston VA Hosp., 1978-92; asst. vis. pathologist Univ. Hosp., Boston, 1986-92; hon. cons. prof. U. Studi, Siena, Italy, 1985; Disting. vis. scientist Armed Forces Inst. Pathology, Washington, 1992—; Disting. vis. prof. U. Utrecht, Netherlands, 1993—; head exptl. pathology dept. Holland Lab. ARC, Rockville, Md., 1992—. Contbr. articles to med. jours., chpts. to books. Recipient rsch. grants HEW, NIH, Nat. Heart, Lung and Blood Inst., Am. Heart Assn, 1978—. Mem. AMA, Am. Heart Assn. (fellow coun. on arteriosclerosis), Swiss Med. Soc., Am. Soc. for Cell Biology, Am. Assn. Pathologists, Internat. Acad. Pathology. Office: Holland Lab ARC 15601 Crabbs Branch Way Rockville MD 20855-2736

HAUEISEN, DAVID C., orthopedic surgeon; b. Columbus, Ohio, Oct. 27, 1954; s. Carl Veit and Freda L. (Kunze) H.; m. Maryellen Haueisen, June 1, 1985; children: Gregory, Michael, Alexander. BA in Chemistry, Coll. Wooster, Ohio, 1976; MD, Case Western Res. U., 1980. Diplomate Am. Bd. Orthopedic Surgeons, added qualifications in hand surgery. Orthopedic surgeon Premier Care Othopedics, St. Louis, 1986—. Mem. Am. Acad. Orthopedic Surgeons, Am. Soc.. Surgery of Hand, St. Louis Met. Med. Soc., Phi Beta Kappa. Home: 304 Wyndmoor Terrace Ct Town and Country MO 63141 Office: Premier Care Orthopedics 12615 Old Tesson Rd Saint Louis MO 63128

HAUGAARD, NIELS, pharmacologist; b. Copenhagen, Denmark, Feb. 25, 1920; came to U.S., 1940, naturalized, 1952; s. Gotfred C. and Karen L. (Pedersen) H.; m. Ella Elizabeth Shwartzman, June 22, 1947 (dec. Feb. 1980); children: David Gregory, Lisa Karen; m. Dorothy Tosi, 1983; children: Gregory, Kimberly, Pamela. Student, U. Copenhagen, 1938-40; A.B. with honors, Swarthmore Coll., 1942; Ph.D. in Biochemistry, U. Pa., 1949. Instr. U. Pa., Phila., 1949-52, asst. prof. rsch. medicine, 1952-54, asst. prof. pharmacology, 1954-60, assoc. prof., 1960-65, prof., 1965-87, emeritus prof., 1987—, mem. Med. Coun., 1972-75, chmn. Grievance Commn., 1986; mem. cardiovascular scis. study sect. NIH, 1978-82. Sect. editor: Chem. Abstracts, 1960-65; editorial bd.: Circulation Research, 1964-69, Molecular and Cellular Biochemistry, 1986—; contbr. articles to profl. jours. Mem. Bristol Twp. (Pa.) Sch. Bd., 1957-60. Guggenheim Found. fellow, 1952; Commonwealth Found. fellow, 1965. Mem. Am. Soc. Biol. Chemists, Am. Soc. Pharmacology and Exptl. Therapeutics (editorial bd. jour. 1965-68), ACLU, AAUP. Home: 129 Maple Ave Bala Cynwyd PA 19004 Office: Urology Rsch Lab Hosp Univ Pa Ravdin Courtyard Bldg Philadelphia PA 19104

HAUGAN, GERTRUDE M., clinical psychologist; b. New Richland, Minn.; d. Henry Albert and Ella Pauline (Gardson) H. BA, George Washington U., 1952, MA, 1956; PhD, U. Md., 1970. Lic. psychologist, D.C., Md. Research psychologist New Eng. Med. Ctr., Boston, 1959-62; intern clin. psychology Hall Psychiat. Inst., Columbia, S.C., 1968-69; fellow in pediatrics Sch. Medicine Johns Hopkins U., Balt., 1970-71; clin. psychologist adloescent program Devel. Services Ctr., Washington, 1971-72, chief children's unit, 1972-85; chief Devel Services Ctr., Washington, 1986-94; cons. in psychology Ea. Shore State Hosp., Cambridge, Md., 1969-71, in child psychology Ctr. for Spl. Edn., Annapolis, Md., 1972-76; instr. in child psychology Montgomery Coll., Rockville, Md., 1977-78. Contbr. articles to profl. jours. Mem. profl. adv. council Easter Seal Soc. for Disabled Children and Adults, Washinton, 1987. Mem. APA, D.C. Psychol. Assn., Am. Assn. on Mental Retardation, Phi Beta Kappa. Home: 4720 S Chelsea Ln Bethesda MD 20814-3720

HAUGH, LARRY DOUGLAS, statistics professor; b. Gary, Ind., June 11, 1944; s. William Edward and Mary Patricia (McFarland) H.; m. Jane Anne Booher, Aug. 21, 1966; children: Wendi Allyn, Joshua Douglas, Jeremy Alan. BA summa cum laude, Wabash Coll., 1966; MA in Math., U. Wis., 1967, MS in Stats., 1970, PhD in Stats., 1972. Asst. prof. stats. U. Fla., Gainesville, 1972-75; faculty assoc. IBM, Burlington, Vt., 1978-81; statistician Shell Research, Amsterdam, The Netherlands, 1981-82; prof. U. Vt., Burlington, 1975—; dir. statistics program, 1990—; lectr. in field, 1981—, U. Tenn., 1985-92; cons. in field. Assoc. editor Technometrics, 1981-86, Jour. Am. Statistics Assn., 1996—; editor Quality Engring., 1996—; mem. editl. bd. Quality Progress, 1992-97; contbr. 60 articles to profl. jours. and 80 profl. conf. papers. Recipient several rsch. grants including NIH, Nat. Inst. Occupl. Safety & Health, Nat. Inst. Disability & Rehab. Rsch., Fulbright-Hays, 1970-71; fellow Woodrow Wilson, 1966, NDEA, 1969-70; NSF trainee, 1966-67. Mem. Am. Statis. Assn. (chair com. on presentation awards 1980-81, chair quality and productivity sect. 1993, Presentation award 1977), Am. Soc. for Quality Control (sr.), Biometric Soc., Internat. Statis. Inst., Royal Statis. Soc. (chartered statistician). Office: U Vt 16 Colchester Ave Burlington VT 05401-1455

HAUGHTON, JAMES GRAY, medical facility administrator, municipal health department administrator, consultant, physician; b. Panama City, Republic of Panama, Mar. 30, 1925; came to U.S., 1942, naturalized, 1953; s. Johnathan Antonio and Alice Eugeney (Gray) H.; m. Vivian Bruna Sodini, July 10, 1982; children—James Gray, Paula Yvette. B.A., Pacific Union Coll., 1947; M.D., Loma Linda U., 1950; M.P.H., Columbia U., 1962; D.Sc. (hon.), U. of Health Scis., Chgo. Med. Sch., 1971. diplomate Am. Bd. Preventive Medicine. Intern Unity Hosp., Bklyn., 1949-50; fellow in abdominal surgery Unity Hosp., 1950-54; resident in preventive medicine N.Y.C. Health Dept., 1960-63, exec. med. dir., 1964-66; first dep. N.Y.C. Health Svcs. Adminstrn., 1966-70; exec. dir. Health and Hosps. Governing Commn. Cook County, Ill., 1970-79; v.p. Drew Postgrad. Med. Sch., Los Angeles, 1980-83; dir. Houston Dept. Health and Human Services, 1983-87; med. dir. Martin. Luther King Jr./Charles Drew Med. Ctr., L.A. Dept. Health Svcs., 1987-93; assoc. dean Drew U., 1989-93; prof. medicine Charles Drew U., 1987—, UCLA, 1987—; assoc. dean Charles Drew U. Medicine and Sci., 1989—; cons. AID Costa Rica Mission, 1982; adj. prof. adminstrv. scis. U. Tex. Health Sci. Ctr., Houston, 1984-87; mem. health svcs. com. Houston Red Cross, 1984-87; mem. Houston Mayor's Task Force on Aids, 1984-87; bd. dirs. Alan Gutmacher Rsch. Inst., 1985-91; AIDS cons. Regional Ministry Pub. Health, Santiago de Compostela, Spain, 1986; sr. investigator Digestive Diseases Ctr., L.A., 1987-91; AIDS med. adv. com. L.A. County Dept. Health Svcs., 1988-91, chair com. on access to health svcs., 1988-91, sr. health svcs. policy advisor, 1993-96, med. dir. pub. health programs & svcs., 1996—; mem. substance abuse coverage study com. Inst. Medicine NAS, 1988-90; mem. Commn. on Future Structure of VA Med. Care, 1990-91; com. study co-adminstrn. svc./rsch. programs of NIH and Alcohol, Drug Abuse and Mental Health Adminstrn. HHS, 1990-91; mem. nat. adv. com. AIDS Svcs. Program, Robert Wood Johnson Found., 1986-91, AIDS Prevention Program, 1987-91; mem. personal health svcs. planning com. L.A. County Dept. of Health Svcs., 1991-93; mem. AIDS adv. com. Alcohol, Drug Abuse, Mental Health Adminstrn., U.S. Dept. Health and Human Svcs., 1991-93; bd. dirs. Calif. Conf. Local Health Officers, 1993—, mem. health info. syss. com., 1993—, co-chair personal health svcs. com., 1996—; bd. dirs. Local Initiative Health Authority LA County, 1996—; hosp. surveyor Consolidated Accreditation and Licensure Survey Program, Calif. Med. Assn./Joint Com. Accreditation Healthcare Orgn., 1992—. Mem. Houston Clean City Commn., 1985-87. Lt. comdr. USN, 1956-58. Recipient Merit award N.Y.C. Pub. Health Assn., 1964, Humanitarian award Nat. Assn. of Health Svc. Execs., 1972, cert. meritorious svc. Health and Hosp. Governing Commn. Cook County, Ill., 1979, Merit award March of Dimes, 1987, Sanville lectureship U.C.L.A. Sch. of Pub. Health, 1992. Fellow Am. Coll. Preventive Medicine (v.p. 1976-78), Am. Pub. Health Assn. (governing council 1965-70, Rosenhaus award 1974); mem. AMA, Inst. Medicine Nat. Acad. Scis., Tex. Med. Assn. (sexually transmitted diseases com. 1984-87), L.A. County Med. Assn., Calif. Med. Assn.; L.A. Acad. Medicine. Democrat. Home: 4259 Palmero Dr Los Angeles CA 90065-4220 Office: King/Drew Med Ctr 12021 Wilmington Ave Los Angeles CA 90059-3019

HAUKENES, GUNNAR CARL, virologist; b. Arendal, Norway, Feb. 2, 1927; s. Jens and Gudrun Marie (Thorbjørnsen) H.; m. Ruth Ellen Gregertsen, Sept. 28, 1951; children: Ellen, Inger, Anne. MD, U. Oslo, 1951; PhD, U. Bergen (Norway), 1962. Med. diplomate. Med. resident Hosps. Sarpsborg and Bergen, Norway, 1953-61; rsch. fellow U. Bergen, 1962-66, prof., 1966—; rsch. fellow U. Rochester, N.Y., 1963-64; head virology diagnostics Univ. Hosp., Bergen, 1966—; cons. physician Hosp. Crippled Diseases, Bergen, 1955-88; head Nat. Ctr. Rsch. in Virology, Bergen, 1988-90. Author: Immunology in Infectious Disease, 1984, Clinical Virology, 1986; author, editor: Clinical Virology, 1989; contbr. 190 articles to sci. jours. Capt. Norwegian mil., 1952-53. Mem. Norwegian Med. Assn., Internat. Taxonomy Com. Viruses. Home: Fantoftveien 17, N-5036 Fantoft Bergen Norway Office: Virus Ctr, N-5020 Bergen Norway

HAUMSCHILD, MARK JAMES, pharmacist; b. West Bend, Wis., Apr. 6, 1951; s. James Harlow and Helen Marie (Bohn) H.; m. Mary Jo Snider, Oct. 15, 1976; 1 child, Ryan James. BA in Chemistry, Fla. Atlantic U., 1973; BS in Pharmacy, U. Fla., 1976; MS in Mgmt., U. South Fla., 1982; PharmD, Mercer U., 1984. Cert. nuclear pharmacist; cert. nutritional support pharmacist. Continuing edn. instr. St. Petersburg (Fla.) Jr. Coll., 1977-81; staff pharmacist Morton F. Plant Hosp., Clearwater, Fla., 1976-78, nuclear pharmacy coordinator, 1978-83, clin. pharmacist, 1984-86, resident, 1984-85; ctr. mgr. Foster Infusioncare, St. Petersburg, 1986-88; gen. mgr. Healthinfusion Inc., St. Petersburg, 1988-95; pres. Pharm D Cons., Largo, Fla., 1984—; regional dir. ops.-Fla. UPC Health Network, Clearwater, Fla., 1995—; adj. instr. Coll. Pharmacy, U. Fla., Gainesville, 1980-86. Mem. Am. Soc. Hosp. Pharmacists, S.W. Soc. Hosp. Pharmacists, Am. Pharm. Assn. (cert. in nuclear pharmacy), Soc. Nuclear Pharmacy, Am. Coll. Hosp. Adminstrs., SW Fla. Soc. Hosp. Pharmacists (cert. nuclear pharmacist), Beta Gamma Sigma, Phi Kappa Phi. Republican. Home: 12494 104th Ter Largo FL 34648-3407 Office: UPC Health Network Ste 1011 13920 58th St N Clearwater FL 34600

HAUPENTHAL, LAURA ANN, clinical psychologist; b. Rochester, N.Y., May 22, 1951; d. Carl Vincent and Helen (Hadden) H.; m. Alvin LaFrance Beers Jr., June 1, 1985. BS, No. Ariz. U., 1976, MA, 1977; EdD, U. No. Colo., 1979. Lic. psychologist, Colo., Calif. Lectr. Arapahoe Community Coll., Littleton, Colo., 1980; asst. prof. stress mgmt. U. No. Colo., Greeley, 1980; clin. psychologist Am. Med. Ctr., Denver, 1980-82, Anaheim (Calif.) Psychol. Assocs., 1986-87, Garden Park Med. Clinic, Inc., Anaheim, 1986-89, CIGNA Healthplans, Fountain Valley, Calif., 1986-88; psychol. cons. Irvine (Calif.) Internal Medicine Assocs., 1987-89; clin. psychologist Van Steenhouse and Assocs., Aurora, Colo., 1989-90, Colo. Family Ctr., Littleton, 1980-85, 90-93; pvt. practice clin. psychology Denver, 1993—; day camp counselor Rochester (N.Y.) Parks and Recreation, 1969; vol. counselor Marc Sch. for Handicapped, Mesa, Ariz., 1973, Cath. Social Svcs., Flagstaff, Ariz., 1976; counselor, house parent Our House, Inc., Greeley, 1977-78. Contbr. articles to profl. publs. Mem. Am. Acad. Behavioral Medicine (diplomate), Nat. Register Health Svc. Providers in Psychology, Am. Psychol. Assn., Colo. Psychol. Assn., Colo. Women Psychologists, Assn. Applied Psychophysiology and Biofeedback, Orange County Psychol. Assn., Am. Soc. of Psychol. Oncology/AIDS. Office: Greenwood Exec Park Bldg 7 Ste 202 6444 S Quebec St Englewood CO 80111-4687

HAUPT, ADRIENNE LYNN, nurse supervisor; b. East St. Louis, Ill., Jan. 6, 1948; d. Dewey Kirk and Glenda Marvell (Barwell) Stafford; 1 child, Daniel. BS in Nursing, U. Md., Balt., 1970; MSEd, U. So. Calif., 1982; postgrad., Southwest Tex. State U., 1982. Commd. 1st lt. U.S. Army, 1970, advanced through grades to lt. col.; staff nurse, pediatrics U.S. Army Hosp., Ft. Knox, Ky., 1970-72; community health nurse William Beaumont Med. Ctr., El Paso, Tex., 1972-73, Tripler Army Med. Ctr., Hawaii, 1973-75; asst. chief, community health nurse U.S. Army Hosp., Ft. Hood, Tex., 1978-81; chief, community health nurse U.S. Army Hosp., Seoul, Korea, 1981-83; asst. chief, community health nurse Walter Reed Army Med. Ctr., Washington, 1983-87; chief nurse Joint Task Force, Bravo Comayagua, Honduras, 1984; community health nurse., supr., asst. supr. U.S. Army Hosp., Ft. Hood, Tex., 1987-89; ret., 1989. Decorated Legion of Merit medal, Meritorious Svc. medal. Mem. Am. Nurses Assn. (cert. in nurse adminstr. and community health nurse), Am. Pub. Health Assn. Home: 5412 E Shaw Butte Dr Scottsdale AZ 85254

HAUSCHILD, DOUGLAS CAREY, optometrist; b. Manchester, Conn., Oct. 3, 1955; s. Vernon Francis and Barbara Gwendolyn (Rose) H.; 1 child, Chelsea Anna. BA in Biology magna cum laude, Wesleyan U., 1977; OD, New Eng. Coll. Optometry, 1981. Clinician Boston Eye Clinic, 1978-81; assoc. Drs. Todd, Todd & Hauschild, Hendersonville, N.C., 1981-84; owner, optometrist Weaverville (N.C.) Eye Assocs., 1984—, Asheville (N.C.) Eye Care Assocs., 1985—; clinician Walter Reed Army Med. Ctr., 1980, West Roxbury VA Med. Ctr., 1981, Newenco Pediatric/Geriatric Sply. Clinic, 1981; nominee Buncombe County Bd. of Health. Contbr. health articles to newsletters. Mem. Henderson County Bd. Health, 1983-85; actor Asheville Community Theatre, 1988—; instr. phys. edn. Evangel. Chapel Christian Acad., Asheville, 1985-86; mem. Bent Creek Bapt. Ch. Choir, Soloist; leader Bent Creek Bapt. Ch. Care Group, 1987-91; choir mem., soloist St. Eugene's Roman Cath. Ch., 1992—. Mem. Am. Optometric Assn., So. Coun. Optometrists, N.C. State Optometric Soc., Mtn. Dist. Optometric Soc., Am. Pub. Health Assn., Lions (past pres.), KC, Elks, Beta Sigma Kappa, Delta Tau Delta. Republican. Office: Weaverville Eye Assocs PO Box 1628 Weaverville NC 28787-1628

HAUSCHKA, THEODORE SPAETH, biologist, researcher, educator; b. Reichenau, Austria, July 31, 1908; came to U.S., 1928, naturalized, 1937; s. Hugo and Carola (Spaeth) H.; m. Elsa Voorhees, Mar. 29, 1938; children—Stephen Denison, Peter Voorhees, Margaret Spaeth. A.B., Princeton U., 1930; M.S. (Harrison fellow), U. Pa., 1941, Ph.D., 1943; Sc.D. (hon.), Bates Coll., 1984. Tchr. biology Chestnut Hill Acad., Phila., 1935-39; instr. U. Pa., 1942-43, Army specialist tng. program, 1943-44; biologist Lankenau Hosp. Research Inst., Phila., 1943-48; sr. mem. Lankenau Hosp. Research Inst., 1949-54; asso. dir. Marine Exptl. Sta., Truro, Mass., 1945-47; sr. mem. Inst. Cancer Research, Phila., 1949-54; cons. cancer research Lederle Lab., Am. Cyanamid Co., 1953-65; dir. biol. research Roswell Park Meml. Inst., Buffalo, 1954-75; cons. Roswell Park Meml. Inst., 1975—; research prof. biology SUNY-Buffalo Grad. Sch., 1954-74; mem. carcinogenesis adv. panel, cons. Nat. Cancer Inst., 1972-74. Contbr. articles to profl. jours. Trustee Med. Found. Buffalo, 1965-69. Fellow AAAS, N.Y. Acad. Sci.; mem. Am. Assn. Tissue Banks, Am. Genetic Assn., Soc. for Developmental Biology, Am. Naturalists, Soc. Exptl. Biology and Medicine, Transplantation Soc., Am. Assn. Cancer Research (v.p. 1958, pres. 1959), Sigma Xi. Home and Office: 333 Fogler Rd Bremen ME 04551

HAUSEN, SCOTT LAURENCE, podiatrist; b. N.Y.C., May 18, 1965; s. Stanley Sherman and Nina (Goldstein) H. BA in Psychology, Brandeis U., 1987; D of Podiatric Medicine, N.Y. Coll. Podiatric Medicine, 1991. Diplomate Am. Bd. Podiatric Physicians and Surgeons. Podiatric residency Med. Coll. Hosps., Elkins Park Campus, Elkins Park, 1991-92; podiatric resident VA Med. Ctr., Montrose, N.Y., 1992-93; assoc. in podiatric practice N.Y.C., 1993-94; pvt. practice New Rochelle, N.Y., 1994—; podiatric cons. VA Med. Ctr., Bronx, 1995—; podiatric attending Our Lady of Mercy Med. Ctr., Bronx, 1995—; co-founder, co-pres. A Step Ahead, Purchase, N.Y., 1995—. Mem. Am. Podiatric Med. Assn., N.Y. State Podiatric Med. Assn., Brandeis U. Alumni Assn., Alumni Admissions Coun., Acad. Ambulatory Foot Surgery (assoc.). Home: 4 Martine Ave #501 White Plains NY 10606 Office: Family Foot Care 466 Main St New Rochelle NY 10801

HAUSER, GEORGE, biochemist, educator; b. Vienna, Austria, Dec. 13, 1922; came to U.S., 1939.; s. Hans Joseph and Juliane Therese (Gleissner) H.; m. Louise Jean Russo, July 2, 1955. BS, Ohio State U., 1949; PhD, Harvard U., 1955. Mem. faculty Harvard Med. Sch., Boston, 1952-55, from rsch. assoc. to prof., 1955-93, prof emeritus, 1993—; from asst. biochemist to biochemist McLean Hosp., Belmont, Mass., 1957-93, sr. biochemist, 1993—; mem. adv. & editorial bds. Jour. Neurochemistry, 1977-86, dep. chief editor, 1986-92; interim dir. Ralph Lowell Labs., McLean Hosp., Belmont, 1983-93; reviewer many sci. jours.; spl. cons. NIH, NSF. Co-editor: Inositol & Phosphoinositides: metabolism & metabolic regulation. Mem., treas. Dem. Ward Com., Newton, Mass., 1976—. With U.S. Army, 1943-48. Grantee Nat. Insts. Health, 1965-92, Nat. Sci. Found., 1980-82; fellow Japan Soc. for the Promotion of Sci., 1988. Mem. Biochem. Soc., Am. Soc. Biochemistry and Molecular Biology, Internat. Soc. Neurochemistry, Am. Soc. Neurochemistry (coun. 1983-87), Soc. Neurosci., Soc. Glycobiol. Democrat. Jewish. Home: 47 Windermere Rd Auburndale MA 02166-2521 Office: McLean Hosp 115 Mill St Belmont MA 02178-1041

HAUSLER, WILLIAM JOHN, JR., microbiologist, educator, public health laboratory administrator; b. Kansas City, Kans., Aug. 31, 1926; s. William John and Clifton (McCambridge) H.; m. Mary Lois Rice, Apr. 19, 1949; children—Cheryl Kaye Johnson, Kenneth Randall, Eric Rice, Mark Clifton. AB in Microbiology, U. Kans., 1951, MA in Microbiology, 1953, PhD in Microbiology, Math., 1958. Diplomate Am. Bd. Med. Microbiology (chmn. 1979-82, Profl. Recognition award 1995). Asst. instr. U. Kans., Lawrence, 1951-56, rsch. asst., 1956-58; assoc. bacteriologist Iowa State Hygienic Lab., Iowa City, 1958-59, asst. dir., prin. bacteriologist, 1959-65, dir., 1965-95; dir. emeritus, 1995—; asst. prof. U. Iowa Coll. Medicine, Iowa City, 1959-66; assoc. prof. U. Iowa Coll. Medicine, 1966-90, prof., 1990—; assoc. prof. U. Iowa Coll. Dentistry, 1966-90, prof., 1990—; cons. to Iran WHO, 1969, U.S. EPA, 1970-72, CDC, 1965—, People's Republic China WHO, 1990, WHO Western Pacific Region, 1991, UNDP India, 1992; cons. to industry. Editor: Standard Methods for the Examination of Dairy Products, 1972, Manual Clinical Microbiology, 3d edit., 1980, 4th edit., 1985, 5th edit., 1991, Compendium of Methods for the Microbiological Examination of Foods, 1980, 2d edit., 1984, Diagnostic Procedures for Bacterial Mycotic and Parasitic Infections, 1981, Laboratory Diagnosis of Infections Diseases: Principles and Practice, 1988; co-editor: Topley & Wilson's Microbiology and Microbial Infections, 9th edit., 1994; mem. editl. bd. various profl. jours.; contbr. articles to profl. jours. Councilman City Govt., University Heights, Iowa, 1966-69; commr. Iowa Air Pollution Control Commn., 1967-74; mem. exec. com. Iowa Dept. Environ. Quality, 1974-80, Nat. Com. for Clin. Lab. Standards, bd. dirs., 1987-93. Lt. comdr. USNR, 1944-67. Recipient Henry Albert Meml. award Iowa Pub. Health Assn., 1974. Fellow APHA, Am. Acad. Microbiology (chmn. 1983-89); mem. Am. Soc. Microbiology, Assn. State and Territorial Pub. Health Lab. Dirs. (pres. 1984-85), Sigma Phi Epsilon, Rotary (Paul Harris fellow). Home: 11 The Woods NE Iowa City IA 52240-7986 Office: U Iowa Hygienic Lab Oakdale Hall Iowa City IA 52242

HAUSMAN, STEVEN JACK, health science administrator; b. Phila., May 20, 1945; s. Leo and Bella Hausman. BA, U. Pa., 1967, MS, 1968, PhD, 1972. Postdoctoral fellow Inst. for Cancer Rsch., Phila., 1972-75; staff fellow Nat. Inst. on Aging, Balt., 1975-77; spl. asst. to assoc. dir. Nat. Inst. Arthritis, Metabolism and Digestive Diseases, Bethesda, Md., 1977-78, dir. ctrs. program, 1978-86; dep. dir. extramural program Nat. Inst. Arthritis and Musculoskeletal and Skin Diseases, Bethesda, 1986-90, dep. dir., 1990—. Mem. AAAS, Am. Assn. Immunologists, Soc. In Vitro Biology, Am. Chem. Soc., Am. Soc. for Cell Biology. Office: NIAMS-NIH Bldg 31 Rm 4C-32 31 Center Dr MSC2350 Bethesda MD 20892-2350

HAUSMAN, WILLIAM, psychiatry educator, consultant; b. N.Y.C., July 25, 1925; s. Jacob Henry and Tillie (Hoffman) H.; m. Lillian Margaret Fuerst, June 12, 1947; children: Steven David, Peter Douglas, Linda Louise Hausman Johnson, Clifford Alan. MD, Washington U., St. Louis, 1947. Diplomate Am. Bd. Psychiatry and Neurology. Commd. capt. U.S. Army, 1949, advanced through grades to col., ret., 1966; intern Coney Island Hosp., Bklyn., 1947-48; resident Worcester (Mass.) State Hosp., 1948-49, Inst. Pa. Hosp., Phila., 1949-50, 51-52; assoc. prof. Johns Hopkins U., Balt., 1966-69; prof. psychiatry, head dept. U. Minn., Mpls., 1969-80, prof. psychiatry, 1980-88, prof. emeritus, 1988—; cons. Levinson Inst., Belmont, Mass., 1975—. Contbr. articles to profl. jours. Fellow Am. Coll. Psychiatrists, Am. Psychiat. Assn., Am. Assn. Social Psychiatry; mem. Nev. Assn. Psychiatric Physicians. Home and Office: 3785 Ranch Crest Dr Reno NV 89509-6871

HÄUSSINGER, DIETER LOTHAR, medical educator; b. Nördlingen, Bavaria, Germany, June 22, 1951; s. Konrad and Margot (Wöhler) H. MD, U. Munich, 1976. Asst. dept. biochemistry U. Munich, 1979; asst. dept. gastroenterology U. Freiburg, Fed. Republic of Germany, 1979-84, pvt. lectr. dept. gastroenterology, 1984-88; prof. U. Hosp Freiburg, 1988—; Heisenberg prof. German Sci. Found., Freiburg, 1985-90, Schilling prof., 1992-94; prof., chmn. dept. internal medicine U. Düsseldorf, 1994—; cons. Inst. for Medizin Prufungen, Mainz, Fed. Republic of Germany, 1989—. Editor: Glutamine Metabolism, 1984, pH Homeostasis, 1988, Mammalian Amino Acid Transport, 1992, Cell Volume and Cell Function, 1993; contbr. numerous articles to profl. jours. Recipient Wewalka price Internat. Soc. Ammonia Metabolism, 1984, Heisenberg award German Sci. Found., 1984, Leibniz-Laureate, 1990, Thannhauser prize Soc. Digestive Diseases, 1989. Mem. Biochem. Soc. London (editor 1991—), Gesellschaft Biolog. Chemie. Lutheran. Office: U Düsseldorf Dept Internal Medicine, Moorenstrasse 5, 4-60225 Düsseldorf Germany

HAVDALA, HENRI SALOMON, anesthesiologist, educator, consultant; b. Minia, Egypt, Apr. 12, 1931; came to U.S., 1957, naturalized, 1963; s. Jacques S. and Regine (Levy) H.; m. Sandra Abrams, Aug. 27, 1961; children—Jack, Debra, Ellen, Michael. B.S. in Sci, St. Mark Coll., 1948; M.B., B.Ch., U. Alexandria, Egypt, 1956. Diplomate: Am. Bd. Anesthesiology. Practice medicine, specializing in anesthesiology Mt. Sinai Hosp., Chgo., 1961—; now chmn. dept. anesthesiology; mem. faculty Chgo. Med. Sch., 1961-74, asst. prof. anesthesiology, 1971-72, assoc. prof., 1972, prof., 1972-74, chmn. dept., 1965-74, acting dean Sch., 1973-74; prof. anesthesiology Rush Med. Coll., 1975-87; prof., chmn. anesthesiology Chgo. Med. Sch./Univ. Health Scis., 1988—; bd. govs. Ill. State Med. Ins. Exchange, 1977; trustee Mt. Sinai Hosp. Anesthesiologists (dir.), 1977; cons. North Chgo. VA, 1992—. Bd. dirs. Council for the Jewish Elderly, Chgo., 1977-87; pres. bd. dirs. Mt. Sinai Cmty. Found., 1995—. Fellow Am. Soc. Anesthesiologists, Inst. Med., Philippine Coll. Anesthesiologists; mem. Ill. Soc. Anesthesiologists (sec. 1971-73, pres. 1976-77), Chgo., Ill. med. socs., AMA, Chgo. Anesthesiology Soc., Internat. Anesthesia Research Soc., Am. Soc. Anesthesiologists (dir.), Am. Soc. Respiratory Therapy, N.Y.C. Acad. Scis., Am. Coll. Chest Physicians, Ill. Council Continuing Med. Edn., Council for Jewish Elderly (dir.), Sigma Xi, Alpha Omega Alpha.; Mem. B'nai B'rith. Office: 2750 W 15th Pl Chicago IL 60608-1704

HAVEKORST, WALTER BENEDICT, dentist; b. San Diego, May 1, 1935; s. Walter Benedict and Margaret Mary (Bostian) H.; children: Walter B. III, Kristilyn. BS, U. Calif., Long Beach; DDS, U. Pacific. Pvt. practice dentistry Newport Beach, Calif., 1964—; prof. U. So. Calif. Dental Sch., 1966—;. Fellow Am. Acad. Gen. Dentistry; mem. Am. Dental Assn., Tri-County Dental Soc., Am. Equilibriation Soc., Newport Harbor Acad. Dentistry, Calif. Dental Assn., Am. Prosthodontic Soc., Am. Acad. Implant Dentistry, Found. for Denture Rsch., Internat. Acad. Gnathology. Republican. Roman Catholic. Home: PO Box 5716 Balboa Island CA 92662

HAVEL, RICHARD JOSEPH, physician, educator; b. Seattle, Feb. 20, 1925; s. Joseph and Anna (Fritz) H.; m. Virginia Johnson, June 28, 1947; children: Christopher, Timothy, Peter, Julianne. BA, Reed Coll., 1946; MS, MD, U. Oreg., 1949. Intern Cornell U. Med. Coll., N.Y.C., 1949-50; resident in medicine Cornell U. Med. Coll., 1950-53; clin. assoc. Nat. Heart Inst., NIH, 1953-54, research assoc., 1954-56; faculty Sch. Medicine, U. Calif., San Francisco, 1956—; prof. medicine Sch. Medicine, U. Calif., 1964—; assoc. dir. Cardiovascular Research Inst., 1961-73, dir., 1973-92; chief metabolism sect., dept. medicine, 1967—; dir. Arteriosclerosis Specialized Center of Research, 1970—; mem. bd. sci. counselors Nat. Heart, Lung and Blood Inst., 1976-80; chmn. food and nutrition bd. NRC, 1987-90. Contbr. chpts. to books, numerous articles to profl. jours.; editor: Jour. Lipid Research, 1972-75; co-editor: Adv. Lipid Res., 1991—; mem. editorial bd.: Jour. Biol. Chemistry, 1981-85, Jour. Arteriosclerosis, 1980—; mem. bd. cons. editors: Am. Jour. Medicine, 1981-86. Established investigator Am. Heart Assn., 1956-61, chmn. coun. on arteriosclerosis, 1977-79. With USPHS, 1951-53. Recipient Disting. Achievement award Am. Heart Assn., 1993, Theobald Smith award AAAS, 1960, Bristol-Myers award for nutrition rsch., 1989. Mem. NAS, Inst. Medicine NAS, Am. Acad. Arts and Scis., Am. Soc. Clin. Nutrition (McCollum award 1993), Assn. Am. Physicians, Am. Soc. for Clin. Investigation, Phi Beta Kappa, Alpha Omega Alpha. Office: U Calif San Francisco Cardiovascular Rsch In San Francisco CA 94143

HAVELIN, LEIF IVAR, orthopaedic surgeon; b. Sör Varanger Finnmark, Norway, Apr. 28, 1949; s. Leif and Marie (Olsen) H.; m. Marit Grönnevet, July 21, 1973; children: Heidi, Gro, Karen. MD, U. Bergen, Norway, 1976, PhD, 1995. Cert. gen. surgery, orthopaedic surgery. Registrar gen. surgery Nordfjord Hosp., Norway, 1978-80; registrar orthopaedic surgery Hagavik Hosp., Norway, 1980-84; registrar gen. surgery Haukeland U. Hosp., Bergen, 1984-87, registrar neurosurgery, 1987-88, registrar orthopaedic surgery, 1988-89, orthopaedic surgeon, 1989—; head Norwegian Arthoplasty Register, Bergen, 1991—. Contbr. articles to profl. jours. With Norwegian Air Force, 1969-70; lt. Norwegian Army, 1981. Mem. Norwegian Orthopaedic Assn., Nordic Orthopaedic Fedn., European Hip Soc. Home: Odinsvei 25, Nesttun, N-5050 Bergen Norway Office: Haukeland Hosp, Dept Orthopaedics, N-5021 Bergen Norway

HAVELUND, TROELS, physician, researcher; b. Herringe, Fyn, Denmark, May 24, 1953; s. Thomas Nørregaard and Eli Kirstine (Havelund) Petersen; m. Christel Work; children: Louise Work, Kathrine Work, Sidsel Work. MB, Odense (Denmark) U., 1980. Specialist gastroenterology, 1994, internal medicine, 1995. Registrar Dept. Surgery and Medicine Fredericia, Denmark, 1980-82; registrar dept. med. gastroenterology Odense, Denmark, 1983-87, registrar dept. medicine, 1988-89, registrar endocrine dept., 1989-90; sr. registrar med. dept. Svenborg, Denmark, 1990-91; sr. registrar dept. med. gastroenterology Odense, Denmark, 1991-93; rsch. asst. Odense (Denmark) U., 1993-94; sr. registrar dept. medicine Herlev, Denmark, 1994-96; staff physician dept. med. gastroenterology Odense U. Hosp., Denmark, 1996—. Contbr. articles to profl. jours. Mem. Danish Soc. Gastroenterology. Home: Sparretornvej 7, DK-5230 Odense M Denmark Office: Dept Med Gastroenterology, Odense U Hosp, DK-5000 Odense Denmark

HAVEN, HOWARD JOEL, psychologist, college dean; b. 1943; married; 3 children. AA, Dutchess Community Coll., 1963; BA cum laude, SUNY, Fredonia, 1965; MA, Bowling Green State U., 1967; PhD, Fla. State U., 1972. Lic. psychologist, Wis. Clerkship Leon County Mental Health Clinic, Tallahassee, 1969, Human Devel. Clinic, Fla. State U., Tallahassee, 1969; clk. Fed. Correctional Instn., Tallahassee, 1969-71, staff psychologist, 1971-72; staff psychologist clin. svcs. unit Milw. Probation and Parole, 1972-73, sr. staff psychologist, 1973-76; chief psychologist, supr. clin. svcs. unit Southeastern Region Probation and Parole, Waukesha, wis., 1976-80; clin. psychologist, dir. Elmbrook Family Counseling, Elmbrook Meml. Hosp., Brookfield, Wis., 1980—; prof. Wis. Sch. Profl. Psychology, Milw., 1984—, dean, 1988—; pvt. practice Clin. Psychology Assocs., Menomonee Falls, Wis.; adj. staff mem. Elmbrook Meml. Hosp.; assoc. mem. psychology staff Charter Hosp., Brown Deer, Wis.; part-time psychologist Sandusky Valley Guidance Ctr., Tiffin, Ohio, 1967; part-time lectr. dept. behavioral scis. Mt. Mary Coll., Milw., 1975-79. Contbr. articles to profl. publs. USPHS fellow, 1968-70. Mem. APA, Wis. Psychol. Assn., Soc. Clin. and Cons. Psychologists, Milw. Area Psychol. Assn., Am. Assn. Correctional Psychologists, Am. Soc. Clin. Hypnosis, Milw. Soc. Clin. Hypnosis (past pres.). Home: 1920 Stardust Ct Waukesha WI 53186-2845

HAVENS, JOE BARNEY, health services administrator; b. Wooster, Ark., Nov. 2, 1931; s. William Edward and Verna Ann (Arthur) H.; m. Grace Marie Wynn, May 10, 1954; children: Cynthia, William, Emmett, Nancy. AA, SUNY, Albany, 1974, BS, 1976. Lic. nursing home adminstr., Tenn. Med. corpsman USN, 1949-70; part-time night adminstr. St. Jude Children's Rsch. Hosp., Memphis, 1969-70; adminstr. Medicenters of Am., Memphis, Jackson, Boston, 1970-71, Americana Nursing Ctr., Cedar Rapids, Iowa, 1971-72; asst. to chmn. Coll. Medicine dept. pathology U. Tenn., Memphis, 1972-76; exec. v.p. Trezevant Episc. Home, Memphis, 1976-92, pres., 1992-95; cons. Lifeblood Mid-South Regional Blood Ctr., Memphis, 1995; v.p. mgmt. divsn. Servicemaster Diversified Health Svcs., Memphis, 1995—; mem. faculty Memphis State U./U. Tenn. Coop. Program in Clin. Nutrition. Author: Desk Reference Nursing Home Adminstration, 1982, Chief Petty Officer, U.S. Navy, 1996, Corpsmen!, 1996; contbr. articles to profl. jours. Appointed to USN Com. for Retired Personnel, 1994—, Gov.'s Com. to Access Requirements for Licensure of Recuperative Ctr., Tenn.; chmn. bd. dirs. Am. Heart Assn.; bd. dirs. Memphis Oral Sch., Memphis Botanic Gardens Found., 1991—, Alzheimers Day Svcs., Memphis, 1995—; pres. Exch. Club East Memphis, 1984-92, Exch. Club Trezevant Manor, Cedar Valley Heart Divsn., Cedar Rapids, Iowa; sec. Arthritis Found. West Tenn. chpt., The Trezevant Found.; cert. preceptor nursing home adminstrs., Tenn.; commr. Memphis City Beautiful Commn., 1988-91; mem. adv. com. Navy Recruiting Dist. Memphis. Decorated Bronze Star, Purple Heart; named Exchangite of Yr. East Memphis Exch. Club, 1983; recipient Disting. Pres.'s award Nat. Exch. Club, Toledo, Ohio, 1984, Nat. Pres.'s award, 1987, Disting. Pres.'s award Arthritis Found. West Tenn. chpt., 1986, Caregiver award Delta Vol. Ombudsman Program, Memphis area, 1994. Fellow Am. Coll. Health Care Adminstrs. (cert. M in Profl. Nursing Home Adminstrn. 1996, chmn. editl. adv. bd. Jour. Long-Term Care, pres. Tenn. chpt., pres. Memphis Coun., nat. chmn. ins. adv. com., Adminstr. of Yr. Tenn. chpt. 1982); mem. Am. Assn. Homes for Aging (Innovator of Yr. 1989), Inst. Pathology Pvt. Practice Assn. U. Tenn. (sec./treas.), Sales and Mktg. Execs. Memphis (bd. dirs.), Tenn. Health Care Assn. (v.p. non-profit coun., Profl. Svc. award 1984, Mem. Emeritus Recognition 1995), Memphis State U. Alumni Health Svcs. Adminstrn. (pres.), Shriners. Republican. Baptist. Home: Homeport Pl 43 Pleasant Valley W Greenbrier AR 72058

HAVENS, LESTON LAYCOCK, psychiatrist, educator; b. Bklyn., July 31, 1924; s. Valentine Britton and Nellie Falk (Laycock) H.; m. Susan Elizabeth Miller, May 19, 1973; 1 child, Emily E.; children by previous marriage: Christopher W., Jeffry B. (dec.), Jennifer F., Sarah B. BA, Williams Coll., 1947; MD, Cornell U., 1952; MA (hon.), Harvard U., 1987; LHD, Mass. Sch. Profl. Psychology, 1993. Intern N.Y. Hosp., 1952-53, asst. resident internal medicine, 1953-54; resident, chief of service Mass. Mental Health Ctr., Boston Psychopathic Hosp., 1954-58, staff visit and asst. clin. dir., 1958-62, prin. investigator studies in visual word perception, 1960-66, program dir. psychiat. rehab. internship program, 1962-68, program dir. med. student teaching, 1964-81; asst. prof. psychiatry Harvard Med. Sch., Boston, 1963-64; assoc. clin. prof. psychiatry Harvard Med. Sch., 1965-71, psychoanalyst, 1967—, prof. psychiatry, 1971—; Cargnegie vis. prof. humanities MIT, 1968; H. B. Williams traveling prof. Australian and New Zealand Coll. of Psychiatrists, 1975; chief psychiat. cons. Mass. Rehab. Commn., 1959-65; mental health adminstr. Region VI, Mass. Dept. Mental Health, 1968-69; dir. of residency tng. Cambridge Hosp., 1987-96. Author: Approaches to the Mind, 1973, Participant Observation, 1977, Making Contact, 1986, A Safe Place: Laying the Groundwork of Psychotherapy, 1989, Coming to Life, 1993, Learning To Be Human, 1994; also articles. Served to 2d lt. AUS, 1944-46. Recipient H.C. Solomon award, 1977, Benjamin Rush award, 1995. Mem. Am. Psychiat. Assn., Soc. Biol. Psychiatry (A.E. Bennett award 1958), Mass. Soc. for Rsch. in Psychiatry (McCurdy prize 1962), Phi Beta Kappa, Alpha Omega Alpha. Home: 151 Brattle St Cambridge MA 02138-2243 Office: Cambridge Hosp 1493 Cambridge St Cambridge MA 02139-1047

HAVERLAND, EDGAR MARION, engineering psychologist; b. Broken Bow, Nebr., Aug. 4, 1925; s. Howard Hobson and Elsie Gertrude (Burke) H.; m. Lillian Edith Hite, May 30, 1952; children: John Howard, Ann Elizabeth (dec.). AB with highest honors, U. Ill., 1949, MA, PhD, 1954. Instr. Ind. U., Kokomo, 1954-55; asst. prof. Augustana Coll., Rock Island, Ill., 1955-58; sr. scientist Human Resources Rsch. Orgn., El Paso, Tex., 1958-65, Alexandria, Va., 1965-77; rsch. psychologist U.S. Army Tropic Test Ctr., Panama Canal Zone, 1977-79; engrng. psychologist U.S. Army Test and Evaluation Command, Aberdeen Proving Ground, Md., 1979-80, U.S. Army Operational Evaluation Command, Alexandria, 1980—; cons. Ill. Dept. Pub. Welfare, Springfield, 1955-58, U.S. Naval Acad., Annapolis, Md., 1968-69. Grad. fellow U. Ill., 1952-54. Mem. APA, Human Factors Soc., Phi Beta Kappa. Home: 8212 Capt Hawkins Ct Annandale VA 22003-4602 Office: US Army Operational Evaluation Command 4501 Ford Ave Alexandria VA 22302-1435

HAVILAND, JAMES WEST, physician; b. Glens Falls, N.Y., July 18, 1911; s. Morrison LeRoy and Mabel Eva (West) H.; children: James Marshall, Elizabeth Bullard, Donald Sherman, Martha Adams Clauser. A.B., Union Coll., Schenectady, 1932; M.D., Johns Hopkins, 1936. Intern medicine Johns Hopkins Hosp., 1936-37, intern, asst. resident, chief outpatient dept. pediatrics, 1937-38, asst. resident medicine, 1939-40; asst. resident medicine New Haven Hosp., 1938-39; instr. medicine Yale Med. Sch., 1938-39, Johns Hopkins Sch. Medicine, 1939-40; chief services crippled children Wash. Dept. Social Security, also Dept. Health, 1940- 42; lectr. medicine U. Wash. Sch. Nursing, 1946-60; practice medicine Seattle, 1946-86; clin. asst. prof., to clin. prof. U. Wash. Sch. Medicine, 1947—, asst. dean, 1949-53, 1954-59, acting dean, 1953-54, asso. dean, 1972-76. Trustee N.W. Kidney Ctr., Seattle Symphony Orch. Served to lt. comdr. M.C., USNR, 1942-46. Fellow Am. Geog. Soc. N.Y.; mem. Wash. State Med. Assn. (sec.-treas. 1948-51), Seattle Acad. Internal Medicine (pres. 1952-53), King County Med. Soc. (pres. 1962), AMA (council med. edn. 1966-76, chmn. 1974-76), Pacific Interurban Clin. Club, AAAS, North Pacific Soc. Internal Medicine, A.C.P. (pres. 1970), Am. Clin. and Climatol. Assn. (pres. 1981-82), Am. Assn. History Medicine, Nat. Acad. Scis. (Inst. Medicine), Phi Beta Kappa, Sigma Xi, Alpha Omega Alpha, Kappa Alpha. Home: 8208 SE 30th St Mercer Island WA 98040-3011

HAW, RICHARD CALVIN, dentist, educator; b. Davenport, Iowa, Mar. 30, 1926; s. William Alfred and Mary Rosella (DeWild) H.; m. Ruth Marie Murphy, Apr. 20, 1924; children: Rebeca Marie, Jeffrey Kent. BS, U. Iowa, 1949, MA in Edn. Sci., 1951, DDS, 1955. Clin. instr. Hawkeye Inst. Tech., Waterloo, Iowa, 1967-94, Hawkeye Cmty. Coll., Waterloo, Iowa, 1994—; mem. dental adv. bd. Hawkeye Cmty. Coll., 1967-96. City councilman City of Sumner, Iowa, 1990-96. With UNS, 1943-46. Fellow Acad. Gen. Dentistry; mem. Iowa Dental Assn. (various coms. 1975-90, Disting. Svc. award 1982), Christian Dental Soc. (exec. dir. 1982-96), Rotary (Paul Harris fellow), Masons, Shrine Club Iowa. Methodist. Office: Christian Dental Soc 113 W First PO 177 Sumner IA 50674

HAWA, ELLEN DENA LEVY, ambulatory pediatrics nurse manager; b. Toronto, Dec. 30, 1961; came to U.S., 1989; d. Naim Ibraham and Cecelia (Shain) Levy; m. Said Hawa, Oct. 14, 1990. BScN, U. Toronto, 1984, MScN, 1989. Cert. nursing adminstrn., PALS. Staff nurse Toronto Hosp. for Sick Children, 1984-85, 86-89; clin. nurse II Meml. Sloan Kettering Cancer Ctr., N.Y.C., 1985-86; teaching asst. faculty of nursing U. Toronto, 1987-88; nurse mgr. ambulatory pediatric nursing N.Y. Hosp. Cornell Med. Ctr., N.Y.C., 1989—. Recipient Open Fellowship, U. Toronto, 1987-88, Florence J. Potts and Anne Blair Shuttleworth Bursary, 1987. Mem. Assn. for the Care of Children's Health, Assn. of Pediatric Oncology Nurses, Registered Nursing Assn. of Ont., Sigma Theta Tau. Office: The New York Hosp 525 E 68th St Rm Ht-506 New York NY 10021-4873

HAWES, RICHARD MANNING, psychologist; b. Portland, Maine, July 19, 1931; s. Willis Manning and Lillian May (Todd) H.; m. Joyce Burdick, Nov. 3, 1956 (div. 1986); children: Karen, Kevin, Christopher, Jennifer; m. Judy Rice, Aug. 1, 1995. BA in Psychology, Colby Coll., Waterville, Maine, 1953; MA in Gen. Psychology, U. of the Pacific, Stockton, Calif., 1960, EdD in Ednl. and Counseling Psychology, 1970. Sch. psychologist, dir. guidance San Juan Unified Sch. Dist., Sacramento, 1959-68; psycholoigst pvt. practice, West Los Angeles, Calif., 1968-88, Greensboro, N.C., 1988-91, Sunset Beach, N.C., 1992—; v.p. Inst. for Reality Therapy, Brentwood, Calif., 1968-88. Contbr. articles to profl. jours. Coach, dir. Little League, Brentwood, 1975-77. With U.S. Army, 1953-55. Mem. Sacramento Psychol. Assn. (pres. 1965), Am. Psychol. Assn., Phi Delta Kappa. Home: 343 Heather Dr Sunset Beach NC 28468-4433

HAWES, SAMUEL PINCKNEY, III, urologist; b. Conway, S.C., May 2, 1941; s. Samuel Pinckney and Jeannette (Malloy) H.; m. Lorene Downs, July 22, 1989; children: Samuel IV, Matthew, Wilson, Erica, Lake.9. BS, Davidson Coll., 1963; MD, Vanderbilt U., 1967. Diplomate Am. Bd. Urology. Intern in surgery U. Va., Charlottesville, 1967-69; resident in urology Duke U., Durham, N.C., 1971-75; pvt. practice urology Charlotte, N.C., 1975—; chmn. urology quality assessment Carolinas Med. Ctr., 1994—; clin. instr. dept. surgery Sch. Medicine U. N.C. Bd. deacons Sharon Presbyn. Ch., Charlotte, 1981-83. Maj. USAF, 1969-71. Fellow Am. Coll. Surgeons. Home: 308 Minden Ln Matthews NC 28105 Office: 1333 Romany Rd Charlotte NC 28204

HAWKEN, PATTY LYNN, nursing educator, dean of faculty; b. Wheaton, Ill., July 13, 1932; d. Leonard William and Betty (Stock) H. BSN, U. Mich., 1956; MSN, Case Western Res. U., 1962, PhD, 1970. Instr. U. Mich., Ann Arbor, 1956-57, Highland Hosp., Oakland, Calif., 1957-59; instr. Case Western Res. U., Cleve., 1960-63, asst. prof., 1963-67, assoc. prof., 1967-69, assoc. prof., assoc. in adminstrn., 1969-71; assoc. prof. Emory U., Atlanta, 1971-72, prof., dir., 1972-74; dean, prof. U. Tex. Health Sci. Ctr. Sch. Nursing, San Antonio, 1974—. Contbr. articles to nursing jours. Bd. dirs. Wesley Community Ctr., San Antonio, 1986, 89; mem. United Way Allocation Com., San Antonio, 1987; mem. adv. com. Trinity U. Health Care Adminstrn., San Antonio, 1984—, VA Dean's Com., San antonio, 1982—. Recipient Nurse of Yr. award Tex. Nursing Assn., San Antonio chpt., 1985, Disting. Alumni award Case Western Res. U., 1991; named to Women's Hall of Fame, Mayor's Commn. on Women, San Antonio, 1986. Mem. ANA (cabinet on edn. 1986-88), Nat. League Nursing (pres. 1989-91, Disting. Svc. award 1991), Am. Assn. Colls. of Nursing (com. on edn. 1986-88), Commns. Grads. Fgn. Nursing Schs. (trustee, pres. 1983-85), Am. Acad. Nursing (bd. govs. 1994—), San Antonio 100 Club, Internat. Women's Forum (San Antonio pres. celebration, Hall of Fame 1994—). Home: 1826 Fallow Run San Antonio TX 78248-2000 Office: U Tex Health Sci Ctr 7703 Floyd Curl Dr San Antonio TX 78284-6200

HAWKES, GLENN ROGERS, psychology educator; b. Preston, Idaho, Apr. 29, 1919; s. William and Rae (Rogers) H.; m. Yvonne Merrill, Dec. 18, 1941; children—Kristen, William Ray, Gregory Merrill, Laura. B.S. in

Psychology, Utah State U., 1946, M.S. in Psychology, 1947; Ph.D. in Psychology, Cornell U., 1950. From asst. prof. to prof. child devel. and psychology Iowa State U., Ames, 1950-66, chmn. dept. child devel., 1954-66; prof. human devel., rsch. psychologist U. Calif., Davis, 1966-89, prof. emeritus, 1990—, acad. coord. Hubert Humphrey fellowship program, 1990—, assoc. dean applied econs. and behavioral scis., 1966-83, chmn. dept. applied behavioral scis., 1982-86, chmn. teaching div., 1970-72, prof. behavioral scis. dept. family practice, Sch. Medicine; acting dir. Internat. Programs, U. Calif., Davis, 1994—; vis. scholar U. Hawaii, 1972-73, U. London, 1970, 80, 86; bd. dirs. Creative Playthings Inc., 1962-66. Author: (with Pease) Behavior and Development from 5 to 12, 1962; (with Frost) The Disadvantaged Child: Issues and Innovations, 1966, 2d edit., 1970; (with Schultz and Baird) Lifestyles and Consumer Behavior of Older Americans, 1979; (with Nicola and Fish) Young Marrieds: The Dual Career Approach, 1984. Contbr. numerous articles to profl. and sci. jours. Served with AUS, 1941-45. Recipient numerous research grants from pvt. founds. and govtl. bodies; recipient Iowa State U. faculty citation, 1965, Outstanding Service citation Iowa Soc. Crippled Children and adults, 1965, citation Dept. Child Devel., 1980, Coll. Agrl. and Environ. Scis., 1983; named hon. lt. gov. Okla., 1966. Home: 1114 Purdue Dr Davis CA 95616-1736 Office: U Calif Internat House 10 College Park Davis CA 95616

HAWKINS, DAVID ROLLO, SR., psychiatrist; b. Springfield, Mass., Sept. 22, 1923; s. James Alexander and Janet (Rollo) H.; m. Elizabeth G. Wilson, June 8, 1946; children: David Rollo Jr., Robert Wilson, John Bruce, William Alexander. B.A., Amherst Coll., 1945; M.D., U. Rochester, N.Y., 1946. Intern Strong Meml. Hosp., Rochester, 1946-48; Commonwealth Fund fellow in psychiatry and medicine U. Rochester, 1950-52; instr. psychiatry U. N.C. Sch. Medicine, 1952-53, asst. prof., 1953-57, asso. prof. psychiatry, 1957-62, prof., 1962-67; prof., chmn. dept. psychiatry U. Va. Sch. Medicine, 1967-77, Alumni prof. psychiatry, 1967-79, asso. dean, 1969-70; psychiatrist-in-chief U. Va. Hosp., 1967-77; prof. psychiatry Pritzker Sch. Medicine, U. Chgo., 1979-90, U. Ill., 1990—; clin. prof. psychiatry U. N.C., Chapel Hill, 1992—; dir. liaison and consultation svcs. dept. psychiatry Michael Reese Hosp., Chgo., 1979-87, chmn., 1987-92; assoc. attending physician N.C. Meml. Hosp., Chapel Hill, 1952-62, attending physician, 1962-67; cons. Watts Hosp., Durham, 1952-67, VA Hosp., Fayetteville, N.C., 1956-67, Eastern State Hosp., Williamsburg, Va., 1971—, VA Hosp., Salem. Va., 1969-79, mem. deans com., 1971-77; spl. rsch. fellow Inst. Psychiatry, U. London, 1963-64, Fogarty internat. rsch. fellow, 1976-77, U.S.-USSR and Romania health exch. fellow, 1978. Rev. editor Psychosomatic Medicine, 1958-70; assoc. editor Psychiatry, 1970-92. Mem. small grants com. NIMH, 1958-62; mem. nursing rsch. study sect. NIH, 1965-67; mem. Gov.'s Commn. Mental, Indigent and Geriatric Patients, 1968-72; mem. rsch. evaluation com. Va. Dept. Mental Hygiene and Hosps., 1970-73; mem. behavioral sci. test com. Nat. Bd. Med. Examiners, 1970-73. Served as capt. M.C., AUS, 1948-50. Fellow Am. Coll. Psychoanalysts (charter bd. regents 1979-81, treas. 1989-91, pres.-elect 1992, pres. 1994), Am. Psychiat. Assn.; mem. AAUP, Am. Psychosomatic Soc. (mem. coun. 1959), AMA, Group for Advancement Psychiatry (bd. dirs. 1987-89), Assn. Am. Med. Colls. (coun. acad. socs. 1973-78), Am. Psychoanalytic Assn., Am. Coll. Psychiatrists, AAAS, Va. Psychoanalytic Soc., Washington Psychoanalytic Soc., Chgo. Psychoanalytic Soc., N.C. Psychoanalytic Soc., Ill. Psychiat. Soc. (coun. 1981-82, pres.-elect 1987, pres. 1988-90), Soc. Neurosci., Am. Assn. Chmn. Depts. Psychiatry (sec.-treas. 1971-73, pres. 1974-75), Sleep Rsch. Soc., Nat. Bd. Med. Examiners (exam. com. 1983-87), Phi Beta Kappa, Sigma Xi, Alpha Omega Alpha. Address: 405 Deming Rd Chapel Hill NC 27514-3207

HAWKINS, DENNIS PATRICK, hospital administrator; b. Shoals, Ind., Mar. 25, 1945; s. Samuel Raymond and Thelma Marinda (Cessna) H.; m. Betty Lou Allen, Oct. 18, 1963; children: Patrick Alan, Miranda Jane. Credit mgr. Sears, Roebuck and Co., Greenwood, Ind., 1967-85; mgr. consumer rels. Community Hosps., Indpls., 1985-86; dir. bus. affairs AMI Culver Union Hosp., Crawfordsville, Ind., 1986-89; dir. patient acctg. Wilcox Meml. Hosp., Lihue, Hawaii, 1989-91; patient acctg. dir. S.W. Med. Ctr., Liberal, Kans., 1991—. Bd. dirs. 1st Christian Ch., Liberal, 1992—, Baker Arts Ctr., 1994—, S.W. Kans. Humane Soc., 1994—. Mem. Healthcare Fin. Mgmt. Assn. (bd. dirs. Sunflower chpt., 1996—), Am. Guild Patient Acctg. Mgrs., Kans. Assn. Patient Account Mgrs. (bd. dirs. 1993-95). Home: PO Box 765 Liberal KS 67905-0765

HAWKINS, NAOMI RUTH, nurse; b. Ft. Smith, Ark., Mar. 8, 1947; d. William Oscar and Sallie Inez (Reynolds) H. BS in Nursing, U. Cen. Ark., 1974. RN, Ark.; cert. pediatric nurse practitioner, Ark. Nurse practitioner Booneville (Ark.) Med. Clinic, 1975-78; lic. practical nurse Greenhurst Nursing Home, Charleston, Ark., 1967-73, RN, 1973-75; pediatric nurse practitioner Ark. Dept. Health, Paris, Ark., 1978—. Fellow Nat. Assn. Pediatric Nurse Assocs. and Practitioners; mem. Ark. Assn. Pediatric Nurse Assocs. and Practitioners, Am. Assn. Christian Counselors, Pub. Health Nurses Assn. Ark., Ark. State Employees Assn. Democrat. Baptist. Home: RR 2 Box 93 Charleston AR 72933-9418 Office: 102 E Academy St Paris AR 72855-4432

HAWKINS, RANDALL A., radiologist; b. Santa Barbara, Calif., Nov. 13, 1949; m. Cynthia Jacquiline Tsang, July 13, 1981; children: James, Julia. AB, Occidental Coll., 1971; MD, U. Calif., Irvine, 1975; MS, UCLA, 1981, PhD, 1985. Diplomate Am. Bd. Radiology, Am. Bd. Nuclear Medicine. From asst. prof. to assoc. prof. UCLA, 1981-93; prof., vice chmn. dept. radiology U. Calif. San Francisco, 1993—. Grantee NIH, 1981—. Office: UCSF 505 Parnassus Ave San Francisco CA 94143

HAWKINS, REGINA ANNETTE KEENER W., critical care nurse; b. Burnsville, N.C., Jan. 17, 1955; d. Jack Lester and Vera Alice (McMahan) Keener; children: Charles Mark, Alice Pauline; m. William Darryl Hawkins, June 19, 1989. AA in Nursing, Asheville-Buncombe Tech. Coll., 1975; BSN, Western Carolina U., 1984. RN, N.C.; cert. CCRN; cert. BCLS instr., ACLS. Charge nurse Haywood County Hosp., Waynesville, N.C., 1975-78; house supr. Canton (N.C.) Nursing Hosp., 1978-81, dir. nursing, 1981-84; charge nurse Meml. Mission Hosp., Asheville, N.C., 1984—; instr. BCLS. Mem. AACN, Nat. Assn. Pro-Life Nurses, Haywood Pro-Life Assn., N.C. Nurses for Life. Baptist. Home: 116 Overlook Dr Waynesville NC 28786-5002

HAWKINS, ROBERT LEE, health facility administrator; b. Denver, Feb. 18, 1938; s. Isom and Bessie M. (Hugley) H.; m. Ann Sharon Hoy, Apr. 28, 1973; children: Robert, Jeanne, Julia, Rose. AA, Pueblo Jr. Coll., 1958; BS, So. Colo. State Coll., 1965; MSW, U. Denver, 1967. Psychiat. technician Colo. State Hosp., Pueblo, 1956-58, 1962-63, occupl. therapist asst., 1964-65, clin. adminstr. psychiat. team, 1969-75, dir. cmty. svcs., 1975-92, asst. supt. clin. svcs., 1992—, supr. vol. services, 1975—, mem. budget com., 1975—; asst. supt. clin. svcs., 1992—; counselor (part-time) Family Svc. Agy., Pueblo, 1968-69, exec. dir., 1969-70; mem. faculty U. So. Colo., 1968-75; ptnr. Human Resource Devel., Inc., 1970-75; mem. Nat. Adv. Com. on Instnl. Quality and Integrity, U.S. Dept. Edn., Washington, 1993—. Mem. Pueblo Positive Action Com., 1970; chmn. adv. bd. Pueblo Sangre de Cristo Day Care Center, 1969-72; chmn. Gov.'s So. Area Adv. Council of Employment Service, 1975-76, chmn. Pueblo's City CSC, 1976-77, Pueblo Cmty. Corrections, 1985-87, Pueblo Civil Svc. Commn., 1988—; commr. Pueblo Housing Authority, 1986—, Colo. Commn. Higher Edn., 1987—, USED Commn. for Ednl. Quality & Integrity, 1993—; mem. gov's. adv. com. Mental Health Stds., 1981—; mem. Colo. Juvenile Parole Bd., 1977; bd. dirs. Pueblo United Fund, 1969-74, pres., 1973; bd. dirs. Pueblo Community Orgn., 1974-76, Spanish Peaks Mental Health Center, 1976—, Neighborhood Health Center, 1977-79, Pueblo Community Corrections, 1983—, Pueblo Legal Svcs., 1983—; mem. Pueblo Colo. 2010 Commn., 1994—, adv. com. YWCA, 1994—, Healthy Pueblo 2000 Task Force, 1993—. Bd. dirs. Posada Shelter for Homeless, 1990—, Boys Girls club, 1991—, ARC, 1994—, pres., 1994—. With U.S. Army 1958-62. Mem. Nat. Assn. Social Workers (nominating com. 1973-76), ACLU (dir. Pueblo chpt. 1980—), NAACP, Broadway Theatre Guild. Democrat. Methodist. Mem. Kiwanis. Home: 520 Gaylord Ave Pueblo CO 81004-1312 Office: Colo State Hosp 1600 W 24th St Pueblo CO 81003-1411

HAWKS, AL NELSON, physician; b. Winston-Salem, N.C., Jan. 17, 1954; s. Al N. Sr. and Sadie B. (Robertson) H.; m. Susan E. Royals, Dec. 17, 1977; children: Stephanie, Matthew, Melissa. AA, Surry C.C., Dobson, N.C., 1973; BS, N.C. State U., 1975; MD, Bowman Gray U., 1979. Diplomate Am. Bd. Family Practice. Resident St. Vincent's Med. Ctr., Jacksonville, Fla., 1979-82; ptnr. High Point (N.C.) Family Practice, 1982—; chmn. bd. Cornerstone Health Care PA, High Point, 1995—; chief of staff High Point Regional Hosp., 1994-95. Bd. dirs. Camp Cheerio YMCA, High Point, Wesley Meml. Meth. Ch., String and Splinter Club. Fellow Am. Acad. Family Physicians (dist. dir. N.C. chpt. 1995-96); mem. Am. Coll. Physician Execs., Alpha Omega Alpha. Republican. Home: 1310 Overland Dr High Point NC 27262 Office: High Point Family Practice 312 N Elm St High Point NC 27262

HAWKS, JANE ESTHER HOKANSON, nursing educator; b. Sac City, Iowa, Apr. 8, 1955; d. Charles Wesley and Esther Pearl (Langbein) Hokanson; m. Edward Harold Hawks, May 24, 1980; 1 child, Jennifer Jane. BSN magna cum laude, St. Olaf Coll., 1977; postgrad., Iowa State U., 1978-79; MSN magna cum laude, U. Nebr., 1981; D in Nursing Sci. summa cum laude, Widener U., 1993. RN, Iowa, Nebr., Minn.; cert. med.-surg. nurse ANA. Nurse Rochester (Minn.) Meth. Hosp., 1976, 77-78; instr. Morningside Coll., Sioux City, Iowa, 1978-79, Jennie Edmundson Sch. Nursing, Council Bluffs, Iowa, 1979-81; instr., asst. prof. Coll. Nursing U. Nebr., Omaha, 1981-86; supr. pvt. duty nursing Family Home Care, Omaha, 1986; instr. Jennie Edmundson Sch. Nursing, Council Bluffs, 1986-83; instr. NCLEX rev. course Stanley H. Kaplan Ednl. Ctr., Omaha, 1986-89; asst. prof. nursing Clarkson Coll., Omaha, 1988-91, assoc. prof., 1991-92; asst. prof. nursing Midland Luth. Coll., Fremont, Nebr., 1992—; mem. Senator Harkin's Nursing Adv. Com., 1989—; mem. edn. com. Omaha Hospice Orgn., 1985-86; bd. dirs. Health Fair Midlands, 1988-95, vice chmn., 1992-94, chmn., 1994-95. Asst. editor Urologic Nursing, 1990—, mem. editorial com., 1988-90; co-author 2 books, several book chpts.; contbr. articles to profl. jours. Bd. dirs. Midwest ARC Regional Blood Svcs., 1992—, sec.-treas., 1995—, mem. nominations com. 1991-94, tissue donor, med. adv. exec. and fin. coms., 1993—; mem. Iowa Gov.'s Task Force on Long Term Care, 1984-85; bd. dirs. Pottawattamie County chpt. ARC, 1987-93, chmn., 1991-92, AIDS edn. speaker, 1988-93, mem. exec. com., 1991-93, mem. steering com., 1991-93, chmn. nursing and health com., 1988-93, facilitator bd. retreat, 1990. Recipient pub. awareness award Pottawattamie County chpt. ARC, 1988, Vol. of Yr. award Council Bluffs, 1989; scholar Evang. Luth. Ch. Am. div. Higher Edn., 1993, Am. Legion 40 and 8, 1991-92, Nurses Ednl. Funds, Inc., N.Y.C., 1991-92; nursing diagnosis rsch. grantee Midwest Nursing Diagnosis Task Force, 1989. Mem. AAUP, ANA, AACN, N. Am. Nursing Diagnosis Assn., Soc. Urologic Nurses and Assocs., Iowa Nurses Found. (bd.dirs., v.p. 1985-90, grant reviewer 1987-90), Iowa Nurses Assn. (state ethics com. 1985-86, state nursing edn. commn. 1989-93, chmn. state nursing rsch. com. 1994—, bd. dirs. dist. 9 1985-91, 9th Dist. Nurse of Yr. award 1983), Sigma Theta Tau (faculty counselor Theta Omega chpt., Leadership award 1996). Lutheran. Home: 514 North St Underwood IA 51576 Office: Midland Luth Coll 900 N Clarkson St Fremont NE 68025-4254

HAWLEY, JOHN L., JR., mental health facility administrator, psychologist; b. Naha, Okinawa, Apr. 2, 1953; naturalized citizen, 1953; s. John L. and Hazel M. (Kinny) H.;m. Cythia Lea Hibbs, Aug. 2, 1975 (div. Jan. 1984); m. Mary Ellen Duzan, Feb. 29, 1992. BA, George Mason U., 1975, MA, 1977; PhD, U. Tenn., 1982. Lic. psychologist, Va. Psychologist Alexandria (Va.) Community Mental Health Ctr., 1980-81, N.W. Community Mental Health Ctr., Reston, Va., 1981-85, Family Counseling Ctr., Reston, 1983-85, Springwood Psychiat. Inst., Leesburg, Va., 1985—; clin. dir. Reston Counseling Ctr., 1985—. Recipient Univ. Svc. award George Mason U., 1975. Mem. APA, Va. Psychol. Assn., Va. Acad. Clin. Psychologists, U. Tenn. Pres.'s Club. Office: Reston Counseling Ctr 131 Elden St Ste 206 Herndon VA 22070-4810

HAWLEY, LINDA JEAN, nurse educator and practitioner; b. Springfield, Mo., Nov. 1, 1951; d. Charles Cornell and Elizabeth Ruth (Anderson) Roberts. BSN, Baylor U., 1973; MSN, Tex. Woman's U., 1978, postgrad., 1988—. RN, Tex.; CNS; FNP; ANCC; cert. addictions RN. Nurse VA Hosp., San Antonio, Houston, Dallas, Fayetteville, Ark., 1973-76; specialist faculty mem., dir. family & adult/geriatric nurse practitioner program U. Tex., Arlington, 1978—; dir. health svcs. Lone Star Steel, Dallas, 1985-87; nurse practitioner Tarrant County Mental Health Mental Retardation, Ft. Worth, 1987—, Salvation Army, Ft. Worth, occupl. health unit USPHS, Ft. Worth. Author: Decision Making in Community Health Nursing, 1978. Recipient PACE award Am. Cancer Soc. Mem. ANA, Am. Assn. Nurse Practitioner Faculty, Tex. Nurses Assn. (One of 100 Gt. Nurses award 1995), Tex. Nurse Practitioners, North Tex. Nurse Practitioners. Episcopalian. Home: 1209 Brittany Ln Arlington TX 76013 Office: U Tex PO Box 19407 Arlington TX 76019

HAWTHORNE, DONALD BRUCE, health care executive; b. L.A., Dec. 31, 1955; s. Donald Claire and Elene Ruth (Roussey) H.; m. Dianne M. Ritter, Oct. 7, 1989; children: Meghan Elizabeth, Sarah Katherine. BS, Harvey Mudd Coll., 1977; MBA, Stanford U., 1981. Fin. planner Westinghouse Electric Corp., Sunnyvale, Calif., 1978-79; fin. analyst, sr. fin. analyst treasury dept. Arco, L.A., 1981-83; sr. fin. analyst corp. planning Syntex Corp., Palo Alto, Calif., 1983-84; fin. planning mgr. ophthalmics divsn. Syntex Corp., Phoenix, 1984-85, divsn. contr., 1985; mgr. fin. and adminstrn. Genelabs Inc., Redwood City, Calif., 1985-87; dir. fin. Genelabs Inc, Redwood City, 1987-89, CFO, 1989-90; v.p. fin. and adminstrn , CFO Oclassen Pharms., Inc., 1990; CFO Biocircuits Corp., Sunnyvale, Calif., 1991—. Trustee Harvey Mudd Coll., Claremont, Calif., 1986-89, pres. student body, 1976-77. Mem. Harvey Mudd Coll. Alumni Assn. (bd. govs. 1981-87, treas. 1982-83, v.p. 1983-84, pres. 1984-86), Assn. Biosci. Fin. Officers (steering com. No. Calif. chpt. 1991-95, pres. 1995, co-chmn. 1992 nat. conf., chmn. 1993 nat. conf.), Pi Sigma Alpha. Republican. Roman Catholic. Home: 260 Windsor Dr San Carlos CA 94070-2822 Office: Biocircuits Corp 1324 Chesapeake Ter Sunnyvale CA 94089-1100

HAWTHORNE, TONYA-KAE, family physician; b. Rockford, Ill., June 17, 1961; d. James and Carla Louise (Head) H. BA, Southeastern Coll., 1983; DO, Kirksville (Mo.) Coll. Osteo., 1992. Emergency med. tech. Lakeland (Fla.) Vol. Dept., 1982-83; youth pastor First Assembly of God, Keystone Heights, Fla., 1983-84; EKG tech. Swedish Am. Hosp., Rockford, 1985-87; emergency physician Sun Coast Hosp., Largo, Fla., 1995—. Mem. Am. Osteopath. Assn., Am. Coll. Osteopathic Family Practitioners. Republican. Office: Enterprise Profl Ctr Largo FL

HAWVER, DENNIS ARTHUR, psychological consultant; b. Millbury, Ohio, Apr. 9, 1940; s. Carl Fullerton and Frances Jewell (Renick) H.; m. Anne M. Augustyn, 1961 (div. Oct. 1974); children: Timothy, Laura, Derek; m. Judith M. Anderson, Jan. 28, 1977. B.A., U. Akron, 1964, M.A., 1965; Ph.D., Temple U., 1970. Dir. research Temple U., Phila., 1964-70, instr. Grad. Sch., 1968-70, internal cons., 1964-70; mng. ptnr. Cardall Assocs., Princeton, N.J., 1970-72; nat. program dir. The RHR Inst., N.Y.C., 1972-80; pres. The Hawver Group, N.Y.C. and Princeton, 1980—. Author: How to Improve Your Negotiating Skills, 1983; contbr. to bus. and profl. jours.; developer research and tng. programs; internat. cons. in exec. identification and devel. and bus. negotiations. Mem. Am. Psychol. Assn., Soc. Indsl. and Organizational Psychology, Internat. Assn. Applied Psychology, Inst. Mgmt. Cons. (CMC), Soc. Assessment Systems Practitioners, Internat. Personnel Mgmt. Assn. Assessment Council, Inst. Mgmt. Cons. Office: Hawver Group 2 Research Way Princeton NJ 08540

HAY, EDWARD LAROCHE, orthopaedic surgeon; b. Charleston, S.C., Jan. 8, 1934; s. Henry Muhler and Pauline Grimbel (Parrott) H.; m. Temple Wright, June 25, 1960; children: Edward L. Jr., Nantce Chase, Temple Wright. BS, Presbyn. Coll., Clinton, S.C., 1956; MD, Med. Coll. S.C., Charleston, 1960. Diplomate Am. Bd. Orthopaedic Surgeons, Am. Soc. for Surgery of Hand, cert. added qualifications in surgery of hand. Intern Grady Meml. Hosp., Emory U. Sch. Medicine, Atlanta, 1960-61; orthopaedic resident Med. U. Hosp. S.C., 1963-67; fellow surgery of hand U. Louisville, 1967; pvt. practice Hand Surgery Ctr. of Charleston, 1968—; clin. asst. in orthopadic surgery Med. U. S.C., 1968—; cons. physician orthopaedic surgery, surgery of hand VA Hosp., 1968—, U.S. Naval Hosp., 1968—; mem. staff Roper Hosp., Charleston, St. Francis Xavier Hosp., Charleston, Med. U. Hosp., Charleston, Baker Hosp., Charleston. Contbr. articles to profl. jours. Mem. AMA, Am. Soc. Surgery of Hand, Am. Acad. Orthopaedic Surgeons, Med. Soc. S.C., Charleston County Med. Soc. Office: Hand Surgery Ctr Charleston Parkshore Centre 1 Poston Rd Ste 200 Charleston SC 29407

HAY, ELIZABETH DEXTER, embryology researcher, educator; b. St. Augustine, Fla., Apr. 2, 1927; d. Isaac Morris and Lucille (Lynn) H. AB, Smith Coll., 1948; MA (hon.), Harvard U., 1964; ScD (hon.), Smith Coll., 1973, Trinity Coll., 1989; MD, Johns Hopkins U., 1952, LHD (hon.), 1990. Intern in internal medicine Johns Hopkins Hosp., Balt., 1952-53; instr. anatomy Johns Hopkins U. Med. Sch., Balt., 1953-56, asst. prof., 1956-57; asst. prof. Cornell U. Med. Sch., N.Y.C., 1957-60; asst. prof. Harvard Med. Sch., Boston, 1960-64, Louise Foote Pfeiffer assoc. prof., 1964-69, Louise Foote Pfeiffer prof. embryology, 1969—, chmn. dept. anatomy and cellular biology, 1975-93; prof. dept. cell biology, 1993—; cons. cell biology sect. NIH, 1965-69; mem. adv. coun. Nat. Inst. Gen. Med. Sci., NIH, 1978-81; mem. sci. adv. bd. Whitney Marine Lab., U. Fla., 1982-86; mem. adv. coun. Johns Hopkins Sch. Medicine, 1982—; chairperson bd. sci. counselors Nat. Inst. Dental Rsch., NIH, 1984-86; mem. bd. sci. counselors Nat. Inst. Environ. Health Sci., NIH, 1990-93. Author: Regeneration, 1966; (with J.P. Revel) Fine Structure of the Developing Avian Cornea, 1969; editor: Cell Biology of Extracellular Matrix, 1981, 2d edit., 1991; editor-in-chief Developmental Biology Jour., 1971-75; contbr. articles to profl. jours. Mem. Scientists Task Force of Congressman Barney Frank, Massach, 1982-92. Recipient Disting. Achievement award N.Y. Hosp.-Cornell Med. Ctrl. Alumni Coun., 1985, award for vision rsch. Alcon, 1988, Excellence in Sci. award Fedn. Am. Socs. Exptl. Biology. Mem. Soc. Devel. Biology (pres. 1973-74), Am. Soc. Cell Biology (pres. 1976-77, legis. alert com. 1982—, E.B. Wilson award 1989), Am. Assn. Anatomists (pres. 1981-82, legis. alert com. 1982—, Centennial award 1987, Henry Gray award 1992), Am. Acad. Arts and Scis., Johns Hopkins Soc. Scholars, Nat. Acad. Sci., Inst. Medicine, Internat. Soc. Devel. Biologists (exec. bd. 1977), Boston Mycol. Club. Home: 14 Aberdeen Rd Weston MA 02193-1733 Office: Harvard Med Sch Dept Cell Biology 220 Longwood Ave Boston MA 02115-5701

HAY, RICHARD CARMAN, retired anesthesiologist; b. Queens, N.Y., June 9, 1921; s. Richard Carman and Frances Pauline (Woodbury) H.; B.S., U. Vt., 1944, M.D., 1946; m. Martha Fambrough, Mar. 2, 1957; children: Richard C., William W., Anne H., Sandra L., Bradford T., Holly K. Practice medicine, specializing in anesthesiology, Houston; ret., 1994. Served with M.C., U.S. Army, 1948-50. Mem. AMA, Tex. Med. Soc., Harris County Med. Soc., Am. Soc. Anesthesiologists, Tex. Soc. Anesthesiologists. Republican. Baptist. Office: 1102 Deerfield Rd Richmond TX 77469-6574

HAY, RICK VANCE, nuclear medicine physician; b. Hailey, Idaho, July 14, 1949; s. Richard and Mary (Griffith) H.; m. Helayne Sherman, Sept. 18, 1988. AB, U. Chgo., 1971, PhD, 1977, MD, 1978. Diplomate Nat. Bd. Med. Examiners, Am. Bd. Nuclear Medicine. Resident anatomic pathology U. Chgo. Hosps. and Clinics, 1978-81; rsch. fellow Biocenter U. Basel, Switzerland, 1981-84; asst. prof. dept. pathology U. Chgo., 1984-91, assoc. prof., 1991-92; clin. fellow in nuclear medicine U. Mich., Ann Arbor, 1992-94; staff physician St. John Hosp. and Med. Ctr., Detroit, 1994—, med. dir. Dept. of Nuclear Med., 1995—; cons. Nat. Heart, Lung and Blood Inst., Bethesda, Md., 1987—. Contbr. articles to profl. jours. Recipient Sheard-Sanford award Am. Soc. Clin. Pathologists, 1979, Nat. Rsch. Svc. award NIH, 1982-84. Mem. Am. Heart Assn. (fellow coun. on arteriosclerosis, coun. on cardiovasc. radiology, Louis N. Katz rsch. prize 1976), Am. Soc. for Investigative Pathology, Am. Soc. Nuclear Cardiology, Soc. Cardiovasc. Pathology, Soc. Nuclear Medicine, Am. Coll. Nuclear Physicians, Ctrl. Soc. Clin. Rsch., Phi Beta Kappa, Alpha Omega Alpha. Office: St John Hosp and Med Ctr 22101 Moross Rd Detroit MI 48236

HAYASHI, HAJIME, immunologist; b. Gifu, Japan, Aug. 26, 1927; came to U.S., 1955.; s. Sho and Masao Hayashi; m. Takeko Kochi, Dec. 21, 1962; children: Masako, Keiko. Diploma in veterinary medicine, Gifu U., 1948; BS, Mich. State U., 1957, MS, 1959, PhD, 1961. Grad. asst. Mich. State U., East Lansing, 1959-61; assoc. Henry Ford Hosp., Detroit, 1961-69; dir. immunology Henry Ford Hosp., 1969—; assoc. prof. Case Western Res. U., Cleve., 1994—. Contbr. articles to profl. jours. Recipient Difco award APHA, 1981. Fellow Am. Acad. Microbiology; mem. AAAS, APHA, Am. Soc. Histocompatibility Immunogenetics, Am. Soc. Microbiology (pres. Mich. br. 1991-92), Electron Microscopy Am., Soc. Analytical Cytology, Soc. Leukocyte Biology, Tissue Culture Assn., N.Y. Acad. Scis., Transplantation Soc. Mich. (adv. bd. 1987—), United Network for Organ Sharing, Sigma Xi. Home: 13322 Borgman Ave Huntington Wd MI 48070-1006 Office: Henry Ford Hosp 2799 W Grand Blvd Detroit MI 48202-2608

HAYASHI, KOZABURO, biomedical engineering educator; b. Nishinomiya, Hyogo, Japan, July 13, 1942; s. Kisaku and Hisako (Tsuchikawa) H.; m. Yoko Wada, Apr. 4, 1970; children: Izumi, Megumi. BA in Engring., Kyoto (Japan) U., 1965, MS in Engring., 1967, PhD, 1970. Rsch. assoc. dept. mech. engring. Kyoto U., 1970-76, rsch. assoc. dept. engring. sci., 1976-79; rsch. fellow dept. artificial organs Cleve. Clinic Found., 1976-78; head lab. cardiac dynamics Nat. Cardiovasc. Ctr. Rsch. Inst., Suita, Osaka, Japan, 1979-82, dept. dir., 1982-87; prof. Hokkaido U., Rsch. Inst. of Applied Electricity, Sapporo, Japan, 1987-93; prof. dept. mech. engring. Faculty Engring. Sci. Osaka U., 1992—. Editor: Progress A New Direction of Biomechanics, 1989, Data Book on Mechanical Properties of Living Cells, Tissues and Organs, 1996, Biomechanics--Functional Adaptation and Remodeling, 1996, Computational Biomechanics, 1996; assoc. editor Jour. Biomech. Engring., 1991—, Clin. Biomaterials, 1990-95, Biomed. Materials and Engring., 1990—. Recipient Japan Soc. Biomed. Engring. prize, 1979, Excellence in Rsch. award Am. Orthop. Soc. Sports Medicine, 1993—, Bioengring. Achievement award Japan Soc. Mech. Engring., 1993. Fellow Am. Inst. for Med. and Biol. Engring.; mem. ASME, World Com. for Biomechanics (sec. gen. 1990—), Internat. Soc. for Artificial Organs, Internat. Soc. Biorheology. Home: 3-44 Hagiwaradai-Nishi, Kawanishi 666, Japan Office: Osaka U, Dept Mech Engring, Faculty Engring Sci, Toyonaka Osaka 560, Japan

HAYASHIDA, MOTOI, psychiatrist, educator; b. Tokyo, Feb. 6, 1932; came to U.S., 1959; s. Toyoji and Takako Hayashida; m. Hiroko Nakagawa, July 16, 1960; children: Tetsu, Naoto. MD, Keio U., Tokyo, 1958, ScD, 1967. Diplomate Am. Bd. Psychiatry and Neurology. Rotating intern Hahnemann U. Hosp., Phila., 1959-60; resident in psychiatry Middletown (N.Y.) State Hosp., 1960-62, Phila. Gen. Hosp., 1962-64; chief alcoholism treatment unit VA Med. Ctr., Phila., 1982-86, sr. psychiatrist addictions treatment unit, 1986-93; dir. Nat. Inst. Alcoholism, Japan, 1993—; adj. prof. dept. psychiatry U. Pa., Phila., 1993—, asst. clin. prof. dept. psychiatry, 1974-88, assoc. clin. prof., 1988-93; hon. prof. dept. neuropsychiatry Keio U., Tokyo, 1993—; cons., speaker on alcoholism; psychiat. cons. Counseling Program N.J. Pa. Hosp., Marlton, N.J., 1986-93. Contbr. articles on alcoholism to med. jours. Recipient Meritorious Svc. award VA, 1987; Fulbright scholar, Tokyo, 1959-62. Mem. Am. Psychiat. Assn. (corresponding), Am. Soc. Addiction Medicine (cert.), N.Y. Acad. Scis., Japanese Med. Soc. Am. (bd. dirs.), Japan-U.S. Garioa/Fulbright Alumni Assn. (adv. coun.), Japanese Med. Soc. Alcohol Related Problems(chmn. bd. dirs. 1995—), Japanese Med. Soc. Alcohol Studeies, Japanese Psychiatric Soc. Alcoholism (mem. coun.). Office: 5-3-1 Nobi Yokosuka-shi, Kanagawa 239, Japan

HAYCOCK, CHRISTINE ELIZABETH, medical educator emeritus, health educator; b. Mt. Vernon, N.Y., Jan. 7, 1924; d. John B. and Madeline (Sears) H.; m. Sam Moskowitz, July 6, 1958. SB, U. Chgo., 1948; MD, SUNY, Bklyn., 1952; MA in Polit. Sci., Rutgers U., 1981. RN, N.J.; diplomate Am. Bd. Surgery. Intern Walter Reed Army Med. Ctr., Washington, 1952-53; resident in surgery St. Barnabas Med. Ctr., Newark, 1954-58, St. John's Episcopal Hosp., Bklyn., 1958-59; pvt. practice Newark, 1959-68; asst. prof. surgery, N.J. Med. Sch. U. Med. and Dentistry N.J.-N.J. Med. Sch., Newark, 1968-75; assoc. prof. surgery, N.J. Med. Sch. UMDNJ, Newark, 1975-89, prof. clin. surgery, 1989-92; prof. emeritus, 1992—; chief GYN Clinic, VA Hosp., East Orange, N.J. Trauma Soc.; pres. Med. Amature Radio Coun., 1981, bd. dirs. (Coun. award 1978); editorial bd. Jour. N.J. Med. Soc., 1979-95, The Physician and Sports Medicine, 1975—, The Main Event, 1987; adv. com. N.J. Phys. Conditioning of the Police Tng. Commn., 1984-96. Editor: Trauma and Pregnancy, 1985, Sports Medicine for the Athletic Female, 1980; contbr. articles to profl. jours. Chmn. bd. Essex County chpt. Am. Cancer Soc., West Orange, N.J., 1978-79, bd. mgrs.,

Livingston, N.J., 1962—, hon. life mem., 1992. With U.S. Army, 1947-86, col. Res. ret. Recipient Outstanding Alumnae award Bloomfield Coll., 1971, Res. Forces Achievement award, 1974, Distinguished Lecturer award Downstate Med. Ctr., 1976, Dr. Frank L. Babbott Meml. award SUNY Alumni Assn., 1982, Pres. Honor Citation, N.J. Assn. Phys. Edn. and Health Tchrs., 1982, Presdl. Citation, N.J. Assn. for Health, Phys. Edn. and Recreation, 1984, Med. Bd. Svc. award Newark City Hosp., 1986; grantee Abbott Labs, 1981-82. Fellow ACS (hon., life, N.J. com. on trauma 1970-91), Am. Coll. Sports Medicine (trustee 1978-80), Photog. Soc. Am. (chmn. video/motion picture divsn. 1993-95); mem. AMA, Am. Med. Women's Assn. (bd. dirs. 1976-86, pres. 1980, hosp. assn. com. 1985—, Silver Medallion award 1980), Zonta Internat., Assn. Women Surgeons (treas. 1989-91, chair found. com. 1991-95, sec. 1995—, Disting. Surgeon award 1990), N.J. Women's Assn. (pres. 1976, treas. 1989-92, Woman of Yr. 19876), Amateur Radio Relay League. Republican. Home: 361 Roseville Ave Newark NJ 07107-1721

HAYDEN, JAMES WALWORTH, emergency physician, medical director; b. Gardner, Ma., Apr. 25, 1942; s. Robert Hawley and Dorothea Wallace (Ward) H.; m. Lauren Shanks, Dec. 10, 1982; children: David Ward, Mark Stevenson. BS in Chemistry, U. N.C., 1963; PhD in Organic Chemistry, U. Kans., 1968; MD, U. Tex., Houston, 1977. Bd. cert. Am. Bd. Forensic Examiners, Am. Bd. Med. Examiners; cert. Am. Assn. Med. Rev. Officers, Am. Soc. Addiction Medicine; cert. ACLS provider and instr., advanced trauma life support provider, BLS instr., pediat. advanced life support provider. Rsch. chemist Shell Devel. Co., Emeryville Rsch. Ctr., Houston, 1968-72; asst. to the dir. Inst. Clin. Toxicology, Houston, 1973-75; sr. rsch. assoc. U. Tex. Med. Sch., Houston, 1975-76; intern and resident Baylor Coll. Medicine, Houston, 1977-78; program physician Inst. Clin. Toxicology Ctrl. Methadone Clinic, Houston, 1978-79, med. dir., 1979-80; emergency dept. physician Gulf Coast Emergency Physicians, St. Luke's Episcopal Hosp., Houston, 1978-79, Houston Emergency Physicians Assocs., Meml. Hosp. Sys., Houston, 1979-80; med. dir. Chem. Dependence Assocs. and Huntsville (Tex.) Clinic, Houston, 1980-87; emergency dept. physician S.E. Tex. Emergency Physicians, West Houston Med. Ctr., 1986-87, Newport (Wash.) Cmty. Hosp., 1989-90; exec. dir. Chem. Dependence Assocs., Priest River, Idaho, 1987—; emergency dept. physician Emergency Physician Svcs., Holy Family Hosp., Spokane, Wash., 1989—; assoc. med. dir., med. rev. officer Cascade Transp. Svcs., Spokane, 1994—; adj. instr. dept. pharmacology U. Tex. Med. Sch., Houston, 1973-77, adj. asst. prof. dept. pharmacology, 1981-88, clin. instr. family practice and cmty. medicine, 1981-88; presenter in field. Contbr. articles to profl. jours. Fellow Am. Acad. Family Physicians; mem. Am. Coll. Emergency Physicians, Assn. Emergency Physicians, Am. Soc. Addiction Medicine, Am. Assn. Med. Rev. Officers, Tex. Med. Assn., Idaho Med. Assn., Bonner County Med. Soc., Wilderness Med. Soc. Home: PO Box 40 Rt 1 Box 111 Priest River ID 83856 Office: Chem Dependence Assocs PO Box 40 Priest River ID 83856

HAYES, ALBERTA PHYLLIS WILDRICK, retired health service executive; b. Blakeslee, Pa., May 31, 1918; d. William and Maude (Robbins) Wildrick; diploma Wilkes Barre Gen. Hosp. Sch. Nursing, 1938-41; student Wilkes Coll., 1953-54, Pa. State U., 1969—; m. Glenmore Burton Hayes, Oct. 9, 1942; children: Glenmore Rolland, William Bruce. Nurse, Monroe County Gen. Hosp., East Stroudsburg, Pa., 1941-44; pvt. duty nurse, 1944-56; with White Haven (Pa.) Center, 1956-82, dir. residential services, 1966-82, ret., 1982. Pres. Tobyhanna Twp. Sch. PTA, 1948-49, Top-o-Pocono Women of Rotary, 1975-76; nurse ARC, 1955; adv. council Luzerne County Foster Grandparent Program, 1977—, Health Services Keystone Job Corps, Drums, Pa., 1977—; active Tobyhana Twp. Zoning Hearing Bd., Pocono Pines, Pa.; coord. Pocono Mountain Chpt. Choral Group, 1993—; chmn. bd. trustees Blakeslee United Meth. Ch. Mem. Am. Assn. Mental Deficiency, Am. Legion Aux. (unit pres. 1946-47), Ea. Star (Lehigh chpt.). Club: Pocono Mountains Women's (Blakeslee, sec. 1993, past pres.). Home: PO Box 11 Blakeslee PA 18610-0011

HAYES, ANDREW WALLACE, II, consumer products company executive; b. Corning, Ark., Aug. 21, 1939; s. Andrew Wallace and Helen (Latimer) H.; m. Sandra Smith, Dec. 28, 1963; children: Andrew Wallace III, Helen Cathleen, Benjamin Bailey. AB, Emory U., 1961; MS, Auburn U., 1964, PhD, 1967. Diplomate Am. Bd. Toxicology, Am. Bd. Forensic Medicine; cert. nutrition specialist. NIH postdoctoral fellow, rsch. assoc. div. toxicology Vanderbilt U. Sch. Med., Nashville, 1966-68; asst. prof. dept. microbiology U. Ala., Tuscaloosa, 1968-71, assoc. prof. dept. microbiology, 1971-75, prof. depts. microbiology and biochemistry, 1975; assoc. prof. dept. pharmacology and toxicology U. Miss. Med. Ctr., Jackson, 1975-76, prof. dept. pharmacology and toxicology, 1976-80, program dir. NIEHS tng. program in environ. toxicology, 1977-80; dir. toxicology rsch. Rohm and Haas Co., Spring House, Pa., 1980-84; dir. regulatory affairs, agrl. chemicals (worldwide) Rohm and Haas Co., Phila., 1984; corp. toxicologist RJR Nabisco Inc., Winston-Salem, N.C., 1984; corp. toxicologist, dir. biochem. and biobehavioral rsch., Bowman Gray Tech. Ctr. R.J. Reynolds Tobacco Co., Winston-Salem, N.C., 1984-86, corp. toxicologist, group dir. biochem. and biobehavioral rsch., 1986-87, corp. toxicologist, v.p. biochem. and biobehavioral rsch., 1987-92; prof. Bowman Gray Sch. Medicine Wake Forest U., Winston-Salem, 1992; v.p. corp. product integrity The Gillette Co., Boston, 1993—; vis. sr. scientist biochemistry dept. Cen. Vet. Lab., New Haw, Weybridge, Surrey, Eng., 1977; disting. lectr. U. Calif., 1979; vis. prof. dept. vet. pub. health, Tex. A&M U., 1979—; rsch. prof. dept. physiology and biophysics, Sch. Dentistry, Temple U., 1981-84, Phila. Coll. Pharmacy and Sci., 1982-84, dept. medicine and toxicology program Duke U., 1986—, dept. pharmacology and toxicology Med. Coll. Va., 1987—, Sch. Vet. Med., Va. Poly. Inst., 1988—, Sch. Pub. Health U. Mass, Armherst, 1994—; mem. faculty Wayne State U., 1987; collaborator Interlab. Collaborative Study for Aflatoxin B1, FDA, 1977, Aflatoxin Check Sample Survey, Internat. Agy. Rsch. on Cancer, 1978; mem. Target Organ Toxicity Conf. Steering Com., 1978-88, Panel on Equivalent Safety Concept of Maritime Hazardous Materials, Nat. Materials Adv. Bd., NAS, 1979-82, Safe Drinking Water Com., Bd. Toxicology and Environ. Health Hazards, NAS, 1979-81, Environ. Health Scis. Rev. Com. NIEHS, 1981-85, Sci. Program Com., Internat. Congress Toxicology, 1982-83, Testing Task Group, CMA, 1981-84, Chem. Systems Lab. Toxin Def. Group Rev. Panel, U.S. Army, 1982, TDB/CIS User Assessment Panel Life Scis. Rsch. Office, FASEB, Bethesda, Md., 1982; alt. del. Internat. Union Toxicology, 1982-83; advisor U.S. Army Med. Command, 1982-84; del. Internat. Union Toxicology, 1984-86; cons. Walter Reed Army Inst. Rsch., 1984-86; mem. Selection Com. Immunotoxicology Found., 1986, Commn. on communications, Internat. Union Toxicology, 1986-89, Program Com., Toxicology Forum, 1986-87, toxicology adv. bd. Raven Press, N.Y.C., 1982-96;. Author: Mycotoxin Teratogenicity, 1981; editor: Toxicology of the Eye, Ear and Other Special Senses, 1985, Extrapolation of Dosimetric Relationships for Inhaled Particles and Gases, 1989, Principles and Methods of Toxicology, 3d edit., 1994, Human and Experimental Toxicology, 1993—; co-author: Loomis's Essentials of Toxicology, 4th edit., 1996; co-editor: Target Organ Toxicity Series, 1989—; founding editor Comments of Toxicology, 1986—; assoc. editor Regulatory Toxicology and Pharmacology, 1986—, Toxicology and Applied Pharmacology, 1980, editor, 1981-86, mem. editl. bd., 1978-80; mem. editl. bd. Archives Environ. Contamination and Toxicology, 1987—, Environ. Toxin Series, 1987—, Toxicology, 1978-83, Jour. Toxicology and Environ. Health, 1979—, Food and Chem. Toxicology, 1987—; mem. editl. coun. Toxicon, 1980-90; contbr. articles to profl. jours., chpts. to books. Mem. adv. coun. Auburn U., 1987—, nat. coun. Fla. Coll., 1980—; trustee Am. Assn. n of Lab. Animal Care, Chgo., 1984-89. Named one of Outstanding Young Men of Am., 1972; named Exec. of Yr. Winston-Salem chpt. Profl. Secs. Internat., 1989-90; recipient Cert. Merit, EPA, 1981, Rsch. Career Devel. award NIH, 1973-78. Fellow Acad. Toxicological Scis. (bd. dirs. 1993-96); mem. Soc. Toxicology (co-chmn. tech. com. 1978, chmn. 1978-79, pres. Mid-Atlantic chpt. 1983-84, v.p. mech. sect., 1981-82, 82-83), Am. Soc. Pharmacology and Exptl. Therapeutics (chmn. com. on environ. pharmacology 1981-82, coun. sect. toxicology), Am. Chem. Soc. (com. on chemistry and pub. affairs task force on TSCA Interagy. Testing Com.'s Preliminary List of Chem. Substances, 1977-80), Am. Inst. Nutrition, Am. Soc. for Microbiology (environ. microbiology com. 1975-76), Internat. Union Pharmacology (sect. on toxicology), Internat. Soc. Regulatory Toxicology and Pharmacology, Sigma Xi. Mem. Ch. of Christ. Office: The Gillette Co Corp Product Integrity Prudential Towers Bldg Boston MA 02199

HAYES, BRIAN EUGENE, orthopedic surgeon; b. Camp Atterbury, Ind., June 24, 1945; s. Edmond Mark and Elma Rose (Chappelle) H.; m. Linda Anne Curley, Apr. 28, 1979; children: Rain Julia, Natalie. BS, U.S. Mil. Acad., 1967; MD, U. Tex., San Antonio, 1976. Diplomate Am. Bd. Orthop. Surgeons. Intern Madigan Army Hosp., Tacoma, Wash., 1976-77; resident in orthop. Madigan Army Hosp., 1978-81, staff orthopedist, 1986-88; chief of orthopedics 121 Evac Hosp., Seoul, Republic of Korea, 1982-84, Womack Army Hosp., Ft. Madigan, N.C., 1984-86; staff orthopedist Mercy Med. Ctr., Roseburg, Oreg., 1988—, Douglas Cmty. Hosp., Roseburg, 1988—. Col. U.S. Army, 1967-88. Recipient multiple medals U.S. Army, 1967-88. Mem. Douglas County Med. Soc. (pres. 1996). Roman Catholic. Office: 1813 W Harvard Ste 201 Roseburg OR 97470

HAYES, CLAUDE QUINTEN CHRISTOPHER, research scientist; b. N.Y.C., Nov. 15, 1945; s. Claude and Celestine (Stanley) H. BA in Chemistry and Geol. Sci., Columbia U., 1971, postgrad., 1972-73; postgrad., N.Y. Law Sch., 1973-75; JD, Western State Law Sch., 1978. Cert. community coll. tchr. earth scis., phys. sci., law, Calif. Tech. writer Burroughs Corp., San Diego, 1978-79; instr. phys. scis. Nat. U., San Diego, 1980-81; instr. bus. law, earth scis. Miramar Coll., 1978-82; sr. systems analyst Gen. Dynamics Convair, 1979-80, advanced mfg. technologist, sr. engr., 1980-81; pvt. practice sci. and tech. cons. Calif., 1979—; instr. phys. sci., phys. geography, bus. law San Diego Community Coll. Dist., 1976-82, 85-90; U.S. Dept. Def. contractor Def. Nuclear Agy., Strategic Def. Initiative Agy., USAF, Def. Advance Rsch. Projects Agy., 1986—, U.S. Army, 1991—; adj. prof. phys. chemistry San Diego State U., 1986-87; bus. and computer sci. def. rsch. contractor to Maxwell Labs., Naval Ocean Sys. Ctr.; tech. cons. Pizza Hut, Inc., Carts of Colo., Smiths Industries. Contbr. articles to profl. jours.; patentee in field. Mem. Am. Chem. Soc., N.Y. Acad. Sci., Am. Inst. Aero. and Astronautics. Home and office: 3737 3rd Ave Apt 308 San Diego CA 92103-4133

HAYES, DAVID ALLEN, internist; b. Roanoke, Va., Aug. 16, 1946; s. Albert A. and Frances (Bagby) H.; m. Katherine Ann Lilly, Aug. 28, 1971; children: Mathew, Allen, Emily Katherine. BS in Chemistry, Roanoke Coll., Salem, Va., 1968; MD, U. Va., 1972. Diplomate Am. Bd. Internal Medicine, Am. Bd. Med. Specialties. Intern U. Mich., Ann Arbor, 1972-73, resident, 1973-75; fellow U. N.C., Chapel Hill, 1977-79; physician Raleigh (N.C.) Internal Medicine, 1979—, pres., 1982-84, 86-94; pres. Cardinal Health Care, Raleigh, 1994—; bd. dirs. Raleigh Cmty. Hosp., 1982-84; chmn. dept. medicine Wake Med. Ctr., Raleigh, 1991, 92. Vol. Am. Cancer Soc., Raleigh; hon. co-chmn. N.C. Lung Assn., raleigh, 1994. Maj. U.S. Army, 1975-77. Fellow Am. Coll. Chest Physicians; mem. ACP, Am. Thoracic Soc. (state councillor 1991-96), N.C. Thoracic Soc. (pres. 1986), N.C. Med. Soc., Raleigh Acad. Medicine (sec.). Office: Cardinal Healthcare 3320 Wake Forest Rd Raleigh NC 27609

HAYES, DAVID RANDALL, health facility administrator; b. Lebanon, Ky., Nov. 20, 1947; s.. Auburn Harold and Virginia Ilene (Weatherford) H.; m. Betty Sue Bewley, Dec. 16, 1967; children: Andrew Stephen, Amy Elizabeth. BS, Campbellsville (Ky.) Coll., 1970. Cert. advanced studies in health svcs. adminstrn. Auditor, audit mgr. HEW and Health Care Fin. Adminstrn., Richmond, Va., 1971-78, Frankfort, Ky., 1971-78; fin. dir., controller Taylor County Hosp., Campbellsville, 1978-86, CEO, adminstr., 1986—. Mem. health care reform Ky. Hosp. Task Force on Health Care Reform, Louisville, 1994-95. Named Outstanding Young Man Am., 1976, Hon. State Treas., Commonwealth of Ky., 1976. Mem. Am. Hosp. Assn., Ky. Hosp. Assn. (bd. dirs.), Campbellsville/Taylor County C. of C., Healthcare Fin. Mgmt. Assn. (officer, bd. dirs., William G. Follmer Merit award 1986), Commn. Ky. Col., Campbellsville Kiwanis (pres.). Democrat. Baptist. Office: Taylor County Hosp 1700 Old Lebanon Rd Campbellsville KY 42718

HAYES, ERNEST M., podiatrist; b. New Orleans, Jan. 21, 1946; s. Ernest M. and Emma Hayes; m. Bonnie Ruth Beigle, Oct. 16, 1970. B.A., Calif. State U., Sacramento, 1969; B.S., Calif. Coll. Podiatric Medicine, San Francisco, 1971, D.P.M., 1973. Resident in surg. podiatry Beach Community Hosp., Buena Park, Calif., 1973-74, dir. residency program, 1974-75; practice podiatry, Anaheim, Calif., 1974-80, Yreka, Calif., 1980—; sr. clin. instr. So. Calif. Podiatric Med. Center, Los Angeles, 1975-78; vice chmn. podiatry dept. Good Samaritain Hosp., Anaheim, Calif., 1978-79; mem. med. staff Mercey Med. Ctr., Mt. Shasta, Calif. Bd. dirs. Little Bogus Ranches Home Owners Assn., 1981-83, pres., 1983-84. Fellow Nat. Coll. Foot Surgeons; mem. Am. Assn. Podiatric Physicians and Surgeons, Am. Coun. Cert. Podiatric Physicians and Surgeons (cert.), Kiwanis. Baptist. Office: 203 Main St Calais ME 04652 also: 19 E Main Machias ME 04652

HAYES, E(VERETT) RUSSELL, anatomist, educator; b. Pomeroy, Ohio, Feb. 5, 1917; s. Everett R. and Mildred (Russell) H.; m. Nancy Padan, Mar. 4, 1946; children: Anne, Alan, Kevin. AB, Ohio U., 1938; PhD, Ohio State U., 1947. Instr. U. Buffalo, 1945-48; asst. prof. Ohio State U., Columbus, 1948-54, assoc. prof., 1954-57; assoc. prof. SUNY, Buffalo, 1957-62, prof. anatomy, 1962-85, prof. emeritus, 1985—. Contbr. articles to profl. publs. Mem. Am. Assn. Anatomists, Am. Soc. Zoologists (assoc. editor Jour. Morphology), Histochem. Soc., Biol. Stain Commn., Am. Soc. Cell Biology. Home and Office: 6599 Bear Ridge Rd Lockport NY 14094-9287

HAYES, GEORGE J., retired neurosurgeon; b. Washington, 1918. MD, Johns Hopkins U., 1943. Diplomate Am. Bd. Neurol. Surgery. Intern Johns Hopkins Hosp., 1944; fellow neurosurgery Lahey Clinic, Boston, 1944-46; chief neurosurgery svc. Walter Reed Gen. Hosp., Washington, 1947-49, 50-51, 55-66; fellow neurosurgery Duke Hosp., 1949-50; chief neurosurg. svc. Brooke Army Hosp., Ft. Sam Houston, Tex., 1953-55; dir. profl. svc. Office Svc. Gen. Dept. Army, 1966-68; prin. dep. asst. sec. def. health & environment Office Sec. Def., 1971-74; clin. prof. neurosurgery George Washington U. Mem. ACS, Inst. Medicine-NAS, Am. Assn. Neurol. Surgeons.

HAYES, JOHN THOMPSON, biology educator, educational administrator; b. Newton, Mass., Sept. 10, 1940; s. William Danforth Jr. and Charlotte Matilda (Thompson) H.; m. Nancy Jean VanDyke, Jan. 30, 1965 (div. Aug. 1978); children: Jonathan VanDyke, Dianne Jellesma; m. Patricia Anne Lynch, Aug. 23, 1980; 1 child, Robert Brennan. BA cum laude, Amherst Coll., 1962; MS, Cornell U., 1966, PhD, 1968. Postdoctoral fellow U. Ga. Savannah River Ecology Lab., Aiken, S.C., 1967-69; mem. faculty Paine Coll., Augusta, Ga., 1969—, prof. biology, 1976—; mgr. for computer-based edn. Med. Coll. Ga., Augusta, 1984-85. Contbr. articles to profl. jours. Mem. Assn. for Ednl. Communications and Tech., Extramural Assocs. NIH, Ga. Acad. Sci., Ga. Assn. for Instructional Tech.. Sigma Xi, Phi Kappa Phi. Unitarian-Universalist. Home: 2409 Persimmon Rd Augusta GA 30904-3354 Office: Paine Coll 1235 15th St Augusta GA 30901-3182

HAYES, JOSEPH THOMAS, preventive medicine physician; b. N.Y.C., Feb. 13, 1953; s. Francis Xavier and Eleanor (Quintilian) H.; m. Mary Valerie Silkowski, Feb. 19, 1994; 1 child, Joseph Thomas Jr. BS, Fairleigh Dickinson U., 1976; MD, Ross U., Dominica, B.W.I., 1980; MPH, Rutgers U., 1986; MBA, N.J. Inst. Tech., 1996. Diplomate Am. Bd. Preventive Medicine. Intern Perth Amboy (N.J.) Gen. Hosp., 1980; family practice John F. Kennedy Med. Ctr., Edison, N.J., 1981; pres., cons. Occupl. Health Assocs., Easton, Pa., 1985—, Metuchen, N.J., 1985—; cons. U.S. Postal Svc., N.Y.C., 1993—, British Oxygen Corp., Winchester, U.K., 1991-93. Mem. Gov. of N.J.'s Coun. on Phys. Fitness and Sports, 1985, Gov.'s Noise Control Coun., 1990. Fellow Am. Coll. Preventive Medicine; mem. Am. Co.. Phys. Execs., Am. Coll. Occupl. and Environ. Medicine. Office: Occupational Health Assocs PO Box 4516 Metuchen NJ 08840-4516

HAYES, LAURA JOANNA, psychologist; b. Winnebeau, N.C., Mar. 26, 1943; d. Victor Wilson and Pansy Lorraine (Springsteen) Hayes; m. Jerry Allen Gladson, June 20, 1965 (div. Mar. 1992); children: Joanna Kaye, Paula Rae. BA, So. Coll., 1965; MEd, U. Tenn., Chattanooga, 1977; EdD, Vanderbilt U., 1985. Lic. psychologist, Ga. Psychol. intern Lakeshore Mental Health Inst., Knoxville, Tenn., 1985-86; counselor, psychologist Tara Heights Enterprises, Atlanta, 1986—; psychologist, owner Assoc. Psychol. Svcs., Inc., Ringgold, Ga., 1990—. Mem. APA, Christian Assn. for Psychol. Studies, Ga. Psychol. Assn. Democrat. Home: 327 Homestead Cir Kennesaw GA 30144-1335 Office: Assoc Psychol Svcs Box 700 5476 Battlefield Pkwy Ringgold GA 30736

HAYES, LYNN NORMAN, health facility administrator; b. Helena, Ark., Sept. 14, 1959; d. Carl Sutton and Helen Faye (Frederick) Norman; m. Gary Randall Pounds, Feb. 10, 1979 (div. 1980); 1 child, Rachel Lynn Pounds; m. David Scott Hayes, Dec. 20, 1991; 1 child, Morgan Brooke. Diploma in nursing, Phillips County C.C., 1986. Staff RN Kidney Care Inc., Clarksdale, Miss., 1986-88; staff/charge RN Meml. Med. Ctr., Savannah, Ga., 1988-92; staff RN U. Tenn. Med. Group, Memphis, 1992-93; charge RN Nephrology Ctr., Statesboro, Ga., 1993-94; adminstr. Total Renal Care, Vidalia, Ga., 1994—. Mem. ANNA. Home: 18106 Sweetwater Ct Statesboro GA 30458 Office: Total Renal Care Nephrology Ctr Vidalia 1806 Edwina Vidalia GA 30474

HAYES, MARK ALLAN, educator, surgeon; b. Bay City, Mich., Oct. 19, 1914; s. Howard Mark and Mildred Marian (Anderson) H.; m. Margaret Mary Rupff, June 23, 1948; 1 son, Mark Allan. A.B., U. Mich., 1937, M.D. cum laude, 1940, Ph.D., 1948, M.S., 1951; M.A. (hon.), Yale, 1961. Diplomate: Am. Bd. Surgery. Intern U. Mich. Hosp., 1940-41, asst. resident surgery, 1941-42, resident surgery, 1942-43, 48-49, demonstrator anatomy, 1942-43, Kellogg fellow anatomy, 1946-47; mem. faculty U. Mich. Med. Sch., 1947-52, asst. prof. sugery, 1951-52; mem. faculty Yale Med. Sch., 1952—; dir. Yale Med. Sch. (Samuel C. Harvey Metabolic Unit), 1952-54, asso. prof. surgery, 1952-61, prof. surgery, 1961-79, prof. emeritus, 1979—. Served to lt. comdr., M.C. USNR, 1942-46. Fellow A.C.S.; mem. Am. Surg. Assn., Am. Gastroenterol. Assn., Frederick A. Coller, New Eng. surg. socs., Soc. Univ. Surgeons, Soc. Surgery Alimentary Tract (a founder), Sigma Xi, Alpha Omega Alpha. Home: 163 Ridgewood Ave North Haven CT 06473-4442

HAYES, MICHAEL ERNEST, psychotherapist, educator; b. N.Y.C., June 28, 1943; s. Raphael and Evelyn (Kaminier) H.; m. Agnes Beatrix Praetorias, May 9, 1967 (div. May 1970); m. Suellen Carroll Croteau, May 16, 1974; children: Elizabeth Carroll Croteau, Sarah Emily English Hayes. AB, Lawrence U., 1965; MA, U. Mich., 1966, MSW, 1969, PhD, 1972. Lic. clin. social worker; bd. cert. diplomate in clin. social work. Asst. prof. cmty. leadership and devel. Springfield (Mass.) Coll., 1972-73; asst. prof. social work U. N.H., Durham, 1973-76; vis. prof. social work U. So. Maine, Portland, 1976-77; assoc. prof. tchg. and adminstrn. Marywood Coll., Dunmore, Pa., 1977-81; assoc. dean arts & sci. U. New Haven, 1981-85; supr. med. social work Vis. Nurse of New Haven, 1985-87; psychotherapist Cmty. Health Care Plan, Branford, Conn., 1987-92; clin. mgr. TeamWorks for Adults Elmcrest Psychiat. Inst., Portland, Conn., 1992-96; dir. dual diagnosis program Stonington Inst., North Stonington, Conn., 1996—; pvt. practice psychotherapist, 1976—. Mem. NASW, Coun. on Social Work Edn., Porsche Club Am., Delta Tau Delta. Office: PO Box 620 Guilford CT 06437-0620

HAYES, MICHELE MARY, optometrist; b. San Diego, Nov. 16, 1960; d. Jude Roger and Arlene Kathrine (George) H. BA in Mammalian Physiology, U. Calif. San Diego, 1983; OD, So. Calif. Coll. Optometry, Fullerton, 1988. Cert. optometrist, Calif. Practice asoc. Valley Optometric Care, Stockton, Calif., 1988-94, Mark Helmus, OD, Stockton, 1989-90; practice assoc. Todd Pickens, OD/Ken Miselis MD, Sutter Creek, Calif., 1990—; optometrist in pvt. practice Sacramento, 1990—. Mem. Am. Optometric Assn., Calif. Optometric Assn. (del. COA cngress 1991-92, participant Vision U.S.A. 1989—), Sacramento Valley Optometric Soc. (advisor Sacramento Vision Project 1995—), So. Calif. Coll. Optometry Alumni. Republican. Roman Catholic. Office: 5601 Florin Rd Sacramento CA 95823-2204

HAYES, OLIVER WESLEY, emergency physician, educator, dean; b. Grayling, Mich., Mar. 5, 1951; s. Oliver Wesley and Patricia Caroline (McKenna) H.; m. Deborah Lee Nethers, Sept. 6, 1975; children: Emily Armstrong, Zachary Gault. BS, Ctrl. Mich. U., 1973; MS, Mich. State U., 1976, DO, 1981; M. Health Svcs. Adminstrn., U. Mich., 1990. Diplomate Am. Bd. Emergency Medicine, Am. Osteopathic Bd. Emergency Medicine, Am. Bd. Med. Mgmt. Intern Botsford Gen. Hosp., Farmington, Mich., 1981-82; resident Ingham Med. Ctr./Sparrow Hosp., Lansing, Mich., 1982-84, chief resident, 1983-84; instr. Mich. State U., East Lansing, 1982-84, asst. prof., 1984-90, assoc. prof., 1990—, acting chmn. dept. biomechanics, 1994-95, interim asst. dean Coll. Osteopathic Medicine, 1993—, project dir. Kellogg Cmty. Univ. Partnership, 1994—; cons. to Bulgaria U.S. Agy. for Internat. Devel., Washington, 1992-95; bd. dirs. Mich. Pub. Health Inst., East Lansing, 1994—; dir. med. edn. Lansing (Mich.) Gen. Hosp., 1992-93, mem.-at-large profl. staff exec. com., 1989-90; med. dir. Mich. State U./ Ingham County Health Dept. Medicaid Manage Care Program, 1993—; project dir. Mich. State U./Cmty./Univ. Health Partnerships, W.K. Kellogg Found. Initiative in Health Professions Edn., 1994—. Contbr. articles to profl. jours. Recipient Hooding award Class of 1987 for Outstanding Tchr., Mich. Stat eU., 1987, Outstanding Svc. award Alumni Assn. of Mich. State U., 1988. Fellow Am. Coll. Emergency Physicians, Am. Coll. Osteopathic Emergency Physicians; mem. Assn. Osteopathic Dir. and Med. Educators (bd. dirs. 1993—), Ingham County Assn. Osteopathic Physicians and Surgeons (pres.-elect 1995), Am. Osteopathic Assn., Univ. Assn. for Emergency Medicine, Mich. Assn. Dirs. Med. Edn., Soc. for Acad. Emergency Medicine, Mich. Assn. for Med. Edn., Am. Coll. Physician Execs., AMA, Pi Kappa Phi, Beta Beta Beta. Democrat. Methodist. Office: Michigan State Univ B 305 W Fee Hall East Lansing MI 48824-1316

HAYES, RICHARD CHARLES, orthodontist; b. N.Y.C., Apr. 26, 1944; s. Harry F. and Fay (Binder) H.; B.S., U. S.C., 1964; D.D.S., Med. Coll. Va., 1968, M.S., 1971. From assoc. prof. to prof. Temple U. Sch. Dentistry, Phila., 1973-95; practice dentistry specializing in orthodontics, Ridley Park, Pa., 1973—; bd. dirs. Medelex, Inc., B And H Assocs. Realty, S and W Assocs. Realty, Atkins Corp., Dani-Elle Fashions, Inc. Contbr. articles to profl. jours. Maj. U.S. Army, 1971-77. Mem. Dental Soc. Chester and Delaware Counties (gov.), ADA, Am. Assn. Orthodontists (coll. diplomates), Am. Bd. Orthodontics, Middle Atlantic Soc. Orthodontists, Pa. Soc. Orthodontists, Pa. Dental Assn., Am. Assn. Dental Editors, Phila. County Dental Soc., Phila. Soc. Orthodontists, Fedn. Dentaire Internat., Franklin Inst., World Affairs Council Phila., Phila. Zoo, Acad. Natural Sci. Phila, Sigma Xi. Republican. Home: 437 Wilde Ave Drexel Hill PA 19026-5253 Office: 101 Dutton St Ridley Park PA 19078-2308

HAYES, RICHARD L., psychology and counseling educator; b. Boston, Feb. 8, 1946; s. John R. and Thelma I. (Pyers) H.; m. Bree A. Botkin, Aug. 18, 1977; children: Jon, Ali, Jessica, Gillian. AB, Harvard Coll., 1968; MEd, Boston U., 1973, EdD, 1980. Lic. psychologist and counselor, Ill., Ga. Tchr. Wellesley (Mass.) High Sch., 1969-77; prof. Colgate U., Hamilton, N.Y., 1977-80, Bradley U., Peoria, Ill., 1980-88, U. Ga., Athens, 1988—. Author: Introduction to the Counseling Profession, 1986, New Directions for Counseling and Human Development, 1988, The Kohlberg Legacy for the Helping Professions, 1991; also articles. Mem. APA, ACA, Assn. for Moral Edn. (pres. 1980-84), Am. Ednl. Rsch. Assn., Assn. for Specialists in Group Work (pres. 1987-88). Office: U Ga 402 Aderhold Hall Athens GA 30602-0001

HAYES, SALLY, mental health nurse; b. Houston, Sept. 7, 1948; d. James Lansdale and Frances Joyce (Seigler) Folmar; 1 child, Logan Lee Blake. BS in Secondary Edn., Tex. A&M U., 1970; BSN, Tex. Woman's U., 1980. Cert. psychiat.-mental health nurse ANA. Charge nurse Acutecare Glenwood Hosp., Midland and Odessa, Tex., 1987-88, Washoe Med. Ctr., Reno, 1988-89; asst. dir. nursing Starlite Village Hosp., Kerrville, Tex., 1989, dir. nursing, 1989-90; charge nurse Acutecare Laurel Ridge Hosp., San Antonio, 1990-91; dir. nursing Alliance Hosp. of Santa Teresa, N.Mex., 1991—; supr. William Beaumont Army Med. Ctr., El Paso, 1991-93; asst. dir. nursing Physicians Hosp., Reno, Nev., 1995; administr., dir. nursing Lynaugh and Ft. Stockton Units Tex. Dept. Criminal Justice, Correctional Healthcare. Mem. Am. Orgn. Nurse Execs., ANA, Tex. Nurses Assn. Home: PO Box 322 Fort Stockton TX 79735-0322

HAYES, STEVEN CHARLES, psychologist, educator; b. Phila., Aug. 12, 1948; s. Charles Aloysius and Ruth Ester (Dryer) H.; m. Angela Fe Butcher (div.); 1 dau., Camille Rose; m. Linda Jean Parrott; children: Charles Frederick, Esther Marlena. BA cum laude in Psychology, Loyola U., Los Angeles, 1970; postgrad. Calif. State U., San Diego, 1971-72; MA in Clin. Psychology, W.Va. U., 1974, PhD, 1977. Lic. psychologist, N.C., Nev. Intern psychology Brown U. Sch. Medicine, Providence, 1975-76; asst. prof. U.

N.C.-Greensboro, 1976-82, assoc. prof., 1982-86; prof. U. Nev., Reno, 1986—, dir. clin. tng., 1986-94, chmn., 1994—. found. prof., W.Va. U. Found. Inc. grantee, 1975; NIMH grantee, 1976-77; U. N.C. grantee, 1976-77, 77-78, 81-82, 82-83, NSF, 1992, NIDA, 1994-96, U. Nev. Found. grantee, 1992-94; named 30th highest impact psychologist in world Inst. Sci. Info., 1986-90. Fellow Am. Psychol. Soc. (sec.-treas. 1988-89), Assn. Applied and Preventive Psychology (exec. com., mem.-at-large, bd. dirs. 1992—, v.p. 1993, pres. 1994-96), Western Psychol. Assn.; mem. AAAS, Am. Psychol. Assn. (divsn. 25 student affairs coord., 1977, 78, continuing edn. chmn. 1980-82, program co-chmn. 1980-82, chmn. long-term planning com. 1982, mem.-at-large 1982-85, pres. 1987, council of reps., 1988-89, fellow divsn. 12, 24, and 25), Assn. Behavior Analysis, Assembly of Sci. and Applied Psychology (sec.-treas. 1987-88), Assn. Advancement Behavior Therapy (student affairs coord. 1978, assoc. program chmn. 1979, program chmn. 1980, chmn. task force student involvement 1980-81), Soc. Exptl. Analysis Behavior (sec. 1985, pres. elect 1996—), Southeastern Assn. for Behavior Analysis (sec. 1985-86), Sigma Xi. Democrat. Author: The Effects of Monthly Feedback, Rebate Billing and Consumer Directed Feedback on the Residential Consumption of Electricity, 1977; Abnormal Psychology, 1979; (with J.D. Cone) Environmental Problems/Behavioral Solutions, 1980; (with D.H. Barlow and R.O. Nelson) The Scientist Practitioner: Research and Accountability in Clinical and Educational Settings, 1984, (with R.O. Nelson) Conceptual Foundations of Behavioral Assessment, 1986, Rule-Governed Behavior, 1989, (with L.J. Hayes) Understanding Verbal Relations, 1992, (with others) Varieties of Scientific Contextualism, 1993, Behavior Analysis of Language and Cognition, 1994, Acceptance and Change, 1994, Scientific Standards of Psychological Practice, 1995; contbr. chpts. to books, articles to profl. jours.; editor APS Observer, 1988-89, The Scientist Practitioner, 1990-92; assoc. editor Jour. Applied Behavior Analysis, 1982-85; editorial bd. Behavioral Assessment, Behavior Modification, Jour. Cons. and Clin. Psychology, The Behavior Analyst, Behaviorism, Jour. Experimental Analysis of Behavior, The Psychological Record. Home: 933 Gear St Reno NV 89503-2729 Office: U Nev Dept Psychology Coll Arts & Sci Reno NV 98557-0062

HAYES, TIMOTHY LEE, analytical chemist, researcher; b. Zanesville, Ohio, Apr. 12, 1955; s. Charles Isaac and Patricia Eileen (Paul) H.; m. Pamela Anne Burns, Aug. 27, 1978; children: Timothy Charles, Abbie Anne. BA, Otterbein Coll., Westerville, Ohio, 1977. Researcher Battelle, Columbus, Ohio, 1977-85, rsch. scientist, 1985-88, prin. rsch. scientist, 1988—; chief chemist Battelle Med. Rsch. and Evaluation Facility, 1986—; presenter poster sessions in field. Contbr. articles to profl. jours. Instr. Support Our Abled Resources Westerville, 1985—; judge Battelle/Otterbein Sci. Fair, 1976-92. Recipient Back to Sch. award Westerville City Schs., 1990-91. Mem. Am. Chem. Soc. Office: Battelle 505 King Ave Columbus OH 43201-2696

HAYES, TIMOTHY LEE, osteopathic family practitioner, educator; b. Dayton, Ohio, Feb. 9, 1949; s. Laurence Grosvenor and Eula Marguerite (Pendergrass) H.; m. Gerrie Woodbury, Jan. 14, 1969 (div. Apr. 1980); children: Christopher Lee, Alexandra Kathleen; m. Leslie Denise Kling, Aug. 13, 1988; 1 child, Lauren Halle. BS in Biology and Microbiology, Wright State U., Dayton, 1976; DO, U. Health Scis., Kansas City, Mo., 1980. Diplomate Am. Bd. Osteo. Family Practice, Am. Bd. Quality Assurance and Utilization Rev. Physicians, Am. Bd. Hyperbaric & Undersea Medicine. Gen. rotating intern Doctors Gen. Hosp., Plantation, Fla., 1980-81; emergency medicine physician Profl. Emergency Svcs., Tavernier, Fla., 1981-88; pvt. practice, Islamorada, Fla., 1988—; assoc. prof. family medicine U. Miami, Fla., 1993—; med. dir. Integracare Med. Ctr., Islamorada, 1994—. Bd. dirs. Redbone Tournament Series To Benefit and Cure Cystic Fibrosis, Islamorada, 1992—. With USN, 1969-73. Mem. Am. Osteo. Assn., Am. Coll. Physician Execs., Am. Coll. Quality Assurance and Utilization Rev. Physicians, Am. Osteo. Coll. Family Practice, Fla. Osteo. Med. Assn. (trustee 1992—). Office: Integracare 83224 Overseas Hwy Islamorada FL 33036

HAYES, WILBUR FRANK, biology educator; b. Rhinelander, Wis., Nov. 10, 1936; s. Wilbur Mead and Evelyn (Stritesky) H.; m. Dawn Olivia Waldorf, July 21, 1979 (div. Feb. 1991); stepchildren: Lynn, Robert, Dana, Richard, Gary, Kevin. BA, Colby Coll., 1959; MS, Lehigh U., 1961, PhD, 1965. Postdoctoral fellow Yale U., New Haven, 1965-67; asst. prof. biology Wilkes Coll., Wilkes-Barre, Pa., 1967-71, assoc. prof., 1971—; vis. prof. Northeastern U., Boston, 1987-88. Contbr. articles to profl. jours. Chmn. bd. dirs. Northeastern Pa. chpt. A. Heart Assn., Wilkes-Barre, 1986-87. Mem. Soc. for Integrative and Comparative Biology, Pa. Acad. Sci., Microscopy Soc. Am., Sigma Xi (pres. Wilkes Coll. chpt. 1976-77, sec.-treas. 1984-87, 88-91). Republican. Congregationalist. Home: 47 Stanley St Wilkes Barre PA 18702-2308 Office: Wilkes U Dept Biology Wilkes Barre PA 18766

HAYES, WILLIAM DANFORTH, III, clinical social worker; b. Worcester, Mass., Oct. 25, 1949; s. William Danforth Jr. and Charlotte (Thompson) H.; m. Margrit Elisabeth Wagner, Oct. 2, 1971; children: Benjamin Burke, Timothy Wagner. BS, Amherst Coll., 1970; MSW, Smith Coll., 1975. Cert. clin. social worker, N.Y.; cert. child abuse instr., N.Y. Child care worker Bonnie Brae Farm for Boys, Millington, N.J., 1970-73; clin. social worker depts. pediatrics and psychiatry Bassett Hosp., Cooperstown, N.Y., 1975—; lectr. dept. sociology Hartwick Coll., Oneonta, N.Y., 1979; co-founding bd. dirs. Nat. Com. to Prevent Child Abuse, 1980, pres. N.Y. chpt., 1994—, sec. exec. com., 1990-91, v.p., 1989-90, 91—, treas., 1988-89; Otsego/Schoharie Perinatal Network, 1993—, regional chmn. early care project N.Y. Health Dept., 1988-90, Otsego Couty LEICC, 1994—; health adv. com. Otsego County Head Start, 1989—, Otsego County Dept. Social Svcs. policy adv. com., 1983-86, Otsego Com. on Child Abuse, 1979—. Fellow Am. Orthopsychiat. Assn.; mem. NASW. Office: Bassett Hosp 1 Atwell Rd Cooperstown NY 13326-1301

HAYFLICK, LEONARD, microbiologist, cell biologist, gerontologist, educator, writer; b. Phila., May 20, 1928; s. Nathan Albert and Edna (Silbert) H.; m. Ruth Louise Heckler, Oct. 3, 1954; children: Joel, Deborah, Susan, Rachel, Anne. BA in Microbiology and Chemistry, U. Pa., 1951, MS in Med. Microbiology, 1953, PhD in Med. Microbiology and Chemistry, 1956. McLaughlin rsch. fellow in infection and immunity, dept. microbiology U. Tex. Med. Br., Galveston, Tex., 1956-58; assoc. mem. Wistar Inst. Anatomy and Biology, Phila., 1958-68; asst. prof. rshc. medicine U. Pa., Phila., 1966-68; prof. med. microbiology Stanford (Calif.) U. Sch. Medicine, 1968-76, senator-at-large, Basic Med. Scis., 1970-73, chmn. gen. rsch. support grant com., 1972-74; sr. research cell biologist Children's Hosp., Oakland, Calif., 1976-81; prof. zoology, prof. microbiology and immunology U. Fla., Gainesville, 1981-87, dir. Ctr. for Gerontol. Studies, Coll. Liberal Arts and Scis., 1981-87; prof. anatomy, cell biology and aging sect. U. Calif. Sch. Medicine, San Francisco, 1988—; mem. subcom. on mycoplasmataceae Internat. Com. Bacteriol. Nomenclature, 1965-78; mem. steering com. cell and devel. biology film program MIT, 1970-73; chmn. Calif. State Com. Health White Ho. Conf. Aging, 1971-72, Calif. state rep., 1972; Nat. Cancer Planning Com. Nat. Cancer Inst., NIH, 1972; chmn., adult devel. and aging rsch. and tng. com. Nat. Inst. Child Health and Human Devel., NIH, 1972-73; non-resident fellow Inst. Higher Studies, Santa Barbara, Calif., 1973—; mem. Argonne Nat. Lab. rev. com. biol. and med. rsch. div. Argonne Nat. Lab., 1973-76; mem. rsch. adv. com. Tchrs. Ins. and Annuity Assn. Am.-Coll. Retirement Equities Funds, N.Y.C., 1974-80; founding mem. Nat. Adv. Coun. on Aging, Nat. Inst. on Aging, NIH, Bethesda, Md., 1975; cons. Office of Dir. Nat. Cancer Inst., Bethesda, 1963-74; vis. scientist Ctr. for Aging Weizmann Inst. Sci., Rehovoth, Israel, 1980, 86; mem. adv. bd. Internat. Exchange Ctr. Gerontology, Fla. Univ. System, Tampa, 1982-86; mem. jury for Sandoz prize in gerontology and geriatrics, 1985-89; bd. dirs. Ctr. for Climacteric Studies, Inc., Gainesville, 1985-88; expert cons. various coms. U.S. Congress, vis. prof. Oita Med. U., Japan, 1991-95, U. Parma, Italy, 1991, Kurume U. Med. Sch., Japan; lectr. in field. Author: How and Why We Age, 1994; editor: Biology of the Mycoplasmas, 1969, Handbook of the Biology of Aging, 1977; sr. editor Biol. Scis. Microfiche Collection Info. on Gerontology and Geriatric Medicine Univ. Microfilms Internat., Ann Arbor, Mich., 1984—; editor-in-chief Exptl. Gerontology, 1984—; asst. editor In Vitro jour. Tissue Culture Assn., 1969-75; editor biol. scis. sect. Jour. Gerontology, 1975-80; assoc. editor Cancer Rsch., 1972-80; mem. editorial bd. Jour. Bacteriology, 1964-72, Jour. Virology, 1967-70, Infection and Immunity jour., 1968-78, Exec. Health Report, 1970—, Mechanisms of Aging and Devel., 1972—, Gerontology and Geriatrics Edn., 1980—, A Revista Portuguesa de Medicina Geriatrica, 1987—; mem. adv. com. Bergey's Manual of Determinative Bacteriology, 1965-78; bd. dirs.. mem. editorial bd. Bollettino Dell Instituto Sieroterapico Milanese, Archivo de Microbiologia ed Immunologia, Milan, Italy, 1968—; contbr. numerous articles in field to profl. jours. Staff sgt. U.S. Army, 1946-48. Recipient Samuel Roberts Noble Found. Rsch. Recognition award, 1984; co-recipient Sandoz prize Internat. Assn. Gerontology, 1991, Biomed. Scis. & Aging award U. So. Calif., 1974, Rsch. Recognition award Samuel Roberts Noble Found., 1984; Karl-Forster lectr. Acad. Sci. and Lit., Mainz, Germany, 1983, Hoffman-LaRoche lectr. Waksman Inst. Microbiology Rutgers U., 1984, Wadworth Meml. Fund lectr. Rush-Presbyn.-St. Luke's Med. Ctr., Chgo., 1984, hon. lectr. Rosenfield Program Pub. Affairs Grinnell Coll., 1989, invited speaker Sandoz lectrs. in Gerontology, Basle, Switzerland, 1986, 92, numerous other lectureships U.S.A., Can. and Europe, 1970—, Career Devel. Cancer Inst., NIH, 1962-70, Lifetime Achievement award Soc. In Vitro Biology, 1996. Fellow AAAS, Gerontol Soc. Am. (program and awards com. 1972-77, chmn., exec. com. biol. scis. sect. 1972-74, com. on internat. rels. 1980-82, pub. policy com. 1980-82, pres. 1982-83, ann. Robert W. Kleemeier award 1972, Brookdale award 1980); mem. Am. Soc. for Microbiology, Tissue Culture Assn. (hon., trustee 1966-68, program com. 1970, mem. coun. 1972-74, v.p. 1974-76, pres. Calif. chpt. 1971-73), Soc. for Exptl. Biology and Medicine (councillor 1984-88), Assn. for Advancement of Aging Rsch. (adv. coun. 1970-71), Am. Aging Assn., Am. Cancer Soc. (virology and cell biology study sect. 1974-76) Internat. Assn. of Microbiol. Standardization (sec. cell culture com. 1963-73, chmn. 1985—, mem. coun. 1987-89), Internat. Orgn. for Mycoplasmology (Presdl. award 1984), Am. Gerontol. Soc. (v.p., coun. 1972-74, 81-83, program com. 1977-79, bd. dirs. 1981-83), Am. Fedn. Aging Rsch. (bd. dirs., exec. com., rsch. adv. com. 1981—, chmn. study sect. 1987—, v.p. 1988—, Leadership award 1983), Fedn. Am. Socs. for Exptl. Biology, Aging Prevention Rsch. Found. (sci. adv. bd. dirs.), Am. Assn. for Cancer Rsch., Am. Soc. Pathologists, Calif. Found. for Biomed. Rsch., Am. Longevity Assn. (sci. adv. bd. dirs. 1981—), Western Gerontology Assn. (coun. 1972-74, bd. dirs. 81-83), Internat. Assn. Gerontology (mem. Am. exec. com. 1972-75, treas., exec. com. 1985-89, co-recipient Sandoz award gerontology 1991), Found. on Gerontology (sci. adv. bd. 1985—), Soc. Medicine & Natural Sci. (U. Parma 1991), Ukrainian Acad. Med. Scis. (fgn.). Office: U Calif 36991 Greencroft Close PO Box 89 The Sea Ranch CA 95497

HAYHURST, JOSEPH WARNER, plastic surgeon; b. Brownfield, Tex., Dec. 23, 1936; s. Watner and Olga (Albright) H.; m. Donna, Dec. 23, 1957; children: Cole, Cort, Dru, Christina, Ryan. BS, U. Okla., 1962, MD, 1968. Plastic surgeon pvt. practice, Oklahoma City, 1976—. With U.S. Army, 1958-60. Recipient Bigger-Lehman award Va. Surg. Soc. Mem. AMA, Am. Soc. Plastic & Reconstructive Surgeons, Okla. State Med. Assn., Oklahoma County Med. Soc., Internat. Soc. Reconstructive Microsurgery (founding). Home: 3112 Norcrest Dr Oklahoma City OK 73121 Office: Presbyn Profl Bldg Ste 609 711 Stanton L Young Blvd Oklahoma City OK 73104

HAYKEN, GERALD DREUX, orthopedic surgeon; b. N.Y.C., Oct. 11, 1949; s. Morris Jay and Dorothy Margaret (McNally) H.; m. Tonette Theresa Farinacci, Aug. 13, 1972; children: Gregory Steven, Valerie Marie. BA in Biology, Hofstra U., 1971; MD, Temple U., 1976. Diplomate Am. Bd. Orthopaedic Surgery. Intern, resident U. Pa. Hosp., Phila., 1976-81; orthop. surgeon Drs. Smolenski, Brill, Hayken and Schwartz, Mt. Laurel, N.J., 1981—; med. advisor Liberty Mutual Ins. Co., Boston, 1994—; treas. So. Jersey Bone and Joint Surgery Inc., Mt. Laurel, 1994-95; bd. dirs. Orthop. Network, Inc. Contbr. articles to profl. jours. Vol. Leather's Playground, Medford, N.J., 1995. Fellow Am. Acad. Orthop. Surgeons; mem. N.J. Orthop. Soc., Phila. Orthop. Soc., Union League Phila. Office: Smolenski Brill Hayken Schwartz PA 204 Ark Rd Mount Laurel NJ 08054

HAYMAKER, DOUGLAS JAMES, psychologist, researcher; b. Evansville, Ind., Oct. 28, 1957; s. James Gallagher and Marjorie Louise (Uber) H.; m. Stephanie Elise Brody, Apr. 4, 1987. BA, Brown U., 1980; MS, U. Fla., 1984, PhD, 1988. Intern Bklyn. VA Med. Ctr., 1986-87; sr. clinician psychologist St. Clares-Riverside Med. Ctr., Denville, N.J., 1987-90; clin. psychologist Ctr. for Evaluation and Psychotherapy Morristown (N.J.) Meml. Hosp., 1989—; clin. psychologist Princeton (N.J.) Psychiatric Recovery Network, 1990-92; field supr. Grad. Sch. of Applied and Profl. Psychology Rutgers U., Piscataway, N.J., 1990—; clin. psychologist, CEO Oldwick (N.J.) Assocs. in Psychotherapy, 1991—. Contbr. articles to profl. jours. NSF fellow, 1978; recipient Recognition award Fla. Dept. Health and Rehab. Svcs., 1986. Mem. APA, N.J. Psychol. Assn. Democrat. Office: Oldwick Assocs in Psychotherapy PO Box 242 Oldwick NJ 08858-0242

HAYMAKER, STEPHANIE ELISE, psychologist; b. Phila., Feb. 21, 1960; d. Martin Robert and Marcia Evelyn (Weinerman) Brody; m. Douglas James Haymaker, Apr. 4, 1987. BS, NYU, 1982; PhD, U. Fla., 1988. Staff psychologist Elizabeth (N.J.) Gen. Med. Ctr., 1987-88; psychologist, managed care resources Medicine and Dentistry of N.J., Piscataway, 1988-93, sr. psychologist, 1993-96; cons. psychologist dept. disability determination N.J. State Dept. Labor, New Brunswick, 1995—; pvt. practice Oldwick, N.J., 1996—. Mem. APA, Phi Beta Kappa. Office: 48 Old Turnpike Rd Oldwick NJ 08858

HAYNES, BOYD WITHERS, JR., surgeon; b. Brandenburg, Ky., July 5, 1917; s. Boyd Withers and Sallie Katherine (Allen) H.; m. Peggy Jane Harrison, May 21, 1955. A.B., U. Louisville, 1939, M.D., 1941. Diplomate Am. Bd. Surgery. Intern Med. Coll. Va., Richmond, 1941-42; research fellow in surgery Med. Coll. Va., 1944-45, resident surgeon, 1945-48, asso. in surgery, 1948-49, asst. prof., 1953-59, asso. prof., 1960-66, prof., 1966, prof., chmn. div. trauma surgery, 1972-82, attending surgeon in charge burn service and gen. surgery service, 1954; assoc. in surgery Baylor U. Coll. Medicine, Houston, 1949-50, asst. prof., 1951-53; cons. gen. surgery McGuire VA Hosp., Richmond, Va., 1966—; mem. Task Force Health Servs. Adminstrn. NIH, 1976; mem. Va. Gov.'s Com. Emergency Med. Servs., 1976-78; bd. dir. M.C.V. Burn Unit, gen. chmn. trauma div., 1972-82. Assoc. editor: Yearbook Plastic and Reconstructive Surgery, 1970-89; contbr. articles on shock, trauma and burns to profl. jours. Served as maj. M.C. AUS, 1953-55. Recipient Harvey Stuart Allen Disting. Ser. award Am. Burn Assn., 1979, commendation for contbn. to burn care Standards, 1977; cert. of recognition NASA, 1978; Disting. Service to Medicine award Med. Coll. Va., 1983; Order of Merit award U. Louisville Alumni Assn., 1983; Year Book medal for disting. service, 1984; Disting. Faculty award Med. Coll. Va. Alumni Assn., 1986, C.P. Artz medal Am. Trauma Soc., 1987. Fellow ACS (Va. pres. 1969-70, gov. 1971-77, chmn. subcom. functions and purposes 1975-77, 2d v.p. 1989—); mem. Am. Burn Assn. (pres. 1969-70, chmn. ad hoc com. care standards 1976-78, chmn. ad hoc com. to trustees on membership 1981-82, chmn. ad hoc com. on archives, 1989—), Soc Univ. Surgeons, Med. Soc. Va., Am. Assn. Surgery of Trauma, Internat. Soc. Burn Injury (U.S. rep. 1965-70 regional rep. The Ams. 1983), Am. Surg. Assn., So. Surg. Assn. (1st v.p. 1986-87), Richmond Acad. Medicine, Surg. Biology Club, Va. Surg. Soc., Univ. Assn. Emergency Med. Svcs. (regional dir. 1976-78), Surg. Infection Soc. (charter mem.), Société Internationale de Chirurgie, Halsted Soc., Alpha Omega Alpha. Home: 6161 River Rd #14 Richmond VA 23226

HAYNES, CATHERINE ANN, wellness educator; b. L.A., May 14, 1944; d. Edgar Thomas Farnum and Irene Bertha (Haynes) Howard. Diploma in nursing, Nebr. Meth. Hosp. Sch. Nursing, 1966; BS, U. Nebr. Med. Ctr., 1973; MS, U. Calif., San Francisco, 1975. Cert. enneagram tchr.; cert. laughter therapy profl. Instr. critical care staff devel. Mills Meml. Hosp., San Mateo, Calif., 1975-76; assoc. program nurse and med. supr. Palo Alto (Calif.) YMCA, 1976-78; clin. coordinator cardiac therapy Loma Linda (Calif.) Med. Ctr., 1978-79; coordinator pacemaker and scanning div. Southwest Monitoring, Houston, 1980-81; asst. prof. nursing U. Ariz., Tucson, 1981-84, U. Tex. Health Scis. Ctr., San Antonio, 1984-86; clin. dir. ICU/Critical Care Unit Meml. Hosp. Natrona County, Casper, Wyo., 1986; expert witness Doug Dalton and Ron Kilgard, Phoenix, 1987; co-owner Haynes Sheppard, 1988—; student health nurse Community Coll. of San Francisco, 1990-91; faculty Samuel Merritt Coll., Oakland, Calif., 1991-92; pvt. healing practice Sebastopol, 1993—; facilitator, cons. U. Ariz. Hosp., Tucson, 1983; mem. staff Ornish Cardiovascular Research Study, Horseshoe Bay, Tex., 1980; lectr. community and profl. orgns. various states, 1978—; expert witness Atty. Ray Speece, Tucson, 1983-85. Chmn. United Way, Tucson, 1982-83. Mem. AACN, Am. Heart Assn. (coun. for cardiovascular nursing 1975-86), Am. Holistic Nurses Assn., Assn. for Enneagram Tchrs., Flower Essence Soc., Internat. Assn. for Human Caring, Sigma Theta Tau. Libertarian. Home and Office: Haynes-Sheppard 5660 Hessel Ave Sebastopol CA 95472-6137

HAYNES, DEBORAH GENE, physician; b. York, Neb., Feb. 18, 1954; d. Gene Eldridge and Margaret Lucille (Manchester) Haynes; m. Russell Larry Beamer, Mar. 3, 1979; children: Staci E. Beamer, Lindsay M. Beamer, Stephanie L. Beamer. BA in Biology cum laude, Wichita State U., 1976; MD, U. Kans., Wichita, 1979. Diplomate Am. Bd. Family Practice; cert. Added Qualifications-Geriatrics. Resident St. Joseph Hosp., Wichita, 1979-82; instr. dept. family and community medicine St. Joseph Family Practice Residency, U. Kans., Wichita, 1982-84, asst. prof. dept. family and community medicine, 1984-85; pvt. family practice Northeast Family Physicians, Wichita, 1985—; clin. asst. prof. U. Kans. Sch. Medicine, Witchita, 1985—; bd. govs. endowment assn. Wichita State U., 1995—; bd. dirs. Via Christi Regional Med. Ctr. Trustee Wichita Collegiate Sch., 1993—. Recipient P.G. Czarlinsky award for Disting. Clin. Svc., U. Kans., 1979, Wichita State U. Gore scholarship, 1992. Fellow Am. Acad. Family Physicians (del. 1991—, commn. on edn. 1991—, task force on procedures, Mead Johnson award 1990-91, chair COD credential com. 1994), Kans. Acad. Family Physicians (pres. elect 1988-89, pres. 1989-90), Kans. Med. Soc., Med. Soc. Sedgwick County (del. 1990-91, chair profl. investigation com. 1993-95), Alpha Omega Alpha. Presbyterian. Home: 1015 N Linden Cir Wichita KS 67206-4075 Office: 8100 E 22nd St N Bldg 2200 Wichita KS 67226-2301

HAYNES, JOHN LENNEIS, healthcare technology consultant; b. Washington, Mar. 25, 1934; s. John L. and Anne F. Haynes; m. Alice Marie Sandi, Sept. 11, 1955; children. BS in Elec. Engring., Cornell U., 1956; MS in Elec. Engring., Stanford U., 1958. Rsch. engr. Stanford Rsch. Inst., Menlo Park, Calif., 1956-61; chief engr. Pacific Communications and Electronics, Redwood, Calif., 1962-65, BD Electronics Lab., Mountain View, Calif., 1965-77; gen. mgr. BD Electronics Lab., Mountain View, 1977-79; assoc. dir. Becton Dickinson Rsch. Ctr., Research Triangle Park, N.C., 1979-92; cons. The O'Donnell Group, 1993—. Contbr. articles to profl. jours. Pres. Oaks Homeowners Assn., Chapel Hill, N.C., 1984. Mem. IEEE (sr.; Grand award 1960), Instrument Soc. Am., Am. Assn. Med. Instruments, Focus Photog. Soc. (pres. 1978). Home and Office: The O'Donnell Group 107 Tweed Pl Chapel Hill NC 27514-6534

HAYNES, MOSES ALFRED, physician; b. Guyana, Nov. 17, 1921; came to U.S., 1947, naturalized, 1955; s. Milton Alphonso and Charlotte Mildred (Alleyne) H.; m. Hazel Louise Edgecombe, July 1, 1951; 1 child, Theresa Sue (Mrs. Larry Law). B.S., Columbia U., 1951; M.D., State U. N.Y., 1954; M.P.H., Harvard U., 1963. Intern St. John's Episcopal Hosp., Bklyn., 1954-55; physician USPHS Indian Hosp., Cheyenne Agy., S.D., 1955-59; asst. prof. community medicine U. Vt., 1959-64; asso. prof. Sch. Pub. Health, Johns Hopkins, 1966-69; prof. preventive and social medicine and pub. health UCLA, 1969-77; asso. dean Drew Postgrad. Med. Sch., Los Angeles, 1969-77; chmn. dept. community medicine Drew Postgrad. Med. Sch., 1969-74, acting dean, 1975-76, dean, pres., 1979-86; dir. Drew/Meharry/Morehouse Consortium Cancer Ctr., 1986-90; pres. SECON Inc., 1977-79; vis. prof. Med. Coll., Trivandrum, Kerala, India, 1964-66; mem. cancer support rev. com. Nat. Cancer Inst. Chmn. health task force Urban Coalition, 1968-69; mem. Pres.'s Com. Health Edn., 1972; exec. dir. Nat. Med. Assn. Found., 1968-69; mem. adv. com. Nat. Ctr. Health Stats., 1974-76; mem U.S. Preventive Svcs. Task Force, 1985-86; mem. bd. sci. counselors, divsn. cancer prevention and control Nat. Cancer Inst., 1989-93, chmn., 1991-93; bd. dirs. Ptnrs. for Prevention, 1991-92; mem. adv. bd. Fogarty Internat. Ctr., 1992-93. With USPHS, 1955-59. Fellow Am. Coll. Preventive Medicine, (pres. 1983-85); fellow AAAS; mem. Inst. Medicine of Nat. Acad. Sci. (internat. health bd., com. human rights 1986-89), Inst. Medicine (council 1983-86), Alpha Omega Alpha. Home: 29249 Firthridge Rd Palos Verdes Peninsula CA 90275*

HAYNES, WILLIAM FORBY, JR., internist, cardiologist; b. Newark, June 6, 1926; s. William Forby and Grace (Brien) H.; BS, U.S. Mcht. Marine Acad., 1946; AB, Princeton U., 1950; MD, Columbia U., 1954; m. Constance Simpson, July 2, 1960; children: William, Suzanne, David; m. Aline Linehan James, Aug. 25, 1984. Intern, St. Luke's Med. Center, N.Y.C., 1954-55, resident, 1957-59, N.Y. Heart Assn. fellow in cardiology, 1959-60; practice medicine specializing in internal medicine and cardiology, Princeton, N.J., 1960—; asst. prof. medicine Robert Wood Johnson Med. Sch., 1972—; cons. internal medicine/cardiology Princeton U., 1968—; sr. attending, ternal medicine Princeton Med. Center, 1960—. Author: A Physician's Witness to the Power of Shared Prayer, 1990, Minding the Whole Person: Cultivating a Healthy Lifestyle from Youth Through the Senior Years, 1994; contbr. articles to profl. jours. Served as ensign USNR, 1944-46, to lt., M.C., 1955-57. Diplomate Am. Bd. Internal Medicine (subcert. in cardiovascular diseases), Nat. Bd. Med. Examiners. Fellow Am. Coll. Cardiology, Am. Coll. Chest Physicians, ACP, Council Clin. Cardiology of Am. Heart Assn.; mem. Phila. Acad. Cardiology, Mercer County Heart Assn. (v.p. 1970, trustee 1964-76, Cardiologist of Yr. 1995), Third Order of St. Francis, Univ. Cottage Club Princeton, Princeton U. Alumni Coun. for Athletics, Princeton Officers Soc., Princeton U. Friends of Swimming (pres. 1975-87), U.S. Masters Swimming Assn. (top ten), Univ. Cottage Club, Nassau Club. Republican. Episcopalian. Co-inventor GI String for detecting intestinal bleeding, 1960. Home: 6 Skyfield Dr Princeton NJ 08540-7403 Office: 281 Witherspoon St Princeton NJ 08540-3210

HAYNIE, ROBERT LEE, internist; b. Cin., Feb. 4, 1945; m. Edweana Robinson. BS in Chemistry, U. Cin., 1967; PhD in Organic Chemistry, Case Western Res. U., 1972, MD, 1978. Lic. physician, Ohio; diplomate Am. Bd. Internal Medicine. Intern Mt. Sinai Med. Ctr., Cleve., 1978-79, resident, 1980-82, dir. internal medicine residency tng. program, 1985-89, dir. Hypertension Control Ctr., 1989—, dir. transitional yr. program, 1990-95, interim med. dir. Ctr. for Urban Health, 1995; asst. prof. Ohio Coll. Podiatric Medicine, Cleve., 1979-80, assoc. prof., 1985— med. cons., 1985—, coord. gen. medicine course for podiatric med. students; instr. organic chemistry Case Western Res. U. Sch. Medicine, Cleve., 1970-72, lectr. organic chemistry, 1972-74, instr. summer prematriculation program, biochemistry, 1974-81, asst. prof. medicine, 1985-88, asst. clin. prof., 1988—, chmn. com. on students, 1993-95, curriculum co-dir. summer prematriculation program, 1988-89, mentor heartwarmers mentor program; asst. prof. chemistry Chgo. State U., 1972-74; med. dir. clin. weight mgmt., Cleve., Cmty. Action Against Addiction, Cleve.; dir. Phase III Core Clerkship in Medicine, Mt. Sinai Med. Ctr./Case Western Res. U., Cleve., 1985-89; adv. bd. mem. Nat. Minority Organ and Tissue Transplant Ednl. Program; mem. profl. edn. com. High Blood Pressure Coun. Greater Cleve.; lectr. various corps., hosps., univs., orgns. Contbr. chpts. to books. Recipient Middleton Lambridge award for med. excellence, 1978, Pres. award Ohio Podiatric Med. Student Assn., Ohio Coll. Podiatric Medicine, 1995, Alumni Svc. award Case Western Res. U. Sch. Medicine, 1995; Spl. sci. fellow, 1971, Ford Found. fellow, 1972. Mem. AAAS, ACP, Nat. Med. Assn. Home: 2403 Traymore University Heights OH 44118 Office: Hypertension Control Ctr Mt Sinai Med Ctr 1 Mt Sinai Dr Cleveland OH 44118

HAYNIE, THOMAS POWELL, III, physician; b. Hearne, Tex., Aug. 9, 1932; s. Thomas Powell, Jr. and Sue Cummings (Gibson) H.; m. Bette Flossel, Mar. 10, 1956; children: David Powell, Amy Cummings, Sue Cummings. Student, U. South, Sewanee, Tenn., 1949-51, U. Tex., Austin, 1951-52; M.D., Baylor U., 1956. Diplomate: Am. Bd. Internal Medicine, also Sub-Bd. Med. Oncology, Am. Bd. Nuclear Medicine. Intern, then resident in internal medicine U. Mich. Med. Center, Ann Arbor, 1956-60; instr. U. Mich. Med. Center, 1960-62; asst. prof. medicine, dir. nuclear med. service U. Tex. Med. Br., Galveston, 1962-65; assoc. prof. medicine U. Tex.-M.D. Anderson Cancer Ctr., Houston, 1965-75; prof. U. Tex.-M.D. Anderson Hosp. and Tumor Inst., Houston, 1975-95, James E. Anderson prof. nuclear medicine, 1988-95, prof. emeritus of nuclear medicine, 1995—, chief sect. nuclear medicine, 1967-84, chmn. dept. nuclear medicine, 1984-93, head dept. internal medicine, 1977-84; adj. prof. radiology Baylor Coll. of Medicine, Houston, 1996—; pres. Am. Coll. Nuclear Medicine, 1993-94; cons. in field. Author articles in field, chpt. in books; editor Jour. Nuclear Medicine, 1985-89. Mem. AAAS, ACP, AMA, Am. Coll. Nuclear Physicians, Am. Coll. Nuclear Medicine, Radiol. Soc. N.Am., Am. Thyroid Assn., Assn. Univ. Radiologists, Soc. Nuclear Medicine, Tex. Med. Assn., Tex. Assn. Physicians in Nuclear Medicine, Am. Coll. Radiology, Sigma Xi, Phi Gamma Delta, Doctor's Club. Episcopalian. Office: 1515 Holcombe Blvd Houston TX 77030-4009

HAYNOR, PATRICIA MANZI, nursing educator, consultant; children: Kelly Christine, Craig; m. Donald C. Maaswinkel. Diploma in nursing, Grasslands Hosp., Valhalla, N.Y.; BSN, Fairleigh Dickinsn U., 1967; MSN in Nursing Adminstrn., U. Pa., 1969; D Nursing Sci., Widener U., 1989. RN, Pa., N.J., N.Y., Del. Asst. dir. surg. nursing Thomas Jefferson U. Hosp., Phila., 1972-74; asst. dir. nursing care depts. Our Lady of Lourdes Hosp., Camden, N.J., 1974-76; assoc. dir. nursing West Jersey Hosp., Camden, 1976-79; dir. nursing West Jersey Health System, Camden, 1979-81, corp. dir. nursing, 1981-82; v.p. nursing Crozer-Chester (Pa.) Med. Ctr., 1982-85; coord. nursing adminstrn. program, asst. prof. Widener U., Chester, 1985-87; v.p. for nursing St. Francis Med. Ctr., Trenton, N.J., 1987-90; asst. prof. U. Del. Coll. Nursing, 1990-92; assoc. prof. Villanova (Pa.) U. Coll. Nursing, Phila., 1992—; cons. Nurse Assocs., Haddon Heights, N.J., 1985—; spkr. in field; abstractor Am. Orgn. Nurse Execs. Leadership Perspectives. Contbr. articles to profl. publs. Mem. adv. bd. Camden County unit Am. Cancer Soc. Mem. AAUP, Am. Orgn. Nurse Execs., Am. Coll. Healthcare Execs., S.E. Pa. Orgn. Nurse Leaders (bd. dirs., chair by-laws). Home: 201 9th Ave Haddon Heights NJ 08035-1632 Office: Villanova U Coll Nursing Villanova PA 19085

HAYRY, PEKKA JUHA, transplant surgeon, immunologist; b. Vihti, Finland, Dec. 13, 1939; s. Olavi K. and Aili (Harjula) H.; 1 child, Valtteri. MD, Univ. Helsinki (Finland), 1965, PhD, 1966. Postdoctoral fellow Wistar Inst., Phila., 1967-70; resident in surgery U. Helsinki Hosp., 1971-73, assoc. chief surgery, 1973-79; asst. prof. immunology U. Helsinki, 1970-79; asst. prof. surgery U. Oulu, Finland, 1973-79; prof. transplantation surgery and immunology U. Helsinki and Helsinki U. Central Hosp., 1979—; vis. prof. U. Rene Descartes, Paris, 1974, Duke U., 1977, U. N.C., 1977, U. Adelaide, Australia, 1981. Contbr. chpts. to books, articles to profl. jours. Served to 1st lt. Finnish Med. Corps, 1960-61, 95. Decorated comdr. Order of Lion (Finland), Order of Agnus Dei (Finland), 1st class of Order St. Mark, (Alexandria), Order of the Phoenix (Greece, commr.), Order of the Holy Sepulchre (Jerusalem), grand comdr. Order of St. Peter and Paul (Antioch); recipient Matti Äyräpää prize Finnish Med. Soc., 1988, Medix prize, 1994; named to Archon Megas Referendarios of Ct. of His All Holiness, the Ecumenical Patriarch, Constantinople. Mem. Finnish Acad. Scis. and Lettres, Scandinavian Soc. Immunology (bd. dirs. 1980-85), Am. Assn. Immunologists, Am. Soc. Transplant Surgeons, Internat. Soc. Heart Transplantation, The Transplantation Soc. (v.p. 1988-90, councillor 1992-94, pres.-elect 1994-96, pres. 1996—), Internat. Soc. Nephrology. Avocations: equestrian sports. sheep breeding, forestry. Office: U Helsinki Transplantation Lab, The Haartman Inst PO Box 21, FIN 00014 Helsinki Finland

HAYS, PEGGY ANN, nurse; b. Chillicothe, Ohio, Mar. 9, 1948; d. Charles Richard and Patricia Ann (Hupp) Maxwell; m. James Bennie Hays, Nov. 12, 1971. RN, Grant Hosp., Columbus, Ohio. RN, 1971; cert. oper. room nurse. Nurse Med. Ctr. Hosp., Chillicothe, 1971-74, operating room supr., 1974-76; pvt. nurse Surg. Specialists Inc., Portsmouth, Ohio, 1976—; dealer Hearthstone Log Timberframe Homes; gen. class falconer. Mem. Ohio Hist. Soc., Hist. Trust for Preservation, Ohio League of Sportsmen. Mem. NRA, Assn. Oper. Rm. Nurses, Ohio Gun Collectors, Nat. Muzzle Loading Rifle Assn., N.Am. Falconry Assn., Ohio Hawk Trust, Nat. Wildlife Fedn. (leader), Wildlife Rehab. Republican. Home: 1832 California Hollow Rd Bainbridge OH 45612-9711

HAYS, THOMAS S., medical educator, medical researcher; b. Winter Haven, Fla., Dec. 20, 1954; married;. BS in Zoology, U. N.C., 1976, PhD in Cell Biology, 1985. Rsch. asst. dept. zoology U. N.C., Chapel Hill, 1975-76; rsch. asst. dept. biol. scis. Duke U., Durham, N.C., 1976-79; asst. instr. quantitative and analytical microscopy Marine Biol. Lab., Woods Hole, Mass., 1981-83; asst. instr. optical microscopy U. Calif., Santa Cruz, 1982; postdoctoral fellow dept. molecular, cellular and devel. biology U. Colo., Boulder, 1985-89; asst. prof. dept. genetics and cell biology U. Minn., St. Paul, 1989-95, assoc. prof. dept. genetics and cell biology, 1995—; external reviewer NSF, 1989—. Reviewer Jour. Cell Biology, Jour. Biol. Chemistry, Molecular Biology of the Cell, Molecular Cellular Biology, Proceedings Nat. Acad. Sci. USA, Cell Motility and the Cytoskeleton, Jour. Cell Sci., Genetics; contbr. articles to profl. jours. Founders scholar Marine Biol. Lab., 1980; H.V. Wilson fellow U. N.C., R.J. Reynolds fellow, 1983; Postdoctoral fellow NIH, 1985-88; recipient Basil O'Connor Scholar award March of Dimes, 1993, Established Investigator award Am. Heart Found., 1996; Tng. grantee NIH, 1991-95, grantee, 1995—; Rsch. Tng. grantee NSF, 1991-95; March of Dimes grantee, 1995—. Mem. Am. Soc. Cell Biology, Genetics Soc. Am. Office: U Minn Biol Sci Ctr Rm 250 1445 Gortner Ave Saint Paul MN 55108

HAYWARD, LINDA F., medical educator. BA, U. Calif., Santa Cruz, 1980; MS, U. Wash., 1984; PhD, Northwestern U., 1990. Rsch. asst. VA Med. Ctr., Seattle, 1984-85; asst. rsch. scientist U. Iowa Dept. Internal Medicine, Iowa City, 1995—; researcher in field. Contbr. articles to profl. jours. Postdoctoral fellow U. Iowa, 1990-94; NIH grantee, 1991-93, Am. Heart Assn. grantee, 1994—. Mem. AAAS, Soc. Neurosci. Office: U Iowa Coll Medicine Dept Internal Medicine 608 MRC Iowa City IA 52242*

HAYWOOD, B(ETTY) J(EAN), anesthesiologist; b. Boston, June 1, 1942; d. Oliver Garfield and Helen Elizabeth (Salisbury) H.; m. Lynn Brandt Moon, Aug. 29, 1969 (div. Aug. 1986); children: Kaylin, Kris Lee, Kelly, Kasy R. BSc, Tufts U., 1964; MD, U. Colo., 1968; MBA, Oklahoma City U., 1993. Intern Wilford Hall AFB, San Antonio, Tex., 1968-69; resident in pediatrics U. Ariz., Tucson, 1971-72, resident in anesthesiology, 1972-74; dir. anesthesia dept. Pima County Hosp., Tucson, 1975-76; staff anesthesiologist South Community Hosp., Oklahoma City, 1977—; staff anesthesiologist Moore (Okla.) Mcpl. Hosp., 1981-94, chief of anesthesia, 1990-94; staff anesthesiologist St. Anthony Hosp., Oklahoma City, 1982—; chief of ethics com. S.W. Med. Ctr., 1996—. Bd. dirs. N.Am. South Devin Assn., Lynnville, Iowa, 1978-86; mem. med. com. Planned Parenthood Okla., 1992—. Lt. col. USAFR, 1968—. Mem. AMA, NAFE (co-dir. Oklahoma City chpt. 1996—), World South Devon Assn. (U.S. rep. 1985, 88—), Tufts U. Alumni Assn. (rep.), Chi Omega (treas. 1963-64). Republican. Presbyterian. Home: 6501 Hunting Hill Oklahoma City OK 73116-3523

HAYWOOD, H(ERBERT) CARL(TON), psychologist, educator; b. Taylor County, Ga., July 2, 1931; s. Howard Chapman and Rosebud (Smith) H.; m. Nancy Patricia Roberts, Oct. 5, 1951 (div. Mar. 1971); children: Carlton, Terence, Elizabeth, Kristin; m. Dona June Wooldridge Tapp, Sept. 6, 1993. A.B., San Diego State Coll., 1956, M.A., 1957; Ph.D., U. Ill., 1961. Mem. faculty George Peabody Coll. (merged with Vanderbilt U. 1979), Nashville, 1962-93; Alexander Heard disting. svc. prof., 1993-94; prof. psychology George Peabody Coll. (merged with Vanderbilt U. 1979), Nashville, 1969-93, prof. spl. edn., 1975-79, prof. emeritus, 1994—, dir. mental retardation research tng. program, 1968-70; dir. Inst. Mental Retardation and Intellectual Devel., 1970-73, Office Research Adminstrn., 1974-76, John F. Kennedy Center Research Edn. and Human Devel., 1971-83; prof. neurology Vanderbilt U. Sch. Medicine, 1971-93, prof. emeritus, 1994—; prof. psychology and edn., dean grad. sch. edn. & psychology Touro Coll., N.Y.C., 1993—; vis. prof. U. Toronto, 1965-66; sr. fellow Vanderbilt Inst. Pub. Policy Studies, 1983-88; chmn. Nat Mental Retardation Research Center Dirs., 1979-82; adv. bd. Ill. Inst. Developmental Disabilities, Chgo., 1970-78, Eunice Kennedy Shriver Center Mental Retardation, Waltham, Mass., 1973-80, Tenn. Dept. Mental Health, 1964-92 ; mem. nat. child health and human devel. council NIH, 1983-88; cons. President's Com. on Mental Retardation, 1968-73; mem. sci. rev. com., health research facilities br., div. edn. and research facilities NIH, 1967-71. Author: (with Brooks and Burns) Bright Start: Cognitive Curriculum for Young Children, 1992; editor: Brain Damage in School Age Children, 1968, Social Cultural Aspects of Mental Retardation, 1970, (with Begab and Garber) Prevention of Retarded Development in Psychosocially Disadvantaged Children, 1981, (with J.R. Newbrough) Living Environments for Developmentally Retarded Persons, 1981, (with D. Tzuriel) Interactive Assessment, 1992, (with S. Friedman) Developmental Follow-Up: Domains, Concepts, and Methods, 1994; editor Am. Jour. Mental Deficiency, 1969-79; mem. editl. bd. Jour. Abnormal Child Psychology, 1973-89, Contemporary Psychology, 1982-85, Acta Paedologica, 1983-87, Jour. Mental Deficiency Rsch., 1984—, Internat. Rev. Rsch. in Mental Retardation, 1982—; contbr. articles on child devel., motivation, and mental retardation to profl. jours. Served with USN, 1950-54. Fellow Am. Assn. Mental Retardation (v.p. psychology 1975-77, 1st v.p. 1978-79, pres. 1980-81), Am. Psychol. Assn. (pres. Div. 33 1978-79, mem. Council of Reps. 1980-82); mem. Internat. Assn. Cognitive Edn. (pres. 1988-92), Soc. Research Child Devel., Inst. Medicine, Psychonomic Soc. Democrat. Episcopalian. Office: Touro Coll 350 5th Ave Ste 1700 New York NY 10118

HAYWOOD, L. JULIAN, physician, educator; b. Reidsville, N.C., Apr. 13, 1927; s. Thomas Woodly and Louise Viola (Hayley) H.; m. Virginia Elizabeth Paige, Dec. 3, 1953; 1 child, Julian Anthony. BS, Hampton Inst., 1948; MD, Howard U., 1952. Intern St. Mary's Hosp., Rochester, N.Y., 1952-53; resident L.A. County Hosp., 1956-58; fellow cardiology White Meml. Hosp., 1959-61; traveling fellow U. Oxford, Eng., 1963; instr. medicine Loma Linda (Calif.) U., 1960-61, asst. prof., 1961-73, assoc. clin. prof., 1973-82, clin. prof., 1982—; asst. prof. medicine U. So. Calif., 1963-67, assoc. prof., 1967-76, prof., 1976—; past dir. comprehensive sickle cell ctr. Los Angeles County/U. So. Calif. Med. Ctr., dir. ECG Dept., 1996—, past dir. coronary care unit, physicians tng. program (Regional Med. Programs), 1970-75; cons. Los Angeles County Coroner, Indsl. Accident Bd. Calif., Health Care Tech. Divsn., USPHS, Nat. Heart and Lung Inst.; past mem. cardiology adv. com. divsn. heart and vascular diseases; bd. dirs., pres. Sickle Cell Diseases Found. Contbr. articles profl. jours.; Mem. editorial bds.: Jour. Nat. Med. Assn. Past pres., hon. mem., bd. dirs. Am. Heart Assn. Greater L.A., 1989—. With M.C. USNR, 1954-56. Recipient award of merit Los Angeles County Heart Assn., 1968, 69, 73, 75, Disting. Alumnus award Howard U., 1982, Louis B. Russel award Am. Heart Assn., 1988, Merit award, 1991, Heart of Gold award Am. Heart Assn./Greater L.A. Affiliate, 1989, Dedicated Svc. award, 1991, 93, award of Achievement in Rsch., 1994, 20th Anniversary Founder's award Assn. Black Cardiologists, 1994; J.B. Johnson Meml. lectr., 1975, 88; honoree Internal Medicine sect. Nat. Med. Assn., 1988; named Alumnus of Yr.-at-Large, Hampton U., 1993. Fellow ACP, AAAS, L.A. Acad. Medicine, Am. Coll. Cardiology, Am. Heart Assn. (coun. on clin. cardiology, coun. on atherosclerosis, exec. com. coun. on epidemiology, long range planning com., dir., past sec., v.p. Greater L.A. affiliate, pres.); mem. AMA, AAUP, Am. Fedn. Clin. Rsch., Western Soc. Clin. Investigation, Assn. Advancement Med. Instrumentation, Nat. Med. Assn. (Charles Drew Med. Soc.), N.Y. Acad. Scis., Hampton Inst. Alumni Assn. (past pres. L.A. chpt.), Med. Faculty Assn. U. So. Calif. Sch. Medicine (past pres.), Assn. Physicians L.A. County Hosp. (pres. 1991—), Western Assn. Physicians, Fedn. Am. Scientists, Assn. Black Cardiologists (Walter Booker Innovation award 1990), Assn. Acad. Minority Physicians (councilor, pres.-elect 1992-93, pres. 1993-94), Alpha Omega Alpha. Home: 3551 Lowry Rd Los Angeles CA 90027-1433 Office: Los Angeles County/So Calif Med Ctr Box 305 1200 N State St Los Angeles CA 90033-4525

HAYWORTH, SCOTT DAVID, physician; b. N.Y.C., Apr. 4, 1956; s. Henry Charles and Anne (Sinnreich) H.; m. Nan Alison Sutter, June 21, 1981; children: William, John. AB, Princeton U., 1978; MD, Cornell U., 1984. Diplomate Am. Bd. Ob/Gyn., Nat. Bd. Med. Examiners. Intern Mt. Sinai Hosp., N.Y.C., 1984-85, resident physician, 1985-87, chief resident, 1987-88; physician Mt. Kisco (N.Y.) Med. Group, 1988—, v.p., 1995-96, pres., 1996—; co-chmn. laser com. No. Westchester Hosp., 1991—, mem. pharmacy and therapeutics com., 1990—. Contbr. chpt. to book and articles to profl. jours. Fellow NIH, 1981, David Barr, 1981. Fellow Am. Coll. Ob-Gyn.; mem. Westchester Obstetrical and Gynecol. Soc. (sec.-treas. 1995-96, co-pres. 1996—), Internat. Soc. Gynecol. Endoscopy, Gynecol. Laser Soc. Office: Mt Kisco Med Group 34 S Bedford Rd Mount Kisco NY 10549-3408

HAZELBAKER, EILEEN GENEVA, medical technologist; b. Decatur County, Kans., Nov. 2, 1928; d. Clint Leonard and Edith Helen (Vermilion) Huff; degree in gen. sci. Ft. Hays (Kans.) State Coll., 1953; m. Fred R. Hazelbaker, Oct. 5, 1974; 1 son by previous marriage, Wayne Leroy Wohler. Intern, Stormont-Vail Hosp., Topeka, 1953; med. technologist hosps. in Kans. and Wash., 1954-67; med. technologist Syringa Gen. Hosp., Grangeville, Idaho, 1967-90. Mem. Am. Soc. Clin. Pathologists, Area Agy. on Aging. Mem. Christian Ch. (Disciples of Christ). Clubs: Extension, Rebekahs. Home: PO Box 225 Grangeville ID 83530-0225

HAZELIP, EDWINA KAY, nurse; b. Louisville, Jan. 25, 1952; d. Edwin O'Neil and Lorraine Esta (Nichols) H.; grad. High Point (N.C.) Meml. Hosp. Sch. Nursing, 1975. Nurses aide Wilkes Gen. Hosp., North Wilkesboro, N.C., 1971-72; day care center worker Child's Kingdom, Wilkesboro, N.C., 1971-72; head nurse coronary and intensive care unit Wilkes Gen. Hosp., North Wilkesboro, 1972-82, pres. nurses' staff, 1976, 78; unit mgr. coronary and intensive care unit Wilkes Gen. Hosp., North Wilkesboro, 1982-84; staff nurse Med. Personnel Pool of the Triad, Greensboro, N.C., 1982-88, personnel com., 1984-87, chmn. personnel com., 1985-87; instr. cardiac defibrillation. Bd. dirs. Wilkes County unit Am. Heart Assn. Cert. instr. CPR; tchr. 2 yr.-old children Weekday Early Edn. of First Baptist Ch., Jamestown, N.C., 1986-87, tchr. 3 yr.-old children, 1987, dir., 1988—, dir. summer day camp; dir. Weekday Early Edn. Presch., Summer Presch., & Day Camp; handbell ringer, 1986—, mem. Chancel Choir, 1985—; Sunday sch. tchr., 1987—, mem. sr. adult ministries com., 1989-93; charter mem. Weekday Early Edn. Assn. N.C. Bapt. Conv., 1995. Mem. ANA, N.C. Nurses Assn. (by-laws com. 1991—, co-chair com. on coms. 1991—, chmn. 1993-94), Greensboro Assn. Edn. of Young Child. Home: 5112 Vickrey Chapel Rd Greensboro NC 27407-9737

HAZEN, TERRY CLYDE, microbial ecologist, educator; b. Pontiac, Mich., Feb. 7, 1951; s. Leo Robert and Phyllis Virginia (Hawley) H.; m. Gayle Kanne Reinecke, June 12, 1972; children—Tracy Heather, Brooks Trevor. B.S. with honors, Mich. State U., 1973, M.S., 1974; Ph.D., Wake Forest U., 1978. Research assoc. Wake Forest U., Winston-Salem, N.C., 1978-79; asst. prof. biology U. P.R., Rio Piedras, 1979-82, assoc. prof., 1982-85, prof., 1985-88 , acting chmn. dept., 1984-85, chmn. grad. studies, 80-84, scientist E.I. DuPont de Nemours Co., Westinghouse Savannah River Lab., Aiken, S.C., 1987—; cons. micro-computer applications in lab.; tchr., cons. in water quality. Head coach Pee Wee Football of P.R., 1983; mem. bd. visitors Wake Forest U. Winner 1st prize Sci. Writing, Puerto Rican Culture Soc., 1983. Mem. Am. Soc. Microbiology, AAAS, Sigma Xi (research award 1977). Republican. Contbr. 110 articles to profl. jours. Home: 2021 Autumn Chase Augusta GA 30907-3185 Office: Westinghouse Savannah River Co Savannah River Technology Ctr Bldg 704-8T Aiken SC 29808

HAZLEHURST, GEORGE EDWARD, physician; b. Jackson, Tenn., Dec. 29, 1928; s. George Edward and Alicia (Davidge) H.; m. Aud Staumo, Oct. 17, 1964; children: Anne Garrard, Edward, Rolf, Alicia. BS, U. Tenn., 1951, MD, 1954. Diplomate Am. Bd. Surgery. Physician Stevens Clinic Hosp., Welch, W.Va., 1962-64, Jackson-Madison County Gen. Hosp., Jackson, Tenn., 1965—; asst. clin. prof. U. Tenn. Family Practice Clinic, Jackson, 1975—. Capt. U.S. Army, 1957-59. Mem. AMA, Tenn. Med. Assn., Soc. Am. Gastrointestinal Endoscopic Surgeons, Am. Soc. for Gastrointestinal Endoscopy, Am. Coll. Gastroenterology. Office: 620 Skyline Dr Jackson TN 38301

HAZLEHURST, JOHN LIVINGSTON, surgeon; b. Wilmington, N.C., July 14, 1931; s. John Livingston Jr. and Elizabeth McLean (Graham) H.; m. Shirley Lord Coxe, Sept. 5, 1953; children: Elizabeth Graham, John L. IV. AB, U. N.C., 1952, MD, 1956. Diplomate Am. Bd. Surgery. Commd. capt. USAF, 1958, advanced through grades to maj., 1964; Pvt. practice surgery Asheville, N.C., 1966—; bd. dirs. Ashville Fed. Savs. & Loan; chief of staff St. Joseph Hosp., Ashville, 1974. Mem. dist. selection com. Morehead Scholarship, 1978-90. Morehead scholar Morehead Found., U. N.C., Chapel Hill, 1952-56. Fellow Am. coll. Surgeions, Southeastern Surgical Congress; mem. N.C. Surgical Assn., AMA, Civitan Club. Republican. Episcopal. Home: 4 Frith Dr Asheville NC 28803-3109 Office: Regional Surg Specialists 16 Mcdowell St Asheville NC 28801-4104

HAZLETT, DONALD ARTHUR, psychiatrist; b. Apollo, Pa., Sept. 17, 1936; s. Charles Clarke and Hilda Ruth (Smith) H.; m. Sandra Mae Garber, June 5, 1962 (div. June 1976); 1 child, Bronweh; m. Mary Ellen Johnson, Oct. 24, 1981; 1 child, Colleen Daniel. BA in English/Chemistry, Greenville Coll., 1962; MD, Washington U. St. Louis, 1967. Commd. ensign USN, 1953, retiredt, 1987; dir. admissions Woodville State Hosp., Carnegie, Pa., 1987-88; assoc. med. dir. Hullside Psychiat. Ctr., McKeesport, Pa., 1988-89; med. dir. Clarion (Pa.) Psychiat. Ctr., 1991—; cons. in field. Decorated Army Commendation medal, Army Achievement medal (2). Mem. AMA, Am. Psychiat. Assn., Am. Acad. Clin. Psychiatrists, World Med. Assn., World Fedn. Mental Health, Nat. Alliance for Mentally Ill, Franklin C. of C. Home: 513 Highland Dr Shippenville PA 16254 Office: Rural Mental Health Assocs 1281 Otter St Franklin PA 16323

HAZLETT, PAUL EDWARD, realtor, information systems executive; b. Gallipolis, Ohio, Dec. 10, 1937; s. Vickers James and Wilma (Dickey) H.; m. Lynn Todd; 1 child, Esther. BBA, Cleve. State U., 1964. Freight sales N.Y. Cen., Cleve., 1964-66; with computer systems dept. Honeywell, Inc., Cleve., 1966-75; investment real estate Cleve., 1975-78; mgr. Fairview Gen. Hosp., Cleve., 1978-96; adj. faculty Cuyahoga Community Coll., Cleve.; cons. in field; real estate agt., Cleve. Bd. mgrs. West Side YMCA, 1987—. Home: 6987 Big Creek Pky Middleburg Heights OH 44130 Office: 13405 Smith Rd Middleburg Heights OH 44130

HAZZARD, WILLIAM RUSSELL, geriatrician, educator; b. Ann Arbor, Mich., Sept. 5, 1936; s. Albert Sidney and Florence Bernice (Woolsey) H.; m. Ellen Bennett Friedman, June 10, 1961; children: Susan Lovejoy Roque, Russell Holden, Rebecca Cornell Oliver, Daniel Bennett. AB, Cornell U., 1958, MD, 1962. Diplomate Am. Bd. Internal Med. Resident in internal medicine U. Wash. Sch. Med. and Affiliated Hosps., Seattle, 1966-67, fellow in endocrinology and metabolism, 1965-66, 67-69; from instr. to prof. medicine U. Wash., Seattle, 1969-82, dir. Northwest Lipid Rsch. Clinic, 1972-78; investigator Howard Hughes Med. Inst., U. Wash., Seattle, 1972-80; prof. medicine, assoc. dir. dept. medicine Johns Hopkins Med. Instns., Balt., 1982-86, dir. ctr. on aging, 1983-86; prof., chmn. dept. internal med. Bowman Gray Sch. Medicine of Wake Forest U., Winston-Salem, N.C., 1986—; dir. J. Paul Sticht Ctr. on Aging of Wake Forest U., Winston-Salem, N.C., 1987—. Editor: Principles of Geriatric Medicine and Gerontology, 1984, 89, 93; contbr. over 100 articles to jours. in field. Lt. USNR, 1963-65. Fellow ACP; mem. Inst. Medicine of NAS, Am. Geriatrics Soc. (bd. dirs. 1988—, pres. 1993), Assn. Profs. Medicine, Gerontol. Soc. Am. (chmn. clin. med. sect. 1984), Am. Heart Assn. (Coun. on Arterosclerosis), Am. Fedn. Clin. Rsch. (mem. emeritus), Am. Soc. Clin. Investigation (mem. emeritus), Assn. Am. Physicians, AM. Clin. and Climatol. Assn., Nat. Inst. on Aging (aging rev. com. 1990-94, Geriatric Medicine Acad. award 1980). Home: 5200 Riverwest Rd Lewisville NC 27023-8121 Office: Bowman Gray Sch of Medicine Dept Internal Medicine Winston Salem NC 27157

HEACOCK, DONALD DEE, social worker; b. Anthony, Kans., Feb. 21, 1934; s. C.W. and Thelma Olive (Hilton) H.; m. Margaret Newberry, Sept. 4, 1953; children: Teresa Ellen, Mark Dee. AB, Washburn U., 1956; BD cum laude, United Sem., 1959; MSW, Barry Coll., 1971. Ordained priest Episcopal Ch., 1965; diplomate in clin. social work. Parish minister St. John's Ch., Clinton, Mich., 1961-66; chaplain, Margarita, Canal Zone, 1966-69; tchr. Christ Ch. Acad. Secondary Sch., Colon, Panama, 1966-69; counselor South Fla. Neighborhood Youth Corp., Miami, 1969-70; chief social service, instr. pediatric comprehensive health care program U. Miami, 1971-72; asst. dir. Alpha House, Dade County, Fla. and field supr. Barry Coll., 1972-73; marriage and family therapist Psychiatric Assocs., Shreveport, La., 1973-75; pvt. practice social work, Shreveport, 1975—; dir. Holy Cross Child Placement Agy., Inc., 1984; lectr. sociology Centenary Coll., 1981-88. With USAF, 1959-61. Mem. Am. Assn. Marriage and Family Therapy, Nat. Assn. Social Workers, Acad. Cert. Social Work, Phi Kappa Mu, Phi Gamma Mu. Lodge: Masons. Home: 748 Thora Blvd Shreveport LA 71106-1824 Office: 929 Olive St Shreveport LA 71104-2103

HEAD, HAROLD DAVID, cardiothoracic surgeon; b. Tampa, Fla., Aug. 11, 1944; s. Harold Sears and Helen Louise H.; m. Frances M. Skowronski Loughnan, Aug. 3, 1966 (div. 1989); children; Chris, Dianna, Cathy, Paul; m. Laura Ellen Witherspoon, June 16, 1990; children; Scott, Allison. BS, Washington and Lee U., 1966; MD, Duke U., 1970. Diplomate Am. Bd. Surgery, Am. Bd. Thoracic Surgery, sub-bd. Surg. Critical Care; lic. physician, Tenn., N.C. Intern Walter Reed Army Med. Ctr., Washington, 1970-71, resident in surgery, 1971-75, resident in thoracic surgery, 1975-77, asst. chief thoracic surgery, 1979-83; fellow in congenital cardiac surgery U. Ala., Birmingham, 1978-79; chief thoracic surgery, program dir. thoracic residence Brooke Army Med. Ctr., San Antonio, 1983-86; thoracic surgeon Valley Cardiovascular and Thoracic Surgeons, Dayton, Ohio, 1990-94; pvt. practice adult and pediatric thoracic surgery Fresno, Calif., 1986-90, Chattanooga, 1994—; assoc. clin. prof. surgery U. Tenn., 1996—, Wright State U., Dayton, 1991-94, U. Calif. San Francisco, Fresno, 1987-90, U. Tex. Health Sci. Ctr., San Antonio, 1984-86, others. Contbr. chpts. to books, articles to profl. jours. Mem. subcom. for disaster preparedness D.C. Mayor's Emergency Med. Svcs., Washington, 1982-83. Served to col. U.S. Army, 1966-86. Decorated Order Mil. Med. Merit, Legion of Merit. Fellow ACS, Am. Coll. Cardiology, Am. Coll. Chest Physicans; mem. AMA, Soc. Thoracic Surgeons, Am. Heart Assn. (cardiac surg. coun.), others. Episcopalian.

HEAD, JONATHAN FREDERICK, cell biologist; b. Syracuse, N.Y., Nov. 23, 1949; s. Arthur Everard and Lillian Myrtle (Hendra) H.; m. Priscilla Catherine Tambone, July 28, 1984; 1 child, Catherine Elizabeth. BS in Zoology, Syracuse U., 1971; MA in Biology, Bklyn. Coll., 1977; PhD in Biology, Fordham U., 1985. Rsch. asst. Naylor Dana Inst. Disease Prevention/Am. Health Found., Valhalla, N.Y., 1974-78, Cornell U. Med. Coll., N.Y.C., 1978; rsch. asst. Mt. Sinai Sch. Medicine, N.Y.C., 1978-84, rsch. assoc., 1984-86, rsch. asst. prof., 1986-87; dir. tumor cell biology Ctr. Clin. Scis./Internat. Clin. Labs., Nashville, 1986-89; pres. Mastology Rsch. Inst., Baton Rouge, 1989—; adj. asst. prof. Tulane U. Sch. Medicine, New Orleans, 1989—; adj. prof. Delta State U., Cleveland, Miss., 1992—; researcher and lectr. in field of cancer. Contbr. articles, abstracts and chpts. to sci. publs. Mem. State of La. Adoption Cmty. Adv. Bd., 1992-95. Mem. AAAS, Am. Assn. Cancer Rsch., Am. Soc. Clin. Oncology, Soc. Biol. Therapy, European Soc. Med. Oncology. Methodist. Home: 6144 Hagerstown Dr Baton Rouge LA 70817-3917 Office: Mastology Rsch Inst 1770 Physicians Park Dr Baton Rouge LA 70816-3222

HEAD, WILLIAM CHRISTOPHER, military officer, health care administrator; b. Clarksville, Tenn., Apr. 24, 1944; s. Asbury Jefferson and Dorothy Lillian (Brown) H.; m. Carolyn M. Bell, July 6, 1990; children: Sara Christine, William Christopher. BS in BA, U. Tenn., Knoxville, 1967; MHA, Duke U., 1969. Commd. USAF, 1969—, advanced through grades to col.; asst. adminstr. USAF Hosp., Homestead AFB, Fla., 1969-72; adminstr. USAF Clinic, Greenham Common, U.K., 1972-74; asst. adminstr. USAF Regional Hosp., Lakenheath, U.K., 1974-77; instr. Sch. Health Care Scis., Sheppard AFB, Tex., 1977-79; health sys. planner Office of Surgeon Gen., Bolling AFB, 1979-80; health sys. analysis Air Firce Med. Svc. Ctr., Brooks AFB, Tex., 1980-82; chief med. sys. divsn. Sch. Health Care Scis., Sheppard AFB, 1982-86; adminstr. 215th Med. Group, Tyndall AFB, Fla., 1986-89, 1st Med. Group, Langley AFB, Va., 1989-91; dir. health care support Office of Command Surgeon, Langley AFB, 1991-92, 92-94; command surgeon Hdqrs. Air Combat Command, Langley AFB, 1992, dep. command surgeon, 1994-95; dep. comdr. 96th Med. Group, Eglin AFB, Fla., 1995—. Mem. cmty. adv. bd. Bay Med. Ctr. Panama City, Fla., 1986-89; mem. regional adv. bd. Am. Hosp. Assn., Chgo., 1982-85; bd. dirs. Young Execs. Healthcare Bus., Wichita Falls, Tex., 1982-86; bd. govs. Career Decision, Inc., 1993-94. Fellow Am. Coll. Healthcare Execs. (chmn. 1994-95, chmn. credentialing task force 1993-94, fin. com. chmn. 1993-94, gov. dist. VIII 1989-93, strategic planning com. 1988-89, gov. dist. VI 1985-86, regional adv. bd. Region 7 1982-85, regent-at-large 1982-85, many other coms., Fed. Excellence in Healthcare Leadership award 1996); mem. Am. Hosp. Assn., Tex. Hosp. Assn. Assn. Mil. Surgeons U.S. (Outstanding Fed. Svc. Adminstrs. award 1995, Ray E. Brown award 1986, Young Fed. Healthcare Adminstr. award 1984), Healthcare Adminstrs. of Tidewater, Royal Soc. Health, Air War Coll. Alumni Assn. (life), Interagy. Inst. for Fed. Health Care Execs., Duke U. Health and Hosp. Adminstrn. Alumni Assn., Profl. Soc. Svcs. Inc. (bd. govs., chmn. 1993-94). Presbyterian. Home: 36 Indian Bayou Dr Destin FL 32541-4447 Office: 96 Medical Group 307 Boatner Rd Ste 114 Eglin AFB FL 32542*

HEADLEY, BARBARA JOAN, physical therapist; b. Livingston, N.J., Mar. 31, 1946; d. Wayne Noel and Alice Elizabeth (Munro) H. BS in Phys. Therapy, Ithaca (N.Y.) Coll., 1968; MS in Phys. Therapy, Boston U., 1974. Phys. therapist Yale-New Haven (Conn.) Hosp., 1968-72, Vt. Ctr., Burlington, 1972-73; clin. specialist burns U. Chgo. Hosp. and Clinics, 1974-76, St. John's Mercy Med. Ctr., St. Louis, 1976-80; clin. and research assoc. burns St. Paul Ramsey Med. Ctr., 1981; dept. head phys. therapy Rehab. Services, Bloomington, Minn., 1982-83, Northwest Rehab. Services, Mpls., 1984-85; dir. biofeedback Primary Beh. Health Clinic, Stillwater, Minn., 1986-88; pvt. practice cons. biofeedback St. Paul, 1988-90; founder Pain Evaluation and Rehab. Ctr., St. Paul, 1988-92. Author: Chronic Pain: Life Out of Balance, 1987, Chronic Pain: A Family Matter, Back in Balance, 1988, Roadblocks to Rehabilitation, 1988, Managing Chronic Pain. You Can Do It, 1989, Play Ball Exercise Program, 1990, Controlling Symptoms At Work, 1995, S.M.A.R.T. The Moves That Matter; contbr. articles to profl. jours.; columnist Advance for Phys. Therapists. Co-founder Pain Edn. and Rsch. Ctr., 1988. Mem. Am. Phys. Therapy Assn. (mem. 2d party payor task force), Am. Pain Soc., Internat. Assn. Study of Pain. Home: 2962 Glenwood Dr Boulder CO 80301 Office: Innovative Sys for Rehab 1711 W Country Rd B # 211 S PO Box 3192 Boulder CO 80307-3192

HEADRICK, CLARK JAY, osteopath; b. San Diego, Aug. 11, 1958; s. Jay and Shirley Joan (Fine) H.; m. Dara Lenore Headrick; 1 child, Ariana Rebecca. BS, U. Calif., Davis, 1980; DO, Coll. Osteo. Medicine Pacific, 1988. Cert. internal medicine, pulmonary medicine, critical care Am. Bd. Osteopathic Internal Medicine. Intern Genesys Health Sys., Genesys Regional Med. Ctr., Flint, Mich., 1988-89, resident in internal medicine, 1989-91, fellow in pulmonary medicine, 1991-93, fellow in critical care medicine, 1994-95; with Mich. Lung Specialists, Flint, 1995—. Fellow Am. Coll. Chest Physicians; mem. Am. Osteo. Acad., Soc. Critical Care Medicine, Genesee County Osteo. Soc. Office: Mich Lung Specialists G-3317 Beecher Rd Flint MI 48532

HEADRICK, DARA LENORE, physician; b. N.Y.C., Mar. 20, 1965; d. David Aaron Kaufman and Carol Elaine (Kent) Butler; m. Clark Jay Headrick, May 16, 1992. BS in Kinesiology, UCLA, L.A., 1986; DO, Coll. Osteo. Medicine Pacific, 1992. Diplomate Nat. Bd. Osteo. Medicine. Tchg. asst. Coll. Osteo. Medicine of the Pacific, Pomona, Calif., 1987-89; undergrad. fellow Coll. Osteo. Medicine, Pomona, 1989-92; intern physician Genesys Health Care-Flint (Mich.) Osteo. Campus, 1992-93; resident physician dept. phys. medicine and rehab. U. Mich. Med. Ctr., Ann Arbor, 1993-96, chief resident dept. phys. medicine and rehab., 1995—; attending physician Phys. Medicine & Rehab. Genesys Regional Health Sys., Grand Blanc, Mich., 1996—. Named Outstanding Young Women of Am., 1991. Mem. AMA, NOW, Am. Osteo. Assn., Am. Acad. Phys. Medicine and Rehab., Assn. Acad. Physiatry, Am. Acad. Osteopathy, Habitat for Humanity, Sigma Sigma Phi. Democrat. Office: Genesys Regional Health System Grand Blanc MI 48439

HEADRICK, LINDA ANN, physician, educator; b. Rolla, Md., Nov. 28, 1955; d. Hubert Harold and Ethel Ruth (Capps) H.; m. David Ray Setzer, Aug. 13, 1977. BA, U. Mo., 1977; MD, Stanford U., 1981. Diplomate Am. Bd. Internal Medicine. Intern in medicine U. Md., Balt., 1981-82, resident in medicine, 1982-84, chief resident in medicine, 1984-85; asst. prof. medicine Sch. Medicine, Case Western Res. U., Cleve., 1985-93, assoc. prof., 1993—; staff physician, primary care clerkship dir. Met. Health Med. Ctr., Cleve., 1985-94. Author: Quality and Cost of Care, 5th edit., 1994, Clinical CQI: A Book of Readings, 1995. Mem. ACP, APHA, Soc. Gen. Internal Medicine, Physicians for Social Responsibility (nat. bd. dirs. 1990-95, pres. N.E. Ohio chpt. 1990-91), Physicians for Human Rights, Amnesty Internat. Home: 6435 Chagrin River Rd Chagrin Falls OH 44022-3540 Office: Met Health Med Ctr 2500 Metrohealth Dr Cleveland OH 44109-1900

HEAGARTY, MARGARET CAROLINE, pediatric physician; b. Charleston, W.Va., Sept. 8, 1934; d. John Patrick and Margaret Caroline (Walsh) H. BA, Seton Hill Coll., 1957; BS, W.Va. Sch. Medicine, 1959; MD, U. Pa., 1961; DSc honoris causa, Iona Coll., 1989. Diplomate: Am. Bd. Pediatrics. Intern Phila. Gen. Hosp., 1961-62; resident in pediatrics St. Christopher's Hosp. for Children, Phila., 1962-64; dir. pediatric ambulatory care services N.Y. Hosp.-Cornell Med. Ctr., N.Y.C., 1969-78; dir. pediatrics Harlem Hosp. Ctr. Columbia U., N.Y.C., 1978—, prof. pediatrics Coll. Physicians & Surgeons, 1987—; cons. Dept. HEW Promotion of Child Health, Washington; mem. Com. Community Oriented Primary Care Inst. Medicine, Washington; mem. Robert Wood Johnson Found. Program for Prepaid Managed Health Care, 1984; mem. governing council Inst. Medicine, Nat. Acad. Scis., 1986. Author: Changing the Medical Car System-Report of an Experiment, 1974, Medical Sociology: A Systems Approach, 1975, Child Health: Basics for Primary Care, 1980. Grantee Commonwealth Found., 1981, Robert Wood Johnson Found., 1983, Ctr. for Disease Control, 1985, Health Rsch. and Svc. Adminstrn., 1988, Nat. Inst. Allergy/Infectious Disease, 1988. Fellow Inst. Medicine (steering group for nat. forum on future of children and their families 1987—); mem. Ambulatory Pediatric Assn. (pres. 1976-77), Soc. Pediatric Research, Am. Pediatric Soc., Am. Acad. Pediatrics (com. on hosp. care 1988—), Assn. Pediatric Program Dirs., Nat. Bd. Med. Examiners. Home: 2520 Kingsland Ave Bronx NY 10469-6108 Office: Columbia U-Harlem Hosp Ctr 506 Lenox Ave New York NY 10037-1802*

HEALEY, JOHN HENRY, orthopaedic surgeon, researcher; b. Lowell, Mass., Aug. 25, 1952; s. Robert Cummings and Ruth Elizabeth (Burckel) H.; m. Paula Olsiewski, Oct. 9, 1977; children: Georgia, Vivian. BS in Biology, Yale U., 1974; MD, U. Vt., 1978. Attending surgeon Meml. Sloan Kettering Cancer Ctr., Hosp. Spl. Surgery, N.Y.C., 1984—, chief orthopaedic surgery, 1991—; assoc. prof. surgery Cornell U. Med. Coll., N.Y.C., 1984—; rsch. exec. bd. mem. Hosp. Spl. Surgery, N.Y.C., 1994-96. Editor: Diagnosis and Management of Pathologic Fractures, 1993. Mem. spl. gifts com. Yale U., New Haven, 1994. NIH grantee; recipient Career Devel. award Am. Cancer Soc., 1986. Mem. Internat. Soc. Limb Salvage (pres. 1995-96), Orthopaedic Rsch. Soc. (bd. dirs. 1994-96), Orthopaedic Rsch. Edn. Found. (Zimmer award Orthopaedic Rsch. 1984). Home: 333 E 68th St New York NY 10021 Office: Sloan Kettering Meml Hosp 1275 York Ave New York NY 10021

HEALY, BERNADINE P., physician, educator, federal agency administrator, scientist; b. N.Y.C., Aug. 2, 1944; d. Michael J. and Violet (McGrath) Healy; m. Floyd Loop, Aug. 17, 1985; children: Bartlett Anne Bulkley, Marie McGrath Loop. AB summa cum laude, Vassar Coll., 1965; MD cum laude Harvard Med. Sch., 1970. Diplomate Am. Bd. Med. Examiners, Am. Bd. Cardiology, Am. Bd. Internal Medicine (bd. dirs. 1983-87); lic. physician, Md., Ohio. Intern in medicine Johns Hopkins Hosp., Balt., 1970-71, asst. resident, 1971-72; staff fellow sect. pathology Nat. Heart, Blood & Lung Inst., NIH, Bethesda, Md., 1972-74—; fellow cardiovascular div. dept. medicine Johns Hopkins U. Sch. Medicine, Balt., 1974-76, fellow dept. pathology, 1975-76, asst. prof. medicine and pathology, 1976-81, assoc. prof. medicine, 1977-82, asst. dean for postdoctoral programs and faculty devel., 1979-84, assoc. prof. pathology, 1981-84, prof. medicine, 1982-84; active staff medicine and pathology Johns Hopkins Hosp., from 1976, dir. CCU, 1977-84; dep. dir. Office Sci. and Tech. Policy, Exec. Office of Pres. White House, Washington, 1984-85; chmn. Rsch. Inst. The Cleve. Clinic Found., 1985-91, sr. health and sci. policy advisor, 1994—; dean Med. Sch. Ohio State U.; dir., NIH, Bethesda, Md., 1991-93; vice chmn. Pres.' Coun. Advisers on Sci. and Tech., 1990-91; mem. Spl. Med. Adv. Group, Dept. Veterans Affairs, 1990-91, chmn. adv. panel for Basic Rsch. for 1990's, Office Tech. Assessment, 1990-91, mem. NHLBI Task Force on Atherosclerosis, 1990; mem. Vis. Com. Bd. Overseers Harvard Med. Sch. and Sch. of Dental Medicine, Boston, 1986-91; councillor Harvard Med. Alumni Assn., 1987-90; mem. Nat. Adv. Bd. Johns Hopkins Ctr. for Hosp. Fin. and Mgmt., 1987-91; mem. Bd. Overseers Harvard Coll., 1989—; chmn. Office of Tech. Assessment Panel New Devels. in Biotech., U.S. Congress, 1986-87; mem. U.S.-Brazil Panel on Sci. and Tech., 1987; mem. White House Sci. Council, 1988-89; cons. Nat. Heart, Lung and Blood Inst., NIH, 1976-91, mem. Adv. Com. to Dir., NIH, 1986-91; chmn. steering com. Post-CABG Clin. Trial, 1987-91; bd. dirs. Medtronic, Inc., Mpls., Nat. City Corp., Cleve., Nova Pharms., Balt.; mem. adv. bd. Bayer Fund for Cardiovascular Rsch., N.Y.C., 1987-89; trustee Edison BioTech. Ctr., Cleve., 1990—; chmn. Ohio Coun. on Rsch. and Econ. Devel., 1989-91. Editorial cons. numerous jours.; abstract reviewer; editorial bd. Jour. Cardiovascular Medicine, 1980-91, Am. Jour. Medicine, 1986-91, Am. Jour. Cardiology, 1981-82, Circulation, 1981—, Jour. Am. Coll. Cardiology, 1982-84. Contbr. articles to profl. jours. Matthew Vassar scholar, 1962-65, Harvard Nat. scholar, 1965-70; Eloise Ellery fellow, 1965-66, Stetler Research fellow, 1976-77; recipient Nat. Bd. Ann. award for Medicine, Med. Coll. Pa., 1983. Mem. Am. Fedn. Clin. Research (pres. 1983-84), Am. Heart Assn. (award 1983-84, 90, pres. 1988-89, fellow Coun. on Clin. Cardiology, Coun. on Circulation, dir. 1983-84), Am. Coll. Cardiology (bd. govs. 1979-82), ACP, Assn. Am. Med. Colls., Internat. Acad. Pathology, Am. Med. Women's Assn., Assn. for Women in Sci., Am. Soc. Clin. Investigation, Am. Bd. Internal Medicine (bd. govs. 1986—), Inst. Medicine, NAS, Johns Hopkins U. Soc. Scholars, Inst. Medicine NAS, Phi Beta Kappa, Alpha Omega Alpha. Office: Ohio State Univ Coll Medicine 254 Meiling Hall 370 West 9th St Columbus OH 43210*

HEALY, DEAN ALAN, physician; b. Long Beach, Calif., Feb. 24, 1953; s. Carl Matthew and Virginia Lucille (Hartman) H.; m. Cynthia Elaine Clipp, May 28, 1983; children: Meredith, Elaine, Douglas. BA, Whittier Coll., 1975; MD, Vanderbilt U., 1980. Diplomate Am. Bd. Surgery with added qualifications in gen. vascular surgery and surg. crit. care. Assoc. prof. Pa. State U. Coll. of Medicine, Hershey, 1989—. Mem. Internat. Soc. Cardiovascular Surgery, Ea. Vascular Soc., Cardiovascular Surgery Coun., Am. Heart Assn. Office: Dept Surgery PO Box 850 Hershey PA 17033

HEALY, JOHN, research scientist; b. Birmingham, Eng., Mar. 15, 1961; s. Edmund Healy and Linda Flynn. Grad., Royal Soc. Chemistry, Stoke-on-Trent, Eng., 1983; PhD, Robert Gordon Inst. Tech./ Rowett Rsch. Inst., Aberdeen, Scotland, 1988. Lab. technician British Indsl. Plastics Ltd., Birmingham, 1979-83; rsch. technician dept. immunology Birmingham U., 1984; post doctoral rsch. fellow Cambridge (Eng.) U., 1988-89; higher sci. officer Health & Safety Lab., Sheffield, London, 1990-95, sr. sci. officer, 1995-96. Contbr. articles to profl. jours. Industry fellow Royal Soc., 1995. Mem. Royal Soc. Chemistry. Home: 126 Oaksfold Rd, Sheffield S5 0TH, England Office: Health & Safety Lab, Broad Ln, Sheffield S3 7HQ, England

HEALY, SONYA AINSLIE, health facility administrator; b. Sudbury, Ont., Can., Apr. 7, 1937; came to U.S., 1949; d. Walter B. and Wilma A. Scott; m. Richard C. Healy, Jr., Dec. 16, 1961. Diploma, Good Samaritan Hosp., West Palm Beach, Fla., 1958; student, U. Mass., 1963-64, NYU, 1964-66; BS, Boston U., 1969, MS in Med.-Surg. Nursing, 1974. Various staff nursing, charge nurse positions, suprs., med.-surg. and obstet. nursing, 1958-69; chmn. jr.-sr. teaching team Sch. of Nursing Melrose (Mass.) Wakefield Hosp., 1969-73; asst. dir. nurses Boston State Hosp., 1973-74; asst. dir., DON Mt. Zion Hosp. and Med. Ctr., 1974-75; asst. dir. patient care svcs., DON St. Elizabeth's Hosp., Boston, 1975-80, St. Joseph's Hosp., Nashua, N.H., 1980-82; adminstr. U. Calif. Med. Ctr., San Diego, 1982-91, corp. chief nursing officer, 1991, assoc. dir. hosp. and clinics, dir. patient care svcs., 1982-93; cons. health care Noyes & Assocs. Ltd., Chgo., 1993—; mem. acad. affairs com., bd. trustees U. San Diego; clin. assoc. U. San Diego, 1984—; mem. adj. faculty San Diego State U.; mem. clin. faculty UCLA Sch. of Nursing; presenter in field. Author: The 12-hour Shift: Is It Viable?-Nursing Outlook, 1984, (handbook) Human Resource Management Handbook, 1987, Human Resources Management Handbook, 1987, Nursing Economics, 1989; mem. editl. adv. bd. dirs. OR Nurse Today, 1989-96; editl. rev. Nursing Economics; contbr. articles to profl. jours. Mem. ASNSA (nominations com. 1978, cert.), Am. Orgn. of Nurse Execs. (bd. dirs. 1990-92, by laws com. 1990-92), Mass. Soc. of Nursing Svcs. Adminstrs. (pres. pres. 1977), Calif. Soc. of Nursing Svc. Adminstrs. (task force on orgns. program com. 1984-85, bd. dirs. 1985-87, mem. com. 1987-88 long range planning com.), San Diego Dirs. of Nurses (sec. 1982-83, pres. 1988-89), Sigma Theta Tau (Zeta Mu chpt.).

HEANEY, DOROTHY PHELPS, nurse, nursing administrator; b. Elmer, N.J., Apr. 8, 1963; d. Joseph Francis and Dorothy Ruth (Andrews) Phelps; m. Bradley George Heaney, June 8, 1985. AS in Nursing, Gloucester County Coll., Sewell, N.J., 1984. Nursing asst. Pine Crest Nursing Home, Sewell, 1982-84, staff nurse, 1984, charge nurse, 1984-85; charge nurse Le Havre Convalescent Hosp., Menlo Park, Calif., 1985-86, dir. staff devel., 1986-87, asst. dir. nursing, 1986, dir. nursing, 1986-87; dir. nursing Hillhaven Convalescent Hosp., Menlo Park, 1987-90, Brookside Convalescent Hosp., San Mateo, Calif., 1990-92; owner, mgr. Friendly Vending, 1992-93; cons. in pvt. practice skilled nursing and geriatric care Mountain View, Calif., 1993—. Home: 148 Promethean Way Mountain View CA 94043-4863

HEARN, RUBY PURYEAR, foundation executive; b. Winston-Salem, N.C., Apr. 13, 1940; c. Mahlon Tasher H. and Ruby Mae (Hamilton) Puryear; m. Robert W. Hearn, Dec. 30, 1961; children: Janna E., Jennifer L. BA., Skidmore Coll., 1960; M.S., Yale U., 1964, Ph.D., 1969. Postdoctoral rsch. assoc. Yale U., New Haven, 1968-69; dir. content devel. Children's TV Workshop, 1972-76; program officer Robert Wood Johnson Found., Princeton, N.J., 1976-80, sr. program officer, 1980-82, v.p., 1983—, sr. v.p. Trustee Meharry Med. Coll., 1981-86; bd. overseers Dartmouth Med. Sch., 1986-92. Recipient Outstanding Alumnae award Skidmore Coll., 1972. Fellow Yale Corp.; mem. AAAS, ABA (pub. mem. accreditation com. 1980-82), Inst. Medicine, Ambulatory Pediatric Assn., Periclean Honor Soc. Home: 7 St Johns Rd Baltimore MD 21210-2121 Office: Robert Wood Johnson Found PO Box 2316 Princeton NJ 08543-2316

HEARN, STEPHANIE ANN, hospital administrator; b. Cin., Mar. 12, 1964; d. Russell Eugene and Ann (Ferneau) Brown; m. John Stephen Hearn, Oct. 2, 1993. BS in Bus., Miami U., Oxford, Ohio, 1986; MHA, Xavier U., Cin., 1989. Diplomate Am. Coll. Healthcare Execs. (cert.). Adminstrv. resident The Christ Hosp., Cin., 1988-89; mgmt. assoc. St. John Hosp., Detroit, 1989-91, assoc. adminstr., 1991—. Campaign chair United Way, Detroit, 1994. Mem. Acad. Med. Adminstrs., Mich. Soc. Healthcare Planning and Mktg. (sec. 1990-93). Office: St John Hosp and Med Ctr 22101 Moross Rd Detroit MI 48236

HEARNE, SANDERS FOWLER, cardiologist; b. Shreveport, La., Aug. 15, 1950; s. George Marion and Mary Elizabeth Hearne; m. Suzanne Bethard, Jul. 29, 1972; children: Sanders Jr., Bethard, Leigh. Student, La. State Univ., 1968-71, MD, 1975. Diplomate Am. Bd. Internal Medicine, Am. Bd. Cardiology. Internship Univ. Ala., Birmingham, 1975-76; residency Mayo Grad Sch. Medicine, 1976-78; fellowship cardiology Mayo Grad. Sch. Medicine, 1978-80; instr. Mayo Medical Sch. Univ. Minn., 1980; assoc. clinical prof. La. State Univ., Shreveport, 1982—; cons. Cardiology Assocs., Shreveport, 1981—; dir. Shreveport Medical Soc., 1987. Contbr. articles to profl. jours. Active Am. Heart Assn., 1980—. Fellow Am. Coll. Cardiology (nat. libr. com. 1991-94), Am. Coll. Physicians; mem. Mayo Alumni Assn., La. State Medical Soc., Shreveport Medical Soc. (bd. dirs. 1987), Alpha Omega Alpha, Am. Soc. Echocardiography. Office: Cardiology Assocs. 851 Olive St Shreveport LA 71104 Home: 743 Hazelwood Shreveport LA 71104

HEARST, BELLA RACHAEL, physician, researcher, artist; b. Pitts.; d. Aba and Bertha (Alpern) H. B.M., Chgo. Med. Sch., 1949, M.D., 1950; postgrad., Johns Hopkins U., 1952-53, Art Inst. Chgo., 1958-68. Rotating intern Norwegian Am. Hosp., Chgo., 1949-50; jr. asst. pathologist Cook County Hosp, Chgo., 1950-52; fellow med. legal pathology U. Md., 1953-54; sr. pathology resident Charity Hosp., New Orleans, 1955-56; spl. cardiac researcher Armed Forces Inst. Pathology, Washington, 1956-57; dir., coordinator pathology dept Hosp. O'Horan Menda Yucatan, Mexico, 1957-58; founder Bertha Hearts Found., Inc., 1958, exec dir., 1958-63; founder Diabetic Inst. Am., Inc., Chgo., 1959, exec. dir., 1959-63; founder Internat. Diabetic Inst., Inc., Chgo., 1963, exec. dir., 1963—; dist. med. dir. compensation U.S. Dept. Labor, Chgo., 1968—; with Chgo. Dept. Health, 1977—, Uptown Neighborhood Health Ctr., 1977-78, Copernicus Multipurpose Ctr., 1978-79, Lakeview Neighborhood Health Ctr., Chgo., 1979—; research dir. Fed. Safety and Fire Council, Chgo.; research assoc. microbiology Stritch Sch. Medicine, Loyola U., Chgo.; staff physician Western Ill. U., 1971-72, assoc. prof., 1971-72. Author: Diabetes and Juvenile Delinquency, 1964, Diabetes and Fitness, 1964, Diabetic Statistical Research Survey, 1961-65, Diabetes and Blood Groups, 1965, Diabetes and Aging, 1965, Diabetes and Newborns; contbr. articles to various publs., art exhibit, Shuster Art Gallery, N.Y., 1966, Internat. Dermatology Congress, Munich, 1967. Recipient 3d prize AMA Conv., Chgo., 1962; recipient testimonial plaque for work sr. citizens Chelsea House, Chgo. Fellow Am. Coll. Angiology, Internat. Coll. Angiology, Am. Geriatric Soc., Royal Soc. Pub. Health; mem. Internat. Acad. Pathology, Am. Women's Med. Assn., Am. Soc. Microbiology, Am. Assn. for Study Neoplastic Diseases, Reticuloendothelial Soc. Home: 514 W Jefferson St Macomb IL 61455-2052 also: PO Box 373 Macomb IL 61455-0373 Office: 8 S Michigan Ave Chicago IL 60603-3302

HEASMAN, PETER ANDREW, restorative dentistry educator, consultant; b. Leeds, Yorkshire, Eng., May 19, 1956; s. Douglas Alvin and Audrey Jane (Chambers) H.; m. Lynne Thompson, July 25, 1987; children: Sophie Rebecca, Christopher James. BDS, U. Newcastle, Eng., 1980, MDS, 1984, PhD, 1993. House surgeon Dental Hosp., Newcastle, 1980-81; demonstrator in oral biology Dental Sch., Newcastle, 1981-83, temporary lectr. restorative dentistry, 1983-85, lectr. restorative dentistry, 1985-94, sr. lectr., hon. cons., 1994—. Author: Drugs, Diseases and the Periodontium, 1992, The Periodontium and Orthodontics in Health and Disease, 1996. Recipient Fish prize in periodontology Brit. Soc. Periodontology, 1987. Fellow Royal Coll. Surgeons and Physicians; mem. Royal Coll. Surgeons Edinburgh (diplomate). Home: 10 Springclose Ebchester, DH8 0QL Durham England Office: Dental Sch, Framlington Pl, NE2 4BW Newcastle England

HEATH, CEDRIC ALEXANDER, nurse, health services administrator; b. St Elizabeth, Jamaica, West Indies, Sept. 3, 1941; came to U.S., 1968; s. Nathaniel David and Ina Ernestine (Williams) H. BS in Nursing summa cum laude, Long Island U., 1973; MPA in Health Svcs. Adminstrn., NYU, 1978, DPA in Health Policy and Mgmt., 1989. Registered nurse, N.Y. From hosp. attendant to Head nurse N.Y. State Hosps., 1969-74; from nurse adminstr. to clinic adminstr. N.Y. State Health Facilities, 1975-80; treatment team leader Manhattan Psychiat. Ctr., N.Y.C., 1980-85; chief of svc. Kirby Forensic Psychiat. Ctr., N.Y.C., 1985-91, Bronx (N.Y.) Psychiat. Ctr., 1991—. Named Gentleman of Distinction, BYKOTA Club of N.Y., 1990; recipient Anne E. Port award 1973. Mem. Am. Soc. Pub. Adminstrn., Soc. Optimates. Home: 3708 Pratt Ave Bronx NY 10466-5929 Office: Bronx Psychiat Ctr 1500 Waters Pl Bronx NY 10461-2723

HEATH, DWIGHT BRALEY, anthropologist, educator; b. Hartford, Conn., Nov. 19, 1930; s. Percy Leonard and Luise (Hosp) H.; 1 child, David Braley. AB in Social Rels., Harvard U., 1952; PhD in Anthropology, Yale U., 1959. Mem. faculty Brown U., 1959—, prof. anthropology, 1970—; dir. Ctr. for Latin Am. Studies, 1984-87, 88-89; vis. prof., U.S. and abroad, cons. in field. Author: A Journal of the Pilgrims at Plymouth, 1963, 86, Land Reform and Social Revolution in Bolivia, 1969, Historical Dictionary of Bolivia, 1972, Contemporary Cultures and Societies of Latin America, 1965, 74, 2d edit., 1988, Cross-Cultural Approaches to the Study of Alcohol, 1976, Alcohol Use and World Cultures, 1980, Cultural Factors in Alcohol Research and Treatment of Drinking Problems, 1981, International Handbook on Alcohol and Cultures, 1995; contbr. articles to profl. jours. With AUS, 1952-54. Grantee Nat. Acad. Scis., 1974, Am. Philos. Soc., 1972, Social Sci. Research Council, 1958, Doherty Found., 1956-57, Nat. Inst. Alcohol Abuse and Alcoholism, 1976-81. Mem. AAAS, Am. Anthrop. Assn., Am. Ethnol. Soc., Am. Soc. Ethnohistory, Royal Anthrop. Inst., Latin Am. Studies Assn. Office: Brown U Dept Anthropology PO Box 1921 Providence RI 02912-1921

HEATH, ELIZABETH ANNE, medical technologist; b. Covington, Ky., Nov. 29, 1960; d. Charles Mentor and Melissa Margaret (Brown) Graves; m. Michael Perry Heath, Aug. 1980 (div. Jan. 1991); children: Michael Shaun, Cory Brent, Matthew Todd. Student, U. Md., College Park, 1979-81, U. Md., Heidelberg, Fed. Republic Germany, 1981-84, Cameron U., 1992—. Cert. med. technologist. Med. technologist Walter Reed Army Inst. Rsch., Washington, 1978-80, Ft. Rucker (Ala.) Gen. Hosp., 1980-81, 140th Sta./ Hosp., Heidelberg, 1981-85, Commanche County Meml. Hosp., Lawton, Okla., 1987-89, Southwestern Med. Ctr., Lawton, 1989—. Bd. dirs., sec. Apache (Okla.) Ambulence Svc., 1995-96. Sgt. U.S. Army, 1978-85. Lutheran. Home: PO Box 649 Apache OK 73006

HEATH, HUNTER, III, endocrinology researcher, administrator; b. Dallas, June 8, 1942; s. Hunter Jr. and Velma M. (Brandon) H.; m. Glenna A. Witt, July 25, 1965; 1 child, Ethan Ford. BA in Chemistry, Tex. Tech Coll., 1964; MD, Washington U., St. Louis, 1968. Intern, then resident in medicine U. Wis. Hosps., Madison, 1968-70; fellow in endocrinology and metabolism Walter Reed Army Med. Ctr., Washington, 1970-72; chief endocrinology sect. Letterman Army Med. Ctr., San Francisco, 1972-74; rsch. fellow in biochemistry and metabolism Grad. Sch. Medicine Mayo Clinic, Rochester, Minn., 1974-76, from asst. prof. to prof. medicine, cons./rschr. endocrinol., 1976-91, head endocrine rsch. unit, 1984-88, assoc. dir., dir. clin. rsch. ctr., 1986-88; dir. for rsch. Mayo Clinic, Scottsdale, Ariz., 1988-90; prof. medicine, chief divsn. endocrinology, metabolism and diabetes U. Utah, Salt Lake City, 1991-96; group leader, endocrinology, med. divsn. Lilly USA Eli Lilly and Co., Indpls., 1996—; mem. adv. com. NIH, Bethesda, Md., 1985-88; pres., bd. dirs. Advances in Mineral Metabolism, Inc., Rochester, 1986-89, treas. 1994-96; mem. select panel of physicians FAA, Washington, 1986-87. Bd. dirs. Utah affiliate Am. Diabetes Assn., 1992-93; bd. dirs. Utah affiliate Arthritis Found., 1993-96; mem. Sch. Dist. Task Force on Lang. Arts Edn., Rochester, 1984. Maj. U.S. Army, 1970-74. Fellow ACP (editl. bd. 1985-88); mem. Am. Soc. for Clin. Investigation, Am. Soc. for Bone Mineral Rsch. (councillor 1985-88), Endocrine Soc. (publs. com. 1985-88), Western Assn. Physicians, Exptl. Aircraft Assn. (chmn. aeromed. adv. coun. Oshkosh, Wis. 1987-89, vice chmn. 1993—). Office: Eli Lilly and Co Lilly Corporate Ctr Indianapolis IN 46285

HEATH, MELISSA LYNN WATERS, nursing educator; b. Thomasville, Ga., May 3, 1961; d. Robert Edward and Rebecca Clyde (Granade) Waters; m. Tommy Lee Heath, June 26, 1982; children: Emily Ann, Matthew Thomas. BSN, Valdosta State Coll., 1983. Cert. BLS, Train the Trainer, Ga. Staff nurse, charge nurse Med. Ctr. of Ctrl. Ga., Macon, 1983-87; instr. CNA Middle Ga. Tech. Inst., Warner Robins, 1987-91, instr. practical nurses, 1991-94; staff devel. coord. Elberta Healthcare, Warner Robins, 1995—; student advisor Vocat. Indsl. Clubs Am. post-secondary, Warner Robins, 1992-93. Office: Elberta Healthcare 419 Elberta Rd Warner Robins GA 31093

HEATHERLEY, MELODY ANN, nursing administrator; b. Dallas, Apr. 15, 1957; d. Harold Ray and Barbara Ann (Roebuck) Jones; m. James Lawrence Heatherley, July 21, 1982. BSN, U. Tex., Arlington, 1979; postgrad., Amber U. RN, Tex., Fla. Surg. nurse St. Paul Hosp., Dallas, 1979, Mesquite (Tex.) Meml. Hosp., 1979-80; charge nurse All Saints Hosp.-Main, Ft. Worth, 1980-87; house supr., charge nurse All Saints Cityview Hosp., Ft. Worth, 1987-88; staff nurse ICU, critical care coord. Hosp. Corp. Am. Med. Plz. Hosp., Ft. Worth, 1986-89; staff nurse ICU, CCU Harris Meth. Hurst, Euless, Bedford, Bedford, Tex., 1989-91; staff nurse rehab. unit Harris Meth. HEB, Bedford, 1991; charge nurse surg. ICU, cardiovascular recovery Humana Hosp.-Lucerne, Orlando, Fla., 1991-93, relief house supr., 1991-93; divsn. supr. nursing adminstrn. St. Paul Med. Ctr., Dallas, 1993-94; adminstrv. supr Baylor Med. Ctr. Ellis County, Waxahachie, Tex., 1994—. Mem. AACN, ANA, NAFE, Assn. Rehab. Nurses, Tex. Orgn. Nurse Execs., Tex. Nurses Assn. Episcopalian. Office: Baylor Med Ctr Ellis County Waxahachie Campus 1405 W Jefferson St Waxahachie TX 75165-2231

HEATHMAN, ADRIENNE MARIE, nursing educator; b. Seattle, Nov. 22, 1926; d. Dennis John and Sophia Frances (Dilg) Healy; m. Dwayne W. Heathman, Sept. 6, 1991; children: Jeanine M. Rosemeau, Barbara A. Caine, Kathryn S. Caine. BSN, Seattle U., 1952; MSN, U. Oreg., Portland, 1968. RN, Oreg. Staff nurse public health Portland (Oreg.) City Bur. Health; supr. med-surg. Woodland Park Hosp., Portland, Oreg.; prof. psychiat. mental health nursing Clark Coll., Vancouver, Wash.; ret. Mem. ANA, AAUW, Am. Assn. Univ. Profs., Am. Psychiat. Nurses Assn., Oreg. Mental Health Assn., Wash. Edn. Assn.

HEATLEY, MARK KEITH, anatomic pathologist, consultant; b. Belfast, No. Ireland; s. James Samuel and Irene Mary Eleanor (Weatherall) H. MB BChir B of Obstetrics, Queens U. Belfast, 1984, MD, 1992. Jr. house officer Ulster Hosp., Dundonald, No. Ireland, 1984-85; sr. house officer Royal Victoria Hosp., Belfast, 1985-88, registrar, 1988-89, sr. registrar, 1990-92; fellow George Washington U., Washington, 1992-93; cons., sr. lectr. U. Sheffield, 1993-95; cons. Taunton & Somerset Nat. Health Svc. Trust, Somerset, 1995—. Contbr. papers to profl. jours. Membership sec. Conservative Party, Sheffield, 1995—. Rsch. fellow CRC/Ulster Cancer Found.,

Belfast, 1989-90, rsch. traveling fellow No. Ireland Coun. for Postgrad. Med. Edn., Washington, 1992; rsch. grantee Royal Victoria Trust Fund, 1989, Wellbeing, 1995, Spl. Trustees of United Sheffield Hosps., 1995. Mem. Royal Coll. Pathologists (London), Internat. Acad. Pathology, Internat. Soc. Gynecol. Pathologists, Pathol. Soc. Office: Taunton & Somerset NHS Trust, Dept Pathology, Taunton Somerset TA1 5DA, England

HEATON, BILLY RAY, chiropractor; b. Princeton, Ky., July 14, 1934; s. Wallace Beckham and Nannie Bell (Cavanah) H.; m. Patsy Ann Stone, July 4, 1957. D of Chiropractic, Palmer Coll., 1959. Pvt. practice Lexington, Ky., 1996—. With U.S. Army, 1953-56, Japan. Mem. Andover Country Club, Campbell House Country Club, Masons. Home: 1756 Bellechasse Dr Lexington KY 40505 Office: 998 New Circle Rd Lexington KY 40505

HEATON, CHARLES LLOYD, dermatologist, educator; b. Bryan, Tex., May 8, 1935; s. Homer Lloyd and Bessie Blanton (Sharp) H. BS, Tex. A&M U., 1957; MD, Baylor U., 1961; MA (hon.), U. Pa., 1973. Diplomate Am. Bd. Dermatology. Intern Jefferson Davis Hosp., Houston, 1961-62; resident Baylor U., 1962-65; sr. attending physician Phila. Gen. Hosp., 1965-69, chief of svc., 1970-77; mem. dept. dermatology U. Pa. Sch. Medicine, 1966-78; assoc. prof. dermatology U. Pa., 1973-78; assoc. prof. dermatology U. Cin., 1978-85, prof., 1985—. Author: Audiovisual Course in Venereal Disease, 1972, (with D.M. Pillsbury) Manual of Dermatology, 1980; contbr. 35 articles to profl. jours., 12 chpts. to books. Served to lt. comdr. USPHS, 1965-67. Fellow ACP, AAD, Coll. Physicians of Phila.; mem. AMA, Soc. Investigative Dermatology, Am. Venereal Disease Assn., Am. Dermatol. Assn., Royal Soc. Medicine (London), Cin. Dermatol. Soc., Alpha Omega Alpha. Home: 5534 E Galbraith Rd Apt 25 Cincinnati OH 45236-2840 Office: U Cin Coll Medicine Dept Dermatology 231 Bethesda Ave Cincinnati OH 45267-0523

HEBER, RUTH R., psychologist, consultant; b. Lodz, Poland, June 27, 1935; came to U.S., 1957; d. Moses Zwi and Ryna (Glucklich) Borenstein; m. Jacob Heber, 1955 (div. 1982); children: Ron, Sheldon, Lorraine; m. Lawrence Walter Kullman, 1987. BA in Psychology, CUNY, 1972; MS in Ednl. Psychology and Guidance, Yeshiva U., 1974, PhD in Devel. Psychology, 1979. Lic. psychologist, N.Y. Staff psychotherapist North Suffolk Mental Health Ctr., N.Y., 1980-82; supervising psychologist, clinic and program coord. Creedmoor Psychiat. Ctr., N.Y., 1982-88; dir. East Side Consultation Ctr., N.Y.C., 1988—; adj. asst. prof. psychology Queens Coll., CUNY; cons., lectr. Humanistic Psychology Ctr., N.Y., 1983-93; lectr. psychiatry Mt. Sinai Sch. Medicine, CUNY, 1990-9 5, asst. clin. prof., 1995—; supr. psychiat. residents Mt. Sinai Med. Ctr., N.Y.C., 1989—; adj. prof. The Union Inst. Grad. Sch. Cin., 1991—; participant, supr. Holocaust Survivors Treatment Program, 1993—; pvt. practice; presenter, guest spkr., workshop leader. Mem. APA (program chmn. humanistic psychology divsn. 1988-89, treas. 1989-92, pres. 1993-94, 95—), Am. Acad. Psychotherapists, Internat. Coun. Psychologists, Internat. Assn. Applied Psychology, Internat. Assn. Cross-Cultural Psychology, Am. Group Psychotherapy Assn., Ea. Group Psychotherapy Assn., N.Y. State Psychological Assn. (disaster/crisis response network 1993—, colleague assistance program com. 1992—), Assoc. Alumni Mt. Sinai Med. Ctr., Phi Beta Kappa, Psi Chi, Kappa Delta Pi, Delta Phi Alpha. Office: 200 E 33rd St Apt 4I New York NY 10016-4826

HEBERT, JAMES CHARLES, surgeon, educator; b. Waterville, Maine, Sept. 25, 1951; s. Joseph Emile and Alyce (Poirier) H.; m. Mary Ellen Sprague, May 31, 1986; children: Molly Elizabeth, Daniel Sprague. AB, Coll. Holy Cross, Worcester, Mass., 1973; MD, U. Vt., 1977. Diplomate Nat. Bd. Med. Examiners, Am. Bd. Surgery; lic. physician, Vt. Resident in gen. surgery U. Vt./Med. Ctr. Hosp. Vt., Burlington, 1978-82, chief resident, 1981-82; asst. prof. surgery U. Vt. Coll. Medicine, Burlington, 1982-88, assoc. prof., 1988-94, prof., 1994—, asst. program dir., 1989-90, program dir., 1990—, chief divsn. gen. surgery, 1994—; attending surgeon Fanny Allen Hosp., Burlington, 1982—, Med. Ctr. Hosp. Vt., Burlington, 1982-94, Fletcher Allen Health Care, Burlington, 1995—;mem. USMLE Part II com. Nat. Bd. Med. Examiners, 1992—. Assoc. editor: Essentials of Surgical Specialties, 1993; contbr. articles to profl. jours., chpts. to books. Mem. med. activities com. Vt. chpt. Am. Cancer Soc., Montpelier, 1985-94, chmn., 1991-94, exec. com., 1991—, bd. dirs., 1991—, v.p., 1994—. Recipient awards W.L. Gore Co., Flagstaff, Ariz., 1985-86, Orthopaedic Rsch. and Edn. Found., Chgo., 1985-86, Nat. Inst. Allergy and Infectious Diseases, Bethesda, Md., 1985-88, Am. Cyanamid Co., Burlington, Mass., 1989-91, Merck Sharp & Dohme, West Point, Pa., 1992, Amgen Corp., Thousand Oaks, Calif., 1992-93, 94. Fellow ACS (mem. com. on applicants 1989—, exec. mem. 1992—, program chmn. Vt. chpt. 1989-91, councilman 1988-91, sec.-treas. 1989-92, v.p. 1992-93, pres. 1993-94); mem. Assn. Surg. Edn. (pres. 1991-92, v.p. 1990-91, sec.-treas. 1988-90, exec. com. 1985—, program com. 1990-92, chmn. curriculum com. 1986-88, vice chmn. 1984-86, com. on issues 1993—), Assn. Surg. Edn. Found. (pres. bd. dirs. 1993—), Assn. Acad. Surgery (membership com. 1988-90, edn. com. 1991-93, chmn. edn. com. 1992-93), John H. Davis Soc. (chmn. local arrangements 1988-89, 93-94, program chmn. 1992-93, sec.-treas. 1994—), Soc. Univ. Surgeons (audit com. 1991), Soc. Am. Gastrointestinal Endoscopic Surgeons (chmn. resident edn. subcom. on curriculum 1990-91), Vt. State Med. Soc. (alt. physicians policy coun. 1992-93, surgery rep. Physicians Policy Coun. 1993-94). Roman Catholic. Office: Fletcher Allen Health Care Dept Surgery Fletcher House 301 Burlington VT 05401

HECETA, ESTHERBELLE AGUILAR, anesthesiologist; b. Cebu City, Philippines, Jan. 1, 1935; came to U.S., 1962, naturalized, 1981; d. Serafin Aguilar and Elsie (Nichols) Aguilar; m. Wilmer G., Heceta, Apr. 5, 1962; children: W. Cristina, W. Elgine, Wuela E. BS Chemistry cum laude, Silliman U., Dumaguete City, Philippines, 1955, BS cum laude, 1956; MD cum laude, U. East Ramon Magsaysay Meml. Med. Center, Quezon City, Philippines, 1961. Diplomate Am. Bd. Anesthesiology, Philippine Bd. Anesthesiology. Intern, Youngstown (Ohio) Hosp. Assocs., 1962-63, resident in anesthesiology, 1963-66; anesthesiologist Salem (Ohio) City Hosp., 1967, St. Joseph's Hosp., Manapla, Philippines, 1967-72; instr. dept. anesthesiology U. Tenn., Memphis, 1972-74; staff anesthesiologist Ohio Valley Med. Ctr., Wheeling, W.Va., 1974—; anesthesiologist Bellaire (Ohio) City Hosp., 1975—; staff anesthesiologist East Ohio Regional Hosp., Martins Ferry, Ohio, 1989—; Joint Conf. Comm. for Profl Affairs, Ohio Valley Med. Ctr., 1992—, mem. exec. comm., sec.-treas. med. dental staff, 1992—, pres.-elect, 1993-94, pres. med. dental staff, 1994-95, physician reviewer Anesthesiology W. Va. Med. Inst., 1992—, mem. Claims Review Panel W. Va. Med. Assn., 1990—; Vol. med.-surg. mission to Philippines, 1982-90. Fellow Am. Coll. Anesthesiology; mem. AMA, Am. Soc. Anesthesiologists, Ohio Valley Philipine Med. Assn. (pres. 1988-90), Tri-State Phillipine-Am. Assn. (pres. 1991-92), Assn. Philippine Physicians in Am., Philippine Soc. Anesthesiologists in Am., W.Va. Soc. Anesthesiologists, Internat. Anesthesia Research Soc., Am. Med. Women's Assn. (organizer, pres. 1983, regional gov. Region IV 1987-89), W.Va. Med. Soc., Ohio County Med. Soc. Presbyterian. Home: 15 Holly Rd Wheeling WV 26003-5656 Office: Ohio Valley Med Ctr Dept Anesthesiology 2000 Eoff St Wheeling WV 26003-3871

HECHT, HAROLD ARTHUR, orchidologist, chiropractor; b. St. Louis, Mo., Apr. 30, 1921; s. William Frederick and Myrtle Regina (Hugo) H.; m. Barbara Evelyne Ross, Nov. 19, 1942. D Chiropractic Medicine, Logan Coll. Sole practice St. Louis, 1942-95, orchidologist, 1950—; judge Orchid Digest Corp., 1959; internat. lectr., photographer in field. Contbr. articles to profl. jours. Mem. World Orchid Cong. (founding com. 1954), Mid-Am. Orchid Cong. (founder, pres. 1959, judge 1968), Am. Orchid Soc. (grand jurist, judge 1968), Mark Twain Orchid Soc. (pres. 1966, 90), Mo. Orchid Soc. (pres. 1959), European Orchid Congress (USA com. 1967). Republican.

HECHT, MANFRED H., psychoanalyst; b. Vienna, Austria, Dec. 6, 1918; came to U.S., 1938, naturalized, 1943; s. Maximilian M. and Ada C. (Spiro) H.; cert. Med. Sch., U. Vienna, 1938; PhD, Columbia U., 1958; Psychoanalytic cert. Postgrad. Ctr. Mental Health, N.Y.C., 1962; m. Marie L. Engel, Aug. 25, 1941; 1 stepchild, Andrew M. Cantor, Congregation B'nai Jeshurun, Newark, 1948-58; leading baritone N.Y.C. Opera, 1948-52; psychology intern VA, 1955-58; fellow Postgrad. Center Mental Health, N.Y.C., 1958-62, assoc. dir. dept. cmty. svc. and edn., dir. pastoral counseling, 1964-80, sr. supr., tng. analyst, 1978—; affiliated profl. staff Berkshire Med. Ctr., Pittsfield, Mass., 1989—; pvt. practice psychoanalysis, N.Y.C., 1960—; supr., cons. Religious Cons. Ctr., Roman Catholic Diocese of Bklyn., 1970-80; mem. adv. bds. various agencies and publs. Served with M.I. U.S. Army, 1943-45. Fellow Coun. Psychoanalytic Psychotherapists; mem. APA, Postgrad. Psychoanalytic Soc. (past pres.), N.Y. State Psychol. Assn. Author various publs. Office: 285 Central Park W New York NY 10024-3006

HECHT, STEVEN LEE, optometrist; b. Englewood, N.J., Oct. 4, 1948; s. Martin Harold and Blanche (Pachman) H.; m. Cheryl Ann Hochstein, July 4, 1971; children: Shana Beth, Samuel Edward. BS, Miami U., 1970; OD, Pa. Coll. Optometry, 1975. Optometrist pvt. practice, Hamilton, Ohio, 1975—. Bd. dirs. ARC, Hamilton, 1977-87. Mem. Rotary. Democrat. Jewish. Office: 39 N "D" St Hamilton OH 45013

HECHTER, MARK LEWIS, otolaryngologist; b. Brookfield, Mo., Dec. 16, 1963; s. George Lewish and Melva Martin (Sheets) H.; m. Lisa Kay Clark, Aug. 9, 1986; children: Danielle, Christina. BS in Biology, Northeast Mo. State U., 1987; DO, Kirksville Coll. Osteo., 1991. Resident Ear, Nose & Throat/Plastic Surgery, Inc., Warrensburg, Mo., 1991-96. Mem. AMA, Am. OSteo. Assn., Am. Acad. Otolaryngology-Head and Neck Surgery, Am. Osteo. Coll. Ophthalmologists Otolaryngologists, Am. Acad. Cosmetic Surgeons, Mo. Assn. Osteo. Physicians & Surgeons. Home: 1407 Summit Crest Warrensburg MO 64093 Office: Plastic Surgery Inc 515 Burkharth Rd Warrensburg MO 64093

HECK, ALBERT FRANK, neurologist; b. Balt., Oct. 9, 1932; s. Albert Franklin and Dorothy Mary (Jirsa) H.; divorced; children: Albert William, Karl Andrew, Robert Conrad, Paul Christopher. A.B., Johns Hopkins U., 1954; M.D., U. Md., 1958. Diplomate: Am. Bd. Psychiatry and Neurology. Intern Mercy Hosp., 1958-59; NIH fellow in neurology U. Md., Balt., 1959-62; faculty, instr. to prof. U. Md., 1964-77; prof., chmn. dept. neurology U. Tenn. Center for Health Scis., Memphis, 1977-82; dir. neurosci. program U. Tenn. Center for Health Scis., 1978-82; prof. neurology W. Va. U., 1982—; vis. prof. Medezinische Hochschule Hannover, W. Ger., 1973-74. Contbr. writings to profl. publs. Served with M.C. U.S. Army, 1962-64. Recipient jr. investigator award NIH, 1965, U.S. sr. scientist award, 1973; Humboldt Found. prize Fed. Republic Germany, 1973-74. Fellow Am. Acad. Neurology, ACP; mem. Am. Neurol. Assn., Stroke Council of Am. Heart Assn., Internat. Coll. Angiology, Alpha Omega Alpha. Home: 325 Southpointe Dr Charleston WV 25314-2471 Office: 1218 Virginia St E Charleston WV 25301

HECK, DAVID ALAN, orthopaedic surgery educator, mechanical engineering educator; b. Syracuse, N.Y., Nov. 20, 1952; s. William C. and Shirley W. (Wolthausen) H.; m. Kimberly Kay North, Sept. 27, 1980; children: William Donald, Andrew David, Daniel Robert. BS in Elect. and Computer Engring. cum laude, Clarkson Coll. Tech., 1973; MD, SUNY, Syracuse, 1977. Cert. Am. Bd. Orthopaedic Surgery. Intern in gen. surgery U. Minn., Mpls., 1977-78; resident in orthpaedic surgery SUNY, Syracuse, 1978-82; resident in orthopaedic biomechanics Mayo Clinic, Rochester, Minn., 1982-83; asst. prof. Ind. U. Sch. Medicine, Indpls., 1983-87, assoc. prof., 1987—; attending physician Ind. U. Med. Ctr., Indpls., 1983—, VA Med. Ctr., Indpls., 1983—, Riley Hosp., 1983—, Wishard Meml. Hosp., 1983—; adj. asst. prof. Sch. Mech. Engring., Purdue U., West Lafayette, Ind., 1984-87, assoc. prof., 1987-96, prof., 1996—; chief orthopaedic surgery sect. VA Med. Ctr., 1993—, medipro advisor, 1986, bd. dirs. Indian Creek Hills, Inc., The Orthopaedic Rev. Course; lectr. various profl. orgns.; dir. Orthopaedic Biomechanics Lab., Ind. U. Med. Ctr., 1984—; mem. residency applicants rev. com. Ind. U., 1983—, orthopaedic chiefs of svcs. com., 1983—, search and screen com., 1984-86, adult ambulatory care com., 1986-90, orthopaedic basic sci. com., 1986-87, chmn. orthopaedic edn. com., 1987—, quality assurance com., 1988-91, med. admissions com., 1989-91, total quality mgmt. chmn., 1993-95. Editl. bd. Jour. Arthroplasty, Jour. Am. Acad. Orthopedic Surgeons; co-editor in chief Electronic Jour. Orthopedics; editl. reviewer Clin. Orthopaedics; contbr. numerous articles to profl. jours. Sports medicine advisor White River Park, 1984-86; bd. dirs. Hand Surgery Rsch. & Edn. Found. Mem. AMA, Am. Acad. Orthopaedic Surgery (outcome com. 1990—, com. on comps. 1988-90), Knee Soc. (ex-officio, com. on evaluation, chmn. outcome com. 1991—, bd. dirs.), Am. Soc. Biomechanics, Ind. Med. Assn., Marion County Med. Soc., Orthopaedic Rsch. Soc., 7th Dist. Med. Soc., Eta Kappa Nu, Tau Beta Pi. Home: 11440 Valley Meadow Dr Zionsville IN 46077-9342

HECK, HENRY D'ARCY, toxicologist; b. Bryn Mawr, Pa., Apr. 18, 1939; s. Harold Joseph and Lydia Suzanne (Holt) H.; m. Mercedes Casanova, Dec. 21, 1984; children: Katherine (Mrs. Daniel Troy), Julia, John Schmitz, Lara (Mrs. Daniel King). AB, Princeton U., 1962; PhD, Northwestern U., 1966. Asst. prof. chemistry U. Calif., Berkeley, 1968-72; chemist Stanford Rsch. Inst., Menlo Park, Calif., 1972-77; scientist Chem. Ind. Inst. Toxicology, Research Triangle Park, N.C., 1977-85, sr. scientist, 1985—; adj. assoc. prof. U. N.C., Chapel Hill, 1983—, Duke U., Durham, N.C., 1987—; cons. in field. Assoc. editor: Fundamental and Applied Toxicology, 1986-1991, editor-in-chief, 1991—. Fellow NSF, NIH, EMBO, 1963-68. Fellow NSF, NIH, EMBO, 1963-68; mem. AAAS, Am. Chem. Soc., N.C. Soc. Toxicology (pres. 1995-96), Soc. Toxicology (Frank Blood award 1983, Inhalation Toxicol. Paper of Yr. award 1987, 93). Home: 1514 Lutz Ave Raleigh NC 27607-6754 Office: Pamlico Plantation Washington NC 27889 Office: Chem Industry Inst Toxicology PO Box 12137 Research Triangle Park NC 27709

HECKER, GERALD ARTHUR, ophthalmologist, historian; b. Montreal, Que., Can., Feb. 11, 1937; s. Smauel F. and Rena Hecker; m. Jocelyne Marie-Louise Chalut, Dec. 7, 1963; 1 child, Pierre. BA, NYU, N.Y.C., 1959; BS, U. Geneva, Switzerland, 1961, MD, 1965. Diplomate Am. Bd. Ophthalmologist. Resident in ophthalmology N.Y. Polyclinic Med. Sch., N.Y.C., 1968-71; fellow oculoplastic surgery Manhattan Eye and Ear Hosp., N.Y.C., 1971-72, attending surgeon, 1972—; pvt. practice, 1972—; clin. instr. Mt. Sinai Med. Sch., N.Y.C., 1985—. Capt. U.S. Army, 1966-68. Deocrated Bronze Star. Mem. N.Y. Acad. Medicine, N.Y. State Ophthal. Soc., Am. Acad. Ophthalmology. Office: 10 W 86th St New York NY 10024

HECKER, WILLIAM PETER, surgeon; b. Phila., July 19, 1957; s. William Peter and Helen Marie (Sweeney) H.; m. Allison Jane Ferrier, Aug. 28, 1993. BS in Biochemistry, Temple U., 1986, MD, 1990. Intern Abington (Pa.) Meml. Hosp., 1990-91; resident in gen. surgery Hahnemann U. Hosp., Phila., 1991-95; fellow in transplant surgery U. Pitts. Med. Ctr. Pitts. Transplant Inst., 1995—. Fellow Am. Cancer Soc., 1989. Mem. AMA, ACS, Philadelphia County Med. Soc., Pa. Med. Soc. Home: 20 Oakland Sq Pittsburgh PA 15213 Office: Pitts Transplant Inst Falk Clinic 3601 5th Ave 4th Fl Pittsburgh PA 15213

HECKING, ERWIN HANS, nephrology educator; b. Karlsruhe, Germany, Mar. 12, 1943; s. Ernst and Grete (Pluecker) H.; m. Ursula Claas; children: Detlef, Ingeborg, Manfred. MD, Freiburg (Fed. Republic Germany) U., 1969. Fellow internal medicine Deutsche Klinik F. Diagnostic, Wiesbaden, Fed. Republic Germany, 1970-72, I. Med. Univ. Clinic, Mainz, Fed. Republic Germany, 1973-75; dr. internal medicine, asst. prof. I. Med. Univ. Clinic, Mainz, 1975-79; chief of nephrological dept. Augusta-Kranken-Anstalt, Bochum, 1980—; chief of dialysis centre Augusta Kranken Anstalt, Bochum, 1980—; nephrological chief transplant dept. Surg. U. Clinic of Bochum, 1992—. Contbr. articles to profl. jours. Mem. Deutsche Gesellschaft Innere Medizin, Deutsche Gesellschaft Nephrologie, Am. Soc. Artificial Internal Organs, Internat. Soc. Artificial Internal Organs. Office: Augusta-Kranken-Anstalt, Bergstr 26, D-44791 Bochum Germany

HECKLER, FREDERICK ROGER, plastic surgeon; b. N.Y.C., Mar. 7, 1942; s. Frances George; children: Jeremy, Michael, Adrienne, Lauren. Student, Tufts U., 1959-62, MD, 1966. Diplomate Nat. Bd. Med. Examiners, Am. Bd. Surgery, Am. Bd. Plastic Surgery with qualification in surgery of the hand. Intern in surgery U. Chgo. Med. Ctr., 1966-67; resident in gen. surgery Tufts New Eng. Med. Ctr., Boston, 1967-69; fellow in surgery Malmo (Sweden) Gen. Hosp., 1969-70; resident in plastic surgery Wilford Hall USAF Med. Ctr., San Antonio, 1973-75; fellow in hand surgery Denver Gen. Hosp., 1976-77; chief surgery USAF Hosp., Taiwan, 1976-77; asst. prof. surgery U. Miss. Med. Ctr., Jackson, 1977-79, chief divsn. plastic surgery, 1979-82; dir. divsn. plastic surgery Allegheny Gen. Hosp., Pitts., 1982—; clin. assoc. prof. plastic surgery U. Pitts. Sch. Medicine, 1982—; active med. staff Miss. Cripple Children's Treatment and Tng. Ctr., Miss., 1981-82; dir. cleft palate clinic Allegheny Gen. Hosp., Pitts., 1982-88; attending physician St. Margaret Meml. Hosp., Pitts., 1984-89, Montefiore Hosp., Pitts., 1986-89, Divine Providence Hosp., Pitts., 1991—, North Hills Passavant Hosp., Pitts., 1993; cons. med. staff Harmarville Rehab. Ctr., Inc., Pitts., 1985; cons. in plastic surgery VA Hosp., Pitts., 1993—, Miss. Meth. Rehab. Ctr., Jackson, 1977-82, VA Hosp., Jackson, 1977-82; dir. burn unit U. Miss. Med. Ctr., Jackson, 1979-82, co-dir. hand surgery svc., 1979-82; mem. med. staff Miss. Crippled Children's Treatment and Tng. Ctr., Jackson, 1981-82; presenter in field. Contbr. numerous articles to profl. publs., chpts. to books; assoc. editor Jour. Plastic and Reconstructive Surgery. Lt. col. USAF, 1972-76. Mem. AMA, ACS, Am. Soc. Plastic and Reconstructive Surgeons, Am. Assn. Plastic Surgeons, Assn. Mil. Plastic Surgeons, Soc. Air Force Clin. Surgeons, Am. Burn Assn., Internat. Soc. for Burn Injuries, Am. Cleft Palate Assn., Plastic Surgery Rsch. Coun., Am. Soc. for Surgery of Hand, Am. Assn. Hand Surgery, Royal Soc. Medicine, Assn. Acad. Chmn. of Plastic Surgery, Lipolysis Soc. N.Am., Allegheny County Med. Soc., Pa. Med. Soc., Ohio Valley Plastic Surg. Soc., Pitts. Surg. Soc. Office: Allegheny Gen Hosp 320 E North Ave Pittsburgh PA 15212-4772

HEDDEN, KENNETH FORSYTHE, chemical engineer; b. Glendale, Calif., Aug. 13, 1941; s. Marion William and Pauline (Forsythe) H.; m. Ann Ellen Young, Jan. 26, 1963 (div. 1990); children: Randolph, Stephen, William; m. Suzanne A. Whitlock, Feb. 10, 1990. BS, U. Calif., Berkeley, 1963; PhD, U. Calif., Davis, 1968; M in Pub. Adminstrn., U. Ga., 1980. Registered profl. engr., sanitarian, specialist microbiologist. Research fellow Tufts U. Med. Sch., Boston, 1968-70; research assoc. Purdue U., Lafayette, Ind., 1970-72; lab. supr. Anheuser-Busch, Inc., Lafayette, 1972-75; sanitary engr. U.S. Army Environ. Hygiene Agy., Aberdeen (Md.) Proving Ground, 1975-78, EPA, Athens, Ga., 1978-83; chem. engr. Environ. Monitoring Systems Lab. EPA, Las Vegas, Nev., 1983-88; environ. engr. Warner Robins Air Logistics Ctr., Robins AFB, Ga., 1988-94, environ. chemist, 1994—. Contbr. articles to profl. jours. Col. USAR. Mem. Conf. Fed. Environ. Engrs., Sigma Xi, Alpha Chi Sigma. Republican. Baptist. Home: RR 3 Box 875 Fort Valley GA 31030-9233 Office: WR-ALC/TIELC 420 2d St Ste 1001 Robins AFB GA 31098-1640

HEDDLES, DONNA J., health facility executive; b. Monte Vista, Colo., July 7, 1937; d. William E. and Hazel M. (Swaggerty) Telinde; m. Donald W. Kelley, Oct. 3, 1955 (div. Dec. 1962); children: Koy A. Glover, Kurt A., Kathi A. Kelley Richards, Kerri A. Kelley Dubas; m. Philip C. Heddles, Mar. 18, 1993. Accredited records technician AHIMA. Med. transcriptionist Sacred Heart Hosp., Lamar, Colo., 1962-64; transcriptionist, receptionist G.W. Eklund, M.D., Lamar, 1964-68; med. records dir. Prowers Med. Ctr., Lamar, 1968—; pres. So. Colo. Med. Record Assn.; mem. nominating com. Colo. Med. Records Assn. Mem. Zonta Club (treas. 1987-89, pres. 1989-90, Zontian of Yr. 1988). Home: 800 West Oak St Lamar CO 81052 Office: Prowers Med Ctr 401 Kendall Dr Lamar CO 81052

HEDGER, RONALD DAVID, osteopathic physician; b. Dickinson, N.D., June 12, 1957; s. David Allen and Sydney Vyonne (Pace) H.; m. Karen Lynn Gibbs; children: Shannon, Christopher, Lindsey. BA, U. Nev., Las Vegas, 1979; DO, Coll. Osteo. Medicine Pacific, Pomona, Calif., 1984. Diplomate Nat. Bd. Osteo. Examiners. Physician Scottsdale (Ariz.) Family Physicians, 1985-87; physician in pvt. practice Scottsdale, 1987-88, Fremont Med. Ctr., Las Vegas, 1988—; pres. Health Quest Prodns., Inc., Henderson, Nev., 1993—. Exec. producer, host TV prodn. Healthquest--The Med. TV Talk Show, 1993—. Mem. Am. Osteo. Assn. Democrat. Office: 5220 E Fremont St Las Vegas NV 89101

HEDGES, MARK STEPHEN, clinical psychologist; b. Chgo., Feb. 15, 1950; s. Norman T. and Doris Mae (Walters) H.; B.S., Purdue U., 1972; M.A., U. S.D., 1974, Ph.D., 1977; m. Janice Finnie, Aug. 16, 1975; children: Anna, Miriam. Psychology intern Western Mo. Mental Health Ctr., Kansas City, 1975-76; dir. children and adolescent svcs., psychologist Northeastern Mental Health Ctr., Aberdeen, S.D., 1977—; chmn. Northeastern Area Local Interagency Team. Mem. adv. bd. Luth. Social Svcs., 1978—, S.D. Mental Health Planning and Coord. Adv. Coun., S.D. Juvenile Justice Adv. Com. Mem. Am. Psychol. Assn., S.D. Assn. Sch. Psychologists, Phi Beta Kappa, Psi Chi, Phi Kappa Phi. Methodist. Office: Northeastern Mental Health Ctr 703 3rd Ave SE Aberdeen SD 57401-4508

HEDGES, RICHARD H., epidemiologist, lawyer; b. Louisville, July 16, 1952; s. Houston and Frances Ruth (Zemo) H.; m. Donna Jean Hough. BA, U. Ky., 1974; MA, Ea. Ky. U., 1975; PhD, U. Ky., 1986; MPA, Ea. Ky. U., 1983; JD, Capital U. Law, 1994. Bar: Ohio 1995. Rehab. specialist Commonwealth of Ky., Somerset, 1976-81; chief health planner Commonwealth of Ky., Frankfort, 1981-82; asst. prof. U. Ky., Lexington, 1985-87; rsch. assoc. dept. med. behavioral sci. U. Ky. Coll. Medicine, Lexington, 1982-85; program adminstr. Rollman Psychiat. Inst., Cin., 1987-88; asst. prof. Ohio U., 1988-92, assoc. prof., 1992—; dir. divsn. on aging Ohio U. Health Promotion and Rsch., 1990-92, MHA Grad Prog. Coord., 1995—. Contbr. articles to profl. jours. Fellow NIMH, 1984-86. Mem. ABA, ATLA, APHA, Ohio Acad. Trial Lawyers, Am. Soc. Law, Medicine and Ethics, Am. Coll. Health Care Execs., Nat. Health Lawyers Assn., Ohio State Bar Assn., Pi Sigma Alpha, Phi Delta Phi. Democrat. Episcopalian. Home: RR 2 Box 14 Mooreland Rd Belpre OH 45714 Office: Ohio U Health Sci 413 Peden Tower Athens OH 45701

HEDIN, MÅNS FREDRIK, dental surgeon, educator; b. Gothenburg, Sweden, Jan. 6, 1941; s. Ernst Gunnar and Eira J.A. (Fredriksson) H.; m. Katarina Bodil Lenárd, Aug. 17, 1985; children: Lisa, Stina. DDS, U. Lund, Sweden, 1964; PhD on Odontics, U. Umeå, Sweden, 1973. Gen. practice Kirvna, Sweden, 1965-66; asst. prof., rsch. fellow Umeå, 1967-75; assoc. prof. Gothenburg, Sweden, 1975-78; chief dental surgeon Gävle, Sweden, 1978—. Contbr. articles to profl. jours. Recipient Peace medal UN, mil. sports medal. Fellow Swedish Soc. Oral Radiology (head 1978-82), Gävle Symphony Choir (head 1984-92), Gefle Rotary (pres. 1989-90). Office: County Hosp, Dept Radiology, S-80187 Gavle Sweden

HEDINGER, CHRISTOPH ERNST, pathologist; b. Basel, Switzerland, Feb. 5, 1917; s. Ernst Rudolf and Mary Valerie (Wetter) H.; m. Annemarie Steck, Aug. 17, 1957; children—Catherine Mary, Bettina Verena. Student U. Geneva, U. Zurich, 1935-41, U. Berlin, 1939; Dr. Med., U. Zurich, 1945; Dr. (honoris causa), Free U. Brussels, Belgium, 1978, U. Paris VI, Pierre et Marie Curie, France, 1981, Deutsche Akademie der Naturforscher Leopoldina, 1985. Head Inst. Pathology, Kantonsspital Winterthur, Switzerland, 1958-66; dir., prof. dept. pathology U. Lausanne, Switzerland, 1966-70; dir., prof. dept. pathology U. Zurich, Switzerland, 1970-87. Editor: Virchows Archiv A., 1968-87, Swiss Med. Jour., 1953-74, Annales de pathologie, Paris, 1981-87. Recipient Virchow's medal, German Soc. Pathology, 1989. Mem. European Soc. Pathology (hon.), Swiss Soc. Pathology, German Soc. Pathology, Internat. Acad. Pathology, French Soc. Pathology (hon.). Home: Attenhogerstrasse 16, 8032 Zurich Switzerland

HEDLEY-WHYTE, JOHN, anesthesiologist, educator; b. Newcastle-upon-Tyne, Eng., Nov. 25, 1933; came to U.S., 1960, naturalized, 1965; s. Angus and Nancy (Nettleton) H.-W.; m. Elizabeth Tessa Waller, Sept. 19, 1959. Student, Harrow Sch., 1947-52; B.A. (Rothschild scholar Clare Coll.), Cambridge U., 1955, M.B., 1958, M.A., 1959, M.D., 1972; A.M. (hon.), Harvard U., 1967. House surgeon St. Bartholomew's Hosp., London, 1958-59; resident in anesthesia Mass. Gen. Hosp., 1960-62, hon. anesthetist, 1977—; clin. asst. anesthesia Harvard U., 1961-63, instr., 1963-65, clin. asso., 1965-67, asso. prof., 1967-69, prof., 1969-76, 1st David S. Sheridan prof. anaesthesia and respiratory therapy, 1976—; prof. dept. health policy and mgmt. Harvard U. Sch. Pub. Health, 1988—; chmn. faculty seminar in health and medicine Harvard U., 1975-76; anesthetist-in-chief Beth Israel Hosp., Boston, 1967-87; chmn. com. on research Beth Israel Hosp., 1976-82; cons. in field; mem. tech. adv. bd. on med. devices tech. Am. Nat. Standards Inst., 1973-83; U.S. del. Internat. Electrotech. Commn., 1989-91, 92—; leader U.S. del. Internat. Orgn. Standardization, Geneva, 1973-89, chmn. com. TC 121, SC 3 on anaesthetic and respiratory equipment, 1978—. Author: Respiratory Care, 1965, Applied Physiology of Respiratory Care, 1976, Continuous Anesthesia Vapor Monitoring, 1990, Operating room and Intensive Care Alarms and Information Transfer, 1992; contbr. articles to profl. jours. Recipient Hichens prize St. Bartholomew's Hosp., London,

1957. Fellow Am. Soc. Testing and Materials (hon., chmn. com. F29 1983-89, Merit award 1994); mem. Am. Physiol. Soc., Abernethian Soc. (past pres.), Am. Soc. Anesthesiologists (chmn. com. mech. equipment 1977-82, chmn. com. on equipment and standards 1982-84), Mass. Soc. Anesthesiologists (pres. 1973-74), Am. Soc. Pharmacology and Exptl. Therapeutics, Roxbury Soc. Med. Improvement (libr. 1970-88, sec.-treas. 1988—), Mass. Med. Soc. (coun. 1975-78), Fairhaven Preservation Assn. (chmn. 1990—), Boodle's Club, The Country Club, Somerset Club, Harvard Club of Boston, Vicarage Club. Democrat. Episcopalian. Home: PO Box 649 Concord MA 01742-0649 Office: VA Med Ctr 1400 VFW Pkwy West Roxbury MA 02132-4927

HED-RAM, DAFNA, physician; b. Jerusalem, Aug. 21, 1965; came to U.S., 1970; d. Eitan and Alicia (Berdichesky) Hed-R. BA Psychology, U. Calif., Santa Barbara, 1988; DO, Nova Southeastern U., 1994. DO. Course instr. sports medicine U. Calif. Santa Barbara Health Edn., Santa Barbara, 1985-87; med. equipment specialist ABL Aerospace, Inc., Valencia, Calif., 1988-90; dir. asst. Area Health Edn. Ctr., Miami, 1992; intern physician Botsford Gen. Hosp., Farmington Hills, Mich., 1994-95; resident physician ob-gyn. San Bernardino (Calif.) County Med. Ctr., 1995—. Med. asst. ARC, Miami, 1993. Mem. AMA, Am. Osteo. Assn., Am. Coll. Gen. Practitioners, Mich. Osteo. Assn., Nat. Osteopathic Women's Physician Assn. (pres. 1991-92), Lambda Omicron Gamma (sec. 1991-92). Home: Apt 3716 1601 Barton Rd Redlands CA 92373-5366

HEDRICK, STEVE BRIAN, psychotherapist; b. Orlando, Fla., Aug. 23, 1958; s. David Warrington and June (Nicholson) H. BA, U. Cen. Fla., 1980, MA, 1988. Lic. mental health counselor, marriage and family therapist, Fla. Child devel. worker Seagrave, Orlando, 1985-86; deinstitutionalization case mgr. Mental Health Svcs. Orange County, Orlando, 1986-88; family therapist, mental health counselor Green House Family Counseling Ctr., Orlando, 1988-92, PruCare of Orlando, Fla., 1993—. Mem. ACA, Am. Mental Health Counselors Assn., Fla. Mental Health Counselors Assn., Fla. Assn. Counseling and Devel., Cen. Fla. Assn. Marriage and Family Therapy, Internat. Assn. Marriage and Family Counselors, Am. Assn. Marriage and Family Therapy (clin. mem.). Democrat. Episcopalian. Office: 3400 Quadrangle Blvd Orlando FL 32817

HEDRICK, WYATT SMITH, pharmacist; b. Roswell, N.Mex., Sept. 28, 1951; s. Wyatt Smith and Roberta Walker (Stuart) H. BS in Pharmacy, U. N.Mex., 1974; MS in Hosp. Pharmacy, U. Houston, 1978. Registered pharmacist, N.Mex., Tex. Pharmacy intern St. Mary's Hosp., Roswell, N.Mex., 1973, Ea. N.Mex. Med. Ctr., Roswell, 1973-74, U-SAVE Drug, Roswell, 1974-75; pharmacy resident U. Tex. Med. Br. Hosps., Galveston, 1977-78; staff pharmacist Meml. Gen. Hosp., Las Cruces, N.Mex., 1978, Columbia Med. Ctr. West, El Paso, Tex., 1978—. Mem. Am. Soc. Health-Sys. Pharmacists, Tex. Soc. Health-Sys. Pharmacists, El Paso Area Soc. Health-Sys. Pharmacists. Home: 1028 Quinault Dr El Paso TX 79912-1223

HEDSTROM, SUSAN LYNNE, maternal women's health nurse; b. Dowagiac, Mich., Jan. 17, 1958; d. Clinton J. and Gloria Anna (Hyink) Moore. ADN, Southwestern Mich. Coll., 1978. RN, Mich., Ind., Calif., Ga., Fla. Staff nurse obstetrics unit Lee Meml. Hosp., Dowagiac, Mich., 1979-81, Meml. Hosp., South Bend, Ind., 1981-90; with MRA Staffing Systems, Inc., Ft. Lauderdale, Fla., 1990-93; staff nurse traveler MUSC, Charleston, S.C., 1990-91; nurse Desert Hosp., Palm Springs, Calif., 1991, Ind. U. Hosp., Indpls., 1992, Valley Med Ctr., Fresno, Calif., 1992; staff nurse post partum/nursery Tallahassee Meml. Regional Med. Ctr., 1993-95, asst. head nurse post partum, 1995—. Mem. Am. Women's Health, Obstetrics and Neonatal Nurses. Office: Tallahassee Meml Reg Hosp Magnolia Dr & Miccosukee Rd Tallahassee FL 32308

HEEREN, MARY L., health facility public relations and developmental officer; b. Alton, Ill., Nov. 19, 1954; d. Leroy Warren and Charlotte Emily (Plegge) H. AA, Lewis & Clark C.C., Godfrey, Ill., 1974; BS, So. Ill. U., 1976. Sec. Owens-Ill. Inc., Godfrey, Ill., 1976-77; reporter Herrin (Ill.) Spokesman, 1977; reporter/mem. advt. sales staff Breese (Ill.) Pub. Co.; dir. pub. rels., devel. officer St. Joseph's Hosp., Breese, 1988—. Mem. Carlyle Lake Audubon Soc., 1975—, pres., 1985—; chair publicity Ill. Ducks Unltd. Adv. Coun., 1992-95, Carlyle Lake chpt., 1989—; com. chair So. Ill. Luth. Singles, 1989—. Office: St Joseph's Hosp 9515 Holy Cross Ln Breese IL 62230

HEESACKER, MARTIN, psychologist; b. Warwick, Va., Apr. 25, 1956; s. Bernard Andrew and Mary (NeCasek) H. BS, U. So. Miss., 1977; MS, U. Mo., 1981, PhD, 1983. Lic. psychologist, Ohio, Fla. Counselor, intern U. Mo., Columbia, 1981-83; asst. prof. psychology So. Ill. U., Carbondale, 1983-86, Ohio State U., Columbus, 1986-89; assoc. prof. to prof. psychology U. Fla., Gainesville, 1989—; cons. Covington Industries, Opp, Ala., 1983-84, North Fla. Evaluation and Treatment Ctr., Gainesville, 1990—, SOAR Am., Inc., Melbourne, Fla., 1990—; lectr. in field. Editorial bd. Jour. Counseling Psychology, 1987-95, Contemporary Psychology, 1995—; editor Profiles of Adjustment, 1994; contbr. articles to profl. jours., chpts. to books. Recipient Grad. Rsch. award Mo. Psychol. Assn., 1982; Fulbright scholar USIA, 1987; Lilly fellow Eli Lilly Endowment, 1988. Fellow APA (counseling psychology divsn., co-chair Gt. Lakes regional conf. 1987-88, new profls. com. 1986-87, Early Career award 1989); mem. Midwestern Psychol. Assn., Soc. Advancement Social Psychology, Soc. Exptl. Social Psychology, Sigma Xi. Office: Dept Psychology U Fla Box 112280 Gainesville FL 32611-2250

HEESTAND, DIANE ELISSA, educational technology educator, medical educator; b. Boston, Oct. 9, 1945; d. Glenn Wilson and Elizabeth (Martin) H. BA, Allegheny Coll., 1967; MA, U. Wyo., 1968; edn. specialist, Ind. U., 1971, EdD, 1979. Asst. prof. communication Clarion (Pa.) State Coll., 1971; asst. prof. learning resources Indiana U. of Pa., 1971-72; asst. prof. communication U. Nebr. Med. Ctr., Omaha, 1972-74; assoc. prof. learning resources Tidewater Community Coll., Virginia Beach, Va., 1975-78; ednl. cons. U. Ala. Sch. Medicine, Birmingham, 1978-81; dir. learning resources, assoc. prof. med. edn. Mercer U. Sch. Medicine, Macon, Ga., 1981-88; asst. dean ednl. devel. and resources Ohio U. Coll. Osteopathic Medicine, 1989-90; assoc. prof. clin. med. edn., dir. biomed. communications U. So. Calif. Sch. Medicine, L.A., 1990-95, acting chair dept. med. edn., 1992-95; dir. office ednl. devel. U. Ark. for Med. Scis., Little Rock, 1995—; cons. Lincoln (Pa.) U., summer, 1975; vis. fellow Project Hope/China, Millwood, Va., summer, 1986. Author (teleplay) Yes, 1968 (award World Law Fund 1968); producer, dir. (slide tape) Finding a Way, 1980 (1st Pl. award HESCA 1981, Susan Eastman award 1981). Grantee Porter Found., 1984. Mem. Health Scis. Comm. Assn. (bd. dirs. 1982-86, pres.-elect 1987-88, pres. 1988-89, Spl. Svc. award 1990), Assn. Ednl. Comm. and Tech. (pres. media design and prodn. div. 1985-86), Assn. Biomed. Comm. Dirs. (bd. dirs. 1993-95). Republican. Unitarian Universalist.

HEFFERN, DEBBI MARIE, dietitian; b. Corona, Calif., May 5, 1956; d. William Anthony Sypniewski and Jacquelyn Agnes Allhoff Shumate; m. Patrick Allen Heffern, June 25, 1977; children: Kevin, Kathy, Michael. BS, Fontbonne Coll., St. Louis, 1978. Registered dietitian, Mo. Sales assoc. Saks Fifth Ave., St. Louis, 1973-77; kitchen supr. St. Mary's Health Ctr., St. Louis, 1977-78; dietetic intern VA Med. Ctr., St. Louis, 1978-79; cafeteria mgr. Our Lady of Lourdes Sch., St. Louis, 1979-80; community coord. LaLeche League Internat., Creve Coeur, Mo., 1983—; dist. advisor Cen. Mo. dist. LaLeche League Internat., 1985-90, dist. coord., 1987-89; state coord. Mo. LaLeche League Internat., 1992—; cons. Human Devel. Corp., St. Louis, 1988-91, Mo. Dept. Health, St. Louis, 1990—, Birthright, St. Louis, 1991—; lectr. in field. Author (booklet): Breast Feeding: What Nature Intended, 1990; contbr. articles to profl. jours. and popular mags. Leader Girl Scouts U.S., St. Louis, 1990-91; coord. Tiger Cub Scouts, St. Louis, 1990-91; contest coord. Creve Coeur Days Festival, 1989—. Mem. NAFE, St. Louis Dietetic Assn., Am. Dietetic Assn., LaLache League Internat., Internat. Lactation Cons. Assn., Lactation Cons. Metro. St. Louis. Home and Office: 11667 Chieftain Dr Saint Louis MO 63146-5463

HEFFLER, KAREN FRANKEL, ophthalmology educator; b. Wilmington, Del., Aug. 4, 1960; d. David Matthew and Lois Sheila (Ableman) Frankel; m. Curt Lewis Heffler, June 28, 1981; children: Lauren, Daniel, Rachel. BA summa cum laude, U. Pa., 1982, MD, 1986. Diplomate Am. Bd. Ophthalmology. Intern in internal medicine Bryn Mawr (Pa.) Hosp., 1986-87; resident in ophthalmology Scheie Eye. Inst., U. Pa., Phila., 1987-90, fellow in cornea and external disease, asst. chief svc., 1990-91; asst. prof. Allegheny U. of the Health Scis., Phila., 1991—, dir. cornea and refractive surgery, 1995—; cons. Laurel Rehab. Svc., 1995—. Contbr. articles to med. jours. Mem. AMA (physician's recognition award 1993—), Am. Acad. Ophthalmology, Pa. Acad. Ophthalmology, Pa. Med. Soc., Women in Ophthalmology, St. George Med. Cancer Soc. (pres. 1983-84), Alpha Omega Alpha. Office: Allegheny U Health Scis 216 N Broad St Philadelphia PA 19102

HEFFLEY, JAMES DICKEY, nutrition counselor; b. Collinsville, Tex., Jan. 12, 1941; s. Floyd F. and Bessie C. (Dickey) H.; m. Betty E. Dozier, Dec. 22, 1963; children: James M., Jon R., David D., Sara E., Anna C. BS, Abilene Christian U., 1964; PhD, U. Tex., 1970. Cert. clin. nutritionist. Rsch. asst., then rsch. assoc. Clayton Found. Bich. Inst., Austin, Tex., 1965-74; lab. supr. Ctr. for Better Health, Austin, 1984—; dir. Nutrition Counseling Svc., Austin, 1974—; cons. Tex. Sch. for Blind, Austin, 1972-74, Tex. Gov.'s Commn. on Aging, Austin, 1976. Contbr. articles to profl. jours. Mem. Internat. Acad. Nutrition and Preventive Medicine (pres. 1994—), Internat. and Am. Assn. Clin. Nutritionists (pres. 1991-95), Clin Nutrition Cert. Bd. (chmn. 1996—). Office: Nutrition Counseling Svc 3913 Medical Pky Ste 101 Austin TX 78756-4016

HEFFNER, PHYLLIS JEAN, child psychiatrist; b. Reading, Pa., Apr. 12, 1958; d. Richard Peters and Helene Mae (Lengel) H.; m. William Robert Toole, Aug. 25, 1984; children: Lauren Ruth, Colin Edward. BA, Franklin and Marshall Coll., Lancaster, Pa., 1982; MD, Pa. State U., Hershey, 1986. Diplomate Am. Bd. Med. Examiners. Intern, then resident in gen. psychiatry N.C. Meml. Hosp., Chapel Hill, 1986-89; fellow in child psychiatry U. Md. Hosps., Balt., 1989-91; staff child psychiatrist Philhaven Hosp., Mt. Gretna, Pa., 1991—. Hermann scholar Franklin and Marshall Coll., 1982, Hammond scholar Pa. State Sch. Medicine, 1983-84. Mem. Am. Psychiat. Assn., Am. Acad. Child and Adolescent Psychiatry, Alpha Omega Alpha, Psi Chi. Episcopalian.

HEFFNER, ROSLYN, rehabilitation counselor; b. Bklyn.; m. Claude H. Heffner, Mar. 12, 1966; children: Steven, Deborah. Diploma in nursing, Buffalo (N.Y.) Gen. Hosp., 1963; BA, San Francisco State U., 1977, MS, 1979. Nurse Pacific Med., San Francisco, 1973-79; nurse, dept. head Mercy Hosp., Roseburg, Oreg., 1979-80; nurse Douglas Community Hosp., Roseburg, 1980-85; rehab. counselor Vocational Planning, Roseburg, 1980-81; dep. dir. services Siskiyou Rehab., Roseburg, 1982-85; rehab. counselor Cooley/Assocs., Roseburg, 1985-86, Richter & Assoc., Portland, Oreg., 1986, Crawford Rehab., Portland, 1987; pvt. practice rehab. counselor, med. case mgr. R. Heffner Vocational Counseling Service, Tualatin, Oreg., 1987—; cons. Adult and Family Svcs., Roseburg, 1984; instr. Gerontology Class, Roseburg, 1982; presenter White House Forest Conf., 1993. Author: The Rehabilitation Nurse's Survival Guide, 1994. Mem. Douglas County Mental Health, Roseburg, 1981-85, Health Systems Agy., Roseburg, 1982-84. Mem. AAUW, Nat. Rehab. Assn., Nat. Rehab. Counseling Assn. Office: R Heffner Vocat Counseling PO Box 1391 Tualatin OR 97062-1391

HEFFRON, WARREN A., medical educator, physician; b. St. Louis, Nov. 7, 1936; s. Willard Page H. and Alma Alberta Revington; m. Rosalee Bowdish, June 10, 1961; children: Kimberly, Wanda, Kara, Arthur. AB, U. Mo., 1958, MD, 1962. Diplomate Am. Bd. Family Practice. Rotating intern U. Calif., Orange, 1962-63; physician Hosp. Castaner (P.R.), 1966-68; resident internal medicine U. N. Mex., Albuquerque, 1968-71, asst. prof., chief divsn., 1971-76; assoc. prof., asst. chair Family Committee and Emergency Medicine, Albuquerque, 1976-82, prof., chmn., 1982-93; chief med. staff U. N. Mex. Hosp., Albuquerque, 1993—; bd. dirs. Am. Acad. Family Physicians, Am. Bd. Family Practice; dir. Family Med. Residency Program, Albuquerque, 1971-82; vis. prof., cons. Dept. Cmty. Health, Punjab, India, Christian Med. Coll., Punjab U., Ludhiana; prof. Dept. Family and Cmty. Medicine, Albuquerque, 1993—. Contbr. numerous articles to profl. jours. Mem. free clinic Albuquerque Rescue Mission. Lt. comdr. USPHS, 1964-66. Recipient Recognition award Am. Med. Assn. Physicians, 1971, 74, 77, 80, 83, 86, 89, 92, 95, N. Mex. Family Physician of the Yr. award, 1990. Mem. N. Mex. Am. Acad. Family Physicians (pres. 1985, N. Mex. Family Dr. of Yr. award, chpt. svc. award 1988), N. Mex. Med. Soc. (pres. 1996, Robbins award Cmty. Svc. 1981), Soc. Tchrs. of Family Medicine (bd. dirs.), Am. Bd. Family Practice. Methodist. Office: U N Mex 2400 Tucker Ave NE Albuquerque NM 87131

HEGARTY, WILLIAM KEVIN, medical center executive; b. Sask., Can., Feb. 14, 1926; came to U.S., 1951; s. William Alexander and Lila (Taylor) H.; m. Doreen Alice Symon, Sept. 8, 1951; children—Kelley, Kerry, Michael. B. Commerce, U. Man., 1949; M.H.A., Northwestern U. 1953. Exec. dir. Calif. Hosp., Los Angeles, 1966-69 v.p. Lutheran Hosp. Soc., Los Angeles, 1969-74; vice chmn. Huntington Meml. Hosp., Pasadena, Calif., 1974-90; ret.; Bd. dirs. Blue Cross of So. Calif. Contbr. articles to profl. jours. Mem. Am. Hosp. Assn., Calif. Hosp. Assn. (pres. 1977, Outstanding Service award), Hosp. Council So. Calif. (pres. 1973), Assn. Am. Med. Colls. Congregationalist. Club: Rotary Internat. Home: 341 Fairway Dr Alisal Ranch Solvang CA 93463

HEGEMAN, GEORGE DOWNING, microbiology educator; b. Glen Cove, N.Y., Aug. 31, 1938; s. George Downing and Bonnie (Blair) H.; m. Sally Lorraine Lofgren, Aug. 26, 1961; children: Susan Elizabeth, Adrian Daniel. AB, Harvard U., 1960; PhD, U. Calif., Berkeley, 1965. Instr. bacteriology and immunology U. Calif., Berkeley, 1965, asst. prof. bacteriology, 1966-72; assoc. prof. microbiology Ind. U., Bloomington, 1972-79, prof. microbiology, 1979—; mem. sci. adv. bd. BioTrol, Inc., Mpls., 1985-90; mem. basic energy scis. adv. com. U.S. Dept. of Energy, 1989—. Mem. editorial review bd. Applied & Environmental Microbiology, 1984—, J. Bacteriol, 1989—; patentee in field; contbr. articles to profl. jours. Mem. Monroe County Health Bd. USPHS fellow, 1962-66; grantee USPHS, NSF. Fellow Am. Acad. Microbiology; mem. AAAS, Am. Soc. Microbiology, Am. Soc. Biochemistry and Molecular Biology, Forest Resources Assn. (past pres., v.p.). Office: Ind U Biology Dept Bloomington IN 47405

HEGVIK, DONNA KAY, psychologist; b. Glenfield, N.D., Apr. 23, 1953; d. Alton and Janice (McDonald) Hegvik; m. Craig Howard Anderson, Dec. 30, 1982; children: Kelsey Craig, Byron Alton, Jillian Joy. LPN, N.D. State Sch. Sci., Wahpeton, N.D., 1973; BS in Psychology, N.D. State U., 1978; PhD in Counseling Psychology, Tex. Tech. U., 1988. Lic. psychologist, Nebr. Asst. coord. Programs for Acad. Support Svcs. Tex. Tech. U., Lubbock, 1981-82; psychiat. nurse Meth. Hosp., Lubbock, 1979-82; psychology intern VA Med. Ctr., Denver, 1982-83; psychotherapist Colo. Neurobehavioral Ctr., Denver, 1986-88; staff psychologist Sherrets and Assocs., Omaha, 1990-91; psychotherapist Sr. Counseling Group, Denver, 1995-96; hypnotherapist Inst. for Clin. Hypnosis, Denver, 1996—. Bear Creek area rep. Jefferson County Dist. Accountability Commn., Golden, Colo., 1993—; co-chair accountability com. Westgate Elem. Sch., Lakewood, Colo., 1992—, legis. chair PTA, 1991—; Pack-o-Gram editor Boy Scouts Am., 1993—. Anderson-Swennson Meml. scholar Tex. Tech. U., 1979, E.V. Estensen Meml. Scholar for outstanding psychology student N.D. State U., 1978, Homewood Meml. scholar Valley City State Coll., 1976, Amidon Meml. scholar, 1976. Mem. N.D. State U. Psychology Club (pres. 1978-79), Psi Chi. Congregationalist.

HEGYELI, RUTH INGEBORG ELISABETH JOHNSSON, pathologist, government official; b. Stockholm, Aug. 14, 1931; came to U.S., 1963; d. John Alfred and Elsa Ingeborg (Sjogren) Johnsson; m. Andrew Francis Hegyeli, July 2, 1966 (dec. June 1982). BA in Scis., U. Toronto, 1958, MD, 1962. Intern Toronto Gen. Hosp., 1962-63; sr. rsch. pathologist Battelle Meml. Inst., Columbus, Ohio, 1967-69; med. officer Nat. Heart and Lung Inst., 1969-73; chief program devel. and evaluation Nat. Heart, Lung and Blood Inst., Bethesda, Md., 1973-76, acting dir. office program planning, 1975-76, asst. dir. internat. relations, 1976-86, assoc. dir. internat. rels., 1986—; mem. sci. adv. bd. Giovanni Lorenzini Found., Inc., N.Y.C., Milan, 1982—, Lorenzini Rsch. Found. Coordinating editor Jour. Soviet Research in Cardiovascular Diseases, 1979-86. Editor: Christopher Columbus Commemorative Book on Discovering New Worlds in Medicine, 1992, also 10 sci. books. Contbr. poetry to nat. anthologies. Bd. dirs. Coun. on Geriatric Cardiology, chmn. internat. com.; nat. adv. bd. Nat. Mus. Women in Arts. Named Hon. Mem. Eagle Tribe of Haida Indians, Queen Charlotte Islands, B.C., Can., 1961; nat. adv. bd. Nat. Mus. Women in the Arts; recipient Outstanding Scientist award Battelle Meml. Inst., Columbus, Ohio, 1966, German Friendship award German Ministry Rsch. and Tech., 1988, Nicolaus Copernicus medal Academica Medica, 1988, Superior Svc. award, HEW, 1975, DHHS, 1991. Fellow Acad. Medicine, Toronto; mem. Am. Soc. Artificial Internal Organs, N.Y. Acad. Scis., Acad. Am. Poets, World Literary Acad., Fed. Exec. Alumni Assn. (policy issues com.). Republican. Avocations: poetry, fiction writing; non-fiction writing; art; music. Home: 24301 Hanson Rd Gaithersburg MD 20882-3501

HEGYI, DOUGLAS FRANK, otorhinolaryngologist, plastic surgeon; b. Aurora, Ill., Mar. 13, 1945; s. Frank Julius and Grace Irene (Dziewior) H.; children: Justin Douglas, Jeffrey Douglas; m. Diane H. Baldwin, Sept. 29, 1990. Diploma Chgo. City Coll., 1968; BS in Psychology, Ill. Inst. Tech., 1971; DO, Chgo. Coll. Osteo. Medicine, 1976. Diplomate Nat. Bd. Examiners, Am. Osteopathic Bd. Otorhinolaryngology (examiner 1992-95, bd. examiner 1995); cert. otorhinolaryngologist, facial plastic surgeon, cosmetic surgeon. Intern, Mt. Clemens Gen. Hosp., Mich., 1976-77; resident in otorhinolaryngology and oro-facial plastic surgery, Pontiac Osteo. Hosp., Mich., 1977-80; staff physician, treas. dept. ophthalmology and otorhinolaryngology, 1980—, mem. teaching staff, 1980—; staff physician, sect. chief otorhinolaryngology Lapeer Gen. Hosp., Mich., 1980—; cons. staff Caro Community Hosp., Mich., 1986—; staff physician Crittenton Hosp., Mich., 1986—; asst. clin. prof. otorhinolaryngology Mich. State U., Coll. Osteo. Medicine, 1980—. Recipient Appreciation cert. Am. Cancer Soc., 1976; named one of Hon. Order Ky. Col., 1987. Fellow Am. Acad. Otolaryngology, Am. Acad. Cosmetic Surgery, Osteo. Coll. Ophthalmology and Otorhinolaryngology, Skin Cancer Found. (hon.); mem. Atlas Club (life, cert. for Outstanding Service and Dedication 1976), Chgo. Coll. Osteo. Medicine Alumni Assn., Am. Osteo. Assn., Am. Acad. Facial Plastic and Reconstructive Surgery, Masons, Order of DeMolay. Episcopalian. Office: 210 W Tienken Rd Rochester MI 48306-4472

HEGYVARY, SUE THOMAS, dean nursing school; b. Dry Ridge, Ky., Nov. 28, 1943. BSN, U. Ky., 1965; MN, Emory U., 1966; PhD in Sociology, Vandebilt U., 1974. Asst. prof. nursing and social Rush U., 1972-74, assoc. prof. mednursing, chair dept., 1974-77; asst. prof. social Rush U. Med. Coll., 1977-80; prof. nursing, assoc. v.p., assoc. dean nursing Coll. Nursing, Rush U., Rush Presbyn.-St. Luke's Med. Ctr., 1977—; assoc. prof. social Med. Coll. Rush U., 1980—; dean, prof. Sch. Nursing U. Wash., Seattle, 1986—; mem. health care adv. com. Rep. Jennifer Dunn, 1993; vis. com. Bd. 50 Emory U. Sch. Nursing, Atlanta, 1990-92; mem. adv. panel outcomes rsch. Nat. Ctr. Nursing Rsch. NIH, 1990-91; external mem. Five Yr. Review com. Coll. Nursing U. Ky., 1989-90; mem. govtl. affairs com. Am. Assn. Colls. Nursing, 1988—; chair planning com. Wash. State Conf. Nursing Shortage, 1989; mem. Wash. State Commn. Nursing, 1989; mem. adv. com. Child Devel. & Mental Retardation Ctr. U. Wash., 1986—; mem. task force nursing shortage Seattle Area Hosp. Coun., 1987-88; vis. prof., ann. lectr. Sch. Nursing U. Va., Charlottesville, 1988; vis. prof. U. Oulu, Finland, 1985; site visitor accreditation schs. nursing Nat. League Nursing, 1977-80; cons. VA Hosp., Miami, Fla., 1968-69, Vanderbilt U., Nashville, 1971-72, Area Health Edn. Sys., Rockford, Ill., 1975, Western Interstate Commn. Higher Edn., Denver, 1975, Andrews U., Berrian Springs, Mich., 1976, dept. nursing studies Nat. Hosp. Inst., Utrecht, The Netherlands, 1976-80, Haukeland Sykehaus, Bergen, Norway, 1976-77, Sch. Nursing Marquette U., Milw., 1977, Wayne State U., Detroit, 1978, Cath. U. Leuven, Belgium, 1980, Walter Reed Army Med. Ctr., Washington, 1979-83, Dalhousie U. Sch. Nursing, Halifax, N.S., 1981, U. Minn., Mpls., 1988, U. Mo., Columbia, 1992. Editl. adv. bd. Nursing Policy Forum, 1995—; editl. cons. Nursing Care Guide Pfizer Corp., 1993; editl. bd. Jour. Nursing & Health, 1993—, Nursing Adminstrn. Quarterly, 1988—; mem. manucscript review panel Jour. Nursing Quality Assurance, 1986—, Nursing Outlook, 1983—, Jour. Rsch. Nursing & Health, 1981—, Nursing Rsch., 1979-89; contbr. chpts. to books and articles to profl. jours. Mem. ANA, Am. Acad. Nursing, Sigma Theta Tau. Office: Univ WA Sch Nursing Box 357260 Seattle WA 98195

HEIAR, JOHN M., medical products company executive; b. Dubuque, Iowa, Feb. 18, 1957; s. Merlin F. and Eileen B. (Savary) H. BS, U. Iowa, 1983. Territory mgr. Boehringer Pharms., Columbia, Mo., 1984-87; radiology cons. Iowa City, 1987-93; imaging specialist Nycomed Corp., Iowa City, 1993—. Mem. U. Iowa Alumni Assn.

HEIBERG, ELISABETH, radiology educator; b. Oslo, May 12, 1945; came to U.S., 1973; d. Erik Lyng and Gerd Augusta (Ursin-Holm) H.; m. J. David Malone, Mar. 25, 1970 (div.); children: Janina, Jonathan. Baccalaureat, Hartvig-Nissen, Oslo, 1964; MD, Royal Coll. Surgeons and Physicians, Dublin, Ireland, 1970. Diplomate Am. Bd. Radiology. Intern in surgery Jervis St. Hosp., Dublin, 1970-71; resident in medicine Nottingham (Eng.) City Hosp., 1971; resident in radiology Washington U., St. Louis, 1975-79; asst. prof. radiology St. Louis U. Hosp., 1979-85, assoc. prof., 1985-92, dir. magnetic resonance imaging, 1991—, prof., 1992—. Contbr. articles to profl. jours. Mem. University City (Mo.) Symphony Orch., 1986—. Mem. AAUP, Am. Coll. Radiology, Am. Assn. Women Radiologists, Greater St. Louis Radiol. Soc., Am. Univ. Radiologists, Radiol. Soc. N.Am., Soc. Magnetic Resonance in Medicine, Norwegian Soc. (sec. 1983, organizer singing group 1983-86), St. Louis Spelemanns Lag. Home: 6959 Waterman Ave Saint Louis MO 63130-4333 Office: St Louis U Hosp Dept Radiology 3635 Vista Ave at Grand Blvd PO Box 15250 Saint Louis MO 63110

HEIDELBAUGH, NORMAN DALE, veterinary medicine educator, consultant, author, inventor; b. Phila., July 29, 1927; s. Milton Harold and Claire Agnus (Dale) H.; m. Judith Sweet Voss, Feb. 16, 1963; children: Clark Hayden, Todd Milton, Lynn Ruth. VMD, U. Pa., 1954; M in Pub. Health, Tulane U., 1958; SM, MIT, 1963, PhD, 1970. Diplomate Am. Coll. Vet. Preventive Medicine; charter diplomate splty. epidemiology; Diplomate Am. Bd. Vet. Pub. Health. Commd. USAF, 1954; vet. officer various locations worldwide; advanced through grades to col., 1972; chief food sci. Lyndon B. Johnson Space Ctr., NASA, Houston, 1970-74; USAF rep. Dept. Def. Research-Devel.-Test and Evaluation Program, Washington, 1974-77; retired USAF, 1977; prof. vet. pub. health Tex. A&M U., College Station, 1977-92, head dept., 1978-90, prof. food sci. and tech., 1977-92; prof. emeritus Tex. A&M U., Coll. Station, Tex., 1994—; mem. vis. com. MIT, Cambridge, 1977-84, cons. UN Devel. Program, N.Y.C., 1979-82; mem. NRC Nat. Acad. Scis., 1984-86. Contbr. 125 articles to profl. jours. Mem. nat. adv. com. on meat and poultry insp., USDA, Washington, 1980-92. Decorated Legion of Merit with 2 Oak Leaf Clusters, USAF; named Tex. Scientist of Yr. Air Force Assn., 1966; Underwood-Prescott meml. lectr. MIT, 1974; recipient Skylab award NASA, 1979. Scroll of Appreciation, U.S. Army Europe and 7th Army, 1984-92; grantee numerous orgns. and govt. Mem. AVMA, (sci. program com. 1982-86, coun. on rsch. 1986—, XII Internat. Vet. Cong. award 1992), Inst. food Technologists, Am. Assn. Food Hygiene Vets (pres. 1983-84, Vet. of Yr. 1986). Office: Tex A&M U Coll Vet Medicine Dept Vet Anat & Pub Health College Station TX 77843-4458

HEIDENDAL, GUIDO ALFONS, nuclear medicine physician; b. Rykevorsel, Antwerp, Belgium, Feb. 15, 1936; s. Felix Heidendal and Emerance Pauwels; m. Martine Jeune, May 6, 1970; children: Carine, Barbara, Philip. MD, U. Louvain, Belgium, 1962; specialist in nuclear medicine, Mayo Clinic, 1972. Bd. cert. nuclear medicine, U.S. Internist City-Hosp., Maaseik, Belgium, 1970, U. Louvain; U. Lyon, France; U. Amsterdam, The Netherlands, 1970; dir. dept. nuclear medicine Free U., Amsterdam, 1972-85, Acad. Hosp., Maastricht, The Netherlands, 1985—; vis. prof. in nuclear medicine Georgetown U., Washington, 1983; mem. Dutch Bd. Nuclear Medicine, 1972-80. Referent: Biologie et Pathologie, 1982, Adrenal Scintigraphy, 1978, Preoperative Pulmonary in Extensive Lung Resection, 1986. Capt. Belgian Army, 1967-68. Fellow Am. Coll. Nuclear Medicine, Royal Soc. Medicine (London); mem. European Union Med. Specialists, Am. Soc. Nuclear Medicine, Belgian Soc. Nuclear Medicine, Netherland's Soc. Nuclear Medicine. Home: Graaf Van Waldeckstraat 20, 6212 AP Maastricht The Netherlands Office: Acad Hosp, P DeByelaan 25, 6202 AZ Maastricht The Netherlands

HEIDENREICH, ARTURO, surgeon; b. Buenos Aires, July 23, 1928; s. Arturo Juan and Matilde (Deurer) H.; m. Maria Celeste Grondona, Sept. 2,

1961; children: Eduardo, Maria Ines, Ana Maria. MD, U. Buenos Aires, 1953. Instr. in surgery U. Buenos Aires, 1963-83, prof. surgery, 1983; surgeon Rawson Hosp., Buenos Aires, 1953-70; chief surg. dept. Salaberry Hosp., Buenos Aires, 1971-77; surgeon German Hosp., Buenos Aires, 1971-89, chief surg. dept., 1990—; pres. VII Argentine Proctologic Congress, 1979. Author: Treatise of Surgery, 1984, Surgical Pathology, 1987, Surgery, 1989, Urgencies in Coloproctology, 1991. Recipient prize Argentine Geriatric Soc., 1977-78, German Medicine Mag., 1980, Argentine Coloproctology Soc., 1988. Fellow ACS; mem. Argentine Proctologic Soc. (pres. 1972-74, prize 1966), Argentine Acad. Surgery. Roman Catholic. Home: Rodriquez Pena 1686, Buenos Aires 1021, Argentina Office: Coronel Diaz 1737, Buenos Aires 1425, Argentina

HEIDINGER, SONIA LYNN, physical therapist; b. Carbondale, Ill., Oct. 20, 1963; d. Roy C. and Bonnie S. (Osman) H. Student, So. Ill. U., 1982-85; BS, U. Puget Sound, 1988; postgrad., U.S. Sports Acad., St. Louis, 1989-90. Lic. phys. therapist, Ill. Shelter caretaker/coord. Appalachian Mountain Club, Gorham, N.H., 1986-87; intern Alaska Native Med. Ctr. and Providence Hosp., Anchorage, 1988; phys. therapist Herrin (Ill.) Hosp., 1988-90; cons. Bi-State Home Health, Anna, Ill.; dir. Harrisburg Med. Ctr. and Work Assesment Ctr., 1990-92; cons. St. Agnes Sport and Spine Ctr., 1992-93; dir. rehab. svcs. The Abbey of Carbondale, Ill., 1993-95; rehab. quality advisor Therapy Mgmt. Innovations, Asheville, N.C., 1995—. Bd. dirs. River to River Runners, 1992-93. Recipient Robert Davis Meml. scholarship So. Ill. U., 1985. Mem. Am. Phys. Therapy Assn., Bus. and Profl. Women. Home and Office: RR4 Box 227 Burnsville NC 28714

HEIFETS, LEONID, microbiologist, researcher; b. Russia, Jan. 5, 1926; came to U.S., 1979; s. Boris and Luba Heifets; m. Seraphima Apsit, Jan. 1955 (div. July 1978); children: Michael, Herman. MD, Med. Inst., Moscow, 1947, PhD, 1953; DSc, Acad. Med. Scis., Moscow. Asst. prof. Med. Inst., Arkhangelsk, Russia, 1950-54, assoc. prof., 1954-57; lab. dir. Mechnikov Rsch. Inst., Moscow, 1957-69; sr. researcher Inst. for Tuberculosis, Moscow, 1969-78; rsch. fellow Nat. Jewish Hosp., Denver, 1979-80; lab. dir. Nat. Jewish Ctr., Denver, 1980—; asst. prof. Colo. U., Denver, 1980-86, assoc. prof., 1986-92, prof. microbiology, 1992—; mem. com. on bacteriology Internat. Union Against Tuberculosis, Paris, 1986—. Author: Effectiveness of Vaccination, 1968; author, editor: Drug Susceptibility, 1991; mem. editorial bd. Antimicrobial Agents and Chemotherapy, Washington; assoc. editor Tubercle; contbr. articles to profl. jours. Mem. Am. Soc. Microbiology. Office: Nat Jewish Ctr Immunology Respiratory Med 1400 Jackson St Denver CO 80206-2761

HEIFETZ, CARL LOUIS, microbiologist; b. Somerville, N.J., Mar. 9, 1935; s. Samuel and Frances Mildred (Potter) H.; m. Sandra Feld, June 28, 1959; children: Jodee Beth, Terry Jay. BS, U. Md., 1957, MS, 1960, PhD, 1964. Registered pharmacist Bd. Pharmacy, Md., 1958. Assoc. rsch. bacteriologist Parke-Davis Pharm. Rsch., Detroit, 1964-68; rsch. microbiologist Parke-Davis Pharm. Rsch., 1968-70, rsch. scientist, 1970-76, rsch. assoc., 1976-78, sr. rsch. assoc., 1978-83; sect. dir. Parke-Davis Pharm. Rsch., Ann Arbor, Mich., 1983-90; dir. infectious diseases Parke-Davis Pharm. Rsch., 1990-92; pres. Micro Doc Cons., Inc., Palm Harbor, Fla., 1992—; clin. prof. med. microbiology and immunology U. South Fla. Med. Sch., 1992—; clin. prof. assoc. health Ea. Mich. U., Ypsilanti, 1986—, adj. prof. biology, 1986—. Editor: New Generation of Quinolones, 1990, Diagnostic Microbiology and Infectious Diseases, 1989-94; contbr. articles to profl. jours.; inventor, patentee in field. Pres. Evergreen Trails Homeowners Assn., Southfield, Mich., 1978; Rep. precinct del., Mich., 1978-80. Fellow Am. Acad. Microbiology; mem. Am. Soc. Microbiology (pres. Mich. br. 1986-87, chmn. div. A 1990-91, councilor 1990-92, alt. 1988-90, councilor Fla. br. 1994—), Brit. Soc. Antimicrobial Chemotherapy, Inter-Am. Soc. Chemotherapy, Sigma Xi, Rho Chi. Republican. Jewish. Office: Micro Doc Cons Inc 5490 Salem Square Dr S Palm Harbor FL 34685-1138

HEIKEN, JAY PAUL, physician; b. N.Y.C., Aug. 31, 1952; s. Martin and Sylvia (Fisher) H.; m. Barbara Ellen Rayburn, Dec. 11, 1976 (div. 1982); m. Francine J. Rosen, Apr. 29, 1990; 1 child, Lauren M. BA, Williams Coll., 1974; MD, Columbia U., 1978. Intern in internal medicine Emory U. Hosp., Atlanta, 1978-79; resident in radiology Columbia-Presbyn. Med. Ctr., N.Y.C., 1979-82; fellow abdominal radiology Mallinckrodt Inst. Radiology, St. Louis, 1982-83; asst. prof. sch. medicine Washington U., St. Louis, 1983-87, assoc. prof. sch. medicine, 1988-93; prof. sch. medicine, 1993—; dir. abdominal imaging Mallinckrodt Inst. Radiology, St. Louis; mem. Washington U. Cancer Ctr. Author, editor: Manual of Clinical Magnetic Resonance Imaging, 1986, 2d edit., 1991; editor: Computed Body Tomography with MRI Correlation, 3rd edit., 1996; contbr. articles to profl. jours. Mem. AMA, Radiol. Soc. N.Am., Am. Roentgen Ray Soc., Am. Coll. Radiology, Greater St. Louis Soc. Radiologists, Soc. Computed Body Tomography, Internat. Soc. Magnetic Resonance in Medicine, Soc. Gastrointestinal Radiologists, Assn. Univ. Radiologists. Home: 1801 Aston Way Chesterfield MO 63005-4579 Office: Mallinckrodt Inst Radiology 510 S Kingshighway Blvd Saint Louis MO 63110-1016

HEILBRUN, M. PETER, surgeon; b. Buffalo, N.Y., 1937. MD, SUNY, Buffalo, 1962. Diplomate Am. Bd. Neurol. Surgery. Intern Barnes Hosp., St. Louis, 1962-63, resident in gen. surgery, 1963-64; fellow in neurosurgery U. Washington, St. Louis, 1966-67; staff U. Utah Med. Ctr., Salt Lake City, 1967—. Mem. AMA. Office: U Utah Medical Center 50 N Medical Dr Salt Lake City UT 84132-1001*

HEILEN, ROBERT JOHN, orthopaedic surgeon; b. N.Y., Oct. 25, 1935. B in Chem. Engring., Cooper Union, 1957; MD, NYU, 1964. Diplomate Nat. Bd. Med. Examiners; bd. cert. Am. Bd. Orthopaedic Surgery. Pvt. practice orthopaedic surgery Washington, 1971-73, Va., 1971—; attending orthopaedic surgery The Fairfax Hosp., Falls Church, Va., 1971—; asst. clin. prof. orthopaedic surgery George Washington U., Washington; courtesy orthopaedic surgery staff Nat. Orthopaedic and Rehab. Hosp., Arlington, Va., The Fair Oaks Hosp., Fairfax, Va., Vencor Hosp. Arlington, Va.; chmn. Area II Regional Com. Med. Costs Per Rev., No. Va., 1988-94, Va. Med. Costs Peer Rev. Statewide Coord. Com. Workers Compensation, Richmond, 1993-94. Capt. U.S. Army Med. Corps, 1966-67, Korea. Fellow ACS, Am. Acad. Orthopaedic Surgery; mem. Washington Orthopaedic Soc. (pres. 1985-86). Home: 813 Lawton St McLean VA 22101 Office: 3289 Woodburn Rd #270 Annandale VA 22003

HEILICSER, BERNARD JAY, emergency physician; b. Bklyn., Jan. 19, 1947; s. Murray and Esther (Dubrow) H.; m. Marcia Cherry, June 2, 1976; children: Micah, Seth, Jacob. BA, SUNY, Binghamton, 1968; MS, Hahnemann Med. Coll., Phila., 1971; DO, Coll. Osteo. Medicine/Surgery, Des Moines, 1976. Diplomate Am. Bd. Emergency Medicine. Instr. anatomy and physiology U. Pa. and Hahnemann Med. Coll., Phila., 1971-73; staff physician Va. Inst. Tech., Blacksburg, 1977-78; asst. prof. emergency medicine Chgo. Coll. Osteo. Medicine, 1979; emergency physician St. Margaret Hosp., Hammond, Ind., 1979-83, Michael Reese Med. Ctr., Chgo., 1989-91, Ingalls Hosp., Harvey, Ill., 1983—; project med. dir. South Cook County Emergency Med. Svc., Harvey, 1984—; mem. faculty Chgo. Osteo. Med. Ctr., 1987—; faculty trauma nurse specialist St. James Hosp., Chicago Heights, Ill., 1980—; preceptor nurse practitioners Purdue U., Hammond, 1981—; fellow MacLean Ctr. Clin. Med. Ethics, U. Chgo., 1993-94; chmn. ethics com., hosp. med. ethicist Ingalls Hosp., Harvey, Ill., 1994—; cons. The Nat. Bd. Osteo. Med. Examiners, Harvey, 1994—. Vol. fireman Flossmoor (Ill.) Fire Dept., 1985—, Matteson (Ill.) Fire Dept., 1980—. Fellow Am. Coll. Emergency Physicians; mem. Am. Osteo. Assn., Nat. Assn. Emergency Med. Svcs. Physicians, Nat. Assn. Emergency Med. Technicians, Prehosp. Care Providers Ill., Sigma Sigma Phi. Jewish. Office: Ingalls Hosp One Ingalls Dr Harvey IL 60426

HEILMAN, JOHN P., JR., public health physician; b. Butler, Pa., July 6, 1939; s. John P. and Marjorie V. (West) H.; m. Peggy Louise Davis, Aug. 8, 1970; children: Mark R., John P. III. BA, Washington and Jefferson Coll., 1960; MD, Jefferson Med. Coll., 1964; MPH, Johns Hopkins U., 1968. Intern Madigan Gen. Hosp., Ft. Lewis, Wash., 1964-65; resident in aerospace medicine Brooks AFB, San Antonio, 1967-70; served to col. U.S. Army, MacDill AFB, Fla., 1965-88; ret. U.S. Army, 1988; dir. Pinellas County Health Dept., St. Petersburg, Fla., 1988—. Bd. dirs. Neighborly Sr. Svcs., St. Petersburg, 1991—. Decorated Legion of Merit with oak leaf cluster, Bronze Star with V, Meritorious Svc. medal with 2 oak leaf cllusters, Air medal with 3 oak leaf clusters. Fellow Am. Coll. Preventive Medicine, Am. Coll. Physician Execs.; mem. Aerospace Med. Assn., Ret. Officers Assn., Am. Pub. Health Assn., Assn. U.S. Army. Office: Pinellas County Health Dept 500 7th Ave S Saint Petersburg FL 33701

HEILMAN, JUNE E., general surgeon; b. Rapid City, S.D., Jan. 29, 1947; d. Henry C. and Edna L. (Baum) H. BA, U. S.D., 1969; MD, NYU, 1973. Diplomate Am. Bd. Surgery. Fellow in trauma U. Wash., Seattle, 1974-75, fellow in cardiothoracic surgery, 1979-80, resident in gen. surgery, 1975-80; intern in surgery Parkland Meml. Hosp., Dallas, 1973-74; attending surgeon Pocatello (Idaho) Regional Med. Ctr., 1980—. Fellow ACS, S.W. Surg. Congress. Office: 333 N 18th Ave Pocatello ID 83201

HEIM, KATHRYN MARIE, psychiatric nurse, author; b. Milw., Sept. 29, 1952; d. Lester Sheldon Wilcox and Laura Dora (Corpie) Wilcox Sears; m. Vincent Robert Gouthro, June 30, 1970 (div. 1976); 1 child, Robert Vincent; m. George John Heim, Sept. 17, 1977 (div. 1988). AS in Nursing, Milw. Area Tech. Coll., 1983; BS in Nursing, NYU, 1986; MS in Mgmt., Cardinal Stritch Coll., 1988; postgrad., Newport U., 1989—. Cert. psychiatric and mental health nurse, AMA. Staff geriatric nurse Clement Manor, Greenfield, Wis., 1983; nurse, health educator Milw. Boys Club, 1983-84; nurse mgr. Milw. County Mental Health Complex, Milw., 1984—, mem. gero-psychiat. inpatient adv. com., 1986-87; RN Psychiat. Acute Care Day Hosp., 1992—; mem. nursing rsch. com. Milwaukee County Mental Health Complex, 1986—; research on loneliness as it relates to mental health, 1989-92. Mem. wellness task force Milw. County Mental Health Complex, 1988-89, chairperson sensory deficit com. Geropsychiatry, 1989-90; active Boy Scouts Am., Milw., 1978-80. Mem. ANA (cert. gerontol. nurse), NAFE (network dir. Milw. chpt. 1982-92), Wis. Nurses Assn., NYU Alumni Assn., Cardinal Stritch Alumni Assn. (class rep. 1986-88), Milw. Area Tech. Coll. Alumni Assn. Home: 351 N 62d St Milwaukee WI 53213 Office: Milw County Mental Health 9455 W Watertown Plank Rd Milwaukee WI 53226-3559

HEIM, TONYA SUE, nurse, small business owner; b. Huntingburg, Ind., Nov. 9, 1948; d. Harold William and Marjorie Elouise (Buse) Rothert; m. James Frederick Heim, Sept. 6, 1969; children: Brian Christopher, Andrea Christine. Diploma, Deaconess Sch. Nursing, Evansville, Ind., 1969. RN, Ind.; cert. HIV/AIDS instr.; cert. in infection control. Oper. rm. staff nurse St. Joseph's Hosp., Huntingburg, 1969-71, emergency rm. staff nurse, 1969-71, staff nurse obstetrics dept., 1971-73, supr. obstetrics dept., 1973-85, dir. obstetrics oper. rm., 1985-88, dir. nursing, 1988-89, dir. obstetrics, oper. rm., infection control sterilizing, 1989-95, dir. surg. svcs., 1995—; owner, operator Holland (Ind.) Toning and Tanning Ctr., 1987—; co-owner Heim Hardware, 1989—. Instr., trainer ARC So. Ind., 1970-92; chmn. health profl. adv. com., mem. exec. com. So. Ind./Ill. chpt. March of Dimes, 1978-92; v.p., chmn. program com., bd. dirs. So. Hills Counseling Ctr., Jasper, Ind., 1988—; event coord. Hoosiers for Safety Belts, Dale, Ind., 1987; troop coleader Girl Scouts Am., Holland, 1986-88; active Southridge Band Boosters, Huntingburg, 1986-91; mem. AIDS coun. S.W. Dubois County Sch. Corp., 1988-94; mem. adv. coun. Prenatal Substance Use Prevention Program, 1989-93; mem. HIV prevention community planning com., Ind. State Dept. Health, 1994-95; chmn. schs. com., chmn. Midwest AIDS Tng. and Edn. Ctr. com., founding co-chmn. Dubois County AIDS Community Action Group, Huntingburg, 1991—; mem. S.W. Dubois County Sch. Bd., 1992—, pres., 1996; active March of Dimes, 1978-90; mem. legis. com. Ind. StateSch. Bd. Assn., 1996. Mem. ANA (bd. dirs.), NAACOG, Ind. Coun. Nurse Mgrs., Assn. for Practitioners in Infection Control (Amelia K. Sloan lectureship Ind. 1992), Assn. Oper. Rm. Nurses, Huntingburg C. of C., Beta Sigma Phi (v.p.). Republican. Lutheran. Home: PO Box 88 403 2nd Ave Holland IN 47541-9757 Office: St Josephs Hosp 1900 Medical Arts Dr Huntingburg IN 47542-9375

HEIM, WERNER G(EORGE), biology educator; b. Muhlheim Ruhr, Germany, Apr. 7, 1929; came to U.S., 1940, naturalized, 1946; s. Fred and Recha (Hirsch) H.; m. Julie I. Blumenthal, June 25, 1961; children: Susan L., David L.; m. Suzanne M. Levine, June 24, 1973; children: Elise B. Ginsburg, Lynn A. Ginsburg. BA in Zoology, UCLA, 1950, MA in Zoology, 1952, PhD in Zoology, 1954. Instr. Brown U., Providence, 1956-57; asst. prof. biology Wayne State U., Detroit, 1957-63, assoc. prof. biology, 1963-67, vice chmn. biology dept., 1961-62, planning coordinator biology bldg. program, 1964-67; mem. faculty Colo. Coll., Colorado Springs, 1967-94, prof. biology, 1967-91, prof. biology spl. sr. status, 1991-94, prof. emeritus, 1994—, chmn. biology dept., 1971-76, 87-90; vis. prof. biophysics and genetics dept. U. Colo. Sch. Medicine, 1978, 86; cons., geneticist divsn. genetic svcs. Children's Hosp., Denver, 1978—, Del., Republican State Conv., Denver, 1982, 84, 86, alt. 1990, 92, 96, USPHS-Nat. Cancer Inst. fellow, 1952-54; NIH grantee, 1958-67, NSF grantee, 1963-70, Am. Cancer Soc. grantee, 1963-65, Colo. Coll. grantee, 1979-83. Fellow AAAS; mem. Soc. Devel. Biology, Internat. Soc. Devel. Biologists, Colo.-Wyo. Acad. Sci. (v.p. 1968-69), Nat. Soc. Genetic Counselors (assoc. mem.), Am. Soc. Human Genetics, Sigma Xi. Contbr. book revs., sci. articles to profl. publs. Office: Colo Coll Dept Biology Colorado Springs CO 80903

HEIMAN, PETER LYND, psychiatrist; b. Iowa City, Nov. 23, 1942; s. Marcel and Silvia (Gabor) H.; m. Marsha Harriet Styler, Mar. 3, 1968; children: Mark Gregory, Erica Michelle. AB, Harvard Coll., 1964; MD, Albert Einstein Coll. Medicine, 1968. Diplomate Am. Bd. Psychiatry and Neurology. Intern Herrick Meml. Hosp., Berkeley, Calif., 1968-69; resident in psychiatry Montefiore Hosp., N.Y.C., 1969-72; staff psychiatrist USPHS, Lexington, Ky., 1972-74; ward supr. Cin. Gen. Hosp., Cin., 1974-78; attending psychiatrist Beth Israel Hosp., N.Y.C., 1979—, N. Cen. Bronx Hosp., N.Y.C., 1987-95; clin. asst. prof. psychiatry Mt. Sinai Sch. Medicine, N.Y.C., 1979-94, Albert Einstein Coll. Medicine, 1994—. Mem. Sine Nomine Singers, N.Y.C. Surgeon USPHS, 1972-74. Mem. Soc. Liaision Psychiatry (treas. 1982-85, pres.-elect 1985-86, pres. 1986-87). Office: 1148 Fifth Ave New York NY 10128-0807

HEIMBACH, DAVID M., surgeon; b. Doylestown, Pa., 1938. MD, Cornell U., 1964. Intern Parkland Meml. Hosp., Dallas, Tex., 1964-65; resident S.W. Hosp., Dallas, 1965-73, fellow, 1968-69; surgeon Harborview Med. Ctr., Seattle, 1975—; prof. surgery U. Wash., Seattle, 1975—. Fellow ACS; mem. Am. Surgeons Assn., Soc. Univ. Surgeons, SSAT. Office: Harborview Med Ctr Dept Surgery ZA 16 325 9th Ave Seattle WA 98104*

HEIMBOLD, CHARLES ANDREAS, JR., pharmaceutical company executive; b. Newark, May 27, 1933; s. Charles Andreas and Mary Joseph (Corrigan) H.; m. Monika Astrid Barkvall, Sept. 22, 1962; children: Joanna, Eric, Leif, Peter. B.A. cum Laude, Villanova U., 1954; LL.B. cum laude, U. Pa., 1960; LL.M., NYU, 1966; postgrad., Hague Acad. Internat. Law, 1959. Bar: N.Y. 1962. Assoc. Milbank, Tweed, Hadley & Mc Cloy, 1960-63; staff atty. Bristol-Myers Squibb Co., N.Y.C., 1963-70, dir. corp. devel., 1970-73, v.p. planning and devel., 1981-84, sr. planning and devel., 1981-84; pres., health care group, 1984-88, pres., health care group and sr. v.p. planning and devel., 1988-89, dir., 1989; exec. v.p. Bristol-Myers Squibb Co., N.Y.C., 1989-92, pres., 1992—, pres. and CEO, 1994—; chmn., pres., CEO, 1995—. Mem. bd. U. Pa.; bd. trustees Internat. House; bd. dirs. Phoenix House; chmn. bd. overseers U. Pa. Law Sch.; trustee Sarah Lawrence Coll. With USN, 1954-57. Mem. Assn. Bar of City of N.Y., Riverside Yacht Club, River Club. Home: Leeward Ln Riverside CT 06878-2409 Office: Bristol Myers Squibb Co 345 Park Ave New York NY 10154-0004

HEIMBURGER, ELIZABETH MORGAN, psychiatrist; b. Atlanta, Apr. 23, 1932; d. Henry Durand and Lillian Elizabeth (Palmour) Morgan; div.; children: Elizabeth Morgan Whitaker, Homer Aggie Whitaker III, Margaret Diane Heimburger, Richard Ames Heimburger Jr., Katherine Durand Heimburger. BS, Ga. State U., 1963; MD, Med. Coll. Ga., 1967. Diplomate Am. Bd. Psychiatry and Neurology. Intern in internal medicine Med. Coll. Ga., Augusta, 1967-68, resident in gen. psychiatry, 1968-70; fellow in child and adolescent psychiatry U. Tex., Galveston, 1970-72; asst. prof. dept. psychiatry U. Tex. Med. Br., Galveston, 1972-73, assoc. prof., dir. residency tng., 1980-87; asst. prof., assoc. prof., dir. psychosomatic svcs. U. Mo. Sch. Medicine, Columbia, 1973-80, clin. assoc. prof. dept. psychiatry, 1987—; pvt. practice specializing in adolescent psychiatry Columbia, 1987—; examiner Am. Bd. Psychiatry and Neurology, Chgo., 1977—; specialist, site visitor residency rev. Coun. Grad. Med. Edn., Washington, 1983—; exec. bd. Am. Assn. Dirs. Psychiat. Residency Tng., 1982-90; exec. coun. Tex. Psychiat. Soc., Austin, 1983-86; dir. confs., workshops on orgnl. and group dynamics. Editorial cons. bd. Am. Psychiat. Assn. Press., Inc., Washington,1 987-90; contbr. articles, scholarly papers to profl. publs. Bd. dirs. Mental Health Assn., Galveston, 1984-87, YMCA, Columbia, 1987-89. Grantee NIMH, 1978-80, 80-83. Fellow Am. Psychiat. Assn.; mem. Am. Soc. Adolescent Psychiatry, Am. Assn. Child and Adolescent Psychiatry (com.), A.K. Rice Inst. (bd. dirs. 1979-85, pres. Cen. States Ctr. 1979-88, bd. dirs. 1979-95), Am. Horticulture Soc. Episcopalian. Home and Office: 814 Hulen Dr Columbia MO 65203-1472

HEIN, DAVID WILLIAM, pharmacology and toxicology educator; b. Faith, S.D., Aug. 17, 1955; s. William K. and Ruth K. (Nordlie) H.; m. Karla J. Raab, Mar. 4, 1978; children: Joshua, Jacob, Isaiah. BS in Chemistry, U. Wis., Eau Claire, 1977; PhD in Pharmacology, U. Mich., 1982. Asst. prof. Morehouse Sch. of Medicine, Atlanta, 1982-85, assoc. prof., 1985-89, prof., 1989, acting chmn., 1983-85, chmn., 1985-89; Chester Fritz Disting. prof., chmn. U. N.D. Sch. of Medicine and Health Scis., Grand Forks, 1989—; mem. rsch. grant peer rev. com. Am. Heart Assn. of Ga., Augusta, 1986-89, spl. rev. com. Nat. Cancer Inst., Bethesda, Md., 1990-92, 95-96. Contbr. articles to Human Molecular Genetics, Toxicology and Applied Pharmacology, Carcinogenesis and other profl. jours. Pres. Sola Scriptura Luth. Ch., Decatur, Ga., 1986-88; sch. bd. mem. River Hgts. Luth. Ch., East Grand Forks, Minn., 1990-94, supt., 1991-95, head elder, 1995—. Recipient Thomas J. Clifford Faculty Achievement award U. N.D., 1992, Burlington No. Faculty Achievement award, 1994; named Chester Fritz Disting. prof. U. N.D., 1993. Mem. Am. Soc. for Pharmacology and Exptl. Therapeutics, Am. Assn. for Cancer Rsch., N.D. Acad. Sci., Grand Forks Master Chorale. Office: U North Dakota 501 N Columbia Rd Grand Forks ND 58202-9037

HEIN, H.A. TILLMANN, physician; b. Olsberg, Germany, Apr. 19, 1946; arrived in U.S., 1982; s. Hanns and Martha Charlotte (Schäfer) H.; m. Rebecca J. Bishop; children: Bettina M.C., H.K. Florian. MD, Freie Univ., Berlin, Germany, 1976, Dr. Med., 1979. Diplomate Am. Bd. Anesthesiology. Instr. Univ. Tex., Dallas, 1985, asst. prof., 1985; assoc. prof. Tex. A&M Univ., Temple, Tex., 1987; assoc. attending anesthesiology Baylor Univ. Medical Ctr., Dallas, 1988, attending anesthesiologist, 1994; clinical assoc. prof. Univ. Tex., Dallas, 1989, clin. prof., 1996—; sec. Met. Anesthesia Cons., Dallas, 1991—. Contbr. articles to profl. jours.; patentee in field. Sec. Dallas Goethe Ctr., 1994, v.p., 1995. Recipient Harriet Cunningham award Excellence, Tex. Medicine, 1986, Cert. Excellence award HESCA, 1993. Mem. Dallas County Anesthesiology Soc. (pres. 1991-92), Dallas County Medical Soc., Texas Soc. Anesthesiologists (chmn. com. econs. 1995—), Tex. Medical Assn., Am. Soc. Anesthesiologists, AMA, Internat. Anesthesia Rsch. Soc., Am. Soc. Regional Anesthesia, Soc. Cardiovascular Anesthesiologists, Deutsche Gesellschaft für Anästhesie und Intensivmedizin. Office: Met Anesthesia Cons 3535 Travis St Ste 210 Dallas TX 75204

HEIN, JOHN WILLIAM, dentist, educator; b. Chester, Mass., Sept. 29, 1920; s. Rudolf Jacob and Mercedes Viola H.; m. Jeannette Marie BeVier, Dec. 16, 1944. B.S., Am. Internat. Coll., 1941; D.M.D., Tufts U., 1944; Ph.D., U. Rochester, 1952; A.M. (hon.), Harvard, 1962; D.Sc. (hon.), Am. Internat. Coll., 1979, Tufts U., 1993. Student instr. oral pathology Tufts Coll. Dental Sch., 1943-44; head div. dental research U. Rochester, 1948-52, sr. fellow dental research, 1949-52, instr. pharmacology, 1951-53, asst. prof. dental research, 1952-55, asst. prof. pharmacology, 1954-55, chmn. dept. dentistry and dental research, 1952-55; instr. anatomy and physiology Eastman Sch. Dental Hygiene, 1950-55, lectr. dental research, 1953-55; research specialist Bur. Biol. Research, Rutgers U., 1955-59; dental dir. Colgate Palmolive Co., 1955-59; prof. preventive dentistry, dean Sch. Dental Medicine, Tufts U., 1959-62; dir. Forsyth Dental Center, 1962-91, sr. mem. staff emeritus, 1995—; prof. dentistry Harvard Dental Sch., 1962-67. Trustee Am. Internat. Coll., 1960-76. Served to capt. AUS, 1942-47. Fellow AAAS, Internat. Coll. Dentists (regent 1967-72, pres. U.S. 1975-76, internat. pres. 1983-84); mem. ADA, Mass. Dental Soc. (pres. 1964-65), Internat. Assn. Dental Research (treas. 1978-82), Am. Assn. Dental Research (treas. 1985-88), Am. Acad. Dental Sci., New Eng. Dental Soc. (hon. pres. 1978), Am. Soc. Dentistry for Children, Assn. Ind. Research Insts. (1st v.p. 1980, pres. 1981-83), Royal Soc. Medicine (hon.), Sigma Xi, Omicron Kappa Upsilon, Delta Sigma Delta. Club: Wellesley. Home: 3 Bridge St Medfield MA 02052-1503 Office: Forsyth Dental Ct 140 Fenway Boston MA 02115-3782

HEIN, KAREN KRAMER, pediatrician, epidemiologist; b. N.Y.C., Feb. 2, 1944; d. Irving W. and Ruth (Eisenberg) Kramer: m. Ralph Dell, Aug. 28, 1983; children: Ethan, Molly. BA, U. Wis., 1966; B of Med. Sci., Dartmouth Med. Sch., 1968; MD, Columbia U., 1970. Intern Bronx Mcpl. Hosp., Bronx (N.Y.) Mcpl. Hosp. Ctr., 1970; resident Bronx (N.Y.) Mcpl. Hosp. Ctr., Bronx, 1971-73; dir. adolescent AIDS program Montefiore Med. Ctr., N.Y.C., 1987-94; prof. pediatrics Albert Einstein Coll. Medicine, N.Y.C., 1991-94, prof. epidemiology and social medicine, 1993-94, clin. prof. pediatrics, epidemiology and social medicine, 1995—; exec. officer Inst. of Medicine, Nat. Acad. of Scis., Washington, 1995—; cons. N.Y.C. Dept. Health, 1980-85, N.Y.C. Bd. Edn., 1987-93; bd. dirs. Dartmouth Med. Sch., Hanover, N.Y. Author: AIDS: Trading Fears for Facts Consumer Reports Books, 1989; contbr. articles to profl. jours. Named Outstanding Physician, Dept. Health and Human Svcs., 1989, Adminstrs. Citation award, 1993. Fellow Am. Bd. Pediatrics; mem. Am. Pediatric Soc., Soc. for Pediatric Rsch., Am. Acad. Pediatrics, Soc. for Adolescent Medicine (pres. 1992-93). Office: Inst Medicine Nat Acad Sci 2101 Constitution Ave NW Washington DC 20418-0007

HEIN, LAVERN EDWARD, medical technologist; b. Crown Point, Ind., July 3, 1941; s. George John and Mathilda Ruth (Seberger) H.; m. Natalie Ruth McGuire, Sept. 5, 1965 (div. Nov. 1970); children: Michelle, Michael; m. Judith Kay Norman, Apr. 8, 1971; children: Kimberly, Kevin. MT and R.T., Am. Acad. of Med. Tech., 1966. Med. technologist Larabida Hosp., Chgo., 1966-68, Broadway Med. Lab., Gary, Ind., 1968-69; med. tech./x-ray tech., EMT U.S. Steel, Gary Works, Gary, 1969—. Contbr. articles to profl. jours. Attendee Lake Co. Planning Com., Crown Point, 1987—, Lake County Bd. of Zoning, 1987—; mem. Citizen Adv. Solid Waste Dist., 1995—; proctor Am. Med. Technologists, 1989—. With U.S. Army, 1962-64. Recipient Citation award Am. Registry Clin., 1972, Disting. Svc. award Radiography Tech., 1973, 74, Disting. Med. Achievement award, 1989. Mem. Am. Med. Technologists (bd. dirs. 1967—), Am. Soc. of Radiol. Tech., Wis. Soc. of Cardiopulmonary Tech., Cath. Order of Foresters. Home: 6060 E 141st Ave Crown Point IN 46307 Office: US Steel Gary Works 1 N Broadway MS 11-1 Gary IN 46402

HEINBERG, NANCY, social worker; b. Columbia, Mo., May 26, 1942; d. John Gilbert and Pauline (Dorsey) H. BA, U. Mo., 1964; MA, U. Wis., 1965, U. Mo., 1980; MSW, U. Md., Balt., 1989. Lic. cert. social worker-clin. Copy editor, reporter The Capital Times, Madison, Wis., 1966-72; copy editor The Washington Post, 1972-73, News-Jour. Papers, Wilmington, Del., 1980-84; social worker Springfield Hosp. Ctr., Sykesville, Md., 1989—; therapist Glass Mental Health Ctrs., Inc., Pikesville, Md., 1990. Mem. NASW, Acad. Cert. Social Workers, Phi Beta Kappa. Democrat. Episcopalian. Home: PO Box 132 Libertytown MD 21762-0132

HEINDEL, CLIFFORD CRAIG, neurosurgeon; b. Chattanooga, Feb. 15, 1939; s. Judson Clifford and Mary (Craig) H.; m. Marie B. Choiniere, July 17, 1981; children—Christian, Stephanie, Clifford, Heather, Justine. B.A., U. N.C., 1960, M.D., 1969; Dip. Edn., Makerere U., Kampala, Uganda, 1962. Diplomate Am. Bd. Neurol. Surgery. Intern N.C. Meml. Hosp., Chapel Hill, 1969-70, resident in neurosurgery, 1970-74, fellowship in neurosurgery, 1974-75; practice medicine specializing in neurosurgery, Kingsport, Tenn., 1975-81, Lewiston, Maine, 1981—; staff Portsmouth Hosp. 1981-94, staff Portsmouth Regional Hosp., N.H., 1994—, Wenthworth Dover Hosp, N.H., Exeter Hosp. Mary's Gen. Hosp., Lewiston. Fellow ACS; mem. Am. Assn. Neurol. Surgeons, Congress Neurosurgeons, Gordon S. Dugger Neurosurg. Soc., Nathan A. Womack Surg. Soc. Home: PO Box 273 New Castle NH 03854-0273 Office: Maine Neurosurg Assocs PO Box 273 New Castle NH 03854-0273

HEINE, JOHN PARKER, urologist, medical administrator; b. San Francisco, Sept. 18, 1944; s. Parker F. and Anne (Bruper) H.; m. Janet K. Nederhus, May 25, 1966; children: David J., Erika L. BS, Loyola U., 1966; MD, U. Calif., San Francisco, 1970. Diplomate Am. Bd. Urology. Intern San Francisco Gen. Hosp., 1971; resident in urology U. Calif. Med. Ctr., San Francisco, 1976; pvt. practice Fremont, Calif.; chief of staff Washington Hosp., Fremont, Calif., 1985; chmn. bd. Mullikin Med. Ptnrs., So. Aldoceda County, Calif., 1995-96; med. dir., 1994-96; pres. Found. Alameda Contra Costa County Med. Assn., 1995-96, pres., 1996—. Maj. USAF NG, 1970-78. Roman Catholic. Office: John P Heine MD 1999 Mowry Ave 2M Fremont CA 94538

HEINECKE, DEBORAH ANN, pediatrics nurse; b. Marcos, Tex., Sept. 8, 1954; d. Casimir J. and Mary L. (Trunk) Bosak; m. James A. Heinecke, June 19, 1976. Diploma, Mercy Hosp. Sch. of Nursing, Pitts., 1972-74; BSN, Duquesne U., 1986, MSN in Nursing Adminstrn., 1994; MS in Human Resource Mgmt., LaRoche Coll., 1994. RN, Pa.; cert. neonatal intensive care nurse. Staff nurse Mercy Hosp., Pitts., 1974-80, Magee Women's Hosp., Pitts., 1981-87; nurse coord. Pediatric Nursing Specialists, Pitts., 1988-89; staff nurse neo-natal ICU Magee-Women's Hosp., Pitts., 1989-91; case coord. ventilator assisted children/home program Children's Hosp. of Pitts., Pitts., 1991—. Mem. Nat. Assn. Neonatal Nurses, Three Rivers Assn. Neonatal Nurses (former sec.), Sigma Theta Tau (former chair mentoring Epsilon Phi chpt.). Home: 243 Meredith St Pittsburgh PA 15210-3946 Office: Children's Hosp of Pitts Pediatric Critical Care 5th Ave At Desoto St Pittsburgh PA 15213

HEINEMANN, STEPHEN F., molecular neurobiologist educator. BS, Calif. Inst. Tech., 1962; PhD, Harvard U., 1967; postgrad., MIT, Stanford U. Prof. molecular neurobiology lab. Salk Inst., dir. molecular neurobiology lab., 1989-95, chmn. of the faculty, 1992-93; adj. prof. U. Calif. Med. Sch., San Diego. Section editor: Jour. Neurosci. Molecular Neurosci.; mem. assoc. editl. bd. Current Opinion in Neurobiology, Proceedings of the Royal Soc. series B, Hippocampus, Cellular and Molecular Neurobiology, Receptors and Channels, Neuron, 1987-91, Jour. Neurosci., 1987-91. Recipient Disting. Achievement in Neurosci. Rsch. award Bristol-Myers Squibb, 1995; named Schmidt. Lectr. U. Pa., Feigen Lectr. Stanford U., Cooper Lectr., Flynn Lectr. Yale U. Mem. NAS (vice-chair com. IBRO), Max-Planck Inst. (external mem.), Soc. Neurosci. (councilor 1992, Grass lectr.). Office: The Salk Inst Molecular Neurobiology Lab 10010 N Torrey Pines Rd La Jolla CA 92037*

HEINER, DOUGLAS CRAGUN, pediatrician, educator; b. Salt Lake City, July 27, 1925; s. Spencer and Eva Lillian (Cragun) H.; m. Joy Luana Wiest, Jan. 8, 1946; children: Susan, Craig, Joseph, Marianne, James, David, Andrew, Carolee, Pauli. BS, Idaho State Coll., 1946; MD, U. Pa., 1950; PhD, McGill U., 1969. Intern Hosp. U. Pa., Phila., 1950-51; resident, fellow Children's Med. Ctr., Boston, 1953-56; asst. prof. pediatrics U. Ark. Med. Ctr., Little Rock, 1956-60; assoc. prof. pediatrics U. Utah Med. Ctr., Salt Lake City, 1960-66; fellow in immunology McGill U., Montreal, 1966-69; prof. of pediatrics Harbor-UCLA Med. Ctr., Torrance, 1969-94; prof. emeritus UCLA Sch. Medicine, 1994—. Author: Allergies to Milk, 1980; mem. editl. bd. Jour. Allergy and Clin. Immunology, 1975-79, Allergy, 1981-88, Jour. Clin. Immunology, 1981-87, Pediat. Asthma, Allergy and Immunology, 1986-94; contbr. over 150 original articles to profl. jours. and chpts. to books. Scoutmaster Boy Scouts Am., Salt Lake City, 1963; com. chmn. Rancho Palos Verdes, 1979-81; high coun. mem. Mormon Ch., Rancho Paos Verdes, 1983-86. 1st lt., MC, U.S. Army, 1952-53, Korea. Recipient Disting. Alumni award Idaho State U., 1987. Fellow Am. Pediatric Soc., Am. Acad. Allergy and Clin. Immunology (food allergy com. 1981—), Am. Coll. Allergy and Immunology; mem. Soc. for Pediatric Rsch., Western Soc. for Pediatric Soc. (Ross award 1961), Am. Assn. Immunologists, Clin. Immunology Soc., Am. Acad. Pediatrics. Republican. Office: Provo Allergy/Immunology Clinic 745 N 500 W Provo UT 84601

HEINICKE, RALPH MARTIN, biotechnology company executive; b. Hickory, N.C., Sept. 3, 1914; s. Martin John and Lydia Sophia (Kurth) H.; m. Sarah Anne Hall, July 31, 1944; 1 child, Mark. BS, Cornell U., 1936; PhD, U. Minn., St. Paul, 1950. Agr. chemist Shell Oil Co., N.Y.C., 1939-43; tech. advisor Jintan-Dolph, Osaka, Japan, 1962-86; assoc. faculty U. Hawaii, Honolulu, 1950-86; chemist Pineapple Rsch. Inst., Honolulu, 1950-55; dir. rsch. Dole Co., Honolulu, 1955-72; v.p. Biol. Control Systems, Honolulu, 1981-86; pres. Biotech. Resources Inc., Clarksville, Ind., 1990-94; cons. various drug cos., 1972—. Inventor, patentee on xeronine; inventor, patentee (pending) on cytoline. Master sgt. U.S. Army, 1942-45, CBI. Democrat. Home and Office: Biotechnology Resources Inc. 1124 Rostrevor Cir Louisville KY 40205-1742

HEINIG, ROBERT E., internist, endocrinologist, educator; b. Tucson, Aug. 22, 1942. BA, U. Ariz., 1964; MD, U. Oreg., 1969. Intern Strong Meml. Hosp., Rochester, N.Y., 1969-70, asst. resident, then assoc. resident in internal medicine, 1970-73, chief resident, 1973-74, instr., then sr. instr. medicine, 1974-77, asst. prof., 1977-82, clin. assoc. prof., 1982-83, clin. prof., 1993—; head endocrinology and metabolism unit Rochester Gen. Hosp., 1977—. Mem. med. bd. St. John's Home, Rochester, 1979-80. Fellow Am. Assn. Clin. Endocrinology; mem. Endocrine Soc., Am. Soc. Nephrology, Monroe County Med. Soc., Rochester Acad. Medicine. Office: Rochester Gen Hosp 1425 Portland Ave Rochester NY 14621

HEINKING, KURT PHILLIP, physician; b. Chgo., Mar. 10, 1965; s. Phillip Karl and Gail Louise (Berg) H.; m. Laura Neman. BS in Biology, No. Ill. U., 1987; DO, Chgo. Coll. Osteo. Medicine, 1994. Intern Chgo. Coll. Hosp. and Med. Ctr., 1994-95, resident, 1995—, instr., 1991—. Contbr. articles to profl. jours. Recipient A.S. McKenzie Rsch grant Ctr. for Osteo. Rsch. and Ednl. Devel., 1996. Mem. Am. Osteo. Assn., Am. Acad. Osteopathy, Ill. Assn. Osteo. Physicians and Surgeons, Am. Coll. Osteo. Family Physicians.

HEINLE, ROBERT ALAN, physician; b. Tarentum, Pa., Oct. 26, 1933; s. Edward William and Mary Alice (Purvis) H.; B.S., U. Pitts., 1955, M.D., 1959; m. Barbara Klimeck, Aug. 23, 1958; children—Richard, Jeffrey, Ronald, Robert, Thomas, Timothy. Intern, U. Pitts. Health Center, 1959-60, resident, 1962-65; research fellow in medicine Peter Bent Brigham Hosp., 1965-67; research asso. in medicine Harvard Med. Sch., 1967-68; asst. prof. medicine U. Rochester (N.Y.) Med. Sch., 1968-71, asso. prof., 1971-75, clin. asso. prof., 1975—; dir. cardiovascular lab. Genesee Hosp., Rochester, 1975—; sr. asso. physician Strong Meml. Hosp., Rochester, 1975—; cons. Am. Heart Jour., 1973—; NIH research fellow, 1965-68. Bd. dirs. Blue Cross in Rochester, Blue Shield in Rochester. Served with U.S. Army, 1960-62. Fellow ACP, Am. Coll. Cardiology; mem. Am. Heart Assn., AMA, Am. Fedn. Clin. Research, Rochester Individual Practice Assn. (dir.), Phi Beta Kappa, Omicron Delta Kappa, Alpha Omega Alpha. Republican. Roman Catholic. Home: 415 Warren Ave Rochester NY 14618-4319 Office: 224 Alexander St Rochester NY 14607-4002

HEINLEIN, WILLIAM EDWARD, psychologist, educator; b. Erie, Pa., Aug. 11, 1951; s. William Peter and Rita (Berchtold) H.; B.A., Gannon U., 1973; M.Ed., Edinboro State Coll., 1974, C.A.G.S., 1975; Ed.D., Va. Poly. U., 1987. Project dir. G.A. Barber Ctr., Erie, 1975-76; psychologist/med. coordinator Erie County Crippled Children's Soc. and Erie County Ctr. Learning Disabilities, Erie, 1977-81; psychologist Elyria Bd. Edn., Cleve., 1981-83; rsch. assoc. Va. Poly. Inst., 1983-85; pvt. practice psychology, Blacksburg, Va., 1985-87; mem. faculty Gannon U., Open U.; cons. S.W. Va. Schs., Blacksburg, 1984-86; sr. psychologist Woodrow Wilson Rehab. Hosp., Fisherville, Va., 1987—; adj. prof. James Madison U., Harrisonburg, Va., 1988-90, Va. Tech. U., Blacksburg, 1988-93; prof. Blue Ridge Community Coll., Weyers Cave, Va., 1988—. Recipient Public Service citation Nat. Easter Seal, 1978; Dept. Public Welfare grantee, 1979-80; Erie Community Found. grantee, 1978-79. Mem. AAAS, Am. Psychol. Assn., Nat. Acad. Neuropsychologists, Nat. Assn., Sch. Psychologists. Rsch. in learning disabilities, hyperactivity, biofeedback; contbr. photographs to various publs. Home: 449 Forest Springs Dr Stuarts Draft VA 24477-9627 Office: Woodrow Wilson Rehab Ctr Dept Psychology & Neurosci WWRC Box 367 Fishersville VA 22939

HEINZE, EVERETT GEORGE, JR., neurologist, educator; b. Mineola, N.Y., Sept. 6, 1937; s. Everett G. and May K. (Zimmer) H.; m. Sara Barthel, June 15, 1963 (div. May 1992); children: Kirsten, Scott, Kenton, Todd; m. Elaine Erwin, June 29, 1996. BA, Cornell U., 1959, MD, 1963. Diplomate Am. Bd. Internal Medicine, Am. Bd. Psychiatry and Neurology. Neurologist Austin (Tex.) Diagnostic Clinic, 1972—; co-med. dir. pain mgmt. program St. David's Hosp., Austin, 1985—, rehab. St. David's Rehab. Ctr., Austin; adj. prof. dept. speech comms., U. Tex., Austin, 1993—. Maj. U.S. Army, 1967-69. Recipient Bronze Star. Mem. AMA, Am. Acad. Neurology, Travis County Med. Soc., Internat. Assn. Study Pain, Am. Congress Rehab. Medicine. Office: Austin Diagnostic Clinic 12221 N Mopac Expy Austin TX 78758

HEINZERLING, THOMAS, pharmacist; b. Kassel, Germany, Feb. 19, 1963; s. Hermann and Johanna (Götte) H. Degree in pharmacy, U. Marburg, Germany, 1987; PhD, Phillips U., Marburg, 1991. Certified pharmacist in pharm. analytical sci., 1992. Rschr. U. Marburg, 1987-92; head labs. Eli Lilly Germany, Giessen, 1992-94, qualified person, 1994—, head packaging, 1994; head global packaging devel. and tech. Lilly Belgium, Mont-Saint-Guibert, 1995—; lectr. Ctr. Profl. Advancement, Amsterdam, The Netherlands, 1996—. Mem. Assn. Pharm. Tech., German Pharmacists Assn. Home: Berensheide 240, 1170 Brussels Belgium Office: Lilly Clin Ops, Rue Granbonpré 11, 1348 Mont-Saint-Guibert Belgium

HEINZMAN, PATRICIA ANN, nurse; b. Wurtzburg, Germany, Feb. 10, 1957; (parents U.S. citizens) d. Peter and Georgia Christina (Hoffman) H. BS in Nursing, U. No. Colo., 1979. Lic. facial specialist Icenhower U. Beauty Arts, Houston, 1982. Nurse The Meth. Hosp.-Tex. Med. Cen., Houston, 1978-83; clin. nurse mgr. Truman Med. Cen., Kansas City, Mo., 1983; orthopaedic nurse clinician & office mgr. Roger W. Hood, MD, Overland Park, Kans., 1983-95; worker's compensation case analyst Yellow Freight Sys., Overland Park, Kans., 1996—; lectr. The Back Cen. and Phys. Therapy Clinic, Overland Park, 1987; co-lectr. Humana Hosp. Overland Park, 1991. Co-author: (manuals) Total Hip Replacement, 1991, Total Knee Replacement, 1991, Humana Hospital Overland Park, 1991. Vol. Hist. Kansas City Found.; preview party chmn. Nat. Wildlife Art Show Ducks Unltd., Kansas City, 1989-92; mem., chmn., mdse. dir. Pomme de Terre chpt. Muskies Inc., Hermitage, Mo., 1989-91. Mem. Am. Acad. Orthopaedic Surgeons (planning com. 1984), Nat. Assn. Orthopaedic Nurses, Am. Assn. Oper. Room Nurses, Women's C. of C. (Am. Royal co-chmn.), Jr. League Kansas City (chmn. cookbook promotions com. 1993-94 cookbook com. stepup 1994-95, thrift shop processor com., 1995—), Zonta (bd. dirs. Kansas City 1986-88, fin. chmn. 1986-88, chmn. status of women com. 1989-91, 91-92), Amelia Earhart (chmn. 1992-96). Home: 12934 W 108th St Shawnee Mission KS 66210-1168 Office: Yellow Freight Sys 5200 W 110th St Overland Park KS 66210

HEISHMAN, STEPHEN JAY, psychology researcher and educator; b. Louisville, Apr. 22, 1953; s. J.W. and Ruth (Seewer) H.; m. Pamela D. Alexander, Oct. 24, 1987; children: Allison Brady, Alexander Tate, Nathaniel Jay. BA, Vanderbilt U., 1975; PhD, U. Louisville, 1985. Asst. prof. psychology St. Anselm Coll., Manchester, N.H., 1982-86; postdoctoral fellow dept. psychiatry sch. medicine Johns Hopkins U., Balt., 1986-88, instr. dept. psychiatry sch. medicine, 1988-94; asst. prof. Johns Hopkins U, Balt., 1994—; staff scientist Nat. Inst. on Drug Abuse Addiction Rsch. Ctr., Balt., 1988-91, rsch. psychologist, 1991—; cons. FAA, 1989—. Contbr. numerous articles to profl. jours. Mem. AAAS, Soc. for Rsch. on Nicotine and Tobacco, Am. Psychol. Assn., Behavioral Pharmacology Soc., Coll. of Problems of Drug Dependence. Democrat. Presbyterian. Office: NIDA Addiction Rsch Ctr PO Box 5180 Baltimore MD 21224-0180

HEISLER, NORMA BOODMAN, psychotherapist; b. N.Y.C., Nov. 11, 1933; d. David Louis and Belle (Hochstein) Boodman; cert. Pratt Inst., 1956; BA in Psychology, Bklyn. Coll., 1972; MSW, NYU, 1977; postgrad. N.Y. Sch. for Study of Psychoanalytic Psychotherapy, 1979-83, Karen Horney Inst. Study Psychoanalysis, 1984-86, postgrad. Erickson Inst., 1992-93, Nat. Inst. Expressive Therapy; m. Arthur Heisler, Aug. 9, 1952; children: Miriam, Daniel. Cert. clin. social worker, art therapist, hynotist/hypnotherapist. Personnel asst. R. H. Miller, N.Y.C., 1952-56; free lance comml. artist Wolf Studios and Lowenstein Studios, 1957-69; tchr. Yeshivab Ohel Moshe, N.Y.C., 1971-72; family counselor, art therapist Lillian Sklar Filler Day Care Ctr., N.Y.C., 1973-76; therapy intern L.I. Coll. Hosp., N.Y.C., 1976-77; tchr. adult edn. Kingsborough C.C., N.Y.C., 1978-79; psychotherapist N.Y. Psychotherapy and Counseling Ctr., 1978-89, also part-time pvt. practice, 1981—; field instr., supr. social work, C.I.H., 1989-92; full time pvt. practice, 1992—; one-woman shows of paintings include Jewish Community House, N.Y.C., 1960; 2-person show Ahda Artzt Gallery, 1969; group shows include Caravan Art Gallery, 1953, 54, 55, Bklyn. Mus. (award), 1956, 57, Duncan Gallery, 1958, Art U.S.A., 1958, Kottler Mus., 1958, Directions Gallery, 1959, Boston Art Festival, 1960, Pa. Acad. Fine Arts, Phila., 1961, St. Louis U., 1962, Ruth Sherman Gallery, 1965, N.Y. World's Fair, Ahda Artz Group, 1970, 71; represented in permanent collection Mapleton Park Hebrew Inst.; contbr. articles to jours. Recipient Latham award for brotherhood, 1954, 55, 56, 57, 59; Grumbacher award of merit, 1960; other art awards. Fellow Soc. Clin. Social Workers; mem. Nat. Assn. Social Workers (diplomate), Am. Assn. Artist Therapists, Nat. Expressive Therapy Assn., Soc. Advancement of Psychoanalytic Developmental Psychology, Am. Orthopsychiat. Assn. Jewish. Home: 2373 E 7th St Brooklyn NY 11223-5434

HEISTAD, DONALD DEAN, cardiologist; b. Chgo., Apr. 2, 1940; m. Sandra J.; children: Wendy, Dean. BS, U. Ill., 1959; MD, U. Chgo., 1963. Asst. prof. medicine U. Iowa Coll. Medicine, Iowa City, 1970-73, assoc. prof. medicine, 1973-76, prof. medicine, 1976—, prof. pharmacology, 1987—; dir. cardiovascular divsn. U. Iowa Coll. Medicine, 1995—; bd. dirs. Iowa Ctr. on Aging; chair Coun. on Circulation, Am. Heart Assn., 1996—. Editor: Cerebral Blood Flow: Effects of Nerves, 1982; assoc. editor: Hypertension, 1989-93, Circulation Rsch., 1980-85; contbr. 332 papers to profl. jours. and chpts to books. Pres. U. Iowa Faculty Senate, Iowa City, 1980-81; vice-chair coun. on circulation Am. Heart Assn., 1994-96. Capt. U.S. Army, 1967-70. Recipient Irving S. Wright award Stroke Coun., 1976, Harry Goldblatt award Coun. for High Blood Pressure Rsch., 1980, Merit award 1987, Disting. Lecture award Coun. on Thrombosis, Disting. Alumni award U. Chgo., 1991. Fellow Coun. for High Blood Pressure Rsch., Am. Soc. for Clin. Investigation, Assn. Am. Physicians, Coun. for Geriatric Cardiology, Assn. Univ. Cardiologist, Am. Physiol. Soc. (chair cardiovascular sect. 1995-96). Democrat. Office: U Iowa Coll Medicine Dept Medicine Iowa City IA 52242

HEISTEIN, ROBERT KENNETH, obstetrician and gynecologist; b. Newark, Oct. 14, 1940; s. Samuel M. and Elizabeth M. (Jellinek) H.; B.A., U. Vt., 1962, M.D., 1966; m. Vallery Gubner, Aug. 26, 1967; children—Jonathan, Erica, Michael. Intern, Newark Beth Israel Med. Center, 1966-67, resident in ob-gyn 1967-70, attending staff, 1972—; asst. chief, dept. ob-gyn Patuxent River Naval Hosp., Md., 1970-72; pvt. practice medicine, specializing in ob-gyn Millburn, N.J., 1972—; mem. staffs St. Barnabas Med. Ctr., Livingston, N.J., Newark Beth Israel Med. Center, Overlook Hosp., Summit, N.J. Served with USNR, 1970-72. Diplomate Am. Bd. Ob-Gyn. Fellow Am. Coll. Obstetricians and Gynecologists, ACS, Internat. Coll. Surgeons, Am. Fertility Soc., N.J. Acad. Medicine, Am. Soc. Abdominal Surgeons; mem. AMA, Pan Am. Med. Assn., N.J. Med. Soc., Essex County Med. Soc., Am. Assn. Gynecol. Laparoscopists, Royal Soc. Medicine. Office: 68 Essex St Millburn NJ 07041-1611 also: 23 Green Village Rd Madison NJ 07940-2540

HEIZER, DAVID EUGENE, health information management educator; b. Sidney, Nebr., Aug. 24, 1946; s. Clifton Edwin and Verna Rose (Davison) H.; m. Bonnie Elizabeth Alsbury, Feb. 14, 1986 (div. Feb. 1996); children: Bradley John, Kurt Clifton. BS, Coll. St. Mary, 1974; MPA, U. Mo., 1989. Supr. Archbishop Bergen Mercy Hosp., Omaha, 1974-75; cons. pvt. practice, Omaha, 1975-77; rsch. asst. Health Info. Tech. Svcs., Omaha, 1977-79; coord. med. audit St. Joseph Hosp., Omaha, 1979-83; dir. St. Joseph (Mo.) State Hosp., 1984-93, St. Francis Hosp., Maryville, Mo., 1993-95; asst. prof. Mo. Western State Coll., 1995—. Donor Dream Factory, 1994, 95, 96. Mem. Am. Health Info. Mgmt. Assn., Mc. Health Info. Mgmt. Assn., Masons, U. Mo. Kansas City Alumni Assn. Republican. Office: Mo. Western State Coll 4525 Downs Dr Saint Joseph MO 64507-2246

HEJNA, WILLIAM FRANK, orthopedic surgeon, company executive; b. Chgo., May 13, 1932; s. William H.; m. Eva Lee Goodale, June 11, 1955; children: William, David, Michael, Susan. B.A., Grinnell Coll., 1954, D.Sc., 1974; M.D., Washington U., St. Louis, 1958. Diplomate: Am. Bd. Orthopedic Surgery (examiner 1969-74). Intern Presbyn.-St. Luke's Hosp., Chgo., 1958-59; coordinator orthopedic clinics and med. sch. tng. Presbyn.-St. Luke's Hosp., 1963-70, dir. electromyography lab., 1963-70, asst. chmn. dept. orthopedic surgery, 1965-70, assoc. attending surgeon, 1967-70, sr. attending surgeon, 1971—; resident in orthopedic surgery U. Ill. Research and Ednl. Hosps., Chgo., 1959-63; assoc. dean Office Surg. Scis. and Services, Rush-Presbyn.-St. Luke's Med. Center, 1970-73; v.p. med. affairs, dean Rush Med. Coll., 1973-76; sr. v.p. Rush U., 1976-84, also prof. orthopedic surgery; pres. BioService Corp., 1977-80, Bus. Cons., Inc., 1970-89, Biotech. Maintenance and Repair Corp., 1978-82, Affiliated Med. Arts, Inc., 1984-90, Met. Orthopedic Surgeons, 1985-90, Combined Orthopedic Resources, Inc., 1984-89; mng. ptnr. Orthopaeic Assocs., 1983-86, U. Orthopaedics, 1986-92; chmn. bd. trustees Anchor HMO, 1980-85; mng. ptnr. PRCC, 1993—; cons. Whittaker Corp., 1978-84; chmn. physician adv. bd. Smith Labs., 1980-83; pres. Coun. Med. Deans, Ill., 1974-76; chmn. Rush Faculty Coun., 1973-76; trustee, chmn., asst. sec.-treas., mem. exec. com. Orthopaedic Rsch. and Edn. Found., Park Ridge; chmn. bd. dirs. Valley Bank Svcs. Corp., St. Charles, Ill., 1992—; pres. Univ. Practice Mgmt., 1988-92. Contbr. articles to profl. jours.; editorial bd. Health Care Mgmt. Rev., 1982—. Bd. dirs. MacNeal Meml. Hosp., 1982—; trustee Ripon Coll., 1982-89, mem. exec. com., 1985—. Fellow ACS, Am. Acad. Orthopedic Surgeons; mem. AMA, Ill. Med. Soc., Chgo. Med. Soc., Chgo. Surg. Soc., Inst. Medicine, Orthopedic Research Soc., Clin. Orthopedic Soc. Club: Econs. (Chgo.). Home: 321 N Delaplaine Rd Riverside IL 60546-1853 Office: 1725 W Harrison St Chicago IL 60612-3828

HEJTMANCIK, MILTON RUDOLPH, medical educator; b. Caldwell, Tex., Sept. 27, 1919; s. Rudolph Joseph and Millie (Jurcak) H.; B.A., U. Tex., 1939, M.D., 1943; m. Myrtle Lou Erwin, Aug. 21, 1943; children: Kelly Erwin, Milton Rudolph, Peggy Lou; m. 2d, Myrtle M. McCormick, Nov. 27, 1976. Resident in internal medicine U. Tex., 1946-49, instr. internal medicine, 1949-51, asst. prof., 1951-54, assoc. prof., 1954-65, prof. internal medicine, 1965-80, dir. heart clinic, 1949-80, dir. heart sta., 1965-80; chief of staff John Sealy Hosp., 1957-58; chief staff U. Tex. Hosps., 1977-79; prof. medicine Tex. A&M Coll. Medicine, 1981-82; cardiologist Olin E. Teague VA Hosp., Temple, Tex., 1981-82, VA Clinic, Beaumont, Tex., 1982-86. Served from 1st lt. to capt., M.C., AUS, 1944-46; ETO. Recipient Ashbel Smith Outstanding Alumnus award U.Tex. Med.Br., 1991, Titus Harris Disting. Svc award, 1992. Diplomate in cardiovascular diseases Am. Bd. Internal Medicine. Fellow ACP, Am. Coll. Chest Physicians, Am. Coll. Cardiology; mem. Am. (fellow council clin. cardiology), Tex. (pres. 1979-80), Galveston Dist. (pres. 1956) heart assns., AMA (Billing's Gold medal 1973), Am. Fedn. Clin. Research, AAAS, Tex. Acad. Internal Medicine (gov. 1971-73, v.p. 1973-74, pres. 1976-77), N.Y. Acad. Scis., Tex. Club Cardiology (pres. 1972), Galveston County (pres. 1971), Tex. (del. 1972-80) med. assns., Am. Heart Assn. (pres. Tex. affiliate 1979-80), Phi Beta Kappa, Sigma Xi, Alpha Omega Alpha, Phi Eta Sigma, Mu Delta, Phi Rho Sigma. Contbr. articles to profl. jours. Home: 500 N Spruce St Hammond LA 70401-2549

HELD, NANCY B., perinatal nurse, lactation consultant; b. Winchester, Mass., Sept. 4, 1957; d. Ann and Laurence Babine; m. Lew Held, May 22, 1976; children: David, Jessica. BSN, NYU, 1979; MS, U. Calif., San Francisco, 1992. Cert. lactation and childbirth educator, Am. Soc. Psychoprophylaxis Obstetrics. Labor/delivery nurse Pascack Valley Hosp., Westwood, N.J., 1979-83; obstetrics educator Drs. Pinski, Wiener & Grasso, Westwood, N.J., 1982-85; ob/gyn office nurse Drs. Power Hagbom Holter & Clark, San Francisco, 1986-87; asst. to dir. maternity svcs. Women's Health Assn., Greenbrae, Calif., 1987-89; perinatal edn. and lactation ctr. clin. coord. Calif. Pacific Med. Ctr., San Francisco, 1989—; owner North Bay Lamaze, 1988—; speaker and cons. in field. Recipient Founders Day award, NYU. Fellow Am. Coll. Childbirth Educators; mem. Assn. Women's Health Obstetric and Neonatal Nursing (spkr. nat. con. 1993, nat. rsch. utilization team 1993), Am. Soc. Psychoprophylaxis (chpt. co-pres.), Nurses Assn. of Am. Coll. Ob/Gyn, Internat. Childbirth Educators Assn., Internat. Lactation Cons. Assn., Sigma Theta Tau.

HELFAND, ARTHUR E., podiatrist; b. Phila., Jan. 12, 1935; s. Nathan H. and Esther (Farbman) H.; m. Myra Werner, May 23, 1976; children—Jennifer Bess, Lewis Aaron. D.Podiatric Medicine, Temple U., 1957. Diplomate Am. Bd. Podiatric Orthopedics, Am. Bd. Podiatric Pub. Health, Am. Bd.Podiatrics and Primary Podiatric Medicine (bd. dirs. 1992-95). Pvt. practice Phila., 1957—; active staff James B. Giuffre Med. Ctr., Phila., 1958-89, coord. dept. podiatry, 1959-68, co-chief, 1968-78, chief, 1978-89, dir. podiatric edn., 1968-89; dir. clin. rsch. Pa. Coll. Podiatric Medicine, Phila., 1963-64, prof. podiatry, coord. clinics, 1964-70, prof. podiatry, chmn. dept. community health and aging, 1970—, prof. podiatric medicine, podiatric orthopedics; mem. staff Thomas Jefferson U. Hosp., Phila., 1973—; cons. podiatry dept. surgery Phila. VA Hosp., 1973-82, 89-93; adj. prof. medicine Jefferson Med. Coll., Phila., 1976—, adj. prof. orthopedic surgery, podiatry, vis. assoc. prof. cmty. health and preventive medicine, 1977-79; cons. staff Wills Eye Hosp., 1980—; affiliate staff Joslin Ctr. for Diabetes, Boston, 1993—, Joslin Ctr. for Diabetes at Wills and Jefferson, 1993—; cons. Dept. Vets. Affairs, Podiatric Svc., Washington; cons. in field. Mem. editl bd. Rehab. Today, 1990-93; contbr. over 275 articles to profl. jours.; editor five textbooks. Bd. dirs. Pa. Diabetes Acad., 1988—, treas., 1991-93, 95—, chmn. 1993-95. Recipient Lifetime Achievement award Podiatry Mgmt., 1991. Fellow ACP, Am. Pub. Health Assn., Pa. Pub. Health Assn., Royal Soc. Health; mem. AMA, AAUP, Am. Geriatrics Soc., Am. Coll. Foot Orthopedists, Am. Soc. Podiatric Medicine (pres. 1994-95), Am. Podiatry Assn. (pres. 1982-83), Pa. Podiatry Assn., Phila. County Podiatry Soc., Am. Soc. Podiatric Dermatology, Am. Assn. Hosp. Podiatrists, Del. Valley Geriatrics Soc. (bd. dirs. 1989—), Gerontol. Soc., Temple U. Alumni Assn., Internat. Acad. Preventive Medicine, Am. Assn. Diabetes Educators, Am. Assn. Colls. Podiatric Medicine. Office: Pa Coll Podiatric Medicine Race at 8th St Philadelphia PA 19107

HELFAT, LUCILE, social services professional; b. N.Y.C., Apr. 6, 1919; d. Morris and Anna (Katz) Podell; m. Bernard Helfat, June 27, 1943; children: Jonathan, Mark. BS, U. Mich., 1942; MS, Columbia U., 1944. Cert. social worker, psychiatric social worker. Mem. faculty Queens Coll. CUNY, N.Y.C., 1966-76; supr. social work L.I. Jewish Hosp., N.Y.C. Co-author: Child Psychology, 1981; contbr. articles to profl. jours. Chmn. State of N.Y. Northeastern Queens Nature and Hist. Preserve Commn.; mem. Ft. Tolten Redevel. Authority, 1996—. Home: 26-18 West Dr Douglaston NY 11363-1049

HELFENSTEIN, JEFFREY S., physician, medical educator; b. N.Y.C., Nov. 12, 1947; s. Bernard and Edith (Spellman) H.; m. Joan Leslee Rothstein, June 19, 1969; children: Samantha, Margot. BA, Syracuse U.; MD, Med. Coll. Va. Diplomate Am. Bd. Internal Medicine, Am. Bd. Cardiovascular Diseases. Pvt. practice physician Beverly Hills, Calif., 1978—; clin. prof. medicine UCLA, 1981—. Fellow Am. Coll. Cardiology. Office: 436 N Roxbury Dr #222 Beverly Hills CA 90210

HELGEMOE, JANET MARILYN, dietitian; b. Lawrence, Mass., Dec. 25, 1931; d. Wallace Leslie and Emily Meta (Dierig) Galeucia; B.S., U. N.H., 1953; M.Ed., U. N.H., 1982; m. Raymond Albin Helgemoe, May 15, 1955; children—Scott Albin, Eric Wallace, Greg Peter. Adminstrv. dietitian, Scripps Metabolic Clinic, LaJolla, Calif., 1954-55; clin. dietitian Lawrence (Mass.) Gen. Hosp., 1955-56; faculty adult edn. Tacoma Wash., 1969-71, Portsmouth, N.H., 1972-73, Durham, N.H., 1973-74, Concord, N.H., 1975—; dir. consumer info. N.E. Mktg. Assn., 1974-75; columnist Portsmouth (N.H.) Herald, 1972-73; cons. dietitian to long term care facilities, 1976—; pvt. practice Counseling Dietitian Assos., Bow, N.H., 1976-87; instr. Merrimack Valley Coll., 1981-82; adj. prof. U. Sys. N.H. Coll., 1981—; applied nutrition lectr. New Eng. Gerontol. Assn., 1981—. Area 7 coordinator Cons. Dietitians in Health Care Facilities, 1980-82. Named Portsmouth Navy Wife of the Yr., 1971. Mem. N.H. Dietetic Assn. (bull. editor 1974-76, pres. 1976), N.H. Cons. Dietitians Assn. (founder 1978), Am. Dietetic Assn., Am. Assn. Family and Consumer Scis., Am. Personnel and Guidance Assn., New Eng. Hist. Genealogical Soc., N.H. Hist. Soc., Vt. Hist. Soc., Kappa Delta. Address: 3 Woodland Cir Bow NH 03304-3727

HELL, KOURAD THEOPHIL, surgeon, educator; b. St. Gallen, Switzerland, Mar. 26, 1938; s. Konrad and Anny (Meyer) H.; m. Annick Türler; children: Sandra, Viviane, Marc. Physician, Med. Sch. U. Basel, Switzerland, 1963; MD, U. Basel, 1963; cert., Ednl. Coun. for Fgn. Med. Grads., 1963; cert. prof. surgery, U. Basel, 1986. Bd. cert. surgeon FMH. Intern Stamford, Conn., 1964; resident in surgery U. Basel, 1965-75; dep. chief physician Surg. Clinic, Liestal, Switzerland, 1975-85; head of med. info. Roche Basel, 1986-91; instrnl. cons., rschr., 1992—; tchr. medicine and surgery U. Basel, 1967—; v.p. med. commn. Swiss Red Cross, 1980-85. Author: Colon Resection, 1976, Antibiotic Prophylaxis in Surgery, 1989, Surgical Infections, 1991, Risk Factors in Surgery, 1994; editor-in-chief: Swiss Jour. Mil. Medicine, 1980-85; mem. editl. bd. Jour. Coloproctology, 1985-96. Oberstleutnant Swiss Army, 1965-95. Mem. Swiss Soc. Surgeons, JSS/SIC. Home: Dammerkirchstrasse 32, CH-4056 Basel Switzerland

HELLBERG, DAN GUNNAR, obstetrican, gynecologist; b. Uppsala, Sweden, Oct. 11, 1953; s. Gunnar Birger and Kerstin Mariana (Persson) H.; m. Ulla Elisabet Sultan, May 16, 1980 (div. June 1991); children: Marten, Maja. MD, Uppsala U., 1978, PhD, 1987. Jr. physician Falun (Sweden) Hosp., 1978-80, staff physician, 1980-82, ob/gyn. trainee, 1982-87, cons. dept. ob/gyn., 1987-92, scientist, 1992—; cons. Los Alamos (N.Mex.) Nat. Lab./NIH, 1993—, WHO Collaborating Ctr. for STDs and Their Complications, Uppsala, 1993—; collaborator Am. Health Found., N.Y.C., 1984—. Co-author: Genital Papillomavirus Infections and their Sequelae, 1987, Bacterial Vaginosis, 1994; author: On Some Possible Etiological Factors of Cervix and Penis Cancer, 1987; co-author, editl. com.: Sexually Transmitted Diseases, 1994. Uppsala Ctr. for STD Rsch. fellow, 1993—. Fellow Scandinavian Soc. for Travel Medicine, Swedish Soc. Medicine, Internat. Fedn. Obstetricians and Gynecologists; mem. Internat. Fedn. of Cervical Pathology, N.Y. Acad. Sci. Office: Falun Hosp, Dept Obstetrics/ Gynecology, S-791 82 Falun Sweden

HELLER, ABRAHAM, psychiatrist, educator; b. Claremont, N.H., Mar. 17, 1917; s. David and Rose Heller; m. Lora S. Levy, June 16, 1957; 1 child, Judith Rose. BA, Brandeis U., 1953; MD, Boston U., 1957. Diplomate Am. Bd. Med. Examiners, Am. Bd. Psychiatry and Neurology. Resident in psychiatry U. Colo., Denver, 1958-61; chief in-patient psychiatry Denver Gen. Hosp., 1961-65, asst. dir. psychiat. services, 1965-70, assoc. dir. psychiat. services, 1970-73, dir., community mental health services, 1970-72; chief psychiatry, dir. community mental health ctr. Newport (R.I.) Hosp., 1973-77; clin. assoc. prof. psychiatry Brown U., Providence, 1973-77; prof. psychiatry, community medicine Wright State U., Dayton, Ohio, 1977-91, vice chmn. dept., 1980-91, prof. emeritus, 1991—. Fellow Am. Psychiat. Assn., Am. Orthopsychiat. Assn., Am. Assn. for Social Psychiatry. Jewish. Home: 1400 Runnymede Rd Dayton OH 45419-2924 Office: Wright State U Sch Medicine Dept Psychiatry PO Box 927 Dayton OH 45401-0927

HELLER, ARTHUR PAUL, orthopaedic surgeon; b. Bklyn., Feb. 28, 1941; s. Samuel and Sylvia (Curland) H.; m. M. Terry Sovel, June 11, 1969; childrenn: Stephanie E., Michael A. AB, Amherst Coll., 1962; MD, SUNY, Bklyn., 1966. Diplomate Am. Bd. Orthopaedic Sugery. Intern U. Colo. Med. Ctr., Denver, 1966-67, resident in orthopaedic surgery, 1967-71; pvt. practice, Englewood, Colo., 1973—; pres. Arapahoe Med. Found., Englewood, 1986—. Lt. comdr. M.C., USN, 1971-73. Fellow Am. Acad. Orthopaedic Surgeons, Am. Occupl. Med. Soc., Western Orthopaedic Assn.; mem. Colo. Med. Soc., Arapahoe Med. Soc. (treas. 1986—). Office: Orthopaedic Physicians Colo 799 E Hampden Ave Ste 400 Englewood CO 80110

HELLER, BARBARA R., dean, nursing educator. BS, Boston U., 1962; MS, Adelphi U., 1966; EdM, Columbia U., 1971, EdD, 1973; postgrad., U. Md., 1986-90. RN Md., Mass., N.Y., Pa., Va. Chmn. dept. nursing SUNY, Farmingdale; asst. dean acad. programs, Coll. Nursing Villanova U.; prof. and chair dept. edn., adminstrn. and health policy, Sch. Nursing U. Md., Balt., dean Sch. Nursing, 1990—; dir. rsch. and edn. nursing dept., Clin. Ctr., NIH, 1983-84; congl. fellow in health policy and edn. Hon. Constance A. Morella, U.S. House of Reps., 1989-90; vice chair, mem. bd. dirs. Computer Based Patient Record Inst., 1992-94, So. Coun. on Collegiate Edn. for Nurses, So. Regional Edn. Bd., chmn. task force on telecomms., numerous others; cons. in field. Co-editor: (book) Information Management in Nursing and Health Care, 1995; contbr. chpts. to books, articles to profl. jours. Mem. bd. dirs. Paul's Place, Open Gates; chair adv. bd. Gov's. Wellmobile. Recipient Innovative Health Program award Md. Found. for Nursing, 1995, Outstanding Educator of Am. award, Alumni award for Nursing Excellence Boston U., Alumni award for Nursing Practice Tchr's. Coll. Columbia U.; numerous grants. Fellow Am. Acad. Nursing; mem. ANA, Am. Assn. Colls. Nursing, Am. Soc. Med. Informatics Assn., Am. Assn. Higher Edn., Nat. League Nursing, Md. Nurses Assn., Md. Assn. Higher Edn., Gerontological Soc., Nurses in Washington Roundtable, Women's Pol. Caucus Md., Exec. Women's Network Balt., Sigma Theta Tau, Phi Kappa Phi. Home: 22 Bellchase Ct Baltimore MD 21208 Office: Univ of MD Sch Nursing 655 W Lombard St Baltimore MD 21201-1627*

HELLER, DAVID R., osteopath; b. Feb. 7, 1953; s. Samuel E. and Beatrice (Bucks) H.; m. Colleen Ford, Apr. 8, 1989; children: Benjamin, Rachel. BA, U. N.H., 1975; BS, Rutgers U., 1979; DO, Southeastern Coll. Osteo., 1985. Intern Humana Hosp. Palm Beaches, West Palm Beach, Fla., 1985-86; resident La. State U. Med. Ctr.-Charity Hosp., New Orleans, 1986-88; emergency physician, med. dir. Emergency Med. Svc. Exeter (N.H.) Hosp., 1988-95, emergency physician, 1995—. Author emergency med. paper. Recipient Upjohn Achievement award Upjohn Co., 1985. Fellow Am. Osteo. Assn., Am. Coll. Emergency Physicians (v.p. N.H. chpt. 1989-91); mem. N.H. E-911 Task Force (chmn. 1991-92), Sigma Sigma Phi. Office: Exeter Hosp 10 Buzell Ave Exeter NH 03833-2515

HELLER, PEGGY OSNA, poetry therapist, psychotherapist; b. Bklyn., Nov. 21, 1936; d. Charles S. and Miriam (Mendelson) Freundlich; m. Eugene Paul Heller, Aug. 3, 1957 (div. 1986); children: Elise Karen, Meredith Leslie. BA, Bklyn. Coll., 1958; MSW, Cath. U. Am., 1983; PhD, Pacific Western U., 1995. Diplomate Acad. Cert. Social Workers (lic. clin. social worker); registered clin. poetry therapist. Speech correction tchr. N.Y.C. Bd. Edn., 1958-60; program dir., instr., writer test courses Stanley H. Kaplan Ednl. Ctrs., N.Y.C., Washington, 1959-81; clin. social worker D.C. Therapy Group, Washington, 1983-85; bibliotherapist Psychiat. Inst. Washington, 1985-87; pvt. practice Potomac, Md., 1985—; lectr. Create Ctr. for Therapy, Growth and Tng., Bethesda, Md., 1984-92, Cath. U. Am., Washington, 1984-89, Lesley Coll., Cambridge, Mass., 1992, Fla. Internat. U., Miami, 1992; poetry therapy cons. Mt. Vernon Hosp., Alexandria, Va., 1987-90, Dominion Hosp., Falls Church, Va., 1990-92, Psychiat. Inst., Washington, 1992-95; dir. Nat. Ctr. Poetry Therapy Edn., 1993—, Poetry Therapy Tng. Inst., 1995. Mem. editl. staff Jour. Poetry Therapy, 1986—, Jour. Arts in Psychotherapy, 1988—; contbr. articles to profl. jours. Former program dir. Beverly Farms PTA, Potomac, Md., Hoover Cmty. Sch., Potomac; founder Last Friday Playreading Club, Potomac, 1983—. Mem. NASW, Am. Group Psychotherapy Assn., Nat. Assn. Poetry Therapy (pres. 1991-93, Disting. Svc. award 1993), Nat. Assn. Poetry Therapy Found. (v.p. 1993-96, pres. 1996—), Nat. Fedn. Biblio/Poetry Therapy (treas. 1987—), Bibliotherapy Round Table (treas. 1984—), Greater Washington Soc. Clin. Social Work, Mensa. Home and Office: 7715 Whiterim Ter Potomac MD 20854-1775

HELLERSTEIN, DAVID JOEL, psychiatrist, writer; b. Cleve., Dec. 30, 1953; s. Herman Kopel and Mary Leah (Feil) H.; m. Lisa Perry, Oct. 16, 1983; children: Sarah Nicole, Benjamin, Jason Samuel. AB, Harvard U., 1976; MD, Stanford U., 1980. Intern, then resident psychiatry N.Y. Hosp. Cornell Med. Ctr., 1980-84; fellow pub. psychiatry Columbia Presbyn. Med. Ctr.-N.Y. State Psychiat. Inst., N.Y.C., 1984-85; attending psychiatrist Beth Israel Med. Ctr., N.Y.C., 1985—; instr. psychiatry Mt. Sinai Med. Ctr., N.Y.C., 1985-88, asst. prof. psychiatry, 1988-93; physician in charge psychiat. outpatient svcs. Beth Israel Med. Ctr., N.Y.C., 1989—; asst. prof. psychiatry Albert Einstein Coll. Medicine, N.Y.C., 1993—. Author: (novel) Loving Touches, 1987, (essay collection) Battles of Life and Death, 1986, (non-fiction) A Family of Doctors, 1994; contbr. articles to profl. jours.; contbg. editor N.Am. Rev., 1981—, Sci. Digest, 1986-87, 7 Days mag., 1988-90, M.D. Mag., 1990—. MacDowell Colony fellow, 1984, 86, 88. Fellow APA; mem. Am. Psychiat. Assn. (editor N.Y. County Dist. newsletter, 1989—; chmn. publs. com. N.Y. County chpt. 1989—), Author's Guild. Democrat. Jewish.

HELLIGE, JOSEPH BERNARD, psychology educator; b. Ft. Madison, Iowa, Sept. 3, 1948; s. Bernard F. and Mary M. (Moffitt) H.; m. Colleen Staudt, Dec. 18, 1971; children: Erin, Katherine, Bridget. BA, St. Mary's Coll., Minn., 1970; MA, U. Wis., 1972, PhD, 1974. Asst. prof. U. So. Calif., Los Angeles, 1974-80, assoc. prof. psychology, 1980-84, prof. 1984—, assoc. chair dept. psychology, 1984-90, chair dept. psychology, 1992—. Editor/ author: Cerebral Hemisphere Asymmetry, 1983, Hemispheric Asymmetry, 1993. Contbr. articles to profl. jours. Grantee NIMH 1975-76, NSF, 1976—. Mem. Am. Psychol. Assn., Am. Psychol. Soc., Psychonomic Soc., Internat. Neuropsychol. Soc., Sigma Xi. Democrat. Home: 1612 S Crest Dr Los Angeles CA 90035-3316 Office: U So Calif SGM 704 University Park Los Angeles CA 90089

HELLINGER, MICHAEL DAVID, colon and rectal surgeon; b. Boston, Dec. 9, 1962; s. Melvin Jay and Sheila Elaine (Goodman) H. BS, Tufts U., 1983; MD, U. Miami, 1988. Diplomate Am. Bd. Surgery; diplomate Am. Bd. Colon and Rectal Surgery. Resident in gen. surgery Jackson Meml. Hosp., Miami, 1988-93; fellow in colon and rectal surgery Orlando (Fla.) Regional Med. Ctr., 1993-94; asst. prof. clin. surgery U. Miami Sch. Medicine, 1994—. Contbr. articles to profl. jours. Fellow Southeastern Surg. Congress; mem. ACS, Am. Soc. Colon and Rectal Surgeons, Alpha Omega Alpha. Office: U Miami Sylvester Comp Canc Ctr Divsn CRS 1475 NW 12th Ave Rm 3550 Miami FL 33136

HELLINGER, WALTER CHARLES, internist; b. Cleve., Aug. 24, 1955; s. Frank Rudolph and Florence (Wimberly) H.; m. Jeanne-Marie Soeting, Sept. 5, 1980; children: Thomas Adriaan, Christopher Frank, Paul Walter. BA, Amherst Coll., 1977; MD, Case Western U., 1982. Diplomate Am. Bd. Internal Medicine, Am. Bd. Infectious Disease. Internal medicine resident U. Calif. San Diego Med. Ctr., 1982-85; asst. clin. prof. medicine LaJolla VA and U. Calif. San Diego Med. Ctr., 1985-86; infectious diseases fellowship Mayo Clinic, Rochester, Minn., 1986-88; sr. assoc. cons. Mayo Clinic, Jacksonville, Fla., 1988-91, cons., 1991—; hosp. epidemiologist St. Luke's Hosp., Jacksonville, 1991-96. Contbr. articles to profl. jours. Mem. ACP, Infectious Diseases Soc. of Am., Soc. for Healthcare Epidemiology of Am., Phi Beta Kappa. Office: Mayo Clinic Jacksonville 4500 San Pablo Rd Jacksonville FL 32224

HELLMAN, ARTHUR ALLAN, cardiothoracic surgeon; b. Bklyn., Oct. 27, 1946; s. Emanuel M. and Sophie (Pugotch) H.; m. Lora Azizov, Dec. 8, 1983; children: Sarah Leah, Moshe Ze'ev. BS, MIT, 1972; postgrad., Columbia U., 1973; MD, Tulane U., 1978. Diplomate Am. Bd. Surgery, Am. Bd. Thoracic Surgery. Intern Sheba Med. Ctr., Tel Hashomer, Israel, 1979; resident in cardiothoracic surgery Hadassah-Hebrew U. Hosp., Jerusalem, Israel, 1981-82; cardiovasc. surgery fellow Tex. Heart Inst., Houston, 1981-82; gen. surg. intern St. Joseph Hosp., Houston, 1982-83, gen. surg. resident, 1983-87; cardiothoracic and vascular surgery resident Tex. Heart Inst., 1987-89; attending surgeon Pa. Hosp., Phila., 1989-94; co-dir. cardiothoracic surgery Westmoreland Regional Hosp., Greensburg, Pa., 1995—; exec. dir. Open Heart Assocs., Greensburg, 1995—; pres. Open Heart Inst., Phila., 1989—. Contbr. articles to profl. jours. Capt. USMC, 1966-73, Vietnam. Decorated Air Medal, Cross of Gallantry with palm, Vietnam, 1969, Vietnam Svc. medal with one silver star and two bronze stars, Navy Commendation medal with Combat "V", Combat Action ribbon, RVN Campaign medal; Am. Heart Assn. rsch. fellow, 1977; E. Ross Kyger, M.D. rsch. grantee, 1984. Fellow ACS (assoc.), Am. Coll. Cardiology, Am. Coll. Chest Physicians; mem. Am. Coll. Physician Execs., Internat. Soc. Cardiothoracic Surgeons, Soc. Thoracic Surgeons. Home: 6 St Ives Dr Greensburg PA 15601 Office: Open Heart Assocs 60 S Washington Ave Greensburg PA 15601

HELLMAN, RONALD EDWIN, physician, researcher; b. Balt., Jan. 2, 1948; s. David Isadore and Lillian Evelyn (Rothenberg) H. BA, SUNY, Buffalo, 1969; MS, MD, Downstate Med. Ctr., 1975. Diplomate Am. Bd. Psychiatry and Neurology. Resident in psychiatry SUNY, Stony Brook, 1975-78, human sexuality fellow, 1978-79; rsch. assoc. SUNY, N.Y.C., 1979-84; pvt. practice N.Y.C., 1979—; staff psychiatrist South Beach Psychiat. Ctr., Bklyn., 1981—; cons. Enter, Inc. Alcohol Treatment Program, N.Y.C., 1986-87. Mem. AMA, Am. Psychiat. Assn., N.Y. Physicians for Human Rights.

HELLMAN, SAMUEL, radiologist, physician, educator; b. N.Y.C., July 23, 1934; s. Henry Sidney and Anna (Egar) H.; m. Marcia Sherman, June 30, 1957; children: Jeffrey Richard, Deborah Susan. B.S. magna cum laude, Allegheny Coll., 1955, D.Sc. (hon.), 1984; M.D. cum laude, SUNY, Syracuse, 1959, DSc (hon.), 1993; M.S. (hon), Harvard U., 1968. Med. intern Beth Israel Hosp., Boston, 1959-60; asst. resident radiology Yale Sch. Medicine and Grace-New Haven Hosp., 1960-62, postdoctoral fellow radiotherapy and cancer research, 1962-64; postdoctoral fellow Inst. Cancer Research and Royal Marsden Hosp., London, Eng., 1965-66; asst. prof. radiology Yale Sch. Medicine, 1966-68; assoc. prof. radiology Harvard Med. Sch., 1968-70; dir. Joint Center for Radiation Therapy, 1968-83, assoc. prof., chmn. dept. radiation therapy, 1971, prof., chmn. dept., 1971-83, also Alvan T. and Viola D. Fuller-Am. Cancer Soc. prof.; physician-in-chief Meml. Sloan Kettering Cancer Ctr., 1983-88, Benno Schmidt chair in clin. oncology, 1983-88; dean div. biol. sci. and Pritzker Sch. Medicine, v.p. for Med. Ctr. U. Chgo., 1988-93, Pritzker Prof., 1988-93, Pritzker Disting. Svc. Prof., 1993—; chmn. bd. sci. counselors divsn. cancer treatment Nat. Cancer Inst., 1980-84; bd. govs. Argonne Nat. Lab., 1990-93; mem. bd. trustees Brookings Inst., 1992—; bd. dirs. Varian Assn. Inc. Contbr. numerous articles to med. jours. Trustee Allegheny Coll., 1979—, chmn. bd. trustees, 1987-93. Recipient Rosenthal award for cancer research, 1980, award for Outstanding Contbns. to Cancer Care, Assn. Community Cancer Ctrs., 1993. Fellow AAAS; mem. Am. Radium Soc., Am. Soc. Therapeutic Radiologists (pres. 1983), Am. Coll. Radiology, Assn. Univ. Radiologists, Am. Soc. Clin. Oncology (David A. Karnovsky lectr. 1994, pres. 1986), Am. Assn. Cancer Rsch., Am. Soc. Hematology, Am. Cancer Soc., Assn. Am. Physicians, Inst. Medicine NAS, Soc. Chmn. Acad. Radiology Depts., N.Y. Acad. Scis., Phi Beta Kappa, Sigma Xi, Alpha Omega Alpha. Home: 4950 S Chicago Beach Dr Chicago IL 60615-3207 Office: U Chgo Divsn Biol Scis 5841 S Maryland Ave Chicago IL 60637-1463

HELLRIEGEL, KAREN MARIE, nurse; b. Buffalo, Aug. 15, 1959; d. James Carl and Donna Marie (Kramer) H. AA, Floyd Jr. Coll., Rome, Ga., 1985; ADN, West Ga. Coll., 1992, BSN, 1994. RN, Ga. Surg. technician Floyd Med. Ctr., Rome, 1987-88; surg. technician Redmond Regional Med. Ctr., Rome, 1988-92, RN, 1992—. Mem. ANA, Assn. Oper. Rm. Nurses, Sigma Theta Tau. Episcopalian. Office: PO Box 497 Cedartown GA 30125

HELM, PHALA ANIECE, physiatrist; b. Ft. Worth, 1931. MD, U. Tex., Dallas, 1966. Diplomate Am. Bd. Phys. Medicine and Rehab. Intern Baylor U. Med. Ctr., Dallas, 1966-67, resident in phys. med. and rehab., 1967-70; mem. staff Parkland Meml. Hosp., Dallas; prof. physiatry U. Tex. S.W. Med. Ctr., Dallas. Mem. ABA, ADA, Am. Acad. Phys. Medicine and Rehab., Am. Congress Phys. Medicine and Rehab. Office: U Tex Health Sci Ctr 51-104 Sprague Clin Sci Bldg 5323 Harry Hines Blvd Dallas TX 75235-9055*

HELME, JAMES BUCKELEW, retired physician; b. Port Chester, N.Y., Apr. 27, 1924; s. James Buckelew and Mary DeHaven (Van Deren) H.; grad. Choate Sch., 1942; AB, Princeton U., 1947; MD, U. Wash., 1952; m. Josephine Coleman Douglas, May 22, 1953 (div. Sept. 1974); children: Susan Van Deren, Catherine Douglas, Martha Buckelew, John Franklin. Intern, Kings County Hosp., Bklyn., 1952-53, Johns Hopkins Hosp., 1953-54, resident, 1954-55, Vanderbilt U. Hosp., Nashville, 1955-56; practice medicine specializing in pediatrics, Nashville, 1956-68; instr. pediatrics and community health Meharry Med. Coll., 1968-71; pediatrician Davidson County Health Dept., 1971-72; med. dir. Nashville Drug Treatment Ctr., 1972-78, Tenn. State Prison and Hosp., 1978-81; mental health cons., 1981-87; chief pediatrics service Nashville Gen. Hosp., 1956-60. Cons. Tenn. Fine Arts Commn., 1968-70. Pres. Nashville Arts Council, 1963-65; bd. dirs. Tenn. Fine Arts Mus., 1963-65, Theatre Nashville Mgmt., 1973-74. Contbr. to The Yucatan Affair, 1974, Collectors Club jour., 1986-92 (Best Article medal 1986, 1992). Recipient Gold Medal Fedn. Internat. Philatelie, 1989. Served to 1st lt. USMCR, 1943-45. Mem. Nashville Acad. Medicine, AMA, Tenn. Med. Assn., Tenn., Davidson County pediatric socs., Am. Philatelic Soc. (expert com. and writers unit), Middle Tenn. Princeton Alumni Assn. (pres. 1962-65). Clubs: Collectors (N.Y.C.); Colonial (Princeton). Home: 3704 Estes Rd Nashville TN 37215-1719

HELMER, CAROL A., psychologist, school psychologist; b. Newport News, Apr. 24, 1946; d. Frederick Otto and Phyllis Amelia (Calf) Helmer; 1 child, Shannon Helmer Ducey. BA, Roanoke Coll., Salem, Va., 1967; MS, Radford U., Va., 1968; PhD, Hofstra U., 1985. Lic. psychologist, N.Y. Tchr. math. Brentwood (N.Y.) pub. schs., 1968-70, psychologist, 1970-72; psychotherapist Bi-County Cons. Ctr., Amityville, N.Y., 1970-78; psychologist BOCES II, Patchogue, N.Y., 1972-73, Middle Country Schs., Centereach, N.Y., 1973—; psychotherapist North Shore Cons., Smithtown, N.Y., 1978-82; pvt. practice psychology Coram, N.Y., 1986—; supr. interns, Hofstra U., 1980—, Adelphi U., 1985-86, Queens Coll., 1986-87, St. John's U., 1987—. Bd. dirs. Community House, Centreach, 1986-87. Redford U. grad. assistantship, 1967-68. Mem. APA (cert. in treatment of alcohol and other psychoactive substance user disorders), EMDRIA, N.Y. State Psychol. Assn. (pres. sch. divsn. 1994), Suffolk County Psychol. Assn. (sch. psychology com. chmn., exec. bd. mem. 1990-94), Rotary. Office: 1 Freemont Ln Coram NY 11727-3234

HELMICK, CHARLES GARDINER, III, epidemiologist; b. Ann Arbor, Mich., Oct. 14, 1950; s. Charles Gardiner Jr. and Marion (Sharkey) H.; m. April Kristy Harrison, June 19, 1982; children: Benjamin Russell, Julia Clarke, Katherine Ryan. BS, U. Mich., 1972; MD, Johns Hopkins U., 1976. Diplomate Am. Bd. Internal Medicine, Am. Bd. Preventive Medicine. Resident Balt. City Hosps., 1976-79; med. epidemiologist Ctrs. for Disease Control, Altanta, 1979—; med. epidemiologist Pan Am. Health Orgn., Port of Spain, Trinidad, 1982-84, Lassa Fever Rsch. Project, Kenema, Sierra Leone, 1981; mem. epidemic intelligence svc. Ctrs. for Disease Control, Atlanta, 1979-81. Contbr. articles to profl. jours. Bd. dirs. Cliff Valley Preschool, Atlanta, 1987-89. Recipient Physicians Recognition award AMA, 1981, 84, 87, Charlotte S. Leebron Meml. Trust Fund award Okla. Med. Assn., 1983, commendation medal USPHS Commd. Corps, 1989, 90, 92, Outstanding Svc. medal, 1991, Outstanding Unit citation, 1995. Mem. Soc. for Epidemiologic Rsch., Physicians for Social Responsibility, Internat. Physicians for Prevention Nuclear War. Office: Ctrs for Disease Control MS-K51 4770 Buford Hwy NE Atlanta GA 30341-3724

HELMREICH, ROBERT LOUIS, psychologist, educator; b. Kansas City, Kans., Apr. 29, 1937; s. Ralph Louis and Caroline (Sheetz) H. B.A., Yale U., 1959, M.S., 1965, Ph.D., 1966. Mem. faculty U. Tex., Austin, 1966—, prof. psychology, 1972—, chmn. grad. program social psychology, 1973-90; dir. NASA/U. Tex. Aerospace Crew Rsch. Project, 1990—; vis. prof. dept. anesthesiology U. Basel/Kantonsspital, 1995—; pres. Robert Helmreich, Inc., 1973—. Co-author: Groups Under Stress, 1968, Social Psychology, 1973, Masculinity and Femininity, 1978, Cockpit Resource Management, 1993; editor: Jour. Personality and Social Psychology, 1984-85; contbr. articles to profl. pubs. Served to lt. USNR, 1959-63. Recipient Disting. Svc. award Flight Safety Found., 1994; Hovland fellow, 1962; grantee Office Naval Rsch., 1966-69, NASA, 1971—, NIMH, 1973-82, NSF, 1978-82, FAA, 1992—. Mem. APA, NAS (mem. com. on space biology and medicine 1986—, human factors com. 1990—, AAAS, Soc. Exptl. Social Psychology (pres. 1978-79), Am. Psychol. Soc. Clubs: Yale (Austin) (pres. 1979-86). Home: 3811 W Lake Dr Austin TX 78746-1617 Office: U Tex Dept Psychology Austin TX 78712

HELMS, LISA MARIE, pediatric intensive care unit nurse, military officer, air force flight nurse; b. Sioux City, Iowa, Nov. 24, 1962; d. Dean Edward and Betty Lou Victora (Guenther) H. BA in Nursing, Carroll Coll., Helena, Mont., 1986; postgrad., Calif. State U., Sacramento, 1990-92; MSN, Incarnate Word Coll., 1996. Cert. pediatric nurse. Enlisted U.S. Army, 1981, advanced through grades to capt., 1990; nurse U.S. Army, San Francisco, 1986-90, Calif. Nat. Guard, San Francisco, 1990-92, Rio Linda (Calif.) Union Sch. Dist., 1990-92; enlisted USAF, 1992; mem. A.F. Nurse Corps Wilford Hall Med Ctr., Lackland AFB, Tex., 1992—; deployed to Guantanamo Bay, Cuba, July to Oct. 1994 for Operation Sea Signal, Operation Safe Haven; provider med. care to Haitian/Cuban migrants. Vol. Big sister/Big brother program United Way. Decorated Humanitarian Svc. medal, Army Commendation medal. Mem. AACN, Nat. Assn. Flight Nurses and Aerospace Med. Assn., Assn. Nurses in AIDS Care. Roman Catholic.

HELMS, PETER JOSEPH, pediatrician, educator; b. Melbourne, Victoria, Australia, June 26, 1947; arrived in U.K., 1956; s. Joseph and Eileen Dorothea (MacFarlane) H.; m. Kathleen Mary Woodward, Nov. 7, 1970; children: Rachel, Joanna, Matthew, Laura. MBBS, Royal Free Hosp., London, 1972; PhD, Inst. Child Health, London, 1983. Cert. con. pediatrician. House officer London Hosp., Brompton Hosp., Hammersmith Hosp., Great Ormond St. Hosp., Hosp. for Sick Children, London, 1976-77; lectr. pediatrics Charing Cross Hosp., London, 1977-78; rsch. fellow Inst. Child Health, London, 1978-82, sr. lectr., 1985-91; rsch. fellow Cardiothoracic Inst., London, 1982-83; prof. child health U. Aberdeen, Scotland, 1991—; cons. pediatrician Great Ormond St. Hosp., Queen Elizabeth Hosp. Hackney, Royal Aberdeen Children's Hosp. Contbr. articles to profl. jours. Grantee Sports Coun. Eng., London, 1988, Wellcome Trust, Aberdeen, 1993, Nat. Health Svc. U.K., Aberdeen, 1995. Fellow Royal Coll. Physicians of London, Royal Coll. Physicians Edinburgh; mem. Brit. Pediat. Assn., Am. Thoracic Soc. Roman Catholic. Office: U Aberdeen Dept Child Health, Foresterhill, Aberdeen AB25 2ZD, Scotland

HELMS, SHERRON R., physician, oncologist; b. Abbeville, Ala., Oct. 1, 1953; d. Levi Preston and Claudie Selma (Renfroe) H.; m. Stan McNeese, Dec. 23, 1982. BS, U. Ala., 1974, MS, 1975, MD, 1979. Diplomate Am. Bd. Internal Medicine and Med. Oncology. Asst. prof. Case Western Res. U., Cleve., 1985-91; pvt. practice Tex. Oncology, Dallas, 1991—; staff physician Presbyn. Hosp., Dallas, 1991—. Office: Texas Oncology # 320 8230 Walnut Hill Ln Dallas TX 75231

HELMSWORTH, THOMAS FREDERICK, surgeon; b. Cin., Dec. 31, 1955; s. James Alexander Helmsworth; m. Lynn Celest Weiler, Sept. 24, 1983; 1 child, Maxwell Alexander. AA, Cin. Tech. Coll., 1977; BS, U. Cin., 1980; MD, Antigua Sch. Medicine, 1985. Rsch. fellow Jewish Hosp., Cin., 1988-89, resident, 1985-91; clin. fellow Vascular Surgeons Ctrl. Columbus, Ohio, 1991-92; gen./vascular surgeon Med. Ctr. Hosp., Chillicothe, Ohio, 1992—. Contbr. articles to profl. jours. Mem. Soc. Critical Medicine, Wound Healing Soc., Am. Trauma Soc., Internat. Soc. Endovascular Surgery, Soc. Vascular Tech., Ross County Med. Soc. (sec.). Office: Vascular Surgery Chillicoth 4439 State Rt 159 Ste 220 Chillicothe OH 45601

HELSABECK, ERIC H., emergency physician; b. Winston-Salem, N.C.; s. Charles Robert and Ruth Haigler H.; m. Judy Ann Hinkleman; children: Keith, Graham. BS, U. N.C., 1971, MD, 1975. Intern Wilson Meml. Hosp., Johnson City, N.Y., 1975-76, resident in family practice, 1977-78; pvt. practice Bath, N.Y., 1978-82; staff emergency physician Randolph Hosp., Asheboro, N.C., 1983—. Mem. Am. Coll. Emergency Physicians, Am. Assn. Family Practitioners, N.C. Med. Soc. Home: 1607 Brevard Dr Asheboro NC 27203-4105

HEMBARSKY, IRENE P. DRAGANOSKY, nurse; b. Freeland, Pa., Jan. 13, 1936; d. Joseph and Helen (Yencho) Draganosky; m. Myron Hembarsky, Aug. 2 1958 (div.); 1 child, Mark. Diploma in Nursing, Allentown (Pa.) Hosp., 1956; BA in Sociology cum laude, La Salle coll., 1980, MBA in Healthcare Adminstrn., 1985. Cert. profl. healthcare quality nurse, Pa., N.J. Charge nurse Albert Einstein Med. Ctr., Phila., 1969-77, quality assurance nurse coord., 1982-86; coord., dept. head quality assurance program St. Joseph Hosp., Phila., 1977-82; clin. svcs. nurse coord. Spectrum Health Svcs., Phila., 1986; UR nurse coord. Grad. Hosp., Phila., 1988; P.I. coord. Our Lady of Lourdes, Camden, N.J., 1988-94; cons. in nursing, Tech. Adv. Svc. to Attys., Ft. Washington, pa., 1987—; nursing cons. quality assurance, Phila., 1987-89, Greater Atlantic Health Svcs., Phila., 1995. Reviewer books in field; contbr. articles to profl. publs. Chair Youth Aid Panel, Phila., 1988-91; mem. com. Walnut St. Theatre, Phila., 1995—; vol. Betsy Ross House, Walnut St. Vol. Troups, PCT Co., Wilma Theatre, Parish Pastoral Coun.;

tour guide Holy Trinity Ch. Mem. ANA, Pa. Nurses Assn., Hosp. Assn. of Pa., Nat. Assn. Healthcare Quality, Am. Soc. Healthcare Risk Mgmt., Allentown Hosp. Sch. Nursing Alumni (bd. dirs. 1957).

HEMENWAY, DAVID, public health educator; b. N.Y.C., Mar. 14, 1945; s. Henry Harold and Marjorie Sophie (Wilson) H.; m. Nancy Lou Williams, Sept. 12, 1969; 1 child, Brett Turner. BA, Harvard Coll., 1966; MA, U. Mich., 1967; PhD, Harvard U., 1974. Mgmt. intern Office of Sec. Defense, Arlington, Va., 1967-68; Washington correspondent Consumers Union, Washington, 1969; asst. prof. Boston U., 1973-75; prof. Harvard Sch. Pub. Health, Boston, 1975—; dep. dir. Harvard Injury Control Ctr., Boston, 1987—; chair, injury prevention coun. Nat. Assn. for Pub. Health Policy, S. Burlington, Va., 1988—. Author: Industrywide Voluntary Product Standards, 1975, Monitoring and Compliance, 1985, Prices and Choices, 1993, Guns and the Constitution, 1995. Injury Rsch. fellow Pew Found., 1986. Mem. APHA, Am. Econ. Assn., Am. Coun. Consumer Interests, Assn. for Pub. Policy Analysis and Mgmt., Am. Soc. for Health Svcs. Rsch. Home: 28 Adams St Brookline MA 02146-3168 Office: Harvard Sch Pub Health 677 Huntington Ave Boston MA 02115-6028

HEMINGWAY, JANET, molecular biologist, researcher; b. Dewsbury, Eng., June 13, 1957; d. Brian Hemingway and Mollie Ibbotson; 1 child, Charlotte Devon. BS in Genetics, U. Sheffield, 1978; PhD, U. London, 1981. Lectr. U. Calif., Riverside, 1981-82; rsch. fellow London Sch. Hygiene and Tropical Medicine, 1982-84, The Royal Soc., London, 1984-94; prof. U. Wales, Cardiff, 1994—; cons. WHO, Geneva, 1984—, Overseas Devel. Orgn., Sri Lanka, 1985-95. Contbr. numerous papers to profl. jours. Project grantee Wellcome Trust, Med. Rsch. Coun. and Biotech. & Biology Rsch. Coun., 1995-98. Fellow Biochemistry Soc., Royal Soc. Tropical Medicine; mem. Entomol. Soc. Am. Home: Old School House, St Mary Hill, Bridgend CF35 5DT, Wales Office: U Wales, Dept Pure & Applied Biol, PO Box 915, Cardiff CF1 3TL, Wales

HEMMER, JOAN DOROTHY, psychologist, educator, researcher; b. Mpls.; d. Wentworth Robert and Dorothy Adeline (Neff) Carlson; m. Donald Moore (div. 1968); children: Ronald, Daniel, Terrence; m. L. Ladd Hemmer, June 12, 1971; 1 child, Derek M. BA, U. Minn.; MA, U. Colo., 1967, PhD, 1972. Lic. psychologist, Minn., Mass. Tchr. English Adams County Dist. 12, Northglenn, Colo., 1964-66; counselor Boulder (Colo.) Valley Schs., 1966-71; asst. prof., psychologist U. Mass., Amherst, 1971-76; prof. psychology dept. St. Cloud (Minn.) State U., 1976—; cons. psychologist VA Med. Ctr., St. Cloud, 1988—; author grant proposals; invited speaker. Contbr. articles to profl. jours. Mem. consumer bd. SFGI, St. Cloud, 1989-90, active in local, regional and nat. confs. ASEE fellow, 1988-89. Mem. APA, Am. Psychol. Soc., Am. Ednl. Rsch. Assn., Assn. for Women in Psychology, Minn. Women Psychologists, Soc. for Psychophysiol. Rsch., Phi Beta Kappa, Phi Kappa Phi (pres. 1985-86). Office: St Cloud State U Psychology Dept Wh # 102A Saint Cloud MN 56301

HEMMING, VAL G., dean; b. Rexburg, Idaho, July 9, 1937; m. Alice Bell Hemming; children: Heidi, Julie, Jill, Patrick. BA in Entomology, U. Utah, 1962; MD, U. Utah Coll. Medicine, 1966. Diplomate Am. Bd. Pediatrics, Nat. Bd. Med. Examiners. Commd. 2d lt. USAF, 1965, advanced through grades to col.; pediatric intern U. Utah Affiliated Hosps., 1966-67; resident physician in pediatrics Wilford Hall USAF Med. Ctr., Lackland AFB, Tex., 1968-70; staff pediatrician USAF Hosp., Wiesbaden, West Germany, 1970-74; chmn., dir. pediatric residency tng. David Grant USAF Med. ctr., Travis AFB, Calif., 1976-80; assoc. prof. dept. pediatrics Uniformed Svcs. U. of the Health Scis., Bethesda, Md., 1980-84, prof. dept. pediatrics, 1984-87, prof., chmn. dept. pediatrics, 1987-95, from interim dean to dean F. Edward Hebert Sch. of Medicine, 1995—; specialty cons. in pediatrics to Air Force Surgeon Gen., 1983-90; ret. USAF, 1990; cons. in pediatrics to the asst. sec. for health affairs Dept. of Def., 1988-91; adv. coun. Nat. Inst. of Child Health and Human Devel. Contbr. numerous articles to profl. jours. Mem. Am. Acad. Pediatrics, Am. Pediatric Soc., Infectious Disease Soc. of Am., Western Soc. for Pediatric Rsch., Pediatric Infectious Disease Soc., Lancefield Soc., Internat. AIDS Soc., Am. Soc. for Microbiology. Office: Uniformed Svcs U Health Scis F Edward Hebert Sch Medicine Bethesda MD 20814

HEMMY, MARY LOUISE, social work administrator; b. Mpls., Nov. 14, 1914; d. Albert H. and Mary (Scott) H. BS, U. Minn., 1936, MA in Social Wk., 1941. Caseworker Washington U. Med. Ctr., St. Louis, 1937-40, Ill. Svcs. for Crippled Children, Springfield, 1941-42; instr., asst. prof. Sch. Social Wk., Washington U., 1942-45; dir. social wk. dept. Washington U. Med. Ctr., 1945-52; assoc. prof., dir. social wk. Coll. Medicine, U. Ill., Chgo., 1952-53; exec. dir. Am. Assn. Med. Social Workers, Washington, 1953-55; prof. sch. medicine sch. social work U. Pitts., 1956-59; exec. dir. Benjamin Rose Inst., Cleve., 1959-77; mem. spl. med. adv. group VA, 1963-68; mem. Ohio Bd. Examiners Nursing Home Adminstrs., 1973-77. Mem. Nat. Assn. Social Workers (bd. dirs. 1961-63), Am. Assn. Homes for Aging (bd. dirs. 1963-70). Home: 13505 SE River Rd Portland OR 97222-8038

HEMP, JAMES ROBERT, surgeon; b. Riverside, Calif., Oct. 20, 1957; s. Robert Herman and Jean Charlene (Middleton) H.; m. Anne Burnett, Apr. 13, 1980; children: Lucas, Samantha. BS in Biochemistry, U. Calif., 1979; MD, Uniformed Svcs. U., 1983. Diplomate Nat. Bd. Med. Examiners, Am. Bd. Surgery, Am. Bd. Thoracic Surgery. Comdr. U.S. Navy, 1979—; intern in surgery Naval Hosp., Oakland, Calif., 1983-84; resident in surgery Naval Hosp., Oakland, 1985-89; gen. med. officer U.S.S. Carl Vinson, 1984-85, ships surgeon, 1989-90; vascular surgery fellow Rush Presbyn. St. Luke's Med. Ctr., Chgo., 1990-91, resident in thoracic surgery, 1991-93; attending surgeon Naval Med. Ctr., San Diego, 1993—; head divsn. vascular surgery Naval Med. Ctr., San Diego, 1995—. Fellow Am. Coll. Cardiology, Am. Coll. Chest Physicians; assoc. fellow Am. Coll. Surgeons. Lutheran. Office: Divsn Cardiothoracic and Vascular Surgery Naval Med Ctr San Diego CA 92134

HEMPHILL, JOHN MICHAEL, neurologist; b. Vernon, Tex., Aug. 6, 1947; s. Gipson Franklin and Floy Marie (Huntley) H.; m. Caroline Anne Frazzitta, Sept. 13, 1975; children: Kate, Ryan. BA, Baylor U., 1969, MD, 1974. Diplomate Am. Bd. Psychiatry and Neurology, Am. Bd. Pediatrics. Rockefeller fellow Div. Sch. Harvard U., 1972-73; fellow Johns Hopkins Med. Instns., Balt., 1974-80, asst. prof., 1980-81; neurologist Savannah (Ga.) Neurol. Assocs., 1981-93; med. dir. Ga. Neurol. Inst., 1993—; clin. asst. prof. Mercer Sch. Medicine, Macon, Ga., 1991—; clin. assoc. prof. neurology Med. Coll. Ga., Augusta, 1993—; chmn. dept. medicine Meml. Med. Ctr., Savannah, 1990-91, dir. neurol. edn., 1993—, v.p. rehab. svcs., 1994—. Bd. dirs. Savannah Symphony, 1991—, pres., 1996—. Bd. dirs. Savannah Symphony, 1991—. Fellow Am. Acad. Pediatrics, Am. Acad. Neurology; mem. Child Neurology Soc., The Chatham Club, Savannah Yacht Club, The Landings Club, Secession Golf Club, Oglethorpe Club. Republican. Episcopalian. Office: Ga Neurol Inst 4600 Waters Ave Savannah GA 31404-6274

HEMPLING, RANDALL, health care administrator; b. Troy, Ohio, Nov. 26, 1945; s. Lionel and Kress (jordan) H.; m. Donna Sue Miller, Jan. 11, 1966 (div. 1985); 1 child, Shirley Ann; m. Deanna Sue Stainbrook, Jan. 31, 1986. Student, U. Tex., 1963-65; BSE, Midwestern State U., 1969, MA, 1971. Adminstrv. asst. City of Wichita Falls, Tex., 1970-71; dir. health and human resources Nortex Reg. Planning Com., Wichita Falls, 1971-76; exec. dir. Health Planning Assoc. W. Kans., Hays, 1976-81; adminstr. Anderson County Hosp., Garnett, Kans., 1981-83, Eyes of Tex. Clin. & ASC, Odessa, Tex., 1987—, Surgery Ctr. Tex., Odessa, 1987—, Symphony Med. Mgmt., Odessa, 1987—; v.p. div. mgr. Westworld Community Healthcare, Lake Forest, Calif., 1984-87; pres., CEO Dental Am., Inc., Midland, Tex., 1991-93; pres. Stainbrook Hempling and Assocs., 1992—; COO Cmty. Hosp., Phoenix, 1994—. Treas., BiCentennial Commn., Wichita Falls, 1971-76, Am. Diabetic Assn., Odessa, 1989. Mem. Med. Group Mgmt. Assn., Am. Coll. Med. Group Adminstrs., Midland Com., Wichita Falls Jaycees (pres. 1976), Odessa C. of C. Leadership Odessa 1988-89, bd. dirs. 1990—), Rotary. Republican. Presbyterian. Home: 1537 E Montebello Ave Phoenix AZ 85014-2414

HENCH, PHILIP KAHLER, physician; b. Rochester, Minn., Sept. 19, 1930; s. Philip Showalter and Mary Genevieve (Kahler) H.; m. Barbara Joan Kent, July 10, 1954; children: Philip Gordon, John Kahler, Amanda Kent. BA, Lafayette Coll., 1952; MD, U. Pitts., 1958; MSc in Medicine, U. Minn., 1965. Intern U. Colo. Med. Ctr., 1958-59; fellow in medicine and rheumatology Mayo Graduate Sch., Rochester, Minn., 1959-63; with Inst. for Arthritis and Metabolic Diseases, NIH, Bethesda, Md., 1963-64; asst. div. rheumatology Scripps Clinic and Rsch. Found., La Jolla, Calif., 1965-66, assoc., 1966-70, assoc. mem., 1970-74, mem., head, 1974-82, sr. cons., 1982—, adj. asst. mem. dept. neuropharmacology, mem. dept. acad. affairs; asst. clin. prof. U. Calif. Sch. Medicine, San Diego; cons. to pharm. cos.; mem. People to People Mission to China on study of Aging. Contbr. articles on rheumatic diseases, pain and sleep disorders to profl. jours.; mem. editorial com. Rheumatism Revs., 1974-84; editorial reviewer Arthritis and Rheumatism, Jour. Rheumatology, 1985—; bd. spl. cons. Patient Care mag., 1987—. Mem. bd. advisors San Diego Opera; mem. U. Calif. San Diego Police Dept. Sr. Vol. Program. Recipient Arthritis Found. award (6), San Diego chpt., 1971-80; Philip S. Hench scholar Mayo Grad. Sch. Medicine, 1965. Fellow ACP, Am. Coll. Rheumatology (chmn. nonarticular rheumatism study group 1975-82, com. on preventive and rehab. medicine 1984-85, com. on rheumatologic practice 1975-77); mem. AMA, Nat. Soc. Clin. Rheumatologists (sec., treas.) Am. Pain Soc., Calif. Med. Assn., Internat. Assn. for Study Pain, La Jolla Acad. Medicine (pres. 1994-96), Arthritis Found (bd. govs. San Diego chpt., Best Doctors in Am. award 1992-93, 94-95), San Diego Hist. Soc., San Diego Mus. Fine Arts, San Diego Opera (bd. advisors). Republican. Home: 7856 La Jolla Vista Dr La Jolla CA 92037-3530 Office: Scripps Clinic & Rsch Found 10666 N Torrey Pines Rd La Jolla CA 92037-1027

HENCHEY, RUTH A., neurologist, epileptologist; b. Northampton, Mass., Oct. 2, 1958; d. Richard F. and Ann R. (Murphy) H.; m. James David Trifilio, May 1987; 1 child, Erin Ruth. BA in Psychology, Smith Coll., 1980; MD, U. Ariz., 1987. Diplomate Am. Bd. Psychiatry and Neurology. Intern Tucson (Ariz.) Hosps. Med. Ctr., 1988; resident in neurology U. Fla., Gainesville, 1991, fellow in epilepsy and clin. neurophysiology, 1993; neurologist West Fla. Med. Ctr. Clinic, Pensacola, 1993—; med. dir. epilepsy monitoring unit Columbia West Fla. Hosp., Pensacola, 19956. Mem. adv. bd. Epilepsy Soc. N.W. Fla., Pensacola, 1993—. Mem. AMA, Am. EEG Soc., Am. Epilepsy Soc., Am. Acad. Neurology, Am. Med. Women's Assn., Epilepsy Found. Am. Office: W Fla Med Ctr Clinic 8333 N Davis Hwy Pensacola FL 32514

HENDEE, WILLIAM RICHARD, medical physics educator, university official; b. Owosso, Mich., Jan. 1, 1938; s. C.L. and Alvina M. H.; m. Jeannie Wesley, June 16, 1960; children: Mikal, Shonn, Eric, Gareth and Gregory (twins), Lara and Karel (twins). B.S., Millsaps Coll., Jackson, Miss., 1959; Ph.D., U. Tex., 1962; DSc (hon.), Millsaps Coll., Jackson, Miss., 1988. Diplomate Am. Bd. Radiology, Am. Bd. Health Physics. AEC fellow Nat. Reactor Testing Sta., Idaho Falls, Idaho, 1960; asst. prof., then assoc. prof. physics Millsaps Coll., 1962-65, chmn. dept., 1964-65; instr. Miss. State U. (extension), 1963; asst. prof., then assoc. prof. radiology (med. physics) U. Colo. Med. Center, 1965-73, prof., 1974-85, chmn. dept., 1978-85; mem. staff VA Hosp., Denver, 1970-85, Mercy Hosp., 1971-85, Denver Gen. Hosp., 1971-85, Beth Israel Hosp., 1974-85; v.p. sci. and tech. AMA, Chgo., 1985-1991; prof. radiology, biophysics, radiation oncology, bioethics Med. Coll. Wis., Milw., 1991—, clin. prof. radiology and biophysics, 1985-91, sr. assoc. dean, v.p., 1991—, dean grad. sch., 1995—; adj. prof. bioengring. Marquette U., 1993—; vis. lectr. Oak Ridge Assoc. Univs., 1964; adj. prof. radiology Northwestern U. Sch. Medicine, 1986-91. Contbr. articles to profl. jours. Served with USMC, 1957-62. Recipient Disting. Alumnus award Millsaps Coll., 1967, Disting. Svc. award Nat. Wildlife Fedn., 1990, Wright Langham Meml. award U. Ky., 1991; Gilbert X-ray fellow, 1960-62, summer fellow NSF, AEC; campus assoc. Danforth Found. Fellow Am. Coll. Radiology, Am. Inst. Med. and Biol. Engring.; mem. AAAS, Health Physics Soc. (chmn. coms., Elda E. Anderson award 1972), Am. Assn. Physicists in Medicine (pres. 1976-77, Robert S. Landauer Meml. award 1977, William D. Coolidge award 1989), Nat. Wildlife Fedn. (Disting. Svc. award 1990), Soc. Biomed. Engring., (sr. mem.), Soc. Nuclear Medicine (pres. 1980-81, Benedict Cassen Meml. award 1984), Am. Acad. Home Care Physicians (Disting. Svc. award 1991), Omicron Delta Kappa, Theta Nu Sigma. Office: Med Coll Wis 8701 W Watertown Plank Rd Milwaukee WI 53226-3548

HENDERSHOT, CAROL MILLER, physical therapist; b. Lancaster, Pa., July 24, 1959; d. Richard Horace and Joan Marie (Nonnenmocher) Miller; m. Richard A. Hendershot, Dec. 29, 1989; 1 child, Scott Michael. BS in Physical Therapy, Quinnipiac Coll., 1981. Staff phys. therapist Easter Seal Rehab. Ctr., Lancaster, 1981-85, phys. therapy dept. head, 1986-89; staff phys. therapist Community Hosp. of Lancaster, 1985-86, Guilds' Sch. & Neuromuscular Ctr., 1990—. Dir. publicity and pub. rels. Lancaster Dist. United Meth. Women, 1988-89, chmn. ch. and soc. com., 1987, 88, mem. chancel choir, 1981-89, mem. adminstrv. bd., 1975-88; trustee Audubon Pk. United Meth. Ch., 1990-93, mem. chancel choir 1990-92, mem. staff parish rels. com. 1993-94, mem. Jubilee Bell Choir, 1990—; dir. Bethlehem and Joy Bells Handbell Choirs, 1994—. Mem. Neuro-Devel. Treatment Assn., Visiting Nurse Assn. (profl. adv. com. 1987-89), Beta Beta Beta. Democrat. Methodist. Home: 6007 W Hopi Ct Spokane WA 99208-9046

HENDERSON, ALEXANDER SCOTT, psychiatrist, researcher; b. Aberdeen, Scotland, Dec. 7, 1935; s. Alexander and Mary Eleanor (Charlton) H.; m. Priscilla Helen Gill, Feb. 25, 1963; children: Mhairi, Susan, Calum, Catriona, Angus. M.B.Ch.B., U. Aberdeen, Scotland, 1959, MD, 1967; DSc, The Australian Nat. U., 1992. House physician Aberdeen Royal Infirmary, 1959-60; registrar Ross Clinic, Aberdeen, 1960-62, Prince Henry Hosp., Sydney, Australia, 1963-64; sci. staff unit studies on epidemiology psychiat. illness Med. Rsch. Coun./U. Edinburgh, 1965-68; found. prof. psychiatry U. Tasmania, 1969-74; dir. social psychiatry rsch. unit Australian Nat. U., Canberra, 1975—. Author: Neurosis and the Social Environment, 1981, An Introduction to Social Psychiatry, 1988. Office: Australian Nat Univ, NHMRC Social Psychit Rsch, Canberra ACT 0200, Australia

HENDERSON, CAROL MORNER, nurse, educator; b. Milw., Oct. 12, 1941; d. Lester A. and Mildred M. (Ford) Kindschi; children from previous marriage: Alicia, Angela, Shannon. BSN, U. Ala., 1963; MA, U. So. Ala., 1970, MSN, 1987; EdD, Nova U., 1983. Coord. Providence Sch. Nursing, 1963-64; staff nurse Providence Hosp., Mobile, Ala., 1964-65; instr., coord. Mastin Sch. Nursing, Mobile, 1966-73; asst. prof. Coordiate Coll. for Health Professions U. South Ala., Mobile, 1973-74, asst. to dir. Sch. Nursing, 1974-76, assoc. dean Coll. Nursing, 1981-89, asst. mem. grad. faculty Coll. Nursing, 1982-95, prof. Coll. Nursing, 1983-95, dir. grad. studies Coll. Nursing, 1987-88; dir. grad. faculty, Coll. Nursing U. South Ala., 1993-95; prof., chair divsn. nursing Spring Hill Coll., 1995—. Mem. ANA, Nat. League Nursing, Sigma Theta Tau, Phi Kappa Phi (past pres.). Office: Spring Hill Coll Divsn Nursing 4000 Dauphin St Mobile AL 36608

HENDERSON, CHARLES WILLIAM, health and medical publishing executive; b. Fitzgerald, Ga., July 20, 1949; s. Aston Leven Henderson Jr. and Frances Ethel Fortson. Cert. in health and WCI, Emory U., 1971; BA in Journalism and Mass Comms., U. Ga., Athens, 1971. Exec. editor Business Atlanta Mag., Atlanta, 1971; columnist Atlanta Mag., 1972; writer Atlanta Jour./Constitution, Atlanta, 1972; staff corr. Bur. Nat. Affairs, Inc., Washington, 1973-74; editor-pub. Buckhead Atlanta, 1975-76; dir. cmty. affairs divsn. City of Atlanta Dept. Cmty. and Human Devel., 1976-77; dir. pub. rels. and comms. Nat. Bank of Ga., Atlanta, 1977; publicist New World Pictures, L.A., Atlanta, 1977, TriStar Pictures, L.A., Atlanta, 1977-79; v.p. TriStar Studios, L.A., Atlanta, 1979; exec. v.p., exec. prodr. Henderson-Crowe Prodns., Inc., Atlanta, 1980-84; publisher, editor-in-chief C.W. Henderson, Publisher, Atlanta, 1984—. Editor-in-chief: (periodicals) AIDS Weekly, 1985—, AIDS Weekly Plus, 1985—, Cancer Weekly, 1988—, Cancer Rschr. Weekly, 1988—, Cancer Biotech. Weekly, 1988—, Vaccine Weekly, 1993—, Blood Weekly, 1993—, TB Weekly, 1993—, Health Letter on the CDC, 1994—, Gene Therapy Weekly, 1994—, Disease Weekly, 1994—, Hepatitis Weekly, 1995—, Malaria Weekly, 1995—, Antiviral Weekly, 1996—, Health Ins. Weekly, 1996—, (interactive database) NewsFile, 1996—; publisher (book) AIDS Therapies, 1988. Cited by Billboard Mag. as Co-Founder First Nationwide Video Music Programming on Cable TV, 1980; cited by Arbitron TV Ratings as exec. producer of Highest Rated Syndicated Musical Variety Program of 1984; cited by USA Today as One of Six Who Made a Difference on the Impact of AIDS, 1985; cited by N.Y. Times as World's Largest Producer Weekly Health Info., 1995; recipient Eagle Scout award Boy Scouts Am., 1963, Fiftieth Anniversary award Order of the Arrow, 1964, Top Pub. Rels. Mktg. Campaign award News Analysis Inst. Over 100 Club, 1979. Mem. AP, Internat. AIDS Soc., Assn. for Continuing Med. Edn., Newsletter Publishers Assn., U. Ga. Alumni Assn., Journalism Alumni Assn. of the Univ. of Ga., Phi Kappa Theta. Home: PO Box 5528 Atlanta GA 30307 Office: CW Henderson Publisher PO Box 5528 Med Ctr II Atlanta GA 31107

HENDERSON, CLAUDE BROOKS, psychiatric physician; b. Columbia, Pa., June 26, 1925; s. Claude Buller and Marian Emma (Flora) H.; m. Ruth Elizabeth Moore, Sept. 18, 1948; children: Craig Brooks, David Bowers, Carolyn Ruth Henderson Scott. BS cum laude, Franklin & Marshall Coll., 1946; MD, U. Pa., 1950. Diplomate Am. Bd. Psychiatry and Neurology. Staff psychiatrist Alcholic Rehab. Clinic, Jacksonville, Fla., 1956-58; clin. dir. Fla. Alchoholic Rehab. Program, Avon Park, Fla., 1958-63; community psychiatrist Marion County, Ocala, Fla., 1963-72; pvt. practice Ocala, 1972-87; chief mental hygiene clinic VA Med. Ctr., Gainesville, Fla., 1987—; trustee Munroe Regional Med. Ctr., Ocala, Big Sun Health Care, Ocala, 1984-87. Leader Marion dist. Boy Scouts Am., Ocala, 1958-80; bd. dirs. Marion Citrus Community Mental Health, Ocala, 1980-84. Col. USAR, 1977-92. Fellow APA (life); mem. AMA, Fla. Psychiat. Assn. (v.p. 1987), Fla. Med. Assn. (del. 1964-84), Marion County Med. Soc. (pres. 1966). Presbyterian. Office: VA Med Ctr 1601 SW Archer Rd Gainesville FL 32608-1135

HENDERSON, DONALD AINSLIE, public health educator; b. Lakewood, Ohio, Sept. 7, 1928; s. David Alexander and Grace Eleanor (McMillan) H.; m. Nana Irene Bragg, Sept. 1, 1951; children: Leigh Ainslie, David Alexander, Douglas Bruce. BA, Oberlin (Ohio) Coll., 1950, DSc (hon.), 1978; MD, U. Rochester (N.Y.), 1954, DSc (hon.), 1977; MPH, Johns Hopkins U., 1960; LLD (hon.), Marietta (Ohio) Coll., 1978; DSc (hon.), U. Ill., 1979, U. Md., 1980; MD (hon.), U. Geneva, 1977—; LHD (hon.), SUNY, 1981, Johns Hopkins U., 1994, Towson State U., 1994; DSc (hon.), Yale U., 1986, Albany Med. Coll., 1989, Lafayette Coll., 1991, U. Mo., 1992. Diplomate: Am. Bd. Preventive Medicine. Intern, then resident Mary Imogene Bassett Hosp., Cooperstown, N.Y., 1954-55, 57-59; chief epidemic intelligence service Center Disease Control, USPHS, Atlanta, 1955-57; chief surveillance sect. Center Disease Control, USPHS, 1960-66; chief med. officer smallpox eradication WHO, Geneva, 1966-77; dean Johns Hopkins U. Sch. Hygiene and Pub. Health, 1977-90; assoc. dir. Office Sci. and Tech. Policy, Exec. Office Pres. of U.S., Washington, 1991-93; dep. asst. sec. HHS, Washington, 1993-94; sr. sci. advisor Dept. Health and Human Svcs., HHS, 1994-95; prof. Johns Hopkins U. Sch. Pub. Health, Balt., 1995—. Contbr. articles to med. jours. Decorated Commendation medal; recipient Ernest Jung prize, 1976, award Govt. India-Indian Soc. Malaria and Other Communicable Diseases, 1975, Rosenhaus Internat. award for excellence, 1975, George MacDonald medal London Sch. Hygiene and Tropical Medicine, Royal Soc. Tropical Medicine and Hygiene, 1976, Health medal Govt. Afghanistan, 1976, Spl. Albert Lasker Pub. Health Svc. award WHO, 1976; Pub. Welfare medal Nat. Acad. Scis., 1978, Joseph C. Wilson award in internat. affairs, 1978, James D. Bruce Meml. award, 1978; Outstanding Alumnus award Delta Omega, 1980; Disting. Alumnus award Johns Hopkins U., 1982; Internat. Merit award Gairdner Found., 1983; Albert Schweitzer Internat. prize for medicine, 1985; Nat. Medal Sci., 1986; Richard T. Hewitt award Royal Soc. Medicine, 1986, Charles Dana Found. award for Pioneering Achievemnt in Health, 1986; Japan prize in Preventative Medicine, 1988, Health medal 1st Grade People's Republic China, 1988, Medal of Abnegation Uruguay, 1988, Honor award Pan Am. Health Orgn., 1990, Health for All medal WHO, 1990, Abraham Lilienfeld award Am. Coll, Epidemology, 1991, Award of Excellence Ronald McDonald Children's Charities, 1992, Surgeon Gen.'s medallion USPHS, 1992, City of Medicine award, Durham, N.C., 1993, Walter Reed medal Am. Soc. Tropical Medicine and Hygiene, 1993, Merit award Nat. Coun. Internat. Health, 1993; hon. fellow London Sch. Tropical Medicine and Hygiene, 1993, Paul Harris fellow Rotary Internat., 1993, Gold medal Albert B. Sabin Found., 1994, John Stearns award N.Y. Acad. of Medicine, 1995, Oswaldo Cruz Gold medal of merit Govt. of Brazil, 1995. Fellow Nat. Acad. Arts and Scis., Am. Acad. Pediatrics (hon.), Royal Coll. Physicians U.K. (hon.); mem. Inst. Medicine Nat. Acad. Scis., Am. Pub. Health Assn., Internat. Epidemiol. Assn., Royal Coll. Physicians Edinburgh (Eng.), Royal Soc. Tropical Medicine and Hygiene, Indian Soc. Malaria and Other Communicable Diseases. Home: 3802 Greenway Baltimore MD 21218-1825 Office: Johns Hopkins U Sch Pub Health 624 N Broadway Baltimore MD 21205

HENDERSON, GREER F., vice chairman CEO; b. Jersey City, N.J., Jan. 11, 1932. BSin accounting, St. Peter's Coll., 1954; grad., Rutgers U. cert. CPA. Supervising senior Hurdman & Cranstoun C.P.A, N.Y.C, 1952-60; divsn. contr. Merck & Co., N.Y.C, 1960-68; v.p.and contr. US Life Corp., N.Y.C, 1975—, v.p., 1977—, vice chmn., chief exec. officer, 1983; vice chmn., chief fin. officer US Life corp., N.Y.C, 1980—, elected vice chm., chief exec. officer, 1996—. mem. bd. dirs. US Life Insurance Co., us Life Income fund, Inc.(exec. com.). Office: US Life Corp 125 Maiden Ln New York NY 10038-4912

HENDERSON, JAMES TAYLOR, retired psychology educator, minister; b. Akron, Ohio, May 7, 1931; s. Joseph Edward and Elizabeth France (Black) H.; m. Nancy Jean Woodman, Aug. 24, 1954; children: Timothy James, Mark Gregory. BA, Baldwin-Wallace Coll., 1953; STB, Boston U., 1956; MA, U. Md., 1970, PhD, 1972. Ordained to ministry Meth. Ch.; cert. gerontology, death edn. Pastor United Meth. Ch., Clyde, N.Y., Jeromesville and Solon, Ohio, 1959-67; coord. tng. programs in suicidology and crisis intervention NIMH, Washington, 1970-72; assoc. prof. psychology, counseling psychologist Cottey Coll., Nevada, Mo., 1972-77; prof. psychology and human svcs. Wingate (N.C.) Coll., 1977-95; ret., 1995; therapist/counselor Community Counseling Cons., Clinton, Mo., 1973-76; vis. prof. S.W. Mo. State U., Springfield, 1975-77; dir. Wingate-In-London, 1982, 92. Author: (book chpts.) Suicide & Bereavement, 1977, New Directions in Death Education & Counseling, 1981; contbr. articles to profl. jours. Staff tng. Hospice Orgns., Charlotte, Union County and Anson County, N.C., 1979—; bd. dirs. Union County Coun. on Aging, Monroe, N.C., 1983-89; organizer/dir. Wingate Coll. Great Am. Heritage Program, Northeastern U.S.A., 1986-88; allocations com. Union County United Way, 1994—. Capt. USAF, 1956-59. Mem. APA, Southeastern Psychol. Assn., Gerontol. Soc. Am., Assn. Death Edn. and Counseling, East Ohio Conf. United Meth. Ch. Democratic. Home: PO Box 310 140 Burris St Wingate NC 28174-9621 Office: Wingate Coll Burris Hall Wingate NC 28174

HENDERSON, JULIAN CROWDER, pathologist; b. Lawrenceburg, Tenn., Jan. 19, 1938; s. Manning Augustus and Katherine (Kent) H.; m. Merle Frances Masters, Dec. 26, 1961; children: Gregory Stephen, Mary Elizabeth, Katherine Merle. BS, U. North Ala., 1957; MD, Tulane U., 1961. Cert. anatomic and clin. pathology Am. Bd. Pathology. Intern U. Miami (Fla.), 1961-62; resident Tulane U., Charity Hosp., New Orleans, 1962-66; instr. Tulane Med. Sch., New Orleans, 1962-66; assoc. clin. prof. pathology U. Miss. Med. Sch.; pvt. practice anatomic and clin. pathology Jackson, Miss., 1968—; assoc. dir. lab. Meth. Med. Ctr., Jackson, 1968—, Woman's Hosp., Jackson, 1975—; cons. pathologist Meth. Rehab. Hosp., Jackson, 1975—. Capt. USAF, 1966-68. Fellow Am. Coll. Pathology, Am. Soc. Clin. Pathologists (councilor 1973-77); mem. AMA, Miss. State Med. Assn. (ho. of dels. 1973—, trustee 1992-95, vice chmn. bd. trustees 1995—), Ctrl. Med. Soc. (pres. 1990-91), Miss. Assn. Pathologists (pres. 1983-84). Republican. Episcopalian. Home: 2153 Eastover Dr Jackson MS 39211-6720 Office: Sturgis Henderson & Proctor PO Box 4475 Jackson MS 39296-4475

HENDERSON, MAUREEN MCGRATH, medical educator; b. Tynemouth, Eng., May 11, 1926; came to U.S., 1960; d. Leo E. and Helen (McGrath) H. MB BS, U. Durham, Eng., 1949, DPH, 1956. Prof. preventive medicine U. Md. Med. Sch., 1968-75, chmn. dept. social and preventive medicine, 1971-75; assoc. epidemiology Johns Hopkins U. Sch. Hygiene and Pub. Health, 1970-75; prof. epidemiology and medicine U. Wash. Med. Sch., 1975—, asst. v.p. and assoc. v.p. health scis., 1975-81, head cancer prevention rsch. program Fred Hutchinson Cancer Rsch. Ctr., 1983-94; mem. Nat. Inst. Environ. Health Scis. Adv. Coun., 1994—; chmn. epidemiology and disease control study sect. NIH, 1969-82; chmn. clin. trial rev. com. Nat.

Heart Lung and Blood Inst., 1975-79; mem. Nat. Cancer Adv. Bd., 1979-84; mem. bd. Robert Wood Johnson Health Policy Fellowship, 1989-93; bd. on radiation effects rsch. NRC, 1991—. Assoc. editor jour. Cancer Rsch., 1987-88; mem. editorial bd. Jour. Nat. Cancer Inst., 1988—; mem. editorial adv. bd. Cancer Detection and Prevention, 1992—. Recipient John Snow award Am. Pub. Health Assn., 1990; Luke-Armstrong scholar, 1956-57; John and Mary Markle scholar acad. medicine, 1963-68. Mem. Inst. Medicine of NAS (coun. 1981-85), Am. Coll. Epidemiology, Assn. Tchrs. Preventive Medicine (pres. 1972-73), Soc. Epidemiol. Rsch. (chmn. 1969-70), Internat. Epidemiol. Assn. (exec. officer 1971-76), Internat. Coun. Cancer Rsch. (sci. adv. bd. 1989—), Am. Epidemiol. Soc. (pres. 1990-91). Home: 5309 NE 85th St Seattle WA 98115-3915 Office: Fred Hutchinson Cancer Ctr Cancer Prevention Rsch Program 1124 Columbia St Seattle WA 98104-2015

HENDERSON, MELFORD J., epidemiologist, molecular biologist, chemist; b. Birmingham, Ala., Dec. 28, 1950; s. Robert Burton and Rena Henderson; 1 child, Erica. Student, NYU Dental Sch., 1977-79; BS, Bishop Coll., Dallas, 1972; MA, Johns Hopkins U., 1976; MPH, Yale U., 1984. Ordained minister. Research assoc. Bishop Coll., 1972-73; rsch. assoc. Sch. of Pharmacy U. Md., Balt., 1976-77; microbiologist Torigian Labs., Queens, N.Y., 1979-81; pub. health analyst internat. program cardiovascular diseases NIH, Bethesda, Md., 1984; epidemiologist/analyst Task Force on Black and Minority Health, Bethesda, Md., 1985—; epidemiologist D.C. Govt., D.C. Health Dept., 1985-88, U.S. Govt., Agy. for Health Care Policy and Rsch., 1990; epidemiologist, sr. rsch. assoc. Prospect Assocs., 1989; epidemiologist, program ofcl. U.S. Dept. HHS; program ofcl. Mayor's Health Policy Coun. D.C. Govt. Author 17 scholarly sci. publs. Recipient numerous awards in chemistry and pub. health; NIH fellow, 1973-76, USPHS fellow, 1982-84, rsch. fellow Assn. Black Cardiologists, 1984-85. Mem. APHA, Md. Pub. Health Assn., Blacks in Govt., Soc. for Epidemiol. Rsch., Assn. Black Cardiologists, Beta Kappa Chi.

HENDERSON, RALPH HALE, physician; b. N.Y.C., Mar. 5, 1937; s. Ralph Ernest and Clifford West (Sellers) H.; m. Ilze Sarma, May 21, 1966. AB, Harvard U., 1959, MD, 1963, MPH, 1970, M.Pub. Policy, 1972. Intern, then resident in internal medicine Boston City Hosp., 1963-65; joined USPHS, 1965, capt., 1973-81, asst. surgeon gen., 1981-90; svc. in USPHS, U.S. and West Africa, 1965-69; lectr., disting. lectr. Baylor Coll. Medicine, 1995; asst. chief venereal disease br., state and cmty. svcs. divsn. Ctrs. Disease Control, Atlanta, 1972-73; dir. venereal disease control divsn. Bur. State Svcs., 1973-76; program mgr. expanded program on immunization WHO, Geneva, 1977-78, dir. expanded program immunization, 1979-89, asst. dir. gen., 1990—; Lilly lectr. Royal Coll. Physicians, 1989; lectr. disting. lecture series Baylor Coll. Medicine, 1995. Contbr. to med. publs. Trustee Dermatology Found., 1975-77. Recipient Commendation medal USPHS, 1969, Meritorius Svc. medal, 1984, Disting. Svc. medal, 1990, Donald MacKay Meml. medal Royal Soc. Tropical Medicine and Hygiene, 1990, Internat. Child Survival award U.S. Com. UNICEF and the Task Force for Child Survival and Devel., 1992, Ann. Pub. Health Forum award London Sch. of Hygiene and Tropical Medicine, 1994. Mem. Am. Coll. Preventive Medicine. Home: 31 Chemin Moise Duboule, 1209 Geneva Switzerland Office: care WHO, 1211 Geneva 27, Switzerland

HENDIN, BARRY ALLEN, physician; b. St. Louis, Apr. 23, 1942; s. Gus and Lillian (Shanker) H.; m. rita Ellen Scissors, Aug. 2, 1964; children: Julie ann Hendin Thikoll, Lori Beth Hendin Travis, Holly Hendin. AB, Washington U., St. Louis, 1964, MD, 1968. Intern Jewish Hosp., St. Louis, 1968-69; resident in neurology Washington U., 1969-72, instr., 1972; clin. lectr. U. Ariz., 1988-95, clin. prof. of neurology, 1995—; chief neurology svc. Good Samaritan Med. Ctr., Phoenix, 1979—, chmn. Divsn. Neuroscis., 1991-92, vice chief of staff, 1993-95; bd. dirs. Samaritan Health System, 1995—. Contbr. articles to profl. jours. Mem. Gov.'s Coun. on Head and Spinal Cord Injuries, Ariz. State Govt., Phoenix, 1994, 95; mem. Parke-Davis Epilepsy Speakers' Bur., 1992—. Maj. USAF, 1972-74. Fellow Am. Acad. Neurology; mem. Maricopa County Med. Soc., Royal Soc. of Medicine. Office: Phoenix Neurol Assocs 2720 N 20th St # 125 Phoenix AZ 85006

HENDLER, MARK STEPHEN, psychology educator, psychotherapist; b. Newark, Oct. 16, 1948; s. Milton Harold and Gloria (Sonin) H.; m. S. Denise McAfee. AB in Psychology, U. Miami, Coral Gables, Fla., 1971; PhD in Psychology, Saybrook Inst., San Francisco, 1977; MA, Calif. State U., Sacramento, 1976; BS, Columbia Coll. Lic. clin. social worker, S.C.; lic. marriage and family therapist, S.C., N.C., Tex.; lic. profl. counselor, Ga. Adj. faculty Santa Rosa (Calif.) Community Coll., 1974-78, Kennesaw Coll., Univ. Systems Ga., Marietta, 1979-81; psychotherapist Charleston, S.C., 1982-90, 93-95, Greenwood Village, Colo., 1991-92; social welfare planner Am. Coun. Mental Health, Arlington, Va., 1991-92; adj. faculty mem. Counseling and Human Svcs. and Social Work, Limestone Coll., 1990, 93-95; faculty mem. psychology Ctrl. Carolina Tech. Coll., 1995—; pres. Am. Coun. on Mental Health, Arlington, 1985-89. Mem. NASW (assoc.), Am. Assn. Marriage and Family Therapy.

HENDLER, NELSON HOWARD, physician, medical clinic director; b. N.Y.C., Aug. 15, 1944; s. Albert and Winifred (Siff) H.; m. Lee Meyerhoff, Oct. 20, 1974; children: Samuel, Alexander, Lindsay, Josepha. BA, Princeton U., 1966; MD, U. Md., 1972, MS, 1974. Diplomate Am. Bd. Psychiatry and Neurology. Resident in psychiatry Johns Hopkins Hosp., Balt., 1975; asst. prof. neurosurgery sch. medicine Johns Hopkins U., 1975—; owner, clin. dir. Mensana Clinic, Stevenson, Md., 1978—; assoc. prof. physiology sch. dental surgery U. Md., 1986—; pres. Pyramid Farms Crayfish Inc., Cambridge, Md. Author: Diagnosis and Non-Surgical Management of Chronic Pain, 1981; (with others) Coping with Chronic Pain, 1979; editor Diagnosis and Treatment of Chronic Pain, 1982; contbr. 51 articles and 29 chpts. to books and profl. jours.; co-patentee direct current motor protector, 1972. Bd. dirs. Md. Mental Health Assn., Balt., 1976-78, Balt. Zool. Soc., 1978-85; bd. dirs. Am. Orgn. Rehab. through Tng., 1983—, pres. Balt. chpt.; bd. dirs. Am. Technion Soc., 1980-92, pres. Balt. chpt.; with Columbia (Md.) Bank, 1991-94. Falk fellow Am. Psychiat. Assn., 1975. Fellow Acad. Psychosomatic Medicine; mem. Am. Inst. Stress (v.p. 1978-89), Internat. Soc. for Study of Pain, Israeli Pain Soc. (hon.), Princeton U. Alumni Assn. Md. (bd. dirs., pres.), Princeton Club N.Y.C., Suburban Club, Safari Internat. Club, Loch Raven Skeet and Trap Club. Republican. Jewish. Office: Mensana Clinic 1718 Greenspring Valley Rd Stevenson MD 21153

HENDLEY, EDITH DI PASQUALE, physiology and neuroscience educator; b. N.Y.C., Sept. 5, 1927; d. Michael and Rose (Parillo) Di Pasquale; m. Daniel Dees Hendley, Apr. 21, 1952; children: Jane Alice, Joyce Louise, Paul Daniel. AB, Hunter Coll. City N.Y., 1948; MS, Ohio State U., 1950; PhD, U. Ill., Chgo., 1954. Instr. U. Chgo., 1954-56; asst. lectr. U. Sheffield (Eng.), 1956-57; instr., rsch. assoc. Johns Hopkins U. Sch. Medicine, Balt., 1963-72; sr. investigator Friends Med. Sci. Rsch. Ctr., Balt., 1972-73; assoc. prof. U. Vt. Coll. Medicine, Burlington, 1973-83, prof., 1983-94; prof. emeritus, 1994—. Co-author 6 books; contbr. over 60 articles to profl. jours. Rsch. grantee NIH, 1974—, NSF, 1986-89, Vt. affiliate Am. Heart Assn., 1982-83, The Sugar Assn. Inc., 1984-85. Mem. AAAS, Am. Physiol. Soc., Am. Soc. Pharmacology and Exptl. Therapeutics, Soc. for Neurosci. (exec. com., treas. Vt. chpt. 1978—), Assn. for Women in Sci. (treas. 1972-74, exec. com., long-range planning com. 1974-76). Home: 10 Highland Ter S Burlington VT 05403-7601 Office: U Vt Coll Medicine Dept Molecular Phys Bi Burlington VT 05405

HENDON, MARVIN KEITH, psychologist; b. Miami, Fla., Oct. 18, 1960; s. James William and Esther (Holts) H.; m. Deborah Faye Moore, Mar. 17, 1990. BA, U. Fla., 1980, MS, 1982, PhD, 1985. Lic. psychologist Fla. Psychologist Psylab Psychol. Svc., Sarasota, Fla., 1986-87; pvt. practice psychology Sarasota, Fla., 1987—; psychol. cons. Child Protection Team, Sarasota, 1988—; outpatient therapist Mental Health Resource Ctr., Jacksonville, 1984-86; therapist U. Counseling Ctr, U. Fla., Gainesville, 1979-83; adj. prof. Manatee Community Coll., 1985. Columnist Insights into Human Behavior, 1987. Adv. bd. One Ch. One Child, 1990—; mem. sch. bd. Westcoast Sch. for Human Devel., 1987—. Republican. Office: 240 N Washington Blvd Sarasota FL 34236-5929

HENDREN, DEBRA MAE, critical care nurse; b. Belle Fourche, S.D., Apr. 27, 1959; d. Clyde Leslie and Kathryn Ann (Daughters) F.; m. Anthony Ray Martinez, May 21, 1983 (div.); m. Cecil B. Hendren, Nov. 21, 1992. AD, Casper Coll., 1987, cert. EMT, 1990. RN, Colo., Wyo.; CCRN. Nurse Wyo. Med. Ctr., Casper, North Suburban Med. Ctr. (formerly Humana Hosp. Mountain View), Thornton, Colo.; nurse Swedish Med. Ctr., Englewood, Colo., charge nurse ICU, 1993—; asst. nurse mgr. North Suburban Med. Ctr., Thornton, Colo. Mem. Wyo. Nurses Assn., Colo. Nurses Assn., AACN. Home: 5168 E 126th Ct Thornton CO 80241-3001

HENDRICKS, LEONARD D., emergency medicine physician, consultant; b. Chgo., Feb. 29, 1952; s. Leonard D. and Edith V. (Elliott) H.; m. Gail Williams, Aug. 26, 1989. BS in Engring., U. Ill., 1974; MD, U. Wis., 1979. Diplomate Am. Bd. Emergency Medicine, Am. Bd. Forensic Examiners, Am. Bd. Forensic Medicine. Med. dir. Cuyahoga County Corrections Facility; emergency physician Meridia Huron Hosp., East Cleveland, Ohio; asst. dir. emergency medicine Kaiser Permanente Hosp., Parma, Ohio; emergency physician Western Res. Care System, Youngstown, Ohio; dir. emergency medicine St. Joseph Riverside Hosp., Warren, Ohio; med. dir. emergency medicine Allen Meml. Hosp., Oberlin, Ohio; pres., CEO Avatar Healthcare Svcs.; cons. Friedman, Domiano and Smith Law Firm, Cleve.; regional physician mgr. Birman & Assocs.; instr. emergency medicine Case Western Res. U., Cleve., Northeastern Ohio U., Rootstown; instr. ACLS, Am. Heart Assn.; instr. advanced trauma life support ACS; instr. pediatric ALS, neonatal resuscitation, Am. Acad. Pediatrics. Fellow Am. Bd. Forensic Examiners, Am. Coll. Medicine, Am. Coll. Emergency Physicians; mem. Am. Coll. Physician Execs., Soc. Acad. Emergency Medicine.

HENDRICKS, MARVIN BERNARD, molecular biologist, researcher; b. Newnan, Ga., Dec. 4, 1951; s. Jimmy Lee and Margaret Hendricks; m. Helen Porthia Talley, Dec. 26, 1971; 1 child, Bridget Clarissa. BS, MIT, 1973; PhD, Johns Hopkins U., 1980. Postdoctoral fellow Fred Hutchinson Cancer Rsch. Ctr., Seattle, 1980-84; rsch. scientist Integrated Genetics, Inc., Framingham, Mass., 1984-87, sr. scientist, 1987-89; head rsch. group Repligen Corp., Cambridge, Mass., 1989-91; group leader Cambridge NeuroSci., Inc., 1991-95; scientist Brigham and Women's Hosp., Boston, 1995—. Contbr. articles to profl. jours.; patentee in field in U.S. and Europe. Featured in Ebony mag., 1988. Mem. ASME, AAAS, N.Y. Acad. Scis. Home: 21 Perry Henderson Dr Framingham MA 01701-4307

HENDRICKSON, BOYD W., health products executive; b. 1945. With Beverly Enterprises Inc., 1970-75, Care Enterprises Inc., 1975-87, Hallmark Health Svcs., 1987-88; exec. v.p., COO, now pres., COO Beverly Enterprises Inc., Ft. Smith, Ariz., 1988—. Office: Beverly Enterprises Inc 5111 Rogers Ave Ste 40 A Fort Smith AR 72919*

HENDRIKSON, EDWARD CHARLES, environmental health researcher; b. Sioux Falls, S.D., Feb. 18, 1953; s. Oscar Charles Hendrikson and Mary Ruth (Stomburg) Shaw; m. Leslie Andrea Bird, Nov. 1, 1980; children: Aaron Allen, Hollie Andrea, Kyle Thomas. BA in Math., 1975, MS in Pediatric Medicine, 1986; postgrad., Colo. State U., 1989; PhD, Pacific Western U., 1990. Tchr. pub. schs., Colo. and N.Mex.; vol., tchr. U.S. Peace Corps, Lesotho, Swaziland; dir. environ. health Plan de Salud del Valle, Ft. Lupton, Colo.; cons. to NIC, NIH, Nat. Inst. Occupl. Safety and Health; med. dir. Am. Embassy, Central African Republic. Contbr. articles to profl. jours. Recipient award Nat. Inst. Occupl. Safety and Health, NIC. Fellow Am. Assn. Physician Assts., Colo. Assn. Physician Assts. Democrat. Home: 1250 W 152d Ave Brownfield CO 80020 Office: Pan de Salue del Valle 11 15th 2d St Fort Lupton CO 80621

HENDRIX, JOHN EDWIN, educator; b. Van Nuys, Calif., Aug. 30, 1930; s. John E. and Leona (Paul) H.; m. Joan B. Haas, Apr. 10, 1954; children: Janet L., James. A. BS, Fresno (Calif.) State U., 1956, AB, 1960; MS, Ohio State U., 1963, PhD, 1967. Orchard foreman Fresno State, 1959-60; grad. asst. Ohio State U., Columbus, 1960-65, instr., 1965-67; asst. prof. plant physiology Colo. State U., Ft. Collins, 1967-72, assoc. prof., 1972-89, prof., 1989—. Contbr. rsch. articles to profl. jours. Mem. AAAS, Am. Soc. Plant Physiologists (editorial bd. Plant Physiology 1982-92). Home: 3000 Tulane Dr Fort Collins CO 80525-2529 Office: Colo State U Fort Collins CO 80523

HENDRIX, RANDY LEE, psychotherapist; b. Tulsa, July 29, 1956; s. Wayne and Virginia (Davis) H; m. Nancy L. Hall, Nov. 11, 1978. BS in Psychology, Oklahoma Christian Coll., 1978; MEd in Counseling Psychology, U. Okla., 1983. Lic. profl. counselor, Okla., marriage and family therapist. Minister Ch. of Christ, Pittsfield, Mass., 1979-81; psychotherapist Juvenile Treatment Ctr., Tecumseh, Okla., 1983-89; pvt. practice psychotherapy Norman, Okla., 1987—; program coord./therapist adolescent acute care unit Hillcrest Health Ctr., Oklahoma City, 1990-92; therapist, Bethesda Non-Violent Sex Offenders program, Norman, 1986-87. Mem. Am. Assn. Counseling and Devel. Republican. Home: 1728 Brandon Cir Norman OK 73071-2806

HENDRIX, RONALD WAYNE, physician, radiologist; b. St. Louis, June 4, 1943; s. Arthur W. and Lida (Martin) H.; m. Miriam Jensen, June 14, 1969. AB, Wash. U., St. Louis, 1965, MD, 1969. Diplomate Am. Bd. Nuclear Medicine, Am. Bd. Radiology. Intern Wash. U., Barnes Hosp., St. Louis, 1969-70; resident U. Chgo., 1970-73, fellow in nuclear medicine, 1973-74; staff radiologist Symmes Hosp., Arlington, Mass., 1976-77; asst. prof. radiology Northwestern U. Med. Sch., Chgo., 1977-84, assoc. prof. radiology, 1984—; attending physician Northwestern Meml. Hosp., Chgo., 1977—, chief, musculoskeletal radiology, 1977—; dir. radiology Rehab. Inst. of Chgo., 1986—. Contbr. articles to profl. jours.; contbg. author to several books. Pres. LaSalle St. Ch., 1982-84, treas., 1984-86, chmn. fin. com., 1986-92. Lt. comdr. USN, 1974-76. Mem. Radiol. Soc. of N.Am., Am. Roentgen Ray Soc., Assn. of U. Radiologists, Am. Coll. Radiology, Internat. Skeletal Soc. Office: Northwestern Meml Hosp 710 N Fairbanks Ct Chicago IL 60611-3013

HENDRIX, SHERMAN SAMUEL, biology educator, researcher; b. Bridgeport, Conn., June 1, 1939; s. Claude Smith and Olga (Kovachik) H.; m. Carol Ann Seibel, June 10, 1961; children: Marc, Robin. BA, Gettysburg Coll., 1961; MS, Fla. State U., 1964; PhD, U. Md., 1972. Instr. biology Gettysburg (Pa.) Coll., 1964-70, asst. prof., 1970-77, assoc. prof., 1977-90, prof., 1990—, chmn. dept., 1985-90. Contbr. articles to Jour. Parasitology, Zeitschrift für Parasitenkunde, Proc. Helminthological Soc. Washington. Bd. dirs. United Way Adams County, Gettysburg, 1983-86. Interam. fellow in tropical medicine NIH, 1973. Mem. Am. Soc. Parasitologists, Helminthological Soc. Washington (pres. 1984, editl. bd. 1985-93, editor jours. 1993—), Pa. Acad. Sci. (pres. 1990-92), Wildlife Diseases Assn., Am. Malacological Union. Lutheran. Office: Coll Biology Dept Gettysburg Coll Gettysburg PA 17325

HENDRIX, THOMAS JEROME, nurse; b. Queens Village, N.Y., Mar. 7, 1953; s. Carl O. and Madeline P. (O'Connor) H.; m. Valerie R. Hendrix, Mar. 28, 1980; 1 child, Thomas J. II. BSN, U. So. Miss., Hattiesburg, 1983; MSA, Ctrl. Mich. U., 1994; postgrad., Pa. State U., 1995—. RN; Cert. BLS, ACLS. Commd. 2d lt. USAF, 1983, advanced through grades to capt., ret., 1995; staff nurse, med. USAF Hosp. Elmendorf AFB, Anchorage, Alaska, 1988-93; nurse mgr. med.-surg. unit USAF Hosp. Minot AFB, Minot, N.D., 1994-95; rsch. asst. in health policy and adminstrn. Pa. State U., 1995—. Decorated Air Force Commendation medal, Meritorious Svc. meda. Christian. Home: 463 Galen Dr State College PA 16803

HENEBRY, MICHAEL STEVENS, toxicologist; b. Decatur, Ill., Jan. 19, 1946; s. Bernard Stevens and Lucille (Benard) H.; m. Virginia Godelsoson Azuela, Jan. 5, 1984; children: Jeffrey Adams, James Stevens. BA in Biology, Millikin U., Decatur, Ill., 1968; MS in Zoology, Ea. Ill. U., 1978; PhD in Aquatic Toxicology, Va. Poly. Inst. and State U., 1981. Teaching asst. zoology Ea. Ill. U., Charleston, 1974-76; teaching asst. biology U. Mich. Biol. Sta., Pellston, 1977-78; rsch. asst. zoology U. Mich. Biol. Sta., 1976-81; rsch. asst. biology Va. Poly. Inst. and State U., Blacksburg, 1967-80; teaching asst. biology Va. Poly. Inst. and State U., 1979-80; asst. prof. biology Ottawa U., Kans., 1981-82, Clarke Coll., Dubuque, Iowa, 1982-83; aquatic toxicologist/ecologist Ill. Natural History Survey, Champaign, Ill., 1983-88; acquatic toxicologist, lab. supr. ecotoxicology lab. Ill. EPA, Springfield, 1988—; cons. in field; lectr. in field; conductor seminars in field. Contbr. articles to profl. jours. Organizer Citizens Utility Bd., Chgo., 1976—, Am. Fedn. State, County and Mcpl. Workers, Springfield, 1983—. With USAF, 1969-73. Mem. ASTM, Soc. Protozoologists, Am. Microscopical Soc., Soc. Environ. Contamination and Toxicology, Ecol. Soc. Am., Midwest Pollution Control Biologists, Sigma Xi. Roman Catholic. Home: 3345 S 3rd St Springfield IL 62703-4612 Office: Ill Environ Protection Agy 2200 Churchill Rd Springfield IL 62702-3406

HENELY, GERALDINE JOSEPHINE, medical/surgical nurse; b. Spencer, Iowa, Apr. 12, 1950; d. Gerald Joseph and Rita Clara (Becker) Henely; children: Jillian Christine, Christopher Andrew. Diploma in nursing, St. Joseph Mercy Sch. Nursing, Sioux City, Iowa, 1971; BS in Health, Coll. St. Francis, Joliet, Ill., 1984; BSN, U. Phoenix, 1988; cert., Command & Gen. Staff Coll., 1992; M in health scis., Health Svcs. Adminstrn., 1995. RN, Ariz.; cert. oper. rm. nurse; cert. RN first asst. Operating rm. nurse St. Joseph Hosp., Sioux City, Iowa, 1971-74; operating rm. nurse St. Joseph Hosp., Phoenix, 1974-88, staff nurse cardiovascular operating rm., 1988-96, asst. charge nurse cardiovascular surgery, 1996—. Major Ariz. N.G., 1981. Mem. Assn. Operating Room Nurses (preceptor). Home: 1645 W Weldon Ave Phoenix AZ 85015-5524

HENINGER, GEORGE ROBERT, psychiatry educator, researcher; b. L.A., Nov. 15, 1934; s. Owen P. and Rachel (Cannon) H.; m. Julie Hawkes, June 27, 1957; children: Steven, Catharine, Karen, Brian. BS, U. Utah, 1957, MD, 1960. Diplomate Am. Bd. Psychiatry and Neurology. Intern Boston City Hosp., 1960-61; resident in psychiatry Mass. Mental Health Ctr., 1961-63, chief resident, 1963-64; clin. assoc., clin. neuropharmacology rsch. ctr. St. Elizabeth's Hosp. NIMH, Washington, 1964-65; program specialist, office of dir. NIMH, Bethesda, Md., 1965-66; asst. prof. psychiatry, assoc. chief rsch. ward Yale U., New Haven, 1966-71, assoc. prof., 1971-76, chief rsch. ward, 1971-78, prof. clin. psychiatry, 1976-78, prof. psychiatry, dir. Abraham Ribicoff Rsch. Facilities, 1978-93, assoc. chmn. rsch. dept. psychiatry, 1988-93, dir. lab. clin. and molecular neurobiology, 1993—; cons. NIMH, 1975-86, 88-94, NIH, 1987, McGill U., 1989, VA, 1990-94, Nat. Rsch. Coun. Can., 1991-93, Nat. Inst. Aging, 1992-93, Wellcome Trust, 1992-94, Pfizer Inc., Merck, Sharp & Dohme, Inc., The Upjohn Co., Hoffman La Roche, Inc., Burroughs Wellcome Co., Bristol-Meyers Co., Squibb Corp., Kali DuPhar, Inc.; bd. sci. advisors, Neurogen Corp. REviewer manuscripts Archives Gen. Psychiatry, Am. Jour. Psychiatry, Psychiatry Rsch., Biol. Psychiatry, Jour. Affective Disorders, Jour. Clin. Psychopharmacology, Life Scis., Neurochemistry Internat., Psychiatry, Schizophrenia Bull., Psychoneuroendocrinology, Jour. AMA. Sr. asst. surgeon USPHS, 1964-66. Recipient Rsch. Sci. Devel. award Type II, NIMH, 1971, 1st prize Anna Monika Found., 1995; grantee NIMH, 1971, 74, 77, 82, 85, 89, 91. Fellow Am. Coll. Neuropsychopharmacology, Am. Psychiat. Assn.; mem. AAAS, Am. Psychopath. Assn., Soc. Neurosci., Soc. Biol. Psychiatry, Psychiat. Rsch. Soc., N.Y. Acad. Scis., Conn. Psychiat. Soc., Sigma Xi, Phi Kappa Phi, Alpha Omega Alpha. Office: Yale U 34 Park St New Haven CT 06511

HENKELS, RANDY, athletic trainer; b. Dubuque, Iowa, May 1, 1958; s. Thomas Leo and Marjorie Louise (Berns) J.; m. Susan Therese Horton, July 2, 1988; children: Alexandra, Kevin. BS, U. Ill., 1980; MEd, Southwest Tex. State U., 1990. Athletic trainer Parkland Coll., Champaign, Ill., 1980-85, Austin (Tex.) Ind. Sch. Dist., 1985-88, 89—, Health South, Austin, 1988-89. Home: 7107 Mesa Dr Austin TX 78731 Office: LBJ High Sch 7309 Lazy Creek Dr Austin TX 78724

HENKEN, BERNARD SAMUEL, clinical psychologist, speech pathologist; b. Everett, Mass., May 30, 1919; s. Issac Edward and Sarah B. (Shatzman) H.; m. Charlotte Popovsky, Dec. 20, 1953; children: Karen Beth, Donna Michele. Student, Boston Coll., 1938-41; BS, Harvard U., 1947; MS, Purdue U., 1950; D. Sci. in Psychology, Calvin Coolidge Coll., 1955. Lic. psychologist, cert. sch. psychologist, cert. rehab. counselor, lic. speech pathologist, Mass.; diplomate Am. Assn. Clin. Counselors. Psychologist Carney Hosp., Boston, 1950-51; dir. speech pathology, psychologist Audiology Ctr., Lynn, Mass., 1951-56; psychologist, chief clin. counseling svcs. Brusch Med. Ctr., Cambridge, Mass., 1956-80; speech pathologist Mass. Gen. Hosp., Boston, 1951-52; speech pathologist, sch. psychologist Everett Pub. Schs., 1955-85; psychologist Rescue Inc., 1959-71; psychologist, clin. counselor North Shore Children's Hosp., Salem, Mass., 1966-74; v.p. North Shore Children's Hosp., 1972-74; psychologist Medford (Mass.) Pediatric Assocs., 1974-94; prof. psychology Calvin Collidge Coll., Boston, 1958-69; lectr. psychology Lawrence Meml. Hosp., Medford, Mass., 1975-77, univ. extension courses Harvard U., 1960-68; psychologist Alfano Med. Inst., Melrose, Mass., 1956-64; guest lectr. Duke U. Med. Ctr., 1965, 72; co-chair symposium on clin. counseling and medicine Tufts U., 1974. Contbr. articles to profl. jours.; creator Henken Operator Safety Evaluation Technique; editor Clin. Counseling Bulletin, 1970-84. Cpl. M.C. U.S. Army, 1942-45, PTO. With MC U.S. Army, 1942-45. Cpl. M.C., U.S. Army, 1943-45, PTO. Mem. APA (charter mem. divsn. of psychotherapy, cert. forensic psychology), Nat. Assn. Sch. Psychologist Assn. (nat. cert. in sch. psychology), Nat. Acad. Counselors and Family Therapists, Mass. Speech and Hearing Assn. (treas. 1957-59), Am. Assn. Clin. Counselors (pres. 1959-63), Mass. Sch. Psychologists Assn. (pres. 1972-74). Republican. Jewish. Home and Office: 118 Waverly Ave Melrose MA 02176-4217

HENKIN, JACK, research biochemist; b. Wolfratzhausen, Fed. Republic Germany, Dec. 23, 1947; came to U.S., 1949; s. David and Anna (Ruditsky) H.; m. Louise Schaefer Pearson, Sept. 2, 1989; children: Anna J., William A., Jonathan J. BS in Chemistry, CCNY, 1969; PhD in Biochemistry, Brandeis U., 1975. Rsch. fellow Harvard U., Cambridge, Mass., 1975-77; asst. prof. U. Tex. Med. Sch., Houston, 1977-84; sect. head pharm. products divsn. Abbott Labs., Abbott Park, Ill., 1984-94, project leader, 1995—. Contbr. articles to sci. jours. Vol. Lighthouse for Blind, Houston, 1982-84, Evanston (Ill.) Mental Health Assn., 1985-87. Rsch. fellow Jane Coffin Childs Found., 1977, fellow Volwiler Soc., 1992; rsch. grantee NIH, 1978, Am. Cancer Soc., 1979, Welch Found., 1980. Mem. Am. Chem. Soc., Am. Soc. for Biochemistry and Molecular Biology, Am. Assn. Cancer Rsch., Sigma Xi. Jewish. Office: Abbott Labs Dept 48R Abbott Park IL 60064

HENKIN, ROBERT ELLIOTT, nuclear medicine physician; b. Pitts., June 7, 1942; s. Hyman and Nettie (Jaffee) H.; m. Denise Dulberg, June 26, 1966 (dec. 1985); children: Gregory, Joshua, Steven; m. Renae Marley, Nov. 27, 1988. Student, Cornell U., 1960-62; BA, NYU, 1965, MD, 1969. Diplomate Am. Bd. Nuclear Medicine, Nat. Bd. Med. Examiners. Internship gen. surgery Bellevue Med. Ctr. NYU, N.Y., 1969-70, residency diagnostic radiology, 1970-72, residency nuclear medicine, 1972-74, asst. prof. radiology, 1974-76; asst. prof. radiology Loyola U., Maywood, Ill., 1976-78, assoc. prof. radiology, 1978-80, prof. radiology, 1980—, dir. nuclear medicine, 1976—. Mem. AMA, Am. Coll. Nuclear Physicians (pres. 1990), Soc. Nuclear Medicine (trustee 1983-89, v.p. 1995-96). Home: 3651 Red Bud Ct Downers Grove IL 60515-1352

HENLEY, EDGAR FLOYD, JR., pharmacist, consultant; b. Corpus Christi, Tex., Feb. 11, 1940; s. Edgar Floyd and Marzelle (Smalling) H.; 1 son, Michael Paul; m. Sylvia Nesbit, Dec. 26, 1981. BS in Pharmacy, U. Ark. Coll. Pharmacy, 1964; DPharmacy, 1983; PhD, Kensington U., 1985. Registered pharmacist; lic. cons. pharmacist. Intern Murray-Hart Drug Co., Pine Bluff, Ark., 1964-65, pharmacist, 1965-67; owner, Bruce Drugs Inc., Smackover, Ark., 1967-78, pres. Bruce Drugs, Inc., 1978—; cons. pharmacy Smackover Nursing Home, 1975—. Pres. Smackover Band Parents, 1974-76, Smackover Retail Credit Assn., 1973-76; chmn. Union County Dem. Com., 1974-76, Union County Election Com., 1974-76; troop leader Girl Scouts U.S.; packmaster Cub Scouts Am., 1971-74; bd. dirs. Union County chpt. ARC, 1975-79; bd. dirs., sec.-treas. Smackover Devel. Corp., 1970—, Smackover Indsl. Devel. Corp., 1970—; mem. Fed. Wetlands Task Force for Congressman Bonyl Anthony, 1989, Ark. Gov.'s Rural Devel. Study Commn., 1989, Exec. Com. Ark. Mcpl. League, Ark. Drug Abuse Authority, 1975; pres. Ark. State Bd. Health, 1992; mem. alumni adv. coun. U. Ark. for Med. Scis., 1984—, chmn.-elect, 1985—, chmn. adv. coun. cities of second class Ark. Mcpl. League, 1987-88; mem. found. fund bd. U. Ark. Med. Scis., exec. planning com. for chancellor, curriculum com. Coll. Pharmacy, admissions com. Coll. Pharmacy, 1987-88, chmn. Alumni Adv. Council, 1987-88; alderman Smackover City Council, 1983-86; mayor City of Smackover, 1987—; pres. Union chpt. Am. Cancer Soc., 1993-95; bd. dirs. So. Ark. Symphony Bd., 1993-95, pres., 1994-95; active Women Ark. Bd. Health,

1990—. Served with USAF, 1958-61. Recipient Bowl of Hygeia award A.H. Robins, Inc., 1974, MS&D award for Outstanding Achievement in Profession of Pharmacy, 1989, Ark. Pharmacist of Yr. award, 1993; named Key Man, Jr. C. of C., 1986. Fellow Am. Soc. Cons. Pharmacists; mem. Am. Pharm. Assn. (bd. dirs.), Smackover Jaycees (pres.), Ark. Pharm. Assn. (v.p., dir., chmn. Ethical Affairs Com. 1987-88, Ark. Pharm. Community Service award 1974), Health Scis. Edn. Found. South Ark. (pres. 1987-88), Nat. Assn. Retail Druggists, Frat. Order Police, Nat. Rifle Assn., Smackover C. of C. (pres. 1974, dir. 1975-80, treas. 1980—, Outstanding Citizen award 1974), U. Ark. Alumni Assn. (pres. Union County chpt. 1994-95), Acacia. Methodist. Club: Pine Hills Country (past pres.). Lodges: Masons (master), Lions, Shriners, KT. Home: 1101 Cedar Ave Smackover AR 71762-2027 Office: Bruce Drugs Inc 711 Broadway St Smackover AR 71762-1822

HENLEY, RICHARD JAMES, healthcare institution administrator and financial officer; b. Wroclaw, Poland, May 31, 1956; came to U.S., 1959; s. Henry and Lidia (Alper) Horczak. BA and MA summa cum laude, CCNY, 1978. Asst. to v.p. fin. Mt. Sinai Med. Ctr., N.Y.C., 1978-80, dir. fin. planning, 1980-81, assoc. dir. fin., 1982-84, dir. fin. profl. svcs., 1984-85; v.p. fin., treas. Vassar Bros. Hosp., Poughkeepsie, N.Y., 1985-92, sr. v.p., treas., 1992—; treas. VBH Corp., Poughkeepsie, 1986—, Vassar Bros. Hosp. Found., 1986—, VBH Ins. Co., Ltd., 1988-90, pres., 1991—, Riverside Diversified Svces., Inc., 1986-92, pres., 1992—, Riverside Mgmt. Svcs., Inc., 1986-92, pres., 1992—. Contbr. articles to profl. jours. Treas. Bardavon 1869 Opera House, Poughkeepsie, 1986-91, Family Svcs. Dutchess County, Poughkeepsie, 1987-88; com. mem. United Way Dutchess County, 1987—; pres. Hudson Terr. Owners' Corp., Poughkeepsie, 1987-88. Fellow Am. Coll. Healthcare Execs., Healthcare Fin. Mgmt. Assn. (nat. sec. 1996—, nat. dir. 1994-96, cost effectiveness award 1979-80, William G. Follmer Merit award 1986, Robert H. Reeves Merit award 1989, Fredric T. Muncie Mert award 1991, Medal of Honor award 1994); mem. Poughkeepsie Area C. of C. Office: Vassar Bros Hosp Reade Pl Poughkeepsie NY 12601

HENN, JAMES STEVEN, medical facility administrator; b. Indpls., Feb. 18, 1947; s. Charles Fredrick and Esther Grace (Kelly) H.; m. Kathleen Ellen Kelly, Oct. 22, 1988. BS, Xavier U., 1986. Therapist Good Samaritan Hosp., Cin., 1980-84; respiratory therapist C.R. Holmes Hosp., Cin., 1981-85; mgr. anesthesia, surg. rsch. Children's Hosp., Cin., 1980-88; coord. eye & tissue bank Meth. Hosp., Indpls., 1988-90, mgr. organ and tissue procurement, 1990-94, procurement transplant coord., 1994—. Mem. Am. Bd. Transplant Coord., Am. Assn. Tissue Banks, Eye Bank Assn. Am., N.Am. Transplant Care Orgn., United Network of Organ Sharing. Roman Catholic.9. Home: 8518 Sarasota Ct Indianapolis IN 46219-2531 Office: Meth Hosp Ind 1701 Senate Blvd Indianapolis IN 46202-1367

HENN, VOLKER, neurology educator; b. Gotha, Germany, Jan. 22, 1943; s. Walter and Hilde (Leistner) H. MD, U. Berlin, 1968. Asst. prof. Mt. Sinai Sch. Medicine, N.Y.C., 1970-71; lectr. in neurology U. Zürich, Switzerland, 1977-81, prof. of neurology, 1981—; rschr. in field. Author 2 books in field; contbr. over 100 papers to sci. jours. Recipient Nylén-Hallpike medal Bárány Soc., 1990. Mem. Am. Neurol. Assn., Soc. for Neurosci., European Neurosci. Assn., European Brain and Behavior Assn., Swiss Neurol. Soc. Office: U Hosp, Neurology Dept, CH-8091 Zurich Switzerland

HENNAN, FLOYD ARTHUR, osteopath; b. Pomona, Calif., Jan. 2, 1959; s. Arthur William and Mary Belle (Pulliam) H.; m. Laura Ann (LeBlanc) May 30, 1981; children: Caycee, Grant, Stephanie. BS, Okla. Christian Coll., 1984; DO, Kirskville Coll. Osteo. Medicine, 1991. Intern Carson City (Mich.) Hosp., 1991-92; pvt. practice, Ava, Mo., 1992—. Mem. AMA, Am. Osteo. Assn., Am. Coll. Gen. Practitioners, Ava C. of C. (pres. 1995). Home: Rt 1 Box 587 Ava MO 65608 Office: Springfield Clinic Ava Br Hwy 5 Ava MO 65608

HENNESSEY, WILLIAM JOSEPH, physician; b. Troy, N.Y., Mar. 8, 1947; s. Joseph William and Loretta (Brooks) H.; m. Patricia McMahon, Jan. 23, 1983; children: Bridget Marie, Jason William, Matthew Brian, Mark Andrew. BS, Rensselaer Poly. Inst., 1969; MD, Albany Med. Coll., 1973. Cert. Am. Bd. of Ob/Gyn. Resident in ob-gyn Albany (N.Y.) Med. Ctr. Hosp., 1973-76; pvt. practice specializing in ob-gyn, Troy, N.Y., 1976—; mng. ptnr. Ob-Gyn Health Ctr. Assocs., 1985; attending physician Albany Med. Ctr. Hosp., Samaritan Hosp.; treas. med. staff Samaritan Hosp., 1988, sec. med. staff, 1989, v.p. med. staff, 1990, pres., 1991; clin. asst. dept. ob-gyn Albany Med. Ctr. and Albany Med. Coll., 1976—, clin. instr.; chmn. dept. ob-gyn Samaritan Hosp., 1991-95; bd. dirs. PSRO, 1981-85, PRO, 1985-86. Fellow Am. Coll. Ob-Gyn, Am. Fertility Assn.; mem. Am. Chem. Honor Soc., AMA, N.Y. State Med. Soc., Rensselaer County Med. Soc., Northeast Ob-Gyn Soc., Northeastern N.Y. Health Care Consortium, Am. Assn. Gynecol. Laporoscopists, Sampson Soc. (pres.). Republican. Roman Catholic.

HENNESSY, JAMES ROBERT, pediatric cardiologist, internist, educator; b. Shelby, Ohio, Feb. 10, 1943; s. William Richard and Christine Agnes (Fink) Henson; children: Alena Lara, Bridget Kathleen, Cecilia Anne, Deidre Marie, Erin Christine. MD, U. Cin., 1971. Staff assoc. prof. Med. Coll. Ohio, Toledo, 1979—. Maj. U.S. Army, 1975-78. Mem. Acad. Medicine. Office: Med Coll Ohio 3000 Arlington Ave Toledo OH 43699

HENNESSY, MARGARET BARRETT, health care executive; b. Oak Park, Ill., Apr. 16, 1952; d. Bernard Leo and Frances (Madigan) H. BA in Sociology and Psychology, St. Norbert Coll., DePere, Wis., 1974; MS, Rush U., Chgo. Communications specialist Ill. Cancer Coun., Chgo., 1983-84; adminstrv. asst. Rush-Presbyn./St. Luke's Med. Ctr., Chgo., 1984-85; adminstrv. intern Cook County Hosp., Chgo., 1985-86; fin. analyst Loyola U. Med. Ctr., Maywood, Ill., 1986-89; operating officer Howard Brown Meml. Clinic, Chgo., 1989-93; hematology-oncology adminstr. Loyola U. Med. Ctr., Maywood, Ill., 1993-96; assoc. dir. primary care svcs. Lake County Health Dept., Waukegan, Ill., 1996—; guest lectr. Loyola U. Law Sch., 1989-90. Contbr. articles to profl. jours. Tchr. English as a second lang. World Relief Orgn., Chgo., 1989; cons. United Charities Camps, Chgo., 1989. Recipient Foster G. McGaw scholar, Am. Coll. health Care Execs., 1985. Mem. Rush U. Alumni Assn. (pres.), Chgo. Health Execs. Forum, Am. Coll. Healthcare Execs., Assn. Ambulatory Care Adminstrs. Office: Lake County Pub Health Dept 2400 Belvedere Rd Waukegan IL 60085

HENNIG, CHARLES WILLIAM, psychology educator; b. Queens, N.Y., May 7, 1949; s. Charles Joseph and Evelyn Mary (Gerstel) H.; m. Mary Christina Shamrock, Jan. 9, 1982; 1 child, Brian Steve. BA, SUNY, Buffalo, 1971; MS, Tulane U., 1976, PhD, 1978. Grad. teaching asst. Tulane U., New Orleans, 1974-78; vis. asst. prof. psychology U. Okla., Norman, 1978-79, Centre Coll. Ky., Danville, 1979-80; asst. prof. Salem (W.Va.) Coll., 1980-83, assoc. prof., 1983-88, prof., 1988-89, chair psychology, 1983-89; prof., chair psychology McMurry U., Abilene, Tex., 1989—; bd. dirs. African Elephant Rsch. and Survival Ranch, Abilene, 1990—. Contbr. articles to profl. jours. Vol. United Way of Abilene, 1990—; mem. Abilene Zool. Soc., 1990—. With U.S. Army, 1972-74. Mem. APA, Am. Psychol. Soc., Animal Behavior Soc., Psychonomic Soc., Midwestern Psychol. Assn., Southeastern Psychol. Assn., Abilene Psychol. Assn. (sec.-treas. 1990-91, 94-95, pres. 1992-93, 96—), Psi Chi. Republican. Roman Catholic. Home: 4701 Stonehedge Rd Abilene TX 79606-3429 Office: McMurry U Psychology Dept PO Box 86 Abilene TX 79604-0086

HENNIGAR, GORDON ROSS, JR., retired pathologist, educator; b. Halifax, N.S., Can., Dec. 16, 1919; came to U.S., 1946; s. Gordon Ross Sr. and Bonita (Barker) H.; m. Loretta June King, Apr. 5, 1947; children: Donna, Gordon Ross III, Warwick, Randolph, Sandra. BS, Dalhousie U., Halifax, 1941, MD, CM, 1945. Diplomate Am. Bd. Anatomy, Am. Bd. Forensic Pathology. Intern Victoria Gen. Hosp., Halifax, 1944-45, Union Meml. Hosp., Balt., 1946-47; resident South Balt. Gen. Hosp., 1947-48, Johns Hopkins Hosp., Balt., 1948-50; assoc. prof. Med. Coll. Va., Richmond, 1950-57; prof. SUNY, Bklyn., 1957-65; chmn., prof. pathology, lab. medicine, forensic pathology Med. U. S.C., Charleston, 1965-88, prof., chmn. emeritus, 1988—; acting chmn. SUNY, Bklyn., 1959-60; supervising pathologist, dir. labs., Kings County Hosp., Bklyn., 1957-65; cons. VA Med. Ctr., Charleston, 1965—; mem. med. staff Med. U. S.C., 1965—, Charleston Meml. Hosp., 1967—, Roper Hosp., Charleston, 1968—; mem., past chmn. Med. Examiners Commn., Charleston County. Author: (with others) Iatrogenic Drug Toxicity, 1985, Techniques in Nephropathology, 1986, Anderson's Textbook of Pathology, 1990. Pres. Save the Wando Assn., Inc., Mt. Pleasant, S.C. 1972; mem. S.C. Coastal Coun. Conservation League, Charleston, 1989—. With Royal Can. Army Med. Corps, 1944-46. Recipient CCE Commr.'s medal Am. Soc. Pathologists, 1989; Johns Hopkins Soc. Scholars award, 1988, AOA, 1968. Fellow Soc. 1824; mem. Nat. Assn. Med. Examiners (1970-77), Nat. Alumni Coun. Johns Hopkins Med. Sch. (bd. dirs., 1950—), S.C. Soc. Pathologists (1965-89), Internat. Acad. Pathologists, 100 Club Greater Charleston (bd. dirs., 1988—). Home: 265 Coinbow Dr Mount Pleasant SC 29464-2535 Office: Med U SC 171 Ashley Ave Charleston SC 29425-0001

HENNINGER, POLLY, neuropsychologist, researcher and clinician; b. Pasadena, Calif., Apr. 1, 1946; d. Paul Bennett and Mary (MacNair) Johnson; m. Richard Henninger Jr., 1966 (div. 1983); children: Marguerite, Nathan; m. Clyde Pechstedt, 1985 (div. 1992). BA, Ind. U., 1967, Pomona Coll., 1977; MA, U. Toronto, 1969, PhD, 1982; PhD (respecialization), Fuller Theol. Sem., 1995. Registered psychologist, Ont., Can. Postdoctoral fellow Calif. Inst. Tech., Pasadena, 1982-84; doctoral respecialization in clin. psychology Fuller Theol. Sem., Pasadena, 1991-95; asst. prof. Pitzer Coll., Claremont, Calif., 1984-87, Brock U., St. Catharines, Ont., 1987-91; vis. assoc. divsn. biology Calif. Inst. Tech., Pasadena, 1984-94; asst. dir. neuropsychol. svcs. Ctr. for Aging Resources, Fuller Theol. Sem., Pasadena, 1991-92; psychology intern Boston VA Med. Ctr. and New Eng. Med. Ctr., 1994-95; neuropsychology fellow Tufts Med. Sch., Boston, 1995-96; staff neuropsychologist Fall River Outpatient Clinic Braintree Rehab. Hosp., 1995—; rsch. assoc. Harvard Med. Sch., Boston, 1996—. Contbr. chpts. to books, articles to profl. jours. Recipient fellowships and grants. Mem. APA (div. 40 chair rsch. selection 1986-89), Nat. Acad. Neuropsychology, Can. Psychol. Assn., Internat. Neuropsychol. Soc. Democrat. Episcopalian. Home: 220 Jamaica Way 16 Jamaica Plain MA 02130 Office: VA Med Ctr Psychology Svc 116B 150 S Huntington Dr Boston MA 02130

HENRICHS, W(ALTER) DEAN, dermatologist; b. Smith Center, Kans., Oct. 26, 1939; s. Walter George and Mildred (Kubias) H.; m. Barbara Ann Bremer, Apr. 7, 1967; children: Matthew, Mark, Jonathan. BA, U. Kans., 1961, MD, 1965. Diplomate Am. Bd. Dermatology, Am. Bd. Dermotopathology. Commd. ensign USN, 1964, advanced through grades to capt.; chmn. dept. dermatology Winston-Salem (N.C.) Health Care Plan, 1984—. Methodist. Office: Winston Salem Health Care 250 Charlois Blvd Winston Salem NC 27103

HENRICKS, ROGER LEE, social services administrator; b. Wauseon, Ohio, May 16, 1943; s. Clifford Seldon and Annabelle Mae (Perkins) H.; m. Judith Ann Shimp, Aug. 28, 1966 (div. Mar. 1981); children: Wendy, Craig, Joel; m. Helen Elizabeth Dennis, June 6, 1986. BA, Adrian (Mich.) Coll., 1966. Welfare caseworker Dept. Social Svcs., Adrian, Mich., 1966-68, protective svcs. caseworker, 1968-78, supr. protective svcs., 1978-94; exec. dir. Family Awareness Ctr., Adrian, 1994—; instr. Ea. Mich. U., Ypsilanti, 1977-82, Siena Heights Coll., Adrian, 1987—, Parent Nurturing Program, Adrian, 1985—; co-founder Family Awareness Ctr., Adrian, 1982-84; presenter in field. Founder, pres. Child Abuse and Neglect Coun., Adrian, 1977—, Sexual Abuse Task Force, Adrian, 1988—; pres., bd. dirs. Call Someone Concerned, Adrian, 1972-86, hon. bd. dirs., 1986—. Recipient Nancy Nichols award Office Substance Abuse, 1983, Mich. Pub. Servant of Yr. award Govt. Adminstrs. Assn. Found, 1988, Ray Helfer award Mich. Commn. for Prevention Child Abuse, 1989. Office: Family Awareness Ctr 199 Broad St Adrian MI 49221

HENRICKSON, MARK, psychotherapist, director, counselor, priest; b. Wilmington, Del., Nov. 28, 1955; s. Bruce and Elaine Mary (Fowler) H.; m. T. A. Bennett, Jan. 15, 1982. BA, Trinity Coll., 1977; MDiv, Episcopal Div. Sch., 1980; MSW, U. Conn., 1990; PhD, UCLA, 1996. Ordained priest, Episc. Ch., 1981. Curate Trinity Episcopal Ch., Torrington, Conn., 1980-82; chaplain resident Hartford (Conn.) Hosp., 1982-83; priest-in-charge St. Monica's Episcopal Ch., Hartford, 1983-85; pvt. practice Hartford, 1985-91; NIMH, AIDS rsch. tng. fellow UCLA, 1992-94; field unit supervisor immunization program L.A. County Dept. Health Svcs., 1995-96; HIV divsn. dir. Northeast Valley Health Corp., 1996—; dir. AIDS/HIV program Hartford Health Dept.; field supr. U. Conn., Hartford, 1988-91; mem. Permanent Task Force on AIDS, Conn., 1989-91; cons. AIDS Ministries Regional Care Team, Hartford, 1990-91; mem. adj. faculty St. Joseph's Coll., Hartford, 1991. Contbr. articles to profl. jours. Mem. Conn. Coalition for Lesbian/Gay Civil Rights, Hartford, 1986—. Mem. NASW, Social Work AIDS Network. Office: 14860 Roscoe Blvd Panorama City CA 91402

HENRIKSON, KATHERINE POINTER, research scientist; b. Erie, Pa., Oct. 4, 1939; d. Leon Royce and Katherine (Hermen) Pointer; m. Ray C. Henrikson, Oct. 29, 1966; children: Charles, Andrew. BA in Chemistry, U. Rochester, 1961; MA in Med. Scis., Harvard U., 1962, PhD in Biol. Chemistry, 1967. Rsch. scientist Commonwealth Scientific and Indsl. Rsch. Orgn., Sydney, Australia, 1967-69; postdoctoral fellow Pathology dept. Columbia U., N.Y.C., 1970-71; asst. prof., biochemistry Fairleigh Dickinson Sch. Dentistry, Hackensack, N.J., 1974; rsch. assoc. to asst. prof. Albany (N.Y.) Med. Coll., 1976-79; rsch. scientist Wadsworth Ctr., State Health Dept., Albany, 1979—; asst. prof. SUNY Sch. Pub. Health, Albany, 1986-93, assoc. prof. 1993—; ad hoc reviewer NSF, Washington, 1988—; speaker in field. Mem. AAAS, Am. Soc. Biochemistry and Molecular Biology, Endocrine Soc., N.Y. Acad. Scis., Phi Beta Kappa. Home: 4 Oldox Rd Delmar NY 12054-2904 Office: Wadsworth Ctr Lab & Rsch NY State Health Dept PO Box 509 Albany NY 12201-0509

HENRIKSON, RAY CHARLES, anatomy educator; b. Worcester, Mass., May 22, 1937; s. Sigurd and Theresa (Edlin) H.; m. Katherine Pointer, Oct. 29, 1966; children: Charles A., Andrew J. BSc, U. Mass., 1959; MSc, Brown U., 1961; PhD, Boston U., 1966. Instr. Boston U. Med. Sch., 1966-67; scientist Commonwealth Sci. and Indsl. Rsch. Orgn., Australia, 1967-69; asst. prof. Columbia U., N.Y.C., 1969-76; assoc. prof. Albany (N.Y.) Med. Coll., 1976-89, prof., 1989—; mem. com. Nat. Bd. Med. Examiners, 1985-88. Author: Key Facts in Histology, 1986. Mem. Am. Assn. Anatomists, Am. Soc. Cell Biology, Assn. Devel. of Computer-Based Instrn. Systems. Office: Albany Med Coll Anatomy Dept (A-135) Albany NY 12208

HENRY, ERNEST NOEL, nephrologist; b. Sunderland, Eng., Jan. 12, 1960; came to U.S., 1988; s. Patrick and Celine (O'Shaughnessey) H.; m. Loretto Teresa Doyle, Aug. 16, 1958; children: Sarah, Neil, Shane. MB, BAD, BCH, Cork (Ireland) Med. Sch., 1983. MRCPI Royal Coll. Physicians of Ireland; diplomate Am. Bd. Internal Medicine. Resident in internal medicine U. Coll., Cork, Ireland, 1983-87; fellow in nephrology U. Coll., Cork, 1982-88; resident in internal medicine Georgetown U. Ctr., Washington, 1988-90, fellow in nephrology, 1990-92; cons. in nephrology Johnson Meml. Hosp., Abingdon, Va., 1992—; internist, nephrologist Russel County Meml. Ctr., Lebanon, Va., 1992—. Mem. Royal Coll. Physicians Ireland. Home: 19174 Triple Crown Dr Abingdon VA 24211 Office: Lebanon Med Group Russell County Med Ctr. PO Box 3600 Lebanon VA 24266

HENRY, GREGORY LEE, emergency physician; b. Trent, Mich., Dec. 25, 1946; s. John Norman and Delores Viola (Bergren) H.; m. Margene Ann Trojan, May 24, 1969; children: Christopher Stephen, Sara Elizabeth, Allison Ann. BA, U. Mich., 1969, MD, 1973. Intern St. Joseph Mercy Hosp., Ann Arbor, Mich., 1973-74; resident Mary Hitchcock Hosp., Dartmouth Med. Sch., Hanover, N.H., 1975-76; chief dept. emergency medicine Oakwood Hosp.-Beyer Ctr., Ypsilanti, Mich., 1978—; v.p. Emergency Physicians Med. Group, Ann Arbor, Mich., 1978—; pres. Am. Physicians Assurance Soc., Ltd., Barbados, West Indies, 1986—; CEO Med. Practice Risk Assessment, Ind., Ann Arbor, 1986—; clin. assoc. prof. dept. surgery, sect. emergency svc. U. Mich., Ann Arbor, 1992—; vis. lectr., keynote spkr. The Australasian Coll. and Soc. Emergency Medicine, 1989; C.C. Roussi Meml. lectr. Akron (Ohio) Gen. Med. Ctr., 1989. Co-author: Neurologic Emergencies-A Symptom Oriented Approach, 1985; editor-in-chief Emergency Medicine Risk Management: A Comprehensive Review, 1991; reviewer, cons. Annals of Emergency Medicine, 1982—; editl. bd. dirs. Emergency Medicine Mag., 1985—. Bd. mem. Huron Valley Ambulance, Ann Arbor, 1984-90; co-chmn. profl. giving Washtenaw County United Way, Ann Arbor, 1992; bd. trustees Emergency Medicine Found., 1991—. Recipient Standing Ovation award/Outstanding Lectr. Mid-Am. Trauma Symposium, Grand Rapids, Mich., 1986. Fellow Am. Coll. Emergency Physicians (councillor Mich. chpt. 1987-90, treas. 1988-90, pres.-elect 1994-95, nat. pres. 1995—); mem. AMA, Am. Acad. Med. Adminstrs., Soc. Acad. Emergency Medicine, Mich. State Med. Soc., Washtenaw County Med. Soc. Home: 1850 Washtenaw Ann Arbor MI 48104 Office: Emergency Physicians Med Group 2000 Green Rd # 300 Ann Arbor MI 48105

HENRY, HECTOR HIMEL, II, pediatric urologist; b. Charlotte, N.C., Oct. 26, 1940; s. Hector H. and Yvonne (Vincent) H.; m. Marjorie Temple Benbow, Apr. 27, 1992; children: Hector III, Brannan, Parr Vincent. BS in Chemistry, U. N.C., 1961; MD, Tulane U., 1965. Diplomate Am. Bd. Urology. PGY 1 Charity Hosp., New Orleans, 1965-66; PGY 2-PGY 3 Ochsner Found./Hosp., New Orleans, 1966-68; PGY 3-PGY 5 Ochsner Found., New Orleans, 1968-71; pvt. practice Cabarrus Urology, Concord, N.C., 1971-82, 83—. Contbr. articles to Jour. Urology. Bd. dirs. orthop. hosp. State of N.C., Gastonia, 1973-77, nursing home adminstrn. State of N.C., Raleigh, 1978-82, 83-86; mem. N.C. Med. Bd., Raleigh, 1986—; mem. city coun. City of Concord, N.C., 1977—; pres. Boys Club, Concord, 1977. Col. U.S. Army, 1990-91. Fellow in pediatric urology Hosp. for Sick Children, London, 1982—. Fellow ACS, Am. Acad. Pediat.; mem. Am. Urol. Assn. (Southeastern sect.), Brit. Assn. Urol. Surgeons (corres.), N.C. Med. Assn. Democrat. Office: Cabarrus Urology Clinic 102 Lake Concord Concord NC 28025

HENRY, JOSEPH LOUIS, university dean; b. New Orleans, May 2, 1924; s. Varice S. and Mabel (Mansion) H.; m. Dorothy L. Whittle, July 28, 1954 (dec. 1991); children: Joseph Louis, Ronald Maurice, Joan Alison, Leilani Cecile (Mrs. P. Smith), Peter Donald. D.D.S., Howard U., 1946; B.S., Xavier U., 1948, Sc.D., 1975; M.S., Ill. U., 1949, Ph.D., 1951; D.H.L., Ill. Coll. Optometry, 1973; M.A. (hon.), Harvard U., 1975. Diplomate Am. Bd. Oral Medicine. Instr. oral medicine Coll. Dentistry, Howard U., Washington, 1946-48, assoc. prof. oral medicine, 1951-53, supt. clinics, 1953-65, prof. oral medicine, 1958-66, dir. clinics, 1965-66, dean, 1966-75, dean emeritus, 1981—; chmn., prof. oral diagnosis and radiology Sch. Dental Medicine, Harvard U., 1975—, prof. emeritus, 1995, assoc. dean, 1978-93, interim dean, 1990-91; nat. adv. coun. dental rsch., HHS, 1991—; Joseph N. Pew Charitable Trust health prof. com. adv. panel for dent., 1991—; nat. adv. coun. on health professions edn. HHS, 1990-92, IOM Commn. on Educating Dentists for Future 1993-95, Nat. Affairs Commn., 1993—; minority audit panel mem. Clinton Health Care Program, 1993; rsch. fellow U. Ill.; extern U. Ill. Rsch. and Ednl. Hosp., Chgo., 1948-51; cons. Freedmen's Hosp., 1951—, Tuskegee VA Hosp., 1951—, Crownsville (Md.) State Hosp., 1960—; trustee Ill. Coll. Optometry, 1972—, chmn. bd. trustees, 1982-86; cons. Essex Community Coll., 1972, Roxbury Med.-Tech. Inst., 1969—, Bakers Dozen Youth Center, Project Headstart, Peace Corps, Mt. Altoe Vets. Hosp.; bd. govs. D.C. Gen. Hosp., 1971-72; mem. dental editorial award com. William J. Gies Found. Advancement Dentistry; mem. adv. panel for dentistry Pew Health Professions Commn., 1991—; mem. nat. adv. coun. for dental rsch. HHS, 1991—. Contbr. to: Optometry: Education for the Profession, 1973, Optometric Education, A Summary Report, 1973, also articles in profl. jours. Mem. White House Conf. Internat. Relations, 1965; cons. White House Conf. Employment Handicapped, 1967, Nat. Urban Coalition, 1971, Nat. Commn. on Optometry, 1971-72; sponsor Boys Town, 1955—; life mem. NAACP; sponsor Urban League, 1953—; program dir. YMCA, 1950-51; mem. St. Gabriel's PTA, 1960—; trustee D.C. div. Am. Cancer Soc., Ill. Coll. Optometry; bd. dirs. Inst. Myofunctional Therapy, 1973, Symposia and Seminars, Inc., 1974; mem. Commn. Ednl. Credit Am. Council Edn., 1974; trustee Roxbury Latin Sch.; bd. dirs. W.E.B. DuBois Inst. Harvard U. Afro-Am. Research, 1976. Served to 2d lt. ASTP, 1942-43. Recipient Student Body and Student Council Faculty award, 1964, Achievement award Howard U. Dental Coll., 1967, Wisdom award Honor, 1970, Dental Alumni award, 1971, Inter-Alumni award United Negro Coll. Fund, 197O, Pub. Service award Urban League, 1970, awards Nat. Dental Assts., 1970, awards Nat. Naval Dental Sch., 1971, awards Roxbury Med.-Tech. Inst., 1972, Founders award Nat. Optometric Assn., 1973, Triennial award Nat. Dental Assn., 1973, award services D.C. govt., 1975, AADS award, OTOD award; named Dentist of Year D.C. Dental Soc., 1973. Fellow AAAS (v.p., chmn. sect. on dentistry, mem.-at-large sect. dentistry), Internat., Am. Coll. Dentists, Royal Soc. Health; mem. Nat. Dental Assn. (Achievement award 1967, dentist of year award 1972, Presdl. award 1976), ADA (Quiz bowl champion trophy 1970, chmn. sect. periodontics ann. meeting 1976), Am. Acad. Oral Medicine (Robert T. Freeman award 1972, numerous others), Inst. Medicine, D.C. Dental Soc., Maimonides Dental Soc., Internat. Assn. Dental Research, Nat. Acad. Scis., Washington Acad. Sci., N.Y. Acad. Scis., Am. Acad. Polit. and Social Scis., Am. Assn. Tchrs. Practice Adminstrn. (pres., v.p., mem. exec. com.), Greater Washington Periodontal Soc. (pres. 197O), Am. Acad. Periodontology, AAUP, Am. Assn. Dental Schs., Acad. Dental Practice Adminstrn. (chmn. profl. liaison com. 1972), Acad. History of Dentistry, Am. Coll. Health Orgn., Howard U., U. Ill., Xavier U. alumni clubs, Sigma Xi, Alpha Eta Epsilon, Alpha Kappa Mhi Delta Mu, Chi Lambda Kappa, Omicron Kappa Upsilon. Roman Catholic. Office: Harvard U Sch Dental Med 188 Longwood Ave Boston MA 02115-5819

HENRY, KATHERINE SAVAGE, physician; b. Marietta, Ga., Aug. 30, 1944; d. James Ernest and Audrey Louise (Armstrong) Savage; BA, Birmingham-So. Coll., 1966; MD, Emory U., 1971. Intern, resident in internal medicine Ga. Bapt. Hosp., Atlanta, 1971-73; emergency room physician Baylor Med. Ctr., Dallas, 1973-74; family physician The Family Clinic, Garland, Tex., 1974; family practice medicine, Richardson, Tex., 1974—; chmn. dept. family practice Richardson Gen. Hosp., 1975; cons. health care Richardson YWCA; exec. com. Richardson Med. Ctr., 1975-78; first physician, designer health service U. Tex., Dallas, 1974-76; chairperson med. adv. com. Dallas Hospice, Inc.; asst. clin. prof. Dept. Community Medicine and Family Practice Southwestern Med. Sch. Diplomate Am. Bd. Family Practice. Columnist The Texas Woman's News. Recipient Physicians Recognition award AMA. Fellow Am. Acad. Family Physicians, Am. Coll. Cryosurgery, Am. Soc. Sports Medicine; mem. AAUW, Am. Coll. Physician Execs., Am., Tex. acads. family practice, Dallas County Med. Soc., Tex. Soc. Sports Medicine, Tex. Med. Assn., Am. Med. Women's Assn. (charter pres. Dallas chpt. 1980). Home: 16007 Ranchita Dr Dallas TX 75248-3834 Office: 721 W Arapaho Rd Ste 2 Richardson TX 75080-4155

HENRY, MICHAEL FITZROY, psychotherapist; b. Port of Spain, Trinidad, Sept. 14, 1949; came to U.S., 1970; s. Francis and Vilma R. (Haynes) H.; m. Margaret J. Baker, May 30, 1976; 1 child, Anthony. AA, Walla Walla (Wash.) C.C., 1972; BA, Whitman Coll., 1975, Whitworth Coll., 1983; PhD, Pacific Western U., 1994. Counselor Carondalet Psychiat. Ctr., Richland, Wash., 1976-78, Luth. Family Svcs., Kennewick, Wash., 1989—; pvt. practice Richland, 1989—; cons. Juvenile Justice Ctr., Kennewick, 1983—; cons., tchr. Leadership Inst. Seattle, 1991-92. Mem. NAACP, Tri Cities, Wash., 1984—. Mem. Am. Assn. Marriage and Family Therapy, Am. Counseling Assn., Nat. Assn. of Drug and Alcohol Counseling, Assn. for the Treatment of Sex Abusers, Exch. Club Am. (Mem. of Yr. award 1993). Office: 750 Swift Blvd Ste 3 Richland WA 99352-3521

HENRY, OLGA ELAINE, nursing educator, health care trainer; b. London, Ont., Can., Aug. 29, 1943; came to U.S., 1979; d. Andrej and Agafia (Schur) Olejar; m. Ronald John Chapchuk, June 4, 1965 (div. July 1980); children: Timothy Jon, Robin Anne Marie; m. Gilbert Armstrong Henry, Dec. 18, 1984; children: Douglas Richard, Valerie Jean, Pauline Michelle. RN, Atkinson Sch. Nursing, Toronto, Ont., 1965; BSN, U. Western Ont., London, 1966; MBA, cert. health svcs. adminstrn., Nova Southeastern U., Ft. Lauderdale, Fla., 1988. Cert. home health nurse, cert. corp. trainer, cert. continuing edn. provider. Dir. edn. Mississauga (Ont.) Hosp., 1974-79, North Ridge Hosp., Ft. Lauderdale, Fla., 1980-84; adminstr. Barna Inst., Inc., Ft. Lauderdale, 1984-85; coord. health care City of Ft. Lauderdale, 1985; supr. nursing Maxicare Home Health, Ft. Lauderdale, 1985-88; dir. nursing All-Care Health Svcs., Lauderhill, Fla., 1988-90, Enteral & Parenteral Support Svc., Sunrise, Fla., 1990; supr. nursing Mederi of Broward County, Inc., Coral Springs, Fla., 1991-93; coord. staff edn. Mederi of Broward County, Inc., 1993—; adj. prof. Broward C.C., Ft. Lauderdale, 1993—; cons., corp. trainer Ednl. Dynamics, Coral Springs, 1984—. Mem. South Fla. Dem. Club, Hollywood, 1996. Mem. ANA, NAFE, The Profl. Woman Spkrs. Bur., Fla. Nurses Assn., Nova Southeastern U. Sch. Bus.

Alumni Assn. (bd. dirs. Broward County chpt. 1995—). Office: Ednl Dynamics Ste 403 10343 Royal Palm Blvd Coral Springs FL 33065

HENRY, PAUL RALEIGH, physician, insurance company executive; b. Cin., Apr. 23, 1928; s. Andrew Raleigh and Margaret (Clifford) H.; m. Betty Dean, June 7, 1952; children: Diane, Stephen, Paula, R. Todd, Leslie. BA, U. Cin., 1949, MD, 1953. Diplomate Am. Bd. Family Practice. Physician Tulare (Calif.) Family Practice Med. Group; treas. Norcal Mutual Ins. Co., San Francisco, 1975—, also bd. dirs. Republican. Roman Catholic. Home: 149 E Woodward Dr Tulare CA 93274-1926 Office: Tulare Family Practice Med Group 922 N Cherry St Tulare CA 93274-2210

HENRY, RICHARD JOSEPH, JR., nursing home management executive; b. Melrose, Mass., Sept. 1, 1954; s. Richard Joseph and Janet Louise (Behrie) H.; m. Diane Marrianne Rael, June 20, 1987; children: Alaimdia, Joseph. ABA, Chattanooga Community Coll., 1976; ThB, So. Coll., Collegedale, Tenn., 1980; postgrad., George Washington U., 1980-81. Cert. nursing home adminstr. Asst. adminstr. Care More, Inc., Chattanooga, 1980-81; dir. devel./adminstrn. Macon (Ga.) Health Care Ctr., 1981-82; adminstr. Sierra Health Care Ctr., Truth or Consequence, N.Mex., 1982-84, Belen (N.Mex.) Health Care Ctr., 1984-85; asst. dir. ops./adminstrn. West Mesa Health Care Ctr., Albuquerque, 1985-86; adminstr. Hobbs (N.Mex.) Health Care Ctr., 1986-87; dir. adminstrv. svcs. Care More, Inc., Macon, 1987-88; adminstr., exec. dir. Aloha Health Care Ctr., Kaneohe, Hawaii, 1988—; sr. v.p. Aloha Mgmt. Co., Kaneohe, Hawaii, 1990-93, 1993—; registered preceptor Hawaii Adminstr.-in-Tng. Program, 1989—; sr. v.p. Aloha Mgmt. Co., 1994—. Mem. Hawaii Joint Tech. Adv. Com., Honolulu, 1989—; v.p., bd. dirs. Po'Ailani Mental Health Ctrs., Honolulu, 1989—; pub. rels. com. Kaneohe Bus. Group, 1988—. With USAF, 1972-74, USNG, 1974-78. Named Adminstr. of the Yr. Care More, Inc., 1985. Fellow Am. Coll. Health Care Adminstrs. (pres., sec. 1989-91), Hawaii Long Term Care Assn. (pres. 1992-94), Rotary (pres.-elect Windward Oahu chpt., dir. cmty. svcs. 1988—, Rotarian of Yr. award 1990, Disting. Svc. award 1995). Republican. Home: 1344 C Kamahele St Kailua HI 96734-3342 Office: Aloha Mgmt Co Ste 309 45-545 Kamehameha Hwy Kaneohe HI 96744-1943

HENSGEN, HERBERT THOMAS, medical technologist; b. Cin., May 28, 1947; s. Herbert and Carolyn Elizabeth (Stites) H. BS, U. Cin., 1973, MS, 1978; AAS, Cin. Tech. Coll., 1981. Reg. med. technologist. Grad. teaching asst. U. Cin., 1976-77; instr. Edgecliff Coll., Cin., 1977-78; tech. Our Lady of Mercy Hosp., Cin., 1979-81, med. lab. tech., 1981-84, med. technologist, 1984-86; rsch. asst. Children's Hosp. Med. Ctr., Cin., 1986—; instr. Cin. Tech. Coll., 1984-85. Contbr. article to Gen. and Comparative Endocrinology; co-author abstracts for Soc. for Pediatric Rsch., Endocrine Soc. Deacon Madisonville Bapt. Ch., Cin., 1977. Mem. Am. Soc. Clin. Pathologists, Triple Nine Soc., Am. Mensa, Ltd., N.Y. Acad. Scis. Home: 7420 Drake Rd Cincinnati OH 45243-1422 Office: Children's Hosp Med Ctr Dept Endocrinology 3333 Burnet Ave Cincinnati OH 45229-3026

HENSLER, TERRANCE, clinical engineer; b. Milw., Apr. 22, 1959; s. Robert G. and Virginia (Sullivan) H.; m. Patricia M. Stingl, July 17, 1982; children: Thomas R., Joseph P. BS in Biomed. Engring., Marquette U., Milw., 1981. Anesthesia technician Milw. County Med. Complex, 1981, biomed. equipment technician, 1981-84; mgr. clin. engring. N.C. Bapt. Hosp., Winston-Salem, 1984-86, Med. Coll. Wis., Milw., 1986-91, Children's Hosp. Wis., Milw., 1991—; med. equipment cons., Milw., 1985—. Mem. Am. Coll. Clin. Engring., Am. Soc. Hosp. Engrs., Assn. for Advancement of Med. Instrumentation. Office: Childrens Hosp of Wis PO Box 1997 9000 W Wisconsin Ave Milwaukee WI 53201-1997

HENSLEY, ROSS CHARLES, dermatologist; b. Oklahoma City, Dec. 23, 1946; s. Ralph and Winona Marie (Clark) H.; m. Melba Carol Holliman, Apr. 11, 1968; children: Jason Scott, Jeffrey Alan. BS, Southwestern State U., 1968; MD, U. Okla., 1972. Dermatologist pvt. practice, Lawton, Okla., 1978—. Maj. U.S. Army, 1976-78. Recipient Roche award U. Okla. Sch. Medicine, 1971., Florence C. Kelly award, 1972. Baptist. Office: 4417 W Gore Blvd Ste 7 Lawton OK 73505

HENSLEY, SHARON QUAN, medical education consultant; b. Chgo., Apr. 11, 1947; d. Emmett Daniel and Mary Rita (Brennan) Quan; children: Brennan, Gabe, Patrick. Student, Loyola U., Rome, 1967-68; BA, Loretto Heights Coll., Denver, 1969; BS, MBA, Am. Grad. Sch. Internat. Mgmt., Glendale, Ariz., 1971. Adj. prof. bus. studies Midland Coll., 1976-88; owner, mgr. Gooseberry Pie, Midland, Tex., 1982-87; chief ops. officer Oakwood Med. Ctr., Midland, 1989-90; dir. mktg. Primary Med. Clin., 1990-92; dir. Permian Basin Tech. Prep Consortium, 1992-95; with spl. projects Capital Area Teca-Pres/Sch.-to-Work Consortium, 1996—; initiator comprehensive wellness program. Author: Jake the Great, The American Businessman in France. Bd. dirs. Jr. Achievement, Midland, 1983-89, bus. cons., 1986-87; mem. adv. com. Midland Coll., 1986-88; pres. Trinity Parents Assn., Midland, 1989-90; bd. dirs. Dongying-Midland Sister Cities; mem. City of Midland Task Force for Ams. with Disabilities Act, 1992-93; v.p. Permian Basin Sch.-to-Work Alliance. Recipient Gov.'s Proclamation Outstanding Family, 1987; named Midland's Family of Yr., 1987. Mem. Internat. Bus. Women's Club, Women's Forum, Bull and Bear Investment Club (pres. 1981-86). Republican. Home: 2010 Princeton 6305 Bexton Cir Austin TX 78745

HENSON, BLAIR W., health facility administrator; b. Memphis, May 9, 1964; s. James C. and Cassandra E. (Ellis) H.; m. Kathryn S., July 25, 1984; children: Kohl S., Clay E. BBA, Memphis State U., 1986; MHA, St. Louis U., 1989. V.p. United Hosp. Corp., Memphis, 1989-94; pres. United Florala (Ala.), Inc., 1994—. Home: 1802 Huntington Niceville FL 32578

HENSON, KENNETH IRVIN, general surgeon; b. Winchester, Va., Nov. 2, 1962; s. J. Richard Henson and Barbara B. (Howell) Lumadue; m. Kathryn A. Garber Austin, July 5, 1986 (div. Dec. 26, 1989); m. Laura A. Zellers, June 3, 1995. BA, Bridgewater Coll., 1984; MD, Med. Coll. of Va., 1988. Diplomate Am. Bd. Surgery. Commd. 2d lt. USAF, 1985, advanced through grades to major, 1994; intern in surgery U. Tex. Health Sci. Ctr., San Antonio, 1988-89, residency in gen. surgery, 1989-93; staff surgeon 51st Med. Group, Osan AFB, Korea, 1993-94, 96th Med. Group, Eglin AFB, Fla., 1994-96; assoc. Wampler, White and Farr, Ltd., Manassas, Va., 1996—; chmn. Infection Control Com., Eglin AFB, 1994-96. Maj. USAF, 1985—. Fellow ACS (assoc.); mem. J. Bradley Aust Surg. Soc., Pensacola Surg. Soc. Methodist. Home: 308 Falmouth St Warrenton VA 22186 Office: Wampler, White and Farr, Ltd 8709 Digges Rd Manassas VA 22110

HENSON, O'DELL WILLIAMS, JR., anatomy educator; b. Kansas City, Mo., Jan. 11, 1934; s. O'Dell Williams and Natalie (Smith) H.; m. Miriam Morgan, Aug. 1, 1964; 1 child, Phillip William. BA, U. Kans., 1957, MA, 1960; PhD, Yale U., 1964. From instr. to assoc. prof. Dept. Anatomy, Yale U., New Haven, 1964-74; prof. Dept. Cell Biology and Anatomy U. N.C., Chapel Hill, 1974—. Chmn. Commn. Anatomy, N.C., 1982—. Recipient Phi Sigma award 1960, Alexander Von Humbolt award 1982, Cen. Carolina Bank Excellence in Teaching award 1982, NIH-Nat. Inst. Deafness and Other Communicative Disorders Claude Pepper award, 1989. Fellow AAAS. Home: 317 Reade Rd Chapel Hill NC 27516-1509 Office: U NC Dept Cell Biology and Anatomy Taylor Hall CB 7090 Chapel Hill NC 27599

HENTGES, DAVID JOHN, microbiology educator; b. LeMars, Iowa, Sept. 18, 1928; s. Romaine Francis and Geneva Mae (Kruger) H.; m. Kathleen Edwina Mullan, Dec. 28, 1957; children: Stephen Edward, Kathleen Marie, Margaret Ann. BS, U. Notre Dame, 1953; MS, Loyola U., Chgo., 1958, PhD, 1961. Asst. prof. Creighton U. Sch. Medicine, Omaha, 1964-67, assoc. prof., 1967-68; assoc. prof. U. of Mo. Sch. of Medicine, Columbia, 1968-72, prof., 1972-81, interim chmn., 1976-79; prof., chmn. Tex. Tech. U. Sch. Medicine, Lubbock, 1981-96, vice provost for rsch., dean grad. sch. biomed. scis., assoc. dean basic scis., 1996—; interim dean grad. programs and vice provost rsch. Tex. Tech. U. Health Scis. Ctr., Lubbock, 1996—. Editor: Human Intestinal Microflora, 1983, Medical Microbiology, 1986—, Microbiology and Immunology, 2d edit., 1995; regional editor Microbial Ecology in Health and Disease, 1987—; editorial bd. Infection and Immunity, 1983-92; contbr. chpts. to books and articles to profl. jours. Lay gen. chmn. Diocesan Cath. Appeal, Lubbock, 1989, steering com., 1985—. Named Knight Comdr., Order of the Holy Sepulchre, 1995. Fellow Am. Acad. of Microbiology; mem. Am. Soc. Microbiology, Assn. for Gnotobiotics, Soc. for Microbial Ecology and Dis. (pres. 1987-89), Serra Internat. (dist. gov. 1987-88, Serran of Yr. 1988), Sigma Xi. Republican. Roman Catholic. Home: 4601 88th St Lubbock TX 79424-4107 Office: Tex Tech U Health Sci Ctr Dept Microbiology Lubbock TX 79430

HENTSCHEL, UWE, psychology educator; b. Greifswald, Pommern, Germany, Jan. 23, 1940; arrived in The Netherlands, 1987; s. Wilhelm Rudolf and Elsa (Anderson) H.; m. Henriette Streffer, Oct. 19, 1962 (div. June 1987); children: Caterin, Ludger; m. Marleen van der Voort, Sept. 16, 1987; children: Mayke, Anouk. Diploma in psychology, U. Giessen, Fed. Republic Germany, 1964; Dr. Philosophy, U. Freiburg, Fed. Republic Germany, 1969; postdoctoral, U. Mainz, Fed. Republic Germany, 1977; Doctorate (hon.), U. Tbilisi, Republic of Georgia, 1995. Researcher Marplan, Frankfurt, Fed. Republic Germany, 1965-67; research dir. McCann, Hamburg, Fed. Republic Germany, 1971; research asst. Max Planck Inst. for Psychiatry, Munich, 1974-75; asst. prof. U. Mainz, 1975-81, prof., 1981-87; prof., head dept. psychology of personality Rijksuniversiteit te Leiden, The Netherlands, 1987—. Editor: Experimentelle Persönlichkeitspsychologie, 1980, Persönlichkeitsmerkmale und Familienstruktur, 1984, The Roots of Perception, 1986, Experimental Research in Psychosomatics, 1993, The Concept of Defense Mechanisms in Contemporary Psychology, 1993; contbr. articles to profl. jours. Research grantee Deutsche Forschungsgemeinschaft, Lund, Sweden, 1972-73. Fellow Internat. Coll. Psychosomatic Medicine; mem. Deutsche Gesellschaft für Psychologie, Soc. for Psychotherapy Rsch., Gesellschaft zur Förderung persönlichkeits-und sozialpsychologischer Forschung (chmn. 1984). Office: Rijksuniversiteit te Leiden, Wassenaarseweg 52, 2333 AK Leiden The Netherlands

HENTZ, VINCENT R., surgeon; b. Jacksonville, Fla., Aug. 29, 1942. MD, U. Fla., 1968. Intern Stanford (Calif.) Hosp., 1968-69, resident in plastic surgery, 1969-74, now hand surgeon; fellow in hand surgery Roosevelt Hosp., N.Y.C., 1974-75. Office: Stanford Univ Dept Hand Surgery 900 Blake Wilbur Dr Palo Alto CA 94304-2205*

HENZ, BEATE MARIA, dermatologist, educator; b. Bochum, Germany, Feb. 12, 1941; d. Alfred H. and Emma H. (Stadler) C. BS, Barat Coll., Lake Forest, Ill., 1966; MD, Marquette U., Milw., 1970. Intern and resident dermatology Met. Gen. Hosp., Cleve., 1970-74; fellow allergy and immunology Johns Hopkins U., Balt., 1974-76; Humboldt fellow immunology U. Mainz, Germany, 1976-77; dermatologist U. Munster, Germany, 1977-86; dir. clin. rsch. dermatology Hoffmann La Roche, Basel, Switzerland, 1986-90; prof. dept. dermatology Virchow Clinic, Humboldt Univ. Berlin, Germany, 1990—. Author: Urticaria, 1986; contbr. articles to profl. jours. Office: Humboldt U Berlin Hautklinik G Virchow Clinic, Augustenburger Platz 1, D 13353 Berlin Germany

HEPNER, BETTY SHORE, social worker; b. Pitts., Mar. 29, 1927; children: Jane, Allen. BS, U. Pitts., 1948, MSW, 1950. Dir. vol. action ctr. United Way, Pitts., 1970-83; cons. John J. Kane Hosp., Pitts., 1983-84, Presbyn. Assn. on Aging, Pitts., 1988; exec. dir. Self Help Group Network, Inc., Pitts., 1983—; field instr. sch. social work U. Pitts. Contbr. articles to profl. jours. Chairperson consumer adv. bd. Peoples Natural Gas Co., Pitts., 1986. Recipient Salute in Volunteerism Triangle Corner, Ltd., 1982; named one of six women chosen to tape 60-second vignettes in celebration of Women's History month (Mar.), Greater Pitts. Commn. for Women, 1992. Mem. NASW (div. chairperson Pa. chpt. 1984-89, Social Worker of Yr. award SW Pa. chpt. 1992), Pa. Assn. for Volunteerism (Harriet Naylor Meml. award 1987), Acad. Cert. Social Workers, U. Pitts. Sch. Social Work Alumni Assn. (Disting. Alumna award 1995). Office: Self Help Group Network 1323 Forbes Ave Ste 200 Pittsburgh PA 15219-4725

HEPTINSTALL, ROBERT HODGSON, physician; b. Keswick, Eng., July 22, 1920; s. James A. and Mabel (Sanders) H.; m. Ann Enraght Porter, Jan. 25, 1950; children: Bridget, Gillian, Jonathan, James, Caroline, Christopher. MB, BS, London U., 1944, MD, 1948. Intern, house surgeon Charing Cross Hosp., London, 1944; jr. lectr. pathology St. Mary's Hosp., London, 1947-50, sr. lectr. pathology, 1950-60; vis. prof. pathology Washington U., St. Louis, 1960-62; assoc. prof. pathology Johns Hopkins Med. Sch., Balt., 1962-67, prof. pathology, 1967-69, 88—, Baxley prof. pathology, dir. dept., 1969-88; pathologist in chief Johns Hopkins Hosp., 1969-88; disting. svc. prof. pathology, 1992—; pathology study sect. NIH, 1963-67, pathology tng. com., 1967-71; sci. adv. bd. Nat. Kidney Found., 1969-73. Author: Pathology of the Kidney, 1966, 4th edit., 1991; editor Lab. Invest, 1976-81; mem. editorial bd. Kidney Internat., Lab Investigation. Served with M.C., Royal Army, 1944-47. Recipient gold medal Danish Surg. Soc., 1984, David M. Hume Meml. award Nat. Kidney Found., 1986. Mem. Am. Assn. Pathologists, Internat. Acad. Pathology, Renal Assn., Am. Soc. Nephrology (pres. 1972-73, Joh P. Peters award 1993), Internat. Soc. Nephrology (v.p. 1981-84). Office: Johns Hopkins Hosp Dept Pathology Baltimore MD 21205

HERB, EDMUND MICHAEL, optometrist, educator; b. Zanesville, Ohio, Oct. 9, 1942; s. Edmund G. and Barbara R. (Michael) H.; divorced; children—Sara, Andrew; m. Jeri Herb. O.D., Ohio State U., 1966. Pvt. practice optometry, Buena Vista, Colo., 1966—; past prof. Timberline campus Colo. Mountain Coll.; past clin. instr. Ohio State U. Sch. Optometry. Mem. Am. Optometric Assn., Colo. Optometric Assn. Home: 16395 Mt Princeton Rd Buena Vista CO 81211-9505 Office: 115 N Tabor St Buena Vista CO 81211 also: Leadville Colorado Med Ctr Leadville CO 80461

HERBER, STEVEN CARLTON, physician; b. L.A., Aug. 25, 1960; s. Raymond and Marilyn Joyce (Dart) H.; m. Katherine Carol Jones, Apr. 23, 1989. BS, Pacific Union Coll., 1982; Dr.med., Loma Linda U., 1986. Diplomate Nat. Bd. Med. Examiners, 1987. Resident surgeon Med. Ctr. Loma Linda (Calif.) U., 1986-90; resident plastic surgery Yale U., New Haven, Conn., 1990-92; asst. prof. surgery Loma Linda (Calif.) U., 1993—. Contbr. articles to profl. jours. NIH grantee, 1988, MacPherson Soc. Clin. Sci. fellow, 1992; recipient Leadership award, AMA, 1991. Mem. ACS, Am. Soc. Plastic and Reconstructive Surgeons, Am. Cleft Palate, Craniofacial Assn., Calif. Med. Assn., San Bernardino County Med. Soc. Republican. Adventist. Office: Loma Linda Univ 11118 Anderson St Loma Linda CA 92354

HERBERS, JEROME EDWARD, JR., internist; b. Memphis, May 17, 1953. BA, Johns Hopkins U., 1975; MD, U. Tenn., Memphis, 1979. Diplomate Am. Bd. Internal Medicine, Am. Bd. Geriatrics. Commd. as capt. U.S. Army, 1979, advanced through grades to lt. col., 1992; intern Walter Reed Army Med. Ctr., 1979-80, resident in internal medicine, 1980-82; fellowship in gen. internal medicine Walter Reed Army Med. Ctr. and Uniformed Svcs. U., 1985-87; chief gen. internal medicine svc. Walter Reed Army Med. Ctr., Washington, 1992-95; resigned, 1995; asst. chief med. svc. VA Med. Ctr., Washington, 1995—; assoc. prof. medicine Uniformed Svcs. U., 1992—, Georgetown U., 1995—. Fellow ACP; mem. Soc. Gen. Internal Medicine. Office: VA Med Ctr Med Svc (111) 50 Irving St NW Washington DC 20422

HERBERT, FRANK LEONARD, dentist educator; b. New Orleans, Dec. 18, 1926; s. Frank Leonard and Dorothy Mary (Klein) H.; m. Rita Maria Winter, May 27, 1950; children: Stephanie Lee, Susan Marie, Edward Francis, Frank L. Jr., Robert Frederick, Martin Winter. DDS, Loyola U., 1948. Lic. dentist, La. Dental intern Charity Hosp. of La., New Orleans, 1948-49; dental officer USN, 1949-54; staff dentist S.E. La. Hosp., Mandeville, 1954-55; dentist pvt. practice Jefferson Parish, La., 1954-61; pediatric dentist pvt. practice Jefferson Parish, 1961-79; clin. asst. prof. Loyola U. Sch. Dentistry, New Orleans, 1964-69; clin. asst. prof. La. State U. Sch. Dentistry, New Orleans, 1970-72, assoc. prof., 1979-87, prof., 1987—. Co-author: The Answer Book, 1984, (book chpt.) Clinical Dentistry, 1987; co-author, editor: (videotape) Child Abuse Alert, 1981; contbr. articles to profl. jours. Mem. Ad Hoc Planning Com. to Establish East Jefferson Gen. Hosp., Jefferson Parish, 1967; founding trustee St. Mary Magdalen Cath. Parish, Jefferson Parish, 1955. Fellow Internat. Coll. Dentists (regent 1981-87), Am. Coll. Dentists, Pierre Fouchard Acad.; mem. ADA, Am. Acad. Dental Practice Adminstrn. (pres. 1979-80), Am. Soc. Dentistry for Children (pres. 1984-85, ASDC "Great" 1990), La. Soc. Dentistry for Children (pres. 1961), La. Dental Assn. (Disting. Svc. award 1995), La. Acad. Pediatric Dentistry (pres. 1977), New Orleans Dental Assn. (pres. 1975, Honor Dentist award 1993), Blue Key Frat. Republican. Roman Catholic. Office: La State U Sch Dentistry Box 127 1100 Florida Ave New Orleans LA 70119

HERBERT, JAMES DALTON, psychology educator; b. Alice, Tex., June 20, 1962; s. Jim Dalton and Gracye Lee (Cates) H.; m. Ruth M. Weisberg, May 20, 1995; children: Aaron J., Talia G., Sylvia L., Elliott B. BA, U. Tex., 1983; MA, U. N.C., Greensboro, 1986, PhD, 1989. Lic. psychologist, Pa. Rsch. asst. U. N.C., Greensboro, 1983-88, asst. dir. Psychology Clinic, 1987-88; psychology intern Beth Israel Med. Ctr., N.Y.C., 1988-89; asst. prof. psychiatry Med. Coll. Pa., Phila., 1989-93, co-dir. Behavior Therapy clinic, 1989-93; dir. psychol./student mental health svcs., asst. prof. Allegheny U., Phila., 1993—. Contbr. articles to profl. jours. Rsch. grantee Sigma Xi, 1988. Mem. Am. Psychol. Assn. (Dissertation grantee 1988), Am. Psychol. Soc., Assn. for Advancement Behavior Therapy, Am. Assn. Applied and Preventive Psychology, Phila. Behavior Therapy Assn. (mem.-at-large 1990—, exec. bd.), Phi Beta Kappa, Psi Chi. Home: 1029 Montgomery Ave Narberth PA 19072-1804 Office: Allegheny Univ Mail Stop 988 Broad And Vine St Philadelphia PA 19104

HERBIN, JOSEPH T., physician; b. Forest City, Pa., May 20, 1937; s. Michael and Anna (Pauley) H.; m. Marilyn Smith, Apr. 12, 1969; children: Sarah, Rachel, Melissa, Catherine. BS, Duquesne U., 1959; MD, U. Zürich, Switzerland, 1965. Diplomate in geriat. medicine Am. Bd. Internal Medicine. Intern St. Vincent Hosp., Bridgeport, Conn., 1966-67; med. resident St. Vincent Hosp., Bridgeport, 1967-70; fellow in infectious diseases U. Vt., Burlington, 1970-71; pvt. practice, 1971—; active staff St. Vincent's Med. Ctr., 1971, chmn. med./nursing svc. liaison com., 1973-75, infection control com., 1975—, chief divsn. infectious disease, 1975—, exec. com., 1985-86; courtesy staff Bridgeport Hosp., 1971—; asst. clin. prof. medicine Yale U. Sch. Medicine, New Haven, Conn., 1981—; med. dir. Cambridge Manor, Fairfield, Conn., 1989—. Contbr. articles to profl. jours. Mem. ACP, AMA, Am. Soc. for Microbiology, Am. Geriat. Soc., Infectious Diseases Soc. Am., Conn. State Med. Assn., Fairfield County Med. Assn. Office: 2228 Black Rock Tpke Fairfield CT 06430

HERBST, ARTHUR LEE, obstetrician, gynecologist; b. N.Y.C., Sept. 14, 1931; s. Jerome Richard and Blanche (Vatz) H.; m. Lee Ginsburg, Aug. 10, 1958. A.B. magna cum laude, Harvard Coll., 1953, M.D. cum laude, 1959. Diplomate Am. Bd. Ob-gyn. (bd. dirs. 1985-93, dir. div. gynecol. oncology 1989-91). Intern Mass. Gen. Hosp., Boston, 1959-60; resident Mass. Gen. Hosp., 1960-62; resident in obstetrics and gynecology Boston Hosp. for Women, 1962-65; instr., assoc. prof. obstetrics-gynecology Mass. Gen. Hosp. and Harvard U. Med. Sch., Boston, 1965-76; Joseph B. DeLee prof. obstetrics and gynecology U. Chgo., 1976-84; chmn. dept. obstetrics-gynecology Chgo. Lying In Hosp., 1976—; Joseph B. DeLee Disting. Service prof. U. Chgo., 1984—; chmn. exec. com. U. Chgo. Hosps. and Clinics, 1980-84; dir. Dentsply Internat. Mem. editorial bd. Jour. Gynecol. Oncology; contbr. articles to profl. jours. Fellow Royal Coll. Obstetricians and Gynecologists (hon.), Inst. Med., Nat. Acad. Scis.; mem. AMA, ACS, Am. Coll. Obstetricians and Gynecologists, Am. Gynecol. and Obstet. Soc., Am. Assn. Profs. Ob-Gyn, Ctrl. Assn. Obstetricians and Gynecologists, Chgo. Gynecologists Soc., Soc. Pelvic Surgeons, Endocrine Soc., Infertility Soc., Soc. Gynecologic Oncologists. Fellow Royal Coll. Obstetricians and Gynecologists; mem. AMA, ACS, NAS (Inst. of Medicine), Am. Coll. Obstetricians and Gynecologists, Am. Gynecol. and Obstet. Soc., Am. Assn. Profs. Ob-Gyn., Ctrl. Assn. Obstetricians and Gynecologists, Chgo. Gynecologic Soc., Soc. Pelvic Surgeons, Endocrine Soc., Infertility Soc., Soc. Gynecologic Oncologists. Home: 1234 N State Pky Chicago IL 60610-2219 Office: U Chgo Med Ctr 5841 S Maryland Ave Chicago IL 60637-1463

HERBST, JOHN JOSEPH, pediatric gastroenterologist; b. Cin., July 18, 1935; s. Harry George and Frances (Brueggemann) H.; m. Diana, June 10, 1961; children: John J. Jr., Melissa Ann. BS, Xavier U., 1957; MD, St. Louis U. Sch. Medicine, 1961. Diplomate Am. Bd. Pediatrics, Bd. Pediatric Gastroenterology. Intern, resident pediatrics Cin. Gen. Hosp., 1961-64; lt. cmdr. USPHS Indian Health Svc., Phoenix, 1964-66; fellow in pediat. gastroenterology Stanford U., Palo Alto, Calif., 1966-69; from asst. prof. to prof. Utah Med. Ctr., Salt Lake City, 1969-85; prof. La. State Med. Ctr., Shreveport, 1985—. Vice chmn. Nat. Cystic Fibrosis Found., Bethesda, Md., 1981-83, chmn., 1984-86, med. adv. coun., 1984-86. Mem. Am. Soc. Gastroenterology, Am. Pediat. Soc., Soc. Pediat. Rsch., So. Soc. Pediat. Rsch., N.Am. Soc. Pediat. Gastroenterology. Roman Catholic. Office: LSUMC Dept Pediat 1501 Kings Hwy Shreveport LA 71130

HERD, JOHN KENNETH, pediatrics educator; b. New Brunswick, N.J., Jan. 12, 1929; s. Edmund John Moffat and Edith Marion (Venn) H.; m. Kathryn Estelle Mitchell, Mar 3, 1956 (dic. Sept. 1989); children: Jeffrey Brian, Daniel Gordon, Barbara Allison. BS, Rutgers U., 1950; MD, Cornell U., 1954. Pediatric intern U. Rochester, N.Y., 1954-55, asst. resident pediatrics, 1955-56, assoc. resident pediatrics, 1959-60, postdoctoral fellow, 1960-63; asst. resident pathology in pediatrics Babies Hosp., N.Y.C.; asst. pathologist Columbia U. Coll. Physicians and Surgeons, N.Y.C., 1956-57; asst. prof. pediatrics, Buswell fellow SUNY, Buffalo, 1963-67, rsch. asst. prof. pediatrics, 1969-72; spl. NIH fellow pediatrics U. Chgo., 1967-69, assoc. prof. pediatrics Creighton U., Omaha, 1972-76, prof. pediatrics, 1976-78; prof. pediatrics East Tenn. State U., Johnson City, 1978—; apptd. grad. faculty East Tenn. State U., Johnson City, 1983-89, adj. prof. biophysics, 1985-89; vis. clin. fellow in pediatric rheumatology New Enland Med. Ctr. Hosps., Boston, 1989; cons. in field. Contbr. articles to profl. jours. Chmn. med. adv. com. Nebr. chpt. Arthritis Found., 1974-76, mem. governing bd., N.Y.C., 1975-76. Served to capt. M.C., U.S. Army, 1957-59. Recipient Bausch & Lomb Sci. award, 1946, Rutgers U. Oakley Van der Poel prize, 1950; Arthritis and Rheumatism Found. postdoctoral fellow, 1960-63, NIH spl. fellow, 1967-69; NIAMD grantee, 1972-75, others. Fellow Am. Acad. Pediatrics, Am. Coll. Rheumatism (formerly Am. Rheumatism Assn., founding fellow); mem. AAUP, AAAS, Midwest Soc. Pediatric Research, Soc. Complex Carbohydrates, Tissue Culture Assn., Omaha Midwest Clin. Soc., Fedn. Am. Scientists, Soc. for Exptl. Biology and Medicine, N.Y. Acad. Sci., Sigma Xi. Democrat. Home: 715 Judith Dr Johnson City TN 37604-1924 Office: E Tenn State U Dept Pediatrics PO Box 70578 Johnson City TN 37614-0578

HERD, PAUL, physician; b. Albany, N.Y., Nov. 19, 1941; s. Jack Morris and Yetta Herd; m. Norma Herd; children: Tessa, Leah. BA, Syracuse U., 1963; PhD, UCLA, 1970; MD, Brown U., 1978. Diplomate in internal medicine and geriatrics Am. Bd. Internal Medicine. Intern, resident in medicine Emory U. Hosps., Atlanta, 1978-81; internist in pvt. practice Atlanta, 1981—; med. dir. Canterbury Ct. Nursing Facility, Atlanta, 1993—, Hosp. Vascular Lab., Atlanta, 1989—. Mem. AAAS, ACP, Am. Soc. Internal Medicine, Am. Geriatric Soc. Home: 2687 Briarlake Woods Way NE Atlanta GA 30345-3905

HERDEG, HOWARD BRIAN, physician; b. Buffalo, Oct. 14, 1929; s. Howard Bryan and Martha Jean (Williams) H.; m. Beryl Ann Fredricks, July 21, 1955; children: Howard Brian III, Erin Ann Kociela. Student Paul Smith's Coll., 1947-48, U. Buffalo, 1948-50, Canisius Coll., 1949; DO, Phila. Coll. Osteopathic Medicine, 1954; MD, U. Calif.-Irvine Coll. Medicine, 1962. Diplomate Am. Acad. Pain Mgmt. Intern, Burbank (Calif.) Hosp., 1954-55; practice medicine specializing in gen. medicine, surgery and pain mgmt., Woodland Hills, Calif., 1956—; chief med. staff West Park Hosp., Canoga Park, Calif., 1971-72, trustee, 1971-73; chief family practice dept. West Hills Regional Med. Center (formerly Humana Hosp. West Hills, 1982-83, 84-85, 88-89), mem. exec. com., 1984-85, 88-89, Mem. Hidden Hills (Calif.) Pub. Safety Commn., 1978-82; bd. dirs. Hidden Hills Community Assn., 1971-73, pres., 1972; bd. dirs. Hidden Hills Homeowners Assn., 1973-75, pres., 1976-77; bd. dirs. Woodland Hills Freedom Season, 1961-67, pres., 1962; mem. Hidden Hills City Council, 1984—, mayor pro tem, 1987-90, mayor, 1990-92. Recipient disting. service award Woodland Hills Jr C. of C., 1966. Mem. Woodland Hills C. of C. (dir. 1959-68, pres. 1967), Theta Chi, Gamma Pi. Republican. Home: 24530 Deep Well Rd Hidden Hills CA 91302-1210 Office: 22600 Ventura Blvd Woodland Hills CA 91364-1414

HERDEWIJN, PIET ANDRÉ MAURITS MARIA, medicinal chemistry educator; b. Aalst, Belgium, Sept. 18, 1954; s. Maurits and Julia (Snoeck) H. Grad., St. Jozef Coll., Aalst, 1972; Pharm. Degree, U. Leuven, Belgium, 1977, PhD, 1981, Dr.Sci., 1990. Rsch. asst. Nat. Funds Scientific Rsch., 1977-81, sr. rsch. asst., 1982-84, rsch. assoc., 1984-90, sr. rsch. assoc., 1990; lectr. Cath. U. Leuven, 1984-90, assoc. prof., 1990-93, prof., 1993—; assoc. prof. State U. Ghent, 1988—. Contbr. articles to profl. jours. Lt. Belgium Air Force, 1982-83. A. Von Humboldt fellow, 1984-85, 88; recipient Van Dyck award, 1990, Smith-Kline Beecham award, 1995. Mem. Royal Acad. Medicine. Office: Rega Inst, Minderbroedersstraat 10, 3000 Leuven Belgium

HERIC, BLAINE RICHARD, surgeon; b. London, Oct. 27, 1956; s. William John and Kathleen Norah (Morris) H. BS, Stanford U., 1979; MD, Cornell U., 1982. Diplomate Am. Bd. Surgery, Am. Bd. Thoracic Surgery. Commd. 2d lt. U.S. Army, 1982, advanced through grades to lt. col., 1988; intern Walter Reed Army Med. Ctr., Washington, 1983-83, gen. surgery resident, 1983-87; staff gen. surgeon Frankfurt (Fed. Republic Germany) Army Med. Ctr., 1987-90; clin. asst. prof. surgery Uniformed Svcs. U. of Health Scis., Bethesda, Md., 1987—; resident in cardiothoracic surgery, Cleve. Clinic Found., 1990-93; staff cardiothoracic surgeon, Madigan Army Med. Ctr., Tacoma, 1993—, chief cardiothoracic surgery svc. Contbr. articles to profl. publs. Scholar, Kilworth Found., 1974, William H. Nichols Found., 1977. Fellow Internat. Coll. Surgeons; mem. ACS. Republican. Episcopalian. Home: 4806 Old Stump Dr NW Gig Harbor WA 98332 Office: Cardiothoracic Surgery Svc Madigan AMC Tacoma WA 98431

HERIS, TONI, psychologist, psychotherapist; b. Chgo., Feb. 28, 1932; d. Nicholas John and Mildred (Mangani) H.; m. Stan Harrison, Aug. 25, 1972. BA, Queens Coll., N.Y.C., 1954; MA, NYU, 1981, PhD, 1987, postdoc., 1990—. Lic. psychologist, N.Y. Advt. cons./writer N.Y.C., 1971-86; career counselor NYU, N.Y.C., 1979-88; staff psychotherapist Ctr. for Marital & Family Therapy, N.Y.C., 1985-88; asst. prof. Baruch Coll., N.Y.C., 1988-93; pvt. practice psychology N.Y.C., 1987—; dir. career devel. Nat. Inst. for the Psychotherapies, N.Y.C., 1987—. Mem. Am. Psychol. Assn., Am. Assn. Counseling, Kappa Delta Pi.

HERMAN, BRUCE CHARLES, internist, geriatrician; b. Des Moines, Nov. 17, 1950; s. Murray and Evelyn (Gruenberg) H.; m. Laurie Lynn Frenkel, Dec. 23, 1979; children: Benjamin, Jonathan, Rachel. BA with honors, U. Wis., Milw., 1973; MD, Med. Coll. Wis., 1977. Diplomate Am. Bd. Internal Medicine, Am. Bd. Geriatric Medicine; cert. BCLS, ACLS. Physician Mequon-Thiensville (Wis.) Med. Clinic, 1980-83; ptnr. physician Ozaubee Med. Ctr., Thiensville, 1983—; dir. Arthritis Ctr. Sports Medicine and Knee Surgery Clinic, Milw., 1987-92; cons. CHIRON-Rehab., Madison, Wis., 987—, Blue Cross/Blue Shield, Milw., 1996—; chmn. sect. gen. medicine St. Michael Hosp., Milw., 1990-94; exam. reviewer Am. Bd. Internal Medicine. Mem. exec. com. Milw. Jewish Coun., 1995—; v.p. Zionist Orgn. Am., Milw., 1990—, Congregation Anshe Sfard, Milw., 1980-83. Recipient AMA commendation, 1993. Fellow ACP. Office: Ozaukee Med Ctr 407 N Main St Thiensville WI 53091

HERMAN, CARL DAVID, psychiatrist; b. Phila., May 12, 1931; s. Albert and Sadye (Jaspan) H.; m. Florence Sokoloff, June 7, 1953; children: Sheri Herman Karr, Lisa Abramowitz. BA, U. Pa., 1952; MD, U. Buffalo, 1957. Diplomate Am. Bd. Psychiatry and Neurology. Internship Albert Einstein Med. Ctr., Phila., 1957-58, residency, 1960-61, attending psychiatrist, 1961—; residency Norristown (Pa.) State Hosp., 1958-60; staff psychiatrist Moss Rehab. Hosp., Phila., 1961—; clin. asst. prof. Sch. of Medicine Temple U., Phila., 1968—; pres. med. staff Moss Rehab. Hosp., Phila., 1979-81. Contbr. articles to profl. jours. Mem. Am. Psychiat. Assn., Nat. Rehab. Assn. Democrat. Jewish. Office: Moss Rehab Hosp 1200 W Tabor Rd Philadelphia PA 19141-3019

HERMAN, DAVID JAY, orthodontist; b. Rome, N.Y., Oct. 4, 1954; s. Maurice Joseph and Bettina S. (Stiener) H.; m. Mary Beth Appleberry, Apr. 11, 1976; children: Jeremiah D., Kellin A. BA in Biology, San Jose State U., 1976; DDS, Emory U., 1981; MS in Orthodontics, U. N.C., 1992, MPH, 1992. Comdr. USPHS, 1990; advanced gen. practice resident Gallup (N. Mex.) Indian Med. Ctr., 1983-84; clin. service specialist Ames Co., Santa Clara, Calif., 1976-77; service unit dental chief Keams Canyon (Ariz.) Service Unit USPHS Indian Health Service, 1981-82; staff dental officer Crownpoint (N. Mex.) Service Unit, 1982-83; service unit dental program chief Winslow (Ariz.) Service Unit, 1984-86; Navajo area dental br. chief Window Rock, Ariz., 1986-89; mem. grad. residency com. U. N.C., Chapel Hill, 1990-91; Navajo area orthodontic specialist Shiprock, N. Mex., 1992—; mem. health adv. bd. Navajo Reservation Headstart, 1986-89; health promotion/disease prevention cons. USPHS-Indian Health Svc. Navajo Area, Window Rock, 1986-89; cons. Ariz. IHS Periodontal Health Task Force, 1986-90. Asst. wrestling coach Winslow (Ariz.) H.S., 1984-86, Gallup High Sch., 1987-89, Chapel Hill H.S., 1991-92, Farmington H.S., 1992—; mem. Farmington Youth Wrestling Program, 1992—. Recipient Healthy Mothers/Healthy Babies Disease Prevention award, 1988, USPHS Achievement medal, 1985, Headstart Achievement award, 1989, Ariz. Pub. Health Assn. Hon. award, 1989; Nat. Health Svc. Corp. scholar Emory U., 1977-81. Mem. ADA, Am. Assn. Pub. Health Dentists, Commd. Officers Assn., Am. Assn. Orthodontists, Rocky Mountain Soc. Orthodontists, Navajo Area Dental Soc. (pres. 1985), Am. Assn. Dental Rsch., Am. Assn. Mil. Orthodontists (sec.-treas. 1992, v.p. 1993-94, pres. 1995—).

HERMAN, KENNETH, psychologist; b. Englewood, N.J., Mar. 4, 1927; s. Joseph and Rose (Sattenstein) H.; m. Benita Saievetz, June 7, 1959; children: Michael Robert, Deborah Lynn, Joseph Todd, Rebecca Jane. A.B., Fla. So. Coll., 1950; M.Ed., Boston U., 1952; Ed.D., Columbia U., 1955, N.Y. U., 1956. Diplomate Am. Bd. Clin. Psychology; cert. sex therapist; fellow Acad. Clin. Psychology. Research Bergen County Dept. Probation, Hackensack, N.J., 1948; investigator Child Welfare Home, Hackensack, 1948; psychometrist Student Clinic, Fla. So. Coll., Lakeland, 1948-50; clin. psychologist Mass. Gen. Hosp., Boston, 1951-54; research psychologist Med. Sch., Harvard, 1952-53; psychologist Speech Clinic, Boston U., 1952-53; research asst. State U. Iowa, 1954; founder Psychol. Service Center, Teaneck, N.J., 1955; dir. Psychol. Service Center, 1955—; dir. Reading Clinic, Child Study Center, 1965-66; chmn. bd., pres. Child Growth and Devel. Corp., 1969. Contbr. articles to profl. jours. Dir. Antipoverty Program, Garfield, N.J., 1965-66; bd. examiners Internat. Assn. Counseling Services, 1973-80; dir. Center Sexual and Relationship Enrichment, 1978—, Psycom Corp., 1980, 2d Self Discovery Program, 1980; cons. Hackensack Juvenile Counseling Program, 1974-76, N.Y. and N.J. Council of Chs., 1979—, participant radio and TV programs. Served with AUS, 1945-46. Mem. Am. Soc. Clin. Hypnosis, Soc. Clin. Exptl. Hypnosis, N.J. Personnel and Guidance Assn., Eastern Psychol. Assn., N.J. Clin. Psychologists, Nat. Council on Family Relations, Bergen County Sch. Psychologists Assn., Psychologists Interested in Advancement Psychotherapy, Am. Group Psychotherapy Assn., Psychologists Interested in Pvt. Practice, Am. Assn. Sex Educators, Counselors and Therapists, Nat. Vocat. Guidance Assn., Acad. Psychologist Marital Counseling, Am. Personnel and Guidance Assn., Am. Speech and Hearing Assn., N.J. Speech Assn., Tau Epsilon Phi, Kappa Delta Pi, Pi Gamma Mu, Omicron Delta Kappa. Home: 342 Orchard Rd Wyckoff NJ 07481-2208 Office: 175 Cedar Ln Teaneck NJ 07666-4315

HERMAN, MARTIN NEAL, neurologist, educator; b. Washington, July 19, 1939; s. Karl and Zina (Bratt) H.; m. Sydney Beryl Epstein, July 1, 1962; children: Kenneth Dayan, Heidi Felice. AA, George Washington U., 1960; BS, Northwestern U., 1961, MD, 1964. Diplomate Am. Bd. Electroencephalography, Am. Bd. Psychiatry and Neurology, Nat. Bd. Med. Examiners; lic. N.J. Intern Georgetown U./D.C. Gen. Hosp., Washington, 1964; resident psychiatry U. Rochester (N.Y.)/Strong Meml. Hosp., 1964; resident neurology U. Va., Charlottesville, 1967-70; rsch. fellow clin. neurophysiology NIH, Bethesda, Md., 1970-71; asst. prof., dir. electroencephalography N.J. Coll. Medicine and Dentistry, Newark, 1971-74; dir. neurology Monmouth Med. Ctr., Long Branch, N.J., 1974—; asst. clin. prof. Hahnemann Med. Coll. and Hosp., 1974-91; clin. assoc. prof. Pa. U., Hahnemann U., 1991—; attending physician Martland Hosp., Newark, 1971-74, East Orange (N.J.) VA Hosp., 1971-74, Riverview Med. Ctr., Red Bank, N.J., 1983—. Contbr. chpts. in books and articles to profl. jours. Mem. AMA, Am. Acad. Neurology, Am. Med. Electroencephalographic Soc., Am. Clin. Neurophysiology Soc., N.J. Med. Soc., N.J. Acad. Medicine, Ea. Assn. Electroencephalographers, Phi Eta Sigma. Home: 58 Palmer Ave West Long Branch NJ 07764 Office: Neurology Med Ctr 107 Monmouth Rd West Long Branch NJ 07764

HERMAN, MARY MARGARET, neuropathologist; b. Plymouth, Wis., July 26, 1935; d. Elmer Fredolein and Esther Lydia (Bross) H.; m. Lucien Jules Rubinstein, Jan. 31, 1969. BS in Med. Sci., U. Wis., 1957, MD, 1960. Diplomate Nat. Bd. Med. Examiners, Am. Bd. Anatomic Pathology, Am. Bd. Neuropathology. Rotating intern Mary Hitchcock Meml. Hosp., Hanover, N.H., 1960-61; resident in neurology U. Wis. Hosps., 1961-62; intern in pathology Yale U., New Haven, 1962-63, asst. resident in pathology, 1963-64, fellow neuropathology, 1964-65, rsch. assoc. pathology, 1967-68; fellow neuropathology Stanford U., Palo Alto, Calif., 1965-66, fellow, acting instr. neuropathology, 1966-67, asst. prof. pathology, 1967-74, assoc. prof. (with tenure), 1974-81; prof., co-dir. div. neuropathology U. Va. Sch. Medicine, Charlottesville, 1981-91, prof. div. clin. pathology, 1991-92; spl. expert neuropathology in clin. brain disorders br. NIMH, Washington, 1991—; neuropathologist NIMH Brain Collection, 1992—, Stanley Fund Brain Collection, 1992—; vis. asst. prof. Albert Einstein Coll. Medicine, Bronx, N.Y., 1971-72; mem. program project rev. com. Nat. Inst. Neurol. and Communicative Diseases, NIH, 1973-77; cons. lab. svc. VA Hosp., Salem, Va., Ctrl. Va. Tng. Ctr., Lynchburg, 1982-92, ad hoc mem. pathology A study sect., 1986-91; cons. neuropathologist D.C. Med. Examiner's Office, Washington, 1992—, D.C. Gen. Hosp., 1992—. Mem. edit. bd. Jour. Neuropathology and Exptl. Neurology, 1989-93; contbr. over 130 articles to profl. jours. Recipient Rsch. Career Devel. award NIH, 1967-72. Faculty Devel. award Merck Found., 1969. Mem. AAAS, Am. Assn. Neuropathologists (Weil award 1974), Am. Soc. for Investigative Pathology, Soc. for Devel. Biology, Internat. Soc. Neuropathology, Am. Soc. Cell Biology (rsch. fellowship program, mentor scientist summer tchr. 1994), Internat. Acad. Pathology, Am. Tissue Culture Assn., Soc. Neurosci. Home: 125 S Reynolds St J-501 Alexandria VA 22304-3152 Office: NIMH Neurosci Ctr at St Elizabeths Clin Brain Disorders Br Washington DC 20032

HERMAN, MICHAEL EDWARD, pharmaceutical company executive; b. N.Y.C., May 31, 1941; s. Harris Abraham and Sally (Ruzga) H.; m. Karen May Kuivinen, May 29, 1966; children—Jolyan Blake, Hamilton Brooks. B.Metall. Engring., Renaselaer Poly. Inst., Troy, N.Y., 1962; M.B.A., U. Chgo., 1964. Sr. bus. analyst W.R. Grace & Co., N.Y.C., 1964-66; asst. to pres., v.p. corp. devel. subs. Nuclear Fuel Service, Washington, 1966-68; v.p. Laird, Inc., N.Y.C., 1968-70; founding gen. partner Dryden & Co., N.Y.C., 1970-74; exec. v.p., chief fin. officer, mem. Office of Pres., dir. Marion Labs., Inc., Kansas City, Mo., 1974-90; pres. Ewing Marion Kauffman Found., 1985-90, Kansas City Royals Baseball Team, 1993—; bd. dirs. Janus Capital Corp. Boatmen's Bank, Kansas City, Mo. Seafield Capital, Aquroun Pharm.; vis. lectr. U. Kans. Grad. Sch. Bus.; assoc. prof. Rockhurst Coll. Grad. Sch. Bus. Trustee Kansas City Royals Baseball Club Profit Sharing Trust; chmn. pension com. Maj. League Baseball Players Rels. Com.; chmn. investment com. Ewing Marion Kauffman Found. Mem. Pharm. Mfrs. Assn. (dir., mem. fin. steering com.), Kansas City Club, N.Y. Athletic Club, Hallbrook Country Club. Carriage Club, Mission Hills Country Club. Jewish. Home: 6201 Ward Pky Kansas City MO 64113-1518 Office: Ewing Marion Kauffman Found 4900 Oak St Kansas City MO 64112

HERMAN, PETER SIMON, dermatologist; b. Melbourne, Victoria, Australia, Sept. 10, 1938; came to U.S., 1968; s. Paul Aaron and Helene (Rein) H.; m. Tova Boski, Jan. 16, 1968; children: Karen Leora, Ronith Eleanora, Michael Paul. B in Medicine and Surgery, Melbourne U., 1962; MSc, U. Minn., 1971. Diplomate Am. Bd. Dermatology. Asst. prof. Centre Hospitalier Universitaire, Sherbrooke, Que., Can., 1971-73; dermatologist Norte Vista Med. Ctr., Hobbs, N.Mex., 1973-75; pres. Peter S. Herman, M.D., P.A., El Paso, Tex., 1975—. Author: Soap Photodermatitis: Photosensitivity to Halogenated Salicylanilides, 1973. Fellow Am. Acad. Dermatology. Office: 2100 N Mesa St El Paso TX 79902-3312

HERMAN, STEVEN DAVID, cardiologist, educator, researcher; b. Springfield, Mass., Dec. 7, 1960; s. Mark and Roslyn Marcia (Slavin) H. BS summa cum laude, Tufts U., 1981, MS, 1982; MD, U. Mass., Worcester, 1986. Diplomate Am. Bd. Internal Medicine, Am. Bd. Cardiovasc Diseases. Resident in internal medicine Med. Ctr. Ctrl. Mass., Worcester, 1986-89; fellow in cardiology Brown U., Providence, 1989-92, asst. prof. medicine, 1993—; rsch. fellow Am. Heart Assn., Providence, 1992-93; dir. CCU, Meml. Hosp. R.I., Pawtucket, 1993-94, dir. nuclear cardiology, 1994—. Contbr. articles to med. jours. Fellow Am. Coll. Cardiology; mem. ACP, AMA, Am. Soc. Nuclear Cardiology (founding), Soc. Nuclear Medicine (rsch. recognition award 1993), Am. Heart Assn. (grant-in-aid 1994). Office: Meml Hosp RI 111 Brewster St Pawtucket RI 02860

HERMAN, STEVEN DOUGLAS, cardiothoracic surgeon, educator; b. Budapest, Hungary, Apr. 7, 1945; came to U.S., 1949; s. Frank Elroy and Marta (Fischer) H.; m. Jacqueline Lee Forman, Aug. 14, 1983; children: Andrew Scott, Rebecca Sue. Student, Cornell U., 1962-64; BA, Johns Hopkins U., 1966, MD, 1969. Diplomate Am. Bd. Surgery, Am. Bd. Thoracic Surgery. Intern, resident, chief resident surgery N.Y. Hosp.-Cornell Med. Ctr., N.Y.C., 1969-75, resident, chief resident cardiovascular and thoracic surgery, 1975-77; asst. prof., attending surgeon adult and pediatric cardiothoracic surgery Hahnemann Med. Sch. and Hosp., Phila., 1977-79; chief cardiovascular and thoracic surgery St. Vincent's Med. Ctr., Bridgeport, Conn., 1979-90; attending cardiothoracic surgeon St. Michael Med. Ctr., Univ. Hosp., Newark, 1990—; clin. asst. prof. surgery Univ. Medicine and Dentistry N.J., Newark, 1991-94, clin. assoc. prof., 1994—; instr. surgery med. coll. Cornell U., N.Y.C., 1974-77; cons. cardiothoracic surgery Milford (Conn.) Hosp., 1979-90; attending surgeon cardiothoracic surgery Bridgeport Hosp., 1979-84, Park City Hosp., Bridgeport, 1989-90, Clara Maass Med. Ctr., Belleville, N.J., 1991—, Mountainside Hosp., Montclair, N.J., 1992—, St. Barnabas Med. Ctr., Livingston, N.J., 1992—; mem. courtesy staff cardiothoracic surgery Park City Hosp., 1978-89, Bridgeport Hosp., 1984-90, Univ. Medicine and Dentistry N.J.-Univ. Hosp., 1990—; mem. cardiovascular task force Health Systems Agy, Fairfield County, Conn., 1980-81; mem. exec. com. St. Michael's Med. Ctr., 1993—; presenter in field. Contbr. articles to profl. jours. Trustee Congregation Ahavath Achim, Fairfield, Conn., 1983-90, Hillel Acad. Sch., 1984-87. Thoracic Surgery fellow Meml. Hosp., Sloan-Kettering Cancer Ctr., 1975. Fellow ACS, Am. Coll. Cardiology, Coll. Physicians Phila.; mem. Am. Heart Assn. (mem. cardiovascular coun., bd. dirs. Fairfield County br. 1980-83, program chmn. Ea. Fairfield County region 1985), N.Am. Soc. Pacing and Electrophysiology, N.J. Soc. Thoracic Surgeons, N.Y. Acad. Scis., N.J. Med. Soc., Essex County Med. Soc. (mem. speakers bur. com. 1992—), Greater Bridgeport Med. Soc., Soc. Thoracic Surgeons, Internat. Soc. Cardiothoracic Surgeons, Internat. Soc. Heart Transplantation, Internat. Assn. Cardiac Biol. Implants, Assn. Acad. Surgery, C. Walton and Richard C. Lillehei Surg. Soc., Johns Hopkins Med. & Surg. Soc. Republican. Jewish. Home: 160 E Linden Ave Englewood NJ 07631-3622 Office: 268 Dr Martin Luther King Newark NJ 07102

HERMAN, THOMAS E., pediatric radiologist; b. St. Louis, Apr. 13, 1949; s. Glen Bernard and Maurine M. H.; m. Paula A. Thoman, Apr. 27, 1985; children: Peter, Nicholas, Philip, Claire. AB, Dartmouth Coll., 1971; MD, Johns Hopkins U., 1975. Pediatric radiologist Mass. Gen. Hosp., Boston, 1981-89, Mallinckrodt Inst. Radiology, St. Louis, 1989—. Contbr. articles to profl. publs. Mem. Am. Coll. Radiology, Radiol. Soc. N.Am., Am. Roentgen Ray Soc., Soc. for Pediatric Radiology, Friends of Ukrainian Radiology. Office: St Louis Children's Hosp 510 S Kingshighway Blvd Saint Louis MO 63110

HERMAN, ZBIGNIEW STANISŁAW, pharmacologist, educator; b. Tluste, Poland, Dec. 17, 1935; s. Leopold and Maria (Fedorow) H.; m. Anna Ludwika Dyaczynska, Apr. 29, 1972. MD, Silesian Acad. Medicine, Katowice, Poland, 1958, PhD, 1963, ScD, 1970; hon. doctorate, Silesian U. Sch. Medicine, 1993. Asst. Silesian Acad. Medicine, 1958-63, chief asst., 1963-70, assoc. prof., 1970-78, prof. pharmacology, 1978—, chmn. dept. pharmacology and clin. pharmacology, 1970—, dean med. faculty, 1978-80, rector, 1980-82. Editor, co-author: Clinical Pharmacology, 1986, 92, Pharmacotherapy of Cardio-vascular Diseases, 1985, 95; author: Pharmacotherapy in Surgery, Anesthesiology and Intensive Care, 1991, 93; co-editor Internat. Jour. Clin. Pharmacology, 1988—; contbr. articles to profl. jours. Mem.-initiator Solidarity, Katowice, 1980. Riker Found. fellow 1966; WHO vis. prof., 1972; recipient 1st Grade Sci. Achievments awards Polish Ministry of Health, 1975, 80, 85, 92. Mem. Polish Pharmacol. Soc. (sec. 1970-73, 1st Grade Sci. award 1972, pres. com. exptl. therapy 1980, mem. nat. sci. com. 1991-94, editor pol. jour. Pharmacol. Pharm. 1987—), Polish Acad. Scis. & Letters, N.Y. Acad. Scis. Roman Catholic. Home and Office: Ordona 14/59, PL 40-16 Katowice Poland

HERMANN, ROBERT EWALD, surgeon; b. Highland, Ill., Jan. 28, 1929; s. Ewald E. and Erna (Pabst) H.; m. Barbara Bower, Aug. 23, 1952 (dec. Aug. 1980); m. Polly Dreher, Mar. 8, 1986; childrn: Robert Jr., Barry, Monty. AB cum laude, Harvard U., 1950; MD, Washington U., St. Louis, 1954. Diplomate Am. Bd. Surgery. Intern, resident Univ. Hosps., Cleve., 1954-61; chmn. gen. surgery Cleve. Clinic, 1969-94, emeritus cons. dept. gen. surgery, 1994—; clin. prof. surgery Case Western Res. Sch. Medicine, Cleve., 1970—; dir. Am. Bd. Surgery, Phila., 1975-81; mem. Residency Rev. Com., Chgo., 1975-81. Author: Surgery of Gall Bladeer, Bile Ducts, Pancreas, 1979, Surgical Practice of Cleveland Clinic, 1985; contbr. over 180 articles to med. jours., 53 chpts. to books. Trustee Cleve. Clinic Found., 1976-77. Capt. M.C. U.S. Army, 1956-57. Recipient Roswell Park Gold medal Buffalo Surg. Soc., 1993. Mem. ACS (gov. 1981-87, v.p. 1996—, Disting. Svc. award 1994), Am. Surg. Soc., Internat. Surg. Soc., Internat. Coll. Surgeons (hon.), Soc. Surg. Oncology, Soc. Surgery Alimenatary Tract (pres. 1988-89), Assn. Program Dirs. Surgery (pres. 1979-81), Ea. Surg. Soc. (pres. 1985-86), Pan-Pacific Surg. Assn. (v.p. 1991-93). Republican. Home: 1 Bratenahl Pl 1403 Bratenahl OH 44108 Office: Cleve Clinic A-80 9500 Euclid Ave Cleveland OH 44195

HERMANN, WILLIAM HENRY, retired hospital administrator, consultant; b. Hillsboro, Ill., Apr. 6, 1924; s. Fred William and Mearle Hermann (Reinecke) H.; m. Loretta Pfister, July 28, 1956; children—Karen Elise, Diane Ellen. B.A., U. Mo., 1951; M.S., Yale U., 1953. With Arabian-Am. Oil Co., Dhahran, Saudi Arabia, 1953-58; adminstr. Dhahran Health Ctr., 1956-58; mem. staff Touro Infirmary, New Orleans, 1958-67, dir., 1962-64, exec. dir., 1965-66; coordinator program in hosp. adminstrn. Tulane U. Med. Sch., 1965-68; sr. v.p. Mary I. Bassett Hosp. and Clinics, Cooperstown, N.Y., 1968-90, ret. sr. vp. and now cons., 1990—; cons. The Clark Found., N.Y.C., 1990—; adj. asst. prof. pub. health and adminstrv. medicine Columbia U. Sch. Medicine; bd. dirs. Cmty. Health Plan, Latham, N.Y.C., 1986-90, Valley Health Svcs., Herkeimer, N.Y. Pres. Templeton Found., Cooperstown; bd. dirs. Clara Welch Thanksgiving Home, Cooperstown, 1975—, Fernleigh Found., N.Y.C., Hospice Inc., Oneonta, N.Y.; vestryman Episcopal Ch. With M.C., USNR, 1945-47. Mem. Am. Coll. Hosp. Adminstrs. (life), Yale Club (N.Y.C.), Pi Kappa Alpha (life). Office: Leatherstocking Corp 16 Main St Cooperstown NY 13326-1331

HERMANS, HUBERT JOHN, psychologist, researcher; b. Maastricht, Limburg, The Netherlands, Oct. 9, 1937; s. Mathias John and Jeannette Maria (Spronck) H.; m. Petronella Cornelia Jansen, Nov. 28, 1961; children: Matthieu, Désirée. B, Cath. U. Nijmegen, The Netherlands, 1962, MA, 1965, D in Psychology, 1967. Asst. psychologist Asthma Ctr., Groesbeek, The Netherlands, 1963-65; staff mem. Psychol. Lab., Nijmegen, 1965-72, lectr., 1972-80, prof. psychology, 1980—; vis. prof. Louvain (Belgium) U., 1975, Duquesne U., Pitts., 1979; chmn. adv. com. Han Fortmann Ctr. Human Growth, Nijmegen, 1982—. Author: (test-constrn.) Achievement Motivation Test for Adults, 1967, Achievement Motivation Test for Children, 1971, (assessment procedure) Self-Confrontation Method; contbr. personality theory and valuation theory to profl. jours. With The Netherlands mil., 1958-60. U.S. travel grantee Dutch Orgn. Advancement Pure Rsch., The Hague, The Netherlands, 1968; fellow Netherlands Inst. Advanced Studies in the Humanities and Social Sci., Wassenaar, The Netherlands, 1976-77. Mem. Soc. for Personology (1st internat. mem.), Dutch Orgn. Psychologists. Home: Bosweg 18, 6571 CD Berg en Dal The Netherlands Office: Cath U Nijmegen, Montessorilaan 3, 6525 HR Nijmegen The Netherlands

HERMSMEYER, REX, recruitment company executive; b. Litchfield, Ill., Nov. 28, 1947; children: Laura Alms, Ryan. BS, So. Ill. U., 1970, MA, 1972. Pres., owner Hitchens & Foster, Inc., St. Louis, 1982—. Mem. Nat. Assn. Physician Recruiters (bd. dirs. 1991-95, v.p. 1992, pres. 1993). Office: Hitchens & Foster Inc Pines Office Ctr One Pines Ct Saint Louis MO 63141

HERNANDEZ, ENRIQUE, gynecologist, educator; b. Vega Baja, P.R., Oct. 25, 1951; s. Nathaniel and Ana Luisa (Lopez) H.; children: David Enrique, Daniel Antonio. BS, U. P.R., Rio Piedras, 1973, MD, 1977. Diplomate Am. Bd. Med. Examiners, Am. Bd. Ob-Gyn, Am. Bd. Gynecol. Oncology. Resident in ob-gyn Johns Hopkins Hosp., Balt., 1977-81, fellow in gynecol. oncology, 1981-83; instr. ob-gyn Johns Hopkins U., Balt., 1981-82, asst. prof., 1982-83; chief gynecol. oncology service Tripler Army Med. Ctr., Honolulu, 1983-87, asst. dir. intern tng., 1984-87; assoc. prof. Allegheny U. Health Scis Ctr., Phila., 1987-89, prof., 1989—; dir. divsn. gynecologic oncology Med. Coll. Pa./Hahneman Univ., Phila., 1987—; pres. med. and dental staff Med. Coll. Pa. Hosp., 1992-93. Author: Manual of Gynecologic Oncology, 1989; editor: Clinical Gynecologic Pathology, 1995; contbr. articles to profl. jours. Bd. dirs. Allegheny Health, Edn. and Rsch. Found., 1992-93. Maj. U.S. Army, 1983-87. Recipient Bristol award P.R. Med. Assn., 1977. Fellow ACS (treas. met. Phila. chpt. 1995—), Am. Coll. Ob-Gyns.; mem. Am. Soc. Clin. Oncology, Soc. Gynecologic Oncologists, Obstet. Soc. Phila. (sec. 1994-96, pres.-elect 1996—), Beta Beta Beta, Alpha Omega Alpha (pres. 1976-77 P.R. chpt.). Roman Catholic. Office: Med Coll Pa 3300 Henry Ave Philadelphia PA 19129-1121

HERNANDEZ, WANDA GRACE, rehabilitation counselor, sales manager; b. Detroit, Apr. 23, 1942; d. Harry Lee and Lillian Delores (Williams) Williams; m. Ignacio Heriberto Hernandez, Nov. 25, 1969 (div. April 1979); 1 child, Heriberto Alejandro. BS, Wayne State U., 1973, MA, 1977; BS in Nutrition, Am. Holistic Coll. Nutrition, Birmingham, Ala., 1994; MS in Nutrition, Am. Holistic Coll. Nutrition, 1995. Substance abuse counselor Boniface Community Action Corp., Detroit, 1972-73; vocations rehab. counselor Mich. Rehab. Svcs., Detroit, 1974—. Named Disting. Rehab. Profl., Nat. Disting. Service Registry Library of Congress, 1987. Fellow Nat. Rehab. Assn.; mem. Smithsonian Assocs., Confedn. Chivalry, Rails-to-Trails Conservancy, Nat. Parks and Conservation Assn., Mus. Heritage Soc., Am. Assn. Retired Persons. Moslem. Home: 9056 Patton St Detroit MI 48228-1622 Office: Mich Rehab Svcs 30 E Canfield St Detroit MI 48201-1804 also: PO Box 205 New South Wales, Manly 2095, Australia

HERNANDEZ, WILBERT EDUARDO, physician; b. Progreso, Mex., Mar. 17, 1916; s. Alonso C. and Adolfina (Camara) H.; came to U.S., 1947, naturalized, 1949; B.S., U. Yucatan, 1937; M.D., Hahnemann Med. Coll. Phila., 1941; m. Jayne Rhodes, Oct. 4, 1941; children: Mary Jayne (Mrs. Clarence Delbridge), Patricia (Mrs. James Wheeler). Intern, Wyoming Valley Hosp., Wilkes-Barre, Pa., 1941-42; gen. practice medicine, Merida, Mex., 1942-46, Allentown (Pa.) State Hosp., 1947-48, Wilkes-Barre, 1948-51; specialized in anesthesiology St. Catherine's Hosp., Bklyn., 1955-57; chief dept. anesthesia Wyoming Valley Hosp., 1957-82; assoc. in anesthesiology Geisinger Med. Group, Geisinger Wyo. Valley Med. Ctr., 1982-83; med. dir. Blue Cross of Northeastern Pa., 1970-87; ret., 1987. Served as capt. M.C., AUS, 1951-53. Fellow Am. Coll. Anesthesiologists; mem. AMA, Pa. Med. Soc., Luzerne County Med. Soc., Am. Soc. Anesthesiologists, Pa. Soc. Anesthesiologists. Author: The Blood of the Conquistador, 1967. Contbr. articles to profl. jours. Home: 1172 Scott St Wilkes Barre PA 18705-3722

HERNANDEZ-TRUJILLO, JUAN MANUEL, pediatrician; b. Matanzas, Cuba, Nov. 22, 1944; came to U.S. 1962; s. Juan Jenaro and Carmelina (Lamothe) Hernandez-T.; m. Magaly Faustina Fernandez, June 18, 1966; children: Vivian Pilar, David Anthony, Daniel Juan. AS, Mo. Western Coll., St. Joseph, 1966; BS, Wayne State U., Detroit, 1968; MD, Universidad de Zaragoza, Spain, 1975. Diploamte Am. Bd. Pediatrics. Resident in pediatrics Bridgeport (Conn.) Hosp., 1975-78; pvt. practice medicine specializing in pediatrics Bridgeport, 1978-79; pvt. practice pediatrics Bridgeport-Monroe Pediatric Group, P.C., Bridgeport and Monroe, 1979—; sr. attending pediatrician Bridgeport Hosp., 1978; mem. active staff St. Vencent Med. Ctr., Bridgeport, 1995—. Bd. dirs. S.W. Cmty. Health Ctr., Bridgeport, 1979—, Make-A-Wish Found. of Conn., 1993; vice chmn. bd. Selective Svc. Sys., Conn., 1985—; mem. Cuban Lyceum of Bridgeport.

Fellow Am. Acad. Pediatrics; mem. Conn. State Med. Soc., Fairfield County Med. Assn., Greater Bridgeport Med. Assn. Republican. Roman Catholic. Office: Bridgeport Pediatric Group 2475 North Ave Bridgeport CT 06604-2337 also: Monroe Pediatric Group 450 Monroe Tpke Monroe CT 06468-2343

HERNDON, ALICE PATTERSON LATHAM, public health nurse; b. Macon, Ga.; d. Frank Waters and Ruby (Dews) Patterson; m. William Joseph Latham, July 21, 1940 (dec. Apr. 1981); children: Jo Alice Latham Miller, Marynette Latham, Lauruby Cathleen Beach; 1 adopted child, Courtney Marie Herndon; m. Sidney Dumas Herndon, Apr. 26, 1985. diploma, Charity Hosp. Sch. Nursing, New Orleans, 1937; student George Peabody Coll. Tchrs., 1938-39; BS in Pub. Health Nursing, U. N.C., 1954; MPH, Johns Hopkins U., 1966. Staff pub. health nurse assigned spl. venereal disease study USPHS, Darien, Ga., 1939-40; county pub. health nurse Bacon County, Alma, Ga., 1940-41; USPHS spl. venereal disease project, Glynn County, Brunswick, 1943-47; county pub. health nurse Glynn County, 1949-51, Ware County, Waycross, 1951-52; pub. health nurse supr. Wayne-Long-Brantley-Liberty Counties, Jesup, 1954-56 dist. dir. pub. health nursing Wayne-Long-Appling-Bacon-Pierce Counties, Jesup, 1956-70; dist. chief nursing S.E. Ga. Health Dist., 1970-79, organizer mobile health services, 1973—. Exec. dir. Wayne County Home Health Agy., 1968-80; exec. dir. Ware County Home Health Agy., 1970-79, mem. exec. com., 1978-85; mem. governing bd. S.E. Ga. Health Systems Agy., 1975-82; mem. governing bd. Health Dept. Home Health Agy., 1978—, also author numerous grant proposals. Bd. dirs. Wayne County Mental Health Assn., 1959, 60, 61, 81, 82, Wayne County Tb Assn., 1958-62; a non-alcoholic organizer Jesup group Alcoholics Anonymous, 1962-63; mem. adv. coun. Ware Meml. Hosp. Sch. Practical Nursing, Waycross, Ga., 1958; mem. Altar Guild, St. Paul's Episc. Ch., 1979-86, vestrywoman, 1981-82; mem. Altar Guild St. Marks Episcopal Ch., Brunswick, Ga., 1994—. Recipient recognition Gen. Service Bd., Alcoholics Anonymous, Inc. Fellow APHA; mem. ANA, 8th Dist. (pres. 1954-58, sec. 1958-60, dir. 1960-62, 1st v.p. 1962), Ga. Nurses Assn. (exec. bd. 1954-58, program rev. continuing edn. com. 1980-86. Dist. 21 Excellence in Nursing award 1994), Ga. Pub. Health Assn. (chmn. nursing sect. 1956-57), Ga. Assn. Dist. Chiefs Nursing (pres. 1976). Contbr. to state nursing manuals, cons. to Home Health Svc. Agys. Home: 192 Bluff Dr Brunswick GA 31523

HERNDON, RHONDA DIANNE, dietitian; b. Milan, Tenn., Aug. 28, 1960; d. William Jennings Jr. and Avinell (Sproles) H. AA, St. Petersburg Jr. Coll., 1980; BS, Fla. State U., 1982, MS, 1986. Project asst. Leon County Coop. Extension Svc., Tallahassee, 1985-87; area program mgmt. specialist dept. edn. State of Fla., Tallahassee, 1987-89, adult care food program coord. dept. edn., 1989-92; dietary svcs. supr. Heritage Health Care Ctr., Tallahassee, 1992; pub. health nutrition cons. Fla. Dep. Corrections., 1992-95; pub. health nutritionist supr. Leon County WIC Program, Tallahassee, 1995—. Mem. Am. Dietetic Assn.

HERNDON, ROBERT MCCULLOCH, experimental neurologist; b. Richmond, Va., May 29, 1935; s. Lee Roy and Lois Ruth (McCulloch) H.; m. Kathryn Lucille Stearns, June 11, 1955; children: Robert McCulloch, William, Cynthia. B.A., U. Chgo., 1955; M.D., U. Tenn., 1958. Diplomate: Am. Bd. Psychiatry and Neurology. Intern, then resident in neurology Wayne State U. Hosp., Detroit, 1959-61; fellow in neuropathology Montreal (Que., Can.) Neurol. Inst., 1962-63; fellow in anatomy Harvard U. Med. Sch., 1965-66; asst. prof. neurology Stanford U. Med. Sch., 1966-69; neurologist, then chief neurology Palo Alto (Calif.) VA Hosp., 1966-69; assoc. prof. Johns Hopkins U. Med. Sch., 1969-77; prof. neurology Center Brain Research, U. Rochester (N.Y.) Med. Center, 1977-88, chmn., 1977-87; chief neurology Good Samaritan Hosp., Portland, Oreg., 1988-94; prof. neurology Oreg. Health Scis. U., Portland, 1988—; chief, chairperson neurological svcs. dept. Legacy Portland Hosps., 1993-94; dir. Multiple Sclerosis Soc. Clinic, Rochester, 1978-88; mem. med. adv. bd. Multiple Sclerosis Soc. U.S., Internat. Fedn. Multiple Sclerosis Socs. Pres. Consortium of Multiple Sclerosis Ctrs., 1993-94. With USAF, 1963-65. Fellow Am. Acad. Neurology; mem. Am. Neurol. Assn., Am. Acad. Sci., Am. Assn. Neuropathologists (Arthur Weil award 1969, 72, Moore award 1983), Soc. Exptl. Neuropathology (pres. 1988-91), Soc. Neurosci., Sigma Xi, Alpha Omega Alpha. Office: Good Samaritan Hosp 1015 NW 22nd Ave Portland OR 97210-3025

HERNDON, WILLIAM ALFRED, pediatric orthopedic surgeon; b. Gainesville, Fla., July 6, 1947; s. Paul Clifford and Virginia May (Mead) H.; m. Judith Virginia Williams; children: Virginia Lin, Robin Elizabeth. AA, U. Fla., 1968, MD, 1972. Diplomate Am. Acad. Orthop. Surgery. Commd. USN, 1969-93, advanced through grades to capt.; orthop. surgeon Naval Hosp., P.R., 1976-78; fellow orthop. surgery Children's Hosp., Boston, 1978-79; pediatric orthop. surgeon Naval Hosp., Portsmouth, Va., 1979-83; prof. orthop. surgery U. Okla., Oklahoma City, 1983—. Contbr. articles to profl. jours. Fellow Am. Acad. orthop. Surgeons; mem. Pediatric Orthop. Soc. N.Am., Scoliosis Rsch. Soc., Soc. Mil. Orthop. Surgeons. Office: 940 NE 13th St Oklahoma City OK 73104

HERNRIED, LUCY S., physician; d. H. Peter Hernreid (dec. Mar. 1987); 2 sons. BA, Swarthmore Coll., 1953; MD, N.Y. Med. Coll., 1957. Pediat. assoc. dir. pulmonary sect. Good Samaritan Hosp., Phoenix, 1970-74, dir. pediat. pulmonary sect., 1974-82; sect. chief pediat. pulmonology Phoenix Children's Hosp., 1982-87, mem. pulmonary sect., 1987-95, dir. Cystic Fibrosis Ctr., 1974-95, chmn. dept. medicine, 1986-88, 92-94; sr. clin. lectr. in pediats. U. Ariz., Tucson, 1987-95; ret., 1995. Fellow Am. Acad. Pediats. (chest sect.); mem. Am. Thoracic Soc., Maricopa County Pediat. Soc., Ariz. Pediat. Soc. Office: Phoenix Childrens Hosp 909 E Brill St Phoenix AZ 85006-2513

HEROLD, RICHARD CARL, developmental biology educator; b. Butler, Pa., June 13, 1927; s. Carl Theodore and Charlotte Emma (Black) H. BS in Zoology, Pa. State U., 1950, MS in Zoology, 1951; PhD in Biology, U. Pa., Phila., 1961. Chemist Aeroprojects Inc., Westchester, Pa., 1953-57; jr. rsch. fellow Inst. Coop. Rsch., Phila., 1957-63; hon. rsch. fellow Univ. Coll., London, U.K., 1983-84; prof. devel. biology U. Pa., Phila., 1963—; dir. Swans Island Marine Lab., Minturn, Maine, 1966-89. Contbr. articles to profl. jours.; patentee in field. Founding mem. French Creek Assn., Chester Springs, Pa. Sigma Xi grantee NIH, Washington, 1986-91. Fellow Royal Hort. Soc., Royal Microscopical Soc.; mem. Electron Microscope Soc. Home: RR 1 Phoenixville PA 19460-9801

HEROS, ROBERTO COSME, neurosurgeon; b. Havana, Cuba, Aug. 27, 1942; m. Deborah O. Heros; children—Elsa, Roby, Carlos. M.D., U. Tenn.-Memphis, 1968. Diplomate Am. Bd. Neurol. Surgery. Surg. Intern Mass. Gen. Hosp., Boston, 1968-69, asst. resident gen. surgery, 1969-70, resident in neurosurgery, 1972-77, asst. in neurosurgery, 1976-77; attending neurosurgeon Presbyn. U. Hosp., Pitts., 1977-79, assoc. chief neurosurgery, 1979-80; attending neurosurgeon Children's Hosp. of Pitts., 1977-80, Montefiore Hosp., Pitts., 1977-80; cons. neurosurgeon VA Hosp., Pitts., 1977-80; dir. neurovascular surgery Mass. Gen. Hosp., Boston, 1980; asst. prof. neurosurgery U. Pitts., 1977-80, dir. neurosurg. residents ednl. program, 1979-80; asst. prof. surgery Harvard Med. Sch., Boston, 1980-83, assoc. prof. surgery, 1983-89, prof. surgery, 1989-90; Lyle A. French prof., chmn. dept. neurosurgery U. Minn., 1990-95; prof., chair dept. neurol. surgery U. Miami, 1995—; dir. U. Miami Internat. Health Ctr. Chmn. editorial bd. Neurosurgery, 1988; contbr. articles to profl. jours. Chmn. Brain Attack Nat. Coalition, Neurovasc. coun. World Fedn. Neurosurg. Soc. Recipient Medal of Surgery, U. Tenn., 1968, Dean's medal, 1968. Fellow ACS; mem. Neurosurg. Soc. Am., New Eng. Neurosurg. Soc., Am. Assn. Neurol. Surgeons, Congress of Neurol. Surgeons (v.p. 1986-87), Am. Acad. Neurol. Surgeons, Alpha Omega Alpha. Office: U Miami Med Sch 1501 NW 9th Ave Miami FL 33136

HERR, JOHN MERVIN, JR., biology educator; b. Charlottesville, Va., July 26, 1930; s. John Mervin and Mary Belva (Bryd) H.; m. Annie Sue Highfield, Aug. 30, 1952 (div. May 1973); children: Susan Rebecca, Rachel Lynn; m. Lucrecia Linder, Dec. 30, 1974; 1 stepchild, Frederick Brent Wahl. BA in Biology, U. Va., 1951, MA in Biology, 1952; PhD in Botany, U. N.C., 1957. Instr. biology Washington & Lee U., Lexington, Va., 1952-54; Fulbright (Found.) postdoctoral fellow U. Delhi, India, 1957-58; asst. prof. Pfeiffer Coll., Misenheimer, N.C., 1958-59; asst. prof. U. S.C., Columbia, 1959-63, assoc. prof., 1963-69, prof., 1969—; prof. emeritus, 1993—. Contbr. chpt. to: Embryology and Taxonomy, 1984; contbr. articles to sci. jours. NSF grantee, 1961-63; AEC grantee, 1959-61. Mem. Bot. Soc. Am., Internat. Soc. Plant Morphologists (mem. editorial bd. 1985-90), Assn. Southeastern Biologists (pres. 1976-77, Meritorious Teaching award 1989), So. Appalachian Bot. Club (pres. 1992-93). Home: 3611 Foxhall Rd Columbia SC 29204-3716 Office: Univ SC Dept Biol Scis Columbia SC 29208

HERRELL, JAMES MILTON, psychologist; b. Austin, Tex., Feb. 17, 1943; s. James Ray and Georgia Maxine (Porter) H.; m. Ileana Collado, June 26, 1965; children: Christine, Robert. BA in Psychology, U. Tex., 1963; MA in Psychology, U. Md., 1965, PhD in Psychology, 1967; MPH, Johns Hopkins U., Balt., 1992. Lic. psychologist, Md., D.C.; cert. mental health adminstr. Dir. mental health Dept. Health, Montgomery County, Md., 1972-86; dir. spl. programs Dept. Addiction Victim and Mental Health Svcs., Montgomery County, 1985-93; chief exec. officer Psychol. Systems Internat., Potomac, Md., 1985—, dir. divsn. child and adolescent svcs., 1994-96; program analyst Ctr. Substance Abuse Treatment, 1996—; part-time faculty St. Mary's U., San Antonio, 1968, Our Lady of the Lake Coll., San Antonio, 1968, U. Md., 1969-81, George Washington U., 1970-73, George Mason U., Fairfax, Va., 1979; cons. Pan Am. Health Orgn., Washington, 1980—, WHO, Geneva, 1989, USIA, Washington, 1985, Fundacion Convivir, Buenos Aires, 1989. Author: Drug Abuse Prevention, 1985; contbr. articles to profl. jours. Mem. Community Action Bd., Montgomery County, 1987-94, Commn. for People with Disabilities, 1987-94, Cancer Prevention Task Force, 1990-94, Mental Health Adv. Com., 1972-85, Commn. on Aging, 1987-96. Capt. U.S. Army, 1966-71. Decorated Bronze Star medal. Mem. APA, APHA, Assn. Mental Health Adminstrs., Md. Gerontol. Assn., Assn. Health Svcs. Rschrs., Delta Omega. Home: 8717 Belmart Rd Rockville MD 20854-1610

HERRERA, GUILLERMO ANTONIO, pathologist; b. Havana, Cuba, Mar. 16, 1952; came to U.S., 1967; s. Guillermo S. and Olga (Del Castillo) H.; m. Elba A. Turbat, Dec. 23, 1972; 1 child, Marlene F. Student, U. Miami, 1970; MD cum laude, U. P.R., 1975. Diplomate Am. Bd. Pathology, cytopathology added qualification bd.; lic. physician Fla., N.Mex., Ala., Miss., La. Intern categorical pathology Brooke Army Med. Ctr., Ft. Sam Houston, Tex., 1975-76, resident pathology, anatomic and clin., 1975-79, chief resident, 1978-79; asst. prof. dept. pathology Sch. Medicine and Dentistry U. Ala., Birmingham, 1982-87, scientist II Nephrology Rsch. and Tchr. Ctr. Sch. Medicine, 1982-88, dir. nephropathology Schs. Medicine and Dentistry, 1987-88, assoc. prof. dept. pathology, 1987-88, prof. pathology, head surg. pathology, 1991-95, sr. scientist Comprehensive Cancer Ctr., 1991-95; prof., chmn. dept. pathology La. State U.-Shreveport Sch. Medicine, Jackson, 1996—; head surg. pathology, attending pathologist VA Hosp., Birmingham, 1991-95; acting med. dir. Sch. Cytotech. U. Ala., Birmingham, 1991-93, faculty mem. Grad. Sch., 1991-95; sr. scientist, co-dir. EM Core Facility Comprehensive Cancer Ctr. Ala., 1991-95; chmn. dept. pathology La. State U., Shreveport, 1996—; assoc. pathologist Palm Beach Pathology, Good Samaritan Hosp., West Palm Beach, Fla., 1988-89; faculty Grad. Sch. U. Miss., 1989-91; cons. pathologist VA Hosp., Jackson, 1990-91; attending pathologist, head surg. pathology VA Hosp., Birmingham, 1991-95; acting med. dir. Sch. Cytotech., U. Ala., Birmingham, 1991-93, acting head cytopathology, 1991-93, faculty mem. Grad Sch., 1991-95; sr. scientist Comprehensive Cancer Ctr. Ala., co-dir. EM Core facility, 1991-95; prof., chair dept. pathology La. State U., Shreveport, 1996—. Mem. editl. bd. Ultrastructural Pathology and Pathology Case Revs, 1995—; manuscript reviewer Applied Pathology, Diagnostic Cytopathology, Am. Jour. Medicine, Am. Jour. Kidney Diseases, Archives Pathology and Lab. Medicine, Ultrastructural Pathology, Stain Tech. and Histochemistry, Am. Jour. Clin. Pathology, Pathobiology, Human Pathology, Cancer, Kidney Internat., Pathology Rsch. and Practice and Annals of Saudi Medicine; contbr. articles to profl. jours., chpts to books. Maj. M.C., U.S. Army, 1974-82, col. USAR, 1988—. Grantee U. P.R., 1972-75, Brooke Army Med. Ctr., Ft. Sam Houston, 1978-79, U. Ala., Birmingham, 1983-86, 87-88, Universita Degli Studi di Milano, 1984, VA, 1986—, Nat. Cancer Inst., 1991—, NIH, 1992—, Ala. Kidney Found., 1992-93. Mem. Internat. Acad. Pathology, Am. Soc. Clin. Pathology, Armed Forces Soc. Lab. Scientists, Electron Microscopy Soc. Am., Soc. Ultrastructural Pathology (sec. 1988-91, tras. 1991—), Am. Soc. Nephrology, Arthur Purdy Stout Soc. Surg. Pathologists, Tex. Electron Microscopy Soc., Birmingham Soc. Pathologists (v.p. 1987-88). Roman Catholic.

HERRERIAS, CARLA TREVETTE, epidemiologist, manager; b. Chgo., Apr. 8, 1964; d. Ludvik Frank and Carlotta Trevette (Walker) Koci; m. Jesus Herrerias, Feb. 25, 1989; children: Elena Mikele, Coco Trevette. BS in Med.Tech., Ea. Mich. U., 1987; MPH in Molecular and Hosp. Epidemiology, U. Mich., 1991. Med. clk. hydramatic divsn. GM, Ypsilanti, Mich., 1983-86; researcher, staff dept. human genetics U. Mich., Ann Arbor, 1987-91; program mgr. Am. Acad. Pediatrics, Elk Grove Village, Ill., 1991—. Project mgr., contbr.: Clinical Practice Guideline: Otitis Media with Effusion in Young Children, 1994. Mem. APHA, Ill. Pub. Health Assn., Assn. for Health Svcs. Rsch., U. Mich. Alumni Soc., U. Mich. Club Chgo. Office: Am Acad Pediatrics 141 Northwest Point Blvd Elk Grove Village IL 60007

HERRICK, KATHLEEN MAGARA, social worker; b. Mpls., Oct. 18, 1943; d. William Frank and Mary Genevieve (Gill) Magara; m. John Middlemist Herrick, Feb. 5, 1966; children: Elizabeth Jane, Kathryn Mary. BA in Social Work and French, Coll. St. Benedict, St. Joseph, Minn., 1965; MSW (Mildred B. Erickson fellow 1975), Mich. State U., E. Lansing, 1976. Social worker II, Carver County Social Services, Chaska, Minn., 1965-70; therapist St. Lawrence Community Mental Health Center, Lansing, Mich., 1974-75; sch. social worker Ingham Intermediate Sch. Dist., Mason, Mich., 1975-76; home/sch. coordinator Eaton Intermediate Sch. Dist., Charlotte, Mich., 1976-81, sch. social worker, 1994—; caseworker St. Vincent Home for Children, Lansing, 1979-80; tchr. cons. for severely emotionally impaired, 1981-83; behavior disorder cons., 1983-85; sch. social work cons., 1985-87, prevention specialist prof. and program svcs., 1987-94. Chairperson bd. dirs. Eaton County Child Abuse and Neglect Prevention Council, 1986—; Democratic precinct del.; bd. dirs. Catholic Social Services, Lansing; specialist substance abuse prevention region XIII SAPE, 1987-94. Mem. NEA, Nat. Platform Assn., Mich. Edn. Assn., Nat. Assn. Social Workers, Nat. Assn. Retarded Citizens, Am. Orthopsychiat. Assn., Mich. Assn. Sch. Social Workers, Mich. Assn. Emotionally Disturbed Children, Eaton County Assn. Retarded Citizens, Nat. Platform Assn., NOW, Nat. Women's Health Network, Amnesty Internat., Mich. Assn. Suicidology, Glasser Inst. for Reality Therapy and Choice Theory, Phi Kappa Phi, Phi Alpha. Democrat. Roman Catholic. Home: 2113 Long Leaf Trl Okemos MI 48864-3210 Office: 1790 E Packard Hwy Charlotte MI 48813

HERRIN, FRANCES SUDOMIER, retired volunteer social worker; b. Hamtramck, Mich., Dec. 1, 1914; d. Wesley Valentine and Anna Theresa (Langowski) Sudomier; widowed. Grad., high sch., 1933. Sec. Parke Davis & Co., Detroit, 1946-47; assembler Gen. Motors, Detroit, 1947, Chrysler Corp., Hamtramck, 1950-57; vol. social worker, mem. adv. com. Detroit Area Agy. on The Aging, Detroit, 1981-92; spkr. St. Theresa Guild, 1981-92, Golden Agers, 1981-92, Polish-Am. Sr. Citizens, 1981-90; precision-tool tested parts of B-29 bomber planes in World War II, Henry Ford Aircraft Bldg., River Rouge Plant. Active in Dem. and Rep. election campaigns; mem. St. Florian's Hist. Commn., Hamtramck, 1985—; sr. citizen activist several sr. orgns., Washington; mem. ret. sr. vol. program Cath. Social Svcs., Wayne County, 1986-87; mem. Presdl. Task Force for Pres. Reagan; patron Cath. orgns. where missionaries provide relief of food, clothing and edn. to children, especially orphaned children of devasted countries. Recipient Medal of Merit from Pres. Reagan. Mem. St. Theresa's Guild. Roman Catholic.

HERRIN, JOHN THOMAS, pediatrician; b. Rutherglen, Australia, Feb. 19, 1936; arrived in Australia, 1968; s. Raymond John and Ellen Rita (Henshaw) H.; m. Patricia Ann Miller, Dec. 16, 1961; children: Catherine Mary Gorecki, Stephen James, Elizabeth Ann, Peter Andrew. MBBS, U. Melbourne, 1961. Jr. resident med. officer St. Vincent Hosp., Melbourne, Australia, 1962-63; jr. resident med. officer Royal Childrens Hosp., Melbourne, 1963-64, pathology registrar, 1964-65, med. registrar, 1966-67; rsch. fellow Mass. Gen. Hosp./Shriner Burn Inst., Boston, 1968-70; chief pediatric nephrology Mass. Gen. Hosp., Boston, 1974-94; chief pediatrics Shriner Burns Inst., Boston, 1986-94; dir. clin. svcs. divsn. nephrology Childrens Hosp., Boston, 1994—; acting dir. Pediatric Renal Dialysis Transplant Program, State of Vic. Australia, 1985. Med. stds. com. End Stage Renal Disorder, 1985-88; med. adv. bd. Nat. Kidney Found., 1987—; bd. dirs. End Stage Renal Disorder, 1991—; mem. chmn. nominating com. Suffolk Med. Soc., Boston, 1994. Mem. Am. Soc. Nephrology, Am. Burn Soc., Suffolk Dist. Med. Soc., Mass. Med. Soc. (alt. del. legis. com. 1991), Internat. Soc. Nephrology, Internat. Soc. Pediatric Nephrology, Am. Soc. Transplant Physicians. Office: Divsn Nephrology HUN 3 Childrens Hosp 300 Longwood Ave Boston MA 02115

HERRING, BERNARD DUANE, physician; b. Massillon, Ohio, Jan. 27, 1929; s. James and Eva (Lancaster) H.; m. Odessa Mae Appling, Sept. 6, 1950; children: Kevin, Duane, Terez, Sean. BS magna cum laude, Kent State U., 1952; MD, U. Cin., 1956; LLB, LaSalle Extension U., 1964. Real estate broker, Calif.; diplomate Am. Coll. Forensic Examiners, Am. Bd. Forensic Medicine; bd. cert. in family practice, geriatrics. Intern San Francisco Gen. Hosp., 1956-57; resident internal medicine VA Hosp., Bklyn., 1957-58, Cleve., 1958-59; asst. clin prof. medicine U. Calif. Med. Sch., San Francisco, 1982—. Fellow Am. Coll. Legal Medicine; mem. AMA, Am. Soc. Internal Medicine, ASCAP, Am. Geriat. Soc. Home: 712 Longridge Rd Oakland CA 94610-2325 Office: PO Box 10286 Oakland CA 94610-0286

HERRING, SAMUEL ALFONSO, physician assistant; b. St. Petersburg, Fla., Aug. 18, 1940; s. William Aubrey and Christian Daisy (Pierce) H.; m. Shelda Delores Dorn, May 23, 1964; children: Michelle Rene, Latrecia Montez. Student, Paine Coll., 1965-69; cert. in psychiatry, Duke U., 1973. Cert. addiction specialist. Physician assoc. N.C. Dept. Mental Health, Butnor, 1972-77, State of Tenn. Dept. Mental Health, Memphis, 1977-92; physician asst. Dept. VA, Memphis, 1992—; exec. dir. Mid-Town Med./Counseling Ctr., Memphis, 1987-92. Young Life Urban Com. Mem., Memphis, 1995; bd. dirs. Harbor House, Inc., 1995. Sgt. U.S. Army, 1960-65. Mem. Soc. for Internat. Tng. and Rsch. Democrat. African Methodist Episcopalian. Home: 484 Haynes St Memphis TN 38111 Office: VA Med Ctr 1030 Jefferson Ave Memphis TN 38104

HERRLICH, PETER ALBERT, genetics educator; b. Munich, Nov. 10, 1940; m. Christiane Goertz, 1966; children: Andreas, Christian, Bettina. MD, U. Munich, 1964; Habilitation, Free U. Berlin, 1972, prof. degree, 1977. Intern viral diagnosis lab. Inst. Tropical Medicine U. Munich, 1964-65; intern rotating Cook County Hosp., Chgo., 1965-66; intern obstetrics and surgery Univ. Hosp. Munich, 1966; fellow Max-Planck-Inst. für Biochemie, Munich, 1967-68, Rockefeller U. N.Y., 1969-70; sr. staff mem. Max-Planck-Inst. fur Molekulare Genetik, Berlin, 1970-73; group leader Max-Planck-Inst. für Molekulare Genetik, Berlin, 1973-77; prof. genetics U. Karlsruhe, Fed. Republic Germany, 1977—; dir. Inst. Genetics Forschungszentrum, Karlsruhe, 1993—; vis. prof. U. Calif. San Diego, La Jolla, 1986-87; cons. and peer reviewer study sects. German Sci. Found., 1977—, Nat. Sci. Found. U.S., 1986—, various European founds., various sci. jours. Mem. editl. bd. Molecular Carcinogenesis, 1989—, Internat. Jour. Cancer, 1990—, The New Biologist, 1991-92; editor Carcinogenesis, 1990-94. Mem. Gesellschaft für Biologische Chemie, Gesellschaft Deutscher Naturforscher und Ärzte, Deutsche Ärztekammer, Karlsruher Chemische Gesellschaft, AAAS, Am. Soc. for Microbiology, European Molecular Biology Orgn. Home: Vogelsang 8, D-76229 Karlsruhe Germany Office: Kernforschungszentrum, Karlsruhe PO Box 3640, D-76021 Karlsruhe 1, Germany

HERRMANN, CHRISTIAN, JR., medical educator; b. Lansing, Mich., 1921; s. Christian and Agnes (Bauch) H. A.B., U. Mich., 1942, M.D., 1944. Diplomate Am. Bd. Psychiatry and Neurology. Intern Harper Hosp., Detroit, 1944-45; asst. resident medicine Henry Ford Hosp., Detroit, 1945-46; resident neurology Neurol. Inst., N.Y.C., 1948-50; research asst. neurology Neurol. Inst., 1950-51, chief resident neurology, 1951-52, asst. neurology, 1950-51, 51-52, asst. attending, 1953-54; mem. faculty U. Calif. at Los Angeles Med. Sch., 1954—, prof. neurology, 1969-86, prof. neurology emeritus, 1986—, vice chmn. dept. Neurology, 1970-86. Vice chmn. Calif. chpt. Myasthenia Gravis Found., 1966—, chmn. med. adv. bd., 1968-72, pres. 1972-74, chmn. nat. med. adv. bd., 1983-85. Served as lt. (j.g.) M.C. USNR, 1946-48. USPHS research fellow neurology Columbia Coll. Phys. and Surg., 1952-54. Office: U Calif Dept Neurology Reed Neurol Research Center Los Angeles CA 90095

HERRMANN, HOWARD CRAIG, cardiologist; b. N.Y.C., Dec. 6, 1955; m. Deborah R. Herrmann; children: Stephanie, Jessica. AB, Harvard Coll., 1977; MD, Harvard Med. Sch., 1981. Intern, then resident Mass. Gen. Hosp., Boston, 1981-84, fellow in radiology, 1984-87; dir. interventional cardiology Hosp. U. Pa., Phila., 1993—; mem. staff. U. Pa., 1987—; assoc. prof. medicine U. Pa. Sch. Medicine, Phila., 1993—. Office: 3400 Spruce St Philadelphia PA 19104

HERRMANN, JOHN BELLOWS, surgery educator; b. Cin., Nov. 21, 1932; s. Louis George and Marion (Bellows) H.; m. MaryJane Gaiser, Sept. 3, 1960; children: Christian L., Karen, Mark E. AB, Dartmouth Coll., 1954, cert. medicine, 1955; MD, Harvard U., 1957. Diplomate Am. Bd. Surgery, Nat. Bd. Med. Examiners. Surg. intern Mass. Gen. Hosp., Boston, 1957-58, surg. resident, 1958-62; rsch. surgeon Walter Reed Army Inst. Rsch., Washington, 1962-64; asst. in surgery Mass. Gen. Hosp., Boston, 1964-65; from. asst. prof. to assoc. prof. Georgetown U., Washington, 1965-72; prof. surgery U. Mass., Worcester, 1972—; chief of surgery Worcester City Hosp., 1972-83; vice chair surgery U. Mass. Med. Sch., Worcester, 1972—. Co-author: Case Studies in General Surgery, 1987; contbr. articles to profl. jours. Bd. dirs. local community group, Worcester, 1989—. Fellow Am. Coll. Surgeons; mem. Mass. Med. Soc., Worcester Dist. Med. Soc. (councilor 1988—), New Eng. Surg. Soc., New Eng. Soc. for Vascular Surgery (v.p. 1990-91), Soc. for Surg. Edn., Assn. Program Dirs. in Surgery, Assn. for Acad. Surgery. Office: U Mass Med Ctr 55 Lake Ave N Worcester MA 01655-0002

HERRMANN, KENNETH JOHN, JR., social work educator; b. Lackawanna, N.Y., Apr. 13, 1943; s. Kenneth John and Alice Jane (Gray) H.; m. Kathleen Wolf, Oct. 1969 (div. 1986); m. Kathleen T. Morris-Costanza, 1994; children: Aaron Kim-Eui, Gabe Sang-Koo, Mark Hoi-Duk, Rachele Hoi-Im, Ruth Myung-Hee, Joseph Costanza. BA, Canisius Coll., 1972; MSW, SUNY, Buffalo, 1975. Tchr. St. Monica's Sch., Buffalo, 1963-67; sr. caseworker Erie County Child Welfare, Buffalo, 1969-73; family therapist Wyndham Lawn Home for Children, Lockport, N.Y., 1975-77; dir. children's svcs. Dept. Social Svc. County of Genesee (N.Y.), 1977-78; assoc. prof. social work SUNY, Brockport, 1978—; pvt. practice psychotherapy East Pembroke, N.Y., 1975—; adoption social worker Dillon Children's Svcs. Intercountry Adoption Program, 1982-84; internat. adoption social worker New Beginnings Child and Family Svcs., 1989—; exec. dir. Vets. Svcs. Ctr. of West N.Y., Batavia, 1991-94, YWCA Domestic Violence group therapist, 1995—; mem. state bd. for social work N.Y. State Edn. Dept., 1984—; cons. UN Children's Fund, U.S. Senate, U.S. Congress; radio and TV appearances, lectr., cons. on children's rights, child abuse and neglect, fmaily violence. Author: I Hope My Daddy Dies, Mister, 1975, I'm Nobody's Child, 1982; author studies on internat. children's issues; contbr. articles to profl. jours. With U.S. Army, 1967-69. Mem. NASW, VFW, Def. for Children Internat., Vietnam Vets. Am., OURS, Bertha Capen Reynolds Soc. Home: 2614 E Main Rd East Pembroke NY 14056 Office: SUNY Faculty Office Bldg Brockport NY 14420

HERROD, HENRY GRADY, III, allergist, immunologist; b. Oakland, Calif., Apr. 30, 1945. MD, U. Ala., 1972. Cert. allergy and immunology; cert. pediats. Intern U. Wash., Seattle, 1972-73, resident in pediats., 1973-74; resident rsch. assoc. in allergy and immunology NIH, Bethesda, Md., 1974-76; fellow in allergy and immunology Duke U., Durham, 1976-78; physician Le Bonheur Childrens Med. Ctr., Memphis; prof. U. Tenn., Memphis. Mem. AAAI, AAI, AAP, APS. Office: Le Bonheur Health Sys Corp Office 850 Poplar Ave Memphis TN 38105*

HERROLD, KENNETH FREDERICK, psychologist, educator; b. Lewisburg, Pa., Aug. 23, 1913; s. Benton Elijah and Millie (Else) H.; m. Elizabeth McMahan, June 21, 1941 (dec. Feb. 1994); children: Carolann, Edmund,

William, John. A.B., Bucknell U., 1936; M.P.H. (fellow), U. Mich., 1940; Ed.D., Columbia U., 1948. Instr. biology Bucknell U., 1936-39, asst. prof. physiology, 1940-42; research asst. Mich. Med. Coll., 1939-40; mem. faculty dept. psychology and edn. Tchrs. Coll., Columbia U., 1947-78, prof., 1956—; pres. Herrold Assos., 1956—; research asso. Inst. Psychol. Research, 1950-54; profl. asso. Human Interaction Research Inst., Edward Glaser Assos., 1963-73; cons. in field. Mem. editorial bd. Jour. of Social Issues; contbr. articles to profl. jours., chpts. to books. Bd. elders Madison Ave. Presbyn. Ch., N.Y.C., West Side Presbyn. Ch., Ridgewood, N.J. Served with USN, 1941-44. Recipient award Phi Sigma-AAAS, 1935; Leader's award Harlem Prep, 1971; grantee U.S. Air Force Human Factors Operation Research Lab., 1953, 54, Hogg Found., 1956, USPHS, 1956, NIH, 1958, NDEA, 1962, Dept. Labor, 1965, 66, 67, AID, 1966, N.J. Edn. Commn., 1972, 73. Fellow Am. Psychol. Assn., Am. Sociol. Assn.; mem. AAAS, N.Y. Acad. Sci., AAUP, Am. Personnel and Guidance Assn. (chmn. membership com.). Home: The Ledge PO Box 24 Burlington PA 18814-0024

HERSCHBERG, SEYMOUR NATHAN, physician; b. N.Y.C., June 28, 1937; s. Jacob and Lena Molly (Kimel) H.; m. Phyllis Carol Burger, June 30, 1966; children: Mark Allan, Michael Bruce. BA, NYU, 1957; MD, U. Medicine and Dentistry N.J., 1961. Diplomate in internal medicine and geriatrics Am. Bd. Internal Medicine. Intern L.A. County Harbor Gen. Hosp., Torrance, Calif., 1961-62; resident in internal medicine VA Hosp., Bklyn., 1964-66; clin. rsch. fellow Inst. for Cancer Rsch., Fox Chase, Phila., 1966-67; chief of medicine Fordham Hosp., Bronx, N.Y., 1968-76; chief of primary care Mt. Sinai Hosp., Chgo., 1976; dir. medicine Lincoln Hosp., Bronx, 1977-79; assoc. prof. med., dir. divsn. gen. internal medicine Chgo. Med. Sch., 1979-85; dir. medicine and med. residency St. Francis Med. Ctr., Trenton, N.J., 1985-90; med. dir. HMO Blue Health Ctrs., Trenton, N.J., 1990—; mem. alumni bd. trustees U. of Medicine and Dentistry N.J.-N.J. Med. Sch., 1986—; clin. assoc. prof. medicine U. Medicine and Dentistry of N.J.-Robert Wood Johnson Med. Sch., 1987-90; clin. asst. prof. primary care Rutgers U. Sch. of Related Health Scis., 1987-90; lectr. in field. Reviewer jour. Gen. Internal Medicine, 1987—, Am. Coll. of Physicians Self-Learning Series, Jour. Clin. Outcomes Mgmt., 1995—; mem. editorial bd. Managed Care Medicine, 1996—; contbr. articles to profl. jours. Mem. task force West Windsor-Plainsboro (N.J.) Sch. Bd., 1986-92; advisor West Windsor Commn. on Aging, 1986-91, West Windsor Bd. of Health, 1987. Fellow Am. Coll. Physicians; mem. AMA, Am. Coll. Physician Execs., Nat. Assn. Managed Care Physicians. Office: HMO Blue 416 Bellevue Ave Trenton NJ 08618-9961

HERSEY, MARIA RUSSO, health facility administrator; b. Balt., June 3, 1943; d. Paul A. and Joanna (Basso) Russo; m. Roscoe Monroe Hersey III, Jan. 3, 1942; children: Sara, Christopher. BA, Loyola Coll., Balt., 1965; MSW, U. Md., Balt., 1970. Clin. social worker Johns Hopkins Hosp., Balt., 1967-68, U. Rochester (N.Y.) Med. Ctr., 1970-72; tng. cons. Rochester Sch. Dist., 1972-75; program mgr. Colo. Perinatal Care Coun., Denver, 1977-79; assoc. program coord. Polyclinic Med. Ctr., Harrisburg, Pa., 1979-84; owner Image Assocs., Hershey, Pa., 1984-86; corp. trainer Pa. Blue Shield, Camp Hill, 1986-88, policy analyst, 1988—; cons. Pa. State U., Harrisburg, 1984-86. Vol. San Joaquin County Com. Action Agy., VISTA, Stockton, Calif., 1965-66, Gov.'s Com. Human Svcs., VISTA, St. Croix, U.S.V.I., 1966-67; bd. dirs. Planned Parenthood, Harrisburg, 1980-84, Infant Devel. Program, Harrisburg, 1983-84, Hershey Pub. Libr., 1981-83. Mem. Am. Soc. Tng. and Devel. (v.p. tech. skills tng. and devel. 1987—). Mem. Soc. of Friends.

HERSH, NELSON MARK, othodontist; b. Detroit, Mar. 18, 1956; s. Jerry Norman and Elaine Rita H.; m. Susan Hersh, Aug. 10, 1980; children: Michelle, Jessica, Rebecca. BS, U. Mich., 1977, DDS, 1981; MS, St. Louis U., 1993. Pvt. practice Commerce Twp., Mich., 1981—; physician Sinai Hosp., Detroit, 1993—. Mem. ADA, Am. Assn. Orthodontists, Mich. Assn. Orthodontists, Mich. Dental Assn., Detroit Dental Assn., Alpha Omega (Fred Garber award 1981). Home: 7239 Silver Leaf Lane West Bloomfield MI 48322-3329

HERSH, ROBERT LAWRENCE, psychotherapist; b. Bridgeport, Conn., Oct. 28, 1954; m. Sherri Lynn Schwartz, Nov. 25, 1979; children: Carrie Michelle, Hilary Isabel. BA, U. Miami, 1975, MEd, 1977; MS, Miami (Fla.) Inst. Psychology, 1987, D in Clin. Psychology, 1989. Lic. mental health counselor, Fla.; cert. forensic specialist; cert. master addiction counselor. Childcare worker Miami Children's Hosp., Fla., 1973-78; clin. supr. Village South Residential Treatment Ctr., Miami, 1977-78; clin. dir. Metatherapy Inst., Inc., Naranja, Fla., 1978-87, also chmn. bd. dirs.; pvt. practitioner Coral Gables, Fla., 1982—; mem. family svcs. protection team Metatherapy Inst., Inc., Naranja, 1995-96; cons. Gulliver Prep. Sch., Miami, 1982—; doctoral internship Dade County Juvenile Justice Ctr. and South Fla. Evaluation and Treatment Ctr., Miami, 1988-89; dir. counseling svcs. Internat. Fine Arts Coll., Miami, 1992—; pres., CEO Kahill Enterprises, Inc., Internat. Game Devel. Bd.; mem. Family Svcs. Planning Team, Dade County, Fla. Motion picture screenwriter. Bd. Trustees Internatl. Fine Arts Coll. Mem. AACD, APA, Am. Edn. and Rsch. Assn., Internat. Platform Assn., Nat. Assn. Forensic Counselors, Masonic Lodge. Office: 1390 S Dixie Hwy Ste 1309 Miami FL 33146-2944

HERSH, SHELDON PAUL, physician; b. Germany, Dec. 23, 1947; came to U.S., 1949; s. Fred and Sarah (Cytrin) H.; m. Helen Rosenbaum, Aug. 3, 1969; children: David, Joshua, Jennifer. BA, Yeshiva U., 1969; MD, N.Y. Med. Coll., 1978. Intern Brookdale Hosp. Med. Ctr., Bklyn., 1978-79; resident Manhattan Eye, Ear, and Throat Hosp., N.Y.C., 1979-82. Contbr. articles to profl. jours. Fellow ACS, Am. Bd. Otorhinolaryngology, Am. Acad. Otolaryngology; mem. Am. Rhinologic Soc., N.Y. State Med. Soc., Queens Med. Soc. Office: 11011 72nd Ave Flushing NY 11375-4946 also: 949 Central Ave Woodmere NY 11598-1204

HERSH, STANLEY BLAIR, ophthalmologist; b. Pitts., Jan. 15, 1943. BS, Bethany Coll., 1964; MD, Chgo. Med. Sch., 1969. Diplomate Am. Bd. Ophthalmology. Intern Jackson Meml. Hsop., Miami, Fla., 1969-70; resident in ophthalmology Yale-New Haven Hosp., New Haven, 1976; ophthalmologist Ophthalmic Surg. Assocs., Waterbury, Conn., 1976—; mem. staff in ophthalmology Waterbury Hosp., St. Mary's Hosp., Yale-New Haven Hosp., Waterbury, 1976—; clin. asst. prof. ophthalmology Yale-New Haven Hosp., New Haven, 1976—; cons. West Haven Vets. Hosp., West Haven, 1976—. Mem. AMA, Conn. State Med. Soc., New Haven County Med. Soc., Waterbury Med. Soc., Alpha Omega Alpha,. Office: Ophthalmic Surg Assocs 1201 W Main St Waterbury CT 06708-3105

HERSH, STEPHEN PETER, psychiatrist, educator; b. N.Y.C., Aug. 11, 1940; s. Joseph Harrison and Lillian (Berk) H.; m. Jean Ann Lehrke, Apr. 10, 1969; children: Damon, Katharine, Justin, Tessa. BA, Amherst Coll., 1962; MD, NYU, 1967. Diplomate Am. Bd. Psychiatry and Neurology. Pediatric intern NYU-Bellevue Med. Ctr., N.Y.C., 1967-68, fellow in child psychiatry, 1970-72; resident in psychiatry U. Pa., Phila., 1968-70; chief Ctr. for Studies in Child and Family Mental Health, NIMH, Rockville, Md., 1972-73, spl. asst. to dir., 1973-74, asst. dir., 1975-79; dir. div. children and youth St. Elizabeths Hosp., Washington, 1981; co-founder, co-dir., chmn. bd. Med. Illness Counseling Ctr., Chevy Chase, Md., 1982-94, exec. and med. dir., 1995—; behavioral health and medicine cons. Marriott Internat., 1996—; clin. prof. psychiatry and pediat. George Washington U. Med. Ctr., Washington, 1989—; cons. pediatric br. Nat. Cancer Inst., Bethesda, Md., 1972—; mem. nat. adv. coun. Nat. Anthrop. Film Ctr., Smithsonian Instn., Washington, 1979-81; chmn. sci. adv. bd. St. Jude Children's Rsch. Hosp., Memphis, 1980-82; attending physician, 1993-94, 95—; dir., prin. investigator HIV R&D project Nat. Cancer Inst., 1988—; med. staff clin. ctr., NIH, 1992—. Author: The Executive Parent, 1979, The Physician and the Mental Health of the Child, 1981; contbg. editor Journeys, 1994—; contbr. chpts. to books. Mem. svcs. com. Am. Cancer Soc., Washington, 1974-79; mem. com. on traffic Somerset (Md.) Town Coun., 1975-78; bd. dirs. Barker Found., Washington, 1984-87; mem. med. bd. Lupus Found. Greater Washington, 1988—, My Image After Breast Cancer, 1995—; bd. med. advisors Multimedia Med. Syss., 1996—. Recipient spl. award Nat. Consortium for Child Mental Health Svcs., 1979. Fellow Am. Psychiat. Assn. (commendation 1983, Significant Achievement award 1993); mem. AAAS, Am. Pain Soc., Am. Acad. Child and Adolescent Psychiatry (com. chmn. 1974-76). Democrat. Home: 421 Kent Square Rd Gaithersburg MD 20878-5711 Office: Med Illness Counseling Ctr 2 Wisconsin Cir Bethesda MD 20815-7003

HERSHBERG, PHILIP ISAAC, physician, electrical engineer, investment advisor; b. Albany, N.Y., Aug. 5, 1935; s. Ben B. and Ann (Gewirtzman) H.; m. Elena Sue Simon, Dec. 25, 1958; children: Jeffrey Aaron, Janet Rose, Matthew Charles. BEE, Rensselaer Poly. Inst., 1957; M Engring., Yale U., 1958; MD, SUNY, Bklyn., 1966. Registered profl. engr., Mass., N.Y.; registered investment advisor SEC. Engr. Norden-Kitay Corp., Milford, Conn., 1957-58, ITT Labs., Nuley, N.J., 1958-59; rsch. assoc. Maimonides Med. Ctr., Bklyn., 1962-66; assoc. in medicine Brigham & Women's Hosp., Boston, 1968-73; rsch. assoc., asst. prof. Harvard U. Sch. Pub. Health, Boston, 1968-73; rsch. assoc. Lahey Clinic Found., 1967-75; asst. prof. Boston U. Sch. Medicine, 1973-81; dir. rsch. NEICO Co., Hopkington, Mass., 1981-83; v.p. INVOCOM, Inc., Hopkinton, Mass., 1983-85; investment advisor Deermont Market Ctr., Wellesley, Mass., 1985—; pvt. practice medicine, Lynn, Mass., 1987-93; assoc. med. dir. Worcester County Hosp., Boylston, Mass., 1990-93; cons. physician USAF, Bedford, Mass., 1992-93. Contbr. articles to med. and tech. jours.; patentee in biomed. field. 1st lt. USAF, 1959-62; surgeon USPHS, 1966-67. Fellow Royal Coll. Health (Eng.), 1963. Mem. IEEE, Am. Coll. Preventive Medicine, B'nai B'rith (pres. Needham-Wellesley 1986-88, svc. award 1985). Home: 43 Harris Ave PO Box 332 Needham MA 02192 Office: Deermont Market Ctr 70 Walnut St Wellesley MA 02181-2102

HERSHEY, ALFRED DAY, geneticist; b. Owosso, Mich., Dec. 4, 1908; s. Robert Day and Alma (Wilbur) H.; m. Harriet Davidson, Nov. 15, 1945; 1 son, Peter. B.S., Mich. State U., 1930, Ph.D. in Chemistry, 1934, D.M.S., 1970; D.Sc. (hon.), U. Chgo., 1967. Asst. bacteriologist Washington U. Sch. Medicine, St. Louis, 1934-36; instr. Washington U. Sch. Medicine, 1936-38, asst. prof., 1938-42, asso. prof., 1942-50; mem. staff, genetics research unit Carnegie Inst. of Washington, Cold Spring Harbor, N.Y., 1950-62; dir. Carnegie Inst. of Washington, 1962-74; ret., 1974. Contbr. articles to profl. jours. Recipient Nobel prize in Medicine (joint), 1969; Albert Lasker award Am. Pub. Health Assn., 1958; Kimber Genetics award Nat. Acad. Scis., 1965. Mem. Nat. Acad. Scis. Address: 1640 Moores Hill Rd Syosset NY 11791

HERSHEY, GERALD LEE, psychologist; b. Detroit, Mar. 7, 1931; s Von Waltz and Clementine H.; m. Shirley Gauld, Oct. 2, 1954; children: Bruce, Dale, James. Student, UCLA, 1949-54; B.A. with honors, Mich. State U., 1957, M.A., 1958, Ph.D., 1961. Asst. instr., research assoc. Mich. State U., East Lansing, 1958-61; mem. faculty dept. psychology Fullerton Coll., Calif., 1961—, prof., 1965—, chmn. dept., 1980—; vis. prof. Chapman Coll., Calif., 1962-69. Co-author: Human Development (2d edit.), 1978, Living Psychology (3d edit.), 1981. Served to 1st lt. AUS, 1954-56. Mem. Am. Psychol. Assn., Assn. Humanistic Psychology, NEA. Lodge: Lions. Office: Fullerton College 321 E Chapman Ave Fullerton CA 92632-2011

HERSHEY, LINDA ANN, neurology and pharmacology educator; b. Marion, Ind., Jan. 15, 1947; d. Matthew John and Janice Elaine (Moody) Kwolek; m. Charles Owen Hershey, May 1, 1976; children: Edward, William, Erin. BS, Purdue U., 1968; PhD, Washington U., St. Louis, 1973, MD, 1975. Diplomate Am. Bd. Psychiatry and Neurology. Resident in neurology Barnes Hosp., St. Louis, 1976-78; fellow in clin. pharmacology Strong Meml. Hosp., Rochester, N.Y., 1978-80; asst. prof. neurology Case Western Res. U., Cleve., 1980-86; assoc. prof.neurology and pharmacology SUNY, Buffalo, 1986-94, prof. neurology and pharmacology, 1994—; chief neurology svc. Buffalo VA Med. Ctr., 1986—; mem. neurology adv. group VA, Washington, 1994—. Co-author: Handbook of Dementing Illnesses, 1994; mem. editl. bd. Clin. Pharmacology and Therapeutics, 1993—, Stroke, 1995—; contbr. articles to profl. jours. Co-dir. Alzheimers Disease Assistance Ctr., Buffalo, 1994—; elder Univ. Presbyn. Ch., Buffalo, 1995-96. Grantee Sterling-Winthrop Co., 1992-96, Lorex Pharms., 1995-96, Nat. Inst. Neurol. and Communicative Disorders and Stroke, 1994—, Parke-Davis, 1996—. Fellow Am. Acad. Neurology, Am. Neurol. Assn.; mem. Ctrl. Soc. for Neurol. Rsch., Am. Soc. Clin. Pharmacology and Therapeutics, Am. Heart Assn. (mem. exec. com. stroke coun. 1993—, chmn. program com. 1995—). Office: Buffalo VA Med Ctr 3495 Bailey Ave Buffalo NY 14215

HERSHEY, NATHAN, lawyer, educator; b. N.Y.C., Apr. 28, 1930; s. Harry and Hannah (Horwitz) H.; m. Carol Fine, July 13, 1958; children—Suzanne, Madeleine. A.B., N.Y. U., 1950; LL.B., Harvard U., 1953. Bar: D.C. 1953, Pa. 1977. Individual practice law N.Y.C., 1955-56; research assoc. in health law U. Pitts., 1956-58, asst. prof., 1958-63, assoc. prof., 1963-68, prof., 1968—; mem. Pa. Bd. Med. Edn., 1974-80; of counsel Markel, Schafer, and Goldman P.C., Pitts., 1977—, Post & Schell, Phila., 1984-94; cons. Pa. State Com. on Public Health and Welfare, 1973-80. Author: (with others) Hospital Law Manual, 1959, (with Robert D. Miller) Human Experimentation and the Law, 1976, Hospital-Physician Relations, 1982; editor: Hosp. Law Newsletter; contbr. articles to profl. jours. Bd. dirs. Women's Health Services, 1976-91, bd. v.p., 1982-91; Bd. dirs. Hill House Assn., Pitts., 1964-71. Served with U.S. Army, 1953-55. Mem. Inst. Medicine-NAS, Am. Soc. Hosp. Attys. (past pres.), Soc. Hosp. Attys. Western Pa. (dir. 1974-85, past pres.), Am. Pub. Health Assn. Democrat. Jewish. Home: 5423 Northumberland St Pittsburgh PA 15217-1128 Office: 1120 Grant Pittsburgh PA 15219-1906

HERSHKOWITZ, JAY, retired physician; b. N.Y.C., Mar. 18, 1922; s. Gustave and Ida (Osheyack) H.; m. Dorothy Frances Feinstein, June 28, 1947; children—Robin Marcia, Helene Lee, Sheryl Beth, Ona Lela. Student liberal arts Bklyn. Coll., 1939-42; A.B., Temple U., 1944; M.D., NYU, 1949. Diplomate Am. Bd. Family Practice. Intern Jewish Meml. Hosp., N.Y.C., 1949-50; practice medicine specializing in family practice, Bronx, 1950-89; med. dir. Bainbridge Nursing Home, Bronx, 1979-89, Wayne Nursing Home, Bronx, 1979-89; ret., 1989. Served to 1st lt. USAF, 1952-53. Fellow Am. Acad. Family Practice; mem. AMA, N.Y. State Acad. Family Practice, N.Y. State Med. Soc., Physicians Square Clubs Am. Avocations: stamps; photography; coins; Royal Doulton figures. Home: 3 Founders Ln East Hampton NY 11937-3303

HERSHMAN, JACK IRA, urologist; b. Bklyn., Oct. 7, 1955; s. Seymour and Sonia Elaine (Kamins) H.; m. Ingrid Gail Bernstein, Aug. 25, 1986; children: Melissa Paige, Jennifer Whitney, Neil Ross. BA in Biology magna cum laude, U. Rochester, 1977; MD, Mt. Sinai Sch. Medicine, 1981. Diplomate Am. Bd. Urology. Resident in surgery Lenox Hill Hosp., N.Y.C., 1981-82; resident in urology Montefiore Med. Ctr., Bronx, N.Y., 1983-86; chief urology Phelps Meml. Hosp., North Tarrytown, N.Y., 1986—; attending urologist Dobbs Ferry (N.Y.) Hosp., 1986—, Westchester County Med. Ctr., Valhalle, N.Y., 1986—; clin. instr. urology N.Y. Hosp., N.Y.C., 1987—; chief section urology Phelps Meml. Hosp., North Tarrytown, 1990—. Fellow Am. Coll. Surgeons; mem. Am. Urologic Soc., N.Y.S. Urologic Soc., N.Y. State Med. Soc., Westchester County Med. Soc., Phi Beta Kappa. Office: 777 N Broadway Ste 309 North Tarrytown NY 10591

HERSHON, LEE EDWARD, orthodontist, educator; b. N.Y.C., June 27, 1944; s. Martin and Betsy (Marks) H.; m. Nina Marcia Haskins, June 5, 1977; children: Lawrence, Marissa, Danielle. AB, Rutgers U., 1966; DDS magna cum laude, U. Md., Balt., 1970; cert., Harvard U., Boston, 1974. Diplomate Am. Bd. Orthodontics. Rsch. fellow Harvard U. and Forsyth Dental Ctr., Boston, 1972-744; asst. prof. Med. Coll. Va., Richmond, 1974-75; pvt. practice, Charleston, S.C., 1975—; assoc. clin. prof. Med. U. S.C., Richmond, 1974-75; mem. staff Trident Regional Hosp., Charleston, 1975—, VA Med. Ctr., Charleston, 1975—. Bd. dirs. Charleston Concert Assn., 1983-87, Charleston Symphony, 1985-90 Cpat. USAF, 1970-72. Fellow Internat. Coll. Dentists; mem. ADA, Am. Assn. Orthodontists, S.C. Assn. Orthodontists (pres. 1995-96), Rotary, Omicron Kappa Upsilon. Office: Orthodontic Assocs Charleston PA 86 Rutledge Ave Charleston SC 29401

HERSKOWITZ, IAN CAIN, physician, medical educator; b. Bklyn., Mar. 14, 1962; s. Herman and Lola (Levinson) H. BS, CCNY, 1984; MD, SUNY, Buffalo, 1986. Cert. diabetes educator Nat. Cert. Bd. Diabetes Educators. Intern then resident SUNY/Buffalo Affiliated Hosps., 1986-89; fellow in endocrinology and metabolism Washington U. and Barnes Hosp., St. Louis, 1989-91; asst. prof. medicine Med. Coll. Ga., Augusta, 1992—; mem. med. staff U. Hosp., Augusta, Ga., 1991—, Internal Medicine and Endocrine Assocs., Augusta, 1991—. Contbr. articles to profl. jours. bd. dirs. Juvenile Diabetes Found., Augusta, 1995—; mem., health care rep. Ricmond County Adv. Coun., Augusta, 1996—. Am. Assn. Diabetes Educators grantee, 1995. Fellow Am. Coll. Endocrinology; mem. ACP, Am. Diabetes Assn., Am. Assn. Clin. Endocrinology, Greater Augusta Diabetes Educators (pres. 1994-95). Office: Internal Med & Endocrine Assocs Augusta PC Ste 7A 820 Saint Sebastian Way Augusta GA 30901

HERSKOWITZ, IRA, educator, molecular geneticist; b. Bklyn., July 14, 1946. BS in Biology, Calif. Inst. Tech., 1967; PhD in Microbiology, MIT, 1971. From asst. to full prof. biology U. Oreg., Eugene, 1972-81; assoc. Inst. Molecular Biology, U. Oreg., Eugene, 1972-81; prof. dept. biochemistry and biophysics U. San Francisco, 1981—, chmn. dept., 1990-95, head divsn. genetics, 1981—; mem. genetics study sect. NIH, Bethesda, Md., 1986-90; mem. sci. rev. bd. in genetics Howard Hughes Med. Inst., Bethesda, 1986-94, mem. med. adv. bd. 1995—; vis. prof. Coll. de France, Paris, 1992; sci. adv. bd. Tularik, Inc., 1992-96; mem. sci. adv. com. Inst. Cancer Rsch., Fox Chase Cancer Ctr., 1995—, bd. sci. counsellors Nat. Cancer Inst., 1996—. Assoc. editor Virology, 1976-81, Genetics, 1982-87, Ann. Rev. Genetics, 1984-89; editor Jour. Molecular Biology, 1982-86, assoc. editor 1986-87; mem. editl. bd. Molecular and Cellular Biology of the Cell, 1989—, Trends in Genetics, 1990—; mem. bd. reviewing editors Sci., 1991-96. Mem. vis. com. for dept. biology MIT, 1982—. Recipient Eli Lilly award Am. Soc. Microbiology, 1983, Disting. Tchg. award U. Calif., San Francisco, 1984, medal Genetics Soc. Am., 1988, Howard Taylor Ricketts award, U. Chgo., 1992, Disting. Alumni award Calif. Inst. Tech., 1994; named Streisinger lectr. U. Oreg., 1984, Harvey Soc. lectr., 1986, Mendel lectr. Genetical Soc. Gt. Britain, 1991, Bateson lectr. John Innes Inst., Norwich, UK. Fellow AAAS, MacArthur Found., Am. Acad. Arts and Scis., Am. Soc. Microbiology; mem. Nat. Acad. Scis. (sci. reviewing award 1985), Genetics Soc. Am. (pres. 1985). Office: U Calif San Francisco Dept of Biochem & Biophys 513 Parnassus Ave San Francisco CA 94122-2722

HERSKOWITZ, MORTON STANLEY, psychiatrist; b. Trenton, N.J., May 23, 1918; s. Harry and Cecelia May (Krueger) H.; m. Frankie Kimmelman, 1946 (div. 1957); m. Karen Ann Tuttle, 1957; 1 child, Robin Ray. BA, Temple U., 1938; DO, Phila. Coll. Osteopathic Medicine, 1943. Diplomate Am. Osteo. Bd. Psychiatry. Analyst, trainee of Wilhelm Reich, 1949-52; pvt. practice psychiat. orgone therapy Phila., 1952—; clin. prof. psychiatry Phila. Coll. Osteo. Medicine, 1966-94, prof. emeritus, 1994—. Author: Human Armoring, 1990. Fellow Am. Coll. Neuropsychiatrists. Home and Office: 2132 Pine St Philadelphia PA 19103-6535

HERTLEIN, FRED, III, industrial hygiene laboratory executive; b. San Francisco, Oct. 17, 1933; s. Fred and Herta (Komning) H.; m. Clara Kam Fung Tse, Apr. 1958 (div. Apr. 1982); children: Fritz, Hans Wernher, Lisa Marie, Gretel Marga. BS in Chemistry, U. Nev., 1956; postgrad., U. Hawaii, Manoa, 1956-58. Cert. profl. chemist, indsl. hygienist, safety profl., hazard control mgr., bldg. insp. and mgmt. planner, biol. safety profl. Grad. teaching ast. in chemistry U. Hawaii, Honolulu, 1956-58; air pollution sampling sta. operator Truesdail Labs., Honolulu, 1957; chemist oceanographical research vessels Dept. Interior, 1957-59; with Bechtel-Hawaiian Dredging, 1959; co-owner marine survey co. Honolulu, 1959-60; radiochemist Pearl Harbor (Hawaii) Naval Shipyard, 1959-62, indsl. hygienist med. dept., 1962-69, head indsl.hygiene br., 1969-72; indsl. hygiene program mgr. Naval Regional Med. Clinic, Pearl Harbor Naval Sta., 1972-78; pres., dir. lab. and indsl. hygiene, co-owner Indsl. Analytical Lab., Inc., Honolulu, 1978—; pres. F. Hertlein & Assocs., 1970-78; asst. clin. prof. U. Hawaii Sch. Pub. Health, 1973—. Contbr. articles to profl. jours. Named Outstanding Male Fed. Employee, Honolulu Fed. Exec. Council, 1967, Citizen of Day citation Sta. KGU76, Honolulu, 1972, cert. of achievement Toastmasters Internat., 1974, expression of appreciation U. Hawaii Sch. Pub. Health, 1985. Fellow Am. Inst. Chemists (life); mem. Am. Acad. Indsl. Hygiene, Am. Chem. Soc., Am. Indsl. Hygiene Assn., Gesellschaft fü Aerosolforschung, Profl. Assn. Diving Instrs. (instr. emeritus), Tubists Universal Brotherhood Assn. (life). Home: 1493 Kaweloka St Pearl City HI 96782-1513 Office: Indsl Analytical Lab Inc 3615 Harding Ave Ste 305 Honolulu HI 96816-3759

HERTNEKY, RANDY LEE, optometrist; b. Burlington, Colo., Jan. 9, 1955; s. Harry Francis and Darleen Mae (Walters) H.; m. Laura Ann Ciaccio, Nov. 28, 1981; children: Lisa Kay, Erin Elizabeth. BA, U. Colo., 1977; OD, So. Calif. Coll. Optometry, Fullerton, 1981. Pvt. practice optometry Yuma, Colo., 1982—. Precinct committeeman Yuma County Rep. Com., 1986—; mem. bd. rev. Boy Scouts Am., Yuma, 1982—; chmn. bldg. com. Yuma H.S., 1987-89; bd. dirs. Yuma Hosp. Found., 1990—, vice chmn., 1994—; chmn. Yuma Sch. Curriculum Com., 1993. Mem. APHA, Am. Optometric Assn. (coord. Colo. Polit. Action Com. 1995—), Colo. Optometric Assn. (trustee 1989-90, vice chmn. legis. com. 1994—, nominee Optometrist of Yr. 1996), Coll. Optometrists in Vision Devel. (assoc.), Lions (treas. 1987-88, pres. 1991-92, Lion of Yr. award 1992), KC (sec. 1990-95, dep. grand knight 1995—). Roman Catholic. Office: 107 S Main St Yuma CO 80759-1913

HERTZ, ILONA H., radiologist; b. N.Y.C., July 8, 1947; d. Ben and Frances Judith (Ramer) H.; m. Howard Martin Rubenstein, Sept. 1, 1969; children: Tara Jo, Benjamin David. BS, CCNY, 1969; MD, SUNY, Bklyn., 1973. Diagnostic radiologist Beranbaum, Khilnani, Neistadt, Jacobs, Hertz & Sherman MDs, N.Y.C., 1984—, MRI of Manhattan, N.Y.C., 1989—, N.Y. Women's Partnership for Health, N.Y.C., 1995—. Fellow Am. Coll. Gastroenterology; mem. Radiologic Soc. N. Am., Am. Med. Womens' Assn., Soc. Breast Imaging. Office: NY Womens Partnership for Health 121 E 60th St New York NY 10022

HERTZBERG, MICHAEL, psychiatrist; b. N.Y.C., Sept. 17, 1945; s. Philip and Edith (Kohn) H.; m. Deborah Asher, Jan. 14, 1984; children: Jeremy Asher, Ethan Daniel. BS, CCNY, 1967; MD, SUNY, Syracuse, 1971. Diplomate Am. Bd. Psychiatry and Neurology. Dir. inpatient svcs. Mt. Vernon Ctr. for Cmty. Mental Health, Alexandria, Va., 1976-78; pvt. practice Alexandria, 1977—; clin. asst. prof. psychiatry Georgetown U. Med. Ctr., Washington, 1978—. Lt. comdr. USPHS, 1972-74. Mem. Am. Psychiat. Assn., Med. Soc. Va., Washington Psychiat. Soc., Alexandria Med. Soc. Office: 803 Franklin St Alexandria VA 22314

HERTZBERGER, DONALD PAUL, cardiologist, researcher; b. Amsterdam, The Netherlands, Mar. 22, 1947; s. Menno and Dora (Haverkamp Begemann) H.; m. Janine A. Van Huls Van Taxis; children: Maurits R., Fleur W., Arnout J. MD, U. Leiden, The Netherlands, 1975; degree in cardiology, U. Amsterdam, 1980. Cert. ECFMG, cardiologist. Cardiologist dept. cardiology U. Amsterdam, 1980; chief of staff dept. cardiology Canisius-Wilhelmina Hosp., Nijmegen, 1981—; cons. St. Maartens Kliniek, Nijmegen, The Netherlands, 1982—. Pres. Beroeps Belangen Commissie, 1989-94. 1st lt. Med. Corps, 1975-76. Mem. NVVC (bd. dirs. 1989-94), KNMG, Dutch Soc. Cardiology (bd. dirs. 1989-94). Home: Theresiaweg 4A, 6523 ND Nijmegen The Netherlands Office: Canisius-Wilhelmina Hosp, Weg Door Jonkerbos 100, 6532 SZ Nijmegen The Netherlands

HERZ, MARVIN IRA, psychiatrist; b. N.Y.C., Dec. 24, 1927; s. Jules Edward and Vivian M. (Becker) H.; m. Beatrice Leslie Mittelman, Sept. 13, 1952; 3 children. B.A., U. Mich., 1949; M.S. in Psychology, Yale U., 1950; M.D., Chgo. Med. Sch., 1955; cert. in psychoanalysis, Columbia U., 1968. Diplomate Am. Bd. Psychiatry and Neurology (sr. examiner). Intern U. Ill. Research and Ednl. Hosps., 1955-56; resident in psychiatry Michael Reese Hosp., Chgo., 1956-59; dir. inpatient service div. psychiatry Montefiore Hosp., N.Y.C., 1961-63; dir. Westchester Sq. Day Hosps., N.Y.C., 1963-65; asst. prof. psychiatry Albert Einstein Coll. Medicine, N.Y.C., 1963-65; asso. in psychiatry Columbia U., 1965-68, asst. prof. clin. psychiatry, 1968-72, asso. prof., 1972-77; ward adminstr. Washington Heights Community Service, N.Y. State Psychiat. Inst., 1965-68; asst. attending psychiatrist Vanderbilt Clinic, Presbyn. Hosp., N.Y.C., 1965-68; dir. Washington Hts. Community Service, 1968-72; dir. community services N.Y. State Psychiat. Inst., 1972-77, acting clin. dir., 1975-76; med. dir. Ga. Mental Health Inst., Atlanta, 1977-78; dir. ops. research, 1977-78; prof. psychiatry Emory U., 1977-78; prof., chmn. dept. psychiatry SUNY Sch. Medicine, Buffalo, 1978-91; dir. psychiatry Erie County Med. Center, Buffalo, 1978-91; head dept. psychiatry Buffalo Gen. Hosp., 1978-91; prof. U. Rochester, N.Y., 1991—; cons. in psychiatry VA Hosp., Buffalo, 1978-91; sr. sci. advisor to dir. NIMH, 1989-91, cons. psychiatry edn. br., 1978; cons. Robert Wood Johnson Found., 1992; cons. Nat. Heart and Lung Inst., Task Panel of

Pres.'s Commn. on Rsch. in Mental Illness, 1977; chmn. psychiat. com. N.Y. State Office Mental Health, 1980-87. Contbr. articles to med. jours. Served to lt. comdr. USNR, 1959-61. Recipient award for outcomes rsch. World Assn. for Psychosocial Rehab., U.S. Br., 1994, Heinz Lehmann rsch. award N.Y. State Office Mental Health, 1994. Fellow Am. Psychiat. Assn. (chmn. com. to develop practice guidelines for schizophrenia 1992—, prize in hosp. psychiatry rsch. 1988, chair rsch. prize com. 1996—), Am. Coll. Psychiatrists (bd. regents 1990-93, 2d v.p. 1994-95, v.p. 1995, pres. elect 1996, Dean award for rsch. in schizophrenia 1993), Am. Coll. Psychoanalysts (treas. 1991-95, v.p. 1996—); mem. Assn. for Clin. Psychosocial Rsch. (pres. 1993-95), Assn. Psychoanalytic Medicine (chmn. com. on comm. psychiatry 1975-76), Am. Psychopathol. Assn., Psychiat. Inst. Am., Alpha Omega Alpha. Home: 5 Vineyard Hill Fairport NY 14450-4601 Office: U Rochester Med Ctr 300 Crittenden Blvd Dept of Psychiatry Rochester NY 14642

HERZ, SYLVIA BEATRICE, clinical and community psychologist; b. N.Y.C., May 1, 1930; d. Jacob and Minnie (Glucksman) Schnipper; m. Jean A. Herz, Apr. 29, 1955; 1 child, Howard Todd Jaffe. BS, Hunter Coll., 1940; MS, NYU and Oreg. State U., Corvallis, 1945; PhD, NYU, 1964. Lic. psychologist; diplomate Am. Bd. Family Psychology, Am. Bd. Sexology. Clin. psychologist cmty. and pvt. practice, N.J., 1964—; pres. Essex County Coun. on Drug Addiction, N.J., 1975-85; chmn. Essex County Mental Health Bd., 1970-76; cons. N.J. Dept. Health, 1972-93; mem. adv. bd. Gov.'s Commn. on Children and Families, 1970-80; mem. N.J. Bd. Psychology Examiners, 1980-90; cons., advisor Gov.'s Task Force on Children and Families, 1980-94. Editor Jour. Family Psychology, 1970-80; contbr. articles to profl. jours. Recipient Nat. Rohrer award APA, 1990, award N.J. Pub. Health Assn., 1985, others. N.J. Pub. Health Assn. (pres. 1989-94). Home: 220 Tillou Rd South Orange NJ 07079

HERZENBERG, JOHN ERIC, medical educator; b. Springfield, Mass., Apr. 13, 1955; s. Jerry S. and Helen (Chernaik) H.; m. Merrill S. Chaus, June 18, 1979. BA, MD, Boston U., 1979. Intern in gen. surgery Montefiore-Einstein Hosps., Bronx, N.Y., 1979-81; resident in orthopaedic surgery Duke U., Durham, N.C., 1981-85; fellow in pediatric orthopaedics Hosp. for Sick Children, Toronto, Ont., Can., 1985-86; instr. U. Mich., Ann Arbor, 1986-88, asst. prof., 1988-91; assoc. prof. U. Md., Balt., 1991—; co-dir. Md. Ctr. for Limb Lengthening and Reconstrn., Balt., 1991—; dir. med. edn. Kernan Hosp., Balt. Mem. Am. Acad. Orthopaedic Surgeons, Assn. for Study of Application of Methods of Ilizarov, Assn. Bone and Joint Surgeons, Royal Coll. Surgeons, Can. Orthopaedic Assn., Pediatric Orthopaedic Soc. of North Am. Office: 2200 Kernan Dr Baltimore MD 21207-6650

HERZFELD-KIMBROUGH, CIBY, mental health educator; b. Mobile, Ala., Oct. 10, 1941; d. Julius Sr. and Nettie (Fraizer) Herzfeld; m. Charles C. Kimbrough, Nov. 28, 1964; children: Carolos R., Choron F. BS, U. Mo., 1970; MA, Wash. U., 1980; MAT, AGC, Webster U., 1982. Cert. tchr., Mo. Coord. children-adolescent svcs. Metro Comprehensive Mental Health Ctr., St. Louis; cons. C. Kimbrough and Assocs.; instr. minority mental health Wash. U., St. Louis; founder, exec. dir. Creative Inovative and Behavioral Experences, CIBE; mng. dir. CKAN Ltd., Nigeria; project coord. Children's Devel. Ctr., Lagos, Nigeria; intervention specialist, counselor Ferguson Florissant Schs.; adj. instr. St. Louis U.; developer Children's Treatment Program; established Metroties Day Treatment Sch., 1987. Knoxville Coll. acad. scholarship, 1961; NIMH fellow, 1979; recipient Outstanding Leadership award Woman's Collaboration Conf., 1985, Exceptional Tchr. award INROADS Pre-Coll. Inst., 1986, Devel. award MTS, Lagos, Nigeria. Mem. Nat. Black Child Devel. Inst. (pres. St. Louis affiliate, Outstanding Svc. award), St. Louis Assn. of Black Psychologists (membership chair), St. Louis Mental Health Assn. (children's svcs. coun., membership chair), Mo. Psychol. Assn. (St. Louis network for women psychologists sec.), Nigerian Field Soc. (membership chair), Internat. Platform Soc., 100 Black Women, Nigerian Federated Women, Am. Woman's Club. Home: 11752 Russet Meadow Dr Saint Louis MO 63146-4231

HERZIG, DAVID JACOB, pharmaceutical company executive and licensing director, immunopharmacologist; b. Cleve., Dec. 13, 1936; s. Marvin Laurence and Lillian Gertrude (Blaine) H.; m. Phyllis Glicksberg, Sept. 2, 1962; children—Michael, Pamela, Roberta, Karen. BA, Oberlin Coll., 1958; PhD in Chemistry, U. Cin., 1963. Vis. scientist NIH, Bethesda, Md., 1963-65, staff fellow, 1965-67; sr. rsch. assoc. NYU Sch. Medicine, N.Y.C., 1967-68, Warner Lambert, Parke-Davis Co., Ann Arbor, Mich., 1968-77, dir. immunopharmacology, 1977-81, dir. sci. devel., 1981-94, v.p. drug devel. and sci. devel. Mich. Biotechnology Inst., also bd. dirs. Contbr. articles to profl. jours. Bd. dirs. Mich. Ctr. High Tech., 1992-95. Fellow Damon Runyon Meml. Fund. Mem. AAAS, Am. Soc. Pharmacology and Exptl. Therapeutics, Am. Acad. Allergy Immunology, Mich. Biotech. Assn. (bd. dirs. 1993-96, pres. 199496), N.Y. Acad. Scis., N.Y. Fencers Club (bd. dirs. 1970-77), Sigma Xi. Avocations: squash, fencing, furniture building. Home: 3540 Windemere Dr Ann Arbor MI 48105-2842 Office: Warner Lambert Parke-Davis 2800 Plymouth Rd Ann Arbor MI 48105-2430

HERZOG, BERNARD MAURICE JEAN, radiology educator; b. Nancy, Meurthe et Moselle, France, Dec. 28, 1935; s. Eugène and Elisabeth (Dufour) H.; m. Anne-Marie Vlasak (div. 1974); children: Xavier, Bertrand, Hedwige; m. Christine Renaud, 1984; 1 child, Irvin. Licencié-ès sciences, Faculté des sciences, Nancy, 1961; Doctorat en Médecine, Faculté de Médecine, Nancy, 1961; nat. degree in electroradiology, Paris, 1963. Biophysics research chief Faculté de Médecine, Nancy, 1961-63; asst. electroradiologist Faculté de Médecine, Grenoble, France, 1964-66; prof. electroradiology Faculté de Médecine, Nantes, France, 1966—; head radiology depts. Nantes Hosp. System, 1966—; consistent research in med. pathology and immunology, Nancy, 1959-64, musicotherapy and psychoanalysis, Nantes, 1975—. Author: Death, Love and Dreams, 1987, The Cancerous Imaginary, 1987; exhibited artist (oil paintings, stained glass, lithography, charcoal) throughout Europe.

HERZOG, GARY L., radiologist; b. N.Y.C., Apr. 26, 1958; s. Irwin Arnold and Beverly (Stein) H. BA, Emory U., 1979; DO, N.Y. Coll. Osteopathic Med., 1994. Attending physician Staten Island (N.Y.) Univ. Hosp., 1991-95; dir. dept. nuclear medicine Good Samaritan Hosp., West Islip, N.Y., 1995-96. Mem. Am. Coll. Radiologists, Radiol. Soc. N.Am., Soc. Nuclear Med., RRS.

HERZOG, KATHRYN WEDEL, health care administrator, hospice consultant; b. Des Moines, Nov. 10, 1955; d. Herman J. and Evelyn K. (Kempker) Wedel; m. Benjamin David Herzog, May 16, 1981; children: Sarah, Kate. BSN, U. Iowa, 1978; MSN, U. Tex., 1980. Staff nurse U. Iowa Hosp., Iowa City, 1977-79; head nurse, supr. Seton Med. Ctr., Austin, Tex., 1980-83; asst. dir. nursing Sacred Heart Med. Ctr., Chester, Pa., 1983-84; Nat. Standard Seminar Instr., hospice surveyer Joint Commn. on Accreditation of Healthcare, Orgns., Chgo., 1983-89; exec. dir. Del. Hospice, Wilmington, 1984-85; dir. nursing Bapt. Hosp., Beaumont, Tex., 1986-89; guest lectr. Lamar U., 1988-89; dir. cancer programs Houston Hosp.-Clear Lake, 1989-92; nat. hospice cons., 1983—; bd. dirs. Del. Hospice. Author of monthly continuing edn. program for nurses, Cancer Awareness, 1983; rsch. presentation at Nat. Conf. on Nursing Adminstrn. Rsch., 1981; manuscript reviewer; contbr. articles to profl. jours. Co-faciliator I Can Cope program, Am. Cancer Soc., Austin, 1981-83, 89—, instr. self breast exam Austin, Wilmington, Del., Houston, 1980-92, pres. Bay Area unit Am. Cancer Soc., Houston, 1990-92, Triple Crown awards, 1991-92; CPR Instr. Am. Heart Assn., Austin, Wilmington, Houston, 1979—; lectr. on women and cancer to local hosp. and community groups, Austin, Wilmington, Houston, 1980—; mem. long range planning com. Del. Hospice, 1994—, Sanford Sch., 1993—; Mem. St. Mary's Parish Coun., 1994—, exec. com., 1995-96. Nominated for Outstanding Young Alumnus U. Iowa, 1983. Mem. Tex. Nurses Assn. (dist. 5 first v.p. 1981-82), Oncology Nursing Soc. (convention del. 1982), Del. State Hospice Orgn. (state rep. 1984-85), Nat. Hospice Orgn. (nat. convention workshop instr. 1983—), Am. Heart Assn., Am. Nurses Assn., Wilmington Women in Bus., Young Exec. Club, Phi Kappa Phi, Sigma Theta Tau. Avocations: china painting, reading, swimming. Home: 31 Slashpine Cir Hockessin DE 19707-9206

HERZOG, NORBERT KARL, molecular biology and virology educator; b. Belo Horizonte, Brazil, Feb. 11, 1955; came to U.S., 1960.; s. Karl Heinz and Elisabeth Herzog; m. Jean Talmage, Dec. 29, 1979. BA in Bacteriology, UCLA, 1976; MS in Biology, Calif. State U., Northridge, 1979; PhD in Microbiology, U. Tex., 1985. Teaching asst. dept. biology Calif. State U., Northridge, 1978-79; teaching asst. dept. microbiology U. Tex., Austin, 1980-81, rsch. asst. dept. microbiology, 1981-85, Nat. Cancer Inst. graduate trainee, dept. microbiology, 1982-85, Welch Found. postdoctoral fellow, dept. microbiology, 1986; postdoctoral rsch. fellow, dept. molecular biology Scripps Clinic and Rsch. Found., La Jolla, Calif., 1986; postdoctoral rsch. fellow, dept. molecular pathology M.D. Anderson Cancer Ctr., Houston, 1987, Welch Found. postdoctoral fellow, dept. molecular pathology, 1988, NIH postdoctoral fellow, dept. molecular pathology, 1988; asst. prof., depts. of pathology and microbiology U. Tex. Med. Br., Galveston, 1989—; mem. WHO Collaborating Ctr. for Tropical Diseases, 1994—. Contbr. articles to profl. jours. Grantee U.S. Army, John Sealy Meml. Endowment Fund, U. Tex. Med. Br. Retrovirus Rsch. Ctr. Mem. Am. Soc. for Microbiology, Tissue Culture Assn. Tex. br., Am. Assn. for the Advancement Sci., Phi Kappa Phi, Sigma Xi. Office: Dept Pathology 0609 U Tex Med Br Galveston TX 77555-0609

HESLEP, GRANT DANIEL, ophthalmologist; b. LaCrosse, Wis., Feb. 7, 1962; s. George Herbert and Eileen Jean (Tweten) H.; m. Lori Tyler, Oct. 22, 1988; children: Kristin, Daniel. BS with high honors, U. Fla., 1984, MD, 1987. Intern La. State U., Shreveport, 1988, resident, 1988-91, chief resident, 1991; chief ophthalmology Owatanna (Minn.) Clinic, 1991—; clin. instr. U. Minn., Mpls., 1992—; cons. VA Hosp., Mpls., 1992—; pres. Owatonna Hosp., 1996, v.p. med. staff, 1995. Wentworth scholar, U. Liberal Arts U. Fla., 1981, 82. Fellow Am. Acad. Ophthalmology; mem. AMA (del. 1984), Am. Soc. Cataract and Refractive Surgery, Minn. Med. Assn. (del. 1993-96), Minn. Ophthalmologic Soc. (sec. 1994, 96), Steele County Med. Soc. (pres. 1992—), Contact Lens Assn. Ophthalmologists, Lions, Phi Beta Kappa. Office: Owatonna Clinic 134 Southview Owatonna MN 55060

HESS, DARLA BAKERSMITH, cardiologist, educator; b. Valparaiso, Fla., June 4, 1953; d. James Barry and Irma Marie (Baker) Bakersmith; m. Leonard Wayne Hess, July 20, 1988; 1 child, Ever Marie. BS, Birmingham So. Coll., 1975; MD, Tulane U., 1979. Diplomate Am. Bd. Internal Medicine, Am. Bd. Cardiovascular Disease. Commd. ensign USN, 1979, advanced through grades to lt. comdr., 1988; resident in internal medicine Portsmouth (Va.) Naval Hosp., 1979-82, cardiologist, head non-invasive cardiology, 1986-88; fellow in cardiology San Diego Naval Hosp., 1982-84; cardiologist, head med. officer in charge ICU Camp Lejeune (N.C.) Naval Hosp., 1984-85; asst. prof. medicine U. Miss. Med. Ctr., Jackson, 1988-91, asst. prof. ob/gyn., 1990-91; dir. adult echocardiography, co-dir. fetal echocardiography U. Mo., Columbia, 1991—, co-dir. Adult Cogenital Heart Disease Clinic, 1991—, asst. prof. medicine, asst. prof. ob/gyn., 1991—. Author: (with others) Obstetrics and Gynecology Clinics, 1992, Clinical Problems in Obstetrics & Gynecology, 1993, General Medical Disorders During, 1991; contbr. articles to So. Med. Jour., Ob/Gyn. Clinics N.Am., So. Med. Assn. Annual Meeting, Soc. Perinatal Obs., Jour. Reproductive Medicine. Fellow Am. Coll. Cardiology; mem. Am. Heart Assn. (fellow stroke coun.), Am. Soc. Echocardiography, Am. Assn. Nuclear Cardiology, Phi Beta Kappa, Alpha Omega Alpha. Republican. Episcopalian. Home: PO Box 10200 Columbia MO 65205-4003 Office: U Mo Health Sci Ctr 1 Hospital Dr Columbia MO 65212-5276

HESS, EVELYN VICTORINE (MRS. MICHAEL HOWETT), medical educator; b. Dublin, Ireland, Nov. 8, 1926; came to U.S., 1960, naturalized, 1965; d. Ernest Joseph and Mary (Hawkins) H.; m. Michael Howett, Apr. 27, 1954. MB, BChir BA in Obstetrics, U. Coll., Dublin, 1949; MD, 1980. Intern West Middlesex Hosp., London, Eng., 1950; resident Clare Hall Hosp., London, 1951-53, Royal Free Hosp. and Med. Sch., London, 1954-57; rsch. fellow in epidemiology of Tb Royal Free Med. Sch., London, 1955; asst. prof. internal medicine U. Tex. Southwestern Med. Sch., 1960-64; assoc. prof. dept. medicine U. Cin. Coll. Medicine, 1964-69, McDonald prof. medicine, 1969—, dir. div. immunology, 1964-95; sr. investigator Arthritis and Rheumatism Found., 1963-68; attending physician Univ. Hosp., chief clinician Arthritis Clinic, 1965—; attending physician VA Hosp.; cons. Children's Hosp., Cin., 1967—, Jewish Hosp., Cin., 1968—; mem. various coms., mem. nat. adv. coun. NIH; mem. various coms. FDA, Cin. Bd. Health. Contbr. articles on immunology, rheumatic diseases to jours., chpts. to books. Active Nat. Pks. Assn., Smithsonian Instn., others. Recipient Arthritis Found., 1973, 78, 83, Am. Lupus Soc., 1979, Am. Acad. Family Practice, 1980, award for AIDS work State of Ohio, 1989, Spirit of Am. Women award, 1989; travel fellow Royal Free Med. Sch., Scandinavia, 1956, Empire Rheumatism Coun., 1958-59. Master ACP; fellow Am. Acad. Allergy, Royal Soc. Medicine; mem. Heberden Soc., Am. Coll. Rheumatology, Pan-Am. League Assns. for Rheumatology, Ctrl. Soc. Clin. Rsch., Am. Fedn. Clin. Rsch., Am. Assn. Immunologists, Am. Soc. Nephrology, Am. Soc. Clin. Pharmacology and Therapeutics, Transplantation Soc., Reticuloendothelial Soc., N.Y. Acad. Scis., Soc. Exptl. Biology and Medicine, Rheumatological Soc. Colombia (hon.), Rheumatological Soc. Peru (hon.), Rheumatological Soc. Italy (hon.), Clin. Immunol. Soc. Japan (hon.), Alpha Omega Alpha. Home: 2916 Grandin Rd Cincinnati OH 45208-3418 Office: U Cin Med Ctr Cincinnati OH 45267

HESS, LOIS K., lawyer; b. Belleville, Ill., Aug. 1, 1951; d. Sidney and Jane Ann (Litowicz) Katz; m. Paul Patrick Hess, Jr., Jan. 14, 1973; children: Mark Robert, Abby Moran. BA, Ind. U., 1973, degree in nursing, 1976; JD, Ill. Inst. Tech., 1982. Bar: Ky., Ill., Md.; RN. Charge nurse orthopedics Bloomington (Ind.) Hosp., 1976-77; staff nurse Jewish Hosp., Louisville, 1977, Methodist-Evang. Hosp., Louisville, 1977-79; atty. Altman & Assocs., Belleville, 1983-84; asst. state's atty. St. Clair County, Ill., 1984-85; dir. med. legal svcs. St. Louis Univ. Hosp., 1985-90; atty. healthcare sect. Wyatt, Tarrant & Combs, Louisville, 1990-92; assoc. gen. counsel to counsel Jewish Hosp. Healthcare Svcs., Inc., Louisville, 1992—; instr. St. Louis U., 1987-90, spl. apptd. instnl. review bd., 1989-90. Bylaws com. chair Pine View Sch. PTO, New Albany, Ind., 1993—, 2d. v.p., 1993, 94. Mem. Am. Acad. of Healthcare Attys., Nat. Health Lawyers' Assn., Louisville Bar Assn., Ky. Bar Assn., Alpha Club, Family and Children's Agy. (bd. dirs.). Home: 1302 Ridgeway Ave New Albany IN 47150 Office: Jewish Hosp Health Care Svc 217 E Chestnut St Louisville KY 40202

HESS, PATRICIA ALICE, nursing educator, geriatrics nurse consultant; b. N.Y.C., Apr. 25, 1938; d. Frederic and Anne (Goldman) H. BSN, Case Western Reserve U., 1961; MS, U. Colo., 1966; PhD, Walden U., 1982; cert. geriatric nurse practitioner, U. Calif., San Francisco, 1986. Cert. gerontol. nurse. Staff nurse Univ. Hosps., Cleve., 1961-62; head nurse Mt. Sinai Hosp., Cleve., 1962-65; instr. U. Mich., Ann Arbor, 1966-67; prof. nursing San Francisco State U., 1967—, U. Calif. Berkeley, 1977-85. Contbr. articles to profl. jours. Recipient Book of Yr. award Am. Jour. Nursing, 1977, 82, 86, 90, 94. Mem. Gerontol. Soc. Am., Am. Soc. on Aging, Nat. League for Nursing, Nat. Acad. Practice. Home: 1341 27th Ave San Francisco CA 94122-1508 Office: San Francisco State U Sch Nursing 1600 Holloway Ave San Francisco CA 94132-1722

HESS, WALTER OTTO, surgeon; b. Zurich, Canton, Switzerland, July 26, 1918; s. Walter and Hermine (Schäublin) H.; m. Charlotte Schmidlin, May 17, 1947 (dec. Feb. 1974); children: Gerhard Walter, Claudia Renate. MD, U. Zurich, 1944. Lic. MD, Switzerland. Resident pathology Swiss Rsch. Inst., Davos, Switzerland, 1945-46; resident Surgical Clinic U. Basle, Switzerland, 1946-49, first resident, 1950-57; resident Surgical Clinic U. Heidelberg, Fed. Republic of Germany, 1949-50; prof. surgery Alexandria (Egypt) U., 1957-59; pvt. practice Zurich, Switzerland, 1960-81; prof. Surgery U. Basle, Switzerland, 1964-85; leading physician Inst. Med. Experts, Zurich, 1988-93. Author: Chirurgie des Pankreas, 1950, Operative Cholangiographie, 1954, Erkrankungen der Gallenweg und des Pankreas, 1959, 2d edit., 1986-93 (prize 1960), Textbook of Bilio-pancreatic Diseases, 4 vols., 1996. Dep. Cantonal Parliament, Zurich, 1968-81; del. Internat. Red Cross, Geneva, 1969-72; Counsellor Community Coun., Kilchberg, Switzerland, 1975-79. Capt. Swiss Army, 1951-54. Named Hon. Mem. Italian Soc. Surgery, Rome, 1972, Acad. Lancisiana, Rome, 1973, Surgical Assn. Cuba, Havana, 1974, Acad. Peruana de Cirugua, 1975, Colegio Brasiliero de Clrugioes, 1975, Acad. de Ciencias Medicas de Cordoba, 1977, Hon. Prof. U. Ica, Peru, 1978. Mem. Swiss Med. Assn., Swiss Soc. Surgery, Swiss Soc. Gastroenterology, Internat. Hepato-pancreatoI-biliary Assn. (hon.), Masons (W. master 1984-90 In Labore Virtus, Grand Officer Swiss Grand Lodge). Mem. Liberal Party. Home: Chalberweidstrasse 47, Canton Zurich, CH-8127 Forch Switzerland

HESSE, GRETE ANNA ERNA, psychologist; b. Botersen, Kreis, Rotenburg, Federal Republic of Germany, Aug. 2, 1933; came to the U.S, 1955; d. Adolf Friedrich and Katharina Margarete (Dierks) H. BA in Psychology, Rutgers U., 1970; MA in Clin. Psychology, Fairleigh Dickinson U., 1972; PhD in Clin. Psychology, Union Inst., 1989; MS in Interdisciplinary Studies in Human Devel., U. Pa., 1989. Lic. psychologist, N.J., Pa. Intern psychology N. J. Dept. Inst. and Agencies, Trenton, 1972-73; psychologist Cumberland County Guidance Ctr., Millville, 1974-80, Ancora Psychiatric Hosp., Hammonton, 1980—; pvt. practice Gloucester Twp., N.J., 1992—; adj. mem. faculty Rutgers U., Camden, N.J., 1989—. Bd. dirs. Internat. Fund AIDS Rsch. and Edn. Mem. German Soc. Pa. Lutheran. Home: 19 Aspen Rd Country Oaks Sicklerville NJ 08081 Office: Ancora Psychiatric Hosp Spring Gardens Rd Hammonton NJ 08037-2704

HESSE, STEFAN, neurologist, consultant; b. Tuebingen, Germany, May 23, 1960; s. Fritz and Gerda (Minsseu) H.; m. Beate Brandl; children: Felix, Stefanie. MD, Tech. U. Munich, 1985. Rsch. asst. Tech. U. Munich, 1985-90; cons. neurologist Berlin, 1990—. Contbr. articles to profl. jours. Home: Kastanienallee 32, 14050 Berlin Germany Office: Klinik Berlin, Kladows Damm 223, 14089 Berlin Germany

HESSEL, DOROTHY ELIZABETH, business administrator; b. Queens, N.Y., Mar. 30, 1963; d. John S. and Mary C. (Manning); m. Joseph James Hessel, Aug. 4, 1990. BS in Mktg., Providence Coll., R.I., 1985; MBA, U. Maine, 1995. Med. sales rep. Pfizer, Inc., Yonkers, N.Y., 1985-88; hosp. rep. Pfizer, Inc., New Haven, Conn., 1988-89; ast. regional mgr. Pfizer, Inc., Clifton, N.J., 1989-90; hosp. rep. Pfizer, Inc., Gainesville, Fla., 1990-91; bus. mgr. Ariz. Cardiovascular Ctr., Phoenix; mem. North Fla. Soc. Hosp. Pharmacists, Gainesville, Fla., 1990-91, Nat. Assn. Female Execs., Gainesville, 1990—. Recipient Rookie of Yr., Pfizer Mgmt., Westchester, N.Y., 1987, Top Hosp. Rep. in U.S., Pfizer Mgmt., New Haven Conn., 1988. Mem. Jr. Med. Guild. Roman Catholic. Home: 5850 N 46th St Phoenix AZ 85018 Office: 515 W Buckeye Rd #306 Phoenix AZ 85003

HESSION, TIMOTHY JOHN, orthodontist; b. Nyack, N.Y., Nov. 28, 1954; s. James Francis and Anna (Buhrman) H.; m. Suzanne Marie Licht, May 24, 1981; Rebecca, Richard, Timothy P. BS, Villanova U., 1976; DDS, SUNY, Buffalo, 1980; MS in Orthodontics, U. Iowa, 1982. Chief of orthodontics USAF, Eielson AFB, Ark., 1982-85; orthodontist Orthodontic Assocs. of Ctrl. N.Y., P.C., Oneida, 1986—; cons. cleft palate clinic SUNY, Syracuse, N.Y. 1993-96. V.p. Bd. of Edn., Oneida, 1994-95, pres., 1996; bd. dirs. United Way of Greater Oneida, 1990-93; pres. PTA, Oneida, 1993-96. Mem. Am. Assn. Orthodontics, Dental Soc. State N.Y. (bd. dirs. 5th dist. 1993-96), Madison County Dental Soc. (chair children's dental health 1988-93, gov. 1986—), Orthognathics Study Group Ctrl. N.Y. (chmn. 1991-92), Rotary (past pres.). Home: 472 Main St Oneida NY 13421 Office: Orthodontic Assocs Ctrl NY 131 Main St Oneida NY 13421

HESTON, LEONARD LANCASTER, psychiatry educator; b. Burns, Oreg., Dec. 16, 1930; s. Alexander Wiley and Florence Mary (Woodhouse) H.; children—William L., Steven, Diane, Gwendolyn, Barbara, Ardis. B.S., U. Oreg., 1955, M.D., 1961. Diplomate Am. Bd. Psychiatry and Neurology. Intern Bernalito County Hosp., Albuquerque, 1961-62; resident in psychiatry U. Oreg., Portland, 1962-65; guest worker Inst. Psychiatry, London, 1965-66; assoc. prof. psychiatry U. Iowa, Iowa City, 1966-70; dir. adult psychiatry U. Minn., Mpls., 1966-70, prof., 1970—. Author: The Medical Casebook of Adolf Hitler, 1979, Dementia, 1983, Mending Minds: A Guide to Modern Psychiatry, 1989; assoc. editor Clin. Psychiatry, 1980—. Served with U.S. Army, 1950-52. NIH fellow, 1965. Fellow Am. Psychiat. Assn., Am. Psychopath. Assn. (Hoch award 1987); mem. Am. Psychol. Assn., Behavior Genetics Assn. (pres., Dobzansky award 1984), Psychiat. Research Soc., Soc. for Study Social Biology (v.p. 1982—), Alzheimers and Related Diseases Assn. (med. and scientific adv. bd., 1980—, nat. bd. 1987—), Nat. Inst. Drug Abuse (adv. council, 1987—). Office: U Wash Box 356560 Seattle WA 98195-6560

HETH, DIANA SUE, therapist; b. Robinson, Ill., Sept. 25, 1948; d. Quentin Wilson and Marguerite (Byrd) Abraham; m. Kenneth Lewis Greider, Aug. 16, 1970 (div. Mar. 1985); children: Kathryn Elizabeth, Susan Nicole, Jonathan Abraham; m. Harold Eugene Heth; children: Joseph Brockwell, Kiley Joy, Mark Quentin. BSE, Eastern Ill. U., 1970; MSW, U. Ill., 1992. Lic. clin. social worker. Exec. dir. Nat. Assn. Downs Syndrome, Chgo., 1976-77, Heartland Hospice, Effingham, Ill., 1983-88; office adminstr. Am. Family Life Assurance, Effingham, Ill., 1988-90; sec. design enging. dept. Fedders N.Am., Effingham, Ill., 1990; co-owner H&S Vending, 1990—; therapist sexual abuse Heartland Human Svcs., Effingham, Ill., 1992-94; child welfare specialist II Ill. Dept. of Children and Family Svcs., Olney, 1994—; mem. Profl. Adv. Com. for Hospice Lincolnland. Author: One Gift to the Next, 1983, Sundance Lady, 1990. Vol. Belleville (Ill.) Hospice, 1981-83; co-chmn. svc. and rehab. com. Am. Cancer Soc.; mem. parent adv. bd. Ill. State U., 1996—; social work cons. Effingham County Health Dept., 1995; mem. parent adv. bd. Ill. State U., 1996—. Mem. NASW, Ill. State Hospice Orgn. (bd. dirs. 1985-86), Ill. Pub. Health Assn., County Orgn. SVc. Providers, Newcomers Club (pres. 1984-85), Compassionate Friends Club (bd. dirs. 1985-86), Topnotcher's 4-H Club (leader), Ill. State U. Parents Assn. (mem. adv. bd. 1996—). Republican. Methodist. Home: RR 1 Box 63 Shumway IL 62461-9722 Office: Olney Field Office Ill Dept Child/Family Svcs 1102A S West St Olney IL 62450-1321

HETTEL, STEPHANIE MARTHA, health facility administrator; b. Phila., Aug. 30, 1934; d. Thomas Francis and Mary Michael (Joanni) M.; m. William Joseph Hettel, Oct. 3, 1953; children: William, Robert, Philip, Stephen. BS, Temple U., 1979; MSHA, St. Joseph's U., 1982. Dir. med. record dept. Oxford Hosp., Phila., 1979-80, St. Mary Hosp., Phila., 1980-82, Thomas Jefferson U. Hosp., Phila., 1982—; mem. steering com. Keystone Peer Rev., Pa., 1993-94. Contbr. articles to profl. jours. Tranition facilitator Phila. City Govt., 1991; campaign vol. Re-elect Ed Rendell, Phila., 1995. Mem. Southeastern Pa. Health Info. Assn. (pres. 1985-86), Pa. Health Info. Mgmt. Assn. (pres. 1990-91, Disting. Mem. 1994), Am. Health Info. Nursing Assn. (chmn. profl. conduct com. 1994—, clin. supr. 1982—). Roman Catholic. Home: 2313 Stanwood St Philadelphia PA 19152 Office: Thomas Jefferson U Hosp 111 S 11th St Philadelphia PA 19107

HEUBLUM, MICHAEL, neurologist; b. Tel Aviv, Nov. 3, 1960; came to U.S., 1968; s. Arie Ludwig and Ahuva H.; m. Laurie Meckler; children: Harry Alexander, Jack Edward. BA, U. Pa., 1982; MD, SUNY, Bklyn., 1986. Diplomate Am. Bd. Psychiatry and Neurology, Am. Bd. Electrodiagnostic Medicine, Am. Bd. Internal Medicine. Attending neurologist Beth Israel Med. Ctr., N.Y.C., 1993—, Cabrini Med. Ctr., N.Y.C., 1993—, Hosp. for Joint Diseases, N.Y.C., 1993—, N.Y. Eye and Ear Infirmary, N.Y.C., 1994—; clin. instr. Mt. Sinai Med. Ctr., N.Y.C., 1995—, attending neurologist, 1996—; clin. instr. Albert Einstein Med. Ctr., Bronx, N.Y., 1995—. Fellow Am. Assn. Electrodiagnostic Medicine; mem. Am. Acad. Neurology, Peripheral Neuropathy Inst., N.Y. City Epilepsy Soc., Am. Soc. Internal Medicine. Office: 247 Third Ave #203 New York NY 10010

HEUER, MARVIN ARTHUR, physician, research and industry consultant; b. Mankato, Minn., Mar. 11, 1947; s. Marvin Ernst and Elaine Olive (Melahn) H.; children: David Walter, Michael Arthur. BA, Mankato State U., 1969; BS, U. Minn., Mpls., 1973, MD, 1973. Intern, resident family practice St. John's Hosp., St. Paul, 1973-80; ptnr. Family Med. Group practice Park Rapids (Minn.)/Walker Clin. LTD, 1980-81; assoc. med. dir. Smith Kline & French Corp., Phila., 1981-82, group dir. clin. rsch., 1982-84, acting v.p. worldwide ops., 1984-87; v.p. med. affairs, v.p. clin. rsch. worldwide Am. Home Products, N.Y.C., 1987-89; v.p. R&D Wallace Labs., Cranbury, N.J., 1989-92; v.p., dir. clin. rsch. Worldwide Smithkline Beecham Corp., London, 1992—; CEO Heuer Assocs., North Oaks, Minn., 1992—; physician Westview Clinic, West Saint Paul, Minn., 1991—; dir. clin. rsch. Allina Corp., Mpls., 1993; clin. asst. prof. Robert Wood Johnson Med. Sch., Dept. of Family Medicine, New Brunswick, N.J., 1981-91; clin. assoc. prof. U. Minn. Med. Sch., Dept. of Family Practice, 1992—; mem. biotech. adv. bd. Mankato State U.; mem. drug utilization rev. panel Dept. Health, Minn., 1992—. Contbr. 12 articles on drugs to profl. jours., tng. manual, Med.

Monitors Guide 1983. Dir. youth activities St. Matthews Luth. Ch., Moorestown, N.J., 1981-86, trustee 1983-92, coun. mem., 1984-87, alt. bd. mem. 1986; fin. com. Incarnation Luth. Ch., St. Paul, Minn., 1991—, property com., 1991—. Fellow Am. Bd. Family Practice; mem. AMA, ACP, Am. Assoc. Physician Execs., Am. Acad. Family Physicians, Minn. Med. Soc., Pharm. Mfrs. Assn., Minn. Acad. Family Practice, Am. Coll. Cardiology, Am. Rheumatol. Assn., Med. Alley Assn., Nat. Geog. Soc., Drug Info. Assn., Soc. Clin. Trials. Republican. Home: 855 Village Ctr Dr Ste 170 North Oaks MN 55127-6512 Office: Westview Clinic 156 Emerson Ave W Saint Paul MN 55118-2125

HEUER, MICHAEL ALEXANDER, dean, endodontist educator; b. Grand Rapids, Mich., Apr. 27, 1932; s. Harold Maynard and Gwendolyn Ruth (Kremer) H.; m. Barbara Margaret Naines, Nov. 23, 1955; children—Kristan M., Karin E., Katrina A. D.D.S., Northwestern U., 1956; M.S., U. Mich., 1959. Practice dentistry specializing in endodontics Chgo., 1959-86; asst. prof. Northwestern U., 1960-66; asso. prof. Loyola U., Chgo., 1968-73; prof., chmn. dept. endodontics Northwestern U., 1974-83, assoc. dean acad affairs, 1983-88, sr. assoc. dean, 1988-93, dean, 1993—; dir. Am. Bd. Endodontics, 1971-77, sec.-treas., 1973-76, pres., 1976-77; chmn. subcom. Am. Nat. Standards Inst.; mem. com. on advanced edn. Commn. on Accreditation of Dental Edn., 1974-77, endodontic cons., 1986-91, curriculum cons., 1986-92. Contbr. articles in field to profl. jours. Served with USNR, 1956-58. Fellow Am. Coll. Dentistry (sec.-treas. Ill. sect. 1986-92, vice chair 1992-94, chair 1994-96), Internat. Coll. Dentistry, Am. Assn. Endodontists (exec. coun. 1967-71, sec. 1979-84, v.p. 1984-85, pres.-elect 1985-86, pres. 1986-87); mem. AAAS, ADA (coun. dental materials and devices 1972-78, chmn. 1977-78), Sci. coun. 1980—, Internat. Assn. Dental Rsch., Am. Assn. Dental Schs., Chgo. Odontographic Soc. (pres. 1982-84), Edgar D. Coolidge Endodontic Soc. (charter sec. 1961, pres. 1964, trustee), Phi Eta Sigma, Omicron Kappa Upsilon, Chi Psi, Delta Sigma Delta. Home: 156 Timber Ridge Lake Barrington Shores Barrington IL 60010 Office: Northwestern U Dental Sch Chicago IL 60611

HEUPEL, CAROL COLLINS, community health and womens health nurse educator; b. Wilmington, Del., Apr. 10, 1935; d. Herbert Deakyne and Marian Elizabeth (Vance) Collins; m. Hermann Wilhelm Heupel, June 4, 1955; children: Ursula, Renata, Douglas, Emily, Michele. BSN, U. Minn., 1976, MPH, 1978, PhD, 1986. RN, Minn.; cert. pub. health nurse; cert. ob-gyn. nurse practitioner. Instr. obstetrics nursing Deaconess Sch. Nursing, 1978-80; asst. prof. med.-surg. nursing Mankato (Minn.) State U., 1980-86, assoc. prof. cmty. health nursing, 1986—; staff nurse in emergency dept. Fairview Southdale Hosp., 1971-72, in obstetrics, 1979-80. Contbr. articles to profl. jours.; presenter in field. Vol. Teenage Med. Ctr., 1977-78, Bloodmobile, ARC, 1986-91; mem. Ch. Coun., 1994—. Mem. AWHONN, Nat. Assn. Nurse Practitioners in Reproductive Health, Minn. Nurses Assn. (del. state conv. 1980, 88, 89), Minn. Politically Involved Nurses (vice chmn. bd. dirs. 1988-90), Midwest Nursing Rsch. Soc., Sigma Theta Tau (v.p. Mu Lambda chpt. 1990-91). Lutheran. Home: 516 9th St NE Waseca MN 56093-3623 Office: Mankato State U Sch Nursing PO Box 8400 Mankato MN 56002-8400

HEWES, ROBERT CHARLES, radiologist; b. Balt., Feb. 14, 1953; s. Gordon Cecil and Gladys Dorothy (Barringham) H.; m. Judith Renee Lacy, Mar. 23, 1975; children: Christy, Amy, Jeremy. Student, Columbia Union Coll., 1973, Kettering Coll. of Med. Arts, 1971; BS, Loma Linda U., 1976, MD. Diplomate Am. Bd. Med. Examiners, Am. Bd. Radiology. Resident in radiology Loma Linda (Calif.) U., 1978-81, asst. prof. radiology, 1983-84; fellow in orthopedic radiology Hosp. for Spl. Surgery Cornell U. Med. Ctr., N.Y.C., 1981-82; fellow in interventional radiology Johns Hopkins U. Hosp., Balt., 1982-83; assoc. prof. Wright State U.; mem. staff Kettering (Ohio) Med. Ctr., vice chmn. dept. radiology, 1985-87, chmn., 1988-95; pres. Kettering Radiologists, Inc., 1987-95, med. dir., 1996—; pres. Patient First Imaging Network, 1994-95; bd. dirs. Spring Valley Acad. Contbr. articles on radiology to profl. jours. Recipient Cert. of merit Am. Roentgen Ray Soc., 1983, Disting. Alumnus award Kettering Coll. of Med. Arts, 1990. Mem. AMA, Radiol. Soc. N.Am., Soc. Cardiovascular and Interventional Radiology, Miami Valley Radiol. Soc. (pres. 1994), Alpha Omega Alpha (award). Republican. Adventist. Office: Kettering Med Ctr Dept Radiology 3535 Southern Blvd Dayton OH 45429-1221

HEWITT, BENJAMIN ATTMORE, psychologist; b. Westerly, R.I., Dec. 20, 1921; s. Benjamin Henry and Anne Mildred (Wangelin) H. BA, Yale U., 1943, MA, 1950, PhD, 1952. Lic. psychol., Conn. Pres. Psychol. Svcs., Inc., New Haven, Conn., 1958-70; rsch. assoc. Yale U., New Haven, 1960-68; cons. psychologist New Haven, 1969-92; furniture cons. Wakefield, R.I.; guest curator Work of Many Hands; Card Tables in Fed. Am. Yale U. Art Gallery, New Haven, 1981-82; furniture researcher, 1965—. Author: The Work of Many Hands: Card Tables in Federal America, 1982. With U.S. Army, 1943-46, PTO. Mem. APA, Conn. State Psychol. Assn. (coun. 1960-64, ethics com. 1983-84), Friends of Am. Arts at Yale (sec. 1969-83, exec. com. 1969-92).

HEWITT, JOHN MICHAEL, internist; b. Hong Kong, Aug. 23, 1952; came to U.S., 1991; s. Walter John and Laura (Tang) H. MB BChir, U. Newcastle-Upon-Tyne, Eng., 1975. Diplomate Am. Bd. Internal Medicine, Am. Bd. Critical Care. House officer (surgery) Cumberland (Eng.) Infirmary, 1975-76; house officer (medicine) St. Georges Hosp. Group, London, 1976-77; sr. house officer (renal) St. Helier Hosp. Carshalton, Surrey, Eng., 1977-78; registrar medicine King's Coll. Hosp., Dulwich, London, 1978-79; sr. medicine Health Scis. Ctr., Winnipeg, Can., 1979-81; internist, gastroenterologist Court Med. Ctr., Winnipeg, Can., 1981-91; internist, intensivist Kern Med. Ctr., later Mesa West Med., Bakersfield, Calif., 1991—; CFO Mesa West Med., Bakersfield, Calif., 1993-95, CEO, 1995—. Fellow Royal Coll. Physicians (Can.), Royal Soc. Medicine; mem. Royal Coll. Physicians (U.K.). Home: PO Box 6337 Bakersfield CA 93386-6337 Office: Mesa West Medical 2020 Troxton Ave Bakersfield CA 93301

HEWITT, NANCY ARLENE, social worker; b. Chambersburg, Pa., July 13, 1946; d. Erskine Enoch and Phyllis Athelia (McLaughlin) H. BA, Thiel Coll., 1968; MSW, Simmons Coll., 1977. Lic. ind. clin. social worker. Clinician, supr. North Shore Community Mental Health Ctr., Salem, Mass., 1978-83; pvt. practice North Bay Counseling and Cons., Salem, 1981—; clinician, supr. Salem Hosp. Mental Health Ctr., 1983-87; adj. asst. prof. Simmons Coll. Sch. Social Work, Boston, 1989-94. Mem. NASW, Pvt. Practice Colloquium. Office: North Bay Counseling & Consultation Assocs 70 Washington St # 322 Salem MA 01970-3520

HEWITT, ROBERT LEE, surgeon, educator; b. Paducah, Ky., Nov. 2, 1934; s. Lee A. and Donis (Brown) H.; m. Patricia M. Stewart, May 1, 1965; children—Heather Edgeworth Hewitt Daniel, Robert Stewart, Whit Butler, Brooke Lee. Student, U. Louisville, 1952-55; M.D., Tulane U., 1959. Diplomate: Am. Bd. Surgery, Am. Bd. Thoracic Surgery. Intern Charity Hosp., Tulane U., New Orleans, 1959-60; resident Tulane U., 1960-66; faculty Sch. Medicine, 1960—, asst. prof. surgery, 1968-70, asso. prof., 1970-75, prof. surgery, 1975-76, clin. prof. surgery, 1976—; bd. dirs. Tulane U. Hosp.; mem. staff Charity, So. Bapt., Tulane U. hosps., Touro Infirmary, all New Orleans, bd. govs. Tulane Med. Ctr., 1991—; cons. several hosps. Contbr. articles to profl. jours. Mem. leadership forum Met. Area Com. New Orleans, 1971; bd. govs. Tulane U. Med. Ctr. With M.C., U.S. Army, 1966-68. Fellow ACS; mem. Soc. Univ. Surgeons, Am. Assn. Thoracic Surgery, So. Surg. Assn., Oscar Creech Surgical Soc., Alton Ochsner Surgical Soc., New Orleans surg. socs., Southeastern Surg. Congress, Soc. Vascular Surgery, Soc. Thoracic Surgeons, Internat. Cardiovascular Soc., So. Assn. Vascular Surgery, Assn. Acad. Surgeons, AMA, La., Orleans Parish med. socs., Assn. Mil. Surgeons, New Orleans Grad. Med. Assembly, Alpha Omega Alpha, Omicron Delta Kappa, Phi Kappa Tau, Phi Chi. Episcopalian. Home: 1207 Webster St New Orleans LA 70118-6030 Office: Tulane Med Ctr Dept Surgery 1430 Tulane Ave New Orleans LA 70112-2699

HEYDORN, WILLIAM HOWARD, physician, medical director; b. Schenectady, N.Y., Feb. 10, 1934; s. William August Heydorn and Lucille H. (Furbeck) Stillwell; m. Joan Gloria Kilian, Sept. 1956; children: Barbara Ann, Kathryn, William A. BA, Hope Coll., 1955; MD, Yale U., 1959. Diplomate Am. Bd. Surgery, Am. Bd. Thoracic Surgery. Commd. officer U.S. Army, 1960, advanced through grades to col.; med. officer U.S. Army, Germany, 1960-62; resident surgery U.S. Army/Letterman Army Med. Ctr., San Francisco, 1962-66; hosp. comdr. 44th Surg. Hosp., Korea, 1966-67; chief surgery 5th Gen. Hosp., Stuttgart, Germany, 1967-70; resident thoracic surgery Letterman Army Med. Ctr., San Francisco, 1970-72; staff surgeon Fitsimmons Army Med. Ctr., Denver, 1972-75; chief surgery Letterman Army Med. Ctr., San Francisco, 1975-85, comdr., 1986; discharged U.S. Army, 1989; med. dir. Brookside Hosp, San pablo, CA, 92—; field rep. accreditation coun. grad. med. edn., 1989-91; assoc. med. dir. Calif. Med. Review, Inc., 1991-92; ; dir. continuing med. edn. Mountain Med. Inst., Oakland, Calif., 1996—; clin. prof. surgery Uniformed Svcs. U. Health Scis., U. Calif., San Francisco. Co-author: Thoracic Surgery: Continuing Education Review, 1980; contbr. chpts. to books and articles to profl. jours. Decorated Legion of Merit, Meritorious Svc. medal, Order of Mil. Med. Merit, Profl. Svc. ribbon U.S. Army. Fellow ACS, Am. Coll. Physician Execs.; mem. Soc. Thoracic Surgeons, Am. Assn. for Thoracic Surgery, San Francisco Surg. Soc., Bohemian Club. Home: 40 Geldert Dr Tiburon CA 94920 Office: Brookside Hosp 2000 Vale Rd San Pablo CA 94806

HEYEN, BEATRICE J., psychotherapist; b. Chgo., June 23, 1925; d. Carl Edwin and Anna W. (Carlson) Lund; m. Robert D. Heyen, June 16, 1950 (dec. Feb. 1981); children: Robin, Jefferson, Neil; m. Robert Christiansen, Nov. 24, 1984. BS, U. Chgo., 1949. Instr. Boone (Iowa) Jr. Coll., 1959-64, Rochester (Minn.) Jr. Coll., 1967-68, Winona (Minn.) State Coll., 1965-68; dir. social svc. State Clinic, Kirksville, Mo., 1968-71; supr., dir. Family Counseling Agy., Joliet, Ill., 1971-85; pvt. practice Muskegon, Mich., 1985—; cons. Homes for Aged, Programs for Aged, Winona, 1965-68, Spl. Programs and Individuals in Psychotherapy, Muskegon, 1984—; dir. Christiansen Fine Art Gallery, North Muskegon. Mem. Gov.'s Com. on Status of Women, Iowa, 1957-62, Gov.'s Com. on Aging, Minn., 1966-68. Grantee for Pilot Projects in Svc. to Women 1971-84. Mem. NASW, Acad. Cert. Social Workers, C.G. Jung Inst. (Chgo.). Methodist. Home: 1610 N Weber Rd Muskegon MI 49445-9629

HEYLIGER, JOYCE THOMAS, nursing administrator; b. St. Thomas, V.I., July 23, 1942; d. Edward Nathaniel and Jennie Belsina (Rabsatt) Thomas; m. Anselmo R. Heyliger, Sept. 16, 1967; children: Riva Jeannette, Anselmo R. Jr. Diploma, St. Luke's Episcopal Sch., Ponce, P.R., 1962; BS in Nursing, Mich. State U., East Lansing, 1967; MS in Nursing, Boston U., 1975; MPH, San Diego State U., 1989. Cert. nurse adminstr. Staff and pub. health nurse V.I. Dept. Health, St. Croix, 1962-67, nurse supr., 1967-78, nurse cons., 1978-80, assoc. dir. nursing, 1980-90, chmn. nursing, 1990—, rsch. nurse, 1991—; cons., policy bd. mem. Head Start Program; clin. instr. U. V.I. Recipient Pub. Health Nurse Leadership award, 1989; grantee Maternal-Child Health Implement Program. Mem. ANA, Am. Nurses Credientialing Ctr. (nursing adminstrn. test devel. com.), Fed. Health Cons., V.I. Nurses Assn., Beta Sigma Nu. Home: PO Box 272 Frederiksted VI 00841

HEYMAN, JOSEPH MARTIN, obstetrician, gynecologist; b. Bklyn., May 21, 1942; s. Ezekiel and Elaine Olga (Adelman) H.; m. Laurel Ann Taylor, June 10, 1967; children: Eve Renata, Todd Sanford. BS, CCNY, 1963; MD, SUNY, Bklyn., 1967. Diplomate, Am. Bd. Ob.-Gyn. Intern USPHS Marine Hosp., Staten Island, N.Y., 1967-68; chief outpatient dept., venereal disease control officer USPHS Northern Navajo Indian Hosp., Shiprock, N.Mex., 1968-70; resident in ob.-gyn. Sinai Hosp., Balt., 1970-73; staff ob.-gyn. Women's Health Care, West Newbury, Mass., 1973—; pres. Women's Health Care, 1984—; pres. med. staff Anna Jaques Hosp., Newburyport, Mass., 1990-92; bd. dirs. Tufts Associated HMO, Waltham, Mass., 1986—; exec. com. bd. trustees Anna Jaques Hosp., 1995—. Contbr. articles to profl. publs. Pres., West Newbury PTA, 1978. Fellow Am. Coll. Ob-Gyn; mem. AMA (coun. on med. scis. 1996—, ho. dels.), Mass. Med. Soc. (exec. bd. 1983—, spkr. ho. dels. 1992-94, v.p. 1994-95, pres.-elect 1995-96, pres. 1996—), Whittier Ind. Practice Assn. (pres. 1985-95, exec. bd. 1985—). Democrat. Home: 163 Middle St West Newbury MA 01985-1922 Office: Womens Health Care 291 Main St West Newbury MA 01985-1416

HEYMAN, MELVIN BERNARD, pediatric gastroenterologist; b. San Francisco, Mar. 24, 1950; s. Vernon Otto and Eve Elsie Heyman; m. Jody Ellen Switky, May 8, 1988. BA in Econs., U. Calif., Berkeley, 1972; MD, UCLA, 1976, MPH in Nutrition, 1981. Diplomate Am. Bd. Pediatrics, Am. Bd. Pediatric Gastroenterology. Intern, resident Los Angeles County-U. So. Calif. Med. Ctr., 1976-79; fellow UCLA, 1979-81; asst. prof. U. Calif., San Francisco, 1981-88, assoc. prof., 1988-94, prof., 1994—, chief pediatric gastroenterology, hepatology and nutrition, 1990—; assoc. dir. Pediatric Gastroenterology/Nutrition, San Francisco, 1986-89; mem. cons. staff San Francisco Gen. Hosp., Natividad Med. Ctr., Salinas, Calif., Scenic Gen. Hosp., Modesto, Calif., U. Calif., Davis Med. Ctr. Contbr. articles to profl. jours. Chmn. scientific adv. com. San Francisco chpt. Crohn's and Colitis Found. Am., 1987-94, bd. dirs., 1986—. Rsch. grantee Children's Liver Found., 1984-85, John Tung grantee Am. Cancer Soc., 1985-89. Office: U Calif Dept Pediatrics Box 0136 San Francisco CA 94143-0136

HEYNEMAN, DONALD, parasitology and tropical medicine educator; b. San Francisco, Feb. 18, 1925; s. Paul and Amy Josephine (KLauber) H.; m. Louise Davidson Ross, June 18, 1971; children: Amy J., Lucy A., Andrew P., Jennifer K., Claudia G. AB magna cum laude, Harvard U., 1950; MA, Rice U., 1952, PhD, 1954. Instr. zoology UCLA, 1954-56, asst. prof., 1956-60; head dept. parasitology U.S. Navy Med. Research unit, Cairo; also co-dir. U.S. Navy Med. Research unit, Malakal, Sudan, 1960-62; assoc. research parasitologist Hooper Found. U. Calif., San Francisco, 1962-64, assoc. prof., 1966-68, prof., 1968-91, prof. emeritus, 1991—, asst. dir. Hooper found., 1970-74, acting chmn. dept. internat. health, 1976-78; assoc. dean Sch. Pub. Health U. Calif., Berkeley and San Francisco 1987-91, assoc. dean emeritus, 1991—, chmn. joint med. program, 1987-91, chmn. emeritus, 1991—; research coordinator U. Calif. Internat. Ctr. Med. Research and Tng., Kuala Lumpur, Malaysia, 1964-66; cons. physiol. processes sect. NSF, 1966-91; environ. biology div. NIH, 1968-91; mem. tropical medicine and parasitology study sect. NIAID-NIH, 1973-76; mem. adv. sci. bd. Gorgas Meml. Inst., 1967-90; cons. WHO, 1967, mem. sci. tech. rev. com. on Leishmaniases, 1984; cons. UN Devel. Program, 1978-91, US-AID, others; panel reviewer Internat. Nomenclature of Diseases, 1984—; Am. cons. and U.S. prin. investigator U. Linkage Project, Egypt-U.S., 1984—; mem. Calif. Health Adv. Com., 1983—. Author: (with R. Boolootian) An Illustrated Laboratory Text in Zoology, 1962, An Illustrated Laboratory Text in Zoology, A Brief Version, 1977, International Dictionary Medicine and Biology, (with R. Goldsmith) Textbook of Tropical Medicine and Parasitology, 1989;co-author, contbg. editor Phytolacca dodecandra: Endod, 1984, Endod II, 1987; contbr. articles to jours., chpts. to books.; editorial cons. Am. Jour. Tropical Medicine and Hygiene, Jour. Parasitology, Jour. Exptl. Parasitology, Sci., 1968—, other jours. Served with AUS, 1943-46. NIH grantee, 1966-85. Mem. Am. Soc. Parasitologists (council 1970-74, pres. 1982-83), Am. Micros. Soc. (exec. com. 1971-75), Am. Soc. Tropical Medicine and Hygiene (councilor 1981-84), So. Calif. Parasitol. Soc. (pres. 1957-58), No. Calif. Parasitologists (sec.- treas. 1969-72, pres. 1977-78), Phi Beta Kappa. Home: 1400 Lake St San Francisco CA 94118-1036 Office: U Calif Dept Epidemiology and Biostatistics Box 0560 San Francisco CA 94143

HEYS, STEVEN DARRYLL, surgeon; b. Accrington, Lancashire, Eng., July 5, 1956; s. Keith and Alice (McNamee) H.; m. Margaret Susan Proctor, Dec. 1, 1984; children: Simon Alexander, Adam Matthew, Julia Michelle. B.Med. Biology, B.Surgery, B.Medicine, Aberdeen (U.K.) U., 1978, MD, 1981, PhD, 1992. Accredited in gen. surgery Joint Com. on Higher Surg. Tng., U.K. Sr. house officer Aberdeen U., 1982-84, registrar in surgery, 1984-87, lectr. surgery, 1989-92, sr. lectr. surgery, 1992—, dir. surg. nutrition and metabolism unit, 1994—; Wellcome rsch. fellow Rowett Inst., Aberdeen, 1987-89, hon. rsch. fellow, 1989—; cons. surgeon Aberdeen Royal Infirmary, 1992—; tutor in minimal access surgery Scottish Royal Coll., 1994—. Contbr. 90 articles to profl. jours. Capt. M.C. Royal Army, 1985-89. Rsch. grantee Wellcome Trust, London, 1987, Scottish Hosps. Rsch. Trust, 1989, 95. Fellow Royal Coll. Surgeons; mem. Surg. Rsch. Soc. of U.K., Brit. Assn. Surg. Oncology. Roman Catholic. Home: Westhill, 12 Mains View, Aberdeen Scotland Office: Univ of Aberdeen, Dept Surgery, Aberdeen Scotland

HEYSSEL, ROBERT MORRIS, physician, retired hospital executive; b. Jamestown, Mo., June 19, 1928; s. Clarence D. and Meta and (Reusser) H.; m. Maria McDaniel, Aug. 7, 1955; children: James Olin, Maria Lisa, Robert Morris, Kurt Frederick, Helen Perrier. B.S., U. Mo., 1951; M.D., St. Louis U., 1953, D.Sc. (hon.), 1985; LHD, John Hopkins U., 1992. Postgrad. tng. St. Louis U. Hosp., 1953-56, Barnes Hosp., St. Louis, 1953-56; hematologist, acting dir. dept. medicine Atomic Bomb Casualty Commn., Nagasaki and Hiroshima, Japan, 1956-58; mem. faculty Sch. Medicine, Vanderbilt U., Nashville, 1959-68; dir. div. nuclear medicine Sch. Medicine, Vanderbilt U., 1962-68, assoc. prof. medicine, 1964-68; assoc. dean Sch. Medicine, Johns Hopkins U., Balt., 1968-72; dir. health care programs and outpatient services Sch. Medicine, Johns Hopkins U., 1968-72, prof. medicine, 1971—, prof. health care orgn., 1972-83; exec. v.p., dir. Johns Hopkins Hosp., 1972-83, pres., CEO, 1983-92; pres., chief exec. officer Johns Hopkins Health System, Balt., 1986-92; trustee Johns Hopkins U.; bd. dirs. Signet Bank Corp., Signet Bank of Md., Monsanto Co.; chmn. Commonwealth Fund on Acad. Health Ctrs., 1983. Contbr. articles to profl. jours. Mem. gen. assembly Assn. Am. Med. Colls., 1974-80, mem. exec. council, 1978, chmn. council teaching hosps., 1978-80, chmn. 1983-84; chmn. com. on emergency med. services Nat. Acad. Scis., 1973-76; mem. Joint Commn. on Prescription Drugs, 1976, Gov's Commn. on High Tech., 1983-86; numerous other local, state and nat. coms. on health, medicine and med. edn.; bd. dirs., trustee St. Louis U., 1989. Recipient USPHS Career Devel. award, 1962; Distinguished Alumnus award U. Mo., 1972. Fellow ACP, Am. Coll. Physician Execs., Internat. Soc. Hermatology; mem. Inst. Med. of NAS, Assn. Am. Physicians, Soc. Med. Adminstrs., numerous other sci. assns. Club: Elk Ridge (Balt.). Home: 230 Stony Run Ln Baltimore MD 21210-3035 Office: Johns Hopkins Health System 600 N Wolfe St Baltimore MD 21205-2110

HIATT, HOWARD H., physician, educator; b. Patchogue, N.Y., July 22, 1925; s. Alexander and Dorothy (Askinas) H.; m. Doris Bieringer, Nov. 29, 1947; children—Jonathan, Deborah, Frederick. M.D., Harvard U., 1948. Intern, then resident medicine Beth Israel Hosp., Boston, 1948-50; research fellow Cornell U. Med. Coll., 1950-53; clin. investigator USPHS, 1953-55; mem. faculty Med. Sch., Harvard U., 1955—, H.L. Blumgart prof. medicine, 1963-72, prof. medicine, 1972—, prof. medicine Sch. Pub. Health, 1984-92, dean Sch. Pub. Health, 1972-84; physician-in-chief Beth Israel Hosp., 1963-72; sr. physician Brigham Women's Hosp., boston, 1984—. Mem. NAS Inst. Medicine, Am. Soc. Clin. Investigation, Assn. Am. Physicians, Am. Acad. Arts and Scis. (sec. 1992—, dir. Initiatives for Childrens 1992—), Alpha Omega Alpha. Home: 130 Mt Auburn St Cambridge MA 02138-5757 Office: Brigham and Womens Hosp Boston MA 02115

HIBL, DAVID J., dentist, orthodontist; b. Boreman, Mont., Aug. 22, 1952; s. Joseph John and Mary Ann Elizabeth Hibl; m. Kay L. Hibl, June 5, 1976; children: Molly, Peter. BA in Biology, U. Colo., 1975, DDS, 1978; MS in Orthodontics, St. Louis U., 1985. Resident St. Louis U. Med. Ctr., 1983-85; pvt. practice Boulder/Louisville, Colo., 1985—. Chmn. safety edn. com. Rocky Mountain Rescue Group, Inc., Boulder, 1985-96. Capt. USNR, 1978-83. Mem. ADA, Am. Assn. Orthodontists. Office: 1760 Centennial Dr # B Louisville CO 80027-1302

HIBNER, RAE A., insurance company official, nurse; b. Libertyville, Ill., Jan. 31, 1956; d. Richard Douglas and Raelene Ann (Warren) Lyons; m. John Paul Hibner, June 21, 1986; children: Kevin John, Thomas Ivan. Diploma, Luth. Gen. Hosp. Sch. Nursing, Park Ridge, Ill., 1979; BS in Nursing, U. Ill., Chgo., 1984; MS, No. Ill. U., 1987. RN. Staff nurse Cardiac Telemetry Luth. Gen. Hosp., 1979-81, staff nurse CCU, 1981-82; staff nurse coronary ICU U. Ill. Hosp., Chgo., 1982-83, asst. head nurse coronary ICU, 1983-86, head nurse coronary ICU, 1986-88, staff nurse coronary-med. ICU, 1988-90; coord. utilization rev. Parkside Health Mgmt. Corp., Chgo., 1989-91; asst. dir. utilization mgmt. U. Ill., Chgo., 1991-93; risk mgr. Rush-Presbyn.-St. Lukes Med. Ctr., Chgo., 1993-96; claims cons. CNA Ins. Cos., Chgo., 1996—. Mem. ASHRM, HCRMSC. Republican. Roman Catholic.

HICKEY, GREGORY JOSEPH, priest, educational administrator; b. Darby, Pa., Aug. 10, 1947; s. Joseph Thomas and Helen Gertrude (Lockard) H. BA, Temple U., 1973; MDiv, St. Charles Sem., 1979; MA, Villanova U., 1989. Ordained priest Roman Cath. Ch., 1979. Tchr. St. Patrick Grade Sch., Norristown, Pa., 1969-74; mem. ednl. testing staff Montgomery County I.U., Norristown, 1972-73, Phila. I.U., 1974-75; asst. pastor Sts. Simon & Jude Ch., Westtown, Pa., 1979-81, St. Augustine Ch., Bridgeport, Pa., 1981-82, St. Leo Ch., Phila., 1982-87; tchr. Cardinal Dougherty High Sch., Phila., 1987-88; campus minister Bishop Conwell High Sch., Levittown, Pa., 1988-90; dir. studies St. Hubert High Sch., Phila., 1990-91; tchr. Cardinal Dougherty High Sch., 1991-92; dir. guidance and psychology Roman Cath. High Sch., 1992-96; prin. Kennedy-Kenrick Cath. H.S., Norristown, Pa., 1996—. Mem. Nat. Assn. Secondary Sch. Prins., ASCD, Nat. Cath. Edn. Assn., Ancient Order Hibernians, Kappa Delta Pi. Republican. Home: 3160 Gaul St Philadelphia PA 19134-4447

HICKEY, PATRICIA WIEGAND, nursing educator; b. July 4, 1943. BS in Nursing, Calif. State U., 1982; M in Nursing, U. Calif., L.A., 1985. Asst. nursing prof. Calif. State U., L.A., 1987-89; prof. Cypress (Calif.) Coll., 1989—. Author: Nursing Process Handbook, 1990. Mem. NEA, Am. Soc. of Pain Mgmt. Nurses.

HICKEY, SISTER JOAN, physician assistant; b. Providence, R.I., BS in Edn., Cath. Tchrs. Coll., 1957; MS in Biology, Coll. of St. Rose, 1970; AS, Essex C.C., 1981. Lic. physician asst., Md. Tchr. various schs., Providence, Newport, R.I., 1952-59; tchr., vice prin. St. Catherine Acad., Belize City, Belize, 1959-63, 64-72; tchr., prin. Inst. San Vicente de Paul, San Pedro Sula, Honduras, 1963-64; tchr. St. Xavier Acad., Providence, 1972-77; nursing asst. Kent County Nursing Home, Warwick, R.I., 1977-79; physician asst. W.P. Benson, M.D., Balt., 1981-94, St. Joseph Med. Ctr., Balt., 1994—; head dept. biology St. Catherine Acad., 1959-63, 64-72; head Spanish dept. St. Xavier Acad., 1974-76. Roman Catholic.

HICKEY, WILLIAM FRANCIS, retired surgeon, medical consultant; b. Watertown, Mass., May 8, 1915; s. William Francis and Edna (Smith) H.; m. Alice J. Mahern, Apr. 25, 1942; children: Margery M., Virginia K. AB cum laude, Harvard U., 1936, MD, 1940. Diplomate Am. Coll. Surgeons. Gen. surgeon Winchester, Mass. and various hosps., 1946-77; cons. Am. Mut. Ins. Co., 1948—, also bd. dirs.; med. dir. vocat. rehab. Mass. Dept. Edn., 1950-65. Mem. Croydon Sec. Planning Bd., N.H., 1980—; bd. dirs. Newport Home Health Agy., N.H., 1980—. Mem. AMA, Mass. Med. Soc. Republican. Roman Catholic. Clubs: Lake Sunapee (N.H.) Yacht; Winchester (Mass.) Country. Home: Reeds Mill Road Newport NH 03773-9518

HICKIE, IAN BERNARD, psychiatrist; b. Australia, Aug. 4, 1959. B. Medicine and surgery, U. N.S.W., Sydney, 1982, MD, 1990. Resident med. officer Westmead Hosp., 1982-83; registrar in psychiatry Prince of Wales and Prince Henry Hosp., 1984-87; rsch. fellow in psychiatry N.S.W. Inst. Psychiatry, 1987-89; sr. registrar in psychiatry Prince of Wales Hosp./U. N.S.W., 1987-89; staff specialist in psychiatry Prince Henry Hosp., 1989-91; lectr. U. N.S.W., 1989-91, sr. lectr. psychiatry, 1991-93, assoc. prof., 1994—; Harkness fellow Commonwealth Fund, Sydney, 1993-94; dir. dept. psychiatry St. George Hsop. and Cmty. Svcs., Kogarah, N.S.W., 1995—; vis. assoc. prof. dept. psychiatry Duke U. Med. Ctr., Durham, N.C., 1994; cons. psychiatrist Mood Disorders unit Prince Henry Hosp., 1989-94; St. George rep., exec. Southeastern Sydney Area Mental Health Svcs., 1995—. Contbr. numerous articles to profl. jours., chpts. to books. Grantee Royal Australian and New Zealand Coll. Psychiatrists, 1988, Prince Henry Hosp., 1990, 91, ME Soc. of N.S.W., 1991, Nat. Health and Med. Rsch. Coun., 1991-93, 1992, 93-95, 95—, 96, Roche Pharms., 1992, Clive and Vera Ramaciotti Found., 1996; N.S.W. Inst. Psychiatry Rsch. fellow, 1987-89. Fellow Australian and New Zealand Coll. Psychiatrists (Maddison medal 1989, Organon Jr. Rsch. award 1992); mem. Australian Soc. for Psychiat. Rsch. (treas. biol. psychiatry sect. 1992-93), Internat. Psychogeriatric Assn., Psychoneuroimmunology Rsch. Soc., Australian Behavioural Immunology Group, Coast Med. Assn. (sec., convenor sci. programme 1990, sec. Tow Prize com. for med. rsch. 1990-93, Tow Prize for clin. rsch. 1988). Office: St George Hosp & Cmty Svcs, Acad Dept Psychiatry, 7 Chapel St, Kogarah 2217, Australia

HICKLING, WILLIAM HENRY, child neurologist; b. Oneonta, N.Y., Sept. 30, 1952; s. William Frederick and Barbara June (Abt) H.; m. Mary Elizabeth Kuhns, Aug. 6, 1977; children: Robert Tyson, Christopher Webb, William Matthew. BS in Life Scis., MIT, 1973; MD, Cornell U., 1978. Diplomate Am. Bd. Pediatrics with subspecialty in child neurology. Resident in pediatrics Children's Med. Ctr., Dallas, 1978-81; resident in neurology/child neurology U. N.C., Chapel Hill, 1981-84, fellow in clin. neurophysiology, 1984-85, instr. neurology, 1984-85, clin. assoc. prof. pediatrics and neurology, 1985—; dir. CSHS Clinic/Moses Cone Hosp, Greensboro, N.C., 1985—; ptnr., staff neurologist Wendover Park Neurol. Assocs., Greensboro, 1985-93; ptnr. Guilford Neurologic Assocs., Greensboro, 1993—; clin. adv. bd. Epilepsy Assn. Greater Greensboro, 1988—, Home Care of Ctrl. N.C., Greensboro, 1986-92. Elder Guilford Park Presbyn. Ch., Greensboro, 1987-89; coach Greensboro Youth Soccer, Greensboro, 1988—; asst. scoutmaster Boy Scouts Am., Greensboro, 1993—. Named Physician of the Yr. Mayor's Coun. Handicapped, Greensboro, 1988; recipient Family Practice Teaching award Class 1995, Greensboro, 1995. Mem. AMA, N.C. Med. Soc., Am. EEG Soc., Greater Greensboro Med. Soc., Am. Acad. Neurology, Child Neurology Soc., Phi Lambda Upsilon. Presbyterian. Office: Guilford Neurologic Assocs 1910 N Church St Greensboro NC 27405

HICKMAN, LINDA MARIE, physician; b. Ada, Okla., Nov. 10, 1953; d. Charlie Lewis and Bertha Mae (Vinson) Phelps; m. Ronnie Clarence Hickman, May 26, 1972; 1 child, Dustin Jake. RN, Cushing (Okla.) Mcpl. Hosp., 1974-75; AS, Okla. State U. Tech. Inst., 1974; BSN with honors, Cen. State U., Edmond, Okla., 1990; MD with distinction, U. Okla., 1994. Staff nurse Cushing Mcpl. Hosp., 1974-75; pub. health nurse Payne County Health, Cushing, 1975-78, 84-88; nurse cons. Care Manor, Stroud, Okla., 1982-83; house supr. Cushing Regional Hosp., 1982-83, asst. dir. home health service, 1983-84; communicable disease nurse Payne County Health Dept., Cushing, 1985-88; intern U. Okla., 1994-95, resident in internal medicine, 1994—. Author: Cushing Regional Hospital Home Health Service Policy and Procedure Manual, 1984. Self breast exam. instr. Am. Cancer Soc., 1984-88. Cushing Bus. and Profl. Women's Club sr. scholar, 1972, named Career Woman of Yr., 1976. Mem. Okla. Pub. Health Assn. Democrat. Avocations: boating, skiing, camping, ceramics, woodworking. Home: 902 S Kings Hwy Cushing OK 74023-9182

HICKMAN, MAXINE VIOLA, social services administrator; b. Louisville, Miss., Dec. 24, 1943; d. Everett and Ozella (Eichelberger) H.; m. William L. Malone, Sept. 5, 1965 (div. 1969); 1 child, Gwendolyn. BA, San Francisco State U., 1966; MS, Nova U., 1991; postgrad., Calif. Coast U., 1991—. Lic. State of Calif. Dept. Social Svcs. IBM profl. mechanic operator Wells Fargo Bank, San Francisco, 1961-65; dept. mgr. Sears Roebuck & Co., San Bruno, Calif., 1966-77; adminstr. Pine St. Guest House, San Francisco, 1969-88; fin. planner John Hancock Fin. Svcs., San Mateo, Calif., 1977-81; chief exec. officer Hickman Homes, Inc., San Francisco, 1981—; cons. BeeBe Meml. Endowment Found., Oakland, Calif., 1990—, Calif. Assn. Children's Home-Mems., Sacramento, 1989—. Mem. NAACP, San Francisco. Named Foster Mother of Yr., Children's Home Soc. Calif., 1985, Woman of Yr., Gamma Nu chpt. Iota Phi Lambda, 1991. Mem. Foster Parents United, Calif. Assn. Children's Homes, Nat. Bus. League, Order of Ea. Star, Masons (worthy matron), Alpha Kappa Alpha. Democrat. Baptist. Office: Hickman Homes Inc 67 Harold Ave San Francisco CA 94112-2331

HICKOK, PATRICIA ANN, medical technologist; b. Marion, Ohio, Oct. 12, 1939; d. Robert Charles Hickok and Edna Marzetta (Allen) Hickok-Carlisle-Grymonprez. Student, Elkhart U. of Med. and Dental, Technique, Ind., Mansfield (Ohio) Bus. Coll. Gen. med. technologist Indpls., 1958-59, St. Joseph's Hosp., Aberdeen, Wash., 1959-61, Knott Heart Street Clinic, Portland, Oreg., 1961-63, High Hoyt Street Clinic, Portland, 1963-65, People's Hosp., Mansfield, 1965, Mansfield Gen. Hosp., 1966-79; nursing aide, asst. Mansfield Meml. Homes, 1980-87; ins. examiner, 1989-96. Asst. vol. Fibromyalgia Support Groups, Florence, S.C., 1995-96. Mem. Soroptimists.

HICKS, ALLEN MORLEY, hospital administrator; b. Toronto, Iowa, May 11, 1928; s. Perle and Grace (Mowry) H.; m. Sue Hicks; children by previous ma rriage: David, Dennis, Wendy, Patricia. Student, Long Beach City Coll., 1949-50; B.S., U. Iowa, 1952, M.S., 1954. Adminstrv. resident St. Lukes Hosp., Davenport, Ia., 1953-54; adminstr. Schmitt Meml. Hosp., Beardstown, Ill., 1954-57, Pekin (Ill.) Meml. Hosp., 1957-63, Ill. Masonic Hosp. and Med. Center, Chgo., 1963-72; pres. Community Hosp., Indpls., 1972-84, Meth. Health Care Systems, Memphis, 1984-85, VHA Enterprises, 1985-90; adminstr. Midwest Med. Ctr., Indpls., 1991-93; sr. advisor St. Vincent's Hosp. and Health Care Corp.; chmn. bd. Vol. Hosps. Am., 1980-84, Multi-Mut. Ins. Cos. of Bermuda and Cayman Islands; bd. dirs. Am. Coll. Testing, Ind. Blue Cross, Am. Health Capital, Indpls. Conv. Ctr.; preceptor masters degree program in health and hosp. adminstrn. U. Iowa; chmn. com. extended care Coun. on Assn. Svc., 1963; pres. Chgo. Hosp. Coun., 1970-71. Campaign chmn., bd. dirs., chmn. indsl. div. United Fund, Pekin, Ill., 1959-64; pres. Tazewell County United Cerebral Palsy, 1960-61; chmn. Cancer Crusade, Pekin, 1960-61; service chmn. Tazewell County, 1958-60; chmn. bd. Tomahawk dist. Creve Coeur council Boy Scouts Am., 1963-64, bd. dirs. Crossroads council; bd. dirs. Cancer Soc., Hosp. Research and Devel. Inst., Inc.; pres. Meth. Health Systems Memphis, 1984-85. H, Served with USNR, 1945- 49, 51-52. Recipient Outstanding Young Man of Year award State Ill., 1960; Distinguished Service award Pekin Jr. C. of C., 1960; Boss of Year award Marquette chpt. Nat. Secs. Assn., 1962. Fellow Am. Coll. Health Adminstrn.; mem. Am. Hosp. Assn. (del. 1971—, chmn. com. community relations), Ill. Hosp.Assn. (trustee, chmn. com. personnel relations), Am. Coll. Hosp. Adminstrs., Am. Assn. Maternal and Infant Health, Ill. Welfare Assn., Ill. C. of C., Am. Legion, Am. Vets., 500 Assn., Beta Gamma Sigma. Presbyterian (elder, trustee). Clubs: Mason, Elks, Kiwanis (bd. dirs. Internat. Found. 1981-85, pres. local chpt. 1983). Office: St Vincents Hosp PO Box 40970 2001 W 86th St Indianapolis IN 46260-0970

HICKS, BARRY A., surgeon; b. Louisville, Ky., Oct. 7, 1957; s. Patricia LeBlanc Hicks, Mar. 12, 1982; children: Laura Elizabeth, Matthew Christopher. BA, Vanderbilt U., 1980; MD, Ind. U., Indpls., 1984. Diplomate Am. Bd. Surgery, Am. Bd. Pediatric Surgery. Resident Vanderbilt Med. Ctr., Nashville, 1984-91; fellow in pediatric surgery Columbia-Presbyn. Med. Ctr., N.Y.C., 1991-93; pediatric surgeon U. Tex. Southwestern Med. Ctr., Dallas, 1993—. Office: U Tex Southwestern Med Ctr Childrens Med Ctr Dallas 1935 Motor St Dallas TX 75235

HICKS, CLAYTON N., optometrist; b. Columbus, Ohio, May 2, 1943; s. Amos Nathaniel and Augusta (Asby) H. BS in Microbiology, Ohio State U., 1964, OD, 1970. Microbiologist Ohio Dept. Health, 1964-70; clin. instr. Ohio State U. Coll. Optometry, Columbus, 1970—; practice medicine specializing in optometry Columbus, 1970—; vision cons. Ohio Dept. HHS, Columbus, 1976—; conv. planner, Columbus, 1982—. Mem. Martin Luther King Jr. Holiday Commn., 1986—, Driving Park Mental Health Comm., 1985—, Nat. Black Leadership Roundtable, 1984—; mem. nat. adv. council United Negro Coll. Fund. Named one of Outstanding Young Men of Am., 1961; recipient Polit. Leadership award 29th Dist. Citizen's Caucus, 1986. Mem. Nat. Optometric Assn. (pres. 1983-85, Optometrist of Yr. 1982), Neighbor House House Inc. (pres. 1978-81), Alpha Phi Alpha (pres. Columbus chpt. 1981-83, Outstanding Service award 1981). Lodge: Lions (pres. Columbus inner city club 1977-80). Home: 4961 Wintersong Ln Westerville OH 43081-4439 Office: 1489 E Livingston Ave Columbus OH 43205-2931

HICKS, FRAN, nurse, educator; b. Wasco, Calif., Jan. 1, 1937; d. Clifford L. and Laura Elizabeth (Collins) H. Nursing cert., Okla. Bapt. Hosp., Muskogee, 1957; BS, Northwestern State U. of La., 1960; MS, Case Western Res. U., 1964; PhD, North Tex. U., 1977. RN, Okla. Staff nurse Valley View Hosp., Ada, Okla., 1957, Okla. Bapt. Hosp., Muskogee, 1957-58; clin. instr. Muskogee Bapt. Hosp., 1959-60; evening med. supr. Muskogee Gen. Hosp., 1960-61, asst. hosp. adminstr., 1964; dir. sch. nursing Confederate Meml. Med. Ctr., Shreveport, La., 1964-71; asst. prof., asst. dean Tex. Woman's U., Denton, 1971-77; prof., asst. dean. U. So. Miss., Hattiesburg, 1977-78; prof., asst. dean U. Portland, Oreg., 1978-89; prof. U. Portland, 1989—; cons. in field; mem. Acad. Senate, 1992-95, chair, 1993-95. Contbr. articles to profl. jours.; reviewer nursing texts, 1986—. Active Statewide Master Planning Commn., Portland, 1985—, Oreg. Health 2000 Team, Portland, 1987—. Mem. ANA (nat. bd. dirs. 1987-92, fin. com. 1990-92), Am. Nurses Found. (sec. 1989, treas. 1990-92, pres. 1993—), Oreg. Nurses Assn. (pres. 1984-86), Am. Assn. Higher Edn., Am. Nurses Credentialing Ctr. (sec. 1990), Am. Ednl. Rsch. Assn., Sigma Theta Tau, Portland Future Focus. Democrat. Baptist. Home: 5393 Green Mountain Rd Woodland WA 98674 Office: U Portland Sch Nursing 5000 N Willamette Blvd Portland OR 97203-5743

HICKS, JESSIE DENEICE, pharmacist; b. Palestine, Tex., Sept. 29, 1959; d. Booker T. and Bedella (Booker) Sloan; m. Thomas Hicks, Dec. 8, 1982; children: Sereca Autumn, Arielle Summer. BS in Pharmacy, U. Houston, 1982; postgrad., U. North Tex., Ft. Worth, 1992—. Registered phrmacist, Tex. Pharmacist, cons. Eckerd Drugs, Ft. Worth, 1982—. Drug abuse counselor E.M. Daggett Elem. Sch., Ft. Worth, 1982—. Grantee U. North Tex. Health Sci. Ctr., 1992-94. Mem. Nat. Pharmacy Assn., Am. Coll. Family Practitioners, Nat. Orgn. Women Physicians, Tex. Osteo. Med. Assn., Sigma Sigma Phi. Baptist. Home: 7521 Blue Sage Cir Fort Worth TX 76123

HICKS, JOCELYN MURIEL, laboratory medicine specialist; b. Leamington Spa, Warwickshire, Eng., Aug. 17, 1937; came to U.S., 1965; d. Harold Archie and Muriel Ellen (Cumberland) Bingley; m. John Geoffrey Hicks, Aug. 15, 1959 (div. Nov. 1965); m. Melvin Blecher, May 1, 1973. BS, U. London, 1959, MSc, 1962; PhD, Georgetown U., 1971. Fellow Georgetown U. Med. Ctr., Washington, 1969-71; dir. clin. chemistry Children's Hosp. Nat. Med. Ctr., Washington, 1971-75, chmn. dept. lab. medicine, 1975-90, chief of lab. medicine and pathology, 1990-95, dir. clin. support svcs., 1995—; asst. prof. George Washington U. Med. Ctr., Washington, 1972-74, assoc. prof., 1975-81, prof., 1981—; mem. profl. staff The Hosp. for Sick Children, Washington, 1984—; pres. Children's Faculty assocs. Children's Hosp., Washington, 1989-90, chmn. bd. dirs., 1990-93, chmn. exec. com., 1994-95; clin. affiliate Cath. U. Am., Washignton, 1982-94; cons. Johnson and Johnson Clin. Diagnostics, Bayer Diagnostics, i-State Corp. Author: Selected Analyses of Clinical Chemistry, 1984, Textbook of Clinical Chemistry, 1984, Textbook of Clinical Chemistry, 1984, Directory of Rare Analyses, 1986, 87, 90, 92, 94, The Neonate, 1974, Pediatric Reference Ranges, 1995; co-author: Biochemical Basis of Pediatric Disease, 1992, 2d edit., 1995; contbr. articles to profl. jours. Recipient Kone award Assn. Clin. Biochemists, 1987. Mem. Am. Assn. for Clin. Chemistry (bd. dirs. 1978-81, pres. 1981-82, chmn. publs. commn. 1982-87, Joseph H. Roe award 1976, Bernard Gerulat Meml. award 1983, Fisher award 1984, cert. of honor, Van Slyke award 1988, Miriam Reiner award 1991, Outstanding Contbns. to Clin. Chemistry 1993), Acad. Clin. Lab. Physicians and Scientists, Assn. Clin. Biochemistry (U.K.). Home: 4329 Van Ness St NW Washington DC 20016-5625 Office: Childrens Nat Med Ctr 111 Michigan Ave NW Washington DC 20010*

HICKS, JUDITH EILEEN, nursing administrator; b. Chgo., Jan. 1, 1947; d. John Patrick and Mary Ann (Clifford) Rohan; m. Laurence Joseph Hicks, Nov. 22, 1969; children—Colleen Driscoll, Patrick Kevin. B.S. in Nursing, St. Xavier Coll., Chgo., 1969; M.S. in Nursing, U. Ill.-Chgo., 1975. Staff nurse Mercy Hosp., Chgo., 1969-70, nursing supr., 1970-73; cons. continuing edn. Ill. Nurses Assn., Chgo., 1974-75; dir. obstetrics and gynecology nursing Northwestern Meml. Hosp., Chgo., 1975-81; v.p. nursing Children's Meml. Hosp., Chgo., 1981-86; pres. Children's Meml. Home Health, Inc., 1986—, Children's Meml. Nursing Services, 1986—; pres. Allied & Children's Home Health and Nursing Services, 1988, CM Healthcare Resources, Inc., 1988—, The Pediatric Place, Inc., 1994—; dir. Near North Health Corp., Chgo., 1982-85; pres. Pediatric Excellence Program Svc.; bd. dirs. Infant Welfare Soc. Chgo., Nat. Breast Cancer Assn. Mem. Ill. Hosp. Assn. (chmn. Council on Nursing 1982-83), Inst. Medicine, Am. Soc. Nursing Adminstrs., Women's Health Exec. Network (pres. 1984-85). Roman Catholic. Home: 2206 Beechwood Ave Wilmette IL 60091-1508 Office: CM Health Care Resources 1181 Lake Cook Rd Deerfield IL 60015-5210

HICKS, LEA FRANCA, hospital administrator; b. Newman, Ga., July 12, 1945; d. Roy and Louise Elizabeth (Johnson) Flournoy; m. Jody B. Hicks, Nov. 10, 1971 (div. June 1979); 1 child, Christopher Lee. Diploma in Nursing, Grady Meml. Hosp., Atlanta. Cert. in infection control and healthcare quality, diplomate Am. Bd. Quality Assurance and Utilization Review. Staff nurse ob-gyn. Tanner Hosp., Carrollton, Ga., 1966-67; supr. ob-gyn. Tanner Hosp., Carrollton, 1968-69; staff nurse ob-gyn./surgery Villa Rica (Ga.) City Hosp., 1969-71, head nurse ICU, 1971-75, head edn., infection control, 1975-77, profl. activities coord., 1977-92, profl. activities dir., 1992—. Mem. Am. Assn. Utilization Mgmt. Nurses, Nat. Assn. Health Care Quality, Ga. Assn. Health Care Quality, Ga. Assn. Healthcare Tng. and Edn., Am. Bd. Quality Assurance and Utilization Rev., Am. Assn. Infection Control Practitioners, Ga. Soc. Utilization Rev. Democrat. Office: Tanner Med Ctr/Villa Rica 601 Dallas Hwy PO Box 638 Villa Rica GA 30180

HICKS, MICHAEL LAWRENCE, physician assistant; b. Menomonie, Wis., Sept. 24, 1950; s. Stephen L. and Marion M. (Lynch) H.; m. Helen Ruth Berecz, June 13, 1971 (div. June 1988); children: Michael Shannon, Justin Joseph; m. Janice Elizabeth Nunn, Jan. 21, 1990; 1 stepchild, Elise N. Robles. BA, So. Coll., 1972; AAS, Kettering Coll. Med. Arts, 1979. Resident in emergency medicine U. Iowa, Iowa City, 1983; physician asst. Durand, Wis., 1979-80, FEMA Cuban Refugee Camps, 1980-82, Shiocton, Wis., 1982-83, Ashton Hosp., West Yellowstone, Mont., 1983-86, Kaiser Permenente, Fontana, Colton, 1986—; chmn. Kaiser Office Positive Response Team, 1993—; instr. Kaiser Minor Surgery Techniques Classes, 1994—. Republican. Home: 10326 Stone Ct Mentone CA 92359

HICKS, PHYLLIS ANN, medical, surgical nurse; b. Croghan, N.Y., July 4, 1935; d. Leonard B. and Doris A. (Schack) Bush; m. Patrick Clare, Aug. 1, 1953 (dec. Jan. 1976); m. Charles L. Hicks, May 26, 1979; children: Michael Clare, Maureen (dec.), Martin (dec.); stepchildren: Lynn, Melinda, Kevin. ADN, St. Elizabeth's Hosp., Utica, N.Y., 1988; cert. pharmacology, Bd. Coop. Ednl. Svcs., Verona, N.Y., 1989, phlebotomy cert., 1994; student, Mercy Hosp. Sch. Nursing, Watertown, N.Y., 1952-53. RN, N.Y. Nurse med.-surg. unit Rome (N.Y.) Murphy Meml. Hosp., 1988-90; head nurse geriatrics Stonehedge Nursing Home, Rome, N.Y., 1990; nurse I Mohawk Valley Psychiatric Ctr., Utica, N.Y., 1990-91; charge nurse ventilator unit Oneida (N.Y.) City Hosp., 1993—. Home: 10276 State Rt 26 Ava NY 13303 Office: Oneida Health Care Assn 321 Genesee St Oneida NY 13421

HIER, DANIEL BARNET, neurologist; b. Chgo., Mar. 23, 1947; s. Stanley W. and Jean (Schrager) H.; m. Myra Goldberg, Aug. 30, 1981 (dec. Jul. 1995); children: Benjamin Philip, David Samuel. BA, Harvard U., 1969, MD, 1973. Medical intern Bronx Mcpl. Hosp., N.Y.C., 1973-74; neurology resident Mass. Gen. Hosp., Boston, 1974-77, neurology fellow, 1977-79; neurologist Michael Reese Hosp., Chgo., 1979—, chmn. neurology, 1987-89; head neurology U. Ill., Chgo., 1989—, assoc. prof. neurology, 1989-91; prof. Ul. Ill., 1991—. Fellow Am. Acad. Neurology, Am. Heart Assn. (stroke council). Home: 641 W Willow St Chicago IL 60614-5176

HIESHIMA, GRANT BUNJI, radiology and neuroradiology educator; b. July 21, 1942; s. Asaichi Shimidzu and Yoshi Alice (Machikawa) H.; m. Donna Marie Yankowski, Mar. 25, 1974; children: Glenn, Michael. MD with honors, Tulane U., 1969. Intern in surgery Harbor/UCLA Med. Ctr., Torrance, 1969-70, resident in radiology, 1970-73, fellow in neuroradiology and nuclear medicine, 1973-74, asst. prof. radiology, 1974-80, assoc. prof. radiology, 1980-85; fellow in neuroradiology UCLA Ctr. for Health Scis., 1974-75, prof., 1985-86; prof. radiology and neurol. surgery U. Calif., San Francisco, 1986-93, clin. prof. radiology and neurol. surgery, 1993—. Contbr. about 150 articles to sci. publs., over 50 chpts. to books. Recipient Surg. award Oscar Creech Soc., 1968. Mem. Alpha Omega Alpha. Office: U Calif PO Box 0628 San Francisco CA 94143

HIGGINBOTHAM, A. C., retired pharmacist; b. Bienville, La., July 27, 1927; s. Alfred C. and Tallie (Farley) H.; m. Maxine Wiggins, June 10, 1944; children: Rodney Gerald, Leara Anne. BS in Pharmacy, Loyola U., New Orleans, 1949, PharmD, 1982. Registered pharmacist, La., Tex., Ark. Pharmacist Burnham Drug, Cullen, La., 1949, Allen Drug, Henderson, Tex., 1950; pharmacist, pres. H&B Drug Inc., Springhill, La., 1950-89; pres. Med. Save Inc., Springhill, 1975-85; ret., 1989; part-time relief pharmacist, 1989—. Alderman Springhill City Coun., 1970-74. With U.S. Army, 1946-47, Japan. Recipient Sound Citizen award Springhill Jaycees, 1972, Melvin Jones award Leona Found., 1996. Mem. Am. Pharm. Assn. (life), Nat. Assn. Retail Druggists, La. Pharmacists Assn. (life), Springhill C. of C. (pres. 1958, Civic Svc. award 1959-60, bd. dirs. 1995—), La. Lions League for Crippled Children (life), Lions (bd. dirs., sec.-treas. 1951-52, v.p. 1953-54, 96-97, bd. dirs. membership chmn. 1992—, bd. dirs. 1996-97, 45 Yr. Mem. award), Masons, Springhill Amateur Radio Club, Inc. (pres. 1995—). Democrat. Baptist. Home: 805 N Arkansas St Springhill LA 71075-2203

HIGGINBOTHAM, EVE JULIET, ophthalmologist, educator; b. New Orleans, Nov. 4, 1953; d. Luther Aldrich and Ruby Edith (Clark) H.; m. Frank Christopher Williams, June 7, 1986. BSChE, MS in Engring., MIT, 1975; MD, Harvard U., 1979. Intern Pacific Med. Ctr., San Francisco, 1979-80; resident La. State U. Eye Ctr., 1980-83; fellow Mass. Eye and Ear Infirmary, Boston, 1983-85; asst. prof. U. Ill., Chgo., 1985-90; assoc. prof. U. Mich., Ann Arbor, 1990-94; prof. U. Md., Balt., 1994—. Co-editor: Management of Difficult Glaucoma, 1994; contbr. articles to profl. jours; mem. editl. bd. Jour. of Glaucoma, 1990-93, Archives of Ophthalmology, 1994—. Bd. dirs. Prevent Blindness Am., Schaumburg, Ill., 1990—, chair publs. com., 1990-95, chair scientific adv. com., 1995—. Fellow Am. Acad. Ophthalmology (trustee 1992-95); mem. Women in Ophthalmology (bd. dirs. 1990—), Assn. Univ. Profs. Ophthalmology, Assn. in Rsch. in Vision and Ophthalmology. Office: U Md 22 S Greene St Baltimore MD 21201

HIGGINS, ELLEN M., physician assistant; b. Balt., Sept. 18, 1949; d. Kenneth J. and Helen A. (Hagerty) Coughlin; m. William J. Higgins, Oct. 16, 1971; children: Daniel, Bridget, Aileen. BA, Emmanuel Coll., 1971; MS, U. Colo., 1987. Cert. physician assistant. Physician asst. Ptnrs. in Pediatrics, Englewood, Colo., 1988—; clin. instr. U. Colo. Health Scis. Ctr., Denver, 1985-95, asst. clin. prof., 1995—; med. adv. bd. Mother's Milk Bank, Denver, 1986-91. Mem. Colo. Assn. Physician Assts. Office: Ptnrs in Pediat 8100 S Quebec Unit B-10 Englewood CO 80112

HIGGINS, GEORGE HERMAN, JR., radiologic technologist; b. Easton, Md., Sept. 29, 1954; s. George Herman and Margaret (Jones) H.; m. Sue Swanhaus, Feb. 15, 1976; children: Sean Herman, Sarah Margaret. Cert. radiologic tech., Easton Meml. Hosp., 1974, Bowman Gray Sch. Medicine, 1980. Registered diagnostic med. sonographer; cert. MRI. Diagnostic radiographer Forsyth Meml. Hosp., Winston-Salem, N.C., 1974-75, spl. procedures technician, 1976-78, radiology supr., 1978-80; mobile sonographer Diagnostic Imaging, Winston-Salem, 1980-82; mobile computerized axial tomography Med. Diagnostics, Winston-Salem, 1982-86; mobile computerized axial tomography Maxum Health Corp., Dallas, 1986-89, supr. magnetic resonance imaging project, 1989—. Mem. Am. Soc. Radiologic Technologists, Md. Soc. Radiologic Tech. Home: 29468 Corbin Pky Easton MD 21601-4834 Office: Maxum Health Corp 14850 Quorum Dr 14850 Quorum Dr Dallas TX 75240-7531

HIGGINS, ROBERT PRICE, zoologist; b. Denver, Oct. 8, 1932; s. Jay and Amy (Gates) H.; m. Gwendolyn Ailene Litherland, Aug. 15, 1954; children: Kent Eric, Scott Edwin (dec.), Kim Ailene. BA, U. Colo., 1956, MA, 1958; PhD, Duke U., 1961; DSc (hon.), U. Copenhagen, 1993. Asst. prof., then assoc. prof. Wake Forest U., Winston-Salem, N.C., 1961-68; resident systematist Marine Biology Lab., Woods Hole, Mass., 1968; dir. Mediterranean Sorting Ctr. Smithsonian Inst., Kherreddine, Tunisia, 1969-71; dir. oceanography and limnology program Smithsonian Inst., Washington, 1971-74, sr. zoologist oceanographic sorting ctr., 1975-78, curator invertebrate zoology Nat. Mus. Natural History, 1978-93; adj. prof. biology We. Carolina U., Cullowhee, N.C., 1989—; disting. adj. prof. biology U. N.C., Charlotte, 1993-94; rsch. assoc. Baruch Inst. for Marine Biology and Coastal Rsch., Columbia S.C., 1974—; adj. rsch. prof. U. N.C., Asheville, 1994—. Co-editor: Introduction to the Study of Meiofauna, 1988; editor proc. Internat. Symposium on Tardigrades, 1974; contbr. articles to profl. jours. Master sgt. USMCR, 1950-52. Grantee NSF, 1964, 68, NATO, 1988; James B. Duke fellow, 1959-61. Fellow AAAS, Explorer's Club; mem. Internat. Assn. Meiobenthologists (chmn. 1980-81), Am. Soc. Zoologists (chmn. div. invertebrate zoology 1969-70 , chmn. div. ecology 1975-76), Am. Microscopical Soc. (pres. 1979-80, assoc. editor 1966-69), Soc. Systematic Zoology (program officer 1967-68), Biol. Soc. Washington, Sigma Xi (pres. Wake Forest chpt. 1966-67). Republican. Presbyterian. Home: 2 Pond Ln Asheville NC 28804-1745

HIGGINS, THOMAS LEO, physician; b. Everett, Mass., Feb. 27, 1955; s. Louis Joseph and Mary Ann (Marino) H.; m. Suzanne Marguerite Furlong, July 11, 1981; children: Amy, Matthew, William. BA, Boston U., 1978, MD, 1978. Diplomate Am. Bd. Internal Medicine, Am. Bd. Anesthesiology; cert. critical care. Staff physician Whidden Hosp., Everett, Mass., 1983-84; resident Mass. Gen. Hosp., Boston, 1984-86, chief resident, 1986-87; dir. cardiothoracic ICU Cleve. Clinic, 1987-94, dir. outcomes rsch., 1994-95; pres. Med. Strat Rsch., Bratenahl, Ohio, 1995-96; dir. adult critical care Baystate Med. Ctr., Springfield, Mass., 1996—; cons. in field. Editor: The High Risk Patient, 1995; contbr. articles to profl. jours. Lt. USPHS, 1981-83. Fellow ACP, Am. Coll. Cardiology, Am. Coll. Critical Care Medicine. Roman Catholic. Home: 126 Williamsburg Dr Longmeadow MA 01106

HIGH, KATHERINE MARY, family therapist, social worker; b. Balt., Mar. 6, 1957; d. Lloyd and Rita (Pagano) H. BS, Towson U., 1984; MSW, U. Md., 1987. Lic. social work, Md.; cert. alcoholism counselor, Md. Mental health worker Sheppard Pratt Hosp., Balt., 1979-81, alcohol counselor, 1981-86, social worker, 1988—; social worker St. Francis Med. Ctr., Pitts., 1987-88. Democrat. Roman Catholic. Home: 11 Burwood Ct Lutherville Timonium MD 21093-3503 Office: 21 West Rd Ste 150 Baltimore MD 21204

HIGHFIELD, MARTHA ELLEN FARRAR, nursing educator; b. Nashville, May 21, 1954; d. Henry Cheiers and Grace Angeline (Johnson) Farrar; m. Ronald Curtis Highfield, Dec. 30, 1977; children: Nathanael, Matthew David. BSN, U. TEnn., 1976; M of Nursing Sci. in Med./Surg. Nursing, U. Ark., Little Rock, 1981; PhD in Nursing, Tex. Woman's U., Denton, 1989. RN, Calif.; cert. oncology nurse. Staff and charge nurse, surg. ICU Meth. Cen. Hosp., Memphis, 1976-77; staff float nurse White County Meml. Hosp., Searcy, Ark., 1980, 81; assoc. instr. nursing Harding U. Sch. Nursing, Searcy, 1977-81; clinician II, surg. urology UT MD Anderson Cancer Ctr., Houston, 1982-83, clnician II, gen. surgery, 1984; instr. nursing Prairie View A&M U. Coll. Nursing, Houston, 1984-86; pvt. duty profl. nurse Ofcl. Registry Profl. Nurses, Houston, 1986-87; nursing instr. Vets. Affairs Med. Ctr., Houston, 1987-89; nursing instr. Wadsworth Div. Vets. Affairs Med. Ctr., L.A., 1989-90, assoc. chief nursing svc. for edn., 1990-95; assoc. prof nursing Calif. State U., Northridge, 1996—; lectr., researcher in field. Contbr. articles to med. jours. Mem. children's ednl. ministry Bering Dr. Ch. of Christ, Houston, 1981, 83, blood dr. ministry, 1983-88, mem. nursery svcs. ministry, 1986-87, nurse mem. interdisciplinary task force on AIDS, 1987-89; vol. World Stars Gymnastics Tng. Ctr., 1993—. ACT scholar Harding U., 1971; Kellogg fellow U. Ark., 1981; winner essay contest Houston Tex. Med. Ctr., 1989; nominated Excellence in Sci. award Nursing Rsch. Roundtable Greater Houston, 1989. Mem. Calif. Nurses Assn., Nat. Oncology Nursing Soc. (coord. focus group on spirituality 1989, coord. spiritual care spl. interest group 1990-93, bd. dirs. Channel Islands chpt.), Sigma Theta Tau.

HIGHMAN, BARBARA, dermatologist; b. Washington; d. Benjamin and Helen (Wienshienk) H. Student, Northwestern U., 1960-63; MD, U. Mich., 1967. Diplomate Am. Bd. Dermatology. Intern Baylor U. Affiliated Hops., Houston, 1967-68; dermatology residency Henry Ford Hosp., Detroit, 1968-71; fellow in dermatology Johns Hopkins U., Balt., 1971-72; pvt. practice Laurel, Md., 1972—; staff North Charles Hosp., Balt., 1972-77, Greater Laurel-Beltsville Hosp.; cons. in dermatology U.S. Army, Ft. Myer, Va., 1972-77. Fellow Am. Acad. Dermatology (continuing med. edn. award 1978-80, 80-83, 83-86, 86-89, 89-92, 95-95, 95—); mem. AMA (physicians recognition award 1971-74, 74-77, 77-80, 80-83, 83-86, 85-89, 88-90, 90-92, 92-95, 95—), Soc. for Investigative Dermatology, Nat. Found. for Dermatology, Anne Arundel County Med. Soc., Med. and Chirugical Soc. State of Md., Laurel Med. Soc., Prince George's Women's Med. Soc. Office: 3335 Old Line Ave Laurel MD 20707-2234

HIGHSMITH, WANDA LAW, retired association executive; b. Cleveland, Mo., Oct. 25, 1928; d. Lloyd B. and Nan (Sisk) Law; student U. Mo., 1954-56; 1 child, Holly. Legal sec., firms in Mo. and D.C., until 1960; various staff positions Am. Coll. Osteopathic Surgeons, 1960-72, asst. exec. dir., conv. mgr., Alexandria, Va., 1974-94; ret., 1994. Mem. NAFE, Profl. Conv. Mgmt. Assn., Washington Soc. Assn. Execs., Am. Soc. Assn. Execs. Republican. Methodist. Home: 4835 Martin St Alexandria VA 22312-1838

HIGHTOWER, ROBERT BRIAN, osteopath; b. Ada, Okla., Dec. 18, 1966; s. Robert Bingham and Karen Louise (Fortelney) H.; m. Laura Anne Margotta, June 12, 1993; 1 child, Robert Bingham. BS, Okla. State U., 1989, DO, 1993. Mem. Young Republicans, Tulsa. Mem. Am. Osteopathic Assn.

HIGLEY, BRUCE WADSWORTH, orthodontist; b. Iowa City, Dec. 1, 1928; s. Lester Bodine and Harriet (Wadsworth) H.; m. Marta Beatriz Velasco, Sept. 23, 1966. D.D.S., State U. Iowa, 1952, M.S., 1953; student, Grinnell Coll., 1946-48, orthodontic certificate, 1953. Research, instr. Iowa Dental U., 1952-53; practice dentistry, specializing in orthodontics South Miami, Fla., 1955—; Owner, chmn. bd. M.B.H. Enterprises, Inc., Miami, Fla., 1960—. Vice chmn. dist. council Boy Scouts Am., 1959-62; Mem. Personnel Bd., South Miami, 1959. Served as 1st lt. Dental Corps AUS, 1953-55. Mem. Am. Assn. Orthodontics, Fla. Orthodontic Soc., So., Miami socs. orthodontists, Fla., Am. socs. dentistry for children, Fla., Fla. East Coast, Miami dental socs., Am., S. Dade dental assns., Fedn. Dentaire Internat., English Royal Acad., C. of C. (past dir., sec., treas.), Psi Omega, Omicron Kappa Upsilon. Presbyn. (deacon). Clubs: Rotarian (pres. 1961-62), Elk, Coral Reef Yacht, Coral Gables Country, Royal Palm Tennis; Bankers, Executive (Miami); Army-Navy. Home: 2000 Brickell Ave Miami FL 33129-1721 Office: 7210 S Red Rd Miami FL 33143-5321

HIILLOS-VUORINEN, RIITTA HELENA, psychodrama trainer, family therapist; b. Tampere, Finland, Sept. 10, 1942; d. Lauri Aukusti and Hilja Maria (Ylänen) Hiillos; m. Ilpo Joonas Vuorinen, Aug. 27, 1964; children: Hanna Matleena, Pauliina Mirjami. MDiv, U. Helsinki, Finland, 1967. High sch. tchr. Kuopio, Finland, 1969-73, family therapist, 1980; pvt. practice Turku, Finland, 1980-90; dir. Finnish Moreno Inst., Turku, 1990—. Author: Vuorovaikutus ja yhteistyö, 1985; dir. television programs, 1978-96; contbr. articles to profl. jours. and newspapers. Mem. Finnish Psychodrama Assn. (pres. 1987-89, mem. tng. bd. 1987-92), Zonta Club. Lutheran. Home: Vadstenankatu 7, SF-21100 Naantali Finland Office: The Finish Morens Inst, Yliopistonkatu 10 C, SF-20110 Turku Finland

HILDEBRAND, DAVID FLOYD, educator, geneticist; b. Bethesda, Md., Mar. 12, 1955; s. Floyd C. and Suzanne Hildebrand; m. Atsuko Yokoyama, May 5, 1984. BS in Chemistry and Agronomy, U. Md., 1977; MS in Agronomy, U. Ill., 1980, PhD in Agronomy, 1982. Exch. scientist Kyoto (Japan) U., 1982; asst. prof. U. Ky., Lexington, 1982-88, assoc. prof., 1988—. Contbr. over 100 rsch. pubs. to profl. jours. USDA grantee. Mem. AAAS, Crop Sci. Soc. Am., Plant Molecular Biology Assn., Am. Oil Chemists Soc., Am. Soc. Plant Physiologists. Office: U Ky Dept Agronomy Lexington KY 40546

HILDEBRAND, DAVID WILLIAM, psychotherapist, marketing professional; b. Pottstown, Pa., Oct. 10, 1951; s. Harry and Marie (Jacquot) H.; m. May 21, 1983; children: Grant, Sarah. BA, Millersville U., 1976. Cert. employee assistance profl., Pa. Dir. outpatient care Creative Health Svcs., Pottstown, 1979-86; mktg. rep. Eugenia Hosp., Lafayette Hill, Pa., 1984-93; ptnr., chief exec. officer Innovative Counseling Assocs., Pottstown, 1984—; regional mktg. dir. Progression Health Sys., Blue Bell, Pa., 1993—. With USMC, 1971-74. Mem. AACD, Employee Assistance Profl. Assn., Soc. for Human Resources, N.J. Assn. of Alcohol and Drug Counselors, Pa. Assn. Student Assistance Profls., Tri-County C. of C. Republican. Lutheran. Home: 677 Beechwood Ave Pottstown PA 19464-4303 Office: Innovative Counseling Assoc 1200 E High St Pottstown PA 19464-4948

HILDEBRAND, REINHARD FRIEDRICH HANS, anatomist, medical historian, educator; b. Berlin, Germany, Jan. 18, 1943; s. Reinhard Rudolf and Else (Hölscher) H.; m. Johanna Stephania Farwick, May 7, 1981; children: Annette Sophie, Friederike Louise. MD, Westfälische Wilhelms U., Muenster, Fed. Republic Germany, 1972, habil., 1979. Asst. prof. Anatomisches Inst. Westfaelische-Wilhelms U., Muenster, 1979-80; assoc. prof. Anatomisches Inst. Bayerische Julius Maximilians U., Wuerzburg, Fed. Republic Germany, 1980-84, Anatomisches Inst. U. zu Köln, Koeln, Fed. Republic Germany, 1984-87; prof. Inst. Anatomie Westfaelische-Wilhelms U., Muenster, 1987—; head Inst. Anatomie, dept. Anatomy, Histo- and Cytochemistry, Muenster, 1987—. Fellow Royal Microscopical Soc.; mem. Gesellschft Histochemie, British Soc. for Hist. of Sci., Scottish Hist. Soc., Gesellschaft fuer Wissenschaftsgeschichte (corresponding), Anatomische Gesellschaft. Home: Lortzingstrasse 8, D-48145 Muenster Germany Office: Inst Anatomie, Vesaliusweg 2-4, D-48149 Muenster Germany

HILDEBRANDT, OSCAR ALLEN, veterinarian; b. Kiel, Wis., June 7, 1934; s. Oscar H. and Clara I. (Hagenow) H.; m. Mary E. Wuest, Nov. 24, 1962; children: Hugh H., Denise J., Kurt E. BS, U. Minn., 1956, DVM, 1958. Lic. veterinarian, Wis., Minn. Vet. Medford (Wis.) Vet. Clinic, 1958-60, vet., owner, 1960-90; owner, technician Outdoor Svcs., Medford, Wis., 1990-95; fin. advisor OAH Consulting, Tomahawk, Wis., 1990—; chmn. bd. dirs. Medford Nat. Bank, Royale Energy Corp., San Diego; mink advisor Wis. Dept. Agr., Madison, 1980—, vet.-tech. advisor, 1975-80; mem. vet. exam bd. State of Wis. Dept. Regulation, Madison, 1972-78; seminar presenter. Contbr. articles to profl. jours. Mem. sch. bd. Medford Area Schs., 1965-88, past pres.; mem. mayor's adv. com. Medford, 1970-73. Recipient Outstanding Sch. Bd. award Wis. Dept. Edn., 1986. Mem. AVMA, Wis. Vet. Med. Assn. (pub. health com. 1988-92, Vet. of Yr. 1990), N.C. Wis. Mink Assn., Wis. Jaycees (officer 1959-65, Outstanding Jaycee 1965, Outstanding Cmty. Leader 1970), Ctrl. Wis. Vet. Assn. (officer 1959-90). Republican. Office: OAH Consulting PO Box 259 Tomahawk WI 54487

HILDING, MARIA BIRGITTA, orthopedic surgeon, consultant; b. Stockholm, Feb. 20, 1958; d. Sven H. and Ingeborg A. B. (Aulin) H.; m. Bengt O. Bäckbro, Sept. 9, 1986. MD, Karolinska Inst., Stockholm, 1982, PhD, 1995. Cert. specialist in orthopedic surgery Nat. Bd. Health Care, Sweden. Intern Köping Hosp., Sweden, 1982-84; registrar Cen. Hosp. Västerås, Sweden, 1984-88, sr. registrar, 1988-93, cons., 1994—; head rsch. program PhD, Karolinska Inst., Stockholm, 1988-95, Lund (Sweden) U., 1988-95. Contbr. articles and papers to profl. publs. Recipient Rsch. prize Odd Fellow Found., 1994. Mem. European Soc. Biomechanics, Nordic Orthopedic Soc., Swedish Orthopedic Soc. Home: Akademivågen 11, S-72217 Vasteras Sweden Office: Cen Hosp, Dept Orthopedics, S-72189 Vasteras Sweden

HILDRETH, EUGENE A., physician, educator; b. St. Paul, Mar. 11, 1924; s. Eugene A. IV and Lila K. (Clator) H.; m. Dorothy Anne Myers, Mar. 23, 1946; children: Jeffrey Reed, William Myers, Anne Sarver, Katherine Clator. BS, Washington Jefferson Coll., 1943; MD, U. Va., 1947. Diplomate: Am. Bd. Internal Medicine (mem. 1969-72, 75-82, cons., com. mem. 1972-75), Am Bd. Allergy and Immunology (founding com. 1970, mem. 1970-72, 1st co-chmn.). Intern Johns Hopkins, 1947-48; resident in medicine Hosp. U. Pa., 1948-49, USPHS Postdoctoral Research fellow in cardiovascular disease, 1949-51, chief resident in medicine, 1953-54, fellow in allergy and immunology, 1954-58, faculty, 1954-69, 71—; instr. medicine U. Pa., Phila., 1953-54; asso. medicine U. Pa., 1954-55, asst. prof. medicine, 1955-60, assoc. prof., 1960-69; assoc. dean U. Pa. (Sch. Medicine), 1964-69, prof. clin. medicine, 1971-90, prof. emeritus, 1990—, acting chmn. dept. research medicine, 1960-64; chmn. dept. medicine Reading (Pa.) Hosp. and Med. Center.; Cons. project site visits USPHS, 1965-70 ; cons. VA Hosp. Phila., 1955—; nat. adv. com. Medic Alert Found. Internat., 1964-83; cons. Citizens' Com. to Study Grad. Med. Edn., 1966; Am. Bd. Med. Spltys: rep. of subsplty. Bd. Allergy and Immunology of Am. Bd. Internal Medicine, 1969-72; chmn. certifying exam. com. Am. Bd. Internal Medicine, 1978-81, mem. core exam. com., 1986—, mem. exec. com., 1978-82, chmn., 1981-82; mem. rep. Am. Bd. Med. Spltys., 1976-83, chmn. nominating com., 1979-80, mem. med. adv. bd. Lupus Found. Del. Valley, 1979—; chmn. Federated Council Internal Medicine; appeals bd. liaison Council of Grad. Med. Edn., 1980—. Co-author: Low Fat Diet, 1953, also research articles, chpts. in textbooks.; Editorial bd.: Annals Internal Medicine, 1960-68, Postgrad. Medicine, 1969-75, Jour. Berks County Med. Soc, 1969-73, Internal Medicine Digest, 1971-75. Served with USNR, 1943-45, 51-53. John and Mary R. Markle scholar in acad. medicine, 1958-63; USPHS Research grantee. Master, fellow ACP (mem. bd. regents 1985—, chmn. bd. dirs. 1989-91, pres. 1991-92, immediate past pres. 1992—, mem. ethics com. 1986-90, chmn. com. to dilineate privileges of med. procedures); fellow Am. Clin. and Climatologic Assn., (hon.) Acad. Medicine of Singapore; mem. AAAS, Peripatetic Soc., Fedn. Am. Socs. for Exptl. Biology, N.Y. Acad. Scis., Inst. Medicine of NAS (mem. nominating com. 1982—, mem. coun. 1986-90, chmn. nominating com. for coun. memberships 1989-90, mem. fin. com. 1988-90), Phila. Art Mus., Am. Acad. Allergy, Federated Coun. Internal Medicine, Royal Soc. Medicine, ACGME (mem. residency rev. com. internal medicine, mem. working group on disability of U.S. presidents 1994—). Home: RR 3 Box 3960 Mohnton PA 19540-9265 Office: Reading Hosp and Med Ctr PO Box 16052 Reading PA 19612-6052

HILGEMANN, DONALD WILLIAM, medical educator; b. Postville, Iowa, Aug. 20, 1952; married. Student, U. Iowa, 1972; MS in Biology, Univ. Tübingen, Germany, 1977, PhD in Pharmacology & Physiology, 1980. Rsch. and tchg. asst. Dept. Pharmacology U. Tübingen, 1977-80; rsch. assoc. Merrell Internat., Strasbourg, France, 1980-81; asst. rsch. physiologist UCLA Sch. Medicine, 1981-87; asst. clin. prof. nursing UCLA Sch. Nursing, 1982-87; asst. prof. Dept. Physiology U. Tex. Southwestern Med. Ctr., Dallas, 1988-91, assoc. prof., 1991—; tchr., lectr. UNISEF, 1992, Univ. Kaiserlautern, 1994; vis. rsch. fellow Oxford U., Eng., 1985-88; invited spkr. Kyoto u., Japan, 1993-94, Northwestern U., Chgo., 1994, U. Konstanz, Germany, 1994, Johns Hopkins U., Balt., 1994, Tokyo Med. Coll., 194, Univ. Laussane, Switzerland, 1994, Pa. U., Phila., 1994, Oreg. Health Sci. Ctr., Portland, 1995, N.Y. Acad. Scis., Woods Hole, Mass., 1995, Rush Med. Ctr., Chgo., 1995, Swiss Fed. Inst. Tech., Zurich, 1994, Tel Aviv U., Israel, 1995. Fellow Binational Israeli-USa Found., Japan Soc. for Promotion Sci.; mem. Biophys. Soc., Soc. Neurosci., Soc. Gen. Physiologists, Physiol. Soc. Office: U Tex Southwestern Med Ctr Dept Physiology Dallas TX

HILKEMEYER, RENILDA ESTELLA, nurse; b. Martinsburg, Mo., July 29, 1915; d. Henry Gerard and Anna Marie (Bertels) Hilkemeyer. Diploma in nursing, St. Mary's Hosp., St. Louis U, 1936; B.S. in Nursing Edn., George Peabody Coll. for Tchrs., Nashville, 1947; postgrad., U. Minn., 1950, U. Tex. Sch. Nursing, 1981; D of Pub. Svc. (hon.), St. Louis U., 1988. Staff nurse oper. rm. St. Mary's Hosp., Jefferson City, Mo., 1936-37; dist. pub. health nurse Mo. Div. Health, Jefferson City, 1937-40, cons. nursing edn., Mo., 1950-55; asst. dir. nursing Gen. Hosp. No. 1, Kansas City, Mo., 1947-49; asst. exec. sec. Mo. Nurses Assn., Jefferson City, 1949-50; dir. nursing U. Tex. System Cancer Ctr., Houston, 1955-77, asst. to pres. nursing resources, 1977-79, staff asst. to pres., prof. oncology nursing, 1979-84; mem. grant rev. com. NIH Nat. Cancer Inst, 1979-83, program rev. com., 1975-77, cons., 1982—; cons. NIH Nat. Heart, Blood and Lung Inst., 1983—, Worker's Inst. Safety, Health, 1983—; chmn., mem. scholarship and professorship com. Cancer Soc., 1980—, mem. nursing adv. com., 1963-80, 85—, profl. edn. com., 1984—; chmn. nursing adv. com., mem. adminstrv. bd. Renilda Hilkemeyer Child Care Ctr., U. Tex. Med. Ctr., 1969—. Book reviewer Am. Jour. Nursing, 1982; contbr. articles to profl. jours, chpts. to books. Pres. Braes Interfaith Ministries, 1991, 94, 95. Recipient Outstanding Profl. Women's award Tex. Fedn. Houston Profl. Women, 1983, outstanding contbns. Award, Nat. Cancer Inst., 1983, Disting. Svc. award Am. Cancer Soc., 1981, Nurse of Yr. Award, Houston Area League Nursing, 1973, Matrix Award, Theta Sigma Phi, Houston, 1963, Disting. Merit award Internat. Soc. Nurses in Cancer Care, 1986; new child care ctr. at U. Tex. Med. Ctr. Houston, named in her honor, 1981 (1st ctr. established 1969); grantee HEW, 1974-77, Am. Cancer Soc., 1974-75, Tex. Fedn. and Profl. Women's Club, 1977-83, Am. Cancer Soc. 1st Nat. Nursing Leadership award, 1989. Achievement: pioneer in cancer nursing. Mem. ANA, Oncology Nursing Soc. (hon. 1991), Tex. Nurses Assn. (pres. 1962-64, bd. dir. 1964-66, 71-75, Nurse of Yr. award 1979, dist. 9 svc. award 1970), Am. Med. Writers Assn. (Houston-Galveston sect. 1983-84), Sigma Theta Tau, Altrusa Club (pres. 1983-84, Houston). Home: 3707 Murworth Dr Houston TX 77025-3531

HILKERT, FRED GEORGE, psychiatrist, psychoanalyst; b. N.Y.C., Dec. 22, 1929; s. August and Alma (Mayan) H.; m. Margaret Ann McNamara, July 4, 1953; children: Tyree August, Elizabeth Paige. BA cum laude, Syracuse U., 1951; MD with distinction, George Washington U., 1955; grad., Washington Psychoanalytic Inst, 1976. Diplomate in psychiatry Am. Bd. Psychiatry and Neurology. Intership Walter Reed Army Hosp., Washington, 1955-56, residency in psychiatry, 1957-59; pvt. practice psychiatry and psychoanalysis, 1963—; assoc. clin. prof George Washington U., Washington, 1963—; instr. Washington Sch. Psychiatry, 1976—; tchr. Georgetown U. med. students Sibley hosp., Washington, 1978—; teaching analyst Washington Psychoanalytic Inst., 1986—; cons. U.S. Dept. Def., 1968—, Internat. Student House, 1972—, Nuclear Regulatory Commn., 1980—, Va. Theol. Sem., 1980-85, Episcopal Ch. House, 1982—. Major U.S. Army, 1955-62. Fellow Am. Psychiat. Assn.; mem. AMA, D.C. Med. Soc., Washington Psychiat. Soc., Am. Psychoanalytic Assn., Washington PSA Soc., Internat. Psychoanalytic Assn., Cosmos Club, Alpha Omega Alpha. Democrat. Episcopalian. Home and Office: 2928 Garfield Ter NW Washington DC 20008-3507

HILL, ALLISON ROSS, physician, educator; b. Bangor, Maine, Nov. 27, 1949; s. Allison Kincade and Katharine Ross (MacKenzie) H.; m. Elaine Ingrid Tuomanen, May 28, 1977 (div. July 1990); 1 child, Laura Kirsi Tuomanen Hill. BA, McGill U., Montreal, Que., Can., 1971, MD, 1975. Resident in internal medicine Montreal Gen. Hosp., 1975-78; resident in respiratory medicine McGill U. Tchg. Hosps., 1978-80; Parker B. Frances fellow U. Va., Charlottesville, 1980-82; attending physician Phila. VA Med. Ctr./Med. Coll. of Pa., 1982-84; attending physician Kings County Hosp., Bklyn., 1984—, med. dir. chest clinic, 1992—; asst. prof. SUNY Health Sci. Ctr., Bklyn., 1984-94, assoc. prof., 1994—. Contbr. numerous articles to profl. publs., chpts. to books. Fellow ACP; mem. Am. Thoracic Soc. Office: SUNY Health Sci Ctr 450 Clarkson Ave Box 19 Brooklyn NY 11203

HILL, BEVERLY ELLEN, health sciences educator; b. Albany, Calif., May 20, 1937; d. Bert E. and Catherine (Doyle) H. BA, Coll. Holy Names, 1960; MS in Edn., Dominican Coll., 1969; EdD, U. So. Calif., 1978. Producer, dir. Health Scis TV U. Calif., Davis, 1966-69, coordinator Health Scis. TV, 1969-73; asst. dir. IMS U. So. Calif., Los Angeles, 1973-76, asst. dir. continuing edn., 1976-80, dir. biocommunications, 1976-80; dir. Med. Ednl. Resources Program Ind. U. Sch. Medicine, Indpls., 1980—; acting asst. dean continuing med. edn. Ind. U. Sch. Medicine, 1991-95; Presenter Cath. U. Nijmegen, Netherlands, 1980, 81, European Symposium on Clin. Pharmacy, Brussels, 1982, Barcelona, Spain, 1983. Contbr. articles to profl. jours. Pres. Indpls. Shakespeare Festival, 1982-83; mem. subcom. Ind. Film Commn., Indpls., 1984—. Recipient first place in rehab. category 4th Biannual J. Muir Med. Film Fest., 1980. Mem. Assn. Biomed. Communications (bd. dirs. 1985—), Health Scis. Com. Assn. (bd. dirs. 1976-79, First Place Video Festival, 1979), Assn. for Edn. Communications and Tech. Home: 5249 W 59th St Indianapolis IN 46254-1109 Office: Med Ednl Resources Program BR 156 1226 W Michigan St Indianapolis IN 46223

HILL, CLARA EDITH, psychology educator; b. Shivers, Miss., Sept. 13, 1948; d. Fletcher Von and Anna (Teich) H.; m. James Gormally, May 25, 1974; children: Kevin, Katherine. BA, So. Ill. U., 1970, MA, 1972, PhD, 1974. Lic. psychologist, Md. Asst. prof. dept. psychology U. Md. College Park, 1974-78, assoc. prof. dept. psychology, 1978-85, prof. dept. psychology, 85—. Author: Therapist Techniques and Client Outcomes, 1989, Working With Dreams in Psychotherapy, 1996; editor Jour. Counseling Psychology, 1994—; contbr. articles to profl. jours. Grantee NIMH, 1983-92. Fellow Am. Psychol. Assn.; mem. Soc. Psychotherapy Rsch. (pres. N.Am. chpt. 1990, pres. internat. orgn. 1994-95). Office: U Maryland Dept Psychology College Park MD 20742

HILL, DAVID MICHAEL, cardiologist; b. Frankfurt, Germany, Dec. 29, 1950; came to U.S., 1953; s. Harold Weymouth and Jacqueline Francis (Wilson) H.; m. Chantal Leslie Underwood, Sept. 11, 1982; children: Nicole Jennifer, Kristiane Michele. BS in Chemistry, Presbyn. Coll., Clinton, S.C., 1972; MD, Med. Coll. Ga., Augusta, 1976. Diplomate Am. Bd. Internal Medicine in cardiovascular diseases. Categorical medicine intern Naval Hosp. San Diego, 1976-77, resident internal medicine, 1977-79, fellow cardiovascular disease, 1979-81; staff cardiologist Naval Hosp. Long Beach, Calif., 1982-85; chief internal medicine Naval Hosp. Long Beach, 1985-87; chief cardiology Naval Hosp. Oakland, Calif., 1987-92; bd. dirs. Critical Air Medicine, Inc., San Diego, 1979—; CEO Spectrum Environ., Inc., Reno, Nev., 1995—; bd. dirs. San Diego Cardiovascular Network, 1995—, San Diego Cardiovascular Assocs., 1995—. Contbr. articles to profl. jours. Comdr. USN, 1972-92. Recipient Meritorious Svc. medal Pres. U.S., Oakland, 1992. Fellow Am. Coll. Cardiology; mem. Calif. Med. Assn., San Diego County Med. Soc. Republican. Presbyterian. Office: San Diego Cardiovascular Assocs Ste 100 351 Sante Fe Dr Encinitas CA 92024

HILL, DONAL DEAN, osteopathic physician; b. Fairfield, Iowa, Aug. 16, 1953; s. Gerald R. and Nada Lavelle (Hanna) H.; m. Mary Mieko Williams, Apr. 9, 1977; children: Heather Ellen, Holly Marie. BS cum laude, Iowa Wesleyan Coll., 1976; DO with honors, U. Osteo. Medicine and Health Scis., Des Moines, 1979. Cert. lay spkr. First United Meth. Ch. Intern, Des Moines Gen. Hosp., 1979-80; ptnr. Med. Arts Clinic, Fairfield, Iowa, 1980—; mem. staff U. Osteo. Medicine and Health Scis., Des Moines, 1981-82; vice chmn. staff Jefferson County Hosp., 1983, chief of med. staff, 1984; mem. Pub. Health Adv. Bd. Bd. dirs. Southeast Iowa Blood Bank, 1986-92, Mahaska Investment Co. Recipient Outstanding Freshman award Iowa Wesleyan Coll., 1977; Charles Reed award U. Osteo. Medicine and Health Scis., 1979, Gov. Health Task Force Iowa award, 1990. Mem. Iowa Maternal/Infant/Child Advising Bd., 1988-91. Mem. Iowa Osteo. Med. Assn. (exec. com. 1995—, trustee 1990-95), Am. Osteo. Assn., Osteo. Nat. Alumni Assn., Iowa Acad. Family Physicians, Jefferson County Med. Soc. (chmn. 1984), S.E. Iowa Osteo. Med. Soc. (pres. 1982-84), Iota Phi (hon.), Beta Beta Beta Soc. Republican, Golf & Country Club, Country (Fairfield). Home: 401 Heatherwood Cir Fairfield IA 52556-3888 Office: Medical Arts Clinic 408 S Maple Fairfield IA 52556

HILL, DOUGLASS ORVILLE, retired internist; b. Oaklette, Va., Oct. 4, 1922; s. Edgar Garlicke and Verlinda (Newcombe) H.; m. Roberta Wildman, June 21, 1952; children: Douglass Orville Jr., Geoffrey Lee, Mark Randolph. BS in Chemistry, Randolph-Macon Coll., 1944; MD, Med. Coll. of Va., 1947. Resident in internal medicine Norfolk (Va.) Gen. Hosp., 1947-49, VA Med. Ctr., Richmond, 1949-51; pvt. practice Winchester (Va.) Pulmonary and Internal Medicine, P.C., 1951-93. Mem. adv. bd. Salvation Army, ARC; chmn. bd. trustees Market St. United Meth. Ch. Col. Va. Army N.G., 1948-71. Melvin Jones fellow, 1994. Fellow Am. Coll. Angiology, Am. Geriatrics Soc.; mem. AMA (hosp. med. sect. 1988-92), ACP (life), Am. Coll. Chest Physicians, Va. Soc. Internal Medicine (past pres.), Lions (past pres., Bryan Stotler Eye Sight award, Melvin Jones fellow 1993, 94), Omicron Delta Kappa, Kappa Alpha Order. Democrat. United Methodist. Home: 143 Hawthorne Dr Winchester VA 22601-3318

HILL, ELLEN BROWN, emergency medicine and gerontology professional; b. Pitts., Dec. 21, 1944; d. F. Gordon and Muriel Edith (Dunkerley) Brown. Diploma in nursing, St. Francis Gen. Hosp., Pitts., 1969; AA magna cum laude, Butler County Community Coll., Butler, Pa., 1982; BSN, La Roche Coll., Pitts., 1986; postgrad., Slippery Rock (Pa.) U., 1987. Cert. sch. nurse, EMT, pre hosp. trauma technician. Trauma technician Richland Emergency Med. Svc., Gibsonia, Pa., 1983—; sch. nurse substitute Mars (Pa.) Area Sch. Dist.; gerontology staff nurse St. Barnabas Free Home, Gibsonia, Pa., 1970-76; head athletic trainer BCCC, 1981-84; head athletic trainer Mars (Pa.) Area Sch. Dist., 1984-86, sch. nurse substitute, 1984—; staff and emergency rehab. nurse Olsten Kimberly Quality Care, Greentree, 1986—; test adminstr. for nursing assts. in long-term care facilities Pa. state cert., 1990-92; profl. tractor-trailer driver for Storming Eagle Transport, Inc., Gibsonia, Pa., 1992—; instr. CPR and first aid. Disaster health svcs. specialist, shelter mgr. ARC, 1976—. Recipient Thanks for Helping award ARC, 1983. Mem. Emergency Nurses Assn., Pa. Assn. EMTs, St. Francis Gen. Hosp. Alumni Assn., Phi Theta Kappa. Home: 122 Butler Street Ext Valencia PA 16059-1606

HILL, FRED GENE, psychotherapist; b. Port Arthur, Tex., Dec. 17, 1933; s. Fred G. and Mary Edith (Culp) H.; m. Linda D. Brazzell, Aug. 13, 1983; children: Frederick, Sonya, Scott, Angela. Student, Tex. A&M U., 1952-53; BA, Baylor U., 1956; postgrad., Southwestern Theol. Sem., 1956-57; MSW, U. Tex., 1960. Lic. advanced clin. social work practitioner, Tex., marriage and family therapist, profl. counselor. Sr. psychiat. social worker Child Guidance Ctr., Amarillo, Tex., 1960-67; dir. Catholic Family Svc., Amarillo, 1966-69; pvt. practice Amarillo, 1967-74; 1980—; dir. Family Svc. Amarillo, 1974-80; Mem. Tex. State Bd. Examiners Social Psychotherapy, 1975-82 (sec. 1978-79, v. chmn. 1980-82). Clin. mem. Am. Assn. Marriage and Family Therapists (approved tng. supr.); mem. Am. Acad. Psychotherapists. Unitarian-Universalist. Home and Office: 5610 W 41st Ave Amarillo TX 79109-5214

HILL, GRAHAM LANCELOT, surgeon, educator; b. Dunedin, Otago, New Zealand, Oct. 24, 1939; s. Thomas Graham Campbell and Margaret Iris (Arthur) H.; m. Bartha Finna de Bres, Feb. 1, 1964; children: Andrew, Philip, Douglas. MBChB, Otago U., Dunedin, 1964, ChM, 1973; MD, U. Leeds, Eng., 1980. Intern Dunedin Hosp., 1964, resident surgery, 1965-68; med. missionary Nethersole Hosp., Hong Kong, 1969-70, Immanuel Hosp., Bandung, Indonesia, 1970-71; lectr. surgery Otago U., Dunedin, 1972, Leeds (U.K.) Gen. Inf., 1973; asst. prof. surgery U. Tex. Med. Sch., Houston, 1974-75; asst. dir. gen. infirmary dept. surgery U. Leeds, 1975-80; prof. surgery Auckland (New Zealand) Hosp.-U. Auckland, 1980—; dir. health rsch. coun. program Health Rsch. Coun. New Zealand, Auckland, 1985—. Author: Ileostomy, 1976, Disorders of Nutrition and Metabolism in Clinical Surgery, 1992; editor: Nutrition and the Surgical Patient, 1981, Nutrition and Metabolism in Patient Care, 1988, Tutorials for Junior Students of Surgery, 1990. Elder Presbyn. Ch. New Zealand, Auckland, 1981—. Surg. traveler James IV Assn. Surgeons, 1982; J. Mitchell Crouch fellow Royal Australasian Coll. Surgeons, 1984, Hunterian prof. Royal Coll. Surgeons Eng. Corr. fellow Assn. of Surgeons, Gt. Britain and Ireland, Surg. Rsch. Soc.; mem. Am. Soc. Parenteral and Enteral Nutrition (Jonathan Rhoads lectr. 1992), European Soc. Parenteral and Enteral Nutrition (Cuthbertson lectr. 1994), Assn. Acad. Surgeons, Soc. Internat. Chirurgie. Home: Mount Roskill, 121A Parau St, Auckland 3, New Zealand Office: U Auckland Dept Surgery, Auckland Hospital Park Rd, Auckland 1, New Zealand

HILL, HELEN LEHEW, psychologist, researcher; b. St. Louis, July 19, 1913; d. Lester Bryan and Josephine Naomi (Arntzen) LeH.; m. Donald M. Hill, July 1, 1964 (dec.); children: Pat Dally, Nancy, Marie Moulton, John J. BA, Harris Tchrs. Coll., 1936; MA, Washington U., St. Louis, 1939; postgrad., San Diego State Coll., 1944, L.A. State Coll., 1947-48. Tchr. St. Louis Pub. Schs., 1938-39, demonstration tchr., 1939-40, prin., 1940-41, sch. psychologist, 1941-42, dir. div. tests and measurements, 1942-43; sch. psychologist San Diego Pub. Sch., 1943-64, clinic psychologist, 1952-58; pvt. practice San Diego, 1969—. Rschr. on gifted children, also social and emotional devel. Republican. Home and Office: 627 Rosemont St La Jolla CA 92037-6147

HILL, HUGH FRANCIS, III, lawyer, physician; b. Roanoke, Va., Mar. 15, 1949; s. Hugh Francis Jr. and Beatrice (Wray) H.; m. Sandra I. Read, Aug. 31, 1974; children: Hugh F. IV, Andrea Read. BS, Washington and Lee U., 1971; MD, Med. Coll. Va., 1975; JD, U. Va., 1979. Bar: Va. 1980, D.C. 1981. Intern PG Y-1 Med. Ctr.; pvt. practice Washington, 1980—; pres. Legal Medicine Ctr., Bethesda, Md., 1992—; med. dir. Montgomery Hospice, 1996—. Author: Pennsylvania Medical Malpractice, 1988; editor Emergency Dept. Law, 1989-91; contbr. chpts. to books. Recipient President's award Am. Coll. Legal Medicine, 1988. Fellow Am. Coll. Emergency Physicians, Am. Bd. Legal Medicine, Am. Bd. Emergency Medicine (examiner), Nat. Health Lawyers Assn. Democrat. Office: 6915 Radnor Rd Bethesda MD 20817-6328 also: Legal Medicine Ctr 5603 Roosevelt St Bethesda MD 20817-6739

HILL, JEFFREY HOWARD, physician; b. Columbus, Ohio, Feb. 10, 1949; s. Howard Russell and Carolyn Jo Anne (Tilley) H.; m. Betsy Plotle, June 18, 1972; children: Daniel Eben, Heather Rebecca. BS in Biochemistry, Ohio State U., 1971; MD, U. Chgo., 1978, PhD in Pathology, 1978.

Diplomate Am. Bd. Internal Medicine, Am. Bd. Pediat., Am. Bd. Pediatric Critical Care Medicine. Rsch. assoc. U. Conn., Hartford, 1971-72; intern/resident U. Colo., Denver, 1978-81; fellow in allergy and immunology Nat. Jewish Hosp., Denver, 1981-83; fellow pediat. crit. care Denver Children's Hosp., 1983-84; asst. prof. pediatrics Rainbow Babies and Children's Hosp., Cleve., 1984-88; dir. pediat. crit. care St. Joseph's Hosp. and Med. Ctr., Phoenix, 1988—; chmn. pharmacy and therapeutics St. Joseph's Hosp. and Med. Ctr., Phoenix, 1993—; v.p., bd. dirs. Ariz. Pediatric Sub-Specialists, IPA, Phoenix, 1995—; pres. Pediatric Critical Care of Ariz., Ltd., 1990—. Bd. dirs., v.p. Drowning Prevention Coalition of Cen. Ariz., Phoenix, 1992—; founding mem. and incorporating officer, Firearm Safety Coalition of Ariz., Phoenix, 1994—. Fellow Am. Assn. Immunology; mem. Am. Coll. Physician Execs., Soc. Critical Care Medicine. Office: Pediatric Crit Care Ariz Ste 890 2828 N Central Ave Phoenix AZ 85004

HILL, JIM TOM, association executive; b. Cushing, Okla., Apr. 27, 1939; s. Wilburn C. and Susie (Ruckman) H.; m. Linda J. Archer, Aug. 30, 1963; children—Sheri, David, Susan. B.S. in Chemistry, Abilene Christian U., 1961; M.S. in Biochemistry, U. Tenn., 1964, Ph.D., 1968. Sr. research scientist E.R. Squibb & Sons, New Brunswick, N.J., 1968-69, Lakeside Labs., Milw., 1969-75; sr. research specialist Monsanto, St. Louis, 1975-78; dir. chemistry Hazelton Labs. Am., Vienna, Va., 1978-80; mgr. toxicology Phelps Dodge, Washington, 1980-81; dir. sci. affairs Chem. Specialties Mfrs. Assn., Washington, 1981-86, dir. product ingredient rev. program, 1987—. Contbr. articles to profl. jours. Mem. Am. Coll. Toxicology, Am. Soc. Pharmacology and Exptl. Therapeutics, Environ. Mutagen Soc., Am. Chem. Soc., Soc. Toxicology, Sigma Xi. Home: 2477 Freetown Dr Reston VA 22091-2527 Office: 1913 I St NW Washington DC 20006-2106

HILL, JOE M., public health service officer. BS, Ark. Bapt. Coll., 1974; grad. basic police training, Ark. Law Enforcement, 1970; postgrad., Ouachita Bapt. Univ., 1974. Field investigator Ark. Alcohol Beverage Control Bd., 1970-71; transport truck loader Colonial Baking Co., 1971-74; exec. dir. G.W. Carver YMCA, 1975-87, Cmty. Orgn. Poverty Elimination Pulaski & Lonoke Countries, 1987-91; dir. Bureau of Alcohol and Drug Abuse Prevention, 1991—; sr. dir. status Mid-Am. Region YMCA, 1982, exec. dir.'s training Cmty. Action Agencies, Kirkwood, Mo., 1989. V.p. drug abuse issues Nat. Assn. State Alcohol & Drug Abuse Dirs.; state dir.; bd. dirs. United Way of Pulaski County; exec. com. Little Rock Fighting Back Program; coord. com. Ark. Alcohol & Drug Abuse; commn. Ark. Minority Health; bd. dirs. New Futures for Little Rock Youth, Little Rock Futures Commn., Little Rock Civil Svc. Commn.; co-chmn. Little Rock 2000 Election Com.; pres. Ark. Cmty. Action Agencies Assn., 1990-92; bd. dirs. Interest on Lawyers Trust Acct.; trustee, bd. dirs. Pilgrim Valley Bapt. Ch. Sunday Sch. Tch. of Sr. Adult class; adv. bd. Ark. Children's Hosp. Early Childhood Initiative. With U.S. Army, 1967-69, Vietnam. Recipient Equal Opportunity award Dept. Army and Air Force Nat. Guard, 1990, Employer of Yr. award Ark. Lighthouse for the Blind, 1990, Cmty. Svc. award Miles Chapel C.M.E. Chr., 1985, Cert. of Appreciation award Hands Across Am. Steering Com., 1986, United Way Gold award, 1984, Martin Luther King Jr. award Hoover United Meth. Ch., 1983. Home: 1821 Fair Park Blvd Little Rock AR 72204*

HILL, JOHN, geneticist, educator; b. Birmingham, Eng., Aug. 2, 1937; s. Alexander James and Doris Ethel (Burman) H.; m. Ann Mary Isaac, June 7, 1969; children: Anna Louise, Stephen Andrew, Rebecca Maree. BS with honors, U. Nottingham, Eng., 1959; PhD, U. Birmingham, 1962. Rsch. worker biometrical genetics unit Agrl. Rsch. Coun., Birmingham, 1962-66; sci. officer Welsh Plant Breeding Sta., Aberystwyth, Wales, 1966, sr. sci. officer, 1966-73, prin. sci. officer, 1973-87; vis. lectr. Royal Vet. and Agrl. U., Copenhagen, Denmark, 1991—; mem. editorial bd. Jour. Euphytica. Contbr. articles to profl. publs. Recipient medal Acad. Scis. Russia, 1991. Mem. AAAS, Brit. Genetical Soc. (mem. plant and animal breeding com. 1975-78), European Assn. Rsch. Plant Breeding (chmn. biometrics sect. 1984—).

HILL, JOHN HEMMINGSON, virologist, plant pathologist; b. Evanston, Ill., Feb. 19, 1941; S. Robert Kermit and Adelaide (Nyden) H.; m. Laani May Fong, Aug. 5, 1967; children: Brent, Bryce, Bjork. BA, Carleton Coll., 1963; MS, U. Minn., St. Paul, 1966; PhD, U. Calif., Davis, 1971. Asst. prof. Iowa State U., Ames, 1972-78, assoc. prof., 1978-82, prof., 1982—. Asst. scoutmaster Boy Scouts Am., Ames, 1982-95; session mem. Collegiate Presbyn. Ch., Ames, 1987-90. Fellow Am. Phytopathological Soc.; mem. Am. Soc. Virology (Am. type culture collection exec. com. 1986—), N.Y. Acad. Scis., Am. Type Culture Collection (bd. dirs. 1992—), Sigma Xi, Gamma Sigma Delta. Home: 2800 Duff Ave Ames IA 50010-4710 Office: Iowa State U Dept Plant Pathology 403 Bessey Hall Ames IA 50011

HILL, JOHN V., orthopedic surgeon; b. Cedar Falls, Iowa, July 23, 1939; s. Caroyl Vance and Kathryn Camilla (Johnsen) H.; m. Barbara Sue Foley, Apr. 15, 1969; children: Kristin Ann, Scott James. BA, State U. Iowa, 1961, MD, 1964. Diplomate Am. Bd. Orthopedic Surgery. Intern L.A. County Hosp., 1964-65; med. officer U.S. Navy, 1965-67; orthopedic resident L.A. County/U. So. Calif. Med. Ctr., 1967-71; pvt. practice orthopedic surgery Ventura, Calif., 1971—. Fellow Am. Acad. Orthopedic Surgeons (bd. councilors 1995—); mem. Ventura County Med. Soc. (pres. 1996), Alpha Omega Alpha. Office: Ventura Orthopedic Med Grp 3525 Loma Vista Rd Ventura CA 93003

HILL, LAWRENCE KING, urologist; b. Greenville, S.C., June 21, 1954; s. Lawrence King and Margaret Oliphant (Donald) H. BS in Chemistry, Hampden Sydney Coll., 1977; MD, U. S.C., 1981. Diplomate Am. Bd. Urology. Resident in surgery U. Hosp., Jacksonville, Fla., 1981-83; resident in urology George Washington U., Washington, 1983-86; fellow in urology Baylor Coll. Medicine, Houston, 1986-87; pvt. practice urology Greenville, S.C., 1987—; med. staff dept. urology Greenville Meml. Hosp. and St. Francis Hosp., Greenville, 1987—, chmn. urology dept., 1996—. Fellow ACS; mem. Am. Urologic Assn., Southeastern Soc. Am. Urologic Assn., S.C. Med. Assn., Greenville County Med. Soc., Am. Fertility Soc., Phi Beta Kappa. Episcopalian. Home: 211 Michaux Dr Greenville SC 29605 Office: Upstate Urology Ste 6 8 Mem Med Ct Greenville SC 29605

HILL, LISA MARIE, psychotherapist; b. Phoenix, Sept. 24, 1956; d. Donn E. and Freda (Scardino) H.; div. 1986; children: Nicholas, Michael. BA in Theology cum laude, U. Steubenville, Ohio, 1978; postgrad., Duquesne U., 1981; neuro-linguistic programming student, Genesee Hosp., 1987-88. Founder, dir. The LightHeart Inst., Rochester, N.Y., 1987—; pub. speaker in field. Office: The LightHeart Inst 500 Helendale Rd # 130 Rochester NY 14609-3109

HILL, MURRAY WILLIAM, dentist educator; b. Perth, Australia, Jan. 28, 1945; s. Arthur William and Lillian Edith (Thornbury) H.; children: Andrew William, Catherine Jean. BDSc, U. Western Australia, Perth, 1968; MSc, U. London, 1972, PhD, 1977. Cert. Dental Bd. Western Australia. Sr. demonstrator Dental Sch. U. Western Australia, Nedlands, 1968-70; rsch. fellow London Hosp. Med. Coll., 1972-75, lectr., 1975-77; asst. prof. dept. oral pathology U. Iowa, Iowa City, 1977-79, assoc. prof. Dows Inst. for Dental Rsch., 1979-85, prof., 1985-88; prof. Dental Sch. U. Western Australia, Nedlands, 1988-94, dean of dentistry, 1988-91, head of Dental Sch., 1988-90, chmn. acad. bd., 1991-92, prof. emeritus, 1995—; sr. dental officer edn. Health Dept. We. Australia, Como, 1995—; sci. reviewer NH and MRC, Australia, 1990-94, Med. Rsch. Coun., Can., 1984, Archives of Oral Bioloy, Jour. Dental Rsch., Australian Dental Jour., Jour. Oral Pathology, 1978—; mem. Dental Bd. We. Australia, 1990-93. Editor Archives of Oral Bioloy, 1986-88; editor, contbr. (book) The Effect of Aging in Oral Mucosa and Skin; author 12 book chpts.; contbr. over 40 articles to profl. jours. Recipient Brit. Coun. Acad. Links Interchange Scheme award, 1989, Merit award Am. Soc. of Dentistry for Children, 1967, Australian Soc. Periodontology prize; NIH, Nat. Health and Med. Rsch. Coun. (Australia), 1981-91; Wellcome Rsch. fellow, 1975-77. Mem. Australian Dental Assn. (councillor 1988-91), Internat. Assn. for Dental Rsch. (pres. Iowa chpt. 1982-83, pres. Perth chpt. 1990-91), Internat. Assn. Oral Pathology, Am. Assn. Dental Schs., Am. Acad. for Oral and Maxillo-Facial Pathology, Royal Soc. Medicine, Sigma Xi, Omicron Kappa Upsilon. Office: Health Dept, Dental Svcs, Como WA 6152, Australia

HILL, RICHARD M., academic administrator. Dean Coll. Optometry Ohio State U., Columbus, 1988—. Office: Ohio State U Coll of Optometry Columbus OH 43210

HILL, RONALD CHARLES, surgeon, educator; b. Parkersburg, W.Va., Sept. 4, 1948; s. Lloyd E. and Margaret (Pepper) H.; m. Lenora Jane Rexrode, June 12, 1971; children: Jeffrey, Mandy. BA, W.Va. U., 1970, MD, 1974. Lic. physician W. Va., N.C.; diplomate Am. Bd. Surgery (recert.), Am. Bd. Thoracic Surgery. Intern dept. of surgery Duke U. Med. Ctr., Durham, N.C., 1974-75; resident in surgery Duke U., Durham, N.C., 1974-85, rsch. assoc., 1976-79, tchg. scholar, 1984-85; asst. prof. surgery W.Va. U., Morgantown, 1985-90, assoc. prof., 1990-96, prof. surgery, 1996—; cons. VA Med. Ctr., Clarksburg, W.Va., 1985—; dir. surg. rsch. dept. surgery W.Va. U., 1986-88, student coord. dept. surgery, 1986—; mem. ad hoc com. Merit Rev. Bd. for Cardiovasc. Studies, VA, Washington, 1988-90. Contbr., co-contbr. numerous book chpts. and articles to profl. publs. Mem.-at-large adminstrv. bd. Drummond Chapel Unified Meth. Ch., Morgantown, 1987-89, 93-95. Recipient Lange Med. Book award, 1971, 73, 74, Merck Med. Book award, 1974, Roche Med. award, 1972, Sowers award Duke U., 1992. Fellow ACS, Southeastern Surg. Congress, Assn. Acad. Surgery, Sabiston Soc., Am. Coll. Cardiology, Am. Coll. Chest Physicians, Am. Coll. Angiology, So. Thoracic Surg. Assn., Soc. Thoracic Surgeons; mem. Am. Heart Assn., (v.p., pres. elect, pres. W. Va. affiliate 1994-96), Soc. Univ. Surgeons, Am. Assn. Thoracic Surgery, Internat. Surg. Soc., So. Surg. Assn., W. Va. Med. Assn., Mended Hearts, Lakeview Country Club, Pines Country Club, Phi Beta Kappa, Alpha Omega Alpha, Alpha Epsilon Delta. Republican. Home: 10 Flegal St Morgantown WV 26505-2240 Office: WVa U Med Ctr Dept of Surgery Medical Center Dr Morgantown WV 26506

HILL, SAMUEL RICHARDSON, JR., medical educator; b. Greensboro, N.C., May 19, 1923; s. Samuel Richardson and Nona (Sink) H.; m. Janet Redman, Oct. 28, 1950; children: Susan Hill Lindley, Samuel Richardson III, Elizabeth Hill Humphreys, Margaret Hill Cohn. BA, Duke U., 1943; MD, Bowman Gray Sch. Medicine, 1946; DSc (hon.), U. Ala., 1975, Wake Forest U., 1979. Intern medicine Peter Bent Brigham Hosp., Boston, 1947-48; asst. resident medicine Peter Bent Brigham Hosp., 1948-49, asst. medicine, 1949-50; teaching fellow medicine Harvard Sch. Medicine, 1948-49, research fellow medicine, Dazian Med. Found. research fellow, 1949-50; chief resident medicine N.C. Bapt. Hosp., instr. medicine Bowman Gray Sch. Medicine, 1950-51; asst. medicine Harvard Sch. Medicine, also Peter Bent Brigham Hosp., 1953-54; asst. prof. medicine, dir. metabolic and endocrine div. Med. Coll. Ala., also chief metabolic div. VA Hosp., Birmingham, 1954-57; assoc. prof. medicine, dir. metabolic and endocrine div. U. Ala. Med. Ctr. and VA Hosp., Birmingham, 1957-62; prof. medicine, dean U. Ala. Sch. Medicine, Birmingham, 1962-68; prof. medicine U. Ala. Med. Coll., Birmingham, 1968-94; v.p. for health affairs, dir. Med. Ctr., 1968-77; pres. U. Ala., Birmingham, 1977-87, Disting. prof., 1987-93, Disting. prof. emeritus and cons., 1994—; dir. med. edn. program U. Ala. System, 1972-79; bd. dirs. Birmingham br. Fed. Res. Bank Atlanta, 1981-83, chmn. Birmingham br., 1983. Contbr. articles to med. jours. Bd. regents Nat. Library Medicine, 1978-80, chmn. bd. regents, 1979-80. Served to maj. M.C., USAF, 1951-53. Fellow ACP (Willard O. Thompson Meml. traveling scholar 1960), AAAS, Royal Soc. Medicine; mem. Soc. Exptl. Biology and Medicine, Am. Fedn. Clin. Research (pres. 1961-62), Endocrine Soc., Am., Ala. diabetes socs., Mass., Jefferson County med. socs., Am. Thyroid Soc., AMA, Inst. Medicine of Nat. Acad. Scis., So. Soc. Clin. Investigation, Med. Assn. State Ala. (councillor), Assn. Am. Med. Colls., Assn. for Acad. Health Centers (pres. 1972), Sigma Xi, Alpha Omega Alpha. Episcopalian. Home: 3337 E Briarcliff Rd Birmingham AL 35223-1306 Office: U Ala Birmingham Dept Ed Birmingham AL 35294-2010

HILL, STEPHEN A., physician, adminstrator; b. Colorado Springs, Colo., 1950; s. Ross H. and Betty M. (Shafer) H.; m. Cynthia A. Sweeney, May 22, 1982; children: Meghan, Donovan, Caelin, Evan. AB, Dartmouth Coll., 1972; MD, Southwestern Med. Sch., 1976. Diplomate Am. Bd. Psychiatry and Neurology, Am. Bd. Electrodiagnostic Medicine. Intern U. Minn., Mpls., 1976-77; resident in neurosurgery Ohio State U., Columbus, 1977-81, fellow in biochem. neuropathology, 1979-80, mem. neurosurgery faculty, 1981-83; pvt. practice Columbus, 1983-85; resident in neurology Med. Coll. Ga., Augusta, 1985-88; pvt. practice Mansfield (Ohio) Neurology, 1988—; med. dir. inpatient rehab. Mansfield (Ohio) Gen. Hosp., 1991—. Contbr. articles to profl. jours. Dep. coroner Richland County, Ohio, 1994—. Traveling fellow Internat. Coll. Surgeons, 1981—. Fellow Am. Assn. Electrodiagnostic Medicine; mem. Am. Assn. for Neurology, Ohio State Med. Assn., Am. Soc. for Neurorehab., Am. Assn. Physicians and Surgeons, Japanese Aikido Assn., Am. Shorin-Ryu Karate Assn. Office: Mansfield Neurology 222 Marion Ave Mansfield OH 44903

HILL, VALERIE CHARLOTTE, nurse; b. Shaftsbury, Vt., Dec. 2, 1932; d. William Henry Harrison and Angeline Margaret Stella (Fuller) Hill; m. Edward Joseph Klanit (dec. July 1984); 1 child, Joyce Ellen Klanit Artadi. Grad., The Mount Sinai Hosp. Sch. of Nursing, 1955. RN, N.Y. Staff nurse The Jack Martin Respiratory Ctr. of The Mt. Sinai Hosp., N.Y.C., 1955-57; v.p. Chauffeurs Unlimited, Inc., N.Y.C., 1957-77; staff nurse Rusk Inst., N.Y.C., 1957-58, Beth Israel Med. Ctr., N.Y.C., 1978-79; owner, mgr. Powers Fish Market, Inc., N.Y.C., 1977-84; tchr. Techs. for Creating, Albany, N.Y., 1983—; staff nurse Doctors Hosp., N.Y.C., 1984-86; pvt. duty nurse Personal Health Care Services, Albany, N.Y., 1987-88; nurse Albany Med. Ctr. Hosp., 1987-95; real estate sales assoc. Century 21-Stanley Major Ltd., West Sand Lake, N.Y., 1988, Century-21 Home Towne Properties, Albany, 1989-92. Author numerous poems. Recipient Outstanding Service to Community award Mayor Koch City of N.Y., 1983. Mem. Alumnae Assn. Mt. Sinai Hosp. Sch. Nursing (bd. dirs. 1968). Democrat. Home: 70 2nd St Albany NY 12210-2517

HILL, WALTER LEONARD, JR., mental health services administrator, educator, social worker; b. Balt., June 15, 1946; s. Walter Leonard and Eleanor (Myers) H.; m. Susan G. Hill, Aug. 24, 1968; 2 children. BA, Western Md. Coll., 1968; MDiv, Yale U., 1972; MSW, Smith Coll., 1975. Lic. social worker, Conn. Staff social worker Yale Psychiat. Inst., New Haven, 1975-77, supervising social worker, 1977-78, admissions officer, 1978-82, asst. dir. social work, 1980-85, dir. social work, 1985—, coord. family therapy program, 1983—, dir. community svcs., 1986-92, dir. tng., 1992—; bd. dirs. Parents Found. for Transitional Living, Inc., New Haven. Fellow Am. Orthopsychiat. Assn.; mem. NASW, Conn. Soc. Clin. Social Work. Office: Yale Psychiat Inst PO Box 208038 Haven CT 06520-8038

HILL, WILLIAM DAVID, health facility administrator; b. Richmond, Ind., July 15, 1950; s. Harold Dillard and Marjorie Ellen (McCain) H.; m. Iris Lynn Clark, Oct. 5, 1975; children: Jacob Alan, Jo Ellen. BS in Edn., Ind. U., 1973; MA in Health Sci., Ball State U., 1986. Cert. in quality healthcare. Therapist Richmond State Hosp., 1973-77, program coord. acute intensive treatment, 1977-79, asst. dir. acute intensive treatment, 1979-81, AIT dir., 1981-86, coord. quality assurance, 1986-91; dir. quality rev. Perry Meml. Hosp., Princeton, Ill., 1991—; bd. dirs. In Home Care Vis. Nurse Assn., Princeton, Ill., chair, 1995—. Mem. Nat. Assn. Healthcare Quality. Office: Perry Meml Hosp 530 Park Ave E Princeton IL 61356

HILL, WILLIAM JACKSON, health organization consultant; b. Nashville, Sept. 6, 1956; s. William Jackson and Julia Pearl (Devenport) H.; m. Teresa Jo Beyers, Apr. 17, 1982; 1 child, William Alexander. BA, Taylor U., 1979; MBA, Ball State U., 1984; postgrad., Wharton Sch., 1989—. Multi-line ins. Sentry Ins., Stevens Point, Wis., 1980-84; third party adminstr. Key Benefit Adminstrs., Indpls., 1984-89; staff Healthplus of Mich., Flint, 1989-92; med. stop loss staff Washington Nat., Evanston, Ill., 1992-94; cons. Health Resource Orgn., Wheaton, Ill., 1994—. Author: Electronic Data Interchange: The Physicians' Guide, 1995. Mem. Chgo. Health Execs. Forum (task force 1993—), Integrated Healthcare Delivery Sys., Inc., Self-Funding Acad. Republican. Office: Omega Healthcare Corp 219 South Erie Wheaton IL 60187

HILLBERRY, SHEILA MARIE STUEHRENBERG, microbiologist; b. Breckenridge, Minn., Apr. 19, 1945; d. Henry Ernest Fredrick and Marian Violet (Sandberg) Stuehrenberg; B.S., Moorhead State U., 1966; M.S., Purdue U., 1970; m. Joseph Hillberry, June 25, 1967; children—Russell Henry, Joseph Martin. Tchr. jr. high. sci. Wausau (Wis.) Public Schs., 1966-67; tchr. sci. Robert G. Cole High Sch., San Antonio, 1967-68; substitute tchr. Rapid City (S.D.) Schs., 1970-71; supr. clin. microbiology sect. Rapid City Regional Hosp., 1971—; adj. prof. S.D. Sch. Mines and Tech., 1979-80. Organist, dir. choir, chmn. bd. edn. Lutheran Ch. Mem. Am. Soc. Clin. Pathology, Am. Soc. Microbiology, Black Hills Soc. Med. Technology. Home: 1309 38th St Rapid City SD 57702-3101 Office: 353 Fairmont Blvd Rapid City SD 57701-7375

HILLEBRAND, PATRICIA, health services administrator; b. Kittanning, Pa., Apr. 19, 1941; d. Martin L. Wilson and Arabelle P. (Beck) Wilson Reed; m. Rudolph Peter HIllebrand, June 21, 1963; children: Michael, Dennis, Steven. Diploma in nursing, Temple U., 1962; BS in Profl. Arts, St. Joseph's Coll., 1978; MEd in Counseling Edn., Pa. State U., 1980. RN, Pa.; cert. mental health adminstr., counselor Nat. Bd. Cert. Counselors. Contbr. articles to profl. publs., chpt. to books. Fellow Am. Coll. Healthcare Execs.; mem. Assn. Mental Health Adminstrs., Am. Coll. Hearlthcare Execs., Ind. County Mental Health Assn., Ind. Hosp. Nursing Alumni, Southwestern Pa. Orgn. Nurse Execs. (exec. com.), Zonta, Delta Mu Sigma, Phi Kappa Phi, Sigma Theta Tau. Office: Ind Hosp Hospital Rd PO Box 788 Indiana PA 15701

HILLEMAN, MAURICE RALPH, virus research scientist; b. Miles City, Mont., Aug. 30, 1919; s. Robert A. and Edith (Matson) H.; m. Lorraine Witmer, Aug. 3, 1963; children—Jeryl Lynn, Kirsten Jeanne. BS, Mont. State U., 1941, DSc (hon.), 1966; DSc (hon.), U. Md., 1968, Washington and Jefferson Coll., 1992; D hon. causa (hon.), U. Leuven, 1984; PhD, U. Chgo., 1944. Asst. bacteriologist U. Chgo., 1942-44; research asso. virus labs. E.R. Squibb & Sons, 1944-47, chief virus dept., 1947-48; chief research and diagnostic sects. virus and rickettsial diseases Army Med. Service Grad. Sch., Walter Reed Army Med. Center, 1948-56, asst. chief lab. affairs, 1953-56; chief respiratory diseases Walter Reed Army Inst. Research, Washington, 1956-57; dir. virus and cell biol. research Merck Inst. Therapeutic Research, Merck & Co. Inc., 1957-66, exec. dir., 1966-71, v.p., 1971-78, sr. v.p., 1978-84; dir. Merck Inst., 1984—; dir. virus and cell biology research v.p. Merck, Sharp & Dohme Research Labs., 1970-78, sr. v.p., 1978-84; vis. investigator Hosp. of Rockefeller Inst. for Med. Rsch., 1951; vis. prof. bacteriology U. Md., 1953-57; adj. prof. virology pediatrics Sch. Medicine U. Pa., 1968—; cons. Children's Hosp. of Phila., 1968—; mem. coun. divsn. biol. scis. Pritzker Sch. Medicine, 1977-95; John Herr Musser lectr. Musser-Burch Soc., Tulane U. Sch. Medicine, 1969, 19th Graugnard lectr., 1978; mem., spl. cons. panel respiratory and related viruses USPHS, 1960-64; mem. Nat. Cancer Inst. primate study group, 1964-70; mem. coun. analysis and projection Am. Cancer Soc., 1971-76; mem. expert adv. panel on virus diseases WHO, 1952—; bd. dirs. W. Alton Jones Cell Sci. Ctr., Lake Placid, N.Y., 1980-82, Am. Liver Found. (hon.), 1986—, Am. Type Culture Collect, 1992-95, Nat. Found. Infectious Diseases, 1987—, Nat. Cancer Inst. Bd. Sci. Counselors, 1990-95, Bd. Sci. Counselors Paul Erlich Found. (Frankfurt, Germany), 1993—; bd. dirs. Jos. J. Stokes Rsch. Inst. U. Pa.; mem. overseas med. rsch. labs. com. Dept. Def., 1980; mem. virology dept. rev. com. Am. Type Culture Collection, 1980; mem. Ad Hoc Vaccine Subcom. AIDS Program NIH, 1991, AIDS Rsch. and Devel. Vaccine Working Group, 1992—, panel 1995—, Panel Internat. Task Force NIH Strategic Plan, 1992; mem. vaccine design and evaln. group, NIAID, NIH, 1995—; bd. trustees Internat. Vaccine Inst., Korea. Editorial bd.: Internat. Jour. Cancer, 1964-71, Inst. Sci. Information, 1968-70, Am. Jour. Epidemiology, 1969-75, Infection and Immunity, 1970-76, Excerpta Medica, 1971—, Proc. Soc. Exptl. Biology and Medicine, 1976—, Jour. Antiviral Research, 1980—, Vaccine, 1983, Virus Genes, 1986, Vaccine Research, 1990; contbr. 460 articles to sci., profl., med. jours. Phi Kappa Phi fellow, 1941-42, Koessler fellow, 1943-44; Recipient Howard Taylor Ricketts prize, 1945, 83, Distinguished Civilian Service award Sec. Def., 1957, Walter Reed Army Med. Incentive award, 1960, Dean M. McCann award, 1970, Procter award, 1971, Lasker Med. Rsch. award, 1983; Achievement award Indsl. Research Inst., 1975, Joseph E. Smadel award, 1984, Alumni medal, U. Chgo., 1987, Albert B. Sabin medal, 1988, Nat. medal Sci., U.S., 1988, San Marino award, 1989, Robert Koch Gold medal, 1989. Fellow Am. Acad. Microbiology; mem. Am. Acad. Arts and Scis., Nat. Acad. Sci., Inst. of Medicine of Nat. Acad. Sci., Am. Soc. Microbiology, Soc. Exptl. Biology and Medicine (mem. editl. and publs. com. 1977—), Tissue Culture Assn. (mem. coun. 1977—), Am. Assn. Immunologists, Am. Assn. Cancer Rsch., Infectious Diseases Soc., Permanent sect. Microbiol. Standardization Internat. Assn. Microbiol. Socs., Internat. Vaccine Inst. (UN bd. trustees 1995—), Russian Acad. Biotechnology (hon. fgn. mem.), L'Acadèie Nationale de Pharmacie (fgn. corr.). Office: Merck Rsch Labs WP53C 350 West Point PA 19486

HILLER, MICHAEL SCOTT, anesthesiologist; s. Stan and Carolyn Hiller. BA in Biology, U. Tex., 1984; MD, U. Tex.-Southwestern Med. Sch., Dallas, 1988. Diplomate Am. Bd. Anesthesiology. Intern U. Ala., Birmingham, 1984-85; resident in anesthesiology U. Ala. Hosps., Birmingham, 1988-92; staff anesthesiologist Irving (Tex.) Healthcare Sys., 1992—, Columbia Surgery Ctr., Las Colinas, Tex., 1993—; ptnr. Providers Capital Cons., Dallas, 1993—; cons. EEAC Fin. Svcs. Co., White Plains, N.Y , 1996; dir. DFW Anesthesia Assocs., P.A., Dallas, 1995—; pres. Las Colinas Pain Treatment Ctr., P.A., Irving, 1992—; co-founder Synergen Healthcare Strategies, LLC, 1996—; pres. house staff U. Ala. Hosps., 1990-92. Mem. AMA (parliamentarian resident physicians sect. 1992), Am. Soc. Anesthesiology, Tex. Med. Assn., Dallas County Med. Soc., Dallas County Anesthesia Soc., Tex. Soc. Anesthesiologists, U. Ala.-Birmingham Alumni Assn. (bd. dirs. 1990-92), U. Tex. Southwestern Alumni Assn. (bd. trustees 1992—). Republican. Home: 1533 Bonham Ct Irving TX 75038 Office: DFW Anesthesia Assocs 4431 Gloster Rd Dallas TX 75220-6411

HILLERT, GLORIA BONNIN, anatomist, educator; b. Brownton, Minn., Jan. 25, 1930; d. Edward Henry and Lydia Magdalene (Luebker) Bonnin; m. Richard Hillert, Aug. 20, 1960; children: Kathryn, Virginia, Jonathan. BS, Valparaiso (Ind.) U., 1953; MA, U. Mich., 1958. Instr. Springfield (Ill.) Jr. Coll., 1953-57; teaching asst. U. Mich., Ann Arbor, 1957-58; instr., dept. head St. John's Coll., Winfield, Kans., 1958-59; asst. prof. Concordia Coll., River Forest, Ill., 1959-63; vis. instr. Wright Jr. Coll., Chgo., 1974-76, Ill. Benedictine Coll., Lisle, 1977-78, Rosary Coll., River Forest, 1976-81; prof. anatomy and physiology Triton Coll., River Grove, 1982-92, prof. emeritus, 1992—; vis. asst. prof. Concordia U., 1993—; vis. instr. Wheaton (Ill.) Coll., 1988; advisor Springfield Jr. Coll. Sci. Club, 1953-57, Concordia Coll. Cultural Group, 1959-62; program dir. Triton Coll. Sci. Lectr. Series, 1983-87; participant Internat. Educators Workshop in Amazonia, 1993. Dem. campaign asst., Maywood, Ill., 1972, 88; vol. Mental Health Orgn., Chgo., 1969-73, Earthwatch, St. Croix, 1987, Costa Rica, 1989, Internat. Med. Care Team, Guatemala, 1995. Mem. AAUW, Ill. Assn. Community Coll. Biol. Tchrs., Nat. Assn. Biol. Tchrs. Lutheran. Home: 1620 Clay Ct Melrose Park IL 60160-2419 Office: Triton Coll 2000 N 5th Ave River Grove IL 60171-1907

HILLESTAD, DONNA DAWN, nurse; b. Merrill, Wis., May 13, 1938; d. Martin T. and Edna (Frederick) Dietrich; m. John Curtis Hillestad, July 18, 1959; children: Dori Jean, David Jeffrey. BSN, Mankato U., 1962. RN, Minn. Office nurse Fairmont (Minn.) Clinic, 1963-65, pvt. duty, pub. health nurse, 1965-67; charge nurse, supr. Lakeview Meth. Health Care Ctr., Fairmont, 1967—; nurse ins. phys. for numerous ins. cos., 1980—. Active Fairmont Community Concert Assn.; host fgn. exch. students, 1989, 90, 91, 92. Mem. AAUW (pub. rels. com. 1986-87, historian 1982-84, bull. editor 1985-86, chmn. hospitality 1987-88, mem. cultural interests com. 1980-81, Internat. Rels. award 1991), Bus. and Profl. Women (chmn. internat. rels. 1986, emblem chmn. 1982-83, pub. rels. com. 1984-85, found. com. .1990, historian 1976, nominating sunshine com. 1989-90, auditing com. 1986-87, sec. 1985-86, 88-89), Holiday Travel Club (founder), Friendship Force (So. Minn. chpt. sec. 1995—), Tourist Club, Cmty. Club, Garden Club. Lutheran. Home: 803 S Hampton St Fairmont MN 56031-4308

HILLIARD, KIRK LOVELAND, JR., osteopathic physician, educator; b. Phila., Mar. 9, 1941; s. Kirk Loveland and Lillian Adele (Hinkle) H.; m. Janet Louise Moyer, Aug. 29, 1970; children: Michael Spence, Stephen Matthew, Allison Day. AB, Haverford Coll., 1963; DO, Phila. Coll. Osteo. Medicine, 1967. Diplomate Am. Coll. Osteo. Internists, Internal Medicine and Med. Diseases of Chest. Intern Doctors' Hosp., Columbus, Ohio, 1967-68, resident, 1970-72, sr. attending, 1977—, dir. respiratory svcs., 1978—; fellow Hahnemann Hosp., Phila., 1972-74; pvt. practice Columbus, 1974-95, part time practice pulmonary medicine, 1996—; asst. prof. Ohio U., Athens, 1979-88, assoc. prof., 1988—; med. dir. CP Home care, Columbus, 1986—; acting dir. Med. Edn. Doctors Hosp., Columbus, Ohio, 1991-92; bd. trustees Doctors Hosp., 1995, program dir. internal medicine, 1994-95; v.p. med. edn. Doctors Hosp., 1995—. Capt. M.C., U.S. Army, 1968-70, Vietnam. Fellow Am. Coll. Osteo. Internists; mem. Am. Osteo. Assn., Assn. Osteo. Dirs. Med. Edn., Am. Lung Assn., Am. Legion, Masons, Shriners. Office: Doctors Hosp 1087 Dennison Ave Columbus OH 43201

HILLIS, FREDRICK ALLEN, surgeon; b. Logansport, Ind., Apr. 10, 1945; s. Lowell Joseph and Helen (Kunkel) H.; m. Margey Michelle Morris, July 29, 1967; children: Erin, Lisa. AB, Ind. U., 1967; MD, Ind. U., Indpls., 1970. Diplomate Am. Bd. Surgery. Intern Ind. U. Hosps., Indpls., 1970-71; resident in surgery Miami Valley Hosp., Dayton, Ohio, 1971-75; staff surgeon Meml. Hosp., Logansport, Ind., 1977—; pvt. practice Logansport Surg. Assocs. P.C., 1977—; county health officer Cass County, Logansport, 1979—. Maj. USAF, 1975-77. Fellow ACS; mem. Soc. Am. Gastrointestinal Endoscopic Surgeons, Am. Soc. Gastrointestinal Endoscopy, Am. Soc. Gen. Surgeons. Office: Logansport Surg Assocs PC PO Box 299 820 Fulton St Logansport IN 46947

HILL-LEFFLER, PAMELA JEAN, pharmacist; b. Indpls., Nov. 4, 1958; d. Cecil Johnnie and Marguerite Alice (Budrech) H.; m. John O. Leffler II. BS, Butler U., 1982, MSc in hosp. pharmacy, 1988. Lic. pharmacist, Ind. Staff pharmacist Ind. U. Hosps., Indpls., 1983-85; resident, 1983; dir. pharmacy services Care Mark Home Health Care of Am., Indpls., 1985-86; pharmacist, cons. PH Cons. 1986—; nutrition cons. Care Mark Home Health Care of Am., 1985-86; faculty Coll. Pharmacy Butler U., 1988-90, Devington Career Ctr., 1989-91; regional dir. Home Nutritional Support, 1989-90; chief pharmacist Supervalu, Inc. 1993—. Author: Nutritional Handbook Indiana University Hospitals, 1985; (with others) Help! I'm Parenting My Parent, 1987; producer videotape series, Corinthian Pharmacy; author, prodr. (videotape) Techniques in IV Admixture Preparation; contbr. articles to profl. jours.; regular guest cable TV Golden Horizons. Office: Cub Pharmacy 3639 S Keystone Ave Indianapolis IN 46227-3507

HILLMAN, ALAN L., internist, educator, researcher; b. N.Y.C., July 12, 1956; s. Herman David and Edith (Geilich) H.; m. Janice Kubo, July 9, 1983; children: Jennifer, Abigail. BA cum laude, Cornell U., 1978, MD, 1981; MBA, U. Pa., 1986. Intern in internal medicine N.Y. Hosp., 1981-82, asst. resident in internal medicine, 1982-84; dir. clin. programs Hosps. of U. of Pa., Phila., 1986-90, med. dir. Health Pass, 1987-90; assoc. dir. med. group U. Pa., Phila., 1987-90, sr. scholar clin. epidemiology, 1990—, dir. Ctr. for Health Policy, 1990—, mem. comprehensive cancer ctr., 1992; assoc. prof. health care Wharton Sch., U. Pa., Phila., 1993—; assoc. prof. medicine Sch. of Medicine, U. Pa., Phila., 1993—; assoc. dean health svcs. rsch. U. Pa., Phila., 1995—; asst. instr. dept. of medicine N.Y. Hosp.-Cornell Med. Ctr., N.Y., 1981-84; asst. prof. of medicine and health care mgmt. Sch. of Medicine and The Wharton Sch., U. Pa., Phila., 1986-93, assoc. prof., 1993—; mem. Inst. for Human Gene Therapy, U. Pa. Med. Ctr., Phila., 1995—; discharge planning com. Hosp. of Univ. of Pa., 1986-88, drug use effects com., 1990-91; admissions and awards com. Health Care Mgmt. Dept., The Wharton Sch., 1990-92; exec. com. The Leonard Davis Inst. of Health Econs., 1990—; co-dir. Health of the Pub. Program, Sch. of Medicine, 1991-92; com. on jud. ethics U. Pa., 1993—; ctr. for bioethics adv. com. Sch. of Medicine, 1994—, faculty senate, 1994—, master's program in med. ethics adv. com. Coll. of Arts and Scis., 1995—, com. on health svcs. rsch. Sch. Medicine, 1995—, com. on multiculturalism in rsch. Inst. on Aging, 1995—; cons. U. Mo. Sch. of Medicine, Columbia, 1994, UNISYS Corp., Blue Bell, Pa., 1993, Prudential Ins. Co., Atlanta, 1993—, PACC Bd. of Dirs., Clackamas, Oreg., 1993, Gate Pharms., Kulpsville, Pa., 1994-95, Exogen Co., Princeton, N.J., 1994—, Forest Labs., N.Y.C., 1994—, VidaMed Corp., Palo Alto, Calif., 1993-95, Health Industry Mfrs. Assn., Washington, 1993—, Proctor & Gamble, Morris Plains, N.J., 1993, Syntex, 1993—, Eli Lilly Corp., Indpls., 1993-95, Amgen, Thousand Oaks, 1993—, Rhone-Poulenc Rorer, Antony Cedex, France, 1992—, Abbott Labs., Abbott Park, Ill., 1991—, and all others. Contbr. numerous articles to profl. jours. Recipient Young Investigators award Assn. for Health Svcs. Rsch., 1993. Fellow ACP, Am. Bd. Internal Medicine; mem. Group Health Assn. of Am., Internat. Soc. of Tech. Assessment in Health Care, Soc. of Gen. Internal Medicine, Phila. Coll. of Physicians, Internat. Soc. for Econ. Evaluation of Medicines, Am. Fedn. for Clin. Rsch., Assn. for Health Svcs. Rsch., Physicians for Social Responsibility, Soc. of Gen. Internal Medicine, Am. Soc. for Clin. Investigation, Alpha Omega Alpha. Office: U Pa 3641 Locust Walk Philadelphia PA 19104-6218

HILLMAN, BRUCE JAY, radiologist, researcher, consultant, educator; b. Miami, Apr. 16, 1947; s. Henry and Mildred (Semel) H.; m. Diane Gartner, June 12, 1948; 1 child, Aaron Gartner. BA, Princeton U., 1969; MD, U. Rochester, 1973. Diplomate Am. Bd. Radiology. Med. intern George Washington U. Med. Ctr., Washington, 1973-74; radiology resident Peter Bent Brigham Hosp., Boston, 1974-78; NIH clin. rsch. fellow Harvard U., Boston, 1975-78; asst. prof. U. Ariz., Tucson, 1978-81, assoc. prof., 1981-85; Pew Health Policy fellow Rand Corp., Santa Monica, Calif., 1984-85; prof. radiology, vice-chmn. radiology dept. U. Ariz., 1985-92; prof. radiology U. Va., Charlottesville, 1992—, chmn. radiology dept., 1992—; sr. scholar Va. Health Policy Ctr., Charlottesville, 1992—; cons. Rand Corp., Santa Monica, 1985—, United Mine Workers of Am. Health and Retirement Funds, Washington, 1989—. Author: Imaging and Hypertension, 1981; contbr. more than 120 articles to profl. jours., 47 chpts. to books, revs., and editls.; editor-in-chief Investigative Radiology, 1989-94, Academic Radiology, 1994—. Mem. Princeton Schs. Commn., Charlottesville, 1993—. Recipient 4 major fellowships, 16 honorary or named lectures. Fellow Am. Coll. Radiology; mem. Soc. Uroradiology (pres. 1994), Soc. Health Svcs. Rsch. in Radiology (pres. 1995—), Assn. Univ. Radiologists (pres.-elect 1996—), Soc. Chairmen of Acad. Radiology Depts. (councillor 1994-96), Acad. Radiology Rsch. (exec. com. 1995-96), Ea. Radiol. Soc. (pres. 1994). Office: Univ Va Health Sci Ctr Dept Radiology Box 170 Charlottesville VA 22908

HILLMAN, GILBERT R., medical educator; b. New Haven, Conn., May 1, 1943; s. Jacob D. and Clara (Rothschild) H.; m. Rachel Read, Aug. 27, 1965; child: Laura. BA, Harvard, 1965; PhD, Yale, 1969. Asst. prof. Brown U., 1970-76; assoc. prof. U. Tex. Med. Br., Galveston, 1976-82, prof., 1982—. Contbr. articles to profl. jours. Grantee NIH, 1976—. Office: U Tex Med Br Dept of Pharmacology Galveston TX 77555-1031

HILLMAN, HAROLD HYRAN, retired physiologist; b. London, Surrey, U.K., Aug. 16, 1930; s. David and Annie H.; m. Elizabeth Holland, Oct. 23, 1973; children: Alexander, Rachel, Benedict, Sophia. MB/BChir, Middlesex Hosp., London, 1956, MRCS, 1956; BS in Physiology, U. Coll., London, 1958; PhD in Biochemistry, Inst. Psychiatry, London, 1963. Rsch. asst., lectr. Inst. Psychiatry, London, 1958-62; rsch. fellow, docent Inst. Neurobiology, Goteborg, Sweden, 1962-64; lectr. Inst. Neurology, London, 1964-65; sr. lectr. Battersea Coll., London, 1965-68; reader in physiology U. Surrey, Guildford, Eng., 1968-95, dir. unity lab., 1970—; med. adviser Inst. Biol. Psychiatry, Bangor, Wales, 1990-93; sec. London Med. Postgrad., 1985—. Author: Certainty and Uncertainty in Biochemical Techniques, 1972, Living Cell, 1980, Cellular Structure Mammalian Brain, 1986, Atlas of Cellular Structure Human Central Nervous System, 1991, The Case for New Paradigms in Cell Biology and Neurobiology, 1991. Exec. mem. Brit. Amnesty, London, 1970-80; senator U. Surrey, Guildford, 1979-89; chmn. Surrey Assn. Univ. Tchrs., Guildford, 1978-89. Recipient medal Free U. Brussels, 1975. Fellow Royal Soc. Medicine; mem. Physiol. Soc., Brit. Med. Assn. (chmn. Guildford divsn. 1995—). Home: 3 Merrow Dene, 76 Epsom Rd, Guildford GU12BX, England

HILLS, WILLIAM JOHNSTON, surgeon; b. Colorado Springs, Colo., Nov. 8, 1922; m. Lavonne E. Hills, Sept. 1945; children: Karen, Barbara, Marcia, Greg, Jim. BA, U. Denver, 1944; MD, U. Colo., Denver, 1946. Diplomate Am. Bd. Surgery, Am. Bd. Med. Specialists. Intern Corwin Hosp. and Clinic, Pueblo, Colo., 1948; resident Robert B. Green Hosp., San Antonio, 1954; fellow M.D. Anderson Hosp., Houston, 1967; ptnr. Surg. Assocs., San Antonio, 1958-94; pvt. practice San Antonio, 1994—; clin. prof. surgery U. Tex. Med. Sch., San Antonio, 1967—. Maj. M.C. U.S. Army, 1943-46, 48-51. Decorated Bronze Star, Purple Heart. Mem. AMA, Tex. Med. Assn., Bexar County Med. Soc., San Antonio Surg. Soc., Tex. Surg. Soc., Soc. of Head and Neck Surgeons. Office: 414 Navarro #1026 San Antonio TX 78205

HILLSMAN, REGINA ONIE, orthopedic surgeon; b. N.Y.C., June 2, 1955; d. David Oka and Laettia Louise (Miller) H.; m. Peter Michael Schmitz, Mar. 18, 1982; children: Michelle, Julien Pierre, Christophe-Gerard Philippe. BA cum laude, Bryn Mawr Coll., 1972; MD cum laude George Washington U., 1977. Diplomate Am. Bd. Orthopaedic Surgery, 1990. Intern Beth Israel Hosp., Boston, 1977-78; resident in surgery Montefiore Hosp., Bronx, N.Y., 1978-79; resident in orthopedics U. Pa., Phila., 1979-81; chief resident Howard U., Washington, 1981-82; practice med. specializing in orthopedics Los Angeles, 1983-87, N.Y.C., 1987—; clin. liaison Martin Luther King, Los Angeles, Calif. Fellow Am. Acad. Orthopaedic Surgeons; mem. ACS, AMA, Am. Med. Women's Assn., Am. Orthopaedics, N.Y. Acad. Scis., N.Y. State Med. Soc., Westchester Polit. Women's Caucus, Westchester Conservatory Music, Phi Delta Epsilon. Roman Catholic. Home: 3614 Post Rd W Ste 238 Westport CT 06880-4754 Office: 1183 New Haven Rd Naugatuck CT 06770

HILLSON, JAN LESLIE, rheumatology researcher and educator; b. Norwich, Conn., Oct. 3, 1952; d. Joseph Stanley and Muriel Anne (Vecker-elli) H.; m. David Robert Haynor, June 18, 1983; children: Samuel Joseph, Benjamin Paul. BS, Mich. State U., 1973; MS, Scripps Inst. Oceanography, 1976, Calif. Inst. Tech., 1976; MD, Stanford U., 1980. Diplomate Am. Bd. Internal Medicine, 1983, Am. Bd. Rheumatology, 1990. Resident in internal medicine U. Wash. Med. Ctr., Seattle, 1980-83, acting instr. medicine, 1984-85, fellow biochemistry and rheumatology, 1985-89, acting asst. prof. rheumatology, 1989-91; asst. prof. rheumatology, 1991—; attending physician U. Wash.; speaker in field. Contbr. sci. articles to profl. jours. NIH fellow, 1986-89, recipient First award, 1989. Mem. AAAS, ACLU, Am. Coll. Rheumatology, Amnesty Internat., Sigma Xi. Democrat. Home: 2446 Warren Ave N Seattle WA 98109-2024 Office: U Wash Med Ctr 1945 NE Pacific St Seattle WA 98195-0004

HILLYARD, IRA WILLIAM, pharmacologist, educator; b. Richmond, Utah, Mar. 23, 1924; s. Neal Jacobsen and Lucille (Duce) H.; m. Venice Lenore Williams, July 10, 1945 (dec.); children: Christine, Kevin, Eric; m. Norma Larsen, May 1, 1970. B.S., Idaho State U., 1949; M.S., U. Nebr., 1951; Ph.D., St. Louis U., 1957. Pharmacologist Mead Johnson Co., Evansville, Ind., 1957-59; sr. pharmacologist, sect. leader Warner-Lambert Research Inst., Morris Plains, N.J., 1959-69; assoc. prof. pharmacology Idaho State U. Coll. Pharmacy, Pocatello, 1969-73, 77-79, dean, 1979-87, prof. pharmacology, 1979-91, prof. emeritus 1991—; dir. pharmacology and toxicology ICN Pharms., Irvine, Calif., 1973-77, cons., 1977-80; cons. Pennwalt Pharm. Co., Rochester, N.Y., 1978-83. Contbr. articles to profl. jours. Served with USN, 1943-45, 51-53. Decorated Purple Heart Fellow Am. Found. Pharm. Edn.; mem. Western Pharmacology Soc., Am. Assn. Colls. Pharmacy, Am. Soc. Pharmacology and Exptl. Therapeutics, N.Y. Acad. Scis., Sigma Xi, Rho Chi, Phi Delta Chi. Lodge: Rotary. Home: 2750 Mt Borah Pl Pocatello ID 83201-2637 Office: Idaho State U Dept Pharmacology Pocatello ID 83209

HILTON, HELEN MCCLEAN, physician assistant; b. Balt., Mar. 17, 1949; d. George Walter and Edna (Schall) McClean; m. Thomas Arnold Hilton, Aug. 25, 1973; children: Brian McClean, Sarah Elizabeth. BS in Medicine, Alderson-Broaddus Coll., 1973, BA in Psychology, 1973. Cert. physician asst. Physician asst. Joseph Reed MD, Buckhannon, W.Va., 1973, Joseph Wilson Health Ctr., Rochester, N.Y., 1974-78; asst. prof. Alderson-Broaddus Coll., Philippi, W.Va., 1978-80; physician asst. Weston State Hosp., Weston, W.Va., 1980-83, Total Life Clinic, Backhannon, W.Va., 1983-85; physician asst. Vet. Adminstrn., Clarksburg, W.Va., 1985-87, Coatesville, Pa. 1987—; promoted to chief grade VA Med. Ctr., Perry Point, Md., 1995—. Mem. ACLS, VA Physician Assts. Baptist. Office: VA Med Ctr Bldg 361 Coatesville PA 19320

HIMATHONGKAM, THEP, endocrinologist; b. Bangkok, Thailand, Aug. 29, 1942; s. Chan and Payia H.; m. Jitrapa Kantabutra, Dec. 12, 1970; children: Tanya, Tarin, Tinapa. BA, U. Calif., Berkeley, 1963; MD, U. Wis., 1969. Diplomate Am. Bd. Internal Medicine. Fellow in endocrinology Peter Bent Brigham Hosp. Harvard U. Med. Sch., Boston, 1972-74; asst. prof. endocrinology Ramathibodi Med. Sch. Mahidol U., Bangkok, 1974-78, assoc. prof., 1979-82, prof., 1983-85, prof. emeritus, 1986—; dir. Theptarin Diabetes Ctr., Bangkok, 1985-90; cons. endocrinologist Phyathai Hosp., Bangkok, 1976-91, Samitivej Hosp., Bangkok; bd. dirs. Phyathai Hosp., Theptarin Gen. Hosp., Bangkok (chmn. 1991—). Author: (book) Disease of the Thyroid, 1984. Dir. Duangprateep Foundn., Bangkok, 1990—. Fellow Am. Coll. Physicians; mem. Royal Coll. Physicians Thailand. Home: 3850 Rama IV, Prakanong, Bangkok 10110, Thailand Office: Theptarin Hosp, 3850 Rama IV, Prakanong, Bangkok 10110, Thailand

HIMELSTEIN, MONROE, surgeon; b. Lebanon, Conn., Jan. 18, 1924; s. Max A. and Dorothy J. (Malkin) H.; m. Faith Freedman, Apr. 26, 1953; children: Mary H. Cohn, Jane H. Sheehan. AB, Wesleyan U., Middletown, Conn., 1947; MD, Columbia U., 1951. Diplomate Am. Bd. Surgery, Nat. Bd. Med. Examiners. Intern Hartford (Conn.) Hosp., 1951-52, surgical resident, 1952-56, clin. asst. to sr. surgeon, 1956—; asst. clin. prof. Dartmouth Med. Sch., Hanover, N.H., 1984—; assoc. clin. prof. surgery U. Conn. Sch. of Medicine, Farmington, 1970—; cons. in surgery Inst. for Living, Hartford, 1977—, Rocky Hill Vet.'s Hosp., Rocky Hill, Conn., 1968—; bd. dirs. Capital Area Health Consortium, Hartford; chief of staff Hartford Hosp., 1986-89, bd. dirs. and exec. com., corporator; lectr. in field. Contbr. articles to profl. jours. Lt. (j.g.) USNR, 1943-46, PTO. Fellow Am. Coll. Surgeons; mem. Conn. Soc. Am. Bd. Srugeons, New Eng. Surgical Soc. (sr. mem.), AMA, Conn. Med. Soc., Hartford County Med. Assn. (bd. dirs. 1986-92), Hartford Med. Soc. (chmn. bd. censors and adv. bd.). Jewish. Office: 85 Seymour St Hartford CT 06106-5501

HIMELSTEIN, PHILIP NATHAN, psychology educator; b. N.Y.C., Sept. 25, 1923; s. Isidore and Martha (Feinberg) H.; m. Peggy Donn, June 1, 1952; children: Steven Mark, Carol Sue, Roger Alan. AB, NYU, 1949, AM, 1950; PhD, U. Tex., 1955. Diplomate Am. Bd. Profl. Psychology. Clin. psychologist Salem (Va.) VA Hosp., 1955-56; rsch. psychologist USAF, 1956-58; mem. faculty U. Ark., Fayetteville, 1958-63; assoc. prof. N.Mex. State U., Las Cruces, 1963-65; prof. psychology U. Tex., El Paso, 1965-90, prof. emeritus, 1990—, chmn. dept., 1966-71; clin. psychologist El Paso Psychiat. Clinic, 1971-78; clin. assoc. prof psychiatry Tex. Tech. U. Sch. Medicine, 1978-80; adj. prof. Sch. Psychology, Fla. Inst. Tech., Melbourne, 1977—; chief psychologist El Paso State Ctr., 1995—. Co-editor: Readings on the Exceptional Child, 1962, 2nd edit., 1972, Handbook of Gestalt Therapy, 1976. With USAAF, WWII. Mem. Fellow APA, Soc. Personality Assessment, Am. Psychol. Soc.; mem. El Paso Psychol. Assn. (pres. 1971-72), El Paso County Psychol. Soc. (pres. 1990-91), Sigma Xi, Phi Kappa Phi. Home: 331 Rainbow Cir El Paso TX 79912-3717

HIMES, GEORGE ELLIOTT, pathologist; b. Huntington, W.Va., Jan. 5, 1922; s. Connell Bradley and Elizabeth (Skeans) H.; m. Rita T. Wasniewski (dec. July 1993); children: Rita Ann Brust, Susan Ruth Burger, George Elliott Jr., Brent Lee; m. Barbara A. Cunningham, Dec. 21, 1994. Student, U. Cin., 1939-42; DO, Chgo. Coll. Osteo. Medicine, 1942-45. Intern Lamb Mem. Hosp., Denver, 1945-46; resident pathology Chgo. Osteo Hosp., 1946-48; asst. prof. pathology Chgo. Coll. Osteo Med., 1948-56; asst. lab. dir. Chgo. Osteo Hosp., 1948-51; dir. of labs Flint (Mich.) Osteo Hosp., 1951-87, dir. of labs and nuclear med., 1957-80; assoc. prof. pathology Coll. Osteo Med., Des Moines, 1968-89; adj. prof. pathology Coll. Osteo. Medicine Mich. State U., East Lansing, Mich., 1974-84; dir. sch. med. tech. Flint (Mich.) Osteo Hosp., 1975-85; mem. radiation, chem. & biol. safety com. Mich. State U., 1978—; mem. Am. Osteo. Bd. Pathology, 1959-68, Am. Osteo. Bd. Nuclear Medicine, 1974-84. Bd. dirs. ARC, Flint, 1963-74, United Way, 1964-72; pres. Flint Civitan Club, 1954. Mem. AMA, AAAS, Am. Osteo. Coll. Pathologists (past pres. and sec.-treas. 1954-72), Am. Osteo. Assn., Am. Assn. Blood Banks, Mich. Assn. Osteo. Physicians and Surgeons, Coll. Am. Pathologists, Am. Soc. Clin. Pathologists, Soc. Nuclear Medicine, Mich. Soc. Pathologists, Genesee Country Osteo. Assn., Flint Golf Club. Home: 444 Luce Ave Flushing MI 48433-1411 Office: Flint Osteopathic Hosp 3921 Beecher Rd Flint MI 48532-3602

HIMES, JAMES ALBERT, veterinary medicine educator emeritus; b. Lucas, Ohio, Aug. 12, 1919; s. Albert Merle and Nina Grace (Galleher) H.; m. Ruth Naomi Banks, Apr. 26, 1958 (div. 1973); children: Leslie Jo, Jillyn Alicia; m. Genia Lee, May 10, 1973. BS, Muskingum Coll., 1941; postgrad., U. Nebr., 1941-42, 46; VMD, U. Penn., 1950; PhD, Cornell U., 1965. Veterinarian Tenn., Va., Fla., 1950-62; rsch. asst. Cornell U., Ithaca, N.Y., 1962-65; from asst. prof. to assoc. prof. U. Fla., Gainesville, 1965-76, dir. vet. medicine edn., 1975-77, prof., 1976-90, from asst. dean to assoc. dean Coll. Vet. Medicine, 1977-90, prof. emeritus, 1990—. Editor: Part X, Spontaneous Animal Models of Human Disease, 1979. Sgt. U.S. Army, 1942-45. Mem. AVMA, Fla. Vet. Med. Assn. (Vet. of Yr. 1987, Exec. Disting. Svc. award 1992), Alachua Vet. Med. Assn. (sec.-treas. 1973-74, pres. 1995), Marion County Vet. Assn. Home: 3716 SW 30th Ter Apt 41C Gainesville FL 32608-3110

HIMES, JOHN HARTER, medical researcher, educator; b. Salt Lake City, July 25, 1947; s. Ellvert Hiram and Mildred Anna (Harter) H.; m. Kathleen Cox; children: Rachel Anne, Matthew Hiram, Sarah Elizabeth. BS, Ariz. State U., 1971; PhD, U. Tex., 1975; MPH, Harvard U., 1982. Rsch., sr. scientist Fels Rsch. Inst., Yellow Springs, Ohio, 1976-79; Fels asst. prof. Wright State U. Sch. Medicine, Dayton, Ohio, 1977-79; sr. analyst, project dir. Abt Assocs., Cambridge, Mass., 1979-82; assoc. prof. CUNY, Bklyn., 1982-87; from assoc. prof. to prof. U. Minn. Sch. Pub. Health, Mpls., 1987—, dir. nutrition coord. ctr., 1995—; expert com physical status WHO, Geneva, Switzerland, 1991-94, expert adv. panel nutrition, 1994—; tech. working group Ctrs. for Disease Control, Washington and Atlanta, 1988—. Author: Parent-specific Adjustment for Assessment of Recumbent Length & Stature, 1981, Antjropometric Assessment of Nutritional Status, 1991; contbr. articles to profl. jours. Recipient Nathalie Masse Meml. prize Internat. Children's Ctr., Paris, 1979. Fellow Human Biology Coun.; mem. Am. Inst. Nutrition, Am. Pub. Health Assn., N.Am. Assn. Study of Obesity, Internat. Assn. Human Auxology, Pan Am. Health Orgn. (tech. adv. nutrition 1994), Nat. Ctr. Health Stats. (tech. working group 1994—), Soc. for Study of Human Biology, Phi Kappa Phi, Sigma Xi, Delta Omega. Office: U Minn 1300 S 2d St Minneapolis MN 55454

HIMMELREICH, ARLENE, occupational health and safety nurse, consultant. RN diploma, Milw. County Gen. Sch. Nursing, 1972; BSN, Alverno Coll., 1985. RN, Wis., COHN. Health svcs. mgr. Miller Brewing Co., Milw., 1973-93; dir. and faculty occupational health Midwest Inst. OEHS, New Berlin, Wis., 1993—; pres. HEALTHCARE Consultants, Milw., 1993—; clin. and weekend coll. assessor Alverno Coll., Milw., 1985—. Instr. ARC, 1975—. Recipient Occupational Health Nurse award Schering Corp., 1987, Creative Practices award S.E. Wis. Assoc. Occupational Health Nurses, 1990, Leadership Occupational Health award Medique, Inc., 1992. Mem. Am. Assn. Occupational Health Nurses (peer review com.), Cen. States Occupational Medicine (edn. liaison 1985—), Wis. State Occupational Health Nurses (edn. chair 1995—), SE Wis. Assn. Occupational Health Nurses (pres. 1986-87, 91-93, various bd. positions 1978—). Office: 4334 N 100 St Milwaukee WI 53222

HINDBAUGH, RONALD C., child therapist, preschool owner; b. Kalamazoo, Mich., Sept. 12, 1940; s. Floyd C. and Loraine M. (Schmidt) H.; m. Matilda K. Hoapli; children: Loretta Ann, Nanette K., Monica June, Katherine L., Allison C., Rebekah E. BS in Sci. Tchg., Ferris State Coll., 1962; MA in Guidance, Western Mich. U., 1968. Lic. profl. counselor, social worker. Tchr. Plainwell (Mich.) Cmty. Sch.; adminstr. Dept. Mental Health, various cities, Mich.; protective svcs. worker Dept. Social Svcs., Coldwater, Mich.; child therapist Branch County Mental Health, Coldwater. Mem., bishop LDS Ch. Republican. Office: Branch County Mental Health 200 Orleans Coldwater MI 49036

HINDER, RONALD ALBERT, surgeon; b. Johannesburg, South Africa, Jan. 14, 1942; came to U.S., 1987; s. Albert Julius and Anna (Ringgenberg) H.; m. Philla Johanna Möller, Nov. 21, 1968; children: Ingrid, Paul, Lisa. MB, BChir, Witwatersrand U., Johannesburg, 1965, PhD, 1976. House surgeon Coronation Hosp., Johannesburg, 1966; houseman Baragwanath Hosp., Johannesburg, 1966; sr. house surgeon in urology, orthop. and paediatric surgery Johannesburg Hosp., 1967, from surg. registrar to prin. surgeon, 1970-86; registrar in pathology South African Inst. for Med. Rsch., Johannesburg, 1968; surg. registrar Whipps Cross Hosp., London, 1969, Bethnal Green Hosp., London, 1969-70; assoc. prof. dept. surgery Creighton U., Omaha, 1987-91, prof. dept. surgery, 1991—; assoc. prof. dept. surgery Witwatersrand U., Johannesburg, 1984-87, bd. faculty medicine, 1977-86, senate animal ethics com., 1978-86, chmn. senate animal ethics com., 1982-83; dir. residency program in surgery Creighton U., Omaha, 1988—, acting dir. surg. rsch., dir. esophageal and gastric function lab., 1990—, grad. med. edn. com., 1988—, exec. com., 1988-90, com. health scis. rsch., 1990—; attending staff VA med. Ctr., Omaha, cons. staff, Lincoln, Nebr.; courtesy staff Bergan Mercy Hosp., Omaha, Luth. Med. Ctr., Omaha; critical care com. St. Joseph Hosp., Omaha., 1988-93, med. policy bd., 1990-91, critical care com., med. policy bd., 1992-93; vis. prof., reviewer, lectr. and spkr. in field. Editor: Problems in General Surgery, 1992, Medical Intelligence Unit Gastroesophageal Reflux Disease, 1993; (with others) Current Problems in Surgery, 1992; co-author: Chest Surgery Clinics of North America, 1995, Seminars in Laparoscopic Surgery, 1995, Current Surgical Therapy Fifth Edition, 1995, Minimally Invasive Surgery of the Foregut, 1995, Operative Laparoscopy and Thoracoscopy, 1994, Practical Endoscopic Surgery for General Surgeons, 1994, Digestive Tract Surgery: A Text and Atlas, 1994, Principles of Laparoscopic Surgery, 1995, Hernia Fourth Edition, 1995, Color Atlas/Text of Advanced Laparoscopy for Surgeons, 1995, Laparoscopic and Thoracoscopic Surgery, 1995, Complications of Laparoscopic Surgery, 1995, Advances in Surgery, 1995, Surgery of the Esophagus, Stomach and Small Intestine, 1995, The Gastrointestinal Surgical Patient, 1994, Laparoscopic Abdominal Surgery, 1993, Perspectives in General and Laparoscopic Surgery, 1993, Problems in General Surgery, 1993, Surgery Annual, 1993, Surgery Clinics of North America, 1992, Current Surgical Therapy, 4th edit., 1991, Ambulatory Esophageal pH Monitoring: Practical Approach and Clinical Applications, 1991, Gastrointestinale Funktionsdiagnostik in der Chirurgie, 1991, Gastrointestinal Motility: Which Test?, 1989; mem. editl. bd. South African Jour. Surgery, 1983-87, Jour. Postgrad. Gen. Practice, 1986-87, Jour. Surg. Laparoscopy and Endoscopy, 1990—, The Mediterranean Jour. Surgery and Medicine, 1994—; contbr. articles to profl. jours. Travelling fellow U. Witwatersrand, 1975, 79, 85; Schweizerische Nationalfonds grantee Stadspital Triemli, Zurich, 1982; recipient numerous rsch. grants. Fellow ACS, Royal Coll. Surgeons, Am. Coll. Gastroenterology, Southwestern Surg. Congress; mem. AMA, Surg. Rsch. Soc. So. Africa (exec. com. 1982-87), South Africa Gastroenterology Soc. (hon. treas. 1978-85), Am. Gastroenterol. Assn., Soc. Internat. Surgery, Assn. Program Dirs. in Surgery, Am. Motility Soc., Soc. Am. Gastrointestinal Endoscopic Surgeons, Colegium Internat. Surgery Digestive, Soc. for Surgery of the Alimentary Tract (auditing com. 1992), Ctrl. Surg. Assn., Assn. for Acad. Surgery, Omaha Mid-West Clin. Soc. (vice-chmn. sect. on surgery 1988, chmn. surg. sect. 1989-90, sci. display awards com. 1991), Met. Omaha Med. Soc., North Ctrl. Cancer Treatment Group, Ea. coop. Oncology Group, Internat. Duodenal Club, Phi Beta Delta. Office: Creighton Univ Dept Surgery 601 N 30th St Ste 3740 Omaha NE 68131

HINDERLICH, HORST KLAUS, health facility administrator; b. Langewahl, Germany, Dec. 17, 1942; s. Herbert Heinz and Else Frieda (Liepe) H.; m. Hilde Johanne Scharf, June 14, 1969; 1 child, Hauke. BBA, U. Bremen, 1971. Bd. mem. HAG Gen. Foods, Bremen, Germany, 1969-86; cons. John Stark & Ptnr., Frankfurt, Germany, 1986-87; mng. dir. R&B Food Handels GmbH, Bremen, 1988-89, Rotes-Kreuz-Krankenhaus, Bremen, 1990—; instr. Bus. Acad. Bremen, 1969—; bd. dirs. Bremen Hosp. Assn., Hosp. Dirs. Assn. Contbr. articles to profl. jours. Chmn. C. of C. Bremen, 1970—; hon. judge Labor Ctr., Bremen, 1972—. Col. German Air Force, 1963—. Recipient Life Saving medal City of Berlin, 1956, Hon. Cross in Gold Ministry Def., 1991, Silver Cross KNBLO, 1995. Mem. German Pers. Assn., German Mil. Res. Assn., Press Club Bremen, Golf Club Worpswede. Lutheran. Home: Birkenheide 14, 27711 Osterholz Scharmbeck Germany Office: Red Cross Hosp, St Pauli Deich 24, 28199 Bremen Germany

HINDLE, PAULA ALICE, nursing administrator; b. Cambridge, Mass., Feb. 26, 1952; d. Edward Adam and Geraldine Ann (Donahue) H. BSN,

Fitchburg State Coll., 1974; MSN, Duke U., 1980; MBA, Simmons Coll., 1988. Staff nurse Mt. Auburn Hosp., Cambridge, Mass., 1974-75; staff nurse U. Hosp., Boston, 1975-77, head nurse, 1977-79; staff nurse Duke U. Med. Ctr., Durham, N.C., 1979-80, clin. instr., 1980-81, area mgr., 1981; nurse leader, clin. dir. New Eng. Med. Ctr., Boston, 1981-87; cons. Ctr. for Nursing Case Mgmt., Boston, 1984-87; v.p. nursing Faulkner Hosp., Boston, 1987-94; v.p. nursing and support svcs. Alexandria (Va.) Hosp., 1994—; mem. adv. com. Regis Coll. Nursing, 1993; mem. planning and resource com. Simmons Coll., 1993-94; mem. affiliate faculty George Mason U., 1994-95. Active Am. Heart Assn. Mem. Am. Orgn. Nurse Execs., Va. Orgn. Nurse Execs., Mass. Orgn. Nurse Execs. (treas. 1991-93), Humane Soc., Simmons Coll. Grad. Sch. Mgmt. Alumni Assn. (bd. dirs. 1991-93, pres. 1992-93), Sigma Theta Tau. Democrat. Roman Catholic. Home: 5908 Munson Ct Falls Church VA 22041-2444 Office: Alexandria Hosp 4320 Seminary Rd Alexandria VA 22304-1500

HINDSON, DAVID ALAN, endocrinologist; b. Albany, N.Y., Dec. 9, 1946; s. George Norman Hindson and Helen (Fessler) Jardine; m. Mary Catherine Cremin, July 25, 1970; children: Joshua Alan, Stephanie Valens. BA, Bowdoin Coll., 1968; MD, Case Western Reserve U., 1972. Diplomate Am. Bd. Internal Medicine, Am. Bd. Endocrinology and Metabolism. Intern, then resident in internal medicine Maine Med. Ctr., 1972-75; staff physician VA Med. Ctr., Boise, Idaho, 1976—; med. student coord. U. Wash., Seattle, 1980-86; asst. chief med. svc. VA Med. Ctr., Boise, 1982-85, chief med. svc., 1985—; clin. prof. medicine U. Wash. Sch. Medicine, Seattle, 1991—, program dir. internal med., 1982—. Fellow ACP (gov. Idaho chpt. 1992-96); mem. Am. Diabetes Assn. (pres. 1982-95), Assn. VA Chiefs of Medicine (treas.-sec. 1992-95). Home: 1361 Rimrock Ct Boise ID 83712 Office: Boise VA Med Ctr 500 W Fort St Boise ID 83702

HINER, GLADYS WEBBER, psychologist; b. Mt. Park, Okla., Mar. 10, 1907; d. Santford and Erie Emma (Rose) Webber; m. Wayman Hiner, Aug. 11, 1927 (dec. Mar. 1967); children: Waynel Cook, Sandra Homer. BS, U. Okla., 1934, MS, 1955, PhD, 1962; HHD (hon.), Wagon Wheel Found., McCloud, Okla., 1973. Bd. cert. devel. psychologist. Tchr. Okla. City Pub. Schs., 1953-61; dir. Dale Rogers Tng. Ctr., Okla. City, 1962-63; prof. Okla. City U., 1963-72, Rose State Coll., Okla. City, 1972-86; cons. Wagon Wheel Sch. McLoud, Okla., 1962-82, pvt. practice, Okla. City, 1986—. Supr. Sunday Sch. Trinity Baptist Ch., Okla. City, 1940-72; bd. dirs. Okla. State Assn. for Mentally Retarded Children, 1963-67, Youth and Child Coun. Okla. U. Med. Sch., 1966-69, Bridge Builders, Okla. City; Dem. state del., 1986. Fellow Okla. Psychol. Assn., Am. Assn. on Mental Deficiency; mem. The Acad. Ret. Profls., Okla. Hist. Soc., DAR, Colonial Dames, Psi Chi, Phi Theta Kappa. Home: 400 Canadian Trails Dr Apt #3 Norman OK 73072

HINES, EDWARD LLOYD, orthopedist; b. Washington, Apr. 29, 1943; s. Sidney L. and Mildred (Wechsler) H.; m. Sharon Eileen Cooper, Aug. 31, 1975; children: Jason, Seth, Susan. Student, Northwestern U., Evanston, Ill., 1960-63; DDS, Columbia U., 1967; MD, George Washington U., 1970. Diplomate Am. Bd. Ortho Surgery. Pvt. practice Burlington (N.C.) Orthop. & Hand Surgery, 1976—. Fellow Am. Coll. Surgery. Home: 247 Coachlight Tr Burlington NC 27215 Office: Edward L Hines MD S#2300 1236 Huffman Mill Rd PO Box 209 Burlington NC 27216-0209

HINES, GEORGE LAWRENCE, surgeon; b. Bklyn., June 10, 1946; s. Frank and Ruth (Katzman) H.; m. Helene Anne Reitman, Aug. 23, 1969; children: Brian, Jennifer. BA, Boston U., 1969, MD, 1969. Diplomate Am. Bd. Gen. Surgery, Am. Bd. Thoracic Surgery, Am. Bd. Gen. Vascular Surgery. Intern Maimonides Med. Ctr., Bklyn., 1969-70; resident Sinai Hosp., Detroit, 1970-71; to chief resident L.I. Jewish Med. Ctr., N.Y.C., 1971-74; cardiothoracic resident NYU Med. Ctr., N.Y.C., 1974-76; attending physician Winthrop U. Hosp., Mineola, N.Y., 1976—; pvt. practice Mineola; chief div. vascular surgery Winthrop U. Hosp., Mineola, N.Y., 1995—. Maj. U.S. Army Res., 1970-79. Fellow Am. Coll. Surgeons; mem. Am. Assn. for Thoracic Surgery, Soc. of Thoracic Surgeons, Internat. Soc. for Cardiovascular Surgery. Democrat. Jewish. Office: Winthrop Cardiothoracic Vascular Surgery Group 120 Mineola Blvd Mineola NY 11501-2545

HINES, PATRICIA, social worker; b. Watertown, N.Y., Nov. 4, 1947; d. Arthur and Bella (O'Neil) Hines; BS, SUNY, Oswego, 1969; MSW, SUNY, Buffalo, 1975; M in Pub. Adminstrn., Fairleigh Dickinson U., 1982. Lic. clin. social worker. Supr. social work Ocean County Bd. Social Services, Toms River, N.J., 1973-77, adminstrv. supr. social work, 1977-83, dep. dir., 1983—; social work cons. Ocean County Vis. Homemaker Svc., Inc., Toms River, 1975-80, Cmty. Meml. Hosp., Toms River, 1978-79, Manchester Manor, Lakeview Manor, Bartley Manor Convalescent Ctr., Ocean Convalescent Ctr., Barnegat Nursing Facility, Burnt Tavern Convalescent Ctr., Jackson Health Care Ctr., Logan Manor, Medicenter, Freehold Convention Ctr., Emery Rehab., So. Ocean; prin. in Sr. Care Planning Assocs.; instr. social work Georgian Court Coll., Lakewood, 1975—. Chmn. Ocean County Title XX Coalition, 1977-82; bd. dirs. Ocean County Family Planning Program, Toms River, 1969-73, Mental Health Bd., 1983-84; mem. exec. bd. United Way, 1983-96; mem. Aging Network Svc., 1992—. Cert., Dr. Thomas Gordon Parent Effectiveness Trainer. Mem. Acad. Cert. Social Workers, Nat. Assn. Social Workers (nat. register clin. social workers, diplomate clin. social work, lic. clin. social worker). Home: 13 Bay Harbor Blvd Brick NJ 08723-7303 Office: 1027 Hooper Ave Toms River NJ 08754

HINES, ROBERTA L., medical educator; b. Manchester, N.H., Sept. 18, 1952. BA, U. N.H., 1974; MD magna cum laude, Dartmouth U, 1978. Diplomate Am. Bd. Anesthesiology, critical care cert.; lic. physician, Conn. Intern surgery Yale-New Haven Med. Ctr., 1978-79, asst. resident surgery, 1979-81, asst. resident anesthesiology, 1981-83, chief resident, 1982-83, cardiovascular fellow, 1983-84, assoc. physician, 1983-84, attending physician, 1984—, dir. recovery rm., 1984-87, dir. cardiothoracic ICU, 1984—, chief dept. anesthesiology, 1995; instr. anesthesiology Yale U. Sch. Medicine, 1982-83, asst. prof., 1984-90, assoc. prof., 1990-94, acting chair, 1994, prof., chmn., 1994—; assoc. examiner Am. Bd. Anesthesiologists, 1991—; lectr., vis. profs. various univs. and hosps. Mem. editl. bd. Soc. Cardiovascular Anesthesia, 1985-89, Jour. Clin. Anesthesia, 1992, 93, 94, 95, Seminars in Anesthesia, 1995; editor Heart Failure, 1988-92; editl. cons. Anesthesia and Analgesia, 1992, 93, 94, 95, Anesthesiology, 1992, 93, 94, 95, Am. Soc. Obstetrics and Gynecology, 1993, 94, 95; reviewer, editl. cons. Clin. Anesthesia, 1993, 94, 95; reviewer Critical Care Medicine, 1992, 93, 94, 95, Jour. Clin. Monitoring, 1992, 93, 94, 95; editor: (with C. Blitt) Monitoring in Anesthesia and Critical Care, 1994; contbr. articles to profl. jours., chpts. to books. Mem. Soc. Edn. in Anesthesia, Internat. Anesthesia Rsch. Soc., Am. Soc. Anesthesiologists (clin. circulation subcom. 1990, 91, critical care medicine subcom. 1991), Soc. Critical Care Medicine (program chair 1994, 95), Soc. Cardiovascular Anesthesiologists (program com. 1990, 91, 92, editl. bd. 1983-88), Assn. Univ. Anesthesiologists, Am. Soc. Critical Anesthesiologists, Conn. State Soc. Anesthesiologists. Office: 333 Cedar St PO Box 208055 New Haven CT 06520-8055*

HINES-MARTIN, VICKI PATRICIA, nursing educator; b. Louisville, Aug. 18, 1951; d. William Adolphus Hines and Mary Iris Bailey; m. Kenneth Wayne Martin, Dec. 30, 1978; 1 child, Michelle Hines Martin. BSN, Spalding Coll., 1975; MA in Edn., Spalding U., 1983; MSN, U. Cin., 1986; PhD, U. Ky., 1994. Cert. clin. specialist in adult psychiat. mental. Staff nurse Norton Hosp., Louisville, 1978-81; instr. critical care Sts. Mary & Elizabeth Hosp., Louisville, 1981-82; asst. chief nursing svcs. VA Med. Ctr., Cin., 1983-85; nursing instr. Jefferson Community Coll., Louisville, 1985-87; head nurse mgr. VA Med. Ctr., Louisville, 1987-88; asst. prof. nursing Ind. U. S.E., New Albany, 1989-95, U. Ky., Lexington, 1995—; bd. dirs. Seven Counties Mental Health Svcs.; mem. steering com. on practice parameters Ky. Health Policy Bd. Contbr. articles to profl. jours. Nurses Scholar/Fellow, Lucy Zimmerman scholar, 1982, Estelle Massey Osborne Meml. scholar, 1983-84, trainee U. Cin., 1983, grad. scholar, 1983; named to Outstanding Young Women of Am., 1986; recipient Rsch. award Ky. Nurses Found., 1992, Nursing Excellence award Jefferson County Ky., 1995, Psychiatric Mental Health Nurse of the Year Ky. Nurses Assn., 1995; Elizabeth Carnegie scholar, 1991, Am. Nurses Found. scholar, 1992; Fellow U. Ky., 1988, grad. fellow, 1992,; postdoctoral fellowship in Health Policy ANA Ethnic Minority fellowship program, 1996. Mem. ANA (minority clin. fellow 1991-93), Ky. Nurses Assn. (mental health coun. sec. 1986-88, psych. mental health nurse of yr. award 1995), Kyanna Black Nurses, Inc. (co-founder, past pres.), Nat. Black Nurses Assn., Soc. Edn. and Rsch. Psychiat. Nursing, Sigma Theta Tau. Office: Univ of Kentucky College of Nursing 537 CON Lexington KY 40536

HINGHOFER-SZALKAY, HELMUT G., physiologist, educator; b. Graz, Styria, Austria, Jan. 22, 1948; s. Günther and Hermine (Kundigraber) Hinghofer-S.; m. Irma Leber, Apr. 6, 1979; children: Dagmar, Stephan. MD, U. Graz, 1974, Dozent, 1981. Rsch. asst. Physiol. Inst., Graz, 1970-74, asst. prof., 1974-82, assoc. prof., 1982-84; rsch. scientist NASA/Ames Rsch. Ctr., Moffett Field, Calif., 1984-85; assoc. prof. physiology U. Graz, 1985-95, prof., 1995—; sci. cons. European Space Agy., Paris, 1980—; mem. Austrian-Soviet mission Austromir, 1989-91, RLF, 1993—; sec. IUPS Sat. Cardiovasc. Symposium, Budapest and Graz, 1980; local organizer 3d European Symposium on Life Sci. Space, Graz, 1987, Space for Life Symposium, Vienna, 1992; head Inst. for Adaptive and Spaceflight Physiology, ASM, Graz, 1994—. Mem. Am. Physiol. Soc., Aerospace Med. Assn., Internat. Acad. Astronautics, German Physiol. Soc., Austrian Physiol. Soc. (sec. 1979-83), Sci. Soc. Styrian Physicians (sec. Graz chpt. 1976—), Austrian Soc. for Space Medicine (Vienna, v.p. 1991—). Office: U Graz Dept Physiology, Harrachgasse 21, A-8010 Graz Austria

HINGSON, RALPH W., medical educator; b. July 21, 1948. BA in Internat. Relations, Johns Hopkins U., 1969, ScD, 1974; MPH, U. Pitts., 1970. Prof. dept. Socio-Med. Scis. and Community Medicine and Dept. of Pediatrics Boston U. Sch. of Medicine, 1986—; now dept. chair social behavioral scis. dept. Boston U. Sch. Pub. Health; cons. Nat. Inst. on Alcoholism and Alcohol Abuse, Nat. Ctr. for Substance Abuse Prevention, Nat. Trans. Rsch. Bd.; nat. bd. dirs. MADD; cons. Am. Cancer Soc., others. Contbr. numerous articles to profl. jours. Named one of America's 10 Outstanding Young Men U.S. Jaycees, 1984; recipient Hero award MADD. Home: 4 Louisburg Sq Boston MA 02108-1203 Office: Boston U Sch Medicine Sch Pub Health 85 E Newton St # M840 Boston MA 02118-2340

HINGSON, ROBERT ANDREW, physician, educator, inventor, farmer, poet; b. Anniston, Ala., Apr. 13, 1913; s. Robert A. and Elloree Elizabeth (Haynes) H.; m. Gussie Dickson, Mar. 2, 1940; children: Dickson James, Andrew Tobian, Roberta Ann, Ralph Waldo, Luke Lockhart. AB, U. Ala., 1935, postgrad., 1933-35, LHD (hon.), 1970; MD, Emory U., 1938; LHD, Monrovia (Liberia) Coll., 1962; LLD, William Jewell Coll., 1963, Eastern Bapt. Coll., 1963; LittD (hon.), Hardin-Simmons U., 1965; DSc (hon.), Thomas Jefferson U. Medicine, 1970. Commd. med. officer USPHS, 1938, advanced through grades to sr. surgeon, med. dir., med. officer, med. dir. various ships USCG and USN, 1939-40; fellow anesthesiology Mayo Clinic, Rochester, Minn., 1940-41; chief of dept. anesthesia, U.S. Marine Hosp. USPHS, Staten Island, N.Y., 1941-42; med. dir. reserve USPHS, 1951-78, ret., 1978; dir. rsch. and anesthesiology Lying-in Hosp., Jefferson Med. Coll., Phila., Pa. Hosp., 1943-45; dir., first prof. and founder anesthesiology, U. Tenn., 1945-48; assoc. prof. obstetrics, anesthesiologist dept. obstetrics Johns Hopkins U., 1948-51; prof. anesthesia, founder dept. Case Western Res. U., 1951-68; prof. pub. health, anesthesiology and dental anesthesiology Magee Women's Hosp. U. Pitts. Sch. Medicine, 1968-73; cons. U.S. VA Hosp., Mt. Sinai Hosp., Sunny Acres Hosp., Highland View Hosp., Met. Hosp., St. Anne's Hosp.; sr. cons. Amigos de Honduras Med. Svc. Mission; vis. prof. at univs. in New Guinea, New Zealand, Australia, S. Am., Asia, Africa, Europe, 1958-80; guest faculty numerous colls. and univs. Author: Control of Pain in Childbirth, numerous poems; co-author: Anesthesia for Obstetrics; co-editor: Pitkin's Conduction Anesthesia; contbr. articles to profl. jours., chpts. to books; creator 12 med. motion pictures and video films with subjects relating to nerve block control of pain, mass immunization world epidemics and other subjects in field. Trustee Religious Heritage Found., 1968; chmn. Polio Plus Program Rotary dist. 692, Ga.; pres., founder Edn. and Relief Found., World Fedn. Soc. Anesthesiologists, 1960-8; 1st pres., founder Brother's Brother Found., med. dir., vaccination programs Operation Brother's Brother, Liberia, 1962; dir. med. survey Ctrl. Am. nations, 1967; deacon local Bapt. ch.; dir. Bapt. World Alliance Interdenominationsl, Inter-Racial Med. Mission Survey of Asia-Africa, 1958. Named Man of Yr. in Medicine Pitts. Acad. Medicine, 1974, 75, one of Ten Outstanding Young Men Am. U.S. Jaycees, 1947, Knight Grand Comdr. Humane Order African Redemption, 1962, Man of Distinction Pitts. Bapt. Assn., 1980, Man of Yr. Rotary of Ocilla, 1985, Humanitarian Svc. to Mankind award, 1989, Kiwanis humanitarian award, 1963; named to Gen. Francisco Morizan, 1968, Order Ruben Dario, 1968, Order Rodolfo Robles, 1974; recipient Service citation Costa Rica, 1967, service citation govts. of Nicaragua, Guatemala, Republic of Panama, El Salvador, Peru, Honduras, Dominican Republic, Haiti, Venezuela, Colombia, Cuba, Jamaica, Hadassah Service award Israel, 1968, Dahlberg Peace award Am. Bapt. Chs., 1977, Human Rights award UN Assn. Pitts., 1978, William O McQuiston Lectureship award Ill. Soc. Anesthesiologists, 1978, Paul Harris Fellowship award Rotary, 1978, Gaston Labat award Am. Soc. Regional Anesthesia, 1981, U.S. Pres.' award Internat. Volunteerism, 1987, Gov.'s Humanitarianism award, 1987, Gov. Clinton's Arkansas Travelers award, 1988, Rep. Presdl. Legion of Merit award, 1994, citation Outstanding Ga. Citizen Sec. State Ga., 1993, Heritage Achievement award U. Ala., 1993; Hingson Day named in his honor, Oxford, Ala., 1985. Fellow Internat. Coll. Anesthesia, William Crawford Gorgas Med. Soc., Am. Soc. Anesthetists, Internat. Coll. Surgeons, Royal Coll. Surgeons (faculty anesthesiology), Am. Coll. Anesthesiology; mem. Coll. Physicians and Surgeons, Republic of Costa Rica (hon.), N.J. Acad. Sci., Internat. Research Soc. (v.p.), Am. Soc. Anesthesiologists (bd. dirs. 1947-56), Rotary (internat. speaker), Sigma Xi, Pi Kappa Alpha. Home: PO Box 525 Ocilla GA 31774-0525 Office: Bros Bro Found 1501 Reedsdale Ste Ste 305 Pittsburgh PA 15233-2341 also: 801 S Irwin Ave Ocilla GA 31774

HINKES, CLIFFORD, orthopedist; b. Washington, Nov. 10, 1952; s. Harry R. and Marian Jean (Rutkin) H.; m. Hope Elaine Green, Jan. 21, 1991; children: David, Brian, Michelle. BA, U. Va., 1974; MD, Howard U., 1978. Diplomate Am. Bd. Orthopedic Surgery. Orthopedic surgeon, pres. Montgomery Orthopedics, PA, Rockville, Md., 1983—; dir. Physician Health Plan Divsn. Mid Atlantic Med. Svcs. Inc., Rockville, 1994—, Montgomery Surgery Ctr., Rockville, 1990—. Fellow Am. Acad. Orthopedic Surgeons; mem. AMA, Montgomery Med. Soc., Phi Delta Epsilon (treas. 1990—). Office: Montgomery Orthopedics 4701 Randolph Rd Rockville MD 20852

HINKLE, DONNA DIANE, medical surgical nurse; b. Abilene, Tex., Aug. 18, 1964; d. Dannis Arthur and Barbara Jean (Worden) Mettam; m. David Rollin Hinkle, June 18, 1988; children: David Rollin Jr., Joshua Lee, Jacob Donald. ADN, Joliet (Ill.) Jr. Coll., 1993. RN, Ill. Staff nurse, med. surg. Hammond-Henry Hosp., Geneseo, Ill., 1993—. Ill. Health Improvement Assn. scholar, 1991, 1992. Lutheran. Home: 233 N Center Geneseo IL 61254 Office: Hammond-Henry Hospital 210 W Elk St Geneseo IL 61254

HINMAN, ALAN RICHARD, public health administrator, epidemiologist; b. New Orleans, Mar. 23, 1937; s. E. Harold and Katharine Ellen (Fradenburgh) H.; m. Donna Virgene Graham, Dec. 21, 1959 (div. 1962); m. Lucy Winkler Householder, May 30, 1965; children: Johanna Mary, Katharine Emily. BA, Cornell U., 1957; MD, Western Res. U., 1961; MPH, Harvard U., 1969. Intern in internal medicine Cleve. Met. Hosp., 1961-62, resident, 1962-64, chief resident, 1964-65; with USPHS, 1965-69, 77—; advanced through grades to asst. surgeon gen., 1988; epidemic intelligence svc. officer Ctr. for Disease Control, Calif. State Dept. Health, 1965-66; regional evaluation officer Malaria Eradication Program, Ctr. for Disease Control, Atlanta, 1966-67, San Salvador, El Salvador, 1967-68; asst. chief viral diseases br. Epidemiology Program, Ctr. for Disease Control, Atlanta, 1969-70; dir. Bur. Epidemiology, N.Y. State Dept. Health, Albany, 1970-71; asst. commr. epidemiology and preventive health svcs. N.Y. State Dept. Health, 1971-75; asst. commr., dir. Bur. Preventive and Med. Svcs., Tenn. Dept. Pub. Health, Nashville, 1975-77; dir. Divsn. Immunization Ctr. for Prevention Svcs., Ctr. for Disease Control, Atlanta, 1977-88; coord. Nat. Vaccine Program Office of Asst. Sec. for Health, 1987-90; asst. surgeon gen. USPHS, 1988—; dir. Nat. Ctr. for Prevention Svcs. Ctrs. for Disease Control, 1988-95; sr. advisor to dir. Ctrs. for Disease Control and Prevention, 1995—; adj. asst. prof. preventive and cmty. medicine Albany Med. Coll., Union U., 1970-75; adj. asst. prof. pub. health Rensselaer Poly Inst., 1971-75; assoc. clin. prof. dept. preventive medicine Vanderbilt U., 1975-77; clin. asst. prof. dept. cmty. medicine Divsn. Healthcare Svcs., U. Tenn., 1975-77; clin. asst. prof. dept. family and cmty. health Meharry Med. Coll., 1975-77; clin. assoc. prof. dept. preventive medicine-cmty. health Emory U. Sch. Medicine, Atlanta, 1978-90; vis. prof. Case Western Res. U. Sch. Medicine, 1984; adj. prof. Emory U. Sch. Pub. Health, 1990—; vis. lectr. Shanghai 1st Med. Coll., 1981. Contbr. over 250 articles to profl. jours. Decorated D.S.M.; recipient Indian Health Svc. Dir. Spl. Excellence award, 1992. Fellow ACP, APHA (mem. gov. coun. 1975-77, mem. program devel. bd. 1984-86, mem. nominating com. 1984-86, chair 1985-86, chair-elect epidemiology sect. 1985-87, chair sect. 1987-89, past chair 1989-91, mem. exec. bd. 1991-95, spkr. governing coun. 1995—), Am. Acad. Pediat., Am. Coll. Epidemiology (mem. exec. bd. 1990-94, v.p. 1991-92, pres. 1992-93), Am. Coll. Preventive Medicine (regent 1974-75, 77-81, v.p. for pub. health 1975-76); mem. AMA, Am. Epidemiol. Soc., Am. Soc. Tropical Medicine and Hygiene, Am. Venereal Disease Assn. (bd. dirs. 1972-75, sec.-treas. 1975-77), Assn. Tchrs. Preventive Medicine, Infectious Diseases Soc. Am., Internat. Epidemiol. Assn., Physicians for Social Responsibility, Soc. Epidemiol. Rsch., Soc. Med. Decision Making. Home: 2194 Creek Park Rd Decatur GA 30033-2714

HINMAN, EDWARD JOHN, healthcare administrator; b. New Orleans, Nov. 10, 1931; s. E. Harold and Katharine (Fradenburgh) H.; m. Emma Jean Richmond, June 15, 1954; children—Cynthia, Alan, David. B.A., U. Okla., 1951; M.D., Tulane U., 1955; M.P.H., Johns Hopkins U., 1971. Diplomate: Am. Bd. Preventive Medicine. Intern USPHS Hosp., New Orleans, 1955-56, resident, Balt., 1958-61; dir. spl. research and devel. project Nat. Center Health Service Research, Rockville, Md., 1973-74; asst. surgeon gen., dir. div. hosps. and clinics USPHS, 1974-78; exec. dir. Group Health Assn., Washington, 1978-83; pres. Risk Control Services, Washington, 1984-86; med. dir. PruCare of Washington, 1986-89; regional med. dir. Lincoln Nat. Health Plan, Washington, 1990-92; v.p. med. affairs Total Health Care, Inc., Balt., 1992—; bd. dirs. Am. Assn. Med. Systems and Informatics, 1980-89, pres., 1985-86; bd. dirs. Coop. League U.S.A., Washington, 1982-85. Contbr. articles in field to profl. jours. Bd. dirs. Greater Southeast Community Hosp. Found., 1983-92. Served with USPHS, 1955-78. Recipient Bronze Letzeiser medal U. Okla., 1951; Meritorious Service award USPHS, 1976; Outstanding Achievement award Md. chpt. Federally Employed Women, 1976. Fellow ACP, Am. Coll. Med. Informatics, Am. Coll. Preventive Medicine (v.p. 1976-77), Am. Pub. Health Assn., Soc. Advanced Med. Systems (dir. 1968-82, pres. 1976-77), Am. Fedn. Clin. Research, Phi Beta Kappa. Home: 2225 Cape Leonard Dr Saint Leonard MD 20685-2445 Office: Total Health Care Inc 2305 N Charles St Baltimore MD 21218

HINNANT, CLARENCE HENRY, III, health care executive; b. Richmond, Va., June 7, 1938; s. Clarence Henry Jr. and Billie Louise (Chewning) H.; m. Barbara Ann Livingston, June 10, 1966 (div. Feb. 1971); children: C.H. IV, W.W. Tuck. BS, Va. Poly. Inst. and State U., 1961; BS magna cum laude, Med. Coll. Va., 1981. Math. tchr. Hopewell (Va.) High Sch., 1961-64; staff mem. Harper & Row Pub., N.Y.C., 1964-67; stockbroker Merrill Lynch & Co., Richmond, Va., 1967-71; pres. Lancaster Corp., White Stone, Va., 1971-81; v.p., treas. Westminster Canterbury, Lynchburg, Va., 1981-89; pres. Westminster Canterbury of Blue Ridge, Charlottesville, Va., 1989—; faculty Am. Coll. Healthcare Adminstrn., Washington, 1982-84. Contbr. articles to profl. jours. Rep. del. to State Conv., Richmond, 1973. Fellow Am. Coll. Healthcare Adminstrs.; mem. Va. Assn. Non-Profit Homes for Aging (bd. dirs. 1983-84), S.R., Country Club of Va. (Richmond), Rotary. Republican. Episcopalian. Home: 407 Key West Dr Charlottesville VA 22911-8423 Office: Westminster Canterbury Blue Ridge 250 Pantops Mountain Rd Charlottesville VA 22911

HINOJOSA, FEDERICO CASAS, physician assistant; b. Taft, Tex., Oct. 23, 1942; s. Federico R. and Rebecca (Casas) H.; m. Georgeanna Zbuka, July 1, 1981 (div. Aug. 15, 1985); children: Rod, Derek, Angela. AA, L.A. City Coll., 1973; Cert. Physician Asst., UCLA, 1973. Lic. physician asst., Calif. Physician asst. Migrant Farmworkers Clinic, Brawley, Calif., 1973-74, Drew-UCLA Ambulatory Rev., L.A., 1974-75, Migrant Clinic, Toppenish, Wash., 1975-76; med. practice investigator Wash. State Lic. Dept., Olympia, 1976; family practice physician asst. Hanford (Calif.) Med. Clin., 1976-79; physician asst., indsl. medicine Fresno (Calif.) Indsl. Clinic, 1979-80; family practice physician asst. Zapanta Med. Group, Monterey Park, Calif., 1980-85, Casas Med. Clinic, W. Covina, Calif., 1986—. Pres. Flying Doctor's Orgn., 1985, vol. relief effort for Mexico earthquake, 1985. With U.S. Army, 1960-66, Germany, Korea, Vietnam. Home: 1419 Apollo West Covina CA 91790 Office: Casas Med Clin 1901 W Bavillo West Covina CA 91790

HINOJOSA, RAUL, physician, ear pathology researcher; b. Tampico, Tamulipas, Mexico, June 18, 1928; came to U.S., 1962, naturalized, 1968; s. Raul Hinojosa-Flores and Melida (Prieto) Hinojosa; m. Berta Ojeda, Sept. 25, 1953; children—Berta Elena, Raul Andres, Jorge Alberto, María de Lourdes. B.S. in Biology, Inst. Sci. and Tech., Tampico, 1946; M.D., Nat. Autonomous U. Mexico, Mexico City, 1954. Asst. prof. U. Chgo, 1962-68, assoc. prof., 1968—, dir. temporal bone program for ear rsch., 1962—, rsch. assoc., 1968-88; rsch. fellow biophysics Harvard U., Boston, 1963; rsch. assoc. in neuropathology, Harvard U., 1964, rsch. fellow in anatomy, 1965. Editor temporal bone histopathology update Am. Jour. of Otolaryngology, 1989-94. Recipient Rsch. Career Devel. award NIH, 1962-65, rsch. grantee, 1962—, hearing rsch. study sect. grantee, 1988-92. Mem. AAAS, Microscopy Soc. Am., Midwest Soc. Electron Microscopists, Assn. Rsch. in Otolaryngology, Am. Otological Soc., N.Y. Acad. Scis. Home: 5316 S Hyde Park Blvd Chicago IL 60615-5706 Office: U Chgo 5841 S Maryland Ave Chicago IL 60637-1463

HINSHAW, ADA SUE, health facility administrator; b. Arkansas City, Kans., May 20, 1939; d. Oscar A. and Georgia Ruth (Tucker) Cox; children: Cynthia Lynn, Scott Allen Lewis. BS, U. Kans., 1961; MSN, Yale U., 1963; MA, U. Ariz., 1973, PhD, 1975; DSc (hon.), U. Md., 1988, Med. Coll. of Ohio, 1988, Marquette U., 1990, U. Nebr., 1992; D Sci. (hon.), Mount Sinai Med. Ctr. Instr. Sch. Nursing U. Kans., 1963-66; asst. prof. U. Calif., San Francisco, 1966-71; prof. U. Ariz., Tucson, 1975-87; dir. nursing rsch. U. Med. Ctr., Tucson, 1975-87; dir. Nat. Inst. Nursing Rsch. Pub. Health Svc., Dept. Health and Human Svcs., NIH, Washington, 1987—. Contbd. articles to profl. jours. Recipient Kay Schilter award U. Kans., 1961, Lucille Petry Leone award Nat. League for Nursing, 1971, Wolanin Geriatric Nursing Rsch. award U. Ariz., 1978, Alumni of the Yr award Sch. Nursing U. Kans., 1981, Disting. Alumni award Sch. Nursing Yale U., 1981, Alumni Achievement award U. Ariz., 1990, Disting. citation Kans. Alumni Assn., 1992, Health Leader of the Yr. award PHS, 1993, Centennial award Columbia Sch. Nursing, 1993. Mem. ANA (Nurse Scientist of the Yr. award 1985), Coun. on Nursing Rschrs. (Nurse Scientist of the Yr. award 1985), Md. Nurses Assn., Western Soc. for Rsch. in Nursing, Am. Acad. Nursing, Nat. Acad. Practice, Inst. Medicine, Sigma Xi, Sigma Theta Tau (Beta Mu Chpt. award of Excellence in Nursing Edn., 1980, Elizabeth McWilliams Miller award, 1987), Alpha Chi Omega. *

HINSHAW, DAVID B., SR., hospital administrator; b. 1923. Grad., Loma Linda U., 1947, post grad., 1947-48. Intern White Meml. Hosp., L.A., 1946-47; resident gen. and vascular surgery VA Hosp., U. Oreg., 1950-54; pvt. practice, 1954—; instr. Sch. Medicine, Loma Linda U., Calif., 1954-83; pres. Loma Linda Faculty Med. Group, 1973—, Adventist Health System Loma Linda Inc., Loma Linda, Calif., 1982—, Loma Linda U. Med. Ctr., Calif., 1983—, Loma Linda Mecantile Inc., Loma Linda, Calif., 1988—. With U.S. Army, 1948-50. Office: Loma Linda U Med Ctr PO Box 2000 Loma Linda CA 92354-0200*

HINSHAW, DAVID B., JR., radiologist; b. L.A., Dec. 28, 1945; s. David B. Sr. and Mildred H. (Benjamin) H.; m. Marcia M. Johns, Aug. 7, 1966; children: Amy, John. BA in German and Pre Medicine, Loma Linda U., Riverside, Calif., 1967; MD, Loma Linda U., 1971. Diplomate Am. Bd. Radiology in diagnostic radiology and neuroradiology. Intern Loma Linda U. Med. Ctr., 1971-72, resident diagnostic radiology, 1972-74; neuroradiologist 2d Gen. Army Hosp., Landstuhl, Fed. Republic Germany, 1975-77; asst. prof. Loma Linda U. Sch. Medicine, 1975-80, assoc. prof., 1981-85, prof., 1986—, vice chmn. dept. radiation scis., 1988-90, chmn. dept. radiology, 1990—; pres. med. staff Loma Linda U. Med. Ctr., 1994-95; dir. sect. magnetic resonance imaging, Loma Linda, 1983—; cons. U.S. Army Med. command, Europe, 1976-77, Jerry L . Pettis Meml. VA Hosp., 1980—. Contbr. numerous articles to profl. jours., book chpts. in field of radiology. Maj. U.S. Army, 1975-77. Recipient Pres's. award Loma Linda U., 1971, Donald E. Grggs award Internal Med. Fellow Am. Coll. Radiology, Walter

E. McPherson Soc. (Outstanding Faculty Research award 1987); mem. AMA (Physicians Recognition award 1980-83, 84—), Am. Soc. Neuroradiology (sr., program com. 1989, chmn. pub. rels. com. 1989-90), Western Neuroradiol. Soc., Radiol. Soc. N.Am., Calif. Med. Assn., San Bernadino County Med. Assn., Inland Radiol. Soc. (pres. 1989-90), Calif. Radiol. Soc., Assn. Univ. Radiologists, Soc. Magnetic Resonance Imaging, Soc. Magnetic Resonance in Medicine, Fedn. Western Socs. Neurol. Scis., Am. Roentgen Ray Soc., Am. Soc. Head and Neck Radiology, L.A. Radiol. Soc., Soc. Chmn. Acad. Radiology Depts., Alpha Omega Alpha (pres. Epsilon chpt. 1987). Republican. Seventh-day Adventist. Office: Loma Linda U Med Ctr Dept Radiology 11234 Anderson St Loma Linda CA 92354-2804

HINSON, JACK ALLSBROOK, research toxicologist, educator; b. Mullins, S.C., Aug. 18, 1944; s. Layton Liston and Will (Allsbrook) H.; m. Joanne Edwards Kidd; children: Edward Thomas, Richard William. BS, Coll. of Charleston, 1966; MS, U. S.C., 1968; PhD, Vanderbilt U., 1972. Postdoctoral fellow Nat. Inst. of Health, Bethesda, Md., 1972-75, sr. staff fellow, 1975-80; rsch. toxicologist Nat. Ctr. Toxicological Rsch., Jefferson, Ark., 1980-90, chief biochem. mechanisms br., 1989-90; adj. prof. U. Ark. Med. Sci., Little Rock, 1980-90; prof., dir. div. toxicology U. Ark. Med. Sci., Little Rock, 1990—; dir. interdisciplinary toxicology program, occupational and environ. health program U. Ark. Med. Sci., 1990—; chmn. Ark. Toxicology Symposium, 1992—; adj. assoc. prof. U. Tenn. Ctr. for Health Scis., Memphis, 1982-90; vis. fellow Middlesex Hops. Med. Sch., London, 1982; vis. prof. U. Leiden, The Netherlands, 1986. Contbr. chpts. to books and articles to profl. jours. Mem. Soc. Toxicology (pres. South Ctrl. chpt. 1990-92), Am. Soc. Pharmacology and Exptl. Therapeutics, Internat. Soc. for Study of Xenobiotics, Am. Indsl. Hygiene Assn. Episcopalian. Home: 8 Piedmont Ln Little Rock AR 72212-2232 Office: U Ark Med Sci Divsn Toxicology 4301 W Markham Slot 638 Little Rock AR 72205

HINSON, PHILLIP WADE, pharmacist; b. Lancaster, S.C., Apr. 22, 1957; s. Wade Croxton and Lois Marian (Hunter) H.; m. Deborah Jean Taylor, Sept. 7, 1985; children: Daniel Wade, Lauren Taylor. BS, U. S.C., 1980. Registered pharmacist, S.C. Asst. mgr. Revco D.S., Inc., Pageland, S.C., 1980-84, Lancaster, S.C., 1984; staff pharmacist Springs Meml. Hosp., Lancaster, S.C., 1984-90, asst. dir. pharmacy, 1991—. Vice pres. bd. dirs. Palmetto Citizens Against Sexual Assault, Lancaster, Chester, and Fairfield Counties, 1990-92, pres. bd. dirs., 1992-94; bd. dirs. Lancaster Rape Crisis Ctr., 1988-90. Mem. Sixth Dist. Pharm. Assn. (pres. 1989, v.p. 1988), Carolina Gamecock Club. Baptist. Office: Springs Meml Hosp 800 W Meeting St Lancaster SC 29720-2202

HINSON, WAYMON RAY, psychology educator; b. Cleveland, Tex., Oct. 3, 1949; s. James Luther and Bula Mae (Vann) H.; m. Charla Sue Nichols, May 22, 1970; children: Joshua Don, Micah Paul. BA, Lubbock Christian Coll., 1972; MTh, Harding Grad. Sch., Memphis, 1976; PhD, U. Miss., 1982. Youth minister North Loop Ch. of Christ, El Paso, Tex., 1976-77, White Station Ch. of Christ, Memphis, 1977-82; counselor Memphis Counseling Ctr., 1980-82; intern psychology Psychol. Assocs., Parkersburg, W.Va., 1983-84; dean students Ohio Valley Coll., Parkersburg, 1982-84; prof., chair dept. marriage and family therapy Abilene (Tex.) Christian U., 1984—; psychologist Big Country Family Therapy Assocs., Abilene, 1985—. Editor Teenage Christian Mag., 1980-82. Com. mem. Abilene Mental Health-Mental Retardation Ctr., 1987; bd. mem. West Tex. Boys Ranch, San Angelo, 1988-90. Named Outstanding Faculty Mem. Coll. Bibl. Studies, Abilene Christian U., 1991. Mem. APA, Am. Assn. Marriage and Family Therapy (approved supr.), Tex. Assn. Marriage and Family Therapy (chair ethics. com. 1990, strategic planninc com. 1994, bd. dirs. 1994—), Christian Assn. Psychol. Studies, Tex. Psychol. Assn. Home: 810 Canyon Ct Abilene TX 79601-5412 Office: Abilene Christian U PO Box 8444 Abilene TX 79699

HIPP, LARRY LEE, medical association administrator; b. Holgate, Ohio, Oct. 1, 1936; s. Raymond H. and Marvelle M. (Rettig) H.; m. Julia Heidorn, Sept. 23, 1962; children: Anthony, Eric, Karen. BSc, Ohio State U., 1958, MD, 1962, MSc, 1970. Diplomate Am. Bd. Preventive Medicine; bd. cert. occupl. medicine. Intern Denver Presbyn. Hosp., 1962-63; pvt. practice Granville, Ohio, 1965-68; resident Ohio State U., Columbus, 1968-70; assoc. med. dir. Western Elec. Mfg. and Devel. Ctr., Columbus, 1970; med. dir. Hawthorne Works Western Elec., Chgo., 1970-78; assoc. gen. med. dir. Western Elec. Corp., Greensboro, N.C., 1978-85; pvt. practice cons. occupl. medicine Greensboro, 1985-87; med. dir. Works Western Elec., Columbus, 1987-89; corp. med. dir. AT&T, Basking Ridge, N.J., 1989-96; v.p. for managed care Joint Commn. for Accreditation of Healthcare Orgn., Oakbrook Terrace, Ill., 1996—; bd. dirs. FACCT, Portland, Oreg. Contbr. articles to profl. jours. Major USPHS, 1963-65, Shiprock, N.Mex. Fellow Am. Coll. Preventive Medicine, Am. Coll. Occupl. and Environ. Medicine; mem. Am. Coll. Physician Execs. Home: 2543 Monticello Pl Westchester IL 60154 Office: Joint Commn for Accreditation Healthcare Orgn One Renaissance Blvd Oakbrook Terrace IL 60181

HIPPE, ERNST ERIK DURELL, hematologist, educator; b. Frederiksberg, Denmark, Feb. 12, 1939; s. Ernst Edvin Durell and Iris Margit (Christoffersen) H.; m. Elisabeth Winkel, June 16, 1962; children: Martin, Merete, Pernille. MD, U. Copenhagen, 1964, DMS, 1973. Specialist in internal medicine, haematology. Resident Torsby Hosp., Sweden, 1964-65, Naestved Hosp., Denmark, 1965-67; sr. resident Glostrup Hosp., Denmark, 1967-68, Bispebjerg Hosp., Copenhagen, 1968-76; head dept. internal medicine Gentofte Hosp., Copenhagen, 1976-91; cons. dept. haematology Herlev Hosp., Copenhagen, 1992—; med. adviser Medi-Lab., Copenhagen, 1970-74, Test Ctr. Health, Copenhagen, 1988-91; asst. prof., lectr. internal medicine U. Copenhagen, 1984—, dir. Med. Sch., 1993—. Author: Akutte Medicinske Tilstande, 4th edit., 1990, Laboratorie Undersogeler, 2d edit., 1995; contbr. numerous articles to profl. jours. Named Best Tchr. of Yr. Faculty Medicine Copenhagen County, 1991, 95. Mem. Danish Soc. Haematology (bd. dirs. 1975-78, 93—). Office: Herlev Hosp, Dept Haematology, 2730 Herlev Denmark

HIRAI, DENITSU, surgeon; b. Yokkaichi, Mie, Japan, July 27, 1943; came to U.S. 1969; s. Denyomu and Shizuo (Tanaka) H.; m. Fumiko Hada, June 14, 1969; 1 child, R. Lisa. MD, U. Tokyo, 1968. Diplomate Am. Bd. Surgery, Am. Bd. Quality Assurance and Utilization Review Physicians, Am. Bd. Surg. Critical Care. Intern and residency Waterbury (Conn.) Hosp., 1969-74; fellow Mt. Sinai Hosp., 1974-75; asst. chief surgery VA Med. Ctr., Lincoln, Nebr., 1975-80; chief surgery VA Med. Ctr., Lincoln, 1981—; asst. clin. prof. surgery Creighton U., Omaha, 1982-84, asst. prof. surgery, 1984—; clin. instr. U. Nebr., Omaha, 1986-88, clin. asst. prof. surgery, 1988—. Author: Brain Ticklers (Japanese), 1983. Mem. AAAS, AMA, ACS, Am. Soc. Parenteral and Enteral Nutrition, Soc. Am. Gastrointestinal Endoscopic Surgeons, Southwestern Surg. Congress, Soc. Critical Care Medicine, Assn. VA Surgeons. Office: VA Med Ctr 600 S 70th St Lincoln NE 68510-2451

HIRANO, ARLENE AKIKO, neurobiologist, research scientist; b. L.A., Oct. 24, 1962; d. Yasuo and Toyoko (Fujimori) H. BS, U. Calif., Irvine, 1984; PhD, Rockefeller U., 1991. Grad. fellow Rockefeller U., N.Y.C., 1984-91, postdoctoral fellow, 1991; rsch. assoc., postdoctoral fellow Cornell U. Med. Coll., N.Y.C., 1991—. Recipient Nat. Rsch. Svc. award USPHS, 1984-90, Excellence in Rsch. award U. Calif., Irvine, 1984, Postdoctoral Nat. Rsch. Svc. award Nat. Eye Inst., 1993-95; Regents scholar U. Calif., Irvine, 1980-84; Lucille P. Markey Charitable Trust fellow, 1984-90, Rockefeller U. fellow, 1984-91, David Warfield fellow in Ophthalmology, N.Y. Cmty. Trust/N.Y. Acad. Medicine. Mem. AAAS, Soc. for Neuroscience. Office: Cornell Univ Med Coll 1300 York Ave New York NY 10021-4805

HIRANO, ASAO, neuropathologist; b. Tomioka, Gunma, Japan, Nov. 26, 1926; s. Yoshiro and Miyoe Hirano; m. Keiko Okubo, May 23, 1959; children—Michio, Ikuo, Yoko, Shigeo. B.D., Kyoto U., 1952. Chief resident neurology Montefiore Hosp., Bronx, 1957-58; vis. scientist NIH, 1959-65; head div. neuropathology Montefiore Med. Ctr., Bronx, 1965—, Harry M. Zimmerman prof. neuropathology, 1995; prof. pathology Albert Einstein Coll. Medicine, 1971—, prof. neurosci., 1974—; vis. prof. Kansai Med. U., Osaka, Japan, 1985, Nippon Med. Sch., Tokyo, 1993. Author: A Guide to Neuropathology, 1981, Metastatic Tumors of the Nervous Systems, 1982, Color Atlas of Neuropathology, 1988; editor: Neuropsychiatric Disorders in the Elderly, 1983, Patholoy of the Myelinated Axon, 1985; mem. internat. editorial bd. Sec. 5 Excerpta Medica, 1976—; mem. editorial com. Neurol. Medicine, 1978—; mem. adv. bd. Jour. Neuropathology and Exptl. Neurology, 1971-81, mem. editorial bd., 1981-84; mem. editorial bd. Progress in Computerized Tomography, 1978—, Annals of Neurology, 1983-89, Acta Neuropathologica (mem. editorial bd.), 1991—; mem. adv. bd. Clinical Neuropathology, 1982—, Neuropathology and Applied Neurobiology, 1983—; hon. editor Brain Tumor Pathology, 1993—, Neuropathology, 1994—. Recipient Billings Silver medal AMA, 1959, Key to Osaka City, Japan, 1977, Royal Coll. Lectr. award Can. Assn. Neuropathologists, Royal Coll. Physicians and Surgeons Can., 1980, 1st Jack Prichard Meml. Lectr. award Queen's U., Belfast, 1981, 1st Endowment Lectr. of Neuropathology in memory of Mrs. Rajan Bharati and 150th Yr. Celebration of Madras Med. Coll., 1984, Commendation award Hon. Ben Blaz, 1992, Plaque, U.S. Ho. Reps., 1992. Mem. Am. Assn. Neuropathologists (pres. 1977-78, Weil award 1968, award for meritorious contbn. to neuropathology 1995), Am. Neurol. Assn., Assn. for Rsch. in Nervous and Mental Diseases, Am. Soc. Cell Biology, Internat. Soc. Neuropathology, Am. Acad. Neurology (assoc.), Japanese Neuropathol. Assn. (councilor 1984—), Western Pacific Neurol. Soc. (hon.), Australian and New Zealand Soc. for Neuropathology (hon.), Brit. Neuropathologists, World Fedn. Neurology (rsch. com. 1978), Japanese Soc. Neurosurgery, (sr. mem.), Japanese Soc. Neurology (hon.). Office: Montefiore Med Ctr 111 E 210th St Bronx NY 10467-2490

HIRAYAMA, CHISATO, retired healthcare facility administrator, physician, educator; b. Kajiki, Kagoshima, Japan, Nov. 6, 1923; s. Shigeki and Hide (Kokusho) H.; m. Utako Nishimura June 10, 1989; children from previous marriage: Toko, Tomoo. M.D., Kyushu U., Fukuoka, Japan, 1947, Ph.D., 1956. Intern Kyushu U. Hosp.; asst. Kyushu U., 1953-62, asst. prof., 1962-66, assoc. prof., 1966-76; prof. medicine Tottori U., Yonago, Tottori, Japan, 1976-89 , dean Sch. Medicine, 1986-88 ; dir. Tottori U. Hosp., 1984-86; dir. Saiseikai Gotsu Hosp., Gotsu, Shimane, Japan, 1989-95. Author: Diseases of the Liver, 1977; editor: Plasma Proteins, 1979; Treatment of Hepatobiliary Diseases, 1980; Pathobiology of Hepatic Fibrosis, 1985. Recipient prize Japan Soc. Electrophoresis, 1968. Fellow Japan Soc. Internal Medicine (bd. dirs. 1985-87), Japan Soc. Gastroenterology; mem. Japan Soc. Hepatology (dir. 1980-88), Internat. Assn. Study Liver, N.Y. Acad. Scis.

HIRES, WILLIAM LELAND, psychologist, consultant; b. South Orange, N.J., July 5, 1918; s. Harrison Streeter and Christine B. (Leland) H.; m. Karen Reynolds Perrott, July 12, 1975; 1 child, Jennifer Leland. BS, Haverford Coll., 1949; PhD, U. Pa., 1972. Asst. to dean of admissions, asst. dir of scholarships U. Pa., 1952-55; supr. psychol. svcs., spl. classes, asst. supt. Office Supt. Chester County (Pa.) Schs., 1956-59; assoc. prof. West Chester Coll., 1960-61; adminstrv. asst. Office of Pres., asst. to sec. U. Pa., 1961-64; assoc. Edward N. Hay & Assocs., 1964-65; asst. supt. pub. schs. Chester County, 1966-68, pvt. cons., 1968-75; dir. diagnostic and consultative svc. Chester County Intermediate Unit, 1975-76, pvt. practice psychology, 1976-78; dir. pupil svcs. Upper Darby (Pa.) Sch. Dist., 1978-81; dean acad. studies Curtis Inst. Music, Phila., 1981-86; ptnr. Hires Assocs., Phila., 1987—. With USMC, 1942-46; with AUS, 1941-42, 50-52; lt. col. AUS ret.; col. Pa. Army N.G. ret. Mem. AAAS, APA, Soc. of Cin. (bd. dirs.), Welcome Soc., Geneal. Soc. Pa., Hist. Soc. Pa. (bd. dirs.), 1st Troop Phila. City Cavalry (hon.), Soc. Colonial Wars Pa. (bd. dirs.), Harvard Club, Penn Club (bd. dirs.), Phila. Club, Merion Cricket Club, The Rabbit.

HIRN, DORIS DREYER, health service administrator; b. N.Y.C., Dec. 3, 1933; d. James Howard and Dorothy Van Nostrand (Young) Dreyer; student Colby Jr. Coll., 1950-51, Hofstra U., 1953-56; m. John D. Hirn, Oct. 27, 1956; children—Deborah Lynn, Robert William. Owner, Dutchlands Farm, Albany, N.Y., 1957-62, Hickory Hill Farm, Galena, Ill., 1965-75; adminstr. Home Health Service, Chgo., 1972-74, exec. dir. Suburban Home Health Service, 1974-87; exec. dir. Home Health Svc. Chgo. North, 1987-95; v.p., pub. Caregivers Inc., 1995—; exec. dir. Columbia Home Care, 1996—; ptnr. Candor Assocs.; pres. Hirn Assocs. Ltd.; dir. Nat. Health Delivery Systems, Serengeti Prodns., Inc.; bd. dirs. Lifeline Pilots, Inc., NAHC, Fin. Mgrs. Forum, Ill. Long Term Task Force, Ill. Homecare Coun., BBH Assocs., Inc. Author: Survey Process in Home Health Manual; contbr. nat. seminars on quality assurance, rehab., long term care, reimbursement legislation; also articles to Caring Mag., Elder Svcs. Directory, Jour. Am. Geriatric Soc. Served with WAVES, 1951-52. Recipient Ill. Govs. award for Excellence Home Care Agy., 1989. Mem. ICHA, Nat. Assn. Home Care. Clubs: Chgo. Yacht. Home: 5747 N Sheridan Rd Chicago IL 60660-4755

HIRNLE, PETER, gynecologist, obstetrician, radiation oncologist, cancer researcher; b. Aug. 29, 1953; 1 child, Christoph. MD, Bonn (Germany) U., 1983; PhD, Tübingen (Germany) U., 1991. Cert. Med. Sci. Project leader U. Bonn Konrad-Adenauer Grant, 1982-83, U. Tübingen Mildred Scheel Grant, 1983-88; head lymphol. lab. U. Tübingen; assoc. prof. gynecology U. Tübingen, 1991—. Author: (with others) Lymph Stasis, 1991; chief editor: Our Opinion, Wroclaw, 1981; co-editor: Lymphology, European Jour. Lymphology and Related Problems; contbr. articles to profl. jours. German Rsch. Soc. grantee Tübingen, 1985, Erwin Riesch grantee Tübingen, 1988. Mem. AAAS, Am. Assn. Cancer Rsch., European Soc. Therapeutic Radiology and Oncology, Internat. Soc. Lymphology, N.Y. Acad. Scis., others. Roman Catholic. Home: Ursrainer Ring 104, 72076 Tübingen Germany Office: Dept Gynecology, U Schleichstrasse 4, 72076 Tübingen Germany

HIROSE, MUNETAKA, anesthesiologist; b. Kyoto, Japan, Mar. 9, 1962; s. Nobuhiko and Kazuko (Hiiragi) H.; m. Junko Kawanishi; children: Yuina Hirose. MD, Kyoto Prefectural U. Medicine, 1987, PhD, 1993. Diplomate Japanese Bd. Anesthesiology. Resident Kyoto Prefectural U. Medicine, 1987-88, Kyoto 1st Red Cross Hosp., 1988-89; chief anesthesiologist Maizuru Nat. Hosp., Kyoto, 1993-95; staff anesthesiologist Kyoto Prefectural U. Medicine, 1995-96, chief anesthesiologist, 1996—; rsch. fellow Mass. Gen. Hosp., Boston, 1992-93. Contbr. articles to med. jours. Mem. Japan Soc. Pain Clinicians (diplomate), Japan Soc. Anesthesiologists, Am. Soc. Anesthesiologists. Home: 3-4-6 Minegadc-cho Goryo, 610-11 Nishikyoku Kyoto, Japan Office: Kyoto Prefec U Medicine, Dept Anesthesiology, 602 Kamigyoku Kyoto, Japan

HIRSCH, GLENN STUART, psychiatrist; b. N.Y.C., Apr. 30, 1954; s. Harry N. and Lee (Kessler) H.; m. Reva J. Eisenberg, Feb. 19, 1977; children: Melanie, Jesse, Jamie, Sabrina, Emily. BA, Yeshiva U., 1975, MD, 1979. Diplomate Am. Bd. Psychiatry and Neurology, Am. Bd. Child Psychiatry. Resident in psychiatry N.Y. Hosp. Westchester, White Plains, N.Y., 1979-82; fellow in child psychiatry Columbia Presbyn. Med. Ctr., N.Y.C., 1982-84; asst. unit chief Hillside Hosp., Glen Oaks, N.Y., 1984-85, unit chief, 1985-88; child and adolescent psychiatrist Schneider Children's Hosp., New Hyde Park, N.Y., 1988-96; asst. prof. clin. psychiatry NYU Sch. of Medicine, 1996—; dep. dir. divsn. child & adolescent psychiatry NYU Med. Ctr., 1996—; physician in charge ambulatory svcs. L.I. Jewish Med. Ctr., New Hyde Park, 1988-96; asst. prof. psychiatry Albert Einstein Coll. Medicine. Author: (with others) Handbook of Clinical Assessment of Children and Adolescents, 1988. Mem. Am. Psychiatric Assn., Am. Acad. Child and Adolescent Psychiatry, N.Y. Coun. on Child Psychiatry. Jewish. Office: NYU Med Ctr 550 First Ave NB21E7 New York NY 10016

HIRSCH, HENRY DAVID, cardiologist; b. N.Y.C., Mar. 24, 1943. BS, U. Fla., 1964; MD, U. Miami, 1970. Diplomate Am. Bd. Internal Medicine, Am. Bd. Cardiovascular Disease, Am. Bd. Geriatrics. Intern, then resident Jackson Meml. Hosp., Miami, Fla., 1970-72; chief resident Jackson Meml. Hosp., 1972-73, fellow in cardiology, 1973-75; pvt. practice Hollywood, Fla., 1975—; clin. assoc. prof. medicine U. Miami, 1984-90, clin. prof. medicine, 1990—. Fellow Am. Coll. Cardiology, Council on Clin. Cardiology Am. Heart Assn., Am. Coll. Chest Physicians; founding mem. Council on Geriatric Cardiology Am. Coll. Cardiology; mem. Am. Coll. Physicians. Office: Internal Medicine Assocs 750 S Federal Hwy Hollywood FL 33020-5424

HIRSCH, IRMA LOU KOLTERMAN, nurse, association administrator; b. Clay Center, Kans., June 11, 1934; d. Arthur Henry and Mildred (Peterson) Kolterman; m. William A. Hirsch, June 8, 1958; children: David William, Brian Duane. BS in Nursing, U. Kans., 1957; M in Nursing, U. Washington, Seattle, 1961. R.N. Mo. Instr. Duke U., Durham, N.C., 1961-64; nurse clinician U. Kans. Med. Ctr., Kansas City, 1968-70; project dir., cons. Mo. Regional Med. Program, Kansas City, 1970-74; project dir., program coordinator Am. Nurses' Assn., Kansas City, 1974-79, policy devel., 1981-92; supr. VA Med. Ctr., Kansas City, 1979-81; dept. dir., 1981-83, policy devel., 1983-92; cons. nursing edn. Joint Commn. on Accreditation of Hosps., Chgo., 1973; cons. for project devel. Am. Nurses Found., Kansas City, 1974; cons. nursing standards Health Standards Directorate, Ottawa, Ont., Can., 1978, Mid-Am. Coalition on Health Care, 1993—. Editor: Guidelines for Review of Nursing Care at the Local Level, 1976, Nursing Quality Assurance Management/Learning System, 1982, Peer Review in Nursing, 1982, Issues in Professional Practice, 1985, Classification Systems for Describing Nursing Practice, 1989. Mem. Friends of Art, Kansas City, 1975—, Internat. Relations Council, Kansas City, 1980—, 2d Presbyn. Ch., Kansas City, elder, deacon, strategic planning chmn.; chpt. pres. Am. Field Svcs., Kansas City, 1978-79; mem. adv. com. Nancy Whalen Nursing Found., 1992—; mem. evaluation com. Heart Am. United Way, 1993—; trustee Presbyn. Manors Mid-Am., 1979-86, Kansas City Manor, 1992—, chair adv. com., 1995—, Nursing Heritage Found., 1994—, pres. 1995—. Mem. ANA (pres. Mo. dist. 1980-81), Kans. U. Nurses Alumni Assn. (pres. 1964-66), Sigma Theta Tau. Home: 1035 W 57th Ter Kansas City MO 64113-1163

HIRSCH, JAY G., psychiatrist, educator; b. Cleve., Aug. 6, 1930; s. Abe and Bertha (Gusman) H.; m. Renee B. Schwartz, Oct. 10, 1962; children—Deborah, David, Lauren, Susan. B.S., U. Cin., 1950, M.D., 1954. Intern Phila. Gen. Hosp., 1954-55; resident U. Ill. Hosps., 1957-60; pvt. practice specializing in psychiatry and child psychiatry Chgo., 1960-70, Highland Park, Ill., 1970—; resident Inst. Juvenile Research, Chgo., 1960-62; research child psychiatrist Inst. Juvenile Research, 1962-66, chief div. preventive psychiatry, 1966-70; dir. Melampus Ltd.; mem. faculty U. Ill. Coll. Medicine, Chgo., 1959—, asso. prof. psychiatry, 1970-74, prof., 1974-95, prof. emeritus, 1995—; interim chief div. child and adolescent psychiatry U. Ill. Coll. Medicine, 1990-92, dir. edn. in child psychiatry and related disciplines, 1973-77; cons. to agys., schs.; mem. Ill. Mental Health Planning Bd., 1967-69, Ill. Comprehensive Health Planning Agy. Bd., 1971-74. Bd. editors Jour. Child Psychiatry, 1972-77; contbr. articles to profl. jours., chpts. to books. Vice pres. Kenneth P. Montgomery Found., Chgo., 1965-71; bd. dirs. Dr. Martin L. King Family Center, 1969-74, Urban Dynamics/ Inner City Fund, 1970-75. Served to capt. USAF, 1955-57. Fellow Am. Psychiat. Assn., Am. Acad. Child and Adolescent Psychiatry, Am. Orthopsychiat. Assn.; mem. AMA, AAAS, Phi Beta Kappa, Alpha Omega Alpha. Home: 591 Stonegate Ter Glencoe IL 60022-1435 Office: 1971 2d St Highland Park IL 60035-3134 also: U Ill Dept Psychiatry 912 S Wood St Chicago IL 60612

HIRSCH, JOSEPH ALLEN, neuropsychologist, psychologist; b. N.Y.C., Aug. 30, 1950; s. Robert Theodore and Gertrude (Bernstein) H.; 1 child, Jason Mathew; m. Karen Weinberg, Jan. 1995. BS in Chemistry, Bklyn. Coll., 1972; BS in Pharmacy summa cum laude, Columbia U., 1975; PhD in Pharmacology, Downstate Med. Ctr., Bklyn., 1979; cert. in counseling, Postgrad. Ctr. Mental Health, 1989; postgrad., Psychotherapy Study Ctr., 1989-91; MS in Edn. in Psychology, Pace U., 1993, PsyD in Psychology, 1995. Diplomate Am. Bd. Forensic Examiners; lic. pharmacist; cert. counselor. Postdoctoral fellow neurosci. MIT, Cambridge, Mass., 1979-81; rsch. assoc. neurosci. Med. Coll. Cornell U., N.Y.C., 1981-83; asst. prof. St. John's U., Jamaica, N.Y., 1984-88; sr. editor McGraw Hill, N.Y.C., 1988-89; dir. profl. rels. Park Row Pubs., N.Y.C., 1989-91; assoc. prof. N.Y. Coll. Podiatric Medicine, N.Y.C., 1991-92; adj. asst. prof. then assoc. prof. L.I. U., Bklyn., 1984—; adj. asst. prof. Coll. of Dentistry, NYU, N.Y.C., 1989—; intern, extern in neuropsychology Hosp. for Joint Diseases, N.Y.C., 1993-95; adj. asst. prof. Coll. of Dentistry, NYU, N.Y.C., 1989—; adj. instr. psychology Pace U., N.Y.C., 1991—, adj. assoc. prof. biology and psychology, 1993—, postdoctoral fellow neuropsychology Comprehensive Epilepsy Ctr., Hosp. Joint Diseases, 1995-96; adj. prof. Western scis. New Ctr. for Wholistic Health Edn. and Rsch., Syosett, N.Y., 1994—. Freelance med. writer; contbr. articles to profl. jours. in neuropsychology. Recipient award for excellence in pharmacology Merck Sharp and Dohme, 1975, Florence L. Denmark Grad. Rsch. award, 1995. Fellow Prescribing Psychologists' Register (mem. profl. adv. bd., mem. curriculum devel. com.); mem. APS, APA, AAAS, N.Y. Acad. Sci., Am. Orthopsychiat. Assn., Am. Psychol. Soc., N.Y. Neuropsychology Group, Internat. Platform Assn., Psi Chi. Office: Pace U Dept Psychology 41 Park Row New York NY 10038-1508

HIRSCH, JULES, physician, scientist; b. N.Y.C., Apr. 6, 1927. Student, Rutgers U., 1943-45; MD, U. Tex., 1948; DSc (hon.), SUNY, 1988. Intern pathology and medicine Duke Hosp., N.C., 1948-50; from asst. resident to resident coll. medicine SUNY, Syracuse, 1950-52; asst. prof., assoc. physician Rockefeller U., N.Y.C., 1954-60, assoc. prof., physician, 1960-67, prof., sr. physician, 1967—; Sherman Fairchild prof. Rockefeller U., 1988—; physician-in-chief Rockefeller U. Hosp., 1992-96. Recipient Robert H. Herman award, 1994, McCollum award, 1984. Fellow Royal Coll. Physicians Edinburgh; mem. AAAS, NAS (Inst. Medicine), Am. Soc. Clin. Investigation, Am. Soc. Clin. Nutrition, Assn. Am. Physicians, Am. Fedn. Clin. Rsch., Harvey Soc. Office: Rockefeller U 1230 York Ave New York NY 10021-6399

HIRSCH, LORE, psychiatrist; b. Mannheim, Fed. Republic of Germany, July 8, 1908; came to U.S., 1940; d. Erwin Hirsch and Marie Kiefe; m. Eugene Hesz, Jan. 25, 1958 (div. Oct. 1968). MD, Karl Ruprecht U., Heidelberg, Fed. Republic Germany, 1937. Diplomate Am. Bd. Neurology and Psychiatry. Intern Greenpoint Hosp., Bklyn., 1942-43; resident Bellvue Hosp., N.Y.C., 1943-48; sect. chief VA Hosp., Bronx, N.Y., 1949-54; dir. psychiatry Wayne County Gen. Hosp., Mich., 1954-55; dir. outpatient services Northville (Mich.) Regional Hosp., 1955-58; practice medicine specializing in psychiatry Dearborn, 1958—. Contbr. numerous articles to profl. jours. Fellow Am. Psychiat. Assn. (life); mem. AMA (life), Mich. Med. Soc., Wayne County Med. Soc., Mich. Psychiat. Soc. Unitarian-Universalist. Home: 212 S Melborn St Dearborn MI 48124-1455 Office: 2021 Monroe St Dearborn MI 48124-2926

HIRSCH, PAUL J., orthopedic surgeon, educator; b. Bklyn., Oct. 12, 1937; s. Morris M. and Dorothy (Wolitzer) H.; 1 child, Jeremy S. BA in English, Roanoke Coll., 1957; MD, U. Va., 1961. Diplomate Am. Bd. Orthopedic Surgery. Intern NYU-Bellevue Med. Ctr., N.Y.C., 1961-62, resident, 1964-68; chief orthopedic surgery Raritan Valley Hosp., Green Brook, N.J., 1969-71; pvt. practice orthopedic surgery Bridgewater, N.J., 1971—; clin. prof. orthopaedic surgery Seton Hall Sch. Grad. Med. Edn.; pres. Orthopaedic Healthcare Network, Lawrenceville, N.J.; active staff, chief orthopaedic svc. Somerset (N.J.) Med. Ctr.; courtesy staff Robert Wood Johnson U. Hosp., New Brunswick, N.J.; clin. asst. prof. orthopedic surgery Rutgers Med. Sch., 1971-79; clin. instr. orthopedic surgery NYU-Bellevue Med. Ctr., 1969-79; clin. assoc. prof. orthopedic surgery N.J. Med. Sch., 1980—; clin. prof. orthopedic surgery Seton Hall Sch. Postgrad. Medicine; trustee, treas. Jour. Bone & Joint Surgery; mem. participating physicians adv. group Nat. Com. Quality Assurance. Chmn. publs. com. Jour. Med. Soc. N.J., 1980-85; contbr. articles, editor profl. jours.; mem. editorial bd. N.J. Medicine. Trustee Rutgers Prep. Sch., pres. bd. trustees, 1983-86; trustee Ruritan VAlley C.C.; bd. dirs. N.J. Med. Polit. Action Com., 1983—, chmn. N.J. Com. for Quality Orthopedic Care; bd. trustees Orthopaedic Rsch. and Edn. Found., 1989-94. Mem. ACS, AMA, Am. Orthopaedic Assn., Am. Acad. Orthopaedic Surgeons (bd. councilors 1982-88), Am. Coll. Physician Execs., Eastern Orthopaedic Assn. (trustee 1981-84), N.J. Orthopaedic Soc. (pres. 1979-80), Med. Soc. N.J. (chmn. orthopaedic sect. 1977-78, ho. of dels. 1976—, treas. 1982-86, 2d v.p. 1986-87, 1st v.p. 1987-88, pres. elect 1988-89, pres. 1989-90, trustee 1982-91), Somerset County Med. Soc., Acad. Medicine of N.J. (chmn. orthopaedic sect. 1975-78, trustee 1978-91, pres. elect 1982-83, pres. 1983-84), Am. Trauma Soc. (pres. ctrl. Jersey unit 1977-81), Internat. Soc. Orthopaedic Surgery and Traumatology, N.J. Health Scis. Group (treas. 1982-83), N.J. Hosp. Assn. (trustee 1986-89), N.J. Assn. Med. Splty. Socs. (pres. 1979-80, dir. 1981-85), Ind. Sch. Chmn. Assn., Med. Inter-Ins. Exch. N.J. (bd. govs. 1987-90), N.J. State Med. Underwriters, Inc. (bd. dirs. 1990—, vice chmn. bd. dirs. 1991—, bd. trustees Jour. Bone and Joint Surgery 1994—). Office: 720 US Highway 202 206 Bridgewater NJ 08807-1746

HIRSCH, PHILIP FRANCIS, pharmacologist, educator; b. Stockton, Calif., June 24, 1925; s. Harold and Elsa (Frohman) H.; m. Eugenia Isaeff, Sept. 21, 1956; children—Steven, Lisa, Kenny, Nancy. B.S. in Chemistry, U. Calif., Berkeley, 1950, Ph.D. in Physiology, 1954. Lectr. physiology U.

Calif., Berkeley, 1954-55; instr. pharmacology Sch. Dental Medicine, Harvard U., Boston, 1955-57; asso. in pharmacology Sch. Dental Medicine, Harvard U., 1957-63, asst. prof. pharmacology, 1964; physiologist Lawrence Livermore Lab., 1964-66; asso. prof. pharmacology Sch. Medicine, U. N.C., Chapel Hill, 1966-70; prof. Sch. Medicine, U. N.C., 1970-92; dir. dental research ctr. U. N.C., 1975-83, prof. dental ecology Sch. of Dentistry, 1988-92, prof. emeritus, 1992—; mem. gen. medicine B study sect. NIH, 1974-78, clin. scis. study section, 1981-85. Contbr. articles to profl. jours. Bd. dirs. YMCA, Chapel Hill, 1981-83. Served with AUS, 1943-46. Mem. AAAS, Am. Soc. for Bone and Mineral Rsch., Endocrine Soc., Am. Soc. Pharmacology and Exptl. Therapeutics, Sigma Xi. Home: 2008 S Lakeshore Dr Chapel Hill NC 27514-2031 Office: U NC Dental Research Ctr Cb # 7455 Chapel Hill NC 27599

HIRSCH, RONALD LAUREN, internist; b. Columbus, Ohio, Sept. 21, 1959; s. Rudolph Leopold and Betty (Richer) H.; divorced. BS, UCLA, 1982; MD, Chgo. Med. Sch., 1988. Diplomate Am. Bd. Internal Medicine. Asst. mgr. athletic ticket office UCLA, 1982-84; resident in internal medicine Kaiser Permanente Med. Ctr., L.A., 1988-91; pvt. practice, Lake in the Hills, Ill., 1991—; physician Bd. Health, Elgin. Mem. adv. bd. AIDS Support Coalition, Crystal Lake, Ill., 1992—; sec. exec. com. HIV Coalition, Mt. Prospect, Ill., 1994-95, bd. dirs., 1995-96. Fellow ACP. Office: Key Med Group 2250 W Algonquin Rd Ste 105 Lake in the Hills IL 60102

HIRSCHBERG, BESSE BRYNA, social worker; b. N.Y.C., Aug. 12; d. Sigmund and Lottie (Popick) H. BA, Hunter Coll.; postgrad. various including, Columbia U., Fordham U., Yale, U., Rutgers U., L.I. U., Cornell U., 1952-72. Cert. social worker, tchr., N.Y. Various to social worker and supr. social svc. caseworkers N.Y. City Dept. Social Svcs., 1965-76; cons. Community Svcs. and Resources, N.Y.C., 1976—; participant TV dramatizations and progs. in field; lectr./cons. in field. Recipient Personal citation Bronx Borough Pres., 1965, Outstanding Profl. Woman of Yr., Dist. I N.Y. State Bus. and Profl. Clubs, 1981. Mem. Am. Soc. Psychodrama and Group Therapy, North Am. Assn. Alcoholism Progs., N.Y. League of Bus. and Profl. Women (pres., other offices), others.

HIRSCHBERG, BRENDON COTTER, surgeon; b. San Diego, Nov. 23, 1945; . James Cotter and Jeanne (Parkison) H.; m. Shannon Lee Heft, June 8, 1968; childen: Ryan, Erin. BS, U. Redlands, 1967; MD, U. Kans., 1971. Diplomate Am. Bd. Surgery, Am. Bd. Critical Care Surgery. Commd. ensign USN, 1969, advanced through grades to capt., 1986; intern Maricopa Med. Ctr., Phoenix, 1971-72; gen. med. officer U.S. Navy, Yokosuka, Japan, 1972-75; gen. surgery resident USN, San Diego, 1975-79, staff surgeon, 1979-80; pvt. practice Flagstaff, Ariz., 1980—; ret. USN, 1991; bd. dirs. Mutual Ins. Co. of Ariz., Phoenix; chief of staff Flagstaff Med. Ctr., 1995; med. dir. Guardian Air Transport, Flagstaff, 1984—. Mng. ptnr. Physicians and Surgeons Bldg. Partnership, Flaggstaff, 1987—. Fellow ACS; mem. Soc. of Gen. Surgeons. Office: No Ariz Surg Assn 77 W Forest Ave #202 Flagstaff AZ 86001

HIRSCHFELD, ROBERT M.A., psychiatrist; b. Alexandria, La., Feb. 9, 1943. BS, MIT, Cambridge, 1964; MD, U. Mich., Ann Arbor, 1968; MS, Stanford (Calif.) U., 1972. Diplomate Am. Bd. Psychiatry & Neurology. Rsch. scientist NIMH, Rockville, Md., 1972-77, head depression sect., clin. rsch. br., 1977-78, chief ctr. for studies of affective disorders, Clin. Rsch. Branch, 1978-85, chief mood, anxiety & personality disorders rsch. branch, Divsn. Clin. Rsch., 1985-90; Titus Harris disting. prof. & chair, Dept. Psychiatry & Behavioral Scis. U. Tex. Med. Branch, Galveston, 1990—; mem. bd. dirs. Am. Suicide Found., N.Y., 1991—, v.p. 1995—; mem. bd. dirs. Anxiety Disorders Assn. Am., Washington D.C., 1990—, Nat. Depressive & Manic Depressive Assn., Chgo., 1989—. Recipient Adminstr's. award for meritorious achievement ADAMHA, 1979, Commd. Corps. Outstanding Svc. medal, 1987, Commendation medal Pub. Health Svc., 1990, Gerald Klerman award for panic disorder World Psychiatric Assn., 1993, Jan Fawcett Humanitarian award Nat. Depressive and Manic Depressive Assn., 1996. Fellow Am. Psychiat. Assn., Am. Coll. Psychiatry, Am. Coll. Neuropsychiatry; mem. Am. Assn. Chmn. Dept. of Psychiatry (chair rsch. com.). Office: U Tex Med Branch 301 University Blvd Galveston TX 77555

HIRSCHFIELD, ROBERT EDWARD, orthodontist; b. Cleve., Aug. 22, 1946; s. Harold R. and Ruth (Yanowitz) H.; m. Sheri Ann Suskin, Aug. 31, 1974; children: Jodi, Jennifer. DDS, Emory U., 1970; MS in Oral Biology, Case Western Res. U., 1972, cert. in orthodontics, 1972. Pvt. practice Miami, Fla., 1972—. Contbr. articles to profl. jours. Recipient Rsch. award Am. Soc. Dentistry for Children. Mem. Am. Assn. Orthodontists, ADA, U.S. Inst. for Orthodontics and Maxillofacial Rsch. and Edn. (pres. 1985—), South Fla. Acad. Orthodontics, West Dade Dental Soc. (editor), East Coast Dist. Dental Soc. (chmn. pub. edn.), Alpha Epsilon Upsilon. Office: 11545 N Kendall Dr Miami FL 33176

HIRSCHHORN, KURT, pediatrics educator; b. Vienna, Austria, May 18, 1926; came to U.S., 1940, naturalized, 1945; s. Emanuel and Helen (Mayberger) H.; m. Rochelle Reibman, Dec. 20, 1952; children—Melanie D., Lisa R., Joel N. Student, U. Pitts., 1944; B.A., N.Y. U., 1950, M.D., 1954, M.S. (Bergquist fellow), 1958. Intern Bellevue Hosp., N.Y.C., 1954-55; resident Bellevue Hosp., 1955-56; fellow N.Y. U., 1956-57, U. Upsala, Sweden, 1957-58; instr. N.Y. U. Sch. Medicine, 1956-58, asst. prof., 1958-63, asso. prof., 1963-66; Arthur J. and Nellie Z. Cohen prof. genetics and pediatrics Mt. Sinai Sch. Medicine, City U. N.Y., 1966-76, Herbert H. Lehman prof., chmn. pediatrics, 1977-95, prof. pediatrics and human genetics, 1995—; adj. prof. biology N.Y. U., 1966-74; Established investigator Am. Heart Assn., 1960-65; career scientist N.Y.C. Health Research Council, 1965-75. Author numerous sci. publs.; editor: (with Harry Harris) Advances in Human Genetics, 1969-95, (now with Robert J. Desnick) 1995—; editl. bd. 16 sci. jours. Mem. council Village Community Sch., 1968-73, chmn., 1972-73. Served with AUS, 1944-47. Recipient Rudolph Virchow medal, 1974, Alumni Achievement award NYU Sch. Medicine, 1982, Jacobi medallion Mt. Sina Med. Ctr., 1993, Wm. Allan award Am. Soc. Human Genetics, 1995. Fellow AAAS, Am. Acad. Pediats., N.Y. Acad. Medicine; mem. Inst. Medicine of NAS, Am. Coll. Med. Genetics, Am. Soc. Clin. Investigation, Am. Assn. Physicians, Am. Pediat. Soc., Am. Soc. Human Genetics (pres. 1969, dir. Allan award 1995, William Allan award 1995), Pediat. Travel Club, Am. Assn. Immunologists, Harvey Soc. (v.p. 1979-80, pres. 1980-81, coun. 1981-84), Genetics Soc. Am., Environ. Mutagen Soc. (coun. 1969-76), Am. Soc. Pediat. Chmn. (coun. 1983-86), Am. Cancer Soc. (coun. 1989-92), Alpha Omega Alpha, Phi Beta Kappa, Sigma Xi. Home: 29 Washington Sq W New York NY 10011-9180 Office: Mt Sinai Sch Medicine 1 Gustave L Levy Pl New York NY 10029-6504

HIRSCHHORN, ROCHELLE, genetics educator; b. Bklyn., Mar. 19, 1932; d. Hyman and Anna Reibman; m. Kurt Hirschhorn; children: Melanie D., Lisa R., Joel N. BA, Barnard Coll., 1953; MD, NYU, 1957. Intern NYU-Bellevue Med. Divsn., N.Y.C., 1958-59; rsch. fellow, teaching asst. NYU Sch. Medicine, N.Y.C., 1963-65, assoc. rsch. scientist, 1965-66, instr. in medicine, 1966-69, asst. prof. medicine, 1969-74, assoc. prof. medicine, 1974-79, prof. medicine, 1979—, head divsn. med. genetics, 1984—; hon. fellow Galton Lab. Human Genetics & Biometry Univ. Coll., London, 1971-72; assoc. attending physician in medicine Bellevue Hosp., N.Y.C., 1969-80, Univ. Hosp., NYU Sch. Medicine, 1974-81; attending physician Bellevue Hosp., 1980—, Univ. Hosp., 1981—; mem. numerous NIH coms. & study sects., 1973—; vis. prof. Harvard U., 1995, U. Calif. San Francisco, 1995. Senatur NYU Senate, mem. pediatrics search com., 1987-89, human subjects instl. rev. bd., 1989-94, co-dir. second year med. genetics course, 1989-93, NYU appointments and promotions com. 1995—; trustee AIDS Med. Found./AMFAR; judge Westinghouse Nat. Sci. Talent Search; founding mem. Village Cmty. Sch. Fellow AAAS, Am. Coll. Rheumatology, Am. Coll. Med. Genetics (founder); mem. NAS, Inst. Medicine, Am. Soc. for Clin. Investigation, Assn. Am. Physicians, Am. Assn. Immunologists, Am. Soc. Human Genetics (cert. 1987), Interurban Clin. Club (pres. 1987-88), Peripatetic Soc., Soc. for Inherited Metabolic Diseases, Harvey Soc. (coun. 1989-92), Alpha Omega Alpha (councillor Delta of N.Y. 1982—). Office: NYU Med Ctr 550 1st Ave New York NY 10016-6481

HIRSCHMANN, RALPH FRANZ, chemist; b. Fuerth, Bavaria, Germany, May 6, 1922; came to U.S., 1937; s. Carl and Alice (Buchenbacher) H.; m. Lucy Marguerite Aliminosa, Mar. 9, 1951; children—Ralph F., Carla M. Hirschmann Hummel. A.B., Oberlin Coll., 1943, D.Sc. (hon.), 1969; M.A., U. Wis., 1948, Ph.D., 1950. Asst. dir. Merck Sharp & Dohme Research Labs., Rahway, N.J., 1964-68, dir., 1968-71; sr. dir. Merck Sharp & Dohme Research Labs., West Point, Pa., 1972-74, exec. dir., 1974-76; v.p. Merck Sharp & Dohme Research Labs., Rahway, 1976-78, sr. v.p., 1978-87; research prof. chemistry U. Pa., Phila, 1987—; prof. biomed. research Med. U. S.C., Charleston, 1987-94, Makineni prof. bioorganic chemistry, 1994—; mem. N.J. Gov.'s Commn. on Sci. and Tech., 1984; mem. adv. com. NSF, 1985; mem. com. to survey opportunities in chem. scis. NRC, 1982; Romanes lectr. U. Edinburgh, Eng., 1985; Charles D. Hurd lectr. Northwestern U., 1985; mem. com. on chem. and pub. affairs Am. Chem. Soc. Contbr. numerous articles to profl. jours.; patentee in field. Trustee Oberline Coll., 1986-93. Served with U.S. Army, 1943-46, PTO. Recipient Nichols medal, 1988, Chem. Pioneer award Am. Inst. Chemists, 1992, Gold medal Max Bergman Kreis, 1993, Alfred Burger award Am. Chem. Soc., 1994. Fellow AAAS, ACS (Medicinal Chemistry award 1986, Carothers award Del. sect. 1994); mem. Am. Acad. Arts and Scis., Am. Soc. Biol. Chemists. Home: 740 Palmer Pl Blue Bell PA 19422-1725 Office: U Pa Dept Chemistry 231 S 34th St Philadelphia PA 19104-3803*

HIRSCHOWITZ, BASIL ISAAC, physician; b. Bethal, South Africa, May 29, 1925; came to U.S., 1953, naturalized, 1961; s. Morris and Dorothy (Drieband) H.; m. Barbara L. Burns, July 6, 1958; children: David E., Karen, Edward A., Vanessa. BSc, Witwatersrand U., Johannesburg, 1943, MB, B of Surgery, 1947, MD, 1954. Intern, resident Johannesburg Gen. Hosp., 1948-50; house physician Postgrad. Med. Sch., London, Eng., 1950; registrar Central Middlesex Hosp., London, 1951-53; instr., asst. prof. U. Mich., 1953-56; asst. prof. Temple U., 1957-59; assoc. prof. medicine U. Ala. Med. Center, Birmingham, 1959-64; prof. medicine U. Ala. Med. Ctr., 1964-95, emeritus prof., 1995; prof. physiology U. Ala. Med. Center, 1970—; Disting. faculty lectr. U. Ala., 1988; chmn. faculty coun. U. Ala. Sch. Medicine, 1989-90; dir. div. gastroenterology medicine U. Ala. Hosp. and Clinics, 1959-87; chmn. exec. com. U. Ala. Hosp., 1986-88. Recipient Charles F. Kettering Prize, Gen. Motors Cancer Found., 1987, Seale Harris award So. Med. Assn., 1992; named to Ala. Acad. Honor, 1991. Fellow AAAS, ACP (Laureate award 1989), Royal Coll. Physicians (Edinburgh), Royal Coll. Physicians (London), Royal Soc. Medicine (hon.), Royal Philatelic Soc., (London); mem. AMA, Assn. Am. Physicians (hon.), South African, Brit., Ala. Med. Assns., Med. Rsch. Soc. Gt. Britain, Am. Fedn. Clin. Rsch., So. Soc. Clin. Investigation, Am. Physiol. Soc., Biophys. Soc., Am. Gastroent. Assn. (Friedenwald medal 1992), Am. Soc. Gastro-Intestinal Endoscopy (Schindler medal 1974, Disting. lectr. 1994), Am. Coll. Gastroenterology (Disting. Sci. Achievement award 1982), Brit. Soc. Gastro-Intestinal Endoscopy (hon.), Brit. Soc. Gastroenterology (Founders lectr. 1988), Italian Soc. Gastroenterology (corr.), William Beaumont Soc. (Eddy Palmer award for contbns. to endoscopy 1976), Soc. Exptl. Biology and Medicine, Sigma Xi, Alpha Omega Alpha. Office: U Ala at Birmingham Med Ctr Birmingham AL 35294

HIRSCHY, JAMES CONRAD, radiologist; b. Kalaupapa, Hawaii, July 6, 1938; s. Ira Dwight and Florence (Moeller) H.; m. Jill Spiller, Oct. 5, 1965; children: Philip, Julia, Thomas. AB, Princeton U., 1960; MD, Jefferson Med. Coll., 1964. Diplomate Am. Bd. Radiology. Intern Pa. Hosp., Phila., 1965; resident N.Y. Hosp., N.Y.C., 1965-68, asst. radiologist, 1968—; radiologist, out-patient dept. Hosp. for Spl. Surgery, N.Y.C., 1968—; ptnr., pvt. practice N.Y.C. and Bronx, 1968—; cons. Squibb Corp., Union Carbide, N.Y.C., 1968-88, Exxon Corp., N.Y.C., 1968-90, N.Y. Telephone Co., N.Y.C., 1970-94, Life Extension Inst., 1992-94. Author: (with others) Computed Tomography of Spine, 1983; contbr. articles to profl. jours. Capt. USAR, 1965-72. Fellow N.Y. Acad. Medicine, Am. Coll. Chest Physicians; mem. N.Y. State Radiol. Soc. (del.), Met. Opera Club (pres. 1990-92), N.Y. Roentgen Soc. Republican. Roman Catholic. Office: Univ Diagnostic Med Imaging 1733 Eastchester Rd Bronx NY 10461-2315

HIRSHBERG, GARY EDWARD, anesthesiologist; b. Quincy, Mass., Jan. 4, 1946; s. Sumner Donald and Molly Barbara (Carliner) H.; m. Martha Jane Schumacher, May 22, 1976; children: Amanda, Jonathan, Peter. AB, Princeton U., 1968; MD, Hahnemann Med. Coll., 1972. Diplomate Am. Bd. Anesthesiology. Intern Barnes Hosp. Washington U., St. Louis, 1972-73, resident in surgery, 1973-74, 76-77, resident in anesthesiology, 1977-79; rsch. fellow Washington U., 1974-76, asst. prof., 1980-88; fellow in pediatric anesthesia and critical care Children's Hosp. Phila., 1979-80; staff anesthesiologist, asst. clin. prof. Jewish Hosp., Wash. U., 1988-92, Shriners Hosp., 1992; anesthesiologist-in-chief, assoc. prof. St. Louis Children's Hosp. Washington U., 1992—; dir. divsn. pediatric anesthesia Washington U., 1992—. Mem. Soc. Pediatric Anesthesiology, Am. Soc. Anesthesiologists, Internat. Anesthesia Rsch. Soc., Am. Acad. Pediatrics (sect. on anesthesia). Office: Washington U Divsn Pediatric Anesthesia 1 Childrens Pl Saint Louis MO 63110

HISE, MARK ALLEN, dentist; b. Chgo., Jan. 17, 1950; s. Clyde and Rose T. (Partipilo) H. AA, Mt. San Antonio Coll., Walnut, Calif., 1972; BA with highest honors, U. Calif., Riverside, 1974; MS, U. Utah, 1978; DDS, UCLA, 1983. Instr. sci. NW Acad., Houston, 1978-79; chmn. curriculum med. coll. prep program UCLA, 1980-85; instr. dentistry Coll. of Redwoods, Eureka, Calif., 1983; practice dentistry Arcata, Calif., 1983—; participant numerous radio and TV appearances. Editor: Preparing for the MCAT, 1983-85; contbr. articles to profl. jours.; speaker in field. Henry Carter scholar U. Calif., 1973, Calif. State scholar 1973, 74, Rgents scholar U. Calif., 1973; Calif. State fellow, 1975, NIH fellow, 1975-79. Mem. AAAS, ADA, Calif. Dental Assn., Acad. Gen. Dentistry, Nat. Soc. for Med. Rsch., North Coast Scuba Club. Roman Catholic. Home and Office: 1225 B St Arcata CA 95521-5936

HISHIDA, TOMI-O, biology educator, reproductive biology researcher; b. Nagoya, Japan, Feb. 17, 1927; s. Mataichiro and Taka Hishida; m. Kiyoko Hiramastu, Feb. 9, 1958; children: Ikuri, Yukito. BSc, Nagoya U., 1949, DSc, 1961. Instr. Nagoya U., 1952-71; Population Coun. postdoctoral fellow dept. ob-gyn-physiology U. Kans. Med. Ctr., Kansas City, 1965-66; prof. biology coll. dentistry Motosu-Gun, Gifu, Japan, 1971-85; prof. biology Asahi U. Motosu-Gun, Gifu, 1985-94, prof. emeritus, 1994—. Grantee Lalor Found., 1966. Office: Asahi U Biol Dept, Hozumi-cho 1851, Motosu-Gun Gifu 501-02, Japan

HISLOP, MERVYN WARREN, health advocate administrator, psychologist; b. Vancouver, B.C., Apr. 26, 1937; s. George and Freda (Wickenden) H.; m. Marilyn Gail Johnson, July 24, 1965; children: Lawren Nyall, Mylene Lorelle. B.A. with honors, U. B.C., 1965; M.A., McMaster U., 1967, Ph.D., 1970. Cert. psychologist, Ont., B.C. cert. health adminstr. Dir. behaviour mgmt. services Surrey Place Centre, Ministry of Health, Toronto, Ont., 1970-73; dir. psychol. services Woodlands Ministry of Human Resources, New Westminster, B.C., 1973-78; coordinator life edn. program New Westminster, 1975-77; exec. dir. Riverview Hosp., Port Coquitlam, B.C., 1978-85, Valleyview Hosp., Port Coquitlam, B.C., 1985-86; dir. legis. and regulatory affairs Mental Health Services Div., B.C. Ministry of Health, 1986-89; physiat. adv. Govt. Alberta, Can., 1989—; research proposal submission cons. Can. Council, 1973; mem. edn. adv. com. Douglas Coll., 1983-86. Demonstration model grantee Province Ont., 1971; province Ont. grad. fellow McMaster U., 1969; recipient David and Jean Bolocan Meml. prize U. B.C., 1965; Nat. Rsch. Coun. Can. scholar, 1965, 66, 67, 68. Mem. Can. Coll. Health Service Execs. (cert.), Can. Inst. Law and Medicine, Coll. Psychologists B.C., Coll. Psychologists Ont. Home: 17203-57 Ave, Edmonton, AB Canada T6M 1B8

HISS, ROLAND GRAHAM, physician, medical educator; b. Newark, Oct. 9, 1932; s. George Crosby and Adrianne (Graham) H.; m. Margaret Barringer McGrath, Aug. 23, 1957; children: John Barringer, Meredith Graham Ketzner. BS, U. Mich., 1955, MD, 1957. Diplomate Am. Bd. Internal Medicine. Intern in medicine Phila. Gen. Hosp., 1957-58; resident in medicine U. Mich. Hosp., Ann Arbor, 1961-64; fellow hematology Simpson Meml. Inst., Ann Arbor, 1964-66; faculty medicine U. Mich. Med. Sch., Ann Arbor, 1966—, chmn. dept. postgrad. medicine, 1982—; coordinator edn. Mich. Diabetes Research and Tng. Ctr., Ann Arbor, 1977—. Contbr. 40 articles to profl. jours. Served to capt. USAF, 1958-61. Recipient Teaching award Kaiser Permanente Found. and U. Mich., 1976. Fellow ACP; mem. Am. Diabetes Assn., AMA, Mich. State Med. Soc. Home: 3551 Chatham Way Ann Arbor MI 48105-2827 Office: U Mich Med Sch Towsley Ctr Box 0201 G-1103 Ann Arbor MI 48109-0201

HITCHINGS, GEORGE HERBERT, retired pharmaceutical company executive, educator; b. Hoquiam, WA, Apr. 18, 1905; s. George Herbert and Lillian (Belle) H.; m. Beverly Reimer, May 30, 1933 (dec. 1985); children: Laramie Ruth (Mrs. Robert C. Brown), Thomas Eldridge; m. Joyce Shaver, Feb. 9, 1989. BS, U. Wash., 1927, MS, 1928; PhD, Harvard U., 1933; DSc, U. Mich., 1971, U. Strathclyde, 1977; DSc (hon.), N.Y. Med. Coll., Valhalla, 1981, Emory U., Atlanta, 1981, Duke U., Durham, N.C., 1982, U. N.C., Chapel Hill, 1982, Mt. Sinai Sch. Medicine, CUNY, N.Y.C., 1983, Harvard U., 1987, Med. U. of S.C., 1988; DMS (hon.), U. N.C., 1988; DSc (hon.), L.I. U., 1989; DHL (hon.), Hahnemann U., 1990; DSc (hon.), East Carolina U., 1993. Teaching fellow U. Wash., 1926-28; from teaching fellow to assoc. Harvard U., 1928-39; sr. instr. Western Res. U., 1939-42; with Burroughs Wellcome Co., Research Triangle Park, N.C., 1942-75, rsch. dir., 1955-67, v.p., 1967-75, dir., 1968-84, scientist emeritus, 1975-94; ret., 1994; prof. pharmacology Brown U., 1968-80; adj. prof. pharmacology and exptl. medicine Duke U., 1970—; adj. prof. U. N.C., 1972—; Hartung lectr., 1972; Dohme lectr., Johns Hopkins U., 1969; Michael Cross lectr. Cambridge U., Eng., 1974; George Hitchings and Gertrude Elion lectr. N.Y. Acad. Scis., 1992; Castle lectr. U. South Fla., 1992; cons. NRC, 1952-53, USPHS, 1955-60, 74-78, Am. Cancer Soc., 1963-66, Leukemia Soc. Am., 1969-73; vis. lectr. Pakistan, Iran, 1976, Japan, India, 1980, Republic South Africa, 1978, 81, Czechoslovakia, France, Pakistan, 1989, Taiwan, Korea, 1990, Poland, 1993; cons., participant in company roundtables, 1988—. Patentee in fields of chemotherpay, anti-metabolitics, organic chemistry of heterocycles, nucleic acids, antitumor, antimalarial, antiviral and anti bacterial drugs. Mem. Am. Cancer Soc., ARC (bd. dirs. Durham County Chpt., 1972-77, 78-84, 85—); bd. dirs. Durham United Fund; founder Greater Triangle Community Found., pres., 1983-85; bd. dirs. Burroughs Wellcome Fund, 1968-93, pres., 1972-91; mem. rsch. and evaluation adv. com. N.C. State Dept. Corrections, 1974-76, drug devel. com. Nat. Cancer Inst., 1975-78, external adv. com. Duke Comprehensive Cancer Ctr., 1978-84; bd. dirs. Med. Found. N.C. Inc., 1984-87; friend Duke U. Libr. (life), 1987—; mem. Hitchings day and symposium Harvard U., 1992. Recipient Gairdner award, 1968; Passano award, 1969; de Villier award, 1969; Cameron prize practical therapeutics, 1972, Bertner Found. award, 1974, Royal Soc. Mullard medal 1976, Papanicolaou Cancer Soc. award, 1979, Gov.'s award N.C., 1980, C. Chester Stock medal, 1981, Disting. Svc. award U. N.C., 1982, Oscar B. Hunter award, 1984, Alfred Burger award, 1984; Disting. Achievement award Modern Medicine, 1973, Gregor Mendel medal Czechoslovakia Acad., 1968, Purkinje medal, 1971; Medicinal Chemistry award, 1972, Ministry of Health medal, Warsaw, Poland, 1988, Inst. Lekow medal, Warsaw, 1988, Nobel prize in Medicine or Physiology, 1988; Albert Schweitzer Internat. prize for Medicine, 1989, Golden Plate award Am. Acad. Achievement, 1989, City of Medicine award Durham, N.C., 1990, Man of the Century award Hoquiam, 1990, Sagamore of the Wabash State of Ind. Gov.'s award, 1990, N.C. Disting. Chemist award, 1991, Civic Honor award Durham, N.C., 1991, medal of Honor, Tech. U. Gdansk, 1993. Fellow AAAS, Royal Soc. Chemistry (hon., fgn.); mem. NAS, NRC (com. on growth 1952-53), The Royal Soc. (fgn. mem.), Am. Acad. Arts and Scis., Am. Soc. Biol. Chemistry, Internat. Transplantation Soc., Am. Assn. for Cancer Rsch. (hon., award 1989), Soc. Exptl. Biology and Medicine, Royal Soc. Medicine (fgn. mem., dir. Found. 1987—), Phi Beta Kappa, Sigma Xi (pres. Rsch. Triangle Park Club 1991), Phi Lambda Upsilon. Home: 1 Carolina Meadows Apt 102 Chapel Hill NC 27514-8508*

HITE, JUDSON CARY, retired pharmaceutical company executive; b. Canton, Ohio, Oct. 12, 1939; s. Everett Corbett and Dorothy Elizabeth (Caley) H.; m. Mary Kay Woodman, July 14, 1962 (div. Mar. 1970); children: Judson Cary III, Kenneth Woodman; m. Elsie Adeline Lilly, Oct. 1, 1977; 1 child, Julie Christina. BS, Ohio State U., 1962. Mgmt. trainee The Upjohn Co., Kalamazoo, Mich., 1962-64, programming analyst, 1964-67, profl. acct., 1967-70, adminstrv. mgr., 1970-74, gen. audit mgr., 1974-81, dir gen. audit, 1981-85, dir. med. affairs, 1985-89, dir. info. systems, 1989-91, dir. rsch. contracts, 1991-93, dir. office mgmt. svcs., 1993-95; ret., 1995. Mem. Nat. Assn. Accts. (dir., v.p., 1964-74), Inst. Internal Auditors (dir. 1974-85), Lic. Execs. Soc., Sigma Chi (v.p. 1960-61). Republican. Home: 5961 Scenic Way Dr Kalamazoo MI 49009-9112

HITE, MARK, toxicologist, researcher; b. Cambridge, Mass., Feb. 7, 1935; s. Jacob William Hite and Miriam (Gertrude) Cohen; m. Nancy Sue Gordon, June 5, 1960; children: Gary Allen, Deborah Lynn. BCE, Rensselaer Poly. Inst., 1956; ScD, U. Cin., 1960. Diplomate Am. Bd. Toxicology. Div. toxicologist Dow Chem. Co., Freeport, Tex., 1962-64; dir. toxicology and pathology Merck Inst. for Therapeutic Rsch., West Point, Pa., 1964-85; dir. drug safety evaluation Wyeth-Ayerst Rsch., Radnor, Pa., 1985-95; pvt. practice toxicology and drug safety cons. Norristown, Pa., 1995—. Capt. USPHS, 1960-62. Fellow Acad. Toxicol. Scis.; mem. AAAS, Soc. Toxicology (counselor 1982-84), Am.Coll. Toxicology (counselor 1990-92), N.Y. Acad. Scis., Masons, Shriners, Sigma Xi. Republican. Jewish. Home and Office: 628 Northampton Rd Norristown PA 19403-4113

HITT, DAVID HAMILTON, hospital executive; b. Tuscaloosa, Ala., May 14, 1925; m. Frances Ford, Aug. 12, 1949; children: David Hamilton, Kathryn Ann. BS, MS in Commerce and Bus. Adminstrn, U. Ala.; MHA, U. Minn., 1952. Hosp. adminstr. U. Ala. Hosp., 1947-50; various positions, including chief exec. officer Baylor U. Med. Center, 1952-79; sr. v.p. James A. Hamilton Assocs. (hosp. consultants), Dallas, 1979-84; pres., chief exec. officer Meth. Hosps. of Dallas, 1984—, also bd. dirs.; bd. dirs. North Tex. Healthcare Network Inc., Bapt. Med. Ctr., Jacksonville, Fla., Dallas Med. Resource, Dallas Meth. Health Svcs., North Ctrl. Tex. Svcs., Helicopter Ambulance Svc. of North Tex., CareFlite GAE, Inc., North Tex. Health Facilities Inc., Ctrl. Dallas Assn., Swiss Ave. Bank; pres. Dallas Hosp. Coun., 1959; mem. adminstrv. bd. Coun. Tchg. Hosps. of Assn. Am. Med. Colls., 1972-79; assoc. clin. prof. Washington U., St. Louis; adj. assoc. prof. Trinity U., San Antonio. Contbr. numerous articles to profl. jours. Mem. exec. bd. council Boy Scouts Am.; v.p. Community Council Greater Dallas. Recipient Earl M. Collier award Distinguished Hosp. Adminstrn. Tex., 1973, Dean Conley award, Silver Beaver award Boy Scouts Am. Fellow Am. Coll. Healthcare Execs. (Gold medal award for excellence in healthcare mgmt. 1990, past regent, editl. bd. Frontiers Health Svcs. Mgmt. 1991-93); mem. Am. Hosp. Assn. (Citation for Meritorious Svc. 1987, Disting. Svc. award 1992, trustee, past chmn. coun. financing), Tex. Hosp. Assn. (trustee, treas., v.p., pres., chmn. ho. of dels. 1967), Am. Protestant Hosp. Assn. (past trustee), Alumni Assn. U. Minn. Program Hosp. Adminstrn. (past pres.), Marine Corps Assn., Exch. Club (East Dallas, pres. 1957), Dallas Wood and Waters, Masons, Shriners, Grotto, Rotary (Dallas) (bd. dirs., dist. Ethics Bus. award 1993). Home: 7231 Twin Tree Ln Dallas TX 75214-1941 Office: Methodist Hosp Dallas PO Box 655999 Dallas TX 75265-5999

HITT, JOHN MICHAEL, occupational health physician; b. Phoenix, Dec. 21, 1952; s. Woodrow Wilson and Nedra Mae (Holmes) H.; m. Linda Georgene Dase, Jan. 22, 1972; children: Kim Michael, Chani Jooeun, Kia Holly. BAE, Ariz. State U., 1973; MA, No. Ariz. U., 1976; MD, U. Ariz., 1983, MS in Toxicology, 1986. Diplomate Am. Bd. Internal Medicine, Am. Bd. Forensic Examiners. Sci. tchr. Collegio Jorge Washington, Cartagena, Colombia, 1974-75, Mesa (Ariz.) Pub. Schs., 1973, 75-80; intern Tucson Med. Ctr./ Kino Cmty. Hosp., 1984-85; resident U. Ariz. Med. Ctr., 1985-86; founding physician Corp. Med. Ctr., Tucson, 1986-90; med. dir. Helian Occupl. Ctrs., Tucson, 1990-93, corp. med. dir., 1994-96; staff physician IBM, Tucson, 1986-88; pres. Well America, Tucson, 1988-91; med. dir. Physician's Partnership with Russia, Colorado Springs, Colo., 1993-95. Med. missionary Navigators, Russia, 1993-94, Project Mercy, Guatemala, 1995. Named Tchr. of the Yr. Ariz.-Nev. Sci. Tchrs. Assn., 1980. Fellow Am. Bd. Forensic Medicine, Am. Coll. Occupl. and Environ. Medicine, Am. Bd. Ind. Med. Examiners. Republican. Office: PO Box 268 Woodland Park CO 80866-0268

HITTINGER, JANE A., critical care nurse, foundation administrator; b. Beech Grove, Ind., Sept. 11, 1950; d. Robert Harold and Roma Madge (McDaniel) Cleveland; children: Ryan A., Scot R. RN diploma, The Deaconess Hosp., Cin., 1986; student, U. Cin. RN, Ohio. Cashier, bookkeeper Mutual Credit, Cin., 1968-71; realtor assoc. Theodore mayer & Bros. Realtors, Cin., 1975-82; cashier, customer svc. Lazarus, Cin., 1982-91;

nursing attendant Deaconess Hosp., Cin., 1985-86, staff nurse, charge nurse CCU, 1986-93; co-founder, v.p. Tri-State RSD & Chronic Pain Support Group, Cin., 1989—. Mem. Clough Pike Sch. PTO, sec., membership sec., 1978-82, pres. 1981-82. Mem. Assoc. Critical Care Nurses (Cin. chpt.), Unified RSD Rsch. Found. (state rep.). Republican. Presbyterian. Home & Office: 812 Oaks Dr Cincinnati OH 45245-1836

HIXON, JAMES SWANN, gastroenterologist, physician internal medicine; b. Columbus, Ga., Apr. 2, 1948; s. Oliver Swann and Margery (Sasser) H.; m. Kathleen Ann Hall; children: Brittany Anne, Mary Elizabeth. BS, U. Ga., Athens, 1974; MD, Med. Coll. of Ga., Augusta, 1973. Diplomate Am. Bd. Internat. Medicine. Intern Med. Coll. of Ga., Augusta, 1973-74, resident in internal medicine, 1974-76, fellow in gastroenterology, 1976-78; pvt. practice in gastroenterology Anniston, Ala., 1978—. Fellow Am. Coll. Gastroenterology. Office: 901 Leighton Ave Ste 101 Anniston AL 36207

HIXSON, EDWARD GEORGE, general surgeon; b. Oneida, N.Y., Nov. 11, 1941; s. Edward George and Doris Elizabeth (Cummings) H.; m. Karen Agnes Rightmayer, June 13, 1981; children: Edward, Chris. BA, Middleburg (Vt.) Coll., 1963; MD, U. Vt., 1967. Diplomate Am. Bd. Surgeons; lic. N.Y. Gen. surgeon Adirondack Med. Ctr., Saranac Lake, N.Y., 1973-90; surgeon 3d Battalion. 172d Infantry (Mountain) Vt. Army Nat. Guard, Jericho, 1989-96. Editor, author: (book) Winter Sportsmedicine, 1990; author: (with others) (books) Sports Neurology, 1987, Orthopedic Sportsmedicine, 1994. Major U.S. Army Med. Corps, 1972-73. Fellow Am. Coll. Surgeons, Am. Coll. Sports Medicine; mem. AMA, Med. Soc. State of N.Y., Soc. Am. Gastrointestinal Endoscopic Surgeons, Soc. Laparandoscopic Surgeons, Ctrl. N.Y. Surgical Soc., Lake Placid Sportsmedicine Soc. (bd. dirs.). Republican. Episcopalian. Home: Box 278 Lake Clear NY 12945 Office: Adirondack Surgical Group 410 Lake Colby Dr Saranac Lake NY 12983

HIXSON, MARCELLA MARIE, critical care nurse; b. Kansas City, Mo., Aug. 21, 1953; d. Jamaes Leland and Marie M. (Fowler) Kenslow; m. Jim D. Hixson, Nov. 27, 1971; 1 child, Kelly M. AD, Maple Woods C.C., Kansas City, Mo., 1990; BSN, William Jewell Coll., Liberty, Mo., 1993. RN, Mo.; cert. TNCC, ACLS, CNA. Med. tech. John Williams, M.D., Liberty, Mo., 1989-90; CNA Liberty (Mo.) Hosp., 1990-93, RN, 1993—; mem. quality assurance com. Liberty Hosp. Mem. Christian Student Fellowship and Ministries disaster relief svc. mission, 1992; vol. Western Mo. Mental Health Ctr., Kansas City, 1992. Mem. AACN, Sigma Theta Tau Internat. (sec. 1994). Home: 2171 SE 207th St Two Creek Hollow Holt MO 64048

HIYAMA, DARRYL TOSHIO, medical educator; b. Honolulu, Dec. 27, 1957; s. George H. and Hiroko K. (Kataoka) Y.; m. Susan Louise Shellenberger, Nov. 1989; children: Katherine, David, Jennifer. BS in Biology, Seattle U., 1980; MD, U. Hawaii, 1984. Diplomate Am. Bd. Surgery. Asst. prof. surgery UCLA Sch. Medicine, 1990—. Editor: Mont Reid Handbook, 1990. Office: UCLA Sch Medicine Divsn Gen Surgery 10833 Le Conte Ave Los Angeles CA 90095

HIZAWA, KAZUO, pathologist; b. Sapporo, Hokkaido, Japan, Mar. 6, 1930; s. Chiyoji and Ichi (Ogawa) H.; m. Atsuko Sano, May 30, 1959 (div. Sept. 11, 1971); children: Nobuyuki, Takayuki; m. Masako Horiuchi, Mar. 27, 1973. MB, Hokkaido U., Sapporo, Japan, 1953, MD, 1960. Diplomate Japanese Pathologist Soc. Lectr. Tokushima U., Shikoku, Japan, 1959-60, asst. prof., 1960-68, prof., 1968—. Editor Pathology & Medicine, 1983-91, Acta Pathologica Japonica, 1990—; editor: Pathology of Muscle, 1989. Dir. Japan-Germany Soc. Tokushima, 1990—. Fellow Japanese Soc. Pathologists, Japanese Div. Internat. Acad. Pathology; mem. Japanese Soc. Pathologists. Home: 9-41 Kamifukuman, Hachiman cho, Tokushima Shikoku 770, Japan Office: Tokushima U, 18-15 Kuramoto cho 3, Tokushima Shikoku 770, Japan

HLAD, GREGORY MICHAEL, psychometrist, assessment services coordinator; b. McKeesport, Pa., Feb. 14, 1947; s. Michael Gregory Jr. and Helen Delores (Harman) H.; m. Carol Ann Huzinec, July 15, 1972; 1 child, Kristen. BEd, U. Miami, Coral Gables, 1969; MEd, Calif. (Pa.) State U., 1974. Cert. tchr., Fla., Pa.; cert. work evaluator; cert. occupational specialist. Tchr. Wilkinsburg (Pa.) Sch. Dist., 1969-79; asst. prof. Pasco-Hernando Community Coll., New Port Richey, Fla., 1979-83; occupl. specialist Pasco-Pvt. Industry Coun., Fla., 1983-93; assessment coord. Workforce Devel. Authority, Ocala, Fla., 1993-96, Pasco-Hernando C.C., New Port Richey, Fla., 1996—; cons. Xerox Ednl. div. New Haven, 1977-79, Pasco-Hernando Community Coll., 1983—, mem. learning lab. adv. com., 1985-86; v.p. Ednl./Psychol. Assessments Inc. Mem. budget adv. com. Safety Harbor (Fla.), 1986-87. Recipient Cert. of Appreciation Dept. of Corrections, 1982, Appreciation of Service award Boy Scouts Am., 1986. Home: 39 Friendship Ct Safety Harbor FL 34695-2644 Office: Pasco-Hernando CC 10230 Ridge Rd New Port Richey FL 34654-5199

HLATKY, MARK ANDREW, cardiologist, health services researcher; b. Windber, Pa., June 4, 1950; s. George Andrew and Rose Annette (Gonnella) H.; m. Donna Marie Alvarado, May 12, 1984; 1 child, Nicholas Michael. BS, MIT, 1972; MD, U. Pa., 1976. Diplomate in internal medicine and cardiovascular disease Am. Bd. Internal Medicine; lic. physician, Calif., N.C. Intern, resident U. Ariz., Tucson, 1976-79; Robert Wood Johnson clin. scholar U. Calif., San Francisco, 1979-81; fellow in cardiology Duke U., Durham, N.C., 1981-83, asst. prof. medicine, 1983-89, assoc. prof. health rsch. and policy, assoc. prof. medicine, 1989-96; prof. health rsch. and policy, prof. medicine Stanford (Calif.) U., 1996—; attending physician, cardiovasc. medicine svc. Stanford U. Med. Ctr., 1989—; mem. Health Care Tech. Study sect. NIH, Rockville, Md., 1992—. Contbr. more than 90 articles to profl. jours. Sloan scholar, 1972. Fellow Am. Coll. Cardiology; mem. Am. Heart Assn. (fellow coun. on clin. cardiology), Am. Fedn. Clin. Rsch., Internat. Soc. for Tech. Assessment in Health Care, Phi Beta Kappa. Home: 168 Rinconada Ave Palo Alto CA 94301 Office: Stanford U Sch Medicine HRP Redwood Bldg Rm 150 Stanford CA 94305

HO, ALLEN C., vitreoretinal surgeon, educator; b. Mpls., Mar. 13, 1962; m. Heather MacMaster; children: Christine, Alexandria, Elizabeth. BA with highest distinction, Cornell U., 1984; MD, Columbia U., 1988. Ophthalmology resident Wills Eye Hosp., Phila., 1992; retina fellow Manhattan Eye and Ear Hosp., N.Y.C., 1994; asst. prof. ophthalmology U. Pa., Phila., 1994—; vitreoretinal surgeon Scheie Eye Inst, Phila., 1994—. Mem. editl. bd. Jour. Ophthalmic Surgery and Lasers, Boston, 1995—. Vision rsch. grantee Assn. Rsch. in Vision and Ophthalmology, Bethesda, Md., 1994, eye rsch. grantee McCabe Found., Phila., 1995. Mem. Pa. Acad. Ophthalmology, Vitreous Soc., Am. Acad. Ophthalmology, Heed-Knapp soc. Fellows. Office: Scheie Eye Inst 51 N 39th St Philadelphia PA 19104

HO, RODNEY JIN YONG, educator, medical researcher; b. Rangoon, Burma, May 21, 1959; came to U.S., 1977; s. David Shoon-Khat and Po-Kin (Paw) H.; m. Lily S. Hwang, July 10, 1988; children: Beatrice Eirene, Martin Theodore. BS, U. Calif., Davis, 1983; MS, U. Tenn., 1985, PhD, 1987. Teaching asst. U. Tenn., Knoxville, 1984-85, rsch. asst., 1985-87; postdoctoral fellow, assoc. investigator Stanford (Calif.) U. Sch. Medicine, 1987-90; assoc. prof. pharmaceutics U. Wash., Seattle, 1990-96, assoc. prof. pharmaceutics Sch. Pharmacy, 1996—, affiliate investigator Wash. Primate Rsch. Ctr., 1996—; affiliate investigator of pharmacology Fred Hutchinson Cancer Rsch. Ctr., Seattle, 1991—. Author: Liposomes as Drug Carriers, 1988, Topics in Vaccine Adjuvant Research, 1991, Trophoblast Research, Vol. 8, 1994, Placental Toxicology, 1995, Vaccine Design: The Subunit and Adjuant Approach; patentee immunoliposome assays, composition and treatment for herpes simplex; contbr. numerous articles on infectious diseases, pharmaceutical sciences, virology, immunology band biochemistry to sci. jours. Mem. AAAS, Am. Assn. Coll. Pharmacy, Am. Assn. Pharm. Scientists, Am. Chem. Soc., Biophys. Soc., Internat. Soc. Antiviral Rsch., N.Y. Acad. Sci. Office: U Wash Sch Pharmacy Dept Pharms Box 357610 Seattle WA 98195

HOANG, DUC VAN, theoretical pathologist, educator; b. Hanoi, Vietnam, Feb. 17, 1926; came to U.S. 1975, naturalized 1981; s. Duoc Van and Nguyen Thi (Tham) H.; m. Mau-Ngo Thi Vu, 7 children. M.D., Hanoi U. Sch. Medicine, Vietnam, 1952; DSc, Open Internat. U., Sri Lanka, 1989. Dean Sch. Medicine Army of the Republic of Vietnam, Saigon, 1959-63; dean Minh-Duc U. Sch. Medicine, Saigon, 1970-71; clin. prof. theoretical pathology U. So. Calif. Sch. Medicine, L.A., 1978—; ret.; adj. prof. Emperor's Coll. Traditional Oriental Medicine, Santa Monica, Calif., 1988—. Author: Towards an Integrated Humanization of Medicine, 1957; The Man Who Weights the Soul, 1959; Eastern Medicine, A New Direction", 1970; also short stories; translator: Pestis, introduction to the work of Albert Camus, Vietnamese translation of La Peste; editor: The East (co-founder); jour. Les Cahiers de l'Asie du Sud-Est. Founder, past pres. Movement for Fedn. Countries S.E. Asia; co-founder, past v.p. Movement for Restoration Cultures and Religions of Orient; active Vo-Vi Meditation Assn. Am.; mem. The Noetic Inst., 1988—, Internat. Found. for Homeopathy, 1987; founder, pres. Intercontinental Found. for Electro-Magnetic Resonance Rsch., 1989—; coord. Unity and Diversity World Health Coun., 1992—. Named hon. dean The Open Internat. U. of Complementary Medicines, Sri Lanka, 1989; Unity-and-Diversity World Coun. fellow, 1990—. Mem. AAUP, Assn. Clin. Scientists, Am. Com. for Integration Eastern and Western Medicine (founder), Assn. Unitive Medicine (founder, pres.), U. So. Calif. Faculty Member Club (L.A.). Republican. Roman Catholic. Home: 3630 Barry Ave Los Angeles CA 90066-3202

HOBACK, FLORENCE KUNST, retired psychiatrist; b. Grafton, Wv., Oct. 26, 1922; d. G H A and Mary (Conaway) Kunst; m. John Holland Hoback, Oct. 27, 1945 (dec.); children: Holly Hoback Clark, Conaway K. AB, W.Va. U., 1944; MD, U. Md., Balt., 1948. Pvt. practice medicine Huntington, W.Va., 1950-55; internal medicine VA Hosp., Huntington, 1955-60; resident psychiatry Med. Coll. VA, Richmond, 1960-65; pvt. practice psychiatry Huntington; ret. Police commn. City of Huntington, 1975-77. Fellow Am. Psychiatric Assn., mem. AMA, W.Va. Med. Assn., Am. Women's Med. Assn. Home: 2658 3rd Ave Huntington WV 25702-1302

HOBBINS, WILLIAM BELL, surgeon; b. Madison, Wis., Aug. 16, 1924; s. William Suhr and Audrey (Bell) H.; m. Meredith Larson, May 7, 1946 (div. Aug. 1972); children: William Krist, Deborah, Cynthia, Teodore, Richard; m. Paul M. Todd, Aug. 8, 1975; children: Kelly, Tracy, Derik, Harrison. BS, U. Wis., 1945; MD, Northwestern U., Chgo., 1946. Sr. surg. resident Cook County Hosp., Chgo., 1946-51; pvt. practice Christian Med. Ctr., Madison, Wis., 1953—; asst. clin. prof. surgery U. Wis., Madison, 1958-67; dir. Woman's Breast Care Ctr., Madison, 1964—, Madison Pain Diagnostic Ctr., 1982—; founder, pres. Wis. Breast Cancer Detection Found., Madison, 1974—. Contbr. chpts. to books. Councilman Maple Bluff, Wis., 1958-60; admiral Mendota Yatch Club, Madison, 1968-70; pres. Wis. Ballet Co., Madison, 1969-76. Capt. U.S. Army, 1951-53, Korea. Named Outstanding Thermographer, Am. Hershel Soc., Jacksonville, Fla., 1991, Hon. Founder Korean Thermography Svc., Seoul, 1992. Mem. Am. Holistic Med. Soc., Christian Med. Dental Soc. (asst. del. 1976-83), Am. Infared Imaging Soc. (founder, pres. 1986—), Madison Club, U. Wis. Alumni. Democrat. Home: 7602 New Washburn Way Madison WI 53719 Office: Christian Med Ctr 5510 Med Ctr Madison WI 53719

HOBBS, NED PETER, optometrist; b. Worden, Ill., Dec. 26, 1921; s. Kermit L. and Marie (Massa) H.; m. Kathryn S. Stonecypher, Dec. 1942; children: Steven, Karen, Michael. OD, No. Ill. Coll., 1947; postgrad., U. Ala., 1993. Lic. optometrist, S.C. Pvt. practice, Darlington, S.C.; mem. staff Wilson Hosp. Darlington; former pres. Am. Optometric Found. Mem. Darlington County Bd. Health, 1987—, councilman City of Darlington, 1950-52; commr. Darlington County, 1962, coroner, 1968; former pres. S.C. Cemetery Assn. Capt. Med. Adminstrv. Corps, AUS, 1942-45, PTO. Named Citizen of Yr., Darlington, 1950. Fellow Am. Acad. Optometry, S.C. Optometric Assn. (Hall of Fame), Royal Soc. Health; mem. So. Coun. Optometry (past pres., Amb. of Yr. award), Lions (pres. 1994—, Lion of Yr. award, 1950). Baptist. Office: 139 Cashua St Darlington SC 29532

HOBBS, NEDDA MARIE, pediatrician; b. Cambridge, Mass., July 21, 1956; d. J. David and Rose-Marie (Delgrego) H. BS, MIT, 1978; MD, U. Mass., 1982. Diplomate Am. Bd. Pediatrics. Resident in pediatrics Children's Hosp. of Phila., 1982-86; fellow devel. disabilities R.I. Hosp., Providence, 1986-88; chief of pediatrics Lakeville (Mass.) Hosp., 1988-91; pediatrician coordinated care svc. Children's Hosp., Boston, 1991-94, co-dir. coordinated care svc., 1994—, pediatrician, myelodysplasia program, 1992—. Fellow Am. Acad. Pediatrics, Soc. Devel. Pediatrics; mem. Mass. Med. Soc., Soc. Mayflower Descs. (life), Phi Beta Kappa. Office: Children's Hosp 300 Longwood Ave Boston MA 02115

HOBBS, ROBERT EDWARD, cardiologist; b. Danville, Pa., Aug. 30, 1948; s. Robert Emmett and Florence (Ciszek) H.; m. Alyce J. Granito, Aug. 12, 1972. BS in Biology, St. Joseph's U., Phila., 1970; MD, Jefferson Med. Coll., Phila., 1974. Diplomate Am. Bd. Internal Medicine and Cardiovascular Disease. Intern and resident Lankenau Hosp., Phila., 1974-77; staff cardiologist Cleve. Clinic, 1979—. Contbr. articles to profl. jours. Fellow ACP, Am. Coll. Cardiology, Am. Coll. Chest Physicians, Am. Heart Assn. Soc. Cardiac Angiography. Office: Cleve Clinic 9500 Euclid Ave Cleveland OH 44195

HOBBY, KENNETH LESTER, psychology educator; b. Searcy, Ark., Jan. 9, 1947; s. James Alvin and Georgia Alice (Pruett) H.; m. Ann Elizabeth Adair, Aug. 20, 1967; children: Anessa, Jared, Tianna, Gerren. BA, Harding U., 1969; MA, Ea. N.Mex. U., 1970, Edn. Specialist, 1971; PhD, Okla. State U., 1981. Lic. psychologist, Ark., Okla. Teaching fellow Ea. N.Mex. U., Portales, 1969-71; sch. counselor Clay County Schs., Orange Park, Fla., 1971-72; sch. psychologist Clay County Schs., Green Cove Springs, Fla., 1972-76; sch. psychometrist Regional Edn. Svc. Ctr., Grove, Okla., 1976-81; sch. psychologist Craig County Spl. Edn. Coop., Vinita, Okla., 1981-82; clin. dir., psychologist Okla. Dept. Health/Child Guidance, Jay, Okla., 1982-85; chief psychologist Grand Lake Mental Health Ctr., Nowata, Okla., 1985-89; prof. psychology Harding U., Searcy, 1989—; cons. psychologist Clearview Psychiat. Hosp., Searcy, Searcy Police Dept. and Fire Dept.; examiner for disability determination Social Security Svc., Little Rock. Mem. Am. Psychol. Soc. Republican. Mem. Ch. of Christ. Home: 65 Mohawk Dr Searcy AR 72143-5935 Office: Harding U PO Box 2260 Searcy AR 72145-2260

HOBGOOD, MITZI JENELL CORBETT, hospital administrator; b. Greenville, N.C., Dec. 18, 1956; d. Jesse Lathan and Doris Lenell (McRoy) Corbett; m. Ronnie Vann Hobgood, June 11, 1978; children: Jessica Carol, Joshua Thomas. BS, East Carolina U., Greenville, N.C., 1978. Asst. dir. med. records Edgecombe Gen. Hosp., Tarboro, N.C., 1978-79; mgr. rehab. records Pitt County Meml. Hosp., Greenville, N.C., 1979-82; data abstractor U. N.C., Chapel Hill, 1983-84; ur coord. Lenoir Meml. Hosp., Kinston, N.C., 1984, asst. mgr. med. records, 1985-93, mgr. health info., 1993—; rev. specialist Med. Rev. N.C., Raleigh, 1984. Mem., pianist First Free Will Bapt. Ch., Greenville, 1988—, tchr. H.S. Sunday sch. class, 1994—; advancement coord. Boy Scouts Am., Winterville, N.C., 1995—; mem. adv. com. HIT Pitt C.C., Greenville, 1993—; mem. adv. com. med. office tech. Lenoir C.C., Kinston, 1994—. Mem. Am. Health Info. Mgmt. Assn., N.C. Health Info. Mgmt. Assn. (mem. region X 1978—, coord. region X 1992). Republican. Home: 107 Essex Dr Winterville NC 28590 Office: Lenoir Meml Hosp 100 Airport Rd Kinston NC 28503-1678

HOBSON, HARRY E., JR., health care administrator; b. Piqua, Ohio, Mar. 17, 1948; s. Harry Elvin and Nancy R. (Brunetto) H.; children: Christopher, Lauren, Andrew. BSBA, Columbus U., 1970; MBA, Central Mich. U., 1976, M Health Care Adminstrn., 1982. Lic. nursing home adminstr. Budget analyst Chem. Abstracts Svc., Columbus, Ohio, 1970-72; dir. fiscal ops. Mt. Carmel Hosps., Columbus, 1972-80; pres. 1st Community Village, Columbus, 1980—; bd. dirs. nursing home adv. bd. Ohio State U., Columbus, 1987—. Author newspaper column Senior Insights. Trustee, Mershon Ctr. Comm. for Social Policy on Aging, Columbus, 1986—, Upper Arlington (Ohio) Commn. on Aging, 1988—; mem. legis. adv. coun. Ohio Ho. of Reps., Columbus, 1988; coach Little League sports. Recipient Award of Honor Ohio Nursing Home Assn., 1995, Resolution of Appreciation Upper Arlington City Coun., 1988; named New Profl. of Yr. Ohio Nursing Home Assn., 1987, Bus. Person of Yr. Upper Arlington C. of C., 1991. Mem. Healthcare Fin. Mgmt. Assn. (pres. 1983-84), Am. Coll. Healthcare Adminstrs., Assn. Ohio Philanthropic Homes for Aged (treas., trustee 1982-94), Athletic Club, Rotary (bd. dirs. 1990-92). Home: 2715 Collinford Dr Apt E Dublin OH 43017-8655 Office: 1st Community Village 1800 Riverside Dr Columbus OH 43212-1855

HOBSON, JOHN ALLAN, psychiatrist, researcher, educator; b. Hartford, Conn., June 3, 1933; s. John Robert and Anne Barnard (Cotter) H.; m. Joan Merle Harlowe, June 18, 1956 (div. Jan. 1993); children: Ian, Christopher, Julia; m. Lia Cesarea Silvestri, May 19, 1995; children: Andrew, Matthew. BA, Conn. Wesleyan U., 1955; MD, Harvard U., 1959. Diplomate Am. Bd. Psychiatry and Neurology; lic. physician, Mass. Intern, Bellevue Hosp., N.Y.C., 1959-60; resident in psychiatry Mass. Mental Health Ctr., Boston, 1960-61, 64-66; NIMH spl. fellow dept. physiology U. Lyon, France, 1963-64; research assoc. dept. physiology Harvard Med. Sch., Boston, 1964-67, instr. psychiatry, 1966-67, assoc. in psychiatry, 1967-69, asst. prof., 1969-74, 74-78, prof. psychiatry, 1978—, prof. psychiatry (neurosci.), 1983—; sr. psychiatrist Mass. Mental Health Ctr., Boston, 1965-67, dir. lab. neurophysiology, 1967, prin. psychiatrist, 1967—, dir. group psychotherapy tng. program, 1972-80; lectr. psychiatry Brown U., Providence, 1972-74; clin. assoc. NIMH, Bethesda, Md., 1961-63; vis. sci., lectr. U. Bordeaux, France, 1973; Sandoz lectr. U. Edinburgh, Scotland, 1975; lectr. Italian Nat. Health Research Inst., Rome, 1978; vis. prof. Istituto di Psicologia, U. degli Studi, Rome, 1983; participant internat. confs.; mem. sci. adv. bd. NIMH Intramural program, NIH, Bethesda, 1981-84, Max Planck Inst. Psychiatry, Munich, 1985—; scholar in residence Rockefeller Study Ctr., Bellagio, Italy, 1987; Decade of the Brain lectr. Soc. Neurosci. 1991, Am. Acad. Neurology, 1993; Joseph P. Erlanger Disting. lectr. Am. Physiol. Soc. Author: The Dreaming Brain, 1988, Sleep, 1989, The Chemistry of Conscious States, 1994; mem. editorial bd. Jour. Cellular and Molecular Neurobiology, 1980—, Archives Itallienes de Biologie, 1983—; contbg. editor Sleep Revs., 1970-72, assoc. editor, 1972-73, editor-in-chief, 1973-74, book rev. editor, 1975-76; sect. editor Neuroreport, 1990—, Psychophysiology, 1993—; contbr. articles to profl. jours. Olin scholar, 1951. Mem. AAAS, Assn. Psychophysiol. Study of Sleep, Soc. Neurosci. (program com. 1974-76, chmn. museum adv. group 1976), Boylston Med. Soc., Mind-Body Network, John D. and Catherine T. MacArthur Found., Sigma Xi. Club: Thursday. Office: Harvard Med Sch 74 Fenwood Rd Boston MA 02115-6113

HOBSON, ROSS SHERWOOD, orthodontist, educator; b. Belfast, No. Ireland, Aug. 6, 1958; s. Sherwood and Muriel (Ross) B.; m. Sally Elizabeth Artindale, June 31, 1982; children: Peter, Simon. B.Dental surgery, Newcastle-upon-Tyle U., Eng., 1984, M.Dental Surgery, 1990. House officer Birmingham (Eng.) Royal Hosp., 1984, Newcastle Dental Hosp., Newcastle-upon-Tyne, 1985; demonstrator in oral biology Newcastle-upon-Tyne U., 1985-87, lectr. orthodontics, 1992—; registrar Glasgow Dental Hosp., 1987-90; registrar in orthodontics Dundee (Scotland) Dental Hosp., 1990-92; developer computer assisted programs Dept. Health, 1994—. Contbr. articles to profl. jours. Huston scholar, 1994; Shore Project Grant Med. Rsch. Coun., 1994-95. Fellow Royal Coll. Physicians and Surgeons; mem. Internat. Assn. Dental Rsch., Brit. Orthodontic Soc. (stds. com. 1995—), Brit. Dental Assn. (dental sch. rep. 1993—). Office: U Newcastle upon Tyne Dental Sch, Framlington Pl, Newcastle upon Tyne NE2 6BW, England

HOCH, DAVID H., electrophysiologist, cardiologist; b. Bklyn., Nov. 1, 1960; s. Oscar and Rhoda (Goldschley) H.; m. Lori R. Hollman, Mar. 24, 1985; children: Jordan, Ethan, Douglas. BS in biological scis., Mass. Inst. Tech., 1981, BSEE, 1981, MS in biomedical engring., 1981; PhD in membrane physiology, Albert Einstein Coll., 1985, MD, 1986. Intern gen. surgery and internal medicine Bronx Mcpl. Hosp. Ctr. and Montefiore Medical Ctr., 1986-87; resident internal medicine Montefiore Medical Ctr., 1987-89; cardiology fellowship Yale-New Haven Hosp., 1989-90, cardiac electrophysiology fellowship, 1990-91, instr. cardiac electrophysiology, 1991-92; assoc. dir. arrhythmia and pacemaker ctr. St. Francis Hosp., Roslyn, N.Y., 1992—; instr. membrane physiology Albert Einstein Coll., 1984-86; tutor for medical sch. courses in physiology, neurobiology, neuroanatomy, 1984-86; attending cardiology electrophysiology St. Francis Hosp. Contbr. articles to profl. jours. Mem. Eta Kappa Nu. Democrat. Jewish. Home: 1 Norden Dr Brookville NY 11545 Office: St Francis Hosp 100 Port Washington Blvd Roslyn NY 11576

HOCHBERG, IRVING, audiologist, educator; b. Bklyn., Apr. 17, 1934. BA, Bklyn. Coll., 1955; MA, Tchrs. Coll., Columbia, 1957; PhD in Audiology, Pa. State U., 1962. Prof. audiology NYU, 1962-70; prof. Bklyn. coll. CUNY, 1970—, exec. officer speech and hearing sci. grad. sch., 1974—, dir. ctr. rsch. speech and hearing sci. grad. ctr., 1979—; with Danforth Assoc., 1968-71. Fellow Am. Speech and Hearing Assn., Acoustical Soc. Am., Inst. Soc. Audiology, Acad. Rehab. Audiology. Office: City University of New York 33 W 42nd St New York NY 10036-8003

HOCHBERG, MARTIN N., obstetrician, gnecologist; b. Bklyn., Oct. 22, 1937; s. Lew A. and Bess A. (Solovei) H.; m. Lois J. Robins, Mar. 5, 1967; children: Leigh Robert, Lauren K. BS, Union Coll., 1958; MD, N.Y. Med. Coll., 1963. Diplomate Am. Bd. Ob/Gyn. Intern Brookdale Hosp. Ctr., Bklyn., 1963-64, resident in ob./gyn., 1966-70; physician Obstetric and Gynecol. Assocs. of Ridgewood, N.J., 1970—; dir. dept. ob.-gyn. The Valley Hosp., Ridgewood, 1996—; assoc. dir. dept. of Ob/Gyn, The Valley Hosp., Ridgewood, 1984-91. Lt. USN, 1964-66. Fellow Am. Coll. Ob/Gyn; mem. Am. Fertility Soc., Am. Assn. Gynecol. Laporoscopists, N.J. Med. Soc., N.J. Ob/Gyn Soc., AMA. Office: Obstetric & Gynecol Assocs 550 N Maple Ave Ridgewood NJ 07450-1632

HOCHENEGG, LEONHARD, physician; b. Innsbruck, Austria, Jan. 24, 1942; s. Hans and Annemarie (Grass) H.; m. Fatima Rendon, Nov. 4, 1976; children: Fatima, Anni, Hans, Franz, Dominick, Clara, Theres, Eugen. Grad., U. Innsbruck, 1967, MD, 1972. Intern U. Hosp., Innsbruck, Austria, 1967-75; asst. in Pharmacological Inst. U. Innsbruck, 1967-69; practice medicine mental hosp. U. Hosp., Hall, Austria, 1969-72; practice in psychiatric clinic St. Gallen, Switzerland, 1972; psychiatristin clin. U. Innsbruck, 1972; pvt. practician neurology and psychiatry Hall, 1980—. Editor: Heiltees, 1987, Die Kunst Nicht Krank zu Werden, 1988, Das Wunder der Heilung, 1994, Das Geheimnis der Geistigen Heilung, 1994; contbr. articles on psychiatry to profl. jours.

HOCHSCHILD, ANN, molecular biologist; b. Urbana, Ill., Jan. 20, 1955; d. Gerhard P. and Ruth Hochschild; m. James Oliver Schwartz, Aug. 26, 1978; children: Eli N., Daniel A. AB, Radcliffe Coll., 1978; PhD, Harvard U., 1986. Asst. prof. Harvard Med. Sch., Boston, 1989-95, assoc. prof., 1995—. Recipient Established Investigator award Am. Heart Assn., 1996. Office: Harvard Med Sch Dept Microbiology 200 Longwood Ave Boston MA 02115*

HOCHSCHILD, RICHARD, medical instruments executive, researcher; b. Berlin, Germany, Aug. 28, 1928; came to U.S., 1939; s. Paul and Ann Ida (Schosstag) H.; m. Carroll Corinne Shepherd, July 25, 1959; children: Christopher Paul, Stephen Shepherd. BA in Physics, Johns Hopkins U., 1950; MA in Physics, U. Calif., Berkeley, 1957. Tech. adv. U.S. Atomic Energy Commn., N.Y.C., 1951-53; chief 300 area U.S. Atomic Energy Commn., Hanford, Wash., 1953-54; pres. Metrol, Inc., Pasadena, Calif., 1957-60; asst. to v.p. Budd Co., Phoenixville, Pa., 1960-61; pres. Microwave Instruments Co., Corona del Mar, Calif., 1962-74; chief exec. officer Hoch Co., Corona del Mar, 1975—; developer computerized med., physiol. and psychol. testing and measuring instruments; specialist in biomarkers of aging; cons. in field. Patentee and author in field. Office: Hoch Co 2915 Pebble Dr Corona Del Mar CA 92625-1518

HOCHSTRASSER, DONALD LEE, cultural anthropologist, community health and public administration educator; b. Taylorsville, Ky., June 10, 1927; s. Emil John and Mary E. (Schad) H.; m. Marie Emlen, Apr. 9, 1960; 1 child, Letitia Cope; stepchildren—Eloise Q. Hatch, Laura A. Hatch. B.A., U. Ky., 1952, M.A., 1955; postgrad. (univ. fellow) Northwestern U., 1955-56; Ph.D. in Anthropology, U. Oreg., 1963; M.P.H., U. Calif.-Berkeley, 1969. Research asst. dept. rural sociology U. Ky., Lexington, 1954-55, instr. dept. anthropology, 1956-57, 1959-60, instr. dept. community medicine, 1961-63, asst. prof., 1963-66, assoc. prof., 1966-73, prof., 1973-80, assoc. dir. Ctr. Developmental Change, 1970-73, prof. community health Coll. Allied Health, prof. anthropology Coll. of Arts and Scis., prof. pub. adminstrn. Grad. Ctr. Pub. Adminstrn., 1980—; teaching fellow dept. anthropology U. Oreg., Eugene, 1957-58, instr., 1958-59, NSF research fellow, 1960-61;

USPHS spl. research fellow Sch. Pub. Health, U. Calif.-Berkeley, 1968-69; chmn. state family planning rev. com. Ky. State Comprehensive Health Planning Council, 1972-74; mem. state family planning task force Council Health Services, Ky. State Dept. Human Resources, 1974-78; cons., adv. numerous orgns.; vis. scholar dept. adminstrv. and social health scis. Sch. Pub. Health, U. Calif.-Berkeley, 1979; dir. Bluegrass Regional Birth Planning Council, Inc., Lexington, 1978-81, Lexington Planned Parenthood, Inc., 1982-89; mem. adv. coun. Ctr. of Creative Living/Adult Care Program of Lexington-Fayette County Health Dept., 1989. Mem. Union of Concerned Scientists, Am. Farmland Trust, Wilderness Soc. Served with USN, 1946-47. Grantee pub. health, family planning, sickle cell anemia, Tb control and occupational health-risk factors. Fellow Am. Anthrop. Assn., Soc. Applied Anthropology; mem. Soc. Med. Anthropology (founding), Am. Pub. Health Assn. (founding mem. population sect.), Assn. Tchrs. Preventive Medicine, AAAS, AAUP, Phi Beta Kappa, Sigma Xi, Alpha Kappa Delta, Delta Omega. Democrat. Clubs: Univ. Faculty, Alumni. Contbr. numerous articles to profl. publs. Home: 953 Holly Springs Dr Lexington KY 40504-3119 Office: Univ Ky Med Ctr 208A Annex 2 208A Annex 2 Lexington KY 40536

HOCKEL, JACK LEWIS, dentist; b. Menomonee, Wis., July 18, 1933; m. Judie Miner, Jan. 23, 1960; 6 children. Student, San Jose (Calif.) State U., 1951-52, U. Calif., San Francisco, 1952-55; DDS, U. Calif., San Francisco, 1959. Assoc. dentist San Francisco, 1959-60; gen. practice dentistry Berkeley, Calif., 1960-62, Concord, Calif., 1962-76, Walnut Creek, Calif., 1976—. Editor: Orthopedic Gnathology. Master Acad. Gen. Dentistry; mem. Internal Acad. Gnathology, Am. Acad. Gnathological Orthop. (pres. 1983-85, diplomate 1986), Cranial Acad., Am. Equilibration Soc., Fedn. Orthodontic Assns. (diplomate 1978). Office: 2651 Oak Grove Rd Walnut Creek CA 94596-2815

HOCKENBERGER, SUSAN JANE, nurse educator; b. Toledo, Apr. 18, 1948; d. Addison James and Jane Elizabeth (Murray) H. Diploma, St. Vincent Hosp. Sch. Nursing, 1969; BSN, Mary Manse Coll., 1973; MSN, Med. Coll. Ga., 1975; EdD, Vanderbilt U., 1991. Clin. nurse specialist, dean Lansing Sch. Nursing Bellarmine Coll., Louisville; bd. dirs. Am. Cancer Soc., Louisville, NCJW Parkside Adult Day Care, Louisville. Editor ethics dept. Plastic Surg. Nursing; contbr. articles to profl. jours. Mem. speakers bur. Am. Cancer Soc., Louisville. Named for Disting. Svc. to Am. Soc. Plastic and Reconstructive Surg. Nursing, 1993, Life Saver Am. Cancer Soc., 1994; recipient Phoebe Kandel Rohrer Disting. Alumni award Med. Coll. Ga., 1995. Mem. ANA (CS), AORN, Ky. Nurses Assn., Am. Soc. Plastic and Reconstructive Surgery (CPSN), Sigma Theta Tau. Democrat. Roman Catholic. Home: 756 Yorkwood Pl Louisville KY 40223-3569 Office: Bellarmine Coll Newburg Rd Louisville KY 40205-0671

HOCKETT, SHERI LYNN, radiologist; b. Cleburne, Tex., Apr. 20, 1953; d. Dale and Rosamond (Prater) Hockett; BA, So. Meth. U., 1974; MD, Southwestern Med. Sch., 1978; m. David Alexander Campbell, Apr. 22, 1978; children: Courtney Michelle, Jonathan David. Resident diagnostic radiology St. Paul Hosp., Dallas, 1978-81, chief resident, 1980-81; fellow, 1981-82; chmn. dept. radiology Baylor Med. Ctr. Garland, Tex. Diplomate Am. Bd. Radiology. Mem. Am. Assn. Women Radiologists, Am. Coll. Radiology, Radiol. Soc. N.Am., Tex. Radiol. Soc., AMA, Dalls-Ft. Worth Radiol. Soc. Office: 2300 Marie Curie Dr Garland TX 75042-5706

HODAS, ARNOLD JAY, psychiatrist; b. Bklyn., Apr. 4, 1933. AB, Colgate U., 1954; MD, New York Med. Coll., 1958. Diplomate Am. Bd. Psychiatry and Neurology. Intern U.S. Naval Hosp., St. Albans, N.Y., 1958-59; resident in psychiatry Manhattan State Hosp., N.Y.C., 1961-64, cons. sr. psychiatrist, 1964-73; asst. attend. psychiatrist N.Y. Psychiat. Inst., N.Y.C., 1970-73; collaborating psychoanalyst Columbia U., Coll. Physicians and Surgeons, N.Y.C., 1972-74; pvt. practice N.Y.C. 1964-73, Scarsdale, N.Y., 1970—. Lt. M.C., USN, 1958-61. Mem. Am. Psychiat. Assn. Office: 235 Garth Rd Ste E1J Scarsdale NY 10583

HODESS, ARTHUR BART, cardiologist; b. N.Y.C., Jan. 15, 1950; s. Samuel and Dora (Rosenkrantz) H.; m. Carol Yasuna, Aug. 31, 1969 (div. May 1985); children: Joshua David, Jeremy Scott; m. S. Christina Ellsworth, Dec. 23, 1987; children: Jonathan Ellsworth, Jason Dorian, Jordan Gottier. BA, Boston U., 1970; MD, Columbia U., 1974. Intern Hosp. of U. Pa., Phila., 1974-75, resident in medicine, 1975-77, fellow in cardiology, 1977-79; asst. instr. dept. medicine Hosp. U. of Pa., Phila., 1974-79; instr. physiology, dept. animal biology U. Pa., Sch. Veterinary Medicine, Phila., 1977-78; clin. assoc. dept. medicine U. Pa., Phila., 1979-81; attending cardiologist Brandywine Hosp., Coatesville, Pa., 1979—; dir. critical care Brandywine Hosp., Coatesville, 1989—, chief of cardiology, 1990—, chmn. dept. medicine, 1991-95; pres. Brandywine Valley Cardiovascular Assocs., Thorndale, Pa., 1991—. Contbr. articles to profl. jours. V.p. Chestnut Hollow Homeowners Assn., West Chester, Pa., 1990-94, bd. dirs. 1995; bd. dirs. Beth Israel Congregation, Chester County, 1991-96. Fellow Clin. Coun. Cardiology Am. Heart Assn. Fellow ACP, Am. Coll. Cardiology, Am. Coll. Chest Physicians; mem. Am. Soc. Echocardiography, Phila. Acad. Cardiology, Drinker Soc. for Critical Care in Phila., Cardiac Electrophysiology Soc., Soc. Critical Care Medicine. Office: Brandywine Valley Cardio 3025 Zinn Rd Thorndale PA 19372-1131

HODGE, JACQUELYN ROBERTS, health information executive; b. Balt., Mar. 3, 1956; d. James R. and Leila E. (Brown) Roberts; m. Sherman M. Hodge, Dec. 18, 1976; children: Lynsey M., Alexis D. AA, Cmty. Coll. Balt., 1976; BA, Coll. Notre Dame of Balt., 1995, postgrad., 1996—. Cancer registrar Greater Balt. Medical Ctr., 1977-79; medical records supr. Union Meml. Hosp., Balt., 1980-81; med. records supr. U. Md., Balt., 1981-82; coder Northwest Hosp., Randallstown, Md., 1983-85; coder Mercy Medical Ctr., Balt., 1985-89, patient info. mgr., 1989—; training site mgr. for MRT student affiliations Cmty. Coll. Balt., 1986—. Contbr. articles to profl. jours. Cmty. rep. Stevensonswood Inprovement Assn., Randallstown, Md., 1995—. Recipient Mercy Excellence award Mercy Medical Ctr., 1993-95. Mem. Md. Health Info. Mgnt. Assn. (date quality com.), Health Infom Mgmt. Systems Soc., Am. Health Info. Mgmt. Assn. Office: Mercy Medical Ctr 301 Saint Paul Pl Baltimore MD 21202

HODGE, WARREN WISE, preventive medicine physician; b. Martinsville, Va., Apr. 29, 1934; s. Charles Spurgeon and Mildred Mae (Wise) H.; m. Irene Ann Vasil, June 29, 1961; children: Charles Wesley, Dana Elise. BS, U. Louisville, 1955, MD, 1958; MPH, Harvard U., 1964. Diplomate Am. Bd. Preventive Medicine. Commd. ensign USN, 1958, advanced through grades to capt., 1973, ret., 1985; intern U.S. Naval Hosp., Portsmouth, Va., 1958-59; resident Naval Aerospace Med. Inst., Pensacola, Fla., 1964-66; physician Escambia County Health Dept., Pensacola, 1986-87, Sacred Heart Hosp., Pensacola, 1987-89, Bapt. Health Care, Pensacola, 1989—. Contbr.: (textbook) Naval Flight Surgeon Manual, 1968. Dist. adminstr. USSF Soccer Referees, Fla., 1985—. Capt. M.C. USN, 1958-85. Decorated Navy Commendation medal, Meritorious Svc. medal (2). Fellow Am. Coll. Preventive Medicine, Aerospace Med. Assn.; mem. Assn. Mil. Surgeons U.S. Home: 120 Nandina Rd Gulf Breeze FL 32561 Office: North Davis Family Med Ctr 6330 N Davis Hwy Pensacola FL 32504-6953

HODGES, MARK KENNETH, physician, medical educator; b. Birmingham, Ala., May 8, 1955; s. James D. and Carolyn Ann (Duke) H.; m. Cindy Ann Buehler, Sept. 15, 1984; children: Caitlin Alexandra, Austin Bradley. BS, Auburn U., 1977; MD, U. South Ala., 1981. Resident U. South Ala., Mobile, 1984-85; physician Baton Rouge Clinic, 1988—; asst. clin. prof. La. State U. Sch. Medicine, Baton Rouge, 1988—; mem. exec. com. Baton Rouge Clinic, 1995—; chief pulmonary divsn. Baton Rouge Gen. Med. Ctr., 1994—; assoc. med. dir. Ascension Hosp., Baton Rouge, 1994—. Sponsor YMCA, Baton Rouge, 1996. Pulmonary divsn. fellow Harvard Med. Sch./Brigham & Womens Hosp., Boston, 1985-88. Fellow Am. Coll. Chest Physicians; mem. Am. Thoracic Soc., Bocage Racquet Club, Phi Kappa Phi. Office: Baton Rouge Clinic 8415 Goodwood Blvd Baton Rouge LA 70806

HODGE-SPENCER, CHERYL ANN, orthodontist; b. Dorchester, Mass., Apr. 1, 1952; d. Herbert Thomas and Edwina Catherine (Morey) Hodge; m. John Lawrence Spencer, June 10, 1978; children: Devin Thomas, Ian Nicholas. BS in Biology cum laude, Boston Coll., 1974; DMD, Tufts Sch. Dental Medicine, 1977; MPH, Harvard U. Sch. Pub. Health, 1981; Cert. in Orthodontics, Harvard Dental Sch., 1983. Orthodontist Brockton/Bridgewater, Mass., 1984—; orthodontic cons. Mass. Hosp. Sch., Canton, Mass., 1990—; vice chmn. Bd. of Investment, Bridgewater Savs. Bank, 1989-92; asst. coach Duxbury Youth Hockey Bantam Team, 1993-94. Lt. Dental Corps USN, 1977-80. Recipient Johnson & Johnson Dentistry award, 1977. Mem. Am. Assn. Orthodontists, Mass. Dental Soc., South Shore Dist. Dental Soc. (sec. 1990-92, peer rev. bd. 1990-92), Northeastern Soc. Orthodontists, Harvard Club Boston, Harvard Soc. Advancement Orthodontics, Metro South C. of C., Rotary (bd. dirs. charitable and ednl. fund 1989-92), Pierre Fouchard Acad., Ma. Amateur Hockey Assn. (intermediate patched hockey coach). Roman Catholic. Office: 572 Pleasant St Brockton MA 02401-2515

HODGES-ROBINSON, CHETTINA M., nursing administrator; b. Roosevelt, N.Y., Mar. 12, 1963; d. Clifford and Janice (Revis) Hodges-Jones; m. Darrell K. Robinson, Mar. 17, 1991. BSN, NYU, 1986. Cert. med.-surg. nurse basic life support and advanced cardiac life support. Staff nurse NYU Med. ctr., N.Y.C., 1986-87, Christ Hosp., Jersey City, 1986-87; cardiothoracic recovery rm. and post-anesthesia nurse, staff nurse Lenox Hill Hosp., N.Y.C., 1987-94; asst. nurse mgr. critical care/intensive/coronary care unit Good Samaritan Hosp., West Islip, L.I., N.Y., 1994—; staff nurse cardiovasc. ICU U. Hosp. at Stony Brook, N.Y., 1995—; field nurse Staff Builders, Medford, N.Y., 1995—; asst. head nurse Jewish Home and Hosp. for the Aged, Bronx, N.Y., 1996—. Mem. Luth. Ch. of the Good Shepherd, Roosevelt, N.Y. Mem. ANA, N.J. Nurses Assn., Black Nurses Assn. (L.I. chpt.), Zeta Alpha Beta. Home: 119 S 28th St Wyandanch NY 11798-2813

HODGKIN, SIR ALAN LLOYD, biophysicist; b. Feb. 5, 1914; s. G.L. and M.F. (Wilson) H.; m. Marion de Kay Rous, 1944; 1 son, 3 daus. Student, Trinity Coll.; (fellow), Cambridge U., 1936, M.A., Sc.D.; M.D. (hon.), univs. of Berne, Louvain; D.Sc. (hon.), univs. of Sheffield, Newcastle-upon-Tyne, East Anglia, Manchester, Leicester, London, Nfld., Wales, Rockefeller U., Bristol, Oxford; LL.D., U. Aberdeen, Cambridge. Sci. officer radar Air Ministry, also Ministry Aircraft Prodn., 1939-45; lectr., then asst. dir. research Cambridge U., 1945-52; Foulerton research prof. Royal Soc., 1952-69; John Humphrey Plummer prof. biophysics U. Cambridge, 1970-81; master Trinity Coll., Cambridge, 1978-84; mem. Med. Research Council, 1959-63; chancellor U. Leicester, 1971-84. Author: Conduction of the Nervous Impulse, 1963, Chance and Design, 1992; also sci. papers on nature of nervous conduction, muscle, and vision. Devised (with Andrew Huxley) system of math. equations describing nerve impulse; worked with giant nerve fibers of squid, proving that electricity was direct causal agt. of impulse propagation. Decorated knight Order Brit. Empire, 1972, Order of Merit, 1973; recipient Baly medal, 1955, Nobel prize for medicine or physiology (with A.F. Huxley, J.C. Eccles), 1963, Lord Crook Medal, 1983. Fellow Royal Soc. (Royal medal 1958, Copley medal 1965, pres. 1970-75), Imperial Coll. Sci., Indian Nat. Sci. Acad. (hon.) Girton Coll., Cambridge (hon.); mem. Physiol. Soc. (fgn. sec. 1960-67), Nat. Acad. Scis., Am. Acad. Arts and Scis. (fgn. hon.), Royal Danish Acad. Scis. (fgn.), Leopoldina Acad., Royal Swedish Acad. Scis. (fgn.), Am. Philos. Soc. (fgn.), Royal Irish Acad. (hon.), USSR Acad. Scis. (fgn.), Marine Biol. Assn. U.K. (pres. 1966-76). Address: 18 Panton St, Cambridge CB2 1HP, England

HODGKIN, JOHN E., pulmonologist; b. Portland, Oreg., Aug. 22, 1939; s. Williard E. and Dorothy (Rigsby) H.; m. Jeanie Walker, Sept. 6, 1980; children: Steve, Kathryn, Carolyn, Jonathan, Jamie. BS, Walla Walla Coll., 1960; MD, Loma Linda U., 1964. Fellow in pulmonology Mayo Clinic, Rochester, Minn., 1970-72; chief pulmonary sect. Loma Linda (Calif.) U., 1974-80; clin. prof. medicine U. Calif., Davis, 1983—; med. dir. respiratory care St. Helena Hosp., Deer Park, Calif., 1983—, med. dir. pulmonary rehab., 1983—, med. dir. ctr. for health promotion, 1983-96; med. dir. Adventist Health No. Calif., Roseville, Calif., 1995—, Calif. Med. Found., 1995—. Editor: Chronic Obstructive Pulmonary Disease: Current Concepts, 1987, Respiratory Care: A Guide to Clinical Practice, 1991, Pulmonary Rehabilitation: Guidelines to Success, 1993, Lung Sounds: A Practical Guide, 1996. Decorated bronze star U.S. Army, 1968. Fellow Am. Assn. Cardiovas. & Pulmonary Rehab. (pres. 1995-96), Am. Coll. Chest Physicians, Am. Coll. Physicians, Am. Thoracic Soc., Nat. Assn. Med. Direction of Respiratory Care, Am. Assn. Respiratory Care (bd. med. advisors). Home: 1330 Crestmont Dr Angwin CA 94508 Office: Saint Helena Hosp Lloyd Bldg Ste 502 Deer Park CA 94576

HODGSON, CLAGUE PITMAN, molecular biologist; b. Rochester, Minn, July 6, 1946; s. Corrin Haley and Florence Mary (Pitman) H.; m. Kristi Kay Lauruhn; children: Corrin William, Riley Clague. BS, U. Minn., 1976, PhD in Cell and Devel. Biology, 1983. Teaching asst. U. Minn., Mpls., 1976-78; predoctoral fellow Mayo Grad. Sch. Medicine, Rochester, 1978-83; postdoctoral fellow Baylor Coll. Medicine, Houston, 1983-85; asst. prof. molecular and devel. biology Ohio State U., 1985-91; assoc. prof., chief divsn. cancer biology, gene therapy lab. Creighton U. Sch. Medicine, Omaha, Nebr., 1991—; reviewer grants and contracts NIH, 1986—; chief exec. officer Nature Tech. Corp., Omaha, 1988—; cons. NIH, various cos., 1985—. Author: Retro-Vectors for Human Gene Therapy, 1995; sect. editor: Current Sci., 1993—, Expert Opinion in Therapeutic Patents; contbr. numerous articles to profl. jours. Recipient Nat. Rsch. Svc. award NIH, 1983-85, fellow, 1983-85, First Ind. Rsch. and Transition award NIH, 1989-93, NIH Shannon Dirs. award, 1995, Inventor's Network Trialon award, 1991, John C. Kenefick award, 1991. Mem. AAAS, Am. Soc. for Cell Biology, Am. Soc. Microbiology, Human Genome Orgn. Home: 109 S 54th St Omaha NE 68132-3401 Office: Creighton Cancer Ctr Calif At 24th St Omaha NE 68178

HODGSON, DAVID, hospital administrator, medical technologist; b. Athol, Mass., Mar. 12, 1935; m. Mary Ann Veilleux, Sept. 13, 1959; children: David, Daniel, Donald, Darin. BBA, Lamar U., 1981, M in Pub. Adminstrn., 1986. Cert. med. tech. Am. Soc. Med. Technologists, Health Care Financing Agy. Hosp. corpsman USN, 1953-57; chief med. technologist Lakes Region Gen. Hosp., Laconia, N.H., 1959-68; dir. referral lab. Hodgdon Clin. Lab., Concord, N.H., 1968-78; lab. mgr. Mid-Jefferson County Hosp., Nederland, Tex., 1978-83; lab. mgr., asst. adminstr. Park Place Hosp., Port Arthur, Tex., 1983-87; productivity mgmt. cons. Am. Med. Internat. S.W. Region, Dallas, 1987-88; COO Doctors Hosp. Laredo, Tex., 1988-93; CEO Doctors Hosp. Laredo, 1993—. Contbr. articles to Am. Jour. Med. Tech. With USN, 1953-57, Korea. Mem. Am. Soc. Med. Technologists, Health Care Fin. Agy., Rotary Club. Home: 113 Lam Rick Cir Laredo TX 78043 Office: Doctors Hosp Laredo 500 E Mann Rd Laredo TX 78041-2699

HODGSON, ERNEST, toxicology educator; b. Durham, Eng., July 26, 1932; came to U.S., 1955; s. Ernest Victor and Emily (Moses) H.; m. Mary Kathleen Devlin, Dec. 21, 1957; children: Mary Elizabeth, Audrey Catherine, Patricia Emily Devlin, Ernest Victor Felix. B.Sc. with honors, Kings Coll. U. Durham, Eng., 1955; Ph.D., Oreg. State U., 1959. Rsch. fellow Oreg. State U., Corvallis, 1955-59, U. Wis., Madison, 1959-61; asst. prof. N.C. State U., Raleigh, 1961-63, assoc. prof., 1963-65, prof. toxicology, 1965—, William Neal Reynolds prof., 1977—, chmn. toxicology dept., 1982—, Disting. Alumni Rsch. prof., 1987-90; mem. adv. panel U.S. EPA, Washington, 1982-85; mem. toxicology study sect. NIH, Washington, 1985-89, mem. NIEHS study sect., 1992—, chmn. 1994—; pres. Toxicology Comm., Raleigh, 1982—; vis. scientist U. Wash., Seattle, 1975. Author, editor: Introduction to Biochemical Toxicology, 1980, 2d edit., 1994, Modern Toxicology, 1987, Dictionary of Toxicology; editor: Reviews in Biochemical Toxicology, 1979—, Reviews in Environmental Toxicology, 1984—, Jour. Biochemical Toxicology; mem. editorial bd. Chemico-Biol. Interactions, Jour. Toxicology and Applied Pharmacology; contbr. articles to profl. jours. Chmn. policy rev. com. Gov.'s Waste Mgmt. Bd., Raleigh, 1984. NIH grantee, 1962—. Mem. AAAS, Soc. Toxicology (edn. com. 1984—, Edn. award 1984, Merit award 1994, pres. mechanisms sect. 1991-92, pres. N.C. chpt. 1984-85), Am. Soc. Pharmacology (drug metabolism com. 1981-84), Am. Chem. Soc. (Burdick and Jackson Internat. award in pesticide chemistry), Internat. Soc. Study Xenobiotics (coun. 1986-89, sec.-elect 1990-92, sec. 1992-94, pres.-elect 1996—), Sigma Xi (chpt. pres. 1974). Democrat. Office: NC State U Dept Toxicology Box 7633 Raleigh NC 27695

HODGSON, PAUL EDMUND, surgeon; b. Milw., Dec. 14, 1921; s. Howard Edmund and Ethel Marie (Niemi) H.; m. Barbara Jean Osborne, Apr. 22, 1945; children: Ann, Paul. BS summa cum laude, Beloit Coll., 1943; M.D. cum laude, U. Mich., 1945. Diplomate: Am. Bd. Surgery. Intern U. Mich. Hosp., 1945-46, resident in surgery, 1948-52; mem. faculty dept. surgery U. Mich., 1952-62, assoc. prof., 1956-62; prof. surgery U. Nebr. Coll. Medicine, Omaha, 1962-88; prof. emeritus U. Nebr. Coll. Medicine, 1988—, asst. dean for curriculum, 1966-72, chmn. dept. surgery, 1972-84; Trustee Beloit Coll., 1977-80. Served to capt. M.C. U.S. Army, 1946-48. Mem. A.C.S., Frederick A. Coller Surg. Soc., Soc. Univ. Surgeons, Central Surg. Assn., Soc. Surgery Alimentary Tract, Am. Assn. Surgery Trauma, Western Surg. Assn., Am. Surg. Assn. Presbyterian. Office: U Nebr Med Ctr 600 S 42d St Omaha NE 68198-3280

HODGSON, W(ALTER) JOHN B(ARRY), surgeon; b. Middlesborough, England, Sept. 17, 1939; came to U.S., 1975; s. Walter Aggett and Constance Lillian (Nelson) H.; m. Jean C. Morgan, Apr. 20, 1967; children: Sean, Russell, Miranda. MB, BS, Charing Cross Med. Sch., London, 1964; M of Surgery, London U., 1976. Rotating intern, resident London U., 1964-75; surgeon Bronx (N.Y.) VA Med. Ctr., 1975-78, asst. chief surg. service, 1977-82; pvt. practice specializing in surgery Mt. Sinai Hosp., N.Y.C., 1978-81; chief gastro-intestinal surgery Westchester Med. Ctr., Valhalla, N.Y., 1981—; prof. surgery N.Y. Med. Coll., Valhalla, 1987—, course organizer for laparoscopic surgery, 1990-92, prof. cell biol. and anatomy, 1993—; clin. prof. surgery NYU, 1995—. Contbr. articles to profl. jours.; editor: Liver Tumors: Multidisciplinary Management, 1987; inventor cavitron surg. technique for liver tumor surgery. Organizer, coach Larchmont Jr. Soccer League, 1977; mem. Larchmont Rep. Com., 1985. Cavitron Co. grantee, 1978, Cavitron Lasersonics grantee, 1987. Fellow ACS, Am. Coll. Gastroneterology; mem. N.Y. Sur. Soc. for Acad. Surgery, Am. Assn. Clin. Anatomists. Episcopalian. Club: Larchmont Yacht. Office: NY Med Coll Dept Surgery Munger Pavilion Valhalla NY 10595

HODSON, CHARLES ANDREW, medical educator; b. Mason City, Iowa, Aug. 9, 1947; s. Ralph A. and Ruby (Olsen) H.; m. Patricia Stavrakas, June 4, 1984; children: Emma Jane, Hannah Louise. BS, Iowa State U., 1969, MS, 1971, PhD, 1975. Rsch. assoc. Mich. State U., Lansing, 1975-78; asst. prof. East Carolina U., Greenville, N.C., 1978-83, assoc. prof., 1983-93; prof., 1993—. Author book chpts; contbr. articles to profl. jours. Capt. USAR, 1972-84. Rsch. grant NIH, 1981-84. Mem. Endocrine Soc., Am. Physiol. Soc., Assn. of Profs. of Ob-Gyn, Sigma Xi. Office: E Carolina U Sch Medicine Dept Ob-Gyn Greenville NC 27834

HOEBEL, BARTLEY GORE, psychology educator; b. N.Y.C., May 29, 1935; s. Edward Adamson and Frances (Gore) H.; m. Cynthia A. Eney, June 22, 1962; children—Valerie, Carolyn, Brett. AB, Harvard, 1957; PhD, U. Pa., 1962; PhD (hon.), Cath. U., Louvain, France, 1991. Mem. faculty psychology dept. Princeton, 1962—, prof, 1970—; sci. adv. bd. Interneuron Pharm. Co., 1993—. Contbg. author: S.S. Stevens Handbook of Experimental Psychology, 1988; contbr. articles to tech. jours. and books. Fellow AAAS, APA (pres. physiol. and comparative psychol. divsn. 1994), Am. Psychol. Soc.; mem. Soc. Neurosci., Soc. Study Ingestive Behavior (pres. 1995), Ea. Psychol. Assn. Unitarian. Home: 207 Hartley Ave Princeton NJ 08540-5615

HOEFFER, BEVERLY, nursing educator, researcher; b. Spokane, Wash., June 14, 1944. BS, U. Wash., 1966; MS, Rutgers U., 1969; D of Nursing Sci., U. Calif., San Francisco, 1979. Cert. clin. specialist adult psychiat./mental health nurse. Assoc. to prof., chmn. dept. mental health nursing Oreg. Health Scis. U., Portland, 1980—; asst. clin. prof., dept. mental health/community nursing U. Calif., San Francisco, 1979-80; clin. nurse specialist Mission Community Mental Health Ctr., San Francisco, 1974-75; presenter confs. in field. Contbr. articles to profl. jours. Recipient Geriatric Mental Health Acad. award NIMH, 1984-87, rsch. grants in field. Fellow Am. Acad. Nursing; mem. ANA (exec. com. psychiat./mental health nursing 1986-88, chmn. coun. of specialists), Phi Beta Kappa.

HOEFLER, HEINZ KARL, physician; b. Fürstenfeld, Austria, Jan. 7, 1949; arrived in Fed. Republic Germany, 1989; s. Alois and Anna (Ruck) H.; m. Heidemarie, Oct. 8, 1974. Diploma, U. Graz, Austria. MD Inst. Pathology, Graz, rsch. fellow, asst. prof., assoc. prof., prof.; dir. Inst. Pathology, Munich, 1989—, prof., dir., 1989—; bd. dirs. Ctr. Environ. and Health, Munich. Author books in field; contbr. articles to profl. jours.; editor jours. in field. Recipient awards from several med. soc., Austria, Fed. Republic Germany. Mem. numerous scientific orgns. Roman Catholic. Home: Ismaninger Strasse 64, 81675 Munich Germany Office: Inst of Pathology, Ismaninger Str 22, 81675, 8000 Munich Federal Republic Germany

HOEFS, JOHN J., health plan administrator; b. Mpls., Sept. 9, 1948; s. LeRoy and Kathryn (Koppi) H.; m. Debra Lynn Nystrom, Jan. 19, 1974; children: Michael, Jeffrey, David, Anna. BS, SUNY, Saratoga Springs, 1989; MS, Sage Grad. Sch., 1994. V.p. HMO oper. Blue Cross Blue Shield Minn., Eagan, 1974-85; divsn. v.p. alt. delivery Sys. Empire Blue Cross Blue Shield, Albany, N.Y., 1985-87; exec. dir., CEO Ctrl. Minn. Group Health Plan, St. Cloud, 1989—; chmn. Minn. Coun. HMO's, St. Paul, 1995—; bd. dirs. Region 3 Health Care Coord. Bd., Ctrl. Minn., 1993—. Pres. Cathedral Athletic Assn., St. Cloud, 1992—; bd. dirs. Cathedral Edn. Found., St. Cloud, 1993—. Mem. Group Health Assn. Am., Med. Group Mgmt. Assn., Nat. Rural Health Assn. Roman Catholic. Office: Ctrl Minn Group Health Plan 1245 15th St North Saint Cloud MN 56303

HOEFT, CARL EDWARD, chemist; b. Mankato, Minn., Mar. 6, 1966; s. Jeffrey Lynn and Marlys Jean (Hoffman) H.; m. Judith Irene Vacek, Aug. 23, 1986; children: Jared Corwin, Summer Rose. BA in Chemistry, Hamline U., 1988; MSChemE, Wash. State U., 1992, PhD in Chem. Engring., 1994. Quality assurance technician Hutchinson (Minn.) Tech., Inc., 1984, chem. technician, 1985-86; tech. aide 3M Care Specialties Lab., St. Paul, 1987-89; tchg./rsch. asst. Wash. State U., Pullman, 1990-94; sr. rsch. chemist Dionex Corp., Sunnyvale, Calif., 1994—. Mem. coun. on ministries Simpson United Meth. Ch., Pullman, 1993. Melvin M. Smith scholar, 1992, 93, 94, 3M scholar, 1985, 86, 87, Hutchinson Tech., Inc. scholar, 1984-88. Mem. Am. Chem. Soc. (sec. student chpt. Hamline U. 1987-88). Methodist. Office: Dionex Corp 1228 Titan Way PO Box 3603 Sunnyvale CA 94086

HOEFT, THEA MARIE, college administrator, therapist, educator; b. Milw., Feb. 9, 1950; d. Peter Kazin and Renate Katherine (Kaniewski) Zidonowitz. B.S. in Recreation, U. Wis.-LaCrosse, 1972; M.S. in Leisure Studies, U. Utah, 1973; EdD in Ednl. Adminstrn., Va. Poly. Tech. Inst. and State U., 1979; postgrad., U. Ark., 1994. Playground dir. Watertown (Wis.) Dept. Parks and Recreation, 1969; dir. Bluffview playground LaCrosse Dept. Parks and Recreation, 1970; instr. Ind. State U., Terre Haute, 1973-74; day camp dir. Vigo County Extension Service, Terre Haute, Ind., 1974; instr. Radford (Va.) U., 1974-75; phys. edn. tchr. St. Patrick Cathedral Sch., Harrisburg, Pa., 1975; receptionist crisis worker Holy Spirit Hosp. Community Mental Health Center, Camphill, Pa., 1975; adj. faculty U. So. Miss., Hattiesburg, 1976; master recreational therapist Ellisville (Miss.) State Sch. for Mentally Ill and Retarded, 1976; instr. Radford U., 1976-77; mental retardation profl. Hearthside Rehab. Ctr., Brown Deer, Wis., 1979; asst. prof., coord. therapeutic recreation curriculum Ariz. State U., Tempe, 1979-83; master therapist Mt. Sinai Med. Ctr. Geriatric Inst. Alzheimer Disease Day Hosp./Phys. Rehab. Hosp., Milw., 1983-84; therapist spinal cord injury unit VA Hosp., Milw., 1984-85; asst. dir. evening coll. and extension programs Milw. Sch. Engring., 1985-88, assoc. dir. admissions and retention, 1988-90, dir. parttime enrollment, 1990, sr. lectr. bus. and mgmt. systems, 1988-90; dir. acad. advising, mem. commn. on the status women U. Ark.-Little Rock, 1990—, pres. commn. status women, 1991-92; pres. Ark. Acad. Advising Network, 1995-96, internat. officer, 1996—; cons. 4-H, 1976, Crippled Children's Hosp., Va., 1978, others; mem. Ark. Act Adv. Coun.; bd. dirs. Life Skills, Inc. Mem. editl. bd. Ark. Area Health Edn. Ctrs., 1991—, U. Ark. Med. Scis. Ctr. Rural Health Newsletter, 1992—; contbr. articles to profl. jours. Mem. Miss. Com. Spl. Olympics, 1976; rep. United Way Ariz., 1979; mem. Mayor's Adv. Drug Com., 1972; bd. dirs. Youth Treatment and Evaluation Ctr., Phoenix, 1979-82; mem. Phoenix spl. populations adv. coun. on recreation, 1980-82; vol. Phoenix Panhellenic Coun., 1982; mem. Ariz. State U. Centennial Com., 1981-83, chairperson disabled students svcs. adv. bd., 1981-83; vol. Pinnacle Mt. State Park, 1990. Wis. Leadership grantee, 1968; recipient Disting. Svc. award Montgomery County Cardiac Therapy Ctr., 1979, United Way, 1980, Recreation Com. U. Wis.,

LaCrosse, 1971, 72; H. Roe Bartle Recruiting award, 1981. Mem. Am. Camping Assn., Ariz. Parks and Recreation Assn., Va. Parks and Recreation Assn., Nat. Recreation and Park Assn., Therapeutic Recreation Assn. Greater Milw. (pres. 1983-84), Am. Assn. Adult and Continuing Edn., AAHPERD (editorial bd.), Nat. Leadership Inst., Nat. Acad. Advising Assn. (book reviewer 1990, mem. commn. acad. advising adminstrs. 1991—, Ark. rep. region 7 1990—), Phi Delta Kappa, Phi Delta Chi (advisor 1986-90, mem. grad. program coun. 1986-90), Sigma Kappa Sigma, Sigma Lambda Sigma, Gamma Sigma Sigma, Alpha Sigma Lambda, Delta Kappa Gamma. Roman Catholic. Home: 30714 Bandy Rd Little Rock AR 72211-9388 Office: U Ark-Little Rock Ross Hall 406 2801 S University Ave Little Rock AR 72204-1000

HOEHN, JAMES GURNEY, plastic surgeon; b. Detroit, Feb. 8, 1938; s. Vincent Henry and Frances Margaret (Pallai) H.; m. Barbara Louise Kegler, Aug. 18, 1962; children: James, Jr., Melissa. BS, Georgetown U., 1960; MD, Northwestern U., 1964. Diplomate Am. Bd. of Plastic Surgery, Am. Bd. of Surgery. Intern Chgo. Wesley Meml. Hosp., 1964-65; residency in gen. surgery Mayo Clinic, Rochester, Minn., 1965-69, residency in plastic surgery, 1969-71; plastic surgeon, sec. Albany Plastic Surgeons Associated, P.C., Albany, N.Y., 1971-84; plastic surgeon, pres. James G. Hoehn, M.D., James A. Edmond, M.D., P.C., Albany, 1984-87; head divsn. plastic surgery Albany Med. Coll., 1987-91; vice chmn. dept. surgery edn. Albany (N.Y.) Med. Coll.; 1988-92, tng. program dir. Divsn. Plastic Surgery, 1993—; bd. dirs. and chmn. Med. Dental staff The Child's Hosp., Albany, 1985-87. Author: Illustrated Buyers Guide to Jaguars, 1987, 2d edition; contbr. articles to profl. jours. Vice chmn. Tricentennial Celebration Com., Inc., Albany, 1986; bd. dirs. Hist. Cherry Hill, Albany, 1987-90. Served to maj. USAR, 1965-75. Fellow ACS (bd. govs. 1986-88), Am. Assn. Plastic Surgeons; mem. AMA (ho. of dels., RBRVS update com.), Am. Soc. Plastic and Constructive Surgeons (bd. dirs. 1988—, pres. 1992-93, Presdl. Citation 1988), Am. Assn. Hand Surgery (pres. 1983-84, Disting. Svc. award 1985), Am. Soc. Aesthetic Plastic Surgery, Am. Soc. Surgery Hand (residency rev. com. for plastic surgery 1993—), Ft. Orange Club (trustee 1988-94), Schuyler Meadows Club, Steuben Athletic Club. Republican. Roman Catholic. Home: Woodland-Pheasant Ln Menands NY 12204 Office: One Executive Park Dr Albany NY 12203

HOEHN-SARIC, RUDOLF, psychiatrist; b. Graz, Austria, Feb. 5, 1929; came to U.S., 1959; s. Werner and Wilhelmine (Wiltschnig) H.-S.; m. Evanne Loh, Oct. 14, 1960; children: Christopher, Edward, Alexander. MD, U. Graz, 1954; diploma in psychiatry, McGill U., Montreal, Que., Can., 1959. Resident in psychiatry Allan Meml. Inst. and Verdun Protestant Hosp., Montreal, 1956-58; fellow in clin. pharmacology Sch. of Medicine Johns Hopkins U., Balt., 1958-59, mem. Phipps Psychotherapy Rsch. Unit, Sch. Medicine, 1962-74, instr. in psychiatry, 1962-64, asst. prof., 1964-71, assoc. prof., 1972-92; prof., 1992—; dir. psychiat. outpatient svcs. Johns Hopkins U., Balt., 1977—, dir. anxiety clinic, 1978—, co-dir. behavioral medicine clinic, 1977—; resident in neuropsychiatry U. Vienna, 1959-60; rsch. psychiatrist Springfield State Hosp., 1960-61; mem. editorial bd. Jour. Anxiety Disorders; cons. Embassy of Fed. Republic Germany, Washington. Contbr. articles to profl. publs. Grantee NIMH. Fellow Am. Psychiat. Assn., Am. Psychopathol. Assn.; mem. AAAS, Med.-Chirurgical Faculty Md., Soc. Biol. Pshcyiatry, Am. Psychosomatic Soc. Office: Johns Hopkins Hosp 115 Meyer Blvd Baltimore MD 21205

HOEKSTRA, PHILIP THEODORE, urologist; b. Grand Rapids, Mich., Feb. 3, 1949; s. Theodore James and Harriett Martha (VanDyke) H.; m. Sharon Jean Alofs, May 25, 1973. AB, Calvin Coll., 1971; MD, U. Iowa, 1975. Diplomate Am. Bd. Urology. Intern Butterworth Hosp., Grand Rapids, Mich., 1976, resident in urology, 1981; pvt. practice Grand Rapids, Mich., 1981—; assoc. clin. prof. Mich. State U., Grand Rapids, 1980—. Recipient traveling fellowship award Am. Urologic Assn. (north ctrl. sect.), 1983. Mem. West Mich. Urology (pres. 1993-95, pres. emeritus 1995—). Republican. Reformed Church of America. Office: Michican Med Urology Divsn 21 Michigan Ste 750 Grand Rapids MI 49503

HOELTGE, GERALD ADRIAN, pathologist; b. Cin., Apr. 12, 1945; s. Elmer J. and Mary L. (Planitz) H.; m. Susan Cheryl Krieg, May 12, 1967; children: Christopher, Evan, Jason. AB, Wabash Coll., 1967; MD, Case-Western Res. U., 1971. Diplomate Am. Bd. Pathology. Intern, resident in lab. medicine Cleve. Clinic Found., 1971-75, mem. profl. staff, 1977—, chmn. dept. blood banking, 1982-91; chmn. med. adv. btr. No. Ohio region ARC, 1993—; lectr. in field. Author peer-reviewed articles, book chpts., monographs, abstracts. Maj. M.C. U.S. Army, 1971-77. Fellow Coll. Am. Pathologists, Am. Soc. Clin. Pathology; mem. AMA, Am. Assn. Blood Banks, Am. Soc. Histocompatibility and Immunogenetics, Ohio Assn. Blood Banks (pres. 1990-92), Case Western Res. U. Med. Sch. Alumni Assn. (trustee 1988-91, 96—), Phi Beta Kappa. Home: 17310 Old Tannery Trl Chagrin Falls OH 44023-2120 Office: Cleve Clinic Found 9500 Euclid Ave Cleveland OH 44195-0002

HOELTING, THOMAS LUDWIG, surgeon, researcher; b. Borghorst, Germany, July 8, 1956; s. Ludwig Albert and Ursula Ana (Rolfes) H.; m. Heike Antje Popken, Sept. 5, 1987; children: Marieke, Kristin, Lisanne. Student, Univ. Muenster, Kiel, Heidelberg, Germany, 1977-83; MD, PhD, Univ. Heidelberg. Gen. surgeon Univ. Heidelberg, 1985—; rsch. fellowship Univ. Calif., San Francisco, 1992-93; asst. prof. Univ. Heidelberg, 1994—; cons. prof., 1994—. Contbr. articles to profl. jours. Recipient sr. rsch. grant Univ. Heidelberg, 1995, Thyroid Fellowship award Endocrine Soc., 1992. Mem. Am. Assn. Cancer Rsch., Endocrine Soc. Am., Am. Thyroid Assn. Roman Catholic. Office: U Heidelberg Dept Surgery, Im Neuenheimer Feld 110, 69120 Heidelberg Germany

HOEMAN, SHIRLEY POLLOCK, medical educator, researcher, administrator and consultant; b. St. Charles, Mo., Oct. 15, 1942; d. Laurence J. and Bernadine Pollock; m. Richard D. Hoeman; children: Christopher, Timothy, Jonathan. BS in Nursing, U. Mo., 1964; MPH, U. Minn., 1974; MA, Rutgers U., 1982, PhD, 1984. RN, N.J.; cert. in advanced nursing adminstrn., cert. in rehab. nursing, cert. case mgr. Dir. nursing Sister Kenny Inst., Mpls., 1970-72; asst. prof. nursing U. Minn., Mpls., 1974-75; supr., cons. Minn. Dept. Health, Mpls., 1974-76; asst. prof. community Creighton U., Omaha, 1976-78; asst. prof. community health Rutgers U., Newark, 1978-81; dir. home health agy. Middlesex Hosp., New Brunswick, N.J., 1981-82; dir. rsch. and edn. Kessler Inst. for Rehab., West Orange, N.J., 1983-88; assoc. prof. pediatric rehab. Thomas Jefferson U., Phila., 1988-90; adminstrv. dir. Ctr. for Human Devel. & Rehab. Morristown (N.J.) Meml. Hosp., 1990-92; clin. assoc. prof. Coll. Physicians and Surgeons, Columbia U., N.Y.C., 1991-93; assoc. prof. Pa. State U., University Park, 1993-95, Fairfield (Conn.) U., 1995—; pres., cons. Health Systems Consultations, Long Valley, N.J., 1983—; cons. Project HOPE Armenia, USSR, 1989; del. leader to China, 1992; cons. Ctrl. Europe Project HOPE, 1993; numerous nat. and internat. presentations in field; prin. investigator various fed. and state grants. Author: Rehabilitation/Restorative Care in Community, 1990, Rehabilitation Nursing, 1995; mem. editl. bd. Rehab. Nursing Jour., 1990-96; contbr. articles to profl. jours. Vol. Homeless Shelter, Morristown, N.J., 1988-91; mem. profl. adv. com. Hospice Morris County, 1988-96. Scholar NSF, 1960-64, Fulbright scholar U. Athens, Greece, 1992; RNF rsch. fellow, 1996; USPHS Title II trainee, 1972-74, numerous other grants for projects and rsch., 1980. Fellow Soc. for Applied Anthropology; mem. APHA, ANA, Assn. Rehab. Nurses (pres. N.J. state chpt. 1992-94), Am. Congress Rehab. Medicine (chmn. pediatric rehab. task force), Am. Anthropol. Assn. Home and Office: 6 Camp Washington Rd Long Valley NJ 07853-3163

HOEPRICH, PAUL DANIEL, physician educator; b. Alliance, Ohio, Jan. 3, 1924; s. Michael and Katharina (Wagner) H.; m. Muriel Lucy Blackwell, July 11, 1948; children: Martha Sue Kennedy, Paul Daniel Jr., Thomas Eric, Kurt Lincoln. Student, Harvard Coll.; MD, Harvard Med. Sch., 1947. Diplomate Am. Bd. Internal Medicine. Instr. medicine Johns Hopkins Sch. Medicine, Balt., 1956; instr. epidemiology Johns Hopkins Sch. Hygiene & Pub. Health, Balt., 1956; asst., assoc. prof. medicine U. Utah Coll Medicine, Salt Lake City, 1957-67, asst., assoc. prof. pathology, 1959-67; prof. medicine U. Calif. Sch. Medicine, Davis, 1967-91, emeritus, 1991—, prof. pathology, 1968-86, chief med. mycology, 1986-91; cons. physician in field. Editor, author: The Fluids of Parenteral Body Cavities, 1959, Infectious Diseases, 1972-94; editor The Infectious Diseases Newsletter, 1985-90; contbr. chpts. to books. Capt. U.S. Army M.C., 1950-53. Recipient Soma Weiss award Harvard Med. Sch., 1947, Disting. Faculty award U. Calif. Davis Med. Ctr., 1986; Fogarty sr. fellow NIH, 1976. Fellow Am. Coll. Physicians, Infectious Disease Soc. Am.; mem. AAAS, Am. Soc. Clin. Investigation, Assn. Am. Physicians.

HOERAUF, KLAUS HEINRICH, anesthetist, researcher; b. Ludwigshafen, Germany, Feb. 1, 1962; s. Emil and Ursula M. (Gotz) H. Student, U. Heidelberg, U. Mainz; DrMed, U. Muenster, 1989. Rsch. fellow Univ. Hosp., Muenster, Germany, 1986-92; rsch. fellow Univ. Hosp., Regensburg, Germany, 1992-94, cons., rschr., 1994-96; cons. Univ. Hosp. Vienna, Austria, 1996—; lectr. in field. Contbr. numerous articles to profl. jours. Mem. Internat. Anesthesia Rsch. Soc., Soc. Cardiovascular Anesthesiologists, Soc. Pediatric Anesthesia, Soc. Ambulatory Anesthesia, Deutsche Gesellschaft Anasthesie und Intensivmedizin, Deutsche Gesellschaft Wehrmedizin und Wehrpharmazie, Berufsverband Deutscher Anasthesisten.

HOERSTING, WENDY SCHUBERT, cardiovascular intensive care nurse; b. Dayton, Ohio, Oct. 24, 1969; d. Gary Melvin and Amy Louise (Gerber) Trowman; m. Robert Andrew Hoersting, Aug. 21, 1993. BSN, Bowling Green (Ohio) State U., 1992. RN, S.C.; cert. CCRN, ACLS instr., ACLS, BLS. Staff nurse cardiovascular ICU Greenville (S.C.) Hosp. System, 1992—. Vol. nurse Greenville Jr. League, 1992-94. Mem. AACCN.

HOFF, CHARLES JAY, geneticist; b. Newark, Oct. 28, 1937; s. Kenneth Albert and Edythe Mae (Walker) H.; m. Marcia Jane Lasswell, July 10, 1977. BS in Math., Pa. State U., 1961, MA in Anthropology, 1968, PhD, 1972; diploma in human biology, U. Oxford, Eng., 1968. Computer programmer IBM Corp., Endicott, N.Y., 1962-64; teaching and research asst. Pa. State U., State College, 1964-67, instr., 1968-69, research assoc., 1969; asst. prof. U. Oreg., Eugene, 1970-76; assoc. prof. U. South Ala. Coll. Medicine, Mobile, 1976-86, prof. med. genetics, 1986—; grant reviewer NSF, Nat. Found. March-of-Dimes Clin. Research Grants, Nat. Geographic, Am. Philos. Soc., Wenner-Gren Found.; manuscript and book reviewer Am. Jour. Phys. Anthropology, Human Biology, Am. Jour. Human Genetics, Am. Jour. Clin. Genetics. Contbr. articles and abstracts to profl. publs. Wenner-Gren fellow Oxford U., 1967-68; NIH grantee 1979-81, 86-88; recipient Acad. Yr. award, 1971-72, 75-76, Summer Research award, 1972, Group Yr. award, 1972-73, Univ. Oreg. Fellow Am. Coll. Epidemiology; mem. Am. Soc. Human Genetics, Am. Soc. Histocompatibility and Immunogenetics, So. Genetics Group, Am. Fedn. Clin. Research, Soc. Epidemiologic Research, Am. Pub. Health Assn., Human Biology Council, Am. Assn. Phys. Anthropologists, Am. Dermatoglyphics Assn., Oxford Soc. Democrat. Home: 1121 Greenway Dr W Mobile AL 36608-4220 Office: Univ Southern Alabama Dept Med Genetics 210 CCCB Mobile AL 36688

HOFF, JULIAN THEODORE, physician, educator; b. Boise, Idaho, Sept. 22, 1936; s. Harvey Orval and Helen Marie (Boraas) H.; m. Diane Shanks, June 3, 1962; children—Paul, Allison, Julia. B.A., Stanford U., Calif., 1958; M.D., Cornell U., N.Y.C., 1962. Diplomate Am. Bd. Neurol. Surgery (sec. 1987-91, chmn. 1991-92). Intern N.Y. Hosp., N.Y.C., 1962-63; resident in surgery N.Y. Hosp., 1963-64, resident in neurosurgery, 1966-70; Asst. prof. neurosurgery U. Calif., San Francisco, assoc. prof. neurosurgery, 1974-78, prof. neurosurgery, 1978-81; prof. neurosurgery U. Mich., Ann Arbor, 1981—; head sect. neurosurgery U. Mich., 1981—; mem. Am. Bd. Neurol. Surgery, 1986-92, chmn., 1991-92; mem. bd. sci. councillors Nat. Inst. Neurol. Diseases and Stroke-NIH, 1993-97. Editor: Practice of Neurosurgery, 1979-85; Current Surgical Management of Neurological Diseases, 1980; Neurosurgery: Diagnostic and Management Principles, 1992, Mild to Moderate Head Injury, 1989; contbr. articles to profl. jours. Served to capt. US Army, 1964-66. Recipient NIH Tchr.-Investigator award, 1972-77, Javits neurosci. investigator award NIH, 1985-99; Macy Faculty scholar, London, 1979. Fellow ACS; mem. Am. Assn. Neurol. Surgeons (v.p. 1991-93, pres.-elect 1992-93, pres. 1993-94), Am. Surg. Assn., Congress Neurol. Surgeons (v.p. 1982-83), Am. Acad. Neurosurgeons (treas. 1989-92, sec. 1992—, pres. elect 1995-96), Cen. Neurosurg. Soc. (pres. 1985-86). Republican. Presbyterian. Home: 2120 Wallingford Rd Ann Arbor MI 48104-4563 Office: U Mich Hosp TC 2128 Ann Arbor MI 48109

HOFFER, AXEL, psychiatrist; b. Gablonz, Bohemia, Czechoslovakia, July 23, 1936; came to U.S., 1937; s. Otto and Elsa H.; m. Anita Panenka; children: David, Daniel. Student (Konrad Adenauer fellow), U. Munich, 1955-56; BA magna cum laude, Harvard U., 1957, MD cum laude, 1961. Diplomate Am. Bd. Psychiatry and Neurology. Med. intern Mass. Gen. Hosp., Boston, 1961-62; resident in psychiatry Mass. Mental Health Ctr., Boston, 1962-64, fellow in child psychiatry, 1964-66; clin. assoc. NIMH, Bethesda, Md., 1966-68; asst. clin. dir. Mass. Mental Health Ctr., Boston, 1968-75, assoc. dir., 1975-76, dir. in-patient svcs., 1977—; pvt. practice of psychoanalysis & psychiatry Boston, 1975—; asst. clin. prof. psychiatry Harvard Med. Sch.; mem. faculty, tng. and supervising analyst Psychoanalytic Inst. New Eng. East, supervising analyst, faculty Mass. Inst. Psychoanalysis. Co-translator: A Phylogenetic Fantasy (by Freud), 1987; editorial bd. Jour. Am. Psychoanalytic Assn. Lt. Comdr. USPHS, 1966-68. Recipient Jour. prize Am. Psychoanalytic Assn., 1984. Mem. Boston Psychoanalytic Soc., Phi Beta Kappa, Alpha Omega Alpha. Home: 14 Welland Rd Brookline MA 02146-4518

HOFFER, DIANE LYNN, psychologist; b. Coral Gables, Fla., Dec. 29, 1953; d. Harold Herman and Charlotte May (Bernstein) H.; m. Joseph Merydith Hawlik, 1989; children: Matthew, Michael. BA in Sociology, U. Miami, 1974; MEd in Psychology, Counseling and Psychol. Svcs., Ga. State U., 1975; D in Psychology, Nova U., 1981. Practicum student Community Mental Health S. Dade, Dade County, Fla., 1978-79; clin. psychology intern Univ. Health Services U. Mass., Amherst, 1980-81; psychologist in pvt. practice, Coral Gables, 1981—; asst. prof. Dept. Family Medicine U. Miami, Fla.; co-owner Jazz Workout, dance and exercise studio, 1982-84; dance instr. Lic. marriage and family therapist, mental health counselor, clin. psychologist. Mem. Am. Psychol. Assn., Am. Psychoanalytic Assn., Fla. Psychol. Assn, Friends of Fla. Psychoanalytic Soc., Soc. for Personal Assessment. Democrat. Jewish. Contbr. articles to profl. jours. Office: 6851 Yumuri St Suite 17 Coral Gables FL 33146

HOFFER, ERIC ROBERT, physician; b. Bklyn., Jan. 18, 1947; s. Joseph Samuel and Mae (Goldfarb) H.; m. Gail Linda Richard; children: Sharon Lynn, Lori Beth. MD, Med. Coll. Va., 1972. Sr. attending dept. medicine North Shore U. Hosp. Forest Hills, N.Y.C., 1976—, program dir. residency programs, 1993—; clin. asst. prof. medicine Cornell Med. Sch., N.Y.C., 1978—. Editor: Update Your Medicine, 1980—, Cyber Med, 1994—. Fellow ACP, Am. Coll. Utilization Rev. Physicians. Office: North Shore Univ Hosp 102-01 66 Rd Forest Hills NY 10709

HOFFERT, PAUL WASHINGTON, surgeon; b. N.Y.C., Feb. 22, 1923; s. Charles and Rose (Isaacs) H.; m. Rosolyn Sheiman, Apr. 20, 1947; children: Marvin Jay, Renee Beth, Deborah Susan. AB with honors, Columbia U., 1942; MD, cum laude, Yale U., 1945. Diplomate Am. Bd. Surgery, Am. Bd. Abdominal Surgery. Intern New Haven (Ct.) Hosp., 1945-46; fellow radiology Hosp. U. Pa., 1948-49; resident surgery VA Hosp., Bronx, N.Y., 1949-53; pvt. practice medicine specializing in gen. and vascular surgery, Yonkers, N.Y., 1953—; attending surgeon Yonkers Gen. Hosp., 1953—, chief of surgery, 1987—; sr. gen. and vascular surgeon St. Joseph's Hosp., 1953—; assoc. vascular surgeon Montefiore Hosp., 1965—; asst. prof. surgery Albert Einstein Coll., 1955—. Contbr. articles to profl. jours. Capt. U.S. Army Med. Corps, 1946-48. Recipient citation Am. Cancer Soc., 1960. Fellow Am. Coll. Surgeons (pres. Westchester, N.Y. chpt.), Am. Coll. Angiology N.Y. Acad. Medicine, Westchester Acad. Medicine (charter), Clin. Soc. N.Y. Diabetes Assn.; mem. N.Y. Surgical Soc., N.Y. Soc. Cardiovascular Surgery, Am. Zionist Orgn. (life) (past pres. Lincoln Park, Yonkers region), Phi Beta Kappa, Alpha Omega Alpha, Phi Delta Epsilon, Masons. Home: 26 Indian Cove Mamaroneck NY 10543-4439

HOFFMAN, ALLAN SACHS, chemical engineer, educator; b. Chgo., Oct. 27, 1932; s. Saul A. and Frances E. (Sachs) H.; m. Susan Carol Freeman, July 29, 1962; children: David, Lisa. B.S. in Chem. Engring, MIT, 1953, M.S. in Chem. Engring, 1955, Sc.D. in Chem. Engring, 1957. Instr. chem. engring. MIT, Cambridge, 1954-56; asst. prof. MIT, 1958-60, assoc. prof., 1965-70; research engr. Calif. Research Corp., Richmond, 1960-63; asso. dir. research Amicon Corp., Cambridge, 1963-65; prof. bioengring. and chem. engring. U. Wash., Seattle, 1970—; asst. dir. Center for Bioengring., 1973-83; cons. to various govtl., indsl. and acad. orgns., 1958—; UN adviser to Mexican govt., 1973-74. Author: (with W. Burlant) Block and Graft Copolymers, 1960; author numerous articles and book chpts. on chem. engring. and biomaterials; patentee in field. Kimberly Clark fellow, 1954-55, Visking fellow, 1955-56, Fulbright fellow, 1957-58, Battelle fellow, 1970-72; Festschrift in honor of 60th birthday 8 issues of Jour. Biomaterials Sci., Polymer Edn., 1993. 94. Mem. Am. Chem. Soc., Am. Inst. Chem. Engrs., Am. Soc. for Artificial Internal Organs, Internat. Soc. Artificial Internal Organs (trustee, bd. dirs. 1987-1990), Soc. for Biomaterials (pres. 1983-84, Clemson award for biomaterial sci. lit., 1985), Controlled Release Soc. (Excellence in Guiding Grad. Rsch. award 1989), Japan Biomaterials Soc. (Biomaterials Sci. prize 1990). Home: 4528 W Laurel Dr NE Seattle WA 98105-3841 Office: U Wash Box 352255 Seattle WA 98195

HOFFMAN, ALLEN LEE, surgeon; b. Pitts., Mar. 26, 1958; s. Ralph and Beatrice Miriam (Shapiro) H.; m. Carolyn Peltin, Sept. 12, 1963. BS, U. Pitts., 1980, MD, 1984. Cert. Am. Bd. Surgery, surg. critical care. Intern, resident Strong Meml. Hosp., Rochester, N.Y., 1984-87; resident, rsch. fellow U. Pitts., 1987-91; liver transplant/hepatobiliary fellow Cedars-Sinai Med. Ctr., L.A., 1991-93, asst. dir. liver transplantation, 1993—. Author: Atlas of Organ Transplantation, 1991, 2d edit., 1995, Handbook of Transplantation Management, 1991, 95, Support of the Acutely Failing Liver, 1994, Principles and Practice of Gastroenterology and Hepatology, 1995; mem. editl. bd. Transplantation Sci., L.A., 1994—. Recipient Merck award, 1980; Lederle traveling fellow, 1989, 90. Fellow ACS; mem. AMA, Assn. Acad. Surgery, Am. Soc. Transplant Surgeons, Southwestern Surg. Congress, L.A. Surg. Soc. Office: St Vincent Med Ctr Profl Office Bldg Ste 500 201 S Alvarado St Los Angeles CA 90057

HOFFMAN, ANDREW PAUL, surgeon; b. Bethlehem, Pa., Oct. 28, 1960; s. Allen Paul and Joyce Ida (Moser) H.; m. Teri Jane Lippowitch (div. May 1993). BS, Muhlenberg Coll., Allentown, Pa., 1982; MD, Hahnemann U., Phila., 1986. Gen. surgery resident Allentown Affiliated Hosps., 1986-89, Nat. Naval Med. Ctr., Bethesda, Md., 1989-92; gen. surgery resident St. Joseph Hosp., Houston, 1993-94, chief surg. resident, 1994-95; gen. surgeon St. Luke's Hosp., Bethlehem, Pa., 1995—. Contbr. articles to profl. jours. Election coord. Northampton County Rep. Com., Bethlehem, Pa., 1992. Lt. comdr. USNR, 1989-92. Recipient Acad. Achievement award St. Joseph Hosp., 1994, 95. Fellow ACS (assoc.); mem. AMA, Soc. of Laparoendoscopic Surgeons. Lutheran.

HOFFMAN, ARLENE FAUN, podiatric medicine educator, physiologist; b. N.Y.C., Nov. 23, 1941; d. Abraham S. and Pearl Tootsie (Weiss) H. BS, CUNY, 1962; PhD in Physiology, SUNY, Bklyn., 1966; D of Podiatric Medicine, Calif. Coll. Podiatric Medicine, San Francisco, 1976. Instr. CUNY, N.Y.C., 1964-66; assoc. prof. basic scis. Calif. Coll. Podiatric Medicine, 1967-68, prof., 1969—, asst. dir. basic scis., 1967-69, dir., 1969-75, assoc. dean curricular affairs, 1972-75, assoc. prof. podiatric medicine, 1978-81, prof., chief non-invasive vascular lab., 1981—; postdoctoral fellow immunophysiology Stanford U. Med. Sch., Palo Alto, Calif., 1966-67; mem. physiology sect. Nat. Bd. Podiatry Examiners, 1967-76; mem. tng. grant rev. com., heart and cardiovascular sect. Nat. Heart, Lung and Blood Inst., 1976-77; cons. Vascular Evaluation Cos., 1986—; mem. Bd. Podiatric Medicine, 1985-92; bd. dirs. Am. Bd. Podiatric Orthopedics and Primary Medicine, 1992—. Editor: Yearbook of Podiatric Medicine & Surgery, 1979, Lower Extremity, 1994—; editor, mem. adv. bd. Jour. Am. Podiatric Med. Edn., 1971-75, editor (adv. bd.) Jour. Am. Podiatric Med. Assn., 1971-92; author: The Podiatry Curriculum, 1970; contbr. articles to profl. jours. Bd. dirs. Lyon-Martin Womens Alternative Med. Svcs., San Francisco, 1980-82, Nat. Ctr. for Lesbian Rights, San Francisco, 1989-93. USPHS fellow, 1962-66. Fellow Am. Assn. Podiatric Dermatology, Am. Soc. Podiatric Medicine, Am. Coll. Foot and Ankle Orthopedics and Primary Podiatric Medicine, Nat. Acad. Practice; mem. Am. Podiatric Med. Assn. (editor jour. 1970—, Meritorious Svc. citation 1996). Office: Calif Coll Podiatric Medicine 1835 Ellis St San Francisco CA 94115-4003

HOFFMAN, DONALD BERTRAND, forensic toxicologist, educator, consultant; b. N.Y.C., May 3, 1939; s. David and Tillie (Miller) H. B.A. in Chemistry, NYU, 1959; M.A. in Chemistry, 1960, Ph.D. in Chemistry, Columbia U., 1967. Diplomate Am. Bd. Forensic Toxicology; cert. clin. toxicologist. Rsch. assoc. Jewish Chronic Disease Hosp., N.Y.C., 1967-68; NIMH postdoctoral fellow dept. psychiatry NYU Med. Ctr., 1968-69; sr. chemist Office Chief Med. Examiner, N.Y.C., 1969-87; rsch. scientist, 1987—; asst. prof. dept. forensic medicine, NYU Med. Ctr., 1977—; adj. asst. prof. John Jay Coll. Criminal Justice, N.Y.C., 1976—; mem. adv. bd. Fire Sci. Inst. John Jay Coll.; pvt. cons. in forensic toxicology; lectr. in field. Contbr. articles to profl. jours. Recipient Cert. Appreciation Victor Collymore Inst., N.Y.C. Fire Dept., 1981. Mem. Am. Acad. Forensic Scis., N.Y. Acad. Scis., Soc. Forensic Toxicologists (sec. 1975-76, charter mem.), Internat. Assn. Forensic Toxicologists, N.Y. Soc. Forensic Scis., Rsch. Soc. Sigma Xi, Soc. Med. Jurisprudence, Phi Beta Kappa. Jewish. Avocation: reading. Home: 1939 Grand Concourse Bronx NY 10453-4917 Office: Dept Toxicology Office of Chief Med Examiner 520 1st Ave New York NY 10016-6402

HOFFMAN, ELLENDALE MCCOLLAM, psychologist, pastoral counselor; b. Alexandria, La., Apr. 3, 1951; d. William and Hope Flower (Joffrion) McCollam; m. Charles L. Hoffman, Nov. 27, 1976. AA, Briarcliff Coll., 1971; BA, Manhattanville Coll., 1973; MDiv, Episcopal Div. Sch., 1976; DMin, Andover Newton Theol. Sch., 1978. Ordained priest Episcopal Ch., 1977, deacon, 1976; lic. psychologist, Mass.; cert. marriage and family therapist, Conn. Clin. supr. Pastoral Inst. Tng. in Alcohol Problems, Cambridge, Mass., 1976-78; dir. growth and learning ctr. Marion (Mass.) Ctr. for Human Svcs., 1978-79; clin. dir. Cape Counseling Ctr., Hyannis, Mass., 1979-82; pvt. practice psychology and pastoral counseling, Falmouth, Mass., 1976-88, Old Saybrook, Conn., 1988—. Chairperson commn. on today's families Diocese of Mass., 1980-82; pastoral assoc. Grace Episc. Ch., 1989—. Roothbert fellow, 1976-78; Epis. Women's scholar, 1976-78. Fellow Am. Assn. Pastoral Counselors (profl concerns com.); mem. Am. Psycol. Assn., Am. Assn. Marriage and Family Therapists (clin.), LWV. Author course Driver's Alcohol Education Curriculum. Home and Office: 8 Sharon Ln Old Saybrook CT 06475-2037

HOFFMAN, GEORGE CHAROL, surgeon, educator; b. Newburgh, N.Y., July 8, 1943; s. Charol and Eleanor (Van derverre) H.; m. Kathleen Coll, May 21, 1977. BS, Boston U., 1965; MD, Tufts U., 1969. Diplomate Am. Bd. Surgery. Intern Roosevelt Hosp. Columbia U., N.Y.C., 1969-70, resident, 1970-74; asst. clin. prof. surgery Columbia Sch. Medicine, N.Y.C., 1972-75; fellow in surgery Lahey Clin. Found., Boston, 1974-75, Nat. Health Systems, Bristol, Eng., 1976-77; asst. prof. surgery Ea. Va. Med. Sch., Norfolk, 1977-88, assoc. prof. surgery, 1988—. Author: Oncology for Stuents and Practitioners, 1983. Bd. dirs. Berwick Boys Found., Brocton, Mass., 1977—. Fellow ACS, Royal Coll. Surgeons; mem. Tidewater Assn. Med. and Surg. Specialists (bd. dirs. 1993—), So. Soc. Clin. Surgeons, So. Surg. Assn. Roman Catholic. Home: 1225 Gates Ave Norfolk VA 23502 Office: Norfolk Surg Group 6160 Kempsville Circle Norfolk VA 23502

HOFFMAN, GWENDOLYN L., surgeon; b. Muskegon, Mich., 1942. MD, Mich. State U., 1976. Intern Butterworth Hosp., Grand Rapids, Mich., 1976-77, resident, 1977-79, surgeon; assoc. prof. Mich. State U. Mem. ACEP, AMA, SAEM. Office: Butterworth Hosp Grand Rapids MI 49503*

HOFFMAN, HOWARD STANLEY, experimental psychologist, educator; b. N.Y.C., May 23, 1925; s. Melvin Leo and Henrietta (Rosenthal) H.; m. Alice Marie Cruikshank, June 7, 1961; children: Randall, Gwendolyn, Russell, Franklin, Daniel, Martha. BA, New Sch. for Social Research, N.Y.C., 1952; MA, Bklyn. Coll., 1953; PhD, U. Conn., 1957. Rsch. fellow in auditory perception U. Conn., 1953-56, instr. dept. stats., 1956-57; asst. to prof. psychology Pa. State U., 1957-70; prof. psychology Bryn Mawr Coll., 1970-92, prof. emeritus, 1992—. Bd. editors: Jour. Exptl. Analysis Behavior, 1966-69, Jour. Exptl. Psychology, Animal Behavior Processes, 1974-84; reviewer: Jour. Comparative and Physiol. Psychology. Served with AUS, 1943-45. Fellow AAAS, Am. Psychol. Assn., Am. Psychol. Soc.; mem. Eastern Psychol. Assn., AAUP, Sigma Xi, Phi Kappa Phi, Psi Chi. Home:

Apt 3211 3300 Darby Rd Haverford PA 19041-1070 Office: Bryn Mawr Coll Dept Psychology Bryn Mawr PA 19010

HOFFMAN, JULIEN IVOR ELLIS, pediatric cardiologist, educator; b. Salisbury, South Rhodesia, July 26, 1925; came to U.S., 1957, naturalized, 1967; s. Bernard Isaac and Minrose (Bermant) H.; m. Kathleen Lewis, 1986; children: Anna, Daniel. B.Sc., U. Witwaterstrand, Johannesburg, South Africa, 1944; B.Sc. Hons., 1945, M.B., B.Ch., 1949, M.D., 1970. Intern, resident internal medicine South Africa and Eng., 1950-56; research asst., postgrad. Med. Sch., London, 1956-57; fellow pediatric cardiology Boston Children's Hosp., 1957-59; fellow Cardiovascular Research Inst., San Francisco, 1959-60; asst. prof. pediatrics, internal medicine Albert Einstein Coll., N.Y., 1962-66; assoc. prof. pediatrics U. Calif. at San Francisco, 1966-70, prof., 1970—, prof. physiology, 1981-88, prof. emeritus, 1994; sr. mem. Cardiovascular Research Inst., U. Calif. at San Francisco, 1966—; mem. bd. examiners, sub-bd. pediatric cardiology Am. Bd. Pediatrics, 1973-78, subbd. pediatric intensive care, 1985-87; chmn. Louis Katz Award Com., Basic Sci. Council, Am. Heart Assn., 1973-74; George Brown Meml. lectr. Am. Heart Assn., 1977; George Alexander Gibson Meml. lectr. Royal Coll. Physicians (Edinburgh), 1978; Lilly lectr. Royal Coll. Physicians (London), 1981; Isaac Starr lectr. Cardiac Systems Dynamics Soc., Eng., 1982; John Keith lectr., 1985; Disting. Physiology lectr. Am. Coll. Chest Physicians, 1985; Nadas lectr. Am. Heart Assn., 1987; 1st Donald C. Fyler lectr. Children's Hosp., Boston, 1990. Recipient Bayer Cardiovascular Mentor award, 1989. Fellow Royal Coll. Physicians; mem. World Congress Pediatric Cardiology and Cardiac Surgery (hon. joint pres. Paris 1993), Am. Physiol. Soc., Am. Pediatric Soc., Soc. Pediatric Rsch. Home: 925 Tiburon Blvd Belvedere Tiburon CA 94920-1525 Office: U Calif Med Ctr 1403 Hse Dept Phyiology San Francisco CA 94143

HOFFMAN, LOIS WLADIS, psychologist, educator; b. Elmira, N.Y., Mar. 25, 1929; d. Gustave and Etta (Wladis) Wladis; m. Martin Leon Hoffman, June 24, 1951 (div.); children—Amy Gabrielle, Jill Adrienne.; m. Herbert Zimiles, Oct. 25, 1981. B.A. cum laude, U. Buffalo, 1951; M.S., Purdue U., 1953; Ph.D., U. Mich., 1958. Asst. study dir. Survey Research Center, 1954-55; research asst. Research Center for Group Dynamics, 1955-56, research asso., 1956-60, cons. psychol. clinic, 1959-60; lectr. psychology, 1967-72, asso. prof., 1972-75, prof., 1975—, chairwoman devel. psychology, 1986-92. Author: (with F. IVan Nye) The Employed Mother in America, 1963, Working Mothers, 1974, (with S. Paris, E. Hall and R. Schell) Developmental Psychology Today, 5th edit., 1986, (with S. Paris and E. Hall) 6th edit., 1993; editor: (with Martin L. Hoffman) Review of Child Development Research, vol. 1, 1964, vol. 2, 1966 (Family Life Book award Child Study Assn. Am. 1965), (with Mednick and Tangri) Women and Achievement, (with Gandelman and Shifman) Parenting, its Causes and Consequences; articles. Mem. APA (pres. devel. div. 1990-91), Soc. Rsch. in Child Devel., Soc. Psychol. Study of Social Issues (pres. 1983-84), Phi Beta Kappa, Phi Kappa Phi. Address: 1307 Baldwin Ave Ann Arbor MI 48104

HOFFMAN, MADELYN KAY, psychoanalyst, social worker; b. Waco, Tex., Jan. 28, 1948; d. Nathan and Evelyn (Giniger) H.; m. Ira Finkelstein, May 31, 1982; 1 child, Sarah Rebekah. AB in Psychology, Rutgers U., 1969; MSW, Yeshiva U., 1973; grad. in psychoanalysis, Nat. Psychol. Assn., 1991. With Community Cons. Ctr., N.Y.C., 1971-72; social work trainee Albert Einstein Med. Ctr., Jacobi Hosp., Bronx, N.Y., 1972-73; social worker Cornell Med. Ctr., The N.Y. Hosp., N.Y.C., 1973-77; coord. social work student internship program Cen. Westchester Mental Health Clinic, White Plains, N.Y., 1977-84; dep. coord. Day Treatment Ctr. Ctrl. Westchester Mental Health Clinic, White Plains, 1978-79; faculty advisor Adelphi Univ. Sch. Social Work, L.I., N.Y., 1986-87; pvt, practice, N.Y.C., 1986—; specialist in treatment of bereavement, trauma and adults with attention deficit disorder or dyslexia. Contbr. articles to profl. jours. Office: 2 W 86th St New York NY 10024-3666

HOFFMAN, MARILYN GRACE, nurse practitioner; b. New Castle, Pa., Nov. 14, 1941; s. John Ashley and Frieda May (McConnell) Brown; m. Stanley Frank Hoffman, July 5, 1966 (div. 1988); children: David Todd, Marilyn Elizabeth. RN, Alleghney Hosp. Sch. Nursing, 1962; grad. in Neonatal Nursing Care, Youngstown State U., 1985; student, W.Va. U., 1985; student Graceland Coll., 1995—. cert. neonatal nurse practioner. Staff nurse neonatal ICU, Western Pa. Hosp., 1966-76, Denver Gen. Hosp., 1980-81, Meml. Hosp., Colorado Springs, Colo., 1981-82, West Pa. Hosp., Pitts., 1982-83, Magee Women's Hosp., Pitts., 1983-96, Allegheny Gen. Hosp., 1996—. Home: 148 Queenston Dr Pittsburgh PA 15235-5428 Office: Magee Womens Hosp Pittsburgh PA 15213

HOFFMAN, MARTIN DEAN, physician, researcher; b. Kansas City, Mo., Apr. 30, 1956; s. Raymond Paul and Alice Lee (Kasselhute) H.; m. Julia Elizabeth Chapman, July 31, 1982; children: Alek Gabriel, Ryan Nathaniel. BSChE, U. Mo., Rolla, 1978; MD, St. Louis U., 1983. Diplomate Am. Bd. Phys. Medicine and Rehab. Intern, resident in phys. medicine and rehab. Med. Coll. Wis. Affiliated Hosps., Milw., 1983-86; assoc. prof. Med. Coll. Wis., Milw., 1994—; med. dir. Cardiopulmonary Prevention and Rehab. Clinic-VA, Milw., 1995—; interim chief Phys. Medicine and Rehab. Svc.-VA, Milw., 1994; team physician U.S. Biathlon Team, Lake Placid, N.Y., 1988—. Mem. editl. bd. Wis. Med. Jour., 1994-96; assoc. editor Archives of Phys. Medicine and Rehab., 1996—; contbr. articles to profl. jours. Recipient 2d prize Nat. Student Design Contest, AIChE, 1978, grant Dept. Vet. Affairs, 1995. Fellow Am. Coll. Sports Medicine, Am. Acad. Phys. Medicine and Rehab.; mem. Am. Med. Soc. for Sports Medicine. Methodist. Office: VA Med Ctr 5000 W National Ave 111R Milwaukee WI 53295

HOFFMAN, MARTIN LEON, psychology educator; b. Bayonne, N.J., Mar. 20, 1924; s. Nathan D. and Ann E. (Goldberg) H.; m. Lois Norma Wladis, June 24, 1951 (div. 1981); children: Amy, Jill; m. Elizabeth Ann Mercer, June 4, 1989. BSEE, Purdue U., 1945; MS in Psychology, U. Mich., 1948, PhD in Social Psychology, 1951. Asst. prof. Purdue U., Lafayette, Ind., 1949-53; sr. rsch. assoc. Merrill-Palmer Inst., Detroit, 1953-65; prof. U. Mich., Ann Arbor, 1965-85; prof. psychology NYU, 1985—. Editor: Review of Child Development Research, Vol. 1, 1964, Vol. 2, 1966 (Book of Yr. award Child Study Assn.), (series) Social and Emotional Development; editor: Merrill-Palmer Quar., 1955-80, 80—; contbr. numerous articles to profl. jours. Ens. USN 1943-46. Founds. Fund for Psychiatry grantee, 1953-55, NIMH grantee 1957-70. Fellow Am. Psychol. Assn. (assoc. editor Devel. Psychology jour. 1980-82, editor Psychol. Rev. 1982-88), AAAS, Soc. Rsch. in Child Devel.; mem. AAUP. Office: NYU FAS Dept Psychology 6 Washington Pl New York NY 10003-6634

HOFFMAN, PATRICIA LOU, health, fitness, and recreational facility director; b. Buffalo, Feb. 2, 1954; d. Norman Richards and Evelyne (Ghnassia) H. BS, Canisius Coll., 1976; MA, Adelphi U., 1973; postgrad., SUNY, Buffalo, 1978-79. Pool supr. Town of Tonawanda Recreation Dept., Kenmore, N.Y., 1973-77; grad. asst. Adelphi U., 1977-78, SUNY, Buffalo, 1978-79; health and phys. edn. asst. Jewish Ctr. of Greater Buffalo, 1979-80, supr., 1980-81, asst. dir. health and phys. edn., 1981-83, assoc. dir. health and phys. edn., 1983-86, dir. health, fitness and recreation, 1986—; cons. Computer Task Group, Buffalo, 1984—; lectr. on fitness; profl. golf instr. Contbr. articles to profl. jours. Grantee JM Found., N.Y.C., 1978, grantee Erie County Svcs. to Srs., 1995, grantee N.Y. State Mary Laskey Heart Inst., 1995, 96. Mem. AAHPERD, U.S. Golf Assn., Internat. Dance Exercise Assn., Am. Coll. Sports Medicine, N.Y. State Assn. for Health Phys. Edn. Recreation and Dance (pres. recreation/leisure sect. 1988—), Assn. Jewish Ctr. Workers (chair ea. states chpt. 1981-83), Canisius Coll. Phys. Edn. Alumni Assn. (pres. 1975-76). Republican. Jewish. Home: 1420 Maple Rd Apt 7 Buffalo NY 14221-3543

HOFFMAN, RICHARD GEORGE, psychologist; b. Benton Harbor, Mich., Oct. 6, 1949; s. Robert Fredrick and Kathleen Elyce (Watts) H.; m. Julia Ann May, Dec. 18, 1970; children: Leslie Margaret, Michael Charles, Angela Lynn, Jennifer Elizabeth. BS with honors, Mich. State U., 1971; MA in Psychology, Long Island U., 1974, PhD in Clin. Psychology, 1980. Lic. con. psychologst. Instr. pediatrics U. Va., Charlottesville, 1977-80; asst. prof. pediatrics and family med. U. Kans., Wichita, 1980-84; asst. prof. behavioral sci. U. Minn., Duluth, 1984-90, assoc. prof. behavioral sci., 1990—, dir. neuropsychology lab., 1986—, co-dir. hypothermia and water safety lab., 1987—, co-dir. neurobehavioral toxicology lab., 1990—; vis. sr. fellow in human clin. neuropsychology U. Okla. Health Scis. Ctr., 1995-96; assoc. dir. Child Evaluation Ctr., Wichita, 1981-82; dir. adminstrn. Comprehensive Epilepsy Clinic, Wichita, 1983-84; cons. psychologist U. Assocs., P.A., Duluth, 1984—. contbr. articles to profl. jour. Pres. Home and Sch. Assn., St. Michael's Sch., Duluth, 1986. Rsch. grantee NIH, 1985, USCG, 1986, Sch. Medicine U. Kans., 1984, U. Minn., 1984, U.S. Army Med. Rsch. Command, 1988—, U.S. Naval Med. Rsch. Command, 1988, Gt. Lakes Protection Fund, 1991—, Agy. for Toxic Substances and Disease Registry, 1992-95, 95—. Fellow Am. Psychol. Soc., Am. Assn. Applied and Preventive Psychology; mem. APA, Nat. Acad. Neuropsychologists. Democrat. Roman Catholic. Home: 219 Occidental Blvd Duluth MN 55804-1365 Office: U Minn Dept Behavioral Scis Duluth MN 55812

HOFFMAN, RONALD, medical educator, physician; b. Passaic, N.J., June 17, 1945; s. Morris and Sarah (Wishna) H.; m. Laura Provisor, July 7, 1968; children: Judith Helaine, Michael Nathaniel. B.A., NYU, 1967, M.D., 1971. Diplomate: Nat. Bd. Med. Examiners, Am. Bd. Internal Medicine, Am. Bd. Hematology. Intern Montreal Gen. Hosp., 1971-73; resident in medicine Stanford U. Hosp., Palo Alto, Calif., 1973-74; fellow in hematology Mt. Sinai Hosp., N.Y.C., 1974-76; spl. hematology research fellow Mt. Sinai Hosp, N.Y.C., 1976-77; assoc. prof. Yale U. Sch. Medicine, New Haven, 1977-80, assoc. prof. medicine, 1980-82; prof. medicine Ind. U. Sch. Medicine, Indpls., 1982-93, prof. pathology, 1990-93; v.p. rsch. Systemix, Palo Alto, Calif., 1993-95; Eileen Lindsay Heidrick prof. oncology U. Ill. Coll. Medicine, Chgo., 1995—. Contbr. numerous articles to profl. jours. Recipient Daniel P. Statz Mt. Sinai Hosp, 1976; recipient Outstanding paper presentation N.Y. Blood Club, 1977, research career devel. NIH, 1980-85. Mem. Am. Fedn. Clin. Research, Am. Soc. Hematology (chmn. erythropoietin and cell proliferation subcom 1982); mem Internat. Soc. Exptl. Hematology; mem. AAAS, Am. Soc. Clin. Investigation, Am. Assn. Physicians, Phi Beta Kappa, Sigma Xi. Democrat. Jewish. Office: U Ill at Chgo (734) Rm 3150 MBRB 900 S Ashland Ave Chicago IL 60612

HOFFMAN, RONALD STUART, physician; b. Detroit, June 22, 1950; s. William and Shirley (Samet) H.; (div.); children: Jessica, Lindsey. BS, U. Mich., 1972; MD, Wayne State U., 1976. Diplomate Am. Bd. Internal Medicine. Pvt. practice Altamonte Springs, Fla., 1979—. Fellow ACP. Home: 2284 Springs Landing Blvd Longwood FL Office: 220 N Westmonte Altamonte Springs FL 32714

HOFFMAN, SAUL, plastic surgeon; b. Edmonton, Alta., Can., Feb. 17, 1931; came to U.S., 1964; s. Joseph and Gertrude (Caushansky) H.; m. Alice Hoffman, June 18, 1967; children: Daniel Paul, Jeffrey Michael. BS, U. Alta., 1951, MD, 1955. Pvt. practice N.Y.C., 1964—; clin. prof. Mt. Sinai Med. Sch.; attending plastic surgeon Mt. Sinai and Beth Israel Hosps.; chief plastic surgery Beth Israel Hosp. North, 1982-88, Dr.'s Hops., 1988—. Contbr. numerous articles to profl. jours. Fellow ACS; mem. Am. Assn. Plastic Surgeons, Am. Soc. Plastic and Reconstructive Surgeons. Home: 301 Hudson Ave Tenafly NJ 07670-1127 Office: 102 E 78th St New York NY 10021-0302

HOFFMAN, THOMAS EDWARD, dermatologist; b. L.A., Oct. 14, 1944; s. David Maurice and Ann (Corday) H.; m. Donna Madison, 1973 (div. 1977); m. Linda L., Feb. 20, 1979; children: David, Jay. AB, U. So. Calif., 1966; MD, Tulane U., 1970. Dermatologist pvt. practice, Menlo Park, Calif., 1976—; clin. assoc. prof. dermatology Stanford (Calif.) U. With USPHS, 1971-73. Recipient Achievement award Tulane U., 1970. Fellow Am. Coll. Physicians, Am. Acad. Dermatology, Am. Soc. Dermatology, Am. soc. Dermatologic Surgery, Am. Soc. Laser Medicine & Surgery. Office: Menlo Dermatology Med Group 888 Oak Grove Ave Menlo Park CA 94025

HOFFMAN, WILLIAM KENNETH, retired obstetrician, gynecologist; b. Milw., Jan. 18, 1924; s. William Richard and Marian (Riegler) H.; student U. Wis., 1942-43; student U. Pa., 1943-44, postgrad, 1954-55; MD, Marquette U., 1947; m. Peggy Folsom, July 28, 1952; children: Janet Susan, Ann Elizabeth. Intern, Columbia Hosp., 1947-48, resident in obstetrics and gynecology, 1948-49, mem. staff, 1949-91; ret., 1991; preceptor R.E. McDonald, MD, Milw., 1949-50; resident in ob-gyn U. Chgo., 1950-51; practice medicine specializing in ob-gyn, Milw., 1955-74; mem. staff, Columbia Hosp.; dir. health service U. Wis.-Milw., 1974-91, cons. Sch. Nursing, 1976-77, clin. assoc. prof., 1979-91, vice chmn., mem. instl. rev. bd., 1976-91, mem. instl. safety and health com., 1981-91, chmn., 1984-88; ret., 1991. Bd. dirs. Wis. sect. Am. Cancer Soc., 1983-88. Mem. Am. Coll. Ob-Gyn, Am. Coll. Health Assn., Am. Coll. Sports Medicine, Royal Soc. Medicine, Am. Cancer Soc. (bd. dirs. Wis. div. 1983-88, public edn. com. Milw. div.). Home: 4629 N Murray Ave Milwaukee WI 53211-1259

HOFFMANN, WILLIAM FREDERICK, III, psychiatrist; b. N.Y.C., Oct. 26, 1940; s. William Frederick Jr. and Mary Angela (McDonnell) H.; m. Robin Lynn Zuckerman; children: William, Lisa, Keith. AB, Coll. of the Holy Cross, 1962; MD, Georgetown U., 1966. Diplomate Am. Bd. Psychiatry and Neurology. Physician Project Concern, Vietnam, 1969-71; pvt. practice in psychiatry N.Y.C., 1971-75, 78-84; resident in psychiatry St. Luke's Hosp., N.Y.C., 1975-78; pvt. practice N. Dartmouth, Mass., 1978—; unit chief Kings County Hosp., Bklyn., 1978-82; dir. behavioral scis. Family Practice Dept., Downstate Med. Ctr., Bklyn., 1981-83; chief, dept. psychiatry Newport (R.I.) Hosp., 1984-88; chief dept. of neuropsychiatry Carlton (Mass.) Meml. Hosp., 1991-93; clin. asst. prof. psychiatry Brown U., Providence, 1986—. Contbr. articles to profl. jours. and lay publs. Member exec. com. Friends of Sakonnet, Portsmouth, R.I., 1988-90. Capt. U.S. Army, 1967-69, Vietnam. Recipient Exemplary Psychiatrist award Nat. Alliance for Mentally Ill, 1993. Mem. AMA, Am Psychiat. Assn. (fellow, pres. 1993-94), R.I. Psychiat. Soc. (sec., treas. 1988—, pres. elect 1991—). Democrat. Roman Catholic. Home: 30 Ann Hutchinson Ct Portsmouth RI 02871-3815 Office: 74 Faunce Corner Rd North Dartmouth MA 02747-1209

HOFFMEISTER, JANA MARIE, cardiologist. MD, SUNY Upstate Med. Ctr., Syracuse, 1976. Diplomate Am. Bd. Internal Medicine, Am. Bd. Cardiovascular Diseases. Intern Albany (N.Y.) Med. Ctr., 1976-78, resident, 1978-80, fellow div. cardiology, 1981-83; fellow div. cardiology Emory U., Atlanta, 1984; fellow coronary angioplasty and interventional cardiology Emory U. Hosp., 1985-86; presenter numerous cardiology confs. Contbr. numerous articles to profl. jours. Mem. ACP, AMA, Cardiac Soc. Upstate N.Y., N.Y. State Soc. Internal Medicine, Am. Soc. Cardiovascular Interventeion. Home: 7 Reddy Ln Albany NY 12211-1632

HOFFMEISTER, MARC A., physician assistant; b. Topeka, Kans., Nov. 1, 1961; s. Richard O. and Lorene M. (McClelland) H.; m. Margaret F. Vining, Aug. 13, 1983; children: Cole, Lane, Heath. AA/AS, York Coll., 1982; BS, Okla. Christian Coll., 1984; B in Health Scis., Wichita State U., 1986. Physician assistant Pine River Valley Clin., Bayfield, Colo., 1986-87, Tricities Med. Clin., Wewoka, Okla., 1987-91, Cherryvale (Kans.) Clinic, 1991—. Fellow Am. Acad. Physician Assts.; mem. Kans. Acad. Physician Assts., Cherryvale Cmty. Club (pres. 1996). Office: Cherryvale Clinic 216 E 4th Cherryvale KS 67335

HOFFNUNG, AUDREY SONIA, speech and language pathologist, educator; b. N.Y.C., Mar. 15, 1928; d. Nathan and Gussie (Karp) Smith; BA cum laude, Bklyn. Coll., 1949; MA, Columbia U., 1950; PhD, City U. N.Y., 1974. Cert. and lic. speech pathologist, N.Y.; m. Joseph Hoffnung, Nov. 26, 1950; children: Bonnie Fern, Tami Lynn. Rehab. therapist Ridgewood Cerebral Palsy Ctr., 1949-50; dir. speech therapy Kingsbrook Med. Ctr., Bklyn., 1950-55; therapist and cons. Morris J. Solomon Clinic, Bklyn., 1956-58; therapist Speech and Hearing Ctr. Bklyn. Coll., 1958-62, 63-64; pvt. practice speech therapy Hewlett (N.Y.) Med. Ctr., 1961-63; pvt. practice speech therapy, Oceanside, N.Y., 1964-71; cons. on staff for aphasic patients Phys. Medicine and Rehab. Ctr., South Nassau Cmtys. Hosp., 1964-65; part-time lectr. Speech and Hearing Ctr., Queens (N.Y.) Coll., 1970-72; adj. lectr. dept. speech Bklyn. Coll., 1973-74, asst. prof. speech and lang. pathology, 1974-77; asst. prof. dept. speech comm. and theatre St. John's U., Jamaica, N.Y., 1977-80, assoc. prof., 1980-91, prof., 1991—, chair, 1992-95; guest lectr. N.Y. Orton Soc., 1979, Brookdale Med. Ctr., 1978; mem. profl. adv. bd. Vis. Home Health Svcs. of Nassau County, 1973—. Author: (with Valletutti and McKnight) Facilitating communication in young children with handicapping conditions; (with Valletutti and Bender) A Functional Curriculum for Teaching Students With Disabilities Noverbal and Verbal Communication, 1996. Mem. Am. Speech-Lang.-Hearing Assn., N.Y.C. Speech, Hearing and Lang. Assn., N.Y. State Speech Lang. and Hearing Assn. (chairperson student activities 1978-79), L.I. Speech, Lang. and Hearing Assn., Nat. Student Speech-Lang.-Hearing Assn. (hon. advisor 1988), Aphasia Study Group of N.Y.C., N.Y. Acad. Scis. Contbr. articles on speech pathology to profl. jours. Home: 3282 Woodward St Oceanside NY 11572-4527 Office: St John's U Dept Speech Comm Scis and Theatre 800 Utopia Pkwy Jamaica NY 11439

HOFFSTEIN, HERBERT, dentist; b. N.Y.C., Jan. 24, 1928; s. Max and Flora (Lichtenstein) H.; m. Myra Jacobs, Feb. 28, 1976. B.A., N.Y. U., 1950, D.D.S., 1955. Intern in oral surgery Mt. Sinai Hosp., N.Y.C., 1955-56; pvt. practice dentistry, N.Y.C., 1956—; mem. staff Mt. Sinai Hosp., N.Y.C., instr. celestial nav. N.Y. Power Squadron, adminstrv. officer, 1969-71, exec. officer, 1971-73, comdr., 1973-75. Served with AUS, 1945-47. Fellow Am. Coll. Dentists, Internat. Coll. Dentists, Acad. Gen. Dentistry (pres. N.Y. State, past nat. chmn. council on constn. and by-laws); mem. 1st Dist. Dental Soc. (legis. commn., lectr. oral pathology 1970—), West Side Dentists Assn., Inst. Grad. Dentists (past trustee), Inst. Clin. Oral Pathology, Omicron Kappa Upsilon, Beta Lambda Sigma, Mu Chi Sigma. Clubs: N.Y. Met. Study, Midhattan Study, N. Home: 80 Central Park W New York NY 10023-5204

HOFKIN, GERALD ALAN, gastroenterologist; b. Balt., July 4, 1936; m. Phyllis Hofkin, Aug. 23, 1959; children: Leah, Stephen, Karen. AB, MA, Johns Hopkins U., 1957; MD, U. Md., 1961. Diplomate Am. Bd. Internal Medicine, Am. Bd. Gastroenterology. Intern U. Md. Hosp., Balt., 1961, resident in medicine, 1962-63, 64-65; resident in medicine Sinai Hosp., Balt., 1963-64, 65-66; resident in gastroenterology Letterman Hosp., San Francisco, 1966-67; pvt. practice Balt., 1969-91; staff Sinai Hosp., Balt., 1991—; chmn. med. exec. com. Sinai Hosp. Med. Staff, Balt., 1989, pres., 1992-93. Contbr. articles to profl. jours. Maj. U.S. Army, 1966-69. Named Disting. Physician, Sinai Hosp., 1992. Fellow ACP, Am. Coll. Gastroenterology; mem. Am. Gastroenterol. Assn., Md. Soc. Gastrointesinal Endocscopy (pres. 1995—), Balt. Amateur Radio Club (v.p. 1978-79), Balt. Radio Amateur TV Soc., Alpha Omega Alpha. Office: Sinai Hosp 2435 W Belvedere Ave Baltimore MD 21215

HOFMAN, WENDELL FAY, educator; b. Grand Rapids, Mich., Oct. 28, 1942; s. Carl and Harriet (Schut) H.; m. Karen Lee DeYoung, May 4, 1942; children: Stephanie Joy, Stacy Lynne, Shanna Leigh. AB, Hope Coll., 1962; BS and MA in Biology, Western Mich. U., 1966; PhD in Physiology, Mich. State U., 1970. Rsch. assoc. Endocrine Rsch. U., Mich. State U., East Lansing, 1969-70; asst. prof. Med. Coll. of Ga., Augusta, 1970-77, assoc. prof., 1977-91, prof., 1991—; prof. Vascular Biology Ctr., Augusta, 1995—. Cmty. vol. Richmond County Pub. Sch., Augusta, 1990. Rsch. grant Am. Heart Assn. 1977, 86, NIH, 1988-93, Ga. Lung Assn., 1985, 91. Mem. Am. Physiology Soc., N.Am. Vascular Biology Soc. Republican. Presbyterian. Home: 825 Park Chase Dr Evans GA 30809 Office: Vascular Biology Ctr Med Coll of Ga Augusta GA 30912

HOFMANN, FRIEDER KARL, biotechnologist, consultant; b. Eppstein, Hessen, Fed. Republic Germany, June 15, 1949; came to U.S., 1984; s. Friedrich Karl and Anna Johannette (Heist) H.; m. Sigrid Marianne Thomae, Sept. 5, 1975. MS, J.W. Goethe U., Frankfurt, Fed. Republic of Germany, 1977, PhD, 1981. Staff scientist, asst. prof. J.W. Goethe U., Frankfurt, 1977-81; sci. mgr. Brunswick Corp., Eschborn, Fed. Republic of Germany, 1982-84; tech. dir. Biotechnetics, San Diego, 1984-90; pres. Hofmann & Co., Oceanside, Calif., 1990—, Ctr. for Continuous Edn., Oceanside, Calif., 1992—. Author: (with others) Scale-Up and Downstream Processing of rDNA Products, 1991, GMP Production of Monoclonal Antibodies, 1991; contbr. over 40 articles to profl. jours. Recipient Senckenberg prize Senckenberg Rsch. Soc., Frankfurt, Fed. Republic of Germany, 1977; Kirkpatrick Chem. Engring. Achievement Honor award, Chem. Engring., 1989, Parenteral Drug Assn. Jour. award, Parenteral Drug Assn., Pa., 1985. Mem. Am. Chem. Soc., Am. Inst. Chem. Engrs., Tissue Culture Assn., European Soc. for Animal Cell Tech. Office: Hofmann & Co 2360 Autumn Dr Ste C Oceanside CA 92056-3528

HOFMANN, MARK CHARLES, rehabilitation physician; b. Gardena, Calif., Sept. 18, 1961; s. Charles Michael and Nauku (Nakamura) H.; m. Dagmar Soccoro Estrada, June 28, 1986; children: Natalie, Brandon. BS in biochemistry, U. Calif., Davis, 1983; MD, St. Louis U., 1987. Diplomate Am. Bd. Phys. Medicine and Rehab. Resident in phys. medicine and rehab. Med. Coll. Wis., Milw., 1987-91; staff physician Genesis Rehab. Hosp., Jacksonville, Fla., 1991—, pres. med. staff, 1992-94, chmn. infection control com., 1995—; mem. pharmacy and therapeutics com. Meml. Med. Ctr., Jacksonville, 1995. Recipient Award for outstanding contbns. and dedicated svc. Med. Coll. Wis., 1991. Mem. AMA, Am. Paraplegia Soc., Am. Acad. Phys. Medicine and Rehab., Duval County Med. Soc., Fla. Med. Assn., Phi Kappa Phi. Office: Physical Med Specialists Ste 103 3901 University Blvd S Jacksonville FL 32216*

HOFMANN, MARTHA ANN, nursing educator; b. Madisonville, Ky., June 22, 1954; d. James Dennis and Mary frances (Hicklin) Bowles; m. Michael David Hofmann, June 18, 1976; children: Elizabeth, Jonathan. AAS, Madisonville C.C., 1974; BSN cum laude, Murray (Ky.) State U., 1992; MSN, U. Evansville, Ind., 1996. Staff nurse Hopkins County Hosp., Madisonville, 1974-75; psychiat. nurse Pennroyal Mental Health Ctr., Madisonville, 1975-80; nurse educator Regional Med. Ctr., Madisonville, 1980-83, childbirth educator, 1985-89; nursing instr. Madisonville C.C., 1989—; lectr. in field. Asst. organist First Presbyn. Ch., Madisonville, 1986—; accompanist Joyful Noise Singers, Madisonville, 1980—; soloist Hopkins County Cmty. Chorus, Madisonville, 1970—. Bus. and Profl. Women scholar Arthritis Found., 1995. Mem. Maroon Band Boosters, Sigma Theta Tau. Presbyterian. Home: 410 Stagecoach Rd Madisonville KY 42431 Office: Madisonville Community Coll 2000 College Dr Madisonville KY 42431

HOFMANN, MARTIN JOHN, science foundation director, chemist; b. Bristol, Avon, Eng., Jan. 4, 1957; s. Karl Johann and Audrey (Smith) H.; m. Cathryn Elizabeth Wright, Sept. 9, 1977 (div. 1993); 1 child, Joseph; m. Rachel Mary Pillar; children: Alfie, George. BS, Aston U., Birmingham, Eng., 1978; MS, Wolverhampton Polytech., Birmingham, 1983; PhD, Birmingham U., 1990. Chartered chemist. Biochemist Dudley Rd. Hosp., Birmingham, 1978-80; chemist analyst Pub. Analysts, Birmingham, 1980-83; rsch. chemist Birmingham U., 1983-86; applications mgr. Amicon, Stonehouse, Eng., 1986-94; rsch. mgr. Viva Sci., Stonehouse, 1994-95; sci. dir. Euroflow/Chromaflow Europe, Stonehouse, 1995—; cons. Pharmacia Biotech., Uppsala, Sweden, 1995—. Patentee in field. Sec. Labor Party, Cheltenham, Eng., 1987. Recipient SMART award Dept. Tech. and Industry, 1995, 96. Mem. Royal Soc. Chemistry, Assn. Clin. Biochemists. Office: Euroflow UK Ltd Unit 33, Stroud Bus Ctr Stonedale Rd, Stonehouse GL10 3RQ, England

HOFMANN, PAUL BERNARD, health care consultant; b. Portland, Oreg., July 6, 1941; s. Max and Consuelo Theresa (Bley) H.; m. Lois Bernstein, June 28, 1969; children: Julie, Jason. BS, U. Calif., Berkeley, 1963, MPH, 1965, DPH, 1994. Research assoc. in hosp. adminstrn. Lab. of Computer Sci., Mass. Gen. Hosp., Boston, 1966-68; asst. dir. Lab. of Computer Sci., Mass. Gen. Hosp., 1968-69; asst. adminstr. San Antonio Community Hosp., Upland, Calif., 1969-70; assoc. adminstr. San Antonio Community Hosp., 1970-72; dep. dir. Stanford (Calif.) U. Hosp., 1972-74, dir., 1974-77; exec. dir. Emory U. Hosp., Atlanta, 1978-87; exec. v.p., chief ops. officer Alta Bates Corp., Emeryville, Calif., 1987-91; cons. Alta Bates Corp., Emeryville, 1991-92, Alexander & Alexander, San Francisco, 1992-94; disting. vis. scholar Stanford (Calif.) U. Ctr. for Biomed. Ethics, 1993—; sr. fellow Stanford (Calif.) U. Hosp., 1993-94; sr. cons. stragetic healthcare practice Alexander & Alexander Cons. Group, San Francisco, Calif., 1994—; instr. computer applications Harvard U., 1968-69; lectr. hosp. adminstrn. UCLA, 1970-72, Stanford U. Med. Sch., 1972-77; assoc. prof. Emory U. Sch. Medicine, Atlanta, 1978-87. Contbr. articles to profl. jours. Served with U.S. Army, 1959. Fellow Am. Coll. Hosp. Adminstrs. (recipient Robert S. Hudgens meml. award 1976); mem. Am. Hosp. Assn., Assn. Univ. Programs in Health Adminstrn., U. Calif. Alumni Assn.

HOFMANN, POLLY A., physiology educator; b. Dixon, Ill., July 8, 1960; married; 1 child. BS in Biology, U. Ill., 1982; PhD in Physiology, U. Pitts., 1987. Postdoctoral fellow dept. physiology U. Wis., Madison, 1987-91; asst. prof. dept. physiology and biophysics U. Tenn., Memphis, 1991—; mem. prof. search com. Dept. Physiology and Biophysics, U. Tenn., 1991-92, grad. program tng. com., 1992-93, 95—, student progress and promotions com. biomed. sci. Coll. of Medicine, 1992-94, chmn. search com. Dept. Preventive Medicine, 1993-94, chmn. grad. program tng. com. Dept. Physiology and Biophysics, 1993-95, student progress and promotions com. for biomed. sci. Coll. of Medicine, 1994-96, Alma and Hal Reagan fellowship selection com. Coll. Grad. Health Scis., 1994—, mem. conflict resolution coun. of student mistreatment program Coll. of Medicine, 1995—. Ad hoc reviewer Am. Jour. Physiology, Jour. Pharmacology and Exptl. Therapeutics; contbr. articles to profl. jours. Predoctoral fellow NIH, 1983-87, Postdoctoral fellow, 1989-92, grantee, 1992—; Postdoctoral fellow Am. Heart Assn., 1988-89, recipient Dave McClain Rsch. award, 1988, Established Investigator award, 1995, grantee, 1992-93. Mem. Am. Physiol. Soc. (career opportunities in physiology com. 1995—), Biophys. Soc., Internat. Soc. Heart Rsch. (Upjohn Young Investigator award 1990), Sigma Xi. Office: U Tenn Dept Physiology & Biophysics 894 Union Ave Memphis TN 38163

HOFMEYR, GEORGE JUSTUS, medical educator, researcher; b. Johannesburg, South Africa, July 23, 1950; s. Reinald Theodor and Adele (Botha) H.; m. Carol Wynne Baker, Jan. 30, 1976; children: Graeme Peter, Robert Mark. MBBCh, U. Witwatersrand, 1973; MRCO9, Royal Coll. of Obstetrics and Gynecology, 1980. Intern, MO Johannesburg Hosp., South Africa, 1974-75; MO Baragwanath Hosp., Johannesburg, 1975-76, Holy Cross Hosp., Transkei, 1977-78; registrar, cons. Johannesburg Hosp., 1978-88; prof. Coronation Hosp., Johannesburg, 1988—. Contbr. chpts. to books in field; contbr. articles to profl. jours. Recipient Rand Mines scholar, 1968; Overseas Rsch. fellow Witwatersrand U., 1983. Office: Dept O&G U Witwatersrand, 7 York Rd, Parktown 2193 Johannesburg South Africa

HOFNUNG, MAURICE JACKY, microbiologist, educator; b. Arles, France, Feb. 3, 1942; s. Salomon Nathan and Rose (Korn) H.; m. Michèle Guillaume, Dec. 14, 1979; children: Clovis, Virgile, France. Degree in engring., Poly. U., Paris, 1963; PhD, U. Paris, 1972. Rsch. dir. CNRS, Paris, 1988—; prof. Inst. Pasteur, Paris, 1988—; unit dir. CNRS, 1979, Inst. Pasteur, 1980. Contbr. articles to sci. publs. Lt. French armed forces, 1962-65. Recipient Sci. prize League Against Cancer, Paris, 1978, 84; decorated Chevalier, Ordre du Mérite, Paris, 1989. Mem. French Acad. Sci. (corr.), French Genetic Toxicology Soc. (pres. 1985-88). Home: 5 place d'Alleray, 75015 Paris 75015, France Office: Inst Pasteur, 25 rue du Dr Roux, 75015 Paris France

HOFSTETTER, JOHN MICHAEL, research pharmacist; b. Toledo, Sept. 18, 1954; s. Robert Graydon and Doris Lou (Austin) H.; m. Nancy Lee Meyer, Oct. 6, 1982; children: Erin, Amy. BS in Computer Sci., U. Toledo, 1984; BS in Pharmacy, U. Okla., Oklahoma City, 1987, MS in Pharm. Sci., 1989, postgrad., 1989-92. Registered pharmacist, Okla.; cert. pharmacy dr. Nat. Assn. Retail Druggists. Pharmacist Bapt. Med. Ctr., Oklahoma City, 1986-92; rsch. pharmacist Abbott Labs., Abbott Park, Ill., 1992-96, sr. rsch. pharmacist, 1996—, internal cons., 1994-95; rsch. asst. U. Okla. Coll. Pharmacy, 1989-91. Inventor dual compartment wet/dry syringe, prefilled-2 constitutent syringe, syringe sys. containing 2 separate prefilled containers. Softball coach Vernon Hills (Ill.) Park Dist., 1992-96. Mosier scholar U. Okla. Coll. Pharmacy, 1985-87. Mem. Am. Assn. Pharm. Scientists, Mortar and Pestle Soc., Sigma Xi, Kappa Psi, Rho Chi. Office: Abbott Labs 100 Abbott Park Abbott Park IL 60064

HOGAN, CHARLES CARLTON, psychiatrist; b. Quincy, Ill., Oct. 5, 1921; s. Carlton Monta and Maryanne (Henry) H.; m. Nina Harriet Redman; children: Matthew P., Carlton H., Noelle N. Student, Bradley U., 1939-41, Ul Ill., 1941-42; MD, Columbia U., 1945, D Med. Sci., 1952. Diplomate Am. Bd. Psychiatry and Neurology. Intern Phila. Gen. Hosp., 1945-46; rsch. asst. neurology dept. Columbia U., N.Y.C., 1948-50, lectr. Ctr. for Psychoanalytic Tng., 1979—, psychoanalytic candidate Ctr. for Psychoanalytical Tng., 1948-52; resident N.Y. State Psychiatric Inst., N.Y.C., 1949-50; asst. physician Presbyn. Hosp., N.Y.C., 1951-54, asst. attending psychiatrist, 1954-60; asst. vis. psychiatrist Bronx (N.Y.) Mcpl. Hosp., 1960—; asst. clin. prof. psychiatry Albert Einstein Coll. Medicine, Bronx, 1960—; chmn. profl. adv. com. Riverdale Mental Health Clinic, Bronx, 1969-77; cons. Wiltwyck Sch. for Boys, Yorktown Heights, N.Y., 1971-77. Author: Psychosomatics, Psychoanalysis and Inflammatory Disease of the Colon, 1995; editor: Fear of Being Fat, 1985, Psychodynamic Technique in the Treatment of Eating Disorders, 1992, The Psychoanalytic Treatment of Patients with Inflammatory Bowel Disease in the Psychoanalytic Approach to Psychosomatics and Eating Disorders, 1990; contbr. articles to profl. jours., chpts. to books on psychosomatic disorders. Treas. Physicians for Social Responsibility, N.Y.C., 1968. Capt. U.S. Army, 1946-48. Fellow Am. Psychiat. Assn. (life); mem. AMA, Am. Psychoanalytic Assn. (life), N.Y. State Med. Assn., Am. Psychosomatic Soc. (emeritus), N.Y. Acad. Scis., Pan Am. Med. Assn., Assn. for Psychoanalytic Medicine (life), World Mental Health Assn., Undersea and Hyperbaric Med. Assn., Archaeol. Inst. Am., Riverdale Yacht Club (bd. govs.). Home: 6 Ploughman's Bush Bronx NY 10471-3541 Office: 119 E 83d St New York NY 10028

HOGAN, DAVID ELDEN, physician; b. Fredonid, Kans., Aug. 9, 1957; s. Aden Ellsworth and Maxine Ruth (Buchanan) H.; m. Sharolyn Gay Hutton, June 6, 1976; children: Robert, Roslyn, Roshelle. BS, Pitts. State U., 1979; DO, Kirksville (Mo.) Coll., 1980-84. Diplomate Am. Bd. Ermegency Medicine. Commd. 2d lt. U.S. Army, 1980, advanced through grades to maj., 1994; chief emergency med. svc. Ft. Leonardwood (Mo.) Army Hosp., 1985-87; chief resident emergency medicine Darnall Army Hosp., Ft. Hood, Tex., 1989-90, asst. chief dept. emergency medicine, 1990-92; asst. prof., dir. disaster emergency med. svcs. U. Okla., Oklahoma City, 1992—; med. dir. paramedic course Ctrl. Tex. Coll., Killeen, 1990-92; asst. prof. emergency medicine Tex. A&M U., College Station, 1990-92. Contbr. numerous articles to profl. jours. Mem. Disaster Com., Oklahoma City, 1994-95; med. dir. Hazardous Material Team, Oklahoma City, 1994—. Recipient Admiral Eske Rsch. award Assn. Mil. Osteo. Physician, 1990; Emergency Med. Found. fellow, 1992-93. Fellow Am. Coll. Emergency Physicians (chmn. edn. pub. rsch. com. disaster sect. 1995, sec.-treas. Okla. chpt. 1994); mem. Internat. Ctr. Disaster Rsch. Republican. Office: U Okla PO Box 26307 Rm EB319 Oklahoma City OK 73126

HOGAN, JOSEPH THOMAS, podiatrist; b. Cooperstown, N.Y., Nov. 25, 1943; s. James H. and Ann M. (Keery) H. DPM, Ill. Coll. Podiatric Medicine, 1975; BA, U. Notre Dame, 1966. Diplomate Am. Bd. Podiatric Surgery (credentials com. 1987-88), Am. Bd. Podiatric Orthopedics, Am. Bd. Quality Assurance Utilization Rev. Physicians, Am. Bd. Primary Podiatric Medicine (mem. case documentation com.); m. Kathleen Mary Sullivan, July 22, 1978; children: Kathleen, Margaret, Joseph II, Thomas, John, Mary Claire. Resident, St. Mary Hosp., Phila.; staff Lourdes Hosp. (Wound care ctr), 1994, staff podiatrist diabetic foot clinic Wilson Meml. Hosp., Binghamton, N.Y., 1979—, dir. orthopedics, 1995—; clin. instr. dept. orthop. SUNY Health Sci. Ctr., Syracuse, 1979—; ptnr., pvt. practice podiatric medicine and surgery, Binghamton, 1976—; adj. clin. prof. N.Y. Coll. Podiatric Medicine; surg. staff Lourdes Meml. Hosp., Wilson Meml. Hosp., Binghamton Gen. Hosp.; mem. faculty Penn. Podiatric Med. Assn. ann. surg. seminar, 1985-88, instr. bd. rev. course, 1986-88; clin. instr. family practice residency program United Health Svcs., 1980—, dir. dept. podiatric medicine and surgery, 1994—. Bd. dirs. Our Lady of Lourdes Meml. Hosp. Found.; chmn. United Way, 1981-82; v.p. N.Y. So. Tier chpt. Am. Diabetes Assn., 1978-83, bd. dirs., 1984—, bd. dirs, Rod Sterling Found., 1996—, bd. dirs. coun. med. sch. affiliated affiliated Podiatrists, 1995— Ch.; mem. Utilization Rev. Com. United Health Svcs., Lourdes Meml. Hosp. Found. Bd.; trustee N.Y. State Podiatric Med. Assn., 1990-92. With U.S. Army, 1967-70. Fellow Am. Assn. Hosp. Podiatrists, Am. Coll. Forensic Examiners and Ankle, Am. Coll. Foot Surgeons, Nat. Soc. Conscious Sedation, Am. Coll. Podiatric Med. Review, Am. Coll. Foot and Ankle Orthopedics and Medicine; mem. APHA, Am. Coll. Podopediatrics, Am. Soc. Podiatric Angiology, Broome County Hist. Soc., Am. Podiatric Med. Assn., N.Y. State Podiatric Med. Soc. (chpt. pres. 1980-82), Am. Diabetes Assn., N.Y. Acad. Scis., Am. Assn. Colls. Podiatric Medicine, Am. Legion, Am. Bd. Quality Assurance and Utilization Rev. (co-founder, diplomate), Am. Acad. Pain Mgmt. (diplomate), N.Y. State Podiatric Med. Assn. (co-chmn. So. tier div. ann. seminar. 1981-88, mem. sci. com. ann. clin. conf. 1989—, podiatric med. div. 1987—, legis. action com. 1990-92, bd. dirs. 1990-92, Excellence in Action award 1992), Edward Frederick Sorin Soc., Pa. Podiatric Med. Assn Surgeons (seminar 1985-87, credentials com. 1987—), Sorin Soc. Roman Catholic. Clubs: Elks, Ancient Order Hibernians, Notre Dame of Triple Cities (pres. 1982-84, editor newsletter, Winner of Yr. award 1991), NYSPMA special achievement award, 1996. Home: 608 Dartmouth Dr Vestal NY 13850-2926 Office: 41 Oak St Binghamton NY 13905-4627

HOGE, MARLIN BOYD, surgeon; b. Ft. Smith, Ark., Oct. 16, 1914; s. Arthur Franklin and Lillie Belle (Boyd) H.; m. Martha Nell Greenwood, Aug. 16, 1948 (dec. Sept. 1983); children: Catherine Nell, Marlin B. Jr., Rollins G. BS, Tulane U., 1937, MD, 1940. Intern Touro Infirmary, New Orleans, 1940-41; bn. surgeon 35th Combat Engrs. Alaska Hwy., 1941-42; asst. chief med. br. N.W. Svc. Command, 1942-43; surgeon Sta. Hosp., Edmonton, Alta., Can., 1943-44, 22 Evacuation Hosp. ETO, 1944-45, St. Edward Mercy Med. Ctr., Ft. Smith, 1945-50; pres. Hoge & Hoge Profl. Assn., Ft. Smith, 1960-87; bd. dirs. Ft. Smith Heritage Found., Friends of Libr.; chief staff and surgery St. Edward Mercy Med. Ctr., 1955-56, chief surgery, 1984-85, mem. adv. bd., 1975-78; bd. dirs. City Nat. Bank, Ft. Smith, 1956-91, chmn. bd., 1981-82. Historian, bd. dirs. Old Fort Mus., 1987-93; chmn. devel. commn. Ft. Smith Heritage Found., 1993—, Friends of Libr., 1993-95. Fellow ACS (pres. Ark. chpt. 1955-57), S.W. Surg. Congress; mem. AMA, Sebastian County Med. Soc. (pres. 1953), Noon Civics Club (pres. 1955). Home: 5501 S Cliff Dr Fort Smith AR 72903-4725

HOGE, PATRICIA PATTEN, human services organization administrator; b. Newton, Mass., Mar. 6, 1945; d. Robert Ross and Jean Barnes (Smith) Patten; m. Thomas Philip Seward, Oct. 2, 1965 (div. Mar. 1987); children: Amy, William; m. Philip A. Hoge, Mar. 5, 1988. Diploma in Nursing New Eng. Bapt. Hosp. Sch. Nursing, 1965; B.S. in Psychology, SUNY, 1979; M.S. in Edn., Elmira Coll., 1981; M.S. in Human Services, Cornell U.. 1983, Ph.D. in Human Services, 1983. Registered nurse, N.Y., Mass., Del. Staff nurse New Eng. Bapt. Hosp., Boston, 1965-66, 1970-71; nurse. tchr. health Post Sch. Dist., Corning, N.Y., 1973-79; project coordinator Steuben-Alleg BOCES Painted Post, N.Y., 1979-81; teaching asst., lectr. Cornell U., Ithaca, N.Y., 1981-83; exec. dir. ARC, Elmira, N.Y., 1983-87; exec. v.p. Del. div. Am. Cancer Soc., Wilmington, 1987—; cons. N.Y. State Edn. Dept., Albany, 1983, Corning-Painted Post Sch. Dist., Corning, 1981-82. Author: Me, My Baby and Blubber, 1980; A Teacher's Guide to Divorce, 1981, Teacher's Guide to Helping Children of Divorce, 1982. Mem. alumni bd. Coll. Human Ecology. sec., N.Y. State div. Am. Cancer Soc., 1982, bd. dirs. 1979 (recipient Voice of Hope award 1979). Mem. AAUW, N.Y. State Fedn. Profl. Health Educators (pres. 1983), N.Y. State Acad. Scis. Republican. Episcopalian. Avocation: hiking. Home: 12 Breeze Hill Rd PO Box 4057 Wilmington DE 19807 Office: Am Cancer Soc Del Div 92 Reads Way New Castle DE 19720-1631

HOGNESS, JOHN RUSTEN, physician, academic administrator; b. Oakland, Calif., June 27, 1922; s. Thorfin R. and Phoebe (Swenson) H. Student, Haverford Coll., 1939-42, D.Sc. (hon.), 1973; B.S., U. Chgo., 1943, M.D., 1946; D.Sc. (hon.), Med. Coll. Ohio at Toledo, 1972; LL.D., George Washington U., 1973; D.Litt., Thomas Jefferson U., 1980. Diplomate: Am. Bd. Internal Medicine. Intern medicine Presbyn. Hosp., N.Y.C., 1946-47; asst. resident Presbyn. Hosp., 1949-50; chief resident King County Hosp., Seattle, 1950-51; asst. U. Wash. Sch. Medicine, 1950-52, Am. Heart Assn. research fellow, 1951-52, mem. faculty, 1954-71, prof. medicine, 1964-71, med. dir. univ. hosp., 1958-63, dean, chmn. bd. health scis., 1964-69, exec. v.p. univ., 1969-70; dir. Health Scis. Ctr., 1970-71; pres. Inst. Medicine, Nat. Acad. Scis., 1971-74; prof. medicine George Washington U., 1972-74; pres. U. Wash., Seattle, 1974-79, pres. emeritus, 1979—; prof. medicine U. Wash., 1974-79; pres. Assn. Acad. Health Ctrs., 1979-88; disting. professorial lectr. dept. medicine Georgetown U., 1983-88; prof. Sch. Pub. Health, U. Wash., 1989-92; provost Hahnemann U., 1992-93; mem. commr.'s adv. com. on exempt orgns. IRS, 1969-71; mem. adv. com. for environ. scis. NSF, 1970-71, adv. com. to dir. NIH, 1970-71; mem. Nat. Cancer Adv. Bd., 1972-76, Nat. Sci. Bd., 1976-82; trustee China Med. Bd., 1965-92; mem. selection com. for Rockefeller pub. service awards Princeton U., 1976-82; chmn. med. injury compensation study steering com. Inst. Medicine, NAS; mem. council for biol. scis. Pritzker Sch. Medicine, U. Chgo., 1977-89; chmn. adv. panel on cost-effectiveness of med. techs. Office Tech. Assessment, U.S. Congress, 1978-80, chmn. study sect. for health care tech. assessment Nat. Ctr. for Health Svcs. Rsch. and Health Care Tech. Assessment, 1985-88; pres. Sun Valley Forum on Nat. Health, 1986-94; dir. Inst. for Health Policy Edn. and Rsch., U. Tex. Health Sci. Ctr., Houston, 1988; mem. Council Health Care Tech., HEW; adv. panel for study fin. grad med. edn. Dept. Health and Human Services, 1980-87; chmn. com. to evaluate the artificial heart, Inst. Medicine, NAS, 1990-91. Contbr. articles to profl. jours. Trustee Case Western Res. U., 1972-73. Served with AUS, 1947-49. Johns Hopkins U. Centennial scholar, 1976; recipient Disting. Service award Med. Alumni Assn. U. Chgo., 1966, Profl. Achievement award Alumni Assn. U. Chgo., 1973; Convocation medal Am. Coll. Cardiology, 1973; Cartwright medal Columbia U. Coll. Physicians and Surgeons 1978; Carel C. Koch Meml. award Am. Acad. Optometry, Toronto, 1986. Fellow AAAS, ACP (regent 1987-90), Am. Acad. Arts and Scis.; mem. NAS, Inst. Medicine, Assn. Am. Physicians, Assn. Am. Med. Colls. (exec. council, chmn.-elect coun. of deans 1968-69), Alpha Omega Alpha. Office: 514 Lost River Rd Mazama WA 98833-9700

HOHENWARTER, MARK WILLIAM, clinical pharmacist, drug research executive; b. Lancaster, Pa., Oct. 28, 1955; s. William Francis and Lucille (Stork) H.; m. Susan Barbara Menendez, Nov. 27, 1982; children: Emily Elizabeth, Marian Rose. B.S. in Pharmacy, U. N.C., 1978; Pharm. D., Med. U. S.C., 1981. Lic. pharmacist, Ala., N.C., S.C. Clin. asst. prof. Med. U. S.C., 1982-84; pharmacy clin. coordinator Roper Hosp., Charleston, S.C., 1982-84; clin. pharmacist Mobile Infirmary Med. Ctr., Ala., 1984-85, pharmacy clin. coordinator, 1985-87; exec. v.p. Serotonin Industries, Inc., Charleston, 1984-91; pres. IV Therapy Assocs., 1987-94, Horizon Bus. Group, 1995—; cons. in field. Contbr. articles to profl. jours. and chpt. to book; patentee in field. Recipient Burroughs Wellcome Hosp. Pharmacy Research award N.C. Soc. Hosp. Pharmacists. Greensboro Drug Club Aux. scholar, 1975; Am. Soc. Hosp. Pharmacists fellow, 1981. Mem. Am. Soc. Hosp. Pharmacists, Am. Soc. Parenteral and Enteral Nutrition, Pharmacists, Rho Chi. Roman Catholic. Club: YMCA. Avocations: sailing; scuba diving; skiing. Home and Office: 8 Rush St Beaufort SC 29902-1722

HOHL, HANS RUDOLF, biology educator; b. St. Gall, Switzerland, Aug. 23, 1933; s. Hans and Rosli (Leicht) H.; m. Marianne E. Sennhauser, May 2, 1959; children: Andreas, Barbara, Markus. Diploma natural sci., Fed. Inst. Tech., Zürich, Switzerland, 1957, PhD, 1961. Rsch. assoc. U. Wis., Madison, 1961-63; from asst. prof. to assoc. prof. U. Hawaii, Honolulu, 1963-69; from assoc. prof. to prof. U. Zürich, 1969—; dean faculty of sci. U. Zurich, 1988-90; chmn. Intercomty. Sch., Zumikon, Zurich, 1985-94. Editor: Fungal Spore, 1981; editor Botanica Halvetica Jour., 1980-95; contbr. articles to profl. jours. Pres. Zumikon Sch. Bd., 1974-82. Lt. Swiss Army, 1953-88. Grantee NSF 1964—. Home: Tobelgasse 10, CH-8126 Zurich Switzerland Office: Inst Plant Biology U Zürich, Zollikerstr 107, CH-8008 Zurich Switzerland

HOHLE, BETH MARIE, public health nurse; b. Grygla, Minn., Mar. 1, 1921; d. Otto and Martha (Paulick) H. Diploma, Ancker Hosp. Sch. Nursing, 1943; BS, Vanderbilt U., 1949; MA in Journalism, U. Minn., 1952; MS in Nursing, UCLA, 1965. Sch. nurse Willmar (Minn.) Pub. Schs., 1950-51; nurse supr. Children's Hosp., L.A., 1953-56; pub. health nurse County of L.A., 1956-79; weekend nurse supr. Congress Convalescent Hosp., Pasadena, Calif., 1983-92. Contbr. articles to profl. jours. 1st lt. nurse corps. U.S. Army, 1944-46. Recipient Mary M. Roberts award Am. Jour. Nursing Co., 1966. Mem. AAUW, NOW, ANA, Calif Nurses Assn., Griffith Park Women's Golf Club, Women's Pub. Links Golf Assn. So. Calif., L.A. County Women's Golf Assn. Democrat. Home: 321 Cameron Pl Apt 15 Glendale CA 91207-2031

HOHN, THOMAS, molecular biologist; b. Duisburg, Germany, May 16, 1938; s. Hans and Grete (Luckmann) H.; m. Barbara Hohn, Sept. 15, 1962; children: Andreas, Michael. Diploma, Max-Planck Inst. Virology, Tübingen, 1962, PhD, 1966. Postdoctoral researcher Stanford (Calif.) U., 1968-71; project leader Basel (Switzerland) U., 1971-78; assoc. prof. microbiology U. Basel, 1973—; group leader Friedrich Miescher Inst., Basel, 1979—. Editor: Plant Gene Research, Virus Genes. Active Amnesty Internat., Basel, 1974-84. Mem. EMBO, Acad. Europea. Office: Friedrich Miescher-Inst, PO Box 2543, Basel CH-4002, Switzerland

HOJAT, MOHAMMADREZA, psychologist, psychological researcher; b. Mashad, Iran, Dec. 22, 1947; s. Mohammad-Bagher Hojat and Fakhri (Ashtiani) Hojat; m. Maymanat Moini-Nazeri, June 25, 1982; children: Arian, Anahita, Roxana. BA, U. Shiraz, Iran, 1971; MA, U. Tehran (Iran), 1973; PhD, U. Pa., 1981. Lic. psychologist. Rsch. supr. Inst. of Psychology, Tehran, 1971-73; prin. researcher Air Force Office of Counseling & Psychol. Svcs., Tehran, 1974-75; demographic rsch. supr. Sch. of Social Work, Tehran, 1975; instr. The Free U. of Iran, Tehran, 1975-76; rsch. assoc. Jefferson Med. Coll., Phila., 1979-83; dir. longitudinal study, rsch. assoc. prof. psychiatry and human behavior Jefferson Med. Coll., Thomas Jefferson U., Phila., 1984—. Contbr. numerous articles to profl. jours. Mem. APA, Am. Ednl. Rsch. Assn., World Fedn. Mental Health. Office: Jefferson Med Coll 1025 Walnut St Philadelphia PA 19107-5083

HOKENSTAD, ALENE ANNE, policy analyst; b. Sioux Falls, S.D., Sept. 18, 1964; d. Merl Clifford and Dorothy Jean (Tarrell) H.; m. Bruce Lawrence Kluger, Oct. 30, 1993; 1 child, Bridgette Anne. BA, Kalamazoo Coll., 1986; MS, Mandel Sch. Applied Social Sci, 1990. Sr. group worker Merrick House Settlement, Cleve., 1987-89; intern Children's Defense Fund, Columbus, Ohio, 1989-90; asst. deputy dir. Mayor's Office Ops., N.Y.C., 1990-94; dir. home care innovations United Hosp. Fund, N.Y.C., 1994—. Home: 309 W 86th Apt 3A New York NY 10024 Office: United Hosp Fund 350 5th Ave New York NY 10118

HOKENSTAD, MERL CLIFFORD, JR., social work educator; b. Norfolk, Nebr., July 21, 1936; s. Merl Clifford and Flora Diane (Christian) H.; m. Dorothy Jean Tarrell, June 24, 1962; children: Alene Ann, Laura Rae, Marta Lynn. B.A. summa cum laude, Augustana Coll., 1958; Rotary Found. fellow, Durham (Eng.) U., 1958-59; M.S.W., Columbia U., 1962; Ph.D., Brandeis U., 1969, Inst. Ednl. Mgmt., Harvard U., 1977. With Lower East Side Neighborhood Assn., N.Y.C., 1962-64; community planning assoc. United Community Services, Sioux Falls, S.D., 1964-66; instr. Augustana Coll., Sioux Falls, 1964-66; research assoc. Ford Found. Project on Community Planning for Elderly, Brandeis U., Waltham, Mass., 1966-67; prof., dir. Sch. Social Work, Western Mich. U., Kalamazoo, 1968-74; prof., dean Sch. Applied Social Scis., Case Western Res. U., Cleve., 1974-83; Ralph and Dorothy Schmitt prof. Sch. Applied Social Scis., Case Western Res. U., 1983—, chmn. PhD program, 1990-94; prof. internat. health Sch. of Medicine, 1994—; vis. prof. Inst. Sociology, Sotckholm U., 1978, Fulbright lectr., 1980; vis. prof. Nat. Inst. Social Work, London, 1981, Sch. Social Work, Stockholm U., 1982-86, Eotvos Lorand U., Budapest, Hungary, 1992, 95, 96, London Sch. Econs., 1994; Fulbright rsch. scholar Inst. Applied Social Rsch., Oslo, 1989; fellow U. Canterbury, Christchurch, New Zealand, 1994. Author: Participation in Teaching and Learning: An Idea Book for Social Work Educators; Elder Care in Sweden: Services and Support During an Era of Social Transition, 1996; editor: Meeting Human Needs: An International Annual, Vol. V, Linking Health Care and Social Services: International Perspectives; editor-in-chief Internat. Social Work Jour., 1985-87; co-editor: Profiles in Internat. Soc. Work, 1992, (internat. issue) Jour. Gerontol. Social Work, 1988, (internat. mental health issue) Jour. Sociology and Social Welfare, 1990, Jour. Social Policy and Adminstration, 1993, Jour. Aging Internat., 1994, Jour. Applied Social Scis., 1996; contbr. articles to profl. jours., chpts. to books. Mem. alcohol tng. rev. com. Nat. Inst. Alcoholism and Alcohol Abuse, 1974-78; workshop leader Am. Assn. State Colls. and Univs., 1974; chmn. U.S. com. XVIII Internat. Congress Schs. Social Work, 1976; chmn. Kalamazoo County Cmty. Mental Health Svcs. Bd., 1971, vice chmn., 1972; mem. edn. and tng. task force Mich. Office Drug Abuse and Alcoholism, 1972-73; mem. Mich. Assn. Mental Health Bds., 1972; bd. dirs. Cleve. United Way Svcs., 1982-84, del. assembly, 1974-82, mem. periodic rev. oversight com., 1982, mem. leadership devel. com., 1978, cmty. resources com., 1988—; bd. dirs. Kalamazoo United Way, 1968-72; trustee Cleve. Internat. Program for Youth Workers and Social Workers, chmn. program com., 1985-87; mem. program devel. com. Cleve. Center on Alcoholism, 1976; trustee Alcoholism Services Cleve., Inc., 1977-86, v.p., 1982-85; trustee Cmty. Info./Vol. Action Ctr., 1982-88, chmn. leadership devel. com., 1984-86, chmn. unmet needs com., 1986-88, exec. com., 1985-88, v.p., 1986-88; exec. com. Western Reserve Geriatric Edn. Ctr., 1995—; mem. adv. com. Coun. for Internat. Exch. Scholars, 1991-93, Fedn. for Cmty. Planning Coun. on Older Persons, 1991—, chmn. caregiver support program initiative, 1995-96; mem. task force of social transition in Soviet Union, U.S. State Dept. Bur. Human Rights and Humanitarian Affairs; mem. UN NGO Com. on Aging, 1996—. Named Outstanding Alumnus, Augustana Coll., 1980, Ohio Soc. Worker of the Yr., 1992; Fulbright Research fellow; NIMH trainee, 1960-62; Vocat. Rehab. trainee, 1966; Gerontology trainee, 1967; Rotary Found. fellow, 1958-59. Mem. NASW (internat. com. 1989-93, chmn. 1992-93), Acad. Cert. Social Workers, Internat. Assn. Schs. Social Work (exec. bd. 1978-92, treas. 1978-86, v.p. N.Am. 1988-92), Internat. Coun. on Social Welfare (dir. U.S. com. 1982-92), Coun. on Social Work Edn. (del. 1972-75, 77-83, chmn. ann. program meeting 1973, chmn. com. on nat. legis. and adminstrv. policy 1975-79,. nominating com. 1978-81, internat. com. 1980-86, chmn. com. 1982-84, dir. 1979-82, exec. com. 1986-89, pres. 1986-89), Nat. Conf. on Social Welfare (bd. dirs. 1978-80, chmn. sect. V. program com. 1977-78), World Future Soc. (area coord. 1972-74), Fulbright Assn. (v.p. N.E. Ohio chpt. 1990-91), Nat. Coun. on Aging (bd. dirs. 1991—, internat. com. 1991—, pub. policy com. 1992—, co-chmn. 1993—). Democrat. Episcopalian. Home: 2917 Weymouth Rd Cleveland OH 44120-2234 Office: Case Western Res U 10900 Euclid Ave Cleveland OH 44106-7164

HOLBERTON, PHILIP VAUGHAN, biotechnology company executive; b. N.Y.C., Sept. 29, 1942; s. Robert Maynard and Charlotte Metcalf (Stone) H.; m. Gale Russell, May 16, 1970 (div. 1980); children: Matthew Russell, Alexandra; m. Anne Meigs Blodget, June 6, 1987; 1 child, Philip Vaughan Jr., Tod. A.B. in Acctg., Franklin and Marshall Coll., Lancaster, Pa., 1964. CPA, N.Y. Auditor Hurdman and Cranstoun CPAs, N.Y.C., 1964-72; mgr. audit svcs. Peat Marwick CPAs, N.Y.C., 1975-79; investment profl. McDonald & Co., N.Y.C., 1972-75; asst. contbr. Becton Dickinson & Co., Franklin Lakes, N.J., 1979-81; group contbr. Becton Dickinson & Co., Paramus, N.J., 1981-85; v.p. fin. Gen. Cinema Theatres, Chestnut Hill, Mass., 1985-91; v.p. fin. and adminstrn., CFO Cambridge, Neuroscience, Inc., Cambridge, Mass., 1991-95; founder Holberton and Co., Lincoln, Mass., 1995—; outside dir. Mgmt. Decision Lab., NYU, 1981-84. Chmn. strategic planning panel United Way of Bergen County, Paramus, 1983-85; dir. Poppenhusen Inst., College Point, N.Y., 1981-83; sr. warden St. Anne's in the Fields, Lincoln, Mass., 1994-96. Mem. AICPA, Fin. Execs. Inst. (pres. bd. dirs. Boston chpt. 1995-96). Office: Holberton & Co PO Box 254 Lincoln MA 01773

HOLBROOK, JOHN HAMILTON, internist, educator; b. Salt Lake City, Sept. 17, 1940; s. Raymond Brimhall and Esther Ruth (Hamilton) H.; m. Judith Ruth Morris, July 10, 1964; children: David, Jennifer, Julie, Mary, Matthew, Ruth, John. BS, U. Utah, 1964, MD, 1967. Diplomate Am. Bd. Internal Medicine. Med. intern U. Utah, Salt Lake City, 1967-68, instr. in medicine, 1972-73, asst. prof. medicine, 1973-79, assoc. prof. medicine, 1979-88, prof. medicine, 1988—, divsn. chief gen. medicine, 1988—; med. resident Washington U./Barnes Hosp., St. Louis, 1968-70; med. officer USPHS, Rockville, Md., 1970-71; med. staff dir. Nat. Clearinghouse for Smoking, Rockville, 1970-71; attending physician Univ. Hosp., Salt Lake City, 1972—; cons. Surgeon Gen., USPHS, Rockville, 1972—, mem. Agy. for Healthcare Policy for Guideline Devel., 1994—, mem. Inter-Agy. Coun. on Smoking, 1985-89; mem. exec. com. faculty orgn. U. Utah Sch. Medicine, 1994—. Editor Surgeon Gen.'s Report on Smoking, USPHS; editor-in-chief Med. Knowledge Self-Assessment Program XI Am. Coll. Physicians; contbr. to med. publs. Recipient Cert. Appreciation, Surgeon Gen. Koop, 1990, Disting. Svc. award Utah Med. Assn., 1994. Fellow ACP (regent 1988-94, rep. to AMA Internal Medicine sect. coun. 1987-94, chair pub. policy com. 1990-94); mem. AMA, Am. Fedn. Clin. Rsch., Soc. Gen. Internal Medicine. Home: 2797 E Commonwealth Ave Salt Lake City UT 84109 Office: U Utah 4B129 University Hosp Salt Lake City UT 84132

HOLBROOK, JOHN MARSHALL, pharmaceutical educator; b. Austell, Ga., Mar. 10, 1945; s. Alonzo Newell and Lois Idell (Reeves) H.; m. Geraldine Pearson, June 1, 1968; children: John Russell, Amy Kathleen. BS in Pharmacy, Mercer U., 1969; PhD in Pharmacology, U. Miss., 1974. Asst. prof. biomed. scis. Mercer U. Sch. Pharmacy, Atlanta. 1974-77, assoc. prof. biomed. scis., 1978-85, prof. pharm. scis., 1986—; co-dir. postgrad. mental health pharmacy residency program Ctrl. State Hosp., Milledgeville, Ga., 1979-81, co-dir. postgrad. residency in alcoholism and substance abuse Fulton County Alcoholism Treatment Ctr., Atlanta, 1980-82, dir. Ctr. for Substance Abuse Edn. and Rsch., 1994—; adj. faculty Dept. Cardiopulmonary Scis., Ga. State U., Atlanta, 1976-91, lectr. in toxicology, Dept. Chemistry, 1982-83, adv. bd. dept. nutrition and dietetics, chmn. 1980-81, Sch. Nurse Anesthetists, Ga. Baptist Med. Ctr., Atlanta, 1976-85; adj. faculty U. Coll. Mercer U., 1993, 94; cons. on drugs of abuse to Composite State Bd. Medicine and Dentistry, Office of Sec. of State, Atlanta. Co-author: Nutrition Principles and Clinical Practice, 1980; contbr. articles to profl. jours., chpts. to books; dir. numerous pharmacy doctorate rsch. projects. bd. dirs. Met. Atlanta Coun. on Alcohol and Drugs; judge for Ga. Sci. and Engring. Fair, Athens, 1980,88, 90; therapeutic cons. Fulton County Alcoholism Treatment Ctr., Atlanta, 1979-1982. Recipient commendation USN and USMC, Atlanta, for svc. in alcohol and drug abuse edn., 1982. Mem. Am. Assn. Colls. of Pharmacy, Am. Assn. Lab. Animal Scis., Soc. of Forensic Toxicologists, Inc., Am. Found. Pharm. Edn. (E. Mead Johnson fellow), SE Assn. of Lab. Animal Scis., Berry Coll. Excelsior Club, Phi Kappa Phi, Rho Chi, Phi Lambda Sigma, Kappa Epsilon. Office: Mercer Univ Sch Pharmacy Dept Pharmaceutical Scis 3001 Mercer Univ Dr Atlanta GA 30341

HOLBROOK, NORMA JEANNETTE, nursing educator; b. Napton, Mo., Oct. 26, 1939; d. R. Milton and Thelma M. (Miller) Cochran; m. Ralph E. Holbrook, June 30, 1961; children: Tamara M., Jennifer L. BS in Nursing, Cen. Mo. State U., 1965; M of Nursing, Kans. U., 1982. Staff nurse Menorah Med. Ctr., Kansas City, Mo., 1965-66, head nurse, 1966-67; instr. nursing Met. Community Coll., Kansas City, 1967-68; staff nurse Independence (Mo.) Med. Ctr., 1971-73; staff nurse St. Francis Hosp., Topeka, 1975-80, 84-89, mem. continuing edn. com., 1988—; instr. nursing Washburn U., Topeka, 1981-85, asst. prof., 1986-89; edn. coord. St. Francis Hosp. and Med. Ctr., 1989-91, 93—, clin. nurse specialist in gerontology, 1991-93; chair nursing rsch. com., 1990-96; mem. nursing quality assurance com. Stormont Vail Regional Med. Ctr., Topeka, 1982-83, mem. task force for improved implementation nursing care plans, 1983, mem. nursing svc. stds. com., chair procedures com., mem. std. care plan com., 1989—, mem. editorial bd. Kansas Nurse, 1990-95. Mem. nursing adv. com. ARC, Capital area chpt., Topeka, 1980-90, chmn. 1982-83, 88-89. Presentor ednl. programs on nursing process and care planning, gerontology, stress mgmt. for caregivers, positive communicating with patients with Alzheimer's Disease. Contbr. articles to profl. jours. Mem. ANA (Kansas State Nurses Assn. coun. continuing edn. 1987-89), Nat. Gerontol. Nursing Assn., Alzheimer's Assn. (bd. dirs. Topeka chpt., mem. edn. com. 1994-96), Sigma Theta Tau Internat. (pres. Eta Kappa chpt. 1990-92, Excellence in Writing award 1993). Republican. Methodist. Office: St Francis Hosp and Med Ctr 1700 SW 7th St Topeka KS 66606-1674

HOLDCROFT, ANITA, anesthetist, educator. MB BChir, Sheffield (Eng.) U., 1969, MD, 1983. Sr. registrar, hon. tutor in anesthesia Hammersmith Hosp. and Royal Postgrad. Med. Sch., London, 1974-77; sr. lectr. in anesthesia Charing Cross Med. Sch., London, 1977-80; prof. anesthesia Jos Univ. Med. Sch., Nigeria, 1980-87; sr. lectr. in anesthesia Royal Postgrad. Med. Sch., London, 1988—. Author: Body Temperature Control in Anesthesia, Surgery and Intensive Care, 1980. Fellow Royal Coll. Anesthetists, West African Coll. Surgeons. Office: Hammersmith Hosp, Royal Postgrad Med Sch, Dept Anesthesia, London W12 OHS, England

HOLDEMAN, NICKY RAY, medical ophthalmologist; b. Perryton, Tex., Mar. 23, 1952; s. Carl Ray and Lena Mae (Smith) H.; m. Lisa Kell Greer, June 11, 1983. AS, Amarillo (Tex.) Coll., 1972; BS, U. Houston, 1974, OD, 1976; MD, Tex. Tech. U., Lubbock, 1987. Optometrist Drs. Dean, Bowen & Holdeman, Lubbock, 1977-83; chief med. svcs., chair residency program, exec. dir. U. Houston, 1989—; exec. dir. Univ. Eye Inst., Houston; chmn. systemic disease sect. Nat. Bd. Examiners in Optometry, Chevy Chase, Md., 1991—; state bd. dirs., med. advisor Prevent Blindness Tex., Houston, 1991—. Contbr. chpts. to books. Recipient Eldon Ourrett scholarship Amarillo Coll., 1972, Lange award Lange Pubs., 1987, Recognition for career accomplishments City of Houston, 1991, 93. Mem. AMA, Assn. Clinic Dirs., Am. Coll. Physician Execs., Tex. Med. Assn., Harris County Med. Soc., Houston Acad. Medicine. Republican. Baptist. Office: U Houston 4901 Calhoun Houston TX 77204-6052

HOLDEN, DAVID MORGAN, medical educator; b. Bronx, N.Y., Jan. 29, 1938; s. James Francis and Lois (Morgan) H.; m. Carolyn Cleaves Chadbourne, Dec. 20, 1959 (div. Nov. 1971); children: David Chadbourne, James Morgan, Katherine VanTassel; m. Susan Elizabeth Garner, Dec. 23, 1971 (div. Mar. 1985); 1 child, Hannah Garner; 1 adopted child, Erin Elizabeth; m. Carol Ann Battaglia, Apr. 12, 1985. BS, Tufts U., 1959; MD, Yale U., 1963. Diplomate Am. Bd. Pediatrics, Nat. Bd. Med. Examiners, Am. Bd. Family Practice. Intern in pediatrics Yale New Haven Med. Ctr., 1963-64; resident in pediatrics Babies Hosp. Columbia Presbyn. Med. Ctr., N.Y.C., 1964-66; med. epidemiologist Ctr. Disease Control USPHS, Atlanta and Manila, 1966-69; clin. instr. Emory U. Sch. Medicine, Atlanta, 1969-73; assoc. prof. family medicine U. N.D. Med. Sch., Minot, 1973-75; prof. family medicine, asst. dean Coll. Human Medicine U. Wyo., Laramie, 1976-77; prof. family medicine Coll. Human Medicine Mich. State U., East Lansing, 1977-80, asst. dean coll. human medicine, 1977-80; prof. family medicine, pediatrics sch. medicine U. Kans., Wichita, 1980-83; prof., chmn. dept. family medicine SUNY Sch. Medicine, Buffalo, 1983-93; prof. family medicine SUNY Downstate Sch. Medicine, Bklyn., 1993—; dir. ambulatory care L.I. Coll. Hosp., Bklyn., 1993-94, chmn. family practice, 1993—; dir. N.W. N.D. Area Health Edn. Ctr., Minot, 1973-75; residency rev. com. Family Practice, 1991—, chmn., 1994—. Contbr. articles to profl. jours; chpts. to books. Fellow Am. Acad. Pediatrics, Am. Acad. Family Physicians; Soc. Tchrs. Family Medicine, County chpt. Am. Acad. Family Physicians, N.Y. chpt. Am. Acad. Family Physicians. Republican. Episcopalian. Office: LI Coll Hosp Family Care Ctr 165 Cadman Plz E Brooklyn NY 11201-1402

HOLDEN, KENTON ROY, neurology educator, pediatrics educator; b. Balt., Apr. 28, 1943; s. Alfred Charles and Alice Anita (Posadski) H.; m. Patricia E. Chisholm, Aug. 14, 1965; children: Kenton R. Jr., W. Blake. BA, U. Va., 1964; MD, Med. Coll. Va., 1968. Diplomate Am. Bd. Pediat.; cert. Nat. Bd. Med. Examiners, Md. Bd. Med. Examiners, S.C. State Bd. Med. Examiners. Pediat. resident Johns Hopkins Hosp., Balt., 1968-70, 72-73, instr. pediat. and neurology, 1973-76, asst. prof. pediat. and neurology, 1976-90; child neurology fellow NIH, Bethesda, 1970-72; pvt. practice pediat. and neurology Drs. Sigler, Roskes, Holden, et al, Balt., 1973-90; assoc. prof. pediat., assoc. prof. neurology Med. U. S.C., Charleston, 1990-95; prof. neurology, professor pediat., 1996—; asst. dir. Pediat. Seizure Clinic, Johns Hopkins Hosp., Balt., 1973-90; staff cons., perinatla rsch. Nat. Inst. Neurol. Diseases and Stroke-NIH, Bethesda, Md., 1943-90; clin. dir. pediat. neurology Med. U. S.C., Charleston, 1990—; bus. mgr., treas. Drs. Sigler, Roskes, Holden & Schuberth, P.A., Balt., 1982-90; lectr. in field. Contbr. articles to profl. jours. Med. missionary Episcopal Ch., Honduras, 1991, 92, 93, 95, 96; bd. dirs. Low Country Epilepsy Assn., Charleston, 1992—; dir. neurology symposium Guinyard-Butler Middle Sch., Barnwell, S.C., 1992—. Lt. comdr. USPHS, 1970-72. Fellow Am. Acad. Pediat.; mem. Am. Epilepsy Soc., S.C. chpt. Am. Acad. Pediat., So. Med. Assn., Johns Hopkins Med. and Surg. Assn., Alpha Omega Alpha. Office: Childrens Hosp MUSC Rm 511 171 Ashley Ave Charleston SC 29425

HOLDEN, LISA ROSE, physical therapist; b. Pitts., Jan. 17, 1962; d. William Thomas and Dorothy Rita (Palombo) H. BA in Human Movement, Lake Erie Coll., Painesville, Ohio, 1983; AS in Phys. Therapist Asst., C.C. Allegheny County, Monroeville, Pa., 1990; M in Phys. Therapy, Duquesne U., 1994. Lic. phys. therapist, Pa. Mental health and mental retardation specialist Siffrin Assn., Canton, Ohio, 1983-84, Idlewood Ctr., Pitts., 1985-90; phys. therapy aide The Phys. Therapy Ctr., Pitts., 1986-90, phys. therapist asst., 1990-94, phys. therapist, 1994—; instr. N.E. C.C., Canton, 1983-85. Mem. Am. Phys. Therapy Assn., Pa. Phys. Therapy Assn., Phi Theta Kappa.

HOLDEN, RAYMOND HENRY, clinical psychologist; b. Providence, Feb. 21, 1924; s. James Herbert and Martha (Sutcliffe) H. AB magna cum laude, Brown U., 1947; AM, Yale U., 1949; EdD, Boston U., 1960. Cert. psychologist R.I., Mass. Asst. in psychology Yale U., New Haven, 1947-48; dir. dept. psychology Meeting St. Sch., Providence, 1952-62; dir. child testing unit Brown U., Providence, 1957-70; dir. learning ctr. R.I. Coll., Providence, 1970-72, prof. dept. psychology, 1970-87, prof. emeritus, 1995—; chief psychologist Vocat. Resources, Inc., Providence, 1965-95, Tavares Pediatric Ctr., Providence, 1989—; vis. scientist Nat. Inst. Neurol. Disease and Strokes, NIH, Bethesda, Md., 1968-69; cons. Fuller Meml. Hosp., South Attelboro, Mass., 1977-85, Johnston (R.I.) Sch. Dept., 1977-91, Dartmouth (Mass.) Sch. Dept., 1986-87. Contbr. articles to profl. publs.; author test revs. Served as tech. sgt. U.S. Army, 1943-46, PTO. Fellow Am. Psychol. Assn., Am. Orthopsychiatric Assn.; mem. Phi Beta Kappa, Sigma Xi, Phi Delta Kappa. Home: 9 Cambria Ct Pawtucket RI 02860-5117 Office: Tavares Pediatric Ctr 101 Plain St Providence RI 02903

HOLDER, SANDRA SUE, X-ray technician; b. Washington, Nebr., July 17, 1938; d. Myron William Melton and Verona Lucille (Nelsen) Melton-Klipp; m. N. Gaylord Holder, Feb. 13, 1960; children: Stacey, Jennifer, Debra, Steven, Kirk. RT, Presbyn. Hosp. Sch. X-Ray Tech, 1958; AA, Aims C.C., 1988, AS in Criminal Justice, 1994; BA, U. No. Colo., 1990, MA, 1993; postgrad., Widener U. Sch. of Law, 1996—; cert. paralegal, Denver Paralegal Inst., 1995. Registered x-ray technician. Staff X-ray tech. St. Lukes Hosp., Denver, 1958-61; office nurse, X-ray tech. Drs. Monty & Chisholm, Denver, 1962-65; staff X-ray tech. St. Anthony North Hosp., Westminster, Colo., 1970-74; reading aide Sch. Dist. 27J, Brighton, Colo.; computer entry clk. Sch. Dist. 27J, Brighton, 1976-79; co-owner maid svc., 1979-81; ins. agt. Oestman Ins. Agy., Brighton, 1982-84; food svc. worker United Air Lines, Denver, 1984-86; vol. library aide Sch. Dist. 27J, Brighton, 1974-76; vol. reading program Sch. Dist. 27J, 1975-76. Mem. Budget Com. Sch. Dist. 27J, Brighton, 1974, Goals Com., 1974; chmn. Parent Adv. Coun., Brighton, 1975; organizer Community Resource File, Brighton, 1976. Mem. APA, Am. Registry X-Ray Technologists. Episcopalian. Home: 914 Cherrytree Ln # 10 Claymont DE 19703

HOLDSWORTH, JANET NOTT, women's health nurse; b. Evanston, Ill., Dec. 25, 1941; d. William Alfred and Elizabeth Inez (Kelly) Nott; children: James William, Kelly Elizabeth, John David. BSN with high distinction, U. Iowa, 1963; M of Nursing, U. Wash., 1966. RN, Colo. Staff nurse U. Colo. Hosp., Denver, 1963-64, Presbyn. Hosp., Denver, 1964-65, Grand Canyon Hosp., Ariz., 1965; asst. prof. U. Colo. Sch. Nursing, Denver, 1966-71; counseling nurse Boulder PolyDrug Treatment Ctr., Boulder, 1971-77; pvt. duty nurse Nurses' Official Registry, Denver, 1973-82; cons. nurse, tchr. parenting and child devel. Teenage Parent Program, Boulder Valley Schs., Boulder, 1980-88; bd. dirs., treas. Nott's Travel, Aurora, Colo., 1980—; nurse Rocky Mountain Surgery Ctr., 1996—; instr., nursing coord. ARC, Boulder, 1979-90, instr., nursing tng. specialist, 1980-82. Mem. adv. bd. Boulder County Lamaze Inc., 1980-88 ; mem. adv. com. Child Find and Parent-Family, Boulder, 1981-89; del. Rep. County State Congl. Convs., 1972-96, sec. 17th Dist. Senatorial Com., Boulder, 1982-92; vol. Mile High ARC, 1980; vol. chmn. Mesa Sch. PTO, Boulder, 1982-92, bd. dirs., 1982-95, v.p., 1983-95; elder Presbyn. ch. Mem. ANA, Colo. Nurses Assn. (bd. dirs. 1975-76, human rights com. 1981-83, dist. pres. 1974-76), Coun. Intracultural Nurses, Sigma Theta Tau, Alpha Lambda Delta. Republican. Home: 1550 Findlay Way Boulder CO 80303-6922 Office: Rocky Mountain Surgery Ctr 2405 Broadway Boulder CO 80304

HOLDSWORTH, ROBERT LEO, JR., emergency medical services consultant; b. Boston, Sept. 30, 1959; s. Robert Leo and Anne Marie (Walsh) H. Student, U. Hartford, West Hartford, Conn., 1977-80; cert. paramedic, Combined Hosps. Program, Hartford, Conn., 1986. Emergency room technician St. Francis Hosp., Hartford, 1981-82; EMT, L&M Ambulance Corp., Hartford, 1981-85; correctional paramedic State of Conn., Hartford, 1981-84; paramedic L&M Ambulance Corp., Hartford, 1983-85, gen. mgr., 1985-87; dir. emergency med. svcs. Lawrence and Meml. Hosp., New London, Conn., 1987-89; pres. Holdsworth & Assocs., East Berlin, Conn., 1988—; chmn. Ea. Regional Mobile Intensive Care Com., Norwich, Conn., 1987-89; pub. rels. dir. Conn. C.I.S.D. team, 1989-92. Author: Multiple Casualty Exercises, 1990, Guidebook on Occupational Exposure to Blood-borne Pathogens, 1992; co-author: TB Infection Protection, 1994; writer, producer: (video) The Alternative. Mem. Nat Assn. EMT's, Nat. Soc. Emergency Med. Svc. Adminstrs., Nat. Soc. Emergency Med. Svc. Instrs., Nat. Soc. Paramedics, Conn. Soc. Emergency Med. Svc. Instrs., Kiwanis (chmn. pediatric tng. seminar Norwich 1990). Office: 1224 Mill St East Berlin CT 06023-1152

HOLDWAY, DOUGLAS ALAN, toxicologist, consultant; b. Montreal, Que., Can., Jan. 23, 1954; arrived in Australia, 1986; s. Charles Edward and Jeanette (Menzie) H.; m. Tracey Ann Monkhouse, June 11, 1983; children: Nathanial Edward, Jazmin Adryanna Hedy, Morgan Alexander Douglas. BSc with honors, U. Guelph, Ont., Can., 1976, MSc, 1978, PhD, 1983. Rsch. asst., tutor U. Guelph, 1976-78, 80-83; sci. subvention researcher Fed. Fisheries Rsch. Sta., St. Andrews, New Brunswick, 197880; NRC/Can. rsch. assoc. U. Waterloo, Ont., Can., 1983-85; Can. Govt. Lab. vis. fellow Environment Can., Burlington, Ont., 1985-86; rsch. scientist, head aquatic toxicology dept. Office of the Supervising Scientist, Jabiru, N.T., 1986-88, sr. rsch. scientist, head aquatic toxicology dept., 1988-89; chief environ. toxicologist Royal Melbourne (Victoria, Australia) Inst. Tech., 1989—, assoc. prof., 1993—; head Oil Spill Rsch. Group, 1995—; mem. auditor rev. panel EPA, Melbourne, 1990-92, head oil spill rsch. group, 1995—; head environ. effects group, mem. rev. task force Jaakko Poyry Oy/Alberta Rsch. Coun., Helsinki, Finland, 1990; Australian expert aquatic toxicology OECD Test Guidelines Program, Canberra, 1991—. Author numerous book chpts. and sci. papers. Regional editor Spill Sci. & Tech.; author: numerous book chpts. and sci. papers. Govt. of Ont. scholar, 1972, 77-79; EPA grantee, 1990—, Commonwealth Pulp and Paper Rsch. Adv. Bd. grantee, 1991—, Australian Rsch. Coun. grantee, 1991—. Mem. ASTM, Nat. Geog. Soc., Soc. Environ. Toxicology and Chemistry (editl. bd. 1988-90), Environ. Inst. Australia, Australian Soc. Ecotoxical, Australian Inst. Biology, Australian Soc. Limnology, Australasian Soc. Clin. and Exptl. Pharmacology and Toxicology (rgional editor Australasia and Japan, Spill Sci. and Tech. Bull. 1996—). Office: RMIT Univ, Dept Appl Biol Biotechnol, Melbourne Vic 3001, Australia

HOLE, SUSAN AUSTIN, physician; b. Live Oak, Fla., Aug. 22, 1949; d. Wilson Towles and Carlie Evelyn (Baker) Austin; m. Winston Winfield Scott, July 9, 1966 (div. June 1974); children: Winston Winfield Jr., Alvin Austin; m. Robert Eugene, June 11, 1978; 1 child, Patrick Eugene. ASN, Daytona (Fla.) Beach C.C., 1971; BA, Stephens Coll., 1978; MEd, U. So. Miss., 1986; DO, U. Osteo. Medicine Health Sci., Des Moines, 1992. Diplomat Am. Bd. Family Practice. Resident in family practice Iowa Luth Hosp., Des Moines, 1993-95; emergency dept. physician Adair County Hosp., Greenfield, Iowa, 1994-95; dep. med. examiner Polk County, Iowa, 1993-95; pvt. practice Edgewater, Fla., 1995—; med. dir. Ocean View Nursing Home, New Smyrna, Fla., 1996—; mem. med. staff Bert Fish Med. Ctr., New Smyrna, 1995—, Halifax Hosp., Daytona Beach, 1996—. Maj. flight surgeon USNG, 1991-96. Mem. AMA, Fla. Acad. Family Physicians, Fla. Med. Assn., Volusa County Med. Soc., Phi Delta Epsilon. Democrat. Office: 601 E Indian River Blvd Edgewater FL 32000

HOLEVAR, MICHELE RENEE, trauma surgeon, emergency medicine physician; b. Detroit, Sept. 25, 1954; d. Andrew George and Dorothy Ann Holevar; m. James Boyer Ebert. Student, U. Mich., 1972-74, MD, 1978. Surg. resident U. Chgo., 1980, U. Ill., Chgo., 1983; attending emergency physician Hyde Park Hosp., Chgo., 1983-86, Jackson Park Hosp., Chgo., 1985-89; trauma fellow Carraway Meth. Med. Ctr., Birmingham, Ala., 1990; dir. trauma surgery Olympia Fields (Ill.) Med. Ctr., 1990-92; assoc. dir. trauma Christ Hosp. and Clinics, Oak Lawn, Ill., 1992—; asst. prof. surgery U. Ill., Chgo., 1995—; legal cons., 1994—. Contbr. chpt. to book. Fellow ACS (mem. med. com. on trauma); mem. Am. Coll. Emergency, Ea. Assn. for the Surgery Trauma, Western Trauma Assn., Chgo. Met. Trauma Soc. Office: Christ Hosp 4440 W 95th St Oak Lawn IL 60453

HOLFORD, THEODORE RICHARD, biostatistician, educator; b. Columbus, Ohio, May 19, 1947; s. Charles Richard and LaVern Lucille (Lukens) H.; m. Maryellen Hutchinson Holford, Dec. 21, 1969; children: Matthew Edwin, Lesley Erin. BA in Math and Chemistry, Andrews U., 1969; PhD in Biometry, Yale U., 1973. Rsch. staff Yale U., New Haven, Conn., 1972-73, asst. prof., 1974-79, assoc. prof., 1979-89, prof., 1989—, head divsn. biostatistics, 1990—; dir. cancer biostats. tng. NCI. Editor: Statistical Methods in Medical Research, 1992—; assoc. editor Am. Jour. Epidemiology, 1989—, Biometrics, 1984-88; contbr. articles to profl. jours. Mem. Consensus Devel. Conf. on Health Implications of Smokeless Tobacco, Washington, 1986, Epidemiology & Disease Control Study Section, Washington, 1986-89, Epidemiology Adv. Subcom. Oak Ridge (Tenn.) Assn., 1988-93. Recipient Wakeman award, 1990, numerous NIH grants. Mem. Am. Statis. Assn., 1973—, Biometric Soc., 1973—, Soc. for Epidemiologic Rsch., 1978—. Office: Yale U 60 College St New Haven CT 06510

HOLINGER, LAUREN DRAKE, surgeon; b. Chgo., Aug. 9, 1942; s. Paul H. and Julia Campbell (Drake) H.; children: Christopher, Elizabeth. BS, Union Coll., 1964; MD, Chgo. Med. Sch., 1971. Diplomate Am. Bd. Otolaryngology, Am. Bd. Med. Examiners. Resident gen. surgery U. Colo. Affiliated Hosps., 1971-72, resident otolaryngology, 1972-75; fellowship Rush-Presbyn.-St. Luke's Med. Ctr., 1975-76, Children's Meml. Hosp., 1975-76, U. Ill. Eye and Ear Infirmary, Chgo., 1975-76; prof. otolaryngology-head and neck surgery Northwestern U. Med. Sch., Chgo.; head divsn. of pediatric otolaryngology and dept. of communicative disorders The Children's Meml. Hosp.; active attending otolaryngologist divsn. of pediatric otolaryngology, sect. head and active attending bronchologist, sect. of bronchoesophagology; attending physician Northwestern Meml. Hosp., Chgo., Rush-Presbyn.-St. Luke's Med. Ctr., Chgo. Editl. bd. Archives of Otolaryngology-Head and Neck Surgery, Annales d' Otolaryngologie et de Chirurgie Cervico-Faciale, The Child's Doctor, Operative Techniques in Otolaryngology-Head and Neck Surgery, Jour. of Bronchology; editl. rev. bd. Otolaryngology-Head and Neck Surgery, The Laryngoscope, Archives of Otolaryngology-Head and Neck Surgery; contbr. chpts. to books and articles to profl. jours. Adv. bd. Horizon Hospice, 1979—; bd. dirs. The Children's Meml. Hosp., 1982-86, 88-92; bd. trustees Latin Sch. of Chgo., 1984-90; chmn. annual giving campaign, 1986-87, chmn. centennial celebration com., 1987-89. Fellow ACS (coun. 1985—, com. on applicants 1984—, young surgeons rep. 1983), Am. Acad. of Otolaryngology, Head and Neck Surgery (nat. and internat. stds. com. 1989—, other coms.), Am. Acad. of Pediatrics, Am. Broncho-Esophagological Assn. (coun. 1982—, sec. 1985-91, pres. 1992-93, chmn. long range planning com. 1993-94, chmn. thesis and awards com. 1994-95), Am. Laryngological Assn. (coun. 1995—), Am. Laryngological, Rhinological, and Otological Soc., Am. Soc. for Head and Neck Surgery, Soc. for Ear, Nose and Throat Advances in Children; mem. Am. Soc. of Pediatric Otolaryngology, Chgo. Laryngological and Otological Soc. (coun. 1986-87, program com. 1986-87), Chgo. Med. Soc., Ill. Med. Soc., Ill. Pediatric Surg. Assn. (affiliate, bd. dirs. 1983-87, sec.-treas. 1983-84, pres. 1985-87), Inst. of Medicine of Chgo., Internat. Broncho-Esophagological Soc., Pan Am. Assn. of Oto-Rhino-Laryngology and Head and Neck Surgery, Soc. of Med. History of Chgo. Home: 2300 Lincoln Park West Chicago IL 60614 Office: Children's Meml Hosp Box 25 2300 Children's Plaza Chicago IL 60614

HOLKUM, VICKI LYNNE, health information manager; b. Ada, Okla., Oct. 2, 1965; d. James Edward and Willa Mae (Davenport) H.; 1 child, Delaney Renee. BS in Health Info. Mgmt., East Ctrl. U., 1994. Chief med. records Fed. Bur. Prisons USPHS, Ft. Worth, 1994-95; escrow asst. Pope and Assocs., Grand Prairie, Tex., 1995; mgr. med. records Primary Care Group Hillcrest Med. Group, Tulsa, 1995-96; med. records coder Pauls Valley (Okla.) Gen. Hosp., 1996—; instr. med. records Pontotoc Area Tech. and Vocat. Sch., Ada, Okla., 1996—; tchr. Mid-Am. Vo-Tech. Sch., Wayne, Okla. Recipient Hazardous Duty Ribbon USPHS, 1995. Mem. Am. Health Info. Mgmt. Assn. (registered rec. adminstr.), Okla. Health Info. Mgmt. Assn. Republican. Baptist. Home: Rt 7 Box 173H Ada OK 74820

HOLL, JAMES ANDREW, prehospital care administrator; b. Jersey City, Sept. 15, 1961; s. Charles J. Jr. and Alice M. (Kearney) H. Cert. paramedic, N.J. Coll. Dentistry/Medicine, 1981; AS in Nursing, Atlantic C.C., 1986; BA in Nursing Mgmt., Stockton State Coll., 1991; postgrad. flight nurse prog., USAF Sch. Aerospace Medicine, 1993. Cert. emergency nurse, flight nurse. Firefighter, EMT instr. Brigantine (N.J.) Fire Dept., 1979-96, firefighter, instr. dep. coord emergency mgmt., 1987—; paramedic mobile intensive care West Jersey Health System, 1982-83, Underwood Meml. Hosp, 1980—; forensic med. investigator Atlantic County Med. Examiners Office, 1982-86; nurse dept. intensive care, emergency Shore Meml. Hosp., 1986—. Mem. 714th Aeromed. Squad USAF, 1991—. Recipient citation Senator Dan Dalton. Mem. Nat. Flight Nurses Assn., Nat. Registry Emergency Med. Technicians, N.J. State Emergency Med. Technician Instrs., Emergency Nurses Assn., Emergency Med. Svcs. Physicians Assn. (assoc.), Internat. Assn. Firefighters, Atlantic County Firefighters Assn. Office: 1417 W Brigantine Ave Brigantine NJ 08203-2147

HOLLAND, CLINTON RUSSELL, JR., medical products executive; b. South Kingstown, R.I., May 15, 1949; s. Clinton Russell Sr. and Esther Jeanette (Montecalvo) H.; m. Christine Lynn Jones, June 26, 1971; 1 child, Caitlin Alexis. BS in Chem. Engring., U. R.I., 1971; MBA, Boston U., 1983. Mktg. specialist Nalco Chem. Co., Oakbrook, Ill., 1971-77; product specialist Millipore Corp., Bedford, Mass., 1977-81; dir. sales Memtek-Filterite Corp., Timonium, Md., 1981-85; chmn., CEO Ember Product, Inc., Totowa, N.J., 1985-89; dir. sales Koch Membrane Corp., Wilmington, Mass., 1989-91; founder, pres., CEO, COO Medtek/Buffalo Filter Co., Inc., Buffalo, N.Y., 1991—; cons. Zenon Membrane, Burlington, Ont., Can., 1990-91; bd. dirs. Medtek Devices, Inc., Buffalo. Inventor in field. With U.S. Army Nat. Guard, 1970-71. Mem. AIChE, Am. Filtration Soc. (founding dir. 1985, chpt. pres.), Inst. Environ. Scis. (sr.), Nat. Assn. Corrosion Engrs. Republican. Roman Catholic. Home: 8388 Bridlewood Dr East Amherst NY 14051 Office: MEDTEK/Buffalo Filter 6000 N Bailey Ste 9 Buffalo NY 14226

HOLLAND, GARY NORMAN, ophthalmologist, educator; b. Long Beach, Calif., July 30, 1953; s. Richard L. and Edith (Hewson) H. MD, UCLA, 1979. Diplomate Am. Bd. Ophthalmology, Nat. Bd. Med. Examiners; lic. MD, Calif., Ga. Intern in internal medicine UCLA, 1979-80; resident in ophthalmology Jules Stein Eye Inst., L.A., 1980-83; fellowship in uveitis rsch. Proctor Found. U. Calif. San Francisco, 1983-84; cornea fellowship Emory U. Med. Sch., Atlanta, 1984-85; prof. ophthalmology Jules Stein Eye Inst. UCLA, 1985—. Assoc. editor Am. Jour. of Ophthalmology, 1993-96. Mem. Am. Uveitis Soc. (chmn. edn. and rsch. com. 1994—). Office: UCLA Jules Stein Eye Inst 100 Stein Plz Los Angeles CA 90095-7003

HOLLAND, JOY, health care facility executive; b. N.Y.C., Oct. 24, 1946; d. Harry Walson and Edna May (Simmons) H.; m. Chesley Roderick Richardson, Sept.21, 1985; children: Carl Allen Fields, Craig Anthony Fields. AA in Nursing, Olive-Harvey Coll., 1972; BS, St. Joseph Coll., Bklyn., 1976; M in Health Adminstrn., C.W. Post Coll., 1978. Staff nurse U. Chgo. Hosp. and Clinics, Chgo., 1972; head nurse N.Y. Hosp., N.Y.C., 1972; clinic adminstr. Morrisania-Montefiore Hosp., Bronx, N.Y., 1973; head nurse, supr. Pilgrim Psychiat. Hosp., Brentwood, N.Y., 1974, assoc. dir. staff devel., 1974-76, dir. nursing, 1976-78; surveyor, cons Joint Commn. on Accreditation of Hosps., Chgo., 1978-82; dir. Ypsilanti (Mich.) Regional Psychiat. Hosp., 1986-90, Clinton Valley Ctr., Pontiac, Mich., 1990-93, Huron Valley Ctr., Ypsilanti, Mich., 1993—; dep. commr. dept. mental health State of Ohio, 1980-82; cons. Joint Commn. Accreditation of Hosps.; adj. lectr. Sch. Nursing, U. Mich.; cons. specialist, bd. dirs. Holland-Richardson Assocs., Detroit. Contbr. author (book) Guide to J.C.A.H. Nursing Standards, 1985, 86 edits. Bd. dirs. Women in Crisis, Inc., N.Y.C., 1979-85, Washtenaw County (Mich.) ARC; bd. dirs. psychiatry dept. Chelsea (Mich.) Hosp., 1989-91. Mem. N.Y. Acad. Sci. (life), Bus. and Profl. Women, Inc., Masons, Order Ea. Star, Alpha Kappa Alpha, Sigma Theta Tau. Republican. Office: Huron Valley Center 3511 Bemis Rd Ypsilanti MI 48197-9307

HOLLAND, LOUIS EDWARD, II, virologist; b. Kansas City, Mo., Nov. 15, 1948; s. Louis Garratt and Evelyn (Plunkett) H.; m. Mary Lynn Lambert, Apr. 21, 1977; children: Michael, Jeffrey. BS, Baker U., 1970; PhD, U. Calif., Irvine, 1979. Postdoctoral fellow U. Mich., Ann Arbor, 1979-84; sr. molecular biologist So. Rsch. Inst., Birmingham, Ala., 1984-88;

sr. virologist IIT Rsch. Inst., Chgo., 1988—. With U.S. Army, 1970-72. Mem. Am. Soc. Microbiology, Am. Soc. Virology, Internat. Soc. Antiviral Rsch., Internat. AIDS Soc. Office: IIT Rsch Inst 10 W 35th St Chicago IL 60616-3799

HOLLAND, MALVERN CARLYLE, physician; b. Simpsonville, S.C., Nov. 27, 1926; s. Samuel Townes and Isola (McHugh) H.; m. Ann Nicholson, Mar. 1, 1952; children: Malvern Carlyle Jr., Timothy, Ruthann, Carolyn, Elizabeth. BS cum laude, U. S.C., 1948; MD, Duke U., 1951. Diplomate Am. Bd. Ophthalmology. Pvt. practice Greenville, S.C., 1960—. Sgt. U.S. Army, 1944-46, USPHS, 1951-60, WWII. Fellow Am. Acad. Ophthalmology, Internat. Coll. Surgeons; mem. AOA, SCMA, AMA, ASCRS. Republican. Office: 612 Grove Rd Greenville SC 29605-4209

HOLLAND, MARIE T., physician; b. D.C., Aug. 5, 1956; d. Pierre Paul and Dorothy Leake Tulou; m. John R. Holland, Mar. 29, 1980; children: Eric, Christopher. BS, U. Mich., 1978; MD, Eastern Va. Med. U., 1981. Diplomate Am. Bd. Neurology. Asst. prof. neurology Eastern Va. Med. Sch., Norfolk, 1981—; cons. Muscular Dystrophy Assn., Norfolk, 1991—. Contbr. articles to profl. jours. Mem. Am. Assn. Electrodiagnostic Medicine (assoc.), Am. Acad. Neurology, Tidewater Neurol. Soc., Myasthenia Gravis Soc. (med. adv. bd. Va. chpt. 1995—).

HOLLAND, MELISSA MARTIN, medical office manager; b. Birmingham, Ala., Jan. 25, 1959; d. Waymon Franklin and Doris Faye (Bennett) Martin; m. Thomas Lee Holland, Aug. 16, 1985; children: James Robert III, Martin Dawson. BS in Chemistry-Sociology, Birmingham So. Coll., 1981; BS, U. Ala., Birmingham, 1985. Asst. lab. technician microbiology U. Ala., Birmingham, 1981-83; physicians asst. neonatology nursery Med. U. S.C., Charleston, 1985-86; office mgr. Andrew Burch, MD, Mobile, Ala., 1986-89, Huntsville Neonatology, Huntsville, Ala., 1989—. Baptist. Office: Huntsville Neonatology PC 115 Manning Dr A202 Huntsville AL 35801

HOLLAND, PETER MARC, ophthalmologist; b. N.Y.C., Apr. 7, 1944; s. George and Estelle (Alpert) H.; m. Merle Lumish, May 26, 1968; children: Matthew David, John Michael. BA, Clark U., 1965; MD, N.Y. Med. Coll., 1969. Diplomate Nat. Bd. Med. Examiners, Am. Bd. Ophthalmology. Med. intern Montefiore Hosp. & Med. Ctr., Bronx, N.Y., 1969-70; resident in ophthalmology Duke U. Eye Ctr., Durham, N.C., 1972-75; asst. prof. dept. ophthalmology George Washington U. Med. Ctr., Washington, 1976-77; clin. asst. prof. Baylor Coll. Medicine, Houston, 1977-90, clin. assoc. prof. dept. ophthalmology, 1990—; ophthalmologist Bayshore Eye Assocs., Pasadena, Tex., 1977—; clin. assoc. prof. Dept. Ophthalmology U. Tex. Med. Br. Galveston, 1996—; cons. space shuttle flights #1 and #2, NASA, Houston, 1978-81; chmn. inst. rev. com. Bayshore Med. Ctr., Pasadena, 1984-93; mem. com. for appointment and promotion Baylor Coll. Medicine, Dept. Ophthalmology, Houston, 1988-92. Contbr. articles to profl. jours. Lt. comdr. USPHS, 1970-72. Mem. Houston Ophthalmologic Soc. (pres. elect 1993-94, pres. 1994-95, exec. com. 1983-86, 93-95), Tex. Med. Assn., Tex. Ophthalmologic Assn. (chmn. Diabetes 2000 com. 1993-94), Tex. Ophthalmology & Otolaryngology Soc., Harris County Med. Soc., Am. Acad. Ophthalmology, Am. Diabetes Assn., Alpha Omega Alpha. Office: Bayshore Eye Assocs 3320 Plainview St Pasadena TX 77504-1906

HOLLAND, ROBERT CAMPBELL, anatomist, educator; b. Bushnell, Ill., Aug. 16, 1923; s. Harvey Howard and Lois Sarah (Campbell) H.; m. Hilda P. Burgi, Sept. 26, 1946 (dec. 1980); children: Jonathan Robert, Heather; m. Elaine M. Probst, Sept. 1, 1988; 1 child, Judith Ashley. BS, U. Wis., 1948, MS, 1949, PhD, 1955. Instr. Dental Sch. Northwestern U., 1949-51; asst. prof. anatomy Sch. Medicine U. N.D., 1955-60; assoc. prof. Sch. Medicine U. Ark., 1960-66; prof. chmn. dept. anatomy Mahidol U., Bangkok, 1966-76; prof., chmn. dept. anatomy Morehouse Sch. Medicine, Atlanta, 1976-90, prof. emeritus dept. anatomy, 1990—; mem. staff Rockefeller Found., 1966-76; vis. prof. UCLA Sch. Medicine, 1976. Author research pubs. on the brain. With M.C., U.S. Army, 1943-46. Fellow Wis. Alumni Rsch. Found., 1951-54, Nat. Found. for Infantile Paralysis, 1957-58; NIH grantee, 1959-88. Mem. Am. Assn. Anatomists, Am. Acad. Neurology, Soc. Exptl. Biology and Medicine, Soc. Neurosci., Sigma Xi.

HOLLANDER, CHARLES SIMCHE, physician; b. N.Y.C., Aug. 25, 1934; s. Bernard and Beatrice (Bobrowsky) H.; m. Joan Simon, Dec. 17, 1972; children: Ellen, Ruth, Barbara. A.B., Columbia U., 1955, M.D., 1959. Intern Bellevue Hosp., N.Y.C., 1959-60; research fellow in medicine Johns Hopkins U., Balt., 1960-62, 65-66; sr. resident Peter Bent Brigham Hosp., 1962-63; research asso. metabolism br. Nat. Cancer Inst., NIH, 1963-65; asso. physician in medicine, chief endocrinology Rochester (N.Y.) Gen. Hosp.; asso. prof. medicine U. Rochester, 1966-69; asso. prof. medicine N.Y. U. Med. Center, 1969-74, prof. medicine, 1974—, chief endocrine div., 1969—, dir. clin. research unit, 1969-91, dir. endocrine research and reference labs., 1991—; asst. in medicine Harvard Med. Sch., 1962-63; asst. physician in medicine Johns Hopkins Hosp., 1965-66; asso. physician Strong Meml. Hosp., Rochester, 1966-69; attending physician N.Y. U. Hosp., 1969—, Bellevue Hosp., 1969—; cons. Manhattan VA Hosp., 1969—; mem. Clin. Research Centers Study Sect., 1979-81, chmn., 1981-82; mem. metabolism panel Health Research Council, N.Y.C., 1969-75; ad hoc cons. Alcohol Abuse and Alcoholism and Drug Abuse, NIH, 1978, VA merit rev., 1978; chmn. workshop com. on advances in neuroendocrinology Div. Research Resources NIH, 1981; mem. alcohol biomed. research rev. com. Nat. Inst. Alcohol Abuse and Alcoholism, 1983-87. Served with USPHS, 1963-65. Mem. A.C.P. (Council Specialized Socs.), Assn. Am. Physician, Am. Soc. Clin. Investigation, Am. Fedn. Clin. Research, Harvey Soc., Endocrine Soc. (mem. manpower liaison com. 1981—, chmn. 1982—), Am. Thyroid Assn. (bd. dirs. Program Dirs. Assn. 1979—, pres. 1980-81), AAUP, N.Y. Acad. Scis., Phi Beta Kappa, Phi Delta Epsilon. Home: 411 W End Ave New York NY 10024-5719 Office: NYU Sch Medicine 550 1st Ave New York NY 10016-6481

HOLLANDER, DANIEL, gastroenterologist, medical educator; b. Mar. 3, 1939. Student, UCLA, to 1960; MD, Baylor U., 1964. Diplomate Am. Bd. Internal Medicine, Am. Bd. Gastroenterology. Intern Phila. Gen. Hosp., 1964-65; resident in internal medicine Med. Ctr., U. Kans., Kansas City, 1965-67; NIH rsch. fellow in gastroenterology U. Wash., Seattle, 1967-69; asst. prof. medicine Albany (N.Y.) Med. Coll., Union U., 1971-73, assoc. prof., 1973; assoc. prof. medicine, head div. gastroenterology Wayne State U., Detroit, 1973-77, prof. medicine, head div. gastroenterology, 1977-78; prof. medicine, head div. gastroenterology U. Calif., Irvine, 1978-94, prof. physiology and biophysics, 1981-94, assoc. dean for rsch. and program devel. Coll. Medicine, 1984-85, assoc. dean for acad. affairs, 1985-89, sr. assoc. dean for clin. affairs, 1989-91, chief gastroenterology Irvine Med. Ctr., 1979-94; exec. dean Sch. of Medicine U. Kans., Kansas City, 1994-95; attending physician, attending gastroenterologist Albany Med. Ctr. Hosp., 1971-73; chief gastroenterology svc., attending physician Harper Hosp., Detroit, 1973-78; cons. in gastroenterology Children's, Detroit Gen. and VA hosps., 1973-78; chief gastroenterology VA Med. Ctr., Long Beach, Calif., 1978-80; chmn. Gastrointestinal Gerontology Rsch. Group, 1988-89; vis. scientist dept. molecular medicine U. Auckland, New Zealand, 1990-91; vis. prof., invited speaker numerous other univs., profl. meetings, confs. Author: (with G. Gitnick, N. Kaplowitz, I.M. Samloff, L.J. Schoenfield) Principles and Practice of Gastroenterology and Hepatology, 1988, (with A. Tarnawski) Gastic Cytoprotection—A Clinician's Guide, 1989, (with Porro G. Bianchi) Treatment of Digestive Disease with Sucralfate, 1989; mem. editl. bd., reviewer Can. Jour. Gastroenterology; contbr. numerous articles, revs. to profl. jours., book chpt. With USAF, 1969-71. Calif. Heart Assn. rsch. fellow, 1960; Fogarty Sr. Internat. fellow Oxford (Eng.) U., 1984-85; grantee NIH, Nat. Inst. on Aging, Nat. Insts. Arthritis, Metabolism and Digestive Diseases, Skillman Found., VA, Goldsmith Found., Internat. Pharm. Products. Mem. ACP (A. Blaine traveling scholar 1973), Am. Fedn. for Clin. Rsch. (pres. Midwestern sect. 1979-80), Am. Gastroent. Assn., Am. Physiol. Soc., Am. Soc. for Clin. Investigation, Orange County Gastroenterology Assn. (pres. 1986-87), Brit. Soc. Gastroenterology, European Assn. Gastroenterology, Western Assn. Physicians, Western Gut Club (pres. 1981-82), Alpha Omega Alpha. Office: Univ Kans Sch of Medicine 3901 Rainbow Blvd Kansas City KS 66160-0001

HOLLANDER, EDWIN PAUL, psychologist, educator; b. Rochester, N.Y., Aug. 15, 1927; s. Victor and Lillian (Kravetz) H.; m. Patricia Ann Harrington, Apr. 18, 1959; 1 son, Peter Andrew. BS, Western Res. U., 1948; MA, Columbia U., 1950, PhD, 1952. Asst. prof. psychology Carnegie Inst. Tech., Pitts., 1954-58; asso. prof. psychology Washington U., St. Louis, 1958-60; asso. prof. internat. communication and social psychology Sch. Internat. Service, Am. U., Washington, 1960-62; prof. psychology SUNY-Buffalo, 1962-89, provost social scis. and adminstrn., 1971-73, dir. social psychology doctoral program, 1962-68, 73-76; vis. prof. Baruch Coll. and Univ. Grad. Ctr., CUNY, N.Y.C., 1987-89, Univ. Disting. prof. psychology, 1989—; study dir. NAS, NRC, 1979-80; vis. faculty U. Istanbul, Turkey, 1957-58, U. Wis., 1961, Inst. Am. Studies, Paris, 1966-67, Harvard U., 1969-70, Oxford (Eng.) U., 1973; cons. NSF, 1965-68, HEW, 1967-72, NAS, NRC, Space Sci. Bd., 1969-70; prin. investigator research projects Office Naval Research, 1955-69, 76-79, NIMH, 1962-64. Author: Leaders, Groups and Influence, 1964, Principles and Methods of Social Psychology, 1967, 4th edit., 1981, Leadership Dynamics, 1978; co-editor: Current Perspectives in Social Psychology, 1963, 4th edit., 1976, Classic Contributions to Social Psychology, 1972; mem. editorial bd.: Jour. Abnormal and Social Psychology, 1962-64, Jour. Personality Social Psychology, 1965-67, Brit. Jour. Social and Clin. Psychology, 1967-79; Leadership Quarterly, 1989-91; editorial bd.: Sociometry, 1969-72, asso. editor, 1971-72; editorial bd., asso. editor: Internat. Rev. Applied Psychology, 1975-79; contbr. articles to profl. jours., chpts. to books, papers at internat. congresses and profl. meetings. Served with AUS, 1946-47; from ensign to lt. USNR, 1951-54. Fulbright fellow Turkey, 1957-58; NIMH sr. fellow Tavistock Inst. Human Rels., London, 1966-67; recipient Disting. Achievement award Psychol Assn. Western N.Y., 1983, Kurt Lewin award social psychology N.Y. State Psychol. Assn., 1986. Fellow Am. Psychol Soc., N.Y. Acad. Scis. (adv. com. psychology sect. 1990—), AAAS (sec. psychology sect. 1974-78), APA (chmn. com. psychology nat. internat. affairs 1962-63, coun. reps. 1965-66, 68-70, 79-81, 83-86, mem. bd. social and ethical responsibility for psychology 1975-78, com. on internat. rels. psychology 1981-84, pres. div. gen. psychology 1980-81), Soc. Indsl. and Orgnl. Psychol.; mem. AAUP (pres. Carnegie Tech. chpt. 1956-57), Soc. Exptl. Social Psychology (chmn. exec. com. 1969-70), Ea. Psychol. Assn. (bd. dirs. 1982-85, 91-94, pres. 1988-89), Soc. Psychol. Study Social Issues (coun. 1968-70), Internat. Assn. Applied Psychology (exec. com. 1975-86, U.S. treas. 1980-82), Internat. Soc. Polit. Psychology (gov. coun. 1985-87, v.p. 1988-90), Am. Assn. Univ. Adminstrs., Acad. Mgmt., Authors Guild, Sigma Xi, Omicron Delta Kappa, Psi Chi. Clubs: Cosmos (Washington), Harvard (N.Y.C.). Home: 330 E 39th St Apt 19L New York NY 10016-2122 Office: CUNY Baruch Coll & U Grad Ctr Box G-1126 17 Lexington Ave New York NY 10010-5526

HOLLANDER, ERIC, psychiatrist, educator, researcher; b. L.A., June 19, 1957; s. Irwin and Nina (Serser) H.; m. Beth Fein, June 16, 1985. BA, Brandeis U., 1978; MD, SUNY, Bklyn., 1982. Diplomate Am. Bd. Psychiatry and Neurology. Med. intern Mt. Sinai Hosp., N.Y.C., 1982-83, resident and chief resident in psychiatry, 1983-86; attending psychiatrist Columbia-Presbyn. Med. Ctr., N.Y.C., 1986-93; rsch. psychiatrist N.Y. State Psychiat. Inst., N.Y.C., 1986-93, dir. obsessive-compulsive disorder studies, 1988-93; asst. prof. psychiatry Columbia U. Coll. Physicians and Surgeons, N.Y.C., 1988-92; assoc. prof. psychiatry Coll. Physicians and Surgeons, Columbia U., N.Y.C., 1992-93; vice chmn., dir. clin. psychopharmacology, assoc. prof. Mt. Sinai Sch. Medicine, N.Y.C., 1993-95, prof. psychiatry, clin. dir. autism rsch. ctr., dir. psycho-pharmacology, dir. compulsive, impulsive and anxiety disorders program, 1995—. Contbr. articles to profl. med. jours.; editor of 6 books. Recipient Marcel Heiman award, M. Ralph Kaufman prize Mt. Sinai Hosp., 1986, CINP Rsch. Fellowship award, 1990; NIMH grantee 1988-93, FDA grantee 1993—. Mem. Am. Psychiat. Assn. (Pennwalt Rsch. award 1986, Wisniewski Young Psychiat. Rsch. award 1990), Soc. for Biol. Psychiatry, Group for Advancement of Psychiatry (Ginsburg fellow 1985-87). Jewish. Home: 380 Orienta Ave Mamaroneck NY 10543 Office: Mt Sinai Sch Medicine 1 Gustave Levy Pl Box 1230 New York NY 10029

HOLLANDER, IRWIN JOEL, pathologist, educator; b. Bayonne, N.J., May 29, 1949; s. Max Leo and Miriam Hilda (Berger) H.; m. Aileen Rhonda Sosnow, June 21, 1970; children: Lori, Sheri, Eric. BS, Pa. State U., 1970; MD, Thomas Jefferson U., 1972. Diplomate Am. Bd. Internal Medicine, Am. Bd. Pathology. Intern in medicine Mt. Sinai Hosp., N.Y.C., 1972-73; resident in pathology Hosp. of U. Pa., Phila., 1973-75; resident in medicine Thomas Jefferson. U. Hosp., Phila., 1975-77, resident in pathology, 1977-79; assoc. pathologist Grand View Hosp., Sellersville, Pa., 1979-81, dir. labs., 1981—; adj. clin. assoc. prof. pathology Thomas Jefferson U., 1994—. Fellow ACP, Coll. Am. Pathologists, Am. Soc. Clin. Pathologists; mem. Bucks County Med. Soc. (pres. 1989). Home: 1519 Fulton Dr Maple Glen PA 19002 Office: Grand View Hosp 700 Lawn Ave Sellersville PA 18960-1548

HOLLANDER, MELVYN ARNOLD, psychologist; b. Newark, July 26, 1941; s. Benjamin and Beatrice (Leder) H.; m Emily Louise Browning, Sept. 20, 1964; children: Julie, Lauren. BA in Psychology, U. Mo., 1963; MA in Psychology, Bowling Green (Ohio) State U., 1965; PhD in Psychology, U. Okla., 1968. Lic. psychologist, N.Y. Asst. supt. N.J. Dept. Corrections, Newark, 1964-65; staff cons. Okla. Dept. Health, Oklahoma City, 1967-68; postdoctoral fellow Yale Med. Sch. and Conn. Valley Hosp., New Haven, 1969; unit adminstr. Bronx (N.Y.) State Hosp., 1969-70; asst. prof. NYU, N.Y.C., 1970-72; prof. psychology CUNY, N.Y.C., 1972—; dir. Ctr. Behavioral Psychotherapy, White Plains, N.Y., 1972—; pres. Hollander Psychol. Cons., P.C., White Plains, 1991—, Paramount Behavioral Health Sys., Inc., White Plains, 1995—. Author: Three Psychotherapies, 1975; author, writer film Managing Stress, Anxiety and Frustration, 1981. Fundraiser Make-A-Wish, N.Y., 1988-91. Recipient Cert. of Svcs. Appreciation NIMH, Washington, 1973; clin. fellow Behavioral Therapy and Rsch. Soc., Phila., 1972. Office: Ctr Behavioral Psychotherapy 23 Old Mamaroneck Rd White Plains NY 10605

HOLLEMAN, JANELLE PEALE, health information management professional; b. Tuscaloosa, Ala., Mar. 29, 1971; d. William Wayne and Clarissa (Sellers) Peale; m. Linton Baskins Holleman IV, Mar. 11, 1995. MD, Med. Coll. Ga., 1994. Registered record adminstr. Intern Charter Med. Corp., Macon, Ga., 1989-94; health info. mgmt. dir., med. staff coord. HealthSouth Rehab. Hosp., Charleston, S.C., 1994—; utilization rev. coord. HealthSouth Rehab. Hosp., Charleston, 1994—. Vol. United Way, 1995—. Mem. Am. Health Info. Mgmt. Assn., S.C. Health Info. Mgmt. Assn. Home: Apt 11Q 2235 Ashley Crossing Dr Charleston SC 29414 Office: Health South Rehab Hosp 9181 Medcom St Charleston SC 29406

HOLLEMAN, VERNON DAUGHTY, physician, internist; b. Brownwood, Tex., Oct. 1, 1931; s. Vernon Edgar and Olene Nollie (Reece) H.; m. Shirley Eyvonne Roberts, April 26, 1961; children: Richard, Joel, Douglas. BA in Chemistry and Biology, Howard Payne Coll., Brownwood, 1952; MD, Baylor U., 1958. Mem. med. staff Santa Fe Meml. Hosp, 1962-83; pres. med. staff Santa Fe Meml. Hosp., 1979-83; mem. med. staff Scott and White Hosp., 1962—; asst. chief physician Santa Fe Employees Hosp. Assn., 1962-85, med. dir., 1985—; intern Scott and White Clinic and Hosp., Temple, Tex., 1958-59, resident in internal medicine, 1959-62; dir. div. gen. internal medicine Santa Fe Ctr., Temple, Tex., 1985—; assoc. prof. internal medicine Tex. A&M Coll. Medicine, Temple, 1982—; adj. faculty clinician Ohio Coll. of Podiatric Medicine, Cleveland, 1982-86. Illustrator: Aesculapian, 1957; contbr. photography to books, including Colorados Biggest Bucks and Bulls, Boone and Crocket Books, Awesome Antlers, Records of North American Mule Deer; author: articles on health, preventive medicine, and numerous others. Bd. dirs Santa Fe Meml. Found. Recipient Centennial award Santa Fe Meml. Found., 1991. Mem. Nat. Assn. Retired and Vet. Railway Employees (hon. life), AMA, Am. Socc. Internal Medicine, Tex. Med. Assn., Tex. Med. Found., Am. Heart Assn. (cardiopulmonary coun.), Am. Assn. Ry. Physicians, World Med. Assn., Tex. Diabetes and Endocrine Soc., N.Y. Acad. Scis., So. Med. Assn. (life), Am. Coll. Occupational Medicine, Am. Acad. Pain Mgmt. (diplomate), Boone and Crockett Club (charter assoc.), Alpha Chi, Phi Chi. Baptist. Office: Scott and White Clinic 600 S 25th St Temple TX 76504-5371

HOLLENBACH, ROBERT L., optometrist; b. Harrisburg, Pa., Nov. 27, 1963; s. Clarence R. and Rosalla M. (Thompson) H. BS in Biology and Chemistry, East STroudsburg (Pa.) U., 1985; BS in Visual Sci., Pa. Coll. Optometry, Phila., 1990, OD, 1990. Lic. optometrist, Pa. Pvt. practice Lancaster, Pa. Mem. Am. Optometric Assn., Lancaster County Optometric Assn., Pa. Optometric Assn., East Petersburg Lions (pres. 1993-94). Republican. Home: PO Box 395 East Petersburg PA 17520

HOLLENBERG, MARTIN JAMES, university dean, anatomy educator; b. Winnipeg, Man., Can., June 30, 1934; s. Abraham and Minnie (Pitkowski) H.; m. Vivian Tannis, June 18, 1959; children: Andrew, Lesley. M.D., U. Man., 1958, B.Sc., 1958; M.Sc., Wayne State U., 1964, Ph.D., 1965. Intern U. Man., 1958-59; trainee in surgery and anatomy U. Minn., 1959-65, Wayne State U., 1959-65; asst. prof. anatomy U. Western Ont., London, 1965-68, assoc. prof., 1968-71, prof., 1978—, dean of medicine, 1978—; prof. anatomy U. B.C., Vancouver, 1971-75, hon. prof. ophthalmology, 1972-75; prof., head morphological sci. U. Calgary, Alta., 1975-78; dir. J.P. Roberts Research Inst., London, Ont., Can., 1983—. Contbr. articles on ultrastructure of eye to profl. jours. Fellow Royal Coll. Physicians Can.; mem. Can. Assn. Anatomists (pres. 1979-81), Am. Assn. Anatomists, Can. Med. Assn., Ont. Med. Assn., Council Ont. Faculties of Medicine (chmn. 1983). *

HOLLENBERG, NORMAN KENNETH, medical educator; b. Winnipeg, Manitoba, Can., Oct. 9, 1936; came to U.S., 1965; BS in Medicine, MD, U. Manitoba, 1960, PhD in Pharmacology, 1965; MS, Harvard U., 1976. Lic. Med. Mass. From rsch. assoc. to prof. Harvard U., Boston, 1965—. Assoc. editor: New England Jour. Medicine, 1975-89; editor of 14 books; contbr. over 400 articles to profl. jours. Isbister scholar, 1953-56, Adalstein Kristjamson Meml. travel scholar, 1961; recipient Govnrs. Gen. Gold medal, 1956, Prowse prize and medal Clin. Rsch., 1965, Royal Coll. Physicians Gold medal and prize, 1969. Mem. Am. Heart Assn., Am. Soc. Nephrology, Am. Soc. Pharm. Therapeutics, Am. Soc. Clin. Investigation, Hypertension Coun.

HOLLENBERG, PAUL FREDERICK, pharmacology educator; b. Phila., Sept. 18, 1942; s. Frederick Henry and Catherine (Dentzer) H.; m. Emily Elizabeth Vanootighem, May 6, 1967; children: Kathryn Mary, David Paul. BS in Chemistry, Wittenberg U., 1964; MS in Biochemistry, U. Mich., 1966, PhD in Biochemistry, 1969. Postdoctoral fellow U. Mich., Ann Arbor, 1969, U. Ill., Urbana, 1969-72; asst. prof. Northwestern U., Chgo., 1972-81, assoc. prof., 1981-84, prof. pathology and molecular biology, 1984-87; prof. pharmacology, chmn. dept. Wayne State U. Sch. Medicine, Detroit, 1987-94, U. Mich. Med. Sch., Ann Arbor, 1994—; mem. pharmacology test com. Nat. Bd. Med. Examiners; mem. Chem. Pathology Study Sect. NIH, 1987-91. Co-founder, assoc. editor Chem. Rsch. in Toxicology, 1988—. Schweppe Found. research fellow, 1974-77; NIH research grantee, 1974—. Mem. Am. Chem. Soc., Am. Soc. Biochemists and Molecular Biologists, Am. Soc. Pharmacology and Exptl. Therapeutics, Am. Assn. for Cancer Rsch., Soc. Toxicology, Internat. Soc. for Study of Xenobiotics. Home: 1968 Woodlily Ct Ann Arbor MI 48103 Office: Univ Mich 2301 MSRB III Sch Medicine 1150 W Medical Center Dr Ann Arbor MI 48019-0632

HOLLENBERG, STEVEN MICHAEL, physician, researcher; b. Alexandria, Va., May 13, 1957; s. Jack Earl and Judith Ann H.; m. Susan Ann Colilla, Aug. 6, 1994. BA cum laude, Amherst Coll., 1978; MD magna cum laude, Emory U., 1984. Diplomate Am. Bd. Internal Medicine, Am. Bd. Crit. Care Medicine, Am. Bd. Cardiovasc. Disease. Intern, resident in internal medicine N.Y. Hosp., 1984-87; fellow in critical care medicine NIH, Bethesda, Md., 1987-89; fellow in cardiology Johns Hopkins U., Balt., 1989-90; sr. staff fellow NIH, Bethesda, 1990-93; asst. prof. med. cardiology and critical care medicine Rush Med. Coll., Chgo., 1993—. Author: (with others) Harrison's Principles of Internal Medicine, 1996, Surgical Intensive Care, 1993; contbr. articles to profl. jours. Lt. comdr. USPHS, 1989-93. Recipient Career Devel. award Schweppe Found., 1995. Fellow Am. Coll. Cardiology; mem. ACP, Am. Heart Assn., Soc. Critical Care Medicine, Am. Fedn. Clin. Rsch., Alpha Omega Alpha. Office: Rush Med Coll 1653 W Congress Pky Chicago IL 60612

HOLLEY, LAUREN ALLANA, psychologist; b. Balt., Oct. 9, 1948; d. Winston Willouby and Mary Elizabeth (Hart) Holley BS, Morgan State U., 1976; MA in Psychology, Antioch U., 1978. Lic. psychiatrist asst. Mental health and behavioral cons. Cmty. Resource Team, Developmental Disabilities Adminstrn., Balt.; dir., psychologist, assoc. Community Team; asst. psychiatrist Glass Mental Health-Commerce Ctr., Pikesville, Md., 1991—, EHP Behavioral Svcs. Union Meml. Hosp., Balt. Mem. Huber Meml. United Ch. of Christ. Office: Johnston Med Ctr Union Meml Hosp EHP Behavioral Svcs 3333 N Calvert St Baltimore MD 21218-2867 also: Glass Mental Health 1777 Reisterstown Rd Pikesville MD 21208-1313

HOLLI, BETSY BIGGAR, nutrition educator; b. Burlington, Vt., May 17, 1933; d. Walter Thomas and Ruth Jane (Ball) Biggar; m. Melvin G. Holli, Aug. 12, 1961; children: Susan, Steven. BS, U. Mass., 1955; MS, Ohio State U., 1959; EdD, No. Ill. U., 1981. Registered dietitian; cert. family and consumer sci. Clin. dietitian Univ. Hosp., Columbus, Ohio, 1956-58; clin. dietitian Univ. Hosp., Ann Arbor, Mich., 1959-62, asst. dir. dietetics, 1962-65; health ctr. nutritionist Rush Presbyn.-St. Lukes Med. Ctr., Chgo., 1966-69; asst. prof. U. Ill. Med. Ctr., Chgo., 1969-70; prof. nutrition Rosary Coll., River Forest, Ill., 1970—. Author: Communication and Education Skills: The Dietitian's Guide, 1986, 2d edit., 1991; author: (with others) Encyclopedia of World Biography, 1988, Historical Dictionary of the Progressive Period, 1988; contbr. articles to profl. jours. Mem. Am. Dietetic Assn., Am. Assn. Family & Consumer Sci., Soc. for Nutrition Edn., Ill. Dietetic Assn. (chair divsn. edn. and rsch. 1986-89), Ill. Assn. Family & Consumer Sci., Dietetic Educators and Practitioners, Phi Kappa Phi, Kappa Omicron Nu. Office: Rosary Coll 7900 Division St River Forest IL 60305-1066

HOLLIDAY, PETER OSBORNE, JR., dentist; b. Macon, Ga., July 9, 1921; s. Peter Osborne and Martha Elizabeth (Riley) H.; m. Mary Lucille Dozier, Nov. 12, 1949; children: Peter III, Lucy, Lindsay, Mary. DDS, Emory U., 1945; postgrad., U. Mich., 1947-48. Pvt. practice dentistry Macon, 1947—; mem. Gov. Carter's Dental Adv. Com., Atlanta, 1972. Head dental div. United Givers Fund, Macon, 1956; mem. bicycle com. Macon-Bibb County Planning & Zoning Commn., 1995—. With USNR Dental Corps, 1945-47, China. Fellow Am. Coll. Dentists, Internat. Coll. Dentists (dep. regent for Ga. 1983-85); mem. ADA (alt. del. 1978), Ga. Dental Assn. (sec.-treas. 1971-76, v.p. 1977, pres. 1978-79), Ga. Acad. Dental Practice (charter), Hinman Dental Soc., Ctrl. Dist. Dental Soc. (pres. 1963, Dentist of Yr. 1962), Pierre Fauchard Acad., League of Am. Wheelmen, So. Bicycle League. Democrat. Unitarian. Home: 744 Forest Hill Rd Macon GA 31210-4202 Office: Holliday Dental Assocs 360 Spring St Macon GA 31201-6739

HOLLIE, GLADYS MIRIAM, nurse; b. Coupland, Tex., Nov. 2, 1932; d. John Charles and Cora Rebecca (Atkinson) H.; m. Simon Jackson Davis, Oct. 25, 1956 (div. 1961); 1 child, Harold Gene Holli Johnson. AD, McClennen Community Coll., Waco, Tex., 1980. Vocat. nurse St. Paul Hosp., Dallas, 1955-58, Tex. Children's Hosp., Dallas, 1958-60, Long Beach (Calif.) VA Med. Ctr., 1960-77, VA Med. Ctr., Waco, 1977-82; RN VA Med. Ctr., Fresno, Calif., 1982-95, ret., 1995. Vol. Am. Cancer Soc., Fresno, 1991, YWCA, Fresno, 1991, Ch. Women United. Mem. Order Ea. Star (asst. matron 1983—). Democrat. Mem. African Methodist Episcopal Ch.

HOLLIER, LARRY HAROLD, vascular surgeon; b. Crowley, Louisiana, Apr. 18, 1943; s. Villere Joseph and Agnes (Cuidry) H.; m. Diana Gayle Johnson, Jan. 25, 1964; children: Larry Jr., Michelle Ann. BS, La. State U., 1965, MD, 1968. Diplomate Am. Bd. Surgery, spl. qualifications invascular surgery. Intern Charity Hosp. La., New Orleans, 1968-69, gen. surgery resident, 1969-75; vascular surgery fellow Baylor U. Med. Ctr., Dallas, 1973-74; chief vascular surgery La. State U. Med. Sch., New Orleans, 1975-80, Mayo Clinic, Rochester, Minn., 1980-87; chmn. dept. surgery Ochsner Clnic, New Orleans, 1987-93; med. dir. HCI Internat. Med. Centre, Glasgow, Scotland, 1993—; founder divsn. vascular surgery Mayo Clinic, Rochester, 1983; bd. mgmt. Ochsner Clinic, New Orleans, 1989-93; exec. dir. clin. affairs HCI Internat. Med. Centre, Glasgow, 1993-96. Editor: Vascular Surgery - Basic Science in Clinical Correlations, 1994, Haimovici's Vascular Surgery, 1995. Maj. USAF, 1970-72. Fellow ACS (young surgeons rep. 1979, pres. La. chpt. 1989); mem. Soc. Vascular Surgery (chmn. membership com. 1985-86), Soc. Clin. Vascular Surgery (pres. 1995), So. Assn. Vascular Surgery (pres. 1995), Midwestern Vascular Soc. (pres. 1988).

HOLLIMAN, DAN CLARK, biology educator; b. Birmingham, Ala., Aug. 25, 1932; s. Murray and Kathleen (Hyde) H.; m. Mary Agnes Brooks, July 26, 1958; 1 child, Diane Carol. BS, U. Ala., 1957, MS, 1959, PhD, 1963. Prof. biology Birmingham (Ala.)-So. Coll., 1961—. Contbr. articles to profl. jours. Mem. The Wildlife Soc., Sigma Xi. Democrat. Presbyterian. Home: 3476 Birchtree Dr Birmingham AL 35226-2104 Office: Birmingham So Coll Box 549005 Birmingham AL 35254

HOLLINGER, CHARLOTTE ELIZABETH, medical technologist, tree farmer; b. Meadville, Miss., June 29, 1951; d. John Fielding and Irene Elizabeth (Mullins) H. BS in Biology, U. So. Miss., 1973. Cert. med. Technologist ASCP. Staff med. technologist U. Miss. Med. Ctr., Jackson, 1974-76, Grady Hosp., Atlanta, 1976, Atlanta ARC, 1976-78; staff med. technologist I Emory U. Hosp., Atlanta, 1978-85, staff med. technologist II, 1985-88, asst. chief technologist, 1988-94; del. Blood Bank Del. to People's Republic China, People-to-People, Seattle, 1988. Supporter numerous civic orgns. Mem. Am. Assn. Blood Banks, Am. Soc. Clin. Pathologists, NOW, Forest Farmers Assn., Habitat for Humanity, People for Ethical Treatment Animals, People-to-People, Miss. Forestry Assn., Cousteau Soc., Ga. Pub. TV, U. So. Miss. Alumni Assn., Delta Zeta, Pi Tau Chi. Roman Catholic. Home: 2490 Silver King Dr Grayson GA 30221-1470

HOLLINGER, MANNFRED ALAN, pharmacologist, educator, toxicologist; b. Chgo., June 28, 1939. BS, North Park Coll., Chgo., 1961; PhD, Loyola U., Chgo., 1967. Postdoctoral fellow Stanford U., Palo Alto, Calif., 1967-69; prof., chmn. dept. med. pharmacology and toxicology U. Calif., Davis, 1969—. Author: Respiratory Pharmacology and Toxicology, 1985, Yearbook of Pharmacology, 1990, 91, 92; asst. editor, field editor Jour. Pharm. Exptl. Therapy, 1978—; cons. editor CRC Press, Boca Raton, Fla., 1989—. Mem. Yolo County Grand Jury, Woodland, Calif.; bd. dirs. Davis Little League. Burroughs-Wellcome fellow Southampton U., U.K., 1986; Fogarty sr. fellow NIH, Heidelberg (Germany) U., 1988. Office: U Calif Dept Pharmacology and Toxicology MSI A Rm 4453 Davis CA 95616-5224

HOLLINGSWORTH, MEREDITH BEATON, enterostomal therapy clinical nurse specialist; b. Danvers, Mass., Oct. 5, 1941; d. Allan Cameron and Arlene Margaret (Jerue) Beaton; m. William Paul Hollingsworth, Nov. 19, 1983; stepchild, Brendon R. Diploma, R.I. Hosp. Sch. Nursing, Providence, 1968; BS in Nursing, U. Ariz., 1976; MS in Human Resource Mgmt., Golden Gate U., 1984; postgrad., U. Tex., 1988; EdD, U. N.Mex., 1995, postgrad., 1996—. Cert. enterostomal therapy nurse, health edn. specialist. Commd. ensign USN, 1968, advanced through grades to lt. comdr., 1979; charge nurse USN, USA, PTO, 1968-88; command ostomy nurse, head ostomy clinic Naval Hosp. Portsmouth, Va., 1985-88; pres., chief exec. officer Enterostomal Therapy Nursing Edn. and Tng. Cons. (ETNetc) Rio Rancho, N.Mex., 1989—; mgr. clin. svcs. we. area Support Systems Internat., Inc., Charleston, S.C., 1990-92; pres., CEO Paumer Assocs. Internat., Inc., Rio Rancho, N.Mex., 1992—; sr. cons. enterostomal therapy nursing, edn., & tng. cons.; provost N.Mex. Sch. Enterostomal Nursing, Rio Rancho, 1996—; enterostomal therapy nurse, clin. nurse specialist, educator Presbyn. Health Care Svcs., Albuquerque, 1992-95; sr. cons. Enterstomal Therapy Nursing Edn. & Tng. Cons. A Divsn. of Paumer Assocs., Rio Rancho, N. Mex., 1995—. Mem. adminstrv. bd. Baylake United Meth. Ch., Virginia Beach, 1980-83; chmn. bd. deacons St. Paul's United Ch., Rio Rancho; active Am. Cancer Soc. Mem. Wound, Ostomy and Continence Nurses Soc. (nat. govt. affairs com., govt. affairs com. Rocky Mountain region, pub. rels. com., regional pres. 1989-93, nat. sec. 1994-95), United Ostomy Assn., World Coun. Enterstomal Therapists, N. Mex. Health Care Assn., N. Mex. Assn. for Home Care, N. Mex. Assn. for Continuity of Care. Republican. Office: PO Box 44395 Rio Rancho NM 87174-4395

HOLLINSHEAD, ARIEL CAHILL, research oncologist; b. Allentown, Pa., Aug. 24, 1929; d. Earl Darnell and Gertrude Loretta (Cahill) H.; m. Montgomery K. Hyun, Sept. 27, 1958; children: William C., Christopher C. Student, Swarthmore Coll., 1947-48; AB, Ohio U., 1951, DSc (hon.), 1977; MS, George Washington U., 1955, PhD, 1957. Asst. prof., fellow in virology Baylor U. Med. Ctr., 1958-59; asst. prof. pharmacology George Washington Med. Ctr., 1959-61, asst. prof. medicine, 1961-64, assoc. prof. medicine, head lab. virus and cancer rsch., 1964-73, prof., dir. lab. virus and cancer rsch., 1974-89; on sabbatical leave 1990, prof. medicine emeritus, 1991—; pres. HT Virus and Cancer Rsch., 1991—; clin. rschr. trials in oncology and virology; cons. to biotech. cos. Contbr. over 250 articles on active immunotherapy and immunochemotherapy of cancer and virus diseases to sci. jours. Bd. dirs. Nat. Women's Econ. Alliance, Ohio U., Med. Coll. Pa., Nat. Arthritis Found.; mem. bd. The Women's Inst., 1994—. Named Med. Woman of Yr. Joint Bd. Am. Med. Colls., 1975-76, one of Outstanding Woman of Am., 1987, Outstanding Alumnus of Yr., Ohio U., 1990; recipient Cert. merit Med. Coll. Pa., 1975-76; decorated Star of Europe, 1980. Fellow Washington Acad. Sci., Am. Acad. Microbiology, AAAS; mem. N.Y. Acad. Sci., Am. Acad. Microbiology, Grad. Women in Sci. (nat. pres. 1985-86, bd. dirs. 1986-92), Internat. Soc. Preventive Oncology, Nat. Soc. Exptl. Biology and Medicine (Disting. Scientist award 1985), Am. Soc. Microbiology, Am. Assn. Cancer Research, Am. Assn. Immunologists, Clin. Immunology Soc., Internat. Soc. Antiviral Research, Am. Soc. Clin. Oncology, Internat. Assn. Study Lung Cancer, Internat. Union Against Cancer, Am. Med. Writers Assn., Phi Beta Kappa (alumnus 1990). Clubs: Kenwood Country, Blue Ridge Mountain Country, Washington Forum (pres. 1987, 91). Home: 3637 Van Ness St NW Washington DC 20008-3130

HOLLIS, BRUCE WARREN, experimental nutritionist, industrial consultant; b. Elyria, Ohio, May 29, 1951; s. Warren Eugene and Evelyn Katherine (Jabbusch) H.; m. Betsy Eberle Yount, Aug. 16, 1980. B.S., Ohio State U., 1973, M.S., 1976; Ph.D., U. Guelph, Ont., 1979. Postdoctoral fellow Case Western Res. U., Cleve., 1979-82, asst. prof. nutrition, 1982-86; assoc. prof. pediatrics Med. U. S.C., Charleston, 1986-94; assoc. prof. biochemistry and molecular biology, 1989-94, dir. gen. clin. rsch. ctr. lab., 1990-95, prof. pediatrics, biochemistry and molecular biology, 1994—. Med. researcher, indsl. cons. Contbr. chpts. to books, articles to sci. jours. Recipient NIH awards, 1980, 82, Mead Johnson Nutritionals award The Am. Inst. of Nutrition, 1991. Mem. Endocrine Soc., Am. Soc. Bone and Mineral Research, Am. Inst. Nutrition, Sigma Xi. Republican. Home: 810 N Channel Ct Charleston SC 29412-4938 Office: U SC Med Dept Pediatrics Charleston SC 29425

HOLLISTER, LEO EDWARD, physician, educator; b. Cin., Dec. 3, 1920; s. William Baker and Ruth Victoria (Appling) H.; m. Louise Agnes Palmieri, Feb. 1, 1950 (div. Oct. 1966); children: Stephen, David, Cynthia, Matthew. BS, U. Cin., 1941, MD, 1943. Diplomate Am. Bd. Internal Medicine. Intern Boston City Hosp., 1944; residence in medicine VA Med. Ctr., San Francisco, 1947-49; chief med. service VA Med. Ctr., Palo Alto, Calif., 1953-60, assoc. chief staff, 1960-70, med. investigator, 1970-82, sr. med. investigator, 1982-86; prof. medicine Stanford U., Palo Alto, 1970—; dir. U.S. Pharmacopeia, Rockville, Md. Mem. editorial bd. Clin. Pharmacology Therapeutics, 1962-85; author: Chemical Psychoses, 1968, Clinical Use of Psychotherapeutic Drugs, 1972, Clinical Pharmacology Psych Drugs, 1978; numerous articles. Served to comdr. USNR, 1945-46, 50-52. Recipient Meritorious Service award VA, 1960, Middleton award VA, 1966. Fellow ACP (Menninger award 1985); mem. Am. Soc. Clin. Pharm. Therapeutics (pres. 1972), Am. Coll. Neuropsychopharmacology (pres. 1974), Coll. Internat. Neuropsychopharmacology (pres. 1978). Presbyterian. Home: 1111 Bering Dr Apt 1304 Houston TX 77057-2321 Office: Harris County Psychiat Ctr PO Box 20249 Houston TX 77225-0249

HOLLMAN, JAY L., cardiologist; b. Hillsboro, Oreg., July 26, 1949; s. Edward Ralph and Elsie Wilhelmia Hollman; m. Charlotte Marie Anderson, May 31, 1986; children: David Scott, Peter John, James Andrew. BS in Chemsitry cum laude, Seattle Pacific Coll., 1971; MD, U. Oreg., 1975. Diplomate Nat. Bd. Med. Examiners, Am. Bd. Internat Medicine; lic. physician, La. Intern then resident Emory U. Hosps., 1975-78, clin. cardiology fellow, 1978-81, rsch. fellow in cardiology, 1981-83; staff physician Cardiology Cleve. Clinic Found., 1983-90, dir. interventional cardiology, 1983-88; dir. interventional cardiology Ochsner Clinic Baton Rouge, 1990—, chmn. rsch. and edn. com., 1993-94; adj. assoc. prof. medicine La. State U., 1993—; Lloyd G. Wilkins Meml. lectr. Cuyahoga Falls Gen. Hosp., 1984, Jean Smith Heart lectr., 1985; Hugo Roesler Meml. lectr. Temple U., 1985. Author: (with others) Clinical Essays on the Heart, 1983, Invasive and Nichtinvasive Angiologische Diagnostik: Perkutane Transluminale Arteriendilation: Technik and Ergebniase Therapeutiache Embolisation, 1984, Angioplasty, 1986, Coronary Angioplasty, 1986, Anesthesia and the Heart Patione, 1989, Coronary Artery Graft Disease: Mechanisms and Prevetion, 1994, Treatment of Severe Dyslipproteinemia in the Prevetion of Coronary Heart Disease, 1992; mem. editorial bd. Am. Jour. Cardiology, 1984; contbr. numerous articles to profl. jours. Fellow AAAS, Am. Heart Assn. (coun. clin. cardiology), Am. Coll. Cardiology, Am. Sci. Affiliate; mem. AMA, La. Med.Soc., East Baton Rouge Parish Med. Soc., Phoenix Internat. Med. Ministries, Inc. (adv. bd.), Christian Med. Soc., Sociedad Argentine de Cardiologia (hon.), Friends of China (internat. coun. reference), Med. Ctrs. West Africa (adv. coun.), Christian Med./Dental Soc. (commn. internat. med. ednl. affairs). Evangelican. Home: 4412 Lake Lawford Ct Baton Rouge LA 70816 Office: Ochsner Clinic Baton Rouge 16777 Med Ctr Dr Baton Rouge LA 70816

HOLLOMAN, JOHN LAWRENCE SULLIVAN, JR., physician; b. Washington, Nov. 22, 1919; s. John Lawrence Sullivan and Rosa Victoria (Jones) H.; m. Patricia Ann Tatje, May 11, 1969; children: Charlotte W., Paul S., Karin E., Laura A., Ellen V. B.S. in Chemistry, Va. Union U., 1940, D.Sc. (hon.), 1983; M.D., U. Mich., 1943; LHD (hon.), SUNY, 1995. Rotating intern Harlem Hosp., N.Y.C., 1943-44; resident in internal medicine Harlem Hosp., 1947-48, mem. med. staff, various dates, 1982—; pvt. practice medicine N.Y.C., 1948—; med. dir. Riverton Labs., N.Y.C., 1947-74, H.I.P. Multiphasic Health Testing Center, 1970-72; med. staff Sydenham Hosp., N.Y.C., 1950-58; asst. med. dir. Diagnostic Labs., N.Y.C., 1969-74; asst. v.p. Health Ins. Plan Greater N.Y., 1972-74; pres., dir., chief exec. officer N.Y.C. Health and Hosps. Corp., 1974-77; med. dir. William F. Ryan Community Health Ctr., 1981—; med. cons. H. Lassitter, Inc., 1971-74; assoc. vis. physician Logan Hosp., N.Y.C., 1965-79; clin. prof. adminstrv. medicine NYU, 1974-78; instr. urban health New Sch. Social Research, N.Y.C.; vis. prof. health adminstrn. U. N.C., Chapel Hill, 1977-78; lectr. numerous univs.; chmn. Health Manpower Devel. Program, 1972-75; mem. profl. staff ways and means subcom. U.S. Congress, 1979-80; regional med. officer region II FDA, Dept. Health and Human Services, 1981-87. Mem. Mayor's Emergency Control Bd., 1974-77; bd. dirs. Am. Com. on Africa, Group Health, Inc., Consumers Assembly N.Y., Nat. Sharecroppers Fund, Nat. Planned Parenthood, N.Y. Epilepsy Found., 1969-75, Community Health, Inc., Blue Haven Farm, 1969-77, Harlem Drug Fighters, Inc., 1969-77, Sex Info. and Edn. Council U.S., Inc., 1968-78; pres., trustee Va. Union U., Richmond, 1962-82; trustee SUNY, 1968-95; mem. adv. com. N.Y. State Health Planning Commn., Cmty. Coun. Greater N.Y. Health Task Force, 1968-78, health adv. resources com. N.Y. Dept. Correctional Svcs., 1970-75, N.Y. State Bd. for Profl. Med. Conduct, 1983—, N.Y.State Govs. Med. Adv. Bd., 1987—; chmn. AIDS Task Force of Nat. Assn. of Cmty. Health Ctrs. Served with M.C., AUS, 1944-46. Recipient Haven Emerson award Pub. Health Assn., 1972, Ernst P. Boas award for advancement social medicine, 1975, Frederick Douglas award N.Y. Urban League, 1975, N.Y. Social Security Bar Assn. Forensic Medicine, 1990; elected mem. Inst. Medicine; elected mem. Nat. Acad. Scis., 1972. Fellow Am. Soc. Internal Medicine, Am. Pub. Health Assn. (mem. adv. com. Mound Bayou bd. monitors 1972-75); mem. AMA, Nat. Med. Assn. (pres. 1966-67, award for pub. service in medicine and pub. health 1975), Student Nat. Med. Assn. (adv. bd.), Nat. Assn. Cmty. Health Ctrs. (Sam Rogers award 1991), Student Am. Med. Assn. (adv. bd.), Physicians Forum (nat. chmn. 1970-71, Paul Cornelly award 1990), Am. Cancer Soc. (dir. N.Y.C. div. 1971—), Pub. Health Assn. N.Y.C. (dir. 1971-77), Am. Hosp. Assn. (dir. 1974-78), N.Y. State Hosp. Assn. (dir. 1974-78), Group Health Assn., Am., N.Y. Acad. Medicine, Herman Biggs Soc. Home: 27-40 Ericsson St East Elmhurst NY 11369-1942

HOLLOWAY, BARBARA R., health science association administrator; b. Bloomfield, N.J., Aug. 4, 1947; married; 2 children. BA in English and History, Siena Coll., 1969; MPH, Emory U., 1979. With La. Health Planning Coun., Baton Rouge, 1969-70; office mgr. Office of Resources Devel. Ga. Inst. Tech., Atlanta, 1970-72; tchr. Gwinnett County (Ga.) High Schs., 1973-75; edn. specialist, chief consultation and tng. sect., program svcs. br., tuberculosis control divsn. Ctr. Disease Control, Atlanta, 1975-79, pub. health advisor hosps. infections br., bacterial diseases divsn. Bur. Epidemiology, 1979-81, asst. dir. ops. divsn. surveillance and epidemiologic studies Epidemiology Program Office, 1981-86, asst. dir. program ops. Epidemiology Program Office, 1986-88, dep. dir. Epidemiology Program Office, 1988—. Home: 1517 Harts Mill Rd Atlanta GA 30319 Office: HHS Ctrs Disease Control 1600 Clifton Rd NE Atlanta GA 30329-4018

HOLLOWAY, EDWARD OLIN, human services manager; b. Rochester, N.Y., July 3, 1944; s. Charles Robert and Chrystal Gertrude (Darling) H.; m. Hama Elizabeth Farris, Dec. 23, 1967. AA, Palm Beach Jr. Coll., Lakeworth, Fla., 1964; BA, Lenoir Rhyne Coll., 1967; MS in Pub. Health, U. N.C., 1975. From sanitarian I to sanitarian supr. I Palm Beach County Health Dept., West Palm Beach, Fla., 1969-73; from emergency med. svcs. coord. to exec. dir. dist. IX Health Planning Coun., Inc., West Palm Beach, 1975-89; sr. health and human svcs. planner bd. county commrs. Palm Beach County Dept. Community Svcs., West Palm Beach, 1989—; faculty Pub. Health Physician Residency Program, 1990—; steering com. Fla. Atlantic Univ. Inst. Govt., 1992—, vice chmn., 1994. Chmn. dist. 9 adv. coun. Dept. Helath and Rehab. Svcs., West Palm Beach, 1990-92; pres. Fla. Assn. Health Planning Agys., Inc., 1984-89; mem. planning unit steering com. Leadership Palm Beach County, 1991; chmn. health care dist. feasibility subcom. Palm Beach County, 1989-90; mem. Palm Beach County data collection com. Health and Human Svcs. Planning Assn., 1992—; mem. Interagy. Planning Group, 1994—; mem. Palm Beach Gardens Cmty. H.S. Adv. Com., 1994—. With U.S. Army, 1967-69, Vietnam. Decorated Bronze Star, Purple Heart, Army Commendation medal, Cross of Gallantry (Vietnam); recipient Outstanding Svc. award Fla. Assn. Health Planning Agys., 1989, Outstanding Achievement award Bd. County Commrs. Palm Beach County Citizens Adv. Com. on Health and Human Svcs., 1995; planning grantee Regional Emergency Med. Svcs., 1975. Mem. ASPA (chpt. 102 coun. mem. 1989—), APHA, Nat. Environ. Health Assn., U. N.C. Sch. Pub. Health Alumni Assn. (bd. dirs. 1994—). Democrat. Lutheran. Office: Bd County Commrs Palm Beach Dept Community Svcs 810 Datura St West Palm Beach FL 33401-5204

HOLLOWAY, FRANK ALBERT, JR., psychologist, educator; b. Houston, Jan. 1, 1940; s. Frank Albert Sr. and Margaret Adelaide (Buel) H.; m. Joan Arlyne Buchanan, Aug. 19, 1967; children: Karen Justine, Benjamin Scott, Jason Luke. BS, U. Houston, 1961, MA, 1964, PhD, 1966. From instr. to assoc. prof. U. Okla. Health Sci. Ctr., Oklahoma City, 1966-77, prof., dir. biopsychology program, 1977-91, 92—, vice-chair dept. psychiatry & behavioral scis.; pres., dir. Okla. Ctr. for Alcohol and Drug-Related Studies, Oklahoma City, 1992—. Contbr. articles to profl. jours. Fellow APA; mem. AAAS, Am. Psychol. Soc., Soc. for Neurosci., Psychonomic Soc., N.Y. Acad. Scis., Sigma Xi. Office: U Okla Health Scis Ctr Rsch Bldg 306R Oklahoma City OK 73190

HOLLOWAY, HARRY, aerospace medical doctor. Diploma Sch. Medicine, U. Okla., 1958. Chief neuropsychiatry SEATO Med. Rsch. Lab., Bangkok; dir. neuropsychiatry Walter Reed Army Inst. Rsch.; chmn. dept. psychiatry Uniformed Svcs. U. Health Scis., acting dean Sch. Medicine, 1990-92, dep. dean, 1992-93; assoc. adminstr. life and microgravity scis. applications, 1993-96; chmn. aerospace medicine adv. com. NASA, 1988-93; cons. World Health Orgn. Recipient Dist. Pub. Svc. award NASA, 1992. Office: NASA Life and Microgravity Sciences and Applications 300 E St NW Washington DC 20546-0001

HOLLOWAY, RICHARD LAWRENCE, marriage and family therapist, college administrator, researcher; b. Buffalo, May 18, 1949; s. Robert Lee and Aurelia (Muresan) H.; m. Julie Ann Sianko, Sept. 26, 1987; 1 child, Evan Richard. AB in Speech and Theater, Heidelberg Coll., Tiffin, Ohio, 1971; MS in Instrnl. Des. Devel. and Evaluation, Syracuse U., 1974, PhD in Instrnl. Des. Devel. and Evaluation, 1976; postgrad. in marriage and family therapy, Coll. Medicine Baylor U., 1987-90. Asst. prof. ednl. measurement Coll. Pharmacy U. Minn., Mpls., 1977-78; asst. prof. family medicine Sch. Medicine U. Minn., Mpls., 1978-82, assoc. prof., 1982-84; assoc. prof., head com. resources Minn. Ext. Svc., St. Paul, 1985-86; prof. Coll. Medicine Baylor U., Houston, 1986-91; prof., rsch. dir. Coll. Medicine Baylor U., 1991-92; prof., assoc. dean student affairs, vice chair, divsn. chief Med. Coll. Wis., Milw., 1992—, assoc. dean for student affairs, 1996—; vis. prof. Syracuse (N.Y.) U., 1981. TV host Campus Closeup, One Step Ahead, Mpls., 1984-86; contbr. chpts. to books, articles to profl. jours. Bd. dirs. Milw. Ave. Homeowners Assn., Mpls., 1976-83. Recipient E.B. Knight Jour. award NACTA, 1977; vis. scholar U. Mich., 1983. Mem. APA, Am. Assn. Marriage and Family Therapy, Am. Ednl. Rsch. Assn. (Recognition award 1985), Soc. Tchrs. Family Medicine (bd. dirs. 1989-95, pres. 1993-94, Recognition award 1982). Democrat.

HOLM, JOY ALICE, psychology educator, art educator, artist, goldsmith; b. Chgo., May 21, 1929; d. Alvin Herbert and Willette Eugenia (Miller) H. BFA, U. Ill., 1952; MS in Art Edn. Inst. Design, Ill. Inst. Tech., 1956; PhD in Edn., U. Minn., 1967. Tchr. art, Eng. West Chgo. H.S., 1952-54; instr., tchr. art J.S. Morton H.S. & Jr. Coll., Cicero, Ill., 1954-65; asst. prof. art & design Mankato (Minn.) State U., 1965-66; asst. prof. art Ill. State U., Normal, 1966-69; assoc. prof. art & design So. Ill. U., Edwardsville, 1969-71; assoc. prof. art, art edn. Winona (Minn.) State U., 1971-75; assoc. prof., chmn. dept. art St. Mary's Coll. of Notre Dame, Ind., 1975-76; assoc. prof. art & design, secondary, continuing edn. U. Wis., Eau Claire, 1976-78; assoc. prof. art & design Sch. Art & Design Kent (Ohio) State U., 1978-80; lectr. Jungian studies C.G. Jung Inst., Evanston, Ill., 1980-82; adj. assoc. prof. art edn. Sch. Art and Design, Sch. Edn. U. Ill., Chgo., 1981-82; lectr. U. Calif. Ext., Santa Cruz, 1983—; adj. prof. art edn., design San Jose (Calif.) State U., 1983-84; owner bus. designer-goldsmith Oak Park, Ill., 1980-82, Carmel, Calif., 1982-87; owner bus. designer-goldsmith Atelier XII, Winona, 1988—; curriculum cons. North Ctrl. Assn. Accreditation Team State of Ill., Edwardsville, 1970; regional cons. Supt. Pub. Instrn., Springfield, Ill., 1970; juror exhbns.; panelist, spkr., presenter confs., meetings. Contbr., cons. Alternative Medicine: A Definitive Guide, 1994; contbr. articles to profl. jours; one-woman shows: J. Sterling Morton H.S. & Jr. Coll., 1963, Russell Art Gallery, Bloomington, 1968, Owatonna (Minn.) Art Ctr., 1980, 86; exhbns. include La Grange (Ill.) Art League (Best of Show, 1st Place award prints), 1963, 64, Minn. Mus. Art, 1974, 75, Craft & Folk Art Mus., L.A., 1978, The Gallery Kent State U., 1978, 79, Saenger Nat. Small Sculpture and Jewelry Exhibit, 1978, Diamonds Internat., N.Y., 1978, Inst. Design Alumni, 1988, Internat. Biographical Ctr. Congress Exhbn., Edinburgh, Scotland, 1994, others. Fellow World Lit. Acad.; mem. AAUP, Nat. Art Edn. Assn. (rep. Wis. Women's Caucus Houston Conf. 1978, higher edn. divsn. 1961—), Am. Assn. Higher Edn., Coll. Art Assn., Soc. N.Am. Goldsmiths, Internat. Sculpture Ctr., Gemological Inst. Am., C.G. Jung Inst. (Chgo., San Francisco), Hon. Soc. Illustrators (hon.), Internat. Soc. Study of Subtle Energies and Energy Medicine, Assn. Transpersonal Psychology, Inst. Noetic Scis., Alpha Lambda Delta (hon.), Phi Kappa Phi (hon.). Methodist. Home: PO Box 183 Winona MN 55987-0183 Office: Atelier XII PO Box 183 Winona MN 55987-0183

HOLM, LARS-ERIK, science foundation administrator; b. Mörsil, Sweden, Apr. 30, 1951; s. Lars Bertil Knut and Alice Maria (Wiklander) H. MD, Karolinska Inst., Stockholm, 1977, PhD, 1980. Assoc. prof. Karolinska Hosp., Stockholm, 1982-92; dir. Nat. Inst. Pub. Health, Stockholm, 1992-95; dir. gen. Swedish Radiation Protection Inst., Stockholm, 1996—; Swedish del. UN Sci. Com. on Effect of Atomic Radiation, 1984—. Capt. Swedish Air Force, 1982-88. Mem. Swedish Soc. Radiotherapy (sec. 1981-85), Nordic Soc. Radiotherapy (pres. 1983-86), Internat. Commn. of Radiation Protection. Office: Swedish Radiation Prot Inst, 17116 Stockholm Sweden

HOLMAN, HALSTED REID, medical educator; b. Cleve., Jan. 17, 1925; s. Emile Frederic and Ann Peril (Purdy) H.; m. Barbara Marie Lucas, June 26, 1949 (div. July 9, 1982); children: Michael, Andrea, Alison; m. Diana Barbara Dutton, Aug. 10, 1985; 1 child, Geoffrey. Student, Stanford U., 1942-43, UCLA, 1943-44; MD, Yale U., 1949. Med. resident Montefiore Hosp., N.Y.C., 1952-55; staff physician Rockefeller Inst., N.Y.C., 1955-60; prof. medicine Stanford (Calif.) U., 1960—, chmn. dept. medicine, 1960-71, co-chief divsn. family and community medicine, 1987—, dir. clin. scholar program, 1969—, dir. Multipurpose Arthritis Ctr., 1977—; pres. Midpeninsula Health Svc., Palo Alto, Calif., 1975-80; mem. adv. bd. Calif Health Facilities Commn., Sacramento, 1978-81, Office Tech. Assessment, U.S. Congress, 1979-81, Inst. Advancement of Health, N.Y.C., 1982—; Guggenhime prof. medicine, 1960—. Author 1 book; assoc. editor Arthritis and Rheumatism, 1995—; contbr. articles to profl. jours. Recipient Bauer Meml. award Arthritis and Rheumatism Found., N.Y., 1964. Master Am. Coll. Rheumatology; fellow ACP (Laureate award no. Calif. chpt. 1994), AAAS (coun. 1974-79); mem. Assn. Am. Physicians, Am. Soc. Clin. Investigation (pres. 1970), Western Assn. Physicians (pres. 1966). Democrat. Home: 747 Dolores St Stanford CA 94305-8427 Office: Stanford U Stanford Arthritis Ctr 100 Welch Rd Ste 203 Palo Alto CA 94304

HOLMAN, LARRY DEAN, health care administrator; b. Lincoln, Nebr., Nov. 1, 1940; s. Clarence Woodford and Ethel Elizabeth (Remmenga) H.; m. Setsuko Umekawa, Dec. 5, 1960 (div. Aug. 1978); children: Lori Akiko, Yuko Donna; m. Debbie Joan Berkowitz, Dec. 8, 1980; children: Andrew Joseph, Jodi Michelle, Matthew Jacob. AA, Palomar Community Coll., San Marcos, Calif., 1971; BS, George Washington U., 1974; MBA, LaSalle U., 1989, MS, 1990. Enlisted USN, 1958, advanced through grades to lt. comdr., ret., 1982, hosp. corpsman, 1958-71; with USN Med. Service Corps, 1971-82; purchasing dir. St. Francis Country House, Darby, Pa., 1982-85; bus. mgr. Stapeley Hall, Phila., 1985-86; bus., program mgr. Seaman's Ch. Inst., Phila., 1986-87; buyer Grad. Hosp., Phila., 1988-89, Grad. Health System, Phila., 1989; purchasing agt. Shriners Hosps., Phila., 1989-91; purchasing mgr. Jeanes Hosp., Phila., 1991—. Mem. Assn. Mil. Surgeons U.S., Am. Soc. Mil. Compts., VFW, AMVETS, Non-Commd. Officers Assn., Vietnam Vets. Am., Navy League, Fleet Res. Assn., Navy Seabee Vets. Am., Vietnam Era Seabees, Ret. Officers Assn., Naval Res. Assn., Vets. Vietnam War, Jewish War Vets. U.S., Am. Legion. Jewish. Home: 6746 Souder St Philadelphia PA 19149-2208 Office: Jeanes Hosp Purchasing Dept 7600 Central Ave Philadelphia PA 19111-2402

HOLMAN, PAUL DAVID, plastic surgeon; b. Waynesboro, Va., Mar. 13, 1943; s. Wallace D. and Rosalie S. Holman. BA, U. Va., 1965; MD, Jefferson Med. Coll., 1968. Intern, George Washington U. Hosp., Washington, 1968-69, resident in gen. surgery, 1969-70, 72-74; resident in plastic surgery Phoenix Plastic Surgery Residency, 1974-76; practice medicine specializing in plastic surgery, Phoenix, 1977—; mem. staff Good Samaritan Hosp., Phoenix, St. Joseph's Hosp., Phoenix, Phoenix Children's Hosp. Served to lt. comdr. USNR, 1970-72. Diplomate Am. Bd. Surgery, Am. Bd. Plastic Surgery. Mem. AMA, ACS, Am. Soc. Plastic and Reconstructive Surgeons, Phi Beta Kappa. Office: 2111 E Highland Ave Ste 105 Phoenix AZ 85016-4732

HOLMAN, RALPH THEODORE, biochemistry and nutrition educator; b. Mpls., Mar. 4, 1918; s. Alfred Theodore and May Carlia Anna (Nilson) H.; m. Karla Calais, Mar. 26, 1943; 1 child, Nils Teodor. AA, Bethel Jr. Coll., 1937; BS, U. Minn., 1939; MS, Rutgers U., 1941; PhD, U. Minn., 1944. Instr., div. of biochemistry U. Minn., Mpls., 1944-46; NRC-Nat. Acad. Scis. fellow Med. Nobel Inst., Stockholm, Sweden, 1946-47; Am. Scandinavian Found. fellow U. Uppsala, Sweden, 1947; assoc. prof. biochemistry and nutrition Tex. A&M U., College Station, 1948-51; assoc. prof. biochemistry Hormel Inst., U. Minn., Austin, 1951-56, prof., 1956—, exec. dir., 1975-85; emeritus prof. Hormel Inst., U. Minn., 1988—; also prof. biochemistry Mayo Med. Sch., Rochester, Minn., 1977—; mem. nutrition study sect. NIH, 1959-63; pres., organizer Golden Jubilee Internat. Congress on Essential Fatty Acids and Prostaglandins, 1980; mem. adv. bd. Deul. Conf. on Lipids, 1960-86; Sinclair Meml. lectr. Third Internat. Congress on Essential Fatty Acids and Eicasanoids, Adelaide, 1992. Founding editor Progress in Lipid Research, 1951—; editor Lipids, 1974-85; mem. editl. bd. Jour. Nutrition, 1962-66; contbr. 420 publs. on nutritional biochemistry of lipids; current rsch. on essentiality of omega 3 fatty acids. Pres. Mower County Coun. Churches., Austin, 1953-57; mem. Hormel Found., Austin, 1979-86. Recipient Fachini award Italian Oil Chemists, Milan. Fellow Am. Inst. Nutrition (Borden award 1966); mem. NAS, Am. Chem. Soc., Am. Oil Chemists Soc. (pres. 1974-75, Lipid Chemistry award 1979), Am. Soc. Biol. Chemists, Am. Orchid Soc. (rsch. com. 1980-85), Am. Heart Assn. (bd. dirs. Minn. affiliate 1991-93). Democrat. Congregationalist. Home: 1403 2nd Ave SW Austin MN 55912-1609 Office: U Minn Hormel Inst 801 16th Ave NE Austin MN 55912-3679

HOLMAN, WILLIAM BAKER, surgeon, coroner; b. Norwalk, Ohio, Mar. 22, 1925; s. Merlin Earl and Rowena (Baker) H.; m. Jane Elizabeth Henderson, June 24, 1951; children: Craig W., Mark E., John S. BS, Capital U., 1946; MD, Jefferson Med. Coll., 1950. Intern, St. Luke's Hosp., Cleve., 1950-51, resident in gen. surgery, 1951-52, 55-57; practice medicine specializing in surgery, Norwalk, 1957-92; coroner Huron County, Norwalk, 1962-95, health commr., 1985-95; asst. clin. prof. surgery Med. Coll. Ohio at Toledo, 1984-92; Bd. dirs. REMSNO, Toledo, 1974-92, Norwalk Profl. Colony, 1983-92 ; mem. exec. com. Huron County Republican Com., Norwalk, 1980; bd. dirs. Fisher-Titus Med. Ctr., 1977-82, chmn., 1982; bd. dirs. Norwalk Area Health Svcs., Inc., 1987-92, 94—; mem. Norwalk City Sch. Bd. Edn., 1962-78, pres., 1964, 67-71, 78. Served to 1st lt. U.S. Army, 1952-54; Korea. Fellow ACS; mem. AMA, Ohio State Med. Assn., Huron County Med. Soc. (pres. 1978), Ohio State Coroners Assn., Nat. Assn. Med. Examiners. Lutheran. Avocations: boating; photography; stamp collecting; gun collecting. Home: 39 Warren Dr Norwalk OH 44857-2447 Office: Huron County Health Dept 180 Milan Ave Norwalk OH 44857-1168

HOLMES, FREDERIC LAWRENCE, science historian; b. Cin., Feb. 6, 1932; m. Harriet Holmes, 1959; 3 children. B.S., MIT, 1954; M.A., Harvard U., 1958, Ph.D., 1962. Asst. prof. history of sci. MIT, 1962-64; asst. prof. to assoc. prof. Yale U., New Haven, 1964-72, prof., chmn. sect. history of medicine, 1979—, master Jonathan Edwards Coll., 1982-87; prof. history of sci., chmn. dept. history of medicine and sci. U. Western Ont., 1972-79. Author: Claude Bernard and Animal Chemistry, 1974, Lavoisier and the Chemistry of Life, 1985, Eighteenth Century Chemistry as an Investigative Enterprise, 1989, Hans Krebs: The Formation of a Scientific Life, 1991, Hans Krebs: Architect of Intermediary Metabolism, 1993; contbr. articles to profl. jours. Rsch. grantee NIH, 1963-67, NSF, 1968-70, 88—, Can. Coun., 1973-74. Mem. History of Sci. Soc. (pres. 1981-83), Am. Assn. History Medicine, Can. Soc. Hist. and Philos. Sci. Office: Yale U Sch Medicine Dept Hist Med PO Box 208015 New Haven CT 06520-8015*

HOLMES, GEORGE EDWARD, molecular biologist, educator; b. Chgo., May 8, 1937; m. Norreen Ruth Petersen, Mar. 12, 1967; children: George Petersen, Norreen Eliza. BS in Biology and Chemistry, Wiley Coll., 1960; MS in Natural Sci., Chgo. State U., 1967; postgrad., U. Calif., Davis, 1967-68; PhD in Molecular Biology, U. Ariz., 1973. Med. technologist DePaul Hosp., St. Louis, 1961, Chgo. Hosp., 1961-67; tchr. Chgo. Bd. of Edn., 1965-67; rsch. assoc. Rockefeller U., N.Y.C., 1973-74; asst. prof. dept. microbiology Coll. of Medicine Howard U., Washington, 1974-82, assoc. prof., 1982—. Contbr. articles to Nature, Jour. Virology, Virology, Molecular and Gen. Genetics, Jour. Gerontology, Jour. Mutation Rsch. NIH fellow in molecular biology, 1968-73; Nat. Inst. on Aging grantee, 1982-87, Am. Soc. Biol. Chemistry and Molecular Biology Travel grantee, 1990. Mem. AAUP (chpt. pres.), Am. Soc. Biochemistry and Molecular Biology (invitee The Gordon Conf. on Biology of Aging 1986), Am. Soc. Virology, Am. Inst. Chemists, Am. Men and Women in Sci. and Medicine, Gerontol. Soc. Am. Lutheran. Office: Howard U Coll of Medicine Dept Microbiology Washington DC 20059

HOLMES, KING KENNARD, medical educator; b. St. Paul, Sept. 1, 1937. AB, Harvard Coll., 1959; MD, Cornell U., 1963; PhD in Microbiology, U. Hawaii, 1967. Diplomate Am. Bd. Internal Medicine, infectious diseases. Resident U. Wash., Seattle, 1967-68, chief resident, 1968-69, from instr. to assoc. prof. medicine, 1969-78, vice chmn. dept. medicine, 1984-89, prof. medicine, 1978—, dir. Ctr. AIDS and Sexually Transmitted Diseases, 1989—; head divsn. pulmonary diseases USPHS Hosp., Seattle, 1969-70, asst. chief dept. medicine, 1969-83, head divsn. infectious diseases, 1970-83; dir. Sexually Transmitted Disease Clinic, Harborview Med. Ctr., 1972-79, chief med., 1984-89; mem. numerous adv. coms. Nat. Inst. Allergy & Infectious Diseases, NIH, USPHS, WHO, NAS; prin. investigator NIH, Nat. Cancer Inst., Nat. Inst. Allergy & Infectious Diseases, Nat. Inst. Child Health & Human Devel., Ctrs. Disease Control, 1983—. With USN, 1965-67. Recipient Squibb award Infectious Disease Soc. Am., 1978, Thomas Parran award Am. Veneral Disease Assn., 1983. Fellow ACP, Royal Coll. Physicians Eng.; mem. AMA, Inst. Medicine-NAS, Assn. Am. Physicians, Am. Epidemiol. Soc., Am. Fedn. Clin. Rsch. Office: U Wash Harborview Med Ctr 325 9th Seattle WA 98104*

HOLMES, LEONARD GEORGE, psychologist; b. Roanoke, Va., May 31, 1954; s. George Washington and Mary Maxine (Templeton) H.; m. Susan Rose Tankersley, June 19, 1976; children: Allison Gayle, Mary Kathleen. BA in Psychology and Religious Studies with high distinction, U. Va., 1976; MS in Clin. Psychology, Fla. State U., 1979, PhD, 1981. Lic. clin. psychologist, Va. Psychology intern William S. Hall Psychiat. Inst., Columbia, S.C., 1980-81; lectr., clin. psychologist Ctr. for Psychol. Services, Coll. of William and Mary, Williamsburg, Va., 1981-88, asst. dir., 1984-88; practice clin. psychology, Williamsburg, 1984—; adj. asst. prof. psychology Coll. William and Mary, 1991—; cons. V.A. Med. Ctr., Hampton, 1985-90, coord. behavioral physiology lab., 1990—; psychologist Sentara Psychol. Group, Newport News, Va., 1988-90; clin. psychologist Behavioral Medicine Inst., 1990—. Univ. fellow Fla. State U., 1977-78, 79-80. Mem. Am. Psychol. Assn., Internat. Soc. Study Dissociation, Phi Kappa Phi. Avocations: gardening, computers, fishing, hiking. Home: 102 Barlows Run Williamsburg VA 23188-9326 Office: Behavioral Medicine Inst 640 Denbigh Blvd Newport News VA 23602-4404

HOLMES, RANDALL KENT, microbiology educator, physician, university administrator; b. Muskegon, Mich., Nov. 7, 1940; s. Scott Travis and Helen Marie (Rosell) H.; m. Kathryn Louise Voelker, June 16, 1962; children: Rebecca Kathryn, Elisabeth Marie. AB, Harvard U., 1962; MD, PhD in Microbiology, NYU, 1968. Diplomate Am. Bd. Internal Medicine, Am. Bd. Infectious Diseases. Intern, then resident Beth Israel Hosp., Boston, 1968-70; research assoc. NIH, Bethesda, Md., 1970-72; instr. medicine U. Tex. Southwestern Med. Sch., Dallas, 1972-73, asst. prof., 1973-75, assoc. prof., 1975-76; prof., chmn. microbiology and immunology Uniformed Services U. Health Scis., Bethesda, 1976-95, assoc. dean for acad. affairs, 1984-93, acting chmn. biochemistry, 1993-95; prof., chmn. microbiology U. Colo. Sch. Medicine, Denver, 1995—; mem. adv. com. vaccines and related biol. products Nat. Ctr. for Drugs and Biologics, Bethesda, 1983-87; mem. cholera panel NIH, 1987-92; mem. bacteriology and mycology 1 study sect. NIH, 1993-95. Contbr. articles to profl. jours. Served to surgeon USPHS, 1968-70. Recipient Research Career Devel. award NIH, 1975-76. Fellow ACP, Infectious Diseases Soc. Am.; mem. Am. Acad. Microbiology (bd. govs. 1992-95), Am. Soc. for Clin. Investigation, Am. Soc. for Microbiology (editorial bd. Infection and Immunity 1978-86, Microbiol. Revs. 1983-88, mem. steering com. postdoctoral rsch. assoc. program 1993-95, chmn. 1996—, awards com. 1995—), Nat. Bd. Med. Examiners (mem. microbiology test com. 1984-86, chmn. 1987-93, mem. U.S. med. licensing exam. step I com. 1990-92, mem. U.S. med. licensing exam. composite com. 1992-95), Phi Beta Kappa, Alpha Omega Alpha. Republican. Office: U Colo Health Scis Ctr Dept Microbiology Campus Box B 175 4200 E 9th Ave Denver CO 80262

HOLMES, RUSSEL PORTER, corporate professional; b. N.Y.C., June 12, 1939; s. John Pharr and Pattie (Porter) H.; m. Susan Bolles; 1 child, Susan Elisabeth; m. Rose Anne Reagan; 1 child, Reagan. BA, Dartmouth Coll.; MBA, Amos Tuck Sch. Sr. staff Arthur Andersen, N.Y.C., 1967-69; mgr. audits Squibb Corp., 1970; group controller Beechnut Corp., 1971-72; controller, dir. Telley Tea, Eng., 1970-71; v.p., controller Cooper Labs., 1972-73; pres. Sparta Instruments, 1974-76, Med. Devises Group, 1977-78; owner, CEO Holmed Corp., 1979—; part-owner, v.p. fin. Riley Med., 1985—. Lt. U.S. Army, 1962-64. Mem. Shelter Island Yacht Club (commadore 1978-80), Gardner's Bay C.C. Office: Holmed Corp 40 Norfolk Ave Easton MA 02375-1913

HOLMSTROM, HANS ERIK EDWARD, plastic surgeon; b. Lund, Sweden, Feb. 28, 1939; divorced; 2 children. MD, Goteborg (Sweden) U., 1967, PhD, 1973. Head dept. plastic surgery, prof. Sahlgrenska Univ. Hosp., Goteborg, 1987—. Mem. Swedish Assn. Plastic Surgery (pres. 1996-99), Internat. Assn. Plastic Surgery (Swedish del. 1995, pres.-elect). Office: Sahlgrenska Univ Hosp, Plastic Surgery Dept, S-41345 Goteborg Sweden

HOLMSTRUP, PALLE, periodontology educator, researcher; b. Frederiksberg, Copenhagen, Denmark, Nov. 4, 1945; s. Holger Lars and Ellen Maria Sogaard (Lund) H.; m. Grete Bankov, Nov. 14, 1975; children: Christian Tobias, Niels Mikkel. DDS, Royal Dental Coll., Copenhagen, 1971, PhD, 1976, Dr. odont., 1985. Cert. Bd. Oral Surgery, 1983. Rsch. assoc. Royal Dental Coll., Copenhagen, 1972-77; clin. asst. prof. U. Hosp., Copenhagen, 1977-85; assoc. prof. oral medicine Royal Dental Coll., Copenhagen, 1985-88, acting prof., 1988-89; prof. periodontology, Sch. Dentistry U. Copenhagen, 1989—, assoc. dir. Sch. Dentistry, 1996—, prof. and chmn.; vice dean Royal Dental Coll., Copenhagen, 1988-92. Recipient Dandy award Dandy Co., 1988, Ingeborg & Leo Dannins Award for Rsch. 1991. Mem. Internat. Assn. Dental Rsch. (pres. Danish sect., Scandinavian divsn. 1987-92), European Acad. Periodontology, Scandinavian Soc. Oral Medicine and Pathology. Office: Dept Periodontology Sch Dentistry U Copenhagen, 20 Norre Alle, DK 2200 Copenhagen Denmark

HOLSTEIN, BRUCE JAY, psychiatrist; b. Pitts., Aug. 2, 1947; s. Nathan and Lillian (Solow) H.; m. Alice Andrea Cihat, July 25, 1970; children: Abigail Catherine, Anne Elizabeth. BA, Conn. Wesleyan U., 1970; MD, Boston U., 1974. Diplomate Am. Psychiatry and Neurology. Med. dir. Stoney Brook Counseling Ctr., Chelmsford, Mass., 1979-87; pvt. practice, Lexington, Mass., 1983—; staff psychiatrist Chelmsford Med. Assocs., 1987-88, Harvard Community Health Plan, Chelmsford, 1988—. Mem. Am. Psychiat. Assn., Mass. Psychiat. Assn. Office: 35 Bedford St Ste 17 Lexington MA 02173-4400

HOLSTEIN, DAVID, psychotherapist, management consultant; b. N.Y.C., Apr. 9, 1934; s. Morris and Esther (Newman) H.; m. Anita Elizabeth Morell, Sept. 8, 1957; children: Gregory Andrew, Christopher Daniel, Carrie Jacqueline. BA, CCNY, 1955; MA, Lehigh U., 1957. With IBM, 1957-87; numerous mktg. and product devel. positions IBM, White Plains, 1957-70; dir. planning system corp. staff IBM, Armonk, N.Y., 1971-72; dir. planning, market devel., product evaluation IBM, White Plains, 1973-75, dir. market research Gen. Bus. Group, 1975-79, dir. strategic mgmt. Gen. Bus. Group, 1980-81, dir. Somers project office Info Sys and Support Group, 1982-85; v.p. mgmt. services Entry Systems div. IBM, Boca Raton, Fla. and Montvale, N.Y., 1985-86; dir. Somers project office Infosystem and Support Group IBM, White Plains, 1987; bus. cons. White Plains, 1987-88; founder, pres., exec. dir. The Hudson Ctr., Cornwall-on-Hudson, N.Y., 1988—. Author: (books) Management Systems, 1976, Digital Computers in Engring., 1977; Contbr. articles to profl. jours. Pres., trustee Cornwall Bd. of Edn., Cornwall, N.Y., 1976-78; trustee Mt. St. Mary Coll., Newburgh, N.Y., 1978-85, Orange County Hospice, Goshen, N.Y., 1985—, Orange County Family Counseling, Newburgh, 1986—. Mem. Am. Assn. for Counseling and Devel., Am. Psychol. Assn. Democrat. Roman Catholic. Home: 3 Idlewild Park Dr Cornwall On Hudson NY 12520-1047 Office: Hudson Ctr 276 Hudson St Cornwall On Hudson NY 12520-1016

HOLSTEIN, RUSSELL MARC, psychologist; b. Pitts., Nov. 6, 1942; s. Nathan and Lillian (Solow) H.; m. Barbara Becker, June 26, 1966; children: Jessica, Justin. BA, U. Pitts., 1964; MA, Wesleyan U., Middleton, Conn., 1966; PhD, Boston U., 1971. Lic. psychologist, N.J. Cons. psychologist Beverly (Mass.) Hosp. Psychiat. Consultation Svc., 1970-71; sr. staff psychologist Pollak Clinic, Monmouth Med. Ctr., Long Branch, N.J., 1971-72; dir. counseling ctr. Monmouth Coll., West Long Branch, N.J., 1972-82; pvt. practice Loch Arbour, N.J., 1973-84, Long Branch, N.J., 1984—. Mem. APA, Ea. Psychol. Assn., N.J. Psychol. Assn. (chair coun. on legis. affairs 1994), Monmouth-Ocean County Psychol. Assn. (pres. 1975-76), N.J. Coalition Mental Health Profls. and Consumers (chair legis. com. 1994—). Democrat. Jewish. Home: 603 E Edgemere Dr Allenhurst NJ 07711 Office: 170 Morris Ave Long Branch NJ 07740-6660

HOLSTIUS, ELVIN ALBERT, former medical school consultant; b. Woonsocket, R.I., Feb. 9, 1921; s. Albert Reinhold and Mary (Elpe) H.; m. Eleanor Christine Andeen, Mar. 28, 1942; children: Faith Eleanor Carlson, Mark Elvin. BS, U. R.I., 1943; MS, Purdue U., 1949, PhD, 1950. Registered pharmacist. Rsch. pharmacist Burroughs Wellcome Co., Tuckahoe, N.Y., 1945-47; sr. chemist Merck & Co. Inc., Rahway, N.J., 1950-53; prof. U. Kansas City (Mo.), 1953-56; dir. pharm. R&D Geigy Pharms., Ardsley, N.Y., 1956-66; tech. dir. Endo Labs., Garden City, N.Y., 1966-67; dir. pharm. R&D Burroughs Wellcome Co., Research Triangle Park, N.C., 1967-84; cons. East Carolina U. Med. Sch., Greenville, N.C., 1983-91. Patentee in field. With Med. Corps, U.S. Army, 1943-45, ETO. Scholar State of R.I., 1939, 40, Emerson scholar U. R.I. Coll. Pharmacy, 1941, 42; fellow Am. Found. Pharm. Edn., Purdue U., 1947-49, fellow Sharpe & Dohme, Phila., 1949-50. Mem. Am. Chem. Soc., Am. Pharm. Assn., Acad. Pharm. Scis., Rho Chi, Sigma Xi, Kappa Psi. Republican. Lutheran. Home: 4A Dogwood Ct Orange City FL 32763-6105

HOLT, FRIEDA M., nursing eduucator, former academic director. BSN with honors, U. Colo., Boulder, 1956; MS in cmty. health nursing, Boston U., 1969, EdD, 1973. RN, Ariz., Calif., Colo., Mass., Md., Pa., Wash., Liberia, W. Africa. Instr., dir. of nursing Cuttington Coll., Liberia, Africa, 1964-67; teaching fellow sch. of nursing Boston U., 1969, asst. prof. sch. of nursing, 1969-74; assoc. prof. sch. of nursing U. Md., 1975-77, assoc. prof., assoc. dean for grad. studies sch. of nursing, 1975-77, dean's dep. sch. of nursing, 1975-86, prof., assoc. dean for grad. studies sch. of nursing, 1977-86, acting dean sch. of nursing, 1978, acting asst. dean sch. of nursing, 1981-82, acting chmn. sch. of nursing, 1983-84, acting dean sch. of nursing, 1986-87, prof., assoc. dean for grad. studies, dean's dep. sch. of nursing, 1987-88, prof., exec. assoc. dean. sch of nursing, 1988-89, acting dean, prof. sch. of nursing, 1989-90, prof. sch. of nursing, 1990-91, dir. sch. of nursing, 1992-94, prof. sch. of nursing, 1994—; project dir. Primary Care Adult Nurse Practitioner Leadership grant, 1976-82, Preparation for Tchrs. in Maternal Child Nursing, judge U. Md. grad. sch. rsch. awards, 1979-84; NLN vis. for Accreditation of Baccalaureate and Masters Nursing Program, SREB/SCCEN Task Force on Grad. Edn., presenter of numerous seminars, conferences and workshop. Contbr. of articles to profl. jours. Recipient Vet. Administrn. Commendation award, 1990, Charter Trustee award Found. for Nursing of Md., 1990, Martin Luther King, Jr. Humanitarian award, 1990. Mem. ANA, ANA Coun. of Nurse Rschr., Nat. League for Nursing, Am. Pub. Health Assn., Am. Edn. Rsch. Assn., Am. Edn. Rsch. Assn., Am. Assn. U. Prof., Md. Assn. for Higher Edn., Md. Nurses Found. Bd. Dirs. (v.p. 1988—), Soc. for Rsch. in Nursing Edn., Sigma Theta Tau. Home: 328-B Sellers Ln RD 1 Port Matilda PA 16870 Office: Pa State Univ 303A Health and Human Devel E University Park PA 16802-1503

HOLT, SUSAN LYNNE, mental health counselor; b. Columbus, Ohio, Sept. 28, 1954; d. Robert Charles and Faith Margaret H. Cert. in nonviolent crisis intervention. Counselor L.A. Gay and Lesbian Cmty. Svc. Ctr., 1987-89, acting asst. dir. counseling svcs. dept., 1990-91, mental health clinician, 1990—, clin. tng. coord., 1991—; group counselor U. Judaism, L.A., 1986-90, mgr. support group facilitator program, 1988-90; counselor rep., mem. counseling adv. bd. L.A. Gay and Lesbian Cmty. Svc. Ctr., 1988-93, chmn. clin. svcs. and tng., 1990-93, mem. planning and adminstrn. com., 1991-92. Mem. Coun. on Jewish Life, Commn. on Cmty. Outreach, Jewish Fedn. Coun. of L.A., 1985-88, chmn. spkr. bur., 1985-88; presenter Domestic Violence Hearings, Office of Criminal Justice Planning, State of Calif., L.A., 1992; mem. GLLSC Domestic Violence Task Force, L.A., 1993—, City of West Hollywood, Calif. Domestic Violence Task Force, 1996—. Mem. Am. Counseling Assn., Am. Mental Health Counselors Assn. Office: 1625 Schrader Blvd Los Angeles CA 90028-9998

HOLTER, ARLEN ROLF, cardiothoracic surgeon; b. Sullivan's Island, S.C., Feb. 1, 1946; s. Arne and Helen (Soderberg) H.; m. Elizabeth Anne Reid, Nov. 9, 1974; children: Matthew Arlen, Peter Reid, Andrew Douglas. BS, Stanford U., 1968; MS, U. Chgo., 1971, MD, 1973. Diplomate Am. Bd. Thoracic Surgery; Am. Bd. Surgery. Intern in surgery Mass. Gen. Hosp., Boston, 1973-74, resident in surgery, 1974-78; sr. registrar in cardiac surgery Southampton Chest Hosp., Eng., 1978; resident in cardiac surgery Yale U., New Haven, 1978-80; pvt. practice medicine specializing in cardiothoracic surgery Mpls., 1980—; instr. surgery Yale U., 1979-80. Contbr. articles to profl. jours. Recipient Franklin McLean rsch. award U. Chgo., 1973. Fellow ACS, Am. Coll. Cardiology, Am. Coll. Chest Physicians; mem. Soc. Thoracic Surgeons, Am. Heart Assn., Mpls. Acad. Medicine, Pan Pacific Sur. Soc. Lutheran. Office: Cardiac Surg Assocs 920 E 28th St Ste 420 Minneapolis MN 55407

HOLTGREWE, HENRY LOGAN, urologist; b. Springfield, Ill., Nov. 25, 1930; s. Edgar Henry and Harriet (Logan) H.; m. Virginia Ann Lightfoot, Aug. 25, 1954; children: Kent Logan, Sally Ann Welch. BA, Kans. U., 1951, MD, 1955. Diplomate Am. Bd. Urology. Intern Hosp. of U. Pa., Phila., 1955-56; asst. resident gen. surgery Duke U. Hosp., Durham, N.C., 1956-57; resident in urology Kans. U. Med. Ctr., Kansas City, 1959-62; mem. med. staff Anne Arundel Med. Ctr., Annapolis, Md., 1962—; chief urology Anne Arundel Med. Ctr., Annaplis, Md., 1966-76, pres. med. staff, 1973-75; assoc. prof. urology Johns Hopkins U. Sch. Medicine, Balt.; trustee, sec.-treas. Am. Bd. Urology, 1992—; mem. Nat. Kidney and Urol. Disease Info. Clearing House, NIH, Bethesda, Md., urology program group to Nat. Inst. Diabetes and Digestive and Kidney Diseases; mem. panel Agy. for Health Care Policy and Rsch., USPHS, Washington; mem. internal sci. com. on benign prostatic hypertrophy WHO, Paris, chmn. com. on internat. econs. benign prostatic hypertrophy; presenter, lectr. in field. Contbr. numerous articles to profl. publs., chpt. to books. Treas. Am. for Urol. Disease, 1986-91, bd. dirs. 1992-93; chmn. judiciary selection comm. Anne Arundel County, 1988; bd. trustees Anne Arundel Med. Ctr., Annapolis, Md., 1973-81. With USNR, 1957-59. Recipient William P. Burpeau award Acad. Medicine N.J., 1993. Fellow ACS; mem. AMA, Am. Urol. Assn. (chmn. arrangements ann. meeting in Spain, 1973, sec. Mid-Atlantic sect. 1976-81, exec. com. 1984-86, treas. 1986-91, pres. elect. 1991-92, pres. 1992-93, chair health policy coun. 1994—) Am. Assn. Genitourinary Surgeons (trustee), Am. Assn. Clin. Urologists, Soc. Internat. D'Urologie, Md. Urol. Assn. (pres. 1970-75), Anne Arundel Med. Soc. (pres. 1966-68), Med. Surg. Faculty Md., Ala. Urol. Soc. (hon.), Fla. Urol. Soc. (hon.), Sigma Nu, Nu Sigma Nu, Alpha Omega Alpha. Home: 473 Fair Oaks Dr Severna Park MD 21146-3107 Office: Conte Bldg 116 Defense Hwy Ste 200 Annapolis MD 21401-7040

HOLTHAUS, ANNE FELTMAN, nurse midwife, public health service officer; b. Austell, Ga., Apr. 15, 1957; d. Conis Horace Feltman and Marie Doby Giera; m. Brian James Holthaus, Sept. 18, 1993; 1 child, Natalie Rose-Jean. ADN, Santa Fe C.C., Gainsville, Fla., 1978; BSN, SUNY, Albany, 1987; MN, MPH, Emory U., 1994. LPN, RN, cert. nurse midwife. Nurse midwife St. Luke's Hosp., Kansas City, Mo., 1994—. Mem. Kansas City Pub. Health Assn., Kansas City Assn. Cert. Nurse Midwives, Mo. Perinatal Assn. Home: Ste A 9201 Thomashaw Ln Lenexa KS 66219 Office: Nurse Midwife Assocs 4320 Wornall Rd Ste 328 Kansas City MO 64111

HOLTKAMP, DORSEY EMIL, medical research scientist; b. New Knoxville, Ohio, May 28, 1919; s. Emil H. and Caroline E. (Meckstroth) H.; m. Marianne Church Johnson, Mar. 20, 1942 (dec. 1956); 1 son, Kurt Lee, 1 stepchild; m. Marie P. Bahm Roberts, Dec. 20, 1957 (dec. 1982); 2 stepchildren; m. Phyllis Laurence Bradfield, Sept. 1, 1984; 3 stepchildren. Student, Ohio State U., 1937-39; AB, U. Colo., 1945, MS, 1949, PhD, 1951, student Sch. Medicine, 1941-42, 46-49. Sr. rsch. scientist biochemistry sect. Smith, Kline & French Labs., Phila., 1951-57, endocrine-metabolic group leader, 1957-58; head endocrinology dept. Merrell-Nat. Labs. div. Richardson-Merrell, Inc., Cin., 1958-70, group dir. endocrine clin. rsch., med. rsch. dept., 1970-81; group dir. med. rsch. dept. Merrell Dow Pharms. subs. Dow Chem. Co., Cin., 1981-87; ind. cons. in med. rsch. Lebanon, Ohio, 1987—. Contbr. articles to profl. publs. U. Colo. Med. Sch. fellow, 1946, biochemistry rsch. fellow, 1948-51. Fellow AAAS; mem. AMA (affiliate), Am. Soc. Clin. Pharmacology and Therapeutics, Endocrine Soc., Am. Fertility Soc., Am. Chem. Soc., Am. Soc. Pharmacology and Exptl. Therapeutics, N.Y. Acad. Sci., Soc. Exptl. Biology and Medicine, Am. Assn. Lab Animal Scis., Internat. Soc. for Reproductive Medicine, Pacific Coast Fertility Soc., Reticuloendothelial Soc., Internat. Platform Assn., Sigma Xi, Nu Sigma Nu. Republican. Presbyterian. Home and Office: 130 S Liberty Keuter Rd Lebanon OH 45036-9333

HOLTON, SUSAN A, psychologist, educator; b. Columbus, Ohio, Apr. 24, 1948; d. William C. and Mary (Floyd) H.; 1 child, Christopher L. Holton-Jablonski; m. Joe Snyders, Aug. 4, 1991. BS, Miami U., Oxford, Ohio, 1970; MA, Case Western Res. U., 1973, PhD, 1976. Dir. Gabriel Ames Assocs., Framingham, Mass., 1975—; asst. to pres., asst. prof. Bridgewater (Mass.) State Coll., 1984-88, dept. chair., assoc. prof., 1988-90, prof., 1990—, asst. to pres., 1991-92; bd. dirs. Profl. Orgn. in Higher Edn.; coord. Mass. Faculty Devel. Consortium, 1988-90; chair., nominating com. Unitarian Universalis Assn., Boston, 1987-89; cons. Alban Inst., 1989—. Author: The Mad Madonna, 1987, Under the Influence of Life; contbr. articles to profl. jours. Dir. Ch. the Larger Fellowship, Boston, 1987-91; founder FOCUS on Gifted and Talented, Framington, Mass. Mem. Speech Communication Assn., Boston Area Assn. Psychol. Type (founder), N.E. Assn. Psychol. Type, AAUW, Ea. Communications Assn., Communications Assn. Mass., Alban Inst., AAUP, Am. Assn. for Higher Edn. Office: Bridgewater State Coll Maxwell Libr Bridgewater MA 02325

HOLTZ, HOWARD ALAN, physician; b. Long Branch, N.J., July 30, 1954; s. Walter and Ruth Sylvia (Weinkofsky) H.; m. Laura Marie Prato, Jul. 16, 1978; children: Angela, Alex. BA, Rutgers Coll., 1975; MD, Univ Med & Dentistry of N.J., 1981. Diplomate Am. Bd. Internal Medicine. Resident internal medicine Univ. Medicine & Dentistry of N.J., 1981-83; clinical instr. Univ. Medicine & Dentistry of N.J. N.J. Medical Sch., Newark, N.J., 1984-86; physician Nat. Health Svc. Corps., Newark, 1984-87; asst. prof. Univ. Medicine & Dentistry of N.J., N.J. Medical Sch., 1986-91, assoc. prof. clinical medicine, 1991—; assoc. chmn. medicine St. Barnabas Medical Ctr., Livingston, N.J., 1991—; chief resident in internal medicine Univ. Medicine & Dentistry of N.J., 1984; residency review com. internal medicine St. Barnabas Medical Ctr., 1994, mem. grad medical edn. com., 1991, mem. dept. medicine housestaff and students com., 1991; chair critical appraisal focus group N.J. Medical Sch. Curriculum task force, 1989; dir. N.Y. Medical Sch. bd. review course in internal medicine, 1983; chair medical ctr. inpatient geriatric task force St. Barnabas Medical Ctr., 1994, prognosis com., 1994, pharmacy and therapeutics antibiotic subcom., 1991, quality resource mgmt. com., 1991, quality assurance com. UMDNJ Univ. Hosp., 1985. Author books, book chpts.; contbr. articles to profl. jours. Dir. Domestic Violence Prevention Project, 1988. Recipient Cert. Appreciation Gov.'s Adv. Coun., 1988, Jersey Battered Women's Svc. Vol. Recognition award 1988; numerous rsch. grants. Fellow Am. Coll. Physicians; mem. Soc. Gen. Internal Medicine, AMA, Medical Soc. N.J., Essex County Medical Soc., N.J. Coalition for Battered Women, N.J. ACP Exec. Coun., Essex County Medical Soc., Alpha Omega Alpha. Home: 39 Hickory Dr Maplewood NJ 07040 Office: Saint Barnabas Medical Ctr Old Short Hills Rd Livingston NJ 07039

HOLTZ, NOEL, neurologist; b. N.Y.C., Sept. 13, 1943; s. Irving and Lillian H.; m. Carol Sue Smith, June 9, 1968; children: Pamela Wendy, Aaron David, Daniel Judah. BA, NYU, 1965, MD, U. Cin., 1969. Diplomate Am. Bd. Psychiatry and Neurology. Intern Cin. Gen. Hosp., 1969-70; resident in internal medicine and neurology Emory U., Atlanta, 1970-71, 73-76; pvt. practice medicine specializing in neurology, Marietta, Ga., 1977—; mem. faculty Emory U. Coll. Medicine, Atlanta, 1977—, asst. prof. dept. neurology, 1977—, assoc. prof., 1987; mem. staffs Kennestone Hosp.; dir. neurodiagnostics unit; mem. staff Grady Meml. Hosp.; cons. Ga. Med. Care Found. Neurology. Co-author: Conceptual Human Physiology, 1985. With USN, 1971-73. Mem. Am. Acad. Neurology, Ga. Neurol. Soc. (sec.-treas., pres. 1990-92), Alpha Omega Alpha. Office: 522 North Ave Marietta GA 30060-1125

HOLTZMAN, ROBERT NEIL NEHEMIAH, neurosurgeon, neurologist; b. Bklyn., Aug. 11, 1941; s. Sidney and Filia (Ravitz) H.; m. Pamela Helen Freeman, Aug. 24, 1973; children: Maia Merav, Jonathan Nisson, Matthew Isaac. BA, Harvard U., 1964; MD, Columbia U., 1969. Rotating intern Harlem Hosp. Center, N.Y.C., 1969-70; resident in neurology Neurol. Inst. N.Y., N.Y.C., 1970-72, resident in neurosurgery, 1973-77; resident in gen. surgery Harbor Gen. Hosp., Torrance, Calif., 1972-73; practice medicine specializing in neurosurgery and neurology, N.Y.C., 1977—; asst. attending in neurosurgery Beth Israel Med. Ctr., 1978—, Columbia-Presbyn. Med. Ctr., N.Y.C., 1991; assoc. attending in neurosurgery Harlem Hosp., N.Y.C., 1977—, Lenox Hill Hosp., N.Y.C., 1987—; asst. clin. prof. in neurosurgery Coll. Physicians Columbia U., N.Y.C., 1991. Co-dir. Stonwin Med. Conf. Editor: Surgery of the Diencephalon, 1989, Surgery of the Spinal Cord: The Potential for Regeneration and Recovery, 1992, Spinal Instability, 1993, Endovascular Interventional Neuroradiology, 1995; editor and contbr.: The

Tethered Spinal Cord, 1985; contbr. articles to med. jours. Diplomate Am. Bd. Psychiatry and Neurology, Am. Bd. Neurol. Surgery. Mem. Am. Acad. Neurology, Am. Assn. Neurol. Surgeons, N.Y. State Neurosurg. Soc., N.Y. Soc. Neurol. Surgery. Democrat. Jewish.

HOLTZMAN, WAYNE HAROLD, psychologist, educator; b. Chgo., Jan. 16, 1923; s. Harold Hoover and Lillian (Manny) H.; m. Joan King, Aug. 23, 1947; children: Wayne Harold, James K., Scott E., Karl H. B.S., Northwestern U., 1944, M.S., 1947; Ph.D., Stanford, 1950; L.H.D. (hon.), Southwestern U., 1980. Asst. prof. psychology U. Tex., Austin, 1949-53; assoc. prof. U. Tex., 1953-59, prof., 1959—; dean Coll. Edn., 1964-70, Hogg prof. psychology and edn., 1964—; assoc. dir. Hogg Found. Mental Health, 1955-64, pres., 1970-93, spl. counsel, 1993—; dir. Social Sci. Rsch. Coun., 1957-63, Centro de Investigationes Sociales, Mex., 1960-70; cons. USAF, also mem. sci. adv. bd., 1969-71; mem. com. basic rsch. com. NRC, 1968-71; mem. behavioral sci. study sect. USPHS, 1957-59, mem. mental health study sect., 1960, chmn. personality and cognition rsch. rev. com., 1968-72; mem. rsch. adv. panel Soc. Security Adminstrn., 1961-62; mem. L.Am. adv. bd. IBM, 1985-89; dir. WHO Collaborating Ctr. in Mental Health for Tex. and Mex., 1993—. Author: (with B.M. Moore) Tomorrow's Parents, 1964, Computer Assisted Instruction Testing and Guidance, 1971, (with R. Diaz-Guerrero and J. Swartz) Personality Development in Two Cultures, 1975, Introduction to Psychology, 1978; (with K.A. Heller and S. Messick) Placing Children in Special Education, 1982, (with T. Bornemann) Mental Health of Immigrants and Refugees, 1990, School of the Future, 1992; editor: Jour. Ednl. Psychology, 1966-72. Trustee Ednl. Testing Service, Princeton, 1972-74, 77-80, 83-86, J.W. and Cornelia Scarborough Found., 1977-82, Ctr. for Applied Linguistics, 1978-80, Salado Inst. Humanities, 1980-85, Population Inst., 1979-85, Menninger Found., 1982—, Population Resource Ctr., 1980—; dir. Sci. Research Assocs., 1975-88; pres., bd. dirs. S.W. Ednl. Devel. Lab., 1974-75; mem. adv. com. computing activities NSF, 1970-73; mem. computer sci. and engring. bd. Nat. Acad. Scis., 1971-73, chmn. panel on selection and placement of mentally retarded students, 1979-82; chmn. interdisciplinary cluster on social and behavioral devel. Pres.'s Biomed. Research Panel, 1975-76; bd. dirs. Found.'s Fund for Research in Psychiatry, 1973-77, chmn., 1976-77; dir. Conf. of S.W. Found., 1976-84, pres., 1978-79; mem. nat. adv. mental health council Alcohol, Drug Abuse, and Mental Health Adminstrn., 1978-81; mem. acad. info. systems adv. council IBM, 1982-85. Served to lt. (j.g.) USNR, 1944-46. Faculty Research fellow Social Sci. Research Council, 1953-54; Faculty Research fellow Center Advanced Study Behavioral Scis., 1962-63. Fellow APA, AAAS; mem. Tex. Psychol. Assn. (pres. 1957), S.W. Psychol. Assn. (pres. 1958), Am. Statis. Assn., InterAm. Soc. Psychology (pres. 1966-67), Am. Ednl. Rsch. Assn., Internat. Union Psychol. Scis. (sec.-gen. 1972-84, pres. 1984-88, exec. com. 1988-92), Philos. Soc. Tex. (pres. 1982-83), Sigma Xi. Methodist. Home: 3300 Foothill Dr Austin TX 78731-5823

HOLWOOD, DAVID, histopathologist, researcher; b. Stockport, Cheshire, Eng., Apr. 7, 1936; s. John and Hilda (Bennett) H.; m. Irene Fraser; children: Iain, Eileen, Scott. BS, Leeds (Eng.) U., 1958, MB BChir, 1960, PhD, 1968, MD, 1972. Sr. house officer Gen. Infirmary, Leeds, 1961-62; lectr. anatomy U. Leeds, 1962-68, U. Nottingham, Eng., 1968-72, U. Dundee, Scotland, 1973-76; sr. lectr., cons. U. Dundee, 1976-84, reader, cons., 1984—. Asst. editor: Histochem. Jour., 1974—. Fellow Royal Coll. Pathologists, Royal Microscopical Soc. (com. mem. 1986—); mem. Brit. Soc. Gastroenterology (com. mem. 1992—), Pathol. Soc. Home: 8 The Logan, Liff Dundee DD2 5P5, Scotland Office: Ninewells Hosp, Pathology Dept, DD1 95Y Dundee Tayside, Scotland

HOLYOKE, EDWARD AUGUSTUS, anatomy educator, consultant; b. Madrid, Nebr., Mar. 10, 1908; s. Edward Augustus and Mary (Holdrege) H.; m. Lois Carse (dec. 1976); children: Edward Augustus Jr., Thomas Turner; m. Frances Brockmeier, Feb. 28, 1981. BS, U. Nebr., 1930, MA, 1932, MD, 1934, PhD, 1938. Instr. anatomy U. Nebr. Coll. Medicine, Omaha, 1932-38, asst. prof., 1938-43, assoc. prof., 1943-46, prof., 1946-86, chmn. dept., 1960-73, prof. emeritis, 1986—. Contbr. articles to profl. jours. Mem. Am. Assn. Anatomists, Anatomy Soc., Great Britain and Ireland, Kiwanis, Sigma Xi, Alpha Omega Alpha. Presbyterian. Home: 1513 S 97th St Omaha NE 68124-1135

HOLZ, GEORGE G., IV, research scientist; b. Santa Monica, Calif., May 8, 1953; s. George G. and Mignon M. (Kiproff) H. BS, Cornell U., 1975; PhD, U. Ill., 1984. Rsch. fellow Tufts U. Med. Sch., Boston, 1984-89; rsch. assoc. Howard Hughes Med. Inst., Boston, 1990-93; asst. prof. medicine Mass. Gen. Hosp.-Harvard Med. Sch., Boston, 1994—; asst. prof. Harvard Med. Sch., 1994—. Corp. mem. Marine Biol. Lab., Woods Hole, Mass. Recipient Rsch. award Am. Diabetes Assn., 1996; N.Y. State Regents scholar Cornell U., 1971-75. Mem. AAAS, Soc. for Neurosci., Endocrine Soc. Home: PO Box 288 West Falmouth MA 02574-0288

HOLZBACH, RAYMOND THOMAS, gastroenterologist, author, educator; b. Salem, Ohio, Aug. 19, 1929; s. Raymond T. and Nelle A. (Conroy) H.; m. Lorraine E. Cozza, May 26, 1956; children—Ellen, Mark, James. BS, Georgetown U., 1951; MD, Case Western Res. U., 1955. Diplomate Nat. Bd. Med. Examiners, Am. Bd. Internal Medicine. Intern, asst. resident U. Ill. Research and Edn. Hosps., Chgo., 1955-56; sr. asst. resident medicine Cleve. Met. Gen. Hosp., 1959-60; asst. chief gastroenterology Case Western Res U., 1961-63; physician Gastroenterology Unit U. Hosps. of Cleve., 1961-63; instr. medicine Case Western Res. U. Sch. Medicine, Cleve., 1961-64; clin. instr. medicine Case Western Res. U. Sch. Medicine, 1964-71; head gastrointestinal research unit, assoc. physician div. medicine St. Luke's Hosp., Cleve., 1967-73; dir. div. gastroenterology St. Luke's Hosp., 1970-73; head gastrointestinal research unit dept. medicine Cleve. Clinic Found., 1973—; vis. prof. numerous instns. including Mayo Med. Sch., 1974, U. Calif., San Diego, 1977, U. Heidelberg, 1978, U. Pa., 1979, U. Zurich, 1980, U. Munich, 1982, U. Minn. Med. Ctr., 1985, med. ctrs., numerous Japanese univs., 1985, 92, Karolinska Inst., 1986, Royal Soc. London, 1987, Pa. State U. Sch. Med., U. Helsinki, RWTH-Aachen, Düsseldorf, Fed. Republic of Germany, U. Groningen, Utrecht, U. Amsterdam, The Netherlands, 1989, U. Perugia, Italy, Va. Commonwealth U.-Med. Coll. Va., Richmond, Christ Ch. Sch. Medicine, U. Otago, New Zealand, SUNY, Buffalo Sch. Medicine, 1990, Pontifical/Cath. U. Chile Sch. Medicine, 1991, Hiroshima U. Sch. Medicine, 1992, Kyoto U. Sch. Medicine, 1992, Sch. Medicine U. Jikei, Tokyo, 1992, Tel Aviv U., Israel Sch. Medicine, 1995, U. Leipzig, Germany, 1996, U. Heidelberg, Germany, 1995; lectr. in field. Mem. editl. bd. Gastroenterology jour., 1984-89; contbr. revs. and articles to med. jours. Served to capt. USAF, 1957-59. Recipient Alexander von Humboldt Found. Spl. Program award, 1978, 82. Fellow ACP; mem. ABA, Am. Gastroent. Assn. (rsch. com. 1976-79), Ctrl. Soc. Clin. Rsch., Am. Assn. for Study of Liver Diseases, AAAS, Am. Soc. Biol. Chemists, Am. Physiol. Assn., Biophys. Soc., Internat. Assn. Study of Liver, Am. Fedn. Clin. Rsch., Midwest Gut Club, Am. Soc. Clin. Nutrition, Ohio State Med. Assn., Sigma Xi. Unitarian. Home: 39251 Lander Rd Chagrin Falls OH 44022-2146 Office: Cleve Clin Found 9500 Euclid Ave Cleveland OH 44195-0001

HOLZBAUR, ERIKA L., medical educator. BS in Chemistry and History with honors, Coll. William and Mary, 1982; PhD in Biochemistry, Pa. State U., 1987. Rsch. fellow, teaching asst. Dept. Molecular and Cell Biology, Pa. State U., 1982-87, postdoctoral scientist, 1987-88; asst. prof. Dept. Animal Biology, Sch. Vet. Medicine, U. Pa., Phila., 1992—. Contbr. articles to profl. jours., chpts. to books. Grad. Sch. fellow Pa. State U., 1984-85, 85-86; Postdoctoral fellow NIH, 1988-92; recipient Established Investigator award Am. Heart Assn., 1996. Mem. Am. Soc. Cell Biology, Pa. Muscle Inst., U. Pa. Cancer Ctr., Phi Beta Kappa, Phi Zeta. Office: U Pa 143 Rosenthal Bldg 3800 Spruce St Philadelphia PA 19104-6046

HOLZMAN, LEWIS C., orthopedic surgeon; b. N.Y.C., Nov. 11, 1941; s. Miriam (Crager) H.; m. Laura Jacobs, Apr. 23, 1983; children: Sara, Lila. BA, U. Rochester, 1962; MD, NYU, 1966. Diplomate Am. Bd. Orthopedic Surgery. Orthopedic surgeon Kaiser-Permanente, Harbor City, Calif., 1974—. Maj. USAF, 1971-74. Fellow Am. Acad. Orthopedic Surgeons; mem. Western Orthopedic Assn. Office: Kaiser-Permanente 25825 S Vermont Harbor City CA 90710

HOLZMAN, PHILIP SEIDMAN, psychologist, educator; b. N.Y.C., May 2, 1922; s. Barnet and Natalie (Seidman) H.; m. Hannah Abarbanell, Sept. 18, 1946; children: Natalie Kay, Carl David, Paul Benjamin. BA, CCNY, 1943; PhD, U. Kans., 1952. Diplomate: Am. Bd. Examiners Profl. Psychology. Psychology intern Topeka VA Hosp., 1946-49; psychologist Topeka State Hosp., 1949-51, cons., 1951-58; psychologist Menninger Found., Topeka, 1949-68; dir. research tng. Menninger Found., 1963-68; prof. psychiatry and psychology U. Chgo., 1968-77; prof. psychology dept. psychology Harvard U., 1977-92; prof. dept. psychiatry Med. Sch., 1977-92; Esther and Sidney R. Rabb prof. psychology Harvard U., 1984-92, prof. emeritus, 1992; chief Lab. of Psychology McLean Hosp., Belmont, Mass., 1977—; tng. and supervising psychoanalyst Boston Psychoanalytic Soc. and Inst., 1977—; vis. prof. U. Minn., 1965, U. Kans., 1966, Boston U., 1973, Jefferson Med. Coll., 1981, U. Pa., 1987; Thomas William Salmon lectr. N.Y. Acad. Medicine, 1994; mem. small grants com. NIMH, 1960-64, clin. projects research rev. com., 1964-68, clin. program projects research rev. com., 1970-74, treatment devel. and assessment rev. com., 1982-86; cons. Ill. State Psychiat. Inst., 1970-77; mem. adv. coms. classification of mental disorders WHO. Author: (with others) Cognitive Control, 1959, Psychoanalysis and Psychopathology, 1970, (with Karl Menninger) The Theory of Psychoanalytic Technique, rev. edit, 1973; editor: (with Merton M. Gill) Psychology Versus Metapsychology, 1975, (with Mary Hollis Johnston) Assessing Schizophrenic Thinking, 1979; bd. editors: Psychol. Issues, 1968—, Contemporary Psychology, 1969-76, Bull. of Menninger Clinic, 1961—, also Psychoanalysis and Contemporary Thought, Jour. Psychiat. Rsch., 1980-92; assoc. editor Schizophrenia Bulletin, Schizophrenia Rsch.; contbr. articles to profl. jours. Mem. Topeka Mayor's Com. on Human Rels., 1963-68; chmn. bd. dirs. Founds.' Fund for Rsch. in Psychiatry; mem. program adv. com. MacArthur Found., sci. adv. bd. NIMH, 1986-92; bd. trustees Menninger Found., 1978—; mem. sci. coun. Nat. Alliance Rsch. Schizophrenia and Depression, 1989—. With AUS, 1943-46. Recipient Career Scientist award NIMH, 1974-77, 92—; Stanley Dean award Am. Coll. Psychiatrists, 1984, Lieber prize Nat. Alliance for Rsch. in Schizophrenia and Depression, 1988, Joseph Zubin award Soc. Rsch. in Psychopathology, 1994; Townsend Harris medal CCNY. Fellow APA, AAAS, Am. Acad. Arts and Scis., Am. Coll. Neuropsychopharmacology; mem. Am. Psychoanalytic Assn., Boston Psychoanalytic Soc., Am. Psychopath. Assn., Inst. Medicine of NAS, Sigma Xi. Office: Harvard U William James Hall Cambridge MA 02138 also: McLean Hosp Lab Belmont MA 02178

HOMANT, ROBERT, psychology educator; b. Petoskey, Mich., Oct. 27, 1944; s. Lawrence Oliver and Jane (Case) H.; m. Susan Lapointe, May 27, 1972; children: Michael, Katherine. AB, U. Detroit, 1966; MA, Mich. State U., 1968, PhD, 1971. Psychologist Mich. Dept. of Corrections, 1970-74; chief psychologist Wis. Dept. Corrections, 1974-78; prof. criminal justice Univ. Detroit, 1978—, chmn. dept. criminal justice and human svcs., 1993—; psychologist Oakland Psychol. Clin., Mich., 1993—. Editorial bd. Security Jour., 1994—; editor: Advances in Police and Law Enforcement, 1984-87 (vols. 3, 4, 5); contbr. articles to profl. jours. Bd. dirs. Southfield Little League, Mich., 1989-92; coach baseball/softball St. Michael of Southfield, 1989—. Mem. Am. Correctional Assn. Office: U Detroit Mercy Dept of Criminal Justice PO Box 19900 Detroit MI 48219-0900

HOMBURGER, FREDDY, physician, scientist, artist; b. St. Gall, Switzerland, Feb. 8, 1916; came to U.S., 1941, naturalized, 1952; s. Ludwig and Cécile (Gaille) H.; m. Regina Thûrlimann, Nov. 8, 1939. Student, U. Vienna, Austria, 1936-37; M.D., U. Geneva, Switzerland, 1941. Diplomate Nat. Bd. Med. Examiners., Am. Bd. Toxicology. Rsch. fellow, intern pathology Yale Med. Sch. and New Haven Hosps., 1941-43; intern, rsch. fellow in medicine Harvard Med. Sch., Thorndike Meml. Lab., Boston City Hosp., 1943-45; fellow in medicine Meml. Hosp., N.Y.C., 1946-48; chief clin. investigation Sloan-Kettering Inst. Cancer Research, N.Y.C., 1945-48; instr. medicine Cornell U. Med. Coll., 1946-48, rsch. prof. medicine; dir. cancer rsch. and control unit Tufts U. Sch. Medicine, Boston, 1948-57; mem. courtesy staff Mt. Desert Island Hosp., Bar Harbor, Maine, 1955-73, Eastern Meml. Hosp., Ellsworth, Maine, 1957-60; sci. assoc. Jackson Lab., Bar Harbor, 1951-60; rsch. prof. oncology, div. basic scis. Sch. Grad. Dentistry, Boston U., 1973—; rsch. prof. pathology Sch. Medicine, 1974—; mem. sci. staff Mallory Inst. Pathology, Boston City Hosp., 1979—; mem. Grad. Sch. Faculty Boston U., 1981—; Mem. corp. Gesell Inst. Child Devel., 1960-78; chmn. adv. com. Am. Students U. Geneva; pres., dir. Bio-Research Inst., Inc., 1957-90, Bio-Research Cons., Inc., 1957-95 ; pres. Trenton Exptl. Lab. Animal Co., Bar Harbor, 1969-81; treas., dir. Cambridge Coordinating Com. Drugs, 1972-74; hon. consul of Switzerland in Boston, 1964-86; neutral mem. mixed med. commn. War Dept., 1944-46. Author: The Medical Care of the Aged and Chronically Ill, 3d edit., 1973, The Biological Basis of Cancer Management, 1957; editor: The Physiopathology of Cancer, 3d edit., 1974-76, Progress in Experimental Tumor Research, vols. I-XXXII, 1960-89, The Rational Use of Advanced Medical Technology With the Elderly, 1994; sr. editor: Symposia on Research Advances Applied to Medical Practice, Current Concepts in Toxicology; exhibited paintings in one-man shows, N.Y.C., Paris, Zurich, Geneva, Boston. Mem. overseers com. to visit Harvard U., 1965-71, 76-82; bd. dirs. Cambridge Soc. Early Music, 1970—; trustee Opera Co., Boston, 1967-84; chmn. Friends Busch-Reisinger Mus., 1974-85; visitor paintings Boston Mus. Fine Arts, 1974-91; mem. adv. bd. Lachaise Found.; bd. overseers Mt. Desert Island Biol. Lab., 1985-88, trustee 1988—; bd. dirs. Copley Soc. Boston, 1986-91, Longy Sch. Music, Cambridge, 1984-93, Coun. for the Arts at MIT, 1991-94; exec. sec. Friends of Switzerland, Boston, 1986—. Recipient Julius Adams Stratton prize for cultural achievement, 1991. Fellow AAAS, N.Y. Acad. Scis. (ednl. adv. com. 1967), Acad. Toxicol. Scis.; mem. Nat. Hypertension Assn. (nat. adv. council 1978—), AMA, Endocrine Soc., Am. Assn. Cancer Research, Am. Fedn. Clin. Research, N.Y. Acad. Medicine, Soc. Exptl. Biology and Medicine, Am. Assn. Pathologists, Soc. Toxicology, Am. Soc. Pharmacology and Exptl. Therapeutics, Royal Soc. Health, Brit. Soc. Toxicology, Soc. Pharmacol. and Environ. Pathologists, Endocrine Soc., New Eng. Soc. Pathologists, Cambridge C. of C. (dir. 1969-73), Sigma Xi. Clubs: Harvard (Boston); Cosmos (Washington). Home: 25 Marion St Ph 1-2 Brookline MA 02146-4966 Office: 675 Massachusetts Ave Cambridge MA 02139-3309

HOMER-VANNIASINKAM, SHERVANTHI, vascular surgeon; b. Colombo, Sri Lanka, Apr. 21, 1958; arrived in U.K., 1985; d. Joseph and Cohaneesveri (Thuraiappa) H. BSc, Bangalore (India) U., 1976; M.B.B.S., Mysore Med. Coll., 1981. Rotating intern Govt. Hosp., Mysore, India, 1981-82; sr. house officer cardiology Christian Med. Coll. Hosp., Vellore, 1982, sr. house officer pediatric surgery, 1982, sr. house officer nephrology, 1983, sr. house officer neurosurgery, 1983, registrar gen. surgery, 1983-84; sr. house officer accident and emergency Northampton (U.K.) Gen. Hosp., 1985, sr. house officer orthop. surgery, 1985-86; sr. house officer paediatric surgery Royal Liverpool Children's Hosp., 1986-87; surg. tng. North Staffs Royal Infirmary, Stoke-on-Trent, 1987-88; registrar gen. surgery Bradford Royal Infirmary and St. Luke's Hosp., 1988-90; rsch. registrar Gen. Infirmary at Leeds and Biomed. Scis./U. Bradford, 1990-91; hon. registrary in surgery Yorkshire Regional Health Authority; mid. grade registrar Gen. Infirmary at Leeds and assoc. hosps., 1991-93; sr. registrar No. and Yorkshire Health Authority, 1993-95; cons. vascular surgeon United Leeds Teaching Hosps., 1995—; hon. sr. clin. lectr. vascular surgery U. Leeds; hon. sr. rsch. fellow biomed, scis. U. Bradford; co-dir. vascular rsch. unit U. Bradford and Gen. Infirmary at Leeds; collaborating scientist vascular rsch. divsn. dept. pathology Brigham and Women's Hosp. and Harvard Med. Sch., Boston; lectr. in field; vis. rsch. fellow divsn. vascular surgery U. Toronto, Ont., Can., 1991; vis. rsch. scholar U. Mich., Ann Arbor, 1993. Contbr. numerous articles and abstracts to profl. jours. Surg. Rsch. Soc. travelling fellow, 1993, Anglo-Canadian travelling fellow Royal Soc. London, 1991, Ethicon found. travelling fellow, 1991, Moynihan travelling fellow, 1996; winner Internat. Union Angiology Sci. award, 1992, 95, Gold medal Registrar'r prize Leeds Regional Surg. Club, 1992, Founders' prize York Med. Soc., 1993. Fellow Royal Coll. Surgeons of Edinburgh (named James Syme Prof. 1993); mem. Surg. Rsch. Soc. (Patey prize 1992), Internat. Soc. for Applied Cardiovascular Biology, Internat. Soc. for Endovascular Surgery. Office: Gen Infirmary at Leeds, Dept Vascular Surgery, Great George St, Leeds LS1 3EX, United Kingdom

HOMESTEAD, SUSAN E. (SUSAN FREEDLENDER), psychotherapist; b. Bklyn., Sept. 20, 1937; d. Cy Simon and Katherine (Haas) Eichelbaum; m. Robert Bruce Randall, 1956 (div. 1960); 1 child, Bruce David; m. George Gilbert Zanetti, Dec. 13, 1962 (div. 1972); m. Ronald Eric Homestead, Jan. 16, 1973 (div. 1980); m. Arthur Elliott Freedlender, April, 1, 1995. BA, U. Miami-Fla., 1960; MSW, Tulane U., 1967. Diplomate Am. Bd. Clin. Social Work; Acad. Cert. Social Workers, 1971, LCSW, Va., Calif. Psychotherapist, cons., Richmond, Va., 1971—, Los Altos, Calif.; pvt. practice, Piedmont Psychiatric Ctr., P.C. (formerly Psychol. Evaluation Rehab. Cons., Inc.), Lynchburg, Va., 1994—; cons. Family and Children's Svcs., Richmond, 1981—, Richmond Pain Clinic, 1983-84; Health Internat. Va., P.C., Lynchburg, 1984-86, Franklin St. Psychotherapy & Edn. Ctr, Santa Clara, Calif., 1988-90; pvt. practice, 1971—; Santa Clara County Children's Svc., 1973-75, 86-88; co-dir. asthma program Va. Lung Assn., Richmond, 1975-79, Loma Prieta Regional Ctr.; chief clin. social worker Med. Coll. Va., Va. Commonwealth U., 1974-79; field supr. 1980 Census, 1981-87. Contbr. articles to profl. jours. Active Peninsula Children's Ctr., Morgan Ctr., Coun. for Community Action Planning, Community Assn. for Retarded, Comprehensive Health Planning Assn. Santa Clara, Mental Health Commn., Children and Adolescent Target Group Calif., Women's Com. Richmond Symphony, Va. Mus. Theatre, mem. fin. com. Robb for Gov.; mem. adv. com. Va. Lung Assn.; mem. steering com. Am. Cancer Soc.(Va. div.), Epilepsy Found., Am. Heart Assn. (Va. div.), Cen. Va. Guild for Infant Survival. Mem. NASW, Va. Soc. Clin. Social Work, Inc. (charter mem., sec. 1975-78), Internat. Soc. Communicative Psychoanalysis & Psychotherapy, Am. Acad. Psychotherapists, Internat. Soc. for the Study of Dissociation, Am. Assn. Psychiatric Svcs. for Children.

HOMMA, MORIO, microbiology educator; b. Fukushima, Japan, Oct. 9, 1930; s. Toma and Shige (Kakudate) H.; m. Mitsuko Endo, Mar. 29, 1955; children: Naoki, Yukari, Akihiko. MD, Tohoku U., Sendai, Miyagi Prefecture, Japan, 1955, DMS, 1961. Med. diplomate. Rsch. assoc. Tohoku U. Sch. Medicine, Sendai, 1956-68, asst. prof., 1968-73; prof., chmn. dept. bacteriology Yamagata (Japan) U. Sch. Medicine, 1973-83; prof., chmn. dept. microbiology Kobe (Hyogo Prefecture, Japan) U. Sch. Medicine, 1983-94, dean, 1989-93; prof. faculty of home econs. Kobe Women's U., Japan, 1994—. Contbr. articles to rsch. jours. Recipient Kojima Meml. Prize, Kojima-Fukumi Commemoration Inst., Tokyo, 1984. Mem. Soc. Japanese Virologists (pres. 1989-90). Home: Kita-ku Naruko 2 chome 6-10, Kobe 651-11, Japan Office: Kobe Women's U Faculty Home Econs, 2-1 Aoyama, Higashisuma Suma-ku Kobe Hyogo 650, Japan

HON, DAVID C., physician, surgeon; b. Singapore, Oct. 29, 1955; s. Sin Yuen and Hee Lan (Foo) H.; m. Elaine Hon, Nov. 28, 1992; 1 child, Christopher. BA, Rutgers U., 1981; MD, Oral Roberts U., 1986. Diplomate Am. Bd. Surgery. Intern St. Francis Med. Ctr., Trenton, 1986-91, surgical Sresident; attending surgeon Loma Linda (Calif.) Cmty. Hosp., 1991-95, San Bernardino (Calif.) Cmty. Hosp., 1991-96, Ridgecrest Hosp., Clayton, Ga., 1995—, Rabun County Hosp., Clayton, Ga., 1995—, Toccoa (Ga.) County Hosp., 1995—. Fellow ACS (assoc.); mem. Soc. Gen. Surgeons. Methodist. Home: 705 Plum Lane Clarkesville GA 30523 Office: Ridgecrest Hosp 392 Ridgecrest Cir Clayton GA 30525

HON, JOHN WINGSUN, physician; b. Canton, China, Aug. 21, 1947; s. Yuen-Pak and Yuk-Ying (Chan) H. BA, CUNY, 1972; MA, SUNY, Buffalo, 1975; DO, Kirksville Coll. Medicine, 1979. Diplomate Am. Coll. Emergency Physicians; bd. cert. emergency medicine and family practice. Enlisted U.S. Army, 1975, advanced through ranks to capt., 1979; intern, resident Tripler Army Med. Ctr., Honolulu, 1979-80; gen. med. officer U.S. Army Med. Corps, Honolulu, 1979-80; intern Tripler Army Med. Ctr., Honolulu, 1979-80; gen. med. officer U.S. Army Med. Corps, Korea, 1980-81, U.S. Mil. Acad., West Point, 1981-83; attending physician Woodhull Hosp., Bklyn., 1983-86; pvt. practice Woodside, N.Y., 1983—; attending physician Bronx Lebanon Hosp., 1987—, Astoria (N.Y.) Gen. Hosp., 1983—, St. John Hosp., Elmhurst, N.Y., 1992—, N.Y. Hosp. Dept. Medicine, 1996; clin. asst. prof. family practice N.Y. Coll. Osteo. Medicine, 1994—. Fellow Am. Coll. Emergency Physicians; mem. Am. Osteo. Assn., N.Y. State Osteo. Med. Soc., Am. Coll. Legal Medicine. Home: 148 Cat Rock Rd Greenwich CT 06807-1302 Office: 30-96 51st St Flushing NY 11377-1457 also: 86-08 Elmhurst Ave Elmhurst NY 11373

HONAKER, CHARLES RAY, health facility administrator; b. Charleston, W.Va., Jan. 13, 1947; s. Charles Frederick and Avis Linda (McCarthy) H.; m. Sarah Powers, Aug. 30, 1969; children: Charles Erik, Cara Powers, Katherine Powers, Erin Powers. BA, U. Del., 1977; M in Health Sci., Johns Hopkins U., 1981. Cert. nursing home adminstr., cert. healthcare exec.; diplomate Am. Coll. Healthcare Execs. Dir. residential treatment Gov. Bacon Health Ctr.-State of Del., Delaware City, 1975-80; sr. health planner State of W.Va., Charleston, 1980-83; assoc. hosp. adminstr. Pinecrest State Hosp., Beckley, W.Va., 1983-84; nursing home adminstr. Arthur B. Hodges Ctr., Charleston, W.Va., 1984-86, Carondelet Holy Family Ctr., Tucson, 1986-89; hosp. adminstr. Carondelet Holy Cross Hosp., Nogales, Ariz., 1989—; bd. mem., v.p. So. Ariz., Am. Cancer Soc., 1989-94; chair, bd. mem. Office of Rural Health, U. Ariz., Tucson, 1990—; chmn. bd. Ariz. Rural Health Assn., Phoenix. Bd. mem. Sahuarita (Ariz.) Unified Sch. Dist., 1987-91, C. of C., Nogales, 1995. Fellow Am. Acad. Med. Adminstrs., Am. Coll. Health Care Adminstrs., U.S.-Mexico Border Health Assn., Ariz.-Sondra Commn. (pub. health coms.). Republican. Roman Catholic. Home: 17211 S La Canada Dr Sahuarita AZ 85629 Office: Cardondelet Holy Cross Hosp 1171 W Target Range Rd Nogales AZ 85621

HONAKER, RICHARD ALBERT, physician; b. Atlanta, Apr. 6, 1951; s. Albert Newton and Virginia Pearl (Fisher) H.; 1 child, Michele Nicole. BA, U. Va., 1973, MD, 1977. Intern Mt. Carmel Med. Ctr., Columbus, Ohio, 1978-79; physician City of Austin (Tex.) Health Dept. Minor Emergency Center, 1979-82; resident in family practice St. Paul's Hosp. and Parkland Meml. Hosp., Dallas, 1982-84; physician 1st Tex. Med. Group, Carrollton, 1984-87; practice medicine specializing in family practice Carrollton, Tex., 1987—. Mem. AMA, Tex. Med. Assn., Am. Acad. Family Physicians, Phi Beta Kappa, Phi Sigma. Office: 4333 N Josey Ln Ste 100 Carrollton TX 75010-4620

HONAMAN, J. CRAIG, health facility administrator; b. Montclair, N.J., June 15, 1943; s. Richard Karl and Gloria (McElwain) H.; m. Dee Dee Toerpe, Dec. 31, 1971; children: Justin Craig Jr., Garman Grayson. BS, N.C. State U., 1965; MS, U. Ala., 1971. Sr. v.p. Bapt. Hosp., Pensacola, Fla., 1970-79; exec. v.p. Tallahassee (Fla.) Meml. Hosp., 1979-89; adminstr. Quorum Health Resources/Leesburg (Fla.) Regional Med. Ctr., 1989-91; v.p., adminstrn. home health care Meth. Med. Ctr., Jacksonville, Fla., 1991-92; pres. Kellogg Healthcare, Inc., Jacksonville, 1992-93, KNH Healthcare, Jacksonville, 1993-95; exec. dir. HomeCare Alliance of Ga., Inc., Atlanta, 1994—; cons. in field, Jacksonville, Fla., 1991—. Contbr. articles to profl. jours. Active Boy Scouts Am., ARC, Am. Cancer Soc., Ronald McDonald House. Capt. U.S. Army, 1966-69, Vietnam. Recipient Nat. Golden Hour award MBB Helicopter, 1988. Fellow Am. Coll. Healthcare Execs., Rotary. Episcopalian. Home: 560 Cambridge Way Atlanta GA 30328 Office: HomeCare Alliance Ga Ste 101 5825 Glenridge Dr NE Bldg 3 Atlanta GA 30328-5387

HONDA, KAZUO, pharmacologist; b. Miyako, Iwate, Japan, Sept. 19, 1949; s. Kou and Nobu (Fujiwara) H.; m. Hiroko Hotta, Nov. 2, 1975; children: Kouichirou, Hirotsugu, Kei. BS, U. Tokyo, 1974, PhD, 1985. Pharmacologist Mitsubishi Chem. Industry, Yokohama, Japan, 1979—; sr. pharmacologist Yamanouchi Pharm. Co. Ltd., Tokyo. Mem. Japanese Pharm. Soc., Am. Chem. Soc., Am. Soc. for Pharmacology and Experimental Therapeutics. Office: Yamanouchi Pharm Co Ltd, 21 Miyukigaoka, Tsukuba-shi Ibaraki 305, Japan

HONET, JOSEPH CECIL, rehabilitation medicine physician; b. Albany, N.Y., Feb. 28, 1933; m. Diana Lynn, Feb. 3, 1958; children: James, Roger, Jennifer. Student, Union Coll., Schenectady, 1950-53; MD, Union Coll., 1957; MS, U. Minn., 1962. Diplomate Am. Bd. Phys. Medicine and Rehab. (bd. dirs. 1990—). Intern Albany Hosp., 1957-58; resident phys. medicine & rehab. Mayo Clinic, 1959-62; chmn. phys. medicine and rehab. Sinai Hosp., Detroit, 1967—; v.p. med. affairs Rehab. Inst. Mich., Detroit, 1989—. Lt. comdr. M.C., USN, 1962-64. Mem. AMA (chmn. residency rev. com. for phys. medicine & rehab. 1990—), Am. Acad. Phys. Medicine and Rehab. (pres. 1979-80, Disting. Clinician award 1986, Zeiter lectr. 1990), Am. Assn. Electrodiagnostic Medicine (pres. 1975-76), Mich. Acad. Phys. Medicine and Rehab. (pres. 1974-75), N.W. Assn. Phys. Medicine and Rehab. (pres. 1967-68), Sigma Xi. Office: Sinai Hosp 6767 W Outer Dr Detroit MI 48235-2893*

HONEY, RICHARD DAVID, psychology educator; b. Millcreek Twp., Pa., Dec. 24, 1927; s. Bennett Vincent and Eleanor Violet (Will) H. A.B., Transylvania Coll., 1957; Ph.D., U. Chgo., 1962. Prof. psychology, clin. psychologist Transylvania U., Lexington, Ky., 1964-91; Sr. psychologist Psychiat. Inst., Municipal Ct., Chgo., 1961, prin. psychologist, 1962-64; Clin. cons. VA Hosp. Served with AUS, 1952-54, Korea. Woodrow Wilson fellow, Danforth fellow; named to Hon. Order of Ky. Cols. Mem. APA, Sigma Xi, Psi Chi, Phi Kappa Tau, Omicron Delta Kappa (Lampas Cir.). Home: PO Box 101 Gerry NY 14740-0101

HONG, RICHARD, pediatrician, educator; b. Danville, Ill., Jan. 10, 1929; s. William and Louise (See) H.; m. Marion Shaw Taylor, May 31, 1952; children—Susan, Steven, Andrew, Laura. B.S., U. Ill., 1949, M.D., 1953. Diplomate Am. Bd. Pediats., Am. Bd. Allergy and Immunology. Intern Cook County Hosp., Chgo., 1953-54; resident Children's Hosp., Cin., 1957-60; research asso. immunology dept. pediatrics Coll. Medicine, U. Cin., 1957-65; asst. prof. pedidatrics U. Minn., 1965-67, prof., 1967-69; prof. pediatrics U. Wis. Med. Sch., Madison, 1969-92; assoc. dean U. Wis. Med. Sch., 1971-75; prof. pediatrics U. Vt. Med. Sch., Burlington, 1992—. Served with USAF, 1954-57. Recipient Immune Deficiency Found.'s Outstanding Achievement award, 1995. Mem. Soc. Pediatric Rsch., Am. Assn. Immunologists, Am. Soc. Clin. Investigation, Am. Pediatric Soc., Soc. for Exptl. Hematology, Reticuloendothelial Soc., Clin. Immunology Soc., Ctrl. Soc. for Clin. Rsch. Midwest Soc. for Pediatric Rsch., Phi Beta Kappa, Phi Kappa Phi. Home: RR 1 Box 1272G Stockbridge Rd Charlotte VT 05445-9720 Office: Vt Regional Cancer Ctr U Vt Genetics Lab 32 N Prospect St Burlington VT 05401*

HONIG, GEORGE RAYMOND, pediatrician; b. Chgo., May 5, 1936; s. Joseph C. and Raymonde S. (Moses) H.; m. Karen R. Jacobson, Dec. 18, 1960 (dec.); children: Sharon, Debra, Robert. BS in Liberal Arts and Sci., U. Ill., 1959, MD, 1961, MS in Pharmacology, 1961; PhD in Biochemistry, George Washington U., 1966. Diplomate Am. Bd. Pediatrics, Nat. Bd. Med. Examiners. Intern Johns Hopkins Hosp., Balt., 1961-62, fellow in pediatrics, 1961-63, asst. resident in pediatrics, 1962-63; rsch. assoc. Nat. Cancer Inst. NIH, 1963-66; fellow in pediatric hematology U. Ill., Chgo., 1966-68, asst. prof. pediatrics, 1968-69, assoc. prof., 1969-74, prof., 1974-75, attending physician, 1968-75, dir. pediatric hematology svc., 1972-75, prof., head dept. pediatrics Coll. Medicine, 1984—; prof. pediatrics Northwestern U., Chgo., 1975-83; attending physician, dir. div. hematology Children's Meml. Hosp., Chgo., 1975-83. Contbr. numerous articles to profl. jours. Mem. AAUP, Am. Acad. Pediatrics, Am. Assn. Cancer Rsch., Am. Soc. Biochemistry and Molecular Biology, Am. Soc. Hematology, Am. Pediatric Soc., Soc. Pediatric Rsch., Alpha Omega Alpha. Office: U Ill Coll Medicine 840 S Wood St Chicago IL 60612-7317

HONOR, STEPHEN, neuropsychologist; b. N.Y.C., Jan. 5, 1942; m. Gayle Honor Sackett, June 14, 1964; children: Kimberly, Jennifer. BA, NYU, 1963; MA, Western Mich. U., 1965; PhD, Hofstra U., 1971. Diplomate Am. Bd. Clin. Neuropsychology, Am. Bd. Profl. Disability Cons., Am. Bd. Forensic Psychology, Am. Bd. Med. Psychotherapy, Am. Bd. Profl. Psychology, Am. Bd. Disability Analysis, Am. Bd. Forensic Examiners, Am. Acad. Behavioral Medicine, Am. Bd. Forensic Medicine; lic. psychologist N.Y. State. Forensic and neuropsychological pvt. practice pvt. practice, Smithtown, N.Y., 1972—; adj. assoc. prof. psychology Hofstra U., C.W. Post Coll.; cons. in field; lectr.in field; seminar leader in field. Contbr. articles to profl. jours. Recipient Outstanding Achievement award Suffolk County Bar Assn., 1989; named First Bd. Cert. Forensic Neuropsychologist in Suffolk County. Mem. APA, Acad. Psychosomatic Medicine, Am. Acad. Behavioral Medicine, Am. Acad. Bd. Cert. Psychologists, Am. Acad. Family Counselors and Mediators, N.Y. Soc. Clin. Psychologists, Am. Coll. Forensic Psychology, Assn. for Advancement Psychology, Behavioral Neuropsychology Spl. Interest Group, Internat. Acad. Law and Mental Health, Nat. Acad. Neuropsychology, Am. Neuropsychiat. Assn., Nassau County Psychol. Assn. Office: 222 Middle Country Rd Smithtown NY 11787-2814

HOOCK, NANCY CAROL, forensic psychiatry nurse; b. Hackensack, N.J., Apr. 12, 1960; d. Joseph Patrick Sr. and Aina Margaret (Ottoson) H. BS, Rutgers U., Newark, 1982. Cert. in psychiat.-mental health nursing; nat. cert. massage therapis. Staff nurse Pascack Valley Hosp., Westwood, N.J., 1982, Bergen Pines Hosp., Paramus, N.J., 1982-84; head nurse Rockland Psychiat. Ctr., Orangeburg, N.Y., 1985-88; staff nurse adolescent psychiatry Westchester County Med. Ctr., Valhalla, N.Y., 1988-89; staff nurse forensic unit Westchester County Jail, Valhalla, N.Y., 1989-96; staff nurse adult psychiatry Westchester County Med. Ctr., Valhalla, N.Y., 1996—; apptd. to clin. ladder IV. Mem. Am. Massage Therapy Assn. Home: 616 Schaefer Ave Oradell NJ 07649-2520

HOOD, ANTOINETTE FOOTE, dermatologist; b. Honolulu, 1941. MD, Vanderbilt U., 1967. Cert. dermatology. Intern Vanderbilt Affiliated Hosps, 1967-68; resident dermatology Harvard U., 1975-76; resident dermatology-pathology Mass. Gen. Hosp., Boston, 1976-78; fellow dermatology Harvard U., 1973-75. Office: Ind U Outpatient Ctr 3240 Dept Dermatology 550 N University Blvd Indianapolis IN 46202-5267*

HOOD, JAMES, internist, consultant; b. Leslie, Fife, Scotland, Sept. 5, 1930; came to U.S., 1966; s. James and Mary J. (Keith) H.; m. Margaret Ferguson Goodman, Aug. 21, 1953; children: James Derek, Margaret Lesley. M.B., Ch. B., U. of Edinburgh, Scotland, 1952. Diplomate Am. Bd. Internal Medicine, Am. Bd. of Nutrition. Registrar in medicine and chest diseases Newmarket Gen. Hosp., Suffolk, Eng., 1958-60; med. registrar, clin. tutor Edinburgh Ea. Gen. Hosp., 1960-62; sr. med. registrar Hampstead Gen. Hosp., Royal Free Hosps. Med. Sch., London, 1962-63; clin. researcher Med. and Biol. Rsch. div. Sandoz Inc., Basle, Switzerland, 1964-66; fellow in clin. nutrition, instr. in medicine U. Hosps., Iowa City, Iowa, 1966-70; staff internal medicine St. Luke's and Mercy Hosps., Cedar Rapids, Iowa, 1970-88, Mid Mich. Regional Med. Ctr., Midland, 1989—; assoc. Midland Internal Medicine Assocs., 1989-93; internist, consultant pvt. practice, Midland, Mich., 1993—; advisor drug evaluations AMA, Chgo., 1971. Author: (with others) Current Therapy, 1975; contbg. editor: Nutrition Revs., 1967-70; contbr. articles to New Eng. Jour. Medicine, Am. Jour. Clin. Nutrition, Jour. Clin. Investigation, Vitamins and Hormones, Am. Jour. Hosp. Pharm. Surgeon lt. Royal Naval Vol. Res., 1954-56. Fellow ACP, 1970, Royal Coll. of Physicians of Edinburgh, 1971, Am. Coll. Nutrition, 1988. Mem. Am. Soc. Internal Medicine, Fedn. of Am. Socs. for Exptl. Biology, Am. Soc. for Nutritional Scis., Am. Soc. Clin. Nutrition, Am. Fedn. Clin. Rsch., European Assn. Internal Medicine, Mich. Med. Soc., Midland County Med. Soc., Rotary. Presbyterian. Home: 5907 Harwood Dr Midland MI 48640-2742 Office: Ste B 4915 Hedgewood Dr Midland MI 48640

HOOD, JOHN SUDLER, orthopaedic surgeon; b. Clearwater, Fla., Feb. 9, 1943; s. Jennings Sudler and Katharine Ann (Borden) H.; m. Lindsay Cocks, July 18, 1970; children: James Sudler, David Charles. BS, MIT, 1965; MD, Columbia U., 1969. Diplomate Am. Bd. Orthopaedic Surgery. Surg. intern Columbia Presbyn., 1969-70, surg. resident, 1970-71; orthop. resident Lahey Clinic/Boston U., 1971-75; pvt. practice Clearwater, 1977-95; physician Orthopaedic Specialties, Clearwater, 1996—; chief of orthopaedics Morton Plant Hosp., Clearwater. Contbr. chpt. to book. Maj. USAR, 1975-77. Recipient Fellowship award Soc. St. Luke, 1964. Mem. Sigma Xi, Phi Lamba Upsilon. Office: Orthopedic Specialities 1011 Jeffords St C Clearwater FL 34616

HOOD, LEROY EDWARD, molecular biologist, educator; b. Missoula, Mont., Oct. 10, 1938; s. Thomas Edward and Myrtle Evylan (Wadsworth) H.; m. Valerie Anne Logan, Dec. 14, 1963; children: Eran William, Marqui Leigh Jennifer. B.S., Calif. Inst. Tech., 1960, Ph.D. in Biochemistry, 1968; M.D., Johns Hopkins U., 1964. Med. officer USPHS, 1967-70; staff scientist Pub. Health Svc., Bethesda, Md., 1967-70; sr. investigator Nat. Cancer Inst., 1967-70; asst. prof. biology Calif. Inst. Tech., Pasadena, 1970-73, assoc. prof., 1973-75, prof., 1975-92, Bowles prof. biology, 1977-92, chmn. div. biology, 1980-89; Gates prof. molecular biotech., chmn. bd. U. Wash. Sch. Medicine, Seattle, 1992—; dir. NSF Sci. and Tech. Ctr. for Molecular Biotech., 1989—. Author: (with others) Biochemistry, a Problems Approach, 1974, Molecular Biology of Eukaryotic Cells, 1975, Immunology, 1978, Essential Concepts of Immunology, 1978, The Code of Codes: Scientific and Social Issues in the Human Genome Project, 1992; co-editor: Advances in Immunology, 1987. Co-recipient, Albert Lasker Basic Medical Research Award, 1987, recipient Scientist of the Year Award, 1993, R&D Magazine. Mem. NAS, Am. Assn. Immunologists, Am. Assn. Sci., Am. Acad. Arts and Scis., Sigma Xi. Office: U of Washington Molecular Biotechnology Box 35 7730 Seattle WA 98195-7730*

HOOD, M. MICHELLE, hospital administrator; b. Kokomo, Ind., Nov. 12, 1956; d. Cornelius Harold and Mary Delores (Dulle) Buersmeyer; m. Russell A. Hood, Oct. 6, 1979; children: Ryan Russell, Elizabeth Mary Claire. BS, Purdue U., 1978; M Healthcare Adminstrn., Ga. State U., 1981. Dir. material svcs. Emory U. Hosp., Atlanta, 1981-82, asst. hosp. dir., 1982-90, assoc. hosp. dir., 1990-93; assoc. faculty Emory U., Atlanta, 1984-93, Washington U., St. Louis, 1994—, U. Ala. at Birmingham Sch. Professions, 1994-95; exec. v.p., COO St. Vincent's Hosp., Birmingham, 1993—; mem. lab. adv. coun. Dept. Human Resources, Atlanta, 1980-93. Bd. dirs. Muscular Dystrophy Asns. Greater Ala., 1995. Mem. Am. Coll. Healthcare Execs. (regents adv. coun. Ga. 1988-93, regents adv. coun. Ala. 1994—), Ga. Assn. Healthcare Execs. (chmn.), Sunrise Rotary Club of Birmingham. Office: St Vincents Hosp 833 Saint Vincents Dr PO Box 12407 Birmingham AL 35202

HOOD, WILLIAM BOYD, JR., cardiologist, educator; b. Sylacauga, Ala., Mar. 25, 1932; s. William Boyd and Katherine Elizabeth (Anderson) H.; m. Katherine Candace Todd, May 5, 1972; 1 son, Jefferson Boyce. B.S. summa cum laude, Davidson Coll., 1954; M.D., Harvard U., 1958. Intern Peter Bent Brigham Hosp., Boston, 1958-59, resident in internal medicine, 1959-60, 62-63; from asst. prof. to assoc. prof. medicine Harvard U., 1967-71; from assoc. prof. to prof. medicine Boston U., 1971-82; chief cardiology Boston City Hosp., 1973-82; prof. medicine U. Rochester (N.Y.), 1982—; head cardiology unit Strong Meml. Hosp., Rochester, 1982—; cons. NIH, 1975—. Mem. editorial bd.: New Eng. Jour. Medicine, 1974-81, Circulation, 1980-83, Circulation Research, 1982-89, Jour. Clin. Investigation, 1984-89; contbr. articles, revs. and editorials on cardiovascular physiology to profl. jours., chpts. to books. Served to capt. USAF, 1953-65. Research grantee NIH, 1971—; grantee Am. Heart Assn., 1971-76. Fellow ACP; mem. Am. Soc. Clin. Investigation, Assn. Am. Physicians, Am. Heart Assn., Am. Physiol. Soc., Assn. Profs. Cardiology (past pres.), N.Y. Cardiol. Soc. (past pres.), Phi Beta Kappa, Alpha Omega Alpha. Office: U Rochester Cardiology Unit Box 679 601 Elmwood Ave Rochester NY 14642-0001

HOOGS, KENNETH E., urologist; b. Oakland, Calif., Nov. 5, 1940; m. Sharon Hoogs. MD, Wake Forest U., 1969. Diplomate Am. Bd. Urology. Intern, resident Health Sci. Ctr. SUNY, Syracuse, 1969-74; pvt. practice, Syracuse, N.Y., 1975—. Mem. AMA, N.Y. State Med. Soc., Onondaga County Med. Soc. Office: Brighton Commons 100 Intrepid Ln Syracuse NY 13205-2546

HOOGWERF, BYRON JAMES, physician; b. Sioux Falls, S.D., Feb. 8, 1945; s. Henry (dec.) Hoogwerf and Nellie (Verbrugge) Hoogwerf-Christians; m. Judith Anne Barrett, Aug. 16, 1966 (div. 1985); children: Jennifer Anne, Byron James II; m. Heidi Ellen Gaenslen, Dec. 21, 1985; 1 child, Rebecca Alexandra. BA, Calvin Coll., 1967; MD, U. Minn., 1971. Cert. diabetes edn. Intern Hennepin County Med. Ctr., Mpls., 1971-72, resident internal medicine, 1976-78; fellow, endocrinology Univ. Minn., Mpls., 1978-81, asst. prof., 1981-85; staff physician Cleve. Clinic Found., 1985—, chmn., endocrinology, 1988-91. Contbr. chpts. to books and over 50 articles to profl. jours. Bd. dirs. Diabetes Assn. Greater Cleve., 1986-95, pres. bd. dirs., 1992-93; bd. dirs. Camp Ho Mito Koda, Cleve., 1986—. Recipient Tng. grant NIH, U. Minn., 1978-79, Nat. Rsch. Svc. award NIH, U. Minn., 1979-81, Spl. Emphasis Rsch. Career award NIH-Nat. Inst. Aging, U. Minn., 1982-85, NIH Post CABG Trial award, 1987-95. Fellow ACP; mem. AAAS, Am. Assn. Clin. Endocrinologists, Am. Diabetes Assn. (chmn. publs. com. coun. on nutritional scis. and metabolism 1988-91, 96—, profl. practice com. 1992-94, chmn. coun. on nutritional scis. and metabolism 1996—), Endocrine Soc., Soc. for Clin. Trials. Presbyterian. Home: 2237 Demington Dr Cleveland OH 44106-3320 Office: The Cleveland Clinic Found 9500 Euclid Ave Cleveland OH 44195-0001

HOOK, EDWARD WATSON, JR., physician, educator; b. Sumter, S.C., Aug. 10, 1924; s. Edward and Theola (Brogdon) H.; m. Jessie Dale Thurecht, June 14, 1949; children: Edward Watson III, Susan Dale, Margaret Jane, Robert Randall. Student, Yale U., 1943-44; BS, Wofford Coll., Spartanburg, S.C., 1946; MD, Emory U., 1949; DMS (hon.), Med. Coll. Pa., 1986. Diplomate: Am. Bd. Internal Medicine (mem. 1979-85). Intern Univ. Hosps., Mpls., 1949-50; jr. asst. resident in medicine Grady Meml. Hosp., Atlanta, 1950-51; sr. asst. resident Grady Meml. Hosp., 1953-54, chief resident, 1954-55; fellow dept. medicine Emory U. Sch. Medicine, Grady Meml. Hosp., 1955-56; practice medicine, specializing in internal medicine and infectious diseases Charlottesville, Va., 1969—; instr. medicine Johns Hopkins Sch. Medicine, Balt., 1956-58; asst. prof. Johns Hopkins Sch. Medicine, 1958-59; assoc. prof. medicine Cornell U. Med. Coll., 1959-64, prof., 1964-69, vice chmn. dept. medicine, 1969; assoc. attending physician N.Y. Hosp., 1959-64, attending physician, 1964-69, mem. med. bd., 1967-69; prof. honorario U. Bahia Sch. Medicine, Salvadore, Brazil, 1966; Henry B. Mulholland prof., chmn. dept. medicine U. Va. Sch. Medicine, Charlottesville, 1969-90, Henry B. Mulholland prof. medicine, 1990—, dir. Program of Humanities in Medicine, 1991-96; physician-in-chief U. Va. Hosp., 1969-90. Contbr. articles profl. jours.; Editor: Antimicrobial Agents and Chemotherapy, 1972-81; editorial bd.: Am. Jour. Medicine, 1974-80. Pres. Va. Ptnrs. of Americas, 1974-76; bd. dirs. Robert Wood Johnson Clin. Scholars Program, 1976-88, chmn. bd., 1978-88, mem. adv. bd. Robert Wood Johnson Minority Faculty Devel. Program, 1991—; mem. del. U.S.-Japan Coop. Med. Sci. Program, 1984-95, emeritus, 1995—. Served with M.C., AUS, 1943-46, 51-53. Fellow ACP (gov. for Va. 1975-79, coun. subsplty. socs. 1977-78, coun. med. splty. socs. 1976-82, residency rev. com. for internal medicine 1977-84, regent 1980-87, pres.-elect 1984-85, pres. 1985-86, pres. emeritus 1987, master 1986, Stengel award 1990), Royal Coll. Physicians of Australia (hon.); mem. Inst. Medicine of NAS, Am. Fedn. Clin. Rsch., Am. Thoracic Soc., AMA, Albemarle County Med. Soc., Soc. for Exptl. Biology and Medicine, Am. Soc. Clin. Investigation, So. Soc. Clin. Investigation, Royal Soc. Tropical Medicine and Hygiene, Am. Assn. Immunologists, Am. Clin. and Climatology Assn. (coun. 1979-83, 90-95, v.p. 1984-85, pres., 1990-91), N.Y. Med. and Surg. Assn., Infectious Diseases Soc. Am. (pres. 1975-76), Assn. Profs. Medicine (coun. 1977-83, pres. 1981-82), Assn. Am. Physicians, Internal. Coll. Tropical Medicine, Sigma Xi, Alpha Omega Alpha. Home: 1203 Hilltop Rd Charlottesville VA 22903-1222 Office: U Va Hosps Jefferson Park Ave Charlottesville VA 22908

HOOK, WILLIAM FRANKLIN, radiologist; b. Williston, N.D., May 26, 1935; s. Charles Ellis and Ann (Franklin) H.; m. Margo Joanne Booth, June 21, 1958 (div. Sept. 1968); children: William, Christopher, Paul; m. Merry Jean Schimke, Nov. 26, 1968 (div. 1987); 1 child, Kari Ann; m. Linda Marie Rohrich, Aug. 18, 1988. AB, Stanford U., 1957; MD, Jefferson Med. Coll., 1961. Diplomate Am. Bd. Radiology, Am. Bd. Nuclear Medicine. Staff radiologist Q&R Clinic, Bismarck, N.D., 1969-74; dir. nuclear radiology Q&R Clinic, Bismarck, 1983—; chmn. dept. radiology, 1990—; chief dept. radiology Bismarck Hosp., 1970-74; dir. dept. radiology Mandan (N.D.) Hosp., 1974-81; staff radiologist Meth. Hosps., Dallas, 1981-83, Med. Ctr. One, 1984—; co-dir. Regional MRI Ctr., Bismarck, 1987-92; asst. clinical prof. U. N.D., 1978—. Author: Common Sense and Modern First Aid, 1967; contbr. articles profl. jours. Lt. USNR, 1961-64, col. res.; comdr. USAR hosp., Persian Gulf, 1991-92. Mem. AMA (Physician's Recognition award 1983-86, 86-92), Am. Coll. Radiology, Soc. Nuclear Medicine, N.D. State Radiol. Soc., 6th Dist. Med. Soc. Lutheran. Home: RR 5 Box 145A Bismarck ND 58501-9805 Office: Q&R Clinic 222 N 7th St Bismarck ND 58501-4436

HOOKER, JOHN HENRY, retired radiologist; b. Dixon, Mo., Sept. 30, 1924; s. Henry Greenleaf and Grace Frances (Wells) H.; m. Betty Lou Wells, Apr. 26, 1952; 1 child, Jennifer Lou. Student pre-medicine, U. Mo., 1942-45; MD, U. Tenn., 1949; cert. radiology, St. Louis City Hosp., 1961. Cert. Am. Bd. Radiology. Radiologist Alton (Ill.) Meml. Hosp., 1961-69, dir. dept. radiology, 1969-94; ret., 1994—; past pres. med. staff Alton Meml. Hosp., Cmty. Meml. Hosp., Madison County Med. Soc. Served to capt. U.S. Army, 1955-57. Mem. AMA, Am. Coll. Radiology, Radiol. Soc. N.Am., Am. Inst. Ultrasound in Medicine. Republican. Presbyterian. Home: 19 Fairmount Dr Alton IL 62002-3216

HOOKER, JOHN PATRICK, neurosurgeon, neurologist; b. Frost, Tex., Sept. 5, 1926; s. Rea Ferdinand and Ada (Walker) H.; m. Mariam Adellon Squires, Apr. 8, 1972 (dec.); m. Mary Katherine Donahue, July 29, 1978. BA, U. Tex., 1950; MD, U. Tex. Sch. Medicine, 1954. Diplomate Am. Bd. Neurol. Surgery. Intern U. Miami, 1954-55, resident in surgery, 1955-56; fellow in neurosurgery Mayo Clinic, Rochester, Minn., 1956-58, Ochsner Found., New Orleans, 1958-61; pvt. practice med./surgical neurology El Paso, Tex., 1961—. SErved with AUS, 1944-46. Fellow ACS, Am. Coll. Angiology, Am. Coll. Geriatrics, Internat. Coll. Surgeons, Internat. Coll. Angiology, Royal Soc. Health (U.K.), Royal Soc. Medicine (U.K.), Southwestern Surg. Congress; mem. Am. Acad. Clin. Neurophysiology, Am. Acad. Neurology, Am. Electroencephalographic Soc., Computerized Med. Imaging Soc., Congress Neurol. Surgeons, Harvey Cushing Soc., Pan Am. Med. Assn., Pan-Pacific Surg. Assn., So. Neurosurg. Soc. Republican. Episcopalian. Home: 8012 Big Bend Dr El Paso TX 79904

HOOKER, OLIVIA J., psychologist, educator; b. Muskogee, Okla., Feb. 12, 1915; d. Samuel David and Anita Juliette (Stigger) H. BS, Ohio State U., 1937; MA, Columbia U., 1947; PhD, U. Rochester, N.Y., 1962. Cert. sch. psychologist, N.Y. Elem. tchr. Columbus (Ohio) Pub. Schs., 1937-45; clin. psychologist dept. mental hygiene State of N.Y., Albion, 1948-51, Bedford Hills, 1951-57, Rochester, 1955-57; research psychologist dept. mental hygiene State of N.Y., Letchworth Village, 1957-61; sch. psychologist Bur. Child Guidance, N.Y.C., 1951-52; psychologist Kennedy Child Studies Ctr., N.Y.C., 1961-64, dir. psychol. svcs., 1964-83; assoc. prof. Fordham U., Bronx, N.Y., 1974-85; cons. St. Benedicts's Day Care Ctr., N.Y.C., 1976—, Fred S. Keller Sch., Yonkers, N.Y., 1987—. Trustee Terence Cardinal Cooke Health Svcs. Coun., N.Y.C., 1984-91; mem. adv. bd. Child Life program Westchester County Med. Ctr., Valhalla, N.Y., 1985—; v.p. White Plains NAACP, 1985-87, White Plains Sr. Pers. Employment Coun., 1987—; tutor Literacy Vols. Am., 1987—; bd. dirs. White Plains Child Day Care Assn., 1988-94, Vis. Nurse Assn. Westchester, 1988-94; chmn. adminstrv. bd. Trinity United Meth. Ch., 1985-87. Served with women's res. USCG, 1945-46. U. Rochester fellow, 1955-56; recipient Women's award Women's History Assn., 1986. Fellow APA (div. on devel. disability), Am. Assn. Mental Deficiency (chmn. constn. com.). Office: Fordham U Dept Psychology Bronx NY 10458

HOOPER, ROBERT EARLE, psychologist; b. Youngstown, Ohio, May 7, 1954; s. Walter Earle and Irene McKinley (Peterson) H.; m. Teresa Ann McCarty, Dec. 13, 1975; children: Erika Elisabeth, Matthew Earle. AB in Psychology, Youngstown State U., 1976; MA in Counseling, Covenant Theol. Sem., 1978; PhD in Counseling Psychology, U. Ga., 1988. Lic. counseling psychologist, S.C. Counselor, psychometrist Counseling Svcs. Ohio, Youngstown and Akron, 1978-81; rsch. asst., Coll. Edn. U. Ga., Athens, 1981-85; psychologist, owner, dir. Columbia (S.C.) Counseling Ctr., Behavioral Medicine, P.A., 1988—. Bd. dirs. Bethany Christian Svcs., Columbia, 1988-90. Capt. U.S. Army, 1985-88. Mem. S.C. Psychol. Assn., Christian Assn. for Psychol. Studies, Am. Assn. Christian Counselors. Republican. Presbyterian. Home: 349 Catawba Trl Lexington SC 29072-9571

HOOPER, STEPHEN RAY, child psychologist; b. Altoona, Pa., Sept. 6, 1954; s. Ralph Carr and Virginia Rebecca (Beers) H.; m. Mary Anne Mullen, Aug. 6, 1989; children: Lindsay Rae, Madeline Grace. BS, Juniata Coll., 1976; MA, Western Ky. U., 1978; PhD, U. Ga., 1984. Lic. psychologist; cert. sch. psychologist, N.C. Asst. prof. dept. psychiatry Sch. Medicine, Pa. State U., Hershey, 1986-87, Sch. Medicine, U. N.C., Chapel Hill, 1987-94; head. psychology sect., dir. child neuropsychology Clin. Ctr. for the Study of Devel. and Learning, Chapel Hill, 1987—; assoc. prof. U. N.C., Chapel Hill, 1994—. Author: Learning Disability Subtying, 1989; co-author: Advances in Child Neuropsychology, 1994, Pediatric Traumatic Brain Injury, 1994; editor: Assessment Issues in Child Neuropsychology, 1988, Child Psychopathology, 1992, Developmental Disorders, 1992. Mem. APA, NASP, Internat. Neuropsychol. Soc., Nat. Acad. Neuropsychologists, Coun. for Exceptional Children. Office: U NC BSRC CDL CB #7255 Chapel Hill NC 27599

HOOPER, SUSAN JEANNE, obstetrical and gynecological nurse practitioner, midwife; b. Rapid City, S.D., Aug. 4, 1950; d. Hugh McNiell and Bertha Regina (Mahlberg) Thomas; m. John D. Lanham, Oct. 6, 1976 (div. Aug. 1979); m. Robert Edward Hooper, Feb. 21, 1981; children: Cassandra, Robert Brian. Diploma, Presbyn. Sch. Nursing, 1971; BS in Psychology, U. Dubuque, 1973; cert. midwife, Frontier Nursing Svc., 1975; MS in Nursing, Vanderbilt U., 1979. RN, Colo., Mo. Staff RN, asst. head nurse Presbyn. Med. Ctr., Denver, 1971-72; dir. student health U. Dubuque, Iowa, 1972-73; dist. RN, preceptor family nurse practitioner clin. inst. Frontier Nursing Svc., Hyden, Ky., 1973-75; staff nurse St. Joseph Hosp., Florence, Colo., 1975-76; home health nurse Custer County Health Dept., Westcliff, Colo., 1975-76; commd. 1st lt. U.S. Army, 1976, advanced through grades to lt. col., 1992; nurse, midwife U.S. Army, Ft. Campbell, Ky., Ft. Hood, Tex., Frankfurt, Fed. Republic Germany, 1976-79, 79-83, 83-86; head nurse mother-baby care unit U.S. Army, Ft. Riley, Kans., 1986-89; head nurse labor and delivery U.S. Army, Ft. Riley, 1989-90; ob-gyn. nurse practitioner, nurse midwife Gen. Leonard Wood Army Community Hosp., Ft. Wood, Mo., 1990-94; chief nurse midwifery svc. Blanchfield Army Cmty. Hosp., Ft. Campbell, Ky., 1994-96; ret. U.S. Army, 1996; pediatric nurse practitioner Custer County Health Dept., Westcliff, Colo., 1975-76; nurse practitioner Phelps County Health Dept., Rolla, Mo., 1996. Mem. AWHONN, ANA, Mo. Nurses Assn., Am. Coll. Nurse Midwives. Roman Catholic. Home: 24450 Red Oak Rd Waynesville MO 65583 Office: 200 N Main Rolla MO 65451

HOOSIN, JANICE, social worker; b. Chgo., June 22, 1942; d. Herbert and Ruth Jean (Rubenstein) Lapine; B.A., U. Ill., 1964; M.S.W., Jane Addams Grad. Sch. Social Work, 1966; postgrad. U. Utah, summer, 1977. Cert. mental health adminstr., psychiat. social worker, Ill., lic. clin. social worker. Psychiat. social worker New Trier Twp. High Sch., East Winnetka, Ill., 1966-70; dir. day hosp. St. Vincent's Hosp., N.Y.C., 1970-73; psychotherapist (part-time) New Trier East High Sch., Winnetka, 1973-74; dir. psychiat. day hosp. dept. psychiatry Evanston (Ill.) Hosp., 1974-78, dir. partial hospitalization, 1978-88; pvt. practice, 1988—; clin. assoc., field work supr. U. Chgo. Sch. Social Svc. Adminstrn., 1974—; cons. in field; pvt. practice marital and individual psychotherapy, specializing in co-dependency and additions, 1975—. NIMH fellow, 1964-66. Mem. Nat. Assn. Social Workers, Assn. Mental Health Adminstrs. Jewish. Home: 2638 N Burling St Chicago IL 60614-1514 Office: 636 Church St Ste 715 Evanston IL 60201-4587

HOOVER, BENJAMIN ANDREW, II, internist, geriatric physician; b. York, Pa., Sept. 24, 1937; s. Philip Abram and Elizabeth Jane (Fles) H.; m. Anne Bruen Cramer, June 22, 1963; children: Benjamin Andrew III, Kathryn Anne Barclay, Jonathan Rush. AB, Princeton U., 1959; MD, U. Pa., 1963. Diplomate Am. Bd. Internal Medicine, Am. Bd. Geriatrics. Intern York Hosp., 1963-64, resident in internal medicine, 1964-67, active staff, 1970—, chief div. internal medicine, 1987-95, pres. med. staff, 1982-83; pvt. practice York, 1970—; bd. dirs., pres. York-Adams chpt. Am. Heart Assn., 1971-77; mem., chmn. med. adv. com. Internat. Assn. Fire Chiefs, Washington, 1974-79. Contbr. articles to med. jours. Chmn. Firemen's Civil Svc. Bd., York, 1971-84; bd. dirs., pres. York Symphony Assn., 1974-79, York Found., 1976-86; ruling elder 1st Presbyn. Ch., York, 1976-79, 93-96; trustee York Coll. Pa., 1977—, chmn. bd., 1993—; bd. dirs., pres. Strand-Capitol Performing Arts Ctr., York 1986-92; bd. dirs. Strand-Capitol Found., York 1993—, pres., 1995—. Fellow ACP; mem. AMA, Am. Soc. Internal Medicine, Am. Geriatrics Soc., Pa. Med. Soc., York County Med. Soc. (bd. dirs. 1973-84), Rotary (bd. dirs. York 1976-78, pres. 1979-80). Republican. Office: Brockie Int Med Consultants 924B Colonial Ave York PA 17403-3430

HOOVER, DEBORAH, critical care, medical and surgical nurse; b. Bay St. Louis, Miss., Apr. 1, 1958; d. Donald Terence and Mary Mauvereen (Graham) Ball; m. Harold Hoover, Jan. 16, 1982; children: Harold Ryan, Carolyn Mauvereen. BSN, Miss. Coll., Clinton, 1991; LPN, Jones Jr. Coll., Ellisville, Miss., 1980; AA, Jones Jr. Coll., 1982. Pvt. duty nurse Upjohn

Health Care, Baton Rouge, 1984; charge nurse Zachary (La.) Manor Nursing Home, 1984; staff nurse Hinds Gen. Hosp., Jackson, Miss., 1982-83, Jones County Community Hosp., Laurel, Miss., 1979-82; 3-11 supr. Clinton (Miss.) Country Manor, 1983-84, 85-86; charge nurse Tracehaven Nursing Home, Vicksburg, Miss., 1986-87; staff nurse Vicksburg (Miss.) Med. Ctr., 1987-91; nurse mgr. ICU Vicksburg Med. Ctr., 1991—, nurse mgr. emergency rm., 1992—, asst. chief nursing officer, critical care coord., 1994, critical care and emergency dept. dir., 1996—. Mem. AACN, ANA, Miss. Nurses Assn., Student Nurses Assn., Emergency Nurses Assn., Miss. Coll. Nursing Honor Soc., Vicksburg Bus. and Profl. Women's Club, Lions, Sigma Theta Tau, Alpha Chi. Baptist. Home: 120 Post Oak Ln Vicksburg MS 39180-7686

HOOVER, DONALD BARRY, pharmacology educator; b. Sunbury, Pa., July 20, 1950; s. Robert Theodore and Helen Velma (Bartholomew) H.; m. Joyce Ann Mettler, June 19, 1971; children: Bryan Patrick, Jeffrey Logan. BS, Grove City Coll., 1972; PhD, W.Va. U., 1976. Postdoctoral fellow NIMH, Bethesda, Md., 1976-78; asst. prof. dept. pharmacology East Tenn. State U., Johnson City, 1978-84, assoc. prof., 1984-90, prof., 1990—. Mem. Soc. Neurosci., Am. Soc. Pharmacology and Exptl. Therapeutics, Am. Heart Assn. (Tenn. affiliate). Office: E Tenn State U Dept Pharmacology Johnson City TN 37614

HOOVER, EDDIE LEE, cardiothoracic surgeon, educator; b. Charlotte, N.C., Sept. 16, 1944; s. Arthur John and Geneva (Phifer) H. BA, U. N.C., 1965; MD, Duke U., 1969. Diplomate Nat. Bd. Med. Examiners, Am. Bds. Surgery and Thoracic Surgery. Intern Duke U., Durham, N.C., 1969-70, resident in gen. surgery, 1970-71; resident in gen. surgery N.Y. Hosp. Cornell U., N.Y.C., 1973-75, resident in cardiothoricic surgery, 1976-78; asst. prof. surgery Cornell U. Med. Ctr., N.Y.C., 1978-80; assoc. prof. surgery SUNY, Bklyn., 1980-87; prof. surgery Meharry Med. Coll., Nashville, 1987-90; prof., chmn. surgery SUNY, Buffalo, 1990—. Author surg. sci. manuscripts. Bd. mem. Urban League, Buffalo, 1991—. Lt. comdr. USN, 1971-73; PTO. Mem. Nat. Med. Assn., Am. Surg. Assn., Soc. Univ. Surgeons, Am. Assn. Thoracic Surgery, Sigma Pi Boule. Home: 7557 Greenbush Rd Akron NY 14001 Office: Erie County Med Ctr 462 Grider St Buffalo NY 14215-3075

HOOVER, JOHN EDWARD, pharmacist, biomedical consultant; b. Middletown, Ohio, July 24, 1929; s. Lloyd Melangthon and Gertrude (Snider) H.; m. Marcia Lavanish, May 15, 1971; children: Elizabeth A., Crawford. BSc in Pharmacy, Ohio State U., 1952. Lic. pharmacist, Pa., Ohio. Community pharmacist various orgns. Middletown, 1954-58; profl. rep. Upjohn Co. and Merck Sharp & Dohme, Middletown, 1954-58; mgr. spl. svcs. Mack Pub. Co., Easton, Pa., 1960-66; dir. adminstrn. and communications Phila. Coll. Pharmacy and Sci., 1958-60, 66-78; cons. biomed. communications Swarthmore, Pa., 1956—; communications cons. to pres. Delmont Labs., Inc., Swarthmore, 1978—. Mng. editor Remington's Pharm. Scis., 1958—, Am. Jour. Pharmacy, 1966-94; editor: Dispensing of Medication, 8th edit., 1976. Lt. U.S. Army, 1952-54, Korea. Mem. Am. Pharm. Assn., Am. Med. Writers Assn., Coun. Biology Editors, Am. Inst. History Pharmacy. Home and Office: 363 Riverview Rd Swarthmore PA 19081-1219

HOOVER, PEARL ROLLINGS, nurse; b. LeSueur, Minn., Aug. 24, 1924; d. William Earl and Louisa (Schickling) Rollings; m. Roy David Hoover, June 19, 1948 (dec. 1987); children: Helen Louise, William Robert (dec.). Grad. in nursing, U. Minn., 1945, BS in Nursing, 1947; MS in Health Sci., Calif. State U., Northridge, 1972. Dir. affiliate nursing sch. Mooselake (Minn.) State Hosp., 1948-49; nursing instr. Anchor Hosp., County Hosp., St. Paul, 1949-51; student nurse supr. and instr. Brentwood VA Hosp., L.A., 1951-52; sch. nurse L.A. Unified City Schs., 1963-91, substitute sch. nurse, 1991-96. Camp nurse United First Meth. Ch., winter and summer past 35 yrs. Mem. L.A. Coun. Sch. Nurses, Calif. Sch. Nurses Orgn. Democrat. Methodist. Home: 17851 Lull St Reseda CA 91335-2237

HOOYDONK, HANS VAN, biomedical engineer; b. The Hague, The Netherlands, Aug. 15, 1946; s. Francois van and Johanna Hooydonk; m. Meta van Driel, Aug. 16, 1975; children: Stephan, Martine. D, U. Rotterdam, The Netherlands, 1976. Engr. Rotterdam, 1977-91; pres. Im-Bellmed, Heerlen, The Netherlands, 1992-94; owner, pres. Electromed, Rotterdam, 1994—; cons. Technomed, Heerlen, 1994—. Author: The New Generation of Operating Tables, 1986, The Use of Ultrasound for Removing of Cancer Cells, 1993; 1st introduction of Neodimium-Ytrium Aluminium Garnet laser for surg. purpose in Netherlands, 1980.

HOPF, FRANK RUDOLPH, dentist; b. N.Y.C., Sept. 1, 1920; s. Rudolph Aldridge and Jennie Victoria (Fusco) H.; B.S., Purdue U., 1942; postgrad. Middlesex U. Sch. Medicine, 1943-44; D.D.S., N.Y. U., 1953, postgrad., 1957-61; M.A., Columbia, 1953, M.P.H., 1955; m. Elsie Hedlund, Sept. 10, 1949; children—Christine, Frank, Victoria, William, Robert. Asst. dir. Bur. Dental Health, N.Y. State Dept. Health, Albany, 1956-57, regional dental dir., White Plains, 1967-90; pvt. practice dentistry specializing in periodontics, Rye, 1957—. Research asso. dept. periodontics, N.Y. U. Coll. Dentistry, 1958-61; clin. asst. prof. dept. periodontics N.J. Coll. Medicine and Dentistry, Jersey City, 1962-67; adj. asst. prof. dept. community dentistry Columbia Sch. Dental and Oral Surgery, N.Y.C., 1971-76; vis. prof. dept. preventive dentistry, Pitts. U. Sch. Dentistry, 1967-72. Pres., Country Ridge Home Owners Assn., Rye Brook, N.Y., 1960-62. Served with USNR, 1944-46. NIH grantee, 1957. Fellow Am. Public Health Assn., Am. Sch. Health Assn., N.Y. Acad. Dentistry, Am. Coll. Dentists; mem. ADA, N.Y. State Public Health Assn. (pres. 1970-72), Westchester Shore Dental Study Club (pres. 1960-61), Royal Soc. Health, North Eastern Soc. Periodontics, AAAS, Westchester Acad. Medicine, Am. Soc. Dentistry for Children, Federation Dentaire Internationale. Roman Catholic. KC (4 deg.). Club: Westchester Country (Rye, N.Y.). Contbr. articles to profl. publs. Home: 42 Rockinghorse Trl Rye Brook NY 10573-1038 Office: 33 Cedar St Rye NY 10580-2137

HOPKINS, DAVID LEE, medical manufacturing executive; b. Marietta, Ohio, Nov. 5, 1937; s. David Russel and Bonnie Grace (Adams) H.; m. Marcia Loretta Hopkins, Oct. 12, 1957; children: Tamara, Theresa, Tracey, David, Heidi, Wendy, Jeremy. Student, U. Dayton, 1955-57, Lorain (Ohio) C.C., 1959; BS, Ohio State U., 1960. Sales mgr. Am. Hosp. Supply, Columbus, Ohio, 1957-75; divsn. mgr. Baxter Healthcare, Stone Mountain, Ga., 1975-80; owner Hosp. Sterile Products, Stone Mountain, Ga., 1980-84; owner Angio Systems, Inc., Ducktown, Tenn., 1984—, also chmn. bd.; bd. dirs. Dalore, Inc., Ducktown, Ashfield Med., Cumbernauld, Scotland. Elder His Kingdom First Ministries. Mem. Rotary (pres. 1968-87, bd. dirs. 1990-91, Presdl. Citation 1987, Paul Harris fellow 1988), Copper Basin Area C. of C. (bd. dirs., pres.). Office: Angio Systems Inc PO Box 760 7 Hopkins Pl Ducktown TN 37326

HOPKINS, DAVID STEPHEN PRINCE, health care executive; b. Pasadena, Calif., Sept. 15, 1943; s. Prynce Charles Hopkins and Fay (Cartledge) Rowell; m. Rosemary Pusey, June 18, 1965; children: Michelle, Susan, Julie, David. AB, Harvard U., 1964; MS, Stanford (Calif.) U., 1967, PhD, 1969. Prin. adminstrv. analyst U. Calif., Berkeley, 1969-70; from staff assoc. to sr. staff assoc. Stanford U., 1971-78, asst. dean for adminstr. med. sch., 1978-80, dir. analysis and planning med. ctr., 1980-86, asst. v.p. for mgmt. and fin. planning, 1986-90; dir. corp. affiliation and policy Stanford U. Hosp., 1990-94; v.p. Internat. Severity Info. Sys., 1994-95; ind. health care cons., 1995; dir. health info. improvement Pacific Bus. Group on Health, 1996—. Co-author: Planning Models for Colleges and Universities, 1980 (Lanchester prize 1981), Clinical Practice Improvement, 1994; contbr. articles to profl. jours. Dir. Fair, Isaac & Co., Inc., 1994—, Alan Guttmacher Inst., N.Y.C., 1975=93; bd. dirs. Planned Parenthood Assn. Santa Clara County, Calif., 1973-80, also several offices. Postdoctoral fellow Stanford U., 1970-71. Fellow AAAS; mem INFORMS, Assn. for Health Svcs. Rsch. Republican. Episcopalian. Clubs: Fox (Cambridge, Mass.); Palo Alto (Calif.) Golf and Country. Home: 954 Laurel Glen Dr Palo Alto CA 94304-1322 Office: Pacific Bus Group on Health Ste 1450 33 New Montgomery St San Francisco CA 94105

HOPKINS, DONALD ROSWELL, public health physician; b. Miami, Fla., Sept. 25, 1941; s. Joseph Leonard and Iva (Major) H.; m. Ernestine Mathis, June 24, 1967. BS, Morehouse Coll., 1962; MD, U. Chgo., 1966; MPH, Harvard U., 1970; DSc (hon.), Morehouse Coll., 1988, Emory U., 1994. Intern San Francisco Gen. Hosp., 1966-67; resident U. Chgo. Hosps., 1970-72; med. officer program planning and evaluation Ctrs. for Disease Control, Atlanta, 1972-74, dep. chief environ. health service div., 1974, asst. dir. ops., 1977-80, asst. dir. internat. health, 1980-84; sr. cons. Global 2000 Inc., Carter Presdl. Ctr., Atlanta, 1987—; dep. dir. Ctrs. for Disease Control, 1984-87; cons. Carter Ctr. Global 2000 Program, Atlanta; asst. prof. tropical pub. health Harvard U., Boston, 1974-77; chmn., advisor on internat. health research Dr. Peter Bourne, White House, Washington, 1977; mem. U.S. del. World Health Assembly, Geneva, Switzerland, 1977-78, 80-86; mem. global adv. group on immunization WHO, Geneva, 1978-79, mem. steering com. epidemiology working group, 1980-83. Author: Princes and Peasants-Smallpox in History, 1983. Recipient Commd. Corps Disting. Service medal USPHS, 1986; recipient Joseph Mountin Lecture award Ctrs. for Disease Control, 1981, Excellence in Environ. Health Rsch. award Lovelance Insts., 1995; Order of Bifurcated Needle WHO, 1977, MacArthur fellow, 1995. Mem. Am. Soc. Tropical Medicine and Hygiene, Inst. Medicine Nat. Acad. Sci., Phi Beta Kappa. Democrat. Episcopalian. Office: Global 2000 Inc Carter Presdl Ctr 1 Copenhill Ave NE Atlanta GA 30307-1400

HOPKINS, LINTON C., neurologist, educator; b. Atlanta, Nov. 22, 1939; m. Priscilla Hopkins; children: Laura Elizabeth, Linton Stephens. BA, Davidson Coll., 1961; MD, U. Va., 1966. D1plomate Am. Bd. Internal Medicine, Am. Bd. Pyschiatry and Neurology, Am. Bd. Electrodiagnostic Medicine. Intern Strong Meml. Hosp., Rochester, N.Y., 1966-67; jr. resident Strong Meml. Hosp., Rochester, 1967-68; sr. resident Emory U. Sch. of Medicine, Atlanta, 1970-71, resident divsn. neurology, 1971-73, chief resident, 1974, asst. prof. neurology, 1974-1980, asst. prof. pathology, 1974-89, assoc. prof. pathology, 1989, assoc. prof. neurology, 1980-89; dir. electromyography lab., muscle pathology lab. depts. neurology and pathology Emory U. Sch. Medicine, Atlanta, 1974—; dir. Dalton (Ga.) Neuromuscular Clinic, 1974—; vis. fellow in muscle pathology, med. neurology br., NIH, Bethesda, Md., 1972, in electromyography, Mayo Clinic, Rochester, Minn., 1974. Contbr. numerous articles to profl. jours. Mem. AMA, Am. Acad. Neurology (chair consortium neurologg clerkship dirs, mem. subcom. for edn. non-neurologists), Ga. Neurolog. Soc., Am. Assn. Electromyograpy and Electrodiagnosis, Atlanta Neurolog. Soc. (pres. 1980), Myasthenia Gravis Found. (mem. med. adv. bd., pres. 1978—, exec. com., chmn. profl. and pub. info. com. 1992—, vice chmn. found. 1994, Doctor's award, 1994), Med. Assn. Ga., Charcot-Marie-Tooth Assn. (mem. med. adv. bd.), Alpha Omega Alpha. Home: 95 Wakefield Dr Atlanta GA 30309 Office: Emory Clinic 1365 Clifton Rd NE Atlanta GA 30322

HOPKINS, PATRICIA ANN, nursing administrator, educator; b. Cedartown, Ga., July 14, 1950; d. Ellen May (Fincher) Deeds; m. James R. Hopkins, Apr. 12, 1968; children: Barbara Hopkins, Ann Marie Fincher, April Hopkins Fincher. A in Nursing, Floyd Coll., Rome, Ga., 1990. LPN, Ga.; CPR instr., ACLS. CNA Polk County Nursing Home, Cedartown, 1979-80, DON, 1993-94; emergency room nurse Polk County Hosp., Cedartown, 1980-81; clin. nurse Floyd Hosp., Rome, 1981-88, Humana Hosp., Cartersville, Ga., 1988-90; recovery outpatient nurse Humana Hosp., Cartersville, 1990-93; clin. nurse Humana Hosp., Destin, Fla., 1993; dir. student health Shorter Coll., Rome, 1993—; care coord. Quality Care, Atlanta, 1988-89; clin. nurse Anneewakee, Rockmart, Ga., 1988-89; CNA instr. Coosa Valley Tech., 1993-95. Home: 302 Jud Brazier Rd Cedartown GA 30125 Office: Shorter Coll 315 Shorter Ave Rome GA 30165

HOPP, CARA LYNN, psychological examiner, consultant; b. Lexington, Mo., Dec. 31, 1964; d. Frank Kriehn III and Alice June (Holloway) Johnson; m. David Hopp, Aug. 10, 1985. BS, Ark. State U., 1987, M of Rehab. Counseling, 1989, postgrad., 1989—. Cert. psychol. examiner, Ark.; cert. profl. counselor, Ark. Psychol. asst. Greenleaf Hosp., Jonesboro, Ark., 1990-91, interim coord. psychol. svcs., 1991-92, coord. adult psychiat. unit, 1992-96; pvt. practice cons. Mem. APA (assoc.), Ark. Psychol. Assn., Psi Chi (treas. 1986-87). Home: 4000 Cobblestone Jonesboro AR 72401 Office: 500 W Washington Ste 200 Jonesboro AR 72401

HOPPENSTEIN, JAY MARSHALL, surgeon; b. Dallas, Sept. 6, 1938; s. Joel Manuel and Stella (Mosesmon) H.; m. Carole Ann Fine, June 11, 1961; children: Jeffrey, Laura, Russell. BA in Zoology, U. Tex., 1960; MD, Southwestern Med. Sch., Dallas, 1964. Diplomate Am. Bd. Surgery. Internship U. Minn. Hosp., Mpls., 1964-65; resident in surgery W.Va. U. Med. Ctr., Morganstown, 1965-69, burn unit resident, 1967, chief resident surgery, 1968-69; resident in surgery Clarksburg (W.Va.) VA, 1968; staff surgeon USAF Regional Hosp., Carswell AFB, Tex., 1969-70, chief of surgery, 1970-71; assoc. attending surgeon Parland Meml. Hosp., 1971-90; attending surgeon Baylor U. Med. Ctr., 1971-90, Presbyn. Hosp., Dallas, 1971—; surgeon Med. City Hosp., Dallas, 1974—, chief gen. surgery, 1977-79; cons. surgeon Baylor U. Med. Ctr., 1990—; clin. instr. U. Tex. Southwestern Med. Sch., Dallas, 1971-75, clin. asst. prof. surgery, 1975, clin. assoc. prof. surgery, 1976; teaching staff VA Hosp., Dallas, 1974-77. Lectr. Am. Assn. Med. Asst., Dallas County Chpt., 1975, 76, 77, Jewish Community Ctr., Dallas, 1977, Lions Club Am., Dallas, 1975; contbr. articles to Contemporary Surgery, W.Va. Med. Jour., Annals of Surgery, others; presenter to Am. Coll. Surgeons, Tex. Surg. Soc., Dallas Soc. Gen. Surgeons, others. Med. adv. com. mem. Golden Acres Home for the Aged, 1979-80, El Centro Community Coll., 1980; med. audit com. Baylor U. Med. Ctr., mortality review com. profl. standards com.; Med. record com. mem. Presbyn. Hosp. of Dallas, 19876, vice chmn., 1988—; surg. adv. com. mem., 1989—. Fellow ACS (trauma com., liaison on cancer, chmn. program com. North Tex. chpt. sci. session 1976, chmn. pub. rels. 1977—, pres. 1971-72, 89-90, 91-92); mem. Ft. Worth Surg. Sco. (hon.), Southwestern Surg. Congress, Dallas So. Clin. Soc. (sec. 1977), Dallas Soc. Gen. Surgeons (chmn. program com. 1979-80), Dallas County Med. Soc., Tex. Surg. Soc. Office: 8220 Walnut Hill Ln Ste 414 Dallas TX 75231-4417

HOPPER, GENE S., director telemedicine center; b. Rockford, Ill., Feb. 1, 1963; d. Richard E. and Dolores H. (Betker) Soderstrom; m. Thomas E. Hopper; 1 child, Alexandra Jan. BA in Comm., U. Tex., 1986. New accounts rep. DBG & H, Dallas, 1985-86; higher edn. rep. Apple Computer, Dallas, 1986-93; dir. Ctr. for Telemedicine, U. Okla. Health Sci. Ctr., Okla. City, 1992—, bd. dirs., 1992—; mem. steering com. Okla. Telemedicine Network, Okla. City, 1993-95; chair healthcare com. Okla. Strategic Plan, 1994-95; mem. adv. bd. Rural Health Rsch., Okla. City, 1994-95. Mem. Big Brothers and Sisters, Dallas, Okla. City, 1984—; speaker Senator Mike Snyer, Washington, 1994; mem. taskforce pub. health info., Ctr. for Pub. Svc., Washington, 1994, adv. bd. Okla. Commn. on Women, Okla. City, 1996. Mem. NAFE, ComNet Soc. (charter),.

HOPPER, WILLIAM CLAYTON, JR., orthopedic surgeon; b. Memphis, Sept. 23, 1943; s. William C. and Julia (Spencer) H.; m. Ann Malone, June 21, 1947; children: Julie, Courtney. BA, U. Miss., 1966, MS, 1968; MD, U. Miss., Jackson, 1971. Diplomate Am. Bd. Orthop. Surgery. Ptnr. Gulf Coast Orthop. Clinic, Gulfport, Miss., 1979—. Contbr. articles to profl. jours. Lt. comdr. USN, 1977-79. Pediat. Orthop. fellow Scottish-Rite Hosp., Atlanta, 1977. Fellow Am. Bd. Orthop. Surgeons, Am. Acad. Orthop. Surgeons; mem. AMA, Nat. Assn. Spine Surgery, Hoke Soc. Office: Gulf Coast Orthop Clinic 1500 45th Ave Gulfport MS 39501

HOPPING, RICHARD LEE, college president; b. Dayton, Ohio, July 26, 1928; s. Lavon Lee and Dorothy Marie (Anderson) H.; m. Patricia Louise Vance, June 30, 1951; children: Ronald, Debra, Jerrold. Student, Chaffey Coll., 1947-48, U. Dayton, 1948-49, Sinclair Coll., 1948-49; BS, So. Coll. Optometry, 1952, OD, 1952, DOS (hon.), 1972; DSc (hon.), SUNY, 1995. Practice optometry Dayton, Ohio, 1953-73; pres. So. Calif. Coll. Optometry, Fullerton, 1973—; mem. Nat. Acads. of Practice, 1983—; chmn. Nat. Acad. Practice in Optometry, 1985-89; chmn. 13th dist. med. quality rev. com., State of Calif. Bd. Med. Quality Assurance, 1985-93; advisor St. Jude Hosp. Adv. Bd., 1985—; nat. spokesperson Better Vision Inst., 1988—; cons. in field. Contbr. numerous articles on vision and health care to profl. publs. V.p. Orange County (Calif.) coun. Boy Scouts Am., 1977-79, mem. adv. coun., 1979-94; mem. Coun. Assocs. of Red Cross, North Orange County Svc. Ctr., 1978-80; mem. adv. coun. YWCA, North Orange County, 1984-92. Named Optimist of Yr. Dayton View Optimists, 1956; recipient Orange County Retinitis Pigmentosa award of Excellence in field of vision care, 1988, award of Excellence VisionAmerica, 1991, Dirs. Choice award Optical Labs. Assn., 1995, Leo award of Excellence in Global Eye Care Nat. Eye Rsch. Found., 1995. Fellow APHA (Vision Care Disting. Achievement award 1984), Am. Acad. Optometry (chmn. primary care optometry sect. 1973-79, chmn. awards com. 1981-90); mem. Am. Optometric Assn. (pres. 1971-72, chmn. task force on practical enhancement 1982-84, chmn. profl. enhancement adv. com. 1982-89, Optometrist of Yr. 1988, chair industry rels. com. 1989-95, cons. comm. ctr. exec. com. 1989-95, chair nat. ednl. summit conf. 1990-91, chair Nat. Optometric Edn. Summit com. 1991-92, Scope of Optometric Practice Conf. 1992, Dr. Raymond I. Meyers award 1990, Disting. Svc. award 1993), Calif. Optometric Assn. (hon. life, jud. coun., Optometrist of Yr. 1988, acad. rels. com. 1990-93, chair Optometrist of Yr. award com. 1990-91), Assn. Ind. Calif. Colls. and Univs. (trustee 1973—), Optometric Ext. Programs Found. (hon. life), Assn. Schs. and Colls. of Optometry (pres. 1983-85), Ohio Optometric Assn. (pres. 1964-65, Optometrist of Yr. 1962, hon. life), Retinitis Pigmentosa Internat. (adv. exec. com. 1984-88), Dayton C. of C. (Man of Yr.), Lincoln of Orange County Club (chmn. ethics com. 1988-92). Office: So Calif Coll Optometry 2575 E Yorba Linda Blvd Fullerton CA 92631-1615

HOPPLE, JANET LYNETTE, medical technologist; b. Clyde, Ohio, Nov. 10, 1942; d. Clarence A. and Gretta I. (Baker) Ferree; m. C. Earl Hopple, Apr. 4, 1964; children: Kent E., Cory E. Med. Lab. Technician, Carnegie Coll., 1961, Med. Technologist, 1964. Mem. Am. Med. Technologists. Med. lab. technician St. Joseph's Hosp., Warren, Ohio, 1961-62, Mercy Hosp., Tiffin, Ohio, 1962-64, Samuel H. Williams, MD, Alexandria, Va., 1964-65; med. technologist Mercy Hosp., Tiffin, 1965-73; med. technologist/lab. mgr. Doctor's Park Clin. Lab., Lake Jackson, Tex., 1975-79; med. technologist Chandler (Ariz.) Med. Surg. Group, 1983-85; med. technologist/lab. mgr. Casa Grande (Ariz.) Clinic, 1984-89; med. technologist/sr. technician, lab. newsletter editor Casa Grande Regional Med. Ctr., 1989—. Mem. Am. Med. Technologists (del. Reno, Nev. 1994), Ariz. State Soc. of Am. Med. Technologists (state conv. com. 1994-95, Disting. Achievement award 1995), Ariz. State Am. Motors Club (treas. 1994-96), Casa Grande 4 Wheelers Club. Republican. Home: 19325 W Hopi Dr Casa Grande AZ 85222 Office: Casa Grande Regional Med Ctr 1800 E Florence Blvd Casa Grande AZ 85222

HORAN, MARY ANN THERESA, nurse; b. Denver, July 4, 1936; d. John Paul and Lucille (Somma) Perito; m. Stephen F. Horan, Sr., Dec. 28, 1957; children: Seanna, Dana, Michelle, Annette, Stephen Jr., Christine, David. BSN, Loretto Heights Coll., Denver, 1958; postgrad, Pima Community Coll., 1982. RN, Ala. Staff nurse Med. Ctr. Hosp., Huntsville, Ala., 1978-79, Crestwood Hosp., Huntsville, 1980-81, St. Joseph Hosp. Eye Surgery, Tucson, 1981—; v.p. Success Achievement Ctr., Tucson, 1987—; Amway distbr. Horan and Assocs., 1992—. Contbr. articles to nursing jours., poetry to lit. jours. Republican. Roman Catholic. Home: 8311 E 3rd St Tucson AZ 85710-2550

HORCH, KENNETH WILLIAM, neurobiologist, educator; b. Cleve., Dec. 18, 1942; s. George A. and Marian (Turner) H.; m. Sandra C. Cameron, June 26, 1965; children: Kevin, Eric; m. Mary Louisa Stewart, Jan. 18, 1987. BS, Lehigh U., 1965; MPhil, Yale U., 1968, PhD, 1971. Instr., Purdue U., West Lafayette, Ind., 1970-71; instr. U. Utah, Salt Lake City, 1973-75, asst. prof., 1976-81, assoc. prof., 1981-93, prof., 1993—, assoc. chmn. dept. bioengring., 1991—, assoc. prof. dept. physiology, 1986-92, prof., 1992—; vis. prof. U. Grenoble, France, 1986; cons. NIH, NSF, FDA, BIOSIS, 1976—. Bd. editors Jour. Electrophysiol. Tech., 1983-87; contbr. articles, revs. to profl. jours., chpts. to books. League pres., dir. coaching Utah Youth Soccer, Salt Lake City, 1981-83. Grantee NIH, NSF, Nat. Geog., NIHR, NIDRR, 1974—; U. Utah NIH postdoctoral fellow, 1971-74. Mem. AAAS, IEEE, N.Y. Acad. Scis., Soc. for Neurosci., Biomed. Engring. Soc., Sunderland Soc., Sigma Xi (sec. U. Utah chpt. 1986-89), Tau Beta Pi. Home: PO Box 581215 Salt Lake City UT 84158-1215 Office: U Utah Dept Bioengring 2480 Meb Salt Lake City UT 84112-1180

HORI, RYOHEI, pharmaceutics educator; b. Shingu, Wakayana, Japan, June 6, 1929; s. Akira and Iwae; m. Sumie Hori, Mar. 3, 1956; children: Wakabayashi Hiroko, Haruko. BS in Pharmacy, Kyoto (Japan) U., 1953, PhD in Pharmacy, 1958. Instr. faculty pharm. sci. Kyoto U., 1962-65, lectr., 1965-66, prof., dept. pharmacy, faculty medicine, 1978-93, prof. emeritus, 1993—; assoc. prof. faculty pharm. sci. Hokkaido U., Sapporo, Japan, 1966-72; prof. faculty medicine Hiroshima (Japan) U., 1972-78; prof. pharm. rsch. & tech. inst. Kinki U., Osaka, Japan, 1993—; chmn. hosp. pharmacy sect. Fedn. Asian Pharm. Assn., Manila, 1982-94. Editor 6 books, author 64 revs. in field of pharmacy. Leader Kyoto U. Bhutan Himalaya Expdn. (the first ascent of Mt. Masagang), 1980; mem. medicinal coun. Ministry Health and Welfare, Tokyo, 1985-91. Fulbright postdoctoral fellow U. Wis., Madison, 1959-61; recipient Hosp. Pharmacy award Japanese Soc. Hosp. Pharmacists, Tokyo, 1990, Acad. prestigious Prize, Pharm. Soc. Japan, Tokyo, 1991, Japan Sports prize Yomiuri Newspaper Co., Tokyo, 1990, Prince Chichibu Meml. prize Japan Soc. for the Promotion of Sci., 1992, FAPA award Fedn. Asian Pharm. Assn., 1994. Fellow Am. Assn. Pharm. Scientists (mem. editl. adv. bd. 1986—); mem. Japan Soc. Therapeutic Drug Monitoring (chmn. bd. dirs. 1991-95, bd. dirs. 1991—), Japan Assn. Hosp. Pharm. (bd. dirs. 1993—, pres. 1994), Japanese Soc. for Study of Xenobiotics (bd. dirs. 1985-93, councillor 1985—), Membrane Soc. Japan (councillor 1977—, mem. editl. bd. 1988—), Japanese Soc. Clin. Pharmacology and Therapy (councillor 1982—), Acad. Pharm. Sci. and Tech. (councillor 1985—, award 1990), Japanese Soc. Nephrology (councillor 1989—), Acad. Alpine Club Kyoto (pres. 1987-92). Home: 12-75 Ito-cho Saga Ukyo-ku, Kyoto 616, Japan Office: Kinki U Pharm Rsch & Tech Inst, 3-4-1 Kowakae, Osaka 577, Japan

HORISBERGER, MICHEL ANDRÉ, pharmaceutical company researcher; b. Neuchâtel, Switzerland, Dec. 29, 1941; s. Robert Auguste and Nadine (Bourgeois) H.; m. Laure Gabrielle Cuendet, Oct. 23, 1976; children: Anne-Pascale, Cyril André, Aurèle Timothée, Florence Séverine. Licence s Scis., Univ. Neuchâtel, 1964; PhD, Swiss Inst. for Cancer Rsch., Lausanne, 1966. Postdoctoral fellow Harvard Med. Sch., Boston, 1967-69; rschr. Pharmaceuticals Rsch., Ciba-Geigy Ltd., Basel, Switzerland, 1970—. Recipient Alfaferone prize Ismunit/Roma Italia, 1989. Mem. Am. Soc. for Microbiology, Internat. Soc. for Interferon Rsch., Swiss Soc. for Cell Biology, Molecular Biology and Genetics, N.Y. Acad. Scis. Office: Ciba Pharmaceuticals Rsch, Postfach, CH-4002 Basel Switzerland

HORIUCHI, ATSUSHI, physician, educator; b. Tsuru, Yamanashi, Japan, Nov. 12, 1929; s. Masashige and Suzuyo Horiuchi; m. Dec. 1, 1961 (dec. June 1977); 1 child, Tadashi; m. Mar. 30, 1981. MD, Nihon U., Tokyo, 1956, D in Med. Sch., 1961. Clin. fellow Sch. Medicine Nihon U., 1957-62; rsch. fellow Sch. Medicine Yale U., New Haven, 1962-64; instr. Sch. Medicine Nihon U., 1964-73, assoc. prof., 1973-74; prof. Sch. Medicine Kinki U., Osaka, Japan, 1974—. Office: Kinki U Sch Medicine, Osakasayama377-2 Ohnohigashi, Osaka 589, Japan

HORLICK, ROBERT ALLAN, molecular biologist; b. Cheverly, Md., Mar. 2, 1956; s. Max and Ruth (Rosenstock) H. BS, U. Md., 1978; cert. of completion, Internat. Sci. Sch. Weizmann, Rehovot, Israel, 1978; PhD, Johns Hopkins U., 1986. Biochemist Nat. Cancer Inst., Bethesda, Md., 1981-86; sr. rsch. scientist E.I. DuPont de Nemours & Co., Wilmington, Del., 1986-90; DuPont Merck Pharm. Co., Wilmington, 1991-96, Pharmacopeia, Inc., Cranbury, N.J., 1996—. Mem. AAAS, Am. Soc. Microbiology, N.Y. Acad. Sci., Del. Sci. Alliance. Democrat. Jewish.

HORN, LYLE WILLIAM, physiology educator, scientist; b. St. Paul, July 22, 1943; s. James Lyle and Julie Ann (Shermeta) H.; m. Jacqueline E. DeBaptiste, 1970 (dec.); m. Nancy Harrison, 1994. BS, U. Colo., 1966; PhD, Johns Hopkins U., 1973. Rsch. assoc. fluid mechanics Johns Hopkins U., Balt., 1973-74; asst. prof. U. Md. Sch. Medicine, Balt., 1974-81; assoc. prof. physiology Temple U. Sch. Medicine, Phila., 1982—. Referee various sci. jours.; contbr. articles to sci. jours. Founder, pres. Vols. Opposing Leakin Park Expressway, Inc., Balt., 1970. NIH grantee, 1976—. Mem. AAAS, Biophys. Soc., Soc. Gen. Physiologists. Office: Temple U Sch Medicine 3223 N Broad St Philadelphia PA 19140-5096

HORN, ROBERTA CLAIRE, psychotherapist, photographer; b. New Brunswick, N.J.; d. John and Ruth (Holden) Teitscheid. BA cum laude, U. Calif., Berkeley, 1985; MA in Psychology, New Sch. for Social Rsch., N.Y.C., 1992; postgrad., Mass. Sch. Profl. Psychology, 1993—. Owner

Roberta Horn Photography, Kennebunkport, Maine, 1983-93; exec. dir. Hospice Vols. of Saco Valley, Biddeford, Maine, 1988-90; psychology intern Wayland (Mass.) Mid. Sch., 1993-94, Boston U. Mental Health Ctr., 1994-95, Mass. Gen. Hosp./Chelsea Meml. Health Ctr., 1995-96, Mass. Gen. Hosp./Shriners Burns Inst., 1996; mental health worker Cambridge Hosp./Fresh Pond Day Treatment Ctr., 1995; counselor Rehoboth McKinley House of Hope, N.Mex., 1996; cons. History of Print exhbn. Xerox Corp., 1978. One-woman show (photography) Portraits of Serenity, Manchester, N.H., 1988. Mem. acquisition bd. for Am. Collection, Am. Sch. in London Libr., 1976-78; mem. condominium bd. San Francisco, 1981-84; bd. dirs. Caring Unltd. Family Violence Shelter, Sanford, Maine, 1986-88; student trainee Headstart, South Bronx, N.Y., 1990-91, Bensonhurst Day Hosp. Bklyn., 1991-92; program specialist children's summer camp Bishopswood, Camden, Maine, 1990. Recipient awards for photography. Mem. APA, N.Y. State Psychol. Assn., Dirs. of Vol. Orgns., Maine State Hospice Assn., York Art Assn., Art Guild of the Kennebunks (former v.p.), Maine Women in the Arts (former pres.), Psi Chi. Office: 5 Mendum St Roslindale MA 02131-1613

HORNBEIN, THOMAS FREDERIC, anesthesiologist; b. St. Louis, Nov. 6, 1930; s. Leonard and Rosalie (Bernstein) H.; m. Gene Schwartz (div. 1968); children: Lia, Lynn, Cari, Andrea, Robert; m. Kathryn Mikesell, Dec. 24, 1971; 1 child, Melissa. BA, U. Colo.; MD, Wash. U. Diplomate Am. Bd. Anesthesiology. Intern King County Hosp., Seattle; resident in anesthesiology Wash. U., St. Louis, USPHS postdoctoral residency; instr. anesthesiology div. Wash. U., 1960-61; asst. prof. U. Wash., Seattle, 1963-67, assoc. prof., 1967-70, prof., 1970—; vice chmn. Dept. Anesthesiology, U. Wash., Seattle, 1972-74, asst. chmn. research 1974-77, chmn. 1978-93, research affiliate Primate Ctr., 1980. Author: Everest the West Ridge, 1966. Mem. bd. trustees Little Sch., Bellevue, Wash., 1982-89. Served to lt. comdr. USN, 1961-63. Recipient George Norlin award U. Colo., Denver, 1970, Alumni Centennial Symposium award 1975, Disting. Teaching award U. Wash., 1982. Fellow AAAS; mem. Am. Physiol. Soc. (editor 1967-73), Am. Soc. Anesthesiologists (Rovenstine lectr. 1989), Assn. Univ. Anesthetists (treas. 1969-72, pres. 1974-75), Soc. Acad. Anesthesia Chairmen, Inst. of Medicine, Phi Beta Kappa, Alpha Omega Alpha. Office: U Wash Sch Medicine Dept Anesthesiology Box 356540 Seattle WA 98195-6540

HORNBERGER, ROBERT HOWARD, psychologist; b. Trenton, N.J., Jan. 26, 1933; s. Jennings Howard and Leah Margaret (Lewis) H.; m. Anne Deshon Lyman, June 11, 1958; children: Lynn Diane, Todd Lyman. BA, Amherst Coll., 1954; MA, U. Iowa, 1957, PhD, 1957. Lic. psychologist, Fla.; cert. Family Mediator, Fla.; cert. family mediator. Instr. to assoc. in med. psychology U. Nebr. Coll. Medicine, Omaha, 1958-62; staff psychologist Nebr. Psychiat. Inst., Omaha, 1958-62; chief psychologist Drs. Young, Wigton & Aita, Omaha, 1962-65; dir. Eastern Maine Guidance Ctr., Bangor, 1965-68; assoc. dir. The Counseling Ctr., Bangor, 1968-69; lectr. in psychology U. Maine, Orono, 1966-69; dir. psychology tng. VA Med. Ctr., Gainesville, Fla., 1969-81; asst. to assoc. adj. prof. U. Fla., Gainesville, 1969—; staff psychologist VA Med. Ctr., Gainesville, 1981—; bd. advisors Fla. Mental Health Inst., Tampa, 1987-95; psychologist pvt. practice, Gainesville, 1976-85, 90—. Contbr. articles to profl. jours. Founder, 1st pres. Sugarfoot Cmty. Improvement Assn., 1972; pres. Mental Health Assn. Alachua County, Gainesville, 1981, Mental Health Assn. Fla., Tallahassee, 1987, Planned Parenthood Nebr., Omaha, 1963; comdr. Gainesville Power Squadron, 1995-96. Mem. Fla. Psychol. Assn. (pres. north ctrl. chpt. 1996). Democrat. Unitarian. Home: 4056 NW 23rd Cir Gainesville FL 32605-2683 Office: DVA Med Ctr Psychology Svc # 116B Gainesville FL 32608

HORNE, W. MARK, internist; b. Laurel, Miss., Mar. 16, 1962; s. Willus M. and Bettie Fay (Farmer) H.; m. Danita Kay Culbertson, Oct. 17, 1992. AD, Jone County Jr. Coll., Elliesville, Miss., 1982; BS in Biology, Miss. Coll., 1984; MD, U. Miss., Jackson, 1988. Diplomate Am. Bd. Internal Medicine. Internist Internal Medicine Clinic, Laurel; med. dir. Comfort Care Hospice, Laurel, 1993—, Osteoporosis Ctr., Laurel, 1995—. Deacon, Sunday sch. tchr. 1st Bapt. Ch. of Laurel, 1995. With U.S. Army. Decorated Bronze Star. Mem. ACP, AMA, So. Med. Assn., Am. Acad. Hospice Physicians, Rotary, Hon. Order of St. Barbara. Republican. Home: 100 Pearl Dr Laurel MS 39440 Office: Internal Medicine Clinic 1203 Jefferson St Laurel MS 39441

HORNE-BROWN, DIANN, health information services administrator; b. Golinda, Tex., May 21, 1958; d. Peleton Horne and Inez (Lang-Horne) Daniels; m. Robert D. Brown, Nov. 2, 1992; 1 child, Deetria S. Horne. AS in Med. Records Tech., Tarrant County Jr. Coll., Hurst, Tex., 1980; BS in Med. Records Adminstrn., Tex. Woman's U., 1992; postgrad., Amber U., 1996—. Dir. med. records Richland Hosp., North Richland Hills, Tex., 1987-94, Dallas/Fort Worth Med. Ctr., Grand Prairie, Tex., 1994-95; dir. health info. svcs. THC-Fort Worth, 1995—; mem. adv. com. med. record tech. program Tarrant County Jr. Coll., 1980-96. Mem. Tex. Health Info. Mgmt. Assn. (conv. bd. liaison 1996—), Tex. Health Info. Mgmt. Assn. (pres. dist. 13 1993-94), Fort Worth Area Health Info. Mgmt. Assn. Baptist. Office: THC-Fort Worth 7800 Oakmont Blvd Fort Worth TX 76132

HORNER, ALTHEA JANE, psychologist; b. Hartford, Conn., Jan. 13, 1926; d. Louis and Celia (Newmark) Greenwald; children: Martha Horner Hartley, Anne Horner Benck, David, Kenneth. BS in Psychology, U. Chgo., 1952; PhD in Clin. Psychology, U. So. Calif., 1965. Lic. psychologist, N.Y., Calif. Tchr. Pasadena (Calif.) City Coll., 1965-67; from asst. to assoc. prof. Los Angeles Coll. Optometry, 1967-70; supr. Psychology interns Pasadena Child Guidance Clinic, 1969-70; pvt. practice specializing in psychoanalysis and psychoanalytic psychotherapy. N.Y.C., 1970-83; supervising psychologist dept. psychiatry Beth Israel Med. Ctr., N.Y.C., 1972-83, coordinator group therapy tng., 1976-82, clinician in charge Brief Adaptation-Oriented Psychotherapy Research Group, 1982-83; assoc. clin. prof. Mt. Sinai Sch. Medicine, N.Y.C., 1977-91, adj. assoc. prof., 1991—; mem. faculty Nat. Psychol. Assn. for Psychoanalysis, N.Y.C., 1982-83; sr. mem. faculty Wright Inst. Los Angeles Postgrad. Inst., 1983-85; pvt. practice specializing in psychoanalysis and psychoanalytic psychotherapy L.A., 1983—; clin. prof. dept. Psychology UCLA, 1985-95. Author: (with others) Treating the Oedipal Patient in Brief Psychotherapy, 1985, Object Relations and the Developing Ego in Therapy, 1979, rev. edit., 1984, Little Big Girl, 1982, Being and Loving, 1978, 3d edit. 1990, Psychology for Living (with G. Forehand), 4th edit., 1977, The Wish for Power and the Fear of Having It, 1989, The Primacy of Structure, 1990, Psychoanalytic Object Relations Therapy, 1991; mem. editorial bd. Jour. of Humanistic Psychology, 1986—, Jour. of the Am. Acad. of Psychoanalysis; contbr. articles to profl. jours. Mem. AAAS, APA, Calif. State Psychol. Assn., Am. Women Sci., Am. Acad. Psychoanalysis (sci. assoc.), So. Calif. Psychoanalytic Soc. and Inst. (hon.). Home: 3579 E Foothill Blvd # 256 Pasadena CA 91107

HORNER, DEBRA KAY, healthcare administrator; b. Independence, Kans., Jan. 8, 1953; d. Phillip Ronald Payne and Helen Marie (Saubers) Tredway; m. Jerry L. Horner, June 6, 1970; children: Peder E., Todd A. BS in Med. Tech., Wichita State U., 1978; MS in Mgmt., Baker U., 1992. Med. technologist Newman Hosp., Emporia, Kans., 1978-82; lab. mgr. St. Mary's Hosp., Emporia, 1982-85; lab. mktg. rep. Stormont-Vail Regional Med. Ctr., Topeka, Kans., 1985-89, dir. physician rels., 1989—. Bd. dirs. ARC, Topeka, 1994—; com. chair, com. vol. Vol. Ctr. of Topeka, 1994, 95. Mem. Am. Soc. Clin. Pathologists (cert.), Am. Hosp. Assn., Am. Coll. Healthcare Execs. (affiliate, diplomate). Office: Stormont-Vail Regional Med Ctr 1500 SW 10th Ave Topeka KS 66604-1353

HORNICK, FREDERIC RICHARD, medical technologist; b. Asmara, Ethiopia, June 25, 1950; s. Richard Lester and Alice Marie (Gould) H.; m. Joanna Cooke, Nov. 2, 1972; children—John, Joseph; 1 stepson, Jacob. B.S. in Biology, U. S.C., 1978, B.A. in Anthropology, 1978; M.S., 1983. Med. Technologist Moncrief Army Hosp., Fort Jackson, Columbia, S.C., 1971—; instr. parasitology U. S.C., 1982-84; parasitology cons. Riverbank Zoo. Served with U.S. Army, 1968-71. Mem. Am. Soc. Biologists, Southeastern Soc. Parasitologists, Am. Soc. Parasitology, Am. Soc. Clin. Pathologists, Sigma Xi. Republican. Roman Catholic. Office: Moncrief Army Hosp PO Box 484 Columbia SC 29202-0484

HORNOR, STEPHEN DAVID, athletic trainer; b. Puerto Rico, Dec. 7, 1953; s. Carl Edwin and Mary Kathleen (Allman) H.; m. Patricia Joanne Tuggle, Sept. 17, 1977; 1 child, Bethany Kathleen. BS, U. Oreg., 1977; MA, Calif. State U., Chico, 1995. Head athletic trainer Washington Diplomats Profl. Soccer, 1977-81, Yuba C.C., Marysville, Calif., 1981-96, Ark. Tech. U., Russellville, 1996—; trainer 1987 Pan Am. Games, Indpls., 1987, Nat. Sports Festivals, 1983, 85, U.S. Olympic Tng. Ctr., Colorado Springs, Colo., 1982. Author: (manual) The Use of Physical Therapy Facilities for Independent Exercise Programs, 1995. V.p. Christian Assistance Network, Yuba City, 1988-89. Mem. Nat. Athletic Trainers Assn. (cert.), Phi Kappa Phi. Office: Ark Tech U Stroupe Bldg Russellville AR 72801

HORNSTEIN, OTTO PAUL, dermatologist, educator; b. Munich, Germany, Jan. 22, 1926; s. Eugen and Anna (Förtsch) H.; m. Ingeborg Jessberger, Sept. 25, 1955; children: Brigitte, Christopher. MD, U. Würzburg, Bavaria, Fed. Republic of Germany, 1952. Med. diplomate (approbation). Lectr. U. Würzburg, 1958, U. Bonn, 1958-63; assoc. prof. U. Düsseldorf (Fed. Republic of Germany), 1964-67; full prof., chmn. dept. dermatology U. Erlangen-Nuremberg, Erlangen, Fed. Republic of Germany, 1967-95; bd. dirs. U. Erlangen-Nuremberg, 1967-95. Author, editor 9 books on dermatology, Dermatotherapie, 1985, Oral Medicine, 1966, 2d edit. 1974, 3d edit. 1996; contbr. articles to med. jours. Hon. mem. Bundesverdienstkreuz, 1993, Humboldt U., Berlin, 1994. Mem. Dermatol. Soc. Hungary (hon.), Dermatol. Soc. Argentina (hon.), Dermatol. Soc. of Japan (hon.), Dermatol. Soc. of Czechoslovakia (hon.), Dermatol. Soc. France (corr. mem.), numerous med. socs. for dermatology, rheumatology, oral pathology, and gen. pathology. Office: Dermatolog Universitaetsklinik, Hartmannstr 14, 91052 Erlangen Germany

HOROSZEWICZ, JULIUSZ STANISLAW, oncologist, cancer researcher, laboratory administrator; b. Warsaw, Poland, Jan. 4, 1931; came to U.S., 1961; s. Tytus Michal and Stefania (Domanska) H.; m. Hanna Urszula Kubik, Jan. 12, 1969; children: Nike Joanna, Peter Juliusz. D of Medicine summa cum laude, Acad. of Medicine, Lodz, Poland, 1954, DMSc. 1960. Teaching asst. dept. bacteriology Acad. of Medicine, Lodz, 1950-55, asst. prof., 1955-59, assoc. prof., 1959-61; cancer rsch. scientist Roswell Park Meml. Inst., Buffalo, 1962-64, sr. cancer rsch. scientist, 1964-67, assoc. cancer rsch. scientist, 1967-76, prin. cancer rsch. scientist, 1976-86; assoc. chief oncological urology rsch. N.Y. State Dept. Health, Roswell Park Meml. Inst. Div., Buffalo, 1986-88; dir. exptl. cancer ctr. Millard Fillmore Hosp., Buffalo, 1988—; dir. electron microscopy lab. viral oncology, 1963-66, dir. human fibroblast interferon program Roswell Park Meml. Inst., 1976-82; chmn. Pleuro-Pneumonia Like Organisms subcom. human cancer virus task force Nat. Cancer Inst., Bethesda, Md., 1963-64, mem. Nat. Prostatic Cancer Project working cadre, 1972-74; assoc. rsch. prof. microbiology SUNY, Buffalo, 1966—; rsch. prof. biology Canisius Coll., Buffalo, 1968—, Niagara U., Niagara Falls, N.Y., 1968—; sci. cons. Cytogen Corp., Princeton, N.J., 1990—, Pacific NW Rsch. Found., Seattle, 1993—. Mem. editl. bd. The Prostate, 1994—; contbr. more than 100 articles to profl. jours.; patentee on specific monoclonal antibody for diagnosis and treatment of human prostate cancer. Rockefeller Found. fellow, 1961-62; Rsch. grantee Nat. Cancer Inst., 1979-82, Phi Beta Psi, 1987—; named Citizen of Yr. Am.-Polish Eagle, Buffalo, 1967. Mem. AAAS, Am. Assn. Cancer Rsch., Am. Soc. Microbiology, Polish Soc. for Bacteriology, Am. Cancer Soc., Am. Assn. for Clin. Rsch., N.Y. Acad. Scis. Roman Catholic. Home: 2210 N Forest Rd Buffalo NY 14221-1357 Office: Millard Fillmore Hosp 3 Gates Cir Buffalo NY 14209-1120

HOROWITZ, BEN, medical center executive; b. Bklyn., Mar. 19, 1914; s. Saul and Sonia (Meringoff) H.; m. Beverly Lichtman, Feb. 14, 1952; children: Zachary, Jody. BA, Bklyn. Coll., 1940; LLB, St. Lawrence U., 1940; postgrad. New Sch. Social Rsch., 1942. Bar: N.Y. 1941. Dir. N.Y. Fedn. Jewish Philanthropies, 1940-45; assoc., ea. regional dir. City of Hope, 1945-50, nat. exec. sec., 1950-53, exec. dir., 1953-35, gen. v.p., bd. dirs., 1985—, bd. dirs. nat. med. ctr., 1980—; bd. dirs. Beckman Rsch. Inst., 1980—. Mem. Gov.'s Task Force on Flood Relief, 1969-74. Bd. dirs., v.p. Hope for Hearing Found., UCLA, 1972-96; bd. dirs. Forte Found., 1987-92, Ch. Temple Housing Corp., 1988-93, Leo Baeck Temple, 1964-67, 86-89, Westwood Property Owners Assn., 1991—. Recipient Spirit of Life award, 1970, Gallery of Achievement award, 1974, Profl. of Yr. award So. Calif. chpt. Nat. Soc. Fundraisers, 1977; Ben Horowitz chair in rsch. established at City of Hope, 1981. City street named in his honor, 1986. Jewish. Formulated the role of City of Hope as pilot ctr. in medicine, sci., and humanitarianism, 1959. Home: 221 Conway Ave Los Angeles CA 90024-2601 Office: City of Hope 208 W 8th St Los Angeles CA 90014-3208

HOROWITZ, ESTHER, speech pathology educator, retired; b. N.Y.C., Dec. 17, 1920; d. Israel and Dora (Altschuler) H. BA, Bklyn. Coll., 1940; MA, U. Wis., 1949; PhD, Columbia U., 1959. Cert. mem. Am. Speech, Hearing, Lang. Assn. Speech clinician Queens (N.Y.) Coll. Speech Clinic, 1944-46; tchr. of speech improvement N.Y.C. Pub. Schs., Bklyn., 1946-50; from instr. to prof. of speech Hofstra U., Hempstead, N.Y., 1950-81, dir. speech clinic, 1953-67. Co-author: Guidelines to Better Speech, 1965; contbr. articles to profl. jours. Recipient cert., The Arts in Britain Today, U. London, 1950. Avocations: music, theatre, arts and crafts. Democrat. Jewish. Home: 14707 Charter Rd Jamaica NY 11435-1285

HOROWITZ, FRED L., dentist, administrator, consultant; b. Chgo., June 10, 1954; s. Jacob and Celia (Morgenstern) H. BA, Washington U., St. Louis, 1976, DMD, 1979; cert. of residency, Sinai Hosp. Detroit, 1980. Gen. practice dentistry Chgo., 1981-92; chief dental cons. Charter Barclay Hosp., Chgo., 1985-89; mem. med. teaching staff Ravenswood Hosp., Chgo., 1983-92, Michael Reese Hosp., Chgo., 1984-90; mem. med. staff St. Francis Hosp., Evanston, 1987-91; exec. v.p. Dental Benefit Providers, Bethesda, Md., 1995—; pres., CEO, TDC, Chgo. and St. Louis; v.p. Employers Health Ins. Co., Green Bay, Wis., 1995; cons. Humana HMO, 1992-94; trustee Coun. on Dental Benefit Processing Stds., 1992; CEO The Amherst Group, Ltd., 1993-94. Contbg. author: EDI Primer for the Dental Office, 1995; contbr. articles to Ravenswood Hosp. publs. Mem. ADA, Am. Assn. Hosp. Dentists, Health Ins. Assn. of Am. (dental rels com.), Acad. Gen. Dentistry, Chgo. Dental Soc., Nat. Assn. Prepaid Dental Plans (bd. dirs., treas. 1994, vice-chair 1995, chair pub. rels. commn. 1996), Ill. Ambs., Alpha Omega (Leadership award 1979). Office: Dental Benefit Providers 30 N La Salle St Ste 3908 Chicago IL 60602 also: Dental Benefit Providers 7200 Wisconsin Ave Ste 800 Bethesda MD 20814

HOROWITZ, HARRY I., podiatrist; b. Astoria, N.Y., Nov. 8, 1915; s. Jacob and Fannie (Singer) H.; student CCNY, 1932-34; Pod.G, First Inst. Podiatry, N.Y.C., 1937; D in Podiatry, L.I. U., 1946; DPM, N.Y. Coll. Podiatric Medicine, 1967 LHD (hon.), 1982; m. Sylvia Glaser, Feb. 11, 1940; children: Marc, Susan. Diplomate Am. Bd. Ambulatory Foot Surgery (hon.). Practice medicine specializing in podiatry, Astoria, N.Y., 1937-76, Belleair, Fla., 1976-95; ret., 1995; mem. podiatry practice com. Workmen's Compensation Bd. N.Y. State, 1953-66, chmn. com., 1966-76; chief podiatry dept. Queens Hosp. Ctr.-L.I. Jewish Hosp., Jamaica, L.I., 1958-76; dir. Foot Clinics of N.Y., 1970-71; chmn. bd. Suncoast Orthotic Labs., Clearwater, Fla., 1978-83; podiatry panel Dept. Welfare N.Y.C.; arbitrator between Am. Bd. Foot Surgery and Am. Bd. Ambulatory Foot Surgery, 1982; cons. Sch. Podiatric Medicine Barry U., 1988-89. Mem. citizens com. Union Free Sch. Dist. 29, Merrick, N.Y., 1957; mem. library com. dist. 29, 1964; founder Fund for Advancement Podiatry Edn., 1958; hon. pres. Fund for Podiatry Edn. and Rsch., 1963—, sec., 1963-66; chmn. Task Force on Podiatry, Health and Hosp. Corp., N.Y.C., 1976-78; trustee N.Y. Coll. Podiatric Medicine, 1973-74, cons., 1981-84; chmn. Commn. to Study and Evaluate Foot Clinics of N.Y., 1980-81; chmn. ADL, Clearwater Lodge, 1985-87, B'nai Brith, Fla.; vol. tutor North Sch. Pinellas County Schs., Fla., 1987—. With U.S. Maritime Svc., 1943-45. Recipient award Jour. Podiatry, 1948, Apple from the Tchr. award Pinellas Classroom Tchrs., 1989, 90; Podiatrist of Year Queens County Podiatry Soc., 1956, 71, Podiatry Soc. State N.Y., 1957, 61, testimonial N.Y. Coll. Podiatric Medicine, 1971; named Disting. Practitioner, Nat. Acads. Practice, 1992. Mem. APHA, Am. Podiatry Assn. (exec. council, trustee 1955-62, award 1963, Disting. Svc. award 1982, Spl. Svc. award 1983), Am. Assn. Hosp. Podiatrists, Fla. Public Health Assn. (chmn. podiatric sect. 1983-85), Acad. Podiatry, Physicians for Social Responsibility, Nat. Peace Found. Clubs: Masons, B'nai B'rith (outstanding svc. award 1988). Home: 100 Oakmont Ln Clearwater FL 34616-1984

HORRIGAN, THOMAS H., retired physician; b. Waterbury, Conn., Feb. 21, 1926; s. Thomas Henry and Kethryn (Sullivan) H.; m. Rosemary Fitch, May 6, 1950; children: Christine, Kathleen, Kevin, Craig, Michael, Lisa. BS, Yale U., 1946; MD, NYU, 1949. Pvt. practice gen. medicine East Hartford, Conn., 1952-70; emergency physician St. Francis Hosp. and Med. Ctr., Hartford, 1970—; physician-in-chg. St. Francis Hosp. & Med. Ctr., 1975-80, acting dir. emergency med. dept., 1980-86, assoc. dir. emergency medicine, 1986-94, emeritus mem. staff, 1994—; now ret. Capt. U.S. Army, 1950-52. Fellow Am. Coll. Emergency Physicians; mem. Hartford County Med. Assn., Conn. Med. Soc., Hartford Med. Soc. Republican. Roman Catholic. Home: 54 Neck Rd Madison CT 06443

HORSKY, TIMOTHY, physician; b. Chester, Pa., Nov. 10, 1961; s. Nicholas Basil and Nina (Homka) H.; divorced; 1 child, Timothy, Jr. BA in Biology, West Chester U., 1986; DO, Phila. Coll. Osteo. Medicine, 1991. Paramedic Sacred Heart Hosp., Chester, 1982-84, Taylor Hosp., Ridley Park, Pa., 1984-89; intern Hosp. of Phila. Coll. of Osteo. Medicine, 1991-92, gen. surgery resident, 1992-96; fellow in cardiothoracic surgery Deborah Heart and Lung Hosp., Browns Mills, N.J., 1996—. Mem. Am. Osteo. Assn., Pa. Osteo. Med. Assn., Am. Coll. Osteo. Surgeons. Republican. Roman Catholic. Office: 4150 City Ave Philadelphia PA 19131

HORSTMANN, DOROTHY MILLICENT, physician, educator; b. Spokane, Wash., July 2, 1911; d. Henry J. and Anna (Hunold) H. AB, U. Calif., 1936, MD, 1940; DSc (hon.), Smith Coll., 1961; MA (hon.), Yale, 1961; D Med. Scs. (hon.), Women's Med. Coll. of Pa., 1963. Intern San Francisco City and County Hosp., 1939-40, asst. resident medicine, 1940-41; asst. resident medicine Vanderbilt U. Hosp., 1941-42; Commonwealth Fund fellow, sect. preventive medicine Sch. Medicine, Yale U., New Haven, 1942-43; instr. preventive medicine Sch. Medicine, Yale U., 1943-44, 45-47, asst. prof., 1948-52, assoc. prof., 1952-56, assoc. prof. preventive medicine and pediatrics, 1956-61, prof. epidemiology and pediatrics, 1961-69, John Rodman Paul prof. epidemiology, prof. pediatrics, 1969-82; John Rodman Paul prof. epidemiology, prof. pediatrics emeritus, sr. research scientist Sch. Medicine Yale U., 1982—; instr. medicine U. Calif., San Francisco, 1944-45. Recipient Albert Coll. award, 1953, Gt. Heart award Variety Club Phila., 1968, Modern Medicine award, 1974; James D. Bruce award ACP, 1975, Thorvald Madsen award State Serum Inst. (Denmark), 1977, Maxwell Finland award Infectious Disease Soc.-Am., 1978, Disting. Alumni award U. Calif. Med. Sch., 1979, NIH fellow Nat. Inst. Med. Rsch., London, 1947-48. Master ACP; fellow Am. Acad. Pediatrics (hon.); mem. NAS, Infectious Disease Soc. Am. (pres. 1975), Am. Soc. Clin. Investigation, Am. Epidemiol. Soc. (v.p. 1974-75), Am. Pediatric Soc., Am. Soc. Virology (coun. 1983-84), Soc. Epidemiol. Rsch., Internat. Epidemiol. Assn., Royal Soc. Medicine (hon., epidemiology/preventive medicine sect.), Conn. Acad. Sci. and Engring., European Assn. Against Virus Diseases, South African Soc. Pathologists (hon.), Cuban Soc. Hygiene & Epidemiology (hon.), Sigma Delta Epsilon (hon.). Home: 11 Autumn St New Haven CT 06511-2220 Office: Yale U Sch Medicine Epidemiology and Pub Health PO Box 208034 New Haven CT 06520-8034

HORTEN, BRUCE C., pathologist; b. Nashua, N.H., May 10, 1943; s. Carl Frank and Alice Jeannette (Yereance) H. BA, Drew U., 1965; MD, Duke U., 1969. Diplomate Am. Bd. Pathology, Am. Bd. Anatomic Pathology, Am. Bd. Neuropathology, Am. Bd. Clin. Pathology; lic. MD, surgeon, N.Y. Asst. pathologist Meml. Sloan-Kettering Cancer Ctr., N.Y.C., 1976-77, 78-80; asst. prof. pathology U. Calif., San Francisco, 1977-78; attending pathologist Lenox Hill Hosp., N.Y.C., 1982-94; med. dir. Impath Labs., N.Y.C., 1994—; asst. prof. pathology Cornell U. Med. Coll., N.Y.C., 1976-77, 78-80; assoc. prof. pathology N.Y. Med. Coll., Valhalla, 1983-89; med. cons. Gerard Barnes Lambert Found., N.Y.C., 1986—. Contbr. articles to profl. jours., chpt. to book. Mem. Save Venice, Met. Opera Club. Mem. Am. Soc. Clin. Pathologists, Am. Assn. Neuropathologists, Coll. Am. Pathologists, Internat. Acad. Pathology, N.Y. Pathol. Soc., Arthur Purdy Stout Soc., The Med. Strollers of N.Y.C. Office: Impath 1010 3d Ave New York NY 10021

HORTON, CHARLES EDWIN, plastic surgeon; b. Purdy, Mo., June 27, 1925; s. Ray B. and Beatrice (McCraw) Lewis; m. Gerry O'Brien, Sept. 29, 1950; 5 children. BA, U. Ark., 1945; BS, U. Mo., 1946; MD, U. Va., 1947. Diplomate Am. Bd. Plastic Surgery. Pvt. practice Dr. Charles E Horton, MD, Norfolk, Va., 1955—; chmn. dept. plastic surgery Ea. Va. Med. Sch., 1978—; dir. Ea. Va. Grad. Sch. Medicine, 1980-90. Editor: Reconstructive Surgery of the Genital Area, 1979; contbr. over 300 articles to profl. jours. Pres. Physicians for Peace. Lt. (j.g.) USN, 1950-52. Recipient 1st Citizen award, Norfolk, 1990, Highest Civilian award King Hussein of Jordan, Spl. Achievement award Am. Soc. Plastic Surgery, 1989, Dieffenbach medal German Plastic Surgery Soc., 1996. Fellow Am. Assn. Plastic Surgery (hon.); mem. Am. Soc. for Aestetic Surgery (past pres.), Found. Am. Soc. Plastic Surgery (past chmn.), Southeastern Soc. Plastic Surgery (past pres.), Am. Bd. Plastic Surgery (past chmn.), Royal Coll. Surgeons (Glasgow, hon.), Israeli Plastic Surgeons Soc. (hon.), Turkish Plastic Surgery Soc. (hon.), Syrian Plastic Surgery Soc. (hon.), Jordanian Plastic Surgery Soc. (hon.), Can. Plastic Surgery Soc. (hon.), South African Plastic Surgery Soc. (hon.), Rotary (past pres.). Episcopalian. Office: E Va Sch Med Dept Plastic Sur Norfolk VA 23510

HORTON, DONALD, neurosurgeon; b. Oklahoma City, Aug. 27, 1957; s. Ira Earl and Mary (Height) H.; m. S. Shaun, July 1, 1984; children: Michael Ryan, Sarah Michelle, Mary Alexandra. BS, Ctrl. State U., 1979; MD, U. Okla., 1983. Intern, resident neurol. surgery Oklahoma Health Sci. Ctr., Oklahoma City, 1983-90, asst. prof., 1990-95; pvt. practice Oklahoma City, 1995—. Mem. AMA, Am. Assn. Neurol. Surgeons, Royal Soc. Spina Bifida & Hydrocephalus. Office: Neurol Assocs 3366 NW Expy Ste 500D Oklahoma City OK 73112

HORTON, GWENDOLYN, nursing educator emeritus; b. Moose Jaw, Sask., Can., June 7, 1914; came to U.S., 1919; d. Orville A. and Myrtle (King) H. AA, L.A. City Coll.; BS, Calif. State U., L.A., 1968, MS, 1974. RN; cert. pub. health. Policewoman L.A. Police Dept., 1940-45; prof. nursing L.A. City Coll., Trade Teck Coll., East L.A. Coll., Harbor Coll.; prof. nursing L.A. Pierce Coll., 1972-83, prof. emeritus, 1983—. Mem. Descanso Gardens Guild, LaCanada, Calif., 1953-56, San. Fernando Valley Bd. Realtors, Van Nuys, Calif., 1980-91; bd. dirs. Owners of Subsidized Housing; pres. L.A. Garden Club, 1988-90. Mem. Water and Power Assocs. L.A. (bd. dirs. 1989-94), Apt. Assn. Greater L.A. (v.p. 1990-91, bd. dirs.), Calif. Nurses Assn., L.A. Cinema Club, L.A. Breakfast Club (emergency aid com.), Los Feliz Rep. Women Federated, So. Calif. Rep. Women, Calif. Rep. Women. Home: 2041 N Vermont Ave Los Angeles CA 90027-1952

HORTON, JAMES DAVID, critical care and emergency nurse; b. Johnson City, Tenn., Sept. 11, 1962; s. William M. and Judith Ann (Myron) H. BS in Spl. Edn., East Tenn. State U., Johnson City, 1985, BSN, 1989. Nat. cert. EMT; cert. trauma nurse core course, basic trauma life support, advanced trauma life support, pre-hosp. trauma life support, ACLS, BCLS instr./trainer. Staff nurse surg. ICU Vanderbilt U. Med. Ctr., Nashville, 1989-91, 95—; primary nurse I surg. intensive care Johnson City (Tenn.) Med. Ctr. Hosp., 1991-92; staff nurse Cross Country Healthcare Profls., 1992-93; unit coord. skilled wing Grey Stone Health Care Ctr., Blountville, Tenn., 1993-94; staff nurse surg. intensive care unit Vanderbilt U. Med. Ctr., Nashville, 1995—; Mem. surg. intensive care unit Fleet Hosp. 15, Jubail, Saudi Arabia, 1991. Lt. (j.g.) Nurse Corps, USNR, 1989-92. Mem. ANA, AACN, Emergency Nurses Assn., Am. Trauma Soc., Assn. Mil. Surgeons U.S., Navy Nurse Corps Assn.

HORTON, JAMES MARVIN, internist; b. Lincoln, Nebr., Jan. 6, 1952; s. Marvin Dean and Janet Elizabeth (Hunt) H.; m. Kathleen Marie Reardon, Apr. 22, 1978; 1 child, Sarah. MD, Duke U., 1977. Resdient U. Fla., Gainesville, 1977-80; fellow Ochsaer, New Orleans, 1980-82, U. Colo., Denver, 1985-84; pvt. practice Charlotte, N.C., 1984-90; faculty Carolinas Med. Ctr., Charlotte, 1990—. Episcopal. Office: Carolinas Med Ctr Dept Internal Medicine Charlotte NC 28232

HORTON, JOHN, academic physician; b. Sheffield, England, June 25, 1934; came to U.S., 1957; s. Leonard and Myra (Gilman) H.; children: Nicholas John, Danielle Alexia. MBChB, U. Sheffield Med. Sch., 1957.

Asst. prof. medicine Albany (N.Y.) Med. Coll., 1960-65, assoc. prof., 1966-72, prof. medicine, 1973—; head div. oncology Albany Med. Coll., 1972-87. Editor, author: Clinical Oncology, 1973; contbr. articles to profl. jours. Pres. Am. Assn. Cancer Edn., U.S.A., 1986, Am. Cancer Soc., N.Y. State Div., 1984. Recipient State Scholarship U.K. Govt., 1952, U. Sheffield Travel scholarship U. Sheffield, 1957. Fellow Am. Coll. Physicians, Am. Assn. Cancer Edn.; mem. Am. Assn. Cancer Rsch., Am. Soc. Clin. Oncology. Home: 1145 Shipwatch Cir Tampa FL 33602-5786 Office: Albany Med Coll Albany NY 12208

HORTON, MARK B., human services administrator. MD, St. Louis U., 1972; MS in Pub. Health, U. N.C., 1976. Pediat. resident Children's Meml. Hosp., Chgo.; pediat. fellow Duke U. Med. Ctr.; dir. ambulatory & pediats., asst. prof. pediats. U. Nebr. Med. Ctr., 1976-78; pediatrician Nat. Health Svcs. Corps, New Bern, N.C., 1978-81; pediatrician, med. cons. hearing impaired team Boys Town Nat. Rsch. Hosp., 1981-90; dir. gen. ambulatory & pediats. Creighton U. Med. Ctr./ St. Joseph Hosp., 1990-91; dir. Nebr. Dept. Health, Lincoln, 1991—. Office: Nebr Dept Health PO Box 95001 301 Centennial Mall S Lincoln NE 68509-5007

HORTON, PAUL CHESTER, psychiatrist; b. Cin., Jan. 29, 1942; s. Paul Chester Sr. and Elizabeth Pauline (Rice) H.; m. Mary Kathryn Kuphal, Sept. 11; children: Paul Andrey, Alexander Robert. BA, U. Minn., 1964; MD, &, 1968. Diplomate Am. Bd. Psychiatry and Neurology. Rotating intern U. Cin., 1969; resident in psychiatry Yale U., New Haven, 1972; staff psychiatrist Guidance Clinic of Camden County, West Collingswood, N.J., 1972-74, Milford (Conn.) Family and Child Guidance Clinic, 1974-77; mem. faculty Sch. Medicine Yale U., New Haven, 1974-76; pvt. practice Meriden, 1974—; cons. psychiatrist Child Guidance Clinic Cen. Conn., Meriden, 1980—; med. dir., 1994—; mem. faculty U. Conn. Sch. Medicine, Farmington, 1978-79; cons. Caring for Children, San Francisco, 1989—; reviewer Am. Jour. Psychiatry, 1980—, and others. Author: Solace, 1981, Solace, paperback edit. 1983, Solace, Japanese edit., 1985; sr. editor: The Solace Paradigm, 1988; contbr. articles to profl. jours. Big Brother Big Bros. Orgn., Mpls., 1964-68. Lt. comdr. USN, 1972-74. Mem. Am. Psychiat. Assn., Meriden Wallingford Med. Assn., Gridiron Club. Home: 18 Metacomet Dr Meriden CT 06450-3568 Office: 234 Hobart St Meriden CT 06450-4307

HORTON, SUSAN RAYE, cardiovascular clinical nurse; b. Lynn, Mass.; d. Raymond E. and Mary C. (McGovern) Berthiaume; m. Joseph Matthew Horton; children: Brian Joseph, Benjamin Matthew III. Diploma in Nursing, Salem (Mass.) Hosp., 1974; BSN, St. Anselm Coll., 1978; MSN, U.R.I., 1980. CCRN. Intensive care staff nurse Salem Hosp., 1974-80, critical care unit leader, 1980-81; infirmary nurse St. Anselm Coll., Manchester, N.H., 1977-78; rsch. asst. U.R.I., Kingston, 1979; dir., cardiac rehab. Cath. Med. Ctr., Manchester, 1981-91; cardiac clinic nurse N.H. Heart Inst., 1991—; rsch. coord. Gusto Clin. Trial, 1991-93, Amlodipine Clin. Trial, 1992-94, Fluvastatin Clni. Trial, 1993-94, Mevacor Clin. Trial, 1994-96. Contbr. articles to profl. jours. Chmn. sch. site program, Am. Heart Assn., 1988-95, ann. meeting pub. program, 1985-88, bd. dirs., 1988-95, sec. N.H. affiliate, 1991-93; bd. dirs. Greater Manchester Heart Coun., 1986-94. Recipient grant-in-aid N.H. Heart Assn., Manchester, 1984, Time Feeling Focus award Am. Heart Assn., 1990. Mem. AACN, Sigma Theta Tau (Nursing Leadership award 1993). Home: 817 Maple St Manchester NH 03104-3214 Office: Cath Med Ctr 100 Mcgregor St Manchester NH 03102-3730

HORVATH, STEVEN M., physiologist, biomedical engineer, educator; b. Cleve., Sept. 15, 1911; s. Steven Michael and Mary (Pinka) H.; m. Elizabeth Dill Sept. 2, 1940 (dec.); children: Aletha Mary Crowder, Steven Michael, Peter Joseph. Student, Oberlin Coll., 1930; BA in Chemistry and Phys. Edn., Miami U., Ohio, 1934, MS in Physiology, 1935; postgrad., Ohio State U., 1935-37; PhD in Physiology and Biology, Harvard U., 1942. Research asst. Woods Hole Biol. Lab., 1936; instr. Miami (Ohio) U., 1937-39; research asst. Harvard U. Fatigue Lab., Boston, 1939-42, tutor in biochem. scis., 1940-42; dir. physiol. research Met. State Hosp. for the Insane, Waltham, Mass., 1939-42; asst. prof. phys. medicine U. Pa., Phila., 1946-47, 1948-49; assoc. prof. physiology State U. Iowa, Iowa City, 1949-50, prof., 1951-58, acting dir. Inst. Gerontology, 1951-57; attendant in physiology VA Hosp., Des Moines, Iowa, 1952-58; vis. prof. U. Copenhagen, 1958-59; dept. head physiology Lankenau Hosp., Phila., 1958-61; vis. prof. in physiology Jefferson Med. Coll., Phila., 1959—; prof. physiology and biomedical engring. U. Calif., Santa Barbara, 1962-96, prof. emeritus, 1996—, chmn. dept. ergonomics and occupational health scis., 1979-80; rschr. Sansum Med. Rsch. Found., Environ. Stress Lab, Santa Barbara, Calif., 1980—; cons. in field; com. mem. Dept. Energy Health Effects Working Group on Coal Techs., EPA, Gordon Conf. on the Chemistry of Aging (chmn.), Gov's. Com. on Aging (Iowa), Nat. Health Council (N.Y.), Nat. Inst. Occupational Safety and Health, NIH, Nat. Research Council, Nat. Social Welfare Assembly. Contbr. articles to profl. jours.; mem. editorial bd. Am. Jour. Physiology, Jour. Applied Physiology, Jour. Gerontology, Sci. and Medicine in Sports; reviewer for Am. Rev. Respiratory Disease, Climatic Change, Jour. Clin. Investigation, Jour. Neurophysiology, Jour. Occupational Medicine, Jour. of the Autonomic Nervous System Sci. Fellow AAAS, Am. Coll. Cardiology, Am. Coll. Sports Medicine, N.Y. Acad. Scis.; mem. AHA, Am. Physiol. Soc., Am. Pub. Health Assn., Gerontological Soc., Inst. Radio Engrs., Pan Am. Med. Assn., Phila. Physiol. Soc., Soc. Experimental Biology and Medicine, Undersea Med. Soc. Home: 5210 Austin Rd Santa Barbara CA 93111-2931 Office: Sansum Med Rsch Found 2219 Bath St Santa Barbara CA 93105 also: U Calif Neurosci Rsch Inst Environ Stress Lab Santa Barbara CA 93113

HORVATH, WILLIAM LOUIS, physician; b. New Brunswick, N.J., Apr. 13, 1943; s. Louis and Florence V. (Bonosoro) H.; m. Susan Williams, Aug. 14, 1965; children: William L. II, Laura E. BA, Johns Hopkins U., 1965; MD, Temple U., 1969; Fellow, Johns Hopkins U., 1969-71; Fellow in Hematology and Oncology, U. N.C., 1971-73. Diplomate Am. Bd. Internal Medicine, Am. Bd. Hematology/Oncology. Ptnr. Hematology/Oncology Assocs., Toledo, 1975—; chief of staff St. Vincent Med. Ctr., Toledo, 1991-94; chmn. bd. St. Vincent PHO, Toledo; clin. assoc. prof. Med. Coll. of Ohio, Toledo, 1975—; adj. prof. of pharmacy, U. Toledo, 1989—, med. dir. oncology, St. Vincent Med. Ctr., Toledo. Contbr. articles to profl. jours. Adv. bd. Wellness Community, Toledo, 1995—. Mem. Am. Soc. Hematology, Am. Soc. Clin. Oncology, AMA, Ohio State Med. Assn., Am. Cancer Soc. (bd. dirs. 1996—).

HORVITZ, ABRAHAM, retired surgeon; b. Providence, Feb. 2, 1911. AB, Brown U., 1932; MD, Columbia Med. Sch., 1936. Diplomate Am. Bd. Surgery. Fellow ACS; mem. AMA, Providence Surg. Soc., Providence Med. Assn., R.I. Med. Soc.

HORVITZ, HOWARD ROBERT, biology educator, researcher; b. Chgo., May 8, 1947; s. Oscar and Mary Horvitz; m. Martha Constantine-Paton, May 2, 1993; 1 child, Alexandra Constantine. BS in Math. and Econs., MIT, 1968; MA in Biology, Harvard U., 1972, PhD in Biology, 1974. Postdoctoral fellow Med. Rsch. Coun. Lab. Molecular Biology, Cambridge, Eng.; asst. to assoc. prof. biology MIT, Cambridge, 1978-86, prof., 1986—, career devel. assoc. prof. biology, Whitehead Inst., 1982-85, mem. sci. adv. bd. Howard Hughes program in neurosci., 1984-88, investigator Howard Hughes Med. Inst., 1988—; neurobiologist (neurology), geneticist (medicine) Mass. Gen. Hosp., Boston, 1989—; advisor dept. biochemistry and molecular biology Harvard U., 1984-90; mem. neurobiology adv. bd. Cold Spring Harbor Lab., 1984—; mem. sci. adv. bd. Hereditary Disease Found., 1987—, Jane Coffin Childs Meml. Fund for Med. Rsch., 1989—; sci. adv. bd. Com. on Scholarly Comm. with People's Rep. of China, U.S. NAS, 1987—, Ain-Shams Med. Genetics Ctr. Cairo, 1990—; co-organizer Gordon Conf. on Devel. Biology, 1985; organizer biennial meeting Cold Spring Harbor Internat. Conf., 1985, coms., 1981, 87; mem. organizing com. biennial meeting Ea. Coast C. elegans, Cambridge, 1988, 90; mem. sci. rev. com. Amyotrophic Lateral Sclerosis Assn., 1990—, co-organizer meetings 1991, 92; lectr. Harvey Soc., 1989; macrofil steering com. spl. programme for esch and tng. in tropical diseases, WHO, 1992—; adv. bd. Umea (Sweden) Ctr. Molecular Pathogenesis, 1993—. Author: (with others) The Role of Intercelluar Signals: Navigation, Encounter, Outcome, 1979, Genetic Maps, Vol. 1, 1980, Nematodes as Biological Models, 1980, Development of the Nervous System, 1981, Repair and Regeneration of the Nervous System, 1982, The Nematode Caenorhabditis elegans, 1988; mem. editorial bds. Jour. Neurogenetics, 1982-88, Jour. Neurosci., 1984-89, Devel. Biology, 1985—, Genes and Devel., 1986—, Cell, 1987—, Trends in Genetics, 1987—, Neuron, 1987-90, The New Biologist, 1989—, Genetic Analysis: Techniques and Applications, 1990—, Current Opinion in Neubiology, 1990—, Current Biol., 1992—, Annual Rev. Genetics, 1993—; contbr. numerous articles to profl. jours. Mem. adv. bd. World Health Orgn. Spl. Programme for Rsch. and Tng. in Tropical Diseases, Microfil steering com., 1992—. Recipient Rsch. Career Devel. award NIH, 1981-86, Spencer award in Neurobiology, Columbia U., 1986, Warren Triennial prize Mass. Gen. Hosp., 1986, Molecular Biology award U.S. Steel Found., 1988, V.D. Mattia award Roche Inst. Molecular Biology, 1993, Hans Sigrist award, 1994, Charles A. Dana award for pioneering achievements in health and edn. Inst. Medicine NAS, 1995; Woodrow Wilson fellow, 1968, NSF predoctoral fellow, 1968-72, Muscular Dystrophy Assn. postdoctoral fellow, 1974-77. Fellow AAAS; mem. Am. Assn. Cancer Rsch., U.S. Nat. Acad. Scis., Am. Acad. Arts and Scis., Genetics Soc. Am. (membership com. 1984-86, bd. dirs. 1990-92, organizer ann. meeting 1989, v.p. 1994, pres. 1995), Soc. Devel. Biology (nominations com. 1989), Soc. Nematologists, Soc. Neurosci. (pub. info. com. 1993-95), Am. Soc. Cell Biology (organizing com. ann. meeting 1992, pub. policy com. 1993—, joint steering com. pub. policy 1994—), Am. Soc. Microbiology, Helminthological Soc. Washington. Office: MIT Dept Biology 77 Massachusetts Ave Cambridge MA 02139-4301

HORWATH, EWALD J., psychiatrist; b. Koflach, Steiermark, Austria, Apr. 12, 1953; s. Jacob and Julianna (Schendlinger) H.; m. Glaucia K. Santos; children: Juliana, Elena. AB, U. Chgo., 1975, MD, 1979; MS, Columbia U., 1988. Diplomate Am. Bd. Psychiatry and Neurology. Intern Overlook Hosp., Summit, N.J., 1979-80; psychiatry resident N.Y. State Psychiat. Inst., N.Y.C., 1980-83, attending psychiatrist, 1983—, dir. ICU, 1985—; fellow Columbia U. Psychiat. Epidemiology Tng. Program, 1983-85. Mem. Am. Psychiat. Assn. Office: 616 E Palisade Ave Englewd Clfs NJ 07632-1825

HORWITZ, ALAN FREDRICK, cell and molecular biology educator and researcher; b. Mpls., Oct. 26, 1944; s. Burt and Helen (Bolnick) H.; m. Carole Joanne Rosen, Nov. 26, 1972; children: Jeremy J., Rachel T. BA in Chemistry with honors, U. Wis., 1966; PhD in Biophysics, Stanford U., 1969; MA (hon.), U. Pa., 1978. NIH postdoctoral fellow Lab. Chem. Biodynamics, U. Calif., Berkeley, 1970-72, chemist P-5, 1972-73; scientist Biozentrum der Universitat Basel, Switzerland, 1973-74; asst. prof. dept. biochemistry and biophysics Sch. Medicine, U. Pa., Phila., 1974-78, assoc. prof., 1978-84, prof., 1984—; prof., head dept. cell and structural biology U. Ill., Urbana, 1987-95, chmn. biophysics program, 1978-85, assoc. dir. med. scientist tng. program, 1986-87, dir. cell and molecular biology tng. program, 1988-92; mem. commn. on cell and membrane biophysics Internat. Union Pure and Applied Biophysics, 1975-82; mem. sci. adv. com. biochemistry and chem. carcinogens Am. Cancer Soc., 1977-81; mem. spl. study sects. Nat. Inst. Gen. Med. Scis. NIH, 1980—, mem. rev. com. cellular and molecular basis of disease Nat. Inst. Gen. Med. Sci., 1984-88; mem. spl. study sects. Nat. Inst. Aging, Nat. Cancer Inst. Nat Inst. Gen. Med. Sci., 1980—, mem. biotech. rev. panel, 1988, mem. adv. coun., 1994; mem. innovative aging rsch. com. VA, 1983; lectr. various nat. and internat. symposia; steering com. Howard Hughes Inst. Med. Rsch., U. Pa., adv. com. for H.M. Watts, Jr. Neuromuscular Disease Rsch. Inst., U. Pa., 1986. Mem. editl. bd. Jour. Cell Biology, 1989—, Jour. Cell Sci., 1990—, Cell Adhesion and Comm., 1992—, Trends in Cell Biology, 1994—, Current Opinion in Cell Biology, 1995—; assoc. editor: Devel. Biology, 1989-95; sect. editor Current Opinion in Cell Biology, 1994; contbr. articles to profl. jours. Recipient Dr. William Daniel Stroud Established Investigator award Am. Heart Assn., 1975-80, NIH Merit award, 1992; prin. investigator, grantee in field, 1974. Mem. Biophys. Soc., Am. Soc. Biol. Chemists, Am. Soc. Cell Biology (pub. policy com. 1986—, nominating com. 1988, program com. 1995), Am. Assn. Anatomy Chmn. Home: 3410 S Persimmon Cir Urbana IL 61802-7128 Office: U Ill Dept Cell & Structural Biology Urbana IL 61801

HORWITZ, RALPH IRVING, internist, medical educator, epidemiologist; b. Phila., June 25, 1947; s. Sidney and Sara (Altus) H.; m. Sarah McCue, Aug. 5, 1970; 1 child, Rebecca Margaret Taylor. BS, Albright Coll., 1969; MD, Pa. State U., 1973. Diplomate Am. Bd. Internal Medicine. Intern McGill U., Royal Victoria Hosp., Montreal, Que., Can., 1973-75; postdoctoral tng. in epidemiology, clin. scholars program Yale U. Sch. Medicine, New Haven, Conn., 1975; sr. resident Harvard U., Mass. Gen. Hosp., Boston, 1977-78; co-dir. clin. scholars program Yale U. Sch. Medicine, New Haven, Conn., 1978—, asst. prof. medicine, 1978-82, assoc. prof. medicine and epidemiology, 1982-88, prof., 1988—, chief gen. internal medicine, 1982-94; vice chmn. internal medicine, 1993-94, chmn. internal medicine, 1994—, Harold H. Hines Jr. Prof. Medicine and Epidemiology, 1991—; mem. nat. selection com. faculty scholar program Henry J. Kaiser Family Found., Menlo Park, Calif., 1987-90; mem. com. allocating resources in biomed. rsch. Inst. of Medicine, Washington, 1988-89; mem. profl. standards rev. orgn., Woodbridge, Conn., 1980-82; editorial bd. The Lancet, 1991—. Contbr. over 100 articles to profl. jours. Recipient Faculty Scholar award Kaiser Family Found., 1981-86. Fellow ACP, AAAS, Am. Coll. Epidemiology, Pa. State U. Alumni Assn.; mem. Am. Soc. Clin. Investigation, Assn. Am. Physicians, Am. Epidemiol. Soc., New Haven Lawn Club, Mory's. Jewish. Home: 130 Deepwood Dr Hamden CT 06517-3452 Office: Yale U Sch Medicine 333 Cedar St New Haven CT 06510

HOSHIKO, MICHAEL, speech pathologist, consultant, educator; b. Surrey, Can., Apr. 8, 1921; s. Tsunehachi and Toshiye (Kuroda) H.; m. Rose Dege, Apr. 7, 1955; children: Cecily, Sumi, Lance. Student, Sir George Williams U., Montreal, Que., Can., 1942-45; BA, Heidelberg Coll., 1948; MA, Bowling Green (Ohio) State U., 1949; PhD, Purdue U., 1957. Asst. instr. U. Kans., Lawrence, 1949-50; intern Peoria (Ill.) State Hosp., 1950; psychology asst. Ill. State U., Normal, 1950-51; intern Ill. Inst. Tech., Chgo., 1951; psychologist Prep Sch., Montreal, 1951-52; rsch. psychologist med. sch. U. Toronto, Ont., Can., 1952-55; prof. communication disorders So. Ill. U., Carbondale, 1957—; prof. behavioral sci. med. sch. MacMaster U., Hamilton, Ont., Can., 1981. Vol. examiner FCC Am. Radio Relay League, Newington, Conn., 1983—. Grantee NIH, 1958-67, Am. Cancer Soc., 1959-62, Ill. Dept. Mental Health, 1962-64. Mem. APA, Psycholphysiol. Rsch. Soc., Am. Speech, Lang. and Hearing Assn. (mem. multicultural bd. 1991—), Japanese Am. Citizens League (bd. dirs. St. Louis chpt. 1988—). Democrat. Home: 7754 El Pine Est Edwardsville IL 62025-3038 Office: So Ill U Clin Ctr Carbondale IL 62901

HOSKIN, SANDRA RUBLE, medical equipment company executive, nurse; b. Chgo., Apr. 21, 1935; d. Robert Adrian and Hallie Jane (Pence) Ruble; m. Ronald Alan Budgett, Dec. 30, 1960 (div. 1973); 1 child, Laura Adrianne; m. James William Hoskin, May 20, 1974. RN, Ill. Masonic Hosp., Chgo., 1957; BSA, Coll. of St. Francis, 1979; MBA, Houston Bapt. U., 1983. RN, Ind., Tex. Staff, head nurse Meml. Hosp., South Bend, Ind., 1960-72; dir. nursing Carlysle Nursing Home, South Bend, 1972-78, Healthwin Hosp., South Bend, 1978-80; surgical supr. The Meth. Hosp., Houston, 1980-82; relief supr. Polly Ryon Hosp., Richmond, Tex., 1982-84; pres. Am. Med. Equipment Co., Houston, 1984—; pres., CEO Am. Med., Inc., 1993—; pres. Sandy's Med. Warehouse, Inc., 1992—. Named one of Houston's Top 50 Women-Owned Bus. Owners, 1995, 96. Mem. Am. Quarter Horse Assn., Nat. Assn. Med. Equipment Dealers, Tex. Assn. Med. Equipment Dealers, Internat. Tex. Longhorn Assn. Republican. Methodist. Home: Running S Ranch PO Box 69 Dobbin TX 77333 Office: Am Med Equipment Co 1841 Old Spanish Trl Houston TX 77054-2001

HOSKIN, WILLIAM DICKEL, physician; b. Akron, Ohio, Jan. 24, 1920; s. Robert E. and Margaret (Dickel) H.; m. Lois Black, June 1, 1951; children: Mark, Ned, David. AB, Hiram Coll., 1942; MD, Western Res. U., 1947; MA in English, SUNY, Brockport, 1990. Intern, U.S. Naval Hosp., San Diego, 1951-52; practice medicine specializing in occupational medicine, 1954-83; instr. physics Hiram (Ohio) Coll., 1943; asst. supt. St. Luke's Hosp., Cleve., 1947-51; staff. physician Eastman Kodak Co., Rochester, 1954-69, asst. dir., 1969-70, med. dir. Kodak Park div., 1970-83; clin. assoc. preventive medicine and community health U. Rochester, 1974-75; mem. N.Y. State Senate Adv. Com. on Alcoholism, 1977-81. Contbr. articles to med. jours. and poetry to lit. jours.; mem. editorial bd., Hiram Poetry Rev, guest editor, 1995. Pres. bd. trustees Norman Howard Sch.; bd. dirs. Park Ridge Chem. Dependency, 1979-83, Writers and Books, N.Y. State Literary Center; trustee Hiram Coll. Served as lt. USNR, 1951-54. Recipient Hiram Coll. Alumni Assn. Ann. award for Outstanding Achievement, 1972; Mrs. F. Ritter Shumway award for disting. vol. service in community health, 1980. Diplomate Am. Bd. Preventive Medicine. Fellow Am. Occupational Med. Assn., Am. Acad. Occupational Medicine, Am. Coll. Preventive Medicine, Garfield Soc.; mem. Indsl. Med. Assn. Upstate N.Y. (pres. 1969-70), Rochester Rehab. Center, Genesee Valley Heart Assn. (dir. 1965-76), N.Y. State Heart Assembly, Nat. Council Alcoholism, Health Assn. Rochester, Monroe County Learning Disabilities Assn. (bd. dirs. mental health chpt.), N.Y. State Bd. Profl. Med. Conduct, Rochester Poetry Soc. Club: U. Rochester Faculty. Home: 1563 East Ave Rochester NY 14610-1614

HOSKINS, GERALDINE, hospital nursing administrator; b. Maysville, Ky., Aug. 15, 1940; d. Vernon Garrett Hoskins and Ivetti Hoskins Candy. Cert., Christ Hosp. Sch. Nursing, Cin., 1961; AA, U. Cin., 1975. Cert. nursing adminstr. Staff nurse, evening supr. Adams County Hosp., West Union, Ohio, 1961-63; staff nurse, then head nurse, then supr. Christ Hosp., Cin., 1963-69; asst. supr., then supr. med. nursing Bethesda Hosp. Oak, Cin., 1969-70; dir. emergency and intensive care Bethesda Hosp. North, Cin., 1970-71, mgr., 1971-72, asst. v.p., 1972-80; ind. contractor, securities salesperson, Fla., 1980-81; v.p. Jewish Hosp., Cin., 1981, sr. v.p., 1981-90; v.p. Naples (Fla.) Cmty. Hosp., 1990-94; assoc. cons. Compass Group Inc., Cin., 1994—; dir. nursing CommuniCare of Clifton, Cin., 1994-96; spl. asst. Berger Hosp., Circleville, Ohio, 1996—; ind. neighborhood nurse practitioner, Cin., 1972-90; career counselor U. Cin.; mem. adv. bd. co-op. edn. dept. Coll. Mt. St. Joseph on the Ohio, 1982-89, mem. adv. bd. dept. bus., 1982-88; presenter in field. Mem. Am. Orgn. Nurse Execs. Republican. Avocations: travel, spectator and participatory sports, swimming, reading, music. Home: 1970 Berkshire Club Dr Cincinnati OH 45230-2438

HOSKINS, WILLIAM JOHN, obstetrician, gynecologist, educator; b. Harlan, Ky., May 10, 1940; s. Lonnie S. and Joanne (Huff) H.; m. Betty Jean Gay, Sept. 10, 1960 (div. 1985); children: Tonya J., William John Jr.; m. Iffath Abbasi Ahson, Nov. 9, 1985; children: Ahad A., Mariya A. BA, U. Tenn., Knoxville, 1962; MD, U. Tenn., Memphis, 1965. Diplomate Am. Bd. Ob-Gyn., Am. Bd. Gynecol. Oncology. Commd. lt. USN, 1966, advanced through grades to capt.; intern Jacksonville (Fla.) Naval Hosp., 1966-67; med. officer Destroyer Squadron 8 USN, Mayport, Fla., 1967-68; resident in ob-gyn Oakland (Calif.) Naval Hosp., 1968-71; mem. staff, dept. ob -gyn Pensacola (Fla.) Naval Hosp., 1971-74; fellow in gynecol. oncology U. Miami, Fla., 1974-76; dir. Gynecol. Oncology Nat. Naval Med. Ctr., Bethesda, Md., 1976-86; assoc. prof. ob-gyn Uniformed Svcs. U., Bethesda, 1976-86; ret. USN, 1986; assoc. chief gynecology svc. Meml. Sloan-Kettering Cancer Ctr., N.Y.C., 1988-90, chief gynecology svc., 1990—, 1990—; assoc. prof. ob-gyn Cornell U. Med. Ctr., N.Y.C., 1986-90; prof. ob-gyn. Cornell U. Med. Coll., N.Y.C., 1990-94, vice chmn. protocol com. gynecol. oncology group, 1993-94, vice chmn. gynecologic oncology group, 1993—; Avon chair gynecologic oncology rsch. Meml. Sloan-Kettering Cancer Ctr., N.Y.C., 1995-96, dep. physician in chief disease mgmt. teams, 1996—; chmn. ovarian com. Gynecol. Oncology Group, Phila., 1984-89. Editor: Principles and Practice of Gynecology & Oncology, 1992, Cancer of the Ovary, 1993; contbr. 224 articles to profl. jours., also chpts. to books. Fellow Am. Coll. Obstetricians and Gynecologists (v.p. Navy sect. 1982-83), ACS; mem. Am. Gynecol. and Obstet. Soc., Soc. Gynecol. Oncologists (sec.-treas. elect 1992, sec.-treas. 1994—, coun. mem. 1988-91), Soc. Gynecol. Surgeons, Internat. Gynecol. Cancer Soc., Am. Radium Soc., Am. Assn Cancer rsch., 1996—. Republican. Muslim. Office: Meml Sloan-Kettering Cancer Ctr 1275 York Ave Dept ObG New York NY 10021-6007

HOSLEY, BRETT DALE, neurologist; b. Kansas City, Mo., May 9, 1960; s. Ray Howard and Nelda Kay (Austin) H.; m. Machele Renee Davis, Oct. 4, 1986; children: Alyx Nicole, Blake Austin. BA, Drury Coll., 1982; DO, U. Health Scis., Kansas City, 1988. Diplomate Am. Acad. Neurology. Resident in neurology St. Louis U. Hosp., 1988-92, fellow in clin. neurophysiology, 1992-93; neurologist Hannibal (Mo.) Clinic, Inc., 1993—; asst. med. dir. spl. care unit Maple Lawn Nursing Home, Palmyra, Mo., 1994—; asst. clin. prof. neurology St. Louis U. Hosp., 1994—. Mem. AMA, Mo. State Med. Assn., N.E. Mo. County Med. Soc. (pres. 1993—), Am. Acad. Neurology.

HOSTETTER, ABRAM MARTIN, psychiatrist; b. Kinzer, Pa., Oct. 10, 1929; s. Isaac Eby and Ruth (Martin) H.; m. Patricia Ann Lerch, Aug. 7, 1954; children: David, Rebecca, Samuel. AB, Goshen Coll., 1953; Dr.med., Thomas Jefferson U., 1957. Diplomate Am. Bd. Psychiatry and Neurology. Intern Meth. Epsicopal. Hosp., Phila., 1957-58; resident in psychiatry Norristown (Pa.) State Hosp., 1958-61; med. dir. Philhaven Hosp., Lebanon, Pa., 1969-71; asst. prof. Hershey (Pa.) Med. Ctr., 1971-73; pvt. practice Hershey, 1973—; clin. prof. U. Miami, Fla., 1975—. V.p. Tri County United Way, Harrisburg, Pa., 1982-86; chmn.-elect capital region United Way, 1989-90, chmn., 1990-91. Am. Coll. Psychiatrists fellow, 1985. Fellow Am. Psychiatric Assn. (area rep. 1975), Pa. Psychiatric Soc. (pres. 1975-76); mem. Pa. Med. Soc., Lebanon Rotary. Republican. Presbyterian. Office: Hershey Psychiatric Assocs 20 Briarcrest Sq Ste 205 Hershey PA 17033-2359

HOSTNIK, WILLIAM JOHN, plastic surgeon; b. Charleroi, Pa., July 21, 1928; s. Charles and Bertha (Wagner) H.; m. Susan Hostnik; children: Charles, Heidi, Stephen, John, Susan. AB in Chemistry, Johns Hopkins U., 1950, MD, 1954. Intern in gen. surgery Johns Hopkins Hosp., Balt., 1954-55, asst. resident, 1957-58; resident in gen. surgery Albany (N.Y.) Hosp., 1958-62; resident and fellow in plastic surgery Barnes Hosp., St. Louis, 1962-64; pvt. practice New London, Conn., 1964—. Contbr. articles to profl. jours. Mem. bd. finance, Old Lyme, Conn., 1987-95. Lt. USN, 1955-57. Fellow ACS; mem. Am. Soc. Plastic and Reconstructive Surgeons, Am. Soc. Awsthetic Plastic Surgeons, New Eng. Soc. Plastic Surgeons (sec., v.p., pres. 1974-79), Conn. Soc. Plastic and Reconstructive Surgeons (pres. 1990-91). Office: 325 Montauk Ave New London CT 06320

HOTCHNER, BRADLEY ROSS, orthopedics surgeon; b. St. Louis, Aug. 22, 1955; s. Selwyn Ross and Beverly June (Novack) H.; children: Jeremiah Selwyn, Justin Noel. BS in Zoology, U. Wis., 1977; MD, St. Louis U., 1981. Intern in gen. surgery St. Louis Univ. Group Hosps., 1981-82, resident in orthopedic surgery, 1982-86; fellow in sports medicine Toronto Orthopedic and Arthritis Hosp.; orthopedic surgeon Palm Springs (Calif.) Med. Ctr., 1986, San Bernardino County (Calif.) Med. Ctr., 1987-91; chief orthopedics Kaiser Permanente, Riverside, Calif., 1991—. AO fellow, Basel, Switzerland and West Berlin, Germany, total joint fellow Cen. DuPage Hosp. Fellow: Am. Acad. Orthopedic Surgery; mem. Assn. Study Applications Flizarov, Phi Beta Kappa, Phi Kappa Phi, Phi Eta Sigma. Office: Kaiser Permanente 10800 Magnolia Riverside CA 92505

HOTELLING, DAVID RAWSON, physician, educator; b. Riverside, Calif., Feb. 26, 1938; s. Kenneth Hotelling and Elizabeth (Gute) Rowland; m. Rebecca Riter, June 22, 1966; children: Kirstin, Kimberly. BA, Reed Coll., 1960; MD, U. Cin., 1964. Diplomate Am. Bd. Internal Medicine. Intern San Francisco Gen. Hosp.; resident VA Hosp., U. Calif. San Francisco, Boston City Hosp.; fellow in endocrinology Beth Israel Hosp., Boston; attending physician Maine Med. Ctr., Portland, 1971—, Mercy Hosp., Portland, 1971—, Brighton Med. Ctr., Portland, 1971—; asst. clin. prof. medicine U. Vt., Burlington, 1990—. Lt. comdr. USNR, 1965-70. Mem. Am. Assn. Clin. Endocrinologists, Am. Assn. Internal Medicine, Am. Assn. Diabetes. Office: 190 Pine St Portland ME 04102

HOTES, CATHERINE LYNN, nursing administrator; b. Cleve., June 24, 1967; d. Thomas Arthur and Coletta Ann (Viancourt) H. Diploma with honors, Idabelle Firestone Sch. Nsg., 1989. RN, Ohio; cert. clin. transplant coord. Staff nurse Akron (Ohio) Hosp., 1989-92, transplant coord., 1992—. Bd. dirs., drug chmn. Kidney Found. of Summit County, Akron, 1993—. Deaconess Hosp. scholar, 1988. Mem. Nat. Orgn. Transplant Coordinators, Transplant Recipient Internat. Orgn. Roman Catholic. Home: 2964 Heatherwood Ct Stow OH 44224

HOTZ, CHARLES LEROY, medical technologist; b. Burke, S.D., June 15, 1957; s. Henry Charles and Iris Myrtle (Teel) H. BS, U. S.D., 1984. Cert. lab. asst. Gregory (S.D.) Cmty. Hosp., 1977-80, U. S.D. Student Health, Vermillion, 1980-83; cert. lab. asst., med. technologist Sacred Heart Hosp.,

Yankton, S.D., 1984-85, IHS Hosp., Rosebud, S.D., 1985—; infection control coord. IHS Hosp., Rosebud, 1986—, S.D. State Infection Control Coun., Pierre, S.D., 1993-94. Mem. Am. Soc. Clin. Pathologists, S.D. Coun. Infection Control Practitioners (adv. com. 1993-94). Home: Box 2 Burke SD 57523 Office: IHS Hosp PO Box 400 Rosebud SD 57570-0400

HOU, KENNETH CHAING, biochemical engineer; b. Wousih, Peoples Republic of China, Apr. 22, 1929; came to the U.S., 1956; s. Nai-Chio and Kun-Jun Hou; m. Catherine Feng, Sept. 5, 1965; children: Howard, Salina. MS in Chem. Engrng., U. Idaho; PhD in Phys. Chemistry, U. Tex. Postdoctoral fellow Pa. State U., University Park, 1962-64, Cornell U., Ithaca, N.Y., 1964-66; sr. rsch. chemist Celanese Chem. Co., Summit, N.J., 1966-73; sr. rsch. engr. CUNO AMF Inc., Meriden, Conn., 1973-79, rsch. dir., 1979-84, 95-98, v.p. R&D, 1984—; indsl. advisor biotech. ctr. U. Conn., Storrs, 1989-91. Contbr. articles to Biochimica et Biophysica Acta, Artificial Organs, Biotechnology and Applied Biochemistry. Mem. Am. Chem. Soc., Phi Lambda Epsilon, Sigma Chi. Office: CUNO Inc 400 Research Pky Meriden CT 06450-7172

HOU, PING WEN, psychiatrist; b. Lu-Kang, Taiwan, Oct. 2, 1940; m. Tsai-Yueh Chen, Sept. 4, 1967; children: Ernest, Bernard. MD, Kaohsiung (Republic of China) Med. Coll., 1966. Intern St. Vincent's Med. Ctr. of Richmond, Staten Island, N.Y., 1968-69; resident N.Y. Med. Coll. Met. Hosp. Ctr., N.Y.C., 1969-72; attending psychiatrist Brookdale Med. Ctr., Bklyn., 1972-74, chief psychiatrist immediate treatment services, 1974-75; unit dir. Bernstein Inst.-Beth Israel Med. Ctr., N.Y.C., 1975-77; assoc. attending psychiatrist Mt. Sinai Services-City Hosp. at Elmhurst, Queens, N.Y., 1977—, dir. psychiat. emergency services, 1988—; clin. asst. prof. psychiatry Mount Sinai Sch. Medicine, N.Y.C., 1988—. Translator: Bertrand Russell's Best, 1959, The Search Within, 1967. Fellow Am. Acad. Psychoanalysts; mem. Am. Psychiat. Assn., Soc. Med. Psychoanalysts, N.Y. Acad. Sci. Office: City Hosp Ctr at Elmhurst Dept Psychiatry 79-01 Broadway Elmhurst NY 11373-1329

HOUCHIN, JOHN FREDERICK, SR., human services administrator; b. Oak Park, Ill., Nov. 1, 1945; s. O. Boyd and Mary Ruth (Schroke) H.; m. Bette Louise Arnold, July 9, 1969; children: John Jr., David Locke. AA, Kemper Mil. Sch. & Coll., Boonville, Mo., 1966; BS, Ohio State U., 1968; EdD, U. Mass., 1987. Prog. dir. Cuyahoga County Assn. Retarded Citizens, Cleve., 1973-75; resdl. dir./asst. supt. Ohio Dept. Mental Health & Retardation, Broadview Devel. Ctr, Broadview Heights, Ohio, 1975-80; reg. mental retardation coordinator Mass. Dept. Mental Health, Region IV A, Watertown, Mass., 1980-83; dir. developmental svcs. Mass. Dept. Mental Health, Belchertown State Sch., 1983-86; asst. reg. dir. Conn. Dept. Retardation, Region 6, Waterford, 1986-91; chief executive officer G.B. Cooley Svcs. for Retarded Citizens, West Monroe, La., 1991—; lectr. in field. Contbr. book: Supported Employment Implementation, 1988. Mem. state adv. coun. Conn. Dept. Rehab. Svcs., Hartford, 1988-91; mem. regional adv. coun. Region 8 Office Mental Retardation, 1992-94, chmn., 1993; mem. Monrie Beautification Bd., 1996—; mem. Twin Cities Mayors Com. on Disabled, 1994—. Cpat. U.S. Army, 1969-72. Mem. Internat. Platform Assn., Internat. Freelance Photographer Assn., Monroe C. of C., N.E. La. Camera Club (pres. 1993-94). Episcopalian. Office: GB Cooley Svcs 364 Cooley Rd West Monroe LA 71291-8800

HOUDAS, YVON JULES, physiologist, educator; b. Oran, Algeria, Mar. 8, 1932; s. Robert Henri and Josephine (Gonzalez) H.; m. Claudette Michelle Heyraud, July 17, 1958; children: Michel, Sophie, Christophe. MD, Faculty of Medicine, Lyon, France, 1956. Rsch. specialist French Air Force, Paris, 1959-66; prof. physiology Faculty of Medicine, Lille, France, 1966—, dean, 1975-78. Author: La Fonction Thermique, 1977, Human Body Temperature, 1982, Physiologie CardioVasculaire, 1990; editor: New Trends in Thermal Physiology, 1978. Office: Cardiologic Hosp, Blvd Leclercq, Lille France 59037

HOUGH, EDYTHE S. ELLISON, dean. BS in Nursing cum laude, U. Conn., 1961; MS in Psychiat. Nursing, Yale U., 1963; EdD in Early Childhood & Devel. Studies, UCLA, 1979; cert., Harvard U., 1984, Albert Einstein Med. Sch. Leadership Inst., 1984. Instr. sch. nursing U. Conn., Storrs, 1964-65; instr. sch. nursing UCLA, 1965-68, asst. prof., 1968-69; asst. prof. dept. nursing Mt. St. Mary's Coll., L.A., 1972-75; asst. prof. dept. psychosocial nursing U. Wash., Seattle, 1978-84, assoc. prof. dept. psychiatry & behavioral sci., 1984-85; fellow Harborview Med. Ctr., Seattle, 1984-85; assoc. prof., head dept. psychiat. nursing U. Ill., Chgo., 1985-86, chief psychiat. clin. svcs., 1985-86, assoc. dean acad. affairs Coll. Nursing, 1986-87, assoc. prof., 1987-88; assoc. v.p., assoc. dean Coll. Nursing Rush-Presbyn.-St. Luke's Med. Ctr., Chgo., 1988-92; assoc. dean edn. Coll. Nursing Rush Univ., 1991, prof. dept. med. nursing, 1992-93; dean, prof. Coll. Nursing Wayne State U., Detroit, 1993—; cons. Brentwood VA Hosp., L.A., 1969, Martin Luther King Hosp., L.A., 1973, Am. Inst. Rsch. Behavioral Scis., Palo Alto, Calif., 1977, YMCA Latchkey Child program, Seattle, 1978, King's Fund Ctr. King Edward's Hosp. Fund, London, 1983, Coll. Nursing Rush U., 1987; presenter in field. Contbr. articles to profl. jours. Mem. gov. bd. Cmty. Psychiat. Clinic, 1979-84, v.p., 1983-84, chair long-range planning com., 1983-84; gov. bd. Keystone Resources, 1982-84, Arbor Housing Assocs., 1983-84; mem. Wash. State Social Skills Consortium, 1983-85, Fourth Presbyn. Ch. Literacy Tutoring project, 1986-89, Women's Health Exec. Network, 1991-92, Sch. Medicine Charter Com. Ctr./Inst. Health Care Effectiveness, 1994—; bd. trustees Detroit Visiting Nurses Assn.; bd. dirs. Visiting Nurse Assn. Southeast Mich., 1993—, Greater Detroit Area Health Coun., Inc., 1993—. Recipient Nat. Rsch. Svc. award, 1978, Child Mental Health Faculty Devel. award NIMH, 1984, Women's Action New Direction award Women Healing the World, 1995; UCLA grantee, 1977. Fellow Am. Acad. Nursing; mem. NOW (Chgo. chpt.), ANA (coun. nurse rschrs., coun. nursing adminstrn.), Am. Psychiat. Nurses Assn., Ill. Orgn. Nurse Execs., Mich. Assn. Colls. Nursing (treas. 1993—), Mich. Nurses Assn., Midwest Nursing Rsch. Soc., Sigma Theta Tau, Soc. Edn. Rsch. Psychiat. Nursing, Transcultural Nursing Soc. Home: 1012 Audubon Grosse Pointe Park MI 48230 Office: Wayne State Univ Sch Nursing 112 Cohn Bldg 5557 Cass Ave Detroit MI 48202*

HOUGH, JACK VAN DOREN, otologist; b. Lone Wolf, Okla., Sept. 12, 1920; s. Chapman Ernest and Hazel (Van Doren) H.; m. Joan Ingle, Dec. 29, 1943; children: Ted Chapman, Jack Van Doren Jr., Timothy Ingle, David Alliston. BS, Southeastern State U., 1939; MD, U. Okla., 1943. Diplomate, Am. Bd. Otorhinolaryngology. Intern USN Hosp., Farragut, Idaho, 1944; resident, then fellow in otolaryngology U. Okla. Hosps., Oklahoma City, 1946-50; clin. instr. otorhinolaryngology U. Okla. Health Scis. Ctr., Oklahoma City, 1950-51; now clin. prof. otorhinolaryngology, head and neck surgery U. Okla. Health Scis. Ctr.; pvt. practice Oklahoma City, 1951—; bd. dirs. MAP Internat., Inc.; developer surg. techniques and instruments for hearing restoration and middle ear reconstrn., electromagnetic hearing devices, cochlear implants. Contbr. sci. articles and textbook chpts. to med. publs. Past ruling elder, Cen. Presbyn. Ch., Oklahoma City; founder, Covenant Community Ch. Oklahoma City, 1980, now session moderator. Decorated Bronze Star medal; recipient Presidential Unit citation, Navy Dept. citation for heroism, Harris P. Mosher award, Triologic Soc., numerous awards from profl. orgns.; inducted into Okla. Hall of Fame, 1991. Mem. AMA, Am. Bd. Otolaryngology, Am. Acad. Otolaryngology-Head and Neck Surgery, Am. Otological Soc. (past pres., award of merit), Head and Neck Surgery Am., Am. Triological Soc., Head and Neck Surgery of Am., Otosclerosis Study Group, Oklahoma County Med. Assn., Okla. Med. Assn., Okla. Acad. Medicine, Osler Soc., Am. Acad. Ophthalmologic and Otolaryngologic Allergy, Christian Med. Soc., Christian Soc. Otolaryngology (founder, pres.), Head and Neck Surgeons, MAP Internat. (founder), Otosclerosis Study Group (past pres.), Audiology Soc., Van Berkesy Soc. (past pres.), Pan-Am. Assn. Otorhinolaryngology and Bronchoesophagology, Politzer Soc., Am. Sci. Affiliation, Von Bekesy Soc., numerous other profl. orgns. Office: Hough Ear Inst 3400 NW 56th St Oklahoma City OK 73112-4452

HOUGH, MARK TAYLOR, hospital executive; b. Providence, June 3, 1949; s. William Henry and Elinor Stewart (Taylor) H.; m. Nancy Gregg O'Brien, Sept. 15, 1973; children: Alden Gregg, Randall Sayles. BA, Muhlenberg Coll., 1971; MBA, Bryant Coll., 1974. Project assn. Hosp. Assn. R.I., Providence, 1972-74; asst. adminstr. Cranston (R.I.) Gen. Hosp., 1974-76; asst. corp. adminstr. St. Joseph Hosp., North Providence, R.I., 1976-79; v.p. Providence unit St. Joseph Hosp., South Providence, R.I., 1979-84; sr. v.p. Fatima unit St. Joseph Hosp., North Providence, 1984—; sr. v.p. St. Joseph Health Svcs. R.I., 1995—; mem. R.I. Gov.'s Adv. Coun. on Cancer, 1987—; mem. faculty Salve Regina Coll., Newport, R.I., 1983—, Bryant Coll., Smithfield, R.I., 1985—. Mem. Am. Hosp. Assn., Cath. Hosp. Assn., Am. Coll. Health Care Execs. (cert., regent coun. 1986—), Health Care Mgmt. Assn. Mass., R.I. Health Care Mgmt. Assn. (bd. dirs., treas. 1983-85), Hosp. Assn. R.I., North Cen. C. of C. (bd. dirs. 1984—), Agawam Hunt Club (Rumford, R.I.), Sakonnet Golf Club (Little Compton, R.I.). Home: 243 Lincoln St Seekonk MA 02771-1715 Office: St Joseph Hosp 200 High Service Ave Providence RI 02904-5113

HOUGHLAND, PAUL, JR., association executive; b. Oakland City, Ind., Sept. 21, 1935; s. Paul and Ruth (Sumners) H.; m. Jane Stevens, Sept. 30, 1947; children: Cia Anne, Paul III. BSE, Oakland City Coll., 1958; MS, Ind. U., 1962. Cert. assn. exec. Classroom tchr. Seymour (Ind.) Cmty. Schs., 1960-70; assoc. exec. sec. Optimist Internat., St. Louis, 1970-87; exec. dir. Engring. Soc., St. Louis, 1987-88, Am. Dental Assts. Assn., Chgo., 1988-90, Opticians Assn. Am., Fairfax, Va., 1990—. Assessor, Redding Twp., Ind., 1966-70; chmn. Jackson County Red Cross, Ind., 1968-69. Cpl. U.S. Army, 1994-95, Guam. Mem. Am. Soc. Assn. Execs., NRA. Home: 9519 Stevebrook Rd Fairfax VA 22032 Office: Opticians Assn Am 10341 Democracy Ln Fairfax VA 22030

HOUGHTON, IVAN TIMOTHY, anesthesiologist; b. Leamington, England, Feb. 23, 1942; s. Arnold Cecil and Enid (Cyriax) H.; m. Teresa Wan, June 17, 1978. BA with honors, Cambridge U., 1963, MB BChir, 1966, MA, 1967; LLB with honors, London U., 1987; MD, Chinese U. Hong Kong, 1993. Cons. anesthesiologist British Mil. Hosp., Munster, 1980-81, Hong Kong, 1982-85; sr. cons. anesthesiologist British Mil. Hosp., Munster, 1985-87, Hong Kong, 1987-94; sr. cons. anesthesiologist Rinteln, 1994—; comdg. officer BMH Rinteln, 1996—; hon. lectr. Chinese U. Hong Kong, 1982-85, 87-94; clin. tutor British Mil. Hosp., Hong Kong, 1992-94. Mem. Territorial Army Vol. Res., 1960-72. Col. Royal Army Med. Corps, 1972—. Recipient Charles Box surgery prize, St. Thomas Hosp., London, 1964, Marshall Webb Mil. Adminstrn. prize and medal, 1973, Alexander prize and Gilt medal, 1989. Fellow Hong Kong Coll. Anesthesiologists; mem. British Med. Assn., Assn. Anesthesiologists, Gt. Britain and Ireland, Soc. Anesthesiologists Hong Kong, Army and Navy Club. Office: c/o Lloyds Bank, 355 Stratford Rd, Shirley B90 3BP, England

HOUK, JAMES CHARLES, physiologist, educator; b. Northville, Mich., June 3, 1939; s. James Charles and Elowene (Tower) H.; m. Antoinette Iacuzio, Dec. 28, 1963; children: Philip, Nadia, Peter. BSEE, Mich. Tech. U., 1961; MSEE, MIT, 1963; PhD, Harvard U., 1966. Instr. Harvard U. Med. Sch., 1967-69, asst. prof., 1969-73; lecturer Mass Inst. Tech., 1971-73; assoc. prof. Johns Hopkins U. Med. Sch., 1973-78; adjunct assoc prof. Univ. of North Carolina, 1975; prof., chmn. dept. physiology Northwestern Univ. Med. Sch., 1978—. Co-author: Medical Physiology 14th edit., 1980, Handbook of Physiology--The Nervous System II, 1981, Encyclopedia of Neuroscience, 1987, Models of Information Processing in the Basal Ganglia, 1995; contbr. chpts. to books. Recipient Javits award NIH, 1984-92. Mem. IEEE, AAAS, Soc. for Neurosci., Am. Physiol. Soc., European Neurosci. Assn., Assn. of Chmn. of Dept. of Physiology, Internat. Neural Network Soc. Office: Northwestern U 303 E Chicago Ave Chicago IL 60611-3008

HOUNSFIELD, GODFREY NEWBOLD, radiation scientist; b. Aug. 28, 1919; s. Thomas H. Ed., City and Guilds Coll., London; diploma, Faraday House Elec. Engring. Coll., London; M.D. (hon.), U. Basel, 1975; D.Sc. (hon.), City U., 1976, U. London, 1976; D. of Tech. (hon.), U. Loughborough, 1976; DHC, Cambridge U., 1992. Joined EMI Ltd., Hayes, Middlesex, Eng., 1951, head med. systems sect., cen. research labs., 1972-76, sr. staff scientist, 1977—; professorial fellow in imaging scis. Manchester U., 1978—. Contbr. articles to sci. jours. Recipient Nobel prize in Physiology or Medicine, 1979; MacRobert award, 1972; Wilhelm-Exner medal Austrian Indsl. Assn., 1974; Ziedses des Plantes medal Physikalishe Medizinische Gesellschaft, Würzburg, 1974; Prince Philip Medal award CGLI, 1975; ANS Radiation Industry award Ga. Inst. Tech., 1975; Lasker award Lasker Found., 1975; Duddell Bronze medal Inst. Physics, 1976; Golden Plate award Am. Acad. Achievement, 1976; Reginald Mitchell Gold medal Stoke-on-Trent Assn. Engrs., 1976; Churchill Gold medal, 1976; Gairdner Found. award, 1976; decorated comdr. Order Brit. Empire, 1976, knight, 1981. Fellow Royal Soc. Office: Thorn EMI Research Labs, Dawley Rd, Hayes Middlesex UB3 1HH, England*

HOUPT, JEFFREY LYLE, psychiatrist, educator; b. Phila., Aug. 13, 1941; s. H. Lyle and Elizabeth (McAlpine) H.; m. Corinne A. Anderson, Dec. 28, 1964; children—Brian Jeffrey, Eric Robert. B.S. in Zoology, Wheaton Coll., 1963; M.D., Baylor Coll. Medicine, 1967. Diplomate Am. Bd. Psychiatry and Neurology. Intern Boston City Hosp., 1967-68; resident in psychiatry Yale U., New Haven, 1968-71; staff med. officer Oak Knoll Naval Hosp., Oakland, Calif., 1971-73; adj. asst. prof. psychiatry Presbyn. Hosp., San Francisco, 1973-75; asst. prof. to prof. psychiatry Duke Med. Ctr., Durham, N.C., 1975-83; prof. psychiatry, chmn. dept. Emory U. Sch. Medicine, Atlanta, 1983-90, dean Sch. Medicine, 1988-96. Author: The Importance of Mental Health Services for General Health Care, 1979; contbr. articles to med. jours. Served to lt. comdr. USN, 1971-73. Fellow Am. Coll. Psychiatry (1st v.p.), Am. Psychiat. Assn. Home: 3612 Tuxedo Rd NW Atlanta GA 30305-1047 Office: Emory U Sch Medicine 408 Woodruff Health Scis Ctr 1440 Clifton Rd NE Atlanta GA 30307-1053

HOUPT, WAYNE EDISON, JR., psychiatrist; b. L.A., Jan. 16, 1951; s. Wayne E. Sr. and Winifred E. (Metzler) H. BS, Georgetown U., 1973; BA in Chemistry, Wright State U., Dayton, Ohio, 1976; MD, U. Ctrl. del Este, San Pedro, Dominican Republic, 1980. Lic. physician, Ohio. Intern Met. Gen. Hosp., Cleve., 1981-82; resident psychiatry Cleve. Clinic, 1983-87; asst. med. dir. psychiat. emergency rm. St. Vincent-Charity Hosp., Cleve., 1987-91; asst. med. dir. Lake County Mental Health Ctr., Mentor, Ohio, 1988-95; med. dir. N.E. Mental Health Ctr., Cleve., 1996—. Office: NE Mental Health Ctr 15735 Euclid Ave Cleveland OH 44112

HOURANI, LAUREL LOCKWOOD, epidemiologist; b. Carmel, Calif., Sept. 10, 1950; d. Eugene Franklin and Katherine Ruth (Miller) Betz; m. Ghazi Fayez Hourani, Feb. 28, 1984; children: Nathan, Danna, Lisa. BA, Chico State U., 1977; MPH, Am. Univ. Beirut, 1983; PhD, U. Pitts., 1990. Prog. evaluator Community Hosp. Monterey Peninsula, Carmel, Calif., 1978-81; instr./researcher Am. Univ. Beirut, 1981-85; predoctoral fellow U. Pitts., 1985-89; researcher, cons. V.A. Med. Ctr., Pitts., 1988-90; dir., tumor registry Med. Ctr. U. Calif. Irvine, Orange, 1990-92; epidemiologist Naval Health Rsch. Ctr., San Diego, 1993-95; head divsn. health scis., 1995—; cons. Nat. Devel. Commn. South Lebanon, 1981-83. Author: No Water, No Peace, 1985; contbr. articles to profl. jours. Bd. dirs. Am. for Justice in Middle East, Beirut, 1982-85, Nat. Devel. Com., South Lebanon, 1983-85. Recipient grant V.A., Pitts., 1989, rsch. grant U. Rsch. Bd., Beirut, 1985. Mem. Am. Psychol. Assn., Am. Pub. Health Assn., Soc. for Epidemiologic Rsch. Office: Naval Health Rsch Ctr Divsn Epidemiology PO Box 85122 San Diego CA 92186-5122

HOUSE, JAMES STEPHEN, social psychologist, educator; b. Phila., Jan. 27, 1944; s. James Jr. and Virginia Miller (Sturgis) H.; m. Wendy Fisher, May 13, 1967; children: Jeff, Erin. BA, Haverford Coll., 1965; PhD, U. Mich., 1972. From. instr. to assoc. prof. sociology Duke U., Durham, N.C., 1970-78; assoc. prof. sociology/assoc. rsch. scientist Survey Rsch. U. Mich., Ann Arbor, 1978-82, assoc. chair dept. sociology, 1981-84, prof. sociology, rsch. scientist Survey Rsch. Ctr., 1982—, chair dept. sociology, 1986-90, dir. Survey Rsch. Ctr., Inst. Social Rsch., 1991—. Author: Work Stress and Social Support, 1981; co-editor: Sociological Perspectives on Social Psychology, 1995; assoc. editor Social Psychology Quar., 1988-91 N.Am. editor Work and Stress, 1985-88; contbr. articles to profl. jours., chpt. to book. Guggenheim fellow, 1986-87. Fellow AAAS, Soc. Behavioral Medicine; mem. Am. Sociol. Assn., Acad. Behavioral Medicine Rsch., Soc. for Psychol. Study of Social Issues, Soc. for Epidemiol. Rsch. Office: Univ Mich Inst Social Rsch PO Box 1248 Ann Arbor MI 48106-1248

HOUSE, KAREN SUE, nursing consultant; b. San Francisco, July 16, 1958; d. Mathas Dean and Marilyn Frances (Weigand) H. Casa Loma Coll., 1985; AS in Nursing, SUNY at Albany, 1987. Psychiat. charge nurse Woodview Calabasas (Calif.) Hosp., 1985-87, Treatment Ctrs. Am., Van Nuys, Calif., 1987-88; cons., RN Valley Village Devel. Ctr., Reseda, Calif., 1988; plastic surg. nurse George Sanders, M.D., Encino, Calif., 1986—; nurse New Image Found., 1989—, Mid Valley Youth Ctr., 1991—; dir. nursing Encino Surgicenter (Sanders), 1992—; dir. nursing Devel. Tng. Svcs. for Devel. Disabled, 1988—; nurse cons. New Horizons for Developmentally Disabled, 1993. Instr., vol. ARC. Recipient Simi Valley Free Clinic Scholarship. Mem. Encino C. of C. Home: 29748 Saguaro St Santa Clarita CA 91384-3567 Office: 16633 Ventura Blvd Ste 110 Encino CA 91436-1834

HOUSE, STEPHEN LAWRENCE, surgeon; b. Atlanta, Apr. 1, 1944; s. Earl Lawrence and Grace Ruth (Moore) H.; m. Alice Arias, June 29, 1970 (div. Aug. 10, 1980); children: Stephen, Peter; m. Diane Zimmerman, Oct. 26, 1984; children: Christopher, Jessica, Meredith. AB, Hamilton Coll., 1965; MD, McGill U., 1969. Diplomate Am. Bd. Surgery, Am. Bd. Thoracic Surgery. Surgeon Blessing Hosp., Quincy, Ill., 1982-86, Charleston (W.Va.) Area Med. Ctr., 1986-87, Sarah Bush Lincoln Health Care Ctr., Matton, Ill., 1987—. Lt. comdr. USN, 1975-77. Fellow ACS, Alpha Omega Alpha, Phi Beta Kappa, Am. Coll. Chest Physicians; mem. Soc. for Clin. Vascular Surgery. Democrat. Presbyterian. Home: 20 S Country Club Rd Matton IL 61938 Office: Coles County Surg Assn 104 Profl Pla Matton IL 61938

HOUSEL, CYNTHIA ANNE, osteopath; b. Charleroi, Pa., Jan. 28, 1962; d. Edward Joseph and Annette Joan (Hetzel) Poska; m. James Edward Housel, Oct. 19, 1991. BS, U. Pitts., 1984; DO, U. Osteo. Medicine, Des Moines, 1988. Intern Detroit Osteo. Hosp., BiCounty Cmty. Hosp., 1988-89, resident in internal medicine, 1989-92, chief resident, 1991-92; staff physician Mt. Clemens (Mich.) Gen. Hosp., 1992—; ptnr. MaComb Internal Medicine Assocs., P.C., Clinton Twp., Mich., 1995—; chmn. critical path steering com., Mt. Clemens, 1994-96; physician advisor Older Adult Svcs., Mt. Clemens, 1992—. Mem. Am. Coll. Osteo. Internists, Mich. Assn. Osteo. Physicians and Surgeons, Am. Osteo. Assn., MaComb County Osteo. Soc. Roman Catholic. Office: MaComb Internal Medicine Assocs PC 15520 19 Mile Rd Ste 480 Clinton Township MI 48038

HOUSER, BETTY JEAN, public health nurse consultant; b. Knoxville, July 20, 1959; d. Lannie and Dorothy Jean (Wolfenbarger) Owens; m. Roger Douglas Houser, May 19, 1995. Diploma in Nursing, East Tenn. Bapt. Hosp., 1980. Staff nurse East Tenn. Bapt. Hosp., Knoxville, 1980-81, Ft. Sanders Med. Ctr., Knoxville, 1981-83, U. Tenn. Med. Ctr., Knoxville, 1983-88; health adminstr. Knoxville Cmty. Svc. Ctr., 1988-90; dir. nursing Tenn. Prison for Women, Nashville, 1990-91; staff devel. coord. Tenn. State Prison, Nashville, 1991-92; quality improvement coord. Deberry Spl. Needs Facility, Nashville, 1992-94; state quality improvement coord. Tenn. Dept. Corrections, Nashville, 1994-95; pub. health nurse cons. Tenn. Dept. Health, Knoxville, 1995—. Elem. grade Sunday sch. tchr. West End United Meth. Ch., Nashville, 1991-95, worker Christmas Bazaar Booth, 1991-93; mem. ch. orgn. tng. Nashville Together, 1993-95. Recipient Nursing award ARC, 1980, Cert. of Appreciation, Tenn. Dept. Corrections, 1994. Mem. Nat. Assn. Health Care Quality (cert. profl. health care quality), Tenn. State Employee Assn. (bd. dirs. 1991, plaque 1993), Assn. for Practitioners in Infection Control, Tenn. Pub. Health Assn. Office: Tennessee Dept Health East Tenn Regional Office 1522 Cherokee Trail Knoxville TN 37920

HOUSER, HAROLD BYRON, epidemiologist; b. North Liberty, Ind., Nov. 22, 1921; s. Edgar Allen and Gladys Chloe (Stillson) H.; m. Clara Jane Goin, Sept. 18, 1944; children: Cristene, Edgar, John, Susan, James. A.B., Ind. U., 1942, M.D., 1944. Intern U.S. Marine Hosp., New Orleans, 1944-45; resident Crile VA Hosp., Cleve., 1947-49; asst. prof. medicine SUNY, Syracuse, 1952-58; asst. prof. medicine and community health Case Western Res. U., 1958-64, assoc. prof., 1965-74, prof. epidemiology, 1974-92, prof. emeritus, 1992—, chmn. dept. biometry, 1975-85, chmn. dept. epidemiology and biostats., 1985-92; cons. in field. Contbr. numerous articles to profl. jours. Served with U.S. Army, 1945-47, 49-52. Recipient Group Lasker award Am. Pub. Health Assn., 1954, Disting. Civilian award Dept. Def., 1973. Fellow Infectious Diseases Soc.; mem. Am. Epidemiol. Soc. (pres. 1991). Home: 10409 E Windflower Ct Sun Lakes AZ 85248-9289

HOUSTON, FRANK MATT, dermatologist; b. New Orleans, Dec. 15, 1939; s. Matt Francis and Amanda Vallie (Welch) H.; m. Helen Butler, Apr. 24, 1965; children: F. Matt, Catherine E.C., Amanda J.B. BS, La. State U., 1960, MD, 1964. Diplomate Am. Bd. Dermatology. Intern Johns Hopkins U., Balt., resident; physician, dermatologist Greensboro (N.C.) Dermatology Assocs., 1970—; cons. Moses H. Cone Hosp., Greensboro, N.C., Wesley Long Hosp. Greensboro, 1970—; asst clin. prof. dermatology U. N.C. Sch. of Medicine, Chapel Hill, 1980—. Bd. dirs. Greensboro Hist. Mus., Greensboro Preservation Soc., Greensboro Symphony Soc., Greensboro Opera Co. Capt. U.S. Army, 1965-71. Fellow Am. Acad. Dermatology; mem. AMA. N.C. Soc. Medicine, Royal Coll. of Physicians, Am. Coll. Physicians, Am. Skin Assn., Greensboro City Club. Republican. Episcopalian. Office: Greensboro Dermatology 1030 Professional Village Greensboro NC 27401

HOUSTON, WILLIAM ROBERT MONTGOMERY, ophthalmic surgeon; b. Mansfield, Ohio, Nov. 13, 1922; s. William T. and Frances (Hursh) H.; B.A., Oberlin Coll., 1944; M.D., Western Res. U., 1948; m. Marguerite LaBau Browne, Apr. 25, 1968; children: William Erling Tenney, Marguerite Elisabeth LaBau, Selby Cabot Truitt Vanderbilt. Intern, Meth. Hosp. Bklyn., 1948-49, Ill. Eye and Ear Infirmary, Chgo., 1949-50; resident N.Y. Eye and Ear Infirmary, 1950-52; practice medicine specializing in ophthalmic surgery, Mansfield, 1952—; fellow retinal vascular disease NYU, 1968-69; mem. staffs Mansfield Gen. Hosp., Peoples Hosp., Mansfield, N.Y. U. Bellevue Med. Center, N.Y.C.; assoc. prof. clin. ophthalmology N.Y. U. Sch. Medicine. Pres. Mansfield Symphony Soc., 1965-68, Mansfield Civic Music Assn., 1965; mem. Mansfield City Sch. Bd., 1962-65, v.p., 1965. Served to capt. M.C. USAF, 1952-55. Diplomate Am. Bd. Ophthalmology. Recipient Honor award Acad. Ophthalmology. Fellow Internat. Coll. Surgeons; mem. SR (color guard 1961-71), Nat. Geneal. Soc. (award of Merit), Ohio Hist. Soc. (life), Western Res. Hist. Soc. (life fellow), N.Y. Geneal. and Biog. Soc. (life), Ohio Geneal. Soc. (trustee 1955—). Editor, Ohio Records and Pioneers Families, 1970—. Address: 456 Park Ave W Mansfield OH 44906-3118

HOUTS, LARRY LEE, osteopathic medicine educator; b. Three Rivers, Mich., Oct. 1, 1942; s. Elmer S. and Hilma M. (Pulver) H.; m. Karen Anne Priddle, Apr. 28, 1973; children: Willem Paul, Carrie Rena. BA in Zoology, Rockford (Ill.) Coll., 1964; MS in Biology, Fla. State U., 1966; PhD, SUNY, Albany, 1976; DO, West Va. Sch. Osteo. Medicine, 1986. Instr. Winthrop Coll., Rock Hill, S.C., 1966-69; rsch. assoc. VA Hosp., Albany, N.Y., 1974-76; asst. prof. Bethany (W.Va.) Coll., 1976-81, Wheeling (W.Va.) Coll., 1981-82; intern Garden City (Mich.) Osteopathic Hosp., 1986-87; resident in internal medicine Garden City Hosp.; pvt. practice, Three Rivers, Mich., 1988-95; assoc. prof. family practice W.Va. Sch. Osteo. Medicine, Lewisburg, 1995—; cons. East Cen. Coll. Consortium, Alliance, Ohio, 1979; presenter, lectr. in field. Coun. mem. Town Council, Bethany, W.Va., 1978-80; elder 1st Presbyn. Ch., Three Rivers, 1989. Mem. Sigma Sigma Phi Osteo. Honor Soc., Sigma Xi. Office: WVa Sch Osteo Medicine Clinic 400 N Lee St Lewisburg WV 24901

HOVENGA, TRENT LAVERN, surgeon; b. Estherville, Iowa, July 29, 1958; s. LaVern Bernard and Jeradine Marian (Laidig) H.; m. Lisa Marie Borkowski, May 20, 1983; children: Bard Parker, Claire Marie, Hunter Halsted, Madeline Kay. AB, Washington U., St. Louis, 1980; MD, U. Iowa, 1984. Commd. 2d lt. U.S. Army, 1980, advanced through grades to maj., 1990; gen. surgery resident Fitzsimons Army Med. Ctr., Aurora, Colo., 1984-89; staff surgeon Landstuhl (Germany) Army Regional Med. Ctr., 1989—, Evans Army Community Hosp., Fort Carson, Colo., 1992—. Fellow ACS. Republican. Presbyterian. Home and Office: 110 Rugely Ct Colorado Springs CO 80906-5954

HOVEY, LESLIE MORRIS, plastic surgeon, educator; b. Anaheim, Calif., Aug. 6, 1936; s. Morris and Georgia M. (Guss) H.; m. Loretta (Szluk) Hovey, June 8, 1963; children: Kevin A., Christopher A., Jason D., Justin D. BA in Physiology, U. Calif., Berkeley, 1959; MD, George Washington

U., 1963. Diplomate Am. Bd. Surgery, Am. Bd. Plastic Surgery. Intern Tripler Army Med. Ctr., Hawaii, 1963-64, surgery resident, 1964-68; commdg. officer 43rd Surgical Hosp., Korea, 1968-69; fellow head & neck surgery Walte Reed Army Med. Ctr., Washington, 1969-70; resident plastic surgery U. Miami Sch. of Medicine, Fla., 1971-72; plastic surgeon U.S. Army, 1972-76; pvt. practice San Francisco, 1977-87; clinical assoc. prof. plastic surgery Stanford U., Palo Alto, Calif., 1987—; chief of staff St. Francis Med. Hosp., San Francisco, 1985-87; bd. dirs. Plastic Surgery Ednl. Found., Chgo., 1986-92. Mem. of surgical teams to fgn. countries Reconstructive Surgery Found., 1977—. U.S. Army Res. Fellow ACS; mem. Am. Soc. Plastic & Reconstructive Surgery, Am. Burn Assn., Calif. Soc. Plastic Surgery, Soc. Head & Neck Surgeons, Santa Clara County Med. Assn. Office: Santa Clara Vly Med Ctr Divsn Plastic Surgery 751 S Bascom Ave San Jose CA 95128

HOVIJITRA, SUTEERA TANTITEERACHART, dentist, researcher; b. Bangkok, Aug. 3, 1944; came to U.S., 1972; d. Tienchai and Sae I. Tantiteerachart; m. Chamnan Hovijitra, Aug. 15, 1972; children: Ray S., Norman T. DDS cum laude, Mahidol U., 1968, postgrad. cert., 1970; MSD, Ind. U., 1976, DDS, 1981. Diplomate Am. Bd. Prosthodontics. Instr. Mahidol U., Bangkok, 1970-72; grad. asst. Ind. U., Indpls., 1972-74, asst. prof., 1974-76; asst. prof. U. Ky., Lexington, 1976-79; assoc. prof. Ind. U. Sch. Dentistry, Indpls., 1979—; vis. prof. Chiangmai (Thailand) U., Prince Songkla U., Chulalongkorn U., Thailand. Fellow Am. Coll. Prosthodontists; mem. Am. Acad. Fixed Prosthodontics, West Side Study Club, Ind. U. Alumni Assn., John F. Johnston Soc. (pres. 1994). Home: 4504 Hidden Orchard Ln Indianapolis IN 46208-3025 Office: 3750 Guion Rd Indianapolis IN 46222-1669 also: Ind U Dental Sch 1121 W Michigan St Indianapolis IN 46202-5211

HOVNANIAN, H. PHILIP, biomedical engineer; b. Aleppo, Syria; s. Philip and Rosa (Jebejian) H.; m. Siran Norian, June 10, 1948; children: Rosemary Janice, Joan Anita, John Philip. B.S., Am. U., Beirut, 1942, postgrad., 1945-47; postgrad., Brown U., 1947-49; M.S., State Coll., Boston, 1951; Ph.D., U. Beverly Hills, Calif. Registered profl. engr., N.Y., Mass.; chartered physicist (U.K.). Prin. investigator, rsch. grant Nat. Heart Inst., NIH; faculty dept. physics Am. U., Beirut, 1942-47, Brown U., 1947-49; sr. engr. Western Electric Co., Haverhill, Mass., 1951-52; asst. chief engr. Calidyne Co., Winchester, Mass., 1952-54; sr. physicist, project head, asst. rsch. dir. Boston Electronics div. Norden-Ketay Corp., 1954-56; ptnr., R & D dir. physics Neutronics Rsch. Co., Waltham, Mass., 1956-58; sr. staff scientist Avco Corp., 1958, dir. med. sci. dept., 1959-66; mgr. lunar biosci. NASA, Washington, 1966-67; mgr. biomed. engring. and biophysics Kollsman Instrument Corp., Syosset, N.Y., 1967-68; v.p., dir. biomed. products Cavitron Corp. (and its successors Cooper Lasersonics, Cooper Med. Corp., Cooper Vision, Inc.), 1969-85; dir. scientific devel. Vital Signs Inc., Totowa, N.J., 1990—; corp. dir. Vital Signs Corp.; v.p. rsch. Sonokinetics Inc., Hoboken, N.J.; cons. rsch. scientist BEI Med. Sys., Hackensack, N.J., 1993—; cons. Parkell Co., Farmingdale, N.Y., 1996—; guest lectr. biomed. engring. Northeastern U., MIT-Harvard Study Group on Biomed. Engring.; rsch. assoc. in surg. rsch. Lahey Clinic Found.; mem. workshop interaction between industry and biomed. engring. NAE; former mem. ob-gyn. devices panel and panels on ophthalmic, ear, nose and throat devices and dental devices FDA. Contbr. tech. papers to profl. jours.; patentee in field. Trustee Haigazian U. Coll. of Beirut, Lebanon. Fellow Inst. Physics (chartered, Brit.), Am. Soc. Laser Med. and Surgery, Am. Acad. Dental Electrosurgery (hon.); mem. Optical Soc. Am., Am. Inst. Physics, IEEE (life mem., profl. group engring. biology and medicine), Internat. Fedn. Med. Electronics, Biomed. Engring. Soc., Rsch. Soc. Am., Internat. Microscopy Assn., Am. Inst. Ultrasound in Medicine, Am. Soc. Microbiology, N.Y. Acad. Scis., AAAS, Assn. for Advancement Med. Instrumentation, Am. Dental Trade Assn. (stds. & materials) ADA (standards coms. dental UV curing lights and electrosurgery devices), Am. Inst. Biol. Scis., Armenian Missionary Assn. of Am. (pres. and/or chmn. bd. dirs.), Sigma Xi. Congregationalist (United Ch. of Christ) (chmn. bd. trustees, deacon, moderator). Lodge: Masons. Home and Office: Unit 1B 3902 Manhattan College Pky Bronx NY 10471-3924

HOWARD, CECIL BYRON, pediatrician; b. Wallins, Ky., Apr. 16, 1927; s. William Knott and Maggie (Cawood) H.; m. Rebekah Ann Buckley, Mar. 4, 1931; children: Mark Byron, Sally Ann Howard Truxal, Maggie Elizabeth Howard Ray. BA, Vanderbilt U., 1949, MD, 1953. Intern U. Va. Hosp., Charlottesville, 1953-54; resident U. Tex. Med. Br., Galveston, 1954-56; pediatrician pvt. practice, Maryville, Tenn., 1956-95. Dir. Christian Ch. Found. Handicapped, 1983-95; elder 1st Christian Ch., Maryville, 1961-96. With U.S. Army, 1945-47. Fellow Am. Acad. Pediatrics; mem. Blount County Med. Soc. (pres. 1973), Maryville Optimist Club (pres. 1973). Republican. Office: 849 E Lamar Alexander Pky Maryville TN 37804-5013

HOWARD, CLIFTON MERTON, psychiatrist; b. Quincy, Mass., Aug. 11, 1922; s. Clifton Merton and Ruth Gilkey (Henderson); m. Margaret Carroll, June 16, 1951 (div. Aug. 1964); children: Kristen, Lauren, Siri; m. Susan D. Krex., May 30, 1965; children: Michael Scott, Jonathan, Robert. SB, Harvard U., 1944, AM, 1947; MD, Columbia U., 1963. Diplomate Am. Bd. Med. Examiners. Rsch. physicist divsn. of Atomic Energy Com. Brookhaven Nat. Lab., 1947-48; founder Waveforms, Inc., 1951-53; pres., chief exec. officer Electronic Workshop, Inc., 1951-59, Sound Workshop, Inc. and E.W. Assocs., Inc., 1953-59; intern Mt. Sinai Hosp., N.Y.C., 1963-64; psychiat. resident Columbia-Presbyn. Med. Ctr., 1964-65, N.Y. State Psychiat. Inst., N.Y.C., 1965-66; sr. psychiat. resident Drug Rsch. Svc., 1966-67; dir. evening Psychiat. Clinic, Mt. Carmel Guild, Union City, N.J., 1964-67; asst. attending psychiatrist Vanderbilt Clinic, Columbia Presbyn. Med. Ctr., 1969-75; cons. in psychiatry Columbia Presbyn. Med. Ctr., 1969-75, assoc. attending psychiatrist, psychiat. drug rsch. unit, 1971-75; pvt. practice N.Y.C., 1967—, N.J., 1980—; instr. engring. dept., Harvard Coll., 1946; instr. physics dept. CCNY, 1948-50, NYU, 1948-54, instr. psychiatry dept. Columbia Coll. of P&S, 1967-71, assoc. in psychiatry dept., 1971-75. Staff writer APPLE computer mag., 1982-85; founder, pres., CEO S&H Software, Inc.; Apple computer cert. software developer lic. to Reader's Digest, D.C. Heath Co., John T. Wiley & Sons, and others. Lt. USNR, 1943-46, PTO. Mem. APA, Ams. of Armorial Ancestry, Ancient and Hon. Artillery Co. of Mass., Baronial Order of Magna Charta, Flagon and Trencher, Gen. Soc. Mayflower Descs. (surgeon gen. N.J. soc. 1978-84), Nat. Geneal. Soc., New Eng. Hist. and Geneal. Soc., Old Bridgewater Hist. Soc., Order Founders and Patriots of Am., Order of the Crown of Charlemagne, Soc. Descs. of Colonial Clergy, Soc. Ams. Royal Descent, Descs. of Illegitimate Sons and Daus. of Kings and Queens of England (aka Royal Bastard Soc.), Soc. Colonial Wars, Sons of Revolution, SAR. Home: 105 Lakeview Dr Old Tappan NJ 07675-7065 Office: 300 Central Park W Ste 1K New York NY 10024-1513

HOWARD, HOMER LAMAR, JR., medical clinic administrator; b. Greenwood, Miss., May 11, 1939; s. Homer Lamar and Inez (Bailey) H.; m. Linda Lee Covington, Mar. 15, 1969; children: Lisa Anne, Homer Lamar III. BA, U. Miss., 1962; MBA, Miss. Coll., 1970. Project dir. family planning U. Miss. Med. Ctr., Jackson, 1970-74; health maintenance orgn. dir. Mercy Hosp., Vicksburg, Miss., 1974; adminstr. Smith County Gen. Hosp., Raleigh, Miss., 1974-76; dist. adminstr. Miss. State Bd. Health, Greenville, 1976-78; adminstr. Gamble Bros. and Archer Clinic P.A., Greenville, 1978—. Active Delta coun. Greenville United Way; bd. dirs. Chickasaw Coun., Boy Scouts Am., Memphis; adminstrv. bd. 1st United Meth. Ch. Lt. USN, 1961-67, comdr. USNR, 1989, ret. Mem. Med. Group Mgmt. Assn., Am. Coll. Med. Practice Exec., Am. Assn. Med. Assts., Navy Res. Assn., Am. Acad. Med. Adminstrs., Med. Group Mgmt. Assn. of Miss., Res. Officer Assn., Am. Legion. Greenville C. of C., Pi Kappa Alpha. Home: 1526 Woodcrest Cv Greenville MS 38701-6935 Office: Gamble Bros and Archer Clinic 344 Arnold Ave PO Box 1277 Greenville MS 38701

HOWARD, JAMES LAWRENCE, psychiatric scientist, researcher; b. Glen Ellyn, Ill., Nov. 30, 1941; s. Ralph Orson and June Virginia (Underwood) H.; m. Judith Anne Bennett, Aug. 25, 1963; children: David Lawrence, Erin Kendra. BA, U. N.C., 1963; MS, Tulane U., 1966, PhD, 1968. Asst. prof. psychiatry dept. U. N.C., Chapel Hill, 1968-74; sr. rsch. scientist Burroughs Wellcome Co., Research Triangle Park, N.C., 1974-95; sr. ptnr. Howard Assocs., Research Triangle Park, N.C., 1995—; adj. prof. N.C. State U., Raleigh, 1978—; sci. cons. N.C. Alcohol Rsch. Authority, Chapel Hill, 1975-89. Contbr. 11 chpts. to books, over 130 articles to profl. jours. NDEA fellow, 1964-68. Fellow APA (coun. rep. 1985-87), Am. Psychol. Soc.; mem. Soc. Stimulus Properties of Drugs (pres. 1983-84), Soc. for Neuroscis., Am. Soc. Pharmacology and Exptl. Therapeutics, Carolina Sailing Club (sec.-treas. 1990-93, commodore 1994). Republican. Presbyterian. Home: 8240 Morrow Mill Rd Chapel Hill NC 27516-7397 Office: Howard Assocs MCB/HLB Complex Box 12195 Rsch Triangle Inst Research Triangle Pk NC 27709

HOWARD, JED LEE, ophthalmologist; b. N.Y.C., Jan. 4, 1934; s. Leo and Claire Lee (Fischer) H.; m. Mary Ellen Ford, July 18, 1971; children: Jed Lee Jr., Karen Rachel, Michael David. BA, Johns Hopkins U., 1954; MD, Harvard Med. Sch., 1959. Diplomate Am. Bd. Ophthalmology. Intern U. Oreg., Portland, 1960-62; resident in ophthalmology Mass. Eye & Ear, Boston, 1963-64; asst. prof. Baylor U. Coll. Med., Houston, 1966—; pvt. practice Pasadena, Tex.; dir. Infocus, Houston; pres. Sightsavers of Tex., Houston. Dir. Orton Dyslexia Soc., Houston. Maj. USAF, 1963-65. USPHS fellow, 1956-57. Mem. Am. Acad. Ophthalmology, Tex. Med. Assn., Harris County Med. Soc., Houston Ophthal. Soc. (past pres.). Home: 5218 Braesheather Houston TX 77096 Office: 4018 Fairmont Pkwy Pasadena TX 77504

HOWARD, JOHN MALONE, surgeon, educator; b. Autaugaville, Ala., Aug. 25, 1919; s. Fontaine Maury and Mary Lorena (O'Brien) H.; m. Nina Lyman Abernathy, Dec. 22, 1943; children: John Malone Jr., Robert Fontaine, Nina Louise, George Glenn, Susan Elaine, Laura Leigh. BS, Birmingham So., 1941; MD, U. Pa., 1944. Resident in surgery U. Pa., 1945-50; mem. faculty Baylor U., Houston, 1950-55; prof., chmn. Emory U., Atlanta, 1955-57; chair surgery Hahnemann Med. Coll., Phila., 1958-62; dir. emergency med. svcs. Med. Coll. Ohio, Toledo, Ohio, 1974-78, prof. surgery, 1974—; pvt. practice surgery Toledo, 1990-95; dir. U.S. army surg. rsch. team Korean War. Editor: Studies of Battle Casualties in Korea, vol. III, 1953, vol. I, 1955, vol. II, 1955, vol. IV, 1955 (with others) Surgical Diseases of the Pancreas, 1960, 2nd edit., 1996, The Chemistry of Trauma, 1963, Cardiovascular Surgery-Supplement to Circulation, 1963, Septic Shock. Clinical and Experimental Experiences, 1964, Studies of Ultraviolet Irradiation: Its Efficiency in Preventing Infections in Operative Wounds, 1964; contbr. chpts. to books, more than 400 articles to profl. jours. Capt. U.S. Army Med. Corps., 1951-53. Decorated Legion of Merit; recipient Distinction award Nat. Rsch. Coun., Disting. Achievement award Am. Trauma Soc. Mem. Royal Coll. Surgeons Edinburgh (hon.), Brazilian Coll. Surgeons (fgn.). Home: 11004 Winslow Rd Whitehouse OH 43571

HOWARD, KENNETH IRWIN, psychology educator; b. Chgo., Oct. 19, 1932; s. Simon and Florence (Bergman) H.; m. Michele R. Krauss, Oct. 1, 1995; children by previous marriage: Deborah, Peter, Lisa, David, Rebecca, Matthew. BA, U. Calif., Berkeley, 1954; PhD, U. Chgo., 1959. Prof. psychology Northwestern U., Evanston, Ill., 1967—. Contbr. over 150 articles to profl. publs.; author 5 books in field. 1st lt. U.S. Army, 1954-56. NIMH rsch. scientist, 1991-96; recipient Disting. Rsch. Career award Soc. for Psychotherapy Rsch., 1991. Recipient Disting. Contbn. Profession Psychology Ill. Psychol. Assn., 1994, Disting. Profl. Contbns. Knowledge award APA, 1995. Democrat. Jewish. Office: Northwestern U Dept Psychology Evanston IL 60208

HOWARD, KEVIN L., osteopath; b. Big Rapids, Mich., Dec. 3, 1962; s. Darroll Z. and Sally K. (Korhonen) H.; m. Mary C. Lee, July 28, 1984; children: Amy L., Ashley E. BS, U. Mich., 1985; DO, Mich. State U., 1996. CLU, ChFC, Pa. Agt. The Equitable, East Lansing, Mich., 1985-90, asst. mgr., 1990-92; owner Advanced Benefit Concepts, East Lansing, 1990-92; intern Mich. Capital Med. Ctr., Lansing, 1996—. Sunday Sch. tchr., East Lansing, 1995-96. Mem. Am. Osteo. Assn., Mich. Assn. Osteo. Physicians and Surgeons.

HOWARD, MARK W., surgeon; b. San Jose, Calif., Mar. 7, 1959; s. Berwyn Jones and Anne Linnea (Madsen) Howard-Kwder; m. Kristina M. Athanas, Aug. 25, 1986; children: Mark Christopher, Tyler Joseph Berwyn. AB in Physiology, U. Calif., Berkeley, 1981; MD, Harvard Med. Sch., 1985. Diplomate Am. Bd. Orthopedic Surgery. Intern, resident UCLA Med. Ctr., Torrance, Calif., 1985-90; fellowship in spinal surgery UCLA Med. Ctr., Westwood, Calif., 1990-91; active staff Community Hosp. of Monterey Peninsula, Monterey, Calif., Salinas Valley Meml. Hosp., Calif. Contbr. articles to profl. jours. and publs. Mem. AMA, Am. Acad. Orthopaedic Surgeons, N.Am. Spine Soc., Calif. Med. Assn., Calif. Orthopaedic Assn., Monterey County Med. Assn., Phi Beta Kappa.

HOWARD, RICHARD RALSTON, II, medical health advisor, researcher, financier; b. Winnfield, Kans., May 26, 1948; s. Richard Ralston and Ione (Mayer) H. BBA, Loyola U., New Orleans, 1970; MPH, Tulane U., 1977, MS, 1984, DrPH, 1988. Researcher Loyola U., 1973; educator Dominican Coll., New Orleans, 1977; educator Sch. Pub. Health Tulane U., New Orleans, 1978-82, researcher Sch. Medicine, 1979-88; med. health advisor Howard Med. Clinic, Slidell, La., 1982-91; founder The Inst. Econ. Tech. Rsch., New Orleans, 1993—. NIH grantee, 1979; VA grantee, 1984. Mem. Internat. Platform Assn., Am. Assn. Individual Investors, Beta Beta Beta. Home: 3531 Nashville Ave New Orleans LA 70125-4339

HOWARD, RONALD EUGENE, chaplain; b. Fairfield, Ala., Aug. 5, 1955; s. Forney Talent and Merry Alma (Grubbs) H.; m. Deborah Sue Tennyson, June 7, 1975; children: Melissa Diane, Jonathan Blake. BA, Samford U., Birmingham, 1977; MDiv, Southeastern Sem., Wake Forest, N.C., 1981. Chaplain resident Bapt. Med. Ctrs., Birmingham, 1981-82; dir. pastoral care and social svc. BMC Cherokee, Centre, Ala., 1982-86; chaplain Golden Triangle Reg. Med. Ctr., Columbus, Miss., 1986-88; chaplain/pastoral counselor DCH Reg. Med. Ctr., Tuscaloosa, Ala., 1988—. Bd. dirs. Cherokee-Etowah-DeKalb Reg. Alcoholism Coun., Gadsden, Ala., 1984-86; pres. Coun. Community & Health Svcs., Centre, 1983-86; advisor County Multidisciplinary Child Protective Team, Centre, 1984-86; dir. Camp Bluebird Adult Cancer Camp, Tuscaloosa, 1989—; chmn. Rural Devel. Com., Centre, 1985. Lt. USN, 1987—. Mem. Civitans Internat., Am. Assn. Clin. Pastoral Edn. Democrat. Baptist. Office: DCH Regional Med Ctr 809 University Blvd E Tuscaloosa AL 35401-2029

HOWARD, THOMAS CLEMENT, surgeon; b. Austin, Tex., May 7, 1943; s. Walter Burke and Virginia Kentucky (Freeman) H.; m. Paula Cheryl Greenwald, June 7, 1969; children: Jennifer, Michael. BA, Stanford U., 1965; MD, Yale U., 1969. Diplomate Am. Bd. Surgery. Intern in surgery Yale-New Haven Hosp., 1969-70, resident in surgery, 1970-74; instr. surgery Yale Med. Sch., New Haven, 1973-74; asst. prof. surgery U. Nebr. Med. Ctr., Omaha, 1976-80; pvt. practice surgery Clarkson Hosp., Omaha, 1980—; pres. Surg. Svcs. of the Great Plains, Omaha, 1991—. Maj. M.C., U.S. Army, 1974-76. Fellow ACS; mem. Midwestern Vascular Surg. Soc., Internat. Soc. for Cardiovascular Surgery (N.Am. chpt.), Southwestern Surg. Soc. Congregationalist. Home: 1750 S 85th Ave Omaha NE 68124-1336 Office: Surg Svcs Great Plains 270 Doctors Bldg N Tower Omaha NE 68131

HOWARD, THOMAS K., surgeon; b. Pitts., June 15, 1935; s. Charles Wooster and Edna Elizabeth (Greene) H.; m. Joan Clement, Dec. 19, 1959; children: Thomas, Jr., Kelley, Clement, Christine Joan, Steven Charles. BS, U. Del., 1956; MD, Jefferson Med. Coll. of Phila., 1960. Diplomate Am. Acad. Orthopedic Surgeons. Active staff Carroll County Gen. Hosp., Westminster, Md., 1968-70, Gettysburg (Pa.) Hosp., 1968-75; chief of staff Elizabethtown (Pa.) State Crippled Children's Hosp., 1975-76; chmn. credential com. Hanover Gen. Hosp., 1988-94, chief of surgery, 1982-84; practicing orthopaedic surgeon Hanover (Pa.) Ortho. Assocs., 1968—; chief of staff Hanover Gen. Hosp., 1990-92. Bd. dirs. YMCA, Hanover, 1973. Lt. USN, 1961-64. Fellow Am. Acad. Ortho Surgeons (bd. councilors 1982-86); mem. Pa. Orthopaedic Soc. (pres. 1980-81), Pa. Med. Soc., Jefferson Orthopaedic Soc., Orthopedic Surgeons and Trauma Soc. (pres. 1995-97), Hanover Jr. Soc. Republican. Methodist. Home: 14 Holly Court Hanover PA 17331 Office: Hanover Ortho Assoc Inc 100 Penn St Hanover PA 17331

HOWARD, THOMAS W., physician; b. Beckley, W.Va., May 28, 1951. MD, W.Va. U., 1978. Diplomate Am. Bd. Internal Medicine, Am. Bd. Rheumatology. Pvt. practice in rheumatology Charleston, W.Va., 1990—. Fellow Am. Coll. Rheumatology; mem. Alpha Omega Alpha. Baptist. Office: 100 Tracy Way Charleston WV 25311

HOWARD, WILLARD HOWE, III, osteopath; b. Kalamazoo, Nov. 8, 1962; s. Willard Howe Jr. and Marguerite (Van Blaricum) H.; m. Vicki Marie Sanford, June 23, 1983; children: Willard Howe IV, Chloe Rochelle. BS, U. Ark., 1990; DO, Kirksville Coll. Osteo., 1990. Intern Osteo. Med. Ctr. Tex., Ft. Worth, 1995—. Vol. tchr. Seventh-day Adventist Ch., Keene, Tex., 1995-96. Mem. Undergrad. Am. Acad. Osteo. (v.p. 1992-93), Am. Osteo. Assn., Ark, Osteo. Med. Assn., Student Osteo. Med. Assn., Kirksville Osteo. Alumni Assn.

HOWARD, WILLIAM ALLEN, physician; b. New Orleans, July 12, 1912; s. Allen and Kate (Elgin) H.; m. Marion McAlpine Rowcliffe; children: Marion McNeill, Alison Rowcliffe, William Rowcliffe. MD, Tulane U., 1934. Diplomate Am. Bd. Pediatrics, Am. Bd. Allergy and Immunology. Pvt. practice Chevy Chase, Md., 1938-88; intern in pediatrics Univ. Hosp., Iowa City, Iowa, 1934-36; asst. resident in pediatrics Strong Meml. Hosp., Rochester, N.Y., 1936-37; chief resident in pediatrics Children's Hosp., Washington, 1937-38; fellow in pediatrics Hosp. Med. Ctr. Georgetown U. Hosp., Washington, 1938-39, asst. prof. pediatrics, 1946-58, chmn., prof., 1958-67, clin. prof. pediatrics, 1967-84, chmn. prof. emeritus in pediatrics, 1984—; Mem. Bd. Pediatric Allergy, 1961-71, chmn., 1967-71; co-chmn. Am. Bd. Allergy and Immunology, 1972. Contbr. articles to profl. jours. and text books. Lt. Col. USMC, 1942-46, ETO. Fellow Am. Acad. Pediatrics (dist. chmn. 1964-70, Bret Ratner award 1978), Am. Acad. Allergy (v.p. 1961); mem. Am. Pediatric Soc., AMA, Soc. Med. Cons. to Armed Forces (pres. 1965), Chevy Chase Club. Episcopalian. Home: 3308 Shepherd St Bethesda MD 20815-3226

HOWARD, WILLIAM JAMES, health facility administrator; b. Little Rock, Sept. 1, 1938; m. Barbara V. Howard; 3 children. BA, Haverford Coll., 1960; MD, U. Pa., 1964. Diplomate Am. Bd. Internal Medicine; lic. physician, Ariz., D.C., Pa. Intern Hosp. the U. Pa., Phila., 1964-65, resident in medicine, 1965-66, fellow in metabolic diseases, 1966-67; fellow in metabolic diseases Duke U. Med. Ctr., Durham, N.C., 1967-68, fellow in clin. endocrinology, 1968-69; dir. Endocrine-Metabolic Outpatient Clinic/Walter Reed Gen. Hosp., Washington, 1969-72; asst. dir. Gen. Clin. Rsch. Ctr./Phila. Gen. Hosp., 1972-76; from dir. med. residency program to dir. med. edn. Good Samaritan Med. Ctr., Phoenix, 1976-88; dir. Medlantic Prevention & Rsch. Clinics, Washington, 1988-92; sr. v.p., med. dir. Washington Hosp. Ctr., Washington, 1992—; asst. chief U. Pa. Med. Svc./Phila. Gen. Hosp., 1973-75, dir. house staff tng., 1973-76, assoc. chief, 1975-76; house staff com., pharmacy and therapeutic com., rsch. and publ. com. Phila. Gen. Hosp., 1973-76, chmn. patient care com., long range planning com. of med. staff., 1974-76; med. com. Good Samaritan Med. Ctr., Phoenix, 1976-80, program dirs. subcom., 1976-85, med. edn. com. 1977-88, rsch. and publ. com., 1979-87, dir. transitional residency program, 1980-88, acting dir. med. edn., 1980-81, chmn. program dirs. subcom., 1981-88, sr. adminstr., 1984-88, exec. com. 1985-88; dir. clin. rsch. Medlantic Rsch. Found., Washington, 1988-92, v.p. med. programs, 1991-92; chief sect. endocrinology Washington Hosp. Ctr., 1990-92, grad. med. edn. com., 1988—, ethics com., 1990—, continuing med. edn. com., 1994—; rsch. and devel. com. VA Med. Ctr., Phoenix, 1980-88; chmn. med. edn. com. Greater Phoenix Affordable Health Care Found., 1984-88; chmn. bd. dirs. Palms Clinic and Hosp. Corp., 1985-88; chmn. Greater Phoenix Alliance Med. Educators, 1986-88; bd. dirs. Washington Regional Transplant Consortium; exec. com. Washington Hosp. Ctr. Med. and Dental Staff, 1992—; profl. affairs, quality assurance com., strategic planning com. Medlantic Healthcare Group Bd. Dirs., Washington, 1992—; exec. com. of med. staff Nat. Rehab. Hosp., Washington, 1993—. Assoc. editor Diabetes Care, 1990-92; contbr. articles to Jour. Neurochemistry, Jour. Urology, Jour. Biol. Chem., Atherosclerosis, Jour. Cell Physiol., Am. Jour. Clin. Nutrition. Pres. Parents Booster Club All Saints Episcopal Day Sch., Phoenix, 1978-79, bd. govs., 1979-82, vice-chmn., bd. govs. 1980-81, chmn., bd. govs., 1981-82; chmn. key club com. Camelback Kiwanis Club, pack com. Cub Scouts, Phoenix, 1981-83; bd. dirs. ARC, Ariz., 1984-88. Maj. U.S. Army M.C., 1969-72. Nat. Merit scholar, 1956-60, Nat. Found. scholar, 1960-64. Fellow ACP (gov.-elect Ariz. chpt. 1987-88); mem. Am. Heart Assn. (bd. dirs. 1989—), Am. Diabetes Assn. (chmn. profl. edn. com. Ariz. chpt. 1978-80, pres.-elect. 1981-83, pres. 1983-85, edn. program rev. panel, 1991-94), Endocrine Soc., Acad. Medicine, D.C. Med. Soc. (med. dirs. forum 1994—), Alpha Omega Alpha. Home: 9120 Willow Gate Dr Bethesda MD 20817 Office: Washington Hosp Ctr Physicians Office Bldg 121 106 Irving St NW Washington DC 20010

HOWARD, WILLIAM PERCY, physician; b. Canton, Miss., Dec. 29, 1947; s. John Wesley Griffin and Ann (Wallace) H.; m. Nancy Rose Moyers, May 25, 1980; children: John W.G. II, Ann Skidmore, Ashley Elizabeth. BS in Chem. Engring., Miss. State U., 1970; MD, U. Miss., 1979. Chem. engr. Miss. Chem. Corp., Yazoo City, 1970-75; resident U. Med. Ctr., JAckson, Miss., 1979-82; staff physician emergency physician MEA Med. Sys., JAckson, Miss., 1982-90, clin. staff physician, 1990—. Fellow Am. Acad. Family Practitioners; mem. AMA, Miss. State Med. Assn. Republican. Methodist. Office: MEA Med Clinic 5606 Old Canton Rd Jackson MS 39211

HOWARDS, STUART S., physician, educator; b. Milw., Mar. 29, 1937; s. Harvey H. and Anne (Levin) H.; m. Carter N. Howards, Aug. 20, 1966; children: Penelope P., Hugh N. BA, Yale U., 1959; MD, Columbia U., 1963. Intern in surgery Peter Bent Brigham Hosp., Boston, 1963-64, resident in urology, 1968-71; resident in surgery Childrens Hosp., Boston, 1964-65; rsch. assoc. NIH, Bethesda, Md., 1965-68; asst. prof. urology and physiology U. Va., Charlottesville, 1971-74, assoc. prof., 1974-76, prof., 1976—, chief divsn. pediat. urology, 1986—; chmn. exam com. Am. Bd. Urology, 1985-91, pres., 1992-93. Editor: Infertility in the Male, 1991, 2d edit., 1990, Adult and Pediatric Urology, 1991, 3d edit., 1995; editor Jour. Urology, 1983—. Maj. USPHS, 1965-68. Recipient Career Investigation award NIH, 1973-78. Fellow Am. Acad. Pediats.; mem. Am. Urologic Assn. (Golden Cystoscope award 1981, Scott award 1990, Hugh Young award 1991), Clin. Soc. Genitourinary Surgeons, Am. Fertility Soc. (bd. dirs. 1994—), Soc. Andrology, Genitourinary Surgeons, Am. Assn. GU Surgeons (sec.-treas. 1992—). Home: 1150 W Leigh Dr Charlottesville VA 22901-7706 Office: U Va Hosp Jefferson Park Ave Charlottesville VA 22908

HOWARTH, HUGH COLLINS, oral surgeon; b. Phila.; s. Benjamin Wesley and Elizabeth Dewees (Collins) H.; m. Marian McClea, May 31, 1958; children: Thomas Robert, Susan Maureen, Hugh Patrick. BA, U. Pa., 1957, DDS cum laude, 1960; MSc in Dentistry, Boston U., 1971. Diplomate Am. Bd. Oral and Maxillofacial Surgery. Dental officer USN, 1960-69, capt., chief dental svc. and oral surgeon, 1972-80; pvt. practice Warwick, R.I., 1980—; cons. Naval Regional Med. Ctr., Newport, R.I., 1980-84, VA Hosp., Providence, R.I., 1981—, R.I. Hosp., Providence, 1981-89, Kent County Hosp., Warwick, 1980—, South County Hosp., South Kingstown, 1980—, Roger Williams Hosp., Providence, 1981—; asst. prof. U. P.R., San Juan, 1974-76; adj. clin. faculty Bristol C.C., Fall River, Mass., 1978-80, U. R.I., Kingston, 1980-90. Fellow Acad. Dentistry Internat., 1990. Fellow Am. Assn. Oral and Maxillofacial Surgeons (R.I. del.), Am. Coll. Oral and Maxillofacial Surgeons, R.I. Soc. Oral and Maxillofacial Surgeons (pres. 1992-93); mem. ADA, R.I. Dental Assn. (Kent County del. 1994—), Kent County Dental Assn. (pres. 1993-94), Alpha Epsilon Delta, Omicron Kappa Upsilon, Pierre Fauchard Acad. Methodist. Office: 222 Jefferson Blvd Warwick RI 02888

HOWATT, SISTER HELEN CLARE, human services director, former college library director; b. San Francisco, Apr. 5, 1927; d. Edward Bell and Helen Margaret (Kenney) H. BA, Holy Names Coll., 1949; MS in Libr. Sci., U. So. Calif., 1972; cert. advanced studies Our Lady of Lake U., 1966. Joined Order Sisters of the Holy Names, Roman Cath. Ch., 1945. Life teaching credential, life spl. svcs. credential, prin. St. Monica Sch., Santa Monica, Calif., 1957-60, St. Mary Sch., L.A., 1960-63; tchr. jr. high sch. St. Augustine Sch., Oakland, Calif., 1964-69; tchr. jr. high math St. Monica Sch., San Francisco, 1969-71, St. Cecilia Sch., San Francisco, 1971-77; libr. dir. Holy Names Coll., Oakland, Calif., 1977-94; activities dir. Collins Ctr. Sr. Svcs., 1994—. Contbr. math. curriculum San Francisco Unified Sch. Dist., Cum Notis Variorum, publ. Music Libr., U. Calif., Berkeley. Contbr. articles to profl. jours. NSF grantee, 1966, NDEA grantee, 1966. Mem. Cath. Libr.

Assn. (chmn. No. Calif. elem. schs. 1971-72). Home and Office: 2550 18th Ave San Francisco CA 94116-3005

HOWE, DEBBIE KAY, health facility administrator; b. Roswell, N.Mex., Feb. 9, 1961; d. Billy Ray Howe and June Annette (Stephenson) Blevins. BS, Southwestern Okla. State U., 1983. Bus. mgr. Okeene (Okla.) Mcpl. Hosp., 1984-91, adminstr., CEO, 1995—; dir. bus. svcs., CFO Craig Gen. Hosp., Vinita, Okla., 1991-95. Mem. Healthcare Fin. Mgmt. Assn., Am. Coll. Healthcare Execs. (assoc.). Democrat. Office: Okeene Mcpl Hosp 207 E F St Okeene OK 73763

HOWE, JOHN FRANTZ, neurosurgeon, educator; b. Oakland, Calif., May 14, 1945; s. Donnell Conde and Margaret (Frantz) H.; m. Cynthia Russell, May 18, 1974; children: Beth, Emily, Nathaniel. BA, Lawrence U., 1967; MD, Case Western Res. U., 1971; degree in neurosurgery, U. Wash., 1977. Diplomate Am. Bd. Neurol. Surgeons. Instr. neurosurgery U. Wash., Seattle, asst. prof. neurosurgery, 1979-82, clin. asst. prof., 1982—; neurosurgeon Group Health, Seattle, 1982—, chief neurosurgery, 1993—. Contbr. articles to profl. jours. Served to maj. U.S. Army, 1977-79. Fellow Am. Bd. Neurosurgery; mem. AMA, Am. Assn. Neurosurgery, Joint Session Spinal Sect. (program com. 1986), ACLU. Democrat. Home: 6 Holly Ln Mercer Island WA 98040-3900 Office: 200 15th Ave E Seattle WA 98112-5260

HOWE, JOHN PRENTICE, III, health science center executive, physician; b. Jackson, Tenn., Mar. 7, 1943; s. John Prentice and Phyllis (MacDonald) H.; children: Lindsey Warren, Brooke Olmsted, John Prentice IV. BA, Amherst Coll., 1965; MD, Boston U., 1969. Diplomate Am. Bd. Internal Medicine, internal medicine and cardiovascular disease. Research assoc. cellular physiology Amherst Coll., 1963-64; research assoc. cardiovascular physiology Boston U. Sch. of Medicine, 1966-67, lectr. medicine, 1972-73; intern Boston City Hosp., 1969-70, asst. resident, 1970-71; research fellow in medicine Harvard U., 1971-73, Peter Bent Brigham Hosp., 1971-73; survey physician Framingham Cardiovascular Disease Study, Nat. Heart and Lung Inst., 1971; asst. clin. prof. medicine U. Hawaii, 1973-75; asst. prof. medicine U. Mass., 1975-77, assoc. prof., 1977-85, vice chmn. dept. medicine, 1975-78, asst. dean continuing edn. for physicians, 1976-78, assoc. dean profl. affairs and continuing edn., 1978-80, acad. dean, 1980-85, vice chancellor, 1980-85, acting chmn. dept. anatomy, 1982-85; pres., prof. medicine U. Tex. Health Scis. Ctr., San Antonio, 1985—; assoc. chief div. medicine U. Mass. Hosp., 1975-78, dir. patient care studies dept., 1975-80, chief of staff, 1978-80. Mem. editorial bd. Archives Internal Medicine, 1991—; contbr. numerous articles to profl. jours., chpts. to books. Trustee S.W. Found. for Biomed. Rsch., San Antonio Med. Found., S.W. Rsch. Inst. Maj. M.C, U.S. Army, 1973-75. Alfred P. Sloan scholar Amherst Coll., 1962-65; recipient Ruth Hunter Johnson award Boston U. Sch. of Medicine, 1969. Fellow ACP, Am. Coll. Cardiology, Am. Coll. Chest Physicians; mem. AMA (del. ho. of dels. 1995—, coun. on sci. affairs 1993—), Am. Heart Assn. (fellow coun. clin. cardiology), Tex. Med. Soc. (coun. med. edn. 1986—, ho. of dels. 1989—), Tex. Soc. Biomed. Rsch. (pres.), Bexar County Med. Soc. (exec. com. 1985—, pres. 1996), Alpha Omega Alpha, Omicron Kappa Epsilon.

HOWE, SUSAN MCCLAINE, medical technologist; b. Wisconsin Rapids, Wis., June 6, 1949; d. Buddy R. and Mary Elizabeth (Hunter) McClaine; m. David T. Howe, May 5, 1984. Diploma, U. Wis., Eau Claire, 1969, LaSalle Inst. Tech., Mpls., 1971. Cert. Am. Med. Technologist. Med. technologist Plantation (Fla.) Hosp., 1971-74; med. technologist Deaconess Hosp., Milw., 1974-75, Lakes Region Gen. Hosp., Laconia, N.H., 1975—. Office: Lakes Region Gen Hosp Highland St Laconia NH 03246

HOWE, WARREN BILLINGS, physician; b. Jackson Heights, N.Y., Oct. 25, 1940; s. John Hanna and Francelia (Rose) H.; m. Hedwig Neslanik, Aug. 7, 1971; children: Elizabeth Rose, Sarah Billings. BA, U. Rochester, 1962; MD, Washington U., St. Louis, 1965. Diplomate Am. Bd. Family Practice with CAQ in Sports Medicine, Nat. Bd. Med. Examiners. Intern Phila. Gen. Hosp., 1965-66; resident physician Highland Hosp./U. Rochester, 1969-71; family physician Family Medicine Clinic of Oak Harbor (Wash.), Inc., PS, 1971-92; student health physician, univ. team physician We. Wash. U., Bellingham, 1992—; team physician Oak Harbor High Sch., 1972-92; head tournament physician Wash. State High Sch. Wrestling Championships, Tacoma, 1989—; attending physician Seattle Goodwill Games, 1990; clin. asst. prof. U. Wash. Sch. Medicine, 1975-82. Contbr. articles to profl. jours. and chpts. to books. Bd. dirs. Oak Harbor Sch. Dist. #201, 1975-87; chmn. Oak Harbor Citizen's Com. for Sch. Support, 1988-90. Lt. comdr. USN, 1966-69, Vietnam. Recipient Disting. Svc. award City of Oak Harbor, 1984; Paul Harris fellowship Oak Harbor Rotary Club. Fellow Am. Coll. Sports Medicine (chair membership com.), Am. Acad. Family Physicians; mem. AMA, Wash. State Med. Assn., Am. Med. Soc. for Sports Medicine, Am. Coll. Health Assn. Presbyterian. Home: 4222 Northridge Way Bellingham WA 98226-7804 Office: WWU Student Health Ctr 25 High St Bellingham WA 98225-5942

HOWELL, CHARLES MAITLAND, dermatologist; b. Thomasville, N.C., Apr. 14, 1914; s. Cyrus Maitl and Lilly Mae (Ammons) H.; m. Betty Jane Myers, Feb. 12, 1949; children—Elizabeth Myers, Pamela Jane. B.S., Wake Forest U., Winston-Salem, N.C., 1935; M.D., U. Pa., 1937. Intern Charity Hosp., New Orleans, 1937-38; resident in medicine Burlington County Hosp., Mt. Holley, N.J., 1938-39; sch. physician Lawrenceville (N.J.) Sch., 1939-42; resident in pathology N.C. Baptist Hosp., Winston-Salem, 1947-48; resident in dermatology Columbia-Presbyn. Med. Ctr., N.Y.C., 1948-50; resident in allergy Roosevelt Hosp., N.Y.C., 1950-51; practice medicine specializing in dermatology Winston-Salem, 1951—; mem. staff N.C. Bapt., Forsyth Meml. hosps.; mem. faculty Bowman Gray Sch. Medicine, Wake Forest U., 1951-86, head. sect., 1984-86, prof. dermatology, 1967-84, prof. emeritus, 1984, head sect., 1961-86, acting head sect., 1984-86. Served as officer M.C. AUS, 1942-46. Fellow Am. Acad. Dermatology, Am. Acad. Allergy; mem. N. Am. Clin. Dermatol. Soc., N.Y. Acad. Scis. Democrat. Baptist. Clubs: Old Town (Winston-Salem); Bermuda Run Country (Clemmons, N.C.). Home: 1100 E Kent Rd Winston Salem NC 27104-1116 Office: 340 Pershing Ave Winston Salem NC 27103-2513

HOWELL, EMBRY MARTIN, researcher; b. Bethesda, Md., Nov. 18, 1945; d. David Grier and Louise (McMichael) Martin; m. Joseph Toy Howell III, Dec. 28, 1965; children: Andrew Martin, Jessica Ramsey. AB, Barnard Coll., 1968; MSPH, U. N.C., 1972; PhD, George Washington U., 1991. Computer programmer Corp. Trust Co., N.Y.C., 1968; computer programmer dept. city and regional planning U. N.C., Chapel Hill, 1969-70; summer intern State Bd. Health, Raleigh, N.C., 1972; rsch. asst. dept. obgyn Georgetown U. Hosp., Washington, 1972-73; health planner, biostatistician Health Systems Agy. No. Va., Falls Church, 1973-75; biostatistician Nat. Capital Med. Found., Washington, 1975-79; dir. SysteMetrics, Inc., Washington, 1979-92; v.p. Mathematica Policy Rsch., Washington, 1992—; dir. Nat. Evaluation Healthy Start Program; sprk. in field. Contbr. numerous articles to profl. jours. Vol. Children's Hosp. Hospice. USPHS trainee, 1971-72; recipient Agy. for Health Care Policy and Rsch. Dissertation Rsch. grant, 1990-91. Mem. Am. Pub. Health Assn., Assn. for Social Scis. in Health, Assn. for Pub. Policy Analysis and Mgmt., Am. Evaluation Assn., Phi Beta Kappa.

HOWELL, GREGORY JACK, neurologist; b. St. Paul, Mar. 12, 1950; s. Buckley Leroy and Anna Juanita (DeHart) H.; married; children: Meghan, Lindsay, Kristen, Natalie. BS, U. Fla., 1972, MD, 1976. Intern Charlotte (N.C.) Meml. Hosp., 1976-78; resident in neurology U. Fla., Gainesville, 1978-81; neurologist Ocala (Fla.) Neurodiagnostic Ctr., 1981—; speaker in field. Mem. Am. Acad. Neurology. Republican. Methodist. Office: Ocala Neurodiagnostic Ctr 2203 SW 3d Ave Ocala FL 34471

HOWELL, JIMMY FRANK, cardiovascular surgeon, educator; b. Winnfield, La., Sept. 10, 1932; s. Burley Desota and Maggie P. (Collins) H.; m. Roberta Percy Blankenstein; children: Elizabeth Annette Howell, LeNoble, Roberta Elise Howell Houren, Celia Deann Dettling, Jennifer Howell Karaman, James Frank, Robert Collins. BS, Lamar U., 1954; MD, Baylor Coll. Medicine, 1957. Intern Jefferson Davis Hosp., Houston, 19575-58; resident Baylor Coll. Medicine Affiliated Residency Program, Houston, 1958-63; asst. prof. surgery Baylor Coll. Medicine, Houston, 1964-71, assoc. prof., 1971-75, prof., 1975—. Mem. ACS, Am. Coll. Cardiology, Soc. for Vascular Surgery, Soc. Thoracic Surgeons, Internat. Cardiovascular Soc. Office: 6535 Fannin St # 802A Houston TX 77030-2705

HOWELL, JULIUS AMMONS, plastic surgeon; b. Thomasville N.C., Apr. 14, 1914; s. Cyrus Maitland and Lillie Mae (Ammons) H.; m. Octavia Anne Southern, Oct. 29, 1951; children: Anne, Karen, Robin. LLB, Wake Forest U., 1935, BS, 1940; MD, U. Pa., Phila., 1943. Diplomate Am. Bd. Plastic & Reconstructive Surgery, Am. Bd. Otolaryngology. Chief plastic surgery sect. Bowman Gray Sch. Medicine, Winston Salem, N.C., 1959-84, prof. emeritus plastic surgery, 1984—; lectr. Sch. Law Wake Forest U., Winston Salem, N.C., 1978-94; pvt. practice Winston Salem, N.C., 1984—; mem. medico-legal com. N.C. Med. Soc., Raleigh, 1960-93, South Soc. Plastuc Surgery; mem. adv. com. N.C. Indsl. com., Raleigh, 1976-86; trustee Blue Cross/Blue Shield, Chapel Hill, 1964-68. Co-author: Plastic Surgery, 1979. Julius Ammons Howell Endowed Chair Surgery named in his honor Bowman Gray Sch. Medicine, 1995. Mem. ACS; Am. Soc. Plastic & Reconstructive Surgery (medicolegal com.), Am. Assn. Plastic Surgeons. Baptist. Office: 480 Forsyth Med Pk Winston Salem NC 27103

HOWELL, LEONARD LEE, behavioral pharmacologist, biomedical researcher; b. Marietta, Ga., Mar. 10, 1956; s. Ralph Edward and Clara (Welch) H.; m. Madeleine Elizabeth Pearce, Aug. 12, 1983. AA, Oxford Coll., 1976; BA, Emory U., 1978; MS, Ga. Inst. Tech., 1982, PhD, 1985. Postdoctoral rsch. fellow Harvard U., Boston, 1985-86; rsch. assoc. Emory U., Atlanta, 1987-89, assoc. scientist, 1989-93, rsch. scientist, 1993-96, asst. rsch. prof., 1996—, asst. prof. pharmacology 1993—, asst. prof. psychiatry & behavioral scis., 1995—; cons. Battelle Meml. Inst., Columbus, Ohio, 1989. Contbr. articles to profl. jours. Biol. Scis. Tng. grantee NIMH, 1985-86, Biomed. Rsch. grantee Nat. Inst. Drug Abuse, 1989—. Mem. APA (Young Psychopharmacologist award 1990), Am. Soc. Pharmacology & Exptl. Therapeutics, Behavioral Pharmacology Soc., Soc. for Neuroscience (Atlanta chpt.), Sigma Xi (Rsch. award 1993). Office: Emory U Yerkes Regional Primate Rsch Ctr Atlanta GA 30322

HOWELL, RALPH RODNEY, pediatrician, educator; b. Concord, N.C., June 10, 1931; s. Fred Lee and Grace Mary (Blackwelder) H.; m. Sarah Vosburg Esselstyn, Nov. 19, 1960 (dec.); children: Grace Meyer, Elizabeth Eriksson, John Esselstyn. BS, Davidson Coll., 1953; MD, Duke U. 1957. Intern Duke U., 1957-58, resident in pediatrics, 1958-59, research fellow in pediatrics and medicine, 1959-60; clin. assoc. and staff NIH, Bethesda, Md., 1960-64; assoc. prof. pediatrics Johns Hopkins U., Balt., 1964-72 pediatrician-in-chief Univ. Children's Hosp. at Hermann, Houston, 1972-87; chmn. med. bd. Univ. Children's Hosp. at Hermann, 1972-87; David Park prof. U. Tex. Med. Sch., Houston, 1972-89, chmn. dept. pediatrics, 1972-87; prof., chmn. dept. pediatrics U. Miami Sch. Medicine, 1989—; sec. med. staff Jackson Meml. Hosp., Miami, 1992-93, v.p. med. staff, 1993-96; cons. pediatrics M.D. Anderson Hosp. and Tumor Inst., 1972-89; mem. metabolism study sect. NIH, 1973-77, chmn. maternal and child health adv. com., 1983-86; mem. exec. com. Nat. Practitioner Data Bank; mem. nat. clin. adv. com. Nat. Found. March of Dimes, 1973-79; mem. nat. med. adv. bd., bd. dirs. Muscular Dystrophy Assn., chmn. sci. adv. bd.; vis. prof. Inst. Molecular Genetics, Baylor Coll. Medicine, Houston, 1988; chief pediatrics Childrens Hosp., U. Miami-Jackson Meml. Med. Ctr., 1989—. Author: (with G.H. Thomas) Selected Screening Tests for Genetic Metabolic Diseases, 1973, (with F.H. Morriss, L.K. Pickering) Role of Human Milk in Infant Nutrition, 1986; contbr. articles to profl. jours. Trustee Jackson Lab. Bar Harbor, Maine; dir. Caldwell B. Esselstyn Found., Troy, N.Y., 1987-92, pres., 1992—; bd. dirs. Congl. Ch. Found., Coconut Grove, Fla. Served to sr. surgeon USPHS, 1960-64. Fellow Am. Acad. Pediatrics (com. on genetics); mem. AMA, Am. Pediatric Soc.,Soc. Pediatric Rsch., Houston Pediatric Soc. (pres. 1978-79), Tex. Med. Assn., Soc. Inborn Errors of Metabolism (pres. 1981), Miami Pediatric Soc., Fla. Med. Assn., Am. Coll. Med. Genetics (bd. dirs. 1991—, treas. 1995—), Pi Kappa Alpha, Banker's Club (Miami), Cosmos Club (Washington). Home: L'Hermitage Villa 66 2000 S Bayshore Dr Miami FL 33133 Office: U Miami Sch Medicine Dept Pediatrics D-820 PO Box 016820 Miami FL 33101-6820

HOWELL, ROBERT EDWARD, hospital administrator; b. Marietta, Ohio, Jan. 19, 1949; married; 3 children. BS, Muskingham Coll., 1971; MS in Hosp. and Health Svcs. Adminstrn., Ohio State U., 1977. Assoc. dir. U. Minn. Hosps. and Clinics, Mpls., 1980-86; exec. dir. Med. Coll. Ga. Hosps. and Clinics, Augusta, 1986-94; dir., CEO, U. Iowa Hosps. and Clinics, Iowa City, 1994—; mem. fin. and audit com. Univ. Hosp. Consortia. Mem. Coun. Tchg. Hosps. (past chmn.), Assn. Profs. Medicine (co-chmn. ad hoc task force), Am. Assn. Med. Colls. (exec. com., audit com., mem. nominating com.), Am. Hosp. Assn. (coord. com. med. edn.), Univ. Health System Consortium (exec. com.). Office: U Iowa Hosps and Clinics 200 Hawkins Dr Iowa City IA 52242-1009*

HOWELL, ROBERT JAMES, psychology educator; b. Salt Lake City, Sept. 13, 1925; s. Elmer Virgil and Stella Myrtle (Knight) H.; m. Mary Winnie Raiford, Aug. 16, 1946; children: Carol Ann, Peggy Lynne, Robert Bruce. Student, Wash. State U., 1944; BA, U. Utah, 1948, MA, 1949, PhD, 1951. Instr. psychology Fresno State Coll., 1951-52; faculty Brigham Young U., Provo, Utah, 1952—; prof. psychology Brigham Young U., 1960—, chmn. dept., 1961-68, dir. clin. tng., 1968-89; sr. psychologist Utah State Hosp., 1958-60, cons., dir. psychol. tng., 1960-61, cons., 1961—; cons. Utah State Prison, 1961—; staff psychologist Patton State Hosp., 1965-66; rsch. specialist Center for Tng. in Community Psychiatry, L.A., 1968-69; adminstrv. dir. Timpanogos Mental Health Center, Provo, 1973-74; mem. Am. Bd. Forensic Psychology, 1979—, corr. sec., 1980-81, pres., 1981-82, nat. chair exams. 1982-89, rec. sec., 1989-90. Mem. ethics com. Am. Bd. Profl. Psychology, 1993—. With USAAF, 1943-45. Fellow APA, Utah Psychol. Assn. (pres. 1963-64, ethics com. 1989—); mem. Rocky Mountain Psychol. Assn., Sigma Xi, Phi Kappa Phi, Psi Chi. Home: 2761 Iroquois Dr Provo UT 84604-4319

HOWELL, ROBERT SPENCER, pathologist; b. Atlanta, Sept. 21, 1943; s. Robert Spencer and Emma Grace (Moore) H.; m. Catherine Elizabeth Bendell, Dec. 22, 1967 (div. Feb. 1981); children: Kurt William Spencer, Justin Moore; m. Ada Mesana, May 15, 1981; children: Robert Spencer, Gregory Stephen. Student, Emory U., 1961-64; MD, U. Miami. 1968. Diplomate Am. Bd. Pathology, Am. Bd. Nuclear Medicine. Resident in pathology Duke U. Hosp., Durham, N.C., 1968-70, U.S. Naval Hosp., Portsmouth, Va., 1970-72; pathologist U.S. Naval Hosp., Jacksonville, Fla., 1972-74, Catawba Meml. Hosp., Conover, N.C., 1974-75, Doctors' Hosp. of Hollywood, Fla., 1975, Mercy Hosp., Miami, Fla., 1975—. Lt. cmmdr. USN, 1970-74. Fellow Coll. of Am. Pathologists, Am. Soc. Clin. Pathologists; mem. AMA, Am. Assn. for Clin. Chemistry, Fla. Med. Assn., D.C. Med. Assn. Home: 113 Gavilan Ave Coral Gables FL 33143 Office: Mercy Hosp 3663 S Miami Ave Miami FL 33133

HOWELL, ROY ALLEN, JR., physician; b. Charleston, S.C., June 7, 1925; s. Roy Allen and Julia (Hanley) H.; m. Betty Jean Faris, June 12, 1954; children: Denise, Lisa, Linda, Roy Allen III. BS, Coll. Charleston, 1946; MD, Med. Coll. S.C., 1948. Diplomate Am. Bd. Internal Medicine. Intern St. Louis City Hosp., 1948-49, resident in internal medicine, 1949-52; asst. in medicine Washington U. Sch. Medicine, St. Louis, 1950-52; teaching fellow in medicine Med. U. S.C., Charleston, 1952-53, rsch. fellow in medicine, 1953-54; pvt. practice Marlboro Gen. Hosp., Bennettsville, S.C., 1954-55, 57-83, Marlboro Park Hosp., Bennettsville, 1983-92; assoc. prof. medicine Med. U. S.C., Charleston, 1992—. Contbr. articles to med. jours. Capt. U.S. Army, 1943, 55-57. Named Young Cath. Man of Yr., Cath. Youth Orgn., 1960. Fellow Am. Coll. Physicians (gov. 1974-78); mem. AMA, S.C. Med. Assn., Am. Heart Assn. (Bronze svc. medal 1970), Am. Soc. Internal Medicine (pres. 1971-73, 88-90); Rotary Club (pres. 1973), Marlboro County Med. Soc. Home: 12 Harleston Pl Charleston SC 29401-1264 Office: Med U SC Ambulatory Care Ctr 30 Bee St Charleston SC 29403-5847

HOWLAND, WARREN WAYNE, medical products company executive; b. St. Cloud, Minn., Aug. 6, 1946; s. Wayne LeRoy and Elinor Edna (Danyluk) H.; divorced; children: Eric, Nikkole. BA, U. Minn., 1972. Scientist, sr. scientist Mills Chems., Mpls., 1968-86; tech. devel. mgr. Henkel Corp., Mpls.; sr. scientist Lamaur, Inc., Fridley, Minn., 1986-87; sr. staff scientist Medtronic, Inc., Fridley, 1987-92; pres. Joats, Inc., Champlin Minn., 1985—; dir. hydrogel devel. LMI Med., Grand Rapids, Mich., 1994-95. Contbr. articles to profl. jours.; patentee in field. Mem. ACS, Am. Soc. Cosmetic Chemists. Office: LMI Medical 4275 Airwest Dr SE Grand Rapids MI 49512-3949

HOWLEY, PETER MAXWELL, pathology educator; b. New Brunswick, N.J., Oct. 9, 1946; s. Bartholomew Maxwell and Grace (Size) H.; m. Ann Margaret McElwee, Aug. 23, 1969; children: Cristin, Megan, Maura. AB, Princeton U., 1968; M Med. Sci., Rutgers U., 1970; MD, Harvard U., 1972. Diplomate Am. Bd. Pathology. Intern Mass. Gen. Hosp., Boston, 1972-73; commd. lt. USPHS, 1973, advanced through grades to capt., 1985; rsch. assoc. NIH, Bethesda, Md., 1973-75; resident in pathology Nat. Cancer Inst., Bethesda, 1975-77, prin. investigator, 1977-84, lab. chief, 1984-93; ret., 1993; George Fabyan prof. comparative pathology, chmn. dept. Harvard Med. Sch., Boston, 1993—; mem. sci. adv. bd. ONYX Pharm. Co., Richmond, Calif., 1992—, Baxter Internat., Deerfield, Ill., 1995—. Editor: The Molecular Basis of Cancer, 1995, Virology, 3d edit., 1995; contbr. over 180 articles to med. jours. Recipient Wallace P. Rowe award Nat. Inst. Allergy and Infectious Diseases, 1986, Meritorious Svc. award USPHS, 1989, Paul Ehrlich-Ludwig Darmstaedter prize Govt. of Germany, 1994. Fellow Am. Acad. Microbiology; mem. NAS, Inst. Medicine, Am. Acad. Arts and Scis. Office: Harvard Medical Sch 200 Longwood Ave Boston MA 02115-5701

HOWSON, AGNES WAGNER, health educator; b. Lebanon, Pa., May 9, 1940; d. Lester Frederick and Mary Elizabeth (Engle) Wagner; AS, Becker Jr. Coll., 1960; AA in Education, Brookdale C.C., 1971, AAS in Nursing, 1975, BS in Human Svcs., Thomas A. Edison State Coll., N.J., 1988; MA in Edn., Georgian Ct. Coll., 1995; m. Robert Douglas Howson, Mar. 25, 1961; children: R. Douglas, Geoffrey F., Eric M., Stephen M. RN, N.J., Cert. Diabetes Educator, Health Edn. Specialist. Substitute sch. nurse Middletown (N.J.) Twp., 1976-82; staff nurse Riverview Hosp., Red Bank, N.J., 1977-78, 80-81; clinic supr., counselor Planned Parenthood of Monmouth County, Shrewsbury, N.J., 1978, 87; staff community health nurse MCOSS Nursing Svcs., Red Bank, N.J., 1983-89; nurse health educator Family Health Resource Ctr. Riverview Med. Ctr., Red Bank, N.J., 1989-92; health educator Blue Cross/Blue Shield Health Ctr., Eatontown, N.J., 1994-95; RN, diabetes educator Wellness Ctr. Jersey Shore Med. Ctr., Neptune, N.J., 1996—. Mem. Am. Assn. Diabetes Educators, Am. Assn. Health Educators. Home: 128 Bruce Rd Red Bank NJ 07701-5605

HOYE, ROBERT EARL, higher education educator, health care consultant; b. Warwick, R.I., Jan. 12, 1931; s. S. Earl and Alice (Landry) H.; m. Patricia Buswell, Aug. 20, 1955; children: Robert Earl Jr., Joanne D., Peter M., Kathleen B. BA, Providence Coll., 1953; MS, St. John's U., N.Y.C., 1955; PhD, U. Wis., Madison, 1973. Instr. St. John's U., 1953-55; dir. guidance Middleboro (Mass.) Pub. Schs., 1955-56, Rutland (Vt.) Pub. Schs., 1956-57; dean Champlain (Vt.) Coll., 1957-58; supt. Frontier Regional Sch. Dist., Deerfield, Mass., 1958-60; New Eng. dir. Sci. Rsch. Assocs. subs. IBM, Chgo., 1960-65; nat. dir. Learning Systems div. Xerox Corp., N.Y.C., 1965-66; dir. Instrnl. Media Lab. U. Wis., Milw., 1966-73; asst. v.p. U. Louisville, 1974-81, prof. urban policy, coord. grad. program in health systems, 1981—, prof. edn., 1992—; cons. to mgmt., Louisville, 1966—. Author: Index to Computer Based Learning, 1973; editor Edn. Jour., 1968-73; also articles. Recipient cert. of merit San Diego State U., 1983, Grad. Teaching Excellence award U. Louisville, 1984, gold medal Project Innovation, 1984. Fellow Am. Acad. Med. Adminstrs. (diplomate, chmn. editl. bd. 1986-94), Royal Soc. Health (Statesman in Healthcare Adminstrn. award 1992). Democrat. Roman Catholic. Home: 2238 Wynnewood Cir Louisville KY 40222-6342 Office: U Louisville School Of Education # 329 Louisville KY 40292

HOYER, JOHN RICHARD, pediatrician; b. Mpls., May 13, 1938; s. Ludolf Julius and Inez (Fuglesteen) H.; m. Carol E. Anderson, Aug. 20, 1983; children: Rolf William, John Steen. BA, Grinnell (Iowa) Coll., 1960; MD, Harvard U., 1964. Diplomate Am. Bd. Pediatrics. Intern in pediatrics U. Minn. Hosps., Mpls., 1964-65, resident in pediatrics, 1965-67, fellow in pediatric nephrology, 1970-73; med. researcher Phila.; asst. prof. pediatrics U. Minn., Mpls., 1973-74, Cornell Med. Coll., N.Y.C., 1974-76, Harvard Med. Sch., Boston, 1976-79; prof. pediatrics UCLA, 1979-83, U. Pa. Sch. Medicine, Phila., 1983—; vis. lectr. biol. chemistry Harvard Med. Coll., 1973-74; assoc. prof. medicine U. Pa., 1983-88, prof. medicine, 1988—; vis. scientist Dept. Medicine, U. Cambridge, 1989-90; established investigator Am. Heart Assn., 1974-79. Maj. U.S. Army, 1967-69. Mem. Phi Beta Kappa. Home: 9 Hathaway Cir Wynnewood PA 19096-1901 Office: Children's Hosp of Phila 34th St And Civic Ctr Blvd Philadelphia PA 19014

HOYER, MARK H., pediatric cardiologist; b. Columbus, Ohio, Sept. 11, 1959; s. Dieter H. and Wilma S. (Steinhauer) H.; m. Maureen A. Connolly, Aug. 21, 1982; children: Brigitte, Michael, Brian. BS, U. Notre Dame, 1981; MD, Ohio State U., 1985. Diplomate Am. Bd. Pediatrics. Resident in pediatrics Wright-Patterson Air Force Med. Ctr., Dayton, Ohio, 1985-88; fellow in pediat. cardiology Children's Hosp. Pitts., 1988-91; chief pediat. cardiology Wilford Hall Air Force Med. Ctr., San Antonio, 1991-95; asst. prof. pediatrics U. Tex. Health Sci. Ctr., San Antonio, 1995—; clin. instr. pediat. cardiology Children's Hosp. Pitts., 1988-91; clin. asst. prof. pediatrics Uniformed Svcs. Univ. Health Scis., Bethesda, Md., 1993-95; pediatric cardiologist, dir. pediat. cardiac catheterizaiton Children's Heart Network, San Antonio, 1995—. Choir mem. St. Francis of Assisi Ch., San Antonio, 1996. Fellow Am. Acad. Pediatrics, Am. Coll. Cardiology; mem. Am. Heart Assn., Tex. Med. Assn., Bexar County Med. Soc., San Antonio Pediat. Soc. Roman Catholic. Office: Children's Heart Network 1901 Babcock Rd #301 San Antonio TX 78229

HOYLE, KENNETH SAMUEL, psychiatrist; b. Austin, Tex., Oct. 20, 1953; s. Vinton Asbury Hoyle, Jr. and Martha Hunter (Byrd) Roberts. BA in History, Duke U., 1975; MD, U. Tenn., 1978. Diplomate, Am. Bd. Psychiatry and Neurology. Commd. ens. USN, 1975, advanced through grades to capt., 1996; intern Nat. Naval Med. Ctr., Bethesda, Md., 1979; resident psychiatry Nat. Naval Med. Ctr., Bethesda, 1980-83; staff psychiatrist Naval Hosp., Beaufort, S.C., 1983-86; staff psychiatrist Nat. Naval Med. Ctr., Bethesda, 1986-91, asst. chmn. dept. psychiatry, 1989-91; fellow in forensic psychiatry U. Md., Balt., 1991-92; chmn. dept. psychiatry Great Lakes Naval Hosp., Great Lakes, Ill, 1992—. Mem. Am. Acad. Psychiatry and the Law, Am. Psychiat. Assn. Episcopalian. Home: 6855 September Blvd Long Grove IL 60047 Office: Naval Hosp Great Lakes IL 60088

HOYME, HAROLD EUGENE, geneticist; b. Dell Rapids, S.D., 1950. MD, U. Chgo., 1976. Diplomate Am. Bd. Pediatrics; Am. Bd. Molecular Genetics, CCyt Genetics, Am. Bd. Molecular Genetics CGen. Faculty mem. dept. pediatrics, med. and molecular genetics U. Ariz, Tucson. Office: U Arz Health Sci Ctr Dept Pediatrics 1501 N Campbell Ave Tucson AZ 85724*

HOYNE, THOMAS TEMPLE, dentist; b. Salina, Kans., May 13, 1935; s. John Thomas and Opal Louise (Fisher) H.; m. Naomi Jeannette Nelson, June 21, 1961. BS in Chemistry, U. Kans., 1957; DDS cum laude, U. Kansas City, Mo., 1963. Gen. practice dentistry Stover, Mo., 1963—; cons. Handicapped Dental Patients of Mo., 1980-83. Contbr. articles on archeology to profl. jours. Scoutmaster to council exec. bd. Boy Scouts Am., Stover, 1963—. Served to 1st lt. U.S Army, 1957-59. Recipient Silver Beaver award Boy Scouts Am., 1972, Silver Lamb award Boy Scouts Am. and Luth. Ch., 1976. Mem. ADA, Soc. Am. Mil. Engrs., Mo. Dental Assn., Royal Soc. Health, U. Kans. Chemistry Dept. Alumni Assn., State Mo. Archeol. Soc. (trustee 1987—, chmn. bd. trustees 1990-93, dep. bd. chmn. trustees 1995, 96), West Ctrl. Mo. Archeol. Soc. (pres. 1986, 87, 95, 96, trustee 1989—), Morgan County Archeol. Soc. (pres. 1963-68), Greater St. Louis Archeol. Soc., Ctrl. States Archeol. Socs. Inc., SAR, Phi Kappa Sigma Alumni Assn. (Beta Beta chpt.), Psi Omega Alumni Assn. Republican. Lutheran. Lodge: Lions. Home: Woodland Dr And Hughes Ave Stover MO 65078 Office: Mimosa Hwy # 52 Stover MO 65078

HRACHOVINA, FREDERICK VINCENT, osteopathic physician and surgeon; b. St. Paul, Minn., Sept. 2, 1926; s. Vincent Frank and Beatrice (Funda) H.; m. Joan Halverson, July 2, 1955. BA in Chemistry, Macalester Coll., St. Paul, Minn., 1948; DO, Kirksville Coll. Osteo. Medicine, Mo., 1956. Chemist Mpls.-St. Paul area, 1948-51; intern Clare Gen. Osteo. Hosp., Mich., 1956-57; pvt. practice Mpls. Minn., 1957-84; asst. prof. osteo.

principles and practices Southeastern Coll. Osteo. Medicine, North Miami Beach, Fla., 1985-88; founder, pres. Physician Placement Svc., Fla. and Minn., 1973—; med. dir. Associated Bioscience, Inc., Mpls., 1992, Sera-Tec Biologicals Inc., Jacksonville, Fla., 1993-94; staff physician Allegheny Biologicals, Inc., Jacksonville, 1995—; med. dir. Serologicals, Jacksonville, 1996; contract physician Portamedic of Fla. and Minn. divsn. Hooper Holmes, Inc., 1996—; lectr. Internat. Acad. Osteo. Medicine, Brussels, 1984; mem. Northlands Regional Med. Program, Inc., 1971-73; mem. Health Svcs. Devel. Com., Regional Adv. Group; founder, faculty advisor Fla. Acad. Osteopathy Student Assn., Southeastern Coll. Osteo. Medicine, North Miami Beach, Fla., 1987. Author: Microscopic Anatomy, 1952; Methods of Development of New Osteopathic Medical Colleges in the Next Millennium, 1977. Contbr. articles to profl. jours. Mem. Sr. Citizen Assn., Garrison, Minn., 1991—, Deerwood Civic and Commerce Assn., Deerwood, Minn., 1992—. Grantee Smith Kline & French Labs., 1973, 89, Hill Labs, Gusman Med. Equipment, 1987. Mem. Am. Osteo Assn. (coun. fed. health programs, drug enforcement adminstrn. prescribers working com. 1974-75), Am. Acad. Osteopathy (life), Am. Assn. Sr. Physicians, Am. Osteo. Acad. Sports Medicine (life), Am. Blood Resources Assn., Am. Assn. Blood Banks, Minn. State Osteo. Assn. (pres. 1965-66, exec. dir. 1966-74, pub. rels. dir. 1974-75), Assn. Osteo. State Exec. Dirs. (pres. 1970-71, dir. 1971-74, founder nat. legis. sem. 1974), Fla. Soc. Coll. Osteopathic Family Practice (lectr. Mo. soc.), Fla. Acad. Osteopathy (bd. trustees, chmn. audit and membership com.), Fla. Osteo Found. (v.p.), Ga. Osteopathic Med. Assn. (chmn. Olympic com. 1995—), Fla Osteo. Med. Assn. (Dade county chpt. chmn. osteo. lit. com., conv. chmn. dist. two 1994, dist. #7 Sarasota County), Internat. Acad. Osteo. Medicine (bd. trustees), Minn. Gymnastic Assn. (founder 1962-72), Fla. Acad. Osteopathy Student Assn. at Southeastern Coll. Osteopathic Medicine (originator, advisor), Dade-Broward Osteopathic Med. County Soc., Duval County Osteopathic Soc., Twin-City Model A Ford Club, Pierce Arrow Soc. (sec. Fla. region 1988, news reporter Arrow Driver Midwest region, Mpls., life, founder Midwest region, 1983, dir./treas., 1983-84, gen. chmn. Midwest region swapmeet, Golden Valley, 19990, nat. dir. 1983-84, contbr. articles to Arrow Jour.), Cadillac LaSalle Club (founder 1978, treas. North Star region 1978-83), Classical Car Club Am. (life, membership chmn. Minn. upper midwest region 1977, sec. 1978, Gold Coast region-Fla.), Antique Auto Club. Am. (life Capital City chpt., Minn. region, Ft. Lauderdale region, Jacksonville region, Venice chpt., Lemon Bay region), Breakfast club Mpls., Y.E.S. Club 1st Nat. Bank Deerwood (Minn.), Scottish Rite, Valley of St. Paul, Lions (Bay Lake, Minn. del. to internat. conv., Miami, Fla., 1989), Optimist (dir. Mpls. 1959-62, 69-72, pres. 1970-71, gen. chmn. fl. exercise Olympic gynmastic program 1959-65), Masons (life, Capitol City #217, St. Paul), Shriners (life mem. Zuhrah Shrine Temple, Mpls., fund raising com.), Phi Sigma Gamma (life, nat. pres. 1987-89, pres. grand coun. and found. 1987-89, grand coun. advisor and chmn. bd.), Arlingtonshire Club (Jacksonville), Cummer Gallery of Art and Gardens, Arlington Preservation Soc. (Jacksonville). Home: 1238 Lucaya Ave Venice FL 34292

HRIBERNIK, STEVEN JOSEPH, oral and maxillofacial surgeon; b. Staunton, Ill., Oct. 20, 1958; s. Michael John and Kathryn Mary (Hoehn) H.; m. Sandra Kay Harmer, June 27, 1981; children: Erin Elizabeth, Steven John. BS in Pharmacy, St. Louis Coll. Pharmacy, 1981; DMD, So. Ill. U., Alton, 1987; cert. in oral and maxillofacial surgery, U. Louisville, 1991. Diplomate Am. Bd. Oral and Maxillofacial Surgery. Resident in oral and maxillofacial surgery U. Louisville Dental Sch., 1987-91; pvt. practice, St. Louis, 1991—. Fellow Am. Assn. Oral and Maxillofacial Surgeons, Mo. Assn. Oral and Maxillofacial Surgeons; mem. ADA, Mo. Dental Assn., Rho Chi, Omicron Kappa Upsilon. Roman Catholic. Office: Affiliated Oral &Maxillofacial Sur 9911 Kennerly Rd Ste E Saint Louis MO 63128

HRICENIAK, JUDITH, nursing administrator; b. Thomaston, Conn., July 30, 1938; d. Enos and Helen (Krayeski) Ptachcinski; m. John Hriceniak, Nov. 26, 1959; 1 child, Kim Marie. BS in Nursing, Boston U., 1960; MS in Edn., Ctrl. Conn. State Coll., 1968; MS in Nursing, U. Conn., 1982, PhD, 1984. Dir. home care svcs. Bristol (Conn.) Hosp., Inc., 1970-90; faculty Ctrl. Conn. State U., New Britain, 1973-80, chmn. dept. nursing, 1980-94, chmn. dept. health & human svcs. professions, 1994—. Mem. ANA, N.E. Orgn. for Nursing, Nat. League Nursing, Conn. Assn. for Home Care (bd. dirs.), Conn. Nurses Assn. (pres. 1991-93), Sigma Theta Tau, Phi Delta Kappa, Phi Lambda Theta.

HRISO, EMMANUEL, psychiatrist, neurologist, medical director; b. Paris, Jan. 4, 1958; came to the U.S., 1970; s. Omiros and Rena (Mangasaryan) H.; m. Carol Lynn Chaney, May 28, 1995. BS, St. Peter's Coll., Jersey City, 1978; MD, U. Ctrl. del Este, San Pedro, Dominican Republic, 1982. Diplomate in psychiatry, neurology, geriatric and addiction psychiatry Am. Bd. Psychiatry and Neurology. Intern, resident in psychiatry Temple U., Phila., 1982-86, resident in neurology, fellow in behavioral neurology, 1986-89; psychiatrist Essex County Hosp. Ctr., Cedar Grove, N.J., 1989-92, Jersey City Med. Ctr., 1991-94; attending neurologist St. Vincent's Med. Ctr., N.Y.C., 1992-94; psychiatrist Palisades Gen. Hosp. Counseling Ctr., North Bergen, N.J., 1993-96; med. dir. Ctr. for Behavioral Medicine Meml. Med. Ctr., South Amboy, N.J., 1993—; v.p., med. dir. Ctr. for Behavioral Medicine Meml. Med. Ctr., South Amboy, 1995—; med. dir. Endeavor House, Keyport, N.J., 1994—. Contbr. articles to profl. jours. Mem. APA, Am. Acad. Neurology. Office: Meml Med Ctr 540 Bordentown Ave South Amboy NJ 08879

HRNA, DANIEL JOSEPH, pharmacist, lawyer; b. Taylor, Tex., March 19, 1940; s. Stephan Peter and Anna Ludmilla (Baran) H.; BS, U. Houston, 1963, JD, 1970; m. Velma Isobel Lesson, Sept. 3, 1963 (dec. Jan. 1994); children: Anna Marie, Daniel Steven, Brian Keith. Bar: Tex. 1972. In mgmt., Gunning-Casteel Co., El Paso, Tex., 1963-65; dir. pharmacy svcs. Tex. Inst. Rehab. & Rsch., Houston, 1966-79; dir. pharmacy Alief Gen. Hosp., Belhaven Hosp., Houston, 1979-85, West Houston Med. Ctr., 1985-88; mem. faculty Baylor U. Coll. Medicine, 1977-79, Sharpstown Gen. Hosp., 1988-94; with Owen Healthcare, Inc at Sharpstown Gen. Hosp., 1990-94; pvt. practice, 1994—. Mem. ABA, Am. Pharm. Assn., Tex. Pharmacy Assn., State Bar Tex., Tex. Soc. Hosp. Pharmacists, Am. Soc. Pharmacy Law, Am. Hosp. Assn., Harris County Pharm. Assn., Houston Bar Assn., Galveston-Houston Pharm. Hosp. Assn., Czech Heritage Soc. Tex. (legal adv., trustee), Profl. Photographers Guild Houston (hon.), Delta Theta Phi, Kappa Psi, Phi Delta Chi. Roman Catholic. Office: 11920 Beechnut St Houston TX 77072-4034

HRUBETZ, JOAN, nursing educator; b. Collinsville, Ill., June 1, 1935; d. Frederick and Josephine (Nepute) H. RN, St. John's Hosp., St. Louis, 1956; BSN, St. Louis U., 1960, MA, 1970, PhD in Edn. and Counseling, 1975. Staff nurse St. John's Hosp., St. Louis, 1956-59; instr. med./surg. nursing St. Louis Mcpl. Sch. Nursing, 1960-63; asst. dir. nursing svc. Barnes Hosp., St. Louis, 1963-65; asst. dir. sch. nursing Barnes Hosp., 1965-68, ednl. cons., 1968-70, dir. sch. nursing, 1970-74; dir. undergrad. mprog. nursing St. Louis U., 1975-82, asst. to assoc. prof. nursing, 1975—, assoc. prof. pastoral health care, 1986—, dean Sch. Nursing, 1982—; lectr. in field. Contbr. articles to profl. jours. Bd. dirs. Paraquad, Inc., Ctr. Independent Living, 1985-87, hon. mem., 1987—; bd. dirs. Kenrick-Glennon Seminar, 1988, sec. bd., 1989-90; mem. adv. com. project on Clin. Edn. in Care of Elderly, 1989. Group Health Found. grantee, 1987-88, 88-89, St. Louise U. Hosps. grantee, 1980-83, others. Mem. Mo. Assn. Adminstrs. of Baccalaureate and Higher Deg. Progs. in Nursing, St. Louis Assn. Deans and Dirs. of Schs. Nursing, Am. Assn. Colls. of Nursing (adv. com. to baccalaureate data project), Am. Nurses Assn., Mo. Nurses Assn., 3rd Dist. Mo. Nurses Assn., Nat. League Nursing, Mo. League for Nursing, St. Louis Reg. League for Nursing, Midwest Alliance in Nursing (governing bd. 1985-87, chair 1986-87, resolutions com. 1987-89), Conf. Jesuit Schs. Nursing, St. Louis Met. Hosp. Assn. Office: St Louis U 3525 Caroline Blvd Saint Louis MO 63103*

HRUSHESKY, WILLIAM JOHN MICHAEL, internist, oncologist, chronobiologist, inventor, educator; b. Poughkeepsie, N.Y., Nov. 9, 1947; s. William Michael and Mary Margaret (Burns) H.; m. Donna M. Turchetti; m. Patricia A. Wood, June 28, 1985; 1 child, Cassandra Marie Nicole. BA in Philosophy with honors Syracuse U., 1969; MD U. Buffalo, 1973. Diplomate Am. Bd. Internal Medicine, Am. Bd. Med. Oncology. Assoc. cancer scientist Roswell Park Meml. Hosp., Buffalo, 1971-73; fellow Johns Hopkins U., Balt., 1973-74; intern Balt. City Hosp., 1973-74; clin. assoc. Nat. Cancer Inst. NIH, Bethesda, Md., 1974-76; resident U. Minn.-Mpls., 1976-78, research fellow, 1978-79, asst. prof., 1979-86, assoc. prof., 1986-89; prof. internal medicine microbiology/Immunobiology Albany Med. Coll., 1989—; prof. chem. engring. R.P.I., 1989—; sr. attending oncologist Stratton VAMC, 1989—; prof. pharmaceutics Albany Coll. Pharmacy, 1989—, prof. dept. biomedical scis. SUNY, Albany; cons. various tech. med. sci. instrument cos., 1982—; pres., chmn. Sine-o-graph Corp., Mpls., 1984—; pres., chmn., founder Info-Med Corp., 1985—; women's health advisor FDA, Nat. Acad. Scis., Pres.'s Cancer Panel. Author: Temporal Control of Drug Delivery, 1991, Circadian Cancer Therapy, 1994; mem. editorial bd. Chronobiology jour., Oncology jour.; patentee in field; contbr. over 500 articles to profl. jours. Adv. to special asst. to gov., St. Paul, 1984. Served to lt. comdr. USPHS, 1975-76. Grantee Union Internationale Contre le Cancer, India, 1979, NIH, 1982—, Nat. Cancer Inst., 1982—, Nat. Inst. Heart, Lung and Blood, 1985, Nat. Inst. on Aging, 1985, Varags, VA Merit Review, 1991—. Fellow ACP; mem. Internat. Soc. Chronobiology, Am. Soc. Clin. Oncology, Am. Assn. Cancer Research, Am. Fedn. Clin. Research. Club: Calhoun Beach (Mpls.), Cosmos club (Wash D.C.). Achievements include discovery and devel. of a simple urine test to predict kidney transplant rejection, devel. of only useful model for human kidney cancer; discovery of circadian dependence of the toxic/therapeutic ratio of cancer chemotherapy in human patients, timing of breast cancer resection within the menstrual cycle determines its cure frequency and the survival of young women with this common disease, computer based method of quasi-instantaneously measuring cardiovascular health/aerobic capacity; discovery and devel. of only useful cheotheraphy program for metastatic kidney cancer. Home: Head Of Ford Ave Troy NY 12180-5847 Office: Stratton VA Med Ctr 113 Holland Ave Albany NY 12208-3410

HSIA, JUDITH ANN, physician; b. Boston, Jan. 29, 1954; d. David Yi-Yung and Hsio Hsuan (Shih) H.; m. Ernest Jay Isenstadt, Jan. 28, 1983; children: Jill, Ruth. AB, Harvard Coll., 1974; MD, U. Ill., Chgo., 1978. Diplomate Am. Bd. Internal Medicine. Intern, resident Tufts-New Eng. Med. Ctr., 1978-81; asst. prof. medicine George Washington U., Washington, 1988-93, assoc. prof. medicine, 1993—. Author: (chpt.) Cardiology and Co-Existing Disease, 1994, (chpt.) Primary Health Care for Women, 1995. Recipient Louis N. Katz award Am. Heart Assn., 1984, Pfizer Scholar's award Pfizer Pharm., 1987. Fellow Am. Coll. Cardiology; mem. Alpha Omega Alpha. Office: George Washington Univ 2150 Pennsylvania Ave NW Washington DC 20037

HSIAO, CHIE-FANG, neuroscientist; b. Chi-Yei, Taiwan, Jan. 15, 1945; came to U.S., 1983; s. Zu-Chin and Chiao (Ching) H.; m. Shu-Lan Lin, Jan. 29, 1976; children: Kathryne, Amy. BS in Pharmacology, Taipei (Taiwan) Med. Coll., 1976; PhD in Med. Sci., Osaka (Japan) U., 1983. Rsch. assoc. SUNY, Stony Brook, 1983-85, U. Colo., Boulder, 1985-89; rsch. instr. U. Mo., Kansas City, 1989-92; neuroscientist U. Calif., L.A., 1992—; lectr. U. Mo., Kansas City, 1988-89; rsch. instr. Osaka U. Med. Sch., 1981-83, U. Calif., L.A., 1992—. Advisor Taipei Med. Sch. Alumni, Calif., 1993, Taiwanese Assn., Colo., 1985. Recipient Nat. Rsch. Svc. award NIH, 1992, fellowship Fight for Sight Inc., 1984, scholarship Japan Rotary, 1982. Mem. AAAS, Soc. for Neurosci., Naturalistic Soc. USA. Home: 1437 S Westgate Ave Apt 12 Los Angeles CA 90025-2250 Office: Univ Calif 405 Hilgard Ave Los Angeles CA 90024-1301

HSIEH, LING-LING, public health educator; b. Taiwan, Mar. 1, 1955; d. P. S. and Y. C. (Chiou) H. B in Pub. Health, Nat. Taiwan U., Taipei, 1977, MPH, 1979; DrPH, Columbia U., N.Y.C., 1985. Teaching asst. Nat. Taiwan U., 1978-79; lectr. Nat. Def. Med. Ctr., Taipei, 1979-82; teaching asst. Columbia U., 1982-83, grad. rsch. asst., 1983-85; postdoctoral rsch. scientist Columbia U., N.Y.C., 1985-90, instr., 1986-90; assoc. prof., head pub. health dept. Chang Gung Med. Coll., Tao-Yuan, Taiwan, 1989—. Mem. Am. Assn. Cancer Rsch., Soc. Chinese Bioscientists in Am., N.Y. Acad. Scis., Harvey Soc. N.Y., Phi Tau Phi. Office: Chang Gung Med Coll, 259 Wen-Hwa 1 Rd, Tao-Yuan 33332, Taiwan

HSU, CHUNG YI, neurologist; b. Taipei, Taiwan, China, Oct. 14, 1944; s. Huo and Jane (Wu) H.; m. Amy Yang, Sept. 27, 1974; children: Alice L., Virginia, Charles Y. MD, Nat. Taiwan U., Taipei, 1970; PhD, U. Va., 1975. Diplomate Am. Bd. Psychiatry and Neurology. NIH fellow Diabetes Rsch. Ctr., U. Va., Charlottesville, 1975-77; fellow dept. pharmacology Med. U. S.C., Charleston, 1977, intern dept. medicine, 1977-78, resident dept. neurology, 1978-80, chief resident dept. neurology, 1980-81, fellow clin. neuropharmacology, 1981, dir. neuropharmacology dept. neurology, 1981-89; dir. neuropharmacology div. restorative neurology Baylor Coll. Medicine, Houston, 1989-93; head cerebrovascular disease sect., dept. neurology Washington U. Sch. Medicine, St. Louis, 1993—; mem. adv. panel on drug info. U.S. Pharmacopeial Conv., Rockville, Md., 1985-90; mem. CNS adv. panel Eastman-Kodak/Sterling, Malvern, Pa., 1988-94; mem. study sect. Nat. Inst. Neurol. Disease and Stroke, NIH, 1988—. Mem. editl. bd. Stroke, Jour. Cerebral Blood Flow and Metabolism, Jour. Neurotrauma; mem. guest editl. bd. Jour. Formosan Med. Assn.; editor 2 monographs; contbr. articles to profl. jours. Pres. Taiwanese Assn., Charleston, 1984-85. 2d lt. Taiwan Navy, 1970-71. Grad fellow U.Va. Sch. Medicine, Charlottesville, 1971-75; recipient Nat. Rsch. Svc. award USPHS, 1977, 81, NIH Tchr. Investigator Devel. award 1983-88, NIH Javits Neurosci. Investigator award, 1991—, Disting. Rschr. award Vivian L. Smith Found., 1993-94. Fellow Am. Acad. Neurology; mem. Am. Heart Assn. (fellow stroke coun., chair brain rev. com. 1996—), Am. Neurol. Assn., Taiwan Stroke Soc., Taiwan Neurol. Soc., Internat. Soc. Cerebral Blood Flow and Metabolism, Neurotrauma Soc. (pres. 1992-93), N.Am. Taiwanese Prof. Assn. (pres.-elect 1994-95, pres. 1995-96, past pres. 1996—), Dana Alliance for Brain Initiatives. Home: 538 Conway Village Dr Saint Louis MO 63141-5807 Office: Washington U Sch Medicine Dept Neurology Box 8111 660 S Euclid Ave Saint Louis MO 63110

HSU, GREGORY SHOOU-REN, osteopath; b. L.A., June 12, 1963; s. Paul and Shirley H. BS in Biology, U. Calif., Irvine, 1985; DO, Coll. Osteo. Med. the Pacific, 1990. Diplomate Am. Bd. Osteo. Ophthalmology, Am. Bd. Ophthalmology. Intern Ohio U., Dayton, 1990-91; resident in ophthalmology Ohio U., Athens, 1991-94; pvt. practice Nev. Eye and Ear, Las Vegas, 1994—; assoc. clin. prof. U. Nev. Coll. Medicine, Reno, 1994; asst. clin. prof. Coll. of Osteo. Medicine Pacific, 1994; clin. instr. Ohio U., 1992. Dep. sheriff Montgomery County, Ohio, 1991, dep. coroner, 1992. Mem. Am. Osteo. Assn. Office: Nev Eye and Ear 600 Whitney Ranch Rd Henderson NV 89014

HSU, ZUEY-SHIN, physiology educator; b. Shining, Taiwan, Republic of China, Dec. 13, 1930; s. Kua and Mun Mei (Kuo) H.; m. Pan Tsu Wu, Feb. 1, 1964; 1 child, Sheng Chin. MD, Nat. Taiwan U., 1956; D in Physiology (hon.), London Inst. Applied Rsch., 1991. Intern in internal medicine Nat. Taiwan U., 1956-57; asst. Kaohsiung Med. Coll., Kaohsiung City, Republic of China, 1957-59, instr., 1959-62, assoc. prof. legal medicine, 1962-68, assoc. prof. physiology, 1968-72, prof. physiology, 1972—, acting dir. dept. pharmacology, 1972-73, dir. dept. pharmacology, 1973-74, dir. dept. physiology, 1972-85; prof. H.S. Rsch. Alliance Universelle pour la Paix pa la Connaissance, 1991. Inventor method of detoxicating heterologous blood for transfusion, 1978; a new immunological method for desensitizing allergic individuals, 1981, preparation of tumor vaccine 1987. Nat. Sci. Council of Taiwan grantee, 1967. Fellow Inst. Med. Sci., Tokyo U., Internat. Biographical Assn. (life); mem. Internat. Parliament for Safety and Peace, Maison Internationale des Intellectuels and Academi Midi, Formosan Med. Assn., Chinese Physiol. Soc., Chinese Soc. Immunology, Endocrine Soc. of Republic of China, Chinese Pharmacological Soc. Home: Fl 8 No 153, Min Tsu Rd, Taichung Taiwan Office: Kaohsiung Med Coll, 100 Shih-Chuan 1st Rd, Kaohsiung 80708, Taiwan

HU, EDNA GERTRUDE FENSKE, pediatrics nurse; b. Arlington, S.D., June 11, 1922; d. Walter O. and Therese (Kautz) Fenske; m. Patrick P.C. Hu, Nov. 26, 1954; children: Lou Anne Hu Yee, Mark C., Lawrence P. BS in Nursing, U. Colo. Sch. Nursing, 1954. RN, Colo. Staff pediatrics nurse Colo. Gen. Hosp., Denver, 1954-63, night nursing supr., 1963-65; staff nurse alcohol withdrawal unit Denver Gen. Hosp., 1971-73; staff surg. nurse Fitzsimons Army Hosp., Denver, 1973-79; staff nurse VA Hosp., Allens Pk., Mich., 1979-81, Drug and Alcohol Withdrawal and Rehab. Ctr., Ft. Dodge, Iowa, 1981-83; researcher Ft. Collins, Colo., 1988—; researcher effects on memory following long term residence in another culture; instr. English, health care, Asia. Recipient Disting. Alumna award Class of 1954. Mem. ANA, Colo. Nurses Assn., Non-practicing and Part-time Nurses Assn. Home: 2518 Timber Ct Fort Collins CO 80521-3120

HU, FUNG-RONG, ophthalmologist, medical researcher; b. Taichung, Taiwan, Sept. 1, 1956; s. Hui-Te and Chan-Chin (Chan) H.; m. Shan-Chwen Chang; children: Hao-Chun Chang, Hao-Yun Chang. MD, Nat. Taiwan U., 1981. Intern Nat. Taiwan U. Hosp., Taipei, 1980-81, resident, 1981-85, attending staff, 1985—, lectr. ophthalmology, 1985-93; postdoctoral fellow Harvard Med. Sch., Boston, 1988-89; fellow in ophthalmology Mass. Eye and Ear Infirmary, Boston, 1988-89; assoc. prof. Nat. Taiwan Univ., Taipei, 1993—; chief cornea sect. dept. ophthalmology Nat. Taiwan U. Hosp., 1996—; cons. Lo-Ton (Taiwan) Po-Ai Hosp., 1985—, Cathay Gen. Hosp., Taipei, 1990—. Contbr. articles to profl. jours. Mem. Ophathlmol. Soc. of Republic of China (supr. 1994—, exec. gen. acad. com. 1991-93, exec. gen. fin. com. 1991-93), Formosan Med. Assn., Am. Acad. Ophthalmology. Office: Nat Taiwan Univ Hosp, No 7 Chung-Shan South Rd, Taipei Taiwan

HUANG, ANDREW J.W., ophthalmologist; b. Taipei, Taiwan, June 22, 1955. MD, Nat. Taiwan U., 1981; MPH, Johns Hopkins U., 1982. Diplomate Am. Bd. Ophthalmology. Postdoctoral fellow Johns Hopkins U., Balt., 1982-84; rsch. fellow Harvard U., Boston, 1984-86; from resident in ophthalmology to corneal Bascom Palmer Eye Inst., Miami, 1987-91; asst. prof. U. Miami, 1991—. Fellow Am. Acad. Ophthalmology (editor 1996—); mem. Assn. Rsch. for Vision and Ophthalmology. Office: Bascom Palmer Eye Inst 900 NW 17th Miami FL 33136

HUANG, CHUONG CHUN, psychiatrist, educator, neuroscientist; b. Taipei, Taiwan, July 1, 1936; came to U.S., 1963; s. Tseng Chien and Wang Shih (Yu) H.; m. Mei Fun Wu, Dec. 28, 1968; children: Elbert S., Frederick Y. MD, Nat. Taiwan U., 1962; PhD, UCLA, 1968. Intern Nat. Taiwan U. Hosp., 1961-62; resident in psychiatry Mo. Inst. Psychiatry, U. Mo., Columbia, 1973-75, U. Iowa Hosps. and Clinics, 1975-77; postgrad. physiologist Brain Rsch. Inst., UCLA, 1968-69, asst. rsch. physiologist, 1969-70; asst. prof. psychiatry U. Mo.-Columbia, St. Louis, 1970-73; asst. prof. psychiatry Med. Coll. Wis., Milw., 1977-87, assoc. prof., 1987—; med. dir. socio-psychiatry unit Milw. Med. Complex, 1986-90; mem. med. record com. Milw. Mental Health Complex, 1978—. Contbr. articles to profl. publs. 2d lt. Taiwan Air Force, 1962-63. Recipient Disting. Svc. to Community award Internat. Biographic Ctr., 1988. Mem. AMA (Physician Recognition award 1971, 77, 81, 84, 87, 90, 93, 96), Am. Psychiatry Assn., N.Y. Acad. Scis., Soc. Neurosci., Formosa Club. Buddhist. Home: 3304 S 123rd St West Allis WI 53227-3813 Office: Milw Mental Health Complex 9455 W Watertown Plank Rd Milwaukee WI 53226-3559

HUANG, ENG-SHANG, virology educator, biomedical engineer; b. Chia-Yi, Taiwan, Republic of China, Mar. 17, 1940; came to U.S., 1968; s. Juong-Sun and King-fa (Ong) H.; m. Shu-Mei Huong, Dec. 26, 1965; children: David Y., Benjamin Y. BS, Nat. Taiwan U., Taipei, Taiwan, 1962, MS, 1964; PhD, U. N.C., 1971. Asst. prof. U. N.C., Chapel Hill, 1973-78, assoc. prof., 1978-86, prof., 1986—; virology program leader Cancer Rsch. Ctr., Chapel Hill, 1979-91; mem. virology study sect. DRG/NIH, Bethesda, Md., 1978-82; mem. AIDS basic rsch. rev. com. Nat. Inst. Allergy & Infectious Diseases/ NIH, 1988-90; chmn. Internat. Sci. Promotion Com., U.S. chpt., 1988—. Contbr. articles to Molecular Biology of Human Cytomegalovirus, Devel. Abnormality Induced by Cytomegalovirus Infection, Interaction between Cytomegalovirus and Human Immunodeficiency Virus. Chmn. membership com. Soc. Chinese Bioscientists in Am., Washington, 1988-89. Lt. ROTC, 1964-65. NIH fellow, 1971-73, Rsch. Career Devel. award NIAID, NIH, 1978-83; grantee in field. Mem. AAAS, Am. Soc. Microbiology, N.Y. Acad. Sci., Am. Cancer Rsch. Democrat. Office: U NC Lineberger Cancer Ctr Chapel Hill NC 27599

HUANG, JACOB CHEN-YA, physician, city official; b. Chia-Yi, Taiwan, Dec. 25, 1937; came to U.S., 1966, naturalized, 1974; s. Chang-Chiang and Agenes Cheng-Jen H.; m. Vivian Lin, Oct. 3, 1970; children: Phyllis, Albert, Edward. Intern, Taipei City Hosp., 1964-65, house officer in pediatrics, 1965-66; fellow in clin. pathology Albert Einstein Coll. Medicine-Lincoln Hosp., 1968-70; chief drug diagnostic sect. N.Y.C. chief med. examiner, 1968-79; resident in family medicine Lutheran Med. Center, N.Y.C., 1970-71; clin. asso. prof. NYU, 1972-76; dist. health dir. N.Y.C., Dept. Health, 1971-76; med. dir. Paterson City (N.J.) Health Dept., 1977—; chmn. dept. family practice Dover (N.J.) Gen. Hosp. and Med. Center, 1980—; trustee N.J. Passaic PRO, 1987—; bd. dirs. ambulatory care adv. bd. Beth Israel Hosp., N.Y.C., 1972-76, cmty. adv. bd. ambulatory svcs. St. Vincent Med. Ctr., N.Y.C., 1972-76, COMED-IPA Inc., N.J., 1980—; bd. dirs. Mount Olive City (N.J.) Bd. of Health, 1993—. Recipient Physician's Recognition award AMA. Diplomate Am. Bd. Family Practice. Fellow Am. Coll. Preventive Medicine, Am. Acad. Family Physicians; mem. Am. Public Health Assn., Am. Chinese Med. Assn. N.J. (pres., founder), N.J. Am. Acad. Family Physicians (trustee 1994—, bd. dirs. 1994—, exec. bd. dirs. 1995—), Chinese Am. Med. Soc. (bd. dirs.), Columbia U. Sch. Pub. Health Alumni Assn. (exec. bd. 1992—). Home: 3 Walnut Hill Dr Chester NJ 07930-3006 Office: Bartley Sq Rte 206 Flanders NJ 07836

HUANG, SHOEI K. STEPHEN, physician; b. Hualien, Taiwan, Dec. 7, 1947. MD, Nat. Taiwan U., 1972. Diplomate Am. Bd. Internal Medicine. Asst. prof. medicine U. Ariz. Sch. of Medicine, Tucson, 1982-88; assoc. prof. medicine U. Mass. Med. Sch., Worcester, 1988-92, prof. medicine, 1992—; dir. cardiac electrophysiology and pacing, U. Ariz. Health Scis. Ctr., Tucson, 1982-88, U. Mass. Med. Ctr., Worcester, 1988-96. Editor: Radiofrequency Catheter Ablation of Cardiac Arrhythmias, 1994; inventor in field. Founder/Svc. award Mass. Electrophysiology Soc., 1993; grantee NIH, Bethesda, 1985, 88, VA, Washington, 1986, Am. Heart Assn., Dallas, 1985. Fellow Am. Heart Assn., Am. Coll. Physician, Am. Coll. Cardiology, Am. Fedn. for Clin. Rsch.; mem. N.Am. Soc. Pacing and Electrophysiology.

HUANG, TIEN-SHANG, medical educator; b. Tainan, Taiwan, Aug. 17, 1949; s. Zu-Ren and Tsai-Hua (Chang) H.; m. Su-Hui Lee, Jan. 10, 1978; children: Steve, Elise, Jean, Helen. MD, Nat. Taiwan U., 1974. Resident dept. medicine Nat. Taiwan U., Taipei, 1976-79, chief resident dept. medicine, 1979-80, asst. prof. med. coll., 1986-89; assoc. prof. med. coll. Nat. Taiwan U., 1989-93, prof., 1993—; dir. office med. edn. Nat. Taiwan U. Hosp; fellow Sch. Medicine UCLA, 1981-86; adj. instr. sch. medicine UCLA, 1982-86. Contbr. articles to profl. jours. Lt. Taiwan Army, 1974-76. Mem. AMA, The Endocrine Soc., Am. Thyroid Assn., N.Y. Acad. Sci., Am. Fedn. Clin. Rsch., European Thyroid Assn. Office: Nat Taiwan U Hosp, 7 Chun-Shan S Rd, Taipei 106, Taiwan

HUANG, TIM HUI-MING, cytogeneticist, educator; b. Tainan, Taiwan, Nov. 6, 1957; came to U.S., 1982; s. Chiu-hui and Chin-Ying (Mu) H.; m. Susan Leu, Sept. 6, 1986; children: Victor, Deren. PhD, U. Calif., Davis, 1989; postgrad., Baylor Coll. Medicine, 1991. Diplomate Am. Bd. Med. Genetics. Dir. cytogenetics Ellis Fischel Cancer Ctr., Columbia, Mo., 1991—; asst. prof. U. Mo., Columbia, 1991—. Contbr. articles to med. jours. Mem. Am. Soc. Human Genetics, Am. Assn. Cancer Rsch. Office: Rm 2007 115 Business Loop I-70W Columbia MO 65203

HUBBARD, JACK EDWARD, neurologist; b. Cleve., Mar. 18, 1944; s. Jack Edward and Mary Jane (Bowman) H.; m. Kathleen Ann Kroening, Nov. 2, 1968; children: Kristin Lynn, Alicia Ann, Mark Aaron. BA, North Ctrl. Coll., Naperville, Ill., 1967; PhD, Loyola U. Chgo., 1971; MD, U. Louisville, 1977. Diplomate Am. Bd. Psychiatry and Neurology, Am. Bd. Pain Medicine. Intern Hennepin County Med. Ctr., 1977-78; resident U. Minn., 1978-81; med. dir. Rehab. Assocs. pain mgmt. program Mpls. Clinic of Neurology Ltd., 1981—; clin. asst. prof. neurology U. Minn., Mpls.; asst. prof. anatomy U. Louisville, 1971-74; mem. med. staff Fairview Ridge Hosp., chief of staff, 1991-92. Contbr. articles to profl. jours. John Walker Moor scholar, 1976. Mem. Am. Acad. Thermology (treas. 1992-93, program chmn. 1986, 96, Pres.'s award 1984), Minn. Pain Study Group (chmn. 1993—). Lutheran. Office: Minneapolis Clin Neurology 305 E Nicollet Blvd #185 Burnsville MN 55337

HUBBARD, LINCOLN BEALS, medical physicist, consultant; b. Hawkesbury, Ont., Can., Sept. 8, 1940; s. Carroll Chauncey and Mary Lunn (Beals) H.; came to U.S., 1957; m. Nancy Ann Krieger, Apr. 3, 1961; children: Jill, Katrina. B.S. in Physics, U. N.H., 1961; Ph.D., MIT, 1967. Diplomate Am. Bd. Radiology; cert. health physicist Am. Bd. Health Physics. Postdoctoral appointee Argonne Nat. Lab., 1966-68; asst. prof. math. and physics Knoxville Coll. (Tenn.), 1968-70; asst. prof. physics Furman U., Greenville, S.C., 1970-74; chief physicist Mt. Sinai Hosp., Chgo., 1974-75, 79—, Cook County Hosp., Chgo., 1975-88; ptnr. Fields, Griffith, Hubbard & Broadbent, Inc., 1978-93; pres. Hubbard, Broadbent & Assoc., Ltd., 1993—; assoc. prof. med. physics, Rush U., 1986— . Mem. Am. Assn. Physicists in Medicine, Am. Coll. Radiology, Am. Phys. Soc. Author: (with S.S. Stefani) Mathematics for Technologists, 1979, (with G. B. Greenfield) Computers in Radiology, 1984. Home and Office: 4113 W End Rd Downers Grove IL 60515-2307

HUBBARD, MARGARET ANNA, medical sonographer; b. Erie, Pa., May 4, 1947; d. John and Lucy (Love) Hamilton; m. William John Hubbard, June 12, 1965 (div. 1978); children: William John II, Michelle Renee. Grad., Genesee Hosp. Sch., Rochester, N.Y., 1980. Sonographer Strong Meml. Hosp., Rochester, 1980; radiologic tech. and sonographer Wilson Health Ctr., Rochester, 1981, IDE Radiology, Rochester, 1982-84; sonographer Copland, Hyman and Shackman, Balt., 1984-85, George Washington U., Washington, 1985-87, Washington Ultrasound, 1987-89, South Bay Radiology, San Diego, 1989; prin. Ultrasound Assocs., San Diego, 1989—. Vol. with abused children, San Diego, 1989—. Mem. Am. Registry Radiologic Techs., Soc. Diagnostic Med. Sonographers. Roman Catholic. Home and Office: 11219 Provencal Pl San Diego CA 92128-3670

HUBBARD, OSCAR EDWIN, retired psychiatrist; b. Ithaca, N.Y., Nov. 14, 1903; s. George David and Edna Elmira (Rugg) H.; widowed; 1 child, George David II. AB, Oberlin Coll., 1925; MD, Johns Hopkins U., 1930. Diplomate, Am. Bd. Psychiatry and Neurology. Intern Church Home and Infirmary, Balt., 1930-31; resident Strong Meml. Hosp., Rochester, N.Y., 1931-32, Yale U. Inst. Human Rels., New Haven, 1932-34; psychiatrist Fairfield State Hosp., Newtown, Conn., 1934-35; fellow in child psychiatry Louisville Child Guidance Clinic, 1935-36; instr. psychiatry U. Louisville Med. Sch., 1936-37; dir. Child Guidance Clinic Buffalo, 1937-41; psychiatrist US VA, Dallas, then Houston, 1946-51, Rikers Island, City of N.Y., 1974-91; chief mental health div., Territory of Alaska, 1953-57; prof. psychiatry, U. Miss., Jackson, 1957-69; electroencepahlographer, Bronx State Hosp., 1969-74. Lt. col. USAF, 1941-46, 51-53. Fellow Am. Psychiat. Soc., N.Y. Acad.Scis. Democrat. Home: 1 Pond St Apt 10-i Winthrop MA 02152

HUBBARD, RICHMOND CHASE, psychiatrist; b. Saylesville, R.I., June 19, 1916; s. Carleton Waterbury and Katharine (Chase) H.; m. Jeanne Marie Pawloski, Sept. 12, 1965; children: David, Ruth, Brenda. AB in Social Sci., Antioch Coll., 1940; MD, U. Cin., 1946. Diplomate Am. Bd. Psychiatry and Neurology. Instr. social sci. Antioch Coll., Yellow Springs, Ohio, 1940-42; resident in psychiatry Elgin (Ill.) State Hosp., 1949-54; pvt. practice Bethel, Conn., 1954—. Pres. Eagle Hill Hosp. Corp., 1977; chmn. Med. Rsch. Modernizaiton Com., 1984-87. Capt. M.S., U.S. Army, 1942-49. Office: 233 Greenwood Ave Bethel CT 06801-2114

HUBBARD, RONALD E., physician; b. Little Rock, Ark., June 16, 1940; m. Linda Hubbard. BS, Hendrix Coll., 1962; MD, U. Ark., 1966. Diplomate Am. Bd. Otolaryngology. Intern St. John's Hosp., Tulsa, Okla., 1966-67; resident in surgery VA Hosp., Memphis, 1970-71; resident in otolaryngology U. Tenn., Memphis, 1971-74; physician Shea Hubbard & Futrell, Memphis, 1974—; assoc. staff Bapt. Meml. Hosp., VA Hosp., Meth. Hosp., St. Joseph Hosp., LeBonheur Children's Hosp., St. Francis Hosp., City of Memphis Hosps.; consulting staff Mid-South Hosp., Germantown Cmty. Hosp.-Meth. East; asst. clin. prof. dept. otolaryngology and maxillofacial surgery U. Tenn. Ctr. for Health Scis. Contbr. articles to profl. jours. With USN, 1967-70. Mem. AMA, So. Med. Assn., Am. Acad. Ophthalmology and Otolaryngology, Am. Rhinologic Soc., Am. Coll. Surgeons, Am. Acad. Facial Plastic and Reconstructive Surgery, Pituitary Found., Am. Acad. Otolaryngic Allergy, Memphis and Shelby County Med. Soc., Memphis So. Otolaryngology and Maxillo-Facial Surgery, Tenn. Acad. Otolaryngology, Univ. Jour. Club, Memphis Mid South Jour. Club. Office: Shea Hubbard and Futrell 6027 Walnut Grove Ste 411 Memphis TN 38120

HUBBARD, RUTH, biology educator; b. Vienna, Austria, Mar. 3, 1924; came to U.S., 1938; d. Richard and Helene (Ehrlich) Hoffmann; m. Frank Twombly Hubbard, Dec. 26, 1942 (div. 1951); m. George Wald, June 11, 1958; children: Elijah, Deborah Hannah. AB, Radcliffe Coll., 1944, PhD, 1950; DSc (hon.), Macalester Coll., 1991, U. Toronto, Ont., Can., 1991; LHD (hon.), So. Ill. U., Edwardsville, 1991. Lab. technician Tenn. Pub. Health Service, Chattanooga, 1945-46; fellow U. Coll. Hosp. Med. Sch., London, 1948-49; Guggenheim fellow Carlsberg Lab., Copenhagen, Denmark, 1952-53; research fellow Harvard U., Cambridge, Mass., 1950-52, 54-58, research assoc., lectr., 1958-74, prof., 1974-90, prof. emerita, 1990—; vis. prof. M.I.T., Cambridge, 1972; cons. Boston Women's Healthbook Collective 1982—. Author: (with Margaret Randall) The Shape of Red: Insider/Outsider Reflections, 1988; author: The Politics of Women's Biology, 1990, (with Elijah Wald) Exploding the Gene Myth, 1993, Profitable Promises: Essays on Women, Science and Health, 1995; editor: Women Look at Biology Looking at Women, 1979, Genes and Gender II, 1979, Biological Woman--The Convenient Myth, 1982, Woman's Nature: Rationalizations of Inequality, 1983, Reinventing Biology: Respect for Life and the Creation of Knowledge, 1995; contbr. more than 150 articles on sci. and women's issues to profl. and lay books and jours. Adv. coun. mem. Nat. Women's Health Network, Washington, 1980—; bd. dirs. Coun. Responsible Genetics, Boston, 1982—; mem. adv. bd. Boston Women's Fund, 1983-85; mem. adv. bd. Civil Liberties Union of Mass., 1990-91, 95—, bd. dirs., 1991-95. Recipient Paul Karrer medal Swiss Chem. Soc., 1967, Peace and Freedom award Women's Internat. League for Peace and Freedom, 1985, Feminist Marathoner award Boston chpt. NOW, 1991, Disting. Svc. award Am. Inst. Biol. Sci., 1992. Fellow AAAS; mem. Marine Biol. Lab. (trustee 1973-78, trustee emerita 1990—), Soc. Biol. Chemists, Nat. Women's Studies Assn., Phi Beta Kappa, Sigma Xi. Office: Harvard U Dept Biology 16 Divinity Ave Cambridge MA 02138-2020

HUBBARD, STEVE GARY, cardiac surgeon; b. Henryetta, Okla., Dec. 23, 1948; s. Floyd T. and Norma E. (Johnson) H.; m. Judy A. Phillips, June 16, 1983; 1 child, Matthew. BS, U. Okla., 1971; MD, U. Okla., Okla. City, 1974. Diplomate Am. Bd. Thoracic Surgery. Staff surgeon Deaconess Hosp., Billings, Mont., 1982-93, St. Vincent Hosp., Billings, 1982-93, East Ala. Med. Ctr., Opelika, Ala., 1994—; bd. dirs. Mont. Associated Physicians, Inc., Billings, 1989-92; chmn. utilization rev. East Ala. Med. Ctr., Opelika, Ala., 1995-96. Co-author (book) Recovering from Coronary Bypass, 1992. Fellow ACS; mem. AMA, Am. Coll. Physician Execs., Ala. Med. Soc., No. Plains Vascular Soc., Rocky Mt. Vascular Surg. Soc., Internat. Soc. Cardiovascular Surgery, SOc. Thoracic Surgeons. Office: E Ala Cardiac & Thoracic Surgery 2000 Pepperell Pkwy Opelika AL 36802

HUBBARD, VAN SAXTON, career medical officer, pediatrics educator; b. Middletown, N.Y., Mar. 1, 1945; s. W. Saxton and M. Elizabeth (Van Fleet) H.; m. Linda Dell Rucker, May 21, 1974; children: Brian S., Kevin S. BS, Union Coll., Schenectady, N.Y., 1967; MD, Va. Commonwealth U., Richmond, 1974, PhD, 1974. Diplomate Nat. Bd. Med. Examiners, Am. Bd. Nutrition, Am. Bd. Pediatrics; lic. U.S. ind. user of radionucleotide, AEC; cert. of radionucleotide use in patients, AEC; med. lic. Minn., D.C. Commd. surgeon USPHS, 1976—, advanced through grades to med. dir., 1988; intern, then resident in pediatrics U. Minn. Hosps., Mpls., 1974-76; fellow, clin. assoc. pediatric metabolism br. NIH, Bethesda, Md., 1976-78, med. officer pediatric metabolism br., 1978-83, dir. nutrient metabolism program, 1983-90, dir. clin. nutrition rsch. units program, 1983—; chief nutritional scis. br. NIDDK, 1993—, acting dir. divsn. nutrition rsch. coordination, 1993-94; dir. divsn. nutrition rsch. coordination, 1995—; mem. staff pediatric dept. Nat. Naval Med. Ctr., Bethesda, 1979—; asst. rsch. prof. child health and devel. George Washington U., Washington, 1981-86, assoc. rsch. prof. child health and devel., 1986—; dir. obesity, eating disorders and energy regulation program NIH, Bethesda, 1983-95, dir., project officer U.S.-Japan coop. med. sci. program, 1983-94, dir. gastrointestinal digestion program, 1988-90, chmn. nutrition coord. com., 1993—; spl. govt. employee expert FDA, 1978-84; human studies rev. com. USDA, 1986-93, policy adv. com., 1987-96; interagy. osteoporosis working grup NHANES III, 1987-95; interagy. com. on human nutrition rsch., 1987-90, 93—; nutrition policy bd. DHHS, 1994—; fish oil test materials adv. com., 1987—; mem. Bethesda Campus Disaster Med. Assistance Team, 1987—, dep. chief med. officer, 1989-90, comdr., 1990-93; dep. comdr. disaster med. assistance team PHS, 1993—; external rev. com. Ctr. Nutritional Scis., Va. Commonwealth U., 1988-91; internat. adv. bd. med. nutrition edn. project U. N.C., Chapel Hill, 1993—. Asst. editor Am. Jour. for Clin. Nutrition, 1981-86; mem. editorial bd. Jour. Nutritional Biochemistry, 1989—, Jour. Parental and Enteral Nutrition, 1991—; reviewer various jours.; contbr. articles to profl. jours. Decorated USPHS Commendation medal; recipient Outstanding Svc. medal USPHS; named Disting. Alumnus Sch. of Basic Health Scis., Va. Commonwealth U., 1989. Fellow Am. Acad. Pediat. (nutrition com. 1988—), Am. Coll Nutrition; mem. Am. Inst. Nutrition, Am. Fedn. for Clin. Rsch., Am. Gastroent. Assn. (rsch. com. 1988—, animal rsch. task force 1989-91), Am. Soc. for Clin. Nutrition (chmn. nominating com. 1987-88, ann. meeting program com., continuing nutrition edn. com. 1987-90, tellers com. 1990-92, membership com. 1992-96, chmn. 1995-96), Am. Soc. for Parenteral and Enteral Nutrition (rsch. and data com. 1984—), Nat. Cystic Fibrosis Found. (rsch. and rsch. tng. com. 1980-83, conf. com. 1980-83), Cystic Fibrosis Found. (cons. ad hoc com. 1978, med. program com. 1980-90, trustee 1981-87), N.Y. Acad. Scis., N.Am. Assn. for Study Obesity (councilor 1993-96), N.Am. Soc. Pediat. Gastroenterology and Nutrition, Soc. for Pediat. Rsch., Inst. Alumni Assoc. (fed. health care exec.), Sigma Xi. Home: 5022 Acacia Ave Bethesda MD 20814-2890 Office: NIDDK NIH Natcher Bldg Rm 6AN-18 45 Center Dr Bethesda MN 20892-6600

HUBBARD, WILLIAM NEILL, JR., pharmaceutical company executive; b. Fairmont, N.C., Oct. 15, 1919; s. William Neill and Mary Emma (Fenegan) H.; m. Elizabeth Terleski, Dec. 28, 1945 (dec. Mar. 1984); children—William Neill III, Michael J., Mary E., Elizabeth A., Susan E.; m. Joyce Elaine Wixson, Apr. 3, 1987. A.B., Columbia, 1942; postgrad., U. N.C. Sch. Medicine; M.D., N.Y. U., 1944. Mem. house staff 3d med. div. Bellevue Hosp., N.Y.C., 1944-50; instr. medicine N.Y. U., 1950-53, asst. prof., 1953-59; asst. dean, then assoc. dean N.Y. U. Coll. Medicine, 1951-59; dean U. Mich. Med. Sch., 1959-70, assoc. prof. internal medicine, 1959-64, prof., 1964-70; dir. U. Mich. Med. Center, 1969-70; gen. mgr. pharm. div., v.p. Upjohn Co., 1970-72, exec. v.p., 1972-74, pres., 1974-84, dir., 1968-91; dir. Johnson Controls, Inc., Consumers Power; bd. dirs. Pharm. Mfrs. Assn., 1978-80, 81-84, chmn. bd., 1980-81; chmn. coun. health care tech. Inst. Medicine of NAS, 1986-90; cons. USPHS; trustee N.Y. Acad. of Medicine, 1994—; bd. dirs. Pan-Am. Health and Edn. Found., 1996—. Mem. Nat. Adv. Commn. on Libraries, 1966-68; med. adv. com. W.K. Kellogg Found., 1959-67, trustee, 1979-92; mem. Gov.'s Adv. Com. on Edn. Health Care, 1965-69; trustee Bronson Meth. Hosp., 1970-84; chmn. Gov.'s Action Com. on Corrections, 1972-73; mem. panel ednl. consultants Commn. on Edn. for Health Adminstrn., 1973-75; mem. com. on med. edn. Brown U., 1974-77; mem. nat. sci. bd. NSF, 1974-80, cons. to bd., 1980-83; bd. dirs Family Health Internat. (formerly Internat. Fertility Research Program), 1981-90; mem. bd. sci. and tech. for internat. devel. Nat. Acad. Scis., 1978-80, Council on Sci. and Tech. for Devel., 1978-83; bd. visitors in East Asian studies U. Mich., 1976-80; bd. overseers Morehouse Coll., 1976-81; bd. dirs. Nat. Med. Fellowships, Inc., 1973-75, Nat. Fund. Med. Edn., 1962-75; trustee Kalamazoo Coll., 1973-78, Columbia U., N.Y.C., 1981-89; mem. bd. regents Nat. Library of Medicine, 1963-67, 72-76, chmn., 1965-67, 74-75, cons., 1976-84; bd. dirs. Am. Near East Refugee Aid, 1977-82; dir. devel. council U. Mich., 1979-87; mem. population adv. panel Office of Technology Assessment, U.S. Congress, 1979-81; chmn. bd. visitors Med. Ctr. U. Mich., 1989—; bd. visitors U. Mich. Sch. of Nursing, 1995—, Columbia U. Sch. Nursing, 1990—. Fellow ACP, Am. Acad. Arts and Scis., Royal Soc. Medicine; mem. AMA, Inst. Medicine of NAS, Harvey Soc., N.Y. Acad. Medicine, Soc. Alumni Bellevue Hosp., Mich. Med. Soc. (coun. 1960-62), Kalamazoo Acad. Medicine, Am. Soc. Clin. Pharmacology and Therapeutics, Assn. Am. Med. Colls. (pres. 1966-67), Jamestown Soc., Sigma Xi, Alpha Omega Alpha. Home: 4630 E Gull Lake Dr Hickory Corners MI 49060-9503

HUBBELL, FLOYD ALLAN, physician, educator; b. Waco, Tex., Nov. 13, 1948; s. F.E. and Margaret (Fraser) H.; m. Nancy Cooper, May 23, 1975; 1 child, Andrew Allan. BA, Baylor U., 1971, MD, 1974; MS in Pub. Health, UCLA, 1983. Diplomate Am. Bd. Internal Medicine. Intern, then resident Long Beach med. program U. Calif., Irvine, 1975-78, asst. prof. medicine, 1981-89, assoc. prof. medicine and social ecology, 1989—, dir. primary care internal medicine residency, 1992—, chief civsn. gen. internal medicine and primary care, 1992—, dir. Ctr. for Health Policy and Rsch., 1993—. Contbr. articles to profl. jours. Recipient Outstanding Tchr. award U. Calif., Irvine, 1985, 89. Fellow ACP; mem. APHA, Soc. Gen. Internal Medicine, Am. Fedn. for Clin. Rsch. Democrat. Office: U Calif Irvine Med Ctr 101 The City Dr S Orange CA 92668-3201

HUBEL, DAVID HUNTER, physiologist, educator; b. Windsor, Ont., Can., Feb. 27, 1926; s. Jesse Hervey and Elsie (Hunter) H.; m. Shirley Ruth Izzard, June 20, 1953; children: Carl Andrew, Eric David, Paul Matthew. BSc, McGill U., 1947, MD, 1951, DSc (hon.), 1978; AM (hon.), Harvard U., 1962; DSc (hon.), U. Man., 1983; DHL (hon.), Johns Hopkins U., 1990; DSci, U. Western Ont., 1993; DSc, Oxford U., 1994, Gustavus Adolphus Coll., 1994, Ohio State U., 1995. Intern Montreal Gen. Hosp., 1951-52; asst. resident neurology Montreal Neurol. Inst., 1952-53, fellow clin. neurophysiology, 1953-54; asst. resident neurology Johns Hopkins Hosp., 1954-55; rsch. fellow Walter Reed Army Inst. Rsch., Washington, 1955-58; sr. fellow neurol. scis. group Johns Hopkins U., 1958-59; faculty Harvard U. Med. Sch., 1959—, George Packer Berry prof. physiology, chmn. dept., 1967-68, George Packer Berry prof. neurobiology, 1968-82, John Franklin Enders univ. prof., 1982—; George H. Bishop lectr. exptl. neurology Washington U., St. Louis, 1964; Jessup lectr. biol. scis. Columbia, 1970; James Arthur lectr. Am. Mus. Natural History, 1972; Ferrier lectr. Royal Soc. London, 1972; Harvey lectr. Rockefeller U., 1976; Weizmann meml. lectr. Weizmann Inst. Sci., Rehovot, Israel, 1979; George Eastman prof. Oxford, Eng., 1991-92; Eastman prof., Oxford, Eng., 1991-92; Fenn lectr. 30th internat. congress Internat. Union Psychol. Sci., Vancouver B.C., Can., 1986; rschr. brain mechanisms in vision; bd. syndics Harvard U. Press, 1979-83; Brookhart lectr. Oreg. Health Scis., 1992, Murlin lectr. U. Rochester, 1992, Thurston lectr. Washington U., 1992; 1st ann. George A. Miller lectr. Cognitive Neurosci. Soc., 1995; keynote spkr. plenary session Am. Assn. for Lab. Animal Sci., Balt., 1995; Hoyt lectr. U. Calif. Sch. Medicine, San Francisco, 1995. Speaker in field. Served with AUS, 1955-58. Recipient Trustees award Rsch. to Prevent Blindness, 1971, Lewis S. Rosentiel award for disting. work in basic med. rsch., 1972, Karl Lashley prize Am. Philos. Soc., 1977, Louisa Gross Horwitz prize Columbia U., 1978, Dickson prize in medicine U. Pitts., 1979, Ledile prize Harvard U., 1980, Nobel prize, 1981, Outstanding Sci. Leadership award Nat. Assn. for Biomed. Rsch., 1990, City of Medicine award, 1990, Glen A. Fry medal Coll. Optometry, Ohio State U., 1991, Charles F. Prentice medal Am. Acad. Optometry, 1993, Helen Keller prize Helen Keller Eye Rsch. Found., 1995; fellow Harvard Soc. Fellows, 1971—, Royal Soc. Medicine, 1991, First Ann. George A. Miller lectr. Cognitive Neurosci. Soc., Gerald award Soc. Neurosci., 1993. Fellow AAAS, Am. Acad. Arts and Scis.; mem. NAS, Am. Physiol. Soc. (Bowditch lectr. 1966), Deutsche Akademie der Naturforscher Leopoldina, Soc. for Neurosci. (Grass lectr. 1976, Gerard award 1993), Assn. for Rsch. in Vision and Ophthalmology (Friedenwald award 1975), Johns Hopkins U. Soc. Scholars, Am. Philos. Soc. (Karl Spencer Lashley prize 1977), Royal Soc. London, Acadmica Europaea (fgn. mem.), Sigma Xi. Home: 98 Collins Rd Newton MA 02168-2235 Office: Harvard U Med Sch Dept Neurobiology 220 Longwood Ave Boston MA 02115-5701

HUBEL, KENNETH ANDREW, medical educator; b. N.Y.C., Nov. 11, 1927; s. G. Andrew and Madeline Barbara (Rudinger) H.; m. Janis Margaret Greer, May 19, 1957; children: Wendy, Nancy, Adam. A.B., U. Rochester, 1950; M.D., Cornell U., 1954. Resident in medicine SUNY-Syracuse, 1954-56, 59-60; assoc. med. dir. Bristol Labs., Syracuse, 1956-59; assoc. in physiology George Washington U., Washington, 1960-62; asst. prof. then assoc. prof. medicine U. Iowa, Iowa City, 1962-74, prof., 1974—. Mem. editorial bd. Am. Jour. Physiology, 1982-85. Pres. Unitarian Universalist Soc., Iowa City, 1966-68, 81-83; chmn. U. Iowa Faculty Senate, 1974-75, Coll. Medicine Exec. Com., 1973-74. With USNR, 1945-46. NIH grantee, 1965-91; N.Y. State scholar, 1950-54, Teagle Found. scholar, 1950-54. Fellow ACP; mem. Am. Physiol. Soc. (GI steering com. 1974-76), Am. Gastroenterological Assn. (sec. 1977-83), Am. Fedn. Clin. Rsch., Gastroenterology Research Group (steering com. 1983-85), Central Soc. Clin. Research, Nat. Inst. Digestive Disease and Kidney Disease Gen. Medicine A Study Sect. (chmn. 1986-88), Sigma Xi, Alpha Omega Alpha. Democrat. Unitarian-Universalist. Avocations: jazz alto saxophone, photography, history, bicycling. Office: Dept Med Univ Hosp Iowa City IA 52242

HUBER, DOUGLAS CRAWFORD, pathologist; b. S. Charleston, W.Va., June 11, 1939; s. Abram Paul and Mary Ashley (Grow) H.; m. Deena Rae Freedman, Aug. 8, 1969; children: Adam Crawford, Laura Kristen; m. Angelika Madelon Pohl, June 3, 1961 (div. 1965); 1 child, Heidemarie Jutta. Student, Harvard U., 1958, 59; AB, Emory U., Atlanta, 1960; MD, Emory U. Sch. of Med., Atlanta, 1964. Assoc. pathologist Baldwin County Hosp., Milledgeville, Ga., 1971-72, Leary Lab., Boston, 1972-73; lab. dir. Homer D. Cobb Mem. Hosp., Phenix City, Ala., 1973-79; gen. practitioner Leonard Morse Hosp., Natick, Mass., 1979-80; lab. dir. Promina Douglas Hosp., Douglasville, Ga., 1980—; med. dir. Roche Biomedical Lab., Atlanta Div., Tucker, Ga., 1989-93; deputy state commr. Coll. Am. Pathologists Lab. Inspection Program, Skokie, Ill., 1976-79; v.p. Ala. Assn. Pathologists, Birmingham, 1979. Pres. Nam Vets of Ga., 1982-85; capt. with U.S Army, 1965-67. Fellow Coll. Am. Pathologists, Am. Soc. Clinical Pathologists.

HUBER, GERD, psychiatrist; b. Stuttgart, Germany, Dec. 3, 1921; s. Fritz and Elizabeth (Hartmann) H. Dr. med., U. Heidelberg, Germany, 1948, priv. doz. (Habilitation), 1957, extraordinary prof., 1961; Dr.med. h.c., U. Asunción, Paraguay, 1991. Prof. psychiatry U. Bonn, Germany, 1962; ordinary prof. U. Ulm, Germany, 1968-74; dir. Akademisches Krankenhaus U. Ulm, Weissenau, 1968-74; ordinary prof., chmn. U. Lübeck, Germany, 1974-78; call ordinary prof., chmn. U. Munich, 1977; ordinary prof., chmn., dir. Psychiat. Univ. Clin., Bonn, 1978-87; ordinary prof. emeritus U. Bonn, 1987—; vis. prof. univs. Asunció, Buenos Aires, Minas Gerais, Brazil. Author 45 books; contbr. more than 380 articles to profl. jours.; editor-in-chief Neurology Psychiatry and Brain Rsch. Decorated Bundesverdienstkreuz (Germany); recipient Pres. Kuratorium K. Schneider-Sci. award, Pres. Kurat. H. Weitbrecht Sci. award. Mem. European Psychiat. Soc. (hon.), Am. Psychiat. Soc. (hon.), Soc. Rsch. on Psychoses (pres.). Office: U Bonn, Nervenzentrum Venusberg, D-53105 Bonn Germany

HUBER, THOMAS WAYNE, microbiologist; b. Eddy, Tx., Sept. 2, 1942; s. Albert Frederick and Flora Hildegard (Hinze) H.; m. Doris Marie Weise, Sept. 7, 1963; children: Mollie Marie, Samuel Thomas, Laura Emily. BA, U. Texas, 1964, PhD, 1968. Posdoctoral fellow Ctrs. for Disease Control, Atlanta, 1968-70; asst. prof. U. Tex. Med. Sch., San Antonio, 1970-74; vis. assoc. prof. U. Tex. Sch. Pub. Health, Houston, 1974-81; chief lab. Houston Health Dept., 1974-81; assoc. prof. Tex. A&M U. Coll. Medicine, Temple, 1981—; microbiologist Olin E. Teague VA Med. Ctr., Temple, Tex., 1981—; adj. prof. Baylor U., Waco, Tex.; cons. HouTex Med. lab., Houston, 1981; reviewer Annals Saudi Medicine; faculty senator Tex. A&M U., 1994—. Co-author Pathogenic Microbiology, 1978. Named visiting prof., microbiology, Burroughs-Wellcome Found., Prarie View A&M U., 1991. Fellow Am. Acad. Microbiology; mem. Am. Soc. for Microbiology (Texas councillor 1990-91), Texas branch Am. Soc. for Microbiology (v.p. 1988, pres. 1989), Southwestern Assn. Clinical Microbiology (area dir. 1987-89, pres. 1996-97), Sigma Xi. Lutheran. Home: 4809 Arrowhead Dr Temple TX 76502-1451 Office: Olin E Teague Lab Svcs 1901 S 1st St Temple TX 76504-7451

HUBER, VIDA S., nursing educator; b. West Liberty, Ohio, Mar. 27, 1937; d. L.L. and Nanna V. (Bender) Swartzentruber; m. Harold E. Huber, June 6, 1970; 1 child, Heidi Marie. Diploma, Milford Meml. Hosp., 1959; BSN, Eastern Mennonite Coll., 1961; MA in Nursing Edn., Columbia U., Tchrs. Coll., 1966, EdD, 1970. Staff nurse Milford Meml. Hosp., Del., 1959-60; nursing supr. County Rest Home, Greenwood, Del., 1959-60, 61-65; instr. nursing Milford Meml. Hosp., Del., 1961-64, ednl. dir., 1964; chmn., prof. Eastern Mennonite Coll., Dept. Nursing, Harrisonburg, Va., 1967-84; vis. prof. U. Va. Sch. Nursing, Charlottesville, Va., 1984-86; exec. dir. Va. Soc. Profl. Nurses, Harrisonburg, Va., 1987-88; prof., dept. head nursing James Madison U., Harrisonburg, Va., 1988—; speaker in field; bd. dirs. County Rest Home, Greenwood, Del., 1970-81, pres., 1980-81. Contbr. articles to profl. jours. Named Outstanding Young Women Am., 1973, Outstanding Educator AM. 1973, 75; recipient Women's Caucus Award for Svc., 1992. Mem. ANA, Am. Assn. Colls. Nursing, Nat. League Nursing, Va. Assn. Colls. Nursing, Mennonite Nurses Assn. (project dir. 1988), Kappa Delta Pi, Pi Delta Kappa, Pi Lambda Theta.

HUBER-STEMICH, FELIX, physician; b. Lucerne, Switzerland, Dec. 26, 1956; m. Martina Stemich; 1 child, Niels. MD, U. Berne, Switzerland, 1982. Med. dir. Swisscare HMO-Gesundheitszentrum, Zurich, 1990—. Contbr. articles to profl. jours. Office: HMO Praxis, Zweierstrasse 136, 8003 Zurich Switzerland

HUBERT, HELEN BETTY, epidemiologist; b. N.Y.C., Jan. 22, 1950; d. Leo and Ruth (Rosenbaum) H.; m. Carlos Barbaro Arostegui, Sept. 11, 1976 (div. May 1987); 1 child, Joshua Daniel Hubert. BA magna cum laude, Barnard Coll., 1970; MPH, Yale U., 1973, MPhil, 1976, PhD, 1978. Rsch. assoc. Yale U., New Haven, 1977-78; rsch. epidemiologist Nat. Heart, Lung and Blood Inst., Bethesda, Md., 1978-84; rsch. dir. Gen. Health, Inc., Washington, 1984-87; sr. rsch. scientist Stanford (Calif.) U., 1988—. Peer rev. Am. Jour. Epidemiology, Am. Jour. Pub. Health, Chest, Jour. AMA (JAMA), Archives Internal Medicine; contbr. articles to profl. jours., chpts. to books. Mem. APHA, Am. Heart Assn. (Coun. on Epidemiology), Am. Coll. Epidemiology, Soc. Epidemiol. Rsch., Arthritis Health Profls. Assn., Phi Beta Kappa, Sigma Xi (grant-in-aid for rsch. 1978). Office: Stanford Univ Med Ctr Dept Health Rsch and Policy Rm T210 Stanford CA 94305

HUBNER, KARL FRANZ, physician, consultant; b. Striegau, Silesia, Germany, Jan. 20, 1934; s. Willy A. and Elisabeth M. (Meissner) H.; m. Sibyll M. Weissenborn, Aug. 5, 1960; children: Christian A., Karl-Philipp. MD, U. Heidelberg, Germany, 1959. Diplomate Am. Bd. Nuclear Medicine. Intern 2d Gen. U.S. Army and 86th Air Force Hosp., Germany, 1960-61; resident in nuclear medicine Oak Ridge (Tenn.) Inst. Nuclear Studies, 1962-64; resident in pediat. U. Tubingen, Germany, 1964-67; rsch. scientist Oak Ridge Associated Univs., 1967-79; dir. nuclear medicine Med. & Health Scis. Divsn., Oak Ridge Assoc. U., 1975-84; dir. radiation medicine Radiation Emergency Assistance Ctr., Oak Ridge, 1977-82; asst. chmn. Med. & Health Scis. Divsn., Oak Ridge, 1982-84; dir. radiology rsch. and nuclear medicine U. Tenn. Med. Ctr. at Knoxville, 1984-91, dir. clin. rsch. dept. radiology, 1991—; mem. com. on radiation rsch. and poligy Office of Sci. and Tech. of Exec. Office of Pres., Washington, 1984—; cons. Oak Ridge Assoc. U./Dept. of Energy, 1984—. Editor: The Medical Basis for Radiation Accidents, 1980, Clinical Positron Emission Tomography, 1991. Mem. AMAA, Soc. Nuclear Medicine, Tenn. Med. Assn., Radiol. Soc. N.Am., Am. Roentgen Ray Soc., Inst. for Clin. PET. Home: 500 Mellen Rd Knoxville TN 37919 Office: UTMCK Dept Radiology 1924 Alcoa Hwy Knoxville TN 37920

HUBSMITH, ROBERT JAMES, surgeon; b. Passaic, N.J., Sept. 16, 1930; s. Edward A. and Gertrude Frances (Boffard) H.; m. Lois Abbey Landrie Hubsmith, Sept. 28, 1957; children: Robert J., Diane C., Edward J. BA, Cornell U., 1952; MD, Cornell U. Med. Coll., 1956. Cert. Am. Bd. Surgery, 1965, Am. Coll. Surgeons, 1967. Post grad. surgical St. Luke's Hosp., N.Y.C., 1956-58; residency Hackensack (N.J.) Hosp., 1961-64; surgeon pvt. practice, Butler, N.J., 1964—; instr. of surgery U. Med. and Dentistry of N.J., N.J. Med. Sch., Newark, 1991-94, asst. prof. clin. surgery, 1994—; emeritus staff Chilton Meml. Hosp., Pompton Plains, N.J., 1991—; fire surgeon Kinnelon (N.J.) Vol. Fire Dept., 1976—; pres. med.-dental staff Chilton Meml. Hosp., Pompton Plains, N.J., 1977. Bd. elders The Community Ch. of Smoke Rise, 1985-87, 90-92. Fellow ACS; mem. Soc. Surgeons of N.J., Kinnelon Jaycees. Home: 706 Orchard Rd Kinnelon NJ 07405-2701 Office: 1395 State Rt 23 Butler NJ 07405-1736

HUCHTON, PAUL JOSEPH, JR., pediatrician; b. El Paso, Tex., Mar. 15, 1934; s. Paul Joseph Sr. and Eugenia Cregor (Kimbrough) H.; m. Sheila Ann Borsian, June 1, 1963; children: Hadley Ann Bernhard, David Morgan, Amy H. Anderson, Caren. BA, U. Tex., 1954; MD, Vanderbilt U., 1958. Diplomate Am. Bd. Pediat. Pvt. practice specializing in pediat. El Paso,

1963—. Pres. El Paso Parents vs. Drugs, 1981. Mem Tex. Med. Assn. (del., counsellor 1970-93), El Paso County Med. Soc. (pres. 1985), Rotary Club El Paso (pres. 1980, Paul Harris award 1983). Republican. Episcopalian. Office: 1515 N Oregon El Paso TX 79902

HUCK, JOHN LLOYD, pharmaceutical company executive; b. Bklyn., July 17, 1922; s. John Lloyd and Adrienne (Warner) H.; m. Dorothy Bertha Foehr, Nov. 20, 1943; children: Lloyd E., Jeanne Huck Leslie-Hughes, Virginia Huck Stalcup. B.S. in Chemistry, Pa. State U., 1946. Research chemist Hoffmann-LaRoche, Nutley, N.J., 1946, sales rep., 1948, dir. sales tng., 1951, asst. gen. sales mgr., 1955, dir. product devel., 1958; dir. mktg. Merck Sharp & Dohme Div., West Point, Pa., 1958; v.p. mktg. planning MSD div., 1966, v.p. sales and mktg., 1968, exec. v.p., 1969, exec. v.p., gen. mgr., 1972, pres., 1973; sr. v.p. Merck & Co., Rahway, N.J., 1975, exec. v.p., 1977, dir., 1977-86, pres., chief operating officer, 1978-85; chmn. bd. Merck & Co., 1985-86; chmn. bd., chief exec. officer Nova Pharm. Corp., Morristown, N.J., 1986-88; chmn. bd. Nova Pharm. Corp., 1988-91. Patentee in field. Trustee Pa. State U., 1977-92, v.p., 1985-88, pres. bd., 1988-91; trustee Morristown Meml. Health Found., Inc., N.J., 1979-96, chmn. bd., 1986-88; trustee Geraldine R. Dodge Found. 1st lt. USAAF, 1942-46. Alumni fellow Coll. Medicine Pa. State U., 1980, Coll. of Sci., 1983. Mem. Morris County Golf Club, Piper's Landing Golf Club. Republican. Presbyterian. Home: 1 Carriage Hill Dr Morristown NJ 07960

HUCKABEE, CAROL BROOKS, psychologist; b. Marion, Ohio, Aug. 2, 1945; d. William Richard and Marjorie (Beal) Brooks; m. Roy M. Huckabee, Dec. 22, 1967; 1 child, Lear Elizabeth. BA, U. Colo., 1967; MS, NYU, 1982, PhD, 1985. Lic. psychologist, N.Y., Conn. Psychology intern Downstate Med. Ctr., Bklyn., 1982-84; staff psychologist Blythedale Children's Hosp., Valhalla, N.Y., 1984-86; dir. psychol. svcs. Arms Acres Hosp., Carmel, N.Y., 1986-88, cons., 1988-89; cons. psychologist Putnam Community Hosp., Carmel, 1988—; pvt. practice Carmel, 1987—; sch. psychologist N.Y.C. Bd. Edn., 1984—. NIMH clin. tng. grantee, 1980-81, 81-82. Mem. Am. Psychol. Assn., N.Y. State Psychol. Assn., Conn. State Psychol. Assn. Democrat. Office: Carmel Psychol PC Stoneleigh Ave Carmel NY 10512

HUCKABEE, MICHAEL JOSEPH, physician assistant; b. Burley, Idaho, Apr. 23, 1958; s. Rupert Joseph and Dorothy Jean (Barclay) H.; m. Nancy Sue Yost, Apr. 23, 1983; children: Tyler Joseph, Tanner Michael, Bailey Sue, Emily Marie. BA in Edn., N.W. Nazarene Coll., 1980; BS in Health Scis., U. Nebr., Omaha, 1983; postgrad., U. Iowa, 1988-89. Cert. physician assn. Lab. technician Mercy Med. Ctr., Nampa, Idaho, 1978-81; physician asst. Grant (Nebr.) Med. Clinic, 1983-87; asst. dir. physician asst. program U. Iowa, Iowa City, 1987-90; physician asst. Family Med. Specialties, Inc., Holdrege, Nebr., 1990—; Chmn. membership com. Assn. Physician Asst. Programs, 1989-90. Fellow Am. Acad. Physician Assts.; mem. Nebr. Acad. Physician Assts., Iowa Physician Assts. Soc. (pres. 1989-90), Christian Med. and Dental Soc. Evangelical Free Ch. Office: Family Med Specialties Inc 414 East Ave Holdrege NE 68949

HUCKSTEP, RONALD LAWRIE, traumatic and orthopaedic surgery educator, consultant; b. Chefoo, China, July 22, 1926; (parents English citizens), arrived in Australia, 1972; s. Herbert George and Agnes (Lawrie-Smith) H.; m. Margaret Ann Macbeth, Jan. 2, 1960; children: Susan, Michael, Nigel. MA, MB BChir, Cambridge U., Eng., 1952, MD, 1957; MD (hon.), U. New South Wales, Australia, 1988. Chief asst. orthopaedic dept. St. Bartholomews Hosp., London, 1959-60; prof. orthopaedic surgery Makerere U., Kampala, Uganda, 1960-71; found. prof., head dept. traumatic and orthopaedic surgery U. New South Wales, Sydney, Australia, 1972-92, chmn. sch. surgery, 1972-92, emeritus prof., 1993—; dir. accident svcs., chmn. orthopaedic surgery Prince of Wales Hosp., Sydney, Australia, 1972-92; hon. cons. orthopaedic surgeon Mulago and Mengo Hosps. and Round Table Polio Clinic, Kampala, 1960-72; hon. orthopaedic surgeon to all govt. and mission hosps., Uganda, 1960-72; adviser orthopaedic surgery Ministry Health, Uganda, 1960-72; hon. adviser to Rotary Internat., The Commonwealth Found., WHO, UN, 1970—; travelling prof. Commonwealth Found., London, 1970, 78, 82-83; sr. med. disaster comdr. Dept. Health, New South Wales, chmn., mem. various disaster and emergency coms., Australia, 1972; founder, hon. mem. World Orthopaedic Concern, 1973-96; cons. orthopaedic surgeon royal S. Sydney and Sutherland Hosps., Sydney, 1974-92; hon. dir. Orthopaedics Overseas, U.S., 1978-94; cons. Archives of Orthopaedic Surgery, 1984; vis. prof. dept. surgery U. Sydney, 1995—. Author: Typhoid Fever and Other Salmonella Infections, 1962, A Simple Guide to Trauma, 1970, 5th edit., 1995, Italian edit., 1978, Japanese edit., 1982, Poliomyelitis Including Appliances and Rehabilitation, 1975, A Simple Guide to Orthopaedics, 1993, Picture Tests Orthopaedics and Trauma, 1994; contbr. chpts. to books; corr. editor: Brit. and Am. Jours. Bone and Joint Surgery, 1965-72; inventor in field. Recipient Melsome Meml. prize, 1948, Raymond Horton Smith prize, 1957, Irving Geist award Internat. Soc. for Rehab. of Disabled, 1969, James Cook medal Royal Soc. New South Wales, 1984, Humanitarian award Orthopaedics Overseas, 1991; Paul Harris fellow and medal Rotary Internat. and Rotary Found., 1987. Fellow Royal Coll. Surgeons Edinburgh, Royal Coll. Surgeons Eng., Royal Australasian Coll. Surgeons Australia, Australian Acad. Technol. Scis. and Engring. (K.L. Sutherland medal 1986), Australian Orthopaedic Assn. (v.p. 1982, Betts Meml. medal 1983), Brit. Orthopaedic Assn., Western Pacific Orthopaedic Assn. (hon.), Assn. Surgeons Uganda (hon.); mem. Coast Med. Assn. (pres. 1986), Med. Soc. U. New South Wales (patron), Australian Club. Home and Office: 108 Sugarloaf Crescent, Castlecrag, Sydney NSW 2068, Australia

HUDAK, THOMAS MICHAEL, plastic surgeon; b. Akron, Ohio, May 16, 1937; s. Rudolph Michael and Muriel (Creighton) H.; m. Anne Elizabeth Verhey, Aug. 11, 1963 (div.); m. Mary Louise Schmidt, Aug. 16, 1974; children: Michael, Stephen, Allison. BA, U. Mich., 1959, MD, 1963. Diplomate Am. Bd. Plastic Surgery. Intern U. Md. Hosp., Balt., 1963-64, resident gen. surgery, 1964-68; resident in plastic surgery U. Mich., Ann Arbor, 1968-70; pvt. practice Phoenix, 1970—. Mem. Phoenix Thunderbirds, 1976—, Ariz. Acad., 1991—; pres. The Heart Mus., Phoenix, 1989-91. Recipient Outstanding Paper award Nat. Residents' Conf., Salt Lake City, 1970. Mem. NCCJ (bd. dirs. 1983-88), Am. Soc. Plastic and Reconstructive Surgery, Am. Sc. Aesthetic Plastic Surgery, Reed O. Dingham Soc., Frederick A. Coller Soc., Am. Assn. Hand Surgery., Men's Art Coun., Phoenix Country Club. Republican. Roman Catholic. Address: 5219 N Casa Blanca Dr Paradise Valley AZ 85253-6999*

HUDD, NICHOLAS PAYNE, physician; b. Romford, Essex, Eng., Oct. 11, 1945; s. Harold Payne and Marguerita Eva (Clarke) H.; m. Gwendeleen Mary Johnstone, Oct. 11, 1969; children: Alastair Payne, Anne Marguerita Jane, Robert Nicholas Harold. BA, Sidney Sussex Coll., Cambridge, Eng., 1967, MB, 1970, B. Surgery, 1970, MA, 1971. House surgeon Westminster Children's Hosp., 1970; house physician Princess Alexandra Hosp., Harlow, Essex, Eng., 1971; sr. house officer Orsett Hosp., Grays, Essex, Eng., 1972; med. registrar Basildon (Eng.) Hosp., 1972-74; pathology registrar Orsett Hosp., Grays, 1974-76; sr. med. registrar Manchester Royal Infirmary, Eng., 1976-78; sr. med. registrar Benenden Hosp., 1978-79, cons. physician, 1980—. Chmn. Romney Marsh Hist. Chs. Trust, 1988-96; pres. The Rising Mercury Soc.; churchwarden St. Mildred's Ch., Tenterden, 1983-88; condr. Benenden Hosp. Choir. Fellow Royal Soc. Medicine, Royal Coll. Physicians; mem. Brit. Diabetic Assn. Kent County Cricket Club, Tenterden Golf Club, Royal Nat. Rose Soc. Anglican. Home: 13 Elmfield, Tenterden TN30 6RE, England Office: 54 Wimpole St, London W1M 7DF, England

HUDDLE, ROBERT H., JR., thoracic surgeon; b. Elmira, N.Y., July 16, 1947; s. Robert H. and Ellen (Bird) H.; m. Kathleen J. Mullen, June 20, 1970; children: Christine, Katherine, Megan, Molly. BS, U. Notre Dame, 1969; MD, U. Buffalo, 1973. Diplomate Am. Bd. Gen. Surgery, Cardiothoracic Surgery. Resident in gen. surgery U. Rochester, N.Y., 1973-77, thoracic surgeon, 1977-79; pvt. practice Elmira, N.Y., 1979—. Fellow Am. Coll. Surgeons; mem. Soc. Thoracic Surgeons, Cen. N.Y. Surg. Soc., Upstate Thoracic Surg. Soc. Office: Elmira Surg Assn 304 Hoffman St Elmira NY 14905-2263

HUDDLESTON, JOHN FRANKLIN, obstetrics and gynecology educator; b. Jacksonville, Fla., June 26, 1942; s. Paul Mc Kisson and Mary Rebecca (Robinson) H.; m. Kathryn Ann Welch, Dec. 30, 1982; children: Suzanne Marie, Edward Ryan, John Stuart, Mary Kathryn, Ryan Mc Kisson. BS, U. Fla., Gainesville, 1963; MD, Duke U., 1967. Diplomate Am. Bd. Ob-Gyn, Am. Bd. Maternal-Fetal Medicine. Dir. maternal-fetal medicine Sch. of Medicine, U. Ala., Birmingham, Ala., 1963-86; pvt. practice Jacksonville, Fla., 1986-89; prof., dir. maternal-fetal medicine Sch. of Medicine, Emory U., Atlanta, 1989—. Contbr. to profl. jours., articles, and book chpts. Surgeon USPHS, 1969-71. Mem. Ctrl. Assn. Obstetricians and Gynecologists, Am. Gynecologic and Obstetrics Soc., Soc. Perinatal Obstetricians, South Atlantic Assn. Obstetricians and Gynecologists. Office: Emory U Divsn Maternal Fetal Med 69 Butler St Atlanta GA 30303

HUDGENS, RICHARD WATTS, psychiatry educator; b. Greenville, S.C., Jan. 10, 1931; s. Robert Watts and Eleanor (Furman) H.; m. Alletta Wood Jervey, June 21, 1952; children: peter, Mary, Helen; m. Carol Ann Brown, May 5, 1973; 1 child, Jonathan; m. Shirley Ann Baron, Mar. 27, 1982. BA, Princeton U., 1952; MD, Washington U., 1956. Cert. in psychiatry Am. Bd. Psychiatry and Neurology. Intern U. Va. Hosp., Charlottesville, 1956-57, resident internal medicine, 1957-58, resident psychiatry, 1958-59; resident psychiatry N.C. Meml. Hosp., Chapel Hill, 1959-61; assoc. dean for curriculum Washington U. Sch. Medicine, St. Louis, 1967-73; faculty dept. psychiatry Wsahington U. Sch. Medicine, St. Louis, 1963—, clin. prof., 1974-89, prof., 1989—, vice chmn. for clin. affairs, 1992—. Author: Psychiatric Disorders of Adolescents, 1974, Practical Psychiatry, 1993; contbr. articles to profl. jours. Capt. USAF, 1961-63. Named to Alpha Omega Alpha Washington U. Sch. Medicine, 1966. Fellow Am. Psychiat. Assn.; mem. AMA. Democrat. Episcopalian. Home: 13 Algonquin Wood Saint Louis MO 63122-2013 Office: Washington U Sch Medicine 24 S Kingshighway Saint Louis MO 63108

HUDGINS, PATRICIA MONTAGUE, biology educator; b. Buckhannon, W.Va., Jan. 31, 1938; d. Richard Wells and Clella (Barger) Montague; m. Guy Hugh Bond, June 30, 1975; children: Leslie, Audrey, Monica. BS, W.Va. U., 1959, MS, 1960, PhD, 1966. Instr. pharmacology Med. Coll. Va., Richmond, 1966-68, asst. prof., 1968-72, assoc. prof., 1972-75; assoc. prof. Kirksville (Mo.) Coll. Osteo. Medicine, 1975-80, prof. physiology, 1980-90; prof. pharmacology W.Va. Sch. Osteo. Medicine, Lewisburg, 1990—. Mem. Am. Soc. for Pharmacology and Exptl. Therapeutics. Office: WVa Sch Osteo Medicine 400 N Lee St Lewisburg WV 24901-1128

HUDIK, MARTIN FRANCIS, hospital administrator, educator; b. Chgo., Mar. 27, 1949; s. Joseph and Rose (Ricker) H.; 1 child, Theresa Abraham. BS in Mech. and Aerospace Engring., Ill. Inst. Tech., 1971; BPA, Jackson State U., 1974; MBA, Loyola U., Chgo., 1975; postgrad. U. Sarasota, 1975-76. Cert. health care safety mgr., hazard control mgr., hazardous materials mgr., OSHA hazardous materials response instr., hazardous materials incident comdr., disaster coord., police instr., Ill., security certification instr., Ill. With Ill. Masonic Med. Ctr., Chgo., 1969—, dir. risk mgmt., 1974-79, asst. adminstr., 1979—; part-time sr. lt. tng. divsn. Cicero (Ill.) Police Dept., sr. lt. Tng. and Internal Affairs Divsn., 1971—; instr. Nat. Safety Coun. Safety Tng. Inst., Chgo., 1977-85; cons. mem. Coun. Tech. Users Consumer Products, Underwriters Labs., Chgo., 1977—; instr., lt. U.S. Def. Civil Preparedness Agy. Staff Coll., Battle Creek, Mich., 1977-85; liaison officer to Cook County, asst. dir. Emergency Svcs. and Disaster Agy., Town of Cicero, 1988—; pres. bd. dirs. Cook County Emergency Mgmt. Coun., 1991-92; mem. bd. dirs. Cook County Emergency Mgmt. Agy., 1992—; bd. dirs. Northside Cmty. Fed. Credit Union, 1992-93; mem. exec. bd., sec. U.S. Postal Svc. Postal Customer Adv. Coun., Cicero, Ill., 1996—. Pres. sch. bd. Mary Queen of Heaven Sch., Cicero, 1977-79, 84-86; pres. Mary Queen of Heaven Ch. Coun., 1979-81, 83-86; pres. I.M.M.C. Employee Club, 1983-86. Ill. State scholar, 1969-71; recipient Meritorious Svc. award Town of Cicero, 1990, Spl. Svc. award Underwriters Labs., 1992, Outstanding Svc. award Cook County Sheriffs Dept., 1993. Mem. Am. Coll. Healthcare Execs., Am. Soc. Hosp. Risk Mgmt., Nat. Fire Protection Assn., Am. Soc. Safety Engrs. (profl.), Am. Soc. Law and Medicine, Ill. Hosp. Security and Safety Assn. (co-founder 1976, founding pres. 1976-77, hon. dir. 1977-82), Cath. Alumni Club Chgo. (bd. dirs. 1983-84, 86), Mensa, Masons (Berwyn, Ill. chpt.), Pi Tau Sigma, Tau Beta Pi, Alpha Sigma Nu. Republican. Roman Catholic. Lodges: KC (Cardinal coun.), Masons. Home: 2116 S 51st Ct Cicero IL 60650-2345 Office: Ill Masonic Med Ctr 2116 S 51st Ct Chicago IL 60650-2345

HUDSON, BETTY ANN, medical products executive; b. Atlanta, Feb. 28, 1937; d. Harlen Dupree and Carolyn Jean (Louis) Sellers; m. Loni Thompson, Dec. 6, 1954; children: Catherine Norwood, Kim Brown, Jeffrey Hoffman. Grad. high sch., Orlando, Fla. Pres., owner Rockaway Chairs, St. Monroe, La., 1988—. Bd. dirs. Birmingham (Ala.) Concert Chorale, 1969-88; pres. Allegro Music Club, Birmingham, 1981-88. Republican. Seventh day Adventist. Home: 111 Alexander Rd #11 West Monroe LA 71291 Office: Rockaway Chairs 111 Alexander Rd #11 West Monroe LA 71291

HUDSON, CHRISTOPHER GILES, social worker, educator; b. Casper, Wyo., June 24, 1949; s. Benjamin and Jean (Barlow) H.; m. Barbara Berger, Dec. 10, 1983; children: Daniel, Elisabeth. BA, U. Chgo., 1971, MA, 1974; PhD, U. Ill., Chgo., 1983. Cert. by Acad. Cert. Social Workers. Psychiatric social worker Northeast Hosps., Chgo., 1974-75; sch. social worker Bd. Edn., Chgo., 1975-76; caseworker Jewish Family Svc., Chgo., 1977-80; asst. prof. social work George Williams Coll., Downers Grove, Ill., 1983-86, East Carolina U., Greenville, N.C., 1987; assoc. prof. Salem (Mass.) State Coll., 1987-92, prof., 1992—; bd. dirs. Family Network, Salem, 1989—, Northshore Mental Health Bd. Dept. Mental Health, Mass., 1989—. Mem. editl. bd. Jour. Ind. Social Work; editor Dimensions of State Mental Health Policy, 1991; contbr. articles to profl. jours. Fellow NIMH, 1981, 82. Mem. NASW (Mass. chpt., bd. dirs. 1990—), Coun. on Social Work Edn., Acad. Cert. Social Workers. Office: Salem State Coll 352 Lafayette St Salem MA 01970-5348

HUDSON, LEONARD DEAN, physician; b. Everett, Wash., May 7, 1938; s. Marshall W. and Blanche V. (Morgan) H.; m. Louise Eleanor Vik, Dec. 30, 1961; children: Sean Marshall, Sherry Elizabeth, Kevin Arthur. B.S., Wash. State U., Pullman, 1960; M.D., U. Wash., Seattle, 1964. Diplomate: Am. Bd. Internal Medicine (pulmonary disease). Intern Bellevue Hosp. Center, N.Y.C., 1964-65; resident in internal medicine N.Y. Hosp., 1965-66, U. Wash. Hosps., 1968-69; chief resident Harborview Med. Center, Seattle; also instr. U. Wash. Med. Sch., 1967-70; Am. Thoracic Soc. fellow in pulmonary diseases U. Colo. Med. Center, 1970-71, instr., then asst. prof. medicine, 1971-73; mem. faculty U. Wash. Med. Center, 1973—, assoc. prof. medicine, 1976-82, prof., 1982—, head pulmonary critical care medicine div., 1985—; chief pulmonary critical care medicine div., med. dir. MICU Harborview Med. Center, 1976-86; chmn. Tb adv. com. Wash. Dept. Social and Health Services. Author papers, revs. in field. Served with USPHS, 1966-68. Named Outstanding Resident, Harborview Med. Center. Fellow ACP, Am. Coll. Chest Physicians (state gov. 1980-87); mem. Am. Fedn. Clin. Rsch., Am. Thoracic Soc. (sec.-treas. 1983-84, v.p. 1993-94, pres.-elect 1994-95, pres. 1995-96), Western Soc. Clin. Rsch., Assn. Am. Physicians, Wash. Lung. Assn. (dir., Vol. Hall of Fame 1977), Wash. Thoracic Soc., Phi Beta Kappa. Democrat. Club: Seattle Flounders Soccer. Office: 325 9th Ave Seattle WA 98104-2420

HUDSON, LINDA, health care executive; b. Tuscaloosa, Ala., Feb. 12, 1950; d. Elvin and Clara (Duke) Hudson; m. Charles Garrett Kimbrough, May 26, 1984. BS in Edn., U. Ala., 1971; MS in Psychology, U. So. Miss., 1984. Lic. profl. counselor. Recreational therapist West Ala. Rehab. Ctr., Tuscaloosa, 1971-72; flight attendant Delta Air Lines, Miami and New Orleans, 1972-80; pvt. practice psychotherapist Hattiesburg (Miss.) and Atlanta, 1984—; program dir. Eating Disorders Adventist Health System/Wedst, Atlanta, 1985-88, regional dir./cons., 1986-87, exec. dir. mental health svcs., 1988-89; owner Hudson Cons. Assocs., 1989—, nat. cons., 1986—. Contbr. articles to profl. jours. Mem. Covington Jr. Svc. League, La., 1981-83; co-chmn. St. Tammany Rep. Polit. Action Com., 1980-81; coord. United Way of St. Tammany Parish, 1979-80. Mem. Women Healthcare Execs., Ga. Mental Health Counselors Assn., Nat. Coun. Sexual Addiction and Compulsivity (bd. dirs., v.p.). Democrat. Office: Ste 238 1090 Northchase Pkwy Marietta GA 30067-6402

HUDSON, RAY TRUMAN, pharmacist; b. Hickory, N.C., Dec. 5, 1929; s. Bruce Allen and Fannie Belle (Brittain) H.; children: Melissa Rae Archer, Constance Lynn Motlow, Tina Marie Browning. BS in Pharmacy, U. N.C., 1951. Pharmacist Statesville (N.C.) Drug Co., 1951-55; pharmacist, ptnr. So. Drug Co., Charlotte, N.C., 1955-60; pharmacist, treas. Akers Pharmacy, Gastonia, N.C., 1960—; ptnr. Forrest, Hudson, Holland, 1980—; bd. dirs. N.C. Mut. Wholesale Drug Co., Durham, N.C. Pres. Akers Ctr. Mcht. Assn., Gastonia, 1965; asst. scout commr. Piedmont Boy Scouts Coun., Gastonia, 1969-72; bd. dirs. N.C. Pharmacy Polit. Action, Chapel Hill, N.C., 1986-91. Named Eagle Scout, Boy Scouts Am., 1945. Mem. Gaston County Pharmacy Assn. (pres. 1991), Gaston County Pharmacy Soc. (pres. 1975), U. N.C. Pharmacy Alumni Assn. (bd. dirs. 1986-89), Phi Delta Chi (pres. 1951, bd. dirs. 1985). Republican. Baptist. Office: Akers Pharmay Inc 1595 E Garrison Blvd Gastonia NC 28054-5138

HUDSON, ROBERT PAUL, medical educator; b. Kansas City, Kans., Feb. 23, 1926; s. Chester Lloyd and Jean (Emerson) H.; m. Olive Jean Grimes, Aug. 1, 1948 (div. 1963); children: Robert E., Donald K., Timothy M.; m. Martha Isabelle Holter, July 10, 1965; children: Stephen, Laurel. BA, U. Kans., 1949; MD, 1952; MA, Johns Hopkins U., 1966. Instr., U. Kans.-Kansas City, 1958-59, assoc. in medicine, 1959-63, asst. prof., 1964-69, assoc. prof., 1969—, prof., chmn. history of medicine, 1969-95; ret. Author: Disease and Its Control, 1983; contbr. articles to profl. jours. mem. editorial bd. Bull. History of Medicine, Balt., 1981-94. 1st lt. U.S. Army, 1953-55. Fellow ACP; mem. Am. Assn. for History of Medicine (pres. 1984-86), Am. Osler Soc. (bd. govs., pres. 1987-88). Home: 12925 S Frontier Rd Olathe KS 66061-9676 Office: Kans U Med Ctr 39th and Rainbow Blvd Kansas City KS 66160

HUDSON, ROY DAVAGE, retired pharmaceutical company executive; b. Chattanooga, June 30, 1930; s. Roy and Everence (Wilkerson) H.; m. Constance Joan Taylor, Aug. 31, 1956; children: Hollye Lynne, David Kendall. BS, Livingstone Coll., 1955; MS, U. Mich., 1957, PhD, 1962; MA, Brown U., 1968; LL.D., Lehigh U., 1974, Princeton, 1975. Prof. pharmacology U. Mich. Sch. Medicine, 1961-66; prof. med. sci. Brown U. Sch. Medicine, 1966-70, assoc. dean grad. sch., 1966-69; pres. Hampton U., 1970-76; dir. rsch. planning and coordination Parke, Davis Pharm. Co., Ann Arbor, Mich., 1976; v.p. rsch. planning Warner Lambert/Parke-Davis Pharm. Rsch. Divsn., Ann Arbor, 1977-79; mgr. sci. liaison Upjohn Co., Kalamazoo, Mich., 1979-81; mgr. CNS diseases rsch. Upjohn Co., 1981, dir. CNS diseases rsch., 1985-87; v.p. pharm. rsch. divsn. Europe Upjohn Co., Brussels, 1987-90; corp. v.p. pub. rels. Upjohn Co., Kalamazoo, 1990-92, ret., 1992; adj. prof. Black Americana studies Western Mich. U., Kalamazoo, 1993; interim exec. dir., CEO Guidance Clinic, Kalamazoo, 1993; interim pres. Livingstone Coll., Salisbury, N.C., 1995-96; dir. Parke-Davis & Co., United Va. Bank-Citizens and Marine, Unied Va. Bankshares, Comerica Bank-Mich., Chesapeake and Potomac Telephone Co. of Va. Contbr. articles to profl. jours., chpts. to books. Mem. screening com. Danforth Grad. Fellowships, 1962—; mem. adv. council Danforth Grad. Fellows program Danforth Found., 1972—; chmn. Va. Com. on Selection Rhodes Scholars, 1973; mem. Commn. on Fed. Relations, Am. Council on Edn., 1972—, bd. dirs., 1973—; mem. adv. council to dir. NIH, 1974—; Mem. R.I. Commn. Econ. Devel., 1967-69, R.I. Urban League scholarship com., 1966-70; mem. inst. policy commn. So. Regional Edn. Bd.; bd. dirs. Afro-Am. Soc. Conn. Coll., Mich. Ctr. Found., Spelman Coll, Kalamazoo Area Math and Sci. Ctr., Kalamazoo Area Academic Achievement Program, ARC; bd. dirs., v.p. Nat. Assn. Equal Opportunity in Higher Edn.; trustee Brown U., Livingstone Coll., Peninsula United Community Services, Spelman Coll. Served with USAF, 1948-52. Recipient Disting. Alumni award Livingstone Coll.; Outstanding Civilian Service award U.S. Army.; Danforth Grad. fellow, 1955-61. Mem. Am. Soc. Pharmacology and Exptl. Therapeutics, Peninsula C. of C., NAACP (life, Golden Heritage), AAAS, N.Y. Acad. Scis., Sigma Xi, Phi Kappa Phi, Phi Sigma, Beta Kappa Chi, Kappa Delta Pi, Omega Psi Phi, Gamma Alpha, Kappa Delta Pi. Home: 7057 Oak Highlands Dr Kalamazoo MI 49009-7508

HUDSON, W. GAIL, social worker; b. Waxahachie, Tex., Apr. 15, 1953; d. Billy M. and Sarah W. (Bowen) H.; m. Garry H. Gillan, Sept. 7, 1991; 1 child, Logan Thomas Gillan. BS, S.W. Tex. State U., 1975, MA, 1976; PhD, So. Ill. U., 1979; MSW, U. Tex., Arlington, 1989. Lic. master social worker, advanced clin. practitioner. Asst., assoc. prof. Millikin U., Decatur, Ill., 1978-87; dept. chair communications Millikin U., Decatur, 1984-87; adj. faculty U. Tex., Arlington, 1987-89; social work fellow M.D. Anderson Hosp., Houston, 1988; social work intern U. Houston Counseling, 1989; social worker U. Houston Counseling & Testing, 1989-92, dir. employee assistance program, 1992—; rep. AIDS Consortium of Tex., 1991; tng. cons. Caterpillar Tractor Co., Decatur, 1979-81; planning com. Nat. Conf. Against Sexual Assault, 1994; cons. Profl. Devel. Program, Decatur, 1979-81; adj. grad. faculty dept. counseling psychology U. Houston, 1991—. Cons. Houston Area Planning Commn. for Substance Abuse Program, 1990-91; treas. ERA Decatur, 1978-82; vol. Coalition Against Domestic Violence, Decatur, 1979-81. Cons. Houston Area Planning Commn. for Substance Abuse Program, 1990-91; prin. investigator/dir. prevention of substance abuse, U. Houston and Higher Edn. Consortium, Houston/Galveston, 1991-94. Grantee U.S. Dept. Edn. Mem. NASW, NOW, Am. Coll. Personnel Assn. (bd. dirs. 1991, 94), Am. Assn. Counseling and Devel.. Home: 1123 Burning Tree Rd Humble TX 77339-3933 Office: U Houston Counseling 4800 Calhoun Rd Houston TX 77004-2610

HUDSPETH, ALBERT JAMES, biomedical researcher, educator; b. Houston, Nov. 9, 1945; s. Chalmers Mac and Demaris (DeLange) H.; m. Ann Maurine Packard, Feb. 12, 1977; children: James Chalmers, Ann Maurine Demaris. BA, Harvard U., 1967, MA, 1968; PhD, 1973, MD, 1974. Mem. biology faculty Calif. Inst. Tech., Pasadena, 1975-83; prof. physiology U. Calif., San Francisco, 1983-89; prof. cell biology and neurosci. U. Tex. Southwestern Med. Ctr., Dallas, 1989—. Recipient W. Alden Spencer award N.Y. Acad. Scis., 1985, Cole award Biophys. Soc., 1991, Dana award Charles A. Dana Found., 1994. Mem. NAS, Phi Beta Kappa, Alpha Omega Alpha. Office: U Tex Southwestern Med Ctr 5323 Harry Hines Blvd Dallas TX 75235-7200*

HUDZINSKI, LEONARD GERARD, social worker; b. Aug. 14, 1946. BA in Psychology and Sociology, Findlay (Ohio) Coll., 1968; MSW, U. Mich., 1971; PhD, U. Pitts., 1975. Diplomate Clin. Social Work Examiners. Teaching asst. dept. sociology Findlay Coll., 1966-68; psychology specialist Lyster Army Hosp., Ft. Rucker, Ala., 1969-70; psychiat. social worker Toledo (Ohio) Mental Health Ctr., 1972; instr. in applied social rsch. and social work Med. Coll. Ohio, 1974-77; head divsn. clin. social work Ochsner Med. Instns., New Orleans, 1977—; dir. Ochsner Ctr. for Elimination of Smoking; asst. clin. prof. psychiatry La. State U. Med. Ctr.; asst. clin. prof. Tulane Med. Ctr.; program dir., adminstr. State of Ohio Epilepsy Deinstitutionalization Assistance Program, 1976-77. Contbr. articles to profl. jours.; mem. editorial bd.: Headache Quar., 1989—. Bd. dirs. Biofeedback Certification Inst. Am., Wheat Ridge, Colo., 1995. Served with U.S. Army, 1968-70. Fellow Am. Assn. for Study of Headache; mem. Assn. for Advancement of Behavior Therapy, Assn. Applied Psychophysiology and Biofeedback, La. Assn. Applied Psychophysiology and Biofeedback (past pres.), Am. Assn. for Study of Headache, NASW, La. Assn. for Clin. Social Work Vendorship (bd. dirs., treas., pres.), ACSW, Am. Fedn. for Clin. Rsch. Home: 274 Garden Rd River Ridge LA 70123-1953 Office: Ochsner Med Instns 1514 Jefferson Hwy New Orleans LA 70121-2429

HUEBBERS, CARL GEORGE, JR., pharmacist; b. Buffalo, Oct. 23, 1952; s. Carl George and Geraldine Irene (Suwalski) H.; m. Elsie Lynne Fraley, June 8, 1974; children: Carl George III, Justin James. BA in Biology, Canisius Coll., 1974; BS in Pharmacy, U. Okla., 1977. Registered pharmacist, Okla., Colo., N.Y. Staff pharmacist Bapt. Med. Ctr. Okla., Oklahoma City, 1978-80, pharmacy supr., 1981-85; dir. pharmacy St. Mary's Hosp. and Med. Ctr., Grand Junction, Colo., 1985-88, Rome (N.Y.) Hosp. and Murphy Meml. Hosp., 1988-89, Genesee Hosp., Rochester, N.Y., 1989—. Cubmaster Boy Scouts Am., Grand Junction, 1986-88. Mem. Am. Soc. Hosp. Pharmacists, N.Y. State Coun. Hosp. Pharmacists. Republican. Roman Catholic. Office: Genesee Hosp 224 Alexander St Rochester NY 14607-4002

HUERTA, SERGIO A., osteopath; b. El Paso, Tex., Aug. 3, 1954; s. Adalberto and Joan Caroline (Graham) H.; m. Lora Huerta, June 4, 1992;

children: Sergio, Nick, Luke. BS in Biology, U. Tex., El Paso, 1976; DO, Mich. State U., 1980. Med. dir. Carrizozo (N.Mex.) Health Ctr., 1981, La Clinica de Familia, San Miguel, N.Mex., 1982-84; pvt. practice Las Cruces, N.Mex., 1984—; chmn. dept. family practice Meml. Med. Ctr., Las Cruces, 1992-93. Bd. dirs. N.Mex. Med. Rev. Assn., Albuquerque, 1993—, N.Mex. Med. Found., Albuquerque, 1993—. Mem. Am. Osteo. Assn., N.Mex. Osteo. Assn., Dona Ana County Med. Assn. Office: Family Med Ctr 1605 El Paseo Las Cruces NM 88001

HUETER, DIANA T., health facility executive; married; 2 children. BBA, Lamar U., 1973, MBA, 1974. Fin. specialist, bus. office mgr., materials mgmt. buyer Humana Beaumont (Tex.) Med.- Surg. Hosp., 1975-78; CFO Carrollton (Tex.) Med. Ctr., 1978-79; sr. v.p., v.p., asst. v.p./ops. interim exec. dir. Baylor Inst. Rehab., asst. v.p./fin., ins. mgr., discharged patient accounts mgr. Baylor Health Care Sys., Baylor U. Med. Ctr., Dallas, 1979-94; exec. v.p./COO St. Vincent Infirmary Med. Ctr., Little Rock, 1994-95, pres., CEO, 1995—; adj. prof. health adminstrn. Grad. Program U. Ark., Little Rock, 1996—; bd. dirs. Ctrl. Ark. Radiation Therapy Inst., 1996—. Chair healthcare svcs. divsn. Pulaski County United Way Campaign, 1995; mem. Ark. Women's Leadership Forum; bd. dirs. Nat. Family Partnership of Ark., 1994-95; vol. St. Vincent Aux., Ctrs. Youths & Families. Named one of Outstanding Young Women of Am., 1986, Top 100 Women in Ark., 1995, 96. Mem. Am. Hosp. Assn., Am. Coll. Healthcare Execs. (del.), Tex. Hosp. Assn. (bd. dirs. edn. com. 1982-88, chair edn. com. 1986-87, bd. dirs. 1989-93, v.p. 1992, pres. 1993, bd. dirs. com. affiliated socs. 1993, state bd. coun. policy devel. 1993), Healthcare Fin. Mgmt. Assn. (nat. com. patient accounting 1988, nat. matrix bd. coun. profl. excellence 1988). Office: St Vincent Infirmary Med Ctr 2 St Vincent Cir Little Rock AR 72205-5499

HUETIG, ROGER DEAN, microbiologist; b. Belden, Nebr., Dec. 5, 1947; s. Harold Dean and Lula (Fiscus) H.; m. Becky Jo Schroder, Apr. 30, 1971; children: Wendy, Patricia. BS, Morningside Coll., 1970. Rsch. technician Ft. Dodge (Iowa) Labs., 1974-80, bioprodn. supr., 1986-89, cell lab. sect. head, 1989—. Webster County Rep. chmn., Ft. Dodge, 1987-91. With U.S. Army, 1971-73, Vietnam. Office: Ft Dodge Labs 800 5th St NW Fort Dodge IA 50501-7425

HUFF, CYNTHIA FAE, medical and orthopedic nurse; b. Albany, Ga., Jan. 3, 1950; d. Henry and Mary Catherine (Vannell) Piedmont; m. Michael Brian Shumaker, June 24, 1972 (div. 1979); 1 child, Brian Michael; m. Byron Lee Huff, Apr. 15, 1983. Diploma, Stuart Circle Hosp., Richmond, Va., 1970. RN, Va. Staff nurse St. Mary's Hosp., Richmond, 1970-71, asst. head nurse orthopedics, 1971, staff nurse emergency room, 1971-72, 73-74, head nurse orthopedics, 1972-73; office nurse Richmond, 1978-82; staff nurse Urology Ctr., Richmond, 1983-84; owner Sesroh Farm-Registered Quarterhorses, Powhatan, Va., 1984-89; nurse-technician for veterinarian for large and small animals, Midlothian, VA., 1986-90; staff nurse Amelia (Va.) Nursing Ctr., 1993—; nurse technician Edda C. Eliasson, D.V.M., Amelia, 1995—; bd. dirs. Amelia Patrons for Animal Welfare. Mem. Nat. Assn. Physicians' Nurses, Am. Heart Assn. (CPR instr.). Republican. Methodist. Home: 3009 Moyer Rd Powhatan VA 23139-7220

HUFF, JIMMY LAURENCE, nurse; b. La Junta, Colo., Feb. 16, 1950; s. Russell Loyal Huff and Pauline Ellen (Porter) Kibler; m. Julia Ann Belden, Jan. 20, 1973 (div. Aug. 1982); 1 child, Anessa. AA, North Platte Coll., 1970; student, Nebr. Western Coll., 1970-71; diploma, West Nebr. Gen. Hosp. Sch. Nursing, 1973; AAS, ITT Tech., Nashville, 1989; B in Applied Sci. Electronics Engring., ITT Tech., Indpls., 1990. Charge nurse, surgical/orthopedic unit West Nebr. Gen. Hosp., Scottsbluff, 1973-74, assoc. dir. nursing, 1974-76; assoc. charge nurse med. ward USAF Med. Ctr., Wright-Patterson AFB, Ohio, 1976-78; OIC spl. med. equipment, flight nurse 9th Aeromedical Evacuation Sqdn., Clark AB, Philippines, 1978-80, flight clin. coord., 1980-81; asst. charge nurse-multisvc. ward USAF Hosp., Blytheville AFB, Ark., 1981-82, charge nurse, outpatient svcs., 1982-84, OIC emergency svcs., 1984-86; night charge nurse orthopedic unit HCA Donelson Hosp., Inc., Nashville, 1986-89; staff nurse orthopedics St. Vincent Hosp., Indpls., 1989-90, staff devel. cons. orthopedics, 1990-91; clin. analyst Mgmt. Info. Systems Bapt. Hosp., Nashville, 1991—; clin. advisor sch. nursing, West Nebr. Gen. Hosp., 1973-76; cons. Lifeflight, Memphis, 1984-86. Maj. USAFR, mobilized Desert Shield/Storm, 1991. Mem. IEEE, Nat. Assn. Orthopedic Nurses, Air Force Assn., Am. Legion. Lutheran. Home: 120 Tomarand Rd Antioch TN 37013

HUFF, LEARAYE, nursing administrator; b. Denver, Sept. 9, 1946; d. Richard Squires Collinson and LaVonia Mae (Jones) Watkins; m. Clifford Udell Huff, Aug. 16, 1988; children: Jessica Lynn Jenks, Rebecca Marie Morgan, Laura G. Morgan. ADN, C.C. Denver, 1979; BSN, Met. State Coll., Denver, 1989. Payroll coord. Ideal Cement Co., Denver, 1967-71; lic. practical nurse Med. Personnel Pool, Denver, 1978-79; ob-gyn nurse Rocky Mountain Hosp., Denver, 1979-86, clin. mgr., ob-gyn, 1986-87, circulating nurse, 1987-88; labor and delivery nurse Humana Mountain View Hosp., Thornton, Colo., 1988-89; clin. instr. Front Range C.C., Westminster, Colo., 1990, C.C. Denver, 1990; charge nurse antepartum and gynecol./oncology floor P/SL, Denver, 1991; perinatal nurse adminstr. Tokos Clin. Svc's., Denver, 1991-94; utilization rev. coord./case mgmt. Antero HealthPlans, Denver, 1994—. Colo. scholar. Mem. Nurses Assn. of the Am. Coll. Ob-Gyn.

HUFF, THOMAS ALLEN, medicine educator; b. Washington, Oct. 9, 1935; s. Thomas Marx and Gladys (Allen) H.; m. Anne Hixon, June 27, 1959; children: Laura Anne, Thomas Allen Jr., Joseph Hixon, David Knox. BA, Southwestern U., Memphis, 1957; MD, Emory U., 1961. Intern, resident Grady Meml. Hosp., Atlanta, 1961-63; fellow endocrinology Duke Med. Ctr., Durham, N.C., 1965-71; asst. prof. to prof. medicine Med. Coll. Ga., Augusta, 1971—. Office: Med Coll Ga Augusta GA 30912

HUFFMAN, DELTON CLEON, JR., pharmaceuticals executive; b. St. Louis, Feb. 18, 1943; s. Delton Cleon and Kathryn (Saegesser) H.; m. Judy Hill, Aug. 11, 1962; children—Kimberly Lea, Jeffrey Keith. B.S. in Pharmacy (Archer Drug Co. scholar), U. Ark., 1966; Ph.D., U. Miss., 1971. Pharmacist Crank Drug Co., Inc., Little Rock, 1966-67; asst. prof., dir. div. pharmacy adminstrn. U. Tenn. Coll. Pharmacy, Memphis, 1970-73; asso. prof., chmn. dept. pharmaceutics U. Tenn. Coll. Pharmacy, 1973; exec. v.p. Am. Coll. Apothecaries, 1971—, also prof., chmn. dept. pharmacy, 1974-89, vice chancellor adminstrn., 1984-89; exec. dir. NARD Mgmt. Inst., Alexandria, Va., 1989—, sr. v.p. practice and mgmt., 1992—. Contbr. articles to profl. lit. Recipient Lederle Faculty award, 1971; NDEA fellow, 1967-70; Am. Found. for Pharm. Edn. fellow, 1967-70. Fellow Am. Coll. Apothecaries; mem. AAAS, Am. Assn. Colls. Pharmacy, Am. Pharm. Assn., Tenn. Pharm. Assn., Okla. Pharm. Assn. (hon.), Ark. Pharm. Assn. (hon. life), Am. Soc. Assn. Execs., Nat. Assn. Retail Druggists, Kappa Psi, Rho Chi. Home: 6020 Willoughby Oak Ln Bartlett TN 38135-1464 Office: Ste 206 5788 Stage Rd Bartlett TN 38134

HUFFMAN, MARK ALAN, family physician; b. Carroll, Iowa, Aug. 23, 1958; s. Stephan Lee Huffman and Kaye Frieda (Arthand) Waters. BSc, U. Iowa, 1981; MD, U. Tech. Santiago, 1984; JD cum laude, LaSalle U., Mandeville, La., 1994. Diplomate Am. Bd. Family Practice. Intern St. Mary's Med. Ctr., Milw., 1984-85; family medicine resident St. Mary's Med. Ctr./Med. Coll. Wis., 1985-87; paramedic Johnson County EMS, Iowa City, Iowa, 1979-81; emergency physician St. Mary's Med. Ctr., Milw., 1987-89, emergency physician, dir., 1989-91; med./legal. cons. Milw., 1991—; fellow in addiction medicine/psychiatry Med. Coll. Wis., Milw., 1994, asst. clin. prof. family medicine, emergency medicine, 1987-91, fellow in addiction medicine, 1994—; EMS med. dir. Milw. Fire Dept., 1988-91; chmn. life support com. St. Mary's Med. Ctr., 1989-91; med. advisor AIDS Resource Ctr. Wis., Milw., 1988—, bd. dirs., exec. sec., 1988-91. Bd. dirs. St. Mary's IPA, Milw., 1990-91; med. dir. Brady St. STD Clinic, Milw., 1987-89. Capt. U.S. Army, 1983-93. Mem. AMA, AAFP, Am. Coll. Emergency Physicians (co-chair Wis. EMS com. 1988-91), Am. Bd. Forensic Examiners, Am. Soc. Law and Medicine. Roman Catholic. Office: Medical Legal Consultants 4421 N Maryland Shorewood WI 53211

HUFFMAN, WILLIAM RAYMOND, emergency physician; b. Nashville, Dec. 9, 1946; s. Raymond W. and Elizabeth (Charlton) H.; m. Janet Richards Bailey, Aug. 19, 1972; children: Alan Drew, Mandie Elaine. BS in Biology, Tenn. Tech. U., 1969; MD, U. Tenn., 1972. Diplomate Am. Bd. Emergency Medicine. Intern, resident US Naval Hosp., San Diego, 1972-74; dir. emergency medicine Miller Hosp., Nashville, 1976-77; emergency physician Bapt. Hosp., Nashville, 1977—, chmn. emergency dept., 1981-83; pres. emergency dept. Mid Tenn. Emergency Phys. PC, Nashville, 1980-86; dir. emergency med. svcs. Rutherford County, Murfreesboro, Tenn., 1984-88. Fellow Am. Coll. Emergency Physicians. Home: 2500 N Berrys Ch Rd Brentwood TN 32027 Office: Mid Tenn Emergency Phys PC 1920 Church St Nashville TN 37203

HUFFORD, DAVID CLINTON, microbiologist, educator, medical technologist; b. Wichita, Kans., Dec. 13, 1945; s. Clinton Jasper and Mary Evelyn (Price) H.; m. Cheryl Earlene Wesbrooks, Aug. 8, 1970 (div. Oct. 1983); 1 child, Kara Vonne; m. Lucy Marie French, Dec. 6, 1983. BS, Ft. Hays State U., 1969; MS, U. Okla., 1973; PhD, U. Ark. Med. Scis., 1980. Cert. med. technologist Am. Soc. Clin. Pathologists; cert. clin. lab. scientist NCA. Med. technologist St. Francis Hosp., Wichita, 1968-70; instr. med. lab. tech. Northern Okla. Coll., Tonkawa, 1972-75; asst. prof. clin. lab. scis. Ferris State U., Big Rapids, Mich., 1978-83; chmn., program dir. dept. med. tech. U. So. Miss., Hattiesburg, 1983-87; assoc. prof. W.Va. Sch. Osteo. Medicine, Lewisburg, W.Va., 1987-91; dir. depts environ. health sci., clin. lab. sci. and med. svcs. tech. Ea. Ky. U., Richmond, 1991—, med. svc. tech. Contbr. articles to profl. jours. Mem. Am. Soc. for Clin. Lab. Sci., Am. Soc. Microbiology, Clin. Lab. Mgmt. Assn., Artist-Blacksmiths' Assn., Sigma Xi, Phi Kappa Phi. Office: Ea Ky U Dizney # 220 Richmond KY 40475

HUFNAGEL, LINDA ANN, biology educator, researcher; b. Teaneck, N.J., Nov. 7, 1939; d. Ernest Albert and Frances Marie (Hrbek) H.; m. Dov Jaron, 1969; children: Shulamit, Tamara; m. Robert Van Zackroff, June 1984. BA, U. Vt., 1961, MS, 1963; PhD, U. Pa., 1967. Lectr. U. Pa., Phila., summer 1967; NSF postdoctoral fellow Yale U., New Haven, 1967-69; rsch. assoc. Columbia U., N.Y.C., 1970; asst. prof. Oakland Community Coll., Farmington, Mich., 1970; rsch. assoc. Wayne State U., Detroit, 1971-73; lectr. biology U. R.I., Kingston, 1973-75, asst. prof., 1975-79, assoc. prof., 1979-86, prof., 1986—, dir. cen. electron microscope facility, 1973-95. NSF rsch. grantee U. R.I., 1975, Am. Heart Assn. rsch. grantee, 1979; Steps fellow Marine Biol. Lab., Woods Hole, Mass., 1978, 79. Office: U Rhode Island Dept Biochm Microbio/Mol Gn Kingston RI 02881

HÜFNER, MICHAEL, internist; b. Dessau, Germany, Sept. 25, 1940. Prof. medicine, endocrinologist U. Heidelburg, Med. Policlinic, Germany, 1971-90, U. Goettingen, Germany, 1990—; chief endocrinology sect. Med. Coll. U. Goettingen, 1990—. Contbr. articles to profl. jours. Mem. German Endocrinology Soc., European Thyroid Assn. Office: Med Clinic U, Robert Koch Str, 34 Goettingen Germany

HUG, CARL CASMIR, JR., pharmacology and anesthesiology educator; b. Canton, Ohio, Dec. 20, 1936; s. Carl Casmir and Aimee Cecelia (McArdle) H.; m. Marilyn Ann France, May 12, 1956; children: Patricia Ann, Michael Stephen, Joan Marie, Mary Lynn, Lori Renee. BS in Pharmacy summa cum laude, Duquesne U., 1958; PhD in Pharmacology, U. Mich., 1963, MD with distinction, 1967. Diplomate Am. Bd. Anesthesiology. From instr. to assoc. prof. pharmacology U. Mich., Ann Arbor, 1963-71; from assoc. prof. anesthesiology and pharmacology to prof. Emory U. Sch. Medicine, Atlanta, 1972—, dep. chmn. for rsch., 1987-95, dep. chmn. for acad. affairs, 1995—; vis. rsch. prof. U. Leiden, The Netherlands, 1982; dir. Am. Bd. Anesthesiology, 1984—, v.p., 1990-92, pres., 1992-93. Author: Alfentanil: Pharmacology and Uses in Anesthesia, 1984; editor Pharmacokinetics of Anaesthesia, 1984; editor Anesthesiology, 1979-88. Chmn. St. Francis Sch. Bd., Ann Arbor, 1967-71; coach Little League, Ann Arbor, 1967-71; various lay positions Corpus Christi Cath. Ch., Stone Mountain, Ga., 1972—; pres. Assn. Univ. Anesthetists, 1983-87. Named Tchr. of Yr. Emory U. Anesthesiology, 1989, hon. lectr. at multiple Univs. Fellow Royal Coll. Anaesthetists (Eng.) (hon.), Australian and New Zealand Coll. Anaesthetists (hon.); mem. Belgian Soc. Anesthesia and Reanimation (hon.), Am. Soc. Anesthesiologists (mem., chmn. various coms. 1976—), Found. for Anesthesiology Edn. and Rsch. (bd. dirs. 1993—, v.p. 1995—). Republican. Office: Emory Univ Hosp Dept Anesthesiology 1364 Clifton Rd NE Atlanta GA 30322-1104

HUGET, EUGENE FLOYD, dental educator, researcher; b. Flint, Mich., Sept. 20, 1931; s. Leonard John and Dorothy (Makey) H.; m. Barbara Claire Wisniewski, June 22, 1957; children: Kirby Gene, Kristen Claire Huget Byrnes, Kathy Claire, Jason Gene, Huget Rather. BS in Chemistry, Alma (Mich.) Coll., 1953; DDS, U. Mich., 1961; MS in Dental Materials, Georgetown U., 1967; MBA, Rensselaer Poly. Inst., 1983, MS in Mgmt., 1986. Enlisted man, radar and guided missile technician U.S. Army, Balt., 1953-55; commd. 1st lt. U.S. Army, 1961, advanced through grades to col., 1978; gen. dentist U.S. Army, Schofield Barracks, Hawaii, 1961-65; guest researcher Nat. Bur. Standards, Washington, 1968-74; rsch. dental officer U.S. Army Inst. Dental Rsch., Washington, 1968-74, chief div. dental materials, 1974-80; indsl. chemist Chevrolet Motor Co., Flint, Mich., 1955-57; dir. rsch. J.M. Ney Co., Bloomfield, Conn., 1980-87; prof dentistry U. Tenn., Memphis, 1987—. Contbr. numerous monographs on dental biomaterials and articles to profl. jours., chpts. to 9 textbooks. Mem. policy coun. Shelby County Headstart Program, Memphis, 1989—. Chancellor's instrnl. devel. grantee U. Tenn., 1989, alumni rsch. grantee Coll. Dentistry, 1990, 93. Mem. Internat. Assn. for Dental Rsch., Am. Assn. for Dental Rsch. (pres. Memphis chpt. 1990), Sigma Xi. Republican. Presbyterian. Home: 2539 Brachton Ave Memphis TN 38139-6409 Office: U Tenn Coll Dentistry 875 Union Ave Memphis TN 38103-3513

HUGGINS, CHARLES BRENTON, surgical educator; b. Halifax, N.S., Can., Sept. 22, 1901; s. Charles Edward and Bessie (Spencer) H.; m. Margaret Wellman, July 29, 1927; children: Charles Edward, Emily Wellman Huggins Fine. BA, Acadia U., 1920, DSc (hon.), 1946; MD, Harvard U., 1924; MSc, Yale U., 1947; DSc (hon.), Washington U., St. Louis, 1950, Leeds U., 1953, Turin U., 1957, Trinity Coll., 1965, U. Wales, 1967, U. Mich., 1968, Med. Coll. Ohio, 1973, Gustavus Adolphus Coll., 1975, Wilmington (Ohio) Coll., 1980, U. Louisville, 1980; LLD (hon.), U. Aberdeen, 1966, York U., Toronto, 1968, U. Calif., Berkeley, 1968; D of Pub. Service (hon.), George Washington U., 1967; D of Pub. Service (hon.) sigillum magnum, Bologna U., 1964. Intern in surgery U. Mich., 1924-26, instr. surgery, 1926-27; with U. Chgo., 1927—, instr. surgery, 1927-29, asst. prof., 1929-33, assoc. prof., 1933-36, prof. surgery, 1936—, dir. Ben May Lab. for Cancer Research, 1951-69, William B. Ogden Disting. Service prof., 1962—; chancellor Acadia U., Wolfville, N.S., 1972-79; Macewen lectr. U. Glasgow, 1958, Ravdin lectr., 1974, Powell lectr., Lucy Wortham James lectr., 1975, Robert V. Day lectr., 1975, Cartwright lectr., 1975. Trustee Worcester Found. Exptl. Biology; bd. govs. Weizmann Inst. Sci., Rehovot, Israel, 1973—. Decorated Order Pour le Mérite Germany; Order of The Sun Peru; recipient Nobel prize for medicine, 1966, Am. Urol. Assn. award, 1948, Francis Amory award, 1948, AMA Gold medals, 1936, 40, Société Internationale d'Urologie award, 1948, Am. Cancer Soc. award, 1953, Bertner award M.D. Anderson Hosp., 1953, Am. Pharm. Mfrs. Assn. award, 1953, Gold medal Am. Assn. Genito-Urinary Surgeons, 1955, Borden award Assn. Am. Med. Colls., 1955, Comfort Crookshank award Middlesex Hosp., London, 1957, Cameron prize Edinburg U., 1958, Valentine prize N.Y. Acad. Medicine, 1962, Hunter award Am. Therapeutic Soc., 1962, Lasker award for med. research, 1963, Gold medal Virchow Soc., 1964, Laurea award Am. Urol. Assn., 1966, Gold medal Worshipful Soc. Apothecaries of London, 1966, Gairdner award Toronto, 1966, Chgo. Med. Soc. award, 1967, Centennial medal Acadia U., 1967, Hamilton award Ill. Med. Soc., 1967, Bigelow medal Boston Surg. Soc., 1967, Disting. Service award Am. Soc. Abdominal Surgeons, 1972, Sheen award AMA, 1970, Sesquicentennial Commemorative award Nat. Library of Medicine, 1986; Charles Mickle fellow, 1958. Fellow ACS (hon.), Royal Coll. Surgeons Can. (hon.), Royal Coll. Surgeons Scotland (hon.), Royal Coll. Surgeons England (hon.), Royal Soc. Edinburgh (hon.), La Academia Nacional de Medicina (Mexico, hon.); mem. NAS (Charles L. Meyer award for cancer research 1943), Am. Philos Soc. (Franklin medal 1985), Am. Assn. Cancer Rsch., Can. Med. Assn. (hon.), Alpha Omega Alpha. Home: 5807 S Dorchester Ave Chicago IL 60637-1729*

HUGGINS, ELAINE JACQUELINE, nurse, retired army officer; b. San Jose, Calif., Mar. 26, 1954; d. William Burr and Edith Gwendolyn (Schindler) Moreland; m. Bruce Carlton Allanach, Oct. 8, 1976, (div. Oct. 1989); stepchildren: Dawn Louise, Christopher Bruce, Jeffrey Scott, Sean Michael; m. Michael Henry Huggins, Dec. 8, 1991; children: Phoebe Marie, Chloe Anne; stepchildren: Abbey Rose, Jamin Michael. BS in Nursing, U.Md., 1976; MS in Nursing, Med. Coll. Ga., 1988; postgrad., Calif. Inst. Integral Studies. RN, Ga., Md., Calif. Commd. 2d lt. Nurse Corps, U.S. Army, 1972, advanced through grades to maj., 1986; staff nurse gen. medicine-oncology Walter Reed Army Med. Ctr., Washington, 1976-78, team leader gen. medicine-oncology, 1978-79, head nurse med. splty. ward, 1979-80; asst. head nurse gynecol. oncology unit Tripler Army Med. Ctr., Honolulu, 1980-81, head nurse med. splty. clinic, 1981-83; staff nurse orthopedics Eisenhower Army Med. Center, Ft. Gordon, Ga., 1983-84, patient edn. coord., 1984-85, head nurse recovery room, 1985-86; head nurse oncology/neurology unit Letterman Army Med. Ctr., Presidio of San Francisco, 1988-89, clin. nurse psychiat. unit, 1989-90, chief nursing adminstrn. E/N, Letterman Army Med. Ctr. Presidio of San Francisco, 1990-92, ret., 1992; casemanager Vis. Nurses Pomona, Claremont, Calif., 1993-94; nursing supr. Vis. Nurses Assn./Hospice of Pomona, San Bernadino, Calif., 1994-95, quality risk resource mgr., 1995—; mem. adj. faculty Sch. Nursing U. Phoenix-So. Calif. Campus, 1995-96; lectr. in field. Contbr. articles to nursing, mil., and med. publs. Mem. pub. edn. com. Am. Cancer Soc., Honolulu, 1982. Recipient Humanitarian Svc. medal, 1990. Mem. Am. Diabetes Assn., Am. Assn. Diabetic Educators, Grad. Student Nurses Assn. (sec. 1986-87), Am. Nurses Assn., Mensa, Sigma Theta Tau. Avocations: reading, walking, beach combing. Home: 7343 Stonebrook Pl Rancho Cucamonga CA 91730-7271 Office: Vis Nurses Assn Hospice of Pomona Claremont CA 91711

HUGHES, ABBIE ANGHARAD, visual neurophysiologist; b. Whiston, Lancashire, Eng., Mar. 28, 1940; c. Rowland Evan and Kathleen Elsa (Elder) H.; ptnr. Gurli Margrethe Anker, 1962; children: Thorben Lewis, Julian Thorkil. BA, MA, Oxford U., 1963; Diploma of Imperial Coll., U. London, 1966; PhD, Edinburgh (Scotland) U., 1968, DSc, 1982. MRC scholar Imperial Coll., London U., 1963-64; asst. lectr. dept. physiology Edinburgh U., 1964-68; univ. demonstrator univ. lab. physiology Oxford U., 1968-72; extra-ordinary lectr. New Coll., Oxford, 1969; postdoctoral fellow JCSMR, Australian Nat. U., Canberra, Australia, 1972-74, sr. rsch. fellow, 1974-82; dir., prof. Nat. Vision Rsch. Inst. Australia, Melbourne, 1982-90, U. Melbourne, 1982-90; vis. fellow RSPhysS, Inst. Advanced Studies, Canberra, 1990—; chair, founder RCH Eye Bank Com., Canberra, 1978-82; bd. dirs. Victorian Coll. Optometry, Melbourne, 1983-90; co. sec., bd. dirs. Nat. Vision Rsch. Found., Melbourne, 1984—. Mem. editorial bd. Behavioural Brain Rsch., 1986—, Clin. Vision Sci., 1987—; topic editor Vision Rsch., 1988—; author: (with others) The Handbook of Sensory Physiology Vol. VII/5 The Visual System in Vertebrates, 1977, Progress in Retinal Research, Vol. 4, 1985, Visual Neurosciences, 1986, Vision: Coding and Efficiency, 1990; contbr. articles to profl. jours. Rsch. scholar Med. Rsch. Coun., UK, 1963; project grantee NH&MRC, ARC, Australia, 1975—. Fellow Optical Soc. Am., Am. Acad. Optometrists; mem. Physiol. Soc. (London), Australian Neurosci. Soc., Australian Physiol. and Pharmacological Soc., Am. Neurosci. Soc., Australian Med. Writers Assn. (affiliate), Women in Sci. and Tech. Home and Office: ANU Ctrs for Optical & Visual Scis, Outlook Dr, Eaglemont 3084, Australia

HUGHES, ANN NOLEN, psychotherapist; b. Ft. Meade, Md.; d. George M. and Georgie T. Nolen; m. Edwin L. Hughes, Oct. 21, 1961; 1 child, Andrew G. BS in Psychology, Rollins Coll., 1985, MA in Counseling, 1986; student in pub. speaking and human rels., Dale Carnegie Inst., 1981; student, Duke U., 1950-52. Lic. mental health counselor; nat. cert. counselor; nat. cert. gerontol. counselor. Supr. top secret control, audio/visual small parts supply U.S. Army, Continental U.S. and Tokyo; adminstrv. sec. Sys. Devel. Corp., Rand Corp., Santa Monica, Calif.; adminstrv. asst., editor, exec. sec., adminstrv. sec. Aerospace Corp., El Segundo, Calif.; staff therapist Circles of Care, Melbourne, Fla.; developer program for leading divorce support groups for Brevard Women's Ctr. Various leadership positions PTA, Pittsford, N.Y., Brookfield, Wis., 1968-81; mem. Brevard Cmty. Chorus; docent Space Coast Sci. Ctr., 1991-92. Mem. ACA, Assn. for Adult Devel. and Aging, Space Coast PC User's Group, Nat. Geneal. Soc., Geneal. Soc. South Brevard, Suntree Country Club, Brevard County Alumnae Assn., Kappa Kappa Gamma, Kappa Kappa Gamma. Presbyterian. Home: 447 Pauma Valley Way Melbourne FL 32940-1918 Office: PO Box 410162 Melbourne FL 32941-0162

HUGHES, BARBARA ANN, dietitian, public health administrator, nutritionist; b. McMinn County, Tenn., July 22, 1938; d. Cecil Earl and Hannah Ruth (Moss) Farmer; BS cum laude in Home Econs. Carson Newman Coll., Jefferson City, Tenn., 1960; MS in Instl. Mgmt., Ohio State U., Columbus, 1963; MA (Adonarium Judson scholar), So. Bapt. Theol. Sem., 1968; MPH, U. N.C., Chapel Hill, 1972; postgrad. in nutrition U. Iowa, 1974, U. N.C., 1975-85, Case Western Res. U., 1979, Walden U.; PhD 1988; m. Carl Clifford Hughes, Oct. 13, 1962. Registered, lic. nutritionist, dietitian. Instr., clin. dietitian Riverside Meth. Hosp., Riverside Whitecross Sch. Nursing, Columbus, 1963-66; consulting dietitian Mount Holly Nursing Home, Ky. Dept. Mental Health, 1966-68, eastern region N.C. Bd. Health, Raleigh, 1968-73; dir. Nutrition and Dietary Services br., Div. Health Services, N.C. Dept. Human Resources, Raleigh, 1973-89, also dir. Women-Infants-Children Program; pres. B.A. Hughes and Assocs., 1990—; asst. to Rep. Karen Gottovi 14th Dist. N.C. Ho. of Reps., Gen. Assembly N.C., 1994; adj. instr. Case Western Res. U., Cleve., 1988-89; adj. asst. prof. dept. nutrition Sch. Public Health, U. N.C., Chapel Hill, 1975-89; mem. adv. bd. Hospitality Edn. program N.C. Dept. Community Colls., 1974-80, adv. com. Ret. Senior Vol. Program, Raleigh and Wake County, N.C., 1975-79, N.C. Network Coordinating Council for End-Stage Renal Disease, 1975, Nat. Adv. Council on Maternal, Infant, and Fetal Nutrition, Spl. Supplemental Food Program for Women, Infants, and Children, Dept. Agr., 1976-79, adv. com. Nutrition Edn. and Tng. program N.C. Dept. Pub. Instrn., 1978-80; mem.-at-large adv. leadership coun. N.C. Cooperative Ext. Svc., 1994—; advisor com. to Wake County N.C. Cooperative Ext. Svc., 1992—, chair. adv. coun., 1994-96; coord. undergrad. program in gen dietetics East Carolina U.; adv. council N.C. Gov.'s Office Citizen Affairs; cons. dietitian Augusta Victoria Hosp. and Jerusalem (Israel) Crippled Childrens Center, 1968; witness U.S. congressional and Senate hearings in field. Active edn. programs Pullen Memorial Bapt. Church, Raleigh, deacon, 1976-80, 94—, area ministry capt., 1977-78, personnel com., 1978-80; bd. dirs. Community Outreach, 1989-92, futuring com., 1995—, coordinating coun. vice-chair, 1996—; dietitian/dir. food service archeol. expedition to Israel, 1968; bd. dirs. N.C. Literacy Assn. 1978-83, 93—, pres., 1981-83; v.p. Wake County Literacy Council, 1986-87; trustee Gardner-Webb Coll., Boiling Springs, N.C., 1979-82, chmn. curriculum com., 1981-82; chmn. Coalition Pub. Health Nutrition, 1983-85; del. various Democratic Convs., 1981-84, precinct sec.-treas., 1981-83, 1st vice chmn., 1983-85, 2nd vice chmn., 1993—, chair, 1985-87; chmn. adv. bd. dept. home econs. Carson-Newman Coll.; area coord. (N.C.) Pacific Intercultural Exch., 1990—; chair Wake County Affiliate food festival com., 1991-92, chair edn. and community program com., 1992—, Am. Heart Assn., bd. dirs., 1992-94; precinct coord. Ruth Cook for N.C. Senate, Dist. 14, 1994; chair chronic disease com. Wake County Bd. Health, 1995-96; pres. State N.C. Coun. Social Legislation, 1993—; dir. N.C. Bds. of Health, 1994—; del. Altrusa Internat., Inc. to 4th World Conf. on Women, Beijing, China, 1995; nutrition staff writer Sr. Source, Raleigh Extra, Durham Morning Herald. Named Woman of Yr., Wake County, 1975, N.C. Outstanding Dietitian of Yr., 1976, N.C. Outstanding Dietitian, Southeastern Hosp. Conf. for Dietitians, 1978; recipient Disting. Alumna award Carson-Newman Coll., 1983, Eleanor Roosevelt Humanitarian award Altrusa Internat., 1995. Fellow N.C. Inst. Polit. Leadership; mem. AAUW (life, pres. Raleigh br. 1971-75, 91-93, pres. N.C. div. 1978-80, coordinator Wake Women Celebrate, 1995, coord. partners for heart disease and stroke prevention 1995, nat. bd. dirs. 1980-82, area rep. 1980-82, nat. edn. found. bd. dirs. 1987-91, edni. equity roundtable 1992), Am. Dietetic Assn. (del. 1971-74, 87-89, pres assn. 1976-77, N.C. network legis. coordinator 1978-81, 92—, nat. nominating com. 1979-80, nat. chmn. council on practice 1982-83, nat. chair legislation and pub. policy com. 1985-87, nat. area coord. Ho. of Dels. 1989-92, Commn. Dietetic Registration assessment devel. com. for credential of FELLOW program 1994, 95, nat. mem. bylaws com. 1989-90, 91-92, chair resolutions com. 1990-91), APHA (exec. com. So. br. 1977-87, sec.-treas. 1979-80, 1st v.p. 1980-81, Catherine Cowell award 1994, chair award com. 1995—), So. Health Assn. (pres. 1982-83, chair nominating com. 1985-86, 91-92, awards com. 1992-93, Spl. Meritorious award 1989), Assn. State and Territorial Pub. Health Nutrition Dirs. (pres. 1977-79, dir. 1981-89, liaison to Assn. Faculties Grad. Program in Pub. Health Nutrition, chair legis. and pub. policy com. 1984-89, Commendation award 1989), N.C. Assn. Bds. of Health, N.C. Council Foods and Nutrition (dir. 1976-78, chmn. membership 1975, nominating com. 1979). N.C. Council Women's Orgns. (mem. at large, bd. dirs. 1989-92, leadership com. 1991—, chair nutrition subcom., Wellness in State Employees adv. bd. 1989-91), Am. Acad. Health Adminstrn., Soc. Nutrition Edn., Nutrition Today Soc., N.C. Acad. Public Health, Ohio State U. Alumni Assn. (life), U. N.C. Gen. Alumni Assn. (life), U. N.C. Public Health Alumni Assn. (life), Altrusa Internat. (pres. Raleigh club 1973-74, 93-96, dir. 1976-78, 90—, 1st vice gov. 1978-79, chmn. nomination com. 1980-82, gov. dist. Three, 1979-80, internat. vocat. services chmn. 1977-79, 1st v.p. 1985-87, pres.-elect 1987-89, pres. 1989-91), Altrusa Internat. Found. (1st v.p. 1985-87, chmn.-elect 1990-92, chmn. 1992—, bd. dirs. 1993—), Greater Raleigh C. of C. (mem. west area bus. coun., chair legis. com., rep. leadership Raleigh 10 1994—, bd. dirs. leadership Raleigh Alumni Assn.), Women's Forum N.C. (young leadership award com. 1989-90, 92—, newsletter editor bd. dirs. 1992—, adminstr. 1995—), Kappa Omicron Nu. Achievements include olympic torchbearer. Co-author: Diet and Kidney Disease, Assn. for N.C. Regional Med. Program, 1969; contbr. numerous papers, articles to symposia, periodicals in field, vol. areas. Home: 4208 Galax Dr Raleigh NC 27612-3714

HUGHES, BARBARA BRADFORD, nurse; b. Bragg City, Mo., Jan. 21, 1941; d. Lawrence Hurl Bradford and Opal Jewel (Prater) Puttin; m. Robert Howard Hughes, Dec. 9, 1961; children: Kimberly Ann Hayden, Robert Howard II. ASN, St. Louis Community Coll., 1978; student, Webster U., 1980. RN, Mo. Med. surg. nurse Alexian Bros. Hosp., St. Louis, 1979-80; staff nurse Midwest Allergy Cons., St. Louis, 1980; nurse high altitude Aviation Nurse, Ltd., St. Louis, 1980-81; cardiac telemetry staff nurse Jefferson Meml. Hosp., Crystal City, Mo., 1992-94; pvt. practice real estate mgmt., 1962—. Vol. Luth. Hosp., St. Louis, 1967-70; mem. Mo. Bot. Garden, St. Louis, 1976—, Mo. Hist. Soc., 1993—, St. Louis Zoo Friends Assn., 1986-87, Nat. Trust for Hist. Preservation, 1990—; Channel 9-Ednl. TV, St. Louis; vol. blood drive ARC, St. Louis, 1980; vol. health tchr. Spartan Aluminum Products, Sparta, Ill., 1984. U. Mo. scholar, 1959. Mem. Mo. Pilots Assn., Women in Aviation Internat. (charter), U.S. Pilots Assn., Tyospaye Club. Republican. Home: 736 Windsor Harbor Rd Imperial MO 63052-2503

HUGHES, CHARLES E., III, plastic surgeon; b. Chgo., Mar. 19, 1943; s. Charles E. and Jane Wittig (McClintock) H.; m. Ellen Alice Schowe, Nov. 1, 1963; children: Kristian, Chad, Adnrew, Polly. BS, Northwestern U., Chgo., 1966, MD, 1969. Diplomate Am. Bd. Plastic Surgery. Fellow in surg. oncology Am. Cancer Soc., Chgo., 1973-74; resident Northwestern U., 1974-76; asst. prof. plastic surgery Ind. U., Inspls., 1976-82; pvt. practice Geech Grove, Ind., 1983—. Contbr. articles to profl. jours. Fellow ACS (fgn. lang. editor jour. 1974-88); mem. Lipoplasty Soc. (pres. 1995—), Am. Soc. Plastic and Reconstructive Surgeons, Am. Soc. Aesthetic Plastic Surgery, Cleft Palate Soc. Office: 1500 Albany St Beech Grove IN 46107

HUGHES, CHRISTINE MARIE, management consultant; b. Janesville, Wis., July 22, 1952; d. Whilden Bradstreet Jr. amd Patricia Jane (Barry) H. BA, U. Wis., 1976. Salesperson Roerig divsn. Pfizer, N.Y.C., 1976-78; with sales and supplies Proctor & Gamble, Oakbrook, Ill., 1979-81; with sales and supplies Seamless divsn. Dart Kraft Co., Chgo., 1981-83; salesperson U.S. Surg. Corp., Norwalk, Conn., 1983, Chgo., 1983; mgr. Med. Products Mktg. Svc. divsn. Lloyd Johnson Assocs., Northfield, Ill., 1983-85; dir. bus. devel. and market planning Internat. Imaging Inc., Bannockburn, Ill., 1985-87; prin. Hadley Hart Group, Chgo., 1987—; mem. adv. bd. Mirex-NMHCC, Burlington, Mass., 1995-96; bd. dirs. Chgo. Lung Assn., 1984-85, Internat. Trade Club Chgo., 1987-88. Mem. editl. adv. bd. Radiology Econ. Strategies, San Francisco, 1993-94; econ. editor Adminstrv. Radiology Jour., Glendale, Calif., 1990-96; contbr. articles and reports to profl. jours. Mem. Univ. Club Chgo. Office: Hadley Hart Group 8 S Michigan Ave Chicago IL 60603

HUGHES, COLLEEN CARRIS, nursing educator; b. Akron, Ohio, Mar. 2, 1937; d. Albert Virgil and Lois Lillian (Potter) Carris; m. Harold Hughes, Aug. 11, 1964 (dec.); children: Sharon, Thomas, Michael, Joe, Timothy, Gregory, Jeremy, Anandi. RN, Akron Gen. Hosp. Sch. Nursing, Ohio, 1957; BS, U. Oreg., Portland, 1963, MS, 1966; PhD, Oreg. State U., Corvallis, 1980. Asst. prof. health care adminstrn., health Oreg. State U., Corvallis, 1976-79; cons. maternal-child health nursing State of Idaho Bur. Child Health, Boise, 1981-86; assoc. prof., coord. Boise MS Satellite Program Boise MS Satellite Program, Idaho State U., Pocatello, 1986-90; exec. dir. Mountain Health Clinics, Inc., Boise, Idaho, 1990-96, maternal-child health cons., 1990—; state cons. Idaho State Sch. and Hosp., 1991-94; utilization review nurse, 1991-96; assoc. dir. Washo County Health Dept., Reno, 1996—; state health edn. chair Idaho March of Dimes, 1982-87; cons. Nat.-Regional Headstart, 1980—; presenter nationwide workshops in maternal-child health, gerontology, SIDS, cultural diversity, death, dying and ethics; mem. nat. bd. dirs. Career Nursing Asst.'s Program, 1995—. Mem. APHA (gov. councilor 1985-93, chair, coun. on affiliates 1992-94, mem. editl. bd. Nations Health 1992-94, nominations com. 1993-94, chair nominations com. 1994, pub. health nursing sect. counselor 1992-95, pub. health nursing rsch. co-chair 1991—, exec. bd. 1995—), Idaho Pub. Health Assn. (pres. 1984-86), Phi Kappa Phi, Phi Delta Kappa, Sigma Theta Tau. Home: 4930 W View Dr Meridian ID 83642-6463

HUGHES, GEORGE MAXWELL KNIGHT, pharmaceutical company executive, retired; b. Wallasey, Eng., July 10, 1928; came to U.S., 1954; s. Arthur Trevor and Gwendolyn Mary (Jones) H.; m. Christine Anne Rofe, Sept. 21, 1954; children: Jane K., Mark K. BA, Cambridge U., Eng., 1950, PhD, 1954. Rsch. chemist, asst. to v.p. rsch., then dir. rsch. adminstrn. Pfizer-Rsch., Groton, Conn., 1959-69; dir. systems and planning Pfizer Pharms., N.Y.C., 1969-72, v.p. adminstrn., 1972-75; v.p. diagnostics products Pfizer Pharms., Columbia, Md., 1980-81; v.p. systems and communications Pfizer Pharms., N.Y.C., 1981-89; v.p., gen. mgr. Pfizer Med. Systems, Columbia, 1975-80; ret., 1992; vis. prof. Coll. Info. Sci. and Tech., Drexel U., Phila., 1990-92, rsch. prof., 1992—; mem. panel on healthcare tech. assessment Inst. Medicine, Washington, 1986-90. Patentee in chemistry; contrb. papers to numerous publs. Capt. U.K. Army, 1946-48. Home: 59 Oak Knoll Dr Berwyn PA 19312-1283 Office: Drexel Univ Coll Info Sci and Tech Philadelphia PA 19104

HUGHES, GEORGE SAMUEL JR., pharmacologist; b. Pitts., Nov. 13, 1952; s. George Samuel and Kate (Parker) H.; m. Martha Reeder, Mar. 29, 1980; children: Stephanie, Cynthia, Neil. BS, U. Richmond, 1974; MD, Med. Coll. Va., 1978. Diplomate Am. Bd. Internal Medicine, Am. Bd. Clin. Pharmacology. Asst. prof. medicine East Carolina U. Sch. Medicine, Greenville, N.C., 1981-85; fellow in pharmacology Med. U. S.C., Charleston, 1985-87; clin. rsch. mgr. The Upjohn Co., Kalamazoo, Mich., 1987-94; assoc. clin. rsch. dir. Pharmacia & Upjohn, Kalamazoo, 1994—; cons., spkr. A.E. DuPont de Nemours, Wilmington, Del., 1983-85, Key Pharms., Miami, 1983-85, G.D. Searle, Chgo., 1986-87. Fellow Am. Coll. Physicians; mem. AMA (physician recognition award 1996), Am. Fedn. Clin. Rsch., Am. Assn. Blood Banks.d.

HUGHES, GWILYM, occupational physician; b. Wales, Jan. 18, 1937; s. William and Catherine Elizabeth (Lloyd) H.; m. Maureen Ann Day, Feb. 24, 1962; children: William Lloyd, Rhodri Owain. MB, BS, U. London, 1961. Various positions U.K. Nat. Health Svc., London, 1961-65; pvt. practice Pinner Middlesex, Eng., 1966-75; occupational medicine advisor Kodak Ltd. P6MA Ltd., Rockware Glass Co., London, 1968-75; med. advisor Kodak Ltd., Harrow, London, 1975-82; deputy chief med. officer Brit. Telecom, London, 1982-84, chief med. officer, 1984-92; vice-chmn. internat. group Am. Coll. Occupational Medicine, 1991-94; chmn., coord. to European Post and Telecom cos. European adv. Physicians Group, 1982-92; vis. lectr., assoc. clin. prof. occupational medicine U. Utah, 1992—; med. advisor Prudential Assurance Co., London, 1993—. Contbr. articles to profl. jours. Mem. health and safety policy com. CBI, London, 1986-92; health and safety advisor Commonwealth Univs. Bd., London, 1986-92. Fellow Royal Soc. Medicine London, Am. Coll. Occupational Medicine, Royal Coll. Physicians, Faculty Occupational Medicine); mem. Royal Coll. Surgeons, Inst. Pers. Mgmt., Soc. Occupational Medicine (chmn. London group 1990-91), Assn. Clin. Biochemists. Methodist.

HUGHES, J. DEBORAH, health care administrator; b. Pitts., Mar. 24, 1948; d. James Francis and Margaret Veronica (Wiullmier) H. Diploma, Columbia Sch. Nursing, Pitts., 1969; BSN, La Roche Coll., 1987; M of Pub. Mgmt., Carnegie-Mellon U., 1988. Cert. nursing adminstr., med. staff coord., profl. in healthcare quality. Staff nurse Forbes Health Sys., Pitts., 1969-78, head nurse recovery, 1978-79, supr. nursing, 1979-84, clin. asst. to med. dir., 1984-88, dir. med. staff svcs., 1988-90; quality tracking mgr. Humana Inc., Louisville, 1990-91; regional quality mgmt. dir. Galen Healthcare, Inc., Louisville, 1991-92; sr. cons. quality and resource mgmt. Metri Cor, Inc., Louisville, 1992-94; mgr. accreditation svcs. and performance improvement HCIA, 1994—. Mem. Am. Soc. for Quality Control, Nat. Assn. healthcare Quality, Ky. Assn. Quality Assurance Profls., Ky. Soc. Healthcare Risk Mgmt., Nat. Assn. Med. Staff Svcs., Internat. Soc., Quality Assurance, Sigma Theta Tau. Office: HCIA 462 S 4th Ave Ste 405 Louisville KY 40202-2941

HUGHES, JAMES MITCHELL, epidemiologist; b. Pitts., Pa., Aug. 11, 1945; s. James Paul and Adelaide (Mitchell) H.; m. Pamela Mary Parsons, June 12, 1971; children: Andrew Saban, Mitchell Parsons. BA, Stanford U., 1966, MD, 1971. Diplomate Am. Bd. Preventive Medicine, Am. Bd. Internal Medicine, Am. Bd. Infectious Diseases. Intern U. Wash., Seattle, 1971-72; fellow infectious diseases U. Va., Charlottesville, 1976-78; epidemic intelligence svc. officer Ctr. for Disease Control, Atlanta, 1973-75; resident internal medicine U. Wash., Seattle, 1972-73, 75-76; chief water-related diseases activity, asst. chief enteric diseases br. Bur. Epidemiology, Ctr. for Disease Control, Atlanta, 1978-81; chief surveillance and prevention br., asst. dir. med. sci. hosp. infections program Ctr. for Infectious Diseases, Ctrs. for Disease Control, Atlanta, 1981-83, dir. hosp. infections program, 1983-88; dep. dir. Ctr. for Infectious Diseases, Ctr. for Disease Control, Atlanta, 1988-92; dir. Nat. Ctr. for Infectious Diseases Ctr. for Disease Control and Prevention, 1992—; clin. assoc. prof. Emory U., Atlanta; clin. asst. prof. div. geographic medicine, dept. medicine, U. Va., Charlottesville, 1979-82; clin. asst. prof. div. infectious dieases, dept. medicine Emory U., Atlanta, 1981-93; staff physician Atlanta VA Hosp., 1989—. Contbr. articles to profl. jours., chpts. to books. Baseball coach North Decatur (Ga.) Youth Assn., 1981-90; pres. Westchester Sch. PTA, Decatur, 1986-87. Asst. surgeon gen. USPHS, 1973-75, 76—. Recipient Meritorious Svc. medal USPHS, Atlanta, 1986, Outstanding Svc. medal, 1989. Fellow ACCP, Infectious Diseases Soc.; mem. AAAS, APHA, Am. Soc. Microbiology, Am. Soc. Tropical Medicine and Hygiene, Internat. Epidemiol. Assn., Royal Soc. Tropical Medicine and Hygiene, Soc. Epidemiol. Rsch. Soc., U. So. Calif. Alumni Assn. (bd. govs. 1995—), Stanford U. Alumni Club Ga. (pres. 1980-82), U. So. Calif. Alumni Club Ga. Office: Nat Ctr Infectious Disease MS C12 Ctrs Disease Control and Prevention 1600 Clifton Rd NE Atlanta GA 30329-4018*

HUGHES, JAMES PAUL, physician; b. Wilkinsburg, Pa., Apr. 9, 1920; s. Paul S. and Sara C. (Coleman) H.; m. Adelaide C. Mitchell, June 21, 1944; 1 son, James Mitchell. B.S., U. Pitts., 1944, M.D., 1945; D. Indsl. Medicine, U. Cin., 1952. Diplomate: Am. Bd. Preventive Medicine. Intern St. Francis Hosp., Pitts., 1945-46; resident in pathology Univ. Hosps., Cleve., 1948-49; fellow in indsl. medicine Kettering Lab. U. Cin., 1949-51; physician The Tex. Co., 1951-52, The Ethyl Corp., Cin., 1952-57; chief Bur. Indsl. Health Dept. Health City of Cin., 1952-55; med. dir. Kaiser Aluminum & Chem. Corp., Oakland, Calif., 1957-82; sr. ptnr. Hughes-Lewis Assocs., Oakland, Calif., 1982-88; asst. prof. indsl. medicine U. Cin., 1952-55; asso. prof. preventive medicine Ohio State U., 1955-57; exec. v.p., dir. Kaiser Found. Internat., 1967-76; project dir. U.S. Peace Corps Health projects, W. Africa, 1966-68, USAID med. relief project, Port Harcourt, Nigeria, 1970-72, Health Services on Bandama River project, Kossou, Ivory Coast, 1970-72; v.p. health sers. Kaiser Industries Corp., 1972-74; clin. assoc. prof. occupational medicine U. Calif., San Francisco, 1979—; med. dir. occupational health services Merritt Peralta Med. Ctr., Oakland, Calif., 1982-86; mem. hearing bd. Bay Area Air Quality Mgmt. Dist., Calif., 1989—. Author: (with N.H. Proctor) Chemical Hazards of the Workplace, 1978, 4th edit., 1996; editor-in-chief Health Hazards of the Workplace Report, 1989-91. Chmn. com. for Industry Council Tropical Health Harvard U. Sch. Public Health, 1969-76. Served to capt. U.S. Army, 1946-48. Decorated Officier de l'Ordre Nat. Ivoirien Abidjan, 1972. Fellow ACP, Am. Coll. Occupational and Environ. Medicine (past pres., Health Achievement award 1972, Kehoe award 1982, Knudsen award 1996); mem. Inst. Medicine/NAS, Am. Indsl. Hygiene Assn. Home: 124 Guilford Rd Piedmont CA 94611-3805

HUGHES, JEFFREY BRIAN, healthcare management consultant; b. New Britain, Conn., May 25, 1957; s. Thomas Francis and Martha Lorraine Hughes; m. Barbara Elaine McGovern, Aug. 11, 1990; children: Moura McGovern, Jonathan McGovern. BA, Boston U., 1979; MPH, Yale U., 1983. Adminstrv. resident Newport (R.I.) Hosp., 1983-84, planning coord., 1984-86; dir. planning Danbury (Conn.) Hosp., 1986-90, dir. ops., 1990-91; sr. assoc. Coopers & Lybrand, Hartford, Conn., 1991-93, mng. assoc. health car emgmt. cons. svcs., 1993—. Selectman Town of Southbury, Conn., 1995—; vice chmn., bd. dirs. Danbury Regional Commn. on Child Care Rights & Abuse, 1986-91; mem. career adv. network Boston U.; bd. dirs., treas. Child Care Connectins, 1989-91; mem. adv. bd. Conn. Forum; bd. liaison to PTO, Pomperaug Elem. Sch., 1990-91; mem. regional ednl. adv. bd. Region 15 Sch. Dist., 1993-94. Mem. Am. Coll. Healthcare Execs., Am. Hosp. Assn., Soc. for Hosp. Planning and Mktg., New Eng. Healthcare Assembly (evaluation coun.), New Eng. Soc. for Hosp. Planning and Mktg., Healthcare Fin. Mgmt. Assn., Yale Alumni in Pub. Health (bd. dirs. 1988-91). Office: Coopers and Lybrand LLP 100 Pearl St Hartford CT 06103

HUGHES, JOE DON, gynecologist, obstetrician; b. Munday, Tex., Feb. 21, 1933; s. George Elbert and Bethel (Mae) H.; m. Easter Ann McGough, June 14, 1958; children: Joe B., Donna Kay, George D. BA, U. Tex., Austin, 1955; MD, U. Tex., Galveston, 1959. Intern U. Tex. Med. Br./John Sealy Hosp., Galveston, 1959-60, resident, 1960-64; ob-gyn. Rutherford (N.C.) Hosp., Rutherfordton, 1964—; pvt. practice Rutherfordton, 1964—. Fellow Am. Coll. Ob-Gyn.; mem. AMA, South Atlantic Assn. Ob-Gyn., N.C. Ob-Gyn. Soc., Gynecol. Laser Soc., So. Med. Soc., Am. Soc. for Reproductive Medicine, Am. Soc. for Laser Medicine and Surgery Inc. Home: RR 4 Box 238 Rutherfordton NC 28139-9244 Office: Rutherford Ob-Gyn Assoc PA PO Box 1208 Rutherfordton NC 28139-1208

HUGHES, LAUREL ELLEN, psychologist, educator, writer; b. Seattle, Oct. 30, 1952; d. Morrell Spencer and Eleanore Claire (Strong) Chamberlain; m. William Henry Hughes Jr., Jan. 27, 1973; children: Frank, Ben, Bridie. BA in Psychology, Portland State U., 1980, MS in Psychology, 1986; D in Clin. Psychology, Pacific U., 1988. Lic. psychologist, Oreg. Counselor Beaverton (Oreg.) Free Meth. Ch., 1982-85; psychotherapist Psychol. Svc. Ctr., Portland, Oreg., 1986, Psychol. Svc. Ctr. West, Hillsboro, Oreg., 1987-89; pvt. practice Beaverton, 1990—; adj. mem. faculty Portland C.C., 1990-91, U. Portland, 1992—, CU/Seattle, 1993-95; vis. asst. prof. U. Portland, 1991-92; psychol. cons. children's weight control group St. Vincent's Hosp., Portland, 1991. Author: How to Raise Good Children, 1988, How to Raise a Healty Achiever, 1991, Beginnings and Beyond, 1996; contbr. articles to profl. jours. Tchr. Sunday sch. Beaverton Free Meth. Ch., 1983-88; mother helper Walker Elem. Sch., Beaverton, 1988-90, 92-93; foster parent Washington County, Oreg., 1976-77, 79-80; vol. disaster mental health svcs. ARC, 1993—. Mem. APA, Oreg. Psychol. Assn. (bd. dirs. 1990-91, editor jour. 1990-91). Office: 4320 SW 110th Ave Beaverton OR 97005-3009

HUGHES, MARK BRIAN, dentist; b. Highland, Ill., Jan. 25, 1956; s. Oliver John Jr. and Lois Marilyn (Schultze) H.; m. Kris Allison Cordts, Aug. 6, 1977; children: Brooke, Brean, Lauren, Shannon. BA, U. Kans., 1979; DDS, U. Mo., 1984. Pvt. practice dentistry Phoenix, 1984—. Mem. Phoenix Art Mus., 1988, Citizens for Better Dental Health, Phoenix, 1988. Mem. ADA, Ariz. State Dental Assn. (state chmn. children's dental health month), Ctrl. Ariz. Dental Soc. (com. peer rev. 1988, com. membership 1987, bd. dirs. 1990—, treas. 1994—), N.W. Phoenix C. of C. (bd. dirs. 1990, v.p. 1992), Westside Study Club, Rotary (program chmn. 1987). Republican. Lutheran. Office: 15648 N 35th Ave Ste 107 Phoenix AZ 85023-3862

HUGHES, MICHAEL JOSEPH, counselor, psychologist; b. Scranton, Pa., Jan. 20, 1951; s. Michael Robert and Mary Catherine (Race) H.; m. Patricia Staley, Sept. 26, 1987. BS, U. Scranton, 1972, MS, 1974; EdD, W.Va. U., 1977. Lic. counselor, psychologist W.Va., Ohio. Counselor Clarks-Summit (Pa.) State Hosp., 1974-75; counselor, instr. W.Va. U., Morgantown, 1975-77; dir. clin. svcs. Prestera Ctr., Huntington, W.Va., 1977-90; cons. VA Med. Ctr., Huntington, 1984-91; counselor Shawnee State U., Portsmouth, Ohio, 1990—; cons. Shawnee Mental Health Ctr., Portsmouth, 1990-95. Mem. APA, ACA, Am. Coll. Counseling Assn., Ohio Mental Health Counselors Assn., W.Va. Psychol. Assn., W.Va. Counseling Assn., W.Va. Mental Health Counselors Assn., Am. Mental Health Counselors Assn., Ohio Counseling Assn. Roman Catholic. Office: Shawnee State U 940 2nd St Portsmouth OH 45662-4347

HUGHES, PETER MICHAEL, urologist; b. Glens Falls, N.Y., Apr. 26, 1952; s. Richard A. and Betty L. (Voelker) H.; m. Ann M. Poulos. MD, Autonomous U. Guadalajara, Mexico, 1978. Intern in surgery Case Western Reserve, Cleve., 1980, resident in urology, 1981-84; chief resident in urology Mt. Sinai Hosp. Med. Ctr., Chgo., 1984-85; pvt. practice Glens Falls. Mem. Am. Urol. Assn., N.Y. State Med. Soc., Warren County Med. Soc. Office: 17 Baywood Dr Queensbury NY 12804

HUGHES, PHILIP ROYAL, optometrist; b. Colebrack, N.H., Nov. 9, 1937; s. Richard and Carolyn (Alls) H.; m. Jeannine Dumont, Sept. 2, 1957; children: Richard, Mark, Stephen, Lisa. D of Optometry, Mass Coll. Optometry, 1958. Optometrist pvt. practice, Md., 1959-64, Springfield, Vt., 1964—. Mem. Am. Optometric Assn., Va. Optometric Assn. Home: 6 Lakewood Rd Springfield VT 05156 Office: 48 Main St Springfield VT 05156

HUGHES, SEAN PATRICK FRANCIS, orthopaedic surgery educator; b. Farnham, Surrey, Eng., Dec. 2, 1941; s. Patrick (dec.) and Kathleen Ethel (Bigg) H.; m. Felicity Mary Anderson, Jan. 22, 1972; children: Sarah Jane, Emily Anne, John Patrick. MB, BS, U. London, 1966, MS, 1976. Asst. lectr. anatomy St. Mary's Hosp. Med. Sch., London, 1967; med. officer Save the Children Fund, Nigeria, 1968; surg. registrar Hammersmith Hosp., London, 1970-73; sr. registrar The Middlesex and Royal Nat. Orthopaedic Hosp., London, 1974-76; rsch. fellow Mayo Clinic, Rochester, Minn., 1975-76; sr. lectr. Royal Postgrad. Med. Sch., London, 1977-79, prof. orthopaedic surgery, 1991—; chief orthopaedic svcs. Hammersmith Hosps., 1993—; prof. orthopaedic surgery U. Edinburgh (Scotland), 1979-91; hon. civilian cons. orthopedic surgery Royal Navy, 1986—; hon. cons. Nat. Hosp. Queens Square; Aris and Gale lectr. Royal Coll. Surgeons Eng., 1976. Editor: Astons Short Textbook of Orthopaedics and Traumatology 1980, 83, 89, 96; co-editor : Basis and Practice of Orthopaedics, 1980, Principles and Practice of Musculoskeletal Surgery, 1987, Musculoskeletal Infections, 1986. Recipient Seddon prize Royal Nat. Orthopaedic Hosp., London, 1976; grantee Action Rsch./Crippled Child, 1988-97, Med. Rsch. Coun., 1985-91, Wellcome Trust, 1978-84, 95—, ARC, 1993—. Fellow Royal Soc. Medicine, Brit. Orthopaedic Assn. (coun. 1989-91), InterCollegiate Bd. Orthopaedic Surgery (chmn. 1992-95), Royal Coll. Surgeons Edinburgh (coun. 1985-94, v.p. 1994—); mem. Internat. Soc. Lumbar Spine, Orthopaedic Rsch. Soc., Brit. Orthopaedic Rsch. Soc. (hon. sec. 1985-88, pres. 1995-97), Assn. Rsch. Circulation (v.p.), World Orthopaedic Concern U.K. Office: Royal Postgrad Med Sch Hammersmith Hosp, Orthopaedic Dept DuCane Rd, London W12 ONN, England

HUGHES, THOMAS ARTHUR, endocrinologist; b. Iowa City, Iowa, Mar. 18, 1949; s. Thomas William and Clara Ann (McCue) H.; m. Suzanne M. Harvath, June 3, 1972; children: Teresa Suzanne, Catherine Christine, Jennifer Marie, Thomas Robert. MD, Wash. U., 1975. Diplomate Am. Bd. Endocrinologist, Am. Bd. Internal Medicine. Instr. U. Ala., Birmingham, 1981-82, asst. prof., 1982-86, dir. rsch. unit, 1984-86; asst. prof. U. Tenn., Memphis, 1987-89, assoc. prof. dept. of medicine and pharmacology, 1989—; dir. Lipid Metabolism Clinic, Regional Med. Ctr., Memphis, 1987—; diabetes edn. faculty Bristol-Myers Squibb, 1995—. Mem. ACP, Am. Heart Assn. (peer rev. com., Cora Louise Carson award 1989, Grant-in-Aid, 1979-91), Am. Diabetes Assn. (mgmt. faculty). Office: U Tenn Rm 340M 951 Court Ave Memphis TN 38163

HUGHES, VINCENT PATRICK, radiologist; b. Fremont, Ohio, Mar. 14, 1927; s. George Francis and Margaret Josephine (O'Connor) H.; m. Joan Catherine Fitz, June 21, 1952; children: Mark, Fr. Benedict, Francis, Marie, Fr. Brendan, Sheila Strain, Theresa Drahman, Sr. M. Emmanuel, Martin, Monica. BS, Notre Dame U., 1948; MD, Ohio State U., 1952. Diplomate Am. Bd. Radiology. Gen. med. practice Port Clinton, Ohio, 1953-62; radiology resident Ohio State U. Hosps., Columbus, Ohio, 1962-65; radiologist Hoffman, Birmingham Assocs., Tiffin, Ohio, 1965-76, Modern Med. Imaging, Spokane, Wash., 1976-93; clin. assoc. Med. Coll. Ohio, Toledo, 1970-76; dir., chief cons. Breast Screening Ctr., Spokane, 1987-93; chief radiologist Deer Park Health Ctr. and Hosp., 1981—; cons. VA Hosp., Spokane, 1977-88, 92—. Contbr. articles to profl. jours. Mem. Spokane Radiol. Soc. (pres. 1987), Spokane Med. Soc., Wash. State Med. Assn., Am. Coll. Radiology, Radiol. Soc. N. Am. Republican. Roman Catholic. Home: 9305 N Gerlach Rd Spokane WA 99207-9301 Office: 220 E Wellesley # 109A Spokane WA 99207-1422

HUGHES, W. JAMES, optometrist; b. Shawnee, Okla., Oct. 15, 1944; s. Willis J. and Elizabeth Alice (Nimohoyah) H. B.A. in Anthropology, U. Okla., 1966, M.A. in Anthropology, 1972; O.D., U. Houston, 1976; M.P.H., U. Tex., 1977. Lic. Optometrist, Okla., Tex., W. Va. commd. med. officer USPHS, 1966; advanced through the grades to capt./optometrist, USPHS, 1993; physician's asst., Houston, Dallas, 1969-70; teaching asst. in clin. optics U. Houston, 1973-74, contact lens research asst., 1974; Wesley Jessen Contact Lens Rep., 1974-76; extern eye clinic Tuba City Indian Hosp., 1975; teaching fellow pub. health optometry U. Houston, 1975-76; Indian Health Service optometrist, Eagle Butte, S.D., 1976; optometrist vision care project Crockett Ind. Sch. Dist., 1977; vision care program dir. Bemidji Area Indian Health Service, 1977-78; optometrist Navajo Area Indian Health Service, Chinle Health Ctr., 1978-79; adj. prof. So. Calif. Coll. of Optometry, Los Angeles, U. Houston Coll. of Optometry, 1978—, So. Coll. Optometry, Memphis, 1980—; optometrist Shiprock USPHS Indian Hosp., 1979—; chief vision care program Northern Navajo Med. Ctr., 1994—; dir. eye clinic USPHS Northern Navajo Med. Ctr., Shiprock, N.Mex.; Navajo area Indian Health Service rep. to optometry career devel. com. USPHS. Sgt. U.S. Army, 1966-69, Capt. USPHS 1993—. Decorated Bronze Star, Purple Heart. Recipient House of Vision award 1974; Community Health Optometry award 1976; Better Vision scholar, 1973-76. Mem. Am. Pub. Health Assn., Am. Optometric Assn., Tex. Optometric Assn. Commd. Officers Soc., Assn. Am. Indian Physicians, Beta Sigma Kappa. Democrat. Roman Catholic. Contbr. articles to profl. jours.

HUGHES, WAUNELL MCDONALD (MRS. DELBERT E. HUGHES), retired psychiatrist; b. Tyler, Tex., Feb. 6, 1928; d. Conrad Claiborne and Bernice Oletha (Smith) McDonald; B.A., U. Tex. at Austin, 1946; M.D., Baylor U., 1951; m. Delbert Eugene Hughes, Aug. 14, 1948; children—Lark, Mark, Lynn, Michael. Intern VA Hosp., Houston, 1951-52; resident Parkland Hosp., Dallas, 1964-67; practiced gen. medicine in Tyler, Tex., 1952-64; acting chief psychiatry service VA Hosp., Dallas, 1967-68, asst. chief, 1968-73, chief Mental Hygiene Clinic and Day Treatment Center, 1973-82, unit chief acute inpatient psychiatry Med. Center, 1982-88; clin. instr. psychiatry Southwestern Med. Sch., U. Tex. Health Sci. Center, Dallas, 1968-88; psychiat. cons. Dallas Family Guidance Clinics, 1990. Chmn. pre-sch. vision and hearing program Pilot Club, Tyler, 1960-64. Mem. Am. Med. Women's Assn. (pres. Dallas 1980-81), Am. Psychiat. Assn., Am. Group Psychotherapy Assn., (pres. Dallas chpt. 1984-86), North Tex. Soc. Psychiat. Physicians (co-chair Mental Health Mental Retardation pro bono clinic com. Dallas chpt. 1989-91, mem. patient advocacy com. 1992—), Dallas Area Women Psychiatrists (archivist 1985—), Alpha Epsilon Iota (pres. 1950-51). Home: 3428 University Blvd Dallas TX 75205-1834

HUGHES, WILLIAM L., health delivery system administrator; b. Richmond, Ky., July 23, 1952; s. Paul and Joann (Broaddus) H. BS, Ea. Ky. U., 1974, MS, 1976; MPH, Tulane U., 1985, MBA, 1985. Adminstrv. fellow Allegheny Health Svcs., Pitts., 1985; asst. v.p. Bristol Meml. Hosp., Bristol, Tenn., 1985-86; v.p. fin. and chief fin. officer The Hosp. of the Good Samaritan, L.A., 1986-92; v.p. fin., CFO U. Colo. Hosp., Denver, 1992-95; v.p., chief fin. officer M.D. Anderson Cancer Ctr. Outreach Corp., Houston, 1995—; bd. dirs. U. Colo. Perinatal Inst. Chmn. med. support com. Calif. Spl. Olympics, 1988-90. Capt. U.S. Army, 1976-81. Mem. Am. Hosp. Assn., Healthcare Fin. Mgmt. Assn., Am. Coll. Healthcare Execs., Rotary Club of Houston, Colo. Perinatal Found. (bd. dirs.), Med. Group Mgmt.

Assn. Republican. Episcopalian. Office: MDACC Outreach Corp 7505 South Main Ste 500 Houston TX 77030

HUGO, NORMAN ELIOT, plastic surgeon, medical educator; b. Beverly, Mass., Sept. 23, 1933; s. Victor Joseph and Helen Bernadette (Box) H.; m. Geraldine P. Tonry, Oct. 10, 1959; children: Helen, William, Geraldine, Norman, Catherine. BA, Williams Coll., 1955, DSc (hon.), 1989; MD, Cornell U. Med. Coll., 1959. Intern, resident Cornell U. Surg. Svc., Bellevue Hosp., N.Y.C., 1959-63, resident N.Y. Hosp.-Cornell Med. Ctr., 1963-65, univ. instr. surgery, 1965-66; asst. prof. Ind. U.; asst. chief plastic surgeon Walter Reed Army Med. Ctr., 1967-69, assoc. prof. U. Chgo., 1969-71; chief plastic and reconstructive surgery Michael Reese Hosp., Chgo., 1969-71, Passavant Hosp., Chgo., 1971-79; assoc. prof. Northwestern U., Chgo., 1971-82; dir. plastic surgery Lakeside VA Hosp., 1971-77; chief plastic and reconstructive surgery Columbia U.-Presbyn. Med. Ctr., N.Y.C., 1982-95; prof. Columbia U. Coll. Physicians & Surgeons, 1982—. Maj. M.C., AUS, 1967-69. Diplomate Am. Bd. Plastic Surgery, dir., 1982-88, vice chmn., 1987-88, residency review com., accreditation coun. grad. med. edn., 1994—. Mem. ACS, Am. Soc. Plastic & Reconstructive Surgeons (trustee 1981-84, historian 1982-84, v.p. 1985-86, pres. elect 1986-87, pres. 1987-88, bd. dirs. Ednl. Found.), Am. Assn. Plastic and Reconstructive Surgery (trustee 1982-84), Am. Soc. Aesthetic Plastic Surgery (sec. 1979-82), Chgo. Soc. Plastic Surgery (sec. 1979-81, v.p. 1981-82), Plastic Surgery Research Council, Am. Cleft Palate Soc., Assn. Acad. Surgery, Soc. Head and Neck Surgeons, N.Y. Acad. Sci., AMA (del. 1983-88), Am. Burn Soc. Clubs: Williams, Union (N.Y.C.); University (Chgo.). Home: 37 Carriage Ln New Canaan CT 06840-4401 Office: Columbia U Coll Physicians and Surgeons 161 Ft Washington Ave New York NY 10032-3713

HUGUIER, MICHEL ALPHONSE, surgeon; b. Paris, Mar. 2, 1937; s. Jacques and Micheline (Decoux) H.; m. Geneviève Verdonck, June 30, 1960. BS, Lycée Carnot, Paris, 1962. Intern Hosp. Paris, 1960; prof. U. Paris VI, 1971-81, prof. digestive surgery, 1981—; head dept. surgery Hosp. Tenon, Paris, 1983—; dir. Diplome d'Etudes Approfondies e/ Chirurgicales, France, 1985—; adviser French Minister of Health, Paris, 1976-79. Editor: Digestive Diseases, 1986, Med. Writing, 1989, Pancreatic Carcinoma, 1991. Named to Ordre Legion d'honneuz, France, 1993. Mem. Assn. Francais de Chir., Assn. Argentina de Cirugia, Soc. de Cirugia Uruguay, Internat. Gastrosurg. Club, N.Y. Acad. Scis. (vice-chmn. for Europe). Home: Passage Gambetta 10, 75020 Paris France Office: Rue de le Chine 4, 75020 Paris France

HUHN, DIETER, medical educator; b. Germany, Nov. 15, 1935. MD, U. Freiburg, Fed. Republic Germany, 1960. Prof. internal medicine U. Munich, 1978—; chief dept. hematology and oncology Free U. Berlin, 1983—. Address: Heruler Weg 5, 1000 Berlin 20, Germany

HUHTANIEMI, ILPO TAPANI, physiology educator; b. Hämeenlinna, Finland, May 22, 1947; s. P. Tapani and Marjatta A. (Nykänen) H.; m. Päivi M. Helminen, May 29, 1971; children: Marianna, Otto. MB, U. Helsinki, Finland, 1968, MD, 1972, DMS, 1974. Lic. physician, Finland. Intern Helsinki U. Ctr. Hosp., 1972; postdoctoral fellow dept. ob-gyn. U. Calif., San Francisco, 1975-76; resident dept. clin. chemistry U. Oulu, Finland, 1976-79; vis. assoc. NIH, Bethesda, Md., 1979-80; sr. fellow Acad. Finland, Helsinki, 1981-83; instr. med. biochemistry U. Helsinki, 1972-75, assoc. prof. dept. clin. chemistry, 1984-85; prof., chmn. dept. physiology U. Turku, Finland, 1986—; vis. prof. U. Heidelberg, Fed. Republic of Germany, 1990-91. Contbr. articles to profl. jours. Lt. med. staff Finnish Army. Grantee Acad. Finland, NIH, Fogarty Found., other pvt. founds., 1975-95. Mem. Internat. Soc. Andrology (sec. 1989—), Finnish Endocrine Soc. (chmn. 1988-90), Am. Endocrine Soc., Brit. Endocrine Soc., Finnish Med. Assn., Finnish Acad. Sci. and Letters. Office: U Turku Dept Physiology, Kiinamyllynkatu 10, 20520 Turku Finland

HUHTIKANGAS, AARRE ERKKI, research professor; b. Helsinki, Finland, May 8, 1938; s. Huugo Juho and Martha Julia Margareta (Sjostedt) H.; m. Leena Riitta Suontaa, May 30, 1963; children: Elina, Ulla, Anna, Matti. B in pharm., U. Helsinki, 1963, MS in pharm., 1967, D in pharm., 1976, docent, 1977. Lic. pharmicist. Asst. Inst. Pharmacy U. Helsinki, 1967-77, assoc. prof., 1978-79; assoc. prof. U. Kuopio, Finland, 1979-83; prof. pharm. chem. U. Kuopio, 1983-92; rsch. prof., 1993—; scientific cons. Havulinna Oy Ltd., Helsinki, 1968-79. Patentee in field; contbr. articles to profl. jours. Lutheran. Home: Kela Svarvars, 02400 Kirkkonumm Finland

HUI, KOON-SEA, neuroscientist; b. Hong Kong, Sept. 21, 1948; came to U.S., 1976; s. Yuk-Tat and Kiu (Lau) H.; m. Maria Po-Ping Cheung, Aug. 27, 1974; children: Jacqueline, Electra Y. BSc with honors, Chinese U. of Hong Kong, 1971; MPhil, Hong Kong U., 1974; PhD, U. Sask., Saskatoon, Can., 1976. Demonstrator Chinese U. of Hong Kong, 1971-72; teaching asst. Hong Kong U., 1972-74; lab. scientist Sask. Govt., Saskatoon, 1974-76; rsch. scientist Ctr. Neurochemistry, N.Y.C., 1976-83; lab. chief Nathan S. Kline Inst., Orangeburg, N.Y., 1983—; reviewer NSF, Washington, 1983—, Jour. Biol. Chemistry, Rockville, Md., 1989—; cons. Bioputa Ltd., Stevenage, Eng., 1988—; asst. rsch. prof. NYU, N.Y.C., 1980-92, assoc. rsch. prof., 1992—. Contbr. chpts. to books. Mem. Affirmative Action Com., Orangeburg, 1987—. Grantee WHO, 1972, 80, BRSG, 1980, 88, NSF, 1979, NIH, 1978—, NIDA, 1991—. Mem. AAAS, Am. Soc. Biochemistry and Molecular Biology, Internat. Soc. Neurochemistry, Internat. Brain Rsch. Orgn., N.Y. Acad. Scis., Am. Soc. Neurochemistry, Hong Kong Soc. Neurosci. Office: Nathan S Kline Inst Orangeburg Rd Orangeburg NY 10962

HUIGENS, DANIEL DEAN, dentist; b. Osmond, Nebr., May 16, 1953; s. Mickey Helen (White) H.; m. Linda Sue Wilbourn, May 19, 1982 (div. 1991); 1 child, Matthew Blake. BA, U. LaVerne, 1975; BS, U. Okla., 1979, DDS with honors, 1982. EMT Community Ambulance Svc., San Dimas, Calif., 1971-74; emergency room technician San Dimas Community Hosp., San Dimas, Calif., 1974-77; physician assoc. Muskogee Bone and Joint Clinic, 1979-82; dentist Drs. Huigens and Hanawalt, LaVerne, Calif., 1986-94; pvt. practice LaVerne, 1994—; mem. part time staff UCLA Coll. Dentistry. Mem. ADA, Acad. Gen. Dentistry, Calif. Dental Assn., Tri County Dental Soc., Pomona Valley Amateur Astronomers Assn., LaVerne C. of C., Assn. Flying Dentists, Aircraft Owners and Pilots Assn., Omicron Kappa Upsilon. Office: 2187 Foothill Blvd Ste E La Verne CA 91750

HUKILL, PETER BIGGS, pathologist; b. Lucerne, Switzerland, Feb. 3, 1927; s. George Raymond and Helen Naudain (Biggs) H.; m. Nancy Nelms, July 9, 1950 (div. 1969); 1 child, Anne Hukill Yeager. AB, Harvard U., 1947; MD, Yale U., 1953. Diplomate Am. Bd. Pathology. Intern Yale New Haven Hosp., 1953-54, resident, fellow, 1957-60; instr., asst. prof., then assoc. prof. pathology Yale U., New Haven, 1958-68; prof. pathology U. Ala., Birmingham, 1968-69, U. Conn., Farmington, Conn., 1969-77; clin. prof. U. Conn., Farmington, 1977—; attending pathologist, dir. labs. Charlotte Hungerford Hosp., Torrington, Conn., 1977-93, cons. pathologist, 1993—; assoc. clin. prof. Yale U., 1977—; cons. various Conn. hosps., 1977—; dir. Conn. Dermatopathology Lab., Torrington, 1977—. Contbr. articles to sci. jours. Capt. M.C. USAF, 1954-56. Fellow Am. Coll. Pathologists; mem. Am. Soc. Dermatopathology, Conn. Soc. Pathologists (pres. 1965-66). Office: Charlotte Hungerford Hosp 540 Litchfield St Torrington CT 06790-6600

HUKINS-RODRIGUE, DANA ANN, community health nurse; b. Raceland, La., Nov. 1, 1964; d. Herman Cecil and Diana Ann (Chiasson) H. BSN, Nicholls State U., Thibodaux, La., 1986. RN, La. Nurse II, staff pediatrics nurse South La. Med. Ctr., Houma, 1986-88; nurse, pub. health nurse III Lafourche Parish Health Unit, Thibodaux, 1988—. Mem. Nicholls State U. Nursing Honor Soc., Sigma Theta Tau.

HULETT, CAROL LEE, orthopaedic surgerin; b. Flint, Mich., Jan. 16, 1952; d. Raymond Harvey and Treva Evelyn (Wagamon) H. BA, Albion Coll., 1974; MD, Wayne State U., 1978. Diplomate Am. Bd. Orthopaedic Surgeons. Intern St. John Hosp., Detroit, 1978-79, resident, 1979-80; resident Wayne State U. Affiliated Hosp., Detroit, 1980-83; orthopaedic surgeon pvt. practice, Clinton Twp., Mich., 1983—. Team physician Grosse Pointe (Mich.) North High Sch., 1979-84, Mt. Clemens (Mich.) High Sch., 1984—; cmty. liaison Gilr Scouts Am., Clinton Twp., 1991—. Named Vol. of Yr. Macomb County Bd. Suprs., 1992. Fellow Am. Acad. Orthopaedic Surgeons; mem. Mid. Am. Soc. Orthopaediac Surgeons, Detrout Acad. Orthopaedic Surgeons. Office: 15520 19 Mile Rd Ste 430 Clinton Township MI 48038

HULKA, BARBARA SORENSON, epidemiology educator; b. Mpls., Mar. 1, 1931; d. Herbert Fritchof and Mable (Alquist) Sorenson; m. Jaroslav Fabian Hulka, Nov. 13, 1954; children: Carol Ann, Gregory Fabian, Bryan Herbert. BS, Radcliffe Coll., 1952; MS, Juilliard Sch. Music, 1954; MD, Columbia U., 1959, MPH, 1961. Diplomate Am. Bd. Preventive Medicine; Lic. physician, Pa., N.C. Research asst. prof. U. Pitts., 1966-67; asst. prof. U. N.C., Chapel Hill, 1967-71, assoc. prof., 1972-76, prof., 1977—, chmn. dept. epidemiology, 1983-93, Kenan prof., 1987—; adj. prof. medicine Duke U. Med. Ctr., Durham, N.C., 1982—; chmn. epidemiology and disease study sect. NIH, 1979-83, mem. Endpoint Rev. Safety Monitoring and Adv. Com., Breast Cancer Prevention Trial, Nat. Surg. Adjuvant Breast and Bowel Project, 1992—; bd. sci. counselors Nat. Cancer Inst., 1980—; mem. Inst. of Medicine com. toxic shock syndrome Nat. Acad. Sci., 1981-82; mem. Sci. Rev. and Evaluation Bd. subcom. VA, 1983—; mem. subcom. on long-term effects of short-term exposure to chem. agts. Nat. Acad. Scis., 1985—; mem. preventive medicine and pub. health test com. Nat. Bd. Med. Examiners, 1985—; mem. consensus conf. on smokeless tobacco Nat. Cancer Inst. Panel, 1986; chair WHO steering com. of Task Force on Safety and Efficacy of Fertility Regulating Methods, 1990—; counsellor Internat. Soc. for Environ. Epidemiology, 1990—; mem. Pres.' Cancer Panel Spl. Commn. on Breast Cancer, Nat. Cancer Inst., 1992-93; mem. bd. scientific counselors divsn. cancer etiology, Nat. Cancer Inst., NIH, 1992—; chair WHO steering com. of task force Epidemiologic rsch. in reproductive health, WHO, 1990—. Mem. editorial bd. Postgrad. Medicine, 1985—; assoc. editor Cancer Epidemiology, Biomarkers and Prevention, 1995; contbr. articles to profl. jours., chpts. to books. Bd. dirs. Am. Cancer Soc., 1993—. Recipient Disting. Achievement award Am. Soc. Preventive Oncology, 1991; Health Resources Adminstrn. grantee, 1975-77; tng. grantee in cancer epidemiology Nat. Cancer Inst., 1980—; prostate cancer grantee Nat. Cancer Inst., 1983-85; travel study fellow WHO, 1978. Fellow Royal Soc. Medicine; mem. APHA (governing coun. 1976-78, chmn. epidemiol. sect. 1976-77), NAS (Inst. Medicine 1988, mem. com. crossroads nuclear test 1994, mem. commn. antiprogestins 1992-93, mem. com. passive smoking 1985—), Am. Coll. Epidemiology (Abraham Lilienfield award 1994), Soc. Epidemicl. Rsch. (pres. 1975-76, exec. com. 1973-77), Am. Epidemiol. Soc., N.C. Pub. Health Assn. (award for excellence, stats. and epidemiology sect. 1975), Am. Coll. Preventive Medicine (bd. regents 1986), Delta Omega. Home: 2317 Honeysuckle Dr Chapel Hill NC 27514 Office: U NC Sch Pub Health McGavran-Greenburg Hall CB #7400 Chapel Hill NC 27599

HULL, ANN FITZSIMONS, medical social worker, entrepreneur; b. Cleve., Aug. 20, 1962; d. Harry Fiske and Joan Margaret (Miller) H. BA in Psychology cum laude, U. Colo., 1983; MSW, Columbia U., 1986. Lic. ind. social worker, Ohio. Social worker Queensboro Soc., Queens, N.Y., 1986-89, MetroHealth Med. Ctr., Cleve., 1989-94, Univ. Hosps., Cleve., 1992-94, Cuyahoga County Dept. Human Svcs., Cleve., 1990-93, Vis. Nurse Assn., Cleve., 1992-94, Cleve. Clinic Found., 1994—; clin. preceptor Case Western Res. U. Sch. Medicine, Cleve., 1993—; chair Cleve. Clinic Task Force on Domestic Violence, 1994—. Contbr. articles to profl. jours. Com. chair Cleveland Heights (Ohio) Bd. Edn., 1992. Mem. NASW. Home: 1060 Roanoke Rd Cleveland Heights OH 44121

HULL, JANE LAUREL LEEK, retired nurse, administrator; b. Ontario, Calif., July 4, 1923; d. William Abram and Susan Bianca (Pethick) Leek; R.N., Columbia Presbyn. Sch. Nursing, 1944; B.A., Redlands U., 1977; ; m. James B. Hull, Oct. 10, 1944 (dec.); children—James W., William P., Kenneth D. Supr. obstetrics Mid-Valley Hosp., Peckville, Pa., 1945-46; sch. and surg. nurse acute nursing Scranton (Pa.) State Hosp., 1947-52; nurse San Antonio Community Hosp., Upland, Calif., 1953-55; office nurse H.L. Archibald, Upland, 1965; vis. nurse Pomona West End Inc., continuity of care coordinator, Claremont, Calif., 1968-73, exec. dir., 1973-92 (named pres. 1991); tchr. ARC nursing course to high sch. students; cons. Livingston Meml. Vis. Nurse Assn. Ventura, Calif. Recipient Woman Achiever award, Pomona Valley, 1983, Excellence in Edn. award Nat. Assn. Home Care, 1988. Treas. PTA, Pomona, Calif.; vol. exec. dir. Inland Hospice Assn., 1979-80, accreditation commn., 1988-89. Nat. Found. for Hospice/Home Care, 1988. Mem. Am. Assn. Retired Persons (local coord.), Calif. Nurses Assn. (pres. dist. 53 1958), Calif. Assn. for Health Services at Home (dir.), Calif. League Nursing, Nat. Homecaring Council (dir.). Home Care Aide Assn. Am. (chmn.), bd. mem. Nat. Assn. of Home Care. Republican. Club: Zonta (Ontario, Upland, pres., 1976). Organizer Homemaker Dept. in Vis. Nurse Assn., 1972, pres., 1991; developer (with Don Baxter Corp.) plugs for in-dwelling Foley catheters, 1963. Home: 543 W F St Ontario CA 91762-3117

HULL, JOSEPH DANIEL, osteopath; b. Springfield, Mo., June 29, 1948; s. Joseph Seymour Jr. and Nannie Frances (Gohn) H.; m. Evelyn Sue Rankin, Feb. 12, 1983; children: Joseph Robert, Stephen Daniel. Student, U. Mo., 1966-68; BS in Zoology, Tex. A&M U., 1970; DO, U. Health Scis., Kansas City, Mo., 1977. Diplomate Am. Osteo. Coll. of Preventive Medicine; cert. in occupational and environ. medicine. Rotating intern Green Cross Gen. Hosp., Cuyahoga Falls, Ohio, 1977-78; instr. dept. gen. practice U. Health Scis. Coll. Osteo. Medicine, 1978-80; pvt. practice, Kansas City 1978-80, Poplarville, Miss., 1980, Long Beach, Miss., 1981-84, Gulfport, Miss., 1984—; chief staff Garden Park Comty. Hosp., Gulfport, 1989-93. Mem. Am. Osteo. Assn., Am. Osteo. Coll. Preventive Medicine (bd. trustees 1994—), Am. Coll. Gen. Practitioners in Osteo. Medicine and Surgery, Am. Coll. Occupational Medicine, Miss. Osteo. Med. Assn., La. Occupational Med. Assn., Assn. Former Students Tex. A&M U. Baptist. Office: Primary Care Assocs 11163 Highway 49 Gulfport MS 39503-4142

HULL, PAMELA JEAN, nurse administrator; b. Mpls., Apr. 11, 1959; d. Orin Curtis and Mae Inga (Gjovik) Paulson; m. Randolph Scott Hull, ug. 13, 1983; children: Anna Mae, Samuel Randolph, Jonathan Orin. AS, Normanale Cmty. Sch., Bloomington, Minn., 1983. Cert. profl. healthcare quality. LPN, Mercy Hosp., Anoka, Minn., 1978-83; vis. nurse Nursing Care Svc. Profls., Burnsville, Minn., 1983-84; nurse case mgr. Optional Care Sys., St. Paul, 1984-91; nurse mgr. continuous quality improvement and edn. HealthEast Optional Care, St. Paul, 1991—, strategic planning facilitator, cons., 1995—; nurse mgr. continuous quality improvement and edn. HealthEast Hospice, St. Paul, 1995—; mem. adv. bd. St. Paul Vocat.-Tech. Sch., 1995—. Mem. Minn. Home Care Assn. (co-chmn. stds. of practice 1995—). Home: 6507 41st Ave N Crystal MN 55427 Office: HealthEast Optional Care 2577 Territorial Rd Saint Paul MN 55114

HÜLLEMANN, KLAUS-DIETHART, internist, psychotherapist, sports physician; b. Eisenach, Germany, Apr. 5, 1938; s. Siegfried and Thekla H.; m. Brigitte Schube, May 16, 1975; children: Niko, Philipp, Mirko. Student, Frankfurt U., Fed. Republic Germany, 1958; MD, Heidelberg U., Fed. Republic Germany, 1964. Intern Psychiat. Hosp. Heidelberg, 1964-65; resident Gen. Hosp. Konstanz, 1966-67; with Ludolf-Krehl-Klinik, Heidelberg, 1968-75; dir. dept. medicine Höhenried (Fed. Republic Germany) Hosp., 1975-77; med. dir. St. Irmingard Hosp. European Pilot Hosp., WHO, Prien, Fed. Republic Germany, 1977—; prin. investigator German Cardiovascular Prevention Study, Bergen, 1979-91; prof. internal medicine, 1975, Munich U., 1978—; dir., prof. Dr.med. Klaus-D. Hüllman GmbH; coord. German Network of Health Promoting Hosps., WHO, 1995—. Author, editor: Quo vadis-Medicine?, 1989, The Part and the Whole in Medicine, 1990, Fitness and Wellbeing, 1992; contbr. over 250 articles to profl. jours. Mem. Hartmannbund, Kennedy Inst. Med. Ethics, Internistenverband, Deutscher Sportärztebund. Office: Saint Irmingards Hosp, Osternacher Strasse 103, 83209 Prien am Chiemsee Germany

HULLEY, RAYMOND JEFFREY, physician assistant; b. Cin., Nov. 12, 1951; s. Roland James and Joy Marie (Banes) H.; divorced. AAS, Cin. Tech. Coll., 1973; BS with honors, U. Cin., 1979; MS with honors, Calif. State U., L.A., 1987. Cert. physician asst. Physician asst. West Mitchell Med. Ctr., Cin., 1973-75; mgr. lab. svcs. U. Cin. Med. Ctr., 1975-79; dir. med. svcs. Alpha Therapeutic Corp., L.A., 1980-89; pres., CEO First Coast Plasma, Inc., Jacksonville, Fla., 1989-93; nat. sales dir. IMC Healthcare, Inc., Jacksonville, 1993-95; mng. ptnr. Apex Med. Group, Jacksonville, 1995—; cons. Fla. Bur. Profl. Regulation, Tallahassee, 1995-96; assoc. prof. Calif. State U., L.A., 1987-89. Fellow Am. Acad. Physician Assts., Fla. Acad. Physician Assts. Home and Office: 1052 W Plantation Oaks Jacksonville Beach FL 32250

HULLINGS, JOANNE ELENA, osteopath; b. Bristol, Pa., Apr. 7, 1957; d. Ernest and Sophia Elena (D'Emidio) H.; m. John Walter Potok, Sept. 12, 1987 (div. Dec. 1994). BA in Spanish, Lycoming Coll., 1979; postgrad., Rider Coll., 1990-92; DO, Phila. Coll. Osteo. Medicine, 1996. Cert. ACLS, EMT, Pa., field hockey ofcl. Tchr. Bristol (Pa.) H.S., 1979-86; fin. contr. Delaware Valley Med. Ctr., Langhorne, Pa., 1985—; registrar Lower Bucks Hosp., Bristol, 1980-84, Helene Fuld Med. Ctr., Trenton, N.J., 1984-85; instr. BLS Am. Heart Assn., 1994—. Recipient Cmty. Svc. award Ciba-Geigy Pharms., 1994. Mem. Student Osteo. Med. Assn. (nat. treas. 1994-95, nat. membership chairperson 1993-94, local pres. 1993-94), Lambda Omicron Gamma (1st v.p. 1994-94). Home: 824 Radcliffe St Bristol PA 19007

HULTGREN, HERBERT NILS, cardiologist, educator; b. Santa Rosa, Calif., Aug. 29, 1917; s. Adolf W. and Hilda (Hakanson) H.; m. Barbara Brooke, Aug. 7, 1948; children—Peter B., Bruce H., John B. Jr. certificate, Santa Rosa Jr. Coll., 1937; A.B., Stanford, 1939, M.D., 1942. Intern San Francisco Gen. Hosp., 1942-43; resident medicine Stanford Hosp., 1943-44, resident pathology, 1946-47; fellow cardiology Thorndike Meml. Lab., Boston, 1947-48; instr. medicine Stanford Med. Sch., 1948-51, asst. prof., 1951-55, asso. prof., 1955-67, prof., 1967—; chief cardiology Service Palo Alto VA Hosp., 1969-88; Chmn. Subspeciality Bd. Cardiovascular Disease, 1972-75 ; co-chmn. VA Coop. Study Surgery in Coronary Artery Disease, 1972—. Contbr. articles to profl. jours. Served from 1st lt. to capt., M.C. AUS, 1944-46, ETO. Markle scholar in med. sci., 1951-56. Mem. Western Soc. Clin. Research (pres.), Western Assn. Physicians (pres.), Assn. U. Cardiologists (pres.), Phi Beta Kappa. Home: 827 San Francisco Ct Palo Alto CA 94305-1021 Office: Palo Alto VA Hosp Palo Alto CA 94304

HUMBER, RICHARD ALAN, microbiologist; b. San Francisco, May 9, 1947; s. Merrill Roy and Jeanette (Boynton) H.; m. Amy Doyle, June 19, 1977; children: Noel Andrew, Emily Rose. AB in Biol. Scis., Stanford U., 1969; MS in Botany, U. Wash., 1970, PhD in Botany, 1975. Postdoctoral fellow, faculty assoc. dept. entomology U. Maine, Orono, 1976-78; postdoctoral fellow dept. plant pathology Cornell U., Ithaca, N.Y., 1978-79; rsch. assoc. Boyce Thompson Inst., Ithaca, N.Y., 1979-82; adj. assoc. prof. dept. plant pathology Cornell U., Ithaca, N.Y., 1988—; mycologist, microbiologist USDA Agrl. Rsch. Svc., Ithaca, N.Y., 1982—. Mem. editl. bd. Mycologia, 1988-92, Jour. Invertebrate Pathology, 1985-87. Recipient Steven Fox Meml. award Stanford U., 1969, Grad. Rsch. prize Mycological Soc. Am., 1975, Soc. for Evolutionary Protistology. Mem. Mycol. Soc. Am. (editor newsletter 1991-94), Soc. Invertebrate Pathology (chairperson jour. adv. com. 1986-87), Soc. Evolutionary Protistology. Office: USDA Agrl Rsch Svc Soil & Nutrition Lab Tower Rd Ithaca NY 14853-2901

HUMBER, WILBUR JAMES, psychologist; b. Winnipeg, Man., Can., June 21, 1911; came to U.S., 1922; s. Arthur W. and Annie Humber; m. Jean Adriansen, May 25, 1945; children: Philip, Scott, Michael. BA, Macalester Coll., 1930; MA, U. Chgo., 1937; PhD, U. Minn., 1942. Diplomate clin. psychology. Dean Kalamazoo (Mich.) Coll., 1941-43; prof. Lawrence U., Appleton, Wis., 1943-46; psychologist Rohrer, Hibler & Replogle, Chgo., 1947-52; sr. ptnr. Humber, Mundie & McClary, Milw., 1952—; bd. dirs. Hopkins Savs. & Loan, Milw., Pope Sci. Corp., Menomonee Falls, Wis. Co-author: Development of Human Behavior, 1951, Introduction to Social Psychology, 1968; editl. bd. Jour. of Consultation. Bd. dirs. Lakeside Children Ctr., Milw., 1966-86; pres. Wis. Mental Health Assn., Milw., 1962-63. Fellow APA, N.Y. Acad. Sci., AAAS; mem. Wis. Psychol. Assn. (founder, 1st pres., Disting. Contbn. award 1984), Milw. Club, Milw. Country Club. Congregationalist. Home: 4012 W Canterbury Ct Mequon WI 53092 Office: Humber Mundie & McClary 111 E Wisconsin Ave Ste 1950 Milwaukee WI 53202-4809

HUMBLE, JOSEPH ELGIN, ophthalmologist; b. Shreveport, La., June 17, 1953; s. Graham Lacy and Addie Belle (Boggs) H.; m. Sylvia Kosmitis, Dec. 27, 1981; children: John Randolph, Melinda Catherine. BA, NE La. U., 1974; MD, La. State U., New Orleans, 1978. Diplomate Am. Bd. Ophthalmology. Intern La. State U. Med. Ctr., Shreveport, 1979-80; pvt. practice, West Monroe, La., 1983—; resident in ophthalmology La. State U. Med. Ctr., Shreveport, 1980-83; med. missionary Med. Benevolence Found.; chief staff NE Surg. Ctr., 1985-90; v.p. La. Eye Found., Shreveport, 1988-90; assoc. Rsch. To Prevent Blindness, 1989-91. Fellow Am. Acad. Ophthalmology; mem. Am. Soc. of Cataract and Refractive Surgery. Presbyterian. Office: Eye Assocs NE La 1804 N 7th St West Monroe LA 71291-4414

HUMENICK, SHARRON SMITH, nursing educator, research administrator; b. Ft. Collins, Colo., Dec. 14, 1937; d. Donald Walter and Cecile Helen (Weeks) S.; m. Michael J. Humenick, June 18, 1960; children: Christine, Michael J. III. Student, Albion Coll., 1955-57; BS in Nursing, U. Mich., 1960; MPH, U. Calif., 1969; PhD, U. Tex., 1979. RN; cert. childbirth edn. Pub. health nurse Alameda County, Oakland, Calif., 1961-64, Contra Costa County, Richmond, Calif., 1964-65; sch. nurse Richmond Sch. Dist., 1966-69; asst. prof. nursing U. Tex., Austin, 1971-81; assoc. prof. nursing U. Wyo., Laramie, 1981-88, asst. to dean health scis., 1985-86, prof. nursing, 1988—; bd. dirs., cert. faculty childbirth edn. ASPO/Lamaze, Washington, 1976-78; chair univ. program accreditation com., 1992-95, chair rsch. com., 1995—. Editor nursing text Analysis of Current Assessment, 1982 (Am. Jour. Nursing Books of Yr. award 1983); co-editor text Practice Theory and Research in Childbirth Edn., 1988 (Am. Jour. Nursing Books of Yr. award), Adolescent Pregnancy: Nursing Perspectives on Prevention, 1991 (Am. Jour Nursing Book of the Year award 1992); mem. editl. bd. Birth, Berkeley, Calif., 1981-89; mem. rev. panel Western Jour. Nursing Rsch., 1984-92, Maternal Child Nursing, N.Y.C., 1983-90, Jour. Human Lactation, 1989—; contbg. editor Jour. Perinatal Edn., 1992-95, editor, 1995—; contbr. articles to profl. jours. Bd. dirs. Campfire Girls, Richmond, 1965-68. Predoctoral fellow Dept. Health Edn. Welfare, Washington, 1978-79; rsch. grant Dept. Health Human Svcs., Washington, 1984-86, NIH, 1991-95. Fellow Am. Acad. Nursing; mem. ANA, APHA, NAACOG, Wyo. Nurses Assn. (treas. dist. 12, 1985-89), Coun. Nurse Researchers (Wyo. legis. rep. 1982-86), Faculty Women's Club (Laramie). Office: U Wyo PO Box 3065 Laramie WY 82071-3065

HUMES, H(ARVEY) DAVID, nephrologist, educator; b. Honolulu, Nov. 20, 1947; s. William and Nancy Humes; m. Dolores Humes; 1 child, Michael David. BA, U. Calif., Berkeley, 1969; MD, U. Calif., San Francisco, 1973. Diplomate Am. Bd. Internal Medicine. Intern Moffit Hosp. and U. Calif. Hosps., San Francisco, Calif., 1973-74; resident U. Calif. Hosps., San Francisco, 1974-75; clin. fellow nephrology U. Pa. Hosp., Phila., 1975-76; rsch. fellow lab. kidney & electrolyte physiology Peter Bent Brigham Hosp., Boston, Mass., 1976-77; instr. Harvard U., Boston, Mass., 1977-78; asst. prof. medicine Harvard U., Boston, 1978-79; asst. prof. internal medicine U. Mich., Ann Arbor, 1979-82, assoc. prof. internal medicine, 1982-86, prof. internal medicine, 1986—, John G. Searle prof.; founder, gen. ptnr., mgr. EpiGenesis, LLC; founder, dir., pres. Nephros Therapeutics, Inc.; cons. Sandoz Pharm., Bristol-Myers-Squibb, Sterling-Winthrop, AmGen.; instr., asst. prof. Peter Bent Brigham Hosp., Boston, 1977-79; dir., chief Nephrology Rsch. Labs., U. Mich., Ann Arbor, 1980-81, chmn. dept. internal medicine, 1996—; chief med. svc. VA Med. Ctr., Ann Arbor, 1983-96. Contbr. articles to profl. jours. Grantee Nat. Kidney Found., 1981-83, 84-85, 87-88, PHS, 1982-93, 87—, VA, 1982-83, 83-87, 87-90, 90-93, 93—, Am. Heart Assn., 1982-87, 94-95. Fellow, ACP; mem. AAAS, Am. Physiol. Soc., Am. Soc. Biol. Chemists, Am. Soc. Renal Chemistry & Metabolism, Am. Soc. Clin. Investigation, Am. Heart Assn., Am. Soc. Nephrology, Am. Fedn. Clin. Rsch., Internat. Soc. Nephrology, Nat. Kidney Found., Nat. Kidney Found. Mich. (pres.'s award), Ctrl. Soc. Clin. Rsch., Alpha Omega Alpha, Phi Beta Kappa. Office: U Mich Med Ctr 3101 Taubman Box 0368 1500 E Medical Ctr Dr Ann Arbor MI 48109-0368

HUMMEL, KAY JEAN, physical therapist; b. Cleve., Apr. 24, 1943; d. Lloyd Elmer and Olive Agnes (Latou) Hetherington; m. Charles William Hummel (div. Feb. 1984); children: Patrick H., Robin E. BA, Miami U.,

Oxford, Ohio, 1965; cert. in phys. therapy, Columbia U., N.Y., 1966. Lic. phys. therapist, La.; cert. ofcl. Games Uniting Mind and Body. Staff phys. therapist St. Joseph's Hosp., Chgo., 1966-68, Wrightwood Extended Care Facility, Chgo., 1967-68, Suburban Hosp., Bethesda, Md., 1969, Holy Cross Hosp., Silver Spring, Md., 1969-70; asst. chief phys. therapist Community Gen. Hosp., Syracuse, N.Y., 1970-76; itinerant phys. therapist Caddo Parish Schs., Shreveport, La., 1976—; pvt. practice Shreveport, 1985—; bd. dirs. Games Uniting Mind & Body, Inc. Mem. U.S. Cerebral Palsy Athletic Assn. (regional classifier), Presbyn. Women's Club of Shreveport, Kappa Delta Alumni Assn. Office: Caddo Exceptional Sch 3202 William Ave Shreveport LA 71103-4246

HUMMEL, ROBERT PAUL, surgeon; b. Bellevue, Ky., Sept. 17, 1928; s. Robert Paul and Clara (Rechtin) H.; m. Helen Beam, June 26, 1954; children—Claire, Molli, Robert Paul. B.S., Xavier U., 1947; M.D., U. Cin., 1951. Diplomate Am. Bd. Surgery. Intern Duke U. Hosp., Durham, N.C., 1951-52; resident in surgery Cin. Gen. Hosp., 1952-54, 56-59, chief resident in surgery, 1959-60; instr. surgery U. Cin., 1959-63, asst. prof. surgery, 1963-67, assoc. prof. surgery, 1967-76, prof. surgery, 1976—, vice chmn. dept. surgery, 1984—; asst. attending surgeon Cin. Gen. Hosp., 1959-64, clinician, surg. out-patient dept., 1960—, attending surgeon, 1965—; attending surgeon Children's Hosp. Cin., 1964—; chief of staff Univ. Hosp., 1992—; mem. staff Univ. Hosp., Our Lady of Mercy Hosp.; mem. courtesy staff Bethesda Hosp., Christ Hosp. Served with U.S. Army, 1954-56. Mem. ACS (gov. 1979-85), AMA, Am. Surg. Assn., Am. Assn. Surgery of Trauma, Am. Burn Assn., So. Surg. Halsted Soc., Soc. Surgery Alimentary Tract, Cen. Surg. Assn. (treas. 1978-81), Ohio Med. Assn., Cin. Acad. Medicine (sec. 1977, pres. 1981), Cin. Surg. Soc. (pres. 1977), U. Cin. Grad. Surg. Soc. (pres. 1985-91), queen City Club, Cin. Country Club, Commonwealth Club, Sigma Xi, Alpha Omega Alpha. Republican. Roman Catholic. Office: U Cin Med Ctr 231 Bethesda Ave Cincinnati OH 45229-2827

HUMPHREY, CHESTER BOWDEN, cardio-thoracic surgeon; b. Marblehead, Mass., July 29, 1939; s. Leonard Graves and Mary Louise (Bowden) H.; m. Joyce Claire Jazwinski, Mar. 20, 1971; 1 child, Andrew Bowden. BS, Dickinson Coll., 1961; MD, Temple U., 1965. Diplomate Am. Bd. Thoracic Surgery, Am. Bd. Surgery. Intern Hartford Hosp., 1965-66, resident in gen. surgery, 1966-71; resident in thoracic and cardiovascular surgery Naval Regional Med. Ctr., San Diego, 1973-75; cardio-thoracic surgeon Hartford (Conn.) Thoracic & Cardiovascular Group, 1976—. Adv. com. Town of West Hartford (Conn.) Paramedics, 1989—. Comdr. USN, 1970-76. Fellow Am. Coll. Surgeons, Am. Coll. Cardiology, Am. Coll. Chest Physicians; mem. Soc. for Thoracic Surgeons, Denton Cooley Surg. Soc., New England Soc. for Vascular Surgery. Office: Hartford Thoracic & Cardiovascular Group 85 Seymour St Ste 325 Hartford CT 06106-5522

HUMPHREY, EDWARD WILLIAM, surgeon, medical educator; b. Fargo, N.D., Dec. 6, 1926; s. Edward W. and Minnie (Ramstad) H.; m. Noreen Sander, Sept. 23, 1950; children: Katherine Lisa, Joan Karen. B.A., U. Minn., 1948, M.D., 1951, Ph.D. in Physiology, 1959. Mem. faculty U. Minn. Med. Sch., Mpls., 1958-94, prof. surgery, 1965—, interim chair, 1993-94; mem. staff VA Hosp., Mpls., 1958-94; chief surg. svc. VA Hosp., 1962-93. Author: Manual of Pulmonary Surgery, 1982, (with D. McQuarrie) Reoperative General Surgery, 1992; contbr. articles to profl. jours. Mem. A.C.S., Minn. Surg. Soc., Am., Central surg. assns., Soc. Univ. Surgeons, Am. Physiol. Soc., Am. Soc. Cell Biology, Am. Assn. Thoracic Surgery, Soc. Internat. De Chirurgie, Soc. Exptl. Biology and Medicine, Sigma Xi, Alpha Omega Alpha. Home: 95 Harbour Passage Hilton Head Island SC 29926

HUMPHREY, FREDERICK JAMES, II, educator, child psychiatrist, psychoanalyst; b. Upper Darby, Pa., May 13, 1940; s. George Henry and Catherine Dorthea (Cragg) H.; m. Barbara Lynn Mohr, Aug. 19, 1963; children: Frederick James III, Ian Woodington. BS, Allegheny Coll., 1962; DO with highest honors, Phila. Coll. Osteo. Medicine, 1966. Diplomate Am. Bd. Psychiatry and Neurology in Adult and Child Psychiatry, Am. Osteo. Bd. Neurology and Adult and Child Psychiatry. Fellow adult and child psychiatry Phila. Mental Health Clinic, 1967-70; resident in adult psychiatry Embreeville (Pa.) State Hosp., 1967-68; resident in child psychiatry Hahnemann Med. Coll., Phila., 1970-72; resident in adult psychiatry Milton S. Hershey (Pa.) Med. Ctr. Pa. State U., 1972-74, asst. prof., 1974-78, vice. chmn., dir. clin. programs, 1976-86, assoc. prof., 1978-86, clin. prof., 1988—; dean, prof. psychiatry Sch. Osteo. Medicine U. Medicine and Dentistry N.J., Stratford, 1986—; psychiat cons. Get Set and Head Start Program, Phila., 1970-72, Devereux Found., 1970-72, Sports Medicine Program Pa. State U., Hershey, 1976-86; child psychiat. cons. Lebanon (Pa.) County Mental Health, 1974-78, Harrisburg (Pa.) Sch. System, 1974-84, Capital Area Intermediate Unit, Lemoyne, Pa., 1974-84, Dept. Child Welfare, Lebanon County, 1976-86; cons. Cen. Pa. Psychiat. Inst. Pa. State U., 1986—. Contbr. numerous articles to profl. jours. Col. USAR, 1990—. Recipient Linback scholarship award Phila. Coll. Osteo. Medicine, 1965, 66. Fellow Coll. Physicians of Phila.; mem. Am. Psychiat. Assn., Am. Osteo. Assn. (chair bd. govs. 1995—), Am. Assn. Colls. Osteo. Medicine (treas. 1990—), Soc. Profs. Child Psychiatry, N.J. Psychiat. Assn., N.J. Assn. Osteo. Physicians and Surgeons, Phila. Assn. Psychoanalysis. Mem. Soc. of Friends. Home: 124 E Main St Moorestown NJ 08057-2949 Office: UMDNJ Sch Osteo Medicine One Med Ctr Dr Ste 305 Stratford NJ 08084-1156

HUMPHREY, ROGER LEA, general surgeon; b. Galveston, Tex., Nov. 9, 1950; s. Thomas Roger and Sarah Ruth (Morgan) H.; m. Patricia Humphrey; children: Sarah, Morgan, Conner. BS in Elec. Engring. with highest honors, U. Calif., Berkeley, 1973; MD, U. Tex. Health Sci. Ctr., Dallas, 1977. Pvt. practice Vancouver, Wash., 1983-90; surgeon Vancouver Gen. Surgeons, Wash., 1990-94, Columbia Surgical Group, Vancouver, Wash., 1994—. Fellow ACS; mem. AMA, Am. Soc. Gastrointestinal and Endoscopic Surgeons, Soc. Am. Gastrointestinal and Endoscopic Surgeons, Phi Beta Kappa.

HUMPHREYS, JAMES MACK, JR., obstetrician, gynecologist; b. Wilmington, N.C., Feb. 10, 1943; s. James Mack and Barbara Urban (Clark) H.; B.A., Baylor U., 1965; M.D., U. Tex., Dallas, 1969; m. Marian Pittman Stephens, 1982; children—Loyd, Robert, Earl, Adrienne, Stephania Stephens, Christopher Stephens. Intern in surgery, then resident in ob-gyn Bexar County Hosp. Dist., 1969-73; practice medicine specializing in ob-gyn Midland (Tex.) Women's Clinic Assocs., 1973-86; v.p. med. affairs Midland Meml. Hosp., 1986-93; dir. Midland City/County Health Dept., 1978-95; mem. quality assurance Com. Tex. Med. Found., 1985-89. Trustee Midland Meml. Hosp., 1984-86. Served with USAFR, 1970-76. Decorated AF Commendation medal. Diplomate Am. Bd. Ob-Gyn. Mem. Midland County Med. Soc., Tex. Med. Assn., AMA. Baptist. Home: 4504 Princeton Ave Midland TX 79703-4710 Office: 2200 W Illinois Ave Midland TX 79701-6407

HUMPHRIES, JOAN ROPES, psychologist, educator; b. Bklyn., Oct. 17, 1928; d. Lawrence Gardner and Adele Lydia (Zimmermann) Ropes; m. Charles C. Humphries, Apr. 4, 1957; children: Peggy Ann, Charlene Adele. BA, U. Miami, 1950; MS, Fla. State U., 1955; PhD, La. State U., 1963. Part-time instr. psychology dept. U. Miami, Coral Gables, Fla., 1964-66; prof. behavioral studies dept. Miami-Dade C.C., 1966—. Registered lobbyist State of Fla. Presenter in field. Prodr., prin. host (videos) Strategies in Global Modern Academia: Issues and Answers in Higher Education, 1993-94; prodr. and host (video) Strategies in Global Modern Academia: Issues and Answers in Higher Education, II, 1995. Mem. Biofeedback Delegation to the People's Republic of China and Hong Kong, 1995. Mem. AAUP (past v.p. and sec., pres. Miami-Dade C.C. chpt. 1986—, past v.p. Fla. conf., 1986-88, mem. exec. bd. Fla. conf. 1989-90, mem. Nat.), AAUW (life, former v.p. Tamiami branch 1983-88, Appreciation award 1977) Biofeedback Soc. of Am. (pres. 1989—), Biofeedback Assn. Fla. (pres. 1990—), Internat. Platform Assn. (gov. 1979—, Silver Bowl award 1993), APA, Am. Psychol. Soc. (charter), Fla. Psychol. Assn., Mexico Beach C. of C. (bus. 1991—), North Campus Speaker's Bur. (award for community lecture series), Physicians for Social Responsibility, Internat. Soc. for Study Subtle Energies and Energy Medicine (charter), Inst. Evaluation, Diagnosis and Treatment (past v.p. 1975-87, pres. 1987—, former bd. dirs.), Dade-Monroe Psychol. Assn., Assn. Applied Psychophysiology and Biofeedback, Noetic Scis., Colonial Dames 17th Century, N.Y. Acad. Scis. (life), Regines in Miami, Soc. Mayflower Descs. (elder William Brewster colony), Hereditary Order of Descendants of Colonial Govs., Phi Lambda (founder's plaque 1976, appreciation award 1987), Phi Lambda Pi. Democrat. Clubs: Country of Coral Gables (life), Jockey (life). Editorial staff, maj. author: The Application of Scientific Behaviorism to Humanistic Phenomena, 1975, rev. edit., 1979; researcher in biofeedback and human consciousness. Home: 1311 Alhambra Cir Coral Gables FL 33134-3521 Office: Miami Dade CC North Campus 11380 NW 27th Ave Miami FL 33167-3418

HUMPHRIES, JOHN ELLIOTT, internist, pathologist, researcher; b. Balt., June 8, 1958; s. John O'Neal and Mary (Cregan) H.; m. Anne Wood, June 2, 1982; children: Shelley Rebecca, Erin O'Neal. BA, Middlebury Coll., 1980; MD, Johns Hopkins U., 1984. Internal medicine resident Johns Hopkins U. Hosp., Balt., 1984-87; fellow in hematology U. Va., Charlottesville, 1987-90, instr. dept. internal medicine, 1990-92, asst. prof. dept. internal medicine, 1992—, asst. prof. dept. pathology, 1992—; assoc. dir. spl. coagulation lab., U. Va., 1991—, dir. hemostasis and thrombosis clinic, U. Va., 1994—; mem. hemophilia adv. bd. State of Va., Richmond, 1990—. Fellow ACP. Home: 4350 Old Fields Rd Free Union VA 22940 Office: Univ Va Health Scis Ctr Box 513 Charlottesville VA 22908

HUMPHRIES, LAURIE LEE, child and adolescent psychiatrist, researcher; b. Atlanta, Apr. 26, 1944; d. Olin Price and Laurie (Baggarly) L.; m. Asa Alan Humphries Jr., July 22, 1972; 1 child, Laura Catherine. BA, Emory U., 1966, MD, 1973. Diplomate Am. Bd. Psychiatry and Neurology. Resident in psychiatry Emory U. Sch. Medicine, Atlanta, 1973-75, fellow in child psychiatry, 1975-77, asst. prof., 1978-81; asst. prof. U. Ky., Lexington, 1981-87, assoc. prof., 1987-92, prof., 1992—. Recipient of Child-Adolescent Acad. award NIMH, 1989-94, Disting. Alumni award Westminster Schs., 1990. Fellow APA, Am. Acad. Child and Adolescent Psychiatry, Kappa Kappa Gamma (Nat. Alumni award, 1988). Office: U Ky Dept Psychiatry 820 S Limestone St Lexington KY 40508-3223

HUMPRHEY, PETER RONALD, neurologist; b. London, Mar. 19, 1946; m. Gillian Pearson, Feb. 23, 1974; children: Rachel Anna, Mark Daniel Charles. MA, U. Oxford, Eng., 1972, BM BCh, 1972; DM, U. Oxford, 1980. Sr. house officer, registrar Southampton (Eng.) Gen. Hosp., 1974-78; rsch. registrar Nat. Hosp. for Neurology and Neurosurgery, London, 1978-80, sr. registrar, 1980-83; cons. neurologist Walton Ctr. for Neurology and Neurosurgery, Liverpool, Eng., 1983—. Contbr. articles to profl. jours., chpts. to books. Recipient various awards Med. Rsch. Coun., 1986—. Fellow Royal Coll. Physicians; mem. Assn. Brit. Neurologists (sec. 1995—), Stroke Assn. (R&D com. 1995—, awards). Office: Walton Ctr Neurology, Rice Ln, Liverpool L9 1AE, England

HUNGERFORD, DAVID SAMUEL, orthopedic surgeon, educator; b. Rochester, N.Y., May 4, 1938; s. Francis Samuel and Marjorie Ellen (Wilson) H.; m. Uta-Heide Jung, July 20, 1962; children: Marc Wilson, Kyle Sasha, Lars Daniel. BA, Colgate U., 1960; MD, U. Rochester, 1964. Diplomate Am. Bd. Orthopaedic Surgery. Asst. prof. orthopaedic surgery Johns Hopkins U., Balt., 1972-78; chief orthopaedic surgery VA Hosp., Balt., 1975-80; chief orthopaedic surgery Good Samaritan Hosp., Balt., 1972—, chief div. arthritis surgery, 1979—; assoc. prof. orthopaedic surgery Johns Hopkins U. Sch. Medicine, Balt., 1978-86, prof. orthopaedic surgery, 1987—; cons. Balt. City Hosp., 1972-85, Children's Hosp., 1972-80, East Balt. Med. Ctr., 1972-78. Author: Progress in Orthopaedics, 1977, Ischemia and Necroses of Bone, 1980, Total Knee Arthroplasty: A Comprehensive Approach, 1984, Total Hip Arthroplasty: A New Approach, 1984, Bone Circulation, 1984, Disorders of the Patello Femoral Joint, 1990, Videobook of Total Knee Arthroplasty, 1994; editor Jour. Arthroplasty, 1985-93. Elder Cen. Presbyn. Ch., Balt., 1974—. Maj. U.S. Army, 1969. Recipient George Hoyt Whipple award, 1965; Colgate U. scholar, 1956-59, GM scholar, 1956-59, U. Rochester scholar, 1959-61, Girdlestone Meml. scholar Oxford U., Eng., 1969-70; fellow USPHS fellow, Paris, 1961-62, Carl Berg traveling fellow, 1973. Mem. Johns Hopkins Med. and Surg. Soc., Md. Orthopaedic Soc., Arthritis Found., Md. Soc. Rheumatic Diseases, Am. Rheumatism Assn., Orthopaedic Rsch. Soc., Hip Soc., Am. Assn. Orthopaedic Surgeons, Am. Assn. Hip Knee Surgeons, Soc. Internat. de Chirurgie Orthopedique et de Traumatologie, Knee Soc. (pres. 1994). Republican. Home: 10715 Pot Spring Rd Cockeysville Hunt Valley MD 21030-3019 Office: Good Samaritan Hosp Profl Office Bldg G-1 5601 Loch Raven Blvd Baltimore MD 21239-2905 also: Johns Hopkins U Sch Medicine Dept Orthopaedic Surgery Baltimore MD

HUNGUND, BASALINGAPPA LINGAPPA, neurochemist; b. Muddebihal, Karnataka, India, July 16, 1942; came to U.S., 1969; s. Lingappa B. and Shawantrewwa (Wali) H.; m. Luisa Lagura, Oct. 13, 1972; children: Jaya, Raj, Vivek. BS, Karnataka U, Dharwar, India, 1962, MSc, 1964; PhD, Nat. Chem. Lab., Poona, India, 1968. Research assoc. Stevens Inst. Tech., Hoboken, N.J., 1969-72; sr. research assoc. Worcester Fedn. Exptl. Biology, Shrewsbury, Mass., 1972-74; research scientist III N.Y. State Psychiat. Inst., N.Y.C., 1975-76, research scientist IV, 1984—; research scientist IV L.I. Research Inst., Stony Brook, N.Y., 1976-84; asst. prof. dept. psychiatry Columbia U., N.Y.C., 1994—; assoc. research scientist Columbia U., N.Y.C., 1984—; asst. prof. SUNY Stony Brook, 1977-84; pres. Asia Soc. N.Y. State Psychiat. Inst., 1986-87. Contbr. more than 70 papers to profl. jours. Jr. rsch. fellow Coun. Sci. and Indsl. Rsch., India, 1964-68; Biomed Rsch. Suppor grantee N.Y. State Psychiat. Inst., 1986-87, NIH grantee, 1985-86, 91-94.; vis. scholar Stanford U., Palo Alto, Calif., 1981-82. Mem. AAAS, Internat. Soc. for Biomed. Rsch. on Alcohol, Am. Oil Chemists Soc., Basava Internat. (v.p. 1980—), Rsch. Soc. Alcoholism, Am. Soc. Neurochemistry, N.Y. Acad. Scis., N.Y. State Health Rsch. Coun. Home: 5 Claudia Ct Tappan NY 10983-1936 Office: NY State Psychiat Inst 722 W 168th St New York NY 10032-2603

HUNKER, FRED DOMINIC, internist, pulmonary medicine consultant; b. Montgomery, Ala., Nov. 13, 1947; s. Joseph Frederick and Frances Cecelia (Armbruster) H.; m. Edith Margaret McCulloch, Sept. 25, 1976; children: Marie Elizabeth, Emily Kathleen, Jacob Dominic. BA in English, Creighton U., 1969; MD, U. Nebr., 1974. Diplomate Nat. Bd. Med. Examiners, Am. Bd. Internal Medicine (SEP com. 1992-96), subspeciality pulmonary medicine (mem. self-evaluation process com. for pulmonary disease 1992-96); lic. physician Ala. Intern U. Ala. Sch. Medicine, Birmingham, 1974-75, resident, chief resident and instr. medicine, 1975-77, 78-79, fellow in pulmonary medicine, 1977-78, clin. asst. prof., 1979-93, clin. assoc. prof., 1993—; founder Montgomery Pulmonary Cons., P.A., 1979; pres. med. staff St. Margaret's Hosp., 1986-88; chmn. coun. on animal and environ. health Ala. Bd. Pub. Health, 1983-86; regional adv. bd. Mutual Assurance Inc., Birmingham, 1990—; chmn. dept. medicine Bapt. Med. Ctr., 1982-84, chmn. ICU com. 1987-91, exec. com., 1982-84; exec. com. St. Margaret's Hosp./ Humana Montgomery, 1988—, credentials com., 1985—. Contbr. articles to profl. jours. Bd. dirs. Am. Lung Assn. Ala., 1984—, exec. com. 1990—, v.p., 1996—, chmn. awards and grants com. 1984-96; Montgomery adv. bd. S.E. Health Plan, 1985-88; physician vol. Maceio, brazil, 1973; bd. dirs. Queen of Mercy Elem. Sch., 1986-91, Combined Montgomery Cath. Schs., 1992—; founding mem., bd. dirs. Endowment Found. for Queen of Mercy Sch.; chmn. Physician's divsn. United Way Campaign, 1987-88; charter mem., bd. dirs. Physicians and Dentists Charities, Montgomery, 1988-91, Leadership Montgomery Class X, 1993-94; mem. coalition for Tobacco Free Ala. Knight Comdr. of the Equestrian Order of the Holy Sepulchre, 1990—. Fellow Am. Coll. Chest Physicians; mem. AMA, ACP (assoc.), Am. Thoracic Soc. (coun. of chpt. reps., state rep. 1988-94, tng. and continuing med. edn. com. 1992-94), Ala. Thoracic Soc. (pres. 1986-87), Nat. Assn. Med. Dirs. of Respiratory Care, Am. Soc. Internal Medicine, Med. Assn. State of Ala. (controlled substances adv. com. 1992-93, coun. on med. edn. 1991-95), Med. Soc. Montgomery County (pres. 1988-89, bd. censors 1989-96), Montgomery C. of C., KC (3d degree), Capital City Club. Roman Catholic. Home: 1595 Gilmer Ave Montgomery AL 36104-5619 Office: Montgomery Pulmonary Cons 1440 Narrow Lane Pky Montgomery AL 36111-2654

HUNSAKER, DON, II, biology educator; b. Ft. Worth, Apr. 6, 1930; s. Don and Thelma (Mumford) H.; m. Barbara Hunsaker, Dec. 23, 1952; children: Robert, Don III, Holly, Russell. BA, Tex. Tech U., 1952, MS, 1957; PhD, U. Tex., 1960. Asst. prof. San Diego State U., 1960-66, prof., 1967—; assoc. research biologist Zool. Soc., San Diego, 1966—; coordinator tech. rep. U.S. Peace Corps, 1969-71; vis. prof. U. Ariz., Tucson, 1971-72. Editor: Biology of Marsupials, 1970. Bd. trustees Santee Sch. Dist., Calif., 1965-71, Grossmont High Sch., La Mesa, Calif., 1977—; pres. Calif. Sch. Bds. Assn., Sacramento, 1984. Fellow San Diego Mus. Natural History (pres. 1970-71); mem. Am. Soc. Ichthyologists and Herpetologists, San Diego Herpetologists Soc. (pres. 1978-79), Nat. Sch. Bds. Assn. (bd. dirs. 1988-92). The Environ. Trust (pres. 1990-96). Democrat. Home: 11458 Meadow Creek Rd El Cajon CA 92020-8274 Office: San Diego State U Dept Biology San Diego CA 92182

HUNSAKER, LEROY WILLIAM, orthopedic surgeon; b. Porterville, Calif., June 30, 1929; s. Loyd Kay and Emma Hazel (Gobby) H.; m. Peggy Jean Smith, Mar. 24, 1948; 1 child, Tara Lynn. BS, U. Calif. San Francisco, 1962, MD, 1965. Diplomate Am. Bd. Orthopedic Surgery. Intern San Diego Gen. Hosp., 1965-66; resident orthop. surgery U. Calif. San Diego, 1966-70; ptnr., CEO Alvarado Orthop. Med. Group, Inc., San Diego, 1970—; owner, proprieter LeRoy's Maple Shop, Porterville, 1950-57; bd. dirs. Found. for Med. Care, San Diego, San Diego Blood Bank, Alvarado Assocs.; supr. Alvarado Hosp., San Diego, 1972-96; bd. govs. Alvarado Cmty. Hosp., San Diego, chmn.; asst. clin. prof. U. Calif. San Diego. Mem. AMA, We. Orthop. Assn., Calif. Med. Assn., San Diego County Med. Assn., Alpha Gamma Sigma. Republican. Office: Alvarado Orthop Med Group 5555 Reservoir Dr #104 San Diego CA 92120

HUNT, ALBERT CHARLES, consultant pathologist; b. Croydon, Surrey, Eng., Dec. 26, 1927; s. Albert Edward and Ethel Olivia (Sherborne) H.; m. Enid Annie, 1951 (div. 1973); children: Matthew S., Paul S., Benjamin S.; m. Josephine Carol Whitney, Mar. 23, 1987. MB BS, London Hosp., 1949, MD, 1952. Med. diplomate. Intern then resident London Hosp., 1949-52; reader in forensic pathology U. Bristol (Eng.), 1959-69, reader in histopathology, 1969-71; pathologist Plymouth (Eng.) Health Authority, 1971-92. Contbr. articles to profl. jours. Pres. Assn. Clin. Pathologists, U.K., 1985-86; v.p. World Assn. Socs. of Pathology, 1986-89. Fellow Royal Coll. Pathologists (v.p. 1986-89), Brit. Assn. Forensic Medicine. Anglican. Home: 13 College St, Stratford upon Avon England

HUNT, DIANA DILGER, health care administraton; b. Ridgewood, N.J., Feb. 25, 1953; d. Daniel G. Dilger and Ruth M. Wheeler; m. Douglas Gordon Hunt, Nov. 1, 1987; children: Daniel Gordon, Kevin Douglas. BS, Quinnipiac Coll., 1975; MPA, L.I. U., 1996. Staff therapist Bergen Pines Hosp., Paramus, N.J., 1976-81; sr. occupational therapist Rockland Childrens Psychiatric Ctr., Orangeburg, N.Y., 1981-82; program dir. psychiatry Bergen Pines Hosp., Paramus, N.J., 1985-87, dir. occupational therapy, 1982-91; dir. rehab. svcs. Ramapo Ridge Hosp. of the Christian Health Care Ctr., Wyckoff, N.J., 1991—; program dir., adolescent day treatment program Ramapo Ridge Hosp. of the Christian Health Care Ctr., 1993—; adj. instr. Dominican Coll., Orangeburg, N.Y., 1995—. Mem. Am. Occupational Therapy Assn., N.J. Occupational Therapy Assn. (award of merit adminstrn. 1987, award of merit for practice 1995, pres. 1992-94), Profl. Health Adminstrn. Assn., Am. Coll. Healthcare Execs., Pi Alpha Alpha. Home: 8 Windsor Ter Mahwah NJ 07430-2815

HUNT, MARGARET ANN, medical technologist, laboratory supervisor; b. Crookston, Minn., Sept. 1, 1938; d. Angus George and Dorothy Ernestine (Wills) McLean; m. Thomas H. Hunt, Sep. 1, 1960; children: Michele, Gregory, Colette, Elizabeth, Patrick (dec.), Charles. cert. med. technologist, Am. Med. Technologists. Bench technologist Bennett Clarkson Mem. Hosp., Rapid City, S.D., 1960-61; bench technologist Massa-Berry Clinic, Sturgis, S.D., 1963-75, lab. supr., 1975—. Mem., officer St. Frances Assisi Ch., Sturgis, 1960—, Sturgis Jaycees, 1963-73. Mem. Am. Med. Technologist, Nat. Certification Agy., Am. Soc. for Clin. Lab. Sci., S.D. Soc. of Med. Technologists (sci. cons. chair 1995-96), Phi Alpha Gamma. Republican. Roman Catholic. Office: Massa-Berry Clinic 981 E Main St Sturgis SD 57785

HUNT, OLIVER RAYMOND, JR., thoracic and cardiovascular surgeon; b. Darlington, S.C., Apr. 23, 1923; s. Oliver Raymond Sr. and Annie Reid (Muldrow) H.; m. Eleanor Margaret Morgan, Dec. 16, 1944; children: David Morgan, Margaret Muldrow, Rebecca Elaine, Sarah Fredricka. AB, Berea Coll., 1947; MD, U. Louisville, 1951. Diplomate Am. Bd. Surgery, Am. Bd. Thoracic and Cardiac Surgery. Asst. in anatomy U. Louisville, 1950; intern Edward W. Sparrow Hosp., Lansing, Mich., 1951-52; fellow in surgery Mayo Found., Rochester, Minn., 1954-58, fellow in thoracic surgery, 1958-60; staff surgeon VA Hosp., Oteen, N.C., 1960-61; clin. assoc. SUNY, Buffalo, 1963-64, asst. prof. surgery, 1964-69, asst. dean, assoc. dean clin. affairs, 1965-67, 67-69; clin. asst., assoc. prof. surgery U. N.C., Chapel Hill, 1969-91; pvt. practice surgery Wilmington, N.C., 1969-91; CEO Regal Tomaoes Internat. Ltd., Nev., 1991—; v.p., bd. dirs. Jugoso Y Pulpas de San Gerado S.A., Costa Rica, 1989—; v.p. med. staff Cape Fear Hosp., Wilmington, 1978, 79, pres., 1980-81, chief of staff, 1972, exec. com., 1978-82; cons. med. edn. Nat. U., Asuncion, Paraguay, 1965-67. Contbr. numerous articles to profl. jours. Bd. dirs. New Hanover Bank, Wilmington, 1972-75, Planters Nat. Bank, Wilmington, 1976-87, Wilmington Devel. Corp., 1981-87, Wilmington Concert Assn., 1970-94; civil svc. commn. City of Wilmington, 1972-81. Lt. USNR, 1943-46. Named Rsch. scholar Dept. Chemistry U. Louisville, 1948-51; recipient Mosby prize for Scholarship, U. Louisville, 1948; named Hon. Prof., Nat. U. Asuncion, 1967. Mem. AMA, N.C. Med. Soc., New Hanover Med. Soc., Soc. Thoracic Surgery, N.Y. Acad. Sci., N.C. Lung Soc., Alpha Omega Alpha, Phi Kappa Phi.

HUNT, PETER TRUE, psychologist; b. Ithaca, N.Y., June 13, 1951; s. Gordon Ellsworth and Patricia (Rudd) H.; m. Sue Triplett, July 14, 1979 (div.); m. Sarah Ivins, Sept. 22, 1990; 1 child, Ian. AB, Antioch Coll., 1974; PhD, Columbia U., 1979. Lic. psychologist, Conn. Psychologist Regional Dept. of Pediatrics, Waterbury, Conn., 1979-81, Conn. Children's Med. Ctr., Glastonbury, 1981—. Mem. Am. Psychol. Assn. Home: 7 Newberry Ln Glastonbury CT 06033-2062 Office: Conn Childrens Med Ctr 181 E Cedar St Newington CT 06111-1539 also: 2906 Main St Glastonbury CT 06033

HUNT, ROBERT G., medical consultant, oral and maxillofacial surgeon; b. San Diego, July 10, 1945; s. Harvey E. and Pauline A. (Nazarovic) H.; m. Diane G. Hunt, Apr. 26, 1975; 1 child, Christine G. AA, Mesa Coll., San Diego, 1971; BS in Medicine, U. nebr., 1979, MD, 1979; DDS, U. So. Calif., 1976. Diplomate Am. Bd. Oral and Maxillofacial Surgery, Nat. Bd. Med. Examiners; lic. physician, Calif., Nebr.; lic. dentist, Calif., Nebr. Oral and maxillofacial surgeon in pvt. practice San Diego, 1981—. With USAF, 1965-70. Fellow Am. Assn. Oral and Maxillofacial Surgeons, Am. Coll. Oral and Maxillofacial Surgeons, Internat. Coll. Surgeons, Internat. Soc. Plastic, Aesthetic and Reconstructive Surgery, Am. Coll. Oral Implantology; mem. AMA, ADA, So. Calif. Acad. Oral Pathology, Mensa, Omicron Kappa Upsilon, Phi Kappa Phi, Alpha Tau Epsilon, Delta Sigma Delta, others. Home: 2240 Sunset Blvd San Diego CA 92103

HUNT, ROBERT MCPHAIL, JR., gastroenterologist; b. Stuart, Fla., Mar. 15, 1943; s. Robert McPhail Sr. and Irene Rosa (Shirley) H.; m. Catherine Annie Germaine Veyrat (divorced); children: Robert McPhail III, Laura Victoria Alexandra, Charlotte Amalie Veyrat. Student, Vanderbilt U., 1961-63, U. Tenn., Knoxville, 1963-64; BA, U. Tenn., Knoxville, 1964; student, U. Tenn. Coll. Medicine, Memphis, 1964-68, MD, 1968. Diplomate Am. Bd. Internal Medicine, Am. Bd. Gastroenterology. Intern U. Tenn. Meml. Rsch. Ctr. and Hosp., Knoxville, 1969-70, resident in internal medicine, 1970-72; gastroenterologist, internist Morristown, Tenn., 1974—. Fellow in Gastroenterology The Cleve. Clinic, 1972-74. Office: 830 W 4th North St Morristown TN 37814-3813

HUNT, ROY TERRY, psychologist, educator; b. Pitts., May 17, 1951; s. Roy A. Hunt Jr. and Sara Harris (Bankson) Stenson; m. Gale Stuart; children: Evan McMasters, Avery Stuart, Oliver Burton. BA, Harvard U., 1973; EdD, Boston U., 1980. Cert. in bioenergetic analysis; lic. psychologist, Mass. Mem. faculty Lesley Coll., Cambridge, Mass., 1981-83, Omega Inst., Rhinebeck, N.Y., 1982—, Esalen Inst., Big Sur, Calif., 1984—; pvt. practice Boston, 1980—; bd. dirs. Ctr. for Psychology and Social Change, Cambridge. Author: Emotional Healing, 1989, Secrets to Tell, Secrets to Keep, 1994. Mem. APA, Assn. Transpersonal Psychology, Assn. Humanistic Psychology, Internat. Assn. for Bioenergetic Analysis, Mass Psychol. Assn. Home: 36

Larchwood Dr Cambridge MA 02138-4606 Office: 214 Market St Brighton MA 02135-1946

HUNT, WAYNE PHILIP, psychologist; b. Balt., Feb. 4, 1947; s. Henry Adus and Nancy Hanna H.; m. Janice Lee Staples; 1 child, Scott Waldo. BS, Mars Hill Coll., 1969; MS, Johns Hopkins U., 1974; EdD, George Washington U., 1982. Lic. psychologist; Nat. Cert. Sch. Psychologist. Cons. psychologist Cmty. Residential Facility for Youth, Balt., 1974; investigator Pre-Trial Release-Supreme Bench Baltimore City, 1973-76; intern psychologist Psychol. Services, Bd. Edn. Baltimore County, 1976; counseling psychologist Glass Mental Health Clinic, Balt., 1977-78; mental health counselor Health and Welfare Coun. Central Md., Balt., 1975-78; coord. counseling svcs. Counseling and Consultation Services, Balt., 1978-80; psychologist St. Francis Sch. Spl. Edn., Balt., 1978-83; cons. psychologist Chestnut Hill Devel. Center, Inc., 1982-84, bd. dirs., 1983-84; clin. psychologist Youth Diagnostic Ctr., State of Del., Wilmington, 1983-84; chief psychologist Md. divsn. correction Reception-Diagnostic and Classification Ctr., State of Md., Balt., 1984—; psychologist Balt. Police Dept. Crisis Negotiation Team, 1989—, mem. critical incident stress debriefing team, 1991—; vis. assoc. staff Taylor Manor Hosp., 1989—; staff affiliate, clin. psychologist dept. psychiatry and behavioral scis. The Johns Hopkins Hosp., 1990—; instr. dept. psychiatry Sch. Medicine Johns Hopkins U., 1992—, faculty assoc. Sch. Continuing Studies, 1993—. Lt. U.S. Army, 1969-72. Mem. Am. Psychol. Assn., Md. Psychol. Assn., Md. Sch. Psychologists Assn., Am. Correctional Psychologists Assn., Phi Delta Kappa. Club: Johns Hopkins. Home: 708 Dunkirk Rd Baltimore MD 21212-2004 Office: Psychology Dept 550 E Madison St Baltimore MD 21202-4295

HUNTER, DAVID GEORGE, physician, researcher; b. Boston, Oct. 28, 1957; s. Donald George and Marie Ann Hunter; m. Michele Trucksis, Oct. 5, 1990; 1 child, Adam J. BSEE, Rice U., 1979; PhD in Cell Biology, Baylor Coll. Medicine, 1984, MD, 1987. Diplomate Am. Bd. Ophthalmology. Intern Framingham (Mass.) Union Hosp., 1987; resident in ophthalmology Mass. Eye & Ear Infirmary, Harvard Med. Sch., Boston, 1988-91; asst. prof. ophthalmology and biomed. engring. Johns Hopkins U., Balt., 1991—. Author: Last Minute Optics, 1996; contbr. articles to profl. jours. Fellow Am. Acad. Ophthalmology; mem. Am. Assn. for Pediat. Ophthalmology and Strabismus, Assn. for Rsch. in Vision and Ophthalmology, IEEE. Democrat. Home: 1008 Rolandvue Ave Baltimore MD 21204 Office: Johns Hopkins Hosp Wilmer B1-35 600 N Wolfe St Baltimore MD 21287-9009

HUNTER, GARY RICHARD, exercise physiology educator, researcher; b. Pontiac, Mich., Aug. 16, 1943; s. Richard W. and Rosealee (Wright) B.; m. Rebecca Ann Shoup, Jan. 29, 1966; children: Robin Elizabeth, Heather Lynn. BS, Ea. Mich. U., 1966; MA, Mich. State U., 1974, PhD, 1978. Coach, excercise physiologist Country of Bahrain, 1978-80; instr. U. Wis., Madison, 1980-84; asst. prof. U. Ala., Birmingham, 1984-89, assoc. prof. exercise physiology, 1989-95, prof., 1995—. Contbr. over 130 articles to profl. jours. Fellow Am. Coll. Sports Medicine; mem. AAHPERD, Nat. Strength and Conditioning Assn. (Sport Scientist of Yr. 1994). Office: U Ala Rm 205 ED Bldg Birmingham AL 35294

HUNTER, HARLEN CHARLES, orthopedic surgeon; b. Estherville, Iowa, Sept. 23, 1940; s. Roy Harold and Helen Iola (King) H.; m. JoAnn Wilson, June 30, 1962; children: Harlen Todd, Juliann Kristin. BA, Drake U., 1962; DO, Coll. Osteo. Medicine and Surgery, Des Moines, 1967. Diplomate Am. Osteo. Bd. Orthopedic Surgery, Am. Osteopathic Acad. Sports Medicine, 1988. Intern Normandy Osteo. Hosp., St. Louis, 1967-68, resident in orthopedics, 1968-72, chmn. dept. orthopedics, 1976-77; founder, orthopedic surgeon Mid-States Orthopedic Sports Medicine Clinics of Am., Ltd., SPORTS Med. Ctrs., Chesterfield, Mo., Fairview Hts., Ill., Jerseyville, Ill., Herman, Mo., Arnold, Mo., 1977—, Hunter Trauma Team, 1988-92; founder, pres. Life Style Health Systems, 1992; assoc. prof. orthopaedics Kansas City Coll. Osteopathy, 1993; mem. staff Outpatient Surgery Ctr., St. Louis, Lutheran Med. Ctr.; clin. instr. Kirksville Coll. Osteo. Medicine; orthopedic cons., team physician to high schs.; pres. Health Specialists, Inc.; program dir. sports medicine Family Physicians, 1993, 94; mem. med. adv. bd. Mo. Athletic Activities Assn.; cons. sports medicine Sports St. Louis newspaper; founder Ann. Sports Medicine Clinic for Trainers and Coaches, 1 yr. fellowship in sports medicine; nat. lectr. various social, profl. orgns.; adj. clin. assoc. prof. Coll. Osteo. Surgery, Des Moines; orthopedic surgeon Iowa State Boys Basketball Tournament, 1966-85; founder Mobile Sports Medicine Semi Truck, 1988, Hunter Sports Med. Clinic, Belleville, Ill.; sponsor U.S. Biathalon Assn., 1989, annual Outstanding Soccer Player of Yr. award Mo. Athletic Club., Hunter 100 Stock Car Race, Peveley, Mo. Contbr. articles to profl. publs. Co-author: Motorsports Medicine, 1992; staff photographer Indpls. Motor Speedway, 1973—. Recipient Clinic Speaker award Iowa High Sch. Baseball Coaches Assn., 1982, 83, Hall of Fame award Mo. Athletic Trainers Assn., 1987. Fellow Am. Coll. Osteo. Surgeons, Am. Osteo. Acad. Orthopedics (past chmn. com. on athletic injuries); mem. Am. Osteo. Assn., Mo. Assn. Osteo. Physicians and Surgeons (medallion award 1990), Am. Coll. Sports Medicine, Am. Orthopedic Soc. Sports Medicine (del. sports medicine exchange program to China 1985), AMA, Am. Coll. Occupational Medicine, St. Louis Met. Med. Assn., Sports Car Club Am. (med. dir. pro racing 1989-91), World Congress Motorsport Scis., St. Louis Auto Racing Club (Ambassador award 1989, 91), adv. bd. Motorsport Rsch. Group Human Performance Internat., Daytona Beach, Fla., 1990—, 500 Old Timers Club, The Butler Soc., Masons, Shriners. Republican. Methodist. Harlen C. Hunter Sports Complex named in his honor Lindenwood Coll, St. Charles, Mo., 1988. Home: 1230 Walnut Hill Farm Dr Chesterfield MO 63005-4524 Office: Hunter SPORTS Med Ctr 13355 Olive Street Rd Chesterfield MO 63017-5735

HUNTER, HARRY LAYMOND, physician, pharmaceutical company executive; b. Girard, Kans., Mar. 7, 1923; s. Adolphus Osborne and Mary Elizabeth (White) H.; m. Louise R. Leone, Aug. 19, 1949 (dec. July 1982); children—John Patrick, Mary Anne; m. Emily F. Esau, Oct. 19, 1985. A.B., U. Ill., Urbana, 1944; B.S., U. Ill.-Chgo., 1944, M.D., 1946. Diplomate: Am. Bd. Internal Medicine. Intern Gorgas Hosp., C.Z., 1946-47, resident in internal medicine, 1947-48; resident Ill. Central Hosp., Chgo., 1949-50, U. Mich., Ann Arbor, 1950-51; assoc. chief medicine Blanchard Valley Hosp., Findlay, Ohio, 1951-52; dir. exec. health Ill. Central Hosp., Chgo., 1953-57, assoc. chief medicine, 1957-64, chief med. officer, 1968-74; clin. assoc. prof. medicine U. Ill. Coll. Medicine, Chgo., 1953-76; assoc. dir. clin. pharmacology Abbott Labs., North Chicago, Ill., 1965-67, med. dir., 1975-76; dir. clin. studies Mead Johnson & Co., Evansville, Ind., 1976-83, dir. med. services, 1984-88. Contbr. numerous articles to profl. jours.; patentee med. devices. Bd. dirs. Ill. Council on Alcoholism, Chgo., 1970-74, Am. Cancer Soc., Evansville, 1978-80. Served to capt. U.S. Army, 1946-49; Panama. Fellow ACP, Am. Soc. Clin. Oncology, Chgo. Soc. Internal Medicine, Chgo. Inst. Medicine; mem. AMA. Home and Office: 5600 Albia Rd Bethesda MD 20816-3303

HUNTER, JAMES EDWARD, toxicologist; b. Phila., May 4, 1945; s. James Bruce and Ruth Moyer (Lenker) H.; m. Marilyn Kay Jones, Aug. 24, 1968; children: Melanie Kay, Timothy Edward. BS in Chemistry, Lehigh U., 1967; MS in Biochemistry, U. Wis., 1969, PhD in Biochemistry, 1974. Staff nutritionist Procter & Gamble Co., Cin., 1974-92, staff toxicologist, 1992-95, staff toxicologist regulatory affairs, 1995—; mem. biol. subcom. of tech. com. Inst. of Shortening and Edible Oils, Inc., Washington, 1981-93, chmn. biol. subcom., 1985-93; mem. human nutrition bd. of sci. counselors USDA, Washington, 1990-92; mem. oral health com. and subcom. on fatty acids and health Internat. Life Scis. Inst., Washington, 1985-92. Editor: (booklet) Food Fats and Oils, 5th edit., 1982, 6th edit., 1988, 7th edit., 1994; contbr. numerous articles to profl. jours. including Jour. Am. Oil Chemists Soc., Am. Jour. Clin. Nutrition. V.p., chmn. fundraisers St. Xavier H.S. Music Promoters Bd., Cin., 1992-94; sec., mem. com. mgmt. Powel Crosley Jr. YMCA, Cin., 1980-86, sec., 1982-86; cubmaster Boy Scouts Am., Cin., 1985-87. With U.S. Army, 1969-71. Mem. Am. Oil Chemists' Soc. (bd. dirs., treas. local chpt. 1990-93), Am. Chem. Soc. (chair various local coms.), Am. Inst. Nutrition, Runners' Club Greater Cin. (v.p. 1994-95, sec. 1995—), Phi Beta Kappa, Sigma Xi, Tau Beta Pi. Office: Procter & Gamble Co 11511 Reed Hartman Hwy Cincinnati OH 45241-9974

HUNTER, KATHLEEN CARNEY, psychologist; b. Louisville, Sept. 7, 1941; d. John Ambrose and Bessie Rose (Bayens) Carney; m. Howard E. Hunter III, June 15, 1978; children: Richard Oney, Lori, Howard E. IV, Sarah E. MA, U. Louisville, 1974; D in Psychology, Spalding U., 1994. Lic. clin. psychologist, Ky. Psychologist Landmarks Seven Counties Svcs., Louisville, 1993—. Mem. APA. Unitarian. Office: Landmarks SCS 3717 Taylorsville Rd Louisville KY 40207

HUNTER, KENNETH WILLIAM, JR., immunologist, parasitologist, educator; b. Phoenix, June 30, 1950; s. Kenneth W. and Mary Elizabeth (Wells) H.; m. Carol Lynn Nesbitt, June 6, 1970; children: Matthew Scott, Michael Middleton. BA, Ariz. State U., 1972, MS, 1973; ScD, Johns Hopkins U., 1977. Postdoctoral fellow Uniformed Svcs. U. Med. Sch., Bethesda, Md., 1978-79; asst. prof. USUHS Med. Sch., Bethesda, Md., 1979-82, assoc. prof., 1982-86; chief scientist Westinghouse Bio-Analy Systems Co., Madison, Pa., 1985-89; pres. Biotronic Systems Corp., Rockville, Md., 1986-89, chmn. bd., 1989—; prof. U. Nev., Reno, 1989—, assoc. v.p. for rsch., grad. dean, 1989—, v.p. rsch., grad. dean, 1995—; mem. adv. bd. Gov.'s Office, State of Md., Annapolis, 1989; mem. adv. bd. Montgomery County Ctr., Johns Hopkins U., 1989; trustee Nev. Innovation, Tech. and Entrepreneur Coun., Reno, 1990. Editor: Immunoparasitology: Principles and Methods in Schistosomiasis and Malaria Research, 1983; contbr. articles to profl. jours. Advocate Md. Conf. on Small Bus., 1988-90; mem. Gov.'s Task Force on Regional Econ. Devel., Md., 1988; mem. Nev. Industry, Sci., Engring. and Tech. Task Force, 1990. NIH predoctoral fellow, 1974. Mem. Am. Assn. Immunologists, Am. Soc. Tropical Medicine and Hygiene, Am. Soc. Clin. Pathology, Assn. Ofcl. Analytical Chemists. Republican. Lutheran. Office: U Nev Reno Grad Sch Reno NV 89557-0035

HUNTER, MARVIN THOMAS, plastic surgeon; b. Chattanooga, May 3, 1942; s. Marvin Thomas and Mildred Marie (Hackney) H.; m. Libby Leff, June 16, 1963 (div. 1976); children: Steven, Edward; m. Nancy Jean Zanzinger, Sept. 24, 1976; children: Adam, Mark. AB in Physics, Temple U., 1964; MD, Hahnemann U., 1968. Diplomate Am. Bd. Plastic Surgery. Intern in surgery Hahnemann Hosp., Phila., 1968-69; resident in surgery Abington (Pa.) Hosp., 1969-70, 72-73; resident in plastic surgery Georgetown U., Washington, 1973-75; pvt. practice Plastic Surgery Assocs. Ltd., Doylestown, Pa., 1975—; chief plastic surgery, chmn. dept. surgery Doylestown Hosp., 1976—, Med. Coll. Hosp. Bucks County Campus, Warmininster, Pa., 1988—. Maj., flight surgeon USAF, 1970-72. Mem. AMA (OHMS rep. 1991—, alt. del. 1995), ACS, Pa. Med. Soc., Am. Soc. Plastic and Reconstructive Surgeons, Am. Soc. Aesthetic Plastic Surgery, Internat. Microsurgery Assn., N.E. Plastic Surgery Soc., Robert Ivy Soc., So. Med. Assn., Phila. Soc. Plastic Surgery, Bucks County (Pa.) Med. Soc. (v.p. 1994, pres.-elect 1995, pres. 1996), Pa. Physician Healthcare Plan, Inc. Office: Cosmetic Surgery Ctr Ste 2-3 S Atrium 301 S Main St Doylestown PA 18901-4870 also: Plastic Surgery Assocs Ltd 301 S Main St # 2-3S Doylestown PA 18901-4870

HUNTER, NADENE DENISON, physician; b. Quincy, Ill., June 2, 1918; d. Walcott and Blanch Nadene (Babb) Denison; m. Harold Wallace Hunter, Oct. 19, 1944; children: Wallace Jr., Josiah W., Nadene B., Melville W., Sara E., James W., Helen C., Martha L., Walcott W. BS, Wash. State U., Pullman, 1939; MS, Tulane U., New Orleans, 1940, MD, 1944. Med. intern Charity Hosp., New Orleans, 1944-45; psychiatrist N.Y. State Dept. Mental Health, West Brentwood, 1946-48; pvt. practice psychiatry Central Islip, N.Y., 1949-59, Sonyea, N.Y., 1963-67; sr. supervising psychiatrist N.Y. State Dept. Mental Health, Brentwood, 1947-48, Sonyea, 1965-68; supervising psychiatrist, 1968-71; asst. dir. Craig Colony, Sch., 1971-76; dir. Hosp. Craig Devel. Ctr., 1976-82; med. dir. Livingston County Health Dept., Mt. Morris, N.Y., 1986—; mem. adv. bd. Univ. Affiliated Program DD, Rochester, 1984-90; exec. bd. Genesee coun. Boy Scouts Am., Batavia, N.Y., 1968—. Author: Parasite Diagnosis, 1942, Chagas Disease Preliminary Studies, 1942-43. Chmn., mem. Mental Health Bd., Livingston County, N.Y., 1968-78; mem. Cmty. Svcs. Bd., Livingston County, 1987—; vestry, warden St. John's Ch., Mt. Morris, 1977—, Diocesan Coun. Episcopal Diocese Rochester, 1985-89, 94—, chair dept. congl. devel., 1993-95, commn. on ministry, 1996—. Recipient Silver Faun award Boy Scouts Am. Genesee coun., 1973, Physician of the Yr. award N.Y. State Legis./Med. Soc. State of N.Y., 1991. Mem. Livingston County Med. Soc. (pres. 1972, sec.-treas. 1978—), AMA, Am. Psychiatric Assn., Am. Acad. Family Physicians, Eastern Star (matron 1977, 84, dist. rep. grand matron 1986), Amaranth (royal matron 1987-89), Neuron Club (Rochester, N.Y., sec.). Republican. Anglican. Home: 9930 S Dansville Rd Dansville NY 14437-9429

HUNTER, PATRICIA PHELPS, physician assistant; b. Nyack, N.Y., Oct. 11, 1952; d. Everett Edward and Evelyn Phelps; m. George Patton Hunter, June 26, 1982; children: Eric I., Kurt A. BA in Psychology & Spanish magna cum, Oneonta State U., 1974; BS in Physician Asst., Hahnemann Med. U., 1981; MS in Pub. Health, West Chester U., 1984. Rsch. asst. Oneonta (N.Y.) State U., 1973-74, Dartmouth Med. Sch., Hanover, N.H., 1974-76; paramedic San Francisco Ambulance, 1977-79; physician asst. Montgomery Hosp., Norristown, Pa., 1981—. Fellow Am. Acad. Physician Assts. (cert.); mem. Assn. for Retarded Citizens, Nat. Orgn. Rare Disorders, Nat. Orgn. Apraxia and Dyspraxia, Easter Seal Soc. Parents Group (co-chairperson 1994-95). Home: 331 Collegeville Rd Collegeville PA 19426 Office: Montgomery Hosp Clinic 15 W Wood St Norristown PA 19401

HUNTER, RICHARD GRANT, JR., neurologist, executive; b. San Antonio, Aug. 22, 1938; s. Richard Grant Hunter Sr. and Elton (Hall) Samouce; m. Margaret Jenkins (div. Dec. 1984); m. Sandra K. Miesel-Conrad; children: Richard Grant III, Brandon Scott. BS, Ga. Inst. Tech., 1960; MBA, U. Pa., 1961; MD, U. Va., 1968. Diplomate Am. Coll. of Physicians, Am. Soc. Neuroimaging, Am. Bd. Internal Medicine, Am. Bd. of Psychiatry and Neurology. Systems analyst N.C. Nat. Bank, Charlotte, 1962-63; ops. rsch. analyst U.S. Geol. Survey, Washington, 1963-64; med. intern Grady Meml. Hosp., Atlanta, 1968-69; resident medicine Emory U. Hosps., Atlanta, 1969-71; resident psychiatry Emory U. Hosp., Atlanta, 1971-72, 89-91; resident neurology U. Va. Hosp., Charlottesville, 1972-75; neurologist U. Va. Hosp., Martha Jefferson Hosp., Charlottesville, 1975-83; chief of neurology Gwinett Med. Ctr., Atlanta, 1983-89; pres. Dixon Biotherapeutics Inc., Atlanta, 1985-86, neuropsychiatrist, behavioral neurologist, 1989—; pres. Charlottesville Neurology Inc., 1975—; bd. dirs., pres. Dixon Biotherapeutics Inc., Atlanta, Plantation at Lenox; bd. dirs. Charlottesville Neurology Inc. With U.S. Army, 1961-62. Fellow Am. Acad. Neurology, ACP; mem. AMA, Behavioral Neurology Soc., Med. Sco. Va., Med. Assn. Ga., Va. Neurol. Soc., Ga. Neurol. Soc., Am. Psychiat. Assn., Am. Neuropsychiat. Assn., Ga. Psychiat. Assn., Am. Soc. Neuroimaging, So. Clin. Neurology Soc., Transcultural Psychology, Farmington Country Club, Farmington Hunt Club, River Bend Gun Club, Milrock Gun Club, Alpha Omega Alpha, Med. Honor Soc., Engring. Honor Soc. Episcopalian.

HUNTER, TIM BRADSHAW, radiologist, educator; b. Balt., Aug. 15, 1943; s. Leo Lauren and Naomi (Bradshaw) H. BA, DePauw U., 1966; MD, Northwestern U., Chgo., 1968; BS, U. Ariz., 1980. Diplomate Am. Bd. Radiology. Fellow, Dept. Radiology, Coll. Medicine U. Ariz., Tucson, 1975, from asst. prof. to assoc. prof. radiology, 1975-87, prof., 1987—, dir. Tucson Breast Ctr., 1986-90; dir. Divsn. of Abdominal Imaging, Tucson, 1987-90; chief of staff Univ. Med. Ctr., Tucson, Ariz., 1993-94; chmn. Soc. for Computer Applications in Radiology, Harrisburg, Pa., 1989; pres. Ariz. Radiological Soc., 1982. Editor: The Computer in Radiology, 1986; sr. editor: Radiologic Guide to Medicial Devices and Foreign Bodies, 1994. Pres. Internat. Dark-Sky Assn., Tucson, 1988—, Tucson Amateur Astronomy Assn., 1989-91. Lt. USN, 1961-71, Vietnam. Am. Coll. Radiology fellow, 1991. Mem. Phi Beta Kappa, Alpha Omega Alpha. Republican. Office: Univ Ariz Dept Radiology AHSC 1501 N Campbell Ave Tucson AZ 85724

HUNTINGTON, PETER PERIT, cardiologist; b. Columbus, Ohio, Sept. 18, 1935; s. John W.P. Huntington and Mary Peters Larsen. MD, Ohio State U., 1961. Diplomate Am. Bd. Cardiovascular Disease. Intern Cin. Gen. Hosp., 1961-62, resident, 1962-65, fellowship in cardiovascular disease, 1964-65; dir. med. intensive care St. Joseph's Hosp., Syracuse, N.Y., 1990—. Maj. U.S. Army, 1965-68. Fellow Am. Coll. Cardiology. Avocations: skiing, gardening. Home: 418 Long Rd Tully NY 13159-9414 Office: 5100 W Taft Rd Ste 2J Liverpool NY 13088

HUNTLEY, DIANE E., dental hygiene educator; b. Concord, N.H., Oct. 1, 1946; d. George Williams and Esther A. (Gadwah) H. AS, Fones Sch. Dental Hygiene, Bridgeport, Conn., 1966; BA, U. Bridgeport, Conn., 1968; MA, SUNY, Buffalo, 1971; PhD, Kans. State U., 1985. Registered dental hygienist. Dental hygienist various gen. practice dentists Conn., Colo., 1966-76; clin. instr. Fones Sch. Dental Hygiene, 1971-74; asst. prof. U. Colo. Dental Sch., Denver, 1974-76; asst. prof. dental hygiene Wichita (Kans.) State U., 1976-82, assoc. prof., 1982—; vol. hygienist Good Samaritan Clinic, Wichita, 1989-90, 92—. Contbr. articles to profl. jours. Mem. dental adv. bd. United Meth. Urban Ministries, Wichita, 1990-92; mem. P.A.N.D.A. Coalition of Kans. Exec. Com., 1995—. Mem. AAUP (Wichita State U. chpt. sec.-treas. 1988-91), Am. Assn. Dental Schs., Wichita Dental Hygienists' Assn. (pres. 1982-83, treas. 1988-90, trustee 1990-91), Kans. Dental Hygienists' Assn. (del 1989-93), Am. Dental Hygienists' Assn. (editl. dir. 1983-85, historian 1993—), Phi Kappa Phi, Alpha Eta. Office: Wichita State U 1845 Fairmount St Wichita KS 67260-0144

HUNTLEY, ROBERT ROSS, physician, educator; b. Wadesboro, N.C., Sept. 6, 1926; s. George W. and Louise (Ross) H.; m. Joan Cornoni, Apr. 10, 1976; children: Katherine, Robert, Julia, Elizabeth, Jeffress. B.S. in Chemistry, Davidson Coll., 1947; M.D., Bowman-Gray Sch. Medicine, 1951. Diplomate: Am. Bd. Preventive Medicine (trustee 1974-78), Am. Bd. Family Practice. Intern U. Mich. Hosp., Ann Arbor, 1951-53; resident, fellow N.C. Meml. Hosp., Chapel Hill, 1959-62; pvt. practice medicine Warrenton, N.C., 1953-58; from instr. to assoc. prof. medicine and preventive medicine U. N.C., Chapel Hill, 1959-68, adj. prof. health policy and adminstrn. Sch Pub. Health, 1989—; asso. dir. Nat. Center for Health Services Research, HEW, 1968-70; prof., chmn. dept. community and family medicine Georgetown U., 1970-89, prof. emeritus, 1989—; pres. Georgetown U. Community Health Plan, Inc., 1972-80; chmn. health care tech. study sect. HEW, 1978-82. Editor various profl. books; contbr. articles to profl. jours. Served with USN, 1945-46. Mem. APHA, Assn. Tchrs. Preventive Medicine, D.C. Med. Soc., N.C. Med. Soc., Acad. Medicine Washington. Democrat. Methodist.

HUNTZBERRY, LARRY STEPHEN, family therapist, educator; b. Hagerstown, Md., Nov. 30, 1943; s. Raymond E. and Anna Louise (Stevens) H.; m. Catherine Moore, Aug. 16, 1965; children: Martin, Damian, Kurtis. AB, Lebanon Valley Coll., Annville, Pa., 1965; MDiv, United Theol. Sem., Dayton, Ohio, 1968; ThM, Princeton Theol. Sem., 1974; PhD, Walden U., Mpls., 1982. Cert. Addictions Counselor, Pa. Teaching fellow Antioch Coll., Yellow Springs, Ohio, 1967-68; dir. residential treatment Today, Inc., Newtown, Pa., 1970-75; family therapist Bristol-Bensalem Mental Health/Mental Retardation Clinic, Bristol, Pa., 1975-78; individual practice marital and family therapy, Phila., 1975-78; clin. dir. outpatient svcs. Achievement Through Counseling and Treatment, Phila., 1978-85; assoc. dir., Family Guidance Ctr., Inc., Yardley, Pa., 1985—; sr. clin. instr. Hahnemann U., Phila. Mem. Am. Assn. Marriage and Family Therapy (clin. mem., approved supr.), Family Inst. Phila. (faculty). Home: 295 Cinnabar Ln Yardley PA 19067 Office: Family Guidance Ctr 301 Oxford Valley Rd Morrisville PA 19067-7706

HUNZIKER, ERICH, pharmaceutical company executive; b. Berne, Switzerland, Sept. 15, 1953; s. Paul and Johanna (Winzeried) H.; m. Brigitte Irene. Dipl.-Ing., Swiss Fed. Inst., Zurich, 1978, Dr.sc.techn., 1983; student Sr. Mgmt. Program, MIT, 1991. Chief asst. Dept. Mgmt. and Indsl. Engring. of ETH, Zurich, 1979-83; dir. bus. devel. pharm. Boehringer Mannheim, Zug, 1983-88; mng. dir. Boehringer Mannheim, Rotkreuz, Switzerland, 1988-92, pres. bd. dirs., 1990-92; mem. exec. bd. Boehringer Mannheim GmbH, Germany, 1992-94; chmn. exec. bd. Boehringer Mannheim GmbH, 1994-95, pres. therapeutic divsn., mem. exec. com., 1995—; chmn. exec. bd. Corange Deutschland Holding GmbH, 1995—; bd. dirs. Swiss Student Travel Office, Zurich, 1977-83, pres. of bd. dirs., 1980-83; active VCI Fin. Coun., VCI Handelspolitischer AssuchuB, European Coun. Fin. Dirs. Author: Auslandmarktstrategien, 1983; contbr. articles tp o profl. jours. Pres. of faculty coun. Dept. Mechanical Engring, ETH, Zurich, 1980-82. Mem. Brit. Soc. Strategic Planning, Swiss Soc. Future Rsch., Swiss Soc. Support R&D, SwissSoc. Indsl. Engrs. (bd. dirs. 1982-92, pres. 1989-92). Office: Boehringer Mannheim GmbH, Sandhofer StraBe 176, D-68298 Mannheim Germany

HUON, HUBERT JOHN, psychiatrist, neurologist; b. Douarnenez, France, June 6, 1936; s. Frank Allen and Mary Ann (Simon) H.; m. Mikaelle Huon, Mar. 31, 1964; children: Nathalie, Renaud, John-Christopher, Valerie. BS, Coll. St. Francois Xavier, Vannes, France, 1953; MD, Faculty Medicine, Paris, 1971; Cert. in Psychiatry, Pediatrics, Faculty Medicine Paris, 1971-72; Cert. in Neurophysiology, Faculty Medicine, 1973. Intern, resident, asst. prof. biochemistry Hosps. of Paris, 1966-70; prof. asst. neurophysiology, psychiatry U. Paris, 1968-72; prof. asst. psychiatry Hosp. Brest, France, 1972-74; chief psychiat. service Ctr. Hosp. Specialise de St. Ave, Vannes, France, 1977—; dir. sleep lab. Ctr. Hosp. Specialise de St. Ave, 1980—; dir. clin. teaching Hosp. Rennes, France, 1977—; cons. neurologist, Paris; expert ct. of justice, Rennes, 1973; clin. expert Ministry of Health, 1973; French del. World Council for Gifted and Talented Children, 1981-83; mgr. house constrn. firm. Author: The Children's Sleep, 1974; contbr. chpt. to book and med. research articles to profl. publs. Served as sgt. French armed forces, 1957-60, col. res. Mem. Sleep Research Soc., European Sleep Research Soc., French Soc. EEG and Neurophysiology, French Soc. Epidemiol. Psychology, Mensa. Roman Catholic. Lodge: Rotary. Home: Kerjaffre, 56610 Arradon France Office: Hospital, 56896 Saint Ave Britany France

HUOT, RACHEL IRENE, biomedical educator, research scientist; b. Manchester, N.H., Oct. 16, 1950; d. Omer Joseph and Irene Alice (Girard) H. BA in Biology cum laude, Rivier Coll., 1972; MS in Biology, Cath. U. Am., 1976, PhD in Biology, 1980. Sr. technician Microbiol. Assocs., Bethesda, Md., 1974-77; chemist Uniformed Svcs. Univ. of Health Scis., Bethesda, 1977-79; biologist Nat. Cancer Inst., Bethesda, 1979-82; postdoctoral fellow S.W. Found. for Biomed. Rsch., San Antonio, 1982-85, asst. scientist, 1985-87, staff scientist, 1987-88; instr. U. Tex. Health Sci. Ctr., San Antonio, 1988-89; asst. prof., dir. basic urologic rsch. La. State U., New Orleans, 1990-96; judge sr. div. Alamo Regional Sci. Fair, San Antonio, 1989-90. Contbr. articles to profl. jours. Vol. ARC; active Stephen Ministry. NSF grantee, 1972-74; recipient NIH Rsch. Svc. award, 1983-86, Searle Young Investigator award, 1994. Mem. AAAS, LWV, AAUW, AMA, Am. Soc. for Microbiology, Am. Assn. Cancer Rsch., Am. Soc. Cell Biology, Fedn. Am. Scientists, Sci. Club (pres. 1971-72), Soc. for In Vitro Biology, N.Y. Acad. Scis., St. Vincent De Paul Soc., Sierra Club, Fedn. Am. Soc. Experiment Biology, Sigma Xi, Iota Sigma Pi, Delta Epsilon Sigma. Democrat. Roman Catholic. Home: 701 Merrick St Shreveport LA 71104

HURAIB, SAMEER OMAR, medical educator; b. Taif, Saudi Arabia, Oct. 15, 1954; s. Omar Ali and Sabah Mohammed H.; m. Maha Mohammed Habeeb. MBBS, King Saud U., Riyadh, Saudi Arabia, 1979. Diplomate Am. Bd. Internal Medicine. Demonstrator dept. medicine King Saud U., Riyadh, Saudi Arabia, 1980-81, asst. prof., 1987-91, assoc. prof., 1991-95, prof. medicine, 1995—; resident in medicine U. Toronto, Can., 1982-85, fellow in clin. nephrology, 1985-87; cons. internist, nephrologist King Khalid U. Hosp., Riyadh, 1987-93, head nephrology divsn., 1993-95, King Fahad Nat. Guard Hosp., Riyadh, 1995—. Editor 3 jours.; contbr. over 70 papers to nat. and internat. jours. Fellow Royal Coll. Physicians Can., Am. Coll. Physicians. Moslem. Office: King Fahad Nat Guard Hosp, PO Box 22490, 11426 Riyadh Saudi Arabia

HURD, ERIC RAY, rheumatologist, internist, educator; b. Columbus, Kans., July 5, 1936; s. Myron Alexander and Isobel (Moore) H.; m. Beverly Jean Button, June 14, 1962; children: Sherryl Lynn, Susan Rae, Brent Eric. BS, U. Tulsa, 1958; MD, U. Okla., 1962. Intern St. John's Hosp., Tulsa, 1962-63, resident in internal medicine, 1963-65; research fellow U. Tex., Dallas, 1965-67, instr. internal medicine, 1967-68, asst. prof., 1968-73, assoc. prof., 1973-80, prof., 1980—; cons. rheumatologist, attending physician Parkland, VA Hosps.; dir. John Peter Smith Hosp. Arthritis Clinic, Ft. Worth; chief rheumatology VA Hosp., 1982—, mem. immunology research merit rev. bd.; assoc. Baylor Arthritis Ctr., 1981—; mem. med. and sci. com. North Tex. Arthritis Found., bd. med. dirs., 1988—, chmn. profl. edn. com.; traveling guest lectr. Tex. Med. Assn., Belgium and Fed. Republic Germany, 1990. Contbr. articles to profl. jours. Served to maj. U.S. Army, 1963-74. Recipient Clin. Scholar award Arthritis Found., 1975-77; named Outstanding Cons. Faculty Mem. John Peter Smith Hosp., 1983-84, Outstanding Part-time Clin. Prof. John Peter Smith Hosp., 1989-90. Mem. ACP, Am. Assn. Immunologists, Am. Fedn. Clin. Research, Am. Rheumatism Assn.

(cooperating clinics com. 1968-74, Founding Fellow 1986), Tex. Rheumatism Assn. (sec.-treas. 1976-79, 2d v.p. 1979-80), Tex. Med. Soc., Dallas County Med. Soc., Phi Eta Sigma. Democrat. Methodist. Office: Arthritis Ctrs of Tex 712 N Washington Ave Ste 200 Dallas TX 75246-1632

HURD, RICHARD NELSON, pharmaceutical company executive; b. Evanston, Ill., Feb. 25, 1926; s. Charles DeWitt and Mary Ormsby (Nelson) H.; m. Jocelyn Fillmore Martin, Dec. 22, 1950; children: Melanie Gray, Suzanne DeWitt. BS, U. Mich., 1946; PhD, U. Minn., 1956. Chemist, Gen. Electric Co., Schenectady, 1948-49; research and devel. group leader Koppers Co., Pitts., 1956-57; research chemist Mallinckrodt Chem. Works, St. Louis, 1956-63, group leader, 1963-66; group leader Comml. Solvents Corp., Terre Haute, Ind., 1966-68, sect. head, 1968-71; mgr. sci. affairs G. D. Searle Internat. Co., Skokie, Ill., 1972-73, dir. mfg. and tech. affairs, 1973-77, rep. to internat. tech. com. Pharm. Mfrs. Assn., 1973-77; v.p. tech. affairs Elder Pharms., Bryan, Ohio, 1977-81; v.p. research and devel. U.S. Proprietary Drugs & Toiletries div. Schering-Plough Corp., Memphis, 1981-83; v.p. sci. affairs Moleculon Inc., Cambridge, Mass., 1984-88; v.p. regulatory affairs Pharmaco-LSR, Inc., Austin, Tex., 1989-94; prin. Hurd & Assocs., Inc., Evanston, Ill., 1994—. Contbr. articles to profl. jours. Mem. Ferguson-Florissant (Mo.) Sch. Bd., 1964-66; bd. dirs. United Fund of Wabash Valley (Ind.), 1969-71. Served with USN, 1943-46, 53-55. E. I. DuPont de Nemours & Co., Inc. fellow, 1956. Mem. Am. Acad. Dermatology, Am. Soc. Photobiology, Am. Chem. Soc., N.Y. Acad. Sci., Am. Pharm. Assn., Am. Assn. Pharm. Scientists, AAAS, Sigma Xi. Achievements include 4 patents in field; co-devel. of Ralgro and Oxsoralen; research on thioamides as a class of organic compounds, devel. of macrocyclic synthetic routes for natural products, devel. of psoralens for photochemotherapy of dermatologic disorders. Presbyterian. Club: Mich. Shores (Wilmette, Ill.).

HURD, SUZANNE SHELDON, federal agency health science director; b. Elmira, N.Y., Dec. 17, 1939; d. Victor Sheldon H. BS, Bates Coll., 1961; MS, U. Wash., 1963, PhD, 1967. Post-doctoral fellow U. Calif., Berkeley, 1967-69; grants assoc. NIH, Bethesda, Md., 1969-70; health sci. adminstr. Nat. Heart, Lung and Blood Inst., Bethesda, 1970-78, dep. dir. div. lung diseases, 1979-84; dir. div. lung diseases Nat. Heart, Lung and Blood Inst., Bethesda, 1984—; acting dir. Nat. Inst. Nursing Rsch., Bethesda, 1994-95. Mem. Am. Thoracic Soc. Office: NIH/NHLBI/DLD/OD Two Rockledge Ctr Ste 10018 6701 Rockledge Dr MSC 7952 Bethesda MD 20892-7952

HURLBUT, RICHARD WADE, psychologist; b. Stevens Point, Wis., Oct. 23, 1950; s. Kenneth Edward and Elizabeth (Swan) H.; m. Connie Haack-Hurlbut, Sept. 17, 1977. BS, U. Wis., 1972, MS, 1976, PhD, 1979. Lic. Psychologist. Intern in psychology Wis. Div. of Corrections, Madison, 1979-80, staff psychologist, 1980-82, sr. staff psychologist, 1982-83; gen. practice psychology Mid-Wis. Psychotherapy Assocs., Stevens Point, 1981—; adj. prof. U. Wis., Stevens Point, 1984-86; cons. Homme Home for Boys, Wittenberg, Wis., 1984-87, Luth. Social Svc., Shawno, Wis., 1984-89, Assoc. Cons. Svcs., Marshfield, Wis., 1984—; co-owner, pres. Health Maintenance Svcs., Wausau, Wis., 1983-93. Mem. APA, Soc. Clin. and Cons. Psychologists (pres. 1984-85), Wis. Psychol. Assn. (pres. 1989-91, fed. advocacy network coord. 1991-96, mem. organizing com., initial v.p. 1995—). Democrat. Office: Mid Wis Psychotherapy Assocs 100 Bremmer St Stevens Point WI 54481-6032

HURLBUT, ROBERT HAROLD, health care services executive; b. Rochester, N.Y., Mar. 9, 1935; s. Harold Leroy and Martha Irene (Fincher) H.; m. Barbara Cox, June 14, 1958; children: Robert W., Christine A. Student, Coll. Hotel Adminstrn., Cornell U., 1953-56. Adminstr., dir. Pillars Nursing Home, Rochester, 1956—, Elmcrest Nursing Home, Churchville, N.Y., 1960—, Elm Manor Nursing Home, Canandaigua, N.Y., 1960—, Penfield Nursing Home, Rochester, 1963—, Avon (N.Y.) Nursing Home, 1964—, Newark (N.Y.) Nursing Home, 1965—, Lakeshore Nursing Home, Rochester, 1972—; bd. dirs. Marine Midland Bank, Blue Cross/Blue Shield Rochester, Living Ctrs. of Am.; organizer, adminstrv. dir. hdqrs. Rohm Svcs. Corp., Rochester, 1964—; organizer, pres. hdqrs. Vari-Care Inc., Rochester, 1969-93; commr. N.Y. State Ins. Fund; mem. Cornell U. Hotel Sch. Adv. Coun. Mem. bd. trustees St. John Fisher Coll., Eastman Dental Ctr.; pres. Hurlbut Trust, 1994; mem. bd. govs. Strong Meml. Hosp. Fellow Am. Coll. Health Care Adminstrs.; mem. Greater Met. C. of C. (past chmn. bd. dirs.), Genesee Valley Club, Oak Hill Club, Cornell Club, Lambda Chi Alpha. Home: 200 Sheldon Rd Honeoye Falls NY 14472-9316 Office: Hurlbut Trust 277 Alexander St Ste 800 Rochester NY 14607-1920

HURLBUT, TERRY ALLISON, pathologist; b. Richmond, Va., Nov. 24, 1957; s. Terry A. and Evelyn I. (Randlette) H. BS, Yale Coll., 1980; MD, Baylor Coll. Medicine, 1985. Pathology residency Vanderbilt Univ., 1986-89; fellowship pathology Dartmouth Medical Sch., 1989-91; pathology residency Monmouth Medical Ctr., Long Branch, N.J., 1991-93; clinical pathologist Kimball Medical Ctr, Lakewood, N.J., 1993-95; dir. informatics Lakewood Pathology Assn., Lakewood, N.J., 1993—; clinical pathologist Meml. Hosp. Burlington County, Mt. Holly, N.J., 1996—. Co-author: The Laboratory Consultant, 1992; contbr. article to profl. jours. Fellow Coll. Am. Pathologists. Baptist. Office: Lakewood Pathology Assocs 1200 River Ave # 10E Lakewood NJ 08701

HURLEY, ALLYSON KINGSLEY, dentist; b. Buffalo, June 15, 1949; d. Norman and Marion (Legler) Kingsley; m. Lawrence Joseph Hurley, May 28, 1977; children: Michael William, Kathryn Elizabeth. Student, Barat Coll., 1967-68; degree in dental hygiene, Marquette U., 1970, BS, 1971; DDS, Howard U., 1977. Pvt. practice dental hygiene, Washington, 1971-77; resident VA Hosp., Lyons, N.J., 1977-78; gen. practice dentistry, Chatham, N.J., 1978—; attending dentist Overlook Hosp., Summit, N.J., 1979—, dir. resident adminstrn., 1980-85, mem. edn. com., 1981-86; clin. instr. dental hygiene Union County Tech. Inst., Scotch Plains, N.J., 1979-81, mem. selection com. for dental dept., 1987; coord. kindergarten-4th grades dental health program Chatham Boro Sch. System, 1978—; active oral cancer screening program Chatham Boro Jr. Women's Club, 1980-82. Editor, contbg. author newsletter Word of Mouth, 1981—; author: (booklet) Your Child's Teeth, 1984. Alumni recruiter Marquette U., Morris County, N.J., 1977-83; bd. dirs. Am. Cancer Soc., Morris County, 1981-83; chair Scholarship Found. of the Chathams, Inc., 1985—. Master Acad. Gen. Destistry; mem. ADA, Am. Acad. Cosmetic Dentistry, Tri-County Dental Soc. (bd. dirs. 1982-83), Internat. Platform Assn., N.Y. Acad. Scis., Columbia U. Dental Study Club, No. N.J. Women's Study Club (pres. 1980-82, 86—, sec. 1983-86), Newcomer's Club Chatham Township. Republican. Roman Catholic. Office: Allyson Kingsley Hurley DDS 585 Main St Chatham NJ 07928-2104

HURLEY, HARRY JAMES, JR., dermatologist; b. Phila., Oct. 10, 1926; s. Harry James and Margaret (McHenry) H.; m. Jeanne Florence Geiger, July 15, 1950; children: Susan, Harry James III, Jeffrey, Marilyn, Nancy. Student, St. Joseph's Coll., Phila., 1943-45; MD, Jefferson Med. Coll., Phila., 1949; DSc in Medicine, U. Pa., 1958. Diplomate Am. Bd. Dermatology (bd. dirs., examiner 1974-83, exec. com. 1978-79, chmn. edn. com. 1979-84, v.p. 1982-83, pres. 1983-84, asst. exec. dir. 1985-92, exec. dir. 1993—, Disting. Svc. award 1984). Rotating intern Fitzgerald-Mercy Hosp., Darby, Pa., 1949-50, resident in ob-gyn., 1950-51; resident in dermatology and syphilogy U. Pa. Hosp., 1951-53; rsch. fellow USPHS, 1955-56; mem. faculty U. Pa. Sch. Medicine, 1956-59, 62—, assoc. prof. dept. dermatology, 1962-68, prof. clin. dermatology, 1978—; prof. dermatology, chief sect., chief dermatol. sect. coll. hosp. Hahnemann Med. Coll., Phila., 1959-62; chief dermatology Phila. Gen. Hosp., 1962-73; attending dermatologist Fitzgerald-Mercy Hosp., 1956-80, Bryn Mawr Hosp., 1956-75, Am. Oncologic Hosp., Phila., 1960-62, U. Pa. Hosp., 1962-80; chmn. adv. bd. Nat. Program Dermatology, 1974-75; pres. Dermatology Found., 1975-76; cons., advisor in field. Contbr. numerous articles to profl. jours.; editor: Jour. Geriatric Dermatology, 1993—; bd. editors Modern Dermatology, 1968, Dermatology Forum, 1984; editorial cons. Annals Internal Medicine, 1982-84. Capt. M.C., USAR, 1953-55. Recipient Rsch. Recognition award Phila. chpt. Nat. Cystic Fibrosis Found., 1959, Clarence E. Shaffrey medal and award St. Joseph's U., 1980, Finnerud award Dermatol. Found., 1991, Everett Fox lectr. and award Am. Acad. Dermatology, 1994. Fellow ACP (chmn. self-assessment program sect. dermatology 1976); mem. Am. Acad. Dermatology (bd. dirs. 1972-75, chmn. coun. govtl. liaison 1974-75, mem. nominating com. 1977-80, chmn. audit com. 1988-89), AMA (chmn. residency rev. com. 1979-82), Am. Dermatol. Assn. (bd. dirs. 1977-82, pres. 1983-84, chmn. nominating com. 1987), Soc. Investigative Dermatology, Pa. Acad. Dermatology (pres. 1969-70, Disting. SVc. commendation 1973), Pa. Med. Soc., Delaware County Med. Soc., Coll. Physicians Phila., Phila. Dermatol. Soc. (pres. 1970-71, editor. proc. 1968-69), Overbrook Golf Club (Bryn Mawr, Pa.; bd. dirs. 1988—, v.p. 1993), Alpha Epsilon Delta. Home: 4119 Echo Valley Ln Newtown Square PA 19073-1623 Office: 39 Copley Rd Upper Darby PA 19082-2511

HURLEY, LAURENCE HAROLD, medicinal chemistry educator; b. Birmingham, U.K., Jan. 29, 1944; s. Harold Harcourt and Mary (Cottrell) H.; children: Bridget, Nicole. BPharm, U. Bath, U.K., 1967, DSc, 1996; PhD, Purdue U., 1970. Apprentice pharmacist Boots the Chemist, Birmingham, 1963-64; hosp. pharmacist Birmingham Gen. Hosp., 1967; postdoctoral fellow U. B.C., Vancouver, 1970-71; asst. prof. U. Md., Balt., 1971-73; from asst. to assoc. to full prof. U. Ky., Lexington, 1973-80; prof. U. Tex., Austin, 1981—, Henry Burlage prof., 1983-86, James Bauerle prof., 1986-88, George Hitchings prof. drug design, 1988-91, George Hitchings regents chmn. drug design, 1992—; cons. Upjohn Co., Kalamazoo, 1979—, Smith Kline French, Phila., 1984-87, Abbott Labs., 1992-94; mem. sci. adv. bd. Sun Pharm. Corp.; chmn. bioorganic and natural products study sect. NIH, 1986-88; dir. Chemistry Inst. Drug Devel., San Antonio. Sr. editor Jour. Medicinal Chemistry; contbr. numerous articles to profl. jours. Recipient George Hitchings award in innovative drug design, 1988, Volwiler Rsch. Achievement award, 1989, Rsch. Achievement award in medicinal chemistry Am. Pharm. Assn., 1992; named Outstanding Investigator Nat. Cancer Inst., 1989, 94. Fellow AAAS; mem. Am. Chem. Soc. (Medicinal Chemistry award 1994). Democrat. Home: 5915 Northwest Pl Austin TX 78731-3660 Office: U Tex Coll Pharmacy Austin TX 78712

HURLEY, STEVEN RAY, health program administrator; b. Tacoma Park, Md., July 10, 1947; s. Robert Warren and Stella Lavern (Burroughs) H.; m. Sharon Lynn Westfall, July 22, 1972; children: Samara Marie, Shannon Nicole. AS, Orange County Community Coll., Middletown, N.Y., 1969; BS, SUNY, New Paltz, 1970; MS, EdS, SUNY, Albany, 1974. Cert. guidance counseling. Probation officer Schoharie County Probation Dept., Schoharie, N.Y., 1974-79; investigator Office Profl. Med. Conduct, Albany, 1979, Office Health Systems Mgmt., Albany, 1979; sr. personnel adminstr. Office Mental Health, Albany, 1979-83; project dir. Office Mental Health, 1983-84; sr. pers. adminstr. N.Y. State Health Dept., Albany, 1984-89; health program administr., dir. staff ops. N.Y. State AIDS Inst., Albany, 1989—; instr. Gov.'s Office Employee Rels., Albany, 1984—. Founder, chmn. bd. dirs. Crisis Intervention Schoharie County, Schoharie, 1973-77; chmn. Zoning Bd. Appeals, Schoharie, 1973-83; mem. Schoharie County Dem. Com., 1979—, Schoharie Sch. Bd. Edn., 1989-92; counselor Schoharie County Correctional Facility, 1987-92. With USNR, 1964-71. Mem. Internat. Pers. Mgmt. Assn. (pres. 1987-88, Irv Handler Meml. award 1982), Orgn. Mgmt. Confidential Employees Assn. (adv. bd.), N.Y. State Sch. Bds. Assn., Am. Legion, Kiwanis. Democrat. Mem. Soc. of Friends. Home: RR 1 Box 174 Howes Cave NY 12092-9738 Office: NY State Dept Health AIDS Inst Rm # 359 Corning Towers Albany NY 12237

HURLEY, SUSAN FAY, health services reseracher; b. Perth, Australia, Feb. 6, 1954; d. Matthias John and Beryl (Murdew) O'Connell; children: Clare Hurley, Elle Hurley. B Pharmacy, Victorian Coll. Pharmacy, Melbourne, Australia, 1973, M Pharmacy, 1986; PhD, Monash U., Melbourne, 1991; MS, U. Wash., 1994. Dep. dir. pharmacy Preston & Northcote Hosp., Melbourne, 1980-86; rsch. fellow Monash U., 1986-87, sr. rsch. fellow, 1991-92; epidemiologist Anti-Cancer Coun. of Victoria, Melbourne, 1987-91; Neil Hamilton Fairley fellow U. Wash., Seattle, 1992-94, U. Melbourne, 1994—; mem. working party on age-related issues in mammographic screening Nat. Health & Med. Rsch. Coun., 1992; cons. Econ. Evaluation of Nat. HIV/AIDS Stragegy, Canberra, Australia, 1994. Contbr. articles to profl. publs. Neil Hamilton Fairley fellow Nat. Health and Med. Rsch. Coun., Australia, 1992, fellow in hosp. pharmacy Merck, Sharp & Dohme, Australia, 1984; Travenol Labs. scholar, 1982. Mem. Soc. for Med. Decision Making, Soc. for Epidemiologic Rsch., Statis. Soc. Australia. Home: 64 McArthur Rd, E Ivanhoe Queensland 3079, Australia Office: U Melbourne, 200 Berkeley St, Carlton 3053, Australia

HURNEY, LEE MAURICE, podiatrist; b. Flushing, N.Y., Jan. 13, 1950; s. Joseph Paul and Wilma (Berlitski) H.; m. Aug. 15, 1981; children: Evan, Christine. BS, St. John's U., Jamaica, N.Y., 1971; DPM, Ill. Coll. Podiatric Medicine, 1978. Diplomate Am. Bd. Podiatric Surgery. Podiatric physician West Haven (Conn.) Podiatry Assocs., P.C., 1979-89; prin. Lee M. Hurney, P.C., Branford, Conn., 1989—; surg. cons. West Haven VA Hosp., 1980-91; prof. N.Y. Coll. Podiatric Medicine, N.Y.C., 1980—, Coll. Podiatric Medicine, U. Iowa, Des Moines, 1984—. Fellow Am. Coll. Foot Surgeons; mem. Am. Podiatric Med. Assn., Conn. Podiatric Med. Assn., New Haven County Podiatric Med. Assn. (pres. 1988-90), Rotary (sgt. at arms 1983-85). Office: 97 E Main St Branford CT 06405-3707

HURST, CHRISTINA MARIE, respiratory therapist; b. San Diego, Jan. 29, 1955; d. Harvey Joseph Breighner and Doris Romaine March-Breighner; children: Heather Erin, Ian Richard. AAS, Del. Tech. Coll., 1989. Cert. and registered respiratory therapist Perinatal and Pediatric Registry. Respiratory therapist Med. Ctr. Del., Christiana, 1989—, Perinatal Pediat. Registry, Lenexa, Kans., 1995—; mem. Nat. Bd. Respiratory Care; instr. basic cardiopulmonary resuscitation, Wilmington, Del., 1989-90; spkr. Senate Labor Rels. Com., 1987. Vol. preschool asthma program Am. Lung Assn. Del., Wilmington, 1989, Del. Epilepsy Found. Wilmington, 1988-90; exec. coun. State Adv. Coun. for Svcs. to Handicapped, Dover, Del., 1989-90; charter mem. parent support group Children with Epilepsy, Wilmington, 1988-90. Mem. Am. Assn. for Respiratory Care, Epilepsy Found. Am., Phi Theta Kappa. Home: 518 Pheasant Run Bear DE 19701-2720 Office: Med Ctr Del Stanton Ogletown Rd Newark DE 19713

HURST, DANIEL LEE, child neurologist; b. Cin., Oct. 14, 1952; s. Charles C. and Edna M. (Bullock) H.; m. Mary Jane Gaines, June 5, 1974; 1 child, Katherine Jane. BA in Chemistry, Denison U., 1974; MD, Ohio State U., 1977. Diplomate Nat. Med. Bd., Am. Bd. Neurology. Commd. 2d lt. U.S. Army, 1974, advanced through grades to lt. col., 1990; pediatric intern Mich. State U., Kalamazoo, 1977-78; pediatric resident Walter Reed Army Med. Ctr., Washington, 1978-79, neurology resident, 1979-82; child neurologist Fitzsimons Army Med. Ctr., Aurora, Colo., 1982-86, Tex. Tech. U. Health Sci. Ctr., Lubbock, 1986—; adult neurologist U.S. Army, Desert Storm, 1991; cons. Tex. State Bd. Med. Examiners, 1993-94. Mem. AIDS Task Force, Lubbock, Tex., 1993-94; mem. adminstrv. coun. St. John's United Meth. Ch., Lubbock, 1992-93. Decorated Army Commendation medal. Fellow Am. Acad. Pediatrics; mem. Child Neurology Soc. Home: 5006 94th St Lubbock TX 79424-4814 Office: Tex Tech U Health Scis Ctr 3601 4th St Lubbock TX 79430-0001

HURST, JOSEPHINE MARIE, cancer researcher; b. Phila., May 14, 1938; d. Russel F. and Josephine (Carlin) H. AB, Immaculata Coll., 1960; MS, St. John's U., 1962, PhD, 1965. Grad. asst. St. John's U., Jamaica, N.Y., 1960-62, instr., 1963-65, asst. prof., 1966-71; rsch. asst. NYU, 1962-63; rsch. assoc. Holt Radiation Labs., Manchester, Eng., 1965, U. Bristol Med. Sch., England, 1965-66, N.Y. Ocean Sci. Lab., Montauk, 1971-72; dir. cancer diagnostic lab. North Ridge Gen. Hosp., Ft. Lauderdale, Fla., 1983-85; dir. Biotherapeutics Assocs., Plantation, Fla., 1987-88; rsch. assoc. Goodwin Inst. for Cancer Rsch., Plantation, 1979-92, dir. rsch., 1992-96. Contbr. chpts. to books and articles to profl. jours. Rsch. grantee NCI, 1980-82, ACS (div. Fla.), 1983-85. Mem. Internat. Assn. Breast Cancer Rsch., Am. Assn. Can. Rsch.

HURST, KENNETH LANDIS, physician, educator, health facility administrator; b. Lancaster, Pa., June 29, 1949; s. Lester Martin and Bertha (Landis) H.; m. Janice Marlene Martin, Aug. 1, 1970; children: Kristin Elisa, Jeremy Estel, Hans Erik. BA in Biology and Chemistry with honors, Messiah Coll., 1970; MD, U. Pa., 1975. Diplomate Nat. Bd. Med. Examiners, Am. Bd. Family Practice. Resident family practice program The Williamsport (Pa.) Hosp., 1975-78; clin. preceptor family practice residency program The Williamsport Hosp./Divine Providence Hosp., 1978-90, staff physician, 1978-90; physician co-founder, mem. Cornerstone Family Health, P.C., Williamsport, 1978-90; staff physician Lancaster Gen. Hosp./St. Joseph's Hosp. & Med. Ctr., 1990—; co. physician Armstrong World Industries, Inc., Lancaster, 1990-93; asst. dir., asst. clin. prof. family practice program Lancaster Gen. Hosp., 1990-95; physician mem. Leola (Pa.) Family Health Ctr., 1993—; med. dir. Hospice of Lancaster County, 1991—; med. dir. Community Home Care Svcs., Inc., Williamsport, 1987-90; founder, med. dir. St. Anthony's Free Med. Clinic, Williamsport, 1987-90. Contbr. chpt. Health Care for the Poor, 1990; editor, columnist Lycoming Medicine, 1981-90; columnist Lancaster Medicine, 1992-93. Vol. clin. asst. prof. dept. family practice and comty. health Temple U. Sch. Medicine and Pa. State U., Hershey Sch. Medicine; active med. missions Raleigh Fitkin Meml. Hosp., Manzini, Swaziland, 1975, Project Help, Pierre Payen, Haiti, 1983, 85, Med. Group Missions, San Jose de Las Matos, Dominican Republic, 1991; founding pres. Physicians and Clergy Peace Initiative, Williamsport, 1986-89; hon. chmn. Lycoming County Cropwalk, Williamsport, 1987. Recipient Cert. of Appreciation, St. Anthony Free Med. Clinic, 1990, Williamsport Hosp. Family Practice/Cornerstone Family Health, P.C. residency, 1990. Fellow Am. Acad. Family Physicians, Pa. Acad. Family Physicians; mem. AMA, Acad. Hospice Physicians, Family Rsch. Coun., Mennonite Med. Assn., Lancaster County Med. Soc., Pa. Med. Soc., Christian Med. and Dental Soc. (state del. 1980-88, 92—). Republican. Office: Leola Family Health Ctr 146 E Main St Leola PA 17540

HURST, MICHAEL WILLIAM, psychologist; b. Medford, Oreg., Dec. 9, 1947; s. William George and Betty Muriel (Stevens) H.; m. Patricia C. Scully, Aug. 22, 1970 (div. 1981); 1 child, Michelle P.; m. Renee Catherine Sancoff, Aug. 20, 1988; children: Rachel C., James M., Elizabeth R. BS, MIT, 1970; MEd, Boston U., 1972, EdD, 1974. Lic. psychologist, Mass., N.H.; cert. employee assistance profl. Rsch. assoc. Powell Assocs., Inc., Cambridge, Mass., 1970-72; rsch. and teaching fellow dept. counselor edn. Boston U., 1972-73, post-doctoral fellow and instr. dept. psychosomatic medicine, 1973-74, asst. prof. psychiatry, 1974-80, assoc. prof. psychiatry, 1980—; attending psychologist Univ. Hosp., Boston, 1978—; pres. Hurst Assocs., Inc., Boston, 1978-91; cons. to numerous orgns., 1978—; v.p. Am. PsychMgmt./Hurst Assocs., Inc., 1991-92; managed behavioral health care cons., 1992-93; pres. InStream Corp. (formerly Med. Comm. Tech., Inc.), 1993—, Nat. Leadership Coun., Inst. Behavioral Healthcare, 1994—. Cons. editor: Behavioral Medicine, 1982-91; patentee in field; contbr. articles to profl. jours. Bd. dirs. treas. Mass. Spl. Needs Assn., Inc., Groton, 1973-76; bd. dirs., steering com. Mass. Psychol. Health Plan Inc., Groton, 1979-82; pres., v.p. Pine Acre Park Assn., Hampstead, N.H., 1982-85. Fellow Mass. Psychol. Assn.; mem. APA, Am. Psychopathological Assn. (Morton Prince prize 1978), N.Y. Acad. Scis., Phi Delta Kappa, Delta Upsilon Alumni Assn. (bd. dirs. 1979-82). Republican. Episcopalian. Home: 3 Eastwood Dr Windham NH 03087-1638

HURTEAU, WILLIAM JAMES, hospital administrator, consultant; b. Iowa City, Iowa, June 14, 1943; s. William Winfield and Francis (Walling) H.; m. Peggie Jean Craig, May 27, 1980; children—Melissa, William F. B.S. in Bus. Mgmt., Ind. U., 1968; M.H.A., Washington U., 1971. Facility planner Health Planning Council, Omaha, 1971-73; asst. adminstr. Lutheran Med. Ctr., Omaha, 1973-74, Mercy Hosp., Des Moines, 1974-78; assoc. adminstr. Lapeer County Hosp., Mich., 1978-80; adminstr. Mason Dist. Hosp., Havana, Ill., 1980-85, Anderson Hosp., Maryville, Ill., 1985—, TCA Northwest Ind., Hammond; cons. small rural hosps., Ill., Ind., 1984, Am. Hosp. Assn., Chgo., 1984. Contbr. articles to profl. jours. Bd. dirs. Methodist Ch., Havana, 1982, Art Council, Havana, 1984. Served with U.S. Army, 1968-73. Mem. Am. Coll. Hosp. Adminstrs., Ill. Hosp. Assn. (various positions 1981—), C. of C. Lodge: Rotary (pres. 1980—). Avocations: collecting toy trains, hunting. Office: TCA Northwest Ind 100 Burns Farm Blvd Edwardsville IL 62025

HURVITZ, ARTHUR ISAAC, pathologist, researcher; b. Newton, Mass., Nov. 29, 1939; m. Gail Joy Hurvitz; children: John, Tad. BS, Mich. State U., 1964, DVM, 1964; PhD, U. Calif., Davis, 1967. Diplomate Am. Coll. Vet. Pathologists. Asst. prof. Rockefeller U., N.Y.C., 1969-71; dir. rsch., chmn. dept. pathology Animal Med. Ctr., N.Y.C., 1971—, also trustee, 1987—; vis. prof. U. Maine, Orono, 1975-82; adj. asst. prof. Coll. Physicians and Surgeons Columbia U., N.Y.C., 1973—; chmn. sci. adv. bd. Cambridge Biotech Corp., 1982—, chmn., 1990-93. Contbr. articles to profl. jours. Mem. N.J. Bd. Health, 1977-82. Grantee Morris Animal Found., USPHS, 1969-85; recipient Proficiency in Small Animal Medicine award Upjohn, 1964, Small Animal Rsch. award Ralston Purina, 1983, Disting. Vet. Alumnus award Mich. State U. Coll. Vet. Medicine, 1990, Alumni Achievement award U. Calif. Sch. Vet. Medicine, 1994; named Astor Chair of Comparative Medicine, Astor Found., 1981. Fellow N.Y. Zool. Soc. Office: The Animal Med Ctr 510 E 62nd St New York NY 10021-8383

HURVITZ, S. ALLAN, thoracic and cardiovascular surgeon; b. Pitts., Dec. 19, 1929; s. Nathan N. and Belle S. (Gold) H.; m. Barbara F. Hurvitz, Dec. 22, 1963; children: Nathan, Lawrence, Robert. BS, UCLA, 1951; MD, Boston U., 1955. Diplomate Am. Bd. Surgery, Am. Bd. Thoracic Surgery. Pvt. practice thoracic surgery L.A., 1964—. Contbr. articles to profl. jours. Lt. cmmdr. USN, 1960-62. Fellow Am. Coll. Angiology; mem. Soc. for Neurovascular Surgery, Soc. of Thoracic Surgeons, Western Thoracic Surgical Assn. Office: S Allan Hurvitz MD 1801 Ave of Stars Ste 640 Los Angeles CA 90067

HURWITZ, ISRAEL SAMUEL, orthopedic surgeon; b. Boston, Feb. 22, 1930; s. Albert and Ada (Godinski) H.; m. Eleanor Phyllis Moran, Feb. 17, 1957; children: Amy Gutschenritter, Nancy Beth, Arthur Andrew. AB, Cornell U., 1952; MD, Tufts U., 1956. Diplomate Am. Bd. Orthopedic Surgery. Intern New Eng. Med. Ctr., 1957-58, resident in gen. surgery, 1958-60; resident in orthopedics Boston VA Hosp., 1960-63; pres. Orthopedic Asscs. of Marlboro, Mass., 1962—; bd. dirs. Marlborough Savs. Bank, Marlborough Hosp.; pres. Marlborough Hosp. Med. Staff, 1978-80. Bd. dirs. Mass. PRO, Waltham, 1988—. Capt. U.S. Army, 1958-60. Recipient Resident's prize Boston Orthopedic Club, 1962. Fellow Am. Acad. Orthopedic Surgeons (bd. councillors 1984-91); mem. Mass. Orthopedic Assn. (pres. 1988-89), New Eng. Orthopedic Soc., Boston Orthopedic Club, Middlesex West Med. Soc. (pres. 1983-85), Mass. Med. Soc. (exec. bd./alt. 1981-93), Alpha Omega Alpha. Home: 15 Metacomet Way Sudbury MA 01776-2317 Office: 65 Fremont St Marlborough MA 01752-1271

HURWITZ, ROGER A., medical educator; b. Cleve., Sept. 1, 1934; s. Maurice and Gladys L. (Hertz) H.; m. Francine R. Rosenblatt, July 9, 1959; children: Andrew, Valerie Goldblatt. BA, Dartmouth Coll., 1956; MD, Northwestern U., Evanston, Ill., 1960; MS, UCLA, 1968. Intern L.A. County Hosp., 1960-61; resident in pediat. Children's Meml. Hosp., Chgo., 1961-63; USPHS pediatric cardiology trainee UCLA, 1965-67, clin. asst. prof., 1967-68; asst. prof. Ind. U. Med. Ctr., Indpls., 1968-71; assoc. prof. Ind. U. Med. Ctr., 1971-76, prof. pediat., 1976-81, prof. pediat. and radiology, 1981—; vis. prof. Children's Hosp. Med. Ctr., Boston, 1980-81. Contbr. chpts. to books. Capt. U.S. Army, 1963-65. Grantee Susan Murphy Fund Riley Meml. Assn., Indpls., 1994; named Phillip Murray Prof. Ind. U. Med. Ctr. Riley Meml. Assn., 1996. Fellow Am. Acad. Pediat. (chair cardiology sect. 1968-96), Am. Coll. Cardiology; mem. Am. Heart Assn., Dartmouth Club INd. (acting pres. 1985—). Office: Pediatric Cardiology RR 104 702 Barnhill Dr Indianapolis IN 46202

HURYK, WILLIAM HENRY, JR., chiropractor; b. Newark, Dec. 5, 1948; s. William and Stella Frances (Oberc) H.; m. Laurie Sue Weiner, Sept. 20, 1975; 1 child, Dawn Francesca. AS, Essex C.C., Newark, 1971; BA, Rutgers U., 1973; DC, Western States Chiropractic, Portland, 1980; fellow, Internat. Acad. Acupuncture, 1995. Diplomate Nat. Bd. Chiropractic Examiners. Assoc. Phillips Chiropractic Clinic, Vancouver, Wash., 1981-83; owner Broadway Chiropractic Clinic, Portland, Oreg., 1983-90; pvt. practice William ŽSid' Huryk, D.C., Denver, 1991—; owner Chiro Relief Svcs., Denver, 1991—; officer, sec.-treas., v.p., pres., dist 2 Chiropractic Soc. Oreg., Portland; dir. The BACA Inst. for Vibratory Studies Inc., Denver, 1991-94; lectr. in field. Bd. dirs. Western States Chiropractic Coll. Alumni Assn., Portland, 1987, 88, 89, 90, Garfield Montessori Sch., Denver, 1994, 95. Fellow Internat. Acad. Clin. Acupuncture; mem. Colo. Chiropractic Assn.

HURYN, JOSEPH MICHAEL, maxillofacial prosthodontist, dental oncologist; b. N.Y.C., Aug. 13, 1951; s. Joseph Thomas and Helen (Kibalo) H.; m. Laryssa Ulana Magun, Aug. 4, 1974; children: Laryssa Anastasia,

Melanie Alexandra. BA, NYU, 1973, DDS, 1976. Resident in gen. dentistry VA Med. Ctr., Bklyn., 1976-77; staff dentist VA Outpatient Clnic, Bklyn., 1977-81, chief dental svc., 1981-84; resident in gen. prosthodontics Meml. Sloan-Kettering Cancer Ctr., N.Y.C., 1984-86, fellow in maxillofacial prosthetics, 1986-87, attending dentist, 1987—. Contbr. articles to profl. jours. Recipient Spl. Contbn. award VA, 1984; Am. Cancer Soc. clin. fellow, 1985-87. Fellow Greater N.Y. Acad. Prosthodontics, Am. Acad. Maxillofacial Prosthetics (assoc.); mem. ADA, N.Y. Head and Neck Soc., Am. Prosthodontic Soc., Am. Coll. Prosthodontists (assoc.). Office: Meml Sloan-Kettering Cancer Ctr 1275 York Ave New York NY 10021

HUSAR, WALTER GENE, neurologist, neuroscientist, educator; b. Jersey City, Sept. 24, 1956; s. Walter and Ksenia H. (Dawybida) H. BS in Biology summa cum laude, St. Peter's Coll., Jersey City, 1978; MS in Microbiology, Rutgers U., 1982; MD, UMDNJ-N.J. Med. Sch., 1988. Diplomate Nat. Bd. Med. Examiners; lic. physician, N.J., N.Y. Adj. instr., then adj. lectr. microbiology St. Peter's Coll., 1979-84; intern in neurology and internal medicine U. Medicine and Dentistry N.J., Newark, 1988-89, resident, then adminstrv. chief resident in neurology, 1989-92; instr. dept. neuroscis. U. Medicine and Dentistry N.J., 1992—; attending physician dept. neuroscis. U. Hosp. U. Medicine and Dentistry N.J., Newark, 1992—; staff/attending physician Dept. VA Med. Ctr., East Orange, N.J., 1992—; cons. physician dept. medicine divsn. neurology Holy Name Hosp., Teaneck, N.J., 1992—, staff neurologist Bernard W. Gimbel Multiple Sclerosis Comprehensive Care Ctr., 1992—; quality assurance physician rep. neurology svc., mem. geriatrics com., mem. patient's health edn. exec. com., 1992—, mem. utilization rev. coun., 1994—, mem. surg. and invasive procedure rev. com., 1992-94; Dept. VA Med. Ctr. mem. long term utilization care subcom., 1992-93. Mem. bd. health Twp. of East Hanover, N.J., 1993—, v.p., 1996—; mem. stroke coun. Am. Heart Assn., 1992—. Fellow Acad. Medicine N.J.; mem. AMA, Med. Soc. N.J., Essex County Med. Soc., Am. Acad. Neurology (assoc.), Am. Assn. Electrodiagnostic Medicine (assoc.). Home: 10 Christine Dr East Hanover NJ 07936-3039 Office: VA Med Ctr 385 Tremont Ave East Orange NJ 07018-1095

HUSMANN, DOUGLAS A., urologist, educator; b. Grad March, Nebr., Sept. 19, 1953; s. Kenneth Reher Husmann and Donna Frances (McGee) Madson; m. Pamela Jean Husmann, July 3, 1976; children: Caleb McGee, Jennie Jean. BS, U. Nebr., 1975; MD, U. Nebr. Med. Ctr., 1979. Diplomate Am. Bd. Urology, Radiation. Asst. prof. urology U. Tex. Southwestern, Dallas, 1987-91; assoc. prof. urology Mayo Clinic, Rochester, Minn., 1991—. Office: Mayo Clinic Dept Urology 200 1st St SW Rochester MN 55905

HUSSAIN, M. MAHMOOD, medical educator. BSc, Osmania U., Hyderabad, India, 1976, MSc in Biochemistry, 1978; MPhil in Enzymology, U. Hyderabad, India, 1979; PhD in Biochemistry, Okla. State U., 1984; Lic. Med. in Biochemistry, U. Copenhagen, 1986. Danida fellow Panum Inst., U. Copenhagen, 1980-81; grad. rsch. asst. dept. biochemistry Okla. State U., 1981-84; rsch. assoc. sect. molecular genetics Boston U. Med. Ctr., 1984-87; postdoctoral fellow Gladstone Found. Labs. for Cardiovascualr Disease, U. Calif., San Francisco, 1987-88, staff rsch. investigator, 1988-91; asst. prof. depts. pathology and biochemistry Med. Coll. Pa., Phila., 1991-95, assoc. prof., 1995—; reviewer grants for extramural funding by Am. Heart Assn., Southeastern Pa. affiliate, 1995—. Reviewer Jour. Biol. Chemistry, European Jour. Clin. Investigation, Jour. Lipid Rsch., Arteriosclerosis and Thrombosis, Biochim. Biophys. Acta, Lipids; contbr. articles to profl. jours., chpts. to books. Recipient Nat. Merit scholarship Govt. India, 1976-78, Rsch. award Boston U. Sch. Medicine, 1986; Danish Internat. Devel. fellow, 1980-81; grantee Am. Heart Assn., Southeastern Pa. affiliate, 1993—, NIH, 1995—. Mem. AAAS, Am. Heart Assn. (Coun. on Arteriosclerosis), N.Y. Acad. Scis., Phi Lambda Upsilon. Home: 2245 County Line Rd Ardmore PA 19003 Office: Med Coll Pa 2900 Queen Ln Philadelphia PA 19129*

HUSSAR, DANIEL ALEXANDER, pharmacy educator; b. Phila., Feb. 12, 1941; s. Alexander and Anna (Nagel) H.; m. Suzanne Rose Fix, Aug. 26, 1967; children—Eric Fix, Christopher Nagel, Timothy Daniel. B.S. in Pharmacy, Phila. Coll. Pharmacy and Sci., 1962, M.S., 1964, Ph.D., 1967. Mem. faculty Phila. Coll. Pharmacy and Sci., 1966—, prof. pharmacy, 1971—, dir. dept., 1971-75, Remington prof., 1975—, dean faculty, 1975-84; Fellow Am. Found. Pharm. Edn., 1962-64, NSF, 1964-66. Author articles, chpts. in books. Mem. Am. Pharm. Assn. (trustee 1977-80), Pa. Pharm. Assn. (pres. 1975-76), Am. Soc. Hosp. Pharmacists, Pa. Soc. Hosp. Pharmacists, Drug Info. Assn. (pres. 1977-78). Home: 1 Boulder Creek Ln Newtown Square PA 19073-1703 Office: Phila Coll Pharmacy and Sci 600 S 43rd St Philadelphia PA 19104-4495

HUSSEY, JOHN FRANCIS, physician, geriatrician; b. Richmond Hill, N.Y., Jan. 6, 1951; s. John F. Sr. and Jean (Peczynski) H.; m. Ann Pelley, Sept. 10, 1979; children: Leo, Nicholas. BS in Biology, St. Johns U., 1972; MD, Creighton U., 1976. Pvt. practice Augusta, Maine, 1982-90; med. cons. Augusta Mental Health Inst., 1990-95; geriatrician, psychology cons. Togus (Maine) VA Hosp., 1995—. Capt. USPHS, 1979-82. Fellow Am. Acad. Family Physicians; Am. Geriat. Soc., Kennebec County Med. Assn. (treas. 1995-96, pres. 1996—). Office: VA Hosp 1 VA Ctr 171 Togus ME 04330

HUSTED, RUSSELL FOREST, research scientist; b. Lafayette, Ind., Apr. 4, 1950; s. Robert Forest and Miriam Ruth (Jackson) H.; m. Nancy Lee Driscoll, Oct. 25, 1969 (div. Feb. 1986); children: Jacqueline Marie, Randall Forest; m. Ruth Elaine Hurlburt, Nov. 12, 1988. BS in Chemistry with highest distinction, Colo. State U., 1972; PhD in Pharmacology, U. Utah, 1976. Post-doctoral fellow dept. medicine U. Iowa, Iowa City, 1976-79, rsch. scientist dept. medicine, 1979-81, 1982—; asst. prof. U. Conn. Sch. Medicine, Farmington, 1981-82. Contbr. articles to profl. jours. Mallinckrodt scholar Colo. State U., 1968. Mem. AAAS, Am. Soc. Nephrology, Am. Physiol. Soc., Soc. Gen. Physiology, N.Y. Acad. Sci., Sigma Xi. Democrat. Methodist. Office: Univ Iowa 317 Medical Laboratories Iowa City IA 52242

HUSTON, DIANE THERESA, critical care nurse; b. Morris, Ill., Nov. 4, 1954; d. Daniel Theodore and Theresa Ella (Koppleman) Zilm; 1 child, Steven Michael. AAS in Nursing, Waubonsee Community Coll., 1985; BSN, Aurora U., 1990; MSN, U. Tex., San Antonio, 1995—. RN, Ill., Tex., Calif. Staff nurse MICU St. Mary's Hosp., Kankakee, Ill., 1982-83; staff nurse Sunnyhill Nursing Home, Joliet, Ill., 1983-85; staff, charge nurse ICU Morris Hosp., 1985-86; clinician II Louis A. Weiss Meml. Hosp., Chgo., 1986-90; commd. capt. USAF, 1990; nurse anesthetist 75th Med. Ops. Group, Hill AFB, Utah. Mem. AACN, Am. Assn. Nurse Anesthetists, Phi Theta Kappa, Alpha Chi, Sigma Theta Tau. Home: 875 E Maple St Ogden UT 84403-1923

HUSTON, KENT ALLEN, rheumatologist; b. Wichita, Kans., May 14, 1944; s. George W. and Elizabeth (Nordyke) H.; m. Janet Kay Heims, June 12, 1968 (div. 1985); children: Kent K., Heather J., Elizabeth K.; m. Susan Jolene Held, Dec. 2, 1990; 1 child, Boris H. BA, U. Kans, lawrence, 1966; MD, U. Kans, Kansas City, 1970. Diplomate Am. Bd. Internal Medicine and Rheumatology. Intern Wesley Med. Ctr., Wichita, 1970-71; resident in internal medicine Mayo Clinic, Rochester, Minn., 1971-75, fellow in rheumatology, 1975-77; pres. Mid-Am. Med. Cons., Kansas City, Mo., 1977-91, Ctr. Rheumatic Disease, Kansas City, 1991—; preceptor U. Kans. Sch. Medicine, 1978—; clin. assoc. prof. U. Mo.-Kansas City Med. Sch., 1982—; mem. organizing com. Mid-Am. Rehab. Hosp.; dir. Mo. State Regional Arthritis Ctr., 1988—. Contbr. to profl. publs. Bd. dirs. Western Mo. chpt. Arthritis Found., 1980-90, chmn. med. and sci. com., 1984-87; mem. Mo. Arthritis Adv. Bd., Jefferson City, 1984—. Capt. USAF, 1971-73. Fellow ACP; mem. AMA, Am. Soc. Internal Medicine, Am. Coll. Rheumatology, Southwest Clin. Soc., Kansas City Met. Med. Soc., Kansas City Rheumatism Soc. (pres. 1991—). Office: Ctr Rheumatic Disease 4330 Wornall Rd Kansas City MO 64111-3201

HUTCHENS, TYRA THORNTON, physician, educator; b. Newberg, Oreg., Nov. 29, 1921; s. Fred George and Bessie (Adams) H.; m. Betty Lou Gardner, June 7, 1942; children: Tyra Richard, Robert Jay, Rebecca (Mrs. Mark Pearsall). BS, U. Oreg., 1943, MD, 1945. Diplomate: Am. Bd. Pathology, Am. Bd. Nuclear Medicine. Intern Minn. Gen. Hosp., Mpls., 1945-46; AEC postdoctoral research fellow Reed Coll., Med. Sch. U. Oreg., 1948-50; NIH postdoctoral research fellow Med. Sch. U. Oreg., 1951-53; mem. faculty Oreg. Health Scis. U., 1953—, prof., chmn. dept. clin. pathology, 1962-87, prof. emeritus, 1987—, prof. radiotherapy, 1963-71, allied health edn. coordinator, 1969-77; vis. lectr. radiobiology Reed Coll., 1955, 56. Mem. adv. bd. Oreg. Regional Med. Program, 1968-75; mem. statuatory radiation adv. com. Oreg. Bd. Health, 1957-69, chmn., 1967-69; founding trustee Am. Bd. Nuclear Medicine, 1971-77, 82-84, sec., 1973-75, 84-85 ; voting rep. Am. Bd. Med. Specialties, 1973-78, chmn. com. long range planning, 1976-78; mem. sci. adv. bd. Armed Forces Inst. Pathology, 1978-83; chmn. Portland Com. on Fgn. Affairs, 1990-91. Lt. (j.g.) M.C., USNR, 1946-48. Charter mem. Acad. Clin. Lab. Physicians and Scientists, Soc. Nuclear Medicine (de Hevesey Nuclear Medicine Pioneer award 1995), Am. Coll. Nuclear Physicians; mem. Oreg. Pathologists Assn. (pres. 1968), Pacific N.W. Soc. Nuclear Medicine (pres. 1958), AMA, Coll. Am. Pathologists (bd. govs. 1967-74, pres. 1977-79, chmn. commn. on internat. affairs 1979-83, chmn. planning com. 1987 World Congress Pathology), Am. Soc. Clin. Pathologists (bd. registry med. technologists 1967-71), World Assn. of Socs. of Pathology (bur. of pathology 1981-87, 89-93, v.p. 1985-87, pres. 1989-91, chmn. commn. on world stds. 1981-86, Gold Headed Cane award 1995), World Pathology Found. (pres. 1987-89, trustee 1989-91), Assn. Clin. Pathologists (hon.), Italian Soc. Lab. Medicine (hon.), Phi Beta Kappa, Sigma Xi, Alpha Omega Alpha. Home: 15385 SW Petrel Ln Beaverton OR 97007-8182 Office: Oreg Health Scis U 3181 SW Sam Jackson Park Rd Portland OR 97201-3011

HUTCHERSON, KAREN FULGHUM, healthcare consultant; b. Winston-Salem, N.C., Oct. 1, 1951; d. John Fulghum and Viola Sprinkle Shaw; m. Victor J. Hutcherson, Dec. 18, 1970; children: Shannon Renae, Ashley Michelle. Diploma, N.C. Bapt. Hosp. Sch. Nursing, 1972; BSN, N.C. A&T State U., 1981; MBA, Wake Forest U., 1990. RN. Staff nurse N.C. Bapt. Hosp., Winston-Salem, 1972; oncology nurse clinician Cancer Ctr., Wake Forest U., Winston-Salem, 1972-81; oncology nurse educator Bowman Gray Sch. of Med., Wake Forest U., Winston-Salem, 1981-87, dir. nursing cancer ctr., 1982-87; asst. dir. clin. support svcs. Bowman Gray Sch. Medicine, Winston-Salem, 1987-96; cons. healthcare and orgnl. devel. Hayes Consulting and Tng. Group, Inc., Winston-Salem, 1996—; curriculum coord., primary inst. Cancer Ctr., 1980-87; mem. spkrs. bur. A.H. Robbins Pharms. Co., 1983-88; cons. S.E. Cancer Control Consortium, Winston-Salem, 1987-90. Author: Patient Education in Understanding Cancer: An Introductory Handbook, 1986; co-author: Understanding Cancer Treatment: A Guide for You and Your Family, 1988, Cancer Chemotherapy Guidelines, 5th edit., 1985. Chmn. western div. nursing com. N.C. Am. Cancer Soc., 1981-82, speakers' bur., 1982, bd. dirs. 1988-92.; mem. spl. rev. com. clin. community oncology program Nat. Cancer Inst., Bethesda, Md., 1987. Recipient Leadership award Babcock Grad. Sch. Mgmt., Wake Forest U., 1992. Mem. ANA, Am. Acad. Ambulatory Nursing Adminstrn., Med. Ctr. Nursing Assn., Piedmont Oncology Assn. (numerous coms.), Oncology Nursing Soc. (mem. com.), Nat. League for Nursing, Am. Orgn. Nursing Execs., Med. Group Mgmt. Assn., S.E. Cancer Control Consortium, N.C. Nurses Assn. (legis. com. 1989, vice chmn. commun. health coun., del. conv. 1987, 88, 89, 90, 91), Sigma Theta Tau. Home: 754 Lacock Ave Rural Hall NC 27045-9742 Office: Hayes Cons & Training Group Inc Ste 301 4400 Silas Creek Pkwy Winston-Salem NC 27104

HUTCHESON, ELDRIDGE TILMON, III, laboratory administrator; b. Atlanta, Tex., Dec. 23, 1942; s. Eldridge Tilmon Hutcheson and Maree (Walls) Proctor; m. Janet Faye Shope, Jan. 22, 1966 (div. 1982); 1 child, Kelly; m. Jennie Etta Mitchell, Aug. 23, 1987. BS in Chemistry, S.W. Tex. State Coll., 1966, MA in Chemistry, 1968; PhD in Chemistry, U. Tex., 1971. Diplomate Am. Bd. Clin. Chemistry. Sr. researcher Flow Labs., Rockville, Md., 1971-72; asst. prof. biochemistry Sch. Health Sci., U. Tenn., Memphis, 1972-75; chief biochemistry VA Med. Ctr., Salem, Va., 1975-82; pres. Biolabs, Roanoke, Va., 1982-91; tech. dir. Nat. Health Labs. (name now LabCorp), San Antonio, 1991-93; supr. clin. chemistry Tex. Dept. Health, Austin, 1994—. Office: Tex Dept Health 1100 W 49th St Austin TX 78756-3101

HUTCHINS, KAREN LESLIE, psychotherapist; b. Denver, Sept. 9, 1943; d. Kimball Frederick and Bonnie Illa (Small) H.; divorced; 1 child, Alec Klinghoffer. BA, U. Denver, 1965; MA, George Washington U., 1972. Lic. profl. counselor clin. hypnotherapist; cert. clin. hypnotherapist; cert. chem. dependency specialist; registered sex offender treatment provider. Tchr. Washington D.C. Sch., 1966-70; asst. housing adminstr. George Washington U., Washington, 1970-72; counselor/instr. No. Va. C.C., Annandale, Va., 1972-77, Austin (Tex.) C.C., 1977-80; co-owner Hearts Day Care, Austin, 1980-81; supr./therapist MaryLee Resdl. Treatment, Austin, 1981-82; child protective svc. worker Dept. Human Resources, Austin, 1982-84; probation officer Adult Probation Travis County, Austin, 1984-90; lead therapist Cottonwood Treatment Ctrs., Bastrop, Tex., 1990-91; psychotherapist Austin, 1991—. Author conf. presentation: Beyond Survival, 1990-92, Why Me? vs. Spirtuality, 1993, Integrating the Wounded Soul, 1994, Ritually Abused Children, 1994, Recognizing PTSD Symptoms in Children, 1996. Vol. trainer Hotline, Austin, 1993—. Mem. ACA, Internat. Soc. Trauma and Stress Studies, Tex. Assn. Alcoholism and Drug Abuse Counselors. Democrat. Jewish. Office: Cicada Recovery Svcs 3004 S 1st St Austin TX 78704-6373

HUTCHINS, KENNETH RAYMOND, urologist; b. Highland Park, Mich., Jan. 13, 1938; s. Sherwood Warren and Dorothy Ida (Bez) H.; m. Marcia Lynne Hutchins, Mar. 12, 960; children: Heidi, Kelly, Kristin, Kenneth, Scott, Eric, Becky, Brett. BS, Alma Coll., 1960; MD, U. Mich., 1963. Diplomate Am. Bd. Urology. Intern U.S. Naval Hosp., Bethesda, Md., 1963-64; commd. ensign USN, 1963, advanced through grades to lt. comdr., 1967, ret., 1972; urologist Nalle Clinic, Charlotte, N.C., 1972—. Fellow ACS; mem. N.C. Med. Soc., Mecklenburg County Med. Soc., N.C. chpt. ACS. Home: 4704 Titleist Dr Charlotte NC 28277 Office: Nalle Clinic 1918 Randolph Rd Charlotte NC 28277

HUTCHINSON, HARRY F., retired physician; b. Asbury Park, N.J., Oct. 16, 1919; s. Harry Louis and Nellie Eames (Bowne) H.; m. Catherine May Briggs, Nov. 27, 1947; children: H. Brian, Dean L., Mark B., Kurt B. BS in Biology, Rutgers U., 1942; MD, Hahnemann U., 1945. Diplomate Am. Bd. Ob-Gyn. Intern. Fitkin Hosp., Jersey Shore Med. Ctr., 1946; assoc. attending Pt. Pleasant (N.J.) Gen. Hosp., 1948-50, 52; asst. attending Obs-Gyn dept. Fitkin Hosp, 1948-50; resident City Hosp., Akron, Ohio, 1950-51, Shreveport (La.) Charity Hosp., 1951-52; full attending Obs-Gyn, 1960; dir. dept. Obs-Gyn Jersey Shore Med. Ctr., 1972-76; emeritus Obs-Gyn Jersey Shore Med. Ctr., 1985. Contbr. articles to profl. jours. Mem. Am. Cancer Soc., Allenhurst, N.J., 1965-85. Capt. Med. Corp, 1946-48. Fellow ACS (emeritus 1986), Am. Coll. Obs-Gyn (life mem. 1958—); mem. Am. Coll. Obs-Gyn. Republican. Home: 213 Bayside Dr Venice FL 34285-1414

HUTCHINSON, JAMES RICHARD, pharmacist; b. Davenport, Iowa, Oct. 28, 1936; s. Carroll John and Kathryn I. (Dahly) H.; m. Carol Mae Weber, Oct. 29, 1960; children: Christine D., Cheryll A., Gregory J., Cathleen M., Geoffrey J. BS in Pharmacy, U. Iowa, 1959. Registered pharmacist. Pharmacist Ford Hopkins Co., Chgo., 1959-60, 62-65; pharmacist Skouland Pharmacy, Fox River Grove, Ill., 1965-70; pharmacist, owner Algonquin Pharmacy, Algonquin, Ill., 1970-93; pharmacy mgr. Eagle Foods, Algonquin, Ill., 1993-95, Albertson's, Sarasota, Fla., 1996—; mem. Family Drug Ctr. Adv. Bd., Melrose Park, Ill, 1976-82; chmn. bd. Midwest Family Drug Ctr. Assn., Melrose Park, 1982-85. Pres. Algonquin Bus. Assn., 1973-74; chmn. Econ. Devel. Commn., Village of Algonquin, 1981-84. With U.S. Army, 1960-62. Recipient Meritorious Svc. award Family Drug Ctr., Melrose Park, 1985. Mem. Nat. Assn. Retail Druggists, Lions (pres. Algonquin chpt. 1977-78, cabinet officer Lions Club Internat. Dist. 1-J 1978-94, Multiple Dist. 1 state chmn. Lions Club Internat. 1983-89. Dist. Gov. Dist. 1-J 1991-92, Melvin Jones fellow Lions Clubs Internat. Found. 1988, Ext. award Lions Club Internat. 1988, Internat. Pres. Leadership award 1989, Internat. Pres. award 1990, Internat. Pres. Cert. Appreciation Lions Club Internat. 1981, 88), Moose (charter gov. Algonquin chpt. 1974-75). Roman Catholic. Home: 410 Lake of the Woods Dr Venice FL 34293-9679

HUTCHISON, LOYAL DWAYNE, pharmacist; b. Stockton, Calif., Jan. 3, 1933; s. Lester and Muriel (Van Nortwick) H.; m. Jean E. McColl, Jan. 26, 1961; children: Michael, Donald. BS in Pharmacy, U. Pacific, 1966. Pharmacist Fifth St. Pharmacy, Stockton, 1966-76, prin., 1976—; prin. Hutchison Pharmacies Inc., Stockton, 1976—, McKinley Pharmacy, Stockton, 1976—, Lathrop (Calif.) Pharmacy, 1976—. Served with U.S. Army, 1957-59. Fellow Am. Coll. Apothecary; mem. Calif. Pharmacists Assn. (Pac Silver Circle), Am. Pharmacists Assn. Home: PO Box 1737 Stockton CA 95201-1737 Office: Hutchison Pharmacies Inc 1839 S El Dorado St Stockton CA 95206-2025

HUTTENLOCHER, PETER RICHARD, child neurologist; b. Lahnstein, Germany, Feb. 23, 1931; came to U.S., 1948; s. Richard E. and Else (Lamparter) H.; m. Janellen Burns, June 13, 1954; children: Daniel, Anna, Carl. BA summa cum laude, U. Buffalo, 1953; MD magna cum laude, Harvard U., 1957. Diplomate Am. Bd. Pediats., Am. Bd. Neurology and Psychiatry. Intern in medicine Peter Bent Brigham Hosp., Boston, 1957-58; rsch. assoc. in neurophysiology NIH, 1958-60; jr. resident in pediats. Children's Med. Ctr., Boston, 1960-61; jr. resident in neurology Mass. Gen. Hosp., Boston, 1961-62, resident in pediat. neurology, 1962-63, fellow in neuropathology, 1963-64; instr. in pediat. neurology Harvard Med. Sch. and Mass. Gen. Hosp., Boston, 1964-66; attending pediatrician Yale-New Haven Hosp., Mass., 1964-74; asst. prof. pediat. neurology Yale U. Med. Sch., 1966-68; assoc. prof. pediats. and neurology Yale U. Sch. Medicine, Cambridge, Mass., 1968-74; prof. pediats. U. Chgo., 1974-76; chief pediat. neurology svc. Wyler Children's Hosp., U. Chgo. Hosps. and Clinics, Chgo., 1974—; prof. pediats. and neurology, mem. com. neurobiology U. Chgo., 1976—; mem. neuroscis. and behavioral scis. study sect. DRG, NIH, 1983-85; chmn. human devel. and aging study sect. III, NIH, 1990-92; mem. awards com. John Merck Scholars Program, 1990—; mem. faculty awards com. U. Chgo., 1991—. Mem. editl. bd. Neuropediats., 1981—, Pediat. Neurology, 1981-91; contbr. numerous articles to profl. jours. Trustee Easter Seal Rsch. Found., 1978-84; med. adv. bd. Nat. Tuberous Sclerosis Assn., 1985—. With USPHS, 1958-66. Recipient Brenneman award Chgo. Pediat. Soc., 1990; Philip R. Dodge lectr. Washington U., 1992, John Barlow lectr. Mass. Gen. Hosp., 1993. Mem. Am. Acad. Neurology (chmn. program com., pediat. neurology sect. 1990, 91), Am. Neurol. Assn., Soc. for Neurosci., Am. Pediat. Soc., Child Neurology Soc. (Hower award for rsch. relevant to pediat. neurology 1984, councillor 1981-93), Chgo. Neurol. Soc. (pres. 1988-89), Internat. Brain Rsch. Orgn. Office: U of Chgo Pritzker Sch of Medicine 5841 S Maryland Ave Chicago IL 60637-1463

HUTTER, ADOLPH MATTHEW, JR., cardiologist, educator; b. Fond du Lac, Wis., Feb. 22, 1937; s. Adolph Matthew and Janet (Kay) H.; m. Sylvia H. Murray, June 18, 1960; children: Janice Marie, Adolph Joseph, Elizabeth Kay, Matthew Murray, Jonathan James. BS summa cum laude, Georgetown U., 1959; MD, U. Wis., 1963. Diplomate Am. Bd. Internal Medicine, Am. Bd. Cardiovascular Diseases; lic. physician, Mass. Med. intern Strong Meml. Hosp., Rochester, N.Y., 1963-64; clin. assoc. Nat. Cancer Inst., Bethesda, Md., 1964-66; asst. resident Strong Meml. Hosp., 1966-67, assoc. resident, 1967-68; fellow in medicine (oncology) Georgetown U. Sch. Medicine, Washington, 1965-66; clin. and rsch. fellow in cardiology Mass. Gen. Hosp., Boston, 1968-70; instr. medicine Harvard U. Med. Sch., Boston, 1970-72, asst. prof., 1972-76, assoc. prof., 1976—; vis. prof. 70 univs. and med. ctrs., 1979-96; asst. in medicine Mass. Gen. Hosp., 1970-72, asst. physician, 1972-76, assoc., 1976-84, physician, 1984—, assoc. dir. CCU, 1970-81, dir., 1981-86, chmn. med. intensive care coord. com., 1986—; cardiologist Boston Bruins hockey team, 1972—, New Eng. Patriots football team, 1982—. Contbr. over 100 articles to med. jours. Recipient Howard H. Blakeslee award Am. Heart Assn., 1974. Fellow ACP, Coun. on Clin. Cardiology of Am. Heart Assn. (mem. com. on postgrad. edn. 1972-75, mem. com. on sci. sessions program 1973-75, mem. sci. sessions com. 1979-81, vice chmn. com. on cardiovasc. disease of elderly 1987-89), Am. Coll. Cardiology (chmn. 1987-90, v.p. 1990-91, pres. 1992-93, past pres. 1993-94, mem. program com. on sci. sessions 1975-76, mem. credentials com. 1976-83, chmn. 1981-83, asst. sec. 1981-82, sec. 1984-85, mem. long-range planning com. 1981-83, mem. ACCEL com. 1982-90, mem. ACCEL edn. bd. 1987-90, 93—, mem. strategic planning com. 1988-92, mem. exec. com. 1990-94, trustee 1981-85, 87-95, chmn. govt. rels. com. 1984-90, chmn. chpt. rels. com. 1993—, mem. chmn. award com. 1993-95), European Soc. Cardiology, AAAS; mem. Am. Clin. and Climatol. Assn., U. Wis. Med. Alumni Assn., Mass. Med. Soc., Alpha Omega Alpha. Roman Catholic. Office: Mass Gen Hosp Ambulatory Care Ctr 15 Parkman St Ste 467 Boston MA 02114-3117

HUTTER, JOHN JOSEPH, JR., pediatric hematologist and oncologist, educator; b. Queens, N.Y., Jan. 26, 1943; s. John Joseph and Dorothy (Bey) H.; m. Maureen J. Lynch, June 17, 1967; children: Catherine, Carolyn. BS in Biology with honors, Manhattan Coll., Riverdale, N.Y., 1963; MD magna cum laude, SUNY, Bklyn., 1967. Diplomate Am. Bd. Pediatrics, sub-bds. hematology and oncology; lic. physician, Calif., Colo., Ariz. Intern, resident in pediatrics Stanford U. Med. Ctr., Palo Alto, Calif., 1967-69; resident in pediatrics U. Colo. Med. Ctr., Denver, 1969-70, NIH trainee in pediatric hematology, 1972-73, instr. pediatrics, 1973-76; assoc. dir. oncology ctr. Children's Hosp., Denver, 1973-76; from asst. prof. to prof. pediatrics U. Ariz. Health Scis. Ctr., Tucson, 1976—, dir. pediatric clin. oncology, 1976—, chief sect. pediatric hematology/oncology, 1991—, dir. Mountain States Regional Hemophilia Ctr., 1990—. Contbr. chpts. to textbooks, articles to profl. jours.; author revs. Trustee Ronald McDonald House, 1979-87, v.p., 1981-83; mem. Tucson Emergency Svcs. Coordinating Coun., 1982-85; trustee Am. Cancer Soc., 1984-85; mem. Angel Charity for Children, 1984—; mem. adv. bd. Children-to-Children, 1991—. Fellow Am. Acad. Pediatrics; mem. Am. Soc. Hematology, Am. Soc. Clin. Oncology, Am. Soc. Pediatric Hematology/Oncology, Am. Acad. Home Care Physicians, Hemophilia Rsch. Soc., We. Soc. for Pediatric Rsch., Alpha Omega Alpha. Home: 5770 N Camino Real Tucson AZ 85718-4214 Office: U Ariz Dept Pediatrics 1501 N Campbell Ave Tucson AZ 85724-0001

HUTTON, JOHN EVANS, JR., surgery educator, retired military officer; b. N.Y.C., Sept. 9, 1931; s. John Evans and Antoinette (Abbott) H.; m. Barbara Seward Joyce, Apr. 15, 1961; children: John III, Wendy, James, Elizabeth. BA, Wesleyan U., 1953; MD, George Washington U., 1963. Diplomate: Am. Bd. Surgery, Am. Bd. Med. Examiners. Commd. 2d lt. USMC, 1953, advanced through grades to capt., 1962; discharged USMCR; commd. capt. U.S. Army, 1963, advanced through grades to brig. gen., 1989; intern, resident in gen. surgery Walter Reed Army Med. Ctr. U.S. Army, Washington, 1963-68, fellow vascular surgery, 1969-70, asst. chief vascular surgery, 1970-71, mem. staff gen. surgery svcs., 1969-71, chief dept. surgery, 1981-84, White House physician, 1984-86, physician to the Pres., 1987-89; chief surgeon 91st Evacuation Hosp. U.S. Army, Vietnam, 1968-69, chief vascular surgery, asst. chief gen. surgery, 1971-74; chief gen. and vascular surgery, program dir., gen. surgery residency Letterman Army Med. Ctr. U.S. Army, San Francisco, 1975-80; comdr. 47th Field Hosp., Honduras, 1984; commanding gen. Madigan Army Med. Ctr. U.S. Army, Tacoma, Wash., 1989-92; ret., 1992; prof. clinical surgery, chief div. gen. surgery, dept. surg. Uniformed Svcs. U. Health Scis., Bethesda, Md., 1992—, mem. faculty senate, 1996—; assoc. clin. prof. surgery U. Calif., San Francisco, 1978-81; assoc. prof. surgery, vice chmn. dept. surgery Uniformed Svcs. U. Health Scis., Bethesda, 1981-84, prof. clin. surgery, 1985—; clin. prof. surgery Tulane U. Sch. Medicine, 1988—, George Washington Sch. Medicine, Washington, 1985—. Contbr. articles, photographs to profl. publs. Mem. men and boys choir Grace Cathedral, San Francisco, 1971-75. Decorated D.S.M., Bronze Star, Meritorious Svcs. medal with oak leaf cluster, Army commendation medal, Navy Commendation medal, Joint Svc. Commendation medal, Vietnam Honor medal 1st class, Vietnam Cross of Gallantry; recipient Barron Dominique Larrey award for excellence in surgery; named to Mil. Order of Med. Merit, 1982; named Prominent Alumnus, George Washington U., 1990. Fellow ACS; mem. Internat. Cardiovascular Soc., Soc. Clin. Vascular Surgery, Am. Assn. for the Surgery of Trauma, Soc. Mil. Vascular Surgery, Chesapeake Vascular Soc., Bay Surg. Soc. (hon.), U.S. Naval Acad. Sailing Squadron, St. Francis Yacht Club (membership com. 1978-81). Republican. Episcopalian. Home: 1707 Priscilla Dr Silver Spring MD 20904-1610 Office: Uniformed Svcs U Health Scis Dept Surgery 4301 Jones Bridge Rd Bethesda MD 20814-4712

HUTTON, JOHN JAMES, medical researcher, medical educator; b. Ashland, Ky., July 24, 1936; s. John James and Alice (Virgin) H.; m. Mary Labach, June 13, 1964; children: Becky, John, Elizabeth. AB, Harvard U., 1958, MD, 1964. Diplomate Am. Bd. Internal Medicine. Sect. chief Roche Inst., Nutley, N.J., 1968-71; prof. medicine U. Ky., Lexington, 1971-79, U. Tex., San Antonio, 1980-84; prof. pediatrics U. Cin., 1984-87, dean Coll. Medicine, 1987—. Editor Internal Medicine, 1983; contbr. articles to profl.

jours. Mem. Am. Soc. Hematology, Assn. Am. Physicians, Am. Soc. Clin. Investigation, NIH (biochemistry study sect.). Office: U Cin Coll of Medicine PO Box 670555 Cincinnati OH 45267-0555

HUTTON, M. JOAN, health facility administrator; b. Windsor, Ont., Can., May 27, 1941; came to U.S., 1964; d. John William and Jeanetta Eleanor (Touscany) Spray; m. Clifton J. Hutton, Oct. 12, 1964 (div. Aug. 1971); 1 child, J. Scott; m. Danny Goldstein, Apr. 12, 1981. Dipl. nursing, St. Joseph Sch. Nursing, Windsor, 1963, U. Windsor, 1964; BA, Marygrove Coll., Detroit, 1973. RN; cert. pers. cons. Clin. instr. Harper Hosp. Sch. Nursing, Detroit, 1964-68, St. Joseph Hosp., Windsor, 1968-69; supr., nurse Children's Hosp., Detroit, 1970-74; dir. ins. edn. Columbia Med. Hosp., Detroit, 1974-75; dir. nursing Renaissance Continuing Care Ctr., Detroit, 1975-76; dir. nursing, COO Park Cmty. Hosp., Detroit, 1976-77; sr. v.p. Harper Assocs., Farmington Hills, Mich., 1977-90; pres., CEO The Hutton Group Inc., Vero Beach, Fla., 1991—; chair curriculum adv. com. Baker Coll., Flint, Mich., 1987-90, Ferris State U., Big Rapids, Mich. Creator, educator Jobs Career Tng., Vero Beach, 1995—. Mem. Nat. Assn. Healthcare Quality (chair task force 1990-91), Fla. Assn. Healthcare Quality (del. 1993, 94, 95). Roman Catholic. Office: The Hutton Group Inc 3675 20th St Ste F Vero Beach FL 32960

HUVOS, ANDREW, internist, cardiologist, educator; b. Budapest, Hungary, Apr. 23, 1930; came to U.S., 1950; s. Julian Gyula and Magdolna (Matyas) H.; m. Monique Chatriot, June 8, 1959; children: Christine, Anne, Philip. Student, Free U. Brussels, 1948-50, Harvard U., 1951; MD, Boston U., 1955. Diplomate Am. Bd. Internal Medicine, Am. Bd. Cardiovascular Disease. Resident in medicine Yale-New Haven Med. Ctr., 1955-59; fellow in cardiology Mass. Gen. Hosp., Boston, 1961-63; physician-in-charge cardiac catheterization lab. Univ. Hosp., Boston, 1963-70; chief cardiology Faulkner Hosp., Boston, 1970-74, chief medicine, 1974—; lectr. medicine Harvard Med. Sch., Boston, 1974-86; lectr. medicine and physiology Boston U. Sch. Medicine, 1976—; prof. medicine Tufts U. Sch. Medicine, Boston, 1985—; dir. Tufts Assoc. Health Plan, 1979-81. Contbr. articles to med. jours., chpts. to books. Chmn. bd. trustees Ecole Bilingue, Inc., Arlington, Mass., 1970-74; trustee Boston Med. Libr., 1981-85. Capt. M.C., U.S. Army, 1959-61. Recipient Excellence in Teaching award Boston U. Sch. Medicine, 1974; USPHS grantee, 1977-83. Fellow ACP, Am. Coll. Cardiology, Am. Coll. Chest Physicians (pres. New Eng. States chpt. 1981-83); mem. Am. Heart Assn. (fellow couns. clin. cardiology and circulation), Dorchester Med. Club, Roxbury Clin. Record Club, Alpha Omega Alpha. Presbyterian. Office: Faulkner Hosp Boston MA 02130

HUVOS, CHRISTOPHER L., psychologist; b. Budapest, Hungary, June 18, 1946; came to U.S., 1956; s. Kornel and Anna Maria (Ledniczky) H.; m. Sally Brewster Moulton, Aug. 7, 1982; 1 child, Emma Brewster Moulton Huvos. AB, Harvard U., 1968, MAT, 1972; PsyD, Mass. Sch. Profl. Psychology, 1983. Lic. psychologist. Mental health assoc. VA, Boston, 1979-80; psychologist Milton (Mass.) Acad., 1981-85; prin. psychologist Met. State Hosp., Waltham, Mass., 1985-88, chief psychologist, 1988-92; pvt. practice Arlington, Mass., 1983—; inst., dept. psychiatry Harvard Med. Sch., Boston and Cambridge, 1986—; psychologist Westborough State Hosp., 1992-95; Tewksbury Hosp., 1995—; trustee Mass. Sch. Profl. Psychology, Dedham, 1986—. Editor: Mass. Psychol. Assn. Newsletter, 1984-89. Fellow Mass. Psychol. Assn. (bd. dirs. 1987-89); mem. Am. Psychol. Assn. Office: 94 Pleasant St Arlington MA 02174-6535

HUXLEY, SIR ANDREW (FIELDING), physiologist, educator; b. London, Nov. 22, 1917; s. Leonard and Rosalind (Bruce) H.; m. Jocelyn Richenda Gammell Pease, July 5, 1947; children: Janet Rachel, Stewart Leonard, Camilla Rosalind, Eleanor Bruce, Henrietta Catherine, Clare Marjory Pease. BA, Cambridge (Eng.) U., 1938, MA, 1941, ScD (hon.), 1978; MD (hon.), U. Saar, 1964; D.Sc. (hon.), U. Sheffield, Eng., 1964, U. Leicester, Eng., 1967, London U., 1973, U. St. Andrews, Scotland, 1974, U. Aston, Birmingham, Eng., 1977; LL.D. (hon.), U. Birmingham, 1979, Marseille U., 1979, York U., 1981, U. Western Australia, 1982, NYU, 1982, Oxford U., 1983, U. Pa., 1984, Dundee U., 1984, Harvard U., 1984, U. Keele, 1985, East Anglia U., 1985, Humboldt U., East Berlin, 1985, Md. U., 1987, Brunel U., 1988, U. Hyderabad, 1991, Glasgow U., 1993, Ulm U., 1993. Mem. research staff Anti-Aircraft Command, 1940-42, Admiralty, 1942-45; fellow Trinity Coll. Cambridge, Cambridge, 1941-60, 90—; hon. fellow Trinity Coll., Cambridge, 1967-90, master, 1984-90, dir. studies, 1952-60; demonstrator Cambridge U., 1946-50, asst. dir. research, 1951-59, reader exptl. biophysics, 1959-60; Jodrell prof. physiology U. Coll. London, 1960-69, Royal Soc. research prof., 1969-83, hon. fellow, 1980; emeritus prof. physiology U. London, 1983—; Herter lectr. Johns Hopkins U., 1959; Jesup lectr. Columbia U., 1964; Forbes lectr., 1966; Croonian lectr. Royal Soc., 1967, Florey lectr., 1982, Blackett Meml. lectr., 1984; Fullerian prof. Royal Inst., London, 1967-73; Hans Hecht lectr., Chgo., 1975; Sherrington lectr. Liverpool U., 1976-77; Centenary Colloquium lectr. Berlin Inst. Physiology, 1977; Cecil H. and Ida Green vis. prof. U. B.C., 1980; 6th annual Darwin Lecture, 1982, Romanes Lecture, Oxford U., 1983; Tarner lectrs. Trinity Coll., Cambridge, 1988; Maulana Abul Kalam Azad Meml. Lecture, New Delhi, 1991; C.G. Bernhard lecture, Stockholm, 1993. Author: Reflections on Muscle, 1980; editor: Jour. Physiology, 1950-57, chmn. bd. Publs. on analysis of nerve conduction (with Hodgkin), physiology of striated muscle, devel. of interference microscope and ultramicrotome. Trustee Brit. Mus. (Natural History), 1981-90, Sci. Mus., 1984-88. Created knight bachelor, 1974; decorated Order of Merit, 1983; recipient (with A.L. Hodgkin and J.C. Eccles) Nobel prize for physiology or medicine, 1963; Imperial Coll. Sci. and Tech. hon. fellow, 1980; Queen Mary and Westfield Coll. fellow, 1987. Fellow Royal Soc. (Copley medal 1973, council 1960-62, 77-79, 80-85, pres. 1980-85), Royal Acad. Engring. (hon.), Inst. Biology (hon.), Royal Soc. Can. (hon.), Royal Soc. Edinburgh (hon.), Indian Nat. Sci. Acad. (fgn.); mem. Physiol. Soc. (hon., rev. lectr. on muscular contraction 1973), Internat. Union Physiol. Scis. (pres. 1986-93), Brit. Biophys. Soc., Royal Acad. Scis., Letters and Fine Arts Belgium (assoc.), Muscular Dystrophy Group Gt. Britain and No. Ireland (chmn. med. research com. 1974-81, v.p., 1981—), Royal Instn. Gt. Britain (hon.), Anat. Soc. Gt. Britain and Ireland (hon.), Am. Philos. Soc., Brit. Assn. Advancement Sci. (pres. 1976-77), NAS (U.S.) (fgn. assoc.), Royal Acad. Medicine Belgium (assoc.), Dutch Soc. Scis. (fgn.), Am. Soc. Zoologists (hon.), Royal Irish Acad. (hon.), Japan Acad. (hon.), Nature Conservancy (coun. 1985-88). Home and Office: Manor Field, 1 Vicarage Dr Grantchester, Cambridge CB3 9NG, England*

HUXLEY, HUGH ESMOR, molecular biologist, educator; b. Birkenhead, Eng., Feb. 25, 1924; s. Thomas Hugh and Olwen (Roberts) H. BA, Christ's Coll., Cambridge (Eng.) U., 1948, MA, 1950, PhD, 1952, ScD, 1964; DSc (hon.), Harvard U., 1969, U. Chgo., 1974, U. Pa., 1975, U. Leicester, 1989. Rsch. student molecular biology unit Med. Rsch. Coun., Cavendish Lab., Cambridge, 1948-52, sci. staff, 1954-55; external staff, Med. Rsch. Coun., dept. biophysics U. Coll., London, 1956-61, Med. Rsch. Coun. Lab. Molecular Biology, Cambridge, 1962-87, dep. dir., 1977-87; Commonwealth fund fellow dept. biology Mass. Inst. Tech., Boston, 1952-54; fellow Christ's Coll., Cambridge U., 1954-56, hon. fellow, 1981, fellow King's Coll., 1961-67, fellow Churchill Coll., 1967-87; prof. biology Rosensteil Basic Med. Scis. Rsch. Ctr., Brandeis U., Waltham, Mass., 1987—, dir., 1988-94. Radar rsch. officer RAF, 1943-47. Decorated mem. Order Brit. Empire, 1948; recipient Feldberg prize, 1963, Hardy prize, 1965, Louisa Gross Hurwitz prize, 1971, Internat. Feltrinelli prize, 1974, Gairdner award, 1975, Baly medal Royal Coll. Physicians, 1975, Royal medal Royal Soc. London, 1977, E.B. Wilson medal Am. Soc. Cell Biology, 1983, Albert Einstein award World Cultural Council, 1987, Franklin medal, 1990, Disting. Scientist award Electron Microscopy Soc. Am., 1991. Fellow Royal Soc., 1960; mem. Physiol. Soc., Brit. Biophys. Soc., European Molecular Biology Orgn.; hon. fgn. mem. Am. Acad. Arts and Scis., Danish Acad. Scis., Leopoldina Acad., NAS (hon. fgn. assoc.). Editor: Progress in Biophysics and Molecular Biology, 1960-66; editorial bd. Jour. Cell Biology, 1959-63, Jour. Molecular Biology, 1962-70, 79-86, 90-93, Jour. Cell Sci., 1966-70. Research, publs. on ultrastructures of striated muscles, especially by electron-microscopy and X-ray diffraction leading to sliding filament theory of contraction (with Jean Hanson; simultaneously proposed by A.F. Huxley and R. Niedergerke), subsequently studying detailed mechanisms of motor proteins: studies on electron microscopy of viruses, ribosomes and other nucleic-acid containing structures. Home: 349 Nashawtuc Rd Concord MA 01742-1616

HUXSTER, HOWARD KNIGHT, psychiatrist; b. Balt., Dec. 25, 1924; s. Howard Leslie and May Eda (Knight) H.; m. Evelyn Rachel Intenzo, Aug. 16, 1961, (div. 1978); children: Peter Knight, Robert Hugh. Student, U. Pa., 1942-43, 46-47, various including U. Nebr., 1943-44, Drexel U., 1946-47; MD, Jefferson Med. Coll., 1952. Diplomate Am. Bd. Psychiatry and Neurology. Intern Walter Reed Army Med. Ctr., Washington, 1952-53; resident Norristown (Pa.) State Hosp., 1954-57; dir. Tri-County Mental Health Clinic, Norristown, Pa., 1958-61; psychiatric cons. Rehab. Ctr., U. Pa. Hosp., 1965-70; pvt. practice, Bala Cynwyd, Pa., 1961-70; dir. Phila. Psychoanalytic Clinic, 1970-80; pvt. practice Phila. and Newark, Del., 1970-88; psychiatrist Coatesville (Pa.) VA Med. Ctr., 1988—; cons. Bucks County Sch. Dist., 1960-70, U. Pa. Student Health Svcs., Phila., 1970-79. Fellow Am. Psychiatric Assn. (life); mem. Am. Psychoanalytic Assn., Internat. Psychoanalytical Assn., Phila. Psychoanalytic Soc. (sec. 1981-83), Phila. Psychoanalytic Inst., Del. Psychiatric Soc. Office: Media VA Outpatient Clinic 1489 Baltimore Pike Ste 107 Springfield PA 19064-3958

HUYSMAN, ARLENE WEISS, psychologist, educator; b. Phila.; d. Max and Anna (Pearlene) Weiss; BA, Shaw U., 1973; MA, Goddard Coll., 1974; Ph.D., Union Inst. Grad., 1980; m. Pedro Camacho; children: Pamela Claire, James David. Actress, dir. Dramatic Workshop, N.Y.C., 1956-68; music and drama critic and columnist Orlando (Fla.) Sentinel Star, 1966-68; psychodramatist Volusia County Guidance Center, Daytona Beach, Fla., 1966-68; free-lance journalist, 1968-70; psychodramatist Psychiat. Inst., Jackson Meml. Hosp., Miami, 1972-77, dir. Adult Day Treatment Center, 1974-77, dir. Lithium Clinic, 1976-77; psychodramatist South Fla. State Hosp., Hollywood, 1971-72; psychotherapy supr., Neurosci. program coord. Miami Heart Inst., 1984—, clin. dir. Family Workshop, 1985—, clin. dir. Adult Day Treatment Ctrs., 1987—; founder, dir. Geriatric Adult Day Treatment Ctrs.; adj. asst. prof. Med. Sch., U. Miami, 1976—; adj. prof., Union Inst., 1992—, Antioch U., 1995—; specialist in Bi Polar Disorders, U. Wis., 1980—; mem. adv. panel Fine Arts Council Fla., 1976-77; mem. Fla. Gov.'s Task Force on Marriage and the Family Unit, 1976, 89-90; vol. Rec. for Blind, 1974—. Recipient Best Dirs. award and Best Actress award Fla. Theatre Festival, 1967. Mem. Am. Psychol. Assn., Fla. Psychol. Assn., Dade County Psychol. Assn. (bd. dirs.), Mental Health Assn. Dade County, Internat. Assn. Group Psychotherapy, Union Inst. Grad. Alumni Assn. (bd. dirs., southeastern rep., pres.-elect), Am. Soc. Aging, Am. Assn. Group Psychotherapy and Psychodrama, Moreno Acad., Fedn. Partial Hospitalization Study Groups, World Fedn. Mental Health, Fla. Assn. Practicing Psychologists (bd. dirs., pres.). Office: Ctr Psychol Growth 3050 Biscayne Blvd Miami FL 33137-4143

HWANG, KOU MAU, pharmaceutical executive; b. Kaoshiung, Taiwan, Sept. 5, 1940; came to U.S., 1966; s. Tien C. and Zui C. (Yu) H.; m. Sue H. Cheng, Sept. 5, 1969; children: Sandy, Carol, Nancy. BS, Kaohsiung Med. Coll., 1964; MS, Ohio State U., 1969, PhD, 1972; postgrad., Yale U., 1974. Teaching asst. Duquesne U., Pitts., 1965-66, Ohio State U., Columbus, Ohio, 1967-71; rsch. fellow Yale Med. Sch., New Haven, 1972-76; asst. prof. M.D. Anderson Hosp./Univ. Tex., Houston, 1976-77, U. So. Calif., L.A., 1977-79; sr. investigator Nat. Cancer Inst., Frederick, Md., 1980-83; sr. scientist Cetus Inc., San Francisco, 1984; sr. dir. Genelabs Inc., Redwood City, Calif., 1985-93; pres. Sintong Pharm. U.S. Inc., Hayward, Calif., 1993—; vis. prof. Rutger U., Piscataway, N.J., 1985-88; educator Internat. AIDS Confs., U.S., China, 1989; cons., lectr. Kaushiung Med. Coll., Taiwan, 1991-92. Patentee AIDS Therapy, 1989, New Therapy for Herpes Simplex, 1992; inventor in field; contbr. numerous articles to profl. jours. Cultural exch. person Taiwanese Prof. Assn., 1990—. 2nd lt. Taiwanese Army, 1964-65. Rsch. grantee Welch Found., Houston, 1977, Am. Cancer Soc., L.A., 1977-80; sml. bus. grantee U.S. Govt., San Carlo, Calif., 1987-88; recipient Nat. Drug Discovery grants NIAID, Redwood City, 1988-91. Mem. Am. Assn. Cancer Rsch., Am. Chem. Soc., AAAS, Rho Chi. Home: 220 Stanbridge Ct Danville CA 94526-2630 Office: Sintong Pharm US Inc 3401 Investment Blvd Hayward CA 94545-3801

HWANG, PETER LAM HUM, endocrinologist, educator; b. Hong Kong, May 11, 1945. B in Medicine, B in Surgery, U. Singapore, 1969; PhD, McGill U., Montreal, Can., 1973. Diplomate Am. Bd. Internal Medicine and Endocrinology. Resident in internal medicine Royal Victoria Hosp., Montreal, Can., 1975-78; fellow in endocrinology Mayo Clinic, Rochester, Minn., 1978-80; asst. prof. medicine Meml. U. Newfoundland, St. John's, 1980-83; assoc. prof. physiology Nat. U. Singapore, 1983-91, prof. physiology, 1991—, also head dept. physiology, 1984—; assoc. staff Nat. U. Hosp., Singapore, 1992—; vis. cons. Nat. U. Hosp., Singapore, 1991—, Singapore Gen. Hosp., 1995—. Mem. Endocrine Soc. Office: Nat Univ Singapore, 10 Kent Ridge Cres, Singapore 119260, Singapore

HWANG, YONG SEUNG, medical educator; b. Pusan, Korea, Oct. 27, 1950; s. Namsi Hwang and Kyuyeon Shin; m. Inryu Choi, Feb. 17, 1975; children: Pilğyu, Junğyu. MD, Seoul (Korea) Nat. U., 1975, PhD, 1983. Diplomate Korean Bd. Pediatrics. Intern Seoul Nat. U. Hosp., 1975-76, resident in pediatrics, 1976-80, instr., 1983-85, asst. prof., 1985-90, assoc. prof., 1990-95, prof. medicine, 1995—; fellow in pediatric neurology U. Minn., Mpls., 1985-87; Editor-in-chief Korean Child Neurology Assn., Seoul, 1993—. Maj. Korean Presdl. Security Forces, 1981-83. Home: 75-705 Hyundai Apt, Abgujung Dong, 135-110 Seoul Korea Office: Seoul Nat U Hosp, 28 Yongon Dong Chongrogu, 110-744 Seoul Korea

HYATT, KATHY LOUISE, cardiac, telemetry nurse; b. Asheville, N.C., Aug. 31, 1955; d. J.C. and Nelle Louise (Tessner) H. AAS in Emergency Med. Sci., Asheville-Buncombe Tech. C.C., 1984, ADN, 1993. RN, N.C.; cert. BLS, ACLS, TNCC. Charge nurse cardiac/telemetry unit Haywood County Hosp., Clyde, N.C., 1993—; staff nurse emergency rm. St. Luke's Hosp., Columbus, N.C. N.C. Nurse Program scholar N.C. State Edn. Assistance Auth., Chapel Hill, 1991-92, 92-93, All-Am. Scholar U.S. Achievement Auth., Lexington, Ky., 1993, James G.K. McClure Ednl. scholar, Fairview, N.C., 1991; recipient Nat. Collegiate Nursing award U.S. Achievement Auth., 1993. Mem. ANA, N.C. Nurses Assn. Democrat. Baptist. Home: 184 Deaver St Asheville NC 28806 Office: Haywood County Hosp 90 Hosp Dr Clyde NC 28721

HYATT, ROSEMARY JANE, community mental health nurse; b. Johnson City, N.Y., Oct. 4, 1949; d. Robert and June (Adams) Clute; m. Harold Hyatt, May 31, 1981; children: Robert, Jaime. AAS, Ulster Community Coll., Stone Ridge, N.Y., 1981; BSN, SUNY, New Paltz, 1984; MSN in Community Health Nursing, Pace U., 1987. RN, N.Y. Staff nurse Kingston (N.Y.) Hosp., 1981-84; health/nutrition coord. Ulster Community Action-Head Start, Kingston, 1984-87; community mental health nurse Ulster DDSO-Wassaic, Kingston, 1987-94; nurse administr. N.Y. State Wassaic Devel. Ctr., 1990-91; mem. Office Mental Retardation and Devel. Disabilities Nurses; PRI assessor, screener N.Y. State Mini fellowship in Aging and Devel. Disabilities. Mem. surrogate decision making com. panel for N.Y. State, 1995-96. Mem. ANA (cert. in devel. disabilities nursing), N.Y. State Nurses Assn., Sigma Theta Tau.

HYER, BETTY MARIE, medical technologist; b. Austin, Ohio, Aug. 13, 1929; d. William Taylor and Clara Elizabeth (Koch) H.ollar; m. Ralph Corliss Hyer, Oct. 29, 1947; children: Corliss, Wendell, Janice, Mitchell, Angela, Donna, Donald, Rosena, John. cert. med. technologist, Am. Med. Technologists. Med. technologist hematology, chemistry, urinalysis, blood bank banking Fayette County Meml. Hosp., Washington Court House, Ohio, 1967-96, hematology mgr., 1973-93; ret., 1996. Office: Fayette County Meml Hosp 1430 Columbus Ave Washington Court House OH 43160

HYERS, THOMAS MORGAN, physician, biomedical researcher; b. Jacksonville, Fla., June 16, 1943; s. John and Joan (Clemens) H.; m. Elizabeth Mclean, June 12, 1965; children: Justin, Adam. BS, Duke U., 1964, MD, 1968. Diplomate Am. Bd. Internal Medicine, Am. Bd. Pulmonary Diseases. Intern in medicine Cleve. Met. Gen. Hosp., 1968-69; asst. chief Nat. Blood Resource Br., Nat. Heart, Lung and Blood Inst., NIH, 1971-72, pulmonary disease adv. com., 1983-86; resident in medicine U. Wash., Seattle, 1972-74; chief resident, instr. medicine, 1974-75; fellow in pulmonary diseases U. Colo. Health Scis. Ctr., Denver, 1975-76, research fellow Cardiovascular Pulmonary Research Lab., 1976-77, asst. prof. medicine, staff physician respiratory care, assoc. investigator, 1977-82; research assoc. Denver VA Med. Ctr., 1979-82; assoc. prof. medicine, dir. div. pulmonary diseases St. Louis U. Med. Ctr., 1982-85, prof. medicine, 1985—; dir. NIH Specialized Ctr. Research in Adult Respiratory Failure, 1983—. Contbr. articles to profl. jours. Served to comdr. USPHS, 1969-71. Named hon. Ky. col. grantee NIH, Nat. Heart, Lung and Blood Inst. Fellow ACP, Am. Coll. Chest Physicians; mem. Am. Heart Assn. (mem. councils on thrombosis and cardiopulmonary disease), Internat. Soc. Thrombosis and Haemostasis, Am. Lung Assn. (Eastern Mo. chpt.), Am. Fedn. Clin. Research, Am. Physiol. Soc., Western Soc. Clin. Investigation, Am. Thoracic Soc., Phi Beta Kappa. Office: Pulmonary Div St Louis U Sch Medicine 1325 S Grand Blvd Saint Louis MO 63104

HYLE, JACK OTTO, orthomolecular psychologist; b. Allentown, Pa., Oct. 19, 1929; s. Lewis Calvin Hyle and Martha Elizabeth (Werft) Hart; m. Anna Louise LeCompte, July 29, 1950; children: Marsha, Jay, Bruce, Susan, Beth. BS in Edn., Bob Jones U., 1959; M in Edn., Temple U., 1961; PhD, Manahath Edn. Ctr., 1967; PMD, Fla. Inst. Tech., 1981. Toll switchman Bell Telephone Co., Harrisburg, Pa., 1950-56; tchr. math. Cen. Dauphin High Sch., Harrisburg, 1959-64; psychologist Narramore Found., Harrisburg, 1964-69; pvt. practice Harrisburg, 1969-89; instr. Pa. State U., 1963-64; prof. of behavioral medicine Fla. Inst. Tech., Melbourne, 1982-85. Contbr. to book, Out of Mighty Waters, 1982; pioneer Orthomolecular Procedure. Scoutmaster Boy Scouts Am., Altoona, Pa., 1947-55; commr., Harrisburg, Pa., 1960-61; Sunday sch. tchr. Grace Brethren Ch., Harrisburg, 1960-70, 89-96. Sgt. USNC, 1947-50. Recipient Hon. Trophy Boy Scouts Am., 1954; named Eagle Scout, 1946. Mem. NEA (life), Internat. Acad. Preventive Medicine, Orthomolecular Med. Soc., Occidental Inst. Rsch. Found., Inst. for the Study of Optimal Nutrition. Republican. Home: 5840 Longview Rd Harrisburg PA 17112-3130

HYLTON, STEVEN CARTER, pharmacist; b. Grundy, Va., Nov. 9, 1965; s. Samuel Wade Jr. and Anna Lee (Niswander) H. BS, East Tenn. State Univ., 1989; PharmD, Mercer U., 1996. Reg. pharmacist, med. technologist. Med. technologist Buchanan Gen. Hosp., Grundy, 1989-92, Promina-Gwinnett, Lawrenceville, Ga., 1992-96; pharmacist RX-Inc, Grundy, 1996—. Mem. Am. Pharmaceutical Assn., Am. Soc. Health Sys. Pharmacists, Nat. Assn. Retail Druggists. Home: 115 Watkins St PO Box 535 Grundy VA 24614

HYMAN, ABRAHAM, electrical engineer; b. Bklyn., Mar. 8, 1934; s. Rubin and Regina (Holzman) H.; m. Marianne Daniel, June 19, 1955; children: Debra Hyman Rathauser, Lori, Karen. BEE, Poly. Inst. Bklyn., 1945; MS, Newark Coll. Engring., 1954. Registered profl. engr., N.Y. Chief elec. engr. Mech. Equipment Research and Devel. Lab., Fort Totten, N.Y., 1955-64; head lab. Office Naval Research, Port Washington, N.Y., 1964-66; tech. adminstr. AEC, Upton, N.Y., 1966-71; supr. indsl. hygienist U.S. Dept. Labor, Westbury, N.Y., 1971-80, regional indsl. hygienist, N.Y.C., 1980-84; mgr. health and safety Unisys Corp., Great Neck, N.Y., 1984-95; safety and health cons., New Hyde Park, N.Y., 1995—; cons. Poison Control Ctr., East Meadow, N.Y., 1981—; adj. assoc. prof. Staten Island Coll., N.Y., 1983-91; lectr. Queensborough C.C., Queens, N.Y., 1991—. Patentee in field. Bd. dirs. Am. Lung Assn., East Meadow, 1974—. Mem. IEEE, Am. Acad. Environ. Engrs. (dimplomate), Nat. Soc. Profl. Engrs., Am. Conf. Indsl. Hygienists, Sci. Research Soc. Am., Sigma Xi. Avocations: photography; swimming; bicycling. Home and Office: 142 Claudy Ln New Hyde Park NY 11040-1635

HYMAN, ALBERT LEWIS, cardiologist; b. New Orleans, Nov. 10, 1923; s. David and Mary (Newstadt) H.; m. Neil Steiner, Mar. 27, 1964; 1 son, Albert Arthur. BS, La. State U., 1943; MD, 1945; postgrad., U. Cin., U. Paris, U. London, Eng. Diplomate: Am. Bd. Internal Medicine. Intern Charity Hosp., 1945-46, resident, 1947-49, sr. vis. physician, 1959-63; resident Cin. Gen. Hosp., 1946-47; instr. medicine La. State U., 1950-56, asst. prof. medicine, 1956-57; asst. prof. Tulane U., 1957-59, assoc. prof., 1959-63, assoc. prof. surgery, 1963-70, prof. research surgery in cardiology, 1970—, prof. clin. medicine Med. Sch., 1983—, adj. prof. pharmacology Med. Sch., 1974—; dir. Cardiac Catheterization Lab., 1957—; sr. vis. physician Touro Hosp., Touro Infirmary, Hotel Dieu; chief cardiology Sara Mayo Hosp.; cons. in cardiology USPHS, New Orleans Crippled Children's Hosp., St. Tammany Parish Hosp., Covington La. area VA, Hotel Dieu Hosp., Mercy Hosp., East Jefferson Gen. Hosp., St. Charles Gen. Hosp.; electrocardiographer Metairie Hosp., 1959-64, Sara Mayo Hosp., Touro Infirmary, St. Tammany Hosp.; cons. cardiovascular disease New Orleans VA Hosp.; cons. cardiology Baton Rouge Gen. Hosp.; Barlow lectr. in medicine U. So. Calif., 1977; mem. internat. sci. com. IV Internat. Symposium on Pulmonary Circulation, Charles U., Prague. Mem. editorial bd. Jour. Applied Physiology; contbr. over 250 articles to profl. jours. Recipient award for rsch. of the Hadassah, 1980, Vis. Scientist award Wellcome Found., Univ. Coll., London, 1991, Disting. Achievement award Am. Heart Assn., 1992, 93, Dickinson-Richards lectr., 1990. Fellow ACP, Am. Coll. Chest Physicians, Am. Coll. Cardiology, Am. Fedn. Clin. Rsch.; mem. AAUP, Am. Heart Assn. (fellow coun. on circulation, fellow coun. on clin. cardiology, mem. coun. on cardiopulmonary medicine, regional rep. coun. clin. cardiology, chmn. sci. com. cardiopulmonary coun. 1981, chmn. cardiopulmonary coun., rsch. com. bd. dirs., editl. bd. mem. Circulation Rsch., edit. bd. mem. Am. Jour. Physiology, Heart Disease and Stroke, Jour. Applied Physiology, Dickinson Richards Meml. Lectr. 1986, 92, Disting. Sci. Achievement award 1993), La. Heart Assn. (v.p. 1974, Albert L. Hyman Ann. Rsch. award, Wellcome Rsch. Found. Vis. Scientist award Univ. Coll. London 1992, Disting. Achievement award outstanding sci. contbns. to cardiopulmonary medicine), Am. Soc. Pharmacology and Exptl. Therapeutics, So. Soc. Clin. Investigation (chmn. membership com.), So. Med. Soc. (Seale-Harris award 1988), Am. Physiol. Soc., N.Am. Soc. Pacing and Electrophysiology, Orleans Surg. Soc. (hon.), New Orleans Surg. Soc. (hon.), N.Y. Acad. Scis., Nat. Am. Heart Assn. (vice-chmn. rsch. com.), Alpha Omega Alpha. Home: 5467 Marcia Ave New Orleans LA 70124-1052 Office: 3601 Prytania St New Orleans LA 70115-3610

HYMAN, ALLEN IRWIN, physician; b. N.Y.C., Dec. 5, 1933; s. Louis and Lena (Skolnick) H.; m. Valerie A. Kravitz, Oct. 15, 1961; children: Joshua, Andrew, Jonathan. Baccalaureate, Columbia Coll., N.Y.C., 1955; MD, Albany Med. Coll., 1959. Asst. anesthesiologist Columbia-Presbyn. Med. Ctr., N.Y.C., 1965-67, asst. prof., 1967-73, assoc. prof., 1973-86, prof., 1986—; assoc. attending Columbia-Presbyn. Med. Ctr., 1973-86, acting chmn. anesthesia, 1985-86, vice-chmn. anesthesia, 1986—, attending, 1986—. Health aide to Senator Bob Dole, Washington, 1988. Health policy fellow Robert Wood Johnson Found., 1988. Office: Columbia Presbyn Med Ctr 622 W 168th St New York NY 10032-3784

HYMAN, ARNOLD, psychology educator, consulting psychologist; b. Bklyn., Mar. 15, 1931; s. Louis and Sadie (Levine) H.; m. Gertrude Lapidus, June 26, 1966; 1 child, Simeon. B.A., Bklyn. Coll., 1952, M.A., 1953; M.S., CCNY, 1961; Ph.D., U. Cin., 1966. Lic. psychologist, Conn. Tchr. mentally retarded, pub. elem. sch., N.Y.C., 1953-57; research asst. Columbia U., N.Y.C., 1958-61, research worker, 1963-67; research assoc. Bklyn. Jewish Hosp., 1968-71; asst. prof. psychology U. New Haven, 1971-74, assoc. prof., 1974, prof., 1984—; pvt. practice cons. psychology, New Haven, Conn., 1981—. Author teaching aid and book: Learning Statistics Empirically, 1972; co-author: (software) Learning to Use Money, A Program for the Developmentally Disabled, 1992; also articles. Mem. Am. Psychol. Assn., AAAS, N.Y. Acad. Scis., Psychonomic Soc., Sigma Xi. Jewish. Avocations: fishing; skiing; playing string bass; gardening. Home: 30 Bromley Ct Hamden CT 06514-1702 Office: U New Haven 300 Orange Ave New Haven CT 06516-1916

HYMAN, BRUCE DAVID, internist; b. L.A., Oct. 30, 1962; s. Barry Stephen and Rhoda Marcia (Karan) H.; m. Joanne Carol Litwack, Aug. 13, 1988; children Zachary Redmond, Samantha Ariel. BA, U. Calif., San Diego, 1985; MA, Boston U., 1987; MD, Rush Med. Coll., Chgo., 1991. Diplomate Am. Bd. Internal Medicine, Nat. Bd. Med. Examiners; lic. physician and surgeon, Ill. Resident in internal medicine Rush-Presbyn. St. Luke's Med. Ctr., Chgo., 1991-94, chief resident, 1994-95, asst. attending, dept. internal medicine, 1995—; pvt. practice Chgo., 1994—; asst. prof. Rush Med. Coll., 1995—. Mem. ACP, AMA, Ill. State Med. Soc., Chgo. Med. Soc., Alpha Omega Alpha. Home: 1240 Eaton Ct Highland Park IL 60035 Office: Univ Assocs in Internal Med 1725 W Harrison St #352 Chicago IL 60612

HYMAN, BRUCE MALCOLM, ophthalmologist; b. N.Y.C., May 22, 1943; s. Malcolm A. and Sylvia S. H.; AB, Columbia U., 1964; MD, NYU, 1968. Intern in surgery Albert Einstein Coll. Medicine/Bronx Mcpl. Hosp., 1968-69; resident in ophthalmology Manhattan Eye, Ear and Throat Hosp., N.Y.C., 1971-74; pvt. practice medicine specializing in ophthalmology, N.Y.C., 1974—; tchr. attending surgeon Manhattan Eye, Ear and Throat Hosp., 1974—; med. cons. U.S. Seaplane Pilots Assn., 1975—, Health Ins. Plan Greater N.Y., 1977—; ophthalmologist to Hotel Trades Coun., Hotel Assn. N.Y.C., 1974—; attending ophthalmologist Roosevelt Hosp., N.Y.C., 1979—, dir. adult outpatient ophthalmology, 1980—; police surgeon N.Y.C., 1977—, dep. chief police surgeon, 1978—; attending ophthalmologist Doctors Hosp., 1979—, Le Roy Hosp., 1979—, St. Luke's Hosp., 1980—; outpatient ophthalmologist N.Y. Hosp., 1975-77; clin. ophthalmologist Columbia Coll. Physicians and Surgeons, 1981—. Served with USPHS, 1969-71. Diplomate Am. Bd. Ophthalmology. Fellow ACS; mem. N.Y. State, N.Y. County med. socs., Am. Acad. Ophthalmology and Otolaryngology. Contbr. articles to profl. jours. Office: 133 E 64th St New York NY 10021-7045

HYMAN, EDWARD SIDNEY, physician, consultant; b. New Orleans, Jan. 22, 1925; s. David and Mary (Newstadt) H.; m. Jean Simons, Sept. 29, 1956; children: Judith, Sydney, Edward David, Anne. BS, La. State U., 1944; MD, Johns Hopkins U., 1946. Diplomate: Am. Bd. Internal Medicine. Intern Barnes Hosp., Washington U., St. Louis, 1946-47; fellow in medicine Stanford U., San Francisco, 1949-51, asst. resident in medicine, 1950-51, Peter Bent Brigham Hosp., Boston, 1951-53; teaching fellow in medicine Harvard U., Boston, 1952-53; practice medicine specializing in internal medicine, New Orleans, 1953—; dir. kidney unit Charity Hosp., New Orleans, 1953-55; investigator Touro Research Inst., New Orleans, 1959; dir. Hyman Corp.; mem. staff Sara Mayo Hosp., 1954-79, chief of staff, 1968-70, trustee, 1970-78; mem. staff Touro Infirmary, New Orleans, St. Charles Hosp.; panelist Pres.'s Commn. on Health Needs of Nation, 1952; cons. water quality New Orleans Sewerage and Water Bd., 1978; mem. research adv. com. Cancer Assn. New Orleans, 1976—, La. Bd. Regents, 1983. Contbr. articles to profl. jours. NIH grantee, 1960-81; Am. Heart Assn. grantee, 1962-65. Fellow ACP; mem. Am. Fedn. Clin. Rsch., Am. Soc. Artificial Internal Organs, Am. Physiol. Soc. Biophys. Soc. (chmn. local arrangements 1971, 77, 81, 87), Am. Soc. Microbiology, AAAS, Pvt. Drs. Am. (co-founder 1968, v.p. 1968—, Dist. Svc. award 1981), Orleans Parish Med. Soc. (gov. 1972-80), La. State Med. Soc. (ho. of dels. 1970-81). Jewish. Subspecialties: Internal medicine; Biophysics. Current work: Clincial internal medicine, biochemistry, biophysics, nephrology, artificial organs, water quality, government in medicine, cause of death in renal failure, significance of bacteria in urine. Isolated aldosterone, 1949; patentee sheet plastic oxygenator (artificial heart), oil detection device; inventor telephone transmission of electrocardiogram, early data transmission; inventor hydrogen platinum detection of heart shunts, Method for detection of bacteria in urine, Systemic Coccal Disease, Desert Storm Syndrome (following the Persian Gulf War) as a bacterial disease (SCD), Silicone Implant Disease as a bacterial disease. Office: 3525 Prytania St Ste 200 New Orleans LA 70115-3549

HYMAN, HARRIS, medical educator; b. N.Y.C., Apr. 11, 1930; s. Harris Jr. and Helen-Aimee (Eppenstein) H.; m. Barbara Hirsberg, Mar. 30, 1958; children: Harris IV, Wendy Hyman Jacobs, Susan E. BA, Yale U., 1951; MD, Harvard U., 1955. Diplomate in internal medicine. Clin. prof. medicine Tulane U., New Orleans, 1975—. With USPHS, 1958-60. Fellow ACP, Am. Coll. Gastroenterology, Am. Gastroenterol. Assn., Am. Soc. Gastrointestinal Endoscopy. Home: 1300 Nashville Ave New Orleans LA 70115 Office: Ste 526 3525 Prytania St New Orleans LA 70115

HYMAN, IRWIN A., psychologist; b. Neptune, N.J., Mar. 22, 1935; Henry Meltzer and Harriet (Greenitz) H.; m. Nada Pospishil (div.); children: Nadine, Deborah; m. Susan Brown, June 16, 1985; 1 child, Rachael. BA, U. Maine, 1957; MEd, Rutgers U., 1961, EdD, 1964. Lic. psychologist, N.J., Pa.; cert. sch. psychologist, N.J., Pa. Tchr. Millstone Twp. (N.J.) Schs., 1957-61; sch. psychologist Lawrence Twp. (N.J.) Schs., 1962-66; chief of clin. svcs. Tng. Sch. at Vineland, N.J., 1966-67; prof. spl. edn., chief clin. psychologist Keane Coll., Union, N.J., 1967-68; prof. sch. psychology Temple U., Phila., 1968—, dir. Nat. Ctr. for Study of Corporal Punishment, 1977—; cons. sch. psychologist Pennington (N.J.) Sch., 1986-95; cons. childrens mag., 1986-89, ACLU, 1977—, U.S. Ho. Reps., Washington, 1990, U.S. Senate, Washington, 1984; tech. specialist Chinese Univs. Project, World Bank, 1987. Author: Reading Writing and the Hickory Stick, 1990; co-editor: Corporal Punishment in American Education, 1979, School Consultation; cons. editor Sch. Psychology Review, 1985-87; contbr. articles to profl. jours. Recipient Pres.'s award Nat. Assn. Sch. Psychologists, 1994. Fellow Am. Psychol. Assn. (pres. div. 16 1977-78, Disting Svc. to Sch. 1986), Internat Soc. for Rsch. on Aggression; mem. Nat. Assn. for Advancement of Sci., Soc. for Traumatic Stress Studies, Coun. for Exceptional Children, Am. Ednl. Rsch. Assn., Phi Delta Kappa. Democrat. Jewish. Office: Temple U 255 Rita Philadelphia PA 19103

HYMAN, NEIL HYMAN, surgeon, educator; b. N.Y.C., Mar. 21, 1958; s. Abe N. and Serene J. Hyman; m. Jennifer S. Shapiro, Sept. 6, 1986; children: Eric, Seth. BA, U. Pa., 1980; MD, U. Vt., 1984. Diplomate Am. Bd. Gen. Surgery, Am. Bd. Colorectal Surgery. Intern Mt. Sinai Med. Ctr., N.Y.C., 1984-85, surg. resident, 1984-89; fellow in colon and rectal surgery Cleve. Clinic, 1989-90; from asst. to assoc. prof. surgery U. Vt. Coll. Medicine, Burlington, 1990—; surgeon Fletcher Allen Health Care, Burlington, Vt., 1990—. Office: Fletcher Allen Health Care 3 Timber Ln South Burlington VT 05403

HYNAN, LINDA SUSAN, psychology educator; b. Ft. Sill, Okla., Nov. 20, 1953; d. Christy J. and Barbara Jean (Camp) Genzel; m. Edward F. Hynan, Feb. 3, 1973; 1 child, Patrick Shane. MS, U. Ill., 1982, PhD, 1993. Tchg. asst., rsch. asst. dept. psychology U. Ill., Urbana, 1980-91; rsch. asst. dept. psychology Del. State Coll., Dover, 1983—; asst. prof. dept. psychology, neurosci., inst. grad. stats. Baylor U., Waco, Tex., 1991—; cons. Infosphere Devel. Systems, Waco, Tex., 1986—; reviewer Allyn & Bacon/Simon & Schuster, Needham Heights, Mass., 1992, 95, Harcourt Brace Coll. Publs., 1994, Worth Pubs., Inc., 1995. Contbr. chpt. to book Cognitive Bias, 1990, articles to profl. jours.; spl. reviewer jour. Behavior Rsch. Methods Instruments and Computers. Fellow U. Ill., 1988-89. Mem. APA, Am. Ednl. Rsch. Assn., Am. Psychol. Soc., Am. Statis. Assn., McLennan County Psychol. Assn., Midwestern Psychol. Assn., Psychometric Soc., Soc. for Judgement and Decision-Making, Soc. for Applied Multivariate Rsch., Soc. for Math. Psychology, Southwestern Psychol. Assn., Ctrl. Tex. Women's Alliance, Thyroid Found. Am., Inst. Math. Statistics, Am. Radio Relay League, Am. Numismatic Assn., Phi Kappa Phi. Home: 1312 Western Ridge Dr Waco TX 76712-8709 Office: Baylor Univ Psychology and Neurosci PO Box 97334 Waco TX 76798-7334

HYNNE, HANS, anesthesiologist, consultant; b. Florø, Norway, July 14, 1957; s. Paul Henrik and Sylvi (Knudsen) H.; m. Astrid Synneve Bjørnerheim, Apr. 3, 1982; children: Ragnhild Bjørnerheim, Ingrid Bjørnerheim, Sigrid Bjørnerheim. MD, U. Bergen, 1984. Anesthesiologist Regional Hosp., Trondheim, Norway, 1986—. Office: Regional Hosp, 7006 Trondheim Norway

HYSLOP, NEWTON EVERETT, allergist, immunologist; b. Newton, Mass., 1935. MD, Harvard U., 1961. Diplomate Am. Bd. Allergy and Immunology, Am. Bd. Internal Medicine. Intern Mass. Gen. Hosp., Boston, 1961-62, resident in medicine, 1962-63, fellow in infectious disease, 1966-68; resident in medicine Peter Bent Brigham Hosp., Boston, 1965-66; with Tulane U. Med. Ctr., New Orleans; prof. medicine Tulane U. Mem. ACP, Am. Assn. Immunologists, Am. Soc. Microbiology, Infectious Disease Soc. Am. Office: Tulane U Med Ctr Dept Infectious Diseases 1430 Tulane Ave New Orleans LA 70112-2699*

HYSON, MORTON ISAAC, neurologist, vocalist; b. Detroit, July 10, 1949; s. Aaron Hyson and Betty (Berman) Ellias; m. Nicole Claire Baillargeon, June 6, 1982; 1 child, Kimberley. MD, Wayne State U., 1979. Diplomate Am. Bd Psychiatry and Neurology; lic. physician Nev., N.Y., Tex. Intern McGill U./Montreal (Quebec, Can.) Neurol. Hosp., 1980-81, resident in neurology, 1982-83; pvt. practice Arlington Tex., 1983-90, Las Vegas, 1990—; weekend coord. emergency rm. Potsdam (N.Y.) Gen. Hosp., 1981-83; clin. assoc. prof. dept. neurology U. Tex. Southwestern Med. Sch., Dallas. appeared in Tosca, Nev. Opera Theatre, 1994, Butterfly, 1993, Amahl, 1993, The Marriage of Figaro, 1991, Il Turco in Italia, Opera Piccola Bremen, Germany, 1991, The Gondoliers, The Lyric Opera, 1990. Cleve. Inst. Music scholar, 1969. Mem. AMA, Am. Assn. Neurologists, Clark County Med. Soc., Nev. State Med. Assn., Muscular Dystrophy Assn. (med. dir. Las Vegas 1991—). Office: 2020 Goldring Ave Ste 402 Las Vegas NV 89106-4000

IACOBELLI, JOAN WEBER, surgeon; b. New Haven, Conn., Jan. 4, 1954; d. Thomas George and Agnes Frances (Hauptly) Weber; m. Anthony Joseph Iacobelli, July 31, 1976; children: Katrina Michelle, Nicholas Peter. BS, U. Conn., 1976; MD, U. Tenn., 1986. Diplomate Am. Bd. Surgery; cert. physicians asst. Intern U. Tenn., 1986-87, resident, 1987-91; surgeon Surg. Arts, P.C., Cullman, Ala., 1991—; chief surgery Woodland Cmty Hosp., Cullman, 1992; chmn. cancer com. Cullman Regional Med. Ctr., 1996. Bd. dirs. Cullman Swim Team, 1996. Fellow ACS; mem. Assn. Women Surgeons, Med. Assn. State Ala., Cullman Med. Soc. Home: 1738 Morning Dr NE Cullman AL 35055 Office: Surg Arts PC 1930 Alabama Hwy 157 Cullman AL 35055

IACOBELLI, MARK ANTHONY, dentist; b. Cleve., Aug. 27, 1957; s. Anthony Peter and Irene Margaret (Pordash) I.; m. Theresa Louise West, Aug. 8, 1991. BS, Case Western Res., 1979, DDS, 1982. Dentist, co-owner Iacobelli & Iffland, Canton, Ohio, 1982-85. gen. practice dentistry North Royalton, Ohio, 1985—; co-lectr. Jamison Cons. and Midwest Implant Inst. Named one of Outstanding Young Men Am., 1982. Fellow Acad. Gen. Dentistry; mem. ADA, Ohio Dental Assn., Cleve. Dental Assn., Am. Assn. Functional Orthodontics (Achievement award 1982), Padua Franciscan Alumni Assn. (chmn. devel. drive 1986, chmn. 1989, 90). Republican. Roman Catholic. Home: 4480 Oak Ridge Dr North Royalton OH 44133-2069 Office: 8030 Corporate Cir North Royalton OH 44133-1245

IACONO, JAMES MICHAEL, research center administrator, nutrition educator; b. Chgo., Dec. 11, 1925; s. Joseph and Angelina (Cutaia) I.; children: Lynn, Joseph, Michael, Rosemary. BS, Loyola U., Chgo., 1950; MS, U. Ill., 1952, PhD, 1954. Chief Lipid Nutrition Lab. Nutrition Inst. Agrl. Rsch. Svc. USDA, Beltsville, Md., 1970-75; dep. asst. adminstrv. nat. program Agrl. Rsch. Svc. USDA, Washington, 1975-77, assoc. adminstr. office human nutrition, 1978-82; dir. Western Human Nutrition Rsch. Ctr. Agrl. Rsch. Svc. USDA, San Francisco, 1982-94; adj. prof. nutrition Sch. Pub. Health UCLA, 1987—. Author over 100 rsch./tech. publs. and chpts. in books relating to nutrition and biochemistry and lipids. With U.S. Army, 1944-46. Recipient Rsch. Career Devel. award NIH, 1964-70. Fellow Am Heart Assn. (coun. on arteriosclerosis and thrombosis), Am. Inst. Chemists; mem. Am. Inst. Nutrition, Am. Soc. Clin. Nutrition, Am. Oil Chemists Soc. Office: USDA ARS Western Human Nutrition Rsch Ctr PO Box 29997 San Francisco CA 94129-0997

IAMMARINO, RICHARD MICHAEL, pathologist, student support services director; b. Cleve., Aug. 17, 1926; s. Salvatore M. and Corinne Marie (De Paul) I.; m. Therese Margaret Dolan, Aug. 9, 1952. BS in Natural Sci., John Carroll U., 1949; MD, Stritch Sch. Medicine, Chgo., 1953. MS in Counseling Psychology, West Va. U., 1990. Diplomate Am. Bd. Pathology, subsplties. in anatomic and clin. pathology; lic. M.D. Ohio, Pa., W.Va. Intern St. Vincent Charity Hosp., Cleve., 1953-54; resident in internal medicine Crile VA Hosp., Cleve., 1954-55, resident in pathology, 1955-56; resident-fellow in pathology U. Kans. Med. Ctr., Kansas City, 1956-58; rsch. fellow in pathology Cleve. Met. Gen. Hosp., 1958-59; assoc. in pathology to assoc. prof. pathology U. Pitts. Sch. Medicine, 1962-79; prof. pathology W.Va. U., Morgantown, 1979-88, emeritus prof. pathology, 1989—, dir. Health Profl. Support Svc., 1989—; dir. program in med. tech., U. Pitts., 1966-69, pathologist cons. to dept. med. tech., 1969-79; med. dir. program in med. tech., W.Va. U., 1979-88, adj. prof. pathology, 1988-89, acting med. dir. blood bank, 1988-89. Contbr. numerous articles to profl. jours., chpts. to books. Mem. adv. com. to Med. Lab. Tech. Dept., Allegheny Cmty. Coll., 1967-79; founding mem., past chmn. bd. dirs., Western Pa. Montessori Sch., Inc., 1964-79; mem. blood svcs. com. Morgantown chpt. ARC, 1980-84; mem. parish coun. St. Johns U. Parish, 1980-82; bd. mem. Morgantown Hospice, Inc., 1982-88, acting pres., 1981-82, pres., 1982-83, profl. adv. coun., 1983-86, hon. life bd. mem., 1989, recipient appreciation award 1993. Recipient various rsch. grants; fellow in pathology Western Reserve U. Fellow Coll. Am. Pathologists; mem. Acad. Clin. Lab. Physicians and Scientists, W.Va. Med. Soc., Monongalia County Med. Soc. Office: WV Univ Med Ctr PO Box 9122 Morgantown WV 26506

IANNONE, ANTHONY M., physician, neurologist; b. N.Y.C., July 11, 1925; s. Donato and Antoinette (Iannone) I.; m. Mary Iannone, Jan. 11, 1955 (dec. Jan. 1996); children: Antoinette, Mary Ann, Susan, Michael, James, Anthony, Peter (dec.). AB, Columbia U., 1945, MD, 1948. Diplomate in neurology Am. Bd. Psychiatry and Neurology. Instr. neurology U. Buffalo, 1957, U. Minn., Mpls., 1957-60; asst. prof. neurology Stanford U., Palo Alto, Calif., 1960-63, assoc. prof., 1963-68; prof., chmn. dept. neurology Med. Coll. Ohio, Toledo, 1968-70, prof., co-chmn., 1970-85, prof., 1985—; guest rschr. NIH, Bethesda, Md., 1986. Contbr. articles to profl. jours.; presenter in field. Capt. USAF, 1951-53. Mem. AMA, AAAS, Am. Acad. Neurology, Am. Physiol. Soc., Ohio State Med. Assn., Soc. for Neurosci. Home: 139-30 Lake Dr Monroe MI 48161 Office: Med Coll Ohio Divsn Neurology 3000 Arlington Ave Toledo OH 43614

IBANEZ, JANE BOURQUARD, stress management consultant, lecturer; b. New Orleans, Oct. 11, 1947; d. Albert John and Josephine (Vachetta) Bourquard; m. Manuel Luis Ibanez, Oct. 16, 1970; children: Juana, Vincent, William, Marc. BS, U. New Orleans, 1970. Lab. researcher in organic chemistry U. New Orleans, 1967-68, genetics lab. instr., 1968-69, fitness instr., 1972-90, yoga and meditative instr., 1972-90, stress mgmt. instr., 1980-90; profl. lectr., stress mgmt. cons., 1972—; bd. examiners Tex. Supreme Ct., 1993—; guest lectr. U. New Orleans, Tex. A&M, Kingsville, ABWA Conv., South Tex. Banker's Assn., others. Author producer: (audiotapes) Childhood Stress, 1985, Yoga Workout, 1985, Jane's Way Mini Workout, 1986. Chmn. Tex. A&M U.-Kingsville Fund for Instnl. Advancement, Kingsville, 1989—, also presdl. asst.; pres Am. Cancer Soc., Kingsville, 1992-94; mem. devel. bd. Spohn Kleberg Hosp., Kingsville, 1990—, trustee, vice chmn., 1991-93; chmn. devel. bd. Am. Heart Assn., Kingsville, 1990—; bd. dirs. Corpus Christi Women's Shelter, 1991-95; trustee South Tex. Ranching and Heritage Festival, 1992—. Mem. AAUW, Kingsville Garden Club, U. New Orleans Fitness Club (pres. 1975-89). Roman Catholic. Home: 905 N Armstrong Ave Kingsville TX 78363-3687 also: 2319 Prentiss Ave New Orleans LA 70122-5309

IBBOTSON, SALLY HELEN, dermatologist; b. Newcastle-on-Tyne, Eng., Feb. 18, 1962; d. Roy Hugh and Margaret Doreen (Trotter) I. BS with 1st class honors, Leeds (Eng.) U., 1983, MB BChir with honors, 1986, MD with commendation, 1994. House officer Leeds Gen. Infirmary, 1986-87, tchrs. fellow medicine, 1987-89, rsch. fellow, 1989-92; registrar dermatology Royal Victoria Infirmary, Newcastle-on-Tyne, 1992-94, sr. registrar dermatology, 1994—. Contbr. papers to profl. jours. Recipient Travel award Psoriasis Assn., 1996-97; rsch. fellow Harvard U., 1996-97. Mem. Royal Coll. Physicians Glasgow, Brit. Assn. Dermatologists (travel award 1996-97, Peel Med. award 1996-97), Brit. Soc. Photobiologists, Am. Soc. Photobiologists. Home: 21 Hartside Gardens Tesmond, Newcastle on Tyne NE2 2JR, England Office: Royal Victoria Infirmary Dept Dermatology, Queen Victoria Rd, Newcastle on Tyne NE1 4LP, England

IBEZIM, FRANCIS, JR., medical auditor; b. Orlu, Imo, Nigeria, Oct. 12, 1956; m. Roselynne Nne Egele, June 5, 1990; 1 child, Chizitam Francis. BBA in Health Care Mgmt., Marshall U., 1990; MPA in Gen. Pub. Adminstrn., S.W. Tex. State U., 1994. Med. records analyst St. David's Hosp., Austin, Tex., 1990-93; mgmt. auditor Tex. Dept. Health, Austin, 1992—, sec., sec.-elect. cultural awareness com., 1994—. Mem. Am. Coll. Health Care Execs. (assoc.), Am. Coll. Health Care Adminstrs. Office: Tex Dept Health 1100 W 49th St Austin TX 78756

IDDINS, BRENDA WALKER, nurse; b. Birmingham, Ala., Aug. 26, 1958; d. Eddie Clyde and Sybil Lucille (Lusk) Walker. Assoc. in Nursing, Jefferson State Jr. Coll., 1979; BSN, U. Ala., Birmingham, 1985, MSN, 1987; postgrad. cert. FNP, U. Ala., 1995. Cert. clin. specialist in med.-surg. nursing, family nurse practitioner. Staff RN Univ. Ala. Birmingham Hosp., 1979-80, charge nurse, 1980-85, part time staff RN, 1985-86, part time transport RN, 1983-84, part time rsch. nurse, 1985, clin. nurse specialist, 1987-92, lung transplant coord., 1992-93; rsch. coord., 1993-95; dir. student health svcs. Samford U., 1995—; item writer Nat. Coun. Licensure Examination for Registered Nursing, 1992; mem. test devel. com. ANCC, 1992-96. Mem. ANA, Am. Acad. Nurse Practitioners, Sigma Theta Tau.

IDLIBI, OMAR M., pathologist; b. Aleppo, Syria, May 3, 1955; came to U.S., 1982; s. Mohammad Amin and Nadima (Al Hariri) I.; m. Mayado O. Al Heib, Sept. 15, 1977; children: Mohammad, Osama, Mojahed, Hazem, Lujain. MD, Aleppo U., 1979. Diplomate Am. Bd. Pathology. Chief resident William Beaumont Hosp., Royal Oak, Mich., 1988-89; pathologist, chief chemistry Grace Hosp., Detroit, 1989-90; dir. residency Lansing (Mich.) Sparrow Hosp., 1990-93; med. dir. Lab. Corp. Am., Charlotte, N.C., 1993—; med. dir. Cytology Sch., Charlotte, 1993—. Author: Medicine and Marriage, 1979. Fellow Coll. Am. Pathologists; mem. N.C. Med. Soc., N.C. Soc. Cytologists. Home: 9112 Bertram Ct Huntersville NC 28078 Office: Lab Corp 3600A Woodpark Blvd Charlotte NC 28206

IDZIKOWSKI, JAN ROGER, physician assistant; b. Milw., Apr. 6, 1953; s. Leonard Anthony and Eleanore Barbara (Kuczynski) I.; m. Doreen Somers, Aug. 16, 1991; children: Sydney, Collin. BS in Physician Asst., U. Wis., 1977. Cert. Nat. Comm. Cert. Physician Asst. Physician asst. Cardiac Surgery Ltd., Milw., 1977-78, Rice Clinic/Orthopaedics, Stevens Point, Wis., 1978-92, Vail (Colo.) Orthopaedics & Sports Medicine, 1992—; mem. phys. adv. bd. U. Wis., Madison, 1980-85, preceptor, assoc. faculty physician asst. program, 1979-92. Contbr. articles to profl. jours. Fellow Am. Acad. Physician Assts. (contbg. editor jour. 1989—), Colo. Acad. Physician Assts. Home: PO Box 332 Edwards CO 81632 Office: Vail/Summit Orthopaedics 181 W Meadow Dr Ste # 800 Vail CO 81657

IENATSCH, GAYLEEN ELIZABETH, nursing educator; b. Mt. Horeb, Wis., May 20, 1940; d. Gerhard Palmer and Mayme Eileen (Grim) Steensrud; m. Grant Peter Ienatsch, June 3, 1962; children: Britt Christine Leach, Peter Jay, Perry Lee. Diploma in nursing, Madison (Wis.) Gen. Hosp. Sch. Nursing, 1961; BSN, Tex. Tech U., 1987, MSN, 1991. RN, Tex.; cert. BCLS instr. Staff nurse CCU Midland (Tex.) Meml. Hosp., 1979-85; staff nurse ICU Med. Ctr. Hosp., Odessa, Tex., 1985-86; program dir., supr. cardiac rehab. for out-patients CardioCentral, Odessa, 1986-92; nursing instr. Tex. Tech. U. Health Sci. Ctr. Sch. Nursing, Odessa, 1992-94, acting regional dean, 1994-95, regional dean, 1995—; cons. CardioCentral, Odessa, 1992—; mem. adv. com. Odessa Coll. Sch. Nursing, 1994—; bd. dirs. Am. Heart Assn. Tex. Affiliate, Austin, also network mem., 1993—. Author chpt. to book; mem. editl. bd. Tex. Jour. Rural Health, 1994—. Mem. cmty. adv. bd. Jr. League of Odessa, 1994—. Recipient Disting. Svc. award Am. Heart Assn., 1990. Mem. APHA, Tex. Nurses Assn., Tex. Rural Health Assn., Sigma Theta Tau. Presbyterian. Home: 1524 Tanglewood Odessa TX 79761 Office: Tex Tech U Health Sci Ctr 800 W 4th St Odessa TX 79763

IERARDI, STEPHEN JOHN, physician; b. Honolulu, July 5, 1960; s. Ernest John and Robert Ann (Hackett) I.; m. Erica Ewing, May 28, 1989; children: Daphne Alexandra, Weston Eric. BA in Biology, Williams Coll., 1982; MD, U. Rochester, 1986. Diplomate Am. Bd. Family Physicians. Intern U. Calif. at Irvine Med. Ctr., Orange, 1986-87, resident, 1987-89, chief resident, 1988-89; physician Laguna Hills, Calif., 1989—; med. dir. Lake Forest Nursing Ctr., 1993—; chief of medicine Saddleback Meml. Med. Ctr., 1996, chmn. family practice, 1994-96. Recipient UCI Care awards Univ. Calif. at Irvine Med. Ctr., 1986-89. Fellow Am. Acad. Family Physicians; mem. AMA (Physician Recognition award 1996), Assn. Am. Family Physicians (assoc.), Orange County Med. Assn. Home: 49 Saint Kitts Monarch Beach CA 92629-4130 Office: Ste 334 23961 Calle De La Magdalena Laguna Hills CA 92653-3665

IFFY, LESLIE, medical educator; b. Budapest, Hungary, May 17, 1925; came to U.S., 1969; s. Zoltan and Rozsa (Lantos) I.; m. Maureen B. Deeney. MD, U. Budapest, Hungary, 1949; MD (hon.), Semmelweis U., Budapest, 1993. Diplomate Am. Bd. Ob-Gyn. Resident, fellow Országos Testnevelési és Sportegészségügyi Intézet Hosp. Ministry of Health, Budapest, 1951-56; fellow U. Wash., Seattle, 1964; asst. prof. Temple U., Phila., 1969-70; assoc. prof. U. Ill., Chgo., 1971-72, Jefferson Med. Coll., Phila., 1972-73; prof. U. Medicine and Dentistry of N.J., Newark, 1974—; dir. obstetrics U. Hosp., Newark, 1974—. Contbr. over 170 articles to profl. jours. and chpts. to books; editor: Perinatology Case Studies, 1978, 85, Obstetrics and Perinatology, 1981 (in English and Spanish), Operative Perinatology, 1984 (in English, Spanish and Japanese), Operative Obstetrics, 2d edit., 1992. Recipient Dr. Robert Jardine Rsch. prize U. Glasgow, 1963, Ford Found. rsch. fellowship, Seattle, 1964, hon. fellowship Hungarian Obstet. Soc., 1986. Fellow Am. Coll. Ob-Gyn., Royal Coll. Surgeons (Can.); mem. Cen. Assn. Ob-Gyn. (life), Chgo. Gynecol. Soc., Am. Coll. Legal Medicine (bd. dirs. 1989-95), Royal Coll. Physicians (Edinburgh, Scotland, licentiate), Royal Faculty Physicians and Surgeons (Glasgow, Scotland, licentiate), Romanian Obstet. Gynecol. Soc. (hon.). Home: 5 Robin Hood Rd Summit NJ 07901-3718 Office: NJ Med Sch UMDNJ 150 Bergen St Newark NJ 07103-2406

IGARASHI, PETER, nephrologist, educator, researcher; b. L.A., Dec. 31, 1956; married; 2 children. BS in Biomed. Scis. with highest honors, U. Calif., Riverside, 1978; MD, UCLA, 1981. Diplomate Am. Bd. Internal Medicine. Intern & resident dept. internal medicine Davis Med. Ctr. U. Calif., Sacramento, 1981-84; postdoctoral fellow nephrology dept. internal medicine Sch. Medicine Yale U., New Haven, 1984-87, asst. prof. medicine dept. internal medicine, 1987-92, assoc. prof. medicine, 1992—; attending physician Yale-New Haven Hosp., 1987—, Vets. Affairs Conn. Health Care Systems, West Haven, 1987—; dir. nephrology fellowship recruitment/selection Yale U., 1992—; chmn. renal physiology-molecular biology physiol. processes abstractr review com. Am. Soc. Nephrology, 1990; ad hoc mem. NIH Gen. Medicine B study sect., 1996; spkr. in field. Editl. bd. Am. Jour. Physiology: Renal, Fluid and Electrolyte Physiology, 1996—; contbr. articles to profl. jours. Recipient Merck Med. Book award, 1981, Lange Med. Book award, 1981, Physician-Scientist award NIH, 1985-90; grantee NIH; Carl Fuglie Meml. scholar, 1978. Mem. AAAS, Am. Heart Assn. (kidney coun., New Eng. regional peer review com. 1991-94, rsch. com. Conn. affiliate 1994—, New Investigator award 1990-93, Established Investigator award 1995—, grantee), Am. Soc. Nephrology, Nat. Kidney Found. (fellowship review com. 1988-91), Am. Soc. Biochemistry & Molecular Biology, Am. Physiology Soc., Salt and Water Club, Phi Beta Kappa, Alpha Omega Alpha. Office: Yale U Sch Medicine Dept Nephrology 2073 333 Cedar St PO Box 208029 New Haven CT 06520-8029

IGLAR, ALBERT FRANCIS, environmental engineer, educator; b. New Kensington, Pa., July 17, 1939; s. Albert Francis and Mary (Harouse) I.; m. Loretta Ruth Streich, Aug. 2, 1964; children: David Alan, Deborah Ruth. BS, Carnegie-Mellon U., 1961; MPH, U. Minn., 1966, PhD, 1970. Registered profl. engr., Minn. San. engr. Pa. Dept. Health, Meadville, Harrisburg, 1961-65; prof. environ. health East Tenn. State U., Johnson City, 1970—. Mem. Nat. Environ. Health Assn. (registered environmentalist, various offices), Tenn. Edn. Assn., Kiwanis. Office: East Tenn State U PO Box 70682 Johnson City TN 37614

IGLE, DIANE CHRISTINE, nurse, nursing services administrator, psychotherapist; b. Wilmington, Del., Apr. 21, 1946; d. Edward A. Igle and Mary Vincent (Caruso) Sassi. Diploma in registered nursing, St. Mary's Sch. of Nursing, 1967; BS, Seton Hall U., 1969; MS, Columbia U., 1971. Staff nurse psychiatry Bergen Pines County Hosp., Paramus, N.J., 1968-69; nurse clinician in psychiatry Hackensack (N.J.) Hosp. and Community Mental Health Ctr., 1971-74; psychiatric nurse therapist Jefferson County Mental Health Ctr., Lakewood, Colo., 1974-77, program mgr. emergency in-patient service, 1977-81; head nurse adolescent unit Denver Health & Hosps., 1981-83; substitute instr. psychiatric nursing Denver Auraria Community Coll., 1983-85; asst. nursing service adminstr. Ft. Logan Mental Health Ctr., Denver, 1983-84, nursing service adminstr., 1984—; pvt. practice psychotherapist, Lakewood, 1982—; mem. planning com. 4th ann. Inst. for Psychiatric Nurse Clinicians, 1982. Author and presenter: Cost Effectiveness of the

Emergency/In-Patient Program, 1981; presenter nat. day treatment forum on Clin. Supervision: Process and Problems, 1983. Mem. Am. Nurse Assn. (item writer cert. exam in psychiatric nursing), Colo. Nurse Assn., Colo. Soc. for Clin. Specialists in Psychiatric Nursing (legis. com.). Democrat. Roman Catholic. Office: Colo Mental Health Inst at Ft Logan 3520 W Oxford Ave Denver CO 80236-3108

IGLEHART, J. DIRK, surgeon, oncologist; b. San Fransisco, Apr. 2, 1949; s. James Albert and Carolyn Ash Iglehart; m. Elizabeth Armstrong; children: Jamie, Liz, Annie, Max. MD, Harvard U., 1975. Intern, 1975-76, resident, 1976-84; from asst. to assoc. prof. Duke U., 1984-93, prof., 1994—; dir. Spore on Breast Cancer, NCI-NIH, 1996. Office: Duke U Med Ctr Box 3873 Durham NC 27710

IGNASH, TIMOTHY J., healthcare executive search consultant; b. Port Austin, Mich., Apr. 12, 1947. BA, Lawrence Tech. U., 1974; MBA, Wayne State U., 1978. Asst. clin. adminstr. Henry Ford Health Sys., Detroit, 1970-77; assoc. clin. adminstr. Detroit Med. Ctr., 1977-80; sr. assoc. Bernie Hoffmann Assocs., Southfield, Mich., 1980-91; pres., owner Aegis Group, Novi, Mich., 1991—. Mem. Mich. Assn. Personnel Svcs., Mich. Soc. Healthcare Planning and Marking, Southeastern Mich. Health Execs. Forum. Office: Aegis Group 23875 Novi Rd Novi MI 48375

IGOU, RAYMOND ALVIN, JR., orthopedic surgeon; b. Esterville, Iowa, Dec. 2, 1933; s. Raymond Alvin Sr. and Pearl Mildred (Christiansen) I.; m. Barbara Igou, Jan. 17, 1958 (div. June 10, 1980); children: Raymond Alvin III, Yvette Sharon; m. Jane Ann Leboda, Jan. 4, 1991. BS, N.Mex. State U., 1955; MD, Boston U., 1965. Diplomate Am. Bd. Orthopedic Surgery; lic. mortgage broker, Fla. Surg. internship Univ. Hosp., Boston, 1965-66; orthopedic resident Boston U. Sch. of Medicine, 1971-75; owner, operator Grant Buie Med. Ctr., Hillsboro, Tex., 1966-71; assoc. dir. dept. orthop. surgery, chief scoliosis clinic Boston City Hosp., 1975—, dir. rehab. svcs. City of Boston dept. health and hosps., 1975-80; asst. prof. ortho surg. Boston U. Sch. Medicine, 1979; med. dir. dept. rehab. svcs. New Eng. Meml. Hosp., Stoneham, Mass., 1979-95; chief orthopedic surgery, trustee New Eng. Meml. Hosp., Stoneham, 1987—, chief of staff, 1989-90; orthopedic surgeon in pvt. practice, Stoneham, 1975—; chmn. dept. surgery Boston Regional Med. Ctr. (formerly New Eng. Meml. Hosp.), Stoneham, 1995; sr. staff mem. Boston City Hosp., Univ. Hosp.; gen. ptnr. New Eng. MRI, L.P., 1989—; pres. Med Ptnrs. Ltd., 1988—; mem. Coun.-Boston Regional Med. Ctr., 1987, Gov.'s Adv. Coun. Indsl. Accidents, 1995; mng. gen. ptnr. WCPR Hartford Data Dispatch Ptnrs. Host talk show WALE, Providence, 1995-96; contbr. articles to profl. jours. Mem. Zoning and Planning Commn., Hillsboro, Tex., 1969-71; city councilman, Hillsboro, 1967-71; mem. Indsl. Found., Hillsboro, 1969-71. Fellow Am. Acad. Orthopedic Surgeons; mem. Mass. Med. Soc., Boston Orthopedic Club, Freemasons, York Rites, Scottish Rites, Shriners. Republican. Home: 611 Revere Beach Blvd Revere MA 02151-4709 Office: Ortho Surgery and Sports Medicine Inc 3 Woodland Rd Ste 322 Stoneham MA 02180-1713

IHDE, DANIEL CARLYLE, health science executive; b. Parsons, Kans., July 10, 1943; m. Mary Katherine Nanninga, 1968; children: Steven C., Douglas H. BS summa cum laude, Ea. N.Mex. U., 1964; MD, Stanford U., 1969. Diplomate Nat. Bd. Med. Examiners, Am. Bd. Internal Medicine. Intern, then resident The N.Y. Hosp., N.Y.C., 1969-71; fellow in med. oncology Meml. Hosp., N.Y.C., 1971-73; clin. assoc. medicine br. Nat. Cancer Inst., Bethesda, Md., 1973-75, sr. investigator VA Med. Ctr., 1975-81, dep. chief, head clin. investigations sect. Nat. Naval Med. Ctr., 1981-91, dep. dir., 1991-94; asst. prof. medicine Georgetown U., Washington, 1978-82, clin. asst. prof, 1982-83; assoc. prof. medicine Uniformed Svcs. U. Health Scis., Bethesda, 1981-85; prof. medicine U. Health Scis., Bethesda, 1985-91, dir. divsn. hematology/oncology, dept. medicine, 1987-90; chief med. oncology, prof. medicine Washington U., St. Louis, 1994—; dir. Cancer Ctr. Planning Grant, 1995—; cons. in med. oncology VA Med. Ctr., Washignton, 1982-83; cons., mem. oncology drugs adv. com. FDA, 1990-91, 91-95, 95—; mem. splty. bd. med. oncology Am. Bd. Internal Medicine, 1991—; mem. clin. rsch. subpanel Nat. Cancer Inst., 1978-80, mem. drug decision network com., 1979-83, mem. promotion/tenure rev. panel, 1983-85. Editor-in-chief Jour. Nat. Cancer Inst., 1989-94; assoc. editor Cancer Treatment Reports, 1979-84, Cancer Investigation, 1988-93, Cancer Rsch., 1989-90, Clin. Cancer Rsch., 1994—; mem. editorial bd. Clin. Oncology, 1992-94; guest editorial bd. Japanese Jour. Clin. Oncology, 1992—; assoc. editor European Jour. Cancer, 1995—; contbr. articles to profl. jours. With USPHS, 1973-85. Recipient Med. Alumni Rsch. award Stanford U., 1969, Outstanding Alumni award Ea. N.Mex. U., 1980, USPHS Commendation medal, 1984, Merit award NIH, 1992. Fellow ACP; mem. Am. Soc. Clin. Oncology (ad joc com. FDA liaison 1988-89, chairperson ann. meeting 1989, chair nominating com. 1990-91, chair lung/head and neck/CNS sect. program com. 1991-92), Am. Assn. Cancer Rsch. (program com. 1985-86, 91-92, chair ann. meeting 1985, 96, 92), Internat. Assn. Study Lung Cancer (chair worldwide conf. 1980, 85, 88, 91, 94). Office: Barnard Cancer Ctr Washington U Sch Medicine 660 S Euclid Ave Saint Louis MO 63110-1010

IKE, ROBERT WILLIAM, internal medicine educator; b. Grand Rapids, Mich., Sept. 4, 1952; s. Richard and Marion Lela (Slater) I.; m. Kathryn Irene Clark, Oct. 4, 1986. BS, U. Mich., 1974, MS, 1975; MD, U. Chgo., 1979. Diplomate Am. Bd. Internal Medicine, Am. Bd. Rheumatology. Intern Barnes Hosp., St. Louis, 1979-80, resident in internal medicine, 1980-82; physician emergency room DePaul Hosp., St. Louis, 1982-83; house physician Christian Hosps. N.E and N.W., St. Louis, 1982-83; fellow in rheumatology U. Mich. Med. Sch. and Rackham Arthritis Rsch. Unit, Ann Arbor, 1983-85; instr. internal medicine U. Mich. Med. Sch., Ann Arbor, 1985-91, asst. prof., 1991-94, assoc. prof. (tenured), 1994—. Fellow Am. Coll. Rheumatology; mem. Mich. Rheumatism Soc. (sec.-treas. 1988-90, v.p. 1991-92, pres. 1993-94, sec.-treas. 1994—). Methodist. Home: 1611 Harbal Dr Ann Arbor MI 48105-1815 Office: U Mich Rheumatology Div 1500 E Med Ctr Dr Ann Arbor MI 48109-0358

IKEDA, SHIGEMASA, anesthesiologist; b. Okayama, Japan, Aug. 7, 1937; came to U.S., 1969; s. Tamakichi and Kimika (Hatano) I.; m. Kazuko Yamana, Aug. 16, 1968; children: Megumi, Ken Kiyoshi, Hiroshi Daniel. MD, Okayama U., 1965, PhD, 1972. Diplomate Am. Bd. Anesthesiology. Clin. rsch. assoc. U. Vt., Burlington, 1969-72; instr. Okayama U., 1972-73; asst. instr. SUNY, Syracuse, 1973-75; asst. prof. St. Louis U., 1975-85, assoc. prof., 1985-91, prof. anesthesiology, 1991—; with St. Louis VA Med. Ctr.; mem. U.S.-Japan Coop. Sci. Program NSF, 1971; chief anesthesiology svc. St. Louis VA Med. Ctr. Fellow Am. Coll. Anesthesiologists. Office: Anesthesiology Svc St Louis VA Med Ctr 915 N Grand Blvd Saint Louis MO 63106

IKUZAWA, MASAO, psychology educator; b. Kyoto, Japan, Sept. 18, 1927; s. Tojiro and Yoshie (Okunaka) I.; m. Yoko Yukiyama, Mar. 26, 1954; children: Nobuko, Masato. BA, Kyoto U., 1950, D in Lit., 1972. Clin. psychologist Kyoto City Govt., 1950-52; lectr. Osaka (Japan) Shiritsu U., 1952-55, asst. prof., 1955-63, assoc. prof., 1963-73, prof., 1973-91, head computer ctr., 1973-77, head gen. edn. course, 1981-83, dean faculty of letters, 1985-87; prof. Kobe (Japan) Gakuin U., 1991—. Author: A Latent Class Analysis of Mental Developments, 1976, The Kyoto Scale of Psychological Development, 1985. Mem. Com. for Health Promotions of Osaka area, 1985-88. Fellow Behaviometric Soc. Japan; mem. Japanese Psychol. Assn., Internat. Soc. for Study of Behavioral Devel. Buddhist. Office: Kobe Gakuin U, Nishi-Ku, Kobe 651-21, Japan

ILANIT, TAMAR, psychologist; b. Tel Aviv, May 5, 1929; d. Aharon and Ada (Berman) Pougatch; came to U.S., 1950, naturalized, 1970; grad. Levinski Tchr. Sem., 1949; Ph.D., U. So. Calif., 1959; m. Apr. 15, 1948; children—Rona, Gill. Research dir. United Cerebral Palsy Assn., Los Angeles, 1959-61; instr. Pepperdine U., Los Angeles, 1962-64; spl. cons. White Meml. Med. Center, Los Angeles; pvt. practice clin. psychology, Los Angeles, 1963—; mem. disability evaluation panel Social Security Adminstrn., 1961-85. Mem. Am. Psychol. Assn., Los Angeles County Psychol. Assn., Sigma Xi, Phi Beta Kappa, Phi Kappa Phi. Jewish. Contbr. articles to profl. jours. Office: 1964 Westwood Blvd Ste 430 Los Angeles CA 90025-4651

ILIFF, NICHOLAS TAYLOR, oculoplastic surgeon, educator; b. Balt., Jan. 19, 1947; s. Charles Edwin and Elizabeth Jackson (Haines) I.; m. Paula Rebecca Bender, May 27, 1972; children: Nicholas Taylor Jr., Benjamin William. BA, Williams Coll., 1968; MD, Johns Hopkins U., 1972. Diplomate Am. Bd. Ophthalmology. Intern surgery Johns Hopkins U., 1972-73, resident in ophthalmology Wilmer Inst., 1974-77; asst. prof. ophthalmology Johns Hopkins Sch. Medicine, Balt., 1979-86, asst. prof. plastic surgery, 1985-86, assoc. prof. ophthalmology and plastic surgery, 1987—; bd. dirs. div. oculoplastic surgery Wilmer Inst. of Johns Hopkins U. Sch. Medicine, Balt. Co-author: Oculoplastic Surgery, 1979. Fellow Am. Acad. Ophthalmology; mem. AMA, Med. and Chirurgical Faculty Md., Balt. City Med. Soc., Am. Ophthal. Soc., Annapolis Yacht Club, Md. Club. Office: Maumenee 127 Wilmer Inst Wilmer Inst 600 N Wolfe St Baltimore MD 21287-9218

ILLIGER, HANS JOCHEN, oncologist; b. Magdeburg, Germany, July 20, 1939; s. Johannes and Melitta (Meese) I.; m. Helga Fischer, June 27, 1974; children: Carola, Dirk-Thorsten. MD, U. Heidelberg (Germany), 1967; Prof., U. Bonn (Germany), 1986. Med. diplomate. Med. asst. Kantonsspital, Zurich, Switzerland, 1970-73, Medizinische U., Bonn, 1974-82; head dept. hematology and oncology Clinic Internal Medicine, Oldenburg, Germany, 1982-87, med. dir., 1988—; mem. extended dirs. Berufsverband Dt Internisten, Wiesbaden, 1988—, mem. exec. com., 1992—; speaker Sect. Hematology and Oncology, 1988—; dir. Wilsede Sch. Oncology and Hematology, Wilsede, 1989—; mem. directory German Soc. Senology, Hamburg, 1989-91; head Cancer Ctr. Weser Ems, Oldenburg, 1986-93; cons. several working communities of govt. Author: Drug Interactions, 3d edit., 1995; editor: Testicular Cancer, 1982; contbr. more than 100 articles to profl. jours. German Govt. grantee, Bonn, 1976—. Mem. Working Community for Internal Oncology (mem. presidency 1981-87), European Soc. Med. Oncology (German rep. ednl. com. 1990—), German Cancer Soc., German Soc. Hematology and Oncology, German Soc. Internal Medicine. Office: Clinic Internal Medicine II, City of Oldenburg, Dr Edenstr 10, 26133 Oldenburg Germany

ILLINGWORTH, ROBERT DAVID, neurosurgeon; b. London, Oct. 17, 1935; s. Robert and Gertrude (Jackson) I.; m. Jean Margaret Jackson; children: Christopher David, Peter James. B Medicine B Surgery, U. London, 1958. Sr. registrar Nat. Hosp. for Nervous Diseases, London, 1967-70; rsch. fellow Notre Dame Hosp., Montreal, Que., Can., 1970-71; cons. neurosurgeon Ctrl. Middlesex Hosp., London, 1972-85, Charing Cross Hosp., London, 1974—; chmn. Riverside Dist. Med. Com., 1987-91; mgr. Regional Neurosci. Ctr., 1990-92; med. dir. Riverside Hosps., 1992-94. Contbr. numerous articles to profl. jours., chpts. to books. Officer RAF, 1960-63. Fellow Royal Soc. Medicine, Med. Soc. London; mem. Soc. Brit. Neurol. Surgeons. Office: Charing Cross Hosp, Fulham Palace Rd, London W6 8RF, England

ILLNER-CANIZARO, HANA, physician, oral surgeon, researcher; b. Prague, Czechoslovakia, Nov. 2, 1939; came to U.S., 1968; d. Evzen Pospisil and Emilie (Chrastna) Pospisilova; m. Pavel Illner, June 14, 1963 (div. 1981); children: Martin Illner, Anna Illner; m. Peter Corte Canizaro, Nov. 1, 1982. MD, Charles U., Prague, 1961. Diplomate State Bd. Oral Surgery, 1963. Resident in oral surgery Inst. of Health, Pribram, Czechoslovakia, 1961-63; attending physician Oral Surgery Clinic, Prague, 1963-68; rsch. assoc. dept. surgery U. Tex. Southwestern Med. Sch., Dallas, 1969-72, instr. surgery, 1972-74; instr. surgery U. Wash. Sch. Medicine, Seattle, 1974-77; asst. prof. surgery Cornell U. Med. Coll., N.Y.C., 1977-81, assoc. prof. surgery, 1981-83; assoc. prof. surgery Tex. Tech U. Health Scis. Ctr., Lubbock, 1984-88, prof. surgery, 1988—; site visitor NIGMS Postdoctoral Tng. Grant, Bethesda, Md., 1987. Mem. editorial bd. Circulatory Shock, N.Y.C., 1981—; manuscript reviewer Surgery, Gynecology and Obstetrics, Chgo., 1985—; contbr. chpts. to books, numerous articles to profl. jours. NIH grantee, 1979-83, 87-92; Tex. Tech U Health Scis. Ctr. grantee, 1985, 86; U.S. Dept. of Army grantee, 1988-90; Fogarty Sr. Internat. fellow, 1991-92. Mem. Shock Soc. Home: 4622 8th St Lubbock TX 79416-4722 Office: Tex Tech U Health Scis Ctr 3601 4th St Lubbock TX 79430-0001

ILLUZZI, ANGELO, physician; b. N.Y.C., Aug. 22, 1955; s. Angelo and Santa (Lepore) I.; m. Matilda Illuzzi, June 13, 1981; children: Jessica, Andrew. DO, Coll. Osteo. Medicine and Surgery, Des Moines, 1981. Diplomate Am. Bd. Internal Medicine. Attending physician Mid-Atlantic Med. Specialists, Galax, Va., 1987-94; dir. respiratory therapy Twin County Cmty. Hosp., Galax, Va., 1987-94; attending physician-pulmonary DuBois (Pa.) Regional Med. Ctr., 1994—; dir. Sleep Lab., DuBois Regional Med. Ctr., 1996. Fellow Am. Coll. Chest Physicians; mem. AMA, Am. Thoracic Soc., Pa. Osteo. Nephrology Assn., Pa. Med. Soc., Jefferson County Med. Soc. Home: 39 Brown St DuBois PA 15801 Office: Ste 202 145 Hospital Ave DuBois PA 15801

IM, YUNG KOOK, physician; b. Kwangju, Chon-nam, South Korea, Sept. 3, 1928; came to U.S., 1957; s. Dong-shik and Nam-Ae (Cho) I.; m. May, 1963 (widowed Apr. 1977). MD, Chon-nam Uc., Kwangju City, 1952. Diplomate Am. Bd. Pathologist. Intern St. Elizabeth Hosp., Covington, Ky., 1959; resident in pathology Louisville Gen. Hosp., 1959-63; assoc. pathologist St. Elizabeth Hosp., Covington, 1963-78, Booth Meml. Hosp., Florence, Ky., 1980-82; dir. Pathology Lab., Erlanger, Ky., 1982—. Capt. Republic of Korea Air Force, 1952-57. Fellow Am. Soc. Clin. Pathologists, Am. Coll. Pathologists; mem. Kenton-Campbell County Med. Soc., Ky. Soc. Pathologists, Ohio Soc. Pathologists, Ind. Soc. Pathologists. Home: 2512 Rardin Ct Covington KY 41017-1121

IMAMURA, TORU, molecular cell biologist; b. Kagoshima, Japan, Feb. 25, 1956; s. Hiroshi and Eiko (Ishikawa) I.; m. Reeko Urabe, Mar. 15, 1986; children: Mayumi, Ryota. BS, Tokyo U., 1979, MS, 1981, PhD, 1984. Researcher Fermentation Rsch. Inst., Tsukuba, 1984-88; vis. scientist ARC, Rockville, Md., 1988-90, 92-93; biotech. cons. Ministry Internat. Trade and Industry, Chiyoda and Tokyo, 1991-92; sr. scientist, group leader Ctr. of Excellence project Nat. Inst. Biosci. and Human Tech., Tsukuba, 1993—; chmn. radiation safety com. Fermentation Rsch. Inst., 1987-88, chmn. pollution prevention com., 1990-91; contact person Japan-U.S. aggreement in sci. and tech. Mechanism of Growth Signaling, 1992—, adj. prof. Sci U Tokyo, 1995—. Contbr. articles to profl. jours. Recipient Tsukuba Encouragement prize, 1996. Mem. AAAS, N.Y. Acad. Scis., Am. Soc. for Cell Biology, Japan Biochem. Soc., Japan Cell Biology Soc., Japanese Soc. Molecular Biology. Home: 2-20-12-1301, Senju-Azuma, Adachi 120, Japan Office: Nat Inst Biosci & Human Tech, 1-1 Higashi, Tsukuba 305, Japan

IMBEAU, STEPHEN ALAN, allergist; b. Portland, Oreg., Nov. 25, 1947; s. David A. and Marjory Anne (Jacobsen) I.; m. Shirley Ruth Burke, Aug. 18, 1979; children: Stephanie Frances, Andrew Paul, Charles Burke. BA, U. Calif., Berkeley, 1969; Dr.med., U. Calif., San Francisco, 1973. Diplomate Am. Bd. Internal Medicine, Am. Bd. Allergy. Intern U. Wis., Madison, S.C., 1973-74; resident in internal medicine U. Wis., Madison, 1974-75, resident in allergy, 1976-78, resident in infectious diseases, 1978-79; pvt. practice Florence, S.C., 1980—; mem. S.C. budget and control bd. S.C. Data Oversight Coun., 1993—. Contbr. articles to profl. jours. Chmn. Florence Symphony Orch., 1985-91; bd. dirs. Big Bros., 1989-92, Am. Lung Assn., 1982-86, Florence County Progress, chmn. 1993-95. Fellow ACP; mem. AMA (S.C. alt. del. 1992—), Am. Acad. Allergists, S.C. Med. Soc. (trustee 1988-90, sec. bd. 1990-94, treas. 1995—, S.C. Ambassador of the Yr. 1995), Florence County Med. Soc. (pres. 1984-85), Lions (pres. 1987-88). Home: 950 Park Ave Florence SC 29501-5734 Office: 901 E Cheves St #440 Florence SC 29503

IMBEMBO, ANTHONY LOUIS, surgeon, educator, educational administrator; b. N.Y.C., Nov. 8, 1942; s. Emil Anthony and Theresa (Rippert) I. AB, Columbia U., 1963, MD, 1967. Diplomate Am. Bd. Surgery Am. Bd. Thoracic Surgery, Nat. Bd. Med. Examiners. Intern Mass. Gen. Hosp., 1967-68, resident, 1968-73; asst. prof. surgery Johns Hopkins U., 1973-77, assoc. prof., 1977-83, surgeon, 1973-83; prof. surgery, vice chmn. dept. Case Western Res. U., 1983-88; dir. dept. surgery Cleve. Met. Gen. Hosp., 1983-88; prof. surgery, chmn. dept. U. Md., 1988—; surgeon-in-chief, U. Md. Hosp., 1988—; cons. Walter Reed Army Med. Ctr., 1982-83; dir. dept surgery Cleve. Met. Gen. Hosp., 1983-88. Johns Hopkins Hosp. grantee, 1976; recipient George J. Stuart award Johns Hopkins U. Sch. Medicine, 1977-84, Dean's Spl. Recognition award, 1983. Fellow ACS; mem. Am. Surg. Assn., Soc. Univ. Surgeons, Assn. Surg. Edn. (pres. 1982-83), Soc. Surgery of the Alimentary Tract, Internat. Cardiovascular Soc., Assn. Acad. Surgery, N.Y. Acad. Sci., Ea. Assn. Surg. Trauma, Cen. Surg. Assn., Halsted Soc. Home: 13815 Cuba Rd Cockeysville Hunt Valley MD 21030-1206 Office: U Md Hosp 22 S Greene St Baltimore MD 21201-1544

IMBER, RICHARD JOSEPH, physician, dermatologist; b. Darby, Pa., Apr. 9, 1944; s. Joseph and Geraldine (Frances) I.; m. Helen Lee Stick, Nov. 18, 1971. BS, U. Dayton, 1966; MD, Temple U., 1970. Diplomate Am. Bd. Dermatology. Intern Denver Presbyn. Med. Ctr., 1970-71; resident dept. dermatology U. Colo. Health Sci. Ctr., 1971-74; chief of dermatology USAF Acad., Colorado Springs, 1974-76; sr. staff dermatologist Colo. Permanente Med. Group, Denver, 1976-83; dermatologist Denver Skin Clinic, 1983—; asst. clin. prof. dermatology U. Colo. Med. Sch., Denver, 1974—. Contbr. articles to profl. jours. Maj. USAF, 1974-76. Fellow Am. Acad. Dermatology; mem. Pacific Dermatologic Assn., Colo. Med. Soc., Denver Med. Soc., Colo. Dermatologic Soc. (sec.-treas. 1980, v.p. 1981, pres. 1982). Home: 4020 S Bellaire Englewood CO 80110 Office: Denver Skin Clinic 2200 E 18th Ave Denver CO 80206

IMBESI, JOSEPH THOMAS, physician, hospital administrator; b. Newark, Sept. 20, 1942; s. Frank Charles and Vita Josephine (Giardina) I.; m. Catherine Antoinette Imbesi, Aug. 14, 1965; children: Joseph M., Catherine M. BA, Sexton Hall U., 1964; DO, Chgo. Coll. Osteo. Medicine, 1969. Diplomate Am. Bd. Emergency Medicine. Intern Union (N.J.) Hosp., 1969-70; pvt. practice Ortley Beach, N.J., 1970, Union, 1970-71; house physician Union Hosp., 1970-71, emergency rm. physician, 1971-74, dir. emergency dept., 1974-94, med. dir., co-founder mobile ICU, 1976, pres. med. staff, 1989-91; affiliation faculty mem. N.J. chpt. Am. Heart Assn. Bd. dirs. N.J. State Gov.'s Coun. on Emergency Med. Care., N.J. Com. on Trauma, Nat. Burn Victim Found., N.J. Dept. Health Poison Info. and Edn. Sys.; mem. steering com. Inter-Agy. Commn. on Emergency Med. Care; adminstrv. mem. Tri-County M.I.C.U. Consortium; adminstrv. com. mem. Union Coll. Paramedic AB Degree Program; establisher Rape Crisis Intervention; chmn., developer N.J. State Guidelines for Hosp. Diversion, 1988; appointed N.J. Med. Dir. EMT Tng., 1994. Mem. Am. Coll. Emergency Physicians (bd. dirs. N.J. chpt.), Am. Coll. Osteo. Emergency Physicians (fellow award 1986), N.J. Assn. Osteo. Physicians and Surgeons (health svcs. planning coun.), Am. Osteo. Soc., Union County Osteo. Soc. Office: Multicare Health Ctr 100 Commerce Pl Clark NJ 07066

IMBODEN, JOHN BASKERVILLE, psychiatry educator; b. Morrilton, Ark., Sept. 17, 1925. MD, Johns Hopkins U., Balt., 1950. Diplomate Am. Bd. Neurology and Psychiatry; lic. physician, Md. Intern Cin. Gen. Hosp., 1950-51; resident Johns Hopkin's Hosp., 1951-52, 54-56; pvt. practice psychiatry Balt., 1963—; chief dept. psychiatry Sinai Hosp. of Balt., 1969-90; assoc. prof. psychiatry Johns Hopkins U., Balt., 1963—. Co-author: Practical Psychiatry in Medicine; contbr. articles to profl. jours, chpts. to books. With U.S. Army, 1952-54. Fellow Am. Psychiat. Assn.; mem. Am. Psychoanalytic Assn. Office: 600 Wyndhurst Ave Baltimore MD 21210-2425

IMBURG, IRVING JEROME, dentist; b. Richmond, Va., July 7, 1924; s. Samuel and Nettie (Meyers) I.; m. Clare Cardozo, Dec. 20, 1948 (dec. Apr. 1986); children: Catherine, Susan, Nancy; m. Jeanne Ross, Dec. 28, 1986. Cert., Washington U., 1944; DDS, Med. Coll. Va., 1948. Pvt. practice dentistry Richmond, Va., 1948-50; attending dentist Richmond Public Schs., Richmond, 1949, Va. Dept. Corrections, 1950; co-founder, dir. Wm. Byrd Free Dental Clinic, Richmond, 1948-50; ptnr., dentist Falls Church Med. Ctr., Falls Church, Va., 1953-58; pres. dental group Imburg, Coleman, Rock et al, Falls Church, 1965-82; pvt. practice dentistry Falls Church, 1953—; postgrad. lectr. Med. Coll. Va., Richmond, Georgetown U., Washington, U. Md., 1975-77. Trustee Am. Jewish Hist. Soc., Waltham, Mass., 1987-92; pres. Beth El Hebrew Congregation, Alexandria, Va., 1963-65, MacArthur Elem. 1967, Alexandria, Howard Mid. Sch., Alexandria, 1968, TC William High Sch., Alexandria, 1969; bd. dirs. So. Jewish Hist. Soc., 1990-93; trustee Washington Jewish Social Svc. Agy., 1990-92. Capt. USAF, 1950-53. Fellow Internat. Coll. Dentists, Va. Dental Assn. (mem. ho. of dels. 1989-90, 94, 95), Am. Coll. Dentists; mem. No. Va. Dental Soc. (chmn. com. dental care programs 1994-95, pres. 1973-74), Fairfax County Dental Soc. (pres. 1964), Commonwealth Dental Soc. (pres. 1959-60), Univ. Club Washington. Independent. Jewish. Home: 6805 Willow Wood Dr Boca Raton FL 33434 Office: Irving J Imburg DDS 7 Corners Med Arts Bldg 2946 Sleepy Hollow Rd Falls Church VA 22044-2003 also: 774 Walker Rd Great Falls VA 22066

IMGRUND, BERNADINE WOJTANOWSKI, nurse educator; b. Connellsville, Pa., Mar. 13, 1936; d. Joseph S. and Wanda V. (Zielinski) Wojtanowski; m. David J. Imgrund, Oct. 8, 1960; children: David K., Kristi-Anne. Nursing degree, Mercy Sch. of Nursing, Pitts., 1956; BS, Boston Coll., 1960; EdM, Columbia U. Tchrs. Coll., 1969. Coord. West Jersey Sch. Nursing, Camden, N.J., 1960-61; instr. St. Joseph's Hosp. Sch. Nursing, Paterson, N.J., 1962-64, Hackensack (N.J.) Hosp. Sch. Nursing, 1964-69; asst. prof. nursing Widener U., Chester, Pa., 1978-79; health coord. Coll. DuPage, Glen Ellyn, Ill., 1984-85; pub. health nurse DuPage County Health Dept., Wheaton, Ill., 1989-90; nursing instr. Coll. DuPage, Glen Ellyn, fall 1993, Triton Coll., River Grove, Ill., fall 1994; nurse educator Morton Coll., 1995. Com. precinct person Dem. Party. Mem. AAUW (leader peace and nat. security group 1982-84, state com. women's equity 1984), Great Decisions Group (facilitator, leader 1982-89, pub. libr. liaison), Dist. Ill. Nurses (bd. dirs. 1986-88), Ill. State Nurses Assn. (bd. dirs. Dist. 19), Pi Lambda Theta. Roman Catholic. Home: 1239 Elizabeth Ave Naperville IL 60540-5719

IMHOF, HERWIG, radiologist; b. Pressburg, Slovakia, Feb. 9, 1943; arrived in Austria, 1945; s. Ernst and Margarethe (Schiefer) I.; m. Ilse Rummelhardt, Aug. 24, 1968; children: Klaus, Andrea. MD, U. Vienna, Austria, 1968. Cert. Austrian Bd. Physicians. Asst. physician I. Med. Klinik/U. Vienna AKH, 1968-71; asst. physician radiology I. Med. Klinik/U. Vienna Allgem Krankenhaus, 1972-75; asst. physician II Surgic Clinic/Allgem Krankenhaus-Radiology, 1971-72; asst. prof. radiology U. Chgo., 1975-76; dozent Zentr Inst. Radiology U. Vienna - Allgem Krankenhaus, 1976-87, leiter, prof. MR Inst., 1987—, leiter, prof. osteology, 1991—; spkr. med. faculty Kuriensprecher, 1992—. Office: U Klinik f Radiodiagnostik AKH Vienna, Waehringerstr 18-20, A-1090 Vienna Austria

IMIG, JOHN DAVID, medical educator; b. Bloomington, Ill., Nov. 20, 1962; m. Melinda L. Peel, June 9, 1984; 1 child, Allyson E. BA in Biology magna cum laude, Blackburn Coll., Carlinville, Ill., 1985; PhD in Physiology, U. Louisville, 1990. Postdoctoral fellow Med. Coll. Wis., Milw., 1990-93; instr. rsch. physiology Tulane U. Sch. Medicine, New Orleans, 1993-95, rsch. asst. prof. physiology, 1995—. Various editorial positions with profl. jours.; contbr. articles to profl. jours. LeRoy Edn. Assn. scholar, 1981, faculty Blackburn Coll. scholar, 1982, 84; Merck Sharp & Dohme fellow, 1992, NIH fellow, 1992-95. Mem. Am. Physiol. Soc., Am. Heart Assn. (coun. kidney in cardiovascular diseases, coun. high blood pressure rsch.), Micorciruclatory Soc., Golden Key. Home: 3702 E Grandlake Blvd Kenner LA 70065 Office: Tulane U Med Ctr Dept Physiology 1430 Tulane Ave New Orleans LA 70112-2699

IMMEDIATO, BARBARA DIANNE, social services administrator; b. Oakridge, Tenn., Aug. 20, 1950; d. Kenton and Dorothy Louise (Tiffany) Neville; m. James J. Immediato, Sept. 21, 1973. AS, Pace U., 1972; BSW, Adelphi U., 1974, MSW magna cum laude, 1975. Lic. social worker, N.Y. Dir. social svcs. King's Harbor Health Care Facility, Bronx, 1976-86; coord. community support svcs. Bronx-Lebanon Hosp., Bronx, 1986-88; clin. coord. White Plains (N.Y.) ARC, 1988-89; adminstr. social work United Cerebral Palsy of N.Y., Manhattan, 1989-94; social work chair Richmond Childrens Ctr., Yonkers, N.Y., 1994—. Mem. NASW, Westchester Trails Assn., Appalachian Mountain Club. Home: 311 Chatterton Pky Hartsdale NY 10530-1815 Office: Richmond Childrens Ctr 919 N Broadway Yonkers NY 10701-1206

IMPARATO, ANTHONY MICHAEL, vascular surgeon, medical educator, researcher; b. N.Y.C., July 29, 1922; s. Silverio and Olga (Santilli) I.; m. Agatha Maria Petriccione, Dec. 19, 1943; children: Maria April Imparato

Phillips, Karen Elsa Imparato Cotton. AB, Columbia U., 1944; MD, NYU, 1946. Diplomate Am. Bd. Surgery; cert. spl. qualifications in gen. vascular surgery. Intern U.S. Naval Hosp., Bklyn., 1946-47; fellow in anatomy NYU Med. Sch., 1949-50; successively intern, asst. resident in surgery, resident, chief resident in surgery NYU Med. Center Bellevue Hosp., 1950-56; mem. faculty NYU Med. Center, 1956—, dir. div. vascular surgery, 1975-92, prof. surgery, 1975—; cons. Norwalk (Conn.) Hosp., Patterson (N.J.) Gen. Hosp., Manhattan VA Hosp.; leader People-to-People delegation in vascular surgery: western Europe 1982, Soviet Union, 1985; ops. com. "Cooperative VA Study on Asymptomatic Carotid Stenosis", 1983-87 and Nascet, 1987-92. Author articles in field, chpts. in textbooks. Served as officer M.C. USNR, 46-49, 50. Grantee NIH, 1976-81. Fellow ACS, Am. Coll. Cardiology; mem. Am. Heart Assn. (fellow Stroke Coun.), Am. Surg. Assn., Soc. for Vascular Surgery (pres. 1984-85), Internat. Cardiovascular Soc., Soc. Clin. Vascular Surgery, Soc. Angiologia Uruguay, Royal Australasian Coll. Surgeons (hon.), Soc. Internat. Chirurgie, N.Y. Regional Vascular Soc. (co-founder, pres. 1982-84), N.Am. Soc. Pacing and Electrophysiology (founding mem.), James IV Assn. Surgeons (dir., treas.), Alpha Omega Alpha. Office: NYU Faculty Practice Area 530 1st Ave Ste 6-f New York NY 10016-6402

IMPERATO, PASCAL JAMES, physician, health administrator, author, editor, medical educator; b. N.Y.C., Jan. 13, 1937; s. James Anthony and Madalynne Marguerite (Insante) I.; m. Eleanor Anne Maiella, June 4, 1977; children: Alison Madalynne, Gavin Humbert, Austin Clement. BS, St. John's U., 1958, DSc (hon.), 1977; MD, SUNY, Downstate Med. Ctr., 1962; M in Pub. Health and Tropical Medicine, Tulane U., 1966, DSc (hon.), 1996. Diplomate Am. Bd. Preventive Medicine, Nat. Bd. Med. Examiners. Fgn. fellow Assn. Am. Med. Colls., Kenya, Tanzania, Uganda, 1961; intern dept. internal medicine L.I. Coll. Hosp., 1962-63, resident dept. medicine, 1963-65; fgn. rsch. fellow Tulane Univ.-U. del Valle, Cali, Colombia, 1965; N.Y. Acad. Medicine/Glorney Raisebeck fellow Tulane U., New Orleans, 1965-66; med. epidemiologist smallpox eradication-measles control program Ctrs. Disease Control/USPHS, Mali, 1966-72; dir. Bur. Infectious Disease Control, N.Y.C. Dept. Health, 1972-74, prin. epidemiologist, dir. immunization program, 1972-74, 1st dep. commr., 1974-77, dir. pub. health residency tng. program, 1974-77; chmn. N.Y.C. Swine Influenza Immunization Task Force, 1976-77; med. cons. Africa Bur., U.S. AID, 1974; commr. health N.Y.C., 1977-78; chmn. N.Y.C. Bd. Health, 1977-78; chmn. bd. N.Y.C. Health and Hosps. Corp., 1977-78; chmn. exec. com. N.Y.C. Health Systems Agy., 1977-78; acting health services adminstr. N.Y.C., 1977-78; clin. instr. dept. medicine Cornell U. Med. Coll., N.Y.C., 1972-74, asst. clin. prof., 1974-78, asst. clin. prof. dept. pub. health, 1974-77, assoc. clin. prof., 1977-78, adj. prof., 1979—; clin. assoc. prof. dept. preventive medicine & community health SUNY Health Sci. Ctr. at Bklyn., 1974-77, lectr., 1977-78, prof. and chmn., 1978-94; disting. svc. prof. and chmn., 1994—; mem. staff N.Y. Hosp. 1972-78, L.I. Coll. Hosp., 1973—, State U. Hosp., 1978, Kings County Hosp., 1978—; lectr. dept. cmty. medicine Mt. Sinai Sch. Medicine, CUNY, 1974-90; lectr. dept. health adminstrn. Sch. Pub. Health, Columbia U., 1982-89; cons. N.Y. State Dept. Edn., 1982-87, NAS, 1985, dept. cmty. health svcs. and ambulatory care Brookdale Hosp. Med. Ctr., 1987-96; cons. program for appropriate tech. in health U.S. AID, 1985-89; med. dir. R&D and Epidemiology Island Peer Rev. Orgn., 1991—; bd. dirs. Primary Care Devel. Corp., 1995—. Author: Doctor in The Land of the Lion, 1964, (with Osa Johnson) Last Adventure, 1966, Bwana Doctor, 1967, The Treatment and Control of Infectious Diseases in Man, 1974, The Cultural Heritage of Africa, 1974, A Wind in Africa, 1975, What To Do About the Flu, 1976, African Folk Medicine, 1977, Historical Dictionary of Mali, 1977, 3d edit., 1996, Dogon Cliff Dwellers: The Art of Mali's Mountain People, 1978, Medical Detective, 1979, (with wife) Mali: A Handbook of Historical Statistics, 1982, The Administration of a Public Health Agency, 1983, Buffoons, Queens and Wooden Horsemen, 1983, (with Greg Mitchell) Acceptable Risks, 1985, (with Robert I. Goler) Early American Medicine, 1987, Arthur Donaldson Smith and the Exploration of Lake Rudolf, 1987, Acquired Immunodeficiency Syndrome: Current Issues and Scientific Studies, 1989, Mali: A Search for Direction, 1989, (with wife) They Married Adventure: The Wandering Lives of Martin and Osa Johnson, 1992; contbr. articles to profl. jours.; cons. editor: N.Y. State Jour. Medicine, 1983, dep. editor, 1983-86, editor, 1986-93; editor Jour. Community Health, 1985—; editl. bd. Explorers Jour., 1979-88, The Am. Jour. of Chinese Medicine, 1985—, The Pharos, 1995—; mem. med. adv. bd. The Med. Herald, 1992—. Bd. dirs. Pub. Health Rsch. Inst., 1977-78, Cmty. Coun. Greater N.Y., 1977-78, Med. Health and Rsch. Assn., 1977-78, Greater N.Y. Hosp. Assn., 1977-78, N.Y. Heart Assn., 1983-84, Primary Care Devel. Corp., 1995—; bd. dirs. Milton Helpern Libr. Legal Medicine, 1977-89, hon. trustee, 1989—; trustee Martin and Osa Johnson Safari Mus., 1964—; mem. adv. bd. Physicians for Social Responsibility, 19.Y. State Bd. Medicine, 1985-95, vice chmn., 1990-93, chmn., 1993-95; mem. bd. zoning and appeals Village of Plandome Heights, N.Y., 1986-90, trustee, 1990-92; mem. sci. adv. bd. Explorers Club, 1988-93; chmn. N.Y.C. Met. Area Task Force on Syphilis, 1990-91; mem. bd. regents L.I. Coll. Hosp., 1992—; mem. N.Y.C. Mayor-Elect Giuliani's Health Care Adn. Group, 1993; mem. N.Y. State Coun. on Grad. Med. Edn., 1994—; co-chmn. adv. commn. on pub. health N.Y.C. Coun., 1994—; mem. N.Y. State Bd. for Profl. Med. Conduct, 1994—. Lt. comdr. USPHS, 1966-69. Recipient Meritorious Honor award and medal Dept. State, 1971, US AID Meritorious Honor award and medal, 1970, Outstanding Alumnus award Tulane U., 1978, Delta Omega Nat. Merit award, 1978, Frank Babbot award SUNY, 1980, Disting. Alumni Achievement award, and medal SUNY, 1987, Spl. Service award for smallpox eradication USPHS, 1987; Fulbright scholar, North Yemen, 1985. Fellow ACP, Royal Soc. Tropical Medicine and Hygiene, Royal African Soc., Am. Coll. Epidemiology, Am. Coll. Preventive Medicine; mem. Am. Soc. Tropical Medicine and Hygiene, N.Y. Soc. Tropical Medicine (v.p. 1976-77, pres. 1989-90), East African Wildlife Soc., African Studies Assn., Author's Guild, Explorers Club, Delta Omega, Alpha Omega Alpha. Roman Catholic. Office: Box 43 450 Clarkson Ave Brooklyn NY 11203

IMPERATO-MCGINLEY, JULIANNE LEONE, endocrinologist, educator; b. N.Y.C., Sept. 22; d. Thomas and Marian (Crispinelli) Imperato; m. Patrick W. McGinley, Aug. 27, 1966; children: Alexandra Claire, Ian Patrick McGinley. BS in Chemistry cum laude, Coll. Mt. St. Vincent, 1961; MD in Pub. Health with honors, SUNY, 1965. Intern in internal medicine St. Vincent's Hosp. and Med. Ctr., N.Y.C., 1965-66, resident in internal medicine, 1966-68; fellow in reproductive endocrinology NYU and Lenox Hill Hosps., N.Y.C., 1968-69; NIH fellow in endocrinology Cornell U. Med. Coll., N.Y.C., 1969-72; asst. physician The N.Y. Hosp., N.Y.C., 1969-72, physician to out-patient dept., 1972-75, asst. attending, 1975-81; from instr. in medicine to asst. prof. medicine Cornell U. Med. Ctr., N.Y.C., 1972-81; assoc. attending physician The N.Y. Hosp., N.Y.C., 1982—; assoc. prof. medicine Cornell U. Med. Coll., N.Y.C., 1982-93, assoc. dir. Gen. Clin. Rsch. Ctr., 1991-93, chief sect. androgen physiology divsn. endocrinology, 1992—, dir. Gen. Clin. Rsch. Ctr., 1993—, chief divsn. endocrinology, 1993—, prof. medicine, 1993—; cons. prof. Nat. U. Pedro Henriquez Urena, Santo Domingo, Dominican Republic, 1987, St. Vincent's Hosp. and Med. Ctr., N.Y.C., 1978—; mem. internat. adv. bd. 3d Internat. Conf. on Geriatric Nephrology and Urology, 1991-92; expert ad hoc grant reviewer behavioral medicine study sect. NIH, 1984, ad hoc mem. biopsychology study sect., 1982, ad hoc mem. site visit team biophysiology study sect., 1981; organizing com. Serono Symposium on Sexual Differentiation, 1982; plenary lectr. Merck Med. Adv. Coun. Meeting, St. Andrews, Scotland, 1991, European Soc. for Paediat. Endocrinology, Vienna, Austria, 1990; mem. Gordon Rsch. Conf., Plymouth, N.H., 1986; Macomber lectr. in human sexuality Harvard Med. Sch., Dept. Ob-Gyn., Boston, 1980. Assoc. editor Jour. Clin. Endocrinology and Metabolism, 1993—, mem. editl. bd., 1993—; reviewer: Acta Endocrinologica, Archives of Internal Medicine, Clin. Endocrinology, Endocrine Revs., Endocrinology, Jour. Andrology, Jour. Clin. Endocrinology and Metabolism, Jour. Urology, New Eng. Jour. Medicine; contbr. over 100 articles to profl. jours. NIH fund rschr.; active fundraising and drug donations The Robert Reid Cabral Children's Hosp., Santo Domingo, 1988—. Recipient award for outstanding clin. rsch. Dominican Pediat. Endocrine Soc., 1988, Rsch. award 1st prize Am. Acad. Pediats., sect. urology, 1984, Nicholas Pichardo award and lectr. for outstanding rsch. contbns. to advancement of medicine in Dominican Republic, Santo Domingo, 1980, also numerous rsch. grants; acad. scholar Coll. Mt. St. Vincent, 1961. Mem. AAAS, Am. Fedn. for Clin. Rsch., Endocrine Soc. (chair, lectr. symposium on steroid 5a-reductase ann. meeting San Antonio 1992, membership com. 1989-91, chair membership com. 1991-92, chair meetings 1984-88), N.Y. Acad. Sci., Soc. for Study of Reprodn., Harvey Soc., Women in Endocrinology, Kappa Gamma Pi. Roman Catholic. Office: NY Hosp-Cornell U Med Ctr Divsn Endocrin/Gen Clin Rsc 525 E 68th St New York NY 10021-4873

IMRE, PAUL DAVID, mental health administrator; b. N.Y.C., May 30, 1925; s. Maximilian and Bluma (Datz) I.; BS, U. Ill.-Urbana, 1950; MA, N.Y. U., 1951; MPH, Johns Hopkins U., 1963; lic. psychologist, Md. m. Jo Ellen Varner, Aug. 16, 1956; children: David Maximilian, Robert Bruce. Extern City Hosp., Welfare Island, N.Y., 1951-52; intern Springfield State Hosp., Sykesville, Md., 1952-53; chief psychologist Cherokee Mental Health Inst., Iowa, 1953-54; staff and chief psychologist Spring Grove State Hosp., Catonsville, Md., 1954-62; rsch. assoc. Johns Hopkins U., 1964-72; dir. mental health ctr. Balt. County Dept. Health, Catonsville, 1970-88 ; cons. Md. State Dept. Health and Mental Hygiene, 1954-70, Children's Guild of Md., 1962-70, Jewish Child and Family Svc., Balt., 1957-62; pvt. practice psychology, Columbia, Md. and Balt., 1951—. Served with inf., AUS, 1943-46; ETO.; recipient Purple Heart, 3 Battle Stars with Arrowhead, 2 Presdl. Unit citations PRCHT Wings Combat Inf. badge; Nat. Register Platinum award. Lic. psychologist, Md. Mem. APA, APHA, Md. Psychol. Assn. (pres. div. II 1982-83, cert. of recognition 1978). Club: Johns Hopkins (Balt.). Home: 10418 Green Mountain Cir Columbia MD 21044-2456

IMSANDE, JOHN DAVID, geneticist, researcher, educator; b. Grass Range, Mont., June 14, 1931; s. Louis H. and Freda M. (Dengel) I.; m. Elizabeth Blanchard, June 2, 1956 (div.); children: Carol Imsande Batastini, Louis D.; m. Marica F. Doerschug, Aug. 13, 1976. BA in Math. and Edn., U. Mont., 1953; MS in Chemistry, Mont. State U., 1956; PhD in Biochemistry, Duke U., 1960. Postdoctoral fellow U. Calif. Berkeley, 1960-61; lectr., postdoctoral fellow Princeton (N.J.) U., 1961-62; asst. prof. Case Western Res. U., Cleve., 1962-64, assoc. prof. dept. biology, 1964-69; assoc. prof. genetics and biochemistry Iowa State U., Ames, 1969-73, prof. genetics, 1973-86, prof. agronomy and genetics, 1990—; vis. scientist U. Edinburgh, Scotland, 1968-69; vis. prof. U. Calif., San Diego, 1976-77; vis. prof. dept. agriculture U. Queensland, Brisbane, Australia, 1986-87, 90-91. Author: (chpt.) The ENZYMES-Pyrophosphorylases, Methods in Enzymology, 1961, Biology of the Rhizobiaceae, 1981; contbr. over 50 articles to profl. jours. Cpl. U.S. Army, 1953-55. NIH fellow USPHS, 1957-60, 60-62; grantee NIH, USDA. Mem. Crop Sci. Soc. Am. Democrat. Home: 5422 Arrasmith Trl Ames IA 50010-9720 Office: Iowa State U Dept Of Agronomy Ames IA 50011

INABINET, LAWRENCE ELLIOTT, retired pharmacist; b. Orangeburg, S.C., June 15, 1933; s. Boysie Benjamin and Alrona Minerva (Robinson) I.; m. Velma Vincent Ferguson (div.); children: Rhett Elliott, Bonny Susan Murphy. BS in Pharmacy, U. S.C., 1963. Registered pharmacist. Retail pharmacist chain and ind. drug stores, 1963-69; staff hosp. pharmacist S.C. State Hosp., Columbia, S.C., 1969-71; staff pharmacist Hawthorne Pharmacy, Columbia, S.C., 1971-72, Hemingway (S.C.) Pharmacy, 1990-93, Revco Drug Stores, Marion, S.C., 1993-95; pharmacy supr. S.C. Dept. Corrections, Columbia, 1972-79; retail pharmacist Ind. Drug Stores, 1979-84; hosp. pharmacist Baker Hosp., North Charleston, S.C., 1984-86; asst. dir. pharmacy Marion (S.C.) Meml. Hosp., 1986-90. Author: (text) Civilian-Military Time Converter; patentee medicating device for animals; contbr. poems to pubs. Deacon Bapt. ch. With USN, 1954-58. Mem. Am. Legion, Masons (past master, masonic knight templar), Kappa Psi. Home: 1-B Greenwood Park Marion SC 29571-9406

INAGAMI, TADASHI, biochemist, educator; b. Kobe, Japan, Feb. 20, 1931; m. Masako Araki, Nov. 12, 1961. B.S., Kyoto U., Japan, 1953, D.Sc., 1963; M.S., Yale U., 1955, Ph.D., 1958. Research staff Yale U., New Haven, 1958-59, research assoc., 1962-66; research staff Kyoto U., Japan, 1959-62; instr. biochemistry Nagoya City U., Japan, 1962; asst. prof. biochemistry Vanderbilt U., Nashville, 1966-69, assoc. prof., 1969-74, prof. biochemistry, dir. hypertension rsch. ctr., 1975-95, Stanford Moore prof. biochemistry, 1991—, prof. medicine, 1992—. Contbr. numerous articles to profl. jours. Fulbright fellow, 1954-55; recipient Roche Vis. Prof. award, 1980, Humboldt Found. award, 1981, Ciba award Am. Heart Assn., 1985, Spa award Belgium Nat. Funds Sci. Rsch., 1986, Sutherland prize Vanderbilt U., 1990, Okamoto award Japan Vascular Disease Rsch. Found., 1995, award for excellence in cardiovascular rsch. Brostil Meyers Squibb, 1996, award Japan Acad., 1996. Fellow High Blood Pressure Rsch. Coun.; mem. Am. Soc. Biol. Chemists, Am. Physiol. Soc., Endocrine Soc., Am. Chem. Soc., Am. Heart Assn., Am. Soc. Cell Biology, Soc. Neurosci., Japan Endocrine Soc. (hon.). Office: Vanderbilt U Sch Medicine Dept Biochemistry 23d Ave S and Pierce Ave Nashville TN 37232-0146

INCAGNOLI, THERESA MARIE, clinical neuropsychologist; b. N.Y.C., June 22, 1949; d. Thomas Marcel and Marie Incagnoli. B.A. cum laude, Bklyn. Coll., 1970; Ph.D., St. John's U., 1978. Diplomate in clin. neuropsychology Am. Bd. Profl. Psychology. Psychologist, St. Vincent's Med. Ctr., N.Y.C., 1973-79; postdoctoral fellow in clin. neuropsychology U. Okla. Health Scis. Ctr., 1979-80; asst. prof. dept. psychiatry (psychology) Sch. Medicine SUNY-Stony Brook, 1982—. Editor textbook: Clinical Application of Neuropsychological Test Batteries, 1986. NIMH fellow, 1979-80. Mem. Am. Psychol. Assn., Internat. Neuropsychol. Soc., Nat. Acad. Neuropsychologists, Brain Injury Assn. Office: 240 Central Park S New York NY 10019

INCAPRERA, FRANK PHILIP, internist; b. New Orleans, Aug. 24, 1928; s. Charles and Mamie (Bellipanni) I.; BS, Loyola U. of South, 1946; MD, La. State U., 1950; m. Ruth Mary Duhon, Sept. 13, 1952; children: Charles, Cynthia, James, Christopher, Catherine. Diplomate Am. Bd. Internal Medicine. Intern, Charity Hosp., New Orleans, 1950-51, resident, 1951-52; resident VA Hosp., New Orleans, 1952-54; practice medicine specializing in internal medicine, New Orleans, 1957—; med. dir. Internal Medicine Group, New Orleans, 1973—; med. dir. Owens-Ill. Glass Co., New Orleans, 1961-85, Kaiser Aluminum Co., Chalmette, La., 1975-84, Tenneco Oil Co., Chalmette, 1978-84, Lutheran Nursing Home, 1990—; assoc. med. dir. Cigna Health Plan of La., 1991—; co-founder Med. Ctr. E. New Orleans, 1975; clin. assoc. prof. medicine Tulane U. Sch. Medicine, 1971-87, clin. prof. medicine, 1987—; clin. prof. medicine La. State U., 1994—; med. dir. Luth. Nursing Home, 1990—; adv. bd. Healthcare New Orleans, 1991—; mem. New Orleans Bd. Health, 1966-70. Bd. dirs. Meth. Hosp., 1971—, sec., 1992—, Lutheran Home New Orleans, 1976-80, Chateau de Notre Dame, 1977-82, New Orleans Opera Assn., 1975—; mem. New Orleans Human Relation Com., 1968-70; bd. dirs. Emergency Med. Svcs. Coun., 1977-86, pres., La. southeastern region, 1979-81; bd. dirs. New Orleans East Bus. Assn., 1980-95, v.p., 1981-83; bd. dirs. Luth. Towers, 1988-89, Peace Lake Towers, 1988-89, La. State U. Med. Ctr. Found. Bd., 1989-91; mem. pastoral care adv. com. So. Bapt. Hosp., 1982-83; mem. pres's. adv. bd. coun. Loyola U. of South, 1989—. Capt. USAF, 1955-57. Fellow ACP, Am. Geriatrics Soc.; mem. AMA, Am. Coll. Physician Execs., Am. Coll. Physicians (gov 1995—, Laureate award 1993), La. Med. Soc. (v.p. 1975-76), Orleans Parish Med. Soc. (sec. 1972-74), New Orleans Acad. Internal Medicine (pres. 1969), La. Occupl. Medicine Assn. (pres. 1971-72), La. State Med. Soc. (v.p. 1975-76), La. Soc. Internal Medicine (exec. com. 1975—, pres. 1983-85), New Orleans East C. of C. (dir. 1979-85), La. State U. Med. Sch. Alumni Assn. (pres. 1989-90), Order of St. Louis, Blue Key, Delta Epsilon Sigma, Optimists Club (bd. dirs. 1964-69, New Orleans). Home: 2218 Lake Oaks Pky New Orleans LA 70122-4345 Office: 5640 Read Blvd New Orleans LA 70127-3140

INCAVO, STEPHEN JOSEPH, orthopaedic surgeon; b. Bologna, Italy, Aug. 4, 1957; came to U.S., 1959; s. Joseph Francis and Noreen (Pezzullo) I.; m. Kerry Ryan, May 27, 1983; children: Daniel, Stephanie, Caroline, Kristine. AB, Colgate U., 1979; MD, SUNY, Syracuse, 1983. Intern gen. surgery U. Vt., Burlington, 1983-84, resident orthop. surgery, 1984-88, fellow orthop. surgery, 1988-89, asst. prof. orthops., 1989-96, assoc. prof. orthops., 1996—; Mem. adv. bd. New Eng. Organ Bank, 1991—. Mem. editl. bd. Jour. Orthop. and Sports Phys. Therapy; contbr. articles to med. jours.; inventor Component Knee Replacement, 1995; mem. design team hip replacement component, 1995. Leader Cub Scout Pack 610, South Burlington, Vt., 1993-95. Charles Dana scholar Colgate U., 1979 Fellow Am. Acad. Orthop. Surgeons; mem. Am. Assn. Hip and Knees Soc., New Eng. Orthop. Soc., Vt. State Orthop. Soc., Acad. Orthop. Soc., Phi Beta Kappa. Republican. Roman Catholic. Home: 55 Butler Dr South Burlington VT 05403 Office: U Vt Dept Orthop and Rehab Stafford Hall 428A Burlington VT 05405

INDICK, BENJAMIN PHILIP, pharmacist, writer; b. Elizabeth, N.J., Aug. 11, 1923; s. Charles Indick and Sarah (Gechtberg) Indick Goldrich; m. Janet Suslak, Aug. 23, 1953; children—Michael Cory, Karen Leigh Indick Maizel. B.S. in Biology, Rutgers U., 1947; B.S. Pharmacy cum laude, Ohio State U., 1954. Registered pharmacist N.J., N.Y. Pharmacist Fruchtman's Prescription Ctr., Summit, N.J., 1954-61, Wald's Drugs, Plainfield, N.J., 1961-63, Cross-Hill Pharmacy, Bronx, N.Y., 1963-77; co-owner Ferben Prescriptions, Inc., Bronx, 1977-92, Wakefield Pharmacy, Bronx, 1978—. Author plays published in Plays Mag. and The Player (many prize winning plays performed). Author essays on writers of sci. fiction, fantasy and horror, included in numerous anthologies: Bok, 1974, Fear Itself, 1982, The Dark Barbarian, 1984, Kingdom of Fear, 1986, Penguin Encyclopedia of Horror and the Supernatural, 1987, Reign of Fear, 1988, Ben's Beat, 1982, Ray Bradbury, Dramatist, 1989, George Alec Effinger: From Entropy to Budayeen, 19993; editor and pub. IBID mag., 1973-89, Onyx mag. 1980-89, Alumni sec., OSU pharmacy mag. Spur, 1972-84. Mem. Dramatist Guild, Horror Writers of America, Phi Lamda Upsilon, Rho Chi. Address: 428 Sagamore Ave Teaneck NJ 07666-2626

INDIVERI, FRANCESCO, internal medicine educator; b. Monopoli, Bari, Italy, Jan. 25, 1939; s. Giacomo and Antonietta (Biasi) I.; m. Amina Di Munno, Dec. 10, 1966; children: Giacomo, Giovanni. MD, U. Genoa (Italy), Genova, Italy, 1964. Asst. prof., internal medicine U. Sassari (Italy), 1966-70; asst. prof., internal medicine U. Genoa, 1970-82, assoc. prof., clin. immunology, 1982-86; prof., internal medicine U. Palermo (Italy), 1986-89, U. Genoa, 1989—; vis. prof. pathology Columbia U., N.Y.C., 1980-83; vis. investigator dept. immunology Scripps Clinic and Rsch. Found., LaJolla, Calif., 1977-80. Editor: Biological Response Modifiers Applications in Clinical Medicine, 1990, New Aspects of Glucocorticold Therapy in Immunological Disorders, 1993; contbr. 270 scientific articles to profl. jours. Internal Medicine fellow U. Genoa, 1964-66, Itlaian-Am. Med. Assn. fellow, 1977, Fogharthy fellow, 1977-79; C.N.R. grantee, 1974-95, AIDS grantee, 1989-95. Mem. Fedn. Italian Soc. Immunology, Italian Soc. Internal Medicine, Am. Assn. Immunology, Internat. Soc. Immunopharmacology, European Acad. Allergies Clin. Immunology, Internat. Soc. Interferon Rsch., Am. Soc. Clin. Immunologists. Office: U Genoa, V le Benedetto XV 6, 16132 Genoa Italy

INDOW, TAROW, psychology educator; b. Tokyo, Aug. 22, 1923; came to U.S., 1980; s. Sahei and Atsuko Indow; m. Minako Kawamura, Oct. 14, 1953. BA, Keio U., Tokyo, 1945, PhD, 1959. Prof. Keio U., 1961-79; research fellow Harvard U., Cambridge, Mass., 1963-66; vis. mem. Inst. for Advanced Study, Princeton, N.J., 1971-72; prof. U. Calif., Irvine, 1980-92, prof. emeritus, 1993—. mem. editorial bd. Jour. Mathematical Psychology, Color Research & Application; contbr. articles to profl. jours. Fellow Soc. Exptl. Psychologists; mem. Assn. Internat. de la Couleur (pres. 1973-77). Office: U Calif Sch Social Scis Irvine CA 92697

INDRABHAKTI, INDRASONG, health facility administrator; b. Bangkok, June 28, 1922; s. Damrong and Sa-nguan Hieng (Apananda) I.; m. Saowanee Maria Bernadette Bhanthumchinda, Aug. 23, 1957; children: Angil, Indranee, Saowanin. BSc in Pharms., Mahidol U., Bangkok, 1945, MD, 1952, cert. in hosp. adminstrn., 1994; MPH, U. N.C., 1957; cert. in food tech., Cen. Food Tech. Rsch. Inst., Mysore, India, 1966. Pharmacist Dr. Paiboon (pvt. clinic), Haadyai, Thailand, 1947; health officer City Health Div., Bangkok, 1953-55; provincial health officer Phisnuloke, Petchboon, Thonburi, Thailand, 1957-59; chief med. officer Provincial Adminstrn., Cholburi, Thailand, 1975; med. dir. Pathanavech Hosp., Bangkok, 1982—; cons. FDA, Bangkok, 1959-68. Recipient Citation award Assn. Excellent Adminstrs., 1995.Fulbright Ednl. Found. grantee (Thailand), 1955. Mem. AAAS (life), N.Y. Acad. Scis. Buddhist. Home: 2600 Charernkrung Rd, Yannawa Bangkok 10120, Thailand Office: Pathanavech Hosp, 662 664 Sukhumvit 71 Rd, Bangkok 10110, Thailand

INDRITZ STOIKES, MARY ELOISE, pharmacy researcher; b. Madison, Wis., May 23, 1960; d. Gerald Leonard and Dorothy Jane (Dunn) S. BS in Pharmacy, Drake U., 1983; MS in Pharmacy Practice, N.D. State U., 1985; postgrad., U. Minn., 1994—. Resident VA Med. Ctr., Fargo, N.D., 1983-85; staff pharmacist Strong Meml. Hosp., Rochester, N.Y., 1985-86; staff pharmacist Park Ridge Hosp., Rochester, 1986-88, clin. coord., 1988-89; supr. clin. svcs. Sisters of Charity Hosp., Buffalo, 1989-91; dir. pharmacy St. Francis Med. Ctr., Buffalo, 1989-91; clin. pharmacist A.O. Fox Meml. Hosp., Oneonta, N.Y., 1991-92; pharmacy supr. St. Joseph's Hosp., St. Paul, 1992-94. Contbr. articles to profl. jours. E.R. Squibb & Sons scholar, 1985; recipient Albert P. Prescott/Glaxo Leadership award, 1993, Albert B. Prescott Leadership award; N.Y. State Rsch. and Edn. Found., 1990. Fellow Am. Soc. Health-Sys. Pharmacists; mem. AAUW, APHA, Am. Sociol. Assn., Am. Pharm. Assn., N.Y. State Coun. Hosp. Pharmacists (pres. 1990-92), Rochester Area Soc. Hosp. Pharmacists (pres. 1987-89), Minn. Soc. Hosp. Pharmacists, Am. Soc. Hosp. Pharmacists (com. 1991—), N.D. Soc. Hosp. Pharmacists, Minn-Dakota Soc. Hosp. Pharmacists (sec. 1984-85), Gamma Phi Beta, Lambda Kappa Sigma, Rho Chi. Home: Unit E 421 Bayless Ave Saint Paul MN 55114

INFANTINO, SALVATORE, physician; b. Siracusa, Italy, Apr. 9, 1945; came to U.S. 1946.; s. Joseph and Maria (Musco) I.; m. Patricia I., Jan. 14, 1979; children: Damian, Dorian, Julian. BA, Rutgers U.; U. of Rome (Italy). Lic. physician Italy 1972, N.Y. 1976, N.J. 1982, Calif. 1983. Intern U. of Rome, Italy, 1972, Cabrini Med. Center, N.Y.C., 1973; intern, then resident N.Y. Med. Coll., N.Y.C., 1974-76; fellow in cardiology N.Y. Med. Coll., 1976-78; pvt. practice Rome, 1978-82; cardiology attending instr. Bergen Pines County Hosp., Paramus, N.J., 1982-84; pvt. practice Hohokus/Fair Lawn, N.J., 1983—; attending physician Valley Hosp., Ridgewood, N.J., 1983—, Bergen Pines, 1983—; cons., dir. cardiology labs for various facilities, Rome, Latina, Italy, 1978-82. Fellow Am. Coll. of Angiology, Internat. Coll. Angiology; mem. N.Y. Acad. of Med., N.Y. Cardiol. Soc. Office: Med Multi A Pa 11-26 Saddle River Rd Fair Lawn NJ 07410-5708

INFANTOLINO, PHILIP LOUIS, cardiologist; b. Newark, N.J., Mar. 23, 1942; s. Joseph and Mary (Testa) I.; m. Alberta Barrasso, June 3, 1966; children: Joseph, Dena. BA, Rutgers U., 1964; MD, N.J. Coll. Medicine, 1968. Diplomate Am. Bd. Cardiology. Intern Harlem Hosp., N.Y.C., 1968-69, resident in medicine, 1969-71, resident in cardiology, 1971-73; pvt. practice in cardiology, 1973—; assoc. chief staff Point Pleasant (N.J.) Hosp., 1991-93, chief staff, 1993-95; sec. med. staff Point Pleasant Hosp., 1989-91, trustee, 1989-95. Fellow Am. Coll. Cardiology; mem. AMA, Internat. Game Fishing Assn. (record holder Blue Marlin 1986). Roman Catholic. Office: 2640 Highway 70 Manasquan NJ 08736-2609

INFELD, DONNA LIND, medical educator, dean; b. Portland, Oreg., June 3, 1949; d. Arthur Lind and Arlene (Hochman) Krall; m. Marcel David Infeld, June 29, 1986. BS in Psychology, Portland State U., 1972; PhD in Social Welfare, Brandeis U., 1978. Rsch. asst. Portland State U., 1975-78; asst. prof. dept. health svc. mgmt. George Washington U., Washington, 1978-82, assoc. prof., 1982-90, dir. doctoral programs, 1984-87, prof., 1990—, assoc. dean, 1991-92. Editor: Cases in Long Term Care Management, 1995, Hospice Care and Cultural Diversity, 1995; contbr. articles to profl. jours. Fellow Gerontol. Soc. Am. (treas. 1993—); mem. Nat. Hospice Orgn. (editor jour. 1994—). Office: George Washington Univ Dept Health Svcs. Mgmt Washington DC 20052

ING, CLARENCE SINN FOOK, preventive medicine physician, surgeon; b. Stockton, Calif., Oct. 1, 1938; s. Clarence S. and Isabel L. (Low) I.; m. May Chan, July 9, 1991; children: Michael, Stephen, Jeffrey, Daniel, Michelle. BA, La Sierra U., 1959; MD, Loma Linda U., 1963, MPH, 1990. Diplomate Am. Bd. Ophthalmology, Am. Bd. Preventive Medicine. Intern San Joaquin Gen. Hosp., Stockton, Calif., 1963-64; dir. emergency med. svc. Cmty. Hosp. San Gabriel, Calif., 1967; resident ophthalmology Hollywood Presbyn. Hosp., L.A., 1967-70; med. missionary Bella Vista Hosp., Mayaguez, P.R., 1970-78; staff physician Wildwood (Ga.) Sanitarium & Hosp., 1978-81; med. missionary, chief staff Armer Ishoda Meml. Hosp., Majuro, Marshall Islands, 1981-82; med. missionary Youngberg Adventist Hosp., Singapore, 1982-89; resident preventive medicine Loma Linda U. Med. Ctr., 1990-91; med. missionary, dir. Wellness Ctr. Youngberg Adventist Hosp., Singapore, 1992—. Capt. U.S. Army, 1964-66. Fellow Am. Acad. Ophthalmology; mem. Am. Coll. Preventive Medicine. Home and Office: 309 Upper Serangoon Rd, 347693 Singapore Singapore

INGAGLIO, DIEGO AUGUSTUS, dentist; b. Phila., Dec. 4, 1922; s. Salvatore and Maria Concetta (Giordano) I.; D.D.S., U. Pa., 1947; m. Geraldine Jean Capizzi, July 11, 1948; children: Marie, Francene. With Phila. Mouth Hygiene Dept., 1947-50; asst. clin. dir. Emerson R. Sausser Med. Dental Clinic, Jefferson Hosp., Phila., 1950-51; pvt. practice dentistry, Drexel Hill, Pa., 1953—; staff Suburban Gen. Hosp., Norristown. Mem. Congressional Adv Bd. Editor-in-chief U. Pa. Dental Jour., 1945-47. With AUS, 1943-45, 51-53. Past pres. mature adults Resurrection Ch., Marmora, N.J., lector for mass readings, mem. Friends for Life com. Fellow Acad. Gen. Dentistry, Acad. Dentistry Internat., Royal Soc. Health; mem. ADA, AAAS, Pa. Dental Assn., Chester-Delaware County Dental Assn., Am. Internat., Philadelphia County Socs. Clin. Hypnosis, Nat. Space Inst., Phila. Physhodontontic Soc. (past pres.), Royal Soc. Hygiene, Nat. Assn. Federally Lic. Firearms Dealers, Nat. Rifle Assn., Serra Internat. Group, Omicron Kappa Upsilon, Psi Omega. Address: 670 Breckley Rd Marmora NJ 08223-1158

INGALL, MICHAEL ALEXANDER, psychiatrist, educator; b. Boston, July 8, 1940; s. Morris and Bessie (Gottler) I.; m. Carol Linda Krepon, June 18, 1961; children: Marjorie Beth, Andrew Morris. AB, Harvard U., 1961; MD, Chgo. Med. Sch., 1966. Diplomate Am. Bd. Psychiatry and Neurology, Am. Bd. Geriatric Psychiatry. Straight med. intern Univ. Hosp., Boston, 1966-67; resident in psychiatry Boston U. Med. Ctr., 1967-69, 71-72, fellow in child psychiatry, 1971-72; med. dir. Providence Mental Health Ctr., 1972-84; chief psychiat. svcs. Harvard Community Health Plan/N.E., Warwick, R.I., 1984-93; clin. assoc. prof. of psychiatry Brown U. Med. Sch., Providence, 1978—; forensic psychiatrist Atty. Gen.'s Office of R.I., Pub. Def. Office of R.I.; cons. psychiatrist Whitmarsh House, Providence. Singer: Providence Singers, 1987—, R.I. Civic Chorale, 1986-88; East Coast Editor, The Fessenden Review, 1988-89; author of several scientific and popular articles. Physican Traveler's Aid Homeless Van, Providence, 1987-92; bd. dirs. Solomon Schechter Sch. Providence, 1980-88, R.I. Youth Guidance Ctr., Providence, 1976-80. Lt. comdr. USN, 1968-70. Recipient Alumni Assn. Award, Chgo. Med. Sch. 1966, Roche Award, 1966. Fellow Am. Psychiatric Assn. (Falk Fellowship award 1972); mem. Am. Group Psychotherapy Assn., Physicians for Soc. Responsibility, R.I. Psychiatric Soc. (pres. 1979-80), Alpha Omega Alpha. Office: 20 Eighth St Providence RI 02906

INGALLS, JOHN K., federal investigator, consumer safety officer; b. Beverly, Mass., July 1, 1946; s. Kenneth Leslie and Ruth (Dwinell) I. BS, Springfield (Mass.) Coll., 1969; MS, Bucknell U., Lewisburg, Pa., 1971; MA, Boston U., 1975. Rsch. asst. Harvard's Primate Rsch. Ctr., Southboro, Mass., 1972-76; generalist U.S. FDA, Stoneham, Mass., 1976-86, drug and device specialist, 1986—. Mem. Nat. Woodcarvers, Soc. Indsl. Microbiology, New Eng. Woodcarvers. Home: 11 Prospect St Topsfield WA 01983 Office: US FDA Stoneham MA 02180

INGBAR, DAVID H., physician, researcher; b. Boston, Aug. 1, 1953; s. Sidney H. and Mary Lee (Mach) I.; m. Mary E. Meighan, Oct. 14, 9191. BA, Reed Coll., 1974; MD, Harvard Med. Coll., 1978. Intern then resident U. Wash., Seattle, chief resident; pulminary fellow Yale U., New Haven, 1982-85, asst. prof. medicine, 1985—; assoc. prof. medicine U. Minnesota, Minneapolis; dir. med. ICU and respiratory care Yale New Haven Hosp., 1986—. Office: U MN Pulmonary & Critical Care Dept Medicine Box 276 UMHC 420 Delaware St SE Minneapolis MN 55455*

INGEBRIGTSEN, CATHERINE WILLIAMS, rehabilitation consultant, health education specialist; b. Lake Charles, La., May 28, 1955; d. Thomas Humphrey and Jane Catherine (Caldwell) Williams; 1 child, Jennifer Catherine Bittle. BS, Old Dominion U., 1978, MS summa cum laude, 1983; diploma profl. nursing, Norfolk Gen. Hosp., 1978. Intensive care unit nurse DePaul Hosp., Norfolk, Va., 1979-80; cons. Internat. Rehab. Assn., Virginia Beach, Va., 1980-82; ptnr., pres., cons. OccuSystems, Norfolk, 1982-85; prin., pres. Cathy Bittle & Assocs., Norfolk, 1985—; health edn. cons. Peninsula Health Dept., Newport News, Va., 1985—, dir. grant writing program, 1985-86; educator Diabetes Inst., Virginia Beach, 1984-88; speaker in field. Com. mem. Tidewater Health Fair Task Force, Norfolk, 1983. LCDR Nurse Corps Res. Program USN, 1988—. Mem. Am. Assn. Counseling and Devel., Am. Assn. Phys. Health, Edn., Recreation and Dance, Old Dominion U. Grad. Student Assn. (pres. 1982-83), Phi Kappa Phi. Republican. Roman Catholic. Avocations: sailing, biking, skiing, running, rollerskating. Home: 3241 River Rd Green Cove Springs FL 32043 Office: Case Mgmt Enterprises Inc PO Box 2281 Orange Park FL 32067-2281

INGLE, JOHN IDE, dental educator; b. Colville, Wash., Jan. 19, 1919; s. John James and Jessie Belle (Ide) I.; m. Joyce Ledgerwood, July 11, 1940; children: John Geoffrey, Leslie Ide Ingle Moxley, Schuyler Neal. Student, Wash. State U., 1936-38; D.D.S., Northwestern U., 1942; M.S.D., U. Mich., 1948. Diplomate: Am. Bd. Endodontics, Am. Bd. Periodontology. Asst. Northwestern U., 1942-43; asst. prof. endodontics and periodontology Sch. Dentistry, U. Wash., 1948-51, assoc. prof., 1951-59, prof., 1959-64, exec. officer dept., 1956-64; dean Sch. Dentistry, U. So. Calif., Los Angeles, 1964-72; dir. div. internat. health, sr. profl. asso. Inst. Medicine Nat. Acad. Scis., 1973-78; pres. Palm Springs Seminars, 1978-92; sr. lectr. UCLA, 1979; vis. lectr. Loma Linda U., 1983; attending staff exec. com. Los Angeles County/ U. So. Calif. Med. Center, 1964-72; cons. Nat. Bd. Dental Examiners, 1964-68; endodontics, asst. surgeon gen. U.S. Army, 1969-70, Nat. Naval Med. Center, 1973; mem. adv. com. dental health Office Sec. HEW, 1970-72; mem. rev. com. on dental edn. NIH, 1970; mem. adv. panel on nat. health ins. U.S. Ho. of Reps. Ways and Means Com., 1975. Author: (with others) Endodontics, 1965, 2d edit. (with E.E. Beveridge) 1976, 3d edit., 1985, 4th edit. (with L.K. Bakland), 1994, (with A.L. Ogilvie) An Atlas of Pulpal and Periapical Biology, 1965; editor: (with P. Blair) International Dental Care Delivery Systems, 1978. Bd. dirs. Los Angeles United Way Crusade, 1967-69. Served with Dental Corps AUS, 1943-46. Recipient Northwestern U. Alumni Merit award, 1966. Fellow AAAS, Internat., Am. colls. dentists; mem. Internat. Assn. Dental Research, Am. Assn. Endodontists (past pres., Ralph F. Sommer research award 1987), Am. Acad. Periodontology, Am. Dental Assn. (cons. dental therapeutics), Los Angeles Dental Soc. (sec. 1968-71), Am. Assn. Dental Schs., Alpha Omega (hon. mem., Achievement medal 1985). Club: Cosmos (Washington). Home: 18755 W Bernardo Dr # 1231 San Diego CA 92127

INGLOT, ANNA DUBOWSKA, virologist; b. Wilno, Poland, Sept. 10, 1933; d. Józef Dubowski and Natalia (Knopf) Pietrzak-Dubowska; m. Inglot, June 29, 1957; children: Tomasz, Dorota. MD, U. Med. Sch., Wroclaw, Poland, 1957; PhD, Polish Acad. Scis., 1962. Rsch. asst. Lab. Virology, Wroclaw, 1956-74; chief lab. virology L. Hirszfeld Inst. Immunology and Experimental Therapy, Wroclaw, 1974—; prof. Polish Acad. Scis., Wroclaw, 1987—; expert state com. for scientific rsch., Warsaw, 1992—; cons. TORF Corp., Pharm. Factory, Wroclaw, 1991—. sect. editor Archivum Immunologiae et Therapiae Experimentalis, Wroclaw, 1979-82, editor-in-chief, 1991—; edit. bd. mem. Jour. Interferon Rsch., N.Y.C., 1980-84; contbr. articles to profl. jours. Mem. Solidarity, Wroclaw, 1980—. Mem. Internat. Soc. Cytokine Interferon and Cytokine Rsch. (nat. coun. 1983-86), Internat. Congress Virology (nat. adv. com. 1986—), Polish Soc. Microbiology (coun. mem.), Polish Soc. Immunology. Roman Catholic. Home: Czarnieckiego 38 m 4, 53-651 Wroclaw Poland Office: L Hirszfeld Inst Immunology/Experiment Therapy, Czerska 12, 53-114 Wroclaw Poland

INGORDO, VITO, medical officer; b. Taranto, Puglia, Italy, July 1, 1954; s. Abramo Ingordo and Santa Tabo; m. Gabriella Conte. Dec. 11, 1982; children: Ilaria, Irene. MD, U. Pisa, Italy, 1979; specialization in Dermatology and Venereology, U. Naples, 1983; specialization in Leprology and Tropical Dermatology, U. Genoa, 1990. Chief med. svc. Lt. Navy Ship "Perseo", La Spezia, Italy, 1979-81; med. dermatology asst. Italian Navy Hosp., La Spezia, 1981-85, chief dermatologic dept., 1985-89; dermatology med. asst. and chief infectious dept. Italian Navy Hosp., Taranto, 1989-94; asst. chief med. svc. Italian Navy Enlistment and Drilling Ctr., Taranto, 1995-96; chief dermatologic dept. Italian Navy Hosp., Taranto, 1995—; monitor G.I.S.D., Italy, 1991—; mem. Net of STD Surveillance-Superior Inst. Health, 1990—; tchr. Military Health Gen. Direction-HIV Infection Officer's Tng. Program, Italy, 1996. Author: (book) L'Aerobiologia Nella Practica Allergologia, 1994; contbr. articles to profl. jours. Recipient citation Admiral of Navy Dept., 1991. Mem. S.I.D.E.V., A.D.O.I., A.M.I.D.E.V. Home: Via Bwandamura 31/C, 74100 Taranto Italy Office: Italian Navy Hosp, Via Pupino 1, 74100 Taranto Italy

INGRALDI, PETER ANTHONY, surgeon; b. Flushing, N.Y., Aug. 31, 1963; s. Richard Francis and Emily Mina (Lasalde) I.; m. Barbara Noreen Ayala, Sept. 12, 1992; children: Jacqueline, Christina. BS, CCNY, 1986; MD, SUNY, Stony Brook, 1988. Resident in gen. surgery, surg. critical care fellow Lincoln Med. and Mental Health Ctr., Bronx, N.Y., 1988-94; sec./ treas. Com. of Interns and Residents, N.Y.C., 1993-96. Mem. Med. Soc. of the State of N.Y., Queens County Med. Soc. Roman Catholic. Home: 34 Warren Ave Tuckahoe NY 10707 Office: Queens Hosp Ctr Dept of Surgery 82-68 164th St Jamaica NY 11432

INGRAM, ALVIN JOHN, surgeon; b. Jackson, Tenn., Mar. 31, 1914; s. Alvin Hill and Margaret (Gallagher) I.; m. Catherine Davis, Feb. 7, 1943; children: Mildred Ingram Dyer, Catherine Ingram Doyle, Peggy Ingram Tagg. BS, U. Tenn., 1939, MD, 1939, MS in Orthopaedic Surgery, 1947. Diplomate Am. Bd. Orthopaedic Surgery (dir. 1972-78, v.p. 1976, pres. 1976-78; mem. residency rev. commn. orthopedic surgery 1972-76, chmn. 1975-76). Intern Univ. Hosp., Ann Arbor, Mich., 1939-40; asst. resident surgery Univ. Hosp., 1940-41; fellow orthopaedic surgery Campbell Clinic, Memphis, 1941-42, 46-47; mem. staff Campbell Clinic, 1947-90; ret., dep. chief of staff, 1967-69, chief of staff, 1970-78, chief of staff emeritus, 1979—; pvt. practice orthopaedic surgery Memphis, 1947-83; med. dir. Crippled Children's Hosp., 1948-61, chief staff, 1961-70; orthopaedic cons. Smith and Nephew Richards, 1984-92; med. dir. Les Passes Cerebral Palsy Treatment Center, 1953-56; med. adv. com. Memphis and W. Tenn. chpt. Nat. Found. Infantile Paralysis, 1947-57, chmn., 1947-55; med. adv. com. Shrine Sch. Crippled Children, 1947-56; med. adv. bd. Variety Club Convalescent Hosp., 1952-56; assoc. prof. orthopaedic surgery U. Tenn. Coll. Medicine, 1960-71, prof., chmn. dept., 1971-79, prof. emeritus, 1979—; mem. staff Bapt. Meml. Hosp., exec. com. med. staff, 1969-70, chmn. orthopaedic dept., 1970-74, pres. med. staff, 1973; mem. staff St. Joseph Hosp.; cons. orthopedics Richards Med. Co., 1983-90; mem. staff LeBonheur Children's Hosp. (trustee 1968-71); cons. staff Meth. Hosp. Program; chmn. 2d Tenn. Conf. Handicapped Children, 1958; chmn. med. div. United Fund Shelby County, 1961, mem. budget com., 1963-65; dir. at large Nat. Assn. Blue Shield Plans, 1965-70; mem. Gov. Tenn. Adv. Bd. Crippled Children's Service, 1961-77, chmn., 1967-77; mem. exec. com. Am. Bd. Med. Specialties, 1980-83; mem. Tenn. Bd. Med. Examiners, 1981-86, adv. council on Orthopaedic Resident Edn., 1982-86. Contbr. to books. Mem. ofcl. bd. St. John's Meth. Ch., 1952—, vice chmn. ofcl. bd., 1965, 66, 69, 70, chmn., 1971-72, gen. chmn. every mem. canvass, 1955-57, 63, pres. men's club, 1958, sec. stewardship, 1964-65; bd. dirs. Front St. Theatre, Memphis, 1963-64; mem. adminstrv. bd. Christ Meth. Ch., 1982-85, 88—, trustee, 1984-85. Maj. M.C., AUS, 1942-46. Mem. Am. Acad. Orthopaedic Surgeons (chmn. program com. 1954, 71, mem. manpower com. 1974-81), Am. Orthopaedic Assn. (chmn. program com., pres. 1973), Central Orthopaedic Club (charter), Tenn. Orthopaedic Soc. (pres. 1963-64), Willis C. Campbell Club (pres. 1967), Internat. Soc. Orthopaedics and Traumatology, So. Orthopaedic Assn. (Disting. So. Orthopaedic Surgeon award 1989), Am. Acad. Cerebral Palsy (chmn. program com. 1955, publs. com. 1957, exec. com. 1958, pres. 1958-59), Pediatric Orthopedic Soc. (pres. 1973), Pediatric Orthopedic Soc. N.Am. (Disting. Pioneer award 1990), ACS (mem. grad. edn. com. 1974-76), AMA (ho. of dels. 1961-64, trustee 1964-70, sec. treas. 1968-70, sec. bd. trustees 1968-70), So. Med. Assn., Tenn. Med. Assn., Memphis and Shelby County Med. Soc. (pres. 1962, bd. censors 1963-65, ho. of dels. 1965), Nat. Acad. Sci. Inst. Medicine (council 1972-75), Memphis Ind. Practice Assn. (med. dir. 1983-84), U.S. C. of C. Home: 190 Belle Meade Ln Memphis TN 38117-3018

INGRAM, ARTONYON S., mental health professional, therapist; b. Fremont, N.C., Dec. 2, 1962; s. Gliffie and Doris Ingram. BS, Atlantic Christian Coll., 1985; cert. in drugs and alcohol abuse, Pierce Coll., Steilacoom, Wash., 1993, AA, 1993; MEd, City U., Bellevue, Wash., 1995; cert. parent educator, Clover Pk. Tech. Coll., 1995. Teaching parent Onslow Mental Health Ctr., Jacksonville, N.C., 1987-89; social svcs. asst. Rainer Vista Health Care, Puyallup, Wash., 1990-91, Lakewood Health Care, Tacoma, Wash., 1990-91; group life counselor Jessie Dyslin Boys Ranch, Tacoma, Wash., 1991-92; case mgr. Puget Sound Ctr., Tacoma, Wash., 1991; counselor intern Dotters Counseling Ctr., Puyallup, Wash., 1992-93, Cross Rd. Treatment Ctr., Tacoma, 1993; instr. Clover Pk. Tech. Coll., Tacoma, 1993—. Counselor First Bapt. Ch., Jacksonville, N.C. With USNG, 1981-88. Army Nat. Guard scholar, 1978-81, L.N. Forbes scholar, Boeing Engrng. scholar, 1993. Mem. Nat. Assn. Alcoholism and Drug Abuse Counselors, Chem. Dependency Profls. Home: 3910 B 70th Ave NW Gig Harbor WA 98335 Office: Dept Correction Pierce County MacNiel Island 510 Tacoma Ave S Tacoma WA 98402

INGRAM, ROLAND HARRISON, JR., physician, educator; b. Birmingham, Ala., Mar. 10, 1935; s. Roland Harrison and Florence (Emerson) I.; m. Marguerite Lewis Colville, June 25, 1961; 1 child, Mary Elizabeth. BS, U. Ala., 1957; MD cum laude, Yale U., 1960; MA (hon.), Harvard U., 1980. Intern Peter Bent Brigham Hosp., Boston, 1960-61; resident Barnes Hosp., St. Louis, 1963, 64, Yale U. Med. Center, 1964-65; from asst. prof. to assoc. prof. medicine Emory U. Sch. Medicine, 1968-70, prof. medicine, 1970-73, 92—; asso. prof. medicine Harvard Med. Sch., 1973-79; dir. respiratory divsn. Brigham and Women's Hosp., Boston, 1973—; dir. respiratory div. Beth Israel Hosp., Boston, 1980-85; Parker B. Francis prof. medicine Harvard Med. Sch., 1979-89; vice chmn. dept. medicine U. Minn., 1989—; chief internal medicine Hennepin County Med. Ctr., Mpls., 1989-92; chief internal medicine Emory Crawford Long Hosp., 1992—, chief pulmonary critical care divsn., 1992—. Assoc. editor Jour. Clin. Investigation, 1983-85; mem. editorial bds.: New England Jour. of Medicine, 1974-77, Jour. of Applied Physiology, 1978-84, Am. Rev. of Respiratory Diseases, 1980-87; contbr. numerous articles to profl. jours. Served with USPHS, 1961-63. Recipient Rsch. Career Devel. award Nat. Heart and Lung Inst., 1968-73, Edward Livingston Trudeau medal Am. Lung Assn., 1996. Mem. ACP, Am. Soc. Clin. Investigation, Assn. Am. Physicians, Am. Physiol. Soc., Am. Thoracic Soc. (pres. 1983-84), Am. Clin. Climatol. Assn., Phi Beta Kappa, Alpha Omega Alpha. Home: 811 Clifton Rd NE Atlanta GA 30307-1223

INGRUM, DAVID ALAN, physician, health facility administrator; b. Detroit, Oct. 27, 1946; s. Harlan Glen and Emily Ingrum; m. Violet Ann Ingrum, Aug. 1, 1980; children: Jennifer Diane, Elizabeth Violet. BS in Chemistry, U. Mich., 1968, MD, 1972. Diplomate Am. Bd. Preventive Medicine; cert. in occupl. medicine. Commd. ens. USN, 1972, advanced through grades to capt.; intern Naval Hosp. USN, Oakland, Calif., 1973; med. officer Underwater Demolition/SEAL USN, Coronado, Calif., 1974-80; med. officer, comdr. Submarine Group Five USN, San Diego, 1980-84; intensive resident in occupl. medicine U. Calif., San Francisco, 1982; resigned USN, 1984; occupl. physician Scripps Clinic, La Jolla, Calif., 1985-95, occupl. health med. dir., 1996—; mem. panel for treatment paramaters Indsl. Med. Coun., L.A., 1995—; lectr. in occupl. medicine San Diego State U., 1979—. Mem. sci. adv. panel San Diego City Coun., 1986-87. Capt. USNR, 1984—. Fellow Am. Coll. Preventive Medicine; mem. Am. Coll. Occupl. and Environ. Medicine, Calif. Med. Assn. (mem. workers' compensation com. 1993—, asst. sec. sci. adv. panel 1996—), San Diego County Med. Soc., West Occupl./Environ. Med. Assn. (chair edn. com. 1996—).

INKLEY, SCOTT RUSSELL, hospital administrator, physician, educator; b. Cleve., Mar. 8, 1921; s. Edwin A. and Isabella Bell (Russell) I.; m. Josephine Newcomer, Feb. 13, 1943; children: Josephine Christian, Leslie Logan, Scott Russell Jr., Sabrina Ann. Student, Harvard U., 1942; MD, Western Res. U., 1945. Intern Univ. Hosps. of Cleve., 1945-46, asst. resident, 1948-49, teaching fellow in medicine, 1949-50, chief med. resident, 1950-51, asst. physician in medicine out-patient dept., 1951-56, asst. physician dept. medicine, 1955-66, assoc. physician, 1966-68, physician, 1968-78, physician-in-charge pulmonary function lab., 1962-77, dir. inhalation therapy dept., 1966-78, chief pulmonary diseases, 1968-78, chief of staff, 1978-82, pres., chief exec. officer, 1982-86, cons., 1986—; instr. dept. medicine Case Western Res. U., Cleve., 1951-54; sr. instr. Case Western Res. U., 1954-55, asst. prof., 1955-56, assoc. clin. prof., 1966-73, assoc. prof., 1973-76, prof., 1976-91, prof. emeritus, 1991—; ret. dir. Huntington Nat. Bank. Contbr. articles to profl. jours. Past pres. Cleve. Med. Libr. Assn.; past trustee Judson Park Retirement Cmty.; trustee Cleve. Mus. Natural History, U. Hosps. of Cleve. (hon.); chmn. bd. trustees Univ. Cir. Inc., 1989—; mayor Hunting Valley Village, 1996—. Capt. M.C. U.S. Army. Fellow ACP, Am. Coll. Chest Physicians; mem. AMA, Am. Heart Assn., Am. Thoracic Soc., Cen. Soc. Clin. Research, Ohio State Med. Assn., Cleve. Acad. Medicine, Sigma Xi. Republican. Episcopalian. Clubs: Union, Tavern, Chagrin Valley Hunt; Harvard (N.Y.C.). Home: 13500 County Line Rd Chagrin Falls OH 44022-4000

INMAN, WILLIAM HOWARD WALLACE, pharmacoepidemiology educator; b. London, Aug. 1, 1929; s. Wallace Mills and Maude Mary (Andrews) I.; m. June Evelyn Maggs, July 21, 1962; children: Stella Evelyn Downey, Rosemary June Bullough, Charlotte Elizabeth. MA, Cambridge (Eng.) U., 1950, MB, BChir, 1956. Various positions Addenbrooke's Hosp., Cambridge, 1956-59; med. advisor I.C.I. Ltd., Manchester, Eng., 1959-64; prin. med. officer Com. on Safety in Medicine, London, 1964-80; prof. pharmacoepidemiology U. Southampton, Eng., 1980—, dir. drug safety rsch. unit, 1980-93. Author: Monitoring for Drug Safety, 1984. Fellow Royal Coll. Physicians (London). Address: Southcroft House, Winchester Rd, Botley Hampshire S032 2BX, England

INNISS-BREWER, YVONNE, nurse, insurance company administrator; b. Sanicholas, Aruba, Netherlands Antilles, Mar. 10, 1948; came to U.S., 1975.; d. William Conrad and Ruby Marion (Edwards) I. BS in Human Services, N.H. Coll., 1984; MS in Urban Studies, So. Conn. State U., 1986; Lic. Practical Nurse, John Radcliffe Sch. of Nursing, Oxford, Eng., 1969; MALS, Wesleyan U., 1990. Asst. charge nurse Churchill Hosp., Oxford, Eng., 1970-73; claims reviewer Aetna Life and Casualty, Hartford, Conn., 1975-77; lic. processor Hartford Steam Boiler, 1977-79, supr. claim services, 1979-82, mktg. asst., 1982-87, 88, exec. asst., 1988—. Mem Wadsworth Atheneum, Hartford, 1986—; mem. town com. A Conn. Party, 1992-93, sec., 1990-92. Mem. Internat. Platform Assn. Anglican. Home: 71 Imlay St # B Hartford CT 06105-3609 Office: Hartford Steam Boiler Inspection and Ins Co One State St Hartford CT 06012-3001

INNS, HARRY DOUGLAS ELLIS, optometrist; b. Tryconnel, Ont., Can., June 4, 1922; s. Thomas Henry and Eleanor (Ellis) I.; children from previous marriage: Susan Elizabeth, Douglas Michael; m. Helen Lynne Mitchell. Student, U. Toronto, 1946-48; grad., Ont. Coll. Optometry, 1950, OD, 1958. Practice optometry specializing in contact lenses, Brantford, Ont., 1963—. Contbr. articles to profl. jours.; patentee Inns extension disc to facilitate corneal measurements. Served to lt. with RCAF, 1941-45. Fellow Assn. Contact Lens Practitioners Eng., Am. Acad. Optometry, Royal Soc. Health, Heraldry Soc. Can. (bd. dirs.); mem. Internat. Soc. Contact Lens Specialists (congress chmn.), Ont. Optometrical Assn., Can. Assn. Optometrists, Internat. Optometric and Optical League, Ont. Assn. Optometrists (Edn. Program award 1976, Contact Lens Program award 1978, Internat. Lecture award 1979, Appreciation award 1980, Disting. Service award 1981), Better Vision Inst., Nat. Eye Research Found., Can. Public Health Assn., Am. Optometric Assn., Brantford C. of C., Internat. Platform Assn., Am. Soc. Contact Lens Specialists (sec.), Waterloo Alumni Assn., Monarchist League Can., 78th Fraser Highlanders (maj.), Royal Can. Mil. Inst., Royal Can. Air Force Assn., Beta Sigma Kappa. Clubs: Anglican Men's, Kiwanis (Brantford, Ont.). Home: 67 Tutela Heights, Brantford, ON Canada N3T 1A4 Office: 36 King George Rd, Brantford, ON Canada N3R 5K1

INOKUCHI, SUGURU, orthopedic surgeon; b. Hiroshima, Japan, Oct. 11, 1945; s. Hisashi and Takiko (Shiraishi) I.; m. Mie Shibata; children: Sayaka, Tsuyoshi. MD, Keio U., Tokyo, 1970, PhD, 1982. Resident Keio U., 1970-76, asst. prof., 1990—; rsch. fellow Karolinska Inst., Stockholm, 1977-78; mem. med. staff Tokyo Denryoku Hosp., 1979-83; chief surgeon Tokyo Senbai Hosp., 1983-90; vis. asst. prof. Dokkyo Med. Coll., Tochigi, Japan, 1987-89. Mem. editl. bd. jour. The Foot, 1994—. Grantee Japan-Sweden Found., 1977. Mem. Japanese Orthopedic Assn., Japanese Soc. Foot Surgery, Am. Orthopedic Foot and Ankle Soc., European Soc. Foot & Ankle Surgeons, Coll. Internat. Medicine & Chirurgie Pied. Home: 6-6-7 Honkomagome Bunkoku, Tokyo 113, Japan Office: Keio U Med Sch, 35 Shinanomachi Shinjukuku, Tokyo 160, Japan

INOUÉ, SHINYA, microscopy and cell biology scientist, educator; b. London, Eng., Jan. 5, 1921; came to U.S, 1948, naturalized, 1989; s. Kojiro and Hideko (Yano) I.; m. Sylvia McCandless, July 18, 1952; children: Heather C., Jonathan H., Christopher W., Stephen K., Theodore D. Rigakushi, Tokyo U., 1941; MA, Princeton U., 1950, PhD, 1951; MA (hon.), Dartmouth Coll., 1959, U. Pa., 1966. Instr. U. Wash. Med. Sch., Seattle, 1951-53; asst. prof. Tokyo Met. U., 1953-54; rsch. assoc., assoc. prof. U. Rochester, N.Y., 1954-59; instr. Marine Biol. Lab., Woods Hole, Mass., 1961—, NATO Summer Schs., Cannes, Stressa, Szeged, 1967, 70, 75; prof., chmn. Dartmouth Med. Sch., Hanover, N.H., 1959-66; prof. U. Pa., Phila., 1966-89; Disting. Scientist Marine Biol. Lab., Woods Hole, 1980—; cons. Am. Optical Co., 1954-60, NSF, 1962-65, NIH, 1965-70, Hamamatsu Photonics K.K., Hamamatsu City, Japan, 1988—, Nikon Corp., Tokyo, 1994—; pres. Universal Imaging Corp., Falmouth, Mass., West Chester, Pa., 1984-87, chmn. bd. dirs., 1987-93. Author: Video Microscopy, 1986; co-editor: Molecules and Cell Movement, 1975; contbr. articles to profl. jours.; mem. editorial bd. several sci. jours., 1964—; ad hoc reviewer, advisor on sci. and tech. NSF, NIH, many univs., founds.; patentee in optics. Trustee Marine Biol. Lab., 1970-77, 81-85, 92, mem. sci. coun., 1993—. Recipient Rosenstiel award Brandeis U., 1988, Brown-Hazen award State of N.Y., 1988; Guggenheim Found. fellow, 1971-72; cancer rsch. scholar Am. Cancer Soc., N.Y.C., 1955-58. Fellow AAAS, Am. Acad. Arts Scis., Royal Microscopial Soc. (hon.); mem. NAS, Biophys. Soc. (coun. 1968-71), Soc. Gen. Physiologists (coun., pres. 1962-065, 69-70), Am. Soc. Cell Biology (coun. 1970-73, E.B. Wilson award 1992), Optical Soc. Am., Microscopy Soc. Am. (Disting. Scientist award 1995). Home: 40 Shore St Falmouth MA 02540-3146 Office: Marine Biol Lab 7 MBL St Woods Hole MA 02543

INOUE, TAKESHI, psychiatrist; b. Kumamoto, Japan, Sept. 3. 1932; s. Tatsuichi and Shigeye (Matsushita) I.; M.D., Kumamoto U., 1957, Ph.D., 1962; m. Michiko Takeshita, Oct. 8, 1961; children: Hiroko, Takao. Lectr. dept. biochemistry Kumamoto U. Med. Sch., 1957-61; lectr. U. Calif. Med. Sch., San Francisco, 1961-73, postdoctoral fellow, 1968; postdoctoral fellow dept. biochemistry Temple U. Med. Sch., Phila., 1968-70; asst. prof. dept. neuropsychiatry Kumamoto U. Med. Sch. (Japan), 1971-83; dir. Minamata Hosp., 1983-85, dir., 1985-93; dir. Kohsei Hosp., 1993—. Mem. AAAS, Japanese Neurochem. Soc., N.Y. Acad. Scis., Sigma Xi. Home: 16-15 2 Chohme Musashigaoka, Kumamoto 862, Japan Office: 1125-2 Shimoharadamachi, Hitoyoshi 868, Japan

INSCHO, EDWARD WILLIAM, physiology educator; b. Owego, N.Y., July 25, 1954. BA in Biology, Mercyhurst Coll., 1976; MS in Biology and Exptl. Medicine, St. Thomas Rsch. Inst., 1978; PhD in Physiology, U. Cin., 1987. Rsch. asst. Biology and Cancer Rsch. Lab. Mercyhurst Coll., Erie, Pa., 1972-76; grad. rsch. asst. dept. biology St. Thomas Rsch. Inst., Cin., 1976-78; lab. asst. dept. neurophysiology Inst. Devel. Rsch., Cin., 1978-80; grad. rsch. asst. dept. physiology and biophysics U. Cin. Coll. Medicine, 1980-87, lab. instr. dept. physiology, 1983-86, med. tutor dept. physiology, 1984-85; physiology lectr. U. Ala., Birmingham, 1988; rsch. instr. dept. physiology Tulane U. Sch. Medicine, New Orleans, 1989-91, rsch. asst. prof. dept. physiology, 1991-92, asst. prof. dept. physiology, 1992—. Reviewer Am. Jour. Physiology: Renal, Heart, Regulatory, Hypterion, Jour. Clin. Investigation, Mineral and Electrolyte Metabolism, Jour. Hypertension; contbr. articles to profl. jours. Recipient Rsch. fellowship NIH, 1984-87, 87, 88, Univ. Rsch. Coun. Travel award U. Cin., 1984, 85, Eckstein Meml. Fund Travel award, U. Cin., 1984, Amgen Young Investigator award Nat. Kidney Found., 1992, 93. Mem. Am. Physiol. Soc. (travel award 1993), Am. Heart Assn. (coun. kidney and cardiovasc. disease, travel award 1989, Established Investigator award 1995—). Office: Tulane Univ Sch Medicine Dept Physiology SL # 39 1430 Tulane Ave New Orleans LA 70112-2699*

INSCHO, JEAN ANDERSON, social worker; b. Camden, N.J., Oct. 31, 1936; d. George Myrick and Alfrida Elizabeth (Anderson) Hewitt; m. James Ronald Inscho, June 4, 1955 (div. Mar. 1982); children: James Ronald Jr.,

Cynthia Ann, Michael Merrick. BA, Fla. Atlantic U., 1971; MA in Coll. Teaching, Auburn U., 1974. Lic. bachelor social worker. Instr. So. Union State Jr. Coll., Wadley, Ala., 1973-75; social worker Jefferson County Dept. Human Resources, Birmingham, Ala., 1976-77, Shelby County Dept. Human Resources, Columbiana, Ala., 1977-78, Houston County Dept. Human Resources, Dothan, Ala., 1978—; adj. instr. Troy State U., Dothan, 1982—. Bd. dirs., v.p. Adolescent Resource Ctr., 1992-93, sec., 1993-95; mem. Alzheimer's Assn., Dothan Area Bot. Gardens. EPDA fellow Auburn U., 1973, 74. Mem. Ala. State Employees Assn. (v.p. Wiregrass chpt. 1987-91, bd. dirs. 1996—), Dist. 7 State Employees Assn. (polit. action com. rep., 1994-96), Ala. Master Gardeners (bd. dirs.), Wiregrass Master Gardeners (pres. 1994-95), Am. Daffodil Soc., Ala. Gerontol. Soc. Episcopalian. Office: Houston County Dept Human Resources 1605 Ross Clark Cir Dothan AL 36301-5438

INSELMAN, LAURA SUE, pediatrician; b. Bklyn., Nov. 2, 1944; d. Alexander M. and Rae (Bloom) Inselman. BA, Barnard Coll., 1966; MD, Med. Coll. Pa., 1970. Diplomate Am. Bd. Pediatrics, Am. Bd. Pediatric Pulmonology. Intern and resident St. Lukes Hosp. Ctr., N.Y.C., 1970-73; fellow in pediatric pulmonary disease Babies Hosp., N.Y.C., 1973-76; chief pediatric pulmonary div. Interfaith Med. Ctr., Bklyn., 1976-81; chief pediatric pulmonary div. North Shore Univ. Hosp., Manhasset, N.Y., 1981-86; clin. dir. pediatric pulmonary div. Newington Con. Children's Hosp., 1987-92; pulmunologist, med. dir. dept. respiratory care A.I. duPont Inst., Wilmington, Del., 1992—; asst. prof. pediatrics Cornell U. Med. Coll., N.Y.C., 1981-86; asst. clin. prof. pediatrics, Yale U. Sch. Medicine, New Haven, 1987-92; asst. prof. pediatrics, U. Conn. Health Ctr., Farmington, 1987-92; assoc. prof. pediatrics, Jefferson Med. Coll. Thomas Jefferson U. Hosp., Phila., 1992—; mem. staff Good Samaritan Hosp., West Islip, N.Y., 1982-87. Bd. dirs. Am. Lung Assn. Nassau-Suffolk, East Meadow, N.Y., 1983-86, Del., 1992—. Fellow Am. Acad. Pediatrics, Am. Coll. Chest Physicians; mem. Am. Thoracic Soc., Am. Fedn. Clin. Research, N.Y. Acad. Medicine, Harvey Soc., Soc. Pediatric Research. Office: AI DuPont Inst 1600 Rockland Rd Wilmington DE 19803-3607

INTELISANO, RONALD GEORGE, osteopath; b. Queens, N.Y., Dec. 28, 1961; s. George and Ines (Magri) I.; m. Maria Mercante, May 19, 1990. BS, C.W. Post Ctr. L.I. U., 1983, MS, 1984; DO, N.Y. Coll. Osteo. Medicine, 1989. Intern Peninsua Hosp. Ctr., Queens, N.Y., 1989-90; resident in internal medicine Kennedy Hosp./U. Medicine & Dentistry of N.J., Stratford, N.J., 1990-93, fellow in gastroenterology, 1993-95; pres. South Jersey Med. Assocs., P.A., Blackwood, N.J., 1994—. Recipient Mildred Marengo award C.W. Post/L.I. U., 1983. Mem. Am. Osteo. Assn., Am. Acad. Osteopathy, Am. Coll. Osteo. Internists., Nat. Italian-Am. Found., AHEPA. Republican. Roman Catholic. Office: South Jersey Med Assocs PA 1504 Blackwood-Clementon Rd Blackwood NJ 08012

INTRAVIA, JOHN ANDREW, gastroenterologist; b. N.Y.C., July 28, 1950; s. Lawrence and Irene (Bisagni) I.; m. Margaret Irene Ryan, June 14, 1975; children: John Thomas, Marissa Kathryn. BS, Georgetown U., 1971; MD, St. Louis U., 1975. Diplomate Am. Bd. Internal Medicine in internal medicine and gastroenterology, Nat. Bd. Med. Examiners. Intern St. Vincent's Hosp. and Med. Ctr., N.Y.C., 1975-76, resident in internal medicine, 1976-78; fellow gastroenterology U. Conn.-Farmington and affiliated hosps., 1978-80; pvt. practice gastroenterology Middletown, Conn., 1980—. Mem. AMA, ACP, Am. Soc. Internal Medicine, Conn. State Med. Soc., Middlesex County Med. Assn. (pres. 1990-92), Alpha Omega Alpha. Roman Catholic. Office: 520 Saybrook Rd Middletown CT 06457 also: 1353 Boston Post Rd Madison CT 06443-3445

INTRIERE, ANTHONY DONALD, physician; b. Greenwich, Conn., May 9, 1920; s. Rocco and Angelina (Belcastro) I.; m. Carol A. Yarmey, Aug. 1, 1945; children: Sherry Shoemaker, Michael, Nancy M., Lisa A. MD, U. Mich., 1944. Intern, New Rochelle (N.Y.) Hosp., 1944-45; pvt. practice, Greenwich, Conn., 1947-53, Olney, Ill., 1956-61, Granite City, Ill., 1961-74, San Diego, 1975—; fellow in internal medicine Cleve. Clinic, 1953-55; fellow in gastroenterology Lahey Clinic, Boston, 1955-56. Capt. M.C., AUS, 1945-47. Fellow Am. Coll. Gastroenterology (assoc.); mem. AMA, ACP (assoc.), Am. Soc. Internal Medicine, Fifty Yr. Club Ill. State Med. Soc. Home: 9981 Caminito Chirimolla San Diego CA 92131-2001

INUI, THOMAS SPENCER, physician, educator; b. Balt., July 10, 1943; s. Frank Kazuo and Beulah Mae (Sheetz) I.; m. Nancy Stowe, June 14, 1969; 1 child, Tazo Stowe. BA, Haverford Coll., 1965; MD, Johns Hopkins U., 1969, ScM, 1973. Diplomate Am. Bd. Internal Medicine. Intern Johns Hopkins Hosp., Balt., 1969-70, resident in internal medicine, 1970-73; clin. scholar Johns Hopkins U., Balt., 1971-73, chief resident, instr., 1973-74; chief of medicine USPHS Indian Hosp., Albuquerque, 1974-76; chief gen. medicine, dir. health svc. rsch. Seattle VA Med. Ctr., 1976-86; dir. Robert Wood Johnson clin. scholars program U. Wash., Seattle, 1977-92, prof. dept. medicine and health svcs., 1985-92, head div. gen. internal medicine, 1986-92; prof., chmn. of dept. ambulatory care and prevention Harvard Med. Sch. and Harvard Community Health Plan, Boston, 1992—. Contbr. articles to profl. publs. Surgeon USPHS, 1974-76. Fellow ACP; mem. APHA (mem. coun. 1988-90), Soc. Gen. Internal Medicine (pres. 1988-89, mem. coun. 1983-89), Am. Fedn. Clin. Rsch., Assn. Health Svcs. Rsch., Soc. Tchrs. of Family Medicine, Inst. Medicine, Phi Beta Kappa, Alpha Omega Alpha.

INVERSO, MARLENE JOY, optometrist; b. Los Angeles, May 10, 1942; d. Elmer Encel Wood and Sally Marie (Sample) Hirons; m. John S. Inverso, Dec. 16, 1962; 1 child, Christopher Edward. BA, Calif. State U., Northridge, 1964; MS, SUNY, Potsdam, 1975; OD, Pacific U., 1981. Cert. doctor optometry, Wash., Oreg. English tchr. Chatsworth (Calif.) High Sch., 1964-68, Nelson A. Boylen Second Sch., Toronto, Ont., Can., 1968-70, Gouverneur (N.Y.) Jr.-Sr. High Sch., 1970-74, 76-77; reading resource room tchr. Parishville (N.Y.) Hopkinton Sch., 1974-75; coordinator learning disability clinic SUNY, Potsdam, 1975-77; optometrist and vision therapist Am. Family Vision Clinics, Olympia, Wash., 1982—; mem. adv. com. Sunshine House St. Peter Hosp., Olympia, 1984-86, Pacific U. Coll. Optometry, Forest Grove, Oreg. 1986. Contbr. articles to profl. jours. Mem. Altrusa Svc. Club, Olympia, 1982-86; tchr. Ch. Living Water, Olympia, 1983-88, Olympia-Lacey Ch. of God, 1989—, sec. women's bd., 1990; bd. advisors Crisis Pregnancy Ctr., Olympia, 1987-89; den mother Cub Scouts Am. Pack 202, Lacey, Wash., 1987-88; vol. World Vision Countertop ptnr., 1986—. Fellow Coll. Optometrists in Optometric Devel.; mem. Am. Optometric Assn. (sec. 1983-84), Assn. Children and Adults with Learning Disabilities, Optometric Extension Program, Sigma Xi, Beta Sigma Kappa. Home: 4204 Timberline Dr SE Olympia WA 98503-4443

INWOOD, DAVID GERALD, psychiatrist; b. Bklyn., Mar. 15, 1946; s. Louis Robert and Evelyn (Glasser) I.; m. Linda Rae Avayou, June 22, 1969; children: Shoshanah, Benjamin, Jonathan. BA, Temple U., 1969; MD, U. Autonoma de Guadalajara, Mexico, 1975. Diplomate Am. Bd. Psychiatry and Neurology, Am. Bd. Child and Adolescent Psychiatry. Resident in psychiatry Downstate Med. Ctr., Bklyn., 1977-79; fellowship in child psychiatry Downstate Med. Ctr., 1979-81; dir. tng. child and adolescent psychiatry SUNY, Health Sci. Ctr., Bklyn., 1984-92; attending psychiatrist Maimonides Med. Ctr., Bklyn., 1981—; pvt. practice, Bklyn. Editor: Spectrum Post-Partum Disorders, 1985; contbr. chpts. to books. CEO Parents Assn.ofo Child Sch., 1989-92. Mem. Am. Psychiat. Assn., Am. Acad. Child and Adolescent Psychiatry, N.Y. Coun. Child and Adolescent Psychiatry (pres. 1992-93), N.Y. Postgrad. Psychotherapy Inst. for Child and Adolescent Psychiatrists (treas. 1993—). Jewish. Office: 95 Pierrepont St Brooklyn NY 11201-2704

IOB, IVO, neurosurgeon; b. Rovereto, Trento, Italy, Jan. 10, 1950; s. Giocomo and Iole (Gollino) I.; m. Clara Salafia, Aug. 11, 1974; children: Davide, Irene, Angela. BA in Medicine, U. Padova, Italy, 1975, postgrad., 1979-89. Fellow Inst. Neurosurgery U. Padova, 1974-80, riceratore comtermato, 1980—, prof. spine surgery Postgrad. Sch. Neurosurgery, 1987—; vis. prof. Boston U., 1995. Contbr. over 200 articles to med. publs.; patentee artificial disk for human spine. Mem. Italian Soc. Neurosurgery. Home: Via Aganoor 26, 35123 Padova Italy Office: Inst Neurosurgery, Via Giustiniani 5, 35123 Padova Italy

IODICE, ARTHUR ALFONSO, biochemist, experimental cardiologist; b. Rome, N.Y., Nov. 7, 1928; s. Gaetano and Loretta (Pace) Iodice. AB, Columbia U., 1950; PhD, SUNY, Syracuse, 1958. Postdoctoral fellow U. Calif., Berkeley, 1958-60, rsch. assoc., 1960-62; rsch. assoc. Inst. Muscle Disease, N.Y.C., 1962-65, asst. mem., 1965-69, assoc. mem., 1969-74; rsch. scientist Masonioc Med. Rsch. Lab., Utica, N.Y., 1975—. Contbr. articles to profl. jours. Jane Coffin Childs Meml. med. rsch. postdoctoral fellow, Yale U., U. Calif., 1958-60. Mem. AAAS, Electrophysiol. Soc., Am. Heart Assn., N.Y. Acad. Scis. Office: Masonic Med Rsch Lab 2150 Bleecker St Utica NY 13501-1714

IOLI, JAMES PETER, podiatrist; b. N.Y.C., Mar. 13, 1951; s. Fredrick and Dolores (Domino) I.; m. Debbie Lyn Wood, Aug. 2, 1975; 1 child, Jennifer Lyn. BS in Biology, SUNY, Albany, 1973; D. of Podiatric Medicine, Ohio Coll. Podiatric Medicine, 1978. Diplomate Am. Bd. Podiatric Surgery, Am. Bd. Podiatric Orthopedics and Primary Podiatric Medicine. Resident Cen. New England Podiatry Residency Program, Fitchburg, Mass., 1978-80; pvt. practice Fitchburg, 1980-82; podiatrist Mass. Gen. Hosp., Boston, 1982-86; pvt. practice Stoughton, Mass., 1986—; mem. attending staff Braintree (Mass.) Hosp., 1982—; mem. attending staff Good Samaritan Med. Ctr., 1986—, chief divsn. podiatry, 1994—; cons. examiner Mass. Bd. Registration Podiatry, 1980-88. Contbr. articles to profl. jours. Fellow Am. Coll. Foot and Ankle Surgeons, Am. Coll. Foot and Ankle Orthopedics and Medicine, Am. Soc. Podiatric Medicine, Am. Coll. Foot and Ankle Pediatrics (pres. 1990-92), Am. Soc. Podiatric Medicine, Am. Podiatric Med. Assn., Mass. Podiatric Med. Soc. (edn. com. 1983-88). Office: 907 Sumner St Ste M-209 Stoughton MA 02072-3374

IPSEN, CAROL ANNE, psychiatrist, educator; b. Schenectady, N.Y., Jan. 9, 1951; d. Peter Grover and Joan Stevens (Wilson) I.; m. James Donald Alpert, Aug. 14, 1976; 1 child, Kathryn Ipsen Alpert. BS, U. Mich., 1972; MD, U. Rochester, N.Y., 1978. Diplomate Am. Bd. Psychiatry and Neurology. Intern U. Colo. Med. Ctr., Denver, 1978-79, resident in psychiatry, 1979-82; staff psychiatrist Ft. Logan Mental Health Ctr., Denver, 1982-84; pvt. practice, Denver, 1982-85, Albany, N.Y., 1985—; clin. asst. prof. Albany Med. Coll., 1986—. Mem. Am. Psychiat. Assn. (ethics com. Albany chpt. 1988—). Home: 92 McGarr Ln Voorheesville NY 12186-9757 Office: 12 Colvin Ave Albany NY 12206-1203

IQBAL, S. MOHAMMED, psychologist; b. Udaipur, India, July 9, 1932; came to U.S., 1970; s. Fazluddin and Fatima (Fazluddin) Ameri; m. Maryam Iqbal, Aug. 4, 1963. BA, U. Karachi, Pakistan, 1967, MA, 1969; MA, Pepperdine U., L.A., 1970; PhD, U.S.I.U., San Diego, 1975. Diplomate Am. Bd. Med. Psychotherapists, Am. Bd. Profl. Disability Cons., Am. Bd. Cert. Managed Care Providers, Am. Bd. Forensic Examiners, Am. Bd. Disability Analysts; cert. sr. disability analyst. Telecommunication engr. Govt. of Pakistan, Karachi, 1950-69; clin. psychologist Gov. Beacon Health Ctr., Delaware City, Del., 1978-80; clin. psychologist Del. State Hosp., New Castle, 1974—, chief psychologist forensic svc., 1987—; pvt. practice psychology, Del., Md., Pa.; rsch. psychologist Psychol. Corp. Fellow Md. Psychol. Assn.; mem. APA, Ea. Psychol. Assn., Del Psychol. Assn., Phila. Neuropsychology Assn., Islamic Soc. (founder 1971), Islamic Soc. Del. (founder, pres. 1978). Home: 109 Dutton Dr New Castle DE 19720-5408 Office: Del State Hosp Forensic Svc New Castle DE 19720

IRBY, ALFRED THARP, nursing home administrator, minister; b. Huntington, W.Va., Jan. 27, 1936; s. Alfred T. and Violet C. (Rogers) I.; m. Marjorie F. McSavoney, Mar. 29, 1958; children: Karen, Donald, Stephen. BA in Psychology, Ohio State U., 1957; MDiv, Andover Newton Theol. Sem., 1961. Ordained minister United Ch. of Christ; lic. nursing home adminstr. Pastor Grace United Ch. of Christ, Canton, Ohio, 1967-77, St. John's United Ch. of Christ, Dover, Ohio, 1977-84, Pilgrim United Ch. of Christ, Toledo, 1984-93; adminstr. Heartland Health Care Ctr., Ionia, Mich., 1993—. Mem. Rotary. Home: 2237 Westover Dr Ionia MI 48846 Office: Heartland Health Care Ctr 814 E Lincoln Ave Ionia MI 48846

IRBY, B(ENJAMIN) FREEMAN, obstetrician, gynecologist; b. Birmingham, Ala., June 13, 1938; s. Benjamin Freeman and Frances (Stone) I.; m. Mary Elizabeth Sharp, Dec. 28, 1960; children: Robert, Anne, Joy. AA, Jacksonville (Fla.) U., 1959; degree, Emory U., 1960, MD, 1964. Diplomate Am. Bd. Obstetrics and Gynecology. Commd. 2d lt. U.S. Army, 1963, advanced through grades to maj., 1969; intern Fitzsimmons Gen. Hosp., Denver, 1964-65; resident in ob-gyn. Fitzsimmons Gen. Hosp., 1966-69; resident in gen. surgery Martin Army Hosp., Ft. Benning, Ga., 1965-66; chief prof. svc. U.S. Army, Ft. McPherson, Ga., 1969-72; resigned U.S. Army, 1972; pvt. practice Jacksonville, Fla., 1972—; chmn. dept. ob-gyn Meml. Med. Ctr., Jacksonville, 1985-91; med. staff officer Meml. Med. Ctr., 1991-96, med. staff pres., 1997—. Fellow Am. Coll. Obstetricians and Gynecologists; mem. AMA, Duval County Med. Soc., Fla. Med. Assn., Am. Fertility Soc., Jacksonville Ob-Gyn. Soc. (pres. 1988), Am. Soc. Law and Medicine, Am. Coll. Physician Execs. Office: N Fla Ob-Gyn Assocs Meml Divsn 3627 University Blvd S Ste 200 Jacksonville FL 32216-4256

IREY, NELSON SUMNER, pathologist; b. Lewisburg, Pa., July 18, 1911; s. Philip Musser and Blanche Sarah (Sechler) I.; B.S., U. Pitts., 1935, M.D., 1938; m. Mary Ellen Sproat, Dec. 21, 1940; children—Ellen Jane, Janet Kathryn, Mary Sarah, Nelson Sumner. Commd. 2d lt. M.C., U.S. Army, 1940, advanced through grades to col.; resident in pathology Fitzsimons Gen. Hosp., Denver, 1946-47, Letterman Gen. Hosp., San Francisco, 1948; chief pathology service Valley Forge (Pa.) Gen. Hosp., 1949-50, 97th Gen. Hosp., Frankfurt, W. Ger., 1950-54, Letterman Gen. Hosp., 1954-60; comdg. officer 65th Med. Group, Korea, 1960-61; chief pathology service Walter Reed Gen. Hosp., 1961-65; ret., 1965; chmn. dept. environ. and drug induced pathology Armed Forces Inst. Pathology, Washington, 1965—; clin. prof. pathology George Washington U. Sch. Medicine, Uniformed Services U. Health Sci. Diplomate Am. Bd. Pathology. Fellow Am. Soc. Clin. Pathologists, Coll. Am. Pathologists, A.C.P., Am. Acad. Forensic Scis.; mem. Washington Soc. Pathologists (pres. 1969), Soc. Pharmacological and Environ. Pathologists (pres. 1974), Internat. Acad. Pathology, Drug Info. Assn. Baptist. Contbr. chpts. to med. books, articles to profl. jours.; editorial bd. Jour. Environ. Pathology and Toxicology, Drug Nutrient Interaction. Office: Armed Forces Inst Pathology Washington DC 20306

IRFAN, MUHAMMAD, pathology educator; b. Lahore, Punjab, Pakistan, Apr. 22, 1928; parents Muhammad and Sadar (Begum) Noman; m. Tahira Irfan, Dec. 10, 1970; children: Soma Sadaf, Ali Khurram, Asad Kaleem, Uzma Naheed. B.V.Sc., Punjab. Vet. Coll., Lahore, 1948; PhD, U. of London, 1958; MA, Trinity Coll., Dublin, Ireland, 1963. Cert. in vet. pub. health, Germany. Lectr. in pathology U. Khartoum, 1959-60; lectr. in pathology Trinity Coll., Dublin, 1960-63, sr. lectr., 1966-68; prin. rsch. officer Ghana Acad. Scis., Accra, 1963-66; prof. of pathology U. of Agrl., Faisalabad, Pakistan, 1968-72, 77-79, 83-88, acting vice chancelor, 1979, dean, 1970-72, 79, 83-88; prin. Coll. Vet. Scis., Lahore, 1972-76, 79-82; animal husbandry commr. Govt. of Pakistan, Islamabad, 1976-77; cons. U. Agr., 1988-94. Author: Curriculum Development, 1988, (textbook) Veterinary General Pathology, 1996; editor varius textbooks, 1988-95; editor-in-chief Pakistan Vet. Jour., 1982-88; author, editor monographs, sci. papers in field. Vice pres. Agrics Housing Soc., Lahore, 1980-96. Fellow Pakistan Acad. Med. Scis., 1987; recipient Tamgha-e-Pakistan award Govt. of Pakistan, 1971, Golden Star award Nat. Farm Guide Coun., Pakistan, 1987, Cert. of Honor, Pakistan Poultry Assn., 1991. Fellow Royal Coll. Vet. Surgeons, 1965. Home: 84-H Gulberg-III, Lahore 54660, Pakistan Office: U Agr, Faculty Vet Scis, Faisalabad Pakistan

IRIBAR, MANUEL R., internist; b. Guantanamo, Cuba, July 27, 1953; s. Jose Orlando and Ana Emilia (Coda) I. AA, Miami Dade Community Coll., 1973; MD, U. Autonoma de Guadalajara, Mexico City, 1977. Diplomate Nat. Bd. Med. Examiners. Intern U. Miami/Jackson Meml. Hosp., Miami, Fla., 1980-81; resident internal medicine U. Miami/Jackson Meml. Hosp., 1981-83; surg. asst. Coral Gables Hosp., Fla., 1978-79; emergency rm. physician Mexican Red Cross Emergency Rm., Ciudad Juarez, Mexico, 1979; surg. asst. South Shore Hosp., Miami Beach, Fla., 1979-80; med. dir., internist Internat. Med. Ctr. #1, Miami, 1983-84, Kings Point Med. Ctr., Delray Beach, Fla., 1984-87, Omni Med. Ctr., Miami, 1984—; exec. med. dir., owner E. Hollywood (Fla.) Med. Ctr.; mem. Quality Assurance Com Aventura Hosp. and Med. Ctr., Miami, Fla., 1993—, Credentials Com. Humana Health Care Plans, Miramar, Fla., 1994—. Mem. leadership council Cuban Am. Nat. Found., Miami, 1988—; trustee Miami Children's Hosp. Found., 1996—. Recipient Mejor Alumno award, U. Autonoma de Guadalajara, Mexico, 1974-77. Mem. AMA, Fla. Med. Assn., Dade County Med. Assn., Am. Geriatrics Soc., Am. Internal Medicine Soc., ACP, Am. Coll. Medicine, Am. Coll. Physician Execs., So. Med. Assn. Republican. Roman Catholic. Home: 8132 NW 164th Ter Hialeah FL 33016-6195

IRION, GLENN LINDSEY, physical therapist, educator; b. Phila., Sept. 30, 1955; s. Walter Frank and Jean Elaine (Reilly) I.; m. Jean Marie Schulte, June 7, 1980; children: Lindsay Marie, Kyle Andrew, Christina Louise, Phillip Reilly, Connor David. BA in Psychology, Temple U., 1977, MEd in Exercise Physiology, 1982, PhD in Physiology, 1985; BS in Phys. Therapy, U. Ctrl. Ark., 1993. Registered phys. therapist, Ark. Asst. prof. health scis. U. Ctrl. Ark., Conway, 1990-93, asst. prof. phys. therapy, 1993-94, 95-96, assoc. prof. phys. therapy, 1996—; staff phys. therapist U. Ark. for Med. Scis., Little Rock, 1994-95; diabetes educator Univ. Hosp., Little Rock, 1995—, cystic fibrosis rehab. cons., 1995—. Contbr. articles to profl. jours. Soccer coach Conway (Ark.) Youth Soccer Assn., 1994—. Grantee Am. Heart Assn., 1986. Mem. Am. Phys. Therapy Assn., Am. Physiol. Soc., Am. Assn. Cardiovascular and Pulmonary Rehab., Am. Heart Assn. Rsch. Coun. Office: U Ctrl Ark Phys Therapy Dept 201 S Donaghey Conway AR 72035

IRION, LEA V., nurse, mental health care coordinator; b. Dec. 30, 1958; d. Jose E. and Jesusa (Teves) Villanueva; m. William H. Irion, Apr. 10, 1987. BSN, Silliman U., Dumaguete City, 1980; postgrad., Hunter Coll., CUNY, 1986, SUNY, Stony Brook, 1994—. RN, N.Y.; cert. psychiat./ mental health nurse. Staff nurse Seaview Hosp. and Home, N.Y.C., 1983-85; staff nurse Met. Hosp., N.Y.C., 1985-86, head nurse, 1986-88; staff nurse Mt. Sinai Hosp., N.Y.C., 1988-92; teaching and rsch. nurse Stony Brook Hosp., 1992-94, care coord., 1994—; RN, N.Y.; cert. psychiat./mental health nurse; cert. in healthcare utilization and quality mgmt. Mem. ANA, N.Y. State Nurses Assn., United Univ. Profls., Silliman U. Alumni Assn. (pub. rels. 1993-96, v.p. 1996—). Office: Stony Brook Univ Hosp Stony Brook NY

IRISH, GARY GENE, health systems executive; b. Lancaster, Wis., Sept. 17, 1951; s. Clyde Gene and Florence Adele (Haudenshield) I.; m. Karen L. Seinhart, Aug. 18, 1974. BA, Andrews U., 1973; MPH, Loma Linda U., 1975; MBA, UCLA, 1980. Asst. health planner Inland Counties Comprehensive Health Planning Coun., San Bernardino, Calif., 1975; adminstrv. resident Corona (Calif.) Community Hosp., 1976; health planner Inland Counties Health Systems Agy., Riverside, Calif., 1977-78; dir. resource mgmt. and planning Loma Linda (Calif.) U. Med. Ctr., 1978-82; exec. dir. Loma Linda Gyn-Ob Med. Group, 1982-83; asst. v.p. Adventist Health System/North, Hinsdale, Ill., 1983-85, v.p. Adventist Health System/North, Eastern and Middle Am., Hinsdale, 1986-87, pres. Glendale Heights Community Hosp., 1987-88, Glenoaks Med. Ctr., 1989-95, v.p. Hinsdale Hosp. and Health Sys., 1995-96; pres. Pinnacle Managed Healthcare Cons. Ltd.; regional v.p. Prime Care Med. Group Network, Inc. Editor Healthcare Innovation. Am. Hosp. Assn., Am. Coll. Healthcare Execs., Am. Managed Healthcare Orgn (sec.). Home: 9340 S Madison St Hinsdale IL 60521-6824 Office: Med Group Mgmt Assn Midwest Regional Bd 1415 W 22d St Oak Brook IL 60521

IRISH, MICHAEL SHAWN, surgeon; b. Shawnee Mission, Kans., Jan. 14, 1964; s. Gary Don and Barbara (Ley) I.; m. Dawn Voigt, Sept. 16, 1995; 1 child, Amanda. BS, Tulane U., 1986; MD, U. Kans., 1990. Resident, chief resident gen. surgery The Mayo Clinic, Rochester, Minn., 1990-95; rsch. fellow in pediat. and fetal surgery Children's Hosp. Buffalo, 1995—. Home: 166 Ivyhurst Rd Amherst NY 14226 Office: Children's Hosp Buffalo 219 Bryant St Buffalo NY 14222

IRVING, GEORGE WASHINGTON, JR., health science association administrator; b. Caribou, Maine, Nov. 20, 1910; s. George Washington Sr. and Adelaide Louise (Butman) I.; m. Frances Catherine Connell, June 4, 1938; children: George Washington III, Mary Constance Fitzpatrick. BS, George Washington U., 1933, MA, 1935, PhD, 1939; postgrad., USDA Grad. Sch., 1933-35, U. Ill., 1937. Rsch. fellow George Washington U. Med. Sch., 1935-38; rsch. fellow Med. Coll. Cornell U., N.Y.C., 1938-39; asst. in chemistry Rockefeller Inst. Med. Rsch., N.Y.C., 1939-42; head protein rsch. USDA, New Orleans, 1942-44; div. head USDA, Beltsville, Md., 1944-47; asst. chief Bur. of Chemistry USDA, Washington, 1947-54, br. chief agrl. mktg. svc., 1954, dep. adminstr. agrl. rsch. svc., 1954-64, assoc. adminstr. agrl. rsch. svc., 1964-65, adminstr. agrl. rsch. svc., 1965-71; rsch. assoc. Fed. Am. Soc. Exptl. Biology, Bethesda, Md., 1972-85; lectr. in antibiotics USDA Grad. Sch., Washington, 1946-52; lectr. in biochemistry George Washington U. Med. Sch., 1947-53; exec. v.p. Agrl. Rsch. Inst., Bethesda, 1982-84; v.p. Internat. Life Sci. Inst., Washington, 1985-87; freelance cons. in field; v.p., mem. grad. coun. George Wash. U., 1956, mem. governing bd., 1959-60; chmn. sci. adv. bd. Sugar Rsch. Found., N.Y., 1967-71; lectr. in field; trustee Nutrition Found., N.Y., 1965-84, chmn. bd., 1983-84; mem. food additives com. NRC, 1985-89; dir. Friends Agr. Rsch., Beltsville, 1985—; mem. adv. bd. Emeritus Scis. Mathematicians, Engrs., 1990—. Contbr., co-contbr. numerous articles to profl. jours. and books; patentee in field. Witness U.S. Congress, Washington, 1947-71; vol. sci. tchr. D.C. Pub. Schs., 1990-95; primary lectr. 1st Internat. Congress of Food Sci. and Tech., London, 1962, 3d Congress, Washington, 1970. Fellow AAAS (v.p., chair agr. sect. 1962, mem. at large 1963-67), Wash. Acad. Sci. (del rep. Inst. Food Tech. 1946-48, Phys. Scis. award 1946, pres. 1955), Alpha Chi Sigma (pres. Washington chpt. 1948-49, assoc. editor nat. mag. Indpls. 1970-84, Svc. award 1968, Man of Yr. 1975); mem. Am. Chem. Soc. (cons. 1978-88), Chem. Soc. Wash. (pres. 1953, Svc. award 1973), Am. Soc. Biochemistry and Molecular Biology, Am. Inst., Chemists, Toastmasters, Cosmos Club (pres. 1974-75), Sigma Xi, Tau Kappa Epsilon. Republican. Roman Catholic. Home and Office: 9707 Old Georgetown Rd Bethesda MD 20814-1727

IRVING, JAN LOUISE, nursing educator; b. Salem, Oreg., Aug. 5, 1952; d. Steve Dwaine and Margery Mae (Campbell) I. BSN, Oreg. Health Scis. U., 1976; MS, U. Portland, 1984; PhD, Oreg. State U., 1995. Asst. head nurse Salem (Oreg.) Hosp.; instr. nursing Chemeketa Community Coll., Salem. Contbr. articles to profl. jours. Grantee Oreg. Dept. Vocat. Edn., 1979-81, Helene Fuld Inst., 1989, 91, 94. Mem. Oreg. Coun. Assoc. Degree Programs, Sigma Theta Tau.

IRWIN, DAVID HERMAN, JR., cardiologist; b. Tupelo, Miss., Apr. 24, 1950; s. David Herman Sr. and Billie Dale (Easterling) I.; m. Jenny Suzanne Shultz, June 1, 1975; children: Jordan Elizabeth, Catherine Dale. BS, Miss. State U., 1972; MD, U. Miss., Jackson, 1975. From intern to resident Ochsner Found. Hosp., New Orleans, 1975-78; staff mem. Cardiology Assocs. of North Miss., P.A., Tupelo, 1978; staff physician North Miss. Med. Ctr., Tupelo, 1978-83, staff cardiologist, 1986—; fellow in cardiology Univ. Hosp. Univ. Med. Ctr., Jackson, 1984-85; cons. physician Saltillo (Miss.) Clinic, 1978—. Fellow Am. Coll. Cardiology (cert.); mem. AMA, ACP (cert.), Miss. State Med. Assn. (sec. 1986-89), Masons. Methodist. Office: PO Box 2519 Tupelo MS 38803-2519

IRWIN, GERALD PORT, physician; b. Muncie, Ind., July 11, 1945; s. Francis Inlow and Helen Marcella (Morgan) I.; m. Martha Sue Vincent, Mar. 10, 1946; 1 child, Tamara Suzette. AB in Biol. Sci., Ind. U., 1968; MD, Ind. U., Indpls., 1972. Diplomate Am. Bd. Family Physicians. Intern and resident Ball Meml. Hosp., Muncie, Ind., 1972-73; pvt. practice Alexandria, Ind., 1973—. Med. dir. Richland Twp. Fire Dept., Anderson. Mem. AMA (physician recognition award 1992-95), Am. Assn. Family Physicians, Ind. State Med. Assn., Ind. Assn. Family Physicians, Lions, Elks. Methodist. Office: PO Box 124 State Rd 9 S Alexandria IN 46001

IRWIN, JAMES ROBERT, surgeon; b. Pitts., Oct. 11, 1940; s. James Walter and Nelle Isabelle (Moore) I.; m. Frances Darlene Herrett, June 12, 1964; children: Paul Eugene, Timothy Robert. BA, Sterling Coll., 1962; MD, U. Kans., 1967. Intern Deaconess Hosp., Spokane, Wash., 1968; resident Iowa Meth. Hosp., Des Moines, 1967-72; chief surgery Naval Hosp., Oak HArbor, Wash., 1972-74, Ganta (Liberia) Meth. Hosp., 1974-75; surgeon pvt. practice, Colville, Wash., 1975-78, NE Wash. Med. Group, Colville, 1978-88, pvt. practice, Moses Lake, Wash., 1988—; pres. med. staff Mt. Carmel Hosp., Colville, 1985-88, Samaritan Hosp., Moses Lake, 1993,

94. Lt. comdr. USN, 1972-74, capt. med. corps. Fellow Am. Coll. Surgeons; mem. Wash. State Med. Assn. (trustee 1995—, chair grievance com. 1985—), Grant County Med. Assn. (pres. 1991), Kiwanis. Presbyterian. Home: 5582 Rd J SE Moses Lake WA 98837 Office: 605 Coolidge Dr 202 Moses Lake WA 98837

IRWIN, MARTIN, psychiatrist; b. N.Y.C., Oct. 15, 1949. BA, Cornell U., 1967; MD, U. Pa., 1971. Resident in psychiatry U. Chgo., 1975-79, fellow in child psychiatry, 1977-79; dir. psychiat. in-patient unit Children's Meml. Hosp., Chgo., 1979-82; dir. child neuropsychiatry in-patient unit, dir. tng. Tulane U. Med. Ctr., New Orleans, 1982-84; chief children's in-patient unit, dir. med. student edn. Badley Hosp./Brown U., Providence, 1984-88; dir. div. child and adolescent psychiatry, assoc. prof. SUNY Health Sci. Ctr., Syracuse, 1988—; vis. prof. Ben Gurion U., Beersheva, Israel, 1994-95. Author: Psychiatric Hospitalization of Children, 1982, ADHD: A No-Nonsense Guide for Primary Care Physicians, 1996; contbr. articles to profl. jours. Mem. Am. Psychiat. Assn., Am. Acad. Child Psychiatry, Soc. for Biol. Psychiatry, Profs. Child Psychiatry. Office: SUNY Health Sci Ctr 750 E Adams St Syracuse NY 13210-2306

IRWIN, MICHAEL HENRY KNOX, physician; b. London, June 5, 1931; came to U.S., 1957; s. William Knox and Edith Isabel Mary (Collins) I.; m. Miriam Elizabeth Naumann, Nov. 1, 1958 (div. Nov. 1982); children: Christina Susan, Pamela Elizabeth, Diana Jennifer; m. Frederica Todd Harlow, Apr. 9, 1983 (div. July 1991); m. Patricia Lady Walters, May 13, 1994. M.B.B.S., St. Bartholomew's Hosp. Med. Coll., London, 1955; M.P.H., Columbia U., 1960. Intern and resident Prince of Wales Hosp., London, 1955-56; med. officer UN, N.Y.C., 1957-61, dep. resident rep. UN Devel. Program, Pakistan, 1961-63; sr. med. officer UN, N.Y.C., 1963-69, med. dir., N.Y.C., 1969-73, dir. div. personnel UN Devel. Program, 1973-76; rep. UNICEF, Bangladesh, 1977-80, sr. adviser UNICEF, N.Y.C., 1980-82, med. dir. UN, UNICEF, UN Devel. Program, N.Y.C., 1982-89; dir. health svcs. dept. World Bank and Internat. Monetary Fund, 1989-90, adviser Action Aid, 1990-91, dir. Westside Action, 1991-93; vice-chmn. UN Assn., 1995—; chmn. Vol. Euthanasia Soc., 1996—; sr. cons. Internat. Yr. of Disabled Persons, 1981; cons. Am. Assn. Blood Banks, 1984-90. Author: Check-Ups: Safeguarding Your Health, 1961; Overweight: A Problem for Millions, 1964; Travelling Without Tears, 1964; Viruses, Colds and Flu, 1966; Blood: New Uses for Saving Lives, 1967; What Do We Know About Allergies?, 1972; Aspirin: Current Knowledge About an Old Medication, 1983; Can We Survive Nuclear War?, 1984; Nuclear Energy: Good or Bad?, 1984; The Cocaine Epidemic, 1985, AIDS: Fears and Facts, 1986, Risks to Health and Safety on the Job, 1987, (novel) Talpa, 1990, Peace Museums, 1991. Pres. Assistance for Blind Children Internat., 1978-85; mem. exec. bd. Internat. Agy. for Prevention Blindness, 1979-83. Recipient Officer Cross Internat. Fedn. Blood Donor Orgns., 1984. Milbank Meml. Fund fellow, 1959. Fellow Royal Soc. Medicine. Address: 15 Hovedene, 95 Cromwell Rd, Hove, Sussex BN3 3EH, England

IRWIN, PATRICIA MARIE, health educator, consultant; b. N.Y.C., Aug. 8, 1938; d. Edmond Joseph and Olga Marie (Chomitz) I. Diploma, Bellevue Sch. Nursing, N.Y.C., 1959; BS in Health Care Adminstrn., St. Joseph's Coll., Windham, Maine, 1993, postgrad., 1993—. Staff nurse Bellevue Hosp. Ctr., N.Y.C., 1959-60, head nurse, neurology, 1960-61, supr. neurology, 1961-85, clin. specialist, quality assurance, 1985-88, asst. dir. quality assurance/risk mgmt., 1988-93; cons. in primary care Mary Immaculate Hosp., Jamaica, N.Y., 1994, cons. edn. of vols., 1994—; vol. sr. edn. Cath. Charities, N.Y.C. Contbr. articles to profl. jours. Mem. Am. Hort. Therapy Assn. Office: Irwin Assocs 104-30 106th St Ozone Park NY 11417

IRWIN, PETER JOHN, orthopaedic surgeon; b. East St. Louis, Ill., July 7, 1934; s. Peter and Anne (Sokalski) Iwasyszyn; m. Kathryn Swanson, June 15, 1960; children: Kathryn Linda, Mary Elizabeth, Amy Marie, Kenneth John, James Patrick. BS in Biology, St. Louis U., 1955, MD, 1959. Diplomate Am. Bd. Orthopaedic Surgery. Intern, Creighton Meml. St. Joseph Hosp., Omaha, 1959-60; resident orthopaedic surgery U. Ark. Med. Ctr., 1961-65, teaching staff, 1965—; practice medicine specializing in orthopaedic surgery, Fort Smith, Ark., 1965—; mem. staff St. Edward Mercy Med. Ctr., 1965—; mem. staff Sparks Regional Med. Ctr., 1965—, chief of staff, 1979, bd. dirs., 1980-87. Lt. comdr. M.C., USN, 1966-68. Fellow Am. Acad. Orthopaedic Surgeons (councillor 1983-89), ACS; mem. AMA, So. Med. Assn., Sebastian County Med. Soc., Ark. Orthopaedic Assn. (pres. 1976-77), Mid-Am. Orthopaedic Assn. (founding mem., pres. 1993-94), Clin. Orthopaedic Soc., Inc., Mid-Central States Orthopaedic Soc. (pres. 1979-80), So. Orthopaedic Assn., Am. Orthopaedic Soc. for Sports Medicine, Am. Soc. Sports Medicine, Ark. Hand Club. Office: 1500 Dodson Ave Fort Smith AR 72901-5128

IRWIN, RICHARD STEPHEN, physician, scientist, educator; b. New London, Conn., Nov. 15, 1942; s. Harold H. and Sylvia Rowena (Hendel) I.; m. Diane Hazel Northrop, June 21, 1969; children: Rachel Helen, Sara Beth, Catherine Jamie, Rebecca Susan. BS, Tufts U., 1964, MD, 1968. Diplomate Am. Bd. Med. Examiners, Am. Bd. Internal Medicine, Am. Bd. Pulmonary Disease; spl. cert. in critical care medicine. Intern Tufts New Eng. Med. Ctr., Boston, 1968-69, jr. asst. resident in medicine, 1969-70; fellow in pulmonary disease Columbia-Presbyn. Hosp., N.Y.C., 1970-72, 1970-72; dir. med. ICU R.I. Hosp., Providence, 1974-79; asst. prof. medicine Brown U., Providence, 1974-79; assoc. prof. medicine U. Mass. Med. Sch., Worcester, 1979-82, prof. medicine, 1982—; dir. pulmonary and critical care medicine U. Mass. Med. Ctr., Worcester, 1979—; dir. Respiratory Care Dept., U. Mass. Med. Ctr., Worcester, 1979—, Pulmonary Nursing Svc., 1989—, Pulmonary Rehab., 1986—, Asthma Self-Mgmt. Program, 1990—. Co-editor: (textbook) Intensive Care Medicine, Jour. Intensive Care Medicine, 1986—; contbr. over 100 articles to profl. jours., over 125 chpts. to books. Maj. USAF, 1972-74. Fellow Am. Coll. Physicians, Am. Coll. Chest Physicians (gov. Mass. chpt.); mem. Am. Thoracic Soc. (ea. sect. pres. 1980-81), Nat. Assn. Med. Dirs. Respiratory Care. Office: U Ma Med Ctr 55 Lake Ave N Worcester MA 01655-0002

IRWIN-OBREGON, VIRGINIA ANN, internist; b. Paterson, N.J., Oct. 24, 1964; d. John A. and Dolores J. (Jansen) I. ADN, Ocean County Coll., 1985; BS in Biology with distinction, Stockton State Coll., 1989; DO, U. Medicine and Dentistry N.J., 1993. Intern Kennedy Meml. Hosp./Univ. Med. Ctr., Stratford, N.J., 1993, resident in internal medicine, 1994-96; fellow in nephrology Kennedy meml. Hosp./Univ. Med. Ctr., Stratford, N.J., 1996—. Lutheran. Home: 3402 Sagemore Dr Marlton NJ 08053 Office: Kennedy Meml Hosp E Laurel Rd Stratford NJ 08084

ISAAC, ALAN S., speech and language pathologist; b. Queens, N.Y., Mar. 7, 1962; s. Alvin M. and Rita (Gill) I. AS, Agrl. and Tech. Coll., Farmingdale, N.Y., 1982; BS, SUNY, Geneseo, 1985; MA, Hofstra U., 1989. Speech-lang. therapist Bd. Coop. Ednl. Svcs., Dix Hills, N.Y., 1985—; audiologist Gt. Neck (N.Y.) Audiol. Assn., 1990—. Scoutmaster Deer Park (N.Y.) area Boy Scouts Am., 1986—. Mem. Am. Speech-Lang.-Hearing Assn., L.I. Speech-Lang.-Hearing Assn. Office: BOCES III 507 Deer Park Rd Dix Hills NY 11746-5207

ISAAC, CHARLES ARNOLD, urologist; b. Santa Barbara, Calif., June 11, 1925; s. Arnold Gerhard and Alice Florence (Kizler) I.; m. Anita Mae Landrum, July 9, 1950 (div. Feb. 1969); children: Kathryn, James Arnold, Carol Ann; m. Mary Carolyn Roop, June 9, 1969; 1 child, Amy Beth Langenhorst. BA, Westminster Coll., 1947; MD, Kans. U., 1949. Diplomate Am. Bd. Urology. Intern Madison (Wis.) Gen. Hosp., 1949-50; resident urology Kans. U., Kansas City, 1952-55; urologist Axtell Clinic, Newton, Kans., 1955-96. Lt. USN, 1950-52. Fellow ACS, Kans. Chpt. ACS (pres. 1990-92); mem. AMA, Kans. Med. Soc., Harvey County Med. Soc., South Ctrl. Sect. Am. Urol. Assn., Am. Urol. Assn. Home: 929 Emmaline Ave Newton KS 67114 Office: Axtell Clinic 203 E Broadway Newton KS 67114

ISAAC, WALTER LON, psychology educator; b. Seattle, May 31, 1956; s. Walter and Dorothy Jane (Emerson) I.; m. Susan Victoria Wells. BS, U. Ga., 1978; MA, U. Ky., 1983; postgrad., U. Ga., 1988-89; PhD, U. Ky., 1989. Advanced EMT Athens (Ga.) Gen. Hosp., 1977-79; teaching asst., rsch. asst. U. Ky., Lexington, 1979-87, instr. gifted student program, 1985, 87; instr. evening classes U. Ga., Athens, 1988, temp. asst. prof., 1989; asst. prof. psychology, mem. grad. faculty East Tenn. State U., Johnson City, 1989—; reviewer McGraw-Hill Pub. Co., Cambridge, Mass., 1990—. Contbg. author: Aging and Recovery of Function, 1984; contbr. articles to profl. jours. Bd. dirs. Upper East Tenn. Sci. Fair, Inc., 1992—; advisor to Gamma Beta Phi Honor Soc., 1994—. Mem. AAAS, Am. Psychol. Soc., Am. Assn. Lab. Animal Sci., Southeastern Psychol. Assn., Soc. for Neurosci., Sigma Xi (grantee 1987). Home: 905 Carroll Creek Rd Johnson City TN 37601-2401 Office: East Tenn State U Dept Psychology PO Box 70649 Johnson City TN 37614-0649

ISAACS, JOHN HENRY, JR., medical educator, otolaryngologist; b. St. Louis, Dec. 12, 1949; s. John Henry and Patricia Agnes (Novy) I.; m. Rita Marie Joost, July 25, 1981 (dec. Feb. 1996); children: Christine Marie, Lisa McGuan. BA, U. Notre Dame, 1971; MD, U. Ill., Chgo., 1975. Diplomate Am. Bd. Med. Examiners, Am. Bd. Otolaryngology. Intern dept. surgery U. Fla., Gainesville, 1975-76, resident dept. surgery and otolaryngology, 1976-80; chief div. otolaryngology U. Hosp., Jacksonville, Fla., 1980-82; asst. prof. otolaryngology Sch. of Medicine U. Fla., Gainesville, 1982-87; chief, otolaryngology VA Med. Ctr., Gainesville, 1985-87, Augusta, Ga., 1987-90; assoc. prof. Med. Coll. Ga., Augusta, 1987-90; chief of otolaryngology, assoc. prof. Med. Ctr. U. Fla., Jacksonville, 1990—. Home: 2316 Miller Oaks Dr N Jacksonville FL 32217-3531 Office: U Fla Dept Surgery 655 W 8th St Jacksonville FL 32209-6511

ISAACS, KENNETH S(IDNEY), psychoanalyst, educator; b. Mpls., Apr. 7, 1920; s. Mark William and Sophia (Rai) I.; m. Ruth Elizabeth Johnson, Feb. 21, 1951 (dec. 1967); m. Adele Rella Bodroghy, May 17, 1969; children: Jonathan, James; stepchildren: John, Curtis, Peter and Edward Meissner. BA, U. Minn., 1944; PhD, U. Chgo., 1956; postgrad., Inst. Psychoanalysis, 1957-63. Intern Worcester State Hosp., Mass., 1947-48; trainee VA Mental Hygiene Clinic, Chgo., 1948-50; chief psychologist outpatient clinic system Ill. Dept. Pub. Welfare, 1949-56; research assoc., assoc. prof. U. Ill. Med. Sch., Chgo., 1956-63; practice psychoanalysis Evanston, Ill., 1960—; supr. psychiat. residency program Evanston Hosp., Northwestern U., 1972-81, Northwestern Meml. Hosp.; pres. Chgo. Ctr. Psychoanalytic Psychology, 1984-87; cons. to schs., hosps., clinics, pvt. practitioners and industry; sr. cons. Beta Consulting Ltd.; pres. Kenisa Drilling Co., Kenisa Securities Co., Kenisa Oil Co. Author: (book) Again with Feeling, 1989, (syndicated newspaper column) A Psychologist's Notebook; contbr. articles to profl. publs. Served with AUS, 1943-45, ETO. Mem. AAAS, APA (bd. dirs. divsn. pschoanalysis), Chgo. Psychoanalytic Soc., Am. Bd. Psychoanalysis (chair bd. dirs.), Am. Bd. Profl. Psychology (bd. trustees 1994—), N.Y. Acad. Sci., Sigma Xi.

ISAACSON, NORMAN HARRY, physician, educator; b. N.Y.C., Apr. 9, 1922; s. Louis and Pauline (Sanders) I.; m. Estelle Ettman, June 29, 1947; children: Paul (dec.), Dale, Lee. BA, NYU, 1941, MD, 1944. Diplomate Am. Bd. Surgery. Intern Jewish Hosp. Bklyn., 1944-45, asst. resident in pathology, 1945-46; surg. resident George Washington U. Med. Ctr., Washington, 1948-52; clin. prof. surgery George Washington U. Med. Sch., Washington, 1952-95, prof. emeritus in residence, 1995—. Author text chpts.; contbr. over 60 articles to profl. jours. Fellow Am. Coll. Surgeons, Internat. Coll. Proctology; mem. AMA, D.C. Med. Soc., Internat. Coll. Surgeons, Soc. Am. Gastrointestinal Endoscopic Surgeons, Jacobi Med. Soc., Washington Acad. Surgery. Democrat. Jewish. Home: 6537 NW 40th Ct Boca Raton FL 33496 Office: U Med Ctr Dept Surgery 2150 Pennsylvania Ave NW Washington DC 20037

ISAACSON, ROBERT LEE, psychology educator, researcher; b. Detroit, Sept. 26, 1928; s. Emil Alfred and Evelyn (Johnson) I.; m. Susan Doherty, Dec. 16, 1956 (div. 1972); children—Gunnar, Lars, Mary Ingrid, Mary Christina; m. Ann W. Braden, Dec. 31, 1974; stepchildren—Richard, Milly Braden. A.B. in Psychology, U. Mich., 1950, M.S. in Psychology, 1954, Ph.D. in Psychology, 1958. Co-dir. U. Fla. Ctr. for Neurobiol. Sci., Gainesville, 1970-78; grad. research prof. U. Fla., Gainesville, 1977-78; disting. prof. psychology SUNY, Binghamton, 1978—; dir. SUNY Ctr. for Neurobehavioral Sci., Binghamton, 1978-88. Author: Limbic System, 2d edit., 1982; editor: (with others) Expression of Knowledge, 1982, The Hippocampus, vols. 3-4, 1986, The Vulnerable Brain and Environmental Risks, vols. 1-2, 1992, vol. 3, 1994. Pres. Alachua County Assn. for Retarded Children, Gainesville, 1973-75; chmn. dist. III Human Rights Advocacy Com., Gainesville, 1975-77. Served with USN, 1950-53, Korea. Holloway fellow U.S. Navy, 1946-50; grantee NSF, NIH, U.S. Army Surgeon Gen. Fellow APA, AAAS; mem. Internat. Behavioral Neurosci. Soc. (councilor 1991-95), Soc. for Neurosci. (pres. cen. N.Y. chpt. 1982-84), Assn. Neurosci. Depts. Programs, Am. Physiol. Soc., Sec. Health Rehab. Svcs. State of Fla. (mem. Blue Ribbon com. 1976). Office: SUNY Dept Psychology Binghamton NY 13902-6000

ISAACSON, SIDNEY, pediatrician; b. Bklyn., Mar. 1, 1928; s. Abraham and Florence (Soloff) I.; BA, NYU, 1949; MD, Berne U., 1955; m. Harriet Kempler, Dec. 21, 1952 (dec. 1986); m. Marilyn Rosen, Dec. 12, 1989; children: Arlene Isaacson Werner, Marsha Lois Lerman. Intern Queen's Hosp. Center, 1955-56, resident in pediatrics, 1956, sr. resident, chief pediatrics, 1957-58; practice medicine specializing in pediatrics, Wantagh, N.Y., 1958—; dir. pediatrics Brunswick Gen. Hosp., Amityville, N.Y., 1972-81; clin. asst. prof. pediatrics Cornell Med. Sch., 1973—; attending North Shore Univ. Hosp., Manhasset, N.Y., 1973—; pres. Wantagh Pediatric Assos., P.C., 1971—. Served with M.C., AUS, 1946-47. Diplomate Am. Bd. Pediatrics. Fellow Am. Acad. Pediatrics; mem. AMA, N.Y. State, Nassau County med. socs., Nassau Pediatric Soc. Office: 2415 Jerusalem Ave Ste 204 North Bellmore NY 11710-1857

ISACHI, IULIUS, radiologist; b. Panciu, Vrancea, Romania, Nov. 1, 1955; s. Nicolae and Sofia (Balan) I.; m. Bogdana Miron, June 29, 1986. MD, Gen. Medicine Faculty, Iasy, Romania, 1983. Bd. cert. diplomate health dept.; radiodiagnosis specialist. Physician radiodiagnosis Bicaz (Romania) Hosp., 1992—. Lt. Romanian Army Res. Mem. Christian and Democratic Nat. Peasant Party. Office: Bicaz Hosp, Barajului, Bicaz Romania

ISACOFF, MARK, psychologist; b. Bklyn., Mar. 2, 1953; s. David and Hannah (Zwirn) I.; m. Mindy Schwartzman, Aug. 28, 1977; children: Adam, Amy. BA in Psychology, Bklyn. Coll., 1975, MS of Edn. in Sch. Psychology, 1977, advanced cert. in sch. psychology, 1977; advanced tng. Clin. Biofeedback, Inst. for Psychosomatic Research, 1982; PhD, Hofstra U., 1987. Nationally cert. sch. psychology; lic. psychologist, N.Y. Cons. psychologist N.Y.C. Bd. Edn. 1977, 78-80; adj. asst. prof. Queens Coll., CUNY, 1978-79; psychol. counselor Bklyn. Coll., CUNY, 1978-79, adj. lectr. sch. edn. and grad. studies, 1979-80, adj. lectr. dept. psychology, 1979-81; staff psychologist Howard Beach Child Guidance and Family Counseling Ctr., Queens, N.Y., 1979-90; psychologist Kings County Hosp. Ctr., Bklyn., 1980-86, dir. treatment in child psychiatry, 1982-86, clin. adminstrn. dir. Program for Adolescent Devel., 1986—; clin. instr. psychiatry SUNY Downstate Med. Ctr., 1980-83, clin. asst. prof. psychiatry, 1983—. Contbr. articles to profl. jours. Pres. Assn. of Sch. Psychologists Bklyn. Coll., 1976-77. Fellow Am. Orthopsychiat. Assn., Am. Bd. Med. Psychotherapists (diplomate), Am. Bd. Psychotherapists and Psychodiagnosticians (diplomate); mem. APA, Nat. Assn. Sch. Psychologists (com. ethics and profl. conduct 1983-86), Bklyn. Psychol. Assn. (bd. dirs. 1978-86), Bklyn. Coll. Alumni Assn. (bd. dirs. 1974-84), Nat. Assn. Watch and Clock Collectors, Soc. Am. Magicians, Internat. Soc. Study Dissociation. Office: Kings County Hosp Ctr 451 Clarkson Ave Brooklyn NY 11203-2054

ISADA, CARLOS MANUEL, physician; b. Syracuse, N.Y., May 13, 1959; s. Nelson M. and Beatriz (Manuel) I.; m. Loretta Roach, May 6, 1989. BA, SUNY, Buffalo, 1981, BS, 1982, MD, 1986. Intern Cleve. Clinic Found., 1986-87, resident in internal medicine, 1987-89, chief resident, spl. fellow dept. internal medicine, 1989-90, spl. fellow dept. infectious diseases, 1990-92, clin. assoc. dept. infectious diseases, 1992-93, staff physician, 1993—, dir. fellowship program dept. infectious diseases, 1994—; Editor, author: Infectious Disease Handbook, 1994. Mem. AMA, ACP, Infectious Diseases Soc. Am. Office: Cleve Clinic Found 9500 Euclid Ave Cleveland OH 44195

ISAY, RICHARD ALEXANDER, psychiatrist; b. Pitts.; s. Milton and Jeanette (Myers) I.; children: David, Joshua. AB, Haverford Coll., 1952-56; MD, U. Rochester, 1957-61; postgrad. psychoanalysis, Western New England Inst., New Haven, 1969-73. Cert. in psychiatry, 1969, psychoanalysis, 1974. Resident in psychiatry Yale U., New Haven, 1962-65; asst. clin. prof. psychiatry Yale U. Sch. Medicine, New Haven, 1967-75; pvt. practice psychiatry and psychoanalysis New Haven, 1967-81; assoc. clin. prof. psychiatry Yale Child Study Ctr., New Haven, 1975-81, Cornell U. Med. Coll., N.Y.C., 1981—; mem. faculty Ctr. for Psychoanalytic Tng. and Rsch., Columbia U., N.Y.C., 1981—; assoc. clin. prof. psychiatry Cornell U. Med. Coll., N.Y.C., 1981-88, clin. prof. psychiatry, 1989—; pres. Western New England Psychoanalytic Soc., New Haven, 1979-81. Assoc. editor: Models of the Mind, Their Relationship to Clinical Work, 1985; author: Being Homosexual, Gay Men and Their Development, 1989, Becoming Gay: The Journey to Self-Acceptance, 1996; contbr. articles to profl. jours. Bd. dirs. Nat. Lesbian and Gay Health Assn., 1987—, v.p., 1992—; bd. dirs. Hetrick Martin Inst., 1992-95. Lt. comdr. USN, 1965-67. Fellow Am. Psychiat. Assn. (gay, lesbian and bisexual issues com. 1987-93, chmn. 1991-93); mem. Am. Psychoanalytic Assn. (cert., chmn. program com. 1981-84), Internat. Psycho-Analytical Assn. (chmn. Am. program com. 1979-81), Phi Beta Kappa. Office: 55 E End Ave New York NY 10028-7928

ISBELL, ROBERT GRINDLEY, radiologist; b. Toledo, Aug. 25, 1937; s. Robert Henry and Winifred Margaret (Grindley) I.; m. Susan Preston Steele, June 12, 1965; children: Deborah, Laura, Lynn. AB (cum laude), Princeton U., 1960; MD, U. Mich., 1964. Diplomate Am. Bd. Radiology, Am. Bd. Nuclear Medicine. Internship St. Joseph's Mercy Hosp., Ann Arbor, Mich., 1964-65; resident Mayo Grad. Sch., Rochester, Minn., 1965-69; radiologist pvt. practice Stern, Drake, Isbell & Assocs., Tampa, Fla., 1969—; assoc. prof. radiology U. South Fla. Coll. Medicine, Tampa, 1976—; chmn. bd. Physicians' Health Plan, Tampa, 1984-85. Mem. United Way of Greater Tampa, Inc., 1983—, Tampa Mus., 1983—. Mem. AMA, Fla. Med. Assn., Hillsborough County Med. Assn. (pres. 1983-84), Am. Coll. Radiology, Am. Coll. Nuclear Medicine, Tampa Yacht and Country Club. Presbyterian. Office: 4516 N Armenia Ave Tampa FL 33603-2732

ISBISTER, WILLIAM HUGH, surgeon; b. Manchester, Eng., Apr. 7, 1934; s. William and Eleanor Gwyneth (Pritchard) I.; m. Magdalena Richter, Mar. 29, 1961; children: William, Gwyneth-Ann, Michael. M.B.,Ch.B., Manchester U., 1958, MD, 1964. From house surgeon to clin. asst. in surgery Manchester Royal Infirmary, 1958-64; resident surg. officer Park Hosp., Davyhulme, 1965-67; sr. surg. registrar Manchester Regional Hosp. Bd., 1967-69; rsch. fellow in surgery and John M. Wilson Meml. scholar Cleve. Clinic Found., 1969-70; sr. surg. registrar, prof. surg. unit Manchester Regional Hosp. Bd., 1970-71; sr. lectr. surgery U. Queensland, Brisbane, 1972-75; from Found. prof. surgery to dep. dean Wellington Sch. Medicine, 1975-90; sr. specialist colorectal surgeon Wellington Hosp., 1975-90, chmn. dept. gen. surgery, 1981-88, 89-90; specialist colorectal surgeon and chmn. dept. surgery King Faisal Specialist Hosp. and Rsch. Ctr., Riyadh, Saudi Arabia, 1990—; mem. Dept. Vets. Affairs Assessing Panel, Australia and N.Z. Jour. Surgery Rev. Panel, Anti-Cancer Coun. of Victoria Nat. Coun. Assessing Panel; cons. in field; lectr. in field. Contbr. numerous articles to profl. jours. Fellow Am. Soc. Colon and Rectal Surgeons; mem. Brit. Med. Assn., Surg. Rsch. Soc. Australasia (life mem., past pres.), Internat. Soc. Univ. Colon and Rectal Surgeons, Saudi Gastroenterology Assn., The Wellington Club, Riyadh Surg. Club, Riyadh Gastroenterol. Club. Home and Office: King Faisal Specialist Hosp, PO Box 3354, Riyadh 11211, Saudi Arabia

ISCHIROPOULOS, HARRY, medical researcher, educator; b. May 26, 1961; m. Patricia Nikitin; 1 child, Constantinos. BS in Chemistry, Wagner Coll., 1984; MS in Pathology, N.Y. Med. Coll., 1987, PhD in Pathology, 1989. Rsch. fellow dept. anesthesiology U. Ala. Sch. Medicine, Birmingham, 1990-92; rsch. assoc. Inst. Environ. Medicine U. Pa. Sch. Medicine, 1992-94, sr. investigator Inst. Environ. Medicine, rsch. asst. prof. biochemistry and biophysics, 1995—. Contbr. articles to profl. jours., chpts. to books; ad hoc reviewer Am. Jour. Physiology, Jour. Applied Physiology, Circulation, Jour. Leukocyte Biology, Chem. Rsch. in Toxicology, Neurosci. Letters, Biochem. Pharmacology, Respiratory Physiology; mem. editl. bd. Free Radical Biology and Medicine, 1996—; presenter in field. Recipient Am. Inst. Chemists award, 1984, Established Investigator award Am. Heart Assn., 1996—; Parker B. Francis fellowship in Pulmonary Rsch., 1993-96; Dr. Frederic Valergakis Grad. grantee, 1988-89. Mem. AAAS, Internat. Soc. for Free Radical Rsch. (young investigator award 1994), Oxygen Soc. (young investigator award 1995). Office: U Pa Sch Med One John Morgan Bldg 3620 Hamilton Walk Philadelphia PA 19140-6068*

ISEL, DEBRA ANNE, nurse; b. Ft. Worth, Nov. 5, 1956; d. John William and Grace Ann (Murphy) I. BS in Nursing, Tex. Christian U., 1979. RN, Tex. Staff nurse St. Joseph's Hosp., Ft. Worth, 1979-80, Tarrant County Nephrology Ctr., Ft. Worth, 1980-81; staff nurse Providence Hosp., Anchorage, 1981—, asst. mgr. thermal unit, 1984-86, edn. coord. thermal unit, 1986-88, thermal outreach coord., 1986-88, thermal case mgr., 1988-93, staff nurse, emergency dept., 1993—. Mem. Am. Burn Assn., Alaska Sled Dog and Racing Assn., Sigma Theta Tau. Home: 3041 Brookridge Cir Anchorage AK 99504-4180 Office: Providence Hosp Thermal Unit 3200 Providence Dr Anchorage AK 99508-4615

ISELE, FRANK WILLIAM, clinical psychologist; b. Scranton, Pa., Dec. 28, 1944; s. Francis Joseph and Annamae Louise (Hauser) I.; m. Rosemary Gayle Sposato, June 24, 1967; children: Dana Lynn, Frank Anthony, Nicholas Joseph. BA, Seton Hall U., 1966; MA magna cum laude, Fairleigh Dickinson U., 1969; PhD, U. Mont., 1971. Lic. clin. psychologist, N.Y.; diplomate Am. Bd. Med. Psychotherapists and Psychodiagnosticians; diplomate Am. Acad. Pain Mgmt.; cert. neurotherapist. Staff psychologist Warren-Washington County Community Mental Health Ctr., Glens Falls, N.Y., 1971-79, clin. psychologist, dir. child and adolescent svcs., 1979-83; instr. in Psychiatry Albany (N.Y.) Med. Coll., 1973-74; clin. asst. prof. Psychology SUNY, Albany, 1973-84; clin. psychologist in pvt. practice Glens Falls and Saratoga Springs, N.Y., 1983-89; clin. psychologist, dir. Adirondack Psychol. Health Svcs. of Glens Falls, Saratoga Springs, 1989—; cons. psychologist N.Y. State Dept. Social Svcs. Bur. Disabilities Determinations, Albany, 1974-84; panel psychologist N.Y. State Office for Vocat. Rehab., Albany, 1977-84; cons. psychologist Marriage Tribunal, Diocese of Albany, 1977-84; psychologist N.Y. States Workers Compensation Bd. Author (book chpt.) Biofeedback & Hypnosis: Multifaceted Approaches in the Management of Pain, 1990; contbr. articles to profl. jours. Basketball coach St. Clement's Sch., Saratoga Springs, 1983-87. Mem. APA, Soc. for Clin. and Exptl. Hypnosis, Internat. Soc. for Hypnosis, Coun. for Nat. Register of Health Svc. Providers in Psychology, N.Y. State Psychol. Assn., Am. Bd. Med. Psychotherapists and Psychodiagnosticians, Am. Acad. Pain Mgmt., Am. Assn. Behavioral Therapists, Soc. Pediat. Psychology, Acad. Cert. Neurotherapists. Home: 5 Hillcrest Ln Saratoga Springs NY 12866-8528 Office: Adirondack Psychol Health Svcs 478 Glen St Glens Falls NY 12801-2926

ISENBERG, JON IRWIN, gastroenterologist, educator; b. Chgo., Mar. 21, 1937; s. Lucien and Roselle (Moss) I.; m. Laury Lipman, Dec. 16, 1962; children: Nancy Beth, Noah William, Rebecca Moss. BS with honors, U. Ill., 1959; MD, U. Ill., Chgo., 1963. Diplomate Am. Bd. Internal Medicine, Am. Bd. Gastroenterology. Assoc. prof. in residence UCLA, 1973-78, prof. medicine in residence, 1978-79; key investigator Ctr. for Ulcer Rsch. and Edn./UCLA, 1979—; prof. medicine U. Calif., San Diego, 1979—, divsn. head, 1979-94; vis. scientist Karolinska Hosp. and Inst., Stockholm, 1982-83, U. Uppsala Biomed. Inst., Sweden, 1991-92; sci. com. mem. 5th Internat. Conf. on Peptic Ulcer, Boston, 1985; mem. study sect. GMA-2, NIH, 1988-92. Author: Physicians Guide to Computers and Computing, 1985; editor: Peptic Ulcer Disease: Clinics in Gastroenterology, 1984. Served to maj. U.S. Army, 1968-70. NIH grantee, 1984—. Fellow ACP; mem. Western Assn. Physicians (counselor 1981-85, pres. 1989-90), So. Calif. Soc. Gastroenterology (pres. 1978-79), Am. Gastroenterology Assn. (councilor 1993-96), Am. Assn. Physicians, Am. Soc. Clin. Investigation. Democrat. Jewish. Home: 1588 Nautilus St La Jolla CA 92037-5639 Office: UCSD Med Ctr Div Gastroenterology 200 W Arbor Dr San Diego CA 92103-1911

ISHII, AKIRA, medical parasitologist, malariologist, allergologist; b. Kochi, Japan, July 11, 1937; s. Katsuhiko and Fusae Ishii; m. Fuyuko Ishii, Mar. 20, 1968; children: Ken, Shin, Taku. MD, U. Tokyo, 1964, D Med. Sci., 1969; MSc, U. London, 1970. Cert. malaria advanced epidemiology. Rsch.

assoc. Inst. Infectious Disease, U. Tokyo, 1969-74; asst. prof. Toyko Med. and Dental U., 1974-78, Inst. Med. Sci., U. Tokyo, 1978-79; prof. Miyazaki (Japan) Med. Coll., 1979-84, Okayama (Japan) U. Med. Sch., 1984-90; dir. dept. parasitology NIH, Tokyo, 1990-95; prof. Jichi Med. Sch., 1995—; com. mem. Japanese Internat. Coop. Agy., Tokyo, 1978-89; panel mem. U.S.-Japan Coop. Med. Program Parasitic Diseases, 1991-95, China-Japan Parasitology Seminar. Mem. editorial bd. Nettai, Japanese Jour. Parasitology, Japanese Jour. Tropicial Medicine and Hygiene, Japanese Jour. Pub. Health. Fellow Am. Soc. Tropical Medicine and Hygiene, Royal Soc. Tropical Medicine and Hygiene; mem. Japanese Soc. Parasitology (exec. bd., councilor, Koizumi prize), Japanese Soc. Tropical Medicine (exec. bd., councilor), Japanese Soc. San. Zoology (Soc. prize), Japanese Soc. Allergologists (councilor), Japanese Soc. Infectious Disease (councilor), Japanese Soc. Internat. Health (mem. exec. bd.), German-Japan Assn. for Protozoan Diseases (coun. mem.), Med. Ent. Zool. Home: 1-18-16-102 Matsubara, Setagayaku Tokyo 156, Japan

ISHIKAWA-FULLMER, JANET SATOMI, psychologist, educator; b. Hilo, Hawaii, Oct. 17, 1925; d. Shinichi and Onao (Kurisu) Saito; m. Calvin Y. Ishikawa, Aug. 15, 1950; 1 child, James A.; m. Daniel W. Fullmer, June 11, 1980. BE, U. Hawaii, 1950, MEd, 1967; MEd, U. Hawaii, 1969, PhD, 1976. Diplomate Am. Acad. Pain Mgmt. Instr. Honolulu Bus. Coll., 1953-59; instr., counselor Kapiolani Community Coll., Honolulu, 1959-73; prof., dir. counseling Honolulu Community Coll., 1973-74, dean of students, 1974-77; psychologist, v.p., treas. Human Resources Devel. Ctr., Inc., Honolulu, 1977—; cons. United Specialties Co., Tokyo, 1979, Grambling (La.) State U., 1980, 81, Filipino Immigrants in Kalihi, Honolulu, 1979-84, Legis. Ref. Bur., Honolulu, 1984-85, Honolulu Police Dept., 1985; co-founder Waianae (Hawaii) Child and Family Ctr., 1979-92. Co-author: Family Therapy Dictionary, 1991, Manabu: The Diagnosis and Treatment of a Japanese Boy with a Visual Anomaly, 1991; contbr. articles to profl. jours. Commr. Bd. Psychology, Honolulu, 1979-85; co-founder Kilohana United Meth. Ch. and Family Ctr., 1993—. Mem. APA, ACA, Hawaii Psychol. Assn., Pi Lambda Theta (sec. 1967-68, v.p. 1968-69, pres. 1969-70), Delta Kappa Gamma (sec., v.p., scholarship 1975, Outstanding Educator award 1975, Thomas Jefferson award 1993, Francis E. Clark award 1993). Home: 154 Maono Pl Honolulu HI 96821-2529 Office: Human Resources Devel Ctr 1750 Kalakaua Ave Apt 809 Honolulu HI 96826-3725

ISHIZAKI, JOSEPH YOSHIKI, pathologist; b. Yasu, Shigra-ken, Japan, Feb. 28, 1925; s. Tsunejiro and Tsuru (Imabayashi) I.; m. Sachixyo Clare Uyeda, July 30, 1969. MD, Kobe (Japan) Med. Coll., 1949; PhD in Medicine, U. Kobe, 1960. Diplomate Am. Bd. Pathology. Instr. pathology Med. Coll. Va., Richmond, 1958-60; asst. pathologist City of Hope Med. Ctr., Duarte, Calif., 1960-63; dir. labs. Kaiser Found. Hosp., Fontana, Calif., 1963-64; dir. Ishizaki Clinic and Labs., Neyagawa, Japan, 1965—. Fellow Coll. Am. Pathologists; mem. Japanese Med. Assn. Home: 22-31 Higashi, Osaka 572, Japan

ISHIZAKI, TATSUSHI, physician, parasitologist; b. Tochigi, Japan, Mar. 8, 1915; s. Takaji and Satoko I.; M.D., Tokyo (Japan) U., 1939, Ph.D., 1951; diploma pub. health, Singapore U., 1959; m. Yuriko Sase, Nov. 5, 1946; children: Terumi, Michiharu. With U. Tokyo Sch. Medicine, 1939, sr. asst. dept. phys. therapy and medicine, 1946-55; chief 2d div. dept. parasitology Nat. Inst. Health, Japan, 1953-67, chief dept., 1967-74; mem. emeritus, 1980—; lectr. clin. allergy U. Tokyo Sch. Medicine, 1956-71; prof. clin. immunology Dokkyo U. Sch. Medicine, 1973-82, prof. emeritus, 1982—, chmn. clin. profs., 1978-80; panelist Japan-U.S.A. Coop. Study Parasitology, 1965-74. Hon. fellow Am. Coll. Allergists; mem. Japanese Soc. Allergy (exec. com., pres., hon. fellow 1981—), Korean Soc. Allergy (hon.), Japanese Soc. Tropical Medicine (hon. fellow, exec. com.), Japan-German Assn. Protozoan Diseases (pres.), Research, publs. on skin tests for various antigens; standardization of criteria of positive skin test basic phenomena of skin reaction especially mast cell degranulation mechanism analysis of onset of asthma attacks especially related to air pollution, weather; analysis of mechanisms of occupational allergy, others. Home: 8-15 Torimachi Mibumachi, Tochigi Japan

ISLEMAN, MICHAEL ALLEN, medical technologist; b. Nashville, Dec. 31, 1954; s. Richard Lee and Shirley Ann (Williams) I.; m. Kathleen Ann Parker, Dec. 15, 1982; children: Spencer, David, Jessie, Michele. BA in History, Eastern Ky. U., 1992. Med. lab. technician Vanderbilt U., Nashville, 1985-87, Ctr. for Clin. Sci., Nashville, 1987-88, SmithKline Beecham Labs., Lexington, Ky., 1989-92; med. technologist U. Louisville, 1993—. Asst. scoutmaster Boy Scouts Am., San Diego, 1973. With U.S. Army, 1974-79. Mem. Am. Med. Technologist (cert.), Phi Alpha Theta. Republican. Mem. LDS Ch. Office: U Louisville Hosp 530 S Jackson St Louisville KY 40292

ISLEY, R(OBERT) ARNOLD, pediatrician; b. Greensboro, N.C., June 23, 1947; s. William Robert and Annie Rebecca (Isley) I.; m. Loretta Jean Piechocki, Oct. 5, 1974; children: Leanne Jeanette, June Caroline, Rachel Marie. AB, U. N.C., 1969; MPH, 1979; MD Johns Hopkins U., 1973. Diplomate Am. Bd. Pediatrics. Intern Children's Med. Ctr., Dallas, 1973-74, resident in pediatrics, 1974-76; pediatrician USPHS Nat. Health Service Corps, Guntersville, Ala., 1976-78; med. cons. div. health services HHS, Region IV, Atlanta, 1979-81; practicing medicine specializing in pediatrics, Snellville (Ga.) Pediatrics, 1981-94, Georgetown Pediatrics, 1994-96. Mem. Johns Hopkins Med. and Surg. Assn., Am. Acad. Pediatrics, Delta Omega. Office: Georgetown Pediatrics 1700 Tree Ln Rd Ste 110e 200 Snellville GA 30278-3708

ISMAIL, YAHIA HASSAN, dentist, educator; b. Egypt, Jan. 20, 1938; came to U.S., 1961; s. Hassan Kareem and Horia (Soloman) I.; m. Launa Lutz, Sept. 5, 1968; children: Alan Kareem, Zane Ziad. D.D.S., Cairo U., 1959; M.S., U. Pitts., 1965, D.M.D., 1973, Ph.D., 1973. Instr. Dental Sch. Cairo U., 1959-62; asst. prof. prosthodontics U. Pitts., 1962-68, assoc. prof., 1968-70, prof., 1970—, dir. prosthodontic grad. program, 1970—, chmn. dept. prosthodontics, 1973-95; prof., chmn. dept. prosthodontics, dir. acad. affairs Dental Medicine, U. Pitts., 1995—; vis. prof., Paris and Marseille, France, Cairo and Alexandria, Egypt; prof. of implantology and prosthodontics, European U., Brussels; mem. staff VA Hosp., Montefiore Hosp., Univ. Med. Center Hosp., St. Margaret's Hosp. Contbr. articles to profl. jours., textbooks. Bd. dirs. Ridgewood Civic Assn., 1969-73; cubmaster Allegheny Trails council Boy Scouts Am.; coach Youth Soccer League Allegheny County. Fellow Internat. Coll. Dentists, Am. Coll. Dentists, Royal Soc. Medicine, Am. Coll. Oral Implantologists, Internat. Congress Oral Implantologists, Am. Acad. Implant Prosthodontics (pres. elect 1989-90, pres. 1990-92); mem. ADA, Internat. Assn. Dentofacial Abnormalities (bd. dirs., sec., treas. 1973-77), Internat. Congress Oral Implantologists (v.p. 1985-86, pres. 1988-89), Am. Prosthodontic Soc. (internat. circuite courses humanities citation), Pa. Prosthodontic Assn. (past pres.), Prosthodontic Soc. Western Pa. (past pres.), Dental Soc. Western Pa. (bd. dirs.), Am. Coll. Oral Implantologists (pres. 1984-86), Am. Coll. Prosthodontists, Am. Assn. Dental Schs., Internat. Assn. Dental Rsch., Royal Coll. Physicians, Omicron Kappa Upsilon. Republican. Club: Univ. Office: U Pittsburgh Sch Dental Medicine Pittsburgh PA 15261

ISOBE, JAMES HAJIME, general and vascular surgeon; b. Kahului, Hawaii, Mar. 29, 1942; s. Harry U. and Vivian H. (Tsue) I.; m. Sheryl H. Nakamura, Aug. 16, 1966; children: Teresa, Laura, Kristina, James. BA, Drake U., 1964; MD, U. Iowa, 1967. Intern Phila. Gen. Hosp., 1967-68; resident in surgery U. Ala., Birmingham, 1968-73; gen. surgeon Salter/Gillis, P.C., Birmingham, 1976-79, The Surgeon's Group, Birmingham, 1979-93, Simon Williamson Clinic, Birmingham, 1993—. Mem. Leadership Birmingham, 1993. Lt. col. U.S. Army Med. Corps, 1973-76. Fellow ACS; mem. Jefferson County Med. Soc. (pres. 1993). Baptist. Office: Simon Williamson Clinic 833 Princeton Ave SW Birmingham AL 35211

ISOM, VIRGINIA ANNETTE VEAZEY, nursing educator; b. Tallapoosa County, Ala., Nov. 19, 1936; d. Jimmy L. and Bessie (Pearson) Veazey; m. William G. Isom, May 1959; children: William Gary, Marleah, James Leland. BSN, Tuskegee Inst., 1959; MSN, Syracuse U., 1974; doctoral candidate, Howard U., 1984—, postgrad., 1994. Cert. in nursing adminstrn. Am. Nurses' Credentialing Ctr. Asst. prof. med. surg. nursing Howard U. Coll. Nursing, Washington, 1975-86; edn. and tng. quality assurance coord. Howard U., Washington, 1986-87; patient care coord. Howard U. Hosp., Washington, 1987-88, coord. for spl. projects, 1988-90; prof. nursing Prince George's C.C., Largo, Md., 1992—. Contbr. articles to profl. jours. Mem. ANA (cert. clin. specialist med. surg. nursing), D.C. Nurses' Assn., Sigma Theta Tau. Home: 534 Round Table Dr Fort Washington MD 20744-5638 Office: Prince George's C C Dept Nursing Largo MD 20772

ISRAEL, JACOB SAMUEL, anesthesiologist, educator; b. N.Y.C., Mar. 23, 1926; s. Flora (Shapiro) I.; m. Alice Jacobson, June 16, 1946 (div. 1973); children: Robert, Janet Rauscher, John; m. Judith Cohn, Apr. 18, 1982. BA, Columbia U., 1946; MD, NYU, 1949. Intern Lincoln Hosp., Bronx, N.Y., 1950-51; asst. prof. anesthesiology SUNY, Syracuse, 1954-75, dir. respiratory therapy, 1968-73; prof. clin. anesthesiology Columbia Presbyn. Hosp., N.Y.C., 1975-80; prof. anesthesiology Albert Einstein Coll. Medicine, Bronx, N.Y., 1980—; dir. anesthesiology Montefiore Affiliated North Cen. Bronx Hosp., 1990—. Editor: The Recovery Room, 1988; contbr. articles to profl. jours.; author: (with others) Anesthesiology for Medical Students, 1991. Pres. Sakier Charity Found., N.Y.C., 1989—. Comdr. USNR, 1944-54, 88-94. Recipient Centrum award Cen. N.Y. Respiratory Care, 1974. Mem. N.Y. State Soc. Anesthesiologists (dist. dir. 1983-91, Cert. Appreciation 1990), Am. Soc. Anesthesiologists (del. 1988-91, rep. armed svcs. com. 1990-92, appointee nat. bd. respiratory care 1991—, appointee bd. med. advisors assn. respiratory care 1984-90). Home: 65 Severn St Scarsdale NY 10583-6848 Office: North Ctrl Bronx Hosp 3424 Kossuth Ave Bronx NY 10467-2410

ISRAEL, MARGIE OLANOFF, psychotherapist; b. Atlantic City, Apr. 30, 1927; d. Herman and Mary (Salter) Olanoff; m. Allan Edward Israel, Sept. 20, 1953; 1 child, Janet. Student U. Miami, 1945-46, 50, Am. Acad. Dramatic Arts, 1946-47; BA in Psychology cum laude, Hunter Coll., 1970; MSW with honors in fieldwork, Hunter Sch. Social Work, 1972; psychoanalytic tng. N.Y. Soc. Freudian Psychologists, 1965-70, Manhattan Ctr. for Advanced Psychoanalytic Studies, 1972-74, 76. Bd. cert. diplomate in clin. social work Am. Bd. Examiners of Clin. Social Workers. Celebrity interviewer Lunchin' with Marge radio show Sta. WFPG, Atlantic City, 1947-48; co-host Steel Pier Midnight radio show, 1949; publicity writer Hy Gardner Astor Hotel, N.Y.C., 1948; writer theatrical interviews Miami (Fla.) Daily News, 1950-51; sec. to exec. dir. Hebrew Old Age Ctr., Atlantic City, 1951-55; sec. to dir. TV-films and radio Nat. Office, Am. Cancer Soc., N.Y.C., 1959-66, asst. to dir. TV-films and radio,1966-70; social worker Bellevue Hosp., N.Y.C., 1972-76; field instr. socialworkN.Y. U., 1975-76; pvt. practice psychotherapy, N.Y.C., 1973—, Providence, 1991—, Wilmington, N.C., 1996—. Fellow N.Y. State Soc. Clin. Social Work, Am. Orthopsychiat. Assn.; mem. NASW (diplomate), Nat. Fedn. Socs. Clin. Social Work (com. on psychoanalysis), Acad. Cert. Social Workers, N.Y. Acad. Scis., Psi Chi. Home and Office: 5711 Andover Rd Wilmington NC 28403

ISRAELSKY, BRAD RICHARD, pharmacist; b. Bklyn., July 11, 1955; s. Irving Harold and Janice (Weinisch) I.; m. Roberta Lynn Schwartz, June 24, 1984; children: Erica, Evan. BSc, Phila. Coll. Pharmacy, 1978. Registered pharmacist, N.J., Pa., Fla. Pharmacist Rite Aid Corp., Phila., 1978-82, The Mill Pharmacy, Mt. Laurel, N.J., 1982-85, Woodcrest Pharmacy, Cherry Hill, N.J., 1985-87; pharmacy mgr. The Rx Place, Stratford, N.J., 1987—. Mem. N.J. Pharm. Assn., Am. Pharm. Assn. Democrat. Jewish. Home: 425 Hialeah Dr Cherry Hill NJ 08002-2037

ISSELBACHER, KURT JULIUS, physician, educator; b. Wirges, Germany, Sept. 12, 1925; came to U.S., 1936, naturalized, 1945; s. Albert and Flori (Strauss) I.; m. Rhoda Solin, June 22, 1955; children: Lisa, Karen, Jody, Eric. AB, Harvard U., 1946, MD cum laude, 1950. Intern, then resident Mass. Gen. Hosp., Boston, 1950-53; investigator NIH, 1953-56; chief gastrointestinal unit Mass. Gen. Hosp., 1957-89, chmn. com. rsch., 1967, dir. Cancer Ctr., 1987—; prof. medicine Harvard Med. Sch., 1966—, chmn. exec. com. depts. medicine, 1968—, Mallinckrodt prof. medicine, 1972—, chmn. univ. cancer com., 1972-87; mem. governing bd. NRC, 1987-90; mem. sci. bd. FDA, 1993. Editor-in-chief: (Harrison) Principles of Internal Medicine, 1976, 91—. Recipient Award for Disting. Achievement in Nutrition Bristol-Myers Squibb, 1991, Sci. Bd. FDA, 1993—. Fellow ACP (John Phillips award for Disting. Achievement in Clin. Medicine 1989), Am. Acad. Arts and Scis.; mem. NAS (chmn. food and nutrition bd. 1983-88, mem. exec. com., mem. coun. 1987-90, chmn. com. on risk assessment of hazardous air pollutants 1991-94), Am. Gastroenterology Assn. (pres. 1974-75, Julius Friedenwald medal for outstanding achievement in gastroenterology 1985), Assn. Am. Physicians Pres. 1977-78). Home: 20 Nobscot Rd Newton MA 02159-1323 Office: Cancer Ctr Mass Gen Hosp 139 13th St Charlestown MA 02129-2023

ISTRICO, RICHARD ARTHUR, physician; b. Bklyn., Oct. 18, 1951; s. Arthur Ralph and Gloria Rose (Petrocelli) I.; m. Candace P. Conforti, July 20, 1974; children: Jonathan Richard, Daniel Robert. BS, Pace U., 1973; DO, Phila. Coll. Osteo. Medicine, 1978. Cert. ringside physician USA Olympic Boxing; cert. of comptence sports medicine Am. Osteo. Acad. Sports Medicine. Chief intern Interboro Hosp., 1978-79; resident in family practice Baptist Med. Ctr., 1979-80, chmn. utilization review com., 1981-82, mem. pharmacy formulary com., 1981-82; panel physician N.Y. State Athletic Commn., 1981—; team physician USA Boxing, Olympics Com., Colorado Springs, Colo., 1981—, chmn. edn. com., 1993—; med. dir. N.Y. Golden Gloves, 1986—, N.Y. Met. Boxing Assn., Daily News Golden Hoops Basketball Tournament, 1988—; attending physician Little Neck (N.Y.) Cmty. Hosp., 1980—, Parkway Hosp., Forest Hills, N.Y., 1989—; mortality and morbidity com. Deepdale Hosp., Little Neck, 1990-91; with Cath. Med. Ctr., 1981—; chief physician Ultimate Fighting Championship, 1995—. Mem. AMA, Am. Osteo. Assn. (bd. cert.), Am. Coll. Sports Medicine, Am. Osteo. Acad. Sport Medicine (bd. cert.), Am. Coll. Gen. Practitioners (cert.), Fla. Osteo. Med. Soc., Beta Beta Beta. Republican. Roman Catholic. Office: 15801 Crossbay Blvd Howard Beach NY 11414-3137

ISWARA, KADIRAWEL, gastroenterologist; b. Kalmanai, Sri-Lanka, Dec. 1, 1944; came to U.S., 1970; s. Periyathamby Kadirawelpillai and Grace Rasanayagam; m. Geetha Somanader, Dec. 15, 1976; children: Shalini, Sanjeevan. MBBS, U. Ceylon, Sri-Lanka, 1968. Bd. cert. internal medicine, gastroenterology. Intern in medicine Coney Island Hosp., Bklyn., 1970-71, resident in medicine, 1971-72; resident in medicine Vets. Hosp., Bronx, N.Y., 1972-73; fellow in gastroenterology Maimonides Med. Ctr., Bklyn., 1973-76, assoc. dir. gastroenterology, 1976-80, attending gastroenterologist, 1976—; staff gastroenterologist St. Vincent Med. Ctr., Staten Island, N.Y., 1980—, Baylay Seton Hosp., Staten Island, 1980—; clin. asst. prof. medicine Health Sci. Ctr. Downstate SUNY, Bklyn., 1976—. Contbr. articles to profl. jours. Pres. Assn. of Tamil in USA, 1983-84. With USAR, 1983—, lt. col. Desert Storm, 1990-91, Saudi Arabia. Decorated Nat. Def. medal, Army Commendation medal, N.Y. State Cross medal N.Y. State. Fellow ACP, Am. Coll. Gastroenterology, Am. Coll. Internat. Physicians (pres. N.Y.-N.J. chpt. 1990-92); mem. Am. Gastroenterology Assn., Am. Liver Found., Ilietis Colitis Foun. Methodist. Office: 2560 Ocean Ave Brooklyn NY 11229-4507

ITAMI, JINROH, physician; b. Mitsu, Okayama, Japan, Feb. 21, 1937; s. Yoshito and Kinuko (Takahashi) I. MD, PhD, Okayama U., 1963. Lic. oncologist. Physician Kobe Clinic, Kobe City, Japan, 1974-83, Kurashiki Meml. Hosp., Kurashiki City, Japan, 1984-86, Shibata Hosp., Kurashiki City, 1986—. Author: Meaningful Life Therapy, 1988; producer Subliminal tape for cancer treatment. Mem. Japanese Med. Assn., Japan Soc. Cancer Therapy, Japanese Congress Morita Therapy, Assn. Meaningful Life Therapy (pres. 1986—). Office: Shibata Hosp, 6108 Tamashima-Otoshima, Okayama Kurashiki 713, Japan

ITANI, ABDUL L., neurologist; b. Beirut, Lebanon, Oct. 9, 1941; came to U.S., 1973; m. Catriona Rosalind, Dec. 21, 1973; children: Zena, Stuart, Fiona. BS, Am. U. Beirut, 1963, MD, 1967. Physician As-Salama Hosp., Saudi Arabia, 1968-69; neurosurgeon Nat. Hosp. for Nervous Disorders, 1969; registrar neurosurgery Atkinson Morely Hosp., London, 1972-73; resident gen. surgery Hamot Med. Ctr., Erie, Pa., 1973-74; resident neurosurgery U. Md. Hosp., Balt., 1974-79; pvt. practice Northeastern Ohio Neurosurgeon Assocs., Inc., Cleve., 1979—; chmn. surg. care com. quality assurance program Lake Hosp., Willoughby, Ohio, 1992—. Contbr. articles to profl. jours. Mem. AMA, Am. Assn. Neurol. Surgeons, Congress Neurol. Surgeons, Ohio State Neurosurg. Soc., Ohio State Med. Assn., Northeast Ohio Neurosurg. Soc., Acad. Medicine of Cleve. Office: Northeastern Ohio Neurosurg Assocs Inc 34900 Chardon Rd #107 Willoughby OH 44094

ITAYA, STEPHEN KENJI, neuroanatomist, educator; b. Cleve., Jan. 11, 1947; m. Patricia Williams, Mar. 24, 1973; children: Catherine, Michael. BA, Washington U., St. Louis, 1968; PhD, U. Tenn. Ctr. Health Sci., 1974. Postdoctoral fellow U. Tenn. Ctr. for Health Sci., Memphis, 1974-76; postdoctoral fellow U. Iowa, Iowa City, 1976-78, asst. prof., 1978-84; asst. prof. U. Ill., Chgo., 1984-87; assoc. prof. U. South Ala., Mobile, 1987—, chair biomed. sci., 1993—. Contbr. articles to profl. publs. Bd. dirs. Exploreum Mus. Sci., Mobile, 1994—. Recipient Ednl. Pathway for Minority Sci. Students award NIH, 1993—. Mem. Soc. for Neurosci. Home: 4133 Ursuline Dr Mobile AL 36608 Office: U South Ala Dept Biomed Sci UCOM6000 Mobile AL 36688

ITO, RYUTA, pharmacologist, educator; b. Kure, Hiroshima, Japan, Mar. 4, 1922; s. Junzo and Tokuko Ito; m. Ruriko Kajiwara, Mar. 17, 1957; children: Yoshiaki, Michie. MD, U. Tokyo, 1946, D Med. Sci., 1956. Asst. internal medicine U. Tokyo, 1946-48, asst. pharmacology, 1948-55; rsch. fellow Iatrochem. Inst., Tokyo, 1958-55; assoc. prof. pharmacology Sch. Medicine, Toho U., Tokyo, 1955-64, prof. pharmacology, 1964-87; prof. therapeutics Sch. Pharmacy, Toho U., Tokyo, 1981-87, prof. emeritus, 1987—. Chief editor dictionary: Japan Medical Terminology, 1975, 2d edit., 1991; contbr. articles to profl. publs. Riker fellow Internat. Union Physiol. Sci., 1961, Niwa prize Japanese Info. Sci. Terminology, 1969, Immunochemotherapy award Soeda Found., 1986, Grand prize for Med. Essay, 1987. Mem. Japanese Assn. Med. Sci. (chmn. com. med. terminology 1964-89), Japanese Coun. Sci. (mem. com. info. sci. 1988—), Yokosuka Inst. Applied Pharmacology (bd. dirs. 1973-91), Japanese Pharmacol. Soc. (hon.). Home: Sanno 2-4-1-406 Ota-ku, Tokyo 143, Japan Office: Teijin Lab Applied Pharm, Higashidaira 656, Matsuyama Saitama 355, Japan

ITO, THOMAS YUTAKE, urologist, entrepreneur; b. Honolulu, Apr. 25, 1946; s. Takao Ito and Haru Watanabe; m. Jean Chizue; 1 child, Darin. BA in Biology, Stanford U., 1968; MD, U. Chgo., 1972; postgrad. in gen. surgery, U. Calif., Irvine, 1972-74, postgrad. in urology, 1974-77. Diplomate Am. Bd. Urology. Chmn. dept. urology Kuakini Hosp., Honolulu, 1982-86; chmn. bd. dirs. Kuakini Med. Plz., Honolulu, 1986-88; med. dir. Kidney Stone Ctr. of the Pacific, Honolulu, 1993—; pvt. practice Honolulu, 1977—; Mem. med. staff Kuakini Hosp., Queen's Hosp., St. Francis Hosp., Pali Momi Hosp., Rehab. Ctr. of the Pacific; mem. exec. com. Kuakini Med. Ctr., 1982-86, peer rev. com. Queen's Hosp., 1987-92, various other hosp. coms.; bd. dirs. Pacific Health Care HMO, 1985-92; chmn. med. oversight com. Kidney Stone Ctr. of the Pacific, 1986-93, med. dir., 1993—; assoc. clin. instr. U. Hawaii Sch. Medicine; chmn., owner Hawaiin Jiffy Inc. franchise of Jiffy Lube (3 stores), 1987—. Contbr. articles to profl. jours.; designer software programs. Mem. Zoning Bd. Appeals City and County of Honolulu, 1981-85, chmn., 1982-85; chmn. Med. Com. Kuakini Capital Fund Drive, 1986. Mem. Am. Bd. Urology, Hawaii Urol. Soc. (Western sect., sec.-treas. 1979, v.p. 1980, pres. 1981). Home: 1850 Laukahi St Honolulu HI Office: 321 N Kuakini St Ste 612 Honolulu HI 96817

ITO, YOICHIRO, pathologist; b. Osaka, Japan, Dec. 22, 1928; came to U.S., 1968, naturalized, 1978; s. Taichi and Ai (Kubota) I.; m. Ryoko Tanioka, Dec. 23, 1963; children—Koichi, Shin. M.D., Osaka City U., 1958. Rotating intern U.S. Yokosuka (Japan) Naval Hosp., 1958-59; resident in pathology Cleve. Met. Gen. Hosp., 1959-61, Michael Reese Hosp., Chgo., 1961-63; instr. physiology Osaka City U. Med. Sch., 1963-68; vis. scientist Nat. Heart, Lung and Blood Inst., NIH, Bethesda, Md., 1968-78, med. officer, 1978—. Mem. N.Y. Acad. Scis., Kenshinkai. Recipient 1st place award ann. sci. research presentation at Cleve. Met. Gen. Hosp., 1960, Tech. Excellence award for devel. blood cell separator, 1979; Fulbright exchange scholar, 1959-63; WHO Research Tavel Fund grantee Nat. Inst. Med. Research, London, 1968. Research on innovation in separation sci., including continuous devel. of countercurrent chromatography, cell separation methods; initiated and developed countercurrent chromatography; patentee coil planet centrifuge, rotating-seal-free flow-through centrifuge, PH-zone-refining countercurrent chromatography. Office: NIH 9000 Rockville Pike Bldg 10 Room 7n-322 Bethesda MD 20892

ITUARTE, ELOY ALFONSO, internist; b. Pasadena, Calif., July 24, 1949; s. Frank Alfonso and Mary (Macias) A.; m. Mary Margaret Harrigan, July 24, 1971 (div. Nov. 1978); 1 child, Michelle; m. Margaret Battin, Oct. 27, 1984; children: Thomas, Catherine. BS, St. Mary's Coll. Calif., Moraga, 1971; MD, U. So. Calif., 1975. Diplomate Am. Bd. Internal Medicine. Intern, resident Huntington Meml. Hosp., Pasadena, Calif., 1975-78; mem. staff student health svc. U. So. Calif., L.A., 1978; staff physician emergency dept. Garfield Med. Ctr., Monterey Pk., Calif., 1979-80; pvt. practice Newport Beach, Calif., 1979-81; mem. staff student health svc. Claremont (Calif.) Colls., 1981-82, U. Calif., Irvine, 1982-84; physician emergency dept. Western Med. Ctr., Anaheim, Calif., 1984-89; fellow in endocrinology VA Wadsworth Hosp-UCLA, 1983-85; pvt. practice Reno, Nev., 1989—; asst. prof. in residence medicine UCLA, 1985-88; dir. diabetes ctr. Doctor's Med. Ctr., Modesto, Calif., 1989-90, Diabetes Treatment Ctrs. Am., Reno, 1983-84; referee Annals of Internal Medicine, 1984-85, Calcified Tissue Internat., 1985; presenter in field. Contbr. over 30 papers to profl. jours. Mem. Am. Diabetes Assn. Profl. Sect., Nat. Osteoporosis Found. Recipient Disting. Svc. award U. So. Calif., 1985, Career Devel. award VA, L.A., 1985; Calif. State scholar, 1968-71. Mem. ACP, AAAS, Am. Soc. Bone and Mineral Rsch., Am. Fedn. Clin. Rsch., Masons, Rotary (Reno). Episcopalian. Office: 343 Elm St Ste 408 Reno NV 89503

IVANHOE, HERMAN, dentist; b. Russia, Aug. 18, 1908; came to U.S., 1912, naturalized, 1930; s. Samuel and Rose (Kelmenson) I.; BS, Columbia, 1929, DDS, 1931; LLD (hon.), Chosun U., Korea, 1979; m. Lynn Rugof, Mar. 6, 1943; children: Eliot Richard, Cindy Beth. Practice gen. dentistry, Bklyn., 1931—; acting attending in charge dept. dentistry Maimonides Hosp., Bklyn., 1959; mem. surgical staff Caledonia, Samaritan, Community Hosps.; guest of Chilean Govt. to help dental profession, 1968; cons. orthodontics Edn. Alliance N.Y.; hon. dean Sch. Dentistry, Chosun U., Korea, 1973; mem. orthodontic panel N.Y.C. Bd. Health. Served with USAAF, 1943-46. Recipient Conspicuous Alumni Service medal Columbia U., 1974, commendation State Dept.-AID, Pres'. Vol. Action award George Bush, 1991. Fellow Internat. Coll. Dentistry, Am. Coll. Dentists; mem. Am. Soc. Study Orthodontics (cert.), Am. Dentists for Fgn. Service (founder, bd. dirs, Pres.), ADA (life), Assn. Dental Alumni Columbia (pres. 1966-67, recipient meritorious award 1972), Pierre Fauchard Acad. Club: B'nai B'rith (pres. Jordan lodge). Contbr. to profl. publs. Introduced topical fluoridation program Carribbean area, 1974—. Established over 3000 dental clinics in 50 fgn. indigent countries; active promoting dental practice fgn. countries; equipped 11 fgn. dental schs., Korea, Peru, Honduras, Uruguay, Chile, Ecuador, China, Egypt, Philippines, Israel, Bolivia. Home: 1151 E 7th St Brooklyn NY 11230-4007 Office: 619 Church Ave Brooklyn NY 11218-3203

IVER, ROBERT DREW, dentist; b. Miami, Fla., Feb. 6, 1947; s. William Henry and Jeanette (Minden) I.; m. Lisa Marie Stettner-Iver, May 5, 1974. Student, Ohio State U., 1965-66, U. Miami, 1966-68; DDS, Georgetown U., 1972. Pvt. practice dentistry Miami Beach, Fla., 1974—. Lt. USNR, 1968-81. Fellow ADA; mem. Fla. Dental Assn., East Coast Dist. Dental Soc., Acad. Gen. Dentistry, Miami Beach Dental Soc., Gold Coast Acad. Gen. Dentistry, Am. Radio Relay League, N.Am. Fishing Club, Dade Radio Club Miami, Everglades Amateur Radio Club. Office: 1205 Lincoln Rd Ste 203 Miami FL 33139-2365

IVERIUS, PER-HENRIK, physician, educator; b. Stockholm, Sept. 26, 1942; s. Karl Gösta and Märta Christina (Engelbert) I. B in Med. Sci., U. Uppsala, Sweden, 1963, PhD in Med. Biochemistry, 1971, MD, 1975. Diplomate Am. Bd. Internal Medicine, Am. Bd. Endocrinology and Metabolism. Intern, resident Emmanuel Hosp., Portland, 1978-80; asst. prof. med. biochemistry U. Uppsala, 1972-74; sr. research fellow U. Wash., Seattle, 1980-82, acting instr. medicine, 1982-85; mem. staff VA Med. Ctr. and U. Utah Hosp., Salt Lake City, 1985—; asst. prof. medicine U. Utah, Salt Lake City, 1985-92, assoc. prof. medicine, 1992—. Contbr. articles to profl. jours. Recipient Research Career Devel. award Swedish Med.

Research Council, 1971-74; fellow Arthritis Found., 1975-78. Mem. AAAS, ACP, Am. Fedn. Clin. Rsch. (sr.), Am. Heart Assn., Am. Diabetes Assn., N.Y. Acad. Scis. Office: VA Med Ctr 500 Foothill Dr Salt Lake City UT 84148

IVERSON, ROBERT LOUIS, JR., internist, physician, intensive care administrator, medical educator; b. Borden, Ind., Sept. 3, 1944; s. Robert L. and Agnes Maxine (Knight) I.; m. Elsa Maschmeyer, Sept. 3, 1967 (div. 1982); children: Nathan, Kirsten; m. Deborah A. Budd, June 16, 1984; children: Richard, Colin. Student, Wabash Coll., 1962-64; BA, Ind. U., 1970, MD, 1974, Intern, 1974-75. Diplomate Am. Bd. Internal Med., diplomate in critical care medicine, Am. Bd. Internal Med. Resident (internal med.) Methodist Hosp., Indpls, 1975-77; fellow in critical care med. U. So. Calif. Shock Rsch. Unit, Ctr. for Critically Ill, L.A., 1977; visiting lectr. U. So. Calif., L.A., 1977; co-dir. critical care, teaching staff, Dept. of Med. Methodist Hosp., Indpls, 1977-84; asst. prof. Med. Wayne State U., Detroit, 1984—; vice chief med. staff Hutzel Hosp., 1995—, dir. med. affairs, 1996—; mem. bd. Rudgate Neighborhood Assocs., Bloomfield Hills, Mich. 1996—, assoc. dir. Intensive Care, Harper Hosp., Detroit, 1984-86; dir. Intensive Care Unit Hutzel Hosp, Detroit, 1986—, chief Dept. Critical Care Med., 1988—; participant Ind. Malpractice Review Panels, 1981-85. Author: (with others) Respiratory Care of the Neurosurgical Patient, 1983, Septic Shock in Critical Care Clinics, 1988; established adminstrv. core curriculum for intensivists Critical Care Clinics, 1993; contbr. abstracts and articles to profl. jours. Med. advisor to Ind. Coun. Emergency Response Teams, 1980-85, mem. (singing) Ind. Symphonic Choir, 1970-84, trustee, 1983-84; hon. dep. sheriff Marion County Sheriff's Dept., 1982-84; bd. dirs. City of Bloomfield Hills, Mich., Rudgate Neighborhood Assn., 1996—. With U.S. Army, 1964-67, Vietnam. Fellow Am. Coll. Physicians, Am. Coll. Chest Physicians; mem. AMA, Soc. Critical Care Med., Soc. for Parenteral and Enteral Nutrition, Mich. Area Radio Enthusiasts, Wayne County Med. Soc. (elected del. 1990-91), Phi Beta Kappa. Home: 165 Harlan Dr Bloomfield Hills MI 48304-3316 Office: Hutzel Hosp Dept Critical Care Med 4707 Saint Antoine St Detroit MI 48201-1427

IVEY, ALLEN EUGENE, psychologist, educator. AB with great distinction, Stanford U., 1955; Fulbright scholar, U. Copenhagen, Denmark, 1955-56; EdD, Harvard U., 1959. Cert. Am. Bd. Profl. Psychology. Prof. psychology and edn. Boston U., 1957-68, Bucknell U., 1957-68, Colo. State U., 1957-68, U. Hawaii, 1957-68; prof. counseling, psychology and edn. U. Mass., Amherst, 1968-91, disting. prof., 1991—; Fulbright lectr. Flinders U., Australia, 1981-82. Contbr. over 200 articles to jours., chpts. to books, and books (21 books translated into 14 langs.). Named Counselor Educator of Yr. Am. Mental Health Counseling Assn., 1990. Mem. APA, ACA (profl. devel. award 1992), ACES (publ. award 1991). Baptist. Home: 2 Cranberry Ln Amherst MA 01002-2802 Office: U Mass Amherst MA 01003

IVIE, SHIRLEY BRIDGES, nurse anesthetist; b. Gaffney, S.C., Mar. 28, 1936; d. Taylor Eugene Bridges and Thelma Lucille (Cabaniss) King; divorced; children: William Patrick Raftery Jr., Kelly Raftery Humphries, Theresa Anne Raftery Wilkes. Nurse diploma, Portsmouth (Va.) Gen. Hosp., 1957; anesthesia diploma, Norfolk Gen. Sch. Anesthesia, 1973. R.N., Va.; cert. R.N. anesthetist. Staff nurse Portsmouth Gen. Hosp., 1957-61, 68-72, Quantico (Va.) Naval Hosp., 1962-64; head pediatric nurse Bakersfield (Calif.) Meml. Hosp., 1958-60; head obstetrics nurse Oceanside (Calif.) Hosp., 1960-61; office nurse Pediatric Assocs., Edgewater, Md., 1964-67; staff anesthetist Meml. Med. Ctr., Savannah, Ga., 1973-84, King Fahad Hosp., Riyadh, Saudi Arabia, 1985, Candler Meml. Hosp., Savannah, 1985-86; chief anesthetist Charlton Meml. Hosp., Folkston, Ga., 1989-92; chief anesthetist, coord. risk mgmt., edn. quality assurance Appling Gen. Hosp. System, Baxley, Ga., 1992—; Appling Health Care System, 1992-95; chief nurse, anesthetist, dir. operative svcs. Appling Health Care System, Baxley, Ga., 1995—; lectr. to health care profls., Savannah, 1979-86. Danforth scholar, 1954, Portsmouth Gen. Hosp. Alumni scholar, 1954. Mem. Am. Assn. Nurse Anesthetists (editorial adv. bd. 1984-85), Assn. Operating Room Nurses (assoc.), Ga. Assn. Nurse Anesthetists (sec.-treas. 1982-83, 86-87, continuing edn. coord. dist. 7, 1979-88), Order Eastern Star, Ladies Shrine. Democrat. Episcopalian. Home: 47 Dunns Lake Rd Baxley GA 31513-2903 Office: Appling Healthcare System Appling Hosp Systems Baxley GA 31513

IVY, JOHN L., medical educator, researcher; b. Portsmouth, Va., Dec. 26, 1946. BS in Phys. Edn., Old Dominion U., 1970; MA in Exercise Physiology, U. Md., 1974, PhD in Exercise Physiology, 1976. Phys. edn. and sci. tchr. Thomas Eaton Jr. H.S., Hampton, Va., 1970; biology and physiology tchr., asst. football coach, head golf coach Kecoughtan H.S., Hampton, Va., 1971-73; asst. prof. biokinetics rsch. lab. dept. phys. edn. Temple U., Phila., 1976-77; rsch. assoc. human performance lab. Ball State U., Muncie, Ind., 1976-77; postdoctoral fellow dept. preventive medicine Washington U. Sch. Medicine, St. Louis, 1978-80; asst. prof. dept. phys. edn. Coll. Health and Sch. Medicine dept. pharmacology U. S.C., Columbia, 1980-82; asst. prof. dept. kinesiology and health edn. Coll. Edn. U. Tex., Austin, 1982-84, assoc. prof. dept. kinesiology and health edn. Coll. Edn., 1984-89, prof., dir. exercise scis. labs. dept. kinesiology and health edn. Coll. Edn. and divsn. pharmacology Coll. Pharmacy, 1989—; cons. clin. diabetes and nutrition sect. NIH, Phoenix, 1985-87; cons. com. mil. nutrition rsch. U.S. Army, 1987-88; mem. adv. bd. performance team Women's Athletic Dept. U. Tex., 1988—; cons. Sports and Cardiovasc. Nutritionists, 1989-92, outside mem. long range planning com., 1989-90; cons. Shaklee U.S., Inc., 1988—; mem. adv. bd. Q Health Club, 1994-96; cons. U.S. Olympic Com. Sports Medicine com. nutrition, 1992-94; mem. com. mil. nutrition and rsch. rev. panel NAS, 1995—. Contbr. articles to profl. jours., chpts. to books; jour. reviewer: Am. Jour. Physiology, Endocrinology and Metabolism, 1993—, Jour. Optimal Nutrition, 1993—, Diabetes, 1987-88, Internat. Jour. Sports Nutrition, 1995—; sect. editor physiology Rsch. Quar. for Exercise and Sport, 1988-91; mem. editl. bd. Medicine and Sci. in Sports and Exercise, 1987—; reviewer: Jour. Applied Physiology, Am. Jour. Physiology, Medicine and Sci. in Sports and Exercise, Internat. Jour. of Sports Medicine, Rsch. Quar., Am. Jour. Clin. Nutrition, Diabetes, Jour. Clin. Investiagation, Internat. Jour. Sports Nutrition; presenter in field. Recipient Nat. Rsch. Svc. award NIH, 1978-80; grantee NIH, Tex. Heart Assn., Ross Products, Pfizer, Inc., Shaklee U.S., Inc., U.S Olympic Rsch. Com. Fellow Am. Coll. Sports Medicine (midwest chpt. 1977-79, southeast chpt. 1980-82, Tex. chpt. bd. trustees 1985-86, 92-95, Tex. chpt. exec. dir. 1986-91, bd. trustees rep. for basic and applied sci. 1986-89, ambassador 1986—, mem. rsch. rev. com. 1991-95, organizer, chair symposium diabetes and exercise I regulation of muscle glucose metabolism acute and chronic effects of exercise 1988); mem. Am. Physiol. Soc., Am. Diabetes Assn. (mem. nutrition scis. and metabolism coun., mem. exercise coun., sec. exercise coun. 1991-93, program chair exercise coun. 1993, organizer, chair symposium role of exercise and phys. activity in the prevention of type II diabetes 1992, organizer, chair symposium exercise through the ages, 1994, grantee, rsch. award 1996), Am. Inst. Nutrition, Am. Soc. Clin. Nutrition, Inc., Phi Epsilon Kappa, Sigma Xi. Office: U Tex Dept Kinesiology Austin TX 78712*

IWAOKA, TEIKI, pharmaceutical company executive; b. Karumai, Iwate, Japan, Mar. 23, 1944; s. Hidezo and Fumi (Sato) I.; m. Yumiko Goto, Apr. 13, 1969; children: Tadaki, Shino, Toshiki. BS, Tohoku U., Sendai, Japan, 1966, MS, 1968, PhD, 1971; cert. in internat. bus. negotiation, Sophia U., Tokyo, 1989. Cert. chemist. From sr. researcher to sect. leader Sankyo Co. Ltd., Tokyo, 1971-85, group dir., 1985-93; exch. prof. U. Calif., Riverside, 1983-85; dep. dir. Rsch. Inst., 1993—; vis. scientist Kyoto (Japan) U., 1968-69; invited seminar speaker Ibaragi U., Mito, Ibaragi, 1977, Nicolet Co., Tokyo, 1988, Tohoku U., Sendai, 1990. Author: Toxicological Biochemistry, 1989; patentee in field. Chmn. ESL program com. North High Sch., Riverside, 1984; com. mem. Com. for the Revision of Japan Indsl. Standard, 1989-90. Mem. Chiba Assn. Internat. Translators (translator 1988—), Japan Soc. for Analytical Chemistry, Soc. for Applied Spectroscopy (chmn. Tokyo meeting, 1990), Chem. Soc. Japan, Pharm. Soc. Japan, Soc. Biophysics Japan, Ski Assn. Japan (instr. 1990—). Home: 238-9 Sonno-cho Inage-ku, Chiba City Chiba 263, Japan Office: Sankyo Co Ltd, 1-2-58 Hiromachi, Shinagawa-ku Tokyo 140, Japan

IWASAKI, KOUICHI, molecular geneticist; b. Yokosuka, Kanagawa, Japan, Jan. 10, 1961; came to U.S., 1986; s. Yukio and Mayako Iwasaki. BS, Kyoto (Japan) U., 1984, MS, 1986; PhD, U. Wis., 1991. Rsch. assoc. Washington U., St. Louis, 1991-94, U. Wash., Seattle, 1994—. Contbr. articles to profl. jours. Recipient Keck award W. Keck Found., 1992. Mem. AAAS, Soc. for Neurosci. Office: U Wash Dept Genetics Mail Box 357360 Seattle WA 98195

IWATA, JAN LEI, pharmacist, consultant; b. Torrance, Calif., Jan. 22, 1959; d. John Takashi and Sally Ann (Tomomitsu) I. PharmD, U. of the Pacific, 1980; MS, U. Md., 1982; D Osteo. Medicine, Chgo. Coll. Osteo. Medicine, 1990; cert. in fashion merchandising, ICS, Scranton, Pa., 1990; cert. in color consultation, 1984. Resident in hosp. pharmacy Johns Hopkins Hosp., 1980-82; project coord. John Hopkins Hosp., 1982-83; asst. dir. pharmacy, clin. asst. prof. Spring Grove Hosp. Ctr., U. Md., Balt., 1984-85; mgr. pharmacy John Hopkins Health Plan, 1986-88; mgr. Rite Aid Pharmacy, 1988-89; mgr. pharmacy, Matthew Thornton Health Plan Dartmouth-Hitchcock Clinics, Nashua, N.H., 1989-90; resident in internal medicine and ophthalmology, 1990—; cons. Pharmatec, Cambridge, Mass., 1988-90. Recipient E.R. Squibb award, 1987, Merch Sharp and Dome award, 1987, Past Pres's. award, 1987, Cora E. Craven award, 1978, Sapha Svc. award, 1976. Fellow AAUW, 1994-95; mem. Md. Soc. Hosp. Pharmacists (asst. editor 1983, sec. 1984, pres.-elect 1986, pres. 1986-87, chmn. bd. dirs. 1988, chmn. pharmacist rehab. com. art auction 1987), Balt. Tibetan Buddhist Group (asst. dir. 1989), Japanese Am. Fellowship League, N.H. Pharmacists Assn., N.H. Soc. Hosp. Pharmacists (bd. dirs.), Am. Soc. Hosp. Pharmacists (apptd. nat. coun. on edn. affairs 1990—), Pan Pacific Fedn. Buddhist, Md. State Bd. Pharmacy (institutional pharmacy subcom. 1986-89), mem. Chgo. Coll. Pharmacy admission com., 1992-93, Psychoneuroimmunology Rsch. Soc. 1992—, Cranial Acad. 1992—, Internat. Soc. of Subtle Energy and Energy Medicine 1993—, Am. Med. Holistic Assn. 1993—, IAOPS com. profl. affairs, trustee 1995—. . Buddhist. Home: 4518 N St Louis Ave Chicago IL 60625

IWATANI, YOSHINORI, physician, educator, researcher; b. Osaka, Japan, May 16, 1952; s. Nobuyuki and Teruko Iwatani; m. Atsuko Iwatani, Sept. 24, 1982; children: Shuko, Kento. MS, Kyushu U., Fukuoka, Japan, 1979; DMS, Osaka U., 1983. Rsch. fellow Univ. Toronto, Can., 1984-86; rsch. asst. Osaka Univ. Med. Sch., 1983-84, 86-89, asst. prof., 1989-93, assoc. prof., 1993-94, prof., 1994—. Mem. Japanese Soc. Clin. Pathology (specialist, councilor 1989—), Japanese Soc. Clin. Immunology (councilor 1991—), Japan Endocrine Soc. (councilor 1989—), Japan Thyroid Assn. (councilor 1988—, Shichijo prize 1989), Am. Endocrine Soc., Am. Thyroid Assn. (century mem. 1991—). Home: 3-13-9 Nagaremachi, Hirano-ku Osaka 547, Japan Office: Osaka Univ Faculty Medicine, Clin Lab Sci 1-7 Yamadaoka, Suita Osaka 565, Japan

IWER, HERBERT WILLIAM, health services administrator; b. Chgo., Nov. 15, 1955; s. Herbert W. II and Victoria Sylvia (Patelski) I.; children: Krista, Herbert IV. BS in Pharmacy, U. Ariz., 1979. Registered pharmacist, Ariz. Pharmacist Plaza del Rio Pharmacy, Phoenix, 1979-80, pharmacy mgr., 1980-83; pharmacy mgr. Medisave Pharmacy, Ltc., Phoenix, 1983-85; clin. svcs. mgr. Super X Pharmacies L.T.C., Phoenix, 1985-87; pharmacy mgr. Vencor Hosp., Phoenix, 1987-92; corp. pharmacy svc. coord. Vencor Hosp., nationwide, 1990—; CEO Vencor Hosp., Youngtown, Ariz., 1990-95, Phoenix, 1992-95; CEO Health-Care Solutions and Info. Systems, Phoenix, 1995—; com. of fin. mem. Ariz. Hosp. Assn., Phoenix, 1994-95; participant healthcare adminstrs. forum, HAFA, Phoenix, 1994-95. Asst. scoutmaster Boy Scouts Am., 1993-95. Home: 11050 N Biltmore Dr # 374 Phoenix AZ 85029 Office: 5805 W Bell Rd # 16-128 Glendale AZ 85308

IZADIDEHKORDI, MOHAMMAD, orthodontist; b. Isfahan, Iran, Aug. 12, 1966; came to U.S., 1984; s. Javad and Ozra (Haraji) I. Student, Essex C.C., Balt., 1984-86, Howard U., 1986-88; DDS, Howard U., 1992, orthodontic cert., 1994. Cert. orthodontist. Lab. technician Preferred Dental Lab., Silver Spring, Md., 1986-88; dentist Loch Raven Dental Assocs., Towson, Md., 1992-94; orthodontist Drs. Solomon, Greenwald, Kyser, Balt., 1994—; orthodontist Dr. Greenwald, Kyser, Riger, Catonville, Md.; 1995—, Dr. Martin, Pasadena, Md., 1995—, Dr. Riger, Lutherville, Md., 1995—; lectr. in field. Inventor in field. Mem. ADA, Am. Assn. Orthodontists, D.C. Dental Soc., Am. Cancer Soc., Md. Dental Soc., Phi Beta Kappa. Office: Drs Solomon Greenwald Kyser 1103 N Pt Blvd #401 Baltimore MD 21224

IZENSTARK, JOSEPH LOUIS, radiologist, physician, educator; b. Chgo., Mar. 29, 1919; s. Paul and Flora (Berger) I.; m. Elizabeth Kaplan, June 25, 1944; 1 child, Susan Rebecca. B.A., U. Calif., Berkeley, 1948; M.D., U. Calif., San Francisco, 1951. Diplomate: Am. Bd. Radiology, Am. Bd. Nuclear Medicine. Intern USPHS, Chgo., 1951-52; resident Kern Gen. Hosp., Bakersfield, Calif., 1952-53; resident in radiology Cedars of Lebanon Hosp., Los Angeles, 1955-56; chief radiology resident Los Angeles County Harbor Gen. Hosp., Torrance, Calif., 1957-58; practice medicine Inglewood, Calif., 1953-55; practice radiology Bakersfield, 1971—; dir. radiology Imperial Hosp., Inglewood, 1959-60; asst. prof. radiology Tulane U., 1960-62, asso. prof., 1963; asso. prof. radiology Emory U., 1963-67, dir. nuclear medicine, 1963-67; prof. radiology U. So. Calif., 1969-72; prof. health scis. Bakersfield State Coll., 1973-83; chief nuclear medicine Cedars of Lebanon Hosp., 1968-71; med. dir. edn. Bakersfield Meml. Hosp., 1983-87; spl. cons. radiol. health USPHS, Calif. Bur. Radiol. Health, U.S. Army; mem. La. Atomic Energy Adv. Council; dir. nuclear medicine Crawford W. Long Meml. Hosp.; mem. USPHS Commn. on Radiation Exposure Evaluation; Med. Bd. Calif., 1982-91. Author: Anatomy and Physiology for X-ray Technicians, 1961; contbr. articles to profl. jours. With AUS, 1941-45. Recipient Cert. of Merit, City of New Orleans, 1962, Physician of Yr. award Bakersfield Meml. Hosp., 1988, Outstanding Physician Contbns. to Medicine award Calif. State Assembly, 1992. Fellow Am. Cancer Soc., Am. Coll. Radiology; mem. Soc. Nuclear Medicine (pres. So. Calif. chpt. 1976), So. Valley Radiol. Soc. (pres. 1975), Kern County Med. Soc. (pres. 1978, Outstanding Physician Contbns. to medicine award with Calif. State Assembly 1992). Office: 3535 San Dimas St # 2 Bakersfield CA 93301-1688

IZQUIERDO, RICARDO, plastic surgeon; b. La Habana, Cuba, Sept. 23, 1955; came to U.S., 1961; BA, Northwestern U., 1977; MD, Loyola U., 1980. Diplomate Am. Bd. Surgery, Am. Bd. Plastic Surgery. Resident in gen. surgery Loyola U. Med. Ctr., Maywood, Ill., 1980-85, resident in plastic surgery, 1985-88; fellow in microsurgery Tulane U. Med. Ctr., New Orleans, 1988-89; instr. surgery Loyola U., Maywood, 1988-89, asst. prof., 1989-94; assoc. prof. Loyola U., Maywood, Ill., 1994—; ptnr. Plastic Surgeons Associated, Palos Heights, Ill., 1994—. Contbr. articles to profl. jours., chpts. to books. Com. mem. Tech. Com. Walker Sch., Clarendon Hills, Ill., 1995-96. John Keely Travelling fellow, 1988. Fellow Am. Coll. Surgeons; mem. Am. Soc. Plastic and Reconstructive Surgeons, Am. Soc. Reconstructive Microsurgery, Plastic Surgery Rsch. Coun. Office: Plastic Surgeons Assocs 11952 S Harlem Ave Palos Heights IL 60463

JABALEY, MICHAEL ELLIS, plastic, reconstructive and hand surgeon; b. Copperhill, Tenn., July 12, 1934; m. Mary Abbay Galbreath, June 10, 1959; children: Mary Powel, Michael Ellis Jr., Elizabeth Irwin, John William, Kate Galbreath. BA, Vanderbilt U., 1957; MD, Johns Hopkins U., 1961. Intern surgery Johns Hopkins Hosp., Balt., 1961-62, resident plastic surgery, 1966-68; resident gen. surgery Mass. Gen. Hosp., 1962-66; asst. chief plastic surgery William Beaumont Hosp., Beaumont, Tex.; chief plastic surgery 3d Field Hosp., Vietnam; prof. surgery Johns Hopkins U., Balt., 1970-72; prof. surgery, plastic and orthopaedic U. Miss. Med. Sch., Jackson, 1972—; pvt. practice plastic and reconstructive surgery U. Miss. Med. Sch.; sr. ptnr. Plastic Surgery Assocs., 1991—; v.p. Am. Bd. Plastic Surgery, 1987. Contbr. articles to profl. jours. Maj. U.S. Army, 1968-70, Vietnam. Recipient numerous rsch. grants. Mem. Am. Assn. Hand Surgery, Am. Soc. Surgery of the Hand (pres. 1986-87), Am. Assn. Plastic Surgeons (v.p. 1994, res. 1996—), Am. Found. for Surgery of Hand (pres. 1987-88), Sunderland Soc. (pres. 1995—). Office: Plastic Surgery Assocs 971 Lakeland Dr Ste 1250 Jackson MS 39216

JABBOUR, JOSEPH MITCHELL, plastic surgeon; b. Bklyn., May 23, 1950; s. Joseph Mitchell and Elizabeth Kathryn (Condron) J.; m. Louise Vincenti, May 29, 1972; children: Suzanne, Michelle. BS, Fordham U., 1972; MD, NYU, 1976. Diplomate Am. Bd. Plastic Surgery, Am. Bd. Surgery. Intern St. Vincent's Hosp., N.Y.C., 1976-77, resident in surgery, 1977-81; plastic surgery resident NYU Med. Ctr., N.Y.C., 1981-83, microsurgery fellow, 1983-84; surgery attending physician St. Vincent's Hosp., N.Y.C., 1984—, Manhattan Eye, Ear and Throat Hosp., N.Y.C., 1984—. Fellow ACS; mem. Am. Soc. Plastic and Reconstructive Surgery, Am. Lipoplasty Soc., Am. Soc. Aesthetic Plastic Surgeons (candidate mem.). Roman Catholic. Office: 2 Fifth Ave New York NY 10011

JABRE, JOE F., neurologist, electromyographer; b. Beirut, Lebanon, Jan. 5, 1947; came to U.S., 1972; s. Farid Y. and Lody (Abou-Rizk) J.; m. Helen A. Perry, Oct. 6, 1974; children: Frederick, Monique, Christopher. B.Math., Christian Bros. Coll., Beirut, 1964; MD with honors, French Faculty Medicine, Beirut, 1972. Diplomate Am. Bd. Psychiatry and Neurology, Am. Bd. electrodiagnostic Medicine. Intern Boston City Hosp., 1972-73; resident Case Western Res. U., Cleve., 1973-77; fellow Cleve. Clinic Found., 1977-78; asst. prof. neurology La. State U. Med. Ctr., New Orleans, 1978-82; attending neurologist Med. Ctr. East New Orleans, 1982-83; assoc. prof. neurology Boston U., 1983—, dir. electromyography, 1983—, rsch. assoc. prof. sch. engring., 1985—; attending neurologist Boston VA Med. Ctr., 1983—; invited guest lectr. numerous countries, 1989—. Author: EMG Manual, 1983. Fellow Am. Assn. Electrodiagnostic Medicine; mem. Am. Lebanese Med. Assn. (pres. 1994), Société de Neurophysiologie Clinique de Langue Française. Office: Boston VA Med Ctr 150 S Huntington Ave Boston MA 02130

JACINTO, GEORGE ANTHONY, social worker, educator, consultant; b. Gilroy, Calif., Dec. 21, 1949; s. George Peter and Isabelle Agnes (Joseph) J. BS in Criminology-Corrections, Calif. State U.-Fresno, 1974; postgrad. Wash. Theol. Union, 1975, U. Wis., 1980, Boise State U., 1981; MEd in Guidance and Counseling-Gen. Personnel Services, Albertson Coll. of Idaho, 1982; MSW in Clin. Social Work, Fla. State U., 1990. Cert. rehab. counselor; lic. clin. social worker. Youth minister Ch. St. Michael, Olympia, Wash., 1976-77; dir. youth ministry St. James Congregation, Franklin, Wis., 1977-80; diocesan youth dir. Cath. Diocese of Boise, Idaho, 1980-83; intern. counselor drug and alcohol Salvation Army, Boise, 1982; dir. religious edn. St. Andrew Ch., Orlando, Fla., 1983-84; intern Orange County Dept. Soc. Svcs., Orlando, Fla., 1988; vocat. rehab. counselor DLES, State of Fla., Orlando, 1984-88, vocat. rehab. cons., 1988-89; social worker Fla. Hosp./Rebound, Orlando, 1989-91; vocat. program specialist Fla. Hosp. Med. Ctr., Orlando, 1991-92; mental health specialist Orange County Cmty. Corrections Dept., Orlando, 1992-96; adj. faculty Fla. State Univ. Sch. Social Work, Orlando, 1994-95, U. Ctrl. Fla., Orlando, 1994-96 clin. instr., 1996—; part-time home health social worker Olsten Health Svcs., Winter Park, Fla., 1991-92—; fair hearings officer Orange County Dept. of Social Svcs., Orlando, 1991-92; part-time youth minister Good Shepherd Ch., Orlando, 1985-88; founder Am. Life Planning Assocs., Orlando, 1985—; social worker, career and life planning cons., youth programming cons. Active diversion program Union St. Ctr., Olympia, Wash.; campaign leader for children's toys Indo-China Refugee Relief, Milw.; mem. adv. community agys. concerned with youth issues; coord. community svc. program for young people, Franklin, Wis.; chair Dept. of Social Work Adv. Coun. U. Cen. Fla., 1991-92. Mem. NASW (chair Cen. Fla. unit 1990-92, bd. dirs. Fla. chpt. 1990-92, del. assembly, 1993, Nat. HIV task force Fla. Chpt. Liaison, central unit social worker of the year 1993, del. assembly 1996), World Future Soc., Nat. Rehabilitation Assn., Inst. Noetic Scis., New Age Network. Home: PO Box 533154 Orlando FL 32853-3154 Office: U Ctrl Fla Sch Social Work PO Box 163358 Orlando FL 32816-3358

JACK, MINTA SUE, hospital department head; b. Huntsville, Tex., Aug. 24, 1935; d. Clinton Orrin and Dorris Eugenia (Pierce) Bunn; m. Samuel Garred Jack, Jr., June 8, 1957 (div. 1984); children: Samuel Garred III, Paul Alan. BA with distinction, U. N.Mex., 1957. Cert. secondary educator. High sch. tchr. Albuquerque Pub. Schs., 1957-58; bd. dirs. Delta Delta Delta, Reno, 1962-63; com. chmn. Tustin (Calif.) Sch. Dist. PTO, 1965-70, Red Hill Luth. Sch., Tustin, 1970-74; bd. dirs. Assistance League of Tustin, 1972-83, Performing Arts Ctr. Guilds, Orange County, Calif., 1983-88; bd.d irs. Delta Delta Delta, Orange County, Calif., 1987-91; dir., vol. Western Med. Ctr., Santa Ana, Calif., 1986—. Vol. leader Boy Scouts/Little League, Tustin, 1966-72; vol. Olympic Organizing Com., L.A., 1984; assoc. Mexican Am. Nat. Women, Santa Ana, 1988-90; mem. Freedom Found./Valley Forge, Santa Ana, 1988-90. Recipient Writing award, 1989, Newsletter award, 1991, Community Svc. award Disneyland, 1981, Amelia Earhart award U. Calif., 1989, Ernestine Grigsby award Delta Delta Delta, 1989; named Woman of Yr. nominee Panhellenic Assn., 1989. Mem. AAUW, So. Calif. Assn. Dirs. of Vol. Svcs. (bd. dirs. 1987-91), Am. Soc. Dirs. Vol. Svcs. (membership com. 1989), Assistance League of Tustin (pres. 1980-81), Westmed Gold Club (membership com. 1986-92), Chapman Univ. Music Assocs. (bd. dirs. 1987-92), Mortar Bd., Delta Delta Delta (pres. 1988-89, bd. dirs. 1988-91), Dirs. Vols. in Agencies, Phi Kappa Phi, Phi Alpha Theta, Pi Lambda Theta. Episcopalian. Home: 7634 Appaloosa Trail Orange CA 92669 Office: Western Med Ctr 1001 N Tustin Ave Santa Ana CA 92705

JACKLIN, CAROL NAGY, psychology educator; b. Chgo., Feb. 23, 1939; d. Albert Elmer and Lee (Black) Nagy; children: Beth Carol, Phillip Albert. BA, U. Conn., 1960, MA, 1961; PhD, Brown U., 1972. Instr. psychology U. Conn., Waterbury, 1961-63, San Jose (Calif.) City Coll., 1964-68; rsch. assoc. Stanford (Calif.) U., 1972-76, sr. rsch. assoc., 1976-83; chmn. SWMS program U. So. Calif., L.A., 1983-86, prof. psychology, 1983-89, prof., chmn. psychology dept., 1990-92, dean div. social scis. and communication, 1992-95; dean faculty of arts and scis. Coll. of William and Mary, Williamsburg, Va., 1995—. Co-author: The Psychology of Sex Difference, 1974; editor: The Psychology of Gender vols. I-IV, 1992; contbr. articles to profl. jours. NIH Post-Dortoral fellow Stanford U., 1971-72. Fellow Am. Psychol. Assn., Am. Psychol. Soc.; mem. Soc. Rsch. Child Devel., Soc. Rsch. Adolscence. Home: 3218 Deerfield Rd Williamsburg VA 23188 Office: College of William & Mary Dean Faculty Arts & Scis Ewell Hall Williamsburg VA 23187

JACKMAN, JAY M., psychiatrist; b. Bklyn., June 4, 1939; s. James Jeremiah and Dora (Emmer) J.; m. Judith Gail Meisels, Nov. 23, 1963 (div. Sept. 1987); children: Tenaya, Rashi, Jason Scott; m. Myra Hoffenberg Strober, Oct. 21, 1990. BA, Columbia U., 1960; MD, Harvard U., 1964. Diplomate Am. Bd. Psychiatry and Neurology. Rotating intern San Francisco County Gen. Hosp., 1965; psychiat. resident Stanford U., 1969; asst. dir. community psychiatry Mt. Zion Hosp., San Francisco, 1969-70; dir. drug treatment programs Westside Community Mental Health Ctr., San Francisco, 1970-74; pvt. practice San Francisco, 1969-74; dir. Lanakila Clinic Kalihi-Palama Community Mental Health Ctr., Honolulu, 1974-75; pvt. practice specializing in forensic psychiatry, Honolulu, 1975-90, Stanford, Calif., 1990—; cons. Salvation Army Addiction Treatment Facility, Honolulu, 1974-81; chmn. Task Force on Drugs, Nat. Coun. Community Mental Health Ctrs., 1971-75; chmn. no. sect. Calif. Assn. Methodone Programs, 1973-74. Contbr. articles on substance abuse to profl. jours. Trustee Foothill-DeAnza C.C. Bd., 1993—; active Mayor's Adv. Com. on Drug Abuse, Honolulu, 1975-77. Mem. Am. Psychiat. Assn. (commn. on drugs 1973-77), Am. Acad. Psychiatry and Law, Am. Coll. Forensic Psychiatrists, No. Calif. Psychiat. Soc., Santa Clara County Bar Assn. (vol., lay mem. fee arbitration com. 1992), Calif. Attys. for Criminal Justice. Democrat. Jewish.

JACKOBS, MIRIAM ANN, dietitian; b. Sioux City, Iowa, Apr. 8, 1940; d. Abraham and Mary (Wadedo) Kaled; m. John Joseph Jackobs, Aug. 28, 1965; children: Mark James, Daniel Michael, Thomas Vincent. Student, St. Louis U., 1962; BS, Briar Cliff Coll., 1963; MS, Iowa State U., 1965. Lic. in dietetics, Ohio. Instr. nutrition Ariz. State U., Tempe, 1965-67, Willoughby (Ohio) Eastlake Sch., 1967-69; clinical dietitian Migrant Clinic of Seneca County, Tiffin, Ohio, 1969-75; nutrition instr. Heidelberg Coll., Tiffin, 1969-75; founder, cons. dietitian Nutrition Cons. Svcs., 1974—; oncology dietitian Hall Radiation Ctr., Cedar Rapids, 1983-87; nutrition instr. Mt. Mercy & Coe Colls., Cedar Rapids, 1976-87; clinical dietitian The Brethren's Home, Greenville, Ohio, 1987-89; dir. dietary dept. Washington Manor Retirement Ctr., Centerville, Ohio, 1989-90; instr. Kettering (Ohio) Adult Sch., 1988-90, Mt. St. Joseph Coll., 1989—; adj. asst. prof. Wilmington Coll., 1990—. Author: (book) Food Prep Manual, 1968, Diet Manual, 1988; contbr. articles on nutrition to prof. jours. Com. chmn. LWV, Ohio and Iowa, 1970-82; fund raising chmn. PTA, Cedar Rapids, 1984-86; unit leader dist. coun. Boy Scouts Am., 1973-88; organizer Greenville Summer Symphony, Ohio, 1988. Recipient Silver Beaver award Boy Scouts Am., St. George award Archdiocese Dubuque, 1985; Gen. Foods Found. fellow Iowa State U., 1965. Mem.

Am. Dietetic Assn., Ohio Dietetic Assn., Ohio Cons. Dietitions (newsletter editor 1988—), Greater Cin. Dietetic Assn., Greater Cin. Cons. Dietitians, Gerontology Practice Group, Cedar Rapids Youth Orch., Coe Woman (pres. 1977-78). Roman Catholic. Home and Office: Nutrition Cons Svcs 7733 Westwind Dr Cincinnati OH 45242-5027

JACKSON, A(ASE) OSA LITTRUP, physical therapy educator; b. Copenhagen, Jan. 3, 1950; d. Gunnar and Gerda (Petersen) Littrup; 1 child, Marius. BS, U. Mich., 1972, MA in Ednl. Adminstrn., 1973, PhD, 1979; student, Hartford Family Inst., 1980, Feldenkrais Practioner Tng. Program, 1981-84. Dir. rehab. Roseville (Mich.) Nursing Home, 1973-74, St. Joseph Nursing Home, Hamtramck, Mich., 1972-75; asst. clin. prof. NYU, N.Y.C., 1975-77; dir. rehab. Hartford Hosp., 1977-79; ptnr. Glastonbury (Conn.) Health Assocs., 1980; founder, pres. Geriatric Inst, Inc., Glastonbury, 1980-81; vis. prof. dept physiotherapy U. Queensland, Brisbane, Australia, 1983-85; assoc. prof., chmn. div. kinesiological scis. Oakland U., Rochester, Mich., 1986-89, assoc. prof. phys. therapy, 1989—; adj. faculty dept. phys. therapy U. Conn., Stoors, 1978-79; asst. prof. dept. phys. therapy U. Md., 1980; lectr. dept. family medicine U. Conn., Farmington, 1981, Diakonissehusets Nursing Sch., Oslo, 1982-85, Oslo Sch. Physiotherapy, 1983-85, Andrew U., Berrien Springs, Mich., 1987—; adj. asst. prof. dept. phys. therapy U. Pitts., 1984—; cons. in field; asst. trainer Feldenkrais, 1989. Author: Physical Therapy of the Geriatric Patient, 1983, Therapeutic Considerations for the Elderly, 1987, Natural Ease For Work-Can You Move To Get The Job Done?, 1994; co-editor Jour. of Geriatric Phys. and Occupational Therapy, 1980-81; mem. editorial bd. Jour. Gerontology and Geriatric Edn., 1980-83, Internat. Phys. Therapy, 1984—; contbr. articles to profl. jours. Mem. Am. Gerontol. Soc., Am. Geriatric Soc., Norwegian Phys. Therapy Assn. (faculty 1983-85, program devel. 1985—), AAUP, Am. Phys. Therapy Assn. (del. 1978-80, pres. Conn. chpt. 1981, chmn. sect. on geriatrics 1982, Joan Mills award 1987, Clin. Excellence award 1995), Am. Heart Assn. (chmn. cardiac rehab.). Home: 1800 Campus Ct Rochester Hls MI 48309-2158 Office: Oakland U Sch Health Scis Rochester MI 48309

JACKSON, BENJAMIN TAYLOR, surgeon, educator, medical facility administrator; b. Jacksonville, Fla., Apr. 28, 1929; s. Julian Harold and Helen Louise (Blasingame) J.; m. Alda Jean Davis, June 18, 1953; children: Benjamin Taylor Jr., Jean Leigh, Kimberly Louise, Jillian Davis. MD, Duke U., 1954; MS, Brown U., 1982. Diplomate Am. Bd. Surgery. Instr. Med. Coll. of Va., Richmond, 1963-64; asst. prof. Sch. of Medicine Boston U., 1964-67, assoc. prof. Sch. of Medicine, 1967-75, prof. Sch. of Medicine, 1975-80; vis. surgeon U. Hosp., Boston, 1975-80; prof. Brown U. Sch. Medicine, Providence, 1980—; chief surg. svc. VA Med. Ctr., Providence, 1980—. Contbr. articles to profl. jours. Capt. U.S. Army, 1955-57. Mem. ACS, Soc. Univ. Surgeons, Soc. for Gynecologic Investigation. Methodist. Home: 11 October Ln Weston MA 02193-1724 Office: VA Med Ctr Davis Pk Providence RI 02908

JACKSON, CARMAULT BENJAMIN, JR., physician; b. Newton, Mass., Apr. 19, 1924; s. Carmault Benjamin and Mabel (Robbins) J.; m. Lynda D. Shaneman; children—Carmault Benjamin, III, Thomas J., Molly Ann. M.D., U. Pa., 1952. Intern Hosp. of U. Pa., 1952-53, resident, 1953-56; internal medicine specialist U.S. Air Force, NASA Space Task Group, 1958-61; practice medicine specializing in internal medicine San Antonio, 1961-76; asso. dir., asso. prof. medicine M.D. Anderson Hosp. and Tumor Inst., Houston, 1977-79; adminstr. Met. Gen Hosp., San Antonio; med. adv. H. B. Zachry Co., San Antonio, Tower Life Ins. Co.; vice chmn. Tex. Health Coordinating Council. Served with U.S. Army, 1942-45; Served with USAF, 1956-61. Decorated Purple Heart with 2 oak leaf clusters, U.S.A.F. Commendation medal. Mem. AMA, So. Med. Assn., Tex. Med. Assn., Tex. Soc. Internal Medicine, Am. Soc. Internal Medicine, Tex. Acad. Internal Medicine, Am. Occupational Medicine Assn., Bexar County (Tex.) Med. Soc., Inst. Medicine, Nat. Acad. Scis.

JACKSON, CHRISTOPHER WILLIAM, emergency medicine physician; b. Joplin, Mo., Feb. 17, 1963; s. Layton McRey Jackson and Barbara Ann (Horn) Bryan; m. Tracey Lynn Landwehr; children: Joshua David, Tyler Geoffrey, Rachel Lea. BS, U. Mo., 1986; DO, U. Health Scis., Kansas City, Mo., 1992. Resident in emergency medicine Ohio U.-Doctors Hosp., Columbus, 1993-96; chief resident, 1995—. Capt. U.S. Army, 1981-96. Mem. Am. Coll. Osteo. Emergency Physicians, Am. Coll. Emergency Physicians, Emergency Medicine Residents Assn. (rep. 1995-96). Mem. United Ch. of Christ. Home: 38 Hunter's Ridge Dr Labadie MO 63055 Office: DePaul Health Ctr 12303 DePaul Dr Bridgeton MO 63044

JACKSON, DAVID B., retired laboratory director; b. Fairland, Okla., Feb. 10, 1928; s. Green B. and Earlora (Cain) J.; m. Betty J. Handley, Dec. 21, 1946; 1 child, Lee David. BS, U. Okla., 1951; diploma, USN Hosp. Corp Sch., 1951, USN Med. Tech. Sch., 1952. cert. med. technologist. Med. and radiographic technologist USN, 1952-53, Cushing (Okla.) Hosp., 1954-67; dir. lab. and radiology dept. Okla. State U. Health Ctr., Stillwater, 1967-93; ret., 1993; guest lectr. Okla. State U., 1978-84. Contbr. numerous articles to profl. jours. With USN, 1951-53. Mem. Am. Med. Technologists, Okla. Soc. Am. Med. Technologists (named Technologist of the Yr., 1969-70), Am. Registry of Radiographic Technologists, Masons. Home: 127 Orchard Stillwater OK 74074

JACKSON, DOROTHY FAYE GREENE, nursing educator; b. Marlin, Tex., Mar. 18, 1947; d. Shellie Tom and Ruby Lee (O'Neal) Greene; m. David Lee Jackson, Jr., Dec. 20, 1967; children: David Lee III, Danese. AAS, Odessa Coll., 1967; BSN, West Tex. State U., 1977; MSN, U. Tex., Galveston, 1980. RN, Tex. Staff nurse Med. Ctr. Hosp., Odessa, Tex., 1967-68, charge nurse CCU, 1968-72, mgr. quality assurance and infection control, 1979-80, dir. nursing, critical care and edn., 1980-81, bd. mgrs. Med. Ctr. Hosp., 1988-89; instr. nursing Odessa Coll., 1972-79, 81-93, dept. chair, 1993; asst. prof. Sch. Nursing Tex. Tech. U. Health Scis. Ctr., Odessa, 1993—; advanced practice nurse Sch. Medicine Family Practice Ctr. Tex. Tech. Health Scis. Ctr., Odessa, 1994—; mem. adv. bd. Head Start, Odessa, 1981—; cons. to long term care facilities, Odessa, 1991-93, clin. specialist in gerontological nursing, 1994—; v.p. Seabury Nursing Home, 1985—; presenter Nat. Conf. on Gerontol. Nursing Edn., Norfolk, Va., 1992. Contbr. articles to jours. in field. Bd. dirs. Odessa Cultural Coun., 1989-93, Midland-Odessa Symphony and Chorale, 1991-94. Mem. ANA, Jr. League Odessa, Phi Delta Kappa, Sigma Theta Tau, Alpha Kappa Alpha. Episcopalian. Home: 410 E 42nd St Odessa TX 79762-6856 Office: Tex Tech U Univ Health Scis Ctr 800 W 4th St Odessa TX 79763

JACKSON, EARL, JR., medical technologist; b. Paris, Ky., Sept. 4, 1938; s. Earl Sr. and Margaret Elizabeth (Cummins) J. BA, Ky. State U., 1960; postgrad., U. Paris, 1978. Clin. rsch. coord. Harvard U., Boston, 1962-64; chem. devel. specialist Electro-Power Pacs, Corp., Cambridge, Mass., 1964-67; sr. rsch. tech. Mass. Gen. Hosp., Boston, 1967-81, med. tech. specialist, 1991-95; retired, 1995. Contbr. articles to profl. jours. Mem. AAAS, NY. Acad. Scis., Am. Assn. Clin. Chemistry, Am. Soc. Clin. Microbiology, N.E. Assn. for Microbiology and Infectious Disease. Democrat. Home: 89 Oxford St Somerville MA 02143-1617 Office: Mass Gen Hosp Fruit St Boston MA 02114-2620

JACKSON, EDGAR B., JR., medical educator; b. Rison, Ark., May 30, 1935; m. Thelma Jackson, 1957; children: Gary, David, Michael, Laura. BA, Case Western Res. U., 1962, MD, 1966. Intern Cleve. Met. Gen. Hosps., 1966-67, chief resident medicine, 1969-70; from sr. instr. medicine to asst. prof. to asst. clin. prof. Case Western Res. U., 1970-83, assoc. clin. prof., 1983-86, clin. prof. medicine, 1986—; asst. dean Case Western Res. U., 1971-74, asst. prof. comty. medicine, 1974-79, comty. health, 1977-88. Contbr. numerous articles to profl. jours. With U.S. Army, 1959-61. Carnegie Common Wealth Clin. scholar, 1970-72. Mem. APHA, Am. Sickle Cell Anemia Assn. Inc. Office: Univ Hosp 2074 Abington Rd Cleveland OH 44106*

JACKSON, FRANCIS CHARLES, physician, surgeon; b. Rutherford, N.J., Sept. 2, 1917; s. Frank Emil and Margaret Charlotte (Kuhn) J.; m. Joan Gloria Mortenson, Sept. 1, 1949; children: Geoffrey P., Bradford M., Gregory C., Donna E. B.A., Yale U., 1939; M.D., U. Va., 1943. Diplomate Am. Bd. Surgery, Nat. Bd. Med. Examiners. Intern N.Y. Hosp.-Cornell Med. Center, 1944, asst. resident surgery, 1945, from asst. resident surgery to 1st asst. chief resident surgeon, 1947-49, chief resident surgeon, 1950; practice medicine specializing in gen. and vascular surgery Pitts., 1952-70; cons., chief surgeon Arabian Am. Oil Co., Dhahran, Saudi Arabia, 1951; asst. chief surg. service VA Center, Togus, Maine, 1952; chief surg. service, dir. Gen. Surg. Residency Program, VA Hosp., Pitts., 1952-70; dir. surg. service VA Central Office, Washington, 1970-72; spl. asst. to chief med. dir. for emergency and disaster med. services VA Central Office, 1972-73, dir. emergency and disaster med. services staff, 1973-75; mem. cons. staff Presbyn.-Univ. Hosp., Pitts., 1959-70; asst. in surgery Sch. Medicine Cornell U., 1946-49, asst. in anatomy, 1946, instr. surgery, 1950; asst. prof. surgery Sch. Medicine U. Pitts., 1953-60, assoc. prof surgery, 1961-65, prof. surgery, 1965-70, sec. exec. com. dept. surgery, 1964-70, MEND coordinator, 1967-68; clin. prof. surgery Georgetown U. Sch. Medicine, George Washington U. Sch. Medicine, Washington, 1970-75; chmn. dept. surgery Sch. Medicine Tex. Tech U., Lubbock, 1975-80; prof. surgery Sch. Medicine Tex. Tech U., 1975—, assoc. dean clin. edn., 1980-82; med. dir. S. Plains Emergency Med. Services, 1978—; prof., chmn. emeritus dept. of surgery Tex. Tech. Med. Sch. Medicine, 1996; cons. Carnegie-Mellon Inst., 1969-71, Westinghouse Electric Corp. (Health Systems), AVCO Corp.; chmn. local com. VA Adj. Cancer Chemotherapy Study, 1957-70; chmn. exec. com. Operation Prep. Pitts. Annual Med.-CD Disaster Drill, 1958-60; mem. ad hoc com. disaster med. surveys, div. med., vice chmn. com. emergency med. services Nat. Acad. Scis.-NRC, 1964-74; mem. surg. drugs adv. com. FDA, 1971-75; mem. panel on physicians asst. CSC, 1971-73; cons. on emergency and disaster services USPHS, 1965-72; VA rep., alternate observer, nat. health resources adv. com. Office Preparedness, 1972-75; VA rep., mem. interdepartmental com. on emergency med. services HEW, 1974-75; mem. ad hoc com. on emergency med. services communications, interdepartmental adv. com. on radio communications Office Telecommunications Policy, 1973-75. Author: Role of Medicine in Emergency Preparedness, 1968; contbr. articles to surg. jours.; creator surg. exhibits. Trustee Peddie Sch., 1972-74. Served as lt. (j.g.) USNR, 1945-46, to lt. comdr., M.C. 1953-55. Recipient Pfizer award of merit U.S. CD Council, Mpls., 1960, Key to City Louisville, 1964, Billings Gold Medal award AMA, 1966. Fellow A.C.S. (past chmn. residents program com. Southwestern Pa. chpt.; chmn. subcom. disaster, surgery and communications of trauma com., trauma com. 1966-78, exec. com. 1976-78, pres. Southwestern Pa. chpt. 1970, gov. 1970-74); mem. AMA (chmn. com. disaster med. care, Council Nat. Security 1958-67), Pa. Med Soc. (chmn. commn. on emergency med. services), Allegheny County Med. Soc., Soc. Biol. Research U. Pitts. Sch. Medicine, Pitts. Surg. Soc., Am. Assn. Surgery of Trauma, So. Surg. Assn., Assn. VA Surgeons (founding), Central Surg. Assn., Soc. Surgery Alimentary Tract, Assn. Mil. Surgeons U.S. (Stitt award 1968), Pitts. Acad. Medicine (Man of Year award 1969), D.C. Med. Soc., Am. Surg. Assn., Société Internat. de Chirurgie, Tex. Surg. Soc., Tex. Med. Assn. (chmn. surg. sect. program com. 1981-82, subcom. on accreditation of continuing med. edn. programs 1983-92, com. on continuing edn. 1959-92, cons.), Lubbock Surg. Soc., Lubbock-Crosby-Garza County Med. Soc., Alpha Omega Alpha. Lodge: Rotary. Office: Dept of Surgery Sch Medicine Tex Tech U Lubbock TX 79430

JACKSON, GARY LYNN, osteopath, internist, pulmonologist; b. Sept. 9, 1949; m. Vickie S. Williams, 1982; children: Heather L., Elizabeth M. BA, U. Kans., 1971; BS, Pittsburg State U., 1973; DO, U. Health Scis. Coll. Osteo., Kansas City, Mo., 1978. Diplomate Nat. Bd. Osteo. Med. Examiners, Am. Bd. Internal Medicine. Intern U. Hosp.-Coll. Osteo. Medicine, Kansas City, Mo., 1978-79; pvt. practice Blue Valley Med. Group Corp. Offices, Overland Pk., Kans., 1979-82; gen. med. officer gen. med. clinic Fitzsimons Army Med. Ctr., Aurora, Colo., 1982-83; resident in internal medicine Fitzsimons Army Med. Ctr., 1983-86, fellow in pulmonary disease svc., 1986-88; dir. med. intensive care unit, chief pulmonary disease svc. William Beaumont Army Med. Ctr., El Paso, Tex., 1989-90; pvt. practice Alamogordo, N.M., 1990—; vice chief profl. staff Lincoln County Med. Ctr., Ruidoso, N.M., 1992, 93, pulmonary cons. to med. staff dir. of cardio-pulmonary svcs., 1990—; dir. cardio-pulmonary svcs. Gerald Champion Meml. Hosp., Alamogordo, 1993—; pulmonary cons. Eastern N.M. Med. Ctr., Roswell, 1990-92; presenter in field. Contbr. articles to prcfl. jours. Maj. U.S. Army, 1982-90, res., 1990—. Fellow Am. Coll. Chest Physicians (assoc.); mem. ACP, Am. Osteo. Assn. (alt. ho. dels. 1988, del. 1989), Assn. Mil. Osteo. Physicians and Surgeons (program chmn. continuing med. edn. 1989, v.p. 1989-90), N.M. Soc. Med. Assts. (physician cons. 1994—), Beta Beta Beta, Alpha Chi Sigma, Theta Chi, Rho Sigma Chi. Home: PO Drawer 3535 HS 208 Mountain Shadow Rd Ruidoso NM 88345 Office: 923 9th St Ste A Alamogordo NM 88310

JACKSON, GILCHRIST L., surgeon; b. Dayton, Ohio, Sept. 30, 1948; s. William Hughes Jr. and Margaret Langhorne (Alexander) J.; m. Katina Ballantyne, Nov. 28, 1970; children: Marina, Alex, Scott, George. BA, Vanderbilt U., 1970; MD, U. Louisville, 1974. Fellow U. Tex. M.D. Anderson Cancer Ctr., Houston, 1979-80, faculty, 1980-81; active staff Kelsey-Seybold Clinic, Houston, 1981—; active staff St. Luke's Episc. Hosp., Houston, 1981—, Meth. Hosp., Houston, 1981—, VA Hosp., Houston, 1981-83, Ben Taub Hosp., Houston, 1981—; courtesy staff Tex. Children's Hosp., Houston, 1981—; mem. dir. Crump Cancer Ctr., Houston, 1984-95, Kelsey-Seybold Cancer Program, 1994—; prin. investigator Tex. Cmty. Oncology Network, Nat. Surg. Adjuvant Breast and Bowel Project, 1986-95. Contbr. articles to profl. jours. Active student recruitment com. Vanderbilt U., 1991, Mus. Fine Arts, Houston, 1995, Mus. Natural Sci., Houston, 1995; bd. dirs. West Univ. Little League, Houston, 1990, 91. Mem. Am. Cancer Soc. (pres. 1987-89, v.p. 1985-87), Thyroid Soc. Am. Republican. Presbyterian. Office: Kelsey Seybold Clinic 6624 Fannin Ste 1700 Houston TX 77030

JACKSON, GREGORY WAYNE, orthodontist; b. Chgo., Sept. 4, 1950; s. Wayne Eldon and Marilyn Frances (Anderson) J.; m. Nora Ann Echtner, Mar. 17, 1973; children: Eric, David. Student, U. Ill., 1968-70; DDS with honors, U. Ill., Chgo., 1974; MSD, U. Wash., 1978. Practice dentistry specializing in orthodontics Chgo., 1978—; instr. orthodontic dept. U. Ill. Coll. Dentistry, Chgo., 1978-81. Coach Little League Baseball, Oak Brook, Ill., 1986-89. Served to lt. USN, 1974-76. Mem. ADA, Ill. State Dental Soc., Chgo. Dental Soc., Am. Assn. Orthodontists, Midwestern Soc. Orthodontists, Ill. Soc. Orthodontists, Omicron Kappa Upsilon. Evangelical. Office: 6435 S Pulaski Rd Chicago IL 60629-5148

JACKSON, HARPER SCALES, JR., healthcare executive; b. Ft. Smith, Ark., Feb. 23, 1951; s. Harper S. and Adele (Graves) J.; m. Virginia Kay Stack, June 4, 1976; children: Laura Elizabeth, Kathrin Ann, Susan Virginia. BSBA, U. Ark., 1973; M in Health Adminstrn., Washington U., 1979. Mgr. Neiman-Marcus Co., Dallas, 1973-77; adminstrv. asst. to Michael E. DeBakey, M.D. Baylor Coll. of Medicine, Houston, 1979-81; asst. v.p. The Meth. Hosp., Houston, 1981-83, v.p., 1983-85, sr. v.p. support svcs., 1985-89, sr. v.p. patient svcs., 1989-93, sr. v.p. surgery svcs. and clin. support, 1993-95, sr. v.p. prof. and surg. svcs., 1995—; bd. dirs. LifeGift, mem. exec. com. 1994—, chmn. 1996—, sec. 1995—; bd. dirs. Vis. Nurse Assn., Houston; bd. dirs. Washington U. Alumni Assn., chmn.-elect, 1994-96, bylaws com., 1992—, chmn., 1996—; adj. faculty Washington U. Sch. Medicine, St. Louis, 1992—. Adminstrv. bd. First United Meth. Ch., Sugarland, Tex., 1988-91, facility assess com., 1995-96; chmn. healthcare campaign coun. United Way of Tex. Gulf Coast, Houston, 1988; adv. coun. Ft. Bend (Ind.) Sch. Dist. Sch.-Bus. Partnership; bd. trustees AORN Found., 1992-94, v.p., 1992-93, chmn. policy com., 1993-94; bd. dirs. Am. Heart Assn., East Ft. Bend divsn., 1990—, pres., 1993-94, chmn. nominating com., 1995, mem. quality improvement network #1 Healthcare Forum. Recipient Cert. of Appreciation, Am. Heart Assn., 1984. Fellow Am. Coll. Healthcare Execs. (mem. Houston chpt., chmn. mem. com. 1996—); mem. Am. Hosp. Assn., United Weslayan Hosp. Assn., Tex. Hosp. Assn. (ad hoc com. corp. values and ethics, leadership forum, del. to 1992 conv.), U. Ark. Alumni Assn., Drs. Club Houston, Sweetwater Country Club, Omicron Delta Kappa, Beta Gamma Sigma, Sigma Iota Epsilon, Phi Gamma Delta (life). Office: The Meth Hosp 6565 Fannin St Houston TX 77030-2704

JACKSON, HERMOINE PRESTINE, psychologist; b. Wilmington, Del., Mar. 11, 1945; d. Herman Preston and Ella Brooks (Roane) Jackson. BA, Elizabethtown (Pa.) Coll., 1967; MA, Ohio State U., 1979, PhD, 1991. Tchr. Wilmington (Del.) pub. sch. sys., 1967-68, Phila. Pub. Sch. Sys., 1968-74; psychologist Midland (Mich.) Hosp., 1979-81, Cen. Mich. U., Mt. Pleasant, 1979-81, West Seneca (N.Y.) Devel. Ctr., 1981-90, N.Y. State Div. for Youth Buffalo Residential Ctr., 1990-94, Tryon Girls Ctr., 1994, Va. Dept. Youth and Family Svcs., Beaumont, 1994—; mem. admissions/discharge com. St. Augustine Ctr., Buffalo, 1983-90. Co-author test manual: Manual of Assessment Instruments for the MR/DD Population, 1978. Mem. Planning Coun., Buffalo, 1989-94. Named Outstanding Instr., Cen. Mich. U., 1981. Mem. APA, Am. Assn. on Mental Retardation, Psychol. Assn. Western N.Y., Coalition of 100 Black Women (corr. sec. 1988-91). Home: 7407 Sandlewood Dr Richmond VA 23235-5664 Office: Va Dept Youth and Family Svcs PO Box 491 Beaumont VA 23014

JACKSON, JEANNETTE HELEN, osteopath, nurse; b. Mt. Clemens, Mich., Oct. 24, 1966; d. Robert Fairfield and Charlette Jeanine (Selvy) J. ADN, Mercy Coll. of Detroit, 1989, BSN, 1990; DO, Mich. State U., 1996. RN, Mich. Cert. EMT, AEMT. Basic EMT-A dispatcher Mich. Ambulance Svc., Detroit, 1986-87; EMT-A/AEMT dispatcher Paragon Ambulance Svc., Detroit, 1987-89; x-ray asst., emergency rm. asst. Beaumont Hosp., Troy, Mich., 1987-89; nurse intern Mt. Clemens (Mich.) Gen. Hosp., 1988-90; shift nurse, emergency rm. St. John Hosp. and Med. Ctr., Detroit, 1989—; intern, family practice, spl. emphasis track Bi-County Cmty. Hosp./Henry Ford Hosp., Detroit, 1996—. USPHS scholar, 1994. Mem. Am. Osteo. Assn., Am. Acad. Osteopathy, Am. Coll. Family Physicians. Roman Catholic. Home: 44770 Kemp St Sterling Heights MI 48314

JACKSON, LARRY ARTHUR, family practice physician; b. Lincoln, Nebr., Jan. 2, 1946; s. Lawrence R. and Verna M. (Wagner) J.; 1 child, Sasha Laurel. BA, Andrews U., 1968; MD, Loma Linda U., 1972, MPH, 1979. Intern Riverside (Calif.) Gen. Hosp., 1972-73; physician Westmoreland Med. Clinic, Eugene, Oreg., 1973-80; pvt. practice Springfield, Oreg., 1980—; bd. dirs. Family Svcs. Coun., Eugene, 1982-85, Emmanuel Credit Counseling, Eugene, 1986-89. Republican. Seventh-Day Adventist. Home: 84973 N Cloverdale Creswell OR 97426 Office: 175 W B St Springfield OR 97477

JACKSON, MARION LEROY, agronomist, soil scientist; b. Reynolds, Nebr., Nov. 30, 1914; s. Cleve L. and Belle Josephine (Hanson) J.; m. Chrystie Marie Bertramson, Sept. 2, 1937; children—Marjorie Lee, Virginia Lynn (Mrs. Bruce P. Conlon), Stanley Bertram, Douglas Mark. B.S. maxima cum laude with high distinction, U. Nebr., 1936, M.S., 1937, D.Sc. (hon.), 1974; Ph.D., U. Wis., 1939. Land classification aide U.S. Dept. Agr., Lincoln, Nebr., 1936-37; grad. research asst. U. Wis., Madison, 1937-39; postdoctoral fellow U. Wis., 1939-41, instr., 1941-42, asst. prof., 1942-45, asso. prof., 1946-50, prof., 1950-74, Franklin Hiram King Disting. prof., 1974—; chemist Purdue U., 1945-46; vis. prof. Cornell U., 1959; disting. vis. prof. U. Wash., Seattle, 1973; mem. panel on disposition radioactive wastes Nat. Acad. Scis., 1976-77; lectr. U.S., Canadian govts., numerous univs. Author: Soil Chemical Analysis, 1958, Soil Chemical Analysis-Advanced Course, 1956, 2d edit., 1969; contbr. articles to profl. jours. Troop chmn. Four Lakes council Boy Scouts Am., 1965, scoutmaster, 1966. Recipient Soil Sci. Achievement award, 1958. Fellow AAAS, Am. Soc. Agronomy, Nat. Acad. Sci., Soil Sci. Soc. Am. (past pres.; Disting. Mem. award 1983, Career award 1986), Mineral Soc. Am.; mem. Clay Minerals Soc. (past pres., Disting. Mem. award 1977), Internat. Soc. Soil Sci., Mineral Soc. London, Phi Beta Kappa, Sigma Xi, Phi Lambda Upsilon, Alpha Zeta, Gamma Sigma Delta, Pi Mu Epsilon. Home: 309 Ozark Trl Madison WI 53705-2534 Office: U Wis 1525 Observatory Dr Madison WI 53706-1207

JACKSON, MARY L., health services executive; b. Phila., June 25, 1938; d. John Francis and Helen Catherine (Peranteau) Martin; m. Howard Clark Jackson III, Dec. 17, 1954; children: Michael, Mark, Brian. Student Bucks County Community Coll., 1977-83. Asst. mgr. retail div. Sears Roebuck & Co., Bensalem, Pa., 1972-77; educator, adminstr., dir. Trevose Behavior Modification Program, Pa., 1975—, leadership tng. workshops, 1979—; participant rsch. studies in field; salesman Makefield Real Estate, Morrisville, Pa., 1977-78; mortgage fin. cons. Tom Dunphy Real Estate, Feasterville, Pa., 1978-81; weight loss cons., Hulmeville, Pa., 1984—, also TV and radio appearances on behavior modification for weight loss and maintenance. Co-author: The Official Calorie Book; pub., columnist monthly newsletter The Modifier, 1977—. Recipient Chapel of Four Chaplain award, 1977. Mem. Assn. Advancement of Behavior Therapy, Bucks County Bd. Realtors, Hulmeville Hist. Soc. (a founder, charter mem.). Democrat. Presbyterian. Avocations: reading, classical music, speed walking, knitting, fishing. Home: 218 Main St Langhorne PA 19047-5635

JACKSON, NICK CURTIS, health facility administrator, educator; b. Emporia, Kans., Jan. 26, 1966; s. John A. and Roberta Kay (Moehlman) J. BA, U. Kans., 1988, MA, 1991, PhD, 1994. Acting adminstr. Countryside Health Ctr., Topeka, 1995-96; exec. dir. Kelly House Residential Facilities, Topeka, 1995-96; asst. prof. apllied psychology Eastern Wash. U., 1996—; adj. prof. Washburn U., Topeka, 1995—; rsch. asst. gerontology ctr. Kans. U., Lawrence, 1994; cons. Douglas County Sr. Svcs., Lawrence, 1992-94. Counselor Hdqs. Crisis Intervention Ctr., Lawrence, 1993-94. Grad. trainee fellow NIH, 1993-94. Mem. APA, Nat. Profl. Nursing Home Adminstrs. Assn., Alzheimers Assn. (VIP award Topeka chpt. 1995). Unitarian. Home: 23 W 15th Ave Spokane WA 99203 Office: Eastern Wash U 135H Martin Hall Cheney WA 99004

JACKSON, RAYMOND CARL, cytogeneticist; b. Medora, Ind., May 7, 1928; s. Thornton Comadore and Flossie Oliva (Booker) J.; m. T. June Snyder, Oct. 24, 1947; children: Jeffrey Wayne, Rebecca June. AB, Ind. U., 1952, AM, 1953; PhD, Purdue U., 1955. Instr. to asst. prof. U. N.Mex., Albuquerque, 1955-58; asst. prof. of Botany U. Kans., Lawrence, 1958-60, assoc. prof. of Botany, 1961-64, prof. of Botany, 1964-71, prof. and chmn. Botany, 1969-71; prof. and chmn. biol. scis. Tex. Tech U., Lubbock, 1971-78, Horn prof. of Biol. Scis., 1990—; chmn. interdepartmental PhD Program in Genetics, U. Kans., chmn. dept. Botany, U. Kans., 1969-71; speaker and presenter in field. Contbr. numerous articles to profl. jours. Staff sgt. USAF, 1946-49. Mem. Genetics Soc. Am., Genetics Soc. of Can., Soc. for the Study of Evolution, Botanical Soc. of Am. (BSA Merit award 1992), Am. Soc. Plant Taxonomists, Internat. Orgn. of Plant Biosystematists, Delta Phi Alpha, Sigma Xi, Phi Sigma. Republican. Home: 7922A Aberdeen Ave Lubbock TX 79424-2808 Office: Dept Biol Scis Tex Tech Univ Lubbock TX 79409

JACKSON, RICHARD JOSEPH, epidemiologist, public health physician, educator; b. Newark, Oct. 23, 1945; s. Robert Joseph Jackson and Dorothy C. (Devine) Connolly; m. Joan M. Guilford, June 21, 1975; children: Brendan, Devin, Galen. AB in Biology, St. Peter's Coll., Jersey City, 1969; M in Med. Sci., Rutgers Med. Sch., 1971; MD, U. Calif. San Francisco, San Francisco, 1973; MPH in Epidemiology, U. Calif. Berkeley, Berkeley, 1979. Diplomate Am. Bd. Pediats., Am. Bd. Preventive Medicine, Nat. Bd. Med. Examiners; lic. MD, Calif. Intern, resident U. Calif., San Francisco, 1973-74, 77-78; resident San Francisco Gen. Hosp. U. Calif., 1974-75; officer Epidemic Intelligence Svc. U.S. Pub. Health Svc., Albany, N.Y., 1975-77; spl. epidemiologist World Health Orgn., Bihar State, India, 1976; chief pesticide unit Epidemiol. Studies Sect. Calif. State Dept. Health Svcs., Berkeley, 1979-82, chief, 1982-91, 92-94; chief divsn. communicable disease control U. Calif., San Francisco, 1992-94; dir. Nat. Ctr. Environ. Health, Disease Control and Prevention, Atlanta, 1994—; acting chief office environ. health hazard assessment, pub. health med. officer III Calif. State Dept. Health Svcs., Sacramento, 1988-90; chief hazard identification and risk assessment br., pub. health med. officer III Calif. State Dept. Health Svcs., Berkeley, 1990-91; chief hazard identification and risk assessment br. office environ. health hazard assessment, pub. health med. adminstr. I Calif. EPA, Berkeley, 1991-92; chief divsn. communicable disease control Calif. State Dept. Health Svcs., 1992-94; dir. Nat. Ctr. Environ. Health Ctrs. Disease Control and Prevention, Atlanta, 1994—; adj. lectr. U. Calif. San Francisco, 1980—, asst. clin. prof., 1986—, U. Calif. Davis, 1982-86, 87—; attending pediatrician Children's Hosp. Med. Ctr., Oakland, Calif., 1978-85; adj. asst. clin. prof. pediatrics Albany (N.Y.) Med. Coll., 1975-78. Editl. bd. mem. Am. Jour. Indsl. Medicine, 1994—, Environ. Rsch., 1988—; contbr. articles to profl. jours. Lt. comdr. USPHS, 1975-77. Recipient Cert. of Appreciation Agy. for Toxic Substances and Disease Registry, 1990, Surgeon Gen.'s Cert. of Appreciation, 1987. Fellow Am. Acad. Pediatrics; mem. APHA, Physians for Social Responsibility, Soc. Occupational and Environ. Health, Epidemic Intelligence Svc. Alumni Assn., Rutgers Med Sch. Alumni Assn., U. Calif. San Francisco Alumni-Faculty Assn. Office: Nat Ctr Environ Health Ctrs Disease Control (F-29) 4770 Buford Hwy NE Atlanta GA 30341-3724

JACKSON, RICHARD THOMAS, medical scientist, pharmaceutical consultant; b. Detroit, Jan. 19, 1930; s. Frank James and Jennie Hedwig (Bloom) J.; m. Astrid Karin Tindall, May 25, 1956; children: Keith Richard, Neil Thomas. BS, U. Detroit, 1952, MS, 1954; PhD, Fla. State U., 1960. Teaching fellow U. Detroit, 1952-54; instr. Fla. State U., Tallahassee, 1956-58; assoc. prof. Loyola U., New Orleans, 1958-63; rsch. dir. otolaryngology Emory U., Atlanta, 1966—; prof. surgery Emory Univ. Sch. Med., Atlanta, 1976—; rsch. physiologist VA Med. Ctr., Atlanta, 1988—; cons. Proctor & Gamble, Storz Janssen, Merrell-Dow, 1990—; head Balance Disorder Lab., Emory Clinic, 1988—. Contbr. articles to profl. jours. Recipient Ga. Lions award Ga. Lions Lighthouse, Atlanta, 1985-91; Japan Rhinological Soc. fellow, 1987, Public Health Svc. fellow Washington, 1965. Mem. Assn. Rsch. in Otolaryngology (membership chmn., 1977), Am. Acad. Otolaryngology (com. on drugs and rsch., 1974-79, Honor award 1980). Office: Emory Clinic 1265 Clifton Rd NE Atlanta GA 30307-1231

JACKSON, SHARON JUANITA, management consultant; b. Modesto, Calif., Sept. 21, 1938; d. H. Edward and Beatrice C. (Wright) Melin; m. John L. George, Apr. 27, 1956 (div. 1974); children: Terri A., Tami L., Timothy J., Tobin E. BS in Edn. magna cum laude, Calif. State U., Hayward, 1965; MEd Guidance and Counseling, Hardin-Simmons U., 1976; MBA in Mgmt., Golden Gate U., 1984. Cert. elem. edn., Calif., elem., secondary counseling, Tex. Tchr. elem. Hayward (Calif) Unified Sch. Dist., 1965-73; tchr. diagnostics, group therapist Tex. Youth Coun., Brownwood, 1974-75; assoc. dir. New Directions Psychiat. Half Way House, Abilene, Tex., 1975-77; exec. dir. Mental Health Assn., Abilene, 1977-78, San Francisco, 1979-84; pres. Health Mktg. & Mgmt., San Francisco, 1983—; exec. dir., cons. Vision of Am. At Peace, Berkeley, Calif., 1984, Oakes Children's Ctr., San Francisco, 1985-87; mktg. dir. Mental Health Providers of Calif., 1987-90; prin., v.p. health care devel. Sakhalin region, Russia Health Marketing and Mgmt., 1990-92; instr. managed care U. San Francisco, 1994; sr. assoc. Behavioral Health Alliance dir. nat. practice 1991-92; founding exec. dir., v.p. adminstrn. Planet Live Earthbeat TV, Inc.; bd. dirs. PL Enterprises, Inc.; vis. lectr. McMurry Coll., Abilene, 1976-78; cons. Dyess AFB, Abilene, 1976-78, Abilene Youth Ctr., 1976-78; founder, pres. Health Mktg. & Mgmt.; speaker in field, 1979—. Chair Commn. on Status of Women of Marin County, Calif., 1985—; mem. adv. con. Displaced Homemaker Project, Sacramento, 1985-90; founder, Children's Mental Health Policy Bd., 1984-90; pres. Artisans Gallery, Mill Valley, Calif., 1984—. Grantee Fed. Dept. Justice, Brownwood, 1975, pvt. community founds., Calif., 1979-87. Mem. NAFE, Council of Calif. Mental Health Contractors, Am. Soc. Profl. Exec. Women. Avocations: travel, gourmet cooking, hiking, public speaking. Home and Office: PO Box 2392 Mill Valley CA 94942-2392

JACKSON, STANLEY WEBBER, psychiatrist, medical historian; b. Montreal, Que., Can., Nov. 17, 1920; came to U.S., 1952; s. Clarence Stanley and Ada D. (Webber) J.; m. Joan Katherine Currie, Aug. 12, 1946. BCom, McGill U., 1941, MD, CM, 1950; MA, Yale U., 1975. Diplomate Am. Bd. Psychiatry and Neurology. Gen. med. intern Royal Victoria Hosp., Montreal, 1950-51; resident in psychiatry Provincial Mental Hosp, Essondale, B.C., Can., 1951-52; resident in psychiatry Pinel Hosp., Seattle, 1952-54, staff psychiatrist, acting med. dir., 1954-57; diploma San Francisco Psychoanalytic Inst., 1962, Seattle Psychoanalytic Tng. Ctr., 1962; pvt. practice Seattle, 1957-64; rsch. fellow Yale U., New Haven, 1964-66, asst. prof., assoc. prof. psychiatry and history of medicine, 1966-75, prof., 1975—, exec. dir. Yale Psychiat. Inst., 1987-89. Author: Melancholia and Depression: From Hippocratic Times to Modern Times, 1986; editor: Observations on Maniacal Disorders (William Pargeter), 1988, Jour. of History of Medicine and Allied Scis., 1992—; contbr. numerous articles to book revs. to med. jours., chpts. to books. Flying officer RCAF, 1941-45, ETO, PTO. Fellow Am. Psychiat. Assn. (life); mem. Am. Assn. for History Medicine, Am. Hist. Assn. Home: 72 Downs Rd Bethany CT 06524-3616 Office: Yale U Sect History of Med 333 Cedar St New Haven CT 06510-3206

JACKSON, STEPHANIE ANN, nurse; b. Thomasville, N.C., Jan. 2, 1960; d. Ellis Wade and Nancy (Myers) J. BSN, East Carolina U., 1982. Staff nurse Pitt County Meml. Hosp., Greenville, N.C., 1981-83, N.C. Bapt. Hosp., Winston-Salem, N.C., 1983-87, Duke U. Med. Ctr., Durham, N.C., 1987-91, Rex Hosp., Raleigh, N.C., 1991-94; nurse clinician Health Infusion, Morrisville, N.C., 1994; nurse clinician Coram Health Care (formerly Health Infusion), Morrisville, N.C., 1995, infusion care mgr. Goldsboro and Kinston brs., 1995—. Republican. Home: 4616 Bayspring Ln Raleigh NC 27613

JACKSON, SUZANNE ELISE, health education coordinator; b. Webster, Mass., Mar. 1, 1942; d. John Edward and Marguerite Emmaline (Plante) Baczek; m. Dale Lynne Bagby, Sept. 28, 1968 (div. July 1975); m. Stephen Harvey Jackson, July 12, 1975; 1 child, Gabrielle Benette. Diploma, Henry Heywood Hosp., 1963; BA, U. Redlands, 1975. RN Calif. Clin. instr. surgery Henry Heywood Hosp., Gardner, Mass., 1963-64; asst. head nurse Los Gatos/Santa Clara County Valley Med. Ctr., San Jose, Calif., 1964-68; head nurse oper. rm. Good Samaritan Hosp., San Jose, Calif., 1970-76; corp. officer SHJ Corp., San Jose, Calif., 1976—; health edn. coord. Ac. Medicine Symposium, Monte Sereno, Calif., 1980—; design cons. Suzanne Jackson Designs, Monte Sereno, Calif., 1986—; pres. Calif. Med. Assn. Alliance, 1994-95, bd. dirs., 1986-96. Bd. dirs. Santa Clara County Med. Assn. Aux., San Jose, 1980—, pres. 1985-86; leader, sch. coord. Girl Scouts U.S., Los Gatos, 1983-89; fundraiser Hillbrook Sch., Los Gatos, 1983-90; bd. dirs LWV, Los Gatos, 1986-90; mem. Monte Sereno City Coun., 1994—. Recipient Gilbert & Sullivan Soc. Gypsy Robe, 1984. Mem. Brandies U. Women, Capitol Club Silicon Valley. Republican. Office: 15984 Grandview Ave Monte Sereno CA 95030-3118

JACKSON, WILLIAM BRUCE, biology educator; b. Milw., Sept. 10, 1926; s. Walter Raleigh and Dorothy (Greene) J.; m. Shirley Jean Slentz, Sept. 6, 1952; children: Beth, Mark, Craig. BA, U. Wis.-Madison, 1948, MA, 1949; ScD, Johns Hopkins U., 1952. Registered sanitarian; cert. pub. pesticide operator. Biologist, Am. Mus. Natural History, C.Z., 1952 NRC, U.S. Trust Ter., 1955-57; sr. asst. scientist USPHS, Atlanta, 1952-55; from asst. prof. to prof. biol. scis. Bowling Green State U., Ohio, 1957-84, Univ. prof., 1981—, emeritus, 1985—, dir. Environ. Studies Ctr., Ctr. Environ. Rsch., 1970-84; pres. Rodent Mgmt. Inc., 1982-85; pres., chmn. Biocenotics, Inc., 1985—; sec. Internat. Pest Mgmt. Cons.; cons. WHO, FAO of UN, Rockefeller Found., food processing industries US-AID, NRC, pest conrol industry. Editor conf. procs. Contbr. articles to profl. publs. Served to lt. USPHS, 1952-55. Recipient S.S. Casper Disting. Faculty award Bowling Green State U., 1968, Disting. Svc. award Health Planning Assn., 1980, Ann. Educator award Ohio Alliance Environ. Edn., 1983, hon. Alumnus Bowling Green State U., 1989, Lifetime Achievement Wildlife Damage Mgmt. award Jack H. Berryman Inst. Utah State U., 1995. Fellow Ohio Acad. Sci. (v.p.), AAAS; mem. ASTM (com. chmn.), Sigma Xi, Omicron Delta Kappa (Man of Yr. 1985), Pi Chi Omega (exec. dir. 1980—). Home: 315 Donbar Dr Bowling Green OH 43402-2716 Office: Bowling Green State U Dept Biol Scis Bowling Green OH 43403

JACOB, FRANÇOIS, biologist; b. Nancy, France, June 17, 1920; s. Simon and Therese (Franck) J.; m. Lysiane Bloch, Nov. 27, 1947 (dec. 1984); children: Pierre, Laurent, Odile, Henri. M.D., Faculty of Medicine, Paris, 1947; D.Sc., Faculty of Scis., Paris, 1954; D.Sc. (hon.), U. Chgo., 1965. Asst. Pasteur Inst., 1950-56, head dept. cellular genetics, 1960-92, pres., 1982-88; prof. cellular genetics Coll. of France, 1964-92. Author: The Logic of Life, 1970; The Possible and the Actual, 1981, The Statue Within, 1987. Recipient Charles Leopold Mayer prize, 1962; Nobel prize in physiology and medicine (with A. Lwoff and J. Monod), 1965. Mem. Académie des Sciences (Paris); fgn. mem. Royal Danish Acad. Scis. and Letters, Am. Acad. Arts and Scis., Nat. Acad. Scis. (U.S.), Am. Philos. Soc., Royal Soc. (London), Académie Royale de Médecine de Belgique, Acad. Scis. Hungary, Royal Acad. Scis. Madrid. Office: Pasteur Inst, 25 Rue du Dr Roux, 75724 Paris Cedex 15, France

JACOB, JOHN DEWITT, retired orthodontist, state official; b. Columbus, Ohio, Sept. 4, 1938; s. John George and Lucille (Young) J.; m. Saundra Anne, July 30, 1966; children: Sharon Sue, James John. DDS, Ohio State U., 1963, MS, 1966. Pediatric dentistry intern Eastman Dental Ctr., Rochester, N.Y., 1963-64; orthodontist Worthington (Ohio) Orthodontic Ctr. Inc., 1966-75; pvt. practice Worthington, 1975-91; ret., 1991; vice chmn. Ohio Unemployment Compensation Bd. Rev., Columbus, 1993—; instr. Ohio State U., Columbus, 1967-70, asst. prof. 1970-75. Chmn. condrs. com. Columbus Symphony Orch., 1970-71; mem. bd. control Ohio Agr. R & D Ctr., Wooster, 1975-82; trustee Ohio State U., Columbus, 1975-84, chmn. bd., 1983-84. Fellow Internat. Coll. Dentists; mem. ADA, Columbus Dental Soc. (Disting. Svc. award 1970), Ohio Dental Assn., Am. Assn. Orthodontists, Gt. Lakes Soc. Orthodontists (chmn. pub. rels. 1972), Ohio State U. Dental Alumni Assn. (bd. govs. 1984-89), Worthington Jaycees (pres. 1969-76), Columbus Dental Vets. (pres. 1988-89), Rotary (Paul Harris fellow). Home: 2384 Tremont Rd Columbus OH 43221-3726 Office: 145 S Front St Columbus OH 43215-4116

JACOB, ROBERT ALLEN, surgeon; b. Cleve., July 25, 1941; s. John B. and Elaine Irene (Puleo) J.; m. M. Elaine Sheppard, Aug. 23, 1980; children: Kristen Elizabeth, Alexandra Elaine. BA, Case Western Res. U., 1963; MSc, Ohio State U., 1966, MD, 1969. Diplomate Am. Bd. Orthopaedic Surgeons, Am. Acad. Pain Mgmt. Orthopaedic surgeon Bluegrass Orthop. Group PSC, Louisville, 1976—; pres. med. staff Sts. Mary & Elizabeth Hosp., Louisville, 1991—; med. dir. Ky. Pain Therapy Ctr. Contbr. articles to profl. jours. Local fundraising chmn. Orthop. Edn. and Rsch. Found., Sts. Mary & Elizabeth Hosp., 1990-91; bd. dirs. Kentuckiana Hemophilia Found., 1987-89, Hosp. Found., 1991-93. Maj. U.S. Army, 1974-76. Recipient Outstanding Svc. award Kentuckiana Hemophilia Found., 1986, Cert. of Recognition, 1987. Fellow Am. Acad. Orthopaedic Surgeons; mem. Ky. Med. Assn., Southern Med. Assn., Jefferson County Med. Assn., Louisville Orthopaedic Assn., Louisville Soc. Physicians and Surgeons (v.p. 1980, pres. 1984). Republican. Roman Catholic. Home: 7512 Chestnut Hill Dr Prospect KY 40059-9484 Office: Bluegrass Orthop Group 1900 Bluegrass Ave Ste 203 Louisville KY 40215-1144

JACOBEY, JOHN ARTHUR, III, surgeon, educator; b. Albuquerque, Oct. 27, 1929; s. John Arthur Jr. and Zelma Mae (Wolfe) Jacobey Mann. AB, Dartmouth Coll., 1951; postgrad., U. Colo., 1951-53; MD, Harvard U., 1956. Diplomate Am. Bd. Surgery, Am. Bd. Thoracic Surgery. Intern Jefferson Davis Hosp., Baylor U., Houston, 1956-57; resident Boston City Hosp., 1957-58, Dartmouth Med. Ctr., Hanover, N.H., 1958-59, Peter Bent Brigham Hosp., 1962-63, St. Mary's Hosp., London, 1963-64, Baylor Affiliated Hosp., Houston, 1964-65; rsch. fellow Harvard Med. Sch., 1959-62; pvt. practice medicine specializing in cardiovascular and thoracic surgery Denver, 1965-71, 72-76; staff surgeon Cheyenne (Wyo.) VA Med. Ctr., 1971-72; asst. prof. clin. surgery SUNY, Stony Brook, 1977-83; pvt. practice medicine specializing in cardiovascular and thoracic surgery Dover, N.J., 1984-89; active cardiothoracic surg. staff Robert Wood Johnson U. Hosp., New Brunswick, N.J., 1992—; clin. instr. surgery U. Colo., Denver, 1965-69; clin. assoc. prof. surgery U. Medicine and Dentistry of N.J., Robert Wood Johnson Med. Sch., New Brunswick, 1984—; leader cardiothoracic surg. delegation to China, Citizen Amb. Program of People to People Internat., 1994. Prin. investigator, author publs. on synchronous assisted circulation, superior mediastinal exploration. Lay reader, chalice bearer Episcopal Ch., Manhasset, N.Y., 1976-83, Mountain Lakes, N.J., 1984-90, Westfield, N.J., 1990—. Fellow Am. Coll. Chest Physicians; mem. AMA, Soc. Thoracic Surgeons, Am. Thoracic Soc., N.J. Soc. Thoracic Surgeons, N.Y. Soc. Thoracic Surgery, N.J. Acad. Medicine, Am. Heart Assn., N.J. Med. Soc., Mass. Med. Soc., Harvard Club (Boston), Univ. Club (Denver). Republican. Office: 406B Durham Ctr 4 Ethel Rd Edison NJ 08817

JACOBO, ELIAS, urologist; b. Panama, Panama, June 18, 1944; s. Joseph and Celia (Doriat) J.; m. Nancy Heger, Nov. 3, 1982; children: Cory, Jason, Sara. MD, U. Mex., Mexico City, 1967. Diploamte Am. Bd. Urology. Gen. surgery intern U. Iowa, 1971-72, prostate cancer fellow, 1975-76; urology resident U. Iowa Hosps. & Clinics, 1972-76; pvt. practice Urology Cons., Longwood, Fla. Office: Urology Consultants Ste 302 515 State Rd 434W Longwood FL 32750-5162

JACOBS, BARUCH, plastic surgeon; b. N.Y.C., Nov. 16, 1956; s. Morris and Sonya Jacobs; m. Robin Jacobs. MD, NYU, 1981. Diplomate Am. Bd. Plastic Surgery, Am. Bd. Surgery. Resident in surgery Boston U. Med. Ctr., 1987; resident in plastic surgery Cleve. Clinic Found., 1987-89; pvt. practice plastic surgery Miami Beach, Fla. Fellow ACS, Am. Soc. Plastic and Reconstructive Surgeons. Office: 524 Arthur Godfrey Rd # 204 Miami Beach FL 33140

JACOBS, BELLA HERTZBERG, gerontologist; b. Bklyn., Mar. 22, 1919; d. Rubin and Pauline (Klaif) Hertzberg; m. Lewis Jacobs; children: Ronald, Paula, Barbara. BA, U. Richmond (Va.), 1940; MA, George Washington U., 1970; EdD, U. So. Calif., 1981. Program asst. Health and Welfare Council, Washington, 1967-68; profl. asst. B'nai B'rith Career and Counseling Service, Washington, 1970-72; sr. program mgr Nat. Council on the Aging, Washington, 1972-88; cons. in field Washington, 1988—; mem. nat. adv. com. later years Am. Found. for Blind, N.Y.C., 1981-83; mem. info consortium Adminstrv. on Aging, Washington, 1983-85. Author: Senior Centers and the At-Risk Older Person, 1980 (with other) A Guidebook for the Educational Goals Inventory, 1984, Organizing a Literacy Program for Older Adults, 1986. Mem. Mont. Co. Commn. on Aging (chair); bd. dirs. Lit. Vols. of Am. (Nat. Capital Area). Mem. Gerontol. Soc., Assn. Adult and Continuing Edn., Assn. Counseling and Devel. Democrat. Jewish. Clubs: Woodmont, Press. Home and Office: 2925 Greenvale Rd Bethesda MD 20815-3126

JACOBS, EDWIN MAX, oncologist, consultant; b. San Francisco, Sept. 9, 1925; s. Edwin Manheim and Floy (Sommer) J. BA, Reed Coll., 1950; MD, Cornell U., 1954. Intern Bellevue Hosp., N.Y.C., 1954-55, resident, 1956-57; resident Meml. Sloan-Kettering Cancer Ctr., N.Y.C., 1955-56, fellow in oncology, 1957-59; instr. medicine U. Calif., San Francisco, 1960-63, head clin. cancer research, 1960-76, asst. prof., 1963-69, assoc. clin. prof., 1969-76; assoc. chief clin. investigations br. Nat. Cancer Inst., Bethesda, Md., 1976-85; assoc. exec. officer No. Calif. Oncology Group, Palo Alto, Calif., 1985—; clin. prof. medicine Cancer Research Inst. U. Calif., San Francisco, 1987—; vis. physician Royal Marsden Hosp., London, 1970; cons. Monsanto Chem. Co., St. Louis, 1985—, G.D. Searle Co., Skokie, Ill., 1985—. Contbr. articles on testicular cancer to med. jours. Bd. dirs. San Francisco Symphony Found., 1968-76. Served with U.S. Army, 1944-46, ETO, PTO. Squibb-Olin fellow Meml. Sloan-Kettering Cancer Ctr., 1965; recipient Spl. Achievment award NIH, 1983. Fellow ACP; mem. AMA (Recognition award 1985—), Am. Soc. Hematology (neoplasia com. 1978-81), Am. Assn. Cancer Research, Am. Soc. Clin. Oncology, Soc. Surg. Oncology, Am. Radium Soc. (v.p. 1978-79), San Francisco Mus.'s Soc. Home: 1860 16th Ave San Francisco CA 94122-4540

JACOBS, ELEANOR, social worker; b. Boston, Oct. 27, 1941; m. Donald M. Jacobs, May 29, 1967. AB, Boston U., 1963; MSW, Simmons Coll., 1965. Cert. social worker; lic. ind. clin. social worker, Mass.; diplomate in clin. social work. Clin. social worker Worcester (Mass.) Youth Guidance Ctr., 1965-67, Jewish Family & Children's Svcs., Boston, 1967-73; sr. clinician Charles River Counseling Ctr., Newton, Mass., 1974-85; dir. group psychotherapy Hahnemann Hosp., Brighton, Mass., 1982-86; family therapist Charles River Hosp., Wellesley, Mass., 1986-94; dir. Charles River Hosp. Outpatient Ctr., 1994—; pvt. practice psychotherapy Needham, Mass., 1975—; staff devel. cons. Community Care Systems, Wellesley, 1975—; social work supr., Needham, 1984—. V.p. Temple Beth Shalom, Needham, 1983-88. Mem. NASW, Am. Group Psychotherapy Assn., Northeast Soc. Group Psychotherapy. Home: 105 Woodbine Cir Needham MA 02194-2140

JACOBS, ELEANOR ALICE, retired clinical psychologist, educator; b. Royal Oak, Mich., Dec. 25, 1923; d. Roy Dana and Alice Ann (Keaton) J. B.A., U. Buffalo, 1949, M.A., 1952, Ph.D., 1955. Clin. psychologist VA Hosp., Buffalo, 1954-83; EEO councelor VA Hosp., 1962-79, chief psychology service, 1979-83; clin. prof. SUNY, Buffalo, 1950-83; speaker on psychology to community orgns. and clubs, 1952—; Mem. adult devel. and aging com. NICHD, HEW, 1971-75. Researcher for publs. on hyperbaric medicine, hyperoxygenation effect on cognitive functions in aged. Recipient Outstanding Superior Performance award Buffalo VA Hosp., 1958, Spl. Recognition award SUNY, Buffalo, Spl. Recognition award SUNY, 1971; W.L. McKnight award Miami Heart Inst., 1972; Adminstrs. commendation VA, 1974; Dirs. commendation VA Med. Center, Buffalo, 1978; Disting. Alumni award SUNY, Buffalo, 1983; named Woman of Yr. Bus. and Profl. Women's Clubs, Buffalo, 1973. Mem. Am. Psychol. Assn., Eastern Psychol. Assn., N.Y. State Psychol. Assn., Am. Group Psychotherapy Assn., Am. Soc. Group Psychotherapy and Psychodrama, Psychol. Assn. Western N.Y. (Disting. Achievement award 1976), Group Psychotherapy Assn. Western N.Y., Undersea Med. Soc., Sigma Xi. Home: PO Box 432, Ridgeway, ON Canada L0S 1N0

JACOBS, ELIAS, colon and rectal surgeon; b. Bklyn., Aug. 26, 1935; s. Harry and Celia (Hornung) J.; children: Anne Kimberly, Alison Paige. AB, Cornell U., 1956; MD, SUNY, Bklyn., 1960; postgrad., St. Mark's Hosp., London, 1969. Diplomate Am. Bd. Colon and Rectal Surgery. Intern in surgery U. Calif. Hosp., San Francisco, 1960-61; resident in gen. surgery U. Calif., San Francisco, 1964-67, VA Hosp., San Francisco, 1963-64; resident in colon and rectal surgery Temple U. Hosp., Phila., 1967-69; pvt. practice colon and rectal surgery Daly City, Calif., 1969—; cons. San Francisco Gen. Hosp., 1970-74, U.S. Naval Hosp., Oakland, Calif., 1972-82; clin. asst. prof. surgery U. Calif., San Francisco, 1976-79; bd. dirs. Am. Bd. Colon and Rectal Surgery, 1986-90; chmn. dept. surgery Seton Med. Ctr., Daly City, 1981-87, sec.-treas. med. staff, 1994-96. Pres. No. Calif. Soc. Colon and Rectal Surgeons, 1977-78. Capt. USAF, 1961-63. Fellow ACS, Am. Soc. Colon and Rectal Surgeons (mem. exec. coun. 1983-86, trustee Rsch. Found. 1982-88), AMA (mem. sect. coun. on colon and rectal surgery 1976-77), San Francisco Surg. Soc., Calif. Med. Assn., San Mateo County Med. Assn. Office: 1800 Sullivan Ave Daly City CA 94015

JACOBS, ERNEST CHRISTOPHER, physician; b. Rochester, N.Y., July 16, 1957; s. Robert Michael and Maria (Kulbieda) J.; m. Elisabeth de Guinald Farre, Aug. 9, 1980; children: Christopher, Michael, Katrina. BS in Chemistry, Carnegie-Mellon U., 1979; MD, U. Pitts., 1982. Resident in pediatrics Mercy Hosp. of Pitts., 1982-83; pvt. practice computer cons. Pitts., 1983-84; med. staff fellow NIH, Bethesda, Md., 1984-86, sr. staff fellow div. computer rsch. and tech., 1986; clin. assoc. Cleve. Clinic Found., 1986-89, asst. staff, 1989-93, assoc. staff, 1993—. Co-author: (chpts.) Surgery of Epilepsy, 1991, Progress in Standardization in Health Care Informatics, 1993; contbr. articles to Cleve. Clinic Jour. of Medicine, Jour. Clin. Monitoring, IEEE Computer and IEEE Transactions in Biomed. Engring. Mem. IEEE, AMA, ASTM (subcom. chmn. 31.16), Am. Med. Informatics Assn., HL7 Tau Beta Pi. Democrat. Roman Catholic. Office: Cleve Clinic Found Dept Neurology S51 9500 Euclid Ave Cleveland OH 44195-5221

JACOBS, GERALD H., neuroscientist; b. Brattleboro, Vt., Sept. 14, 1934. BA, U. Vt., 1956; PhD, Ind U., 1963. Asst./assoc. prof. U. Tex., Austin, 1964-69; prof. U. Calif., Santa Barbara, 1969—, faculty rsch. lectr., 1996. Author: Comparative Color Vision, 1981; contbr. articles to profl. jours. Recipient Rank Prize in Optoelectronics award Rank Prize Found., 1988. Fellow AAAS, Optical Soc. Am.; mem. Am. Physio. Soc., Soc. for Neuroscience, Assn. for Rsch. in Vision and Opthalmology. Office: Univ of Calif Neurosci Rsch Inst Santa Barbara CA 93106

JACOBS, GRETCHEN HUNTLEY, psychiatrist; b. N.Y.C., July 20, 1941; d. Louis Gordon and Gertrude Mary (Eberz) La Pointe; m. Michael Edward Jacobs, Dec. 26, 1965 (div.); children: Dylan Huntley, Danielle La Pointe. BS, Fordham U., N.Y.C., 1963; MD, SUNY, Bklyn., 1968. Diplomate Am. Bd. Psychiatry and Neurology, Am. Bd. Child and Adolescent Psychiatry. Pediatric intern St. Luke's Hosp., N.Y.C., 1968-69; psychiatry resident George Washington U. Hosp., Washington, 1969-71; child psychiatry resident Beth Israel Hosp., Boston, 1972-73, McLean Hosp. Children's Ctr., Waltham, Mass., 1973-74; coord. health and human devel. Martha's Vinyard Sch. Sys., 1974-80; pvt. practice adult and adolescent/child psychiatry Martha's Vinyard, Mass., 1974—; asst. clin. prof. child psychiatry Tufts U. Med. Sch., Boston, 1974—; staff psychiatrist Martha's Vineyard Hosp., 1974—. Contbr. articles to profl. jours. Cons. Mass. Dept. Pub. Health Svcs. to Multi-Handicapped Children, 1974-75; bd. dirs. Mass. Dept. Social Svcs., 1979-83; founding mem., clin. dir. Vineyard Child Assault Prevention Project, 1986, Com. on Rural Child Psychiatry, 1988-92. Mem. Am. Psychiat. Assn., New England Coun. Child and Adolescent Psychiatry, Am. Acad. Child and Adolescent Psychiatry, Mass. Med. Soc., Rotary Internat. (sec. Martha's Vineyard chpt.), Amnesty Internat.. Home and Office: Tashmoo Farm RR1 Box 600 Vineyard Haven MA 02568

JACOBS, JOHN WILLIAM, psychiatrist; b. Washington, Dec. 27, 1943; s. Arthur THeodore and Marcia Alexandria (Fox) J.; m. Peri Pike; 1 child, Seth Jordan; m. Vivian F. Diller, Jan. 11, 1986; children: Jordana, Gideon, Gabriel. BA, Brandeis U., 1965; MD, Albert Einstein Coll. Medicine, 1969. Resident in psychiatry Albert Einstein Coll. Medicine, Bronx, N.Y., 1970-73; fellow in liaison psychiatry Montefiore Med. Ctr., Bronx, 1973-75, dir. outpatient dept., 1977-82; dir. psychiat. residency tng. Montefiore Med. Ctr., 1982-87; dir. postgrad. psychotherapy tng. program Albert Einstein Coll. Medicine, 1987-91; pvt. practice, N.Y.C., 1973—. Author: Fatherhood and Divorce, 1986; contbr. articles to profl. jours. Fellow Am. Orthopsychiat. Assn.; mem. Am. Psychiat. Assn., Acad. Psychosomatic Medicine, Am. Family Therapy Acad. Office: 180 E 79th St Apt 1D New York NY 10021

JACOBS, JONATHAN S., physician, researcher; b. N.Y.C., June 13, 1947; s. Leo H. and Sara (Golshevsky) J.; m. Dale H. Jacobs; children: Jennifer, Allison, Jordan. AB, U. Rochester, 1968; DMD cum laude, Harvard U., 1971; MD, Vanderbilt U., 1973. Oral surgery intern Vanderbilt U. Hosp., Nashville, 1971-73, resident in surgery, 1973-75, 78; resident in surgery Eastern Va. Grad. Sch. Medicine, 1978-79, resident in plastic surgery, 1979-81; asst. prof. dept. plastic surgery Eastern Va. Med. Sch., 1982-90, assoc. prof., 1991—; chief dept. plastic surgery Med. Ctr. Hosps., 1986-89; med. dir. Plastic Surgery Assocs., Inc., 1993—; chief dept. plastic surgery Sentara Health Systems, 1994—. Contbr. articles to profl. jours.; presenter in field. Mem. ACS, AMA, Am. Soc. Maxillofacial Surgeons (pres.-elect), Am. Soc. Plastic and Reconstructive Surgery, Am. Soc. Temporomandibular Joint Surgeons, Southeastern Soc. Plastic and Reconstructive Surgery, Am. Assn. Oral and Maxillofacial Surgeons, Va. Med. Soc., Va. Soc. Plastic Surgeons (past pres.), Norfolk Acad. Medicine, Omicron Kappa Upsilon, others. Office: Plastic Surgery Assocs Inc 935 First Colonial Rd Virginia Beach VA 23454

JACOBS, JOSHUA J., orthopaedic surgeon; b. Chgo., Apr. 6, 1956; s. Abraham F. and Bernice J.; m. Faye Robbins. BS, Northwestern U., 1977; MD, U. Ill., Chgo., 1981. Diplomate Am. Bd. Orthopaedic Surgery. Assoc. prof. orthopaedic surgery Rush Med. Coll., Chgo., 1994—; adj. prof. Northwestern U., Chgo., 1992—. Recipient Career Devel. award Orthopaedic Rsch. & Edn. Found. Fellow Am. Acad. Orthopaedic Surgery, Hip Soc. (Otto award); mem. ASTM (vice chmn.), Soc. Biomaterials. Office: Midwest Orthopaedics 1725 W Harrison 1063 Chicago IL 60612

JACOBS, KAREN LOUISE, medical technologist; b. Kingston, N.Y., May 7, 1943; d. William Charles and Vera Elizabeth (Kelly) Jacobs; BS in Applied Tech., Empire State Coll., 1976; MS in Pub. Service Adminstrn., Russell Sage Coll., 1982. Sr. lab. technician, hosp. lab. supr. City of Kingston (N.Y.) Labs., 1962-68; sr. rsch. asst. Dudley Obs., Albany, N.Y., 1972-75; lab. adminstr. Albany Med. Coll., 1976—, mem. faculty, 1982—; mem. infection control com. and subcoms. on AIDS mgmt. and human immunodeficiency virus universal precautions Albany Med. Ctr. Infection Control, 1987—. Bd. dirs. chpt. Leukemia Soc. Am., 1983-87; judge sci. and tech. summer issue on excellence in Am. U.S. News and World Report; vol. asst. naturalist Five Rivers Environ. Ctr. Mem. Clin. Lab. Mgmt. Assn. (del. citizen amb. program to China 1989), Am. Soc. Clin. Pathologists, Sierra Club, Earthwatch, Nat. Speleological Soc., Helderburg-Hudson Grotto, Hudsonia (bd. dirs. 1995). Home: 11 Eastmount Dr Apt 202 Slingerlands NY 12159-2168 Office: Albany Med Coll Div Hematology and Oncolgy 47 New Scotland Ave Albany NY 12208-3412

JACOBS, KENT FREDERICK, dermatologist; b. El Paso, Tex., Feb. 13, 1938; s. Carl Frederick and Mercedes D. (Johns) J.; m. Sallie Ritter, Apr. 13, 1971. BS, N.Mex. State U., 1960; MD, Northwestern U., 1964; postgrad., U. Colo., 1967-70. Dir. service unit USPHS, Laguna, N.Mex., 1966-67; pvt. practice specializing in dermatology Las Cruces, N.Mex., 1970—; cons. U.S. Army, San Francisco, 1968-70, cons. NIH, Washington, 1983, Holloman AFB, 1972-77; research assoc. VA Hosp., Denver, 1969-70; preceptor U. Tex., Galveston, 1976-77; mem. clin. staff Tex. Tech U., Lubbock, 1977—; asst. clin. prof. U. N.Mex., Albuquerque, 1972—; bd. dirs. First Nat. Bank of Dona Ana County, Las Cruces, N.Mex., 1987—. Author: Breckkan,

1996; contbr. articles to profl. jours. and popular mags. Trustee Mus. N.Mex. Found., 1987—, mem. bd. regents, 1987—, pres., 1989-91, 95—; bd. dirs. Dona Ana Arts Coun., 1992-93, Border Book Festival, 1996—, N.Mex. State U. Found., 1993—. Invitational scholar Oreg. Primate Ctr., 1968; Acad. Dermatology Found. fellow, 1969; named Disting. Alumnus N.Mex. State U., 1985. Fellow Am. Acad. Dermatology, Royal Soc. Medicine, Soc. Investigative Dermatology; mem. AMA, Fedn. State Med. Bds. (bd. dirs. 1984-86), N.Mex. Med. Soc., N.Mex. Bd. Med. Examiners (pres. 1983-84, N.Mex. State U. Alumni Assn. (bd. dirs. 1975-79), Mil Gracias Club (pres. 1972-74) Pres.'s Assocs., Univ. Ambs., Rotary, Phi Beta Kappa, Beta Beta Beta. Democrat. Presbyterian. Home: 3610 Southwind Rd Las Cruces NM 88005-5556 Office: 2525 S Telshor Blvd # 15-106 Las Cruces NM 88011-5071 also: Mus NM PO Box 2087 Santa Fe NM 87504-2087

JACOBS, MARTIN STUART, oral and maxillofacial surgeon; b. Newark, Oct. 26, 1944; s. Julius and Gertrude (Sokolowsky) J.; m. Linda Claire Afflitto, June 16, 1968; children: Jeffrey, Suzanne. AB, Rutgers U., 1966; DMD, Fairleigh Dickinson Sch. Dentistry, 1970. Cert. Am. Bd. Oral & Maxillofacial Surgery, 1978. Intern Newark Beth Israel Hosp., 1970-71; resident in oral and maxillofacial surgery N.J. Coll. Medicine and Dentistry, 1972-75, chief resident, 1975; chief divsn. oral surgery Mountainside Hosp., Montclair, N.J., 1986-87, asst. chief oral surgery, 1994-95; med. adv. com. Roseland (N.J.) Surg. Ctr., 1985—. Fellow Am. Coll. Oral and Maxillofacial Surgeons; mem. Am. Assn. Oral and Maxillofacial Surgeons, N.J. soc. Oral and Maxillofacial Surgeons. Office: 16 Smull Ave Caldwell NJ 07006

JACOBS, MICHAEL AARON, orthopedic surgeon; b. Newark, Oct. 30, 1953; s. Abraham and Minna (Stolar) J.; m. Margaret Berta Bandomir, Oct. 2, 1984; children: Joshua, Benjamin, Matthew. BS, Bowdoin Coll., 1975; MD, Columbia U., 1979. Intern gen. surgery Hosp. U. Pa., Phila., 1979-80; resident gen. surgery Bryn Mawr (Pa.) Hosp., 1980-81; resident orthopedic surgery Combined Harvard Program, Boston, 1981-85; fellow Johns Hopkins U., Balt., 1985-86, asst. prof. Sch. Medicine, 1986-90, 93—; pvt. practice Clin. Assocs., P.A., Balt., 1991—; team orthopedist Balt. Orioles Baseball, Balt. Bandits Hockey. Editorial assoc. Jour. Arthoplasty, 1991—; editorial bd. Jour. Orthopaedic Tech., 1991—. Fellow Am. Acad. Orthopaedic Surgery; mem. Internat. Soc. Orthopaedic Surgery and Traumatology, Assn. Arthritic Hip and Knee Surgery, Md. Orthopaedic Soc., Md. Soc. Rheumatic Diseases. Office: 5601 Loch Raven Blvd Baltimore MD 21239-2905

JACOBS, PAUL ROBERT, psychologist, artist, consultant; b. N.Y.C., Aug. 1, 1948; s. Harold L. and Muriel Gisherman (Gilman) J.;. AB, Rutgers U., 1970; MA, Fairleigh Dickinson U., 1975; postgrad., Tulane U., 1977-79; PhD, Fla. Inst. Tech., Melbourne, 1982. Lic. psychologist, Ga., mental health counselor, Fla. Psychology intern VA Med. Ctr., Tuskegee, Ala., 1981-82; neuropsychologist Highland Park Hosp., Miami, Fla., 1982; psychologist State of La., Jackson, 1983-84; counselor Auburn, Ala., 1985-86; psychologist State of Ga., Atlanta, 1986-95; psychologist, evaluator Merit Behavioral Care, Inc., Ft. Lauderdale, 1994—; CEO, Ctr. for Treatment Depression, Atlana, 1987-93; staff psychiatrist Psychiat. Inst. Atlanta, 1991-93, Ridgeview Inst., Smyrna, Ga., 1991-93, U. Pavillion Hosp., Tamarac, Fla., 1994—; cons. psychologist Howell Indsl. Clinic, Atlanta, 1991-93, Ga. Dept. Human Resources, Browad County (Fla.) Sheriff's Office, 1995; spkr. Mental Health Assn. Atlanta, 1989-91; psychologist Fla. Dept. Corrections, 1994, med. expert social security divsn. Bd. Hearings and Appeals, 1994—. One-man shows include Loyola U., New Orleans. Mem. APA. Home and Office: 4300 N Ocean Blvd Apt 21F Fort Lauderdale FL 33308-5944

JACOBS, RICHARD DOUGLAS, internist; b. St. Louis, June 22, 1951; s. Richard Douglas and Marcia Agnes (Mochle) J.; m. Susan Ellen McGowan, Aug. 25, 1973; children: Jennifer Lynn, Steven Matthew. MD, St. Louis U. Med. Sch., 1976; MBA, U. Phoenix, 1992. From assoc. med. dir. to v.p. health care delivery FHP Healthcare, Inc., Phoenix, 1988-94; pres. Ariz. div. Talbot Med. Mgmt. Corp., Phoenix, 1994—; witness for managed care U.S. House Ways and Means Com., Washington, 1995. Founding pres. West County Christian Sch., St. Louis, 1984-88; bd. dirs. Valley Christian H.S., Tempe, 1988-92; trustee Dobson Ranch Ch., Chandler, Ariz., 1992—; adv. bd. HopeLink Homeless Shelter, Phoenix, 1994—. Lt. cmdr. U.S. Navy, 1979-81, Guam. Mem. Am. Coll. Physicians, Am. Coll. Physician Execs. Republican. Mem. Ch. of the Nazarene.

JACOBS, RICHARD FULLER, pediatrics and pediatric infectious disease educator; b. Arkadelphia, Ark., May 1, 1952; s. Robert Earl and Addye Lou (Fuller) J.; m. Margaret Ann Pennington; 1 child, Robert Fuller. BS, Henderson State U., 1973; MD, U. Ark., 1977. Cert. Am. Bd. Pediatrics, 1982, Ark., Am. Bd. Pediatric Infectious Diseases, 1994. Asst. prof. pediatrics U. Ark. Med. Sci., Little Rock, 1982-85, assoc. prof. pediatrics, 1985-92, prof. pediatrics, 1992—, Horace C. Cabe prof. pediatrics, 1993—. Editl. bd. mem. Infectious Diseases Newsletter, 1989, The Pediatric Infectious Diseases Jour., 1992, Seminars in Respiratory Infections, 1992, Report on Pediatric Infectious Diseases, 1993. Bd. dirs. KLRE Radio Sta., Little Rock, 1985-91, St. James United Meth. Ch., Little Rock, 1986-90; mem. Ark. Advs. for Children, Little Rock, 1986—. Fellow Royal Soc. Pediatrics of the Philippines (hon.); mem. So. Soc. for Pediatric Rsch. (pres./councillor 1985—, instnl. rep. 1988—, Young Investigator award 1982), Am. Acad. Pediatrics (spkr., com. mem. 1989—), Am. Thoracic Soc. (sec./liaison 1984—, nat. nominating com. 1990-93), Pediatric Infectious Diseases Soc. (councillor 1993—, treas. 1994—), Soc. for Pediatric Rsch. Office: Ark Childrens Hosp 800 Marshall St Little Rock AR 72202-3510

JACOBS, RICHARD LEE, orthopedic surgeon, educator; b. Elsberry, Mo., Dec. 29, 1930; s. H. Lee and Hazel (Ruth) J.; m. Anne Schmitt, Sept. 17, 1954; children: Gregory, Hugh, LeAnne. BA, State U. Iowa, 1952, MS, 1962, MD, 1956. Intern Butterworth Hosp., Grand Rapids, Mich., 1956-57; resident in orthopedic surgergy State U. Iowa Hosp., Iowa City, 1959-65; rsch. fellow Harvard U.-Mass. Gen. Hosp., Boston, 1961-62; prof. orthopedic surgery U. Ill., Chgo., 1965-74; prof., head orthopedic surgery Albany (N.Y.) Med. Coll., 1974-96; adj. prof. Rensselaer Poly. Inst., Troy, N.Y.; cons. Ill. State Div. Svcs. for Crippled Children, 1965-74, Union Health Svcs., Chgo., 1966-68; staff physician Presbyn. St. Luke's Hosp., Chgo., 1966-70, Dixon (Ill.) State Sch., 1966-74, West Side VA Hosp., Chgo., 1968-74, Cook County Hosp., Chgo., 1972-74, Community Health Plan, Albany, 1976—, Albany VA Hosp., 1974—, St. Peter's Hosp., Albany, N.Y. State Dept. Disability Found. Contbr. articles to profl. jours. Lt. comdr. USN, 1957-59, USNR, 1959-67. Nat. Found. for Infantile Paralysis fellow, 1954, Arthritis and Rheumatism Found. fellow, 1959-61, Orthopaedic Rsch. and Edn. Found. fellow, 1961-62, NIH fellow, 1962, USPHS fellow, 1965-66. Fellow Am. Acad. Orthopedic Surgeons; mem. Ill. State Acad. Sci., Iowa Orthopaedic Alumni Assn., Orthopaedic Rsch. Soc., AAAS, Lincoln Orthopaedic Soc., N.Y. Acad. Sci., Am. Orthopaedic Foot Soc., Am. Soc. Bone and Mineral Rsch., Am. Orthopaedic Assn., Harvard Combined Orthopaedic Alumni, N.Y. State Orthopaedic Soc., Assn. Orthopaedic Chmn., Sigma Xi. Democrat. Congregationalist. Home: 41 Linda Ct Delmar NY 12054-3516 Office: Albany Med Coll New Scotland Albany NY 12208

JACOBS, RUTH SHEILA, psychologist; b. N.Y.C., June 23, 1949; d. Irwin and Lea (Hillman) Polk; B.A. magna cum laude, N.Y.U., 1970; M.A., Fordham U., 1972, Ph.D., 1976; m. Alan S. Jacobs, June 1, 1969; children: Lisa Nicole, Laurie Jennifer. Psychologist, Rockland County Mental Health Clinic, Orangeburg, N.Y., 1976-78, St. Peters Coll., Englewood Cliffs, N.J., 1979, 82; pvt. practice Englewood, N.J., 1980—; asst. supr., clin. assoc. Ackerman Inst. Family Therapy, N.Y.C., 1982-84; clin. dir. Family Therapy Assocs., Englewood, 1983-88; clin. supr. Willowbrook Outreach Ctr., Wayne, N.J., 1986-88; faculty Family Inst., Ridgefield Park, N.J., 1988-90, Nat. Inst. for Psychotherapies, Inc., N.Y.C., 1989-90; clin. supr. psychol. svcs. Fairleigh Dickenson U., Hackensack, N.J., 1989-92. Fellow Am. Orthopsychiat. Assn.; mem. Am. Psychol. Assn., N.J. Psychol. Assn., N.J. Acad. Psychology, Assn. for Advancement of Family Therapy in N.J. (pres. 1990-94), Bergen County Assn. Lic. Psychologists, Am. Assn. Marriage & Family Therapy (approved supr.), Phi Beta Kappa, Sigma Chi. Office: 75 Grand Ave Englewood NJ 07631-3522

JACOBS, TIMOTHY ANDREW, epidemiologist, international health consultant; b. St. Petersburg, Fla., Nov. 5, 1944; s. W. Andrew and Virginia (Ott) J.; m. Carolyn Martin, Nov. 4, 1972; 1 child, Jenny Thuy Ha. BSN, U. Fla., 1970; MS, PNP, U. Utah, 1976; PhD, Internat. Inst. Advanced Studies, 1979; C.T.M., Liverpool (Eng.) Sch. Tropical Medicine, 1982; cert. hosp. epidemiology, U. Iowa, 1985; MPH, Yale U., 1991. Nat. design and media cons. Nat. Assn. Pediatric Nurse Assocs. and Practitioners, Cherry Hill, N.J., 1977-83; asst. prof., co-coord. community health nursing U. N.D., Grand Forks, 1980; vol. epidemiologist, pub. health specialist Vinh Children's Hosp., Vinh City, Vietnam, 1989; pediatric staff nurse I U. Fla. Pediatric Svc., Shands Teaching Hosp., Gainesville, 1970; instr. pediatric nursing U. Utah Coll. Nursing, Salt Lake City, 1976-77; pvt. cons. Internat. Cmty. Health and Epidemiology, New Haven, 1990-94; med. supr., health svcs. mgr. Brown & Root Logcap Med. Clinic, Port-au-Prince, Haiti, 1994-95; med. tech. proposal cons. UN, Rwanda, Angola, 1995; specialist Home Health Care, Tampa, Fla., 1996—; vol. pub. health scientist, cons. Hanoi (Vietnam) Sch. Pub. Health; cons. epidemiologist Vinh and Hucng Son, Vietnam, 1993; internat. edn. cons. U. Am., New Orleans, 1994. Contbg. editor Episource, 1991, Resources in Epidemiology; contbr. articles to profl. jours.; contbr. to poetry jours. Capt. Nurse Corps, U.S. Army, 1968-73, Vietnam. Recipient Cert. of Achievement in HIV-AIDS Edn., AIDS Project, New Haven, Conn., 1994. Fellow Royal Soc. Tropical Medicine and Hygiene (London), Am. Biog. Inst.; mem. AMA, VFW, Am. Legion, Vietnam Vets. Am., Nat. Assn. Pediatric Nurse Assocs. and Practitioners (com. dir. graphics & logos mil. chpt., former chmn. nat. art and exhibits subcom., former mem. pub. rels. com., Cert. Recognition 1983), Am. Pub. Health Assn. (epidemiology sect., internat. healthsect.), Fla. Pub. Health Assn., Nat. Adolescent Health Promotion Network, Assn. Mil. Surgeons U.S., Ret. Army Nurse Corps Assn., Liverpool Tropical Sch. Assn. (Eng.), Assn. Yale Alumni in Pub. Health, Consortium for Internat. Nursing Edn., Rsch. & Practice, U.S.-Vietnam Friendship Assn., Doctorate Assn. N.Y. Educators, Fleet Marine Force Corpsman Assn. (former Conn. rep., charter mem.), U.S. Navy Corpsmen United Assn., Am. Assn. Navy Hosp. Corpsmen, U.S. Army (Vietnam) 24th Evacuation Hosp. Assn. (com. asv. reunion 1993), Vets. Vietnam Restoration Project, U.S. Com. Scientific Cooperation with Vietnam, N.Y. Acad. of Sci., Sigma Xi, Sigma Theta Tau (charter mem. Gamma Rho chpt.), Phi Kappa Phi. Home: 11333 Calgary Cir Tampa FL 33624-4804

JACOBS, WILLIAM HENRY, financial executive; b. Buffalo, June 2, 1931; s. Walter Jerome and Gwendolyn (Liebman) J.; m. Carolyn Douglas, May 21, 1989; children: William Bradford, Benjamin Douglas. BA, Yale U., 1976, MD, 1980. Diplomate Am. Bd. Internal Medicine, Am. Bd. Infectious Diseases. Intern N.Y. Hosp.-Cornell Med. Ctr., N.Y.C., 1980-81, resident, 1981-83, fellow in infectious diseases, 1983-86, attending physician, 1986—, med. dir. Ctr. Spl. Studies, 1988—, dir. Office AIDS Clin. Program Mgmt., 1990—; assoc. prof. clin. medicine Cornell U. Med. Coll.; financial executive; b. Buffalo, June 2, 1931; s. Eames and Guida (Marx) D.; m. Sept. 17, 1960; children: Kimberly, Matthew, Adam. BA, Yale U., 1953; MA (hon.), 1970; MBA, Harvard U., 1958; LLD (hon.), Webster U., 1992; DPHIL (hon.), St. Lawrence U., 1995, DHL Alfred. U., 1995. Chmn., chief exec. Donaldson, Lufkin & Jenrette, Inc., N.Y.C., 1959-73; undersec. of state U.S. Dept. State, Washington, 1973-74; spl. cons., to v.p. of U.S., Washington, 1974; dean, Beinecke prof. mgmt. Yale Grad. Mgmt. Sch., New Haven, 1975-80; chmn., CEO Donaldson Enterprises, Inc., N.Y.C., 1980-90, 95—; chmn., chief exec. N.Y. Stock Exch., N.Y.C., 1991-95; founder, sr. advisor Donaldson, Lufkin and Jenrette, Inc., 1996—; bd. dirs. Aetna Life & Casualty, Honeywell Inc., Philip Morris Cos. Inc. Trustee, chmn. fin. com. Ford Found., N.Y.C., 1968-80, Yale U., New Haven, 1970-75; bd. dirs. N.Y.C. Partnership, Bus. Coun. of State of N.Y., Lincoln Ctr. for Performing Arts, N.Y.C.; trustee St. Lawrence U., Marine Corps Command and Staff Coll. Found., Carnegie Endowment Internat. Peace, N.Y. Police Found.; chmn. Aetna Found.; gov. Foreign Policy Assn. Served to 1st lt. USMC, 1953-55. Recipient Pres's. Disting. Service award SUNY, 1976; named Businessman of Yr., AP, 1969. Mem. Inst. Chartered Fin. Analysts, N.Y. Stock Exchange (dir. 1972-73), Coun. on Fgn. Rels., Coun. for Econs. Devel. Contbr. articles to sci. publs.; dir. AIDS films. Recipient Humanitarian award East Manhattan C. of C., 1988. Mem. Am. Fedn. Clin. Rsch., Alpha Omega Alpha. Office: Donaldson, Lufkin & Jenrette 277 Park Ave New York NY 10172

JACOBSEN, GRETE KRAG, pathologist; b. Copenhagen, Sept. 27, 1943; d. Per Krag J. and Marie Louise (Gorrison) Hanssen; m. Joachim Knop, Apr. 27, 1987; children: Nikolaj, Filip. MD, U. Copenhagen, 1977, Dr.med., 1985. Lic. pathologist. Jr. registrar Mcpl. Hosp., Dept. Pathology, Copenhagen, 1971-73, Mcpl. Hosp., Dept. Dermatology, Copenhagen, 1974-75; registrar dept. pathology Gentofte Hosp., 1975-76; sr. registrar Herlev Hosp., Dept. Pathology, Copenhagen, 1976-80; asst. prof. pathology Herlev Hosp., Copenhagen, 1980-82; sr. registrar dept. pathology Hvidovre Hosp., Copenhagen, 1982-85; cons., chief pathologist Gentofte Hosp., Copenhagen, 1985—; lectr. in field. Author: Atlas of Germ Cell Tumours, 1989; contbr. articles to profl. jours.; exhibited art in shows, 1976—. Grantee in field, 1976—. Fellow Med. Soc. Copenhagen (v.p.); mem. Danish Soc. Pathology (chmn. 1989-92), others. Home: Bispebjerg Parkallé 11, 2400 NV Copenhagen Denmark Office: Kas Gentofte Dept Pathology, Niels Andersensvej, 2900 Hellerup Denmark

JACOBSON, EDWIN JAMES, medical educator; b. Chgo., June 27, 1947; s. Edwin Julius and Rose Josephine (Jirinec) J.; m. Martha Shanks; 1 child, Emily. BA, U. So. Calif., 1969; MD, UCLA, 1976. Diplomate Nat. Bd. Med. Examiners, Am. Bd. Internal Medicine; lic. physician, Calif. Intern in medicine UCLA Hosp., 1976-77, resident in medicine, 1977-79, fellow in nephrology, 1979-81, chief resident in medicine, 1979-81; asst. clin. prof. of medicine UCLA, 1981-88, assoc. clin. prof. medicine, 1988-94, clin. prof. medicine, 1994—; adj. asst. prof. medicine, UCLA, 1980-81; mem. med. sch. admissions com. UCLA, 1981—, med. staff credentials com., 1984—, med.staff exec. com., 1990-94, med. staff/hosp. adminstrn. liaison com. 1991-94, hosp./med. sch. faculty rels. com., 1991—, nat. kidney found., 1991—, med. adv. bd., 1991—; prin. investigator A/M Group Grant, UCLA Med. Ctr., 1993, Peter Langer Meml. Fund Award, 1993; lectr. in field. Author: Medical Diagnosis: An Algorithmic Approach, 1989; co-author: (with P. Healy) Il Proceso Decisionale nella Diagnosi Medica, 1992; manuscript rev. bd.: Bone Marrow Transplantation, 1988—, Jour. Am. Geriatrics Soc., 1989—; editor for symposia in field; contbr. articles to profl. jours.; editor book chpts. Recipient Upjohn Achievement award, 1977. Mem. ACP, Alpha Omega Alpha. Office: UCLA 100 UCLA Medical Plz # 690 Los Angeles CA 90024

JACOBSON, GERALD, orthodontist; b. Phila., Mar. 15, 1937; s. Simon Louis and Bess (Kirsh) J.; m. Marlene Pechter, Dec. 22, 1963; children: Alicia Sue and Andrew David. BA, Muhlenberg Coll., 1957; DDS, Temple U., 1961; postgrad., U. Pa., 1964. cert. orthodontics, 1964. Orthodontist Atrium Med. Dental Ctr., Cherry Hill, N.J., 1965—; attending dentist Thomas Jefferson U. Hosp., Phila., 1965-78; staff J.F.K. U. Med Ctr, Cherry Hill, 76—; assoc. prof. of orthodontics Temple U., Phila., 1986—; lectr. U. Pa. Sch. Dentistry, Phila., 1968-72; adj. faculty lectr. Camden County Coll., Blackwood, N.J., 1972—, Camden County Tech. Inst., Berlin, N.J., 1972—. Capt. USAF, Robins AFB, 1961-63. Mem. ADA, Am. Assn. Orthodontists, Middle Atlantic Assn. Orthodontists, N.J. Assn. Orthodontists, N.J. Dental Assn., So. Dental Soc, Temple U. Dental Alumni (bd. dirs. 1992—), Greater Phila. Soc. Orthodontics (bd. dirs. 1990—, pres. 1994-95). Office: Atrium Med-Dental Ctr 1910 E Rte 70 Cherry Hill NJ 08003

JACOBSON, HAROLD GORDON, radiologist, educator; b. Cin., Oct. 12, 1912; s. Samuel and Regina (Dittman) J.; m. Ruth Enenstein, Aug. 10, 1941; children: Richard, Arthur. B.S., U. Cin., 1934, M.B., 1936, M.D., 1937. Diplomate Am. Bd. Radiology (trustee 1971-82, chmn. written exams com. in diagnostic radiology 1973-81, co-chmn., mem. 1981—, treas. 1976-78, v.p. 1978-80, pres. 1980-82, mem. residency rev. com. 1976-82, vice-chmn. 1979-80, chmn. 1980-82, exec. com. 1976—). Intern Los Angeles County Gen. Hosp., 1936-38; fellow in pathology Longview Hosp., Cin., 1938; resident Mt. Sinai Hosp., N.Y.C., 1939-41, Associated Hosps. U. Tex., 1941-42; asst. in radiology U. Tex., 1941-42; assoc. radiologist New Haven (Conn.) Hosp.; also instr. Yale U., 1952; asst. chief, asso. radiologist VA Hosp., Bronx, N.Y., 1946-50; chief radiology service VA Hosp., 1950-53, cons., 1958—; asst. clin. prof. N.Y. U., 1952-53, clin. prof., 1953-59, prof. clin. radiology, 1959-64; prof. radiology Albert Einstein Coll. Medicine, 1964-71; prof., chmn. Albert Einstein Coll. Medicine of Montefiore Hosp. and Med. Center, N.Y.C., 1972-85; prof. radiology Albert Einstein Coll. Medicine of Montefiore Hosp. and Med. Center, 1985-86, prof. emeritus, chmn., Disting. Univ. Prof. radiology, 1986—; dir. dept. roentgenology Hosp. for Spl. Surgery, N.Y.C., 1953-55; radiologist-in-chief Montefiore Hosp. and Med. Center, N.Y.C., 1955—; sr. cons. in radiology Nat. Bd. Med. Examiners, 1975—, mem. bd., 1979-83; vis. prof. radiology Inst. Orthopaedics, U. London, 1975—; vis. prof., lectr., UCLA Med. Ctr., 1986, 88, various socs., med. schs., univs. in Israel, Brazil, Finland, Cuba, Eastern Europe; vis. prof., lectr., med. ctrs. Republic of China and guest Chinese Radiol. Soc., 1986; named lectures include Felson Lecture, Carman Lecture, Baylin Lecture, Beeler Lecture, Freedman Lecture, Pfahler Lecture, Chamberlain Lecture, Evans Lecture, Sampson Lecture, Wolf Meml. Lecture, Caffey Lecture, Grubbe Lecture, Myron Melamed Lecture; Double Day lectr. U. Tex., 1992, Spl. lectr. N.Y. Roentgen Soc., 1992; head del. of radiologists to Republic of China, 1984. Author: (with Clarence Schein, William Z. Stern) The Common Bile Duct, 1967, Neuroradiology Workshop, Vol. III, 1968, (with Ronald O. Murray) Radiology of Skeletal Disorders: Exercises in Diagnosis, 1971, 2nd edit. 1977, 3rd edit. 1989; co-author: Bone Disease Syllabus, 1972, 2d series, 1976, 3d series, 1980, 4th series 1989, Index for Roentgen Diagnosis, 3d edit. 1975; co-editor in chief Jour. Internat. Skeletal Soc., 1976—; co-chief editor Skeletal Radiology, 1975; mem. editorial bd. Excerpta Medica, 1974—, Jour. AMA, 1979—, others. Served as maj. M.C. AUS, 1942-46. Recipient Gold medal Assn. Univ. Radiologists, 1982, Gold medal Phi Lambda Kappa, 1983, Spl. Excellence award (in lieu of Hon. Doctorate) U. Cin., 1987, Spl. award N.Y. Roentgen Soc., 1993, Alumni Staff Assn. Montefiore Med. Ctr., 1993; spl. named lecture in his honor Roentgen Soc., 1992. Fellow Am. Coll. Radiology (councilor 1960—, bd. chancellors, chmn. com. on radiol. coding 1967—, mem. commn. on credentials 1968—, chmn. commn. on affairs Am. Inst. Radiology 1971—, co-chmn. com. on diagnostic coding index and thesaurus 1973—, Gold medal 1978, selected for video taping as living legend in radiology), Royal Coll. Radiologists (London) (hon.); mem. Am. Roentgen Ray Soc. (Cert. Appreciation 1983, Gold medal 1989), N.Y. Roentgen Soc. (pres. 1959-60, historian 1967—, spl. lecture 1992), AMA, N.Y. State Med. Soc., N.Y. Med. Soc., Soc. of Chairmen Acad. Radiology Depts. (mem. exec. council 1972—, pres. 1973-74), Radiol. Soc. N.Am. (pres. 1966-67, mem. bd. censors 1968—, Diamond Jubilee lectr. 1989, Gold medal 1972), Royal Soc. Medicine (hon.), Internat. Skeletal Soc. (co-founder, pres. 1974-75, chmn., mem. exec. com. 1976—), Chinese Radiol. Soc. (hon.), Cuban Radiol. Soc. (hon.), Alpha Omega Alpha (Rigler lectr. 1964, 70, Crookshank lectr. London 1974, Holmes lectr. Boston ubleday lectr. Houston 1991). Home: 3240 Henry Hudson Pky Bronx NY 10463-3212 Office: Montefiore Med Ctr Dept Radiology 111 E 210th St Bronx NY 10467-2490

JACOBSON, HOWARD NEWMAN, obstetrics and gynecology educator, researcher; b. St. Paul, Aug. 13, 1923; s. Irvin Oliver and Nora Henrietta (Olson) J.; m. Barbara Jane Dinger, Aug. 20,1961. BSc in Medicine, Northwestern U., Chgo., 1947, BM, 1950, MD, 1951. Intern Presbyn. Hosp., Chgo., 1950-51, resident in ob-gyn, 1951-52; fellow, rsch. fellow in obstetrics, mem. family clinic Harvard Sch. Pub. Health, Boston, 1952-55; resident Boston Lying-In Hosp. and Free Hosp. for Women, Brookline, Mass., 1955-58; obstetrician, physiologist Lab. Neuroanat. Scis., Nat. Inst. Nervous Disease and Blindness, NIH, Bethesda, Md., 1958-60; instr., asst. prof. Harvard Med. Sch., Boston, 1960-65; assoc. prof. U. Calif., San Francisco, Berkeley, 1965-69; dir. Macy program Med. Sch. Harvard U., 1969-74; prof. dept. community medicine Coll. Medicine and Dentistry N.J., Piscataway, 1974-78; dir. Inst. Nutrition, clin. prof. U. N.C., Chapel Hill, 1978-88; rsch. prof. Coll. of Pub. Health Coll. of Pub. Health U. South Fla., 1988—; prof. dept. ob-gyn U. South Fla. Med. Sch., Tampa, 1990—; cons. Children's Bur., HEW, Washington, 1964-73, GAO, Washington, 1974-83, AMA, 1980-82, 88—; mem. food and nutrition bd. NRC/NAS, Washington, 1971-74; prof. dept. biology and Sch. Home Econs., U. N.C., Greensboro, 1978-88, Ellen Swallow Richards lectr., 1978; cons. pregnancy and nutrition study U. Minn., Mpls., 1979—; adj. prof. dept. food, nutrition and instn. mgmt. East Carolina U. Sch. Home Econs., Greenville, 1981-88; mem. nutrition grad. faculty N.C. State U., Raleigh, 1979-88. Contbr. over 130 articles and abstracts to FMA Today, Jour. Nurse-Midwifery, Clin. Nutrition, Contemporary Internal Medicine, Food and Nutrition News, Nutrition Today, New Eng. Jour. Medicine, chpts. to books. Panel vice chmn. White House Conf. on Food, Nutrition and Health, Washington, 1969; chmn. Quality of Life Conf., Mass. Med. Soc., Boston, 1972; mem. hunger com. Episcopal Ch. S.W. Fla., 1990-94; mem. Fla. Health Start Initiative working Group, 1991—. Lt. (j.g.) USNR, 1943-46, PTO. Recipient Agnes Higgins award March of Dimes and APHA, 1987; recipient Career Devel. award NIH, 1963-65. Fellow Am. Coll. Ob-Gyn (assoc.); mem. Am. Soc. Clin. Nutrition, Am. Physiol. Soc., Mass. Med. Soc. (chmn. commn. 1972-74), Fla. Pub. Health Assn. (chmn. sect. 1990-91), Am. Dietetic Assn. (hon.). Democrat. Office: U South Fla Coll Pub Health 13201 Bruce B Downs Blvd Tampa FL 33612-3805

JACOBSON, JOAN, retired speech pathologist, audiologist, educator; b. Hull, Iowa, Apr. 26, 1924; d. Fred and Mary (Hoogschagen) Elsinga; m. John Jacobson, June 1, 1945 (div. 1952). BA, Morningside Coll., 1944; MA, Syracuse U., 1948, PhD, 1958. Cert. of clin. competence in speech pathology and audiology. Speech clinician Brookline Pub. Schs., Mass. Gen. Hosp., 1951-57; rsch. assoc. Syracuse (N.Y.) U., 1957-58; asst. prof. speech pathology and audiology Eastern Ill. U., Charleston, 1958-62; faculty St. Cloud State U., Minn., 1962-92; ret., 1992. Mem. Am. Acad. Rehabilitive Audiology, Am. Cleft Palate Assn., Minn. Speech Lang. and Hearing Assn. (recipient honors 1984), Am. Auditory Soc. Presbyterian. Avocation: tournament bridge. Home: 41212 7th Ave S Saint Cloud MN 56301-4312

JACOBSON, JOHN STEPHEN, corporate healthcare executive; b. Sioux Falls, S.D., May 1, 1945; s. Edwin Gerald Jacobson and Alexandra (Smyrak) King; m. Mary Elizabeth Leander, June 12, 1970; children: Kevin, Anna, Erik, Carrie. BS in Journalism, S.D. State U., 1972; MPA, Calif. State U., 1992. Sports editor Hdqrs. 1st Army, Fort Meade, Md., 1967; news editor STRATCOMEUR, Schwetzingen, Germany, 1968-69; staff writer Argus-Leader, Sioux Falls, 1972-73, state editor, 1973-75, asst. city editor, 1975-76; pub. rels. dir. McKennan Hosp., Sioux Falls, 1976-84; cmty. rels. dir. Mercy Med. Ctr., Redding, Calif., 1984-93; v.p. Flagstaff (Ariz.) Med. Ctr., 1993-96, No. Ariz. Healthcare, Flagstaff, 1996—; founding chmn. Presentation Health Sys. Pub. Rels. Coun., Sioux Falls, 1979-84; founding pres. S.D. Assn. Hosp. Mktg., Sioux Falls, 1981-82; mem. Health Coun. of No. and Ctrl. Calif. Pub. Affairs Com., San Francisco, 1989-92. Author: (booklet) Patient Handbook, 1987; editor (tv comml.) The People of Mercy, 1990 (Telly award 1991), (booklet) Cardiac Care at Mercy, 1992. Chmn. United Way of No. Calif., Redding, 1989; bd. dirs. Norwest Bank, Flagstaff, 1993—, Ariz. for A Healthy Future, Phoenix, 1994, Festival of Sci., Flagstaff, 1995—. Sgt. U.S. Army, 1967-69. Recipient Associated Press News award S.D. Associated Press, 1974, Pres.'s award for pub. rels. Sertoma Internat., 1981, Advt. award S.D. Advt. Fedn., Rapid City, 1983. Mem. Am. Soc. Hosp. Mktg. and Pub. Rels. (cert., presdl. selection com. 1981, region six rep. 1982, presdl. achievement com. 1982, edn. com. 1983, Touchstone award com. 1985), Am. Coll. Healthcare Execs. (assoc.), Rotary, Flagstaff C. of C. (arts, bus. and culture com. 1995—). Office: No Ariz Healthcare 1200 N Beaver Flagstaff AZ 86001

JACOBSON, KRAIG WARREN, allergist; b. Portland, Oreg., July 19, 1949; s. Frank Maurice and Phyllis (Miller) J.; m. Mary Beth Harris, Sept. 13, 1969; children: Sarah Lynn, Timothy Michael. BS, Oreg. State U., 1970; MD, Univ. Oreg., 1974. Diplomate Am. Bd. Internal Medicine, Am. Bd. Allergy and Immunology. Intern/resident Letterman Hosp., San Francisco, 1974-77; fellow Fitzsimons Hosp., Aurora, Colo., 1977-79; assoc. prof. health edn. U. Oreg., Eugene, 1979-88; med. dir. Allergy and Asthma Rsch. Group, Eugene, 1979-96; pvt. practice Allergy and Asthma Assocs., P.C., Eugene, 1979—; med. cons. Alcon Labs., Ft. Worth, Tex., 1994-95; med. dir. MOA program Lane C.C., Eugene, 1995-96, chmn. adv. com., 1986—. Contbr. articles to profl. jours. Bd. dirs. Am. Lung Assn. Oreg., 1982-88; chmn. bd. dirs. Young Life Internat., Eugene, 1988-91. Maj. U.S. Army, 1973-79. Recipient ALA Councilor Am. Lung Assn. of Oreg., 1986; grantee Schering Corp., 1988, 94, E.R. Squibb & Sons, 1988, Glaxo Pharms., 1988, 90, 95, Rhone Poulenc Rorer, 1992, 93, 94, 95, Abbott Labs., 1993, 94, G.D. Searle, 1993, Forest Pharms., 1994, Pfizer Pharms., 1994, Astra USA, Inc., 1994, 3M Health Care, 1995, 96, ZENECA Pharms., 1996. Mem. AMA, Oreg. Med. Assn., Am. Thoracic Soc., Oreg. Thoracic Soc., Am. Acad. Allergy and Immunology, Am. Coll. Allergists, Western Soc. Allergy and Immunology, Assn. for Care of Asthma, Lane County Med. Soc., Oreg. Soc.. Allergy and

Immunology, Rotary, Alpha Omega Alpha. Office: Allergy & Asthma Assocs PC 1488 Oak St Eugene OR 97401

JACOBSON, LLOYD ELDRED, retired dentist; b. Madison, Minn., Mar. 9, 1923; s. Jacob Elton and Hilda Emily (Larson) J.; m. Ruth Solveig Skinsnes, Jan. 26, 1945; children: Rolf, Kathryn, Heidi. Student, St. Olaf Coll., 1943-44, 46-47, U. Chgo., 1945-46; DDS, U. Minn., 1951. Gen. practice dentistry Kenyon, Minn., 1951-91; ret., 1991. Chmn. Am. Luth. Ch. Coun., Mpls., 1972-74; vol. World Brotherhood Exch., Bumbuli, Tanzania, 1965; treas. Kenyon Sch. Bd., 1958-60, Kenyon Devel. Corp., 1955-60. 1st lt. 14th Aif Force (Flying Tigers), USAAF, 1943-45, CBI. Recipient Outstanding Alumni award St. Olaf Coll., 1972, Disting. Alumni award U. Minn. Sch. Dentistry, 1987. Mem. Minn. Dental Assn. (treas. 1980-86), S.E. Dist. Dental Soc. (pres. 1979-80, sec.-treas. 1976-79), Rice County Dental Soc. (pres. 1969). Republican. Lodge: Lions (pres. Kenyon club 1952-54, dist. sec.-treas. 1974, Citizen of Yr. award 1986). Home: 521 Spring St Kenyon MN 55946-1519

JACOBSON, LOUISE GROVES, nutritionist, educator; b. Kittanning, Pa., Oct. 10, 1938; d. Walter and Bessie (Lewis) Groves; m. Gerald Jacobson; children: David Jr., Jeffrey Haushalter. BS in Home Econs., Indiana U. of Pa., 1960; MS in Food and Nutrition, Ind. State U., 1974; postgrad., Memphis State U. Lic. nutritionist and dietitian, Tenn. Dietitian Stouffers Restaurant, Pitts., 1960-61; home econs. tchr. North Hills Sch. System, Pitts., 1961-64; clin. dietitian Bellevue Suburban Hosp., Pitts., 1964-67; nutrition instr. Youngstown (Ohio) State U., 1967-72; food svc. dir. Saga Food Svcs., St. Mary's of the Woods, Ind., 1972-73; home econs. tchr. Normandy Sch. System, St. Louis, 1973-74; assoc. prof. Shelby State Community Coll., Memphis, 1974-81; nutritionist and health edn. coord. Health First Med. Group, Memphis, 1981—; nutritionist nat. health edn. com. Prudential Ins. Co., Roseland, N.J., 1987-88; reviewer Soc. for Nutrition Edn., Oakland, Calif., 1987-88. Author numerous booklets and videos. Active Brooks Art Mus., Memphis, 1983-87; vol. Memphis in May, 1982-95, Ctr. fo So. Folklore, Memphis, 1982-88, Friends of the Orpheum, Memphis, 1982-88, Nat. Ornamental Metal Mus., Memphis, 1984-88, Theatre Memphis, 1982-86. Mem. Am. Dietetic Assn. (edn. chmn. Memphis dist. 1977-78, chmn. scholarship 1981-83, pub. rels. chmn. 1980, long-range planning chmn. 1986, Outstanding Dietitian 1980), Tenn. Dietetic Assn. (state seat 1978-80), Memphis Area Nutrition Coun. (various elected offices 1975-81), Indiana Univ. of Pa. Mid-South Alumni Assn. (chmn.). Home: 6567 S Poplar Woods Cir Apt 1 Memphis TN 38138-3670 Office: 6401 Poplar Ave Ste 150 Memphis TN 38119

JACOBSON, MINDY LEINER, art psychotherapist, educator; b. N.Y.C., July 25, 1954; d. Murray and Joan Lois (Rubenstein) Leiner; m. Christopher Harold Jacobson, Mar. 9, 1980 (div. 1984); 1 child, Stephanie Beth. Student, Union Coll., Schenectady, 1972-74; BA, SUNY, Stony Brook, 1975; MCAT in Creative Arts Therapies, Hahnemann U., 1978; cert. in adminstrn. social svcs., Temple U., 1985. Cert. open water diver. Sr. art psychotherapist Friends Hosp., Phila., 1978—; pvt. practice Phila., 1982—; asst. prof. Hahnemann U. Phila., 1979—, continuing edn. instr., 1990-91; clin. instr., supr. trenton (N.J.) State Coll., 1989; cons. U.S. Naval Regional Med. Ctr., Phila., 1978; faculty mem. Ea. Regional Conf. on Multiple Personality Disorders, 1988-94; articles reviewer Dissociation, 1989, 93, 96; presenter in field. Contbr. articles to profl. jours. Speaker on preventive child abuse Jewish Fedn. Phila., 1988, 89; asst. Brownie leader Girl Scouts U.S.A., Melrose Park, Pa., 1988-91; treas. Phila. Sea Horses, 1990-93. Mem. Am. Art Therapy Assn. (registered profl., editor film-video jour. 1994—), Internat. Soc. for Study Multiple Personality Disorders and Dissociative States (profl.), Delaware Valley Art Therapy Assn. (hon. life, profl., treas. 1979-82, newsletter com.). Democrat. Jewish. Office: Friends Hosp 4641 Roosevelt Blvd Philadelphia PA 19124-2343

JACOBSON, PETER LARS, neurologist, educator; b. Englewood, N.J., Feb. 17, 1951; s. George Pershing and Mona (Friedman) J.; m. Karen Joy Frenkel, June 11, 1972; children: Kersten Jenny, Lars Edward II. BA summa cum laude, Princeton U., 1973; MD, Washington U., 1977. Chief resident in neurology U. N.C. Hosp., Chapel Hill, 1980-81; fellow in electroencephalography Mayo Clinic, Rochester, Minn., 1981-82; pres. Pinehurst (N.C.) Neurology, P.A., 1982—; clin. prof. neurology U. N.C., Chapel Hill, 1982—, adj. prof. journalism, 1990—; chmn. dept. neurology Moore Regional Hosp., Pinehurst, 1985-87. Columnist The Pilot, 1989—. Trustee The O'Neal Sch., Southern Pines, N.C., 1992—. Recipient Lange Med. Book prize Washington U., 1976, Samson F. Wennerman award in surgery, 1977, Cert. of Appreciation, State of N.C., 1987; Mosby scholar, 1977. Fellow Am. Acad. Neurology, Am. EEG Soc.; mem. N.C. Neurol. Soc. (pres. 1990-91), Am. Med. Writers Assn., Alpha Omega Alpha, Phi Beta Kappa. Office: Carolina Headache & Pain Ctr PA PO Box 37 Pinehurst NC 28374

JACOBUS, BRENT ARLYN, JR., physician; b. Dover, N.J., July 23, 1961; s. Arlyn Warren and Marlene (Ribe) J.; m. Elizabeth Carol Johnson, July 28, 1984; children: Brittney Elizabeth, Bethany Marlene. BA, Taylor U., 1983; DO, Kirksville Coll. Osteo. Med., 1987. Intern Grandview Hosp. and Med. Ctr., Dayton, Ohio, 1987-88; resident Grandview Hosp. and Med. Ctr., Dayton, 1988-89; resident in family practice Ball Meml. Hosp., Muncie, Ind., 1989—; staff position Wright Patterson AFB, Dayton, 1988-89; emergency room physician EPP Meml. Hosp., Cin., 1988-89, Mercy Hosp., Ellwood, Ind., 1990—. Mem. AMA, Am. Osteo. Assn., Am. Coll. Gen. Practitioners (bd. cert. 1990, bd. mem. 1990), Am. Acad. Family Physicians, Christian Med. Soc., Ind. Acad. Osteo. Medicine, Ind. State Med. Assn., Ind. Osteo. Assn. Republican. Home: 711 Clover Ln Crown Point IN 46307-2967 Office: Seasons Pla Clinic 9101 E 109th Ave Crown Point IN 46307-8680

JACOBY, ALISON GAIL, critical care nurse, educator; b. Modesto, Calif., Oct. 10, 1960; d. Alfred Lincoln IV and Juanita Gail (Coston) J. BSN, Loma Linda (Calif.) U., 1983; MN, U. Calif., L.A., 1986. RN, Calif. Critical care clin. nurse specialist Humana Hosp. of West Anaheim, Anaheim, Calif., Martin Luther Med. Ctr., Anaheim, Friendly Hills Med. Ctr., La Habra, Calif. Calif. scholar. Mem. AACN, Am. Heart Assn., Sigma Theta Tau.

JACOBY, IRVING, physician; b. N.Y.C., Sept. 30, 1947; s. Philip Aaron and Sylvia (Newman) J.; m. Sara Kay Vartanian; children: James Tyler, Kathryn Aaryn. BS magna cum laude, U. Miami, Coral Gables, Fla., 1969; MD, Johns Hopkins U., 1973. Diplomate Am. Bd. Internal Medicine, Am. Bd. Infectious Diseases, Am. Bd. Emergency Medicine. Intern Boston City Hosp., 1973-74, resident in medicine, 1974-75, chief resident, 1978-79; resident in medicine Peter Bent Brigham Hosp., Boston, 1975-76, fellow in infectious diseases, 1976-78; asst. dir. emergency med. svcs. U. Mass. Med. Ctr., Worcester, 1979-84; asst. dir. dept. emergency med. U. Calif. Med. Ctr., San Diego, 1984—, assoc. prof. med. surgery, 1988-94; prof. med. surgery, 1994—; disaster control officer, assoc. dir. Hyperbaric Med. Ctr., 1985—; vis. physician, cons. infectious diseases Soroka Med. Ctr., Ben Gurion U., Beer-Sheva, Israel, 1980; flight physician New Eng. Life Flight, Worcester, 1982-84, Life Flight Aeromed. Program U. Calif., 1984-87. Sect. editor for disaster medicine Jour. Emergency Medicine; assoc. editor Undersea and Hyperbaric Medicine, 1996—. Comdr. Disaster Med. Assistance Team CA-4. Fellow ACP, Am. Coll. Emergency Physicians; mem. Am. Soc. Microbiology, Infectious Diseases Soc. Am., Soc. Acad. Emergency Medicine, Undersea and Hyperbaric Med. Soc., Johns Hopkins Med and Surg. Assn., Iron Arrow Leadership Soc., Omicron Delta Kappa, Phi Kappa Phi, Alpha Epsilon Delta, Phi Eta Sigma. Office: U Calif Med Ctr 200 W Arbor Dr San Diego CA 92103-8676

JACOBY, JACOB, consumer psychology educator; b. Bklyn., Feb. 17, 1940; s. David and Frances (Berman) J.; m. Renee S. Berkowitz; children: Robin Ann, Jonathan Scott. BA, Bklyn. Coll., 1961, MS, 1963; PhD, Mich. State U., 1966. Prof. consumer behavior Purdue U., West Lafayette, Ind., 1968-81, NYU, 1981—; cons. DuPont, Gen. Electric Co., Gen. Motors. Co., Am. Assn. Adv. Agys., Procter and Gamble, Standard Oil, U.S. Senate, FTC, FDA, others. Author: Brand Loyalty, 1978, Miscomprehension of Televised Communication, 1980, The Comprehension and Miscomprehension of Print Communications, 1987. Served to 1st lt. USAF, 1965-68. Recipient Outstanding Contbn. to Advt. award Am. Acad. Advt., 1991. Fellow APA (pres. divsn. 23 1973-74, Disting. Sci. Rsch. award 1995), Assn. for Consumer Rsch. (pres. 1975); mem. Am. Mktg. Assn. (H.H. Maynard award 1978), Am. Assn. Pub. Opinion Rsch., Advt. Ednl. Found. (bd. dirs.). Jewish. Office: NYU 44 W 4th St New York NY 10012-1126

JACOX, ADA KATHRYN, nurse, educator; b. Centreville, Mich.; d. Leo H. and Lilian (Gilbert) J. BS in Nursing Edn., Columbia U., 1959; MS in Child Psychiat. Nursing, Wayne State U., 1965; PhD in Sociology, Case Western Res. U., 1969. R.N. Dir. nursing Children's Hosp.-Northville State Hosp., Mich., 1961-63; assoc. prof., then prof. Coll. Nursing Univ. Iowa, Iowa City, 1969-76; prof., assoc. dean Sch. Nursing U. Colo., Denver, 1976-80; prof., dir. rsch. ctr. sch. nursing U. Md., Balt., 1980-90, dir. ctr. for health policy rsch., 1988-90; prof. sch. nursing, Independence Found. chair health policy Johns Hopkins U., Balt., 1990-95; assoc. dean for rsch. Wayne State U. Coll. Nursing, Detroit, 1996; co-chmn. panels to develop clin. guidelines for pain mgmt. U.S. Agy. for Health Care Policy and Rsch., 1990-94. Co-author: Organizing for Independent Nursing Practice, 1977 (named Book of Yr., Am. Jour. Nursing); A Process Measure for Primary Care: The Nurse Practitioner Rating Form, 1981 (named Book of Yr., Am. Jour. Nursing). Editor: Pain: A Sourcebook for Nurses, 1977 (named Book of Yr., Am. Jour. Nursing). Chair AIDS study sect. NIH, 1990-92. Recipient Disting. Achievement in Nursing Rsch. and Scholarship, Alumni Assn. Columbia U. Tchrs. Coll., 1975, Disting. Alumna award Ft. Wayne U. Coll. Nursing, 1994, award for spl. achievement Nat. Coalition for Cancer Survivorship, 1994; Carver fellow U. Iowa, 1972. Fellow Am. Acad. Nursing; mem. ANA (dir. 1978-82, 1st v.p. 1982-84), AMA (mem. health policy agenda work group 1983-86), Am. Nurses Found. (pres. 1982-85), Am. Acad. Nursing, Nat. Acad. Scis. (com. on nat. needs for biomed. and rsch. pers. 1984-87), Inst. of Medicine, Wayne State U. Alumni Assn. (Disting. Alumni award 1994). Office: Wayne State U Coll Nursing 5557 Cass Ave Detroit MI 48202

JADVAR, HOSSEIN, physician, biomedical engineer; b. Tehran, Iran, Apr. 6, 1961; came to U.S., 1978, naturalized, 1995; s. Ramezan Ali and Fatemeh (Afzal) J. BS, Iowa State U., 1982; MS, U. Wis., 1984, U. Mich., Ann Arbor, 1986; PhD, U. Mich., Ann Arbor, 1988; MD, U. Chgo., 1993. Rsch. asst. dept. human oncology U. Wis., Madison, 1983-84; rsch. asst. dept. elec. engring. U. Mich., Ann Arbor, 1984-88; sr. rsch. engr. Arzco Med. Electronics, Inc., Chgo., 1988-89; sr. rsch. assoc. Pritzker Inst., Inst. Int. Tech., Chgo., 1989-92; med. intern U. Calif., San Francisco, 1993-94; resident in radiology Stanford (Calif.) U., 1994-96, resident in nuc. medicine, 1996—; reviewer study sect. small bus. innovative rsch. program NIH, 1989; session chmn. IEEE/EMBS 11th Ann. Conf., Seattle, 1989. Contbr. articles to profl. jours., chpts. to books. Recipient Resident Rsch. award NIH, 1994. Mem. AMA, IEEE, Am. Roetgeon Ray Soc., Am. Coll. Radiology, Radiol. Soc. N.Am., Assn. for Advancement of Med. Instrumentation, Biomed Engring. Soc., Computers in Cardiology (local com. organizing mem. 1990), Tau Beta Pi, Sigm Xi, Eta Kappa Nu. Home: 1170 Welch Rd # 734 Palo Alto CA 94304-9999 Office: Stanford Univ Med Ctr Dept Radiology Divsn Nuc Medicine 300 Pasteur Dr Rm H0101 Stanford CA 94305-9999

JAEGER, PHILIPPE, physician, educator; b. Fribourg, Switzerland, Sept. 10, 1949; s. Louis and Jacqueline (Bunge) J.; m. Nicole Baechtold, Oct. 2, 1982; 1 child, Hélène. B of Arts and Scis., Coll. St. Michel, Fribourg, 1968; MD, U. Lausanne, Switzerland, 1975. Diplomate Swiss Bd. Internal Medicine. Rsch. fellow in renal physiology Yale U., New Haven, 1976-77, resident in nephrology, 1982-83; rsch. fellow in hypertension U. Lausanne, 1975-76, resident in internal medicine, 1978-80, chief resident, 1980-82, adj. physician dept. medicine, 1983-88; physician-in-chief U. Berne, Switzerland, 1988—; instr. medicine Univ. Hosp., Lausanne, 1984, asst. prof. nephrology, 1985; prof. medicine, dir. Policlinic of Medicine, Univ. Hosp., Berne, 1988; hon. pres. Internat. Congress on Renal Stone Analysis, Bordeaux, France, 1993. Editor: Métabolisme Electrolytique et Minéral, 1994; editor Praxis, 1990—; contbr. numerous articles and abstracts to New Eng. Jour. Medicine, Kidney Internat., Jour. Bone and Mineral Rsch., Jour. Clin. Investigation, Am. Jour. Physiology, The Lancet, others. Served to capt. Swiss Med. Svc. Recipient prize Swiss Soc. Urology, 1985. Fellow ACP (hon.); mem. European Assn. Internal Medicine (pres.-elect 1994-96), European Fedn. Internal Medicine (v.p. 1996—), Swiss Soc. Internal Medicine (pres.-elect 1993—, prize 1984, 93, 94), French Soc. Nephrology (v.p. 1995—), Swiss Soc. Nephrology (coun. mem. 1991—), Swiss Assn. Against Osteoporosis (coun. mem. 1989—). Roman Catholic. Office: Univ Hosp, 3010 Berne BE, Switzerland

JAEGER, VIVIAN G., health facility administrator; b. Bronxville, N.Y., Aug. 17, 1956; d. Robert S. and Virginia (Lloyd) J. BSN, Skidmore Coll., 1978; MA, NYU, 1985. RN, N.Y. Instr. perioperative svcs. N.Y.H.-C.U.M.C., N.Y.C., coord. perioperative svcs., asst. dir. perioperative svcs.; dir. operating room svcs. Beth Israel Med. Ctr., N.Y.C., chair RWJ-PEW grant; dir. edn. and staff devel. Pascack Valley Hosp.; adj. prof. Dominican Coll. Reviewing editor Aspen Publ. Perioperative Nursing; contbr. articles to profl. pubs. Former v.p. alumni programs Skidmore Coll., Saratoga, N.Y. Mem. ANA, Assn. Operating Rm. Nurses, Am. Assn. Critical Care Nurses, Am. Orgn. Nurse Execs.

JAFEK, BRUCE WILLIAM, otolaryngologist, educator; b. Berwyn, Ill., Mar. 4, 1941; s. Robert William and Viola Mabel (Newstrom) J.; m. Mary Bell Kirkpatrick, Sept. 1, 1962; children: Lynette A., Robert K., Timothy B., Britta C., Kayla E., Kristen M. BS, Coe Coll., 1962; postgrad., U. Omaha, 1962; MD, UCLA, 1966. Instr. dept. otology/laryngology Johns Hopkins Sch. Medicine, Balt., 1971-73; asst. prof. dept. otolaryngology U. Pa. Med. Sch., Phila., 1973-76; prof., dept. chmn. dept. otolaryngology/head and neck surgery U. Colo. Med. Sch., Denver, 1976—. Served with USPHS, 1971-73. Recipient Fowler award Triologic Soc., 1983. Republican. Mem. LDS Ch. Office: U Colo Health Sci Ctr B-205 4200 E 9th Ave # B-205 Denver CO 80220-3706

JAFFA, AYAD A., medical educator, medical researcher. Student, Brunel Tech. Coll., Bristol, Eng., 1975-77; BSc in Biol. Chemistry with honors, U. Essex, Colchester, Eng., 1980, PhD in Biol. Chemistry, 1984. Postdoctoral fellow dept. medicine Med. U. S.C., Charleston, 1984-86, rsch. assoc. dept. medicine, 1986-89, asst. prof. medicine dept. medicine, endocrinology-diabetes-metabolism divsn., 1989-96, asst. prof. pharmacology dept. cell and molecular pharmacology and exptl. therapeutics, 1990-96, mem. grad. faculty, 1991—, assoc. prof. medicine dept. medicine, divsn. endocrinology-diabetes-med. genetics, 1996—, assoc. prof. pharmacology dept. cell and molecular pharmacology and exptl. therapeutics, 1996—; mem. rsch. com. endocrinology-diabetes-med. genetics divsn. Med. U. S.C., Charleston, 1986—; grant reviewer Med. U. Rsch. Com., VA; vis. prof. Cath. U. of Chile, Santiago, 1996; lectr. in field. Manuscript reviewer Am. Jour. Physiology, Kidney Internat., Life Scis., Jour. Pharmacology and Exptl. Therapeutics, Diabetes; contbr. articles to profl. jours. Grantee Med. U. S.C., 1991-92, 92-93, 95-96, VA, 1993—, NIH, 1995—, recipient FIRST award, 1995. Mem. Am. Diabetes Assn. (exec. mem. fund raising com. S.C. affiliate 1992-96, bd. dirs. 1995—, Rsch. and Devel. award 1990, John A. Colwell award 1992, Rsch. award 1996), Am. Fedn. Clin. Rsch. (Henry Christian award 1995). Office: Med U SC Dept Medicine Divsn Endocrinology 171 Ashley Ave Charleston SC 29425

JAFFE, BERNARD MICHAEL, surgeon; b. N.Y.C.; s. Abner I. and Sylvia (Rothman) J.; m. Marlene Lambert, June 4, 1961; children: Mark Allen, Debra Lynn. B.A., U. Rochester, 1961; M.D., NYU, 1964. Diplomate Am. Bd. Surgery (exec. com. 1987-88, rep. to Am. Bd. Med. Specialists 1986-89). Asst. prof. surgery Washington U., St. Louis, 1971-75; assoc. prof. Washington U., 1975-77, prof., 1977-79; prof., chmn. dept. surgery SUNY Health Sci. Ctr. at Bklyn., 1979-92; vice-chmn. dept. surgery, chief div. surg. rsch. Tulane U., New Orleans, 1992—. Author: (with Behrman) Methods of Hormone Radioimmunoassay, 1980; editor in chief Surgical Rounds, 1989—. Served to lt. col. USAF, 1972-74. James IV traveling surg. fellow. Mem. ACS, Assn. Acad. Surgery (pres. 1978-79), Soc. Univ. Surgeons (sec. 1979-82, pres. 1983-84), Am. Surg. Assn., Soc. Clin. Surgery, Surg. Biol. Club I (sec. 1982-85), Am. Soc. Clin. Investigation, Soc. for Surgery Alimentary Tract (pres. 1987-88), So. Surg. Assn., Halsted Soc., Transplant Soc., Soc. for Surg. Oncology, Phi Beta Kappa, Alpha Omega Alpha. Office: Tulane Univ Med Ctr 1430 Tulane Ave New Orleans LA 70112-2699

JAFFÉ, ERNST RICHARD, medical educator and administrator; b. Chgo., Jan. 4, 1925; s. Richard Hermann and Berta (Kohn) J.; m. Anne Jane Sylvestre, Aug. 5, 1950; children: Stephanie Anne Green, Richard Sheridan. BS, U. Chgo., 1945, MD, 1948, MS in Pathology, 1948; DHL (hon.), Yeshiva U., 1987. Diplomate Am. Bd. Internal Medicine, Hematology, Nat. Bd. Med. Examiners; lic. physician, N.Y. Intern Med. Presbyn. Hosp., N.Y.C., 1948-50, resident, 1953-55; postdoctoral fellow Albert Einstein Coll. of Medicine, Bronx, N.Y., 1955-57, instr., asst. prof., 1957-62, assoc. prof., 1962-69, prof. medicine, 1969-84, acting dean, 1972-74, 83-84, sr. assoc. dean, 1974-83, 84-91, disting. univ. prof. medicine, 1984-92, disting. univ. prof. medicine emeritus, 1992—; mem. hematology study sect. Nat. Inst. Health, Bethesda, Md., 1972-82, Hirschl Sci. Adv. Com. I.T. Hirschl Trust, N.Y.C., 1974-92, N.Y. Community Trust Blood Disease Panel, N.Y.C., 1980—; dir. Belfer Inst. for Advanced Biomed. Studies, 1978-92. Co-editor: Seminars in Hematology, 1968—; editor-in-chief Blood, 1975-77; contbr. articles to profl. jours. Nat. bd. govs. ARC, Washington, 1984-90, chmn. blood svcs. com., 1988-90; bd. dirs. Nat. Marrow Donor Program, 1987—. With U.S. Army, 1944-46; capt. USAF, 1951-53. Named Career Scientist, Health Rsch. Coun.; recipient Charles R. Drew award ARC, 1990. Fellow Internat. Soc. Hematology (counselor 1980-88, v.p. 1984-88, historian 1990—); mem. Am. Soc. Hematology (pres. 1983, historian 1993—), Assn. Am. Physicians, Am. Fedn. Clin. Rsch., Am. Soc. Clin. Investigation, Am. Physiol. Soc., Assn. Am. Med. Colls. (emeritus), Coun. Acad. Socs. (adminstrv. bd. 1985-90, chmn. 1989), N.Y. Soc. Study Blood (pres. 1978-80), Soc. for Exptl. Biology and Medicine (pres. 1993-95), U. Chgo. Alumni Assn. (Profl. Achievement citation 1992), U. Chgo. Med. Alumni Assn. (Disting. Svc. award 1981), Phi Beta Kappa, Sigma Xi, Alpha Omega Alpha. Democrat. Lutheran. Office: Albert Einstein Coll Medicine 1300 Morris Park Ave Bronx NY 10461-1926

JAFFE, FREDRICK F., surgeon; b. N.Y.C., June 3, 1942; s. David A. and Mildred C. (Leibner) J.; m. Mary E. Mark, June 14, 1964 (div. Dec. 1994); children: David, Harry; m. Deborah L. Moody, Nov. 5, 1995. BS, Tufts U., 1964, MD, 1968. Diplomate Am. Bd. Orthopedic Surgery. Surg. intern N.Y. Hosp., N.Y.C., 1968-69, surg. fellow, 1969-70; orthopedic resident Hosp. for Joint Diseases, N.Y.C., 1970-73, fellow, 1973-74, attending orthopedic surgeon, 1974—, chief adult reconstructive surgery, 1991-94; attending orthopedic surgeon Beth Israel Med. Ctr., N.Y.C., 1994—, chief adult reconstructive surgery North Divsn., 1994—; dir. Insall, Scott, Kelley Inst. for Orthopaedics and Sports Medicine, N.Y.C., 1994—. Fellow Am. Acad. Orthopedic Surgery, Am. Coll. Surgeons, N.Y. Acad. Medicine; mem. Orthopaedic Rsch. Soc., Ea. Orthopedic Assn., N.Y. State Orthopedic Assn. Office: 401 E 55th St New York NY 10022

JAFFE, HERBERT, ophthalmologist; b. N.Y.C., May 21, 1939; s. Charles and Gertrude Jaffe; m. Madalon Jaffe, Dec. 18, 1960; 1 child, Robyn. MD, U. Louvain, Belgium, 1970. Diplomate Am. Bd. Ophthalmology. Intern Nassau Hosp., Mineola, N.Y., 1971-74; resident ophthalmology U. N.Y. Downstate, Bklyn., 1974; attending in ophthalmology Maimonides Med. Ctr., Bklyn., 1974—, Doctors Hosp., S.I., N.Y., 1993—, Univ. Hosp., S.I., 1991—; dir. ophthalmology Beth Israel Hosp., Bklyn., 1985—. Fellow Am. Bd. Ophthalmology; mem. Am. Assn. Ophthalmology, N.Y. State Ophthal. Soc., Bklyn. Acad. Ophthalmology. Office: 2128 Olean Ave Brooklyn NY 11229

JAFFE, JOHN SAMUEL, urologist; b. Great Bend, Kans., Dec. 22, 1944; s. Matthew Harold and Irma J.; m. Jane Frances Jaffe; children: William, Melissa, Elizabeth. BA, U. Pa., 1966; MD, NYU, 1970. Diplomate Am. Bd. Urology. Resident dept. urology Columbia Presbyn. Med. Ctr., N.Y.C., 1973-77; attending physician Lehigh Valley Hosp., Allentown, Pa., 1977—; courtesy physician Sacred Heart Hosp., Allentown, 1977—; pres. med. staff Lehigh Valley Hosp., Allentown, Pa., 1990-92; exec. med. dir. Lehigh Valley PHO, Allentown, 1994—; mem. adv. med. bd. Planned Parenthood Northeast Pa., Allentown. Contbr. numerous articles to urological jours. Lt. commdr. U.S. Pub. Health Svc., 1971-73. Recipient Soifer Meml. award NYU Sch. Medicine, 1970. Fellow Am. Coll. Surgeons, Coll. of Physicians of Phila.; mem. AMA, Phila. Urologic Soc., Greater Lehigh Valley Ind. Physician Assn. (chmn. 1994—). Office: Urologic Assocs Allentown 1240 S Cedar Crest Blvd Allentown PA 18103

JAFFE, JONATHAN HENRY, physician; b. Chgo., July 4, 1948; s. Jack Howard and Judith Reva (Greenberg) J.; m. Joanne Lenore Lattiff; 1 child, Jonathan Robert. BA, Yale U., 1970; MD, U. Ill., 1974. Diplomate Am. Bd. Family Practice. Family doctor Bedford, N.H., 1978—; clin. asst. prof. dept. family & cmty. medicine Tufts U., 1984—. Bd. dirs. Greater Manchester Childcare Assn., 1978-84. Fellow Am. Acad. Family Physicians; mem. N.H. Med. Soc. Office: River Road Family Health Ct 665 River Rd Bedford NH 03110

JAFFE, MARVIN EUGENE, pharmaceutical company executive, neurologist; b. Phila., July 16, 1936; s. William Reuben and Ida Dorothy (Weiner) J.; m. Joan Sheila Fineman; children: Jonathan, Matthew, Ondria, Joshua. BS, Temple U., 1956; MD, Jefferson U., 1960. Diplomate Am. Bd. Psychiatry and Neurology. Intern, Womack Army Hosp., Ft. Bragg, N.C., 1960-61; resident Jefferson Med. Coll., Phila., 1964-67; neurologist Phila. Gen. Hosp., 1967-70; research physician Merck Sharp & Dohme Research Labs., West Point, Pa., 1970-78, v.p., 1978-87, sr. v.p. 1987-88; pres. R.W. Johnson Pharm. Rsch. Inst., 1988-94; assoc. prof. Jefferson Med. Coll., Phila., 1982—; med. adv. Wilson's Disease Adv. Bd., N.Y.C., 1984—; bd. dirs. Royal Soc. Medicine Found., 1990—, v.p. 1992-95, pres., 1995—; bd. dirs. Chiroscience P.L.C., Immunomedics, Inc., Titan Pharm., Inc. Contbr. articles to profl. jours. Served to capt. U.S. Army, 1960-64, Germany. Fellow Am. Acad. Neurology, Am. Heart Assn. (stroke council); mem. Alpers Soc. for Clin. Neurology (sec., treas. 1982-88), Pharm. Mfrs. Assn. (steering com. 1983-94, chmn. 1993-94), Am. Physician's Fellowship (nat. dir. 1980—). Office: 20 Seagate Dr # 502 Naples FL 33940

JAFFE, RALPH HERMAN, social worker, psychologist, consultant; b. N.Y.C., Sept. 9, 1954; s. Gustave and Sarah (Pollack) J.; m. Andrea Marie D'Asaro, May 4, 1986; 1 child, Daniel Gustave. BA, SUNY, Albany, 1976; MSW, Hunter Coll., 1979; PsyD, Widener U., 1992. Clinician Bedford Stuyvesant Cmty. Mental Health Clinic, Bklyn., 1977-81; clinician, sr. clinician Esther T. Dutton Counseling Ctr., Morristown, N.J., 1981-84; clinician U. Medicine and Dentistry of N.J., New Brunswick, N.J., 1984-87; pvt. practice psychotherapist Phila., 1986—; part-time instr. Temple U. Sch. of Social Adminstrn., Phila., 1988, 89; cons. Olney Vet. Ctr., Phila., 1987—, Chestnut Hill Hosp., Phila., 1990-94; sr. employee assistance counselor PECO Energy Co., 1992—.

JAFFE, RICHARD LOUIS, psychiatrist; b. Phila., Feb. 27, 1952; s. William and Annette (Freilich) J.; m. Terry Dee Glass, May 19, 1974; children: Evan, Brian. BS, Pa. State U., 1972; MD, Thomas Jefferson U., 1974. Diplomate Am. Bd. Psychiatry and Neurology. Intern St. Elizabeth's Hosp., Washington, 1974-75; resident Temple U. Hosp., Phila., 1977; teaching unit asst. dir. Temple Hosp., Phila., 1977-82; assoc. prof. psychiatry Temple U. Sch. Medicine, Phila., 1985—; teaching unit dir. Belmont Ctr., 1982—. Mem. Am. Psychiat. Assn., Phila. Psychiat. Assn., Assn. for Acad. Psychiatry, Assn. for Convulsive Therapy, Coll. Physicians Phila. Office: Belmont Ctr 4200 Monument Rd Philadelphia PA 19131-1625

JAFFE, ROBERT BENTON, obstetrician, gynecologist, reproductive endocrinologist; b. Detroit, Feb. 18, 1933; s. Jacob and Shirley (Robins) J.; m. Evelyn Grossman, Aug. 29, 1954; children: Glenn, Terri. M.S., U. Colo., 1966; M.D., U. Mich., 1957. Intern U. Colo. Med. Ctr., Denver, 1957-58, resident, 1959-63; asst. prof. Ob-Gyn. U. Mich. Med. Ctr., 1964-68, assoc. prof., 1968-72, prof., 1972-74, dir. steroid rsch. unit, 1964-74; prof. U. Calif., San Francisco, 1974—, chmn. dept. ob-gyn and reproductive scis., 1974-96; mem. nat. adv. council, mem. human embryology and devel. and reproductive biology study sect. Nat. Inst. Child Health and Human Devel.; bd. dirs. Population Resource Center. Author: Reproductive Endocrinology: Physiology, Pathophysiology and Clinical Management, 1978, 2d edit., 1986, 3d edit., 1991, Prolactin, 1981, The Peripartal Period, 1985; contbr. numerous articles to profl. jours.; mem. editorial bd. Jour. Clin. Endocrinology and Metabolism, 1971-75, Fertility and Sterility, 1972-78; editor-in-chief Obstetric and Gynecologic Survey, 1991—. Josiah Macy Found. faculty fellow, 1967-70, 81; USPHS postdoctoral fellow, 1958-59, 63-64; Rockefeller Found.

grantee, 1974—; Andrew Mellon Found. grantee, 1978-81. Mem. Endocrine Soc. (coun. 1985-86, sec.-treas. 1994—), Soc. Gynecologic Investigation (pres. 1975-76, Pres.'s Disting. Scientist award 1993), Perinatal Rsch. Soc. (pres. 1973-74), Am. Coll. Obstetricians and Gynecologists (awards), Internat. Soc. Neuroendocrinology, Assn. Am. Physicians, Inst. Medicine Nat. Acad. Scis., Royal Coll. Obstetricians and Gynecologists (ad eundum). Democrat. Jewish. Home: 90 Mt Tiburon Rd Belvedere Tiburon CA 94920-1512 Office: U Calif Med Sch OB-Gyn & Reproductive Sci San Francisco CA 94143

JAFFE, ROSS ALLAN, physician; b. Suffolk, Va., Sept. 12, 1958. AB, Dartmouth Coll., 1980; MD, Johns Hopkins U., 1985; MBA, Stanford U., 1990. Rsch. assoc. Lewin & Assocs., Washington, 1980-81; resident U. Calif. Med. Ctr., San Francisco, 1985-88; physician Redwood Med. Clinic, Redwood City, Calif., 1988-89; clin. instr., attending physician U. Calif. Med. Ctr., 1988-90, 92-95, U. Calif., Irvine, 1990-92; gen. ptnr. Brentwood Assocs., Menlo Park, Calif., 1990—; cons. in field. Contbr. articles to profl. jours. Com. mem. Blue Cross Adv. com. Peninsula Cmty. Found., San Mateo, Calif., 1995—. Office: Brentwood Assocs 2730 San Hill Rd #250 Menlo Park CA 94025

JAFFE, RUSSELL MERRITT, pathologist, research director; b. Albany, N.Y., Jan. 1, 1947. AB cum laude, Boston U., 1972, MD with honors, 1972, PhD in Biochemistry, 1972. Diplomate Am. Bd. Pathology (clin., chem.), Nat. Bd. Med. Examiners. Med. intern Boston U. Med. Ctr., 1972-73; resident in clin. pathology NIH, Bethesda, Md., 1973-75, sr. staff physician clin. pathology dept., 1973-79, chief resident tng. program clin. chemistry sect., 1976-79; fellow health rsch., practice, policy devel. Health Studies Collegium, 1979—; dir. Serammune Physicians Lab., Vienna, Va., 1987—, Princeton BioCenter, 1989-92; prin. faculty Oriental Med. Strategy in Western Med. Practice, HSC, N.Y.C., 1980-85. Assoc. editor The New Physician, 1971-72, sr. assoc. editor, 1972-73. Bd. govs. Light Found., 1980—. Comdr. USPHS, 1973-79. Recipient Nat. Rsch. award Am. Acad. Med. Preventics, 1979, J.D. Lane award USPHS, 1975, Excellence in Rsch. award Mead Johnson, 1969, Man of Yr. award Hillel Found., 1967. Fellow Am. Coll. Nutrition, Am. In-Vitro Allergy/Immunology Soc., Am. Soc. Clin. Pathologists; mem. APHA, Am. Assn. Clin. Chemists, Am. Fedn. Clin. Rsch., Am. Holistic Med. Assn. (chmn. sci. adv. com. 1978-80), Internat. Coll. Applied Nutrition, Acad. Clin. Lab. Physicians and Scientists. Home: 1890 Preston White Dr Reston VA 22091-5430 Office: Serammune Physicians Lab AMSA Bldg 2d Fl 1890 Preston White Dr Reston VA 22091-5430

JAFFIN, JONATHAN HUNTER, surgeon; b. Princeton, N.J., Oct. 2, 1955; s. Charles Leonard and Rosanna Gordon (Webster) J.; m. Annesley Jeanne Williamson, Oct. 22, 1988; children: James Annesley, David Williamson. AB, Princeton U., 1977; MD, Johns Hopkins U., 1981; MMAS, U.S. Army Command Coll., 1991. Commd. 2d lt. U.S. Army, 1977, advanced through grades to lt. col., 1993; resident in gen. surgery Walter Reed Army Med. Ctr., Washington, 1981-86, attending surgeon, 1986-88; group surgeon 5th Spl. Forces Group, Ft. Campbell, Ky., 1988-90; fellow trauma and critical care Washington Hosp. Ctr., 1991-93; chief trauma and critical care Brooke Army Med. Ctr., Fort Sam Houston, Tex., 1993-96; divsn. surgeon 4th Inf. Divsn., Ft. Hood, Tex., 1996—. Decorated Army Commendation medal, Meritorious Svc. medal. Fellow ACS (vice chmn. U.S. Army com. on trauma 1995—); mem. Assn. Mil. Surgeons, Ea. Assn. for Surgery of Trauma, Soc. Critical Care Medicine, Assn. Acad. Surgery. Home: 13823 Crown Bluff San Antonio TX 78216 Office: Divsn Surgeon 4th Inf Divsn Fort Hood TX 76544

JAGLINSKY, KENNETH, laboratory administrator; b. Chgo., Oct. 27, 1950; s. Arthur and Marie (Stepek) J.; m. Marlene Jaglinski, Aug. 26, 1976; children: Kevin, Timothy, Robin. BS, Valparaiso U., 1973; postgrad., U. Wis., Milw., 1985. Cert. med. technician. V.p., gen. mgr. Bayshore Clin. Labs., Milw., 1988—. Chmn. Zoning Bd. Appeals, Whitefish Bay, Wis., 1988—. Mem. Clin. Lab. Mgmt. Assn. (pres. Wis. chpt. 1994-96), Coun. Small Bus. Execs. (CEO Roundtable). Office: Bayshore Clin Labs 4555 W Shroeder Dr Brown Deer WI 53223-1476

JAHIEL, RENE INO, physician; b. Boulogne S/Seine, France, Mar. 29, 1928; s. Richard and Cecile (Lwovsky) J.; m. Deborah Berg, May 8, 1955; children: Abigail, Richard, Beth. French Lycees, Baccalaureat, 1944; BA, NYU, 1946; MD, Downstate Med. Coll., SUNY, 1950; PhD, Columbia U., 1957. Intern, Montefiore Hosp., N.Y.C., 1950-51; resident Mt. Sinai Hosp., N.Y.C., 1952, fellow virology, 1952-55; exptl. immunologist Nat. Jewish Hosp., Denver, 1957-59; asst. attending pathologist, exptl. pathology Mt. Sinai Hosp., 1959-61; asst. prof. pub. health Cornell U. Med. Coll., 1961-66; rsch. assoc. prof. preventive medicine NYU, 1967-70, rsch. prof., 1970-76, rsch. prof. medicine Sch. Medicine, 1976-88, cons. health, svcs. rsch., policy and planning, 1989—; adj. prof. health svcs., rsch. and policy New Sch. for Social Rsch., 1991—; dean faculty of scis. and pub. health Ecole Libr des Hautes Etudes of N.Y., 1991-94, v.p. scis., 1994—; vis. prof. dept. cmty. medicine & health care U. Conn., 1995—; pres. Internat. Health Policy Rsch. Corp., 1995—; med. dir. Southbury (Conn.) Tng. Sch., 1993-95; tchr. met. leadership program U. Coll., NYU, 1969-73; physician Assn. for Help Retarded Children, 1982-88, Young Adult Inst., 1984-89, Assn. for Children with Retarded Mental Devel., 1988-93; cons. Nat. Ctr. for Health Svcs. Rsch., 1983-85. Bd. dirs. N.Y. Scientists Com. Pub. Info., 1974-79, Physicians Forum, 1975-84; mem. interferon adv. com. Am. Cancer Soc., 1985-93; mem. nat. bd. Com. for Nat. Health Svc.,1976-79, coalition, 1980-85. Lt. USNR, 1955-57. USPHS Rsch. grantee, 1966-79. Mem. Am. Public Health Assn. (chmn. com. on health svcs. rsch. 1980-87, governing coun. 1983-85, chmn. homelessness study group 1984-90, chmn. policy com. caucus on disablement 1989-92, founding chmn. caucus on homelessness 1990-91, Med. Care sect. award 1985), Soc. for Social Study of Sci., Assn. Health Svcs. Rsch. (Spl. Recognition award 1986), World Assn. for Psychosocial Rehab. (chmn. com. on mental handicaps 1992-94). Author sci. rsch. articles on tissue culture, virology, interferon, preventive medicine, health policy, health svcs. rsch., sociology of knowledge; editor: Homelessness: A Prevention-Oriented Approach, 1992. Home: 60 E 8th St Apt 19F New York NY 10003-6519

JAHN, LAURENCE ROY, retired biologist, institute executive; b. Jefferson, Wis., June 24, 1926; s. Roy Johaan and Mabel Marie (Kothlow) J.; m. Helen Florence Faville, Sept. 5, 1947; children: Katharine Marie (Mrs. Ronald J. Cook), Richard Alan. B.S., U. Wis., 1949, M.S., 1958, Ph.D., 1965. Aquatic biologist Wis. Dept. Natural Resources, 1949-59; with Wildlife Mgmt. Inst., Washington, 1959-91; v.p. Wildlife Mgmt. Inst., 1971-87, pres., 1987-91, chmn. bd., 1991-92; chmn. bd. United Conservation Alliance, Washington, 1990-92; liaison officer Nat. Assn. Univ. Fisheries and Wildlife Programs, 1992—; mem. Va. bd. Game and Inland Fisheries, 1992—, chmn., 1994-95, sci. adv. bd.; chmn. bd. Dept. Def. Strategic Environ. R&D Program, 1992-94; mem. waterfowl adv. com. U.S. Fish and Wildlife Svc., 1968-76, U.S. Implementation Bd., N.Am. Waterfowl Mgmt. Plan, 1988-91, chmn., 1990-91; mem. spl. adv. panel on water resources rsch. Dept. Interior, 1971-73, chmn., 1973, mem. adv. com. on fish, wildlife and parks, 1975-77, mem. adv. com. on outer continental shelf environ. studies, 1975-77; mem. adv. com. on water data for pub. use and working group on river quality assessment U.S. Geol. Survey, 1972-87; mem. wildlife adv. com. Dept. State, 1972-76; mem. adv. com. on natural resources conservation award Sec. Def., 1973, 76, 80, 85, 86; mem. adv. panel on tuna-porpoise Nat. Marine Fisheries Svc., 1974; mem. environ. adv. bd. U.S. Army C.E., 1979-85, chmn., 1983-85; mem. marine fisheries adv. com. NOAA, 1982-84; mem. bd. agr. and renewable resources Nat. Acad. Scis., 1980-83, mem. exec. bd., 1981-83; mem. adv. bd. on wild horse and burro U.S. Dept. Agr. and Interior, 1986-88, Agr./Conservation Coalition, 1981-91, chmn., 1981-86. Author numerous articles in field.; Editor symposia procs. and books. Pres. Horicon (Wis.) Bd. Edn., 1965-67; bd. dirs. Citizens Com. on Natural Resources, 1970-78; mem. steering com. Nat. Watershed Congress, 1971-90, chmn., 1977-90; tustee N.Am. Wildlife Found., 1972-85, sec.-treas., 1974-85; chmn. program com. N.Am. Wildlife and Natural Resources Conf., 1972-88; bd. dirs. Urban Wildlife Rsch. Ctr., 1972-76; mem. bd. Wildfowl Found., 1972-93, sec., 1975-91. With USNR, 1944-46. Recipient certificate merit Nash Conservation Awards Program, 1953; resolution appreciation Miss. Flyway Council, 1970; Outstanding Civilian Service medal Dept. of Army, 1985. Fellow AAAS; mem. Wildlife Soc. (pres. 1979, Trippensie-McPherson award 1984, spl. recognition award 1986, Aldo Leopold Meml. award 1989), Soil Conservation Soc. (commendation 1969), Am. Water Resources Assn. (interim dir. S. Atlantic dist. 1975), Natural Resources Council Am. (exec. com. 1976-86, sec. 1978-81, vice chmn. 1981-83, chmn. 1983-85, hon. mem. 1985, Barbara Swain award of honor 1991), Nat. Audubon Soc., Wilderness Soc., Internat. Assn. Fish and Wildlife Agencies (life), Am. Forests (life), Nat. Wildlife Fedn. (life), Wis. Acad. Scis., Arts and Letters, Am. Fisheries Soc., Washington Biologists' Field Club, Whooping Crane Conservation Assn. (life), Wilson Ornithol. Soc. (life), Cosmos Club (admissions com. 1985-88, chmn. 1986-88, awards com. 1991-93, chmn. 1992-93), Boone and Crockett Club. Presbyn. Home and Office: 2435 Riviera Dr Vienna VA 22181-3120

JAHNKE, VOLKER, otorhinolaryngologist; b. Stettin, Germany, Sept. 6, 1937; s. Walter and Luise (Schlegel) J.; m. Marie Helene Bourassa, June 24, 1968 (div. 1979); children: Kim, Nina. MD, U. Hamburg, Germany, 1961; MSc, U. Montreal, Can., 1964. Intern U. Hamburg, Germany, 1961-63; rsch. fellow U. Montreal, Can., 1963-64; resident Bellevue Med. Ctr. NYU, 1964-69; asst. prof., assoc. prof. U. Marburg, Lahn, Germany, 1970-73; assoc. prof. U. Munich, 1973-77; chmn. Rudolf Virchow Hosp., Berlin, 1978-87, Univ. Klinikum Rudolf Virchow, Berlin, 1987—. Recipient 1st prize in Otorhinolaryngology rsch., 1968, 2d prize, 1969. Fellow ACS, Am. Acad. Ophthalmology and Otolaryngology, Am. Acad. Facial Plastic and Reconstructive Surgery, Am. Soc. Head and Neck Surgery, Am. Laryngol., Rhinol. and Otolaryn. Soc.; mem. Lions Club Berlin-Dahlem. Home: Bernadottestr 9, 14193 Berlin Germany Office: Virchow-Klinikum Humboldt U, Augustenburger Platz 1, 13353 Berlin Germany also: Universitätsklinikum Charité der Humboldt U, Schumannstr 20/21, 10117 Berlin Germany

JAIN, AMAR SINGH, orthopedic surgeon, consultant; b. Sadlilpur, Rajasthan, India, Jan. 4, 1949; m. Vijaya Jain; children: Anant, Anita. MB, BS, S.M.S. Med. Sch., Jaipur, India, 1971. Clin. lectr. U. Dundee, Scotland, 1984-87; cons. in charge Dundee Limb Fitting Ctr., 1987—; cons. orthop. surgeon DTH NHS Trust, Dundee, 1987—; chmn. clin. placement Nat. Ctr. Tng. and Edn. in Pros/Orthotics U. Strathclyde, Glasgow, Scotland, 1993—, convener exam. bd., 1989—; convener working group Internat. Stds. Orgn., 1992—. Contbr. chpts. in books. Mem. Royal Coll. Surgeons, Internat. Soc. Prosthetics and Orthotics (hon. sec. 1995—), Brit. Orthop. Assn. Office: Dundee Limb Fitting Ctr, 133 Queens St Broughty Fry, Dundee Tayside DD5 1AG, Scotland

JAINDL, JEFFREY JOSEPH, radiologist; b. Allentown, Pa., Nov. 7, 1951; s. Joseph James and Elsie Veronica (Pesarcik) J. BS in Biology, Moravian Coll., Bethlehem, Pa., 1973; DO, Phila. Coll. Osteo. Medicine, 1977. Diplomate Am. Bd. Radiology. Staff radiologist Upstate Carolina Med. Ctr., Gaffney, S.C., 1987—. With USN, 1977-87. Mem. Am. Coll. Radiology, S.C. Radiol. Soc., Am. Osteo. Coll. Radiology. Office: Cherokee Radiological Assoc 111B Tiffany Pk Gaffney SC 29342

JAIVIN, JONATHAN STEVEN, orthopedic surgeon; b. New London, Conn., May 7, 1958; s. Lewis Stanley and Naomi (Dorsky) J.; m. Ann Melissa Halverstadt, Sept. 4, 1988. ScB with honors in Biology, Brown U., 1980; MD, U. Conn., 1985. Diplomate Am. Bd. Orthopedic Surgery, Nat. Bd. Med. Examiners; qualified med. examiner, Calif.; lic. physician, Calif. Intern in gen. surgery Hartford (Conn.) Hosp., 1985-86, resident in gen. surgery, 1986-87; resident in orthop. surgery U. Conn. Combined Program, Farmington, 1987-90; fellow in foot and ankle surgery Baylor Coll. Medicine, Houston, 1990-91; attending surgeon So. Calif. Orthop. Inst., Van Nuys, 1991—; chmn. dept. orthop. surgery Valley Presbyn. Hosp., Van Nuys, 1994—; provisional staff Henry Mayo Newhall Hosp., Valencia, Calif., Motion Picture Hosp., Woodland Hills, Calif., West Hills Med. Ctr., West Hills; lectr. in field. Contbr. articles to profl. jours. Fellow Am. Acad. Orthop. Surgeons; mem. Am. Orthop. Foot and Ankle Soc. Office: So Calif Orthop Inst 6815 Noble Ave Van Nuys CA 91405

JALAL, IBRAHIM MOHAMMAD, pharmaceutical executive; b. Jaffa, Palestine, July 8, 1943; arrived in Jordan, 1948; s. M. I. and Bahiyyah (Rous) J.; m. Nadia S. Tahboub, July 30, 1973; children: Diana, Rania, Shadia, Saba. BS in Pharmacy, U. Alexandria, Egypt, 1967; MSc in Pharmacy, Phila. Coll. Pharmacy & Sci., Pa., 1972; PhD in Pharmacy, U. Wis., Madison, 1978. Prodn. mgr. Arab Pharms., Sult, Jordan, 1967-70, 72-73; teaching asst. U. Wis., 1973-74, rsch. asst., 1974-78; group leader Riker Labs. subs. 3M Ctr., St. Paul, 1978-79; tech. vp. Hikma Internats., Amman, Jordan, 1979—; adj. prof. U. Jordan, 1981-84; mem. com. on MSc exam Yarmouk U., Irbid, Jordan, 1982—; tech. cons. Ministry of Health Amman, 1987-89. Contbr. articles to profl. jours. Mem. Am. Assn. Pharm. Scientists, Jordan Pharm. Assn. Home: PO Box 925554, Amman Jordan Office: Hikma Pharms, PO Box 182400, Amman Jordan

JALKH, ALEX E., ophthalmologist, researcher; b. Beirut, Lebanon, May 22, 1949; s. Edmond and Eugenie (Pollak) J. MD, St. Joseph U. Beirut. Diplomate Am. Bd. Ophthalomolgy. Clin. assoc. scientist Schepens Eye Rsch. Inst., Boston, 1985—; asst. prof. ophthalmolgy Harvard Med. Sch., Boston, 1992—; asst. surgeon Mass. Eye and Ear Infirmary, Boston, 1985—. Fellow Am. Acad. Ophthalmology (hon. award); mem. AMA, RETINA Soc., Macula Soc., New Eng. Ophthalmological Soc. Office: Schepens Retina Assocs 100 Charles River Plaza Boston MA 02114

JALLER, MICHAEL M., retired orthopedic surgeon; b. Zurich, Switzerland, Feb. 25, 1924; came to U.S., 1926; s. Arthur and Anna (Eliash) J.; m. Helen F. Cowan, June 24, 1944; children: David, Daniel, Amy. BA, NYU, 1944; MD, U. Lausanne (Switzerland), 1952. Diplomate Am. Bd. Orthopaedic Surgery. V.p. A. Jaller & Co. Inc., N.Y.C., 1944-61; intern Waterbury (Conn.) Gen. Hosp., 1952-53; surg. resident Bridgeport (Conn.) Gen. Hosp., 1953-54; orthopedic resident U. Hosp. of Cin., Cin. Gen. Hosp., 1954-57; instr. orthopaedic surgery U. Hosp., Cin., 1954-57, chief resident in orthosurgery, 1956-57; rsch. fellow in biophysics Weitzmann Inst., Rehovoth, Israel, 1965; chief cons. VA Hosp., Washington, 1966-71; pres. Greater Washington Orthopaedic Group, Silver Spring, Md., 1967-93; ret., 1993; pres. MHJ Fisheries Inc.; bd. dirs. Rotocast Plastics Inc. Pres. Silver Spring Jewish Ctr., Silver Spring, 1984-91. With U.S. Army, 1942-46. Fellow ACS, Am. Acad. Orthopaedic Surgery, Royal Soc. Health, Washington Art League, N.Y. Acad. Sci., Selby Bay Yacht Club. Republican.

JAMES, BRENT CARL, health care executive, biomedical sciences educator; b. Shelley, Idaho, Dec. 28, 1950; s. John Carl and Barbara Joyce (Hendrickson) J.; m. Karen Anne Stephenson, Nov. 21, 1979 (Sept. 1986); 1 child, Ian Carl. BS in Computer Sci., U. Utah, 1974, BS in Med. Biology, 1975, MD, 1978, M in Statis., 1983. Sr. systems programmer 1st Security Bank, Salt Lake City, 1972-79; asst. dir. cancer dept., dir. computing dept. ACS, Chgo., 1979-83; lectr. Harvard U. Sch. of Pub. Health, Boston, 1984-85, asst. prof., 1985-86; v.p. med. rsch. and continuing med. edn. Intermountain Health Care, Salt Lake City, 1986—; exec. dir. IHC Inst. for Health Care Delivery Rsch., Salt Lake City, 1990—; pres. Health Care Software, Salt Lake City, 1980—; vis. lectr. dept. biostatis. Harvard U. Sch. of Pub. Health, 1986-95; adj. prof. dept. family and preventive medicine U. Utah, Salt Lake City, 1987—; v.p. Interwest Quality of Care, Inc., Salt Lake City, 1990—; vis. lectr. dept. health policy and mgmt. Harvard Sch. Pub. Health, 1995—. Contbr. numerous articles to profl. jours. Capt. USPHS, 1979-80. Nat. Merit scholar, 1969. Mem. Am. Statis. Assn., Am. Assn. for Med. Systems and Informatics, Phi Beta Kappa. Mormon. Office: Intermountain Health Care 36 S State St 16th Fl Salt Lake City UT 84111

JAMES, FRANCIS MARSHALL, III, anesthesiologist; b. Phila., Dec. 22, 1935. MD, Hahnemann U., 1961. Intern Phila. Gen. Hosp., 1961-62; resident Hosp. U. Pa., Phila., 1964-67; attending anesthesiologist N.C. Bapt. Hosp., Winston-Salem; prof., chmn. Wake Forest U. Med. Ctr. Office: Bowman Gray Sch Med Dept Anesthesia Medical Ctr Blvd Winston Salem NC 27157-1009*

JAMES, GREGORY JON, health facility administrator; b. Inglewood, Calif., Jan. 19, 1960; s. John William and Joyce (Branson) J.; m. Carolyn Holly Szabo, June 11, 1988; children: William Anthony, Nicholas Taylor. AA, Manatee Community Coll., 1981; BA in Chemistry, U. South Fla., 1983; DO, Nova Southeatern U., 1988. Resident in family practice then chief resident Sun Coast Hosp., Largo, Fla., 1988-91; mem. teaching staff family practice residency Sun Coast Hosp., 1991—; med. dir. family practice residency clinic Sun Coast Hosp., Largo, Fla., 1994—; family physician Bay Med. Ctr., Dunedin, Fla., 1991-94; ACLS instr. Am. Heart Assn., Largo, 1990—, affiliate faculty, 1994—; asst. prof. family medicine Southeastern U. Health Scis., Kirkville Coll. Osteo. Medicine; vice chmn. dept. family practice Mease Hosp., Dunedin, 1993; chmn. dept. family parctice Mease Hosp., 1994. Mem. Am. Osteo. Assn., Fla. Osteo. Med. Assn., Pinellas County Osteo. Assn., Am. Coll. Family Practitioners (cert.), Sigma Sigma Phi, Phi Theta Kappa. Office: Sun Coast Hosp 2025 Indian Rocks Rd Largo FL 34644

JAMES, KATHLEEN DAWN, mental health facility administrator; b. Hanover, Pa., June 5, 1944; d. David W. and Florence R. (Lucabaugh) Lehigh; children: Benjamin, Elizabeth. BA, Ea. Mennonite Coll., 1967; MSW, Ohio State U., 1970; cert. in pastoral counseling, Pastoral Inst. Lehigh Valley, 1986. Lic. ind. clin. social worker, Mass., marriage counselor, N.J. Caseworker Jewish Family Svc., Columbus, Ohio, 1970-71; social worker Santa Clara County Dept. Social Health Svcs., San Jose, Calif., 1971-72; program dir. Echo Glen Children's Ctr., Snoqualmie, Wash., 1972-78; clin. social work supr. Danvers State Hosp., Hathorne, Mass., 1978-80; pvt. practice, 1980-85; family therapist Pa. Found. for Mental Health, Sellersville, Pa., 1985-86; bereavement coord. Ctr. for Hope Hospice, Roselle, N.J., 1986-88; clin. coord. East Orange (N.J.) Outpatient Mental Health Ctr., 1988—. Author: Psychotherapy, Incest: The Teenagers Perspective, 1977, Coed Residential Milieu, 1980. Democrat. Episcopalian. Office: E Orange Gen Hosp 300 Central Ave East Orange NJ 07018-2819

JAMES, KIMBERLY ANN, medical and surgical nurse; b. Elkhart, Ind., July 13, 1971; d. John Franklin and Esther Marie (Rapp) Houston. BSN, Ind. U., South Bend, 1993. RN, Ind.; cert. BLS. Pediatric nurse extern Meml. Hosp., South Bend, Ind., 1993-94; staff med./surg. nurse Elkhart (Ind.) Gen. Hosp., 1994-95, outpatient surgery nurse, 1995—. Jr. vice comdr. DAV Aux., Ind., 1995-96, comdr. 1996-97. Mem. Profl. Nurses Orgn., Sigma Theta Tau Internat. Republican. Mem. Brethren Ch. Home: 30868 Oaksprings Dr Granger IN 46530

JAMES, MARY SPENCER, nursing administrator; b. London, Ont., Can., July 10, 1949; d. Richard Spencer and Helen Frances (Winterbottom) James; m. Robert Peter Owler, Oct. 4, 1969 (div. June 25, 1975). AA, Norwich U., 1969; Nursing Diploma, Toronto (Ont.) Gen. Hosp., 1973; BA in Psychology, U. Vt., 1975. RN, Calif. Staff nurse Toronto Gen. Hosp., 1973-77, Stanford (Calif.) U. Hosp., 1977-81, B.C. Children's Hosp., Vancouver, 1981-83; sr. staff nurse King Abdul Aziz Mil. Hosp., Tabuk, Saudi Arabia, 1983-84, Charter Med. Ltd./Tawam Hosp., Al Ain, Abu Dhabi, UAE, 1984-87; nurse Dubai Petroleum Co., UAE, 1987-88; nursing dir. Ygia Polyclinic, Limassol, Cyprus, 1988-89; nurse Stat Travelers, Inc., L.A., 1990-91; staff nurse Lucile Salter Packard Children's Hosp. at Stanford, Palo Alto, Calif., 1991-92; case mgr. H.S.S.I. Home Care and Olsten Healthcare, Milbrae and San Francisco, 1992-93; nursing dir. CHS Home Health Agy., San Francisco, 1993-94; liaison nurse coord., pvt. duty supr. United Nursing Internat., San Francisco, 1994-95; nursing supr. Staff Builders Home Care Svcs., Santa Rosa, Calif., 1995; home health coord. Care Home Health Svcs., Sonoma, Calif., 1995—. Home: 340 Channing Way Apt 353 San Rafael CA 94903

JAMES, MAURICE, ophthalmologist; b. Canton, Miss., Dec. 22, 1949; s. Marion Bridford and Wardine (Meeks) J.; m. Mavis L. Parkman, May 17, 1970; children: Mioshi, Maurice P., Maxwell. BS, Tougaloo Coll., 1971; MD, Columbia U., 1975. Diplomate Am. Bd. Ophthalmology. Intern Harlem Hosp., N.Y.C.; resident Harlem Hosp.-Columbia U., N.Y.C.; fellow in vitreo-retinal Vanderbilt U., Nashville, 1980; pvt. practice, Jackson, 1980—; physician, bd. dirs. Miss. Vocat. Rehab. Svc., Jackson, 1980-85; physician, mem. task force Miss. Gov.'s Statewide Comprehensive Planning Studies for Blind and Visually Handicapped Children, Jackson, 1984-85; bd. dirs., vice chmn. Miss. Bd. Health, Jackson, 1992-96. Contbr. articles to med. jours. Fellow Am. Acad. Ophthalmology; mem. Nat. Assn. To Prevent Blindness (bd. dirs. Jackson 1989), Am. Diabetic Assn. (bd. dirs. Jackson 1981-82). Home: 830 Camden Dr Jackson MS 39206 Office: 971 Lakeland Dr Ste 661 Jackson MS 39216

JAMES, MICHAEL CHARLES, urologist; b. Harvey, Ill., Feb. 2, 1957; s. Henry A. and Janet M. (Kline) J.; children: Michael, Robert, Nick, Elizabeth. Student, Knox Coll., 1977; BS cum laude, U. N.D., 1979, MD, 1984. Diplomate Am. Bd. Urology. Intern U. N.D.-VA Hosp., Fargo, 1984-85; resident in gen. surgery So. Ill. U., Springfield, 1985-87, resident in urology, 1987-90; pvt. practice, Mankatot, Minn., 1990—; bd. dirs. Mankato Clinic, 1992-9. Mem. Am. Urol.. Assn., Minn. Med. Assn. (del. Blue Earth County chpt.), Minn. Urol. Assn. Office: Mankato Clinic PO Box 8674 Mankato MN 56002

JAMES, MICHELLE ANNE, orthopaedic surgeon; b. San Francisco, Dec. 30, 1957; d. Preston M. and Beverley F. (Smith) J.; m. David M. Artale, Dec. 13, 1980; 2 children. BA, U. Calif., Berkeley, 1979; MD, U. Calif., San Diego, 1983. Diplomate Am. Bd. Orthopaedic Surgery. Intern then resident U. Calif., San Francisco, 1983-88; fellow Ind. Ctr. for Srugery of The Hand, Indpls., 1988-89; pvt. practice San Francisco, 1989-91; mem. orthopedic and hand surgery staff Shriners Hosp., San Francisco, 1989—, med. dir. rehab., 1991—. Author: (with others) The Child With A Spinal Cord Injury, 1996; contbr. articles to profl. jours. Bd. dirs. Grace Infant Care Ctr., San Francisco, 1992-93, v.p. bd. Montessori Children's House, San Francisco, 1994-96. Fellow Am. Acad. Orthopaedic Surgeons; mem. Am. Soc. Surgery of the Hand, Am. Spinal Injury Assn., Pediat. Orthopaedic Soc. N.Am., Calif. Med. Soc., Calif. Orthopaedic Assn., San Francisco Med. Soc., Ruth Jackson Orthopaedic Soc., Leroy C. Abbott Soc. (bd. dirs. 1993—, pres.-elect bd. 1994—). Office: Shriners Hosp 1701 19th Ave San Francisco CA 94122

JAMES, NANCY CAPLAN, pharmacist, researcher; b. Detroit, May 22, 1959. BS in Pharmacy, U. Mich., 1982, PharmD, 1983. Lic. pharmacist, Mich., N.C. Am. Soc. Hosp. Pharmacists clin. pharmacy resident Health Scis. Ctr. U. Ill., Chgo., 1983-84; clin. drug rsch. fellow clin. pharmacokinetics/dynamics sect. U. N.C. and Burroughs Wellcome Co., Research Triangle Park, 1984-85; clin. trials specialist clin. pharmacokinetics/dynamics sect. Burroughs Wellcome Co., Research Triangle Park, 1985-86, clin. rsch. assoc., 1986-87, clin. rsch. scientist, 1987-88; clin. pharmacokineticist clin. pharmacokinetics dept. Glaxo Inc., Research Triangle Park, 1988-89, group leader bioequivalence, 1989-91, group leader clin. evaluations, 1991, assoc. dir. R & D project planning, 1991-92, head full devel. planning R & D project planning, 1992-94, dir. full devel. planning R & D project planning, 1994-95; internat. dir. anti-infective and antiviral planning Glaxo Wellcome Inc., 1995—; presenter in field. Author: (with others) Clinical Drug Trials and Tribulations, 1988, Antiepileptic Drug Interactions, 1989; contbr. articles to profl. jours. Recipient Outstanding Achievement in Pharmacy award, Merck, Julia E. Emmanuel award U. Mich., 1982, James B. Angell scholarship, 1981-82. Mem. Am. Assn. Pharm. Scientists, Am. Coll. Clin. Pharmacy, Drug Info. Assn., Project Mgmt. Inst., Rho Chi, Phi Lambda Upsilon. Home: 2944 Bally Bunion Way Raleigh NC 27613-5402 Office: Glaxo Wellcome Inc 5 Moore Dr Durham NC 27701-4613

JAMES, THOMAS NAUM, cardiologist, educator; b. Amory, Miss., Oct. 24, 1925; s. Naum and Kata J.; m. Gleaves Elizabeth Tynes, June 22, 1948; children: Thomas Mark, Terrence Fenner, Peter Naum. BS, Tulane U., 1946, MD, 1949. Diplomate Am. Bd. Internal Medicine (bd. govs. 1982-88), Bd. Cardiovascular Diseases (bd. dirs. 1972-78). Intern Henry Ford Hosp., Detroit, 1949-50, resident in internal medicine and cardiology, 1950-53, mem. staff, 1959-68; practice medicine specializing in cardiology, 1953—; mem. staff U. Ala. Hosps., 1968-87; instr. medicine Tulane U., New Orleans, 1955-58, asst. prof., 1959; prof. medicine U. Ala. Med. Ctr., Birmingham, 1968-87, prof. pathology, 1968-73, assoc. prof. physiology and biophysics, 1969-73, dir. Cardiovascular Rsch. and Tng. Ctr., 1970-77, chmn. dept. medicine, dir. divsn. cardiovascular disease, 1973-81, Mary Gertrude Waters prof. cardiology, 1976-87, Disting. prof. of univ., 1981-87; prof. medicine, prof. pathology, pres. U. Tex. Med. Br., Galveston, 1987—, dir. WHO Cardiovascular Ctr., 1988—; mem. adv. coun. Nat. Heart Lung and Blood Inst., 1975-79; pres. 10th World Congress Cardiology, 1986; mem. cardiology del. invited by Chinese Med. Assn. to China, 1978; Campbell orator Queens U., Belfast, No. Ireland, 1982; Mikamo lectr. Japan Circulation Soc., 1982; Sir Thomas Lewis lectr. Brit. Cardiac Soc., 1983, Einthoven lectr. U. Leiden, The Netherlands, 1993, Bailey K. Ashford lectr. U. P.R., 1995. Author: Anatomy of the Coronary Arteries, 1961, The Etiology of Myocardial Infarction, 1963; Mem. editorial bd.: Circulation, 1966-83; mem. editorial bd.: Am. Jour. Cardiology, 1968-76; assoc. editor, 1976-82; mem. editorial bd.: Am. Heart Jour, 1976-79; Contbr. articles on cardiovascular diseases to med. jours. Served as capt. M.C. U.S. Army, 1953-55. Fellow ACP (gov. Ala. 1975-79, master 1983); mem. AMA, Am. Clin. and Climatological Assn. (v.p. 1992-93, councillor 1992-93), Assn. Am. Physicians, Am. Soc. Clin. Investigation, Assn. Univ. Cardiologists (pres. 1978-79), Am. Heart Assn. (pres. 1979-80), Am. Coll. Cardiology (v.p. 1970-71, trustee 1970-71, 76-81, First Disting. Scientist award 1982, chmn. publs. com. 1994—), Am. Soc. Pharmacology and Exptl. Therapeutics, Soc. Exptl. Biology of Medicine, Am. Coll. Chest Physicians, Ctrl. Soc. Clin. Rsch., Internat. Soc. and Fedn. Cardiology (pres. 1983-84), WHO (expert adv. panel on cardiovascular diseases 1988—), So. Soc. Clin. Investigation, Am. Fedn. Clin. Rsch., Ala. Acad. Honor. Philos. Soc. Tex., Phi Beta Kappa, Sigma Xi, Omicron Delta Kappa, Alpha Omega Alpha, Alpha Tau Omega, Phi Chi. Presbyterian. Clubs: Cosmos, Mountain Brook, Galveston Artillery. Office: U Tex Med Br Office of the Pres Galveston TX 77555-0129

JAMES, VERNON LESTER, pediatrician, educator; b. Liberty, N.C., Mar. 12, 1929; m. Dessie Oliver, July, 1976. BS in Zoology, U. N.C., 1951, MD, 1955. Diplomate Am. Bd. Pediatrics; lic. physician, N.C., Mass., Ohio, Kans., Tex. Rotating intern Ohio State U., Columbus, 1955-56, pediatric resident Children's Hosp., 1956-58; rsch. fellow dept. child health Harvard Med. Sch., Boston, 1964-65; tng. fellow Children's Hosp. Med. Ctr., Boston, 1964-65; rsch. fellow pediatrics Boston Lying-in Hosp., 1964-65; dir. ambulatory svcs. dept. pediatrics Coll. Medicine U. Ky., Lexington, 1966-69; dir. Cystic Fibrosis Clinic, Diagnostic and Treatment Ctr. U. Ky. Med. Ctr., Lexington, 1967-75; dir. ambulatory care svcs. Wesley Med. Ctr., Wichita, 1978-79, dir. Child Evaluation Ctr., pediatrician High-Risk Infant Follow-Up Clinic, 1977-79; chief of staff Santa Rosa Children's Hosp.; pvt. practice San Antonio, 1979-95; med. dir., pediatric devel. program Santa Rosa Children's Hosp., San Antonio, 1995—; mem. active staff Santa Rosa Children's Hosp., 1985—, Met. Hosp., 1985-91, Bapt. Med. Ctrs., 1985-95, Women's and Children's Hosp., 1985-95, Meth. Hosp., 1985—; instr. dept. family health care Children's Hosp. Harvard Med. Sch., Boston, 1964-65; asst. prof. dept. pediat. Sch. Medicine U. Ky., Lexington, 1965-71, assoc. prof., 1971-75; prof. dept. pediat. Sch. Medicine U. Kans., Wichita, 1975-79, clin. prof., 1979-85; mem. clin. staff and tchg. panel Wesley Med. Ctr., Wichita, 1975-85; chief pediatric sect. Wesley Med. Ctr., 1984; mem. exec. bd. Med. Soc. Sedgwick County, 1984; clin. prof. dept. pediat. U. Tex. Health Sci. Ctr., San Antonio, 1985—; med. cons., Children Habilitation Ctr., San Antonio; presenter in field. Contbr. articles to profl. jours. Mem. adv. bd. Brighton Sch. Developmentally Delayed Children; child advocate Sedgwick County Dist. Ct.; mem. health adv. com. Wichita Head Start; mem. Sedgwick County Zoological Soc.; mem. governing bd. Santa Rosa Children's Hosp.; mem. San Antonio Botanical Soc.; mem. St. Francis Episcopal Ch. Maj. USAF, 1956-62; col. USAFR, 1962-89. Recipient Outstanding Contbn. award Nat. Coun. Prevention Child Abuse, 1977; grantee Bureau Edn. of Handicapped, 1976, 77, 78, March of Dimes U. Kans. Medicine Endowment Found. for Genetics Clinic, 1977, 78, Wesley Med. Endowment Found., 1984. Mem. AMA, Am. Acad. Pediatrics (Ann. Journalism award 1977), Tex. Acad. Pediatrics, Tex. Pediatric Soc., Tex. Med. Assn., Bexar County Med. Soc., San Antonio Pediatric Soc. (pres. 1991), Wichita State U. Intercollegiate Scholarship Assn., Wichita C. of C. Office: Santa Rosa Children's Hosp 519 W Houston St San Antonio TX 78207

JAMES, WALTER ENNIS, cardiologist; b. Green, S.C., Nov. 30, 1949; s. Walter Ennis and Inez (Hay) J.; m. Drury James, June 19, 1973; children: Leslie, Ennis. BS, Presbyn. Coll.; MD, Med. U. S.C., 1976. Bd. cert. medicine and cardiology. Cardiologist Piedmont Cardiology Assocs., Greenwood, S.C. Office: Piedmont Cardiology Assocs Box 679 Greenwood SC 29648

JAMES, WILLIAM BRUCE, hospital administrator; b. Virginia Beach, Va., Apr. 21, 1958; s. Aubrey Overstreet and Betty Jane (Belvin) J.; m. Terry Lynn Jeter, July 17, 1982; children: Shannon Rebekah, Amanda Lynn, Cameron Bruce. BA, U. Va., 1980; M of Health Adminstrn., Med. Coll. Va., 1983. Asst. adminstr. Humana Hosp., St. Lukes, Richmond, Va., 1983-85, assoc. adminstr., 1985-86; asst. adminstr. Meml. Hosp. Martinsville (Va.) and Henry County, 1986-88; assoc. adminstr. Meml. Hosp. Martinsville (Va.) & Henry County, 1988-90; adminstr., chief exec. officer Alleghany Regional Hosp., Low Moor, Va., 1990-95; CEO No. Hosp. Surry County, Mt. Airy, N.C., 1995—. Mem. Am. Coll. Healthcare Execs., Rotary. Baptist. Home: 109 Quail Run Rd Mount Airy NC 27030 Office: No Hosp Surry County 830 Rockford St Mount Airy NC 27030

JAMES, WILLIAM CHANDLER, periodontist; b. High Point, N.C., Mar. 26, 1948; s. Chandler Carthell and Willie (Crump) J.; m. Linda Jean Webb, July 20, 1974; children: Lauren Nicole, Lindsey Elizabeth, William Chandler James II, Nolan Darwin Smith; BS, U. N.C., 1971, DDS, 1974; MS, 1976. Temporary staff dentist Pub. Health Service, Morgantown, W.Va., 1973 (summer); staff dentist Orange Chatham Comprehensive Health Svc., Chapel Hill, N.C., 1974; practice dentistry specializing in periodontology, Charlotte, N.C., 1976—; ins. cons. Aetna, 1980—; ins. cons. Blue Cross Blue Shield, Durham, 1983—; spl. cons. N.C. Dept. Justice, 1986—. Contbr. articles to periodontology jours. Pres. Charlotte Choral Soc., 1981-82, 85, chmn. bd. dirs., 1982-83, prodn. coordinator 25th, 26th, 30th, and 31st Singing Christmas Tree, 1979, 1980, 84, 85; med. missions vol. United Meth. Ch., 1988—; asst. ch. choir dir. Pineville United Meth. Ch., asst. handbell choir dir., Sunday sch. tchr.; dental missionary to Cap Haitien, Haiti, 1988—; active Christian Missions. Recipient Billy Pennel award So. Acad. Periodontology, 1976. Mem. Am. Acad. Periodontology (mem. com. on dental care programs 1977—, com. vice chmn. 1989-90, chmn, 1990-92, 3d dist. advisor, dental health plans com. 1978—, mem. nominating com. 1987, 89, 91-92, trustee 1989-94, membership com. 1989-90, internat. rels. com. 1989-90, exec. com. 1990-91, cons. CPT-6 1989-90, mem. conflict interest com. 1991-93, sr. dist. trustee 1992-94), Am. Acad. Periodontology Found. (bd. dirs. 1989-94, v.p. 1990-94, conflict of interest com. 1991-93), So. Acad. Periodontology (chmn. dental health plans com. 1978—, sec. 1987-88, pres.-elect 1988-89, pres. 1989-90, exec. coun. 1985-91), N.C. Soc. Periodontists (sec. 1991-92, pres. elect 1992-93, pres. 1993-94), N.C. Dental Soc. (peer rev. com. 1978-81, chmn. 1980-81, 90-93, ins. com. 1992—), Charlotte Dental Soc., Mecklenburg Periodontal Assn., Cabarrus Dental Soc., Country Haven Tennis & Swim Club. Democrat. Avocations: softball, singing, tennis, basketball, white-water rafting. Home: 3711 Spokeshave Ln Matthews NC 28105-7177

JAMESON, CHARLES WILLIAM, chemist; b. LaPlata, Md., Feb. 3, 1948; s. Thomas Jefferson and Mary Adlaide (Cooksey) J.; m. Brenda Marie Stinnett, Aug. 23, 1969 (div. Dec. 1992); 1 child, Charles William, Jr.; m. Barbara Lynne Trotter, Apr. 24, 1993. BS, Mt. St. Mary's Coll., 1970; PhD, Univ. Md., 1975. Chemist Tracor Jitco Inc., Rockville, Md., 1976-79, Nat. Cancer Inst., Bethesda, Md., 1979-80; rsch. chemist Nat. Inst. Environ. Health Scis., Research Triangle Park, N.C., 1980—; cons. WHO, Munich, 1990, London, 1991. Editor: (books) Chemistry for Toxicity Testing, 1981, Chemical Health and Safety for Toxicity Testing, 1981. Pres. North Raleigh (N.C.) Athletic Assn., 1990, 91. Home: 8313 Stryker Ct Raleigh NC 27615-3034 Office: NIEHS/NIH PO Box 12233 Research Triangle Park NC 27709

JAMIESON, DARA GREANEY, neurologist; b. Honolulu, Nov. 18, 1955. BA, George Washington U., 1976; MD, U. Pa., 1982. Diplomate Am. Bd. Psychiatry and Neurology. Resident in internal medicine Presbyn. Med. Ctr., Phila., 1982-83; resident in neurology U. Pa. Hosp., Phila., 1983-86, fellow in cerebrovascular medicine, 1986-89; asst. prof. Temple Hosp., Phila., 1989-93, Pa. Hosp., Phila., 1993—; asst. prof. Thomas Jefferson U., 1993—. Mem. AMA, Am. Acad. Neurology, Am. Soc. Neuroimaging, Am. Heart Assn. (stroke affiliate liaison), Internat. Soc. CBF and Metabolism. Office: Pa Hosp 800 Spruce St Philadelphia PA 19107

JAMISON, DARLENE MARY, university administrator; b. Kansas City, Mo., Nov. 24, 1928; d. Joseph and Caroline E. Broyles; B.A. in Sociology, U. Mo., Kansas City, 1963, M.A., 1969; m. Homer C. Jamison, Feb. 12, 1971; 1 dau., Carolyn Suzanne Love. Mem. adminstrv. staff U. Mo., Kansas City, 1967-74, dir. affirmative action-academic, 1973-74; adminstrv. assoc., affirmative action officer Sch. Optometry, U. Ala., Birmingham, 1974-81, asst. to dean, 1981-89. Mem. Ala. Assn. Women Deans, Adminstrs. and Councelors, Personnel Assn. Birmingham, Nat. Conf. Women in Chambers of Conf. (del. 1979-81), Women's Jr. C. of C. Birmingham (pres. 1981-82), Birmingham Met. Bus. and Profl. Women's Club (v.p. 1979-80), Am. Bus. Women's Assn. (chpt. pres. 1984-85, chpt. Woman of Yr. 1986, One of Top Ten Bus. Women of Yr., 1986). Editor various univ. publs. Home: 3586 Rockhill Rd Birmingham AL 35223-1402 Office: U Ala Sch Optometry Birmingham AL 35294

JAMISON, HUBERT MILTON, optometrist, navy officer; b. Westwood, Calif., Mar. 4, 1946; s. Bert Edward and Ruth Maryetta (Martin) J.; m. Martha Louise Peters, Mar. 21, 1970; children: Hugh Martin, Amy Christine. BS, So. Coll. Optometry, 1968; OD, So. Coll. Opometry, Memphis, 1972; MA, Central Mich. U., 1981. Commd. ens. USN, 1972, advanced through grades to capt., 1989; staff optometrist U.S. Naval Hosp., Charleston, S.C., 1972-74, Roosevelt Roads, P.R., 1974-78, Jacksonville, Fla., 1978-81; head optometry dept. U.S. Naval Hosp., Beaufort, S.C., 1981-85; exec. officer Naval Ophthalmic Support and Tng. Activity, Yorktown, Va., 1985-88; head optometry dept. U.S. Naval Hosp., Charleston, S.C., 1988-92; comdg. officer Naval Ophthalmic Support and Tng. Activity, Yorktown, Va., 1992-95; def. med. standardization bd., 1995—; splty. advisor for optometry U.S. Navy, 1993—. Mem. Armed Forces Optometric Soc., U.S. Naval Inst., Assn. Mil. Surgeons U.S., Am. Optometric Assn. Republican. Home: 5008 Bob White Ct Frederick MD 21703 Office: Def Med Standardization Bd Bldg 1423 Fort Detrick Frederick MD 21702-5013

JAMISON, REX LINDSAY, medical educator; b. Des Moines, July 8, 1933; s. Orin Lindsay and Helen Belle (Buck) J.; m. Dorothy Tufts Lockwood, Mar. 3, 1962; children: Richard Lindsay, John Lockwood. AB, U. Iowa, 1955; BA, U. Oxford, Eng., 1957; MA, U. Oxford, 1961; MD, Harvard U., 1960. Intern Mass. Gen. Hosp., Boston, 1960-61, asst. resident in medicine, 1961-62; sr. asst. resident in medicine Columbia-Presbyn. Med. Ctr., N.Y.C., 1962-63; clin. assoc. Lab. Kidney and Electrolyte Metabolism, NIH, Bethesda, Md., 1963-66; instr. in medicine Washington U. Sch. Medicine, St. Louis, 1966-67, asst. prof. medicine, 1967-71, asst. prof. physiology and biophysics, 1968-71; assoc. prof. medicine Stanford (Calif.) U. Sch. Medicine, 1971-82, co-head div. nephrology, 1971-80, chief div., 1980-87, prof. medicine and physiology, 1982-87, acting chmn. dept. medicine, acting physician-in-chief, 1984-86, prof. medicine, 1992—; Charles A. Dewey prof. medicine, chmn. dept. medicine U. Rochester (N.Y.) Sch. Medicine and Dentistry, 1987-90, prof. medicine and physiology, 1990-92; physician-in-chief Strong Meml. Hosp., Rochester, 1987-90; chief renal div. Jewish Hosp. St. Louis, 1966-71, div. nephrology Stanford U. Hosp., 1971-87; vis. prof. Laboratorie de Physiologie Physico-Chimique Centre d'Etudes, Nucleaires de Saclay, Gif-sur-Yvette, France, 1977-78; mem. external monitoring com. modification of diet in renal disease study Nat. Inst. Arthritis, Diabetes and Digestive and Kidney Diseases, 1989-90; med. adv. bd. Nat. Kidney Found. Upstate N.Y., 1987-91, No. Calif., 1992—; mem. Intersoc. Coun., 1988-92; William C. Smith lectr. UCLA St. Mary Hosp. Author: (with Wilhelm Kriz) Urinary Concentrating Mechanism: Structure and Function, 1982; author, editor: Transplantation in the 1980s: Recent Advances, 1984, (with Serge Jard) Vasopressin, 1991; contbr. numerous articles to profl. jours. Mem. Rhodes Scholar Selection Coms. Vt., Md., Mo., Calif. Dist. V. Rhodes scholar, Markle scholar; John S. Guggenheim Found. fellow; Rsch. Career Devel. grantee USPHS, 1963-66, grantee Calif. Acad. Medicine, Rochester Acad. Medicine. Fellow ACP; mem. Am. Heart Assn. (vice chmn. coun. on cardiovascular disease and the kidney 1986-88, chmn. 1988-92), Am. Physiol. Soc., Am. Soc. Clin. Investigation , Am. Soc. Nephrology (chmn. program com. 1984), Assn. Am. Physicians, Assn. Profs. Medicine, Western Assn. Physicians, Western Soc. Clin. Investigation (councilor 1974-77), Peruvian Soc. Nephrology (hon.), Internat. Soc. Nephrology Commn. on Devel. Countries, Phi Beta Kappa. Episcopalian. Home: 850 Cedro Way Palo Alto CA 94305-1003

JAMPLIS, ROBERT WARREN, surgeon, medical foundation executive; b. Chgo., Apr. 1, 1920; s. Mark and Janet (McKenna) J.; m. Roberta Cecelia Prior, Sept. 5, 1947; children: Mark Prior, Elizabeth Ann Jamplis Bluestone. B.S., U. Chgo., 1941, M.D., 1944; M.S., U. Minn., 1951. Diplomate Am. Bd. Surgery, Am. Bd. Thoracic Surgery. Asst. resident in surgery U. Chgo., 1946-47; fellow in thoracic surgery Mayo Clinic, Rochester, Minn., 1947-52; chief thoracic surgery Palo Alto (Calif.) Med. Clinic, 1958-81, exec. dir., 1965-81; clin. prof. surgery Stanford U. Sch. Medicine, 1958—; mem. council SRI Internat.; chmn. bd. TakeCare Corp.; charter mem., bd. regents Am. Coll. Physician Execs.; mem. staff Stanford Univ. Hosp., Santa Clara Valley Med. Center, San Jose, VA Hosp., Palo Alto, Sequoia Hosp., Redwood City, Calif., El Camino Hosp., Mountain View, Calif., Harold D. Chope Community Hosp., San Mateo, Calif.; pres., chief exec. officer Palo Alto Med. Found.; past chmn. Fedn. Am. Clinics; dir. Blue Cross Calif.; varsity football team physician Stanford U. Author: (with G.A. Lillington) A Diagnostic Approach to Chest Diseases, 1965, 2d edit., 1979; contbr. numerous articles to profl. jours. Trustee Santa Barbara Med. Found. Clinic; past pres. Calif. div. Am. Cancer Soc.; past chmn. bd. Group Practice Polit. Action Com.; past mem. athletic bd. Stanford U.; past mem. cabinet U. Chgo.; bd. dirs. Herbert Hoover Boys' Club; past trustee No. Calif. Cancer Program; past bd. dirs. Core Communications in Health, Community Blood Res., others. Served to lt. USNR, 1944-46, 52-54. Recipient Alumni citation U. Chgo., 1968, Nat. Divsn. award Am. Cancer Soc., 1979, Med. Exec. award Am. Coll. Med. Group Adminstrs., 1981, Russel V. Lee award lectr. Am. Group Practice Assn., 1982, Mayo Disting. Alumnus award, 1991. Mem. Inst. Medicine of Nat. Acad. Scis., ACS, Am. Assn. Thoracic Surgery, Soc. Thoracic Surgeons (past pres.), Western Thoracic Surg. Assn. (past pres.), Western Surg. Assn., Pacific Coast Surg. Assn., San Francisco Surg. Soc. (past pres.), Portland Surg. Soc. (hon.), Doctors Mayo Soc., Am. Coll. Chest Physicians (bd. govs.), Calif. Acad. Medicine, Am. Fedn. Clin. Research, Am. Group Practice Assn. (past pres.), AMA, Calif. Med. Assn., Santa Clara County Med. Assn., Sigma Xi. Republican. Roman Catholic. Clubs: Bohemian, Pacific Union, Commonwealth of California (San Francisco); Menlo Country (Woodside, (Calif.); Menlo Circus (Atherton, Calif.); Stanford (Calif.) Golf; Rancheros Visitadores (Santa Barbara, Calif.). Office: 300 Homer Ave Palo Alto CA 94301-2726

JANACK, MARK A., management consultant, nurse; b. Ogdensburg, N.Y., Feb. 7, 1957; s. Reginald Earl and Helen (Doboze) J.; m. Anne Kariotakis, Feb. 4, 1990; children: Michael Stephen, Matthew Ryan. Diploma in Nursing, St. Lawrence Psychiat. Sch., 1977; BS in Bus., Century U., Calif., MBA. RN, Ohio, N.Y. Staff nurse neurosurgery, psychiatry Cleve. Clinic, 1977-78; staff nurse dept. orthop. surgery St. Luke's Hosp., Cleve., 1978-82; physician asst. Collis, Kim & Assocs., Cleve., 1982-86; adminstrv. dir. The INNOVA Surgery Ctr.; co-dir. Cleve. Spine and Arthritis Ctr.; pres. M & M Adminstrs., Inc., Cleve., M & M Mgmt. and Cons., Inc., Cleve.; staff Luth. Med. Ctr., St. Vincent Charity Hosp. and Health Ctr., Hillcrest Hosp., Geauga Hosp. Contbr. articles to profl. jours. Mem. Med. Group Mgmt. Assn., Am. Acad. Neurol. and Orthop. Surgery, Am. Assn. Neurosci. Nurses, Am. Hellenic Edni. and Progressive Assn., Am. Coll. Health Care Execs. Greek Orthodox. Office: M & M Management Cons Inc 6701 Rockside Rd #200 Independence OH 44131

JANASIE, MARGARET ANN, nurse; b. Elizabeth, N.J., Dec. 20, 1949; d. Frank Harold and Margaret (Maloney) Folinus; m. John J. Jansie, Apr. 3, 1976; children: Theresa Ann, Stephen John, Catherine Marie. Diploma in nursing, Elizabeth Gen. Hosp.; BSN, Kean Coll., 1986. RN, N.J. RN, charge nurse, asst. head nurse Elizabeth (N.J.) Gen. Hosp., 1973-82; nurse office asst. Dr. H. Poch, Elizabeth, 1983-86; sch. nurse Ocean Day Tng. Sch., Toms River, N.J., 1986-87; charge nurse Health South, Toms River, 1987-89; infection control coord. So. Ocean County Hosp., Manahawkin, N.J., 1990—. Mem. funding rev. com. Monmouth Ocean AIDS Consortium, Red Bank, N.J., 1993—; mem. Ocean County AIDS planning group Ocean County Dept. Health, Toms River, 1996. Mem. Assn. for Profls. in Infection Control. Roman Catholic. Office: So Ocean County Hosp 1140 Rt 72 W Manahawkin NJ 08050-2412

JANE, JOHN ANTHONY, neurosurgeon, educator; b. Chgo., Sept. 21, 1931; m. Noella Fortier, Dec. 17, 1960; children: Jane Serrita, Jennie Elizabeth, Katherine Colette, John Anthony Jr. BA cum laude, U. Chgo., 1951, MD, 1956, PhD, 1967. Diplomate Am. Bd. Neurol. Surgeons. Intern Royal Victoria Hosp. McGill U., 1953-56, jr. asst. resident in surgery, 1957-58, sr. fellow and demonstrator in neuropathology, 1959-60; jr. asst. resident in neurosurgery U. Chgo. Clinics, 1957; fellow in neurophysiology Montreal (Can.) Neurol. Inst., NIH, 1958-59; rsch. asst. in neurosurgery St. George's Hosp. and Nat. Hosp., London, 1961; rsch. assoc. dept. psychology Duke U., 1962; sr. resident in neurosurgery, asst. in neurology and neurosurgery U. Ill. Rsch. and Ednl. Hosp. and Ill. Neuropsychiat. Inst., 1963-64; sr. instr. neurosurgery Case Western Res. U. Sch. Medicine, 1965-66, chief neurosurg. div. Cleve. VA Hosp., 1965-66, asst. prof. neurosurgery, asst. neurosurgeon Univ. Hosp. Cleve., chief neurosurg. div. Cleve. VA Hosp., 1967-68; David D. Weaver prof., chmn. dep. neurosurgery U. Va. Health Scis. Ctr., Charlottesville, 1969—; Harry Wilkins lectr. U. Okla., 1983, Samuel Snodgrass lectr. U. Tex. at Galveston, 1983, Herbert Olivecrona lectr. Karolinska Inst. of Stockholm, Sweden, 1985, 29th Ann. Fellows Day lectr. Montreal Neurol. Inst., 1986, Arthur A. Ward lectr. U. Wash., Seattle, 1986, 1st Stuart Rowe lectr. neurosurgery U. Pitts., 1987, E. S. Gurdjian lectr. Wayne State U., Detroit, 1987; mem. neurology B study sect. NIH, 1971-74, neurol. disorders program project rev. B com., 1979-82, spl. study sect. on interdisciplinary studies role of cen. nervous system in hypertension, 1979, sci. adv. com., rev. com. of nat. com. for rsch. on neurol. and communicative disorders, 1981. Author: (with Yashon D.) Cytology of Tumors Affecting the Nervous System, 1969; contbr. numerous articles, abstracts, book chpts. to profl. publs.; editor: (with Winn H.R. and Rimel R.W.) Recent Advances in Neurotrauma Seminars in Neurological Surgery, Jour. Neurosurgery, 1992—; mem. editorial bd. Jour. Neurosurgery, 1984—. Recipient Alumni award for disting. svc. U. Chgo., 1988; grantee NIH.hon guest, Congress of an Neurological Surgeons, 1985. Fellow ACS, Royal Coll. Physicians and Surgeons Can.; mem. Am. Acad. Neurol. Surgery, Am. Assn. Anatomists, Am. Physiol. Soc., Am. Assn. Neurol. Surgeons, AMA, Neurosurg. Soc. Am., Can. Neurosurg. Soc., Rsch. Soc. Neurol. Surgeons (Grass prize and medal 1985), Soc. Neurosci. (chmn. membership com.), Soc. Brit. Neurol. Surgeons, Soc. Univ. Surgeons, So. Neurosurg. Soc., Pavlovian Soc., Med. Soc. Va., Neurosurg. Soc. Virginias, Albemarle County Med. Soc., The Cajal Club. Office: U Va Dept Neurosurgery Box 212 Charlottesville VA 22908-0212

JANES, DONALD WALLACE, biologist, educator, academic administrator, consultant; b. Kansas City, Mo., June 12, 1929; s. H. Wallace and Leila G. (Duncan) Janes; m. Norma Marie Lee, Feb. 21, 1953 (dec. 1978); children: Todd Allan, Jeffrey Wallace, Scott Lee Duncan, Nancy Marie; m. Janina Z. Piorkowska, Nov. 14, 1981. BA, Baker U., 1951; MS, U. Kans., 1956; PhD, Kans. State U., 1962. Instr. biology Washburn U., Topeka, 1957-61; asst. prof. biology Parsons Coll., Fairfield, Iowa, 1962-63; postdoctoral research assoc. Ind. U., Bloomington, 1963, Baylor Coll. Medicine, Houston, 1964, 66, Iowa State U., Ames, 1965; assoc. prof. and dean U. So. Colo., Pueblo, 1966-78, prof. biology, 1978-92; ret., 1992, microbiology cons., 1992—; cons., examiner North Ctrl. Assn. Colls. and Schs., Chgo., 1969-90; vis. prof. U. Colo., Boulder, 1978-79. People to people amb. People's Republic of China, 1989; vice-chair, sec. bd. dirs. Breckenridge Music Inst., 1990—. Fulbright fellow U. Graz, Austria, 1956-57; Acad. Adminstrn. fellow Am. Council on Edn., Washington, 1968-69. Mem. Audubon Club, Pueblo (organizer 1968); Pueblo C. of C. 1968-78; Am. Soc. Microbiology, Soc. for Indsl. Microbiology, Sigma Xi (pres. 1986-88), Breckenridge Ski Touring Soc. (pres. 1993—), Colo. Mountain (Pueblo, chmn. 1973-74), Breckenridge Music Inst. (sec. bd. dirs.). Republican. Clubs: Colo. Mountain (Pueblo) (chmn. 1973-74). Home: PO Box 191 Breckenridge CO 80424-0191

JANES, ROBERT HARRISON, JR., surgeon; b. Little Rock, Nov. 13, 1939; s. Robert Harrison and Fahy Helen (Mathers) J.; B.S., U. Ark., 1965, M.D., 1965; m. Patricia Mayes, June 30, 1962; children: Robert, Clayton, Matthew. Intern surgery U. Ark. Hosps., Little Rock, 1965-66, resident surgery, 1966-70; practice medicine, specializing in surgery Holt-Krock Clinic, Fort Smith, Ark., 1972—; mem. staff Sparks Regional Med. Center, chief surgery, 1977-78, 1982-83; mem. staff St. Edwards Mercy Med. Center; instr. surgery U. Ark., Little Rock, 1969-70, asst. clin. prof. surgery, 1976-90, assoc. clin. prof. surgery, 1990—. Pres. Sebastian County (Ark.) unit Am. Cancer Soc., 1975-76, bd. dirs. Ark. div., pres. Ark. div., 1978-79, 81-82, nat. bd. dirs., 1982-89, exec. com., 1989; bd. dirs. Ft. Smith Symphony, 1979-83, treas., 1980-82, pres., 1982-83; bd. dirs. Broadway Theatre League Ft. Smith, 1981-84. Served to maj., M.C., USAF, 1970-72. Diplomate Am. Bd. Surgery. Fellow ACS (commn. on cancer 1983-89, vice chmn. 1987-88), Southwestern Surg. Congress; mem. AMA, Western Surg. Assn., Soc. Surgery Alimentary Tract, Ark. Med. Soc., Lambda Chi Alpha. Methodist (adminstrv. bd. 1974-77). Clubs: Hardscrabble Country; Red Apple Country (Eden Isle, Ark.); Oaklawn Jockey (Hot Springs, Ark.). Contbr. articles to profl. jours. Home: 6221 Duncan Rd Fort Smith AR 72903-2671 Office: 1500 Dodson Ave Fort Smith AR 72901

JANEWAY, RICHARD, university official; b. L.A., Feb. 12, 1933; s. VanZandt and Grace Eleanor (Bell) J.; m. Katherine Esmond Pillsbury, Dec. 23, 1955; children: Susan Kent, David VanZandt, Elizabeth Anne. AB, Colgate U., 1954; MD, U. Pa., 1958. Diplomate Am. Bd. Psychiatry and Neurology. Intern Hosp. U. Pa., 1958-59; resident N.C. Baptist Hosp., Winston-Salem, 1963-66; mem. faculty Bowman Gray Sch. Medicine Wake Forest U., Winston-Salem, 1966—; prof. neurology Wake Forest U., 1971—, dir. Bowman Gray Sch. Medicine (Cerebral Vascular Research Center), 1969-71, dean Bowman Gray Sch. Medicine, 1971-85, exec. dean Bowman Gray Sch. Medicine, 1985-94, v.p. health affairs, 1983-90, exec. v.p. health affairs, 1990—; mem. exec. com. So. Nat. Bank, Winston-Salem, N.C., 1982-92; bd. dirs., mem. exec. com. So. Nat. Corp., 1989—; mem. nat. adv. coun. regional med. programs HEW, 1974-77; mem.-at-large Nat. Bd. Med. Examiners, 1979-87; mem. N.C. Joint Conf. Com. on Med. Care, Inc., 1983—; dir. N.C. Inst. Medicine, N.C. Biotech. Ctr.; bd. dirs. Castle Springs, Inc., QualChoice of N.C., Inc. Mem. Winston-Salem Forsyth County Bd. Edn., 1970-73; bd. dirs. Nat. Assn. for Biomed. Rsch., 1993—; Ams. for Med. Progress, Inc., 1993-96, Winston-Salem Found., 1994—; trustee Colgate U., 1988-95, Winston-Salem State U., 1991-95. Capt. USAF, 1959-63. USPHS fellow, 1956; Markle scholar, 1968-73. Fellow ACP, Am. Acad. Neurology; mem. AMA, Am. Neurol. Assn., Am. Heart Assn. (coun. on stroke), Assn. Am. Med. Colls. (exec. coun. 1977-86, mem. accreditation coun. on grad. med. edn. 1981-85, chmn. coun. of deans 1982-83, exec. com. 1982-86, chmn. 1984-85), Am. Clin. and Climatol. Assn., Inst. Medicine of NAS, Greater Winston-Salem C. of C. (bd. dirs., chmn. 1992), Soc. Med. Adminstrs., Phi Beta Kappa, Sigma Xi, Alpha Omega Alpha. Clubs: Rotary (dir. 1977-80, v.p. 1981-82, pres. 1982-83), Cosmos. Office: Wake Forest U Bowman Gray Sch Medicine Medical Ctr Blvd Winston Salem NC 27157-1003

JANEWAY, TIMOTHY, orthopedist; b. N.Y.C., May 27, 1933; s. Jacob Jones V and Clara Margaret (McKown) J.; m. Joyce Lily Swartz, Aug. 23,

1968; children: Timothy H.H., Kenneth T., Brant McKown. AB, U. Mich., 1958, MD, 1963. Orthop. surgeon Laing, Coulson & Janeway, Pitts., 1969-86; pvt. practice Pitts., 1987-93; orthop. surgeon Shadyside Orthop. Assocs., Pitts., 1993—; pres. Shadyside Hosp. Med. Staff, Pitts., HealthSouth Med. Staff, Monroeville, Pa.; active med. staff St. Francis Several Hosp., Pitts.; cons. med. staff Forbes Health Sys., Pitts.; bd. dirs. Orthop. Overseas, Washington, vice chmn. Chmn. troop com. Boy Scouts Am., Pitts. Mem. Pitts. Athletic Assn. Republican. Presbyterian. Home: 20 Newgate Rd Pittsburgh PA 15202 Office: Shadyside Orthop Assocs PC 5200 Centre Ave Ste 712 Pittsburgh PA 15232

JANI, SUSHMA NIRANJAN, child and adolescent psychiatrist; b. Gwalior, Madhya, Pradesh, India, Sept. 26, 1959; came to U.S., 1983; d. Kirty Ambalal and Purnima Kirty (Bhatt) Dave; m. Niranjan Natwerial Jani, Mar. 30, 1983; children: Suni Jani, Raja Jani, Roma Jani. Inter Sci., Mithibai Coll., Bombay, India; MB;BS, B.J. Med. Coll., Ahmedabad, India; MD in Adult Psychiatry, Ind. U., 1984; MD in Child Psychiatry, Johns Hopkins U., 1987. Diplomate Am. Bd. Psychiatry and Neurology, sub-bd. Child Psychiatry. Child psychiatrist Johns Hopkins Univ. Hosp., Balt.; asst. clin. prof., dir. child & adolescent psychiatry U. Md., Balt.; chief cons. psychiatrist Balt. Detention Ctr., 1988-89, cons. psychiatrist Vets. Hosp., Indpls., 1986-87. Vol. Radha-Krishna Leprosy Camp, Bombay, 1981-83. Mem. AMA, Am. Acad. Child & Adolescent Psychiatry, Am. Psychiatry Assn., Md. Psychiat. Soc., Columbia Assn., India Assn. Hindu. Home: 10485 Owen Brown Rd Columbia MD 21044-3835 Office: U Md Hosp 701 W Pratt St Baltimore MD 21201-1023 also: Hawthorne Office Pl 10810 Hickory Ridge Rd Columbia MD 21044

JANICKI, ROBERT STEPHEN, retired pharmaceutical company executive; b. Manette, Wash., Dec. 7, 1934; s. Stephen Walter and Elizabeth Caroline (Gorman) J.; m. I. Jane Betcher, Aug. 18, 1956; children: Robert, Beth, David. B.S., Grove City Coll., 1956; M.D., Temple U., 1961. Diplomate: Nat. Bd. Med. Examiners. Intern U.S. Naval Hosp., Phila., 1961-62; resident in occupational medicine USN, 1962-63; assoc. dir. clin. research Dow Pharms., Indpls., 1966-68; assoc. med. dir. Neisler div. Union Carbide Corp., Sterling Forest, N.Y., 1968-69; assoc. med. dir. regulatory affairs Abbott Labs., North Chicago, Ill., 1969-70; dir. clin. research pharm. products div. Abbott Labs., 1970-71, v.p. med. affairs pharm. products div., 1971-79, v.p. research pharm. products div., 1979-83, corp. v.p. R & D pharm. products div., 1983-89, sr. v.p., 1989-90; bd. dirs. Sunpharm Corp., Jacksonville, Fla., Afferon Corp., Wayne, Pa.; cons. New Drug Devel. Contbr. articles profl. to jours. Trustee Grove City (Pa.) Coll. Served to lt. comdr., M.C. USN, 1961-66. Fellow Am. Coll. Clin. Pharm.; mem. Am. Soc. Clin. Pharmacology and Therapeutics, Inst. Medicine Chgo., Coll. Physicians of Phila., Sigma Xi, Alpha Omega Alpha. Home: 318 Fern St Marathon FL 33050-3818

JANIS, RONALD ALLEN, pharmacologist; b. Mossbank, Sask., Can., Oct. 11, 1943; came to U.S., 1968; s. Joseph Aleck and Julia (Romanow) J.; m. Adriana Beukers, Jan. 23, 1968; children: Mary Alice, Joseph Walter. BS in Pharm. Scis., U. B.C., Vancouver, Can., 1966, MS in Med. Chemistry; PhD in Pharmacology, SUNY, Buffalo, 1972. Rsch. fellow U. Alta., Edmonton, Can., 1972-74; asst. prof. Northwestern U. Med. Ctr., Chgo., 1974-80; assoc. prof. Northwestern U., Chgo., 1980; prin. rsch. scientist Miles Inc., West Haven, Conn., 1980-84, prin. staff scientist, 1984—; assoc. prof. dept. medicine U. Conn., Farmington, 1981-89; assoc. clin. prof. U. Conn. Health Ctr., Farmington, 1990-91; spl. reviewer NIH, 1981-87, Med. Rsch. Coun. of Can., 1989-91; reviewer in field. Contbr. over 100 publs. to profl. jours. Med. Rsch. Coun. fellow, 1973; grantee NIH. Mem. Am. Soc. Physiology, Am. Soc. Pharmacology Exptl. Therapy, Biophys. Soc. (One of Most-Cited Authors in world in field of xenobiotics 1981-92). Home: 656 High Ridge Rd Orange CT 06477-1531 Office: Bayer Corp Lead Discovery Rsch 400 Morgan Ln West Haven CT 06516-4175

JANNIGER, CAMILA KRYSICKA, physician; b. Sopot, Poland, July 18, 1959; came to U.S., 1984; d. Stanislaw and Felicja Halina (Kurnatowska) Krysicka; m. Robert A. Schwartz, Dec. 29, 1984; 1 child, Jack Edmund. MD, Med. U. Warsaw, Poland, 1984. Diplomate Am. Bd. Dermatology. Intern Albert Einstein Coll. Medicine/Montefiore Hosp., N.Y.C., 1986-87; resident in dermatology UMDNJ NJ Med. Sch., 1987-90; clin. asst. prof. dermatology and pediat. U. Medicine and Dentistry of N.J.-N.J. Med. Sch., Newark, 1990-95, chief pediat. dermatology, 1990—, clin. assoc. prof. dermatology and pediat., 1995—; mem. adv. bd. Nat. Tuberous Sclerosis Found., 1994—. Mem. editl. bd. Cutis, 1991—, pediat. editor, 1992—. Co-founder student br. Solidarity Movement, Poland, 1980. Republican. Roman Catholic. Home: 100 Glenwood Rd Eaglewood NJ 07631 Office: Univ Medicine and Dentistry NJ Med Sch 185 S Orange Ave Newark NJ 07103-2714

JANOFSKY, JEFFREY STUART, physician; b. Balt., Aug. 12, 1957; s. Arthur M. and Joan S. Janofsky; m. Julie C. Janofsky; children: Jill S., Robin J. Student, Emory U., 1975-77; BA, Johns Hopkins U., 1979, MD, 1982. Diplomate Am. Bd. Psychiatry and Neurology with added qualification in forensic psychiatry, Am. Bd. Forensic Psychiatry. Internship Balt. City Hosps., Balt., 1982-83; residency Johns Hopkins Hosp., Balt., 1983-86; assoc. prof. Johns Hopkins U., Balt., 1994—, dir. psychiatry and law program, 1992—. Book rev. editor Bulletin of the Am. Acad. of Psychiatry and Law. Fellow Am. Psychiat. Assn., Am. Acad. Psychiatry and the Law (Rappeport fellow 1985). Office: 30 E Padonia Rd Ste 206 Lutherville Timonium MD 21093-2308 also: Johns Hopkins Hosp Meyer 101 600 N Wolfe St Baltimore MD 21287

JANORA, DEANNA MARIE, physiatric medicine educator; b. Point Pleasant, N.J.; d. Edward and Joan (Kulakowski) J. BS in Biochemistry, U. Scranton, 1987; MD, Temple U., 1991. Intern Chestnut Hill Hosp., Phila., 1991-92; resident in phys. medicine and rehab. Temple U. Hosp., Phila., 1992-94, chief resident, 1994-95; asst. prof. physiatry U. Medicine and Dentistry N.J. Sch. Osteo. Medicine, Stratford, 1995—. Mem. AMA, Am. Acad. Phys. Medicine and Rehab., Assn. Acad. Physiatrists, Am. Assn. Electrodiagnostic Medicine. Office: UMDNJ Sch Osteo Medicine 42 E Laurel Rd Stratford NJ 08084

JANOSKO, RUDOLPH E. M., psychiatrist; b. Munhall, Pa., Apr. 30, 1930; s. Rudolph E. and Anne (Gerek) J.; m. Audrey M. Nemeth, May 18, 1932; children: Beth, Gwen, Ellen. BS, U. Pitts., 1952, MD, 1956. Cert. in psychiatry Am. Bd. Psychiatry and Neurology. Intern Easton (Pa.) Hosp., 1956-57; resident in psychiatry U. Pitts., 1957-59, 61-62; instr. psychiatry U. Pitts. Sch. Medicine, 1962-65; lectr. U. Pitts. Dept. Spl. Edn., Grad. Sch., 1966-70; clin. asst. prof. psychiatry U. Pitts. Sch. Medicine, 1965-75; mem. attending staff Presbyn.-Univ. Hosp., Pitts., 1962—; faculty Pitts. Psychoanalytic Inst., 1970—; clin. assoc. prof. psychiatry U. Pitts. Sch. Medicine, 1975—; tng. and supervising analyst Am. Psychoanalytic Assn., Pitts. Psychoanalytic Inst., 1979—; pres. Pitts. Psychoanalytic Ctr., 1981-83; dir. Pitts. Psychoanalytic Inst., 1985-86; med. dir. Family Svcs. of Western Pa., Pitts., 1988—; cons. Greater Pitts. Guild for Blind, Bridgeville, Pa., 1964—, Social Security Adminstrn., HHS, Pitts., 1979—. Author in field. Capt. USAF, 1959-61. Recipient Meritorious Distinction award Greater Pitts. Guild for Blind, 1967, Outstanding Tchr. award Western Psychiat. Inst., 1981. Fellow Am Psychiat. Assn.; mem. Am. Psychoanalytic Assn., Pitts. Acad. Medicine, Pitts. Psychoanalytic Soc. (pres. 1983-85), AMA. Republican. Roman Catholic. Home: 2534 Mt Royal Rd Pittsburgh PA 15217-2542 Office: 161 N Dithridge St Pittsburgh PA 15213-2646

JANOUT, VLADIMIR, epidemiologist; b. Prague, Czechoslovakia, Nov. 13, 1939; s. Frantisek J. and Emilie (Kantorová) Janoutová; children: Martina, Marek, Martin, Marketa. MD, Charles U., Prague, 1962; PhD, Czech Acad. Scis., Prague, 1968; Prof., Palacky U., Olomuc, Czech Republic, 1991. Physician Pub. Health Ctr., Česke Budejovice, Czechoslovakia, 1962-63; dir. Pub. Health Ctr., Česke Krumlov, 1970-72, Olomuc, Czechoslovakia, 1972-91; researcher Inst. Epidemiology, Prague, 1963-70; head of dept. Faculty of Medicine, Olomuc, Czech Republic, 1991—; cons. Ministry Health, Czech Republic, 1970—, short term WHO, India, 1974, 76, Somalia, 1978; mem. sci. com. European Sch. Oncology, Vienna. Mem. Internat. Epidemiologic Assn. Office: Palacky U Faculty Medicine, Hnevotinska 3, 77515 Olomuc Czech Republic

JANOWITZ, HENRY DAVID, physician, researcher, medical educator; b. Paterson, N.J., Mar. 23, 1915; s. Sam and Rose (Meyers) J.; m. Adeline R. Tintner, Oct. 31, 1942; children: Mary Rebecca, Anne Francis. B.A., Columbia U., 1935, M.D., 1939; M.S., U. Ill., 1949. Intern Mt. Sinai Hosp., N.Y.C., 1939-41; resident in medicine Mt. Sinai Hosp., 1947-48; practice medicine specializing in gastroenterology N.Y.C., 1956—; head div. gastroenterology Mt. Sinai Hosp., 1958-83, attending physician gastroenterology, 1961-85, now cons. in gastroenterology, 1985—, clin. prof. medicine, 1967-85; emeritus clin. prof. medicine, 1985—; mem. Am. Bd. Gastroenterology, 1966-70; chmn. program project com., div. arthritis and metabolism NIH, 1969-70. Author: (with D.A. Dreiling and C.V. Perrier) Pancreatic Inflammatory Disease, 1965; Inflammatory Bowel Disease: A Clinical Approach, 1994, Your Gut Feelings, 1987, Indigestion, 1992; contbr. 300 articles to profl. jours.; editorial bd.: Proceedings of Soc. for Exptl. Biology and Medicine, 1974-86, Am. Jour. Physiol., 1970-74, Jour. Chronic Diseases, 1966-88. Founder Ileitis and Colitis Found. Am. Served to maj. U.S. Army, 1942-46. Recipient Jacobi medal Mt. Sinai Sch. Medicine, 1974, Clin. Achievement award Am. Coll. Gastroent., 1992. Fellow Royal Soc. Medicine (hon., J. Lester Gabrilove award, 1994); mem. Am. Soc. Clin. Investigation, Assn. Am. Physicians, Am. Phys. Soc., Am. Gastroent. Assn. (pres. 1972-73, Friedenwald medal 1973), N.Y. Gastroent. Assn. (pres. 1968-69), Brit. Soc. Gastroent. (hon.). Office: 1075 Park Ave New York NY 10128-1003

JANSEN, G. THOMAS, dermatologist; b. Manitowoc, Wis., July 16, 1926; s. Gerald M. and Sarah (Grady) J.; m. Frances Bovick, Sept. 6, 1952; children: Mark, Kurt, Anne, Drew, Fran. B.S., U. Wis., Madison, 1948, M.D., 1950. Diplomate: Am. Bd. Dermatology (pres. 1985-86). Intern Med. Coll. of Va., 1950-51; resident in dermatology U. Wis., 1953-54, U. Mich., 1954-56; practice medicine specializing in dermatology Little Rock, 1956—; pres. Little Rock Dermatology Clinic, 1968—; mem. faculty U. Ark. Med. Center, 1956—, prof. dermatology, 1965—, chmn. dept., 1965-82; mem. staff Doctors Hosp., U. Ark. Hosp., St. Vincent Infirmary, Bapt. Hosp.; pres. Am. Dermatology Found., 1980-81. Served as officer M.C. USNR, 1951-54. Recipient Disting. Svc. award Am. Bd. Dermatologists, 1987, Finnerud award Am. Dermatology Found., 1993. Mem. AMA, Am. Dermatol. Assn. (pres. 1993), Am. Acad. Dermatology (asst sec.-treas. 1980-83, sec.-treas. 1983-85, pres.-elect 1987, pres. 1988, hon. 1991, Master in Dermatology 1991, Everett C. Fox Lectureship award 1995), Soc. Investigative Dermatology, Nat. Program Dermatology, Am. Coll. Chemosurgery, So. Med. Assn. (pres. 1976-77, Disting. Svc. award 1991), Ark. Med. Soc., Ark. Dermatol. Soc., Pulaski County Med. Soc., Alpha Omega Alpha. Roman Catholic. Home: 6601 Pleasant Pl Little Rock AR 72205-2868 Office: 500 S University Ave Ste 501 Little Rock AR 72205-5307

JANSEN, SCOTT D., health services administrator, recruiter; b. Omaha, July 31, 1960; s. C.K. and Joan M. (Van Ryckeghem) J.; m. Teresa A. Roepker, Aug. 19, 1988; children: Tony, Haley. BSBA, N.W. Mo. State U., 1982; MBA, U. Nebr., Omaha, 1986; postgrad. in Health Care Adminstrn., U. Minn. Sales rep. Profl. Adminstrv. Svcs., Omaha, 1982-83; sales mgr. Ctrl. Waste Sys., Omaha, 1983-86; clinic adminstr. Family Practice of Grand Island, Nebr., 1986-90, Physicians of Ob/gyn., Omaha, 1990-93; v.p. phys. svcs. St. Francis Med. Ctr., Grand Island, 1993—. Author, developer (computer software) Personnel Works, 1993. Grad. Leadership Tomorrow, Grand Island, 1995. Mem. Grand Island C. of C. (govt. rels. com 1996). Republican. Roman Catholic. Office: St Francis Med Ctr 2620 W Faidley Grand Island NE 68803

JANSING, C. WILLIAM, surgeon; b. Huntsville, Ala., Oct. 1, 1936; s. Carl and Dora Jansing; m. Esther M. Puram, Mar. 12, 1960; children: J. David, Kristin L., James M. AB, Princeton U., 1958; MD, Cornell U., N.Y.C., 1962. Diplomate Am. Bd. Surgery. Intern in gen. surgery Med. Coll. Va., Richmond, 1962-63, resident, 1963-67; pvt. practice, gen., thoracic and vascular surgery, Owensboro, Ky., 1969—; chief staff Owensboro Daviess County Hosp., 1981-82. Pres. bd. dirs. Owensboro Area Mus. Sci. and History, 1988-90; dist. chmn. Audubon coun. Boy Scouts Am., 1992-93; mem. founding bd. dirs. Owensboro Cmty Found., 1994—. Maj. M.C., USAR, 1967-69. Fellow ACS; mem. AMA. Soc. Am. Gastroent. Surgeons, Am. Soc. Gen. Surgeons, Ky. Soc. for Gastrointestinal Endoscopy (bd. dirs. 1994-95), Ky. Med. Assn. (peer rev. com. 2d dist. 1970-90), Daviess County Med. Soc. (pres. 1994-95), Owensboro Daviess County C. of C. (health care com. 1992-95). Presbyterian. Home: 1915 Littlewood Dr Owensboro KY 42301 Office: Surg Group Owensboro 1102 Triplett St Box 1441 Owensboro KY 42302

JANSON, RAINER, radiologist; b. June 13, 1942; s. Ernst and Elisabeth (Remmert) J.; m. Ursula Pletziger, Apr. 2, 1976; children: Nina, Julia, Eva. MD, U. Bonn, Fed. Republic of Germany, 1967. Mem. pathology dept. U. Bonn, 1963-70, mem. radiology dept., 1970-74, radiologist, 1974-76, dr. medicine radiology dept., 1976-80, prof. medicine radiology dept., 1980-83; head radiology dept. Städt. Krankenhaus Leverkusen, Fed. Republic of Germany, 1983—. Contbr. over 100 articles to profl. jours. Office: Städt Krankenhaus Leverkusen, Dhünnberg 60, 5090 Leverkusen Germany

JANSON, SUSAN LEE, nurse, educator; b. Racine, Wis., Mar. 24, 1945; d. Harold G. and Jean A. Janson; children: Andrew, Sarah. BSN, U. Mich., 1967, MS, 1971; D of Nursing Sci., U. Calif., San Francisco, 1983. RN, Calif.; cert. adult nurse practitioner. Head nurse, respiratory clin. specialist U. Colo. Med. Ctr., Denver, 1972-73; clin. nurse specialist U. Calif., San Francisco, 1978-80, prof. Sch. Nursing, 1983—; adj. prof. dept. medicine U. Calif., San Francisco; mem. expert panel on asthma NIH. Contbr. articles to profl. publs. Fellow Am. Acad. Nursing; mem. ANA, Nat. Org. Nurse Practitioner Faculty, Am. Thoracic Soc. (past chair nursing assembly). Home: 10 Azalea Dr Mill Valley CA 94941-1409

JANSYN, GREGORY MARTIN, podiatrist; b. Chgo., Jan. 20, 1958; s. Albin Martin and Dolores Marie (Madura) J.; m. Maureen Ward, June 8, 1986; children: Bryan, Kailey. BS, Loyola U., Chgo., 1981; D Podiatric Medicine, Scholl Coll. Podiatric Med., 1986. Diplomate Am. Bd. Podiatric Orthopedics and Primary Podiatric Medicine. Practice podiatry Glenside Podiatry, Glendale Heights, Ill. Fellow Am. Coll. Foot and Ankle Orthopedics and Medicine. Republican. Roman Catholic.

JÄNTTI, PIRKKO ORVOKKI, geriatrician, consultant; b. Uusikaupunki, Finland, Apr. 8, 1949; d. Kalle Juho and Maire Mirjam (Lehtinen) Mattila; m. Ville Heikki Jäntti, Apr. 10, 1976; children: Kalle, Maria. MD, Tampere (Finland) U., 1993; Licenciate of Medicine, Turku (Finland) U., 1974. Med. officer Lahti Mcpl. Health Ctr., Finland, 1974-76, Turku Mcpl. Health Ctr., 1976-82; ward physician Turku City Hosp., 1982-83; cons. in geriatric medicine Tampere City Hosp., 1983-95; rsch. Royal London Hosp., 1988-89; cons. in geriatric medicine Oulu (Finland) City Hosp., 1995—; asst. tchr. Tampere U., 1986-87, 91-95; physician Nat. Pensions Inst. Rehab. Rsch. Ctr., Finland, 1979-80. Author: Falls in the Elderly, 1993; contbr. articles to profl. jours. Mem. Finland Geriatric Soc. (sec. 1993-95), Brit. Geriatric Soc. Home: Hallitusk 11 A 16, 90100 Oulu Finland Office: Oulu City Hosp, PO Box 265, 90101 Oulu Finland

JANTUNEN, KAUKO ILMARI, physician; b. Ruokolahti, Finland, Aug. 27, 1941; came to U.S., 1970, naturalized, 1978; s. Heimo and Helvi Sivia (Teppana) J.; m. Silvi Ploom, Mar. 11, 1991; children: Pertti Tapio, Timo Juhani, Frank Kari, David Jabez, Karl Edvin, Ken Eduard, Kevin Alex. MD, U. Helsinki, Finland, 1967. Diplomate Am. Bd. Family Practice. Gen. practice medicine Kiihtelysvaara, Finland, 1967-69, Pajala, Sweden, 1969-70; intern St. Luke's Hosp., Fargo, N.D., 1970-71; practice family medicine New York Mills, Minn., 1971-75, Lake Worth, Fla., 1975-92; mem. staff Christian Unity Hosp., Grafton, N.D., 1992—. Fellow Am. Acad. Family Physicians; mem. AMA. Pentecostal. Address: 155 W 14th St Grafton ND 58237-1801

JANUZZI, JAMES LOUIS, physician, internist, gastroenterologist; b. N.Y.C., Feb. 2, 1941; s. Fred and Alexandra (Calogera) J.; m. Louise Marie Carini, June 27, 1964; children: Marisa, James, Louis. AB, St. Peter's Coll., 1962; MD, N.Y. Meml. Coll., 1966. Diplomat of Am. Bd. Internal Medicine and Gastroenterology. pres. med. staff St. Vincent's Hosp., N.Y.C., 1989-91. Bd. Trustees St. Vincent's Hosp., N.Y.C., 1989-93. Capt. U.S. Army, 1968-70. Office: 29 Washington Sq W New York NY 10011-9180

JANZEN, NORINE MADELYN QUINLAN, medical technologist; b. Fond du Lac, Wis., Feb. 9, 1943; d. Joseph Wesley and Norma Edith (Gustin) Quinlan. BS, Marian Coll., 1965; med. technologist St. Agnes Sch. Med. Tech., Fond du Lac, 1966; MA, Cen. Mich. U., 1980; m. Douglas Mac Arthur Janzen, July 18, 1970; 1 son, Justin James. Med. technologist Mayfair Med. Lab., Wauwatosa, Wis., 1966-69; supr. med. technologist Dr.'s Mason, Chamberlain, Franke, Klink & Kamper, Milw., 1969-76, Hartford-Parkview Clinic, Ltd., 1976-94, patient svc. ctrs. supr. Med. Sci. Labs., Wauwatosa, Wis., 1994—; coord. health in bus. Hartford Parkview Clinic, 1990-91, drug program coord., 1991-94; co-chair joint mtg. Clin. Lab. Mgrs. Assn. and Wis. Assn. for Clin. Lab. Scientists, 1993-94. Substitute poll worker Fond du Lac Dem. Com., 1964-65; mem. Dem. Nat. Com., 1973—. Mem. Am. Soc. for Clin. Lab. Scientists (people to people clin. lab. scientist del. to People's Republic of China 1989), Nat. Soc. Clin. Lab. Scientists (awards com. chair 1984-87, 88-91, chmn. 1986-88, nominations com. 1989-92), Wis. Assn. Clin. Lab. Scientists (exec. sec. 1991—, chmn. awards com. 1976-77, 84-85, 86-87, treas. 1977-81, pres.-elect 1981-82, pres. 1982-83, dir. 1977-84, 85-87, Mem. of Yr. award 1982, 95, numerous svc. awards, chair ann. meeting 1987-88), Clin. Lab. Mgmt. Assn. (co-chair joint meeting 1993-94), Milw. Soc. Clin. Lab. Scientists (pres. 1971-72, bd. dir. 1972-73), Communications of Wis. (originator, chmn. 1977-79), Southeastern Suprs. Group (co-chmn. 1976-77), LWV, Alpha Delta Theta (nat. dist. chmn. 1967-69, nat. alumnae dir. 1969-71), Alpha Mu Tau. Methodist. Home: N98w17298 Dotty Way Germantown WI 53022-4618 Office: Med Scis Labs 11020 W Plank Ct Ste 100 Wauwatosa WI 53226

JAPP, NYLA F., infection control services administrator; b. Sterling, Colo., Jan. 8, 1948; d. Leonard W. and Eleanor M. (Barnts) J. Assoc. in Nursing, Garden City Community Coll., 1980; diploma, Pikes Peak Inst. Med. Tech., 1970; BS in Human Resources Mgmt., Friends U., 1992. RN, Kans. With surg. unit St. Catherine Hosp., Garden City, Kans.; sanitarian Finney County Commrs., Garden City; mgr. sterile processing St. Catherine Hosp., Garden City, Kans., mgr. infection control. Mem. Am. Soc. Hosp. Ctrl. Svc. Pers. (regional bd. dirs., chmn. recognition com., mem. tech. cert. com., APIC liaison, AORN liaison, JCAHO liaison, educator of yr., Tom Samuels rsch. award), Great Plains Soc. Hosp. Ctrl. Svc. Pers. (chmn. program com., mem. newsletter com., chmn. nominating com., rsch. com., pres., bd. dirs.), Nat. Inst. for Cert. Healthcare Sterile Processing and Distbn. Pers. (bd. dirs.), Internat. Assn. Hosp. Ctrl. Svc. Mgmt., Assn. Practitioners in Infection Control. Home: 1712 E Fair St Garden City KS 67846-3558

JAQUA, RICHARD ALLEN, pathologist; b. Fort Dodge, Iowa, Apr. 15, 1938; s. John Franklin and Esther Constance (Rossing) J.; m. Mary Joanne Stewart, Dec. 29, 1969. B.A. magna cum laude, Yale U., 1960; M.D., Harvard U., 1965. Diplomate: Am. Bd. Pathology, Am. Bd. Nuclear Medicine. Teaching fellow pathology Harvard Med. Sch., 1965-67; resident clin. pathology NIH, 1967-69; intern pathology Mass. Gen. Hosp., Boston, 1965-66; fellow tumor pathology Meml.-Sloane Kettering Cancer Center, N.Y.C., 1969-70; asst. prof. pathology U. S.D. Sch. Medicine, Vermillion, 1970-73; asso. prof. U. S.D. Sch. Medicine, 1973-74, asso. prof., acting chmn. dept. lab. medicine, 1974-77, prof., chmn. dept. lab. medicine, 1977—; dir. U. S.D. Sch. Medicine (Electron Microscopy Lab. and Clin. Virology Lab.), 1979—; pathologist VA Hosp., Sioux Falls, S.D., 1978—; practice medicine specializing in anatomic and clin. pathology and nuclear medicine Lab. Clin. Medicine, Sioux Falls, 1970—. Served with USPHS, 1967-69. Recipient Outstanding Prof. awards U. S.D. Med. Students, 1971, 75, 77, 90; VA grantee, 1980-82. U. S.D. Faculty Recognition award, 1986. Fellow Coll. Am. Pathologists, Am. Soc. Clin. Pathologists; mem. Electron Microscopy Soc. Am., Am. Assn. Cancer Edn., AAAS, Internat. Acad. Pathology, Soc. Nuclear Medicine, Sigma Xi, Alpha Omega Alpha. Home: 27546 483d Ave Canton SD 57013 Office: USD Health Sci Ctr 1400 W 22nd St Sioux Falls SD 57105

JAQUITH, GEORGE OAKES, ophthalmologist; b. Caldwell, Idaho, July 29, 1916; s. Gail Belmont and Myrtle (Burch) J.; BA, Coll. Idaho, 1938; MB, Northwestern U., 1942, MD, 1943; m. Pearl Elizabeth Taylor, Nov. 30, 1939; children: Patricia Ann Jaquith Mueller, George, Michele Eugenie Jaquith Smith. Intern, Wesley Meml. Hosp., Chgo., 1942-43; resident ophthalmology U.S. Naval Hosp., San Diego, 1946-48; pvt. practice medicine, specializing in ophthalmology, Brawley, Calif., 1948—; pres. Pioneers Meml. Hosp. staff, Brawley, 1953; dir., exec. com. Calif. Med. Eye Council, 1960—; v.p. Calif. Med. Eye Found., 1976—. Sponsor Anza council Boy Scouts Am., 1966—. Gold card holder Rep. Assocs., Imperial County, Calif., 1967-68. Served with USMC, USN, 1943-47; PTO. Mem. Imperial County Med. Soc. (pres. 1961), Calif. Med. Assn. (del. 1961—), Nat., So. Calif. (dir. 1966—, chmn. med. adv. com. 1968-69) Soc. Prevention Blindness, Calif. Assn. Ophthalmology (treas. 1976—), San Diego, L.A. Ophthal. Socs., L.A. Rsch. Study Club, Nathan Smith Davis Soc., Coll. Idaho Assocs., Am. Legion, VFW, Res. Officers Assn., Basenji Assn., Nat. Geneal. Soc., Cuyamaca Club (San Diego), Elks, Phi Beta Pi, Lambda Chi Alpha (Hall of Fame). Presbyterian (elder). Office: PO Box 511 665 S Western Brawley CA 92227-0511

JARA, FERNANDO, cardiac and thoracic surgeon; b. San Jose, Costa Rica, Jan. 2, 1943; came to U.S., 1966; s. Abel and Anita (Vargas) Jara; m. Francine Drozen; 1 child, Ana. MD, Nat. U. Mex., 1966; cert. in cardiac and thoracic surgery, SUNY, Buffalo, 1975. Sr. staff surgeon Henry Ford Hosp., Detroit, 1975-81; cardiac and thoracic surgeon, chief thoracic surgeon McLaren Regional Med. Ctr., Flint, Mich., 1981—. Maj. U.S. Army, 1970-72. Republican. Roman Catholic. Office: G-4568 Beecher Rd Flint MI 48532

JARBOE, EDWARD JOSEPH, medical administrator; b. Memphis, Mar. 14, 1935; s. James A. and Margaret B. (Johnson) J.; AA, Christian Brothers U., Memphis, 1955; BS, U. Memphis, 1957; MD, U. Tenn., 1960; m. Veronica Botti, Aug. 24, 1963; children: E.J., Jeff. Intern, U. Tenn., 1960-61; gen. practice medicine, South Pittsburg, Tenn., 1961-62; resident in surgery VA Hosp., Memphis, 1964-65; resident in otolaryngology U. Tenn., 1965-68; practice medicine specializing in otolaryngology, head and neck surgery New Britain, Conn., 1968-77, 80—; asst. chief surgery Gulf Coast Hosp., Houston, 1977-80; New Britain Gen. Hosp.(hon. staff), 1987-91; chmn. dept. otolaryngology Bristol (Conn.) Hosp., 1987-91; clin. instr. dept. surgery U. Conn., 1980-93. Served as capt. M.C., USAF, 1962-64; chief Air Force Clinic, Zaragoza AFB, Spain. Diplomate Am. Bd. Otolaryngology. Fellow Am. Coll. of Surgeons, mem. Am. Acad. Otolaryngology-Head and Neck Surgery, Am. Acad. Otolaryngologic Allergy, Am. Coll. Physician Exec., AMA (Physician's Recognition award), Hartford County Med. Soc. Medicine (assoc.), Phi Rho Sigma (life). Club: Rotary Internat. Home: 4 Pheasant Hill Farmington CT 06032-1629 Office: Aetna Health Plans Med Rev Unit MC17 151 Farmington Ave Hartford CT 06156

JARCHO, SAUL WALLENSTEIN, retired physician, medical historian; b. N.Y.C., Oct. 25, 1906; s. Julius and Susanna (Wallenstein) J.; m. Irma Seijo, Oct. 24, 1948; children: Thomas, Andrew. AB magna cum laude, Harvard U., 1925; MA, Columbia U., 1926, MD, 1930. Diplomate Am. Bd. Internal Medicine. Asst. house surgeon N.Y. Lying-in Hosp., 1930; intern, house physician Mt. Sinai Hosp., N.Y.C., 1931-33, asst. in pathology, 1933-34, in charge cardiovascular rsch., 1945-51, adj. physician, 1940-48, assoc. attending physician, 1951-70; staff mem. Sch. Tropical Medicine, San Juan, P.R., 1930, 38, 41; asst., instr. pathology Johns Hopkins U., Balt., 1934-36; instr., assoc. in pathology Coll. Physicians and Surgeons, Columbia U., N.Y.C., 1936-42; mem., chmn. history medicine study sect. NIH, 1959-63, mem. history life scis. study sect., 1974-76; mem. Armed Forces Med. Libr. Adv. Group, 1954-56, cons. 1973-78; bd. regents Nat. Libr. Medicine, 1961-65, mem. index medicus com., cons., 1975-88. Author: The Concept of Heart Failure from Avicenna to Albertini, 1980, Quinne's Predecessor: Francesco Torti and the Early History of Cinchona, 1993; translator: The Clinical Consultations of Giambattista Morgagni, 1985, Clinical Consultations and Letters by Ippolito Francesco Albertini, Francesco Torti, and other Physicians, 1989; editor: Human Palaeopathology, 1966; cons. editor in chief, editor Trans. and Studies of Coll. Physicians of Phila., 1979-83; contbr. numerous articles, book revs. to profl. jours. From capt. to lt. col. AUS, 1942-46. Recipient George Urdang medal Am. Inst. History Pharmacy, 1995; named Disting. Mem. Regt. U.S. Army Med. Dept. Regt., 1995. Fellow AAAS, Am. Pub. Health Assn., N.Y. Acad. Medicine (editor bull. 1967-77, acad. plaque 1979); mem. AMA, Am. Coll. Physicians (life), Am.

Assn. Pathologists and Bacteriologists, Am. Assn. for History Medicine (William Welch medal 1963, pres. 1968-70, Lifetime Achievement award 1988), Am. Soc. for Tropical Medicine, Soc. Med. Cons. to Armed Forces, History Sci. Soc., Harvey Soc. (life), Phi Beta Kappa.

JÁRDÁNHÁZY, TAMÁS, neurologist; b. Kiskunmajsa, Hungary, Oct. 11, 1946; s. Jozsef Tivadar and Terezia Judit (Mayer) J.; m. Klara Domonkos, Sept. 11, 1971; 1 child, Anett. MD, Szote U., 1971, dr. habil. med., 1994; PhD, MTA-TMB, 1985. Resident Szote Neurol./Psychiat., Szeged, Hungary, 1971-75, registrar, 1975-84, asst. prof., 1984-90, assoc. prof., 1990—; rsch. fellow AZU-KNF, Utrecht, Holland, 1982-83. Recipient Apathy Istvan medal Szote U., 1971, Medal for Univ. Studies Ministry of Edn., 1971. Mem. MIEOT, Hungarian Soc. Clin. Neurophysiology, World Fedn. Neurology. Office: Szote Dept Neurol/Psychiat, Semmelweis u 6, H-6725 Szeged Hungary

JARDINE, ALAN GEORGE, medical educator, nephrologist; b. Thurso, Scotland, Aug. 27, 1960; s. George Cuthbertson Jardine and Elizabeth (Weir) Mackenzie; m. Catherine Patricia Pickering, Aug. 27, 1986; children: Jennifer, Alan, Johanna. BSc with honors, Glasgow (Scotland) U., 1981, MB ChB, 1984, MD, 1991. Clin. scientist MRC Blood Pressure Unit, Glasgow, 1987-90; registrar in nephrology Western Infirmary, Glasgow, 1990-92; lectr. in medicine Aberdeen U., 1992-93; lectr. in nephrology Glasgow U., 1994—. Contbr. numerous chpts. to books, papers to profl. publs. Mem. Royal Coll. Physicians (U.K.), Am. Soc. Nephrology. Office: U Glasgow, Western Infirmary, Glasgow G11 6NT, Scotland

JARDINE, JAMES QUINTUS, obstetrician, gynecologist; b. Washington, Dec. 2, 1954; s. James C. and Sue (Campbell) J.; m. Deborah Lee Booth, May 4, 1985; children: Bolling Campbell, Katherine Virginia, Ashley Charlotte. BA, Vanderbilt U., 1977; MD, U. Ala., 1981. Diplomate Am. Bd. Obstetrics and Gynecology. Intern in ob-gyn Vanderbilt U. Hosp., Nashville, 1981-82, resident in ob-gyn, 1982-85; practice medicine specializing in ob-gyn Bay Area Physicians for Women, P.C., 1985—; bd. dirs. Springhill Meml. Hosp., Mobile, 1989—, chmn. bd., 1995—. Mem. AMA, ACOG, Am. Fertility Soc., ala. Assn. Obn-Gyn. (bd. dirs. 1992), Am. Soc. Colposcopy and Cervical Pathology, Am. Assn. Gynecol. Laparoscopists, Med. Assn. State of Ala., Med. Soc. Mobile County, Knights of Revelry, Mardi Gras Mystic Soc., Kappa Alpha Order. Office: Bay Area Physicians For Women PC 3715 Dauphin St Ste 3B Mobile AL 36608-1764

JARECKI, HENRY GEORGE, physician, financial executive; b. Stettin, Germany, Apr. 15, 1933; s. Max Jarecki and Gerda Kunstmann; m. Gloria Friedland, 1957; children: Andrew, Thomas, Eugene, Nicholas. MD, U. Heidelberg, Germany, 1957. Diplomate Am. Bd. Psychiatry and Neurology. Dir. Mocatta Metals Corp., N.Y.C., 1970-89, Mocatta & Goldsmid Ltd., London, 1973-89, Mocatta Hong Kong Ltd., 1975-89; chmn. Brody, White & Co. Inc., N.Y.C., 1971—, Brody White Ltd, London, 1989-95, Guana Island Hotel Corp., British Virgin Islands, 1975—, Falconwood Corp., N.Y.C., 1976—, MovieFone, Inc., N.Y.C., 1989—; asst. clin. prof., lectr. dept. psychiatry Sch. Medicine Yale U., New Haven, 1970—; gov. BVI Cmty. Coll., British Virgin Islands, 1989—. Author: Modern Psychiatric Treatment, 1971; contbr. articles to profl. jours. Adv. coun. Princeton U., Yale U. Sch. Medicine Dept. Psychiatry, 1992—; trustee Am. Mus. Natural History, 1991—; bd. dirs. Botanic Soc. Brit. V.I., 1986—, Chgo. Bd. Trade, 1993-96. Mem. Nat. Futures Assn. (bd. dirs. 1979-93), Am. Psychiat. Assn. (Presdl. Commendation 1984). Office: Falconwood Corp 3d Fl 565 Fifth Ave New York NY 10017

JARETT, LEONARD, pathologist, educator, researcher; b. Lubbock, Tex., Aug. 25, 1936; s. Hyman Jerome and Nellie M (Bloomberg) J.; m. Arlene Kramer, June 10, 1962; children: Stacy, Douglas, Jennifer. BA, Rice Inst., 1958; MD, Washington U., St. Louis, 1962; MA, U. Pa., 1982. Diplomate Am. Bd. Pathology. Intern Barnes Hosp., St. Louis, 1962-63, resident, 1963-64; assoc. prof. pathology, head div. lab. medicine Washington U., 1969-73, prof., 1973-80; chmn. dept. pathology and lab. medicine Hosp. U. Pa, Phila., 1980—, Simon Flexner prof., 1983—; dir. Cen. Diagnosis Lab., Barnes Hosp., 1969-79; mem. steering com. Nat. Diabetes Rsch. Interchange, 1980-82; mem. sci.adv. bd. St. Jude's Childrens Rsch. Hosp., 1980-83, mem. med. sci. adv. com. Juvenile Diabetes Found., 1981-85; external adv. com. diabetes and endocrinology rsch. Baylor Coll. Medicine, 1982—; mem. metabolism study sect. Nat. Inst. Arthritis, Diabetes and Digestive Diseases, 1983-86; Reginald Mason Meml. lectr. U. Utah, 1988; plenary speaker 5th Congress ASEAN Fedn. of Endocrine Socs., Singapore, 1989; George Hoyt Whipple lectr. U. Rochester Med. Ctr., Rochester, N.Y., 1993. Editor: Gradwohl's Clinical Laboratory Methods and Diagnosis, 1980; contbr. articles to profl. jours., chpts. to books. With USPHS, 1964-66. Recipient Richard S. Brookings award Sch. Medicine Washington U., 1962, Sheard-Sanford award Am. Soc. Clin. Pathology, 1962, David Rumbough award Juvenile Diabetes Found., 1980, Cotlove award Acad. Clin. Lab. Physicians and Scientists, 1985, Gerald T. Evans award Acad. Clin. Lab. Physicians and Scientists, 1992, 2d Annual E. Clifford Toren Meml. award U. S. Ala., 1992, Van Syke award N.Y. Metropolitan sect. Am. Assn. Clin. Chemistry, 1995; John and Mary Markle scholar, 1967-72. Home: 1024 Great Springs Rd Bryn Mawr PA 19010-1724 Office: U Pa Sch Medicine 36th And Fairmount Ave Philadelphia PA 19104-1999

JARNAGIN, DONALD EDWARD, optometrist; b. Phoenix, Feb. 7, 1945; s. Woodrow Hanchey and Dorothea (Woolard) J.; m. Cheryl Ann Koiser, Aug. 30, 1965 (div. May 1990); children: Pamela, Matthew, Joshua, Rebecca; m. Shawn Lawson, June 25, 1995. Student, Ariz. State U., 1963-66; BS, So. Calif. Coll. Optometry, 1968, OD cum laude, 1970. dir. Ariz. Vision Svcs. Plan; chair Ariz. Eye Care Assocs.; bd. chair Omni Eye Svcs. Phoenix; cmty. adv. bd. Charter Hosp. Glendale. Chair bd. adjustment City of Glendale (Calif.), chair bd. commrs. Glendale Housing Authority, chair review com.; active Boy Scouts Am., Youth soccer, baseball and basketball; sect. chair Am. Cancer Soc.; venture fund panel United Way; adv. com. Ctrl. Ariz. Health Sys. Agy.; charter dir. Ariz. Rep. Caucus; steering com., panel recorder Ariz. Rep. Town Hall; dir., treas. West Valley Alliance; founders com. Ariz. State U. West Campus. Capt. U.S. Army Med. Svc. Corp., 1971-73. Mem. Am. Optometric Assn. (trustee, sec./treas., v.p., pres., various coms.), Ariz. Optometric Assn. (pres., O.D. of Yr.), Ctrl. Ariz. Optometry Soc. (pres., O.D of Yr.), Glendale C. of C. (chair state govt. com., chair govt. affairs com.), Rotary (pres., dir., Paul Harris fellow). Home: 6846 N 4th Ave Phoenix AZ 85013 Office: Ste 106 5334 W Northern Ave Glendale AZ 85301

JAROWSKI, CHARLES IGNATIUS, oncologist; b. Phila., May 5, 1946; s. Charles I. and Winifred Theresa (Ospeck) J.; m. Joan Squillacote, Dec. 25, 1971; children: Charles Leo, Peter Damian. BA, Columbia U., 1968; MD, Cornell U., 1972. Intern N.Y. Hosp., N.Y.C., 1972-73, resident in medicine, 1973-75, fellow in hematology/oncology, 1975-78, asst. attending physician, 1978—; instr. medicine Cornell U. Med. Coll., N.Y.C., 1978-84, clin. asst. prof. medicine, 1984—. Author: Synopsis of Cancer Chemotherapy, 1977, 2d edition, 1985. Mem. Am. Soc. Clin. Oncology, Am. Soc. Hematology. Democrat. Office: 400 E 77th St New York NY 10021-2366

JARRATT, WALLACE CURTIS, medical technologist; b. Flint, Mich., May 20, 1955; s. Curtis Neely and Betty Sue (Haile) J.; m. Sharron Thella Warren Stribling, Jan. 13, 1973 (div. May 1982); 1 child, Tracy Marie Jarratt; m. Lee Ann Taylor, Jan. 24, 1995; 1 child, Joshua Taylor Stanley. Med. technologist Chickaswba Hosp., Blytheville, Ark., 1977-79, 81-92, VA Med. Ctr., Charleston, S.C., 1979-81, United Lab. Assocs., Searcy, Ark., 1992-95; lab. mgr. Newport (Ark.) Hosp., 1995—. With USN, 1973-77. Mem. Am. Med. Technologists, Elks. Home: 50 Stoneybrook Apt 1 Searcy AR 72143 Office: Newport Hosp & Clinic 2000 McLain Newport AR 72112

JARRETT, STEVEN RONALD, physician, physical medicine and rehabilitation; b. Bklyn., Oct. 22, 1944; s. Irving J. and Clara (Rockower) J.; m. Susan Appel, June 15, 1969; children: Joshua, Elizabeth. BS, Muhlenberg Coll., 1965; MD, Chgo. Med. Sch., 1969. Diplomate Am. Bd. Phys. Medicine and Rehab. Intern Michael Reese Hosp., Chgo., 1969-70; resident phys. medicine and rehab. Schwab Rehab. Hosp., Chgo., 1970-73; dir. of clin. svcs. Inst. of Phys. Med. and Rehab., Peoria, Ill., 1973-76; med. dir. Franciscan Hosp. Rehab. Ctr., Rock Island, Ill., 1977-83; chief phys. med. and rehab. Sunnyview Hosp. and Rehab. Ctr., Schenectady, N.Y., 1983—; clin. prof. Albany (N.Y.) Med. Coll., 1996—; survey cons. Commn. on Accreditation of Rehab. Facilities, Tuscon, 1979—; bd. dirs. Sunnyview Hosp. and Rehab. Ctr., Schenectady, 1987—; guest examiner Am. Bd. Phys. Med. and Rehab., 1989, 96; expert cons. N.Y. State Dept. of Health, Office of Profl. Med. Conduct, 1995—. Author: (with others) Conn's Current Therapy, 1989; editl. adv. bd. Medical Rehab Services Management, 1995—. Mem. govs. task force for rehab. needs State of N.Y., 1986-87. Recipient Cert. of Appreciation CARF, 1980. Mem. AMA, N.Y. State Med. Soc., Schenectady County Med. Soc., Am. Geriatric Soc., Am. Assn. of Electrodiagnostic Medicine, Am. Acad. of Phys. Medicine and Rehab. Home: 2155 Lynnwood Dr Niskayuna NY 12309 Office: Sunnyview Hosp & Rehab Ctr 1270 Belmont Ave Schenectady NY 12308

JARRETT, THOMAS EDWARD, physician; b. Anderson, S.C., May 28, 1954; s. Wiley Edward and Sara Elizabeth (Wardlaw) J. BS, Clemson U., 1978; MD, Med. U. S.C., 1978. Diplomate Am. Bd. Internal Medicine. Intern Spartanburg (S.C.) Gen. Hosp., 1978-79; resident New Hanover Meml. Hosp., Wilmington, N.C., 1979-82; active staff High Point (N.C.) Regional Hosp., 1982—; ptnr. Med. Ctr. Internists, High Point, 1983—. Med. dir., bd. dirs. Cmty. Clinic of High Point, 1993-96. Mem. Am. Soc. Internal Medicine, N.C. Med. Soc. (vice councilor 1992-93, councilor 1994-95), High Point Med. Soc. (pres. 1992). Office: Med Ctr Internists PA 624 Quaker Ln Ste 205A High Point NC 27262

JARRETT, WILLIAM HOPE, ophthalmologist; b. Balt., Jan. 1, 1933; s. Edwin Bosley and Dorothy (Duncan) J.; m. Carol Goldsborough, Jan. 3, 1981; children: Laurie Jarrett Rogers, Whitney Jarrett McDonough, William H. Jarrett, III. BA, Yale U., 1954; MD, Johns Hopkins U., 1958. Cert. Am. Bd. Ophthalmology. Intern Osler Med. Svc. Johns Hopkins Hosp., Balt., 1958-59, asst. resident Osler Med. Svc., 1959-60, intern resident Wilmer Inst., 1960-63; fellow retina svc. Mass. Eye and Ear Infirm./Harvard Med. Sch., Boston, 1963-64; chief resident Wilmer Eye Svc. Johns Hopkins Hosp., 1964-65; ophthalmologist and chief Beni Messous Eye Hosp., CARE/MEDICO, Algiers, Algeria, 1965-66; asst. prof., ophthalmology Emory U. Sch. of Medicine, Atlanta, 1966-71; with Eye Cons. of Atlanta, 1971—. Contbr. articles to profl. jours. Bd. dirs. Diabetes Assn. of Atlanta, 1985—; vestry mem. Episcopal Ch., Atlanta, 1972-75. Recipient Florence McDonnell Man of Vision award, Atlanta, 1994. Mem. Ga. Soc. Ophthalmology (pres. 1988-89), Atlanta Ophthalmol. Soc. (pres. 1981-82), Phi Beta Kappa, Alpha Omega Alpha. Office: Eye Consultants of Atlanta Ste 3000 95 Collier Rd Atlanta GA 30309

JÄRVINEN, SEPPO HEIKKI KULLERVO, orthodontist, dentist; b. Wiipuri, Finland, Mar. 15, 1935; s. Eino Henrik and Rauha Rakel (Reponen) J.; m. Leila Irmeli Sjöstedt, Oct. 15, 1960; children: Laura Erika, Klaus Henrik Julius. Lic. in Odontology, U. Helsinki, Finland, 1961, D in Odontology, 1977. Cert. dental specialist in orthodontics and in pub. health dentistry Finnish Med. Health Bd. Chief dentist Mcpl. Health Ctr., Lahti, Finland, 1972—; acting assoc. prof. orthodontics U. Kuopio (Finland), 1977-78, 84-86, lectr., 1979, docent in pedodontics and orthodontics, 1981—, acting prof. dental devel. and orthodontics, 1992-93; docent in pedodontics and orthodontics U. Helsinki (Finland), 1990—; vice dean of dental faculty U. Kuopio, 1978, chairperson coun. edn. of dental faculty, 1978-79; expert adviser in orthodontics Com. Dental Care, State of Finland, 1981-82; cons. Am. Jour. Orthodontics and Dentofacial Orthopedics, 1988—. Decorated Order Suomen Leijonan Ritarikunta, State of Finland. Office: Lahden Sosiaali-Ja Terveysvirasto, Kirkkokatu 8 B, FIN-15140 Lahti Finland

JARVIS, BASIL, microbiologist; b. Derby, Eng., Dec. 8, 1936; s. Sidney Harry and Getrude Alice (Brown) Roberts-Jarvis; m. Marjorie Joan Brown, May 18, 1963; children: Iain Stuart, Sarah Jane. BS, U. Reading, Eng., 1958, PhD, 1967; MS, U. London, 1963. Chartered biologist. Asst. bacteriologist United Dairies Ltd., London, 1958-60; clin. biochemist St. Helier Hosp., Carshalton, Surrey, Eng., 1960-62; from lectr. to sr. lectr. Nat. Coll. Food Tech. U. Reading, Weybridge, 1964-71; chief microbiologist Leatherhead Food Research Assn., Surrey, Eng., 1971-78, dep. dir. sci., 1979-83; dir. research, devel. Express Foods Group Internat. Ltd., Ruislip, Eng., 1983-87; tech. dir. H.P. Bulmer Ltd., Hereford, Eng., 1987-95; microbiologist Ross Bioscis Upton Bishop, Ross-on-Wye, Eng., 1996—; chmn. Regem Ltd., Cardiff, Wales, 1987-90; vis. prof. U. Reading, 1979—; hon. prof. U. Surrey, Guildford, 1985—. Author: Statistical Aspects of Food Microbiology, 1987; editor Food Microbiology and Technology, 1979; patentee Blue Cheese Flavor, 1971; contbr. numerous articles to profl. jours. Mem. various coms. Ministry Agr., Fish and Food Dept. Health, London, 1972—; chmn. course com. food microbiology WHO, 1973—. Research fellow Dept. Sci. Indsl. Research, London, 1962-64, European Molecular Biology Orgn., Oslo, 1968. Fellow Inst. Biology (examiner 1972-77), Inst. Food Sci. (examiner 1976-83, counsellor 1991—); mem. Soc. Applied Bacteriology (pres. 1987-89), Soc. Gen. Microbiology, Rsch. Devel. Soc. (coun. 1985-91). Mem. Conservative Party. Mem. Ch. Eng. Club: Fly Dressers (London) (editor 1980-86). Home: Daubies Farm, Upton Bishop, Ross-on-Wye Herefordshire HR9 7UR, HR4 OLE

JARVIS, DAPHNE ELOISE, laboratory administrator; b. Lithia, Fla., Feb. 18, 1945; d. Grady Edwin and Vera Eloise (Smith) Smith; m. Hubert E. Jarvis, Aug. 1, 1964; 1 child, Jessica Ellen. BS, Blue Mountain Coll., 1966; MA, Spalding U., 1972. Cert. med. technologist with specialist in blood bank. Med. technologist St. Anthony's Hosp., Louisville, 1968-69, Clark County Meml. Hosp., Jeffersonville, Ind., 1969-73; asst. to edn. coord. ARC, Washington, 1973-75; dir. Grace Bapt. Ch. Sch., Bryans Rd., Md., 1978-83; sect. chief blood bank Physicians Meml. Hosp., LaPlata, Md., 1975-76, 83-84; supr. donor blood labs. Southwest Fla. Blood Bank, Tampa, 1984-87, dir., 1987-89; asst. dir. tech. svcs. Ark. Region ARC, Little Rock, 1989-93, dir. tech. svcs./hosp. svcs. Ark. Regional Blood Svcs., 1993-95; mfg. team leader Lifeblood-Midsouth Regional Blood Ctr., Memphis, 1995—; lectr. UAMS Sch. Med. Tech., Little Rock, 1989-95. Children's leader Ingram Blvd Bapt. Ch., West Memphis, Ark., 1995—. Mem. Am. Assn. Blood Banks, South Ctr. Assn. Blood Banks (membership com. 1989-95). Office: Lifeblood Midsouth Reg Blood Ctr 1040 Madison Ave Memphis TN 38104-2106 Office: Lifeblood-Midsouth 1040 Madison Ave Memphis TN 38104-2106

JASIEWICZ, RONALD CLARENCE, physician; b. Suffern, N.Y., June 8, 1964; s. Clarence William and Adele Helen (Rucki) J. AAS in Sci., Math., SUNY, Rockland, 1984; BS in Life Sci., N.Y. Inst. Tech., 1987; DO, N.Y. Coll. Osteo. Medicine, 1992; AAS in Emergency Med. Tech., SUNY, Rockland, 1993. Diplomate Nat. Bd. Osteo. Med. Examiners. Unit asst. Good Samaritan Hosp., Suffern, 1980-87; paramedic Empress Ambulance Svc., Yonkers, N.Y., 1985-86, Nyack (N.Y.) E.M.S., 1986-87; intern in medicine and surgery Wilson Meml. Regional Med. Ctr., Johnson City, N.Y., 1992-93; asst. clin. instr. Stony Brook (N.Y.) Med. Sch., 1993-96; resident in anesthesiology Univ. Med. Ctr., 1993-96; fellow pediatric anesthesiology Children's Hosp. of Buffalo, 1996—. Mem. Am. Soc. Anesthesiologists, Am. Osteo. Coll. Anesthesiologists, Am. Osteo. Assn., Am. Assn. Osteo. Postgrad. Physicians, Sigma Omicron. Roman Catholic. Home: 17 Spindrift Ct Ste 5 Williamsville NY 14221-7874

JASION, ARTHUR RAYMOND, plastic surgeon; b. Balt., Jan. 18, 1936; s. Edward John and Irene (Lekstein) J.; widowed; children: Edward Robert, Jennifer, Arthur W. BS, U. Md., 1957, MD, 1959. Diplomate Am. Bd. Plastic Surgery. Pvt. practice Timonium, Md., 1967—; active staff Franklin Square Hosp., Balt., 1968—; cons. Mercy Hosp., Balt. Home: Valley Garth 1819 Blakefield Cir Lutherville Timonium MD 21093

JASPER, DONALD EDWARD, clinical pathology educator; b. La Grande, Oreg., Dec. 30, 1918; s. Edward Doak and Florence Margaret (MacDonald) J.; m. Elizabeth Ann Miller, May 23, 1943; children: Donald Richard, Jean Ellen Jasper Edwards. Grad., East Oreg. State Coll., 1938; BS, Wash. State U., 1940, DVM, 1942; MS, Iowa State U., 1944; PhD, U. Minn., 1947. Lic. veterinarian. Asst. clinician Iowa State U., Ames, 1942-44; research asst. U. Minn., St. Paul, 1944-47; from asst. prof. to prof. U. Calif., Davis, 1947-89, dean sch. vet. medicine, asst. dir. agrl. experiment sta., 1954-62, chmn. dept. clin. pathology, 1984-89; cons. Pres.'s Adv. Com. on World Food Supply, 1967, Food and Agriculture Orgn. Mex., 1977; mem. vet. drug efficacy com. Nat. Acad. Sci., 1968-69; Fulbright-Hays vis. prof. U.S. Bd. Fgn. Scholarships, Yugoslavia, 1978. Author research publs.; contbr. articles to profl. jours., chpts. to books. Fulbright-Hays Research scholar U.S. Bd. Fgn. Scholarships, New Zealand, 1975-76; recipient numerous grants USDA; recipient Alumni Achievement award Eastern Oreg. State Coll., 1975, Alumni Achievement award Wash. State U., 1980, Research award Am. Diary Sci. Assn., 1987. Mem. Am. Vet. Medicine Assn. (Borden Research award 1967), Nat. Mastitis Council (pres. 1972), Am. Soc. for Vet. Clin. Pathology (pres. 1971), Am. Soc. for Microbiology, Internat. Orgn. for Mycoplasmology (chmn. bovine sect. 1982-88). Republican. Baptist. Office: Univ of Calif Davis Sch of Vet Medicine Dept of Pathology Davis CA 95616

JASPER, DORIS J. BERRY, nurse; b. Banner, Miss., Sept. 12, 1933; d. William Richard and Lena Martha (Gambill) Berry; m. Lyman W. Jasper, Jan. 8, 1949; children: Richard L., Lynn William. Student, Blytheville (Ark.) Sch. Nursing, 1949, Purdue U., Westville, Ind., 1979-80, Lake Mich. Coll., Benton Harbor, 1977-80. Staff nurse St. Anthony's Hosp., Michigan City, Ind., 1951-66; pvt. duty nurse Michigan City, 1962-68; emergency rm. nurse St. Anthony's Hosp., 1968-74; charge nurse, emergency rm. nurse Meml. Hosp., Michigan City, 1974-75; pvt. duty nurse Three Oaks, Mich., 1972-84, Michigan City, 1981-88; staff nurse Alpha Christiansan Registry, New Buffalo, Mich., 1988—; pvt. practice Three Oaks, 1989-90; owner, practitioner Jaspers Health Care, Three Oaks, 1991—; owner, mgr. D.J.'s Frolick Kennel; pvt. practice No. Ind., So. Mich.; co-owner, mgr. grain farm. Mem. Bus. and Profl. Women's Club, Inc. (legis. chair dist. 2 1987-88, rec. sec. dist. 2, exec. bd. mem.), Mich. Fedn. Bus. Profl. Women USA (legis. chair dist. 9), New Buffalo Area Bus. Profl. Women (legis. chair), Tenn. Walking Horse Assn., Smithsonian Inst. Republican. Baptist. Home and Office: 101 Jasper Dr Three Oaks MI 49128

JATLOW, PETER I., pathologist, medical educator, researcher; b. New Brunswick, N.J., Feb. 12, 1936; s. Daniel and Anne (Davis) J.; m. Stephanie Bea Yager, Dec. 22, 1959; children—Allison, Julia. B.S., Union Coll., Schenectady, 1957; M.D., SUNY Downstate Med. Ctr., Bklyn., 1961; M.S. (hon.), Yale U., 1976. Intern Montefiore Hosp., Bronx, N.Y., 1961-62; resident Yale-New Haven Hosp., 1962-66; asst. prof. lab. medicine Yale U., New Haven, 1968-73, assoc. prof. lab. medicine, 1973-76, prof. lab. medicine, 1976—, chmn. dept. lab. medicine, 1984—; cons. FDA, Washington, 1978-82; mem. biomed. research rev. com. USPHS, Nat. Inst. Drug Abuse, Rockville, Md., 1982-86; mem. test material deve. subcom. FLEX Program Nat. Bd. Med. Exam., Philly, 1990-91. Editor: Methodology in Analytical Toxicology, vol. II, 1982; editorial bd. Clin. Chemistry, 1973-83, Selected methods in Clin. Chemistry, 1976-79, Jour. Analytical Toxicology, 1978-79, Therapeutic Drug Monitoring, 1979-86, 90—, Clinica Chimica Acta, 1984-90, Am. Jour. Clin. Pathology, 1988—; contbr. numerous articles to profl. jours. Served to surgeon USPHS, 1966-68. Recipient Irving Sunshine award in clin. toxicology Internat. Assn. Therapeutic Drug Monitoring and Toxicology, 1993. Fellow Coll. Am. Pathologists; mem. AAAS, Acad. Clin. Lab. Physicians and Scientists (pres. 1983-84, Gerald T. Evans award 1988), Am. Soc. Clin. Pathology, Am. Assn. Clin. Chemistry (award for outstanding contbns. to clin. chemistry in selected area of rsch. 1985, award for outstanding contbns. in edn. 1995). Home: 617 Saddle Ridge Rd Orange CT 06477-2024 Office: Yale U Sch Medicine Dept Lab Medicine 333 Cedar St New Haven CT 06510-3206

JATZKEWITZ, HORST WALDEMAR, retired neurochemist; b. Graudenz, Germany, Sept. 1, 1912; s. Ernst Franz and Margarete Johanna (Thies) J.; m. Elsa Adele Brandt, Aug. 5, 1947; children: Till Ernst, Annegret Maria. Diploma in Engring., Tech. U., Berlin, 1938, D. in Engring., 1941. Head. neurochem. div. Max-Planck-Inst. for Psychiatry, Munich, 1956-77; dir. Max-Planck-Inst. for Psychiatry, 1969-77; prof. U. Munich, 1965-77. Author: Neurochemistry an Introduction, 1978; contbr. articles and experiments on errors in sphingolipid metabolism to profl. jours.; adv. bd. Jour. Neurochemistry, 1968-75. Mem. Internat. Soc. for Neurochemistry, Gesellschaft Deutscher Naturforscher u. Ärzte, Gesellschaft für BiologischeChemie.

JAVED, MURID HUSSAIN, embryologist; b. Chak Jhumra, Punjab, Pakistan, May 1, 1960; s. Muhammad and Niamat (Bibi) Amir; m. Ghulam Fatima, Sept. 2, 1972; children: Muhammad Asif, Sajida, Inayat Ullah, Zaka Ullah, Sana Ullah. DVM, U. Agr., Faisalabad, Pakistan, 1981, MS, 1984; PhD, Wash. State U., 1990. Fellow in sci. U. Agr., 1974-76; rsch. officer Pakistan Agrl. Rsch. Coun., Islamabad, 1981-82, sci. officer, 1984-86, sr. sci. officer, 1990—; owner Javed Vet. Hosp.; embryo transfer cons. Agrl. Devel. Bank of Pakistan, Islamabad, 1991—; livestock farming cons., animal health and prodn. cons. Islamabad Capital Ter., 1991—; trainer Embryo Transfer Tech., Pakistan. Mem. Pakistan Vet. Jour.; contbr. articles to profl. jours. Organizer Social Welfare Union, Faisalabad, 1983; gen. sec. Pakistan Students Assn., Pullman, Wash., 1989, pres., 1990. Recipient hon. cert. Vet. Med. Soc. Pakistan, 1978, 80, Best Achievement award PARC Scientists Assn., 1995; FAO fellow to China, 1994, Japan Soc. for Promotion of Sci. fellow, 1996, Islamic Devel. Bank postdoctoral fellow, 1996—Punjab Govt. schlar, 1972-74, U. Agr. scholar, 1974-81, Ministry of Edn. scholar, 1986-90. Mem. Internat. Embryo Transfer Soc., Pakistan Agrl. Scientists Forum, Soc. for Advancement of Sci. in Pakistan, Pakistan Vet. Med. Assn. (life), Parc Scientists Assn. (joint sec. 1992). Home: HNo 262-19 Jinnah St, Shamasabad, Rawalpindi Pakistan Office: Animal Prodn Inst, Islamabad 45500, Pakistan

JAVID, MANUCHER J., neurosurgery educator; b. Tehran, Iran, Jan. 11, 1922; came to U.S., 1944, naturalized, 1957; s. Asdolah and Touba (Ahdiyeh) J.; m. Lida Emma Fabbri, Oct. 19, 1951; children—Roxane, Daria, Jeffrey, Claudia. M.D., U. Ill., 1946. Diplomate: Am. Bd. Neurosurgery. Intern Augustana Hosp., Chgo., 1946-47; resident gen. surgery Augustana Hosp., 1947-48, resident neurosurgery, 1948-49; asst. in neuropathology Ill. Neuropsychiat. Inst., Chgo., 1948-49; fellow in neurosurgery Lahey Clinic, Boston, 1949; resident neurosurgery New Eng. Med. Center, Boston, 1950; clin. research fellow neurosurgery Mass. Gen. Hosp., Boston, 1950; asst. resident Mass. Gen. Hosp., 1951, sr. resident neurosurgery, 1952; teaching fellow in surgery Harvard, 1952; instr. Med. Sch. U. Wis., Madison, 1953-54; asst. prof. Med. Sch. U. Wis., 1954-57, asso. prof., 1957-62, prof. neurosurgery, 1962—, chmn. dept. neurosurgery, 1963-95; cons. neurosurgeon VA Hosp., Madison, 1956—. Contbr. articles profl. jours. Mem. AMA, ACS, AAUP, AAAS, Soc. Neurol. Surgeons, Am. Assn. Neurol. Surgeons, Am. Assn. Med. Colls., Am. Trauma Soc., Pan Am. Med. Assn., Soc. for Neurosci., Central Neurosurg. Soc. (pres. 1964), Internat. Intradiscal Therapy Soc. (treas. 1987-90, pres.-elect 1990—, pres. 1991), N.Y. Acad. Scis., Xeiron, Sigma Xi, Phi Beta Pi, Alpha Omega Alpha.. Mem. Baha'i Faith. Club: Rotarian. Home: 4750 Lafayette Dr Madison WI 53705-4865 Office: Univ Wis Hosp and Clinics 600 Highland Ave Madison WI 53792-0001

JAVID, NIKZAD SABET, dentist, prosthodontics educator; b. Kashan, Iran, May 24, 1934; s. Salam and Pika (Farhang) Javid-S.; m. Mahnaz Zolfaghari, Oct. 22, 1942; children: Nikrooz, Behrooz, Farnaz. DMD, U. Tehran, Iran, 1958; cert., U. Chgo., 1970; MSc, Ohio State U., 1971; MEd, U. Fla., 1981. Asst. prof. U. Tehran, 1959-69, prof., dean, 1975-79; asst. prof. Ohio State U., 1971-73, assoc. prof., 1973-74; assoc. prof. removable prosthodontics U. Fla., 1974-75, prof., 1982; pvt. practice dentistry specializing in prosthodontics, Gainsville, Fla., 1980—; cons. in field; guest lectr. numerous internat. meetings. Author books, including: Stress Breaker in Partial Denture, 1966, Cleft Palate Prosthetics, 1968, Complete Denture Construction, 1974, (with Sara Nawab) Essentials of Complete Denture Prosthodontics, 1988; contbr. numerous articles to profl. jours. Named Outstanding Clin. Instr. of Yr. Student Dental Council, Columbus, Ohio, 1973, Outstanding Tchr. of Yr. 1990, Excellent Clin. Prof., U. Fla., 1994, Most Outstanding Prof. of Yr., 1996. Fellow Internat. Coll. Dentists, Internat. Coll. Prosthodontics, Am. Coll. Prosthodontics, Am. Acad. Maxillofacial Prosthetics, Royal Soc. Health (Eng.); mem. Iranian Dental Assn. (dir. 1975-78), ADA, Internat. Assn. Dental Research (sec.-treas. Iran div. 1978). Lodge: Lions. Home: 3941 NW 67th Pl Gainesville FL 32653 Office: U Fla PO Box 100435 Gainesville FL 32610-0435

JAVIER, AILEEN RIEGO, pathologist; b. Fabrica, Negros Occidental, Philipines, Apr. 4, 1948; d. Filemon Yanson and Alicia Vazquez (Alteros) R.; m. Mark Anthony Navarro Javier, July 15, 1972; children: Martha Francesca, Nadine Ruth. BS, U. Phillipines, 1967, MD, 1972; MHA, Ateneo de Manila U., 1989. Diplomate Philipine Bd. Pathology. Instr.

pathology U. Philipines, Manila, 1972-76, asst. prof., 1976-80, sr. lectr., 1987-94; med. specialist, chmn. dept. Lung Ctr. Philipines, Quezon City, 1987-91; cons., 1991—; lectr. Ateneo de Manila Grad. Sch., Quezon City, 1989—; med. specialist Philipine Children's Ctr., Quezon City, 1981-82, cons. 1986; cons. Polymedic Gen. Hosp., Rizal, Philipines, 1984-86, dept. chmn. 1987-94; med. specialist Nat. Kidney Inst., Quezon City, 1984-87, 91-93, cons. 1987-91, dep. dir., 1994—, Bur. Research and Labs, Manila, 1987—; cons. Cardinal Santos Med. Ctr., 1986—; v.p. Philipine Blood Coordinating Council, 1987-88, pres. 1990; bd. dirs. Fetus as a Patient Inst., Philippines, 1990—. Active Goodwill Industries, Quezon City, 1981; bd. dirs. Rizal chpt. Phillipine Nat. Red Cross, 1994—. Fellow Philippine Soc. Oncologists (sec.-treas. 1990-91); mem. Philippine Med. Assn. (life), Transplantation Soc. of the Philippines (life), Internat. Acad. Pathology, Philippine Soc. Pathologists (treas. 1985-87, pres. 1987-89, bd. pathology, 1994-96), Philippine Bible Soc. (life). Baptist. Office: Nat Kidney & Transplant Inst, East Ave, Quezon City The Philippines

JAVITT, JONATHAN C., physician, health policy analyst; b. N.Y.C., Nov. 7, 1956; s. Norman B. and Suzanne (Markovits) J.; m. Marcia C. Fishman, June 29, 1986; children: Zachary, Matthew, Gabrielle. AB with honors, Princeton U., 1978; MD, Cornell U., 1982; MPH, Harvard U., 1984. Diplomate Am. Bd. Ophthalmology. Instr. Johns Hopkins U., Balt., 1987-90, asst. prof., 1990—; asst. prof. Georgetown U., Washington, 1990-93, assoc. prof., 1993-96, prof. Sch. Medicine, prof. sch. Pub. Policy, 1996—; expert cons. Health Care Fin. Adminstrn., Balt., 1987—; spl. employee The White House Health Reform Task Force, Washington, 1992; cons. The World Bank, Washington, 1993—. Editor Archives of Ophthalmology, 1993—, Ophthalmology Times, 1993—; author numerous books, chpts., articles; patentee in field. Com. chair Nat. Health Policy Coun., Washington, 1992—; cmty. speaker on health care The White House, 1992—. Recipient Cert. of Appreciation, USAF, 1992, Physician Scientist award Nat. Eye Inst., 1988; Kellogg Found. fellow, 1983. Fellow Am. Acad. Ophthalmology (Honor award 1990); mem. AMA, Assn. for Rsch. in Vision and Ophthalmology, Assn. for Health Svc. Rsch., Am. Glaucoma Soc., Royal Ocean Racing Club. Republican. Jewish. Office: Georgetown Med Ctr 3800 Reservoir Rd Washington DC 20007

JAVITT, NORMAN B., medical educator; b. N.Y.C., Mar. 9, 1928; s. Bernard and Zara (Hillman) Jakubovitz; m. Suzanne Markovits, June 5, 1955; children: Jonathan Chaim, Daniel Coleman, Joel Israel, Gail Hannah. AB cum laude, Syracuse U., 1947; PhD in Physiology, U. N.C., 1951; MD, Duke U., 1954. Diplomate Am. Bd. Internal Medicine; lic. physician, N.Y. Predoctoral fellow USPHS, Chapel Hill, N.C., 1949-51; intern Mt. Sinai Hosp., N.Y.C., 1954-55, asst. resident, 1957-58, chief resident, 1959-60, Sara Welt fellow in medicine, spl. USPHS, 1961-62; asst. physician, advanced fellow Am. Heart Assn. Vanderbilt Clinic, Columbia Coll. Physicians and Surgeons, N.Y.C., 1957-58; instr. dept. medicine NYU Sch. Medicine, 1962-64, asst. prof., 1964-68; assoc. prof. Cornell U.Med. Coll., N.Y.C., 1968-73, prof., 1973-83; assoc. attending physician N.Y. Hosp., N.Y.C., 1968-73, attending physician, 1973-83; prof. medicine, prof. pediatrics NYU Med. Ctr., N.Y.C., 1983—, dir. divsn. hepatic diseases, 1983—, assoc. dir. clin. rsch. unit, 1985-90; cons. Meml. Sloan-Kettering Cancer Ctr., N.Y.C., 1970-83; vis. prof. Rockefeller U. Hosp., 1970-76; cons. medicine VA Hosp., Bklyn., 1977-83; chief divsn. gastroenterology Cornell-N.Y. Hosp. Med. Ctr., 1973-81, chief divsn. hepatic diseases, acting chief divsn. gastroenterology, 1981-83; cons. Tisch Hosp., NYU Med. Ctr., 1983—; mem. tng. grant study sect. Nat. Inst. Arthritis, Metabolic & Digestive Diseases, NIH, 1978-85; mem. steering com. Nat. Cooperative Gallstone Study, 1973-80, chmn. clin. mgmt. com., 1974-78; gen. medicine study Section A, NIH, 1976-80. Mem. editl. adv. bd. Hosp. Practice, 1969-93; assoc. editor Jour. Lipid Rsch., 1977-78, 86—, editl. bd., 1983—; author, editor 2 books; contbr. articles to profl. jours. Capt., M.C., U.S. Army, 1955-57. Fellow ACP; mem. Am. Physiol. Soc., Am. Soc. Pharmacology and Exptl. Therapeutics, Am. Fedn. Clin. Rsch., Am. Soc. Clin. Investigation, Am. Assn. Study of Liver Disease, Am. Gastroenterol. Assn., Am. Soc. Clin. Pharmacology and Therapeutics, Am. Soc. Biol. Chemists, Am. Pediatric Soc., Am. Soc. Parenteral and Enteral Nutrition, Harvey Soc., Sigma Xi, Alpha Omega Alpha. Jewish. Home: 501 E 79th St New York NY 10021 Office: NYU Med Ctr Divsn Hepatic Disease New York NY 10016

JAWORSKI, DAVID JOSEPH, pharmaceutical executive; b. Erie, Pa., June 16, 1952; s. Marion Augustine and Jean Dorothy (Januleski) J.; m. Beverly Ann Rosenthal, July 23, 1977; children: Jessica Rose, Andrew David. BS in Microbiology, Pa. State U., 1973; MBA, Syracuse U., 1985. Supr. W.H. Rorer Pharms., Fort Washington, Pa., 1974-76, Abbott Labs., Rocky Mount, N.C., 1976-78; supr. Bristol Labs Div. Bristol Myers, Syracuse, N.Y., 1978-80, dept. supr., 1980-81, plant mgr., 1981-82, dir. prodn., 1982-86; dir. pharm. prodn. Bristol Myers, Barceloneta, PR, 1986-87, Sandoz Pharms., East Hanover, N.J., 1987-88; mgr. Ernst & Young, Metro Park, N.J., 1988-91; dir. mfg. Baker Norton Pharmaceuticals, Miami, Fla., 1991-94; dir. tech. ops. Zenith Goldline Pharmaceuticals, Miami, 1995—; pres. North Wind Charters, Ltd., Syracuse, 1985-89. Contbr. articles to profl. jours. Coach Roxbury Soccer Club, Succasunna, N.J., 1989, 90. Mem. Pa. State Alumni Assn., Internat. Soc. Pharm. Engrs., Am. Mgmt. Assn. Democrat. Roman Catholic. Home: 10798 Nashville Dr Hollywood FL 33026-4900 Office: Zenith Goldline Pharm 8800 NW 36th St Miami FL 33178-2404

JAY, HARVEY H., dermatologist, educator; b. Jersey City, Oct. 24, 1944; s. Jack and Miriam (Stein) J.; m. Phyllis Scheinberg, Dec. 1, 1985; children: David, Laura, Rachel, Rebecca. AB, Columbia Coll., 1966; MD, NYU, 1970. Diplomate Am. Bd. Dermatology. Pvt. practice specializing in dermatology N.Y.C., 1974—; clin. asst. prof. dermatology Cornell Med. Coll., N.Y.C., 1977—. Capt. USAFR, 1971-76. Fellow Am. Acad. Dermatology, Am. Soc. for Laser Medicine and Surgery; mem. AMA, Am. Telemedicine Assn., Med. Soc. of County of N.Y., N.Y. State Med. Soc., N.Y. State Dermatology Soc., Dermatology Soc. Greater N.Y. Office: 45 E 62d St New York NY 10021

JAY, MICHAEL ELIOT, radiologist; b. Bklyn., Nov. 29, 1949; s. Leon and Ruth (Zucker) J.; m. Susan C. Champagne; children: Melissa, Zachary. BS with honors, SUNY, Stonybrook, 1971; MD, Georgetown U., 1975. Diplomate in diagnostic radiology, vascular and interventional radiology Am. Bd. Radiology. Rotating internship Nassau County Med. Ctr., East Meadow, N.Y., 1975-76, resident in diagnostic radiology, 1976-79; fellow in cardiovascular radiology Brigham Woman's Hosp., Boston, 1979-80, staff radiologist, 1980—; assoc. chief dept. radiology West Roxbury (Mass.) VA Med. Complex, 1980—; instr. radiology Harvard Med. Sch., Boston, 1980-86, asst. clin. prof. radiology, 1986—; lectr. in field. Author: Plain Film in Heart Disease, 1992; mem. editl. bd. Jour. Cardiovascular Medicine, 1985-86, Primary Cardiology, 1986-87, Choices in Cardiology, 1987-94; contbr. articles to profl. jours. Mem. New England Cardiovascular Interventional Radiology Soc., Radiology Soc. N. Am. Jewish. Office: VA Med Ctr VFW Hwy Revere MA 02151

JAY, WALTER MICHAEL, ophthalmologist; b. Evergreen Park, Ill., Dec. 31, 1950; m. M. Susan Jay, June 23, 1973; children: Allison Meredith, Hilary Diana. BS with honors magna cum laude, Loyola U. Chgo., 1972; MD, U. Chgo., 1976. Diplomate Am. Bd. Ophthalmology. Asst. prof. ophthalmology Med. Coll. Ga., Augusta, 1980-84, assoc. prof., 1984-85; assoc. prof. U. Ark. Med. Sci., Little rock, 1985-88, prof., 1988-89; prof. and chmn. dept. ophthalmology Loyola U. Chgo., Maywood, Ill., 1989—. Editl. bd. Survey of Ophthalmology, 1990—. Dir. Ill. soc. for Prevention of Blindness, Chgo., 1995—. Fellow Am. Acad. Ophthalmology, Chgo. Ophthalmology Soc. (sec.-treas. 1995—). Office: Loyola Univ Med Ctr Dept Ophthalmology 2160 S First Ave Maywood IL 60153-3304

JAYAKRISHNAN, CHEMMALE, cardiologist; b. Madras, India, Mar. 28, 1948; came to U.S., 1972; s. M. and Padma Nair; m. Ganga Menon, June 27, 1977; children: Asha, Nina, Jay. MBBS, Madras Med. Sch., 1970. Chief medicine St. Charles Parish Hosp., Luling, La., 1984—. Past pres. La. chpt. Am. Assn. Physicians from India, New Orleans, 1991-92. Fellow Royal Coll. Physicians and Surgeons of Can., Am. Coll. Cardiology (assoc.); mem. ACP. Office: St Charles Med Clinic 853 Milling Ave Luling LA 70070

JAYNE, CYNTHIA ELIZABETH, psychologist; b. Pensacola, Fla., June 5, 1953; d. Gordon Howland and Joan (Rockwood) J. AB, Vassar Coll., 1974; MA, SUNY, Buffalo, 1978, PhD, 1983. Lic. psychologist, Pa. Instr. dept. psychiatry Temple U. Sch. Medicine, Phila., 1982-84, asst. prof., 1984-85, asst. dir. outpatient services, asst. dir. residency tng., 1982-85, clin. asst. prof., 1985—; pvt. practice psychology Phila., 1985—; adj. prof. Chestnut Hill Coll., 1994—. Contbr. articles to profl. jours. Soc. for Sci. Study Sex scholar, 1981; Sigma Xi grantee, 1981, Kinsey Inst. Dissertation award, 1983. Mem. APA, Ea. Psychol. Assn., Soc. for Sci. Study Sex (bd. dirs. 1984-86).

JEANES, LINCOLN DOUGLAS, JR., neurosurgeon; b. Shreveport, Feb. 13, 1931; s. Lincoln Douglas Jeanes and Hazel Graves Goins; m. Nina Crisman Vann; children: Lincoln Douglas, Lisa Vann. BA with highest honors, U. Tex., 1952; MD, Harvard Med. Sch., 1960. Diplomate Am. Bd. Neurol. Surgery. Intern surg. Balt. City Hosp., 1959-60; resident neurosurgery Johns Hopkins Hosp., Balt., 1960-66; pvt. practice neurosurgery Austin, Tex., 1966-67, Corpus Christi, Tex., 1967-71, Minot, N.D., 1971-73, San Diego, 1973-78; emergency medicine physician Ft. Stewart Winn Army Hosp., Hinesville, Ga., 1990; physician clinic medicine Primary Care Clinic, Naval Hosp., Jacksonville, Fla., 1990-94. Lt. (j.g.) USN, 1952-55, Korea. Mem. Navy League, Am. Legion, Phi Beta Kappa. Libertarian. Methodist. Home: PO Box 50497 Jacksonville Beach FL 32240

JEAN-PIERRE, PAUL JACQUES, surgeon; b. Gonaives, Haiti, July 25, 1948; came to U.S., 1976; Diplomate in gen. surgery and surg. critical care Am. Bd. Surgery. BA, Petit Seminaire, Port-au-Prince, Haiti, 1968; MD, U. State Haiti, Port-au-Prince, 197; 1974. Diplomate Am. Bd. Surgery. Resident in ob-gyn. U. Hosp. Haiti, Port-au-Prince, 1974-76; intern in surgery Sydenham Hosp., N.Y.C., 1977-78; resident in gen. surgery Franklin Square Hosp., Balt., 1978-83; fellow in surg. critical care Westchester County Med. Ctr., Valhalla, N.Y., 1983-84; pvt. practice, Hollis, N.Y., 1985—; surg. attending emergency room Woodhull Hosp., Bklyn., 1985-86, Brookdale Hosp., Bklyn., 1986-87; surg. house officer St. John's Queens Hosp., Elmhurst, N.Y., 1987-90, dir. surg. ICU, 1990—. Fellow ACS; mem. Soc. Critical Care Medicine, Med. Soc. County Queens. Roman Catholic. Home and Office: 196-02 Hillside Ave Hollis NY 11423

JEANTEUR, PHILIPPE ANDRÉ, molecular biologist; b. Sablé, France, Mar. 4, 1940; s. André and Madeleine (Larcelet) J.; children: Servane, Pierre-Arthur, Matthieu. MD, U. Paris, 1963, PhD, 1969. Rsch. fellow Calif. Inst. Tech., Pasadena, 1966-88; prof. U. Montpellier, France, 1973—; dir. CNRS Genetique Moleculaire, Montpellier, 1974—; dept. head Centre Val d'Aurelle Paul Lamarque, Montpellier, 1977—. Contbr. numerous articles to profl. jours. Head dept. biology and health French Ministry for Rsch. and Tech., 1985-89. Recipient Rosen prize of Oncology, 1987, Prize of Oncology, French Acad. Medicine, 1987, Grand prix Fegefluc, 1992. Mem. European Molecular Biology Orgn. Home: 16 Chemin du Rapatel, 34980 Montferrier France Office: Institut De Genetique Moleculaire CNRS, BP5051 1919 Route De Mende, F-34033 Montpellier Cedex 1, France

JECK, CHARLES N., osteopath; b. Phila., June 3, 1959; s. Saul and Sheila Jeck; m. Sandra Ruth Jeck; children: Evan, Nicole. BS, Temple U., 1981; DO, Phila. Coll. Osteo. Medicine, 1985. Family physician Franciscan Family Care, P.C., Trenton, N.J., 1991—, Whitehorse Med. Assoc.; staff St. Francis Hosp., Trenton; dir. Meadeville N.H., 1995—. Mem. Mercer County Osteo. Med. Soc. (pres. 1985), Lambda Omicron Gamma. Home: 1 Chickory Pl Newtown PA 18940-1253

JEFFER, EDWARD KENNETH, medical administrator; b. Bklyn., Mar. 3, 1940; s. Norman Lee and Rosalind (Tiger) J.; m. Marsha Goldberg, June 19, 1960 (div. 1976); m. Ulrike Erika Seufert, Sept. 23, 1976. BA, UCLA, 1962; MD, U. So. Calif., 1966. Diplomate Am. Bd. Psychiatry and Neurology. Intern L.A. County Gen. Hosp., 1966-67; resident in gen. surgery Wadsworth VA Hosp., L.A., 1967-68; gen. practice Avalon Med. Clinic, L.A., 1968-69; resident psychiatry NPI-UCLA, 1969-70, Letterman Army Med. Ctr., 1970-72; div. psychiatrist, dir. mental hygiene U.S. Army, Wuerzburg, Fed. Republic Germany, 1972-74; coordinator mental hygiene svcs., chief Office Drug & Alcohl U.S. Army Med. Command, Heidelberg, Fed. Republic Germany, 1974-76; chief dept. psychiatry Landstuhl (Fed. Republic Germany) Regional Med. Ctr., 1976-78; div. surgeon, alcohol and drug control officer 1st Armored Div., Ansbach, 1978-81; comdr., 209th gen. dispensary dir. Health Svcs., Hanau (Fed. Republic Germany) Mil. Command, 1981-83; dep. comdr. clin. svcs. Blanchfield Army Community Hosp., Ft. Campbell, Ky., 1983-85; comdr. U.S. Med. Dept. Activity, Ft. Eustis, Va., 1985-88; chief quality assurance div. Office of Surgeon Gen., Falls Church, Va., 1988-91; chief surgeon U.S. Army Nat. Guard, Arlington, Va., 1991—; instr. UCLA Sch. Medicine, 1969-70, U. Calif. Sch. Medicine, Berkeley, 1970-72, Acad. Health Scis., Ft. Sam Houston, Tex., 1983-85, U. Okla. Sch. Pub. Health, Norman, 1984-85; adj. prof. behavioral sci. European div. Ball State U., 1976-78; assoc. clin. prof. Meharry Med. Sch., Nashville; assoc. clin. prof. psychiatry Uniformed U. Health Scis., 1988—; asst. med. dir. L.A. Free Clinic, 1968-69. Contbr. articles to profl. pubs. Col. U.S. Army, 1970-96. Fellow Am. Assn. Social Psychiatry, Am. Psychiat. Assn.; mem. No. Calif. Psychiat. Assn., Assn. U.S. Army, World Psychiat. Assn. (mil. sect.), Assn. Mil. Surgeons, World Conf. Mental Health, Am. Acad. Med. Dirs., Soc. Mil. Surgeons, PHi Beta Kappa, Alpha Omega Alpha.

JEFFERIES, WILLIAM MCKENDREE, internist, educator; b. Richmond, Va., Oct. 1, 1915; s. Richard Henry and Mary Adeline (Harris) J.; m. Jeanne Telfair Mercer, Dec. 28, 1946 (dec. Dec., 1991); children: Richard Mercer, Scott McKendree, Colin Tucker, Leslie McLaurin. BA summa cum laude, Hampden Sydney Coll., 1935; MD, U. Va., 1940. Diplomate Am. Bd. Internal Medicine. Instr. in Math., Physics, Chemistry McGuires Univ. Sch., Richmond, Va., 1936; resident Mass. Gen. Hosp., Boston, 1940-42; flight surgeon San Antonio Aviation Cadet Ctr., 1942; post surgeon India China Div. Air Transport Command, 1943-45, divsn. med. inspector, 1945; rsch. fellow Am. Cancer Soc. Com. on Growth NRC Harvard Med. Sch., Boston, 1946-49; from instr. to asst. prof. medicine Case Western Reserve Med. Sch., Cleve., 1949-92; clin. prof. medicine U. Va. Sch. of Medicine, Charlottesville, 1993—; mem. internship com. Univ. Hosps., Cleve., 1955-65; bd. dirs. Brush Found., 1966-67; mem. com. for human investigation Luth. Med. Ctr., Cleve., 1977-92; chmn. diabetes adv. com. Euclid Gen. Hosp., Cleve., 1979-82. Author: (med. books) Safe Uses of Cortisone, 1981, Safe Uses of Cortisol, 1996; contbr. articles to profl. jours., chpts. to books. Com. mem. Boy Scouts Am., Shaker Heights, Ohio, 1957-68; past chmn. coun. of deacons, bd. of ministry and fellowship Plymouth Ch. of Shaker Heights. Lt. col. med. corps U.S. Army (attached to air force) India Burma Theatre. Fellow Am. Coll. Physicians; mem. AAAS, SAR, AMA, N.Y. Acad. Scis., Abermarle County Med. Soc., Am. Thyroid Assn (Van Meter award 1949), Clin. Immunology Soc., Endocrine Soc., Am. Fertility Soc., Am. Fedn. for Clin. Rsch., Ctrl. Soc. for Clin. Rsch., Friends of Nat. Libr. of Medicine, Am. Legion, Cheshire Cheese Club, Raven Soc., Phi Beta Kappa, Omicron Delta Kappa, Alpha Omega Alpha, Kappa Alpha, Phi Beta Pi.

JEFFORDS, DEXTER LEE, urologist; b. Johnson City, Tenn., June 23, 1944; s. Dexter M. and Elizabeth M. (Mackey) J.; m. Deborah Ann Dyches, June 15, 1991; children: Eric D., Sarah Mackey, Sumner Alexandra. AB, Duke U., 1966, MD, 1970. Diplomate Am. Bd. Urology. Intern, resident in gen. surgery Barnes Hosp.-Washington U. St. Louis, 1970-72; resident in urology U. Minn. Health Scis. Ctr., Mpls., 1974-78; sr. ptnr. North Suburban Urologic Surgeons, Mpls., 1978-87, Island Urology, Hilton Head Island, S.C., 1987—. With USNR, 1972-74. Episcopalian. Home: 89 Harbour Passage Hilton Head Island SC 29926 Office: Hilton Head Clin Inc Urology 35 Bill Fries Dr Ste I Hilton Head Island SC 29926

JEFFREY, CHARLES CAHILL, physician; b. LaJunta, Colo., Mar. 3, 1944; s. George Bernard and Mildred (Measurac) J. BA, So. Conn. State U., 1967; MPH, Yale U., 1969; MD, Case Western Res. U., 1975. Diplomate Am. Bd. Anesthesiology. Instr. health and PE, asst. gymnastics coach So. Conn. State U., New Haven, 1970-71; grad. asst. med. edn. Med. Sch. Case Western Res. U., Cleve., 1972-73; intern medicine Mt. Sinai Hosp., Cleve., 1975-76; resident anesthesia Mass. Gen. Hosp., Boston, 1976-79, asst. anesthetist, 1979-80, 81-93, assoc. anesthetist, 1993—; dir. intensive care Mt. Auburn Hosp., Boston, 1980-81; fellow Harvard U. Med. Sch., 1976-79, instr. anesthesia, 1979—. Trainer U.S. team Gymnastcis-World Championships, Bulgaria, 1974. Named Disting. Alumnus So. Conn. State U., 1991. Mem. Am. Soc. Anesthesiologists, Mass. Soc. Anesthesiologists, Harvard Mus. Assn.

JEFFREY-SMITH, LILLI ANN, biofeedback specialist, educator, administrator; b. Bedford, Ind., 1944; d. Charles Constantine and Adelai (Malon) Jeffrey-Smith. Grad. Ind. Bus. Coll., 1963; B.S., Ind. U., 1973; grad. Psychosomatic Medicine Clinic, Berkeley, Calif. (accredited by Albert Einstein Coll. Medicine); PhD in Behavioral Sci., Kennedy-Western U., 1988. Cert. biofeedback specialist. Project assoc., stress mgmt. clinician City of Indpls., 1973-79; cons. Airport Med. Clinic, Indpls., 1981; outreach coord. Abbot-Northwestern Hosp., Mpls., 1981; dir. biofeedback dept. Sister Kenney Inst., Mpls., 1979-81, Noran Neurol. Clinic, Mpls., 1981-83; instr., dir. Biofeedback Tng. and Treatment Ctr., Edina, Minn., 1979—; pres. Biofeedback Rsch. and Devel. Co. Ltd., Edina, 1983—; cons. to biofeedback depts. St. Joseph Hosp., Mankato, Minn., 1984—, Lakeview Clinic, Waconia, Minn., 1983, Psychiat. Clinic of Mankato, 1983—, Fairview Ridges Hosp., Burnsville, Minn., 1987—. Author, narrator health and wellness tape series. Mem. Republican Presdl. Task Force, 1984—, NSC, 1985; co-chmn. Mayor's Handicapped Task Force, Indpls., 1975; founder, pres. Miss Wheel Chair of Ind., Inc. Named Hon. Lt. Gov., State of Ind., 1978; given Key to the City of Indpls., 1973, Flag of the City of Indpls., 1975. Mem. Am. Inst. Stress, N.Y. Acad. Sci., NAFE, AAAS, AAUW, Edina C. of C., Minn. Women's Network, Biofeedback Soc. Am., Biofeedback Soc. Minn., Am. Assn. Control Tension, Am. Assn. Behaviorial Therapists, Am. Assn. Biofeedback Clinicians, Nat. Assn. Women Bus. Owners, Soc. Open Focus and Tng. Rsch., Am. Assoc. of U. Woman, Nat. Assoc. of Female Execs., Assn. Trainers in Clin. Hypnosis, Internat. Stress and Tension Control Assn., Minn. Assn. Rehab. Providers, Nat. Assn. Exec. Women, Internat. Platform Assn. Avocations: music, stamp collecting, shooting, poetry. Office: Biofeedback Tng & Treatment Ctr 7300 France Ave S Ste 200 Minneapolis MN 55435-4542

JEFFRIES, RICHARD HALEY, physician, broadcasting company executive; b. Harrisburg, Pa., June 7, 1941; s. Richard Lawrence and Jeanette Ruth (Haley) J.; m. Alana Evangeline Straley, Aug. 6, 1966; 1 child, Richard Straley. BS, Pa. State U., 1963; DO, Kirksville Coll. Osteo. Medici, 1968. Diplomate Am. Coll. Osteo. Internists. Intern Cmty. Gen. Osteo. Hosp., Harrisburg, 1968-69, resident in internal medicine, 1969-72, attending staff dept. internal medicine, 1972—, dir. coronary and intensive care units, 1983-86, chmn. dept. medicine, 1986—, v.p. med. staff, 1977-79, pres., chief of staff, 1979-82; pvt. practice Harrisburg, 1972—; founder, pres. Quaker State Broadcasting, Inc., WTPA-FM, Mechanicsburg, Pa., 1982—; founder, sec. Midstate Comm., Inc., 1990—; sr. clin. instr. Phila. Coll. Osteo. Medicine, 1977-81, clin. asst. prof., 1981—; clin. asst. prof. Hahnemann Med. Coll., Phila., 1977—, N.Y. Coll. Osteo. Medicine, N.Y.C., 1981-84; adj. asst. prof. U. Osteo. Medicine and Health Scis., Des Moines, 1990—; regional clin. faculty Kirksville (Mo.) Coll. Osteo. Medicine, 1993; trustee Cmty. Gen. Osteo. Hosp., Harrisburg, 1979-84, mem. staff exec. com., 1974-84, 86—, chmn. staff exec. com., 1979-82; sr. flight surgeon FAA, 1975—; med. dir. Ecumenical Home of Harrisburg, Beverly Preferred Choice Hospice Program, Harrisburg, 1995—. Contbr. articles to profl. jours. Chmn. fundraising dr. Dauphin County Retarded Citizens Assn., 1984; founding mem., bd. dirs., past pres. Dauphin Residences, Inc., 1974-81; mem. Allied Arts Fund, Physicians Divsn., 1992, 93, 94. Mem. Am. Osteo. Assn., Pa. Osteo Med. Assn., Am. Coll. Osteo. Internists, Am. Soc. Critical Care Medicine, Pa. Soc. Critical Care Medicine (founding mem.), Am. Heart Assn. (bd. dirs. South Ctrl. Pa. chpt. 1976-79), Daguerreian Soc., Alpha Chi Sigma. Republican. Methodist. Home: 4600 Custer Dr Harrisburg PA 17110-3208 Office: Bronstein-Jeffries PA 4830 Londonderry Rd Harrisburg PA 17109-5240

JEFFRIES, RICHARD RAY, osteopathic physician; b. Denver, Jan. 20, 1947; s. Fred Owen and Dorothy Marie (Fabling) J.; m. Carol Ann Burkhardt, June 20, 1970; children: Cherie Lynn, Marcia Marie. BA/BS, Coe Coll., 1969; Secondary Teaching Cert., U. Colo., 1972; DO, Coll. Osteo. Medicine, Des Moines, 1979. Diplomate Am. Bd. Family Physicians, Am. Bd. Osteo. Family Physicians. Dir. clin. svcs. USN 29 Palms (Calif.) Hosp., 1982-84; dir. residency tng. USN Naval Hosp., Camp Pendleton, Calif., 1985-91; regimental surgeon 11th Marines USMC Persian Gulf War, 1990-91; divsn. surgeon 1st Marine Divsn. USMC Persian Gulf War, Camp Pendleton, 1991-93; MARFOR/1 MEF surgeon Operation Restore Hope, Somalia, 1992-93; head dept. family practice, residency program dir. Naval Hosp., Camp Pendleton, 1993—. Contbr. articles to profl. jours. Decorated with Bronze Star, 1992. Fellow Am. Assn. Family Practitioners; mem. Am. Osteo. Assn. (chmn. coun. on continuing med. edn. 1993-95, house del. 1985—), Assn. Mil. Osteo. Physicians and Surgeons (pres. 1990, 91, bd. dirs. 1991—). 1st Ch. of Religious Sci. Home: 5938 Rio Valle Dr Bonsall CA 92003 Office: Naval Hosp Family Practice Camp Pendleton CA 92055

JEKEL, JAMES FRANKLIN, physician, public health educator; b. St. Louis, Oct. 14, 1934; s. Oscar Henry and Frances Sarah (Newell) J.; m. Janice Marilyn Clark, Aug. 30, 1958; children: Clifford R., Mark R., Linda F., Timothy W. AB, Wesleyan U., 1956; MD, Washington U., St. Louis, 1960; MPH, Yale U., 1965. House officer Hartford (Conn.) Hosp., 1960-62; epidemiologist Ctrs. for Disease Control, Atlanta, 1962-67; asst. prof. pub. health Yale U. Sch. Medicine, New Haven, 1967-71, assoc. prof., 1971-80, prof., 1980—, C.E.A. Winslow prof. pub. health, 1982—, dir. residency program in gen. preventive medicine, 1975-93; asst. dir. Robert Wood Johnson Clin. Scholar Program Robert Wood Johnson Clin. Scholar Program, New Haven, 1976-95. Pres. Bd. Health Quinnipiack Valley Health Dist., Hamden, Conn., 1986-91. Lt. comdr. USPHS, 1962-67. Fulbright Faculty fellow The Bahamas, 1985-86; recipient various rsch. grants, 1968—. Fellow Am. Coll. Preventive Medicine, Am. Sci. Affiliation; mem. Am. Pub. Health Assn., Christian Med./Dental Soc. Presbyterian. Office: Yale U Sch Med Box 208034 60 College St New Haven CT 06520-8034

JEKŐ, ZSUZSA BENTZIK, chemist; b. Zalaegerszeg, Zala, Hungary, June 5, 1961; d. Ferenc and Éva (Arató) Bentzik; m. József Jekő, Aug. 20, 1983; children: Tamás, Anita. BS, U. Szeged, Hungary, 1984. Rsch. chemist Alkaloida Chem. Co., Tiszavasvári, Hungary, 1984-89, devel. chemist, 1989-95, head pharm. tech. devel., 1995—. Mem. Hungarian Pharm. Com. Home: Élmunkás 4 B, H-4440 Tiszavasvári Hungary Office: Alkaloida Chem Co Ltd, Kabay J 29, H-4440 Tiszavasvári Hungary

JELINEK, JOSEF EMIL, dermatologist; b. Prague, Czechoslovakia, Feb. 12, 1928; came to U.S., 1958, naturalized, 1964; s. Frank and Olga (Frankl) J.; m. Vera Adrienne Schnitzer, June 19, 1960; children—David Frank, Paul William. M.B., B.S., U. London, 1951; postgrad., U. London Postgrad. Sch., 1956, NYU, 1963—. Diplomate Am. Bd. Dermatology. Intern, house surgeon in orthopedics St. Mary's Hosp., London, 1951-52; house physician in internal medicine Harold Wood Hosp., Essex, Eng., 1952, Princess Beatrice Hosp., London, 1955; registrar in internal medicine Royal Victoria Hosp., Bournemouth, Eng., 1955-57, Dulwich Hosp., London, 1957-58; precepteeship in dermatology with Norman B. Kanof, N.Y.C., 1961-62; chief resident dermatology Bellevue Hosp., N.Y.C., 1962-63; chief resident Univ. Hosp., N.Y.C., 1963; cons. VA Hosp., N.Y.C., 1965—; asst. attending physician Bellevue Hosp., N.Y.C., 1965—; attending physician Univ. Hosp., N.Y.C., 1976—; chief skin and cancer unit Univ. Hosp., 1973; clin. prof. dermatology N.Y. U. Sch. Medicine, 1976—; practice medicine specializing in dermatology, 1963—; cons. AMA Council on Drugs and the Dept. of Drugs, 1972. Author: The Skin in Diabetes, 1985; contbr. articles to profl. jours, also chpts. to textbooks. Served to flight lt. RAF, 1952-54. Fellow ACP, Am. Acad. Dermatology; mem. Atlantic Dermatologic Conf. (past chmn.), Dermatologic Soc. Greater N.Y. (past pres.), N.Y. Acad. Medicine (past chmn.), Manhattan Dermatol. Soc. (past pres.), Am. Folk Art Soc. (pres. 1986-91). Office: 15 W 12th St New York NY 10011-8546

JELKS, MARY LARSON, retired pediatrician; b. Galva, Ill., 1929. MD, U. Nebr., 1955. Diplomate Am. Bd. Pediats., Am. Bd. Allergy and Immunology. Intern Johns Hopkins Hosp., Balt., 1955-56, resident, 1956-57, 58-60; resident Grace-New Haven Hosp., 1957; fellow U. Fla. Tchg. Hosp., 1960-61; clin. asst. prof. U. South Fla.; ret. Fellow Am. Acad. Allery and Immunology, Am. Acad. Pediats.; mem. AMA. Home: 1930 Clematis St Sarasota FL 34239-3813

JELLEY, SCOTT ALLEN, microbiologist; b. Tarrytown, N.Y., July 22, 1960; s. Alfred Paul and Nadine Elaine (Scott) J. BS in Biology, Bucknell U., 1982; MS in Microbiology, Va. Poly. Inst., 1985. Grad. teaching asst. Va. Poly. Inst., Blacksburg, 1983-85, lab. specialist, 1985; scientist Pfizer Cen. Rsch., Groton, Conn., 1986-88; microbiologist Findley Rsch., Inc., Fall River, Mass., 1988-90; microbiologist sterilization scis. group Johnson & Johnson Profl., Inc., Raynham, Mass., 1990—. Contbr. articles to Applied and Environmental Microbiology. Mem. Assn. for Advancement Med. Instrumentation (sterilization resuable med. devices com.), Am. Soc. for Microbiology, Soc. for Indsl. Microbiology (N.E. br.), Johnson & Johnson Corp. Office Sci. and Tech. (scientific liaison focused giving program). Office: Johnson & Johnson Profl Inc 325 Paramount Dr Raynham MA 02767-0350

JELLIFFE, ROGER WOODHAM, cardiologist, clinical pharmacologist; b. Cleve., Feb. 18, 1929; s. Russell Wesley and Rowena (Woodham) J.; m. Joyce Miller, June 12, 1954; children: Susan, Amy, Elizabeth, Peter. BA, Harvard U., 1950; MD, Columbia U., 1954. Diplomate Am. Bd. Internal Medicine, Am. Bd. Cardiovascular Disease. Intern Univ. Hosps., Cleve., 1954-56; also jr. asst. resident in medicine; Nat. Found. Infantile Paralysis exptl. medicine fellow Case Western Res. U., Cleve., 1956-58; staff physician in medicine VA Hosp., Cleve., 1958-60; resident in medicine VA Hosp., 1960-61; instr. medicine U. So. Calif. Sch. Medicine, L.A., 1961-63; asst. prof. U. So. Calif. Sch. Medicine, 1963-67, assoc. prof., 1967-76, prof. medicine, 1976—; developer Lab. Applied Pharmacokinetics, 1973—, The USC*PACK Computer Programs, 1973—; cons. Dynamic Scis., Inc., Van Nuys, Calif., 1976-93, Simes S.P.A., Milan, 1979—, IVAC Corp., San Diego, 1983-88, Bionica, Sydney, Australia, 1987-94. Author: Fundamentals of Electrocardiography, 1990; cons. editor Am. Jour. Medicine, 1972-78, Current Prescribing, 1974-79, Am. Jour. Physiology, 1984-91, Computers in Biology amd Medicine, 1994—, Therapeutic Drug Monitoring, 1995—; contbr. articles to profl. jours.; patentee in field. Advanced Rsch. fellow L.A. County Heart Assn., 1961-64. Fellow ACP, Am. Coll. Med. Informatics, Am. Coll. Clin. Pharmacology, Am. Heart Assn. Coun. on Clin. Cardiology; mem. Am. Soc. Clin. Pharmacology and Therapeutics, Am. Fedn. Clin. Rsch., Am. Med. Informatics Assn. Office: U So Calif Sch Medicine CSC 134-B 2250 Alcazar St Los Angeles CA 90033

JELLINEK, MICHAEL STEVEN, psychiatrist, pediatrician; b. N.Y.C., Sept. 30, 1948; s. Kurt and Kate (Jacoby) J.; m. Barbara A. Jellinek, June 14, 1970; children: David M., Abraham R., Isaiah T., Hanna R. BA, Columbia Coll., 1970; MD, Albert Einstein Coll. Medicine, 1973. Diplomate Nat. Bd. Med. Examiners, Am. Bd. Pediatrics; diplomate in psychiatry and child psychiatry Am. Bd. Psychiatry and Neurology. Instr. pediatrics Montefiore Hosp. & Med. Ctr., N.Y.C., 1976-79; chief child psychiat. svcs. Mass. Gen. Hosp., Boston, 1979—, asst. in pediat., 1979-81, asst. pediatrician, 1981-83, dir. outpatient psychiatry, 1984-93, assoc. pediatrician, 1984-86, assoc. psychiatrist, 1984-86, pediatrician. 1986—, psychiatrist, 1986—, asst. gen. dir. ambulatory svcs., 1992—, sr. v.p. ambulatory svcs., 1994—, sr. v.p. adminstrn., 1995—; assoc. prof. psychiatry (pediatrics) Harvard U., Boston, 1987—; asst. instr. Columbia U., N.Y.C, 1970; cons. Shriner Burns Inst., Boston, 1979—. Dir. Camp Rainbow, Croton-on-Hudson, 1977-81. Fellow Am. Acad. Pediat., Am. Acad. Child Psychiatry (treas. 1991-93, Simon Wile award 1993); mem. Soc. Prof. Child Psychiatry, New Eng. Coun. Child Psychiatry, Inst. Soc. Ethics and Life Scis. Democrat. Jewish. Home: 132 Pleasant St Newton MA 02159-1828 Office: Mass Gen Hosp Fruit St WACC 725 Boston MA 02114

JELSEMA, RUSSEL DALE, physician, educator; b. Zeeland, Mich., Apr. 11, 1960; s. Alden Ross and Ruth Elaine (Gras) J.; m. Leann Sue Oosterink, Aug. 14, 1981; children: Rebecca, Sarah, Timothy. BS, Calvin Coll., 1982; MD, Wayne State U., 1986. Diplomate Am. Bd. Obstetrics and Gynecology, Nat. Bd. Med. Examiners. Resident ob-gyn. Butterworth Hosp., Grand Rapids, Mich., 1986-90; fellow maternal-fetal Hutzel Hosp. Wayne State U., Detroit, 1990-92; asst. prof. Mich. State Dept. Ob-Gyn., Grand Rapids, 1992—; assoc. dir. West Mich. Perinatal, Grand Rapids, 1992—. Editl. cons. Obstetrics-Gynecoloy, 1994—; contbr. articles to profl. jours., chpts. to books. Fellow Am. Coll. Surgeons (assoc.), Am. Bd. Obstetrics and Gynecology; mem. AMA, Assn. Profs. Ob-Gyn., Soc. Perinatal Obstetricians (assoc.). Office: West Mich Perinatal 221 Michigan Ste 300 Grand Rapids MI 49503

JEMISON, MELISSA WOODARD, medical administrator; b. Raleigh, N.C., June 12, 1950; d. Moses Washington and Evelyn A. (Lewis) Woodard. BS in History, East Carolina U., 1972. Examiner N.C. Disability Determination Services, Raleigh, 1972-74, examiner II, 1974-75, supr. I, 1975-80, supr. II, 1980-86, med. adminstr., 1986—. bd. dirs. Raleigh Symphony Orchestra. Mem. Nat. Assn. Disability Examiners (v.p. 1978-79, bd. dirs. 1979-80, pres. 1980-81), Nat. Assn. Female Execs., Phi Alpha Theta (local pres. 1972), Gamma Theta Upsilon, Phi Kappa Phi. Office: Disability Determination Services Dept Human Resources PO Box 243 Raleigh NC 27602-0243

JENDEN, DONALD JAMES, pharmacologist, educator; b. Horsham, Sussex, Eng., Sept. 1, 1926; came to U.S., 1950, naturalized, 1958; s. William Herbert and Kathleen Mary (Harris) J.; m. Jean Ickeringill, Nov. 18, 1950; children: Patricia Mary, Peter Donald, Beverly Jean. BSc in Physiology with 1st class honours, Kings Coll. London, 1947; MB, BS with honours, U. London, 1950; PhD in Pharm. Chemistry (hon.), U. Uppsala, Sweden, 1980. Demonstrator pharmacology U. London, 1948-49; lectr. pharmacology U. Calif.-San Francisco, 1950-51, asst. prof. pharmacology, 1952-53; mem. faculty UCLA, 1953, assoc. prof., 1956-60, prof. pharmacology, 1960—, prof. pharmacology and biomath., 1967—, chmn. dept. pharmacology, 1968-89; Wellcome vis. prof. U. Ala., Birmingham, 1984; mem. brain research inst. UCLA, 1961—. Contbr. articles in field. Served to lt. comdr. M.C., USNR, 1954-58. USPHS Postdoctoral fellow, 1951-53, NSF Sr. Postdoctoral fellow; hon. research assoc. Univ. Coll., London, 1961-62; Fulbright Short-Term Sr. Scholar award, Australia, 1983; recipient Univ. Gold medal U. London, 1950. Fellow Am. Coll. Neuropsychopharmacology, West Coast Coll. Biol. Psychology (charter); mem. AAAS, Am. Soc. Pharmacology and Exptl. Therapeutics, Am. Physiol. Soc., Physiol. Soc. (London), Soc. Neurosci., Am. Chem. Soc., Western Pharmacology Soc. (pres. 1970), Assn. for Med. Sch. Pharmacology, Am. Soc. Neurochemistry, Internat. Union Pharmacology. Home: 3814 Castlerock Rd Malibu CA 90265-5625 Office: UCLA Sch Medicine Dept Pharmacology Ctr Health Scis Los Angeles CA 90009-5173

JENKINS, ADELBERT HOWARD, psychology educator; b. St. Louis, Dec. 10, 1934; s. Herbert Crawford and Helen Alma (Howard) J.; m. Betty Jo Lanier, July 5, 1969; 1 child, Christopher Lanier. BA, Antioch Coll., Yellow Springs, Ohio, 1957; MA, U. Mich., 1958, PhD, 1963. Lic. psychologist, N.Y. USPHS postdoctoral fellow Albert Einstein Coll. Medicine, Bronx, N.Y., 1962-64, from asst. instr. to instr., 1964-67; asst. prof. clin. psychology NYU Med. Ctr., N.Y.C., 1967-71; assoc. prof. psychology Faculty Arts and Sci. NYU, 1971—; tng. cons. N.Y. VA Hosp., N.Y.C., 1974—, Bronx VA Hosp., 1975—; M.L. King-Rosa Parks vis. prof. dept. psychology U. Mich., 1987. Author: Psychology and African Americans, 1995. Mem. bd. deacons Riverside Ch., N.Y.C., 1989-90, mem. edn. commn., 1990-92. Ford Found. grantee, 1976, 80; recipient M.L. King Jr. award N.Y. Soc. Clin. Psychologists, 1984. Fellow APA, Soc. for Personality Assessment; mem. Assn. Black Psychologists (chair N.Y.C. chpt. 1970, Scholar of Yr. 1983), N.Y. State Psychol. Assn., Ea. Psychol. Assn., Nat. Register Health Svc. Providers Psychology. Office: NYU 715 Broadway New York NY 10003-6806

JENKINS, DOUGLAS WILLIAM, physician; b. Flint, Mich., Jan. 19, 1944; s. Douglas William Sr. and Bernice Emma (White) J.; m. Linda Kay Woodard, July 11, 1964; children: Douglas Woodard, Patrick Laird. MD, U. Mich., 1967. Diplomate Am. Bd. Internal Medicine, Am. Bd. Quaility Assurance and Utilization Rev. Physicians. Intern Wilford Hall Med. Ctr., San Antonio, Tex., 1967-68, resident in medicine, 1968-71; fellow in pulmonary disease Scott AFB, Ill., 1971-73; pvt. practice Skinner Clin., San Antonio, Tex., 1983—; cons. City Pub. Svc., San Antonio, 1987—; regional med. dir. Tex. Med. Found., San Antonio, 1987-94; dir. utilization mgmt. Bapt. Meml. Healthcare Sys., San Antonio, 1994—. Contbr. articles to profl. jours. Served to col. USAF, 1966-91. Fellow ACP, Am. Coll. Chest Physicians; mem. Bexar County Med. Assn., Tex. med. Assn. Office: Skinner Clin 124 Dallas St San Antonio TX 78205

JENKINS, EDMUND CHARLES, cytogeneticist and clinical researcher, educator; b. Wilkes-Barre, Pa., Sept. 15, 1942; s. Edmund and Mary A. J.; m. Valerie Ann Burhorst, 1983; children: E. Charles Jr., William Henry. BS, King's Coll., Pa., 1964; PhD, Fordham U., 1968. Cert. of Qualification in clin. cytogenetics The City of N.Y. Dept. Health; cert. of qualification in cytogenetics N.Y. State Dept. Health; cert. registry in Cytogenetics State of N.J. Dept. Law and Pub. Safety Divsn. Consumer Affairs, State Bd. Med. Examiners; diplomate Am. Bd. Med. Genetics. NIH trainee developmental cytology Fordham U., 1964-68; rsch. scientist cytogenetics N.Y. State Inst. Basic Rsch. in Developmental Disabilities, S.I., N.Y., 1968—, sr. rsch. scientist, 1969-73, assoc. rsch. scientist, 1973-82, rsch. scientist VI, 1982-90, program coord., 1978—, dir. Lab. of Clin. Cytogenetics, 1979—, chief divsn. cytogenetics, 1982-85; chmn. dept. cytogenetics, 1985-90, chief dept. genetics, 1990-92, chief dept. cytogenetics, 1992—, rsch. scientist VIII, 1990—; adj. prof. biol. rsch. King's Coll., Wilkes-Barre, Pa., 1971-81; dir. cytogenetics, cons. North Shore U. Hosp., 1975-78, 84, 85, 86; lab. dir. Diagenetic Labs., Inc., 1987-89; vis. lectr. cytogenetics various colls., univs., med. ctrs., 1969—; adj. lectr. cytogenetics Manhattanville Coll., Purchase, N.Y., 1974—; adj. assoc. prof. dept. biology Grad. Sch. Arts and Scis., Fordham U., Bronx, 1983—; prof. dept. anatomy and cell biology SUNY Health Sci. Ctr., Bklyn., 1987—; mem. Genetics Task Force of N.Y. State, 1976—, bd. dirs., 1979-81, 91-96; bd. dirs. Rsch. Found. Mental Hygiene, 1980-90, 92—, v.p., 1984-90, 94—; chmn. cytogenetics adv. com. Prenatal Diagnostic Lab. of N.Y.C., mem. policy and rsch. adv. com., 1981—; chmn. Instl. Rev. Bd., S.I. Developmental Ctr., 1982—, Inst. Basic Rsch., 1994—; co-chmn. 4th Internat. Workshop on Fragile X and X-linked Mental Retardation, 1989, co-editor of proceedings, 1990; chmn. various workshops, meetings; editor various proceedings. Recipient Citizenship award VFW, 1957, Regina award for sci., 1964, Humanitarian award Assn. for the Help of Retarded Children, 1979. Fellow Am. Coll. Med. Genetics (founder); mem. Genetics Soc. Am., Soc. of Cryobiology, Coun. of Rsch. Scientists (mem. exec. com. 1978—, sec. 1978-82, chpt. rep. 1982-86, v.p. 1986-93, chairperson 1993—), Teratology Soc., Am. Soc. Human Genetics, Environ. Mutagen Soc., AAAS, Sigma Xi. Contbr. more than 150 articles on rsch. in cytogenetics to sci. jours. and books; rsch. on the fragile X and Down syndromes. Home: 11 Starlight Rd Staten Island NY 10301-4436 Office: NY State Inst for Basic Rsch in Devel Disabilities 1050 Forest Hill Rd Staten Island NY 10314-6330

JENKINS, FLOYD ALBERT, biology educator, priest; b. Los Angeles, Aug. 14, 1916; s. Floyd Ernest and Irma Helena (Luer) J. AB, St. Louis U., 1940, MA, 1942, MS, 1943, PhD, 1954; ThM, Santa Clara U., 1949. Ordained priest Roman Cath. Ch., 1948. Instr. bio. Loyola U., Los Angeles, 1943-45, prof. biol., 1953-87, emeritus prof. biol., 1987—. Mem. Soc. Vertebrate Paleontology, Paleontol. Soc., So. Calif. Acad. Sci., Vatican Philatelic Soc., L.A. Philatelic Soc. Republican. Home: 7900 Loyola Blvd Los Angeles CA 90045-8427

JENKINS, HELEN WILLIAMS, administrative dietitian; b. Marion, N.C., Aug. 1, 1921; d. John Andrew and Ethel W. (Bailey) Williams; m. Marshall D. Jenkins, Feb. 17, 1946; children: Barbara Ann, Ronald Lee. BS cum laude, Carson-Newman, Jefferson City, Tenn., 1944; MA, Emory U., 1974. Registered and Lic. dietitian. Mgr. food svc. Roane Anderson Co., Oak Ridge, Tenn., 1944-45; food svc. asst. dir. Emory U., Atlanta, 1945-55, food svc. dir., 1955-84, dir. dietetic internship, 1967-70, asst. prof. nutrition, 1970-90, food svc. liaison, 1984—; historian Nat. Assn. Coll. and Univ. Food Svc., 1990-91; adv. Vocat. Edn. Bd., Ga. 1965-73; publ. editor nat. Assn. Coll. & Univ. Food Svc., Chgo., 1965-68; pres. Ga. Dietetic Assn., Atlanta 1963-64, Southeastern Hosp. Dietitian Assn., Atlanta, 1959-60. Author: Systems Management in Dietetics, rev. 1988; contbr. articles to profl. jours. Mem. Nat. Assn. Coll. and Univ. Food Svc., Am. Dietetic Assn. (com. chmn. 1965-69), Ga. Nutrition Coun. (pres. 1968-69, nominating com. 1993-94), Dieticians in Coll. and Univ. Food Svc. (nominating com. chmn. 1989-90), Ga. Dietetic Assn. (teller 1994-95), Altrusa Internat. (Atlanta) (pres. 1961-62). Republican. Baptist. Home: 2331 N Decatur Rd Decatur GA 30033-5503 Office: Emory Univ PO Box YY Atlanta GA 30322-1001

JENKINS, JAMES SHERWOOD, JR., pharmacologist; b. Franklin, Tenn., July 25, 1941; s. Jim S. and Martha (Austin) J.; m. Emma E. Smithson, Dec. 21, 1962, (div. Sept. 1987); children: Gregory S., Leah E., Gerald B., Cheryl C., Jason J. BS, David Lipscomb U., 1962; Pharmacy degree, U. Tenn., 1965, PD, 1974; Cert. Geriatic Practice, U. Miss., 1987. Diplomate Am. Acad. Pain Mgmt.; lic. pharmacist, pharmacologist. Clin. practice, rsch., 1969—, pvt. rsch. in hypertension therapy and others, 1980—. Mem. editl. adv. bd. Am. Jour. Pain Mgmt.; contbr. articles to profl. jours. Holder over 40 world and U.S. aviation speed records. Fellow Am. Coll. Apothecaries; mem. Nat. Aeronautic Assn. (life), Phi Delta Chi. Office: Clin Pharmacology Cons PO Box 772 Goodlettsville TN 37070-0772

JENKINS, JAMES WILLIAM, osteopath; b. Columbus, Ohio, May 15, 1953; s. William Harvey and Irene Barbara (Kacsor) J.; m. Deborah Susan Dorrance, June 16, 1987. BA in Biology, Calif. State U., Fullerton, 1976; DO, Coll. Osteopathic Med. Pacific, 1984; diploma in emergency medicine, Ohio State U., 1988. Intern Warren (Ohio) Gen. Hosp., 1984-85; resident in emergency medicine Meml. Osteopathic Hosp., York, Pa., 1985-87; rsch. fellow, clin. instr. Coll. Medicine, Ohio State U., Columbus, 1987-88; clin. emergency physician, med. edn. coord. emergency dept. Dr.'s Hosp., Columbus, 1988-89; med. dir. emergency dept. Greenfield (Ohio) Area Med. Ctr., 1989-93, clin. emergency/trauma physician, 1991-93; med. dir. Chillocothe (Ohio) Correctional Inst., 1993—; emergency med. svc. med. advisor Franklin Twp. Fire Dept., Columbus, 1988-89; clin. asst. prof. Coll. Osteo. Medicine Pacific, Pomona, Calif., 1989. Contbr. articles to profl. publs., chpt. to book. Mem. CPR com. ARC, Santa Ana, Calif., 1978-81; instr. trainer Am. Heart Assn., Santa Ana, 1972-80; instr., course coord. basic trauma life support Am. Coll. Emergency Physicians, Columbus, 1988—. Rsch. grantee Emergency Medicine Found., 1988, Kellogg Found., 1979-80; recipient rsch. fellow award Emergency Medicine Residents Ohio, 1988, Armstrong Lit. award, 1980. Mem. Am. Coll. Emergency Physicians, Am. Osteo. Assn., Beta Beta Beta.

JENKINS, LARRY PARKER, ophthalmologist; b. Knoxville, Tenn., May 21, 1940; s. A.L. and Elizabeth Jenkins; m. Doris G. Jenkins, Juen 23, 1962; children: Laura, Paul, Stephen, Sissy, Mary. MD, U. Tenn., Memphis, 1964. Diplomate Am. Bd. Ophthalmology. Mem. staff Stanley Meml. Hosp., chief of staff; pvt. practice ophthalmology Albemarle. Maj. U.S. Army, 1966-69. Fellow ACS, Am. Acad. Ophthalmology, Stanley Med. Soc. (pres.), Albemarle Rotary Club (bd. dirs.). Republican. Christian. Office: 121 Yadkin St Albemarle NC 28001

JENKINS, LINDA BECKETT, nurse, author; b. Iowa, Mar. 10, 1940; d. Albert H. and Altabel L. Beckett; m. Donovan L. Jenkins, Apr. 14, 1963; children: Renée, Diana. BSN with honors, U. Fla., 1962. Cert. childbirth educator. Author: Pregnancy, Birth and You!, Sexuality and the Pregnant Couple; producer, dir. 3 videos in Spanish: Practicing for Birth, During Labor and Delivery, Giving Birth with Love. Office: 9 Cabernet Ct Lafayette CA 94549-3308

JENKINS, MARK GUERRY, cardiologist; b. Charleston, S.C., July 6, 1957; s. Oliver Hart and Lois (Metze) J.; m. Kathy Ann Moses, June 20, 1980; children: Anne Elizabeth, Andrew Guerry. BA, U. Va., 1979; MD, Med. U. S.C., 1983. Diplomate Am. Bd. Internal Medicine, Am. Bd. Cardiovascular Diseases, Am. Bd. Clin. Cardiac Electrophysiology. Resident in internal medicine U. Va., Charlottesville, 1983-86; fellow in cardiology U. N.C., Chapel Hill, 1986-89; cardiologist Cardiovascular Cons., P.C., Savannah, Ga., 1989—; dir. clin. cardiac electrophysiology Meml. Med. Ctr., 1989—, chief cardiology sect., 1993—. Contbr. articles to profl. jours. Fellow Am. Coll. Cardiology; mem. AMA, AHA (sec. 1st dist. med. soc. 1993—), Savannah Golf Club, Alpha Omega Alpha, Phi Beta Kappa. Office: Cardiovascular Cons PC 4750 Waters Ave Ste 302 Savannah GA 31404-6268

JENKINS, MARLENE, nurse administrator, educator, entrepreneur; b. Elmhurst, Ill., Oct. 16, 1952; d. Lester H. and Ann Marie (Commare) J. ASN, Coll. of the Desert, 1972; BSN, Calif. State U., Dominguez Hills, 1986, MSN in Adminstrn., 1989. RN, Calif.; cert. nurse adminstr. Adminstr. nurse oncology unit; adminstr. nurse, gynecology-oncology unit UCLA Med. Ctr., 1976-89; with Pacific Stat Systems, Inc., L.A., 1985-92; pvt. practice adminstrv. and ednl. cons., Manhattan Beach, Calif., 1989—; lectr., assoc. coord. Calif. State U., Dominguez Hills, 1989—. Co-author, co-prodr. infant and child CPR and choking rescue videotape, 1987. Grantee HHS, 1988. Mem. Calif. Nurses Assn., Am. Orgn. Nurse Execs., Calif. Soc. Nursing Adminstrs., Nat. Nurses in Bus. Assn., Sigma Theta Tau. Home and Office: 429 26th St Manhattan Beach CA 90266-2109

JENNER, FREDERICK ALEXANDER, retired psychiatry educator; b. London, Mar. 15, 1927; s. Frederick James Henry and Marion Wilson (Young) J.; m. Barbara Mary Killick, July 21, 1951; children: Margaret Anne, Mary Elizabeth Chapman-Jenner. MB ChB, U. Sheffield (Eng.), 1954, PhD, 1958. House officer Sheffield Health Authority, 1954-56; lectr. physiology U. Sheffield, 1955-58, lectr. psychiatry, resident, 1958-62; cons. psychiatrist Med. Rsch. Coun. Unit, Birmingham, Eng., 1962-64, physician in charge, 1964-67; hon. dir. Med. Rsch. Coun. Unit, Sheffield, 1967-79; prof. psychiatry U. Sheffield, 1967-92; ret., 1992; vis. prof. U. Concepcion, Chile, 1994—; mem. Com. on Safety of Medicine, London, 1976-85; v.p. Phoenix House Drug Addiction, London, 1980—. Author: Some Ways of Being Human, 1994; editor, translator: Phenomenology & Psychiatry, 1982, Somatology of Periodic Catatonia, 1976; editor, founder Asylum Mag.; contbr. articles to profl. jours. With Brit. Royal Navy, 1945-48. Fellow Royal Coll. Physicians, Royal Coll. Psychiatrists; mem. Royal Soc. Medicine. Labour. Home: Manor Farm Brightholmlee, Ln Wharncliffe Side, Sheffield S30 4DB, England Office: U Sheffield, Western Bank, Sheffield S10 2TN, England

JENNETT, SHIRLEY SHIMMICK, hospice executive, nurse; b. Jennings, Kans., May 1, 1937; d. William and Mabel C. (Mowry) Shimmick; m. Nelson K. Jennett, Aug. 20, 1960 (div. 1972); children: Jon W., Cheryl L.; m. Albert J. Kukral, Apr. 16, 1977 (div. 1990). Diploma, Rsch. Hosp. Sch. Nursing, Kansas City, Mo., 1958. RN, Mo., Colo., Tex., Ill. Staff nurse, head nurse Rsch. Hosp., 1958-60; head nurse Penrose Hosp., Colorado Springs, Colo., 1960-62, Hotel Dieu Hosp., El Paso, Tex., 1962-63; staff nurse Oak Park (Ill.) Hosp., 1963-64, NcNeal Hosp., Berwyn, Ill., 1964-65, St. Anthony Hosp., Denver, 1968-69; staff nurse, head nurse, nurse recruiter Luth. Hosp., Wheat Ridge, Colo., 1969-79; owner, mgr. Med. Placement Svcs., Lakewood, Colo., 1980-84; vol., primary care nurse, admissions coord., team mgr. Hospice of Metro Denver, 1984-88, dir. patient and family svcs., 1988, exec. dir., 1988-94; pres. Care Mgmt. & Resources, Inc., Denver, 1996—; mem. adv. com. Linkages Assn. for Older Adults, Denver, 1989-90. Community liaison person U. Phoenix, 1988-90. Mem. NAFE, Nat. Hospice Orgn. (bd. dirs. 1992-95), Colo. Hospice Orgn. (bd. dirs., pres. 1991-93). Republican. Mem. Ch. of Religious Sci. Office: 2223 S Monaco Pkwy # E6-209 Denver CO 80222

JENNEY, JUDITH ANN, critical care nurse; b. Medina, Ohio, Mar. 2, 1964; d. Guy B. Sr. and Velma L. (Kramer) Page. BSN, U. Akron, 1986. Cert. in intravenous therapy, CPR, emergency cardiac care. Staff nurse, gerontology Altercare, Millersburg, Ohio, 1986-87; staff nurse, med.-surg. Coshocton County Meml. Hosp., Coshocton, Ohio, 1988-89; staff nurse, CCU Bethesda Hosp., Zanesville, Ohio, 1989-95; staff nurse cardiac care unit Mt. Carmel East Hosp., Columbus, Ohio, 1992—. Recipient scholarships and grants. Mem. Ohio Nurses Assn. Home: 7216 Johnstown Rd Johnstown OH 43031

JENNINGS, ANTHONY SCOTT, physician; b. Nashville, June 16, 1945; s. William E. and June (Scarborough) J.; m. Victoria Lee Velter, June 9, 1974; children: Jennifer Lee, Jonathan Scott, Jason Brian. BS, Middle Tenn. State U., 1966; MD, Emory U., 1970. Diplomate internal medicine, endocrinology and metabolism Am. Bd. Internal Medicine. Intern, resident Johns Hopkins Hosp., Balt., 1970-73; fellow endocrinology Vanderbilt U., Nashville, 1973-75; fellow endocrinology U. Pa., Phila., 1977-79, staff physician, 1979-89; staff physician Presbyn. Med. Ctr., Phila., 1989—, endocrine chief, 1989-93; endocrine chief Phila. Naval Hosp., 1975-77. Contbr. articles to profl. jours. Lt. comdr. USN, 1975-77. Rsch. fellow Measey Found., 1979. Mem. Am. Fedn. Clin. Rsch., Am. Diabetes Assn., Am. Thyroid Assn., Endocrine Soc., Alpha Omega Alpha. Office: Presbyn Med Ctr Ste 305 Medical Office Bldg Philadelphia PA 19107

JENNINGS, DONALD ERB, psychologist; b. Chattanooga, July 2, 1939; s. James Robert Jennings and Nell (Erb) Allen; m. Nancy Sue Sells, Feb. 18, 1965; children: Nicole, Beth, Susan. BS, Livingston U., 1964; MEd, U. Tenn., 1968; D.Ed., U. Pa., 1979. Lic. psychologist, Pa. Rehab. psychologist Moccasin Bend Psychiat., 1964-65; rehab. counselor State of Tenn., 1965-66, Commonwealth of Pa., 1966-67; cons. psychologist rehab. unit Pa. Hosp., 1967-69, Nazareth Mental Health Ctr., 1969-72; psychologist Hahnemann Med. Coll. and Hosp., Phila. Prison System, 1980-82; v.p., psychologist Edn. & Vocat. Guidance Consultants, Inc., 1967-81; dir. psychology sect. NE Outpatient and Rehab. Ctr., 1985-87; instr. psychology St. Joseph's U., Phila., 1967—; pvt. practice psychologist Phila., 1967—; cons. Cooper St. Pain Group, 1980-85, pain clinic South Phila. Orthopedic Assocs., 1982-83; presenter in field. Contbr. articles to profl. jours. Mem. Am. Psychol. Assn., Pa. Psychol. Assn. (chair impaired psychologist program, ethics com.), Phila. Soc. Clin. Psychologists, Am. Assn. for the Advancement Psychology, Am. Orthopsychiat. Assn., Am. Psychology-Law Soc., Nat. Acad. Forensic Scientists, Nat. Assn. Rehab. Profls. in Pvt. Sector, Nat. Rehab. Assn., Nat. Forensic Ctr., Internat. Rehab. Inst., Nat. Head Injury Found. (profl.), Am. Bd. Profl. Disability Evaluators, Am. Bd. Med. Psychotherapists. Home: 27 Galena Ct Southampton PA 18966-1125 Office: 826 Bustleton Pike Unit 109 Feasterville PA 19053-6057

JENNINGS, EUGENE EMERSON, health care company executive; b. Phila., July 26, 1953; s. Eugene Emerson and Marlyan (Peterson) J.; m. Deborah Jane Morgan, Sept. 27, 1977. BA, Mich. State U., 1975, MBA, 1979. Bus. analyst Am. Hosp. Supply, Evanston, Ill., 1979-81; product mgr. Am. Hosp. Supply, Evanston, 1981-82; dir. sales and mktg. Medi-Vac div. Am. Hosp. Supply, Evanston, 1982-83; dir. mktg. Pharmaseal Div. supply, Valencia, Calif.; v.p. mktg. Convertors Div. Baxter, Valencia, 1986-87; v.p. mktg.and bus. devel. Baxter Health Care, Ill., 1987-88; pres., chief exec. officer Cardiovascular Imaging Systems, Inc., Sunnyvale, Calif., 1988-90; pres. Endoscopy div. Stryker Corp., 1990-91; cor. v.p. AMSCO Internat., Pitts., 1991-96; chmn., CEO, pres. USML, Southfield, Mich., 1996—. Home: 618 Whispering Pines Dr Pittsburgh PA 15238-1947 Office: Two Chatham Ctr Ste 1100 Pittsburgh PA 15219

JENNINGS, HENRY SMITH, III, cardiologist; b. Atlanta, May 16, 1951; s. Henry Smith Jr. and Elizabeth (Martin) J.; m. Polly Cooper; 1 child, Mary Bailey. BS summa cum laude, Davidson Coll., 1973; MD, Vanderbilt U., 1977. Diplomate Am. Bd. Internal Medicine, subspecialty cardiovascular diseases, Nat. Bd. Med. Examiners; lic. physician and surgeon, Tenn. Intern internal medicine Vanderbilt U. Affiliated Hosps., Nashville, 1977-78, resident internal medicine, 1978-80; fellow clin. cardiology divsn. cardiology dept. medicine Vanderbilt U., Nashville, 1980-82; clin. instr. medicine Vanderbilt U. Sch. Medicine, Nashville, 1982-89, asst. clin. prof. medicine, 1989—; med. dir. Cardiac Rehab. Ctr. St. Thomas Hosp., Nashville, 1984—; mem. active staff St. Thomas Hosp., Nashville; vis. staff Vanderbilt U. Med. Ctr., Nashville; mem. courtesy staff Centennial Med. Ctr., Nashville. Contbr. articles to profl. jours. Bd. dirs. Heart Inst., St. Thomas Hosp., Nashvile, 1992-94, Tenn. Heart Inst., 1989-91. Justin Potter med. scholar Vanderbilt U. Sch. Medicine, Nashville, 1973-77; recipient Physician's Recognition award AMA, 1985-88, 89-92, 92-95, 95—. Fellow ACP, Am. Coll. Cardiology, Am. Coll. Chest Physicians, Coun. Clin. Cardiology Am. Heart Assn., Soc. Cardiac Angiography and Interventions (cert. of proficiency in diagnostic cardiac catheterization and angioplasty 1989-92, 92-95, 96-99), Am. Soc. Cardiovascular Interventionists; mem. Internat. Soc. Heart Transplantation,Am. Heart Assn., So. Med. Assn., Tenn. Med. Assn., Nashville Acad. Medicine, Nashville Soc. Internal Medicine, Nashville Cardiovascular Soc. (bd. trustees 1992—). Methodist. Home: Northumberland 3 Castle Rising Nashville TN 37215-4126 Office: Page-Campbell Cardiology PC Ste 900 4230 Harding Rd Nashville TN 37205-2013

JENNINGS, MARK THOMAS, neurologist, oncologist; b. Chgo., Dec. 21, 1951; m. V. DeVeta Moe; children: Elyse I., Mark-Eamon, Jonathon B. BA,

Coll. Holy Cross, Worcester, Mass., 1973; MD, Loyola U., 1976. Resident in child neurology Mass. Gen. Hosp., Boston, 1980-83; fellow in neuro-oncology Meml. Sloan-Kettering Cancer Ctr., N.Y.C., 1983-85, fellow in tumor immunology, 1983-85; fellow in med. genetics N.Y. Hosp., N.Y.C., 1985-88; staff Vanderbilt U. Med. Ctr., Nashville, 1989—, Blanchfield Army Cmty. Hosp., Fort Campbell, Ky., 1993—, Vanderbilt Stallworth Rehab. Hosp., Nashville, 1993—; staff Meml. Sloan-Kettering Cancer Ctr., N.Y.C., 1985-88, inst. rev. bd., 1987-88; mem. ad hoc special rev. com. Nat. Cancer Inst., 1993, investigator; reviewer Cancer Rsch., Cancer, neurology com. Childrens Cancer Group; neurology rep. sedation task force com. Vanderbilt U., 1992-93, mem. continuing med. edn. com., 1993—; rschr. in field. Patentee in field; Contbr. articles to profl. jours., chpts. to books. Bd. dirs. Dream Makers, Nashville, 1991-93, screening bd., 1991—. Grantee Nat. Inst. Neurological Disorders and Stroke, 1985-91, 92-96, Am. Cancer Soc. Inst., 1986-87, 90, Soc. Meml. Sloan-Kettering Cancer Ctr., 1987-88, Univ. rsch. coun. Vanderbilt Univ., 1989-90; Daland fellow Am. Philos. Soc., 1982, Assoc. for Brain Tumor Rsch. fellow, 1983-85, Clin. Scholars fellow Norman and Rosita Winston Found., 1983-85; recipient Clin. Investigator Devel. award Am. Cancer Soc., 1985 (award declined), Vanderbilt Comm. Svc. award, 1994. Mem. Soc. Neuro-Oncology, Child Neurology Soc. (rsch. com. 1993-96, mem. com. 1995—), Internat. Soc. Neuroimmunology, N.Y. Acad. Scis., Am. Acad. Neurology (selection com. Farber award 1992—, co-chair neuro-oncology basic sci. session 39th annual meeting, 1987, 45th ann. meeting, 1993), N.Am. Neuro-Oncology Soc. Office: Vanderbilt Med Sch 2100 Pierce Ave Nashville TN 37212-3162

JENNINGS, RICHARD HUNTER, III, surgeon; b. Atlanta, Mar. 23, 1956; s. Richard Hunter and Laticia (Sharp) J.; m. Kimberly Hayes, Dec. 15, 1987; children: Alexis Grace, Richard Hunter IV. BS, Davidson Coll., 1978; MD, Emory U., 1982. Diplomate Am. Bd. Surgery, Am. Bd. Surg. Critical Care. Pvt. practice, Chattanooga, 1988—, Ft. Oglethorpe, Ga., 1988—; vice chief suurgery Meml. Hosp., Chattanooga, 1994-96; chief surgery Hutcheson Med. Ctr., Ft. Oglethorpe, 1994—. Fellow ACS; mem. So. Surg. Assn., Christian Med. and Dental Soc., Am. Soc. Gen. Surgery, Chattanooga Acad. Surgery, Med. Assn. Ga., Walker-Dade-Catoosa Med. Soc. (pres. 1994), Phi Beta Kappa, Alpha Omega Alpha. Mem. Ch. of Christ. Office: Hayes Park & Jennings PC PO Box 5398 Fort Oglethorpe GA 30742

JENNINGS, ROBERT BURGESS, experimental pathologist, medical educator; b. Balt., Dec. 14, 1926; s. Burgess Hill and Etta (Crout) J.; m. Linda Lee Sheffield, June 28, 1952; children—Carol L., Mary G., John B., Anne E., James R. B.S., Northwestern U., 1947, M.S., B.M., 1949, M.D., 1950. Diplomate Am. Bd. Pathology (trustee 1976-87, pres. 1986-87). Intern Passavant Meml. Hosp., Chgo., 1949-50; resident pathology Passavant Meml. Hosp., 1950-51; mem. faculty Northwestern U. Med. Sch., 1953-75, prof. pathology, 1963-75, Magerstadt prof. and chmn. pathology dept., 1969-75; prof., chmn. dept. pathology Duke U. Med. Sch., Durham, N.C., 1975-89, James B. Duke prof., 1980—; vis. scientist Middlesex Hosp. Med. Sch., London, 1961-62; cons. VA Rsch. Hosp., Chgo.; mem. attending staff Northwestern Meml. Hosp., Chgo., 1963-75; mem. pathology A Study sect. USPHS, 1960-65; mem. clin. cardiology adv. com. NIH, 1976-80, mem. cardiovascular and renal study sect., 1992-95. Mem. editl. bd. Lab. Investigation, 1967—, Archives Pathology, 1967-95, Jour. Molecular and Cellular Cardiology, 1972-89, Exptl. and Molecular Pathology, 1973—, Circulation, 1988-91, 93—, Circulation Rsch., 1976-82, Histopathology, 1977-92, Am. Jour. Pathology, 1983-92, Jour. Applied Cardiology, 1986—, Cardiosci., 1990-95, Trends in Cardiovascular Medicine, 1991-92, Carciovascular Pathology, 1991-95. Served as lt. (j.g.) USNR, 1951-53. Markle scholar med. scis., 1958-63. Office: Duke U Med Ctr Dept Pathology Durham NC 27710

JENRETTE, JOSEPH MALPHUS, III, radiation oncologist; b. Raleigh, Feb. 24, 1951; s. Joseph Malphus and Helen Bell (Broughton) J.; m. Elizabeth Chandler, Dec. 24, 1954; children: Emma Chandler, Elliott Broughton. BA, U. N.C., 1973; MD, Med. U. S.C., 1979. Diplomate Am. Bd. Radiology. Resident in radiation oncology Med. U. S.C., Charleston, 1979-83, instr. radiation oncology, 1983-86, asst. prof., 1986-89, assoc. prof., 1989—, acting chmn. dept. radiation oncology, 1989-94. Contbr. articles to profl. jours. Pres. S.C. divsn. Am. Cancer Soc., 1989-90; exec. com. Hollings Cancer Ctr., Charleston, 1990—; pres. Charleston Symphony Orch., 1990-92; pres., founder Over the Rainbow Arts, Charleston, 1988—; v.p. Am. Classical Homes Found., N.Y.C., 1993—, Charleston Preservation Soc., 1990-92. Recipient Carolopolis award Preservation Soc., 1989, Pace Leadership awardee Am. Cancer Soc., 1985, Danforth Leadership awardee Danforth Found., 1969. Mem. AMA, S.C. Med. Soc., Am. Coll. Radiation Oncology, S.C. Oncology Soc. (pres. 1992-93), Radiol. Soc. N.Am., Am. Soc. for Therapeutic Radiology and Oncology, Charleston Men's Book Club, Order of Holy Grail. Office: Medical University of SC Dept Radiation Oncology Charleston SC 29425

JENSEN, ANNETTE M., mental health nurse, administrator; b. Albert Lea, Minn., Jan. 16, 1952; d. Oliver H. and Ardis R. (Nelson) J. BSN, Winona (Minn.) State U., 1974; postgrad., Calif. Coll. Health Scis. Staff nurse in adolescent psychiatry C.B. Wilson Ctr., Faribault, Minn., 1974-76, 79-80, Abbott Northwestern Hosp., Mpls., 1981-82; charge nurse in child psychiatry Med. Coll. Ga., Augusta, 1983-87; adminstr. child psychiat. program Charter Hosp. of Augusta, 1987-91; staff educator/quality mgmt. in psychiatry Ga. Regional Hosp. at Augusta, 1990-92; team leader child psychiatry Charter Peachford Hosp., Atlanta, 1992—. Mem. Girl Scouts of Am. Mem. NAFE, AAUW, ANA, Ga. Nurses Assn., Assn. Child/Adolescent Psychiat. Nurses, Am. Camping Assn. Presbyterian. Home: 725 Josh Ln Lawrenceville GA 30245-3157

JENSEN, ERIK HUGO, pharmaceutical quality control consultant; b. Fredericia, Denmark, June 27, 1924; came to U.S. 1950; s. Alfred Marinus and Clara Krista (Sorensen) J.; m. Alice Emy Olesen, Oct. 8, 1949; children: Ian Peter, Lisa Joan, Linda Anne. BS, Royal Danish Sch. Pharmacy, Copenhagen, 1945, MS, 1948, PhD, 1954. Head product development AB Ferrosan, Malmo, Sweden, 1955-57; research scientist Upjohn Co., Kalamazoo, Mich., 1957-62, head quality control, 1962-63, mgr. quality control, 1963-66, asst. dir. quality control, 1966-81, dir. quality control, 1981-85, exec. dir. control devel. and adminstrn., 1985-86; pres., cons. Jensen Enterprises, 1986—. Author: A Study on Sodium Borohydride, 1954; contbr. articles to profl. jours.; patentee in field. Bd. dirs. Kalamazoo Inst. Arts, 1971-73, treas., 1973-74, pres., 1974-75. Mem. Pharm. Mfr.'s Assn. (quality control sect. recorder 1971-78, vice chmn. 1978-80, chmn. 1980-83), Acad. Pharm. Scis. (vice chmn. 1968-69, chmn. 1971-72) Lodge: Kiwanis (treas. 1962-65). Avocations: painting, sculpting, photography.

JENSEN, GERALD OTTO, pediatrician; b. Bklyn, Feb. 10, 1927; s. Emil Adolf and Else Valborg (Sorenson) J.; m. Barbara Rudd, Apr. 19, 1958; children: Neil, Susan, Margaret, David, Sarah. BS in Biology, Columbia U., 1953; MD, N.Y. Med. Sch., 1957; MPH, U. Conn., 1989. Diplomate Am. Bd. Pediatrics. Intern Meth. Hosp., Bklyn, 1957-58; resident in pediatrics Akron (Ohio) Children's Hosp., 1960-62; pvt. practice Bristol, Conn., 1962—; mem. pediatric staff Bristol Hosp., 1962-85, chief of pediatrics, 1971-73, 77-80, 82-83; chmn. Bd. of Health of Bristol-Burlington Health Dist., 1972-93; mem. com. on pub. health Conn. State Med. Soc., chmn. pub. health com. Corporator Bristol Hosp., Wheeler Clinic, Plainville, Conn.; bd. dirs. Hospice: Project Horizon: Inc., Terryville, Bristol Vis. Nurse Assn.; mem. steering com. MPH program U. Conn.; tenor Bristol Choral Soc.; bd. dirs. north ctrl. chpt. ARC, Bristol Symphony Orch. Fellow Am. Acad. Pediatrics, Royal Soc. Health (London); mem. AMA, APHA, MENSA, Conn. State Med. Assn., Hartford County Med. Assn., Bristol Med. Soc., New Eng. Pub. Health Assn. Republican. Lutheran. Home: 116 Belridge Rd Bristol CT 06010-5204 Office: Pediatric Office 780 Farmington Ave Bristol CT 06010-3920

JENSEN, HELENE WICKSTROM, nutritionist, educator; b. Carthage, Mo., Mar. 3, 1929; d. Frank Emil and Lois (Stroup) Wickstrom; m. Robert Gordon Jensen, Dec. 20, 1947; children: Gordon Lee, Jeffrey Alan. BS, U. Mo., 1951; MS, U. Conn., 1983; PhD, Century U., 1996. Registered dietitian; cert. dietitian/nutritionist. Dietitian-in-charge U. Mo., Columbia, 1952-56; therapeutic dietitian Windham Community Meml. Hosp., Willimantic, Conn., 1967, dir. food service, 1967-72; dir. sch. lunch program Windham Pub. Schs., Willimantic, 1963-66; lectr. U. Conn., Storrs, 1972-78, leader ednl. outreach program, 1979-92; cons. Recipient award Met. Life Ins. Co., 1985, Czajowski Nutrition award U. Conn., 1989, Disting. Alumna award U. Conn. Agr. and Natural Resources Alumni Assn., 1989. Mem. Am. Dietetic Assn. (presenter), Am. Sch. Food Svc. Assn (exec. bd. 1989-91, presenter), Soc. Nutrition Edn., Conn. Sch. Food Svc. Assn. (com. mem.), Conn. Nutrition Coun. (presenter), Conn. Dietetic Assn. (presenter, Dietitian of Yr. 1987), Phi Kappa Phi, Gamma Sigma Delta. Home: 186 Chaffeeville Rd Storrs Mansfield CT 06268-2637

JENSEN, JUDY DIANNE, psychotherapist; b. Portland, Oreg., Apr. 8, 1948; d. Clarence Melvin and Charlene Augusta (Young) J.; m. Frank George Cooper, Sept 4, 1983; stepchildren: Pamela Cooper, Brian Cooper. BA in Sociology and Anthropology with honors, Oberlin Coll., 1970; MSW, U. Pitts., 1972; postgrad., U. Wis., 1977. Lic. clin. social worker, marriage and family therapist, Oreg. Social worker Day Hosp. Western Psychiat. Inst. and Clinic, Pitts., 1972-73, South Hills Child Guidance Ctr., Pitts., 1973-74; mem. drug treatment program Umatilla County Mental Health Clinic, Pendleton, Oreg., 1975-77; social worker Children's Services Div. State of Oreg., Pendleton, 1978-80, therapist intensive family services project, 1980—, dir. intensive family services project, 1986—; pvt. practice Pendleton, 1980—. NIMH grantee, 1970-72; NDEA fellow 1977; Gen. Motors scholar Oberlin Coll., 1966-70. Mem. Am. Assn. Marriage and Family Therapists (clin.), Nat. Assn. Social Workers. Home: 325 NW Bailey Ave Pendleton OR 97801-1604 Office: PO Box 752 Pendleton OR 97801-0752

JENSEN, PHILIP BAILEY, urologist; b. Kingston-on-Thames, Surrey, Eng., Apr. 10, 1922; s. Axel P.C. and Mabel (Bailey) J.; m. D. Patricia Riley, Nov. 28, 1953; children: Frances, Charles, Richard. MB, BS, London U., 1952. Diplomate Am. Bd. Urology. House physician Middlesex Hosp., London, 1952-53, Cen. Middlesex Hosp., London, 1953, Royal No. Hosp., London, 1953-54; resident Greenwich (Conn.) Hosp., 1954-56, Columbia Presbyn. Med. Ctr., N.Y.C., 1956-59; pvt. practice Greenwich, 1959-75, Sharon, Conn., 1976—; attending physician Greenwich (Conn.) Hosp., 1959-75, United Hosp., Port Chester, N.Y., 1961-75; attending physician New Milford (Conn.) Hosp., 1977-93, attending physician emeritus, 1993—; attending physician Sharon (Conn.) Hosp., 1977-93, attending physician emeritus, 1993—; instr. urology Coll. Physicians and Surgeons, Columbia U., N.Y.C., 1959-75. Lt. Royal Naval Vol. Res., 1941-46. Fellow ACS. Home: 59 Hilltop Rd Sharon CT 06069-2131

JENSEN, RONALD H., medical educator; b. Chgo., Nov. 25, 1938; s. Gunner Charles and Elizabeth (Rowley) J.; m. Judith Ann Miller, Dec. 27, 1958; children: Montgomery Allen, Gregory Joel, Heather Lee. BS in Chemistry, Lawrence Coll., 1960; PhD in Chemistry, Calif. Inst. Tech., 1964. Rsch. fellow Calif. Inst. Tech., Pasadena, 1964-67; rsch. biochemist Internat. Mineral and Chem. Corp., Libertyville, Ill., 1967-69; sr. investigator Smith Kline and French Lab., Phila., 1970-75; biomed. scientist Lawrence Livermore (Calif.) Nat. Lab., 1975-91; prof. lab. medicine U. Calif., San Francisco, 1991—; biophysicist Lawrence Berkeley (Calif.) Lab., 1994—; mem. sci. adv. coun. Ministry of Health of Russia, Moscow, 1995—; mem. working group NCI Study of Leukemia among Clean-up Workers in Ukraine following Chernobyl, 1993—; sci. advisor Italian-Ukranian Coop. Program on Children's Health following Chernobyl, 1993—; mem. program organizing com. Internat. Soc. for Analytical Cytology Congress, 1993—. Contbr. articles to profl. jours. Grantee NCI, 1992—. Mem. Soc. for Analytical Cytology, Am. Assn. Cancer Rsch. Office: U Calif San Francisco-DMC Box 0808 1855 Folsom San Francisco CA 94143

JENSH, RONALD PAUL, anatomist, educator; b. N.Y.C., June 14, 1938; s. Werner G. and Dorothy (Hensle) J.; m. Ruth Eleanor Dobson, Aug. 18, 1962; children: Victoria Lynn, Elizabeth Whitney. B.A., Bucknell U., 1960, M.A., 1962; Ph.D., Jefferson Med. Coll., 1966. Instr. in anatomy Thomas Jefferson U., Phila., 1966-68, assoc. in radiology, 1966-68, asst. prof. radiology and anatomy, 1968-74, assoc. prof. radiology, 1968-92, assoc. prof. anatomy, 1968-74, prof. anatomy, 1982-94, vice chmn., 1984-94, prof. anatomy, pathology and cell biology, 1994—, assoc. prof. pediatrics, 1992—, chmn. curriculum com., 1987-93; head anatomy div. Coll. Allied Health Scis. Thomas Jefferson U., 1975-88, co-dir. pre-doctoral tng. program, 1971-79, course coord. histology, 1988-93; mem. staff Op. Concern Inc., Cherry Hill, N.J., 1970-72; cons. reproductive biology Bio-Search Inc., Argus Research Lab. Inc., Ortho Research Found. Contbr. articles to sci. jours. Mem. task force com. on communications S. Jersey Methodist Conf., 1974-80; chmn. Learning Resources Ctr., Haddonfield United Meth. Ch. (N.J.), 1976-79. Recipient Christian R. and Mary F. Lindback Found. Disting. Teaching award, 1978, Disting. Alumnus award, 1985, Faculty Achievement award Burlington Northern Found., 1989, Jefferson Med. Coll. Portrait, 1994. Mem. AAAS, Am. Soc. Zoologists, N.Y. Acad. Scis., Teratology Soc. (treas. 1989-92), Behavioral Teratology Soc. (pres. 1985-86), Am. Assn. Anatomists, Soc. Am. Mus. Natural History, Inst. Social Ethics and Life Scis., Jefferson Med. Coll. Alumni Assn. (hon. life), Phi Beta Kappa, Sigma Xi, Psi Chi, Phi Sigma. Home: 230 E Park Ave Haddonfield NJ 08033-1835 Office: 562 Jefferson Alumni Hall 1020 Locust St Philadelphia PA 19107-6799

JERNDAL, SIR JENS, holistic medicine educator, health center promoter; b. Goteborg, Sweden, Jan. 5, 1934; came to Spain, 1968; s. Ebbe and Ingrid M. (Forsberg) J.; children: C. Patrick, J.O. Mathias, J.T. Christofer. MS, Stockholm U., 1958; BA, Uppsala U., 1959; Diploma, Internat. Coll. Acupuncture, Colombo, Sri Lanka, 1982; MD, 1987; DSc. honoris causa, U. Complementary Medicines, Colombo, Sri Lanka, 1988. Attaché Royal Swedish Ministry Fgn. Affairs, 1960-62; embassy sec. Royal Swedish Embassy, Copenhagen, 1962; 1st sec., chargé d'affaires Royal Swedish Embassy, Karachi, Pakistan, 1964; 1st sec. Royal Swedish Ministry Fgn. Affairs, 1965-68; investment broker Real Lanzarote SA, Las Palmas, Spain, 1968-79; founder, pres. Dragon's Head Life Expansion Svcs.; expert del. UN High Commr. for Refugees, Geneva, 1966-67; pres. Cosmosophical Found., Stockholm, 1977-88; lectr. in astrology and alternative medicine; vis. prof., internat. coord. The Open Internat. U. for Complementary Medicine, Colombo, Sri Lanka, 1988, prof. holistic medicine, 1991; mem. faculty World U. Author: Indonesien, 1958; contbr. articles to profl. jours. Fgn. lang. transmission mgr., broadcaster for Radio Sweden, 1956-57; rep. Assn. Swedish Citizens Residing Abroad, Canary Islands, 1972-75. Decorated Knight of Royal Order of Dannebrog His Majesty the King of Denmark, Knight Commdr. of Justice of Sovereign Order of St. John of Jerusalem (Knights of Malta), Knight Grand Cross Ordre Souverain et Militaire de la Milice du Saint Sepulcre, Knight Humanity Sovereign World Order of the White Cross, 1991; recipient Albert Schweitzer Prize for Medicine, 1990. Mem. Cosmosophical Found. (chmn.), World Univ. Roundtable (v.p.), Acupuncture Found. Sri Lanka, Medicina Alternativa (life, vis. lectr.), Commonwealth Inst. Acupuncture and Natural Medicines (founding), Sci. and Med. Network, Inst. Dirs. (London).

JERVEY, HAROLD EDWARD, JR., medical education consultant, retired; b. Charleston, S.C., Dec. 3, 1920; s. Harold Edward and Stella (White) J.; m. Lillian Pearce Hair, July 13, 1946; children: Harold Edward, III, Nancy Middleton, Margaret Pearce, Harriett Beachum, Helen White, Charles Stewart, Lillian Hair. BS, U. S.C., 1941; MD, Med. U. S.C., 1949. Diplomate Am. Bd. Med. Examiners (mem.). Intern Greenville (S.C.) Gen. Hosp., 1949-50; house officer Bapt. Hosp., Columbia, S.C., 1951-54; gen. practice medicine Columbia, 1951-74; acting head health facilities U. S.C., 1968-70; asst. prof. Med. U. S.C., 1970-77; pres. Fedn. State Med. Bd. U.S., Ft. Worth, 1960-61, exec. v.p., sec., 1978-84; sec., treas. Edit. Bull., 1961-78; med. cons. S.C. Law Enforcement Agy., 1958-51, S.C. Vocat. Rehab. Dept., 1961-63, S.C. Indsl. Commn., 1963-68, S.C. Dept. Family Practice, 1971-74; med. adv. S.C. Gov. Health and Social Devel., 1973-75; mem. S.C. Bd. Med. Examiners, 1952-72, sec., 1954-56, vice chmn., 1962-64, bd. dirs. Fedn. Assn. Health Regulatory Bds., 1977-80; mem. adv. bd. Am. Bd. Med. Specialties, 1959-70; pres., chmn. bd. Ednl. Commn. Fgn. Med. Grads., 1978-80; past pres. Gen. Practitioners Club Central S.C., pres.Columbia Med. Club; del. Congress Dels. Am. Acad. Gen. Practitioners, 1958-62. Author articles in field. Contbg. editor: Med. Economics. Episc. lay reader, past vestryman; active Richland County Bd. Health, 1992-93. Lt. comdr. USNR, WWII, 1941-45, capt. M.C., USNR. Decorated Bronze Star, 16 battle stars, Presdl. unit citation. Fellow Am. Acad. Family Practice; mem. AMA (coms.), S.C. Med. Assn., S.C. Med. Soc., S.C. Acad. Family Practice, Columbia Med. Soc., Soc. of Cincinnati, S.C. Hist. Soc., S.C. Writers Workshop, Sertoma, Rotary. Episcopalian. Address: 4819 Quail Ln Columbia SC 29206-4622

JESSEN, RAYMOND JAMES, public health educator, business administrator; b. San Francisco, Nov. 4, 1910; s. James Niels and Millie Marie (Ring) J.; m. Lois Barron, Dec. 24, 1940 (div. 1969); m. Charlotte Sarett, July 9, 1971; children: Tony, Marna, Van. BS, U. Calif., 1937; PhD, Iowa State U., 1943. From research assoc. to prof. stats. Iowa State Coll., Ames, 1938-57, acting dir. statis. lab., 1947-50; agrl. and math. statistician USDA, Ames, 1938-56; project dir. CEIR, Inc., Los Angeles, 1957-62; prof. mgmt. and pub. health UCLA, 1962-78, prof. emeritus, 1978—; tech. dir. allied mission observing Greek election, U.S. Dept. State, Washington and Athens, 1946. Author: Statistical Survey Techniques, 1978; co-author: Basic Statistics for Business and Economics, 1971. Fellow Am. Statis. Assn., Internat. Statis. Inst.; mem. AAAS, Sigma Xi. Home: 327 21st St Santa Monica CA 90402-2417 Office: The Anderson Sch at UCLA 110 Westwood Plz Box 951481 Los Angeles CA 90095-1481

JESTE, DILIP VISHWANATH, psychiatrist, researcher; b. Pimpalagaon, India, Dec. 23, 1944; came to U.S., 1974; naturalized Feb., 1980; m. Sonali D. Jeste, Dec. 5, 1971; children: Shafali, Neelum. B in Medicine & Surgery, U. Poona, India, 1966; D. Psychiat. Medicine, Coll. Physicians and Surgeons, 1970; MD, U. Bombay, 1970. Cer. Am. Bd. Psychiatry and Neurology, 1979; lic. physician, D.C., Md., Calif. Hon. asst. prof. KEM Hosp., G.S. Med. Coll., Bombay, 1971-74; staff psychiatrist St. Elizabeth's Hosp., Washington, 1977-82, chief movement disorder unit, 1982-86; clin. assoc. prof. psychiatry Walter Reed Med. Ctr., Bethesda, Md., 1981-84; assoc. clin. prof. psychiatry and neurology George Washington U., Washington, 1984-86; prof. psychiatry and neuroscis. U. Calif., San Diego, 1986—; chief psychiatry svc. San Diego VA Med. Ctr., San Diego, 1989-92; dir. geriatric psychiatry clin rsch ctr U. Calif. and VA Med. Ctr., San Diego, 1992—; vis. scientist dept. neuropathology Armed Forces Inst. of Pathology, Washington, 1984-86; co-dir. Med. Students' Psychiatry Clerkship Program, 1987-91; ad-hoc mem. Vets. Adminstrn. Neurobiology Grant Rev. Bd., 1984—; participant numerous meeting and confs.; lectr. in field. Co-author: Understanding and Treating Tardive Dyskinesia, 1982; editor: Neuropsychiatric Movement Disorders, 1984, Neurpsychiatric Dementias, 1986, Psychosis and Depression in the Elderly, 1988; contbr. articles to numerous profl. jours, reviewer numerous profl. jours. Mem. Acad. Geriatric Resource Com., U. Calif., 1986-87, mem. com. on joint doctoral program in clin. psychology, 1986-87, mgmt. com. faculty compensation fund com., 1988-89, chmn. Psychiat. Undergrad. Edn. Com., 1987. Recipient Merit award NIMH, 1988; recipient numerous grants in field. Fellow Indian Psychiatric Soc. (recipient Sandoz award 1973), Am. Psychiatric Assn. (co-chmn. Tardive Dyskinesia task force 1984-92), Am. Coll. Neuropsychopharm. (co-chmn. fin. com. 1988-89); mem. Soc. for Neurosci., Internat. Brain Rsch. Orgn., Soc. Biolog. Psychiatry (A.E. Bennett Neuropsychiatric Rsch. award 1981), Am. Acad. Neurology, Am. Geriatrics Soc., Calif. Psychiatric Soc., Am. Assn. Geriatric Psychiatry, West Coast Coll. Biolog. Psychiatry, San Diego Soc. Psychiatric Physicians, Assn. Scientists of Indian Origin in Am. (pres. neurosci. chpt. 1988—, named Outstanding Neuroscientist 1988). Office: Vets Affairs Med Ctr 3350 La Jolla Village Dr V116A San Diego CA 92161

JESTER, MARK A., physician; b. Ft. Belvoir, Va., Mar. 4, 1955; s. Guy Earlscourt and Roberta (Andrews) J.; m. Colleen Ann Parks, Dec. 30, 1978; children: Christopher, Michelle. BS in chem. magna cum laude, Davidson Coll., 1977; MD, Univ. Mo., 1981. Internship, residency Univ. Tex., San Antonio, 1984; staff physician U.S. Navy, Long Beach, Calif., 1984-87; physician Medical Arts Clinic, Ennis, Tex., 1987-88, Northwest Ga. Internal Medicine, Rome, Ga., 1988—. Lay eucharistic minister St. Peter's Episcopal Ch., Rome, 1988—. With U.S. Navy, 1984-87. Mem. AMA, Am. Coll. Physicians, Southern Medical Assn., Ga. Medical Assn., Floyd-Polk-Chattooga Medical Soc. Home: 8 Crestwood Dr Rome GA 30165 Office: 7 John Maddox Dr Rome GA 30165

JEW, HENRY, pharmacist; b. Hong Kong, June 10, 1950. BS in Pharmacy, U. Ga., 1974. Preceptor to externship program So. Sch. of Pharmacy, U. Ga., 1974-78; researcher Brompton's Mixture, 1977-78; pharmacist VA Med Ctr, Decatur, Ga., VNS Inc., Atlanta.

JEWELEWICZ, RAPHAEL, obstetrician, gynecologist, educator; b. Nowogrodek, Poland, Dec. 26, 1932; came to U.S., 1963; s. Chaim and Chaia (Tawricki) J.; m. Ronnie Oved, July 3, 1955; children: Rachel, Dov, Daniel, Dory. MD, Hebrew U., Jerusalem, 1961. Cert. Am. Bd. Ob-gyn. 1971, 89, reproductive endocrinology, 1974. Intern Hadassah Hebrew U. Hosp., Jerusalem; resident NYU Med. Ctr., Bellevue Hosp., N.Y.C.; assoc. prof. ob-gyn. Columbia U., N.Y.C., 1975-92; prof. ob-gyn. SUNY, 1992—; chair. dept. ob-gyn. Memonides Medical Ctr., Bklyn.; bd. dirs. divsn. reproductive endocrinology Columbia U. Coll. Physicians and Surgeons, N.Y.C.; chmn. ob-gyn. Maimonides Med. Ctr.; prof. ob=gyn. SUNY, Bklyn. Author: Clinical Aspects of Cervical Incompetence, 1989, The Menstrual Cycle: Physiology, Reproductive Disorders and Infertility, 1993; editor ob-gyn. investigation: mem. editorial bd. several sci. jours.; contbr. over 100 articles to profl. jours. Mem. Am. Coll. Ob-gyn., Am. Coll. Surgeons, Am. Fertility Soc., Am. Gynecol. & Obstet. Soc., N.Y. Obstet. Soc., N.Y. Gynecol. Soc. (pres. 1994-95), Soc. for Gynecol. Jewish. Home: Church St Alpine NJ 07620 Office: Memonides Med Ctr Dept Ob-gyn 4802 10th Ave Brooklyn NY 11219

JEWETT, CONSTANCE MARIE, health services administrator; b. Tyler, Minn., Sept. 2, 1944; d. Evald A. and Thelma C. (Lybeck) Jorgensen; m. William Lee Jewett, Nov. 11, 1966; children: Dawn Marie Jewett Faerber, Sarah Diane. Diploma, Sioux Valley Hosp. Sch Nursing, 1965; BS, Coll. St. Francis, Joliet, Ill., 1993; MPH in Health Svcs. Adminstrn., U. Minn., 1994. RN, Minn. With Sioux Valley (S.D.) Hosp., 1966; head nurse Brookings (S.D.) Hosp., 1966-67; supr. nursing Sanford Hosp., Farmington, Minn., 1971-83, quality assurance coord., 1983-84; asst. to adminstr. South Suburban Med. Ctr., Farmington, 1983-89, asst. adminstr. patient svc., 1989-94, chief oper. officer, 1995—; mem. adv. bd. Dakota County Pub. Health, Rosemount, Minn., 1993—, Dakota County Sch. Nursing, Rosemount, 1990—, Fairview Home Care and Hospice, Mpls., 1989—. Mem. Grace Luth. Ch., Apple Valley, Minn., 1989—. Mem. Minn. Orgn. Leaders in Nursing (membership com. 1989-95), Dist. F. Nursing Leaders. Home: 15754 Hayes Trail Apple Valley MN 55124 Office: South Suburban Med Ctr 913 Main St Farmington MN 55024

JHIN, MICHAEL KONTIEN, health care executive; b. Hong Kong, Jan. 26, 1950; came to U.S., 1958; s. Paul Y. and Monica J. BSME, Rensselaer Poly. Inst., 1971; MBA, Boston U., 1974. Adminstrv. asst. St. Vincent Hosp., Worcester, Mass., 1974-76; asst. dir. Thomas Jefferson U. Hosp., Phila., 1976-79, assoc. dir., 1979-84; exec. dir., CEO Temple U. Hosp., Phila., 1984-88; exec. v.p. Long Beach (Calif.) Meml. Health Sys., 1988-90; pres., CEO hosp. divsn. St. Luke's Episcopal Hosp., Houston, 1990—, pres., CEO corp., 1995—. Bd. dirs. Houston Hosp. Coun., 1991-96, chmn. bd., 1994-95, Jr. Achievement, 1991—. Fellow Am. Coll. Healthcare Execs.; mem. Rensselaer Alumni Assn. (v.p. 1994-96, pres.-elect 1995-96, pres. 1996—), Am. Hosp. Assn. (regional planning bd. 1992-95), Tex. Hosp. Assn., Young Pres.'s Orgn. Office: St Luke's Episcopal Hosp 6720 Bertner St Houston TX 77030-2604

JIALAL, ISHWARLAL, medical educator; b. Durban, Natal, South Africa, Oct. 13, 1953. B in Medicine, B in Surgery, U. Natal, South Africa, 1976, MD, 1983. Registered med. practitioner, specialist in chem. pathology South African Med. and Dental Coun.; Diplomate Royal Coll. Pathologists (Eng.), Am. Bd. Internal Medicine, Am. Bd. Clin. Chemistry. Intern in medicine and surgery King Edward VIII Hosp., U. Natal Med. Sch., Durban, South Africa, 1977, resident in endocrinology and metabolism divsn., 1978-82; resident dept. chem. pathology U. Natal, 1978-82, sr. lectr./specialist depts. medicine and chem. pathology, 1984-87; fellow divsn. diabetes and metabolism Harvard Med. Sch., E.P. Joslin Rsch. Lab., Joslin Diabetes Ctr., Boston, 1983-84; dir. clin. pathology R.K. Khan Hosp., U. Natal Med. Sch., 1984-87; assoc. prof./sr. specialist dept. chem. pathology and medicine U. Natal Med. Sch., 1987; sr. fellow divsn. metabolism, endocrinology and nutrition, dept. medicine U. Wash., Seattle, 1987-88; asst. prof. depts. clin. nutrition, internal medicine and pathology U. Tex. Southwestern Med. Ctr., Dallas, 1988-92, co-dir. Lipid Clinic, 1990—, assoc. prof. dept. pathology, internal medicine and clin. nutrition, 1992—, dir. clin. chemistry dept. pathology, 1992—, sr. investigator Ctr. Human Nutrition, 1992—; dir. divsn. clin. chemistry Parkland Meml. Hosp.; attending physician, co-dir. Lipid

Disorders Clinic, Parkland Meml. and Aston Ambulatory Care Ctr.; attending physician endocrinology & metabolism Parkland Meml. and Zale Lipshy Hosps.; cons. chem. pathologist VA Med. Ctr., Dallas; vis. scientist dept. chem. pathology and metabolic disorders St. Thomas Hosp. Med. Sch., London, 1984; cons. chem. pathologist Dallas VA Med. Ctr., 1995—. Clin. Rsch. grantee Am. Diabetes Assn., 1996. Home: 7214 Rustic Valley Dr Dallas TX 75248 Office: U Tex Southwestern Med Ctr Dept Endocrinology 5323 Harry Hines Blvd Dallas TX 75235

JICK, BRYAN, gynecologist; b. L.A., Apr. 13, 1957; s. John Joseph and Anita Dora (Overbach) J.; m. Marina Rabinovich, June 10, 1984; children: Andrew, Kevin. BA summa cum laude, UCLA, 1979; MD, U. Calif., San Diego, 1984. Diplomate Am. Bd. Ob-Gyn. Resident, intern dept. ob/gyn. qaiser Found. Hosp., L.A., 1984-88; pvt. practice Glendale, Calif., 1988-89, Pasadena, Calif., 1990—; spkr. in field. Contbr. articles to profl. jours. Fellow Am. Coll. Ob-Gyn. (cognate award for continuing med. edn. 1993, 96); mem. AMA (physician recognition award for continuing edn. 1990, 91, 94), Calif. Med. Assn., Soc. Laparoendoscopic Surgeons, L.A. County Med. Assn., L.A. Ob/gyn. Soc., Phi Beta Kappa, Phi Eta Sigma. Republican. Jewish. Office: 800 S Fairmount Ave # 410 Pasadena CA 91105-3154

JILCOTT, RUPERT WADSWORTH, III, internist; b. Rocky Mount, N.C., Dec. 28, 1947; s. Rupert Wadsworth Jr. and Annie Ruth (McMillan) J.; m. Frances Norfleet Garriss, Apr. 22, 1975; children: Louisa Monroe, Olivia Norfleet. AB in Chemistry, U. N.C., 1970; MD, Emory U., 1974. Diplomate Am. Bd. Internal Medicine. Ptnr. Kinston (N.C.) Internists, 1977-87; pvt. practice Kinston, 1987—; pres. Lenoir-Greene Med. Soc., Kinston, 1980s; dept. medicine chief Lenoir Meml. Hosp., Kinston, 1988. Bd. dirs. Am. Cancer Soc., N.C. chpt., Lenoir County Hist. Assn., N.C. Symphony, Lenoir County chpt. Mem. AMA, Am. Soc. Internal Medicine, N.C. Med. Soc., N.C. Soc. of Medicine, Rotary Club, Phi Beta Kappa, Phi Eta Sigma, Alpha Delta Epsilon. Episcopalian. Home: 1001 Harvey Cir Kinston NC 28501-3642 Office: PO Box 1315 Kinston NC 28503-1315

JILHEWAR, ASHOK, gastroenterologist; b. Nanded, Maharashtra, India, Jan. 30, 1947; came to U.S., 1977; naturalized 1987; BS, Marathwada U., Aurangabad, India, 1970; MB, Marathwada U., 1970; MD, Govt. Med. Coll., Aurangabad, 1970. Diplomate Am. Bd. Internal Medicine, Am. Bd. Gastroenterology, Am. Bd. Geriatric Medicine, Am. Bd. Quality Assurance and Utilization Rev. Physicians. Rotatory intern Med. Coll. Hosp., Aurangabad, India, 1968-70; resident St. Luke's Hosp. and Royal infirmary, Huddersfeild, Bolton, Eng., 1970-72; med. registrar internal medicine Gen. Hosp., Sligo, Ireland, 1973-77; chief resident PG1 and internal medicine U. Health Scis.-Chgo. Med. Sch. and VA Hosp., 1977-79; clin. instr. U. Heath Scis.-Chgo. Med. Sch., 1978-79; fellow in gastroenterology Michael Reese Hosp., Chgo., 1980-81; mem. exec. com. Meth. Hosp., Chgo, 1985-90, chmn. dept. med., 1988-90; mem. staff dept. medicine Grant Hosp., Chgo., 1986—; lectr. preventive and social medicine Med. Coll., Aurangabad, 1970; mem. exec. com. Meth. Hosp. Chgo., 1985-90, v.p. med. staff, 1987-88, treas., sec. 1985-87, chmn. dept. medicine, 1988-90; med. dir. approved homr for intermediace care nursing home, 1986-95; med. advisor Office Hearings and Appeals, HHS, 1985—; med. reviewer Ill. Med. Rev. Orgn., 1993—, Crescent Cmty. Found. for Med. Care, 1994—. Fellow Royal Coll. Physicians Can., Am. Coll. Internat. Physicians; mem. AMA, ACP, Am. Gastroenterol. Assn., Royal Coll. Physicians U.K., Royal Coll. Physicians Ireland, Ill. State Med. Assn., Chgo. Med. Soc. (PRO study com., fee mediation subcom. 1992). Office: North Park Stomach Clinic 5393 N Milwaukee Ave Chicago IL 60630-1251

JIM, EDWARD L.S., surgeon; b. Wailuku, Maui, Hawaii, Sept. 26, 1929; s. A.K. and Ethel (Tam) J.; m. Mardie C. Sughrue, Oct. 8, 1966; children: Edward E., Gregory R. MD, U. Chgo., 1955. Diplomate Am. Bd. Surgery. Intern Kings County Hosp., Bklyn., 1955-56; resident in surgery St. Vincent's Hosp., N.Y.C., 1956-58, 60-62; fellow in cancer surgery Meml. Hosp., N.Y.C., 1962-63; clin. instr. surgery NYU, N.Y.C., 1961-62; asst. clin. prof. surgery U. Hawaii Sch. Medicine, Honolulu, 1967-80, assoc. prof., 1981-93, clin. prof., 1994—; pvt. practice Honolulu, 1963—; mem. staff, chief oncology svc. Queen's Med. Ctr., 1969-70. Capt. USAFMC, 1958-60. Fellow ACS; mem. AMA, Soc. Head and Neck Surgeons, Am. Soc. for Head and Neck Surgery, Hawaii Med. Assn., Hawaiian Surg. Assn. (past pres.), Honolulu Rose Soc. Roman Catholic. Office: PO Box 10431 Honolulu HI 96816

JIMENEZ, ALFONSO FERNANDEZ, family practice physician; b. Mountain View, Calif., May 28, 1963; s. Efren and Gabriela (Fernandez) J.; m. Kimberly Marie Mann, Aug. 24, 1985 (div. Mar. 1994); m. Julie Ann Bruce, Apr. 2, 1994; 1 child, Aaron. BA, So. Calif. Coll., Costa Mesa, 1987; DO, Mich. State U., 1992. Diplomate Am. Bd. Family Practice. Intern Los Angeles County-Harbor UCLA Med. Ctr., Torrance, Calif., 1992-93; resident in famlity practice U. Hawaii, Mililani, 1994-96; physician Homeless Project, Harbor-UCLA Med. Ctr., 1992—; clk. Am. Indian Clinic, Bellflower, Calif., 1992—; student coord. St. John's (Mich.) Clinic, 1990—. Recipient scholarships and fellowships. Mem. AMA, Am. Acad. Family Physicians, Am. Coll. Osteo. Family Physicians, Am. Osteo. Assn., Hawaii Acad. Family Physicians. Office: U Hawaii Dept Family Practice 95-390 Kuahelani Ave Mililani HI 96789

JIMENEZ, KATHRYN FISHER, nurse, patient educator; b. Indiana, Pa., Nov. 23, 1948; d. Homer Leonard Fisher and Ruth Maxine (Foltz) Barclay; m. Adalberto Beltran Jimenez, Apr. 24, 1971; 1 child, Adalberto Jr. AAS in Nursing, Borough Manhattan C.C., 1982. RN, N.Y.; cert. BCLS Am. Heart Assn. Dietary cons. Indiana Hosp., 1966-68; LPN Brookdale Hosp. Med. Ctr., Bklyn., 1970-79, staff nurse, 1982—, asst. head nurse diabetes edn., 1990—; presenter workshops on diabetes mgmt.; presenter at profl. confs. Mem. Am. Assn. Diabetes Educators (cert.), Am. Diabetes Assn. Office: Brookdale Hosp Med Ctr 1 Brookdale Plz Brooklyn NY 11212-3139

JINDRAK, KAREL FRANCIS, pathologist, researcher, educator; b. Merin, Czechoslovakia, Mar. 29, 1926; came to U.S., 1967; s. Frantisek and Marie (Vetesnik) J.; m. Heda Kult, Jan. 6, 1951; 1 child, Heda. MD, Charles U. Med. Sch., Prague, Czechoslovakia, 1950, PhD, 1963. Diplomate Am. Bd. Anatomic and Clinical Pathology. Asst. prof. pathology Charles U. Med. Sch., 1956-65; pathologist Rsch. Inst. for Pharmacy and Biochemistry, Prague, 1965-67; researcher U. Hawaii, Honolulu, 1967-68; resident in pathology Mt. Sinai Hosp., N.Y.C., 1969-71; attending pathologist Meth. Hosp., Bklyn., 1971—; dir. dept. pathology Czechoslovakian Hosp., Vietnam, 1957-60; clin. asst. prof. pathology SUNY, Bklyn., 1973—. Co-author: (with Alicata J.E. Jindrak) Angiostrongylosis in the Pacific and Southeast Asia, 1970, (with H. Jindrak) Sing, Clean Your Brain, and Stay Sound and Sane, 1986. Capt. M.C., Czechoslovakian Army, 1951-56. Recipient Spl. award Czechoslovakian Ministry Health, 1951. Fellow Am. Coll. Pathologists. Office: Meth Hosp 506 6th St Brooklyn NY 11215-3609

JOBE, JARED BRUCE, psychologist; b. Oklahoma City, Feb. 12, 1951; s. James P. and Norma D. (Preston) J.; m. Lynne Toncheff, Aug. 9, 1974 (div. Aug. 1992); 1 child, Jocelyn Catherine; m. Lisa Potts, Jan. 9, 1993; 1 child, James Walter. BA, U. Okla., 1972, MS, 1973, PhD, 1976. Vis. asst. prof. U. Okla., Norman, 1976-77; commd. capt. U.S. Army, 1977; research psychologist Combat Devels. Experimentation Command U.S. Army, Ft. Ord., Calif., 1977-79; research psychologist Research Inst. Environ. Medicine U.S. Army, Natick, Mass., 1979-82; dir. health and performance div. Research Inst. Environ. Medicine U.S. Army, Natick, 1983; ret. U.S. Army, 1983; research psychologist U.S. Army Research Inst., Ft. Knox, Ky., 1984-85; personnel psychologist U.S. Army, Ft. Monroe, Va., 1985-87; dir. collaborative research program Nat. Ctr. Health Statistics, Hyattsville, Md., 1987-95; chief adult psychol. devel. br. Nat. Inst. on Aging NIH, Bethesda, Md., 1995—. Editor Cognition and Survey Measurement, 1987-95; co-editor spl. issue on cognition and surveys Applied Cognitive Psychology, 1991; reviewer Sci., 1976, Annals Internal Medicine, 1982—, Jour. Behavioral Medicine, 1985—, Applied Cognitive Psychology, 1989—, Am. Jour. Pub. Health, 1989—, Jour. Am. Dietetic Assn., 1990—, Psychol. Bull., 1991—, Jour. Aging and Health, 1991—, Pub. Health Reports, 1991—, Am. Jour. Epidemiology, 1994—, Perceptual and Motor Skills, 1994—, Women's Health, 1995—, NSF, 1990—, Nat. Cancer Inst., 1995—; contbr. articles to profl. jours. Mem. APHA, Am. Psychol. Assn. (pres. Div. 19, 1990-91, sec.-treas. 1989), Washington Statis. Soc. (bd. dirs. 1991-94), Soc. Applied Rsch. in Memory and Cognition, Kappa Alpha. Episcopalian. Home: 13423 Rippling Brook Dr Silver Spring MD 20906-5379 Office: Nat Inst on Aging 7201 Wisconsin Ave Rm 533 Bethesda MD 20892-9205

JOBE, ROBERT LEE, cardiologist; b. Laredo, Tex., May 28, 1961; s. Robert E. and Linda B. (Gardner) J.; m. Donna M. Crump, Oct. 1, 1988; children: Robert Tyler, Lydia Audreanna. BS, U. N.C., 1983, MD, 1987. Diplomate Am. Bd. Internal Medicine. Resident in medicine Carolinas Med. Ctr., Charlotte, 1987-90; fellow in cardiology Vanderbilt U., Nashville, 1990-93; assoc. faculty Duke U., Durham, N.C., 1993—; attending physician Cabarrus Meml. Hosp., Concord, N.C., 1993-96, Rex Hosp., Raleigh, N.C., 1996—, Wake Med. Ctr., Raleigh, N.C., 1996—. Fellow Am. Coll. Cardiology; mem. Am. Heart Assn. Office: Capital Heart Assocs 2605 Blue Ridge Rd #320 Raleigh NC 27607

JOE, GEORGE WASHINGTON, clinical researcher, quantitative methodologist; b. Augusta, Ga., Feb. 22, 1943. BS, U. Ga., 1965, EdD, 1969. Rsch. scientist Inst. of Behavioral Rsch./Tex. Christian U., Ft. Worth, 1969-70, asst. prof., 1970-74, assoc. prof., 1974-83; rsch. scientist Tex. Christian U., 1989—; rsch. scientist behavioral rsch. program Tex. A&M U., College Station, 1983-89. Author monographs in field; contbr. articles to profl. jours., chpts. to books. Mem. Am. Edn. Rsch. Assn., Phi Beta Kappa, Phi Kappa Phi, Sigma Xi. Office: Tex Christian U PO Box 298740 Fort Worth TX 76129 also: PO Box 9482 Fort Worth TX 76147-2482

JOEHL, RAYMOND JOSEPH, surgeon, educator; b. Alton, Ill., July 20, 1948; s. Raymond Casper and Barbara Christine Joehl; m. Julia Nelle Garrels, ug. 28, 1970; children: Jacob, Samuel, Hillarie, Sarah, Claudia, Hannah. BA, U. Pa., 1970; MD, St. Louis U., 1974. Diplomate Am. Bd. Surgery. Resident in surgery Pa. State U., Hershey, 1974-79, rsch. fellow, 1979-80, from asst. to assoc. prof. surgery, 1980-85; from assoc. prof. to prof. surgery Northwestern U., Chgo., 1985-91, James R. Hines prof. surgery, 1993—; chief divsn. gen. surgery and dir. residency in surgery, attending surgeon Northwestern Meml. Hosp., Chgo., 1985—, Hershey Med. Ctr., 1980-85; chief surg. svc. VA Lakeside Med. Ctr., Chgo., 1987-95. Fellow ACS, Am. Surg. Assn.; mem. Soc. Univ. Surgeons, Soc. for Surgery Alimentary Tract, Alpha Omega Alpha. Episcopalian. Office: Northwestern Univ Dept Surgery 250 E Superior Ste 201 Chicago IL 60611-2914

JOERGER, JAY HERMAN, psychologist, entrepreneur; b. Freeport, N.Y., Sept. 23, 1957; s. Herman Alexander and Ellen Rose (Becker) J.; m. Diana Botero, Mar. 27, 1993; 1 child, Nicholas Alexander. BS, Union U., 1980; MA, Colgate U., 1981; EdD, Columbia U., 1987. Diplomate Am. Bd. Profl. Disability Cons.; lic. psychologist, N.Y.; cert. addiction specialist, cert. profl. cons.; registered hypnotherapist. Drug abuse counselor Drug Abuse Coun., Norwich, N.Y., 1980-81; vocat. rehab. counselor Community Workshop, Glens Falls, N.Y., 1981-83; assoc. psychologist N.Y. State, Wingdale, N.Y., 1986-96; pres. Mentors Resource and Devel. Corp., 1991—; mem. group practice Ctr. Stress Reduction, 1993—, Carmel Psychol. Assocs., 1993-94; admission and hosp. privileges Four Winds Hosp., Katonah, N.Y., 1995—; cons., Somers, N.Y., 1988—; adj. asst. prof. Iona Coll., 1993-95; adj. prof. Lehman Coll., 1994—. Author: A Participant Manual for Mentally Ill Chemical Abusers, 1989, Living Successfully: A Self-Study Guide, 1993; co-author: The Physical, Psychological and Social Effects of Chemical Abuse—A Clinician's Workbook, 1994. Amateur radio operator, mil. affiliate radio operator Westchester Emergency Comm. Assn., Westchester County, 1983—; bd. dirs. Hudson Valley Fedn., Clintondale, N.Y., 1987-88. Recipient Excellence in Psychology award Med. Staff Orgn., Harlem Valley Psychologists, 1990. Mem. APA, Am. Coll. Forensic Examiners (life), Am. Bd. Profl. Disability Cons. (life), Acad. Profl. Cons. and Advisors, Family Firm Inst., N.Y. State Psychol. Assn. (sec.-treas. addiction divsn. 1993-95, liaison managed care task force 1994-95), Westchester County Psychol. Assn. (pres. indsl. orgn. divsn. 1992-95), Acad. Profl.Cons. and Advisors. Home and Office: Rural Rte 2 120 Krystal Dr Somers NY 10589-9778

JOEST, SUSAN MARIE, health information executive; b. Connersville, Ind., Feb. 6, 1951; d. William Lewis Linke and Fredonna Marie (Roach) Stine; m. Gerald R. Joest, June 29, 1968 (div.); children: David M., Heather N. BS in Med. Rec. Adminstrn., East Ctrl. U., 1982. Registered rec. adminstr. Am. Health Info. Mgmt. Assn. Dir. med. recs. Logan County Health Ctr., Guthrie, Okla., 1982-84, Woodford Hosp., Versailles, Ky., 1984—; cons. med. recs. Wayne County Hosp., Monticello, Ky., 1984-92. Mem. Alpha Ci. Home: 2305 Whitewater Blvd Connersville IN 47331

JOFFE, RALF, health facility administrator; b. Berlin, Germany, Sept. 3, 1950; came to U.S., 1967; s. Arthur and Raisa J. BS in Biology, Aquinas Coll., 1972; MS in Biology, Wayne State U., 1974; MPH, U. Mich., 1982; DO, Coll. Osteo. Medicine, 1987. Instr. biology Wayne County C.C., Detroit, 1974-82; assoc. dir. dept. emergency medicine Highland Hosp., Rochester, N.Y., 1992-93, Lima (Ohio) Meml. Hosp., 1993-95; med. dir. employee health, chmn. dept. emergency medicine St. Francis Hosp., Greenville, S.C., 1995—. Mem. AMA, ACOFP, ACEP, Am. Osteo. Assn., Wild Springs Med. Soc. Home: PO Box 27175 Greenville SC 29616-2175 Office: St Francis Hosp 1 St Francis Way Greenville SC 29601

JOHANNESSEN, LEIF BERTRAM, orthodontist, psychotherapist; b. Oslo, Aug. 25, 1925; came to U.S., 1945; s. Jens W. and Bernthine (Aspevold) J.; m. Berit Hem, Mar. 27, 1947; children: Erik B., Lars, Nils H., Ingrid K., Sigrid L. Examen Artium in Psychology, Hegdehaugen Coll., Oslo, 1944. DMD Mass., Calif., Maine, N.H., Norway. Dir. dental health Norway Pub. Health Svc., Tromsdalen, Norway, 1949-50; intern Forsyth Dental Ctr., Boston, 1951-52; Lt., Norwegian Dental Svc. Norway Royal Navy, Horten, Norway, 1950-51; vis. pedodontist Perkins Sch. for Blind, Watertown, Mass., 1952-60; pvt. practice orthdontist, psychotherapist Needham, Mass., 1952-80; rsch. assoc. Harvard U. Sch. Dental Medicine, Boston, 1957-60; pvt. practice orthdontist, psychotherapist Wakefield, N.H., 1983—. Contbr. articles to profl. jours. Chief fundraiser New Eng. Lutheran Ch., 1965, Boy Scouts Am., Needham, Mass., 1964. Capt. USPHS Dental Corps, 1953-55, Korea. Mem. ADA, Norumbega Lodge Sons of Norway (charter), Omicron Kappa Upsilon. Republican. Lutheran, Congregational. Home and Office: L-B Farm Gage Hill Rd Wakefield NH 03872

JOHANSEN, BARBARA B., social worker, consultant; b. N.Y.C.; d. William R. and Kathleen D. (McGowan) Busse; m. John C. Johansen; children: Kathleen, Paul (dec.). BS, Fordham U., 1956, MSW, 1988; cert. in psychosocial Oncology, Meml. Sloan Kettering Med. Ctr, 1990. Lic. social worker, Conn., N.Y. Coord. family edn. Diocese of Bridgeport, Conn.; exec. dir. Change of Pace Experiences, New Canaan, Conn., 1983-89; med. social worker Bridgeport Hosp., 1986-87, Greenwich (Conn.) Hosp., 1988—; mem. adv. bd. Vol. Ctr., Stamford, Conn., 1986-94, Ctr. for Hope, Darien, Conn., 1990—; mem. com. Hole in the Wall Gang Fund, Inc., New Haven, 1989-94. Mem. social work com. Am. Cancer Soc. of Fairfield County, Westport, Conn., 1988—. Recipient Make a Difference award YWCA, 1986, Golden Rule award J.C. Penney Co., Inc., 1986, Community Leader award Women in Mgmt. Inc., 1986; named Woman of Yr. AAUW New Canaan, 1992. Mem. NASW (diplomate in clin. social work), Am. Assn. Pediatric Oncology Social Workers, Nat. Assn. Oncology Social Workers. Home: 23 Green Meadow Ln New Canaan CT 06840-6823 Office: Greenwich Hosp Perryridge Rd Greenwich CT 06830

JOHANSON, ORIN WILLIAM, social worker, consultant; b. Salt Lake City, June 23, 1946; s. Nephi E. and Margaret (Bauman) J.; m. Agnes Lindstrom, Oct. 8, 1986; children: Chad Zierenberg, Jason Zierenberg, Amanda. BA in Sociology, U. Utah, 1971, MSW, 1973. Lic. clin. social worker, cert. social worker, marriage and family counselor, Utah. Youth counselor Utah Boy's Ranch, Salt Lake City, 1970-73; caseworker Ettie Lee Homes for Boys, Fontana, Calif., 1973-74; social worker Salt Lake City Schs., 1974—, coord. peer leadership team West High Sch., 1986—; assoc. prof. U. Utah Grad. Sch. Social Work, Salt Lake City, 1975-76, Westminster Coll., Salt Lake City, 1988; cons. on drug and alcohol edn., 1977—; prevention specialist Utah Div. Substance Abuse, Salt Lake City, summer 1982; cons. Ctr. for Ednl. Devel., San Antonio, 1980-86, Kans. Sch. Team Tng., Wichita, 1980-86; trainer Improv Teen Theatre, Salt Lake City, 1980—, K-12 Drug and Alcohol Edn., Salt Lake City, 1978—, Parent-Teen Alternative Program, Salt Lake City, 1984—. County and state del. Salt Lake County Dem. Com., 1968-73; bd. dirs. Community Counseling Ctr., Salt Lake City, 1982-85, Utah Assn. for Children's Therapy, 1980. Mem. NEA, Utah Edn. Assn., Salt Lake Tchrs. Assn., Collegiate Assn. for Devel. and Renewal Educators, Kans. Assn. for Prevention Profls. Home: 1226 Moray Ct Park City UT 84060-6901 Office: West H S 241 N 300 W Salt Lake City UT 84103-1120

JOHN, GERALD WARREN, hospital pharmacist; b. Salem, Ohio, Feb. 16, 1947; s. Harold Elba and Ruth Springer (Pike) J.; m. Jean Ann Marie Orris, Nov. 5, 1977; children—Patrick Warren, Jeanette Lynn. B.S.Ph., Ohio No. U., 1970; M.S., U. Md., 1974. Registered pharmacist, Ohio, Md. Staff pharmacist North Columbiana County Community Hosp., Salem, 1970-72; asst. resident in hosp. pharmacy U. Md. Hosp., Balt., 1972-73, sr. resident, 1973-74, chmn. patient care pharmacies, 1974-76; dir. pharmacy Ohio Valley Hosp., Steubenville, Ohio, 1976—; preceptor profl. externship program Ohio No. U. Sch. Pharmacy, 1977—; adj. clin. instr. practical experience program Duquesne U. Sch. Pharmacy, 1976—. Columnist Weirton Daily Times, 1990-94. Trustee, v.p. Valley Hospice Inc., 1985—. Named Hosp. Pharmacist of Yr., Md. Soc. Hosp. Pharmacists, 1976, Outstanding Young Man of Am., U.S. Jaycees, 1977. Fellow Am. Soc. Cons. Pharmacists; mem. Am. Soc. Hosp. Pharmacists, Ohio Soc. Hosp. Pharmacists, Jefferson County Acad. Pharmacy, Southeastern Ohio Soc. Hosp. Pharmacists (pres. 1985-87), Rho Chi, Phi Eta Sigma. Methodist. Mem. adv. bd. Contemporary Pharmacy Practice, 1977-83.

JOHNS, DAVID LEE, psychotherapist; b. Binghamton, N.Y., July 9, 1951; s. Carl Lee and Dorothy (Heron) J.; children from previous marriage: Stefanie Leigh, David Carl; m. Dawn Waldorf, Jan. 15, 1993; 1 child, Tanner Evan. BS, Western Ill. U., 1976, MS in Edn., 1979. Cert. mental health counselor, Fla.; nat. bd. cert. clin. hypnotherapist. Psychotherapist Seminole Community Mental Health Ctr., Altamonte Springs, Fla., 1979-81; psychologist III, Winter Haven (Fla.) Hosp., 1981-86; pvt. practice Winter Park, Fla., 1986—; clin. coord. The Allen Group Employee Assistance Program, 1996; estab. Bereaved Survivors of Homicide Treatment Program, 1991; clin. coord. The Allen Group Employee Assistance Program, 1996. Vice pres. mental health Orange County Assn. for Counseling and Devel., 1991—; mem. Orange County Coalition for Victim Svcs., 1990—. Mem. ACA, Anxiety Disorders Assn. Am. (profl.), Nat. Alliance for Mentally Ill (coord., establisher Sebring Fla. chpt. 1985-86). Democrat. Presbyterian. Office: 1201 Louisiana Ave Winter Park FL 32789-2340

JOHNS, JANET SUSAN, physician; b. Chgo., July 18, 1941; d. Nicholas C. and Doris Ann (Douglas) J.; m. Harlan R. Bullard; children: George, Sam. AB, Ind. U., 1963, MD, 1966. Home: 3510 Woodcliff Dr Lafayette IN 47905 Office: Purdue U Student Health 1826 Push West Lafayette IN 47905

JOHNS, J.C., health facility administrator, internist; b. Cleve., May 2, 1935; s. John I. and Marian F. (Farinacci) J.; m. Stephanie Behrle, Oct. 30, 1981; children: Linda Marie Johns Bradley, John B., Diane Marie Johns Gilger. BS, John Carroll U., 1957; MD, Loyola U., Chgo., 1961. Intern Akron Gen. Hosp., Akron, 1961-62; resident in internal medicine Akron Gen. Hosp., Rochester, N.Y., 1962-65; pvt. practice Akron, 1965-91; v.p., corp. med. dir. Preferred Care, Rochester, N.Y., 1991—; chmn. dept. med. edn. Akron Gen. Med. Ctr., 1970-82; assoc. dean clin. affairs Northeastern Univs. Coll. Medicine, Akron, 1974-91, assoc. prof. medicine, 1976-91; med. dir. Health Guard, Akron, 1982-86; med. dir. for alt. sys. Blue Cross/Blue Shield of Ohio, Cleve., 1986-91. Bd. dirs. Am. Diabetes Assn., Crystal City, Va., 1980-86; mem. Cmty. Tech. Adv. Com., Rochester, 1993. Recipient Quality Achievement award Blue Cross/Blue Shield Assn., Chgo., 1989; named to Soc. Disting. Physicians, Akron Gen. Med. Ctr., 1995. Mem. Fairlawn Country Club, Akron City Club, Rotary. Home: 90 Pebble Brook Dr Mendon NY 14506 Office: Preferred Care 259 Monroe Ave Rochester NY 14607

JOHNS, MICHAEL MARIEB EDWARD, otolaryngologist, academic administrator; b. Detroit, Jan. 27, 1942; s. Trina Lou DelCampo; children: Christina, Michael. BS, Wayne State U., 1964, Grad. Biol. Sci., 1965; MD with distinction, U. Mich., 1969. Diplomate Am. Bd. Otolaryngology. Intern Univ. Hosp., Ann Arbor, Mich., 1969-70, resident in otolaryngology, 1971-75; resident in gen. surgery St. Joseph's Mercy Hosp., Ann Arbor, 1970-71; asst. prof. U. Va. Med. Ctr., Charlottesville, 1977-79, assoc. prof., 1979-82, prof., 1982-84; prof. Johns Hopkins U. Sch. Medicine, Balt., 1984—, dean med. faculty, v.p. medicine, 1990—; co-chmn. Md. Sci. Week Blue Ribbon Panel, Balt., 1992—' chmn-elect Coun. of Deans. Co-author: Head and Neck Cancer, 1990; contbr. articles to profl. jours. Grantee Robert Wood Johnson Found., 1992, NIH, 1995. Mem. Inst. Medicine, Cosmos Club, Ctr. Club. Office: Emory U Robert W Woodruff Health Scis Ctr 1440 Clifton Rd Ste 400 Atlanta GA 30327

JOHNS, RICHARD JAMES, physician, educator; b. Pendleton, Oreg., Aug. 19, 1925; s. James Shanard and Pearl (McKenna) J.; m. Carol Greacen Johnson; children: Richard Clark, Robert Shanard, James Ashmore. BS, U. Oreg., 1947; MD, Johns Hopkins U., 1948. Diplomate Am. Bd. Internal Medicine. Intern Johns Hopkins Hosp., Balt., 1948-49, asst. resident, 1951-53, fellow in medicine, 1953-55, resident, 1955-56, instr., 1955-57, physician, 1956—, asst. prof., 1957-61, assoc. prof., 1961-66, asst. dean admissions, 1962-66, prof. medicine, 1966—, dir. subdept. biomed. engring., 1966-70, mem. adv. bd., prin. profl. staff Applied Physics Lab., 1967—, prof., dir. dept. biomed. engring., 1970-91, disting. svc. prof., 1991—; bd. visitors Sch. Engring., Duke U., 1986—; chmn. adv. com. Divisional Health Scis. and Tech. Harvard-MIT, 1987-92; mem. com. sci., engring. and pub. policy NAS, 1988-90; mem. sci. adv. com. GM, 1991—. Sec., vice chmn., chmn. med. bd. Myasthenia Gravis Found.; trustee Am. Bd. Clin. Engring., pres., 1976-83; bd. dirs. Whitaker Found., 1991-94. Capt. M.C. AUS, 1949-51. Fellow ACP, AAAS, Am. Inst. for Biol. & Med. Engring. (founding), Royal Soc. Medicine; mem. Am. Clin. and Climatol. Assn. (v.p. 1977-78, sec.-treas. 1979-85, pres. 1986-87), Am. Soc. Clin. Investigation, Assn. Am. Physicians, Biomed. Engring. Soc. (bd. dirs. 1972-75, pres. 1978-79), IEEE (pres. group on engring. in medicine and biology 1970-72), Inst. Medicine NAS (coun. 1987-90), Johns Hopkins Med. Soc. (pres. 1968-69), Interurban Clin. Club (pres. 1980-81), Peripatetic Club, Caduceus Club, Sigma Xi, Alpha Omega Alpha, Phi Kappa Psi, Nu Sigma Nu, Tau Beta Pi. Clubs: Annapolis Yacht; Elkridge; Johns Hopkins (v.p. 1969-70). Home: 203 E Highfield Rd Baltimore MD 21218-1105 Office: Johns Hopkins U Sch Med Rm 124 720 Rutland Ave Baltimore MD 21205-2196

JOHNS, WILLIAM HOWARD, psychiatrist, neurologist; b. Hamilton, Ohio, Apr. 18, 1941; s. Howard William and Martha (Sleigh) J.; m. Catherine Marie O'Keefe, May 30, 1982; children: Howard William II, Stephanie Marie. AB, Princeton U., 1963; MS in Anatomy, U. Cin., 1968; DO, Kirksville (Mo.) Coll. Osteo. Medicine, 1973; ed. spl. student program, Topeka Inst. for Psychoanalysis, 1984-90. Instr. anatomy Kirksville Coll. Osteo. Medicine, 1967-73; intern Grandview Hosp., Dayton, 1973-74; resident in neurology Cleve. Clinic Hosp., 1974-77; asst. prof. neurology Ohio U. Coll. Osteo. Medicine, Athens, 1977-78; pvt. practice neurology Dayton, Ohio, 1978-82; resident psychiatry The Menninger Found., Topeka, Kans., 1982-85, psychiatrist, staff psyciatrist, 1985—, asst. team leader, 1985-89; team leader The Menninger Found., 1989—, comprehensive out-patient evaluations, 1985-89; faculty mem. Karl Menninger Sch. Psychiatry, Topeka, 1990-95; pvt. practice psychiatry, 1995—, pvt. practice neurology, 1996—; dir. Psychotic Disorders Study Program, 1993-95, neuropsychiatry consultations, 1992-95; pvt. practice psychiatry, 1996—; clin. asst. prof. neurology Wright State U. Sch. Medicine, Dayton, 1979-82, Ohio U. Coll. Osteo. Medicine, Athens, 1979-82, W.Va. Sch. Osteo. Medicine, Lewisburg, 1979-82. Recipient Outstanding Clin. Faculty award Dayton region Ohio U. Coll. Osteo. Medicine, 1982, Sydney M. Kanev Meml. award Am. Coll. Neuropsychiatrists, 1985, Outstanding Clun. Faculty award Dayton region Ohio Coll. Osteo. Medicine. Mem. Am. Acad. Neurology, Am. Neuropsychiatric Assn. Home: 517 SW Danbury Ln Topeka KS 66606-2229 Office: The Menninger Found PO Box 829 Topeka KS 66601-0829

JOHNSON, A. PATRICIA, nursing administrator; b. Jersey City, Mar. 21, 1945; d. Frank Stanley and Caroline Rose (Penk) Caskey; m. Thomas Peter Johnson, Mar. 2, 1968; children: Wayne, Victoria, Scott. BSN, Syracuse U., 1966; MA in Edn., Seton Hall U., 1976; MA in Nursing, NYU, 1982. Staff nurse Overlook Hosp., Summit, N.J., 1966, N.Y. Hosp.-Cornell Med. Ctr., N.Y.C., 1966-67; instr. Jackson Meml. Hosp. Sch. Nursing, Miami, Fla., 1967-68; instr., dean Muhlenberg Regional Med. Ctr., Plainfield, N.J., 1968-85, v.p. nursing affairs, 1987-92; assoc. clin. prof. Union County Coll., Cranford, N.J., 1975-85; v.p. chief oper. office Ctr. for Health Edn., Inc., Plainfield, 1985-87; v.p. patient care svcs. New Britain (conn.) Gen. Hosp., 1992—; fellow Johnson and Johnson program Wharton Sch., U. Pa. Co-author: Redesign of Patient Care Delivery, 1990. Mem. Am. Orgn. Nursing Exec., N.J. Orgn. Nursing Exec., N.J. State Nurses Assn., N.J. League for Nursing, Sigma Theta Tau (Upsilon chpt.), Kappa Delta Pi (Beta Pi chpt.). Home: 1090 Fallbrook Ln Lewisville NC 27023-8628 Office: New Britain Gen Hosp 100 Grand St New Britain CT 06052-2016

JOHNSON, ALLEN FRANK, psychotherapist; b. Bridgeport, Conn., Sept. 25, 1944; s. Gustav Folke and Alice Helena (Nelsen) J.; m. Lori Haak, May 23, 1992; 1 child, Zachary M. BA, CUNY, 1966; MSW, NYU, 1968; PhD, Smith Coll., 1979. Lic. ind. clin. social worker, marriage and family therapist, Mass. Supervising social worker Salvation Army Family Svc. Bur., N.Y.C., 1968-71; dir. Queens office Big Bros. of N.Y.C., 1971-72; dir. social work tng., supr. Worcester State Hosp. Mass. Dept. Mental Health, 1974-77; dir. Psychol. Collaborative, Worcester, 1977-84, Auburn (Mass.) Family Inst., 1984—; cons. Hubbard Hosp., Webster, Mass., 1975-77; field placement supr. Hunter Coll., 1971-72, Boston Coll., Boston U., U. Conn., 1991-92, Gordon-Conwell Theol.Sem., others; instr. continuing edn. Clark U., Worcester, 1974—. Sr. editor Jour. Pediatric Social Work, 1975-85; editorial bd. Christian Parenting Today, Jour. Psychology and Christianity, 1987—, Jour. Am. Assn. Spinal Cord Injury Psychologists and Social Workers, Psychosocial Process, 1989—; columnist Worcester Telegram and Gazette, 1987—. Mem. Mass. Coalition of Citizens with Disabilities, 1974—; advocate for physically, mentally and emotionally challenged. Fellow Am. Orthopsychiat. Assn.; mem. Internat. Assn. for Pediatric Social Svcs. (pres. 1980-82), Am. Assn. for Marriage and Family Therapy, Christian Assn. for Psychol. Studies, Am. Assn. Christian Counselors, Spina Bifida Assn. Am. Democrat. Office: Auburn Family Inst 6 South Ter Auburn MA 01501-2816

JOHNSON, ALLEN L., health facility administrator; b. Edmonton, Alta., Can.; m. Karen; 4 children. BA in Econs., U. Calgary, Alberta, Can., 1971; MHA, U. Minn., 1974. Hosp. cons., pers. officer, asst. adminstr. Alta., Can.; v.p., COO Henry Ford Hosp. Svcs. Corp., Detroit, 1972-83, also adminstr. external programs; pres., CEO St. Vincent Med. Ctr., Toledo, 1979-85, Farley Health Care Corp., 1982-85, St. Vincent Corp. Svcs. Inc., Toledo, 1982-85, Med. Ctr. Del., 1986—. Chmn. bd. dirs. United Way of Del.; mem. Gov. appointed State Edn. Reform com.; mem. adv. bd. Del. Hospice; sec., mem. exec. com. Premier Health Alliance. Mem. Am. Heart Assn. (chmn. bd. dirs. Del. chpt.), Am. Hosp. Assn., Assn. Del. Hosps. (chmn. bd. dirs., chmn. exec. com.), Del. Roundtable, Inc. (treas.), Can. Coll. Health Svc. Execs. Office: Med Ctr of Del PO Box 1668 501 W 14th St Wilmington DE 19899-1668*

JOHNSON, ANNETTE MADELEINE, health administrator, b. Windsor, Ont., Can., Nov. 17, 1950; d. Walter E.A. and Madeleine St. George (Wilson) J. B.S., Mich. State U., 1972; cert. Tuskegee Inst., 1973; M.S. in Health Edn., Columbia U. Tchrs. Coll., 1977; postgrad. Hunter Coll., 1980-81, Colum doctoral program in health edn. Tchrs. Coll., 1988 Registered dietitian; cert. health edn. specialist. Clin. nutritionist, health educator Whitney M. Young Health Ctr., Albany, N.Y., 1977-80; nutritional cons. N.Y. State Office of Aging, 1980-81; nutritional edn. cons. WIC program N.Y. State Health Dept., 1981-84, dir. edn., 1984-87, edn. coord. AIDS inst., 1984-87, with minority mgmt. devel. fellowship program, 1987-88, met. regional coord. cancer svcs. program, 1988-94, dir. N.Y. state sch. health program, 1994—; nutritional cons. N.Y.C. Council Chs. Ctr. for the City, 1985-87, others. Mem. steering com. Black Women's Health Project, N.Y.C., 1985-86, bd. dirs.; co-chmn. Coalition of Blacks in the Nutrition Profession, N.Y.C., 1983-84; bd. dirs. Self Help for Women with Breast/Ovarian Cancer. Mem. Am. Dietetic Assn., Am. Pub. Health Assn., Nat. Black Caucus Health Workers, Nat. Women's Health Network, Soc. Pub. Health Educators (chpt. del.), Internat. Union Pub. Health and Edn., Phi Delta Kappa, Pi Lambda Theta (chpt. sec. 1977), Nat. Assn. Female Execs., Bus. and Profl. Women USA (dist. chmn. 1986). Democrat. Avocations: travel; reading; collecting ceramics and glass; dance; theatre. Home: 357 Morris St Apt 6 Albany NY 12208-3366 Office: NY State Dept Health Empire State Pla Corning Tower Rm 821 Albany NY 12237

JOHNSON, BARRY LEE, public health research administrator; b. Sanders, Ky., Oct. 24, 1938; s. Otto Lee and Sarah Josephine (Deatherage) J.; m. Billie Reed, Aug. 19, 1960; children—Lee, Clay, Scott, Reed, Sarah. B.S., U. Ky., 1960; M.S., Iowa State U., 1962, Ph.D., 1967. Elec. engr. USPHS, Cin., 1960-70; bioengr. EPA, Cin., 1970-71; bioengr. Nat. Inst. for Occupational Safety and Health, HHS, Cin., 1971-77, rsch. adminstr., 1978-86; asst. adminstr. Agy. for Toxic Substances and Disease Registry, 1986—; also asst. surgeon gen., 1990—. Editor: Behavioral Toxicology, 1974, Neurotoxicology, 1986; editor Neurotoxicology, 1979, Archives Environ. Health jour., 1980, Toxicology and Industrial Health, 1985, Prevention of Neurotoxic Illness, 1987, Advances in Neurobehavioral Toxicology, 1990, Jour. of Clean Tech. and Environ. Scis., 1991. Pres. S.E. Cin. Soccer Assn., 1978-80. Recipient Commendation medal USPHS, 1980, 84, Superior Performance medal USPHS, 1986, Meritorious Svc. award USPHS, 1988, Disting. Svc. medal Asst. Surgeon Gen., 1990; USPHS fellow 1962-65. Mem. Am. Pub. Health Assn., Am. Conf. Govt. Hygienists, Am. Assn. Clin. Toxicology, Internat. Conf. Occupational Health, Am. Coll. Toxicology, Soc. of Occupational and Environ. Health, Nat. Environ. Health Assn., Internat. Assn. for Exposure Analysis. Office: Agy for Toxic Substances and Disease Registry 1600 Clifton Rd NE Atlanta GA 30329-4018*

JOHNSON, BETTY ANNE, nurse; b. Centerville, Iowa, Sept. 14, 1924; d. Delazon Marion and Lucy Glen (Guernsey) Wilson; m. Vern William Johnson (dec. Oct. 1966); children: Richard Hugh, Russell William, John Allen. Grad., St. Joseph Sch. Nursing, Ottumwa, Iowa, 1946; BS in Health Arts, Coll. of St. Francis, Joliet, Ill., 1982. RN, Iowa. Tchr. Albany Sch., Bloomfield, Iowa, 1942-43; nurse Ottumwa Hosp., 1946-49, 78-83, Balboa Hosp., San Diego, 1949-50, Davis County Hosp., Bloomfield, Iowa, 1951-52, 74-78; nurse, pediatrics dept. St. Joseph Hosp., Ottumwa, 1967-73; nurse Glenwood (Iowa) State Hosp. for Retarded, 1973-74; substitute house parent Rainbow Acres, Ranch for Handicapped Adults, Camp Verde, Ariz., 1984-87; supr. Foothills Care Ctr., Cottonwood, Ariz, 1985-87; with Kachine Point Health Ctr., Sedona, Ariz, 1987-89; nurse East Seals East Camp, Va., 1990, Good Samaritan Care Ctr., Ottumwa, Iowa, 1991; day substitute Child Care Ctr., Dallas; RN Vista Woods, Ottumwa, Iowa, 1994-95; residential care nurse Rescare, Brookfield, Iowa, 1996—. Home: 425 S Willard St Ottumwa IA 52501-5032

JOHNSON, BOBBY J., JR., biochemist; b. Sherman, Tex., July 20, 1967; s. B.J. and Beverly Ann (Hines) J.; m. Karen Telschow, May 21, 1989. BS in Biochemistry, Tex. A&M, 1989. EMT-paramedic Wheaton (Md.) Vol. Rescue Squad, 1991-93; tchg. asst. Tex. Coll. Osteo. Med., Ft. Worth., 1994-95, undergrad. tchg. fellow, 1995—. Mem. AMA, Am. Osteo. Assn., Am. Acad. Osteo., Am. Coll. Emergency Physicians, Am. Coll. Osteo. Emergency Physicians., Sigma Sigma Phi, Psi Sigma Alpha. Democrat. Home: 3430 W 4th St # 2 Fort Worth TX 76107

JOHNSON, BRIAN, psychiatrist, psychoanalyst; b. Oceanside, N.Y., Jan. 22, 1952; s. Lauren Theodore and Virginia Loretta (Mutter) J.; m. Letitia Upton. BS, Columbia U., 1972; MD, N.Y. Med. Coll., Valhalla, 1976; Cand. in sychoanalysis, Boston Psychoanalytic Inst., 1980-89. Diplomate Am. Bd. Psychiatry. Intern Hoplem Hosp., 1976-77; resident Met. Hosp., N.Y.C., 1977-78; resident in psychiatry Cambridge (Mass.) Hosp., 1978-81; pvt. practice Newtonville, Mass., 1981—; clin. instr. Harvard Med. Sch., Boston. Contbr. articles to profl. jours. Mem. Am. Med. Soc. for Addictions, Am. Psychiatric Assn., Am. Psychoanalytic Assn., Mass. Psychiatric Soc., Boston Psychoanalytic Soc. Home and Office: 5 Park Pl Newton MA 02160-1910

JOHNSON, B(RUCE) CONNOR, biochemist, educator, consultant; b. Regina, Sask., Can., Apr. 28, 1911; came to U.S., 1937; s. Wilfred Connor and Edna Pearl (Young) J.; m. Elizabeth Marie Peterson, Sept. 1, 1940 (div.); children: Bruce Connor II, Peter Young, Stephen Paine, Elizabeth Carter (dec.), Christina Marie; m. Halina Victoria Bogdanska, Oct. 25, 1966; 1 child, Margaret Edna. BA in Chemistry, McMaster U., 1933, MA in Chemistry, 1934; PhD in Biochemistry, U. Wis., 1940. Chemist Can. Canners, Hamilton, Ont., 1934-37; DuPont fellow U. Ill., Urbana, 1940-42; rsch. biochemist Golden State Co., San Francisco, 1942-43; from asst. prof. to assoc. prof. U. Ill., Urbana, 1943-51, prof. biochemistry, 1951-65; prof., head dept. biochemistry and molecular biology U. Okla. Health Scis. Ctr., Oklahoma City, 1965-79, prof., 1979-82, prof. emeritus, 1982—; disting. career scientist Okla. Med. Rsch. Found., Oklahoma City, 1982—; rsch. scientist Inst. de Chimie Biologique, U. Strasbourg, France, 1971; mem., head biochemistry sect. Okla. Med. Rsch. Found., Oklahoma City, 1966-73, head vitamins and nutrition rsch., 1973-81; rsch. scientist dept. pediatrics Coll. Medicine, U. South Fla., St. Petersburg, 1985-87; mem. nutrition study sect. NIH, 1962-66; cons. Can. Sci. Svc., Winnipeg, Man. and Ottawa, Can., 1952, 64, Armour & C., Cen. Rsch. Labs., Chgo., 1957-63, Agrl. Rsch. Coun., Fedn. Rhodesia and Nyasaland, 1962, N.Mex. State U., Las Cruces, 1975, others; ofcl. U.S. del. Pres. Eisenhower's 2d Atoms for Peace Mission to S.Am., 1956, 2d UN Atoms for Peace Conf., Geneva, Switzerland, 1958, USAF, Dept. of Def. Symposium on Arctic Biology and Medicine, Fairbanks, Alaska, 1965, White House Conf. on Food and Nutrition, Washington, 1969, others; invited participant to numerous symposia including Gordon Conf. on Vitamins & Metabolism, New London, N.H., 1956, Workshop on Vitamin K Function, Internat. Nutrition Congress, San Diego, 1981, Internat. Conf. on Post-Translational Covalent Modification of Proteins for Function, Oklahoma City, 1982. Author: Methods of Vitamin Determination, 1948; editor: Post-Translational Modifications of Proteins, 1983; contbr. chpts. to 25 books, 1955-86; mem. editl. bd.: Jour. Nutrition, 1966-70; mem. sci. adv. bd.: Nat. Vitamin Found., 1953-56; contbr. numerous papers on nutrition and biochemistry to profl. publs. Pres. 1st Unitarian Ch. Oklahoma City, 1972, Alliance Française d'Oklahoma City, 1980. Recipient Nutrition Coun. award Am. Feed Mfrs. Assn., 1960, Purkyne medal Czech Acad. Sci., 1969; Guggenheim Found. fellow U. Reading, Eng., 1955, NSF sr. fellow Inst. de Chimie des Substances Naturelles, Nat. Ctr. Sci. Rsch., Gif-sur-Yvette, U. Paris, France, 1961-62. Fellow Am. Inst. Nutrition (mem. editl. bd. 1966-70, Osborne-Mendel award 1975); mem. AAAS, Am. Assn. Med. Colls., Internat. Haemostasis and Thrombosis Soc., Endocrine Soc., Biochem. Soc. (Gt. Britain), Am. Soc. for Biochemistry and Molecular Biology, Am. Chem. Soc., Soc. Exptl. Biology and Medicine. Office: Okla Med Rsch Found 825 NE 13th St Oklahoma City OK 73104

JOHNSON, CHARLES CHRISTOPHER, JR., consulting environmental engineer; b. Des Moines, Sept. 6, 1921; s. Charles C. and Haley Dale (Evans) J.; m. Betty Jean Tanner, Dec. 25, 1947; children: Charles Christopher III, Teresa Ilene. Student, Dowling Jr. Coll., Des Moines, 1941-42; BS in Civil Engring., Purdue U., 1947, MS, 1957. Diplomate: Am. Acad. Environ. Engrs.; Registered profl. engr., D.C., Md. Commd. jr. grade officer USPHS, 1947, advanced through ranks to asst. surgeon gen., 1968; chief sanitation facilities constrn. br. Div. Indian Health, 1960-66, chief office environ. health, 1966-67; adminstr. consumer protection and environ. health service HEW, 1968-69, adminstr. environ. health service, 1970; asso. exec. dir. Am. Pub. Health Assn., Washington, 1970-72; asst. commr. health for environ. health N.Y.C. Health Dept., 1967-68; v.p. research and devel. Washington Tech. Inst., 1973-74; resident mgr. Malcolm Pirnie, Inc., Washington and Silver Spring, Md., 1974-77; v.p. Malcolm Pirnie, Inc., 1977-79; founder, pres., chief exec. officer CC Johnson and Malhotra, P.C. (environ. engrs.), 1979—; adj. assoc. prof. N.Y. U. Sch. Environmental Medicine, 1967-68; cons. Booz, Allen & Hamilton, N.Y.C., 1967. Contbr. articles to profl. jours. Bd. dirs. Urban Am., Nat. Cath. Found., Episcopal Ch. Am., Washington, Community Health, Inc.; mem. adv. council Sch. Engring. Stanford U., 1970-74; mem. Nat. Capitol Planning Commn., 1971-74; tech. adv. group for municipal waste water systems EPA, 1973-75; mem. adv. council Sch. Engring., Purdue U., 1972-75; Commn. on Edn. for Health Adminstrn., 1972-74; mem., chmn. Nat. Drinking Water Adv. Council, 1975-81; mem. Md. Drinking Water Adv. Council, 1975, Adv. Com. Water Data for Public Use, U.S. Geol. Survey-Dept. Interior, 1979-80. Served with USMCR, 1942-46. Recipient Meritorious Pub. Svc. award Gov. D.C., 1967, Disting. Engring. Alumnus award Purdue U. Sch. Engring., 1969, Walter F. Snyder award Nat. San. Found.-Nat. Environ. Health Assn., 1977, Exceptional Achievement award HHS, 1989. Mem. NAE, Commd. Officers Assn., Am. Pub. Health Assn., Nat. Environ. Health Assn., Am. Waterworks Assn. (Fuller award 1990), Water Pollution Control Fedn. Home: 2801 New Mexico Ave NW Apt 1415 Washington DC 20007-3914 Office: 11510 Georgia Ave Silver Spring MD 20902-1925*

JOHNSON, CHRISTINE ANN, nurse; b. Omaha, Nebr., Aug. 23, 1951; d. Ralph James and Marlene (Marlenee) Matney; m. Timothy Carl Johnson, Aug. 1, 1970; children: Erik Carl, Christine Nicole. Cert. practical nurse, Met. Tech. Community Coll., 1973; BA cum laude, Creighton U., 1989. LPN, Nebr.; cert. pregnancy exercise instr.; cert. lactation cons. EKG technician Bishop Clarkson Meml. Hosp., Omaha, 1971-74, lic. practical nurse, 1978—, instr. pregnancy exercise, 1984-86, instr. sibling preparation, 1985-86, instr. breastfeeding, 1985-95; LPN Cons. in Cardiology, P.C., Omaha, 1974-78; tchr. asst. Creighton U. Dept. Psychology, Omaha, 1987-88; lactation cons. Bergan Mercy Med. Ctr., Omaha, 1994—; teaching asst. dept. psychology, child psychology, adolescent psychology, devel. psychology Creighton U., 1987-88. Assoc. editor (cons.' corner) Jour. Human Lactation, 1994—. Sec. United Meth. Women First United Meth. Ch., 1984-85, chmn. 1985-86; vol. Radio Talking Book, 1985; mem. Omaha Pub. Schs. Superintendent's Task Force on Human Growth and Devel., 1986. Mem. Internat. Lactation Cons. Assn., Psi Chi. Methodist. Home: 4618 N 129th Ave Omaha NE 68164-1708 Office: Bergan Mercy Med Ctr 7500 Mercy Rd Omaha NE 68124

JOHNSON, CHRISTY LYNN RODEHEAVER, nurse; b. Macon, Ga., Nov. 11, 1956; d. Charles Stewart and Dorothy (Roper) Rodeheaver; m. Herbert Clay Johnson Jr., June 5, 1974. ADN, Gordon Coll., 1977; cert. RN 1st asst., Delaware Community Coll., 1989; BA in Health Care Bus., Stephens Coll., 1991; BSN, N.Y. State Regents Coll., 1994. RN first asst., Ga.; cert. nurse oper. rm. Staff nurse med./surg. unit HCA Coliseum Med. Ctrs., Macon, Ga., 1977-79, head nurse med./surg. unit, 1979-82, staff nurse oper. rm., 1982-89, RN 1st asst., 1989—. Mem. Assn. Oper. Rm. Nurses (chair nat. RN First Assts. splty. assembly 1995-96), Southeastern Surg. Nurses Assn., Ga. Nurses Assn., Nat. League for Nursing. Home: 1528 Rumble Rd Forsyth GA 31029-8945

JOHNSON, COLIN DAVID, surgeon and surgical editor; b. Wallsend-on-Tyne, U.K., Apr. 18, 1952; s. Stanley and Gwen (Bannister) J.; m. Anne Jennifer Taylor, May 11, 1974; children: Emma-Louise, Amy, Edward. BA, Cambridge (U.K.) U., 1973, M.B.,B.Chir., 1976, M.Chir., 1984, MA (hon.), 1977. Registrar Brook Hosp., London, 1979-80; MRC traveling fellow INSERM, Marseille, France, 1980-82; registrar various hosps., Bristol, U.K., 1982-85; sr. registrar Westminster Hosp., London, 1986-88; sr. lectr. U. Southampton, U.K., 1988—. European editor Brit. Jour. Surgery, 1990—; editl. bd. Postgrad. Med. Jour., 1993—; editor: Pancreatic Diseases: Progress and Prospects, 1992, Recent Advances in Surgery, vols. 14-20, 1990—; author: Advice to House Surgeons, 1992. Chmn. Burley Primary Sch. Assn., 1990, Burley Twinning Assn., 1993—. Office: Southampton Gen Hosp-F Level, Mailpoint 816, Tremona Rd, Southampton SO16 6YD, United Kingdom

JOHNSON, CRYSTAL DUANE, psychologist; b. Houston, Mar. 2, 1954; d. Alton Floyd and Duane (Mullican) J.; m. Donald Beecher Hart, Mar. 21, 1989. BA, U. Tex., 1983, MS, 1985. Lic. profl. counselor, psychol. assoc., marriage and family therapist; cert. chem. dependency specialist. Student devel. specialist U. Tex., Tyler, 1985-86, intake counselor, 1986-88; staff psychologist Sabine Valley Ctr., Longview, Tex., 1987-88, Mental Health/Mental Retardation Ctr. of East Tex., Tyler, 1988-89; pvt. practice psychologist Tyler, 1989—; counselor Juvenile and Adult Probation Depts., 1988—, ICF/MR Residential Homes, 1991—; spl. edn. counselor, 1990—; counselor Child Protective Svcs., 1991—. Mem. Smith County Humane Soc., Tyler, 1985—, Humane Soc. of the U.S., Washington, 1987—, Am. Soc. Prevention Cruelty to Animals, 1987—, Nat. Wildlife Fedn., 1986—, World Wildlife Fedn., 1986—. Mem. Am. Psychol. Assn., Tex. Psychol. Assn., East Tex. Psychol. Assn.

JOHNSON, DANIEL WOODROW, hospital administrator; b. Magnolia, Ark., Aug. 14, 1952; s. Woodrow Wilson and Licia (Louvier) J.; m. Stephanie Jurisich; children: Amy, John, Erin, Kelly, Katie, Beau, Anna. BA, La. Tech. U., 1977. Cert. profl. counselor; cert. profl. alcohol and drug counselor. Program dir. Compcare/St. Joseph's Hosp., Memphis, 1976-78; asst. adminstr. Charter Med., Memphis, 1978-80; adminstr. Charter Med., Torrance, Calif., 1981-82, Republic, Monroe, La., 1982-85; regional dir. Charter Med., various locations, 1985-89; v.p. ops. CAPS, McLean, Va., 1989-90; CEO DePaul Hosp., New Orleans, 1990-93, Rivernorth/Northgate Hosp., Alexandria, La., 1993—; pres., chmn. Sof-Serve, New Orleans, 1993—; bd. dirs. Ctrl. La. Health Alliance, Alexandria; cons. Egan Healthcare, New Orleans, 1995. Author: Poverty Point People, 1974; co-author: Treatment Planning Library, 1978, Software, 1993. Res. dep. sheriff Rapides Sheriffs Dept., Alexandria, 1993. With USN, 1972-76. Recipient Gov.'s award State of La., 1993, 94. Mem. Pineville C. of C. (mayors task force 1995). Republican. Roman Catholic. Home: 6443 Canal Blvd New Orleans LA 70124 Office: Cmty Health Sys 5505 Shreveport Hwy Pineville LA 71360

JOHNSON, DAVID ALAN, synthetic organic chemist; b. Newton, Mass., Apr. 29, 1954; s. Roy Arnold and Frances Myra (Brown) J.; m. Rose Mary Davis, July 17, 1982; children: Benjamin Davis, Eric David, Matthew Alan. BS in Biology, U. Maine, 1976; MS in Medicinal Chemistry, W.Va. U., 1978; PhD in Organic Chemistry, Dartmouth Coll., 1986. Sr. chemist Mylan Pharm., Inc., Morgantown, W.Va., 1979-80; rsch. chemist Pfizer Ctrl. Rsch., Groton, Conn., 1980-82; Am. Cancer Soc. postdoctoral rsch. assoc. U. Pa., Phila., 1987-88; rsch. scientist Ribi ImmunoChem Rsch. Inc., Hamilton, Mont., 1988-91; sr. rsch. scientist Ribi ImmunoChem Rsch. Inc., Hamilton, 1991-93, head dept. synthetic chemistry, 1993—; adj. prof. chemistry U. Mont., Missoula, 1990—. Contbr. chpt. to book and articles to profl. jours. Samuel M. Graves Meml. scholar Wellesley (Mass.) Tchrs. Assn., 1972. Mem. Am. Chem. Soc., Mont. Acad. Scis., Internat. Endotoxin Soc., Rho Chi. Office: Ribi ImmunoChem Rsch Inc 553 Old Corvallis Rd Hamilton MT 59840-3131

JOHNSON, DAVID ALAN, internist, gastroenterologist, educator; b. Jersey City, July 20, 1954; s. Gustav E. and Mary Carolyn J.; children: Andrew Kessler, Catherine Louise. BA, U. Va., 1976; MD, Med. Coll. Va., 1980. Commd. 2d. lt. USN, 1976, advanced through grades to comdr.; resident Portsmouth (Va.) Naval Hosp., Va., 1980-84; fellow Nat. Naval Med. Ctr., Bethesda, Md., 1984-86, mem. staff, 1986-89; resigned, 1989; pvt. practice, Norfolk, Va.; prof. medicine Ea. Va. Sch. Medicine, Norfolk, 1995—, prof., 1995—; mem. adv. bd. Bard Products, 1995;. Assoc. editor Am. Jour. Gastroenterology, 1988—; contbr. articles to profl. jours., chpts. to books. Recipient Outstanding Acad. award Bethesda Naval Hosp., 1987. Fellow ACP, Am. Coll. Gastroenterolgy (course co-dir. 1994, bd. govs. Va. chpt., 1994—, chmn constl. bylaws com. 1994—, bd. trustees 1995—); mem. Am. Gastroenterolgy Assn., Am. Soc. Gastrointestinal Endoscopy (course co-dir. 1989). Office: Digestive Disease Specialists 844 Kempsville Rd Ste 106 Norfolk VA 23502-3927

JOHNSON, DAVID CURTIS, surgeon; b. Phoenix, Sept. 30, 1953; s. Clarence J. and Mary (Studdard) J.; m. Leslie Ann Dean, Sept. 26, 1984; children: Samuel, Gabrielle, Nathael, Michaela, Luana. BS, Ariz. State U., 1976; MD, U. Ariz., 1982. Diplomate Am. Bd. Surgery. Intern Maricopa Med. Ctr., Phoenix, 1982-83, resident, 1983-87; pvt. practice, Phoenix, Ariz., 1989—. Fellow ACS; mem. Soc. Am. Gastrointestinal Endoscopic Surgeons, Christian Med.-Dental Soc., Phoenix Surg. Soc. Office: 6641 E Baywood Ave #B Mesa AZ 85206-1723

JOHNSON, DAVID WOLCOTT, psychologist, educator; b. Muncie, Ind., Feb. 7, 1940; s. Roger Winfield and Frances Elizabeth (Pierce) J.; m. Linda Mulholland, July 7, 1973; children: James, David, Catherine, Margaret, Jeremiah. BS, Ball State U., 1962; MA, Columbia U., 1964, EdD, 1966. Asst. prof. ednl. psychology U. Minn., Mpls., 1966-69, assoc. prof., 1969-73, prof., 1973—, Emma Birkmaier prof. in ednl. leadership, 1994—; orgnl. cons., psychotherapist. Author: Social Psychology of Education, 1970, (with Goodwin Watson) Social Psychology: Issues and Insights, 1972, Reaching Out, 1972, 5th edit., 1993, Contemporary Social Psychology, 1973, (with F. Johnson) Joining Together, 1975, 5th edit., 1994, (with D. Tjosvold) Porductive Conflict Management, 1983, Circles of Learning, 1984, 4th edit., 1993, (with R. Johnson) Learning Together and Alone, 1975, 4th edit., 1994, Human Relations and Your Career, 1978, 3d Edit., 1991, Educational Psychology, 1979, Cooperative Learning, 1984, 4th edit., 1991, Structuring Cooperative Learning, 1987, Creative Conflict, 1987, Leading the Cooperative School, 1989, 2d edit., 1994, Cooperation and Competition: Theory and Research, 1989, Teaching Students to be Peacemakers, 1991, 3d edit., 1995, also film, 1991, Active Learning: Cooperative Learning in the College Classroom, 1991, Learning Mathematics and Cooperative Learning, 1991, Creative Controlversy, 1992, 3d edit., 1995, (with R. Johnson, E. Holubec) Advanced Cooperative Learning, 1988, 2d edit., 1992, (with R. Johnson, K. Smith) Cooperative Learning: Increasing College Faculty Instructional Productivity, 1991, Cooperation in the Classroom, 6th edit., 1993, Creative Controversy, 1992, Positive Interdependence, 1992, (video) 1992, (with R. Johnson and E. Holubel) The Nuts and Bolts of Cooperative Learning, 1994; editor Am. Ednl. Rsch. Jour., 1981-83; contbr. over 250 articles to profl. jours. Bd. dirs. Walk-In Counseling Ctr., 1971-74. Recipient Gordon Allport award Soc. for Psychol. Study of Social Issues, 1981, Helen Plante award Am. Soc. Engring. Edn., 1984, Outstanding Rsch. award Am. Pers. and Guidance Assn., 1972, Nat. Coun.l for the Social Studies Rsch. award, 1986, Outstanding Rsch. award Am. Assn. Counseling and Devel., 1988, award for Outstanding Contbn. Am. Edn. Minn. Assn. for Supervision and Curriculum Devel., 1990, Outstanding Alumni of Yr. award Ball State U., 1990, Rsch. and Practice award S.W. Ohio Planning Coun. for Insvc. Edn., 1990, Excellence in Tchg. award Dept. Def. Schs., Panama, 1994, Emma Birkmaier Prof. in Ednl. Leadership Coll. Edn. U. Minn., 1994—. Fellow Am. Psychol. Assn.; mem. Am. Sociol. Assn., Am. Ednl. Rsch. Assn. (award for Outstanding Contbn. to Coop. Learning 1996), Am. Mgmt. Assn., Am. Assn. for Counseling and Devel., Nat. Rsch. Coun. Home: 7208 Cornelia Dr Minneapolis MN 55435-4160 Office: U Minn 330 Burton Hall Minneapolis MN 55455

JOHNSON, DEWEY, JR., biochemist; b. Sapulpa, Okla., Sept. 23, 1926; s. Dewey and Maude (Hickey) J.; m. Patricia R. Rodgers, Feb. 14, 1953; children: Joseph D., Paul D., Mary Ann, Richard E. BS, Colo. State U., 1950; MS, U. Conn., 1955; PhD, Rutgers State U., 1958. Nutritionist Limecrest Rsch. Lab., Newton, N.J., 1958-63; biochemist Equitable Life, N.Y.C., 1963-79; biochemist Met. Life, N.Y.C., 1980-90, disability underwriter, 1990-92; chemist EPA, Edison, N.J., 1993—. Contbr. rsch. articles to profl. jours. Home: 12 Barbara Pl Edison NJ 08217

JOHNSON, DEWEY E(DWARD), JR., dentist; b. Charleston, S.C., Mar. 19, 1935; s. Dewey Edward and Mabel (Momeier) J.; A.B. in Geology, U. N.C., 1957, D.D.S., 1961. Pvt. practice dentistry, Charleston, 1964-92, assoc. to Stanley H. Karesh, Charleston, D.D.S., 1970-77, tech. market rschr., designer, Charleston, 1970-90, indsl. designer, various orgns., 1965, 75, 77, 88, 91, 92. Served to lt. USNR, 1961-63. Mem. Royal Soc. Health, Charleston C. of C. (cruise ship com. 1969), ADA, Charleston Dental Soc., Hibernian Soc., Charleston Museum, Internat. Platform Assn., Charleston Library Soc., S.C. Hist. Soc., Gibbes Art Gallery, Preservation Soc. of Charleston, Navy League of U.S., Phi Kappa Sigma, Sigma Gamma Epsilon, Psi Omega. Congregationalist. Club: Optimist. Achievements include various scientific and engineering designs; patent in dental matrix device.

JOHNSON, DONNA LYNN, critical care nurse; b. Bitburg, Fed. Republic Germany, Jan. 31, 1958; d. Bill and Bernice R. (Staudt) J. BSN, Northwestern State U., 1980. RN, La.; CCRN. Nurse SICU Schumpert Med. Ctr., Shreveport, La., 1981-87, adminstrv. supr., 1987-89; relief nurse ICU Riverside Community Hosp., Bossier, La., 1982-83, Minden (La.) Med. Ctr., 1983-86; recovery coord. La. Organ Procurement Agy., Shreveport, 1989-94; dir. critical care La. State U. Med. Ctr., Shreveport, 1994—; preceptor Northwestern State U., Shreveport, 1983-89. Mem. AACN (pres. 1992—), N.Am. Transplant Coord. Orgn., Krew of Aesclepius, Sigma Theta Tau. Home: 448 Huron St Shreveport LA 71106-1648 Office: La State U Med Ctr 1501 Kings Hwy Shreveport LA 71103-4228

JOHNSON, DOROTHY PHYLLIS, counselor, art therapist; b. Kansas City, Mo., Sept. 13, 1925; d. Chris C. and Mabel T. (Gillum) Green; BA in Art, Ft. Hays. State U., 1975, MS in Guidance and Counseling, 1976, MA in Art, 1979; m. Herbert E. Johnson, May 11, 1945; children: Michael E., Gregory K. Art therapist High Plains Comprehensive Mental Health Assn., Hays, Kans., 1975-76; art therapist, mental health counselor Sunflower Mental Health Assn., Concordia, Kans., 1976-78, Pawnee Mental Health Svcs., 1978-91, co-dir. Project Togetherness, 1976-77, coord. partial hospitalization, 1978-82, out-patient therapist, 1982-91; pvt. practice, 1991—; dir. Swedish Am. State Bank, Courtland, Kans., 1960—, sec., 1973-77. Mem. Kans., Am. art therapy assns., Am. Mental Health Counselors Assn., Am. Counseling Assn., Kans. Counseling Assn., Assn. for Humanistic Psychologists, Assn. Transpersonal Psychologists, Assn. Specialists in Group Work, Phi Delta Kappa, Phi Kappa Phi. Contbr. articles to profl. jours. Home: PO Box 200 Courtland KS 66939-0200 Office: 520 Washington St # B Concordia KS 66901-2117

JOHNSON, DOUGLAS HERBERT, ophthalmologist; b. Rochester, Minn., Apr. 17, 1951; s. Herbert Wesley and Betty Lou (Hevle) J.; m. Nancy Lee Schilling, July 19, 1975; children: Emily, Valerie. BA summa cum laude, St. Olaf Coll., Northfield, Minn., 1973; MD, Mayo Med. Sch., 1977. Diplomate Am. Bd. Ophthalmology. Resident in ophthalmology Mayo Clinic, Rochester, 1977-81, cons. in ophthalmology, clin. investigator, 1983—; fellow in ophthalmology Harvard U., Boston, 1981-83, clin. instr. ophthalmology, 1981-83. Group leader Cmty. Bible Study, Rochester, 1990—. Mem. Phi Beta Kappa. Office: Mayo Clinic 200 1st St SW Rochester MN 55905

JOHNSON, EDGAR MCCARTHY, psychologist; b. Jacksonville, Fla., Oct. 29, 1941; s. James Mack Johnson and Dorothy (Vickers) Logue; m. Fatima Nunes, Sept. 9, 1967; children: Victoria C., David M. BS in Applied Psychology, Ga. Inst. Tech., 1964; MS in Exptl. Psychology, Tufts U., 1967, PhD in Exptl. Psychology, 1969. Research psychologist U.S. Army Research Inst., Alexandria, Va., 1970-78, chief human factors sect., 1978-80, dir. systems research lab., 1980-82, tech. dir. U.S. Army Research Inst., 1982-93, dir., 1993—; chief psychologist U.S. Army, 1982—. Served to capt. U.S. Army, 1968-70. NDEA fellow, 1965-67. Fellow Am. Psychol. Assn., Am. Psychol. Soc., Human Factors and Ergonomics Soc., Washington Acad. Sci. (Sci. Achievement award 1980); mem. IEEE (Franklin V. Taylor award 1984), Ergonomics Soc., Sigma Xi. Club: Cosmos (Washington). Home: 5315 Renaissance Ct Burke VA 22015-2194 Office: US Army Rsch Inst 5001 Eisenhower Ave Alexandria VA 22304-4811

JOHNSON, EDWARD ELEMUEL, psychologist, educator; b. Jamaica, B.W.I., July 25, 1926; came to U.S., 1941, naturalized, 1948; s. Edward and Mary Elizabeth (Blake) J.; m. Beverley Jean Morris, Jan. 26, 1955; children—Edward Elemuel, Lawrence Palmer, Robin Jeannine, Nathan Jerome, Cyril Ulric. B.S., Howard U., 1947, M.S., 1948; Ph.D., U. Colo., 1952. Assoc. prof. psychology Grambling Coll., La., 1954-55; prof. So. U., Baton Rouge, 1955-60, prof., head dept. psychology, 1960-69, assoc. dean univ., 1969-72, dir. Regional Head Start Evaluation and Research Ctr.; clin. prof. La. State U. Med. Sch., New Orleans, 1969-72; dir. United Bd. for Coll. Devel., 1972-74; dir. 13 coll. curriculum program So. U., Baton Rouge; clin. prof. psychiatry Emory U. Med. Sch., Atlanta, 1973-74; prof. psychiatry Robert Wood Johnson Med. Sch., Piscataway, N.J., 1974—; cons. collaborative child devel. project; cons. State Indsl. Sch. Scotlandville, La., 1973-74, VA Hosp., Lyons, N.J., 1987; mem. Med. Rev. Panel, State of N.J., 1976—, chmn., 1993; vocat. cons. HEW; mem. mental health adv. group Westinghouse Health Systems, 1978-82; region II mental health coordinator Head Start Program, 1978—; mem. gen. research support rev. com. NIH, 1980—; mem. acad. council Thomas A. Edison Coll. of N.J., 1978-83; mem. adv. bd. Office Pub. Guardian, State of N.J., 1988—; chmn. minority and cultural concerns com. div. Mental Health and Hosps. of State of N.J., 1989—. Bd. dirs. Crossroad Theatre Co., New Brunswick, N.J. Served to 1st lt. AUS, 1951-53. Fellow AAAS; mem. Am. Psychol. Assn. (com. on adv. svcs. for edn. and tng. 1968-69, task group on faculty devel. for minority and non-minority faculty to implement culturally relevant curriculum 1992), N.Y. Acad. Scis. (life), Masons, Sigma Xi, Sigma Pi Phi, Alpha Phi Alpha, Beta Beta Beta, Pi Gamma Mu, Psi Chi. Home: PO Box 597 East Brunswick NJ 08816-0597

JOHNSON, EDWARD MICHAEL, molecular biologist, educator; b. Kenosha, Wis., Apr. 9, 1945; s. Edward and Mary Margaret (Pratch) J.; m. Elizabeth Buckingham Childs, June 14, 1969; 1 son, Nathaniel Livingston. B.A., Pomona Coll., 1967; Ph.D., Yale U., 1971. Postdoctoral fellow Rockefeller U., N.Y.C., 1971-73, asst. prof. molecular biology, 1975-81, assoc. prof., 1981—; research assoc. Sloan-Kettering Cancer Ctr., N.Y.C., 1973-75; adj. assoc. prof. Cornell U. Grad. Sch. Med. Sci., N.Y.C., 1981—; prof. molecular biology and pathology Mt. Sinai Med. Sch., 1984—. Contbr. numerous articles to sci. publs. Jane Coffin Childs fellow in molecular biology, 1971; Leukemia Soc. Am. Spl. Fellow, 1974; recipient Faculty Rsch. award Am. Cancer Soc. Mem. Am. Soc. Biolchem. and Molecular Biology, Am. Soc. for Pharmacology and Exptl. Therapeutics, Am. Soc. for Cell Biology, N.Y. Acad. Scis., AAAS. Home: 531 E 88th St Apt 4B New York NY 10128-7756 Office: Mt Sinai Sch Medicine 1 Gustave L Levy Pl # 1194 New York NY 10029-6504

JOHNSON, ELAINE MCDOWELL, federal government administrator; b. Balt., June 28, 1942; d. McKinley and Lena (Blue) McDowell; m. Walter Johnson; children: Nathan H. Murphy, Michael W. Murphy. BA, Morgan State U., Balt., 1965; MSW, U. Md., 1971, PhD, 1988. Drug abuse adminstr., acting regional dir. State Md. Drug Abuse Adminstrn., Balt., 1971-72; social sci. analyst, pub. health advisor Nat. Inst. Drug Abuse, Rockville, MD, 1972-76, dep. dir., dir. div. community assistance, 1976-82, dep. assoc. dir. for policy devel., 1981-82, dir. div. prevention and communications, 1982-85; exec. asst. to adminstr. Alcohol, Drug Abuse & Mental Health Adminstrn., Rockville, Md., 1985; dep. dir. Nat. Inst. on Drug Abuse, Rockville, MD, 1985-88; dir. Office for Substance Abuse Prevention, 1988-94; acting adminstr. Alcohol, Drug Abuse and Mental Health Adminstrn., Rockville, Md., 1992; acting adminstr. Substance Abuse and Mental Health Svcs. Adminstrn., Rockville, Md., 1992-94, dir. Ctr. Substance Abuse Prevention, 1995—; expert cons. in substance abuse, treatment, and mental health fields. Active Presbyterian Ch., Balt., 1979—. Recipient Secretary's commendation HHS, 1989, Disting. Svc. award, 1990, Pride Bldg. Bridges award, 1991, Nat. Fedn. Parents Nat. Leadership award, 1991, Nat. Coun. on Alcoholism and Drug Dependence Ind., Pres. award for outstanding fed. leadership, 1991, Presdl. Meritorious Exec. Rank award, 1991, Presdl. Meritorious Disting. Rank award, 1993. Mem. NASW, ASPA, Sr. Execs. Assn., Fed. Exec. Inst. Alumni Assn. Office: Ctr for Substance Abuse Prevention Rockwell 2 Bldg 5600 Fishers Ln 9th Fl Rockville MD 20857

JOHNSON, E(LMER) MARSHALL, biology educator, reproductive toxicologist; b. Midlothian, Ill., June 16, 1930; s. Burt and Gertrude Esther (Miller) J.; m. Marlys Claire Van Overstraeten, 1954 (div. 1974); children: Mark Dee, Kim Leah, Erik Marshall, Lora Marlys; m. Sharon Ann Coyle, May 9, 1976. Diploma, Thornton Jr. Coll., 1950; BS, Tex. A & M U., 1953, MS, 1954; PhD, U. Calif., Berkeley, 1958. Grad. teaching asst. Tex. A & M U., College Station, 1952-55; rsch. asst. Tex. A & M Rsch. Found., College Station, 1955; teaching asst. Coll. Medicine U. Calif., Berkeley, 1955-58; instr. Contra Costa Coll., San Pablo, Calif., 1958-59; from instr. to assoc. prof. Coll. Medicine U. Fla., Gainesville, 1960-68, prof., acting chmn., 1968-70; prof. devel. biology, chmn. dept. anatomy Coll. Medicine U. Calif., Irvine, 1970-72; prof., chmn., dir. Danial Baugh Inst. Thomas Jefferson U., Phila., 1972-94, prof. pathology, anatomy and cell biology, 1994—; mem. sci. adv. bd. EPA; mem. sci. com. U.S. Dept. Army; mem. com. for NASA space sta. toxicity NAS, 1992—; founding pres. Argus Rsch. Labs. Contbr. more than 200 sci. articles to profl. jours.; patentee in vitro toxicity test, method of growing hydozoa. Grantee March of Dimes, 1962-69, 75-87, Nat. Inst. Child Health, 1963-85, Nat. Inst. Environ. Health, 1993—. Mem. AAAS, Am. Coll. Toxicology, European Teratology Soc., Mid. Atlantic Soc. Toxicology, Teratology Soc. (charter, pres.), Soc. Xenobiotics (charter), Soc. Toxicology (founding pres. reproduction and devel. specialty, sect. on reproductive toxicology), Am. Assn. Anatomy, Sigma Xi. Home: 2311 Naudain St Philadelphia PA 19146-1119 Office: Jefferson Med Coll 1020 Locust St Philadelphia PA 19107-6731

JOHNSON, FRANK CORLISS, criminal psychologist; b. Taylor Falls, Minn., June 3, 1927; s. Frank August and Julia (Fallt) J.; widower; 1 son, Thomas Christopher. BS, San Diego State U., 1964, MS, 1968; postgrad. Mich. State U., 1970; PhD (hon.), Clinton U., 1974. Asst. commr. correction State Conn., Hartford, 1970-71; exec. dir. Empire State Vets., Staten Island, N.Y., 1979—; exec. dir. Recovered Alcoholics, Staten Island, 1972—; with Alcohol and Drug Control Office U.S. Army, Bklyn., 1972-73; mem. Mayors adv. council on alcoholism City of N.Y., 1972-85; prison psychologist N.Y.C. Health Dept., 1968-89 psycologist Staten Island Hosp. suicide prevention team, 1995—; cons. F. Johnson & Assocs., Staten Island, 1975—. Author: The Invisible Line, 1966. Bd. dirs. Half Way House of Lansing (Mich.), 1969-70, New Haven Council on Alcoholism, 1970-73, Nat. Assn. Recovered Alcoholics, N.Y.C., 1978—; mem. central com. Republican party of Staten Island, 1979-82; asst. commr. Boy Scouts Am., Staten Island, 1983—, troop leader, 1981-83, exec. bd., 1984—. Served with USN, submarine svc. USS Redfish, 1944-46, 50-51. Recipient citation for meritorious service Calif. Gov.'s Com., 1968; cert. of merit, Am. Vets., 1980-81; Unsung Hero award N.Y. Daily News, N.Y.C., 1983. Fellow Am. Personnel and Guidance Assn. (chpt. dir. 1970-72); mem. Internat. Platform Assn., Am. Assn. Marriage Counselors. Republican. Lutheran. Home: 20 Cliff St # 5-d Staten Island NY 10305-3933

JOHNSON, FRANK EDWARD, surgeon, educator; b. Evanston, Ill., Oct. 28, 1943; s. Frank E. and Beryl Madeline (Johnson) J. m. Tamiko Asato, Jan. 24, 1976; children: Mariko, Michael, Eric, David. BA, U. Minn., 1964, MD, 1967. Diplomate Am. Bd. Surgery. Intern, UCLA affiliated hosps., 1967-78; resident in surgery U. Wash., Seattle, 1972-74, U. Colo., 1974-77; research fellow U. Calif.-San Francisco, 1975-76; fellow in surg. oncology Meml. Sloan-Kettering Cancer Ctr., N.Y.C., 1977-79; research prof. Guy's Hosp., London, 1986-87; clin. instr. surgery Cornell U., N.Y.C., 1977-79; asst. prof. surgery St. Louis U. Med. Ctr., 1979-84, assoc. prof. surgery, 1984-89, prof., 1989—. Contbr. articles to profl. jours.; author 10 med. films. Co-founder Children's Heart Fund, Mpls., 1969. Served to lt. commander USN, 1969-71, Vietnam. Decorated Bronze Star; grantee, NIH, Am. Cancer Soc., Royal Coll. Surgeons Found., VA Merit Rev. Mem. Soc. Surg. Oncology, Am. Gastroent. Assn. AMA, Am. Fedn. Clin. Research, Am. Soc. Clin. Oncology, Am. Assn. Cancer Edn., Am. Assn. Cancer Research, ACS, Am. Pancreatic Assn., Am. Radium Soc., Am. Soc. Preventive Oncology, Ctrl. Surg. Assn. (grantee), Radiation Rsch. Soc., Southwestern Surg. Congress, Soc. Head and Neck Surgeons, Am. Physiol. Soc., Soc. Univ. Surgeons, Assn. Acad. Surgeons.

JOHNSON, GARNER PHILIP, surgery educator; b. Winona, Minn., Nov. 6, 1954; s. Howard C. and Rose M. (Simon) J.; m. Kathleen M. Hickey, Oct. 31, 1987; children: Brendan, Caroline. BS, Brown U., 1977; MD, U. Minn., 1982. Diplomate Am. Bd. Surgery, Am. Bd. Colon and Rectal Surgery. Resident in surgery U. Chgo. Med. Ctr., 1982-84, U. Mass. Med. Ctr., Worcester, 1984-87; researcher and fellow in colon and rectal surgery Mayo Grad. Sch. Medicine, Rochester, Minn., 1987-89; clin. asst. prof. surgery Albany (N.Y.) Med. Coll., 1989—. Contbr. articles to profl. jours. Mem. AMA, Am.Soc. Colon and Rectal Surgeons, Assn. for Acad. Surgery. Office: 319 S Manning Blvd Ste 310 Albany NY 12208

JOHNSON, GARY KEITH, pediatrician; b. Chgo., Aug. 26, 1951; s. John Edward and Dorothy Lucille (Rudder) J. AB, Dartmouth Coll., 1973; MD, U. Ill., Chgo., 1979, MPH, 1985. Diplomate Am. Bd. Med. Examiners, Am. Bd. Pediatrics. Intern Columbus Hosp., Chgo., 1980, resident in pediatrics, 1980-83; fellow in ambulatory pediatrics Cook County Hosp., Chgo., 1983-85; dir. ambulatory pediatrics Hurley Med. Ctr., Flint, Mich., 1986-92; clin. pediatrician McCree North Health Ctr., Flint, 1992-95; participant scholars program Mich. Pub. Health Leadership Inst., Flint, 1995-96; med. dir. Genesee County Health Dept., 1995—; asst. prof. pediatrics Mich. State U., East Lansing, 1986—, tchr. med. ednl. program Coll. Human Medicine and U. Affiliated Hosp. of Flint (Mich.), Inc., 1986—; participant Mich. Public Health Leadership Inst. scholars program, Okemos, Mich., 1995-96; presenter in field. Contbr. numerous articles to profl. jours. and cmty. newspapers. Chairperson Early On program Genesee County, 1993-94. Primary Care Faculty Devel. fellow Mich. State U., 1988-89. Fellow Am. Acad. Pediatrics (Mich. chpt. exec. com. cmty. access to child health, state facilitator 1990—); mem. AMA, Chgo. Pediatric Soc., Genessee County Med. Soc., Mich. State Med. Soc., Ambulatory Pediatric Assn., Am. Pub. Health Assn. Democrat. Presbyterian. Home: 5443 Waters Edge Way Grand Blanc MI 48439-9720 Office: Genesee County Health Dept 630 S Saginaw St Flint MI 48502

JOHNSON, GERALD, III, cardiovascular physiologist, researcher; b. Liberty, Tex., Aug. 16, 1945; s. Gerald Jr. and Jimmie Leah (Hensley) J.; m. Delynda Juanice Wall, Sept. 20, 1985. MS, U. Okla., 1971; PhD, U. Okla., Oklahoma City, 1980. NIH stipendiary U. Okla., Oklahoma City, 1972-76, rsch. assoc., 1979-80; electrophysiologist Childrens Med. Ctr., Tulsa, Okla., 1980-82; post-doct. fellow Oral Roberts U. Sch. Medicine, Tulsa, 1982-84, asst. prof., 1984-88; sr. rsch. fellow Jefferson Med. Coll., Phila., 1988-90; assoc. prof. dept. medicine, health scis. ctr. U. Okla., 1990—; dir. cardiovascular lab. W. K. Warren Med. Rsch. Inst., Tulsa, 1990—; cons. McGee Rehab. Inst., Phila., 1990, Dept. Pediatrics City of Faith Hosp., Tulsa, 1982, Aerobics Ctr. Oral roberts U., Tulsa, 1981; rsch. asst. to assoc. VA Hosp., Oklahoma City, 1970-72, Cen. State Hosp., Norman, Okla, 1969-70, U. Okla. Health Scis. Ctr., Oklahoma City, 1979-80; mem. numerous coms. Oral Roberts U., 1984-88. Contbr. numerous articles to profl. jours.; presenter in field. Grantee The Hearst Found., 1981-82, Am. Heart Assn., 1985-86; recipient Travel award Biofeedback Soc. Am., 1981, Citation Paper awards, 1981, 82. Mem. AAAS, Internat. Soc. for Heart Rsch. (Am. sect.), Am. Heart Assn., Am. Physiol. Assn., Am. Soc. Nuclear Cardiology (founding), Fedn. Am. Socs. for Exptl. Biology, Soc. Nuclear Medicine, N.Y. Acad. Scis., Soc. of Sigma Xi, Phi Kappa Phi. Office: W K Warren Med Rsch Inst 6465 S Yale Ave Ste 1010 Tulsa OK 74136-7812

JOHNSON, GINA, psychiatric nurse; b. Bklyn., Feb. 23, 1957; d. Joesph and Emma Bell (Privott) J.; m. Sherman McDonald Jr., Oct. 1, 1976 (div. Dec. 1983); children: Ronnie Alexander Johnson, Sherman McDonald III; m. Maxwell Elliott Key, June 15, 1987. AAS, Tidewater Cmty. Coll., 1987; BS in Psychology, Regents U., 1994. RN, Va. Staff nurse, LPN Jeanne Stuart Meml. Hosp., Hopkinsville, Ky., 1979, Hamot Med. Ctr., Erie, Pa., 1979-82; staff nurse Maryview Med. Ctr., Portsmouth, 1982-89, Maryview Psych. Ctr., Portsmouth, 1987-89, Maryview Nursing Home, Portsmouth, 1982-89; charge nurse, staffing, transp. coord., clin. coord. Pines Residential Treatment Ctr., Portsmouth, 1987-92; med./surg. nurse Oakland Naval Hosp., USN, 1992, divsn. officer, charge nurse, 1992-95; adminstrv. asst. Portsmouth Naval Med. Ctr., 1996 (ret.); ward rep. Jr. Nurse Corp. Coun., Oakland, Calif., 1992-95, task force nursing documentation, 1993-95. Ensign USNR, ret. Holly Hogge Meml. scholarship Tidewater Cmty. Coll., 1986, Commonwealth of Va. grant State of Va., 1986. Mem. Phi Theta Kappa. Southern Baptist. Home: 7940 Pipers Creek Rd # 1521 San Antonio TX 78251

JOHNSON, HERMAN LEONALL, research nutritionist; b. Whitehall, Wis., Apr. 1, 1935; s. Frederick E. And Jeanette (Severson) J.; m. Barbara Dale Matthews, July 3, 1960 (dec. May 1971); m. Barbara Ann Badger, Apr. 3, 1976. BA in Chemistry, North Cen. Coll., Naperville, Ill., 1959; MS in Biochemistry & Nutrition, Va. Poly. Inst. and State U., 1961, PhD in Biochemistry and Nutrition, 1963. Rsch. biochemist S.R. Noble Found., Ardmore, Okla., 1963-65; nutrition chemist U.S. Army Med. Rsch., Denver, 1965-74; nutrition physiologist Letterman Army Rsch., Presidio San Francisco, 1974-80, Western Human Nutrition Rsch. Ctr. USDA, Presidio San Francisco, 1980—. Contbr. numerous articles to profl. jours. Trustee 1st Meth. Ch., Ronnert Park, Calif., 1985-94, mem. fin. com., 1994—. With Med. Svc. Corps U.S. Army, 1954-56. Named one of Outstanding Young Men of Am., 1975; NIH traineeship Va. Poly. Inst. and State U., Blacksburg, 1961-63. Mem. AAAS, Am. Inst. Nutrition, Am. Soc. Clin. Nutritionists, Am. Coll. Nutritionists, Am. Coll. Sports Medicine, Sebastopol Spinners, Sigma Xi, Phi Lambda, Phi Sigma. Republican. Home: 256 Alden Ave Rohnert Park CA 94928-3704 Office: USDA Western Human Nutrition Rsch Ctr PO Box 29997 San Francisco CA 94129-0997

JOHNSON, HORTON ANTON, pathologist; b. Cheyenne, Wyo., Nov. 12, 1926; s. Horton Antonius and Katharine Mary (Tidball) J.; m. Caryl Abell Daly, Nov. 20, 1970; children by previous marriage: Katherine, Kristin, Margaret, Ann, Gregory, Marjorie. AB, Colo. Coll., 1949; MD, Columbia U., 1953. Diplomate: Am. Bd. Pathology. Intern Univ. Hosp., Ann Arbor, Mich., 1953-54; resident in pathology Univ. Hosp., 1954-57, Pondville Cancer Hosp., Walpole, Mass., 1957-58; scientist Brookhaven Nat. Lab., 1958-60, 63-70; asst. prof. pathology U. Utah, 1960-63; prof. pathology SUNY, Stony Brook, 1970-72, Ind. U., 1972-75; prof., chmn. dept. pathology Tulane U., New Orleans, 1975-84; prof. pathology Columbia U., N.Y.C., 1984-91; dir. pathology St. Luke's-Roosevelt Hosp. Ctr., N.Y.C., 1984-91. Served with USNR, 1944-46. Recipient Lederle Med. Faculty award, 1961. Fellow Coll. Am. Pathologists; mem. Am. Assn. Pathologists, Internat. Acad. Pathology, Biophys. Soc., Radiation Research Soc., N.Y. Acad. Scis., Assn. Clin. Scientists, Soc. Health and Human Values, Phi Beta Kappa, Alpha Omega Alpha. Home: 39 N Cove Rd Old Saybrook CT 06475-2538 Office: Three Lincoln Center Plz Ste 28G New York NY 10023-6560

JOHNSON, HOWARD EUGENE (STRETCH JOHNSON), educator, consultant; b. Orange, N.J., Jan. 30, 1915; s. Howard MacPherson and Gertrude Parker (McGinnis) J.; (div. Jan. 1989); children: Wendy Kay, Wini Lorie, Lisa Alin. BS in Comparative Lit., Columbia U., 1966; MA in Sociology, NYU, 1977; postgrad., SUNY, Binghamton, 1989—; HHD (hon.), Honolulu U., 1990. Documentation specialist psychiat. epidemiol. rsch. unit Columbia U. Coll. Physicians and Surgeons, 1966-67, field supr. social scis. rsch. unit, 1968-69; asst. to dir. ethical culture schs., project dir. Fieldston Sch., 1969-71; asst. prof. dept. black studies SUNY, New Paltz, 1971-74, adj. assoc. prof. dept. sociology, 1975-82; tech. advisor to Francis Ford Coppola film The Cotton Club, 1983; vis. lectr. ethnic studies program U. Hawaii, 1986-89. Chmn. Strand Cmty. Orgn. to Rehab. the Environment, Kingston, N.Y., 1978-82; founder, chmn. Hudson Valley Minority Regional Congress, 1979-82; 1st vice chmn. Hudson Valley Econ. Devel. Dist., 1981-82; founder, co-chmn. of Afro-Am. Leadership Conf., Hawaii, 1988; v.p. St. Croix Cmty. Crime Com.; vice chmn. Martin Luther King Jr. Commn., Hawaii. Mem. Assn. for the Study of Afro-Am. Life and History (life), Mil. Order of the Purple Heart (life), Am. Field Svc. Com., NAACP (life), SAG. Address: 1315 25th St Galveston TX 77550

JOHNSON, JANE ELAINE, medical educator. BS in Chemistry magna cum laude, U. Wash., 1983, PhD in Biochemistry, 1988. Postdoctoral fellow Calif. Inst. Tech., 1988-92; asst. prof. dept. cell biology and neurosci. U. Tex. Southwestern Med. Sch., Dallas, 1993—. Contbr. articles to profl. jours. Devel. Biology Predoctoral Tng. grantee NIH, 1984-88; Postdoctoral fellow Muscular Dystrophy Assn., 1989-91; recipient Young Investigator award Neurofibromatosis Found., 1993, Established Investigator award Am. Heart Assn., 1995. Office: U Tex Southwestern Med Ctr 5323 Harry Hines Blvd Dallas TX 75235*

JOHNSON, JEAN ELAINE, nursing educator; b. Wilsey, Kans., Mar. 11, 1925; d. William H. and Rosa L. (Welty) Irwin. B.S., Kans. State U., 1948; M.S. in Nursing, Yale U., 1965; M.S., U. Wis., 1969, Ph.D., 1971. Instr. nursing Iowa, Kans. and Colo., 1948-58; staff nurse Swedish Hosp., Englewood, Colo., 1958-60; in-svc. edn. coord. Gen. Rose Hosp., Denver, 1960-63; rsch. asst. Yale U., New Haven, 1965-67; assoc. prof. nursing Wayne State U., Detroit, 1971-74, prof., 1974-79; dir. Ctr. for Health Rsch., 1974-79; assoc. dir. oncology nursing Cancer Ctr. U. Rochester, N.Y., 1979-93; prof. nursing U. Rochester, 1979-95, prof. emerita, 1995—; Rosenstadt prof. health rsch. Faculty Nursing U. Toronto, 1985; vis. prof. U. Utah Coll. Nursing, 1996. Contbg. author: Handbook of Psychology and Health, vol. 5, 1984; contbr. articles to profl. jours. Recipient Bd. Govs. Faculty Recognition award Wayne State U., 1975, award for disting. contbn. to nursing sci. Am. Nurses Found. and ANA Coun. for Nurse Rschrs., 1983, Grad. Teaching award U. Rochester, 1991, Disting. Rschr. award Oncology Nursing Soc., 1992, Outstanding Contbns. to Nursing and Psychology award divsn. of health psychology APA, 1993; NIH grantee, 1972-95. Fellow AAAS, APA (Outstanding Contbns. to Nursing and Psychology award 1993), Acad. for Behavioral Medicine Rsch., Am. Psychol. Soc.; mem. ANA (chmn. coun. for nurse rschrs. 1976-78, commn. for rsch. 1978-82), Inst. Medicine NAS (com. on patient injury compensation 1976-77, membership com. 1981-86, gov. coun. 1987-89), Sigma Xi, Omicron Nu, Phi Kappa Phi. Home: 1412 East Ave Rochester NY 14610-1619 Office: U Rochester Box 80N 601 Elmwood Ave Rochester NY 14642-0001

JOHNSON, JEANNE MARIE, nurse psychotherapist, clinical nurse specialist; b. N.Y.C.; d. Hector J. and Jean (Bershacht) Streyckmans; 1 child, Robert M. AAS, Queens Coll., 1963; BSN, Adelphi U., 1967, MSN, 1973; postgrad., Karen Horney Inst., N.Y.C., 1981-82. Cert. clin. nurse specialist, 1981. Pub. health nurse Nassau County Dept. Health, Mineola, N.Y., 1963-69; instr. cmty. nursing Molloy Coll., Rockville Centre, N.Y., 1977-78; cmty. mental health nurse, admiinstr., psychotherapist Cmty. Mental Health Ctr. Nassau County, Westchester County, N.Y., 1969-89; nurse psychotherapist Cen. Nassau Guidance and Counseling Svc., Inc., Hicksville, N.Y., 1990-91; geriatric psychotherapist New Hope Guild, 1989; pvt. practice as nurse/psychotherapist and cons., 1988—, clin. nurse specialist, 1981—; substitute sch. nurse Wantagh Sch. Dist., 1991-95, Bethpage Sch. Dist., 1995—; mem. disaster action team ARC, 1979—, Red Cross nurse, 1967—. Mem. ANA (congressional dist. coord.), N.Y. State Nurses Assn., Network of Clin. Nurse Specialists, Sigma Theta Tau. Home: 112 Hawthorn St Massapequa Park NY 11762-2001

JOHNSON, JEROME LINNÉ, cardiologist; b. Rockford, Ill., June 19, 1929; s. Thomas Arthur and Myrtle Elizabeth (Swanson) J.; m. Molly Ann Rideout, June 27, 1953; children: Susan Johnson Nowels, William Rideout. BA, U. Chgo., 1951; BS, Northwestern U., 1952, MD, 1955. Diplomate Nat. Bd. Med. Examiners. Intern U. Chgo. Clinics, 1955-56; resident Northwestern U., Chgo., 1958-61; chief resident Chgo. Wesley Meml. Hosp., 1960-61; mem., v.p. Hauch Med. Clinic, Pomona, Calif., 1961-88; pvt. practice cardiology and internal medicine Pomona, 1988—; clin. assoc. prof. medicine, U. So. Calif., L.A., 1961—; mem. staff Pomona Valley Hosp. Med. Ctr., chmn. coronary care com. 1967-77; mem. staff L.A. County Hosp. Citizen ambassador, People to People; mem. Town Hall of Calif., L.A. World Affairs Coun. Lt. USNR, 1956-58. Fellow Am. Coll. Cardiology, Am. Geriatrics Soc., Royal Soc. Health; mem. Galileo Soc., Am. Heart Assn. (bd. dirs. L.A. County div. 1967-84, San Gabriel div. 1963-89), Am. Soc. Internal Medicine, Inland Soc. Internal Medicine, Pomona Host Lions. Home: 648 Delaware Dr Claremont CA 91711-3457

JOHNSON, JERRY DOUGLAS, biology educator; b. Salina, Kans., Sept. 1, 1947; s. Maynard Eugene and Norma Maude (Moss) J.; m. Kathryn Ann Johnson, May 12, 1973; children: George Walker, Brett Arthur. BS in Zoology, Fort Hays State U., 1972; MS in Biology, U. Tex., El Paso, 1975; PhD in Wildlife Sci., Tex. A&M U., 1984. Teaching asst. biology dept. U. Tex., El Paso, 1973-75; instr. biology El Paso C.C., 1975—; adj. asst. prof. U. Tex., El Paso, 1984—; Piper prof. El Paso Community Coll., 1989-90; councilor bd. scientists Chihuahuan Desert Rsch. Inst., Alpine, Tex., 1991—. Co-author: Middle American Herpetology, 1988; contbr. articles to profl. jours. Bd. dirs. Meml. Park Improvement Assn., 1987—, El Paso Coun. for Internat. Visitors, 1988—, Parks and Recreation Bd., El Paso, 1991-94. Grantee Soc. Sigma Xi, 1974, Theodore Roosevelt Found. Am. Mus. Natural History, 1979, Exline Corp., 1980, NSF, 1992—, NIH, 1992-94; recipient El Paso Natural Gas Faculty Achievement award, 1995-96, NISOD Tchg. Excellence award, 1995-96. Mem. NSF, Nat. Ctr. for Acad. Achievement, Nat. Inst. Gen. Med. Sci., Soc. for Study of Amphibians and Reptiles (elector 1980, assoc. editor Geog. Distbn. Herpetol. Rev. 1993—), Southwestern Assn. Naturalists (assoc. editor 1977-85, bd. govs. 1985-89), Tex. Herpetol. Soc. (v.p., pres. 1995-96), El Paso Herpetol. Soc. (pres. 1993—), Herpetologists League, others. Home: 3147 Wheeling Ave El Paso TX 79930-4321 Office: El Paso CC Biology Dept PO Box 20500 El Paso TX 79998-0500

JOHNSON, JETSIE WHITE, nurse, consultant; b. Newport News, Va., Apr. 7, 1944; d. Breavoid Milton and Jetsie (Johnson) White; m. Henry Johnson Jr., Feb. 24, 1963; children: Cheryl Johnson Holmes, Henry Breavoid, Daryl Jay, Shamala Michelle. AAS magna cum laude, Thomas Nelson Community Coll., Hampton, Va., 1974; BS, Hampton U., 1985, MSN, 1987. RN, Va.; cert. family nurse practitioner, psychiat. clin. nurse specialist. Staff nurse Hampton Gen. Hosp., 1974-77; nurse practitioner Alvin Bryant, M.D., Hampton, 1978-80, VA Med. Ctr., Hampton, 1980-81; staff nurse VA Med.

Ctr., Richmond, Va., 1983-84; nurse practitioner Naval Regional Med. Ctr., Norfolk, Va., 1981-82; nurse supr. Commonwealth Health Care, Hampton, 1982—; staff nurse Med. Coll. of Va., Richmond, 1988; nurse practitioner Ea. State Hosp., Williamsburg, Va., 1984-91; preceptor Old Dominion U., Norfolk, 1981-82, Hampton U., 1988-89; hon. instr. nurse practitioner program Med. Coll. of Va., 1979-80; cons. Alvin Bryant, M.D., 1981-91; mem. adv. coun. Hampton U. Nursing Ctr., 1989-90; pres. Minority Cancer Task Force, Hampton, 1989-92; corr. sec. Dept. Mental Health/Mental Retardation and Substance Abuse Svcs. Nurse Practitioner Practice Group, 1989-91. Co-leader Girl Scouts U.S., Hampton, 1985-86; v.p. La Progressive Ten, Hampton, 1982; pres. Young Profls. of Tidewater, Hampton, 1980-81. Recipient Cert. of Appreciation, Minority Cancer Task Force, 1985; NIMH Tng. grantee Dept. HHS, 1985, 86. Mem. Va. Coun. Nurse Practitioners, Phi Theta Kappa, Sigma Theta Tau. Democrat. Home: 66 Santa Barbara Dr Hampton VA 23666-1638

JOHNSON, JOHN MORRIS, biology educator; b. Boise, Idaho, Mar. 16, 1937; s. Carl Theodore and Fannie Margaret (King) J.; m. Margaret May, June 13, 1959; children: Mori Kay, Stephen Wade. BS, Coll. Idaho, 1959; MS, Oreg. State U., 1961, PhD, 1964; postgrad., U. Chgo., 1965-66. Asst. prof. Cen. Coll., Pella, Iowa, 1964-67, assoc. prof., 1967-69; assoc. prof. biology Western Oreg. State Coll., Monmouth, 1969-74, prof., 1974—, coordinator biology sect., 1969-72, dir. honors program, 1983-85, chmn. divsn. natural sci. and math., 1985-93. Author: Handbook of Uncommon Plants, 1980; contbr. articles to profl. jours. Dist. chmn. Boy Scouts Am., Polk County, Oreg., 1973-77. Recipient Faculty Honors award Western Oreg. State Coll., 1980, Silver Beaver award Boy Scouts Am., 1981. Mem. AAAS, Am. Soc. Cell Biology, Bot. Soc. Am., Oreg. Acad. Sci. (chmn. biology sect. 1981-82, 88-89), Phi Kappa Phi (chmn. local chpt. 1980-81). Democrat. Methodist. Home: 271 Walnut Dr S Monmouth OR 97361-1944 Office: Western Oreg State Coll 345 Monmouth Ave N Monmouth OR 97361-1314

JOHNSON, JOHN PHILIP, geneticist, researcher; b. Wabash, Ind., June 6, 1949; s. Melvin Leroy and Cleo Pauline (Aldrich) J.; m. Sheryl Kay Kennedy, June 3, 1978; children: Craig Eric, Lindsay Sara. BS, U. Mich., 1971, MD, 1975. Diplomate Am. Bd. Pediatrics, Am. Bd. Med. Genetics. Intern, 2d-yr. resident Children's Hosp. Los Angeles, 1975-77; 3d yr. resident in pediatrics U. Utah, Salt Lake City, 1977-78, fellow in genetics, 1980-82, asst. prof. pediatrics, 1982-85; pediatrician Family Health Program, Salt Lake City, 1978-80; assoc. dir. med. genetics, attending/active staff physician Children's Hosp. Oakland, Calif., 1985-92; dir. med. genetics, attending/active staff physician Children's Hosp., Oakland, 1992-94; dir. med. genetics Shodair Children's Hosp., Helena, Mont., 1994—, active mem. staff, 1995—; clinic physician Utah State Tng. Sch., American Fork, 1982-85; attending and staff physician Primary Children's Med. Ctr., Salt Lake City, 1978-80. Contbr. articles to med. jours. Recipient William J. Branstrom award U. Mich., 1967. Fellow Am. Acad. Pediatrics; mem. Am. Soc. Human Genetics, Soc. for Pediatric Rsch., Alpha Omega Alpha. Home: 2604 Gold Rush Ave Helena MT 59601-5625 Office: Shodair Children's Hosp PO Box 5539 Helena MT 59604-5539

JOHNSON, JOHNNY, research psychologist, consultant; b. Clarksdale, Miss., Jan. 10, 1938; s. Eddie B. and Elizabeth (Ousley) J.; children: Tonya, Anita. Student, Coahoma Jr. Coll., 1957, Hunter Coll., 1964, N.Y.U., 1963; BS, Tenn. State U., 1970, MS, 1974; postgrad., Saybrook Inst., 1987-89. Instr. Dept. of the Navy, Millington, Tenn., 1976-80, edn. specialist, 1980-87, curriculum advisor, 1987-88; prof. human resources mgmt. Pepperdine U., L.A., 1975-77; prof. psychology Shelby State C.C., Memphis, Tenn., 1985—. Actor: (films) Elvis, 1989, Memphis, 1990, The Firm, 1993, A Family Thing, 1995; recording artist with releases in jazz, blues and Latino. With USN, 1957-63. Mem. APA (assoc.), Am. Psychol. Soc., Soc. Psychol. Study of Social Issues, Assn. Black Psychologists, Soc. Psychol. Study Gay and Lesbian Issues, Internat. Platform Assn. Home: 773 Margie Dr Memphis TN 38127-2727

JOHNSON, JONAS TALMADGE, otolaryngology educator; b. Ravenna, Ohio, Jan. 3, 1947; s. J. Norman and K. Alice (Harkarader) J.; m. Janis, Dec. 22, 1968; children: Olin T., Rurik C., Ivar N. MD, SUNY, Syracuse, 1972; postgrad., Dartmouth Coll., 1965-68. Asst. prof. U. Pitts., 1979-84, assoc. prof., 1984-87, prof., 1987—, vice chmn., 1982—; active staff Montefoire Hosp., Pitts., 1987—; cons. VA. Med. Ctr., Pitts., 1979-80, Children's Hosp., Pitts., 1980-89. Editor: Antibiotic Therapy in Head and Neck Surgery, 1987, Am. Jour. Otolaryngology, 1992—; co-editor: Tracheotomy, 1985, Instructional Courses, Vols. 1-6, 1988-92; contbr. articles to med. jours. Maj. M.C., USAF, 1977-79. Recipient Ben Shuster award Am. Acad. Facial Plastic and Reconstructive Surgery, 1976. Mem. ACS, Am. Acad. Otolaryngology-Head and Neck Surgery (bd. dirs. 1992-94, coord. for continuing edn. 1995—, Merit award in clin. rsch. 1976, Honor award 1982, Disting. Svc. award 1994), Am. Soc. for Head and Neck Surgery (sec. 1994—), Soc. Head and Neck Surgeons, Am. Laryngol., Rhinol., and Otol. Soc., Am. Diopter and Decibel Soc., Am. Bronchoesophagologic Soc. Office: Eye and Ear Inst UPMC 203 Lothrop St Ste 500 Pittsburgh PA 15213-2548

JOHNSON, KATHERINE ANNE, health research administrator, lawyer; b. Medford, Mass., Apr. 20, 1947; d. Lester and Eileen Anne (Henaghan) J. BS, La. State U., 1969; MSA, George Washington U., 1972; JD, Cath. U., 1985. Bar: Md. 1985. Pub. health adviser HHS, Washington, 1970-76; dir. plan implementation SE Colo. Health Systems Agy, Colorado Springs, 1976-78; sr. mng. assoc. CDP Assocs., Inc., Atlanta, 1978-87, dir. legal affairs, 1986-87; v.p. Cancer CarePoint Inc., Atlanta, 1987; sr. mgr. Salick Health Care, Inc., Bethesda, Md., 1987-89; pvt. practice atty. cons., Potomac, Md., 1989-90; assoc. dir. for adminstrn. San Antonio Cancer Inst., 1990-96; dir. planning and adminstrn. CTRC Rsch. Found., San Antonio, 1996—; speaker in field. Contbr. articles to profl. jours. Vol. Ct.-Apptd. Spl. Adv. for Abused Children. Mem. Md. Bar Assn., Nat. Health Lawyers Assn., Healthcare Attys., Assn. for Health Svcs. Rsch., Leadership Tex. Class of 1996. Office: CTRC Rsch Found 8122 Datapoint Dr Ste 600 San Antonio TX 78229-3264

JOHNSON, KATHERINE HOLTHAUS, health care marketing professional; b. Denver, Mar. 19, 1961; d. William Philip and Barbara Kristine (Nielsen) Holthaus; m. Robert Scott Johnson; children: Katie Maree, Brian David. B in Applied Math. Engring., U. Colo., 1983; MBA, U. Denver, 1992. Acctg. intern Cooper, Haugen & Co., CPAs, Englewood, Colo., 1982-84; market analyst mktg. dept. Porter Meml. Hosp., Denver, 1985-88; account exec. Tallant LaPointe & Ptnrs., Inc., Englewood, 1988-92; advt. mgr. Micromedex, Inc., Denver, 1992-93; mktg. cons. Highlands Ranch, Colo., 1993-96; planner Micromedex, Inc., Englewood, 1996—. Judge, vol. 4-H Clubs, Met. Denver, 1979—; supt. Sunday sch. Ascension Luth. Ch., Littleton, Colo., 1985-87. Recipient 2 Advantage awards Adventist Health System, 1987. Mem. Soc. for Healthcare Planning and Mktg., Am. Hosp. Assn., Acad. for Health Svcs. Mktg., Am. Mktg. Assn., Alpha Chi Omega. Republican.

JOHNSON, KATHRYN LEE, physician; b. Paterson, N.J., July 27, 1952; d. J. Myron and Constance Mary (Blodgett) J.; children: Jonathan Charles, William James, Andrew Seth, Patrick David Moffat. BA. U. conn., 1974; MS, Stevens Inst. Tech., 1978; MD, Uniformed Svcs. U. of U.S., 1981; MPH, U. Conn., 1990. Commd. ensign USN, 1977, advanced through grades to capt., 1996; physician advisor Groton (Conn.) Vis. Nurses Assn., 1987-96. Com. mem. Bd. Edn., Salem, Conn., 1989, 96; Cubscout den leader Boy Scouts Am., Salem, 1991-94, mem. pack com., 1994-96. Fellow Am. Coll. Preventive Medicine, Am. Coll. Occupational & Environ. Medicine; mem. Am. Pub. Health Assn., Conn. Occupational Medicine Assn. Democrat. Roman Catholic. Home: 32 Cedar Hill Ln Salem CT 06420 Office: Electric Boat Corp 75 Eastern Point Rd Groton CT 06340

JOHNSON, KENNETH M., JR., biomedical scientist; b. Houston, Dec. 7, 1944; s. Kenneth M. and Mary E. Johnson; m. Carolyn Johnson; children: Benjamin, Aaron. BS, Stephen F. Austin U., 1967; PhD, U. Houston, 1974. H.S. tchr. Houston Ind. Sch. Dist., 1967-69; predoctoral fellow U. Houston, 1969-74; postdoctoral fellow Med. Coll. Va., Richmond, 1975-79; asst. prof. U. Tex. Med. Br., Galveston, 1977-82, assoc. prof. pharmacology, 1982-87, prof. pharmacology, 1987—, prof. psychiatry, 1995—, mem. John Sealy Meml. Endowment Fund rev. com., 1995—, mem. acad. planning com., 1989-92; mem. pharmacology rev. panel Nat. Inst. Drug Abuse, Rockville, Md., 1988-92. Mem. editl. bd. Jour. Pharmacology and Exptl. Therapeutics, 1991—; contbr. more than 90 articles to profl. jours. Mem. Galveston County Cultural Arts Coun., 1981-82; coach Little League Baseball, Galveston, 1982-89, Bay Area Soccer Assn., Galveston, 1985-88. Mem. Am. Soc. for Neurosci., Internat. Soc. for Neurochemistry, Am. Soc. for Pharmacology and Exptl. Therapeutics. Office: U Tex Med Br 301 University Blvd Galveston TX 77555-1031

JOHNSON, KENNETH PETER, neurologist, medical researcher; b. Jamestown, N.Y., Mar. 12, 1932; s. Kenneth Peter and Nina (Bengtson) Johnson; m. Jacquelyn Johnson, June 23, 1956; children: Peter, Thomas, Diane, Douglas. B.A., Upsala Coll., East Orange, N.J., 1955; M.D., Jefferson Med. Coll., Phila., 1959. Diplomate: Am. Bd. Psychiatry and Neurology. Intern Buffalo Gen. Hosp., 1959-60; resident Hosp. of Cleve., 1963-65; asst. prof. neurology Case Western Res. U., Cleve., 1968-71, assoc. prof., 1971-74; prof. U. Calif., San Francisco, 1974-81; prof., chmn. U. Md., Balt., 1981—; chief neurology VA Hosp., Balt., 1981-83. Editor: Neurovirology, 1984; contbr. numerous articles in field to profl. jours. Served to lt. U.S. Navy, 1961-63. Recipient Weil award Am. Assn. Neuropathology, 1967; recipient Research Ctr. Devel. award NIH, 1968-73; Zimmerman lectr. Stanford U., 1981. Fellow Am. Neurol. Assn.; mem. Am. Acad. Neurology, Am. Soc. Virology, Am. Clin. and Climatol. Assn., Am. Congress Rehab. Medicine, Am. Soc. Neurorehab., Teratology Soc., Soc. for Exptl. Neuropathology, Internat. Soc. for Neuroimmunology. Lutheran. Home: 49 Seminary Farm Rd Lutherville MD 21093-4545 Office: U Md Hosp Neurology Dept N4W46 22 S Greene St Baltimore MD 21201-1544

JOHNSON, KENNETH RUSSELL, medical educator; b. Superior, Wis., Dec. 14, 1945; m. Cathy Woest; children: Todd, Kellie, Stacy, Mark. BS, Wis. State U., Superior, 1968; MD, U. Wis., Madison, 1972. Diplomate Am. Bd. Surgery; lic. physician, Ariz. Resident in gen. surgery UCLA, 1972-74, Tucson Hosps., 1975-77; asst. clin. prof. surgery U. Ariz., Tucson, 1979—; mem. med. staff St. Elizabeth's Hungary Clinic, Tucson, 1977—, Tucson Med. Ctr., St. Joseph's Hosp., Tucson, St. Mary's Hosp., Tucson, El Dorado Med. Ctr., Tucson, Univ. Hosp., Tucson, N.W. Hosp., Tucson. Contbr. articles to profl. jours. Mem. contract maintenance citizen's panel Pima County Transp. and Flood Control Dist., 1984; mem. profl. adv. group Kimberly Home Health Svcs., Tucson, 1987—. Recipient Thomas Leonard award, 1969, Eben J. Carey award, 1969, Michael J. Carey Sr. Svc. award, 1972; Phillip's scholar, 1971. Fellow ACS; mem. AMA, Am. Trauma Soc. (founder), Am. Soc. Gen. Surgeons, Wis. med. Alumni Assn., Calif. med. Assn., Ariz. Med. Assn. L.A. County Med. Assn., Pima County Med. Soc., Tucson Surg. Soc., Student Am. Med. Assn., Student Health Orgn., Med. Student's Assn., U. Assn. Emergency Med. Svcs., Southwestern Surg. Congress, Elks, Sigma Sigma, Alpha Omega Alpha, Phi Chi. Home: 5155 Camino Alisa Tucson AZ 85718 Office: Thomas-Davis Med Ctrs 630 N Alvernon Way Tucson AZ 85711

JOHNSON, LEAYN HUTCHINSON, nursing educator, mental health nurse; b. Elizabeth, Pa., June 3, 1936; d. Ernest Eba and Edna (Caley) Hutchinson; m. Donald E. Johnson, Mar. 10, 1959; children: Donna Lynn, Donald E. Diploma, McKeesport Hosp. Sch. Nursing, 1957; BSN cum laude, Wright State U., 1975; MS, Ohio State U., 1977; PhD in Psychology, U.S. Internat. U., 1987. RN, Calif. From lectr. to asst. prof. U. Hawaii, Honolulu; prin. Ourself Counseling Ctr., Newport Beach, Calif.; asst. prof. Calif. State U., Long Beach; assoc. prof. Mem. ANA, Calif. Nurses Assn., Sigma Theta Tau. Home: 16932 Edgewater Ln Huntington Beach CA 92649-4206 Office: 1400 Quail St Ste 235 Newport Beach CA 92660

JOHNSON, LELAND "LEE" HARRY, social services administrator; b. Moscow Twp., Wis., Jan. 30, 1947; s. Amos Sanford and Bethellen (Otto) J.; m. Susan Chapman, May 28, 1976; children: Najib, Zack, Jessica, Karine. B degree, Gettysburg Coll., 1969; M degree, Ind. U.-Purdue U., 1971. Supr. psychiat. social work Rock County Guidance Clinic, Beloit, Wis., 1971-73; acting adminstr. Rock County Guidance Clinic, Janesville, Wis., 1974; program dir., coord. Rock County Mental Health Svcs., 1974-75; program dir. Columbia County Home & Unified Bd., Portage, Wis., 1975; svcs. program dir. Columbia County Home & Unified Bd., Portage. Wyocena, Wis., 1975-77; dir. human svcs. Columbia County Health Svcs., Portage, 1977; exec. dir. Navajo County Guidance Clinic, Winslow, Ariz., 1977-78, Coconino Community Guidance Ctr. Inc., Flagstaff, Ariz., 1978-85; human svcs. dir Eau Claire (Wis.) County Human Svcs., 1985-89; from dep. dist. adminstr. to dist. adminstr. Fla. Dept. Health & Rehab. Svcs., Jacksonville, 1989—. Mem. NASW, Acad. Cert. Social Workers. Home: 219 Sequoia Saint Augustine FL 32086 Office: Dept Health & Rehab Svcs 5920 Arlington Expy Jacksonville FL 32211-7156

JOHNSON, LEONARD MORRIS, pediatric surgeon; b. Gowanda, N.Y., June 11, 1931; s. Leonard Brynolf and Helen Berdina (Morris) J.; m. Ann Marie Homer, Mar. 30, 1968; children: H. Leif B. Johnson, Nils A.C. Johnson. BA, Haverford Coll., 1954; MD, U. Pa., 1958; MS in Surgery, U. Minn., Mayo Grad. Sch., Rochester, 1966. Diplomate Am. Bd. Gen. Surgery; cert. special competence in pediatric surgery. Intern Colo. Gen. Hosp., Denver, 1958-59; fellow in gen. surgery Mayo Clinic, Rochester, 1959-63; fellow in pediatric surgery Children's Mercy Hosp., Kansas City, Mo., 1964-65; vis. pediatric surgeon Acad. Hosp., Uppsala, Sweden, 1967; registrar in pediatric urology Alder Hel Children's Hosp., Liverpool, Eng., 1967-68; gen. surgeon SS Hope (Project Hope), Guayquil, Ecuador, 1964; gen. and pediatric surgeon SS Hope (Project Hope), Conakry, Guinea, 1965, Nicaragua, Colombia, Sri Lanka, 1965-68; pediatric surgeon Children's Hosp., Oakland, Calif., 1969—; chief of dept. of surgery Children's Hosp., Oakland, 1989-92. Bd. dirs. Children's Hosp., Oakland, Calif., 1982-91; bd. trustees Children's Hosp. Found., Oakland, 1986—; mem. exec. bd. Mt. Diablo-Silverado Coun. Boy Scouts Am., 1996—. Recipient Order Ruben Dario, Pres. Republic of Nicaragua, Managua, 1966; recipient Bronze Bambino award Children's Hosp., Oakland, 1990. Fellow Am. Coll. of Surgeons, Surgical fellow Am. Acad. of Pediatrics; mem. AMA, Am. Trauma Soc. (founding mem.), Am. Pediat.-Surg. Assn., Pacific Assn. Pediatric Surgeons, Brit. Assn. Pediat. Surgeons, Calif. Med. Assn., Alameda-Contra Costa Med. Assn. Republican. Office: Pediatric Surgical Assocs of the East Bay 744 52d St Ste 4100 Oakland CA 94609

JOHNSON, LEONIDAS ALEXANDER, optometrist, minister; b. Chgo., Jan. 16, 1959; s. Leon and Dolores J.; m. Crystal Dwaun Ellington, June 23, 1990. BA in Biology, Ill. Wesleyan U., 1981; BS in Visual Sci., So. Calif. Coll. of Optometry, Fullerton, 1983, OD, 1985; student, Grace Theol. Sem., Long Beach, Calif., 1986-89, Biola U., La Mirada, Calif., 1991—. Registered optometrist; ordained to ministry Bapt. Ch., 1996. Optometrist Larry Gotlieb, O.D., Redondo Beach, Calif., 1985-86, James Moses, O.D., Inglewood, Calif., 1986-87, Eyecare U.S.A., Montclair, Calif., 1987-89, Pearle Visioncare, Brea, Calif., 1989-94, Montebello Med. Eye Ctr., Calif., 1994-95, Watts Health Found., Inc., L.A., 1994—; chief vision care svcs. Watt's Health Found., Inc., L.A., 1996—; mem. quality assurance com. Eyecare U.S.A., 1988-89, Watts Health Ctr., 1996—, United Health Plan, 1996—; investigator Ocular Hypertension Treatment Study. Contbr. article to profl. jour. Min., deacon Friendship Bapt. Ch., Yorba Linda, Calif. Fellow Am. Acad. Optometry; mem. Am. Optometric Assn., Calif. Optometric Assn., Nat. Optometric Assn. Home: PO Box 4434 Diamond Bar CA 91765-0434 Office: Watts Health Ctr 10300 Compton Ave Los Angeles CA 90002-3628

JOHNSON, LINDA DIANNE, optometrist; b. Richland, Miss., Feb. 5, 1954; d. Adam and Gertrude (Williams) J.; m. James Walter Carson Jr., Apr. 28, 1984 (div. July 1988); 1 child, James Walter Carson III. BS, Jackson (Miss.) State U., 1974; OD, Ind. U., 1978. Dir. optometry clinic Jackson (Miss.) Hinds Comprehensive Health Ctr., 1978—. Bd. dirs. Ctrl. Miss. chpt. ARC, Jackson, 1988—, 2d vice chmn., 1991-93, vice chmn., 1993-95, chmn., 1995—. Named Vol. of Month, Ctrl. Miss. chpt. ARC, 1990. Mem. Am. Optometric Assn., Nat. Optometric Assn. (sec. 1989-93, v.p. 1993-95, regional trustee 1983-85, trustee-at-large 1981-83, Optometrist of the Yr. 1993, pres.-elect 1995—), Soc. Coun. Optometric, Miss. Optometry Assn. (chmn. pub. rels. 1991-93, membership chmn. 1993-95, cert. of appreciation 1990), Jackson State U. Jackson Hind Alumni Assn. (reporter 1979-83, v.p. 1983-85, scholarship chmn. 1979-88, Disting. Svc. award 1982). Democrat. Baptist. Home: 2400 Ladd St Jackson MS 39209-3719 Office: Jackson Hinds Comprehensive Health Ctr 4433 Medgar Evers Blvd Jackson MS 39213-5202

JOHNSON, LLOYD P., surgeon, educator; b. Yakima, Wash., Nov. 6, 1931; s. Philip Samuel and Harriet Evangeline (Danielson) J.; m. Joann Nordale; children: Cynthia, Lloyd Philip Jr., Douglas; m. Kathleen Elizabeth Gates; 1 stepchild, Anthony. BS, U. Wash., 1953, MD, 1956. Diplomate Am. Bd. Surgery. Intern San Francisco Hosp./U. Calif. Svc., 1956-57; resident in surgery U. Wash., 1959-64, sr. rsch. fellow in surgery, 1964-65; prof. surgery Pub. Health Coll. Haile Selassi I U., Gondar, Ethiopia, 1965-67; pvt. practice Seattle Surg. Group; clin. asst. prof. surgery U. Wash., Seattle, 1972-77, clin. assoc. prof. surgery, 1978-89, clin. prof. surgery, 1989-96; exec. dir. Scientific Tech. and Lang. Inst., Seattle, 1996—; pres. bd. dirs. Logoc Bookstore, Seattle, 1970-80; prof. surgery Haile Selassie U., Gondar, Ethiopia, 1965-68; mem. lung com. S.W. Oncology Group, 1957—, mem. surg. exec. com., 1975-80, lung cancer study group, 1978-89. Developer intra-tracheal oxygen catheter; contbr. articles to profl. publs. Vis. surgeon World Med. Mission, Mercy Corps., Sci. Tech. and Lang. Inst., India, 1978, Kenya, 1982, Pakistan, 1990, Kyrgystan, 1993. Capt., flight surgeon USAF, 1957-59. Fellow ACS; mem. AMA, Seattle Surg. Soc. (pres. 1991), King County Med. Soc., Wash. State Med. Assn., North Pacific Surg. Assn. (sec.-treas. 1989-95), Pacific Coast Surg. Assn., Sigma Xi, Alpha Epsilon Delta. Presbyterian. Home: 5600 Ann Arbor NE Seattle WA 98105 Office: Scientific Tech and Lang Inst 1833 N 105th Seattle WA 98133

JOHNSON, LORRAINE ALISON, social worker; b. Sharon, Conn., Mar. 3, 1960; d. Frederick John and Maureen Ann (Johnson) Cahill; m. Eric Frank Johnson, June 11, 1983; children: Samuel Frank, Caleb Frederick. BA, Warren Wilson Coll., Swannanoa, N.C., 1982; MSW, Fordham U., 1983. Lic. ind. cert. social worker, Mass. Social worker women's correctional svcs. Salvation Army, N.Y.C., 1983-85, Lincoln Hall, Lincolndale, N.Y., 1985-86, Child and Family Svcs., Newport, R.I., 1986-87; counselor R.I. Student Assistance Program, Warwick, R.I., 1987-89; social worker Berkshire Farm Ctr. and Scs. for Youth, Canaan, N.Y., 1989-90; outpatient counselor Berkshire Coun. on Alcoholism and Addiction, Pittsfield, Mass., 1990-92; chmn. Hillcrest Ednl. Ctrs., Inc., 1992-95; social worker Wide Horizons for Children, Inc., Pittsfield, Mass., 1995—. Mem. Acad. Cert. Social Workers. Home: RR 1 Richmond MA 01254-9802

JOHNSON, LYNN DOUGLAS, psychologist; b. St. George, Utah, Aug. 23, 1946; s. Grant Douglas and Lorriane (Mason) J.; m. Carol Sue Edson, Feb. 7, 1976; children: Christopher, Jeffrey, Catherine, Stephen. BS, Brigham Young U., 1970; MS, U. Utah, 1974, PhD, 1976. Lic. psychologist, Utah. Pvt. practice psychology Salt Lake City, 1977—; dir. Grief Therapy Ctr., Salt Lake City, 1984—; cons. Aetna/Human Affairs Internat., Salt Lake City, 1988—. Author: Psychotherapy in the Age of Accountability, 1995. Mem. APA, Am. Soc. Clin. Hypnosis, Utah Soc. Clin. Hypnosis (pres. 1970-72), Internat. Assn. Near-Data Studies (dir. Utah chpt. 1973—). Office: Grief Therapy Ctr 166 E 5900 S B-108 Salt Lake City UT 84107

JOHNSON, MARIE-LOUISE TULLY, dermatologist, educator; b. N.Y.C., July 26, 1927; d. James Henry and Mary Frances (Dobbins) Tully; m. Kenneth Gerald Johnson, June 10, 1950. AB, Manhattanville Coll., 1948; PhD, Yale U., 1954, MD, 1956. Intern, then resident Yale-New Haven Med. Ctr., 1956-59; asst. prof. medicine, dermatology Yale U., 1961-67, clin. prof. dermatology, 1980—; chief dermatologist med. svc. Atomic Bomb Casualty Commn., Hiroshima, Japan, 1964-67; assoc. prof. dermatology NYU, 1967-70, 74-76, prof. dermatology, 1976-80; assoc. prof. dermatology, coordinator continuing med. edn. Dartmouth Coll., Hanover, N.H., 1971-74; chief dermatology Bellevue Hosp., N.Y.C., 1974-80; dir. med. edn. Benedictine Hosp., Kingston, N.Y., 1980-93; cons. Health and Nutrition Exam. Survey I, II, Health Stats., Washington, 1967-84. Contbg. author: Cecil's Textbook of Medicine, 15th edit., 1979, 16th edit., 1982, 17th edit., 1985, Dermatology in General Medicine, 2d edit., 1979. Mem. Cardinal Cooke Pro-Life Commn., Albany, N.Y., 1986-87; bd. dirs. Maternity and Early Childhood Found., Albany, 1985—, pres., 1987—. Named Disting. Alumna, Manhattanville Coll., 1977. Fellow Am. Acad. Dermatology (master, bd. dirs. 1976-80; mem. Am. Dermatol. Assn. (bd. dirs. 1986-92, v.p. 1991-92), NAS Inst. Medicine, Internat. Physicians for Prevention of Nuclear War (del. 1982, 83, 87, 88, 89). Roman Catholic. Home: 15 Strawberry Bank Rd High Falls NY 12440 Office: Kingston Hosp Med Arts Bldg Ste 202 368 Broadway Kingston NY 12401-5159

JOHNSON, MARILYN, obstetrician, gynecologist; b. Houston, May 7, 1925; d. William Walton and Marilyn (Henderson) J.; B.A., Rice Inst., 1945; M.D., Baylor U., 1950. Intern, New Eng. Hosp. Women and Children, Boston, 1950-51; resident Meth. Hosp., Houston, 1951-53; resident in gynecology M.D. Anderson Tumor Inst., Houston, 1954, fellow, 1955; fellow in gynecol. pathology Harvard Med. Sch., 1952-53; practice medicine specializing in ob-gyn, Houston, 1954-81, Fredericksburg, Tex., 1981—; mem. staffs St. Joseph's, Meml., Meth., Park Plaza, Hill Country Meml. Rosewood, South Austin Community, Comfort (Tex.) Community hosps.; clin. instr. ob-gyn Coll. Medicine, Baylor U., 1954—, Postgrad. Sch. Medicine, U. Tex., 1954—; gynecologist De Pelchin Faith Home, Houston, 1954—, also Rice U., Richmond State Sch.; med. dirs. Birthright, Inc., Houston, 1973—; chief med. staff Hill Country Meml. Hosp., Fredericksburg, Tex., 1990-92; cons. Tex. bd. Blue Cross Blue Shield; pro-life public speaker. Bd. dirs. Right to Life, Houston, Found. for Life. Sandoz Labs. grantee, 1973, 75, Delbay Pharm. Co. grantee, 1977. Fellow Am. Coll. Obstetricians and Gynecologists; mem. AMA, Am. Soc. Colposcopic Pathologists, Tex. Med. Assn., Am. Med. Women's Assn., Internat. Infertility Assn., Harris County Med. Soc., Postgrad. med. Assembly S. Tex., Houston Ob-Gyn Soc., Tex. Folklore Soc. Republican. Baptist. Clubs: Zonta; Fredericksburg Rockhounds. Home: 205 S Orange St Fredericksburg TX 78624-3738 Office: 204 W Schubert St Fredericksburg TX 78624-3847

JOHNSON, MARK ANTHONY, physician, ophthalmic surgeon; b. Seattle, Mar. 18, 1962. BS, U. Miami, 1984; MD, Northwestern U., 1988. Diplomate Am. Bd. Ophthalmology. Intern St. Francis Hosp./Northwestern U., Evanston, Ill., 1988-89; resident U. Colo. HSC, Denver, 1989-92; commd. 2d lt. USAF, 1992, advanced through grades to maj., 1996; ophthalmologist Homestead (Fla.) AFB, 1992, MacDill AFB, Tampa, Fla., 1992—. Mem. Phi Beta Kappa, Alpha Omega Alpha.

JOHNSON, MARK BERNARR, preventive medicine physician; b. Addis Ababa, Ethiopia, June 10, 1953. MD, Loma Linda U., 1980. Diplomate Am. Bd. Preventive Medicine. Intern (rotation) White Meml. Med. Ctr., L.A., 1980-81; resident in preventive medicine Johns Hopkins U., Balt., 1984-86; clin. asst. prof. U. Colo., Boulder, 1986—. Fellow Am. Coll. Preventive Medicine, Royal Soc. Health; mem. AMA, AHPA. Office: Jefferson County Dept Health & Environment 1801 19th St Golden CO 80401-1798

JOHNSON, MARK KEVIN, operating room nurse; b. Camden, N.J., Mar. 22, 1963; s. Charles James and Doris Frances (Dodd) J. Diploma, Meth. Hosp. Sch. Nursing, Phila., 1984; student, Camden County Coll., Blackwood, N.J., 1991-92, St. Joseph's Coll., Windham, Maine, 1993—. Staff nurse surg. unit Meth. Hosp., Phila., 1984-85, staff nurse intravenous therapy dept., 1985-86; staff nurse surg. unit Misericordia Hosp., Phila., 1987-88, staff nurse operating rm., 1988-92; staff nurse oper. rm. West Jersey Hosp., Voorhees, N.J., 1992—; chairperson continuous Quality Improvement Coun., West Jersey Hosp. Operating Rm., Voorhees, N.J., 1994-95; spkr. role of a nurse Jennings Elem. Sch., Oaklyn, N.J., 1991-93. Fellow Assn. Operating Rm. Nurses. Roman Catholic. Home: 929 Merrick Ave Westmont NJ 08108-3229

JOHNSON, MARY B., medical surgical nurse, educator; b. Virginia, Minn., Apr. 28, 1938; d. Walter Frederick and Hazel Olene (Pedersen) Buntrock; m. Paul Erick Johnson; children Molly J. Magnani, Daniel E., Benjamin P. BSN, St. Olaf Coll., 1960; MSN, U. Minn., 1977, PhD, 1988. RN, NLN; OCN, Oncology Nurses Soc. Staff, charge nurse Union Meml. Hosp., Balt., 1961-64; asst. prof. St. Olaf Coll., Northfield, Minn., 1978-90; assoc. prof. St. Olaf Coll., Northfield, 1990—; adv. bd. Allina Helath Sys., Mpls., 1995—; lectr. in field. Feature writer Lutheran Women Today, 1988-96; contbr. book chpts. Care Curriculum for Oncology Nursing, 1992-95; contbr. articles to profl. jours. Provider of healing touch Pathways, Mpls., 1995-96. Lt. Army Nurse Corps, 1960-61. Grantee Pivitol Course Revision St. Olaf Coll., Northfield, 1983-84, rsch., 1995. Mem. ANA, Minn. Nurses Assn., Oncology Nurses Soc., Metro. Minn. Oncolgy Nurses Soc. (dir. at large),

Am. Holistic Nurses Assn., Minn. Holistic Nurses Assn. (treas., rsch. grantee 1995), Nurse Healer Profl. Assn. Lutheran. Home: 3459 Orchard Ln Minnetonka MN 55305 Office: St Olaf Coll. 1520 St Olaf Ave Northfield MN 55057

JOHNSON, MARY FRANCES, biostatistician, consultant; b. Milford, Conn., Nov. 21, 1951; d. Greig Adams and Ann Catherine (Goulding) J.; m. Robert Walter Makuch, Oct. 22, 1990; 1 child, Justine Elise. BS in Maths., Tufts U., 1973, BA in Philosophy magna cum laude, 1973; MPH in Epidemiology, Yale U., 1975, PhD in Biostatistics, 1978. Math. statistician and group leader bur. drugs FDA, Rockville, Md., 1978-86; prin. statistician G.H. Besselaar Assocs., Princeton, N.J., 1986-88; exec. dir. biostatistics G. H. Besselaar Assocs., Princeton, 1988-90; v.p. biostatistics Corning-Besselaar, Inc., Princeton, 1990-95, PharmaNet, Inc., Princeton, 1996—; rsch. cons. Waterford Conservation Commn., 1973-75; invited speaker Pharm. Mfrs. Assn., 1984, Midwest Biopharm. Stats. Workshop, 1988, Regulatory Affairs Profl. Soc., 1989; mem. NIH task force periodontal disease ADA, Chgo., 1984-86; stats. cons. Procter & Gamble Co., Cin., 1986-94, Mylan Pharms., Tampa, Fla., 1990-94, Astra Pharms, Westborough, Mass., 1990-91, Pfizer, Groton, Conn., 1988-90, Upjohn Co., Kalamazoo, 1992, Oncomembrane, Seattle, 1992-96, Searle, Chgo., 1995-96, Gilead Scis., Foster City, Calif., 1996. Editor: Yale Jour. Biology and Medicine, 1975-78; contbr. chpts. to books and articles to profl. jours. Mem. Am. Stats. Assn., Biometric Soc., Drug Info. Assn. (invited speaker), Soc. for Clin. Trials (invited speaker). Home: 171 Sayre Dr Princeton NJ 08540-5813

JOHNSON, MARY MURPHY, social services director, writer; b. N.Y.C., Mar. 5, 1940; d. Richard and Nora (Greene) Murphy; m. Noel James Johnson, Oct. 8, 1961; children: Valerie Johnson Powell, Donna Homan, Noreen Marie Pettitt, Richard. BA in English/History magna cum laude, Jacksonville State U., 1983, BS in Sociology magna cum laude, 1983, MA in History, 1984, B in Social Work magna cum laude, 1988. Cert. gerontology specialist. Asst. activities dir. Jacksonville (Ala.) Nursing Home, 1985-86; social services dir. Beckwood Manor, Anniston, Ala., 1987—; Cons. in field. Editor: Vladivostak Diary, 1987. Mem. Ala. Archaeol. Soc., Coosa Valley Archaeol. Soc. (sec. 1982-87), Soc. Ala. Archivists, Human Svcs. Coun., Vietnam Vets. Am., Soc. for Creative Anachronism (Reeve, Canton of the Peregrine), Phi Eta Sigma, Phi Alpha Theta, Sigma Tau Delta, Omicron Delta Kappa. Russian Orthodox.

JOHNSON, MICHAEL LEWIS, psychiatrist; b. Louisville, May 17, 1941; s. Ralph L. and Bee (Burr) J.; children: Kirstin, Aaron, Jessica; m. Frances Bourne. AB, Earlham Coll., Richmond, Ind., 1963; MD, Ind. U., 1968. Diplomate Am. Bd. Psychiatry and Neurology. Intern Marion County Gen. Hosp., Indpls., 1968-69; resident in psychiatry Wash. U. Barnes Hosp., St. Louis, 1969-72; staff psychiatrist U.S. Naval Hosp., Portsmouth, Va., 1972-74, South Cen. Community Mental Health Ctr., Bloomington, Ind., 1974-80; psychiatrist pvt. practice, Bloomington, Ind., 1974-83; unit dir. Milford-Whitinsville (Mass.) Regional Hosp., 1983-85; staff psychiatrist Harvard Community Health Plan, Cambridge, Mass., 1985—; instr. in psychiatry Harvard Med. Sch., Cambridge, 1985—, Cambridge Hosp., 1985-92, Brigham and Women's Hosp., 1993—. Author: (book chpt.) Psychotherapists Guide to Pharmacotherapy, 1989; subject of docudrama Virtuoso, 1991. Quaker. Office: Harvard Community Health 1611 Cambridge St Cambridge MA 02138-4302

JOHNSON, MURRAY H., optometrist, researcher, consultant, lecturer; b. Montreal, Que., Can., Jan. 29, 1956; came to U.S., 1980; s. William and Leah (Bedzowski) J.; m. Linda Fluxman, Apr. 30, 1978; children: Warren Natan, Tanya Yael, Arielle Carly. Diploma in Optometry, Witwatersrand Coll., Johannesburg, 1977; postgrad., U. Montreal, 1980; BS, U. Houston, 1981, OD, 1981, MSc in Physiol. Optics and Vision Sci., 1984; postgrad., U. Tex. Health Ctr., 1983. Lic. optometrist, Tex., therapeutic lic., Tex.; cert. ocular therapeutics for treatment and mgmt. ocular disease U. Houston. Clin. instr. U. Houston, 1981-85; researcher Inst. contact Lens Rsch., Houston, 1983-88; pvt. practice optometry specializing in contact lenses Eye & Contact Lens Assocs. North Tex., Dallas, 1985—; vis. asst. prof. U. Houston, 1984-85, adj. asst. prof., 1985-89; cons., clin. investigator Metro Optics, Inc., Dallas, 1989—; premktg. clin. evaluator, cons. and investigator to various contact lens and pharm. mfrs., 1989—; clin. investigator Paragon Optical, Mesa, Ariz., 1992; cons. Unilens Corp., Largo, Fla., 1989; bd. dirs. Equitable Bank-Dallas. Contbr. articles to profl. jours. Mem. clin. care com. Global Vision Inst., Global Vision Dallas, 1996—; mem. edn. com. Akiba Acad. Dallas, 1986-88, bd. dirs., 1986—, long range planning com., 1987-88, devel. com., 1993, v.p., treas., 1993-94, budget com., 1993—, scholarship com., 1994—; bd. dirs. Congregation Share Tefilla, Dallas, 1988-92; steering com. B'nai B'rith, 1986-88, treas., 1987-88; bd. dirs., assoc. bd. dirs. Equitable Bank, Dallas, 1994-96. Fellow U. Houston, 1981, grantee 1981, 82; Ezell Rsch. fellow Am. Optometric Found., 1983. Fellow Am. Acad. Optometry; mem. AAAS, Assn. Rsch. in Vision and Ophthalmology, Am. Pub. Health Assn. (vision care sect.), Am. Optometric Assn. (contact lens sect.), Tex. Optometric Assn., Dallas County Optometric Soc., Better Vision Inst., Am. Optometric Found. (Ezell fellows club), Sigma Xi. Jewish. Office: Eye & Contact Lens Assocs N Tex 18111 Preston Rd Ste 180 Dallas TX 75252-5470

JOHNSON, NOEL LARS, biomedical engineer; b. Palo Alto, Calif., Nov. 11, 1957; s. LeRoy Franklin and Margaret Louise (Lindsley) J.; m. Elise Lynnette Moore, May 17, 1986; children: Margaret Elizabeth, Kent Daniel. BSEE, U. Calif., Berkeley, 1979; ME, U. Va., 1982, PhD, 1990. Mgr. bus. devel. critical care products Hosp. Products divsn. Abbott Labs., Mountain View, Calif., 1986—. Contbr. articles to profl. jours. Fellowship NIH 1980-85; rsch. grantee Abbott Labs. 1989. Mem. IEEE, Biomed. Engrng. Soc., Am. Soc. Anesthesiologists, Sigma Xi, Delta Chi (founder, 1st pres. chpt. U. Calif. at Berkeley). Home: 14586 Aloha Ave Saratoga CA 95070 Office: Abbott Labs Hosp Products Divsn 1212 Terra Bella Ave Mountain View CA 94043-1824

JOHNSON, NORMAN JAMES, physician, lawyer; b. Bklyn., Apr. 15, 1921; s. James Henry and Florence Gertrude (Crilley) J.; m. Bernadette Frances Lowe, Jan. 17, 1948; children: Michael Lowe, Christopher Day, Mark HUghes, David Hughes. AB magna cum laude, Fordham U., 1942; MD, SUNY, 1945; JD, U. Ga., 1979. Bar: Ga. 1981; cert. Am. Bd. Pediat., Am. Bd. Emergency Medicine. Intern Kings County Hosp., Bklyn., 1945-46; intern pediatrics The L.I. Coll. Hosp., Bklyn., 1948-49; resident cardiology Irvington House, Irvington-on-Hudson, N.Y., 1949-50; resident pediatrics Cin. Children's Hosp., 1950-51, chief resident pediatrics, 1951-52; assoc. prof. pediatrics U. Ark., Little Rock, 1952-56; chief pediats. Miners Meml. Hosp., Williamson, W.Va., 1956-59; asst. prof. pediatric medicine U. Tenn. Med. Sch., Memphis, 1959-61; from asst. chief to chief pediatrics Met. Hosp., Detroit, 1961-71; practice medicine specializing in pediats. Athens, Ga., 1972-77; clin. dir emergency medicine St. Mary's Hosp., Athens, 1976-86; with emergency medicine Hilton Head Hosp., Hilton Head Island, S.C., 1986-87; with Newton Gen. Hosp., Covington, Ga., 1987-95; instr. pediatrics U. Cin. , 1951-52, assoc. prof. pediatrics U. Ark., Little Rock, 1952-56, asst. prof. pediatrics U. Tenn., Memphis, 1959-61. Contbr. articles to profl. jours. Pres. PTA, Athens, 1975-76, Friends of Ga. Mus. of Art, Athens, U. Ga., 1985-86, 95-96. Capt. U.S. Army, 1946-48, PTO. Mem. ABA, AMA, Am. Acad. Pediatrics, Am. Coll. Emergency Physicians, Irish and Am. Pediat. Soc. Democrat. Roman Catholic. Home and Office: PO Box 305 Watkinsville GA 30677-0305

JOHNSON, PAUL CHRISTIAN, physiologist, educator; b. Ironwood, Mich., Feb. 3, 1928; s. George Herman and Sophia (Kliemola) J.; m. Genevieve Ruth Shanklin, Sept. 3, 1955; children: Ciri, Philip, Christopher. AA, Gogebic Jr. Coll., 1948; BS in Physics, U. Mich., 1951, MA in Physiology, 1953, PhD, 1955; MD (hon.), U. Limburg, The Netherlands, 1986. Instr. dept. physiology U. Mich., Ann Arbor, 1955-56, Case Western Res. U., Cleve., 1956-58; asst. prof. Ind. U., Bloomington, 1958-61, assoc. prof., 1961-67; prof. physiology U. Ariz, Tucson, 1967-94, head dept., 1967-87; adj. prof. bioengrng. U. Calif. San Diego, La Jolla, 1994—; mem. study sect. on physiology NIH, 1968-72. Mem. editorial bd. Am. Jour. Physiology, 1964-70, co-editor, 1976-78; editorial bd. Jour. Applied Physiology, 1964-70, Circulation Rsch., 1971-76, 81-86; contbr. articles to profl. jours. NIH Spl. postdoctoral fellow, 1965-66; rsch. grantee NIH, 1960—. Mem. Am. Physiol. Soc. (chmn. circulation group 1973-74, mem. coun. 1978-82, Wiggers award lectr. 1981, chmn. publs. com. 1985-89), Microcirulatory Soc. (pres. 1967-68, Landis award lectr. 1976), Basic Sci. Coun., Am. Heart Assn. (exec. com. 1973-75, 82-85, rsch. grantee 1960-72), Tucson Sailing Club. Democrat. Home: 2411 El Amigo Rd Del Mar CA 92014-3118 Office: U Calif San Diego Dept Bioengrng La Jolla CA 92093-0412

JOHNSON, PAUL EDWIN, psychologist, psychotherapist; b. Buffalo, Dec. 27, 1933; s. Sidney O.B. and Maggie Juanita Johnson; m. Shirley A. Williams, Sept. 5, 1957; children: Paula Rene, Darryl Edwin, Justin Edwin. BA, Talladega (Ala.) Coll., 1955; MS, Harvard U., 1957; MDiv, Hartford (Conn.) Theol. Sem., 1958; MEd, Auburn (Ala.) U., 1974, EdD, 1980. Lic. counselor, Ala. Assoc. pastor North N.Y. Congl. Ch., Bronx, 1958-61; commd. 2d lt. U.S. Army, 1961, advanced through grades to lt. col., ret., 1972; quality assurance coord. Ala. Dept. Mental Health and Retardation, Montgomery, 1972-93; ret., 1994; pastor, counselor and psychotherapist First Congl. Christian Ch., Montgomery, 1980-85, 88; ret.; chair Ala. Bd. Examiners, Montgomery, 1986-91; cons. Montgomery Bd. Edn., 1986-88; pvt. practice human rels. cons., Ala., 1985—. Bd. dirs. Coun. on Aging, Montgomery, 1983-86, Montgomery United Way, 1983-86, Cen. Ala. Girl Scouts Coun., Montgomery, 1988—, Ptnrs. in Edn., Montgomery, 1987—. Recipient Legis. award Am. Assn. for Counseling and Devel., 1987, Disting. Svc. award, 1987. Mem. Am. Psychol. Assn., Nat. Acad. Clin. Mental Health Counselors, Am. Bd. Cert. Counselors, Internat. Acad. Profl. Counseling and Psychotherapy. Democrat. Home: 118 Elm Dr Montgomery AL 36117-3712

JOHNSON, PAUL RANDALL, cardiovascular, thoracic surgeon; b. Portsmouth, Va., May 12, 1957; s. Walter M. and Gloria C. (Mueller) J.; m. Melinda K. Johnson, Sept. 4, 1994; 1 child, Katherine Morgan. BS in Chemistry/Biochemistry, Worcester Poly. Inst., 1975; MD, U. Mass., 1979. Diplomate Am. Bd. Surgery, Am. Bd. Thoracic Surgery. Gen. surgery resident U. Mass. Med. Coll., Worcester, 1983-88; gen. surg. registrar William Harvey Hosp., Ashford, Kent, Eng., 1988-89; cardiovascular and thoracic surgery resident N.E. Deaconess Hosp., Boston, 1989-91; pvt. practice Bristol County Surg. Assocs., Taunton, Mass., 1991—. Fellow ACS; mem. AMA, Mass. Med. Soc., Am. Soc. for History of Medicine. Office: 895 Prospect St North Dighton MA 02764-1329*

JOHNSON, PAULINE BENGE, nurse, anesthetist; b. London, Ky., May 10, 1932; d. Chester G. and Bertha M. (Hale) Benge; m. Scottie W. Johnson, Apr. 29, 1950 (dec. 1976); children: Rita Johnson, Nita Johnson Yaw, Gina Johnson Carlson. AA, U. Ky., 1968; diploma, U. Cin. Sch. Nurse Anesthesia, 1971; BS summa cum laude, U. Cin., 1974, M., 1977, D., 1981. RN, Ohio, Ky., Tenn., Ind., W.Va., Fla., Tex.; cert. lic. RN anesthetist; cert. RN anesthetist. Staff anesthetist Jewish Hosp., Cin., 1971-72, Mercy North Hosp., Hamilton, Ohio, 1972-86, Ft. Hamilton Hosp., Hamilton, 1972-86, McCullough-Hyde Hosp., Oxford, Ohio, 1986-88; freelance anesthetist multiple hosps. Ohio, Ky., 1982-88; staff anesthetist, ind. contractor Shriner Burn Inst., Cin., 1989; pres., staff anesthetist, ind. contractor multiple hosps. Pauline B. Johnson Co., Inc., Ohio, Ky., Tenn., Ind., W. Va., Fla., Tex., 1989—; provider hosp. anethesia relief svcs. to under-serviced rural hosp. oper. rms., 1990—. Ch. clk. Lindenwald Bapt. Ch., Hamilton, 1955-72, mem. 1955-85, instr., 1955-76; mem. 1st Bapt. Ch., Hamilton, 1985—, NOW, 1978—, nominating com. major polit. party, Hamilton, 1986-89; mem., med. com. Planned Parenthood, Hamilton, 1987—; vol. various rural hosps., 1990—. Scholar U. Cin., 1969-71, 77-81; recipient Spl. Recognition Higher Edn., Laurel County Homecoming, London, Ky., 1988. Mem. Am. Assn. Nurse Anesthetists (speaker nat. conv. 1982, speaker rsch. forum nat. meeting 1989, mem. nominating com. 1978), Ohio State Assn. Nurse Anesthetists (state bd. dirs. 1989-92, 88-90, 79-80, chair bylaws com. 1991-92, 92-93, nominating com. 1993-94, chair edn. com. 1990-91, pres. 1982-84, state editor Highlights 1974-82, co-chair state meeting 1982, pres. dist. 5 Cin. 1978, govt. rels. chpt. Greater Cin. chpt. 1976-87, speaker meetings), Kappa Delta Pi. Home: 128 S F St Hamilton OH 45013-4710

JOHNSON, PETER FINK, prosthodontist, educator, consultant; b. Richmond, Va., July 30, 1945; s. Joel Benjamine and Emma Elizabeth (Fink) J.; m. Marie Bernadette Betts, Oct. 29, 1988; 1 child, Neil Wesley. AB, Princeton U., 1967; DMD, U. Pa., 1971; cert. in prosthodontics, U. So. Calif., 1977. Diplomate Am. Bd. Prosthodontists. Commd. 1st lt. USN, 1971, advanced through grades to capt., 1987; dir. Area Dental Lab. USN, San Diego, 1986-91; ret., 1991; pvt. practice, La Mesa, Calif., 1991—; former asst. prof. Naval Dental Sch., Bethesda, Md.; professorial lectr. Georgetown U., Washington, 1982-87; asst. prof. U. So. Calif. Sch. Dentistry, L.A., 1988-96, assoc. prof., 1996—. Contbr. articles to dental jours. Fellow Am. Coll. Prosthodontists (bd. dirs. 1988—, pres. 1993-94), Internat. Coll. Prosthodontists, Internat. Coll. Dentists; mem. ADA, Calif. Dental Assn., Pacific Coast Soc. Prosthodontists (assoc.), Omicron Kappa Upsilon. Office: Ste 1-110 5565 Grossmont Center Dr La Mesa CA 91942

JOHNSON, PHYLLIS ELAINE, chemist; b. Grafton, N.D., Feb. 19, 1949; d. Donald Gordon and Evelyn Lorraine (Svaren) Lanes; m. Robert S.T. Johnson, Sept. 12, 1969; children: Erik, Sara. BS, U. N.D., 1971, PhD, 1976. Instr. chemistry Mary Coll., Bismarck, N.D., 1971-72; postdoctoral rsch. fellow U. N.D., Grand Forks, 1975-79, chemist, 1977-79; rsch. chemist USDA Human Nutrition Rsch. Ctr., 1979-87, rsch. leader for nutrition, biochemistry and metabolism, 1987-91; assoc. dir. Pacific West Area USDA-ARS, 1991—. Editor: Stable Isotopes in Nutrition, 1984; mem. editorial bd. Jour. Micronutrient Analysis, 1988-91; contbr. articles to profl. jours. Chmn. Parents of Gifted and Talented, 1984-86. Recipient Arthur S. Flemming award Outstanding Sci. Achievement, 1989, Women in Sci. and Engring. award, 1993. Mem. Am. Soc. for Clin. Nurition, Am. Chem. Soc., Am. Inst. Nutrition, Internat. Soc. for Trce Element Rsch. in Humans (sec. 1992-95), Exec. Women in Govt., Sr. Exec. Assoc., Soc. Exptl. Biology and Medicine, Phi Beta Kappa, Sigma Xi. Lutheran. Lodge: Sons of Norway (dist. v.p. 1984-86, dist. pres. 1986-88, internat. bd. dirs. 1988-92). Avocations: cooking, skiing, needlework, camping. Home: 828 Dorset Way Benicia CA 94510-3609 Office: USDA 800 Buchanan St Berkeley CA 94710-1105

JOHNSON, RAYMOND ARD, psychiatrist, educator; b. Lewistown, Pa., Nov. 22, 1942; s. Raymond Ard and Elsie Clara (Sowers) J.; m. Linda R. Johnson; 1 child, Hilary. BS in Speech Therapy, Bloomsburg State U., 1965; MD, Temple U., 1972. Diplomate Am. Bd. Psychiatry and Neurology. Speech therapist Montgomery County Sch. System, 1965-68; intern in internal medicine Hahnemann U., Phila., 1972-73, resident in psychiatry, 1977-80, now asst. clin. instr.; emergency room physician, adminstr. Atlanta Emergency Physicians Group, Riverdale, Fla., 1975-77; pvt. practice Penn Valley, Pa., 1980—; dir. chem. dependence unit The Willough, Naples, Fla., 1995—; dir. addictive svcs. Guiffre Med. Ctr., Phila., 1980-81, program dir. substance abuse unit Fairmount Inst., Phila., 1981-87, Horsham Clinic, Ambler, Pa., 1987-89; med. dir. Malvern (Pa.) Inst., 1989-91; psychiat. cons. Impaired Physicians Com., Lemoyne, Pa., 1988-89, Camden (N.J.) Diocese, 1988-89; bd. dirs. Starting Point, Collingswood, N.J.; speaker in field; mem. complimentary med. staff Northwestern Psychiat. Inst.; exec. mem. Coun. for Compulsive Gambling; assoc. med. dir. addiction svcs. Northwestern Inst. Psychiatry., 1993; active med. staff Hortham Clinic. Contbr. articles to med. jours. Lt. comdr. M.C., USN, 1973-75. Mem. AMA, Am. Psychiat. Assn. (Falk fellow 1980), Am. Soc. Addictive Medicine (cert.), Fla. Psychiat. Assn. Republican. Home and Office: 5260 S Landings Dr Apt 507 Fort Myers FL 33919

JOHNSON, RAYMOND BRUCE, medical educator; b. Sheridan, Wyo., Aug. 25, 1946; s. Charles Raymond and Dorothy Alberta (Fowler) J.; m. Judith Elaine Fisher, Aug. 31, 1968; children: Kristi, Erica. BS, Chadron State Coll., 1968; B of Med. Sci., Emory U., 1973. Lic. physician asst., Wyo. Med. tech. intern. St. John's Hosp., Rapid City, S.D., 1968-69, med. technologist, 1968-70, lab. supr., 1969-70; physician asst. Dr. Mary Fisher Clinic, Pagosa Springs, Colo., 1973-79; asst. prof. family practice, asst. dir. adminstrn. affairs family practice residency program U. Wyo., Casper, 1979—; mem. adv. bd. Wyo. Bd. Medicine, 1980-94; acting dir. Area Health Edn. Ctr., Wyo., 1994—. Contbr. articles to profl. jours. Coroner Archuleta County, Pagosa Springs, 1978-79. Recipient Hernan Alvarez Meml. award Wyo. Heart Assn., 1987; named EMS Profl. of Decade 1980-90 Wyo. Office Emergency Med. Svcs. Fellow Am. Acad. Physician Assts. (Nat. Phys. Asst. of Yr. 1987, profl. practice coun. 1987-94), Wyo. Assn. of Physician Assts. (Physician Asst. of Yr. 1984, 87, pres. 1985-86, v.p. 1983-84, sec. 1982-83). Home: 4036 Bretton Casper WY 82609 Office: Family Practice Residency U Wyo 1522 East A Casper WY 82601

JOHNSON, RICHARD, marketing professional, physician; b. Bethpage, N.Y., Sept. 14, 1958; s. Henry Leonard and J. (Jacobs) J.; m. Nora Anastelli, Aug. 1, 1981. BA magna cum laude, NYU, 1981; MD, Mt. Sinai Sch. of Medicine, 1985. Diplomate Nat. Bd. Med. Examiners. Pres. HTS, St. Louis, 1987-88; dir. clin. rsch. Lederle Labs., Wayne, N.J., 1988-90, dir. mktg., 1990-93; gen. ptnr. The Genesis Fund, Houston, 1993—; CEO, pres. OED Internat., Valhalla, N.Y., 1994—. Contbr. articles to profl. jours. Mem. ACP, N.Y. Venture Capital Club, Houston Venture Capital Assn. Office: OEO Internat 20 Madison Ave Valhalla NY 10595

JOHNSON, RICHARD DEAN, pharmaceutical consultant, educator; b. De Kalb, Ill., July 8, 1936; s. Arthur Dean and Evelyn Alice (Telford) J.; BS, U. Calif., Berkeley, 1960; PharmD, U. Calif., San Francisco, 1961, MS, 1962, PhD, 1965; MBA, Rockhurst Coll., Kansas City, Mo., 1984; m. Paula Marcellus Jennings, Nov. 3, 1942; children: Janet Telford, Julie Tess, Richard Dean, Jr., Jennings Brodie. Pharmacy lic., Calif.; cert. tchr., Calif. Sect. head R & D Allergan Pharms., Irvine, Calif., 1965-67; dir. regulatory affairs Syntex Labs., Inc., Palo Alto, Calif., 1967-73; mng. dir. licensing Marion Labs., Inc., Kansas City, Mo., 1973-79, v.p. licensing, 1980-82, v.p. corp. devel., 1983-87, v.p. bus. alliances, 1987-89; corp. v.p. Marion Merrell Dow Inc., Kansas City, Mo., 1989-91, ret., chmn., CEO KC Pharma, Mo., 1991—; adj. prof. Sch. Pharmacy U. Mo., Kansas City, 1991-95, rsch. coun., 1993—, adj. grad. prof., 1995—; bd. dirs. Dey Labs. Inc., Concord, Calif., Tanabe-Marion Labs., Kans. City, U.S. Biosci. Inc., Blue Bell, Pa., ImmunoPharmaceutics, Inc., San Diego, Lovelace Med. Found., Albuquerque, N.Mex., Micrologix Biotech Inc., Vancouver, B.C.; guest lectr. U. S.C. Coll. Bus. Adminstrn., Columbia, 1975-79. Presdl. exchange exec. White House, Washington, 1970-71, U.S. Pharmacopeia Com. of Rev., 1990-94, 95—; trustee U. Mo., Kansas City Pharmacy Found., 1993—, v.p., 1994-96, pres. 1996—, chmn. devel. com., 1994-96, chmn. exec. and fin. coms., 1996—, dean's adv. bd., 1995—; trustee Kansas City Cmty. Found., 1993—, U. Kansas City Bd., Mo., 1996—; mem. dean's adv. bd. Sch. Pharmacy U. Calif., San Francisco, 1994—, Sch. Pharmacy U. Mo., Kansas City, 1995—; active De La Salle Sch. Devel. Com., 1993—, St. Lukes Hosp. Stroke Com., 1993—, USP Drug Nom. Com., 1990-94, 95—, ARC, Kirkwood Soc. Recipient Grad. award Borden Co., 1962; Am. Found. for Pharm. Edn. fellow, 1962-64; Sir Henry S. Wellcome Meml. fellow, 1962-63; Am. Inst. Chemists fellow, 1965-70. Mem. AAAS, ACS, ARC Kirkwood Soc., Am. Assn. Pharm. Scis., Am. Pharm. Assn., Acad. Pharm. Sci., N.Y. Acad. Sci., Pharm. Mfrs. Assn., Fedn. Internat. Pharmacy, Licensing Exec. Soc., Sigma Xi, Rho Chi, Phi Lambda Sigma. Republican. Clubs: Balboa Bay (Newport Beach, Calif.), Carriage (Kansas City, Mo.), Hallbrook Country Club. Contbr. articles to pharm. jours. Home: 5330 Ward Pky Kansas City MO 64112-2369 Office: KC Pharma LLC 222 W Gregory Blvd Kansas City MO 64114-1127

JOHNSON, RICHARD FREDERICK, psychologist, researcher, educator; b. Boston, July 11, 1943; s. Frederick and Alice Hilda (Kullen) J.; m. Sharyn Lois Doyle, Sept. 11, 1965; children: Wendy Kullen, Adam Bruns. BA with honors, Northeastern U., 1966; MA in Psychology, Brandeis U., 1968, PhD, 1970. Lic. psychologist, Mass. Rsch. psychologist Medfield (Mass.) Found., 1972-76; rsch. psychologist Human Factors and Physiology Group U.S. Army Natick R&D Labs., 1976-83; rsch. psychologist, acting chief Mil. Performance and Neurosci. div. U.S. Army Rsch. Inst. Environ. Medicine, Natick, 1983—; mem. faculty Medfield State Hosp., 1974-76; sr. lectr. psychology Northeastern U., 1971-76, 84—; cons. in field. Editl. cons. Jour. Consulting and Clin. Psychology, 1973-83, Exercise and Sport Sis. Revs., 1985-87, Psychosomatic Medicine, 1987—, Jour. of Aging & Health, 1991—, Human Factors, 1992—, Armed Forces & Soc., 1993—; corr. assoc. commentator The Behavioral and Brain Scis., 1978—; contbr. more than 100 articles to profl. jours., book chpts., tech. reports. Capt. Med. Svc. Corps U.S. Army, 1970-72, with Res., 1966-74. Recipient Milton H. Erickson Sci. Excellence award Am. Soc. Clin. Hypnosis, 1977; grantee Nat. Inst. Mental Health, 1972-76; fellow Brandeis U. 1967-70. Fellow Am. Psychol. Assn. (chmn. conv. program div. gen. psychology 1974-75), Am. Psychol. Soc.; mem. AAAS, Aerospace Med. Assn.,Human Factors and Ergonomics Soc., Soc. Applied Exptl. Engrng. Psychologists, Sigma Xi (chmn. program com., 1989-90, pres.-elect 1990, pres. 1991). Office: US Army Rsch Inst Environ Medicine Mil Performance Neuros Div Natick MA 01760

JOHNSON, RICHARD T., neurology, microbiology and neuroscience educator, research virologist; b. Grosse Pointe, Mich., July 16, 1931; s. Horton and Katharine (Tidball) J.; m. Frances W. Johnson, Sept. 18, 1954; children: Carlton, Erica, Matthew, Nathan. AB cum laude, U. Colo., Boulder, 1953; MD, U. Colo., Denver, 1956. Diplomate Am. Bd. of Psychiatry and Neurology. Intern Stanford U. Hosps., San Francisco, 1956-57; clin. pathologist dept. virus diseases Walter Reed Army Inst. of Research, Washington, 1957-58, asst. chief dept. of virus diseases, 1959; asst. resident in neurology Mass. Gen. Hosp., 1959-60, clin. fellow neuropathology, 1959-61, sr. resident neurology, 1961-62; teaching fellow in neurology Harvard Med. Sch., Boston, 1959-60, teaching fellow neuropathology, 1959-61; teaching fellow neurology Harvard Med. Sch., 1961-62; exchange teaching fellow, 1st asst. in neurology Med. Sch. of King's Coll., U. Durham, Newcastle-Upon-Tyne, 1962; hon. fellow dept. microbiology Australian Nat. U., Canberra, 1962-64; assoc. neurologist Cleve. Met. Gen. Hosp., 1964-69; asst. prof. neurology Case Western Res. U., Cleve., 1964-68, assoc. prof. neurology, 1968-69; assoc. prof. microbiology Johns Hopkins U. Sch. of Medicine, Balt., 1969-74, Dwight D. Eisenhower prof. neurology, 1969-88, prof. microbiology, 1974—, prof. neurosci., 1983—; joint appointment dept. immunology and infectious diseases Johns Hopkins U. Sch. Hygiene and Pub. Health, 1984—; neurologist Johns Hopkins Hosp., Balt., 1969-88, neurologist-in-chief, 1988—, prof., dir. dept. neurology, 1988—; cons. neurology Balt. City Hosps., 1974; vis. prof. U. Peruana Cayetano Heredia, Lima, Peru, 1971, Imperial Coll. of Health Scis., Teheran, Iran, 1974, Inst. fur Virologie und Immunobiologie, U. Wurzburg, 1976; vis. prof. neurology and neuropathology Mahidol U., Bangkok, 1984; vis. scientist Armed Forces Research Inst. of Med. Scis., Bangkok, Thailand, 1984;. Author: (with others) Amotrophic Lateral Sclerosis: Recent Research Trends, 1976, Infections of the Nervous System, 1987, Viral Infections and the Developing Nervous System, 1988; author: Viral Infections of the Nervous System, 1982, Current Therapy in Neurologic Diseases, 1985, Current Therapy in Neurologic Diseases, Vol. 2, 1987, Vol. 3, 1990; mem. editorial bd. 10 profl. jours. Mem. adv. coun. James A. Baker Inst. for Animal Health, Cornell U., 1977-89; program dir. Pew Neurosci. Program, Pew Charitable Trusts, 1985-91; mem. adv. bd. Nat. Multiple Sclerosis Soc., 1971—, exec. com., 1981—, chmn. 1985-89. Recipient Jean Martin Charcot award Internat. Fedn. of Multiple Sclerosis Socs., 1985, Smadel medal Infectious Disease Soc. of Am., 1986, Multiple Sclerosis Soc. medal Assn. of Brit. Neurologists, 1986; comendador Order of Hipolito Unanue, 1981, numerous others. Fellow Am. Acad. of Neurology (2d v.p. 1975-77); mem. Assn. of Am. Physicians, Am. Soc. for Virology, Australian Assn. of Neurologists (hon.), Interurban Clin. Club, Acad. Brasileira de Neurologia, Assn. for Research in Nervous and Mental Diseases, Internat. Brain Research Orgn., Peripatetic Club, Soc. for Neurosci., Soc. Peruana de Psiquiatria, Johns Hopkins Med. Soc. (pres. 1970-71), Balt. Neurol. Soc. (pres. 1973-74), Am. Soc. for Clin. Investigation, Am. Neurol. Assn. (councillor 1977-81, v.p. 1984-85, pres. 1986-87), Am. Assn. of Neuropathologists (assoc.), World Fedn. of Neurology (chmn. research group on neuroimmunology and virology 1979—), Am. Soc. for Microbiology, AAAS, Philippine Neurol. Assn. (hon. fellow), Internat. Soc. for Antiviral Research, Inst. of Medicine of the Nat. Acad. of Sci., Am. Fedn. of Clin. Research, Alpha Omega Alpha, Phi Beta Kappa. Office: Johns Hopkins U Sch Medicine Dept of Neurology 600 N Wolfe St Meyer 6-113 Baltimore MD 21287-7613

JOHNSON, ROBERT EUGENE, physiologist; b. Conrad, Mont., Apr. 8, 1911; s. Arthur D. and Florence May (Disbrow) J.; m. Margaret Hunter, Jan. 11, 1935; children: Thomas Arthur, Charles William, Katherine Helen (dec.). B.S. in Chemistry, U. Wash., 1931; B.A. in Physiology (Rhodes scholar), U. Oxford, Eng., 1934, D.Phil. in Biochemistry, 1935; M.D., Harvard U., 1941. Research asst. advancing to asst. prof. indsl. physiology Harvard Fatigue Lab., 1935-46; expert cons. QMC 3, AUS, 1941-46; dir. U.S. Army Med. Nutrition Lab., Chgo., 1946-49; prof. physiology U. Ill. at Urbana, 1949-73, head dept., 1949-60, dir. univ. honors program, 1959-67, acting dean Grad. Coll., 1952-53; prof. biology Knox Coll., Galesburg, Ill.,

1973-79; coordinator Knox Coll.-Rush U. Med. Program, 1973-79; sci. cons. Presbyn.-St. Luke's Hosp., Chgo., 1973-83; pres. Horn of the Moon Enterprises, Montpelier, Vt., 1980—; vis. prof. physiology U. Vt., 1983—. Co-author: Metabolic Methods, 1951, Physiological Measurements of Metabolic Functions in Man, 1963; author: Sir John Richardson, 1976; also articles in profl. jours. NSF Sr. Postdoctoral Research fellow, 1957-58; Guggenheim Meml. Found. fellow, 1964-65. Mem. Am. Soc. Clin. Investigation, Am. Physiol. Soc., Nutrition Today, History of Sci. Soc., Phi Beta Kappa, Sigma Xi. Home and Office: 5 East Ter South Burlington VT 05403-6145

JOHNSON, ROBERT LEE, JR., physician, educator, researcher; b. Dallas, Apr. 28, 1926; s. Robert L. and Doris (Miller) J.; m. Aileen Johnson, 1952; children: Stephen Lee, Robert Edward. BS, So. Meth. U., 1947; MD, Northwestern U., 1951. Intern Cook County Hosp., Chgo., 1951-52; resident in internal medicine Parkland Meml. Hosp., Phila., 1952-55; fellow nat. foun. infantile paralysis and clin. instr. U. Tex. Southwestern Med. Ctr., Dallas, 1955-56; fellow dept. physiol. and pharmacology Grad. Sch. Medicine U. Pa., Phila., 1956-57; asst. prof. U. Tex. Southwestern Med. Ctr., Dallas, 1959-65, assoc. prof., 1965-69, prof. medicine, 1969—; vis. staff Parkland Meml. Hosp., Dallas, 1957—, Zale Lipshy U. Hosp., Dallas, 1989—; cons. chest diseases VA Hosp., Dallas, 1966—; dir. chest medicine clinic Parkland Meml. Hosp., 1983—; mem. parent rev. com. Nat. Heart, Lung, and Blood Inst. for Spl. Ctrs. of Rsch. proposals, 1983-85; mem. Nat. Heart, Lung, and Blood Rsch. Rev. Com., 1985-89; mem. respiratory and applied physiology study sect. NIH, 1991-94. Assoc. editor: Jour. Clin. Investigation, 1972-77; mem. editl. bd. Jour. Applied Physiology, 1980-82; guest referee editor Jour. Applied Physiology, Am. Jour. Physiology, Chest, Circulation, Circulation Rsch., Am. Rev. Respiratory Disease, Am. Jour. Med. Sci., Jour. Clin. Investigation, Early Human Devel., Kidney Internat.; contbr. articles to profl. jours. With Naval ROTC, 1945-46; with USNR, 1944-46; maj. USAR, 1962. Mem. Am. Heart Assn. (cardiopulmonary coun. exec. com. mem. 1990-92, nominating com. cardiopulmonary coun. 1989—, chmn. 1990-92), Am. Thoracic Soc. (planning com. mem. 1987-90, com. proficiency standards 1985—), Am. Coll. Chest Physicians, Am. Fedn. Clin. Rsch., Am. Physiol. Soc., Am. Soc. Clin. Investigation, Assn. Am. Physicians, Cen. Soc. Clin. Rsch., So. Soc. Clin. Rsch., Soc. Sigma Xi. Office: UT Southwestern Med Ctr 5323 Harry Hines Blvd Dallas TX 75235-7200

JOHNSON, ROBERT WILLIAM GREENWOOD, transplant surgeon; b. Reigate, Surrey, Eng., Mar. 15, 1942; s. Robert William and Suzanne (Mills) J.; m. Carolyn Mary Vooght, July 23, 1942; children: Melanie Jane Johnson, Julian Robert Greenwood Johnson. B Medicine, Durham U., 1965, B Surgery, 1965; M Surgery with distinction, U. Newcastle on Tyne, 1973. Reg. GMS, gen. surgery. House surgeon Royal Victoria Infirmary, Newcastle Upon Tyne, 1965-66; sr house officer, registrar Newcastle Gen. Hosp., Royal Victoria Infirmary, 1966-70; sr. rsch. fellow Newcastle U., 1970-71; sr. registrar Royal Victoria Infirmary, Newcastle, 1971-74; vis. asst. prof. U. Calif.-Moffat Hosp., San Francisco, 1974; cons. surgeon, reader in surgery Manchester Royal Infirmary, Manchester U., 1974—; dir. N.W. Regional Transplant Svc., 1976—. Author: (book) Scientific Foundations of Urology, 1990. Fellow Royal Coll. Surgeons of Edinburgh; mem. Am. Soc. Transplant Surgeons, British Transplantation Soc. (pres. 1995-98), Internat. Transplant Soc. Office: Manchester Royal Infirmary-Renal Transplant Unit, Oxford Rd, M13 9WL Manchester England

JOHNSON, SHELDON ASHLEY, oncologist; b. Poplarville, Miss., June 27, 1948; s. Henry Ashley and Wanda Victoria (Jennings) J.; m. Millicent Ann LeBlanc, Aug. 15, 1970 (div.); children: Lars Adam, Amanda Ellen, Amelia Frances; m. Judith Lutens Rowe, Nov. 27, 1993. BS in Biol. Sci., U. New Orleans, 1970; MD, U. Miss. Med. Sch., 1974. Diplomate Am. Bd. Radiology. Rotating intern William Beaumont Army Med. Ctr., El Paso, Tex., 1974-75; gen. med. officer Fort Polk (La.) Army Hosp., 1975-76; resident in radiation oncology M.D. Anderson Cancer Ctr., Houston, 1976-79; staff radiation oncologist Walter Reed Army Med. Ctr., Washington, 1979-81; staff radiation oncologist Mary Bird Perkins Cancer Ctr., Baton Rouge, 1981-86, med. dir., 1986—; asst. prof. La. State U. Med. Sch., New Orleans, 1981—; adj. asst. prof. nuclear sci. ctr. La. State U., Baton Rouge, 1982—. Editor Cancer Quarterly, 1987-89. Bd. chmn. La. divsn. Am. Cancer Soc., New Orleans, 1990-92, bd. dirs., 1985-92, Greater Baton Rouge unit Am. Cancer Soc., 1982—. Recipient Quality of Life award La. Div. Am. Cancer Soc., 1989. Mem. AMA, Am. Coll. Radiology, Am. Soc. for Therapeutic Radiology and Oncology, Am. Endocurietherapy Soc., Gilbert H. Fletcher Soc., M.D. Anderson Assocs., Ama. Coll. Radiation Oncology. Lutheran. Home: 411 Woodstone Ct W Baton Rouge LA 70808 Office: Mary Bird Perkins Cancer 4950 Essen Ln Baton Rouge LA 70809-3432

JOHNSON, STEPHEN CHARLES, exercise physiology and sport science educator; b. Vancouver, Wash., Sept. 15, 1950; s. Russell Cahles and Jeanne (Stephens) J.; m. Marianne Griffith, Dec. 27, 1971 (div. 1978); m. Kristine McTavish, June 26, 1994. BS in Biology, U. Utah, 1976, PhD in Exercise Physiology, 1985. Vis. asst. prof. dept. exercise and sport sci. U. Utah, Salt Lake City, 1985-87, asst. prof. dept. exercise and sport sci., 1987-91, assoc. prof., 1991—, adj. assoc. prof. dept. bioengring., 1996—; adj. assoc. prof. dept. bioengring. U. Utah, 1996—; adj. asst. prof. div. foods and nutrition U. Utah, 1987—, dir. Human Performance Rsch. Lab., 1987—, adj. assoc. prof., 1993—; dir. physiology U.S. Ski Team, Park City, Utah, 1987-90; dir. sport sci. U.S. Skiing, 1991—; cons. to Health Rider, Inc., Salt Lake City, 1995—, Vetta Sports, Inc., Park City, 1995—, Orthopedic Splty. Hosp., Salt Lake City, 1994—, Utah Sports Found., 1988-91; cons. cardiac rehab. Holy Cross Hosp., Salt Lake City, 1985-90. Author: Coaches Guide to Diet and Weight Control, 1990; contbr. over 100 articles and abstracts to profl. jours. Mem. Utah Gov.'s Coun. on Health and Phys. Fitness, Salt Lake City, 1986-88, chmn. sport medicine, 1988; mem. Mayor's Bicycle Com., Salt Lake City, 1986-89. Grantee Purdue Frederick Co., 1988, U.S. Olympic Com., 1990, HealthRider, Inc., 1994, 95, Nat. Operating Com. on Stds. in Athletic Equipment 1994-95, U.S. Ski Team Found., 1992, 93, 94, others; named U.S. Cycling Fedn. Masters Athlete of Yr., 1989; recipient Outstanding Contbn. to Fitness award Utah Gov. Coun. on Phys. Fitness, 1988. Mem. Am. Coll. Sports Medicine, AAHPERD (chmn. sports medicine S.W. dist.), AAAS, AAUP. Democrat. Home: 10119 S Bell Canyon Rd Sandy UT 84092 Office: U Utah Dept Exercise & Sport Sci 230 E Hper Salt Lake City UT 84112-1184

JOHNSON, SYLVESTER, health services administrator; b. Chesson, Ala., Mar. 20, 1948; s. Taylor and Lula (Elmore) J.; m. Ynetta V. Darden, June 21, 1977 (div. Jan. 1986); children: Anita M., Carlena; m. Anne Bascomb Johnson, Aug. 29, 1986; children: Calenge, Stephanie, Carl, Eric. AS, Alexander Jr. Coll., 1978; diploma data processing, Opelikia Tech. Coll., 1978; student, Friends U., 1995. Chief computer program Tuskegee (Ala.) U., 1978-80; data processing mgr. City of Tuskegee, 1980-83; sr. programmer Van Guard Tech., Charleston, S.C., 1983-84, State of Ala., Auburn, 1984-85; computer system analyst Dept. ov VA, Tuskegee, 1985-87, Waco, Tex., 1987-90; asst. chief info. resources mgmt. svc. Dept. ov VA, Washington, 1990-94; chief info. resources mgmt. svc. Dept. ov VA, Leavenworth, Kans., 1994—; cons. Sylvester Johnson, Tuskegee, 1983; data processing instr. So. Vocat. Coll., Tuskegee, 1985-86. With USAF, 1966-73. Recipient Award Freedom Found., 1968. Mem. Healthcare Info. Mgmt. System soc. Jehovah's Witnesses. Home: 8613 N Beaman Ave Kansas City MO 64154 Office: VA Med Ctr 4101 S 4th Traffic Way Leavenworth KS 66048

JOHNSON, TERRI L., physician assistant; b. Carlisle, Pa., Jan. 8, 1962; d. M. Wayne Neff and Janice T. (Thornton) Sweet; m. David L. Johnson, Nov. 27, 1992; 1 child, Ian David. BS, Gannon U., 1984. Physicians asst. St. Mary's Hosp., Rochester, N.Y., 1985-87, Rochester Gen. Hosp., 1987, Thornton (Colo.) Med. Ctr., 1987-89, Kipling Med. Group, Littleton, Colo., 1989-91, South Denver Physicians Asst. Group, Denver, 1991, Geisinger Med. Ctr., Danville, Pa., 1991-93, Health South Rehab. Hosp., Mechanicsburg, Pa., 1993-95, Colonial Park Family Practice, Harrisburg, Pa., 1995—. Fellow Am. Acad. Physician Assts.; mem. Pa. Soc. Physician Assts. Home: 16 Walnut Ln Camp Hill PA 17011

JOHNSON, THEODORE, physician; b. Ames, Iowa, Apr. 30, 1925; s. Birger Lars and Elizabeth (Schulze) J.; m. Hope Polishuk, Aug. 1951; children: Theodore E., Jeffrey L., Christian E. BS, Mont. State U., 1948; MD, Temple U., 1953. Intern Thomas D. Dee Hosp., Ogden, Utah, 1954; physician Weber County, Ogden, Utah, 1954-59; pvt. practice Ogden, 1955-59; asst. editor JAMA AMA, Chgo., 1959-60; pvt. practice Glenview, Ill., 1964-77; asst. dir. AMA Commn. Cost of Med. Care, Chgo., 1960-63; med. dir. Raleigh Hills Hosp., Spokane, Wash., 1977-84; pvt. practice Spokane, 1977-84; clin. dir. LOU Wash. State Hosp., Medical Lake, 1986-83, clin. dir. ITA, 1990-93; clin. instr. Abraham Sch. Medicine, Chgo., 1975-77; asst. physician Alcohol Treatment Ctr., Luth. Gen. Hosp., Park Ridge, Ill., 1967-77, chmn. dept. family practice, 1969; chmn. med. staff Wash. State Hosp., Medical Lake, 1987-89. Pub. health officer Glenview, Ill., 1964-67. Lt. USN, 1943-46, USNR, 1946-66. Mem. AMA, Wash. Med. Assn., Spokane Med. Soc. (pres. 1985), Am. Assn. Marriage and Family Therapists, Am. Soc. Addiction Medicine. Office: 1924 E 23rd Ave Spokane WA 99203-3802

JOHNSON, THEODORE REYNOLD, biology educator; b. Willmar, Minn., Mar. 20, 1946; s. Harry Reynold and Mildred (Kendall) J.; m. Michelle Rae Flaherty, June 13, 1970; children: Carrie, Eric, Daniel. BA, Augsburg Coll., Mpls., 1968; MS, U. Ill., Chgo., 1970, PhD, 1973. Prof. biology Mankato (Minn.) State U., 1972-77, St. Olaf Coll., Northfield, Minn., 1977—; cons. Donaldson Corp., Bloomington, Minn., 1983-90; dir. Inst. Clin. Immunology, Mpls., 1989-92. Author: Laboratory Experiments in Microbiology, 4th edit., 1995. NIH grantee, 1987-89. Mem. AAAS, Am. Soc. Microbiology, Nat. Assn. Advisors in Health Professions. Home: 5115 Ebert Ct Northfield MN 55057-4372 Office: St Olaf Coll Dept Biology 1520 St Olaf Ave Northfield MN 55057

JOHNSON, THOMAS FRANCIS, allergist; b. Lewiston, Maine, July 29, 1942; d. Thomas Francis and Winifred Emma (Flaherty) J.; m. Carleen G. Tombarello; children: Christopher, Thomas III, Jennifer Lynn, Tiffany Kira. Student Loyola Coll., Montreal, Can., 1959-60; MD, U. Toronto, 1966. Diplomate Am. Bd. Internal Medicine, Am. Bd. Allergy and Immunology. Intern, St. Vincent Hosp., Worcester, 1966-67; resident Mayo Clinic, Rochester, Minn., 1967-69, 71-73, SUNY-Buffalo, 1973-75; organizer, founder New Eng. Allergy and Immunology, P.C., North Andover, Mass., 1975, pres., owner, 1975—; organizer, founder New Eng. Allergy and Immunology Lab., Inc., North Andover, 1973, pres., owner, 1984—. Served to maj. USAF, 1969-71. Teagle Found. scholar, 1962-66. Fellow ACP, Am. Coll. Allergists, Am. Assn. Cert. Allergists, Am. Assn. Clin. Immunologists and Allergists; mem. AMA, Am. Acad. Allergy and Immunology, Mass. Med. Soc. Home: 34 Samoset Dr Salem NH 03079-1532 Office: New England Allergy & Immunology PC 555 Turnpike St North Andover MA 01845-5923

JOHNSON, THOMAS HENRY, dentist; b. Mt. Clemens, Mich., Aug. 4, 1933; s. Jenry T. and Jennie Susan (Kirkbridge) J.; m. Nancy Jean Seydler, Aug. 23, 1958; children: Lisa L., David Alan, Steven Lloyd. DDS, U. Mich., 1959. Diplomate Am. Acad. Pain Mgmt. Pvt. practice Dearborn, Mich., Ann Arbor, Mich. Bd. dirs. YMCA, Dearborn, 1976-83. Capt. U.S. Army, 1954-61. Master Acad. Gen. Dentistry; mem. Mich. Acad. Gen. Dentistry (pres. 1974). Home: 5893 Dutch Hill Dr Ann Arbor MI 48105 Office: 1816 Grindley Pk Dearborn MI 48124

JOHNSON, TRACEY A., health facility administrator; b. Everett, Mass., Aug. 16, 1971; d. Robert James and Kathleen Mary (Boyle) J. BSN, U. Mass., Lowell, 1994. Dir. nursing svcs., home health aide supr. Supportive Care Inc./Supportive Health Svcs. VNA, Lawrence, Mass., 1995—. Roman Catholic. Office: Supportive Care Inc 11 Lawrence St Lawrence MA 02148

JOHNSON, VINCENT GREGORY, anesthesiologist; b. Parkville, Mo., May 20, 1956; s. Noble Harold and Frances (Holmes) J.; m. Kathleen Tirrell, June 19, 1981; 1 child, Tess Tirrell. BS in Biology, Rockhurst Coll., 1978; DO, U. Health Scis., Kansas City, Mo., 1983. Diplomate Am. Bd. Anesthesiology, Am. Bd. Med. Examiners. Intern Suburban Gen. Hosp., Norristown, Pa., 1983-84; commd. 2d lt. USAF, 1984, advanced through grades to maj., 1989; gen. med. officer Hanscom Air Force Clinic, Bedford, Mass., 1984-85, chief acute care clinic, 1985-87; resident anesthesia Wilford Hall USAF Med. Ctr., San Antonio, 1987-89; fellow pediatric anesthesia Harvard-The Children's Hosp., Boston, 1989-90; staff instr. anesthesia Wilford Hall USAF Med. Ctr., San Antonio, 1990-92; med. dir. anesthesiology and pain mgmt. Surgicenter of Kansas City, Mo., 1992—. Contbr. articles to profl. jours. and chpts. to anesthesia texts. Mem. Air Force Soc. Clin. Surgeons, Am. Soc. Anesthesiologists, Internat. Anesthesia Rsch. Soc., AMA, Am. Osteo. Assn. Office: Surgicenter Kansas City 1800 E Meyer Blvd Kansas City MO 64132-1142

JOHNSON, W. TAYLOR, physician; b. Suffolk, Va., Jan. 17, 1936; s. Walter Taylor and Ethel (Storey) J.; m. Bettie Ann Orenduff; children: Elizabeth Ann, Patricia Ellen. Grad., Duke U., 1957, MD, 1961. Diplomate Am. Bd. Dermatology, Am. Bd. Dermatopathology. Intern Nat. Naval Med. Ctr., Bethesda, Md., 1961-62; resident in dermatology U.S. Naval Hosp., San Diego, 1964-66; fellow in dermatopathology Armed Forces Inst. Pathology, Washington, 1967-68; staff physician U.S. Naval Tng. Ctr., San Diego, 1962-64; staff dermatologist Nat. Naval Med. Ctr., Bethesda, 1967-72, asst. chief of dermatology, 1972-78, chief of dermatology, 1978-81; asst. prof. medicine Georgetown U., Washington, 1969-88; pvt. practice Gaithersburg, Md., 1981—. Contbr. articles to profl. jours. Mem. AMA, Assn. Mil. Dermatologists (pres. 1979), Washington, D.C. Soc. Dermatology (pres. 1983), Am. Acad. Dermatology, Am. Soc. Dermatopathology, Assn. Mil. Dermatologists, Montgomery County, Md. Med. Soc., Med. and Chirurgical Faculty of Md., Internat. Soc. for Dermatol. Surgery. Republican. Presbyterian. Home: 12301 Rivers Edge Dr Potomac MD 20854 Office: Ste A-28 19201 Mont Village Ave Gaithersburg MD 20879

JOHNSON, WAINE CECIL, dermatologist; b. Mt. Vernon, Tex., Sept. 30, 1928; s. Tulley Bell and Lizzie J.; m. Deanna Glutz, Dec. 1973; children: Susan Lynn, Carol Ann, Sandra Kay. B.S., E. Tex. State U., 1949; M.D., U. Tex., 1953. Intern Brooke Army Hosp., 1953-54; resident in dermatology Walter Reed Army Hosp., 1955-58; fellow in dermal pathology Armed Forces Inst. Pathology, 1960-61; mem. staff Skin and Cancer Hosp., Phila., 1962-78; asst. dir. lab. Skin and Cancer Hosp., 1962, dir., 1970-78; mem. faculty Temple U. Med. Sch., Phila., 1962-78; prof. dermatology Temple U. Med. Sch., 1970-78; clin. prof. U. Pa. Med. Sch., 1978—; chmn. dept. dermatology Grad. Hosp. U. Pa., 1978—; pres. Johnson & Griffin Dermatology Assns., 1990—. Author numerous papers in field.; Co-editor: Dermal Pathology, 1974. Served to maj. M.C. USAR, 1953-62. Recipient Gold medal sci. exhibit Am. Soc. Clin. Pathologists-Coll. Am. Pathologists, 1962. Mem. AMA, ACP, Am. Acad. Dermatology (chmn. com pathology 1976-80), Am. Dermatol. Assn., Internat. Acad. Pathology, Am. Registry Pathology (sec. 1982-85, treas. 1985), Am. Soc. Dermatopathology (pres. 1988) Soc. Investigative Dermatology, Histochem. Soc., Phila. Dermatol. Soc. (pres. 1979-80, Atlantic Dermatol. Conf. (pres. 1979-80, Coll. Physicians of Phila. (chmn. dermatology sect. 1994—). Home: 744 Crosswicks Rd Rydal PA 19046-3004 Office: 137 S Easton Rd # 8 Glenside PA 19038-4535

JOHNSON, WALTER HARVEY, JR., pediatric cardiologist; b. Spartanburg, S.C., Feb. 15, 1956; s. Walter Harvey and Martha Verna (Burnett) J.; m. Andrea Jane Perry, June 18, 1983; children: Victoria Ellen, Hilary Catherine. BS, Wofford Coll., 1977; MD, Med. U. S.C., 1980. Diplomat Nat. Bd. Med. Examiners, Am. Bd. Pediatrics, Am. Bd. Pediatric Cardiology. Resident in pediatrics Ark. Children's Hosp., Little Rock, 1980-83, chief resident in pediatrics, 1983; fellow in pediatric cardiology U. Minn., Mpls., 1983-86; asst. prof. pediatric cardiology U. So. Ala., Mobile, 1986—. Contbr. articles to profl. jours. Mem. coun. on cardiovascular disease in the young, coun. on basic sci., Am. Heart Assn. Recipient Nat. Rsch. Svc. award tng. grant NIH, 1984-86, grantee Am. Lung Assn., Ala. Affiliate, 1988-90, Am. Heart Assn., Ala. Affiliate, 1990-92. Fellow Am. Acad. Pediatrics (cardiology sect.), Am. Coll. Cardiology; mem: So. Soc. for Pediatric Rsch., Ala. Acad. Pediatrics. Office: Div Pediatric Cardiology Univ So Ala 2451 Fillingim St Mobile AL 36617-2238

JOHNSON, WALTER HENRY, medical research official, physiology educator; b. Montreal, Que., Can., Feb. 9, 1911; s. Robert Ernest and Beatrice Annie (Fowler) J.; BSc, McGill U., 1933; PhD, U. Toronto, 1937; m. Joyce MacKay, Sept. 17, 1982; children: Barbara, David, Melisande. Teaching fellow in physiology McGill U., Montreal, Que., Can., 1937-39; asst. prof. Georgetown Med. Sch., Washington, 1939-44; asst. prof. U. Western Ontario 1945-48; sci. officer Def. Research Med. Labs., Toronto, 1949-64; assoc. prof. faculty medicine U. Toronto, Ont., Can., 1965-76, spl. lectr., 1976—; dir. research otolaryngology St. Michael's Hosp., Toronto, 1956—, dir. research ear, nose, throat, U. Toronto, 1965-76; mem. nominating com. Nobel Prize in medicine and physiology, 1976. Served to Squadron Leader RCAF, 1956-64. Can. Aeron. and Space Inst. fellow, 1988; recipient Tuttle Award in aviation medicine, 1956; NASA Skylab achievement award, 1975; 1st recipient Dr. Wilbur Franks award in aviation medicine, 1983. Fellow Aero-Space Med. Assn. (past v.p.); mem. Am. Otological Soc., Barany Soc. (Sweden), Civil Aviation Med. Assn. (hon.), Internat. Acad. Astronautics, Collegium Otolaryngologicum, Can. Soc. Aerospace Medicine (past pres.). Clubs: Toronto Flying (past pres.), Royal Can. Yacht; Faculty (U. Toronto); Arts and Letters (Toronto). Contbr. over 75 articles to med. jours. Office: St Michael's Hosp, 30 Bond St, Toronto, ON Canada M5B 1W8

JOHNSON, WARREN CHARLES, psychiatrist; b. Seattle, June 8, 1923; s. Leo Edwin and Lina (Knapp) J.; m. Dorothy Marlin; children: Warren C., Jr., Edith Elizabeth. BS, Seattle U., 1944; MD, St. Louis U. Med. Sch., 1947. Diplomate Am. Bd. Psychiatry and Neurology. Intern St. Louis U. Group Hosp., 1947-48; resident in psychiatry St. Louis State Hosp., 1948-50, Johns Hopkins U., Perry Point, Md., 1950-52; chief psychiatry HQ Command Bolling AFB, 1952-54; dir. Juvenile Ct. Guidance Clinic USPHS, Bethesda, Md., 1954-56; dep. med. dir. Am. Psychiat. Assn., D.C., 1956-59; chief psychiatry Police and Fire Surgeons, Washington, 1970-83; assoc. clin. prof. George Washington U. Med. Sch., 1956—; psychiatrist Community Psychiat. Clinic, Wheaton, Md., 1984-95; pvt. practice Washington, 1958-96; chmn. bd. of tellers Washington Psychiat. Soc., 1984-94. Recipient Cert. of Appreciation St. Louis U., 1962, Met. Police Dept., 1979. Fellow Am. Psychiat. Assn., Am. Coll. Pscyhoanalysis; mem. AMA, Med. Soc. of D.C. (chmn. psychoanalytic sect.), Washington Psychiat. Soc., Am. Coll. Psychiatry, So. Psychiat. Assn., Washington Coun. of Child and Adolescent Psychiatry, So. Psychiat. Assn., Am. Psychoanalytic Assn., Am. Acad. Adolescent Psychiatry, Congressional Country Club.

JOHNSON, WARREN DOUGLAS, infectious diseases physician, researcher; b. Mt. Vernon, N.Y., Oct. 9, 1937; s. Warren D. and June Marie (Lavezzi) J.; m. Barbara Florence Bean, June 14, 1969; children: Christopher, Sarah, David, Matthew. BS, Carrol Coll., 1958; MD, Columbia U., 1962. Diplomate Am. Bd. Med. Examiners, Am. Bd. Internal Medicine with subspecialty in infectious diseases. Instr. in medicine Cornell U. Med. Coll., N.Y.C., 1967-69, asst. prof., 1969-74, dir. rsch. and tng. program at U. Bahia, 1969-79, assoc. prof. medicine, 1974-81, prof. medicine, 1981, dir. internat. health svcs., 1986—, chief divsn. internat. medicine, 1986, chief divsn. internat. medicine and infectious diseases, 1995—, B.H. Kean prof. tropical medicine, 1990; from asst. to attending physician N.Y. Hosp., N.Y.C., 1969—; mem. nat. adv. allergy and infectious diseases coun. NIAID, NIH, Washington, 1995—, chmn. micro and infectious diseases rsch. coun., 1987-90; chmn. subspecialty bd. infectious diseases Am. Bd. Internal Medicine, 1996—. Contbr. over 120 sci. articles to profl. publs., chpts. to books. Mem. Demerest (N.J.) Sch. Bd., 1984-90. Capt. USAF, 1964-66. Recipient Emilio Ribas medal in infectious diseases Brazil Soc. Infectious Diseases, 1992; named Prof. Hon. Fed. U. Bahia, Brazil, 1989. Fellow ACP, N.Y. Acad. Scis., Infectious Disease Soc. Am., Royal Soc. Tropical Medicine; mem. Am. Soc. Tropical Medicine, Am. Clin. Climatology Assn., Assn. Am. Physicians. Lutheran. Office: Cornell U Med Coll A421 1300 York Ave New York NY 10021-4805

JOHNSON, WILLIAM HUGH, JR., hospital administrator; b. N.Y.C., Oct. 29, 1935; s. William H. and Florence P. (Seinsoth) J.; m. Gloria C. Stube., Jan. 23, 1960; children: Karen A., William H. III. B.A., Hofstra U., 1957; M.Ed., U. Hawaii, 1969. Commd. 2d lt. U.S. Army, 1957, advanced through grades to lt. col., 1972, health adminstr., world wide, 1957-77, health adminstr., world wide, ret., 1977; chief exec. officer U. N. Mex. Hosp., Albuquerque, 1977—; asst. prof. U.S. Mil. Acad., West Point, N.Y., 1962-65; mem. clin. faculty U. Minn., Mpls., 1980-83; preceptor Ariz. State U., Tempe, 1982-83; pres. Albuquerque Area Hosp. Council, 1980; bd. dirs. Bank Am. of N.Mex., Tri West, Inc. Mem. exec. bd. Albuquerque Com. on Devel.; v.p. Vis. Nurse Svc., Albuquerque, 1979; pres. Magnifico Arts Fiesta; bd. dirs. Goodwill N.Mex.; bd. dirs. Albuquerque Conv. and Visitors Bur., mem. exec. com., 1994—. Decorated Army Commendation Medal with 2 oak leaf clusters, Order of Merit (Rep. of Vietnam), Legion of Merit. Mem. Am. Hosp. Assn. (governing bd. met. hosp. sect. 1982-86, chmn. com. AIDS, mem. regional policy bd. 1982-86, 88—), Am. Coll. Hosp. Adminstrs., Coun. Tchg. Hosps. (bd. dirs.), N.Mex. Hosp. Assn. (bd. dirs. 1983, chmn. 1995—), Nat. Assn. Pub. Hosps. (bd. dirs. Tri West Inc., Vita S.W.), Greater Albuquerque C. of C. (bd. dirs., econ. planning coun., v.p.), N.Mex. Assn. Commerce and Industry (treas.), Albuquerque Conv. and Visitors Bur. (bd. dirs.). Roman Catholic. Home: 7920 Sartan Way NE Albuquerque NM 87109-3128 Office: Univ N Mex Hosp 2211 Lomas Blvd NE Albuquerque NM 87106-2745

JOHNSON, WILLIAM LARRY, orthopedist; b. Kingsport, Tenn., May 9, 1956; s. Haskel Guy and Margaret Emma (Johnson) J.; m. Katherine Marie Barrett, Mar. 29, 1986; children: Sophie, Hannah, Claire. BA in Chemistry, U. Tenn. Knoxville, 1978; MD, U. Tenn. Memphis, 1982. Diplomate Am. Bd. Orthopaedic Surgery. Resident orthop. Fitzsimons AMC, Denver, 1982-87; surgeon orthop. U.S. Army, 1987-93, Blount Orthop. Assoc., Knoxville, 1993—; med. adviser Tenn. Therapy Svc., Knoxville, 1994—. Contbr. articles to profl. jours. Fellow Am. Acad. Orthop. Surgeons, Arthroscopy Assn. N.Am.; mem. Ky. Cols., Am. Legion. Republican. Office: Blount Orthop Assocs 101 Blount Ave #700 Knoxville TN 37920

JOHNSTON, COLIN IVORAO, medical educator; b. Hong Kong, May 28, 1934; s. James Hamilton and Dorothy Eleanor (Shields) J.; m. Susan Bailhache, June 12, 1959; children: Sam, Anna, Amy. MB BS, U. Sydney, Australia, 1957. Residency Royal Prince Alfred Hosp., Sydney, Australia, 1958-64; reader dept. medicine U. Melbourne, Australia, 1971-72, prof. medicine, chmn. Austin Hosp., 1986—; v.p. Austin & Repatriation Med. Ctr., Melbourne, 1973-86; v.p. bd. mgmt. Prince Henry's Hosp., Melbourne, 1982-86; bd. dirs. rsch. found. Royal Children's Hosp., Melbourne; chmn. High Blood Pressure Rsch. Coun. Australia. Fellow Royal Australasian Coll. Physicians (Gold medal 1995); mem. Am. Soc. Hypertension (exec. coun. 1988—, Richard Bright award 1995), Internat. Soc. Nephrology (nominating com. 1986—), Nat. Heart Found. Australia (mem. scientific and edn. com. 1990—), High Blood Pressure Rsch. Coun. Australia (chmn. 1990-93, treas. 1993-95), Internat. Soc. Hypertension (v.p. 1985-90, Franz Volhard award 1992). Home: 6 Berkeley St, Hawthorn, Melbourne VIC 3122, Australia Office: U Melbourn Dept Medicine, Austin & Repatriation MC, Studley Rd, Victoria Heidelberg 3084, Australia

JOHNSTON, DEAN LIVINGSTON, physician; b. Orlando, Fla., Jan. 12, 1953; s. Harold Wilkes and Mary Jane (Torgeson) J.; m. Kathleen Karen Koehnke, May 7, 1988. BA, U. South Fla., 1974; MD, Wake Forest U., 1979. Physician pvt. practice, Lake Mary, Fla., 1987—; chmn. dept. plastic surgery Orlando Regional Med. Ctr., 1990-94. Fellow Am. Coll. Surgeons; mem. AMA, Am. Soc. Plastic and Reconstructive Surgeons, Southeastern Soc. Plastic and Reconstructive Surgery, Fla. Plastic Surgery Soc., Orange County Med. Soc. Office: Ste 212 4106 W Lake Mary Blvd Lake Mary FL 32746

JOHNSTON, FRANK C., psychologist; b. West Hartford, Conn., June 21, 1955; s. Frank C. and Chris (Butler) J.; m. Susan H. Leffert, July 26, 1981. BA, Fairfield U., 1977; MEd, Columbia U., 1979, MA, 1979; PhD, SUNY, Albany, 1984. Sch. psychologist bd. coop. ednl. svcs. Herkimer, N.Y., 1979-80; intern Counseling Ctr., SUNY, Buffalo, 1983-84; psychologist Family Svc. Rochester, N.Y., 1985-87, Child and Youth div. Rochester Mental Health Ctr., 1988; pvt. practice Rochester, 1988—; cons. Brockport (N.Y.) Day Care Ctr., 1989-90, Learning Devel. Ctr., Rochester Inst. Tech., 1989-90; co-founder Behavioral Health Consortium Rochester, 1996. Mem. APA, N.Y. State Psychol. Assn. (managed care task force), Genesee Valley Psychol. Assn. (mem. legal legis com. 1988-90, mem. ins. com. 1990-92, chmn. ins. com. 1990, 93, pres. 1994, past pres. 1995), Rochester Area Assn. Clin. Psychologists, Nat. Register Health Svc. Providers in Psychology. Office: 480 White Spruce Blvd Rochester NY 14623-1608

JOHNSTON, FRANK MARION, general practice physician; b. Macon, Ga., Dec. 6, 1928; s. Thomas Allen and Frances Marion (Driggers) J.; m. Eugenia Elliott, Jan. 10, 1950 (div. 1975); children: Allene, Eugenia, Frank Marion Jr.; m. Margaret Moore, Dec. 31, 1975 (dec. 1989); m. Carol Lasell Hoskins, July 31, 1993. BA, Emory U., Atlanta, 1953; MD, Med Coll. Ga., 1959. Diploamte Am. Bd. Psychiatry and Neurology. Intern Emory U. Hosp., Atlanta, 1959-60; resident Med. Coll. Ga. Hosps., 1960-63; pvt. practice psychiatry and gen. medicine Savannah, Ga., 1965-77; pvt. practice gen. medicine Spring Hill, Fla., 1983—; med. dir. Community Mental Health Ctr. of Middle Ga., Dublin, 1977-80, Charter Broad Oaks Hosp., Savannah, 1972-76; chief of staff H.C.A. Oak Hill Hosp., Spring Hill, Fla., 1986-88. Chmn. bd. trustees H.C.A. Oak Hill Hosp., 1990—. Recipient Mental Health Bell award, Savannah Mental Health Assn., 1973; Paul Harris fellow, 1989. Fellow Am. Psychiat. Assn. (del. 1968-76); mem. Ga. Psychiat. Assn. (pres. 1975-76), Hernando County Med. Soc. (pres. 1989-90), Med. Assn. Ga. (del. 1968-78), Rotary, Masons, Shriners. Democrat. Presbyterian. Office: Woodlands Med Ctr 7211 Hiawatha Pky Spring Hill FL 34606-2542

JOHNSTON, GERALD SAMUEL, physician, educator; b. Johnstown, Pa., Aug. 4, 1930; s. Fleurence Gerald and Lorna Freda (Lawhead) J.; m. Dorothy Anna Jones, June 18, 1956; children: Joy Johnston Biciocchi, Jill A. Verna, Jana S. Moritzkat, Gerald S. Jr., Amy L. Tapparo, Douglas S. BS, U. Pitts., 1952, MD, 1956. Diplomate Am. Bd. Internal Medicine, Am. Bd. Nuclear Medicine. Intern Walter Reed Gen. Hosp., Washington, 1956-57; resident in internal medicine Brooke Gen. Hosp., San Antonio, 1958-61; commd. med. officer U.S. Army, 1955-71, advanced through grades to col., 1971; capt. USPHS, 1971-82; surgeon 358 Gen. dispensary, Seoul, Korea, 1961-62; chief nuclear medicine Walter Reed Gen. Hosp., Washington, Md., 1963-69, Letterman Gen. Hosp., San Francisco, 1969-71, NIH, Bethesda, Md., 1971-82; chief nuclear medicine U. Md., Balt., 1982-93, acting chmn. dept. radiology, 1989-92, prof. medicine, radiology and oncology, 1982-93; chmn. dept. nuclear medicine Washington Hosp. Ctr., 1993—. Author two books; contbr. over 170 articles to profl. jours. Decorated Legion of Merit, 1970. Fellow ACP, Am. Coll. Radiology; mem. AMA, AAUP, Am. Coll. Nuclear Medicine, Soc. Nuclear Medicine, Soc. of Chmn. of Acad. Radiology Depts. Republican. Office: Washington Hosp Ctr 110 Irving St NW Washington DC 20010-2931

JOHNSTON, JEFFREY MONROE, physician, pharmaceutical company executive, researcher; b. Charlotte, N.C., Oct. 15, 1952; s. Joe Monroe and Camille (Newman) J.; m. Margaret B. Wheeler, Apr. 12, 1980; children: Catherine Browning, Joe Monroe. BS, Davidson Coll., 1974; MD, Duke U., 1977. Diplomate Am. Bd. Internal Medicine, Am. Bd. Infectious Diseases. Fellow in rheumatic and genetic diseases Duke U., Durham, N.C., 1978; resident in medicine Vanderbilt U., Nashville, 1978-80; epidemic intelligence service officer Ctrs. for Disease Control, New Orleans, 1980-82; chief resident in medicine U. Utah, Salt Lake City, 1982-83, fellow in infectious diseases, 1983-85, asst. prof. internal medicine, 1985-87; asst. prof. medicine and microbiology U. Tex. Health Sci. Ctr., San Antonio, 1987-88; clin. assoc. prof. medicine U. N.C. Sch. Medicine, Chapel Hill, 1989-94; head clin. immunology Burroughs Wellcome Co., Research Triangle Park, N.C., 1988-95; clin. prof. medicine U. N.C. Sch. Medicine, Chapel Hill, 1994—; sr. clin. program head rheumatology and immunology GlaxoWellcome Inc., Research Triangle Park, N.C., 1995—; clin. asst. prof. La. State U., New Orleans, 1981-82; instr. Tulane U., New Orleans, 1980-82. Contbr. articles to profl. jours. Served with USPHS, 1980-82. Recipient Nat. Research Service awards NIH, Nat. Inst. Gen. Medicinal Scis., 1984, NIH, Nat. Inst. Allergy Infectious Diseases, 1985; Dana scholar Davidson Coll., 1971. Fellow ACP, Infectious Diseases Soc. Am., Am. Coll. Rheumatology; mem.Am. Soc. Microbiology, Am. Fedn. Clin. Rsch., Internat. Soc. Antiviral Rsch., Am. Acad. Pharma. Physicians, Phi Beta Kappa. Democrat. Office: GlaxoWellcome Co 5 Moore Dr Research Triangle Pk NC 27709

JOHNSTON, LYNN FRANCES, dentist; b. Royal Oak, Mich., Mar. 27, 1957; d. Charles A. and A. Joyce (Causey) J.; m. Charles Daniel Staveley, Aug. 13, 1983; children: Bennett Charles Stavely, Daniel Causey Stavely, Michael Cleveland Stavely. BA in Spanish, U. Miss., 1979, BA in Zoology, 1979, DMD, 1983. Bd. Cert. Miss., Fla. Faculty U. Miss., Jackson, 1983-84; dentist, assoc. Family Dental Clinic, Jackson, 1983-85; dentist Johnston and Stavely, Pensacola, Fla., 1985—; faculty Pensacola (Fla.) Jr. Coll., 1989—; bd. dirs., sec. Escamba/Santa Rosa County Dental Soc., Pensacola, Fla., 1990—; pres. Johnston and Stavely DMD, Pensacola, Fla., 1989—; staff mem. Sacred Heart Hosp., Pensacola, 1987—. Contbr. articles to local publs. Mem. Leadership Pensacola Class of 1990, LEAP Alumnae, Liberty Sertoma, 1987-91, past bd. dirs.; past bd. dirs. 90 + 9 Boys Ranch, Cantonment, Fla.; spkrs. bur., bd. dirs. Sacred Heart Found. Mem. Escambia/Santa Rose County Dental Soc. (bd. dirs., treas., v.p., pres.), Five Flags Dental Study Club, Pankey Study Club, Jr. League Pensacola (co-chair cmty. rsch./project devel., chair rsch. evaluation & devel. com), Gaites De Femme (chair rsch. devel. com), Femme Nouvelle (publicity chmn.). Office: Johnston & Stavely DMD 1560 Airport Blvd Pensacola FL 32504-8616

JOHNSTON, MARY ELLEN, nursing educator; b. Roswell, N.Mex., June 4, 1951; d. E. Bernard and Jane (Shugart) J. BSN, Baylor U., 1973; MSN, Oral Roberts U., 1982. Staff nurse crit. care dept. Tucson Med. Ctr., 1973-74; charge nurse med. unit St. Mary's Hosp., Roswell, 1975; instr. nursing Ea. N.Mex. U., Roswell, 1975—. Mem. ANA (cert. med.-surg. nurse), N.Mex. Nurses Assn. (past pres. dist. V), Baylor U. Nurses Alumni Assn., Philanthropic and Ednl. Orgn., Daus. of Am. Colonists, Altrusa Club Roswell, DAR, Sigma Theta Tau. Republican. Methodist. Home: 2715 N Kentucky Ave Apt 16 Roswell NM 88201-5868 Office: Ea NMex U PO Box 6000 Roswell NM 88202-6000

JOHNSTON, MARY HOLLIS, clinical psychologist; b. Woodward, Okla., Oct. 19, 1946; d. James Quincy and Mary Alda (Neighbors) J.; m. Randall R. Rowlett, Mar. 20, 1976 (div. 1982); 1 child, Nathan Rowlett. AB, Carleton Coll., 1968; MA, U. Chgo., 1971, PhD, 1975. Registered psychologist, Ill. Psychologist U. Ill. Med. Sch., Chgo., 1975-81; faculty Erikson Inst., Chgo., 1977-81; pvt. practice psychology Chgo., 1975—; faculty Ctr. for Psychoanalytic Studies, Chgo., 1983-93; lectr. U. Chgo. Med. Ctr., 1993—; adj. faculty Ill. Sch. Profl. Psychology, Chgo., 1993—; cons. Virginia Frank Child Devel. Ctr., Chgo., 1975—. Author: Assessing Thought Disorder, 1976. Mem. APA, Soc. for Personality Assessment, World Assn. for Infant Mental Health, Phi Beta Kappa, Sigma Xi.

JOHNSTON, MELISSA GAIL, nurse; b. Carthage, Miss., Aug. 29, 1971; d. Ralph Maylon and Mary Eileen (Barrett) Johnson; m. Mitchel Johnston, Dec. 3, 1990. Grad., East Ctrl. C.C., Decatur, Miss., 1993; student, Hinds C.C., Raymond, Miss., 1993—. LPN, Miss. Nurse Scott Regional Hosp., Morton, Miss., 1993—. Mem. Nat. LPN Assn. Home: Rte 1 Box 207-2 Lena MS 39094

JOHNSTON, PAMELA MCEVOY, clinical psychologist; b. Forest Hills, N.Y., Mar. 8, 1937; d. Renny T. and Pamela (Sweeny) McE.; m. Percy H. Johnston, Jr. (dec.); children: Michael B. Anderson, Jeffery A. Thomas, Candy L. Watts, Kenneth L. Anderson. BA, U. La Verne, 1978, MS, 1980; PhD, U.S. Internat. U., 1982. Instr. psychology-sociology Allan Hancock Coll., Santa Maria, 1977-78; mental health asst. Santa Barbara City Alcoholism Dept., 1977-78; gen. mgr. Profl. Suites, San Diego, 1978-81; therapist Chula Vista (Calif.) Community Counseling Ctr., San Diego, 1978-85; research asst. U.S. Internat. U., 1979-82; rsch. coordinator Mil. Family research Ctr., San Diego, 1981-82; assoc. dir. Acad. Assoc. Psychotherapists, 1982-86; pvt. practice, San Diego, 1982—; pres. Borrego Springs Med. Clinic, 1987-90, 91—, Family Custody Santa Maria Superior Ct., 1994-95, Santa Barbara County Mental Health Assn., Santa Maria, Calif., 1995—; bd. dirs. Women's Internat. Ctr., 1984-86. Bd. dirs. San Diego County Mental Health Assn., 1978-84, Civic Fedn., 1993-95. State fellow, 1979, 80, 81, 82, Calif. State scholar, 1976-77. Mem. Am. Psychol. Assn., Calif. State Psychol. Assn., Rotary Internat. Republican. Roman Catholic. Home: PO Box 1198 Borrego Springs CA 92004-1198

JOHNSTON, RUBY CHARLOTTE, nurse; b. Freedom, Nebr., Oct. 6, 1918; d. William Murray and Delia Isabel (Morgan) Phillips; student Nebr. Sch. Agr., Curtis, 1932-36, U. Colo., Boulder, summer 1938; R.N., Denver Gen. Hosp., 1945; m. Gerald William Johnston, Sept. 19, 1943; 1 son, Leo F. Rural sch. tchr., 1936-41; sec. supt.'s office Nebr. Sch. Agr., 1941-42; staff nurse Denver Gen. Hosp., 1945-46; office nurse, Cambridge, Nebr., 1946-47; staff nurse St. Catherine's Hosp., McCook, Nebr., 1947-56, LaGrange County Hosp., LaGrange, Ind., 1956-58; obstet. supr. LaGrange County Hosp., 1958-68, dir. nurses, 1968-70; dir. nurses Miller's Merry Manor, LaGrange, 1970-76; county health nurse LaGrange County Health Dept., LaGrange, 1976-80, part-time staff nurse, 1980-95; chmn. exec. com. Ind. Nurses Assn. Geriatric Conf., 1975-77; trustee, elder Presbyn. Ch.; Bd. dirs. N.E. Ind. chpt. Am. Lung Assn., 1981-89; Co-coordinator Focus on Health, LaGrange, 1982-85. Registered Mem. Ind. Nurses Assn., Nurses Assn. Am. Coll. Obstetricians and Gynecologists, Am. Legion Aux. Republican. Clubs: Bus. and Profl. Women's, Eastern Star, River Oaks Extension. Home: 1070E-480 N Howe IN 46746 Office: Court House Annex Lagrange IN 46761

JOHNSTON, THOMAS PATRICK, pharmaceutics educator; b. Chgo., Oct. 16, 1956; s. James Michael and Claire Ann (Fowler) J.; m. Jocelyn Elaine Stanwell, Nov. 28, 1986; 1 child, Gillian Claire. BS, U. Minn., 1980, PhD, 1987. Postdoctoral fellow pediatric cardiology and pharmaceutics U. Mich. Med. Sch., 1987-88; asst. prof. pharmaceutics U. Ill. Coll. Pharmacy, Chgo., 1988-95; assoc. prof. pharmaceutics U. Mo., Kansas City, 1995—; lectr. and presenter in field. Reviewer Jour. Pharm. Sci. and Tech., 1989—; contbr. Internat. Jour. Pharmacy, Jour. Pharm. Sci. and Tech., Jour. Pharm. Sci., Jour. Applied Polymer Sci., Jour. Controlled Release, others. Recipient Rho Chi Rsch. award U. Minn., 1980; Am. Soc. for Artificial Internal Organs Travel fellow, 1988, Theodore J. Rowell fellow, U. Minn., 1983-84. Mem. Am. Assn. Pharm. Sci., Am. Pharm. Assn., Am. Assn. Coll. Pharm., Controlled Release Soc., Parenteral Drug Assn., Minn. State Pharm. Assn., N.Y. Acad. Scis., Rho Chi. Office: U Mo-Kansas City Katz Pharmacy Bldg 5100 Rockhill Rd Kansas City MO 64110

JOHNSTON, WILLIAM DAVID, health care company executive; b. Chgo., Nov. 5, 1944; s. Samuel David and Jeanne (Williams) J.; m. Susan Diane Ward, Aug. 19, 1966; children: Kimberly Dawn Sites, Kirk David, Tiffany Dee Hansen, Kyle Donald, Ryan Daryl. BS in Chemistry, Brigham Young U., 1969, PhD in Organic Chemistry, 1974. V.p. Parish Chem. Co., 1973-75; mgr. materials control Travenol Labs., Inc., 1975-80, group mgr., polymer rsch. and material control, 1980-84, v.p. Material and Membrane Tech. Ctr., 1984-86, v.p. applied scis., 1987-93; v.p., gen. mgr. gene therapy div. Baxter Healthcare Corp., Round Lake, Ill., 1993—; mem. adv. bd. Ill. Jr. Acad. Sci., Springfield, 1984-86; bd. dirs. Ill. Hi-Tech. Assn., 1990-92; mem. adv. bd. Coll. Engring., U. ill., Chgo., 1988-92, dept. chem. engring. Northwestern U., Evanston, Ill., 1989—. Contbr. articles to profl. jours.; patentee in field. Coun. stake pres. LDS Ch., Schaumburg, Ill., 1982-88, stake pres., Buffalo Grove, Ill., 1988—; exec. coun. N.E. Ill. coun. Boy Scouts Am., 1989—; chmn. bd. LDS Social Svcs., Naperville, Ill., 1990—; bd. dirs. Neocrin Co., 1992-96. Brigham Young U. scholarship. Mem. AAAS, Am. Chem. Soc., Internat. Soc. for Artificial Organs, Internat. Soc. Blood Purification (exec. bd. 1991—), Soc. for Biomaterials, Internat. Soc. of Cell Transplantation, Sigma Xi. Home: 20851 W Yorkshire Dr Kildeer IL 60047-7951 Office: Baxter Healthcare Corp Baxter Technology Park Round Lake IL 60073

JOHNSTON, WILLIAM FREDERICK, emergency services administrator; b. Oakridge, Tenn., Mar. 4, 1945; s. Leonard E. and Helene C. (Spicker) J.; m. Kathleen Jo Hotaling, Nov. 17, 1988; 1 child, Lindsey Anne. BS, U. Wash., 1969, MS, 1971, MD, 1974. Diplomate Am. Bd. Emergency Medicine. Med. intern U. Wash. Affiliated Hosps., Seattle, 1974-75; emergency medicine resident Valley Med. Ctr. Fresno/U. Calif. San Francisco, Fresno, 1975-77; pres., CEO N.W. Emergency Physicians, Seattle, 1977-81; med. dir. emergency svcs. N.W. Hosp., Seattle, 1977—. Contbr. articles to med. jours. Fellow Am. Coll. Emergency Physicians. Home: 4731 Beach Dr SW Seattle WA 98116 Office: N W Hosp 1550 N 115th St Seattle WA 98133

JOHNSTON, WILLIAM LESLIE, osteopathic physician, educator; b. Sault Ste. Marie, Ont., Can., Feb. 17, 1921; s. Roy Leslie and Eva Pearl (Osborn) J.; m. Margaret MacFarlane, Jan. 1945; children—Merilyn, Gail; m. Anne McCabe, Mar. 18, 1979. D.O., Chgo. Coll. Osteo. Medicine, 1943. Intern, Mass. Osteo. Hosp., Boston, 1944; pvt. practice medicine, Manchester, N.H., 1945-73; mem. faculty Mich. State U. Coll. Osteo. Medicine, East Lansing, 1973—, prof. biomechanics, 1973-81, prof. dept. family medicine, 1981-90, prof. emeritus, 1990—; vis. prof. Chgo. Coll. Osteo. Medicine, 1986—; cons. staff Lansing Gen. Hosp. Author: Functional Methods, 1994, Chpt. med. text, Contbr. numerous articles to profl. publs. Recipient of the Taylor Still Medallion of (hon), 1996, Mem. Am. Acad. Osteopathy (cert. Osteo. Manipulative Med. , chmn. Conclave of Fellows 1972-74, 1983-84), Am. Osteo. Assn. (editorial adv. bd. Jour. Am. Osteo Assn. 1989—, Louisa Burns Meml. Lectr., 1982, Burroughs Wellcome Gutensohn-Denslow award bur. rsch. 1991), Mich. Assn. Osteo. Physicians and Surgeons, N.H. Osteo. Assn. (pres.). Home: 830 N Harrison Rd East Lansing MI 48823-3021 Office: Mich State U Coll Osteo Medicine B216 W Fee East Lansing MI 48824

JOHNSTON, WILLIAM WEBB, pathologist, educator; b. Statesville, N.C., Aug. 26, 1933; s. Jesse Clyde and Pauline Elizabeth (Massey) J. B.S., Davidson Coll., 1954; M.D., Duke U., 1959. Diplomate Am. Bd. Pathology, Am. Bd. Cytopathology, Internat. Bd. Cytopathology. Intern Duke U., 1959-60, resident in pathology, 1960-63, mem. faculty, 1963—, prof. pathology, 1972—, dir. div. cytopathology and cytotechnology tng. program, 1966—; bd. dirs. Anatomical Pathology Svc.; cons. pathologist Durham VA Hosp., Duncan County Hosp.; chmn. Internat. Bd. Cytopathology, 1992—. Author: (with W.J. Frable) Respiratory Cytopathology, 1974; Diagnostic Respiratory Cytopathology, 1979; (with S.H. Bigner) The Cytopathology of the Central Nervous System, 1981, 2d edit., 1994, Pulmonary Cytology (with James Linder), 1992; assoc. editor Acta Cytologica, 1978—, sr. mem. editorial bd., 1992; editor: Masson Monographs in Cytopathology; mem. editorial bd. Am. Jour. Clin. Pathology, 1986; editorial cons. Masson Publs., N.Y.C.; mem. editorial adv. bd. Jour. Nat. Cancer Inst. Fellow Internat. Acad. Cytology (Maurice Goldblatt award 1995), Am. Soc. Clin. Pathologists, Coll. Am. Pathologists, Royal Soc. Medicine; mem. AMA (del. 1982—), Am. Soc. Cytology (rev. bd., pres. 1981-82, Papanicolaou award 1986), Am. Assn. Pathologists, Arthur Purdy Stout Soc. Surg. Pathology, Internat. Acad. Pathology, Am. Assn. for Cancer Rsch. Republican. Presbyterian (organist). Home: 8200 Bromley Rd Hillsborough NC 27278-9709 Office: Duke U Med Ctr Box 3712 Durham NC 27710

JOHNSTONE, CHAUNCEY OLCOTT, pharmaceutical company executive; b. N.Y.C., Sept. 11, 1943; s. Edmund F. and Janet (Olcott) J.; BA, Jacksonville U., 1965; m. Patricia E. Porter, May 30, 1971; children: Carolyn Ann, Jessica Olcott. Fin. analyst Dun & Bradstreet, Inc., Jacksonville, Fla., 1965-68; co-founder, v.p. Trinity Industries, Inc., Mount Kisco, N.Y., 1968-77; product mgr. Beiersdorf, Inc., Norwalk, Conn., 1978-81, mktg. mgr., 1982—, v.p., mem. mgmt. bd., 1984-88, sr. v.p., mem. mgmt. bd. 1988—; sr. v.p. mem. mgmt./ bd. divsn. mgr. U.S.A. and Can., 1993-96; exec. v.p., COO Beiersdorf-Jobst Inc., Charlotte, N.C., 1996—; mem. adv. bd. Baxter, Inc., Ill., 1990-92. Bd. dirs. Wilton (Conn.) chpt. ARC, 1976-81; charter mem. Wilton Vol. Ambulance Corps, 1976—; corp. mem. Dublin Sch., N.H., 1986— founding mem. Healthcare Mktg. Coun., 1988—. Mem. Wilton (Conn.) Riding Club, Peninsular Yacht Club (Cornelius, N.C.). Home: 19 Hillbrook Rd Wilton CT 06897-1706 Office: Beiersdorf-Jobst Inc PO Box 471048 Carnagie Blvd Charlotte NC 28247-1043

JOHNSTONE, PAULA SUE, medical technologist; b. Springfield, Mo., July 5, 1947; d. Nathan Paul and Ima Louise (Glenn) Johnstone. BS, S.W. Mo. State U., 1969. Cert. med. technologist Am. Soc. Clin. Pathologists. Vol., Cox Med. Ctr., Springfield, 1964-68; lab., office aide Springfield Med. Lab., 1964-68; chief technologist Springfield Gen. Osteo. Hosp., 1969-73; staff technologist St. John's Regional Health Ctr., Springfield, 1973-75, evening supr., 1975-76, asst. adminstrv. dir., 1976-86, clin. lab. coord., 1986-89, lab. computer coord., 1989-96, hosp. LIS coord., 1996—. Dir., Glidewell Bapt. Ch. Tng., Springfield, 1984-85, chmn. budget and fin. com. 1986-87; pres. MER class Broadway Bapt. Ch., 1993-94, 95-96. Mem. NAFE, Am. Soc. for Clin. Lab. Sci., Mo. Soc. Med. Technologists (pres. 1976-77, columnist newsletter 1976-77), S.W. Mo. State U. Alumni Assn. Baptist. Clubs: Nat. Travel, Frommer's Dollarwise Travel Club. Avocations: Internat. travel, reading, knitting, house plants. Home: 1384-A E Arlington Springfield MO 65803-9622 Office: St John's Regional Health Ctr 1235 E Cherokee St Springfield MO 65804-2203

JOINER, NORA LYNN, surgical cardiac and thoracic nurse; b. Russellville, Ky., Apr. 7, 1966; d. Lillian Joyce Bryant; m. Joseph Thomas Joiner, Sept. 25, 1993. BSN, Ga. Coll., 1993. Mem. nursing staff Med. Ctr. Ctrl. Ga., Macon, 1993—. Mem. Profl. Nurse Coun. Home: 121 Kelli Dr Byron GA 31088 Office: Med Ctr Ctrl Ga 777 Hemlock St Macon GA 31201

JOKLIK, WOLFGANG KARL, biochemist, virologist, educator; b. Vienna, Austria, Nov. 16, 1926; s. Karl F. and Helene (Giessl) J.; m. Judith Vivien Nicholas, Apr. 9, 1955 (dec. Apr. 1975); children: Richard G., Vivien H.; m. Patricia Hunter Downey, Apr. 23, 1977. B.Sc. with 1st class honors, U. Sydney, Australia, 1948, M.Sc., 1949; D.Phil. (Australian Nat. U. scholar), U. Oxford, Eng., 1952. Australian Nat. U. research fellow Copenhagen, Denmark, 1953, Canberra, Australia, 1954-56; fellow, 1957-62; assoc. prof. cell biology Albert Einstein Coll. Medicine, Bronx, N.Y., 1962-65; prof. cell biology Albert Einstein Coll. Medicine, 1965-68, Siegfried Ullmann prof. biochem. virology, 1966-68; prof., chmn. dept. microbiology and immunology Duke U. Med. Ctr., Durham, N.C., 1968-92; James B. Duke Disting. prof. microbiology and immunology Duke U. MEd. Ctr., Durham, N.C., 1972-92, James B. Duke prof. microbiology, 1992-96; James B. Duke prof. emeritus Duke U. Med. Ctr., Durham, N.C., 1996—. Sr. author: Zinsser Microbiology, 15th, 16th, 17th, 18th, 19th, 20th edits.; editor-in-chief Virology, 1975-93, Microbiological Rev., 1991-95; contbr. articles to profl. jours. Recipient Sr. U.S. award Alexander Humboldt Found., 1985, ICN Internat. prize for virology, 1991. Mem. NAS, Inst. Medicine of NAS, Am. Soc. Virology (pres. 1982-83), Am. Soc. Microbiology, Am. Soc. Biol. Chemists. Address: Duke U Med Ctr Dept Microbiology Durham NC 27710

JOLISSAINT, STEPHEN LACY, pathologist; b. Honolulu, Oct. 7, 1951; s. John Mire and Joyce Marie (Lacy)) J.; m. Belle Kamille Bowen, Dec. 29, 1988; children: Taylor Elise, Stephen Lacy Jr. BS, La. State U., Baton Rouge, 1973; MD, La. State U., New Orleans, 1976. Intern resident U.S. Army, Fitzsimons Army Med. Ctr., Aurora, Colo., 1976-80; staff pathologist U.S. Army, 1980-82; pathologist Pecot, Padgett & Jolissaint, APMC, Opelousas, La., 1982—; med. dir. dept. pathology Abbeville (La.) Gen. Hosp., 1989—, Abrom Kaplan (La.) Hosp., 1989—, Med. Ctr. of Southwest La., 1993—; mem. adv. bd. Midsouth Nat. Bank, 1984—. Fellow Am. Coll. Pathologists (keyperson 1986-88), Am. Soc. Clin. Pathology; mem. AMA (del. young physicians sect. 1986-91), La. Med. Soc. (del. 1985-88, 90-91, chmn. young physicians com. 1988-91), La. Pathology Soc., St. Landry Parish Med. Soc. (pres. 1985-86), Thoroughbred Owners and Breeders Assn., Alpha Omega Alpha. Roman Catholic. Home: 202 Mill Valley Run Lafayette LA 70508-7052

JOLLIE, WILLIAM P(UCETTE), anatomy educator, department chairman; b. Passaic, N.J., June 27, 1928; s. William Pucette and Katharina (Grau) J.; m. Ludmila Georgieva Jollie, Dec. 28, 1950; children: William P. Jr., Michael Konstantin. BA, Lehigh U., 1950, MS, 1952; PhD, Harvard U., 1959. Sci. instr. Bradford (Mass.) Jr. Coll., 1958-59; lectr. histology/embryology Queen's U. Faculty Medicine, Kingston, Ont., Can., 1959-61; asst. prof. anatomy Tulane U. Sch. Medicine, New Orleans, 1961-65, assoc. prof., 1965-68, prof., 1968-69; prof., chmn. anatomy Med. Coll. Va., Va. Commonwealth U., Richmond, 1969—. Author: (with others) Medical Primatology, 1972, Dysmenorrhea, 1981; co-editor: Biology of the Uterus, 1989; contbr. 75 articles to profl. jours. Fellow Royal Microscopical Soc.; mem. Am. Assn. Anatomists (sec.-treas. 1980-88, pres. 1991-92, exec. officer 1993-94, Centennial award for svc. 1987), Assn. Anatomy Chairmen, Am. Soc. for Cell Biology, Teratology Soc. Home: 8304 River Rd Richmond VA 23229-8419 Office: Va Commonwealth U Med Coll Va, Dept Anatomy PO Box 980709 Richmond VA 22298-0709

JOLLY, ATHENA THEOFILOPOUBU, occupational medicine physician; b. Amalias, Greece, June 14, 1943; came to the U.S., 1970; d. Akekos George and Areti (Rabowilas) T.; m. Gary William Jolly; children: Alexis, Carolina. MD, Athens (Greece) U., 1970; MPH, Johns Hopkins U. Pvt. practice internal medicine Dover, Del., 1973-77, Wilmington, Del., 1977-79; assoc. med. dir. ICI Americas, Wilmington, 1979-91; cons. Occupl. Environ. Health, 1992—; sys. dir. CKHS Ctrs. for Occupl. Health, Media, Pa., 1994—. Environ. occupl. subcom. mem. Adv. Coun. for Cancer Control, Dover, Del., 1996. Fellow Am. Coll. Occupl. and Environ. Medicine, Am. Coll. Preventive Medicine; mem. AMA, ACP, APHA, Del. Med. Soc. (chair environ. pub. health com. 1991—), Del. Nature Soc. (co-chair air resource subcom. 1991—). Office: Ctrs for Occupl Health Rose Tree Corp Ctr 1400 N Providence Rd #212 Media PA 19063

JOLLY, BARBARA LEE, home healthcare professional; b. Central City, Nebr., Dec. 23, 1952; d. Louis Carl and Elizabeth (Mesner) Lindahl; m. William C. Zimmerman, June 2, 1973 (div. Aug. 1986); m. Daniel Ehs Jolly, May 7, 1988 (div. Mar. 1996). BS in Pharmacy, U. Mo., Kansas City, 1976, MPA, 1984. Registered pharmacist. Pharmacy supr. Truman Med. Ctr., Kansas City, Mo., 1976-87; dispensing dept. mgr. Nursing Ctr. Svcs., Hilliard, Ohio, 1988-90; v.p. Pharmacy Systems, Inc., Dublin, Ohio, 1990-96; chief pharmacist Integrity Healthcare Svcs., Inc., Columbus, Ohio, 1996—; trustee Ohio Cancer Pain Initiative, Columbus, 1987—. Bd. dirs. Open Ch., Inc., Columbus, 1991—; mem. social svcs. bd. Salvation Army, Kansas City, 1986-88; co-dir. Siouxland Hotline, Inc., Sioux City, Iowa, 1972-73; med. missionary, Honduras, 1992-96; del. to state conv. Easter Seals of Ohio, Columbus, 1989-91. Recipient Outstanding Vol. award Salvation Army, Kansas City, 1987. Mem. Am. Soc. Hosp. Pharmacists, Ohio Soc. Hosp. Pharmacists, Ohio Pharmacists Assn., Ky. Soc. Hosp. Pharmacists, Midwest Pain Soc., Pi Alpha Alpha (pres. 1983-84). Mem. United Ch. of Christ. Home: 6337 Tamworth Ct Dublin OH 43017

JOLLY, DANIEL EHS, dental educator; b. St. Louis, Aug. 25, 1952; s. Melvin Joseph and Betty Ehs (Koehler) J.; m. Paula Kay Haas, 1972 (div.); 1 child, Farrell Elisabeth Ehs; m. Barbara Lee Lindahl, 1988 (div.). BA in Biology and Chemistry, U. Mo., Kansas City, 1974, DDS, 1977. Resident in hosp. dentistry VA Med. Ctr., Leavenworth, Kans., 1977-78; pvt. practice Newcastle, Wyo., 1978-79; asst. prof. U. Mo., Kansas City, 1979-87; chief restorative dentistry Truman Med. Ctr., Kansas City, 1979-87; dir. dental oncology Trinity Luth. Hosp., 1982-87; assoc. prof., dir. gen. practice residency program Ohio State U., Columbus, 1987—; prof., dir. gen. practice residency program, 1993—; dir. Honduras Clinic Project, 1992—; bd. dirs. Rinehart Found., U. Mo. Dental Sch., Kansas City, 1985-87; cons. Lee's Summit (Mo.) Care Ctr., 1984-87, Longview Nursing Ctr., Grandview, Mo., 1986-87; sec. Combined Hosp. Dental Staff, Columbus, 1989-90, v.p., 1990-91, pres., 1991-92. Author: (manual) Hospital Dental Hygiene, 1984, Hospital Dentistry, 1985, OSU Manual of Hospital Dentistry, 1989-96, (booklet) Nursing Home Dentistry, 1986, Dental Oncology, 1986. Mem. regional coun. Easter Seal Soc., Kansas City, 1985-87, mem. profl. adv. coun. Nat. Easter Seal Soc., 1986-92; sec. bd. dirs. Easter Seal Rehab. Ctr., Columbus, 1990-93. Recipient Alumni Achievement award in dentistry U. Mo., Kansas City, 1995. Fellow Acad. Dentistry Internat., Am. Soc. Dentistry for Children, Am. Assn. Hosp. Dentists (regional v.p. 1993—), Acad. Gen. Dentistry, Am. Soc. Geriatric Dentistry, Acad. Dentistry for Handicapped (pres. 1992), Am. Coll. Dentistry, Pierre Fauchard Acad.; mem. ADA, Internat. Assn. Dentistry for Handicapped (pres. 1994—), Mo. Dental Assn., Internat. Assn. Dental. Handicap, Greater Kansas City Dental Soc., Fed. Spl. Care Orgns. in Dentistry (chmn. 1992-93), Southwest Oncology Group, Internat. Soc. for Oral Oncology, Ohio Dental Assn. Club: Magna Charta Barons. Home: 5322 Bay Meadows Ct Columbus OH 43221-5703 Office: Ohio State U Coll Dentistry 305 W 12th Ave Columbus OH 43210-1249

JONAS, GARY FRED, health care center executive; b. N.Y.C., Apr. 26, 1945; s. Otto and Hilde (Levy) J.; m. Rosalyn Ethel Levy; children: Lauren, Rachel. BS in Ops. Rsch., Columbia U., 1966; MBA, Harvard U., 1968. Mgmt. cons. Fry Cons., Washington, 1968-69; div. dir. Univ. Rsch. Corp. Ctr. Human Svcs., Chevy Chase, Md., 1970-73, exec. v.p., 1973-75, pres., chief exec. officer, 1975-85, chmn., chief exec. officer, 1985-88, also bd. dirs.; pres., chief operating officer The Earle Palmer Brown Cos., Bethesda, Md., 1988-93, also bd. dirs.; pres., CEO 20/20 Laser Ctrs., Inc., Bethesda, 1993—, also bd. dirs.; bd. dirs. Color Me Beautiful Inc., Herndon Va. Contbr.

articles to profl. jours. Mem. Inst. Mgmt. Cons. (cert.), Profl. Svcs. Coun. (past bd. dirs., v.p.), Nat. Contract Mgmt. Assn., Conf. Bd., Am. Soc. Tng. and Devel., Washington Bd. Trade, Young Pres.'s Orgn. (exec. com., chmn. Washington metro chpt. 1987-88), Harvard Club, Harvard Bus. Sch., Woodmont Country Club. Home: 6716 Melody Ln Bethesda MD 20817-3115 Office: 20/20 Lasers Ctrs Inc 6701 Democracy Blvd Ste 200 Bethesda MD 20817-1572

JONAS, RUTH HABER, psychologist; b. Tel Aviv, Aug. 24, 1935; d. Fred S. and Dorothy Judith (Bernstein) Haber; m. Saran Jonas, Sept. 16, 1956; children: Elizabeth, Frederick. AB, Barnard Coll., 1957; MA, New Sch. for Social Rsch., 1977, PhD, 1987. Lic. psychologist, N.Y. 1st and 2d yr. intern clin. psychology NYU Med. Ctr.-Bellevue Hosp., N.Y.C., 1985-87; postdoctoral rsch. fellow NYU Med. Ctr., N.Y.C., 1987-88; clin. instr. psychiatry NYU Sch. Medicine, N.Y.C., 1987, clin. asst. prof. psychiatry, 1991; sr. psychologist forensic svc. Bellevue Hosp., N.Y.C., 1988—; pvt. practice psychology N.Y.C., 1988—. Fellow Am. Orthopsychiat. Assn.; mem. APA, N.Y. State Psychol. Soc., Manhattan Psychol. Assn., Am. Heart Assn. (fellow stroke coun.). Office: 200 E 33rd St Apt 10B New York NY 10016-4827

JONAS, SARAN, neurologist, educator; b. N.Y.C., June 24, 1931; s. Myron and Margaret (Wurmfeld) J.; m. Ruth Haber, Sept. 16, 1956; children: Elizabeth Ann, Frederick Jonathan. B.S., Yale U., 1952; M.D., Columbia U., 1956. Diplomate Am. Bd. Psychiatry and Neurology, Am. Bd. Internal Medicine. Intern Bellevue Hosp., N.Y.C., 1956-57; resident and fellow in medicine and neurology Bellevue Hosp., 1957-62; practice medicine specializing in neurology N.Y.C., 1964—; from clin. instr. to assoc. prof. clin. neurology NYU Sch. Medicine, 1964-77, prof. clin. neurology, 1977—, acting chmn. dept. neurology, 1987-91; assoc. dir. neurology NYU Hosp., 1970-87, dir., 1987-91, dir. electroencephalography, 1969-94; acting dir. neurology Bellevue Hosp., N.Y.C., 1987-91, assoc. dir., 1991—, dir. electroencephalography, 1994—. Served with USN, 1962-64. N.Y. State fellow in rheumatic diseases, 1962-64. Mem. Am. Acad. Neurology, Assn. for Rsch. in Nervous and Mental Diseases, Am. Heart Assn. (Stroke Coun., Epidemiology Coun.), Am. Epilepsy Soc. Office: 530 1st Ave New York NY 10016-6402

JONDERKO, KRZYSZTOF PAWEŁ, physician, researcher; b. Zabrze, Poland, Feb. 8, 1958; s. Gerard Edmund and Monika Janina (Okon) J.; m. Anna Urszula Kasicka, Dec. 17, 1988. Diploma in medicine, Silesian Sch. Medicine, Katowice, Poland, 1982, specialist I in internal medicine, 1985, MD, 1986, specialist II in internal medicine, 1988, DSc, 1994. Intern dept. orthopedics Med. Acad., Rijeka, Yugoslavia, 1979; intern dept. gen. surgery Krankenhaus Thusis, Thusis, Switzerland, 1980; asst. rsch. fellow dept. gastroenterology Silesian Sch. Medicine, 1982-83, rsch. fellow, 1983-85, sr. rsch. fellow, 1985-94; rsch. dir. Inst. Occupl. Med. Environ. Health, Sosnowiec, Poland, 1995—; assoc. prof., head Dept. Physiology Inst. Occupl. Med. Environ. Health, Sosnoweic, Poland, 1995—; researcher dept. pharmacology Nat. Inst. Agronomy Rsch., Toulouse, France, 1990-91; researcher dept. rheumatology St. Josef-Stift, Sendenhorst, Germany, 1989, 90, 91. Contbr. numerous articles to sci. jours. Recipient sci. award Polish Ministry Health and Social Welfare, 1989; rsch. fellow Alexander von Humboldt Found., 1990, European rsch. fellow, 1991; Fournier-Thylmer rsch. grantee Labs. Fournier, Paris, 1989. Mem. Polish Assn. Internal Medicine, Polish Soc. Gastroenterology, Polish Nuclear Medicine Soc., Soc. Humboldtiana Polonorum, N.Y. Acad. Scis. Office: Inst Occupl Medicine &, Environ Health, 13 Koscielna St, Pl-41200 Sosnoviec Poland

JONES, BARBARA EWER, school psychologist, occupational therapist; b. Marion, Ind., Jan. 28, 1942; d. J. Bertrand and Audrey May (Carter) Ewer; m. Jan Alden Fowler. BS, Ind. U., 1965, MS, 1970; MS, Ind. U.-Purdue U., Indpls., 1977; postgrad., U. Indpls., 1986-93. Tchr. Marion Sch. Sys., 1965-66, Decatur Twp. Sch. Sys., Indpls., 1967-71; contract substitute tchr. San Bernardino (Calif.) Sch. Sys., 1967; dir. Univ. Early Childhood Sch., Indpls., 1971-75; psychologist occupl. therapist master level Monroe County Cmty. Sch. Corp., Bloomington, Ind., 1977—, also consultation and insvc. trainer, rschr.; lectr. evening divsn. Butler U., Indpls., 1974-81; mem. com. for study of children of alcoholics in sch. environ., Bloomington, 1990—. Co-editor, author The Special Needs Child in American Schools, 1995; contbr. articles to profl. jours. Recipient awards for photography, sculpture, and watercolors, 1978, 86-89. Mem. Am. Occupl. Therapy Assn., Ind. Occupl. Therapy Assn. Home: RR 2 Box 5 Morgantown IN 46160-9510

JONES, BEVERLY ANN MILLER, nursing administrator, patient services executive; b. Bklyn., July 14, 1927; d. Hayman Edward and Eleanor Virginia (Doyle) Miller. BSN, Adelphi U., 1949; m. Kenneth Lonzo Jones, Sept. 5, 1953; children: Steven Kenneth, Lonnie Cord. Chief nurse regional blood program ARC, N.Y.C., 1951-54; asst. dir., acting dir. nursing M.D. Anderson Hosp. and Tumor Inst., Houston, 1954-55; asst. dir. nursing Sibley Meml. Hosp., Washington, 1959-61; assoc. dir. nursing svc. Anne Arundel Gen. Hosp., Annapolis, Md., 1966-70; asst. adminstr. nursing Alexandria (Va.) Hosp., 1972-73; v.p. patient care svcs., Longmont (Colo.) United Hosp., 1977-93; pvt. cons., 1993—; instr. ARC, 1953-57; mem. adv. bd. Boulder Valley Vo.-Tech Health Occupations Program, 1977-80; chmn. nurse enrollment com. D.C. chpt. ARC, 1959-61; del. nursing adminstrs. good will trip to Poland, Hungary, Sweden and Eng., 1980. Contbr. articles to profl. jours. Bd. dirs. Meals on Wheels, Longmont, Colo., 1978-80, Longmont Coalition for Women in Crisis, Applewood Living Ctr., Longmont; mem. Colo. Hosp. Assn. Task Force on Nat. Commn. on Nursing, 1982; mem. utilization com. Boulder (Colo.) Hospice, 1979-83; vol. Longmont Police Bur., Colo.; mem. coun. labor rels. Colo. Hosp. Assn., 1982-87; mem.-at-large exec. com. nursing svc. adminstrs. Sect. Md. Nurses' Assn., 1966-69; mem. U. Colorado Task Force on Nursing, 1990; vol. Champs program St. Vrain Valley Sch. Dist.; vol. Longmont Police Dept. Mem. Am. Orgn. Nurse Execs. (chmn. com. membership svcs. and promotions, nominee recognition of excellence in nursing adminstrn.), Colo. Soc. Nurse Execs. (dir. 1978-80, 84-86, pres. 1980-81, mem. com. on nominations 1985-86). Home: 853 Wade Rd Longmont CO 80503-7017

JONES, BILLY ERNEST, dermatology educator; b. Daytona Beach, Fla., Jan. 29, 1933; s. Bibb Ernest and Marjorie (Eyre) J.; m. Hannah Warren, June 12, 1958; children: Alan W., Lawrence W., Marjorie E. BS, The Citadel, 1954; MD, Duke U., 1958. Diplomate Am. Bd. Dermatology. Commd. 2d lt. U.S. Army, 1958, advanced through grades to maj., 1964; intern William Beaumont Hosp. U.S. Army, El Paso, Tex., 1958-59; gen. med. officer Henry Barracks U.S. Army, Cayey, P.R., 1959-61; resident in dermatology The Presidio U.S. Army, San Francisco, 1961-64; chief dermatology U.S. Army, Ft. Gordon, Ga., 1964-67; resigned U.S. Army, 1967; practice medicine specializing in dermatology Greenville, N.C., 1967-80; prof. medicine, chief div. dermatology East Carolina U., Greenville, 1980-91, prof. medicine, 1991—. Recipient Clin. Tchr. award Sr. Class, 1983, 84, 88, Teaching Recognition award 1st yr. residents, 1982, 3d yr. residents, 1985 Med. Sch. East Carolina U. Fellow Am. Acad. Dermatology; mem. AMA, N.C. Med. Soc. Republican. Episcopalian. Office: East Carolina U Sch Medicine Greenville NC 27858-4354

JONES, BLANCHE, nursing administrator, orthopaedic and gerontology consultant; b. Edgecombe, N.C., Nov. 11, 1935; d. Cosevelt Ewuell and Evelyn (Jones) Harrison. Diploma, CUNY Hunter Coll., 1971; AAS, CUNY Medgar Evers Coll., 1986; BS in Cmty. Health, Gerontology and Med. Surg. Sci., St. Joseph's Coll., 1990. RN, N.Y.; RN in med.-surg., ANCC. Nurse aide Bellevue Hosp., N.Y.C., 1958-61, lic. practical nurse, 1961-71, staff nurse, 1971-72, head nurse, 1972-77; head nurse Coney Island Hosp., Bklyn., 1978-90, clin. supr., 1990—. Contbr. articles to profl. jours. Bd. dirs. Baisley Park Neighbors Inc., Jamaica, N.Y., 1968—. Mem. Orthopaedic Nurses Assn., N.Y. Nurses Assn. (del. 1972), Bowling League, Fishing Club, Target Pistol Club. Democrat. Baptist. Home: 15026 119th Ave Jamaica NY 11434-2009 Office: Coney Island Hosp 2601 Ocean Pky Brooklyn NY 11235-7791

JONES, CALVIN EMBERT, surgeon; b. Balt., Oct. 21, 1938; s. Calvin Embert and Pearl Laura (Hoffman) J.; m. Dorothy Lou Breneman, May 1, 1971; 1 child, Thomas Randolph. BS, Md. U., 1961, MD, 1965. Diplomate Am. Bd. Surgery, General Vascular Surgery. Assoc. prof. surgery Johns Hopkins U., Balt., 1993—. Capt. U.S. Army, 1966-68, Vietnam. Fellow ACS. Presbyterian. Office: Johns Hopkins Bayview Med Ctr 4940 Eastern Ave Baltimore MD 21224

JONES, CHERYL SCOTT, mental health administrator; b. Memphis, Nov. 14, 1952; d. Elgin L. and Millie L. (Hill) Scott; m. Anthony Jones, June 15, 1986 (div. Sept. 1987); children; Patricia Cheryl, April Elaine Jones-Nichols. BA, Knoxville Coll., 1974; postgrad., Memphis State U., 1977-78; MSSW, U. Tenn., Memphis, 1980. Lic. clin. social worker; cert. forensic examiner. Counselor Rape Crisis Program, Memphis, 1980-82, dir., 1982-83; sexual assault counselor Pvt. Practice Counseling Svcs., Memphis, 1984-86; crisis support specialist Crisis Stblzn. Unit, Memphis, 1986-87; cons. social worker Meth. Outreach, Inc., Memphis, 1990-92, Midtown Counseling Ctr., Memphis, 1986—; forensic examiner Midtown Mental Health Ctr., Memphis, 1984—, program mgr., 1987-92, dep. dir. crisis svcs., 1992—; rsch. ast. dept. psychiatry, spl. problems unit U. Tenn. Ctr. for Health Scis., Memphis, 1977-80; regional rep. Nat. Coalition Against Sexual Assault, 1978-94. Contbr. articles to profl. jours. Troop leader Tenn.-Ark.-Miss. coun. Girl Scouts U.S., 1993. Mem. APHA, Am. Coll. Health Svcs. Execs., Assn. Mental Health Adminstrs., Nat. Assn. Health Svcs. Execs. (sec. 1993—), Delta Sigma Theta. Office: Midtown Mental Health Ctr 152 Beale St Ste 300 Memphis TN 38103

JONES, CHRISTOPHER ERNEST, pharmacologist, toxicologist; b. Clinton, Ind., Nov. 4, 1952; s. William Arthur and Mary Elisabeth (Tippin) J.; m. Catherine Ann Robl, Aug. 5, 1989. BS in Biology, U. Houston, 1973; PhD in Pharmacology, Baylor U., 1979. Diplomate Am. Bd. Forensic Toxicology, Am. Bd. Clin. Chemistry, Am. Bd. Forensic Examiners. Postdoctoral fellow. Northwestern U. Med. Sch., Chgo., Ill., 1979-81; chief clin. pathology USAF Sch. of Aerospace Med., Brooks AFB, Tex., 1982-85, chief toxicology, 1985-87; intern Wilford Hall USAF Med. Ctr., Lackland AFB, Tex., 1987-88; chief comp. clin. path. Armstong Aerospace Med. Rsch. Lab., Wright-Patterson AFB, Tex., 1988-90; dir. chem. and tox. CBC Lab. Svcs., Grand Rapids, Mich., 1990-92; dir. Analytitix, Inc., Englewood, Colo., 1992-94; instr. Butterworth Med. Tech. Internship, Grand Rapids, 1990; dir. Arata Med. Group Lab., Ft. Wayne, Ind., 1990. Contbr. numerous articles to sci. jours. Capt. USAF, 1982. Recipient Commendation medal USAF, 1985, 87, Nat. Rsch. Svc. award NIH, 1980. Mem. Nat. Acad. of Clin. Biochemistry, Am. Acad. of Forensic Sci., Am. Soc. of Clin. Pathologists, Am. Assc. for Clin. Chemistry, Am. Med. Technologists, Aerospace Med. Assc., Am. Chem. Soc. Home: 1511 S Kansas St Wichita KS 67211-3624

JONES, CLYDE WILLIAM, anesthesiologist; b. Barbados, West Indies, Sept. 29, 1929; came to U.S., 1947; s. Lewis F. and Albertha B. (Lewis) J.; m. Norma Anita, Sept. 14, 1963; children: Michael W., Ronald C., Stephen T. BS, City Coll., N.Y.C., 1954; MD, Howard U., 1958. Diplomate Am. Bd. Anesthesiology. Capt. U.S. Navy, 1959-79, med. officer, 1959-63; resident in anesthesiology U.S. Naval Hosp., San Diego, 1963-66; staff anesthesiologist U.S. Naval Hosp., Camp Pendleton, Calif., 1966-67, chief of anesthesiology, 1967-69; chief of anesthesiology 1st Hosp. Co., Danang, Vietman, 1968, U.S. Naval Hosp., Marianas Island, Guam, 1969-71; staff anesthesiologist Naval Regional Med. Ctr., San Diego, 1971-73, chief of anesthesiology, 1973-79; staff anesthesiologist Kaiser Permanente Med. Ctr., San Diego, 1979-81, 87—, chief of anesthesiology, 1981-87. Contbr. articles to profl. jours. Acolyte lay reader, sub Deacon All Sts. Episcopal Ch., San Diego, 1971—; bd. dirs. Bishop's Sch., San Diego, 1980-81, San Diego Civic Light Opera, Inc., 1980-83. Recipient Meritorious Svc. medal, certificate of merit Surgeon Gen. U.S. Navy, 1979. Fellow Am. Coll. Anesthesiologists; mem.Am. Soc. Anesthesiologists (delegate), Assn. Mil. Surgeons of U.S., Am. Soc. Clin. Hypnosis, Internat. Anesthesia Rsch. Soc., Naval Inst., Sigma Pi Phi. Democrat. Home: 5201 Countryside Dr San Diego CA 92115 Office: Kaiser Permanente Med Ctr 4647 Zion Ave San Diego CA 92120

JONES, CYNTHIA MARIE, medical technologist; b. Reno, Nev., Aug. 23, 1958; d. Marvin Kent Segar and Yvonne Vera (Yost) Francis; m. Benjamin Lee Jones, Sept. 1, 1978; 1 child, Rebecca Michelle. BS in medical tech., Western Carolina Univ., 1987. Medical tech./specialist U.S. Army 130th Sta Hosp., Heidelberg, Germany, 1977-79; medical tech. Commanche Meml. Hosp., Lawton, Okla., 1979-80, U.S. Army, Ft. Sill, Okla., 1979-80, Sylva (N.C.) Cmty. Hosp., 1980; lab. supr. Buncombe County Hosp., Asheville, N.C.; medical tech. Swain County Hosp., Bryson City, N.C., 1986, Promina Gwinnett Medical Ctr., Lawrenceville, Ga., 1986—; nat. medical lab. week coord. Am. Medical Technologist, Lawrenceville, 1994-96. Recipient Disting. Achievement award Am. Medical Technologist, 1995. Mem. Ga. State Soc. Am. Medical Technologist (pres. 1994—, bd. dirs. 1992-94, Outstanding Svc. award 1994), Queen Esther Rebekah Lodge, Capitol Theta Rho (pres., v.p. sec., treas. 1968—), Assn. Soc. Clinical Pathologist. Republican. Lutheran. Home: 420 Thorntree Pass Lawrenceville GA 30243 Office: Gwinnett Med Ctr 1000 Med Ctr Blvd Lawrenceville GA 30245

JONES, DAN B., ophthalmologist, educator; b. Raleigh, N.C., June 12, 1936; m. Marilyn Woodall; children: Danny Brigman Jr., Allen Walker. BA, Duke U., 1958, MD, 1962. Diplomate Am. Bd. Ophthalmology. Intern Duke Hosp., Durham, 1962-63; resident in ophthalmology Bascom Palmer Eye Inst., U. Miami (Fla.) Sch. Medicine, 1965-69; fellow in cornea and external disease Moorfields Eye Hosp., Inst. Ophthalmology, London, 1967-68; asst. prof. then assoc. prof. ophthalmology dept. surgery Vanderbilt U. Sch. Medicine, Nashville, 1969-71; assoc. prof. then prof. ophthalmology Cullen Eye Inst., Baylor Coll. Medicine, Houston, 1972-78; Sid W. Richardson prof., chmn. dept. ophthalmology Cullen Eye Inst., Baylor Coll. Medicine, 1981—, Margarett Root Brown chair ophthalmology, 1991—; mem. staff, then chief ophthalmology svc. Ben Taub Gen. Hosp., 1972—, Meth. Hosp., Houston, 1972—; mem. staff St. Luke's Episcopal Hosp., Houston, 1973—, M.D. Anderson Hosp. and Tumor Inst., Houston, 1978—; chief ophthalmology sect. VA Hosp., Houston, 1973-78; mem. sci. adv. com. Knights Templar Eye Found., Inc., 1984—; mem. various coms. and couns. Nat. Eye Inst., 1975—; mem. adv. panel on ophthalmology U.S. Pharmacopeial Conv., 1980-84; mem. ophthalmic drugs adv. com. FDA, 1975-78; cons. in field; vis. prof. to numerous schs., including Johns Hopkins U., Balt., 1975, 79, Washington U., St. Louis, 1975, Tipler Army Hosp., Honolulu, 1974, Yale U., New Haven, 1988, others; lectr. in field. Contbr. numerous articles to profl. jours. Bd. dirs. William C. Connor Found., Tex. Christian U., 1981—, Tex. Soc. to Prevent Blindness, 1981—; bd. dirs. The Lighthouse of Houston, 1981-89, mem. adv. coun., 1989—; mem. exec. med. com. Lions Eye Bank of Tex., 1981—, bd. dirs., 1989—. Epidemic intelligence officer USPHS, 1963-65. Recipient Honor award in Edn. Am. Acad. Ophthalmology and Otolaryngology, 1976; grantee NIH, 1978—, Sid W. Richardson Found., 1977-82. Mem. AMA (mem. program com. sect. ophthalmology 1970-73), Am. Acad. Ophthalmology (mem. faculty of basic and clin. sci. course 1970-76, mem. ophthalmology knowledge assessment com. 1972-80, mem. adv. com. 1973-77, mem. long range planning com. 1976-80, mem. program adv. com. 1986-89, sec. instrn. 1989—, trustee 1989—, Sr. Honor award 1986), Am. Ophthalmol. Soc., Am. Soc. for Microbiology, Assn. for Rsch. in Vision and Ophthalmology, Assn. Univ. Profs. Ophthalmology (chmn. resident and fellowship edn. com. 1986-88, chmn. edn. com. 1988—, trustee 1988—, pres. bd. trustees 1993—), Harris County Med. Soc., Houston Ophthal. Soc. (pres. 1979-80), Ocular Microbiology and Immunology Group, Inc. (exec. sec. 1973-89, bd. dirs. 1989—), Pan Am. Assn. Ophthalmology, Tex. Ophthal. Assn. (mem. bd. councillors 1982-85), Tex. Soc. Infectious Diseases, Baylor Ophthalmology Alumni Assn., Inc., Bascom Palmer Alumni Assn., Phi Beta Kappa, Phi Eta Sigma, Alpha Omega Alpha. Office: Baylor Coll of Medicine Vision Rsch Ctr-Cullen Eye Inst 6501 Fannin NC 200 Houston TX 77030

JONES, DAN LEWIS, psychologist; b. Halifax, Va., Oct. 8, 1951; s. Ernest Lewis and Mary Elizabeth (Francis) J.; m. Temple Kiger Jones, Aug. 17, 1974; children: Natalie Temple, Layla Michelle. BA, Appalachian State U., 1974; MA, West Ga. Coll., 1976; PhD, U. Kans., 1986. Lic. psychologist, N.C., Tenn., Calif., Va.; diplomate in counseling psychology Am. Bd. Profl. Psychology; cert. treatment of alcohol and other psychoactive substance use disorders, APA Coll. of Profl. Psychology. Instr. psychology N.C. Cen. U., Durham, 1976-79; counselor Adult Life Resource Ctr., U. Kans., Lawrence, 1979-84; psychology intern Counseling Ctr. U. Calif., Irvine, 1984-85; acting dir. adult life resource ctr. U. Kans., 1985-86; staff psychologist Counseling Ctr. Utah State U., Logan, 1986-88; psychologist Counseling Ctr. East Tenn. State U., Johnson City, 1988-89; sr. psychologist, dir. tng., asst. dir. Counseling and Psychol. Svcs., Appalachian State U., Boone, N.C., 1989—; part-time pvt. practice; cons. IRS, 1985, Bristol (Tenn.) Mental Health Ctr., 1989, N.C. Ct. Counseling Svcs., 1979. Author: (with others) Counseling Adults, 1985, editor; author (manual) The Stress management Workshop, 1985, (with others) AACD Stress Workshop Manual, 1985. Fellow Acad. of Counseling Psychology; mem. APA (chmn. spl. interest group on coll. counseling ctrs. divsn. 17), Am. Coll. Pers. Assn. (directorate commn. VII), Soc. of Psychotherapy Integration. Democrat. Home: 257 Fawn Boone NC 28607-9804

JONES, DAVID LANCE, nurse; b. Boaz, Ala., Apr. 19, 1967; s. K. David and Barbara (Harris) J. Diploma in practical nursing, Gadsden Tech. Inst., 1987; ADN, Northeast State Jr. Coll., 1990; BS in Mgmt., Internat. Coll., 1994. Cert. ACLS nurse, cert. trauma nurse, cert. in trauma nursing core course. Staff nurse emergency dept. Boaz-Albertville Med. Ctr., 1990-92; emergency rm.-staff nurse St. Thomas (V.I.) Hosp., Virgin Islands, 1992; asst. nurse mgr. progressive care unit St. Joseph Med. Ctr., Port Charlotte, Fla., 1992—; asst. nurse mgr. progressive care unit Bon Secours St. Joseph Hosp., Port Charlotte, 1993-94, adminstrv. rep., 1993-94, 94—; nurse mgr., emergency svc. Walker Meml. Med. Ctr., Wauchula, Fla., 1994; nurse mgr. med./surg./oncology Bon Secours St. Joseph Hosp., Port Charlotte, 1995—. Mem. ANA, Nat. League Nursing, Am. Assembly of Men in Nursing, Emergency Nurses Assn., Ala. Nurses Assn., Marshall County Nurses Soc. (chmn.-elect), Fla. Orgn. of Nurse Execs., Am. Assembly of Men in Nursing, ENA. Republican. Episcopalian. Home: 8316 Island Breeze Ln Tampa FL 33637-1050

JONES, DAVID ROBERT, toxicologist; b. Wrecsam, Clwyd, Wales, Sept. 6, 1955; s. William Derek and Christine Mary (Wright) J.; m. Stephanie Helen Langford, Jan. 3, 1957; children: Rachel Sarah, Amanda Louise. BSc in Chemistry, U.C.W. Aberystwyth, Wales, 1976, BSc with honors in Biochemistry, 1977; MSc in Pharmacology, Hertfordshire, Eng., 1986. Registered toxicologist, Eng.; chartered biologist, European biologist. Toxicologist HRC, Cambridge, Eng., 1978-85, Fisons Pharms., Loughborough, Eng., 1985-95; sr. toxicologist Fisons Respiratory Devel., Loughborough, 1995-96; toxicologist UK Medicines Control Agy., London, 1996—. Ch. warden Ch. of Eng., Coalville, 1994, ch. treas., 1991; sch. gov. Ravenstone CP, Eng., 1992. Mem. Brit. Toxicology Soc., Inst. Biology, Assn. Inhalation Toxicologists. Mem. Ch. of Eng. Home: 7 Hervey Woods Whitwick, Leics LE67 SHH, England Office: Medicines Control Agency, Market Towersž, 1 Nine Elms Ln, London SW8 5NQ, England

JONES, DOROTHY JOANNE, social services professional; b. L.A.; d. Joseph Anthony and Florence (Chaffin) Ghiotto; divorced; children: Teri McKane, Carole Thompson, Christopher Jones. BA, La Verne U., 1980; MS, Calif. State U., Fullerton, 1983. Lic. marriage, family/child counselor. Dep. sheriff L.A. County Sheriff Office, 1972-76; dir. A.I.C., L.A., 1976-80; mgr. McDonnell Douglas, Long Beach, Calif., 1980-93; pvt. practice Los Alamitos, Calif., 1985—; cons. L.A. County, 1993-94. Author: When to SayNo, 1983; contbr. poems to lit. publs. Mem. Ctr. for Performing Arts, L.A., 1976&, Transpacific Mgmt., Long Beach, 1982-83. Recipient Spl. Svc. award Assn. Labor and Mgmt., Orange County, Calif., 1983. mem. Employee Assistance Profls. Assn. (pres. 1980-82), Alcoholism Info. Ctr. (v.p. 1980-91), Counseling Assocs. (v.p. 1976-83), Calif. Assn. Marriage and Family Tehrapists (cons. Los Angeles County 1993—). Democrat. Episcopalian. Office: 10741 Los Alamitos Blvd Ste 201 Los Alamitos CA 90720-5608

JONES, EDWARD GEORGE, anatomy and neurobiology professor, department chairman; b. Upper Hutt, Wellington, N.Z., Mar. 26, 1939; came to U.S., 1972; s. Frank Ian and Theresa Agnes (Riordan) J.; m. Elizabeth Suzanne Oldham, Apr. 27, 1963; children: Philippa Emilie, Christopher Edward. MD, U. Otago, Dunedin, N.Z., 1962; PhD, U. of Oxford, Eng., 1968. Med. and surg. intern Tauranga Hosp., New Zealand, 1963; demonstrator to assoc. prof. dept. anatomy U. Otago Med. Sch., Dunedin, New Zealand, 1964-72; Nuffield Dominions demonstrator and lectr. Balliol Coll., U. of Oxford, Eng., 1964-72; assoc. prof. to prof., dept. anatomy and neurobiology Washington U. Sch. Medicine, St. Louis, 1972-84, George H. and Ethel Ronzini Bishop scholar, 1981-84, dir. div. exptl. neurology, 1981-84; prof. and chmn. dept. anatomy and neurobiology U. Calif., Irvine, 1984—; cons. NIH, 1972—; dir. Neural Systems Lab., Frontier Rsch. Program in Neural Mechanisms of Mind and Behavior, Riken, Japan, 1988-96; vis. sr. rsch. fellow St. John's Coll. at U. Oxford, Eng., 1989-90. Author: The Thalamus, 1984; co-author: The Thalamus and Basal Telencephalon, 1982; co-editor: (book series) Cerebral Cortex, 1984—; author, reviewer numerous sci. and hist. articles, chpts. in books, 1964—. Mem. Pres.'s Adv. Bd. Calif. State U., Long Beach, 1986-90. Recipient Rolleston Meml. prize U. Oxford, 1970; rsch. grantee NIH, 1971—; named one of 1000 most cited biol. scientists, Sci. Citation Index, 1982. Mem. Soc. for Neurosci. (com. chair 1978-81, 88-89), Am. Assn. Anatomists (Cajal medal 1989), AAAS, Anat. Soc. Great Britain and Ireland (Symington Meml. prize 1968). Democrat. Office: U Calif Dept Anatomy & Neurobiology Irvine CA 92697

JONES, EUGENE GORDON, pharmaceutical company executive; b. Lookout, W.Va., June 26, 1929; s. Alphus Raymond and Mona Blanche (Bobbitt) J.; m. Nancy Lee Hall, Aug. 19, 1951; children: Gene Douglas, Michael Gordon, Rebecca Lee, Jody Lynn. BS, Va. Tech. U., 1951. Med. rep. The Upjohn Co., Charlottesville, Va., 1956-60; profl. svcs. mgr. The Upjohn Co., Washington, 1960-63; sr. med. rep. The Upjohn Co., Roanoke, Va., 1963-68; hosp. med. rep. The Upjohn Co., Richmond, Va., 1968-70; dist. sales mgr. The Upjohn Co., Va., 1970-73; tng. specialist The Upjohn Co., Kalamazoo, Mich., 1973-76, tng. mgr., 1976-87, nat. tng. dir., 1987-90; pres. Global Meeting Planners, 1991—; dir. Kalamazoo Speciality Plants, 1991—. Author: (self instrn. course) Managed Health Care, 1985, Arthritis Primer, 1976. Pres. Am. Diabetes Assn., Roanoke chpt., 1967, Richmond chpt., 1971, state del., 1970; bd. dirs. United Way, Kalamazoo, 1990, 91, Mich. Diabetes Assn., Detroit, 1979; deacon River Rd. Presbyn. Ch.; mem. Rep. Presdl. Task Force. Lt. U.S. Army, 1951-53, Korea, capt. USAR, 1953-60. Mem. Nat. Soc. Pharm. Sales Trainers (hon., pres. Western chpt. 1980-81, pres. nat. orgn. 1987-88, dir. 1985-90, founder newsletter 1987), Meeting Planners Internat., Internat. Meeting Planners, Mil. Order World Wars (treas. 1964-68), Kalamazoo Air History Mus., Charles Garfield Group (hon.), Korean War Vets. Assn. Home: 2828 Kalarama Rd Kalamazoo MI 49002-2321

JONES, FLOYD ARDEN, osteopath; b. West Palm Beach, Fla., Feb. 1, 1944; m. Sue Ann Willis, Aug. 21, 1965; children: Bryan, Eric, Justin, Jessica. BS, Simpson Coll., Indianola, Iowa, 1966; postgrad., Drake U., Des Moines, 1966-67; DO, Coll. Osteo. Medicine/Surgery, Des Moines, 1971. Pvt. practice Shenandoah, Iowa, 1971—; dir. Elm Heights/Park Crest, Shenandoah; pres. med. staff Shenandoah Meml. Hosp., bd. dirs. Fellow Am. Acad. Family Physicians; mem. Am. Assn. Physician Specialists, Am. Acad. Osteopathic Physicians, Am. Acad. Family Practice. Home: 15 Applewood Dr Shenandoah IA 51601 Office: 300 Park Ave Shenandoah IA 51601

JONES, FRANK EMERSON, orthopedic surgeon; b. Memphis, June 10, 1934; s. Frank Emerson Jr. and Madeline Victoria (Jackson) J.; m. Audrey Jeanne Wojcik, May 13, 1961; children: Catherine, Ann, Daniel, Patricia. MD, U. Tenn., 1958; MS in Orthopedic Surgery, U. Minn., 1967; MA in French, Vanderbilt U., 1995. Diplomate Am. Bd. Orthopedic Surgery. Intern D.C. Gen. Hosp., Washington, 1958-59; resident in gen. surgery U. Vt., 1959-60; resident in orthopedic surgery Mayo Clinic, Rochester, Minn., 1963-66; fellow in hand surgery Dr. Joseph Boyes, L.A., 1966; orthopedic surgeon Tenn. Orthopaedic Assocs., Nashville, 1967—; assoc. clin. prof. surgery Mehany Med. Coll., Nashville, 1968—; asst. clin. prof. orthopedics and rehab. Vanderbilt U., Nashville, 1972—. Capt. USAR, 1961-63. Fellow ACS; mem. Am. Soc. for Surgery of the Hand, Am. Acad. Orthopedic Surgeons (councilor 1988-94), Tenn. Orthopedic Soc. (pres. 1986), Tenn. Hand Soc. (pres. 1990), Nashville Orthopedic Soc. (pres. 1985), Société Internationale de Chirurgie Orthopédique et de Traumatologie, Socété Francaise de Chirurgie de la Main. Home: 724 Summerly Dr Nashville TN 37209 Office: Tenn Orthopaedic Assocs 301 21st Ave North Nashville TN 37203

JONES, FRANKLIN DEL, psychiatrist, consultant; b. Hereford, Tex., Sept. 22, 1935; s. Oren William and Augusta Virginia (Morris) J.; m. June Suk Kim, Nov. 30, 1957; children: Gregory, Geoffrey, Gresham, Giselle. Student, Baylor U., 1957; MD, Southwestern Tex. U., 1961. Diplomate Am. Bd. Psychiatry and Neurology. Commd. 2d lt. U.S. Army, 1961, advanced through grades to col., ret., 1988; pvt. practice Rockville, Md., 1988—; cons. Fairfax County Mental Health, Annandale, Va., 1968—, Montgomery County Addictions, Rockville, 1972—; cons. in psychopharmacology and behavior therapy Walter Reed Army Med. Ctr., 1988—. Editor: War and Its Aftermath, 1983, Military Psychiatry, 1994, War Psychiatry, 1995, Rehabilitation Methods in Neuropsychiatry, 1996. Pres. Md. Soc. for Autistic Adults and Children, Annapolis, 1984-86; v.p. Cmty. ACTS, Annapolis, 1988-94. Decorated Bronze Star, Legion of Merit. Fellow Am. Psychiat. Assn., Behavior Therapy and Rsch. Soc.; mem. World Psychiat. Assn. (chmn. 1977-83, sec. 1983-89, hon. pres. 1989—). Home and Office: 6508 Tall Tree Ter Rockville MD 20852-3733

JONES, FRANKLIN DOUGLAS, neurosurgeon; b. Wilkes-Barre, Pa., Oct. 6, 1950; s. Franklin and Elizabeth Almeda (Cole) J.; m. Brenda Helen Barr, Aug. 30, 1980; children: Kristin Elizabeth, David Douglas. BA, U. Pa., 1972; MD, Ea. Va. Med. Sch., 1977. Resident U. N.C., Chapel Hill, 1983; asst. prof. divsn. neurosurgery U. N.C. Sch. Medicine, Chapel Hill, 1983-85; clin. asst. prof. East Carolina Sch. Medicine, Greenville, N.C., 1985-90, clin. assoc. prof., 1990—, chief divsn. neurosurgery, 1992—. Bd. dirs. Ronald McDonald House, Greenville, 1987-91. Mem. AMA, Am. Assn. Neurol. Surgeons, N.C. Neurosurg. Soc. (sec./treas. 1988-91, pres. 1991-93), Congress Neurol. Surgery. Office: Eastern Carolina Neurosurg 2325 Stantonsburg Rd Greenville NC 27834

JONES, GALEN EVERTS, microbiologist, educator; b. Milw., Sept. 9, 1928; s. Galen and Grace (Everts) J.; m. Edith Agnes Boehme, July 17, 1954 (div. 1984); children: Galen Randolph, Gwenith Grace, Christopher Thomas; m. Eleonore Angell Barton, June 14, 1986. A.B., Dartmouth Coll., 1950; M.A., Williams Coll., 1952; Ph.D., Rutgers U., 1956. With Scripps Inst. Oceanography, U. Calif., La Jolla, 1955-63, asst. research microbiologist, 1957-63; assoc. prof. biology Boston U., 1963-66; prof. microbiology U. N.H., Durham, 1966—, chmn. dept., 1975-80, prof. emeritus, 1991—; dir. Jackson Estuarine Lab., 1966-72, 83-87; dir. Marine Sci. Labs., Coastal Marine Lab., Anadromous Fish and Aquatic Invertebrate Rsch. facility, 1985-87, interim dir. UNH Sea Grant, 1986-87; vis. prof. U. Liverpool, Eng., 1972-73, Scripps Inst. Oceanographic, U. Calif., La Jolla, 1981; mem. Pres.'s Santa Barbara Oil Spill panel, 1969, adv. com. to biol. oceanography NSF, 1971-72, 74-75, water ecosystems adv. com. Inst. of Ecology to Nat. Commn. on Water Quality, 1974-77, adv. com. for ocean scis. NSF, 1979-80; World Cultural Coun., 1987. Contbr. articles to profl. jours. Recipient Dartmouth Coll. 1950 Class award, 1990. Fellow AAAS, Am. Acad. Microbiology; mem. Am. Soc. Microbiology, The Oceanography Soc., Sigma Xi. Home: 6684 Michaeljohn Dr La Jolla CA 92037-6239

JONES, GALEN RAY, physician assistant; b. Salt Lake City, Feb. 1, 1948; s. Leonard Ray and Veda (Whitehead) J.; m. Patricia Ann Poulson, Jan. 21, 1972; children: Brian, Marci, Natalie. Grad., Med. Field Svc. Sch. Ft. Sam Houston, San Antonio, 1971; BS, U. Utah, 1982. Missionary Ch. of Jesus Christ of Latter Day Saints, Alta., Sask., Can., 1967-69; asst. mgr. Cowan's Frostop Hamburger Stand, Salt Lake City, 1969-70; with Safeway Stores, Inc., Salt Lake City, 1970; o.r. tech. Latter Day Saint Hosp., Salt Lake City, 1973-75; physician asst. Lovell Clinic Inc., Lovell, Wyo., 1975-77, Family Health Care, Inc., Tooele, Utah, 1977-86, West Dermatology and Surgery Med. Grp., Redlands, Calif., 1986-95; maturation lectr. Tooele Sch. Dist., 1978-86; course dir., instr. EMT, North Big Horn County Search and Rescue, 1976; instr. EMT, Grantsville Ambulance Inc., 1979-85; lectr. on skin care and changes to sr. citizen groups, hosp. auxs., health fairs, 1986—; high sch. sophomore sem. tchr. religion, 1991-96. Author: (with others) The P.A. Medical Handbook, 1995. Chmn. County Health Teen Pregnancy Prevention Project, Tooele, 1980-81; adv. bd. State Dept. Health-Rural Health Network, Salt Lake City, 1985-86; health lectr. County Health & Edn. Dept. Progs., Tooele, 1977-86; mormon bishop/pastor Lakeview Ward, Latter Day Saints Ch., Tooele, 1982-86; mem. Utah Acad. Physician Assts. (pres. 1980-81, editor newsletter 1979-80). With U.S. Army, 1971-73. U. Utah grantee, 1966, 67, 69. Fellow Am. Acad. Physician Assts., Calif. Acad. Physicians Assts. Republican. Mem. LDS Ch. Home: 101 Channing St Redlands CA 92373-4862

JONES, GENE ALAN, dental educator, dentist; b. Hodgenville, Ky., Dec. 21, 1924; s. Ben H. and Henritta B. (Baird) J.; m. Dorothy Burdette, Nov. 19, 1944; children—Janene L., S. Mark, Judy L., Timothy G. B.A., Coll. Anathoth, Indpls., 1964; D.D.S., Ind. U.-Indpls., 1962, M.S.D., 1980; B.S., Butler U., 1971. Records clk. Bidgeport Brass Co., Indpls., 1946-53; with purchase dept. Allison div. Gen. Motors Corp., Indpls., 1953-57; gen. practice dentistry, Danville, Ind., 1962-81; asst. prof. Sch. Dentistry, Ind. U.-Indpls., 1978-81; asst. prof. radiology U. Tenn.-Memphis, 1981-87, assoc. prof., 1987-92, prof., 1992—, head sect. dental radiology. Served to sgt. USAAF, 1943-45; PTO. Mem. ADA, Tenn. Dental Assn., Memphis Dental Soc., Am. Assn. Dental Schs., Am. Acad. Dental Radiology. Avocation: travel. Office: U Tenn Coll Dentistry 875 Union Ave Memphis TN 38103-3513

JONES, GEORGE BRYAN, psychologist; b. Scotia, Calif., June 8, 1947; s. George Bryan and Jennie Mildred (Wise) J.; m. Cynthia Louise Chester, Aug. 14, 1976; children: Carrie Beth, Christian Bryan. BS, Pa. State U., 1969; MA, Temple U., 1976, MEd, 1986, PhD, 1987. Lic. psychologist, Pa. Faculty mem. dept. psychiatry Med. Coll. Pa., Phila., 1988-89; comdr. USPHS, 1990—; adj. faculty Dept. Counseling Psychology Temple U., Phila., 1987-89; cons. spl. projects Naval Mil. Pers. Command, Washington, 1982-90; governing bd. mem. Intercommunity Action, Inc., Cmmunity Mental Health/Mental Retardation Ctr., Phila., 1985-90. Coun. mem. Epiphany Luth. Ch., Phila., 1985-90. Comdr. USNR, 1969-90. Mem. ACA, Am. Psychol. Assn., Pa. Psychol. Assn., Naval Res. Assn., Assn. Mil. Surgeons U.S., Res. Officer Assn., Commd. Officer Assn. USPHS. Republican. Home: 264 Fountain St Philadelphia PA 19128-4508 Office: USPHS 5600 Fishers Ln Rockville MD 20857-0001

JONES, GEORGE HERBERT, ophthalmologist; b. Baton Rouge, Mar. 7, 1922; s. George Herbert and Mary Weir (Tucker) J.; m. Klileen Leister, June 16, 1946. BSChemE, La. State U., 1942; MD, La. State U., New Orleans, 1953. Diplomate Am. Bd. Ophthalmology. Cons. engr. La., and Mex., 1946-49; intern New Orleans Charity Hosp., 1953-54; resident in ophthalmology Tulane U., New Orleans, 1955-57; pvt. practice Baton Rouge, 1957—; mem. staff Baton Rouge Gen. Hosp., Our Lady of Lake Hosp., 1957—; asst. prof. Tulane U. Sch. Medicine, New Orleans, 1965-92; pres. Am. Cellphone Inc., Baton Rouge, 1983-92; bd. dirs. Interacel, Inc., Cambridge, Mass.; sec.-treas. Interactive Video of Detroit. Author various ophthalmology books; contbr. articles to profl. jours. Bd. dirs. Baton Rouge Little Theater, 1962-65, Baton Rouge Community Concerts, 1965-80, pres., 1966-70; bd. dirs. State Christian Social Concerns, 1968-72, Baton Rouge Symphony, 1970-73, La. State U. Union, 1973-75. Capt. arty., U.S. Army, 1942-46, ETO. Mem. AMA, La.-Miss. EENT Soc. (pres. 1976-77), La. Ophthalmology Soc. (pres. 1963, 70, 74), Am. Acad. Ophthalmology, La. Med. Soc. (chmn. pub. policy and legis.), Internat. Brotherhood Magicians (local pres.), Nat. Intrafraternity Conf. (bd. dirs. 1984-92, v.p. 1989-90), Masons (32 deg., worshipful master 1991-92), Shriners, Sigma Chi (internat. pres. 1981-83, author history of ritual 1955), Nu Sigma Nu, Alpha Omega Alpha, Omicron Delta Kappa. Republican. Methodist. Home: 2727 E Lakeshore Dr Baton Rouge LA 70808-2151

JONES, GEORGE HUMPHREY, retired healthcare executive, hospital facilities and communications consultant; b. Kansas City, Mo., July 10, 1923; s. George Humphrey and Mary R. (Marrs) J.; m. Peggy Jean Thompson, Nov. 23, 1943; children: Kenneth L., Daniel D., Kathleen Jones Carrigan, Carol R. Jones Johnson, Janet S. Jones Fitts. Student, U. Mo., Kansas City, 1940-43, Wis. State Coll., 1943. Police officer Kansas City (Mo.) Police Dept., 1947-51; elec. contr. Paramount Elec. Svc., Kansas City, 1947-50; electrician Automatic Temp. Control Co., Kansas City, 1951-57; pres., chief ops. George H. Jones Co., Kansas City, 1957-65; sales mgr. Nycon Inc., Lee's Summit, Mo., 1965; design engr. Midland Wright Corp., Kansas City, 1966; dist. sales mgr. Communications Electronics, Kansas City, 1967; plant ops. supr. Research Med. Ctr., Kansas City, 1968-77; dir. plant ops. and communications Research Med. Ctr., 1977-90; hosp. facilities and communications cons. Overland Park, Kans., 1990—; guest lectr. Nat. U., San Diego, 1987. Mem. Met. Emergency Preparedness Coun.; bd. dirs. Camellot Fine arts Acad., 1974-76, v.p. bd. dirs., 1975, 76; vol. program devel. Mid-Am. chpt. Multiple Sclerosis Soc.; vol. emergency svcs. Salvation Army; vol. emergency ops. and comms. Kansas City Area Hosp. Assn.; mem. Confederate Air Force. With USAAF, 1942-46, U.S. Army, 1950-51. Fellow Am. Soc. Hosp. Engring., Healthcare Info. and Mgmt. Systems Soc.; mem. Kansas City Area Hosp. Engrs. (pres. 1985, bd. dirs. 1985-89), Am. Legion, Alpha Phi Omega. Presbyterian. Home and Office: 6022 W 86th St Shawnee Mission KS 66207-1521

JONES, GORDON KEMPTON, dentist; b. Rochester, N.Y., July 22, 1946; s. Joseph Kempton and Eunice (Patten)J.; m. Kathleen Anne FitzSimmons, July 24, 1971; children: Bryan Kempton, Brendan Austin, Graeme Meghan, Michael Cameron, Meredith Hunter, Mallory Sterling. BA in chemistry, U. N. C., 1968; DDS, U. N.C., 1976; MS in Restorative Dentistry, U. Mich., 1984. Lic. dentist, Ill., N.C. Commd. lt. USN, 1976, advanced through ranks to capt., 1993; resident Naval Regional Medical Ctr., Camp Pendleton, Calif., 1977; dentist U.S.S. Holland USN, Holy Loch, Scotland, 1977-80; dentist regional med. ctr. USN, Great Lakes, Ill., 1980-82; head dept. operative dentistry Naval Dental Clinic, Great Lakes, Ill., 1984-90, 93—; head dept. operative dentistry Naval Dental Ctr., Norfolk, Va., 1990-93, dir. managed care, 1993—; cons. operative dentistry Naval Dental Clinic, Great Lakes, Ill., 1984-90, 93-96; dir. managed care Naval Dental Ctr., Great Lakes, Ill., 1993—; dir. branch dental clinic Naval Dental Ctr., 1996—; clinic dir. Naval Dental Ctr., Great Lakes, Ill., 1996—; cons. operative dentistry Naval Dental Ctr., Norfolk, 1990-93; featured spkr. Memphis Dental Soc., 1990, Coastal Carolina Dental Soc., 1992; cons. Naval Hosp. Great Lakes, 1984-86, 93—; asst. clin. prof. Northwestern U. Dental Sch., Chgo., 1985-90, 95—; quality assurance coord., head advanced clin. program in gen. dentistry, Norfolk, 1990-93. Contbr. articles to profl. jours.; speaker in field. Course dir. ARC, Great Lakes, 1984-90. Mem. ADA (USN Operative Dentistry (com. chmn. 1987—, pres. 1996—, exec. coun. 1996—), Acad. Operative Dentistry (mem. jour. editl. bd. 1993-95, 96), Internat. Assn. Dental Rsch., Acad. Gen. Dentistry, Am. Assn. Dental Schs., Am. Legion, Omicron Kappa Upsilon, Alpha Phi Omega, Delta Sigma Delta. Home: 1541 N McKinley Rd Lake Forest IL 60045-1377

JONES, H. JAMES, neurologist; b. Glendale, Calif., Nov. 24, 1954; s. William Wright and Anita Duran (Dussan) J.; m. Linda Marie Galloway, Jan. 5, 1980; children: Ryan James, Lauren Elizabeth. AA, L.A. City Coll., 1976; BS in Phys. Therapy, Calif. State U. Long Beach, 1980; DO, Coll. Osteo. Medicine Pacific, 1992. Diplomate Nat. Bd. Osteo. Examiners; lic. physician, Calif., phys. therapist, Calif. Phys. therapist Huntington Meml. Hosp., Pasadena, Calif., 1980-83, Profl. Health Resources, Tarzana, Calif., 1983-84; supr. phys. therapists Kaiser Permanente, West L.A., 1984-92; neurologist Kaiser Permanente, L.A., 1992—. Contbr. articles to profl. jours. Mem. Am. Osteo. Assn., Am. Acad. Neurology. Office: Kaiser Permanente 1505 Edgemont St Los Angeles CA 90029

JONES, HELENE RASBERRY, nursing educator; b. Weleetka, Okla., Apr. 16, 1940; d. John Milburn and Florence Loretta (King) Rasberry; m. Thomas Graves Jones, June 29, 1974; children: Kimberly Anne, Kendall Lee. BSN, Okla. Bapt. U., 1962; MN, Emory U., 1970. RN, Okla., Miss. Instr. Bapt. Sch. Nursing, Oklahoma City, 1963-66; staff nurse Presbyn. Hosp., Oklahoma City, 1966-67; instr. William Rufus King State Tech. Inst., Selma, Ala., 1967-69; prof. Sch. Nursing U. Miss., Jackson, 1970-80, coord., asst. prof., 1986-90; asst. DON div. staff devel. Univ. Hosp., Jackson, 1990-95; dir. dept. of staff devel. Univ. Hosps. and Clinics, Jackson, 1995—; assoc. prof. U. Tulsa, 1981; asst. dir., coord. divsn. staff devel. Hillcrest Med. Ctr., 1983-86; cons. Miss. Regional Med. Program, Jackson, 1972; chair accreditation rev. com. Schs. Nursing and bd. trustees instns. higher learning, Jackson, 1979-80. Mem. coms. health check and awards, Jackson, 1986-90, Am. Heart Assn., 1986—, PTA, Jenks, Okla. and Jackson, 1970-84; Citizens Better Edn., Jackson, 1978-80. Lt. U.S. Army, 1961-63. Mem. ANA, Miss. Nurses Assn. (dist. #13 nurse educator II award 1993), Sigma Theta Tau. Republican. Baptist. Home: 65 Glenway Pl Brandon MS 39042-2530 Office: UMC Univ Hosp 2500 N State St Jackson MS 39216-4500

JONES, HENRY WALTER, III, internist; b. Balt., Feb. 8, 1948; s. H. Walter Jr. and Elizabeth (DeNiord) J. BA, Pomona Coll., 1970; MD, U. Va., 1974. Diplomate Am. Bd. Internal Medicine. Resident in medicine Pa. Hosp., Phila., 1974-77; fellow in nephrology Stanford (Calif.) U., 1977-78; fellow in medicine Mass. Gen. Hosp., Boston, 1978-80; staff physician Permanente Med. Group, Santa Clara, Calif., 1980-88, Stanford (Calif.) Med. Group, 1988-92, Palo Alto (Calif.) Med. Clinic, 1992—; clin. prof. medicine Stanford U. Sch. Medicine, 1980—; mem. Nat. Bd. Med. Examiners, Phila., 1985—. Recipient Henry J. Kaiser Teaching award and Russell V. Lee Teaching award Stanford U. Fellow ACP. Office: Palo Alto Med Clinic 300 Homer Ave Palo Alto CA 94301

JONES, HERBERT CORNELIUS, III, otolaryngologist; b. 1936. MD, Ind. U., 1961. Intern Brook Gen. Hosp., San Angonio, 1961-62; resident in otolaryngology H&NS U. Ill. Coll. Medicine, 1965-68; mem. staff S.W. Cmty. Hosp., Atlanta; clin. assoc. prof. otolaryngology Morehouse Sch. Medicine. Mem. AAOHNS, NMA. Office: Tenn Valley Authority Water Mgmt Divsn 2600 M L King Dr SW Atlanta GA 30311*

JONES, JAMES CURTISS, surgeon; b. Dillon, S.C., Apr. 25, 1943; s. Samuel and Eunice Irene (Mallett) Jones; m. Dianne McAdams, Oct. 18, 1986; children: Lashawn, James II, Eunicia, Jette, Morgan. BS, Morehouse Coll., 1965; MD, U. Calif., San Francisco, 1969. Diplomate Am. Bd. Surgery, Am. Bd. Thoracic Surgery. Commd. maj. U.S. Army, 1979, advanced through grades to col., 1992; chief thoracic surgery Malcolm Grow USAF Med. Ctr., Andrews AFB, Md., 1979-83; staff thoracic surgeon Landstuhl (Germany) U.S. Army Med. Ctr., 1983-86; chief thoracic surgeon Madigan Army Med. Ctr., Ft. Lewis, Wash., 1986-90; staff thoracic surgeon Letterman Army Med. Ctr., Presidio Army Base, Calif., 1990; chief thoracic surgeon 8th Evacuation Hosp., Saudi Arabia, 1990-91; staff thoracic surgeon Brooke Army Med. Ctr., Ft. Sam Houston, Tex., 1991-92; chief thoracic surgery Womack Army Med. Ctr., Ft. Bragg, N.C., 1992—. Active Friends of Pacific Luth. U., Tacoma, 1987-90, Friends of Weymouth, Southern Pines, N.C., 1995-96. Decorated Army Commendation medals U.S. Army, 1986, 91, 92, 95; Nat. Med.-Sloan fellow Nat. Med. Fellowships, 1965-69. Fellow ACS, Am. Coll. Chest Physicians; mem. Soc. Thoracic Surgeons, So. Thoracic Surg. Assn., Fayetteville Symphony Orch. Assn., Omega Psi Phi. Baptist. Office: Thoracic Surgery Svc Womack Army Med Ctr Fort Bragg NC 28307

JONES, JAMES EDWARD, osteopath; b. Poplar Bluff, Mo., Apr. 17, 1939; s. Arthur Lee and Juanita M. (Huffman) J.; m. June Westaver, Apr. 2, 1966; children—James E., Julie Ann. Student N.E. Mo. State U., 1957-61; Western Ill. U., summer 1961; D.O., Kirksville Coll. Osteo. Medicine, 1966. Intern, Normandy Osteo. Hosp., St. Louis, 1966-67; practice osteo. medicine, St. Peters, Mo., 1967—; chief of staff Barnes-St. Peters Hosp., 1982, 88, also trustee. Mem. AMA, Am. Osteo. Assn., Mo. State Med. Assn., Am. Acad. Family Practice, First Physician Care (bd. dirs., v.p.). Republican. Lutheran. Home: PO Box 10 Saint Peters MO 63376-0010 Office: 327 Mid Rivers Mall Dr Saint Peters MO 63376-1516

JONES, JAMES THOMAS, hospital administrator; b. Glen Dale, W.Va., Nov. 13, 1949; s. James H. and Rose (Antonacci) J.; m. A. Jane Byrne, Sept. 4, 1971; 1 child, Jennifer. BS, W.Va. U., 1971; MHA, U. Minn., 1973. Resident W.Va. U. Hosp., Morgantown, 1972-73; asst. adminstr. Wheeling (W.Va.) Hosp., 1973-79, assoc. adminstr., 1979-90; exec. dir. St. Mary's Hosp., Huntington, W.Va., 1990—; instr. health adminstrn., Wheeling Coll., 1977; lectr. W.Va. U., Wheeling, 1982. Named one of Outstanding Young Men Am., U.S. Jaycees, 1980. Mem. Am. Coll. Health Adminstrs., W.Va. Hosp. Assn., W.Va. Hosp. Edn. and Rsch. Found. (pres. 1984-86), Huntington Area C. of C. (bd. dirs. 1990—). Republican. Roman Catholic. Home: 53 Camelot Dr Huntington WV 25701-5302 Office: St Mary's Hosp 2900 1st Ave Huntington WV 25701

JONES, JANET LOUISE, health services administrator; b. New Haven, Oct. 29, 1944; d. Raymond Burford Kinberly; m. Steven Craig Williams, Sept. 28, 1994; 1 child, James Lyle Cook. BSN, U. No. Fla., 1979, postgrad. RN, Fla. Various nursing edn. and adminstrn. positions, 1967-80; dir. edn. Meth. Hosp., Jacksonville, Fla., 1976-79; staff devel. instr. U. Mass. Med. Ctr., Worcester, 1979-80; mem. faculty Sch. Nursing Valdosta (Ga.) State Coll., 1980-81; exec. dir. Ctrl. Home Health, Inc., Valdosta, 1981-83; clin. coord. med. nursing South Ga. Med. Ctr., Valdosta, 1983-84; dir. Pub. Health Home Health Svcs., Valdosta, 1984-87; patient care adminstr., gen. acting mgr. Hospice Inc. of Dade County, Miami, Fla., 1987-88; adminstr. Mederi Home Health, inc., Miami, 1988; exec. dir. Cath. Hospice, inc., Miami Lakes, Fla., 1988-92, pres., CEO, 1992—; cons. Mederi Home Health, Inc., 1988—; mgmt. cons. Clay County Meml. Hosp., Green Cove Springs, Fla., Ed Fraser Meml. Hosp., Maccleny, Fla., Baker County Nursing Home, Maccleny, Brackford County Hosp., Stark, Fla., 1976-79. Mem. Fla. Cath. Conf. Task Force Against Assisted Suicide, 1992—; co-chair Archbishop of Miami's Task Force Against Assisted Suicide, 1993—; chair ed. and tng. com. Fla. Hospices, Inc., 1992-95, sec., 1995, mem. legis. task force, 1995, mem. ethics com., 1995; mem. Leadership Miami, 1993; mem. gov.'s study/adv. task force on nursing edn. Fla. Commr. Edn., 1978-79. Recipient Bronze medallion for vol. svc. Am. Heart Assn., 1983. Mem. N.W. Fla. Hospice Assn. (charter mem., trainer, mem. ethics com. 1993, chair code of ethics subcom. 1993—, chair survey rev. subcom.), Nat. Hospice Orgn., Internat. Hospice Inst. (bd. dirs.), Am. Acad. Med. Adminstrs., Am. Col.. Oncology Adminstrs. (bd. dirs. 1995—), Greater Miami C. of C., Rotary Internat. (North Dade/North Miami club, treas. 1991-93, pres.-elect 1994, pres. 1995, dist. gov.'s rep. 1996), Sigma Theta Tau. Home: 1020 SW 153d Terr Pembroke Pines FL 33027

JONES, JEFFREY ALLEN, urologist, surgeon, educator; b. Newport News, Aug. 6, 1959; s. Enoch Morse and Gladys Marie (Hemphill) J. BA in Biology/Psychology magna cum laude, Trinity U., San Antonio, 1981; MD, Baylor Coll. Medicine, 1984. Diplomate Am. Bd. Urology; lic. physician, Ind., Tex. Resident in gen. surgery Ind. U. Hosps., Indpls., 1985-87, resident in urology, 1987-91, fellow urologic oncology, 1991-92; asst. prof., chief divsn. urology Tex. Tech. U. Health Scis. Ctr., Lubbock, 1992-94, assoc. prof., 1996—; dir. urology/oncology, asst. med. dir. S.W. Cancer Ctr., Lubbock, 1994—; cancer liaison physician ACS Commn. on Cancer, 1994-96; med. advisor Medically Underserved Cancer Program, 1995-96; med. adv. bd., co-chmn. med. symposium Nat. Kidney Found., 1994-96; founder, med. advisor U.S. TOO Prostate Cancer Support Group, 1993-96; vis. prof. U. Neuvo Leon, Monterrey, Mex., 1994; lectr. in field; active staff Ind. U. Hosps., 1991-92; teaching staff Richard A. Roudebush VA Hosp., 1991-92; staff med. officer Great Lakes Naval Hosp., 1991-92; active staff Univ. Med. Ctr. Hosp., Lubbock, 1992—; courtesy staff Highland Med. Ctr. Hosp., Lubbock, 1994—, St. Mary of the Plains Hosp., Lubbock, 1995; provisional staff South Park Hosp., Lubbock, 1995, R.E. Thomason Hosp., El Paso, Tex., 1995. Jour. reviewer Oncogene, Urology; contbr. numerous articles and abstracts to profl. jours. Pres.-elect, bd. dirs. Am. Cancer Soc., Lubbock; med. dir. Sunshine Kids Children with Cancer Program, State of Tex.; bd. dirs. Women's Protective Svcs., Lubbock; med. advisor Univ. Med. Ctr. Found./UMC Forum, Lubbock; adv. bd. Tex. Cmty. Oncology Network, 1992-94; co-chmn. symposium com., program planning com. Nat. Kidney Found., 1994, 95; vol. Am. Heart Assn., ARC; exec. Nat. Kidney Found. of West Tex., 1995, med. adv. com., 1994-95; mem. Lakeridge United Meth. Ch. Christian Fellowship. Lt. comdr. USNR, 1989—. Recipient Disting. Leadership award for outstanding contbn. in med. edn. and rsch., 1995, Outstanding Vol. Leadership award Nat. Kidney found., 1995; grantee So. Med. Assn., 1985, Am. Found. for Urologic Disease, 1991, Searle, 1992, Audrey B. Jones Cancer Rsch. Fund, 1993, S.W. Oncology Group, 1994, 95, Schering Pharms., 1995. Fellow ACS; mem. AMA, AAAS, Am. Urol. Assn., Am. Assn. Cancer Rsch., N.Y. Acad. Scis., Soc. Urologic Oncology, Soc. Univ. Urologists, Southwestern Surg. congress, Internat. Soc. Study of Comparative Oncology, Am. Inst. Ultrasound in Medicine, Soc. Laparoendoscopic Surgeons, Tex. Urologic Soc., Endourologic Soc., West Tex. Transplant Soc., Soc. for Basic Urologic Rsch., Am. Assn. Clin. Urologists, Tex. Med. Assn., Ind. Med. Assn., Sigma Xi, Alpha Omega Alpha. Methodist. Home: 8406 Vicksburg Lubbock TX 79424 Office: University Urology Assocs 3502 9th St #260 Lubbock TX 79415

JONES, JOHN COURTS, wildlife biologist; b. Washington, Oct. 3, 1913; s. Copeland Page and Marie Louise (Wood) J.; m. Wilma Irene Aho, Feb. 22, 1940 (dec. Feb. 1988); m. Joanne Quear Buehler, Oct. 12, 1991; 1 child, Scott Robert Buehler. BA, U. Minn., 1934; MA, George Washington U., 1937. Cert. hazard control mgr., safety mgr., wildlife biologist. Wildlife biologist U.S. Bur. Biol. Survey, Washington, 1936-37, Bur. of Game, Conservation Dept., Albany, N.Y., 1938-42; animal control biologist U.S. Fish & Wildlife Svc., Washington, 1946-56, safety mgr., 1964-65; staff specialist Bur. Sport Fish & Wildlife, Washington, 1957-63, chief office of safety, 1966-75; dir. BioDynamic Systems, Bethesda, Md., 1975—. Author: Food Habits of the American Coot, 1940, Manual of Rodent Control, 1947, Rat Control Methods, 1947, (with others) The Ruffed Grouse, 1947. Vice-pres. Glen Mar Park Civic Assn., Bethesda, Md., 1974-78. With Sanitary Corps., 1943-46. Recipient Orgn. Award of Honor Nat. Safety Coun., 1972, 73. Mem. Am. Ornithologists Union, Am. Soc. of Mammalogists, Cooper Ornithol. Soc., Nat. Safety Mgmt. Soc., Nat. Safety Mgmt. Soc., The Wildlife Soc., Wilson Ornithol. Soc. Home and Office: BioDyanamic Systems 5810 Namakagan Rd Bethesda MD 20816-2346

JONES, JOIE PIERCE, acoustician, educator, writer, scientist; b. Brownwood, Tex., Mar. 4, 1941; s. Aubrey M. and Mildred K. (Pierce) J.; m. Kay Becknell, June 12, 1965. B.A. (Jr. fellow 1961-63), U. Tex., Austin, 1963, M.A., 1965; Ph.D., Brown U., 1970. Sr. scientist Bolt Beranek & Newman, Inc., Cambridge, Mass., 1970-75; assoc. prof., dir. ultrasonics research lab. Case Western Res. U. Sch. Medicine, Cleve., 1975-77; prof., chief med. imaging, dir. grad. studies, dept. radiol. scis. U. Calif., Irvine, 1977—; cons. acoustics; pres. Computer Sci. Systems, 1978—; founding gen. ptnr. Of Food and Wine, 1982—, Meditherm Assocs., Ltd., 1983-85, Spar Techs., 1987-90, Surgisonics Inc., 1991—; proposal reviewer NSF/NIH, 1974—; appointee sci. and tech. adv. com. Pres. Carter, 1977-81. Author 3 books; mem. editorial bd. Ultrasound in Medicine and Biology, 1976—, IEEE Procs., 1976—, Jour. Clin. Ultrasound, 1977—; contbr. over 200 articles to profl. jours.; 15 patents in field. Active vol. local govt. Fellow Am. Inst. Ultrasound in Medicine; mem. IEEE, AAAS, Acoustical Soc. Am., Am. Phys. Soc., Am. Assn. Physicists in Medicine, Fedn. Am. Scientists, Soc. Calif. Wine and Food Soc., Phi Beta Kappa. Democrat. Home: 2094 San Remo Dr Laguna Beach CA 92651-2628 Office: U Calif Dept Radiol Sci Irvine CA 92717

JONES, KATHLEEN ANN, nuclear medicine technologist; b. Allentown, Pa., July 15, 1964; d. Edward Thomas and Catherine Marie (Steve) Jones. BS in Nuclear Med. Tech. magna cum laude, Cedar Crest Coll., Allentown, Pa., 1986. Cert. in nuclear med. tech. Staff nuclear med. technologist Lehigh Valley Hosp., Allentown, 1986—, clin. coordinator, 1988—. Editor ednl. programs Greater N.Y. chpt. Jour. Nuclear Med. Tech., 1990-93. Mem. Soc. Nuclear Medicine (technolgist sect. bylaws chmn. 1990-91, area councilor 1991-92, technologist sect. treas. Greater N.Y. chpt. 1988-90, pres.-elect 1992-93, pres. 1993-94, awards chmn. 1995), Lehigh Valley Soc. Nuclear Med. Technologists (sec. 1987-88, pres. 1989-90, nominating chmn. 1990-91, bylaws com. 1991—), Del. Valley Soc. Nuclear Medicine Technologists. Democrat. Roman Catholic. Home: 1234 California Ave Whitehall PA 18052-4634 Office: Lehigh Valley Hosp 1200 S Cedar Crest Blvd Allentown PA 18103-6202

JONES, KENNETH BRUCE, surgeon; b. Scottsville, Ky., Apr. 17, 1953; s. Kenneth C. and Betty (Miller) J.; m. Carol Jean Munger, June 28, 1980; children: Daniel, Christopher, Elizabeth. BS, U. Ky., 1974; MD, Vanderbilt U., Nashville, 1978. Diplomate Am. Bd. Surgery; cert. advanced trauma life saving. Surg. intern and resident U. Louisville Med. Sch., 1978-80; resident in surgery East Tenn. U. Med. Sch., Johnson City, 1980-82, chief resident, 1983; surgeon Claiborne Surg. Group, Tazewell, Tenn., 1983-84, N.E. Ark. Surg. Clinic, Jonesboro, Ark., 1984—; sec. med. staff Meth. Hosp., 1986-87, chief of surgery, 1988-90, vice chief of staff, 1989-91, chief of staff, 1992-94; chief of surgery St. Bernard's Regional Med. Ctr., 1996—; asst. clin. prof. surgery U. Ark. Area Health Edn. Ctr., Jonesboro, 1985—; cancer liaison of Am. Coll. Surgeons Commn. on Cancer to St. Bernard's, 1996—. Contbr. articles on surgery to profl. jours. Active sch. bd., 1993—; deacon So. Bapt. Ch. Justin Potter med. scholar, 1974-78. Mem. ACS (cancer liaison physician commn. on cancer), Am. Soc. Gen. Surgery, So. Med. Assn., Ark. Med. Assn., Soc. Am. Gastrointestinal Endoscopic Surgeons, Am. Soc. Bariatric Surgery, NRA, Ark. Wildlife Fedn., Ducks Unltd., Quail Unltd.,

Phi Beta Kappa. Baptist. Home: 2600 Nix Lake Dr Jonesboro AR 72401-8561 Office: NE Ark Surg Clinic 800 S Church St Ste 104 Jonesboro AR 72401-4176

JONES, KEVIN PETER, medical educator; b. Paulton, Somerset, U.K., May 25, 1955; s. Basil Anthony and Josephine Ann (Parfitt) J.; m. Elaine Christina Davidson, July 31, 1981; children: Charlotte Mary Estelle, Adam Christopher Parfitt. BA, Cambridge U., 1976, MA, 1980; M.B.B.S., U. London, 1979; DM, U. Southampton, 1992. Gen. practice trainee West Cambria, U.K., 1985-87; rsch. fellow U. Southampton, 1987-88, lectr., 1988-91, sr. lectr., 1991-93; sr. lectr. U. Newcastle, 1993—; referee for grants Nat. Asthma Campaign, 1990—, Brit. Med. Jour., Brit. Jour. Gen. Practice, Thorax, Quality in Health Care; medicolegal advisor Med. Protection Soc., 1995—; mem. rsch. com. Nat. Asthma Campaign, 1996—; editl. advisor Brit. Med. Jour., 1996—; part-time family physician Oxford Terrace Med. Group, Gateshead, UK. Contbr. articles to profl. jours.; editor Asthma in Gen. Practice, 1992-96. Sch. gov. St. Joseph's, Hexham, U.K., 1995—. Maj. RAMC, 1980-87. Recipient numerous grants, 1987—. Mem. Royal Coll. Gen. Practitioners; mem. Assn. U. Depts. Gen. Practice, Brit. Thoracic Soc. Roman Catholic. Home: Limetree Cottage, Kitty Frisk, Hexham NE46 1UN, England Office: U of Newcastle Sch Health Scis, Framlington Pl, Newcastle NE2 4HH, England

JONES, LARRY MARTIN, surgeon; b. Marion, Ind., July 5, 1952; s. Norman Harvey and helen Louise (Stanley) J.; m. Donna Suzanne Leddy, June 10, 1979; children: Erin Beth, Ashley Brooke, Adam Michael. AB in Zoology, Ind. U., 1974, MD, 1977. Diplomate Am. Bd. Surgery. Intern Miami Valley Hosp., Dayton, 1977-78, resident in gen. surgery, 1978-82; gen. surgeon R.K Finley Jr. & S.F. Miller MD's Inc., Dayton, 1982-87; dir. trauma ctr. The Mercy Hosp. Pitts., Pitts., 1987—, dir. burn unit, 1991—, assoc. chmn. dept. surgery, 1994-96, vice chmn. dept. surgery, 1996—. Author (book chpt.) Clinical Medicine, 1988, Current Therapy in Critical Care Medicine, 1996; contbr. articles to profl. jours. Fellow ACS; mem. ACP Execs., Am. Trauma Soc., Ea. Assn. for the Surgery of Trauma, Pa Soc. of Critical Care Medicine, Internat. Coll. Surgeons, Am. Acad. Med. Dirs., Pitts. Surg. Soc. Home: 117 Old Oak Rd Mc Murray PA 15317-2626 Office: The Mercy Hosp of Pitts 1400 Locust St Pittsburgh PA 15219-5166

JONES, LYLE VINCENT, psychology educator; b. Grandview, Wash., Mar. 11, 1924; s. Vincent F. and Matilda M. (Abraham) J.; m. Patricia Edison Powers, Dec. 17, 1949 (div. 1979); children: Christopher V., Susan E., Tad W. Student, Reed Coll., 1942-43; B.S., U. Wash., 1947, M.S., 1948; Ph.D., Stanford U., 1950. Nat. Research fellow, 1950-51; asst. prof. psychology U. Chgo., 1951-57; vis. assoc. prof. U. Tex., 1956-57; assoc. prof. U. N.C., 1957-60, prof., 1960-69, Alumni disting. prof., 1969-92; rsch. prof., 1992—; dir. L.L. Thurstone Psychometric Lab. U. N.C., 1957-74, 79-92, vice chancellor, dean Grad. Sch., 1969-79; pres. Assn. Grad. Schs., 1976-77; cons. in field. Author: (with others) Studies in Aphasia: An Approach to Testing, 1961, The Measurement and Prediction of Judgment and Choice, 1968, (with others) An Assessment of Research-Doctorate Programs in the United States, 5 vols., 1982, Indicators of Precollege Education in Science and Mathematics, 1985; mng. editor: Psychometrika, 1956-61; editorial com. for psychology, Mc-Graw-Hill, 1965-77; contbr. articles to profl. jours. Mng. trustee J. Mckeen Cattell Fund, 1974—. With U.S. Army Air Corps, 1943-46. Recipient Thomas Jefferson award U. N.C., 1979; fellow Ctr. Advanced Study in Behavioral Scis., 1964-65, 81-82; grantee NIH, 1957-63, NSF, 1960-63, 71-74, 82-84, 93—, NIMH, 1963-74, 79-87. Fellow APA (pres. divsn. 1963-64), Am. Acad. Arts and Scis., Am. Psychol. Soc., Am. Statis. Assn.; mem. Am. Ednl. Rsch. Assn., Nat. Coun. Measurement Edn., Inst. of Medicine, Psychometric Soc. (pres. 1962-63). Home: 6578 US 15-501 N Pittsboro NC 27312-9807 Office: U NC CB 3270 Davie Hall Chapel Hill NC 27599-3270

JONES, LYNNE CHRISTINE HEILENMAN, biological research associate; b. Phila., Dec. 26, 1956; d. Benjamin Franklin and Phyllis Marie (Lindholm) Heilenman; m. Paul Alan Jones, Feb. 18, 1978; children: Amy, Christine. BS, Ursinus Coll., 1977; MS, Towson (Md.) State U., 1987. Rsch. technician Johns Hopkins U., Balt., 1977-78, lab. coord., 1979-84, coord. rsch., 1984-85, rsch. assoc., 1985—; mem. faculty Johns Hopkins Sch. Medicine; adj. faculty Harford Cmty. Coll., 1990; CEO Ctr for Osteonecrosis Rsch. and Edn., 1995—; rsch. cons. Contbr. articles to profl. jours., chpts. to books. Leader Girl Scouts U.S., 1993—. Named one of Outstanding Young Women Am., 1984. Mem. Orthopaedic Rsch. Soc., Am. Soc. Testing and Materials, Soc. Biomaterials, Md. Soc. Med. Rsch. Republican. Lutheran. Home: 3510 Glen Oak Dr Jarrettsville MD 21084-1836 Office: Johns Hopkins U Dept Orthopaedics G-1 Good Samaritan Profl Bldg. Baltimore MD 21239-2905

JONES, MARK MITCHELL, plastic surgeon; b. Atlanta, Mar. 27, 1951; s. Curtis B. and Julia (Mitchell) J.; m. Regine M.F. Heckel, Jan. 10, 1980; children: Céline Julia Micheline, Cédric André Curtis. Student, Oxford (Ga.) Coll., 1971; BA in Chemistry, Emory U., 1973; DBA, U. Canterbury, Christchurch, New Zealand, 1975; BA, MA, Oxford (Eng.) U., 1977; MD, Med. Coll. Ga., 1979. Surg. intern Med. U. of S.C., Charleston, 1979-80; surg. resident Union Meml. Hosp., Balt., 1980-81; resident in otolaryngology Johns Hopkins Hosp., Balt., 1981-84, mem. staff, instr., 1984-85; resident in plastic surgery Stanford U. Med. Ctr., Palo Alto, Calif., 1985-86; chief resident in plastic surgery, 1987-88; assoc. Calif. Ear Inst., 1988-89; chief surgeon Atlanta Plastic Surgery Specialist, 1989—. Fulbright fellow in plastic surgery, Paris, 1986-87. Home: 985 Foxcroft Rd NW Atlanta GA 30327-2621 Office: Atlanta Plastic Surgery Specialist 2001 Peachtree Rd NE Ste 630 Atlanta GA 30309-1476

JONES, MARK WILCOX, neurological surgeon; b. Salt Lake City, Feb. 3, 1955. BS, Brigham Young U., 1978; MD, U. Iowa, 1982. Diplomate Am. Bd. Neurol. Surgery, Am. Bd. Pain Medicine, sub-specialty pain mgmt. Surg. intern SUNY Health Sci. Ctr., N.Y., 1982-83, resident in neurosurgery, 1983-88; hon. registrar-postgrad. fellow U. London, 1988-89; asst. prof. SUNY Health Sci. Ctr., Syracuse, 1989-94; group practice Saginaw Valley Neurosurgery, Saginaw, Mich., 1994—. Mem. Am. Assn. Neurol. Surgeons, World Soc. Sterotactic and Functional Neurosurgery, Internat. Soc. Study of Pain, Congress Neurol. Surgeons. Office: Saginaw Valley Neurosurgery 4677 Towne Centre Rd Saginaw MI 48604

JONES, MARSHALL PAUL, JR., wildlife biologist, government administrator; b. Indpls., Jan. 22, 1947; s. Marshall Paul Jones and Virginia June Spitler; m. Kathleen S. McDonnell, 1968 (div. 1980); 1 child, Erin Kathleen; m. Cornelia Clay Fulghum, June 21, 1988. BA, U. Mich., 1971; MS, Murray State U., 1973; postgrad., Cornell U., 1973-74. Circulation mgr. Atlantic City (N.J.) Press, 1974; tech. writer U.S. Fish & Wildlife Svc., Washington, 1975-76, team leader, 1977-80, office chief, 1988-94, dir. internat. affairs, 1995—; regional specialist U.S. Fish & Wildlife Svc., Atlanta, 1980-83, regional supr., 1984-87; dep. chief U.S. Del. Conv. on Trade in Endangered Species, Lausanne, Switzerland, 1989; chmn. Interagy. Com. to host Conv. on Trade in Endangered Species 9th Conf. on Parties, Ft. Lauderdale, Fla., 1994; head U.S. Del. Conf. on Wetlands of Internat. Importance, Brisbane, Australia, 1996. Author govt. regulation U.S. ivory trade ban, 1989; editor (monthly publ.) Endangered Species Tech. Bull., 1976. With U.S. Army, 1969-71. Recipient W.J. Branstrom prize U. Mich., 1964. Office: US Fish & Wildlife Svc Dept of Interior 1849 C St NW Room 3245 Washington DC 20240

JONES, MARTHA LEE, social worker, consultant; b. Bklyn., Dec. 6, 1945; d. Harold L. and Janet R. (Holcomb) Utts; m. Steve R. Jones; 1 child, Erin R. BS, Juniata Coll., 1967; postgrad., Columbia U., 1967-68; MSW, U. Md., 1972; PhD, Fielding Inst., 1990. Lic. social worker, Pa. Dir. Child Welfare Svcs., Huntingdon, Pa., 1968-70; supr. Child Welfare Svcs., Carlisle, Pa., 1970-75; dir. child care Meth. Children's Home, Mechanicsburg, Pa., 1975-76; pvt. practice Camp Hill, Pa., 1976-78; pres. Common Sense Assoc., Mechanicsburg, 1979-96; exec. dir. Common Sense Adoption Svcs., Mechanicsburg, 1993—; adminstr. Pa. Statewide Adoption Network, Mechanicsburg, 1995—; dir. U. So. Maine Mgmt. Inst., Portland, Maine and Mechanicsburg. Contbr. articles to profl. jours. Office: Common Sense Assoc 5021 E Trindle Rd Mechanicsburg PA 17055-3622

JONES, MELVIN DOUGLAS, JR., pediatrician; b. San Antonio, Apr. 22, 1943. MD, U. Tex., 1968. Diplomate Am. Bd. Pediatrics. Intern U. Colo. Sch. Medicine, Denver, 1968-69, resident in pediatrics, 1969-71, prof., chmn. Dept. Pediatrics; rsch. fellow U. Colo. Med. Ctr., Denver, 1973-75; pediatrician Children's Hosp. Denver, Univ. Hosp. Denver. Mem. Am. Assn. Pediatrics, AHA, APA, Perinatal Rsch. Soc. Office: Children's Hosp BO65 1056 E 19th Ave Denver CO 80218-1007*

JONES, MICHAEL WAYNE, health services administrator; b. Amarillo, Tex., May 10, 1957; s. Robert Edgar and Ginger Louise (Smith) J. BSN, West Tex. State U., 1980; MBA, Wayland Bapt. U., 1987. CNAA; CEN, CCHP. Staff nurse, charge nurse N.W. Tex. Hosp., Amarillo, 1980—; prison health svc. adminstr. Tex. Tech. U. Health Sci. Ctr., Amarillo, 1983-95, dir. utilization mgmt., 1995—; alumnus advisor Kappa Alpha Order, West Tex. A&M U.; presenter Emerging Roles; Nursing in Correctional Instns.; Utilization Mgmt. in Correctional Health, Correctional Facility Nursing; guest lectr. to West Tex. A&M U. Sch. of Nursing. Bd. dirs. Leadership Amarillo; helping one student to suceed mentor Amarillo Ind. Sch. Dist.; bd. dirs. Golden Spread Boy Scouts Am.; loaned exec. United Way; mem. interfraternity adv. bd. West Tex. A&M U.; Institutional Ethics Comm.; N.W. Tex. Healthcare Sys. Mem. SAR, Sons of Confederate Vets., Emergency Nurses Assn., Panhandle Orgn. Nurse Execs. (pres.), Tex. Orgn. Nurses Execs. (state bd. dirs.), Am. Correctional Assoc., Am. Correctional Health Svcs. Assn. (bd. dirs), Tex. Panhandle Alumni (pres. Kappa Alpha Order), Leadership Amarillo Alumni, Sigma Theta Tau. Home: RR 1 Box 419 Amarillo TX 79121-9606 Office: Tex Tech U Health Scis 7120 I 40 W Ste 300 Bldg A Amarillo TX 79106-1708

JONES, MILES JAMES A., pathologist, consultant; b. Abington, Pa., Nov. 22, 1952; s. James. A. and Jessie L. (Brisbane); m. Linda Darlene Ableitner, Oct. 14, 1979; children: Dominick, Jessica. BS in Biochemistry, Princeton U., 1973; MD, Howard U., 1977. Am. Bd. Pathology. Research fellow Washington, 1975; resident in gen. surgery Cleve.Clinic, 1977-78; intern in anatomic & clin. pathology Mayo Clinic, Rochester, Minn., 1978-82; emergency room physician Mt. Sinai Hosp., Mpls., 1979-81; jr. staff pathologist Armed Forces Inst. of Pathology, Washington, 1982-84; pathologist, dir. Herrin (Ill.) Hosp. Lab., 1985-91; pathologist, lab. dir. LaPorte (Ind.) Hosp. and Found., 1991—; lectr. various colls. and univs.; mem. step 1 pathology test com. Nat. Bd. Med. Examiners. Recipient Stowell-Orbison award, 1982. Fellow Am. Soc. Clin. Pathologists, Coll. Am. Pathologists,; mem. Am. Acad. Forensic Scis., AMA, Coll. Am. Pathologists Ho. Delegates, Ill. State Med. Soc., Internat. Acad. Pathology, Internat. Soc. Gynecologic Pathologists, Williamson County Med. Soc., Herrin C. of C. Lodge: Rotary. Home: 144 Dogwood Dr La Porte IN 46350-2809

JONES, MILNOR, surgeon; b. Athens, Tenn., Mar. 14, 1925; s. Cyril William and Billie (Dodson) J.; m. Miriam Conner, Aug. 29, 1953; children: Cyril William III, Miriam Conner, Jonathan Milnor, Camille Chambers. BA, Vanderbilt U., 1945, MD, 1948. Diplomate Am. Bd. Surgery. Intern Grady Meml. Hosp., Emory U., Atlanta, 1948, resident in surgery, 1949-52, chief resident in surgery, 1952-53, instr. surgery, 1952-53; practice medicine specializing in surgery Athens, 1953-89;; bd. dirs. First Nat. Bank of McMinn County, chmn. bd. dirs., 1989-95. Vice chmn. Athen Bd. of Edn., 1967-77, chmn. 1977-89. Fellow ACS (pres. Tenn. chpt. 1988-89), Southeastern Surg. Soc.; mem. Chattanooga Acad. Surgeons, AMA, So. Med. Assn. Democrat. Episcopalian. Home: 127 Highland Ave Athens TN 37303-3223

JONES, NANCY GALE, retired biology educator; b. Gaffney, S.C., Nov. 12, 1940; d. Louransey Dowell and Sarah Louise (Pettit) J. BA, Winthrop Coll., 1962; MA, Oberlin Coll., 1964; postgrad., Duke U. Marine Biology Lab., 1963, Marine Biol. Lab., Woods Hole, Mass., 1964, N.C. State U., 1965, Ohio State U., 1966, Ariz. State U., 1970. Lectr. biology Oberlin (Ohio) Coll., 1964-66; from instr. to asst. prof. zoology Ohio U., Zanesville, 1966-73; media specialist Muskingum Area Vocat. Sch., Zanesville, 1973-74; salesperson Village Bookstore, Worthington, Ohio, 1975. Vol. hortitherapist for mentally disabled adults Habilitation Svcs., Inc. Gaffney, S.C., 1977-80; vol. dir. emergency assistance to needy PEACHcenter Ministries, Gaffney, 1991-94; mem. planned giving adv. coun. Winthrop U. Recipient Winthrop U. Alumni Disting. Svc. award, 1996. Mem. Ohio Retired Tchrs. Assn., Sigma Xi (assoc.). Baptist. Home: 1643 W Rutledge Ave Gaffney SC 29341-1023

JONES, PATRICIA GREGORY, retired dental hygiene adminstrator; b. Pitts., Oct. 26, 1938; d. Harry Knight and Mabel (Shick) Gregory; m. Herman Donald Jones, May 13, 1966; children: Suzanne Marie, Gregory Knight. AS in Dental Hygiene, West Liberty State Coll., 1959, BS in Edn., 1961; MS in Health Edn., W.Va. U., 1965. Registered dental hygienist, W.Va., Pa. Dental hygiene instr. W.Va. U., Morgantown, 1964-66, chairperson dental hygiene, 1966-69; assoc. prof. dental hygiene State Coll., W.Va., 1978-95; chairperson dental hygiene West Liberty (W.Va.) State U., 1978-95, fin. advisor Chi Omega, 1969—; cons. ADA, Allegheny C.C., Cumberland, Md., 1968-69. Mem. W.Va. Dental Hygienists Assn. (treas. 1969-96, pres. 1966-68), Am. Assn. Dental Schs., Sigma Phi Alpha (pres. 1974-95). Republican. Episcopalian. Home: 12 Tierra Rd # 1 Wheeling WV 26003

JONES, PATRICIA RENFRO, health association administrator; b. Lufkin, Tex., Nov. 20, 1954; children: Joseph Franklin Mott, Chase Patrick Mott. ASN, Angelina Coll., Lufkin, 1975. RN, Tex. Staff nurse Grimes County Hosp., Navasota, Tex.; clinic nurse Grimes County Clinic, Navasota, Tex.; homecare nurse Concepts of Care, Brenham, Tex.; homecare supr. Concepts of Care, Lufkin; childbirth educator Meml. Med. Ctr., Lufkin; ind. nursing home cons. Lufkin, Nacogdoches, Tex.; cmty. edn. coord. Meml. Med. Ctr., Lufkin, dir. homecare; reviewer Internat. Childbirth Educators Contact Hours rev. com., 1987-91. Chmn. Leadership Tomorrow, Angelina County C. of C., 1992-96; mem. buyers com. Youth Fair, Angelina County, 1992-96. Named Vol. of the Month Angelina County C. of C., 1995. Mem. Home Health Nurses Assn., Tex. Assn. Homecare (exec. bd. mem., treas. 1995—, chmn. hosp.-based com. 1992-94, mem. govt. affairs com. 1991-96). Baptist. Office: Memorial Med Ctr Homecare 1210 Frank St Lufkin TX 75901

JONES, PAUL KENNETH, biostatistician, educator; b. Des Moines, Jan. 5, 1943; s. Paul Kenneth and Bernice Sylvia (Kurtz) J.; m. Susan Lynn Organ, Dec. 30, 1971. BA, Grinnell Coll., 1964; MS, U. Iowa, 1969, PhD, 1972. ad hoc reviewer NIH, Washington, 1983—, Nat. Cancer Inst., Washington, 1983—, Nat. Inst. Aging, Washington, 1983—, Nat. Inst. Arthritis and Musculoskeletal and Skin Diseases, Washington, 1983—, Nat. Inst. for Nursing Rsch., Washington, 1983—. Mem. Am. Statis. Assn. (sect. tchg. statistics health scis. Cleve. sect. chair 1979, pres. 1985, sec.-treas. 1996), Biometric Soc., Soc. Epidemiologic Rsch. Home: 5240 Austen Ln Richmond Heights OH 44143 Office: Case Western Res U Dept Epidemiology and Biostats 10900 Euclid Ave Cleveland OH 44106-4945

JONES, REGINALD LORRIN, clinical psychologist, consultant; b. St. Petersburg, Fla., Dec. 12, 1951; s. Daniel George Jones and Susie Beatrice (Lewis) W.; m. Helen Elizbeth Lightfoot, Aug. 18, 1984; children: Tammy LeVette McKay, Myla Carmel, Regina Yvonne, Deneale Elizabeth Hand. BA, Clark Coll., 1973; MA, U. Cin., 1977, PhD, 1980. Lic. psychologist, Ohio. Statistician Atlanta Pub. Schs., 1973-74; psychology trainee U. Cin., 1974-80; team leader, supr. Social Skills Program, Cin., 1980-81; psychologist, unit dir. Day-Mont West, C.M.H.C., Dayton, Ohio, 1981-83; field psychologist advisor Ohio Indsl. Commn., Dayton, 1983-87; pvt. practice psychology, Dayton, 1983—; clin. asst. prof. Wright State U., Dayton, 1981—; cons. Adapt Inc., Springfield, Ohio, 1986-94; cons. Sickle Cell Awarness Group, Cin., 1986-90, v.p., 1981. Mem. adv. bd. Drew Sickle Cell Ctr., 1989-92; trustee Family Svc. Assn. Dayton, 1989-92. Named One of Outstanding Young Men of Am., 1984. Mem. APA, Nat. Assn. Black Psychologists, Ohio Psychol. Assn., Dayton Area Psychol. Assn., Am. Soc. Clin. Hypnosis, Dayton Assn. Black Psychologists (pres. 1983-84, Svc. award 1986), Nat. Register Health Svc. Providers in Psychology, Prescribing Psychologist Register. Democrat. Home: 180 Folsom Dr Dayton OH 45405-1108

JONES, REINOLD JOSEPH, thoracic surgeon; b. San Francisco, Nov. 3, 1925; s. Reinold Joseph and Mary C. (Ward) J.; m. Marjorie Ann Smith, June 23, 1964; children: Trish, Ron. B in Mech. Engring., U. Minn., 1946; MD, Creighton U., 1953. Diplomate Am. Bd. Surgery, Am. Bd. Thoracic Surgery. Assoc. clin. prof. surgery U. Calif. Med. Sch., San Francisco, 1970-88; chief of staff Seton Med. Ctr., Daley City, Calif., 1975-76, chmn. dept. surgery, 1987-94; chmn. dept. surgery St. Mary's Hosp., San Francisco, 1984-87. Served to lt. USN, 1953-55. Fellow ACS; mem. soc. Thoracic Surgeons, Western Thoracic Surg. Assn. (founding mem.), San Francisco Surg. Soc. (councilor 1984-88). Roman Catholic. Club: Olympic (San Francisco). Office: 2645 Ocean Ave San Francisco CA 94132-1633

JONES, RENEE KAUERAUF, health care administrator; b. Duncan, Okla., Nov. 3, 1949; d. Delbert Owen and Betty Jean (Marsh) Kauerauf; m. Dan Elkins Jones, Aug. 3, 1972. BS, Okla. State U., 1972, MS, 1975; PhD, Okla. U., 1989. Diplomate Am. Bd. Sleep Medicine. Statis. analyst Okla. State Dept. Mental Health, Okla. City, 1978-80, divisional chief, 1980-83, adminstr., 1983-84; assoc. dir. HCA Presbyn. Hosp., Okla. City, 1984—; adj. instr. Okla. U. Health Sci. Ctr., 1979—; assoc. staff scientist Okla. Ctr. for Alcohol and Drug-Related Studies, Okla. City, 1979—; cons. in field. Assoc. editor Alcohol Tech. Reports jour., 1979-84; contbr. articles to profl. jours. Mem. assoc. bd. Hist. Preservation, Inc., treas. 1994. Mem. APHA, Assn. Health Svcs. Rsch., Alcohol and Drug Problems Assn. N.Am., Am. Sleep Disorders Assn., N.Y. Acad. Scis., So. Sleep Soc. (sec.-treas. 1989-91), Phi Kappa Phi. Democrat. Methodist. Home: 401 NW 19th St Oklahoma City OK 73103-1911 Office: HCA Presbyn Hosp NE 13th at Lincoln Blvd Oklahoma City OK 73104

JONES, ROBERT BROOKE, microbiologist and immunologist educator; b. Knoxville, Tenn., Sept 14, 1942; s. Robert Melvin and Evaleen (Brooke) J.; m. Barbara Burgess McLawhorn, Sept. 7, 1963; children—Julia Ashley, Jonathan Davis, Quinnette Brooke. A.B. in Chemistry, U. N.C., 1964, M.D., 1970, Ph.D. in Biochemistry, 1970. Diplomate Am. Bd. Internal Medicine. Intern U. Wash., Seattle, 1970-71; resident U. Wash., Seattle, 1974-76; fellow in infectious diseases, 1976-78; asst. prof. Ind. U. Sch. Medicine, Indpls., 1978-83, assoc. prof. medicine, microbiology and immunology, 1983-86, prof., 1986—; dir. Ind. Sexually Transmitted Diseases Research Ctr., Indpls., 1983—; mem. NIH bacteriology rev. group, 1987—. Contbr. sci. articles to profl. jours. Served to lt. comdr. U.S. Navy, 1971-74. NIH grantee, 1983. Fellow ACP; mem. Am. Venereal Disease Assn. (bd. dirs. 1983—), Am. Soc. Microbiology, Infectious Disease Soc. Am., Am. Fedn. Clin. Research, Order Golden Fleece, Sigma Xi, Alpha Omega Alpha. Republican. Mem. Society of Friends. Office: Ind U Emerson #435 Dept Medicine Indianapolis IN 46237

JONES, ROBERT EUGENE, physician; b. Bauxite, Ark., Aug. 25, 1926; s. Curtis Whittemore and Rosina (Nelson) J.; m. Frances (Mickey) Harper, June 24, 1949; children: Eric R., Bryant, Gretchen M. Student, Tulane U., 1944-45; BS, U. Ark., Fayetteville, 1947; MD, U. Ark., Little Rock, 1951. Cert. correctional health profl. Intern St. Vincent Infirmary, Little Rock, 1951-52; pvt. practice physician Benton, 1953—; chief of staff Saline Meml. Hosp., Benton, Ark., 1965-66, 68-69; pres. Saline County Med. Soc., Benton, 1965-66, 68-69; med. dir. Ark. Region PHP Health, Pine Bluff, Ark., 1989-90; Benton, 1952—; med. dir. Mid Delta Health Systems. Inc., De Valls Bluff, Ark., 1994—; assoc. dept. community and family medicine U. Ark. for Med. Sci. With USN, 1944-45, 1st lt. Med. Corps, U.S. Army, 1953-55. Fellow Royal Soc. Health. Episcopalian. Home: 723 W Narroway St Benton AR 72015-3653 Office: Mid Delta Health Systems Market St De Valls Bluff AR 72041

JONES, ROBERT LYLE, emergency medical services leader, educator; b. Washington, Feb. 6, 1959; s. Herman Aven and Dorothy Edith (Fisher) J.; m. Cynthia Celia Bogdanowicz, May 15, 1996. B in Gen. Sci., U. Kans., 1982; MA in Adult and Continuing Edn., U. Mo., 1990. Registered paramedic, Kans., Kans. cert. Emergency Med. Svcs. Tng. Officer, 1992—. Paramedic team leader Johnson County (Kans.) Med. Action, 1983-89, dist. supr., 1989-92, edn. supr., 1992—; BCLS instr., 1979-87, affiliate faculty, 1987—, ACLS instr., 1985-88, affiliate faculty, 1988—, PALS instr., 1993—. Served to Capt. USAR, 1979-94. Mem. Nat. Assn. EMTs (prehosp. trauma life support instr. 1986—), Nat. Soc. EMS Adminstrs., Nat. Soc. EMT Paramedics, Assn. Profls. in Infection Control and Epidemiology. Home: 7137 Lowell Dr Shawnee Mission KS 66204-1837 Office: Johnson County Med Action 111 S Cherry St Ste 300 Olathe KS 66061-3441

JONES, ROBERT N., cardiovascular surgeon; b. Chgo., June 23, 1949; s. Phillip and Rebecca M. (Means) J.; m. Mica Moruzzi, July 27, 1974; children: David, Julie. BA in English Lit., Williams Coll., 1971; MD, Rush Med. Coll., 1976. Diplomate Am. Bd. Gen. and Thoracic Surgery. Intern, gen. and thoracic surgery Duke U. Med. Ctr., Durham, N.C., 1977-78, jr. asst. resident, gen. and thoracic surgery, 1978-80, rsch. fellow, cardiaphysiology, 1980-83, sr. asst. resident, gen. and thoracic surgery, 1983-84, chief resident, gen. and thoracic surgery, 1984-85, fellow in cardiac surgery, 1985-86; pvt. practice Great Lakes Cardiovasc. Surgery PC, Saginaw, Mich., 1986—; mem. credentials com. ACS, Saginaw, 1992—; councillor Mich. Soc. Thoracic and Cardiovasc. Surgery, Ann Arbor, 1994—; dist. rep. Am. Coll. Cardiology, Saginaw, 1989-91; mem. com. pub. health Saginaw Med. Soc., 1991—. Contbr. numerous articles to profl. jours. Recipient tng. award Am. Heart Assoc. Rsch., N.C., 1979, rsch. adv. group grant VA, 1986. Fellow ACS, Am. Coll. Cardiology, Am. Coll. Chest Physicians; mem. Internat. Soc. Heart Transplantation, Soc. Thoracic Surgeons, Mich. State Med. Soc. Office: Great Lakes Cardiovasc Surg 4701 Towne Centre Rd #301 Saginaw MI 48604

JONES, ROBERT WAYNE, psychology educator; b. Dallas, Sept. 24, 1937; s. Wilburn Orville and Lorinne (Garvin) J. BS, Tulane U., 1958; MA, La. State U., 1960; PhD, U. Miami, Fla., 1964. Lic. psychologist, Ga.; diplomate Am. Bd. Profl. Psychology, Am. Bd. Neuropsychology. Rsch. assoc. State Colony and Tng. Sch., Pinesville, La., 1959-60; intern St. Elizabeth's Hosp., Washington, 1961; instr. Miami Sch. of Medicine, 1963-66; rsch. assoc. U. Miami, Coral Gables, Fla., 1964-66; asst. prof. child clin. psychology Emory U., Atlanta, 1966-69; assoc. prof. dept. counseling and psychol. svcs. Ga. State U., Atlanta, 1969-72, prof. sch. psychology, 1972—; cons. Coral Gables Acad. of Reading, Anti-Convulsive Clinic, Dept. of Pub. Health, Dade County, Fla., 1962-66, Ga. Rehab. Ctr., Warm Springs, Ga., 1966-69, Ga. Ctr. for Multihandicapped Deaf-Blind, Aidmore Hosp., 1967-70, Ednl. Devel. Ctr. of Pa., Wilkes-Barre, 1967-70, Russell Acad. of Coral Gables Acad. Schs., Atlanta, 1972-83, Children's Ctr., Cobb County Schs., Ga., 1981-85, West Paces Ferry Hosp., 1985-87, Westminster Schs., Atlanta, 1986—, Gables Acad. Internat., Sydney, Australia, and Atlanta, 1987—; spl. edn. cons. Recife Brazil, 1976-82. Co-author: Mental Retardation: Selected Problems in Appraisal and Treatment, 1967, Seminar in Indian Studies, 1974, Hyperactivity, A Meeting of the Minds, 1977, Specialized Education in Today's Secondary Schools, 1978, Attention Deficit Hyperactivity Disorders, 1991, (with P. McKee, RW Jones, RH Barbe) Suicide and the Schools, 1993, 2d edit., 1996; contbr. articles to profl. jours. Mem. Hogansville City Sch. Bd., 1987-90; mem. Troup County Planning Coun., 1988-91; mem. adv. bd. Gables Acads., Miami, 1967-76, Family Learning Ctrs., Atlanta, 1969-72, Russell Acad., Atlanta, 1972-83, Howard Sch., Atlanta, 1975—, Archway Schs., N.Y., 1976-78; Barclay Sch., Atlanta, 1982-87, Decatur (Ga.) City Schs., 1982-87; bd. dirs. Hogansville Hist. Commn., 1989-90. Fellow Ga. Psychol. Assn.; mem. APA, Southeastern Psychol. Assn., Ga. Psychol. Assn. (state ethics com. 1989-94), Nat. Acad. Neuropsychologists, Ga. Sch. Psychology Assn., Ga. Assn. Sch. Psychology Trainers (pres. 1991-92), Am. Bd. Profl. Neuropsychology (founding bd. dirs. 1982-87). Home: 703 E Main St Hogansville GA 30230-1509 Office: Ga State U University Plz Atlanta GA 30303

JONES, RODNEY LEE, anesthesiologist; b. Wichita, Kans.. MD, U. Iowa, 1982. Pres. Kans. Anesthesia Spedialists, Wichita, 1989—; chmn. dept. anesthesiology St. Francis Hosp., Wichita, 1993-94. Mem. Am. Soc. Anesthesia, Kans. Med. Soc., Sedgewick County Med. Soc. (legal com. 1995—). Address: 1040 N Rutland St Wichita KS 67206-3823

JONES, RONALD VANCE, health science association administrator; b. Springfield, Ill., Oct. 7, 1946; s. Dallas Vance and Bertha Henrietta (Bentley) J.; m. Patricia Ann O'Neill, Feb. 1, 1969; children: Devon Vance, Zachary Brice. BS, U. Ill., 1969, MEd, 1972. Tchr. English lang. Ottawa (Ill.) Twp.

H.S., 1969-70; rsch. assoc. U. Ill., Urbana, 1970-73; dir. cmty. programs Ga. Dept. Youth Svcs., Atlanta, 1973-79; dir. planning Ga. Dept. Mental Health, Atlanta; capital project planner Ill. Dept. Mental Health, Springfield, 1979-85; bus. adminstr. Chester (Ill.) Mental Health Ctr., 1985-92; asst. supt. Malcolm Bliss Mental Health Ctr., St. Louis, 1992-96; chief operating officer Met. St. Louis Psychiatric Ctr., 1996—. Editor: tchr. guidebooks for elem. schs., 1971-73. Vice-chmn., bd. dirs. Lullwater Sch. Atlanta; vol. St. Louis Easter Seal Soc., 1987-88. Mem. Ill. Health Facilities Planning Bd., Ill. Hosp. Licensing Bd., Ill. Long Term Care Facilities Bd., Gov's. State Bldgs. Energy Cons. Bd., Kappa Delta Pi, Phi Delta Kappa. Home: 7 Birnawoods Olivette MO 63132 Office: Malcolm Bliss Psychiatric Ctr Dept of Mental Health Saint Louis MO 63112

JONES, RUSSELL WARD, optometrist; b. La Junta, Colo., Dec. 11, 1946; s. William Russell and Josephine Johnny (Mahill) J.; m. Daphne Sue Dean, Dec. 29, 1966; children: Ean Trent, Chian Alicia. BS, U. Colo., 1968; MS, U. Ariz., 1972; OD, Pacific U., Forest Grove, Oreg., 1976. Pvt. practice Flagstaff, Ariz., 1976—. Dir. Big Bros. of Flagstaff, treas., 1988-94. Recipient Silver Medal award Pacific U., 1976. Mem. Am. Optometric Assn. (state lic. regulation com.), Ariz. Optometric Assn. (pres. 1986, Optometrist of the Yr. 1992), Rotary (pres. 1983), Beta Sigma Kappa. Office: Flagstaff Eye Care 410 N San Francisco St Flagstaff AZ 86001

JONES, SCOTT CHRISTOPHER, occupational physician; b. St. Louis, Dec. 17, 1959; s. Don Allen and Joyce Mae (Kitzinger) J. Student, S.W. Mo. State U., 1977, Drury Coll., 1978-79; AB, Washington U., St. Louis, 1981; DO, Kirksville Coll. Osteo. Med., 1985; MPH with great distinction, St. Louis U., 1994. Diplomate Am. Osteo. Coll. Preventive Medicine. Intern Normandy Osteo. Hosps., St. Louis, 1985-86; gen. practice medicine Multicare Med. Group, St. Louis, 1986-88; physician, med. dir. Healthcare Pl., St. Louis, 1988-90, Healthline Ctr. I, St. Louis, 1990-94; physician, med. dir. Healthline Ctr. IV, St. Louis, 1994—, on-call physician, case mgr., 1993—; physician preceptor Healthline Occupational Residency Tng., 1992; physician ambulatory care area DePaul ExpressCare, St. Loius, 1990-93; med. dir. Medi-Fast Weight Loss Clinic, St. Louis, 1987-88; mem. staff Christian Hosps., St. Louis, Deaconss Hosps., St. Louis, DePaul Hosp.; regional cons. physician for Mo. and Ill.,. Mem. APHA, Am. Coll. Gen. Practitioners, Am. Coll. Occupational and Environ. Medicine, Am. Osteo. Assn., Am. Osteo. Coll. Preventive Medicine, Ctrl. States Occupational Med. Assn., Mo. Assn. Osteo. Physicians and Surgeons, Internat. Assn. Machinists (bd. dirs.). Democrat. Methodist. Home: 6239 Washington Ave Saint Louis MO 63130

JONES, STANLEY BOYD, health policy analyst, priest; b. Balt., July 27, 1938; s. Arthur Boyd and Lillian Ailene (Powell) J.; m. Judith K. Miller, Mar. 9, 1981; children—Andrew, Jeffrey, Lisa, Julia. BA, Dartmouth Coll., 1960; postgrad., Yale U., 1960-63. Ordained Episc. priest., 1992. Mem. profl. staff, staff dir. Subcom. on Health, U.S. Senate, Washington, 1970-76; program devel. officer Inst. of Medicine, Nat. Acad. Scis., Washington, 1976-78; v.p. Fullerton, Jones & Wollkstein (Health Policy Alternatives), Washington, 1978-80; v.p. for Washington representation Nat. Assns. Blue Cross and Blue Shield Plans, 1980-83; prin. Health Policy Alternatives, 1983-86; pres. Consol. Healthcare, 1986-89; ind. cons. on health policy Washington, 1989—; clergyman Diocese of W.Va., 1992—; commr. D.C. Gen. Hosp. Fellow Inst. of Soc., Ethics and the Life Scis.; mem. Inst. of Medicine of Nat. Acad. Scis.

JONES, THOMAS BRANCH, JR., retired counselor; b. Richmond, Va., Mar. 13, 1930; s. Thomas B. Sr. and Lucy (Robinson) J.; m. Dorothy W., June 1, 1953; children: Robert, William. Student, Bridgewater Coll., 1946-48. Cert. employee assistance profl., Va.; nat. and internat. cert. alcohol and drug abuse counselor. Engr. sales Broadcast Electronics, Silver Spring, Md., 1974-76; mgr. sales Multronics Inc., Ft. Lauderdale, Fla., 1976-81; asst. to pres. Antenna Research Assocs. Inc., Beltsville, Md., 1981-89. Mem. Suburban Md. Internat. Trade Assn. (bd. dirs. 1984-86, 88-89), Md. Mfrs. Assn. (founding pres. 1983), Nat. Assn. Alcohol and Drug Abuse Counselors, Va. Assn. Alcohol and Drug Abuse Counselors, Amateur Radio Club, Elks, Shriners. Episcopalian. Home: 123 Pennsylvania Ave Shenandoah VA 22849-1536

JONES, THOMAS ROBERT, social worker; b. Escanaba, Mich., Jan. 3, 1950; s. Gene Milton and Alica Una (Mattson) J.; m. Joy Sedlock. BA, U. Laverne, 1977; MSW, U. Hawaii, 1979. Social work assoc. Continuing Care Svcs., Camarillo, Calif., 1973-78; psychiat. social worker Camarillo State Hosp., 1980-84; psychotherapist Terkensha Child Treatment Ctr., Sacramento, Calif., 1984-86; psychiat. social worker Napa (Calif.) State Hosp., 1986-87, Vets. Home Calif., Yountville, 1987—. Mem. Nat. Assn. Social Workers, Soc. Clin. Social Work, Am. Orthopsychiat. Assn., Acad. Cert. Social Workers, Assn. for Advancement Behavior Therapy. Home: PO Box 1095 Yountville CA 94599-1095 Office: Vets Home Calif Yountville CA 94599

JONES, WALTON LINTON, internist, former government official; b. McCaysville, Ga., Dec. 4, 1918; s. Walton Linton and Pearl Josephine (Gilliam) J.; m. Caroline Wells Schachte, June 5, 1943; children—Walton Linton III, Francis Stephen, Kathleen Caroline. B.S., Emory U., 1939, M.D., 1942. Diplomate Am. Bd. Preventive Medicine. Commd. lt. (j.g.) U.S. Navy, 1942, advanced through grades to capt., 1956; rotating intern U.S. Naval Hosp., Charleston, S.C., 1942-43, aerospace medicine, 1944; flight surgeon USMC Aircraft Squadrons, 1944-47; head aero. med. safety Navy Dept., 1947-53; sr. med. officer U.S.S. Randolph, 1953-55; dir. aero. med. ops. and equipment Bur. Medicine and Surgery, Navy Dept., 1955-64; dir. biotech. and human research div. NASA, 1964-66; ret. U.S. Navy, 1966; civilian dir. biotech and human research div. NASA, Washington, 1966-70, dep., dir. life scis., 1970-75, dir. occupational medicine, 1975-82, dir. occupational health, 1982-85; cons. aerospace medicine, 1985—; mem. exec. com. hearing and bioacoustics Nat. Acad. Scis., 1964-85, chmn., 1970, mem. exec. com. on vision, 1964-85; Kober lectr. Georgetown U., 1968. Leader, mem. com. Nat. Capital Area council Boy Scouts Am., Falls Church, Va., 1956-64. Decorated Legion of Merit; recipient Exceptional Service medal NASA, 1979, Outstanding Leadership medal NASA, 1985. Fellow Aerospace Medicine Assn. (Bauer award 1970, pres. 1980), AIAA (assoc., recipient John Jeffries award 1970), Royal Soc. Health; mem. Internat. Astronautics Acad., Assn. Mil. Surgeons (Founders award 1956), Internat. Acad. Aerospace Medicine.

JONES, WANDA CAROL, nurse; b. Riverside, Calif., Jan. 2, 1956; d. Wallace Campbell and Erma Frances (Elliott) Wendelstadt; m. Rodney Jay Shelton, Feb. 16, 1980 (dec.); 1 child from previous marriage, Wendy Mae Cox; m. Jimmy L. Jones, July 30, 1992. Cert. in voc. nursing, United Health Careers, 1982; AS, San Bernardino Valley Coll., 1987. RN, Calif. Tchr. piano Fontana, Calif., 1969-75; underwriter Prudential Ins. Co., San Bernardino, Calif., 1977; newspaper editor Allied Constrn. Ind., San Bernardino, 1979-82; nursing asst. San Bernardino County Med. Ctr., 1982-83; voc. nurse Remedy Health Svcs., San Bernadino, 1983; voc. nurse Kaiser Permanente, Fontana, 1983-87, RN, 1987—. Active Oasis Christian Fellowship. Mem. NAFE, United Nurses Assn. Calif., Grange Club, Order of Rainbow for Girls, Piano and Organ Club, Clinkers Organ Club, Alpha Gamma Sigma.

JONES, WENDELL EMMETT, physician; b. Detroit, Dec. 18, 1958; s. Tom and Lillian (Campbell) J.; 1 child, Angela. BS in Biology, Morehouse Coll., 1980, MD, 1985; MBA in Health Adminstrn., U. Miami, 1991. Diplomate Am. Bd. Internal Medicine. Intern, resident Jackson Meml. Hosp./U. Miami; emergency rm. physician Group Practice, Miami, Fla., 1988; staff physician VA Med. Ctr., Miami, Fla., 1988-93; assoc. chief of staff VA Med. Ctr., Amarillo, Tex., 1993-96, Audie L. Murphy VA, 1996—. Program dir. ACLS; bd. dirs. Am. Cancer Soc., Amarillo, 1993-96. Recipient Alumnus of Yr. award Morehouse Sch. of Medicine, 1994. Mem. AMA, Nat. Med. Assn., Am. Coll. Physicians, Am. Coll. Physician Execs., Kappa Alpha Psi. Office: VA Med Ctr 7400 Merton Minter Blvd San Antonio TX 78284

JONES, WILLIAM HENRY, physician; b. Salisbury, Md., Oct. 12, 1967; s. Robert Dale and Rebecca Leigh (Parker) J.; m. Daniela Marie Bianchi, Apr. 3, 1993. BS, U. Md., 1989; DO, Phila. Coll. Osteopathic Med., 1993. Resident U. Med. Reisdency Svcs., U. Buffalo, 1995—. Computer cons. Sisters of Charity Hope, Buffalo, 1993—; legis. affairs com. Student Osteopathic Med. Assn., Chgo., 1991-92, bd. trustees, 1992-93, bd. dirs., 1991-92, legis. affairs coord., Phila., 1989-90; fundraiser, coord. Phils. Spl. Olympics, 1990. Mem. AMA, Am. Osteopathic Assn., Western Osteopathic Assn. Home: 4990 Daisy Ln Buffalo NY 14219

JONES-VESELENY, TINA MARIE, vascular nurse, consultant; b. Reading, Ohio, Mar. 15, 1955; d. Robert Gregory and Louisa Catherine (Schoenlaub) J.; m. John David Veseleny, Jr., Oct. 2, 1994. BSN summa cum laude, U Cin., 1980. RN, Ohio; RVT, Am. Registry of Diagnostic Med. Sonographers. Staff ICU nurse The Children's Hosp., Cin., 1980-81; vascular nurse supr. Univ. Hosp., Cin., 1981-83; vascular lab. nurse The Christ Hosp., Cin., 1983-84; vascular nurse, tech. dir. Christ Hosp., Cin., 1991-95; vascular nurse dir. Vascular Lab. of Palm Beaches, West Palm Beach, Fla., 1984-86; clin. rsch. assoc. Kendal Rsch. Assocs., Cin., 1986-87; peripheral vascular nurse Jewish Hosp., Cin., 1987-88; staff nurse, tech. dir. Vascu-Sonics Lab., Inc., Cin., 1989-92; cons. vascular nurse Biosound, Inc., Indpls., 1990—, nat. and internat. lectr., 1990—; clin. trial rsch. coord. Univ. Hosp. Med. Ctr.-Sandoz Labs., Cin., 1982-83; guest lectr. Indian Sound, Indpls., 1988-91. Principal author and presenter abstracts and presentations Soc. Vascular Technology, 1984, 86, 89, 90, 92. Founder career orientation program McAuley H.S., Cin., 1988-89; vol. local group for homeless and abused women, Cin., 1994—. Mem. Am. Heart Assn., Soc. Vascular Technology, Tri-State Sonographers' Soc., U. Cin. Alumni Assn., Humane Soc. U.S. Republican. Office: PO Box 62453 Cincinnati OH 45262-0453

JONG, SHUNG-CHANG, mycologist; b. Taipei, Taiwan, Nov. 12, 1936; came to U.S., 1965; m. Chiu-Hwa Kou, Apr. 20, 1965; children: Maria, Cynthia, Victoria. MS, Western Ill. U., 1966; PhD, Washington State U., 1969. Plant pathologist Taiwan Agrl. Rsch. Inst., Taipei, Taiwan, 1961-63; instr. Nat. Taiwan U., Taipei, 1963-65; teaching asst. Western Ill. U., Macomb, 1965-66; rsch. asst. Washington State U., Pullman, 1966-69; sr. mycologist Am. Type Culture Collection, Rockville, Md., 1969-71; curator Am. Type Culture Collection, Rockville, 1971-89, head mycology dept., 1973—, sr. staff scientist, 1989—, dir. mycology and protistology program, 1993—; dissertation dir. George Washington U., Washington, 1975-79; tech. advisor Yamazaki Baking Co., Tokyo, Japan, 1984—; exec. bd. World Fedn. for Culture Collection, 1988-92. Contbr. articles to profl. jours. Recipient Internat. Sci. and Tech. award Ministry of Agr., 1988, Brown Hazen grant Rsch. Corp., 1974-76, NSF grants, 1975-80, 80-85, 85-90, 90-95, 95—. Fellow Am. Acad. Microbiology, Washington Acad. Scis.; mem. World Fedn. for Culture Collections, Internat. Mycol. Assn. (exec. com. 1983-90), Internat. Commn. on Taxonomy of Fungi, Mycol. Soc. of Am. (com. on culture collection 1986-91). Office: Am Type Culture Collection 12301 Parklawn Dr Rockville MD 20852-1776

JONGBLOET, PIET HEIN LEO ARTHUR MICHIEL, pediatrician, health care facility administrator; b. Brugge, Belgium, Feb. 21, 1933; s. Michiel and Laura (Embo) Jongbloet; m. Gisela Maria Anna Van Houtte, July 25, 1964; 1 child, Annekatrien. MD, State U. Gent, Belgium, 1958. Trainee in pediatrics, 1960-64; mem. staff Maria Roepaan Inst. for Mentally Handicapped, Ottersum, Netherlands, 1964-70; med. dir. Maria Roepaan Inst. for Mentally Handicapped, Ottersum, The Netherlands, 1970-93; mem. staff Free U., Amsterdam, The Netherlands, 1975-94, Cath. U., Nijmegen, The Netherlands, 1990—. Author: Mental and Physical Handicaps in Connection, 1970; contbr. 150 articles to profl. jours. Chmn. Algemeen Nederlands Verbond Gelderland, 1984-94; pres. Orde van den Prince Nijmegen, 1978-81, 93—. Mem. Rotary Internat. (chmn. 1984-85). Home: Roepaanstraat 4, 6595 NH Ottersum The Netherlands

JONSEN, ALBERT R., medical ethics educator; b. San Francisco, Apr. 4, 1931; s. Albert R. and Helen (Sweigert) J. BA, Gonzaga U., 1955, MA, 1956; STM, U. Santa Clara, 1963; PhD, Yale U., 1967. Mem. S.J., 1949-76; ordained priest Roman Catholic Ch.; instr. philosophy Loyola U., Los Angeles, 1956-59; asst. in instrn. Yale Div. Sch., 1966-67; asst. prof. theology and philosophy U. San Francisco, 1967-72, pres., 1969-72; prof. med. ethics Sch. Medicine, U. Calif.-San Francisco, 1972-87; adj. assoc. prof. dept. community medicine and internat. health Sch. Medicine, Georgetown U., 1977; prof. med. ethics, chmn. dept. med. history and ethics Sch. Medicine U. Wash., Seattle, 1987—; mem. artificial heart assessment panel Nat. Heart and Lung Inst., 1972-73, 84-86; mem. Am. Bd. Med. Splitys., 1978-81; cons. Am. Bd. Internal Medicine, 1978-82, Am. Coll. Obstetrics and Gyn., 1983-88; mem. Pres.'s Commn. for Study of Ethical Problems in Medicine, 1979-82, Nat. Commn. for Protection Human Subjects of Biomed. and Behavioral Research, HEW, 1974-78; mem. Nat. Bd. Med. Examiners, 1985-87; mem. Commn. on AIDS Rsch., NRA, 1986-92—, Panel on Social Impact of AIDS (chmn.), 1989-91; chmn. nat. adv. bd. Ethics and Reproduction, 1991-96. Author: Responsibility in Modern Religious Ethics, 1968, Patterns of Moral Responsibility, 1969, Christian Decision and Action, 1970, Ethics of Newborn Intensive Care, 1976, Clinical Ethics, 1982, The Abuse of Casuistry: A History of Moral Reasoning, 1987, The New Medicine and the Old Ethics, 1990, The Social Impact of AIDS in the United States, 1993; mem. editorial bd. Jour. Philosophy and Medicine, Jour. Clin. Ethics. Trustee Inst. Ednl. Mgmt., Harvard U., 1971-74, Ploughshares Found., 1980-84; mem. San Francisco Crime Com., 1969-71; bd. dirs. Found. Critical Care Medicine, 1983-86, Sierra Found., 1987—. Fellow Inst. for Soc., Ethics and Life Scis.; mem. Soc. Health and Human Values (pres. 1986-87), Am. Soc. Law and Medicine (bd. dirs. 1986-88), Soc. Christian Ethics, Inst. Medicine of NAS (com. human values 1973, coun. 1983-85, 90-92). Office: Univ Wash Med History and Ethics Box 357120 Seattle WA 98195

JONTRY, RICHARD, psychologist; b. Bklyn., May 5, 1942; s. Henry and Esther (Schor) J.; BA, City U. N.Y., 1964; MA, New Sch., 1966; PhD, Ind. No. U., 1973; m. Sharon Gladson; children: Brie, Ari. Clin. psychology intern N.J. Neuro-Psychiat. Inst., Princeton, 1966-67, rsch. scientist bur. rsch. in neurology and psychiatry, 1967-73; dir. Ctr. Family Interaction, Hatboro, Pa., 1972-74; dir. tng. and edn. bur. substance abuse, div. mental health Del. Dept. Health and Social Svcs., New Castle, 1974-79; dir. Intercept, Oxford, Pa., 1981-85; clin. supr. ARC Counseling Svcs., So. Chester County Med. Ctr., West Grove, Pa.; adj. prof. Washington Coll., Chestertown, Md., 1980-85; clin. cons. Four Winds Addiction Recovery Ctr., N.Mex., 1986-95, Family Crises Ctr., 1987-93; clin. dir. Halvorson House, 1993— cons. Jicarilla Apache Tribe, 1996—; condr. tng. seminars for mental health profls.; dir. San Juan County Community Mobilization Grant; mem. Robert Woods Johnson S.W. N. Mex. Fighting Back Treatment Subcom., San Juan County Com., Cecil County (Md.) Mental Health and Addictions Adv. Bd., 1970-81, Cecil County Anti-Drug Abuse Action Com., 1980-82, Talbot County (Md.) Sch. Health Curriculum Adv. Com., 1980-82; adv. bd. Lincoln (Pa.) U., 1975-79, NE Regional Support Ctr., New Haven, 1976-79, Eastern Area Alcohol Tng. Program, Bloomfield, Conn., 1976-79, Johns Hopkins U. Tng. Inst. Alcoholism Counselors, 1976-79; cons. in field. Mem. Internat. Imagery Assn., Nat. Assn. Alcholism and Drug Abuse Counselors, Employee Assistance Profl. Assn., Am. Counseling, N.Mex. Alcoholism and Drug Abuse Counselors Assn., N.Y. Inst. Gestalt Therapy, Psi Chi. Home: 2416 Ventana Cir Farmington NM 87401-3988 Office: 605 1/2 N Butler Ave Farmington NM 87401-6853

JORDAN, DAVID RANDOLPH, health facility administrator; b. Lovington, N.Mex., May 30, 1958; s. Lacy and Mildred Jordan; m. Leslie Ann Blevins, Oct. 7, 1978; children: Lindsey, Haley, Riley. BS in Health Care Adminstrn., S.W. Tex. State U., 1994; student, St. Joseph Coll., Standish, Mass., 1995—. Dist. supr. Chevron U.S.A., Midland, Tex., 1981-92; asst. adminstr. E.B. Davis Hosp., Luling, Tex., 1993; spl. mgmt. asst. to CEO McKenna Meml. Hosp., New Braunfels, Tex., 1994-95; CEO, adminstr. Shackelford County Hosp. Dist., Albany, Tex., 1995—. Contbr. articles to profl. jours. Chmn. Shackelford Needs Assessment, Albany, 1995—; area rep. Congress Rural Health Care Task Force, Washington, 1995—; co-leader United Way, Midland, Tex., 1992. Mem. Am. Coll. Healthcare Execs. (assoc.), Tex. Hosp. Assn., Mid-Tex. Hosp. Alliance, Albany C. of C., Phi Theta Kappa. Democrat. Baptist. Home: PO Box 1871 541 N 2d St Albany TX 76430

JORDAN, ELKE, molecular biologist, government medical research institute executive; b. Gottingen, Germany, Apr. 8, 1937; came to U.S., 1953, naturalized, 1961; d. Peter Friederich and Elisabeth A.K. (Lehmann) J.; m. Thomas H. Edelson, Aug. 21, 1972 (div. 1991). B.A., Goucher Coll., 1957; Ph.D, Johns Hopkins U., 1962. In various rsch. positions Harvard U., 1962-64, U. Cologne, Fed. Republic Germany, 1964-68, U. Wis., Madison, 1968-69, U. Calif., Berkeley, 1969-72; grants assoc. NIH, Bethesda, Md., 1972-73; coord. for collaborative rsch. Nat. Cancer Inst., NIH, Bethesda, Md., 1973-76; health scientist adminstr. Nat. Inst. Gen. Med. Scis., NIH, Bethesda, 1976-82, assoc. dir., 1982-88; dir. Office of Human Genome Rsch., NIH, Bethesda, 1988-89; dep. dir. Nat. Ctr. for Human Genome Rsch., NIH, Bethesda, 1989—. Contbr. articles on molecular biology of E. coli and bacteriophage lambda to profl. jours. NIH fellow, 1959-65; Helen Hay Whitney Found. fellow, 1965-68. Fellow AAAS; mem. Genetics Soc. Am., Am. Soc. for Human Genetics, Am. Soc. Microbiology. Office: Nat Ctr for Human Genome Rsch NIH 9000 Rockville Pike Bethesda MD 20892-0001

JORDAN, JENNIFER ANNE, medical and surgical nurse; b. Augusta, Maine, Dec. 16, 1970; d. Stephen Francis and Joanne Anita (Wilson) Zayszly; m. Kenneth Leroy Jordan, Aug. 14, 1993. BSN, St. Joseph's Coll., Windham, Maine, 1993. RN, Maine. Med.-surg. nurse Ctrl. Maine Med. Ctr., Lewiston, 1993—. Mem. Sigma Theta Tau. Democrat. Roman Catholic. Home: 7 Skillings Woods Turner ME 04282 Office: Ctrl Maine Med Ctr T3 300 Main St Lewiston ME 04240

JORDAN, JERRY D., cardiologist; b. Alexandria, La., Oct. 8, 1930; s. Edgar Chapman and Marion Dugger J.; m. Frances Brewer Jordan, Dec. 21, 1954; children: Scott, Brian, Lynn, Leigh, Jeffrey. BS, La. Coll., 1951; MD, La. State U., 1955. Intern Confederate Meml. Med. Ctr., Shreveport, La., 1955-56, resident in pediatrics, 1956-57; resident in pediatrics Tex. Children's Hosp., Houston, 1959-60, fellow, 1960-62; pediatric cardiologist Ochsner Clinic/Ochsner Found. Hosp., New Orleans, 1962-67; dir. Divsn. Rsch. Alton Ochsner Med. Found., New Orleans, 1964-67; dir. Cardiovascular Lab. U. South Ala. Med. Ctr., Mobile, 1967-73; cardiologist Cardiovascular Assocs. of Mobile, 1973-89, Mobile Heart Ctr., 1989-95, The Heart Group, 1995—; cons. in pediatric cardiology, Crippled Children's Program, New Orleans, 1962-67; co-dir. dept. pediatrics U. South Ala. Med. Ctr., 1967-73, prof. pediatrics, 1967-73. Fellow Am. Acad. Pediatrics, Am. Coll. Cardiology; mem. Med. Soc. Mobile County, Med. Assn. State of Ala., AMA, Southeastern Soc. of Pediatric Cardiology (sec. 1971), Am. Heart Assn. (v.p. Ala. affil. 1977-78, pres. 1978-79). Republican. Roman Catholic. Home: 4510 Kingsway Dr Mobile AL 36608

JORDAN, JOHN EDWARD, dentist; b. Nashville, Nov. 17, 1930; s. John Edward Jordan and Mary Celess (Mar) Richardson; m. Dec. 26, 1958 (widowed); 1 child, John Edward III. AB in Biology, 1952, DDS, 1957; DDS, Meharry Med. Coll., 1957. Dentist Memphis Health Dept., Wellington Ctr., Head Start Program; pvt. practice Memphis. Editor Hyde Park Newsletter, 1991, 92. V.p. North Memphis Neighborhood Watch, 1990-92; v.p. trustees Med. Bapt. Ch., 1986-92; coord. sec. Memphis Bapt. Laymen, 1991-92; pres. Laymen Med. Bapt. Ch., 1983—, Sanctuary Choir, 1989-92; v.p. laymen West Tenn. Missionary and Edn. Assn., to 1996; pres. Austin St. Neighborhood Watch, 1988-91; exec. dir. Hollywood Block Club, pres., 1992; bd. dirs. Kennedy Dem. Club, Hyde Park Neighborhood Coalition, pres., 1993-96; del. to U.S. Presdl. Inaugural Celebration, 1993. Recipient Plaque, Colgate Dental Health Edn. Adv. Bd., 1990, Shanknon Hills Civic Club, 1991, Northside High Sch., 1991, 30 Year Participation in Dentistry plaque, Svc. cert. Middle Bapt. Ch., 1993; recipient Martin Luther King award for Civil Rights, 1992. Mem. Shelby County Dental Soc. (v.p. Memphis chpt., chmn. dental health month, Plaque 1986), Evergreen Optimist Club (v.p., sec., treas. 1987-90, v.p. 1992), Kappa Alpha Psi (Germantown Chpt.). Home and Office: 2154 Chelsea Ave Memphis TN 38108-2205

JORDAN, JUDITH VICTORIA, clinical psychologist, educator; b. Milw., July 28, 1943; d. Claus and Charlotte (Backus) J.; m. William M. Redpath, Aug. 11, 1973. AB, Brown U., 1965; MA, Harvard U., 1968, PhD, 1973. Diplomate Am. Bd. Profl. Psychology. Psychologist Human Relations Service, Wellesley, Mass., 1971-73; assoc. psychologist McLean Hosp., Belmont, Mass., 1978-93, psychologist, 1993—, dir. women's studies program, 1988—, dir. tng. in psychology, 1991, dir. Women's Treatment Network, 1992—; vis. scholar Stone Ctr. Wellesley Coll., 1985—; asst. prof. psychiatry Harvard Med. Sch., 1988—; cons. in field. Author: Empathy and Self Boundries, 1984, Women's Growth in Connection, 1991, (with others) The Self in Relation, 1986; editor, author: Relational Self in Women. Mem. Am. Psychol. Assn., Mass. Psychol. Assn. (bd. dirs. 1983-85), Phi Beta Kappa. Office: McLean Hosp 115 Mill St Belmont MA 02178-1041

JORDAN, ROBIN HALL, physician assistant; b. Branford, Conn., Aug. 25, 1953; d. Stanley Hotchkiss and Helen Summers (Clark) H.; m. Robert Paul Jordan, Sept. 21, 1985; children: Heather, Christopher. BA in Biology, Hamilton Coll., 1974; BS (magna cum laude), Duke U., 1979, M in Health Sci., 1993. Physician asst. Cherry Hosp., Goldsboro, N.C., 1979-85; physician asst., rsch. assocs. U. Miami, 1985-88; physician asst. U.S. Army/NATO Hosp., Mons, Belgium, 1989-91; physician asst. for pvt. physician Enon, Ohio, 1995—. Vol. art appreciation Pub. Schs., Ohio, 1993-95, Sumter, S.C., 1995-96, ARC, Belgium, Calif., Ohio, 1988-93, Girl Scouts USA, Ohio, 1994-95. Mem. Am. Acad. Physician Assts., N.C. Acad. Physician Assts. (bd. dirs. 1982-85). Home and Office: 705 Haile Dr Sumter SC 29150

JORDAN, SUSAN JEAN, health services administrator; b. Staunton, Ill., July 12, 1963; d. Arnold Gene and Roseanne (Moruskey) Franke; m. Patrick Miles Jordan, Dec. 28, 1985; children: Preston, Sydney. BSN, Ill. Wesleyan U., 1985; MA, Webster U., 1993. RN. Critical care unit nurse Methodist Med. Ctr., Peoria, Ill., 1985-86; nurse coord. Deaconess Hosp, St. Louis, 1986-88; utilization mgr. White County Meml. Hosp., Monticello, Ind., 1988-89; from nursing dept. head to quality performance supervisor Lafayette (Ind.) Home Hosp., 1989—. Mem. Nat. Assn. Healthcare Quality, Ind. Assn. Healthcare Quality. Republican. Roman Catholic. Home: 262 NSR 39 Monticello IN 47960 Office: Lafayette Home Hosp 2400 South St Lafayette IN 47904-3027

JORGE, JOÃO CARLOS SANTANA, biochemist, researcher; b. Lisbon, Portugal, Aug. 21, 1961; s. Alfredo Dores and Maria Isabel (Santana) J.; m. Isabel Nascimento Augusto, Apr. 16, 1988; children: Jorge, Goncalo. Grad., U. Lisbon, 1984. Bd. cert. diplomate; chemistry diplomate Br. Biochemistry and Organic Chemistry. Bursery FLAD, Lisbon, 1987-89; superior technician INETI, Lisbon, 1989-96, rsch. asst., 1996—; Portuguese expert E.C.-C.A.P. Drug Targeting Cancer Treatment, 1991. Contbr. articles to profl. jours.; patentee in field. Mem. Portuguese Soc. Biochemistry, Biochem. Soc., Spanish-Portuguese local chpt. Controlled Release Soc. Home: R Bernardo Santareno 33 6C, 2855 Corroios Portugal Office: INETI-IBQTA D B, Azinhaga dos Latieiros, 1600 Lisbon Portugal

JORGENSEN, ANDERS FJENDBO, physician; b. Rodding, Viborg, Denmark, Feb. 28, 1950; s. Hans and Kristina (Nielsen) J.; m. Kirsten Nohr, Apr. 4, 1974; children: Jonas Nohr, Anna Katrine Nohr. MD, U. Aarhus, Denmark, 1979. Physician, cons. Danish Health Ministry, Aarhus, 1979-80; physician Nykoing, Denmark, 1983-84, Danish Health Ministry, Odense, Denmark, 1989—, Danish Vol. Svc., Sivonga, Zambia, 1980-83, Danish Internat. Aid Agy., Qacha's Nek, Lesotho, 1984-86, Rigshopitalet, Copenhagen, 1987-88, Dar es Salaam, Tanzania, 1988-89; cons. infectious diseases Odense U. Hosp., 1994—; physician Dept. Infectious Diseases, Odense, 1988-95; advisor Danida, Nat. AIDS Control, Tanzania, 1995—; dir. H-Consult, Odense, 1989—. Author: (booklets) AIDS, 1988, Ukimwi, 1989, Contbr. articles to profl. jours. Office: c/o Royal Danish Embassy, Sonder Blvd, PO Box 9231 Dar es Salaam Tanzania

JORGENSEN, GERALD THOMAS, psychologist, educator; b. Mason City, Iowa, Jan. 15, 1947; s. Harry Grover and Mary Jo (Kollasch) J.; m. Mary Ann Reiter, Aug. 30, 1969; children—Amy Lynn, Sarah Kay, Jill Kathryn. B.A., Loras Coll., Dubuque, 1969; M.S., Colo. State U., Ft. Collins, 1970, Ph.D., 1973. Lic. psychologist, Iowa; cert. health svc. provider Iowa; ordained to ministry Roman Cath. Ch. as deacon, 1979. Psychology intern Counseling Ctr., Colo. State U., Ft. Collins, 1971-72, VA Hosp., Palo Alto, Calif., 1972-73; psychologist Loras Coll., 1973-76, Clarke Coll., Dubuque, 1973-76; asst. prof. psychology, Loras Coll., 1976-80, assoc. prof., 1981-93, dir. Ctr. for Counseling and Student Devel., 1977-86, assoc. dean of students, 1985-86, dean of students, v.p. for student devel., 1986-93; cons.

and supervising psychologist Dubuque/Jackson County Mental Health Ctr., 1977—; assoc. med. staff Mercy Health Ctr., Dubuque, 1989—; asst. dir. for formation Office of Permanent Diaconate, Archdiocese of Dubuque, 1979-93, dir., 1993-96, auditor. consulting psychologist Met. Tribunal, 1993—; chairperson Iowa Bd. Psychology Examiners, Des Moines, 1984-90, continuing edn. coordinator, 1983. Contbr. articles to profl. jours. Treas. Dubuque County Assn. Mental Health Inc., Dubuque, 1975-82. NDEA fellow, 1969-72. Mem. Am. Coll. Pers. Assn. (chmn. com. VII 1980-82), Am. Assn. Counseling Devel., Am. Psychol. Assn., Iowa Psychol. Assn. (mem. exec. coun., highest honors 1990), Assn. State and Provincial Bds. (exec. com. 1986-89, pres. 1989-92), Nat. Assn. Permanent Diaconate Dirs. (sec. 1983-85, treas. 1985-90, award 1991), Canon Law Soc. Am., Iowa Student Pers. Assn., Fedn. Assns. Reg. Bds. (v.p. 1993-94, 96—, pres. 1994-96), Delta Epsilon Sigma, Phi Kappa Phi, Sigma Tau Phi. Democrat. Roman Catholic. Home: 2183 St Celia St Dubuque IA 52002-2742 Office: Archdiocesan Ctr 1229 Mount Loretta Ave Dubuque IA 52003-7826

JORGENSEN, JOHN, nursing administrator; b. San Francisco, Apr. 10, 1949; s. Erik and Anna Jean (Siverts) J.; m. Bret Brengle, Dec. 18, 1972; children: Heather, Cory, Jeffrey. B Psychiatry, Sonoma State U., Rechnart Park, Calif., 1972; AS in Nursing, Santa Rosa (Calif.) Coll., 1977; AA, Coll. of Marin, Kentfield, Calif., 1979; MPA, Pa. State U., Middletown, 1987. ACLS provider instr. Am. Heart Assn. Psychiat. technician Keokuk Hosp., Petaluma, Calif., 1974-77; nurse mgr. ER/ICU Sonoma Valley Hosp., 1977-82; clin. mgr., systems coord., staff nurse Pa. State U., Hershey, 1982-88; nurse mgr. Harrisburg (Pa.) Hosp., 1988-90, St. Mary's Med. Ctr., Knoxville, Tenn., 1990-91, Ft. Sanders Parkwest Med. Ctr., Knoxville, 1991-95; ops. leader Ft. Sanders Health Sys., Knoxville, 1995—. Bd. mem. Farrasal Baseball, Inc., Farragut, Tenn., 1995-96. Home: 348 Sweetgum Dr Farragut TN 37922 Office: Ft Sanders Health System 1901 Clinch Ave Knoxville TN 37916

JORGENSEN, JUDITH ANN, psychiatrist; b. Parris Island, S.C.; d. George Emil and Margaret Georgia Jorgensen; BA, Stanford U., 1963; MD, U. Calif., 1968; m. Ronald Francis Crown, July 11, 1970. Intern, Meml. Hosp., Long Beach, 1969-70; resident County Mental Health Services, San Diego, 1970-73; staff psychiatrist Children and Adolescent Services, San Diego, 1973-78; practice medicine specializing in psychiatry, La Jolla, Calif., 1973—; staff psychiatrist County Mental Health Services of San Diego, 1973-78, San Diego State U. Health Services, 1985-87; psychiat. cons. San Diego City Coll., 1973-78, 85-86; asst. prof. dept. psychiatry U. Calif., 1978-91, assoc. prof. dept. psychiatry, 1991-96; chmn. med. quality rev. com. Dist. XIV, State of Calif., 1982-83. Mem. Am. Psychiat. Assn., San Diego Soc. Psychiat. Physicians (chmn. membership com. 1976-78, v.p. 1978-80, fed. legis. rep. 1985-87, fellowship com. 1989), Am. Soc. Adolescent Psychiatry, San Diego Soc. Adolescent Psychiatry (pres. 1981-82), Calif. Med. Assn. (former alternate del.), Soc. Sci. Study of Sex, San Diego Soc. Sex Therapy and Edn. (cert. sex therapist), San Diego County Med. Soc. (credentials com. 1982-84). Club: Rowing. Office: 470 Nautilus St Ste 211 La Jolla CA 92037-5970

JØRGENSEN, KARSTEN EJSING, otorhinolaryngologist, educator; b. Horsens, Denmark, Aug. 1, 1937; s. Hakon Ejsing and Dagny (Eriksen) J.; m. Birgit Bøge Henriksen, Nov. 28, 1964; children: Morten, Annegrethe, Sofie. MD, U. Aarhus, 1964, postgrad. degree, 1974. Chief ear-nose-throat dept. Univ. Hosp. Odense, Denmark, 1977—; prof. Inst. Oto-rhino-laryngology U. Odense, 1987—. Contbr. papers to profl. publs. Lt. Danish air force, 1966-67. Mem. Dahanca. Home: Platanvej 43, 5230 Odense M, Denmark Office: Univ Hosp Odense, Sdr Blvd 29, 5000 Odense C, Denmark

JORGENSEN, LOU ANN BIRKBECK, social worker; b. Park City, Utah, May 14, 1931; d. Robert John and Lillian Pearl (Langford) Birkbeck; student Westminster Coll., 1949-51; B.S., U. Utah, 1953, M.S.W., 1972, D.S.W., 1979; grad. Harvard Inst. Ednl. Mgmt., 1983; m. Howard Arnold Jorgensen, June 9, 1954; children: Gregory Arnold, Blake John, Paul Clayton. Social work adminstr. nursing home demonstration project, dept. family and community medicine U. Utah Med. Ctr., Salt Lake City, 1972-74; mental health ednl. specialist Grad. Sch. Social Work, U. Utah, 1974-77, 77-80, asst. prof., 1974-80, assoc. prof., 1980-94, prof., 1994—, dir. doctoral program, 1984-89, assoc. dean, 1986-94; regional mental health cons. Bd. dirs. Info. and Referral Ctr., 1975-82, United Way of Utah, 1976-82, Pioneer Trail Parks, 1977-83, Rowland Hall-St. Marks Sch., 1980-86; Salt Lake County housing commr., 1980-86, Utah State Health Facilities Bd., 1991—, chair, 1994; pres. Human Svcs. Conf. for Utah, 1979-80; bd. dirs. Alzheimer Assn., Utah chpt., 1990—, Salt Lake County Coalition Bus. and Human Svcs., 1990-94, Town Club 1990-93, bd.; mem. Valley Mental Health Bd., 1990—. Mem. Coun. on Social Work Edn., Commn. Women in High Edn., Nat. Assn. Social Workers (pres. Utah chpt. 1978-79), Adminstrs. of Public Agys. Assn., Human Svcs. Assn. Utah, Jr. League of Salt Lake City, Phi Kappa Phi. Republican. Episcopalian. Clubs: Town. Author: Explorations in Living, 1978, Social Work in Business and Industry, 1979; Handbook of the Social Services, 1981; contbr. articles to profl. jours. Home: 1458 Kristianna Cir Salt Lake City UT 84103-4221 Office: U Utah Grad Sch Social Work Social Work Bldg 324 Salt Lake City UT 84112-1182

JOSE, SHIRLEY ANN, nurse, critical care educator; b. Pueblo, Colo., Mar. 26, 1934; d. William Henry and Mildred Dorothy (Sanders) Priest; m. Laurent A. Jose, June 13, 1958; children: Steven William, Lauren Michele. BSN, Loma Linda U., 1957; MS, U. Colo., 1969. RN Colo. Staff nurse White Meml. Hosp., L.A., 1957-58, West Covina (Calif.) Hosp., 1958-59; sr. instr. Colo. State Hosp., Pueblo, 1960-62; charge nurse Swedish Med. Ctr., Englewood, Colo., 1965-68; asst. prof. Union Coll., Lincoln, Nebr., 1969-74; nursing coord. Porter Meml. Hosp., Denver, 1974-77; critical care nurse Dept. Vets. Affairs Med. Ctr., Denver, 1977-80, nursing instr., 1980-91, critical care educator, 1991-95, ADP clin. coord., 1995—; asst. clin. prof. Sch. Nursing, U. Colo. Health Sci. Ctr., 1984—, mem. access com., 1987-88; reviewer Critical Care Nurse, 1986—; instr. ACLS, Am. Heart Assn., Denver, 1989—. Author of poems. Mem. citizens adv. com. Denver C.C., 1981-95, chmn., 1991. Recipient Golden Poet award, 1991, Editor's Choice award Outstanding Achievement in Poetry, 1995. Mem. AACN, NNSDO, Hosp. Staff Devel. Network (program planning com. 1990-91), Sigma Theta Tau. Office: Dept VA Med Ctr 1055 Clermont St Denver CO 80220-3808

JOSEFSSON, GÖRAN ERIK, orthopedic surgeon, administrator; b. Ljusne, Sweden, Dec. 26, 1933; s. Georg Axel and Helga Cecilia (Norén) J.; m. Elisabet Barbro Oldenburg, Aug. 12, 1958 (div. 1988); children: Torun, Jonatan, Maria, Fredrik; m. Anna Margareta Edlund, Aug. 5, 1989. MD, Royal Karolinska Inst., Stockholm, 1963; PhD, U. Lund, Sweden, 1980. Cert. specialist in gen. and orthopedic surgery. Asst. chief surgeon dept. orthopedic surgery Gävle (Sweden) Hosp., 1972-78, chief surgeon dept. orthopedic surgery, 1978—, head dept. orthopedic surgery, 1986-95; assoc. prof. orthopedic surgery U. Lund, 1991; asst. med. chief of staff Gävel, 1983-85; med. advisor to gen. ins., Gävleborg. Author: The Hip, The Hip Society, 1977, Acta Orthop Scand, 1990, Excerpta Medica Amsterdam, 1983. Capt. Naval M.C., 1955-65. Recipient fin. support King Gustav V:s Found., 1978, Ulla and Gustaf af Ugglas Found., 1979, Swedish Med. Rsch. Coun., 1979. Mem. European Bone and Joint Info. Soc., European Hip Soc., Rotary. Lutheran. Home: Lexevägen 20, S-806 27 Gavle Sweden Office: Gävle Hosp, Dept Orthopedic Surgery, S-801 87 Gavle Sweden

JOSEFSSON, PER OLOF, orthopedic surgeon, consultant; b. Virserum, Sweden, July 19, 1948; s. Josef Verner and Karin Marie (Israelsson) S.; m. Ingrid Margareta Nilsson, 1975 (div. 1986); children: Charlotta, Helena, Sofia; m. Eva Marianne Berggren; children: Hanna, Carolina. MD, Lund (Sweden) U., 1973, PhD, 1987. Resident in gen. surgery and anesthesia Oskarshamn, 1973-77; resident in orthopedic surgery Kalmar, 1977-79; resident in orthopedic surgery U. Hosp., Malmö, 1979-81, cons. in orthopedic surgery, 1981—. Mem. Swedish Orthopedic Assn., Nordic Orthopedic Assn., European Soc. for Surgery of Shoulder and Elbow. Home: Allansgatan 43, S-21565 Malmo Sweden Office: U Hosp Malmö, S-20502 Malmö Sweden

JOSEPH, ANTHONY BARNETT, psychiatrist; b. Bristol, England, Feb. 11, 1955; came to U.S., 1965; s. Bertram Leon and Ada Emilie (Goldschmidt) J.; m. Karen Beverly Spinks, June 20, 1980; m. James Edward, Oliver Charles. BA, CUNY, 1975, MA, 1975; BA, U. Oxford, Oxford, England, 1978; M.B., B. Chir., U. Cambridge, Cambridge, England, 1980. Diplomate Am. Bd. Psychiatry and Neurology. House surgeon Hillingdon Hosp., London, 1981; house physician Ashford Hosp., London, 1981-82; resident in psychiatry St. Elizabeth's Hosp., Boston, 1982-85; Asst. pschiatrist Inst. Law and Psychiatry, McLean Hosp., Belmont, Mass., 1985-86; dir. neuropsychiatry clinic Mass. Mental Health Ctr., Boston, 1985-89; clin. instr. psychiatry Harvard Med. Sch., Boston, Mass., 1986-88; assoc. med. dir. Medfield State Hosp., Medfield, Mass., 1986-90; sr. cons. forensic psychiatrist Mass. Dept. Mental Health, Boston, 1988-91; asst. clin. prof. psychiatry Harvard Med. Sch., Boston, 1988-95, assoc. clin. prof., 1995—, mem. continuing med. edn. faculty, 1988—; med. dir. Core Mgmt., Inc., Lexington, Mass., 1989-93, Ctr. Neurobehavioral Rehab., Waltham, Mass., 1990—; profl. adv. bd. neurobehavioral unit McLean Hosp., Belmont, Mass., 1987-90. Contbr. articles to profl. jours.; reviewer Jour. Clin. Psychiatry, 1987—. Fellow Royal Soc. Medicine; mem. Royal Soc. Chemistry, Am. Psychiat. Assn., Boston Soc. Neurology and Psychiatry, Am. Neuropsychiat. Assn. Office: Ctr Neurobehavioral Rehab 775 Trapelo Rd Waltham MA 02154-7915

JOSEPH, RICHARD SAUL, cardiologist; b. N.Y.C., Mar. 27, 1937; s. Charles Irving and Lillian (Horowitz) J.; m. Frances B. Rappaport, Jan. 27, 1963; children: Lauryl, James, Alisa, Jennifer. BA magna cum laude, Hofstra Coll., 1958; MD, Albert Einstein U., 1962. Intern U. Utah Affiliated Hosp., Salt Lake City, 1962-63; resident in chest medicine Bronx Mcpl. Hosp., Bronx, N.Y., 1963-64; resident internal medicine Mt. Sinai Hosp., N.Y.C., 1966-68; fellow in cardiology Nassau County Med. Ctr., East Meadow, N.Y., 1968-69; pvt. practice cardiology Huntington (N.Y.) Hosp., 1969—, chief cardiology, 1981-90, attending cardiology, 1973—; asst. prof. clin. medicine (Cardiology) SUNY, Stony Brook, 1973—; cons. in cardiology Kings Park (H.Y.) Hosp., 1971—; electro cardiographer Huntington Hosp., 1971—, co-dir. cardiac stress lab., 1975—; dir. Huntington Cardiac Rehab., 1977-94; adj. attending cardiologist St. Francis Hosp., Roslyn, N.Y., 1993—. Contbr. articles to profl. jours. Speaker med. adv. bd. Suffolk County Heart Assn., Blue Point, N.Y., 1971-73; speaker med. dir. Huntington (N.Y.) YMCA, 1973-77. Lt. USN, 1964-66. Recipient Pres. prize Hofstra Coll., Uniondale, N.Y., 1954; named Valedictorian Hofstra Coll., Uniondale, N.Y., 1958. Fellow Am. Coll. Cardiology; mem. Alpha Omega Alpha. Hebrew. Office: 205 E Main St Huntington NY 11743-2923

JOSEPH, SMITH, pharmacist; b. Saint-Louis du Nord, Haiti, June 15, 1961; came to U.S., 1979; s. Constantin and Jeannette Joseph; m. Eltha Souffrant, May 13, 1989; children: Euclide Fabien, Bénoushkah Dominique. AA, Miami Dade Cmty. Coll., 1987; PharmD, Fla. A&M U., 1991; postgrad. in Medicine, Nova Southeastern U., 1994—. Registered pharmacist Fla., N.J. Clin. lab. specialist U. Miami, 1983-87; staff pharmacist Walgreen's Pharmacy, Miami, 1990-92; clin. pharmacist Miami Heart Inst., 1992-94; bd. dirs. Ann-Marie Adker Overtown Cmty. Health Ctr., Miami. Mem. Haitian-Am. Civic Assn., Inc. (bd. dirs.), Soc. Haitian-Am. Profls. (co-founder, interim chmn.), Beta Kappa Chi.

JOSEPH, STEPHEN C., health sciences administrator; b. N.Y.C., Nov. 25, 1937; m. Elizabeth Preble; children: Denise Ellen, Tara Anne. BA, Harvard Coll., 1959; MD, Yale U., 1963; MPH, Johns Hopkins U., 1968. Intern pediats. Boston Children's Hosp., 1963-64, asst. resident, 1966-67; fellow comprehensive child care project dept. pediats. Johns Hopkins Sch. Medicine, 1967-68; prof. pediats. and comty. health Univ. Ctr. Health Sci., Yaounde, Cameroon, 1971-73; dir. med. edn. & planning, cons. to pres. U. Wyo., Washington, 1973-74; asst. med. Children's Hosp. Med. Ctr., 1974-78; dep. asst. adminstr. human resources devel. Bur. Devel. Support, Agy. Int. Devel., 1978-81; cons., lectr. Int. Devel. Rsch. Ctr., Can., 1981-82; chief pediats. Grenfell Regional Health Svc., St. Anthony, Can., 1982-83; spl. coord. child health & survival UN Health, U. Minn., 1991-93; asst. sec. def. for health affairs Dept. of Def., Washington, 1993—; dir. Office Int. Health Programs, Harvard Sch. Pub. Health, 1974-78, lectr. dept. maternal and child health, 1974-78; mem. Nat. Coun. Int. Health, 1975-78; acting asst. adminstr. Bur. Devel. Support, Agy. Int. Devel., 1981; bd. trustees U.S. Conf. Local Health Officers, 1987-78; mem. Nat. Adv. Com. HIV Ctrs. Disease Control, 1988-91; Sol Fleischman vis. prof. medicine Harvard Comty. Health Plan, 1990. Author: Dragon Within the Gates: The Once and Future AIDS Epidemic, 1992. Recipient Pub. Svc. for Medicine award ACP, 1989. Fellow APHA, Am. Acad. Pediats.; mem. Inst. Medicine-NAS. Office: Dept of Def Rm 3E-3 Washington DC 70301*

JOSEPHS, EILEEN SHERLE, mediator, financial consultant; b. Johnstown, Pa.; d. David and Freda (Beerman) Venetsky; m. Gerald Lisowitz, June 27, 1953 (div. 1968); children: Mara Lisowitz, Carlyn Lisowitz Walker; m. Marvin Josephs, May 25, 1969 (div. 1988); m. Michael N. Berger, Aug. 28, 1993. BS cum laude, U. Pitts., 1956, MA, 1969. Cert. mediator. Tchr. Pitts. Pub. Schs., 1958-59; tchr. mil. Ft. Lee, Va., 1960; docent edn. staff Carnegie Inst., Pitts., 1971-77; real estate developer, sales rep. Equity Real Estate, Pitts., 1977-79; women's div. buyer and retail cons. Coach House Stores, Pitts., 1980; ptnr., mediator Divorce and Separation Ctr., 1980—; ptnr. Mediation Masters, Pitts., 1992—; guest lectr. U. Pitts., 1982-88, Duquesne U., 1995-96, C.C. Pitts., 1988-91; co-owner Michael Berger Gallery, 1995—. Author: Landmark Mediations-Long Term Marriage, 1992, Divorce Agreements and Landmark Adoption Mediation Resulting in Shared Parenting, 1993, Expanding Non-Adversarial Dispute Resolution in Business Practice, 1993, Advance Mediation in Profl. Practices; contbr. articles to profl. jours. Pub. co-chair Three Rivers Arts Festival, Pitts., 1965; found. bd. dirs. Group Against Smog & Pollution, Pitts., 1967-70; bd. dirs. nat. Coun. Jewish Women, Pitts., 1979; vol. Pitts. Mediation Ctr., 1988—; mem. Family Mediation Coun. Bd. Senatorial scholar U. Pitts., Marshall scholar, 1954. Mem. Pitts. Plan Art, Acad. Family Mediators (cons. 1985—, presentor workshops 1988, 89, 90, 92), Family Mediation Coun. Western Pa. (charter, bd. dirs. 1992—), Greater Pitts. Bd. Realtors. Office: Mediation Masters 7514 Kensington St Pittsburgh PA 15221-3224

JOSEPHSON, ALAN SAMUEL, medical educator; b. Bronx, N.Y., Nov. 30, 1930; s. Max and Mildred (Berk) J.; m. Adeline Goldberg, Dec. 24, 1955; children: Michelle, Neil, Debra. AB, NYU, 1952, MD, 1956. Diplomate Am. Bd. Medicine, Allergy and Immunology, Diagnostic Lab. Immunology. Intern III med. div. Bellevue Hosp., N.Y.C., 1956-57, med. resident, 1957-58, chief med. resident, 1960-61; USPHS trainee NYU, 1958-60; instr. Coll. of Medicine U. Cin., 1961-63; asst. prof. SUNY, N.Y.C., 1963-67, assoc. prof., 1967-75; prof. SUNY Downstate Med. Ctr., Bklyn., 1975—; dir. div. allergy and immunology SUNY, Bklyn., 1970—. Fellow ACP, Am. Acad. Allergy and Immunology. Office: SUNY 450 Clarkson Ave # 50 Brooklyn NY 11203-2012

JOSEPHSON, MARK ERIC, cardiologist, electrophysiologist; b. N.Y.C., Jan. 27, 1943; s. Joan Ellen Eisenberg, Aug. 27, 1967; children: Rachel Laurie, Stephanie Paige. BS cum laude, Trinity Coll., 1965; MD, Columbia U., 1969; MA (hon.), U. Pa., 1982, Harvard U., 1992; PhD (hon.), U. Limburg, Maastricht, Netherlands, 1986. Diplomate Am. Bd. Med. Examiners, Am. Bd. Internal Medicine, Am. Bd. Cardiology, Am. Bd. Electrophysiology. Intern Mt. Sinai Hosp., N.Y., 1969-70, resident, 1970-71; fellow in cardiology U. Pa. Sch. Medicine, Phila., 1973-74, research assoc. in cardiology, 1974-75; asst. prof. medicine U. Pa., Phila., 1975-79, Samuel Bellett asst. prof. cardiology, 1978-79, assoc. prof., 1979-81, Robinette Found. assoc. prof. cardiovascular diseases, 1981-84, Robinette Found. prof., 1984-92; prof. Harvard Med. Sch., Boston, 1992—; dir. med. intensive care unit Hosp. of U. Pa., 1975-77, clin. electrophysiology lab., 1975-83, co-dir. med. intensive care unit, 1977-80, chief cardiovascular sect., 1981-91, dir. electrophysiology program, 1991-92; cons. Nat. Heart Lung and Blood Inst., VA.; dir. Harvard-Thorndike Electrophysiology Inst. Beth Israel Hosp., Boston, 1992—. Author: (with S.F. Seides) Clinical Cardiac Electrophysiology: Techniques and Interpretations, 1979, 2d edit., 1992; editor: Ventricular Tachycardia: Mechanisms and Management, 1982 (with H.J.J. Wellens) Tachycardias: Mechanisms, Diagnosis, and Treatment, 1984, Tachycardias: Mechanisms and Management, 1993; guest editor (with A.N. Brest) Sudden Cardiac Death, 1985, editor, 1992; contbr. over 325 articles to profl. jours., Am. Jour. Cardiology, Circulation, Clin. Progress in Pacing and Electrophysiology, Jour. Am. Coll. Cardiology, PACE, Rhythmology, European Journal of Cardiac Pacing and Electrophysiology; editorial cons. Am. Jour. Medicine, Annals of Internal Medicine, Chest, Circulation Research, PACE, Am. Jour. Cardiology, Japanese Heart Journal, European Journal of Cardiology, Am. Jour. Physiology, Jour. of Clinical Investigation; mem. publ. com. Revista Argentina Cardiologia; editorial bd. Journal of Cardiovascular Electrophysiology, European Heart Journal. With USPHS, 1971-73. Recipient Medal for Excellence, Columbia U., N.Y.C., 1982, Century IV Physician of Yr. award, 1982, RESCAR award for Cardiovascular Research, Maastricht, 1986, Sr. Rsch. Investigator award Am. Heart Assn., Southeastern Pa. chpt., NASPE Teaching award, 1996. Fellow ACP, Am. Coll. Cardiology (chmn. electrophysiology/electrocardiography com., mem. cardiology test com. Med. Knowledge Self Assessment Program V), Am. Heart Assn. Council on Clin. Cardiology; mem. Am. Heart Assn. (Mass. affiliate, council on clin. cardiology com. on electrocardiography and cardiac electrophysiology, council on clin. cardiology credentials com., subcom. on computers and electrocardiography), Am. Soc. Clin. Investigation, Assn. Am. Physicians, Cardiac Electrophysiology Group, Am. Fed. for Clin. Rsch., N.Am. Soc. Pacing and Electrophysiology Inc., Mass. Med. Soc., Mass. EP Soc., Assn. Univ. Cardiologists. Office: Beth Israel Hosp 330 Brookline Ave Boston MA 02215-5400

JOSHI, SEWA RAM, toxicologist; b. Baluana, Punjab, India, Oct. 15, 1933; s. Hariram and Mayadevi (Khindria) J.; came to U.S., 1961, naturalized, 1971; B.Vet. Sci., Punjab U., 1954; M.S., Cornell U., 1963, Ph.D., 1965; m. Surinder Sharma, Aug. 1954; 1 son, Ashok Kumar. State veterinarian Punjab, 1954-55; research assoc. Indian Vet. Research Inst., 1955-61; research assoc. pathology, toxicology Children's Cancer Research Found., Harvard U. Med. Sch., 1965-71; sr. staff fellow Nat. Cancer Inst., NIH, Bethesda, Md., 1971-76; physiologist in pharmacology and toxicology Ctr. Drug Evaln. and Rsch., FDA, Rockville, Md., 1976—; assoc. prof. Howard U., Washington, 1972-75. Recipient Career Service Recognition award USPHS, 1982. Mem. Soc. Toxicology, Teratology Soc., Soc. for Study Reprodn., Environ. Mutagen Soc., AAAS, N.Y. Acad. Scis., Sigma Xi. Club: Lake Linganore Country. Co-author: Carcinogenesis-A Comprehensive Survey, vol. 3, 1978. Contbr. tech. articles to profl. jours. Home: 9905 Sunset Dr Rockville MD 20850-3658 Office: FDA (HFD-520) Div Anti-infective Drug Products 5600 Fishers Ln Rm 16B10 Rockville MD 20857-0001

JOSKOW, RENEE W., dentist, educator; b. N.Y.C., Mar. 15, 1960; d. Melvin Lawrence and Eunice Lila (Levine) J. BA, SUNY, Binghamton, 1981; MPH, Columbia U., 1985, DDS, 1985. Cert. Shiatsu practitioner, Am. Oriental Bodywork Therapy Assn. Gen. practice resident Hackensack (N.J.) Med. Ctr., 1985-86; pvt. faculty practice, gen. practitioner Sch. of Dental and Oral Surgery, Columbia U., N.Y.C., 1986-90; asst. prof., dentistry Columbia U., N.Y.C., 1986—, dir. freshman dental courses, 1987—; pvt. practice gen. dentistry N.Y.C., 1990—; cons. alternative delivery sys. Sch. Dental and Oral Surgery, Columbia U., 1985-86, workshop leader, 1993, mem. curriculum com. Ctr. for Alt. and Complementary Medicine; cons. on quality assurance Prudential Ins. Co., 1994—; clin. program coord. health of pub. grant Columbia Sch. Pub. Health, 1987-88; workshop leader Columbia-Presbyn. Med. Ctr., 1993; guest lectr. Inst. for Child Devel.-Cmty. Outreach lectr. oral health Hackensack Med. Ctr., 1986. Mem. Julliard Evening Divsn. Chorale. Recipient L.I. Acad. of Odontology award, N.Y., 1985, Ella Marie Ewell award for Meritorious Svc., Columbia Univ., 1985, Alumni award for Excellence in Preventive Dentistry, Columbia U., 1985. Fellow N.Y. Acad. Dentistry, Acad. Gen. Dentistry; mem. ADA, Am. Assn. Women Dentists (faculty advisor 1986—), 1st Dist. Dental Soc., Columbia U. Alumni Assn. (com. chmn. 1989—), Nat. Assn. Women Bus. Owners, Omicron Kappa Upsilon. Office: 29 W 57th St New York NY 10019-3406

JOSLIN, STUART LORIN, psychiatrist; b. Springfield, Mass., May 1, 1916; s. Lorin Lee and Florence (Mellen) Joslin; m. Dorothy Dennett (dec. Nov. 1988); children: Ellen Johnck, Nancy Fritz, Ernst Laurent. BA, Wesleyan Coll., Middletown, Conn., 1937; MS, Yale U., 1939, MD, 1943. Diplomate Am. Bd. Psychiatry and Neurology. Intern Yale U., New Haven, 1943-44; resident Johns Hopkins U., Balt., 1944-45, N.Y. Hosp., 1945; pvt. practice Fairfield, Conn., 1946—; psychiatrist Yale Dept. Psychiatry, New Haven, 1966-68, Yale Child Study Ctr., New Haven, 1968-70. Lt. (j.g.) USN, 1945-47. Mem. Am. Psychiat. Assn., Am. Acad. Child and Adolescent Psychiatry. Democrat. Congregationalist. Home: 497 Iroquois Ln # A Stratford CT 06497-8246 Office: 1305 Post Rd Fairfield CT 06430-6016

JOSLYN, WALLACE DANFORTH, psychologist; b. Cape Girardeau, Mo., Apr. 13, 1939; s. Lewis Danforth and Margaret Bernice (Gallup) J.; m. Annette Andre, Aug. 27, 1966 (div. Feb. 1969); m. Moreen V. Drescher, May 26, 1979; children: Jonathan David, Sarah Analisa Malathi. BA, U. Va., 1961; MS, U. Wis., 1965, PhD, 1967. Lic. psychologist, Iowa. Rsch. assoc. Oreg. Regional Primate Rsch. Ctr., Beaverton, 1967-71; clin. psychologist Dept. Vets. Affairs Med. Ctr., Knoxville, Iowa, 1972—; adj. asst. prof. U. Oreg. Health Scis. U., 1970; diplomate Viktor Frankl Inst. Logotherapy. Contbr. articles to profl. jours. Mem. Nat. Register for Health Care Providers in Psychology. Fellow NIMH. Home: 802 E Competine Knoxville IA 50138-1955 Office: VA Med Ctr Knoxville IA 50138

JOSSELSON, RUTHELLEN, psychologist; b. Pitts., Dec. 18, 1946. AB in Psychology, U. Mich., 1967, PhD in Clin. Psychology, 1972; postgrad., Harvard U., 1971-72, Johns Hopkins U., 1975—. Lic. psychologist, Md. Clin. psychology intern Psychol. Clinic, Ann Arbor, Mich., 1968-70; clin. fellow psychiatry Harvard Med. Sch., Mass. Mental Health Ctr., Boston, 1970-71; staff psychologist Mass. Mental Health Ctr., Community Mental Health Svc., Boston, 1971-72; pvt. practice psychotherapy Ann Arbor, 1972-73, Balt., 1974—; asst. prof. dept. psychology U. Toledo (Ohio), 1972-73; asst. prof. dept. psychology, dir. clin. concentration Towson State U., Balt., 1975-82, assoc. prof., dir. clin. concentration program, 1982-89, prof., dir. clin. concentration program, 1989—; rsch. asst. U. Mich., 1967-70; tchg. fellow psychology U. Mich., 1968-70; assoc. rsch. scientist The Johns Hopkins U., Ctr. Social Orgn. Schs., Balt., 1973-75; cons. Sheppard Pratt Hosp., 1977, 81-82; Fulbright prof. psychology The Hebrew U., Jerusalem, 1989-90; vis. prof. Harvard Grad. Sch. Edn., 1992-93; Forchheimer prof. psychology Hebrew U., Jerusalem, 1993-94; sr. cons. The Johns Hopkins U. Student Health Svcs.; assoc. A.K. Rice Inst., Washington-Balt. Ctr.; faculty mem. Fielding Inst., 1996—. Author: Finding Herself: Pathways to Identity Development in Women, 1987, The Space Between Us: Exploring The Dimensions of Human Relationships, 1992, Revising Herself: The Story of Women's Identity from College to Midlife; co-editor: The Narrative Study of Lives, Vols. 1-4, 1993-96; mem. editl. bd. Jour. Youth and Adolescence, 1977—; contbr. chpts. to books and articles to profl. jours. Fellow Md. Psychol. Assn. (exec. coun. chmn. ethics com. 1977-79, human resources com. 1976-77); mem. Am. Psychol. Assn. (Md. state rep. to com. on women 1976-79), Am. Group Psychotherapy Assn., Mid. Atlantic Group Psychotherapy Assn., Internat. Soc. Adolescent Psychiatry (coun. dels. 1988—). Office: 600 Wyndhurst Ave Ste 200 Baltimore MD 21210-2425

JOURDEN, MARTIN GREGORY, obstetrician, gynecologist, health administrator; b. Grand Rapids, Mich., May 9, 1952; s. Lawrence Maynard and Yvette (Grossman) J.; m. Renee G. Asher, June 10, 1973; children: Nicole Denise, Samuel Alexander. BS in Psychology, Mich. State U., 1974, MS in Anatomy, 1977; DO, Coll. Osteo. Med. and Surgery, Des Moines, 1980. Diplomate Nat. Osteo. Bd. Examiners. Flexible intern Tripler Army Med. Ctr., Honolulu, 1980-81, resident in ob-gyn., 1981-85; mem. ob-gyn. staff Blanchfield Army Cmty. Hosp., Ft. Campbell, Ky., 1985-86, chief ob-gyn., 1986-88; asst. chief ob-gyn. 34th Gen. Hosp., Augsburg, Germany, 1988-92; chief dept. surgery U.S. Army MEDDAC, Heidelberg, Germany, 1992-93, dep. comdr. clin. svcs., 1993-94; dep. comdr. clin. svcs. U.S. Army-Kenner Army Cmty. Hosp., Ft. Lee, Va., 1994—; mem. resident rev. com. Meharry Med. Coll., Nashville, 1986-88. Dir. girls travel soccer Colonial Heights (Va.) Soccer Assn., 1994-96; v.p., scholarship chair Ctrl. Va. Soccer League, Richmond, Va., 1995—. Lt. col. U.S. Army, 1980—. Decorated Order Mil. Med. Merit. Fellow Am. Coll. Ob-gyn.; mem. Am. osteo. Assn., Assn. Mil. Osteo. Physicians and Surgeons, Jewish War Vets (life). Jewish. Home: 8719 Country View Ln Hopewell VA 23860

JOVE, RICHARD, molecular biologist; b. Barcelona, Cataluna, Spain, Feb. 5, 1955; came to U.S., 1960; s. Ricardo and Maria Rosa (Calmet) J.; m. Hua Yu, June 21, 1984. BA, SUNY, Buffalo, 1977, MS, 1978; M in Philosophy, Columbia U., 1981, PhD, 1984. Postdoctoral fellow Rockefeller U., N.Y.C., 1984-88; asst. prof. U. Mich., Ann Arbor, 1988-94, assoc. prof., 1994-95, dir. molecular oncology program Cancer Ctr., 1992-95; prof. U. So. Fla. Sch. of Med., Tampa, 1995—; dir. Molecular Oncology Program Moffitt Cancer Ctr. and Rsch. Inst., Tampa, 1995—. Recipient John S. Newberry prize

Columbia U., 1984, Jr. Faculty Rsch. award Am. Cancer Soc., 1988-91; Damon Runyon-Walter Winchell Cancer Fund fellow, 1984-87. Mem. The Harvey Soc., Sigma Xi. Office: U So Fla Moffitt Cancer Ctr 12902 Magnolia Dr Tampa FL 33612

JOWERS, RONNIE LEE, university health sciences center executive; b. Columbia, S.C., July 4, 1951; s. Talbert Joseph and Mary Helen (Reed) J.; m. Kay Byars, July 6, 1974; children: C. Ryan, Ivey Amanda. BA, Furman U., 1973; MBA, Clemson U., 1984. Acct., mortgage banker First Piedmont Mortgage Co., Greenville, S.C., 1972-76; fin. mgr. Greenville Hosp. System, 1976-80; bus. mgr. Greenville Gen. Hosp., 1980-81; adminstr., med. edn. Greenville Hosp. System, 1981-87; adminstrv. dept. medicine Emory U., Atlanta, 1987-91, assoc. v.p. for health affairs, 1991—; exec. adminstr. Emory U. System Health Care, 1995—, sec. joint conf. com.; co-mgr. Emory Med. Care Found., Atlanta, 1989-90; chmn. adv. coun. S.C. Consortium of Community Teaching Hosps., Charleston, S.C., 1982-86; adj. asst. prof. Med. U.S.C.;. Transp. chmn. Beat Leukemia Celebrity Classic, 1988—; mem. nat. planning com. Sr. Adminstrn. of Acad. Health Ctr. meetings; Sunday sch. tchr. Smoke Rise Bapt. Ch., Stone Mountain, Ga., 1989-94, deacon, 1991, fin. com. chmn., 1996—; treas. Greenville Hosp. Sys. Credit Union, 1980-84, pres., 1985. Mem. Am. Coll. Healthcare Execs. (assoc.), Acad. Health Ctrs. Assn., Beta Gamma Sigma. Baptist. Home: 810 Eagle Cove Way Lawrenceville GA 30244-5843

JOY, CHARLES RICHARD, psychiatrist; b. Cleve., Jan. 27, 1952; s. Charles Alexander and Esther Mary (Fischle) J.; m. Dawn Elizabeth Coburn, June 4, 1983; children: Nicole Genevieve, Veronica Elizabeth, Gregory Coburn. BA, Fordham U., 1974; MD, U. Pitts., 1978. Psychiat. intern Warren (Pa.) State Hosp., 1982-83; psychiat. resident W.Va. Univ. Hosp., Morgantown, 1983-87, chief psychiat. resident, 1986-87, child psychiatry fellow, 1985-87; psychiatrist Hamot Med. Ctr., Erie, Pa., 1987-88; psychiatrist Ctr. for Personal and Family Growth, Erie, 1988-89, med. dir., 1989-90; pvt. practice child and adolescent psychiatry Erie, 1990—; cons. psychiatrist Harborcreek Youth Svcs., Erie, 1987—. Democrat. Roman Catholic. Home: 4406 Sunnydale Blvd Erie PA 16509-1651 Office: 4 W 34th St Erie PA 16508-2812

JOY, EDWIN DOUGLAS, JR., oral and maxillofacial surgeon, educator; b. Bridgeport, Conn., June 15, 1933; s. Edwin Douglas and Bernadette Rose (Fagan) J.; m. Beverly Edwards, Aug. 29, 1953; children: Edwin Douglas III, David Michael. BA, Yale U., 1954; DDS, U. Pa., 1958. Diploamte Am. Bd. Oral and Maxillofacial Surgery. Intern Phila. Naval Hosp.; resident Med. Coll. Va., 1962-65; pvt. practice Norfolk, Va., 1965-72; assoc. prof. Med. Coll. Va., Richmond, 1972-75; prof. and chmn. oral and maxillofacial surgery dept. Med. Coll. Ga., Augusta, 1975—; cons. U.S. Army, 1975—, USN, 1975—, U.S. VA, 1975—. Contbr. articles to profl. jours. Comdr. USNR, 1955-92. Mem. Augusta Rowing Club (bd. dirs. 1993-95), Augusta Sailing Club (commodore 1990). Office: Med Coll Ga Oral and Maxillofacial Surg Dept 1120 15th St Augusta GA 30912-0004

JOY, MARILYN D., nurse; b. Rockford, Ill., Nov. 29, 1956. BSN, Viterbo Coll., 1978. RN, Ill.; cert. ACLS. Med.-surg., ICU nurse Rockford (Ill.) Meml. Hosp., 1978-80, 86-87; nurse, mgr. Willows Health Ctr., Rockford, 1980-86; cardiac ICU nurse St. Anthony Med. Ctr., Rockford, 1987-90; Medicare/home health nurse St. Therese Med. Ctr., Waukegan, Ill., 1991-95; ICU nurse Centegra No. Ill. Med. Ctr., McHenry, 1995—; resource nurse local ch., Rockford, 1984-86. Author poetry. Fellow Am. Biog. Inst. (award), Internat. Biog. Ctr. (award); mem. NAFE. Home: 4411 Sheffield Ct Gurnee IL 60031

JOYCE, REX MARION, surgeon; b. Garden City, Kans., Mar. 1, 1956; s. Lloyd Everett and Frances Pauline (Greathouse) J.; m. Kathleen LaRae Frazier, June 5, 1982; children: Lora Kathleen, Mary Elizabeth. BA, Kans. State U., 1978; MD, U. Kans., 1982. Diplomate Am. Bd. Surgery. Residency in surgery Mayo Clinic, Rochester, Minn., 1982-87; staff surgeon Rsch. Med. Ctr., Kansas City, Mo., 1987—; staff surgeon Menorrah Park Med. Ctr., Overland Park, Kans., 1994—. Fellow Am. Coll. Surgeons; mem. AMA, Phi Beta Kappa. Office: 6420 Prospect Ste 501 Kansas City MO 64132

JOYNER, CLAUDE REUBEN, JR., physician, medical educator; b. Winston-Salem, N.C., Dec. 4, 1925; s. Claude R. and Lytle (Mackie) J.; m. Nina Glenn Michael, Sept. 21, 1950; children: Emily Glenn, Claude Courtney. B.S., U. N.C., 1947; M.D., U. Pa., 1949. Intern Hosp. U. Pa., 1949-50; resident Bowman Grey Med. Sch., 1950; resident U. Pa., 1954-55, fellow in cardiology; Nat. Heart Inst. trainee, 1952-53; asst. instr. medicine Hosp. U. Pa., Phila., 1951-53; instr. Hosp. U. Pa., 1953-56, assoc. medicine, 1956-59, asst. prof., 1959-64, assoc. prof., 1964-72; prof. medicine U. Pitts., 1972-87; prof. medicine Med. Coll. Pa., 1987—, vice dean, 1989—; chief medicine Allegheny Gen. Hosp., Pitts., 1972—. Contbr. articles to profl. jours. Served to lt. M.C. USNR, 1950-52. Fellow Am. Coll. Cardiology, ACP, Councils on Circulation, Arteriosclerosis and Cardiovascular Radiology of Am. Heart Assn.; mem. AAAS, Am. Heart Assn., Am. Clin. and Climatol. Soc. Home: Pulpit Rock Little Sewickley Creek Rd Sewickley PA 15143 Office: Allegheny Gen Hosp Pittsburgh PA 15212

JOYNER, JO ANN, geriatrics nurse; b. Glenwood, Ga., Mar. 9, 1947; d. Roy and Lucille (Mercer) Powell; m. Henry Gene Lamb, Dec. 3, 1965 (div. 1984); children: Henry G. Lamb, Jr., Roy, Melinda, Jody; m. Robert Eugene Joyner, June 14, 1991. Diploma, Swainsboro Vocat./Tech., 1979; student, Ga. So. Coll., 1980. LPN, Ga. Staff nurse Meadows Meml. Hosp., Vidalia, Ga., 1980-82; staff nurse in ICU and critical care unit Toombs Alcohol and Drug Abuse Ctr., Vidalia, 1982-84; charge nurse Conners Nursing Home, Glenwood, Ga., 1984-85; supr. Bethany Nursing Ctr., Vidalia, 1990-92, charge nurse, 1985-92; nurse Claxton (Ga.) Nursing Home, Toombs Nursing and Intermediate Care Home, Lyons, Ga., 1992-93; staff nurse Laurens Convalescent Ctr., Dublin, Ga., 1994, 1994; staff nurse Meadow Brook Manor, 1994—, Dublin, 1994-95; relief house supervisor Dulinair Healthcare & Rehab. Ctr., Dublin, Ga., 1995-96; mem. ind. nursing registry, Claxton; nurse Meml. Med. Ctr., Savannah, Ga.; office nurse Montgomery County Correctional Inst., Mt. Vernon, Ga., Laurens Convalescent Ctr., 1994-95, Meadowbrook Manor, 1994—; 3-11 relief house supr., supr. medicare spl. unit, 1995-96. Democrat. Apostolic. Home: 315 Clover St Dublin GA 31021-7719

JOYNT, ROBERT JAMES, academic administrator; b. Le Mars, Iowa, Dec. 22, 1925. MD, 1952, PhD, 1963. Diplomate Am. Bd. Psychiatry and Neurology (past pres.). Intern Royal Victoria Hosp., Montreal, Que., Can., 1952-53; chief neurology Strong Meml. Hosp., Rochester, N.Y., 1966-84; assoc. U. Iowa, Iowa City, 1957-58, asst. prof. neurology, 1958-61, assoc. prof., 1961-66; prof., chmn. dept. neurology U. Rochester, 1966-84, dean Sch. Medicine and Dentistry, 1984-89, v.p. and vice provost for health affairs Sch. Medicine & Dentistry, 1989-94. Cambridge U. Fulbright scholar, 1953-54; USPHS neurology fellow, 1954-57. Mem. AMA (chief editor Arch Neurology 1982—), Am. Neurol. Assn. (past pres.), Am. Acad. Neurology (past pres.), Am. Electroencephalographic Soc., Royal Soc. Medicine, Inst. Medicine, Nat. Libr. of Medicine (bd. regents 1992—). Office: U Rochester Sch Medicine and Dentistry Dept Neurology Box 673 Rochester NY 14642

JUAREZ, ANTONIO, psychotherapist, consultant, counselor, educator; b. El Paso, Tex., Nov. 6, 1952; s. Juan Antonio and Amelia (Rivas) J. BS in Psychology, U.Tex.-El Paso, 1976, MA in Clin. Psychology, 1982; postgrad., N.Mex. State U., 1987—, Calif. Coast U., 1990—. Cert. counselor, clin. mental health counselor; lic. profl. counselor, Tex. Caseworker asst. El Paso Mental Health Ctr., 1978-79, caseworker III, 1982-83; clin. specialist S.W. Mental Health Ctr., Las Cruces, N.Mex., 1979-80; therapist, trainer S.W. Community House, El Paso, 1980-81; psychol. cons. El Paso Guidance Ctr., 1981-82, psychotherapist, 1983—, dir. N.E. svcs.; pvt. practice El Paso, 1987—; dir. Cross-Cultural Counseling Ctr., 1988—; instr. psychology El Paso C.C., 1988-90, counselor, cons.; cons. Citizens and Students Together, El Paso, 1983—, group facilitator Tai Chi Chuan Instr., Sun Valley Regional Hosp., El Paso, Tex., 1988; adj. prof. counseling Webster U., Ft. Bliss, Tex., 1995—. Mem. Latin Am. com. N.Mex. State U., 1985. Served with USAF, 1972-76. Fellow N.Mex. State U., 1981. Mem. U.S.-Mex. Border Health Assn., El Paso Psychol. Assn., Tex. Assn. for Counseling and Devel., Tex. Assn. for Children of Alcoholics, Am. Biographical Inst. Rsch. Assn., Golden Key Nat. Honor Soc. (N.Mex. state chpt.), Nat. Bd. For Cert. Counselors, Nat. Acad. For Clin. Mental Health Counselors, Ea. U.S.A. Martial Arts Assn. Democrat. Roman Catholic. Avocations: martial arts, playing stringed instruments. Home: PO Box 1493 Santa Teresa NM 88008-1493 Office: Cross-Cultural Counseling Ctr 2112 Trawood Dr # 3B El Paso TX 79935-3318

JUAREZ, MARETTA LIYA CALIMPONG, social worker; b. Gilroy, Calif., Feb. 14, 1958; d. Sulpicio Magsalay and Pelagia Lagotom (Viacrusis) Calimpong; m. Henry Juarez, Mar. 24, 1984. BA, U. Calif., Berkeley, 1979; MSW, San Jose State U., 1983. Lic. clin. social worker; cert. in eye movement desensitization and reprocessing. Mgr. Pacific Bell, San Jose, Calif., 1983-84; revenue officer IRS, Salinas, Calif., 1984-85; social worker Santa Cruz (Calif.) County, 1985, Santa Clara County, San Jose, 1985—; co-chair Inter-Agy. Coun. of South Santa Clara County. Recipient award Am. Legion, 1972. Mem. NASW, Nat. Coun. on Alcoholism, Assn. Play Therapists, No. Calif. Sandplay Soc., EMDR Network, South County Multidisciplinary Team (co-founder), Calif. Alumni, U. Calif. of Santa Clara County. Democrat. Roman Catholic.

JUAREZ-URIBE, JOEL, cardiologist, internist; b. Acapulco, Mex., Dec. 10, 1948; came to U.S., 1973; s. Joel and Gloria (Juarez-Uribe) Juarez-Guzman; m. Lourdes Sanchez, Sept. 1, 1971 (div. 1993); children: Joel, Jacob, Jessica, Alejandro; m. Mary Zella Jimenez, Feb. 1, 1993; children: Joel Joshua, Joelle-Maryzelle, Jarret Jordan, Joelly-Gloria. MD, U. Mex., Mexico City, 1973. Diplomate Am. Bd. Internal Medicine, Am. Bd. Cardiology. Pvt. practice Chula Vista, Calif., 1983—; cardiologist Sharp Hosp. of Chula Vista, 1983—, Scripps Hosp. of Chula Vista, 1983—, Paradise Valley Hosp., National City, Calif., 1983—. Fellow Am. Coll. Cardiology, Am. Coll. Chest Physicians. Office: Cardiology Med Clinic Ste 14 750 Medical Center Ct Chula Vista CA 91910

JUBALA, JOHN ARTHUR, psychologist; b. Chgo., Apr. 21, 1952; s. Arthur Joseph and Helen Victoria (Lapinski) J.; m. Julie L. Lambert, May 20, 1978; 1 child, Anna Zofia. BA, Ill. Benedictine Coll., Lisle, 1974; MA, Duquesne U., 1976, PhD, 1988. Lic. psychologist, Pa. Staff psychologist Harmarville Rehab. Ctr., Pitts., 1977-82, supr. psychology dept., 1982-85, asst. dir. psychology dept., 1985-87, dir. psychology dept., 1987-89; chief psychol. svcs. Mercy Hosp., Altoona, Pa., 1989—; instr. phys. medicine residency U. Pitts. Med. Sch., 1984-89. Contbr. chpts. to books. Bd. dirs. Am. Cancer Soc., Altoona, 1990. Mem. Am. Psychol. Assn., Pa. Psychol. Assn. (chair membership recruitment com. 1989-90), Cen. Pa. Psychol. Assn., Laurel Mountain Psychol. Assn. Roman Catholic. Home: 2807 Edgewood Dr Altoona PA 16602-3319 Office: Mercy Regional Health Sys 2500 7th Ave Altoona PA 16602-2099

JUDD, CATHERINE RUTH, physician assistant; b. Providence, May 30, 1948; d. William Warren and Ruth Anne (McCrillis) Hunt; m. David P. Judd, Dec. 30, 1972 (div. Aug. 1996). BA in Psychology, U. Maine, 1970; MS in Human Devel. and Counseling, Vanderbilt U., 1976; BS in Health Care Sci., U. Tex. Health Sci. Ctr., Dallas, 1983. Cert. physician asst. Nat. Commn. on Cert. Physician Assts. Psychiat. asst. psychiatry svc. Dallas VA Med. Ctr., 1984, coord. clin. rsch. and phase II clin. drug trials, 1985-87; coord. clin. rsch. Schizophrenia Rsch. Ctr. U. Tex. Southwestern Med. Sch., Dallas, 1987-89, faculty assoc. dept. psychiatry, 1989—, clin. asst. prof. health care sci., 1993—; coord. psychiatry admissions and referrals Zale Lipshy U. Hosp. at Southwestern Med. Ctr., 1989-95; mem. med. staff Zale Lipshy U. Hosp. U. Tex. Southwestern Med. Ctr., 1995—; lectr., spkr., rschr., presenter workshops in field. Contbr. numerous articles, abstracts to profl. publs. Bd. dirs. Women's Ctr. of Dallas, 1985-87; dir. vol. project counseling for battered women Parkland Meml. Hosp., 1985-87, vol. trainer and vol. counselor, 1985-89; mem. physician delegation Citizen to Citizen Ambassador Exch. to People's Republic of China, 1992. Recipient Outstanding Cmty. Svc. Provider award Dallas Alliance for Mentally Ill, 1991, cert. of appreciation Dallas County Mental Health Mental Retardation, 1992, Profl. Provider of Yr. award Tex. Alliance for mentally Ill, 1993. Mem. Am. Acad. Physician Assts. (del. to State of Tex. Ho. of Dels. 1993, 95), Tex. Acad. Physician Assts. (co-chair peer assistance com. 1993—, bd. dirs. 1995—), Nat. Alliance for mentally Ill, Dallas Alliance for Mentally Ill, Mental Health Assn. of Dallas, Coalition for Mentally Ill. Office: Southwestern Med Ctr U Tex 5323 Harry Hines Blvd Dallas TX 75235-9070

JUDD, DAVID EDWARD, therapist; b. Phila., Apr. 24, 1930; s. Edward William and Bertha Emma (Thomann) J.; A.B., Temple U., Phila., 1953; M.A., Am. U., 1959; Ph.D., U. Md., 1974; children—Peter, Erika. Tchr., then adminstr. Montgomery County (Md.) Public Schs., 1955-65, pupil personnel worker, 1965-84; mem. faculty U. Va.; ind. practice marriage and sex counseling. Served to capt. AUS, 1953-55. Fellow Am. Orthopsychiat. Assn.; mem. Am. Assn. Marriage and Family Therapists (clin. mem.), Am. Mental Health Counselors Assn., Am. Assn. Sex Educators, Counselors and Therapists (cert. sex counselor), Internat. Assn. Pupil Personnel Workers (editor jour.). Home and Office: 113 Columbia Ave Swarthmore PA 19081-1615

JUDGE, NANCY E., obstetrician, gynecologist; b. Holyoke, Mass., May 21, 1951; d. Martin P. and Barbara (Blou) J.; m. David B. Wood, Oct. 30, 1982; children: David, William, Elizabeth, Meredith. AB, Smith Coll., 1973; MD, U. Mass., 1977. Staff physician MetroHealth Med. Ctr. Case Western Res. U. Hosps., Cleve., 1981-90; dir. reproductive imaging ctr. Case Western Res. U. Hosps., 1990—, maternal-fetal medicine cons., 1990—; asst. prof. reproductive biology Case Western Res. U., 1981—; obstetrical advisor Regional Perinatal Network, Cleve., 1990—. Contbr. articles to profl. jours. Active Cleve. Art Mus., Playhouse Sq. Assn., Cleve. Children's Mus., Cleve. Garden Ctr. Fellow Am. Coll. Ob.-Gyn.; mem. Cleve. Ob.-Gyn. Soc. (asst. treas. 1994-95, treas. 1995). Office: Case Western Res U Hosp Dept Ob-Gyn 11000 Euclid Ave Ste 1200 Cleveland OH 44105

JUDSON, FRANKLYN NEVIN, physician, educator; b. Cleve., Apr. 14, 1942; s. Franklyn S. and Nancy Elizabeth (Nevin) J.; m. Kathleen A. Thompson, June 24, 1972 (div. 1977); m. Marti J. Sachse, Dec. 10, 1981; children: Jennifer, Rachel. BA, Wesleyan U., 1964; MD, U. Pa., 1968. Intern U. Wis. Hosps., Madison, 1968-69, resident, 1969-70; epidemic intelligence svc. officer Ctrs. Disease Control, Atlanta, 1970-72; fellow in infectious diseases U. Colo., Denver, 1972-74, from asst. prof. to assoc. prof. depts. medicine and preventive medicine, 1976-87, prof., 1987—; dir. Denver Disease Control Service, 1976-86; chief infectious disease service Denver Gen. Hosp., 1982—; dir. Dept. Pub. Health City of Denver, 1986—; pres. med. staff Denver Health, 1996—; chmn. anti-infectial agts. adv. com. FDA, 1993-95. Editor: Diagnosis of Sexually Transmitted Diseases, 1985; assoc. editor Sexually Transmitted Diseases, 1988—; mem. editorial bd. Genitourinary Medicine, 1984-94; contbr. articles to profl. jours. Pres. met. council Colo. chpt. Am. Lung Assn., Denver, 1988-90, bd. dirs.; pres. Coalition for A Tobacco Free Colo., 1995-96. Mem. Am. Veneral Disease Assn. (bd. dirs. 1981—, pres. 1983-85, Outstanding Investigator 1980), Am. Social Health Assn. (bd. dirs. 1983-90, v.p. 1987), Group Against Smokers' Pollution (bd. dirs., v.p. Colo. chpt. 1982—). Soc. of Friends. Home: 662 Josephine St Denver CO 80206-3723

JUENEMANN, SISTER JEAN, hospital executive, nun; b. St. Cloud, Minn., Nov. 19, 1936; d. Leo A. and Teresa M. (Oster) Juenemann. Diploma St. Cloud (Minn.) Sch. Nursing, 1957; student Coll. St. Benedict, 1957-59; BSN cum laude, Seattle U., 1967; MHA, U. Minn., 1977. Joined Order of St. Benedict, Roman Catholic Ch., 1959. Dir. nursing svc. Queen of Peace Hosp., New Prague, Minn., 1963-65, 67-77, asst. adminstr., 1967-77, CEO, 1977—; mem. bd. Bush Med. Fellows Program; spkr. at confs. Chmn. Cmty. Com. for Prevention Chem. Abuse, New Prague, 1975-80; bd. dirs. St. Cloud (Minn.) Hosp., St. Benedict's Coll., St. Joseph, Minn. Named participant Itasca Seminar on Leadership, Mpls. Found., 1979; Bush Found. summer fellow Cornell U., U. Calif., Berkeley, 1982. Fellow Am. Coll. Healthcare Execs.; mem. AAUW (past pres. New Prague chpt.), Am. Hosp. Assn. (CEO of Yr. 1989), Soc. Health care Planning & Mktg., Cath. Hosp. Assn., Women's Health Leadership Trust, New Prague Opportunities, Rotary (pres. New Prague chpt. 1994-95), Sigma Theta Tau. Avocations: working out, cooking.

JUHL, JOHN H., osteopath; b. N.Y.C., Jan. 23, 1960; s. Ernst Otto and Jacqueline (Evans) J. BA in Chemistry summa cum laude, CUNY, 1984; DO with honors, U. Medicine and Dentistry N.J., Stratford, 1988. Diplomate Am. Bd. Family Practice. Carptner, cabinetmaker, constrn. foreman, 1974-82; rotating intern St. Clare's Hosp. and Health Ctr., N.Y.C., 1988-89; resident in family practice St. Peter's Hosp.-U. Medicine and Dentistry N.J., New Brunswick, 1989-92; pvt. practice, N.Y.C., 1993—; lectr., presenter in field; peer reviewer low back pain guidelines AHCPR, 1994. Mem. AMA, Am. Acad. Family Practice, Am. Osteo. Assn., Am. Coll. Gen. Practitioners, Am. Acad. Osteopathy, Am. Osteo. Acad. Sports Medicine, N.J. Assn. Osteo. Physicians and Surgeons. Office: 625 Madison Ave Ste 10A New York NY 10022

JUKES, THOMAS HUGHES, biological chemist, educator; b. Hastings, Eng., Aug. 25, 1906; came to U.S., 1925, naturalized, 1939; s. Edward Hughes and Ann Mary (Barton) J.; m. Marguerite Esposito, July 2, 1942; children: Kenneth Hughes (dec. 1995), Caroline Elizabeth (Mrs. Nicholas Knueppel), Dorothy Mavis (Mrs. Robert Hudson). B.S.A., U. Toronto, 1930, Ph.D., 1933; NRC fellow med. scis., U. Calif. at Berkeley, 1933-34; D.Sc. (honoris causa), U. Guelph, 1972. Instr., asst. prof. U. Calif. at Davis, 1934-42; with pharm. div. Lederle Labs., 1942-45; dir. nutrition and physiology research sect. research div. Am. Cyanamid Co., Pearl River, N.Y., 1945-58; dir. research agrl. div. Am. Cyanamid Co., 1958-59, dir. biochemistry, 1960-62; vis. sr. research fellow in biochemistry Princeton, 1962-63; prof. dept. biophysics and med. physics U. Calif., Berkeley, 1963-91, prof. dept. integrative biology, 1991—, prof. emeritus nutritional scis., 1974—, rsch. biochemist Space Scis. Lab., 1963—, assoc. dir., 1968-70; cons. CWS, AUS, 1944-45, NASA, 1969-70; guest lectr. various univs.; Storer lectr. U. Calif. at Davis, 1973; Fred W. Tanner lectr. Inst. Food Technologists, 1979; vis. prof. U. Wis., River Falls, 1985; plenary lectr. Japanese Molecular Biology and Genetics Socs., Nagoya, 1986; cons. Calif. Cancer Adv. Council, 1981—; invited speaker Internat. Symposium on Evolution of Life, Kyoto, Japan, 1990. Author: B Vitamins for Blood Formation, 1952, Antibiotics in Nutrition, 1955, Molecules and Evolution, 1965; mem. editorial bds., Biochem. Genetics, BioSystems; biog. editor: Jour. Nutrition; assoc. editor: Jour. Molecular Evolution; Contbr. articles to profl. jours. Recipient Borden award Poultry Sci. Assn., 1947, Spencer award Am. Chem. Soc., 1976, Agrl. and Food Chemistry award, 1979, Disting. Svc. award Am. Agrl. Editors Assn., 1978, Cain Meml. award Am. Assn. Cancer Rsch., 1987, Klaus Schwartz commemorative medal Internat. Assn. Bioinorganic Scientists, 1988, Disting. Sci. Achievement award Am. Coun. on Sci. and Health, 1993, Disting. Scientist award Ctr. for Study of Evolution and Origin of Life, 1994. Fellow Am. Soc. Animal Sci., Poultry Sci. Assn., Am. Inst. Nutrition (coun. 1941-45, pub. affairs officer 1978-81, chmn. com. on history 1979-83), Calif. Acad. Scis.; mem. Internat. Coun. Sci. Unions (chmn. biology working group COSPAR 1978-80, chmn. interdisciplinary sci. commn. F 1980-84), Human Genome Orgn., Am. Soc. Biol. Chemists, Soc. for Exptl. Biology and Medicine, Am. Chem. Soc., Trustees for Conservation (San Francisco) (pres. 1970-71), Am. Alpine Club (Golden, Colo.), Explorers Club (N.Y.C.), Chit Chat Club (San Francisco), Sierra Club (San Francisco), Faculty Club (Berkeley, Calif.), Sigma Xi, Delta Tau Delta. Home: 170 Arlington Ave Kensington CA 94707-1135 Office: U Calif Space Scis Lab 6701 San Pablo Ave Oakland CA 94608-1239

JUKKOLA, GEORGE DUANE, obstetrician, gynecologist; b. Aliquippa, Pa., Feb. 28, 1945; s. Waino Helmer and Bedelia (Pyle) J.; m. Gretchen Louise Strom, Feb. 14, 1970 (div. 1984); children: David, Jeffrey; m. Wendee Leigh Bookhart, Apr. 23, 1988 (div. 1993). BA in Psychology, U. Calif., Berkeley, 1970; MD, U. Pitts., 1975. Diplomate Am. Bd. Ob-Gyn., Am. Bd. Quality Assurance Utilization Rev. Physicians. Caseworker Pa. Dept. Welfare, Rochester, 1971; resident in ob.-gyn. Akron (Ohio) Med. Ctr., 1975-78; pvt. practice Riverside, Calif., 1978—; co-founder Family Birthing Ctr., Riverside, 1981-87; mng. ptnr. Parkview Profl. Ctr., Riveside, 1984-93; chief dept. ob-gyn. Parkview Cmty. Hosp., Riverside, 1986-91, vice-chief of staff, 1992-93, chief of staff, 1994-96; chmn. ob-gyn dept. Moreno Valley Med. Ctr., 1991-93, dir. perinatal svcs., 1992-94, mem.-at-large exec. com., 1996, mem. CMA survey team, 1992—; guest lectr. Riverside Cmty. Coll., 1984, 85; health care adv. com. 43d Congl. Dist., Calif., 1994—; mem. Riverside County Fetal-Infant Mortality Com., 1994—. With USAF, 1965-69. Decorated Air medal with 4 oak leaf clusters. Fellow ACOG; mem. AMA, Am. Coll. Physician Execs., Calif. Med. Assn., Riverside County Med. Assn., Am. Assn. Individual Investors, Victoria Club Riverside, Inland Physicians Med. Group (v.p. 1987-88), Mensa. Republican. Unitarian-Universalist. Home: 10252 Victoria Ave Riverside CA 92503-6100 Office: 3900 Sherman Sr Ste F Riverside CA 92503-4062

JUKOFSKY, S. LAWRENCE, ophthalmologist; b. Hackensack, N.J., Mar. 13, 1925; s. I. and Rosella (Meltzer) J.; m. Betsy Anne Cushing, Dec. 1947; children: Michael Alan, Diane Jukofsky Wille. BA, Columbia U., 1944; MD, N.Y. Med. Coll., 1948. Diplomate Am. Bd. Ophthalmology. Resident in ophthalmology Washington U., St. Louis, 1949-51; intern Hackensack (N.J.) Hosp., 1948-49; chief ophthalmology dept. Pascack Valley Hosp., Westwood, N.J., 1959-78; attending ophthalmologist Hilton Head (S.C.) Hosp., 1978-84, cons., 1984—; chief Home Eye Care, Hilton Head, 1990—; participant Ophthalmologists For Vols. In Medicine clinic. Lt. comdr. USNR, 1951-53, Korea. Fellow ACS; mem. Rotary Internat. Republican. Hebrew. Home and Office: 36 Angelwing Dr Hilton Head Island SC 29926-1903

JULANDER, PAULA FOIL, professional society administrator; b. Charlotte, N.C., Jan. 21, 1939; d. Paul Baxter and Esther Irene (Earnhardt) Foil; m. Roydon Odell Julander, Dec. 21, 1985; 1 child, Julie McMahan Shipman. Diploma, Presbyn. Hosp. Sch. Nursing, Charlotte, N.C., 1960; BS magna cum laude, U. Utah, 1984; MS in Nursing Adminstrn., Brigham Young U., 1990. RN, Utah. Nurse various positions Fla. and S.C., 1960-66; co-founder, office mgr. Am. Laser Corp., 1970-79; gen. staff nurseoper. rm. Salt Lake Surg. Ctr., Salt Lake City, 1976-79; self employed Salt Lake City; teaching asst. U. Utah, Salt Lake City; rep. Utah State Legislature Coms., 1989-92; demo. nominee lt. gov., 1992; adj. faculty Brigham Young U. Coll. Nursing, 1987—, clin. asst. prof. of nursing, 1996—; bd. dirs. Block Fin. Svcs.; mem. Utah state exec. bd. U.S. West Comm., 1993-96; bd. regents Calif. Luth. U., 1994. Pres. Utah Nurses Found., 1986-88; mem. Statewide Task Force on Child Sexual Abuse, 1989-90, Utah Nursing Resource Study, 1985-96, State Feasibility Task Force for Nurses, 1985-96, Women's Polit. Caucus, Statewide Abortion Task Force, 1990; bd. dirs. Community Nursing Svc. Home Health Plus, 1992-94; trustee Westminster Coll., 1994—, HCA-St. Mark's Hosp., 1994-95. Mem. ANA (del. conv. 1986-90), LWV, Utah Nurses Assn. (legis. rep. 1987-88, pres.), Nat. Orgn. Women Legislators, Sigma Theta Tau, Phi Kappa Phi (Susan Young Gates award 1991). Home: 1467 Penrose Dr Salt Lake City UT 84103-4466 Office: Utah Nurses Assn 455 E 400 S Ste 402 Salt Lake City UT 84111-3008

JULESZ, BELA, experimental psychologist, educator, electrical engineer; b. Budapest, Hungary, Feb. 19, 1928; came to U.S., 1956; s. Jeno and Klementin (Fleiner) J.; m. Margit Fasy, Aug. 7, 1953. Dipl. Elec. Engring., Tech. U., Budapest, 1950; Dr. Ing., Hungarian Acad. Sci., Budapest, 1956. Asst. prof. dept. communication Tech U. Budapest, Hungary, 1950-51; mem. tech. staff Telecommunication Research Inst., Budapest, 1951-56; mem. tech. staff Bell Labs., Murray Hill, N.J., 1956-64, head sensory and perceptual processes, 1964-83; rsch. head visual perception rsch. AT&T Bell Labs., Murray Hill, N.J., 1984-89; State of N.J. prof. psychology, dir. lab. of vision rsch. Rutgers U., Piscataway, N.J., 1989—; continuing vis. prof. biology dept. Calif. Inst. Tech., Pasadena, 1985-94. Author: Foundations of Cyclopean Perception, 1971, Dialogues on Perception, 1995; author over 200 sci. papers on visual perception; discover computer generated random-dot stereogram technique. Fairchild disting. scholar Calif. Inst. Tech., 1977-79, 87, assoc. Neurosci. Research Progam, 1982; MacArthur Found. fellow, 1983-87; Dr. H.P. Heineken prize Royal Netherlands Acad. Arts and Scis., 1985; Karl Spencer Lashley award Am. Philos. Soc., 1989. Fellow AAAS, Am. Acad. Arts and Scis., Optical Soc. Am.; mem. NAS, Goettingen Acad. Scis. (corr.), Hungarian Acad. Scis. (hon.), Am. Philos. Soc. Home: 30 Valleyview Rd Warren NJ 07059-5229 Office: Rutgers U Lab Vision Rsch Psychology Bldg Busch Campus Piscataway NJ 08854

JULIAN, SYDNEY R., urologist; b. Buffalo, May 28, 1936; s. Sydney Robert and Helen Louise (Miller) J.; m. Ann Sigrid Kalijarvi, Aug. 25, 1956; children: Karen, Robert, Christopher, Jennifer. AB, Columbia U., 1957; MD, U. Tex., 1960. Diplomate Am. Bd. Urology. From intern to chief urology USN, Orlando, 1960-71; pvt. practice urology Fresno, Calif., 1971—. Fellow Am. Coll. Surgeons. Home: 13723 Killarney Dr Madera CA 93638 Office: 1313 E Herndon Fresno CA 93720

JULIANO, RUDOLPH L., medical educator; b. July 18, 1941. BS in Physics, Cornell U., 1963; PhD in Biophysics, U. Rochester, 1971; post grad. dept. experimental pathology, Roswell Park Mem. Inst., 1971-72. Investigator Hosp. for Sick Children, Ont., Can., 1972-78; asst. prof. dept. med. biophysics U. Toronto, Can., 1973-78; assoc. prof. dept. pharmacology U. Tex. Med. Sch., Houston, 1978-82, prof., 1982-86; prof., chair dept. pharmacology U. N.C., Chapel Hill, 1986—; part-time asst. prof. dept. biology SUNY, 1971-72. Author: Drug Delivery Systems: Characteristics and Biomedical Applications, 1981, Biological Approaches to the Controlled Delivery of Drugs, 1987, Targeted Drug Delivery, 1991; co-author: Cell Surface Glycoproteins: Structure, Biosynthesis and Biological Functions, 1979; mem. editl. bd. Jour. Cell Biology, Antisense Rsch. and Devel., Cell Adhesion and Communication, Pharmaceutical Rsch.; editor Advanced Drug Delivery Reviews; assoc. editor Cancer Rsch.; contbr. over 100 articles to profl. pubs. including Life Sci., Biochemistry, Experimental Cell Rsch., others.; contbr. chpts. to books including Adhesion Receptors as Therapeutic Targets, Delivery of Protein Drugs, Prolonged Arrest of Cancer, also others; patentee in field. Tchr., cmty. devel. organizer U.S. Peace Corps., Philippines, 1964-66. NIH fellow in biophysics, 1966-70, Internat. Union Against Cancer Travel fellow, 1978, Fogarty Sr. Internat. fellow Cambridge U., England, 1993; ACS grantee, 1992-95, NIH grantee, 1992-96, 89-94, 92-97, 94-97. Mem. Am. Soc. Cell Biology, Am. Soc. Pharmacology and Experimental Therapeutics, Am. Assn. Cancer Rsch., Assn. Med. Sch. Pharmacology. Home: 408 Lyons Rd Chapel Hill NC 27514*

JULIEN, ROBERT MICHAEL, anesthesiologist, author; b. Port Townsend, Wash., Mar. 24, 1942; s. Frank Felton and Mary Grace (Powers) J.; m. Judith Dianne DeChenne, Feb. 26, 1963; children: Robert Michael, Scott M. BS in Pharmacy, U. Wash., 1965, MS in Pharmacology, 1968, PhD, 1970; MD, U. Calif.-Irvine, 1977. Intern, Good Samaritan Hosp., Portland, Oreg., 1977-78; resident Oreg. Health Scis. U., 1978-80; asst. prof. pharmacology U. Calif.-Irvine, 1970-74, asst. clin. prof., 1974-77; assoc. prof. anesthesiology and pharmacology U. Oreg., Portland, 1980-83; staff anesthesiologist St. Vincent Hosp., Portland, 1983—. Author: Primer of Drug Action, 1975, 7th edit., 1995, Understanding Anesthesiology, 1984., Drugs and the Body, 1987. Recipient Service award Am. Epilepsy Soc., 1975. Mem. Am. Soc. Anesthesiologists, Am. Assn. Pharmacology and Exptl. Therapeutics, Soc. Neurosci., Oreg. Med. Assn., Western Pharmacology Soc. Roman Catholic. Club: Oswego Lake (Lake Oswego, Oreg.). Home: 1212 SW Hessler Dr Portland OR 97201-2807 Office: St Vincent Hosp Dept Anesthesia 9205 SW Barnes Rd Portland OR 97225-6622

JULIUS, STEVO, physician, educator, physiologist; b. Kovin, Yugoslavia, Apr. 15, 1929; came to U.S., 1965, naturalized, 1971; s. Dezider and Jelena (Engel) J.; m. Susan P. Durrant, Sept. 17, 1971; children: Nicholas, Natasha. M.D., U. Zagreb, 1953, Sc.D., 1964; M.D. (hon.), U. Goteborg, Sweden, 1979. Intern, then resident in internal medicine Univ. Hosp., Zagreb, 1953-60; sr. instr. internal medicine Univ. Hosp., 1962-64; research asst. U. Mich. Med. Sch., 1961-62, mem. faculty, 1965—, prof. internal medicine, 1974—, assoc. prof. physiology, 1980-83, prof. physiology, 1983—, chief divsn. hypertension, 1974—. Co-editor: The Nervous System in Arterial Hypertension, 1976; contbr. articles med. jours. Fellow Am. Coll. Cardiology; mem. Internat. Soc. Hypertension (v.p., Astra award 1984), Interam. Soc. Hypertension (treas. 1978-83), Am. Heart Assn. (couns. high blood pressure rsch. and epidemiology, life achievement award coun. for high blood pressure 1994), Am. Physiol. Soc. (adv. bd.), Am. Fedn. Clin. Rsch., Soc. Exptl. Biology and Medicine, Coun. for High Blood Pressure Rsch. (adv. bd.). Office: Univ Mich Med Sch Div Hypertension 3918 Taubman Ctr Ann Arbor MI 48109-0356

JUMA, FRANCIS DOIL, physician, pharmacologist, consultant; b. Busia, We. Province, Kenya, May 5, 1949; s. John Wesonga Sulwe and Tecla Wesonga (Songoro) Nafula; m. Imelda Muramba Aswani, July 11th, 1976; children: Caroline, Miriam, Howard, Tom. MBChB, MBI, Nairobi, 1975; PhD, London, 1980; MIBiol (hon.), Eng., 1981, CBiol (hon.), 1984; MD, MBI, Nairobi, 1996. Med. officer Ministry Health, Kenya, 1975-76, med. officer health, 1976-77; rsch. fellow U. London WHO, 1977-80; rsch. fellow, vis. scholar Cambridge U. WHO, Eng., 1978; rsch. fellow, vis. scholar Johns Hopkins U. WHO, Balt., 1979; from lectr. to prof. U. Nairobi, 1981—; registrar (hon.) Brit. Poison Ctr., London, 1977-80; cons. (hon.) Kenyatta nat. Hosp., Kenya, 1981—; mem. expert panel WHO, Geneva, 1994—. Author: (textbook) Essential Clin. Pharmacology, 1988, Essential Drug List, 1993, African Forum for Health Scientists, 1995; chmn. editl. bd. New African Jour. Medicine, 1994. Mem. Internat. Rescue Com. Physicians, Iisxenobiotics (hon), Socepta (sec. gen. 1989—). Home: Menelik Rd PO Box 48439, Nairobi Kenya Office: Nairobi U Med Sch, PO Box 19676, Nairobi Kenya

JUNG, ANDRÉ, internist; b. Geneva, Oct. 9, 1939; s. Charles and Anna (Schifrin) J.; m. Agnes Sideris, Aug. 6, 1973; children: Michel, Anne. BS in Math., U. Geneva, 1962, MD, 1965. Intern, resident, Geneva, Basle, Berne, Switzerland; chargé de recherche Geneva U., 1977-81; head med. dept. City Hosp., Nyon, Switzerland, 1981—; rsch. fellow Mass. Gen. Hosp., Boston and London. Contbr. numerous articles to profl. jours. Mem. Soc. Internal Medicine, European Soc. Intensive Care Medicine, Swiss Soc. Intensive Care Medicine, Swiss Soc. Tropical Medicine, also others. Mem. Orthodox Ch. Home: 1 Ch de l'Escalade, 1206 Geneva Switzerland Office: Hopital de Zone, Ch Monastier 8, 1260 Nyon Switzerland

JUNG, TIMOTHY TAE KUN, otolaryngologist; b. Seoul, Korea, Dec. 1, 1943; came to U.S., 1969; s. Yoon Yong and Helen Chung-Hyuk (Im) J.; m. Lucy Moon Young, Sept. 10, 1972; children: David, Michael, Karen. BS, Seoul Nat. U., 1966, Loma Linda U., 1971; MD, Loma Linda U., 1974; PhD, U. Minn., 1980. Diplomate, Am. Bd. Otolaryngology. Med. intern Loma Linda (Calif.) U. Med. Ctr., 1974-75; resident in surgery U. Minn. Med. Sch., Mpls., 1975-76; resident in otolaryngology U. Minn. Med. Sch., 1976-80, asst. prof. otolaryngology, 1980-84, clin. asst. prof., dir. prostaglandin lab., 1984-85; assoc. prof., dir. otolaryngology rsch. Loma Linda U., 1985-90, prof., dir. otolaryngology rsch., 1990-92, clin. prof., assoc. dir. otolaryngology rsch., 1992—; mem. deafness and communications disorders rev. com. Nat. Inst. Deafness and Communications, NIH, 1989-92. Bd. editors Annals of Otology, Rhinology & Laryngology, 1994—; contbr. numerous chpts. to med. books, over 100 articles and abstracts to med. jours. Sgt. Korean army, 1966-69. Recipient Edmund Price Fowler award. Fellow ACS, Triological Soc., Am. Acad. Otolaryngology (honor award 1990); mem. AMA, Am. Otol. Soc., Am. Neurol. Soc., Soc. Univ. Otolaryngologists, Assn. Rsch. in Otolaryngology, Centurions, Collegium Otorhinolaryngogicum Amicetiae Sacrum, N.Am. Skull Base Soc., Alpha Omega Alpha. Seventh-day Adventist. Home: 11790 Pecan Way Loma Linda CA 92354-3452 Office: 3975 Jackson St Ste 202 Riverside CA 92503-3947

JUNGNICKEL, PAUL WAYNE, pharmacist; b. Forest Grove, Oreg., Mar. 19, 1949; s. Raymond Harold and Mary Margurette (Fenimore) J.; m. Mariann Ruth Dykstra, Feb. 27, 1982. BS, Oregon State U., 1972; MS, U. Kans., 1975; PhD, U. Nebr., 1993. Registered pharmacist Oreg., Nebr. Clin. pharmacy intern VA Med. Ctr., Portland, Oreg., 1972-73; pharmacy resident U. Kans. Med. Ctr., Kansas City, 1973-75; asst. dir. pharmacy Good Samaritan Med. Ctr., Portland, 1975-77; patient care pharmacist Holladay Park Hosp., Portland, 1977-85; instr. pharmacy U. Nebr. Med. Ctr., Omaha, 1983-85, asst. prof. pharmacy, 1985-95, assoc. prof., 1995—. Contbr. articles to profl. jours., chpts. to books. Mem. Am. Pharm. Assn., Am. Assn. Colls. of Pharmacy (PEP SIG chair 1992-93), Am. Soc. Health System Pharmacists, Assn. for Study of Higher Edn., Phi Kappa Phi, Rho Chi. Office: U Nebr Med Ctr 600 S 42d Omaha NE 68198-6045

JUNOD, DANIEL AUGUST, podiatrist; b. Vandalia, Ill., Sept. 12, 1928; s. Louis August and Nettie Louise (Martin) J.; m. Joanne Alice Denton, Mar. 29, 1952; children: Paul, John, Timothy, David, Stephen. Student, Greenville (Ill.) Coll., 1946-48; DPM, Scholl Coll. Podiatric Med., Chgo., 1952. Lic. podiatric physician, Ill. Pvt. practice podiatrist Greenville, 1952—; staff podiatrist Fair Oaks Nursing Home, Greenville, 1970—, Brauns Terrace, Greenville, 1989—, Faith Countryside Homes Nursing Ctr., Highland, Ill., 1992—, Highland (Ill.) Health Care Ctr., 1993—; staff podiatrist 25 different nursing homes in several south ctrl. Ill. cities, many yrs. Contbr. articles to profl. jours. Home: 511 S 2d St Greenville IL 62246-1742 Office: 309 W College Ave PO Drawer 697 Greenville IL 62246-0697

JURAND, JERRY GEORGE, periodontology educator, researcher; b. Gostyn, Piaski, Poland, Apr. 23, 1923; came to U.S., 1956; s. Piotr and Maria (Mizerska) J.; m. Ruth Edith I. Kujus, 1950; children: Lydia U., Robert B., Darlene S. Diploma, Polish Humanistic Lyceum, Ingolstad, Germany, 1947; Dr.Med.Dent., Friedrich Alexander U., Erlangen, Germany, 1956; DDS, U. Tenn., Memphis, 1965. Cancer rsch. scientist in biochemistry Roswell Park Meml. Inst., Buffalo, 1957-62; rsch. assoc. in immunology St. Jude Children's Rsch. Hosp., Memphis, 1962-65; assoc. prof. periodontology U. Tenn., Memphis, 1965-70, prof. periodontology, 1970—, rsch. dir. in periodontology, 1965-75, clinic dir. in periodontology, 1975-80; cons. in periodontics St. Jude Children's Rsch. Hosp., 1965—. Contbr. to book: Surface Chemistry and Dental Integuments, 1973; contbr. articles to profl. jours. Advisor Boy Scouts Am., Memphis, 1965-75; discussion panelist Amnesty Internat., Memphis, 1982. Capt. Dental Corps U.S. Army, 1953-56. NIH rsch. grantee, 1965-75. Mem. ADA (life), AAAS, Am. Assn. Dental Rsch. (life), Internat. Assn. Dental Rsch. (life), N.Y. Acad. Scis. Office: U Tenn Coll Dentistry 875 Union Ave Memphis TN 38163

JURKA, EDITH MILA, psychiatrist, researcher; b. N.Y.C., Dec. 4, 1915; d. Charles Anton and Edith Dorothy (Schevcik) J. BA, Smith Coll., 1936; postgrad., Charles U., Prague, Czechoslovakia, 1936-38; MD, Yale U., 1944. Diplomate Am. Bd. Psychiatry and Neurology. Intern in children's med. svc. Bellevue Hosp., N.Y.C., 1944-45, asst. alienist, 1947-49; rotating intern Gallinger Hosp., Washington, 1945-46; intern N.Y. State Psychiat. Inst., N.Y.C., 1946-47; asst. psychiatrist Mt. Sinai Hosp., N.Y.C., 1949-51; pvt. practice N.Y.C., 1949—; asst. psychiatrist Roosevelt Hosp., N.Y.C., 1954-57; chief psychiatrist Pleasantville (N.Y.) Cottage Sch., 1961-74; bd. dirs. intuition network Inst. Noetic Scis.; dir. Wind Song Programs. Fellow Am. Orthopsychiat. Assn.; mem. Am. Psychiat. Assn., N.Y. Coun. Child and Adolescent Psychiatry, N.Y. County Med. Soc., N.Y. State Med. Soc., Westchester Psychiat. Soc. Home: 16 Apple Bee Farm Ln Croton On Hudson NY 10520 Office: 116 E 66th St New York NY 10021-6547

JURKIEWICZ, MAURICE JOHN, surgeon, educator; b. Claremont, N.H., Sept. 24, 1923; s. Charles B. and Mary (Ostrowska) J.; m. Mary de Forest Freeman, July 7, 1951; children—Elizabeth de Forest, John Christopher. D.D.S. magna cum laude, U. Md., 1946; M.D., Harvard U., 1952. Diplomate: Am. Bd. Surgery, Am. Bd. Plastic Surgery (mem. bd. 1971-77, chmn. 1977-78). Intern Barnes Hosp., Washington U., St. Louis, 1952-53; resident Barnes Hosp., Washington U., 1953-58, clin. fellow, 1958-59, instr. surgery, 1957-59; mem. staff U. Fla. Hosp., Gainesville; asst. prof. surgery U. Fla., 1959-64, assoc. prof., 1964-67, prof., 1967-71, chief div. plastic and reconstructive surgery, 1959-71; chief of surgery VA Hosp., Gainesville, 1968-71; prof. surgery, chief of plastic and reconstructive surgery Emory Affiliated Hosps., Atlanta, 1971-92; chief surg. services Grady Meml. Hosp., Atlanta, 1972-77; chief of surgery VAMC, Atlanta, 1989-93; cons. in plastic surgery Walter Reed Gen. Hosp., Washington, 1971-91; sci. counselor Nat. Inst. Dental Rsch., 1966-71; chmn. com. on study of evaluation procedures Am. Bd. Med. Spltys., 1979-81; mem. at large Nat. Bd. Med. Exams., 1989-93; commr. Joint Commn. on Accreditation of Health Care Orgns., 1985-94 (sec. 1989-90, treas. 1990-91, vice chmn. 1991-92), Nat. Cons. in Plastic Surgery to the Shriners Hosp., 1995—. Editor: Operative Techniques in Plastic Surgery, 1994—; assoc. editor: Plastic and Reconstructive Surgery, 1972-78, 79-83, co-editor, 1985-89; assoc. editor Am. Surgeon, 1977—. Served to lt. (j.g.) USNR, 1946-48. Fellow Royal Australasian Coll. Surgeons (hon.); mem. AMA, Am. Cancer Soc., Am. Cleft Palate Assn., ACS (bd. regents 1979-88, vice chmn. 1985-88, pres.-elect 1988, pres. 1989-90), Am. Soc. Plastic and Reconstructive Surgeons, Southeastern Soc. Plastic and Reconstructive Surgeons, Ga. Soc. Plastic and Reconstructive Surgeons, Southeastern Surg. Congress, Am. Soc. Head and NEck Surgeons (pres. 1989), Ednl. Founds. Plastic Surgery Coun., Am. Assn. Plastic Surgeons (pres. 1989-81), Am. So, surg assns. (1st v.p. 1993-94), Med. Assn. Ga. Home: 715 Old Post Rd NW Atlanta GA 30328-4758 Office: Emory U Clinic 25 Prescott St NE Atlanta GA 30308-2209

JURTSHUK, PETER, JR., microbiologist; b. N.Y.C., July 28, 1929; s. Peter and Mary (Ferens) J.; m. Rebecca Jones, Jan. 2, 1971; children: Peter, Larissa. A.B., NYU, 1951; M.S., Creighton U., 1953; Ph.D., U. Md., 1957. Asst. prof. pharmacology Bklyn. Coll. Pharmacy, L.I. U., 1957-59; asst. prof. enzyme chemistry U. Wis.-Madison, 1962-63; asst. prof. microbiology U. Tex., Austin, 1963-69; assoc. prof. biology U. Houston, 1970-76, prof., 1976—, dir. program in microbiology, 1990—; mem. vis. biol. program Am. Inst. Biol. Scis., 1969-72. Contbr. chpts. to books. Recipient Disting. Service award Am. Soc. Microbiology, 1982; NIH grantee, 1964-75; NSF grantee, 1986-89. Fellow Am. Acad. Microbiology; mem. Am. Soc. Microbiology (pres. Tex. br. 1972-74), N.Y. Acad. Scis., Am. Soc. Biol. Chemists, Am. Chem. Soc., Sigma Xi (pres. U. Houston chpt. 1979-80). Russian Orthodox. Home: 879 Ramada Dr Houston TX 77062-5607 Office: U Houston Biology Dept Houston TX 77204

JUSKO, WILLIAM JOSEPH, pharmaceutical scientist, educator; b. Salamanca, N.Y., Oct. 26, 1942; s. Joseph Chester and Pauline Helen (Wrona) J.; m. Laura Jean Gillett, May 30, 1964; children: Suzanne, Marjorie, Katherine. BS in Pharmacy, SUNY, Buffalo, 1965, PhD, 1970; Doctor Honoris Causa, Med. Acad. of Cracow, Poland, 1987. Rsch. pharmacologist VA Hosp., Boston, 1969-72; asst. prof. Boston U. Sch. Medicine, 1970-72; asst. prof. SUNY, Buffalo, 1972-74, assoc. prof., 1974-77, prof., 1977—; dir. Clin. Pharmacokinetics Lab., Buffalo, 1972-81; vis. scientist Mario Negri Inst. for Pharmacology, Milan, 1978-79; cons. Wyeth Labs., Radnor, Pa., 1976—, various other cos., 1980—. Editor: (book) Applied Pharmacokinetics, 1980, 2d rev. edit., 1992; contbr. numerous rsch. articles to profl. jours. Recipient Rorer award Am. Coll. Gastroenterology, Toronto, Can., 1980. Fellow AAAS, Am. Assn. Pharm. Sci., Am. Coll. Clin. Pharmacology (Russell Miller award 1988), Am. Coll. Clin. Pharmacy (Disting. Svc. award 1989); mem. Am. Soc. Clin. Pharm. Therapy (Rawls-Palmer award 1987). Office: SUNY Sch Pharmacy Buffalo NY 14226

JUSTESEN, DON ROBERT, psychologist; b. Salt Lake City, Mar. 8, 1930; s. Richard Carvel and Elizabeth Agnes (Gustafson) J.; m. Patricia Ann Larson, Feb. 14, 1957; children: Lyle Richard, Jonille Jacelyn, Tracy Ann, Anthony Ray. BA in Psychology and Philosophy, U. Utah, 1955, MA, 1957, Ph.D., 1960. Asst. prof., chmn. dept. psychology Westminster Coll., Salt Lake City, 1959-62; lectr. to prof. dept. psychology U. Mo.-Kansas City, 1963-75; vis. prof. U. Colo., Boulder, 1965; asst. prof. to prof. dept. psychiatry U. Kans. Sch. Medicine, Kansas City, 1963—; dir. behavioral radiology labs. VA Med. Ctr., Kansas City, 1962-95; cons. Nat. Coun. on Radiation Protection and Measurements, Washington, 1977—, EPA, NAS, NIH, NSF, USN, 1972-95, to assocs. programs NRC/NAS, 1988-94. Contbr. articles to profl. jours.; assoc. editor Jour. Microwave Power and Electromagnetic Energy, 1975-88; editor Spl. Supplements to Radio Sci., Washington, 1977-79; editor in chief Bioelectromagnetics, 1988-93; mem. editorial bd. Bioelectromagnetics Soc., 1979-83, 88-93. Pres. Fountains Homes Assn., Grandview, Mo., 1974-75. Served with USN, 1948-52, ATO; served to lt. USNR, 1962-65. Recipient First Cash prize in psychopharmacology Am. Psychol. Assn., 1968; VA Research Career Scientist, 1980; USPHS grantee, 1971-86. Fellow AAAS, APA, Am. Psychol. Soc.; mem. IEEE (sr.), Soc. for Neurosci., Bioelectromagnetics Soc. (pres. 1984-85), Brit. Soc. Philosophy of Sci., Nat. Acad. Sci., Internat. Union Radio Sci. (U.S. nat. com., commn. on metrology). Home: 12416 Ewing Ave Grandview MO 64030-1834

JUSTICE, (DAVID) BLAIR, psychology educator, author; b. Dallas, July 2, 1927; s. Sam Hugh and Lou-Reine (Hunter) J.; m. Rita Norwood, July 26, 1972; children: Cynthia, David, Elizabeth. BA, U. Tex., Austin, 1948; MS, Columbia U., 1949; MA, Tex. Christian U., 1963; PhD, Rice U., 1966. Diplomate Am. Bd. Med. Psychotherapists. Reporter Ft. Worth Star-Telegram, 1952-55; sci. writer N.Y. Daily News, 1955-56, Ft. Worth Star-Telegram, 1956-64; sci. editor, columnist Houston Post, 1964-73; exec. asst. to Mayor Houston, 1966-72; prof. psychology Sch. Pub. Health, U. Tex., Houston, 1968—; assoc. dean for acad. affairs U. Tex., Sch. Pub. Health, Houston, 1994—; dir. Project Support, Imagery & Immune Function in Breast Cancer, 1993—; co-investigator Alt. Medicine Ctr. for Cancer Rsch. U. Tex. Sch. Pub. Health, Houston, 1995—; co-investigator U. Tex. Ctr. for Alternative Med. Cancer Rsch.; sr. psychologist, group therapist, psychiat. residency faculty Tex. Rsch. Inst. Mental Scis., 1973-85; cmty. assoc. Rice U., Lovett Coll.; cons. child abuse Tex. Dept. Human Resources; faculty assoc. Ctr. for Health Promotion, R & D, U. Tex. Health Sci. Ctr., mem. inter-faculty coun., 1991-92; dir. Ctr. for Prevention of Violence and Injury, 1987-89, chmn. faculty Sch. of Pub. Health, 1990-91, chmn. faculty policy com., 1989-90, faculty marshal, 1990, mem. exec. com., 1991-93, vice chair interfaculty coun., 1992-93; vis. scholar U. Colo., 1990—; founding assoc. Blaffer Gallery U. Houston. Author: Violence in the City, 1969, Detection of Potential Community Violence, 1967, (with Rita Justice) The Abusing Family, 1976, The Broken Taboo: Sex in the Family, 1979, Perspectives in Public Mental Health, 1982, Who Gets Sick: Thinking and Health, 1987, Who Gets Sick: How Beliefs, Moods and Thoughts Affect Your Health, 1988, The Abusing Family, rev. edit., 1990; editor: Your Child's Behavior, 1972; editorial bd.: Internat. Jour Mental Health, 1980—. Gen. chmn. Houston Job Fair, 1967-73; chmn. Houston Manpower Area Planning Council, 1972-74; mem. Tex. Urban Devel. Commn., 1970-72; bd. dirs. Houston Housing Devel. Corp., Tex. Citizens Human Devel., 1979-84, Greater Houston Com. Prevention of Child Abuse, 1982-88; sec. bd. mgrs. Tarrant County Hosp., Dist., 1961-64; pres. Greater Houston Youth Council, 1978-79, Houston Area Council on Sudden Infant Death Syndrome, 1977-78; mem. nat. adv. com. Marine Biomed. Inst., U. Tex. Med. Br., 1971-84; mem. Office of Minority Affairs, Resource Persons Network, HHS, 1988—; mem. community bd. Tex. Youth Council; vestry, chmn. adult edn. St. John The Divine Episc. Ch., 1984-88. Served with USNR, 1945-46. Recipient most outstanding book award Tex. Writers Roundup, 1970, award of recognition City of Houston, 1973, Benjamin Franklin Book award Pubs. Mktg. Assn. Am., 1988, Excellence in Media award Am. Psychol. Assn., 1988, Friends of Fondren Libr. book award Rice U., 1989, 91, Heritage award for child abuse rsch. Child Abuse Prevention Coun., 1989; named One of Five Outstanding Young Men of Tex., 1962; recipient numerous awards for sci. writing; grantee NIH. Fellow Am. Coll. Psychology, Am. Inst. Stress; mem. Nat. Assn. Sci. Writers (life; exec. com. 1965-67), Houston Psychol. Assn. (pres. 1975), Am. Public Health Assn. (chmn. mental health sect. 1980-81, governing council 1983-85, action bd. 1985-87, mental health sect. award 1989), Coun. on Behavioral and Social Scis., Am. Assn. Schs. Pub. Health, Phi Beta Kappa (dir. Houston chpt. 1979-89, pres. Houston chpt. 1982-83), Phi Beta Kappa Assocs. Clubs: Dr.'s of Houston, Knights of the Vine. Home: 6331 Brompton Rd Houston TX 77005-3403 Office: 1200 Hermann Pressler Dr Houston TX 77030-3900

JUSTICE, BRADY RICHMOND, JR., medical services executive; b. Albertville, Ala., Dec. 26, 1930; s. Brady R. and Kate (McEachern) J.; m. Sandra Gearner, Dec. 29, 1956; children: David, Michael, Lori Blankenship, Kathryn Baker. BBA, Baylor U., 1953. CPA, Ind. Ptnr. Arthur Andersen & Co., Dallas, 1953-64, Indpls., 1964-72; exec. v.p. Basic Am. Industries, Inc., Indpls., 1972-83; pres. Basic Am. Med., Inc., Indpls., 1983-92; sr. v.p. Columbia Hosp. Corp., 1992-93; chmn. Heritage Capital Corp., Indpls., 1993—. Mem. Columbia Club, Lions (pres. Indpls. chpt.). Republican. Baptist. Home: 5435 Hedgerow Dr Indianapolis IN 46226-1625 Office: Heritage Capital Corp 6900 Gray Rd Indianapolis IN 46237-3227

JUSTINIANI, FEDERICO ROBERTO, internist, educator; b. Havana, Cuba, Aug. 15, 1929; came to U.S., 1964, naturalized, 1969; s. Federico Luis and Margarita (Longa) J.; BS, De La Salle Coll., Havana, 1947; MD, Havana U., 1954; m. María Suarez, Nov. 29, 1955. Intern, resident in internal medicine Havana U. Hosp., 1955-61; practice medicine, Havana, 1961-64; intern St. Francis Hosp., Miami Beach, Fla., 1965; resident in internal medicine Mt. Sinai Hosp., Miami Beach, 1966-69, program coord. residency in internal medicine, 1969-74; dir. med. edn. Mt. Sinai Med. Center, Miami Beach, 1974—; instr. medicine U. Miami, 1969-72, asst. prof., 1972-82, assoc. prof., 1982-90, prof., 1990—. Diplomate Am. Bd. Internal Medicine (recognized for advanced achievement 1987). Fellow ACP; mem. AMA (Physicians' Recognition award 1969, 72, 76, 79, 82, 85, 88, 91,95), Fla. Med. Assn., So. Med. Assn., Dade County Med. Assn., Am. Soc. Internal Medicine, Am. Geriatrics Soc., Assn. Hosp. Med. Edn., Alliance for Continuing Med. Edn., Assn. Program Dirs. in Internal Medicine, Cuban Med. Assn. in Exile. Contbr. articles to profl. jours. Office: 4300 Alton Rd Miami Beach FL 33140-2849

JUSZKIEWICZ, TEODOR, retired toxicology educator; b. Lida, Poland, Jan. 31, 1922; s. Julian and Helena (Pacewicz) J.; m. Janina Koziolkiewicz, 1953 (dec. Jan. 1977); children: Maria, Lucas, Leon; m. Teresa Szprengier, Dec. 28, 1978. DVM, Lublin (Poland) U., 1950, PhD in Pharmacology, 1955; PhD in Toxicology, Agrl. U., Lublin, 1961. Instr. Faculty Vet. Medicine U., Lublin, 1948-50, assoc. prof., 1950-56; head dept. Nat. Vet. Rsch. Inst., Pulawy, Poland, 1956-93, prof., 1968-74, Disting. prof., 1974-94; ret., 1994; vis. prof. Iowa State U., Ames, 1959-60; mem. Polish Drug Commn., 1970—; nat. rep. Codex Aliment. Com. FAO-WHO, 1985-92. Coauthor: (textbook) Pharmacometrology, 1982; translator: (textbook) Veterinary Toxicology, 1954; chief editor jour. Polskie Archiwum Weterynaryjne, 1964-69. Served with Polish mil., 1942-44. Recipient Polonia Restituta cavalier award Coun. State, Warsaw, 1971, Polonia Restituta officer, 1985; fellow Rockefeller Found. Iowa State U., Ames, 1958-59; Rsch. grantee FAO, Rome, 1978. Mem. Polish Acad. Sci. (vet. com. 1975-96), Polish Soc. Toxicology (hon., v.p. 1980-89), Polish Soc. Pharmacology (sci. coun. 1967—), Polish Pharmacopea Com., Internat. Union Pure and Applied Chemistry (nat. rep. 1977-83), European Assn. Vet. Pharmacology and Toxicology (nat. rep. 1983—), Lublin Sci. Soc., Polish Soc. Vet. Scis., World Assn. Nat. Army. Roman Catholic. Home: Kaniowczykow 6/3, PL24-100 Pulawy Poland

JUTHANI, NALINI VIRENDRA, psychiatrist; b. Bombay, India, Jan. 26, 1946; came to U.S., 1970; d. Kantilal Chotalal and Sushila (Bakhai) Ghevaria; m. Virendra J. Juthani, Mar. 29, 1970; children: Manisha, Kapila, Viral. MBBS, Bombay U., 1971; MD, Albert Einstein Coll. Medicine, 1971. Diplomate Am. Bd. Psychiatry and Neurology; cert. Commn. on Adminstrv. Psychiatry. Resident in psychiatry Bronx (N.Y.) Lebanon Hosp., 1975-78, attending psychiatrist, 1978-79, dir. residency tng., 1979—, assoc. prof., 1993—. Fellow An. Psychiat. Assn., N.Y. Acad. Psychiatry, Am. Assn. Adminstrv. Psychiatry; mem. Am. Assn. Dirs. Psychiat. Residence, Am. Assn. Acad. Psychiatry, Bronx County Med. Soc. Home: 17 Pheasant Run Scarsdale NY 10583-3100 Office: Bronx Lebanon Hosp Psych 1276 Fulton Ave # 4S Bronx NY 10456-3402

KABACK, MICHAEL, medical educator; b. Phila., Sept. 1, 1938. MD, U. Pa., 1963. Diplomate Am. Bd. Med. Genetics, Am. Bd. Pediatrics. Intern Johns Hopkins Hosp., Balt., 1963-64, resident pediatrics, 1966-68; fellow molecular biology and genetics NIH, Bethesda, Md., 1964-66; mem. staff Children's Hosp., San Diego; prof. pediatrics and reproductive medicine U. Calif., San Diego. Recipient William Allan Meml. award Am. Assn. Human Genetics, 1993. Fellow AAAS; mem. AMA, NAS, Inst. Medicine, Am. Acad. Pediatrics, Am. Pediatric Soc., Am. Soc. Human Genetics, Soc. for Pediatric Rsch. Office: Children's Hosp San Diego 8110 Birmingham Way San Diego CA 92123-2758

KABALIN, JOHN NICHOLAS, urologist; b. L.A., Dec. 23, 1958; s. Nicholas Augustin and Mary Jane (Engleman) K.; m. Pamela Grace White, July 11, 1981. BS, Stanford U., 1980; MD, Johns Hopkins U., 1984. Diplomate Am. Bd. Urology. Intern in surgery Stanford U. Med. Ctr., 1984-85, resident in surgery, 1985-86, resident in urology, 1986-90, chief resident in urology, 1989-90; chief urology sect. Va Med. Ctr., Palo Alto, Calif., 1990—; asst. prof. urology Stanford (Calif.) U., 1990—. Contbr. over 75 articles to profl. jours., 12 chpts. in books. Fellow ACS; mem. AMA, Am. Urol. Assn., Am. Soc. for Laser Medicine and Surgery, Soc. Urologic Oncology, Soc. Univ. Urologists, Phi Beta Kappa, Alpha Omega Alpha. Roman Catholic. Home: 719 17th Ave Menlo Park CA 94025 Office: VA Medical Center 3801 Miranda Avenue Palo Alto CA 94304

KABALKA, GEORGE WALTER, chemistry educator; b. Wyandotte, Mich., Feb. 1, 1943; s. Walter George and Rose Marie (Witkowski) K.; m. Beth Ann Swaim, Aug. 31, 1968; children: Stephen, Katherine. BS with honors, U. Mich., 1965; PhD, Purdue U., 1970. Prof. chemistry U. Tenn., Knoxville, 1970—, dir. rsch. biomed. imaging ctr., 1985—; Robert H. Cole prof., 1984—; cons. Oak Ridge (Tenn.) Nat. Lab., 1976—, Oak Ridge Associated Univs., 1977—, Los Alamos (N.Mex.) Nat. Lab., 1987—; bd. advisers Nat. Tritium Facility, Berkeley, Calif., Stable Isotope Resource, Los Alamos Nat. Lab. Contbr. numerous articles to profl. jours. Chancellor's Rsch. scholar U. Tenn., 1984; recipient European lectureship Nat. Acad. Scis., 1978, Sci. Alliance Rsch. award U. Tenn., 1984—, U. Tenn. Alumni Disting. Prof., 1992—. Mem. Am. Chem. Soc., Internat. Isotope Soc. (bd. dirs. 1988—, pres. 1992—), Soc. Nuclear Medicine, Soc. Magnetic Resonance. Democrat. Roman Catholic. Office: U Tenn Med Ctr Biomed Imaging Ctr Knoxville TN 37920

KABARA, JON JOSEPH, biochemical pharmacology educator; b. Chgo., Nov. 26, 1926; s. John Stanley and Mary Elizabeth (Wielgus) K.; m. Virginia Christie (dec. 1974); children: Christie Anne, Mary K., Sheila Jon, Pat Lee; m. Annette Elser Sproudll (dec. 1986); m. Betty Z. Tabor. B.S., St. Mary's Coll., Minn., 1948; M.S., U. Miami, 1950; Ph.D. (Univ. scholar), U. Chgo., 1959. Prof. chemistry U. Detroit, 1957-68; prof., assoc. dean Mich. Coll. Osteo. Medicine, Pontiac, 1967-70; prof. assoc. dean pharmacology Mich. State U., E. Lansing, 1970-71; prof. biomechanics Mich. State U., 1971-89, prof. emeritus, 1989; dir. research and devel. Med.-Chem. Labs., Okemos, Mich., 1957—, Kabe Realtor, 1986—; pres., dir. R&D Lauricidin, Inc., 1989-95; pres. div. research and devel. Galena's Kitchen Chemist, 1989, Tech. Exch. Inc., 1989; pres., dir. R&D Lil Gen. Miniature Golf, 1996; cons. in neurochemistry and microbiology. Contbr. numerous articles to profl. jours.; editor: Cosmetic Preservation and Korkies Cookbook, other books on lipid pharmacology; U.S. and fgn. patentee in field. Pres. Mich. NE PTA, 1959; active Little League, 1973-75. Damon Runyon Cancer fellow, 1949-50; Mt. Sinai fellow, 1949-51; Bishop Heffron awardee St. Mary's Coll., 1970; named Man of Year St. George High Sch. Alumni Club, 1970. Fellow Am. Inst. Chemists; mem. Am. Oil Chem. Soc., N.Y. Acad. Sci., Detroit Physiology Soc., Assn. Analytical Chemists, AAAS, Am. Soc. Clin. Pathologists, Sigma Xi, other orgns. Address: 4350 Chatham Dr Longboat Key FL 34228-2342

KABRIEL, MARCIA GAIL, psychotherapist; b. El Reno, Okla., Jan. 8, 1938; d. Gail Frederick and Katherine (Marsh) Slaughter; m. J. Ronald Kabriel, May 25, 1957 (div. Sept. 1985); children: Joseph Charles, Jeffrey Gail, Jae B. BA, U. Okla., 1965, MSW, 1968; postgrad. Am. U. Psychiat. social worker Dept. Mental Hygiene, N.Y.C., 1968-69; psychiat. social worker Washington Hosp. Ctr., 1970-72, assoc. mem. dept. psychiatry, 1972-75, sr. psychotherapist Counseling Ctr., 1972-75; psychotherapist Md. Inst. Pastoral Counseling, Annapolis, Md., 1972—; chief dept. social svcs. Washington Hosp. Ctr., 1979-82, cons. spl. projects, 1974-82; supr. continuing protective svcs. State Md., 1983-91; supr. rsch. project on child sexual abuse for AACO, 1991-93; forensic social worker Anne Arundel Cir. Ct., 1991—; exec. v.p. Kent Island Transport, Inc., 1985—; field instr. Cath. U., Washington, 1973-75, U. Md., 1976-91; adjunct prof. U. Md. 1992-94. Mem. Nat. Assn. Social Workers, Acad. Cert. Social Workers (bd. cert. diplomate). Democrat. Presbyterian. Home: 1416 Regent St Annapolis MD 21403-1247 Office: 104 Forbes St Suite F Annapolis MD 21404

KACHMAR, ANDREW JEFFREY, healthcare executive; b. Wooster, Ohio, Dec. 20, 1954; s. Andrew David and Marie Ellen (Baker) K.; m. Mary Elizabeth Stoten, Sept. 2, 1984. BA, Coll. of Wooster, 1977; MS, Purdue U., 1982. Project rev. officer State of Ind. Bd. Health, Indpls., 1984-85; HMO devel. specialist Mexicare of Ind., Indpls., 1985-86; sr. contract cons. The Associated Group, Indpls., 1986-89; mgr. provider network devel. CIGNA, Indpls., 1989-91; vol. in mission Donaldina Cameron House, San Francisco, 1992-93; dir. bus. devel. AdminaStar Solutions, Indpls., 1994—; cons. Meth. Hosp., Indpls., 1982-83, CIGNA, 1993-94; ins. agt., Ind., 1986-96. Deacon Fairview Presbyn. Ch., Indpls., 1990—; bd. dirs. The Caring Cmty., Indpls., 1995—. Mem. Am. Assn. Physician-Hosp. Orgns., Healthcare Fin. Mgmt. Assn.

KACZKOFSKY, PETER EARL-DAVID, osteopath, educator; b. Kalamazoo, Mich., Nov. 25, 1966; s. H.W. and Anita Kaczkofsky. BS, Western Mich. U., 1988; DO, Mich. State U., 1993. Intern Metro. Hosp., Grand Rapids, Mich., resident; asst. clin. prof. Coll. Osteo. Medicine Mich. State U., East Lansing, 1995—. Fellow AMA, Am. Osteo. Assn. Republican. Lutheran. Home: 1936 Adams SE Grand Rapids MI 49506 Office: Met Hosp 1919 Boston SE Grand Rapids MI 49526

KAD, SURINDER KUMAR, physician, educator, researcher; b. Patiala, Punjab, India, Nov. 17, 1950; came to U.S. 1974; s. Ram Lall and Sarla Rani (Bhala) K.; m. Joan Mary Peters, Apr. 16, 1977; children: Robert Steven, Elizabeth Mary. Grad. Punjabi U., India, 1968, MB, BS, 1974. Diplomate Am. Acad. Pain Mgmt., Am. Coll. Forensic Examiners; sr. diplomate Am. Coll. Disability Analysts. Resident med. officer Phila. Hosp., Ambala City, India, 1975-77; sr. house officer Royal N. Infirmary, Raigmore, Inverness, Scotland, 1977; clin. instr. phys. medicine and rehab. Med. Coll. Wis., Milw., 1978-79; resident in internal medicine Kingsbrook Jewish Med. Ctr. affiliate SUNY-Downstate Med. Ctr., Bklyn., 1979-82, fellow in nephrology SUNY-Stony Brook, 1982-84; internist, nephrologist PHP Health Ctr. East, Syracuse, N.Y., 1984—; clin. instr. Med. Coll. Wis., Milw., 1978-79; asst. clin. instr. internal medicine SUNY-Stony Brook, 1982-84, clin. instr. dept. medicine SUNY Upstate Med. Ctr., Syracuse, 1984-88; clin. asst. prof. SUNY Health Sci. Ctr., 1988—. Vol. med. officer in rural/underdeveloped area in India, 1973-74. Maj. M.C., USAR, 1991. Fellow Royal Soc. Health; mem. ACP, N.Y. Acad. Scis., Am. Soc. Internal Medicine, Am. Soc. Hypertension, Am. Diabetes Assn., Am. Heart Assn., Am. Soc. Nephrology, Internat. Soc. Nephrology, Am. Fedn. Clin. Rsch. (assoc.), Sigma Xi (assoc.). Republican. Roman Catholic. Club: Limestone Harmonizers. Lodges: Rotary, Kiwanis. Avocations: reading, traveling, music, swimming, tennis, jogging. Home: 100 Cedar Heights Dr Fayetteville NY 13066-9757 Office: PHP Health Ctr E 2803 Erie Blvd E Syracuse NY 13224-1396

KADAKIA, SHAILESH CHANDRAKANT, physician; b. Devgad Baria, Gujarat, India, July 12, 1952; came to U.S., 1975; s. Chandrakant Keshavial and Bhanu Chandrakant (Mody) K.; m. Ami Vimal Shah, Apr. 30, 1950; children: Nirag S., Ashaini S. BS, M.S. Univ., Baroda, Gujarat, 1969; MBBS, Baroda Med. Coll., 1975. Diplomate Am. Bd. Internal Medicine, Am. Bd. Gastroenterology, Am. Bd. Critical Care Medicine. Intern, internal medicine St. Vincent's Med. Ctr., Bridgeport, Conn., 1978-79; resident, internal medicine St. Vincent's Med. Ctr., Bridgeport, 1979-81; fellow, critical care medicine Walter Reed Army Med. Ctr., Washington, 1981-82; staff internist Kimbrough Army Community Hosp., Ft. Meade, Md., 1982-83; fellow, gastroenterology Walter Reed Army Med. Ctr., Washington, 1983-85; asst. prof. medicine Uniformed Svcs. Univ. of Health Sci., Bethesda, Md., 1982-85; chief endoscopy, asst. chief Gastroenterology Svc., Letterman Army Med. Ctr., San Francisco, 1985-88; asst. prof. medicine U. Tex. Health Sci. Ctr., San Antonio, 1988-92; assoc. prof. medicine, 1992—; from asst. chief to chief gastroenterology svc. Brooke Army Med. Ctr., Ft. Sam Houston, Tex., 1988-91, chief gastroenterology, 1991—; program dir. fellowship tng. Brooke Army Med. Ctr., 1991—. Col. USMC, 1995—. Recipient trainee rsch. award William Beaumont Soc. Gastroenterology, 1986, Eddy Palmer endoscopy award, 1993. Christopher White Best Tchr. award, 1987. Fellow ACP, Am. Coll. Gastroenterology, Am. Gastroent. Assn., Am. Coll. Chest Physicians; mem. Am. Gastroent. Assn., Am. Soc. Gastroent. Endoscopy, Gastroent. Rsch. Group. Hindu. Home: 19114 Nature Oaks San Antonio TX 78258-4412 Office: GI Svc Brooke Army Med Ctr Houston TX 78219

KADAR, AVRAHAM, immunologist; b. Rishon Le Zion, Israel, Nov. 13, 1950; s. Yosef and Amalia (Hayon) K.; m. Naomi Carol Prawer, Sept. 2, 1976; children: Maya, Nadav, Einat. BS in Physics, Hebrew U., Jerusalem, 1972; MD, Sackler Sch. Medicine, Tel Aviv, Israel, 1983. Diplomate Am. Bd. Pediatrics, Am. Bd. Diagnostic Lab. Immunology, Am. B. Allergy and Immunology, Am. Bd. Medicine. Intern Tel-Hashomer, Ramat Gan, Israel, 1982; intern Albert Einstein Coll. of Medicine, N.Y.C., 1983, resident, 1984-86, asst. prof., 1989-92, asst. clin. prof., 1992—; fellow NIH, Bethesda, Md., 1986-89; immunology cons. Pediatric HIV Primary Care, N.Y.C., 1989—. Mem. AAAS, N.Y. Acad. Scis. Home: 5 Woodland Ct Bedford NY 10506-2034 Office: 530 Park Ave New York NY 10021 also: 666 Lexington Ave Mount Kisco NY 10549

KADELL, JEROME GILBERT, ophthalmologist; b. N.Y.C., July 6, 1942; s. Herbert Charles and Mildred C. (Schnechter) K.; m. Alyce Jean Dederich, June 27, 1975; children: Abigail, Gabriel. BS, U. Rochester, 1962; MD, U. Wis., 1966. Diplomate Am. Acad. Ophthalmology. Intern Wayne County Hosp., Eloise, Mich., 1966-67; unit dir. USHPS Hosp., Wagner, S.D., 1967-69; ophthalmology resident U. Wis., Madison, 1971-73; ophthalmologist Dean Clinic, Madison, 1973—; assoc. clin. prof. eye dept. U. Wis., Madison, 1973-94. Lt. comdr. USPHS, 1967-69. Fellow AMA, Am. Acad. Ophthalmology. Office: Dean Clinic 3434 E Washington Ave Madison WI 53704

KADIN, MARSHALL EDWARD, hematopathologist, educator; b. Milw., July 19, 1939; s. George and Mildred (Goldberg) K.; m. Martha LuClare Hutchinson, June 15, 1980. B.A., Northwestern U., 1961, M.D., 1965. Diplomate Am. Bd. Pathology. Intern Milw. County Gen. Hosp., 1966; resident in pathology Barnes Hosp., Washington U., St. Louis, 1967-68; NIH fellow in surg. pathology Stanford U., Calif., 1969-70; fellow in clin. hematology U. Calif.-San Francisco, 1972-73; asst. prof. medicine, clin. pathology and research assoc. Cancer Research Inst., 1974-77; assoc. prof. pathology and lab. medicine U. Wash., Seattle, 1977-82, prof., 1982-84, prof. pathology and lab medicine, adj. prof. medicine, 1981-84; mem. Fred Hutchinson Cancer Ctr., Seattle, 1980—; dir. hematology lab. and hematopathology, sr. pathologist Beth Israel Hosp., Boston, 1984—; assoc. prof. pathology Harvard Med. Sch., 1984—; mem. Lymphoma Panel for Clin. Trials NIH, 1985—, Children's Cancer Study Group, 1977—, European Lymphoma Panel Study Group, 1985—, spl. reviewer Pathology B Study Sect., 1994; mem. cutaneous lymphoma project group European Orgn. for Rsch. and Therapy of Cancer, 1990—. Editor: (with Sam Newcom) Diagnosis and Management of Hematologic Malignancies, 1981, (with M. Hanaoka, A. Mikata, S. Watanabe) Lymphoid Malignancy: Immunocytology and Cytogenetics, 1990; mem. editorial bd. Am. Jour. Surgical Pathology, 1983—, Cancer, Human Pathology, Internat. Jour. Hematology; contbr. articles to profl. jours. Served to maj. M.C., U.S. Army, 1970-72. Cancer Rsch. grantee NIH, 1992—; rsch. grantee Am. Cancer Soc., 1990—. Decorated Bronze Star. Mem. Am. Soc. Hematology (sci. subcom. for immunohematology and lymphocyte biology 1995—), Soc. for Hematopathology (charter), European Assn. Hematopathology, Am. Soc. Cytology, Internat. Acad. Pathology, Acad. Clin. Lab. Physicians and Scientists, Soc. Investigative Pathology, Soc. Investigative Dermatology, Boston Cancer Rsch. Assn. (pres. 1993—), N.Y. Acad. Scis., Internat. Soc. for Cutaneous Lymphomas, Phi Beta Kappa. Republican. Jewish. Home: 103 Clinton Rd Brookline MA 02146-5842

KADISH, ALAN HOWARD, internist, researcher; b. Bklyn., Aug. 18, 1956; s. Abraham Samuel and Hilda (Gelber) K.; m. Constance Kadish, Sept. 21, 1984; children: Deborah, Benjamin, Jessica, Neomi. BA, Columbia U., 1977; MD, Albert Einstein Coll. Medicine, 1980. Resident Brigham & Woman's Hosp., Boston, 1980-83; instr. Harvard Med. Sch., Boston, 1980-83, U. Pa., Phila., 1986-87; asst. prof. U. Mich., Ann Arbor, 1987-90; assoc. prof. Northwestern U., Chgo., 1990—, Chester and Deborah Colbey prof. of cardiology, 1993—; mem. sci. adv. bd. Endocardial Solutions, Mpls., 1993—; guest rev. cons. NIH, Bethesda, Md., 1995-96. Editl. bd. Jour. Am. Coll. Cardiology, 1995—; contbr. over 100 articles to profl. jours.; author chpts. in Cardiac Electrophysiology (textbook), 1989-95. Bd. dirs. Young Israel of Northbrook, Ill., 1990—, Arie Crown Day Sch., Skokie, Ill., 1994—. Recipient Young Investigator award N.Am. Soc. for Pacing and Electrophysiology, 1986; Feinberg Inst. scholar, 1990. Mem. Am. Heart Assn., Am. Fedn. Clin. Rsch., Am. Soc. Clin. Investigators. Jewish. Office: Northwestern Univ 250 E Superior #520 Chicago IL 60611-2914

KADISH, LORI GAIL, clinical psychologist; b. Newark, Mar. 6, 1962; d. Gerald Bernard and Marlene (Brodsky) K. BA in Psychology, Emory U., 1984; MS in Clin. Psychology, Fla. Inst. Tech., 1987, PsyD in Clin. Psychology, 1988. Lic. psychologist, N.J., N.Y., Fla.; cert. addiction specialist. Tutor Dekalb County Juvenile Detention Ctr., Atlanta, 1982-83; edn. counselor, interviewer Planned Parenthood, Atlanta, 1983; crisis intervention counselor Helpline, Atlanta, 1982-84; therapist Brevard Community Mental Health Ctr., Melbourne, Fla., 1984-86; therapist adolescent-adult psychiat. unit Wuesthoff Meml. Hosp., Rockledge, Fla., 1986-87; psychology intern South Oaks Hosp., Amityville, N.Y., 1987-88; staff clin. psychologist, team leader Fair Oaks Hosp., Summit, N.J., 1988-92; clin. dir. Outpatient Substance Abuse Ctr., Paramus, N.J., 1993-94; pvt. practice clin. psychology, Summit, 1990-94, Livingston, N.J., 1992-93, Ft. Lee, N.J., 1992—; presenter in field. Vol. recreational and occupational therapist asst. St. Barnabas Hosp., Livingston, 1983; vol. psychiat. nurse asst. Muhlenberg Hosp., Plainfield, N.J., 1983. Mem. APA, N.Y. State Psychol. Assn., N.J. Psychol. Assn., Fla. Psychol. Assn., Soc. Psychologists in Addictive Behaviors, Assn. for Advancement Behavior Therapy, Bergen County Assn. Lic. Psychologists. Office: 2083 Center Ave Ste G Fort Lee NJ 07024-4999

KADNER, CARL GEORGE, biology educator emeritus; b. Oakland, Calif., May 23, 1911; s. Adolph L. and Otilia (Pecht) K.; m. Mary Elizabeth Moran, June 24, 1939; children: Robert, Grace Wickersham, Carl L. BS, U. San Francisco, 1933; MS, U. Calif., Berkeley, 1936, PhD, 1941. Prof. biology Loyola Marymount U., Los Angeles, 1936-78, prof. emeritus, 1978—; trustee Loyola U., Los Angeles, 1970-73. Served to maj. U.S. Army, 1943-46. Mem. Entomol. Soc. Am. (emeritus), Sigma Xi, Alpha Sigma Nu. Republican. Roman Catholic. Home: 8100 Loyola Blvd Los Angeles CA 90045-2639

KAELBER, CHARLES THEODORE, medical research administrator; b. Cardington, Ohio, Feb. 25, 1938; s. Harry Fredrick and Mabel Elizabeth (Behner) K.; m. Nancy Lee Meyer Kaelber, July 23, 1966; children: David Charles, Steven Andrew. BA, Capital U., 1960, BS, 1961; MD, Case Western Reserve U., 1965; MPH, Harvard U., 1967, DrPH, 1969. Intern Johns Hopkins U., Balt., 1965-66; preventive medicine resident Harvard U., Boston, 1966-69; epidemiologist U.S. Army, Washington, 1969-72; NHLBI, 1972-79; med. officer NIAAA, 1979-84, NIMH, 1987—, NIH, Bethesda, Md.; psychiatry resident St. Elizabeths Hosp., Washington, 1984-87; Diplomate Am. Bd. Preventive Medicine, Am. Bd. Psychiatry and Neurology. Contbr. various articles to profl. jours. Fellow Am. Coll. Preventive Medicine, Am. Heart Assn.; mem. Am. Psychiat. Assn., Internat. Epidemiol. Assn., Internat. Soc. and Fedn. Cardiology, USPHS Commn. Officers Assn. (Washington), Harvard Club. Home: 1099 Larkspur Ter Rockville MD 20850-1004

KAERJAE, JUHANI, health facility administrator; b. Kalajoki, Finland, Dec. 25, 1934; s. Matti and Aino (Ojala) K.; m. Leena Niemi, July 31, 1960; children: Taina, Vesa. MD, U. Turku, Finland, 1960; Speciliast in Oto-Rhino-Larynogology, U. Oulu, Finland, 1966, DMS, 1968; Specialist in Audiology, U. Kuopio, Finland, 1979. Asst. demonstrator in oto-rhino-laryngology U. Oulu, 1965-72, asst. chief surgeon in oto-rhino-laryngology, 1973-74, assoc. prof. oto-rhino-laryngology, 1974-75; prof. oto-rhino-laryngology U. Kuopio, Finland, 1975-90; pres. U. Kuopio, 1984-90; med. dir. Pohjois-Savo Hosp. Dist., Kuopio, Finland, 1990—, U. Kuopio Hosp., Finland, 1993—; pres. Finnish Coun. U. Rectors, Finland, 1988-90; chmn. Finnish Coun. Higher Edn., Finland, 1990-91; mem. Sci. and Tech. Policy Coun. Finland, 1990-91. Co-author: Audiology and Audiological Rehabilitation, 1978, 2d edit., 1984; editor: University Research in Finland, 1989; joint editor: Ear Nose and Throat Diseases, 1980, 2d edit., 1984, 3d edit., 1990; contbr. articles to profl. jours. Recipient Best Paper of Yr. award Hemisphere Publ. Corp., U.S.A., 1984. Mem. Collegium Oto-Rhino-Laryngologicum Amicitiae Sacrum. Office: P-S Hosp Dist, SF 70200, SF 70280 Kuopio Finland

KAFKA, MARIAN STERN, neuroscientist; b. Richmond, Va., Mar. 30, 1927; d. Henry Sycle and Adele (Lewit) Stern; m. John S. Kafka, Oct. 3, 1952; children: David Egon, Paul Henry, Alexander Charles. AB in Zoology, Conn. Coll., 1948; PhD in Physiology, U. Chgo., 1952. Rsch. asst. dept. physiol. chemistry Emory U. Sch. Medicine, Atlanta, 1952-53; rsch. assoc. Ill. Neuropsychiat. Inst., U. Ill. Sch. Medicine, Chgo., 1953-54; rsch. asst. dept. internal medicine Yale U. Sch. Medicine, New Haven, 1954-57; USPHS postdoctoral fellow endocrinology br. Nat. Heart, Lung and Blood Inst. NIH, Bethesda, Md., 1965-68, physiologist hypertention-endocrine br., 1968-74; physiologist sect. biochemistry and pharmacology Biol. Psychiatry Br. NIH, Bethesda, 1974-82; physiologist Clin. Neurosci. Br. NIMH, Bethesda, 1982-86; exec. sec. neurobehavioral rsch. rev. subcom., neuroscis. rsch. rev. com. NIMH, Rockville, Md., 1986, exec. sec. cellular neurobiology & psychopharmacology com., 1986-90; chief clin. rev. br. divsn. extramural activities NIMH, Rockville, 1990. Contbr. articles, revs. to sci. publs. Recipient Adminstr.'s award for Meritorious Achievement, ADAMHA, 1989; Marie J. Mergler fellow in physiology, 1950. Mem. AAAS, Am. Physiol. Soc. (mem. pub. affairs and pub. info. com. 1974-79, chair pub. info. com. 1980-84, centennial com. 1979-85), Soc. for Neurosci., Endocrine Soc., Biophys. Soc., Internat. Soc. Chronobiology, Fedn. Am. Soc. for Exptl. Biology (pub. info. com. 1977-82), Phi Beta Kappa, Sigma Xi. Home: 7834 Aberdeen Rd Bethesda MD 20814-1102 Office: NIMH Parklawn Bldg 5600 Fishers Ln Rm 902C Rockville MD 20857-0001

KAGAN, BENJAMIN M., pediatrician; b. Washington, Pa., July 18, 1913; m. Katherine Hamburger, June 2, 1940; children: Christopher, Robert. AB, Washington & Jefferson Coll., 1933; MD, Johns Hopkins U., 1937. Diplomate Am. Bd. Pediatrics (examiner, chmn. written examination com., mem. exec. com. 1967-83), Am. Bd. Nutrition. Intern Sinai Hosp., Balt.; resident Willard Parker Hosp. Infectious Diseases, N.Y.C.; resident in pediatrics Presbyn. Hosp., N.Y.C., 1938-40; instr. Med. Coll. Va., 1941; from assoc. prof. to clin. prof. pediatrics U. Ill., Chgo., 1945-48; prof. Northwestern U., Chgo., 1948-55; dir., chmn. dept. pediatrics Michael Reese Hosp., Chgo., 1945-55; from. clin. prof. to prof., vice-chmn. dept. pediatrics UCLA, 1955-84; dir., chmn. dept. pediatrics Cedars-Sinai Med. Ctr., Los Angeles, 1955-84, sr. cons. pediatrics, dir. pediatric infectious disease unit, 1984—; dir. Cystic Fibrosis Ctr., L.A., 1955-95. Author, editor numerous books in field; contbr. articles to profl. jours. Served to maj. M.C., U.S. Army, 1942-46, MTO. Fellow ACP, Am. Acad. Pediatrics, Am. Coll. Chest Physicians, Infectious Diseases Soc. Am.; mem. Am. Pediatric Soc. (Joseph St Geme MD Meml. award 1993), Soc. Pediatric Rsch., Western Soc. Pediatric Rsch. (award), Western Soc. Physicians, Western Soc. Clin. Rsch., Southwestern Pediatric Soc., L.A. Pediatric Soc., L.A. Acad. Medicine, Phi Beta Kappa, Sigma Xi, Alpha Omega Alpha. Home: 5005 Finley Ave Los Angeles CA 90027-1809 Office: Cedars-Sinai Med Ctr Rm 4314 8700 Beverly Blvd Los Angeles CA 90048-1804

KAGAN, GEORGE IRWIN, dentist; b Brookline, Mass., Aug. 8, 1939; s. Abraham and Sylvia (Coleman) K. BS in Biol. Psychology, U. Chgo., 1961, BS in Dentistry, 1963; DDS, U. Ill., 1965. Technician Cook County Sch. Nursing, Chgo., 1964-65; intern U. Chgo., 1965-66; staff dentist Chgo. Bd. Health, 1966-68, Stickney Twp. Pub. Health Dist., Burbank, Ill., 1969; dental health care provider State of Ill., 1969-79; gen. practice dentistry, Chgo., 1968—; table clinician Chgo. Dental Soc., 1980-85, Ariz. State Dental Soc., Phoenix, 1983-85. Mem. adv. bd. Ill. State Acupucture Assn., 1995—. Served to capt. USAR, 1965-67. Fellow Acad. Gen. Dentistry, Royal Soc. Health; mem. Chgo. Dental Soc., Royal Coll. Dental Surgeons Ont. (licentiate), Ill. State Dental Soc., ADA, Am. Legion (chmn. counter-subversive activities com. 3d dist. 1st div. dept. Ill. 1989-90, chaplain, historian Richard J. Daley Post #1976 1988-90, chmn. program com., 1989-90, Darius-Girenas post #271 1991—, asst. chmn. counter subversive activities com. 1992), Ill. Railway Museum, Cen. Electric Railfans Assn., Assn. U.S. Army, NRA, Ill. Camaro Club, Mil. Order of the World Wars (adv. staff Chgo. chpt. 1989-90, adj. Chgo. chpt. 1990-92), Assn. U.S. Army, Res. Officers Assn. (dental surgeon Chgo. chpt. 1990-91), Ret. Officers Assn. Avocations: railroading, restoration of classic autos, motorsports, touring, history. Office: IIT Rsch Inst Box 91 10 W 35th St Chicago IL 60616-3799

KAGAN, JEROME, psychologist, educator; b. Newark, Feb. 25, 1929; s. Joseph and Myrtle (Liebermann) K. B.S., Rutgers U., 1950; Ph.D., Yale, 1954. Instr. psychology Ohio State U., 1954-55; research assoc. Fels Research Inst., Yellow Springs, Ohio, 1957-59; chmn. dept. psychology Fels Research Inst., 1959-64; asso. prof. psychology Antioch Coll., 1959-64; prof. psychology Harvard U., 1964—; Adv. com. Nat. Inst. Child Health and Devel. Author: (with G.S. Lesser) Contemporary Issues in Thematic Apperceptive Methods, 1961, (with Moss) Birth to Maturity, 1962, (with Mussen, Conger and Hustar) Child Development and Personality, 7th edit., 1990, (with Segal) Psychology, 7th edit., 1991, (with Janis, Mahl and Holt) Personality, 1969, Understanding Children, 1971, Change and Continuity in Infancy, 1971, (with Kearsley and Zelazo) Infancy, 1978, (with Brim) Constancy and Change, 1980, The Second Year, 1981, The Nature of the Child, 1984, Unstable Ideas, 1989, Galen's Prophecy, 1994. Served with AUS, 1955-57. Recipient Lucius Cross medal Yale U., 1981; Phi Beta Kappa scholar, 1988-89. Fellow AAAS, APA (Disting. Sci. Contbn. award 1987, G. Stanley Hall award 1995), Am. Acad. Arts and Scis., Soc. Rsch. Child Devel. (Disting. Sci. Contbn. award 1989); mem. NAS, Inst. Medicine, Ea. Psychol. Assn. Home: 210 Clifton St Belmont MA 02178-2605 Office: Harvard U Dept Psychology William James Hall 22 Kirkland Cambridge MA 02138

KAGAN, STUART MICHAEL, pediatrician; b. Milw., June 22, 1944; s. Harry and Bertha (Pittleman) K.; m. Gloria Jean Glass, Aug. 1, 1971; children: Jennifer Anne, Abigail Elizabeth. BS, U. Wis., 1966; MD, U. Utah, 1969; postgrad., U. Kans., 1995—. Deiplomate Am. Bd. Pediatrics. Intern in pediats. Kans. U. Med. Ctr., Kansas City, 1969-70, resident in pediats., 1970-71, fellow in pediat. cardiology, 1971-73; pvt. practice Overland Park, Kans., 1975-88; occupational medicine physician Employer Health Svc., Kansas City, Mo., 1988—, med. rev. officer, 1994—, acting med. dir., 1994—. Lt. comdr. USN, 1973-75. RecipientKans. Cardiology fellowship Kans. U. Med. ctr., 1972. Mem. Am. Coll. Occupational and Environ. Medicine, Am. Soc. Addiction Medicine, Great Plains Occupational and Environ. Medicine. Office: Employer Health Svcs 8511 Hillcrest Ste 320 Kansas City MO 64138-2776

KAHANA, RALPH JONAH, psychiatrist; b. Winnipeg, Man., Can., May 2, 1924; came to U.S., 1926; s. Irving Edward and Eva (Gershfield) K.; m. Eda Malisoff, July, 28, 1947; children: Irene, Laura. BA, Bard Coll., Annandale on Hudson, N.Y., 1944; MD, N.Y. Med. Coll., 1946. Diplomate Am. Bd. Psychiatry and Neurology. Intern Met. Hosp., N.Y.C., 1946-47; resident psychiatry Cin. Gen. Hosp., 1949-52; staff mem. Beth Israel Hosp., Boston, 1952—; faculty mem. Harvard Med. Sch., Boston, 1952—, Boston Psychoanalytic Inst., 1968—; pvt. practice psychiatry and psychoanalysis Brookline, Mass., 1952—; assoc. clin. prof. psychiatry Harvard Med. Sch., Boston, 1979—; candidate Boston Psychoanalytic Soc. and Inst., 1953-61. Author: (with Grete L. Bibring) Lectures in medical Psychology, 1969; editor: (with Sidney Levin) Psychodynamic Studies in Aging, 1967; co-editor Jour. Geriatric Psychiatry, 1975-95; contbr. chpts. to books, articles to profl. jours. Capt. MC, U.S. Army, 1947-49. Fellow Am. Psychiat. Assn. (life; Weinberg Meml. award 1991); mem. Am. Psychoanalytic Assn. (life), Boston Psychoanalytic Soc. and Inst. (life; pres. 1980-82), Boston Soc. Gerontol. Psychiatry (pres. 1974-78). Democrat. Jewish.

KAHLER, DAVID MARC, orthopaedic surgeon; b. New Haven, Conn., Sept. 20, 1959; s. Richard Lee K. and Diane (Dunn) Richards; m. Victoria Fay Norwood, June 5, 1985. AB, Dartmouth Coll., 1981; MD, Tulane U., 1985. Reisdent Tulane Orthopaedic Surgery, New Orleans, 1990; asst. prof. orthopaedic surgery U. Va., Charlottesville, 1991—; asst. prof. Curry Sch. Edn., Charlottesville, 1993—. Contbr. articles to profl. jours. Fellow Am. Acad. Orthopaedic Surgery; mem. Alpha Omega Alpha. Office: U Va Box 159 Charlottesville VA 22903

KAHLER, ELIZABETH SARTOR (MRS. ERVIN NEWTON CHAPMAN), physician; b. Washington, Oct. 20, 1911; d. Armin Adolphus and Lenore Elome (Sartor) K.; m. Dr. Ervin Newton Chapman, Feb. 24, 1942 (dec. Apr. 1987). B.S., George Washington U., 1933, M.A., 1935, M.D. with distinction, 1940. Intern Gallinger Municipal Hosp. (now D.C. Gen. Hosp.), Washington, 1940-41; resident Children's Hosp., Washington, 1941-42; practice medicine Washington, 1942-78; assoc. univ. physician George Washington U., 1942-50; examining physician YWCA, 1942-45; courtesy staff Washington Hosp. Center, until 1978, George Washington U. Hosp., until 1978; physician for health services br. resources div. Bur. Social Services and Resources Social Services Adminstrn. D.C. Dept. Human Services, 1953-75; sch. physician D.C. pub. schs., 1959-89; mem. cons. com. for practical nursing program D.C. Pub. Schs., 1962-70. Everitt-Pomery trustee Wilson Coll., 1993—; vol. Widowed Persons Svc., 1993—; mem. exec. com. Nat. Voluntary Orgns. for Ind. Living for Aging, 1978-82, liaison from Am. Med. Women's Assn., 1975-82; mem. nat. program com. Camp Fire Girls

Inc.; treas. Women's Assn. of Nat. Presbyn. Ch., 1981-83, fin. chmn., 1983-85, 87-89, asst. treas., 1989-91, chmn. memls., 1985-87, 91-93, cir. leader, 1994-96, nat. pres. ch. memls. com., 1986—, mem. libr. com. 1991—, Stephen min., 1993—. Mem. AMA, Women's Med. Assn. (pres. 1957-58, treas. Past Presidents Coun. 1976-78), Med. Soc. D.C. (life, chmn. com. on medicine and religion 1967-72, aging com. 1985-86, 88, mem. pub. info. and edn. com. 1986), D.C. Assn. Mental Health, Am. Heart Assn., Columbia Women of George Washington U. (life). Republican. Presbyterian. Office: 3601 Davis St NW Washington DC 20007-1428

KAHN, ARNOLD SANFORD, psychology educator; b. Sioux City, Iowa, June 13, 1942; s. Lester and Gladys (Eagles) K.; m. Ronnetta Diane Bisman, Aug. 29, 1964; children: Gregory Howard, Jessica Anne. BA, U. Mo., 1964; MS, So. Ill. U., 1967, PhD, 1969. Asst. prof. psychology Iowa State U., Ames, 1968-72, assoc. prof. psychology, 1972-78, prof. psychology, 1978-84; prof., chmn. dept. psychology James Madison U., Harrisonburg, Va., 1986-88, prof. psychology, 1988—; guest prof. U. Mannheim, Fed. Republic of Germany, summer 1975. Fellow APA (dir. office social and ethical responsibility 1982-86), Am. Psychol. Soc., Soc. for the Psychol. Study of Social Issues (sec.-treas. 1990-92); mem. Soc. for Exptl. Social Psychology, Nat. Women's Studies Assn. Home: 701 Locust Hill Dr Harrisonburg VA 22801-3313 Office: James Madison U Dept Psychology Johnston Hall Harrisonburg VA 22807

KAHN, CARL RONALD, research laboratory administrator; b. Louisville, Jan. 14, 1944; s. David L. and Reva W. (Waldman) K.; m. Susan Becker; children: Stacy, Jeffrey. BA, U. Louisville, 1964, MD, 1968, MS, 1984; MA (hon.), Harvard U., 1984; DSc (honoris causa), U. Louisville, 1984, U. Paris-Pierre and Marie Curie, 1990. Diplomate Am. Bd. Internal Medicine, Am. Bd. Endocrinology and Metabolism. Intern and resident in ward medicine Barnes Hosp., St. Louis, 1968-70; clin. assoc., sr. clin. assoc., clin. endocrinology br. Nat. Inst. Arthritis, Metabolism and Digestive Diseases, NIH, Bethesda, Md., 1970-73; sr. investigator Diabetes Br. NIH, Bethesda, Md., 1973-78, chief diabetes br., 1979-81; rsch. dir Joslin Diabetes Ctr., Boston, 1981—; assoc. prof. Harvard Med. Sch., Boston, 1981-84, prof. medicine, 1984—, Mary K. Iacocca prof. medicine, 1986—; lectr. symposia, meetings, thesis supr., course dir. and devel. numerous med. instns.; admitting and attending physician NIH Clin. Ctr., 1972-81; physician Brigham and Women's Hosp., Boston, 1981, chief div. Diabetes and Metabolism, 1981-92; assoc. staff Endocrinology/Internal Medicine, New Eng. Deaconess Hospital, Boston, 1982, active staff, 1986; clin. assoc. prof. medicine, Uniformed Svcs. U. Health Scis, Bethesda, Md., 1979-81; vis. scientist Centre de Moleculaire, Centre National de la Recherche Scientifique, Gif-sur-Yvette, France, 1979-80; adj. prof. genetics George Washington U., 1980-81; overseas vis. prof. Royal Melbourne Hosp., Australia, 1985; vis. prof. Royal Postgrad. Hosp., London, 1985; Rosemary Sarver vis. prof. in endocrinology and metabolism, The Hosp. of the Good Samaritan, L.A., 1985. Author or co-author over 430 publs. in field; mem. editl. bds. Jour. Clin. Endocrinology and Metabolism, 1977-80, Diabetes, 1977-84, Am. Jour. Medicine, 1979-84, Jour. Clin. Investigation, 1979-84, Jour. Receptor Rsch., 1980-83, Hormone and Metabolic Rsch., 1980-83, Endocrinology, 1981-85, Jour. Biol. Chemistry, 1983-88, Diabetes and Metabolism Revs., 1984, Receptor, 1989—; exec. editor Trends in Endocrinology and Metabolism, 1989-90; cons. editor Jour. Clin. Investigation; assoc. editor Diabetes, 1996—. Mem. Nat. Diabetes Adv. Bd., 1981-85, co-chmn. rsch. com., 1982-85. Recipient David Rumbough Meml award for Sci. Achievement Juvenile Diabetes Found., 1977, CIBA-Geigy Drew award for biochem. rsch., 1981, Mary Jane Kugel award Juvenile Diabetes Found., 1982, AFCR award for Outstanding Clin. Rsch. under Age 40, 1983, Sol Berson Meml. lectureship NIH, 1983, Hehnemann Lectr. in Pharmacology U. Calif.,1984, Pfizer Biomed. Rsch. award, Pfizer inc., 1986, Cristobal Diaz award Internat. Diabetes Fedn., 1988, Banting award Am. Diabetes Assn., 1993, others. Fellow AAAS; mem. Am. Acad. Arts & Scis., Am. Fedn. Clin. Rsch. (award for outstanding clin. rsch. under age 40 1983), The Endocrine Soc. (Edwin B. Astwood lectr. 1987), Am. Diabetes Assn. (Eli Lilly award for rsch. 1980, Otto Brandman award N.J. affiliate 1989, Elliott P. Joslin medal Mass. affiliate), Am. Soc. Clin. Investigation (nat. coun. 1986—, pres. elect 1987-88, pres. 1988-89), Am. Soc. Biol. Chemistry, Assn. Am. Physicians, Sigma Xi, Alpha Epsilon Delta, Phi Kappa Phi, Alpha Omega Alpha. Office: Joslin Diabetes Ctr One Joslin Pl Boston MA 02215

KAHN, CHARLES EDWARD, JR., radiology educator, researcher; b. Chgo., 1958; s. Charles E. Kahn. BA, U. Wis., 1981; MD, U. Ill., Chgo., 1985. Diplomate Am. Bd. Radiology. Resident in radiology U. Chgo., 1985-89, asst. prof., 1989-91; assoc. prof. Med. Coll. Wis., Milw., 1991—, dir. info. and decision scis. dept. radiology, 1994—; adj. assoc. prof. U. Wis., Milw., 1994—; founder, co-dir. MIDAS Consortium, Milw., 1994—; numerous presentations in field at nat. and internat. sci. meetings; Konica vis. scientist Assn. Univ. Radiologists, 1990. Contbr. articles to med. jours.; author, editor World Wide Web resource CHORUS, collaborative hypertext of radiology, 1994—. Bertram A. Richardson scholar U. Ill. Coll. Medicine, 1985; biomed. engrng. rsch. grant Whitaker Found., 1995. Mem. Am. Coll. Radiology, Am. Med. Informatics Assn., Am. Roentgen Ray Soc. (scholar 1993), Radiol. Soc. N.Am., Soc. for Med. Decision Making, Am. Assn. for Artificial Intelligence. Office: Med Coll Wis 9200 W Wisconsin Ave Milwaukee WI 53226

KAHN, CYRUS IRA, ophthalmologist; b. N.Y.C., July 3, 1965; s. Robert and Clara (Polackoff) K.; m. Susan Hope Rieders, July 3, 1965; children: Deborah, Sharon. BA, NYU, Bronx, 1960; MD, NYU, N.Y.C., 1964. Diplomate Am. Bd. Ophthalmology. Intern Montefiore Hosp., Bronx, N.Y., 1964-65; resident in ophthalmology Kings County Hosp., Bklyn., 1966-69; chief ophthalmology U.S. Naval Hosp., Key West, Fla., 1969-71; pvt. practice ophthalmology Great Neck, N.Y., 1971—; chief vision svcs. Parker Jewish Geriatric Ctr., New Hyde Park, N.Y., 1975—; cons. Margaret Tietz Nursing Ctr., Jamaica, N.Y., 1975—. Contbr. chpt. to book: Care of Geriatric Medicine, 1995. Lt. comdr. USNR, 1969-71. Fellow ACS; mem. Am. Acad. Ophthalmology, N.Y. State Med. Soc., Nassau County Med. Soc., L.I. Ophthalmol. Soc., Phi Delta Epsilon (pres. North Shore chpt. 1992-94). Office: 212 Middle Neck Rd Great Neck NY 11021

KAHN, FAITH-HOPE, nurse, administrator, writer; b. N.Y.C., Apr. 25, 1921; d. Leon and Hazel (Cook) Green; RN, Beth Israel Med. Center, N.Y.C., 1942; student N.Y. U., 1943; m. Edward Kahn, May 29, 1942; children: Ellen Leora, Faith Hope II, Paula Amy. First scrub nurse operating room Beth Israel Hosp., N.Y.C., 1942; supr., operating room Hunts Point Gen. Hosp., 1942; gynecol. reconstrn. procedures researcher Phoenixville (Pa.) Gen. Hosp., 1943, Sydenham Hosp., N.Y.C., 1945; supr. ARC Disaster Field Hosp., Queens, N.Y., 1950-51; adminstr., mgr. team coordinator Dr. Edward Kahn, FACOG, Queens Village, N.Y., 1945—. Inventor, publicity chmn. Girl Scouts U.S.A., 1953; exec. dir. publicity Woodhull Schs., 1956-60, pres., 1961-62; exec. dir. publicity N.Y. Dept. Parks Figure Skating, 1956-70; exec. dir. publicity and applied arts St. John's Hosp., Smithtown, N.Y., 1965-66; state advisor N.Y., U.S. Congressional Adv. Bd., Washington, 1981—; nat. adv. bd. Am. Security Council, 1978—; founder Am. Security Found.; bd. trustees, Am. Police Hall of Fame and Mus., 1983—; mem. Republican Presdl. Task Force, 1986, Statue of Liberty and Ellis Island Centennial Commn., N.Y., 1986—. Recipient citation ARC, 1951, Am. Law Enforcement Officers Assn., Bronze medal Am. Security Council Ednl. Found., 1978, spl. recognition award Center Internat. Security Studies, 1979, Meml. Plate, Patriots of Am. Bicentennial, 1976, Great Seal of U.S.A. Plate, cert. Am. Sons Liberty, 1987, Good Smaritan award, 1987, Justice award Cross of Knights, 1987 Knights of Justice award, 1987; named Knight Chevalier Venerable Order of Michael the Archangel, 1987. Fellow, World Lit. Acad. (life), Acad. Nat. Law Enforcement (hon.); mem. Am. Acad. Ambulatory Nursing Adminstrn., Nurses Assn., Nat. League Nursing, Am. Coll. Obstetricians and Gynecologists, Nat. Assn. Physicians' Nurses, Nat. Critical Care Inst., Assn. Operating Room Nurses, AAAS, Nat. Assn. Female Execs., N.Y. Acad. Scis., Am. Police Acad. (cert. appreciation 1979, 83), Am. Fedn. Police, The Retired Officers Assn., Internat. Platform Assn., Security and Intelligence Found. (cert. appreciation 1986), Internat. Intelligence and Orgnd. Crime Investigators Assn., Smithtown Hist. Soc., Nat. Audubon Soc., NRA. Clubs: Tiyospaye, Paul Revere, Sterlingshire Woman's. Author, editor: The Easy Driving Way for Automatic and the Standard Shift, 1954; (with Edward Kahn) The Pelvic Examination, Outline and Guide for Residents, Internes and Students, 1954; (with Edward Kahn) Traction Hysterosalpingography for Uterine Lesions, 1949; contbr. articles profl. and lay jours. Home and Office: 213-16 85th Ave Jamaica NY 11427

KAHN, FREDRICK HENRY, internist; b. L.A., Aug. 26, 1925; s. Julius and Josephine Leone (Langdon) K.; m. Barbara Ruth Visscher, Feb. 14, 1952; children: Susan, Kathryn, William. AB, Stanford U., 1947, MD, 1951. Diplomate Am. Bd. Internal Medicine. Rotating intern San Francisco Gen. Hosp., 1950-51, fellow pathology, 1951-52; resident medicine Los Angeles VA Hosp., 1954-57, sr. resident, 1956-57; asst. clin. prof. medicine UCLA Sch. Medicine, 1957-91; attending physician Cedars Sinai Med. Ctr., L.A., 1957-96, attending physician emeritus, 1996—; attending physician UCLA; med. advisor Vis. Nurse Assn., Los Angeles, 1957-87. Contbr. articles to med. jours.; inventor blow through high altitude chamber; promoter iodine method of personal water disinfection for travelers and hikers. Served with USNR, 1943-46; lt. (M.C.), USNR, 1952-54. Fellow ACP; mem. AMA, Los Angeles County Internal Medicine Soc., Am. Handel Soc. Home: 3309 Corinth Ave Los Angeles CA 90066-1312

KAHN, HOWARD DALE, optometrist, consultant; b. Norfolk, Va., July 5, 1925; s.Louis and Bertha (Leon) K.; m. Dorothy Helen Mollen, July 14, 1946; children: Norman, Nancy Kahn Eberhardt. Student, U. Va., 1943-44, U. Richmond, 1944-45; OD, Pa. Coll. Optometry, Phila., 1950. Pvt. practice optometry Virginia Beach, Va., 1951-66; ptnr. Drs. Kahn and Toscano, Virginia Beach, 1966-79; ptnr. (with son) Drs. Kahn and Kahn, Virginia Beach, 1979-90, cons., 1990—. Author: Video Display Terminals and Vision, 1989; assoc. editor: Current Optometric Information and Terminology, 1974, 2d edit. 1975; contbg. author Nursing mag., 1974. Advisor, hon. life mem. All Vol. Rescue Squad, Virginia Beach, 1952—; key man Virginia Beach Civitan Club, pres., 1962; life bd. dirs. Temple Emanuel, pres., 1967. Lt. (j.g.) USNR, 1943-46; PTO. Recipient Safety Coun. award City of Virginia Beach, 1993. Fellow Coll. Optometrists in Vision Devel., Va. Acad. Optometry (pres. 1970); mem. Am. Optometric Assn. (chmn. edn. com. 1965-68, Edn. Recognition award 1979—), Va. Optometric Assn. (pres. 1965, Disting. Achievement award 1993, Optometrist of Yr. 1967), Tidewater Optometric Assn. (Contbn. to Field of Devel. Optometry award 1989), Virginia Beach Jaycees (life, pres. 1958), Kiwanis (life). Office: Drs Kahn and Kahn 1547 Laskin Rd Virginia Beach VA 23451

KAHN, MARK BENNET, vascular surgeon, educator; b. Harrisburg, Pa., Feb. 11, 1957; s. Hyman Richard and Sara (Margolis) K. BA, Oberlin Coll., 1979; MD, Jefferson Med. Coll., 1983. Diplomate Am. Bd. Gen. Surgery; cert. vascular surgeon. Resident in gen. surgery U. Pitts., 1983-85; chief resident N.J. Med. Sch., Newark, 1985-87, 87-88; staff surgeon J.L. McClellan Meml. Vets. Hosp., Little Rock, 1988-90; resident vascular surgery U. Ark. Med. Scis., Little Rock, 1988-90; asst. prof. surgery & attending surgeon Med. Coll. Pa., Phila., 1990—; asst. prof. surgery Jefferson Med. Coll., 1994—; staff surgeon, co-dir. vascular lab. Phila. VA Med. Ctr., attending surgeon Jeanes Hosp., Fox Chase Cancer Ctr., 1990-94; presenter in field; researcher in field. Contbr. articles to profl. jours. Fellow ACS, Del Val Vascular Soc., Peripheral Vascular Surgery Soc., Internat. Cardiovascular Surgery Soc., Soc. Clin. Vascular Surgeons; mem. AMA, Pa. Med. Soc., Phila. County Med. Soc.

KAHN, MARVIN WILLIAM, psychology educator; b. Cleve., Feb 1, 1926; s. Alexander and Ida (Solowitz) K.; m. Gale C. Carroll, Sept. 10, 1982; children: Karen V. Kahn Dotson, David B. PhD, Pa. State U, 1952. Diplomate Am. Bd. Profl. Psychology; cert. psychologist., Ariz. Instr., asst. prof. Yale U., New Haven, 1952-54; asst. prof., assoc. prof. U. Colo. Sch. Medicine, Denver, 1954-64; prof. Ohio U., Athens, 1964-69; prof. psychology U. Ariz., Tucson, 1969—. Office: U Ariz Dept Psychology Tucson AZ 85721

KAHN, MARY KOBASA, health facility administrator; b. Pitts., July 30, 1963; d. John Kobasa and Karen Louise (Zehr) Jersey; m. Kenneth Benjamin Kahn, Aug. 10, 1991. Diploma, Shadyside Hosp. Sch. Nursing, Pitts., 1987; BS in Nursing, Radford (Va.) U., 1994. RN, Ga.; CPHQ Health Care Quality Bd. Staff nurse Shadyside Hosp., Pitts., 1987-90; admission nurse Montgomery Regional Home Health, Blacksburg, Va., 1990-91, dir. profl. svcs., 1991-93; CQI coord. Montgomery Regional Home Health, Blacksburg, 1993-94; dir. quality improvement/utilization rev. Metro Home Health Svcs., Inc., Atlanta, 1994—. Mem. NAFE, Nat. Assn. Healthcare Quality, Assn. for Profls. in Infection Control, Phi Kappa Phi. Home: 1968 Timothy Dr NE Atlanta GA 30329 Office: Metro Home Health Svcs Inc 2045 Peachtree Rd NE Atlanta GA 30309

KAHN, SANDRA S., psychotherapist; b. Chgo., June 24, 1942; d. Chester and Ruth Sutker; m. Jack Murry Kahn, June 1, 1965; children: Erick, Jennifer. BA, U. Miami, 1964; MA, Roosevelt U., 1976. Tchr. Chgo. Pub. Schs., 1965-67; pvt. practice psychotherapy, Northbrook, Ill., 1976—. Host Shared Feelings, Sta. WEEF-AM, Highland Park, Ill., 1983—; author: The Kahn Report on Sexual Preferences, 1981, The Ex Wife Syndrome Cutting The Cord and Breaking Free After The Marriage Is Over, 1990; columnist Single Again mag. Mem. Ill. Psychol. Assn., Chgo. Psychol. Assn. (past pres. 1990). Jewish. Office: 2970 Maria Dr Northbrook IL 60062-2017

KAHN, SIGMUND BENHAM, retired internist and dean; b. Phila., May 18, 1933; s. Maxwell Louis and Clara (Parris) K.; m. Joanne Pokras, June 11, 1955; children: Marc L., Elissa Kahn Petrosky, Hillary Kahn Roth, Lauren B. BA, U. Pa., 1954, MD, 1958. Diplomate Am. Bd. Internal Medicine; cert. hematology and med. oncology. Rotating intern Albert Einstein Med. Ctr., Phila., 1958-59; resident in internal medicine Hosp. of U. Pa., Phila., 1959-61; fellow in hematology Hosp. of U. Pa., 1961-62, USPHS rsch. fellow dept. hematology, 1962-63; assoc. in hematology medicine Hahnemann U. Hosp., Phila., 1963-66; asst., assoc., then prof. medicine Hahnemann U. Hosp., 1966-94; prof. dept. neoplastic disease Hahnemann Univ. Hosp., Phila., 1978-94; dir. edn., vice chmn. dept. Hahnemann Univ. Hosp., 1978-94; assoc. dean Hahnemann U., Phila., 1986-94; prof. dept. medicine divsn. hematology/ med. oncology Med. Coll. Pa./Hahnemann U., Phila., 1994-95, assoc. dean edn., 1994-95; cons., chmn. dean's com. Wilkes-Barre (Pa.) VA Hosp., 1987-92. Mem. editl. bd. Jour. Cancer Edn., 1988-94, Am. Jour. Clin. Oncology; contbr. articles to profl. jours. Instl. rep. Boy Scouts Am., 1970-75; pres. Temple Beth Sholom, Cherry Hill, N.J., 1977-80; mem. med. bd. Lupus Found., Delaware Valley, 1977-79. Mem. AMA, ACP, Phila. County Med. Soc., Phila. Hematology Soc., Pa. Med. Soc., Am. Fedn. Clin. Rsch., Am. Hematology Soc., Am. Assn. Cancer Rsch., Am. Soc. Clin. Oncology, Am. Assn. Cancer Edn., Am. Cancer Soc. (chmn. patient svc. com. Phila. divsn. 1981-83, chmn. med. subcom. profl. edn. com. 1979-81, fin. com. 1981). Jewish. Home: 324 Surrey Rd Cherry Hill NJ 08002-1540

KAHN, STEVEN EMANUEL, medical educator; b. Durban, South Africa, July 28, 1955; m. Stephanie Berk; 2 children. MB, ChB, U. Cape Town, South Africa, 1978. Diplomate Am. Bd. Internal Medicine. Intern depts. ob./gyn. and medicine Somerset Hosp., Cape Town, South Africa, 1979; resident dept. ob./gyn. 2 Mil. Hosp., Wynberg, South Africa, 1980; resident and coord. dept. ob./gyn., 1981; resident dept. medicine divsn. endocrinology Groote Schuur Hosp., Cape Town, 1982; rsch. fellow diabetes and endocrine rsch. group U. Cape Town, 1983; resident dept. medicine Albert Einstein Med. Ctr., Phila., 1983-86; sr. rsch. fellow divsn. metabolism, endocrinology and nutrition Dept. Medicine U. Wash. Sch. of Medicine, VA Med. Ctr., Seattle, 1986-88; assoc. investigator, staff physician divsn. endocrinology and metabolism Dept. Medicine VA Med. Ctr., Seattle 1988-91, rsch. assoc., staff physician divsn. endocrinology and metabolism Dept. Medicine, 1991-95; acting instr. divsn. metabolism, endocrinology and nutrition Dept. Medicine U. Wash. Sch. of Medicine, Seattle, 1988-92, asst. prof. divsn. metabolism, endocrinology and nutrition Dept. Medicine, 1992-95, assoc. prof. divsn. metabolism, endocrinology and nutrition Dept. Medicine, 1995—. Mem. editl. bd. Jour. Clin. Endocrinology and Metabolism, 1995—; contbr. articles to profl. jours. Amelia Schenkman scholar, 1973-75; named Assoc. Investigator, Dept. VA, 1988, Rsch. Assoc., 1991; recipient Career Devel. award Juvenile Diabetes Found., 1988, Feasibility award Dana Found., 1989, Clin. Investigator award NIH, 1991, New Investigator award Diabetes Rsch. Coun., 1992-94, Rsch. award Am. Diabetes Assn., 1996. Mem. ACP, Am. Diabetes Assn. (bd. dirs. Washington affiliate 1993-94, exec. bd. dirs. 1994—, rsch. grant rev. panel 1994—), Am. Fedn. Clin. Rsch. (chair program com. for metabolism 1994, 96, councillor western sect. 1994-96, pres.- elect western sect. 1996, nat. councillor 1996), Western Soc. Clin. Investigation, Gen. Med. Coun. (U.K.), Endocrine Soc. Office: VA Puget Health Care Sys 1660 S Columbian Way Seattle WA 98108

KAHN, THOMAS, medical educator; b. Offenburg, Germany, June 23, 1938; s. Ludwig and Ellen (Kaufman) K.; m. Si Mi Pak, Nov. 7, 1968; children: Diana, David, Philip. BA, NYU, 1958, MD, 1962. Intern medicine Balt. City Hosps., 1962-63, U. Pitts. Hosps., 1963-64; intern medicine Mt. Sinai, N.Y.C., 1964-65, resident in nephrology, 1965-67; chief renal sect. Bronx VA Med. Ctr., 1979-96; prof. medicine Mt. Sinai Sch. Medicine, N.Y.C., 1988—. Maj. U.S. Army, 1967-69. Office: VA Med Ctr 130 W Kingsbridge Rd Bronx NY 10468-3992

KAHN, WALTER J., ophthalmologist; b. Schotten, Germany, June 21, 1934; came to U.S., 1936; s. Max and Celia (Weil) K.; m. Susan Kahn, July 30, 1969; children: Peter, Mike, Margie. MD, U. Chgo., 1959. Intern Phila. Gen. Hosp., 1959-60; resident in ophthalmology U. Ill., Chgo., 1960-63, surg. instr., 1963-64; asst. clin. assoc. Hahneman Med. Sch., 1985—; pres. med. staff River View Med. Ctr., Red Bank, N.J., 1995—. Pres. Monmouth County Med. Soc., 1991-92. Mem. AMA (alt. del. 1992-96, del. 1996—), Med. Soc. N.J. (vice-spkr. 1992-95, spkr. 1995-96). Office: 70 E Front Red Bank NJ 07701

KAHRILAS, PETER JAMES, medical educator, researcher; b. Culver City, Calif., June 9, 1953; s. Peter Jerome and Leticia (Llorett) K.; m. Elyse Anne Lambiase, Mar. 30, 1984; children: Genevieve Anne, Ian James, Miranda Elyse. Student, Yale U., 1971-75, U. Rochester, N.Y., 1975-79. Resident in medicine U. Hosp. of Cleve., 1979-82; fellow in gastroenterology Northwestern U., Chgo., 1982-84; rsch. fellow Med. Coll. of Wis., Milw., 1984-86, asst. prof. medicine, 1986-90, assoc. prof. medicine, 1990-95; prof. medicine, 1995—; dir. lab. Northwestern Meml. Hosp., Chgo. Contbr. articles to profl. jours. NIH grantee, 1990—. Fellow ACP, Cen. Soc. for Clin. Rsch., Am. Coll. Gastroenterology; mem. Am. Gastroenterol. Assn., Am. Fedn. for Clin. Rsch., Am. Soc. for Gastrointestinal Endoscopy, Am. Motility Soc. Democrat. Home: 203 Columbia Ave Park Ridge IL 60068-4923 Office: Northwestern U 746 Passavant 303 E Superior St Chicago IL 60611-3015

KAIDEN, RICHARD LOUIS, ophthalmologist; b. Bklyn., Feb. 2, 1941; s. Murray and Lillian (Rosenthal) K.; children from previous marriage: Jonathan, Douglas, Amy; m. Ellen Siris, Aug. 23, 1992. BA, Cornell U., 1962; MD, Albert Einstein, 1966. Diplomate Am. Bd. Ophthalmology. Ophthalmologist Dr. Soll & Kaiden, P.A., Westwood, N.J., 1971-75, Westwood Ophthalmology Assocs., P.A., 1975—; bd. trustees Pascack Valley Hosp., Westwood, 1980, 81, pres. gen. active staff, 1980, 81; team ophthalmologist N.J. Giants, N.J. Nets, N.J. Knights, 1984—. Capt. U.S. Army, 1966-67. Mem. Am. Acad. Ophthalmology, Am. Bd. Ophthalmology, Am. Coll. Surgeons, Bergen County Med. Soc., AMA. Office: Westwood Ophthalmology Asso 300 Fairview Ave Westwood NJ 07675-1703

KAIDO, BONNELL DOLORES, medical education administrator; b. Cooperstown, N.Y., Dec. 5, 1951; d. Samuel Wellington and Bernadette Elizabeth (Rafferty) K. AAS in Bus., SUNY, 1972; BS in Bus., Coll. of St. Rose, 1974; MS in Edn., U. Albany, 1978. Bus. educator Sharon Springs Cen. Sch., 1975-80; supr. The Mary Imogene Bassett Hosp., Cooperstown, 1980-82, coord. med. edn., 1982-86, asst. dir. med. edn., 1986—; mem. com. Assn. for Hosp. Med. Edn., 1989—, vice chair mem. com., 1991—, nominating com., 1993-95; dir. Med. Alumni Assn. MIBH, Cooperstown, 1988—; spkr. Alliance for Continuing Med. Edn., 1991, Assn. Hosp. Med. Edn. Spring Inst., 1988-91, 94, N.J. Assn. Med. Edn. New Directions in Med. Edn., 1988, N.J. Med. Soc., Coun. Adminstrn. Direct in Med. Edn. Workshop, 1986, 89, chmn.-elect, 1988-91, chair, 1992-94, immediate past chair, 1994-96; instr. emergency med. svcs. Otsego County Emergency Svcs.; mem. regional EMS faculty N.Y. State Dept. Health, 1995—. Mem. Otsego EMS Coun., 1990—, chair, 1996—; CPR instr. Am. Heart Assn.; capt. Cooperstown Fire Dept. Emergency Squad, 1992-96; mem. Adirondack-Appalachian Regional Emergency Med. Svcs. Coun., 1990—, LWV. Mem. LWC, Delta Kappa Gamma, Delta Pi Epsilon. Democrat. Roman Catholic. Office: The Mary Imogene Bassett Hosp One Atwell Rd Cooperstown NY 13326

KAIL, DEBRA CAROL, family nurse practitioner; b. Brownsville, Tenn., May 10, 1954; d. James and Elizabeth Kail. ADN, Union U., Jackson, Tenn., 1974; FNP cert., U. Ala., 1979; BSN, U. Memphis, 1992; MSN in Adult Health Nursing, Ark. State U., 1995. RN, Ark., Tenn., Miss.; cert. FNP, ANCC; cert. RN practitioner, Ark. Charge nurse Jackson-Madison County Gen. Hosp., 1974-77; evening supr. Parkway Hosp., Jackson, 1977-78; FNP, Lake County Primary Care Ctr., Tiptonville, Tenn., 1979-81; FMP, health educator, nursing supr. East Ark. Family Health Ctr., West Memphis, Ark., 1981—; rehab. specialist, case mgr. Rehab. Mgmt., Little Rock, 1989-91; inscvc. HIV/AIDS presenter. Mem. ANA, NAFE, Am. Acad. Nurse Practitioners, Am. Assn. Diabetes Educators, Ark. Nurses Assn., Sigma Theta Tau. Methodist. Home: 304 N Worthington Dr West Memphis AR 72301

KAIL, KONRAD, physician; b. Iowa City, July 7, 1949; s. Joseph Andrew Kail and Jean Lucille (Peterson) Tienan; m. Jane Marie Petersen, Jan. 5, 1973. BS in Biology, U. Houston, 1974; BS in Medicine, Baylor Coll. Medicine, 1976; ND, Nat. Coll. Naturopathic, Medicine, 1983; DACNFM, Am. Coll. Naturopathic Family, Medicine, 1995. Lic. naturopathic physician. Cardiac-catherization technician St. Luke's/Tex. Children's Hosp., Houston, 1972-75; physician's asst. various clinics, Silver City, N.Mex., 1976-80; dir. Naturopathic Wheeling and Healing Around Country Bike Tour, 1983-84; chmn. bd. dirs. U.S. Complementary Health, Inc., Phoenix, 1995—; dean postgrad. med. edn. S.W. Coll. of Naturopathic Medicine, Phoenix, 1996—; owner, operator Naturopathic Family Care, Phoenix, 1990—; cons. Ins. Cos., Nutrient Supplement Cos., Govt. Agys., 1985—. Editor: Alternative Medicine, 1994; contbr. articles to profl. jours. Bd. dirs. Inst. for Natural Medicine. With USN Res., 1971-76. Fellow Am. Assn. Naturopathic Physicians (chmn. scientific affil. 1986, pres. 1992-94), Am. Coll. Naturopathic Family Practice (chmn., pres. 1995—). Green Party. Office: Naturopathic Family Care Ste C2-4 13832 N 32d St Phoenix AZ 85032

KAISER, FRAN ELIZABETH, endocrinologist, gerontologist; b. N.Y.C., Dec. 6, 1949; d. Philip Francis and Bronia (Weiss) K.; m. T.B. Levine, June 1, 1975 (div. 1987). BS, CCNY, 1970; MD, N.Y. Med. Coll., N.Y.C., 1974. Diplomate Am. Bd. Internal Medicine, Am. Bd. Geriatrics. Intern Beth Israel Med. Ctr., N.Y.C., 1974-75, resident to chief resident, 1975-78; fellow in endocrinology and metabolism U. Minn., Mpls., 1978-81, instr. dept. medicine, 1980-81, asst. prof., 1981-86; asst. prof. in residence UCLA Sch. medicine, 1986-89; assoc. prof. medicine St. Louis U., 1989-94, prof., 1994—, assoc. dir. divsn. geriatric medicine, 1989-94; chief sect. endocrinology and metabolism Dept. Internal Medicine, St. Paul Ramsey Med. Ctr./U. Minn. Hosps., St. Paul, 1981-86; John A. Hartford Geriatric Faculty Devel. award scholar Hartford Found., N.Y.C./UCLA Sch. Medicine, 1986-87; chief geriatric medicine Olive View Med. Ctr./UCLA San Fernando Valley Program, Sylmar, Calif., 1987-89; med. dir. Hosp. Based Home Care, VA Med. Ctr., Sepulveda, 1987-89. Ad hoc reviewer Jour. Clin. Endocrinology and Metabolism, Endocrinology, Jour. AMA, Jour. Am. Geriatrics Soc.; past mem. editl. bd. Am. Geriatric Soc., Internat. Medicine Bull.; cons. editor Am. Health Mag.; contbr. articles to profl. jours. Grantee NIH, 1980-81, Genetech, 1987-89, Syntex Corp. 1990-92, Hoechst-Roussel, 1992-94, Bur. Health Professions, 1991-97, VIVUS, 1993—, Merck, 1994—, Upjohn, 1995—. Mem. AAAS, Am. Diabetes Assn.,Endocrine Soc., Am. Fedn. Clin. Rsch., N.Y. Acad. Sci., Women's Caucus of the Endocrine Soc., Gerontol. Soc. Am., Am. Geriatrics Soc. (past mem. editl. bd. Internal Medicine Bull., Jour. Am. Geriatrics Soc., Jour. Geriatric Nephrology & Urology), Am. Assn. of Home Care Physicians (rsch. com.), Am. Geriatrics Soc. (adv. bd. aging parents project), Impotence Inst. of Am. Office: St Louis U Med Sch 1402 S Grand Blvd # 238M Saint Louis MO 63104-1004

KAISER, GEORGE CHARLES, surgeon; b. Bronx, N.Y., July 30, 1928; s. George P. and Bertha B. (Schwehla) K.; m. Jane Haggart, Nov. 21, 1953; children—Barbara, G. Charles, James H. A.B. in Biology, Lehigh U., 1949; M.D., Johns Hopkins U., 1953. Diplomate: Am. Bd. Surgery, Am. Bd. Thoracic Surgery. Intern in surgery Johns Hopkins Hosp., Balt., 1953-54;

resident in gen. and thoracic surgery Ind. U. Med. Center, Indpls., 1956-61; instr. surgery Ind. U. Med. Center, 1961-63, asst. prof. surgery, 1963; practice medicine specializing in cardiovascular and thoracic surgery St. Louis, 1963—; staff surgeon VA Hosp., Indpls., 1961-63; staff surgeon St. Louis U. Hosps., chief thoracic and cardiovascular surgery, 1975—; mem. staff St. Mary's Health Center, St. Louis City Hosp., chief surgery, 1967-68, cons. surgery, 1968—; cons. surgery John Cochran Va Hosp., 1965—; asst. prof. surgery St. Louis U. Sch. Medicine, 1963-65, asso. prof., 1965-70, prof. surgery, 1970—. Contbr. numerous articles on cardiology and cardiovascular surgery to profl. jours. Served with USPHS, 1954-56. Fellow A.C.S., Am. Heart Assn. Council Cardiovascular Surgery; mem. Am. Assn. Thoracic Surgery, Internat. Cardiovascular Soc., Midwestern Vascular Surg. Soc., Soc. Vascular Surgery, Soc. Thoracic Surgeons, Am. Coll. Cardiology, Am. Coll. Angiology, Am. Surg. Assn., Central Surg. Assn., So. Surg. Assn., St. Louis Thoracic Surg. Soc., Am. Fedn. Clin. Research, So. Thoracic Surg. Soc., St. Louis Cardiac Club, Am. Soc. Artificial Internal Organs, St. Louis Heart Assn. (Arthur E. Strauss award 1981), AMA, Mo. Med. Assn., Mo. Heart Assn., Sigma Xi, Alpha Omega Alpha. Episcopalian. Home: 30 Joy Ave Saint Louis MO 63119-2502 Office: 1325 S Grand Blvd Saint Louis MO 63104-1018

KAISER, MARC CLAUDE, radiologist; b. Luxembourg, Luxembourg, Dec. 16, 1950; s. Marcel R. and Olga (Demuth) K.; m. Dianna N. Barron, May 28, 1995. MD, Grand Duchy of Luxembourg, 1975, Dr. Chirurgie, 1976, Dr. Obstetrique, 1976; Diploma in Radiology, U. Utrecht, The Netherlands, 1980. Intern radiologist Academisch Ziekenhuis, Utrecht, 1976-80; replacement intern radiologist Horacio Oduber Hosp., Aruba, Netherland Antilles, 1979; temp. radiologist Hosp. for Sick Children, Toronto, Ont., Can., 1980-81; staff radiologist Centre Hosp., Luxembourg, 1981-85, Hosp. Free Univ., Amsterdam, Holland, 1985-89, Sacred Heart Hosp., Luxembourg, 1989—. Co-author: (with M. Sperber) Magnetic Resonance Imaging of the Thorax, 1987, (with L. Ramos) MRI of the Spine, 1990, (with L. Ramos) RMN de la Columna Vertebral, 1992; editor: Medizine im Bild, 1994—; contbr. numerous articles and abstracts to profl. jours., chpts. to books. Fellow Royal Soc. Medicine; mem. Brit. Inst. Radiology, Luxembourg Soc. Radiology, Assn. Medecins et Medecins Dentistes Luxembourg, Coll. d'Enseignement Post Univ. de Radiologie. Roman Catholic. Office: Sacred Heart Hosp, 48A Ave Gaston Diderich, L-1420 Luxembourg Luxembourg

KAISER, NINA IRENE, health facility administrator; b. San Diego, Nov. 29, 1953; d. Louis Frederick and Mary Elizabeth (Wright) K.; m. N. Klimist, Aug. 27, 1987; children: Kellen Anne Kaiser, Ethan Andrew Kaiser-Klimist. BSN, BA in Women Studies, San Francisco State U., 1980. RN, Calif. RN Calif. Pacific Med. Ctr., San Francisco, 1980-81, Ralph K. Davies Med. Ctr., San Francisco, 1982-85, Planned Parenthood, San Francisco, 1985-86, Visiting Nurses and Hospice, San Francisco, 1986-88; RN supr. St. Mary's Home Care, San Francisco, 1991-93; RN dir. St. Vincent's Homecare and Hospice, Fremont, Calif., 1993-94, Home Health Link, San Leandro, Calif., 1994—. Pres. Daus. of Bilitis, San Francisco, 1977-78; founding mem. Buena Vista Lesbian and Gay Parents Assn., San Francisco, 1985; treas., bd. dirs. Holladay Ave. Homeowners Assn., San Francisco, 1984-96; bd. dirs. Midrasha High Sch., Berkeley, Calif., 1996. With USN, 1971-74.

KAJI, AKIRA, microbiology scientist, educator; b. Tokyo, Jan. 13, 1930; came to U.S., 1954; s. Kiichi and Chiyo (Hanai) K.; m. Hideko Katayama, Aug. 22, 1958; children: Kenneth, Eugene, Naomi, Amy. BS, Tokyo U., 1953; PhD, Johns Hopkins U., 1958; MS (hon.), U. Pa., 1973. Rsch. fellow Johns Hopkins Hosp., Balt., 1958-59; guest investigator Rockefeller U., N.Y.C., 1959; rsch. assoc. microbiology Vanderbilt Med. Sch., Nashville, 1959-62; vis. scientist Oak Ridge (Tenn.) Nat. Lab., 1962-63; assoc. U. Pa. Med. Sch., Phila., 1963-64, asst. prof. microbiology, 1964-67, assoc. prof., 1967-72, prof., 1972—; permanent mem. bd. sci. councilors Nat. Eye Inst., Bethesda, Md., 1987-92; prof., chair Tokyo U. Faculty Pharm. Scis., 1972-73; vis. prof. Kyoto U. Virus Rsch. Inst., 1985. Contbr. over 200 articles to profl. jours. Recipient Fulbright-Smith-Mundt award, 1954, Helen Hay Whitney award, 1964-69, John Simmon Guggenheim award, 1972-73, Fogarty Internat. Sr. award, 1985-86. Mem. Am. Soc. Biol. Chemistry and Molecular Biology, Am. Soc. Cell Biology, Am. Soc. Microbiology, Am. Soc. Chemistry. Office: U Pa Sch Medicine Dept Microbiology Johnson Pavilion Philadelphia PA 19104

KAJI, HIDEKO KATAYAMA, pharmacology educator; b. Tokyo, Jan. 1, 1932; came to U.S., 1954; d. Sakae and Tsuneko (Matsuda) Katayama; m. Akira Kaji, Aug. 23, 1958; children: Kenneth, Eugene, Naomi, Amy. BS, Tokyo Coll. Pharmacy, 1954; MS, U. Nebr., 1956; PhD, Purdue U., 1958. Vis. scientist Oak Ridge (Tenn.) Nat. Lab., 1962-63; assoc. U. Pa., Phila., 1963-64; rsch. assoc. The Inst. Cancer Rsch., Phila., 1965-66, asst. mem., 1966-76; vis. mem. Max Planck Inst. Molek. Gen., Berlin, 1972-73, Nat. Inst. Med. Rsch., London, 1973; assoc. prof. Jefferson Med. Coll., Phila., 1976-82; vis. prof. Wistar Inst., Phila., 1984-85; prof. pharmacology and structural biology Jefferson Med. Coll., Phila., 1983—; cons. Nippon Paint Co., Ltd., Tokyo, 1990—, Coatesville (Pa.) VA Hosp., 1982-84. Contbr. articles to profl. jours. Fellow NIH (bd. dirs. 1986-89); mem. Am. Soc. Biochemistry and Molecular Biology, Am. Soc. Pharmacol. and Exptl. Therapeutics, Am. Soc. Microbiology, Sigma Xi. Home: 334 Fillmore St Jenkintown PA 19046-4328 Office: Jefferson Med Coll 1020 Locust St Philadelphia PA 19107-6731

KAKATI, DINESH CHANDRA, physician; b. Gauhati, India, Feb. 1, 1941; arrived in Eng., 1969; s. Nara Kanta and Subhandra (Baishya) K.; m. Bhabani Medhi, Mar. 27, 1974; children: Rita, Rishi. MBBS with distinction, Gauhati Med. Sch., 1967; Diploma in Tropical Medicine and Hygiene, Liverpool (Eng.) U., 1970; Diploma in Thoracic Medicine, London U., 1984, Diploma in Cardiac Medicine, 1984; Diploma in Geriatric Medicine, Royal Coll. Physicians, 1985. Sr. house officer Sunderland (Eng.) Health Authority, 1969-70, med. registrar, 1970-72; med. registrar Addinbrook Hosp., Cambridge, Eng., 1972-74, London Hosp., 1974-77; assoc. specialist N.E. Thames region, Hornchurch, Eng., 1977-84, asst. physician in medicine, 1984—. Fellow Royal Soc. Health Eng.; mem. Brit. Med. Assn., Royal Coll. Gen. Practitioners (assoc.), Cultural Assn. of Assam in England (pres.). Home: 99 Ardleigh Green Rd, Emerson Park, Hornchurch, Essex RM11 2LE, England Office: St Georges Hosp, Suttons Ln, London E6 S56, England

KAKIMOTO, YUKIKO, medical researcher. Flight safety rsch. psychologist Behavioral Sci. divsn. Japan Air Self Def. Forces, dir. Editor Traffic Psychology, Aerospace & Environ. Medicine; chief editor Applied Physiology; contbr. articles to profl. jours. Fellow Aerospace Med. Assn. (Raymond F. Longacre award 1996); mem. Aerospace Human Factors Assn., Japan Soc. Aerospace & Environ. Medicine, Japanese Assn. Psychology, Japanese Assn. Ergonomics, Japanese Assn. Applied Psychology, Japanese Assn. Traffic Psychology. *

KAKIZOE, SABURO, surgeon; b. Fukuoka, Japan, June 6, 1958; s. Shinobu and Tamako (Shimura) K.; m. Yumiko Hironaga, May 27, 1990; children: Showtaro, Mayuco. MD, Kurume U., Fukuoka, 1983; PhD, Kyushu U., Fukuoka, 1988. Surg. resident Kyushu U., Fukuoka, 1983-84; vis. fellow dept. pathology Kurume U., Fukuoka, 1984-86; rsch. fellow dept. pathology Wis. U., Madison, 1987-88; fellow dept. pathology Pitts. U., 1988-89, fellow dept. surgery, 1989; staff surgeon Ctrl. Fukuoka Nat. Hosp., 1989-90; fellow surgeon Kyushu U., Fukuoka, 1990-91; staff surgeon Kakizoe Hosp., Hirado, Nagasaki, Japan, 1991-93, chief dept. surgery, 1993—. Contbr. articles to profl. jours. Mem. Japan Surg. Soc., Am. Assn. for Study Liver Disease, Transplantation Soc., Internat. Gasto-Surg. Club, Smithsonian Instn., Porsche Owners Club Japan, Hirado Triathlon Club. Office: Kakizoe Hosp Dept Surgery, Kagamigawa 278, Nagasaki 859-51, Japan

KAKUGAWA, TERRI ETSUMI, osteopath; b. Honolulu, Sept. 16, 1965; d. Paul Katsumi and Ruby Yetsuko (Oshiro) K. BA, U. Hawaii, 1987; DO, Kirksville Coll. Osteo. Medicine, 1992. Diplomate Am. Bd. Osteo. Family Physicians. Intern Cmty. Health Ctr., Branch County, Coldwater, Mich., 1992-93, resident in family medicine, 1993-95; group practice Waianae, Hawaii, 1995—. Mem. Am. Osteo. Assn., Am. Coll. Osteo. Family Physicians, Hawaii Assn. Osteo. Physicians and Surgeons. Democrat. Office: Waianae Coast Comprehensive Health Ctr 87-2070 Farrington Hwy Waianae HI 96792

KALACHMAN, MARVIN STEVEN, physician assistant; b. N.Y.C., Oct. 20, 1949; s. Abraham and Sylvia K. BA, Queens Coll. (CUNY), 1975, CUNY, 1975; MS and EAP certification, St. Joseph's U., 1984. Cert. physician asst. Physician asst. J.C. Rex Thoracic Surg. Group, Allentown, Pa., 1977; physician asst. supervisor St. Luke's Children's Med. Ctr., Phila., 1977-84; from supervisor ambulatory care to adminstrv. dir. inpatient VA Med. Ctr., Providence, R.I., 1984-91; physician asst. Occupl. Health & Rehab., R.I., Mass., 1994; physcian asst. Child & Adolescent Behavioral Health Ctr. Three Springs Inc., Huntsville, Ala., 1995—. Clinician Nat. Depression Screen, Huntsville, 1994, 95; vol. Kidspace Cmty. Program, Huntsville, 1995; coord. Project Heartbeat United Way, Phila., 1980s. Fellow Am. Acad. Physician Assts., VA Physician Assts. Assn., Ala. Soc. of Physician Assts., Am. Acad. Med. Adminstrs., Am. Acad. Healthcare Info. Mgrs.; mem. Am. Coll. Healthcare Execs. Office: Child & Adolescent Health 247C Chateau Dr Huntsville AL 35801

KALAUAWA, ELLIOT JOSEPH, physician; b. Honolulu, Aug. 30, 1953; s. Pastor Ganal and Rebecca Kalauawa; m. Luana Lovey Garcia, Dec. 14, 1991. BA in Biology, Whitman Coll., 1975; MD, U. Hawaii, 1979. Diplomate Am. Bd. Internal Medicine. Flexible intern U. Hawaii, Honolulu, 1979-80, resident in internal medicine, 1981-83, chief resident in medicine, 1983-84; resident in internal medicine Valley Med. Ctr., Fresno, Calif., 1980-81; liaison physician Marshall Islands Govt., Honolulu, 1983-84; pvt. practice Kaneohe, Hawaii, 1984-86; med. dir. Waikiki Health Ctr., Honolulu, 1986—. Mem. ACP. Jehovah's Witness. Office: Waikiki Health Ctr 277 Ohua Ave Honolulu HI 96815

KALAYJIAN, ANIE SANENTZ, educator, international consultant, logotherapeutic psychotherapist, nurse; b. Aleppo, Syria; came to U.S., 1971; d. Kevork and Zabelle (Mardikian) K.; m. Shahé Navasart Sanentz, Dec. 16, 1984. BS L.I. U., 1979; MEd, Columbia U., 1981, EdD, 1985, profl. nurses tng. course, 1984; cert. photography, Pratt Inst., 1979. R.N., N.Y., N.J., Conn.; cert. psychiat. mental health specialist; Dutch diplomate in logotherapy; advanced cert. in Eye Movement Desensitization and Reprocessing, advanced cert. in disaster mgmt. ARC. Psychiat. nurse Met. Hosp., N.Y.C., 1979-84; staff psychiat. mental health nurse Manhattan Bowery Project, N.Y.C., 1978-86; instr. Hunter Coll., N.Y.C., 1980-82; prof. Bloomfield Coll., N.J., 1984-85; lectr. Jersey City Coll., 1985; prof. Seton Hall U., South Orange, N.J., 1985-87; assoc. prof. grad. program St. Joseph Coll., 1987-91; prof. John Jay Coll. Criminal Justice Fairleigh Dickinson U., 1991-92, vis. prof., 1991-92, Pace U., N.Y.C., 1994-95; adj. prof. Coll. Mt. St. Vincent, Riverdale, N.Y., 1995—, disting. lectr., Columbia U., N.Y.C., 1995; spkr. in field; keynote spkr. Mid Am. Logotherapy Inst., 1995, Coll. Mt. St. Vincent, 1995, Hollins Coll., Va., 1995, UN. Active com. for presdl. task force on nursing curriculum Soc. for Traumatic Stress Studies; co-founder, East coast coord. Mental Health Outreach to Earthquake Survivors in Armenia; dir. Julia Richman-Pace Univ.-N.Y. State Bd. Edn.-Visiting Nurse Svc.-Partnership program, 1991-92; UN rep. World Fedn. For Mental Health, mem. mental health/ human rights com. 1996—. Author: Disaster and Mass Trauma: Global Perspectives on Post Disaster Mental Health Management, 1995; contbr. articles to profl. jours, chpts. to books; reviewer: Readings: A Journal of Reviews and Commentary in Mental Health, 1995. Recipient Clark Found. scholarship award, 1985, Outstanding Rsch. award Columbia U., 1993, Disting. Svc. award N.Y. Counties RN Assn., 1994, ABSA Outstanding Achievement award APA, 1995; rsch. grantee Pace U., 1992; Endowed Nursing Edn., Columbia U., scholar, 1984; Armenian Relief Soc. scholar, 1976-77, Armenian Students Assn. Am. scholar, 1976-78, Columbia U. Tchrs. Coll., Outstanding Rsch. award, 1993. Fellow Am. Orthopsychiat. Assn., N.Y. State Nursing Assn. (planning com. nursing edn.); mem. APA (outstanding achievement award 1995), Coun. on Continuing Edn., Psychiat. and Mental Health Nursing (coun.), Am. Psychiat. Nurses Assn., Internat. Coun. Psychologists, Internat. Trauma Counselors, Inst. for Psychodynamics and Origins of Mind, Armenian Students Assn. (treas. 1980-81, pres. 1981-83, scholarship chairperson 1983-85, v.p. Cen. Exec. Com. 1987-88, pres. 1988-89, elected nat. pres. 1988-90), Armenian Info. Profls. (corr. sec., 1992—), Armenian-Am. Soc. for Studies on Stress and Genocide (founder, pres. 1988—), N.Y. Registered Nurses' Assn. (chairperson edn. com., 1989—), World Fed. for Mental Health (UN rep. 1994—, treas., sec., UN com. on human rights, 1994—), Univ. for Peace (cooresponding sec. UN com.), Internat. Soc. Tramatic Stress Studies (v.p. N.Y. chpt. 1993-95, pres. 1995—), N.Y. State Nurses Assn. (coun. Human Rights, 1996—), N.Y. Counties RN Assn. (Jane Delano Disting. Svc. award 1994), N.Y. State Nurses Assn. (coun. on human rights 1995—), Kappa Delta Pi (advisor 1989-90), Sigma Theta Tau (Alpha Zeta chpt. 1981—). Avocations: aerobics, photography, acting. Office: 130 W 79th St New York NY 10024-6477

KALB, DIANE M., psychiatric nurse; b. Shelby, Ohio, June 14, 1962; d. Thomas C. and Ruth E. (Shaeffer) Reffert; m. Gregory A. Kalb, Sept. 6, 1980; children: Douglas A., Joseph B., Rebecca M. ADN, North Ctrl. Tech. Coll., Mansfield, Ohio, 1992. RN, Ohio. Staff nurse Heartland of Bucyrus, Ohio, 1993, Richland Hosp., Mansfield, Ohio, 1993—.

KALBFLEISCH, JOHN MCDOWELL, cardiologist, educator; b. Lawton, Okla., Nov. 15, 1930; s. George and Etta Lillian (McDowell) K.; m. Jolie Harper, Dec. 30, 1961. AS, Cameron A&M U., Lawton, 1950; BS, U. Okla., 1952, M.D., 1957. Diplomate Am. Bd. Internal Medicine, subsplty. bd. cardiovascular disease. Intern U. Va. Hosp., 1957-58; resident and fellow U. Okla. Med. Ctr., 1958-62, instr. medicine, 1964-66, asst. prof., 1966-69, assoc. clin. prof., 1970-78, clin. prof. Tulsa br., 1978—; pvt. practice specializing in cardiology Tulsa, 1969—; pres., chief exec. officer Cardiology of Tulsa, Inc., 1969—; dir. cardiovascular svcs. St. Francis Hosp., Tulsa, 1975—; mem. physician adv. bd. City of Tulsa, 1978-81; bd. dirs. St. Francis Hosp., mem. exec. com., 1987—; treas. Tulsa Med. Edn. Found., 1988-89, v.p., 1990-92, pres., 1992-94; med. dir., chmn. bd. Warren Clinics, 1990—; mem. Okla. Ctr. for Advancement of Sci. and Tech., 1989-95; mem. adv. com. Ctr. for Lasser Devel. and Applications, Okla. State U. Contbr. articles to profl. jours. Served with USPHS, 1962-64. Fellow ACP (gov.-elect Okla. 1990-91, gov. 1991-95, Okla. Laureate award 1995), Am. Coll. Cardiology (gov. Okla. 1978-81); mem. AMA, AAAS, Tulsa County Med. Soc., Okla. State Med. Assn., Am. Heart Assn. (coun. on clin. cardiology), tchg. scholar 1967-69), Okla. Soc. Internal Medicine (v.p., pres.-elect 1983-84, pres. 1985-86), Am. Soc. Internal Medicine, Am. Fedn. Clin. Rsch., Am. Inst. Nutrition, Delta Upsilon. Republican. Presbyterian. Office: 6585 S Yale Ave Ste 800 Tulsa OK 74136-8321

KALEN, VICKI, pediatric orthopaedist; b. N.Y.C., May 15, 1951; d. Marshall and Gladys K.; 1 child, Allegra Faith. BA, U. Pa., 1973; MD, Temple U., 1977. Intern Abington (Pa.) Meml. Hosp., 1977-78; resident Temple U. Med. Ctr., Phila., 1978-82; fellow Stanford U. Med. Ctr., 1982-83; asst. prof. surgery Stanford (Calif.) U. Sch. Medicine, 1983-84; asst. head orthopaedics Palo Alto (Calif.) VA Med. Ctr., 1983-84; dir. spinal & trauma Stanford U. Med. Ctr., 1984; assoc. med. dir. Carrie Tingley Hosp., Albuquerque, 1985-86; asst. prof. U. Fla., Gainesville, 1987-89; orthopaedic faculty U. Hosp., Jacksonville, Fla., 1988—; assoc. prof. U. Fla., 1989—; adj. asst. prof. U. N.Mex. Hosp., Albuquerque, 1985-86; acting med. dir. Carrie Tingley Hosp., 1986; cons. Shriner's Hosp., Tampa, Fla., 1987-93, Nemours Childrens Clinic, Jacksonville, 1990—. Mem. NASA Space Shuttle Med. Support Team, 1989—. Recipient Residents Teaching award U. Fla., 1994. Mem. Am. Acad. Orthopaedic Surgeons, Am. Acad. Cerebral Palsy and Developmental Medicine, Pediatric Orthopaedic Soc. N.Am., Fla. Med. Assn., Scoliosis Rsch. Soc., Ruth Jackson Orthopaedic Soc., Alpha Omega Alpha. Office: U Fla Coll Medicine 1600 SW Archer Rd JHMHC Box 100246 Gainesville FL 32610

KALENSCHER, ALAN JAY, surgeon; b. Bklyn., July 9, 1926; s. Abraham and Julia (Horwitz) K.; BS, Union Coll., Schenectady, 1945; MD, N.Y. U., 1949; m. Hannah Blaufox, June 18, 1949; children: Judith Lynne, Mark Robert. Intern Morrisania City Hosp., N.Y.C., 1949-50; surg. resident Maimonides Med. Ctr., Bklyn., 1950-51, 54; asst., then chief resident Bronx Mcpl. Hosp. Ctr., 1954-56; mem. faculty surgery dept. Albert Einstein Coll. Medicine, 1956-59; practice medicine specializing in surgery, Sacramento, 1959-84; chief med. officer Disability Evaluation Div. Calif. State Dept. Soc. Svcs., 1984—; attending surgeon Sacramento Med. Ctr.; commr. Bd. Med. Quality Assurance Calif.; clin. faculty dept. surgery U. Calif. Coll. Medicine, Davis, 1970-75 . Served with USNR, 1943-45, 51-53; ETO, Korea. Recipient citation N.Y.C. Cancer Com., 1959. Diplomate Am. Bd. Surgery, Nat. Bd. Med. Examiners (examiner 1957-59). Fellow Am. Soc. Contemporary Medicine and Surgery; mem. AAAS, Calif. Med. Assn., Sacramento County Med. Soc., Am. Diabetes Assn., Am. Mensa Ltd.

KALIN, MARCIA FAY, physician; b. N.Y.C.; BA cum laude, Brandeis U., 1976; MD, Mt. Sinai Sch. Medicine, 1980. Resident in internal medicine Overlook Hosp., Summit, N.J., 1980-81; editor Sci. Am., N.Y.C., 1981-83; resident in internal medicine Beth Israel Med. Ctr., N.Y.C., 1983-85, fellow in endocrinology, 1985-88, attending physician in internal medicine, 1988-93, head diabetes sect. divsn. endocrinology dept. medicine, 1993—. Office: Beth Israel Med Ctr 1st Ave at 16th St New York NY 10003

KALINA, IVAN, pediatrician; b. Kosice, Slovak Republic, May 22, 1932; came to U.S., 1965; s. Geza and Helen (Fedorak) K.; m. Vera M., July 1, 1956; children: Peter, Yvette. MD, Charles U., Prague, Czechoslovakia, 1956. Diplomate Am. Bd. of Pediatrics. Pediatrician Children's Univ. Hosp., Kosice, Slovak Republic, 1956-65; resident N.Y.U Hosp., 1965-68; pvt. practice in pediatrics Rocky Point, N.Y., 1968—. Fellow Am. Acad. Pediatrics; mem. Suffolk County Med. Soc., Suffolk County Pediatric Soc., N.Y. State Med. Soc. Republican. Office: 81 Broadway Rocky Point NY 11778

KALINA, ROBERT EDWARD, physician, educator; b. New Prague, Minn., Nov. 13, 1936; s. Edward Robert and Grace Susan (Hess) K.; m. Janet Jessie Larsen, July 18, 1959; children: Paul Edward, Lynne Janet. B.A. magna cum laude, U. Minn., 1957, B.S., 1960, M.D., 1960. Diplomate Am. Bd. Ophthalmology (dir. 1981-89). Intern U. Oreg. Med. Sch. Hosp., Portland, 1960-61; resident in ophthalmology U. Oreg. Med. Sch. Hosp., 1961-62, 63-66; asst. in retina surgery Children's Hosp., San Francisco, 1966-67; Nat. Inst. Neurol. Diseases and Blindness Spl. fellow Mass. Eye and Ear Infirmary, Boston, 1967; instr. ophthalmology U. Wash., 1967-69, asst. prof., 1969-71, acting chmn. dept. ophthalmology, 1970-71, asso. prof., 1971-72, chmn. dept. ophthalmology, 1971—, prof., 1972—; mem. staffs Univ. Hosp., Harborview Hosp., Children's Hosp., Seattle; cons. VA Hosp., Seattle, Pacific Med. Ctr., Seattle, Madigan Hosp., Tacoma; assoc. head divsn. ophthalmology dept. surgery Children's Hosp., Seattle, 1975-86; pres. U. Wash. Physicians, 1990-93. Contbr. author: Introduction to Clinical Pediatrics, 1972, Ophthalmology Study Guide for Medical Students, 1975; contbr. numerous articles to profl. publs. Served to capt., M.C. USAF, 1962-63. Fellow ACS, Am. Acad. Ophthalmology (Sr. Honor award 1989); mem. AMA, Assn. Univ. Profs. Ophthalmology (pres. 1983-84, exec. v.p. 1989-94), Assn. Rsch. in Vision and Ophthalmology, Pacific Coast Oto-Ophthalmol. Soc. (councilor 1972-74), King County Med. Soc., Wash. State Acad. Ophthalmology, Phi Beta Kappa. Home: 2627 96th Ave NE Bellevue WA 98004-2107 Office: U Wash Dept Ophthalmology Box 356485 1959 NE Pacific St Seattle WA 98195-6485

KALINER, MICHAEL ARON, physician, researcher; b. Balt., Apr. 27, 1941; m. Jean A. Andrews, June 17, 1972; children: Aaron F., Matthew E., Leslie S. BS, U. Md., 1963, MD, 1967. Diplomate Am. Bd. Internal Medicine, Am. Bd. Allergy & Immunology. Intern Hosp. U. of Md., 1967-68; resident U. Calif., San Francisco, 1968-70; fellow Harvard U., Boston, 1970-73; scientist NIH, Bethesda, Md., 1975-93; physician Inst. for Asthma and Allergy, Washington, 1993—; bd. dirs. Allergy and Asthma Network, Fairfax, Va.; bd. tech. advisors Warner Lambert Co., Morris Plains, N.J., 1993—; cons. numerous pharm. cos. Editor Allergy and Immunology Internat., 1992-95; contbr. over 400 articles to profl. jours.; holder 3 patents in field. Recipient Outstanding Med. Alumni award U. Md. Med. Sch. 1994, Go West award, 1996; numerous other profl. awards. Mem. Am. Acad. Allergy and Immunology (pres. 1995—), Internat. Assn. Allergy and Immunology (exec. com. 1986—, treas. 1994—). Home: 6515 Hillmead Rd Bethesda MD 20817 Office: Inst for Asthma and Allergy 106 Irving St NW Washington DC 20010

KALIPOLITES, JUNE E. TURNER, rehabilitation professional; b. Grasmere, N.H., Aug. 10, 1932; d. Louis O. and Edith Mae (Allen) Turner; m. Nicholas G. Kalipolites, Feb. 12, 1955; children: George, Stephanie, Athena. AA, Hesser Coll., Manchester, N.H., 1977; B of Gen. Studies, U. N.H., 1980; MS in Rehab. Adminstrn. and Svcs., So. Ill. U., Carbondale, 1982; EdD in Ednl. Adminstrn., Vanderbilt U., 1992. Cert. rehab. counselor. Office mgr. Harris Upham and Co., Inc., Manchester; mgr. Amoskeag Bank & Trust Co.; rehab. counselor Div. Vocat. Rehab., Nashua, N.H.; rehab. cons. N.H. Divsn. Vocat. Rehab., Concord, 1986—, tng. coord., 1993-94; rehab. cons. spl. svcs. N.H. Divsn. Adult Learning and Rehab., Concord, 1995—. Author: Profile of Women in Rehabilitation Administration: A Common Theme, 1992, Projects with Industry: A Unique Concept for Providing Rehabilitation Services to Persons with Severe Disabilities, 1982. LaVerne Noyes scholar. Mem. ACA, Am. Rehab. Counseling Assn., Nat. Rehab. Assn. (nat. bd. dirs. 1994—), Nat. Rehab. Counseling Assn. (bd. dirs. 1986-87), Nat. Rehab. Adminstrn. Assn. (nat. bd. dirs. 1983-87, 92-94), N.E. Rehab. Counseling Assn. (pres. 1987, bd. dirs. 1986-88), N.H. Rehab. Assn. (bd. dirs. 1977—, treas. 1978, 89-92, sec. 1977-78), Nat. Assn. Ind. Living, Rho Sigma Chi, Chi Sigma Iota. Republican. Greek Orthodox. Home: 668 Lake Ave Manchester NH 03103-3538 Office: NH Divsn Adult Learning and Rehab 78 Regional Dr Concord NH 03301-8508

KALKHOF, THOMAS CORRIGAN, physician; b. Wellsville, N.Y., Aug. 12, 1919; s. Arthur Albert and Evelyn (Corrigan) K.; m. Mary E. Jones, Mar. 3, 1946 (dec. 1955); children: Thomas E., Susan A., Mark A., Patricia D.; m. 2d Constance N. McCarthy, Apr. 19, 1958; children: Christopher J., Constance M., Craig Alan. B.S., Gannon U., 1943; M.D., Marquette U., 1946. Intern, resident St. Vincent's Hosp., Erie, Pa., 1946-47; pvt. practice nutritional problems, continued breast cancer rehab. and thermography, gen. geriatrics and psychosomatic, Erie, 1947—; med. dir. Twinbrook Med. Ctr., 1960-84; dir. Iroquois Med. Centre, Erie; staff mem. St. Vincent's Health Ctr., Hamot Med. Ctr., Erie; pres., dir. Small Hosp. Cons., Inc., Erie, 1954—. Past chmn. Pa. Bd. Accreditation Nursing Homes and Related Facilities; past pres. Cath. Social Svcs., Erie; past pres. Erie County Ind. Coun. on Aging.; bd. dirs. Cath. Charities USA Commn. on Aging. With M.C., AUS, 1943-44. Fellow Am. Coll. Health Care Adminstrs., Am. Geriatric Soc., Am. Acad. Family Physicians, Acad. Psychosomatic Medicine; mem. AMA, Pa. Health Care Assn. (past pres.), Acad. Psychomatic Medicine (past pres.), Pa. Acad. Family Physicians (past pres. Erie chpt.), Assn. Physicans in Chronic Disease Facilities (past pres.), Am. Soc. Clin. Hypnosis, Pa., Erie County Med. Socs., Nat. Geriatric Soc. (pres.), Soc. Prospective Medicine, Ind. Coun. on Aging (past pres.), KC (4 deg.), Internat. Transactional Analysis Assn. Republican. Roman Catholic. Home: 3749 E Lake Rd Erie PA 16511-1346 Office: PO Box 7265 4401 Iroquois Ave Erie PA 16516-2219

KALKWARF, KENNETH LEE, academic dean; b. Lincoln, Nebr., Apr. 12, 1946; s. Robert G. and Grace L. (Beck) K.; m. Sharon R. Moore, July 6, 1974; children: Kyle J., Kevin J. Student, U. Nebr., 1964-66, DDS, 1970, MS, 1973. Diplomate Am. Bd. Periodontology. Asst. prof. Univ. Nebr., Lincoln, 1973-78; prof. U. Nebr., Lincoln, 1980-87; assoc. prof. U. Okla., Oklahoma City, 1978-80; prof./assoc. dean U. Tex. Health Sci. Ctr., San Antonio, 1987-88, prof./dean, 1988—; cons. Cen. Regional Dental Testing, Topeka, Kans., 1980-87, VA, Nebr., 1981-87, ADA, Chgo., 1982—; vis. prof. Svc. U. Autonoma de Guadalajara/Mexico, 1980-82. Contbg. author textbooks, 1978—; contbr. articles to profl. jours., rsch. abstracts. Bd. dirs. McAllister Park Little League, San Antonio, 1990-94, mem. Leadership San Antonio, 1989-90. Recipient Alumni Achievement award U. Nebr., 1990, Outstanding Tchr. award U. Okla., 1980. Fellow Internat. Coll. Dentists, Am. Coll. Dentists; mem. ADA, San Antonio Dist. Dental Soc. (bd. dirs. 1988-93), Am. Acad. Periodontology, S.W. Soc. Periodontology (bd. dirs. 1984—, pres. 1993-94), Tex. Soc. Periodontists (bd. dirs. 1988-95), Internat. Assn. for Dental Rsch. Republican. Methodist. Office: Univ Tex Health Sci Ctr 7703 Floyd Curl Dr San Antonio TX 78284-7906

KALL, JOHN G., medical educator; b. Chgo., Feb. 11, 1959; s. John and Delphine Loretta (Beczek) K. BA, Loyola U., Chgo., 1981, MD, 1985. Intern, resident Mayo Clinic, Rochester, Minn., 1985-88; fellow Loyola U. Med. Ctr., Maywood, 1988-92; asst. prof. medicine Loyola U. Chgo., Maywood, 1992-94, U. Chgo., 1994—. Contbr. articles to profl. jours. Mem. Am. Coll. Cardiology, Am. Heart Assn. Office: U Chgo Cardiology Sect 5841 S Maryland Ave Chicago IL 60637

KALLAR, SURINDER KAUR, anesthesiologist; b. Panjab, India, Aug. 16, 1943. MD, Med. Sch., Rohtak, India, 1965. Diplomate Am. Bd. Anesthesiology; lic. physician, Va. Rotating intern, sr. house officer ob-gyn. and pediatrics Rohtak Med. Coll. Hosp., 1966-67; sr. house officer obstetrics St. Andrews, Scotland, 1968-69; sr. house officer anesthesia Gen. Hosp., South Shields, Eng., 1969-70, Macclesfield Gen. Hosp., Cheshire, Eng., 1970-71; fellow cardiac anesthesia, resident anesthesiology Med. Coll. Va., Richmond, 1972-74, asst. prof. anesthesiology, 1975-82, assoc. prof. anesthesiology, 1982-89, tenured prof. anesthesiology, 1989—, vice-chmn. dept. anesthesiology, 1990-92, interim chmn. dept., 1992-95; dir. Obstet. Anesthesia Svc., 1976-81; dir. Preoperative Anesthesia Clinic, Med. Coll. Va., 1988-90, dir. ambulatory anesthesia, 1981—; med. dir. Ambulatory Surgery Ctr., 1992—; organizer nat. continuing edn. confs.; speaker various local, regional and nat. meetings and confs.; internat. lectr. Mem. editorial bd. Anesthesiology Rev., Milestones in Anesthesia, Advances in Anesthesiology; invited reviewer Anaesthesia and Analgesia, Jour. Clin. Anesthesia, Anesthesiology Rev.; contbr. articles to profl. jours., chpts. to books; author videotapes on ambulatory surgery. Fellow Am. Coll. Anesthesiologists; mem. AMA (Acad. Achievement award, Women in Medicine award 1995, extensive clin. rsch. and grant support 1982—), Soc. Ambulatory Anesthesia (sec. 1985-87, pres. 1988-90, chmn. comm. com. 1992—, mem. edn. com. 1992—, ad-hoc devel. com. 1985—, editorial bd. newsletter), Va. Soc. Anesthesiologists (treas. 1986-88), Internat. Janssen Rsch. Coun., Am. Soc. Anesthesiologists (chair subspecialty representation com. 1991—), Med. Soc. Va., Richmond Acad. Medicine, Internat. Anesthesiology Rsch. Soc., Soc. Regional Anesthesia, Soc. Edn. in Anesthesia. Home: 9517 Carterwood Rd Richmond VA 23229-7656 Office: Med Coll Va PO Box 103 Richmond VA 23201-0103

KÄLLÉN, A. J. BENGT, embryology educator; b. Kristianstad, Sweden, June 1, 1929; s. A.O. Yngve and Karin S.M. (Redin) K.; m. O. Ingegerd Mörck, June 14, 1951; children—Anders, Ragnar, Rune, Barbro. Ph.D., Med. Faculty, Lund, Sweden, 1952, M.D., 1958. Assoc. prof. Med. Faculty, Lund, 1952-64, prof. embryology, 1965-94, prof. emeritus, head of Tornblad Inst., 1994—; research fellow Med. Research Council Sweden, 1964-65; research fellow Univ. Coll., London, 1953; Rockefeller fellow Washington U., St. Louis, 1954-55; cons. Nat. Bd. Health, Stockholm, 1964—. Contbr. articles on teratology, embryology, reprodn. epidemiology, immunobiology and cancer research to sci. jours. Home: Galjevångsvägen 26, S-22465 Lund Sweden Office: U Lund Tornblad Inst, Biskopsgatan 7, S-22362 Lund Sweden

KALLEN, LOWELL HART, psychiatrist, health science facility administrator; b. Jersey City, Apr. 1, 1943; s. Arnold Milton and Jessica Yvonne (Eppston) K.; m. Erica Elisabeth Jost, Aug. 22, 1969; children: Jeremy, Joshua, Jonathan. BA, Johns Hopkins U., 1963, MD, 1968; MBA, So. Ill. U., 1974. Diplomate Nat. Bd. Med. Examiners, Am. Bd. Pediatrics, Am. Bd. Psychiatry and Neurology, Am. Bd. Forensic Psychiatry, Am. Bd. Med. Mgmt. Intern pediatrics Johns Hopkins U., Balt., 1968-69; resident pediatrics Naval Regional Med. Ctr., Oakland, Calif., 1969-71, chief resident pediatrics, 1971-72; residency in psychiatry Naval Regional Med. Ctr., Oakland, 1972-74; fellowship child psychiatry Langley Porter Inst. Univ. Calif. Med. Ctr., San Francisco, 1974-76; commd. ensign USN, 1969, advanced through grades to capt., 1982; dir. child and adolescent psychiatry svc. Naval Hosp., Oakland, Calif., 1976-82, dir. psychiatry residency tng., 1978-79, head outpatient psychiatry br., 1981-82; head psychiatry outpatient dept. Naval Hosp., San Diego, 1982-84, dir. child and adolescent pychiatry svc., 1982-84; with Naval Hosp., Newport, R.I., 1984-89; head alcohol rehab. dept. Naval Hosp., Newport, 1984-86, head psychiatry dept., 1985-89, pres. med. staff, 1987-89; retired USN, 1989; chmn. dept. psychiatry Lawrence and Meml. Hosp., New London, Conn., 1989—; asst. clin. prof. Sch. of Medicine U. Calif., San Francisco, 1977—; pres., chief med. officer Shoreline Psychiat. Assocs., Groton, Conn., 1989—; bd. dirs. Cmty. Mental Health Svcs., Southeastern Conn., Norwich, Citizen's Task Force on Substance Abuse in New London County, Psychiat. Options East, Mansfield Ctr., Conn. Bd. dirs. United Way of Southeastern Conn., Inc. Fellow Am. Coll. Physician Execs., Am. Acad. Psychiatry and Law, Am. Acad. Child and Adolescent Psychiatry, Am. Acad. Pediatrics; mem. Am. Psychiat. Assn. Office: Lawrence and Meml Hosp 365 Montauk Ave New London CT 06320-4700

KALLHOVD, ROGER THOMAS, psychiatrist; b. N.Y.C., July 25, 1941; s. Gunstein Grundesen and Aase (Foss) K.; children: Christy, Erik. BS, Tufts U., 1963; MD, SUNY, Bklyn., 1967. Diplomate Am. Bd. Psychiatry and Neurology. Intern Greenwich (Conn.) Hosp., 1968; resident in psychiatry St. Luke's Hosp. Ctr., N.Y.C., 1968-71; psychiat. cons. Lakeland Sch. Dist., Westchester, N.Y., 1973-76, Dominican Sisters, Ossining, N.Y., 1974-78; chief psychiatry Phelps Meml. Hosp. Ctr., North Tarrytown, N.Y., 1980-93; med. dir. Phelps Mental Health Ctr., North Tarrytown, 1980-93; pvt. practice Phila., 1971-73, Briarcliff Manor, N.Y., 1973-80, North Tarrytown, 1980-93; with Croton on Hudson, 1993—; med. dir. Pederson-Krag Ctr., Huntington, 1993—. Lt. comdr. M.C., USN, 1971-73. Mem. Am. Psychiat. Assn.

KALLMAN, BURTON JAY, foods association director; b. N.Y.C., Nov. 1, 1927; s. Leo Melville and Muriel Kallman; m. Ellis Katherine Hachikian, Dec. 12, 1958; children: Lisa, David. BS, Bethany Coll., 1947; MS, U. So. Calif., 1951, PhD, 1958. Research biochemist U.S. Govt., Denver, Los Angeles, 1959-67; mem. profl. staff TRW Systems, Redondo Beach, Calif., 1967-76; sr. scientist Sci. Applications Inc., La Jolla, Calif., 1976-80; prin. Interdisciplinary Sci. Assocs., Torrance, Calif., 1980-82; lab. dir. Applied Biol. Scis., Glendale, Calif., 1982-85; dir. sci. and tech. Nat. Nutritional Foods Assn., Newport Beach, Calif., 1985—; cons. Children's Asthma Research Inst., Denver, 1961-63, Behavioral Health Services, Redondo Beach, 1973-77, Centinela Child Guidance, Inglewood, Calif., 1984-86. Mem. editl. bd. Jour. Applied Nutrition, 1991—, Jour. Optimal Nutrition, 1992—; reviewer sci. books and films, 1978—; contbr. articles to profl. jours. Recipient Merit award NASA, 1976. Mem. Am. Chem. Soc., Sigma Xi. Democrat. Jewish. Home: 23214 Robert Rd Torrance CA 90505-3244 Office: Nat Nutritional Foods Assn Ste 101 3931 MacArthur Blvd Newport Beach CA 92660

KALLSTROM, CHARLES CLARK, dentist; b. Chgo., Jan. 15, 1943; s. Charles Edward and Margaret Jane (Clark) K.; m. Roberta Lou Easterday, June 19, 1965; children: Cynthia Ann, Heidi Lynn, Karen Kristine. BS in Chem. Engring., Purdue U., 1965; DDS, Northwestern U., Chgo., 1971. Project engr. Chgo. Bridge & Iron Co., Oakbrook, Ill., 1965-67; pvt. practice dentistry Geneva, Ill., 1973—; mem. dental staff Cmty. Hosp., Geneva, 1974—, chmn., 1980-81; chmn. Elgin C.C. Dental Assisting Adv. Bd., 1994—. Author, editor: Dental Assisting for the Red Cross Aide, 1971. Bd. dirs. Tri City Family Svcs., Geneva, 1983-90, v.p., 1985-87, pres., 1988-90, chmn. capitol gifts campaign, 1992-93; bd. dirs. Men's Found. Delnor Cmty. Hosp., Geneva, 1979—; pres. Geneva chpt. Am. Cancer Soc., 1986-88. Lt. USN, 1971-73. Fellow Am. Coll. Dentists, Internat. Coll. Dentists; mem. ADA, Acad. Gen. Dentistry, Ill. State Dental Soc. (dental edn. com.1989-92, bd. trustees 1992—, access to care com. 1992-93, fin. and planning com. 1992-95, chmn. annual planning com. 1993-94, dental benefits com. 1994-95, ins. com. 1995—), Fox River Valley Dental Soc. (sec. 1986, treas. 1987, v.p. 1988, bd. dirs. 1988-91, pres. 1989), Ill. Acad. Dental Practice Adminstrn., Geneva Golf Club (sec. 1988, bd. dirs. 1986-88, 92-95, v.p. 1995). Republican. Presbyterian. Home: 615 Carriage Dr Batavia IL 60510-1159 Office: PO Box 488 302 Randall Rd Ste 105 Geneva IL 60134-4203

KALMAZ, GULGUN DURUSOY, physician, scientist; b. Ankara, Turkey, Jan. 2, 1946; came to U.S., 1974; d. Avni H. and Nazime A. (Ipari) Durusoy; BA in Biochemistry, Am. Coll. for Women, Turkey, 1965; MD, U. Istanbul, Turkey, 1974; postgrad. Duke U. Med. Center, 1974-76; m. Ekrem E. Kalmaz, Oct. 3, 1974; children: Phyllis, Denise. Intern in pediatrics and surgery U. Istanbul Sch. Medicine, 1972-73, resident, 1973-74; practice medicine specializing in hematology, 1973—; rsch. assoc. pediatric hematology Zeynep Kamil Children's Hosp., Istanbul, 1973-74; vis. scientist U. Tenn. Meml. Research Center, Knoxville, 1976-78, research asso. dept. med. biology Sch. Medicine, 1978-80; fellow NIH, 1980-83, hematology Shriners Burn Inst., 83-85, dept. internal medicine, div. hematology and oncology U. Tex. Med. Br., Galveston, 85—, asst. prof. medicine, sci. staff mem. Shriners Burns Inst.. Recipient Nat. Svc. award NIH, 1980-83. Mem. AAAS, Am. Chem. Soc., Am. Soc. Hematology, Assn. Exptl. Hematology, Internat. Soc. for Exptl. Hematology, N.Y. Acad. Scis., Tissue Culture Assn., Sigma Xi. Contbr. articles on hematology to profl. jours. and books. Home: 7036 N Holiday Dr Galveston TX 77550-3028 Office: U Tex Med Br Dept Internal 45135 Galveston TX 77555

KALMUS, GERHARD WOLFGANG, biology educator; b. Berlin, Dec. 19, 1942; came to U.S., 1956; s. Werner and Hildegard C. (Schneiderlin) K.; m. Karin C. Biehl, Mar. 18, 1967. AA, Monterey Peninsula Coll., 1965; BA, U. Calif., Berkeley, 1967; MS, Rutgers U., Camden, N.J., 1974; PhD, Rutgers U., 1977. Rsch. asst. U. Pa., Phila., 1967-68; asst. project mgr. Info Intersci. Inc., Phila., 1969-70; biology tchr. Quakertown Community High Sch., Quakertown, Pa., 1972; rsch. asst. Temple U., Phila., 1973-74; rsch. asst. Rutgers U., Camden, N.J., 1973-74, New Brunswick, N.J., 1974-77; asst. prof. E. Carolina U., Greenville, N.C., 1977-83, assoc. prof., 1983-93, prof., 1993—; dir. undergrad. studies E. Carolina U., Greenville, 1981-89, dir. grad. studies, 1989—. Editor CANCAS Jour., Greenville, 1985—; contbr. articles to profl. jours. With USN, 1960-66. G.W. Kalmus Biology scholar East Carolina U. Biology Club, 1981, Teaching Excellence award, 1989. Mem. AAAS, N.C. Acad Sci. (sec. 1980—), Soc. Integrative and Comparative Biology, Soc. in Vitro Biology, Soc. for Devel. Biologists, East Carolina U. Biology Club (life), Alpha Epsilon Delta (hon.), Beta Beta Beta. Republican. Lutheran. Home: RR 3 Box 161 Greenville NC 27858-9316 Office: E Carolina U Dept Biology Greenville NC 27858

KALSNER, STANLEY, pharmacologist, physiologist, educator; b. N.Y.C., Aug. 21, 1936; s. William Louis and Sadie (Feldman) K.; m. Jenny Book, Aug. 4, 1963; children—Lydia, Pamela, Louisa. AB, NYU, 1958; postgrad., SUNY Downstate Med. Ctr., 1959-62; PhD, U. Man., Can., 1966; postgrad., Cambridge (Eng.) U., 1966-67. Asst. prof. pharmacology U. Ottawa, Ont., Can., 1967-72, assoc. prof., 1972-77, prof., 1977-85; prof., chmn. joint dept. physiology and pharmacology CUNY, 1985—; med. rsch. scientist on heart disease and blood vessel function; sci. referee Med. Rsch. Coun. Can., Can. Heart Found. Editor, contbr. chpts. to books, articles to jours.; assc. editor Can. Jour. Physiology and Pharmacology, until 1985; mem. editorial bd.: Jour. Autonomic Pharmacology, Blood Vessels. USPHS fellow, 1960-67; Med. Rsch. Coun.-NRC and Ont. Heart Found. grantee; Am. Heart Assn. grantee, 1987—. Mem. AAAS, AAUP, Can. Pharmacology Soc., Am. Soc. Pharmacology and Therapeutics. Home: 21 Hillcrest Rd Suffern NY 10901-6834 Office: CUNY Med Sch 138th St And Convent Ave New York NY 10031

KALTER, STEVEN PAUL, oncologist; b. Syracuse, N.Y., Feb. 9, 1952; s. Seymour Sanford and Gloria Vivian (Verstein) K.; m. Karen Bridget Reichley, May 26, 1985; 1 child, Benjamin David. BS, Brown U., 1974; MD, Baylor U., 1978. Diplomate Am. Bd. Internal Medicine, Oncology, Hematology. Physician Cancer Therapy and Rsch. Ctr., San Antonio, 1981—. Named Physician of Yr. Humana Hosp., 1994. Fellow ACP; mem. Am. Soc. Hematology, Am. Soc. Clin. Oncology. Office: Cancer Therapy & Rsch Ctr 4450 Medical Dr San Antonio TX 78229

KAM, FREDERICK ANTHONY, internist, physician; b. Port-of-Spain, Trinidad, Feb. 9, 1961; came to U.S., 1979; s. Frederick and Joan Yvonne K.; m. Charlene; children: Brendan, Allison. BS, U. Miami, 1983, MD, 1986. Diplomate Am. Bd. Internal Medicine. Internal medicine resident Jackson Meml. Hosp., 1986-89; co-dir. Gen. Medicine Clinics, JMH dir. U. Miami Sch. Medicine, 1989-92; med. dir., CEO UM Care, Miami, 1992-95; v.p. health delivery sys., corp. med. dir. Collegiate Health Care, Norwalk, Conn., 1995—. Mem. AMA, Am. Coll. Physicians, ACHA, Nat. Assn. Managed Care Physicians. Roman Catholic. Office: Collegiate Health Care 800 Connecticut Ave Norwalk CT 06856-5233

KAMBACK, MARVIN CARL, psychologist; b. Yankton, S.D., July 15, 1939; s. Carl Melvin and Pauline Elizabeth (Albrecht) K.; children: Elizabeth, Christopher. BA in English, U. S.D., 1961, MA in Psychology, 1962; PhD, Vanderbilt U., 1965. Diplomate Am. Coll. Forensic Examiners, Am. Bd. Profl. Disability Conss.; cert. psychologist, Md. Lic. psychologist, Wyo., Calif. Instr. U. S.D., 1962, asst. prof. dept. psychology, physiology, 1967-71; fellow neuro-psychology Stanford (Calif.) U. Med. Sch., 1966-67; psychol. intern Balt. City Hosps., 1971-74, family therapy intern, 1974-78; asst. prof. John Hopkins U. Med. Sch., Balt., 1971-74; assoc. prof. U. Md. Med. Sch., Balt., 1974-78; dir. Washakie County Mental Health Services, Worland, Wyo., 1978-79; dir. psychol. services Raleigh Hills (Calif.) Hosps., 1979-84; clin. psychologist Behavior Therapy & Research Inst., Newport Beach, Calif., 1979-84; pvt. practice neuropsychology, rehab., chronic pain, hypnotherapy, and behavioral medicine; dir psychol. services Alcoholism Program, Advanced Health Services, Newport Beach, 1979-84. NIMH fellow. Mem. APA, AAAS, Nat. Register Health Service Providers in Psychology, Soc. for Gen. Systems Research. Contbr. chpts. to books and articles to profl. jours. Home: 613 Douglas Ave Yankton SD 57078-3528 Office: Yankton Med Clinic 1104 W 8th St Yankton SD 57078-3306

KAMBARA, HIROFUMI, cardiologist; b. Kagawa, Japan, June 1941; married, Apr. 17, 1968; 2 children. MD, Kyoto U., 1966, PhD, 1982. Med. intern U.S. Army Hosp., Camp Zama, Kanagawa, Japan, 1966-67; med. resident Kyoto (Japan) U. Hosp., 1967-68, asst. physician, 1975-84, asst. prof. medicine, 1984-85, assoc. prof. medicine, 1985-88; straight med. intern St. Louis City Hosp., 1968-69; med. resident VA Hosp., New Orleans, 1969-72, chief resident in cardiology, 1972-73; fellow in cardiology Sch. Medicine, Tulane U., New Orleans, 1973-74, lectr., 1974-75; dir. of cardiology Osaka (Japan) Red Cross Hosp., 1992-94, dir. Cardiovasc. Ctr., 1994—; expert advisor WHO, Geneva, 1985—; mem. adv. bd. Internat. Symposium Cardiovascular Pharmacotherapy, Geneva, 1988—. Author: Tissue Plasminogen Activator in Thrombolytic Therapy, 1987; mem. editorial bd. Jour. Cardiology, 1993—; editorial cons. Jour. Interventional Cardiology, 1987—. Fellow Am. Coll. Cardiology. Home: Iwakura, 16-2 Naka-Osagi-cho, Kyoto 606, Japan Office: Osaka Red Cross Hosp, 5-53 Fudegasaki-cho, Osaka 543, Japan

KAMERMAN, SHEILA BRODY, social worker, educator; b. Jan. 7, 1928; d. S. Lawrence and Helen (Golding) Brody; m. Morton Kamerman, Sept. 11, 1947; children: Nathan Brody, Elliot Herbert, Laura Kamerman-Katz. BA, NYU, 1946; MSW, Hunter Coll., 1966; D. Social Welfare, Columbia U., 1973. Social worker N.Y.C. Dept. Social Svcs., 1966-68; social work supr. Bellevue Psychiat. Hosp., 1968-69; assoc. prof. social work Hunter Coll., 1977-79; from rsch. assoc. to sr. rsch. assoc. Columbia U. Sch. Social Work, 1971-79, assoc. prof. social policy and planning, 1979-81; prof. Sch. Social Work Columbia U., 1981—; chmn. NAS-NRC panel on work, family and community, 1980-82; mem. Com. Child Devel. Rsch. and Pub. Policy, 1983-88; mem. com. on prenatal care Inst. Medicine, 1986-88; cons. in field; mem. numerous social welfare coms. and adv. bds.; mem. Gov. Cuomo's Task Force on Poverty and Welfare Reform, 1986-87, adv. com. on Work and Family, 1987-88, UN Expert groups on social welfare and family policies. Author: (with Alfred J. Kahn) Not for the Poor Alone, 1975, Social Services in the United States, 1976, Social Services in International Perspective, 1977, Family Policy: Government and Families in Fourteen Countries, 1978, Child Care, Family Benefits and Working Parents, 1981, Parenting in an Unresponsive Society, 1980, Maternity and Parental Benefits and Leaves, 1980, Helping America's Families, 1982, Maternity Policies and Working Women, 1983, Income Transfers for Families with Children, 1983, Child Care: Facing the Hard Choices, 1987, The Responsive Work Place, 1987, Child Support: From Debt Collection to Social Policy, 1988, Mothers Alone: Strategies for a Time of Change, 1988, Privatization and the Welfare State, 1989, Social Services for Children, Youth and Families in the United States, 1990, Child Care, Parental Leave, and the Under 3's, 1991, A Welcome for Every Child, 1994, Starting Right: How America Neglects Its Youngest Children and What We Can Do About It, 1995; contbr. numerous articles to profl. jours. Recipient Hexter award Hunter Coll. Sch. Social Work, 1977, Nat. Leadership award in Social Policy, Heller Sch. Brandeis U., 1989; named to Hunt Coll. Hall of Fame, 1981; fellow Ctr. Advanced Study in Behavioral Scis., 1983-84. Mem. NASW, Am. Pub. Welfare Assn., Assn. Policy Analysis and Mgmt., Phi Beta Kappa. Home: 1125 Park Ave New York NY 10128-1243 Office: Columbia U Sch Social Work 622 W 113th St New York NY 10025-7982

KAMETANI, HIDEKI, psychologist; b. Kyoto, Japan, July 26, 1951; s. Yoshiki and Reiko Kametani. BA, U. Tokyo, 1976, MA, 1979, postgrad., 1983. Rsch. psychologist Tokyo Met. Inst. Gerontology, 1983-84, Mitsubishi Kasei Inst. Life Scis., Tokyo, 1989-92; rsch. assoc. U. Utah, Salt Lake City, 1985-86; vis. fellow Nat. Inst. Aging, Balt., 1986-89, rsch. sci., 1992-93; prof. Fukuoka Prefectural U., 1993—. Co-author: The Integrative Control Functions of the Brain, 1978, Neural Mechanisms and Biological Significance of Grooming Behavior, 1988; contbr. articles to profl. publs. Mem. AAAS, N.Y. Acad. Scis., Physiol. Soc. Japan, Japanese Soc. Neuropharmacology, Japanese Soc. Animal Psychology. Home: 2-27-24 Hanegi, Setagaya, Tokyo 156, Japan

KAMEYAMA, OSAMU, orthopaedic surgeon, educator; b. Osaka, Japan, July 14, 1950; s. Susumu and Yoshiko (Eguchi) K.; m. Hinako Shimazu, Sept. 2, 1984; children: Tadashi, Akira. MD, Kansai Med. U., 1976, PhD, 1984. Asst. prof., assoc. prof. Kansai Med. U., Osaka, Japan, 1982—; chief surgeon Otokoyama Horp., 1982-85; dir. Rakusai NT Hosp., Kyoto, 1995—; Olympic Sports Dr., Tokyo, 1988—; chief sports dr. Japan Canoe Assn., Tokyo, 1988—. Author: Neural and Mechanical Control of Movement, 1984; contbr. articles to profl. jours. Recipient Arukea award Japan Orthopaedics and Traumatology Found., 1994. Office: Kansai Med Univ, 10-15 Fumizono, Osaka 570, Japan

KAM FOON WING, healthcare company executive, chemist; b. Johor Bahru, Johore, Malaysia, Feb. 5, 1939; s. Kam Chong Ming and Yong Moi; m. Wong Poh Kueen, Sept. 22, 1963; children: Kok Fei, Lai Fong, Lai Yin, Lai Lien. Diploma in chemistry, Poly. U., Singapore, 1963. Chief chemist Singapore Testing Lab., 1963-68; group chmn., mng. dir. Chem. Lab. (S) Pte. Ltd., Singapore, 1969—, Pathology & Clin. Lab. Pte. Ltd., Singapore, 1974—, Kam Holdings (S) Pte. Ltd., Singapore, 1976—, Kampmas Pte. Ltd., Singapore, 1975—, Kampco Corp. (S) Pte. Ltd., Singapore, 1976—, Alfred H. Knight (S) Pte. Ltd., Singapore, 1980—, Chem. Lab. Technologist (S) Pte. Ltd., Singapore, 1982—, Pathlab Healthcare (S) Pte. Ltd., Singapore, 1988—; ceo Kam Holdings Group, Pathlab Group, Chemlab Group. Contbr. articles to profl. jours. Chmn. Inst. of Petroleum, Singapore, 1977, Plastic & Rubber Inst., Singapore, 1979. Fellow Royal Soc. Chemistry (U.K.), Royal Australian Chem. Inst., Inst. Food Sci. and Tech. (U.K.), Plastic and Rubber Inst. (U.K.), Royal Soc. Health (U.K.), Brit. Inst. Mgmt., Lions (hon. Singapore 1976). Home: 12 Jansen Rd, Singapore 548397, Singapore Office: Kam Holdings (S) Pte Ltd, 520 Balestier Rd 06-01 Loong On Bldg, Singapore 329853, Singapore

KAMHOLZ, STEPHAN L., physician; b. N.Y.C., Oct. 16, 1947; s. Sidney Maurice and Sylvia (Goldsmith) K.; divorced; 1 child, Sheryl R.; m. Rosemary Veronica Potucek, May 6, 1978; children: Sandra H., Roger A. BA, NYU, 1968; MD, N.Y. Med. Coll., 1972. Diplomate Am. Bd. Internal Medicine, 1975, Pulmonary Disease, 1978, Advanced Achievement in Internal Medicine, 1987; cert. in critical care medicine, 1987. Med. resident Montefiore Med. Ctr., Bronx, 1972-75, fellow pulmonary disease, 1975-77; asst. prof. Albert Einstein Coll. Medicine, Bronx, 1978-83, assoc. prof., 1983-86, vis. assoc. prof., 1986—; prof. med. SUNY Health Sci. Ctr., Bklyn., 1988—, chief pulmonary disease, 1986-93; interim chmn. dept. medicine SUNY Health Sci. Ctr., 1991-93, chmn. dept. medicine, 1993—; chief pulmonary disease Kings County Hosp. Ctr., Bklyn., 1986-93; vis. prof. SUNY Health Sci. Ctr., 1986-88; bd. dirs. Assn. Pulmonary Program Dirs., 1988-92, Am. Lung Assn. Bklyn., 1988—. Contbr. articles to profl. jours.; editor/contbr. to med. book: Pulmonary Aspects of Neurological Diseases, 1987. Hon. med. officer N.Y.C. Fire Dept., 1987—. Recipient Linn J. Boyd award, N.Y. Med. Coll., 1972. Fellow ACP (gov.-elect N.Y. 1995-96, Downstate II region, gov. 1996—), Am. Coll. Chest Physicians, N.Y. Acad. Medicine, N.Y. Soc. Thoracic Surgery; mem. Am. Thoracic Soc., Am. Fedn. Clin. Rsch., Internat. Heart Transplant Soc., Assn. Profs. Medicine, Assn. Acad. Minority Physicians (councillor 1994—), Sigma Xi (pres. SUNY Bklyn. chpt. 1993-95, sec. 1995—), Alpha Omega Alpha (faculty inductee). Jewish. Office: SUNY Health Sci Ctr 450 Clarkson Ave # 50 Brooklyn NY 11203-2012

KAMINER, BENJAMIN, physician, educator; b. Slonim, Poland, May 1, 1924; came to U.S., 1959, naturalized, 1973; s. Idel and Bluma (Zayoncik) K.; m. Freda Shnitke, Aug. 22, 1948; children—Brian, Lauren. M.B., B.Ch., U. Witwatersrand, South Africa, 1946; diploma child health, Royal Coll. Physicians and Surgeons, Eng. House physician, surgeon Johannesburg (South Africa) Gen. Hosp., 1947-48; registrar Edgeware Hosp., London, 1949-50; lectr. physiology Med. Sch. Johannesburg, 1951-54, sr. lectr., 1955-59; investigator Marine Biol. Lab., Woods Hole, Mass., 1959-69; lectr. Harvard Med. Sch., Boston, 1968-69; prof., chmn. dept. physiology Boston U. Sch. Medicine, 1970—. Rockefeller fellow, 1959-60. Mem. Marine Biol. Lab., Soc. Gen. Physiology, Am. Physiol. Soc., Soc. Cell Biology, Biophys. Soc. Home: 150 Oliver Rd Newton MA 02168-2321 Office: Boston Univ Sch Medicine Boston MA 12118

KAMINSKI, DONALD LEON, medical educator, surgeon, gastrointestinal physiologist; b. Elba, Nebr., Nov. 9, 1940; s. Edwin and Irene (Syntek) K.; m. Maureen M. Cudmore, Nov. 28, 1964; children: Christian, Julie, Jane, Kathryn. B.S., Creighton U., 1962, M.D., 1966. Diplomate: Am. Bd. Surgery. Intern. St. Louis U., 1966-67, resident in surgery, 1967-71; attending surgeon St. Louis U. Hosp., 1972—, dir. gen. surgery, 1982—. Mem. Soc. Univ. Surgeons, Am. Physiol. Soc., Am. Gastroent. Assn., Am. Surg. Assn., Central Surg. Soc., Alpha Omega Alpha. Republican. Roman Catholic. Home: 1025 Joanna Ave Saint Louis MO 63122-1821 Office: St Louis U 3635 Vista at Grand PO Box 15250 Saint Louis MO 63110-0250

KAMINSKI, GERHARD, psychologist, emeritus educator; b. Steinau, Silesia, Germany, Sept. 19, 1925; s. Ernst and Gertrud (Pfeiffer) K.; m. Gerda Bosdorf, Oct. 23, 1954; children: Katharina, Claudia (dec. 1980), Sebastian. Diploma in Psychology, Free U. Berlin, 1952, PhD, 1958, Habilitation, 1968. Sci. asst. psychology dept. Free U. Berlin, 1952-59, acad. councillor, 1959-68, sci. councillor, 1968; prof., head sect. gen. & ecol. psychology U. Tuebingen, Fed. Republic Germany, 1968-90, prof. emeritus, 1990—; various directorships psychology dept. U. Teubingen, 1968-90, dean faculty behavioral social scis., 1979-80; pres. Studienreform-Kommission Psychologie des Landes Baden-Wurttemberg, Stuttgart, Fed. Republic Germany, 1975-76; elected reviewer German Sci. Found., Bonn, 1976-84. Author: Verhaltenstheorie und Verhaltensmodifikation, 1970; editor, author: Umweltpsychologie, 1976, Ordnung und Variabilität im Alltagsgeschehen, 1985; co-author: Kinder und Jugendliche im Hochleistungssport, 1984; contbr. over 90 articles to profl. jours. and readers. Mem. German Assn. for Psychology, Berufsverband Deutscher Psychologen, Internat. Assn. Applied Psychology (div. environ. psychology), Environ. Design Rsch. Assn., Internat. Assn. for People-Environment Studies, Arbeitsgemeinschaft fur Sportpsychologie, Deutsche Gesellschaft fur Humanoekologie (cons. bd. mem.). Home: Steinboesstr 72, D-72074 Tuebingen Germany Office: Psychologisches Inst U Tuebingen, Friedrichstr 21, D-72072 Tuebingen Germany

KAMINSKI, MIKE JOSEPH, family practice physician; b. Seattle, Mar. 13, 1954; s. Michael J. and Ruth L. (Loos) K.; partner Rubén de Anda. BS in Chemistry, U. N.D., 1975, MD, 1979. Diplomate Am. Bd. Family Practice. Intern in surgery Swedish Hosp. Med. Ctr., Seattle, 1979-80, resident in surgery, 1980-81, resident in family practice, 1981-83; group practice-family practice Valley Family Practice Clinic, Renton, Wash., 1982—; vice chief dept. of family practice Valley Med. Ctr., Renton, Wash., 1992-94, chief, 1994-96; chief quality assurance family practice Valley Med. Ctr., Renton, 1992-94. Active in assisting in care of HIV/AIDS patients N.W. AIDS Found., Seattle, 1990—. Fellow Am. Acad. of Family Practice; mem. Wash. State Med. Assn., Wash. Acad. of Family Practice, King County Med. Soc. (alt. del. 1993-95, del. 1996). Office: Valley Family Practice Clinic 4361 Talbot Rd S #100 Renton WA 98055

KAMINSKY, DAVID MICHAEL, psychiatrist; b. Toledo, Ohio, May 12, 1948; s. Jack Harold and Sally (Kale) K.; m. Barbara Ann Wiener, Mar. 6, 1976; 1 child, Rachel. BS, U. Toledo, 1970; MD, Universidad Autonoma Guadalaja, Mexico, 1974. Diplomate Am. Bd. Psychiatry and Neurology. Resident in psychiatry L.I. Jewish-Hillside Med. Ctr., New Hyde Park, N.Y., 1975-78; fellow in child psychiatry N.Y. Hosp./Cornell Med. Ctr., White Plains, 1978-80; pvt. practice psychiatry Great Neck, N.Y., 1980—; staff psychiatrist N.Y. Hosp./Cornell Med. Ctr., White Plains, 1980-81, L.I. Jewish Med. Ctr., 1981—, North Shore U. Hosp., Manhasset, N.Y., 1982-88, 94—, St. Francis Hosp., Roslyn, N.Y., 1986-93; physician-in-charge child psychiatry outpatient dept. Queens Hosp. Ctr. Jamaica, 1983-86; psychiat.

cons. Peninsula Counseling Ctr., Woodmere, N.Y., 1986-93. Recipient Physician Recognition award, AMA, 1980, 83, 86. Mem. AMA, Am. Psychiatric Assn., Am. Acad. Child Psychiatry, N.Y. Council Child Psychiatry, Alpha Epsilon Delta, Psi Chi. Office: 29 Barstow Rd Great Neck NY 11021-2209

KAMPINE, JOHN P., anesthesiologist. MD, PhD, U. Wis. Prof., chair dept. anesthesiology John Doyne Hosp., Milw., 1979—. Mem. Inst. Medicine-NAS. Office: John Doyne Hosp PO Box 150 8700 W Wisconsin Ave Milwaukee WI 53226*

KAMPSCHNIEDER, CAROL ANN, nursing administrator; b. West Point, Nebr., Aug. 16, 1954; d. Florian F. and Norma J. (Nykodem) Bayer; m. Adrian H. Kampschnieder, June 19, 1976; children: Elizabeth, Kathryn, Sara. Diploma, Lincoln Gen. Hosp. Sch. Nursing, 1975; BSN with distinction, U. Nebr. Med. Ctr., 1978; MSN, U. Nebr. Med. Ctr., Omaha, 1995. RN, Nebr. Evening charge nurse/float pool Lincoln (Nebr.) Gen. Hosp., 1975-80; evening staff nurse, evening emergency rm. charge nurse, supr., DON, v.p. clin. and regulatory svcs. St. Francis Meml. Hosp., West Point, 1981—. Mem. Dodge (Nebr.) Booster Club, 1995-96; mem., sec. Parish Coun., Olean, Nebr., 1990—. Mem. Nebr. Nurses Assn. (sec. 1995—), Nebr. Orgn. of Nurse Execs. (sec./treas. 1995—), Sigma Theta Tau. Home: RR 2 Box 65 Howells NE 68641

KAN, YUET WAI, physician, investigator; b. Hong Kong, June 11, 1936; came to U.S., 1960; s. Tong-Po and Lai-Wai (Li) K.; m. Alvera Lorraine Limauro, May 10, 1964; children—Susan Jennifer, Deborah Ann. BS, MB, U. Hong Kong, 1958, DSc, 1980, DSc (hon.), 1987; DSc (hon.), Chinese U., Hong Kong, 1981; MD (hon.), U. Cagliari, Sardinia, Italy, 1981. Investigator Howard Hughes Med. Inst., San Francisco, 1976—; prof. lab. medicine U. Calif., San Francisco, 1977—, Louis K. Diamond prof. hematology, 1991-95; mem. NIDDK adv. coun. NIH, 1991-95; trustee Croucher Found., Hong Kong, 1992—. Contbr. over 225 articles to med. jours., chpts. to books. Recipient Dameshek award Am. Soc. Hematology, 1980, George Thorn award Howard Hughes Med. Inst., 1980, Gairdner Found. Internat. award, 1984, Allan award Am. Soc. Human Genetics, 1984, Lita Annenberg Hazen award for Excellence in Clin. Rsch., 1984, Waterford award, 1987, ACP's award, 1988, Genetic Rsch. award Sanremo Internat., 1989, Warren Alpert Found. prize, 1989, Albert Lasker Clin. Med. Rsch. award, 1991, Christopher Columbus Discovery award, 1992, City of Medicine award, 1992, Excellence 2000 award, 1993, Helmut Horten Rsch. award, 1995. Fellow Royal Coll. Physicians (London), Royal Soc. (London), Third World Acad. Scis., AAAS, Am. Acad. Arts & Scis.; mem. Nat. Acad. Scis. USA, Acad. Sinica (Taiwan), Chinese Acad. Scis. (fgn. mem.), Assn. Am. Physicians, Am. Soc. Hematology (pres. 1990). Office: U Calif U426 3d & Parnassus Aves San Francisco CA 94143-0724

KANAKAMEDALA, RAGHAVAIAH VEERA, physician; b. Penamakoor, India, June 21, 1927; came to U.S., 1970; s. Subbaiah and Bullamma (Movva) K.; m. Jhancy Laxmi, June 11, 1948 (dec. Feb. 1966); children: Jyothi, Ravi, Bhanu; m. Kamala Kumari, Aug. 24, 1967. MBBS, Andhra Med., 1953; MD in Pediatrics, Osmania Med. U., 1953. Diplomate Am. Bd. Pediatrics, Am. Bd. Electrodiagnostic Medicine, Am. Bd. Phys. Medicine & Rehab. Resident Worcester (Mass.) City Hosp., 1970-71, Maricopa County Gen. Hosp., Phoenix, 1971-72, N.Y. Med. Coll. Hosp., N.Y.C., 1972-75; staff psychiatrist Schwab Rehab. Hosp., Chgo., 1975-81, VA Med. Ctr., Long Beach, Calif., 1981—; prof. U. Calif., Irvine, 1989—. Contbr. articles to profl. jours. Mem. Am. Assn. Electrodiagnostic Medicine. Office: VA Med Ctr 5901 E 7th St Long Beach CA 90822-5201

KANAKOUDI-TSAKALIDOU, FLORENCE, pediatrician, immunologist educator; b. Thessaloniki, Greece, Jan. 27, 1940; d. Sterianos and Hellen (Kouyoumtzi) Kanakoudi; m. Dimitrios Tsakalides, Apr. 24, 1971; children: Maria, Venetia. DCH, Thessaloniki U., Greece, 1968, MD, 1970, PhD, 1980. Lectr. U. Thessaloniki, Greece, 1970-80, sr. lectr., 1980-86, assoc. prof., 1986—; rsch. fellow Royal Infirmary, Edinburgh, 1970-71; head immunology lab. Hippokration Hosp., U. Thessaloniki, 1972—, cons. for chronic rheumatic diseases, 1982—. Organizer, leader League Against Pediatric Rheumatism in No. Greece, Thessaloniki, 1989—. Recipient Rotary Club award, 1990, 95, Internat. Women's Orgn. of Greece award, 1991. Mem. Hellenic Pediat. Soc. (bd. dirs. 1996—), Med. Soc. No. Greece, Greek Soc. Immunology (v.p. 1988-91), Brit. Soc. Immunology, Friends Assn. Children with Rheumatic Diseases (pres. 1989—, rep. of Greece in European League Against Rheumatism standing com. on pediatric rheumatology 1990—), Hellenic Soc. Social Pediatrics and Health Promotion. Greek Orthodox. Office: Hippokration Hosp 49 Konstantinoupoleos, 1st Dept of Pediatrics, 546 42 Thessaloniki Greece

KANDARIAN, SUSAN CHRISTINE, medical educator; b. Apr. 10, 1959. BS in Biology cum laude, Albion (Mich.) Coll., 1981; MS in Edn., U. Mich., 1983, PhD in Kinesiology, 1988. Asst. prof. health scis. Boston U., 1988-94, postdoctoral, 1989-91, rsch. asst. prof. physiology, 1991—, rsch. asst. prof. neuromuscular rsch. ctr., 1993—, assoc. prof. health scis., 1994—. Reviewer profl. jours.; contbr. numerous articles to profl. jours. Grantee Boston U., 1989-92, Am. Coll. Sports Medicine Found., 1989-90, Am. Heart Assn. 1992—, NIH, 1992—, Sargent Coll. Accelerated Rsch. Fund, 1994, Nat. Aero. and Space Adminstrn., 1995-96. Fellow Am. Coll. Sports Medicine; mem. AAAS, Am. Physiol. Soc. Office: Boston U 635 Commonwealth Ave Boston MA 02215*

KANDEL, JOAN ELLEN, osteopath; b. L.A., Apr. 6, 1963; d. William Isadore Kandel and Helen Sylvia (Cutler) Abraham; m. Kristin Graziano, July 13, 1996. BA, U. Calif., 1985; DO, Coll. Osteo. Med. Pacific, 1993. Vol. health educator U.S. Peace Corps, Nuapua, Paraguay, 1986-88; resident, chief resident family practice Cmty. Hosp., Santa Rosa, Calif., 1993-96. Mem. Am. Acad. Family Physicians, Am. Acad. Osteopathy, Physicians for a Violence-Free Soc., Gay and Lesbian Med. Assn. Democrat. Jewish.

KANDEL, PAUL DAVID, internist; b. Middletown, N.Y., Feb. 27, 1944; s. Morris and Beatrice Althea (Abramson) K.; m. Linda Beck, Dec. 5, 1970; children: Bree, David. BA in Biologic Scis., SUNY, Buffalo, 1965; MD, U. Bologna, 1970. Diplomate Am. Bd. Internal Medicine. Intern internal medicine Northern Westchester Hosp., Mt. Kisco, N.Y., 1971-72, resident internal medicine, 1972-73; resident internal medicine U. Buffalo Sch. Medicine, 1973-74; pvt. practice internal medicine, 1974-95; intern Northern Westchester Hosp. Ctr., Mt. Kisco, 1971; resident Northern Westchester Hosp. Ctr., Mt. Kisco, N.Y., 1972-73, attending physician, 1974—; resident SUNY Med. Sch. Hosps., Buffalo, 1974; group practice, 1995—; v.p. med. staff Northern Westchester Hosp., 1981-83, med. med. bd., 1986-89, editor newsletter. Police surgeon Mt. Kisco Police Dept., 1985-89. Fellow ACP, Soc. for Vascular Medicine and Biology; mem. Am. Soc. Internal Medicine. Office: 101 S Bedford Rd Mount Kisco NY 10549-3439

KANDELL, HOWARD NOEL, pediatrician. B.S., U. Miami, 1956; M.D., Tulane U., 1959. Diplomate Am. Bd. Pediatrics. Intern, Phila. Gen. Hosp., 1959-60; resident N.Y. Hosp. Cornell Med. Ctr., N.Y.C., 1960-62; practice medicine specializing in pediatrics, Phoenix, 1965—; bd. dirs. Health Maintenance Assocs., Ltd., Phoenix, 1975-82, chief pediatrics, 1977-82; assoc. chmn. dept. pediatrics Maricopa County Hosp., Phoenix, 1965-71, service chief dept. pediatrics, 1972-77; assoc. in pediatrics U. Ariz. Coll. Medicine, 1970-82, clin. instr. 1982-83; asst. prof., 1983-87; chmn. pediatric dept. CIGNA Healthplan of Ariz., Phoenix, 1984-87; adj. faculty mem. Ariz. State U. Coll. Nursing, 1986—; faculty Phoenix Hosps. Affiliated Pediatric Program, 1965—; med. dir. INA Healthplan (CIGNA) South Fla., 1982-83. Capt. MC USAF, 1962-64. Recipient Tchr. of Yr. award dept. pediatrics Maricopa County Gen. Hosp., 1972. Fellow Am. Acad. Pediatrics; mem. Am. Coll. Phys. Exec., Ariz. Pediatric Soc. (treas., exec. com. 1970-76), Phoenix Pediatric Soc. (v.p. 1970-72). Office: 12635 N 42nd St Phoenix AZ 85032-7601 Home: 7257 E Echo Ln Scottsdale AZ 85258-2768

KANE, AGNES BREZAK, pathologist, educator; b. Danbury, Conn., Nov. 3, 1946; d. John Edward and Mary Elizabeth (Hatfield) Brezak; m. David E. Kane, June 22, 1970. BA, Swarthmore Coll., 1968; MD, Temple U., 1974, PhD, 1976. Diplomate Am. Bd. Pathology. Resident Temple U. Hosp., Phila., 1975-76, 77-78; postdoctoral fellow Karolinska Inst., Stockholm, 1976-77; asst. prof. Temple U. Sch. Medicine, Phila., 1977-82; asst. prof. Brown U., Providence, 1982-87, assoc. prof. pathology, 1987-95, prof. pathology, 1995—; mem. merit rev. bd. for basic scis. VA, Washington, 1984-86; cons. R.I. Commn. for Safety and Occupational Health, Providence, 1986—; commr. Commn. to Identify Occupational Diseases, Providence, 1987-88; mem. rev. com. Nat. Inst. Environ. Health Scis., Research Triangle Park, N.C., 1988—. Assoc. editor Am. Jour. of Pathology, 1992—; contbr. articles on exptl. pathology to sci. publs. Lucretia Mott fellow Swarthmore Coll., 1969-71; recipient Rsch. Career Devel. award NIH, 1981-86. Mem. Am. Assn. Pathologists (women's com. 1987—, program com. 1990—), Assn. Women Med. Faculty Brown U. (founder, coord.), Women in Medicine (faculty advisor Brown U. chpt.; Mary Putnam Jacobi award 1986), Phi Kappa, Sigma Xi. Office: Brown Univ Box G Providence RI 02912

KANE, GERALD SAUL, orthopedic surgeon; b. Chgo., Nov. 4, 1932; s. Arthur Lewis and Florence (Minsky) K.; m. Renee Senk, May 30, 1958; children: Susan, Pam, Lisa. BS, U. Ill., 1954; MD, Chgo. Med. Sch., 1958. Intern Michael Reese Hosp., Chgo., 1958-59, resident in orthopedic surgery, 1959-63; pvt. practice Fraerman, Kane, Cohen, M.D.'s P.C., Highland Park, Ill., 1965—; clin. instr. in orthopedic surgery U. Ill., 1965-95; clin. asst. prof. of orthopedic surgery U. Health Scis. at Chgo. Med. Sch., North Chicago, 1979. Capt. USAF, 1963-65. Mem. AMA, Mid Am. Orthopedic Soc., Ill. Orthopedic Soc., Ill. State Med. Soc., Lake County Med. Soc. Home: 333 Moraine Rd a Highland Park IL 60035 Office: Gerald S Kane and Norman J Cohen 1170 Park Avenue West Highland Park IL 60035

KANE, GRACE MCNELLY, maternal, women's health and pediatrics nurse; b. Auburn, Ill., Mar. 31, 1939; d. Irving Benjamin and Ruby Louise (Stinnett) McNelly; m. Robert John Kane, July 23, 1960 (dec. 1994); children: Scott Robert, Timothy Phillip, Pamela Collette, Glenn Randall, Andrew Keith, Bruce Ryan. Diploma, Mem. Hosp. Sch. Nursing, Springfield, Ill., 1960; BS in Profl. Arts, St. Joseph's Coll., North Windham, Maine, 1985. RN, Ill.; cert. in occupational hearing conservation, fetal monitoring I and II; cert. ACLS. Staff nurse nursery-newborn units Walther Meml. Hosp., Chgo., 1962-67; staff nurse rooming-in nursery Luth. Gen. Hosp., Park Ridge, Ill., 1977-85; staff nurse med.-surg. unit Swedish Covenant Hosp., Chgo., 1989; staff nurse occupational clinic Rush-Presbyn-St. Luke's, Elk Grove Village, Ill., 1988; staff replacement nurse Nursefinders, Arlington Heights, Ill., 1989-90; staff nurse newborn nursery Alexian Bros. Med. Ctr., Elk Grove Village, 1990-91; nurse Kingsley Med. Ctr., Arlington Heights, Ill., 1991-92; Turner Family Practice, Elk Grove Village, Ill., 1993. Home: 675D Versailles Cir Elk Grove Village IL 60007

KANE, JACK ALLISON, physician, county administrator; b. Meadville, Pa., Feb. 28, 1921; s. Thomas Emery and Mildred (McMahon) K.; m. Virginia Joanne (Gasque), Sept. 28, 1946; children: Jeffrey, Marsha, Sharman, Cheryl. BS, Allegheny Coll., Meadville, Pa., 1943; MD, Case Western Res. U., 1949. Diplomate Am. Bd. Preventive Medicine. Intern U.S. Naval Hosp., 1949-50; fellow Sch. of Pub. Health U. Mich., 1950-51; med. dir. power train div. Cen. Foundry div. GM, Defiance, Ohio, 1954—; med. dir. Defiance County Health Dept., 1975—; pres. J. Kane MD, Inc., Defiance, 1977—; pres. Defiance County Bd. Health, 1962-82, Defiance County Lung Assn., 1968-78. Lt. USNR, 1952-54. Fellow Am. Coll. Occupl. Medicine, Am. Coll. Occupl. & Environ. Medicine; mem. AMA, Ohio State Med. Assn., Ohio Thoracic Soc. Home: PO Box 501 Defiance OH 43512-0501 Office: GM Powertrain Div PO Box 70 Defiance OH 43512-0070

KANE, LOWELL H., urologist; b. N.Y.C., June 18, 1930; s. Eugene and Ruth K.; m. 1961 (div. 1970); 3 children. BA, Drew U., 1951; MD, N.Y. Med. Coll., 1955. Diplomate Am. Bd. Urology. Intern Bronx Mcpl. Hosp.; resident Bronx Veteran's Hosp., Beth Israel Hosp.; urologist Queens, N.Y., 1962—. Mayor Village North Hills, N.Y., 1978-91. Lt. (s.g.) USN, 1956-58. Fellow Am. Coll. Surgeons. Office: 176-60 Union Tpk Flushing NY 11366

KANE, MICHAEL JOEL, physician; b. Erie, Pa., July 2, 1951. BS, U.S. Naval Acad., 1973; MD, N.J. Med. Sch., 1983. Diplomate Am. Bd. Internal Medicine. Med. intern Thomas Jefferson U. Hosp., Phila., 1983-84, resident in medicine, 1984-86; fellow in neoplastic diseases Mt. Sinai Med. Ctr., N.Y.C., 1986-88; attending physician Jefferson Med. Coll., Phila., 1988-91, Med. Ctr. at Princeton, N.J., 1991—. Served to lt. U.S. Navy, 1969-79. Decorated Navy Achievement medal. Fellow ACP, Acad. Medicine of N.J., Am. Soc. Clin. Oncology, Am. Assn. Cancer Rsch., Am. Soc. Hematology, Oncology Soc. N.J., Med. Soc. N.J. Office: Cancer Inst NJ at Hamilton 5 Hamilton Health Pl Ste 120 Hamilton NJ 08690

KANE, THOMAS JAY, III, orthopaedic surgeon, educator; b. Merced, Calif., Sept. 2, 1951; s. Thomas J. Jr. and Kathryn (Hassler) K.; m. Marie Rose Van Emmerik, Oct. 10, 1987; children: Thomas Keola, Travis Reid, Samantha Marie. BA in History, U. Santa Clara, 1973; MD, U. Calif., Davis, 1977. Diplomate Am. Bd. Orthopaedic Surgery. Intern U. Calif. Davis Sacramento Med. Ctr., 1977-78, resident in surgery, 1978-81; resident in orthopaedic surgery U. Hawaii, 1987-91; fellowship adult joint reconstruction Rancho Los Amigos Med. Ctr., 1991-92; ptnr. Orthop. Assocs. of Hawaii, Inc., Honolulu, 1992—; asst. prof. surgery U. Hawaii, Honolulu, 1993—, chief divsn. implant surgery, 1993—. Contbr. articles to profl. jours. Mem. AMA, Hawaii Med. Assn., Hawaii Orthop. Assn., Am. Acad. Orthop. Surgery, Alpha Omega Alpha, Phi Kappa Phi. Office: Orthopaedic Assocs Hawaii 1380 Lusitana St Ste 608 Honolulu HI 96813-2442

KANEB, ELIZABETH M., nursing home administrator; b. Massena, N.Y., Jan. 16, 1958; d. Edward John and Catherine Margaret (Meinhold) K. BA, St. Lawrence U., 1979; MBA, Clarkson U., Potsdam, N.Y., 1988. Lic. nursing home adminstr. Adminstr. Highland Nursing Home, Inc., Massena, 1983—; sec. Kaneb Corp.

KANEFIELD, MARVIN, psychiatrist; b. Phila., Nov. 18, 1935; s. Albert and Lillian (Bass) K.; m. Isabel Sultan, June 15, 1958; children: Jeffrey, Susan, Karen. BS, Villanova U., 1957; DO, Phila. Coll. Osteopathic Med., 1961. Pres. Psychiatric Cons., Inc., Phila., 1993—. Office: Friends Hosp 4641 Roosevelt Rd Philadelphia PA 19124

KANEKO, YOSHIHIRO, cardiologist, researcher; b. Shizuoka, Japan, Jan. 22, 1922; s. Rokurohei and Yoshino (Momochi) K.; m. Toyo Nozaki, Apr. 8, 1962; children: Kyoko, Eriko, Hiroko. MD, Tokyo U. Med. Sch., Japan, 1945, DMS, 1951. Clin. assoc. dept. internal medicine Tokyo U. Hosp., Japan, 1945-53, instr., 1953-70; rsch. fellow Cleve. Clinic Found., 1958-61, postdoctoral rsch. fellow, 1962-63; asst. prof. 2nd dept. internal medicine Tokyo U. Med. Sch., 1971-73; prof. medicine, chmn. dept internal medicine Yokohama City Univ. Med. Sch., Japan, 1973-87, emeritus prof., 1987—; dir. Yokohama Hypertension Rsch. Ctr., 1987—; prof. emeritus Yokohama City U., 1987—; hon. dir. Nishi-Yokohama Internat. Hosp., 1987-93. Contbr. articles to profl. jours. Com. mem. Pharm. Bur. Japan Ministry Health & Welfare, Tokyo, 1974-87, Med. Affairs Bur., Tokyo, 1976-79. Grantee NIH, 1965-67; recipient award Japanese Kidney Found., 1986, Internat. Soc. Hypertension, 1988. Fellow High Blood Pressure Coun.; mem. Japanese Soc. Hypertension (1st pres. 1978-79, dir. 1978-89), Japanese Soc. Internal Medicine (councilor), Japan Circulation Soc., Japan Soc. Nephrology (dir. 1974-87), Am. Heart Assn. (coun. mem.), Internat. Soc. Hypertension, (coun. 1982-90, chmn. 1988). Home: 2-27-14 Nishishiba, Kanazawa-ku, Yokohama 236, Japan Office: Yokohama Hypertension Rsch Ctr, Deiki 2-8-19-402 Kanazawa-ku, Yokohama 236, Japan

KANENAKA, REBECCA YAE, microbiologist; b. Wailuku, Hawaii, Jan. 9, 1958; d. Masakazu Robert and Takako (Oka) Fujimoto; m. Brian Ken Kanenaka, Nov. 10, 1989; children: Kent Masakazu, Kym Sachiko. Student, U. Hawaii, Manoa, 1976-77; BS, Colo. State U., 1980. Lab. asst. Colo. State U., Ft. Collins, 1979-80; microbiologist Foster Farms, Livingston, Calif., 1980-81; microbiologist Hawaii Dept. Health, Lihue, 1981-86, Honolulu, 1986—. Mem. Am. Soc. Microbiology (Hawaii chpt.), Nat. Registry of Microbiologists, Am. Soc. Microbiology. Clubs: Brown Bag (Lihue) (pres. 1985-86); Golden Ripples (4-H leader). Home: 1520 Liholiho St Apt 502 Honolulu HI 96822-4093 Office: Hawaii Dept Health Lab Hawaii Dept Health Lab 2725 Waimano Home Rd Pearl City HI 96782

KANG, BANN C., immunologist; b. Kyungnam, Korea, Mar. 4, 1939; d. Daeryong and Buni (Chung) K.; came to U.S., 1964, naturalized, 1976; A.B., Kyungpook Nat. U., 1959, M.D., 1963; m. U. Yun Ryo, Mar. 30, 1963. Intern, L.I. Jewish Hosp.-Queens Hosp. Center, Jamaica, N.Y., 1964-65, resident in medicine, 1965-67; teaching assoc. Kyungpook U. Hosp., Taegu, Korea, 1967-70; fellow in allergy and chest Creighton U., Omaha, 1970-71; fellow in allergy Henry Ford Hosp., Detroit, 1971-72; clin. instr. medicine U. Mich. Hosp., Ann Arbor, 1972-73; asst. prof. Chgo. Med. Sch., 1973-74; chief allergy-immunology Mt. Sinai Hosp., Chgo., 1975—; asst. prof. Rush Med. Sch., Chgo. 1975-84, assoc. prof., 1984-86; assoc. prof. U. Ky. Coll. Medicine, 1987-92, prof., 1992—; cons., 1976—, Nat. Heart, Lung, Blood Inst., 1979—; mem. Exptl. Transplantation Adv. Bd., Ill., 1985-86, Diagnostic and Therapeutic Tech. Assessment (AMA), 1987—, Gen. Clin. Rsch. Com. (NIH), 1989-93; adv. com. Ctr. for Biologics and Rsch., FDA, 1993-96; counselor Chgo. Med. Soc., 1984-86, mem. policy com., adv. com. to health dept. Chgo. and Cook County, 1984-86. Recipient NIH award U. Mich., 1972-73. Diplomate Am. Bd. Internal Medicine, Am. Bd. Allergy-Immunology. Fellow ACP, Am. Acad. Allergy; mem. Am. Fedn. Clin. Research, AMA, Inter-Asthma Assn. Contbr. over 50 articles to profl. jours. Home: 2716 Martinique Ln Lexington KY 40509-9509 Office: U Ky Coll Medicine K528 Albert B Chandler Med Ctr 800 Rose St Lexington KY 40536

KANG, JUAN, pathologist; b. Chang-Young, Kyung-Nam, Republic of Korea, Aug. 10, 1935; came to U.S., 1965; s. Bugon and Umchun (Chung) K.; children: Angie, Alex, Erik. PreMed, Kyung-Pook U., Taegu, Republic of Korea, 1955; MD, Kyung-Pook U., 1959. Diplomate Am. Bd. Pathology, Am. Bd. Radioisotopic Pathology, Am. Bd. Hematology, Am. Bd. Dermatopathology. Capt. Med. Corps Republic of Korea Army, 1959-65; intern Watts Hosp., Durham, N.C., 1965-66; resident St. Louis U. Hosp., 1968-70; pathologist Allen Pathology Group, St. Louis, 1971—; clin. asst. prof. St. Louis U. Med. Sch., 1979—. Mem. AMA, Am. Soc. Clin. Pathologists, Coll. Am. Pathologists, Internat. Acad. of Pathologists, Am. Soc. Dermatopathology, Soc. for Hematopathology. Home: 12939 Banyan Town Dr Saint Louis MO 63146-4300 Office: Christian Hosp NE 11133 Dunn Rd Saint Louis MO 63136-6119

KANG, MANJIT SINGH, geneticist, plant breeder; b. Punjab, India, Mar. 3, 1948; came to U.S., 1969, naturalized 1976; s. Gurdit Singh and Parminder Kaur (Brah) K.; m. Georgia Anna Crocker, Feb. 13, 1971. BS in Agr. with honors (India Council Agrl. Research scholar), Punjab Agrl. U., Ludhiana, India, 1968; MS, So. Ill. U., Edwardsville, 1971, MA in Botany, Carbondale, 1977; PhD, U. Mo., Columbia, 1977. Teaching asst. So. Ill. U., Edwardsville, 1969-71; research asst. plant and soil sci. So. Ill. U., Carbondale, 1971-72, preceptor plant and soil sci., 1972-74; grad. research asst. agronomy U. Mo., Columbia, 1974-77; research asso. Ctr. Biology of Natural Systems, Washington U., St. Louis, 1977; sr. plant breeder hybrid corn research sta. Cargill, Inc., St. Peter, Minn., 1977-78, research sta. mgr., 1979; research asso. agronomy U. Mo., 1980; asst. prof. genetics U. Fla. Everglades Rsch. and Edn. Ctr., Belle Glade, 1981-85; assoc. prof. agronomy La. State U., Baton Rouge, 1986-90, prof., 1990—. Author: Applied Quantitative Genetics, 1994; editor: Genotype-By-Environment Interaction, 1990, Genotype-By-Environment Interaction: New Perspectives, 1996. Contbr. articles to profl. jours. Mem. AAAS, Am. Soc. Agronomy, Am. Genetic Assn., Crop Sci. Soc. Am., Am. Soc. Sugar Cane Technologists, Internat. Soc. Plant Molecular Biology, Sigma Xi, Gamma Sigma Delta. Achievements include research on developing resistance to Aspergillus flavus and the carcinogen aflatoxin in maize grain. Home: 2477 Creekside Dr Baton Rouge LA 70810-6966 Office: La State U Dept Agronomy MB Sturgis Hall Baton Rouge LA 70803

KANG, YOOGOO, anesthesiologist; b. Seoul, Korea, Apr. 10, 1946; s. Kiduk and Samkum (Koh) K.; m. Young H. Kim, Nov. 9, 1972; children: Michael N., David H. BS, Seoul (Korea) Nat. U., 1967, MD, 1971. Diplomate Am. Bd. Anesthesiology. Intern in surgery St. Raphael Hosp., New Haven, Conn., 1974-75; resident in surgery Albert Einstein Med. Ctr., Phila., 1975-76; resident in anesthesiology Thomas Jefferson U. Hosp., Phila., 1976-78; fellow in obstetric anesthesia Magee Women's Hosp., Pitts., 1978-79; asst. prof. U. Pitts., 1979-88, dir. hepatic transplantation anesthesiology, 1984—, assoc. prof., 1989-93, prof., 1994—; head Internat. Symposium in Liver Transplantation, Pitts., 1984-88. Editor: Hepatic Transplantation: Anesthetic Management and Perioperative Care, 1985, Anesthesia and Intensive Care for Patients with Liver Diseasae, 1995; assoc. editor Liver Surgery and Transplantation, 1993—; mem. editl. bd. Current Opinions in Organ Transplantation, 1996—. Med. officer Korean Army, 1971-74. Mem. Am. Soc. Anesthesiologists, Internat. Soc. Rsch. in Anesthesiology, Internat. Liver Transplantation Soc. (pres. 1989-93, mem. exec. coun. 1993-95, adv. bd. 1995—), Liver Intensive Care Group Europe. Office: U Pitts-Presbyn Univ Hosp Dept Anesthesiology C-Wing 200 Lothrop St Pittsburgh PA 15213-2546

KANIA, DEBORAH BOZEK, social worker; b. Rowes Run, Pa., Aug. 1, 1954; d. Joseph John and Betty (Petrus) B.; m. Richard John Kania, Sept. 7, 1985; 1 child, Joseph William. BSW, U. California (Pa.), 1976; MSW, U. Pitts., 1981. Diplomate in Clin. Social Work; lic. social worker, Pa. Caseworker McKeesport (Pa.) Neighborhood Ministry, 1976-77, Seton Hill Day Care, Inc., Greensburg, Pa., 1977-80; oncology social worker Westmoreland Hosp., Greensburg, 1980-93; clin. social worker Uniontown (Pa.) Hosp., 1993—; cons. Oak Hill Nursing Home, Greensburg, 1984-86. Active Fayette County Human Svc. Coun., 1995—. Recipient Achievement award for Patient Edn., Hosp. Assn. Pa., 1990. Mem. NASW, Nat. Assn. Oncology Social Workers, Acad. Cert. Social Workers, Kiwanis. Roman Catholic. Home: RR 1 Box 1951 Hopwood PA 15445-9801 Office: Uniontown Hosp 500 W Berkeley St Uniontown PA 15401

KANNANGARA, DON WALTER, infectious disease consultant; b. Bandaragama, Sri Lanka, June 1, 1942; came to U.S., 1975; s. Don Charles and Donna Maggie (Edussuriya) K.; m. Yoges Kanagaratnam, June 20, 1968; children: Nelum, Saman. MB BS, U. Ceylon, Sri Lanka, 1966; MSc in Parasitology, U. London, 1971, PhD in Parasitology, 1974; Diploma in Tropical Medicine, London Sch. Hygiene, 1972. Diplomate, Am. Bd. Internal Medicine, Am. Bd. Infectious Disease. Lectr. in parasitology U. Ceylon, Sri Lanka, 1968-74; asst. prof. medicine Charles Drew Postgrad. Sch. Medicine, L.A., 1979-81, Hahneman U., Phila., 1981—; cons. infectious diseases St. Joseph Hosp., Girard Med. Ctr., Phila., Easton (Pa.) Hosp., St. Lukes Hosp., Bethlehem, Pa., Muhlenberg Hosp., Bethlehem. Contbr. numerous articles to med. jours. Lt. col. M.C., U.S. Army Res., 1982. Mem. Am. Soc. Microbiology, Infectious Disease Soc. Am.

KANNER, ELLEN BARBARA, clinical psychologist; b. Newark, Apr. 22, 1950; d. S. Lee and Elsie (Frumkin) K.; m. Brian R. Donovan, June 10, 1973; children: Gregory Kanner, Rebecca Kanner. BA in Psychology, Smith Coll., 1972; MA in Clin. Psychology, Fordham U., 1974, PhD in Clin. Psychology, 1980. Lic. psychologist N.Y. Psychology aide Behavior Modification Program Northampton (Mass.) State Hosp., 1972-73; psychology intern Kings County Hosp., Bklyn., 1975-76; part time psychology work various clinics, N.Y., 1976-77; psychologist Kings Park (N.Y.) Psychiat. Ctr., 1980-83; pvt. practice Huntington, N.Y., 1983—. Unitarian. Office: 205 E Main St Huntington NY 11743-2923

KANNER, MARTIN ZELIG, physiatrist; b. Chrleston, W.Va., Dec. 12, 1950; s. Harry and Jeannette Rena Kanner. BA, Brandeis U., 1972; MD, W.Va. U., 1976. Diplomate Am. Bd. Phys. Medicine and Rehab., Am. Bd. Electrodiagnostic Medicine, Nat. Bd. Med. Examiners. Intern Sinai Hosp., Balt., 1976-77, attending physician dept. rehab. medicine, 1980-82, resident in rehab. medicine, 1977-79; attending physician dept. rehab. medicine North Charles Gen. Hosp., Balt., 1981-88; chief divsn. rehab. medicine Northwest Hosp. Ctr., Randallstown, Md., 1982—; adj. asst. prof. dept. neurology U. Md., Balt., 1981-95; chmn. subcom., bd. of practices Med.-Chirurgical Faculty of Md., Balt., 1996. Mem. Md. Soc. Orthop. Rehab. and Occupl. Medicine Specialists (sec.-treas., exec. bd. 1984—). Home: 16 Hambleton Ct Pikesville MD 21208 Office: Ste 224 1700 Reisterstown Rd Pikesville MD 21208

KANNOWSKI, PAUL BRUNO, biologist, editor; b. Grand Forks, N.D., Aug. 11, 1927; s. Max Bruno and Frances Eleanor (Burdick) K.; m. Phyllis

Inez Mosher, Apr. 6, 1953; children: Katherine Ann, Mark Allan. BS, U. N.D., 1949, MS, 1952; PhD, U. Mich., 1957. Instr. in biology Bowling Green (Ohio) State U., 1956-57; asst. prof. biology U. N.D., Grand Forks, 1957-60, assoc. prof. biology, 1960-69, prof. biology, 1969-90, prof. emeritus, 1991—, chmn. dept. biology, 1963-70, 82-88, dir. Inst. for Ecol. Studies, 1965-81; adj. curator insects Mus. Zoology, U. Mich., Ann Arbor, 1982—; mem. rev. panel NSF/NATO fellowships, Nat. Acad. Scis., 1976-80; mem. editorial bd. Environ. Entomology, 1972-77, chmn., 1976-77. Author: Wildflowers of North Dakota, 1989; editor (quarterly jour.) Prairie Naturalist, 1968-95; contbr. articles to profl. jours. Mem. N.D. Gov's. Com. on Energy Devel., 1973-76. With USN, 1945-46, PTO. Sr. postdoctoral fellow NSF Smithsonian Tropical Inst., 1966-67; recipient profl. award The Wildlife Soc., 1988. Fellow AAAS, Explorers Club; mem. N.D. Acad. Sci. (pres. 1964-65, chmn. state sci. adv. com. 1972-77), N.D. Natural Sci. Soc. (sec.-treas. 1980-94), The Nature Conservancy (trustee N.D. chpt. 1992—). Home: 1800 Lewis Blvd Grand Forks ND 58203-1642 Office: Univ N D 109 Starcher Hall Grand Forks ND 58202

KANNRY, SYBIL, retired psychotherapist, consultant, b. Tulsa, Okla., Oct. 1, 1931; d. Julius and Celia Bertha (Triger) Zeligson; children: Jeffrey Alan Shames, Erica Leslie Shames, Jonathan Adam Shames. Student U. Colo., 1949-51; BA, U. Okla., 1953; MSW, NYU, 1974. Diplomate in Clin. Social Work; cert. clin. social worker, N.Y., addiction counselor, employee assistance profl., alcoholism counselor, N.Y. Tchr. piano, Tulsa, 1956-61; psychiatric social worker Essex County Hosp., Cedar Grove, N.J., 1974-75, Rockland Psychiat. Ctr., Spring Valley, N.Y., 1975, adult team supr., 1975-78, adult team supr., Haverstraw, N.Y., 1978, clinic supr., Orangeburg, N.Y., 1978-83, clinic dir., Yonkers, N.Y., 1983-84; founder, dir. Indsl. Counseling Assocs., South Nyack, N.Y., 1982-84, Ctr. for Corp. and Cmty. Counseling, South Nyack, 1984-95; founder, pres. Tulsa Assn. for Childbirth Edn., 1957-59; adj. prof. psychology St. Thomas Aquinas Coll., Sparkill, N.Y., 1995. Fellow Soc. Clin. Social Work Psychotherapists; mem. Am. Assn. Marriage and Family Therapy (clin. mem.), Nat. Assn. Social Workers, Am. Orthopsychiat. Assn., Acad. Cert. Social Workers, Employee Assistance Profl. Assn., Soc. Clin. and Exptl. Hypnosis. Avocations: piano, tennis, travel. Home: 340 Glendare Dr Apt E Winston Salem NC 27104

KANOF, NORMAN B., dermatologist; b. N.Y.C., May 31, 1920. AB, CTWU, 1941, MD, 1941; D in Med. Sci., Columbia U., 1949. Diplomate Am. Bd. Dermatology. Clin. prof. dermatology NYU Sch. of Medicine, N.Y.C. Home: 737 Park Ave New York NY 10021 Office: 10 E 70th St New York NY 10021-4913

KANOFF, RICHARD JESS, pediatric neurologist; b. N.Y.C., Sept. 5, 1963; m. Donna M. Guidone, July 12, 1987; children: Michael, Julia. BS, U. Miami, 1985; DO, Nova-Southeastern U., 1990. Resident in pediatrics U. Miami (Fla.)-Jackson Meml. Med. Ctr., 1990-92, resident in adult neurology, 1992-93, fellow in pediatric neurology, 1993-95; pediatric neurologist Duluth (Minn.) Clinic, 1995—; clin. instr. Fla. Coll. Physician Assts., Miami, 1994-95, Nova-Southeastern U., Davie, Fla., 1994, U. Minn., Duluth, 1995—; mem. adv. bd. Lake Superior Epilepsy League, Duluth, 1995—. Mem. Am. Acad. Neurology, AMA, Am. Acad. Pediatrics, Lake Superior Med. Soc., Am. Osteo. Assn. Office: Duluth Clinic Ltd 400 E 3d St Duluth MN 55802

KANOFF, STEVEN J., ophthalmologist; b. Phila., Oct. 13, 1955; m. Audrey Kanoff; children: Sara, Max, Ben. MD, Temple U., 1985. Diplomat Am. Bd. Ophthalmologist. Ophthalmologist Lehigh Valley Eye Physicians, Bethlehem, Pa., 1989—. Fellow Am. Acad. of Ophthalmology; mem. Pa. Acad. Ophthalmology; mem. Pa. Acad. Ophthalmology, Alpha Omega Alpha. Office: Lehigh Valley Ey Physicians 2663 Schoenersville Rd Bethlehem PA 18017

KANOFSKY, JACOB DANIEL, psychiatrist, educator; b. Phila., Apr. 16, 1948; s. Philip and Mollie (Edelstein) K. BA in Physics, Temple U., 1965-69; MD, Thomas Jefferson Med. Coll., Phila., 1974; MPH in Epidemiology, Johns Hopkins U., 1978. Diplomate Am. Bd. Psychiatry and Neurology. Intern Met. Hosp., N.Y.C., 1974-75; resident in psychiatry St. Luke's-Roosevelt Hosp. Ctr., Columbia U., N.Y.C., 1978-80, fellow in psychiat. epidemiology, 1980-82; asst. editor-in-chief Med. Tribune, N.Y.C., 1984-85; ward chief rsch. unit Bronx (N.Y.) Psychiat. Ctr., 1986, assoc. clin. dir., 1986-87, acting clin. dir., 1987, pres. med. staff orgn., 1987-89; assoc. dir. schizophrenia rsch. Albert Einstein Coll. Med./Bronx Psychiat. Ctr., 1989-90, sr. rsch. psychiatrist, 1989—, asst. prof. psychiatry, 1986—; asst. prof. epidemiology and social medicine Albert Einstein Coll. Med., 1993—; lectr. in psychiatry Columbia U., N.Y.C., 1980—; attending psychiatrist St. Luke's-Roosevelt Hosp. Ctr., 1980—; contbg. editor Med. Tribune, 1986—; nutrition cons. Office of Alternative Medicine, NIH, 1992, Time Life Books, 1994—. Consulting editor Jour. of the Am. Coll. of Nutrition, 1990—; contbr. over 50 articles to profl. jours. Fellow Am. Coll. Nutrition; mem. Am. Psychiat. Assn. Jewish. Office: Bronx Psychiat Ctr 1500 Waters Pl Bronx NY 10461-2723

KANOPKA, FRANK LOUIS, community health nurse, lab technologist; b. Bklyn., Feb. 16, 1961; s. John Peter Kanopka and Helen (Tommasso) Picone; m. Lillian Marie McGuire, Sept. 17, 1988; children: Jacquelyn Michelle, Lisa Marie. BSMT, N.Y. Inst. Tech., Old Westbury, 1984; BSN, Fla. Atlantic U., Boca Raton, 1993. RN, Fla. Staff nurse Jackson Meml. Hosp., Miami, Fla., 1993; cmty. health nurse Seminole Tribe of Fla., Hollywood, 1993—. Mem. Fla. Nurses Assn. Republican. Home: 1381 Amaryllis Ln West Palm Beach FL 33415

KANO-SUEOKA, TAMIKO, molecular and cell biology educator, researcher; b. Kyoto, Japan, June 26, 1932; came to U.S., 1956; d. Ikuro and Fumiko (Okada) Kano; m. Noboru Sueoka, Jan. 23, 1957; 1 child, Miki P. MA, Radcliffe Coll., 1960; PhD, U. Ill., 1963. Rsch. asst. Calif. Inst. Tech., Pasadena, 1956-58; rsch. assoc. Princeton (N.J.) U., 1963-67, mem. rsch. staff, 1968-72; asst. prof. molecular and cell biology U. Colo., Boulder, 1973-79, assoc. prof., 1979-85, prof., 1985—. Contbg. author: Biochemical Action of Hormones, 1983; contbr. articles to profl. jours. Predoctoral fellow NIH, 1961-62, fellow Promotion for Cancer Rsch., 1987, 90, 92, 95. Mem. Am. Assn. Cancer Rsch., Am. Soc. for Biochemistry and Molecular Biology, Am. Tissue Culture Assn. Office: U Colo Campus Box 0347 Boulder CO 80309

KANTAROVSKY, ALEXANDER, surgeon; b. Vilnius, Lithuania, June 28, 1955; arrived in Israel, 1972; s. Reuven and Olga Kantarovsky; m. Liora Karniel, Mar. 10, 1983; children: Jony, Shelly. MD, Tel Aviv U., 1983, diploma in surgery, 1991. Intern Assaf Harofe Med. Ctr., Israel, 1982-83; resident in gen. surgery Meir Hosp., Israel, 1984-92, jr. cons., 1992; prin. med. officer Baragwanath Hosp., South Africa, 1992-93; fellow in vascular surgery Ichilov Hosp., Tel Aviv, 1993-96, jr. cons., 1996; dept. chief vascular surgery Hillel Yaffe Med. Ctr., Madera, Israel, 1996—; ATLS instr. Israel Def. Force, 1990—; instr. in surgery Tel Aviv U., 1991—, Witz Med. Sch., South Africa, 1992-93. Maj. Israel Def. Force, 1973-76. Mem. Israel Vascular Surgery Soc., Israel Trauma Soc., Assn. Surgeons South Africa. Office: PO Box 4699, Ramat-Hasharon 47278, Israel

KANTHARAJ, ADISAYAM JOSEPH, pediatrician; b. Rangoon, Burma, May 21, 1931; came to U.S. 1967; m. Lily David, May 12, 1961; children: Mary Sujana, Devaprasad. Student, Am. Coll., Madurai, India, 1946-50; BA, Madras U., 1950, MB, BS, Diploma in Child Health, 1960. Diplomate Am. Bd. Pediatrics. Intern, sr. resident Christian Med. Coll. and Hosp., Vellore, India, 1956-57, 59-60; chief of pediatrics Children's Hosp., Holdsworth Meml. Hosp., Mysore, India, 1960-61; pediatrician Med. Coll. Hosp., Pondicherry, India, 1961-64; med. relief organizer Tibetan Refugee Camp, Bylakuppe, Mysore, India, 1964-66; intern, medicine and pediatrics Roger Williams Hosp., Providence, R.I., 1967-68; resident in pediatrics Roger Williams Hosp., Providence, 1968-69, Grasslands Hosp., Valhalla, N.Y., 1969-70; resident in psychiatry State Hosp., Taunton, Mass., 1970-73; pvt. practice pediatrics Norwich, Conn., 1973—; practice pediatrics and internal medicine Holdsworth Meml. Hosp., Mysore, India, 1966-67. Mem. AMA, Am. Coll. Allergy, Asthma and Immunology, Am. Acad. Pediatrics, Indian Acad. Pediatrics, Conn. Med. Soc., New London County Med. Assn. Mem. Congregationalist. Office: 80 Sherman St Norwich CT 06360-4106

KANTOR, GUY ROBERT, radiation oncologist; b. St. Germain en Laye, France, Mar. 31, 1951; s. Henry Pierre Kantor; m. Sophie Pansieri; children: Pierre, Benjamin. MD, U. Hosp. Stautoine, Paris VI, 1976. Intern Tenan Hosp., Gustave Roimy Inst., Bordeaux, France, 1976-82; chef de clinique A.P., Paris, 1982-84, Coventry Hosp., Bordeaux, 1985; asst. prof Inst. Bergonié, Bordeaux, 1985-89, prof., 1989—; prof. medicine Bordeaux II U.; advisor Pub. Health Faculty, Bordeaux, 1993; advisor Inst. Curie, Paris, 1995; coord. European Programs Bordeaux II U., 1996. Contbr. articles to profl. jours. Recipient French Radiotherapy award Prix Lucien Mallet, 1986. Mem. French Soc. Radiation Oncology (bd. dirs.). Office: Inst Bergonie, 180 rue de St Genes, 33076 Bordeaux France

KANTOR, MEL LEWIS, dental educator, researcher; b. N.Y.C., July 13, 1956; s. Irving and Sarah (Schneider) K. BA in Chemistry and Math., CUNY, 1977; DDS, U. N.C., 1981. Diplomate Am. Bd. Oral & Maxillofacial Radiology. Resident Hennepin County Med. Ctr., Mpls., 1981-82, U. Conn. Health Ctr., Farmington, 1982-84; asst. prof. U. N.C. Sch. Dentistry, Chapel Hill, 1984-88, U. Conn. Sch. of Dental Medicine, Farmington, 1988-92; assoc. prof. N.J. Dental Sch., U. Medicine and Dentistry N.J., Newark, 1993—, clin. assoc. prof. N.J. Med. Sch., 1993—; cons. dental selection criteria panel FDA, 1985-87; test constructor Nat. Bd. Dental Examiners, 1989-93, 96—. Assoc. editor Jour. Dental Edn., 1986—; contbr. articles to Jour. Chem. Physics, Jour. ADA, Jour. Dental Rsch., Oral Surgery, Oral Medicine and Oral Pathology, Jour. Dental Edn. Mem. Internat. Assn. Dental Rsch. (founding mem. diagnostic sys. group, group program chmn. 1993—), Am. Acad. Oral and Maxillofacial Radiology (constitution and bylaws com., long range planning com., splty. recognition com., position paper com.), Am. Assn. Dental Schs. (steering com. competency-based predoctoral edn. initiative), Internat. Assn. Dentomaxillofacial Radiology, Radiol. Soc. N.Am., Soc. for Med. Decision Making, Phi Beta Kappa, Sigma Xi, Omicron Kappa Upsilon. Office: UMDNJ-NJ Dental Sch 110 Bergen St # C827 Newark NJ 07103-2400

KANTOREK, SANDRA SCHWAHL, optometrist; b. Newark, Sept. 18, 1952; d. Charles Richard and Mary (Costabile) Schwahl; m. John Kantorek, Aug. 17, 1974; children: Christopher, Heather, Amy. Student, Rutgers U., 1970-72; OD, Mass. Coll. of Optometry, 1976 Clinical instr. New England Coll. of Optometry, Boston, 1976-78; pvt. practice Union, N.J., 1978—; low vision specialist St. Barnabas Med. Ctr., Livingston, N.J., 1986-93. Mem. adv. bd. Head Start Program, 1985—. Mem. Am. Optometric Assn. (contact lens, low vision sect. mem.), Mid Jersey Optometric Soc. (treas. 1982-89), Tri-County Optometric Soc., Rotary, Beta Sigma Kappa (Silver Medal award). Office: 1485 Morris Ave Union NJ 07083-6332

KANTOUNIS, STRATOS GEORGE, surgeon; b. N.Y.C., Dec. 2, 1931; s. George Stratos and Liberty (Tsarnas) K.; m. Joan Amanda Schuman, Dec. 8, 1956; children: Lizabeth Ann, Stratos Jeffrey. BS, CCNY, 1954 MD, SUNY, Bklyn., 1958. Diplomate Am. Bd. Surgery. Intern Bellevue Hosp., N.Y.C., 1958-59, resident surgery, 1959-61; resident surgery Manhattan VA Hosp., N.Y.C., 1962-64; chief gen. surgery South Nassau Community Hosp., Oceanside, N.Y., 1980-91, pres. med. staff, 1988-90, attending gen. surgeon, 1967—. Capt., M.C. U.S. Army, 1964-67. Fellow ACS, Nassau Acad. Medicine; mem. AMA, Hellenic Med. Soc., Nassau Surg. Soc. (v.p.). Republican. Greek Orthodox. Office: 2 Lincoln Ave Rockville Centre NY 11570-5775

KANTROWITZ, JEAN ROSENSAFT, research program administrator medical products; b. Passaic, N.J., May 27, 1922; d. Nathan and Yetta (Applebaum) Rosensaft; m. Adrian Kantrowitz, Nov. 25, 1948; children: Niki, Lisa, Allen. BS, Rider Coll., 1942; MS, U. N.C., 1945; MPH, U. Mich., 1975. Adminstrv. asst. Maimonides Med. Ctr., Bklyn., 1961-70, Sinai Hosp., Detroit, 1970-78, '80-83; program coord., sr. clin. instr. child psychiatry div. Case Western Reserve U. Sch. Medicine, Cleve., 1978-80; v.p., adminstrv. mgr. L.VAD Tech., Inc., Detroit, 1983—; mgmt. cons. NIH, Washington, 1974—. Mem. Am. Pub. Health Assn., Soc. Rsch. Adminstrs., Am. Soc. Artificial Internal Organs. Home: 70 Gallogly Rd Lake Angelus MI 48326-1227 Office: LVAD Tech Inc 300 River Place Dr # 6850 Detroit MI 48207-4225

KANTZLER, GEORGE WILLIAM, psychiatrist; b. Detroit, July 13, 1924; s. George William and Dolores Marie (Latrau) K.; m. Elizabeth Helen Case, Feb. 7, 1948 (dec. July 1996); children: Mark George, Kris Phillip, Elyse Ann, Kurt William, Cheryl Marielle. Student, U. Detroit, 1947; DO, Chgo. Coll. Osteo. Medicine, 1951; student, Midwest Inst. Alcohol Studies, 1962, Rutgers U., 1963. Diplomate Am. Osteo. Bd. of Neurology and Psychiatry, Am. Bd. Psychiatry and Neurology. Rotating intern Art Ctr. Hosp., 1951-52; pvt. practice Detroit, 1952-70; resident in psychiatry Wayne State U. Sch. Medicine, Lafayette Clinic, Detroit, 1970-73; dir. psychiat. edn., assoc. dir. alcholism unit Detroit Meml. Hosp., 1973-79; pvt. practice Comprehensive Psychiat. Svcs., P.C., Southfield, Mich., 1973-79; adminstrv. dir. Dept. of Psychiatry Mercy-Meml. Hosp., Monroe, Mich., 1978-79; program dir. alcohol and substance abuse program Tampa Bay (Fla.) Neuropsychiat. Inst., 1979-82; dir. psychiat. svcs. Harborside Hosp., St. Petersburg, Fla., 1979-82, 84-85; pvt. practice St. Petersburg, 1979-91, Clearwater, Fla., 1985-91; cons. in field; mem. staff various hosps.; mem. faculty Wayne State U. Sch. Medicine, Dept. Psychiatry, 1973-79; asst. prof. various univs.; psychiat. dir. group therapy dept. and substance abuse out-patient program Bi-County Hosp., 1973-76, Robinwood Clinic, Detroit, 1973-79, Humanity House of Romeo, 1974-79; vice chmn. Dept. Psychiatry Mease Hosp., 1985-86, chmn. 1986; co-chmn. psychiatry, continuing edn. in osteo. medicine Mich. State U., 1975-79; vis. prof. W.Va. Sch. Osteo. Medicine, 1982; chief psychiatry sect. Morton Plant Hosp., Clearwater, 1992. Assoc. editor psychiatry Mich. Jour. Osteo. Medicine, 1974-75. Recipient Disting. Svc. award Mich. Alcohol and Addiction Assn., 1978. Mem. Am. Osteo. Assn., Am. Coll. Neuropsychiatry, Am. Med. Soc. on Alcoholism, Am. Psychiat. Assn., Am. Group Psychotherapy Assn., Fla. Osteo. Med. Assn., Fla. Psychiat. Soc., Pinellas County Osteo. Med. Assn. (sec. 1983-85, pres. 1986), Pinellas County Psychiat. Assn. (sec.-treas. 1989-90, pres. 1990-91).

KANZLER, WALTER WILHELM, biomedical educator; b. Jersey City, Sept. 17, 1938; s. George Hess and Martha (Strasser) K. BA, Montclair State Coll., 1960, MA, 1963; MA, Marshall U., 1964; PhD, U. Cin., 1972. Cert. counselor, N.J. Tchr. biology Union City (N.J.) High Schs., 1960-65; asst. prof. Trenton State Coll., 1965-66; instr. Wagner Coll., S.I., N.Y., 1966-72, asst. prof., 1972-76, assoc. prof., 1976-84, prof., 1984—; adj. prof. St. John's U., S.I., 1989, St. Peter's Coll., Jersey City, 1990—; cons. Scientist's Ctr. Animal Welfare, Washington, 1981—; sr. rsch. assoc. Nat. Ctr. for Biomed. Ethics, Drew U., 1976. Author: Pheromones and Trail Making in Ants. Fellow NASA, 1969-70, NSF, U. Calif., 1971; grantee NSF-Am. Mus. Natural History, N.Y.C., 1994. Mem. AAAS, Nat. Wildlife Fedn., Animal Behavior Soc., Sigma Xi, Beta Beta Beta. Home: 376 New York Ave Jersey City NJ 07307-1105 Office: Wagner Coll Biology Dept 631 Howard Ave Staten Island NY 10301-4428

KAO, SUE FEI, ophthalmologist; b. Taiwan, Apr. 22, 1957. BA, Ind. U., 1978; MD, Ind. U., Indpls., 1982. Diplomate Am. Bd. Ophthalmology. Intern Meth. Hosp., Indpls., 1982-83; resident Med. Coll. Ohio, 1983-86; fellow U. Mich., Ann Arbor, 1986-87; chmn. dept. ophthalmology Milw. Med. Clinic, 1994—. Recipient Physician's Recognition awards Am. Med. Soc., 1989, 93. Fellow Am. Acad. Ophthalmology, Phi Beta Kappa. Office: Milw Med Clinic 3003 W Good Hope Rd Milwaukee WI 53217

KAO, WILLIAM CHISHON, dentist; b. Santiago, Chile, July 10, 1952; s. John S. and Mary Kao; m. Susie M. Moy, June 3, 1978; children: Jonathan, Kristen. BS with high honors, U. Ill., Chgo., 1974, BS in Dentistry with honors, 1976, DDS with honors, 1978. Comprehensive inst. U. Ill. Coll. Dentistry, Chgo., 1978-80; dentist, assoc. Dental Bldg., Oak Lawn, Ill., 1978-83; pvt. practice Carol Stream, Ill., 1978-82; dentist Preventive Dental Group, Glendale Heights, Ill., 1982-86; pvt. practice Roselle, Ill., 1986—. Mem. ADA (presiding chmn. ltd. attendance clinic at midwinter conv. 1980), Am. Acad. Implant Dentistry, U.S. Dental Inst., Ill. State Dental Soc., Chgo. Dental Soc., Ill. Dental Soc., Roselle C. of C., Bloomingdale Study Club, Lake Park Hockey Club (sec.). Office: 1150 Lake St Roselle IL 60172-3365

KAPANDJI, ADALBERT IBRAHIM, orthopedic surgeon; b. Paris, Apr. 17, 1928; s. Mehmet Ibrahim and Roberte Jeanne (Chevalier) K.; m. Lydie Mauricette Richard, Oct. 12, 1950; children: Martine, Thierry. MD, Faculty of Medicine U. Paris, 1960. Externe hosps. Pub. Assistance, Paris, 1951-56, interne hosps., 1956-59, asst. hosps., 1960-65; prof. anatomy Nurses Sch. Paris Hosp., 1959-60; chef de clinique Faculty Medicine, Paris, 1960-65; pres. Clinique de L'Yvette S.A., Longjumeau, France, 1965—; prof. articular physiology Physiotherapists Sch. Necker Hosp., Paris, 1959-65, Physiotherapists Staff Sch., Bois-Larris, France, 1968-70. Author: The Physiology of the Joints, 3 vols., 1960 (translated into English, Italian, Spanish, German, Dutch, and Japanese), Dessins de Mains, Vol. 1, 1988 (translated in Japanese). Mem. French Soc. Angeiology, French Soc. Orthopaedics and Traumatology, French Soc. Hand Surgery (pres. 1987), Italian Soc. Hand Surgery, Rioplatenese Soc. Anatomy (Argentina). Home: Copernic 7, 91160 Longjumeau France Office: Clinique de L'Yvette, Rte de Corbeil 43, 91160 Longjumeau France

KAPELLA, BOHDAN WOJCIECH, physician; b. St. Etienne, France, Nov. 16, 1943; m. Jablonska Danuta, Sept. 18, 1949; children: Adam, Michel, Jean, Anna. MD, Acad. Medicine Poznan, Poland, 1974, U. Paris, 1981. Resident in surgery Centre Hospitalier Régional de Valenciennes, 1974-79; gen. practice medicine Cucq, France, 1983—. Pres. Found. Jean-Paul II France; counsellor Mcpl. de Cucq, 1989—. Mem. Franco Polish Soc., Soc. Polish History and Lit., Polonia Scouting Movement. Roman Catholic. Office: Cabinet Med, 33 Ave de la Poste, 62780 Cucq France

KAPELMANN, BARBARA ANN, physician, educator; b. N.Y.C., Apr. 30, 1949; d. Leonard A. and Helen (Hass) K.; m. Lawrence William Koblenz, Mar. 24, 1979; 1 child, Adam. BA, Barnard Coll., 1970; MS in Microbiology, Yale U., 1972; MD, Yeshiva U., 1975. Diplomate Am. Bd. Internal Medicine, Am. Bd. Gastroenterology. Intern St. Lukes-Rocsevelt Hosp.-Columbia U., N.Y.C., 1975-76, resident, 1976-78; fellow gastroenterology St. Luke's Hosp.-Columbia U., N.Y.C., 1978-80; fellow liver diseases Mt. Sinai Sch. Medicine-CUNY, N.Y.C., 1980-81; asst. attending physician in gastroenterology Beth Israel Hosp., N.Y.C., 1982-88, assoc. attending physician in medicine and gastroenterology, 1988—; clin. instr. in medicine Mt. Sinai Sch. of Medicine, N.Y.C., 1981-87, asst. clin. prof. medicine, 1987—; bd. dirs. Beth Israel Med. Ctr., N.Y.C., 1984—; asst. clin. prof. medicine Albert Einstein Coll. Medicine, N.Y.C., 1994—; attending physician Beth Israel North, Beth Israel Med. Ctr., N.Y.C., 1982—, Hosp. for Joint Diseases-Orthopedic Inst., N.Y.C., 1982—; vis. clin. fellow Columbia U. Coll. Physicians and Surgeons, N.Y.C., 1975-80. Co-author: Gastroenterology for the House Officer, 1989; contbr. articles to profl. jours. Fellow ACP, Am. Coll. Gastroenterology; mem. Am. Women's Med. Assn., Women's Med. Assn. N.Y.C. (officer), Am. Gastroent. Assn., Am. Assn. for Study of Liver Diseases, Am. Soc. for Gastrointestinal Endoscopy, Am. Med. Informatics Assn., N.Y. Acad. Gastroenterology, N.Y. Soc. for Gastrointestinal Endoscopy. Office: 944 Park Ave New York NY 10028-0319

KAPIKIAN, ALBERT ZAVEN, physician, epidemiologist; b. N.Y.C., May 9, 1930; s. Zareh Kaloust and Baizar (Bazikian) K.; m. Catherine Firth Andrews, Feb. 27, 1960; children: Albert Kaloust, Thomas Firth, Gregory Baird. BS cum laude, Queens Coll., 1952; MD, Cornell U., 1956; postgrad., Johns Hopkins U. Sch. Hygiene and Pub. Health, 1961-62, Royal Postgrad. Med. Sch. U. London, 1970. Intern Meadowbrook Hosp., Hempstead, N.Y., 1956-57; commd. med. officer USPHS, 1957, advanced through grades to capt., ret., 1988; with USPHS Civil Svc., 1988-90, USPHS Sr. Exec. Svc., 1990—; with epidemiology sect. Lab. Infectious Diseases, Nat. Inst. Allergy and Infectious Diseases, NIH, Bethesda, Md., 1957—, head epidemiology sect., 1967—; rsch. prof. child health and devel. George Washington U. Sch. Medicine and Health Svcs., 1977—; temporary advisor WHO, 1980-88, 91. Contbr. articles to profl. jours. Recipient Meritorious Svc. medal USPHS, 1970, 74, Disting. Svc. medal USPHS, 1983, Disting. Alumnus award Queens Coll., 1974, Stitt award Assn. Mil. Surgeons, 1974, Kabakjian award Armenian Students Assn. Am., 1974, Diagnostic Virology award (Murex) Pan Am. Soc. for Clin. Virology, 1993. Mem. AAAS, APHA, Infectious Diseases Soc. Am., Am. Epidemiol. Soc. (pres. 1996—), Am. Soc. Microbiology (Behring Diagnostics award 1987), Am. Soc. Virology, Phi Beta Kappa. Mem. Armenian Apostolic Ch. Home: 11201 Marcliff Rd Rockville MD 20852-3631 Office: NIH Lab Infectious Diseases Bethesda MD 20892

KAPISOVSKY, VALENTIN, pediatric surgeon; b. Krucov, Svidnik, Slovakia, Sept. 7, 1950; s. Pavel and Julia (Uramova) K.; m. Eva Kuzmova, July 27, 1974; children: Pavol, Slavomir. MD, U. Kosice, Czechoslovakia, 1974; cert., Acad. Acupuncture, Brno, Czech Republic, 1993. Intern dept. surgery Presov Hosp., Czechoslovakia, 1974-79, gen. surgeon, 1979-85, pediatric surgeon specialist, 1991—; pediatric surgery specialist U. Bratislava, Czechoslovakia, 1985-86; gen. surgery specialist K. el Boughari Algerie, 1987-91; lectr. faculty edn. U. Presov, 1994—. Home: Jarkova 29, 082 21 Velky Saris Presov Slovakia Office: Chirurgicke Oddelenie NsP, Holleho 20, 080 01 Presov Slovakia

KAPITAN, MARY L., retired nursing administrator, educator; b. Lawrence, Mass., July 9, 1920; d. Vincent and Concetta (Tomaselli) Zazzo; m. John A. Kapitan, Sept. 6, 1947. Diploma, Somerville (Mass.) Hosp., 1944; BS in Nursing Edn., DePaul U., Chgo., 1960, MS in Nursing Adminstrn., 1962. RN; lic. health facility adminstr., Ind. Occupational health nurse E. I. duPont de Nemours & Co., Lincolnwood, Ill., Senco Corp., Newtown, Ohio; asst. prof. psychiat. and med. nursing No. Ky. U., Highland Heights; nursing coord. VA Hosp., Butler, Pa.; instr. psychiat. nursing Ohio Valley Community Hosp., McKees Rocks, Pa.; dir. nursing svc. Presbyn. Home, Evanston, Ill., Edgewater Hosp., Chgo., Franklin Blvd Hosp., Chgo. 1st lt. U.S. Army Nurse Corps, 1944-47. Mem. ANA, Am. Assn. Occupational Health Nurses, Am. Coll. Health Facility Adminstrs., Ohio Nurses Assn., Ill. Nurses Assn., Ind. Nurses Assn., Mass. Nurses Assn., Southwestern Ohio Assn. Occupational Health Nurses (chmn. legislation and edn. com.), Women in Mil. Svc. for Am., Women's Meml. Found.

KAPLAN, ABRAHAM IRVING, retired psychiatrist; b. N.Y.C., Dec. 25, 1914; s. Max and Rose (Perlstein) K.; m. Shirley B. Bercovici, Jan. 18, 1942; children: Martin Paul, Richard David. BA, NYU, 1934; MD, Anderson Coll. Med., Glasgow, Scotland, 1939. Diplomate Am. Bd. Psychiatry and Neurology. Internship Jewish Meml. Hosp., N.Y.C., 1940-41; resident Post-Grad. Hosp., N.Y.C., 1942-43; pvt. practice psychiatry Queens Village, N.Y., 1946-51; resident Creedmore State Hosp., Queens, N.Y., 1951-52, Hillside Hosp., Queens, 1952-53; analytic tng. N.Y. Med. Coll., N.Y.C., 1953-56, clin. instr., 1956-58; asst. clin. prof. Med. Sch. Cornell U., N.Y.C., 1970-85; attending psychiatrist L.I. Jewish-Hillside Med. Ctr., Queens, 1965-86, North Shore U. Hosp., Manhasset, N.Y., 1970—. Maj. AUS, 1943-46. Fellow Am. Psychiat. Assn.; mem. Nassau Psychiat. Soc. (pres. 1976-77). Jewish. Home: 3360 S Ocean Blvd Palm Beach FL 33480-5668

KAPLAN, ALLEN P., physician, educator, academic administrator; b. West New York, N.J., Oct. 27, 1940; m. Lee Kaplan, Aug. 22, 1965; children: Rachel, Seth. AB, Columbia U., 1961; MD, Downstate Med. Coll. Diplomate Am. Bd. Internal Medicine, Am. Bd. Rheumatology, Am. Bd. Allergy and Clin. Immunology; cert. in diagnostic lab. immunology. Head allergic disease sect. NIH, Bethesda, Md., 1972-78; prof. medicine, head divsn. allergy rheumatology & clin. immunology SUNY, Stony Brook, 1978-87, chmn. dept. medicine, 1987-94. Editor: Allergy, 1985; contbr. over some 225 articles to profl. jours. Lt. comdr. USPHS, 1972-78. Recipient Commendation medal USPHS, 1976. Mem. Am. Acad. Allergy & Immunology (pres. 1989-90), Clin. Immunology Soc. (pres. 1992-93), Internat. Assn. Allergology and Clin. Immunology (sec. gen. 1991—). Office: SUNY Stony Brook Health Scis Ctr Stony Brook NY 11794

KAPLAN, ALVIN I., internist; b. Phila., Feb. 18, 1930; s. Harry and Dora (Lesack) K.; m. Miriam Kincus; children: Lawrence, Loren, Robert, Sally. BA, Temple U., 1951, MD, 1955. Diplomate Am. Bd. Internat. Medicine. Resident in internal medicine Phila. Gen. Hosp., 1955-59, chief emergency medicine, 1961-62; pvt. practice Bound Brook, N.J., 1962—; mem. staff Somerset Med. Ctr., Somerville, N.J., 1962—, pres. med. staff, 1980-81. Bd. dirs. Cen. N.J. Home for Aged, Somerset, Somerset Enterprise Corp., 1986—. Capt. M.C., USAF, 1959-61. Mem. ACP, AMA, Med. Soc. N.J. Office: 207 W Union Ave Bound Brook NJ 08805-1334

KAPLAN, BARBARA JOAN, geneticist, educator; b. N.Y.C., Sept. 5, 1941. BA, Calif. State U., L.A., 1969; MA in Orgnl. Mgmt., Univ. Phoenix, L.A., 1992. Cert. cytotechnologist Am. Soc. Clin. Pathologists; cert. clin. lab. specialist in cytogenetics, clin. lab. supr. Nat. Certifying Agy. for Med. Lab. Pers. Instr. LAC & USC MC, L.A., 1971-85; dir. Sch. Cytotech., 1981-95; editor Applied Cytogenics (formerly Karyogram), 1979-96; ednl. coord., supr. II Molecular and Cytogenics Labs. LAC & USC MC, L.A. County, 1971—. Mem. Assn. Cytogenic Technologists (bd. dirs., editor jour.), ASPCA, Nature Conservancy, Sierra Club, The Children's Bur. (L.A.). Office: LAC-USC Med Ctr GNH 2840 1200 N State St Los Angeles CA 90033-1078

KAPLAN, BARNARD ALAN, ophthalmologist; b. N.Y.C., Dec. 6, 1949; s. Herbert Wilbur and Blanche (Dorf) K.; m. Amy Mann, Sept. 11, 1976; children: Sarah, Naomi. BA, U. Pa., 1970, MD, 1974. Intern St. Elizabeth's Hosp., Boston, 1974-75; resident Georgetown U. Hosp., 1976-79; resident in ophthalmology Georgetown U., Washington, 1976-79; ophthalmologist Eye Profls, P.A., Cherry Hill, N.J., 1979—; trustee PRO of N.J., Voorhees, 1983—; mem. exec. com. Summit Surg. Ctr., Voorhees, 1990-93. Fellow Am. Acad. Ophthalmology (bd. govs. N.J. chpt. 1990-93); mem. AMA Med. Soc. N.J., Camden County Med. Soc. Office: Eye Profls PA Rte 70 E Gate Dr Cherry Hill NJ 08034

KAPLAN, BERNARD JOSEPH, surgeon; b. New Britain, Conn., Jan. 14, 1918; m. Samuel L. and Ethel (Marcus) D.; m. Hattie Kuniansky, Apr. 9, 1946; children: Sheryl Lynn, Robin Lee. BS, Muhlenberg Coll., 1941; MD, U. Vt., 1949; MS, U. Minn., 1955. Diplomate Am. Bd. Colon and Rectal Surgery, Nat. Bd. Med. Examiners. Intern St. Francis Hosp., Hartford, Ct., 1949-50; resident in gen. surgery U.S. VA Hosp., Newington, Ct., 1950-53; fellow colon and rectal surgery U. Minn. Hosp., Mpls., 1953-55; practice medicine specializing in colon and rectal surgery Hartford, 1955-88, Old Saybrook, Conn., 1991—; attending surgeon St. Francis Hosp., Hartford, 1955-88, mem. emeritus staff, 1988—; attending surgeon Mt. Sinai Hosp., Hartford, 1955-88, mem. hon. staff, 1988—; active staff surgery Middlesex Hosp., Middletown, Conn., 1991—; asst. clin. prof. surgery U. Conn. Med. Sch., Farmington, Conn., 1974-85, assoc. clin. prof. surgery, 1986—; clin. investigator pharm. cos.; vis. surgeon Dempsey Hosp., Farmington, 1973—; program dir. colon and rectal surgery St. Francis Hosp., 1985-88. Contbr. articles to med. and profl. jours. Pres. Hartford unit Am. Cancer Soc., 1970-72, Conn. div. 1977-79, bd. dirs., 1981-89, lifetime bd. dirs. Recipient C. Graham Eddy endoscopic award Biologic Photographic Assn., 1968, med. edn. award, 1970; bronze award and nat. divisional award Am. Cancer Soc., 1983, cert. of merit Conn. div., 1989. Fellow ACS, Internat. Coll. Surgeons, Am. Soc. Colon and Rectal Surgeons (v.p. 1986-87, Hermance plaque 1961, N.Y. Soc. Colon and Rectal Surgeons award 1969), North Eastern Soc. Colon and Rectal Surgeons (pres. 1979-81), New Eng. Soc. Colon and Rectal Surgeons (past pres.), Soc. Am. Gastrointestinal Endoscopic Surgeons (founding); mem. AMA, Conn. Med. Soc., Hartford County Med. Assn. (bd. dirs. 1969-71), Pilot's Point Yacht Club (commodore 1982-83, 88-90). Republican. Jewish. Home: 138 Captains Dr Westbrook CT 06498-1873 Office: 929 Boston Post Rd Old Saybrook CT 06475-2143

KAPLAN, DAVID RAY, immunologist; b. Akron, Ohio, June 14, 1952; s. Robert and Barbara Helen (Rudin) K.; m. Kathleene Anne Smachlo, June 9, 1984; children: Joshua Daniel, Celia Renee. AB, U. Chgo., 1974, PhD, 1979, MD, 1980. Lic. physician, Ohio. Postdoctoral fellow Washington U., St. Louis, 1980-84; asst. prof. immunology Case Western Res. U., Cleve., 1984-91, assoc. prof., 1991—, dir. Immunology Labs., 1984—; chairperson Ohio rsch. com. Am. Cancer Soc. Contbr. articles to profl. jours. Fellow Lederer Found., 1974-80, Hartford Found., 1985-87. Mem. AAAS, Am. Assn. Pathologists, Am. Assn. Immunologists, Am. Soc. Microbiologists, Clin. Immunology Soc. Jewish. Office: Case Western Res U 2109 Adelbert Rd Cleveland OH 44106-2624

KAPLAN, EDWARD STEVEN, neurosurgeon; b. Memphis, Tenn., Nov. 16, 1933; s. Jack and Violet Catherine (Needleman) K.; m. Linda Cecile Stone, July 1, 1958; children: Andrew Stone Kaplan, Jeffery Stone Kaplan. BS, Yale U., 1955; MD, Columbia U., 1959; MS, U. Minn., 1964. Diplomate Am. Bd. Neurosurgery. Clin. neurosurgeon Memphis Neurosurg. Clinic (now Kaplan-Friedman Clinic), Memphis, 1964—; instr. in neurology U. Tenn., Memphis, 1964-73, asst. prof. of neurosurgery, 1973—. Mem. Am. Assn. Neurol. Surgeons, Congress of Neurol. Surgeons, AMA, Memphis-Shelby County Med. Soc., Tenn. Med. Soc., Am. Coll. Surgeons. Jewish. Office: Kaplan-Friedman Clinic PC 910 Madison Ave Memphis TN 38103

KAPLAN, GEORGE WILLARD, urologist; b. Brownsville, Tex., Aug. 24, 1935; s. Hyman J. and Lillian (Bennett) K.; m. Susan Gail Solof, Dec. 17, 1961; children: Paula, Elizabeth, Julie, Alan. BA, U. Tex., 1955; MD, Northwestern U., 1959, MS, 1966. Diplomate Am. Bd. Urology. Intern Charity Hosp. of La. at New Orleans, 1959-60; resident Northwestern U., 1963-68; instr. Med. Sch. Northwestern U., Chgo., 1968-69; clin. prof., chief pediatric urology Sch. Medicine U. Calif., San Diego, 1970—; trustee Children's Hosp. and Health Ctr., San Diego, 1978-90, Am. Bd. Urology, Bingham Farms, Mich., 1991—; del. Am. Bd. Med. Specialties, Evanston, Ill., 1992—. Author: Genitourinary Problems in Pediatrics; asst. editor Jour. Urology, Balt., 1982-89; assoc. editor Child Nephrology and Urology, Milan, Italy, 1988—; contbr. articles to profl. publs. Pres. med. staff Children's Hosp., San Diego, 1980-82. Lt. USN, 1960-63. Recipient Joseph Capps prize Inst. of Medicine, 1967. Fellow ACS (pres. San Diego chpt. 1980-82), Am. Acad. Pediatrics (chmn. sect. on urology 1986); mem. AMA, Soc. for Pediatric Urology (pres. 1993), Am. Urol. Assn., Soc. Internat. Urologie, Soc. Univ. Urologists. Republican. Jewish. Office: Pediatric Urology Assocs 7930 Frost St Ste 407 San Diego CA 92123-2741

KAPLAN, GERALD, chemist; b. N.Y.C., Dec. 21, 1939; s. Louis and Ruth (Waldmen) K.; m. Marilyn Hollander, Dec. 9, 1967; children: Andrew, Michael, Jason, Laura-Anne. BS, Columbia U., 1957, MS, 1961; PhD, Rutgers U., 1968. From rsch. scientist to asst. mgr. Johnson & Johnson Domestic Operating Co., North Brunswick, N.J., 1967-78; from sect. head analytical labs. to mgr. analytical labs. Johnson & Johnson Products, Inc., North Brunswick, 1978-87; from mgr. analytical svcs. to dir. analytical svcs. Johnson & Johnson Health Care Co., North Brunswick, 1987-89; mgr. analytical svcs. Johnson & Johnson Consumer Products, Inc., Skillman, N.J., 1989-94; mgr. oral care R&D Johnson & Johnson Consumer Products Worldwide, Skillman, 1994—, mgr. oral care R & D, 1995—. Mem. Am. Chem. Soc., Rho Chi, Phi Lambda Upsilon. Office: Johnson & Johnson Consumer Products 199 Grandview Rd Skillman NJ 08558-1311

KAPLAN, HAROLD IRWIN, psychiatrist, psychoanalyst, educator; b. Bklyn., Oct. 1, 1927; s. William and Fannie Rose K.; m. Helen Singer, June 20, 1953 (div. 1971); children: Phillip, Peter, Jennifer; m. Nancy Barrett, Dec. 14, 1980. MD, N.Y. Med. Coll., 1949, cert. psychoanalysis, 1954; BA, NYU, 1988. Diplomate Am. Bd. Psychiatry and Neurology (examiner 1961—, assoc. examiner 1983—), Am. Bd. Forensic Medicine, Am. Bd. Forensic Examiners (life mem., fellow); cert. group psychotherapist. Intern Bklyn. Jewish Hosp., 1949-50; resident in psychiatry VA Hosp., Bronx, N.Y., 1950-53; fellow in psychiatry Mt. Sinai Hosp., N.Y.C., 1952; fellow in child psychiatry Jewish Bd. Guardians, N.Y.C., 1953; pvt. practice psychiatry and psychoanalysis, N.Y.C., 1953—; asst. prof. N.Y. Med. Coll., 1957-61, 1961-65; prof. psychiatry, 1965-80, NYU Sch. Medicine, 1980—; attending psychiatrist Bellevue Hosp., 1980—, Univ. Hosp. of NYU Med. Ctr., 1980—; cons. psychiatrist Lenox Hill Hosp., N.Y.C., 1994—; attending and vis. psychiatrist Met. Hosp. and Flower Hosp., N.Y.C., 1954-80; chief psychiat. edn. and tng. N.Y. Med. Coll.-Met. Hosp. Ctr., N.y.C., 1960-80; mem. med. bd. Met. Hosp., 1964-80; specialist in psychiat. tng.; mem. Prep. Commn. on Psychiat. Edn., NIMH-Am. Psychiat. Assn., 1974-75. Co-author: Modern Group Therapy series, 1972, Studies in Human Behavior series, 1972, Comprehensive Group Psychotherapy, 3d edit., 1993, Study Guide and Self-examination Review for Synopsis of Psychiatry, 5th edit., 1994; co-editor: The Sexual Experience, 1975, Modern Synopsis of Comprehensive Textbook of Psychiatry, 4th edit., 1985, Clinical Psychiatry, 1990, Pocket Handbook of Clinical Psychiatry, 1995, Glossary of Psychiatry, 1990 Pocket Handbook of Psychiatric Drug Treatment, 1993, 2d edit., 1995, Pocket Handbook of Psychiatric Emergency Medicine, 1993, Synopsis of Psychiatry, 7th edit., 1994, Comprehensive Textbook of Psychiatry, 6th edit., 1995, Concise Testbook of Clinical Psychiatry, 1996, Pocket Handbook of Primary Care Psychiatry, 1996; contbr. articles to profl. jours. Recipient Scroll of Acad. Achievement in psychiatry Alumni Assn. N.Y. Med. Coll., 1983; Disting. Service award Assn. Psychiat. Outpatient Ctrs. Am. and NYU Postgrad. Med. Sch., 1982; NIMH grantee, 1960-72. Fellow Am. Psychiat. Assn. (life, chmn. com. med. edn. 1973-75, cert. commendation 1976), Acad. Psychoanalysis (cert.), Acad. Psychosomatic Medicine, ACP (life); mem. Am. Psychosomatic Soc., Assn. Research Nervous and Mental Diseases (life), Med. Soc. County and State N.Y., AMA, Am. Geriatric Soc., World Psychiat. Assn., Assn. Advancement Psychotherapy, Am. Med. Writers Assn., Can. Psychiat. Assn., N.Y. Acad. Scis. (life), N.Y. Acad. Medicine (life), AAAS (life), Pan Am. Med. Assn. (diplomate), Royal Soc. Medicine (London), Am. Ortho Psychiat. Assn. (life), Am. Public Health Assn., Assn. Dirs. Psychiat. Residency Tng. Programs, Assn. Acad. Psychiatry, Am. Group Psychotherapy Assn., Soc. Med. Psychoanalysts, Alumni Assn. Bklyn. Jewish Hosp., Alumni Assn. N.Y. Med. Coll., NYU-Bellevue Psychiat. Soc., AAUP, Alpha Omega Alpha. Office: 50 E 78th St New York NY 10021-1809

KAPLAN, HAROLD PAUL, physician, health science facility administrator; b. N.Y.C., Jan. 22, 1939; s. David Benjamin and Sophie (Cohen) K.; m. Barbara Anne Sundstrom, Mar. 28, 1962; children: Todd, Jonathan, Robin, Scott. BS, Tufts U., 1959; MD, Yale U., 1963. Diplomate Am. Bd. Internal Medicine. Physician Internal Medicine Assocs., Meriden, Conn., 1970—; v.p. Internal Medicine Assocs., Meriden, 1974—, med. dir., mng. ptnr., 1985-93; clin. instr. internal medicine Yale U. Sch. Medicine, 1994—; chief of gastroenterology Meriden-Wallingford (Conn.) Hosp., 1976-91, chief of medicine, 1980-82, corporator, 1984—; chief of medicine WWII Vets. Meml. Hosp., 1977-79; corporator Vets. Meml. Med. Ctr., 1991—; bd. dirs. Healthworks, Ltd., Wallingford. Contbr. articles to profl. jours. Pres. Alliance for Edn. of North Haven, Conn., 1974-86, So. Conn. Swim League, 1978-83; chmn. ofcls. tech. com. Conn. Swimming, 1981-85; mem. parents coun. exec. com. Bowdoin Coll., 1988-91. Fellow ACP; mem. Am. Gastroent. Assn., Am. Soc. Gastrointestinal Endoscopy, Am. Soc. Internal Medicine, Farms Country Club of Wallingford (bd. govs. 1981-86). Republican. Office: Internal Medicine Assocs 116 Cook Ave Meriden CT 06451-5540

KAPLAN, HENRY JERROLD, ophthalmologist, educator; b. N.Y.C., Dec. 29, 1942; s. Ralph and Henrietta (Davis) K.; m. Adele Lotner, June 26, 1966; children: Wendi Suzanne, Todd Daniel, Ariane Dev. AB, Columbia U., 1964; MD, Cornell U., 1968. Diplomate Am. Bd. Ophthalmology. Intern in medicine Lakeside Hosp., Univ. Hosps. Cleve., Case-Western Res. U., 1968-69; surg. resident Bellevue Hosp., NYU Med. Ctr., 1969-70; NIH rsch. fellow in immunology U. Tex. (Southwestern) Med. Sch., Dallas, 1972-74; asst. prof. dept. cell biology U. Tex. (Southwestern) Med. Sch., 1974-75; resident in ophthalmology U. Iowa Hosps. and Clinics, Iowa City, 1975-78; retina-vitreous fellow dept. ophthalmology Med. Coll. Wis., Milw., 1978-79; assoc. prof. dept. ophthalmology Emory U. Sch. Medicine, Atlanta, 1979-84, prof., dir. rsch., 1984-88, assoc. prof. dept. microbiology, 1985-88; prof., chmn. dept. ophthalmology and visual scis. Washington U. Sch. Medicine, St. Louis, 1988—; ophthalmologist in chief Barnes Hosp., Washington U. Med. Ctr., 1988—; affiliate scientist in pathology and immunology Yerkes Regional Primate Rsch. Ctr., Atlanta, 1981—; adj. prof. dept. small animal medicine U. Ga., Athens, 1985—; assoc. chief ophthalmology Emory U. Hosp., 1985-88; mem. visual scis. study sect. A-1 NIH, Bethesda, Md., 1985-89, chmn., 1987-89; pres. Barnes Eye Care Network, 1994—. Author, co-author or editor, co-editor more than 150 med. textbooks, chpts. and articles on uveitis and macular degeneration and retinal degeneration pub. in refereed sci. and med. jours., 1974—; mem. sci. jour. rev. bds. Archives Ophthalmology, 1978—, Retina, 1982—, Am. Jour. Ophthalmology, 1983—, Ophthalmology, 1983—, Current Eye Rsch., 1986—, Exptl. Eye Rsch., 1986—; mem. sci. rev. bd. Investigative Ophthalmology and Visual Sci., 1983—, mem. editorial bd., 1990-92; co-editor Ocular Immunology and Inflammation, 1994—. Maj. M.C., USAF, 1970-72. Recipient sci. award Alcon Rsch. Inst., 1987; Olga Keith Weiss rsch. scholar to Prevent Blindness, Inc., N.Y.C., 1984. Fellow ACS, Am. Acad. Ophthalmology (Honor award 1984, Sr. Honor award 1994); mem. AMA, Assn. for Rsch. in Vision and Ophthalmology, Am. Assn. Immunologists, Macula Soc., Am. Uveitis Soc., Retina Soc., St. Louis Ophthal. Soc., St. Louis Met. Med. Soc., Mo. Ophthal. Soc. Jewish. Office: Washington U Sch Medicine Dept Ophthalmology and Visual Scis 660 S Euclid Ave # 8096 Saint Louis MO 63110-1010

KAPLAN, J. DOREENE, social worker; b. San Antonio, Jan. 30, 1943; d. Reginald and Bennie Louise (McCarley) Ormand; m. Sanford Kaplan, July 20, 1964; children: Shawn Eric, Paige Amy. BS, Trinity U., 1964; MSW, Temple U., 1979. Lic. social worker. Ptnr. GKC Assocs., Langhorne, Pa. Mem. United Way. Contbr. articles to profl. jours. Mem. NASW, PATFWA (chmn.).

KAPLAN, JERROLD MARVIN, internist; b. Chgo., Nov. 17, 1938; s. Meyer and Edith (Maltz) K.; m. Henrietta Carolyn Appel, Aug. 19, 1962; children: David P., Brian H. BS, U. Ill., 1960; MD, U. Ill., Chgo., 1963. Diplomate Nat. Bd. Med. Examiners, Am. Bd. Internal Medicine. Intern Letterman Gen. Army Hosp., San Francisco, 1963-64, resident in medicine, 1964-66, sr. resident in medicine, chief med. resident, 1966-67; fellow in cardiology Cedars Sinai Med. Ctr., L.A., 1970-71; pvt. practice internal medicine, cardiology San Bruno (Calif.) Internists Group, 1971—; attending physician cardiology clinic Stanford (Calif.) U. Sch. Medicine, 1972; active staff mem. Peninsula Hosp. and Med. Ctr., Burlingame, Calif., 1971—, instr. physical diagnosis, 1975-87; clin. asst. prof., vol. clin. faculty mem. Stanford U. Sch. Medicine, 1984-87; physician cons. Jour. AMA, 1965-67. Contbr. articles to med. jours. With U.S. Army Med. Corps, 1963-70. Fellow ACP; mem. Am. Soc. Internal Medicine, Calif. Med. Assn., San Mateo County Med. Assn., Alpha Omega Alpha. Office: Unified Med Clinics 1001 Sneath Ln # 300 San Bruno CA 94066

KAPLAN, KENNETH BARRY, psychologist; b. Boston, Mar. 15, 1947; s. Harold Irving and Eleanor (Miller) K.; m. Rhonda I. Sherer; children: David B., Rachel L., Howard D., Amy M. BA, U. Mass., Boston, 1969; EdM in Ednl. Counseling Psychology, Suffolk U., 1972; postgrad., Boston State Coll., 1974-76, Emmanuel Coll., 1974-76, Bridgewater State Coll., 1982-83, Fitchburg State Coll., 1989-90. Lic. cert. social worker, ednl. psychologist, sch. psychologist, tchr., secondary sch. prin. Asst. mgr. S.S. Pierce Co., 1970-71; tchr. Boston Pub. Schs., 1972-82; cons. svc. specialist for retarded individuals Wrentham State Sch., 1972-79; secondary sch. psychologist Bridgewater/Raynham (Mass.) Pub. Schs., 1982—. Chair edn. sector United Way of Greater Taunton, Mass., 1991—, bd. dirs., 1991-93; bd. dirs. Taunton Family. Named Horace Mann Tchr., Mass. Dept. Edn., 1986-87; Alliance Against Drugs grantee, 1993. Mem. NEA, NASW, NASP, Mass. Soc. Psychol. Assn., Mass. Sch. Counselors Assn., Mass. Assn. Social Workers, Mass. Tchrs. Assn., Raynham Edn. Assn. (pres. 1988-94), Bristol County Educators Assn., Bridgewater Raynham Edn. Assn., Plymouth County Educators Assn., Rotary. Home: 2 Sherwood Cir Sharon MA 02067-2262 Office: Bridgewater Raynham Schs 777 Pleasant St Raynham MA 02767-1562

KAPLAN, LAWRENCE RALPH, health system administrator; b. Orlando, Fla., Aug. 24, 1944; s. Ray and Molly Rothella (Luginsky) K.; m. Ann Hough, Apr. 12, 1986; children: Alexander, David. BA, U. Minn., 1966; MD, Einstein Coll. Medicine, N.Y.C., 1973; MPA, Harvard U., 1993. Asst. prof. medicine U. Minn., Mpls., 1977-80; chmn. bd. Aspen Med. Group, St. Paul, 1986-92; pres., CEO Metrowest Med. Ctr., Framingham, Mass., 1994—. Fulbright fellow, India, 1966, internat. fellow Columbia U., N.Y.C., 1968, Bush Found. fellow, Boston, 1992. Home: 8 High Meadow Circle Wellesley MA 02181

KAPLAN, LEE MICHAEL, biomedical scientist, physician, educator; b. N.Y.C., July 1, 1954; s. Bernard and Arlene (Lavender) K. AB, Harvard U., 1974; MD, PhD, Einstein Med. Sch., 1981. Diplomate Am. Bd. Internal Medicine, 1984; subspecialty Gastroenterology, 1987. Medicine intern Mass. Gen. Hosp. Harvard Med. Sch., Boston, 1981-82; resident Mass Gen. Hosp./Harvard Med. Sch., Boston, 1982-84; fellow in gastroenterology Mass. Gen. Hosp. Harvard Med. Sch., Boston, 1984-87; instr. in medicine Harvard Med. Sch., 1987-88, asst. prof. medicine neurosci., 1988—; asst. physician Mass. Gen. Hosp., Boston, 1988-95, assoc. physician, 1995—; assoc. chief gastrointestinal unit Mass. Gen. Hosp., 1993—, chief edn. unit clin. rsch. program, 1996—; sr. fellow Cannon Soc., Harvard Med. Sch., 1990—. Editor Einstein Quarterly Journal of Biology and Medicine, 1981-91. Recipient Pettis Meml. award AMA, Chgo., 1981; named Krancer Rsch. scholar Nat. Found. for Ileitis and Colitis, N.Y.C., 1987, Stuart Rsch. scholar Am. Gastroenterol. Assn., Thorofare, N.J., 1987. Fellow Am. Coll. Gastroenterology; mem. ACP, am. Fedn. Clin. Rsch., Am. Gastroent. Assn., Am. Assn. for Study of Liver Diseases, Am. Soc. Microbiology, Soc. for Neurosci., Endocrine Soc., Alpha Omega Alpha. Jewish. Home: 19 W Cedar St Boston MA 02108-1205 Office: Mass Gen Hosp GI Unit Jackson 802 Boston MA 02114

KAPLAN, MARTIN BERK, ophthalmologist; b. Buffalo, N.Y., Dec. 17, 1939; s. Alexander and Rose (Berk) K.; m. Terry Mae Nolan, Oct. 1965 (div. 1975); children: Bradley, Bryan; m. Carole Ann Goldstein, Dec. 19, 1978; stepchildren: Lisa Fish, Jamie Fish. BA, BS, Univ. Minn., 1960, MD, 1964. Diplomate Am. Bd. Ophthalmology. Internship L.A. County Harbor Gen. Hosp., Torrance, Calif., 1964-65; capt. Flt. surgery USAF, 1965-67; resident surgeon Wills Eye Hosp., Phila., 1967-70; pvt. practice Mpls., 1970—. Mem. Am. Acad. Ophthalmology, Minn. Acad. Ophthalmology (pres. 1992-93, sec. 1989-93), AMA, Wills Eye Soc. Office: Southdale Eye Clinic 6533 Drew Ave S Edina MN 55435

KAPLAN, MARTIN PAUL, pediatrician, educator; b. N.Y.C., Sept. 30, 1946; s. Abraham I. and Shirley (Bercovici) K.; m. Cynthia Gordon, June 21, 1970; children—Benjamin Mark, Dara Beth, Rachel Eve. B.A., U. Pa., 1968; M.D., N.Y. U. 1972; Intern, N.Y. U. Bellevue, N.Y.C., 1972-73, resident, 1973-74; sr. resident in pediatrics Duke Hosp., Durham, N.C., 1974-75; practice medicine specializing in pediatrics, Port Jefferson, N.Y., 1978—; mem. staff St. Charles Hosp.; chief pediatrics , 1994—, John T. Mather Hosp., (both Port Jefferson); clin. asst. prof. SUNY Stony Brook, 1981—. Mem. Brookhaven Youth Bd., Patchogue, N.Y., 1981-88. Served to lt. comdr. USNR, 1975-78. Fellow Am. Acad. Pediatrcis; mem. AMA, N.Y. State Med. Soc., Sufolk Pediatric Soc. (treas. 1984, sec. 1985, v.p. 1986, pres. 1987), Suffolk County Med. Soc. Democrat. Jewish. Office: 12 Medical Dr Port Jefferson Station NY 11776

KAPLAN, MAX, ophthalmologist; b. Winslow, Ind., Mar. 31, 1911; s. David Louis and Kate (Wolf) K.; m. Ethel Fishman, Jan. 28, 1940; children: David William, Catherine Ellen Levinson. AB, U. Rochester, 1933; MD, U. Ill., Chgo., 1937; postgrad., U. Ill., 1950. Diplomate Am. Bd. Pediatrics. Intern St. Anthony De Padua Hosp., Chgo., 1937; intern Michael Reese Hosp., Chgo., 1938-39, asst. resident in pediatrics, 1939-40; resident in pediatrics Children's div. Cook County Hosp., Chgo., 1940; resident Ill. Eye-Ear Infirmary, Chgo., 1950-52; asst. med. supt. children's div. Cook County Hosp., Chgo., 1941-42; pvt. practice medicine specializing in pediatrics Denver, 1946-50, pvt. practice medicine specializing in ophthalmology, 1952—; clin. prof. dept. pediatrics U. Colo., 1946—, clin. prof. dept. ophthalmology, 1952—; acting med. dir. Children's Hosp., Denver, 1978-79. Contbr. articles to profl. jours.; contbr. chpts. to books. Served to lt. col. Med. Corps, U.S. Army, 1942-46. Fellow Am. Acd. Pediatrics; mem. AMA, Am. Acad. Ophthalmology, Colo. Ophthal. Soc., Physicians for Social Responsibility. Jewish. Home: 3066 S St Paul St Denver CO 80210-6761

KAPLAN, MELVIN HYMAN, immunology, rheumatology, medical educator; b. Malden, Mass., Dec. 23, 1920; s. Harry and Rena (Chernoff) K. A.B., Harvard U., 1942, M.D., 1952. Intern Boston City Hosp., 1952; research fellow medicine House of Good Samaritan, Boston; also asst. bacteriology and immunology Harvard Med. Sch., 1953; research assoc. medicine, instr., also established investigator Am. Heart Assn., 1954-57, assoc. bacteriology and immunology, 1957-58; practice medicine, specializing in rheumatology and clin. immunology Cleve., 1958—; asst. prof. medicine Sch. Medicine Western Res. U., 1958-60, assoc. prof., 1960-65, prof., 1965-74; prof. medicine U. Mass., 1974-91, prof. emeritus, 1991—, dir. div. immunology and rheumatology, 1974-82, acting chmn. lab. medicine, 1974-79; assoc. physician Cleve. Met. Gen. Hosp., 1958-62, physician, 1962-74; Cons. allergy and immunology study sect. USPHS, 1964-69; asso. mem. com. streptococcal diseases Armed Forces Epidemiological Bd., 1956-70; temp. adviser WHO Study Cardiomyopathies in Africa, 1965; mem. merit review bd. VA, 1972—; mem. med. adv. bd. Arthritis Found., New Eng. Lupus Found. Assoc. editor: Jour. Lab. and Clin. Medicine, 1963-68, Jour. Clin. and Exptl. Immunology, 1965-71; Contbr. articles to profl. jours. Served with AUS, 1942-46. Recipient Research Career award USPHS, 1964. Mem. Am. Soc. Clin. Investigation, Am. Rheumatism Assn., Am. Assn. Immunologists. Home: 1550 Worcester Rd Apt 519 Framingham MA 01701-8937 Office: 55 Lake Ave N Worcester MA 01655-0002

KAPLAN, PAUL ELIAS, physiatrist, educator; b. N.Y.C., Oct. 26, 1940; m. Candia Starling Post, June 18, 1966; children: Steven Post Hitchcock, Heather, Danielle Kaplan Richards. BA cum laude, Amherst Coll., 1962; MD, UCLA, 1966. Diplomate Am. Bd. Phys. Medicine and Rehab., Am. Bd. Electrodiagnostic Medicine. Intern in internal medicine Ohio State U. Hosp., Columbus, 1966-67; resident in internal medicine Cedars-Sinai Med. Ctr., L.A., 1969-70, UCLA Med. Ctr., 1970-71; NIH fellow, resident in phys. medicine & rehab. U. So. Calif. Med. Ctr., L.A., 1971-73; pvt. practice Beverly Hills, Calif., 1973-74; prof. medicine and internal medicine Inst. of Chgo./Northwestern U., 1974-86; prof., dept. chmn., med. dir. Rusk Rehab. Ctr. U. Mo., Columbia, 1986-89; Bert C. Wiley prof., chair phys. medicine and rehab. Ohio State U., Columbus, 1989—, chmn. dept., 1989-94, dir. residency program, 1992-94. Author several textbooks on phys. medicine and rehab.; editor-in-chief jour. Yearbook of Rehab., 1984-89; alt. editor Archives of Phys. Medicine and Rehab., 1988—; cons. editor Advance and Rehab Management, 1995—; contbr. more than 100 articles to profl. jours. Fellow ACP, Am. Acad. Phys. Medicine and Rehab.; mem. Assn. Acad. Psychiatrists (pres. 1987-89, pres. coun. of chairpersons), Am. Spinal Injury Assn. Office: Ohio State U Dodd Hall Rehab Ctr 480 W 9th Ave Columbus OH 43210-1245

KAPLAN, RANDY KAYE, podiatrist; b. Detroit, Sept. 18, 1954; s. Earl Gene and Renee Joy (Sheftel) K. D of Podiatric Medicine, Ohio Coll., Cleve., 1979. Diplomate Am. Bd. Podiatric Surgery. Resident Kern Hosp., Warren, Mich., 1979-80; pvt. practice specializing in podiatric medicine, surgery Detroit, 1980—; clin. instr., mem. staff Kern Hosp., Warren, 1980—; adj. prof. Ohio Coll. Podiatric Medicine, 1986—, Pa. Coll. Podiatric Medicine, 1986—; mem. staff Providence Hosp., 1995; lectr. in field. Contbr. articles to profl. jours. Co-founder The Great Lakes Conf., 1988. Recipient Earl G. Kaplan award for polit. action excellence, 1994; Inspector Gen's. Integrity award U.S. HHS, 1995. Fellow Am. Coll. Foot Surgeons; mem. Am. Diabetes Assn., Am. Podiatric Med. Assn. (mem. continuing edn. com. 1988-94, mem. labor rels. com. 1990-94), Mich. Podiatric Med. Assn. (bd. dirs. 1985—, 2nd v.p. 1988-90, pres. 1990-91, 92-93, Podiatrist of Yr. Southeastern divsn. 1987-88, Shining Star award for excellence 1992), Kern Hosp. Resident Alumni Assn., Mich. Pub. Health Assn., Phi Alpha Pi (Man of Yr. 1979). Jewish. Office: 20511 Dequindre St Detroit MI 48234-1259

KAPLAN, ROBERT MALCOLM, health researcher, educator; b. San Diego, Oct. 26, 1947; s. Oscar Joel and Rose (Zankan) K.; m. Catherine J. Atkins; children—Cameron Maxwell, Seth William. A.B. in Psychology, San Diego State U., 1969; M.A., U. Calif.-Riverside, 1970, Ph.D., 1972. Lic. psychologist, Calif. Teaching asst. U. Calif., Riverside, 1969-72, vis. assoc. prof. psychology, 1977-78; asst. prof. in residence U. Calif., San Diego, 1973, asst. research psychologist and cons. dept. community medicine div. health policy, assoc. adj. prof., 1980-86, prof., 1986—, chief div. health care scis., 1989—; sr. rsch. assoc. Am. Inst. for Rsch., Palo Alto, Calif., 1972-73; from asst. prof. to prof. psychology San Diego State U., 1974-88, dir. Ctr. for Behavioral Medicine; bd. dirs. NATO Advanced Rsch. Workshop on Behavioral Epidemiology and Disease Prevention; mem. health svcs. rsch. study sect. Nat. Ctr. Health Svcs. Rsch., 1981-85, 88-92, VA Sci. Rev. and Evaluations Bd. for Health Svcs., 1989-91 (chair 1991-92); cons., lectr. in field. Faculty fellow San Diego State U., 1977; epidemiology fellow Am. Heart Assn., 1983; recipient Career Rsch. Devel. award NIH, 1981-86, Alumni and Assocs. Disting. Faculty award San Diego State U., 1982, Exceptional Merit service award San Diego State U., 1984. Fellow APA (bd. dirs., Outstanding Sci. Achievement award health psychology divsn. 1987, pres. 1992-93); mem. AAAS (exec. com. Pacific divsn. 1978-82), Am. Pub.

Health Assn., Soc. Behavioral Medicine (bd. dirs., pres. 1996-97). Office: U Calif-San Diego Sch Medicine Dept. Family Preventive Medicine La Jolla CA 92093-0622

KAPLAN, RONALD IVAN, physician; b. Atlanta, Mar. 12, 1949; s. Arthur Marvin and Frances Faye (Hardman) K.; m. Angelia Spears, Nov. 24, 1986; children: Natalie, Steven, Mark. BA, Tulane U., 1971; MD, Med. Coll. Ga., 1975; JD, Ga. State U., 1992. Bd. cert. Am. Coll. Forensic Examiners. Intern Grady Meml. Hosp., Atlanta; resident Grady Meml. Hosp./Piedmont Hosp., Atlanta; pvt. practice surgery Atlanta, 1980—; advisor Atlanta Police S.W.A.T., 1980-96. Lt. comdr. USNR, 1983-85. Office: Ste 205 2520 Windy Hill Rd Marietta GA 30067-8650

KAPLAN, SAMUEL, pediatric cardiologist; b. Johannesburg, South Africa, Mar. 28, 1922; came to U.S., 1950, naturalized, 1958; s. Aron Leib and Tema K.; m. Molly Eileen McKenzie, Oct. 17, 1952. MB, BcH., U. Witwatersrand, Johannesburg, 1944, MD, 1949. Diplomate: Am. Bd. Pediatrics. Intern Johannesburg, 1945; registrar in medicine, 1946; lectr. physiology and medicine U. Witwatersrand, 1946-49; registrar in medicine U. London, 1949-50; fellow in cardiology, research assoc. U. Cin., 1950-54, asst. prof. pediatrics, 1954-61, assoc. prof. pediatrics, 1961-66, prof. pediatrics, 1967-87, asst. prof. medicine, 1954-67, assoc. prof. medicine, 1967-82, prof. medicine, 1982-87; prof. pediatrics UCLA, 1987—; cons. NIH; hon. prof. U. Santa Tomas, Manila. Mem. editl. bd. Circulation, 1974-80, Am. Jour. Cardiology, 1976-81, Am. Heart Jour., 1981—, Jour. Electrocardiology, 1977-94, Clin. Cardiology, 1979—, Jour. Am. Coll. Cardiology, 1983-87, Progress Pediat. Cardiology, 1990—. Cecil John Adams fellow, 1949-50; grantee Heart, Lung and Blood Inst. of NIH, 1960—. Mem. Am. Pediatric Soc., Am. Soc. Pediatric Rsch., Am. Heart Assn. (med. adv. bd. sect. circulation), Am. Fedn. Clin. Rsch., Am. Coll. Cardiology, Internat. Carviovascular Soc., Am. Acad. Pediatrics, Midwest Soc. Pediatric Rsch. (past pres.), Sigma Xi. Alpha Omega Alpha; hon. mem. Peruvian Soc. Cardiology, Peruvian Soc. Angiology, Chilean Soc. Cardiology, Burma MEd. Assn. Office: UCLA Sch Medicine Dept Pediatric Cardiology Los Angeles CA 90095

KAPLAN, SAMUEL SIMON, orthopedic surgeon; b. N.Y.C., Aug. 31, 1939; s. Arthur Murray and Gertrude K.; m. Brenda Joan, June 10, 1962; children: Kenneth, Karen. AB, N.Y.U., 1961, MD, 1965. Diplomate Am. Bd. Orthopedic Surgery. Intern Kings County Hosp., Bklyn., 1965-66; sugrical resident Albert Einstein Coll. Medicine, Bronx, N.Y., 1966-67; chief surg. services 328th Air Force Base Hosp., Grandview, Mo., 1967-69; resident orthopedic Kans. U. Med. Ctr., Kansas City, 1969-72; pres. Orthopedists Ltd., Scottsdale, Ariz., 1972—; tchr. Maricopa County Med. Ctr., Phoenix, 1986—. Reviewer: Jour. Bone and Joint Surgery 1986—; conbtr. articles to profl. jours. Fellow Am. Acad. Orthopedic Surgeons; mem. Western Orthopedic Assn., Ariz. Orthopedic Assn., Maricopa County Med. Soc., Ariz. Med. Soc., Ariz. Macintosh User Group, Road Runners M.D. Club. Office: Orthopedists Ltd 3501 N Scottsdale Rd Scottsdale AZ 85251-5648

KAPLAN, SANDRA LEE, physical therapist, educator; b. Lakewood, N.J., Jan. 2, 1956; d. Edward S. and Adele (Lee) K. BS, U. Conn., 1978; MS, Ohio State U., 1984; PhD, NYU, 1991. Lic. phys. therapist, Ohio, Conn., W.Va., N.Y. Phys. therapist Maumee Valley Phys. Therapy Svcs., Toledo, 1978-80, Hamilton County Bd. of MRDD, Cin., 1982-82; pvt. practice Columbus, Ohio, 1982-84; instr. Nisonger Ctr., Columbus, 1983-84; acad. coord. clin. edn. W.Va. U., Morgantown, 1984-85; pvt. practice phys. therapy Blyn., 1985-95; assoc. prof. phys. therapy program L.I. U., Blyn., 1987-95, interim co-dir. phys. therapy program, 1988-89; asst. dir., assoc. prof. clin. phys. therapy U. Medicine and Dentistry N.J., Newark, 1995—. Trustee Park Slope Jewish Ctr., Bklyn., 1988-91. Mem. Am. Phys. Therapy Assn., N.Y. Road Runners Club, Phi Kappa Phi. Office: U Medicine and Dentistry N J Dept Phys Therapy 65 Bergen St Newark NJ 07107

KAPLAN, SANFORD ALLEN, internist, allergist; b. Elizabeth, N.J., Feb. 27, 1929; s. Theodore and Rose (Fisher) K.; m. Maxine Jewel Schoenfeld, July 4, 1954; children: Lloyd Austin, Dean Ian, Keith Wayne. BS in Chemistry, Ind. U., 1950; MD, Chgo. Med. Sch./Finch U., 1954. Diplomate Nat. Bd.; charter diplomate Am. Bd. Family Practice, recert.; cert. diplomate Am. Bd. Allergy and Immunology; lic. medicine and surgery, N.Y.; lic. medicine and surgery, Fla.; cert. sch. health inspector N.Y.C. Bd. Edn.; cert. compensation rating CIM; cert. local health officer grade 2, N.Y. Rotating intern Kings County Hosp., Bklyn., 1954-55; pvt. practice specializing in internal medicine and allergy Bronxville, N.Y., 1958—; fellow in allergy Misericordia Hosp. Allergy Clinic, 1963-68; attending in medicine Mt. Vernon (N.Y.) Hosp., 1970—, Lawrence Hosp., Bronxville, 1975—; assoc. attending allergy sect. dept. medicine Westchester County Med. Ctr., 1978—; clin. assoc. prof. medicine N.Y. Med. Coll., 1986—; chmn. utilization com. Cross County Hosp., 1965-75; proctor family practice St. Joseph Hosp. Family Practice Residency Program, 1974-78; mem. med. bd. Mt. Vernon Hosp., 1977-81; clin. cons. for programs administered by N.Y. State Dept. Health; vis. clin. asst. prof. medicine N.Y. Coll. Osteopathic Medicine, 1978—; mem. hosp. bd. Westchester County Med. Ctr., 1974-76, 84—, mem. exec. com., 1986—, sec., 1989—. Contbr. numerous articles to profl. jours. and confs. Dir. Big Bros.-Big Sister Program, Yonkers, N.Y., 1963-74, dir. adv. bd., 1975—; v.p. Big Bros.-Big Sister, Inc., 1972-74; former mem. Yonkers Econ. Devel. Bd.; dir. Milton Budnick Found., 1966, Tax Payers of N.E. Yonkers, 1964-86, Mark Brent Dolinsky Found., 1981—; chmn. Westchester Coord. Com. for Handicapped, 1977-79; apptd. advisor on narcotics to Mayor of Yonkers 1970; chmn. Narcotics Guidance Coun. 1972-75; mem. drug abuse com. Yonkers Bd. Edn., 1979-86. Maj. USAF, 1955-57, res., ret. Recipient Hon. Award of Yr., Big Bros.-Big Sister of Yonkers, 1974, Proclamation for svc. to handicapped Westchester County Exec., 1980, Cert. of Award-Winning for original writing Med. Econs., 1972. Fellow Am. Acad. Family Physicians (charter, Recognition award for active family practice tchg. 1975, 76), Am. Acad. of Allergy, Asthma and Immunology, Am. Assn. Clin. Immunology and Allergy, Am. Coll. Allergy, Asthma and Immunology; mem. AMA, Am. Geriatric Soc. (chmn. drug abuse and alcoholism com. Lawrence Hosp. 1977-80, chmn. med.-nursing liaison com. Mt. Vernon Hosp. 1984-86, mem. disaster com. Lawrence Hosp. 1981—), N.Y. State Allergy Soc., Med. Soc. of State of N.Y. (exec. com. hosp. med. staff sect., legis. com., drug abuse com., geriatric com., councilor 9th dist. 1992-95, 95-98, Presdl. Citation for comty. svc. 1975), Westchester County Med. Soc. (pub. rels. 1966-68, editl. bd. Bull. 1982—, vice chmn. legis. com. 1974-76, chmn. legis. com. 1981-86, pres.-elect 1990, pres. 1991). Home: 6 Greenwood Ct Briarcliff Manor NY 10510 Office: 821 Bronx River Rd Bronxville NY 10708

KAPLAN, STANLEY ALBERT, pharmaceutical research and development executive; b. N.Y.C., Sept. 28, 1938; s. Martin Kaplan and Sara Claire (Meszel) Swerdlow; m. Lois Elaine Haber, Sept. 11, 1960; children: Lisa Joy, Michelle Joanne, Martin William. BS, Columbia U., 1959, MS, 1961; PhD, U. Calif., San Francisco, 1965. Lic. pharmacist, N.Y., Calif. Postdoctoral fellow St. Mary's Hosp. Med. Sch., London, 1965-66; various positions to assoc. dir. therapeutics div. Hoffmann-La Roche, Inc., Nutley, N.J., 1966-84; exec. dir. med. rsch. div. Lederle Am. Cyanamid Co., Pearl River, N.Y., 1984-87; sr. v.p. rsch. and devel. Liposome Tech. Inc., Menlo Park, Calif., 1987-89; pres., chief operating officer Pharmetrix Corp., Menlo Park, 1989-92; sr. v.p. R & D Alpharma, Balt., 1992—. Mem. editorial bd. Clin. Pharmacology and Therapeutics, Pharmacokinetics and Biopharmaceutics, Jour. Pharm. Scis.; contbr. over 60 rsch. and rev. articles, 10 book chpts. Fellow AAAS (chmn. pharm. scis. sect. 1983-84), Am. Assn. Pharm. Scientists, Am. Inst. Chemists, Am. Coll. Clin. Pharmacology and Therapeutics, Am. Soc. for Pharmacology and Exptl. Therapeutics; mem. N.Y. Acad. Scis., Fedn. Internationale Pharmaceutique, B'nai Brith, Sigma Xi. Office: Alpharma 333 Cassell Dr #3500 Baltimore MD 21224-6818

KAPLAN, STANLEY BARUCH, medicine educator, researcher; b. Memphis, Jan. 6, 1931; s. Leon Labe and Henrietta (Schaffer) K.; m. Sue Heidel, Feb. 27, 1977. MD, U. Tenn., Memphis, 1954. Diplomte Am. Bd. Internal Medicine. Intern Jefferson Med. Coll. Hosp., Phila., 1955-56; from asst. resident to chief resident in medicine U. Tenn., Memphis, 1958-61, chief resident in medicine, 1961-62; instr. medicine U. Tenn., 1961-63, asst. prof., 1963-67, assoc. prof., 1967-73, prof., 1973—, dir. clin. tng. divsn. connective tissue diseases, 1986—. Contbr. articles to med. jours. Bd. dirs. Les Passees Rehab. Ctr., Memphis, 1972—; bd. dirs., trustee Leo Levi Arthritis Hosp., Hot Springs, Ark., 1977—; bd. dirs. Tenn. chpt, Arthritis Found., 1962—, chmn. med. and sci. com., 1992—; mem. med. com. Memphis chpt. Lupua Found. Am., 1983—, past chmn. Capt. M.C., U.S. Army, 1956, Korea. Rheumatology fellow U. Tenn., Memphis, 1961-63. Fellow Am. Coll. Rheumatology; mem. AMA, Tenn. Med. Assn., Memphis and Shelby County Med. Soc., Memphis Acad. Memphis (v.p. 1996—), Alpha Omega Alpha. Home: 5105 Winton Pl Memphis TN 38117 Office: U Tenn 956 Court Ave Memphis TN 38163

KAPLAN, STEPHEN ROBERT, medical educator, university dean; b. N.Y.C., May 18, 1937; s. William and Jeanne (Spandorf) K.; m. Marilyn Dubin, August 6, 1961; children: Allison, Seth, Adam. BA, Wesleyan U., 1959; MD, NYU, 1963. Diplomate Am. Bd. Med. Examiners. Intern and resident in medicine Long Island Jewish Med. Ctr., New Hyde Park, NY, 1963-65; fellow in clin. pharmacology Yale New Haven (Conn.) Med. Ctr., 1965-67; instr. Brown U., Providence, 1969-70, asst. prof. med. scis., 1970-76, assoc. prof. medicine, 1976-84, from asst. dean to assoc. dean of medicine, 1982-89, prof. medicine, 1984-88; adj. assoc. prof. Coll. of Pharmacy of U. R.I., Kingston, 1977-88; dean medicine Wright State U. Sch. Medicine, Dayton, Ohio, 1989-90, assoc. v.p. health affairs, 1991; prof. medicine (tenured), dept. head gen. internal medicine SUNY, Buffalo, 1991—; cons. U.S. Pharmacopoeia, 1988—. Contbr. abstracts and articles to profl. pubs. Pres. Temple Habonim, Barrington, R.I., 1976-78; v.p. Bur. Jewish Edn., R.I., 1986-88. Capt. USAF, 1967-69. Fellow ACP; mem. Am. Soc. Clin. Pharmacology and Therapeutics, Am. Rheumatism Assn., AMA, Am. Fedn. Clin. Rsch., Am. Soc. Clin. Oncology, AAAS, Dayton Racquet Club, Engineers Club. Jewish. Home: 24 Stonewood Dr East Amherst NY 14051-1742 Office: Millard Filmore Hosp 3 Gates Circle Buffalo NY 14209

KAPLAN, ZACHARY, dentist; b. Los Angeles, Nov. 11, 1939; s. Harry and Tillie (Cohen) K.; m. Peggy Jean Knibb, June 25, 1966; childen: Scott Matthew, Alison Jean. Student, U. Calif., Santa Barbara, 1957-61; DDS, St. Louis U., 1965. Gen. practice dentistry Ft. Collins, Colo., 1967—; asst. clin. prof. U. Colo., Denver, 1983—. Served to lt. comdr. USN, 1965-67. Mem. ADA, Colo. Dental Assn., Larimer County Dental Soc. (peer rev. com., 1983—, community resource com. 1985—). Democrat. Jewish. Office: 373 W Drake Rd Fort Collins CO 80526-2881

KAPLOWITZ, LISA GLAUSER, physician, educator; b. Phila., Apr. 18, 1951; d. Felix E. and Charlotte (Gordy) Glauser; m. Paul Bernard Kaplowitz, Dec. 28, 1970; children: Joshua Michael, Daniel Steven. BS, U. Mich., 1970; MD, U. Chgo., 1975. Diplomate Am. Bd. Internal Medicine, Am. Bd. Infectious Diseases. Resident U. N.C., Chapel Hill, 1976-78; postgrad. fellow U. N.C., 1978-80, inst. Dept. Medicine, 1980-82; asst. prof. Dept. Medicine Med. Coll. Va., Richmond, 1982-89; assoc. prof. Dept. Medicine Med. Coll. Va., 1989—; dir. HIV/AIDS Ctr. Va. Commonwealth U., Richmond, 1993—; bd. dirs. AIDS Action Coun., Washington, 1995-96. Contbr. (book chpt.) Conn's Current Therapy, 1985, 2d rev. edit., 1988, Principles of Critical Care Medicine, 1992. Mem. adv. bd. Va. League for Planned Parenthood, Richmond, 1993—, Richmond AIDS Ministry, 1988—, Leadership Metro Richmond, 1992-93. Named Woman of Year Va. Commonwealth U., 1995, mem. Va. Women's Hall of Fame Va. Coun. on Status of Women, 1992; health policy fellow Inst. Medicine, 1996—. Fellow ACP, Infectious Disease Soc. Am.; mem. APHA, Am. Soc. Microbiology. Office: HIV AIDS Ctr Va Commonwealth U 1001 E Broad St Ste 125 Richmond VA 23298-0049

KAPLOWITZ, NEIL, physician, educator; b. N.Y.C., Mar. 16, 1943; s. Louis and Henrietta (Schall) K.; m. Fattaneh E. Enayat; children: Hillary C., Gregory D. BS, NYU, 1964, MD, 1967. Intern, resident Bellevue Hosp., 1967-69; resident Albert Einstein Med. Ctr., 1969-70; fellowship Cornell U. Coll. Medicine, 1970-72; guest investigator Rockefeller U., N.Y.C., 1970-71; asst. prof. Cornell U. Med. Coll., N.Y.C., 1972-73; asst. prof. UCLA Sch. Medicine, 1975-77, assoc. prof., 1977-82, prof., 1982-90; prof. U. So. Calif. Sch. Medicine, L.A., 1990—, chief div. gastrointestinal and liver diseases, 1990—; chief gastroenterology Wadsworth VA Hosp., L.A., 1980-90. Editor: Liver and Biliary Diseases, 1992; assoc. editor: Hepatology, 1985-90, Am. Jour. Physiology, 1991—; contbr. over 100 articles to profl. publs Lt. comdr. USN, 1973-75. Recipient Western Gastroenterology Rsch. prize Western Gut Club, 1986. Mem. Am. Assns. Physicians, Am. Soc. Clin. Investigation, Western Soc. Clin. Investigation (pres. 1985-86), Phi Beta Kappa, Alpha Omega Alpha. Office: U So Calif Sch Medicine 2025 Zonal Ave Los Angeles CA 90033-4526*

KAPPAS, ATTALLAH, physician, medical scientist; b. Union City, N.J., Nov. 4, 1926; s. Attie and Sofia (Kozam) K.; m. Oct. 26, 1963; children: Peter, Michael, Nicholas. A.B., Columbia U., 1947; M.D. with honors, U. Chgo., 1950; Sc.D., N.Y. Med. Coll., 1978. Diplomate: Am. Bd. Internal Medicine. Med. intern Univ. Service, Kings County Hosp., N.Y.C., 1950-51; research fellow div. steroid biochemistry and metabolism Sloan Kettering Inst., N.Y.C., 1951-54; asst. resident physician and sr. asst. resident physician Peter Bent Brigham Hosp. Harvard Med. Sch., Boston, 1954-56; assoc. div. steroid biochemistry and metabolism Sloan Kettering Inst., 1956-57; from asst. prof. to assoc. prof. dept. medicine, head div. metabolism and arthritis U. Chgo. Med. Sch., 1957-67; Guggenheim fellow, guest investigator Rockefeller U., N.Y.C., 1966-67; assoc. prof., physician Rockefeller U., 1967-71, sr. physician, 1971-74, prof., 1971-81, Sherman Fairchild prof., 1981—, v.p., 1983-91, physician-in-chief, 1974-91, physician-in-chief emeritus, 1991—; Vincent Astor chair clin. sci. Meml. Sloan-Kettering Cancer Ctr. and Cornell U. Med. Coll., 1979-81, prof. medicine, 1972—, prof. pharmacology, 1972-87; bd. dirs. Russell Sage Inst. Pathology Cornell U., 1977-87; vis. com. div. biol. scis. Pritzker Sch. Medicine, U. Chgo., 1977-86; attending physician N.Y. Hosp., 1972—, Meml. Hosp. Cancer and Allied Diseases, 1977-91; mem. selection com. John A. Hartford Found. Fellowship program in clin. scis., N.Y.C., 1979-83; co-dir. Rockefeller U.-Cornell U. combined MD-PhD program, 1980-85; mem. com. pyrene and selected analogs NRC-Nat. Acad. Sci., Washington, 1981-83, cons. Merck Sharp & Dohme Rsch. Labs., 1974-79, 82-84, Abbot-Ross Labs., 1985-90, Hoffman LaRoche Labs., 1985-87, Glaxo Rsch. Labs., 1988-90; mem. sci. adv. bd. Environ. Scis. Lab. Mt. Sinai Med. Ctr., 1983-87; prof. adj. faculty dept. pediat. Karolinska Inst., Stockholm, 1987-90; disting. vis. prof. U. Vt. Coll. Medicine, Burlington, 1993—. Contbr. articles to profl. jours. Bd. dirs. Vis. Nurse Service N.Y., 1982-86 ; mem. gov.'s com. on rev. sci. studies and devel. pub. policy on problems resulting from hazardous wastes N.Y. State, 1980. Served with U.S. Army, 1945-46. Commonwealth Fund fellow, 1961-62, Guggenheim fellow, 1966-67; recipient Spl. award in clin. pharmacology Burroghs Wellcome Fund, 1973, Disting. Svc. award in med. scis. U. Chgo. Sch. Medicine, 1975, Citation for profl. achievement U. Chgo. Alumni Assn., 1995, 1st Ann. award for excellence in clin. rsch. NIH, 1989; named Sr. Henry Hallet Dale Meml. lectr. and vis. prof. Johns Hopkins Hosp., 1975, Pfizer lectr. clin. pharmacology Peter Bent Brigham Hosp., Harvard Med. Sch., 1977, Pfizer lectr. Pa. State U., 1980, first Rolf Blomstrand lectr. Karolinska Inst., 1988, first Glaxo lectr. Cornell U. Med. Sch., 1984; Gunner and Lillian Nicholson Found. exch. prof. Karolinska Inst., Stockholm, 1985-86; Barowsky Meml. lectr., N.Y. Med. Coll., 1986. Fellow ACP; mem. Assn. Am. Physicians, Am. Soc. Clin. Investigation, Am. Clin. and Climatol. Assn., Am. Soc. Pharmacology and Exptl. Therapeutics (pub. affairs com., award for exptl. therapeutics 1978), Practitioners Soc. N.Y., Harvey Soc., Endocrine Soc., Interurban Clin. Club, Cosmos Club (Washington), N.Y. Athletic Club, Lotos club. Home: 1161 York Ave New York NY 10021-7940 Office: Rockefeller U Hosp 1230 York Ave New York NY 10021-6307

KAPPEN, CLAUDIA THERESE, molecular biologist; b. Remscheid, Germany, Apr. 5, 1958; came to U.S., 1988; d. Hermann-Josef and Ursula Elisabeth (Müller) K. MSc, U. Cologne (Germany), 1983, PhD, 1987. Postdoctoral fellow dept. biology Yale U., New Haven, 1988-90, postdoctoral assoc. dept. biology, 1990-92; asst. prof., assoc cons dept. biochemistry/molecular biology Mayo Clinic, Scottsdale, Ariz., 1992-94; sr. assoc. cons., asst. porf. dept. biochemistry, 1994—; spokesperson for profl. women in sci. and tech. Profl. Women in Sci. and Tech., Germany, 1981-88; invited speaker on topics of sci. and tech. multiple orgns. and instns., 1984-88. Mem. subcom. on women in sci. German Fedn. Univ. Women, Germany, 1984-88. Postdoctoral fellow German Rsch. Soc., 1988-90. Mem. AAAS, Soc. for Devel. Biology, Neurosci. Soc., Phi Sigma Kappa. Roman Catholic. Home: Dr # 338 10080 E Mountainview Lake Dr Scottsdale AZ 85258 Office: Mayo Clinic/Rsch 13400 E Shea Blvd Scottsdale AZ 85259-5404

KAPTIJN, ANDRÉ MARINUS, medical consultant; b. Rotterdam, The Netherlands, Dec. 13, 1928; s. Gysbertus and Cato (Berg) K.; m. Caroline H. Hofstee, July 19, 1942; children: Jan, Marina, Herman, Jeroen. MD, U. Leiden, 1955, pediatrician, 1963, occupational physician, 1981. Govt. dr. Indonesian Govt., 1956-59; asst. pediatrician The Hague, Leiden, Eindhoven, The Netherlands, 1959-64; pediatrician Kampen, Heerlen, The Netherlands, 1964-76; med. dir. Dow Chem. Benelux, Terneuzen, The Netherlands, 1976-91; med. cons. The Netherlands, 1991—; med. cons. Old Peoples Homes, The Netherlands, 1988-92. Capt. Dutch Army, 1955-56. Home: Spuikompark 3, 4553 BC Philippine The Netherlands

KARAFIN, GAIL RHODA, psychologist; b. Phila., May 4, 1946; d. Harry Kleinberg and Sylvia (Greenberg) Kleinberg; m. Fredrick Karafin, Sept. 4, 1966; children: Matthew Scott, Jonathan Sean. BA, Temple U., 1968, MEd, 1970, EdD, 1977. Lic. psychologist, Pa.; cert. sch. psychologist, Pa., N.J.; cert. counselor, Pa.; cert. secondary sch. tchr., Pa. Rsch. asst. Rsch. for Better Schs., Inc., Phila., 1968-74; cert. sch. psychologist Vanguard Schs., Paoli, Pa., 1974-81; pvt. practice Achievement and Guidance Ctrs., Doylestown, Pa., 1982—; cons. psychologist Bensalem (Pa.) Sch. Dist., 1989—, Woods Schs., Langhorne, Pa., 1986-90, Pennsbury Sch. Dist., 1993—; instr. Temple U., Phila. Active Hideaway Hills Civic Assn., Ambler, Pa., 1978—, past pres., 1986-87. Mem. Am. Psychol. Assn., Internat. Coun. Psychologists, Nat. Antivisection League, Pa. Psychol. Assn., Temple U. Alumni Assn., Assn. for Children with Learning Disabilities, Mensa. Home: 1222 Lois Rd Ambler PA 19002-1511 Office: 25 E State St Ste 201 Doylestown PA 18901-6301

KARAFIN, LESTER JUDGE, urology educator; b. Phila., Sept 26, 1926; s. Cyril Israel and Bertha Karafin; m. Aileen Tulsky, Oct. 15, 1950 (div. 1984); children: Karen Ellen, Brian Scott, Ted David; m. Sheila A. Judge, June 29, 1986. BA, Temple U., 1945, MD, 1949, MSc in Urology, 1956. Diplomate Am. Bd. Urology. Intern Mt. Sinai Phila., 1949-50; resident Temple U., Phila., 1953-56, instr., then asst. prof. urology, 1965-60, prof., 1960-93, prof. emeritus, 1993—; prof. surgery (urology) Med. Coll. Pa., Phila., 1961—. Editor: Loose Leaf Textbook of Urology, 1965. Asst. surgeon USPHS, 1951-53. Fellow ACS; mem. Am. Urol. Assn. Republican. Jewish. Home: 717 Tennis Ave Ambler PA 19002 Office: Med Colll Pa 3300 Henry Ave Philadelphia PA 19129

KARAM, DAOUD BOUTROS, physiatrist; b. Ain Kabou, Lebanon, Aug. 4, 1934; came to U.S., 1962; s. Boutros D. and Najla (Maluf) K.; m. Barbara M. Rudolph, Oct. 8, 1966; children: Lisa C., Mina Y. MD, St. Joseph U., Beirut, 1962. Internship Queens Hosp. Ctr., Jamaica, N.Y., 1962-63; residency N.Y. Med. Coll. Physical Medicine and Rehabilitation, 1963066; fellowship Rehabilitation Inst. Montreal, 1966-69; residency Mt. Sinai, Elmhurst, N.Y., 1969-70; assoc. attending Long Island Jewish/Queens Hosp. Ctr. Affiliation, Jamaica, N.Y., 1970-73, attending, 1973-79; dir. rehab. medicine Coler Meml. Hosp., N.Y.C., 1980-87; med. dir. Orthopedic and Rehab. Diagnostic and Treatment Ctr., Jamaica, 1987-92, Island Orthopedic and Sport Medicine, Massapequa, N.Y., 1992—; instr. SUNY, Stony Brook, 1971-73, asst. prof., 1973-79; asst. prof. N.Y. Med. Coll., N.Y.C., 1980—. Contbr. articles to profl. jours. Fellow Am. Acad. Phys. Medicine and Rehab.; mem. AMA, N.Y. Soc. Phys. Medicine and Rehab. (pres. 1987-88, chmn. exec. com. 1988-89). Republican. Maronite. Home: 12 Tower Ct Syosset NY 11791-3623 Office: Island Orthopedic and Sport Medicine 660 Broadway Massapequa NY 11758-2312

KARAM, JIM DANIEL, biochemistry educator; b. Kumasi, Ghana, Jan. 31, 1938; came to U.S., 1960; m. Betty Hoffman; 1 child, Giselle. BS in Biology, Am. U. Beirut, Lebanon, 1958; PhD in Biochemistry, U. N.C., 1965. Rsch. asst. biochemistry Am. Univ. Beirut, 1959-60; predoctoral trainee in genetics U. N.C., Chapel Hill, 1961-65; postdoctoral fellow Cold Spring Harbor (N.Y.) Lab., 1965-67; rsch. asst. prof. genetics and cell biology sect. U. Conn., Storrs, 1967-68; rsch. assoc. and assoc. div. genetics Sloan-Kettering Inst. Cancer Rsch., N.Y., 1968-71; from assoc. prof. to prof. biochemistry Med. U. S.C., Charleston, 1971-91; prof., chmn. dept. biochemistry Sch. of Medicine, Tulane U. Med. Ctr., New Orleans, 1991—; mem. adv. com. NSF, Washington, 1982-85, 89, 90, NIH, 1980, 81, 85, 89, 92, NRC, 1992. Contbr. articles to profl. jours. Recipient Postdoctoral fellowship USPHS-Nat. Inst. Gen. Med. Scis., 1965-67, Rsch. Career Devel. award, 1974-79, NIH grantee, 1988-94, NSF grantee, 1988-93. Mem. Am. Soc. Biochemistry and Molecular Biology, Am. Soc. Microbiology, Genetics Soc. Am. Home: 3317 Coliseum St New Orleans LA 70115-2401 Office: Tulane Univ Med Ctr Dept Biochemistry 1430 Tulane Ave New Orleans LA 70112-2699

KARAMEHMETOGLU, OMER AYDIN, cardiologist, educator; b. Istanbul, Turkey, Oct. 29, 1926; s. Huseyin Avni and Fahrunnisa (Devellioglu) K.; m. Mualla Cokyuksel, May 11, 1956 (dec.); children: Huseyin Avni, Ali Oguz. MD, Istanbul U., 1952. Intern Doctors Hosp., Cleve., 1956, resident in medicine, 1957-58; chief resident medicine St. Alexis Hosp., Cleve., 1959; resident cardiology City Hosp., Cleve., 1960-61; fellow cardiology Montreal Heart Inst., 1962-65; asst. prof. cardiology Hacettepe U., Ankara, Turkey, 1965-75; prof. Hacetrepe U., Ankara, Turkey, 1975-93. Author: Adrenergic Receptors and Related Drugs, 1976; translator: Antiarrythmic Drugs (A.J. Moss), 1973. Mem. Turkish Soc. Cardiology (v.p. 1989-96), European Soc. Cardiology. Home: Cinnah Caddesi No 35/7, Ankara 06680, Turkey Office: Mitatpasa Caddesi No 39/4, Ankara 06420, Turkey

KARASU, T(OKSOZ) BYRAM, psychiatry educator; b. Feb. 11, 1935. MD, U. Istanbul, Turkey, 1959. Jr. intern St. Jeanne D'Arc Hosp., Montreal, Can., 1963-64; sr. intern St. John Gen. Hosp., New Brunswick, Can., 1964-65; resident in psychiatry Fairfield Hosp., 1966-67, Yale-New Haven Med. Ctr., 1967-68, Conn. Mental Health Ctr., 1968-69; fellow in psychiatry Yale U., New Haven, 1969; dir. dept. psychiatry Bronx (N.Y.) Mcpl. Hosp. Ctr., 1975-93; prof. psychiatry Albert Einstein Coll. Medicine, Bronx, 1981—, Silverman prof. psychiatry, 1993—; dep. chmn. Albert Einstein Coll. Medicine-Montefiore Med. Ctr., 1982-93, chmn., 1993—; psychiatrist-in-chief Montefiore Med. Ctr., 1993—; Bicentennial lectr. Harvard U., 1983. Author: Wisdom in the Practice of Psychotherapy, 1992; editor: Psychotherapy Research: Methodological and Efficacy, 1982, The Psychiatric Therapies, Part I, The Somatic Therapies, Part II, The Psychosocial Therapies, 1984, Treatments of Psychiatric Disorders: A Task Force Report, 1989, other books and numerous articles. Fellow Am. Psychiat. Assn. (chmn. commn. 1979-83, task force 1981-90, practice guidelines work group in major depression 1991-93, Disting. Svc. award 1983, Spl. Presdl. award 1988); mem. AMA (diagnostic and therapeutic tech. assessment panel 1983), Assn. for Acad. Psychiatry, Soc. Medico-Psychologique. Home: 2 E 88th St New York NY 10128-0555 Office: Albert Einstein Coll Sch Medicine 1300 Morris Park Ave Bronx NY 10461-1926

KARAVOLAS, HARRY J(OHN), biochemist, educator; b. Peabody, Mass., Feb. 21, 1936; s. John Louis and Maria (Kayavas) K.; m. Barbara A. Katsaras, Aug. 26, 1962; 1 son, Christian Mark. B.S., Mass. Coll. Pharmacy, 1957, M.S. (Am. Found. Pharm. Edn. fellow), 1959; Ph.D. (USPHS fellow), St. Louis U., 1963; postgrad., Harvard U., 1963-66. Research fellow in biol. chemistry Harvard U. Med. Sch., 1963-66, research assoc. instr. biol. chemistry, 1966-68, vis. lectr. biol. chemistry, 1975; tutor biochemical scis. Harvard Coll., 1966-68; asst. prof. physiol. chemistry and endocrinology U. Wis., Madison, 1968-72; mem. endocrinology-reproductive physiology program U. Wis., 1968—, assoc. dir., 1974-85, assoc. prof. dept. biomolecular chemistry, 1972-75, prof., chmn. dept., 1975—; sect. head neuroendocrinology Waisman Center on Mental Retardation and Human Devel., 1972-81; mem. study sect. biochem. endocrinology NIH, 1979-81; vis. prof. Ludwig Cancer Inst., London U., 1983. Editorial bd.: Endocrinology, 1974-78; bd. reviewers: Federation Proceedings, 1972-77; contbr. sci. articles to profl. jours. Chmn. basic sci. chairs caucus Med. Sch., U. Wis., 1989—. Recipient Borden award; Merck award; Rexall award, 1957; Amoco Distinguished Teaching award U. Wis., 1977; Ford Found. research grantee, 1970; NICHD research career devel. awardee, 1972-75; NIH research grantee, 1972. Mem. Am. Assn. Biol. Chemists, Endocrine Soc., Soc. Neuroscience, AAAS, Sigma Xi. Home: 2 Regis Cir Madison WI 53711-

2303 Office: Univ Wisconsin 589 Med Scis Bldg 1300 University Ave Madison WI 53706

KARCHER, DONALD STEVEN, medical educator; b. New Orleans, Aug. 23, 1948. BS, U. New Orleans, 1970; MD, La. State U., 1974. Diplomate Am. Bd. Pathology in hematopathology and anatomic and clin. pathology; lic. physician, D.C. Rotating intern Brooke Army Med.Ctr., Ft. Sam Houston, Tex., 1974-75, resident anatomic and clin. pathology, 1974-78; med. dir. hematopathology sect. dept. pathology/faculty mem. Walter Reed Army Med. Ctr., Washington, 1978-81; asst. prof. pathology La. State U. Med. Ctr., New Orleans, 1981-82, clin. asst. prof., 1982-84; staff pathologist Hotel Dieu Hosp., New Orleans, 1982-84; assoc. med. dir. Am. Bio-Sci. Labs., 1983-84; asst. prof. pathology George Washington U. Med. Ctr., 1984-92, assoc. prof., 1992—, chief hematopathology svc., 1984-93, interim dir. divsn. clin. pathology, 1992-93, dir., 1993-96, dir. labs., 1996—; vis. pathologist Charity Hosp. La., New Orleans, 1981-82; faculty mem. New Orleans Combined Med. Tech. Course, 1981-84; cons. pathologist St. Tammany Parish Hosp., Covington, La., 1982-84, Riverside Med. Ctr., Franklinton, La., 1982-84; lectr. various meetings, orgns., hosps., univs., confs. Mem. editl. rev. panel Human Pathology, 1939—; contbr. articles to profl. jours., chpts. to books. Maj. M.C., U.S. Army, 1974-81. Grantee George Washington U., 1986-87. Fellow Am. Soc. Cln. Pathologists, U.S. and Can. Acad. Pathology; mem. Soc. Hematopathology, Phi Eta Sigma, Alpha Theta Epsilon, Alpha Omega Alpha. Office: U Hosp Dept Pathology 901 23rd St NW Washington DC 20037

KARDOS, GARY GABRIEL, internist, nephrologist; b. Budapest, Hungary, May 23, 1936; came to the U.S., 1938; s. Leslie and Magdolna (Pasternak) K.; m. Zeeva Zaretsky, June 12, 1960; children: Leslie S., Kate D. BA, UCLA, 1957; MD, U. Calif., San Francisco, 1961. Cert. in inernal medicine and nephrology Am. Bd. Internal Medicine. Intern U. Calif., San Francisco, 1961-62; pvt. practice internal medicine and nephrology San Francisco, 1968—; resident, chief resident U. Calif., San Francisco, 1962-65. Capt. U.S. Army, 1965-67. Jewish. Office: CN & MG Inc 45 Castro St #227 San Francisco CA 94114

KARESH, JAMES WINKER, ophthamologist, educator; b. Chgo., June 29, 1948. BA, Case Western Res. U., 1970, MA, 1973, MS, 1973; MD, U. Md., 1979. Diplomate Am. Bd. Ophthalmology; cert. Am. Soc. Ophthalmic Plastic and Reconstructive Surgery. Intern Children's Hosp. Nat. Med. Ctr., Washington, 1979-80; resident in ophthalmology U. Md. Hosp., Balt., 1980-83; fellow U. Ill. Eye and Ear Inst.-Michael Reese Hosp., Chgo., 1983-84; lectr. U. Ill., Chgo., 1983-84; asst. prof. U. Md., Balt., 1984-91, asst. clin. prof., 1991—; asst. prof. Johns Hopkins U., Balt., 1991—; chmn. peer rev. com. med. and chirurgical faculty of state of Md., Balt., 1987—. Contbr. articles on ophthalmology and ophthalmic plastic and reconstructive surgery to profl. jours., chpts. to books; author 1 book. Recipient Honor award Am. Acad. Ophthalmology, 1989. Mem. Md. Soc. Eye Physicians and Surgeons (bd. dirs., treas., newsletter editor 1985—, pres.). Office: Krieger Eye Inst Sinai Hosp Balt 2411 W Belvedere Ave Baltimore MD 21215-5213

KARIBO, JOHN MICHAEL, allergist, immunologist, pediatrician; b. Louisville, Ky., 1930. MD, U. Louisville. Diplomate Am. Bd. Allergy and Immunology, Am. Bd. Pediatrics. Intern St. Joseph Infirmary, 1963-64, resident, 1964-65; resident Children's Hosp., Louisville, 1965-66; fellow Cin., 1966-67. Office: 1261 Goss Ave Louisville KY 40217-1239*

KARKANIAS, GEORGE B., neurologist, educator. BS in Biology, Rutgers U., 1983-87; MS with honors, Albert Einstein Coll. Medicine, 1991, PhD, 1993. Postdoctoral fellow dept. neurosci. Albert Einstein Coll. Medicine, 1993-94, instr., 1994-95, asst. prof., 1995—. Contbr. articles to profl. jours. Rsch. grantee Juvenile Diabetes Found. Mem. AAAS, Am. Diabetes Assn. (rsch. grantee 1995—), N.Y. Acad. Scis., Internat. Brian Rsch. Orgn., Soc. Neurosci. Office: Albert Einstein Coll Medicine 1300 Morris Park Ave F113 Bronx NY 10461

KARKUT, RICHARD THEODORE, clinical psychologist; b. Derby, Conn., Apr. 28, 1948; s. Harry Chester and Mary (Katz) K. AB, William Jewell Coll., 1971; MA, U. Mo., Kansas City, 1976; D Psychology, Forest Inst. Profl. Psychology, 1988. Lic. psychologist, Ohio, Ind.; cert. in biofeedback. Psychology intern Burrell Mental Health Ctr., Springfield, Mo., 1987-88; clin. psychologist Wabash Valley Hosp., Lafayette, Ind., 1989-91, Quinco Cons., North Vernon, Ind., 1991-93; CEO Adkar Assocs., Inc., Bloomington, Ind., 1993—; cons. Div. Family Svcs., Lafayette, 1989-90. Guest editor jour. Ind. Psychologist; contbr. articles to profl. jours. Mem. Am. Psychol. Assn., Soc. Behavioral Medicine, Assn. Applied Psychophysiology and Biofeedback, Am. Pain Soc., Am. Soc. Clin. Hypnosis, Am. Orthopsychiat. Assn., Am. Assn. Counseling and Devel., Am. Mental Health Counselor's Assn., Ind. Psychol. Assn., Ill. Psychol. Assn., Ind. Biofeedback Soc. Anglican. Home: PO Box 1396 Bloomington IN 47402-1396

KARL, ROBERT HARRY, cardiologist; b. Milw., Sept. 4, 1947; s. Max Henry and Anita Rene (Davis) K.; m. Nilza Maria Secomandi, Jan. 14, 1979; children: Daniel, Lara, Kevin. BA, Northwestern U., Evanston, Ill., 1969; MD, Washington U., St. Louis, 1973. Diplomate cardiovascular disease subsplty. Am. Bd. Internal Medicine. Intern internal medicine U. Miami (Fla.), 1973-74, resident internal medicine, 1974-76, cardiology fellow, 1976-78; pvt. practice cardiology Miami, 1978—; asst. clin. prof. U. Miami Med. Sch., 1978-90; chief cardiology Bapt. Hosp. Miami, 1986-88; asst. chief of medicine Bapt. Hosp., 1992-94, chief of medicine, 1994—; pres. Medicard Am., Inc., Miami, Biocard Corp., Miami; v.p. Schoolink, Inc., Miami. Mem. exec. com. South Dade Jewish Fedn., Miami, 1986-89; bd. dirs. Beth David Congregation, Miami, 1985-87, Bet Shira Synagogue, Miami, 1987-88, Child Abuse Prevention Project, 1986—, Aish Hatorah, Miami, 1991—. Fellow Am. Coll. Cardiology (dist. councillor Fla. chpt. 1995—), Coun. Clin. Cardiology of Am. Heart Assn.; mem. ACP, Fla. Med. Assn., Dade County Med. Assn. (peer rev. com. 1980-82), Young Israel of Kendall (v.p. 1995—). Office: 8950 N Kendall Dr Ste 302 Miami FL 33176-2131

KARLAN, ANDREW WARREN (DREW KARLAN), pharmaceutical company executive; b. N.Y.C., May 2, 1944; s. Laurence Jack and Isabelle (Kerner) K.; m. Rosalyn Silverberg, Mar. 1, 1969; children: Mara Lisa, Adam Jason. BA in Biology, Hofstra U., Hempstead, N.Y., 1967; MS in Biology, Adelphi U., Garden City, N.Y., 1972; MBA in Pharm. Mktg., Fairleigh Dickinson U., Teaneck, N.J., 1982. Rsch. assoc. Worthington Biochem. Corp., Freehold, N.J., 1972-73; supr. E.R. Squibb & Sons, Inc., New Brunswick, N.J., 1973-79, sect. head, 1979-82, asst. mgr. of investigational data, 1982-88, regulatory mgr. , 1988-89, sr. regulatory mgr., 1989-91; dir. regulatory affairs Roberts Pharm. Corp., Eatontown, N.J., 1991-94; v.p. worldwide regulatory affairs, 1994—, Howell Jewish Cmty. Ctr., (N.J.), 1980-92, bd. dirs.; pres. Men's Club; vice chmn. United Way-Squibb, New Brunswick, 1982; chmn. Jewish com. on Scouting, 1983-91, dist. vice chmn., 1983-87; cubmaster Monmouth Coun. Boy Scouts Am., Monmouth County N.J., 1989-93. 1st lt. U.S. Army, 1969-71, LTC USAR. 1967-95. Mem. Res. Officers Assn., Parental Drug Assn., Regulatory Affairs Profl. Soc., Drug Info. Assn., Delta Mu Delta. Home: 121 Sargent Rd Freehold NJ 07728-2842 Office: Roberts Pharm Corp Dept Pub Affairs Eatontown NJ 07724

KARLIN, JOEL M., allergist; b. N.Y.C., Oct. 5, 1944; s. Louis and Frances (Weisenberg) K.; m. Caroline McInerney, July 7, 1977; children: Scott, Bradley, Bethany, Becky. BA, NYU, 1964; MD, Washington U., St. Louis, 1968; MS, U. Colo. Med. Sch., 1972. Pres., CEO Denver Allergy & Asthma Assocs., Lakewood, 1972—; bd. dirs. Colo. Physicians' Network; CEO Allergy and Asthma Assocs. Colo., Inc. Maj. USAF, 1970-72. Fellow Am. Acad. Allergy & Immunology, Am. Coll. Allergy & Immunology; mem. AMA (coun. on legis.), Colo. Med. Soc. (pres. 1995-96), Phi Beta Kappa. Office: 8805 W 14th Ave Lakewood CO 80215

KARLIN, MICHELLE RENE, oncology nurse, educator; b. Charlotte, N.C., Sept. 23, 1969; d. Leslie Carrol and Wilma Mae (Nix) Liggett; m. Mark Kevin Karlin, Jan. 22, 1994. BSN, Tex. Tech U., 1993. RN Tex.; cert. BLS instr., ACLS. Staff nurse in oncology Meth. Hosp., Lubbock, Tex., 1992-94; nurse clinician Tex. Oncology, P.A., Mesquite. Mem. Oncology Nursing Soc., Tex. Nursing Assn. Roman Catholic. Home: RR 5 Box 473A Princeton TX 75407-9361

KARLOWSKI, THOMAS RAYMOND, physician; b. Detroit, Jan. 6, 1943; s. Stanley A. and Sophie R. K.; m. Diana M. Lambert, June 21, 1968; children: Thomas, Maria, Christina. BS, Wayne State U., 1966, MD, 1969. Diplomate Am. Bd. Internal Medicine. Intern William Beaumont, Royal Oak, Mich., 1969-70, NIH, Bethesda, Md., 1970-72; resident Mayo Clinic, Rochester, Minn., 1972-74; pvt. practice Waterloo, Iowa, 1974—. Mem. ACP, AMA, Drs. Mayo Soc., Elks, Kiwanis. Office: 2055 Kimball Ste 355 Waterloo IA 50701

KARLSON, ULRICH, soil microbiologist, microbial ecologist; b. Unna, Westphalia, Germany, July 14, 1956; s. Karl Friedrich and Margarete Annemarie (Schoenherr) Gosewinkel; m. Melodie Jayne Karlson, Sept. 1, 1984; 1 child, Safra Noelle. MSc, U. Calif., Davis, 1981, PhD in Soil Microbiology, 1984. Postdoctoral rsch. asst. U. Calif., Riverside, 1985-88, asst. rsch. soil microbiologist, 1988-89; assoc. researcher German Nat. Rsch. Ctr. for Biotech., Braunschweig, 1989-91; sr. scientist Ministry of Environ. & Energy Nat. Environ. Rsch. Inst., Roskilde, Denmark, 1992—; com. testifier Calif. Legis. Assembly, Sacramento, 1987-88. Contbr. articles to sci. jours.; patentee in soil decontamination. Fellow German Nat. Scholarship Found., 1978-85. Mem. Internat. Soc. Soil Sci., Am. Soc. Agronomy, Soil Sci. Soc. Am., German Soc. for Gen. and Applied Microbiology, N.Y. Acad. Scis., Sigma Xi. Office: Nat Environ Rsch Inst, PO Box 358, DK-4000 Roskilde Denmark

KARMALI, RASHIDA ALIMAHOMED, lawyer; b. Uganda, May 12, 1948; came to U.S., 1978; d. Alimahomed and Sakina (Govani) K. BSc, MakerereU., 1971; MSc, Aberdeen U., 1973; PhD, U. Newcastle Upon Tyne, 1976; JD, Rutgers U. Sch. Law, 1993. Bar: N.Y. 1994. Postdoctoral fellow Clin. Rsch. Inst., Montreal, 1976-78; rsch. assoc. E. Carolina U., Greenville, N.C., 1978-80, Meml. Sloan-Kettering Inst., N.Y.C., 1980-84; adj. assoc. prof. Cook Coll., New Brunswick, N.J., 1984-90; law clk., assoc. Hopgood, Calimafde, Kalil, N.Y.C., 1992-94; assoc. Pennie & Edmonds, N.Y.C., 1994-95, Bryan Cave LLP, N.Y.C., 1995—; cons. Meml. Sloan-Kettering Cancer Ctr., N.Y.C., 1990-92, fish oil test material program NIH, Bethesda, Md., 1986—; bd. dirs. Skin Rsch. Found., N.Y.C., 1994—. Grantee NIH, Am. Cancer Soc., others. Mem. ABA, The Assn. of the Bar of the City of N.Y. Office: 245 Park Ave New York NY 10167

KARMAN, PAMELA BETH, podiatrist, educator; b. N.Y.C., Feb. 28, 1953; d. Lillian Demsky. BA, Bklyn. Coll., 1974; MA, NYU, 1975; D in Podiatric Medicine, N.Y. Coll. Podiatry, 1984. Diplomate Am. Bd. Foot Surgeons. Lectr. in behavioral scis. Kingsborough C.C., Bklyn., 1975-84; pvt. practice podiatric medicine and surgery N.Y.C., 1984—; clin. instr. dept. orthopedics Mt. Sinai Hosp., N.Y.C., 1988—. Mem. Affiliated Podiatrists N.Y. Office: 19 E 80 St New York NY 10021

KARNEI, ROBERT FREDERICK, JR., physician; b. San Antonio, Jan. 14, 1934; s. Robert Frederick and Hattie (Albert) K.; m. Karen Zimmermann, Dec. 19, 1964; children: Robert III, Kimberly, Christopher, Susan, Kathleen. BA, Rice Inst., 1956; MD, U. Tex., Galveston, 1960. Commd. ensign USN, 1959, advanced through grades to capt., 1975, bn. surgeon 3d MAR div. FMF, 1961-62; resident in anatomic and clin. pathology Naval Med. Sch. USN, Bethesda, Md., 1962-66; chief, lab. svc. Naval Hosp., Jacksonville, Fla., 1966-70; head anatomic pathology Nat. Naval Med. Ctr., Bethesda, 1972-80; dep. dir. USN Armed Forces Inst. Pathology, Washington, 1980-87, dir., 1987-91; pathologist, med. dir. lab. Wythe County Cmty. Hosp., Wytheville, Va., 1992—; also mem. bd. trustees Wythe County Cmty. Hosp., 1995—; prof. pathology Uniformed Svcs. U. Health Sci., Bethesda, 1976—; splty. adviser Navy Surgeon Gen., Washington, 1980-91. Author: (with others) Otolaryngology Clinics of North America, 1979; contbr. articles to profl. jours. Fellow Armed Forces Inst. Pathology, Washington, 1970-72. Fellow Coll. Am. Pathologists, U.S. Acad. Pathology, Can. Acad. Pathology; mem. Am. Coll. Physician Execs., Am. Assn. of Blood Banks, Assn. Mil. Surgeons U.S. (Edwards Rhodes Stitt award 1989), Acad. Medicine, Washington Soc. Pathologists, Blue Ridge Pathology Assn. Methodist. Home: 105 Hickory Ln Wytheville VA 24382-4114

KARNES, LUCIA ROONEY, psychologist; b. Moncton, N.B., Can., Mar. 9, 1921; d. Charles William and Jean Waring (Robson) Rooney; m. Thomas Campbell Karnes, June 7, 1946; children; Eleanore, Campbell, Timothy, Charles. BS, Ga. State Coll., 1942; MA, Emory U., 1946; PhD, U. N.C., 1967. Tchr. Decatur Girls High, Decatur, Ga., 1942-46; tchr. Summit Sch., Winston-Salem, N.C., 1947; prof. Salem Coll., Winston-Salem, 1949-54, 60-77; lang. therapist Bowman Grey Sch. Medicine, Winston-Salem, 1950-57, Orton Reading Ctr., Winston-Salem, 1957-72; dir. Ctr. for Spl. Edn., Salem Coll., Winston-Salem, 1972-77; pvt. practice psychology Winston-Salem, 1977—; dyslexic cons. Jefferson Acad., Winston-Salem, 1980—, Greenfield Sch., Wilson, 1986—, Wingate (N.C.) Coll., 1988—. Creator Using Computers in Psychology courses, 1972; author (video) Teaching Dyslexics, 1975. Founder, pres. state bd. LWV, Winston-Salem, 1953; pres. state bd. AAUW, Winston-Salem, 1950-54; bd. dirs. YWCA, Winston-Salem, 1950-54; v.p. bd. dirs. Arts Coun., Winston-Salem, 1954-60. Named Outstanding Reading Tchr., Reading Assn., Winston-Salem, 1982; fellow Orton-Gillingham Acad. Mem. APA, Orton Dyslexia Soc. (v.p. bd. dirs. 1960-77), N.C. Psychol. Assn., Assn. for Children with Learning Disabilities (v.p. bd. dirs. 1972—, Orton-Gillingham Acad. fellow), Sorosis Club, Delta Kappa Gamma. Democrat. Presbyterian. Home: 200 Lamplighter Cir Winston Salem NC 27104-3419

KARNES, TIMOTHY JOSEPH, hospital administrator, consultant; b. Buffalo, Feb. 21, 1956; s. John Richard and Margaret Mary (Beck) K.; m. Michelle Jean Suchsland, Oct. 23, 1982; children: Caitlin Marie, Courtney Colleen. BA in Psychology, SUNY, Buffalo, 1979; M in Health Svcs. Adminstrn., George Washington U., 1982. Sys. analyst Health Resources Adminstrn., Hyattsville, Md., 1980-81; adminstrv. resident Richland Meml. Hosp., Columbia, S.C., 1981-82; adminstrv. fellow William S. Hall Inst., Columbia, 1982; asst. adminstr. Cypress Hosp., Hosp. Corp. Am., Lafayette, La., 1982-83; asst. CEO Iredell Meml. Hosp., Statesville, N.C., 1983-85; asst. v.p. profl. svcs. Indian River Meml. Hosp., Vero Beach, Fla., 1985-87; v.p. Meml. Hosp., Danville, Va., 1987-90; sr. v.p. ops. Mercy Med. Ctr., Johnstown, Pa., 1990-93; pres., CEO Good Samaritan Med. Ctr., Johnstown, 1993—; pres., COO Cmty. Health Sys. Meml. Med. Ctr., 1996—; pres. Tommy R. McDougal Symposium on Healthcare Adminstrn., Montgomery, Ala., 1987-88. Recipient Traineeship award U.S. Dept. Health, Edn. and Welfare, 1980, Leadership award Cypress Hosp., 1983, Kidney Dialysis Orgn. Iredelle County, 1985. Fellow Am. Coll. Healthcare Execs.; mem. Rotary (Johnstown club). Republican. Roman Catholic. Home: 150 Peggy Ln Johnstown PA 15904-1236 Office: Good Samaritan Med Ctr 1020 Franklin St Johnstown PA 15905-4109

KARNOVSKY, MORRIS JOHN, pathologist, biologist; b. Johannesburg, South Africa, June 28, 1926; came to U.S., 1955; s. Herman Louis and Florence (Rosenberg) K.; m. Shirley Esther Katz, Aug. 26, 1952; children; David Mark, Nina Jane. BS, U. Witwatersrand, Johannesburg, 1946, MB, BCh, 1950, DSc, 1984; diploma clin. pathology, U. London, 1954; M.A. (hon.), Harvard U., 1965. Prof. pathology Harvard U. Med. Sch., Boston, 1968-72, Shattuck prof., 1972—, chmn. program in cell and devel. biology, 1975-90, chmn. pathology dept., 1991-93. Recipient E.B. Wilson award The Am. Soc. for Cell Biology, Gold Head Care award Am. Soc. for Investgative Pathology, 1994, Maude Abbott award U.S. and Can. Acad. of Pathology, 1994; hon. mem. German Soc. for Cell Biology. Fellow Royal Microscopic Soc.; mem. NAS Inst. Medicine, Am. Soc. Cell Biology (pres. 1983-84), Am. Assn. Pathologists (co-pres. 1978-79, Rous-Whipple award), Am. Soc. for Investigative Pathology (Gold-Headed Cane award 1994), U.S. and Can. Acad. Pathology (Maude-Abbott award 1994). Office: Harvard Med Sch DZ Rm 430 200 Longwood Ave Boston MA 02115-6027

KAROL, MERYL HELENE, immunotoxicology educator; b. N.Y.C., Aug. 10, 1940; m. Paul Jason; children: Darcie, Deverin, Meredith. BS, Cornell U., 1961; PhD, Columbia U., 1967. NIH fellow SUNY-Stony Brook, 1967-68; research assoc. U. Pitts., 1974-76, research asst. prof., 1976-79, assoc. prof., 1979-85, prof. environ. and indsl. health, 1985—; advisor numerous govt. health adv. bds., agys.; lectr. in field. Assoc. editor Jour. Chem. Rsch. in Toxicological Environ. Health, Toxicology and Ecotoxicology News; mem. editl. bd. Methods in Toxicology; contbr. articles to profl. jours. Recipient Women in Sci. award U. Mich., 1986, Rachel Carson award, 1993. Mem. AAAS, Am. Chem. Soc., Am. Thoracic Soc., Am. Conf. Govt. Indsl. Hygienists, Soc. Toxicology (v.p. 1993, pres. 1994, Frank R. Blood award), N.Y. Acad. Scis., Am. Assn. Immunologists. Avocations: sports, decorating, design, travel. Office: U Pitts Dept Environ Occupational Health 260 Kappa Dr Pittsburgh PA 15238-2818

KARP, HOWARD M., physician, osteopath; b. Paterson, N.J., Jan. 11, 1941; s. Max and Bertha (Schwartz) K.; m. Linda Dreishdoon, Dec. 24, 1967; children: Bryan, Sean. BA, Rutgers U., 1961; DO, Kirksville (Mo.) Coll. Osteo. Medicine, 1969. Diplomate Am. Bd. Internal Medicine. Physician Regional Nephrology Assn. P.A., Northfield, N.J., 1974—; pres. med. staff Shore Meml. Hosp., Somers Pt. N.J., 1981, chmn. dept. medicine, 1988-94. Fellow ACP.

KARP, JUDITH ESTHER, oncologist, science administrator; b. San Diego, July 15, 1946; d. Louis Moses and Bella Sarah (Perlman) K.; m. Stanley Howard Freedman, Sept. 21, 1975. BA in Chemistry, Mills Coll., Oakland, Calif., 1966; MD, Stanford U., 1971. Diplomate Am. Bd. Internal Medicine. Intern in medicine, jr. resident in medicine Stanford Hosps., 1971-72; asst. resident in medicine Johns Hopkins Hosp., 1972-73; clin. and rsch. fellow oncology Johns Hopkins Med. Sch., 1973-75, instr. oncology and medicine, 1975-78, asst. prof., 1978-85, assoc. prof., 1985-92; spl. asst. to dir. Nat. Cancer Inst., NIH, 1990-94, asst. dir. applied sci., 1995-96; prof. medicine U. Md. Cancer Ctr. Dept. Medicine, U. Md. Sch. Medicine, 1996—; mem. consensus com. Immuno-compromised Host Soc., 1987-88. Mem. med. adn sci. affairs com. Leukemia Soc. Am., 1995—. Am. Cancer Soc. Jr. clin. faculty fellow, 1976-79; San Diego Heart Assn. grantee, 1965-67; recipient Aurelia Henry Reinhardt prize Mills Coll., 1966, Cancer Rsch. award Washington chpt. Awards for Rsch. Coll. Scientists, 1975, Resolution of Commendation award State of Md., 1982, Recognition award City of Balt., 1984, NIH Dirs. award, 1995. Mem. Am. Soc. Hematology, Am. Soc. Clin. Oncology, Cell Kinetics Soc. (clin. counsellor governing council 1985-87), Am. Soc. Microbiology, Immunocompromised Host Soc., Internat. Soc. Exptl. Hematology, Leukemia Soc. Am. (mem. med. and sci. affairs com. 1995—), Nat. Bd. Med. Examiners, Phi Beta Kappa. Democrat. Jewish. Home: 3422 Manor Hill Rd Baltimore MD 21208-1824 Office: U Md Cancer Ctr 22 S Greene St Rm S9D15 Baltimore MD 21201

KARP, ROBERT, surgeon, educator; b. L.A., Feb. 6, 1934; s. Jacob Hamilton and Myrtle (Aronson) K.; m. Sondra Gayle Price, May 24, 1960; children: Andrew and Gillian (twins). BS, Stanford U., 1954; MD, U. Calif., San Francisco, 1958. Diplomate Am. Bd. Surgery, Am. Bd. Thoracic Surgery. From instr. to prof. surgery U. Ala., Birmingham, 1967-83, assoc. prof. surgery, 1971-74, prof. surgery, 1974-83; prof. surgery, chief cardiac surgery U. Chgo., 1983—. Capt. U.S. Army, 1960-62. Fellow ACS, Am. Coll. Cardiology; mem. Am. Heart Assn., Soc. Univ. Surgeons, Am. Surg. Assn. Home: 219 E Lake Shore Dr Apt 2D Chicago IL 60611-1303 Office: U Chgo Hosp Mc 5040 Chicago IL 60637

KARPA, JAY NORMAN, surgeon; b. Feb. 6, 1935; s. Isador and Dora (Wiener) K.; m. Elizabeth Jane Karpa, Nov. 24, 1960; children: Debra Lynn, Michael David, Lisa Michelle, Jonathan Saul. BS, Johns Hopkins U., 1955; MD, U. Md., 1958. Diplomate Am. Bd. Surgery. Intern Sinai Hosp., Balt., 1958-59, resident, 1959-64; pvt. practice gen. surgery Balt., 1964—; mem. active staff gen. surgery Balt. County Gen. Hosp., Randallstown, Md., 1965—, Sinai Hosp., Balt., 1964—; chief surgery North Charles Gen. Hosp., Balt., 1983-85; cons. disability determination Social Security Adminstrn., Balt., 1980-82. Fellow ACS; mem. Balt. Acad. Surgery. Office: 1700 Reisterstown Rd Ste 217 Baltimore MD 21208-2935

KARPILOW, CRAIG, physician; b. San Francisco, Oct. 23, 1947; s. David and Babette (David) K.; BSc, U. Alta. (Can.), 1967; MA, U. So. Calif., 1970; MD, Dalhousie U., 1974. Diplomate Canadian Coll. of Family Practice. Intern, Dalhousie U., Halifax, N.S., Can., 1974-75; resident in family practice medicine Meml. U. Nfld., St. John's, 1975-77; practice medicine specializing in family medicine and occupational medicine, 1978-95; practice occupational medicine, Snohomish, Wash., 1981-83; med. health officer Storey County, Nev., 1978-80; med. dir. Med. Ctr., Dayton, 1978-81; pres. Internat. Profl. Assocs. Ltd., 1978—; med. dir./clin. N.W. Occupational Health Ctrs., Seattle, 1983-84; ptnr. physician, co-dir. CHEC Med. Ctr., Seattle, 1984-85; head dept. occupational and diagnostic medicine St. Cabrini Hosp., Seattle, 1984-86; med. dir. N.W. Indsl. Health Svcs., 1985-86, Queen Anne Med. Ctr., Seattle, 1985-95, Travel Med. and Immunization Clinic of Seattle, 1986-94; ptnr. Clin. Assocs., 1990-95. Diplomate Am. Bd. Family Practice; licenciate Med. Coll. Can. Author: Occupational Medicine in The International Workplace, 1991, Handbook of Occupational Medicine, 1994. Fellow Am. Acad. Family Practice, Am. Coll. Occupational & Environmental Medicine, Royal Soc. Tropical Medicine, Am. Coll. Occupational Medicine (recorder Ho. of Dels./bd. dirs. 1990-91); mem. AMA, Am. Soc. Tropical Medicine and Hygiene, Wash. State Med. Assn. King County Med. Soc., Wash. Acad. Family Physicians (rsch. collaborative, Com. on Rsch.), Am. Coll. Occupational and Environ. Medicine (chmn. internat. occupational medicine sect.), N.W. Occupational Med. Assn. (bd. dirs. 1985-92, 95—, pres. 1990-91), Can. Soc. for Internat. Health, Can. Pub. Health Assn., Am. Com. Clin., Tropical and Travel Medicine, Can. Soc. of Northwest, Marimed Found. Pacific N.W. (adv. bd.), Seattle Swiss Soc., Finnish Soc., Corinthian Yacht Club, Nature Conservancy, Rotary (bd. dirs., chmn. internat. rels. com., chmn. Hepatis Project, chmn. Malaria Project), U. So. Calif. Alumni assn., Kappa Sigma.

KARPINSKI, PATRICIA ANNE, psychologist; b. Blue Island, Ill., Apr. 25, 1948; d. Edmund James and Elsie Gertrude (Hlavatovich) K. BA, Roosevelt U., Chgo., 1971, MA, 1977; postgrad., Spalding U., Louisville, 1989—. Cert. psychologist. Tchrs. aide Ill. Inst. Visually Handicapped, Chgo., 1975; intern psychology Rehab. Inst. Chgo., 1976-77; therapist River Region Mental Health/Mental Retardation Bd., Louisville, 1977-78; therapist, psychologist Seven Counties Svcs., Louisville, 1978—. Roosevelt U. grantee, Chgo., 1974-75. Mem. APA (assoc.), Am. Psychol. Soc., Ky. Psychol. Assn. (assoc.). Democrat. Unitarian. Home: 1412 Willow Ave Apt 31 Louisville KY 40204-1429 Office: Seven Counties Svcs 2105 Crums Ln Louisville KY 40216-4231

KARPINSKI, RICHARD HENRY STEPHEN, plastic surgeon; b. N.C., Dec. 7, 1945; s. Henry Stephen and Beatrice Dolores (Luczycki) K.; m. Kristina Nordling, Nov. 3, 1973; 1 child, Stefan Gottfrid. BS in Biology with honors, St. Joseph's U., 1967; MD, Harvard Med. Sch., 1971. Diplomate Am. Bd. Surgery, Am. Bd. Plastic Surgery. Intern in surgery Boston City Hosp., 1971-72, resident in surgery, 1972-73; resident in surgery New Eng. Deaconess Hosp., 1973-77; resident in reconstructive plastic surgery NYU Med. Ctr., 1979-81; teaching fellow in anatomy Harvard U., 1974; tutor in surgery U. Aberdeen (Scotland), 1974; instr. in anatomy Harvard U., 1976; clin. fellow in surgery Harvard U., 1976; clin. instr. in surgery Creighton U., 1977; clin. instr. in plastic surgery NYU, 1979; instr. in plastic surgery Columbia P&S, 1981; mem. credentials com. St. Luke's/Roosevelt Hosp., 1990—, ambulatory surgery com., 1988—, infection control com., 1988-89. Presenter in field of plastic surgery, 1978—. Trustee Med. Liability Mutual Ins. Co., N.Y.C., 1992. Maj. USAF, 1977-79. Fellow Am. Coll. Surgeons; mem. Am. Soc. Plastic and Reconstructive Surgeons, N.Y. County Med. Soc. (workers' compensation com. 1983-96, chmn. 1992-96), Med. Soc. N.Y. Office: 200 Central Park S New York NY 10019-1415

KARPMAN, HAROLD LEW, cardiologist, educator, author; b. Belvedere, Calif., Aug. 23, 1927; s. Samuel and Dora (Kastleman) K.; m. Molinda Karpman. Student, UCLA, 1945-46; BA, U. Calif., Berkeley, 1950; MD, U. Calif., San Francisco, 1954. Diplomate Am. Bd. Internal Medicine. Rotating intern L.A. County Gen. Hosp., L.A., 1954-55; cardiovascular trainee Nat. Heart Inst., L.A., 1957-58; asst. resident Beth Israel Hosp., Boston, 1955-57; fellow Wyley Winsor Rsch. Found., L.A., 1958-59; pvt. practice Beverly Hills, Calif., 1958—; clin. instr. medicine U. So. Calif., L.A., 1958-64, asst. clin. prof., 1964-71, assoc. clin. prof., 1971-72; assoc. clin. prof. medicine UCLA Sch. Medicine, 1972-92, clin. prof. medicine, 1992—; attending physician, bd. govs. Cedars-Sinai Med. Ctr., L.A.; attending physician UCLA Med. Ctr., Westside Hosp., L.A., Brotman Med. Ctr., Culver City, Calif.; examiner in cardiovascular diseases Calif. Indsl. Accident Commn., Calif. Dept. Vocat. Rehab.; founder, bd. dirs., chmn. bd. Cardio-Dynamics Labs., Inc., 1969-82; gen. ptnr. Camden Med. Bldg., L.A., 1970-

86; bd. dirs. Mcht. Bank Calif.; bd. dirs. med. rsch. Faberge, Inc., N.Y.C., 1980-84; cardiovascular cons. Delta Air Lines, 1992-94. Author: Your Second Life, 1979, Preventing Silent Heart Disease, 1989; assoc. editor Internat. Medicine Alert, 1992—; contbr. numerous articles to med. jours. Fellow ACP, Am. Coll. Cardiology, Am. Coll. Chest Physicians, Internat. Cardiovascular Soc., Am. Coll. Angiology, Internat. Coll. Angiology, Am. Thermographic Soc. (charter, pres. 1971-72), Am. Acad. Thermology; mem. AMA, Calif. Med. Assn., L.A. Med. Assn., Nat. Cardiovascular Network (exec. com., bd. dirs. 1994—), Western Cardiovascular Network (chmn., med. dir. 1993—), Am. Soc. Internal Medicine, Am. Heart Assn., Calif. Heart Assn., L.A. County Heart Assn., CORDA Med. Care, Inc. (chmn., founder, med. dir.). Office: 414 N Camden Dr Beverly Hills CA 90210-4532

KARPMAN, ROBERT RONALD, orthopedic surgeon; b. Phila., Nov. 18, 1952; s. Sol H. and Tillie C. (Ginsburg) K.; m. Laurel Ann Brody, May 29, 1977; children: Hannah Elizabeth, Jodi Gayle. BA magna cum laude, LaSalle Coll., Phila., 1973; MD, U. Pa., Phila., 1977; MBA, U. Phoenix, 1992. Diplomate Am. Bd. Orthopedic Surgeons. Intern U. Ariz. Health Scis. Ctr., Tucson, 1977-78, resident in orthopedic surgery, 1978-81; gen. surgery intern U. Ariz., Tucson, 1977-78; pvt. practice Phoenix, 1981-86; resident in orthopedic surgery U. Ariz., Tucson, 1978-81; dir. acad. affairs Maricopa Med. Ctr., Phoenix, 1992—; assoc. prof. dept. orthopedic surgery Med. Sch. Mayo; adj. prof. dept. biomed. engring. Ariz. State U., Phoenix, 1991—; clin. prof. surgery Coll. Medicine U. Ariz., Tucson, 1989—. Editor: Musculoskeletal Disorders in Aging, 1989; contbr. 25 articles to profl. jours., 1981. Fellow ACS, Royal Soc. Medicine, Am. Acad. Orthopedic Surgeons; mem. Am. Orthopedic Foot and Ankle Soc., Gerontol. Soc. Am., Acad. Orthopedic Soc. (pres.-elect), Ariz. Geriatrics Soc. (pres. 1990-91). Jewish. Office: Maricopa Med Ctr 2601 E Roosevelt St Phoenix AZ 85008-4973

KARR, DANIEL JOHN, ophthalmologist, educator; b. Albany, N.Y., Aug. 29, 1946; s. William Karashopoff and Beda Evangeline (Addy) Dick; m. Susan Jo Jett, Jan. 2, 1971; children: Emilia, Eli. BA, Fla. Presbyn. Coll. renamed Eckerd Coll., 1968; MD, U. Miami, 1978. Diplomate Am. Bd. Ophthalmology, Nat. Bd. Med. Examiners. Vol. Peace Corps, Nepal, 1968-70; resident in pediatrics U. Wash.-Children's Hosp. and Med. Ctr., Seattle, 1978-81, resident in ophthalmology, 1981-84, asst. prof. ophthalmology, 1986-91, adj. asst. prof. pediatrics, 1986-91; clin. asst. prof. ophthalmology U. Wash.-Children's Hosp. and Med. Ctr., 1991—; chief pediatric ophthalmology U. Wash.-Children's Hosp. and Med. Ctr., Seattle, 1986-91; pediatric ophtholmology fellowship U. Iowa, 1984-85. Contbr. articles to med. jours. K.T. Eye Found. grantee, 1987-88. Fellow Am. Acad. Ophthalmology, Am. Acad. Pediatrics; mem. Am. Assn. Pediatric Ophthalmology and Strabismus, Wash. State Acad. Ophthalmology, Wash. State Soc. Pediatrics. Office: A Children's Eye Clinic 4540 Sand Point Way NE Seattle WA 98105-3941

KARR, REYNOLD MICHAEL, medical educator; b. N.Y.C., June 24, 1942; m. Janet Sue Mahaney; children: Reynold III, Daniel, Tamara, Julianne, Andrew, Diana. BA, Johns Hopkins U., 1964; MD, U. Md., 1969. Diplomate Am. Bd. Internal Medicine, Am. Bd. Allergy and Immunology, Am. Bd. Rheumatology. Intern Orange County Med. Ctr. U. Calif., Irvine, 1969-70, resident, 1970-72; clin. immunology fellow U. Colo. Med. Ctr., Denver, 1972-74; dep. chief allergy sect. Malcolm Grow USAF Med. Ctr., Washington, 1974-76; assoc. prof. dept. medicine Tulane U. Sch. Medicine, New Orleans, 1976-79; clin. prof. medicine U. Wash. Sch. Medicine, Seattle, 1979—; CEO PlasmaLab Internat., Everett, Wash., 1985—; primary rsch. investigator Clin. Rsch., Everett, 1990—. Maj. USAF, 1974-76. Fellow ACP, Am. Coll. Rheumatology, Am. Acad. Allergy and Immunology. Office: Allergy & Arthritis Specialists 3128 Norton Ave Everett WA 98201

KARRER, F. WILLIAM, physician and surgeon; b. Palisade, Nebr., Mar. 9, 1931; s. Frederick Merrill and Echo Elinor (Westervelt) K.; m. Beverley Anne Bush, Aug. 15, 1952; children: Frederick Merrill, Suzan Rae Karrer Rohrig. Student, U. Nebr., 1949-52, 52-56. Diplomate Am. Bd. Surgery; lic. physician, Nebr. Rotating internship Denver Gen. Hosp., 1956-57; resident gen. surgery U. Nebr. Hosp., 1957-61; fellow surg. oncology M.D. Anderson Hosp. and Tumor Instn., 1961-62; clin. asst. prof. U. Nebr. Med. Ctr., 1988, clin. assoc. prof., 1988—; active staff Nebr. Methodist Hosp. Children's Hosp., pres. med. staff, 1984-85; courtesy, cons. staff Clarkson Hosp.; assoc. staff Immanuel Hosp.; vice councillor, councillor Southwestern Surg. Congress, 1988—; mem. N. Ctrl. Cancer Treatment Group, 1988—; prin. investigator Nat. Surg. Adjuvant Breast Cancer Protocols; dir. Howard B. Hunt Tumor Registry presenter infield. Contbr. numerous articles to profl. jours. Chmn. statewide tumor registry Nebr. Med. Found., bd. dirs.; past mem. official bd. 1st Methodist Ch.; past bd. dirs. Douglas Sharpy County; official Nat. AAU Swimming Championships, 1966-67; past mem. Westside Cmty. Coun.; scientific exhibits review colorectal cancer Nebr. Methodist Hosp. Regents scholar U. Nebr., 1949-50; Cancer Fellow U. Nebr. NCI, 1960-61, M.D. Anderson, 1961-62. Fellow Am. Coll. Surgeons (surveyor cancer commn., vice chmn. fields liaison com., pres. Nebr. chpt. 1990-91); mem. Am. Cancer Soc. (past pres., bd. dirs. Douglas Sharpy unit, chmn. profl. edn. com. Nebr. divsn., past pres. Nebr. divsn.), Suburban Rotary, Omaha C. of C., Omaha Westerners, We. Hist. Assn., Nebr. Quarter Horse Assn. (bd. dirs., pres. 1978-79), Regional Veterinary Coun., Westbrook Cmty. Club (past pres.), Hockey Hounds Booster Club, Brownville Fine Arts, Brownville Hist. Soc. Office: Surgery West PC 8111 Dodge St #263 Omaha NE 68114-4118

KARRER, RATHE STEVENS, psychophysiologist, behavioral sciences educator; b. Cleve., Mar. 8, 1930; s. Enoch and Ethel (Walther) K.; m. Nancy Donaldson, Apr. 15, 1951 (div. 1971); children: Dana, Tana; m. Betty MacKune, Aug. 15, 1971 (div. 1991); m. Jennifer West, Nov. 30, 1991. BA, La. State U., 1953; MA, New Sch. for Social Rsch., 1957, PhD, 1966. Lic. psychologist, Ill. Rsch. psychologist Tng. Sch. at Vineland, N.J., 1960-66; sr. rsch. scientist Pediatric Inst., Chgo., 1966-78; assoc. rsch. dir. Ill. Inst. Devel. Disabilities, Chgo., 1979-82, dir. behavioral scis., 1982-94; asst. prof. dept. psychiatry U. Ill., Chgo., 1967-73, prof. dept. psychology, 1975-94, prof. emeritus, 1994—; rsch. prof., sr. scientist Life Span Inst. U. Kans., Kansas City, 1994—; assoc. divsn. psychology and psychiatry Northwestern U., Chgo., 1967-85. Author, editor: Developmental Psychophysiology of Mental Retardation, 1976, Brain and Information, 1984; contbr. articles to profl. jours. Nat. Inst. Child Health grantee, 1971-91, 94—, March of Dimes Found. grantee, 1982, 88. Fellow AAAS, APA, APS; mem. Am. Assn. Mental Retardation, Am. Assn. Applied Psychophysiology, Soc. Psychopysiol. Rsch., Soc. Neurosci., Soc. Child Devel., Sigma Xi. Office: U Kans Med Ctr Smith Rsch Ctr/MRRC 39th & Rainbow Kansas City KS 66103

KARSH, RICHARD BRUCE, diagnostic radiologist; b. Boston, July 14, 1944; s. Seymour Solomon and Frances Loretta (Karsh) K.; m. Sue Patrice Shaffer, Mar. 21, 1970; children: Brice, Frances, Benjamin. BA with honors, Williams Coll., 1965; MD, Duke U., 1969. Diplomate Am. Bd. Pediatrics, Am. Bd. Pediatric Cardiology, Am. Bd. Radiology. Intern in pediatrics Cin. Children's Hosp., 1969-70; resident in pediatrics Duke U. Med. Ctr., 1972-73; fellow pediat. cardiology U. Colo. Med. Ctr., 1973-75; pvt. practice cardiology Knoxville, Tenn., 1975-76; resident in radiology Letterman Army Med. Ctr., 1979-81; pvt. practice radiology Thomasville, Ga., 1983—; chief dept. radiology J.D. Archbold Meml. Hosp., Thomasville, 1987-90; cons. in radiology Moody AFB Hosp., Valdosta, Ga., 1987—, Eisenhower Army Med. Ctr., Augusta, Ga., 1992—. Contbr. articles on cardiology to med. jours. Vice pres. Congregation Beth Israel, Thomasville, 1988—. Lt. col. U.S. Army, 1976-83. Mem. AMA, Radiol. Soc. N.Am., Soc. Cardiovascular and Interventional Radiology, Soc. Breast Imaging, Med. Assn. Ga., Thomas Area Med. Assn. Republican. Home: 100 Glen Eagles Circle Thomasville GA 31792 Office: Radiology Assocs 142 Blue Flax Avon CO 81620

KART, BARRY HAROLD, radiologist; b. Pitts., Dec. 15, 1943; s. Nathan Herbert and Marion Louise (Goldstein) K.; m. Jane Malvin Singer, May 7, 1972; 1 child, Lauren. BA magna cum laude, Washington & Jefferson Coll., Washington, Pa., 1965; MD, Temple U., 1969. Diplomate Am. Bd. Radiology. Rotating intern Cleve. Clinic, 1969-70; resident radiology U. Pitts., 1970-73, 75-76; staff radiologist VA Med. Ctr., Pitts., 1976-78, acting chief radiology svc., 1978-79, chief radiology svc., 1979-91, asst. chief radiology svc., 1991-92, chief radiology svc., 1993—; sec. S.R.T. Radiologists, P.C., Pitts., 1985-90; tchg. fellow U. Pitts. Sch. Medicine, 1970-73, 75-76, asst. prof. clin. radiology, 1976-80, asst. prof. radiology, 1980-91, assoc prof. radiology, 1991—; med. advisor Added Care, 1982-85. Author: (with others) Procedure Manual, 1979, 2d edit., 1983, 3d edit., 1990. Team mem. Pitts. area fundraising The Mercersburg Acad., 1979; bd. dirs. Carriage House Children's Ctr., 1980-81. Maj. USAF, 1973-75. Mem. AMA, Am. Coll. Radiology, Am. Roentgen Ray Soc., Radiol. Soc. N.Am., Pitts. Roentgen Soc., Pa. Radiol. Soc., Pa. Med. Soc., Allegheny County Med. Soc., VA Chief's Radiology Assn., Faculty Assn. Sch. Medicine U. Pitts., Assn. Univ. Radiologists, Phi Beta Kappa, Chi Epsilon Mu, Delta Phi Alpha, Phi Sigma, Alpha Omega Alpha. Republican. Jewish. Home: 17 Davonshire Dr Pittsburgh PA 15238-1509 Office: VA Med Ctr University Dr C Pittsburgh PA 15240-1002

KASAMATSU, ROBERT KEN, podiatric physician, surgeon; b. L.A., June 16, 1962; s. Takao and Lillian (Yuriko) K.; m. Nancy Tam, Aug. 3, 1959. BS in Biology, UCLA, 1985; D of Podiatric Medicine, Ohio Coll. Podiatric Medicine, 1989; MS, Calif. Coll. Podiatric Medicine, 1990. Diplomate Am. Bd. Podiatric Orthopedic, Am. Acad. Pain Mgmt. Resident so. campus program Calif. Coll. of Podiatric Medicine, USC Med. Ctr., 1989-90; podiatry clinic dir. Century Freeway Med. Group, L.A., 1991—; owner Nursing Home Svcs., La Puente, Calif., 1991—, Coast Foot and Ankle, Inglewood, Calif., 1991—; podiatrist Extended Care Podiatry Group, Laguna Hills, Calif., 1995—; mem. staff Robert F. Kennedy Med. Ctr., 1995—, Hawthorne Hosp., 1992—, Surgicenter of South Bay, 1995—. Recipient Recognition award Calif. State Senate, 1990, Recognition award Am. Acad. Family Physicians. Mem. Am. Bd. Podiatric Orthopedics and Primary Podiatric Medicine, Am. Acad. Pain Mgmt., Asian Am. Physicians Assn., Hawthorne Rotary (internat. svc. dir. 1995—). Democrat. Office: Coast Foot and Ankle 330 E Hillcrest Blvd Inglewood CA 90301

KASCHULA, RONALD OTTO CHRISTIAN, pathologist; b. Ciweru, Midlands, Zambabwe, Nov. 11, 1935; arrived in South Africa, 1960; s. Frederich Otto Robert and Anna Johanna Maria (Pretorius) K.; m. Sheila Roberta Darby, Oct. 19, 1963; children: Andrew Russell, Marion Jean, Wendy Anne. M.B.Ch.B., U. Cape Town, South Africa, 1959, M.Med. (Pathology), 1964. Cert. pathologist, South Africa; cert. med. practitioner, Gt. Britain. Intern Groote Schuur Hosp., Cape Town, 1960, registrar/resident, 1961-65; med. officer Cape Town City Hosp., 1961; lectr. U. Cape Town, 1965-67, sr. lectr., 1967-78, assoc. prof., 1978—; paediatric pathologist Red Cross War Meml. Children's Hosp., Cape Town; dir. St. Luke's Hospice, Cape Town, 1982-84; external examiner Nairobi U., Kenya 1993-95. Co-author: Infectious Diseases in Paediatric Pathology, 1989; contbr. articles to profl. jours. Chmn. group and divsn. coun. Boy Scouts Assn. South Africa, Cape Town, 1974-80; treas., chmn. Christian Med. Fellowship of South Africa, Cape Town, 1983-91; mem. mgmt. com. Rusteubrug H.S. for Girls, Cape Town, 1979-85; lay minister Christ Ch., Kenilworth, South Africa, 1984—. Rsch. grantee Med. Rsch. Coun. South Africa, 1983-96, Nat. Cancer Assn. South Africa, 1983-96. Fellow Internat. Paediatric Pathology Assn. (life, sec. 1984-92, pres. 1992-94); mem. Fedn. South African Socs. of Pathology (pres. 1988-90, Internat. Coun. of Socs. Pathology (councillor 1989-92), Internat. Acad. Pathology (v.p.. 1984—), Chilian Soc. Pathology (hon. life), Brit. Med. Assn., Paediatric Pathology Soc. (acting chmn. 1972—), Pathol. Soc. Gt. Britain and Ireland. Mem. ch. of Province of South Africa. Office: Red Cross Childrens Hosp, Kupfontein Rd, Rondebosch 7700, Republican of South Africa

KASHTAN, CLIFFORD ELLIOT, physician; b. Detroit, Nov. 2, 1952; s. Harry Aaron and Doris Bernice (Rabinowitz) K.; m. Judith Finkelstein, Dec. 11, 1977; children: Aaron, Paula, Sarah. BS, U. Mich., 1974; MD, Wayne State U., 1978. Diplomate Am. Bd. Pediatrics; cert. in pediatrics and pediatric nephrology. Resident in pediatrics Boston City Hosp., 1978-81; staff pediatrician Columbia Point Health Ctr., Dorchester, Mass., 1981-83; fellow pediatric nephrology Mass. Gen. Hosp., Boston, 1983-84; fellow pediatric nephrology U. Minn., Mpls., 1984-87, instr. in pediatrics, 1987-89, asst. prof. pediatrics, 1989-95, assoc. prof. pediatrics, 1995—. Contbr. articles to profl. jours., book chpts. Mem. Soc. for Pediatric Rsch., Am. Acad. Pediatrics, Internat. Soc. Nephrology, Internat. Pediatric Nephrology Assn., Am. Soc. Nephrology, Am. Soc. Pediatric nephrology. Office: U Minn Med Sch Box 491 UMHC 515 Delaware St SE Minneapolis MN 55455

KASIMIS, BASIL, oncologist, educator; b. Athens, Greece, June 19, 1946; came to U.S., 1974; s. Spiros and Theoni (Stefanides) K.; m. Katherine Markantonis, July 10, 1975; children: Anna T., Elizabeth J. MD, Nat. U., Athens, 1970, DSc, 1974. Fellow hematology/oncology Boston U., 1977-80; asst. prof. medicine U. Calif., Irvine, 1980-84, U. Medicine and Dentistry N.J., New Brunswick, 1984-86; assoc. prof. medicine U. Medicine and Dentistry N.J., Newark, 1986—; adjunct prof. pharmacology Rutgers U., Piscataway, N.J., 1988—; chief med. oncology U. Medicine and Dentistry N.J., New Brunswick, 1984-86; chief hematology/oncology East Orange (N.J.) VA Med. Ctr., 1986—. Author: (book chpt.) Chemotherapy of GU System, 1982; contbr. articles to profl. jours. Col. U.S. Army. Grantee VA, 1984, 1987, ICI Ams., 1986, 1989. Fellow ACP; mem. AMA, AAAS, Am. Soc. Clin. Oncology. Mem. Eastern Greek Orthodox Ch. Office: East Orange VA Med Ctr Dept Medicine # 111 East Orange NJ 07019

KASIMOS, JOHN NICHOLAS, pathologist; b. Chgo., Jan. 26, 1955; s. Nicholas John and Mia (Panos) K.; m. Helen Papadakis, July 10, 1994. BS in Biology, Loyola U., Chgo., 1978; MS in Biology, Ill. Inst. Tech., 1980; DO, Chgo. Coll. Osteopathic Med., 1984. Diplomate Nat. Bd. Examiners for Osteo. Physicians and Surgeons, Am. Osteo. Bd. Pathologists, Anatomic Pathology and Lab. Medicine. Intern Chgo. Osteo. Health Systems, 1984-85, resident pathology, 1985-89, pathologist, 1989—; asst. prof. pathology Chgo. Coll. Osteo. Medicine, 1989-93; assoc. prof. pathology Midwestern U., 1993—; acad. mentor, advisor Chgo. Coll. Osteo. Medicine, 1989—, dir. residence tng. dept. pathology, dir. deptl. edn./rsch., vice chmn. dept. pathology, 1993—. Fellow Coll. Am. Pathologists, Am. Soc. Clin. Pathologists; mem. Am. Osteo. Assn., Am. Osteo. Coll. Pathologists, U.S. and Can. Acad. Pathologists, Ill. Assn. Osteo. Physicans and Surgeons, Ill. Pathology Soc., Chgo. Pathology Soc. Greek Orthodox Office: Olympia Fields Osteo Hosp & Med Ctr Dept Pathology 20201 Crawford Ave Olympia Fields IL 60461-1010

KASINATH, BALAKUNTALAM S., medical researcher; b. Nov. 9, 1951; m. Uma Kasinath; children: Manasa, Vivek. MBBS in Medicine, Bangalore Med. Coll., India, 1975. With internal medicine Ill. Masonic Med. Ctr., Chgo., 1977-80; with nephrology U. Chgo. Hosps. and Clinics, 1980-83; asst prof. Rush-Presbyn.-St. Luke's Med. Ctr., Chgo., 1983-90; assoc. prof. dept. medicine divsn. nephrology U. Tex. Health Sci. Ctr., San Antonio, 1990—; staff physician Audie Murphy Meml. VA Hosp., San Antonio, chief renal divsn., 1991—. Contbr. articles to profl. jours., chpts in books; lectr. in field. Recipient Henry Christian award for excellence in rsch. Am. Fedn. for Clin. Rsch., 1994, Rsch. award Am. Diabetes Assn., 1995. Mem. AAAS, ACP (assoc.), Am. Soc. Nephrology, Am. Soc. Cell Biology, Internat. Soc. Nephrology, Indian Soc. Nephrology. Office: U Tex Health Sci Ctr Dept Medicine-Nephrology 7703 Floyd Curl Dr San Antonio TX 78284*

KASKA, CHARLES POWERS, psychologist; b. Orange, N.J., Apr. 26, 1943; s. Charles Basil and Florence May (Powers) K.; m. Barbara Perreault, Apr. 4, 1968 (div. June 1986); 1 child, Juliet. AA in Psychology, Monmouth Coll., 1965, BA in Psychology, 1969; MA in Psychology, Newark State Coll., 1972; PsyD, Rutgers U., 1978. Diplomate Am. Bd. Disability Analysts; lic. psychologist, Pa., N.J.; cert. sch. psychologist, Pa., N.J. Sch. psychologist Trenton (N.J.) Pub. Schs., 1971-75, 85—, Alexandria Twp. (N.J.) Schs., 1979-84; clin. psychologist Devereux Found., Devon, Pa., 1984-85; dir. Northover Coop. Sch., Boundbrook, N.J., 1975-76; pvt. practice psychologist Yardley, Pa., 1976-79; child custody expert ATLA, Tech. Adv. Svc. for Attys., TASA, 1994—; child welfare cons. Divsn. Youth and Family Svcs., N.J., 1987—. Editor, pub. The Hawker mag., 1965-66. Prin. organizer Christmas Project, Jackson, Miss., 1965. Vol. Peace Corps, 1966-68. Fellow Profl. Acad. Custody Evaluations; mem. Assn. Family and Conciliation Cts., Profl. Soc. on the Abuse of Children. Office: 55 Lookover Ln Yardley PA 19067

KASLICK, JESSICA HELLINGER, psychiatric social worker; b. N.Y.C., Nov. 9, 1945; d. Joshua and Joan (Nathan) Hellinger; student Elmira Coll., 1963-65; B.A., N.Y. U., 1967; M.S., Columbia U., 1969; m. Ralph S. Kaslick, Oct. 24, 1976. Staff, Mt. Sinai Med. Center, N.Y.C. - Dept. Social Work, Child and Adult Psychiat. Service, 1969—, preceptor of med. students, 1970—, preceptor of social work students, 1978—, psychiat. social worker, 1969-85, pvt. practice, 1985—. Bd. dirs. Columbia U. Sch. Social Work Alumni Assn., 1977-79. Recipient Alpha Delta Kappa award in sociology, 1967; Vol. Service award, United Hosp. Fund, 1968; DAR Citizenship award, 1963, others. Mem. Nat. Assn. Social Workers, Acad. Cert. Social Workers, Soc. Clin. Social Workers. Contbr. chpts. to books.

KASLOW, FLORENCE W., psychologist; b. Phila., Jan. 6; d. Irving and Rose (Tarin) Whiteman; m. Solis Kaslow; children: Nadine Joy, Howard Ian. AB in Sociology with distinction, Temple U., 1952; MA, Ohio State U., 1954; PhD, Bryn Mawr Coll., 1969. Lic. psychologist, marriage and family therapist, Fla.; diplomate in clin., family and forensic psychology, Am. Bds. Profl. Psychology. Pvt. prac., 1964—; dir. Fla. Couples and Family Inst., West Palm Beach, 1982—; adj. prof. med. psychology Duke U. Med. Ctr., Durham, N.C., 1982—; vis. prof. psychology Fla. Inst. Tech., Melbourne, 1985—; disting. vis. prof. Calif. Grad. Sch. Family Psychology, 1989-92; cons. USN Dept. Psychiatry Residency Tng. Programs, San Diego, Portsmouth, Va., Phila., 1976-88, Palm Beach Inst., 1983-90. Editor: Couples Therapy in a Family Context: Perspective and Retrospective, 1988, Voices in Family Psychology, 1990; author: (with L.L. Schwartz) Dynamics of Divorce: A Life Cycle Perspective, 1987, The Military Family in Peace and War, 1993, Handbook of Relational Diagnoses and Dysfunctional Family Patterns, 1996; contbr. articles to profl. jours., chpts. to books; mem. editl. bd. Jour. Marital and Family Therapy, 1976—, Marriage and Family Rev., 1977-92, Jour. Sex and Marital Therapy, 1984—, Jour. Clin. Child Psychology, 1986—. Recipient Disting. Psychology Contbn. award Am. Bd. Profl. Psychology, 1994, Outstanding Family Therapy Contbn. award Am. Assn. Marriage and Family Therapy, 1991; Ohio State U. Grad. Sch. fellow, 1954; NIMH trainee, 1969. Mem. APA (divsn. family psychology pres. 1987, sec. 1983-85, com. mem. 1987—, pres. divsn. media psychology 1993), Am. Bd. Forensic Psychology (pres. 1978-80, bd. dirs. 1978-81), Am. Assn. Marital and Family Therapy, Am. Family Therapy Acad., Coalition Family Diagnosis (chmn. 1989-93), Am. Psychology Law Soc., Am. Assn. Sex Educators, Counselors and Therapists, Internat. Coun. Psychologists, Acad. Family Mediators (bd. dirs. 1982—, treas. 1985-87), Fla. Assn. Profl. Family Mediators (pres. 1984-86). Office: Fla Couples & Family Inst Ste 216 2161 Palm Beach Lakes Blvd West Palm Beach FL 33409

KASLOW, RICHARD ALAN, epidemiologist; b. Omaha, Mar. 1, 1943; s. Benjamin E. and Sophia (Handler) K.; m. Leanne Penelope Davidson, July 18, 1970; children: Jessica, Daniel. BA, Yale U., 1965; MD, Harvard U., 1969, MPH, 1976. Intern, then resident Mt. Sinai Hosp., N.Y.C., 1969-71; med. epidemiologist Ctrs. for Disease Control, Atlanta, 1971-73, chief arthritis, 1976-79; resident U. Calif., San Francisco, 1973-74; fellow in infectious diseases Children's-Beth Israel Hosp., Boston, 1974-76; chief epidemiology and biometry sect. Inst. Allergy and Infectious Diseases, NIH, Bethesda, Md., 1979-88, chief epidemiology and biometry br., 1988-95; prof. epidemiology, medicine and microbiology U. Ala., Birmingham, 1995—; adj. prof. epidemiology Sch. Hygiene and Pub. Health, Johns Hopkins U., 1996—. Editor: Epidemiology of AIDS, 1989, Viral Infections of Humans, 1996; contbr. articles to profl. jours. Active various civic orgns. Capt. USPHS (ret.). Fellow ACP, Infectious Diseases Soc. Am., Am. Coll. Epidemiology; mem. Am. Epidemiologic Soc., Soc. for Epidemiologic Rsch., others. Office: Sch of Pub Health 212 C Tidwell Hall 720 20th St S Birmingham AL 35294-0008

KASPARECK, JOSEPH M., JR., ophtholmologist; b. Plainfield, N.J., Oct. 2, 1954; s. Joseph Matthew Sr. and Marion Grace (Arthur) K.; m. Diane Dorothy Miller, June 16, 1984. BA in Psychology, U. Vt., 1976; MD, Coll. Medicine and Denistry of N.J., 1980. Diplomate Am. Bde. Ophthalmology. Resident in ophthalmology Temple U. Hosp., Phila., 1984-87; ophthalmologist Ctr. Jersey Eye Assocs., Somerville, N.J., 1987—. Mem. Alpha Omega Alpha. Office: Ctrl Jersey Eye Assocs 56 Union Ave Somerville NJ 08876

KASPER, SUSAN KATHRYN, psychologist; b. Irvington, N.J., Sept. 3, 1944; d. Albert Frank and Frances Marie (Coleman) DeFrancisco; m. Ronald S. Kasper, July 16, 1966 (div. May 1982); 1 child, Andrew S. Kasper; m. Joseph Pucilowski, May 5, 1990. BA magna cum laude, Kean Coll., 1966, MA with distinction, 1971; MA, Fairleigh Dickinson U., 1977; PhD, Hofstra U., 1982. Lic. psychologist, N.Y., N.J. Fifth grade tchr. Parsippany (N.J.) Sch. System, 1966-67; adj. asst. prof. gen. and child psychology County Coll. of Morris, Randolph, N.J., 1972-82; mental health profl. crisis intervention Pequannock Mental Health Ctr., Pompton Plains, N.J., 1979-81; sr. clin. psychologist Essex County Hosp. Ctr., Cedar Grove, N.J., 1982-87; cons. Hagedorn Ctr. for Geriatrics, Glen Gardner, N.J., 1987-88, Psychol. Consultants Group, Randolph, 1986-91; pvt. practice psychologist Randolph, 1983—; trainer parent group Pequannock Mental Health Ctr., Pompton Plains, N.J. 1979; adj. faculty child abnormal psychology Fairleigh Dickinson U., Madison, N.J., 1988. Author (rsch.) Psychological Abuse, 1982. Co-founder Morris County Hotline, Denville, N.J., 1970, trainer, 1976-76; vol. occupational therapy Greystone Park (N.J.) Psychiat. Hosp., 1972-73. N.J. Jr. fellow in psychology, 1976-77; recipient Cert. of Appreciation, Vol. Action Coun., Morris County, N.J., 1974, Outstanding Svc. award Nat. Assn. for Mental Health, 1974. Mem. APA, Ea. Psychol. Assn., N.J. Acad. Psychology, N.J. Psychol. Assn. (com. on aging 1986-89, pub. info. com. 1990, com. on legis. affairs 1991-93), Morris County Assn. for Mental Health (bd. dirs. 1973-77, v.p. 1976-77, co-chair vol. tng. com. 1974, Vol. of Yr. 1974, pub. info. com. 1974-75, low cost psychiatry com. chair 1975-76), Morris County Psychol. Assn. (coord. Speakers Bur. 1991-93, Am. Soc. Clin. Hypnosis, Kappa Delta Pi. Home and office: 151 Dover Chester Rd Randolph NJ 07869-1901

KASPERLIK-ZAŁUSKA, ANNA ANTONINA, medical educator, consultant, researcher; b. Warsaw, Poland, Aug. 16, 1933; d. Stanisław and Waleria (Zakrzewska) Kasperlik; m. Józef Roman Załuska, Feb. 8, 1964; 1 child, Andrzej. Grad., Acad. Medicine, Warsaw, 1957, D Med. Scis., 1967. Intern in surgery Inst. Hematology, Warsaw, 1957-58; intern in pediatrics Pediatric Hosp. Nr 1, Warsaw, 1957-58; intern in obstetrics and gynecology Hosp. Gynecology and Obstetrics, Warsaw, 1957-58; intern in internal medicine Inst. Postgrad. Med. Edn., Warsaw, 1957-58, fellow in internal medicine, 1958-60; jr. asst. Bielanski Hosp., Warsaw, 1960-62; jr. asst. Postgrad. Med. Sch., Acad. Medicine, 1963-66, asst. lectr., 1966-69; asst. prof. medicine Ctr. Postgrad. Med. Edn., 1970-80, assoc. prof., 1981-89, prof., 1989—; dist. endocrinology cons. Dept. Health, Warsaw, 1992—. Contbr. numerous articles to sci. jours. Grantee Com. Sci. Rsch., 1992, 94; recipient award Ministry Health, 1977, 87, 92. Fellow Polish Endocrinology Soc. (pres. Warsaw sect. 1990—). Roman Catholic. Home: Gabinska 18/35, 01-703 Warsaw Poland Office: Ctr Postgrad Med Edn, Ceglowska 80, 01-809 Warsaw Poland

KASPERS, GERTJAN JOHANNES L., pediatrician; b. Amsterdam, The Netherlands, Mar. 22, 1963; s. Johannes Q.D.M. and Johanna (Huisman) K.; m. Anna E. Veltman, May 26, 1989; 1 child, Sylvi E.Y. MD, Free U. Hosp., Amsterdam, 1988, PhD, 1993. Pediatrician-in-tng. Sophia's Children's Hosp., Rotterdam, Netherlands, 1989; rsch. fellow Free Univ. Hosp., Amsterdam, 1989-93, pediatrician-in-tng., 1993—, postdoctoral fellow in pediatric hemato-oncology, 1993—; organizer sci. com. Internat. Symposia on Drug Resistance Leukemia and Lymphoma, Amsterdam, 1992, 95; reviewer Blood, 1995—,Biochim. Biophys. Acta, 1995—, Brit. Jour. Cancer, 1993—; reviewer grants Internat. Union Against Cancer, 1995—. Editor: Drug Resistance in Leukemia and Lymphoma, 1993, 96; contbr. articles to med. jours. Comdr. Royal Army Med. Corps, Netherlands, 1988-89. Recipient poster award Deutsche Arbeitsgemschaft fü Oncology, 1991, 94; rsch. grantee Pharmacia BV, 1993. Mem. Dutch Cancer Soc., Am. Assn. Cancer Rsch., Lawn Tennis Club (pres. 1992—). Office: Free Univ Hosp Dept Pediatrics, De Boelelaan 1117, 1081 HV Amsterdam The Netherlands

KASPRENSKI, MATTHEW ANTHONY, health facility administrator; b. Elizabeth, N.J., Feb. 17, 1932; s. Matthew Joseph and Josephine Elizabeth (Murzinski) K.; m. Rosemarie Damweber, Jan. 7, 1956; children: Matthew L., Maria L., Lisa A., Michael D., Kara J., Krista S. BA, St. Vincent Coll., Latrobe, Pa., 1953; MD, Hahnemann U., Phila., 1957. Diplomate Am. Bd. Family Practice. Intern Sacred Heart Hosp., Allentown, Pa., 1957-58; pvt. practice family medicine Whitehall, Pa., 1960-92; med. dir. employee health

Lehigh Valley Health Network, Allentown, 1991-93; med. dir. transitional care facility Sacred Heart Hosp., Allentown, 1994—. Capt., U.S. Army, 1958-59, Germany. Mem. AMA, Am. Acad. Family Practice, Am. Med. Dirs. Assn. (cert.), Am. Geriat. Soc., Am. Acad. Home Care Physicians, Pa. Med. Soc., Pa. Med. Dirs. Assn., Lehigh County Med. Soc., Am. Coll. Occup. and Environ. Medicine. Office: Sacred Heart Hosp 421 W Chew St Allentown PA 18102-3406

KASPRICK, LYLE CLINTON, volunteer, former finacial executive; b. Angus, Minn., Aug. 23, 1932; s. Max Peter and Mary (Taus) K.; BS in Bus. Adminstrn. magna cum laude, U. N.D., 1959. CPA, Minn., N.D.; m. Harriet Susan Lydick, July 14, 1953; children: Susan, Michael, John; m. Kathleen M. Westby, June 4, 1977; 1 stepchild, Kristin. Tax mgr. Arthur Andersen & Co., Mpls., 1959-69; v.p. Search Investments Corp., Mpls., 1969-77; fin. v.p., treas. Tropicana Hotel and Country Club, Las Vegas, 1970-72; chief oper. officer Key Pharms., Inc., Miami, Fla., 1972-76, bd. dir., 1976-86; bd. dir. Search Investments Corp., 1973-77, Mo Am Co Corp., 1975-76; v.p. MEI Corp., Mpls., 1977-86; v.p. MEI Diversified, Inc., Mpls., 1986-88; bd. dirs. IVAX Corp., Miami, Fla., 1987—. bd. dirs. N.Am. Vaccine, Inc., Montreal, Que., Can., Beltsville, Md., 1988—, chmn. bd., 1991-95. Speaker before profl. and civic groups., dist. and city convs. Del. Rep. Com., 1964, 66, 68, 70; bd. dirs. U. N.D. Found., 1993—. With USN, 1951-55. Mem. AICPA, Minn. Soc. CPA's, Am. Legion, U. N.D. Alumni Assn. (bd. dirs. 1993—), U. N.D. Nat. Alumni Leadership Coun., Beta Gamma Sigma. Republican. Roman Catholic. Home: 1067 Linden Ln Orono MN 55364-9754 Office: NAm Vaccine Inc 12103 Indian Creek Ct Beltsville MD 20705-4223

KASSALOW, JORDAN SETH, optometrist; b. New York, Sept. 14, 1961; s. Theodore William and Sandra Clare (Kelberg) K.; m. Erica Gwynn Komisar, May 20, 1995. BA, U. Vt., 1983; OD, New England Coll. Optometry, 1988; MPH, Johns Hopkins U., 1991. Pvt. practice N.Y.C., 1989—; cons. River Blindness Found., N.Y.C., 1991-92, Helen Keller Internat., N.Y.C., 1989-92, dir. Onchocerciasis divsn., 1992—; cons. Morrison Internat., Sarasota, Fla., 1994-96, Pilkington, Barnes Hind, Inc., Sunnyvale, Calif., 1995; mem.nat. program com. Lighthouse Inc., N.Y.C., 1994—; tech. cons. com. African Program Onchocerciasis Control WHO, Geneva, 1996—. Mem. editl. bd. Optometric Mgmt., 1996—. Term mem. Coun. Fgn. Rels. Mem. Am. Optometric Assn., Am. Pub. Health Assn., Am. Acad. Optometry, Soc. Eye Care Specialists (founding). Office: 30 E 60th St Ste 201 New York NY 10022

KASSAN, STUART S., rheumatologist; b. White Plains, N.Y., Nov. 19, 1946; s. Robert Jacob and Rosalind (Suchin) K.; m. Gail Karesh, Apr. 4, 1971; children: Michael Andrew, Merrill Alissa. BA, Case Western Res., 1968; MD, George Washington U., 1972. Diplomate Am. Bd. Internal Medicine, Am. Bd. Rheumatology, Am. Bd. Geriatrics. Intern and resident Grady Meml. Hosp., Altanta, 1972-74; clin. fellow NIH, Bethesda, Md., 1974-76; fellow Hosp. for Spl. Surgery, Cornell Med. Ctr., N.Y.C., 1976-78; head rheumatology clinic VA Med. Ctr., Denver, 1978-80; asst. clin. prof. medicine U. Colo. Health Scis. Ctr., Denver, 1978-84, assoc. clin. prof. medicine, 1984-94, clin. prof. medicine, 1994—; med. dir. rehab unit. Luth. Med. Ctr., Wheatridge, Colo., 1983-87; med. dir. rehab. unit St. Anthony Hosp., Denver, 1987-93; cons. Annals Internal Medicine, Phila., 1986—, Arthritis and Rheumatism, Atlanta, 1995—; vis. alumni scholar George Washington U. Sch. Medicine, 1986; mem. nat. med. adv. bd. Sjögren's Syndrome Found., Port Washington, N.Y., 1987—, bd. dirs., 1996—. Co-editor: Sjögren's Syndrome, 1987; contbr. over 25 articles to profl. jours. Bd. dirs. Rocky Mountain chpt. Arthritis Found., Denver, 1978-80, Polachek fellow, 1976-77; bd. dirs. Lupus Found. Colo., v.p., 1995-96, pres., 1996—. With USPHS, 1974-76. Mem. ACP, Am. Coll. Rheumatology (network physician 1989); mem. Harvey Soc. Jewish. Office: Colo Arthritis Assoc 4200 W Conejos Pl Ste 314 Denver CO 80204-1311

KASSELL, NEAL FREDERIC, neurosurgery educator; b. Phila., Mar. 17, 1946; s. Martin Buddy and Evelyn Abigail (Block) K.; m. Nancy Coffin, Dec. 14, 1967 (div.); children: Natasha Lynn, Lauren Tamara, Nicole Tristan; m. Denise Etheridge, Aug. 30, 1986 (div. 1987); m. Lynn Haire, Mar. 12, 1994. MD, U. Pa., 1972. Diplomate Am. Bd. Neurol. Surgery. Intern Pa. Hosp., Phila., 1972-73, resident in neurology, 1973-74, resident in neurosurgery, 1974-75; resident in neurosurgery U. Western Ont., London, 1975-77; rsch. asst., neurosurgery Pa. Hosp., Phila., 1962-68; rsch. assoc., neurosurgery U. Pa., Phila., 1968-72; fellow Inst. Neurol. Sci., U. Pa., Phila., 1968-70; asst. prof. neurosurgery U. Iowa, Iowa City, 1977-81, assoc. prof. neurosurgery, 1981-82, prof. neurosurgery, 1982-84; prof. and vice chmn. neurosurgery U. Va. Sch. Medicine, Charlottesville, 1984—; pres. Va. Neurol. Inst., 1993—; chmn. bd., founder Multimedia Med. Sys., Inc., 1995—; dir. Coop. Aneurysm Study, 1977—, also other various NIH-Nat. Inst. Neurol. Disorders and Stroke study sects., 1984—. Reviewer Neurosurgery, Jour. Cerebral Blood Flow and Metabolism, 1977—; mem. editl. bd. Stroke, Surg. Neurology; contbr. over 350 papers to profl. jours. Recipient numerous rsch. grants and contracts; recipient McKenzie Meml. award, 1977; honored guest Japanese Stroke Soc., 1985, 87, Japanese Surgery of Stroke Soc., 1988; winner 1996 Grass award. Honored guest Japanese sTroke Soc., 1985, 87, Japanese Surgery of Stroke Soc., 1988; recipient Grass award, 1996; numerous rsch. grants and contracts. Republican. Home: Wingate 2154 Garth Rd Charlottesville VA 22901-8950 Office: U Va Hosps Dept Neurosurgery Box 212 Charlottesville VA 22908

KASSER, JAMES R., medical educator; b. Pitts., Sept. 16, 1949. BSME, Lehigh U., 1971; MD, Tufts U., 1976. Diplomate Am. Bd. Orthop. Surgery; lic. Mass. Intern Tufts Med. Ctr., Boston, 1976-78, resident orthop., 1978-81; fellow pediatric orthop. Alfred I. duPont Inst., Wilmington, Del., 1981-82; instr., asst. prof. orthop. surgery Harvard Med. Sch., Boston, 1982-94, assoc. prof. orthop. surgery, 1994—; asst. orthop. surgery Children's Hosp., Boston, 1982-87, assoc. chief, 1987-94, orthop. surgeon-in-chief, 1994—. Presenter in field; contbr. articles to profl. jours. Mem. AMA, Am. Acad. Orthop. Surgeons (bd. dirs., exam. and evaluation com. 1988-92), Am. Orthop. Assn., Acad. Orthop. Soc., Am. Acad. Cerebral Palsy and Devel. Medicine, Pediatric Orthop. Soc. N.Am., Mass. Orthop. Assn. Home: 8 Washington St Sherborn MA 01770*

KASSEWITZ, RUTH EILEEN BLOWER, retired hospital executive; b. Columbus, Ohio, May 15, 1928; d. E. Wallett and Helen (Daub) Blower; BS in Journalism-Mgmt., Ohio State U., Columbus, 1951; m. Jack Kassewitz, July 28, 1962 (dec.); 1 stepchild, Jack. Copywriter, Ohio Fuel Gas Co., Columbus, 1951-55, Merritt Owens Advt. Agy., Kansas City, Kans., 1955-56; account exec. Grant Advt., Inc., Miami, Fla., 1956-59; account supr. Venn/Cole & Assocs., Miami, 1959-67; dir. communications Ferendino/Grafton/Candela/Spillis Architects & Engrs., Miami, 1967-69; dir. communications Dade County Dept. Housing and Urban Devel., Miami, 1969-72; dir. communications Met. Dade County Govt., 1972-78; adminstr. pub. rels. U. Miami/Jackson Meml. Med. Ctr., 1978-90, ret., 1990. Pres., U. Miami Women's Guild, 1973-74; bd. dirs. Girls Scouts Tropical Fla., 1974-76, 81-83, Lung Assn. Dade-Monroe Counties, 1976-87, Met. YMCA, 1996—; mem. exec. com. Miami-Dade Community Coll. Found., 1984—; pres. Mental Health Assn. Dade County, 1982; mem. Miami Ecol. and Beautification Com., 1978—, also vice-chmn.; bd. govs. Barry U., Miami, 1981-83; trustee Nat. Humanities Faculty, 1981-83; trustee, sec. United Protestant Appeal, 1984-92; treas., past chmn. Health, Edn., Promotion Council, Inc.; adv. bd. Miami's for Me, 1987-88; mem. Coral Gables Cable TV Bd., 1983-86; ch. moderator Plymouth Congl. Ch., 1986-88 (trust. 1995—); community adv. bd. Jr. League Greater Miami, Inc., 1989-92; founding mem. Nat. Honor Roll Women in Pub. Rels., No. Ill. U., 1993. Recipient Disting. Service award Plymouth Congl. Ch., Miami, 1979; Ann Stover award, 1983, Golden Image award Fla. Pub. Rels.Assn, 1987; named Woman of Yr., Plymouth Congl. Ch., U. Miami Med. Sch., 1991. Fellow Public Relations Soc. Am. (pres. South Fla. chpt. 1969-70, nat. chmn. govt. sect. 1973-74, nat. dir. 1974-78; continuing edn. council 1981-83; Silver Anvil award 1973, Assembly del. 1970-73, 86-89, Paul M. Lund Pub. Svc. award 1993, Miami chpt. Lifetime Achievement award, 1995); mem. Women in Comm. (pres. Greater Miami chpt. 1962-63; Clarion award 1973, 75, Community Headliner 1985), Miami Internat. Press Club (bd. dirs. 1986-87, treas. 1992), Greater Miami C. of C. (gov. 1983-86), Rotary Club of Miami (bd. dirs., 1988—, pres. 1993-94). Home: 1136 Aduana Ave Miami FL 33146-3206

KASSIRER, JEROME PAUL, medical educator, editor-in-chief; b. Buffalo, Dec. 19, 1932; s. Irvin D. Kassirer and Belle Fried; m. Geraldine Weinger, June 20, 1957 (div. 1979; children: Amy, Richard, Wendy, Elizabeth; m. Sheridan L. Kassirer, Mar. 25, 1979; children: Winston, Samuel. Grad., U. Buffalo, 1953, MD magna cum laude, 1957; DS (hon.), U. Mass., 1992; D honoris causa, L'Universite Rene Descartes, Paris, 1992; DS (hon.), Thomas Jefferson U., 1994, SUNY, 1995. Diplomate Am. Bd. Internal Medicine (mem. certifying examination com. 1987-89, bd. dirs. 1989-96, mem. exec. com. 1993-96, chmn. 1995-96). Intern, asst. resident in medicine Buffalo Gen. Hosp., 1957-59; fellow in nephrology New Eng. Med. Ctr., Boston, 1959-61, sr. resident in medicine, 1961-62, asst. physician, 1961-65, physician renal svc., 1969-74, assoc. physician-in-chief, 1971-91, acting physician-in-chief, 1976-77; instr. medicine Sch. Medicine, Tufts U., Medford, Mass., 1961-65, asst. prof. medicine, 1965-69, assoc. prof., 1969-74, vice chmn. dept. medicine, 1971-91, acting chmn. dept. medicine, 1974-75, prof. medicine, 1974—, Sara Murray Jordan Prof. Medicine, 1987-91; editor-in-chief New Eng. Jour. Medicine, Boston, 1991—; lectr. in medicine Harvard U., 1991—; lectr. in medicine Harvard U., 1991—; bd. dirs. Postgrad. Med. Inst. Mass. Med. Soc., 1988-91. Editor-in-chief Current Therapy in Internal Medicine, 1990; co-editor Clin. Problem Solving, Hosp. Practice, 1985-91; consultant editor Am. Jour. Medicine, 1976-86; mem. editorial bd. New Eng. Jour. Medicine, 1972-75; co-editor Nephrology Forum, Kidney Internat., 1978-91, Med. Decision Making, 1987-89; editorial advisor Outline of Knowledge, Part 4: Human Life, The New Encyclopaedia Britannica, 1989. Recipient Ednl. Rsch. Found. award AMA, 1993. Master Am. Coll. Physicians (chmn. sci., chmn. 1985-88, gov. Mass. 1985-89, mem. exec. com. bd. govs. 1988-89, mem. health and pub. policy com. 1989-91, bd. regents 1990-91); fellow AAAS, Am. Coll. Med. Informatics; mem. Am. Soc. Nephrology, Am. Fedn. Clin. Rsch., Internat. Soc. Nephrology, Inst. Medicine NAS, Assn of Am. Physicians, Nat. Libr. Medicine (chmn. bd. sci. counselors 1989-90, mem. biomed. journalism award com. 1992—), Mass. Med. Soc., Buffalo Acad. Medicine (hon. life), Soc. Clin. Decision Making (charter mem.). Jewish. Office: New Eng Jour Medicine 10 Shattuck St Boston MA 02115

KASSIRER, MARILYN RITA, neurologist, pain management specialist; b. Buffalo, Aug. 30, 1940; d. Irvin David and Belle (Fried) K.; m. Stanley Robert Wayne, Dec. 2, 1978; 1 child, Martin Isaac Kassirer Wayne. BS, SUNY, Buffalo, 1961, MD, 1970. Diplomate Am. Bd. Psychiatry and Neurology. Intern St. Elizabeth Hosp., Brighton, Mass., 1970-71, asst. med. resident, 1971-72; resident in neurology New Eng. Med. Ctr., Boston, 1972-75; instr. in neurology Boston U. Sch. Medicine, 1975-80; clin. instr. neurology Harvard Med. Sch., Boston, 1975; asst. vis. prof. Boston City Hosp., 1976-80; staff neurologist VA Hosp., Boston, 1976—; asst. clin. prof. neurology Boston U. Sch. Medicine, 1980—; lectr. in neurology Tufts U. Med. Sch., 1982—; pres. med. staff Mattapan (Mass.) Hosp., 1978-79; dir. paine mgmt. team VA PC, Boston, 1981—. Book reviewer Jour. Tropical and Geog. Neurol., Jour. Pain; contbr. articles to profl. jours. Mem. com. Brookline (Mass.) Ct. Centennial, 1982-83; pres. Corey Hill Neighborhood, Brookline, 1985-86. Mem. Am. Pain Soc., Am. Acad. Neurology, New Eng. Pain Soc. (membership chmn. 1987-89, treas. 1989-91), Boston Soc. Neurology and Psychiatry. Office: Vet Adminstrn 251 Causeway St Boston MA 02114

KASTELLA, JANICE MAGNUSSON, retired physician; b. Chisholm, Minn., Apr. 22, 1937; m. P.W. Hardie. BA, Stanford, 1961; MS, U. Wash., 1971. Diplomate Am. Bd. Neurology. Intern, resident U. N.Mex. Affiliated Hosps., Albuquerque, 1978. Home: 3515 Fordham Anchorage AK 99508

KASTENBERG, CHARLES A., osteopath; b. N.Y.C., Apr. 6, 1936; s. Murray Kastenberg and Florence Musikar; children: David, Judy Klein, Stephen. BS, Rutgers U., 1957; DO, Phila. Coll. Osteo. Medicine, 1974. Registered pharmacist, N.J.; lic. osteo. physician, N.J., Pa., Fla. Pharmacist, 1957-61; owner Charles Pharmacy, Morris Plains, N.J., 1965-70; pvt. practice physician Camden and Mt. Holly, N.J., 1975-77, Mt. Holly, 1975—. With U.S. Army, 1968-64. Mem. Am. Osteo. Soc. (del.), N.J. Osteo. Soc. (pres. 1990-92), Camden County Osteo. Soc. (pres. 1986-87),. Jewish. Home: 31 Spring Mill Ln Cherry Hill NJ 08003 Office: Mt Holly Family Practice 1613 Rt 38 Mount Holly NJ 08060

KASTNER, MICHAEL JAMES, dentist; b. Huntington, Ind., Oct. 20, 1954; s. James H. and Barbara A. (Bartrom) K.; m. Kimberly A. Ricke, June 18, 1983; children: Kevin Michael, Ryan James, Derek Edward. BS, Manchester Coll., 1977; DDS, Ind. U., Indpls., 1981. Gen. practice dentistry Toledo, 1981—; asst. dentist Toledo Zoo, 1991—; mem. Ohio Mass Disaster Team, 1995—; asst. Lucas County Coroner's Office, 1987—. Bd. trustees Dental Ctr. Northwest Ohio, 1995—. Mem. ADA (cert. recognition for vol. svc. fgn. country in Dominican Republic, 1987, in Costa Rica, 1990, in Nepal, 1994), Ohio Dental Assn. (humanitarian of yr. award 1995), Toledo Dental Soc. (trustee 1995—), Am. Acad. Cosmetic Dentistry, Am. Soc. Forensic Odontology, Am. Coll. Oral Implantology, Am. Soc. Osseointegration Internat. Congress Oral Implantologists, Mensa. Roman Catholic. Home: 4616 Waterford Ct Toledo OH 43623-2988

KASTOR, JOHN ALFRED, cardiologist, educator; b. N.Y.C., Sept. 15, 1931; s. Alfred Bernard and Ellen Voigt Bentley; m. Mae Belle Eisenberg, July 4, 1954; children: Elizabeth Mae, Anne Sarah, Peter John. BA, U. Pa., 1953; MD, NYU, 1962. With NBC, N.Y.C., 1956-58; intern, asst. resident in medicine Bellevue Hosp., N.Y.C., 1962-64; chief resident physician N.Y. U. Hosp., N.Y.C., 1964-65; clin. and research fellow in medicine Mass. Gen. Hosp., Boston, 1965-68; clin. asst. and asst. in medicine Mass. Gen. Hosp., 1968-69; instr. in medicine Harvard Med. Sch., 1968-69; dir. med. intensive care unit Hosp. U. Pa., Phila., 1969-72; assoc. chief cardiovascular sect. Hosp. U. Pa., 1972-77, chief, 1977-81; physician-in-chief U. Md. Hosp., 1984—; prof. medicine U. Pa. Sch. Medicine, Phila., 1976-83; Theodore E. Woodward prof. medicine, chmn. dept. medicine U. Md. Sch. Medicine, 1984—; vis. prin. fellow Nat. Heart and Lung Inst., London, 1995. Author: Arrhythmias, 1994; founding editor Internat. Jour. Cardiology, 1981-84; contbr. numerous articles on cardiac electrophysiology and gen. cardiology to med. jours. Served with U.S. Army, 1953-55. Fellow ACP, Am. Coll. Cardiology, Coun. Clin. Cardiology Am. Heart Assn.; mem. Am. Fedn. Clin. Rsch., Am. Heart Assn. (bd. govs. Southeastern Pa. chpt. 1975-81, bd. govs. Md. affiliate 1990-93), Assn. Am. Physicians, Assn. Univ. Cardiologists, Assn. Profs. Medicine (bd. govs. 1992-95), Venezuelan Soc. Internal Medicine, Paul Dudley White Soc. (dir. 1977-86), Alpha Omega Alpha. Home: 2415 Boston St Baltimore MD 21224-4733 Office: U Md Hosp 22 S Greene St Baltimore MD 21201-1544

KASULEN, BRENDA LEE, health facility administrator; b. Norwalk, Conn., Apr. 26, 1960; d. Michael Angelo and Carol Elizabeth (Greene) Renzulli; m. Mark Kasulen, Aug. 12, 1995. BSN, Tex. Christian U., Ft. Worth, 1982. RN, Conn. Staff nurse intensive care Norwalk (Conn.) Hosp., 1982-83; staff nurse Greenwich (Conn.) Hosp., 1983-84, Traveling Nurse Corp., various locations, 1984-85; staff nurse intensive care The Stamford (Conn.) Hosp., 1986-93; donation coord. Yale New Haven Transplant Ctr./New Eng. Organ Bank, 1994—; lectr. in field. Disaster nurse ARC, Norwalk, 1994; youth leader Young Life, Wilton, Conn., 1986-91; youth group leader Hope Ch., Wilton, 1992-95. Mem. N.Am. Transplant Coords. Orgn. Home: 42 Whitney Ln Berlin CT 06037 Office: Yale New Haven Transplant 333 Cedar St New Haven CT 06510

KASUYA, MINORU, public health educator; b. Hokkaido, Japan, June 22, 1936; s. Kiyoshi and Mineko (Furusawa) K.; m. Harumi Ban, Mar. 18, 1961; children: Yuichi, Mizuki. MD, Sapporo (Japan) Med. Coll., 1961, D Med. Sci., 1972. Rsch. assoc. dept. physiology Sapporo Med. Coll., 1962-65, rsch. assoc. dept. pub. health, 1966-67, asst. prof., 1967-73, assoc. prof., 1973-78; prof. faculty medicine dept. pub. health Toyama (Japan) Med. and Pharm. U., 1978—. Author: Environmental Toxicology, 1977. Mem. Internat. Commn. on Occupational Health, Singapore, Global Environ. Epidemiology Network, WHO, Geneva; mem. bd. Japan Soc. Hygiene, Sapporo. Home: 3330-6 Nagasawa, Fuchu-Machi 939-26, Japan Office: Toyama Med and Pharm U, Dept Pub Health, 2630 Sugitani, Toyama 930-01, Japan

KASZNIAK, ALFRED WAYNE, neuropsychologist; b. Chgo., June 2, 1949; s. Alfred H. and Ann Virginia (Simonsen) K.; B.S. with honors, U. Ill., 1970, M.A., 1973, Ph.D., 1976; m. Mary Ellen Beaurain, Aug. 26, 1973; children: Jesse, Elizabeth. Instr. dept. psychology Rush Med. Coll., Chgo., 1974-76, asst. prof. dept. psychology, 1976-79; from asst. prof. to assoc. prof. dept. psychiatry U. Ariz. Coll. Medicine, Tucson, 1979-82, assoc. prof. dept. psychology and psychiatry, 1982-87; prof. depts. psychology, neurology and psychiatry, 1987—; chmn. U. Ariz. Commn. on Gerontology, 1990-93, acting head U. Ariz. dept. psychology, 1992-93 ; dir. U. Ariz. Coordinated Clin. Neuropsychology Program; staff psychologist Presbyn.-St. Luke's Hosp., Chgo., 1976-79, Univ. Hosp., Tucson, 1979—; mem. human devel. and aging study sect. div. research grants NIH, 1981-86. Trustee So. Ariz. chpt. Nat. Multiple Sclerosis Soc., 1980-82; mem. med. and sci. adv. bd. Nat. Alzheimer's Disease and Related Disorders Assn., 1981-84; mem. VA Geriatrics and Gerontology Adv. Com., 1986-89, Ariz. Gov.'s Adv. Com. on Alzheimer's Disease, 1988-92; mem. med. adv. bd. Fan Kane Fund for Brain-Injured Children, Tucson, 1980-92. Grantee Nat. Inst. Aging, 1978-83, 89-94, NIMH, 1984-94, Robert Wood Johnson Found., 1986-89. Fellow Am. Psychol. Assn. (Disting. Contbr. award div. 20 1978, pres. clin. geropsychology sect. 1995); mem. Internat. Neuropsychol. Soc., (bd gov's., 1994—), Soc. for Neurosci., Gerontol. Soc. (rsch. fellow 1980). Author 3 books; editorial cons. Jour. Gerontology, 1979-92; mem. editorial bd. Psychology and Aging, 1984-87; The Clin. Neuropsychologist, 1986-96, Clin. Geropsychology, 1994—, Jour. Clin. and Exp. Neuropsychol., 1987-90, Jour Gerontology, 1988-92, Neuropsychology, 1992-93; contbr. articles to profl. jours. Home: 2327 E Hawthorne St Tucson AZ 85719-4944 Office: U Ariz Dept Psychology Tucson AZ 85721

KATCHUR, MARLENE MARTHA, nursing administrator; b. Belleville, Ill., Dec. 20, 1946; d. Elmer E. and Hilda B. (Gutherz) Wilde; m. Raymond J. Katchur, Feb. 22, 1969; 1 child, Nickolas Phillip. BSN, So. Ill. U., 1968; MS in Health Care Adminstrn., Calif. State U., L.A., 1982. RN; cert. critical care nurse. Staff nurse, head nurse, nursing supr. U. So. Calif Med. Ctr. LA County, 1968-81, assoc. dir. nursing, internal medicine nursing, 1981-83, internal medicine nursing info. systems coord., 1983-89, patient-centered info. systems cons., 1989-90, nursing info. systems cons. for pediatrics, psychiatry and ICU, 1990-92, psychiat. nursing svcs. human resources and info. systems, 1992-94; nursing supr. adminstrv. nursing office, 1994-95; nurse mgr. Gen. Hosp., 1995—. Mem. Sheriff's Relief Assn. Mem. AACCN, NAFE, AAUW, Nat. Critical Care Inst. Edn., Am. Heart Assn., So. Ill. U. Alumni Assn. (life), Health Svcs. Mgmt. Forum, Orgn. Nurse Execs. Calif. (membership com.), Am. Soc. Profl. and Exec. Women, Soc. Clin. Data Mgmt. Systems (bd. dirs. 1990-91), Soc. Med. Computer Observers (charter), Am. Legion Aux., Nat. Hist. Soc., Job's Daus. (past honor queen). Office: LA County U So Calif Med Ct U So Calif Med Ctr 1200 N State St Los Angeles CA 90033-4525

KATH, PHILIP D., ophthalmologist; b. Rochester, Minn., June 7, 1950; m. Carolyn Dyer; 1 child, Katherine Elizabeth. BS, U. Minn., 1972; MD, Mayo Med. Sch., 1976. Internship Cleve. Clinic Hosp., 1976-77; residency in ophthalmology Mayo Clinic, Rochester, Minn., 1977-80; physician Morgantown (N.C.) Eye Physicians, P.A., 1981—. Office: Morgantown Eye Physcians PA 335 East Parker Rd Morgantown NC 28655

KATHAN, JOYCE C., social worker, administrator; b. Middletown, Conn., Oct. 28, 1931; d. Herbert G. and Mabel Elizabeth (Lee) Clark; m. Boardman W. Kathan, Aug. 17, 1952; children: Nancy Lee, David Wardell, Robert Boardman. B of Social Work magna cum laude, Southern Conn. State U., 1976. Dir. sr. citizen programs Town Woodbury (Conn.); dist. dir. Coun. Greater Boston Camp Fire Girls; participant Global Assembly of Women and Environ., 1991; mem. adv. bd. VNA health Care, 1985-95. Co-author: Youth Where the Action Is, 1970, (with others) Management of Hazardous Agents, Vol. 2: Social and Political Aspects, 1992. Bd. dirs. Waterbury YWCA, 1977-83, rec. sec.; mem. Prospect Commn. on Aging, Prospect, Conn., 1979-89, chair 1979-87; apptd. mem. Congl. Dist. 5 adv. coun. Conn. Permanent Commnon Status of Women, 1996—. Recipient Outstanding Conn. Women award, 1987. Mem. NASW, AAUW (Conn. chpt., pub. policy chair 1996-98, com. mem. Assn. Pub. Policy Com. 1985-89, mem. local and state coms. 1978-96, Award for Outstanding Cmty. Svc. Conn. chpt. 1994), LWV (pres. Cheshire chpt. 1989-93), Conn. LWV (pub. policy com. 1988—), Conn. Assn. Sr. Ctr. Pers. (charter mem., rec. sec. 1995-97, Svc. award 1986), Wetern Conn. Area Agy. Aging (bd. dirs. 1986-92, pres. 1990-92), Conn. Soc. Gerontology.

KATIMS, ROBERT BERNARD, physician; b. N.Y.C., Aug. 8, 1929; s. Herman S. and Pearl Pauline K.; m. Arlyn Ruth Austin, Sept. 3, 1950 (wid. May 1994); children: Lee, Neil, David. Student, U. Fla., 1946-48; MD, Washington U., 1952. Intern St. Louis City Hosp., 1952-53, asst. resident in medicine, 1953-54; fellow in metabolism Barnes Hosp., 1954; asst. resident in medicine Johns Hopkins Hosp., Balt., 1956-57; fellow in endocrinology The Johns Hopkins Hops., Balt., 1957-59; pvt. practice of endocrinology Miami, 1959—; clin. prof. of medicine U. Miami Sch. of Medicine, 1959—; cons. Fla. Dept. Labor, Miami, 1994—; courtesy staff U. Miami Med. Ctr., 1960-69, exec. com., 1969-71; active staff Cedars Med. Ctr., chief of medicine, 1970-72, pres. med. staff, 1972-73, chief endocrinology sect., 1969-89; active staff Bapt. Hosp.; cons. Jewish Home for the Aged, 1966-95; chmn. State of Fla. Dept. Profl. Regulation, 1989, Probable Cause Panel, 1987—, chmn., 1989-91, 93—, others; mem. Fla. Bd. Medicine, 1979-87. Co-author: (book) Thyroid and Endocrine System Investigations with Radionuclides and Radioassays, 1979; contbr. articles to profl. jours. Lt. USNR, 1954-56. Mem. The Johnson Soc., Tropical Deerstalkers/Sherlock Holmes Soc., Physicians Wine Appreciation Soc. (v.p. 1962—), Fla. Diabetes Assn. (bd. dirs. 1960-79, pres. 1968-69), Dade County Med. Assn. (pres. 1975-76, trustee 1975-79), Fla. State Bd. Med. Examiners (chmn. 1979-80), AMA, Fla. Med. Assn., The Endocrine Soc., Assn. of Clin. Endocrinologists, Fla. Endocrine Soc., others. Office: Endocrinology Assocs 8740 SW 88 St Miami FL 33176

KATKIN, EDWARD SAMUEL, psychology educator; b. N.Y.C., Aug. 15, 1937; s. Nathan and Rosalind (Davis) K.; m. Felice Lapin, Aug. 10, 1958 (dec. 1961); m. 2d Wendy Sue Freedman, Feb. 3, 1963; children: Kenneth, Elizabeth. B.A., CCNY, 1958; Ph.D., Duke U., 1963. Asst. prof. SUNY, Buffalo, 1963-66, assoc. prof., 1966-70, prof. dept. psychology, 1970-86 (chmn. 1980-86); prof. dept. psychology SUNY, Stony Brook, 1986—, chmn. dept. psychology, 1986-92, dean divsn. social and behavioral scis., 1993-96. Fellow Am. Psychol. Soc.; mem. Soc. Psychophysiol. Rsch. (pres. 1983-84), Am. Psychosomatic Soc., N.Y. Acad. Sci. Home: 11 Bayview Ave East Setauket NY 11733-3903 Office: SUNY Dept Psychology Stony Brook NY 11794-2500

KATLIC, MARK R., thoracic surgeon; b. Latrobe, Pa., 1951. MD, John Hopkins U., 1977. Diplomate Am. Bd. Surgery, Am. Bd. Thoracic Surgery. Intern Mass. Gen. Hosp., Boston, 1977-78, resident gen. surgery, 1978-82, resident thoracic surgery, 1982-83; chief thoracic surgeon dept. thoracic surgery Wilkes-Barre Gen. Hosp., Pa., 1985—. Mem. AMA, Am. Coll. Chest Physicians, Am. Cancer Soc., Soc. Thoracic Surgery, Alpha Omega Alpha. Office: Surg Spec Wyoming Vly 200 S River St Wilkes Barre PA 18705-1143 also: Wyoming Vly Surg Assocs 250 Pierce St Kingston PA 18704-5149

KATO, RYUICHI, pharmacology educator; b. Hokkaido, Japan, Feb. 23, 1930; s. Tamakichi and Taka (Matsuda) K.; m. Nagako Okabe, May 28, 1961; children: Shigetaka, Akiko. M.D., Keio U., 1954, D.Med.Sci., 1961; Ph.D., U. Milan, Italy, 1962. Asst. in psychiatry Sch. medicine Keio U., Tokyo, 1955-57, rsch. fellow U. Milan, 1957-62; vis . assoc. NIH, Bethesda, Md., 1962-64; sect. head Nat. Inst. Hygenic Sci., Tokyo, 1964-71; head biol. dept. Fujisawa Research Lab., Osaka, 1971-77, chmn., prof. pharmacology Keio U. Sch. Medicine, Tokyo, 1977-95, emeritus prof. 1995—; mem. new drug devel. com. Ministry Health and Welfare, Japan, 1979—. Author: Drug Metabolism and Action, Toxic, 1968, Clinical Pharmaco Kinetics, 1991. Editor: Microsomes, Drug Oxidations and Drug Toxicity, 1982; Comparative Biochemical Drug Metabolism, 1984. Recipient award Found. Princess Takamatsu Cancer Research, 1982, Decoration Cavalieri Ufficiale Italian Govt., 1984, Med. award japanese Med. Assn., 1993, Soc. award Japan Soc. Pharm. Sci., 1995. Mem. Internat. Soc. Study Xenobiotics (pres. 1986-87), Internat. Union Pharmacology (chmn. sect. drug metabolism 1987-90), Japan Pharm. Soc. (past pres.), Japan Soc. Clin. Pharm. Therapy, (trustee), Japan Toxicological Soc. (trustee). Roman Catholic. Home: 4-26 4-805

Shimomaruko, Ōta-ku Tokyo 146, Japan Office: Keio U Sch Medicine, 35 Shinanomachi, Shinjuku-ku, Tokyo 160, Japan

KATONA, PETER GEZA, biomedical engineer, educator; b. Budapest, Hungary, June 25, 1937; came to U.S., 1956, naturalized, 1962; s. Stephan and Irene (Renner) K.; m. Jaroslava Blanar, Aug. 27, 1966; children—Catherine Iris, Andrew George. B.S. in Elec. Engring, U. Mich., 1960; S.M. in Elec. Engring. (Sloan fellow, 1960-62), M.I.T., 1962, Sc.D. in Elec. Engring, 1965. Asst. prof. elec. engring. M.I.T., 1965-69; assoc. prof. biomed. engring. Case Western Res. U., Cleve., 1969-78; prof. Case Western Res. U., 1978-92, chmn. dept., 1980-87; program dir. biomed. engring. and aiding the disabled NSF, 1989-91; exec. v.p. biomed. engring. The Whitaker Found., 1991—. Editorial bd.: American Jour. Physiology, 1975-81; contbr. articles on cardio-respiratory control and automated drug delivery to profl. jours. Recipient Alexander von Humboldt award, 1987-88. Fellow AAAS, Am. Inst. Med. & Biol. Engring. (founding); mem. IEEE, Am. Physiol. Soc., Biomed. Engring. Soc. (bd. dirs. 1977-80, pres. 1984-85), Am. Soc. Engring. Edn. Office: The Whitaker Found 1700 N Moore St Ste 2200 Arlington VA 22209

KATSONIS, MICHAEL GEORGE, pharmacist; b. Harrisburg, Pa., Nov. 7, 1951; s. George Manuel and Doris Virginia (Geise) K. BS in Pharmacy, U. Pitts., 1974. Lic. pharmacist, Pa., Fla., Colo., Utah. Lift opr. Breckenridge (Colo.) Ski Area, 1985-86, 87-88; asst. mgr. Checker Auto Parts, Denver, 1986-87; staff pharmacist Pharmacy Mgmt. Svcs., Inc., Tampa, Fla., 1988-90, U. Fla. Student Health Ctr., Gainesville, 1990-92; pharmacy mgr. Winn-Dixie, Kissimmee, Fla., 1992-93; with Payless Drug Stores, 1993; staff pharmacist K-Mart Pharmacy, Orem, Utah, 1993-94; pharmacy mgr. K-Mart Pharmacy, Farmington, Utah, 1994—. Mem. United Way Chmn.'s Leadership Club, Gainesville, 1990-91, Rep. Nat. Com., Washington, 1991, Pres.'s Club, Washington, 1992, Campaign Coun., Washington, 1992—, Presdl. Roundtable, Washington, 1992-95; life mem. Rep. Senatorial Inner Circle, Washington, 1992, Rep. Presdl. Task Force, Washington, 1992. Republican Senatorial medal of Freedom 1994. Fellow Nat. Cath. Pharmacists guild; mem. Am. Pharm. Assn., Am. Soc. Pharmacy Law, Fla. Pharmacy Assn. (orgnl. affairs coun. 1990-92), Alachua County Assn. Pharmacists (sec. 1991-92), Ctrl. Fla. Pharmacy Assn. (v.p.-elect 1992), Utah Pharmacy Assn. (life), Utah Elephant Club, Olympus-Crossroads Kiwanis Club Salt Lake City, Gold Spike Leadership Circle (bronze mem. 1992), Mystic Shrine El Kalah Temple (noble 1994, 95, 96), Midvale Lions Club, KC. Home: 3595 S Orion Cir # V West Valley City UT 84119-6130

KATTAH, JORGE, neurologist; b. Bogota, Colombia, Jan. 12, 1948; s. Jorge Y. and Beatriz (Calderon) K.; m. Janet Marie. MD, Coll. Mayor Ntra Sra Rosario, Bogota, 1972. Intern in neurologist Georgetown U. Med., 1976; intern in neurophthalmology Pitts. Eye and Ear Hosp., 1977; assoc. prof. Georgetown U., Washington, 1977—. Mem. Am. Neurol. Assn. Office: Georgetown U 3800 Reservoir Rd Washington DC 20007

KATTAN, KENNETH ROBERT, radiologist; b. Baghdad, Iraq, Feb. 26, 1926; arrived in Israel, 1951; came to U.S., 1966; s. Eliahoo T. and Sabiha (Horesh) K.; m. Daisy Rahima; children: Joseph, Ezra. MD, Hebrew U., Jerusalem, 1953. Diplomate Am. Bd. Radiology. Radiologist Beilinson Hosp., Petah-Tikya, Israel, 1964-66; fellow in radiology U. Cin. Hosp., 1966-68, asst. prof. radiology, 1968-70, assoc. prof., 1970; prof., chief radiology Wright State U., Dayton, Ohio, 1976-85, Veterans Med. Ctr., Dayton, Ohio, 1977-85; radiologist, clin. prof. U. Cin., 1985-95, Veterans Med. Ctr., Cin., 1985-96; cons. Wright Patterson Air Force Base, Dayton, 1977-85. Contbr. 75 articles to profl. jours., 1966-95; editor: Trauma and No Trauma Cervical Spine, 1975; discoverer 12 diagnostic signs in the interpretation of x-ray films. Emeritus fellow Am. Coll. Radiology; mem. Am. Roentgen Ray Soc., Internat. Skeletal Soc. Home: 6741 Meadowridge Ln Cincinnati OH 45237

KATZ, ALAN ROY, public health educator; b. Pitts., Aug. 21, 1954; s. Leon B. and Bernice Sonia (Glass) K.; m. Donna Marie Crandall, Jan. 19, 1986; 1 child, Sarah Elizabeth. BA, U. Calif., San Diego, 1976; MD, U. Calif., Irvine, 1980; MPH, U. Hawaii, 1987; postgrad., U. So. Calif., 1980-81, U. Hawaii, 1982-83. Staff physician emergency medicine L.A. County U. So. Calif. Med. Ctr., 1981-82; staff physician, med. dir. Waikiki Health Ctr., Honolulu, 1983-87; dir. AIDS/STD prevention program Hawaii State Dept. of Health, Honolulu, 1987-88; asst. prof. dept. pub. health scis. U. Hawaii, Honolulu, 1988-94, assoc. prof., 1994—, dir. preventive medicine residency program, 1994—; bd. dirs. Hawaii AIDS Task Group; mem. Chlamydia control workgroup USPHS, 1985-87. Me. Leptospirosis ad hoc com. Hawaii State Dept. Health, Honolulu, 1988—, mem. prenatal screening adv. com., 1992—; mem. com. human subjects U. Hawaii, 1989—. USPHS Chlamydia Prevalence Survey grantee, Hawaii, 1986, Tuberculosis Survey grantee U. Hawaii, 1991; recipient presdl. citation for meritorious teaching, U. Hawaii, 1989, regents medal excellence in teaching U. Hawaii, 1992. Fellow Am. Coll. Preventive Medicine; mem. Am. Pub. Health Assn., Soc. Epidemiologic Rsch., Delta Omega. Office: U Hawaii Sch Pub Health Dept Pub Health Sci 1960 E West Rd Honolulu HI 96822-2319

KATZ, ALFRED DAVID, surgeon, oncologist; b. Long Branch, N.J., Nov. 22, 1925; s. Samuel and Rose Eve (Sandberg) K.; m. Cecelia Eve Rubnitz, July 1, 1952; children: Vern Louis, Debre Katz Weintraub, Maureen Anne, Michelle Mavis. BA, U. Wis., 1949; MD, Yale U., 1951. Diplomate Am. Bd. Surgery. Intern Strong Meml. Hosp., Rochester, N.Y., 1951-52; surg. resident Cedars of Lebanon Hosp., L.A., 1952-55; oncology resident Roswell Park Meml. Inst., Buffalo, N.Y., 1955-57; active staff Cedars-Sinai Med. Ctr., L.A., Midway Med. Ctr., L.A.; asst. clin. prof. surgery U. Calif., Irvine, 1963-71; mem. staff Cedars-Sinai Hosp., 1957—, Midway Hosp., 1958—; vis. cons. City of Hope, Duarte, Calif., 1958-63. Contbr. 40 articles to profl. jours. Bd. dirs. Jewish Fedn. Coun., L.A., 1982-87, 89-96; Pacific regional bd. dirs. Ani-Defamation League B'nai B'rith, 1982-96, fellowship com. Western region, 1982—; chmn. com. on cancer, L.A. County Med. Assn., 1969-74; bd. dirs. Cmty. Cancer Control of L.A., 1977-83; exec. com. L.A. chpt. Am. Cancer Soc., 1968-70, profl. edn. com of Calif., 1972-81; pres. Roswell Park Surg. Soc., 1974-75. Fellow ACS. Office: Ste. 695-W 8635 West Third St Los Angeles CA 90048

KATZ, ALLAN ROBERT, obstetrician, gynecologist; b. N.Y.C., Apr. 1, 1942; s. Milton and Mildred (Pfeffer) K.; m. Judith Kass, June 1, 1964 (div. 1974); 1 child, Robin; m. Patti Jayne Ross, May 23, 1976. BA, NYU, 1963; MD, Med. Coll. Va., 1967. Intern Maimonides Med. Ctr. Kings County Hosp., N.Y.C., 1968; resident Albert Einstein Coll. Medicine, N.Y.C., 1970-74; asst. prof. ob/gyn. U. Tex., Houston, 1975-80, vice chmn. dept. ob/gyn., dir. grad. med. edn., 1980-84; assoc. prof., vice chmn. dept. ob/gyn., reproductive sci., 1984-91, prof., vice chmn. residency program dir., 1991—. Capt. U.S. Army, 1969-70. Decorated Bronze Star, Air medal; recipient Physicians Recognition award AMA, 1974-81, 84. Fellow Am. Coll. Ob-Gyn.; mem. Assn. Profs. Ob-Gyn., Am. Assn. Gynecol. Laparoscopists, So. Perinatal Assn., Gynecologic Laser Soc. Jewish. Office: U Tex Med Sch 6431 Fannin St # 3204 Houston TX 77030-1501

KATZ, ARNOLD MARTIN, medical educator; b. Chgo., July 30, 1932; s. Louis Nelson and Aline (Grossner) K.; m. Phyllis Beck, Apr. 18, 1959; children: Paul, Sarah, Amy, Laura. BA with honors, U. Chgo., 1952; MD cum laude, Harvard U., 1956; D.Med. (hon.), Carol Davila U., 1994. Diplomate Nat. Bd. Med. Examiners. Intern Mass. Gen. Hosp., Boston, 1956-57, asst. res., 1959-60; rsch. assoc. NIH, Bethesda, Md., 1957-59; asst. registrar Inst. Cardiology, London, 1960-61; rsch. fellow dept. medicine UCLA, 1961-64; asst. prof. physiology Columbia U., N.Y.C., 1963-67; asst. physician Presbyn. Hosp., N.Y.C., 1963-67; assoc. prof. medicine and physiology U. Chgo., 1967-69; Philip J. and Harriet L. Goodhart prof. cardiology Mt. Sinai Sch. Medicine, N.Y.C., 1969-77; prof. medicine, head cardiology divsn. U. Conn., Farmington, 1977-95, prof. medicine/divsn. chief emeritus, 1995—; cons. VA, 1970; coord. Problem Area #3, US-USSR Collaboration in Cardiovascular Rsch., 1983-86; mem. adv. com. Chinese Acad. med. Sci., 1982-89; R.T. Hall lectr. Cardiac Soc., Australia and New Aezland, 1991; chair sci. bd. Stanley J. Sarnoff Endowment Cardiovascular Sci. Inc., 1992-93; chair, sci. adv. bd. Patrick, Catherine, Weldon, Donaghue Med. Rsch. Found., 1994—; mem. bd. sci. counsellors Nat. Heart Lung Inst., 1989-92. Author: Physiology of the Heart, 1977, 2d edit., 1992; editor: The Heart and Cardiovascular System, 1986, 91; mem. editorial bd.: Am. Jour. Cardiology, 1970-75, Am. Jour. Medicine, 1971-77, Am. Jour. Physiology, 1966-72, Can. Jour. Cardiology, 1988-91, Cardiology, 1980-85, Cardioscience, 1988—, Cardiovascular Pharmacol., 1979-88, Circulation, 1992—, Circulation Rsch., 1974-80, Jour. Am. Coll. Cardiology, 1983-87, Jour. Clin. Investigation, 1971-76, Jour. Mechanochemistry and Cell Motility, 1970-72, Jour. Molecular and Cellular Cardiology, 1970-92, also editor-in-chief, 1986-92, Life Sciences, 1979-88, Physiol. Rev. 1976-80; reviewer several profl. jours.; contbr. articles to profl. jours. Chair sci. bd. Donaghue Found., 1993—. Served with USPHS, 1957-59. Humboldt fellow Alexander von Humboldt Found., 1975-76, Moseley traveling fellow Harvard U., 1960-61. Fellow ACP, Am. Coll. Cardiology (gov. Conn. 1984-87); mem. Am. Heart assn. (advanced rsch. fellow 1961-63, established investigator 1963-68, v.p. couns. 1992-94, bd. dirs. 1992-94, chmn. coun. affairs com. 1992-94, chmn. exec. com. basic sci. coun. 1990-92, Conn. affiliate bd. dirs. 1986-94, Greater Hartford chpt. bd. dirs. 1977-84, sec. 1982-84, v.p. 1984-86, pres. 1986-88, Rsch. Achievement award 1989, Disting. Achievement award Basic Sci. Coun. 1991, award of Meritorious Achievement 1995, Honoree Louis N. and Arnold M. Katz prize Basic Sci. Coun. 1995), N.Y. Heart Assn. (bd. dirs. 1971-74, 75-77), Am. Physiol. Soc. (mem. circulation group), Cardiac Muscle Soc. (pres. 1969-71), Am. Soc. Pharmacology and Exptl. Therapeutics, Am. Soc. Clin. Investigation, Assn. Am. Physicians, Internat. Soc. Heart Rsch. (pres. Am. sect. 1985), Am. Soc. Biol. Chemists Molecular Biology, Assn. Univ. Cardiologists, Alpha Omega Alpha. Home: PO Box 1048 Norwich VT 05055-1048 Office: U Conn Health Ctr Divsn Cardiology Dept Farmington CT 06030-1305*

KATZ, SIR BERNARD, physiologist; b. Leipzig, Germany, Mar. 25, 1911; s. Max and Eugenie (Rabinowitz) K.; m. Marguerite Penly, Oct. 27, 1945; children: David, Jonathan. MD, U. Leipzig, Germany, 1934; MD (hon.), U. Leipzig, German Dem. Republic, 1990; PhD, U. London, 1938, DSc, 1943; DSc (hon.), U. Southampton, 1971, U. Melbourne, 1971, Cambridge U., 1980; PhD (hon.), Weizmann Inst. Sci., 1979. Beit Meml. Research fellow, 1938-39; Carnegie Research fellow Sydney, Australia, 1939-42; asst. dir. biophys. research U. Coll., London, 1946-50, reader, 1950, prof., head biophysics dept., 1952-78; lectr. univs., socs. Author: Electric Excitation of Nerve, 1939; Nerve, Muscle and Synapse, 1966; The Release of Neural Transmitter Substances, 1969; also articles. Mem. Agrl. Research Council, 1967-77. Recipient Feldberg award, 1965, Copley medal Royal Soc., 1967, Nobel prize in medicine-physiology, 1970, Cothenius medal Deutsche Akademie der Naturforscher Leopoldina, 1989; created knight, 1969. Fellow Royal Soc. (council 1964-65, v.p. 1965, biol. sec. 1968-76), Royal Coll. Physicians (Baly medal 1967); fgn. mem. Royal Danish Acad. Scis. and Letters, Acad. Nat. Lincei, Am. Acad. Arts and Sci., Nat. Acad. Scis. U.S. (fgn. assoc.), Order Pour le Mérite für Wissenschaften und Künste (fgn.). Office: U Coll Dept Physiology, Gower St, London WC1E 6BT, England

KATZ, DANIEL, pediatric neurologist; b. Topeka, Oct. 29, 1952; s Jerome B. and Alma (Mindel) K.; m. Margot Brown, Nov. 25, 1979; children: Benjamin, Jonathan. BA, Kans. U., 1973; MD, U. Tex. Med. Br., 1977. Diplomate Am. Bd. Pediat., Am. Bd. Neurology, Am. Bd. Child Neurology. Intern St. Louis Children's Hosp., 1977-79; resident Okla. Children's Meml. Hosp., Oklahoma City, 1979-80; pediatric neurologist pvt. practice, sacramento, 1984-91; staff nuerologist Menninger, Topeka, 1991—. Neurology fellow U. Cin., 1980-83, neurophysiology fellow U. Tex. Health Sci. Ctr., Dallas, 1983-84. Mem. Am. Acad. Pediatrics, Child Neurology Soc Office: Menninger 5800 6th St SW Topeka KS 66614

KATZ, DAVID M., neurologist. BA, Colgate U., 1983; MD, U. Buffalo, 1988. Resident in neurology Duke U., Durham, N.C., 1988-92; fellow in neuro-ophthalmology U. Mich., Ann Arbor, 1992-93; neurologist in pvt. practice Framingham, Mass., 1993—; neuro-ophthalmologist in pvt. practice Framingham, 1993—. Office: Neurol Svcs PC 463 Worcester Rd Framingham MA 01701

KATZ, ELIOT JOEL, physician, educator; b. Boston, May 30, 1948; s. Gerald and Frances (Belson) K.; m. Sally Ragin, May 10, 1974; children: Rachael, Sarah, Leah. BA, Brandeis U., 1970; MD, St. Louis U., 1974. Diplomate Am. Bd. Internal Medicine, Am. Bd. Endocrinology. Registrar in endocrinology Princess Margaret Hosp., Christchurch, New Zealand, 1979-81; asst. prof. medicine Tex. Tech. U., Amarillo, 1981-83; asst. clin. prof. medicine U. Calif., San Francisco, 1983-88; assoc. chief of staff, acting chief of staff VA Med. Ctr., Fresno, Calif., 1983-88; assoc. consulting prof. medicine Duke U. Med. Ctr., Asheville, N.C., 1988-92; asst. prof. medicine St. Louis U., Health Scis. Ctr., 1992—. Office: VA Med Ctr III/JC Saint Louis MO 63125

KATZ, FRED N., osteopath, radiologist; b. N.Y.C., Apr. 26, 1941; s. Samuel and Molly (Boodman) K.; m. Doris Strauss, June 20, 1964; children: Barrie Gail, Michelle Stacey. BS, L.I. U., 1962; DO, U. Health Scis., Des Moines, 1966. Diplomate Am. Bd. Diagnostic Radiology, Am. Bd Nuclear Medicine. Intern Detroit Osteopathic Hosp., 1966-67, resident radiology, 1969-72; chief diagnostic imaging Northlake Regional Med. Ctr., Atlanta, 1972—; chmn. Am. Osteo. Bd. Radiology. 1988—. Chmn. Israel Bonds, Atlanta, 1988—; bd. dirs. Atlanta Jewish Fedn., 1990, United Jewish Appeal, Northlake Regional Med. Ctr. Decorated Bronze Star. Fellow Am. Osteo. Coll. Radiology (pres. 1986-87, Trenary lectr. 1986), Ga. Osteo. Med. Assn. (pres. 1978-79, Outstanding Physician award 1987). Office: Northlake Regional Med Ctr 1455 Montreal Rd Tucker GA 30084-8100

KATZ, HENRY ALLEN, physician; b. Newark, Feb. 21, 1940; s. Edward K. and Toby (Gross) K.; m. Jeanne M., Feb. 20, 1965; children: Jennifer, Sheryl, Melissa; m. Linda Beth, Mar. 19, 1987. BA, Rutgers U., 1961; MD, Georgetown U., 1965. Pvt. practice internal medicine Parsippany, N.J., 1971—; pres. Morris County Med. Soc., Morristown, 1979-80; faculty U. Medicine and Dentistry, Newark, 1980—; chmn. dept. medicine St. Clare's Hosp., Denville, N.J., Riverside Hosp., Boorton, N.J. Capt. USAF, 1968-70. Jewish. Office: 3699 Rt 46 Parsippany NJ 07054

KATZ, JAY, psychiatry and law educator; b. Zwickau, Fed. Republic Germany, Oct. 20, 1922; came to U.S., 1940, naturalized, 1945; s. Paul and Dora (Ungar) K.; m. Marilyn B. Arthur, June 18, 1989; children from previous marriage: Sally Jean, Daniel Franklin, Amy Susan. BA, U. Vt., 1944, DS (hon.), 1995; MD, Harvard U., 1949; DS (hon.), Northeastern Ohio U., 1994. Intern Mt. Sinai Hosp., N.Y.C., 1949-50; resident Northport (N.Y.) VA Hosp., 1950-51, Yale U., 1953-55; instr. psychiatry Yale U., New Haven, 1955-57, asst. prof., 1957-58, asst. prof. psychiatry and law, 1958-60, asso. prof. law, asso. clin. prof. psychiatry, 1960-67, adj. prof. law and psychiatry, 1967-79, prof., 1979-81, John A. Garver prof. law and psychoanalysis, 1981-90, Elizabeth K. Dollard prof. law, medicine and psychiatry, 1990-93, Elizabeth K. Dollard prof. law, medicine and psychiatry emeritus, Harvey L. Karp Profl. lectr. in law and psychoanalysis, 1993—; tng. and supervising psychiatrist Western New Eng. Inst. for Psychoanalysis, 1972—; cons. to asst. sec. health and sci. affairs HEW, 1972-73, mem. artificial heart assessment panel, 1972-73; active Presdl. Adv. Com. on Ho. Radiation Experiments, 1994-95. Author: (with Joseph Goldstein) The Family and the Law, 1964, (with Joseph Goldstein and Alan M. Dershowitz) Psychoanalysis, Psychiatry and Law, 1967, Experimentation with Human Beings, 1972, (with Alexander M. Capron) Catastrophic Diseases—Who Decides What?, 1975; The Silent World of Doctor and Patient, 1984. Bd. dirs. Family Service of New Haven. Served to capt. M.C. USAF, 1951-53. Recipient Henry K. Beecher award Hastings Ctr. for Ethics and Life Scis., 1993; John Simon Guggenheim Meml. Found. fellow, 1981. Fellow ACP (William C. Menninger award 1983), Am. Psychiat. Assn. (Isaac Ray award 1975), Am. Orthopsychiat. Assn., Am. Coll. Psychiatry, Center for Advanced Psychoanalytic Studies; mem. Inst. Medicine, Nat. Acad. of Scis., Group for Advancement of Psychiatry, Am. Psychoanalytic Assn. Jewish. Home: 27 Inwood Rd Woodbridge CT 06525-2513 Office: Yale Law Sch 127 Wall St New Haven CT 06511-6636

KATZ, JEFFREY IVAN, urologist; b. N.Y.C., Aug. 21, 1943; s. David and Rebecca (Shapiro) K.; BA, Pa. State U., 1965; MD, U. Bologna (Italy), 1970; m. Ethelinda Spiegel, Sept. 29, 1973; children: David, Jennifer. Diplomate Am. Bd. Urology. Intern, N.Y. Med. Coll., 1971-72; resident in surgery Mt. Sinai Hosp., Miami, Fla., 1972-73, resident in urology Albert Einstein Med. Coll., Bronx, N.Y., 1973-76; practice medicine specializing in urology, West Orange, N.J., 1976—; mem. staff St. Barnabas Med. Ctr., Livingston, N.J., chief urology, 1984-89; chief of surgery Irvington (N.J.) Gen. Hosp., 1989-95; mem. med. staff Irvington Gen. Hosp., Kessler Inst. Rehab., West Orange; rschr. in field. Fellow ACS; mem. AMA, N.J. Med. Assn., Essex County Med. Assn., Am. Assn. Clin. Urologists, Am. Urology Assn., N.J. Urology Assn. Jewish. Office: 101 Old Short Hills Rd West Orange NJ 07052-1023

KATZ, JERRY, podiatrist; b. N.Y.C., May 29, 1961; s. David and Eva (Duell) K.; m. Susan Jane Siegel, July 18, 1986; 1 child, Rachel Paige. BA in Biology, CUNY, 1983; D Podiatric Medicine, Ill. Coll. Podiatric Medicine, 1987. Diplomate Am. Bd. Podiatric Surgery, Am. Bd. Podiatric Orthopaedists. Lab. asst. dept. pathology Sch. Medicine, NYU, N.Y.C., 1979-80; rsch. asst. Beth Israel Med. Ctr., Mt. Sinai Sch. Medicine, N.Y.C., 1981-83, animal technician, 1983, rsch. asst. dept. ophthalmology, 1984; mem. staff Wheaton (Md.) Podiatry Assocs., 1989-90; pvt. practice podiatry Randallstown, Md., 1990—; dir. diabetic foot clinic Liberty Med. ctr., Inc., Randallstown; mem. staff Liberty Med. Ctr., Inc., N.W. Hosp. Ctr., Montgomery Gen. Hosp. Contbr. articles to profl. publs. Mem. Am. Podiatric Med. Assn. (vice chmn. 1987-90, liaison to podiatry polit. action com. 1987-89), Md. Podiatric Med. Assn. Jewish. Office: 5310 Old Court Rd Randallstown MD 21133-5243

KATZ, JOSE, cardiologist, theoretical physicist, educator; b. Havana, Cuba, June 6, 1944; s. Lipa and Victoria (Masson) K.; m. Anke Ebsen; children: Susan, David, Rachel, Hannah. BS, U. Ill., 1963, MS, 1964, PhD, 1967; MD, F.U., Berlin, 1980. Rsch. assoc. physicist U. Hamburg, Fed. Republic Germany, 1967-69; instr. physics Purdue U., Lafayette, Ind., 1969-71; asst. prof. physics Free U. of Berlin, West Berlin, Fed. Republic Germany, 1971-74; prof. physics F.U., West Berlin, Fed. Republic Germany, 1974-82; resident in internal medicine Cleve. Met. Gen. Hosp., Mt. Sinai Med. Ctr., Cleve., 1982-85; cardiology fellow Southwestern Med. Sch., Dallas, 1985-88; asst. prof. Columbia U. Coll. Physicians and Surgeons, N.Y.C., 1988-94, assoc. prof. medicine and radiology, 1994—, dir. cardiovasc. MRI spectroscopy, 1988—. Contbr. articles to profl. jours., chpts. to books. Fellow ACP, Am. Coll. Cardiology, Am. Coll. Chest Physicians, Am. Coll. Angiology, Am. Heart Assn. (coun. clin. cardiology, coun. on cardiovascular radiology, coun. on basic scis.), Soc. Magnetic Resonance Imaging, Soc. Magnetic Resonance in Medicine; mem. AMA, Radiol. Soc. N.Am., Soc. Nuclear Medicine, N.Am. Soc. Cardiac Imaging, Sigma Xi, Phi Kappa Phi, Sigma Tau, Pi Mu Epsilon, Tau Beta Pi. Office: Columbia U Divsn Cardiology 630 W 168th St New York NY 10032-3702

KATZ, JULIAN, gastroenterologist, educator; b. N.Y.C., Apr. 3, 1937; s. Abraham M. and Fay (Sher) K.; m. Sheila Moriber, Aug. 18, 1963; children—Jonathan Peter, Sara Katherine. A.B., Columbia U., 1958; M.D., U. Chgo., 1962. Diplomate: Am. Bd. Internal Medicine. Intern U. Chgo. Hosps., 1962-63; resident in medicine Duke U., 1963-65; fellow in gastroenterology Yale U., 1965-67; practice medicine specializing in gastroenterology, internal medicine and geriatrics Phila., 1969—; prof. medicine, lectr. in physiology and biochemistry Med. Coll. Pa., 1970—; prof. medicine Jefferson Med. Coll., 1988—; also lectr. local and nat. groups; chief clin. gastroenterology Med. Coll. Pa. Editor profl. jours.; Contbr. articles to profl. jours. and books. Served with USN, 1967-69. Fellow ACP, Am. Coll. Gastroenterology; mem. Am. Soc. Gastrointestinal Endoscopy, Am. Soc. Study Liver Disease, Am. Gastroenterological Assn., others. Home: 701 Dodds Ln Gladwyne PA 19035-1516 Office: Gastrointestinal Specialists 2 Bala Pla Bala Cynwyd PA 19004

KATZ, KATHY SILVER, psychologist, educator; b. N.Y.C., May 9, 1947; d. Albert M. and Lola (Galvin) Silver; m. Richard J. Katz, June 21, 1970; children; Marisa S., Eliza J. BA, U. Pa., 1968; PhD, Rutgers U., 1974. Lic. Psychologist, Md., D.C. Psychology intern Judge Baker Guidance Ctr., Boston, 1972-73; postdoctoral fellow Children's Hosp. Med. Ctr., Boston, 1974-75; asst. prof. pediatrics Georgetown U. Med. Ctr., Washington, 1975-83, staff psychologist, 1975-83, assoc. prof. of pediatrics, 1983—; dir., infant follow-up Georgetown U. Child Devel. Ctr., Washington, 1978-88, 93—, dir. psychology tng., 1983-94; adj. assoc. prof. psychology Cath. U., Washington, 1983—; cons. in field. Author: Chronically Ill and At Risk Infants, 1989, Headed Home, 1992; contbr. articles to profl. jours. panel mem. Dist. Govt. Task Force on Personnel Preparation for Pub. Law 99-457, Washington, 1989—. Grantee U.S. Dept. Edn., 1985-88, 86-89, 88-91, 89-94, 92—, 93—, March of Dimes, 1988-89. Mem. APA (exec. bd. sect. on clin. child psychology 1995—), Soc. Pediatric Psychology, Am. Assn. Mental Retardation. Office: Georgetown U Med Ctr 3800 Reservoir Rd NW Kober Cogan 415 Washington DC 20007

KATZ, LOIS ANNE, internist, nephrologist; b. Rockville Centre, N.Y., Dec. 1, 1941; d. Irvin Martin and Frances (Berenstein) Fradkin; m. Arthur A. Katz, Aug. 18, 1962; children: David, Brian. BA, Wellesley Coll., 1962; MD, NYU, 1966. Diplomate Am. Bd. Internal Medicine, Am. Bd. Nephrology. Intern medicine Bellevue Hosp., NYU, N.Y.C., 1966-67, resident medicine, 1967-68; sr. resident medicine N.Y. Hosp., N.Y.C., 1968-69; chief resident medicine N.Y. VA Med. Ctr., N.Y.C., 1969-70, fellow nephrology, 1970-71, staff physician, 1970-74, assoc. chief nephrology, 1974—, assoc. chief of staff ambulatory care, 1980—; asst. prof. clin. medicine NYU Sch. Medicine, N.Y.C., 1974-79, assoc. prof., 1979-94, prof. clin. medicine, 1994—. Alumna admission rep. Wellesley-in-Westchester, N.Y.; bd. mem. Women's Med. Assn., N.Y.C., 1986—. Fellow ACP; mem. Am. Soc. Nephrology, Am. Med. Women's Assn., Soc. Gen. Internal Medicine, Women in Nephrology (treas. 1985-89), Am. Soc. Hypertension, Sigma Xi, Alpha Omega Alpha. Jewish. Office: Dept Vets Affairs Med Ctr 423 E 23rd St New York NY 10010-5050

KATZ, MAX, psychiatrist; b. Rosthern, Sask., Can., Feb. 16, 1919; naturalized U.S. citizen, 1964; m. Ellen Speiser; children by previous marriage: Lawrence, Andrea, Shirley, Elaine. BA, U. Sask., 1939; MD, U. Manitoba, Winnipeg, Can., 1942. Pvt. gen. practice B.C., Can., 1946-53; resident psychiatry Temple U. Hosp., Phila., 1953-56; clin. assoc. prof. psychiatry Temple U., Phila. Capt. Royal Can. Army Med. Corps, 1943-46. Mem. Am. Psychiat. Assn., Am. Psychoanalytic Assn., AMA, Phila Psychoanalytic Soc. Home and Office: 2005 Delancey Pl Philadelphia PA 19103-6509

KATZ, MICHAEL, pediatrician, educator; b. Lwow, Poland, Feb. 13, 1928; came to U.S., 1946, naturalized, 1951; s. Edward and Rita (Gluzman) K.; m. Robin J. Roy, July 19, 1986; 1 child, Edward Alexander. A.B., U. Pa., 1949, postgrad. (Harrison fellow), 1950-51; M.D., SUNY, Bklyn., 1956; M.S., Columbia U. Sch. Public Health, 1968. Intern UCLA Med. Center, 1956-57; resident Presbyterian Hosp. (Babies Hosp.), N.Y.C., 1960-62; dir. pediatric service Presbyterian Hosp. (Babies Hosp.), 1977-92, cons., 1992—; hon. lectr. pediatrics Makerere U. Coll., Kampala, Uganda, 1963-64; instr. in pediatrics Columbia U., 1964-65, prof. tropical medicine Sch. Public Health, 1971-92, prof. pub. health emeritus, 1992—, prof. pediatrics Coll. Physicians and Surgeons, 1972-77; Reuben S. Carpenter prof. pediats., 1977-92; prof. pub. health Columbia U., 1977-92, Reuben S. Carpentier prof., 1977-92, Reuben S. Carpentier prof. emeritus of pediatrics, 1992—; v.p. rsch. March of Dimes Birth Defects Found., White Plains, N.Y., 1992—; assoc. mem. Wistar Inst., Phila., 1965-71; asst. prof. pediats. U. Pa., 1966-77; cons. WHO, Guatemala, Venezuela, Egypt, Yemen; mem. U.S. del. 32d World Health Assembly, Geneva, 1979; cons. UNICEF, N.Y.C. and Tokyo, USAID, Egypt, 1982, Poland, 1987; mem. bd. sci. councillors Nat. Inst. Dental Rsch., 1986-90, chmn., 1990-92; vis. prof. U. Würzburg, Fed. Republic Germany, 1988; vis. prof. pediats. U. Negev, Beer Sheva, Israel, 1996. Author: (with others) Parasitic Diseases, 1982, 2d edit., 1989; editor: (with Volker ter Meulen) Slow Virus Infections of the Central Nervous System, 1977; mem. editorial bd. Med. Microbiology and Immunology, 1975-90, Pediatric Infectious Diseases Jour., 1981-92, Vaccines, 1983—; co-editor: Manuals in Pediatrics; contbr. articles to profl. jours. Pres. World Alliance of Orgns. for the Prevention of Birth Defects, Inc., 1995—. Lt. M.C., USNR, 1957-59. NIH grantee, 1968-76; WHO grantee, 1972-76; recipient Jurzykowski Found. award in Medicine, 1983, Alexander von Humboldt Sr. U.S. Scientist award, 1988. Fellow AAAS, Infectious Diseases Soc. Am., Am. Acad. Pediat.; mem. SOc. Pediatric Rsch., Am. Pediatric Soc., Harvey Soc., Am. Soc. Microbiology, Deutsche Gesellschaft für Neuropathologie und Neuroanatomie E.V. (corr.), Am. Soc. Tropical Medicine and Hygiene, N.Y. Soc. Tropical Medicine (pres. 1976-77), Royal Soc. Tropical Medicine and Hygiene (London), Pediatric Infectious Disease Soc., World Alliance of Orgns. for the Prevention of Birth Defects (pres. 1995—), Inst. Medicine of Nat. Acad. Scis., Ea. Soc. for Pediatric Rsch.

(coun.), Sigma Xi. Home: 1040 Park Ave New York NY 10028-1032 Office: March of Dimes Birth Defects Fdn 1275 Mamaroneck Ave White Plains NY 10605-5201

KATZ, MICHAEL JESSE, orthopedic surgeon; b. N.Y.C., Mar. 7, 1956; s. Walter and Thea Katz; m. Sherry Falk, July 4, 1979; children: Jonathan, Judith, Ezra, Daniel. BA, Queens Coll., N.Y.C., 1976; MD, Albert Einstein Coll. Medicine, N.Y.C., 1980. Diplomate Am. Bd. Forensic Examiners, Am. Bd. Orthopedic Surgery. Intern Hosp. U. Pa., 1980-81; resident in orthopedic surgery U. Pa. Hosp., Phila., 1981-85; cons. U.S. Fed. Cts., N.Y., 1994—. Jonas Salk scholar, 1976; faculty fellow U. Pa., 1981. Fellow Am. Acad. Orthopedic Surgeons, Am. Bd. Forensic Examiners; mem. AMA, Nassau County Med. Soc. Jewish. Home: 15 White Dr Cedarhurst NY 11516

KATZ, PHYLLIS ALBERTS, developmental research psychologist; married; 2 children. AB in Psychology summa cum laude, Syracuse U., 1957; PhD in Devel. Clin. Psychology, Yale U., 1961. Assoc. prof. psychology CUNY, 1969-72, chairperson devel. psychology sect. PhD program in edn., 1969-75, acting exec. officer PhD program in edn., 1974-75, prof., 1973-76; dir. Inst. Rsch. on Social Problems, Boulder, 1975—; adj. prof. U. Colo., Boulder, 1980—. Editor: Towards the Elimination of Racism, 1976; co-editor: Eliminating Racism: Profiles in Controversy, 1988, Health Issues for Minority Adolescents, 1995; founding editor: Sex Roles: Jour. Rsch., 1976-91; editor: Jour. Social Issues, 1996-2000; mem. editl. bd. Devel. Psychology, 1992; contbr. chpts. on racism, gender-role rsch., and only-child rsch. to books; also numerous articles. Trustee Colo. Music Festival, 1982-84, pres. bd. trustees, 1984-85; mem. Colo. Women's Forum, 1992—; bd. dirs. Women's Found., Colo., 1986-92. USPHS trainee Yale U., 1956-59; grantee NYU Arts and Sci. Rsch., 1963-66, CUNY Faculty Rsch., 1973, Nat. Inst. Child Health Human Devel., 1966-68, 68-72, 79-81, 81-83, 87-91, 92-97, Office of Child Devel., 1972-75, NIMH, 1977-79. Mem. APA (editor jour. 1974-77, chmn. child advocacy com. 1973, mem. fin. com. 1990-93, coun. rep. 1983-86, 89-92, divsn. pres. 1986-87, fellow divsns. 7, 8, 9, 35 and 45), Soc. Rsch. in Child Devel., Assn. Women in Sci.

KATZ, ROBERT IRWIN, retired physician; b. Springfield, Mass., Dec. 16, 1924; s. Julius Louis and Florence (Greenburg) K. Student, Tufts Coll., 1942-44; MD, Tufts U., 1948. Diplomate Am. Bd. Surgery, Am. Bd. Thoracic Surgery, Nat. Bd. Med. Examiners. Intern Charity Hosp. of La., New Orleans, 1948-49, resident in pathology, 1949-50; resident in gen. surgery Boston City Hosp., 1953-56; resident in surg. oncology Anderson Cancer Ctr. U. Tex., Houston, 1956-57; resident in thoracic surgery VA Hosp., L.A., 1960-61, Children's Hosp., L.A., 1961; chief thoracic surgery V.A. Hosps., Sepulveda/San Fernando, Calif., 1962-70; pvt. practice general and thoracic surgery L.A., 1970-86; head gen. surgery Naval Hosp., Corpus Christie, Tex., 1987; head dept. surgery Naval Hosp., Cherry Point, N.C., 1988-90; surgeon USS New Jersey WES PAC, 1986, 88; ret., 1990; clin. asst. prof. UCLA Med. Ctr., 1969-89, U. So. Calif., L.A., 1964-96. Contbr. articles to profl. jours. Tournament ofcl. So. Calif. Tennis Umpires Assn., L.A., 1972—; commr. Calif. Bd. Medicine, Sacramento, Calif., 1980—. With USN, 1944-45, surgeon USMC, 1950-52, US Merchant Marines, 1953. Recipient clin. fellowship Am. Cancer Soc., Houston, 1957-58. Fellow Am. Coll. Chest Physicians; mem. AAAS, Soc. Thoracic Surgeons, So. Med. Assn., So. Assn. Oncologists, Assn. Mil. Surgeons of U.S., Marine Corps Hist. Soc., Nat. Wildlife Fedn. (life), U.S. Tennis Assn. (life), Naval Res. Assn., M.D. Anderson Assocs. Republican. Jewish. Home and Office: 1733 Centinela Ave Santa Monica CA 90404-4238

KATZ, ROBERT STEPHEN, rheumatologist, educator; b. Balt., July 31, 1944; s. Irving Gilbert and Shirley Ann (Feldman) K.; m. Carlen Jo Levin, Dec. 12, 1972; children: Jeremy, Alexandra, Gena. BA, Columbia U., 1966; MD, U. Md., 1970. Diplomate Am. Bd. Internal Medicine. Fellow in rheumatology Johns Hopkins Hosp., Balt., 1974-76; assoc. prof. medicine Rush-Presbyn. St. Luke's Med. Ctr., Chgo., 1976—; intern Jewish Hosp. St. Louis/Washington U. Med. Ctr., 1970-71, resident in internal medicine, 1971-72; mem., chmn. med. adv. bd. Lupus Found. Ill.; chmn. med. sci. com. No. Ill. chpt. Arthritis Found., 1985-87. Med. editor WBBM-TV, 1991-92, med. editor Fox TV WFLD, 1993—; chmn. Med. Adv. Bd. Chicago Sun-Times Medlife sect.; contbr. articles to profl. jours. Lt. USN, 1970-72. Mem. AMA, Cen. Rheumatism Soc., Am. Coll. Rheumatology, Chgo. Med. Soc. Office: Dept Internal Medicine Rush Presbyn St Luke Med Ctr 1725 W Harrison St Ste 1039 Chicago IL 60612-3828

KATZ, ROGER, pediatrician, educator; b. Menominee, Mich., Feb. 23, 1938; s. Peter W. and Mae C. (Chudacoff) K.; m. Barbara Morguelan, Feb. 6, 1966; children: Carl, Gary, Robyn. BS, U. Wis., 1960; MD, U. Louisville, 1965. Diplomate Am. Bd. Allergy and Immunology, Am. Bd. Pediatric Allergy, Am. Bd. Pediatrics. Clin. prof. pediatrics UCLA, 1978—; spkr. in field; expert legal evaluator. Author and editor sci. books and manuscripts. Maj. U.S. Army, 1970-72. Fellow Am. Acad. Allergy, Asthma and Immunology, Am. Coll. Allergy, Asthma and Immunology (bd. regents 1990-93), Am. Acad. Pediat., Am. Coll. Chest Physicians, Joint Coun. Allergy, Asthma and Immunology (pres. 1986-90). Office: 100 UCLA Med Plz 550 Los Angeles CA 90095-6970

KATZ, SAMUEL LAWRENCE, pediatrician, scientist; b. Manchester, N.H., May 29, 1927; s. Morris and Ethel (Lawrence) K.; m. Betsy Jane Cohan, June 27, 1950; children: Samuel Lawrence Jr. (dec.), John S.L., David L., Deborah Susan, William L., Susan Johanna, Penelope Jennifer; m. Catherine Minock Wilfert, July 23, 1971; stepchildren: Rachel Ann, Katie Claiborne. A.B. magna cum laude, Dartmouth Coll., 1948; M.D. cum laude, Harvard U., 1952; DSc (hon.), Georgetown U., 1996. Intern Beth Israel Hosp., Boston, 1952-53; resident Children's Hosp., Boston, 1953-54, 55-56, Mass. Gen. Hosp., 1954-55; from research fellow to asst. prof. Harvard Med. Sch., 1956-68; prof., chmn. dept. pediatrics Duke Med. Sch., 1968-90, Wilburt C. Davison prof., 1972—; mem. sci. adv. bd. Boston Children's Hosp., Hasbro Children's Found.; chmn. bd. Burroughs Wellcome Fund, Albert Sabin Vaccine Found., Pediat. AIDS Found.; rschr. on virology, virus vaccines and immunization couns. and study sects., pediat. AIDS exec. com. NIH, WHO, Children's Vaccine Initiative; chmn. adv. com. immunization practice Ctrs. for Disease Control, Atlanta, 1985-93. Developer (with John F. Enders) attenuated live measles-virus vaccine; contbr. to books, articles to profl. jours. With USNR, 1945-46. Nat. Found. fellow, 1956-58; NIH Rsch. Career Devel. awardee, 1965-68; recipient Presdl. medal of achievement Dartmouth Coll., 1991. Mem. Am Fedn. Clin. Rsch., Am. Soc. Clin. Investigation, Soc. Pediatric Rsch., Am. Pediatric Soc. (pres. 1986-87, St. Geme award 1988), New Eng. Pediatric Soc., Infectious Diseases Soc. Am. (Bristol award 1988, Soc. citation 1993), Am. Assn. Immunologists, Am. Acad. Pediatrics (Grulee award 1975, Jacobi award 1986), Assn. Med. Sch. Pediatric Dept. Chmn. (pres. 1977-79), Pediatric Infectious Diseases Soc. (Disting. Physician award 1991), Inst. Medicine of NAS. Home: 1917 Wildcat Creek Rd Chapel Hill NC 27516-9786 Office: Duke U Med Ctr PO Box 2925 Durham NC 27715-2925

KATZ, SIDNEY F., obstetrician, gynecologist; b. Detroit, Sept. 5, 1928; m. Sally R. Katz. BS, Wayne State U., 1949; MD, U. Mich., Ann Arbor, 1953. Diplomate Am. Bd. Ob-Gyn. Pvt. practice Dearborn, Mich. Served as capt. USAF, 1954-56. Fellow Am. Coll. Ob-gyn., ACS, Mich. Soc. Gynecologists, So. Mich. Surgical Soc. Office: 4407 Roemer St Dearborn MI 48126-3405

KATZ, STEPHEN ERIC, psychiatrist; b. Topeka, Dec. 23, 1948; s. Jerome Bertram and Alma (Mindel) K.; m. Judith Holiner, May 23, 1971 (div. 1977); m. Jan K. Peimann, June 7, 1980; children: Eric, Natalie, Rachel, Rebecca. MD, U. Kans., Kansas City, 1976. Diplomate Am. Bd. Psychiatry and Neurology. Resident Karl Menninger Sch. Psychiatry, Topeka, 1976-81; staff psychiatrist Meml. Hosp., Topeka, 1979-89, St. Francis Hosp., Topeka, 1981-93, C.F. Menninger Meml. Hosp., Topeka, 1981-93; med. dir. Bloomington Meadows Hosp., 1995—; supr. Karl Menninger Sch. Psychiatry, 1981-93; investigator drug rsch., C.F. Menninger Hosp., 1983-93, cons., 1984-93, chmn. and founder psychopharmacology com., 1984-93. Seeley fellow Menninger Sch. Psychiatry, 1979-80. Democrat. Jewish. Home: 3303 Mulberry Ln Bloomington IN 47401 Office: Meadows Hosp Bloomington IN 47404

KATZ, STEPHEN I., dermatologist; b. Bklyn., Jan. 26, 1941. BA with honors, U. Md., 1962; MD with honors, Tulane U., 1966; PhD in Immunology, U. London, 1974. Diplomate Am. Bd. Dermatology. Chief dermatologist Nat. Cancer Inst./NIH, Bethesda, Md., 1974-95; v.p., rschr. March of Dimes, Fla., 1995—; asst. dermatology Walter Reed Gen. Hosp., Washington, 1970-72; rsch. fellow dept. pathology Royal Coll. Surgeons Eng., London, 1972-74; sr. investigator dermatology Nat. Cancer Inst./NIH, Bethesda, Md., 1974-77, acting chief dermatology br., 1977-80, chief dermatology br., 1980—; Marion B. Sulzberger prof. dermatology Uniformed Svcs. U. Health Scis., Bethesda, 1989-95, acting chmn. dermatology dept., 1993-95; dir. Nat. Inst. Arthritis and Musculoskelatal and Skin Diseases; cons. Georgetown U., 1970-72, Walter Reed Army Hosp., 1975-79, Nat. Naval Med. Ctr., 1976-95, Washington Dermatol. Soc., 1980-81. Editl. bd. Internat. Jour. Dermatology, 1977-81, Jour. Investigative Dermatology, 1979-82, Jour. Am. Acad. Dermatology, 1979-83, Jour. Immunology, 1981-85, Am. Jour. Dermatopathology, Epithelia, 1986-88, Regional Immunology, 1988-95, Medicine, 1992—, Am. Jour. Contact Dermatitis, 1992—, Dermatology Internat., 1992—, Proceedings Assn. Am. Physicians, 1995—, others. Goldberger Summer fellow AMA, 1965, Advanced Tng. fellow Dermatology Found., 1972-74. Mem. Inst. Med.-Nat. Acad. Sci. Office: Nat Cancer Inst Divsn Cancer Biology Diagnosis Ctrs 10 Ctr Dr MSC 1908 Bethesda MD 20892-1908*

KATZ, STEVEN ALAN, urologist; b. N.Y.C., July 19, 1943; s. Eli and Adele (Bottner) K.; m. Meg Katz, June 14, 1988; 1 child, Meghann. BA, NYU, 1965; MD, Buffalo Med. Sch., 1969. Diplomate Am. Bd. Urology. Intern, resident N.Y. Med. Coll., N.Y.C., 1969-76, instr. urology, 1976-77; capt. USAF, Mo., 1970-72; pvt. practice, urology Englewood, N.J., 1977—; chief, dept. urology, Englewood (N.J.) Hosp., 1993—. Mem. Cmty. Chest, Englewood 1994—. Capt., USAF, 1970-72. Fellow ACS; mem. Am. Assn. Clin. Urologists, Am. Urologic Assn., N.J. Med. Soc., Bergen County Med. Soc. Office: 75 South Dean St Englewood NJ 07631

KATZ, STEVEN EDWARD, psychiatrist, state health official; b. Phila., Aug. 10, 1937; s. Benjamin R. and Charlotte (Tomkins) K.; m. Marjorie A. Billstein, June 12, 1960; children: Barri L. Stryer, Stacey J. Herron. BA, Cornell U., 1959; MD, Hahnemann U., 1963. Cert. psychoanalyst, Columbia U., 1972. Diplomate Am. Bd. Psychiatry and Neurology. Intern Montefiore Hosp., Bronx, N.Y., 1963-64; resident Columbia U. N.Y. Psychiat. Inst., N.Y.C., 1966-69; dir. edn. dept. psychiatry Roosevelt Hosp., N.Y.C., 1971-74, assoc. dir., 1974-78; med. dir. dept. psychiatry Bellevue Hosp., N.Y.C., 1979-83; vice-chmn. dept. psychiatry NYU Med. Ctr., 1980-83, prof. psychiatry, 1987—, exec. vice-chmn. dept. psychiatry, 1987-94; commr. N.Y. State Office of Mental Health, Albany, 1983-87; dir. psychiatry Bellevue Hosp., 1987-91, dir. health policy NYU Med. Ctr., 1987-93, med. dir. dept. psychiatry, Tisch Hosp., 1992-94; clin. prof. psychiatry Albany Med. Coll., 1984-87; exec. v.p., med. dir. Jackson Brook Inst., Maine, 1994—; med. dir. Integrated Physician Svcs., Inc., 1994—; clin. prof. Sch. Medicine U. Vt., 1994—; exec. v.p., chief med. officer Cmty. Care Sys., Wellesley, Mass., 1996—. Contbr. articles to profl. jours., publs. and book chpts. Bd. dirs. Facilities Devel. Corp., Albany, 1983-87, Am. Mental Health Fund, 1983—, League Ctr., N.Y.C., 1988—, Vis. Nurse Svc., N.Y.C., 1992—; mem. Bd. Profl. Med. Conduct N.Y. State Health Dept., Albany, 1994—; bd. dirs. York Shelter, Alfred, Maine, 1995—. Capt. U.S. Army, 1964-66. Recipient Pub. Svc. award N.Y. Psychol. Soc., 1984, Pub. Svc. award Suffolk County Mental Health Assn., 1984, Exceptional Achievement award N.Y. State Office Mental Health, 1985, Governing Bd. award Crotona Park Cmty. Mental Health Ctr., 1985, Pub. Svc. award N.Y. State Psychol. Assn., 1986, Pub. Svc. award for outstanding achievement Am. Assn. for Affirmative Action, 1986, Alexander P. Braile award, 1986, Horace M. Kallen Disting. Cmty. Svc. award Am. Jewish Congress, 1987, William E. Byron award N.Y. State chpt. Assn. Mental Health Adminstrs., 1987; Cert. of Recognition Hosp. Assn. N.Y., 1991. Fellow Am. Psychiat. Assn. (commendation 1983), Am. Coll. Psychiatry (chair com. on fin. 1996—); mem. AMA, Group for Advancement of Psychiatry, Am. Assn. Psychiat. Adminstrs. (Disting. Psychiat. Adminstr. award N.Y. regional chpt. 1990), Hosp. Assn. of N.Y. State (cert. of recognition 1991). Democrat. Office: Jackson Brook Inst 175 Running Hill Rd South Portland ME 04106

KATZ, TODD ALAN, ophthalmologist; b. Bklyn., May 15, 1960; s. Bernard and Barbara K.; m. Diane E. Powell, Sept. 6, 1986. BS, SUNY, 1982, MD. Intern, resident Interfaith Med. Ctr., Bklyn.; fellow in vitreoretinal disease Touro Infirmary, New Orleans; ophthalmologist, retinal specialist Eye Associates, Kingston, N.Y., 1991—. Mem. N.Y. State Ophthalmology Soc. (bd. dirs. 1993—), Phi Beta Kappa. Office: Eye Assocs 40 Hurley Ave Kingston NY 12401

KATZ, WARREN ALLEN, rheumatologist; b. Phila., June 20, 1936; s. Milton Sidney and Elizabeth (Abrams) K.; m. Ellen Paul, June 30, 1974; children: Jamie, Heidi, Greg. BA, Temple U., 1957; MD, Jefferson Med. Coll., 1961. Intern Albert Einstein Med. Ctr., Phila., 1961-62; resident Boston City Hosp., 1962-63, Mt. Sinai Hosp., N.Y.C., 1964-65; teaching fellow in rheumatic diseases Tuft's New England Med. Ctr., Boston, 1963-64, NYU Med. Ctr., 1965-66; chief divsn. rheumatology Med. Coll. Pa., Phila., 1974-86; chief divsn. rheumatology Presbyn. Med. Ctr., Phila., 1986—, chmn. dept. medicine, 1988—; clin. prof. medicine U. Pa. Sch. MEdicine, 1988—; mem. adv. bd. NIH Info. Clearinghouse, 1979-81; chmn. Gov.'s Adv. Bd. Arthritis, Pa., 1980-86; pres. Arthritis Assocs., P.C., 1966—, ARthritis Profl. Svcs., 1978—, Med. Cons. Svcs., 1994—, Salitron Dry Mouth Ctrs. Am., 1988; v.p. Medifit of Am., 1985-91; pres., chmn. bd. trustees Internal Medicine Found., 1987—. Author: Diagnosis and Management of Rheumatic Diseases, 1977, 2d edit., 1988. Chpt. del. Nat. Arthritis Found., Atlanta, 1966—, bd. dirs., 1980—; pres. ea. Pa. chpt. Arthritis Found., Phila., 1976-78; arthritis chmn. Gov.'s Task Force, Harrisburg, Pa., 1976-77; bd. dirs. Moss Rehab. Hosp., 1980—, vice chmn., 1985—, chmn. rsch. com., 1985—. Recipient Nat. Vol. Citation Arthritis Found., 1974, 78. Fellow Am. Coll. Rheumatology, ACP (life); mem. AMA, Am. Coll. Physician Execs., Phila. Rheumatism Soc. (pres. 1974-75), Pa. Med. Soc. (ho. of dels. 1983-84), Phila. County Med. Soc. (health care subcom. 1990). Office: Presbyn Med Ctr Phila 39th and Market Sts Philadelphia PA 19104

KATZ, WILLIAM DAVID, psychologist, psychoanalytic psychotherapist, educator, mental health consultant; b. N.Y.C., Sept. 14, 1915; s. Charles and Esther (Dann) K. AB, Bklyn. Coll., 1940; MA, NYU, 1942, PhD, 1953. Diplomate Am. Bd. Med. Psychotherapists (fellow) 1986, Am. Acad. Behavioral Medicine (fellow) 1986. Clin. intern and resident Hillside Hosp., 1950-53; pvt. practice as cons. psychologist and psychotherapist, N.Y., Fla., 1942—; staff psychotherapist Palms West Hosp., Fla., Wellington Regional Med. Ctr., Fla.; cons. psychologist Human Rels. Guidance Ctr., 1946-56; exec. dir. Civic Ctr. Clinic, Bklyn. Assn. Rehab. Offenders, Inc., 1951-55, Play Rsch. Inst., Inc., 1953-57; psychotherapist Group for Community Guidance Ctrs., 1955-57; psychotherapist Mental Health Inst., 1957-59, assoc. dir., 1957, exec. dir., 1958; clin. assoc. Psychol. Svc. Ctr., N.Y.C., 1968—; supr. psychotherapy Met. Ctr. Mental Health, N.Y.C., 1969—; asst. prof. psychology L.I. U., 1958-64, assoc. prof., 1964-70, prof., 1970-82, prof. emeritus, 1982—, asst. chmn. psychology dept., 1963-72, 74-76, acting chmn., 1966, 75; prof. U.S. Army Chaplain Ctr. and Sch., Fort Wadsworth, Fort Hamilton, 1970-77; psychotherapist Counseling & Psychotherapy Associates, 1986-87. Assoc. editor Am. Imago, 1978-83, Am. Psychol. Assn., 1950—; contbr. articles to profl. jours. Recipient Cross of Honor, La Fundacion Internat., Eloy Alfaro, 1964. Fellow Am. Internat. Acad. (cert. and medallion 1957), Assn. Applied Psychoanalysis (exec. sec. 1963-67, 78-79, pres. 1968-69, 74-75); mem. AAAS, Am. Acad. Polit. and Social Scis., Interam. Soc. Psychology, Am. Acad. Psychotherapists, AAUP, Soc. Clin. and Exptl. Hypnosis, Coun. Psychoanalytic Psychotherapists, Am. Psychol. Assn., N.Y. State Psychol. Assn., N.Y. Soc. Clin. Psychologists, Bklyn. Psychol. Assn. (pres. 1971-72), N.Y. Acad. Scis., S.I. Mental Health Soc., Nat. Register Health Services Provider in Psychology, Bklyn. Assn. Mental Health, Pa., Richmond County Psychol. Assn. (pres. 1975), Palm Beach County Mental Health Assn., NYU Alumni Assn., KP Lodge (past chancellor), Shriners, Masons (past master), Psi Chi, Alpha Phi Omega, Tau Delta Phi. Home: 116 Village Walk Dr West Palm Beach FL 33411-2995

KATZBERG, JANE MICHAELS, health care administrator, consultant; b. Bklyn., Apr. 17, 1940; d. David Donn and Shirley (Ingram) Michaels; m. Mitchell Ronald Katzberg, Jan. 19, 1959; children: Michael Loren, Todd Alexander. BS, Adelphi U., 1961; M of Profl. Studies in Health Care Adminstrn., L.I. U., 1975. Cert. home economist, tchr., N.Y. Mgr. quality assurance Suffolk Physicians, Central Islip, N.Y., 1979-81; dir. quality assurance Community Hosp. of Glen Cove, N.Y., 1982-84; dir. intermediate care facilities program United Cerebral Palsy, Commack, N.Y., 1985-86; dir. svcs. for handicapped Town of Huntington, L.I., N.Y., 1986-95; pres., cons. Images, Dix Hills, N.Y., 1985-88; cons. JMK Cons., pres., 1994—; lectr. in field. Mem. Citizen's Adv. Com. for Handicapped, Town of Huntington, 1985-86; mem. selection and steering com. C. of C. Found., 1993-96, Leadership Round Table, Huntington Health and Human Svcs. steering com., 1992-94, Huntington Hosp. Dolan Cmty. Health Ctr. Bd., 1992-96; mem. adv. bd. Dept. Social Svcs., Huntington, L.I., 1986-96, Devel. Ctr., Melville Estates, 1989-96; facilitator Nat. Orgn. Disability award N.Y. State Eleanor Roosevelt award for Town Huntington; pres. Howell Rd. Sch. PTA, North Valley Stream, N.Y., 1973; meeting rep. N.Y. State Advocate for Disabled, 1986-95; mem. divsn. dirs. Cmty. Resource Dept., 1986-89, divsn. dirs. human svcs., 1989-95. Acad. scholar C.W. Post Coll., Greenvale, N.Y., 1974. Mem. Assn. Local Govt. Advocates for Disabled. Republican. Jewish. Home: 81 Buttonwood Dr Dix Hills NY 11746-4804

KATZENELLENBOGEN, BENITA SCHULMAN, physiology and cell biology educator; b. N.Y.C., Apr. 11, 1945; d. Max and Miriam G. (Schulman); 2 children. BA, Bklyn. Coll., 1965; MA, Harvard U., 1966, PhD in Biology, 1970. Rsch. fellow endocrinology NIH, 1970-71; from asst. prof. to prof. U. Ill. Coll. Medicine, Urbana, 1970-82; prof. physiology, cell and structural biology U. Ill., Urbana, 1982—; vis. prof. dept. biochem. and biophys. U. Calif., San Francisco, 1977-78; mem. endocrinology study sect. NIH, 1979-83, biochem. endocrinology study sect., 1995—; mem. sci. bd. Nat. Inst. Diabetes, Digestive and Kidney Diseases, 1983-87; mem. internat. orgn. com. Internat. Congress on Hormones and Cancer, 1987—; co-chmn. Gordon Rsch. Conf. Hormone Action, 1988; mem. Waterman award com. NSF, 1989-91. Recipient Young Scholar award AAUW, 1981, Merit award NIH, 1991—. Fellow Am. Acad. Arts and Scis.; mem. Am. Physiol. Soc., Endocrine Soc. (pubs. com. 1981-83, program com. 1983-87, coun. 1989-92), Am. Assn. Cancer Rsch. (task force endocrinology 1987-89), Soc. Study Reprodn., Internat. Soc. Endocrinology (ctrl. com. 1988—), Am. Cancer Soc. (adv. com. on biochemistry and endocrinology, 1989-93, Ernst Oppenheimer award for meritorious rsch. 1984). Home: 704 W Pennsylvania Ave Urbana IL 61801-4821 Office: Dept Physiol and Biophys U Ill 524 Burrill Hall 407 S Goodwin Ave Urbana IL 61801-3704

KATZMAN, MERLE HERSHEL, orthopaedic surgeon; b. Hartford, Conn., Aug. 28, 1928; s. Samuel Sidney and Bertha (Hirshberg) K.; m. Charna Lytell, June 26, 1955; children: Beth, Amy, Sam, Robert. BS, Trinity Coll., 1950; MD, Jefferson Med. Coll., 1954. Diplomate Am. Bd. Orthopaedic Surgery. Intern Hartford (Conn.) Hosp., 1954-55, resident in surgery, 1957-58; surgeon N.Y. Ortheopaedic Hosp., 1958-61; attending orthopaedic surgeon, chief orthopaedic dept. Englewood Hosp., 1965-80; with Katzman, Tarsney & Feldman, Tenafly, N.J., 1994—; ret., 1994; mem. credentials com., exec. com., chmn. future devel. com., Englewood Hosp. Lt. USNR, 1955-57. Fellow ACS, Am. Acad. Orthopaedic Surgeons, Bergen County Med. Soc. (del., health ins. review com. mem.), N.J. State Med. Soc., N.J. Orthopaedic Soc. (exec. com. pres. 1977-78), Stannard Beach Assn. (exec. com. mem., pres.-elect). Office: Katzman Tarsney & Feldman 111 Dean Dr Tenafly NJ 07670-2708

KATZMAN, ROBERT, medical educator, neurologist; b. Denver, Nov. 29, 1925; s. Maurice and Leah K. (Schnitt) K.; m. Nancy Bernstein, Sept. 2, 1947; children: David Jonathan, Daniel Mark. BS, U. Chgo., 1949, MS, 1951; MD cum laude, Harvard U., 1953. Diplomate Am. Bd. Psychiatry and Neurology. Intern Boston City Hosp., 1953-54; chief resident Neurol. Inst. Columbia Presbyn. Hosp., N.Y.C., 1956-57; faculty mem. Albert Einstein Coll. Medicine, N.Y.C., 1957-84, prof., chmn. neurology dept., 1964-84, dir. Resnick Gerontology Ctr., 1979-84; chmn. dept. neurosci. U. Calif., San Diego, 1984-90, Florence Riford prof. neurosci. and rsch. in Alzheimer's disease, 1984-94, rsch. prof. neurosci., 1994—; mem. clin. rsch. adv. com. Nat. Found. March of Dimes, 1975-76; mem. adv. coun. Nat. Inst. on Aging, 1982-85; chmn. med. and sci. bd. Alzheimer Disease and Related Disorders Assn., Chgo., 1979-85; mem. adv. panel on Alzheimer's disease HHS, 1987-93. Co-author: Brain Electrolytes and Fluid Metabolism, 1973, Neurology of Aging, 1983; co-editor: Basic Neurochemistry, 1972-81, Principles of Geriatric Neurology, 1992, Alzheimer's Disease, 1994. Served with USN, 1944-46, PTO. Recipient Humanitarian Award Alzheimer's Disease and Related Disorders Assn., 1985, Disting. Svc. award, 1989, Allied Achievement in Aging award Allied Signal Corp., 1985, Henderson Meml. award Am. Geriatric Soc., 1986, 7th Ann. Chgo. Rita Hayworth Gala award recipient, Alzheimer's Assn., 1994. Fellow Am. Acad. Neurology (S. Weir Mitchell award 1960, George W. Jacoby award 1989, co-recipient Potamkin prize for Alzheimer's disease rsch. 1992); mem. Assn. for Rsch. in Nervous and Mental Disorders (pres. 1977), Am. Physiol. Soc. (cons.) Inst. Medicine, Am. Neurol. Assn. (pres. 1985-86), Internat. Soc. for Alzheimer's Disease Rsch. (pres. 1996—), Alpha Omega Alpha. Office: U Calif Sch Medicine Dept Neurosci Alzheimers Disease Rsch 9500 Gilman Dr # 0949 La Jolla CA 92093-0949

KATZUNG, BERTRAM GEORGE, pharmacologist; b. Mineola, N.Y., June 11, 1932; m. Alice V. Camp; children: Katharine Blanche, Brian Lee. BA, Syracuse U., 1953; MD, SUNY, Syracuse, 1957; PhD, U. Calif., San Francisco, 1962. Prof. U. Calif., San Francisco, 1958—. Author: Drug Therapy, 1991, Pharmacology, Examination and Board Review, 1995; contbr. to profl. jours. Markle scholar. Mem. AAAS, AAUP, Am. Soc. Pharmacology and Exptl. Therapeutics, Biophysical Soc., Fed. Am. Scientists, Internat. Soc. Heart Rsch., Soc. Gen. Physiologists, Western Pharmacology Soc., N.Y. Acad. Sci., Phi Beta Kappa, Alpha Omega Alpha, Golden Gate Computer Soc. Office: UCSF Dept Pharmacology PO Box 0450 San Francisco CA 94143

KAUDEWITZ, FRITZ, genetics educator; b. Breslau, Germany, Mar. 11, 1921; s. Paul and Aloisia (Sendler) K.; m. Gertrud Wagner, Mar. 24, 1951; children: Peter, Wolfgang. Dr.rer.nat., U. Tübingen, Germany, 1949. Asst. Max Plank Inst. for Biochemistry, Tübingen, 1950-59; habiltation U. Tübingen, 1956; dir. M.P.I. for Erbiol., Berlin, 1960-64; prof., dir. Inst. Genetics U. Munich, 1963-86, prof. emeritus, 1986—. Author 4 books in field; contbr. articles to profl. publs. Recipient Emil V. Behring medal U. Marburg, 1960, Golden Plate award Acad. Achievement, 1960. Roman Catholic. Home: Hermelinweg 5, 81549 Munich Germany Office: Inst Genetics & Microbiol, Maria-Ward Str 1a, 81549 Munich Germany

KAUFENBERG, PATRICIA ANN, health facility administrator; b. Shakopee, Minn., Dec. 14, 1938; d. Clemens H. and Cecelia M. (Pauly) Lenzmeier; m. Ronald M. Kaufenberg, Apr. 8, 1961 (div. 1992); children: Nancy Martinson, Karen Gibney, Liza. Diploma in nursing, St. Mary's Sch. Nursing, 1959; BA in Nursing, Coll. of St. Catherine, 1987. RN, Minn.; cert. nursing adminstr. RN St. Mary's Hosp., Mpls., 1959-62, Sanford Meml. Hosp., Farmington, Minn., 1962-65, River's Edge Clinic, Farmington, 1965-75; nurse Ob.-Gyn. Ltd., Mpls., 1975-76; RN mgr. Meth.-Univ. Family Practice, St. Louis, 1976-78; RN supr. St. Louis Park Med. Ctr., Minnetonka, Minn., 1978-80; RN nursing leader Eden Prairie (Minn.) Family Physicians, 1980-93; RN clinic mgr. Park Nicollet Clinic, Eden Prairie, 1993—. Mem. St. Catherine's Alumni Assn., Am. Acad. Ambulatory Care Nursing, Minn. Nurses Assn., Sigma Theta Tau. Home: 189 Glenmoor Ln Long Lake MN 55356

KAUFFMAN, DANIEL J., psychologist; b. Johnstown, Pa., Apr. 19, 1947; s. John Daniel and Mary Kauffman; m. Bonnie Smith, Aug. 1969 (div. 1981); children: Marsha, Michele; m. Lois J. Kauffman, June 17, 1983. BS in Spl. Edn., Clarion U., 1969; MEd in Counseling, Shippensburg U., 1971; EdD in Spl. Edn., U. Mo., 1976. Psychologist Warren State Hosp., North Warren, Pa. Mem. APA, Am. Assn. on Mental Retardation, Coun. for Exceptional

Children, Am. Assn. on Behl Therapy. Office: Warren State Hosp 33 Main Dr Warren PA 16365-5001

KAUFFMAN, JEFFREY MICHAEL, psychotherapist; b. Phila., Pa., Dec. 29, 1942; s. Raymond and Florence (Packer) K.; m. Hilda Reagan; 1 child, Daniel; 1 stepchild, Will Gorham. MA, New Sch. for Social Rsch., 1977; MSS, Bryn Mawr Sch. of Social Work, 1985; postgrad., Inst. for Psychoanalytic, Phila. Cert. profl. death counselor. Dir. Ctr. for the Care of Community Insts., Upper Darby, Pa., 1988—, Grief Counseling and Support Svcs., Upper Darby, Pa., 1988—; bereavement cons. various groups in Phila. area including Families of Murder Victims, MADD, also numerous retardation ags. Editor: Awareness of Mortality, 1995; contbr. articles to profl. jours. Mem. adv. bd. Job Corps, Phila. br., 1988-91; bd. dirs. Families of Murder Victims, Phila., 1989-93. Recipient Svc. Awd. Leukemia Soc. Southeastern Pa., 1988. Mem. NASW, Assn. for Death Edn. and Counseling (pres. Del.-Pa. chpt. 1989-93), Pa. Soc. Clin. SocialWork (program chmn. 1991-93). Office: Ctr Care Community Instns PO Box 155 Saint Peters PA 19470-0155

KAUFMAN, DAVID I., neuro-ophthalmologist, educator; b. Phila., Apr. 17, 1951; s. Soloman and Molly (Glickstein) K.; m. Laryssa Nahirniak, Aug. 17, 1974; children: Matthew, Sarah. BS, U. Wis., 1973; DO, Phila. Coll. Osteo. Medicine, 1978. Diplomate Am. Bd. Psychology and Neurology. Resident neurology U. Wis., Madison, 1979-82, fellow neuro-physiology, 1982-83; fellow in neuro-ophthalmology Mass. Gen. Hosp., Boston, 1983-84; asst. prof. Mich. State U., East Lansing, 1984-88, assoc. prof., 1988-96, prof., 1996—, dir. neurovisual unit, 1986—; dir. Consortium of Osteo. Residencies in Ophthalmology, East Lansing, 1988—; med. dir. Sparrow Neuroscis., 1993—; rschr. on prognosis and treatment strategy of optic nerve disease. Republican. Jewish. Office: Mich State Univ A-217 MSU Clin Ctr East Lansing MI 48824

KAUFMAN, DAVID MARC, pediatric neurologist; b. Bronx, N.Y., July 10, 1945; s. Harold M. and Edna M. (Markowitz) K.; m. Harriet B. Kaufman, June 30, 1968; 1 child, Jill R. BS, Union Coll., 1967; MD, Boston U. Sch. of Medicine, 1975. Diplomate Am. Bd. Pediatrics. Intern-resident N.Y. Hosp., N.Y.C., 1975-77; resident-fellow Mt. Sinai Med. Ctr., N.Y.C., 1977-80; pvt. practice in pediatrics N.Y.C., 1980—; mem. admissions com. Mt. Sinai Sch. of Medicine, N.Y.C., 1992—, ethics com. Child Neurology Soc., Mpls., 1995—; adv. bd. Winston Prep Sch. Spl. Edn. Sch., N.Y.C., 1990, Young Adult Inst., N.Y.C., 1995—. Author: (with others) The Founders of Child Neurology, 1990. Fellow Am. Acad. Pediatrics; mem. Am. Acad. Neurology, Child Neurology Soc. Office: 3 E 83rd St New York NY 10028

KAUFMAN, DENISE NORMA, psychologist, addictions counselor, educator; b. Trenton, N.J., Feb. 7, 1954; d. Charles Edwin and Luella (Barcroft) Farr; m. Peter Alan Kaufman, May 15, 1986 (div. Nov. 1989). BS, Trenton State Coll., 1976, MEd, 1977; EdD, Temple U., 1983. Cert. tchr. health, driver edn., spl. edn., N.J., cert. sch. psychologist, cert. addictions counselor, cert. in student per. svcs., N.J. Health edn. tchr., dept. dir. Haddon Heights (N.J.) Pub. Schs., 1976-81; tchr. educationally handicapped adolescents Haddon Twp. (N.J.) High Sch., 1984-85; tchr. educationally handicapped adolescents, psychologist Archway Programs, Atco, N.J., 1984-90; tchr., psychologist Ferris Sch. for Boys, Dept. Children, Youth and Families, Wilmington, Del., 1991-92; tchr., cons. psychologist Willingboro (N.J.) Twp. Pub. Schs., 1991-92; pvt. practice psychology, addictions counselor Haddon Heights, 1979—; psychologist Atlantic County Spl. Svcs. Sch. Dist., Mays Landing, N.J., 1992-93; prof., supr. student interns Rowan Coll. of N.J., Glassboro, 1993-95; adj. prof. psychology Camden County Coll., Blackwood, N.J., 1993—; psychologist, coord. mental health Little Neighborhood Ctrs., Phila., 1995-96; behavior specialist United Health and Human Svcs., North Wales, Pa., 1996—; mem. Gov. Brendan Byrne's Smoking and Health Com., 1978-80; assoc. prof. health edn. Mercer County Community Coll., Trenton, 1981; program dir. Phila. (Pa.) Health Mgmt. Corp., 1982; cons. Clearview Regional High Sch., Jr. High Sch. Pub. Sch. Dist., 1986—, Lower Camden County Regional Sch. Dist., 1986—; lectr. Assn. Schs. and Agys. for the Handicapped, 1986—; cons., lectr. Charter Fairmont Inst., Phila., 1991—. Instr. Camden chpt. ARC, S.E. Pa. chpt. Am. Heart Assn.; lectr., cons. Haddon Heights (N.J.) Rotary, 1988—. Mem. APA, ACA, NJCA, Eta Sigma Gamma, Kappa Delta Pi. Home: 1604 Chestnut Ave Haddon Heights NJ 08035-1506 Office: United Health and Human Svcs 1201 Bethlehem Pike Ste 210 North Wales PA 19454

KAUFMAN, ELIZABETH SUITS, internist, electrophysiologist; b. Yonkers, N.Y., Feb. 12, 1960; d. Thomas A. and Alice-Mae (Buell) Suits; m. Stephen Richard Kaufman, Dec. 18, 1983; children: Michael Koch, Evan Thomas. BA in Molecular Biophysics, Biochemistry, Yale U., 1981; MD, Harvard U., 1985. Diplomate Am. Bd. Internal Medicine with subspecialty in cardiovascular disease, clin. cardiac electrophysiology. Resident in internal medicine Columbia-Presbyn. Med. Ctr., N.Y.C., 1985-88, cardiology fellow, 1988-91; sr. instr. Case Western Res. U., Cleve., 1991—; dir. cardiac electrophysiology Metrohealth Med. Ctr., Cleve., 1991—. Recipient Hart Lyman prize for acad. excellence Yale U., 1980. Fellow Am. Coll. Cardiologists; mem. N.Am. Soc. Pacing and Electrophysiology, Am. Heart Assn. (coun. basic sci.), N.E. Ohio Soc. Pacing and Electrophysiology (bd. dirs. 1993—), Phi Beta Kappa. Office: MetroHealth Med Ctr 2500 Metrohealth Dr Cleveland OH 44109

KAUFMAN, HARVEY ISIDORE, neuropsychology consultant; b. Virginia, Minn., May 13, 1937; s. Carl and Marcia (Borkon) K.; m. Glenda Kaufman, Oct. 16, 1971; children: Jason Alexis, Justin Bram. BA, U. Minn., Duluth, 1959, BS cum laude, 1960; MA, U. Minn., Mpls., 1961; PhD, Marquette U., 1967, Southwest U., 1992. Fellow and diplomate Am. Bd. Neuropsychology, Am. Bd. Med. Psychotherapists; Diplomate Internat. Acad. of Behavioral Medicine; cert. in clin. hypnosis. Psychology supr. Winnebago (Wis.) Mental Health Inst., 1971-75; dir. outpatient svcs. Health Care Ctr., Fond du Lac, Wis., 1975-81; neuropsychologist Sharpe Clinic, Fond du Lac, 1983-89, St. Mary's Hosp., Milw., 1986-89; cons. Fond du Lac, 1990—; cons. in neurology Racine, 1992—. Fellow dept. neurology med. sch. U. Wis., 1981-82. Mem. Am. Psychol. Assn., Wis. Psychol. Assn., Nat. Acad. Neuropsychologists, Am. Soc. Clin. Hypnosis, Internat. Soc. Clin. Hypnosis, Internat. Neuropsychol. Soc., Internat. Acad. Behavioral Medicine. Home and Office: 409 Berkley Pl Fond Du Lac WI 54935-5205

KAUFMAN, HERBERT EDWARD, ophthalmologist, educator; b. N.Y.C., Sept. 28, 1931; s. Benjamin and Claire (Krinsky) K.; m. Maija H. Uotila; children: Stephen, Joshua, Claire. A.B. magna cum laude, Princeton U., 1952; M.D. magna cum laude, Harvard U., 1956. Intern Mass. Gen. Hosp., Boston, 1956-57; resident Mass. Eye and Ear Infirmary, Boston, 1959-62; assoc. prof., chief div. ophthalmology Coll. Medicine, U. Fla., 1962-64, prof., chmn. dept., 1964-77, prof. pharmacology, 1970-77; acting dean Coll. Medicine, U. Fla. (Coll. Medicine), 1972; prof., head dept. ophthalmology La. State U. Med. Ctr., 1978—, Boyd prof., ophthalmology, pharmacology, and exceptional therapeutics, 1985—; med. dir. Eye, Ear Nose and Throat Hosp. La., 1978-84; chmn. tng. com. Nat. Eye Inst., 1970-71, mem. nat. eye adv. council, 1978-82, 1993-96; Pocklington lectr. Royal Coll. Surgeons, 1979; Jackson Meml. lectr., 1979, Maxwell K. Bochner Meml. lectr., 1978, Proctor lectr., 1981, Thorpe Meml. lectr., 1982, Jack S. Guyton lectr., 1982, Dunphy Meml. lectr., 1983, Waldert Meml. lectr., 1983, First Wohl Meml. lectr., 1983, Glover-Lisman lectr., 1983, G. Victor Simpson lectr., 1984, Peter Kronfield Meml. lectr., 1984, Irvine lectr., 1986, Earl Padfield Meml. lectr., 1987, Montgomery lectr., 1987, 1st Claes Dohlman lectr., 1991; adv. bd. Dry Eye Inst., 1985—; gen. com. revision U.S. Pharmocopeial Conv., 1985. Editorial bd. Am. Jour. Ophthalmology; editor: Investigative Ophthalmology, 1972-77; contbr. articles profl. jours. Served with USPHS, 1957-59. Recipient Lions Humanitarian award, 1968; R. Townley Payton award, 1983, Lacrima award Dry Eye Inst., 1984, Sr. Honor award Am. Acad. Ophthalmology, 1984, Castroviejo award, 1987, Physician's Recognition award, 1987, Montgomery medal, 1987, Innovator's award Am. Soc. Cataract and Refractive Surgery, 1990. Fellow AAAS, A.C.S., Am. Coll. Clin. Pharmacology; mem Am. Assn. Immunologists, Am. Assn. Ophthalmology, Am. Fedn. Clin. Research, AMA, Am. Soc. Microbiology, Am. Soc. Clin Investigation, Assn. Research Vision and Ophthalmology (pres. 1975), Assn. U. Profs. Ophthalmology (trustee, pres. 1980), Pan Am. Assn. Ophthalmology (mem. council), Am. Soc. Contemporary Ophthalmology (pres.), Am. Acad. Ophthalmology and Otolaryngology, Eye Bank Assn. Am. (dir.), N.Y. Acad. Scis., Eye Bank Assn. Am. (bd. dirs. 1985—), Com. Study Nat. Needs for Biomed. and Behavioral Research Personnel, Contact Lens Assn. Ophthalmologists (pres. 1979), Soc. Exptl. Biology and Medicine, Royal Soc. Medicine, Can. Implant Assn. (hon.), Ophthal. Soc. Finland (hon.) Sigma Xi. Office: La State U Eye Center 2020 Gravier St Suite B New Orleans LA 70112

KAUFMAN, JEFFREY LAWRENCE, surgeon; b. L.A., Oct. 29, 1950; s. Julius A. and Ellen (Schenfield) K.; m. Katherine C. Eisenmenger, July 20, 1986; 1 child, Audrey Anne. BS, MIT, 1972; MD, U. Calif., San Francisco, 1976. Diplomate Am. Bd. Surgery. Asst. prof. surgery Rutgers Med. Sch., UMDNJ, New Brunswick, N.J., 1982-86; assoc. prof. surgery Albany (N.Y.) Med. Coll., 1986-91, Tufts U. Sch. of Medicine, 1991—; surgeon Baystate Med. Ctr., Springfield, Mass., 1991—. Fellow ACS; mem. Internat. Soc. for Cardiovascular Surgery, Mass. Med. Soc., Ea. Vascular Soc. Office: Division Vascular Surgery Baystate Med Ctr Springfield MA 01199

KAUFMAN, JEROME BENZION, neurosurgeon; b. Waterloo, Iowa, July 22, 1934; s. Louis and Dorothy (Rosenbloom) K.; m. Judith Ellen Lasker, June 29, 1967; children: David, Jonathan, Jefferey. BA, Wayne State U., 1955, MD, 1961; postgrad., U. Madrid. Diplomate Am. Bd. Neurol. Surgery, 1975. Rotating intern Michael Reese Hosp. and Med. Ctr., Chgo., 1961-62; resident in internal med. Michael Reeese Hosp. and Med. Ctr., Chgo., 1962-63; resident in gen. surgery VA Hosp., Bronx, 1965-66, resident in neurology, 1966, resident in neurosurgery, 1967, from sr. to chief resident neurosurgery, 1969-70; resident neurosurgery Neurol. Inst. N.Y., Columbia Presbyn. Hosp., 1968; resident neuropathology Mt. Sinai Hosp. and Med. Sch., N.Y.C., 1968; chief resident neurosurgery City Hosp., Elmhurst, N.Y., 1969; chmn. dept. neurosurgery Carle Clinic Assn. and Found. Hosp., Urbana, Ill., 1972—; cons. neurosurgery McKinley Hosp., Urbana, Covenant Hosp., Urbana; asst. instr. internal medicine Chgo. Med. Sch., 1963; clin. assoc. prof. neurosurgery U. Ill. Coll. Medicine, Urbana, 1982—. Contbr. articles to profl. jours. Served to capt. USAF, 1963-65. Fellow ACS, Am. Assn. Neurol. Surgeons (Continuing Edn. award in neurosurgery 1980, 83, 85, 87, 89, 93, 96), Internat. Coll. Surgeons (vice regent) N.Y. Acad. Scis.; mem. AMA (Physicians Recognition award 1980, 82, 85, 89, 93), Ill. Med. Soc., Champaign County Med. Soc., Congress Neurol. Surgeons, Ctrl. Neurosurg. Soc., Assn. Mil. Surgeons U.S., Chgo. Neurol. Soc. Home: 2104 Zuppke Dr Urbana IL 61801-6706 Office: 602 W University Ave Carle Clinic Assn Urbana IL 61801

KAUFMAN, JOHN PEARSE, dermatologist, educator; b. Durham, N.C., Sept. 9, 1944; s. William Henry and Elizabeth (Pearse) K.; m. Linda Sargent, Jan. 29, 1972; children: Elizabeth, William. AB, Duke U., 1966; MD, U. Va., 1970. Intern U. Mich., Ann Arbor, 1970-71, chief dermatology resident, 1973-74; chief cons. dermatologist USAFE, Wiesbaden, Germany, 1974-77; pvt. practice dermatology Roanoke, Va., 1977—; clin. asst. prof., dept. dermatology U. Va. Med. Ctr., Charlottesville, Va., 1977—; cons. staff Community Hosp. of the Roanoke Valley, 1977-92; sec. Roanoke (Va.) Acad. Medicine, 1980-81. Contbr. articles to profl. jours. Maj. USAF, 1974-77. Fellow Am. Acad. Dermatology, Am. Soc. Dermatol. Surgery; mem. AMA, Am. Soc. Dermatologic Surgery, Southwestern Va. Med. Soc. (pres. 1987-88), Med. Soc. Va., Va. Dermatol. Soc. (pres. 1986-87), Assn. Mil. Dermatologists (life), Alpha Omega Alpha.

KAUFMAN, LOUISE SUSAN, pharmaceutical company executive; b. S.I., N.Y., Dec. 4, 1952; d. Santo Michael and Selma Mary (Sidoti) Repage; m. Peter Joseph Kaufman, Sept. 18, 1976. BS, Wagner Coll., 1975, MS, 1978; MBA, St. John's U., 1983. Vet. technician Hylan Animal Hosp., S.I., 1972-75; vet. abstractor Merck & Co., Inc., Rahway, N.J., 1975-78, regulatory affairs asst., 1978-79, sr. regulatory coordinator, 1979-82, mgr. registration, 1982-85; dir. regulatory affairs internat. Warner-Lambert Co., 1985-88, sr. dir., 1988-94, v.p. 1994—. Mem. Pharm. Mfg. Assn. (mem. internat. regulatory affairs com. 1987—, mem. clinical safe surveil com. 1988—), Drug Info. Assn. (publicity dir. 1980-82, treas. 1982-86, gen. chmn. 1st internat. meeting in Rome, Outstanding Acheivement award 1987), N.Y. Acad. Scis. (com. on 25th ann. meeting 1989), Nat. Soc. Microbiology, Am. Vet. Med. Assn. Aux., N.Y.C. Soc. Microbiology. Office: Warner-Lambert Co 201 Tabor Rd Morris Plains NJ 07950-2614

KAUFMAN, MICHELE BETH, clinical pharmacist, educator; b. Perth Amboy, N.J., May 13, 1963; d. Harold Alexander and Elaine Sue (Sommers) K. BS in Pharmacy, U. R.I., 1986; PharmD, Mass. Coll. Pharmacy, 1991. RPh, Mass., N.J., N.Y. Staff pharmacist Robert Wood Johnson U. Hosp., New Brunswick, N.J., 1986-91; product devel. pharmacist Reed & Carnrick Pharm. Co., Piscataway, N.J., 1987-89; poison info. specialist Mass. Poison Control System Children's Hosp., Boston, 1990-92; drug info. specialist U. R.I. Drug Info. Ctr., Providence, 1991-92; asst. clin. prof. pharmacy St. John's U., Jamaica, N.Y., 1992-96; clin. pharmacist coord. Health Ins. Plan Greater N.Y., N.Y.C., 1996—; clin. coord. internal medicine, drug info. specialist L.I. Jewish Med. Ctr., New Hyde Park, N.Y., 1992-96; clin. pharmacist coord. HIP of Greater N.Y.C., 1996—; reviewer Micromedex Info. Systems. Contbr. articles and revs. to profl. jours.; patent pending for pineapple colon electrolyte lavage solution. Active St. John's Univ. Jazz Ensemble, 1992—. Fellow Drug Info., 1992; recipient Indsl. Pharm. Tech. award Am. Pharm. Assn., 1986. Mem. Am. Soc. Health Systems Pharmacists, New Eng. Coun. Health Systems Pharmacists, Am. Soc. Pharmacy Law, Am. Inst. History Pharmacy, N.Y. State Coun. Health-Systems Pharmacists, Lambda Kappa Sigma (pres. Xi chpt. 1985-86, v.p. 1984-85, fundraiser 1983-84), Rho Chi. Home: 97 Preusser Rd Craryville NY 12521 Address: 212-72 73d Ave #3G Bayside NY 11364

KAUFMAN, RAYMOND HENRY, physician; b. Bklyn., Nov. 24, 1925; s. Morris and Anne (Markewich) K.; m. Patrician Ann Judson, June 23, 1946; children: Susan, Wendy, Murri, Elisabeth. Student, Coll. William and Mary, 1942-43, U. N.C., 1943-44; MD, U. Md., 1948. Acting chmn., dept. ob-gyn Baylor Coll. Medicine, Houston, 1968-73, chmn., dept. ob-gyn, 1973-93, prof., dept. pathology, 1973—, prof. dept. ob-gyn, 1973—. Contbr. articles to profl. jours. Capt. USAF, 1953-55. Fellow Am. Coll. Ob-Gyn, Am. Coll. Surgeons; mem. Am. Gyn. and Obstet. Soc. (v.p. 1986), Soc. Gyn. Oncology (v.p. 1983), Tex. Assn. Ob-gyn (pres. 1982-83), Internat. Soc. for Study of Vulvar Disease (pres. 1979). Office: Baylor Coll of Medicine Dept Ob-Gyn 6550 Fannin MS-701 Houston TX 77030

KAUFMAN, RONALD PAUL, physician, school official; b. Hartford, Conn., Nov. 30, 1929; s. Louis Elliot and Sarah K.; m. Beth Winkler, Dec. 28, 1968; children: Ronald Paul, Michael, Karyn, Leesa, Jennifer. BS, Trinity Coll., 1951; MD, U. Pa., 1955. Intern Hartford Hosp., 1955-56, resident in internal medicine, 1956-58, chief resident, 1960-61. Asst. dir. dept. medicine, 1966-70, dir. med. edn. dept., 1967-70; med. dir. George Washington U. Hosp., Washington, 1970-75; asso. dean clin. affairs. Univ. Med. Ctr., 1972-73, dean, 1973-77, acting v.p. for med. affairs, 1975-76, v.p. for med. affairs, 1976-87; v.p. for health scis. Health Scis. Ctr. U. So. Fla., 1987-94, prof. medicine, dir. divsn. health care reform, 94—. Contbr. articles to profl. publs. Mem. D.C. Med. Community com. Mayor's Panel on Human Resources Orgn. and Mgmt. of D.C., 1977. Served to capt. M.C. USAF, 1958-60. Mem. Am. Acad. Med. Dirs., Am. Bd. Med. Mgmt. (treas. 1990, sec. 1991-93, pres.-elect 1993, pres. 1994-95, immediate past pres. 1995-96), ACP, AMA, Am. Soc. Internal Medicine, Assn. Acad. Health Ctrs. (chmn. 1986-87), Assn. Am. Med. Colls., Assn. for Hosp. Med. Edn., D.C. Med. Soc., Nat. Bd. Med. Examiners, Am. Coll. Physician Execs. (pres. 1986), Nat. Acad. Med. Examiners (editl. adv. bd. 1991—), World Access Inc., D.C. Consortium Univ. Health Sci. Ctrs., Soc. Med. Adminstrs. (treas. 1992—), Soc. Med. Assn., D.C. Hosp. Assn., Nat. Assn. Biomed. Rsch. Office: 3500 E Fletcher Ave Ste 510 Tampa FL 33613

KAUFMAN, RUSSELL EUGENE, hematologist, oncologist; b. Kenton, Ohio, Mar. 7, 1946; s. George W. and Eileen M. (Risner) K.; m. Jane Ann Steinman, Sept. 25, 1948; children: Jonathon R., Emily J. BS, Ohio State U., 1968, MD cum laude, 1973. Diplomate Am. Bd. Internal Medicine. Resident medicine Duke U. Med. Ctr., Durham, N.C., 1973-77, chief resident medicine, 1977; rsch. hematologist NIH, Bethesda, Md., 1978-80; asst. prof. medicine Duke U. Med. Ctr., Durham, 1980-86, from asst. prof. to assoc. prof. biochemistry, 1985—, from assoc. prof. to prof. medicine, 1986—, chief div. hematology and oncology, 1989—, vice chair dept. medicine, 1995; mem. sci. adv. com. Am. Cancer Soc., Atlanta, N.Y.C., 1987—; mem. com. Nat. Acad. Sci., Washington, 1983-86; mem. sci. rev. coms. NIH, Bethesda, Md., 1985—. Contbr. articles to profl. jours., chpts. to books. Searle Found. scholar, 1983-86, Leukemia Soc. scholar, N.Y.C., 1986-90. Mem. AAAS, Am. Soc. Biochemistry, Am. Soc. Hematology (head subcom. on red cell 1985-88), Assn. Subsplty. Profs. (exec. coun. 1994), Assn. Hematology/Oncology Program Dirs. (chaiar-elect 1996). Presbyterian. Office: Duke U Med Ctr PO Box 3250 Durham NC 27715-3250

KAUFMAN, STEPHEN LAWRENCE, radiologist, educator; b. Phila., Nov. 7, 1942; s. Abraham S. and Genevieve (Finestone) K. BA, U. Pa., 1963, MD, 1967. Resident in radiology, then fellow in cardiovascular radiology Johns Hopkins Med. Ctr., Balt., 1970-75, asst. prof. radiology, 1975-79, assoc. prof., 1980-88; prof. radiology, dir. cardiovascular and interventional radiology Emory U., Atlanta, 1988—. Author: Techniques in Interventional Radiology, 1982; editor: Biliary Radiology, 1992; contbr. articles to med. jours. Served as lt. comdr. USPHS, 1968-70. Fellow Soc. Cardiovascular and Interventional Radiology; mem. Radiol. Soc. N.Am., Am. Coll. Radiology, Am. Heart Assn., Ga. Radiol. Soc. Avocations: hiking, white-water rafting, golf, computers. Office: Emory U Hosp 1364 Clifton Rd NE Atlanta GA 30322-1059

KAUFMAN, WILLIAM, internist; b. Dec. 31, 1910; s. Leo and Marie Kaufman; m. Charlotte R. Schnee, May 9, 1940. BA, U. Pa., 1931; MA in Chemistry, U. Mich., 1932, PhD in Physiology, 1937, MD cum laude, 1938. Diplomate Am. Bd. Internal Medicine. Intern Barnes Hosp., Washington U. Sch. Medicine, St. Louis, 1938-39; asst. resident, then resident Mt. Sinai Hosp., N.Y.C., 1939-40; Emanuel Libman fellow Yale U. Sch. Medicine, New Haven, 1940-41, Dazian Found. fellow, clin. asst., 1940-42; pvt. practice Bridgeport, Conn., 1940-65; courtesy staff mem. Bridgeport Hosp., 1941-65; courtesy staff St. Vincent's Hosp., Bridgeport, 1941-65; assoc. med. dir. L.W. Frohlich and Co./Intercon Internat. Inc., N.Y.C., 1964-65, med. dir., 1965-67, dir. med. affairs, 1967-68; assoc. med. dir. Klemtner Casey, Inc., N.Y.C., 1969-70, dir. med. affairs, 1970-71; v.p., dir. med. affairs Klemtner Advt., Inc., N.Y.C., 1971, sr. v.p., dir. sci. and med. affairs, 1971-81; pres., chmn. program and pub. edn. coms. Acad. Psychosomatic Medicine, 1953-55; founder fellow, mem. governing coun. Collegium Internationale Allergologicum, 1955-62; chmn. psychosomatic sect. 3d Internat. Congress Allergology, 1958; D. C. Y. Moore Meml. lectr. Manchester (Conn.) Med. Soc., 1967; cons. Family Life Film Ctr. Conn. Inc., 1967-74; mem. screening jury med. edn. sect. Am. Film Festival, 1975. Author: The Common Form of Niacinamide Deficiency Disease (Aniacinamidosis), 1943, The Common Form of Joint Dysfunction: Its Incidence and Treatment, 1949; (drawings) Kaufman's Kritters, 1990; (play) People Like Us, A Bad Day for Spider; contbg. editor Internat. Archives Allergy and Applied Immunology, 1952-54, 67-69, Am. editor in chief, 1954-67; mem. bd. editorial collaborators Psychotherapeutica, Psychosomatica et Orthopaedagogica, 1955-62; contbg. editor Quar. Rev. Allergy and Applied Immunology, 1955; contbr. numerous articles to profl. and popular jours.; exhibited drawings and paintings at Housatonic Community Coll., New Canaan Art Show, others. Mem. adv. bd. Huxley Inst. So. Conn. for Biosocial Rsch., 1980-84. Recipient citation Internat. Assn. Gerontology, 1983, 1st Pl. award Faculty of Fine Arts, Housatonic Community Coll., 1983, Sci. and Math. medal Rensselaer Poly. Inst., 1928, Sternberg Meml. Gold medal, 1938. Hon. fellow Internat. Acad. Preventive Medicine (Tom Spies Meml. award and lectr. 1978); fellow AAAS, Am. Coll. Allergy, Asthma and Immunology (emeritus, chmn. pub. edn. com. 1951-55, chmn. com. on allergy of nervous system 1962, Award of Merit 1981), Am. Coll. Nutrition, ACP (life), Gerontol. Soc. Am. (mem. various sects.), N.Y. Acad. Medicine, Royal Soc. Medicine (London); mem. AMA (life), Am Psychosomatic Soc. (emeritus), Conn. State Med. Soc. (life), Fairfield County Med. Assn. (life), Nat. Assn. Sci. Writers, N.Y. Acad. Scis., Dramatists Guild, Sigma Xi, Alpha Omega Alpha, Phi Sigma, Phi Lambda Upsilon, Phi Kappa Phi. Home: 3180 Grady St Winston Salem NC 27104-4008

KAUFMANN, MARK DAVID, dermatologist; b. N.Y.C., June 17, 1962; s. Paul and Pearl K.; m. Patricia V. Heiden, Jan. 16, 1991; children: Alexandra E., Olivia R. BA, NYU, 1984, MD, 1988. Diplomat Am. Bd. Dermatology. Clin. instr. Montefiore Med. Ctr., Bronx, 1992-94; asst. prof. N.Y. Med. Coll., Valhalla, 1994—; dir. dermatologic surgery Met. Hosp. Ctr., N.Y.C., 1995—; clin. instr. Mt. Sinai Med. Ctr., N.Y.C., 1995—. Mem. Am. Acad. Dermatology, Am. Soc. Dermatologic Surgery. Office: 21 E 90th St New York NY 10024

KAUL, DHANANJAYA KUMAR, physiologist; b. Etawah, India, July 23, 1943; came to U.S., 1974; s. Gopal K. and Kamla (Devi) K. MS, Agra U., Nainital, India, 1963; PhD, Rajasihan U., Jaipur, India, 1969. Lectr. Rajasihan U., Jaipur, 1966-74; staff assoc. Columbia U., N.Y.C., 1974-77; assoc. Albert Einstein Coll. Medicine, Bronx, N.Y., 1978-81, asst. prof. medicine, 1981-88, assoc. prof., 1988-94, prof., 1994—. Fellow WHO, Lyon, France, 1974; rsch. grantee Am. Heart Assn., 1986-93, NIH, Bethesda, Md., 1990—. Mem. Am. Soc. Hematology, Microcirculatory Soc. USA, N.Am. Soc. Biorheologists. Office: Albert Einstein Coll Med Dept Medicine Rm U-917 1300 Morris Park Ave Bronx NY 10461-1926

KAUNITZ, PAUL EHRLICH, psychiatrist; b. N.Y.C., Oct. 6, 1914; s. Julius and Ruth Lillian (Moss) K.; m. Rita Davidson; children: Victoria, Jonathan, Andrew. BA, Columbia U., 1933, MA, 1934; MD, NYU, 1938. Diplomate Am. Bd. Psychiatry and Neurology. Intern Montefiore Hosp., N.Y.C., 1938-39, Jewish Hosp., Bklyn., 1939-41; resident in medicine Mt. Sinai Hosp., N.Y.C., 1945-48, resident in psychiatry, 1948-49; resident in psychiatry Manhattan State Hosp., N.Y.C., 1949-50, N.Y. State Psychiat. Inst., 1950-51; clin. psychiatrist Mt. Sinai Hosp., N.Y.C., 1951-54; asst. prof. psychiatry Yale U. Sch. Medicine, New Haven, Conn., 1955-62, assoc. prof. psychiatry, 1962-72, clin. prof. psychiatry, 1972—; assoc. examiner Am. Bd. Psychiatry and Neurology, 1972-89. Lt. col. U.S. Army Med. Corps, 1941-46, ETO. Decorated Bronze Star. Fellow Am. Psychiat. Assn. (life); mem. Am. Psychoanalytic Assn., Conn. Psychiat. Soc. (pres. 1970-71, Disting. Svc. award 1988), Alpha Omega Alpha. Democrat. Jewish. Home and Office: 7 Admiral Ln Norwalk CT 06851

KAURENE, BRUCE RICHARD, health care computer software executive; b. Phila., Feb. 22, 1955. BSBA, Pa. State U., 1976. Programmer, analyst Eastman Kodak, Rochester, N.Y., 1976-78; project mgr. E. I. duPont, Wilmington, Del., 1978-84; asst. v.p. Erisco, Inc., N.Y.C., 1984—; instr. U. Del., Wilmington, 1979-84. Office: Erisco Inc 1700 Broadway New York NY 10019-5905

KAUTH, BENJAMIN, podiatric consultant; b. N.Y.C., Oct. 20, 1913; m. Bertha Locke. Student, CCNY, 1936-39; D in Podiatric Medicine, N.Y. Coll. Podiatric Medicine, 1939, postgrad., 1944-45, HHD (hon.), 1981. Pvt. practice N.Y.C., 1939-78; podiatric cons., 1960—; co-chief podiatry staff St. Clare's Hosp., N.Y.C.; chief of staff podiatry Jewish Home and Hosp. for Aged, Village Nursing Home of St. Vincents Hosp.; mem. staff French Polyclinic; chief podiatry panel 1199 Nat. Fund; coord. podiatry panel 32 B-J Health Ctr.; mem. med. panel Med. Malpractice Bronx County; trustee, mem. exec. coun. N.Y. Coll. Podiatric Medicine; cons. Podiatrist Local 1199 Health Fund, Equitable Life Assurance Co., various other third-party insurers, pub. rels. firms. Editorial asst. N.Y. Podiatrist Del. to Nat. Conv.; contbr. articles to profl. jours. Bd. dirs. Adams Sch. for Retarded Children, Am. Jewish Distbn. Com. Fellow Nat. Assn. of Professions; mem. Am. Coll. Foot Surgeons (assoc.), Am. Podiatric Med. Assn. (pub. affairs com., editorial asst.), Podiatry soc. of the State N.Y. (spl. asst. to pres., editorial asst. ann. meeting), N.Y. County Podiatry Soc. (sec., exec. bd.), Fair Harbor Yacht Club (sec.), Friars. Home and Office: 302 W 12th St New York NY 10014-6025

KAUTZ, BONNIE MITCHELL, school nurse; b. Millboro, Va., May 28, 1934; d. Terry Glenn and Roasamond Virginia (Loan) Mitchell; m. John Lewis Kautz, June 15, 1957; children: Rosamond Amelia Kautz Learn, John Mitchell, Rachel Ann. BS, Alderson-Broaddus Coll., 1957; M. in Litt. in Nursing Svc. Adminstrn., U. Pitts., 1961; postgrad., Carlow Coll., 1988-89. RN, W.Va., Pa., Va., Ga.; cert. ednl. specialist II, Pa. Charge nurse Presbyn. Hosp., Pitts., 1957; head nurse Magee Hosp., Pitts., 1957-62; adminstrv. asst. dental office Office John L. Kautz, DDS, Apollo, Pa., 1964—; substitute sch. nurse Apollo-Ridge, Kiski Area, New Kensington-Arnold, Highlands sch. dists., Spring Church, 1987—; long term substitute sch. nurse Kiski Area

Sch. Dist., Vandergrift, Pa., 1990-91, 92, sch. nurse, 1993—. Ch. organist, treas. First United Ch. of Christ, Apollo, nurse for ch. camp, 1983—, past mem. ch. consistory, past Sunday sch. supt., past. music dir. and past fin. sec. community vacation bible sch., past youth advisor; mem. past sec., past. pres., past treas. Apollo Area Ch. Women United; treas. for elem. and jr. high PTA; vol. ARC Blood Bank; chmn. Well Baby Clinic; mem. Community Chorus, Sweet Harmony's female barbershop quartet. Mem. ANA, Pa. Nurses Assn., Armstrong County Nurses Assn., Nat. Assn. Sch. Nurses, Pa. Assn. Sch. Nurses (bd. dirs.), Vis. Nurses Assn.-Home Health Svcs. Found. Inc. (chmn. profl. adv. com., sec.), Alderson-Broaddus Coll. Alumni Coun. (chairperson gifts com., sec., pres. 1982-84, 96—, v.p. 1993-94, 94-95), Alumni Assn. of Sch. Home: 309 S 3rd St Apollo PA 15613-1131

KAVALER-ALDER, SUSAN, clinical psychologist; b. N.Y.C., Jan. 31, 1950; d. Solomon and Alice (Zelikow) Weiss; m. Thomas Kavaler, July 12, 1970 (div. 1975); m. Saul Michael Adler, Aug. 14, 1983. PhD in Clin. Psychology, Adelphi U., 1974. Psychologist Beth Israel Hosp., N.Y.C., 1974-76, Manhattan Psychiat. Children's Ctr., N.Y.C., 1977-80; pvt. practice psychotherapy-psychoanalysis, N.Y.C., 1976—, condr. writing and mourning groups; founding dir., supr. faculty, tng. analyst Object Rels. Inst. for Psychotherapy and Psychoanalysis, 1991—; mem. faculty Postgrad. Ctr. Mental Health, N.Y.C., 1984-86, 90—; mem. faculty, supr. Nat. Inst. Pychotherapies, N.Y.C., 1985-91; bd. dirs., supr. Bklyn. Inst. Psychotherapy and Psychoanalysis, 1985-91, mem. psychoanalytic inst. faculty; bd. dirs. Women and Psychoanalysis; adj. prof. Fordham U.; founding exec. dir. Object Rels. Inst. Psychotherpy and Psychoanalysis; pvt. practice in psychotherapy, psychoanalysis; spkr. pvt. seminars, writing groups. Office: 115 E 9th St New York NY 10003-5414

KAWAI, IROKU, psychologist, educator; b. Oita, Japan, Mar. 13, 1928; s. Jiro and Some Kawai; m. Yoshiko Kobayashi, May 30, 1953; 1 child, Tetsuya. BA, Hiroshima (Japan) U., 1951, PhD, 1976. Asst. instr. Hiroshima U., 1951-53, Hiroshima Jogakuin Coll., 1953-62; prof. Hiroshima U., 1980-91, prof. emeritus, 1991—; asst. instr. Oita U., 1962-72, prof., 1973-80; prof. Fukuyama (Japan) U., 1991-94, Fukuyama Heisei (Japan) U., 1994—. Author: A Nurture and Behavior-analysis, 1986, Behavior Management, 1987, School Refusal, 1991; co-author: Educational Psychology, 1989. Mem. Japanese Psychol. Assn. (bd. dirs. 1990—), Japanese Assn. Ednl. Psychology (bd. dirs. 1976—), Japanese Assn. Behavior Analysis (bd. dirs. 1982—). Home: 11-8-1001 Uchikoshi-cho, Nishiku Hiroshima 733, Japan Office: Fukuyama Heisei U, Kami-IWanari Miyuki-Cho, Fukuyama 720, Japan

KAWAKAMI, YUTAKA, biomedical researcher, hematologist; b. Osaka, Japan, Jan. 27, 1956; came to U.S., 1985; s. Kiichi and Etsuko Kawakami; m. Masako Abe, Apr. 29, 1982; children: Yuko, Tadashi, Kazuki. MD, Keio U, Tokyo, 1980, PhD, 1996. Resident Keio U. Hosp., 1980-82; mem. med. staff Nat. Okura Hosp., Tokyo, 1982-84; instr. med. div. hematology Keio U., 1984-85; rsch. assoc. dept. med. microbiology U. South Fla., Tampa, 1985-87; vis. fellow surgery br. Nat. Cancer Inst., NIH, Bethesda, Md., 1987-90, vis. assoc. surgery br., 1990-92, vis. scientist surgery br., 1992—. Contbr. articles to sci. jours. Keio U. Rsch. grantee, 1985; Fogarty Internat. fellow NIH, 1987-90. Mem. AAAS, N.Y. Acad. Sci., Am. Assn. Immunologists, Am. Assn. for Cancer Rsch. Office: Nat Cancer Inst NIH Bldg 10 Rm 2B42 9000 Rockville Pike Bethesda MD 20892-1502

KAWAOA, CHARLES YOICHI, physician; b. Kikuma, Japan, July 19, 1945; came to U.S., 1954; s. Giichi and Mitsu (Wooyenaka) K. BA, Amherst Coll., 1967; MD, Albany Med. Coll., 1971. Diplomate Am. Bd. Ob-Gyn. Resident in ob-gyn. U. Chgo. Hosps., 1971-75; dir. gen. ob/gyn New England Med. Ctr., Boston, 1983-95; program dir., resident in Ob/Gyn Tufts U. Sch. Medicine, Boston, 1988-95; chmn. dept. ob-gyn. Mt. Auburn Hosp., Cambridge, Mass., 1995—; asst. clin. prof. ob-gyn. Harvard Med. Ctr., Boston, 1995—. Fellow Am. Coll. Ob-Gyn., Boston Obstet. Soc.; mem. Mass. Med. Soc., Assn. Profs. Ob-Gyn. Office: Mt Auburn Hosp 330 Mt Auburn St Cambridge MA 02238

KAWATA, PAUL AKIO, health association administrator; b. Salt Lake City, July 24; s. William and Miyeko (Hashima) K. BA, U. Pacific; MA, Antioch U., Seattle. Mem. mayor's staff City of Seattle, 1980-85; exec. dir. Nat. AIDS Network, Washington, 1986-89, Nat. Minority AIDS Coun., Washington, 1989—; cons. WHO, Geneva. Co-author: Everything You Wanted to Know About AIDS. Named hon. citizen City of New Orleans, 1987; recipient Michael Hirsh award Body Positive, N.Y.C., 1990. Mem. Internat. AIDS Orgn. (bd. dirs.). Democrat. Office: Nat Minority AIDS Coun 1931 13th NW Washington DC 20009

KAY, BRUCE G., hospital pharmacy administrator; b. Canndaigua, N.Y., Dec. 26, 1938; s. Samuel and Lillian K.; BA, Syracuse U., 1961; BS, Albany Coll. Pharmacy, Union U., 1966; MS, Bklyn. Coll. Pharmacy, L.I.U., 1971; m. Sally Ann Feldman, Nov. 9, 1968; children: Amy Hillary, David Lawrence. Asst. dir. pharmacy Clifton Springs (N.Y.) Hosp. and Clinic, 1967-72; pharmacy supr. Univ. Hosp., N.Y.U. Med. Center, 1972-75; dir. pharmacy services Kingsbrook Jewish Med. Center, Bklyn., 1975-78, L.I. Jewish-Hillside Med. Center, New Hyde Park, N.Y., 1978—; assoc. clin. prof. pharmacy St. John's U. Coll. Pharmacy; pharm. cons. Community Health Program of Nassau and Queens, Vis. Nurse Service N.Y. Served with USPHS, 1966-67. Fellow Am. Coll. Apothecaries, Am. Soc. Cons. Pharmacists; mem. Am. Pharm. Assn., Am. Soc. Hosp. Pharmacists, N.Y.C. Soc. Hosp. Pharmacists N.Y. State Council Hosp. Pharmacists, Diplomates in Pharmacy, N.Y. Acad. Pharmacy, Internat. Pharm. Fedn. (assoc.), Rho Chi. Contbr. articles to profl. jours., chpt. to book. Home: 750 Kensington Ct Westbury NY 11590-5813 Office: 270-05 76th Ave New Hyde Park NY 11040

KAY, DOUGLAS HAROLD, optometrist, optometry educator; b. Oakland, Calif., Oct. 7, 1949; s. Marvin Jack and Lois Natalie (Bernstein) K. A.B., U. Calif., 1971, B.S. in Optometry, 1973, O.D., 1975. Registered optometrist, Calif. Assoc. Woodland Clin. Med. Group (Calif.), 1975-78; cons. Calif. Vision Service Plan, Sacramento, 1977-82; pvt. practice optometry, Davis, Calif., 1978—; indsl. vision cons. Hunt-Wesson Foods, 1980—; asst. clin. prof. Sch. Optometry, U. Calif., Berkeley, 1983—; chmnsupervisory com. Calif. Optometric Credit Union; chair Calif. Vision Project, 1996—. Bd. dirs. Valley Artist Prodns., Library Assocs., U. Calif.-Davis, Salvation Army, Davis, Econ. Devel. Council of Davis, 1985-87; mem. Davis Comic Opera Co.; chmn. South Davis Traffic Study Com., 1984, Davis 2000 Study Com., 1985. Named Young Optometrist of Yr., Sacramento Valley Optometric Soc., 1981. Mem. Am. Optometric Assn. (chmn. polit. action com. Calif., nat. keyperson coord. 1995-96), Calif. Optometric Assn. (bd. trustees 1993-96, chair polit. action com. 1996—), Sacramento Valley Optometric Soc. (pres. 1985-86), Vision Conservation Inst., C. of C. (dir. membership Davis Area). Democrat. Jewish. Lodge: Rotary (Davis) (asst. sec. 1981-93, sec. 1993—). Office: 1111 Kennedy Pl Ste 6 Davis CA 95616-1266

KAY, GEORGE NEAL, cardiology educator, consultant; b. Battle Creek, Mich., July 17, 1953; s. George Watson and Margaret (Jay) K.; m. Linda Wiltzer, Nov. 4, 1978. BS, Mich. State U., 1975; MD, U. Mich., 1979. Chief resident U. Ala., Birmingham, 1979-83; asst. prof. U. Ala., Birmingham, N.C., 1986-89; assoc. prof. U. Ala., 1989-93, prof., 1993—; cardiology fellow Duke U., Durham, N.C., 1983-86; dir. cardiac electrophysiology U. Ala., 1993. Author: Clinical Cardiac Pacing, 1995, Clinical Management of Cardiac Arythmia, 1988. Mem. Am. Heart Assn., N.Am. Soc. Pacing & Electrophysiology, Am. Coll. Cardiology, Alpha Omega Alpha. Office: U Ala at Birmingham 321 THT Birmingham AL 35294

KAY, GLEN SCOTT, hospital administrator, physician; b. Bklyn., Apr. 27, 1960; s. Gary and Jane K.; m. Karen. BS, Columbia U., 1981; MD, SUNY, 1985. Intern Baystate Med. Ctr., Springfield, Mass., 1985-86; emergency svcs. attending staff Brookdale Hosp., Bklyn., 1986-87; emergency medicine resident L.I. Jewish Med. Ctr., New Hyde Park, N.Y., 1987-90; assoc. dir. emergency dept. St. Luke's Hosp., Newburgh, N.Y., 1990—; computer cons./specialist Emergency Dept. Consultants, Newburgh, 1990—, emergency med. svcs. dir. 1994—. Fellow Am. Coll. Emergency Physicians. Office: EDC 3 Racquet Rd Newburgh NY 12550

KAY, JERALD, child psychiatry educator, researcher; b. Washington, Mar. 26, 1945; s. Max and Miriam (Schwartz) K.; m. Rena Lynn Victor, Aug. 17, 1968; children: Sarah Jennifer, Rachel Hannah, Jonathan Emile. BA, Washington U., 1967; MD, U. Md., 1971; diploma, Cin. Psychoanalytic Inst., 1984. Diplomate Am. Bd. Psychiatry and Neurology. Resident in psychiatry Cin. Gen. Hosp., 1971-73, fellow in child psychiatry, 1973-75; instr. child psychiatry U. Cin. Coll. Medicine, 1971-77, asst. prof. child psychiatry, 1977-82, assoc. prof. child psychiatry, 1982-89, prof. child psychiatry, 1989-90; prof., chair dept. psychiatry Wright State U. Sch. Medicine, Dayton, Ohio, 1990—; dir. med. student edn. U. Cin. Dept. Psychiatry, 1975-82, dir. residency tng., 1982—, dir. med. student edn.; mem. psychiatry com. Nat. Bd. Med. Examiners, 1988-90; specialist site visitor Accreditation Coun. Grad. Med. Edn., 1986—. Editor Jour. Psychotherapy Practice and Rsch., 1990—; mem. editorial cons. bd. Am. Psychiat. Press, Inc., 1987, mem. editorial bd. Acad. Psychiatry; contbr. articles on child and adult psychiatry, psychoanalysis, psychotherapy, ethics, psychiat. and cardiac transplantation edn. to profl. jours. Recipient Golden Apple Teaching award U. Cin. Coll. Medicine, 1979; named Exemplary Psychiatrist, Nat. Alliance for the Mentally Ill, 1994, Educator of Yr. Assn. Acad. Psychiatry, 1996. Fellow Am. Psychiat. Assn. (chmn. med. studies edn. com. 1982-86, coun. med. edn. 1989, career devel. 1986—, chmn. 1989, mem. com. on psychotherapy, program com.); mem. Am. Coll. Psychiatrists, Am. Psychoanalytic Assn., Am. Acad. Child and Adolescent Psychiatry, Am. Assn. Chmn. Depts. of Psychiatry (chmn. edn. com.), Acad. Psychosomatic Medicine, Alpha Omega Alpha. Home: 4192 Rose Hill Ave Cincinnati OH 45229-1421 Office: Wright State U Sch Medicine PO Box 927 Dayton OH 45401-0927

KAY, JEROME, psychiatrist, educator; b. Phila., Feb. 4, 1920; s. Louis and Mattie (Schwartz) Kanevsky; m. Myra Resnick, June 11, 1943; children: Paul, Jonathan, David. AB, U. Pa., 1940, MD, 1943. Diplomate Am. Bd. Psychiatry and Neurology. Intern Einstein Med. Ctr., Phila., 1944; resident in psychiatry Butler Hosp., Providence, 1948-50; med. dir. Gov. Bacon Health Ctr., Delaware City, Del., 1950-52; cons. to health svc. U. Del., Newark, 1952-56; cons. Family Svc. North Del., Wilmington, 1958-62; pvt. practice psychiatry Wilmington and Chadds Ford, Pa., 1952—; asst. prof. dept. psychiatry Jefferson Med. Sch., Phila., 1974-89, clin. prof. Dept. Psychiatry Jefferson Med. Sch., sr. attending physician, 1978—, clin. prof., 1989—. Capt. U.S. Army, 1945-47, Korea. Fellow Am. Psychiat. Assn. (life); mem. AMA, Del. Psychiat. Assn. (pres. 1958-61, svc. award 1983), Am. Psychoanalytic Soc., Phila. Psychiat. Soc., Phi Beta Kappa. Democrat. Jewish. Home: PO Box 64 Chadds Ford PA 19317-0064 Office: 1701 Augustine Cut Off Ste 45 Wilmington DE 19803-4495

KAY, MARGUERITE M., immunologist, geriatrician, medical educator; b. Washington, May 13, 1947; d. Ann Margot. BA in Zoology summa cum laude, U. Calif., Berkeley, 1970; D of Medicine, U. Calif., San Francisco, 1974. Staff fellow Gerontology Rsch. Ctr., Nat. Inst. Child Health and Devel., NIH, Balt. City Hosps., Balt. and Bethesda, Md., 1974, USPHS officer, chief high resolution lab, coord. human immunoepidemilolgy program, 1975-77; chief longitudinal immunology program Nat. Inst. on Aging, NIH, Balt. and Bethesda, 1975-77; chief lab. molecular and clin. immunology, dir. electron microscopy facilty chief lab Geriatric Rsch. Edn. and Clin. Ctr., VA Wadsworth Med. Ctr., L.A., 1977-81; staff geriatrician, rsch. assoc. dept. medicine UCLA, 1977-81; intern UCLA and VA Wadsworth Med. Ctr., 1978, resident in medicine, 1979-80, geriatric fellow, 1981; immunologist, internist, assoc. chief of staff rsch. Olin E. Teague Vets. Ctr., Temple, Tex., 1981-90; dir. div. geriatric medicine Tex. A&M U., College Station, 1981-90, prof. medicine, med. biochemistry, genetics, microbiology and immunology, 1981-90; regent's prof. microbiology, immunology and medicine U. Ariz. Coll. of Medicine, Tucson, 1990—; guest lectr. in basic microbiology Goucher Coll., Towson, Md., 1974-75, guest lab. instr. advanced microbiology, 1975-77; presenter, instr., participant numerous profl. symposia and seminars, 1974—. Author: (with J. Gaplin and T. Makinodan) Aging, Immunity and Arthritic Disease, 1980; (with T. Makinodan) CRC Handbook of Immunology in Aging, 1981; contbr. chpt. to Liver and Aging, 1977, Clinical Immunochemistry, 1978, Geriatric Dentistry, 1986, numerous others; contbr. numerous articles to profl. publs. and jours.; mem. editorial bd., Comprehensive Gerontology sect. editor Mechanisms of Aging and Development, 1985—; spl. issue editor Gerontology, 1985, 90, N.Am. editor, Gerontology, 1987—; author poems. NIH Med. Scientist Tng. fellow U. Calif., San Francisco, Pres.'s Undergrad. fellow, 1971-72, 72-73, 73-74, Edwin Letts Oliver scholar, Finkelstein scholar, Al Holman scholar, 1972-73; recipient Internat. Congress Gerontology Travel award, 1978, Arthur S. Fleming award, 1983; named Register Honoree in Sci. and Tech. Esquire mag., 1985; many other hons. and awards. Mem. Am. Soc. Clin. Investigation, Am. Soc. Biochemistry and Molecular Biology, Am. Assn. Immunologists, Am. Geriatrics Soc., Am. Soc. Cell Biology, Am. Soc. Hematology, Am. Fedn. Clin. Rsch., Gerontol. Soc., Sigma Xi. Home: PO Box 36018 Tucson AZ 85740-6018 Office: U Ariz Health Sci Ctr Dept Microbiology 1501 N Campbell Ave Rm 650 Lsn Tucson AZ 85724-0001

KAY, RICHARD FREDERICK, paleontology and biological anthropology educator; b. N.Y.C., Oct. 21, 1947; s. G. Marshall and Inez (Clark) K.; m. Cheryl Rice, June 5, 1971; children: Elizabeth C., Andrew S. BS, U. Mich., 1969; M in Philosophy, Yale U., 1971, PhD, 1973. Asst. prof. anatomy Duke U. Med. Ctr., Durham, N.C., 1973-78, assoc. prof., 1978-83, prof., 1983-88, prof. biol. anthropology and anatomy, chmn. dept., 1988—. Mem. Am. Assn. Phys. Anthropologists (exec. com. 1986-88), Argentine Paleontology Soc., Soc. Vertebrate Paleontology. Democrat. Home: 1502 Blount St Durham NC 27707-1526 Office: Duke U Med Ctr Dept Biol Anthropology & Anatomy Durham NC 27710

KAY, RICHARD M., physician assistant; b. Oct. 19, 1958. Diploma, Chgo. Urban Skill Ctr., 1984; AAS with honors, Kennedy King Coll., 1988; Physician Assistant, Cook County Hosp., Chgo. CPR instr.; lic. clergyman; nat. certified physician asst. Epidemiologist Dept. Health, Chgo., 1980-81; asst. supr. Cermak Hosp. Cook County Dept. Corrections, Chgo., 1981-85; nurse Hyde Park Community Hosp., Chgo., 1989, Michael Reese In House Registry, Chgo., 1989—; paramedic officer Chgo. Fire Dept., 1985—; asst. supr. EMT's; adj. faculty Kennedy King/Chgo. City Wide Colls., 1987—; mem. physician asst. program MXC/Cook County Hosp., 1995. Named to Dean's List; recipient Superior Achievement in Anatomy and Physiology/Obstetrical Nursing award, Unit Performance award, Paramedic of Valor award. Home: 8858 S Crandon Chicago IL 60617-1222

KAY, SAUL, pathologist; b. N.Y.C., Feb. 13, 1914; s. Wolf and Rose (Savitzky) Kossovsky; m. Grace Calef, Aug. 15, 1940; 1 dau., Deborah. B.A., N.Y. U., 1936; M.D., N.Y. Med. Coll., 1939. Intern Harlem Hosp., N.Y.C., 1939-41; resident Fordham Hosp., 1941-42, N.Y. Postgrad. Med. Sch. and Hosp., 1946-48, Columbia Presbyn. Med. Center, 1948-50; practice medicine specializing in pathology Richmond, Va., 1950—; prof. dept. surg. pathology Med. Coll. Va., 1952-78, emeritus prof., 1978—. Served to maj. AUS, 1942-45. Decorated Bronze Star. Mem. Coll. Am. Pathology, Va. Med. Soc., Richmond Acad. Medicine, Am. Soc. Clin. Pathology, Internat. Acad. Pathology, Am. Assn. Pathologists, Am. Soc. Cytology, AMA, Va. Path. Soc. Home: 322 Charmian Rd Richmond VA 23226-1705 Office: Med Coll Va Richmond VA 23298

KAYATE, ETHEL MAE, physician assistant; b. Albuquerque, Nov. 9, 1939; d. John and Lucy (Kiro) K. Diploma, Regina Sch. Nursing, 1960; AA, U. N.Mex., 1976. Staff nurse St. Joseph Hosp., Albuquerque, 1960-61, USPHS Indian Health Svc. Gallup (N.Mex.) Indian Med Ctr., 1969-71; physician asst. Gallup Indian Med. Ctr., 1974-95. Native Am. Tribal Affiliation: Pueblo of Laguna, N.Mex.; dir. religious edn. St. John Vianney, Gallup, 1995-96. Lt. col. USAF, 1962-69, 72-87. Fellow Am. Acad. Physician Assts., N.Mex. Physician Assts. Roman Catholic. Home: 3610 Zia Dr Gallup NM 87301

KAYE, CLIVE MERVYN, pharmacokineticist; b. London, Feb. 18, 1945. BSc in Chemistry and Human Physiology with distinction, Liverpool (Eng.) U., 1966, BSc in Biochemistry with honors, 1967; PhD in Drug Metabolism, London U., 1971. Chartered chemist. Demonstrator St. Thomas's Hosp. Med. Sch., London, 1967-70, asst. lectr., 1970-72; sr. rsch. biochemist St. Bartholomew's Hosp., London, 1972-76; sect. head DMPK May & Baker Ltd., Dagenham, Eng., 1976-86; unit head DMPK Smith Kline Beecham, Welwyn, Eng., 1986—. Contbr. numerous sci. articles to profl. jours. Fellow Royal Soc. Chemistry (London); mem. Inst. Biology. Home: 61 Wellfields, Essex Loughton IG10 1PA, England Office: Smith Kline Beecham, DMPK Dept, Herts Welwyn AL6 9AR, England

KAYE, DONALD, physician, educator; b. N.Y.C., Aug. 12, 1931; s. Morris and Rose (Hirschtritt) K.; m. Janet Miriam Sovitsky, June 26, 1955; children: Kenneth Marc, Karen Lynne, Kendra Beth, Keith Steven. A.B., Yale, 1953; M.D., N.Y. U., 1957. Diplomate Am. Bd. Internal Medicine, Am. Bd. Infectious Disease. Intern N.Y. Hosp., 1957-58, resident, 1958-60; practice medicine, specializing in internal medicine and infectious diseases N.Y.C., 1961-69, Phila., 1969—; asso. attending physician N.Y. Hosp., 1961-69; physician-in-chief Hosp. Med. Coll. Pa., 1969-95; instr. medicine Cornell U. Med. Coll., 1961-63, asst. prof., 1963-66, asso. prof., 1966-69; prof., chmn. dept. medicine Med. Coll. Pa., Phila., 1969-94; prof., chmn. dept. medicine Med. Coll. Pa. and Hahnemann U. Sch. Medicine, 1994-95, prof., 1995-96; prof. Allegheny U. of Health Scis., 1996—; cons. Phila. VA Hosp., 1969-95; CEO, pres. Med. Coll. Hosp., 1991-94, Med. Coll. Pa. and Hahnemann U. Hosp. Sys., 1994-96, Allegheny U. Hosps., 1996—, Allegheny Integrated Health Group, 1996—; mem. revision com. U.S. Pharmacopeia, 1975-95; mem. VA Merit Rev. Bd. in Infectious Diseases, 1976-78; mem. com. on infectious diseases Am. Bd. Internal Medicine, 1976-84, cons., 1984-86. Author: Urinary Tract Infection and Its Management, 1972, Infective Endocarditis, 1976, Fundamentals of Internal Medicine, 1983, Internal Medicine for Dentists, 1983, 2d edit., 1990, Endocarditis, 1984, Infective Endocarditis, 1992; mem. editorial bd. Aging: Immunology and Infectious Diseases, Gerontology: Med. Sci., Antimicrobial Agts. Chemotherapy; contbr. articles to med. jours. Recipient Distinguished Teaching award Lindback Found., 1972; NIH grantee, 1967-76, 82—; Pharm. Industry grantee, 1965—. Master ACP (gov. Ea. Pa. region 1983-88, pres. Pa. chpt. 1987); fellow Gerontol. Soc. Am., Infectious Disease Soc. Am.; mem. AMA, Pa. Med. Soc. (alt. del to AMA 1991-92), Phila. County Med. Soc. (pres. 1991-92), Am. Soc. for Microbiology, Am. Fedn. for Clin. Rsch., Am. Soc. for Clin. Investigation, Assn. Am. Physicians, Am. Clin. and Climatol. Assn., Phi Beta Kappa, Alpha Omega Alpha, Sigma Xi. Home: 1535 Sweet Briar Rd Gladwyne PA 19035-1216 Office: 3300 Henry Ave Philadelphia PA 19129-1121

KAYE, GAIL LESLIE, healthcare consultant; b. Upland, Pa., Aug. 6, 1955; d. Ronald E. and Doris T. (Welfley) K. BS, W.Va. Welseyan Coll., 1977; MS, Ohio State U., 1982, PhD, 1989. Lic. profl. clin. counselor; registered dietitian. Asst. dir. food svc., chief clin. dietitian Albert Einstein Med. Ctr., Phila., 1983; asst. prof. Ind. State U., Terre Haute, 1983-85; nutrition cons. Ohio State U. Hosp. Clinics, Columbus, 1986-88, grad. rsch. asst., 1986-89; legis. rep. Ohio Assocs. Counseling and Devel., Columbus, 1988-89; rsch. cons. State Dept. Edn., Columbus, 1988-89; lectr. counselor edn. Ohio State U., Columbus, 1989—; program devel. and clin. rschr. Ross Labs., Columbus, 1990-94; pres. Kaye Consultation Svcs., Inc., 1994—. Inventor in field; contbr. articles to profl. jours. Recipient Pres. award Ohio Mental Health Counselors Assn., 1990. Mem. ACA, Am. Mental Health Counselors Assn., Am. Dietetics Assn., Ohio Dietetics Assn. Home and Office: 365 Helmbright Dr Gahanna OH 43230-3290

KAYE, GORDON ISRAEL, pathologist, anatomist, educator; b. N.Y.C., Aug. 13, 1935; s. Oscar Swarz and Rebecca (Schachman) K.; m. Nancy Elizabeth Weber, June 4, 1956; children: Jacqueline Elizabeth, Vivienne Rebecca. AB, Columbia U., 1955, AM, 1957, PhD, 1961. Research asst. cytology Columbia U., N.Y.C., 1953-55, asst. zoology, 1955, asst. anatomy, 1958-61, research assoc. dept. anatomy, 1961-63, assoc. surg. pathology, 1963-66, asst. prof. surg. pathology, 1966-70, assoc. prof., 1970-76, dir. F. Higginson Cabot Lab. Electron Microscopy, 1963-76; research and teaching asst. cytology Rockefeller Inst., N.Y.C., 1957-58; Alden March prof. Albany (N.Y.) Med. Coll., 1976—, chmn. dept. anatomy, 1976-87, prof. pathology, 1981—; prof. biomed. sci. SUNY Sch. Pub. Health, 1986—; pres., CEO Waste Reduction by Waste Reduction, Inc., Troy, N.Y., 1993—; mem. seminar on creative process Wenner-Gren Found., 1964-65; cons. electron microscopy dept. pathology N.Y. VA Hosp., 1965—; Raymond C. Truex Disting. lectr. Hahnemann U., 1987. Co-author: Key Facts in Histology, 1985, Histology: A Text and Atlas, 1995, Atlas der Histologie (in German), 1995; editor: Current Topics in Cellular Anatomy, 1981; assoc. editor: The Anat. Record, 1972—; editorial reviewer: Exptl. Eye Rsch., 1964, Cancer, 1972—, Investigative Ophthalmology, 1973—, Gastroenterology, 1969—; patentee (with Dr. Peter B. Weber) Method for Disposal of Radioactively Labeled Animal Carcasses. Trustee Palisades free Libr., 1965-71; mem. Citizens Adv. Com., Sparkill Palisades Fire Dist., 1968-69; pres. Palisades Free Libr., 1969-71; trustee Orangetown Pub. Libr., 1971-73, Friends of Chamber Music, Troy, N.Y., 1988—; mem. citizens adv. com. Title III Program, S. Orangetown Ctrl. Sch. Dist., 1972-75; chmn. N.Y. State Low Level Waste Group, 1986-95; trustee Rockland Country Day Sch., 1974-78. Recipient Charles Huebschman prize in zoology Columbia U., 1954, Career Scientist award Health Rsch. Coun. N.Y.C., 1963-72, Rsch. Career Devel. award Nat. Inst. Arthritis and Metabolic Diseases, NIH, USPHS, 1972-76, Tousimis prize in biology, 1984; Ford Found. scholar, 1951-55; NSF predoctoral fellow, 1955-56, Nat. Inst. Neurol. Diseases and Blindness predoctoral fellow, 1959-61. Mem. Assn. Anatomy Chairmen (pres. 1980-81), Assn. Am. Med. Colls. (rep. council acad. socs. 1979—, mem. adminstrn. bd. CAS 1985-86), Am. Assn. Anatomists, Electron Microscope Soc. Am., Am. Soc. Cell Biology, Harvey Soc., Assn. Career Scientists Health Research Coun., Internat. Soc. Eye Research, N.Y. Soc. Electron Microscopists (dir. 1964-67), Arthur Purdy Stout Soc. Surg. Pathologists (hon.), Sigma Xi. Club: Waquoit Bay Yacht (Waquoit, Mass.). Office: Albany Med Coll Dept Pathology 47 New Scotland Ave # A-135 Albany NY 12208-3412

KAYE, JANET MIRIAM, psychologist; b. New Haven, Mar. 2, 1937; d. Al and Rose (Marcus) Sovitsky; m. Donald Kaye, June 26, 1955; children: Kenneth, Karen, Kendra, Keith. BS, NYU, 1958, MA, 1960; PhD, Med. Coll. of Pa., 1980. Clin. instr. Med Coll. of Pa., Phila., 1980-82, asst. prof., 1982-86, assoc. prof., 1986-96; prof. Med. Coll. Pa., Phila., 1996—; prof. Allegheny U. of the Health Scis. MCP Hahnemann Sch. of Medicine, East Falls, 1996—. Contbr. articles to profl. jours. Mem. APA, Am. Assn. Cancer Edn., Am. Soc. Clin. Hypnosis, Soc. Health and Human Values, Gerontol. Soc. Am., Am. Soc. Psychiat. Oncology, Coll. Physicians Pa., Internat. Soc. Exptl. Hypnosis. Office: Allegheny Univ of the Health Scis 3300 Henry Ave East Falls PA

KAYE, KEITH WOODHILL, urology educator; b. Cape Town, South Africa, Feb. 8, 1942; arrived in Australia, 1993; s. Josse and Helga (Schlesinger) K.; m. Valda Noreen Goldberg, Oct. 10, 1973; children: Jessica, Deborah, Maxine. BS with honors, U. Witwatersrand, 1964, MB BCh, 1967. Instr. dept. urologic surgery U. Minn., 1979-83, clin. asst. prof., 1983-88, clin. assoc. prof., 1988-92, prof. urology, 1992-93; prof. urology U. Western Australia, Perth, Australia, 1993—; dir. Urological Rsch. Ctr., Perth, Australia, 1993—; presenter in field. Author/editor: Outpatient Urologic Surgery, 1985; contbr. articles to profl. jours.; inventor in field. Recipient Cottrill Meml. prize U. Witwatersrand, Johannesburg, South Africa, 1967. Mem. Australian Prostate Health Coun. (state rep. 1993—), Urological Soc. Australia, Am. Urological Assn., Minn. Urological Soc. (corr. mem.). Jewish. Office: Urological Rsch Ctr, Level 2 M Block Verdun St, Nedlands 6009, Australia

KAYE, NEIL SCOTT, psychiatrist; b. Albany, N.Y., June 1, 1958; s. Jesse J. and Shirley Mae (Poskanzer K.; m. Susan M. Donnelly, July 2, 1988. BA, Skidmore Coll., 1980; MD, Albany Med. Coll., 1984. Diplomate Nat. Bd. Med. Examiners, Am. Bd. Psychiatry and Neurology; lic. med. practitioner, N.Y., Mass., Del.; bd. cert. geriatric psychiatry, 1991. Rotating intern Albany (N.Y.) Med. Ctr. Hosp., 1985, resident dept. psychiatry, 1986-87; with crisis unit coverage Capital Dist. Psychiat. Ctr., Albany, 1986-87; forensic fellow dept. psychiatry Syracuse U.-SUNY Upstate, 1987-88; asst. prof. psychiatry sch. medicine U. Mass., Worcester, 1988-90; evening admissions & continuing treatment unit psychiatrist Worcester State Hosp., 1988-90; dir. consultation and liaison psychiatry Med. Ctr. Del., Christiana Hosp., Wilmington, 1990-92; spl. guest instr. Widener U. Sch. Law, 1991—; asst. prof. dept. psychiatry Thomas Jefferson Sch. Medicine, 1991—; chmn. credentials com. Worcester State Hosp., Worcester; cons. psychiatrist State of N.Y., Auburn (N.Y.) Prison, 1987-88; weekend ward coverage VA Hosp., Albany, 1987-88; supr. jail social worker Rensselaer County Jail, Forensic Svc., Rensselaer County Mental Health Dept., 1987-88; supr. social workers, medication mgmt. for the clinic, Social Security and Disability evalutions, child custody Rensselaer County Mental Health Dept., Unified Svcs., Rensselaer, N.Y., 1987-88; lectr., presenter. Contbr. articles to profl. jours. Rowing referee U.S. Rowing Assn., 1987—; founder and co-chmn. Empire State Regatta, Albany, 1984-87; mem. Downtown Redevel. Commn., Albany, 1984-90, Riverfront Devel. Commn., Albany, 1984-90; at-large mem. bd. dirs. Albany Med. Coll. Aluni Assn., 1985—; vol. driver, attendant, EMT, Saratoga Emergency Corps, 1978-80; house counselor Skidmore Coll, 1979, residence asst., 1980; dir. Camp Shelley Day Camp, New Scotland, N.Y., 1977-82; adv. com. Schaffer Libr. Health Scis., 1981-87. Recipient Mayor's Proclamation for Community Svc., Albany, 1985, Tricentennial Proclamation, Albany, 1986; named Rappeport Fellow nominee, 1987. Mem. AMA (Physicians Recognition award for Continuing Med. Edn.), Am. Psychiat. Assn., N.Y. State Med. Soc., Mass. Med. Soc., Nat. Assn. Sports Ofcls., Am. Acad. Forensic Scis. (com. on ethics 1990—, award for best paper by a forensic fellow 1989), Am. Acad. Psychiatry and the Law (com. on AAPL/APA rels. 1988—, com. on ethics 1988—), Assn. Am. Med. Colls. (faculty 1988—), N.Y. Acad. Scis., Internat. Wine and Food Soc., Am. Acad. Psychiat. Adminstrs., Assn. Compulsive Therapy, Am. Assn. Geriatric. Home: Limestone Hills 3 Hayloft Ct Wilmington DE 19808-1934 Office: Med Ctr Del Dept Psychiatry Dir Consultation and Liaison Psychiatry Wilmington DE 19899 also: Allied Psychiat Svcs 1601 Concord Pike Ste 92-100 Wilmington DE 19803-3613

KAYE, RONALD LEE, physician, educator; b. Toledo, Apr. 15, 1932; s. Philip and Gertrude (Berman) K.; m. Tobye Davidson, June 19, 1955; children: Brian, Todd, Douglas, Jeffrey. BA, U. Mich., 1953, MD, 1957. Diplomate Am. Bd. Rheumatology, Am. Bd. Internal Medicine. Intern Sinai Hosp., Detroit, 1957-58; fellow and staff mem. Mayo Clinic, Rochester, Minn., 1959-63; chmn. dept. rheumatology, dir. med. edn. Palo Alto (Calif.) Med. Clinic, 1963—; clin. prof. medicine Stanford U. Sch. of Medicine, Palo Alto, 1963—. Contbr. articles to profl. jours. Bd. dirs. Am. Mogan David Adom., N.Y.C., 1967—, U.S.-China Ednl. Inst., San Francisco, 1975—, Sino-Judaic Inst., Palo Alto, 1985—. Served to capt. USAF, 1959-61. Fellow ACP; mem. AMA, Am. Soc. Clin. Rheumatology (pres. 1975-80), Arthritis Found. (bd. dirs., Disting. Service award 1974). Jewish. Office: Palo Alto Med Clinic 300 Homer Ave Palo Alto CA 94301-2726

KAYSER, ARND FREDERIK, dentist, educator, researcher; b. Medan, Indonesia, Apr. 23, 1932; arrived in The Netherlands, 1946; m. Henny Fontaine, Jan. 17, 1978; children: Sabine, Stan. DDS, U. Utrecht, The Netherlands, 1956; PhD, U. Nymegen, The Netherlands, 1976. Asst. dentist U. Utrecht, 1956-58; pvt. practice Aruba, Netherlands Antilles, 1958-66; head clinic Dental Sch., Nymegen, 1966-76; prof. dentistry, chmn. dept. oral function U. Nymegen, 1976—; cons. Dental Sch., Free U. of Brussels, 1981-83. Author: (textbook) Crown and Bridge Prosthodontics, 1996, Removable Partial Porsthodontics, 1996. Mem. European Prosthodontic Assn. Home: Prof Vd Grintenstr 1, 6524RG Nymegen The Netherlands Office: P B 9101, 6500 HB Nymegen The Netherlands

KAYSER, KLAUS W., pathologist, researcher; b. Berlin, Aug. 25, 1940; s. Werner and Hildegard (Schultes) K.; m. Maria Consuelo Gatchalian, May 4, 1970; children: Corinna, Gian. PhD, U. Heidelberg, 1965, MD, 1975, Prof. Pathology, 1980. Scientist Bur. Stds., Braunschweig, Ger., 1965-70; med. asst. Inst. Pathology U. Heidelberg (Ger.), 1972-85; head. dept. pathology Thoraxklinik Heidelberg, 1985—. Author: Height and Weight in Human Beings, 1987, Analytical Lung Pathology, 1992, Natural and Synthetic mineral fibers affecting man, 1994; editor: Electronic Journal of Pathology and Histology, 1995—. Mem. European Soc. Pathology (chmn. 1986). Office: Thoraxklinik Dept Pathology, Amalienstr 5, D-69126 Heidelberg Germany

KAYSER, ROBERT JUSTIN, healthcare executive; b. Chgo., Dec. 31, 1946; s. Robert Buttlar and Lorraine A. (Justin) K.; m. Valerie Rose Sommers, Feb. 7, 1976; children: Chad J., Timothy J. BA, Wesleyan U., 1969; MPH, Yale U., 1971. Adminstrv. resident Mary Imogene Bassett Hosp., Cooperstown, N.Y., 1971; asst. hosp. adminstr. Mohawk Valley Gen. Hosp., Ilion, N.Y., 1972-73; nursing home adminstr. Mohawk Valley Nursing Home, Inc., Ilion, 1972-73; assoc. Earl Nicklas, Inc., Cooperstown, 1973-74; rsch. assoc. dept. preventive and community medicine Albany (N.Y.) Med. Coll., 1973-74; area adminstr. N.Y. State Office Health Systems Mgmt., Syracuse, 1974-80; adminstr., chief oper. officer Geneva (N.Y.) Gen. Hosp./Taylor Brown Meml. Hosp., 1980-86; pres., chief exec. officer House of the Good Samaritan Hosp./Samaritan Keep Nursing, Watertown, N.Y., 1986-92, E.J. Noble Hosp.-Alexandria Bay, Alexandria Bay, N.Y., 1991-92; pres. VHA Upstate N.Y., Syracuse, 1992—; adj. prof. health studies program Syracuse U., 1975-80; bd. dirs., mem. exec. com. Finger Lakes (N.Y.) Health Systems Agy., 1980-86; bd. dirs. Chase Lincoln First Bank of No. N.Y. Bd. dirs. upstate N.Y. chpt. Vol. Hosps. of Am., 1986-92. Mem. Ctrl. N.Y. Hosp. Assn. (bd. dirs. 1987-92), Rotary (bd. dirs. Watertown club 1989-92). Home: 8095 Squirrel Corn Ln Manlius NY 13104-9795

KAZAN, ROBERT PETER, neurosurgeon; b. Chgo., Mar. 29, 1947; s. Peter Joseph and Genevieve (Pauga) K.; m. Janet Rae Hoiland, June 21, 1975. BS, Loyola U., Chgo., 1969, MD, 1973. Diplomate Am. Bd. Neurol. Surgeons; lic. physician Ill., Minn. Intern in surgery Mayo Clinic, Rochester, Minn., 1973-74, resident in neurosurgery, 1974-78; neurosurg. cons. West Suburban Neurosurg. Assocs., Hinsdale, Ill., 1978-92; med. dir. neurosci. dept. Hinsdale Hosp., 1992; clin. asst. prof. neurosurgery U. Ill., Chgo., 1983—; various teaching appointments West Suburban Hosp. Dept. Surgery, Chgo. Med. Soc. Midwest Conf., Northwestern U.; staff neurosurgeon Hinsdale Hosp., vice chmn. surgery, 1988-90, chmn. dept. surgery, 1990—, med. dir. neuroscis., 1992. Contbr. articles to profl. jours. Fellow ACS; mem. AMA, DuPage County Med. Soc., Ill. Med. Soc., Mayo Clin. Neurosurg. Soc., Congress Neurosurg. Surgeons, Am. Assn. Neurol. Surgeons, Cen. Neurosurg. Soc., Soc. Med. Cons. Armed Forces U.S., Am. Assn. Neurol. Surgeons (joint sec. trauma and disorders of spine and peripheal nerves), Congress Neurol. Surgeons (joint sect. trauma and disorders of spine and peripheal nerves), Internat. Skullbase Soc., Ill. State Neurosurg. Soc. (membership chmn. 1995). Republican. Roman Catholic. Home: 120 Lakewood Cir Hinsdale IL 60521-6339 Office: West Suburban Neurosurg Assocs 20 E Ogden Ave Hinsdale IL 60521-3543

KAZAZIAN, HAIG HAGOP, JR., medical scientist, physician, educator; b. Toledo, July 30, 1937; s. Haig Hagop and Hermine Adriene (Papelian) K.; m. Lillian Agnes Cleaver, Oct. 13, 1962; children: Haig Hagop III, Sonya Elizabeth. AB, Dartmouth Coll., 1959; MD, Johns Hopkins U., 1962. Asst. prof. pediatrics Johns Hopkins U., Balt., 1969-74, assoc. prof. pediatrics, 1974-77, prof. pediats., 1977-94, prof. biology, 1978-94, prof. ob-gyn., 1985-94, prof. medicine, 1989-94, dir. Ctr. Med. Genetics, 1989-94, Sutland prof. pediat. genetics, 1991-94; chmn. dept. genetics U. Pa. Sch. Medicine, Phila., 1994—; mem. mammalian genetics study sect. NIH, Bethesda, Md., 1981-85; pres. bd. dirs. Citizens for Good Govt., Balt., 1973-75. Author more than 250 sci. papers; editor jour. Human Mutation, 1992. Sr. surgeon USPHS, 1966-68. Grantee NIH, 1968—; recipient Mead Johnson award Am. Acad. Pediatrics, 1976. Mem. Inst. of Medicine, Am. Pediat. Soc., Am. Soc. Human Genetics (bd. dirs. 1982-85), Am. Soc. Clin. Investigation, Assn. Am. Physicians, Alpha Omega Alpha. Democrat. Episcopalian. Home: 1015 Winding Way Baltimore MD 21210-1232 Office: U Pa Sch Medicine 475 Clinical Research Bldg 422 Curie Blvd Philadelphia PA 19104-6145

KAZEMI, HOMAYOUN, physician, medical educator; b. Teheran, Iran, Sept. 28, 1934; came to U.S., 1953, naturalized, 1970; s. Parviz and Irandokht K.; m. Katheryne McNulty, June 7, 1958; children: Paul, Laili. BA, Lafayette Coll., 1954; MD, Columbia U., 1958; MSc (hon.), Harvard U., 1990. Diplomate: Am. Bd. Internal Medicine. Intern M.I. Bassett Hosp., Cooperstown, N.Y., 1958-59; resident in medicine Mass. Gen. Hosp., Boston, 1963; chief pulmonary unit Mass. Gen. Hosp., 1967-89, chief pulmonary and critical care unit, 1989—; assoc. prof. medicine Harvard U., 1971-78, prof., 1979—, prof. medicine Harvard/MIT program in health sci. and tech., 1980—; hon. cons. in internal medicine Shanghai (China) 1st People's Hosp., 1992—; bd. dirs. Boston Tb Assn.; vis. prof. U. Ghent, 1975-76, Peking Union Med. Coll., China, 1992; dir. U.S. Beryllium Case Registry, 1968-78; vis. fellow Hammersmith Hosp., London, 1965; cons. Fed. Aviation Agy., 1987. Author: Disorder of the Respiratory System, 1976, (with L.G. Miller) Manual of Pulmonary Medicine, 1982—, Acute Lung Injury, 1986; mem. editorial bd. New Eng. Jour. Medicine, 1981-90, Respiratory Mgmt., 1989-93; mem. editorial bd. Current Opinion in Pulmonary Medicine, 1993—, Current Opinion in Critical Care, 1993—. dir. Am. Lung Assn. Boston; mem. rsch. evaluation subcom. Am. Heart Assn., mem. cardiopulmonary coun., 1979—, v.p. 1985-87, pres. 1987-89, mem. rsch. rev. com.; bd. trustees Dublin (N.H.) Sch., 1987—. Am. Heart Assn. fellow, 1961-63, Dickinson Richards lectr., 1996; recipient chadwick medal Mass. Thoracic Soc., 1988. Fellow ACP; mem. Am. Fedn. Clin. Rsch., Am. Thoracic Soc. (pres. Ea. sect. 1974-75), Mass. Med. Soc., Am. Physiol. Soc, Am. Soc. Clin. INvestigation, Soc. Occupl. and Environ. Health, Sigma Xi. Office: Mass Gen Hosp Boston MA 02114

KAZEROONI, ELLA ANNABELLE EFFAT, radiologist, educator; b. Sheffield, Eng., Feb. 1, 1965; d. S.A. Majid and Pamela (Hebden) K.; m. Charles Luis Nino, Apr. 30, 1988; 1 child, Charles. BS in Biomed. Scis., U. Mich., 1986, MD, 1988. Diplomate Am. Bd. Radiology. House officer U. Mich., Ann Arbor, 1988-92, lectr., 1992-93, asst. prof., 1993—; fellow Mass. Gen. Hosp., Boston, 1992; manuscript reviewer Am. Jour. of Roentgenology, 1992—. Manuscript reviewer Radiology, 1995—; contbr. articles to profl. jours. U. Mich. grantee, 1994, 95; GEAUR rsch. fellow, 1995—. Fellow Am. Coll. Chest Physicians; mem. Am. Assn. Women Radiologists. Assn. Univ. Radiologists, Am. Roentgen Ray Soc. (program com. 1995—), Soc. Thoracic Radiology, Radiol. Soc. N.Am. Office: Univ Mich Med Ctr 1500 E Medical Center Dr Ann Arbor MI 48109-0326

KAZIM, SUHAIL MOHAMED, physician, consultant, surgeon; b. Dubai, United Arab Emirates, July 9, 1958; s. Mohamed Ahmed and Ziba Abdulrehman (Bookhash) K.; m. Fatma Mohamed Aqil Abbas, Jan. 25, 1989; children: Sumayya, Mohamed. MB, ChB, Baghdad U., Iraq, 1985. Intern Med. City, Baghdad, 1985-86; with Mafraq Hosp., Abu Dhabi, 1985-88; registrar Royal Inverclyde, Glasgow, Scotland, 1989-90; sr. registrar Al-Qasimi Hosp., Sharjah, 1990-91, cons. surgeon, med. dir., 1991—, head of laparoscopy, head of surgery, 1992—, tech. dir., 1991—; mem. sci. surg. adv. com. Ministry of Health and Med. Coll. Al-Ain, Abu Dhabi, 1991—. Contbr. articles to profl. jours. Recipient Sheikh Rashid award for Excellence United Arab Emirates Govt., 1989. Fellow Royal Coll. Surgeons (Edinburgh); mem. Royal Soc. Medicine (London). Home: PO Box 3941, Dubai United Arab Emirates

KAZMIERSKI, SUSAN HEDWIG, family nurse practitioner, nurse midwife; b. Milw., Oct. 20, 1951; d. Albert Fredrick and Louise (Seimers) K. BSN, U. Wis., Milw., 1975; cert. FNP, Stanford U., 1983, cert. nurse midwife, 1985. RN, N.Mex. Nurse, FNP, nurse midwife ARC, Colombia, 1978-81; nurse Migrant Health, Wild Rose, Wis., 1981-82; nurse midwife Rockridge Health Ctr., Oakland, N.Mex., 1984-86; FNP, Health Care No. N.Mex., Coyote, 1986—; bd. dirs. Health Resources No. N.Mex., Albuquerque, 1990-93. Home: PO Box 833 Abicuiu NM 87510 Office: Health Care No N Mex 620 Coronado Cordova NM 87523

KEAGLE, DOUGLAS LEE, physician; b. Elizabeth, N.J., June 9, 1946; s. LeRoy Curtis and Jane Alice (Beckman) K.; m. Donna Theresa Cocola, Sept. 28, 1974; children: Danielle, Dyana, Dana, Douglas. BA, Northeastern U., 1969; DO, Phila. Coll., 1973. Diplomate Am. Bd. Internal Medicine. Intern Fitzgerald Mercy Hosp., Darby, Pa., 1973-74; resident internal medicine Mercy Cath. Med. Ctr., Darby, Pa., 1974-76; assoc. attending physician Huntington Gen. Hosp. and Faulkner Hosp., Jamaica Plain, Mass., 1976-77; staff physician Sacred Heart Gen. Hosp., Chester, Pa., 1977-78; attending physician Mercy Cath. Med. Ctr., Darby, 1978—, Riddle Meml. Hosp., Media, Pa., 1978—; clin. asst. prof. medicine Med. Coll. Pa. Mem. Am. Coll. Physicians, Am. Coll. Osteo. Internists. Republican. Home: 650 Lakeview Cir Newtown Square PA 19073-2608 Office: Mercy Fitzgerald MOB 1501 Landsdowne Ave Ste 301 Darby PA 19023-1333

KEAMY, DONALD GEORGE, otolaryngologist, plastic surgeon; b. Lawrence, Mass., Sept. 23, 1930; s. Mitchell Fadoul and Wadie K.; m. R. Yvonne Hajjar, Sept. 12, 1957; children: Cheryl, Jean, Donald Jr. AB, MIT, 1953; MD, Tufts U., 1957. Pvt. practice pvt. practice, Lawrence, Mass., 1964-70, Chelmsford, Mass., 1970—. Fellow Am. Coll. Surgery, Am. Acad. Facial Plastic and Reconstructive Surgery, Am. Bd. Cosmetic Surgery, Am. Bd. Otolaryngology; mem. New England Otolaryngology Surgery, Am. Acad. Cosmetic Surgeons. Office: 6 Boston Rd Chelmsford MA 01824

KEANE, JOHN FINBARR, pediatric cardiologist; b. Cork, Ireland, Apr. 22, 1937; s. Jeremiah and Christina (Fennell) K.; m. Clare O'Donovan, May 4, 1968; children: John Patrick, Catherine Clare, David Hanley. MB BCh, Nat. U. Ireland, 1960. Intern Charles Wilson Hosp., Johnson City, N.Y., 1963-64; med. resident St. Francis Hosp., Hartford, Conn., 1964-66; fellow in cardiology U. Vt., Burlington, 1966-68; fellow in pediat. cardiology Children's Hosp., Boston, 1970-72, staff cardiologist, 1972—, sr. staff cardiologist. Author chpts. to books; contbr. articles to profl. jours. Lt. col. U.S. Army Med. Corps, 1968-70. Democrat. Roman Catholic. Office: Children's Hosp Cardiology Dept Longwood Ave Boston MA 02115

KEARNEY, WILLIAM F., ophthalmologist; b. Manchester, N.H., Aug. 18, 1933; s. William F. and J. Teresa (O'Connor) K.; m. Barbara M. Dolph, Aug. 24, 1957; children: Patricia Cottiero, Michael, Sheila Bennett, Kevin, Brian, Mary, Karin. BS magna cum laude, Tufts U., Medford, Mass., 1955; MD, Tufts U., Boston, 1959. Diplomate Am. Bd. Ophthalmology. Intern in medicine Boston City Hosp., 1959-60; resident in ophthalmology Cornell U. Med. Ctr.-N.Y. Hosp., N.Y.C., 1960-63, instr., 1963-64; pvt. practice, Manchester, 1964—; pres. med. staff, trustee Elliot Hosp., Manchester, 1984-85. Bd. dirs. YMCA, Manchester, 1985, Manchester Inst. Arts and Scis., 1975. Maj. Army N.G., 1961-67. Mem. Phi Beta Kappa, Alpha Omega Alpha. Republican. Roman Catholic. Home: HC 73 Box 482 Alton Bay NH 03810 Office: NH Eye Assocs 1415 Elm St Manchester NH 03101

KEARNEY NUNNERY, ROSE, nursing administrator, educator, consultant; b. Glen Falls, N.Y., July 8, 1951; d. James J. and Helen F. (Oprandy) K.; m. Jimmie E. Nunnery. BS with honors, Keuka Coll., 1973; M of Nursing, U. Fla., 1976, PhD, 1987. Asst. prof. La. State U. Med. Ctr., New Orleans, 1976-87, U. of South Fla., Tampa, 1987-88; project coord. indigent health care U. Fla., Gainesville, 1984-85; dir. nursing programs SUNY, New Paltz, N.Y., 1988-94; project dir. MS in gerontol. nursing advanced nursing edn. grant U.S. Health Resources and Svcs. Adminstrn. Div. Nursing, 1992-94; head nursing dept. Tech. Coll. of the Lowcountry, Beaufort, S.C., 1995—. Bd. dirs. Ulster County unit Am. Cancer Soc., 1991-94, mem. nursing edn. com., 1990-92; bd. dirs. Mid-Hudson Consortium for Advancement Edn. for Health Profls., 1988-94, mem. nursing edn. com., 1988-92, mem. scholarship com., 1989-93, com. chmn., 1990-93, treas., 1992-94; mem. prof. devel. program SUNY, Albany, 1989-92; mem. adv. coun. Ulster C.C., 1989-94; mem. adv. regional planning group for early intervention svcs. United Cerebral Palsy Ulster County Inc., Children's Rehab. Ctr., 1989-91; mem. Ulster County adv. com. Office for Aging, 1991-94; state del. S.C. Conf. on Aging, 1995; bd. dirs. Beaufort County Coun. on Aging, 1995; mem. cmty. adv. bd. Hilton Head Hosp., 1996—, Hilton Head Med. Ctr. and Clinics, 1996—. Mem. ANA, Sigma Theta Tau. Roman Catholic. Home: 41 S Shore Ct Hilton Head Island SC 29928-7656

KEATING, THOMAS PATRICK, health care administrator, educator; b. Cleve., Jan. 5, 1949; s. Thomas Wilbur and Margaret (Gahllagher) K.; m. Carolyn Elizabeth Kraft, Sept. 4, 1976; children: Jerrod Patrick, Kerri Ann. BS in Bus., Cleve. State U., 1971; MS in Bus., U. Toledo, 1973. Lic. nursing home adminstr.; cert. health care exec. Asst. dir. facilities U. Kans. Med. Ctr., Kansas City, 1977-80; dir. mgmt. svcs. Charleston (S.C.) County Park and Recreation Commn., 1980-84; adminstr. fin., support svcs. Med. U. of S.C., Charleston, 1984—, instr., 1987—, preceptor adminstrv. residency, master health svcs. adminstrn., 1990-93; adj. instr. Cen. Mich. U., Mt. Pleasant, 1979—, Rockhurst Coll., Kansas City, 1979-80, Kansas City (Kans.) Community Jr. Coll., 1978-80, Fayetteville (N.C.) Tech. Inst., 1974-75; accredited cons. SBA, Charleston, 1980-91; adj. prof. Webster U., St. Louis, 1981—, faculty U. Ala., New Coll., 1974; nursing home cons. Charleston County Mental Retardation Bd., Charleston, 1987-88. Contbr. articles to profl. jours. Vol. Driftwood Health Care Ctr., Charleston, 1981-83. Capt. U.S. Army, 1973-77, lt. col. USAR ret. Fellow Am. Coll. Health Care Execs.; mem. Sigma Phi Epsilon (com. chmn. 1970-71), Alpha Kappa Psi (com. chmn. 1972-73), KC. Roman Catholic. Club: Toastmasters (adminstrv. v.p. 1985-86). Home: 898 Farm Quarter Rd Mount Pleasant SC 29464-9518 Office: Med U SC 171 Ashley Ave Charleston SC 29425-0001

KEATING, THOMAS PHILLIP, II, psychotherapist; b. Worcester, Mass., Nov. 4, 1940; s. Phillip Ford and Viola E. (Johnson) K.; m. Lisa Jean Charette, June 8, 1991. BA in Psychology, U. Mass., 1969; MA in Rehab., Assumption Coll., 1979. Social worker Dept. Pub. Welfare, Worcester, Mass., 1969-73; crisis counselor Sch. Dept. Child Study, Worcester, 1973-83; psychotherapist Lipton Ctr., Fitchburg, Mass., 1985—. Author: Fathers, Sons, Mothers and Mercenaries. Mem. Assn. for Tx of Sex Abusers (lectr.), N.H. Assn. Social Workers, N.H. Rehab. Assn. Home: 40 Pikes Hill Rd Sterling MA 01564 Office: Lipton Center 255 Main St Fitchburg MA 01420

KEATON, CHARLES HOWARD, health care administrator; b. Bainbridge, Ga., Oct. 12, 1937; s. Benjamin P. and Annie (Beane) K.; m. Arlene Webb, June 26, 1960; children: Susan K. Parker, C. Benjamin, William H. AB, Mercer U., 1960; MS, Med. Coll. Ga., 1964, Med. Coll. Va., 1990. Sales rep. Parke-Davis, Salisbury, N.C., 1964-68; assoc. dir. Rowan Meml. Hosp., Salisbury, 1968-72; adminstr., chief exec. officer Chester County Hosp., Chester, S.C., 1972-75, Doctors Hosp., Columbus, Ga., 1975-85; pres., chief exec. officer Hughston Sports Medicine Hosp., Columbus, 1983—; trustee Blue Cross/Blue Shield of Ga., Atlanta, 1983—; adj. faculty Tulane U., New Orleans, 1982—. Capt. U.S. Army, 1960-63, Germany. Fellow Am. Coll. Healthcare Execs.; mem. Ga. Hosp. Assn. (chmn. bd. 1990-91), Southeastern Hosp. Assn. (trustee 1991—), Columbus C. of C. (bd. dirs. 1986-90). Republican. Baptist. Office: Hughston Sports Medicine Hosp PO Box 7188 100 Frist Ct Columbus GA 31995-0001

KEATS, CHRISTOPHER JOHN, psychiatrist; b. Phila., Sept. 13, 1943; s. John Cresswell and Margaret (Bodine) K.; children: Leo, Anthony; m. Denise Fort, Aug. 27, 1991. BA, Harvard U., 1970; MD, Temple U., 1973. Diplomate Am. Bd. Psychiatry and Neurology. Staff psychiatrist Chestnut Lodge Hosp., Rockville, Md., 1978—, dir. psychotherapy, 1995—. Co-author (with Thomas H. McGlashan): Schizophrenia: Treatment Process and Outcome, 1989. 1st lt. USAR, 1965-67, Korea. Recipient Edward Bell Krumbhaar prize Coll. Physicians of Phila., 1972. Mem. APA, Washington Psychoanalytic Soc., Am. Psychoanalytic Assn., Alpha Omega Alpha. Office: Chestnut Lodge Hosp 500 W Montgomery Ave Rockville MD 20850-3892

KEATS, MATTHEW MASON, psychiatrist; b. Tokyo, Dec. 10, 1952; s. Theodore Eliot and Margaret (McNamara) K.; m. Anupama Bhardwaj, July 27, 1985. BA, Dartmouth Coll., 1975; MD, U. Va., 1980. Diplomate Am. Bd. Psychiatry and Neurology. Resident psychiatry Cornell Med. Sch., N.Y. Hosp., Westchester div., White Plains, 1981-84; med. dir. Middle Peninsula No. Neck Counseling Ctr., Gloucester, Va., 1984-86; instr. psychiatry Columbia U. Coll. Physicians and Surgeons, N.Y.C., 1986-88; attending psychiatrist Silver Hill Hosp., New Canaan, Conn., 1988-89; assoc. med. dir. chem. dependency unit Tidewater Psychiat. Inst., Virginia Beach, Va., 1989-91, med. dir. Ctr. for Depression, 1992-95; pvt. practice psychiatry Atlantic Psychiat. Svc., Virginia Beach, 1989—; assoc. med. dir. Sentana Mental Health Mgmt., 1995—; asst. prof. clin. psychiatry Med. Coll. Hampton Roads and Psychiat. Ctr., Norfolk, 1991—. Lt. comdr. USPHS, 1984-86. Mem. Am. Psychiat. Assn., Am. Soc. Addiction Medicine, Am. Assn. Psychiatrist in Alcoholism and Addictions. Mem. Unity Ch. Office: Atlantic Psychiat Svcs 780 Lynnhaven Pky Ste 220 Virginia Beach VA 23452-7315

KEATS, THEODORE ELIOT, physician, radiology educator; b. New Brunswick, N.J., June 26, 1924; m. Margaret E. McNamara, Aug. 27, 1949 (dec.); children—Matthew Mason, Ian Stuart B.; m. Patricia L. Hart, Mar. 30, 1974. B.S., Rutgers U., 1945; M.D., U. Pa., 1947. Diplomate: Am. Bd. Radiology (trustee). Intern U. Pa. Hosp., Phila., 1947-48; resident U. Mich. Hosp., Ann Arbor, 1948-51; instr. U. Calif. Sch. Medicine, San Francisco, 1953-54; asst. prof. U. Calif. Sch. Medicine, 1954-56; assoc. prof. U. Mo. Sch. Medicine, Columbia, 1956-59; prof. radiology U. Mo. Sch. Medicine, 1959-63; prof., chmn. dept. radiology U. Va. Sch. Medicine, Charlottesville, 1963-92; vis. prof. Karolinska Hosp., Stockholm, 1963-64; mem. adv. council Greenbrier Clinic. Author: (with Lee B. Lusted) Atlas of Roentgenographic Measurement, 6th edit., 1990, An Atlas of Normal Roentgen Variants That May Simulate Disease, 6th edit., 1995, Self-Assessment of Current Knowledge in Diagnostic Radiology, 2d edit., 1980, An Atlas of Normal Developmental Roentgen Anatomy, 1978, 2d edit., 1988, (with Thomas H. Smith) Radiology of Musculoskeletal Injury, 1990; editor-in-chief Current Problems in Diagnostic Radiology, 1981, Emergency Radiology, 1984, 2d edit., 1989, Applied Radiology, 1989; Am. editor Skeletal Radiology; editor Emergency Radiology, 1993—. Served with AUS, 1943-47; to capt., M.C. AUS, 1951-53. Fellow Am. Coll. Radiology (Gold medal 1995); mem. AMA, Am. Roentgen Ray Soc., Radiol. Soc. N.Am., Assn. Univ. Radiologists, Soc. Pediatric Radiology, So. Med. Assn., Internat. Skeletal Soc. (medal 1995), Soc. Emergency Radiology, Phi Beta Kappa, Sigma Xi, Alpha Omega Alpha. Home: 421 Key West Dr Charlottesville VA 22901-8423 Office: U Va Hosps Jefferson Park Ave Charlottesville VA 22911

KECHIJIAN, PAUL, dermatologist, educator; b. Providence, Mar. 17, 1940; s. Harry Maderos and Annette (Rhia) Paré; m. Janice Ann Kechijian, July 31, 1976; children: Douglas Paul, Lisa Ann. AB in Psychology, Brown U., 1961, SM in Biology, 1964; MD, Albany Med. Coll., 1968. Lic. Nat. Bd. Med. Examiners, N.Y. State Med. Lic.; diplomate Am. Bd. Dermatology, diplomate Dermatopathology Am. Bds. of Dermatology and Pathology. Med. intern, med. resident Barnes Hosp., St. Louis, 1968-69, 69-70; dermatology resident Mass. Gen. Hosp., Boston, 1970, Univ. Miami (Fla.) Sch. of Medicine, 1973-75; dermatopathology fellow NYU Med. Ctr., N.Y.C., 1975-76; instr. clin. dermatology NYU Sch. of Medicine, N.Y.C., 1975-78; clin. asst. prof. of dermatology to clin. assoc. prof. NYU Sch. of Medicine, 1978-84, 84—; asst. attending physician to assoc. attending physician Bellevue Hosp., 1976-81, 81—, NYU Med. Ctr., 1976-84, 84—; asst. attending dermatologist to sr. asst. North Shore Univ. Hosp., 1978-87, 87—; chief inpatient dermatology svc. Bellevue Hosp., 1976-86; cons. Holy Martyrs Armenian Day Sch., 1976—; hon. surgeon (dermatology) N.Y.C. Police Dept., 1981—; chief nail sect. NYU Med. Ctr., 1983—; presenter and lectr. in field. Contbg. editor: Jour. Dermatologic Surgery and Oncology, 1983-85; contbr. reports and articles to profl. jours. and chpt. to book. Fellow ACP, Am. Acad. Dermatology (com. on evaluation 1980-84, coun. on govtl. liaison key contact program 1986—), Am. Soc. Dermatopathology; mem. AMA, N.Y. Acad. Scis., Dermatology Found., Soc. for Investigative Dermatology, Nassau County Med. Soc., L.I. Dermatol. Soc., Soc. for Dermatol. Surgery, Internat. Soc. for Tropical Dermatology, Internat. Soc. Dermatol. Surgery, others. Office: 935 Northern Blvd Great Neck NY 11021-5309

KEDDIE, ROLAND THOMAS, physician, hospital administrator, lawyer; b. Altoona, Pa., Oct. 21, 1928; s. John Barkeley and Jessie E. (Keddie) Isenberg; B.S. cum laude, U. Pitts., 1956, M.D., 1957, J.D., 1970; m. Suzanne M. Seno, Feb. 6, 1978; 1 dau., Dawn Michelle; children by previous marriage: Roland, Thomas, Francis, Robert, Michael, Karen, Andrew, Rosemary. Intern St. Josephs Hosp., Pitts., 1958; practice medicine specializing in emergency medicine and family practice; admitted to Pa. bar, 1970; medico legal cons., 1970—; med. dir. Westmoreland Manor, Greensburg, Pa., 1971; dir. emergency dept. Connemaugh Valley Meml. Hosp., Johnston, Pa., 1976-77, Shadyside Hosp., Pitts., 1978-80, chmn. dept. emergency services McKeesport (Pa.) Hosp., 1980-83, also dir. emergency medicine residency program; pres. EmergiCenters Inc., 1983—; chmn. dept. family practice St. Clair Hosp., Pitts., 1990—; pres. Emergency Med. Services Inst., 1982-85; adj. prof. Sch. Nursing, U. Pitts. Served with USN, 1946-47, 50-52. Diplomate Am. Bd. Family Practice. Mem. Am. Coll. Emergency Physicians (life, bd. dirs. Pa. chpt. 1977-81, 83-86, v.p. 1980-81, pres. 1985-86), Pa. Med. Soc., Hosp. Assn. Pa. (mem. profl. practice com. 1981-82), Allegheny County Bar Assn., AMA (Physicians Recognition award 1974, 77, 80), Allegheny County Med. Soc., Pa. Emergency Health Services Council (dir. 1980), Soc. Tchrs. Emergency Medicine, Beta Beta Beta. Roman Catholic. Home: 45 Meadowcrest Dr Cecil PA 15321-1122 Office: Charters Valley Med Ctr Bridgeville PA 15017

KEDES, LAURENCE H., biochemistry educator, physician, researcher; b. Hartford, Conn., July 19, 1937; s. Sammuel Ely and Rosalyn (Epstein) K.;

m. Shirley Beck, June 15, 1958; children: Dean Hamilton, Maureen Jennifer, Todd Russell. Student, Wesleyan U., 1955-58; BS with distinction, Stanford U., 1961, MD, 1962. Intern Presbyn. U. Hosp., Pitts., 1962-63, asst. resident, 1963-64; rsch. assoc. lab. biochemistry Nat. Cancer Inst. Peterson, 1964-66; sr. asst. med. resident Peter Bent Brigham Hosp., Boston, 1966-67; surgeon USPHS, 1966-68; postdoctoral fellow dept. biology MIT, 1967-68; jr. assoc. in medicine and hematology assoc. Peter Bent Brigham Hosp., Boston, 1967-69; rsch. trainee in embryology Marine Biol. Lab., Woods Hole, Mass., 1967-69; rsch. instr. biology MIT, Boston, 1969-70; asst., assoc. then prof. medicine Stanford U., 1970-89, dir. admissions med. sch., 1978-81; William M. Keck prof. biochemistry and medicine, chair biochemistry, dir. Inst. Genetic Medicine U. So. Calif. Sch. Medicine, L.A., 1989—; staff physician VA, 1970-92; vis. scientist Lab. Molecular Embryology, Naples, Italy, 1969-70, Dept. Animal Genetics, U. Edinburgh, 1970, Imperial Cancer Rsch. Fund, London, 1976-77; instr. embryology Marine Biol. Lab., Woods Hole, 1976; investigator Howard Hughes Med. Inst., 1974-82; founder, dir. IntelliCorp., Mountain View, Calif., 1980-90, chmn., 1982-86. Mem. editorial bd. Jour. Biol. Chemistry, 1982-88, Molecular and Cellular Biology, 1982-89, Jour. Applied Molecular Biology, 1982-85, Oxford Surveys on Eukaryotic Genes, 1983—, Trends in Genetics, 1984-88; assoc. editor Jour. Molecular Evolution, 1982—. Mem. fellowship award com. Am. Cancer Soc., 1978-81; co-principle investigator BIONET, 1984—; mem. rsch. com. Am. Heart Assn., 1987; mem. sci. adv. bd. Muscular Dystrophy Assn. Fellow Med. Found. Boston, 1967-69, John Simon Guggenheim Found. fellow, 1976-77; Leukemia Soc. Am. scholar, 1969-74. Mem. Western Soc. for Clin. Rsch., Am. Soc. Clin. Investigation, Assn. Am. Psysicians, Am. Soc. Microbiology, Am. Soc. Biochemistry and Molecular Biology, Internat. Soc. Devel. Biology, Alpha Omega Alpha. Office: U So Calif 2011 Zonal Ave HMR # 413 Los Angeles CA 90033*

KEEFE, DEBORAH LYNN, cardiologist, educator; b. Oklahoma City, Nov. 23, 1950; d. Stanley William and Gloria Jean (Kelsoe) Denton; m. Richard Alan Keefe, May 14, 1971; children: Jennifer, Colin, Corwin. BA, Rice U., 1973; MD, N.Y. Med. Coll., 1976; MPH, Columbia U., 1990. Diplomate Am. Bd. Internal Medicine, Am. Bd. Cardiovascular Disease, Am. Bd. Critical Care, Am. Bd. Clin. Pharmacology. Intern and resident St. Vincent's Hosp., N.Y.C., 1976-79; fellow in cardiology Stanford (Calif.) Univ. Hosp., 1979-81; dir. CCU Bronx (N.Y.) Mcpl. Hosp., 1981-87; assoc. dir. Am. Cyanamid, Pearl River, N.Y., 1987-88; assoc. mem. Sloan-Kettering Meml. Hosp., N.Y.C., 1988-94, mem., 1994—; asst. prof. medicine Albert Einstein Coll. Medicine, Bronx, 1981-87; assoc. prof. medicine Cornell U., N.Y.C., 1988-95, prof. medicine, 1995—. Assoc. editor Jour. Clin. Pharmacology, 1985-94, editor, 1994—; contbr. articles to Clin. Pharm. Therapeutics, Jour. Cardiovascular Pharmacology, Am. Jour. Cardiology. Fellow Am. Coll. Cardiology, Am. Coll. Chest Physicians, Am. Coll. Angiology, Am. Coll. Clin. Pharmacology (regent 1985-89, 92—, treas, 1992-94); mem. Am. Bd. Clin. Pharmacology, Inc. (sec.-treas. 1994-96). Office: Sloan-Kettering Meml Hosp 1275 York Ave New York NY 10021-6007

KEELER, LYNNE LIVINGSTON MILLS, psychologist, educator, consultant; b. Detroit, Sept. 18, 1934; d. Robert Livingston Mills Staples and Lyda Charlotte (Diehr) Staples; m. Lee Edward Burmeister, July 16, 1955 (div. 1982); children: Benjamin Lee, Lynne Ann; m. Robert Gordon Keeler, Oct. 26, 1986. BS, Ctrl. Mich. U., 1957; MA, U. Mich., 1965; student, Marygrove Coll., Cen. Mich. U., 1971-74. Ltd. lic. psychologist, sch. psychologist; cert. social worker, elem. permanent cons. and tchr. for mentally handicapped. First grade tchr. Shepherd (Mich) Schs., 1957-59; tchr. Kingston (Mich.) Schs., 1959-65; tchr. educationally handicapped Rialto (Calif.) Unified Sch. Dist., 1965-66; tchr., cons. Tuscola Int. Sch. Dist., Caro, Mich., 1966-71; sch. psychologist Huron Int. Sch. Dist., Bad Axe, Mich., 1971-74, Tuscola Int. Sch. Dist., Caro, 1974-89; instr. Delta Coll., University Center, Mich., 1976-88; tchr. spl. day classes Victorville (Calif.) High Sch., 1989; sch. psychologist Bedford (Ind.) Schs., 1990-91; clin. psychologist ACT team and outpatient therapy Sanilac County Mental Health Svcs., Sandusky, Mich., 1991—; cons. sch. psychologist Marlette (Mich.) Schs., 1982-86, Bartholomew Pub. Schs., Columbus, Ind., 1989, Johnson County Schs., Franklin, Ind., 1990; clin. psychologist Thumb Family Counseling, Caro, 1985-88; personnel com. Team One Credit Union, 1993. Conf. presenter in field. Del. NEA-Mich. Edn. Assn. Rep. Assemblies, 1970-89; pres., auction chmn. Altrusa Club, Marlett, 1982-88; style show chmn. Marlette Band Boosters, 1983; mem. exec. bd. Lawrence County Tchrs. Assn., Bedford, 1991; mem. Sanilac Symphonic Band, 1993-94; bd. dirs. Team One Credit Union, 1994—. Fed. govt. grantee Wayne State U., 1968. Mem. Am. Federated State and Mcpl. Employees (chairperson #219 1993, chairperson #15 chpt. 1993-96), Ind. State Tchrs. Assn. (rep. assembly del. 1991), Ind. Assn. Sch. Psychologists (pub. rels. bd. 1990-91), Lions (bd. dirs. 1996—). Democrat. Methodist. Home: 6726 Clothier Rd Clifford MI 48727-9501 Office: Sanilac County Cmty Mental Health 190 N Delaware St Sandusky MI 48471-1009

KEELING, BRENDA LEE, hospital director, charge nurse; b. Pauls Valley, Okla., Nov. 5, 1954; d. William Jack and Ada Cordillia (Carter) Huthchins; m. Ronnie Noel Keeling, Feb. 15, 1982; children: Jamie, Lisa, Robby, Brandon. A Surgical Tech., So. Okla. City Jr. Coll., 1976; ADN, Murray State Coll., Tishomingo, Okla., 1978; BSN, East Ctrl. U., Ada, Okla., 1985. RN, Tex., Okla.; Audiometric cert., Ky.; cert. Intensive Care Neonatal, Okla., Interqual Registration, Tex. Charge nurse labor-delivery Bryan Mem. Hosp., Durant, Okla., 1983-87; staff nurse Baylor Med. Ctr., Dallas, 1987-91; review coord. Okla. Found. Med. Quality, Okla. City, 1989-93; relief nurse supr. Med. Ctr. Southeast Okla., Durant, 1991—, asst. coord. utilization mgmt., 1991-94; dir. utilization mgmt.-physician quality Mem. Hosp., Ardmore (Okla.) Hosp., 1994—; pres. Keeling Med. Legal Cons., Milburn, Okla., 1995—. Team mem. Critical Incident Stress Mgmt., 1995—; vol. ARC, 1995—, Jr. 4-H, Johnston County, 1985—. Mem. Nat. Assn. Healthcare Quality, Am. Assn. Utilization Mgmt. Nurses (accreditation com. 1995-96). Democrat. Baptist. Home: Rt 1 Box 212 Milburn OK 73450 Office: Mem Hosp So Okla 1011 14th NW Ardmore OK 73401

KEELING, ELIZABETH BURFOOT, health facility administrator; b. Wills Point, Tex., Jan. 23, 1959; d. Charles Andrews and Elizabeth Ligon (Wilson) Burfoot; m. Robert Walton Keeling, Aug. 31, 1985. ADN, La. Tech. U., 1983; BSN, N.E. La. U., 1985; MSN, U. Tex. Sch. Nursing, Arlington, 1991. RN, Tex., La. Staff nurse St. Francis Med. Ctr., Monroe, La., 1983-85; staff nurse Valley Bapt. Med. Ctr., Harlingen, Tex., 1985-86, nurse mgr., 1986-88, MIS coord., 1988-89; staff nurse Meth. Med. Ctr., Dallas, 1989-91, asst. dir. nursing, 1991-92, edn. dir., 1992-93, dir. women and children's svcs. and edn., 1993-94; asst. adminstr. patient care svcs. Med. Ctr. Mesquite, Tex., 1994-95; program dir. patient info. systems Meth. Med. Ctr., Dallas, 1996—. Mem. ANA, Tex. Nurses Assn., Tex. Orgn. Nurse Execs., Tex. Soc. Healthcare Educators (bd. dirs. 1992-94), Dallas Area Soc. Healthcare Educators (pres.-elect 1991-92, pres. 1992-94), Healthcare Info. Mgmt. Systems Soc., Sigma Theta Tau. Home: 649 S First St Hewitt TX 76643 Office: Meth Med Ctr PO Box 655999 Dallas TX 75265-5999

KEENAN, RETHA ELLEN VORNHOLT, nurse, educator; b. Solon, Iowa, Aug. 15, 1934; d. Charles Elias and Helen Maurine (Konicek) Vornholt; BSN, State U. Iowa, 1955; MSN, Calif. State U., Long Beach, 1978; m. David James Iverson, June 17, 1956; children: Scott, Craig ; m. Roy Vincent Keenan, Jan. 5, 1980. Publ. health nurse City of Long Beach, 1970-73, 94—, Hosp. Home Care, Torrance, Calif., 1973-75; patient care coord. Hillhaven, L.A., 1975-76; mental health cons. InterCity Home Health, L.A., 1978-79; instr. Community Coll. Dist., L.A., 1979-87; instr. nursing El Camino Coll., Torrance, 1981-86; instr. nursing Chapman Coll., Orange, Calif., 1982, Mt. Saint Mary's Coll., 1986-87; cons., pvt. practice, Rancho Palos Verdes, Calif., 1987-89. Contbg. author: American Journal of Nursing Question and Answer Book for Nursing Boards Review, 1984, Nursing Care Planning Guides for Psychiatric and Mental Health Care, 1987-88, Nursing Care Planning Guides for Children, 1987, Nursing Care Planning Guides for Adults, 1988, Nursing Care Planning Guides for Critically Ill Adults, 1988. Cert. nurse practitioner adult and mental health, 1979; mem. Assistance League of San Pedro, Palos Verdes, Calif. NIMH grantee, 1977-78. Mem. Sigma Theta Tau, Phi Kappa Phi, Delta Zeta. Republican. Lutheran. Avocations: travel, writing, reading. Home: 27849 Longhill Dr Rancho Palos Verdes CA 90275 Office: 2525 Grand Ave Long Beach CA 90815

KEENE, CLIFFORD HENRY, medical administrator; b. Buffalo, Jan. 28, 1910; s. George Samuel and Henrietta Hedwig (Yeager) K.; m. Mildred Jean Kramer (dec.), Mar. 3, 1934; children: Patricia Ann (Mrs. William S. Kneedler), Martha Jane (Mrs. William R. Srpoule), Diane Eve (Mrs. Gordon D. Simonds); m. Mary Oliver Dixon, Dec. 16, 1995. AB, U. Mich., 1931, MD, 1934, MS in Surgery, 1938; DSc, Hahnemann Med. Coll., 1973; LLD, Golden Gate U., 1974. Diplomate Am. Bd. Surgery, Am. Bd. Preventive Medicine (occupational medicine). Resident surgeon, instr. surgery U. Mich., 1934-39; cons. surgery of cancer Mich. Med. Soc. and Mich. Dept. Health, 1939-40; pvt. practice surgery Wyandotte, Mich., 1940-41; med. dir. Kaiser-Frazer Corp., 1946-53; instr. surgery U. Mich., 1946-54; med. adminstrv. positions with Kaiser Industries and Kaiser Found., 1954-75, v.p., 1960-75; v.p., gen. mgr. Kaiser Found. Hosps. and Kaiser Found. Health Plan, 1960-67; med. dir. Kaiser Found. Sch. Nursing, 1954-67; dir. Kaiser Found. Research Inst., 1958-75; pres. Kaiser Found. Hosps. Health Plan, Sch. Nursing, 1968-75, dir., 1960-80; chmn. editorial bd. Kaiser Found. Med. Bull., 1954-65; lectr. med. econs. U. Calif.-Berkeley, 1956-75; mem. vis. com. Med. Sch., Stanford U., 1966-72, Harvard U., 1967-71, 79-85, U. Mich., 1973-78; Mem. Presdl. Panel Fgn. Med. Grads. (Nat. Manpower Commn.), 1966-69. Contbr. papers to profl. lit. Bd. visitors Harvard Bus. Adv. Council, 1972, Charles R. Drew Postgrad. Med. Sch., 1972-79; trustee Amman Civil Hosp., Jordan, 1973, Community Hosp. of Monterey Peninsula, 1983-92. Lt. col. M.C. AUS, 1942-46. Recipient Disting. Service award Group Health Assn. Am., 1974; Disting. Alumnus award U. Mich. Med. Center, 1976; Disting. Alumnus Service award U. Mich., 1985. Fellow ACS; mem. Am. Assn. Indsl. Physicians and Surgeons, Nat. Acad. Scis., Inst. Medicine, Calif. Acad. Medicine, Frederick A. Coller Surg. Soc., Calif., Am. med. assns., Alpha Omega Alpha (editorial bd., contbr. to Pharos mag. 1977—). Home: 3978 Ronda Rd PO Box 961 Pebble Beach CA 93953

KEENE, JACK DONALD, microbiology educator; b. Jacksonville, Fla., June 21, 1947; s. Jack Donald and Stella Collene (Ellis) K.; m. Judy May Keene, Sept. 6, 1969; children: Mike, Lisa. AB, U. Calif., Riverside, 1969; PhD, U. Wash., 1974. Staff fellow NINDS/NIH, Bethesda, Md., 1974-78; asst. prof. Duke U. Med. Ctr., Durham, N.C., 1979-84, assoc. prof., 1984-88, prof., 1988-92, chmn., 1992—; mem. nat. selection and adv. bd. PEW Scholars in the Biomed Scis., 1991—; mem. molecular biology study sect. NIH, 1991-95, chmn., 1993-95; co-chmn. Diversity Biotech. Consortium, Santa Fe, 1994—; dir. basic sci. rsch. Duke U. Comprehensive Cancer Ctr., Duke U. Program in Genetics, Program in Molecular and Cellular Biology. Assoc. editor: Virology, 1983—; editorial bd.: Jour. of Virology, 1985-95, Molecular and Cellular Biology, 1991—; editor: Microbiological Reviews, 1992—, Molecular Diversity, 1995—. Mem. fellowship com. Arthritis Found., 1990-92, mem. rsch. com., arthritus found, 1990-92. Recipient Faculty Rsch. award Am. Cancer Soc., Devil's Bag award Arthritis Found.; Nanaline Duke Faculty Scholar, PEW Scholar in the Biomed. Scis. Fellow Am. Soc. Microbiology; mem. Am. Soc. Virology, Am. Soc. Biochemistry and Molecular Biology, RNA Soc. Office: Duke Univ Med Ctr Box 3020 Microbiol Dept Research Dr/414 Jones Bldg Durham NC 27710

KEENER, ELLIS B., neurosurgeon; b. Murphy, N.C., Nov. 24, 1926; s. Horace Harvey and Nancy Lou (Tindell) K.; m. Margaret Ann Stambaugh, Apr. 24, 1954; children: Jane Mackenzie, E. Barlow, John, Jere, Bill, Jim. BS, Emory U., 1947, MD, 1950; MS, McGill U., Montreal, Can., 1956, diploma in Neurosurgery, 1959. Diplomate Am. Bd. Neurol. Surgeons. Intern, then resident in surgery N.Y. Med. Coll., N.Y.C., 1950-52; clin. clerk in neurology Nat. Hosp. for Nervous Diseases, London, 1954-55; fellow in neuropathology Montreal Neurol. Inst., 1955-56; demonstrator in neuropathology McGill U., 1955-56; resident in neurosurgery Montreal Neurol. Inst., 1956-59; demonstrator in neurosurgery McGill U., 1958-59; fellow in electroencephalography Montreal Neurol. Inst., 1958; instr. to asst. prof. Emory U. Sch. Med., Atlanta, 1959-63; pvt. practice Atlanta, 1963-88; instr. in physiology Emory U. Sch. Med., Atlanta, 1963-66; chief dept. neurosurgery DeKalb Gen. Hosp., Decatur, Ga., 1970-81, chief dept. surgery, 1973-77; chief neurol. scis. St. Joseph's Hosp., Atlanta, 1973-77; clin. assoc. prof. Emory U. Sch. Med., Atlanta, 1988—; pvt. practice Gainesville, Ga., 1988-95; vis. prof. neurosurgery U. Tenn., Memphis, 1975, Temple U., Phila., 1976; cons. Yerkes Regl. Primate Ctr. Emory U., 1966—; pres. Composite State Bd. Med. Examiners, 1992-93. Contbr. numerous articles to profl. jours. 1953—; editor: Clin. Neurosurgery vols. 23-25, 1975-78. Lt. M.C., USNR, 1952-54. Markle scholar in Med. Sci., Emory U., 1961-63. Fellow ACS (sec. Ga. chpt. 1985-91, pres. 1992-94, mem. bd. govs. 1986-92, exec. com. 1989-92, sec. 1990-92, chmn. gov.'s com. to study fiscal affairs 1990-92, mem. bd. regent's finance com. 1990-92); mem. AMA, So. Neurol. Soc., Am. Assn. Neurol. Surgeons (nominating com. 1986-89, mem. profl. conduct com. 1990-92, bd. dirs. 1992-95), Congress Neurol. Surgeons, Soc. Univ. Neurosurgeons (pres. 1974), Am. Acad. Neurol. Surgery (membership com. 1985-87, v.p. 1986-87), Ga. Surg. Soc. (pres. 1996), Ga. Neurosurg. Soc. (pres. 1975), Med. Assn. Ga. (neurosurg. rep. at inter-specialty coun. 1973-92, chmn. peer rev. com. for neurosurgery 1978-81, chmn. interspecialty coun. 1979-89, chmn. sci. assembly com. 1983-86, del. Hall County 1984-89), Atlanta Clin. Soc., Atlanta Neurol. Soc. (treas. 1977-80, pres. 1980—), Sigma Xi. Home: 915 E Lake Dr NW Gainesville GA 30506

KEENEY, ARTHUR HAIL, physician, educator; b. Louisville, Jan. 20, 1920; s. Arthur Hale and Eugenia (Hail) K.; m. Virginia Alice Tripp, Dec. 27, 1942; children—Steven Harris, Martha Blackledge Heyburn, Lee Douglas. B.S., Coll. William and Mary, 1941; MD, U. Louisville, 1944; MS, U. Pa., 1952, DSc, 1955; DSc honoris causa, Bellarmine Coll., 1996. Diplomate Am. Bd. Ophthalmology (assoc. examiner 1960-84, hon. M in Ophthalmic Optics 1992). Intern Louisville Gen. Hosp., 1944-46; resident in ophthalmology Wills Eye Hosp., Phila., 1949-51, ophthalmologist in chief, 1965-73; dir. ophthalmology research U. Louisville, 1952-65, asst. prof. ophthalmology, 1958-63, assoc. prof., 1963-65, prof., dean Sch. Medicine, 1973-80, Disting. prof. ophthalmology, dean emeritus, 1980—; prof., chmn. ophthalmology Temple U., 1966-72; profl. adv. com. Nat. Soc. Prevention of Blindness, 1964-78, dir., 1981-84, exec. com., 1984, regional rep., 1984-86, v.p., 1986-87; Alvaro lectr. S.Am. Univs., 1960; sec.-treas. Nat. Com. Research in Ophthalmology and Blindness, 1964-78; vision study sect. neurol. and sensory disease control program Nat. Ctr. Chronic Disease Control, USPHS, 1966-69; med. cons. Project Head Start, 1968—; chmn. com. on ophthalmic Standards Am. Nat. Standards Inst., 1970-85; chmn. Ky. med. rev. bd. driver limitation program State of Ky., 1974—; med. adv. bd. Recording for Blind, 1976-80, Nat. Aid to Visually Handicapped, 1970-79; hon. pres. 2d symposium Internat. Congress Diagnostic Ultrasound in Ophthalmology, Czechoslovakia, 1967; pres. 4th Internat. Congress Ultrasonography in Ophthalmology, Phila., 1968. Author: Chronology of Ophthalmic Development, 1951, Ocular Examination: Basis and technique, 1970, 2d edit., 1976; co-author: Dictionary of Ophthalmic Optics, 1995; editor: (with V.T. Keeney) Dyslexia: Diagnosis and Management of reading Disorders, 1968, (with K. Gitter, D. Mayer and L.K. Sarin) Ophthalmic Ultrasound, 1969; assoc. editor Am. Jour. Ophthalmology, 1965-81, cons. editor, 1981—; mem. editl. bd. Investigative Ophthalmology, 1969-73, Ophthalmology Excerpta Medica, 1974—, Sight Saving, 1982-86; contbr. articles to profl. jours., chpts. in books. Mem. Phila. Dist. Bd. Health and Welfare Coun., 1967-69, Nat. Coun. to Combat Blindness, 1967-84; mem. adv. bd., assoc. trustee U. Pa. Sch. Social Work, 1968-73; exec. bd. dirs. Old Ky. Home coun. Boy Scouts Am., 1976-79; life trustee James Graham Brown Found., 1978—; bd. dirs. Louisville Orch., 1963-65, Pa. Assn. for Blind, 1965-68, Am. Found. for Blind, 1975-78, The Lighthouse, N.Y.C., 1995—. Served to capt. MC, AUS, 1942-47. Recipient Laureate award Younger Women's Club, 1964, Allstate Safety Crusade award, 1965, Patrick R. O'Connor Meml. award, 1983, 11th Howe medal U. Buffalo, 1973, 21st Beverly Myers Nelson award Am. Bd. Opticianary, 1974, Meritorious Service award Am. Nat. Standards Inst., 1985, Ednl. Achievement award Ky. Med. Assn., 1986, Faculty Dist. Service award U. Louisville, 1987, Disting. Alumnus award U. Louisville Med. Sch. Alumni Assn., 1988, Spirit of Excellence award Ky. Mil. Inst. Alumni Assn., 1992. Fellow Am. Ophthal,. Soc., Am. Acad. Ophthalmology (life, chmn. com. ophthalmic instruments and devices 1977-85, Sr. Merit award 1984, v.p. 1985-87), Coll. Physicians of Phila., Pa. Acad. Ophthalmology and Otolaryngology (v.p. 1973), Am. Soc. Ophthalmic Ultrasound (hon.); mem. AMA, AAAS, Columbian Soc. Ophthalmology, Ky. Eye, Ear, Nose and Throat Soc. (pres. 1958), Hellenic Ophthal. Soc., Joint Commn. Allied Health Pers. in Ophthalmology (v.p. 1985-87, pres. 1987-89), Louisville Acad. Ophthalmology, Ky. Acad. Eye Physicians and Surgeons (pres. 1984), Ky. Surg. Soc., Ill. Soc. Ophthalmology and Otolarynology, Salmagundi Club, Pendennis, Louisville Country Club. Home: 3727 Fairway Ln Louisville KY 40207-1414 Office: 301 E Muhammad Ali Blvd Louisville KY 40202-1511

KEGELES, LAWRENCE STEVEN, psychiatrist; b. Madison, Wis., Feb. 9, 1947; s. Gerson and Bertha (Webber) K.; m. Wendy Carol Winer, Aug. 10, 1987; 1 child, Laura Rosalyn. AB, Princeton U., 1969; PhD in Physics, U. Pa., 1974; MD, Mt. Sinai Sch. Medicine, N.Y.C., 1991. Lic. physician, N.Y. Rsch. assoc. U. Pa., Phila., 1974-76, U. Alberta, Edmonton, Can., 1976-78, Stevens Inst. Tech., Hoboken, N.J., 1978-80; mem. tech. staff AT&T Bell Labs., Murray Hill, N.J., 1981-87; postdoctoral resident Columbia Presbyn. Hosp., N.Y.C., 1991-95, rsch. fellow in psychiatry, 1995—; adj. rsch. faculty Mt. Sinai Sch. Medicine, 1991—. Contbr. 20 articles to profl. jours. Eli Lilly & Co. fellow, 1995; Nat. Alliance for Rsch. on Schizophrenia and Depression grantee, 1995—. Mem. Sigma Xi. Office: Columbia Presbyn Hosp Dept Psychiatry 722 W 168th St New York NY 10032

KEGELES, S. STEPHEN, behavioral science educator; b. Manchester, N.H., June 2, 1925; s. Alex and Jennie (Wilder) K.; m. Jane Ainsworth, Jan. 3, 1948; children: Susan, Martha, Nancy, Robert, Dorothy. BA, Drake U., 1949; MA, Boston U., 1951, PhD, 1955. Rsch. psychologist Boston Psychopathic Hosp., 1950-52, USPHS, Washington, 1954-56; chief social psychol. studies sect. Div. Pub. Health and Resources, USPHS, 1957-62, chief social studies br., 1960-62; rsch. assoc., lectr. U. Mich., 1962-65, assoc. prof. pub. health, asst. dir. pub. health practice, 1965-66, co-dir., doctoral tng. program in pub. health adminstrn., 1966-69, prof. dept. behavioral scis. and community health, 1969—; sr. rsch. scientist Ctr. for the Environ. and Man, Inc., Hartford, Conn., 1970-71; assoc. dir. Conn. Cancer Control Rsch. Unit at Yale, 1986-89; head, behavioral scis., 1986-89; expert cons. WHO, 1969-79; tech. advisor surgeon gens. adv. com.; adv. com. Conn. State Dept. Health Svcs. Contbr. articles to profl. jours., chpts. to books. With USN, 1943-45. Recipient Disting. Sr. Sci. award Behavioral Scientists in Dental Rsch., 1988, numerous grants from various orgns. Fellow Acad. Behavioral Medicine Rsch.; mem. Internat. Assn. Dental Rsch., Am. Assn. Dental Rsch., Am. Pub. Health Assn., Am. Psychol. Assn. Home: 114 N Main St West Hartford CT 06107-1209 Office: U Conn Health Ctr Dept Behavioral Scis Farmington CT 06032

KEGLEY, JOHN FRANKLIN, psychotherapist, educator; b. Evanston, Ill., Mar. 6, 1944; s. Charles William and Elizabeth Euphemia (Meck) K.; m. Mary Frances Gardner, Dec. 28, 1966; children: Carolynn Elizabeth, Geoffrey Gardner. BA, Gettysburg Coll., Pa., 1966; MA, George Washington U., Washington, 1969, EdS, 1970, EDD, 1973. Counselor, tchr. D.C. Pub. Schs., Washington, 1966-72; lectr. in edn. Va. Polytechnic Inst. & SU, Reston, Va., 1974-79; community coord. Montgomery County Pub. Schs., Rockville, Md., 1972-79, supr. of spl. svcs., 1979-81, pupil personnel worker, 1981—; mental health counselor pvt. practice, Rockville, Md., 1979—; speaker WDCA-TV Newsprobe, Washington, 1982; bd. dirs. The C.W. Kegley Lectureship in Political Philosophy, Bakersfield, Calif., 1986—. Founder: Gateway Alternative Sch., 1978; supr. Kaps I-V Keeping All Pupil in Sch., 1973-78; grantsman, supr. Richmond Montgomery Intergroup Rels. Project, 1975; supr. Inward, Outward, Upward 1976; contbr. articles to profl. jours. Recipient The Harry E. Detwiler Meml. award in counseling, The George Washington U., 1977. Mem. ACA, Am. Mental Health Counselors Assn., Internat. Assn. Pupil Pers. Workers, Assn. for Counseling Edn. and Supervision, Phi Delta Kappa, Phi Delta Theta. Lutheran. Home: 9604 Napoleon Way Montgomery Village MD 20879-2160 Office: Dept Alternative Programs Montgomery County Pub Schs 12518 Greenly St Silver Spring MD 20906

KEILL, STUART LANGDON, psychiatrist; b. Binghamton, N.Y., Oct. 5, 1927; s. Kenneth and Dorothy B. (Langdon) K.; m. Joanne Veness, Sept. 2, 1950; children: Elinor Anne Moran, Patricia J., Brian S., Victoria M. Keill Lo Russo. B.A., Princeton U., 1947; M.A., Cornell U., 1948; M.D., Temple U., 1952. Intern Highland Hosp., Rochester, N.Y.; resident in psychiatry N.Y. State Psychiat. Inst., Presbyn. Hosp., Columbia U., N.Y.C., 1955-58; dir. edn., dir. West Side Community Mental Health Ctr., N.Y.C., 1958-71, Roosevelt Hosp., N.Y.C., 1958-71; regional dir. N.Y. State Dept. Mental Health, 1971-75; prof. clin. psychiatry SUNY, Stony Brook, 1975-80; chmn. dept. psychiatry Nassau County Med. Ctr., East Meadow, N.Y., 1975-80; clin. prof. psychiatry SUNY, Buffalo, 1980-86; chief psychiat. service VA Med. Ctr., Buffalo, 1981-86; prof. of psychiatry Sch. of Medicine U. Md., 1986-94, vice chmn. dept. psychiatry, 1986-93, prof. sch. social work, 1993-94, acting chmn., 1991-92; clin. prof. psychiatry Sch. Medicine NYU, 1994—; counselor Advocates Coalition for Psychiat. Patients, 1980-86; med. dir. Inst. for Psychiatry and Human Behavior, 1986-93; mem. adv. com. mental health laws Md. Atty. Gen. Office, 1987—; mem. com. on pub. social policy Fedn. Protestant Welfare Agys., 1974-77; cons. USPHS, Adamaha, 1977-80; mem. faculty NIMH Staff Coll., 1979; sr. rsch. fellow U. Glasgow, Scotland, 1994. Author: (with others) Textbook on Administrative Psychiatry, 1992; also 48 articles; mem. editorial bd. Social Work and Health Care, 1975—, Hosp. and Community Psychiatry; assoc. editor Gen. Hosp. Psychiatry Jour., 1981—. Chmn. Nassau coun. Health Systems Agy., 1977-80; mem. adv. com. Dr. Glory's Children's Theatre, N.Y.C., 1980—; mental health laws adv. com. State's Atty. Gen., 1987. With USN, 1953-55. Recipient Julius T. Marcus award dept. psychiatry SUNY, Stony Brook, 1980. Fellow Am. Coll. Psychiatrists, Am. Psychiat. Assn. (Distinction in Adminstrn. award 1990); mem. MEDIPP Psychiatry Council (dist. chmn. 1981-86), Am. Assn. Psychiat. Adminstrs. (pres. 1981-82), Am. Hosp. Assn. (chmn. psychiat. services sect. 1985), Am. Assn. Gen. Hosp. Psychiatrists (pres. 1985-87), N.Y. Soc. Clin. Psychiatry (pres. 1974-75, chmn. pub. psychiatry com.), Md. Psychiatric Soc. Office: MPC Ward's Island Dept Psychiatry New York NY 10035

KEILLER, DANNY L., urologist, educator; b. Mpls., Apr. 15, 1942; s. Matt and Ivedell (Lee) K.; m. Barbara Booth, May 30, 1964; children: Douglas, Karin. BS in Zoology, U. Ariz., 1964; MD, Baylor U., 1968. Diplomate Am. Bd. Urology, Am. Bd. Family Practice. Pvt. practice, San Diego, 1975—; clin. instr. U. Calif. Med. Sch., San Diego, 1975-79, clin. asst. prof., 1979-85, clin. assoc. prof., 1985—; mem. adv. bd. Planned Parenthood, San Diego, 1980-95; vice chief staff Sharp Cabrillo Hosp., San Diego, 1995—. Contbr. articles to med. jours. Bd. dirs. San Diego Hospice, 1976-80. Maj. M.C., USAF, 1973-75. Fellow ACS, Am. Coll. Physician Execs.; mem. AMA, Am. Urol. Assn., Calif. Med. Assn. (splty. del. 1985-91), Calif. Urol. Assn. (founding bd. dirs. 1988). Unitarian. Office: Urol Physicians 4033 3d Ave Ste 400 San Diego CA 92103

KEILP, MARK JOHN, microbiologist; b. Jersey City, N.J., June 14, 1957; s. John P. and Catherine M. (Wisniewski) K. BS in Microbiology, Rutgers U., 1979, postgrad. in Chemistry, 1979-83. Med. technologist U. Hosp.-U. Medicine and Dentistry of N.J., Newark, 1979-83; microbiologist Cosmair/Loreal-Lancome, Piscataway, N.J., 1983-85, Whitehall/Am. Home Products, Hammonton, N.J., 1985-88, Labs. Serobiologiques, Somerville, N.J., 1988-90, Ciba Corning Diagnostics Corp., Medfield, Mass., 1990—; mem. microbiology com. Cosmetics Toiletries and Fragrances Assn., Washington, 1988-90; mem. Ind. Cosmetic Mfrs. and Distbrs., Palatine, Ill., 1989-91. Asst. dist. staff office USCG Aux., Boston, 1986-95. Mem. Am. Soc. Microbiology. Republican. Roman Catholic. Home: 121 North St # 12 Medfield MA 02052 Office: CIBA Corning Diagnostics 63 North St Medfield MA 02052

KEIM, MICHAEL RAY, dentist; b. Sabetha, Kans., June 8, 1951; s. Milton Leroy and Dorothy Juanita (Stover) K.; m. Christine Anne Lorenzen, Nov. 20, 1971; children: Michael Scott, Dawn Marie, Erik Alan. Student, U. Utah, 1969-72; DDS, Creighton U., 1976. Pvt. practice Casper, Wyo., 1976—. Mem. organizing bd. dirs. Ctrl. Wyo. Soccer Assn., 1976-77; mem. Casper Mountain Ski Patrol, Nat. Ski Patrol System, 1980—, avalanche and ski mountaineering advisor No. Divsn. Region III, 1992—; bd. dirs., dep. commr. for fast pitch Wyo. Amateur Softball Assn., 1980-84; bd. dirs. Ctrl. Wyo. Softball Assn., 1980-84; pres. Wyo. Spl. Smiles Found., 1995-96; mem. organizing com. Prevent Abuse & Neglect thru Dental Awareness Coalition, Wyo., 1996; mem. adv. com. Natrona County Headstart, 1985—. Recipient Purple Merit Star for Saving a Life, 1992. Mem.. ADA, Fedn. Dentaire Internat., Pierre Fauchard Acad., Wyo. Acad. Gen. Dentristry (sec.-treas. 1980-82, pres. 1982-87), Wyo. Dental Assn. (bd. dirs. 1992—, chmn. conv. 1993, ADA alt. del. 1994-95, v.p. 1993-94, pres.-elect 1994-95, pres. 1995-

96), Wyo. Dental Polit. Action Com. (sec.-treas. 1985—), Ctrl. Wyo. Dental Assn. (sec.-treas. 1981-82, pres. 1982-83), Wyo. Dental Hist. Assn. (bd. dirs. 1989-95), Wyo. Donated Dental Svcs. (organizing bd. dirs. 1994, pres. 1995-96), Kiwanis (v.p. Casper club 1988-89, bd. dirs. 1986—, pres.-elect 1989-90, pres. 1990-91, internat. del. 1989-91, chmn. internat. rels. com. 1992—), Creighton Club (pres. 1982-84). Methodist. Home: 58 Jonquil St Casper WY 82604-3863 Office: 1749 S Boxelder St Casper WY 82604-3538

KEIRSEY, KENNETH JEFFREY, optometrist; b. Sikeston, Mo., Jan. 23, 1954; s. John Kenneth and Betty Marie (Holder) K.; m. Angela Kay Shell, Aug. 10, 1975; children: Andrew B., Hannah K., Nathaniel J. BS in Secondary Edn., Southeast Mo. State U., 1977, OD, 1992. Tchr. secondary sch. Scott City (Mo.) Schs., 1977-88; optometrist Insight Eyecare, Warrensburg, Mo., 1992—. Deacon, bible tchr. Grover Park Bapt. Ch., Warrensburg, 1992—. 1st lt. USAFR, 1972—. Mem. Am. Optometric Assn. (polit. action com. 1989-93), Mo. Optometric Assn., West Ctrl. Mo. Optometric Assn. Republican. Home: 420 Lynn Warrensburg MO 64093-2235 Office: Insight Eyecare 602 N Maguire Warrensburg MO 64093

KEISEL, MAURINE LILLEY, rehabilitation nurse; b. Corry, Pa., Oct. 31, 1939; d. Maurice D. and Violet S. (Vettenburg) Lilley; m. Glenn L. Keisel, Apr. 7, 1962; children: G. Adam, Glenda (Sunny), Mark. Diploma in nursing, Hamot Hosp. Sch. Nursing, 1961. RN; CRRN, Rehab. Nursing Certification Bd. RN Bethesda Childrens Home, Meadville, Pa., 1961-62; staff RN Ashtabula (Ohio) Gen. Hosp., 1969-71; coord., supr. restorative nursing program Ashtabula Medicare Ctr., 1975-87; co-owner, cons. Keisel Phys. Therapy, Ashtabula, 1989—; parish nurse, health ministries coord. Bethany Luth. Ch., Ashtabula, 1992—; cons. in field; coord. Faith and Health Partnership Ashtabula County, 1995—; mem. adv. bd. Continuum Home Care Inc., 1995—. Mem. ANA, Ohio Nurses Assn., Assn. Rehab. Nurses, Health Ministries Assn., Nurses Christian Fellowship. Lutheran. Home: 3016 S Ridge W Ashtabula OH 44004 Office: Keisel Phys Therapy 416 W 27th St Ashtabula OH 44004-4975

KEITH, FRASER, surgeon; b. Montreal, Que., Can., Apr. 30, 1948. B.Engring. with honors, McGill U., Montreal, 1970; MD, Queens U., Kingston, Ont., 1976. Diplomate Am. Bd. Surgery. Attending surgeon Henry Ford Hosp., Detroit, 1985-89; assoc. clin. prof. U. Calif., San Francisco, 1989—, dir. cardiopulmonary transplantation, 1989—. Fellow ACS, Royal Coll. Surgeons (Can.). Office: Univ of California M-593 Box 0118 505 Parnassus Ave San Francisco CA 94143-0118

KEITH, HOWARD BARTON, surgeon; b. Enid, Okla., Aug. 23, 1932; s. John A. and Dorothy O. (Murphy) K.; m. Joanne Lee Norman, Mar. 12, 1954; children: Preston Jonathan, Kim Keith Glazier, Shaun Howard, Spencer Norman. Degree, U. Okla., 1953, MD, 1957. Diplomate Am. Bd. Surgery, Am. Bd. Thoracic Surgery. Intern in surgery U. Okla. Med. Ctr., 1957-58, resident in gen. surgery, thoracic, cardiovascular surgery, 1958-63; gen. and thoracic surgeon Newman Meml. Hosp., Shattuck, Okla., 1963-87, chief of staff, bd. dirs., 1963-83; gen. and thoracic surgeon Woodward (Okla.) Hosp. and Health Ctr., 1988—; pres. N.W. Okla. Specialty Clinic, Woodward, 1988-92; assoc. preceptor U. Okla. Med. Ctr., Shattuck, 1963-79, preceptor, 1979-87; preceptor U. Okla. Med. Ctr., Woodward, 1988—; pvt. practice MedWest Physicians Network, Inc., Woodward; clin. asst., prof. surgery U. Okla., 1980—; pres. Newman Med. Ctr., Inc., 1977, 85-87; cons. utilization and peer rev. Region VI Dept. Human Health Svc., 1973—; bd. dirs. Okla. Regional Med. Program, 1964-70; med. dir., bd. dirs. Shattuck Convalescent Ctr., 1964-78; aviation med. examiner FAA, 1967-92; cancer liaison physician Woodward Hosp. and Health Ctr., 1988; gen. surgery cons. Dept. Human Health Svcs., 1979—; presenter in field. Contbr. articles to profl. publs. Trustee Shattuck Hosp. Authority, 1964-76; mem. exec. bd. dirs. Great Salt Plains coun. Boy Scouts Am., 1969-82, mem. fin. com., 1970-82; med. advisor N.W. Okla. chpt. Okla. State TB Assn., 1964-80; bd. edn. Shattuck Pub. Sch. Sys., 1964-71; pres. Lions Club, Shattuck, 1967; bd. dirs. Big Bros-Big Sisters, N.W. Okla., 1986, Woodward Indsl. Found., 1988—, Okla. Found. for Peer Rev., 1981-91, K-101 Classic Bowl, 1989, Grand Nat. Quail Found., 1991, Okla. U. Club of N.W. Okla., 1989-92, Woodward Rotary Club, 1989-92; med. advisor Angel Fire Ski Patrol, 1981-84; mem. adv. bd. Blue Cross Blue Shiels, 1984—; chmn. Shattuck Bus. Devel. Com., 1987; trustee Alumni Assn. Sch. Medicine U. Okla., 1987; advisor to tech. med. direction com. Okla. State Health Dept., 1979-93; bd. govs. Angel Fire Corp., 1980-84; mem. ad hoc adv. com., High Plains adv. com. High Plains Vo-Tech. Sch., Woodward, 1984, mem. supt.'s bd., 1989; chmn. EMS, tech. med. direction com. Okla. State Dept. Health, 1984-93; v.p. Okla. Trauma Soc., 1990; chmn. med. direction subcom. Okla. EMS Adv. Coun., 1990; bd. EMS-C consortum sect. gen. pediatrics U. Okla. Health Sci. Ctr., 1990. Mem. AMA, ACS (liaison fellow commn. on cancer 1968—, mem. coun. 1977—, mem. Okla. cancer com. 1971-77, mem. Okla. trauma com. 1972—, chmn. 1979-89, Okla. adv. com. 1975—, v.p. Okla. chpt. 1980-81, pres.-elect 1982, pres. 1982-83, nat. com. on trauma 1989-95), Nat. Assn. EMS Physicians, Okla. Thoracic Soc. (pres. 1972), Okla. State Med. Assn. (med. advisor N.W. Okla. 1964-80, chmn. peer rev. com. 1965-74), N.W. Counties Med. Soc. (pres. 1965, 82-83), Okla. Surg. Soc. (pres.-elect 1976, pres. 1977), Aerospace Med. Assn., Am. Nuclear Soc., Pan Am. Med. Assn., Am. Soc. for Laser Medicine and Surgery, Soc. Am. Gastrointestinal Endoscopic Surgeons. Home: 2402 Brentford Pl Woodward OK 73801 Office: MedWest Physician Network 908 19th St Woodward OK 73801

KEKATOS, DEPPIE-TINNY Z., microbiologist, researcher, lab technologist; b. Buffalo, Oct. 16, 1960; d. Soter Spyros and Mary Soter (Kassimis) Zarifopoulos; m. Dion Kekatos; 1 child, Mary. BS, CUNY, 1983; MS, St. John's U., Jamaica, N.Y., 1986. Lic. lab. technologist, N.Y. Clin. lab. technologist trainee Booth Meml. Hosp., Flushing, N.Y., 1986-87; clin. lab. technologist L.I. Jewish Hosp., New Hyde Park, N.Y., 1988-89, Elmhurst (N.Y.) Hosp., 1990-95; asst. supr. microbiology United Health Labs., Woodside, N.Y., 1995-96. Mem. Am. Pharm. Assn., St. John's U. Alumni Fedn. Home: 25-34 Crescent St Apt 5K Long Island City NY 11102-2928 Office: United Health Labs 72-34 Calamus Ave Woodside NY 11377

KELALIS, PANAYOTIS, pediatric urologist; b. Nicosia, Cyprus, Jan. 17, 1932; came to U.S., 1960, naturalized, 1969; s. Peter and Julia (Petrides) K.; m. Barbara Wilson, Apr. 8, 1970. Student, U. Edinburgh, 1950-51; M.B.B.Ch., U. Dublin, 1957; M.S. in Urology, Mayo Grad. Sch. Medicine, 1964. Resident in urology Mayo Grad. Sch. Medicine, Rochester, Minn., 1960-64; asst. to staff Mayo Clinic, 1964, cons. urology, 1965—, head sect. pediatric urology, 1975-91, chmn. dept. urology, 1982-91; chmn. dept. urology Mayo Clinic, Jacksonville, Fla., 1991, chair internat. activities, 1991—; prof. urology Mayo Med. Sch., 1975—, Anson L. Clark prof. pediatric urology, 1985—; mem. Residency Rev. Com. for Urology, 1989-95 (chair 1993, 94). Editor: Clinical Pediatric Urology, 2 vols., 1976, 3d ed., 1992; contbr. numerous sci. articles to profl. jours., chpts. in books. Hon. consul Republic of Cyprus. Recipient Edward J. Noble Found. award, 1964; decorated knight Order of St. Andrew. Fellow ACS; mem. Am. Assn. Genito-Urinary Surgeons, Internat. Soc. Urology, Am. Urol. Assn., Soc. Pediatric Urology (pres.), Am. Acad. Pediatrics (pres., chmn. urology sect.), Royal Soc. Medicine, Soc. Univ. Urologists, Sociedad Latino Americana de Urologia Infantile (hon.), Assn. Francaise d'Urologie (hon.), Hellenic Urol. Soc. (hon.), Sociedad Argentine de Urologia (corr.), Venezuelan Urol. Soc. (corr.), Sigma Xi. Office: Mayo Clinic 4500 San Pablo Rd S Jacksonville FL 32224-1865

KELCH, ROBERT PAUL, pediatric endocrinologist; b. Detroit, Dec. 3, 1942; s. Paul and Iona Bertha (Schmitt) K.; m. Jeri Anne Parker, Aug. 17, 1963; children: Randall Paul, Julie Marie. PhB, Wayne State U., Detroit, 1964; MD, U. Mich., Ann Arbor, 1967. Intern then Wyeth pediatric residency fellow U. Mich. Med. Center, 1967-70, research fellow, 1969-70, mem. faculty, 1972-94, prof. pediatrics, 1977-94, acting chmn. dept., 1979-80, chmn. dept., 1981-94; physician-in-chief C.S. Mott Children's Hosp. U. Mich., 1983-94; chief clin. affairs U. Mich. Hosps., 1989-92; NIH trainee pediatric endocrinology U. Calif. Med. Center, San Francisco, 1970-72; prof. pediatrics, dean U. Iowa Coll. Medicine, Iowa City, 1994—. Co-author: A Practical Approach to Pediatric Endocrinology, 1975; contbr. articles med. jours. Served with USNR. Fellow Am. Acad. Pediatrics; mem. Soc. Pediatrics Rsch. (pres. 1988), Am. Bd. Pediatrics (sec.-treas. 1992, chmn. elect 1994, chmn. 1995), Endocrine Soc., Am. Fedn. Clin. Rsch., Am. Soc. Clin. Investigators, Assn. Med. Sch. Pediatric Dept. Chmn. (pres. 1989), Ctrl. Soc. Clin. Rsch., Lawson Wilkns Pediatric Endocrine Soc., Midwest Soc. Pediatric Rsch. (pres. 1983-84). Methodist. Home: 620 Larch Ln Iowa City IA 52245-3435 Office: U Iowa Coll Medicine 212 CMAB Iowa City IA 52242-1101

KELEMEN, JOHN, neurologist, educator; b. Nyíregyháza, Hungary, Apr. 28, 1948; s. Ignac and Anna (Hartman) K. BA, SUNY, Binghamton, 1970; MD, Georgetown U., 1974. Cert. Am. Bd. Psychiatry and Neurology-Neurology, Am. Bd. Electrodiagnostic Medicine. Med. intern Nassau County Med. Ctr., East Meadow, N.Y., 1974-75; neurology resident Nassau County Med. Ctr., East Meadow, 1975-78, staff neurologist, 1980-85, dir. MDA clinic, 1980-85, chief neuromuscular program, 1981-85; neuromuscular fellow Tufts U.-New Eng. Med. Ctr., Boston, 1978-80; pntr. Island Neurol. P.C., Plainview, N.Y., 1985—; clin. asst. prof. neurology NYU Sch. of Medicine, 1996—; clin. asst. prof. neurology Cornell U. Med. Coll., N.Y.C., 1986-95; tchg. residents and med. students Stony Brook U., Cornell U., NYU, Manhasset, East Meadow, 1980—; lectr. in field. Contbr. chpts. to books and articles to profl. jours. Rsch. grantee Muscular Dystrophy Assn., Boston, 1979, Nassau Heart Assn., East Meadow, 1984. Fellow Am. Acad. Neurology. Office: Island Neurol PC 824 Old Country Rd Plainview NY 11803

KELETI, GEORG, retired microbiologist, researcher; b. Michalovce, East Slovakia, Czechoslovakia, May 30, 1925; s. Louis and Lilly (Silberstein) K.; m. Martha Helene Maxian, July 28, 1956; children: Eva, Daniel. Degree in pharmacy, Comenius U., Bratislava, Czechoslovakia, 1950, PhD in Microbiology, 1952; candidate of sci. in biology, Acad. Scis., Bratislava, 1961; cert., Continuing Edn. Physicians, Bratislava, 1963. Asst. prof. microbiology Comenius U., 1950-53, prof.'s asst., 1953-63, assoc. prof., 1963-68; sr. fellow Max-Planck Inst., Freiburg, Fed. Republic of Germany, 1968-70; asst. rsch. prof., then assoc. prof. U. Pitts., 1970-96; sr. scientist Bactex Pitts., 1979-81; cons. in field, 1986—; adj. prof. occupational environ. health Grad. Sch. Pub. Health, U. Pitts., 1986-96, ret., 1996, now part-time assoc. prof. Author: Handbook of Micromethods for the Biological Sciences, 1974; contbr. articles to profl. jours. Patentee Anti-tumor process using a Brucella Abortus preparation, 1989. Served to 1st lt. Czech. Army, 1951-54. Mem. Am. Soc. Microbiology, Allegheny Soc. Microbiology. Home: 5831 Nicholson St Pittsburgh PA 15217-2309

KELFER, HOWARD M., neurologist, pediatrician; b. Boston, Aug. 28, 1950; s. Albert I. and Paula (Bargar) K.; m. Laurie Sarfatti, Sept. 2, 1979; children: Adam, William. BS, Trinity Coll., Hartford, Conn., 1972; BMS, Dartmouth Coll., 1974; MD, Tufts U., 1976. Diplomate Am. Bd. Pediatrics, Am. Bd. Neurology with special qualification in child neurology. Intern in pediatrics New Eng. Med. Ctr., Boston, 1976-77, resident in pediatrics, 1977-79, fellow in child neurology, 1979-82; pvt. practice Ft. Worth Child Neurology Assoc., 1982-93; staff physician in child neurology Cook Physician Network, Ft. Worth, 1994—; chmn. ethics com., mem. credentials com. Cook Children's Med. Ctr. Office: Cook Physician's Network Dept Child Neurology 709 W Leuda Fort Worth TX 76104

KELL, SHERRON HENDERSON, internist, geriatrician; b. Birmingham, Ala., May 10, 1949; d. John Lehman and Ruby Irene (Beranek) Henderson; m. Robert Edward Kell, May 28, 1979. BA, U. Ala., Birmingham, 1972, BS, 1983, MD, 1987, M in Pub. Health, 1993. Graphic designer Campus Crusade for Christ, San Bernardino, Calif., 1972-76; self employed art dir. Birmingham, Ala., 1976-77; sr. art. dir. Luckie & Forney Advt., Birmingham, 1977-80; cons. art dir. Cargill Wilson & Acree Advt., Birmingham, 1981-84; internal medicine resident Bapt. Med. Ctrs., Birmingham, 1987-90; geriatric medicine fellowship U. Ala., Birmingham, 1991-93, asst. prof., 1993—. Contbr. articles to Jour. Am. Geriatric Soc., Jour. Applied Physiology, Jour. Cardiopulmonary Rehab. Recipient Trainee Investigator award Am. Fedn. for Clin. Rsch., 1993, Outstanding Poster award Marion Merrill Dow, L.A., 1994. Mem. AMA, Am. Geriatrics Soc., Gerontolog. Soc. Am. Office: Univ Ala Med Sch 933 S 19th St Rm 219 Birmingham AL 35294

KELLAM, JAMES FRANKLIN, orthopedic surgeon; b. Toronto, June 2, 1945; came to the U.S., 1990; s. Franklin Wilson and Nora Irene (Brown) K.; m. Lynda Maureen Henry, Aug. 19, 1969; children: Lindsay, Stepanie, Paterk. BS, U. Toronto, 1967, MD, 1973. Asst. prof. surgery U. Toronto, 1980-90; vice chmn. dir. orthopedic trauma Carolinas Med. Centre, Charlotte, N.C., 1990—; chmn. edn. com. A.O. N.Am., Paoli, Pa., 1993-96; trustee A.O. Internat., Davos, Switzerland, 1993-96; Kennedy vis. prof. U. Toronto, 1996; vis. prof. Royal Coll. Surgeons, 1994-95. Contbr. chpts. to books. Office: Carolinas Med Ctr 1000 Blyne Blvd Charlotte NC 28232

KELLAM, NORMA DAWN, medical, surgical nurse; b. Benton Harbor, Mich., June 13, 1938; d. Edgar Arnold and Bernice (Cronk) K. AA, San Bernardino Valley Coll., 1958; student, Calif. State Coll., Long Beach, 1961-1964, 1965, 1966, 1967; BS, San Diego State Coll., 1961; MS, Calif. State U., Fresno, 1972. Nursing instr. Porterville (Calif.) State Hosp., 1966-69; staff nurse Northside Psychiat. Hosp., Fresno, 1969-72; nursing instr. Pasadena (Calif.) City Coll., 1972-73; night shift lead Fairview Devel. Ctr., Costa Mesa, Calif., 1973-96; freelance writer, 1996—. Contbr. articles to newspapers. Vol. Spanish translator for Interstitial Cystitis Assn. Recipient Cert. of Appreciation for vol. work Interstitial Cystitis Assn. Mem. Calif. Nurses Assn., Soc. Urologic Nurses and Assocs., Inc., Phi Kappa Phi.

KELLAM, SANDRA, occupational therapist; b. Saginaw, Mich., May 14, 1940; d. I. Lee and Charlotte (O'Neall) Kellam; children: Scott Howe, Rick Howe, Piet Beerends. AA, Stephens Coll., 1960; BS, Coll. of William and Mary, 1962. Occupational therapist Met. Hosp., N.Y.C., 1963-65, Gen. Hosp. of Monterey County, Salinas, Calif., 1965-66; supr. occupational therapy Grant-Cuesta Hosp., Mountain View, Calif., 1968-71; dir. occupational therapy svcs. Kennebec County Regional Health Agy., Waterville, Maine, 1976-82; occupational therapist Eastern Shore Regional Ednl. Continuum, Accomac, Va., 1982-86; registered occupational therapist cons. to spl. learning ctr., Onancock, Va., 23417, 1986—; cons. in field. Chmn. For a Safe Park, Rangeley, Maine, 1973, Citizens for Longley for Gov., Rangeley, 1974; field worker Cohen for Senate, Maine, 1978; organizer Citizens for Responsible Govt., Dresden, 1980; chmn. Citizens for Barrier-free Access, 1986—, Post and Beam Homebuilders Group, 1986. Recipient cert. Merit Occupational Therapy Club. Mem. Am. Occupational Therapy Assn., World Fedn. Occupational Therapists, Orthotics Unltd. (v.p. 1979-80), Eastern shore bike club. Presbyterian. Clubs: Subron Officers Wives (pres. 1967-68) (Rota, Spain); Skiers Anonymous (v.p. 1973-74) (Rangeley).

KELLAWAY, PETER, neurophysiologist, researcher; b. Johannesburg, Republic of South Africa, Oct. 20, 1920; s. Cecil John Rhodes and Doreen Elizabeth (Joubert) K.; m. Josephine Anne Barbieri, Apr. 1957; children: David, Judianne, Kevin, Christina, Jaime. BA, Occidental Coll., 1942, MA, 1943; PhD, McGill U., 1947; MD (hon.), U. Gothenberg, Sweden, 1977. Diplomate Am. Bd. Clin. Neurophysiology. Lectr. physiology McGill U., Montreal, Que., Can., 1946-47, asst. prof. physiology, 1947-43; assoc. prof. Baylor U. Coll. Medicine, Houston, 1948-61, prof., 1961-78, prof. neurology, 1978—, prof. div. neurosci., 1990—, dir. lab. clin. electrophysiology, 1948-65; dir. dept. clin. neurophysiology The Meth. Hosp., Houston, 1948-71, mem. attending staff, 1948—, chief, sr. attending physician Neurology Svc., 1971—; cons., neurophysiologist Hermann Hosp., Houston, 1949-73, dir. dept. electroencephalography, 1955-73; dir. electroencephalography lab. Ben Taub Gen. Hosp., Houston, 1965-79; mem. cons. staff, chief neurophysiology svc. Dept. Medicine Tex. Children's Hosp., Houston, 1972—; mem. cons. staff neurology St. Luke's Episc. Hosp., Houston, 1971-73, mem. cons. staff neurophysiology, chief neurophysiology svc., 1973—; dir. Blue Bird Circle Children's Clinic Neurol. Disorders The Meth. Hosp., 1949-60, dir. Blue Bird Circle Rsch. Labs., 1960-79, chmn. Instnl. Rev. Bd. Human Rsch., 1974-90, dir. Epilepsy Rsch. Ctr., 1975—; chmn. appointment and promotions com. Baylor U. Coll. Medicine, 1968-71, dir. Epilepsy Rsch. Ctr., 1975—, chief sect. neurophysiology Dept. Neurology, 1977—; cons., electrophysiologist VA Hosp., Houston, 1949—; cons. electroencephalography So. Pacific Hosp. Assn., Houston, 1949-57; cons., neurophysiologist M.D. Anderson Hosp. and Tumor Inst., Houston, 1953-62; mem. coun. adminstrs. Tex. Med. Ctr., Houston, 1954-60; cons. electroencephalography sect. NIH, 1961-62; hon. pres. Internat. Congress Clin. Neurophysiology, 1993. Author numerous books; editor Electroencephalography and Clin. Neurophysiology, 1968-71, cons. editor, 1972-75, hon. cons. editor, 1989; mem. editl. bd. Jour. Clin. Neurophysiology, 1995; contbr. over 180 articles to profl. jours. Recipient Sir William Osler medal Am. Assn. History of Medicine, 1946; grantee NIH, NASA; named Grass lectr. Am. Soc. EEG Technologists, 1989; Berger lectr., 1982, 92. Fellow Am. Acad. Pediat. (hon.), Am. Electroencephalographic Soc. (hon., coun. 1954, 64-66, treas. 1956-58, pres.-elect 1962-63, pres. 1963-64, Jasper award 1990); mem. Am. Epilepsy Soc. (sec.-treas. 1955-58, pres.-elect 1959, pres. 1960, Lennox lectr. 1981, Disting. Clin. Investigator award 1989), Am. Physiol. Soc., Am. Physiol. Assn., Am. Acad. Neurology, Am. Neurol. Assn., Can. Physiol. Soc., Internat. Fedn. Clin. Neurophysiology (hon. pres. internat. congress), Internat. League Against Epilepsy (Am. br.), So. Electroencephalographic Soc. (coun. 1953, v.p. 1954, pres. 1955), Ea. Assn. Electroencephalographic Soc., Ctrl. Encephalographic Soc., Houston Neurol. Soc. (v.p. 1957, pres. 1967, chmn. bd. trustees 1970-73), Soc. Neurosci., Child Neurology Soc., Epilepsy Assn. Houston/Gulf Coast (profl. adv. bd. 1985-92). Home: 627 E Friar Tuck Ln Houston TX 77024-5706 Office: Baylor Coll Medicine 1 Baylor Plz Houston TX 77030-3411

KELLEHER, CATHERINE PATRICIA, nursing educator; b. Jersey City, May 3, 1947; d. Vincent John and Kathryn Helen (Petsu) K. BSN cum laude, Georgetown U., 1969; MSN, U. Calif., San Francisco, 1970; MPH, Harvard U., 1979; ScD, Johns Hopkins U., 1985. Staff nurse McAuley Neuropsychiat. Inst. St. Mary's Hosp., San Francisco, 1970-71, 74; postgrad. rsch. nurse/faculty HEW commune health edn. grant San Francisco Med. Ctr. Sch. Nursing U. Calif., 1971-74; mem. faculty San Francisco Med. Ctr. divsn. Continuing Edn. in Nursing U. Calif., 1973-74; dir. video, telemedicine project Thomas A. Dooley Found., N.Y.C., 1975-76; audiovisual supr. Brookdale Hosp. Med. Ctr., Bklyn., 1976, clin. coord., 1976-78; rsch. assoc. Bur. Med. Svcs. USPHS Adminstrn., Hyattsville, Md., 1980; rsch. assoc. Office of Rsch. Balt. USPHS Hosp., 1981, Wyman Park Health Sys., Balt., 1981-83; staff nurse Henry Phipps Psychiat. Clinic Johns Hopkins Med. Instns., Balt., 1979, 84, sr. rsch. assoc. Office Med. Practice Evaluation, 1985; rsch. assoc. Oncology Ctr. Johns Hopkins U. Sch. Medicine, Balt., 1985-91; asst. prof. Sch. Nursing Johns Hopkins U., Balt., 1990-92, asst. prof. Oncology Ctr. Sch. Medicine, 1991-95; asst. prof. dept. health policy and mgmt. Sch. Hygiene and Pub. Health Johns Hopkins U., 1993-95; dir. MSN/MPH joint degree program Schs. Nursing and Hygiene and Pub. Health Johns Hopkins U., 1992-95; faculty assoc. dept. health policy and mgmt. Sch. Hygiene and Pub. Health Johns Hopkins U., 1995—, faculty assoc. Sch. Nursing, 1995—; sr. rsch. assoc./program evaluator Vis. Nurse Svc. of N.Y., Ctr. for Home Care Policy Rsch., N.Y.C., 1995—; adj. instr. Sch. Nursing Georgetown U. Med. Ctr., Washington, 1985-86, Inst. for Health Policy Analysis Sch. Medicine Georgetown U. Med. Ctr., 1985-89; mem. adv. coun. Johns Hopkins U. Sch. Nursing Rsch., 1990-95; mem. Johns Hopkins U. Interdivisional Curriculum Adv. Group, 1992—; mem. generic data elements working group and severity of illness task force Office Clinical Quality Assessment and Rsch. Initiative Johns Hopkins U., 1992-93; cons. State Md. Dept. Health and Mental Hygiene, 1990-95, Divsn. Nursing Indian Health Svc., 1992, Robert Wood Johnson Found., 1989, Health Svcs. Rsch. and Devel. Svc. VA Adminstrn., 1986-88, Ctr. for Home Care Policy and Rsch. Vis. Nurse Svc. of N.Y., 1995, Johns Hopkins U. Sch. Nursing, 1995—, Ramathibodi Sch. Mahidol U. Dept. Nursing Faculty of Medicine, Bangkok, Thailand, 1996—, United Hosp. Fund of N.Y., 1996—; mem. interdivisional working group for Ctr. for Am. Indian and Alaskan Native Health, Sch. Hygiene and Pub. Health Johns Hopkins U., 1992-95, mem. Child and Adolescent Mental Health Svcs. Ctr., 1994-95; presenter in field; adj. prof. NYU Sch. Edn. Divsn. Nursing, 1995—; faculty assoc. dept. health policy and mgmt. Johns Hopkins U. Sch. Hygiene and Pub. Health, 1995—, Johns Hopkins U. Sch. Nursing; mem. adv. bd. Pace U. Leinhard Sch. Nursing. Author: (with others) A Clinical Information System for Oncology, 1989; contbr. articles to profl. jours., chpt. in book. Harvard U. scholar, 1978-79, Johns Hopkins U. scholar, 1979-85; NIH grantee, 1990, USPHS grantee, 1981; recipient Nat. Rsch. Svc. award HHS, Dept. Pub. Health Svcs., HRA, BHP, 1980-84. Mem. ANA, APHA (med. care, internat. health and pub. health nursing sects., chair Masters in Nursing-Masters in Pub. Health joint degree program task force pub. health nursing sect. 1994—, liaison to Assn. Cmty. Health Nursing Educators 1994—, mem. legis. com. 1994-95), NAFE, Am. Hosp. Assn., Assn. for Health Svcs. Rsch., Oncology Nursing Soc., Md. Pub. Health Assn. (mem. program com. 1993-94, bd. dirs. 1994-95), Friends of Nat. Inst. for Nursing, Assn. Cmty. Health Nursing Educators (mem. edn. com. 1994—), Nat. League for Nursing (mem. coun. cmty. health svcs. 1993—), Md. League of Nursing, Md. League for Nursing, Assn. of Cmty. Cancer Ctrs., Nat. Coun. for Internat. Health, Nat. Assn. County and City Health Ofcls., Md. Nurses Assn. (dist. 2, mem. cmtyorce 1993-95), Nursing Honor Soc., Delta Omega (Alpha chpt. Pub. Health Honor Soc. 1985), Sigma Theta Tau (Tau chpt. 1969, Nu Beta chpt. 1992), others. Home: 100 Riverside Dr Apt 1E New York NY 10024-4822 Office: Vis Nurse Svc of NY Ctr for Home Care Policy and Rsch 18th Fl 5 Penn Plz New York NY 10001-1810

KELLEHER, JAMES RAYMOND, health care corporation executive; b. N.Y.C., Sept. 14, 1948; s. James Raymond and Constance (Roche) K.; m. Anne Gilmartin, May 6, 1972; children: Brian James, Michael Patrick. BS, Fairfield U., 1970; MBA, St. John's U., N.Y.C., 1975. Plant controller Gen. Foods, Topeka, 1976-79; owner Rutland Corp., Newport, R.I., 1979-81; asst. controller C.R. Bard-Davol, Cranston, R.I., 1981-83; controller cardiopulmonary div. C.R. Bard, Santa Ana, Calif., 1983-84; v.p., controller cardiosurgery div. C.R. Bard, Billerica, Mass., 1984-88, asst. corp. controller, 1988-94; v.p., gen. mgr. export divsn. C.R. Bard Inc., Murray Hill, N.J., 1994-96; area v.p. Ams. C.R. Bard Inc., Murray Hill, 1996—. Served with U.S. Army N.G., 1970-76. Roman Catholic. Home: 71 Linden Dr Basking Ridge NJ 07920-1963 Office: CR Bard Inc 730 Central Ave New Providence NJ 07974-1139

KELLER, BEN ROBERT, JR., gynecologist; b. Big Spring, Tex., July 9, 1936; s. Ben Robert and Rowena Ward (Gibson) K.; children: Gwenyth Sue Keller Wood, Jennifer Lynn Keller Pleska, Amy Jo Keller Hightower, Ben R. III, Destry S.L. BA, U. Tex., 1959; MD, U. Tex., Dallas, 1961. Diplomate Am. Bd. Obstetrics and Gynecology. Intern Hermann Hosp., Houston, 1961-62, ob-gyn resident, 1962-65; pvt. practice Arlington, Tex., 1967-79, 87—, Glenwood Springs, Colo., 1979-87, Arlington, 1987—; clin. instr. U. Tex., Dallas, 1975-79; assoc. clin. prof. U. Colo., Denver, 1983-86; mem. active staff Arlington Meml. Hosp., 1989—; courtesy staff South Arlington Med. Ctr., 1990—. Bd. dirs. Planned Parenthood North Tex., 1990—; chmn. speakers bur. Am. Cancer Soc., Arlington, 1968-73; mem. Arlington Drug Abuse Com., 1969-72, Glenwood Springs (Colo.) Coun. on Drug Abuse, 1984-87; chmn. bd. elders 1st Christian Ch., Arlington, 1975-76; chmn. Texpac com. Tarrant County, Ft. Worth, 1972-75. Capt. M.C., USAF, 1965-67. Fellow Am. Coll. Ob-Gyn.; mem. Tex. Med. Assn. (del. 1972-79, treas. 1974-79), Tarrant County Med. Soc., Rotary Internat., Sunlight Ski Club (chmn. bd. dirs. 1985-86). Republican. Mem. Christian Ch. (Disciples of Christ). Office: 109 W Randol Mill Rd Ste 101 Arlington TX 76011-4608

KELLER, PHILLIP BURNS, optometrist; b. Balt., Dec. 2, 1938; s. Earl Dwight and Arriette (Trigg) K.; m. Galen Gourley, Jan. 1962 (div. 1970); children: Bruce, Bill; m. Kristine Spaethe, Feb. 7, 1974; 1 child, Cory. BS of Optometry, Ohio State U., 1962. Diplomate Am. Bd. Optometry. Pvt. practice Hudson, Ohio. Pres., bd. dirs. Big Bros./Big Sisters of Akron, 1979-80. 1st lt. USAF, 1963-67. Mem. Am. Optometric Assn., Ohio Optometric Assn. (zone gov. 1970), Summit County Optometric Soc., Hudson Rotary (pres. 1980). Presbyterian. Home: 2401 Danbury Ln Hudson OH 44236 Office: Phillip B Keller OD 126 W Streetsboro St Ste 9 Hudson OH 44236

KELLEY, BRUCE DUTTON, pharmacist; b. Hartford, Conn., Jan. 4, 1957; s. Roger Weston and Elizabeth Morrill (Atwood) K.; m. DawnReneé Cinocco, Jan. 19, 1990. Student, U. Hartford, 1975-77; BS in Pharmacy, U. Colo., 1985; diplomas in Russian, Pushkin Inst., Moscow, 1995; BA in Russian, U. Colo., 1995. RPh, Colo. Various part time jobs while attending school, 1975-85; pharmacist King Soopers, Inc., Boulder, Colo., 1990—; asst. tour leader in Russia U. Tex., El Paso, 1991; Russia asst. guide, U. Ariz., Tucson, 1992 (summer). Vol. Warderburg Student Health Ctr., U. Colo., Boulder, 1981-83, Am. Diabetes Assn. Mem. Am. Fedn. Police, Elks, Nat. Eagle Scout Assn., Am. Legion. Republican. Home: 6152 Willow Ln Boulder CO 80301-5356 Office: King Soopers Inc 6550 Lookout Rd Boulder CO 80301-3303

KELLEY, CAROL LEE, optometrist; b. Hill AFB, Utah, Aug. 30, 1962; d. Stanley Phillip and Momoyo K. BA, U. Calif., Santa Barbara, 1988; OD, So. Calif. Coll. Optometry, Fullerton, 1993. Optician Neil Metus, OD, Montecito, Calif., 1984-89; optometrist, tchg. staff So. Calif. Coll. Optometrists, Fullerton, 1993-95; optometrist San Diego Ctr. Vision Care, 1993—; sec. Achievement Through Vision, San Diego, 1995—; vision care cons. San Diego Rehab. Inst., 1994—. Mem. Am. Optometric Assn., Coll. Optometrists in Vision Devel. (assoc.), Calif. Optometric Assn., San Diego County Optometric Soc., Young Alumni Assn. So. Calif. Coll. Optometry (com. mem. 1993—). Republican. Office: 7898 Broadway Lemon Grove CA 91945

KELLEY, CATHY ANNE, physician assistant; b. Denver, July 8, 1957; d. John B. and Shirley E. (Kirkpatrick) Cross; m. Brian L. Kelley, Mar. 21, 1980; children: Courtney Nicole, Jonathan Dayton. BS in Health Sci., U. Colo. Health Sci. Ctr., 1980. Physician asst. Pediatrix, Phoenix, 1980—; adj. faculty, prof., preceptor Kirksville Coll. Osteo. Medicine, Phoenix, 1995—; mem. adj. faculty, preceptor nurse practitioner program Ariz. State U., Phoenix, 1993—. Author: We Care For Kids, 1985. Bd. dirs. Myasthenia Gravis Found., Phoenix, 1985, Ariz. Partnership for Infant Immunization, Phoenix, 1995; PTSO sec. Oasis Elem. Sch., Peoria, Ariz., 1988-96. Fellow Am. Acad. Physician Assts.; mem. Ariz. State Assn. Physician Assts. (sec. 1981-83, chmn. ethics com. 1990, treas. 1995-97), Acad. Child Health Assocs. Office: Pediatrix 15650 N Black Canyon # 100 Phoenix AZ 85023

KELLEY, JOHN HOYT, orthopedic surgeon; b. Des Moines, Mar. 11, 1924; s. Lawrence Flam and Susan (Gunn) K.; m. Janice Lou Streater, Apr. 14, 1965; children: Scott, Loen, Karen. BS, MD, Northwestern U., 1950. Intern Cook County Hosp., Chgo., 1951-52; resident Mayo Clinic, Rochester, Minn., 1952-55; pvt. practice Des Moines, 1957—; med. dir. Employers Modern Life Co., Des Moines, 1960—; bd. dirs. Employers Mut. Ins. Co., Des Moines. Co-author: Neck & Back Injuries Following Rear End Collisions, 1965; contbr. articles to profl. jours. With U.S. Army, 1943-45, ETO. Mem. Econ. Roundtable Boca Raton. Republican. Congregationalist. Home: 2038 Thatch Palm Dr Boca Raton FL 33432 Office: Des Moines Orthopedic Surge 6001 Westown Pkwy West Des Moines IA 50266

KELLEY, MAURICE LESLIE, JR., gastroenterologist, educator; b. Indpls., June 29, 1924; s. Maurice Leslie and Martha (Daniel) K.; m. Carol J. Povec, Feb. 11, 1967; children: Elizabeth Ann, Mary Sarah. Student, U. Vt., Va. Ply. Inst., Princeton U., 1943-45; M.D., U. Rochester, 1949. Intern, resident Strong Meml. Hosp., Rochester, N.Y., 1949-51; Bixby fellow in medicine Strong Meml. Hosp., 1953-56; fellow in gastroenterology Mayo Clinic, Rochester, Minn., 1957-59; asst. prof. medicine U. Rochester, 1959-64, assoc. prof., 1964-67; practice medicine specializing in gastroenterology Rochester, N.Y., 1959-67; assoc. prof. clin. medicine Dartmouth Med. Sch., 1967-74, prof. clin. medicine, 1974-88; chmn. sect. internal medicine Hitchcock Clinic, 1972-74, chmn. sect. gastroenterology, 1974, 88; prof. medicine emeritus Dartmouth Med. Sch., 1988—; mem. staff Strong Meml. Hosp., Hitchcock Clinic, Mary Hitchcock Meml. Hosp.; cons. Canandaigua VA, Rochester Gen., Genesee hosps., VA. Med. Ctr., White River Junction. Contbr. articles to profl. jours., chpts. to books. Served with AUS, 1942-45; M.C. USAF, 1951-53. Fellow ACP (gov. for N.H. 1974-78, Laureate award 1993), Am. Gastroenterol. Assn.; mem. Am. Soc. Gastrointestinal Endoscopy, AMA (chmn. sect. gastroenterology 1970-71), Am. Physiol. Soc., Alpha Omega Alpha. Home: 15 Ledge Rd Hanover NH 03755-1612 Office: Dartmouth-Hitchcock Med Ctr 1 Medical Center Dr Lebanon NH 03756-0001

KELLEY, MICHAEL JAMES, medical services executive, author; b. Columbus, Ohio, Oct. 27, 1955; m. Linda May Wagner, Mar. 18, 1988. BS, Fla. Atlantic U., 1976, MBA, 1980. Advisor to prime minister Turks and Caicos Islands, Brit. West Indies, 1978-79; chief adminstr. Ft. Lauderdale (Fla.) Eye Inst., 1980-87; v.p. Ambassador Real Estate Equities Corp., Tamarac, Fla., 1984-89, also bd. dirs.; v.p. Ambassador Fin. Group Inc., Tamarac, Fla., 1985-89; exec. dir. Retina Consultants Southwest Fla., Ft. Myers, 1990—; CEO Vision Rehab. Strategies, Ft. Myers, 1994—. Mem. Med. Group Mgmt. Assn. (AO pres. 1996—), Fla. Atlantic U. Alumni Assn. (bd. dirs. 1989-93), Visually Impaired Persons Inc. (adv. bd.). Office: Retina Cons 2668 Winkler Ave Fort Myers FL 33901-9336

KELLEY, ROBERT OTIS, medical science educator; b. Santa Monica, Calif., Apr. 30, 1944; s. David Otis and Onetia May (Nettles) K.; m. Marcia Jean Bell; children: Jennifer Leigh, Karin Michelle, Matthew Philip, Sarah Ann. BS, Abilene Christian U., 1965; MA, U. Calif., Berkeley, 1966, PhD, 1969. Asst. prof. U. N.Mex. Sch. of Medicine, Albuquerque, 1969-74, assoc. prof., 1974-79, prof., 1979—, chmn. dept. anatomy, 1981—; vis. scientist Okazaki (Japan) Nat. Labs., 1984-85, spkr. U. N. Mex. spkrs. bur., 1969—; mem. study sect. NIH, Bethesda, Md., 1982-86, USMLE, Step 1, 1995—; anatomy com. Nat. Bd. mex. Examiners, Phila., 1992—. Author: Basic Histology, 1989; editor Cell and Tissue Rsch., 1970—, Anat. Record, 1970—; contbr. articles to profl. jours. Patroller Nat. Ski Patrol, 1970—. Recipient Rsch. Career Devel. award NIH, 1972-77, Kaiser award U. Calif., Irvine, 1976; Internat. Exch. Scholar NSF; NIH grantee, 1970—;. Mem. Fedn. Am. Socs. for Exptl. Biology (pub. affairs exec. com. 1993—), Am. Soc. Cell Biology, Soc. for Devel. Biology, Electron Microscopy Soc. Am. (bd. dirs. 1987—), Am. Assn. Anatomists (exec. com. 1988—), Assn. Am. Med. Colls. (exec. coun. 1995—), Nat. Caucus of Basic Biomed. Sci. Chairs. Democrat. Protestant. Office: U NMex Sch Medicine Dept Anatomy Albuquerque NM 87131

KELLEY, ROSANNE, medical technologist; b. Cleve., Aug. 18, 1958; d. Vincent Samuel and Dolly (Rodi) Tinnirello; children: Shamus Patrick, Timothy Michael. AAS in Med. Lab. Tech., Cuyahoga C.C., Cleve., 1980; BA in Mgmt., Malone Coll., 1996. Cert. med. lab. technician, Am. Soc. Clin. Pathologists; cert. med. technologist Am. Med. Technologists; cert. clin. lab. scientist, Nat. Certification Agy. Med. technologist St. John Hosp., Cleve., 1980-90; lead technologist St. John Emergency Ctr., Cleve., 1990-94; shift supr., med. technologist St. Vincent Charity Hosp. and Health Ctr., Cleve., 1994-96; lab site supervisor St. John and Westshore Hosp., West Lake, 1996—, mem. safety com., customer satisfaction com., 1996; mem. Continuous Quality Improvement, Cleve., 1995; mem. 130th anniversary com. cmty. events St. Vincent Charity Hosp., Cleve., 1995. Com. chair St. Ignatius H.S. Band Boosters, Cleve., 1993-95; exec. sec. St. Mark Pastoral Coun., Cleve., 1994-96. Roman Catholic. Office: St John & Westshore Hosp 29000 Ctr Ridge Rd Westlake OH 44145

KELLEY, WILLIAM NIMMONS, physician, educator; b. Atlanta, June 23, 1939; s. Oscar Lee and Will Nimmons (Allen) K.; m. Lois Faville, Aug. 1, 1959; children: Margaret Paige, Virginia Lynn, Lori Ann, William Mark. MD, Emory U., 1963; MA (hon.), U. Pa., 1989. Diplomate Am. Bd. Internal Medicine (mem. bd. govs. 1978-86, chmn. 1985-86), Am. Bd. Med. Spltys. (mem. exec. com. 1980-82). Intern in medicine Parkland Meml. Hosp., Dallas, 1963-64, resident, 1964-65; sr. resident medicine Mass. Gen. Hosp., Boston, 1967-68; clin. asso., sect. on human biochem. genetics NIH, 1965-67; teaching fellow medicine Harvard U. Med. Sch., 1967-68; asst. prof. to prof. medicine, asst. prof. to asso. prof. biochemistry, chief div. rheumatic and genetic diseases Duke U. Sch. Medicine, 1968-75; Macy faculty scholar Oxford U., 1974-75; prof., chmn. dept. internal medicine, prof. dept. biol. chemistry U. Mich. Med. Sch., Ann Arbor, 1975-89; Robert G. Dunlop prof. medicine, biochemistry and biophysics U. Pa., Phila., 1989—, dean Sch. Medicine, 1989—; exec. v.p., CEO U. Pa. Med. Ctr. and Health System, Phila., 1989—; metabolism study sect. NIH, 1978-81, adv. coun. Nat. Inst. Arthritis, Diabetes and Digestive and Kidney Disease, 1986-87, human gene therapy subcom., 1986-92, recombinant DNA com., 1988-92, dirs. adv. com., 1992-95; bd. dirs. Merck & Co., Beckman Instruments, Inc., The Phila. Orch. Assn., Greater Phila. First Corp.; bd. dirs., exec. com. Greater Phila. First Partnership for Econ. Devel. Author: (with J.B. Wyngaarden) Gout and Hyperuricemia, 1976, (with I.M. Weiner) Uric Acid, 1979, (with Harris, Ruddy and Sledge) Textbook of Rheumatology, 1981, 4th edit., 1993, (with M. Osterweiss and E.R. Rubin) Emerging Policies for Bio-Medical Research (Health Policy Annual III), 1993, (with Harris, Ruddy and Sledge) Arthritis Surgery, 1994; editor-in-chief Textbook of Internal Medicine, 1989, 2d edit., 1992, Essentials of Internal Medicine, 1994; also articles. Trustee Emory U., Woodruff Health Scis. Ctr., Wistar Inst., Leonard Davis Inst.; bd. dirs. Greater Phila. First Corp., Phila. Orch. Assn.; bd. dirs., mem. exec. com. Greater Phila. First Partnership for Econ. Devel. Recipient C.V. Mosby award, 1963, John D. Lane award USPHS, 1969, Geigy Internat. prize rheumatology, 1969, Rsch. Career Devel. award USPHS, 1972-75, Heinz Karger Meml. Found. prize, 1973, John Phillips Meml. award and medal Am. Coll. Phys., 1990, Nat. Med. Rsch. award Nat. Health Coun., 1993—, Robert H. Williams award Assn. Profs. of Medicine, 1995, Disting. Med. Achievement award Emory U., 1985; Mead Johnson scholar, 1967; Clin. scholar Am. Rheumatism Assn., 1969-72; Josiah Macy Found. scholar, 1974-75. Master ACP; fellow Am. Acad. Arts and Scis., AAAS; mem. Inst. Medicine of NAS (chmn. sect. 4, 1988-90, chmn. membership com. 1990-94, coun. 1996—, exec. com. 1996—), Am. Soc. Clin. Investigation (editorial bd. 1974-79, pres. 1983-84), So. Soc. Clin. Investigation, Central Soc. for Clin. Research (pres. 1986-87), Am. Soc. Biochemistry and Molecular Biology (editorial bd. 1976-81), Am. Fedn. Clin. Rsch. (nat. coun. 1975-80, exec. com. 1975-80, nat. sec.-treas. 1976-78, pres. 1979-80), Assn. Am. Physicians, Assn. Profs. Medicine (nominating com. 1978-79, sec.-treas. 1987-89), Am. Coll. Rheumatology (chmn. membership com., program com., rsch. com., dir. 1975-76, exec. com. 1976-87, editorial bd. 1972-77, sec.-treas. 1982-85, pres. 1986-87, residency rev. ccm., 1986-93, com. chmn. 1990-93), Am. Soc. Human Genetics, Am. Soc. Nephrology, Am. Soc. Internal Medicine, Central Rheumatism Soc. (pres. 1978-79), Sigma Xi, Alpha Omega Alpha. Home: 768 Woodleave Rd Bryn Mawr PA 19010-1709 Office: Univ of Pa Med Ctr & Health Sys 21 Penn Tower 399 S 34th St Philadelphia PA 19104-4385

KELLOGG, DAVID WAYNE, agriculture educator, researcher; b. Seymour, Mo., Aug. 19, 1941; s. Martin David and Lula May (Spurlock) K.; m. Mary Sue Powell, June 7, 1964; children: Kirk David, Susan Joann Franz, Kimberley Annelle Van Vacter, Gregory William. BS, U. Mo., 1963, MS, 1964; PhD, U. Nebr., 1968. Profl. animal scientist. Asst. prof. agriculture N.Mex. State U., Las Cruces, 1967-71, assoc. prof., 1971-78, prof., 1978-81; prof., dept. head U. Ark., Fayetteville, 1981-86, prof., 1986—; cons. AID-N.Mex. State U. Mission, Asuncion, Paraguay, 1971; spkr. Ark. Farm Bur., Little Rock, 1981-90, ORFFA Seminar, Rennes, France, 1995, Breda, Holland, 1996; mem. adv. com Ark. Livestock and Poultry Commn., 1989-94. Mem. editorial bd. Jour. Dairy Science, 1978-84; contbr. chpts. to book and sci. articles to profl. jours. Mem. Am. Registry Profl. Animal Sci. (bd. dirs. 1989-91, pres.-elect 1993-94, pres. 1994-95), Am. Dairy Sci. Assn. (sec. so. sect. 1991, v.p. 1992, pres. 1993), Am. Soc. Animal Sci. (awards com. 1990-92, spkr. symposium on chelated trace minerals, 1996), Am. Grassland and Forage Coun., So. Assn. Agrl. Sci. (bd. dirs. 1993-94), Ark. Registry Profl. Animal Scientists (charter, sec., treas. 1989-93), Ark. Nutrition Coun., Gideons Internat. (trustee 1975-81), Gamma Sigma Delta. Mem. Evang. Free Ch. Am. Office: U Ark Dept Animal Sci Fayetteville AR 72701

KELLY, ANNE MARIE, nurse, quality control manager; b. Tonsberg, Norway, May 9, 1959; d. John William and Susan Celine (de Schaepdryver) K. BS in Landscape Architecture, Purdue U., 1983, ADN, 1983; BSN, U. So. Fla., 1986, MPH, 1994. RN; lic. health care risk mgr., ABQAURP, CPHQ. Staff nurse, diagnostic unit St. Joseph's Hosp., Tampa, Fla., 1983-84; staff nurse, med./gastroenterol. James A. Haley Vets. Hosp., Tampa, 1984-86, staff nurse, med./oncology, 1986-88, QA/UR specialist, 1988-91, assoc. quality assurance coord., 1991; adminstrv. asst. to ACOS for ambulatory care Bay Pines (Fla.) VAMC, 1991-93; action team leader Fla. Med. Quality Assurance, inc., Tampa, 1993-94; dir., quality/risk mgmt. Shriners Hosps., Tampa, 1994—; courtesy instr., U. So. Fla., Tampa, 1995-96; instr. Fla. Risk Mgmt. Inst., Clearwater, 1995—. Co-author: Ednl. Manual, 1988. Mem. Fla. Soc. Healthcare Risk Mgrs., Nat. Assn. Healthcare Quality, Fla. Assn. Healthcare Quality, Sigma Theta Tau, Alpha Lambda Delta. Home: 11808 Branch Mooring Dr Tampa FL 33635 Office: Shriners Hosp for Children Tampa Unit 12502 N Pine Dr Tampa FL 33612

KELLY, BRIAN DAVID, cardiologist; b. Elizabeth, N.J., Jan. 11, 1958; s. George Leo and Marie Helen (Finelli) K.; m. Sharon Marie Kingsmore, Apr. 30, 1988; children: Kevin, Daniel, Joseph, Michael. BA in Biology, U. Del., 1979; DO, Kirksville (Mo.) Coll., 1983. Intern Saddle Brook Gen. Hosp., 1983-84; resident Cooper Hosp. and Univ. Med. Ctr., Camden, N.J., 1984-87, fellow, 1987-90; clin. cardiologist Internal Medicine Group, Orlando, Fla., 1990—. Fellow Am. Coll. Cardiology. Office: Internal Medicine Group 7212 Curry Ford Rd Orlando FL 32822

KELLY, DANIEL JOHN, physician; b. Binghamton, N.Y., June 23, 1940; s. William James and Mary Elizabeth (Schmitt) K.; m. Lois Ann Lanshe, Aug. 21, 1965; children: Britton James, Jeffrey Daniel, Reid William, Piper Ann. AB in History, Yale U., 1962; MD, Jefferson Med. Coll., 1966. Diplomate in Pathology, Nuclear Medicine, Dermatopathology. Intern Naval Hosp., Boston, 1966-67; resident Naval Hosp., Oakland, Calif., 1966-71; asst. chief lab. Naval Hosp., Great Lakes, Ill., 1971-73, chief lab. svcs., 1973-75; co-dir. lab. Highland Park (Ill.) Hosp., 1992—, dir. lab., 1980-89; co-dir. lab. Lake Forest (Ill.) Hosp., 1992—, dir. lab., 1989-91; with Dean, Hoffman & Clark Pathologists S.C., Lake Forest, 1975—; chief of staff elect Highland Park (Ill.) Hosp., 1992-94, chief of staff, 1994-96, also bd. dirs.; mem. med. exec. com. Highland Park Hosp., 1992—, Lake Forest Hosp., 1989-91. Bd. dirs. Lake Forest Hist. Preservation Soc., 1979-80; mem. bldg. rev. bd. City Govt., Lake Forest, 1989-93; mem. clin. lab. and blood bank adv. bd. Ill. Dept. Pub. Health, 1990-95; mem. Am. Pathology Found. Comdr. USNR, 1966-75. Fellow Coll. Am. Pathology, Am. Soc. Clin. Pathology, Internat. Acad. Pathologists, Am. Assn. Clin. Scientists; mem. AMA, Am. Soc. Nuclear Medicine, Ill. Soc. Pathologists, Am. Soc. Microbiology, Am. Soc. Dermatopathology, Internat. Soc. Dermatopathology, Am. Acad. Dermatology, Assn. Military Surgeons. Roman Catholic. Home: 499 E Illinois Rd Lake Forest IL 60045-2364 Office: Pathology and Nuclear Medicine Assocs 101 Waukegan Rd Ste 1250 Lake Bluff IL 60044-1687

KELLY, DANIEL P., cardiologist; b. Oct. 6, 1955; m. Therese J. Michelau; 3 children. BS in Biology, U. Ill., 1978, MD, 1982. Diplomate Am. Bd. Internal Medicine, Am. Bd. Cardiovascular Disease. Intern in medicine Barnes Hosp., St. Louis, 1982-83, asst. resident in medicine, 1983-85; chief med. resident John Cochran VA Hosp., Washington U. Svc., 1984-85; rsch. postdoctoral fellow cardiovascular divsn. and dept. biol. chemistry Washington U. Sch. of Medicine, St. Louis, 1985-87, fellow in clin. cardiology, 1987-89, instr. of medicine cardiovascular divsn., 1989-90, asst. prof. medicine cardiovascular divsn., 1990-95, asst. prof. molecular biology and pharmacology, 1993-95, co-dir. Ctr. Adults with Congenital Heart Disease, 1993—, assoc. prof. medicine and molecular biology & pharmacology, 1995—; lectr. rsch. and clin. fellowship program Washington U. Sch. of Medicine, 1989, lectr. pharmacology and pathophysiology, 1994; attending physician medicine and cardiology svcs. Barnes and Jewish Hosps., St. Louis, 1989. Contbr. articles to profl. jours., chpts. to books. Recipient Lucille P. Markey Scholar award Markey Found., 1989, Basal O'Connor Scholar award March of Dimes, 1991; Rsch. Tng. grantee NHLBI, 1994—, 96—. Fellow Am. Coll. Cardiology; mem. AAAS, Am. Fedn. Clin. Rsch., Am. Heart Assn. (basic sci. coun., Established Investigator award 1995), Internat. Soc. Heart Rsch., Internat. Soc. Adult Congenital Heart Disease, Phi Beta Kappa, Alpha Omega Alpha. Office: Washington U Sch of Medicine Cardiovascular Divsn 660 S Euclid Ave Box 8086 Saint Louis MO 63110

KELLY, DAVID LEE, JR., neurosurgeon, educator; b. Elkin, N.C., Apr. 25, 1935; s. David Lee and Catherine (Church) K.; m. Sarah Brooks Pullen, Aug. 23, 1958; children—Sarah Katherine, David Lee, Mary Brooks, Julia Ann. B.S., U. N.C.-Chapel Hill, 1956, M.D., 1959. Diplomate Am. Bd. Neurol. Surgery; lic. physician, N.C. Instr., Bowman Gray Sch. Medicine, Wake Forest U., Winston-Salem, N.C., 1965-66; asst. prof. Bowman Gray Sch. Medicine, Wake Forest U., 1966-71, assoc. prof., 1971-78, prof. neurosurgery, head sect., 1978—; chmn. com. ednl. requirements Am. Bd. Neurol. Surgery, 1984-86, mem. oral exam. com., 1985-86. Contbr. articles to profl. jours., chpts. to books; editorial bd. Neurosurgery, 1982—, mem. mgmt. com., 1977-82. Bd. dirs. Forsyth County YMCA, Winston-Salem, 1968-75, v.p., 1973, pres., 1974; bd. dirs. Forsyth Country Day Sch., Winston-Salem, 1975-78. Fellow ACS; mem. Am. Acad. Neurol. Surgery (exec. com. 1982-85), Am. Assn. Neurol. Surgeons (fin. com. 1978-83, mem.-at-large bd. dirs. 1980-83, chmn. hon. membership 1982-83, adv. council neurosurgery 1979-83), AMA, Assn. Acad. Surgery, Congress of Neurol. Surgeons (sci. program com. 1967-68, registration com. 1969-70, membership com. 1967-68, 70-71, chmn. residents com. 1971-72, chmn. registration com. 1973-74, sec. 1974-77, pres.-elect 1977-78, pres. 1978-79, chmn. cert. com. 1980—, exec. com. 1982—), Fellowship of Acad. Neurosurgeons, Forsyth-Davie-Stokes County Med. Soc. (chmn. program com. 1970-71), Med. Soc. N.C. (coms.), Neurosurg. Soc. Am. (v.p. 1979-80), N.C. Neurosurg. Soc. (pres. 1976-77, chmn. peer rev. com. 1982-83), So. Neurosurg. Soc. (program com. 1974-76, v.p. 1977-78), Phi Beta Kappa, Alpha Omega Alpha (chpt. counselor 1970-72), Phi Eta Sigma. Presbyterian. Club: Forsyth Country (Winston-Salem). Office: Bowman Gray Sch Medicine 300 S Hawthorne Rd Winston Salem NC 27157-0002*

KELLY, DAVID REID, pathologist; b. Morganton, N.C., Nov. 21, 1947; s. Everett Oree and Paris Dereama (Keever) K.; children: Marie Keever, David Reid Jr. AB, U. N.C., 1970; MD, U. Tenn. Ctr. Health Scis., 1974. Diplomate Am. Bd. Pathology, Clin. and Anatomic Pathology, Am. Bd. Pediatric Pathology. Intern, then resident U. Ala., Birmingham, 1974-78; Am. Cancer Soc. fellow dept. pathology and lab. medicine U. Minn., Mpls., 1978-79; pathologist-in-chief, med. dir. labs. Children's Hosp., Birmingham, 1979—; clin. prof. of pathology U. Ala.-Birmingham, 1985—; pathology cons. Pediatric Oncology Group, Chgo., 1979—. Author: Comprehensive Textbook of Oncology, 1986, Clinical Pediatric Oncology, 1991, Pediatric Neoplasia: Morphology and Biology, 1996; contbr. articles to Cancer, Pediat. Pathology, Am. Jour. Clin. Pathology, Med. and Pediat. Oncology, Kidney Internat. Leader Cub Scouts and Boy Scouts Am., Birmingham, 1988-94. Fellow Am. Soc. Clin. Pathologists, Coll. Am. Pathologists; mem. AMA (physician recognition award 1980, 91, 95), Soc. for Pediat. Pathology, Soc. Hematopathology, U.S. Acad. Pathology, Can. Acad. Pathology, Phi Alpha Theta, Phi Kappa Phi. Baptist. Office: Children's Hosp of Ala 1600 7th Ave S Birmingham AL 35233-1711

KELLY, DENISE MARIE, critical care nurse; b. Staten Island, N.Y., Nov. 16, 1966; d. Edward Augustine and Dorothy Catherine (Ferrante) K. AAS, Coll. of S.I., 1987, BSN, 1989; MS in Adult N.P., SUNY, Stony Brook. Cert. specialist, cardiothoracic surg. nurse practitioner ANCC; CCRN. From staff nurse to critical care nurse, 1989-94; nurse practitioner Univ. Hosp. at Stony Brook, 1994—. Mem. AACN, Nurse Practitioner Assn. L.I. Home: 6 Houston Ct Coram NY 11727-1510

KELLY, DOROTHY HELEN, pediatrician, educator; b. Fitchburg, Mass., July 29, 1944. BS in Nursing magna cum laude, Fitchburg State Co., 1966; BS with distinction, Wayne State U., 1968, MD with distinction, 1972. Diplomate Am. Bd. Pediatrics, Pediatric Pulmonology. Intern Children's Svc. Mass. Gen. Hosp., Boston, 1972-73, resident in pediatrics, 1973-75, fellow in pediatrics pulmonary medicine, 1976-79, assoc. dir. pediatric pulmonary unit, 1988-95; teaching fellow Harvard Med. Sch., Boston, 1973-75, clin. fellow, 1972-75, instr. in pediatrics, 1975-81, asst. prof. pediatrics, 1981-89, assoc. prof. pediatrics, 1989-95; assoc. prof. pediatrics U. Tex., Galveston, 1995—; assoc. dir. S.W. SIDS Rsch. Ctr. Herman Hosp., Houston, 1995—; cons. Bur. Community Health Svcs., NEW, 1979-80, FDA, 1986, 88-92, ECRI, 1987-88, also others; chmn. apnea adv. com. Nat. Sudden Infant Death Syndrome Found., 1979-81; mem. com. anesthesiology and respiratory devices panel Ctr. for Devices and Radiol. Health, FDA, 1990—; chmn. physicians' coun. Nat. Assn. Apnea Profls., 1990-91, also others; reviewer numerous jours. in field. Contbr. numerous articles to profl. jours. Recipient Woman of Vision award Nat. Soc. for Prevention of Blindness, Mass. Affiliate, 1981, First Disting. Alumni award Fitchburg State Coll., 1984, grants in field. Mem. Am. Med. Woman's Assn., Am. Acad. Pediatrics (task force on prolonged apnea 1978), Am. Thoracic Soc., Internat. Pediatric Soc., Assn. for Psychophysiol. Study Sleep, Soc. for Pediatric Rsch., Mass. Thoracic Soc., Ea. Soc. for Pediatric Rsch. Office: SW SIDS Rsch Inst Herman Hosp Houston TX 77030 also: U Tex Med Br-Children's Hosp Galveston TX 77550

KELLY, FRANCIS W., retired psychiatrist; b. Bklyn., May 29, 1913; s. William F. and Mary Ann (McMahon) K.; m. Mary D. Stanton, Feb. 1, 1940 (dec. July 1943); 1 child, William; m. Mary Rose Mackovjak, Dec. 1, 1944; children: Francis, Maureen, Jonathan, Margaret, Kathleen. BS, St. John's U., Jamaica, N.Y., 1939; MD, SUNY, Bklyn., 1939. Diplomate Am. Bd. Psychiatry, Am. Bd. Hosp. Adminstrn. Intern Mary Immaculate Hosp., Jamaica, 1939-40; resident in psychiatry Bklyn. State Hosp., 1940-41; fellow in psychiatry Inst. of Living, Hartford, Conn., 1946-47; supt. Brandon (Vt.) State Sch., 1947-56; physician-in-charge Brigham Hall, Canandaigua, N.Y., 1951-56; pvt. practice psychiatry Rochester, N.Y., 1956-83; retired, 1983; staff psychiatrist U. Rochester Med. Sch., 1956-83; chief psychiatrist St. Mary's Hosp., Rochester, 1968-69, Highland Hosp., Rochester, 1970-78. Maj. USAAF, 1942-46. Fellow Am. Psychiat. Assn. (life), Assn. Mil. Surgsons U.S. (life); mem. Am. Occupational Medicine Assn. (life). Roman Catholic. Home: 8 Log Cabin Cir Fairport NY 14450-1914

KELLY, GAY ANNE, social worker, educator; b. Peoria, Ill., Nov. 13, 1951; d. Walter Reuel and Ada Frances (Dixon) Wright; children: James, N. Jason, Justin; m. Kevin J. Kelly, May 14, 1994. AA, Lincoln Land C.C., 1975; BA in Child Family Comty. Svc., U. Ill. Sangamon campus, 1978; MEd, U. Ill., 1990. Cert. child protective investigator, child devel. specialist II, Ill. Case coord. Jacksonville (Ill.) Area Assn. Retarded Citizens, 1975-76; surrogate parent/ednl. advocate Ill. State Bd. Edn., Vermillion County, 1977-79; child care specialist Parents Anonymous, Champaign, Ill., 1990-91, parent facilitator, 1991-93; child devel. specialist Devel. Svcs. Ctr., Champaign, 1990-94; child protective investigator Ill. Dept. Children and Family Svcs., Urbana, 1994—; parent group facilitator, sponsor Parents Anonymous, Champaign, Ill., 1990-92; vol. EMT Midleford Vol. Ambulance, Potomac, Ill., 1986-89; surrogate parent/ednl. advocate Ill. State Bd. Edn., Vermillion County, 1986-89; grad. rsch. asst. dept. spl. edn. U. Ill., Champaign, 1987-90; v.p., rep. dept. spl. edn. Coun. Grad. Students in Edn., U. Ill., Champaign, 1987-90. Sec. Middlefork Twp. Vol. Ambulance, Potomac, Ill., 1987-89. Grantee Kappa Delta Pi, U. Ill., Champaign, 1990; Hilton-Perkins scholar, 1993. Mem. Coun. Exceptional Children (div. phys. handicaps, div. mental retardation, div. early childhood), Ill. Div. Early Childhood, Kappa Delta Pi. Republican. Mem. LDS Ch. Home: 1706 Nancy Beth Champaign IL 61821 Office: Ill Dept Children and Fam Svcs 508 S Race Champaign IL 61821-2099

KELLY, GREGORY, molecular biologist; b. McKeesport, Pa., Dec. 7, 1954; s. Bernard Paul and Rita L. (Woll) K.; m. Bonita Jean Sowa, May 1, 1976; children: Mark Patrick, Emily Ann. BS, U. Pitts., 1977; PhD, Purdue U., 1983. Postdoctoral fellow U. Iowa Sch. Medicine, Iowa City, 1983-86; staff scientist Inhalation Toxicology Rsch. Inst., Albuquerque, 1986-95; pres. Southwest Sci. Resources, Inc., Albuquerque, 1995—; adj. asst. prof. Purdue U. Sch. Vet. Medicine, West Lafayette, Ind., 1989—; clin. asst. prof. dept. pharmacology U. N.Mex., Albuquerque, 1990—. Contbr. articles to profl. publs. Vol. Boy Scouts Am., Albuquerque, 1973—, United Way of Greater Albuquerque, 1987—, United Way of Greater Pitts., 1974-77. Recipient Nat. Rsch. Svc. award NIH, 1983-86, Young Scientist award L.H. Gray Conf., 1988. Mem. AAAS, Am. Assn. Biochemistry and Molecular Biology, Am. Assn. Cancer Rsch., Nat. Eagle Scout Assn. Democrat. Roman Catholic. Home: 10533 Calle Alba NW Albuquerque NM 87114-5419 Office: Southwest Sci Resources Inc 5300 Sequioa NW #150 Albuquerque NM 87114

KELLY, JAMES PATRICK, lawyer; b. Twin Falls, Idaho, Mar. 25, 1946; s. James Patrick Sr. and Ynes Mary (Alastra) K.; m. Carol Louise White, June 6, 1968; children: Mary Louise, Christopher John. AB, Harvard U., 1968, JD, 1975. Bar: Ga., U.S. Dist. Ct. (no. dist.) Ga., U.S. Ct. Appeals (11th cir.) . Assoc. Kilpatrick & Cody, Atlanta, 1975-80; ptnr. Morris & Manning, Atlanta, 1980-83, Smith, Gambrell & Russell, Atlanta, 1983-85, Asbill, Porter & Churchill, Atlanta, 1985-86; sr. ptnr. Kelly Law Firm, P.C., Atlanta, 1986—. Bd. dirs. Sr. Citizen Services of Met. Atlanta, 1980-83. Served to capt. U.S. Army, 1968-72. Mem. ABA (corp. and banking law sect.), Ga. Bar Assn., Am. Acad. Hosp. Attys., Ga. Acad. Hosp. Attys. (bd. dirs. 1987-89), Nat. Health Lawyers Assn. (bd. dirs. 1993—), Am. Soc. Law and Medicine, Lawyers Club Atlanta, Harvard Alumni Assn. (bd. dirs. 1983-84), Harvard Law Sch. Assn. Ga. (v.p. 1988-89, pres. 1989-91), Cochise Club, Harvard Club (pres. 1982-83, bd. dirs. 1990—), Georgian Club, Commerce Club, World Trade Club, Capital City Club, Kiwanis (pres.). Episcopalian. Home: 3240 Lemons Ridge Dr NW Atlanta GA 30339-4305 Office: 200 Galleria Pky NW Ste 1510 Atlanta GA 30339-5946

KELLY, JAMES PATRICK, JR., retired engineering and construction executive; b. Bklyn., July 19, 1933; s. James Patrick and Marion Rita (Gleason) K.; children: Kathryn, Mark, Lisa Angelique, Trevor, Lisa, James. B.S. in Engring, U.S. Naval Acad., 1955; postgrad., U. Houston, 1968-69. Registered profl. engr., Calif. Asst. site mgr. Pathfinder reactor Allis Chalmers Mfg. Co., Sioux Falls, S.D., 1963-67; nuclear project mgr. Brown & Root, Houston, 1967-69; constrn. project mgr., then asst. v.p. Gibbs & Hill, Omaha and N.Y.C., 1969-75; pres. Dravo Lime Co., Pitts., 1975-77; group v.p. natural resources Dravo Corp., Pitts., 1976-81, sr. v.p. engring. and constrn., domestic and internat., 1982-84; pres., dir. C.F. Braun & Co., Alhambra, Calif., 1984-86; pres., chief exec. officer Hadson Power Systems, Inc., Irvine, Calif., 1986-91, ret., 1991; bd. dirs. Hadson Corp. Bd. dirs. S.D. Mental Health Assn., 1966-67, Western Pa. Sch. Blind Children, 1978-84; active Sioux Falls Bd. Edn., 1965-66, Assn. Retarded Citizens Pitts., 1970—; pres. found. bd. Calif. State U., L.A., 1985-95; pres. Santa Ana Com. for Ednl. and Recreational Redevel. Area, mem. Devel. Disabilities Area Bd. Mem. NSPE, Mensa, Sierra Club. Home: 1413 Franzen Ave Santa Ana CA 92705-6926

KELLY, JOHN PATRICK, JR., pharmaceutical marketing executive; b. Atlanta, Aug. 26, 1957; s. J. Patrick and Jane (Watson) K.; m. Maureen Elizabeth Kelly, July 14, 1984 (div. Feb., 1988); 1 child, Caroline Patricia. BA, Duke U., 1980. Mkt. rsch. assoc. Pfizer, Inc., N.Y.C., 1981-82, product analyst, 1982-83; mktg. assoc. Roerig Div., Pfizer, Inc., N.Y.C., 1983-83, from asst. product mgr. to dir. mktg., 1984-92; v.p. mktg. Roerig divsn. Pfizer, Inc., N.Y.C., 1992-93; group v.p. disease mgmt. Pfizer, Inc., N.Y.C., 1994—. Office: Prizer Inc 235 E 42d St New York NY 10017-5706

KELLY, JOSEPHINE KAYE, social worker; b. Grand Rapids, Mich., May 30, 1944; d. Clark Everet Peterson and Dorothy Jane (Mudd) Schaefer; m. Raymond Luke Kelly, July 19, 1969; children: William Lawrence, Kenneth James. BA with honors, Grand Valley State Coll., 1967; MA, Western Mich. U., 1993. Registered social worker. Exec. dir. Voluntary Action Ctr., Grand Rapids, 1970-77; project coord. Area Agy. on Aging, Grand Rapids, 1977-79; program coord. Aquinas Coll., Grand Rapids, 1979-80; psychiat. social worker Kent Oaks Psychiat. Unit, Grand Rapids, 1980-87; continued care social worker St. Mary's Hosp., Grand Rapids, 1987-88; co-owner Hidden Lake Farm, Conklin, 1969—; med. social worker Alpine Manor Inc., Grand Rapids, 1988-91; coord. Alzheimer's Living Ctr., Birchwood Care Ctr., Horizon Healthcare Corp., Marne, 1994-96; dir. Good Shepherd Home, Resthaven Care Ctr., Resthaven Patrons, Inc., Holland, 1996—. Coord. Alzheimer's Living Ctr., Birchwood Care Ctr., Horizon Healthcare Corp., Marne, 1993—; bd. pres. North West Ambulance, 1993—; bd. dirs. Ottawa County Cmty. Mental Health, 1993—; trustee Chester Twp., 1984-96, mem. canteen svcs. unit, 1984-94; mem. planning bd. St. Mary's Hosp., Grand Rapids, 1981-82; mem. lay adv. bd. Cath. Info. Ctr., Grand Rapids, 1983-85, pres., 1984-85; pres. Coun. on Aging of Kent County, Grand Rapids, 1979-80, mem., 1977—; mem. transp. adv. commn. Coopersville (Mich.) Area Pub. Schs., 1977-81; sec. Conklin Food Coop., 1977-80; bd. dirs. Women's Resource Ctr., Grand Rapids, 1977-79, steering com., 1972-73; mem. Alzheimer's Profl. Devel. Network, 1995—, Interhcange-Orgn. West Mich. Comm. Profls., 1994—. Mem. AAUW, Am. Legion (aux.), Mich. Beefalo Breeders Assn. (sec.-treas. 1982-84, v.p. 1993-95, pres. 1995—), Am. Beefalo World Registry, Vol. Mgmt. Assn. Western Mich. (founder, 1st pres. 1975-76), Conklin Brotherhood Assn., Internat. Beefalo Found. (bd. dirs.). Republican. Roman Catholic. Home: 3616 Coolidge St Conklin MI 49403-9509

KELLY, KATHLEEN ANN, nurse practitioner internal medicine; b. Albany, N.Y., Sept. 28, 1953; d. William Francis and Wilhelmina S. (Stockman) Cain; m. Thomas J. Kelly Jr., June 1, 1974; children: Sean, Brian. BSN, Russell Sage Coll., 1975; Nurse Practitioner Program, Albany Med. Coll., 1977; MS, Russell Sage Coll., 1981. Lic. family nurse practitioner, N.Y. state. Nurse practitioner Dr. David Pankin, Albany, N.Y., 1977-78; instr. Primary Care Nurse Practitioner Program, Albany, N.Y., 1978-81; nurse practitioner clin. coord. Cmty. Health Plan, Latham, N.Y., 1982-89; nurse practitioner Dr. Jeffrey Perkins, Albany, N.Y., 1989—, office mgr., 1991—; cons. N.Y. State Office Profl. Discipline, Albany, 1981—, N.Y. State Health Dept., Albany, 1992—. Mem. Am. Coll. Nurse Practitioners (v.p. 1994-96), N.Y. State Coalition of Nurse Practitioners (treas. 1992-93, pres.-elect 1994, pres. 1995, Nurse Practitioner of Yr. 1993). Roman Catholic. Home: PO Box 201 Newtonville NY 12128

KELLY, KATHRYN ANN, nursing executive; b. Newark, Dec. 21, 1947; d. Harry Aloysius and Gertrude (Cox) K.; m. Gauthier, May 15, 1971 (div. May 1978). BSN, Seton Hall U., 1969; MA, Fairleigh Dickinson U., 1987. RN. Staff nurse Monmouth Med. Ctr., Long Branch, N.J., 1971-73, asst. nurse mgr., 1973-77, adminstrv. coord. nursing dept., 1977-79, nurse mgr. emergency dept., 1980-86, adminstrv. dir. emergency dept., 1986-93, adminstr. emergency & patient access, 1994-95, chief nurse exec., 1995—; mem. adv. bd. Ctrl. Jersey Vis Nurses Assn., Red Bank, N.J., 1995—. Mem. Am. Orgn. Nurse Execs., Sigma Theta Tau. Office: Monmouth Med Ctr 300 2d Ave Long Branch NJ 07740

KELLY, KEVIN A., medical association executive; b. Poughkeepsie, N.Y., Jan. 5, 1956; s. Ronald and Bonnnie (McCreary) K.; m. Jamie Savvas, July 25, 1981; children: Daniel Peter, Michael Ronald. Student, Duke U. ., 1974; BS in Econs., Mich. State U., 1978; MPA, Western Mich. U., 1992. Dir. health facility project rev. Mich. Mid South Health System Agy., Mason, 1978-79; legis. coord. Mich. State Med. Soc., East Lansing, 1979-84, mgr. dept. govt. rels. and membership devel., 1984-87, mng. dir., 1987—; bd. dirs. Mich. Hospice Orgn., 1977-81, Gateway Comty. Svcs., 1989, Sparrow Home Care Network, Am.-Russian Med. Exchange, Mich. Health Policy Forum; mem. Mich. Coalition for Safety Belt Use, pub. policy com. Mich. Transplant Ctr., responseysystem adv. com. Am. Cancer Soc., physician orgns. com. Mich. State Med. Soc., adv. com. Med. Opportunities in Mich., risk mgmt. com. Mich. Physicians Mutual Liability Co.; sec. Health Edn. Found, Mich. Bd. dirs. Mich. Ski for Light, Mich. Youth in Govt., Mich. Festival, chmn. mktg. com. Mich. Festival, 1990, sales com., 1990, pres. 1991, 92; mem. Blue Ribbon Com., Lansing Comty. Coll.; chmn. Green and White Polit. Action Com.; bd. dirs. Concerned Citizens for the Arts; mem. Fine Arts Commn.; chmn. East Lansing City Mgr. Search Com.. Mem. Am. Soc. Assn. Execs., Am. Assn. Med. Soc. Execs., Blue Care Network Health Ctrl. (bd. dirs.), Mich. Pub. Health Assn., Mich. Soc. Assn. Execs. (bd. dirs.), Mich. Soc. Hosp. Risk Mgmt., Capitol Hill Club (Washington), Nat. Rep. Club (Washington), Nat. Dem. Club (Washington), Country Club of Lansing. Office: Mich State Med Soc 120 W Saginaw East Lansing MI 48823

KELLY, LUCIE STIRM YOUNG, nursing educator; b. Stuttgart, Germany, May 2, 1925; came to U.S., 1929; d. Hugo Karl and Emilie Rosa (Engel) Stirm; m. J. Austin Young, Aug. 30, 1946 (div. Feb. 1971); m. Thomas Martin Kelly, 1972; 1 child by previous marriage, Gay Aleta (Mrs. Donald Meyer). BS, U. Pitts., 1947, MLitt, 1957, PhD (HEW fellow), 1965; D in Nursing Edn. (hon.), U. R.I., 1977; LHD (hon.), Georgetown U., 1983; DSc (hon.), Widener U., 1984, U. Mass., 1989; D of Pub. Svc. (hon.), Am. U., 1985; DHL (hon.), SUNY, 1996. Instr. nursing McKeesport (Pa.) Hosp., 1953-57, asst. adminstr. nursing, 1966-69; asst. prof. nursing U. Pitts., 1957-64, asst. dean, 1965; prof., chmn. nursing dept. Calif. State U., Los Angeles, 1969-72; co-project dir. curriculum research Nat. League for Nursing, 1973-74; project dir. patient edn., office consumer health edn., also adj. asso. prof. community medicine Coll. Medicine and Dentistry N.J.-Rutgers Med. Sch., 1974-75; prof. pub. health and nursing Sch. Pub. Health and Sch. Nursing Columbia U., N.Y.C., 1975-90, prof. emeritus Sch Pub. Health, Sch. Nursing, 1990—, assoc. dean acad. affairs Sch. Pub. Health, 1988-90, hon. prof. nursing edn. Tchrs. Coll., 1977-93, acting head div. health adminstrn. Sch. Pub. Health, 1980-81, 86-88; on leave as exec. dir. Mid-Atlantic Regional Nursing Assn., 1981-82; cons. U. Nev., Las Vegas, 1970-72, Ball State U., Ind., 1971, Long Beach (Calif.) Naval Hosp., 1971-72, Travis AFB, Calif., 1972, Brentwood VA Hosp., L.A., 1971-72, Ctrl. Nursing Office VA, Washington, 1971-94, N.J. Dept. Higher Edn., 1974-78, John Wiley Pub., 1974-76, Sch. Nursing Am. U. Beirut; mem. spl. med. adv. group VA Dept. Medicine and Surgery, Washington, 1980-84; cons. nursing com. AMA, 1971-74, Citizen's Com. for Children, N.Y.C.; v.p. Pa. Health Coun., 1968-69; mem. adv. com. physicians assts. Calif. Bd. Med. Examiners, adv. com. Cancer Soc. L.A., 1970-72, com. nursing VA, Washington, 1971-74, regional med. programs, Pa., 1967-69, Calif. 1970-72; mem. spl. adv. coun. on med. licensure and profl. conduct N.Y. State Assembly, 1977-79, mem. nat. adv. com. Encore (nat. YWCA post-mastectomy group rehab. project), 1977-83; assoc. mem. N.Y. Acad. Medicine, 1988-90; mem. ethics com. Palisades Gen. Med. Ctr., 1993—, bd. govs., 1995—; lectr., cons., guest Beijing Med. Coll., China, 1982, Aga Khan U., Pakistan, 1990; bd. visitors U. Pitts. Sch. Nursing, 1986-93; mem. editl. adv. bd. Am. Jour. Pub. Heallth, 1992, chair, 1993—; nat. and internat. lectr. in field; chair adv. com. grad. program in pub. health U. Medicine and Dentistry of N.J., 1995—. Author: Dimensions of Profl. Nursing, 7th edit., 1995, The Nursing Experience: Trends, Challenges, Transitions, 3d edit., 1995; contbg. editor Jour. Nursing Adminstrn., 1975-82; mem. editl. bd. Nurse Practitioner, 1976-82; columnist Nursing Outlook, editor-in-chief, 1982-91; mem. bd. advisors Nurses Almanac, 1978, Nurse Manager's Handbook, 1979, Nursing Administration Handbook, 1992; mem. editl. adv. bd. Am. Health, 1981-91, Nursing and Health Care, 1991-95; contbr. articles to prof. jours. Bd. dirs. ARC, Los Angeles, 1971-72, Vis. Nurse Service N.Y., 1980—, mem. exec. com., chmn. human resources, 1989—; bd. dirs. Concern for Dying, 1983-89; trustee Calif. State Coll. Los Angeles Found., 1971-72, U. Pitts, 1984-90, mem. exec. com. 1988-90; chair bd. visitors U. Pitts. Sch. Pub. Health, 1988; bd. visitors U. Miami Sch. Nursing, 1986—; mem. health services com. Children's Aid Soc., N.Y., 1978-84; v.p. Am. Nurses Found., 1980-82; mem. nat. adv. council on nurse tng. HRA, 1981-85. Named Outstanding Alumna U. Pitts. Sch. Nursing, 1966, Pa. Nurse of Yr., 1967, to Roll of Honor N.J. State Nurses Assn., 1990; recipient Disting. Alumna award U. Pitts. Sch. Edn., 1981, Shaw medal Boston Coll., 1985, Bicentennial Medallion of Distinction, U. Pitts., 1987, R. Louise McManus Medallion for Disting. Svc. to Nursing, Tchrs. Coll. Columbia U., 1987, Dean's Disting. Svc. award Columbia Sch. Pth, 1995, Second Century award in health care, Columbia U. Sch. Nursing, 1996. Fellow Am. Acad. Nursing; mem. ANA (dir. 1978-82, Hon. Recognition award 1992), APHA (Ruth Freeman Pub. Health Nursing award 1993), Pa. Nurses Assn. (pres. 1966-69), Nat. League Nursing (bd. govs. 1991-95), Nurses Ednl. Funds Bd., U . Pitts. Sch. Nursing Alumni (pres. 1959), Am. Hosp. Assn. (com. chmn. 1967-68), Assn. Grad. Faculty Cmty. Health/Pub. Health Nursing (v.p. 1980-81), Sigma Theta Tau (sr. editor Image 1978-81, pres.-elect 1981-83, pres. 1983-85, nat. campaign chair Ctr. for Nursing Scholarship 1987-89, chair devel. com. 1989-95, Mentor award 1985, 93), Pi Lambda Theta, Alpha Tau Delta (Cert. of Merit). Home: 6040 Boulevard E Apt 11G West New York NJ 07093-3809

KELLY, PATRICK JOSEPH, neurosurgeon, educator; b. Lackawanna, N.Y., Sept. 19, 1941; s. Joseph P. and MaryD. (Connor) K.; m. Carol Huey; 1 child, Caitlin M. BS, U. Mich., 1962; MD, SUNY, Buffalo, 1966. Intern U.S. Naval Hosp., Phila., 1966-67; resident Northwestern U., Chgo., 1970-72; resident, asst. prof., assoc. prof. U. Tex. Med. Sch., Galveston, 1972-79; assoc. prof. SUNY, Buffalo, 1979-84; prof., cons. Mayo Med. Sch./Mayo Clinic, Rochester, Minn., 1984-93; prof., chmn. neurosurg. dept. NYU Med. Ctr., 1993—; cons., adv. bd. mem. Jet Propulsion Lab NASA, Pasadena, Calif., 1994—. Author: Tumor Stereotaxis, 1991; co-editor: Computers in Stereotactic Neurosurgery, 1992; mem. editl. bd. Neurosurgery, 1991—, Surg. Neurology, 1990—, Jour. Stereotactic and Functional Neurosurgery, 1986—; contbr. chpts. in books and articles to profl. jours. Lt. comdr. USN, 1968-70. Named Citizen of Yr. Buffalo Evening News, 1982, Best Doctors in Am. Good Housekeeping, 1993, Town & Country, 1992. Fellow ACS; mem. Am. Soc. Stereotactic Neurosurgery (past pres., bd. dirs.), Am. Assn. Neurol. Surgeons (Van Weganan fellow 1977, com. chmn.), Acad. Neurol. Surgery, Soc. Neurol. Surgeons (com.), Societe de Neurochurgic de Lange Francaise. Roman Catholic. Home: 7 Gracie Sq New York NY 10028 Office: NYU Med Ctr 530 First Ave New York NY 10016

KELLY, RALPH WHITLEY, emergency physician, health facility administrator; b. Hernando, Miss., Oct. 13, 1949; s. Leslie Athrel and Nina Earline (Christopher) K.; m. Janet Sue Evans Burns, May 15, 1971 (div. May 1991); children: Rochelle, Angela, Melanie, Christopher; m. Virginia Markle Alfson, Mar. 13, 1993. BS, U. Tex., Arlington, 1972; DO, Tex. Coll. Osteo. Medicine, Ft. Worth, 1976. Diplomate Am. Bd. Emergency Medicine, Am. Bd. Pediat., Am. Bd. Quality Assurance and Utilization Rev. Physicians, Nat. Bd. Examiners. Mem. staff pediat. USAF, Wichita Falls, Tex., 1979-82; med. dir. emergency dept. Fischer-Mangold Group, Pleasanton, Calif., 1982-90, EmCare, Inc., Dallas, 1990-91; chmn. emergency dept. Hillcrest Bapt. Med. Ctr., Waco, Tex., 1990-91; dir. EMS tng. programs Vernon Regional Jr. Coll., Wichita Falls, 1991-95; dir. emergency svcs. Wichita Gen. Hosp., Wichita Falls, 1991-95; pres. Texoma Emergency Assn., Wichita Falls, 1991-95; dir. informatics MEPA, Dallas, 1995—; chmn. emergency dept. Trinity Med. Ctr., Carrollton, Tex., 1995—; bd. dirs. Foster Child Advocacy Svcs., Wichita Falls, 1983-85; mem. faculty Tex. affiliate Am. Heart Assn., Austin, 1985—, course dir. ACLS, 1982—; mem. exec. com. Wichita Gen. Hosp., 1991-95; physician advisor for quality Trinity Med. Ctr., 1996. Rev. editor Tex. Emergency Bulletin of Tex. Coll. Emergency Physicians, 1987-89. Mem. pre-med. adv. com. Midwestern State U., Wichita Falls, 1987-89; mem. child mortality com. DA's Office, Wichita Falls, 1994-95; EMS med. dir. Lifeline EMS, Wichita Falls, 1992-94, AMT EMS, Waco, 1990-91. Major USAF, 1976-82. Recipient Physician Recognition award AMA, 1985. Fellow Am. Coll. Emergency Physicians, Am. Acad. Pediat.; mem. Tex. Med. Assn., Tex. Osteo. Med. Assn., Group Mgmt. Sect. (charter). Republican. Home: 1525 Commerce Dr Plano TX 75093 Office: Trinity Med Ctr 4343 N Josey Ln Carrollton TX 75010

KELLY, STEPHEN EULESS, ophthalmologist; b. Oklahoma City, July 2, 1944; s. Harold Shaw and Mart Will (Euless) K. BS with honors, U. Okla., 1966; MD, Washngton U., St. Louis, 1970. Diplomate Am. Bd. Ophthalmology. Intern Lenox Hill Hosp., N.Y.C., 1970-71; resident in ophthalmology N.Y. Eye and Ear Infirmary, N.Y.C., 1972-75; corneal fellow Manhattan Eye, Ear and Throat Hosp., N.Y.C., 1975-76, attending surgeon, 1976—; pvt. practice Cataract & Corneal Assocs., N.Y.C., 1976—; investigator Excimer Laser-FDA, 1991—. Sec., dir. Microsurg. Rsch. Found., 1976—. Maj. USAR, 1970-76. Fellow ACS, Am. Acad. Ophthalmology (Honor award 1985); mem. AMA (Physician's Recognition award 1990), Am. Soc. of Cataract and Refractive Surgery, Internat. Soc. Refractive Surgery. Office: Cataract & Cornea Assocs 154 E 71st St New York NY 10021

KELLY, THOMAS JESSE, JR., molecular biologist; b. Birmingham, Ala., Nov. 21, 1941; s. Thomas Jesse and Agnes (Allen) K.; m. Mary Lucinda Schwartz, June 25, 1969; children: Mark Thomas, Andrew Samuel. BA with honors, Johns Hopkins U., 1962, PhD in Biophysics, 1968, MD, 1969. Served with USPHS, 1970-72. Postdoctoral fellow Harvard Med. Sch., Boston, 1968, Johns Hopkins U. Sch. Medicine, Balt., 1969-70; staff assoc. Nat. Inst. Health, Bethesda, Md., 1970-72; asst. prof. microbiology Johns Hopkins U. Sch. Medicine, Balt., 1972-75, assoc. prof., 1976-79, Boury Prof. molecular biology and genetics, 1980—, dir. dept., 1982—; chmn. study sect. virology NIH, 1988-90. Mem. editorial bd. Jour. Biol. Chemistry, Jour. Virology, Virus Rsch., Oncogene Rsch., Seminars in Virology. Mem. awards assembly Gen. Motors Cancer Prize; bd. dirs. Passano Found. Recipient Career Devel. award NIH, 1972-77. Fellow Am. Acad. Arts and Sci.; mem. NAS, Am. Soc. Biological Chemists, Am. Soc. Microbiology, Am. Soc. Virology, Phi Beta Kappa, Alpha Omega Alpha. Office: Johns Hopkins U Sch Medicine 725 N Wolfe St Baltimore MD 21205-2185

KELLY, VINCENT MICHAEL, JR., orthodontist; b. Tulsa, Mar. 15, 1933; s. Vincent Michael and Ivy Maria (Phelps) K.; m. Donna Deane Amis, June 1955 (div. 1972); children: Kevin Marie, Leslie Rene, Karen Elizabeth, Carolyn Michelle, Kathleen Ann; m. Aleatha Wilkinson Kelly. BA in Biology, U. Mo., Kansas City, 1954, DDS, 1957, Orthodontist, 1962, MS in Oral Histology, 1963. Diplomate Am. Bd. Orthodontics. Pvt. practice Tulsa, 1963—; asst. prof. orthodontics St. Louis U., 1972-76; assoc. prof. U. Okla., Oklahoma City, 1980-90; bd. dirs. State Bank NA, Tulsa. Nature Works Inc. Patentee in field. Organizer, bd. mem. Arvest Savs. and Loan, Tulsa, 1995. Capt. USAF, 1957-59. Mem. Tweed Found. Orthodontic Rsch. (instr. 1966-79), Am. Assn. Orthodontics, S.W. Soc. Orthodontics, Okla. Orthodontic Assn. (pres. 1976), Tulsa County Dental Soc., Coll. Europeen Orthodontie (hon. life mem.), Soc. Panamena de Orthodoncia Panama (hon. life), Soc. Colombiana de Orthodoncia Colombia (hon. life), Assn. Mex. Orthodoncia Med. (hon.), European Soc. Lingual Orthodontists (hon.), So. Hills Country Club, Arrowhead Yacht Club, Bailli (pres. Tulsa chpt.), Chaîne des Rôtisseurs. Republican. Roman Catholic. Home: 6517 Timberlane Rd Tulsa OK 74136-4520 Office: 4550 S Harvard Ave Tulsa OK 74135-2906 also: 333 W Blue Starr Dr Claremore OK 74017-5810

KELLY, WILLIAM E., psychoanalyst; b. Nashville, Mar. 17, 1914; s. Charles Peck and Alice (Eager) K.; student Antioch Coll., 1932-34; B.S. in Edn., U. Va., 1938, M.D., 1945; m. Martha L. Parks, June 6, 1953; children: Susie Eager Kelly Sayegh, Penelope Ellen Bayley, Benjamin Alexander. Intern, Kings County Hosp., Bklyn., 1945-46; resident psychiatrist U. Va. Hosp., 1946, Inst. Pa. Hosp., Phila., 1948-50; sr. research psychiatrist VA Hosp., Coatesville, Pa., 1950-51; asst. vis. physician Phila. Gen. Hosp., 1951-59; staff psychiatrist Lakeland Mental Hosp., Camden, N.J., 1951-55; practice medicine specializing in psychiatry, Phila., 1951-83; mem. staff Jefferson Hosp., 1951-71; sr. attending staff Inst. Pa. Hosp., 1951-78, pres. staff, 1968-70, cons., 1978-87, hon. cons., 1987—; attending physician VA Hosp., Phila., 1955-66; cons. neuropsychiatrist Graterford Penitentiary, 1954-58; asst. cons. neuropsychiatrist Devereaux Schs., 1956-58; asst. neurologist Wills Eye Hosp., Phila., 1959-71; cons. psychiatry Valley Forge Gen. Hosp., 1965-74; staff psychiatrist Coatesville (Pa.) VA Hosp., 1974-77, dir. profl. edn., 1977-79, asso. chief of staff for edn., 1979-83; staff psychiatrist Western State Hosp., Staunton, Va., 1985-89; assignments Comphealth, Med. Drs. Assn., 1989—; instr. psychiatry U. Pa. Med. Sch., 1951-54; instr. neurology Jefferson Med. Coll., 1951-71, clin. prof. psychiatry, 1974-84, hon. prof. psychiatry, 1984—; asst. clin. prof. psychiatry Med. Coll. Pa., 1971-74; grad. psychoanalysis Phila. Assn. Psychoanalysis, 1964, mem., 1966—, dir. extension sch., 1967-73, mem. faculty, 1970-84, sec., 1976-79, bd. dirs., 1976-84; vis. scholar dept. behavioral medicine and psychiatry U. Va. Sch. Medicine, 1985-89, clin. prof. behavioral medicine and psychiatry, 1989-91. Capt. M.C., AUS, 1946-48. Diplomate Am. Bd. Psychiatry and Neurology. Fellow AMA, ACP, Am. Psychiat. Assn., Phila. Psychiat. Soc., Phila. Coll. Physicians, Am. Coll. Psychiatrists, Am. Coll. Psychoanalysts; Am. Psychoanalytic Assn., Internat. Psychoanalytic Assn. Editor: Barriers to the Efficacy of Psychiatric Treatment, 1981; The Changing Role of Rehabilitation Medicine in the Management of the Psychiatric Patient, 1983; Alzheimer's Disease and Related Disorders, 1984; Posttraumatic Stress Disorder and the War Veteran Patient, 1985. Home and Office: 1026 La Paloma Blvd Fort Myers FL 33903-1343

KELMAN, CHARLES D., ophthalmologist; b. Bklyn., May 23, 1930; s. David and Eva K.; m. Ann Gur-Arie; 1 child: Evan Ari Kelman; children from previous marriage: David, Lesley, Jennifer. B.S., Tufts U., 1950; B.M.S., U. Geneva, Switzerland, 1952, M.D., 1956. Diplomate Am. Bd. Ophthalmology. Intern, Kings County Hosp., N.Y.C., 1956-57; resident, Wills Eye Hosp., Pa., 1956-60; with Manhattan Eye, Ear, Nose and Throat Hosp., N.Y.C., 1967—, N.Y. Eye and Ear Infirmary, N.Y.C., 1983—; clin. prof. N.Y. Med. Coll., Valhalla, 1980—; Arthur J. Bedell Meml. lectr., 1991; hon. pres. elect 1994 World Congress on Lens Implant Surgery. Author: Cataracts-What You Must Know About Them, 1982; Atlas of Cryosurgical Techniques in Ophthalmology, 1966; Phacoemulsification Aspiration-The Kelman Technique of Cataract Extraction, 1975; Through My Eyes, 1985. Contbr. numerous articles to profl. jours. Recipient Gold Plate award Am. Acad. Achievement, 1969, 1st prize for sci. exhibit, Am. Acad. Ophthalmology, 1970, 1st Outstanding Achievement award Am. Soc. Contemporary Ophthalmology, 1981, Physicians Recognition award AMA, Can. Implant Assn. award, 1982, Congl. Salute, U.S. Senate 97th Congress, 1983, 1st Ann. Innovators award Am. Internat. Intraocular Lens Congress, 1985, Am. Acad. Ophthalmology Sr. Honor award, 1986, Binkhorst medal Am. Soc. Cataract and Refractive Surgery, 1989, Ridley medal Internat. Congress Ophthalmology, 1990, Special recognition award Am. Acad. Ophthalmology, Nat. Medal Tech., 1992, Pres. of U.S. Inventor of the Yr. award, 1992, Disting. Svc. award Tufts U., 1992. Fellow Am. Acad. Ophthalmology; mem. AMA, Internat. Assn. Ocular Surgeons, Can. Implant Assn., N.Y. Implant Soc., Am. Soc. for Contemporary Ophthalmology, Am. Soc. for Cataracts and Refractive Surgery (pres.-elect), N.Y. State Soc. Ophthalmology, N.Y. Acad. Medicine (sec. sect. on ophthalmology), European Phaco-Cataract Soc. (hon. life pres.), Soc. for Phacoemulsification and Related Techniques (hon. life pres.). Jewish. Avocations: golf, saxophone, composing, flying, writing. Office: Empire State Bldg 350 Fifth Ave New York NY 10118

KELMAN, DONALD BRIAN, neurosurgeon; b. Brandon, Man., Can., Apr. 3, 1942; came to U.S., 1979; s. Alexander and May Marguerite (Ronayne) K.; m. Joan Ann Thompson, July 10, 1966 (div. Sept. 1985); children: Carl Michael, Melanie Catherine, Leslie Jane, Brian Andrew; m. Cynthia Marie Esser, Mar. 21, 1986; 1 child, Craig Richard. BA in Biology, U. Sask., 1964, MD, 1968. Diplomate Am. Bd. Neurol. Surgery. Jr. rotating intern St. Joseph's Hosp., Victoria, B.C., Can., 1968-69; pvt. practice Victoria, 1969-70; resident in neurosurgery Mayo Grad. Sch. of Medicine, Rochester, Minn., 1970-76; pvt. practice Prince George, B.C., Can., 1976-79; neurosurgeon Marshfield (Wis.) Clinic/St. Joseph's Hosp., 1979—; chmn. neurosurgery dept. Marshfield Clinic, 1984—. Wis. rep. Joint Coun. of State Neurol. Socs., 1990, 91, 92, 93, 94, 95, 96. Mem. AMA, Am. Assn. Neurol. Surgeons, Wis. Med. Soc., Wis. Neurosurg. Soc. (sec., treas. 1987, pres. 1989). Home: 1403 N Broadway Ave Marshfield WI 54449-1321 Office: Marshfield Clinic 1000 N Oak Ave Marshfield WI 54449-5703

KELSEY, EDITH JEANINE, psychotherapist, consultant; b. Freeport, Ill., Oct. 15, 1937; d. John Melvin and Florence Lucille (Ewald) Anderson; divorced; children: Steven Craig, Kevin John. Student, Pasadena Coll., 1955-58; BA in Psychology, Calif. State U., San Jose, 1980; MA in Counseling Psychology, Santa Clara U., 1984. Lic. marriage, family and child counselor. Counselor, cons., cert. trainer Values Tech., Santa Cruz, Calif., 1981—, dir. research, 1982-84; intern in counseling Sr. Residential Services, San Jose, 1983-84; psychotherapist Process Therapy Inst., Los Gatos, Calif., 1983-86, Sexual Abuse Treatment Ctr., San Jose, 1984-87; cons. in field, Santa Clara Valley, 1982—; trainer, cons. Omega Assoc., 1987-88; teaching asst. Santa Clara U., 1987-88; pvt. practice psychotherapy, cons., tng., 1987—. Contbr. articles to profl. jours. Vol. Parental Stress Hotline, Palo Alto, Calif., 1980-85. Mem. Am. Assn. Marriage and Family Therapists, Am. Soc. Aging, Calif. Assn. Marriage and Family Therapists (clin.), Palo Alto C. of C. Democrat. Presbyterian. Home: 431 Casita Ct Los Altos CA 94022-1736 Office: 153 Forest Ave Palo Alto CA 94301-1615

KELSEY, FRANCES OLDHAM (MRS. FREMONT ELLIS KELSEY), government official; b. Cobble Hill, Vancouver Island, Can., July 24, 1914; came to U.S., 1936, naturalized, 1956; d. Frank Trevor and Katherine (Stuart) Oldham; m. Fremont Ellis Kelsey, Dec. 6, 1943; children—Susan Elizabeth, Christine Ann. B.Sc., McGill U., 1934; M.Sc., 1935; Ph.D., U. Chgo., 1938, M.D., 1950. Instr., asst. prof. pharmacology U. Chgo., 1938-50; editorial assoc. AMA, Chgo., 1950-52; assoc. prof. pharmacology U. S.D., 1954-57; med. officer FDA, Washington, 1960—; dir. divsn. sci. investigations Office of Compliance, FDA, Rockville, Md., 1967-95, dep. dir. for sci. and medicine Office of Compliance, 1995—. Author: (with F.E. Kelsey, E.M.K. Geiling) Essentials of Pharmacology, 1960. Recipient Pres.'s award for Distinguished Fed. Civilian Service (refusal to approve coml. distbn. thalidomide in U.S.), 1962. Mem. Am. Soc. Pharmacology and Exptl. Therapeutics, Soc. Exptl. Biology and Medicine, Am. Med. Writers Assn., Teratology Soc., Sigma Xi, Sigma Delta Epsilon. Home: 5811 Brookside Dr Bethesda MD 20815-6669 Office: FDA Office of Compliance 7520 Standish Pl Rockville MD 20855-2737

KELSO, LYNN A., acute care nurse practitioner; b. Pitts., July 11, 1961; d. Harry Gladden and Colette Louise (Franz) K. BSN, W.Va. U., 1984; MSN, Case Western Res. U., 1991; CRNP, U. Pitts., 1993. RN, Pa., Ky.; CCRN, CRNP; cert. ACLS, CS-ACNP. Acute care nurse practitioner liver transplant ICU U. Pitts. Med. Ctr., Pitts., 1993-95; faculty ACNP program Chandler Med. Ctr., U. Ky., 1995—. Mem. ANA, Ky. Nurses Assn., AACN, Internat. Transplant Nurses' Soc., Sigma Theta Tau. Home: 986 Fairhaven Dr Lexington KY 40515-5500

KELTER, RICHARD JOHN, physician; b. N.Y.C., Apr. 6, 1946; s. Joseph John and Viola Giorgia (Ades) K.; m. Louise Carolyn Kohlberg, Sept. 7, 1974; children: Michael Jacob, Stephanie Jill. BA, U. Pa., 1967; MD, U. Louis Pasteur, Strasbourg, France, 1974. Diplomate Am. Bd. Internal Medicine. Intern Bklyn. Hosp. Med. Ctr., 1974-75, resident, 1975-77; mem. staff Tuxedo (N.Y.) Meml. Hosp., 1977-78, Good Samaritan Hosp., Spaine Vally, N.Y., 1978; physician emergency rm. Old Bridge (N.J.) Regional Hosp., 1979-80, mem. staff, 1980-81; mem. staff Centrastate Med. Ctr., Freehold, N.J., 1979—; pvt. practice Manalapan, N.J., 1979—; mem. staff Raritan Bay Med. Ctr., 1996. Mem. Am. Gertiatric Soc., Am. Soc. Internal

Medicine, Med. Soc. N.J., Monmouth County Med. Soc. Office: 368 Union Hill Rd Manalapan NJ 07726

KELTY, PAUL DAVID, physician; b. Louisville, Oct. 2, 1947; s. William Theadore and Mary Frances (Hinton) K.; BEE, U. Louisville, 1970; MS, Ohio State U., 1971; MD, U. Louisville, 1978. Mem. tech. staff Bell Labs., Whippany, N.J., 1970-72; design engr. Gen. Electric Co., Louisville, 1972-74; intern St. Mary's Med. Center, Evansville, Ind., 1978-79, resident in ob-gyn, 1979-82; practice medicine, specializing in ob-gyn, Corydon, Ind., 1982—; clin. instr. Dept. Ob-Gyn U. Louisville (Ky.) Sch. Medicine, 1987— . Mem. AMA, Am. Fertility Soc., Am. Inst. Ultrasound in Medicine, N.Y. Acad. Scis., Sigma Xi, Phi Kappa Phi, Tau Beta Pi, Sigma Tau, Sigma Pi Sigma, Eta Kappa Nu, Gamma Beta Phi, Omicron Delta Kappa. Roman Catholic. Home and Office: 2000 Edsel Ln NW Corydon IN 47112-2030

KEM, MYRON RICHARD, orthopedic surgeon; b. Dayton, Ohio, May 1, 1939; s. Myron Stuart and Bernice Kem; m. Carla Ray, Jan. 24, 1975; children: Crista Beth, Michael D. BA, Northwestern U., 1961; MD, Ohio State U., 1965. Diplomate Am. Bd. Orthopedic Surgery. Intern and resident U. Cin., 1965-67, orthopedic surgery resident, 1969-72; fellow hand surgery U. Louisville, 1972; pvt. practice orthopedic surgery Denver, 1972—; dept. chmn. Mercy Hosp., Denver; asst. chmn. Swedish and Porter Hosps. Capt. USAF, 1967-69. Fellow Am. Acad. Orthopedic Surgeons; mem. Colo. Med. Soc., Denver Med. Soc., Arapaho Med. Soc., Western Orthopedic Assn., Kiwanis Club of South Denver (treas.). Home: 4151 S Ivy Ln Englewood CO 80111 Office: 210 University Blvd #340 Denver CO 80206

KEMBLE, JAMES VICTOR HARVEY, plastic surgeon; b. London; s. James and Dorothy (Wright) K. B Medicine B Surgery, Cambridge (Eng.) U., 1962, MA, 1963. Surg. registrar Middlesex Hosp., London, 1968-70; sr. registrar in plastic surgery Odstock Hosp., Salisbury, Eng., 1973-77, Hammersmith Hosp., London, 1973-77; cons. plastic surgeon St. Bartholomew's Hosp., London, 1977-95, hon. sr. lectr., 1977—; cons. plastic surgeon St. Andrew's Hosp., Billericay, Essex, Eng., 1977—. Co-author: Plastic Surgical and Burns Nursing, Practical Burns Management; contbr. articles to profl. jours. Fellow Royal Coll. Surgeons Eng. (surg. tutor); mem. Brit. Assn. Plastic Surgeons, Brit. Soc. for Surgery of Hand (treas., mem. editl. bd. Jour. of Hand Surgery). Office: Essex Nuffield Hosp, Brentwood, Essex CM15 8EH, England

KEMENY, NANCY ELLEN, physician, medical educator; b. Elizabeth, N.J., Jan. 18, 1945; d. George and Ellen (Sagi) K.; children: Jackie, Vicki, Laura; m. Daniel Libby. BA, U. Pa., 1967; MD, U. Medicine & Dentistry N.J., 1971. Intern and resident St. Luke's Hosp., N.Y.C.; clin. asst. attending physician Meml. Sloan-Kettering Cancer Ctr., N.Y.C., 1976-77, asst. attending physician, 1977-83, assoc. attending physician, 1983-91, gastrointestinal svcs. attending physician, 1991—; asst. prof. medicine Cornell U. Med. Coll., N.Y.C., 1977-82, assoc. prof. clin. medicine, 1982-92, prof. medicine, 1992—; rsch. assoc. Sloan-Kettering Inst., N.Y.C., 1977—. Named Alumni of Yr., Vail-Dean Sch., 1989. Mem. Am. Soc. Clin. Oncology (spl. awards chairperson). Office: Meml Sloan-Kettering Cancer Ctr 1275 York Ave New York NY 10021

KEMERY, WILLIAM ELSWORTH, psychotherapist, hypnotherapist; b. Portland, Oreg., Apr. 16, 1929; s. William Elsworth Jr. and Charlotte Francis (Leydic) K.; m. Norma Mae Ishmael, Nov. 22, 1963 (div. May 1972); children: William M., Robert Z.; m. Marlene Agnes Kwiatkowski, Dec. 15, 1983; children: William E., William M., Robert Z., Bradley E. DD, Episcopal Sem., Balt., 1953; BA, Fresno State U., 1954; PhD (hon.), Hamilton State, 1973; Masters, Newport Internat. U., 1976, PhD, 1979. Cert. psychotherapist, hypnotherapist, sex therapist. Psychotherapist Chula Vista, Calif., 1967—; founding dir. Calif. Hypnotists Examining Coun., L.A., 1974; pres., fellow Acad. Sci. Hypnotherapy, San Diego, 1974—; bishop Holy Episcopal Ch., Chula Vista, 1978—; dir. Assn. of Spiritual Psychology, San Diego, 1968—. Contbr. articles to profl. jours. Named Hon. Mayor, Chula Vist C. of C., 1967, Knight of Grace, Order of St. John of Jerusalem, 1981. Fellow Nutrition and Preventive Medicine Assn.; mem. Internat. Assn. Clin. Hypnotherapy (life), Acad. Orthomolecular Psychiatry, Assn. Huministic Psychology, Internat. New Thought Alliance, Am. Guild Hypnotherapists, Am. Mental Health Counselors Assn., Am. Assn. Sex Educators, Counselors and Therapists. Republican. Home and Office: 379 G St Chula Vista CA 91910

KEMMOTSU, OSAMU, anesthesiologist, educator; b. Tokyo, Mar. 12, 1940; s. Tatsuo and Tatsu Kemmotsu; m. Hiroko Matsuno, May 1965. MD, Sapporo (Japan) Med. Coll., 1965, PhD, 1973. Cert. Japanese Bd. Anesthesiology. Fellow Tufts U., Boston, 1971-73; assoc. prof. Sapporo Med. Coll., 1976-79, Kitasato U., Sagamihara, Japan, 1979-84; prof. Toho U., Tokyo, 1984-85, Hokkaido U., Sapporo, 1985—; dir. ICU Kitasato U. Hosp., 1979-84; dir. ICU Hokkaido U. Hosp., 1991—, dir. critical care unit, 1994—; vis. prof. U. Iowa, 1980-81. Contbr. articles to profl. jours. Fellow Critical Care Medicine, Internat. Coll. Surgeons; mem. Assn. Univ. Anesthesiologists (hon.), N.Y. Acad. Scis. Office: Hokkaido U Sch Medicine, N-15 W-7 Kita-ku, Sapporo 060, Japan

KEMNA, MARGARITA ELISABETH, medical technologist; b. Wiesbaden, Germany, Dec. 21, 1947; d. Robert. I. and Elli E. (Mahler) K. BS in Med. Technology, Hartwick Coll., 1969; cert., United Hosp. Sch. Med. Tech., Pt. Chester, N.Y., 1969. Technologist lab. VA Med. Ctr., Iowa City, 1969-71, Bklyn. Jewish Hosp., 1971-77; sr. instr. microbiology Sch. Med. Tech. Albany (N.Y.) Med. Ctr. Hosp., 1977-82; supr. mycology lab. Wadsworth Ctr. for Labs. and Rsch. N.Y. State Dept. Health, Albany, 1982-93; mgr. mycology reference lab. dept. dermatology Case Western Res. U., Cleve., 1993—, instr. sch. medicine, 1994—; Com. mem., chmn. public employees fedn. health and safety com. Dept. Health, Albany, 1990-93; mem. adv. com. med. tech. program Hudson Valley C.C., Troy, N.Y., 1991-93. Contbr. rsch. articles to sci. jours. and procs. Named one of Outstanding Young Women of Am., 1979. Mem. Internat. Soc. Human and Animal Mycology, Mycology Soc. of the Ams., Am. Soc. Clin. Pathologists (registered med. technologist), Am. Soc. Microbiology, Med. Mycology Soc. of the Ams., Med. Mycol. Soc. N.Y., Omicron Sigma.

KEMP, BASTIAAN, physicist; b. Ede, The Netherlands, Aug. 2, 1951; s. Arie and Cornelia (Van Doorn) K.; m. Hermina M.T. Van Oosten, Sept. 1, 1978. MD, Twente U., Enschede, 1977; PhD, Twente U., 1987. Physicist U. Hosp., Leiden, The Netherlands, 1977—; dir. Dutch Ctr. Sleep-Wake Disorders. Contbr. articles to profl. jours.; patentee radar measurement of neurol. movement disorders. Mem. Dutch Soc. Clin. Physics, Royal Inst. Engrs., Dutch Soc. Clin. Neurophysiology, European Soc. Engring. Medicine, European Sleep Rsch. Soc., Internat. Inst. Elect., Electronic Engrs. Office: U Hosp Dept KNF, Rijnsburgerweg 10, 2333 AA Leiden The Netherlands

KEMP, EJVIND, internist; b. Copenhagen, July 21, 1929; s. Gerhardt and Kirsten (Pedersen) K.; m. Grethe Serup Jorgensen, July 1, 1956; children: Michael, Helene, Kaare. MD, U. Copenhagen, 1956, D in Med. Sci., 1962. Sci. asst. Inst. Exptl. Medicine U. Copenhagen, 1957-61; registrar Bispebjerg Hosp., 1961-64; hon. clin. asst. dept. urology Leeds (Eng.) Gen. Infirmary, 1966-67; sr. registrar Copenhagen U. Hosp., 1964-68; cons. nephrology Odense U. Hosp., 1968, chmn. Lab. of Nephropatology, 1968, prof. internal medicine, 1972—; mem. group for rsch. in transplantation of organs across species EEC, 1991; sec., co-founder Danish xenotransplantation group working with prodn. transgenic pigs, 1996. Author: Hypertension in Poliomyelitis, 1957, To Be or Not To Be, 1975, Xenotransplantation, 1991; mem. bd. Scandinavian Journal of Urology and Nephrology, 1994, Xenotransplantation. With Royal Danish Navy, 1956. Decorated Knight of Denmark; recipient U. Copenhagen Gold Medal, 1955, Odd Fellow prize, 1977, Spies grant of honor, 1990. Mem. Danish Soc. Nephrology, Transplant Soc., Internat. Soc. Nephrology. Home: 8 Hannerupvaenget, DK-5230 Odense M, Denmark Office: Odense U Hosp, Dept Nephrology, DK-5000 Odense C, Denmark

KEMP, GINA CHRISTINE, human services provider; b. New Orleans, June 5, 1968; d. Donald Rue and July Carol (Sallee) K.; m. Patrick E. Hutto, May 15, 1994; 1 stepchild, Patrick B. BA in Psychology, So. Coll., Collegedale, Tenn., 1989; MA in Edn., U. Ga., 1991. Cert. nat. counselor; master addiction counselor; criminal justice specialist. Sociology tchr. So. Coll., 1989; counselor offender rehab., GED examiner IW Davis Detention Ctr., Jefferson, Ga., 1991; counselor offender rehab. drug specialist Alcovy Diversion Ctr., Monroe, Ga., 1991-96; v.p. H&M Sales, Loganville, Ga., 1994—; human svc. provider Rockdale Mental Health, Conyers, Ga., 1996—; boot camp officer Ga. Dept. Corrections. Mem. ACA, Internat. Assn. Addictions and Offender Counseling, Chi Sigma Iota, Psi Chi. Republican. Adventist. Home: 2823 Claude Brewer Rd Loganville GA 30249-4203 Office: Rockdale Mental Health 1429 Business Center Dr Conyers GA 30207

KEMP, JAMES P., allergist, immunologist; b. Charleston, W.Va., June 18, 1936; s. James P. Kemp; m. Judith A. Kemp. BA in Biology, U. Va., 1958, MD, 1962. Diplomate Am. Bd. Pediatrics, Sub-bd. Pediatric Allergy, Am. Bd. Allergy and Immunology. Intern in pediatrics U. Fla., Gainesville, 1962-63; resident in pediatrics Emory U. Grady Meml. Hosp., Atlanta, 1964-65; staff pediatrician U.S. Naval Hosp., San Diego, 1965-67; fellow pediatric allergy and clin. immunology U. Calif., San Francisco, 1967-69; co-dir. pediatric allergy and immunology tng. prog. U. Calif., San Diego, 1969-76; pvt. practice allergy San Diego, 1969—; cons. FDA; clin. prof. pediatrics U. Hosp., Mercy Hosp.; chief div. allergy & immunology, Chilren's Hosp. and Health Ctr., 1988-90; mem. med. staff Grossmont Hosp., Sharp's Meml. Hosp., all in San Diego; mem. pulmonary bd. U.S. Pharmacopeia, 1992—; presenter numerous research papers in field. Mem. editorial bd. Respiratory Medicine Today, 1985—; editorial adv. bd. Clin. Advances in Treatment of Allergic Reactions, 1987—, Am. Jour. Asthma and Allergy for Pediatricians, 1987—, Jour. of Asthma, 1988—; contbr. 150 articles to med. jours. Fellow Am. Acad. Allergy and Immunology (com. on drugs 1970—, chmn., 1987, v.p. 1996, Asthma Mortality Task Force 1986—, Rsch. Coun. 1987—), Am. Coll. Allergy and Immunology, Am. Acad. Pediatrics (exec. com. allergy and immunology sect. 1982-84), Am. Assn. Cert. Allergists, Am. Coll. Chest Physicians (steering com. sect. on allergy and clin. immunology 1989); mem. AMA (drug evaluations cons. 1986), Am. Thoracic Soc., Assn. for the Care of Asthma, Western Soc. Allergy and Immunology, Calif. Med. Assn., Calif. Soc. Allergy and Clin. Immunology (pres. 1972), San Diego County Med. Soc., San Diego Allergy Soc. (pres. 1971), Asthma and Allergy Found. Am. Republican. Home: 3264 Curlew St San Diego CA 92103-5540 Office: Allergy and Asthma Med Group Rsch Ctr APC 9610 Granite Ridge Dr # B San Diego CA 92123-2661

KEMPER, HAN C. G., exercise physiologist, health science educator; b. Amsterdam, The Netherlands, Mar. 20, 1941; m. Bertheke G. Post, Dec. 17, 1985; children: Ilse, Birgit. MS in Phys. Edn., Free U., Amsterdam, 1961; PhD in Phys. Edn., Free U., Brussels, 1968. Tchr. phys. edn. Ignatius Coll., Amsterdam, 1965-74; tchr. exercise physiology Ctrl. Inst. Sports, Overveen, The Netherlands, 1960-70, Acad. Phys. Edn., Tilburg, The Netherlands, 1971-84; asst. prof. U. Amsterdam, 1965-84; prof. Vrye U., Amsterdam, 1984—; dean faculty human movement sci. U. Amsterdam, 1986-90. Author: (textbook) Measuring Physical Activity and Energy, 1996, (monograph) Growth, Health and Fitness of Teenagers, 1985, 96; contbr. articles to profl. jours. Recipient Excellence in Rsch. award Coun. Sports Medicine, 1974. Fellow Am. Coll. Sports Medicine; mem. Nat. Health Coun. (com. mem. 1991-96). Roman Catholic. Home: Meikevermeent 2, 1218 HD Hilversum The Netherlands Office: Vrye U Emgo Inst, v d Boechorstr str 7, 1081 BT Amsterdam The Netherlands

KEMPER, JAMES WILLARD, physician; b. Indpls., May 24, 1927; s. Garvey E. and Elizabeth Mae (Smith) K.; m. Carolyn Jane Allee, June 2, 1952 (div. 1972); children: Katherine Elizabeth, Deborah Ann; m. Julie Beth Catterton, Dec. 31, 1973. BS, Ind. U., 1949, MD, 1952; MS in Medicine, U. Minn., 1956. Diplomate Am. Bd. Internal Medicine. Fellow internal medicine Mayo Clinic, 1953-57; physician, ptnr. Kelsey-Seybold Clinic, P.A., Houston, 1957—; chief exec. officer, 1977-79, 83-94; attending staff St. Luke's Episcopal Hosp., Houston, 1957—, chief rheumatology dept., 1970-86; clin. prof. medicine Baylor Coll. Medicine, Houston. With USAF, 1945-46. Fellow ACP, Am. Coll. Rheumatology; mem. Arthritis Found. (pres. Tex. Gulf Coast chpt. 1966), Tex. Rheumatism Assn. (pres. 1964-65, sec., treas. 1961-64, bd. dirs. 1960-61, 66-67), Houston Soc. Internal Medicine, Nat. Soc. Clin. Rheumatologists (pres. 1994), Alpha Omega Alpha. Office: Kelsey-Seybold Clinic PA 6624 Fannin St Houston TX 77030-2312

KEMPER, WALKER WARDER, JR., dentist, educator; b. Indpls., Aug. 26, 1924; s. Walker Warder Sr. and Margaret Louise (Mast) K.; m. Janet Morene Cottingham, June 10, 1950 (div. Oct. 1973); children—Walker Warder III, Todd Geller; m. Stephanie Ann Brean, June 24, 1978; stepchildren—Jeffrey L., Michael L., Scott L. B.S., Butler U., 1949; D.D.S., Ind. U., 1953, M.Sci. Dentistry, 1965. Clin. instr. Ind. U., Indpls., 1953-65; practice dentistry specializing in prosthodontics, Indpls., 1953—; faculty practitioner, Ind. U., 1979-94; chief dental sect. St. Vincent Hosp. and Health Care Ctr., 1976-86, exec. com., 1976-86; mem. Ind. State Bd. Dental Examiners, 1971-77; dental dir. Marquette Manor Retirement Home, Indpls., 1975—; Peerview Inc. of Ind. Active in Ind. U. Century Club, Indpls., 1968—, Butler U. Pres.'s Club, 1966—; bd. dirs. Little Red Door Cancer Soc., 1970-74, Paul Coble Post, Am. Legion, life mem.; chmn. Boys State, 1978-79. Served to staff sgt. USAF, 1943-46. Decorated Bronze Star. Mem. ADA (life), John F. Johnston Soc. (pres. 1982, exec. com. 1977-86), Ind. State Dental Assn., Indpls. Dist. Dental Assn. (pres. 1970-71, Honor Dentist of Yr., 1988), Am. Coll. Dentists (life, pres. Ind. sect. 1988-89), Am. Acad. Crown and Bridge, Am. Acad. Dental Medicine (life), Am. Coll. Prosthodontics, Pierre Fauchard Acad., East Africa Hunters Assn., Safari Club Internat. (pres. 1982-83 Ind. chapt.), Game Conservation Internat. (life, Game Coin), Adult Firecrafter, Phi Delta Theta, Omicron Kappa Upsilon (Dental hon.), Psi Omega. Republican. Methodist. Clubs: Meridian Hills Country, Columbia (Indpls.). Avocations: big game hunting, fishing, scuba diving, swimming, skiing, golfing. Home: 7574 Morningside Dr Indianapolis IN 46240-2859 Office: 8402 Harcourt Rd Ste 625 Indianapolis IN 46260-2055

KENAGY, JOHN WARNER, surgeon; b. Lincoln, Nebr., May 28, 1945; s. Wyman Black and Sylvia (Adams) K.; m. Barbara Penterman, Feb. 1968 (div. 1975); 1 child, Jennifer; m. Jonell Day, Apr. 21, 1978; children: Susanne, Emma, John Wyman. BS, U. Nebr., 1967, MD, U. Nebr., Omaha, 1971. Diplomate Am. Bd. Surgery; splty. cert. in gen. vascular surgery. Intern, Hosps. of U. Wash., Seattle, 1971-72, resident in surgery, 1971-76; surgeon Longview Surgical Group, Longview, Wash., 1976—; clin. instr. surgery U. Wash., Seattle, 1979-82, clin. asst. prof. surgery, 1982-89, clin. assoc. prof., 1989—; dir. peripheral vascular svcs. St. Johns Hosp., Longview, 1979-88, chmn. credentials com., 1989-90; dir. trauma svcs. St. Johns Med. Ctr., 1990-92; regional v.p. med. divsn. Lower Columbia Regional Health System; regional v.p. med. divsn. Peace Health, 1995—. Editor current concepts in vascular diagnosis St. Johns Vascular Lab., Longview, 1979-88; contbr. articles to profl. jours. Chmn. bd. dirs. Cowlitz Med. Service, Longview, 1985-86. Regents scholar U. Nebr., Lincoln, 1963-67. Fellow ACS, Henry Harkins Surg. Soc. (trustee 1983-84), Seattle Surg. Soc.; mem. Internat. Cardiovascular Soc., Pacific N.W. Vascular Soc. (pres.-elect 1986-87, pres. 1987-88, chmn. com. on standards 1989-91), North Pacific Surg. Soc., Med. Group Mgmt. Assn., Am. Coll. Physician Execs., Alpha Omega Alpha, Theta Nu, Phi Gamma Delta. Republican. Office: Longview Gen & Thoracic Surgery 900 Fir St Ste 1J Longview WA 98632-2544

KENDALL, HARRY OVID, internist; b. Eugene, Oreg., Nov. 29, 1929; s. Edward Lee and Jessie Avis (Giem) K.; m. Katherine Alexander, June 20, 1951 (div. 1957); 1 child, Jessica Gail Gress; m. Barbara Ann Matt, Jan. 21, 1961 (div. June 1, 1977); children: David Lee, Brian Padraic; m. Wanda Eve Helmer, July 2, 1993. AB, U. Redlands, 1952; MD, Yale U., 1955. Diplomate Am. Bd. Internal Medicine, Am. Bd. Pulmonary Disease. Intern in internal medicine UCLA Med. Ctr., 1955-57; resident in internal medicine West L.A. VA Med. Ctr., 1957-59; staff physician U.S. Naval Regional Med. Ctr., San Diego, 1959-62, Tulare-Kings Counties Hosp., Springville, Calif., 1962-63; staff physician, ptnr. So. Calif. Permanente Med. Group, Fontana, Calif., 1963-67, Kaiser Hosp. and So. Calif. Permanente Med. Group, San Diego, 1967—; dir. respiratory care Kaiser Hosp., San Diego, 1967—; attending physician San Bernardino County Hosp., 1964-67; asst. clin. prof. medicine U. Calif. San Diego Med. Ctr., 1976—; com. mem. numerous hosps. and med. clinics. Mem. NAACP, Amnesty Internat., ACLU. Lt. USNR, 1954-56, lt. comdr. 1961, comdr. 1973. Mem. Am. Thoracic Soc., cAlif. Thoracic Soc., San Diego Pulmonary Soc.

KENDALL, JOHN WALKER, JR., medical educator, researcher, university dean; b. Bellingham, Wash., Mar. 19, 1929; s. John Walker and Mathilda (Hansen) K.; m. Elizabeth Helen Meece, Mar. 19, 1954; children: John, Katherine, Victoria. BA, Yale Coll., 1952; MD, U. Wash., 1956. Intern, then resident in internal medicine Vanderbilt U. Hosp., Nashville, 1956-59, fellow in endocrinology, 1959-60; fellow in endocrinology U. Oreg. Med. Sch., Portland, 1960-62; asst. prof. medicine Oreg. Health Scis. U., Portland, 1962-66, assoc. prof. medicine, 1966-71, prof. medicine, 1971—, head divsn. metabolism, 1971-80, dean Sch. Medicine, 1983-92, dean emeritus Sch. Medicine, 1992—; assoc. chief staff-rsch. VA Med. Ctr., Portland, 1971-83, dep. chief of staff, 1993, VA disting. physician, 1993—; cons. Med. Rsch. Found. Oreg., Portland, 1975-83; sec., bd. dirs. Oreg. Found. Med. Excellence, Portland, 1984-89, pres., 1989-91. Lt. comdr. M.C., USN, 1962-64. Mem. AMA (governing coun. med. sch. sect. 1989-93, chair 1991-92, alt. del. 1992-93, Oreg. del. 1994—, rep. Coun. Grad. Med. Edn. 1993-94), Assn. Am. Physicians, Am. Soc. Clin. Investigation, Am. Fedn. Clin. Rsch., We. Soc. Clin. Rsch. (councillor 1972-75), Endocrine Soc., Multnomah County Med. Soc. (treas. 1989, pres. 1991), Med. Rsch. Found. (Mentor award 1992). Presbyterian. Home: 3131 SW Evergreen Ln Portland OR 97201-1816 Office: Oreg Health Scis U Sch Medicine 3181 SW Sam Jackson Park Rd Portland OR 97201-3011

KENDALL, KENNETH RICHARD, optometrist; b. San Gabriel, Calif., Mar. 27, 1964; s. Richard Hunter and Sally Diane (Vannoy) K.; m. Melanie Kay Davis, June 16, 1989; children: Nathan Hunter, Natalie Laura. BS in Visual Sci., So. Calif. Coll. Optometry, 1988; postgrad., Calif. State U., Hayward, 1985-86; DO, Point Coma Coll., 1990. Lic. optometrist, Calif. Pvt. practice Kendall Optometry, Lompoc, Calif., 1990—. Bd. dirs., music leader Trinity Ch. of the Nazarene, Lompoc, 1992—. Mem. Am. Optometric Assn. (contact lens sect.), Calif. Optometric Assn. Republican. Office: Kendall Optometry 437 N H St Apt A-1 Lompoc CA 93436

KENDALL, LEIGH WAKEFIELD, surgeon; b. Brattleboro, Vt., Mar. 8, 1937; s. Irwin Samuel and Laura Eliza (Walbridge) K.; m. Grace Eleanor Fullarton, July 1, 1961; children: William Leigh, Bradley Edward. AB, U. Pa., Phila., 1959; D of Medicine, U. Vt., 1963; MS, U. Ill., Chgo., 1965. Diplomate Nat. Bd. Med. Examiners, Am. Bd. Surgery; cert. ACLS. Intern then resident surgery U. Ill. Hosp., Chgo., 1963-69; rsch. fellow Am. Cancer Soc., Chgo., 1964-65; clin. fellow Am. Cancer Soc., 1968-69; staff surgeon USN Hosp., Great Lakes, Ill., 1969; surgeon USN Hosp. Ships, Vietnam, 1969-70; pvt. practice Lancaster, Pa., 1971-93; medical dir. St. Joseph P.H.O., Lancaster, Berks, 1995—; instr. surgery U. Ill. Hosp., Chgo., 1968-69; active staff St. Joseph Hosp., Lancaster, 1971—, sect. chief gen. surgery, 1981-88, chmn. dept. surgery, 1989-93; mem. courtesy staff Lancaster Gen. Hosp., 1971—; cons. surgery Franklin & Marshall Coll., Lancaster, Masonic Homes, Elizabethtown, Pa., staff physician, Millersville, U., 1993—; staff physician cardiac rehab., Lancaster Gen. Hosp. Health Campus, 1995—. Lt. comdr. USNR M.C., 1959-71, Vietnam. Decorated 1st Class Mil. Honor medal Republic of Vietnam. Fellow ACS, Internat. Soc. Surgeons; mem. AMA, Pa. Med. Soc., Warren H. Cole Soc. (pres. 1994-95), Royal Soc. Medicine (Eng.), Intrepids Club, Sigma Nu. Republican. Episcopalian. Home: 1314 Quarry Ln Lancaster PA 17603-2424 Office: Millersville Univ Witmer Infirmary Millersville PA 17551-0302

KENDIG, EDWIN LAWRENCE, JR., physician, educator; b. Victoria, Va., Nov. 12, 1911; s. Edwin Lawrence and Mary McGuire (Yates) K.; m. Emily Virginia Parker, Mar. 22, 1941; children: Anne Randolph (Mrs. R.F. Young), Mary Emily Corbin (Mrs. T.T. Rankin). B.A. magna cum laude, Hampden-Sydney Coll., 1932, B.S. magna cum laude, 1933, D.Sc. hon., 1971; M.D., U. Va., 1936. House officer Med. Coll. Va. Hosp., Richmond, Bellevue Hosp., N.Y.C., Babies Hosp., Wilmington, N.C., Johns Hopkins Hosp., Balt., 1936-40; instr. pediatrics Johns Hopkins U., 1944; practice medicine specializing in pediatrics Richmond, 1940-94; dir. child chest clinic Med. Coll. Va., 1944-94, prof. pediatrics, 1958—; chief of staff St Mary's Hosp., Richmond, 1966-67; cons. on diseases of chest in children, 1944-94, William P. Buffum orator Brown U., 1978; Abraham Finkelstein Meml. lectr. U. Md., 1983; Derwin Cooper lectr. Duke U., 1984; Renato Ma Guerrero lectr. U. Santo Tomas, Manila, 1984; Bakwin Meml. lectr. NYU-Bellevue Hosp., 1986. Contbr. numerous articles on desease of chest in children to profl. publs.; editor: Disorders of Respiratory Tract in Children, 1967, 72, 77; co-editor: (with V. Chernick) Disorders of Respiratory Tract in Children, 4th edit., 1983, cons. editor to V. Chernick, 5th edit., pub. as Kendig's Disorders of the Respiratory Tract in Children, 1990; (with C.F. Ferguson) Pediatric Otolaryngology, 1972; contbg. editor: (books) Gellis and Kagan Current Pediatric Therapy, 13 edits., 1993, Burg, Ingelfinger, Wall Current Pediatric Therapy, 14th edit., Antimicrobial Therapy, Kagen, 3 edits., Practice of Pediatrics, Kelley, Practice of Pediatrics, Maurer, Allergic Deseases of Infancy, Childhood and Adolescence, Bierman and Pearlman, James, Sarcoidosis and Other Granulomatous Diseases, 1994; former mem. editl. bd. Pediat. Pulmonology; former mem. editl. adv. bd. Pediat. Annals; former mem. editl. bd. Pediat., Alumnews U. Va., 1988. Chmn. Richmond Bd. Health, 1961-63; bd. visitors U. Va., 1961-72; former mem. bd. dirs. Va. Hosp. Svc. Assn.; former ofcl. examiner Am. Bd. Pediatrics; mem. White House Conf. on Children and Youth, 1960; pres. alumni adv. com. U. Va. Sch. Medicine, Charlottesville, 1974-75; past bd. dirs. Maymont Found., Richmond; bd. dirs. Children's Hosp., Sheltering Arms Hosp.; former mem. adv. bd. Ctr. for Study of Mind and Human Interaction, U. Va. Sch. Medicine, 1988; mem. steering com. One Hundred Twenty Fifth Anniversary, Med. Coll. of VA Hosps., 1986; former bd. dirs. St. Mary's Health Care Found., 1990. Recipient resolution of recognition Va. Health Commr., 1978, Obici award Louise Obici Hosp., 1979, Bon Secours award St. Mary's Hosp., 1986, Keating award Hampden-Sydney Coll., 1989; named an Outstanding Alumnus Sch. Medicine U. Va., 1986; The Edwin Lawrence Kendig Jr. Disting Profesorship in Pediatric Pulmonary medicine named in honor Med. Coll. Va. Commonwealth U. Mem. AMA (pediat. residency rev. com.), Am. Acad. Pediat. (past pres. Va. sect., chmn. sect. on diseases of chest, mem. exec. bd. 1971-78, nat. pres. 1978-79, Abraham Jacobi Meml. award with AMA, 1987, cons. com. on internat. child health), Am. Acad. Pediat. for Latin Am. (ofcl. adv. to exec. bd. 1988), Va. Bd. Medicine (former pres.), Richmond Acad. Medicine (pres. 1962, chmn. bd. trustees 1963), Va. Pediat. Soc. (past pres.), Am. Pediat. Soc., So. Med. Assn., So. Soc. Pediat. Rsch., Internat. Pediat. Assn. (cons., standing com., medal 1986), Med. Soc. Va. (editor Va. Med. Quarterly 1982, resolution of recognition), Soc. Cin., Raven, Phi Beta Kappa, Alpha Omega Alpha, Tau Kappa Alpha, Kappa Sigma, Omicron Delta Kappa. Episcopalian. Clubs: Commonwealth, Country of Va; Farmington (Charlottesville). Home: 5008 Cary Street Rd Richmond VA 23226-1643 Office: Va Med Quarterly 4205 Dover Rd Richmond VA 23221

KENDIG, JOAN JOHNSTON, neurobiology educator; b. Derby, Conn., May 1, 1939; d. Frank and Agnes (Kerr) Johnston; children: Scott Johnston Kendig, Leslie Anne Kendig. BA, Smith Coll., 1960; PhD, Stanford U., 1966. Rsch. assoc. Stanford U. Med. Sch., 1968-71, asst. prof. biology in anesthesia, 1971-76, assoc. prof., 1976-86, prof., 1986—; mem. physiology study sect. NIH, 1981-85. NIH neurosci. grantee, 1973—; Javits neurosci. investigator, 1988-95. Mem. Soc. for Neurosci., Assn. U. Anesthesiologists, Am. Pain Soc., Internat. Assn. for Study of Pain. Office: Stanford U Med Sch Dept Anesthesia Stanford CA 94305

KENDRICK, WILLIAM DAVID, physician assistant; b. Carlisle, Ky., July 30, 1951; s. Richard Daniel and Martha M. (Gamblin) K. BS, Ea. Ill. U., 1973, U. Okla., 1986. Cert. physician asst. Faculty asst. Ea. Ill. U., Charleston, 1973-78; commd. chief warrant officer 2 U.S. Army, 1988-95, advanced through grades to 1st lt., 1992, physician asst., 1978-95; physician asst. Ferrell Hosp., Eldorado, Ill., 1995-96, Wirth regional Hosp./Oakland City (Ind.) Clinic, 1996—. Co-author articles contbd. periodical Vorläufer, 1994. Fellow Am. Acad. Physician Assts., Ky. Acad. Physician Assts.; mem. Soc. Army Physician Assts., Soc. European Physician Assts. (life), Am. Chem. Soc., Am. Mensa (life). Home: 2935 Ilsley Rd Madisonville KY 42431 Office: Wirth regional Hospital/Clinic 1201 Pine St Oakland City IN

KENNA, ROY AUSTIN, administrator; b. Kansas City, Mo., Jan. 23, 1927; s. Roy Austin and Sara Elizabeth (Bernard) K.; m. Tescue U. Berry, June 1, 1955; children: John, Bernard, Teresa, Edward, Lisa, Lawrence, Debra. BS, No. Ariz. U., 1953, MA, 1956. Cert. adminstr. Tchr., asst. coach Tucson High Sch., 1953-55; instr. U. Ariz., Tucson, 1955-57, asst. dean, 1968-74; dir. health svcs. dept. family and cmty. medicine Ariz. Med. Ctr. U. Ariz., Tucson, 1968-74; with U.S. Civil Svc., Ft. Huachuca, Ariz., 1961-63; cons. Kenna Assocs., Tucson, 1958-60, 64-67; vis. prof. No. Ariz. U., Flagstaff, 1980-81; dir. adult edn. Affiliation Ariz. Indian Ctrs., Phoenix, 1981-82; counselor Community Counseling Ctr., Winslow, 1982-85; psychologist assoc. State of Ariz., Winslow, 1988-93; ret. Author: Understanding Mathematics, 1963; contbr. articles to profl. jours. Mem. aquatic com. YMCA, Tucson, 1955; mem. Gov.'s Com. on Disability, Phoenix, 1995—; mem. AZ Bridge to Ind. Living Com., Phoenix, 1994—; chmn. Winslow Com. on Disability Awareness, 1992—. Comdr. USN, 1950-52, PTO. Named Outstanding Toastmaster, 1963; recipient Merit award Rotary, 1963, Merit cert. Optimists, 1974, Merit cert. Naval Res. Assn., 1975. Mem. Am. Soc. Pers. Adminstrn., Am. Mgmt. Assn.

KENNEDY, COLLEEN GERALYN, nurse, social worker; b. S.I., N.Y., Feb. 2, 1955; d. James Martin and Eleanor S. (Dehlinger) K.; m. Edward Francis Humphries, July21, 1990; children: Michael J. Carlucci, Stephen Edward Humphries. AAS in Nursing, Coll. S.I., 1976; BSW, Adelphi U., 1982, MSW, 1984. RN, N.Y.; cert. social worker, N.Y. Staff nurse S.I. Hosp., 1976-80, social work asst., 1980-84, clin. social worker, 1984-85; asst. dir. social work Eger Health Care Ctr., S.I., 1985-87; systems analyst program devel. and evaluation St. Vincent's Med. Ctr., S.I., 1987-89; asst. dir. Ctr. Chem. Dependency, Bayley Seton Hosp., S.I., 1989-93; med, coord., managed care, utilization mgmt., quality assurance Bayley Seton Hosp., S.I., 1993-95; dir. health and mem. svcs. Health Plus Prepaid Health Svcs. Plan, Inc., Bklyn., 1995—. Named to Outstanding Young Women of Am., 1984. Mem. NASW, ACSW, NAFE, S.I. Coun. on Domestic Violence. Democrat. Roman Catholic. Office: Health Plus 5800 3d Ave Brooklyn NY 11220

KENNEDY, DAVID WILLIAM, otolaryngologist, educator; b. York, Eng., June 27, 1948; s. Michael Leo and Winifred Pearl (Shepherd) K.; m. Edna Mae Schirmer, Apr. 20, 1978; children: Garrett David, Kirin Suzanne. Ed. pre-med. program, Ampleforth Coll., York, 1962-66; MD, Royal Coll. Surgeons, Ireland, 1972. Diplomate Am. Bd. Otolaryngology, Am. Bd. Head and Neck Surgery; lic. physician Pa., Md. Intern St. Laurence's Hosp., Dublin, Ireland, 1972-73; asst. resident in surgery Johns Hopkins U., Balt., 1973-74, asst. resident in otolaryngology, 1974-77, mem. staff, 1977-91, chief resident in otolaryngology, asst. prof. otolaryngology, 1977-78, asst. prof., 1978-86, assoc. prof. otolaryngology-head and neck surgery, 1986-91, assoc. prof. neurosurgery, 1987-91; mem. staff Loch Raven VA Hosp., Balt., 1980-87, cons. physician, 1987-91; mem. staff Sinai Hosp. Balt., 1981-88; chmn. U. Pa. Med. Ctr., Phila., 1991—; mem. staff VA Hosp., Phila., 1991—; departmental rep. staff conf. com. Johns Hopkins U., 1979-81, chmn. med. student edn. dept. otolaryngology-head and neck surgery, 1980-85, dir. dept. residency tng. program, 1981-91, mem. house staff policy com., 1984-90; chmn. laser com. U. Pa. Med. Ctr., 1991—, chmn. ambularoty care task force, 1992-94, mem. steering com., 1992-93, mem. oversight com., 1992—, vice chairperson med. bd., 1993-94, chairperson med. bd., 1994—, prof., chairperson dept. otorhinolaryngology-head and neck surgery, 1991—; chmn. fin. com. Clin. Practices of U. Pa., 1992—; mem. Md. State Bd. Examiners for Otolaryngologists, 1979-91, Md. State Bd. Examiners for audiologists, 1984-88; cons. Md. State Dept. Health, Balt., 1979-91; vis. prof. ednl. instns., most recently Mayo Clinic, Rochester, Minn., 1993, Duke U. Med. Ctr., Durham, N.C., 1994, U. N.C., Chapel Hill, 1994; vis. Bettinger lectr. U. Minn., Mpls., 1994; John F. Daly vis. prof. NYU Med. Ctr., N.Y.C., 1994; mem. faculty numerous courses at ednl. instns., 1982—; presenter/speaker in field, most recently 6th Internat. Course on Endoscopic Surgery of Paranasal Sinuses, Brussels and Cologne, Germany, 1994, Otolaryngology Symposium, Burlington, Mass., 1994, Nassau Surg. Soc., Manhasset, N.Y., 1994, Conn. Ear Nose Throat Soc., New Haven, 1995; bd. dirs. Internat. Symposium Infection and Allergy of the Nose, pres. bd. dirs., 1989-90, pres. VIIIth Internat. Symposium Infection and Allergy of the Nose, 1989. Contbr. or co-contbr. 13 chpts. to books, including: Rhinitis, 2nd edit., 1991, Diseases of the Nose, Throat, Ear, Head and Neck, 1991, Otolaryngology, 3rd edit., 1991, Surgery for Skull Base Tumors, 1991; contbr. numerous articles to profl. jours.; mem. editl. bd. Ear, Nose and Throat Jour., 1983—, Am. Jour. Rhinology, 1986—, Laryngoscope, 1988—; editor-in-chief (otolaryngology) Am. Jour. Rhinology, 1984—, Current Opinion in Otolaryngology and Head and Neck Surgery, 1992—, Jour. Otolaryngology, 1993—. Recipient Leonard Abrahamson Meml. Gold medal, 1971, Lyons Meml. medal, 1971, gold medal Coombe Lying-In Hosp., 1971, Reuben-Harvey prize, 1972, Coun.'s prize and gold medal, 1972; rsch. grantee Schering Corp., 1981, HHS, 1983-88, Norwich-Eaton Corp., 1984-86, Minn. Mining and Mfg. Co., 1984, Healthtek, 1990-91. Fellow Am. Acad. Otolaryngology-Head and Neck Surgery (mem. hearing subcom. 1985-91, mem. rhinology-paranasal sinus com. 1986-93, mem. CPT com. 1992—, legis. alt. bd. govs. 1991—, mem. adv. coun. on continuing edn. with TV subcom. 1994, instr. endoscopic sinus surgery 1985), Royal Coll. Surgeons (anatomy demonstrator/lectr. 1972-73, vis. prof. 1980-81, Sir William Wheeler Meml. medal 1972, Fitzsimmons Gold medal for surgery 1972, Bronze medal), Royal Coll. Surgeons (Ireland); mem. ACS, AMA (hon.), Am. Rhinologic Soc. (bd. dirs. 1988—, v.p. 1989-90, pres. 1992-93, cons. to bd. dirs. 1987-88), Internat. Symposium on Infection of the Nose (bd. dirs., pres. 1989), Phila. Laryngol. Soc., Assn. Acad. Depts. of Otorhinolaryngology, Soc. Univ. Otolaryngologists (mem. nom-86), Pa. Acad. Otolaryngology, John Morgan Soc., Johns Hopkins Med. and Surg. Assn. Office: Univ Pa Med Ctr 5 Ravdin 3400 Spruce St Philadelphia PA 19104

KENNEDY, HAROLD LEE, physician; b. Amarillo, Tex., Oct. 1, 1948; s. Hugh L. and Marilyn Ruth (Kelley) K.; m. Cynthia Louise Garst; children: Rachael, Nikki, Jason, Megan, Jeremy, James, Josh. La. State Univ., 1969; MD, La. State, 1973. Diplomate Am. Bd. Surgery, Am. Bd. Colon Rectal Surgery. Intern Naval Hosp., Oakland, Calif., 1973-74, gen. surgery residency, 1974-78; staff surgeon Naval Hosp., Bremerron, Wash., 1978-81; colon rectal surgical fellow Univ. Minn., Mpls., 1981-82; colon rectal surgeon Sacramento, Calif., 1982—; founding ptnr. Sacramento Colon Rectal Surgery, set up anal physciology lab., Sacramento, 1987—; lectr. numerous nat. meetings, numerous nat. com. Contbr. articles to profl. jours. Fellow Am. Coll. Surgeons, Am. Soc. Colon Rectal Surgery, Soc. Gastointestinal Endoceapic Surgery; mem. Calif. Medical Assn., Sacramento/El Dorado Medical Soc., Sacremento Surgical Soc., Northern Calif. Soc. Colon & Rectal Surgeons, The Northwest Soc. Colon & Rectal Surgeons, Alpha Omega Alpha. Office: Sacramento Colon Rectal Surgery 1020 29th St #350 Sacramento CA 95816

KENNEDY, JOHN FREDERICK, chemistry educator; b. Streatham, London, Eng., Sept. 17, 1942; s. Ernest Frederick Vincent and Dorothy Ethel (Proctor) K.; m. Linda Lucy Lloyd, Aug. 17, 1988. BSc, U. Birmingham, Eng., 1964, PhD, 1967, DSc, 1973. Lectr. U. Birmingham, 1961-85, sr. lectr., 1985—82; prof. applied chemistry North East Wales Inst., Wrexham, 1984—; cons. biochemist Area Health Authority, Hereford and Worcester, U.K., 1977-80; dir. biochemistry Leacastle Hosp., Kidderminster, Eng., 1980-82; bd. dirs. The Cellucon Trust, Birmingham, Chembiotech. Ltd., Birmingham. Editor Carbohydrate Polymers, 1988—; chmn. editor Polymer Internat., 1984-96; book revs. editor Bioseparation, 1990—; editor of revs. Cellulose, 1992—. Fellow Inst. Mgmt., Royal Soc. Chemistry (Meldola medal 1972, The Tate and Lyle Carbohydrate award 1976), Inst. Biology, Inst. Food Sci. and Tech.; mem. Soc. Chem. Industry (publ. com. 1985—), Rolls Royce Enthusiasts Club. Anglican. Office: Sch Chemistry, Univ Birmingham, Birmingham B15 2TT, England

KENNEDY, JOHN PATRICK, pharmacist and pharmaceutical engineer; b. Washington, N.C., Sept. 9, 1966; s. John Ronald and Shirley (Walker) K. AS, Southeastern Community Coll., 1987; BS Pharmacy with honors, Med. U. of S.C., 1990; PhD in Indsl. Pharmaceutics, Medical U. of S.C., 1995. Farm labor Whiteville, N.C., 1976-85; AKC canine trainer Whiteville, 1983-87; pathology lab. asst. Columbus County Hosp., Whiteville, 1985-86; lab. info. specialist Med. U. S.C., Charleston, 1988-89, lab. instr. Coll. of Pharmacy, 1991-95, acad. v.p. Student Govt. Assn., 1993-94; intern indsl. pharmaceutics Merrell-Dow Rsch. Inst., 1989; renovator Charleston, 1989-90; pharmacist RPh VA Med. Ctr., Charleston, 1990-94; bd. trustees, rep. Med. U. S.C., 1993-95, faculty edn. and student affairs, 1993, chmn. dean's PharmD, PhD and res. coun., 1993, chmn. honor coun., 1992-93. Coord. Charleston County S.C. Recovery and Intervention Pharmacist Team, 1990-92. Recipient Med. U. of S.C. Leadership award, 1993. Fellow Am. Found. Pharm. Edn. (sponsor Glaxo Pharms. 1990, sponsor Bristol Myers Squib 1992-94); mem. Grad. Students Assn. (pres. 1992-93). Methodist. Home: 123 Shanahan Ln Winchester KY 40391 Office: International Processing Corp 1100 Enterprise Dr Winchester KY 40391

KENNEDY, JOSEPH ALOYSIUS, physician; b. N.Y., June 16, 1926; s. Thomas James and Delia Bridget (Sullivan) K.; m. Marilyn Grace Maun, June 16, 1951; children: Elizabeth, Joseph T., John L. BS, Fordham Coll., 1948, MS, 1951; EdD, N.Y.U., 1957; edn. medicine, N.Y. Medical Coll., 1961. Diplomate Am. Bd. Acad. Ophthalmology. With USN, 1944-46. Home: 171 Wampum Ln West Islip NY 11795 Office: 786 Montauk Hwy West Islip NY 11795

KENNEDY, KAREN THERESA, anesthesiologist; b. Manhasset, N.Y., July 25, 1966; d. Donald Joseph and Elizabeth Rosealie (Hesser) K.; m. Rogelio Alberta Brito, Mar. 7, 1992; 1 child, Roger Alexander. BS with honors, Eckerd Coll., St. Petersburg, Fla., 1988; DO with honors Nova Southeastern U., St. Petersburg, Fla., 1992. Transitional intern Fla. Hosp. East Orlando, 1992-93; resident dept. anesthesia U. Miami/Jackson Meml. Hosp., 1993—, chief resident, 1995—. Mem. AMA, Am. Osteo. Assn., Am. Soc. Anesthesiologists, Internat. Anesthesia Rsch. Soc. Home: 1751 SW 11th Terrace Miami FL 33135

KENNEDY, ROBERT MICHAEL, neurologist; b. Chadron, Nebr., May 30, 1948; s. Thomas A. Kennedy and Leora Marie Zeman; m. Pamela Ann Kennedy, June 19, 1973. Student, U. Wyo., 1970; MD, U. Utah, 1974. Diplomate Am. Bd. Internal Medicine, Am. Bd. Psychology and Neurology. Resident in internal medicine U. Mo., Kansas City, 1975-77; resident in neurology U. Kans., Kansas City, 1977-80; pvt. practice Pocatello, Idaho, 1980—; chief of staff Pocatello Regional Med. Ctr., 1991, chmn. hosp. governing bd., 1994-95; mem. adj. faculty Idaho State U., Pocatello, 1993—. Contbr. articles to profl. jours. Fellow ACP; mem. Am. Acad. Neurology, Idaho Neurol. Soc. (v.p. 1993—), Idaho Med. Assn., S.E. Idaho Med. Assn. Office: 755 Hospital Way C-1 Pocatello ID 83201

KENNEDY, WILLIAM JAMES, pharmaceutical company executive; b. Troy, N.Y., Dec. 4, 1944; s. James Francis and Marjorie (Albrecht) K.; m. Mary Monika Silasz, July 22, 1967; children: Susan M., John R., Morgan E. BS, Siena Coll., Loudonville, N.Y., 1966; MA, Clark U., Worcester, Mass., 1969; PhD, SUNY, Buffalo, 1975. Assoc. dir. drug regulatory affairs Pfizer Pharms., N.Y.C., 1977-80; asst. dir. drug regulatory affairs Berlex Labs., Morristown, N.J., 1980-81; dir. drug regulatory affairs Kali Pharma, Elizabeth, N.J., 1981-82, GD Searle & Co., Skokie, Ill., 1982-86; v.p. drug regulatory affairs ICI Pharms. Group, Wilmington, Del., 1986-93, Zeneca Pharms. Group, Wilmington, 1993—; cons. various pharm. cos., 1981-86. Contbr. articles to profl. jours. and chpts. to books. NIH fellow, 1971-75. Mem. Pharm. Mfrs. Assn. (chmn. drug regulatory affairs com. 1991), Del. Valley Regulatory Affairs Forum (chmn. 1988), Nat. Acad. Sci. Home: 116 Marcella Rd Wilmington DE 19803-3411 Office: Zeneca Pharms Group Concord Pike New Murph Wilmington DE 19803

KENNEMORE, DOUGLAS ERVIN, neurosurgeon; b. Greenville, S.C., May 30, 1931; married. BA, Duke U., 1953; MD, Med. Coll. S.C., 1957. Diplomate Am. Bd. Neurol. Surgery. Intern Med. Coll. of S.C., Charleston, 1957-58; asst. resident Med. Coll. Va., Charlottesville, 1958-59; asst. resident U. Va., Charlottesville, 1959-60, resident, 1962-65; neurosurgeon Greenville Neurosurg. Group, P.A., 1965—; cons. sr. assocs. staff in neurosurgery, tchg. staff, Greenville Hosp. System, 1965—; assoc. in neurosurgery, St. Francis Hosp., 1972—; cons. in neurosurgery, Shriners Hosp. for Crippled Children, 1965—, clin. assoc. prof. U. S.C. Sch. of Medicine, 1992—, Med. U. S.C., 1992—; mem. peer rev. panel, S.C. Assn. Neurol. Surgeons; asst. prof. neurosurgery, U. Va. Med. Sch. Contbr. articles to profl. jours. Fellow ACS; mem. AMA, Am. Assn. Neurol. Surgeons, Congress of Neurol. Surgeons, Greenville County Med. Assn., S.C. Assn. Neurol. Surgeons, S.C. Med. Assn., So. Med. Assn., So. Neurosurg. Soc. Office: Greenville Neurosurg Group 27 Memorial Medical Dr Greenville SC 29605-4407

KENNER, CAROLE ANN, nursing educator; b. Cin., Sept. 19, 1953; d. Lester O. and Betty A. Waugh. BSN, U. Cin., 1976; MSN, Ind. U., 1983, D of Nursing Sci., 1988. Staff nurse Children's Hosp. Med. Ctr., Cin., 1978, 81, 83-87, asst. head nurse, 1981-83; prof., dept. chair U. Cin., Cin., 1991—. Instr. CPR, ARC. Fellow Am. Acad. Nursing; mem. Assn. Women's Health, Obstetric, and Neonatal Nurses (ednl. coord. Ohio chpt., coord. Greater Cin. chpt.), Nat. Assn. Neonatal Nurses (bd. dirs., pres.), Sigma Theta Tau. Home: 5678 Pleasant Hill Rd Milford OH 45150-2345

KENNER, WILLIAM DAVIS, III, psychiatrist; b. Kingsport, Tenn., Oct. 3, 1943; s. Kenneth Bynum and Charlotte (Lineback) K.; m. Carole Freeman, May 23, 1970; children: William IV, Mary Clay, Michael. Student, Tulane U., 1961-63; BS, U. Tenn., 1965; MD, U. Tenn., Memphis, 1969. Lic. physician, Tenn., Md. Rotating med. intern Bapt. Meml. Hosp., Memphis, 1969-70; resident in adult psychiatry and fellow child psychiatry Inst. Psychiatry and Human Behavior, U. Md. Hosp., Balt., 1970-73; fellow in child psychiatry Vanderbilt U. Hosp., Nashville, 1975-76; pvt. practice adult and child psychiatry/psychoanalysis Nashville, 1977—; asst. prof. psychiatry Vanderbilt U. Med. Sch., Nashville, 1973-75, 76-77, assoc. clin. prof. psychiatry and child psychiatry, 1977—; dir. Vanderbilt Admission Unit of ctrl. State Hosp., 1973-75; lectr. in field; cons. Fed. Pub. Defender for Middle Dist. of Tenn., Fed. Atty. Gen. State of Tenn., Atty. Gen. State of Tenn., Bd. Profl. Responsibilities of Supreme Ct. Tenn., Dist. Atty. for Davidson County, Tenn., Helen Ross McNabb Cmty. Mental Health Ctr. Forensic Team, Boys Town Home of Md., others; hosp. staff Vanderbilt Child and Adolescent Psychiat. Hosp., Vanderbilt U. Hosp., Centennial Med. Ctr.; cons. staff Bapt. Hosp. Contbr. articles to profl. jours. Mem. quality assurance com. for adolescent unit Centennial Med. Ctr., chmn. ethics com., 1994—, mem. ad hoc com. to write guidelines for impaired physicians, impaired physicians com.; mem. Tenn. dept. Mental Health and Retardation Commn. to Establish Guidelines for Violent Patients, Commn. to Establish Voluntary Admission Procedure, forensic transfer com. Mem. Am. Psychiat. Assn., Nashville Acad. Medicine, Tenn. Acad. Child Psychiatry, Am. Assn. Adolescent Psychiatry, Am. Psychoanalytic Assn. (mem. study groups), Internat. Psychoanalytic Assn. Office: 113 30th Ave N Nashville TN 37203-1325

KENNETTE, JENNIE LAURA FAKES, medical and surgical nurse; b. Hanston, Kans., Jan. 16, 1935; d. Jack Delmont and Bertha Mabel (Law) Fakes; m. Leslie Cleland Koontz, Dec. 4 1958 (dec.); children: Kim, Lynn, Gay, Jan, Jay, Lee; m. Robert Ray Hamill, Oct. 21, 1979 (div.); m. Russell T. Kennette Jr., Nov. 17, 1990. ADN, Barton County Community Coll., 1971; BSN, U. Wyo., 1988. RN; cert. med.-surg. nurse, gerontol. nurse. Staff nurse clin. level III Laramie County Hosp., Cheyenne, Wyo.; asst. head nurse DePaul Hosp., Cheyenne; charge nurse St. Catherine's Hosp., Garden City, Kans.; DON Spearville (Kans.) Dist. Hosp.; charge nurse Meml Hosp. Laramie County, Laramie County Hosp., Cheyenne, Wyo.; supr. Wyo. Retirement Ctr. Mem. ANA, Barton County C.C. Alumni Assn. Home: PO Box 841 Basin WY 82410-0841

KENNISH, ARTHUR, internist, cardiologist; b. N.Y.C., Feb. 28, 1950; s. Howard L. and Betty I. (Friedman) K.; m. Fran Ptazynska, Mar. 11, 1972; children: Brian, Lauren, Lisa. BS, Cooper U., 1971; MD, PhD, Albert Einstein Med. Ctr., 1977. Resident in internal medicine Mt. Sinai Hosp., 1977-80, cardiology fellow, 1980-82; attending physician Mt. Sinai Med. Ctr., N.Y.C., 1982—. Office: 1111 Park Ave New York NY 10128

KENNY, DOUGLAS TIMOTHY, psychology educator, former university president; b. Victoria, B.C., Can., Oct. 20, 1923; s. John Ernest and Margaret Julia (Collins) K.; m. Lucille Rabowski, Apr. 18, 1950 (dec.); children—John Douglas, Kathleen Margaret; m. Margaret Lindsay Little, June 5, 1976. Student, Victoria Coll., 1941-43; BA, U. B.C., 1945, MA, 1947; PhD, U. Wash., 1950; LLD (hon.), U. B.C., 1983. Lectr. U. B.C., Vancouver, 1950-54, asst. prof. psychology, 1954-57, assoc. prof., 1957-64, prof., 1965-89, head dept. psychology, 1965-69, acting dean faculty of arts, 1969-70, dean faculty of arts, 1970-75, pres., vice chancellor, 1975-83, pres. emeritus, 1989—; vis. asso. prof. Harvard., 1963-65; trustee Can. Council, 1975-78, Social Scis. and Humanities Research Council, 1978-83, Monterey Inst. Internat. Studies, 1980-83, Discovery Found., B.C., 1979-83. Contbr. articles to profl. jours. Trustee Vancouver Gen. Hosp., 1976-78; founding mem. bd. govs. Arts, Sics. and Tech. Ctr., Vancouver, 1980; hon. patron Internat. Found. of Learning, 1983—. Recipient Queen's Silver Jubilee medal, 1977, Park O. Davidson Meml. award, 1984. Mem. Can. Psychol. Assn., B.C. Psychol. Assn. (pres. 1951-52), Am. Psychol. Assn., Am. Psychol. Soc., Vancouver Inst. (pres. 1973-74), U. B.C. Faculty Assn. (pres. 1961-62), B.C. Rsch. Coun. (trustee 1975-89), Vancouver Club, U. B.C. Faculty Club, U. B.C. Alumni Assn. (hon. pres. 1975-83).

KENT, ALAN JOSEPH, psychologist; b. N.Y.C., Sept. 12, 1954. BA, U. Rochester, 1976; PhD, DePaul U., 1984. Lic. psychologist, Fla. Therapist Evanston (Ill.) Hosp., 1981-83; dir. emergency svcs. N.W. Dade Ctr., Hialeah, Fla., 1983-85; dir. clin. svcs. Nova U., Ft. Lauderdale, Fla., 1985-89; pvt. practice psychotherapy Tamarac, Fla., 1985—; clin. dir. Am. Biodyne, Miami, Fla., 1989—; assoc. prof. Nova S.E. U., Ft. Lauderdale, 1992—. Schmitt fellow DePaul U., Chgo., 1978. Mem. APA, Fla. Psychol. Assn., Broward County Psychol. Assn., Phi Beta Kappa. Office: U Mental Health Offices 7301 N University Dr Ste 210 Tamarac FL 33321-2935

KENT, BARTIS MILTON, physician; b. Terrell, Tex., June 23, 1925; s. Bartis William and Annie (Smalley) K.; student So. Meth. U., 1942-44; M.D., Baylor U., 1948; m. Ann L. Kiel, July 6, 1954; children—Susan Ruth, Martha Lucille, Bartis Michael. Intern, Jefferson Davis Hosp., Houston, 1948-49; resident pathology Mass. Meml. Hosps., Boston, 1951; resident in internal medicine Baylor U., 1953-56; indsl. physician Humble Oil Co., Houston, 1949-51; instr. dept. medicine U. Iowa, 1956-58; staff physician Iowa City VA Hosp., 1956-58; practice medicine specializing in internal medicine, Muskogee, Okla., 1958—; cons. Muskogee VA Hosp.; clin. asst. prof. medicine U. Okla. Sch. Medicine, 1975—. Chmn., Muskogee County chpt. Am. Nat. Red Cross, 1963-65. Served with USAF, 1951-53. Decorated Air medal. Diplomate Am. Bd. Internal Medicine. Mem. A.C.P., Indsl. Med. Assn., Soc. Nuclear Medicine, Am. Fedn. Clin. Research, Am. Heart Assn., Aerospace Medicine Assn., Am., Okla. socs. internal medicine. Muskogee C. of C. Methodist. Mason (Shriner). Home: 800 N 45th St Muskogee OK 74401-1505 Office: 211 S 36th St Muskogee OK 74401

KENT, DEBORAH WARREN, hypnotherapist, consultant, lecturer; b. N.Y.C., May 6, 1947; d. Fred Warren and Margo (Lefebre) North. BS in Spl. Edn., U. Cin., 1969; MS in Counseling, CUNY, Hunter Coll., 1973; cert. master level hypnotherapist, Am. Hypnosis Tng. Acad., Silver Spring, Md., 1987. Cert. clin. mental health counselor; nat. cert. counselor. Remediation specialist, counselor, psychometrist N.Y.C. Bd. Edn., 1973-79; cons. on assessment and remediation, N.Y.C., 1979-81; prodn. mgr. The Singing Experience, N.Y.C., 1981-83; hypnotherapist Inst. for Hypnotherapy, N.Y.C., 1983-85; pvt. practice hypnotherapy and counseling, N.Y.C., 1985—; conducted workshops and seminars in clin. hypnosis, comm. skills and tng., stress mgmt.; lectr. to bus. and univs.; vocat. specialist Alternatives for Growth, N.J.; cons. vocat. case mgmt. assessment Ams. with Disabilities Act. Author, columnist Ofcl. Map and Guide mag., 1990-91. Action writer Nat. Abortion Rights Action League, Washington, 1987—; co-developer Counselors Legis. Action Support System, 1989; v.p. Joint Coun. for Mental health Svcs., 1989—. Recipient Profl. Svc. award Am. Mental Health Counselors Assn., 1992. Fellow Am. Acad. Pain Mgmt., Am. Assn. Profl. Hypnotherapists (cert.); mem. ACA, ASCD (N.Y.C. br.), Nat. Certified Counselors, Am. Mental Health Counselors Assn., Nat. Bd. Cert. Clin. Hypnotherapists (mem. examining bd.), Acad. Clin. Mental Health Counselors, Cert. Clin. Mental Health Counselors (approved clin. supr.), Nat. Soc. Neurolinguistic Programming (cert.), N.Y. Mental Health Counselors Assn. (legis. rep. 1989—, v.p. 1989-91), N.Y. Counselors Assn. (Legis. Svc. award 1991), Am. Assn. for Assessment in Counseling (bd. dirs. 1995—). Home and Office: 355 S End Ave New York NY 10280-1005

KENT, DONALD CHARLES, physician; b. Bonesteel, S.D., Apr. 26, 1923; s. Charles Alfred and Thelma Marguerite (Wilson) K.; B.S., U. Nebr., 1945, M.D., 1947; m. Anna I. Marshall, May 2, 1953; children: Martha, Michael, Sara, Christopher. Rotating intern Wayne County Gen. Hosp., Eloise, Mich., 1947-48; staff physician in psychiatry Norfolk (Nebr.) State Hosp., 1947; gen. practice medicine, Wahoo, Nebr., 1948-50; physician C. & N.W. R.R., 1948-50; county physician, Madison County, Nebr., 1949-50; physician La. Indsl. Health Office, 1950-51; lt. (j.g.), M.C., USN, 1950, advanced through grades to capt., 1963; regtl. surgeon 1st Marine Divsn., Korea, 1951-52; resident internal medicine, chief allergy clinic U.S. Naval Hosp., Chelsea, Mass., 1952-54; officer-in-charge Cardiopulmonary Lab., U.S. Naval Hosp., St. Albans, N.Y., 1954-56; officer-in-charge U.S. Naval Dispensary, Nice, France, 1956-58; post physician U.S. Consulate, Nice, France, 1956-58; post physician Fgn. Svc. Lang. Sch., Nice, France, 1957-58; chief of medicine, exec. officer U.S. Naval Hosp., Bainbridge, Md., 1958-60; cons. internal medicine U.S. Army Hosp., Aberdeen, Md., 1958-60; fellow pulmonary disease rsch. Cardiovasc. Rsch. Inst., San Francisco, 1960-61; chief pulmonary diseases and infectious disease svc. and cardiopulmonary lab. U.S. Naval Hosp., San Diego, 1961-63, chief of medicine, 1970-71; dir. Cardiopulmonary Technicians Sch., USN, 1961-63; clin. instr. medicine U. Calif., San Francisco, 1960-61; mem. attending staff San Diego County Hosp., 1963; head chest svc., chief oxygen therapy and cardiopulmonary function lab., asst. chief med. svc. U.S. Naval Hosp., St. Albans, 1963-65; cons. VA Hosp., Castle Point, N.Y., 1963-67, Nassau County Tb. Sanatorium, Farmingdale, N.Y., 1963-65; clinician Nassau County Dept. Health Chest Clinics, 1963-65; asst. clin. prof. medicine Downstate Med. Ctr., Bklyn., 1965-67; attending Kings County Hosp., Bklyn., 1964-67, Syosset Hosp. and Manhasset Med. Center Hosps., 1963-65; dir. interns U.S. Naval Hosp., St. Albans, 1964-67, chief of medicine, 1965-67, dir. postgrad. med. edn., 1965-67; med. cons. med. dept. UN, N.Y.C., 1965-67; guest lectr. pulmonary physiology U.S. Naval Sch. Submarine Medicine, Groton, Conn., 1964-67; comdg. officer Naval Med. Rsch. Unit No. 3, Cairo, UAR and Addis Ababa, Ethiopia, 1967-70; guest lectr. Haile Selassie I Med. Sch., Addis Ababa, 1967-70, Cairo U., 1967-70, Ein Shams Med. Sch., Cairo, 1967-70, Am. U. Beirut, 1968-70; post physician Am. Embassy, Cairo, 1967-70; assoc. clin. prof. medicine U. Calif., San Diego Sch. Medicine, 1970-71; ret., US Navy 1971; med. dir. Nat. Tb. and Respiratory Disease Assn., 1971-73; attending physician chest svc. Bellevue Hosp., N.Y.C., 1972-73, 74-82; assoc. prof. clin. medicine N.Y. U., 1972-73, 74-82; dir. medicine Meth. Hosp., Bklyn., 1973-74; clin. prof. medicine SUNY, Downstate Med. Ctr., Bklyn., 1973-74, attending physician, 1973-74; clin. prof. environ. medicine N.Y.U., 1981-82, attending physician U. Hosp. Medicine, N.Y.C., 1976-82; nat. chmn. Nat. Interagy. Coun. on Smoking and Health, 1973-76; med. dir. Life Extension Inst., N.Y.C., 1974-82, v.p., 1974-78, editor Guidelines, 1974-78, sr. v.p., 1975-78; cons. Nat. Lung Assn., 1973-82; med. dir. Electric Boat divsn. Gen. Dynamics Corp., 1982-88, 92-93, cons., 1988—; assoc. med. dir. Pan Am. World Airways, JFK Internat. Airport, N.Y.C., 1988-91, also numerous other cos. in N.Y.C.; staff physician Occupl. Health Ctr., Lawrence and Meml. Hosp., Groton, Conn. 1995—; contract physician Pfizer Ctrl Rsch., Groton, 1995—; cons. IBM, Internat. Paper Co., Continental Can Co., W.T. Grant Co., 1974-82, Gen. Dynamics Corp. and Reactor Plant Svcs., 1988-92, Pan Am. World Airways, 1991, Occupl. Medicine Ctr., Pequot Health Ctr., Lawrence and Meml. Hosp., Groton, Conn., 1995—. Decorated Legion of Merit, Bronze Star, Purple Heart; recipient Meritorious award for disting. svc. Am. Acad. Oral Medicine, 1977. Diplomate Am. Bd. Internal Medicinm. Bd. Pulmonary Diseases. Fellow ACP, Am. Coll. Chest Physicians, N.Y. Acad. Medicine, Royal Soc. Tropical Medicine, Royal Soc. Medicine, Explorers Club; mem. AMA, Bklyn. Thoracic Soc., Am. Lung Assn., Am. Fedn. Clin. Rsch., N.Y. Trudeau Soc. (program chmn. 1966-67), Am. Soc. Tropical Medicine and Hygiene, Tb. and Health Assn. N.Y. State, Am. Public Health Assn., Undersea Med. Soc., Am. Occupational and Environ. Medicine Assn., Nat. Tb. Assn., Assn. Mil. Surgeons (life mem., Stitt award 1971), Soc. Occupational and Environ. Health, Navy League U.S., Med. Execs. N.Y.C., Alpha Omega Alpha. Republican. Roman Catholic. Editor: Clinical Notes of Respiratory Diseases, 1972-77; exec. editor: Basics of RD, 1972-77; contbr. articles to med. jours.

KENT, JAMES GUY, kinesiologist; b. Jacksonville, N.C., Nov. 8, 1952; s. David Wolfe and Lucille (Epstein) K.; m. Rochelle Sue Halfon, June 16, 1979; children: Ashley, Jason, Bryan. BA, Calif. State U., Northridge, 1974; MS, UCLA, 1979; PhD, Pacific Western U., L.A., 1982. Diplomate Am.

Bd. Forensic Medicine, Am. Bd. Forensic Examiners. Dir. Wilshire Phys. Therapy, L.A., 1977-80; pres., founder Integrated Rehab. Corp. and predecessor cos., Marina Del Rey, Calif., 1980-92; clin. assoc. prof. Calif. Coll. Podiatric Medicine, L.A., 1984-85, clin.. instr., 1983-84; co-founder Phys. Therapy Program Coll. Osteo. Medicine Pacific, Pomona, Calif., 1992. Editorial bd. Sports Medicine Digest, 1981-86. Sponsor Student Internships, UCLA, 1979-84; bd. dirs. Switzer Ctr. for Children, Torrance, Calif., 1988-91. Mem. Am. Coll. Sports Medicine, Am. Acad. Forensic Scis., Am. Coll. Forensic Examiners, Am. Congress Rehab. Medicine, Internat. Soc. Biomechanics, N.Am. Soc. Pediat. Exercise Medicine, Soc. Automotive Engrs. Office: 924 Westwood Blvd Ste 800 Los Angeles CA 90024-2929

KENTRA-GOREY, ELIZABETH RENEE, physician; b. Oak Lawn, Ill., Oct. 8, 1961; d. Edward Joseph and Joyce Leigh (Metz) Kentra; m. Rian Mark Gorey, dec. 30, 1984; children: Erin Kathleen, Aidan Christopher. BA, St. Mary's Coll., Notre Dame, Ind., 1983; MD, Loyola U., 1987. Researcher, author Loyola U., Chgo., 1986-87; med. doctor, researcher U. So. Calif., Los Angeles, 1987-92; physician So. Ear, Nose & Throat, P.C., Atlanta, 1992—. Author: (with others) What I Believe, 1985; contbr. articles to profl. jours. Mem. AMA, Am. Acad. Otolaryngology (cert.), Am. Woman Med. Alliance, Am. Med. Students Assn. (v.p. 1984-85), Med. Assn. Ga., Nat. Assn. Residents and Interns. Roman Catholic.

KENYHERCZ, THOMAS MICHAEL, pharmaceutical company executive; b. Youngstown, Ohio, Jan. 6, 1950; s. William Stephen and Goldie Elizabeth (Matica) K.; m. Linda Jane Kostyshak, Mar. 20, 1973; 1 child, Craig Thomas. BS, Youngstown State U., 1971; MS, U. Cin., 1973, PhD in Analytical Chemistry (Lowenstein Schubert Twitchell fellow), 1975; postdoctoral fellow in bioanalytical chemistry, Kissinger fellow, Purdue U., 1975-77. Cert. regulatory affairs profl. Scientist, sr. scientist, mgr. prodn. support labs. Ortho Pharm. Corp., Raritan, N.J., 1977-80; dir., product devel., quality assurance and regulatory affairs Janssen Pharmaceutica Inc., Piscataway, N.J., 1980-85; pres. KROSS, Inc., Hillsborough, N.J., 1985—; founder KROSS Coatings, Inc., 1987—; COO Telluride Pharm. Corp., 1994—; participant FDA approved Orphan Drug Devel. program. Mem. editorial bd. Jour. Automated Chemistry, 1975—. Coach basketball St. Mary's Sr. High Sch., 1979-83. Recipient SBIR Rsch. award EPA Phase I and II for studies of marine contamination, 1987, FDA Orphan Drug designation, 1994. Active Ctr. for Creative Living, Religious Sci. Ch. Princeton. Mem. Am. Mgmt. Assn., Am. Assn. Clin. Chemists, Am. Assn. Anti Aging Med., Am. Chem. Soc., Am. Assn. Pharm. Scientists, Am. Soc. for Quality Control, U.S.-N.I.S. C. of C., Electrochem. Soc., Parenteral Drug Assn., Pharm. Mfrs. Assn., Drug Info. Assn., Regulatory Affairs Profl. Soc., Am. Soc. Pharmacognosy, Western Electroanalytical Theoretical Soc., Licensing Execs. Soc., Aquinas Inst., Controlled Release Soc., Soc. for Biomaterials. Byzantine Catholic.

KEOCHAKIAN, SIMON V., psychologist, educator; b. Madison, Maine, May 13, 1935; s. Vartan S. and Mariam M. (Manoogian) Karchakian; m. Joan Gail Bennett, Aug. 25, 1956; children: Stephen, Gregory, Geoffrey. BS, Springfield Coll., 1958, MS, 1961; EdD, U. Mass., 1970. Lic. psychologist and guidance counselor, Mass.; cert. expressive therapist; bd. cert. forensic examiner. Assoc. dir. clin. svcs. Ctr. Counseling and Academic Devel. U. Mass., Amherst, 1960—, assoc. prof. sch. edn., 1971—, dir. continuing edn. for psychologists, 1989—; vis. lectr. Lesley Coll., Cambridge, Mass., 1979; Fulbright Sr. lectr. Coun. for Internat. Exch. of Scholars, Armenia, 1982. Co-author: Access Policy and Procedure and the Law in Higher Education, 1978. Pres. Amherst chpt. SEIU Local 509 AFL-CIO, 1991—. Mem. Am. Assn. Applied and Preventive Psychology, Nat. Expressive Therapy Assn. (life), Am. Coll. Forensic Examiners (life). Home: 174 West St Amherst MA 01002-2968 Office: U Mass Berkshire House Amherst MA 01003

KEOGH, ANDREW JOHN, neurosurgeon; b. Manchester, United Kingdom, Jan. 9, 1938; s. George Augustine and Theresa (Angler) K.; m. Mary Ruth Newman, Jan. 19, 1967; children: Emma, Victoria, Edward, George. MBChB, U. Glasgow, 1962. Sr. registrar, hon. lectr. U., 1972-78; cons. neurosurgeon Lancashire, United Kingdom, 1978—; clin. dir. for neuroscis. Royal Preston Hosp., 1991—, head dept. neurol. surgery, 1989—. Contbr. articles to profl. jours. Mem. Soc. Brit. Neurol. Surgeons, Brit. Med. Assn. Roman Catholic. Home: Grantham House 21 Beech Gro, Ashton Preston PR2 1DX, England Office: Royal Preston Hosp, Dept Neurol Surgery, Preston PR2 4HT, England

KEON, THOMAS PETER, pediatric anesthesiologist, educator; b. Detroit, June 1, 1936; s. Peter Francis and Mary Irene (McCool) K.; m. Janice Kathleen Lahue, Aug. 18, 1962; children: Peter, Elizabeth, Timothy. BS, St. Patrick's Coll., Ottawa, Ont., Can., 1959; MD, U. Ottawa, 1965. Diplomate Am. Bd. Anesthesiology, Royal Coll. Physicians and Surgeons. Intern Cooper Hosp., Camden, N.J., 1965-66; resident in anesthesia U. of Ottawa/Ottawa (Ont.) Civic Hosp., 1971-74; fellow in pediatric anesthesia and critical care medicine The Children's Hosp. of Phila., 1974-75; pvt. practice Almonte, Ont., 1966-71; dir. ICU Children's Hosp. Ea. Ont., Ottawa, 1975-78; assoc. prof. anesthesia U. Pa. Sch. Medicine, Phila., 1979—; anesthesiologist Children's Hosp. Phila., 1979—. Contbr. articles on anesthesiology to profl. jours., chpts. to books. Mem. AMA, Am. Soc. Anesthesiology, Am. Acad. Pediatrics. Office: Childrens Hosp Phila 34th St Civic Ctr Blvd Philadelphia PA 19104

KEPECS, JOSEPH GOODMAN, physician, educator; b. Phila., Oct. 8, 1912; s. Jacob and Mary (Goodman) K.; m. Joan A. Epstein, Oct. 17, 1944; children—Susan, Jonathan. B.S., U. Chgo., 1935, M.D., 1937; grad., Inst. for Psychoanalysis, Chgo., 1949. Intern Cook County Hosp., Chgo., 1938-39; resident St. Elizabeth's Hosp., Washington, 1940-41; practice medicine, specializing in psychiatry Madison, Wis., 1965—; attending physician dept. psychiatry Michael Reese Hosp., Chgo., 1950-65; prof. psychiatry U. Wis., 1965-84, prof. emeritus, 1984—; lectr. Chgo. Inst. for Psychoanalysis, 1957-60, mem. faculty, 1974—; professorial lectr. dept. psychiatry U. Chgo., 1960-65. Served with AUS, 1941-46. Mem. Am. Psychoanalytic Assn., Wis. Psychoanalytic Study Group (pres. 1979-80), Am. Psychosomatic Soc., Am. Psychiat. Assn., Chgo. Psychoanalytic Soc. (pres. 1964-65). Home: 3580 Lake Mendota Dr Madison WI 53705-1473 Office: 3230 University Ave Madison WI 53705-3540

KEPHART, EARL LAWRENCE, nurse; b. Madera, Pa., Dec. 15, 1919; s. Lawrence and Cora (Lockett) K.; R.N., Pa. Hosp., 1943; B.S. in Edn., U. Pa., 1949; M.Ed., U. Va., 1959; m. Harriet Hosmer, Nov. 29, 1944; 1 child, Larry Herbert. Head nurse, then instr. Pa. Hosp., 1943-49; mem. nursing staff VA, 1949-84; chief nursing service VA Med. Center, Shreveport, 1973-84. Served with AUS, 1944-45. Mem. Assn. Mil. Surgeons U.S., Sigma Theta Tau, Kappa Phi Kappa. Republican. Presbyterian. Author ednl. TV material. Home: 411 N Middletown Rd Apt F124 Media PA 19063-4422

KERBER, DEBORAH LYNN, optometrist; b. Elgin, Ill., Nov. 7, 1964; d. Joseph William Kerber and Coy Ophadell (Phillips) Coonts; m. Jeffrey Thomson rehr, Dec. 17, 1994. BS, S.E. Mo. State U., Cape Girardeau, 1986; OD, U. Mo., St. Louis, 1992. Optometrist, owner Resler Optometry, Inc., Florissant, Mo., 1992—; clin. internship provider optometry U. Mo. St. Louis, 1992—. Mem. Am. Optometric Assn., Mo. Optometric Assn., St. Louis Optometric Soc. (mem.exec. bd. 1995-96), Florissant C. of C., Rotary. Office: Resler Optometry Inc 875 Saint Francois Florissant MO 63031

KERBER, RICHARD E., cardiologist; b. N.Y.C., May 10, 1939; s. Max and Pauline Kerber; m. Linda K. Kaufman; children: Ross, Justin. AB in Anthropology, Columbia U., 1960; MD, NYU, 1964. Diplomate Am. Bd. Internal Medicine, Am. Bd. Cardiology. Med. intern/resident Bellevue Hosp., N.Y.C., 1964-66; med. resident Stanford (Calif.) U. Hosp., 1968-69, cardiology fellow, 1969-71; asst. prof. internal medicine U. Iowa, Iowa City, 1971-74, assoc. prof. internal medicine, 1974-78, prof. medicine, 1978—. Editor: Echocardiography in Coronary Artery Disease, 1988. Capt. U.S. Army, 1966-68. RO1 grant NHLBI, 1995—. Fellow Am. Heart Assn. (award of Meritorious Achievement 1996), Am. Coll. Cardiology (gov. for Iowa 1976-79); mem. Am. soc. of Echocardiology (sec. 1978-80, treas. 1993-95, v.p., pres. elect 1995—), Am. Physiology Soc., Am. Soc. for Clin. Investigation, Assn. of Univ. Cardiologists, Assn. of Am. Physicians. Office: U Iowa Dept Medicine 200 Hawkins Dr Iowa City IA 52242*

KERFOOT, KARLENE M., health facility administrator; b. Newton, Iowa, Sept. 17, 1942; d. Elzy Woodrow and Irene Lavina (Wilson) Mathern; m. William Kerfoot, Apr. 5, 1979; 1 child, Kristopher. BSN, U. Iowa, 1965, MA, 1970; PhD, U. Ill., 1983. Cert. nursing adminstr., advanced CNAA. Chief, Mental Health Assistance/Community Svcs. Div. Linn County Psychiat. Clin., Cedar Rapids, Iowa, 1974-78; asst. prof. Coll. of Nursing U. Iowa, Iowa City, 1979-81; sr. assoc. dir. U. Iowa Hosps. and Clinics, Iowa City, 1981-85; exec. v.p. patient care St. Luke's Episcopal Hosp., Houston, 1985—. Contbr. over 100 articles to profl. books and jours. Fellow Am. Acad. Nursing; mem. Am. Orgn. Nurse Execs. (chmn. bylaws com. 1989), Houston Orgn. Nurse Execs. (pres. 1988, sec. 1990). Home: 3522 Durness Way Houston TX 77025-2516 Office: St Luke's Episc Hosp 6720 Bertner St Houston TX 77030-2604

KERIEAKES, DEAN JAMES, cardiologist; b. Louisville, Jan. 8, 1953; s. James G. and Helen (Christy) K.; m. Anne Sugar, June 20, 1981; children: Jennifer, David, Andrew, Nicholas. BS, U. Cin., 1974, MD, 1978. Diplomate Am. Bd. Internal Medicine, Am. Bd. Cardiology. Intern, resident U. Calif., San Francisco, 1978-80; sr. resident Mass. Gen. Hosp., Boston, 1980-81; chief med. resident H.C. Moffitt Hosp., San Francisco, 1981-82; adult cardiology fellow U. Calif., San Francisco, 1982-84; coronary angioplasty fellow San Francisco Heart Inst., 1984, Sequoia Hosp., Redwood City, Calif., 1984; attending cardiologist The Christ Hosp., Cin., 1985—; med. dir. The Christ Hosp., 1986-95, Carl & Edythe Lindner Ctr. Clin. Cardiovasc. Rsch., Cin., 1995—; prof. clin. medicine U. Cin. Coll. Medicine, 1995—; scientific adv. bd. Schneider-Shiley, Inc., 1989—; clin. adv. bd. Advanced Cardiobascular Systems, Inc., 1987—. Editl. bd. Jour. Invasive Cardiology. Fellow Am. Coll. Cardiology; mem. AMA, Am. Heart Assn., Alpha Omega Alpha, Phi Beta Kappa. Republican. Presbyn. Office: The Ohio Heart Health Ctr 2123 Auburn Ave #139 Cincinnati OH 45219

KERLAN, ROBERT K., JR., interventional radiologist; b. L.A., Oct. 19, 1952; s. Robert Keith and Rachel (Frauenfelder) K.; m. Randi Moklebust, July 29, 1978; children: Keith, Kyle, Kelsey, Kevin. AB, U. So. Calif., 1973, MD, 1977. Diplomate Am. Bd. Radiology, Nat. Bd. Med. Examiners. Intern in internal medicine UCLA Ctr. Health Scis., 1977-78; resident in radiology U. Calif., San Francisco, 1978-80, chief resident, 1980-81, asst. prof., 1981-85; staff radiologist Scripp's Meml. Hosp., La Jolla, Calif., 1985-93; assoc. clin. prof. U. Calif., San Francisco, 1993—; med. adv. bd. Am. Motorcycle Assn., 1995—. Mem. AMA, Soc. Cardiovasc. and Interventional Radiology, Soc. Gastrointestinal Radiologists, Radiol. Soc. N.Am., Western Angiographic Soc. Office: UCSF Mt Zion Med Ctr Dept Radiology C-248 1600 Divisadero San Fransisco CA 94115

KERLIN, PAUL, gastroenterologist; b. Brisbane, Australia, Jan. 24, 1947; s. Arthur William and Catherine Mary (Mahon) K.; m. Rosemary Heath, Jan. 17, 1976; children: Douglas, Beata, Victoria, Amelia. MB, BS with honors, U. Queensland, Australia, 1972, BA, 1973; FRACP, Royal Australian Coll. Phys., Australia, 1979; MD, U. Queensland, Australia, 1983. Resident Royal Brisbane Hosp., Australia, 1973; resident, registrar Royal Canberra Hosp., Australia, 1974-75; registrar The Queen Elizabeth Hosp., Adelaide, Australia, 1976-77; rsch. fellow U. So. Calif., L.A., 1978-79, Mayo Clinic, Rochester, Minn., 1979-81; dir. dept. gastroenterology Princess Alexandra Hosp., Brisbane, 1981-90; clin. prof. U. Queensland, Brisbane, 1991—; cons. gastroenterologist Princess Alexandra Hosp., Brisbane, 1991—. Contbr. 80 articles to profl. jours. Recipient Fulbright Postdoctoral fellowship, 1978-81, Mayo Rsch. fellowship, 1979-81, Rappaport Clinician-Investigator award, 1980. Fellow Royal Australasian Coll. Physicians; mem. Gastroenterology Soc. Australia (coun. 1987—), Australian Med. Assn., Am. Gastroenterol. Assn. Roman Catholic. Office: The Wesley Med Ctr, 40 Chasely St, Auchenflower QLD 4066, Australia

KERMAN, BARRY MARTIN, ophthalmologist, educator; b. Chgo., Mar. 31, 1945; s. Harvey Nathan and Evelyn (Bialis) K.; B.S., U. Ill., 1967, M.D. with high honors, 1970. Diplomate Am. Bd. Ophthalmology; m. Pamela Renee Berliant, Aug. 18, 1968 (div. 1989); children: Gregory Jason, Jeremy Adam. Intern in medicine Harbor Gen. Hosp., Torrance, Calif., 1970-71; resident in ophthalmology Wadsworth VA Hosp., L.A., 1971-74; fellow in diseases of the retina, vitreous and choroid Jules Stein Eye Inst. UCLA, 1974-75; fellow in ophthalmic ultrasonography Edward S. Harkness Eye Inst., Columbia U., N.Y.C. and U. Iowa Hosps., Iowa City, 1975; asst. prof. ophthalmology UCLA, 1976-78, Harbor Gen. Hosp., 1976-78; asst. clin. prof. ophthalmology UCLA, 1978-83, assoc. clin. prof., 1983-95, clin. prof., 1995—, dir. ophthalmic ultrasonography lab., 1976—; cons. ophthalmologist, L.A., 1976—; mem. exec. bd. Am. Registry Diagnostic Med. Sonographers, 1981-87. With USAFR, 1971-77. Fellow Am. Acad. Ophthalmology; mem. Am. Soc. Cataract and Refractive Surgery, L.A. Soc. Ophthalmology, Am. Soc. Ophthalmic Ultrasound, Am. Assn. Ophthalmic Standardized Echography, Societas Internat. Pro Diagnostica Ultrasonica in Opthalmic, Western Retina Study Club. Contbr. articles to profl. jours. Office: 2080 Century Park E Ste 800 Los Angeles CA 90067-2011

KERMAN, JULES, psychiatrist; b. Bklyn., Jan. 9, 1944; B.A., Columbia U., 1964; M.D., Albert Einstein Coll., 1972, Ph.D., 1977. Diplomate Am. Bd. Psychiatry and Neurology. Intern, Einstein/Bronx Mcpl. Hosp., 1972-73; resident in psychiatry, 1973-76; practice medicine specializing in psychiatry, psychoanalysis, N.Y.C., 1976—; mem. staffs Columbia Presbyterian Med. Ctr., 1985—. Mem. Am. Psychoanalytic Assn. Office: 239 Central Park W New York NY 10024-6038

KERMODE, JOHN COTTERILL, pharmacology educator, researcher; b. Changi, Singapore, June 10, 1949; arrived in U.S. 1983; s. Alfred Cotterill and Rose Price (Roberts) K. BA with honors, Cambridge (Eng.) U., 1970, MA, 1974; PhD, London U., 1983. Rsch. scientist U. Coll. Hosp. Med. Sch., London, 1970-74; rsch. biochemist U. Coll. Hosp., London, 1975-83; postdoctoral fellow U. Conn. Health Ctr., Farmington, Conn., 1983-87; postdoctoral assoc. U. Vt., Burlington, 1987-90; rsch. chemist McGuire VA Med. Ctr., Richmond, Va., 1990-93; rsch. asst. prof. Med. Coll. Va., Richmond, 1990-93; asst. prof., dept. pharmacology and toxicology U. Miss. Med. Ctr., Jackson, Miss., 1993—. Mem. editl. bd. Jour. Receptor & Signal Transduction Rsch., 1991—; contbr. articles to profl. jours. Recipient Earnest G. Spivey Meml. Rschr. award, 1994; Cambridge (Eng.) U. scholar, 1967; Am. Heart Assn. grantee, Va., 1991, Miss., 1994. Mem. Am. Soc. Pharmacology & Exptl. Therapeutics, Am. Heart Assn. (coun. basic sci.), N.Y. Acad. Scis. Home: 57 Redbud Ln Madison MS 39110-9615 Office: U Miss Med Ctr 2500 N State St Jackson MS 39216-4505

KERN, ARTHUR STEPHEN, physician; b. Newark, N.J., Dec. 19, 1930; s. Meyer and Fannie (Greenberg) K.; m. Ruth E. Feingold; children: Melissa, Laurence, Deborah. BA, Harvard U., 1952; MD, Tulane U., 1955. Diplomate Am. Bd. Ophthalmology. Ltd. comdr. USN, 1955-62. Office: 90 Millburn Ave Millburn NJ 07041

KERN, DONALD MICHAEL, internist; b. Belleville, Ill., Nov. 21, 1951; s. Donald Milton and Dolores Olivia (Rust) K. BS in Biology, Tulane U., 1973; MD magna cum laude, U. Brussels, 1983. ECFMG cert.; lic. Calif. Intern in surgery Berkshire Med. Ctr., Pittsfield, Mass., 1983-84; intern in psychiatry Tufts New England Med. Ctr., Boston, 1984-85; resident in internal medicine Kaiser Found. Hosp., San Francisco, 1985-87; with assoc. staff internal medicine Kaiser Permanente Med. Group, Inc., San Francisco, 1987-89; assoc. investigator AIDS Clin. Trial Unit Kaiser Permanente Med. Ctr., Stanford U., Nat. Inst. Allergy & Infectious Disease, San Francisco, 1988-90; mem. staff internal medicine Kaiser Permanente Med. Group, South San Francisco, 1989—. Democrat. Roman Catholic. Office: Kaiser Permanente Med Group Inc 1200 El Camino Real South San Francisco CA 94080-3208

KERN, STANLEY ROBERT, physician, forensic psychiatrist; b. Paterson, N.J., Jan. 13, 1928; s. William and Doris (Lunde) K.; m. Allison Kimberg; children: Andrew, Suzanne Gelinas. BA, NYU, 1949; MD, Thomas Jefferson U., 1954. Diplomate Am. Bd. Psychiatry and Neurology, Am. Bd. Forensic Psychiatry. Intern Newark Beth Israel Med. Ctr., 1954-55; resident Phila. Psychiatric Ctr., 1957-60; instr. psychiatry Seton Hall Coll. of Medicine, Jersey City, 1960-61, sr. instr. in psychiatry, 1961-63; clin. asst. prof. psychiatry N.J. Coll. of Medicine, Newark, 1964-71; clin. assoc. prof. psychiatry N.J. Med. Sch., Newark, 1971—; adj. assoc. prof. law Rutgers U. Sch. Law, Newark, 1984—; trustee Forensic Psychiat. Hosp., Trenton, N.J., 1988-94; chief sect. of psychiatry The Hosp. Ctr. at Orange, N.J., 1972-92. Editor: Medical-Legal Digest for New Jersey Psychiatrists, 1979. Bd. dirs. Mental Health Assn. of Essex County, East Orange, N.J., 1981-88. Capt. USAF, 1955-57. Fellow Am. Psychiat. Assn. (life), Am. Acad. Forensic Scis.; mem. AMA (Physician's Recognition award 1971—), Am. Acad. Psychiatry and the Law (sec. 1987-91, v.p. 1991-92), N.J. Psychiatry Assn. (pres. 1986-87), N.J. Psychoanalytic Soc. (pres. 1982-84).

KERNEN, JULES ALFRED, pathologist; b. St. Louis, July 23, 1929; s. Jules Henri and Edna Lina (Aigler) K.; m. Rita Dennehy, Oct. 25, 1981. AB, Harvard U., 1951; MD, Wash. U. Sch. of Medicine, 1955. Diplomate Am. Bd. Pathology. Intern Barnes Hosp., St. Louis, 1955-56; asst. resident Ind. U. Med. Ctr., Indpls., 1956-58; resident Barnes Hosp., St. Louis, 1958-59, Hosp. U. Pa., Phila., 1959-60; chief of pathology 5th Army Med. Lab., St. Louis, 1960-62; pathologist St. Vincent Hosp., Birmingham, Ala., 1962-63, Hosp. of the Good Samaritan, Los Angeles, 1964—; pathologist, ptnr. Clin. Lab Med. Group, L.A., 1964-87; v.p. CLMG Inc., L.A., 1972-84; clin. prof. pathology U. So. Calif. Sch. of Medicine, L.A., 1965-93, prof. emritus, 1993—. Author of numerous published articles in field. Served to capt. U.S. Army, 1960-62. Mem. Los Angeles Soc. of Pathologists (pres. 1979), Coll. of Am. Pathologists, Am. Soc. of Clin. Pathologists, Internat. Acad. of Pathology, Calif. Soc. of Pathologists, Phi Beta Kappa, Alpha Omega Alpha. Republican. Home: 1000 Principia Dr Glendale CA 91206-1524

KERNS, GERTRUDE YVONNE, psychologist; b. Flint, Mich., July 25, 1931; d. Lloyd D. and Mildred C. (Ter Achter) B.; BA, Olivet Coll., 1953; MA, Wayne State U., 1958; PhD, U. Mich., 1979. Sch. psychologist Roseville (Mich.) Pub. Schs., 1958-68, Grosse Pointe (Mich.) Pub. Schs., 1968-86; pvt. practice psychology, Grosse Pointe, 1980—; instr. psychology Macomb C.C., 1959-69. Author: A Second Heartbeat, 1979. Mem. Am. Psychol. Assn., Mich. Psychol. Assn., Lakeshore Psychol. Assn. (pres. 1988-89), Psi Chi. Home: 28820 Grant St Saint Clair Shores MI 48081-3207 Office: 131 Kercheval Ave Ste 140 Grosse Pointe MI 48236-3630

KERR, ALLEN STEWART, psychologist; b. Evanston, Ill., Nov. 13, 1928; s. Charles Allen and Mildred (Latham) K.; m. Charlyn Floyd, July 19, 1952; children: Betsy Kerr Hedding, Chet, Peggy Kerr Ihinger, Cindy Kerr Levesque. BA, Brown U., 1950; D of Psychology, Forest Inst. Profl. Psychology, 1988. Lic. psychologist, Ga. Salesman Sleepeck Printing Co., Bellwood, Ill., 1953-68, v.p. sales, 1968-83; staff psychologist The Bradley Ctr., Columbus, Ga., 1988-94; sr. psychologist The Pastoral Inst., Columbus, Ga., 1994—. Lt. (j.g.) USN, 1950-53. Mem. APA, Ga. Psychol. Assn., Columbus Area Psychol. Assn., Soc. Personality Assessment, Mental Health Assn. Columbus, Ga. (bd. dirs. 1992—, Bell Ringer Award 1995), Rotary (Muscogee charter mem., sec. 1994-95). Methodist. Home: 887 Oakwood Dr Columbus GA 31904 Office: The Pastoral Inst 2022 15th Ave Columbus GA 31901

KERR, CHARLES MORGAN, psychiatrist, educator; b. Perry, Okla., Feb. 14, 1935; s. John Bradley and Eddith Geneva (Thompson) K.; m. Esther Elizabeth Vargo, Oct. 21, 1957 (div. Dec. 1986); children: Charles Morgan II, John Timothy, Christopher Scott, Erik Bradley. BA, Yale U., 1957; MD, Baylor Coll. Medicine, 1963. Diplomate Am. Bd. Psychiatry and Neurology. Rotating intern U.S. Naval Hosp., Portsmouth, Va., 1963-64; resident in psychiatry U. Rochester (N.Y.) and Strong Meml. Hosp., 1967-70, clin. instr., 1970; asst. prof. psychiatry U. Ariz. Coll. Medicine, Tucson, 1970-75, sr. lectr., 1975-90, clin. assoc. prof., 1993—; pvt. practice Tucson, 1975—; cons. So. Ariz. Mental Health Ctr., Tucson, 1970-76, U.S. Indian Health Svc., Tucson, 1971-73, Ariz. Dept. Corrections, Tucson, 1972-76. Bd. dirs., v.p. Tucson South Cmty. Mental Health Ctr., Tucson, 1971-74; sustaining fund drive chmn., committeeman troop 166 Boy Scouts Am., Tucson, 1972; chmn. edn. com. Ariz. Gov.'s Coun. on Health and Fitness, Phoenix, 1980-82; mem. ad hoc com. for gen. budgets Tucson Cmty. Coun., 1982. Lt. M.C., USN, 1963-67. Lit flame for opening ceremonies Winter Olympics, Lake Placid, N.Y., 1980; recipient award for excellence in teaching U. Ariz. Med. Ctr., 1984, 92, 94; Dr. Charles Kerr Day proclaimed by City of Tucson, May 19, 1980. Fellow Am. Psychiat. Assn. (pres. Tucson chpt. 1982-83); mem. AMA, Ariz. Med. Assn., Pima County Med. Soc., Am. Group Psychotherapy Assn., Am. Coll. Sports Medicine, Am. Orthopsychiat. Assn., Am. Assn. Sex Educators, Counselors and Therapists (cert. educator and therapist), Southern Ariz. Roadrunners Assn. (Outstanding Mem. award 1978), Yale U. Alumni Assn. (rep. 1982-85), Yale Club (pres. 1986), Tucson Psychiat. Soc. (pres. 1982-83), Tucson Psychiat. Soc., Ariz. Psychiat. Soc. Republican. Episcopalian. Office: 8230 E Broadway Blvd Ste W2 Tucson AZ 85710-4044

KERR, DAVID JAMES, oncologist; b. Glasgow, Scotland, June 14, 1957; arrived in England; s. Robert and Sarah P. (Hogg) K.; m. Anne M. Young, July 11, 1980; children: Stewart, Sarah, Fiona. BS with 1st class honors, U. Glasgow, 1977, MBChB, 1980, MS in Clin. Pharmacology, 1986, MD, 1987, PhD, 1989. House officer Glasgow Royal Infirmary, 1980-81; sr. house officer Western Infirmary, Glasgow, 1981-83; lectr. in endocrinology U. Glasgow, 1983-84, lectr. in med. oncology, 1984-89, sr. lectr., 1989-92; prof. clin. oncology U. Birmingham, England, 1992—. Co-author numerous books; contbr. articles to profl. jours. Grantee Med. Rsch. Coun., 1994, Cancer Rsch. Campaign, 1992, Regional Health Authority, 1995. Fellow Royal Coll. Physicians Glasgow and London. Mem. Labour Party. Home: 27 Westhill Rd Kings Norton, Birmingham B38 8TL, England Office: CRC Inst for Cancer Studies, U Birmingham, Birmingham England

KERR, STEVEN GEORGE, administrator; b. Story City, Iowa, Oct. 9, 1941; s. John Martin K. and Celia Marie (Corneluisseiy) Bennett; m. Margaret Eleanor Veitch, Aug. 7, 1965; children: Kristin, Steven, Amy. BS, U. Ariz., 1964; MD, U. Tex., 1968. Diplomate Am. Bd. Urology. Intern Baylor Affiliated Hosps., Houston, 1968-69, resident, 1972-76; urologist Wenatchee (Wash.) Valley Clinic, 1976-94, adminstr., 1994—. Capt. U.S. Army, 1970-72. Mem. AMA, Am. Coll. Surgeons, Am. Urological Assn. (western sect.), Wash. State Med. Assn. (bd. dirs. 1986-94). Republican. Lutheran. Office: Wenatchee Valley Clinic 820 N Chelan Wenatchee WA 98801

KERR, WILLIAM B., health facility administrator. Dir. U. Calif. Med. Ctr., San Francisco, 1977—. Office: U Calif San Francisco Med Ctr 505 Parnassus Ave San Francisco CA 94122-2722*

KERR, WILLIAM JOHN STANTON, orthodontist, dental educator; b. Belfast, No. Ireland, July 12, 1941; s. Henry Joseph and Phoebe Stanton (Burns) K.; m. Françoise Contoz, July 3, 1967; 1 child, Sophie. B Dental Surgery, Queen's U., Belfast, 1965, M Dental Surgery, 1976; D Dental Surgery, U. Glasgow, 1992. Gen. dental practice NHS Govt. Health Svc., Bermuda, 1965-72; registrar, sr. registrar Sch. Dentistry, Belfast, 1972-77; sr. lectr. U. Glasgow, 1977-88, reader, 1988-93, prof., 1993—; mem. bd. Faculty Dentistry, RCS, Dublin, 1980-86; mem. specialist adv. com. orthodontics and pediat. dentistry, London, 1983-88, 91-96; mem. dental coun. Royal Coll. Physicians and Surgeons. Co-author: The Design, Construction and Use of Removable Orthodontic Appliances, 1995; contbr. articles to profl. jours. Mem. European Orthodontic Soc., Brit. Dental Assn., Assn. Univ. Tchrs. Orthodontics (chmn. 1989-92), Royal Scottish Automobile Club. Home: 12 Wardlaw Rd Bearsden, Glasgow G61 1AL, Scotland Office: U Glasgow Dental Sch, 378 Sauchiehall St, Glasgow G2 3JZ, Scotland

KERRIGAN, JAMES JOSEPH, physician, neurologist; b. Johnstown, Pa., June 26, 1957; s. James J. and Ann (Solomon) K.; m. Vivianne Mastrogiacomo, Jan. 9, 1982; children: James, Michael Patrick, Sarah, Thomas. BS, U. Notre Dame, 1979; MD, Thomas Jefferson U., 1984. Diplomate Am. Bd. Psychiatry and Neurology, Am. Bd. Clin. Neurophysiology. Resident in internal medicine Mercy Hosp. of Pitts., 1984-85; resident in neurology Thomas Jefferson U. Hosp., Phila., 1985-88, fellow in neurology, 1988-89, chief resident in neurology, 1987; neurologist Neurology Assoc. of Monroe County, East Stroudsburg, Pa., 1989—; vice chief of medicine Pocono Med. Ctr., East Stroudsburg, 1995. Contbr. articles to profl. jours. Mem. adv. bd. Lehigh Valley Epilepsy Fund, Allentown, 1991-94. Mem. AMA, Am. Acad. Neurology, Pa. Med. Soc., Monroe County Med. Soc., Notre Dame Club (treas. Pocono chpt. 1991-95). Roman Catholic. Home: 41 Evergreen

Dr Stroudsburg PA 18360 Office: Neurology Assocs Monroe Co RD 5 Box 5167 East Stroudsburg PA 18301

KERRIGAN, MABEL BAISLEY, peri-operative nurse, educator; b. New Haven, July 13, 1937; d. Melville Mathew and Mary (Werle) Baisley; m. John Francis Kerrigan, June 15, 1968; children: Maureen, Elizabeth, Mary, John, Francis, Mark, William. Diploma, Hosp. St. Raphael, New Haven, 1958; BSN, U. Bridgeport, 1965. RN, cert. operating room nurse. Sch. nurse Branford (Conn.) Pub. Schs., 1980; clin. instr. Hosp. St. Raphael, 1966-68, instr. oper. rm., 1981-95, ret., 1995. Mem. Am. Assn. Operating Room Nurses (1st place writing award 1986).

KERSHAW, CAROL JEAN, psychologist; b. New Orleans, Apr. 11, 1947; d. Neal Howard and Gloria Jackson (Moss) Perkins; m. John William Wade, Aug. 20, 1983; stepchildren: Chris Wade, Stephen Wade, Tiffany Wade. BS in Secondary Edn., U. Tex., 1969; MS in Speech Communication, North Tex. State U., 1971, MEd in Counseling, 1976; EdD in Counseling, East Tex. State U., 1979. Lic. psychologist, Tex. Assoc. prof. DeVry Inst., Dallas, 1971-73; instr., counseling psychologist East Tex. State U., Commerce, 1976-78; counselor, instr. Tarrant County Jr. Coll., Hurst, Tex., 1971-74; dir. spl. svcs. Goodwill Industries, Dallas, 1974-76; marriage and family therapist, cons. mental health clinic Tex. Dept. Mental Health and Retardation, Greenville, 1977-79; asst. prof., dir. grad. program in marriage & family therapy Tex. Woman's U., Denton, 1980-83; coord. child devel. dept. Tex. Woman's U., Houston, 1983-88; pvt. practice Inst. for Family Psychology, Houston, 1986—; co-dir. Milton H. Erickson Inst. Houston, 1986—; bd. dirs. Milton H. Erickson Inst. Tex., Houston, 1986—; internat. presenter in field. Author: Therapeutic Metaphor in the Treatment of Childhood Asthma: A Systemic Approach, Ericksonian Monographs, Vol. 2, 1986, The Couple's Hypnotic Dance, 1992, The Healing Power of the Story, Ericksonian Monographs, Vol. 9, 1994, audio Mind/Body Healing and Hypnosis, 1996; co-author: Learning to Think for an Organ, Bridges of the Bodymind, 1980, Psychotherapeutic Techniques in School Psychology, 1984, Restorying the Mind: Using Therapeutic Narrative in Psychotherapy in Ericksonian Methods, 1994. Sec. Tex. Assn. for Marriage and Family Therapy, 1978-80. Recipient Visionary award, Meritorious Svc. award Tex. Assn. for Marriage & Family Therapy, 1980. Mem. Am. Psychol. Assn, Am. Assn. for Marriage and Family Therapy (clin., approved supr.), Soc. for Exptl. & Clin. Hypnosis, Am. Soc. for Clin. Hypnosis (cons., appointed to ethics com., 1996), Internat. Soc. for Clin. & Exptl. Hypnosis, Psi Chi. Democrat. Methodist. Office: Inst for Family Psychology 2012 Bissonnet St Houston TX 77005-1647

KERSHBAUM, CAROL, family practice physician; b. Phila., Apr. 16, 1942. BS, Temple U., 1963, MEd, 1966; MD, Med. Coll. Pa. Diplomate Am. Bd. Family Practice, Am. Bd. Pain Mgmt. Med. dir. Health Pass-Maxicare, Phila., 1986-88, Behavioral Health and Rehab., Maitland, Fla., 1988-90, Humana Health Plan, Maitland, 1994, Prudential Healthcare, Horsham, Pa., 1995—; pvt. practice Bryn Mawr, Pa., 1986-88, Longwood, Fla., 1991-95; chief clinic physician Cmty. Health Ctr. for Migrant Farm Workers, Apopka and Winter Garden, Fla., 1990-94. Mem. Am. Acad. Family Practice, Am. Pain Soc. Home: 273 Ironwood Cir Elkins Park PA 19027

KERSHNER, MELISSA ANNE, genetic counselor; b. Columbia, S.C., May 7, 1966; d. William Franklin and Mary Elaine (Doyon) K. BS, Dickinson Coll., 1988; MS, U. Pitts., 1990. Genetic counselor Pa. Hosp., Phila., 1990—. Contbr. articles to profl. jours. Mem. Nat. Soc. Genetic Counselors, Am. Soc. Human Genetics. Republican. Roman Catholic. Office: Pa Hosp/Genetrix 800 Spruce St Philadelphia PA 19107

KERTH, JACK D., otolaryngologist; b. Cin., July 28, 1933. MD, Ohio State U., 1958. Intern St. Luke's Hosp., Cleve., 1958-59; resident in otolaryngology Northwestern U., Chgo., 1959-63, fellow in otolaryngology, 1963, assoc. prof.; mem. staff Northwestern Meml. Hosp., Chgo.; pvt. practice otolaryngoloty. Fellow ACP; mem. AMA, AAFRPS, AAOHNS, ABO. Office: 845 N Michigan Ave Chicago IL 60611-2201*

KESAVAN, BRAMAWANDA SWAMY, JR., pediatrician; b. Nagercoil, Tamilnadu, India, Sept. 27, 1946; came to U.S., 1973; s. Bramawanda Swamy and Thanammal K.; m. Geetha S. Kesava; children: Anil, Anita. MB BS, Madurai Med. Sch., Tamilnadu, India, 1970. Chief dept. pediatrics Galesburg (Ill.) Coll. Hosp., 1994—, St. Mary's Hosp., Galesburg, Ill., 1994—. Mem. Knox County Med. Soc. (pres. 1995). Hindu. Home: 1128 Tamarind Dr Galesburg IL 61401 Office: 575 N Kellogg Galesburg IL 61401

KESHAVAN, MATCHERI, psychiatrist; b. Belur, Karnataka, India, May 23, 1953; came to U.S., 1985; s. Matcheri Sannaiyengar and Rama Matcheri Srinivasamurthy; m. Asha Keshavan, June 5, 1981; 1 child, Meghana. MB BS, Mysore Med. Coll., Karnataka, India, 1977; MD, Nat. Inst. of Mental Health, Bangalore, India, 1979. Asst. prof. psychiatry St. Johns Med. Coll., Bangalore, 1979-80; lectr. in psychiatry NIMH, Bangalore, 1980-82; IBRO rsch. fellow Internat Brain Rsch. Orgn., Vienna, Austria, 1982-83; registrar Maudsley Hosp., London, 1984-85; asst. prof. of psychiatry Wayne State U., Detroit, 1986-87; asst. prof. of psychiatry U. Pitts., 1987-91, assoc. prof., 1991—; med. dir. schizophrenia unit Western Psychiat. Inst. and Clinic, Pitts., 1988—. Contbr. over 100 articles to profl. publs.; author 3 books. Recipient Silver Jubilee prize Mysore U., 1977, Young Investigator award NIMH, 1989, Rsch. Scientist Devel. award, 1995—; Schizophrenia Rsch. grantee Scottish Rite Found., 1989; Internat. Brain Rsch. Orgn. scholar, 1982-83. Mem. Royal Coll. Psychiatrists (Gaskell medal 1985), Indian Psychiat. Soc. (Jayaram award), IndoAm. Psychiat. Assn. (Sci. award 1996). Hindu. Home: 2570 Mt Royal Rd Pittsburgh PA 15217-2542 Office: Western Psychiat Inst 3811 Ohara St Pittsburgh PA 15213-2593

KESKINER, ALI, psychiatrist; b. Kirsehir, Turkey, Mar. 10, 1929; came to the U.S., 1963; s. Mustafa and Ayse (Memis) K.; m. Lynne E. Hirz, Oct. 18, 1968 (div. 1982); children: Murad A., Aydin D. MD, Istanbul U., 1955; diploma in psychiatry, McGill U., 1962. Sr. intern psychiatry St. Anne's sect. Queen Mary Vets. Hosp., Montreal, Que., Can., 1958-59, resident psychiatry, 1959-60, sr. asst. resident psychiatry, 1960-61; sr. asst. resident in psychiatry Montreal Children's Hosp., 1961-62; asst. resident medicine-neurology Univ. Hosp., U. Sask., Saksatoon, Sask., Can., 1962-63; sr. rsch. scientist Mo. Inst. Psychiatry U. Mo., St. Louis, 1963-68, prof. psychiatry, 1964-76, chief behavioral rsch., 1968-75; staff psychiatrist, dir. rsch. Anclote Manor Hosp., Tarpon Springs, Fla., 1975-83; dir. rsch., staff psychiatrist VA Med. Ctr., Bay Pines, Fla., 1984-87, chief psychiatry svcs., 1988—; prof. psychiatry U. South Fla. Coll. Medicine, Tampa, 1984—; mem. rsch. com. U. South Fla. Dept. Psychiatry, Tampa, 1989—; mem. exec. com. VA Med. Ctr., 1992—; mem. sr. adv. com. Mo. Inst. Psychiatry, St. Louis, 1970-75. Contbr. chpt. to Therapeutic Studies in Therapy Resistant Schizophrenia, 1966-74; contbr. articles to profl. jours. Capt. Turkish Army, 1956-58. Grantee NIH, 1970-74; recipient Golden Eagle award Coun. on Internat. Non-Theatrical Events, 1975, 1st Place award in community mental health Nat. Mental Health Assn., 1977. Fellow Am. Psychiat. Assn. (life); mem. AAAS, N.Y. Acad. Sci., Fla. Psychiat. Soc. (chair various coms. 1984—), Turkish Am. Neuropsychiat. Assn. (pres. 1981-82). Office: VA Med Ctr Bay Pines FL 33504

KESL, DALE WAYNE, family practice physician; b. Helena, Ark., Sept. 6, 1955; s. James William Kesl and Gwendolyn Dean (Foley) Cole; m. Mary Denise Paine, Aug. 8, 1975 (div. May 1984); m. Peggy Marie Church, June 6, 1984; children: Megan, James, Matthew, (twins) Abigal and Allison. BA, U. Ark., 1978; DO, Kans. City Coll. Osteo. Path., 1982. Diplomate Am. Bd. Family Practice. Staff physician, instr. Univ. Hosp., Kansas City, 1983—. Mem. Am. Coll. Emergency Physicians, Am. Osteopath Assn., Am. Coll. Osteo. Family Physicians, Mo. Assn. Osteo. Physicians & Surgeons. Lutheran. Home: Rt 4 Box 383-A Wausaw MO 65355

KESLER, DARREL J., biochemist, educator; b. Portland, Ind., Sept. 21, 1949; s. D. Gordon and Lucille M. (Bullock) K.; m. Cheryl Scaletta, May 26, 1973; children: Cheralyn Elizabeth, Darrel Phillip Adam. BS, Purdue U., West Lafayette, Ind., 1971, MS, 1974; PhD, U. Mo., 1977. Research asst. U. Mo., 1974-77; asst. prof. U. Ill., Urbana, 1977-81, assoc. prof., 1981—; biochemist Abbott Labs., North Chicago, 1983-84; cons. research scientist CEVA Labs, Overland Park, Kans., 1986—, BallistiVet, Inc., 1988—. Contbr. articles to sci. jour. Mem. AAAS, Am. Soc. Animal Sci. (Midwest Outstanding Young Scientist award 1983), Controlled Release Soc., Am. Chem. Soc. Biochem. Tech., Am. Chem. Soc. Polymeric Materials Sci. and Engring., Soc. Study Reproduction, Sigma Xi. Roman Catholic. Home: 1204 Alderbury Dr Saint Joseph IL 61873-9617 Office: U Ill 1207 W Gregory Dr Urbana IL 61801-3838

KESLER, JAMES L., ophthalmologist; b. Vincennes, Ind., July 8, 1949; s. Richard Kesler and Bonnie L. (Perrott) Treece; m. Jana L. Blake, Aug. 29, 1970; children: Jason, Jessica. BS, U. Ill., 1971; MD, Washington U., 1975. Diplomate Am. Bd. Ophthalmology, Nat. Bd. Med. Examiners. Resident U. Va., Charlottesville, 1975-76, Barnes Hosp./Washington U., St. Louis, 1976-79; ophthalmologist Coastal Carolina Eye Clinic, Wilmington, N.C., 1979—. Fellow ACS, Am. Acad. Ophthalmology (councilor 1996); mem. AMA, N.C. Med. Soc., N.C. Soc. Ophthalmology (pres. 1988), New Hanover-Pender County Med. Soc. (pres. 1991), Nat. Parliamentarian Soc., Phi Beta Kappa, Alpha Omega Alpha. Office: Coastal Carolina Eye Clinic 1120 Med Ctr Dr Wilmington NC 28401

KESLER, KENNETH ALLEN, thoracic surgeon, educator; b. Indpls., Apr. 12, 1953; s. Jack Allen and Jacqueline Rita (Schaeffer) K. AB in Math., Ind. U., 1975; MD, Ind. U., Indpls., 1979. Bd. cert. Am. Bd. Surgery, Am. Bd. Thoracic Surgery. Gen. surgery resident Ind. U., Indpls., 1979-85; thoracic surgery resident St. Louis (Mo.) U, 1985-87; asst. prof. surgery thoracic surgery divsn. Ind. U. Sch. Medicine, Indpls., 1987-93, assoc. prof. surgery thoracic surgery divsn., 1993—; dir. pulmonary transplantation svc. Ind. U., Indpls., 1991—, surg. dir. thoracic oncology program, 1993—; thoracic surgery subcom. Ea. Coop. Oncology Group, 1992—. Contbr. chpts. to books and articles to profl. jours. Recipient Liebig Found. award for original rsch. Soc. Vascular Surgeons, 1985. Fellow ACS; mem. Soc. Thoracic Surgeons, Soc. Surg. Oncology, Gen. Thoracic Surg. Club, U.S. Triathlon Med. Assn., Sigma Xi. Office: Ind U Dept Surgery Thoracic Divsn 545 Barnhill EM #212 Indianapolis IN 46202

KESSEN, WILLIAM, psychologist, educator; b. Key West, Fla., Jan. 18, 1925; s. Herman Lowry and Maria Angela (Lord) K.; m. Marion Lord, June 10, 1950; children: Judith, Deborah, Anne, Peter Christopher, Andrew Lord, John Michael. B.S., U. Fla., 1948; Sc.M., Brown U., 1950; Ph.D., Yale U., 1952. Postdoctoral fellow Child Study Ctr. Yale U., 1952-54, faculty dept. psychology and Child Study Ctr., 1954-76, Eugene Higgins prof. psychology, 1976—, chmn. dept. psychology, 1977-80, prof. pediatrics, 1978—, acting univ. sec., 1980-81; acting master Calhoun Coll., spring 1989. Author: (with G. Mandler) The Language of Psychology, 1959, The Child, 1965, Childhood in China, 1975, (with M.H. Bornstein) Psychological Development from Infancy, 1979; editor: Mussen's Handbook of Child Psychology, vol. 1, 1983, The Rise and Fall of Development, 1990; contbr. articles to profl. jours. Mem. Carnegie Coun. on Children, 1973-77; trustee Barnard Coll., 1983-90. With U.S. Army, 1943-46. Fellow Ctr. Advanced Study Behavioral Scis., 1959-60, Guggenheim fellow, 1970-71, Russell Sage fellow, 1989-90. Fellow Am. Psychol. Assn. (pres. div. 7 1979-80); mem. Am. Psychol. Soc., Soc. Research Child Devel., Soc. Exptl. Psychologists, Am. Acad. Arts and Scis. Home: 30 Halstead Ln Branford CT 06405-5508 Office: Yale U Dept Psychology PO Box 208205 New Haven CT 06520-8205

KESSETE, MIRACH TEWELDEBRHAN, anesthesiology educator; b. Harien, Akeleguzai, Eritrea, Feb. 11, 1946; s. Teweldebrhan Mirach Tesfay and Kidusan Bahibla Debretsion; m. Tebbe Woldemariam Tesfaselassie, Aug. 24, 1985; children: Bethel, Quaanan, Berhane. Diploma in nursing, Menen Sch. Nursing, Asmara, Eritrea, 1967, diploma in nurse/midwifery, 1967; advanced diploma in anesthesia, WHO/Ministry of Health Sch., Addis Abeba, Ethiopia, 1976; BSN, Laroche Coll., 1991. Nurse in charge surg. and maternity wards Mekonnen Hailesellassie Hosp., Harar, Ethiopia, 1967-71; recovery rm. nurse Menen Hosp., Asmara, 1971-72, sr. midwife, 1972-73, surg. head nurse, 1973-74; nurse anesthetist Nekemt (Ethiopia) Hosp., 1976-79; asst. head anesthesia svc. Tikur Anbessa Hosp., Addis Abeba, 1979-82; founder, dir. Sch. of Anesthesia for Nurses, Ministry of Health, Addis Abeba, 1982—. Mem. Ethiopian Assn. Nurses (pres. dist. II 1972-74), Ethiopian Assn. Nurse Anesthetists (pres. 1984-86, 92-96). Home: PO Box 6611, Addis Ababa Ethiopia

KESSINGER, MARGARET ANNE, academic physician; b. Beckley, W.Va., June 4, 1941; d. Clisby Theodore and Margaret Anne (Ellison) K.; m. Loyd Ernst Wegner, Nov. 27, 1971. MA, W.Va. U., 1963, MD, 1967. Diplomate Am. Bd. Internal Medicine and Med. Oncology. Internal medicine house officer U. Nebr. Med. Ctr., Omaha, 1967-70, fellow med. oncology, 1970-72, asst. prof. internal medicine, 1972-77, assoc. prof. 1977-90, prof., 1990—, assoc. chief oncology/hematology sect., 1988-91, chief oncology/hematology sect., 1991—. Contbr. articles to profl. publs. Fellow ACP; mem. Am. Assn. Cancer Edn., Am. Soc. Clin. Oncology, Am. Assn. Cancer Rsch., Internat. Soc. Exptl. Hematology, Am. Soc. Hematology, Sigma Xi, Alpha Omega Alpha. Republican. Methodist. Office: U Nebr Med Ctr 600 S 42nd St Omaha NE 68198-3330

KESSLER, DAVID A., health services commissioner; b. N.Y.C., May 31, 1951; married; 2 children. BA, Amherst Coll., 1973; JD, U. Chgo., 1978; MD, Harvard U., 1979; APC, NYU Sch. Bus. Food and drug law Columbia U. Sch. of Law; med. dir. Einstein-Montefiore Hosp., N.Y.C.; commr. FDA Dept. Health and Human Svcs., Rockville, Md., 1990—; mem. Inst. of Medicine; assoc. prof. pediatrics Einstein Med. Sch. Office: Dept Health and Human Svcs FDA 5600 Fishers Ln Rockville MD 20857-0001

KESSLER, DAVID BRIAN, osteopathic dermatologist; b. Roslyn, N.Y., June 16, 1959; s. Milton and Estelle (Hubelbank) K.; m. Linda Gail Ochital, June 15, 1986; children: Andrew, Eric. BS in Bus. and Econs., SUNY, Oneonta, 1981; DO, N.Y. Coll. Osteo. Medicine, 1986. Diplomate Am. Osteo. Bd. Dermatology. Mem. profl. ski patrol Hunter (N.Y.) Meml. Sik Area, 1981-82; pvt. practice, Mineola, N.Y., 1991-94, Massapequa, N.Y., 1994—. Mem. Am. Osteo. Assn., Am. Osteo. Coll. Dermatology, Suffolk County Dermatology Soc. (sec. 1994-95), Am. Acad. Dermatology, Nassau County Med. Soc. Office: Massapequa Dermatology 20 Hicksville Rd Ste 5 Massapequa NY 11758

KESSLER, JEFFREY T., neurologist; b. Phila., Sept. 4, 1943; s. Irving K. and Behina C. (Chertkoff) K.; m. Lauren Jane Goldberg, Oct. 14, 1973 (dec. 1980); 1 child, James; m. Ilana Camille Hercz, Sept. 1, 1983; children: Andrew, Ian, Victoria. BA, Wesleyan U., 1965; MD, Cornell U., 1969. Diplomate Am. Bd. Internal Medicine. Asst. prof. neurology N.J. Med. Sch., Newark, 1974-76; pvt. practice Great Neck, N.Y., 1976—; cons. Am. Parkinson Assn., N.Y.C., 1974—, L.I. Myasthenia Gravis Found., 1980—, L.I. Multiple Sclerosis Soc., 1980—; clin. assoc. prof. Cornell U. Med. Coll., 1976—; pres. med. staff North Shore U. Hosp., 1988-89. Author: Management of Head and Neck Pain, 1989; contbr. articles to profl. jours. Active Archtl. Rev. Bd., Kings Point, N.Y., 1988-93, Bd. Zoning Appeals, 1993-96; founder Multiple Sclerosis Club North Shore U. Hosp., 1980. Capt. USAR, 1971-77. Fellow Nassau Acad. Medicine; mem. AMA (Physicians Recognition award 1979—), Am. Acad. Neurology, Nassau County Med. Soc. (v.p. 1976—), Med. Soc. State N.Y., Am. Assn. Study Headache. Jewish. Home: 5 Beech Ln Kings Point NY 11024 Office: Neurol Assn LI 179 Community Dr Great Neck NY 11021

KESSLER, MARTIN ELLIOT, surgeon; b. Bklyn., July 19, 1953. BA, Queens Coll., 1976; MD, Cornell U. Med. Coll., 1980. Intern dept. surgery N.Y. Hosp. Cornell Med. Ctr., N.Y.C., 1980-81, jr. asst. resident dept. of surgery, 1981-82, sr. asst. resident dept. of surgery, 1982-83, resident dept. of surgery, 1983-85; fellow hand surgery The Cleve. Clinic, 1985; fellow reconstructive microsurgery U. Louisville Health Ctr., 1986; plastic and reconstructive surgeon pvt. practice Rockville Ctr., N.Y., 1986—; clin. instr. plastic surgery Cornell U. Med. Coll., North Shore U., Hosp., Manhasset, N.Y., 1986—. Grantee N.Y. Lung Assn., 1977, March of Dimes, 1978. Fellow Am. Coll. Surgeons; mem. AMA, Am. Soc. Plastic and Reconstructive Surgeons, AmericanBurn Assn., N.Y. County Med. Soc., Med. Soc. State of N.Y., Nassau County Med. Soc., N.Y. Acad. Scis. Office: Martin E Kessler 242 Merrick Rd Rockville Centre NY 11570

KESSLER, PETE WILLIAM, dentist; b. Paterson, N.J., Feb. 21, 1949; s. Martin and Bernice S. Kessler; m. Sue E. George, Nov. 2, 1988; children: Kasey Martin, Kelly George, Kristopher William. BA, Peabody Conservatory of Music, 1971; BS, U. Md., 1976, MS, 1978, DDS, 1982. Bassist, musician Roberta Flack, Alexandria, Va., 1970-73, Atlantic Records, N.Y.C., 1970-75; pvt. practice Balt., 1982—. Recorded with Fifth Dimension, Friends of Distinction, Freddy Hubbard, Village People, Crystal Gayle, Ronnie Milsap, Hulk Hogan, others. Office: 4801 Ritchie Hwy Baltimore MD 21225-3045

KESTENBAUM, RICHARD, psychologist; b. N.Y.C., Mar. 20, 1942. BA, NYU, 1967, PhD, 1968. Asst. prof. psychology SUNY, Stony Brook, N.Y., 1969-74; assoc. dir. rsch. N.Y. Med. Coll., N.Y.C., 1974-79; sr. supr. Beth Israel Med. Ctr., N.Y.C., 1983-87; pres. Psychol. NEtworks, N.Y.C., 1986—; psychologist pvt. practice, N.Y.C., 1979—; adj. assoc. prof. psychology Columbia U., N.Y.C., 1984—. Contbr. articles to profl. jours. Mem. APA.

KESTIN, WILLIAM I., ophthalmologist, educator; b. N.Y.C., Dec. 15, 1953; s. Sol Israel and Patricia Pearl Kestin. BS, SUNY, Stony Brook, 1974; MD, UMDNJ, 1978. Diplomate Am. Bd. Ophthalmology. Assoc. dir. Kochman Eye Surg. Facility, Bklyn., 1982-90; ptnr. J. Robert Rosenthal MD & William I. Kestin MD, PC, Bklyn., 1990—; clin. asst. prof. ophthalmology NYU Med. Ctr., 1982—. Fellow ACS, Am. Acad. Ophthalmology; mem. Am. Coll. Eye Surgeons, Am. Soc. Cataract and Refractive Surgery, Med. Soc. State N.Y., N.Y. State Ophthalmol. Soc. Office: Drs Rosenthal & Kestin PC 2613 E 16th St Brooklyn NY 11235

KESTLER, HARRY WILLIAM, molecular virologist, educator; b. Rochester, N.Y., Jan. 24, 1956; s. Harry William Kestler Jr. and Helen Judith (Kryk) Farnan; m. Julie Carlson, Aug. 25, 1988; 1 child, Jacob Harry. MS, U. Rochester, 1981, PhD, 1985. Postdoctoral fellow Harvard U., Southborough, Mass., 1986-89, rsch. assoc., 1989-91; instr. Clark U., Worcester, Mass., 1989-91; mem. staff Cleve. Clinic Found., 1991—; judge Worcester Sci. Fair, 1989-91. Contbr. articles to profl. jours. Councilor Camp TaKumta, Am. Cancer Soc., Waterbury, Vt., 1986—. Charles A. King fellow Med. Found. Mass., 1989-91. Mem. AAAS, Am. Soc. Microbiology, N.Y. Acad. Scis. Office: Cleve Clinic Found NC2-146 9500 Euclid Ave # 1 Cleveland OH 44195-0001

KESZELI, ALEXANDER CHARLES, medical educator; b. Phila., Sept. 3, 1963; s. Alexander Robert and Eleonora (Maday) K.; m. Kim Marie Fronczak, June 10, 1995. BA, Franklin & Marshall U., 1985; DO, Phila. Coll. Osteo. Medicine, 1989. Clin. instr. otolaryngology/head and neck surgery SUNY, Buffalo, 1992-95; founder Ear, Nose and Throat Assocs. Chester County, Exton, Pa., 1995—. Contbr. articles to profl. jours. Recipient Nato scholarship for advanced study NSF, Erice, Sicily, 1991, first prize rsch. essay contest ACS, Buffalo, 1994. Fellow Am. Soc. for Laser in Medicine and Surgery; mem. AMA, Am. Acad. Otolaryngology Head and Neck Surgery, Osteo. Coll. of Otolaryngology/Opthomalogy, The Triology Soc. Office: Med Arts Bldg 80 W Welsh Pool Rd Exton PA 19341-1222

KESZLER, MARY LENORE, physician; b. Pottsville, Pa., Jan. 13, 1953; d. Leonard Edward and Helen Elizabeth (Kolet) Gricoscki; m. Martin Keszler, Jan. 2, 1982; children: Andrew, Peter. BS, Chestnut Hill Coll., Phila., 1974; MD, Pa. State U., Hershey, 1979. Diplomate Am. Bd. Pediat., Am. Bd. Neonatology. Intern then resident Akron (Ohio) Children's Hosp., 1979-82; fellow in neonatology U. Md. Hosp., Balt., 1982-83, Georgetown U., Washington, 1983-84. Den leader, chaiperson com. Cub Scouts Am., Bethesda, Md., 1990— (Dean Leader award 1995). Mem. Am. Heart Assn. (regional trainer ACLS state of Md.), Am. Pediatric Soc. (regional trainer ACLS state of Md.), Mont. County Pediatric Soc. Roman Catholic. Home: 8309 River Trail Ln Bethesda MD 20817 Office: Holy Cross Hosp Divsn neonatology 1500 Forest Glen Rd Silver Spring MD 20910

KETCHERSID, WAYNE LESTER, JR., medical technologist; b. Seattle, Oct. 16, 1946; s. Wayne Lester and Hazel May (Greene) K.; m. Wilette LaVerne Mautz, Oct. 6, 1972; 1 son, William Les. BS in Biology, Pacific Luth. U., 1976, BS in Med. Tech., 1978; MS in Adminstrn., Cen. Mich. U., 1990; postgrad. Kennedy Western U., 1996—. Cert. med. technologist; cert. clin. lab. dir. Nat. Cert. Agy. for Med. Lab. Pers. Staff technologist Tacoma Gen. Hosp., 1978-79, chemistry supr., 1979-81, head chemistry, 1981-83; head chemistry Multicare Med. Ctr., 1984-86, mgr., 1986-93, clin. lab. scientist, 1993—. Mem. Nat. Rep. Com. Served with U.S. Army, 1966-68. William E. Slaughter Found. scholar, 1975-76. Mem. Am. Soc. Clin. Lab. Sci. (cert., chmn. region IX adminstrn. 1984-94, nat. del. 1984—, vice chmn. govt. affairs com. 1991-92, chmn. 1992-93, vice chair, 1993-94, bd. trustees polit. action com. 1991—, treas. 1994-96, nat. licensure coord. 1996—, sec./treas. bd. dirs. 1996—, co-chair ann. meeting 1996, nominee Mem. of Yr. 1992, Bd. Dirs. award 1994, Mendelson award 1994, Pres. award 1996), Wash. State Soc. Clin. Lab. Sci. (chmn. biochemistry sect. 1983-86, dist. pres. 1986—, cert. merit 1983, 84, 86, 88, pres. 1988-89, 89-90, mem. of the yr., 1990, chmn. govt. affairs com. 1991-92, chmn. 1992—), Am. Soc. Clin. Pathologists (med. technolgist), N.W. Med. lab. Symposium (chmn. 1986-88, 90, 92), Alpha Mu Tau. Lutheran. Contbr. articles to profl. jours. Office: 2906 S 274th Pl Auburn WA 98001-1803

KETCHLEDGE, KATHLEEN A., nurse; b. Reading, Pa., May 12, 1956; d. Charles C. and Arlene M. (Krommes) T. AS, Reading Area Community Coll., 1977. Staff nurse Community Gen. Hosp., Reading, Leigh Valley Hosp. Ctr., Allentown, Pa.; nurse mgr. skilled unit Laurel Nursing and Rehab. Ctr., Hamburg, Pa., medicare coord. infection control, 1995—. Home: 712 N Warren St Apt 2 Orwigsburg PA 17961

KETTER, TERENCE ARTHUR, psychiatrist; b. Toronto, Apr. 20, 1950; s. Arthur Walde and Patricia Jean (Crozier) K.; m. Vera Hildegard Wegener, Aug. 28, 1971 (div. Sept. 1982); m. Nzeera Amirali Virani, Nov. 3, 1984. BS, U. Toronto, 1973; MS, U. Sydney, 1976; MD, U. Toronto, 1984. Diplomate Am. Bd. Psychiatry & Neurology. Resident in psychiatry U. Calif., San Francisco, 1984-88; sr. staff fellow NIMH, Bethesda, Md., 1988-95; assoc. prof. psychiatry & behavioral scis. Stanford (Calif.) U. Sch. Medicine, 1995—. Fellow Royal Coll. Physicians & Surgeons of Can.; mem. AAAS, Am. Psychiat. Assn., Internat. Soc. Neuroimaging Psychiatry, Am. Soc. Clin. Psychopharmacology, Am. Acad. Clin. Psychiatrists, Soc. Biol. Psychiatry, Am. Epilepsy Soc., Assn. for Convulsive Therapy, Nat. Depressive and Manic Depressive Assn., Nat. Alliance for the Mentally Ill, Am. Neuropsychiat. Assn. Office: Stanford U Sch Medicine Dept Psychiatry Stanford CA 94305-5543

KETTLER, KARL KINAUD, pharmacist; b. New Orleans, Feb. 9, 1943; s. Karl Kinaud and Louise Elizabeth (Morrison) K.; m. Janis Louise Pyka, Feb. 24, 1968 (div. Feb. 1980); children: Laura Lynn, Kristin Marlene; m. Patricia Ann Jekel, Oct. 10, 1992. BS in Pharmacy, Northeast La. U., 1968. Registered pharmacist, Tex., La. Staff pharmacist Brooke Army Med. Ctr., Fort Sam Houston, Tex., 1974-83; clinic pharmacist 574th Med. detachment, Stuttgart, Fed. Republic Germany, 1983-84; staff pharmacist Northeast Bapt. Hosp., San Antonio, 1984, Joint Mil. Med. Command, 1985-91; out patient pharmacist, Wilford Hall USAF Med. Ctr., 1991—. Mem. Soc. Air Force Pharmacists, Ctrl. Tex. Soc. Hosp. Pharmacists (bd. dirs. 1987-89), Wilford Hall Journal Club (v.p.), Kappa Psi. Republican. Roman Catholic. Avocations: motorcycling; hunting; fishing, reading. Home: 1485 N Ellison Dr San Antonio TX 78251-4001 Office: Lackland Afb San Antonio TX 78236-5000

KETTLESON, DAVID NOEL, retired orthopaedic surgeon, timber manager; b. St. Paul, Dec. 20, 1938; s. John Benton and Dorothy S. (Elkins) K.; m. Karen Nordstrom, Aug. 25, 1961; children: Maria, Daniel, Laura. BA, U. Minn., 1960, BS, MD, 1964. Diplomate Am. Bd. Orthopaedic Surgery. Intern St. Mary's Hosp., Duluth, Minn., 1964-65; resident in othopaedic surgery U. Minn. Hosp., Mpls., 1965-69; v.p., sec., treas. Orthopaedic Surgery, Inc., Omaha, 1971-92; pres. Nebr. Spine Surgeons, Omaha, 1992-94; ret., 1994; owner Eagleview Farms, Crosslake, Minn., 1994—; chmn. dept. orthopaedics Immanuel Med. Ctr., Omaha, 1978-82. Served to maj. USAF, 1969-71. Fellow N.Am. Spine Soc.; mem.

AMA, Mid Cen. States Orthopaedic Soc. (sec. 1974-85), Scoliosis Rsch. Soc. Republican. Office: Eagleview Farms PO Box 40 Crosslake MN 56442-0040

KETY, SEYMOUR S(OLOMON), physiologist, neuroscientist; b. Phila., Aug. 25, 1915; s. Louis and Ethel (Snyderman) K.; m. Josephine R. Gross, June 18, 1940; children: Lawrence Philip, Roberta Frances. AB, U. Pa., 1936, MD, 1940, ScD (hon.), 1965; ScD (hon.), Loyola U., 1969, U. Ill., 1981, Mt. Sinai U., 1982, Med. Coll. Pa., 1985, Georgetown U., 1987, Washington U., 1989; MD (hon.), U. Copenhagen, 1979; ScD (hon.), U. Mich., 1991. Intern Phila. Gen. Hosp., 1940-42; NRC fellow Harvard U., 1942-43; instr. to asst. prof. pharmacology Sch. Medicine U. Pa., 1943-48; prof. clin. physiology Grad. Sch. Medicine, 1948-51; scientific dir. Nat. Insts. Mental Health and Neurol. Diseases and Blindness, 1951-56; chief Lab. Clin. Sci. NIMH, 1956-61, 62-67, sr. scientist, 1983—; Henry Phipps prof., dir. dept. psychiatry Sch. Medicine Johns Hopkins U., 1961-62; prof. psychiatry Med. Sch. Harvard U., 1967-80, prof. neurosci. Med. Sch., 1980-83, prof. emeritus neurosci. Med. Sch., 1983—; Thomas Dent Mütter lectr., 1951, Eastman lectr., 1957, William Harvey Tercentenary lectr., 1957, NIH lectr., 1960, Thomas William Salmon lectr., 1961, Alvarenga Prize lectr., 1961, Acad. lectr. Am. Psychiat. Assn., 1961, Saul Korey lectr., 1964, James Arthur lectr., 1966, 3d Mental Health Research Fund lectr., London, 1965, Heinrich Waelsch lectr., 1969, Benjamin Musser lectr., 1970, Edward Mapother lectr., London, 1974, George Bishop lectr., 1975, Harvey lectr. Rockefeller U., 1975, Grass Found. lectr., 1975, Henry Maudsley lectr., London, 1978, Edward Sachar lectr., 1985; vis. prof. Coll. de France, 1966-67; fellow Ctr. Adv. Study in Behaviroal Sci., 1978-79. Editor-in-chief Jour. Psychiat. Research, 1959-83, founding editor, 1983—; hon. editor Jour. Cerebral Circulation and Metabolism, 1980—; contbr. sci. articles to profl. publs. Organizing com. Internat. Neurochem. Symposia, 1952-60; sci. advisory com. Mass. Gen. Hosp., 1956-60; bd. dir. Found. Fund Rsch. in Psychiatry, 1962-65; assoc. Neuroscis. Rsch. Found., 1962-83; trustee Rockefeller U., 1976-85; mem. vis. com. for biology Calif. Inst. Tech., 1972-76; mem. vis. com. for psychology MIT, 1973-76; mem. overview cluster Pres.'s Biomed. Rsch. Panel, 1975-76; chmn. biosci. adv. com. NASA, 1959-60; mem. Pres.'s Panel on Mental Retardation, 1961-62; sr. sci. advisor to adminstr. Alcohol, Drugs and Mental Health Adminstrn., USPHS, 1984-85. Recipient Max Weinstein award, 1954, Disting. Svc. award HEW, 1958, Stanley Dean award, 1962, McAlpin award Nat. Assn. for Mental Health, 1972, William C. Menninger award ACP, 1976, Fromm-Reichman award, 1978, Founds. Fund Rsch. award, 1979, Passano award, 1980, Loretta Bender award, 1980, Thomas W. Salmon medal, 1982, Emil Kraepelin medal, 1984, Mihara Fund award, 1984, Disting. Alumnus award U. Pa., 1985, Ralph Gerard award, 1986, Georg Charles de Hevesy Nuclear Medicine Pioneer award, 1988, Schizophrenia Rsch. award Internat. Congress Rsch. Schizophrenia, 1989, Disting. Scientist award Nat. Assn. Rsch. Schizophrenia and Affective Disorders, 1992, Sarnat Internat. prize 1993, Lifetime Achievement award Internat. Soc. Psychiat. Genetics, 1993. Disting. fellow Am. Psychiat Assn. (Disting. Svc. award 1980), Royal Coll. Psychiatrists London (hon.); fellow Am. Neurological Assn. (hon.); mem. AAAS (Theobald Smith award 1949), Nat. Acad. Scis. (Kovalenko award 1973, Neurosci. award 1988), Am. Philos. Soc. (Lashley award 1992), Assn. Rsch. Nervous Mental Disease (trustee, pres. 1965, 80, Rsch. Achievement award 1980), Am. Psychopath. Assn. (pres. 1965, Paul Hoch award 1973), Soc. for Psychiat. Rsch., Am. Soc. Clin. Investigation, Am. Soc. Pharmacology and Exptl. Therapeutics, Internat. Soc. Cerebral Bld. Flow and Metabolism (hon. pres. 1980—), Soc. for Neurosci. (Grass. Found. award 1975, Ralph Gerard award 1986), Phi Beta Kappa, Sigma Xi, Alpha Omega Alpha. Office: NIH Clin Ctr 4c-110 Bethesda MD 20892

KEUCHER, THOMAS RUDOLPH, neurosurgeon; b. New Haven, Jan. 15, 1948; s. Werner Gerald and Martha Elizabeth (Lewis) K.; m. Jan K. Graves, June 14, 1969; children: Amy, Melissa. BS, Ind. U., Bloomington, 1968; MD, Ind. U., Indpls., 1972. Diplomate Am. Bd. Neurol. Surgery. Intern Wishard Hosp., Indpls., 1972-73; resident in neurological surgery Ind. U. Med. Ctr., Indpls., 1973-78; pvt. practice neurosurgery, South Bend, Ind., 1980—; mem. active staff Meml. Hosp., South Bend, 1980—, St. Joseph's Med. Ctr., South Bend, 1980—, St. Joseph Cmty. Hosp., Mishawaka, Ind., 1985—. Numerous offices Grace United Meth. Ch., South Bend, 1982—. Maj. M.C., USAR, 1978-80. Mem. AMA, Am. Assn. Neurol. Surgeons, Congress Neurol. Surgeons, Ind. Med. Soc. Office: North Ctrl Neurosury Inc 328 N Michigan St Ste 200 South Bend IN 46601

KEVERLINE, PAUL ORVILLE, ophthalmologist; b. Bradford, Pa., Feb. 6, 1943; s. Raymond L. and Kathryn Ila (McCown) K.; m. Greta J. Dunham, July 5, 1965 (div.); children: Jeffrey, Michael, Andrew, Douglas; m. Linda M. Taylor, Jan. 21, 1995. BS in Chemistry, U. Pitts., 1965, MD, 1969. Intern York (Pa.) Hosp., 1969-70; resident Eye & Ear Hosp., Pitts., 1972-75; ophthalmologist W.R. Hill, Inc., DuBois, Pa., 1975-76, Seneca Eye Surgeons, Inc., Warren, Pa., 1976—. Capt. USAF, 1970-72. Mem. AMA, Am. Acad. Ophthalmology, Am. Soc. Cataract & Refractive Surgeons, Am. Coll. Eye Surgeons, Internat. Soc. Refractive Surgery, Contact Lens Assn. Ophthalmologists. Office: Seneca Eye Surgeons Inc 103 Saint Clair St Warren PA 16365

KEY, JAMES EVERETT, ophthalmologist; b. Freeport, Tex., July 19, 1944; s. James Everett and Margaret Ann (Parker) K.; m. Betty Wilson, Dec. 22, 1967; children: Peter Wilson and Courtney Brooke (twins). BA, U. Tex., 1966; MD, Baylor U., 1970. Diplomate Am. Bd. Ophthalmology. Mem. staff Coll. Medicine Baylor U., Houston, 1976-89, clin. assoc. prof. ophthalmology, 1989-93, clin. prof. ophthalmology, 1994—; chief ophthalmology St. Luke's Episcopal Hosp., Houston, 1987—. Contbr. articles to jours., chpts. to books. Trustee U. of South, Sewanee, Tenn., 1991. Lt. USN, 1972-73. Mem. Am. Acad. Ophthalmology; mem. AMA, Contact Lens Assn. Ophthalmologists (past pres.), Harris County Med. Assn., Tex. Ophthal. Assn. (past bd. dirs.), Phi Beta Kappa. Episcopalian. Office: 6624 Fannin St Ste 2100 Houston TX 77030-2333

KEY, PAUL HOWARD, gastroenterologist; b. L.A., Feb. 23, 1943; s. Canon Robert MacLellan and Nira Bavington (Andrews) K.; m. m. Karin Lynn Casper, Oct. 3, 1964 (dec. Nov. 1991); 1 child, Paul Howard II; m. Dianna Grace, Aug. 28, 1993. BA, UCLA, 1969, MD, 1973. Intern, resident Wadsworth VA Hosp., 1973-75, chief resident in medicine, 1975-76; fellow in gastroenterology Cedars Sinai Med. Ctr., 1976-78; pvt. practice L.A., 1978—; assoc. clin. prof. medicine UCLA Sch. Medicine, 1978—. Fellow Am. Coll. Physicians; mem. Am. Gastroenterology Assn., Am. Soc. Gastrointestinal Endoscopy, Assn. for Study of Liver Diseases, So. Calif. Soc. for Gastrointestinal Endoscopy, So. Calif. Soc. Gastroenterology, Calif. Fedn. Digestive Diseases Socs. Office: 9808 Venice Blvd #503 Culver City CA 90232

KEY, SAMUEL NEWTON, III, ophthalmologist; b. Iowa City, Iowa, Sept. 30, 1945; s. Samuel Newton Jr. and Doris Kathleen (Jones) K. BS in Chemistry, Stanford U., 1967; MD, U. Pa., 1971. Diplomate Am. Bd. Ophthalmology. Intern Mayo Grad. Sch. Medicine, Rochester, Minn., 1971-72; resident in ophthalmology U. Calif. Sch. Medicine, San Francisco, 1972-75; fellow in ophthalmic pathology Wilmer Ophthal. Inst./Johns Hopkins Hosp., Balt., 1975-76; chief eye clinic U.S. Army MEDACC Hosp., Ft. Polk, La., 1976-78; pvt. practice Austin, Tex., 1978—. Contbr. chpt. to book, articles to profl. jours. Fellow ACS, Am. Acad. Ophthalmology (honor award 1984), Soc. Head Fellows, Tex. Soc. Ophthalmology and Otolaryngology; mem. Alpha Omega Alpha. Home: 3543 Greystone Dr Apt 2059 Austin TX 78731

KEY, TERRI ALICE, ophthalmologist; b. Lubbock, Tex., Oct. 13, 1958. BS in Pharmacy, U. N.Mex., 1981, MD, 1986. Chief ophthalmology Reno (Nev.) VA Med. Ctr., 1990—. Recipient Disting. Svc. award DAV, 1995. Fellow Am. Acad. Ophthalmology; mem. AMA, Nat. Assn. VA Physicians and Dentists, Assn. VA Ophthalmologists. Office: Va Hospital 1000 Locust St Reno NV 89520-0102

KEYE, WILLIAM RICHARD, JR., physician, educator; b. Mineola, N.Y., Oct. 31, 1943; s. William Richard and Jane Elizabeth (Snell) K.; m. Suzanne Marie Edstrom, Aug. 13, 1965; children: Deborah Sue, Jeffrey Scott. BA, U. Minn., 1965, BS, 1969, MD, 1969. Diplomate Am. Bd. Ob-Gyn, Bd. Reproductive Endocrinology. Intern, U. Minn. Mpls., 1969-70, resident, 1970-72; resident U. Mich., 1972-73, U. Calif., San Francisco, 1973-77; physician Caylor-Nickel Clinic, Bluffton, Ind., 1977-78; asst. prof. U. Utah, Salt Lake City, 1979-84, assoc. prof., 1984-90; dir. divsn. reproductive endocrinology & infertility William Beaumont Hosp., Royal Oak, Mich., 1990—; clin. assoc. prof. U. Mich., 1992—. Editor: Laser Surgery in Obstetrics and Gynceology, 1984, 2nd edit., 1990, PMS, 1988, Infertility: Diagnosis and Treatment, 1995. Contbr. articles to profl. jours. Med. advisor Resolve of Utah, Salt Lake City, 1979-90. Maj. USAF, 1974-76. Fellow Am. Coll. Ob-Gyn, Am. Soc. Reproductive Medicine (dir. 1994—), Soc. Reproductive Endocrinology; mem. Gynecol. Laser Soc., Soc. Reproductive Surgeons (treas. 1990-91, sec. 1991-92, v.p. 1992-93, pres. 1993-94).

KEYES, BENJAMIN B., therapist; b. Alexandria, Va., Sept. 18, 1953; s. Jay F. and Harriet Edith (Champagne) K.; m. Natalie Ann Keyes, Nov. 1, 1989; children: Shawn David, Jasmin Victoria, Sara Danielle, Alyssa Marie, Amanda Beth. MA, U. South Fla., 1978; PhD, Internat. Coll., 1985; ThD., DMin., Zoe Coll., 1985; DD, Reeves Christian Coll., 1987. Lic. profl. counselor, Tex., mental health counselor, Fla., practitioner, cons.; nat. cert. mental health counselor. Psychologist Baker Correctional Instn., Olustee, Fla.; prof. grad. sch. Fla. Beacon Bible Coll., Largo; dir. Charis Inc., Clearwater, Fla.; dir. clin. programs partial hospitalization Rapha Inc., Pasadena, Tex.; clin. dir. Bridgework Ministry, Clearwater; pvt. practice counselor, cons.; evaluator accreditation Dept. Corrections, 1984; dir. Manors Hosp., Largo, Fla.; program dir. Medfield Hosp., Largo; CEO Daylight Partial Hospitalization Programs, St. Petersburg, Fla. Co-author: Family Training Manual, E Ploribus Unum From Many to One; author: Sexuality, Learning and Teaching Modality, Christian Counseling, Substance Abuse Manual, A Christian Approach to Inner Healing No More Turning Away, A Christian Approach to Treating Dissociative Identity Disorder; contbr. articles to profl. jours. Recipient Appreciation cert. ARC, 1980-84, Youth award Trinity United Meth. Ch., 1980-81. Mem. AACC, Am. Mental Health Counselors Assn., Am. Counseling Assn., Assn. Ambulatory Behavioral Healthcare, Am. Rehab. Counseling Assn., Assn. Religious and Value Issues Counseling, Christians Who Do Therapy Assn., Assn. Christian Therapists, Internat. Soc. Study of Dissociation (mem. Tampa Bay chpt.), Internat. Assn. Counselors and Therapists (bd. dirs.), Fla. Ambulatory Partial Hospitalization Assn., Network of Christian Counselors, Upper Pinellas Minsterial Assn. (treas., v.p.), Fla. Rehab. Assn. (past exec. bd.), Fla. Rehab. Counseling Assn. (past regional rep.), Psi Chi. Home: 6095 2d Ave S Saint Petersburg FL 33707

KEYSER, JOHN EDWARD, III, vascular surgeon; b. Dayton, Ohio, June 7, 1954; m. Robin Jowers, June 8, 1985; children: John Brent, Mary Katherine. BS, U. Ill., 1976; MD, U. Ill., Chgo., 1980. Diplomate Am. Bd. Surgeons (added qualifications gen. vascular surgery). Ptnr. Surgical Group of Nashville, 1993—; med. dir. wound care ctr. Bapt. Hosp., Nashville, 1989—. Contbr. articles to So. Med. Jour., Postgrad. Medicine. Fellow ACS; mem. AMA, Tenn. Med. Assn., Nashville Acad. Medicine, So. Assn. for Vascular Surgery. Office: Surgical Group of Nashville 2011 Church St Ste 404 Nashville TN 37203-2011

KHALEF, BACHIR, physician, physicist, educator; b. Constantine, Algeria, Jan. 2, 1937; arrived in France, 1954; s. Mohand Khalef and Zahra Belmoufok; m. Nicole Auge, July 8, 1962 (div.); children: Francois, Anne, Emmanuelle; m. Evelyne Ritaine. Lic. in Math., Faculte des Scie, Bordeaux, France, 1960, Lic. in Physique, 1961, Diplôme d'Etudes Approfondies, 1966; MD, Faculte de Medecine, 1973. Intern Inst. des Scis. & Techniques Nuclaires, Saclay, France, 1964, Hosp. Pellegrin, 1969-71; resident Hosp. Haut Leveque, 1971-73; math. monitor Faculte des Scie, Bordeaux, 1960-62; prof. physics Lycee Montaigne, Bordeaux, 1962-73; chargé d'enseisnement d'anatomie et d'electrologie Institute Des Carrieres de Sante, 1973-78; prof. acupuncture U. Bordeaux, 1979-88; dir. Cabinet Med., Talence, France, 1973—. Author: Approche Mathematique et Thermodynamique de l'Acupuncture, 1978, Vitesse de Reactions Photo Chimique, 1966, Laser en Medecine, 1984, Acupuncture Medecine de L'Energie, 1984, Energie en Medecine Acupuncture Medecine D'Avant-Garde, 1993, Hypnose Renouveau, 1994. Mem. Milton H. Erickson Inst. Paris. Office: Cabinet Med, les Terrasses, 33400 Talence France

KHALIFA, AMAL IBRAHIM, cardiologist, researcher; b. Cairo, Abdeen, Egypt, May 1, 1959; d. Ibrahim Abdel Fatah Khalifa and Nazli Ismail Sedki; m. Ahmed Hesham Reda El Garhi, Jan. 17, 1983; children: Omaya, Mohamed, Abdallah. Gen. cert., Ramses Coll., Cairo, 1976; MB, BCh, Cairo, 1982, M in Cardiology, 1989; MD in Cardiology, Cairo U., 1996. Intern Cairo Univ. Hosp., 1982-83, fellow, 1985-96, resident cardiology dept., 1985-86; resident Tudor Bilharzh Inst., Giza, Egypt, 1983-85; echo specialist Es Salam Internat. Hosp., Cairo, 1986-88; echocardiographic trainer Diagnostic Untrasound Ctr. Cairo U. Hosp., 1989-96, echocardiographic cons., 1989-96; clin. investigator Egyptian Nat. Hypertension Project, Cairo, 1990-93. Author abstracts. Recipient Young Investigator award Pan Arab Conf. Hypertension, 1993. Mem. Egyptian Soc. Cardiology (Young Investigator award 1989), Egyptian Soc. Hypertension (founder), World Hypertension League. Home: 10 Thawra St Dokki, 12311 Giza Egypt Office: Cairo U Hosp Diagnostic Ultrasound Ctr, Kasr El Aini PO Box 139, Cairo Egypt

KHALIL, MUHAMMAD AHSAN KHAN, geneticist, researcher; b. Shahjahanpur, India, July 5, 1918; s. Muhammad Mazharhasan and Kubra Begum Khan Khalil. BSc, Muslim U., Aligarh, India, 1937, MSc, 1939; PhD, U. Minn., 1967; diploma long term planning Fed. Pub. Service Commn. Can., 1976. With forest dept. Govt. United Provinces, Lucknow, India, 1942-50; prof. Pakistan Forest Inst., Peshawar, 1951; dep. conservator forests Govt. Pakistan, 1951-53; prof. Pakistan Forest Inst., Peshawar, 1953-59, prin. silviculturist, 1956-60, dir., 1958-60, dir. Pakistan Forest Research Inst., Chittagong, 1960-63; research assoc. Sch. Forestry U. Minn., St. Paul, 1967-69; asst. prof. Sch. Forestry, Lakehead U., Thunder Bay, Ont., 1969-71; research scientist forest genetics Can. Forestry Service at Nfld. Forest Research Ctr., St. John's, 1971-84; apptd. mem. research bd. advisors Am. Biog. Inst. Inc. Co-author: Conifers for Biomass Production; editor: Pakistan Jour. Forestry, 1956-60; contbr. over 40 articles and papers to profl. jours. Recipient Sci. Gold medal Muslim U.; fellow Truman Found., 1953, FAO, 1955, AID. Avocations: classical Urdu and Persian literature, Islamic culture. Home: 106 Highland Dr, Saint John's, NF Canada A1A 3C5

KHAN, NASIR ALI, psychiatrist, educator; b. London, June 14, 1939; came to U.S., 1965; s. Ahmad A. and Bilquis B. (Khan) K.; m. Kay S. Kraus, May 21, 1967; children: Tahira, Zafar, Alexander. MD, U. London, 1962; Owners & Presidents Mgmt. Program cert., Harvard U., Boston, 1995. Diplomate Am. Bd. Psychiatry and Neurology. Resident in psychiatry Harvard U. Med. Sch., 1965-68, fellow in psychiatry, 1968-69; chief geriatric svcs. Mass. Dept. Mental Health, Boston, 1969-73; supt. Danvers (Mass.) State U., 1974-79; pvt. practice, Newton, Mass., 1970—; dir. Bournewood Hosp., Brookline, Mass., 1979—; asst. clin. prof. psychiatry Tufts U. Med. Sch., Boston, 1986—; bd. dirs., chmn., pres. 1st Psychiat. Planners Inc., Brookline, 1980—; bd. dirs., treas. Newton Psychiat. Group, 1994—; chmn. exec. com. Newton-Wellesley Hosp., 1990, pres. med. staff, 1995. Author: Handbook of Psychiatry, 1972. Coach Newton Youth Soccer, 1982-84. Fellow Am. Psychiat. Assn.; mem. Nat. Assn. Psychiat. Health Sys. (trustee 1995—), Assn. Gen. Psychiatrists (bd. dirs., pres. Brookline 1990-92), Mass. Med. Soc. (councilor 1992—), Mass. Assn. Pvt. Psychiat. Hosps. (bd. dirs., pres. 1990-91), Waquoit Bay Yacht Club (Falmouth, Mass., chmn. race com. 1986-88). Democrat. Home: 18 St Mary's St Newton MA 02162 Office: Bournewood Hosp 300 South St Brookline MA 02167

KHAN, STEVEN SHAHID, cardiologist; b. Rawalpindi, West Pakistan, Mar. 30, 1956; came to U.S., 1960; BS, Northwestern U., 1977; MD, Rush Med. Coll., 1981. Diplomate Am. Bd. Internal Medicine. Resident in internal medicine Cedars-Sinai Med. Ctr., L.A., 1981-84; fellow in cardiology Wadsworth VA Hosp., L.A., 1984-86, rsch. fellow, 1986-87; cardiologist Cedars-Sinai Med. Ctr., L.A., 1987—; asst. prof. Sch. Medicine UCLA, 1988-95, assoc. prof., 1995—. Contbr. chpts. to books, articles to profl. publs. Grantee Am. Heart Assn., 1987. Fellow Am. Coll. Cardiology, Am. Coll. Chest Physicians, Am. Heart Assn. (mem. clin. coun.); mem. AMA, AAAS, Am. Fedn. for Clin. Rsch., N.Y. Acad. Scis., Alpha Omega Alpha. Office: Cedars Sinai Med Ctr 8700 Beverly Blvd Rm 6215 Los Angeles CA 90048-1804

KHANTZIAN, EDWARD JOHN, psychiatrist, psychoanalyst; b. Haverhill, Mass., May 26, 1935; s. John Stephen and Nuvart K.; AB, Boston U., 1958; MD, Albany Med. Coll., 1963; m. Carol Ann DeAndrus, May 17, 1959; children: Nancy Jo, Susan Joyce, Jane Elizabeth, John Stephen. Intern, R.I. Hosp., Providence, 1963-64; resident Mass. Mental Health Center-Boston Psychopathic Hosp., 1964-67; practice medicine specializing in adult psychiatry, 1967—, specializing in addiction psychiatry, Haverhill and Cambridge, Mass., 1973—; chief psychiat. consultation service Cambridge (Mass.) Hosp., 1967-71, dir. drug treatment program, 1971-74, asso. dir. dept. psychiatry, 1976-80, spl. asst. to dir., 1980-82, dir. departmental liaison, 1982-85, prin. psychiatrists for addictions, 1985—, pres. med. staff, 1983-84. dir. drug treatment services Cambridge-Somerville Mental Health and Retardation Center, 1974-76, assoc. dir. clin. services, 1976-80; program dir. 1978-95, instr. psychiatry Harvard Med. Sch., Boston, 1967-73, asst. prof., 1973-78, assoc. prof., 1978-95, clin. prof., 1995—; mem. Drug Rehab. Adv. Bd. Commonwealth Mass., 1973-78, chmn., 1976-78. Served to maj. M.C., U.S. Army, 1967-70. Diplomate Am. Bd. Psychiatry and Neurology. Fellow Am. Psychiat. Assn. (cons. com. drug abuse 1984-86, mem. 1986-89, mem. addiction coun. 1993—, vice chair 1995—); mem. Boston Psychoanalytic Soc. and Inst. (Felix and Helen Deutsch prize 1973), Am. Psychoanalytic Assn., Mass. Psychiat. Soc., North Essex County Med. Soc., Am. Acad. Psychiatrists in Alcoholism and Addictions (v.p. 1989-91, pres. 1993-95), Am. Coll. Psychoanalysts, Group for Advancement Psychiatry (chmn. com. on alcoholism and addictions 1986-91), North Essex Mental Health Assn. (dir., 1st v.p. 1975-77). Assoc. editor Am. Jour. of Addiction, 1989—; mem. editorial rev. bd. Jour. Substance Abuse Treatment, 1984—, Am. Jour. Drug and Alcohol Abuse, 1986—; contbr. articles to profl. jours. Home: 55 King St Groveland MA 01834-1809 Office: 10-12 Phoenix Row Haverhill MA 01830

KHAROUF, JOHN GEORGE, orthodontist; b. Milw., May 15, 1960; s. George John and Ruth Elizabeth (Tareilus) K.; m. Mary C. Malone, Jun. 15, 1985; children: Jacqueline E., John G. Jr. DDS, Marquette Univ. Sch. Dentistry, 1985; cert of GPR, Langley Regional Hosp., 1986; MS, Univ. Iowa, 1992. Gen. dental resident Langley Regional HOsp., Hampton, Va., 1985-86; gen. dental officer Hahn AFB, West Germany, 1986-90; orthodontic resident Univ. Iowa, Iowa City, 1990-92; orthodontic officer Yokota AFB, Tokyo, 1992-95; orthodontist Rapid City, Iowa, 1995—; mem. Tri-Svc. Dental Soc. Japan, Tokyo, 1994-95. Contbr. articles to profl. jours. With USAF, 1985-95. Mem. Am. Dental Assn., Black Hills Dental Soc., South Dakota Dental Assn., Am. Assn. Orthodontists, KC. Roman Catholic. Office: 720 St Anne St Rapid City SD 57701

KHATAIN, KENNETH GEORGE, psychiatrist, former air force officer; b. Seattle, Oct. 11, 1953; s. Edward and LaVerne Mae (Bender) K.; m. Marla Dee Morgan, Aug. 12, 1978; children: Alanna E., Larissa E. AAS, Edmonds Community Coll., Lynnwood, Wash., 1976; BS in Molecular and Cellular Biology, U. Wash., 1978; MD, Wayne State U., 1986. Diplomate Am. Bd. Psychiatry and Neurology with qualifications in geriatric psychiatry, Nat. Bd. Med. Examiners. Resident in psychiatry Wright State U., Dayton, Ohio, 1986-90; commd. capt. USAF, 1986; advanced through grades to maj., 1992; chief inpatient psychiatry mental health svcs. Wilford Hall Med. Ctr., Lackland AFB, Tex., 1990-94; chief inpatient psychiatry VA Med. Ctr., Boise, Idaho, 1994—; guest reviewer AIDS articles Psychiat. Svcs., 1988—; clin. cons. Nat. Tng. Lab. Inst., Bethel, Maine, 1989; workshop presenter, guest speaker in field. Mem. adult edn. com. Westminster Presbyn. Ch., Dayton, 1989. Recipient physician recognition award AMA, 1989, Arnold Allen outstanding resident award Wright State U., 1990. Mem. Am. Psychiat. Assn., Tex. Soc. Psychiat. Physicians, Bexar County Psychiat. Soc., Phi Beta Kappa, Phi Theta Kappa. Office: VA Med Ctr 500 W Fort St Boise ID 83702-4501

KHAZAN, NAIM, pharmacology educator; b. Baghdad, Iraq, Feb. 15, 1921; came to U.S. 1966, naturalized 1973; s. Rahamim adn Tova (Eliezer) K.; m. Evelyn Muallem, Nov. 12, 1952; children: Uri, Ron. PhC in Pharm. Chemistry, Sch. Pharmacy, Baghdad, 1943; PhD in Pharmacology (hon.), Hebrew U., Jerusalem, 1960. Internat. NIMH rsch. fellow UCLA, 1962-63; rsch. asoc. Upjohn Co., Kalamazoo, 1963-64; dept. pharmacology and toxicology Hebrew U., Jerusalem, 1964-66; asst. prof. pharmacology Coll. Pharm. Sci., Columbia U., N.Y.C., 1967-68, Mt. Sinai Sch. Med., N.Y.C., 1968-72; head dept. pharmocology Merrell Nat. Labs., Cin., 1972-73; prof., chmn. dept. pharmacology and toxicology Sch. Pharmacy, U. Md., Balt., 1974-86, Emerson prof., 1976-86, prof. pharmacology, 1986-91, prof. emeritus, 1991—; sr. pharmacologist VA Med. Ctr., Washington, 1991-93. Contbr. over 150 rsch. articles, papers and revs. to Jour. Pharmacol. Exptl. Therapeutics, Neuropharmacology, Neuroscience, Life Science, others in the area of CNS pharmacology and EEG effects of drugs of abuse. NIDA grantee, 1968-88; apptd. eminent scholar Commn. on Higher Edn., State of Md., Annapolis, 1989. Mem. Am. Pharm. Assn., Am. Soc. Pharmacology and Exptl. Therapeutics (nominee Otto Krayer lectr. award 1990), Soc. Neurosci, N.Y. Acad. Sci. Home: 2126 Caves Rd Owings Mills MD 21117-2326

KHAZEI, AMIR MOHSEN, surgeon, oncologist; b. Teheran, Iran, July 21, 1928; came to U.S., 1957; s. Abol Khasem and Esmat (Khaligh-Azam) K.; m. Carmeline Victoria Grace Picardi; children: Alan, Darla, Mia, Lance. BS, U. Lausanne, Switzerland, 1952, MD and Cert. d'Etudes Medicale, 1957. Diplomate Mass. Bd. Medicine, N.H. Bd. Medicine; qualified Am. Bd. Surgery. Intern Mercy Hosp., Pitts., 1957-58, resident in gen. surgery, 1957-62; fellow in surgery Lahey Clinic Found., Boston, 1962-63, assoc. staff mem. surgery and chemotherapy, 1963-67, assoc. dir. surg. rsch. lab., 1967-68; attending surgeon VA Hosp., Manchester, N.H., 1968-70; staff surgeon Cath. Med. Ctr./Elliot Hosp., Manchester, 1971—; pres., chmn. exec. com. of med. staff Cath. Med. Ctr., 1981-82. Mem. editorial bd. Living With Cancer; co-author book; contbr. articles to profl. jours. Bd. dirs., incorporator Cath. Med. Ctr., 1981—, trustee, 1981-90; trustee Fiedlity Health Alliance Bd., Manchester, 1991-93, N.H. Nurses Found., 1991-95; pres. N.H. div. Am. Cancer Soc., 1977-79, nat. del. dir., 1982-91. Recipient St. George medal Am. Cancer Soc., 1982, Golden Apple award Cath. Med. Ctr., 1990, Med. Staff award N.H. Hosp. Assn., 1990. Fellow Am. Coll. Angiology, Internat. Coll. Angiology, Inter-Am. Coll. Physicians and Surgeons; mem. AMA, Am. Fedn. Clin. Rsch., N.H. Med. Soc. (pres., chmn. exec. com. 1986-87, trustee 1992-96, pres., chmn. bd. trustees 1996—), N.Y. Acad. Scis., Orgn. State Med. Assn. Pres.'s (life), Transplantation Soc., Hillsborough County Med. Soc. (pres. 1981-82), Am. Assn. for Cancer Edn., Soc. Laparo-endoscopic Surgeons, Am. Coll. Physician Execs. Office: Bedford Commons Bldg 3 36 Riverway Pl Bedford NH 03110

KHEDDACHE, SUSANNE, radiologist, researcher; b. Västervik, Sweden, June 17, 1949; m. Sid Ali Kheddache, May 30, 1969; children: Yassin, Mimmi, Karim, Miriam. MD, U. Göteborg, Sweden, 1985, PhD, 1991. Bd. cert. specialist in radiology, subspecialized in thoracic radiology. Specialist in radiology dept. radiology Sahlgrenska Hosp., Göteborg, 1985-90, Mölndal, Sweden, 1990-93; specialist in radiology Sahlgrenska Hosp., Kungsbacka, Sweden, 1993-95, Göteborg, 1995—. Author: Digital Chest Radiography with a Large Image Intensifier, 1991; contbr. articles to profl. jours. Mem. Swedish Assn. for Radiology in Medicine, Swedish Radiology Orgn., Swedish Orgn. for Women Radiologists, Swedish Soc. Medicine. Office: Sahlgrenska Univ Hosp, Dept Radiology, 41345 Goteborg Sweden

KHOJASTEH, ALI, medical oncologist, hematologist; b. Shiraz, Fars, Iran, Nov. 10, 1947; came to U.S., 1974; s. Mostafa and Pari Jan (Azimi) K.; children: Artemis, Amitis. Degree, Pahlavi U., Shiraz, 1968, MD, 1974. Vice dean Sch. Medicine Shiraz U., 1980-82, chmn. med. dept. Sch. Medicine, 1982-83; chief med. oncology Ellis Fischel Cancer Ctr., Columbia, Mo., 1983-87, chmn. med. dpet., 1987-90; med. dir. St. Mary Cancer Ctr., Jefferson City, Mo., 1993—; pres. Columbia (Mo.) Comprehensive Cancer Care Clinic, 1990—; assoc. prof. U. Mo., Columbia, 1989—; prin. investigator Ellis Fischel CCOP, Columbia, 1988-90; chmn. Mo. Cancer Pain Initiative, 1991. Contbr. articles to New Eng. Jour. Medicine, Cancer, Am. Jour. Medicine; author: (with others) Immunoproliferative Small Intestinal Disease, 1988. Rsch. grantee Purdue Fredrick Co., Conn., 1984—, Adria Lab., Columbus, 1988—, Glaxo Rsch. Lab., Research Triangle Park, N.C., 1988-91, Ciba-Geigy Co., 1990-93, Merrill Dow Co., 1991-95, Pfizer, 1995—. Fellow AAAS, Am. Coll. Physicians; mem. Am. Soc. Clin. Oncology, Am. Soc. Internat. Medicine, Smithsonian Soc., N.Y. Acad. Sci., Mo. Acad. Scis. (chmn. oncology sect. 1988-89), So. Med. Assn. Zoroastrian. Home: 2801

Greenbriar Dr Columbia MO 65203-3663 Office: Columbia Comprehensive Cancer Care Clinic 500 Keene St Ste 202 Columbia MO 65201-8104

KHOO, BOO-CHAI, plastic surgeon; b. Singapore, Apr. 24, 1929; s. Peng-Seng and Lew-Kee (Lim) K. MB, BS, U. Singapore, 1954. Med. officer, gen. surgery Singapore Gen. Hosp., 1954-58; resident plastic surgery in plastic surgery unit Met. Police Hosp., Tokyo, 1959-61; pvt. practice Khoo Plastic Surgery Clinic, Singapore, 1962—; vis. prof. plastic surgery 3rd Teaching Hosp., Beijing Med. U., 1990—, Shanghai 2nd Med. U., 9th Peoples Hosp., China, 1991—. Author: Cosmetic Plastic Surgery for Orientals, 1993; author, compiler: 25-Yr. Cumulative Index British Jour. Plastic Surgery, 1974; contbr. 5 book chpts. and 40 papers to splty. jours. Fellow Israel Assn. Plastic Surgeons (hon.); mem. Am. Soc. Plastic and Reconstructive Surgeons Inc., N.Y. Acad. Sci., Assn. Plastic Surgeons of India.

KHORANA, HAR GOBIND, chemist, educator; b. Raipur, India, Jan. 9, 1922; s. Shri Ganpat Rai and Shrimati Krishna (Devi) K.; m. Esther Elizabeth Sibler, 1952; children: Julia, Emilie, Dave Roy. BS, Punjab U., 1943, MS, 1945; PhD, Liverpool (Eng.) U., 1948; DSc, U. Chgo., 1967. Head organic chemistry group B.C. Rsch. Coun., 1952-60; vis. prof. Rockefeller Inst., N.Y.C., 1958—; prof. co-dir. Inst. Enzyme Rsch. U. Wis., Madison, 1960-70, prof. dept. biochemistry, 1962-70, Conrad A. Elvehjem prof. life scis., 1964-70; Alfred P. Sloan prof. biology and chemistry MIT, Cambridge, 1970—; vis. prof. Stanford U., 1964; mem. adv. bd. Biopolymers; researcher chem. methods for synthesis of nuccleotides, coenzymes and nucleic acids, elucidation on the genetic code, lab. synthesis of genes, biol. membrane and light-transducing pigments. Author: Some Recent Developments in the Chemistry of Phosphate Esters of Biological Interests, 1961; mem. editorial bd.: Jour. Am. Chem. Soc, 1963—; contbr. numerous articles to profl. jours. Recipient Merck award Chem. Inst. Can., 1958, Gold medal Profl. Inst. Pub. Service Can., 1960, Dannie-Heinneman Preiz Göttingen, Germany, 1967, Remsen award Johns Hopkins U., 1968, Am. Chem. Soc. award for creative work in synthetic organic chemistry, 1968, Louisa Gross Horwitz prize, 1968, Lasker Found. award for basic med. research, 1968, Nobel prize in medicine, 1968; elected to Deutsche Akademie der Naturforscher Leopoldina HalleSaale, Germany, 1968; Overseas fellow Churchill Coll., Cambridge, Eng., 1967. Fellow Chem. Inst. Can., Am. Acad. Arts and Scis.; mem. NAS. Office: MIT Rm 68-680 77 Massachusetts Ave Cambridge MA 02139-4301

KHOSLA, VED MITTER, oral and maxillofacial surgeon, educator; b. Nairobi, Kenya, Jan. 13, 1926; s. Jagdish Rai and Tara V. K.; m. Santosh Ved Chabra, Oct. 11, 1952; children: Ashok M., Siddarth M. Student, U. Cambridge, 1945; L.D.S., Edinburgh Dental Hosp. and Sch., 1950, Coll. Dental Surgeons, Sask., Can., 1962. Prof. oral surgery, dir. postdoctoral studies in oral surgery Sch. Dentistry U. Calif., San Francisco, 1968—; chief oral surgery San Francisco Gen. Hosp.; lectr. oral surgery U. of Pacific, VA Hosp.; vis. cons. Fresno County Hosp. Dental Clinic.; Mem. planning com., exec. med. com. San Francisco Gen. Hosp. Contbr. articles to profl. jours. Examiner in photography and gardening Boy Scouts Am., 1971-73, Guatemala Clinic, 1972. Granted personal coat of arms by H.M. Queen Elizabeth II, 1959. Fellow Royal Coll. Surgeons (Edinburgh), Internat. Assn. Oral Surgeons, Internat. Coll. Applied Nutrition, Internat. Coll. Dentists, Royal Soc. Health, AAAS, Am. Coll. Dentists; mem. Brit. Assn. Oral Surgeons, Am. Soc. Oral Surgeons, Am. Dental Soc. Anesthesiology, Am. Acad. Dental Radiology, Omicron Kappa Upsilon. Club: Masons. Home: 1525 Lakeview Dr Hillsborough CA 94010-7330 Office: U Calif Sch Dentistry Oral Surgery Div 3D Parnassus Ave San Francisco CA 94117-4342

KHOURI, GEORGE GEORGE, ophthalmologist; b. Beirut, Lebanon, May 24, 1957; came to U.S., 1976; BA summa cum laude, Rollins Coll., 1978; MD, Am. U. of Beirut, 1983. Diplomate Am. Bd. Ophthalmology. Intern in internal medicine Am. U. Hosp. and Med. Ctr., Beirut, 1982-83; rsch. fellow in ocular pharmacology and physiology Wilmer Inst., Johns Hopkins Hosp., Balt., 1983-84; resident in ophthalmology U. Chgo. Hosps. and Clinics, 1984-87; clin. fellow Retina Assocs. & Schepens Eye Rsch. Inst. Mass. Eye and Ear Infirmary/Harvard Med. Sch., Boston, 1987-88; asst. prof. Tufts U. Sch. Medicine, Boston, 1988-92; staff ophthalmologist Dept. Vets. Affairs Med. Ctr., Boston, 1988-92, Malden (Mass.) Hosp., 1992-93, Melrose (Mass.)-Wakefield Hosp., 1992-93; pvt. practice West Palm Beach, Fla., 1994—; presenter in field. Contbr. articles to profl. publs. Vol. eye surgeon Aravind Eye Hosp., India, 1993, Lumbini (Nepal) Eye Hosp., 1993, Nepal Eye Hosp., Kathmandu, 1993, Lighthouse for Christ Eye Ctr., Mombasa, Kenya, 1993. Eye rsch. grantee Mass. Lions, 1992-93, VA, 1990-92. Fellow Am. Acad. Ophthalmology. Office: Palm Beaches Eye Ctr Ste 2 2540 Metrocentre Blvd West Palm Beach FL 33407

KHOURY, ADA CELESTE, psychiatrist; b. San Antonio, Jan. 31, 1964; d. Mounir Salem and Nancy Joanne (Whitley) K. BS, Tex. A&M U., 1986, MD, 1988. Diplomate Am. Bd. Psychiatry and Neurology, Forensic Medicine. Officer house staff U. N.C. Hosps., Chapel Hill, 1988-92; med. dir. geropsychiat. svcs. McQuistion Regional Med. Ctr., Paris, Tex., 1992-93; staff psychiatrist Northeast Cmty. Mental Health, Memphis, 1993; acting med. dir. St. Vincent Health Ctr., Erie, Pa., 1993; staff psychiatrist S.W. Va. Mental Health Inst., Marion, 1993-94, Overlook Ctr., Knoxville, Tenn., 1994-95; pvt. practice Asheville, N.C., 1995—. Mem. AMA (Physicians Recognition award 1996), Am. Psychiat. Assn., Am. Group Psychotherapy Assn. Office: 860 Merrimon # 344 Asheville NC 28804

KHOUZAM, HANI RAOUL, psychiatrist, physician, educator; b. Heliopolis, Egypt, June 5, 1950; came to U.S., 1980; s. Raoul Aniss Khouzam and Jeannette (Guindi) Roufael; m. Lynda Margaret Dickerson, Nov. 20, 1982; children: Andrea Adahlia, Andrew Amaris. MB BCh, Faculty Medicine Cairo, Egypt, 1977; MPH, Tulane U., 1981. Diplomate Am. Bd. Psychiatry and Neurology with added qualifications in Geriatric Psychiatry; cert. ednl. commn. fgn. med. grads. Med. house officer Cairo U. Teaching Hosps., 1978-79; psychiatrist Shaalan M.D., Inc., Cairo, 1979-80; rsch. scholar Okla. Med. Rsch. Found., Oklahoma City, 1981-82; nursing asst. Four Seasons Nursing Ctr., Oklahoma City, 1982-83; resident in psychiatry U. Okla. Health Scis. Ctr., Oklahoma City, 1983-87; staff psychiatrist Okla. County Crisis Intervention Ctr., Oklahoma City, 1987-90; med. dir., inpatient psychiatry unit VA Med. Ctr., Oklahoma City, 1990-92; dir. consultation liaison psychiatry VA Med. Ctr., Manchester, N.H., 1992—; asst. prof. psychiatry dept. psychiatry and behavioral scis. Coll. Medicine U. Okla., Oklahoma City, 1987-92; adj. asst. prof. psychiatry Dartmouth Med. Sch., Lebanon, N.H., 1995—; clin. instr. in medicine Harvard Med. Sch., Boston, 1994—. Author: Emergency Psychiatric Interventions, 1988; contbr. to profl. jours. Hubert H. Humphrey fellow in pub. health, USIA, New Orleans, 1980-81. Fellow Egyptian Sci. Soc.; mem. Egyptian Med. Assn., Am. Psychiatric Assn., N.H. Psychiatric Soc. Coptic Catholic Christian. Home: 5 Terrace Rd Concord NH 03301-3138 Office: VA Med Ctr 718 Smyth Rd Manchester NH 03104-4098

KHUBCHANDANI, INDRU TEKCHAND, colon and rectal surgeon; b. Karachi, India; s. Tekchand and Sarsati Khubchandani; m. Lynne Adderley, July 11, 1965; children—Joya, Mona, Sonya. M.D., Grant Med. Coll., Bombay, India, 1956; postgrad. Royal Coll. Surgeons, Eng., 1960. Diplomate Am. Bd. Colon and Rectal Surgeons. Fellowship in gen. surgery New Eng. Hosp., Boston, 1961-62; residency Temple U. Med. Sch., Phila., 1962-64; chief div. colon and rectal surgery Healtheast Teaching Hosps. Allentown, Pa., 1979-93, also program dir. colon and rectal residency, bd. dirs., 1983-93; prof. surgery Pa. State U. Hershey Med. Sch.; bd. dirs. Healtheast, Slate Belt Med. Ctr.; prof. surgery Hanneman U. assoc. U. Pa. Mem. editorial bd. Jour. ColoProctology, 1980—, Phila. Jour. Diseases of Colon and Rectum, Revista Brasileira de ColoProctologia. Pres. Harry E. Bacon Found., 1985; fund raiser Republican Party. Recipinet medal of honor Assn. Latin Americana De Coloproctolgia. Fellow Royal Coll. Surgeons (Edinburgh); mem. Am. Soc. Colon and Rectal Surgeons (chmn. sci. and comml. exhibits 1979-94, Best Paper awards 1970, 81, Rowell award 1985), Am. Gastroenterological Soc., Cuban Soc. Coloproctology (hon.), Assn. Surgeons India, Assn. Colon and Rectal Surgeons India (pres.), Royal Soc. Medicine, N.E. Soc. Colon and Rectal Surgeons (pres.), Pa. Soc. Colon and Rectal Surgeons (pres.), Internat. Soc. Univ. Colon and Rectal Surgeons (dir. gen. 1980—), Chilean Soc. Coloproctology (hon.), Venezuelan Soc. Colon and Rectal Surgeons (hon.), Sociedad Gallegade De Patologia Digestiva, La Coruna, Spain (hon.), Brazilian Soc. Colon and Rectal Surgeons (hon.), Hindu Club, Lehigh Country Club, Contemporary Club, Pa. Soc. Club, Rotary, Masons. Office: 1275 S Cedar Crest Blvd Allentown PA 18103-6207

KIBRICK, ANNE, nursing educator, university dean; b. Palmer, Mass., June 1, 1919; d. Martin and Christine (Grigas) Karlon; m. Sidney Kibrick, June 16, 1949; children: Joan, John. RN, Worcester (Mass.) Hahnemann Hosp., 1941; BS, Boston U., 1945; MA, Columbia Tchrs. Coll., 1948; EdD, Harvard U., 1958; LHD (hon.), St. Joseph's Coll., Windham, Maine, 1973. Asst. edn. dir. Cushing VA Hosp., Framingham, Mass., 1948-49; asst. prof. nursing Simmons Coll., Boston, 1949-55; dir. grad. div. Boston U. Sch. Nursing, 1958-63, dean, 1963-68, prof., 1968-70; chmn. dept. nursing Boston Coll. Grad. Sch. Arts and Sci., 1970-74; chmn. sch. nursing Boston State Coll., 1974-82; dean Sch. Nursing U. Mass., Boston, 1974-88, prof., 1988-93, prof. emeritus, 1993—; cons. div. nursing USPHS, 1964-68; cons. Nat. Student Nurses Assn., 1985-88; mem. nat. adv. council nurse tng. USPHS, NIH, 1968-73; cons. Hebrew U.-Hadassah Med. Orgn., Jerusalem, 1971—; mem. Inst. Medicine of Nat. Acad. Scis., 1972—, mem. steering com. costs of edn. of health professions, 1972-74; mem. Nat. Med. Audiovisual Tng. Center, 1972-76, Gov.'s Com. and Area Bd. Mental Health and Mental Retardation, Nat. Commn. for Study Nursing and Nursing Edn., 1970-73; mem. faculty com., regent's external degree program in nursing SUNY, 1974-82; mem. hosp. mgmt. bd. U. Hosp., U. Mass., 1976-81; dir. Medic Alert, Am. Jour. Nursing Co.; cons. Cumberland Coll. Health Scis., New South Wales, Australia, 1986, Menoufia U., Shibin El Kom, Egypt, 1987. Mem. editorial bd. Mass. Jour. Community Health. Bd. dirs. Brookline Mental Health Assn., Met. chpt. ARC, Children's Ctr. Brookline and Greater boston, Inc., 1984-89, Boston Health Care for Homeless, 1988-90; bd. dirs. Landy-Kaplan Nurses Coun., 1992—, treas., 1994—; mem. Brookline Town Meeting, 1995—; mem. nat. adv. com. Hadassah Nurses Coun., 1996—. Fellow Am. Acad. Nursing; mem. Nat. Mass. Leagues Nursing (pres. 1971-73), Am. Nurses Assn., Mass. Nurses Assn. (dir. 1982-86), AIDS Internat. Info. Found. (founding mem. 1985), Mass. Nurses Found. (v.p. 1983-86), Nat. Acads. of Practice, Mass. Med. Soc. (bd. dirs. postgrad. med. inst. 1983—, exec. com. 1989—), Mass. Blueprint 2000, Sigma Theta Tau, Pi Lambda Theta. Home: 381 Clinton Rd Brookline MA 02146-4146

KICLITER, E(RNEST) EARL, JR., anatomy educator, researcher; b. Fort Pierce, Fla., June 19, 1945; s. Ernest Earl and Betty Lloyd (Winn) K.; m. Nidza Lugo, Aug. 29, 1993; 1 child, Jennifer Alicia. AB, U. Fla., 1968; PhD, SUNY, Syracuse, 1973. Postdoctoral fellow in neurosurgery U. Va., Charlottesville, 1972-74; asst. prof. neuroanatomy and physiology U. Ill., Urbana, 1974-77; assoc. prof. anatomy U. P.R., Med. Scis. Campus, San Juan, 1977-84, prof., 1984—. Fellow NSF, 1967, Ford Found., 1967-68, NIH, 1968-74; grantee: NIH, 1976—, Nat. Acad. Sci., 1976. Fellow AAAS; mem. Am. Assn. Anatomists, Cajal Club, J.B. Johnston Club, Soc. Neuroscience, Sigma Xi. Contbr. articles to profl. jours.; research in comparative structure and function of vertebrate visual systems and color vision. Home: A-8 Argentina St Gardenville Devel Guaynabo PR 00966 Office: Inst Neurobiology Blvd Del Valle 201 San Juan PR 00901

KIDAMBI, ANANTACHARY VENKATACHARY, radiologist; b. Chandrapur, India, May 1, 1946; s. Venkatachary Rangachary and Vasumati (Swamy) K.; m. Hema Jain, Dec. 5, 1973; children: Deepali, Ajay. BSc, Nagpur U., 1963; MB BS, Govt. Med. Coll., Nagpur, India, 1968. Cons. radiologist Altnagelvin Hosp., Londonderry, Northern Ireland, 1977-86, Gen. Hosp., Hartlepool, Eng., 1986—; dir. acute avcs. Hartlepool Health Authority, 1990-94; clin. dir. radiology Hartlepool & Peterlee Hosps. NHS Trust, 1990-96; acting chief exec. Hartlepool Health Unit, 1993. Chmn. Overseas Drs. Assn. Northern Ireland, 1978-86. Fellow Royal Coll. Radiologists; mem. Brit. Med. Assn. Home: 15 Hardwick Ct, Hartlepool TX26 0AZ, England Office: Gen Hosp Hartlepool, Holdforth Rd, Hartlepool TS24 9AH, England

KIDAWA, ANTHONY STANLEY, podiatrist, educator; b. Phila., Apr. 1, 1942; s. Felicia H. (Kopczynski) K.; m. Nancy A. Skokowski, Sept. 20, 1969; children: Kevin, Lori. BS, Villanova U., Pa., 1964; D of Podiatric Med., Pa. Coll. Podiatric Medicine, Phila., 1969. Podiatric cons. We. Jersey Hosp. Central Div., Camden, N.J., 1970-72; active staff Girard Med. Ctr., Phila., 1971-89; courtesy admit staff John F. Kennedy Memorial Hosp., Turnersville, N.J., 1973-89; from chmn. dept. med to section chief Pa. Coll. of Podiatric Med., Phila., 1976—; rotating dir. Foot Health Ctr., Phila., 1981-83; nat. speaker panel Hoechst-Roussel Pharm. Co., Sommerville, N.J., 1987—; dir. pres. Clindialab, Inc., Phila., 1984—; editl. cons. Current Podiatric Med. Publ., N.Y.C., 1982-85; contbg. editor Year Book of Podiatric Med., Chgo., 1984, Podiatry Tracts, Phila., 1987—, manuscript rev. Pan Jour. of Am. Podiatric Med., Bethesda, 1989—. Researcher Clinical Angiology Nerve Block Study, 1984 (Bronze award 1985; author: Articles & Abstract Periph Circulation, 1984; co-author film Toenail Burr Tech., 1987. Organizer Clindialab, Inc., Phila, 1989—; judge Lions Club Miss Am. Prelim, Glassboro, N.J., 1990. Research Grantee Collagen Corp, Phila, 1985, Leggs Corp., 1986, Aris-Isotoner Corp., 1987, Becton-Dickenson Corp, 1988, Zimmer Corp, 1989. Fellow Am. Soc. Podiatric Med.; Mem. Alumni Assn. Pa. Coll. Podiatric Med. (pres. 1973). Roman Catholic. Home: 12 Autumnwood Ln Mount Laurel NJ 08054 Office: PA Coll Podiatric Med 810 Race St Philadelphia PA 19107-2406

KIDD, JAMES MARION, III, allergist, immunologist, educator; b. Baton Rouge, Dec. 15, 1950; s. James Marion Jr. and Germaine Elizabeth (Hunt) K.; m. Carolyn Ann Kelley, Apr. 29, 1981; children: Mackenzie Elizabeth, Katherine Anne. MD, La. State U., 1976. Diplomate Am. Bd. Internal Medicine, Am. Bd. Allergy and Immunology; lic. physician, La., Fla., Wis. Resident physician La. State U. Sch. Medicine, New Orleans, 1977-79; rsch. fellow Med. Coll. Wis., Milw., 1980-82; pvt. practice in allergy and immunology Allergy, Asthma, and Immunology Clinic, Baton Rouge, 1982—; clin. asst., prof. medicine La. Sch. Medicine, New Orleans, 1982—; clin. asst., prof. community medicine and pub. health Tulane U. Sch. Medicine, New Orleans, 1992—. Fellow Am. Coll. Physicians, Am. Acad. Pediat., Am. Acad. Allergy and Immunology, Am. Coll. Chest Physicians; mem. La. Allergy Soc. (pres. 1989-90, exec. sec.-treas. 1992-96), Baton Rouge Allergy Soc. (pres. 1990—), Robary (Paul Harris fellow). Office: James M Kidd III MD 8017 Picardy Ave Baton Rouge LA 70809-3538

KIDD, LYNDEN LOUISE, healthcare consultant; b. Casper, Wyo., May 7, 1959; d. David Thomas and Sally Louise (Noble) K. AA, Stephens Coll., 1979; BA in Polit. Sci., Comm., U. Wyo., 1981, JD, 1986. Adminstrv. dir. Wyo. Med. Ctr., Casper, 1986-92, v.p. med. affairs, 1992-95; consultant Next Iteration, Casper, 1995-96; assoc. APM Inc., Chgo., 1996—. Mem. Wyo. Heritage Soc., 1987-89, Gov.'s Coun. Sports and Fitness, Wyo., 1991-96; chmn., mem. Leadership Casper, 1989-91; bd. dirs., campaign chmn. United Way, Casper, 1989-96, pres., 1994-95; bd. dirs. Casper Classic, Inc., 1989-92. Mem. Am. Coll. Med. Staff Affairs, Nat. Health Lawyers Assn., Am. Coll. Healthcare Execs. (assoc.), Wyo. Hosp. Assn., Casper C. of C. (bd. dirs. 1991-94), Phi Alpha Delta. Home: 480 N McClurg Ct Apt 601 Chicago IL 60611 Office: APM Inc 30 N LaSalle Ste 2200 Chicago IL 60602

KIDD, NANCY VAN TRIES, psychologist, mediator; b. Huntingdon, Pa., June 5, 1933; d. Samuel Musser and Jesse Pauline (Haupt) Van Tries; children: Linda Rowley Tawfik, Joseph J. Rowley III, Bruce W. Rowley; m. 2d Jerome Thomas Kidd, May 23, 1970. BA in Journalism and Fine Arts, Pa. State U., 1955, EdD in Counseling and Psychology, 1977; MEd in Elem. Edn. and Ednl. Psychology, Temple U., 1969. Assoc. prof. psychology and counseling Community Coll. R.I., 1973-82; psychologist Child, Adult and Family Psychol. Ctr., State College, Pa., 1981-83; family mediator, counselor Ariz. Counseling Ctr., Phoenix, 1983; psychologist, mediator, dir. Psychol. and Counseling Resources, Richmond, 1985-96, Psychol. & Mediation Resources, Boalsburg, Pa., 1995—. Contbr. articles to profl. jours. Trustee Pa. State U., 1983—. Fellow Pa. Psychol. Assn; mem. Acad. Family Mediators, R.I. Personnel and Guidance Assn. (exec. bd. 1978-79), Pa. State Alumni Club, Phi Delta Kappa, Pi Lambda Theta, Kappa Kappa Gamma. Office: Psychol & Mediation Resources 173 Indian Hill Rd Boalsburg PA 16827

KIDD, THORNTON LENOIR, JR., allergist; b. San Antonio, Aug. 3, 1932; s. Thornton Lenoir and Lillian Beatrice (Watts) K.; 1 dau., Sharlyn Gail; m. Betty Louise., San Antonio Coll., 1950-51, Trinity U., 1951-52; student U. Tex., 1952-53, MD, 1957. Diplomate Am. Bd. Pediatrics, Am. Bd. Allergy and Immunology, Am. Bd. Allergy. Intern, Brackenridge Hosp., Austin, Tex., 1957-58; resident U. Tex. Med. Br.-Galveston, 1958-60, fellow in allergy, 1960-61 practice medicine specializing in allergy, Austin, 1963-64, Pasadena, Tex., 1964—; mem. staffs Bayshore Hosp., Southmore Hosp. Bd. regents Am. Coll. of Allergy; clin. instr. dept. family practice Health Sci. Dept. U. Tex., Houston; con. El Buen Samaritano, Aquismon, Mex. Served to lt. comdr. USPHS, 1961-63. Mem. Am. Coll. Allergists, Am. Assn. Cert. Allergists, Am. Coll. Chest Physicians, AMA, So. Med. Assn., Houston Allergy Soc. (pres. 1984-86), Asthma and Allergy Found. Am., Internat. Corr. Soc. Allergy, Tex. Med. Assn., Am. Assn. Clin. Immunology and Allergy, Am. Acad. Allergy. Republican. Baptist.

KIDDER, DAVID MONROE, physician; b. Reed City, Mich., Aug. 28, 1950; s. William Kidder and Eula (Johnson) Kidder Grace; m. Linda Lee Patten, Dec. 23, 1973; children: David William, Kristy Lynn. BS, U. S.C., 1968-74; EMT, paramedic III, Grand Valley State Coll., Grandville, Mich., 1974; DO, Phila. Coll. Osteo., 1978. Diplomate Am. Bd. Family Practice. Family physician Ekalaka (Mont.) Clinic & Hosp., 1979-81, Shelby (Mont.) Clinic, 1981-84, Powder River Clinic, Broadus, Mont., 1984-86, Grand Forks (N.D.) Clinic, 1986—. Co-contbr. aticles to profl. jours. Med.-surg. World Med. Missions, The Phillipines, 1982, Mex., 1991, Bangladesh, 1993; humanatarian relief med. Milk & Honey Ministries, Russia, 1992. Fellow Am. Acad. Family Practice; mem. Am. Acad. Family Physicians, Am. Osteo. Assn., Minn. Med. Bd. (discipline com. 1992, 94, drug diversion com. 1994, pres. bd. 1994). Baptist. Home: HCR 75 Box 12 Pitt MN 56623 Office: Northland Clinic 850 East Side Rd Deer Lodge MT 59722

KIEFER, HELEN CHILTON, neurologist, psychiatrist; b. Washington; d. Frank McGlowing and Sue (Stanford) Chilton; m. John Harold Kiefer, Feb. 4, 1961 (div. July 1971); 1 child, Steven Chilton. AB in Chemistry magna cum laude, Cornell U., 1961; MS, U. Chgo., 1971, PhD in Biochemistry, 1971; MD with honors, Northwestern U., 1981. Lic. physician, Ill.; diplomate Nat. Bd. Med. Examiners. Intern psychiatry and internal medicine Michael Reese Hosp. and Med. Ctr., Chgo., 1981-82; resident neurology U. Ill. Med. Sch., Chgo., 1983-85; physicist, computer programmer physics div. Los Alamos (N.Mex.) Sci. Labs., 1965—; asst. prof. dept biochemistry Northwestern U. Med. Sch., Chgo., 1972-78; editor Marcus Acad. Media, Chgo., 1978-81; clin. assoc. prof. dept. biochemistry Loyola Med. and Dental Sch., Chgo., 1978-81; med. staff Charter Barclay Neuropsychiat. Hosp., Chgo., 1983—; pvt. practice Chgo., 1983—; dir. med. rsch. for biotech., assoc. med. dir. high tech. Abbott Labs., Abbott Park, Ill., 1986-89; assoc. ctr. for biotechnology Northwestern U., 1992—; adj. assoc. prof. dept. biomed. engring. and grad. multidisciplinary program in neurosci. Northwestern U., Evanston, Ill., 1989-90, vis. prof., assoc. ctr. for biotech., 1992—; affiliate Internat. Human Genome Mapping Project, 1991—; vis. prof. dept. bioengring. U. Wash., Seattle, 1982-83; mem. presdl. adv. com. NIH, 1976-80; CEO, pres. The Doctor Cooks, Inc., 1995—; mem. numerous program project rev. bds., 1978-80. Woodrow Wilson fellow, NSF fellow, Danforth Found. fellow, NIH postdoctoral fellow. Mem. Assn. Clin. Scientists, N.Y. Acad. Scis., Phi Beta Kappa, Alpha Omega Alpha.

KIEFER, RENATA GERTRUD, pediatrician, economist, international health consultant; b. Lorrach, Baden, Germany, July 4, 1946; came to U.S., 1970; d. Friedrich W. and Gertrud Anna (Keller) K.; m. James C. Bridgman. BA, Stanford U., 1963; MA, U. Calif., Berkeley, 1967; MD, U. Geneva, Switzerland, 1982; MPH, U. Calif., Berkeley, 1990. Diplomate Am. Bd. Pediatrics; cert. in environ. health, Germany. Asst. instr. dissection lab. dept. morphology U. Geneva Sch. of Medicine, Switzerland, 1979-80; interim resident dept. diagnostic radiology Univ. Hosp., Geneva, 1980, intern physician, 1982-83; clin. fellow in pediatrics Harvard Med. Sch., Boston, 1983-85; resident physician Mass. Gen. Hosp., Boston, 1983-85; sr. resident dept. pediatrics U. Calif., San Francisco, 1985-86; attending physician emergency dept. Children's Hosp. Med. Ctr., Oakland, Calif., 1986-94; fellow dept. epidemiology and internat. health U. Calif., San Francisco, 1988-90; German tech. cooperation expert tropical medicine & internat. health Inst. for Health Sci. Rsch., Asuncion, Paraguay, 1990-94, vis. prof. epidemiol. and preventive medicine, 1992—; sci. methods advisor Nat. U. Asuncion, 1994—; chief adv. Health Strategies Internat.; rep. of IICS/Internat. Orgns., cons. and presenter in field. Contbr. numerous articles to profl. jours. Recipient Pub. Health Svc. Nat. Rsch. Svc. award, 1989-90; co-winner Nat. Sci. prize Paraguay Parliament, 1994; ASSU scholar Stanford U., 1962-63, Fulbright scholar, 1962-64, Internat. scholar Swedish Inst., 1968, Internat. Health scholar U. Calif., 1990; AAUW fellow, 1968. Address: 6 Locksley Ave San Francisco CA 94122-3839

KIEFFER, STEPHEN AARON, radiologist, educator; b. Mpls., Dec. 20, 1935; s. Julius Hyman and Anita Elaine (Brudnick) K.; m. Cyrile Frada Kaplan, Dec. 21, 1958; children: Alisa, Mitchell, Stuart, Paula. B.A. summa cum laude, U. Minn., 1956, B.S., 1957, M.D., 1959. Diplomate: Am. Bd. Radiology. Intern Wadsworth VA Hosp., Los Angeles, 1959-60; resident in radiology U. Minn. Hosps., Mpls., 1960-62, 64-65; NIH fellow in neuroradiology, 1966-68; instr. U. Minn. Med. Sch., Mpls., 1966-67; asst. prof. U. Minn. Med. Sch., 1967-68, asso. prof., 1968-72, prof., 1972-74; chief radiology service Mpls. VA Hosp., 1968-74; prof., chmn. dept. radiology SUNY-Health Sci. Ctr., Syracuse, 1974—, chmn. governing bd. clin. practice mgmt. plan, 1985-88; v.p., mem. med. bd., mem. med. exec. com. Univ. Hosp., 1988-93; cons. Syracuse VA Med. Center, Crouse-Irving-Meml. Hosp. Co-author: Introduction to Neuroradiology, 1972; co-editor: An Atlas of Cross-sectional Anatomy, 1979; contbr. numerous articles to profl. jours., also chpts. to books; editl. adv. bd. Radiology, 1980-85, assoc. editor, 1986, cons. to editor, 1987-93; cons. to editl. bd. Am. Jour. Neuroradiology, 1980—; assoc. editor: Yearbook of Radiology, 1981-86; editl. bd. RadiOGraphics, 1987-93. Chmn. tech. adv. subcom. on computed tomography Ctrl. N.Y. Health Systems Agy., 1979-80; mem. tech. adv. com. on computed tomography N.Y. State Office Health Systems Mgmt., 1981; bd. dirs. Syracuse Jewish Fedn., 1975-81, 90-96, v.p., 1990-93; bd. dirs. Academic Health Profls. Ins. Assn., 1991—. Capt. M.C. U.S. Army, 1962-64. Nat. Heart Inst. trainee, 1961-62; Nat. Inst. Neurol. Diseases and Blindness fellow, 1966; James Picker Found. scholar, 1966-68. Fellow Am. Coll. Radiology (councilor 1986-92); mem. AMA, Am. Roentgen Ray Soc. (publs. com. 1979-84), Am. Soc. Neuroradiology (pres. 1978-79, chmn standards for practice subcom. 1992-96, chmn. clin. outcomes rsch. com. 1996—), Assn. Univ. Radiologists (program com. 1985-86), Ctrl. N.Y. Radiol. Soc. (chmn. program com. 1979-82, chmn. socioeconomics com. 1994—), Ea. Neuroradiol. Soc. (pres. 1992-93), Med. Soc. State of N.Y., Minn. Radiol. Soc. (sec. 1974), Neurosurg. Soc. Am., Onondaga County Med. Soc., Radiol. Soc. N.Am. (refresher course com. 1977-82, program com. 1984-91), Soc. Chairmen Acad. Radiology Depts., N.Y. State Radiol. Soc. (v.p. 1985-86, pres. 1987-88), XVI Symposium Neuroradiologicum (v.p.). Jewish. Home: 503 Standish Dr Syracuse NY 13224-2015 Office: 750 E Adams St Syracuse NY 13210-2306

KIEFFER, SUSAN WERNER, management consultant; b. Warren, Pa., Nov. 17, 1942. BS in Physics and Math., Allegheny Coll., 1964; MS in Geol. Scis., Calif. Inst. Tech., 1967, PhD in Planetary Scis., 1971; DSc (hon.), Allegheny Coll., 1987. Postdoctoral research geochemist UCLA, 1971-73, asst. prof. geology, 1973-79; geologist U.S. Geol. Survey, Flagstaff, Ariz., 1979-90; prof. geology Ariz. State U., Tempe, 1988—, Regents prof., 1991-93; prof., dept. geol. sci. U. B.C., Vancouver, Can., 1993-95; co-founder Kieffer & Woo, Inc., Palgrave, Ont., Can., 1996—. Co-editor: (with A. Navrotsky) Microscopic to Macroscopic: Atomic Environments to Mineral Thermodynamics, 1985. Alfred P. Sloan Found. fellow, 1977-79; W.H. Mendenhall lectr., U.S. Geol. Survey, 1980; recipient Disting. Alumnus award Calif. Inst. Tech., 1982, Meritorious Svc. award Dept. Interior, 1986, Spendiarov award Soviet Acad. of Scis., 1990, MacArthur fellow, 1995—, award for excellence in environ. health rsch. Lovelance Inst., Albuquerque, 1995. Fellow Am. Geophys. Union, Am. Acad. Arts and Scis., Mineral. Soc. Am. (award 1980), Geol. Soc. Am. (Arthur L. Day medal 1992), Meteoritical Soc.; mem. NAS. Office: Kieffer & Woo Inc, PO Box 130, Palgrave, ON Canada L0N 1P0

KIENKER, KAREN ANN, physical medicine and rehabilitation physician; b. Kansas City, Mo., Apr. 26, 1951; d. Kenneth Louis and Norma Clare (Innes) K. BA, Cen. Meth. Coll., 1973; MD, U. Ill., Rockford, 1977. Diplomate Am. Bd. Phys. Medicine and Rehab. Intern Columbus-Cuneo-Cabrini Med. Ctr., Chgo., 1978; resident in phys. medicine and rehab. Rehab.

Inst. Chgo., 1978-81; instr. U. Wis. Hosp. and Clinics, Madison, 1981-82, asst. prof., 1982-84; staff physiatrist Iowa Meth. Med. Ctr., Des Moines, 1984—; rehab. med. dir. Integrated Health Svcs., Des Moines, 1995—. Fellow Am. Acad. Phys. Medicine and Rehab.; mem. Am. Pain Soc. Democrat. Unitarian. Home: 8895 Summit Dr Clive IA 50325-5431 Office: Iowa Meth Med Ctr 1200 Pleasant St Y310 Des Moines IA 50309

KIERNAN, JUDITH ANN, health facility administrator, educator; b. South Weymouth, Mass., Nov. 19, 1937; d. Vincent Owen and Eunice (Warner) Kiernan; m. Robert Stanley Graff, Dec. 29, 1973 (div. Oct. 1983). Diploma, Mass. Meml. Hosp. Sch. Nursing, 1958; BSN, Boston U., 1961; MS in Nursing, U. Colo., Denver, 1965; PhD in Health Svcs. Adminstrn., U. Utah, 1992. RN, Utah; cert. nurse adminstr. advanced; cert. alt. dispute resolution. Nurse edn. advisor U.S. Agy. for Internat. Devel., Vietnam, 1969-71; dir. nursing Univ. Hosp., Boston, 1972-74; asst. prof. U. Utah Coll. Nursing, Salt Lake City, 1974-78, asst. prof., coord., 1978-81, clin. asst. prof., 1981-83; nurse cons. Intermountain Health Care, Inc., Salt Lake City, 1982-85; asst. prof. U. Utah Coll. Nursing, Salt Lake City, 1983-85, asst. prof., asst. dean, 1985-86, clin assoc. prof., 1986—; dir. nursing, med./surg. Univ. Hosp., Salt Lake City, 1986—; cons. Intermountain Health Care, Salt Lake City, 1982-83; lectr., speaker various orgns., 1986—. Contbr. articles to profl. jours. Recipient Medal of Civilian Svc., Min. Health, Vietnam, 1971, Danforth Found. nomination. Mem. ANA, Utah Nurses Assn. (Ednl. Adminstrn. award 1981, Excellence in Nurse Adminstrn. award 1995), Western Inst. Nursing (gov. representing nursing practice 1991—), Western Soc. Rsch. in Nursing, Am. Orgn. Nurse Execs. (commr., policy/legis. advocacy), Am. Arbitration Assn. (panelist). Democrat. Episcopalian. Home: 525 2nd Ave Apt 8 Salt Lake City UT 84103-2930 Office: Univ Utah Hosp 50 N Medical Dr Rm 1540 Salt Lake City UT 84132

KIERSCH, THEODORE ALAN, oral surgeon; b. Temple, Tex., Nov. 25, 1943; s. Theodore Alexander and Mary (Omel) K.; m. Malinda Kay Masterson, Aug. 23, 1953; children: Deborah, Tanner, Tiffany. BS, U. Ill., Urbana, 1966; DDS, Chgo. Coll. Dental Surgery, 1970. Diplomate Am. Bd. Oral and Maxillofacial Surgery. Chief dept. oral surgery El Dorado Med. Ctr., Tucson, 1985-87; practice dentistry specializing in oral and maxillofacial surgery Tucson Med. Ctr., St. Joseph's Hosp., Tucson; assoc. prof. of surgery U. Ariz. Med. Sch., Tucson; med. staff mem. Tucson Crippled Children's Clinic; cons. Vets. Hosp., Tucson; assoc. prof. U. Ariz. Med. Ctr. Hosp., Tucson. Contbr. scholarly articles to profl. jours. Fellow Am. Coll. Oral and Maxillofacial Surgeons, Internat. Assn. Oral and Maxillofacial Surgeons; mem. Am. Assn. Oral and Maxillofacial Surgeons, Ariz. Soc. Oral and Maxillofacial Surgeons (pres. 1981-83), ALA, So. Ariz. Dental Soc., Western Soc. Oral and Maxillofacial Surgeons, Rocky Mountain Soc. Oral Surgeons, Alpha Delta Phi, Xi Psi Phi. Office: 801 N Wilmot Rd Tucson AZ 85711-1711

KIERSKI, JOZEF, gynecologist, obstetrician; b. Warsaw, Poland, May 9, 1935; s. Aleksander and Aniela (Brazert) K.; m. Krystyna Widy, Jan. 6, 1961; 1 child, Aleksander. MD, Med. Sch., Warsaw, 1958, PhD, 1969; MS in Med. Demography, London U., 1977. Intern, 1957-58, resident, 1959-66; asst., sr. asst., lectr., sr. lectr. Med. Acad., Warsaw, 1958-71; head family health dept. WHO Inst. Pub. Health, Constantine, Algeria, 1971-75; family heath advisor WHO, Govt. of Fiji, Suva, 1976-79; med. rsch. officer Ministry Health, Warsaw, 1979-81; team leader WHO Sterilization Program, Dhaka, Bangladesh, 1982-84; med. officer Family Health div. WHO, Geneva, 1984-95, ret. Co-author: Obstetrics and Gynecology, 1968, Early Diagnosis of Cervical Cancer, 1969. Fellow Internat. Acad. Cytology; mem. Brit. Soc. Clin. Cytology. Home: 11 Av Krieg, 1208 Geneva Switzerland

KIERULFF, STEPHEN, clinical psychologist; b. Los Angeles, June 17, 1942; s. Charles Taylor and Barbara Phillips K.; m. Carol Winter, June 14, 1970 (div. Nov. 1983); 1 child, Benjamin. B.A. in Cultural Anthropology, U. Calif.-Berkeley, 1963; M.A., William Paterson Coll., Wayne, N.J., 1971-74; Ph.D. in Psychology, U.S. Internat. U., San Diego, 1980. Lic. psychologist, Calif.; lic. marriage and family counselor, Calif. Intern, Wyandotte Gen. Hosp., Mich., 1979-80; asst. prof. Chapman Coll., San Diego, 1980; psychol. asst. Psychology & Psychiatry Ctr., Los Angeles, 1982-83; pvt. practice clin. psychology, Santa Monica, Calif., 1983—; mem. faculty Antioch U., Los Angeles, 1982, Calif. State U., Long Beach, 1983-84, U.S. Internat. U., Glendale, 1984-91, Profl. Sch. Psychology Studies, 1986. Contbr. articles to profl. jours. Recipient State of Calif. Scholarship award, 1959. Mem. APA, Calif. Psychol. Assn., Assn. Humanistic Psychology, Psi Chi. Office: 110 S La Brea Ave Ste 220 Inglewood CA 90301 also: 3201 Wilshire Blvd Ste 201 Santa Monica CA 90403

KIEWRA, GUSTAVE PAUL, psychologist, educator; b. Garden City Park, N.Y., July 25, 1943; s. Gustave Francis and Alice (Kozyrski) K.; m. Donna Elaine Womack, Nov. 29, 1969; children: Amy Marie, Christopher Paul, Jessica Lauren. BA, Franklin Coll., 1967; MA, Ball State U., 1968, EdD, 1972. Instr. psychology Fla. Jr. Coll., Jacksonville, 1968-70; counselor, asst. prof. counselor edn. Western Ky. U., Bowling Green, 1972-76; prof. psychology Piedmont Va. C.C., Charlottesville, 1976—; mem. psychology peer group planning com. Va. C.C. Sys., 1996; mem. bldg. com. Piedmont Va. C.C., 1993-96, planning coun., 1996—. Bd. dirs. Western Albemarle Rescue Squad, Crozet, Va., 1987, 88, Am. Lung Assn., Charlottesville, 1986-88; coord. Neighborhood Watch, Crozet, 1985-96; mem. sch. improvement com. Crozet Elem. Sch., 1990-91; mem. Piedmont (Va.) Cmty. Coll. Planning Coun., 1995-96. Recipient svc. award Piedmont Va. C.C., 1981, 86, 91. Mem. APA, Va. Psychol. Assn., Am. Assn. Marriage and Family Counselors, Va. C.C. Assn. (rep. faculty affairs com. 1990-92), Faculty Profl. Assn., Internat. Platform Assn., Lions (pres. Crozet, Va. 1989-92, Key award 1991, Advancement Key award 1991, Master Key award 1992, 100% Pres. award 1990-92, Dist. Gov. Membership Growth award 1990-92, Va. Multiple Dist. 24 Achievement award 1990-92, Pres. Svc. Appreciation award 1992, Achievement award medal 1992, Melvin Jones fellow Internat. Found.), Phi Delta Kappa, Phi Theta Kappa (hon., faculty advisor 1980-88), Phi Delta Theta. Home: 1440 Birchwood Dr Crozet VA 22932-9441 Office: Piedmont Va CC RR 6 Box 1 Charlottesville VA 22902-9806

KIHARA, YASUKI, cardiology and cellular physiology educator; b. Hiroshima, Japan, Feb. 8, 1955; s. Yasuhiko and Keiko (Yamate) K.; m. Miho Yukitoshi, Oct. 7, 1979; children: Momoko, Yuzuko, Ryo. MD, Kyoto (Japan) U., 1979, PhD, 1986. Jr. resident in medicine Tenri (Japan) Hosp., 1979-81, sr. resident in medicine, 1981-82; clin. fellow Kyoto U. Hosp., 1986; rsch. fellow Harvard Med. Sch., Boston, 1986-87, instr. in medicine, 1987-89; asst. prof. medicine Toyama (Japan) Med. and Pharm. U., 1989-93, Kyoto (Japan) U. Grad. Sch. Medicine, 1993—; dir. inpatient clinic cardiovascular medicine Toyama (Japan) Med. and Pharm. U., 1992—. Contbr. articles to profl. jours. Grantee Yamanouchi Found., 1986, Tamura Found., 1990, Ministry of Edn., Culture and Sci., 1990, 91, 92, 95, 96, Japan Heart Found., 1991; recipient Sagawa Young Investigators award Cardiovascular System Dyamics Soc., 1992. Fellow Am. Coll. Cardiology (assoc.); mem. AAAS, Japanese Soc. Internal Medicine (specialty bd. internal medicine), Japanese Circulation Soc. (specialty bd. cardiology), Am. Heart Assn. (affiliate), Sigma Xi. Roman Catholic. Office: Kyoto U Hosp-Dept Cardiovascular Med, 54 Shogoin, Sakyo, Kyoto 606, Japan

KIKOLER, DAVID JONATHAN, gastroenterologist; b. Detroit; s. Sigmund and Dorothy (Javna) K.; m. Beverly Elaine Katanick, Aug. 22, 1971; children: Jennifer, Jason. BA, Wayne State U., 1969, MS, 1971; DO, Chgo. Coll. Osteo. Medicine, 1976. Pvt. practice Kalamazoo, 1983-87, Ingersoll Diagnostic Ctr., Des Moines, Iowa, 1987-90, Ctrl. Iowa Gastroenterology, Des Moines, Iowa, 1990—; adj. asst. prof. medicine U. Osteo. Medicine and Health Scis., Des Moines, 1988—; chmn. dept. medicine Des Moines Gen. Hosp., 1993-94; chief of medicine Broadlawns Med. Ctr., Des Moines, 1994—; med. dir. at large, Iowa/Nebr. Soc. for Enterol. and Peroral. Nutrition, Des Moines, 1993. Contbr. articles to sci. and profl. jours. Mem. ACP, Am. Soc. Gastrointestinal Endoscopy, Am. Coll. Gastroenterology, Am. Gastroenterol. Assn. Office: Ctrl Iowa Gastroenterology 4116 University Des Moines IA 50311-3533

KIKOVA, VIERA HELGA, medical librarian; b. Bratislava, Czechoslovakia, Jan. 27, 1954; d. Jan and Olga (Pastori) Čík; m. Marian Kika, Sept. 2, 1978; 1 child, Thomas. PhD, Comenius U., Bratislava, 1982. Ref. libr. State Sci. Libr., Banska Bystrica, Czechoslovakia, 1978-80; reference libr. Regional Hosp., Banska Bystrica, Czechoslovakia, 1978-84; chief med. libr. F.D. Roosevelt Hosp., Banska Bystrica, Slovakia, 1984—. Mem. Czech Red Cross/Slovak Red Cross, 1978—. Mem. Soc. Slovak Librs., Slovak Med. Soc. Roman Catholic. Office: F D Roosevelt Hosp, Medical Library, L Svobodu 1, 975 17 Banska Bystrica Slovakia

KIKUCHI, HIDEAKI, molecular geneticist, researcher; b. Yokohama, Kanagawa, Japan, Sept. 3, 1948; s. Yoshiaki and Norkio (Furuno) K.; m. Kyoko Suzuki, Sept. 23, 1948; children: Naoko, Fumiaki. BS, Tohoku U., Sendai, Japan, 1971, MS, 1973, PhD, 1979. Rsch. asst. Rsch. Inst. for TB & Cancer Tohoku U., Sendai, 1973-83; postdoctoral fellow M.D. Anderson Hosp. & Tumor Inst. U. Tex. Sys. Cancer Ctr., Houston, 1983-85; rsch. assoc. Rsch. Inst. for TB & Cancer Tohoku U., Sendai, 1985-87, assoc. prof. Inst. Devel., Aging & Cancer, 1987—. Mem. Japanese Cancer Assn., Japanese Biochem. Soc., Molecular Biology Soc. Japan. Home: Kamo 1-24-9 Izumi-ku, 981-31 Sendai Miyagi, Japan Office: Tohoku U, Inst Devel Aging Cancer, 4-1 Seiryo-machi Aoba-ku, 980-77 Sendai Miyagi, Japan

KILBOURNE, BARBARA JEAN, health and human services consultant; b. Milw., Mar. 21, 1941; d. Burton Conwell and Marjorie Janet (Tufts) K.; m. Kenneth Keith Kauffman, Feb. 10, 1962 (div. 1983). BA, U. Minn., 1972; MBA, Coll. St. Thomas, St. Paul, 1980. Adminstr. Ebenezer Soc., Mpls., 1974-85; v.p., dir. housing Walker Residence and Health Svcs., Inc., Mpls., 1985-88; exec. v.p. Oblate Ministries Health and Aging, West St. Paul, Minn., 1988-94; cons., 1995—; pres. Barbara J. Kilbourne, Ltd., 1996—; bd. dirs. Westminster Resident Svcs. Corp., St. Paul, chmn., 1996—, River Region Health Svcs., Red Wing, Minn., chmn. seminary plaza, 1995—, St. Olaf Residence; mem. commn. on aging Cath. Charities USA, Washington, 1989—; presenter, cons. and spkr. in field. Author: Family Councils in Nursing Homes, 1981. Chmn. bd. dirs. Dakota Inc., Eagan, Minn., 1985-96, Minn. Assn. Homes for Aging, 1991-92, Sem. Plz., Red Wing, 1995; project chair Dialog 2000, Dakota County, Minn., 1988-91. Episcopalian. Home: 1021 Sibley Memorial Hwy Lilydale MN 55118-6100

KILBOURNE, EDWIN DENNIS, virologist, educator; b. Buffalo, July 10, 1920; s. Edwin I. and Elizabeth (Alward) K.; m. Joy Schmid, Dec. 20, 1952; children: Edwin Michael, Richard Schmid, Christopher Norton, Paul Alward. AB, Cornell U., 1942, MD, 1944; DSc honoris causa, Rockefeller U., 1986. Asst. Rockefeller Inst., 1948-51; mem. faculty Tulane U., 1951-55, Cornell U. Med. Coll., N.Y.C., 1955-68; prof. pub. health, dir. div. virus research Cornell U. Med. Coll., 1961-68; prof., chmn. dept. microbiology Mt. Sinai Sch. Medicine, City U. New York, 1968-86, disting. service prof., 1986-92; rsch. prof. N.Y. Med. Coll., 1992—; chmn., bd. dirs. Aaron Diamond AIDS Rsch. Ctr. for the City N.Y., 1989-94. Author: (with Wilson G. Smillie) Human Ecology and Public Health, 4th edit, 1968, Influenza, 1987; Editor: The Influenza Viruses and Influenza, 1975. Mem. Health Research Council N.Y.C., 1968-75. Recipient R.E. Dyer Lectureship award NIH, 1973, Borden award Assn. Am. Med. Colls., 1974, Dowling Lectureship award, 1976, Thomas Francis Lectureship award, 1976, Nat. Acad. Scis. 1977, Harvey Lectureship award, 1978, award of distinction Cornell U. Med. Alumni Assn., 1979, acad. medal N.Y. Acad. Medicine, 1982, Jacobi Medallion award Mt. Sinai Alumni Assn., 1991, Fogarty scholar award NIH, 1992. Fellow N.Y. Acad. Scis., Am. Philos. Soc.; mem. Harvey Soc., Soc. Clin. Rsch., Ctrl. Soc. Clin. Rsch. (emeritus), AAAS, Am. Assn. Immunologists, Am. Acad. Microbiology, Soc. Exptl. Biology and Medicine, Am. Soc. Clin. Investigation (emeritus), N.Y. Acad. Medicine, Am. Pub. Health Assn., Assn. Am. Physicians, Am. Soc. Microbiology, Infectious Diseases Soc. Am. Home: 23 Willard Ave Madison CT 06443-3202 Office: NY Med Coll Dept Microbiology/Immunology Valhalla NY 10595

KILBURN, KAYE HATCH, medical educator; b. Logan, Utah, Sept. 20, 1931; d. H. Parley and Winona (Hatch) K.; m. Gerrie Griffin, June 7, 1954; children: Ann Louise, Scott Kaye, Jean Marie. BS, U. Utah, 1951, MD, 1954. Diplomate Am. Bd. Internal Medicine, Am. Bd. Preventive Medicine. Asst. prof. Med. Sch. Washington U., St. Louis, 1960-62; assoc. prof., chief of medicine Durham (N.C.) VA Hosp., 1962-69; prof., dir. environ. medicine Duke Med. Ctr., Durham, 1969-73; prof. medicine and environ. medicine U. Mo., Columbia, 1973-77; prof. medicine and cmty. medicine CUNY Mt. Siai Med. Sch., 1977-80; Ralph Edgington prof. medicine U. So. Calif. Sch. Medicine, L.A., 1980—; pres. Neurotest Inc., 1988—; pres. Workers Disease Detection Svc. Inc., 1986-95. Editor-in-chief Archives of Environ. Health, 1986—; editor Jour. Applied Physiology, 1970-80, Environ. Rsch., 1975—, Am. Jour. Indsl. Medicine, 1980—; contbr. more than 200 articles to profl. jours. Capt. M.C., U.S. Army, 1958-60. Home: 3250 Mesaloa Ln Pasadena CA 91107-1129 Office: U So Calif Sch Medicine 2025 Zonal Ave Los Angeles CA 90033-4526

KILDAHL, JOHN PHILLIP, clinical psychologist; b. Owatonna, Minn., Dec. 24, 1927; s. Johan Lauritz and Edith Amanda (Glasoe) K.; B.A., St. Olaf Coll., 1949; B.D., Luther Theol. Sem., 1953; Ph.D., N.Y.U., 1957; cert. psychoanalysis Postgrad. Center for Mental Health, 1957; m. Joyce Peterson, Aug. 12, 1951; children—Kent, Margit, Lisa, Karl, Ann. Practice psychotherapy and psychoanalysis, N.Y.C., 1957—; prof. pastoral psychology N.Y. Theol. Sem., 1967-92; mem. faculty Postgrad. Center for Mental Health, 1966—; vis. lectr. univs. Wis., Minn., Colo., Switzerland, Japan, Hong Kong, New Zealand; mem. profl. adv. com. Bklyn. Psychiat. Centers, 1963-67; Mem. edn. com. Town Club, Scarsdale, 1971-75; basketball coach Scarsdale Recreation Dept., 1969-71; trustee N.Y. Theol. Sem., 1969-71; trustee Bklyn. Assn. Mental Health, 1963-67. Served with USN, 1945-46. Grantee, NIMH, Am. Luth. Ch. Mem. Am. Psychol. Assn., N.Y. Psychol. Assn., N.Y. Soc. Clin. Psychology, AAUP. Lutheran. Clubs: Highlands Lakes Country, Tennis of Palm Beach, Fox Meadow Tennis. Author: The Dynamics of Personality, 1970; The Psychology of Speaking in Tongues, 1972, Beyond Negative Thinking, 1989. Office: 120 E 62nd St New York NY 10021-8149

KILDE, SANDRA JEAN, nurse anesthetist, educator, consultant; b. Eau Claire, Wis., June 25, 1938; d. Harry Meylan and Beverly June (Johnson) K. Diploma Luther Hosp. Sch. Nursing, Eau Claire, 1959; grad. anesthesia course Mpls. Sch. Anesthesia, 1967; BA, Met. State U., St. Paul, 1976; MA, U. St. Thomas, 1981; EdD, Nova Southeastern U., 1987. RN, Wis., Minn. Operating room nurse Luther Hosp., Eau Claire, 1959-61, head nurse operating room, 1961-63; supr. operating room Midway Hosp., St. Paul, 1963-66; staff anesthetist North Meml. Med. Ctr., Robbinsdale, Minn., 1967-68, St. Joseph's Hosp., St. Paul, 1992—; program dir. Mpls. Sch. Anesthesia, St. Louis Park, Minn., 1968-96; adj. assoc. prof. St. Mary's U., Winona, Minn., 1982-96, adj. prof., 1996—, program dir. Masters Degree Program, 1984-96, nurse anesthesia cons., 1996—; ednl. cons. accreditation visitor Coun. on Accreditation of Nurse Anesthesia Ednl. Programs, Park Ridge, Ill., 1983-92, elected to coun., 1992—, vice chmn., 1994—; presentations in field. Recipient Good Neighbor award Sta. WCCO, Mpls., 1980, Disting. Alumni Achievement award Nova Southeastern U., 1993. Mem. Am. Assn. Nurse Anesthetists (pres. 1981-82, pres. and bd. dirs. Edn. and Rsch. Found. 1981-83, cert. profl. excellence 1976, Program Dir. of Yr. award 1992), Minn. Assn. Nurse Anesthetists (pres. 1975-76). Lutheran. Avocations: gardening, fishing, photography, choir directing, playing guitar and piano. Home and Office: PO Box 80 Palisade MN 56469-0080

KILDSIG, NANCY EVALINE, consultant pharmacist; b. International Falls, Minn., July 7, 1936; d. Oscar Carl Lundgren and Alta Maude Wetmore Brown; m. Dane Olin Kildsig, Feb. 2, 1958; children: Dane Olin, Douglas Gustav. BS, U. Wis., 1958; MS, Purdue U., 1972. Registered pharmacist. Pharmacist Meth. Hosp., Madison, Wis., 1958-61, Hogan's Pharmacy, Madison, Wis., 1962-64, Bill Long Pharmacy, West Lafayette, Ind., 1974-81; cons. pharmacist Healthcare Prescription Svcs., Indpls., 1982-95; dir. ops. TeamCare, Indpls., 1995—; presenter healthcare seminars, Indpls., 1983—; workshop presenter and facilitator. Vice-chair Salute to Women Banquet, Tippecanoe County, Ind., 1991, chair, 1992. Fellow Am. Soc. Cons. Pharmacists; mem. AAUW (br. pres. 1977-79, 90-92, state pres. 1979-81, dir. Great Leakes region 1989-91, Ind. dir. pub. policy 1991-93), Ind. Pharmacists Assn. (ednl. affairs coun.), Ind. Soc. Cons. Pharmacists (sec.-treas.). Home: 2526 Shagbark Ln West Lafayette IN 47906-4531 Office: Team Care Pharm Svcs 5644 W 74th St Indianapolis IN 46278

KILEY, THOMAS, rehabilitation counselor; b. Mpls., Aug. 18, 1937; s. Gerald Sidney and Veronica (Kennedy) K.; m. Jane Virginia Butler, Aug. 25, 1989; children: Martin, Truman, Tami, Brian. BA in English, UCLA, 1959; MS in Rehab. Counseling, San Francisco State U., 1989. Cert. rehab counselor, nat. and Hawaii. Former rsch. profl., businessman various S.E. Asian cos.; sr. social worker Episcopal Sanctuary, San Francisco, 1986-88; dir. social svcs. Hamilton Family Ctr., San Francisco, 1988-89; rehab. specialist Intracorp, Honolulu, 1989-91; pres. Heritage Counselling Svc., Honolulu, 1991—, Hunter Employment Svc., Yuma, Ariz., 1995. Mem. Am. Counseling Assn., Nat. Assn. Rehab. Profls. in Pvt. Sector, Am. Rehab. Counselors Assn. (profl.), Nat. Rehab. Assn., Rehab. Assn. Hawaii, Rotary, Phi Delta Kappa. Office: Heritage Counselling Svcs PO Box 3098 Mililani HI 96789-0098 also: 2801 S 4th Ave # 114 Yuma AZ 85364

KILGORE, DONALD GIBSON, JR., pathologist; b. Dallas, Nov. 21, 1927; s. Donald Gibson and Gladys (Watson) K.; m. Jean Upchurch Augur, Aug. 23, 1952; children: Michael Augur, Stephen Bassett, Phillip Arthur, Geoffrey Scott, Sharon Louise. Student, So. Meth. U., 1943-45; MD, Southwestern Med. Coll., U. Tex., 1949. Diplomate Am. Bd. Pathology, Am. Bd. Dermatopathology, Am. Bd. Blood Banking. Notary Pub. Intern Parkland Meml. Hosp., Dallas, 1949-50; resident in pathology Charity Hosp. La., New Orleans, 1950-54, asst. pathologist, 1952-54; pathologist Greenville (S.C.) Hosp. System, 1956—, dir. labs., 1985—; dir. labs. Greenville Meml. Hosp., 1972—; cons. pathologist St. Francis Hosp., Shriners Hosp., Greenville, Easley Baptist. Hosp.; vis. lectr. Clemson U., 1963—; asst. prof. pathology Med. U. S.C., 1968—; pres. Pathology Assocs. of Greenville, 1983—. Recipient Disting. Svc. award S.C. Hosp. Assn., 1976. Fellow Coll. Am. Pathologists (life, assemblyman S.C. 1968-71), Am. Soc. Clin. Pathologists (councilor S.C. 1959-62), Am. Soc. Dermatopathology; mem. Am. Assn. Blood Banks (life, adv. coun. 1962-67, insp. committeeman Southeast dist. 1965—), AMA (ho. of dels. 1978-94), So. Med. Assn., S.C. Med. Assn., (exec. coun. 1969-76, 1978-94, pres. 1974-75; A.H. Robins award for Outstanding Cmty. Svc. 1985), Am. Soc. Cytology, Am. Coll. Nuc. Medicine, Nat. Assn. Med. Examiners, S.C. Inst. Med. Edn. and Rsch. (pres. 1974-80), S.C. Soc. Pathologists (pres. 1969-72), Richard III Soc. (co-chmn. Am. 1966-75), Am. Numis. Soc. (life), Soc. Ancient Numismatics (life), Am. Numis. Assn. (life), Blue Ridge Numis. Assn. (life), Royal Numis. Soc. (life), S.C. Numis. Assn. (life), Mensa (life), S.C. Congress Parents and Tchrs. (life), Greenville County Dental Soc. (hon. life), Greater Greenville C. of C., Greenville County Hist. Soc. (life), Hist. Greenville Found. (exec. com. 1994—), Preservation Soc. of Charleston (life), S.C. Hist. Soc. (life), Tex. State Hist. Assn. (life), Thomas Wolfe Soc. (life), Medieval Acad. of Am. (life), Archeol. Inst. Am. (life), Brookgreen Gardens Found. (life), Friends of Tewkesbury Abbey (life), Canterbury Cathedral Trust in Am. (life), Assn. Friends of Lincoln Cathedral (life), U.S. Power Squadron, Confrerie des Chevaliers du Tastevin (chevalier Atlanta chpt.), Soc. Med. Friends of Wine, Wine Acad. Am. (life), Soc. Wine Educators, Les Amis du Vin (life), Confrerie de la Chaine des Rotisseurs (bailli and conseiller de L'Ordre Mondial Greenville chpt.), Epicurean Assn. of Am. (selection com.), Clan MacDuff Soc. Am. (exec. coun. 1980—), St. Andrews Soc. Upper S.C. (bd. govs. 1991-93), So. Meth. U. Alumni Assn. (life), Highland Park H.S. Alumni Assn. (life), Phi Eta Sigma, Phi Chi. Democrat. Presbyterian (ruling elder 1969—). Clubs: Commerce (life), Poinsett (life), Torch (pres. 1964-65), Greenville Country (life), Thirty-Nine (pres. 1981-82), Chandon. Lodge: Rotary (Paul Harris fellow 1988). Home: 129 Rockingham Rd Greenville SC 29607-3620 Office: 8 Memorial Medical Ct Greenville SC 29605-4485

KILGORE, EUGENE STERLING, JR., surgeon; b. San Francisco, Feb. 3, 1920; s. Eugene Sterling and Mary (Kirkpatrick) K.; m. Marilynn Wines; children: Eugene Sterling, Marilynn Ann. BS, U. Calif., Berkeley, 1941; MD, U. Calif., San Francisco, 1949. Intern in medicine Harvard service Boston City Hosp., 1949-50; intern in surgery Roosevelt Hosp., N.Y.C., 1950-51; resident gen. surgery, reconstructive hand surgery Roosevelt Hosp., 1951-55; practice medicine specializing in reconstructive hand surgery San Francisco, 1955—; asso. clin. prof. surgery U. Calif.-San Francisco, 1955-75, clin. prof., 1975-91, prof. emeritus, 1991—; chief hand surgery dept. surgery U. Calif. Hosp., also San Francisco Gen. Hosp., 1965-91; chief hand service Ft. Miley Vets. Hosp., San Francisco, 1965-91, Martinez (Calif.) Vets. Hosp., 1970-91, Livermore (Calif.) Vets. Hosp., 1965-70; chief hand service plastic surgery tng. service St. Francis Meml. Hosp., 1965-91, chief of surgery, 1979—; cons. hand surgery numerous pvt. hosps., San Francisco, 1955—. Author numerous publs. in field. Served to lt. col., inf. AUS, 1941-45. Decorated Bronze Star; recipient Gold Headed Cane, AOA medal; Kaiser award for excellence in teaching U. Calif.-San Francisco Sch. Medicine, 1976, Charlotte Baer Meml. Clin. Faculty award U. Calif., 1993. Mem. AMA, ACS, Am. Assn. Surgery of Trauma, Am. Trauma Soc., Am. Soc. Surgery of Hand, Carribean Hand Soc., San Francisco Surg. Soc. (pres. 1979-80), Pacific Coast Surg. Assn., City Club. Clubs: Rotary; Bohemian (San Francisco).

KILGORE, JAMES RICHARD, physician assistant; b. Birmingham, Ala., May 20, 1953; s. James Edward Kilgore and Mollie Marie (Wood) Key; m. Twila Ann Knowles, Oct. 6, 1973; children: John, Mark. BA, U. Ala., 1976; BMSc, Emory U., 1981; MS, Finch U. Health Scis., 1996. Lab. aide VA Hosp., Birmingham, 1972-73; lab. asst. U. Ala. Med. Ctr., Birmingham, 1973-76, research asst., 1976-79, physician asst., 1982-88; dir. clin. research Simon-Williamson Clinic, Birmingham, 1988—; mem. bd., mem. physician asst. com. Ala. Bd. Med. Examiners, 1987—. Chmn. bd. dirs. Riverchase South Ch., Birmingham, 1987—. Fellow Am. Acad. Physician Assts. (com. mem., bd. dirs., trustee found.); mem. Ala. Soc. Physician Assts. (v.p., pres. 1983, bd. dirs., exec. com. 1987, com. mem., outstanding mem. award 1986, pres.'s award 1987), Riverchase Country Club (Hoover). Republican. Office: Simon-Williamson Clinic 833 Princeton Ave SW Birmingham AL 35211-1311

KILGORE, RANDALL FREEMAN, health information services administrator; b. Birmingham, Ala., June 10, 1955; s. Isaac D.L. and Daisy Jewell (Bray) K. Student, Samford U., Birmingham, 1973-75; BS in Med. Record Adminstrn. with honors, U. Ala., 1978; postgraduate in adult edn., U. Mo., Columbia, 1980—; MRE cum laude, Midwest Bapt. Theol. Sem., Kansas City, Mo., 1991. Registered Am. Health Info. Mgmt. Assn. Asst. dir. health info. mgmt. program Stephens Coll., Columbia, Mo., 1980-82; dir. quality/risk mgmt. svcs. Boone Hosp. Ctr., Columbia, 1982-87; risk mgr. univ. hosp. U. Mo. Hosp. and Clinics, Columbia, 1987-89; coord. mktg. and adminstrv. svcs. McQuilkin, Keeling-Wallace Counseling Assocs., Inc., Columbia, 1991; dir. health info. svcs. Charter Hosp. of Columbia, 1991—; spkr., conf. leader Univ. Hosp. Consortium, 1989, chmn. spl. com. on integration of quality assurance and risk mgmt., 1988-89. Mem. historic sites com. Boone County (Mo.) Hist. Soc.; com. mem. Boone County Commn. Spl. Task Force for preservation of historic and scenic roads; bd. dirs. HHosp. Industry Data Inst., 1985-88; judge Miss Columbia Pageant, 1993. Charles M. Hudson Meml. scholar, 1989, Rotary Internat. graduate fellow, 1979-80, Brandon scholar, 1990-91. Mem. Am. Health Info. Mgmt. Assn., Mo. Med. Record Assn. (nominating com., ad-hoc scholarship com., dir. exec. com. 1983-84, pres.-elect 1984-85), Nat. Alumni Soc. U. Ala. at Birmingham (charter, bd. dirs.), Mo. Symphony Soc., Omicron Delta Kappa. Democratic. Methodist. Home: 201 North Roby Farm Rd Rocheport MO 65279 Office: Charter Behav Health Sys 200 Portland St Columbia MO 65201

KILLEBREW, ELLEN JANE (MRS. EDWARD S. GRAVES), cardiologist; b. Tiffin, Ohio, Oct. 8, 1937; d. Joseph Arthur and Stephanie (Beriont) K.; BS in Biology, Bucknell U., 1959; MD, N.J. Coll. Medicine, 1965; m. Edward S. Graves, Sept. 12, 1970. Intern, U. Colo., 1965-66, resident 1966-68; cardiology fellow Pacific Med. Center, San Francisco, 1968-70; dir. coronary care, Permanent Med. Group, Richmond, Calif., 1970-83; asst. prof. U. Calif. Med. Center, San Francisco, 1970-83, assoc. prof., 1983-93, clin. prof. medicine, Univ. Calif., San Francisco, 1992—. Contbr. chpt. to book. Robert C. Kirkwood Meml. scholar in cardiology, 1970; recipient Physician's Recognition award continuing med. edn., Lowell Beal award excellence in teaching, Permante Med. Group/House Staff Assn., 1992. Diplomate in cardiovascular disease Am. Bd. Internal Medicine. Fellow ACP, Am. Coll. Cardiology; mem. Fedn. Clin. Rsch., Am. Heart Assn. (rsch. chmn. Contra Costa chpt. 1975—, v.p. 1980, pres. chpt. 1981-82, chm. CPR com. Alameda chpt. 1984, pres. Oakland Piedmont br. 1995—). Home: 30 Redding Ct Belvedere Tiburon CA 94920-1318 Office: 280 W Macarthur Blvd Oakland CA 94611-5642

KILLEBREW, FLAVIUS CHARLES, biology educator, academic administrator; b. Canadian, Tex., Apr. 2, 1949; s. Wilbur N. and Nellie M. (Davidson) K.; m. Kathy C. Bartley, Dec. 23, 1981; 1 child, Arian. BS in Biology, West Tex. State Univ., 1971; MS in Biology, West Tex. State U., 1972; PhD in Zoology, U. Ark., 1976. Grad. asst. U. Ark., Fayetteville, 1972-76, mus. asst., 1974-76; asst. prof. biology West Tex. State U., Canyon, 1976-81, assoc. prof., 1981-88, prof., 1988—, grad. dir., 1988-91, grad. dean, 1991-94; dir. regional div. Tex. Engring. Experiment Sta., Canyon, 1991—; provost, v.p. for acad. affairs, 1994—; adj. prof. Tex. A&M U., College Station, 1990—. Sponsor T-Anchor 4-H, Canyon, 1985—, WT Speakers Bur., Canyon, 1986—. Grantee U.S. Army Corps Engrs, 1978, Killgore Rsch. Ctr., 1989-91. Mem. Herpetologists League, Soc. for Study of Amphibians, Am. Soc. Ichthyologists, Assn. Tex. Grad. Schs. (pres. 1993), Masons, Tri Bet, Alpha Chi. Methodist. Office: West Tex A&M U WT Box 727 Canyon TX 79016

KILLELEA, DONALD EDWARD, pediatrician; b. New Orleans, Aug. 25, 1926; s. Edward Joseph and Genevieve (Giuffria) K.; m. Katherine Louise Ferguson, Feb. 5, 1955; children: Katherine, Genevieve, Margaret, Donna, Patricia, Donald Jr., Edward. BA, U. Tex., 1948; MD, Tulane U., 1952. Cert. in pediats., recert.; lic., Miss., La. Pvt. practice Children's Clinic, Natchez, Miss., 1961—; clin. prof. pediats. Tulane Med. Sch., New Orleans, 1980—; chief of staff Jeff Davis Hosp., Natchez, 1966, exec. com., 1995-96. Bd. dirs. Britton Koontz Bank, Natchez, 1976—, Natchez Opera Festival, 1990—, Santa Claus Club, Natchez, 1955—. 1st lt. U.S. Army, 1945-47. Mem. AMA, Am. Acad. Pediats., Homochitto Valley Med. Assn., Natchez C. of C. (bd. dirs. 1970-74), So. Soc. for Pediatric Rsch. Republican. Roman Catholic. Office: Children's Clinic 136 Jeff Davis Blvd Natchez MS 39120

KILLGALLON, CHRISTINE BEHRENS, healthcare administrator; b. Portsmouth, Ohio, June 29, 1958; d. Carl William Behrens and Karin Rita (Roeder) Behrens-Ellis; m. William Casley Killgallon, June 21, 1989. AS in Sci., Brunswick Coll., 1979, AS in Nursing, 1981; BA in Econs., George Mason U., 1987; M in Healthcare Adminstrn., Xavier U., 1989. CCRN. Staff nurse Bath County Community Hosp., Hot Springs, Va., 1981-82; critical care nurse U. Va. Med. Ctr., Charlottesville, Va., 1982-85; med. paralegal Donahue, Ehrmantraut, Montedonico, Washington, 1986; adminstrv. intern U. Va. Med. Ctr., Charlottesville, 1987; adminstrv. resident Alleghany Regional Hosp., Lowmoor, Va., 1989-95; exec.v.p. Odin Co., 1995—; bd. dirs. Odin Co.; v.p. comms. Odin Sys. Internat. Mem. aux. Safe Harbor, St. Simons, Ga., 1991; active Med. Assistance Program, Brunswick, 1990, Rep. Women's Orgn., St. Simons, 1990; mem. found. bd. S.E. Ga. Regional Med. Ctr. mem. AACCN, Am. Hosp. Assn., Am. Coll. Healthcare Execs., Golden Isles Investment Club St. Simons (pres. 1994), Omicron Delta Epsilon Theta. Presbyterian. Home: 1335 Hilltop Rd Charlottesville VA 22903-1224

KILLIAN, EDWARD JAMES, pediatrician; b. Bklyn., Nov. 14, 1927; s. Edward James and Helen Marie (Miller) K.; m. Henriette Marian Sarno, Oct. 26, 1957; children: Christopher Edward, Bryan Alfred, Paul Matthew. BS, St. John's Coll., 1950; MD, SUNY, 1954. Diplomat Am. Bd. Pediatrics, Nat. Bd. Med. Examiners; lic. physician, N.Y. Intern Bklyn. Hosp., 1954-55, resident, 1955-57, attending pediatrician, 1959-61; attending pediatrician Southside Hosp., Bayshore, N.Y., 1961-93; attending pediatrician Good Samaritan Hosp., West Long Island, N.Y., 1961-93, retired, 1994. Capt. USAF Med. Corps, 1957-59. Fellow Am. Acad. Pediatrics; mem. AMA, Med. Soc. State N.Y. (life), Suffolk County Med. Soc. (life), Suffolk Pediatric Soc. (emeritus). Republican. Roman Catholic. Home: 21 Brentwood Rd Apt 27 Bay Shore NY 11706

KILMAN, JAMES WILLIAM, surgeon, educator; b. Terre Haute, Ind., Jan. 22, 1931; s. Arthur and Irene (Piker) K.; m. Priscilla Margaret Jackson, June 20, 1968; children: James William, Julia Anne, Jennifer Irene. B.S., Ind. State U., 1956; M.D., Ind. U., 1960. Intern Ind.U. Med. Ctr., Indpls., 1960-61; resident surgery Ind.U. Med. Center, 1961-66, asst. prof., 1966-69, assoc. prof., 1969-73; prof. surgery Ohio State U. Coll. Medicine, 1973-91, prof. surgery emeritus, 1991—; chmn. dept. thoracic surgery Children's Hosp., 1975-91; attending surgeon Univ. Hosp., Columbus, Ohio; attending staff Children's Hosp., Columbus; pres. staff Children's Hosp., 1978; attending staff Grant Hosp., Riverside Hosp.; cons. surgeon VA Hosp., Dayton; pres. Columbus Acad. Medicine, 1977. Trustee Central Ohio Heart Assn., Acad. Medicine Edn. Found., Children's Hosp., 1978—. Served with USNR, 1951-55. USPHS Cardiovascular fellow, 1963-64; recipient Alumni Achievement award, Ind. State U., 1989. Fellow ACS, Am. Coll. Cardiology, Am. Acad. Pediats., Coll. Chest Physicians; mem. Columbus Surg. Soc. (pres. 1974, hon. mem. 1993), Columbus Acad. Medicine (coun. 1971-73), Am. Surg. Assn., Soc. U. Surgeons, Am. Assn. Thoracic Surgery, Cen. Surg. Assn., Western Surg. Assn., Soc. Vascular Surgery, Internat. Cardiovasc. Soc., Internat. Soc. Surgeons, Chest Club, Cardiovasc. Surgery Club, City Club, Palm Aire Country Club, Faculty Club, Capital Club, Univ. Club, Sigma Xi, Alpha Omega Alpha. Home and Office: 4231 Jackson Pike Grove City OH 43123-9198 Winter Home: 7517 Fairlinks Ct Sarasota FL 34243

KILPATRICK, DAVID CHALMERS, immunologist, researcher; b. Edinburgh, Scotland, Apr. 7, 1950; s. David and Alice Mary (Chalmers) K.; m. Sharon Penelope Gandy (div. 1979); m. Sheila Alison Crofton, Mar. 29, 1980; children: Alan Iain, Laura Emily. BSc, U. Aberdeen, 1972; PhD, U. London, 1975. Rsch. fellow Queen Elizabeth Coll., London, 1975-76, U. Edinburgh, 1976-78; sr. immunologist Royal Infirmary, Edinburgh, 1978-81; sr. immunologist Blood Transfusion Svc., Edinburgh, 1981-84, prin. immunologist, 1984—. Editor: (with others) Lectin Reviews, 1991; contbr. rsch. reports and articles to profl. jours. and books. Rsch. grantee S.H.E.R.T., 1987-89, S.H.H.D., 1989-91, TENOUVS, 1996. Fellow Royal Coll. Pathologists (London); mem. Brit. Soc. Immunology, Brit. Blood Transfusion Soc., Biochem. Soc. Home: 105 St Alban's Rd, Edinburgh EH9 2PQ, Scotland Office: Blood Transfusion Svc, 2 Forrest Rd, Edinburgh EH1 2QN, Scotland

KIM, ANNA H., optometrist, nurse; b. Seoul, Korea, Dec. 9, 1944; came to U.S., 1964; d. Kyo Bong and Ok Boon (Choi) Kim; m. Jack D. Hefley, Oct. 19, 1980 (div. Mar. 1990); 1 child, Julie E. Sur. ADN, U. Hawaii, 1972; BS in Optometry, U. Houston, OD, 1987. Nurse Queens Med. Ctr., Honolulu, 1972-77, VA Med. Ctr., Seattle, Dallas, Houston, 1977-87; optometrist Houston Med. Inst., 1993—; pvt. practice Houston, 1987—. Treas. Korean Am. Voters League, Houston, 1994-95, Korean Am. Reps., Houston, 1992—; dir. Korean Sch., Houston, 1988-91. Mem. ANA, Am. Optometric Assn., Houston Korean Lions (pres., treas., 1994, 95). Buddhist. Office: 10013 Long Point Houston TX 77055

KIM, BRIAN YONGTAE, physician; b. Seoul, Korea, July 18, 1963; s. Che Kol and Mary Kunja Kim; m. Christina Yun Kim, Mar. 17, 1991; children: Zachary KwongJo, Isabelle Aerhyn. BA in psychology, Univ. Md., 1987; DO, U. Osteopathic Med.& Health, 1992. Intern Mich. State Univ., East Lansing, 1992-93; resident The Grad. Hosp., Phila., 1993-96; fellow Buffalo Spine & Sports Medicine, Williamsville, N.Y., 1996—; clinical adv. Am. Running & Fitness Assn., Bethesda, 1996—; medical dir. Fairmont Park Triathlon, Phila., 1995; medical staff U.S Men's Marathon Olympic Trials, Charlotte, N.C., 1996. Contbr. articles to profl. jours. Head physician Nike Nat. Youth Soccer Tournament, Phila., May 1996. Mem. Am. Medical Athletic Assn., Am. Coll. Sports Medicine, Am. Acad. Physical Medical & Rehab., Am. Osteopathic Assn., AMA. Home: 1003 Ashbrook Ct Voorhees NJ 08043 Office: The Grad Hosp 1800 Lombard St Philadelphia PA 19146

KIM, CHARLES WESLEY, microbiology educator; b. Nashville, Mar. 20, 1926; s. Herbert Hyungsik and Kyung Sook (Lee) K.; m. Soo Johung, June 9, 1956; 1 child, Charles W. Jr. BA, U. Calif., Berkeley, 1949; MS in Pub. Health, U. N.C., 1952, PhD in Parasitology and Microbiology, 1956. Instr., asst. prof. N.Y. Med. Coll., N.Y.C., 1956-59, 59-64; assoc. scientist, scientist Brookhaven Nat. Lab., Upton, N.Y., 1965-68, 68-70; assoc. dean basic health sci. SUNY, Stony Brook, 1972-74, assoc vice provost, 1974-83, assoc. prof., 1970-87, prof. microbiology and medicine, 1987—. Author: Microbiology Review, 1962, 11th edit., 1995; editor: Trichinellosis, 1974, 4th edit., 1985; editorial bd. Exptl. Parasitology, 1984—; reviewer Am. Jour. Tropical Medicine and Hygiene, 1990-93. Bd. govs. Friends of Sunwood, Stony Brook, 1973-85, Suffolk Symphonic Soc., Suffolk County, N.Y., 1975-77; mem. devel. com. Museums Stony Brook, 1983-85; moderator elect N.E. Synod Presbyn. Ch., 1996. Tropical medicine fellow La. State U. Sch. Medicine, 1958, USPHS fellow Argonne Nat. Lab., U. Chgo., 1964-65, Royal Soc. Tropical Medicine and Hygiene fellow, London, 1975. Mem. Internat. Commn. Trichinellosis (pres. 1988-93), Am. Soc. Parasitologists (chmn. nominating com. 1987), Am. Soc. Tropical Medicine and Hygiene, N.Y. Soc. Tropical Medicine (pres. 1985-86), Sigma Xi (chpt. pres. 1993-94), Delta Omega. Office: SUNY T-15 080 Health Scis Ctr Stony Brook NY 11794-8153

KIM, DOOHIE, public health educator; b. Taegu, Korea, Sept. 17, 1935; s. Dong-Hoon and Hong-Dahl (Chae) K.; m. Keun-Ok Ahn, Mar. 24, 1959; children: Ji-Eoun, Ji-Kwan, Nah-Youn. BA, Kyungpook Nat. U., 1961, MA, 1963, PhD, 1970. Instr. Sch. Medicine Kyungpook Nat. U., Taegu, Korea, 1968-70, asst. prof., 1970-75, assoc. prof., 1975-78, prof., 1978-95, dir. med. libr., 1978-80, dean Sch. Pub. Health, 1990-92, 94-95, emeritus prof., 1996—; prof. and dean Sch. Medicine Dongguk U., Kyung-ju, Korea, 1995—; com. mem. Provincial Com. for Environ. Contamination, Taegu, Korea, 1975-79; adv. mem. Taegu Supervising Corp. for Korean Indsl. Safety, 1985—. Author: Environmental Sanitation, 1975, Introduction of Health Science, 1989, Practice of School Health, 1979, Making Health for Prolonging Life, 1994. Adv. mem. Provincial Policy Com. of Kyungpook-do Korea, Taegu, 1979-81, Policy Com. Taegu City, 1981-83. Maj. Korean mil., 1964-67. Recipient Letters of Commendation, Prime Ministry Korea, 1963, Minister of Helath and Social Affairs of Korea, Seoul, 1985, Pres. of Kyungpook Nat. U., Taegu, 1987. Mem. APHA, Am. Coll. Preventive Medicine (internat. mem.), Korean Soc. Preventive Medicine (pres. 1987-89, Plaque 1990), Korean Indsl. Health Assn. (leader Kyungpook br. 1974-80), Internat. Commn. Occupl. Health, Korean Soc. Agrl. Medicine and Rural Health (pres. 1994-96). Home: Lombard Mantion 2-101, 1-3 Sooseoung 2ka, Taegu 706-032, Republic of Korea Office: The Dongguk Univ Sch Medicine, 707 Suck-jang Dong Kyung-ju, Kyung 780-714, Republic of Korea

KIM, DUCKSOO, radiologist and educator; b. Seoul, Korea, Aug. 16, 1948; came to U.S., 1977; s. Changkun and Sunchom (Cho) K.; m. Eunjoo Lee, May 22, 1978; children: LeeAnn, SueAnn, Andrew. BS, Cath. U., Seoul, 1969, MD, 1973; postgrad., Stanford (Calif.) U., 1981-83. Diplomate Am. Bd. Radiology; lic. physician, Mass., N.Y., Calif. Intern St. Mary's Hosp., Seoul, 1976-77, McKeesport (Pa.) Hosp., 1977-78; resident in diagnostic radiology Beth Israel Hosp., Newark, 1978-81; NIH fellow in cardiovascular and interventional radiology Stanford (Calif.) U. Med. Ctr., 1981-83; instr. radiology Harvard Med. Sch., Boston, 1983-86, asst. prof. radiology, 1986-92, assoc. prof. radiology, 1992—; staff diagnostic radiologist Beth Israel Hosp., Boston, 1983—, dir. divsn. cardiovascular and interventional radiology, 1986—; vis. prof. radiology U. Zurich, 1987, Nat. Rsch. Ctr. of Surgery, Ministry of Health, Russia, 1992; lectr. in field; rschr. in field. Author: Peripheral Vascular Imaging and Intervention, 1992; reviewer Catheterization and Cardiovascular Diagnosis, 1992-94, Hepatology, 1993; contbr. articles to profl. jours., chpts. in books. Sec. Korean Cath. Community, Boston, 1988-89, v.p., 1989-91, pres., 1991-92. Capt. Korean Army, 1973-76. Cath. U. Med. Coll. scholar, 1969-73; NIH grantee, 1981-83. Fellow Am. Coll. Angiology, Internat. Coll. Angiology, Am. Heart Assn., Soc. of Cardiovascular and Interventional Radiology; mem. AMA, Radiol. Soc. N.Am., Am. Coll. Radiology, New Eng. Soc. for Cardiovascular and Interventional Radiology (pres. 1992-93), New Eng. Korean Med. Soc., Norfolk Dist. Med. Soc., Mass. Med. Soc., Soc. of Magnetic Resonance in Medicine, Soc. of Magnetic Resonance Imaging, New Eng. Alumni Assn. of Cath. U. Med. Coll. (pres. 1991-92). Roman Catholic. Home: 9 Cedar Hill Rd Dover MA 02030-1631 Office: Beth Israel Hosp 330 Brookline Ave Boston MA 02215

KIM, EDWARD WILLIAM, ophthalmic surgeon; b. Seoul, Korea, Nov. 25, 1949; came to U.S., 1957; s. Shoon Kul and Pok Chu (Kim) K.; m. Carole Sachi Takemoto, July 24, 1976; children: Brian, Ashley. BA, Occidental Coll., Los Angeles, 1971; postgrad. Calif. Inst. Tech., 1971; MD, U. Calif.-San Francisco, 1975; MPH, U. Calif.-Berkley, 1975. Diplomate Nat. Bd. Med. Examiners, Am. Bd. Ophthalmology. Intern San Francisco Gen. Hosp., 1975-76; resident in ophthalmology Harvard U.-Mass. Eye and Ear Infirmary, Boston, 1977-79; clin. fellow in ophthalmology Harvard U., 1977-79; clin. fellow in retina Harvard, 1980; practice medicine in ophthalmic surgery, South Laguna and San Clemente, Calif., 1980—; vol. ophthalmologist Eye Care Inc., Ecole St. Vincent's, Haiti, 1980, Liga, Mex., 1989; chief staff, South Coast Med. Ctr., 1988-89; assoc. clin. prof. dept. ophthalmology, U. Calif., Irvine. Founding mem. Orange County Ctr. for Performing Arts, Calif., 1982, dir. at large, 1991; pres. Laguna Beach Summer Music Festival, Calif., 1984. Reinhart scholar U. Calif.-San Francisco, 1972-73; R. Taussig scholar, 1974-75. Fellow ACS, Am. Acad Ophthalmology, Royal Soc. Medicine, Internat. Coll. Surgeons; mem. Calif. Med. Assn., Keratorefractive Soc., Orange County Med. Assn., Mensa, Expts. in Art and Tech. Office: Harvard Eye Assocs 665 Camino De Los Mares Ste 102 San Clemente CA 92673-2840

KIM, HERA, orthodontist; b. Seoul, Korea, May 17, 1964; d. Ilya and Nam Kyoo (Hwang) K.; m. Jamie Joshua Berman, Aug. 9, 1995. BS, SUNY, 1987, DDS, 1991; MSc, Harvard U., 1994. Rsch. fellow Harvard U., Cambridge, Mass., 1991-94; asst. prof. W.Va. U., Morgantown, 1994—; vis. scientist Mass. Inst. Tech., Cambridge, 1991-94. Grantee Nat. Inst. Dental Rsch., 1991-92. Mem. Am. Bd. Orthodontics, Am. Assn. Orthodontists, Internat. Assn. Dental Rsch., Am. Assn. Dental Rsch., Northeast Soc. Orthodontists, Harvard Soc. Advancement of Orthodontics, Southeast Soc. Orthodontists. Office: WVa U Dept Orthodontics PO Box 9480 Morgantown WV 26505

KIM, IH CHIN, pediatrician; b. Seoul, Korea, Aug. 6, 1925; s. Young Whan and Young Ho (Cho) K.; came to U.S., 1953, naturalized, 1965; MD, Seoul Nat. U., 1950; student Yon Sei U., 1944-46; postgrad. U. Pa., 1954-55; m. Helen Fern Wagner, Mar. 15, 1957 (dec.); children: Catherine Joy Kim Smith, Stephen Thomas. Diplomate Am. Bd. Pediatrics. Intern, Transp. Hosps., Seoul and Pusan, Korea, 1950-51; resident in pediatrics Pusan Children's Charity Hosp., 1951-53, Children's Hosp. Phila., 1953-55, fellow in pediatric gastroenterology, 1955-58, research assoc., 1958-67, med. staff, 1963-67; practice medicine, specializing in pediatrics, Easton, Pa., 1965—, Phillipsburg, N.J., 1971—; staff dept. pediatrics Hahnemann Med. Coll. and Hosp., Phila., 1967—, Easton Hosp., 1965—, Warren Hosp., Phillipsburg, N.J., 1966—, chief dept. pediatrics, 1978-90; clin. asst. prof. pediatrics Hahnemann Med. Coll., Phila., 1971—. Contbr. articles to med. jours. Fellow Am. Acad. Pediatrics; mem. AMA. Country Club Northampton County. Presbyterian. n County. Address: 6 Ivy Ct Easton PA 18045-5816 Office: 545 Heckman St Phillipsburg NJ 08865-2600

KIM, JENNIFER JUNG-HEE, dentist; b. Seoul, Korea, June 7, 1963; d. Chang Woo and Kil-Soon K.; m. Min Jae Yu, Aug. 6, 1989; children: Kristin Ye-Jin, David Hyun-Joon. BS, Rutgers U., 1986; DMD, UMDNJ NJ Med. Sch., 1990. Dental asst. Freehold (N.H.) Dental Ctr., 1989-90; dentist Dentistry for Children, Trenton, N.J., 1991-93; pvt. practice dentistry Metuchen, N.J., 1992—. Pianist Trenton Korean Ch., 1987-94. Mem. Am. Dental Assn., N.J. Dental Assn., N.J. Dental Soc. Office: 2 Bridge St Metuchen NJ 08840

KIM, KYU-WON, molecular biology educator; b. Daegu, Korea, July 1, 1952; s. Byung-Hoon and Bok-Hee K.; m. Sou-Joo, Apr. 13, 1985; 1 child, Sun-Jae. BS, Seoul Nat. U., Korea, 1976; MS, Korea Advanced Inst. Sci., Seoul, 1978; PhD, U. Minn., 1985. Researcher Korea Rsch. Inst. Chem. Tech., Daejeon, Korea, 1978-80; rsch. asst. U. Minn., Dept. Biochemistry, Mpls., 1980-85; postdoctoral fellow Dana-Farber Cancer Inst. & Harvard Med. Sch., Boston, 1985-87; assoc. prof. dept. molecular biology Pusan (Korea) Nat. U., 1987—; dir. Rsch. Inst. of Genetic Engring., Pusan Nat. U., 1994—; sect. chief Pusan Nat. U., Inst. Genetic Engring., 1987—. chmn. dept. molecular biology, 1990-92. Editorial bd. Biochemistry News, 1988-89, Molecular Biology News, 1990-95. Recipient Seoul Nat. U. scholarship, 1972, YuHan Found. scholarship, 1973-76, Grant, Fellowship, The Brit. Coun., 1989; grantee The Dae Woo Found., 1988. Mem. Am. Assn. for Cancer Rsch., N.Y. Acad. Sci., Korean Biochem. Soc. (councilor 1988), The Genetics Soc. Korea (dir. 1991), Microbiol. Soc. Korea (dir. 1991), Korean Soc. Molecular Biology, Zool. Soc. Korea. Buddhist. Home: Buk-Gu Manduk-3 Dong 216-7, Greencore 601-607, Pusan Republic of Korea Office: Pusan Nat U, Dept Molecular Biology, Pusan 609-735, Republic of Korea

KIM, MI JA, dean; b. Seoul, Jan. 23, 1940; came to U.S., 1966; d. Si Hyung and Jung Kwon (Ahn) Lee; m. Heung Soo Kim, Jan. 14, 1964; children: Yoon Hi and Joseph. BS in Nursing, Yon Sei U., Seoul, 1962; PhD, U. Ill., Chgo., 1975. Staff nurse Severance Hosp., Seoul, 1962-63; health nurse Am. Embassy, Seoul, 1963-66; asst. prof. Coll. Nursing/Univ. Ill., Chgo., 1975-79, assoc. prof., 1979-84, prof., 1984—, interim assoc. dean for rsch., 1984-86, assoc. dean rsch., dir. grad. studies, 1986-87, assoc. dean acad. affairs, dir. grad. studies, 1987-88, acting dean, 1988-89, prof., dean, 1989—; cons. Levine Assocs., Kensington, Md., 1989—, Bd. Regents Higher Edn., Boston, 1989, Nat. Ctr. Nursing Rsch., Bethesda, Md., 1987—. Named Univ. Scholar, U. Ill., 1985-88, Outstanding Nurse Educator, Korean Nurses Assn., Seoul, 1983; recipient Book of Yr. award Am. Jour. Nursing, 1984, Golden Apple award, students of Coll. Nursing, U. Ill., 1976, 78. Fellow Am. Acad. Nursing; mem. North Am. Nursing Diagnosis (bd. dirs. 1985—), Am. Thoracic Soc., Chgo. Lung Assn. (bd. dirs. 1977—), Chgo. Heart Assn. (bd. govs. 1980-88), Am. Physiol. Soc., Sigma Theta Tau (Disting. Lectr. 1987). Office: U Ill Chgo Rm 310AOB 1737 W Polk M/C 672 Chicago IL 60612*

KIM, SEONG-JUN, anesthesiologist; b. Seoul, Republic of Korea, Feb. 16, 1937; came to U.S., 1965; s. Man-Bong and Duk-Hee (Kang) K.; m. Jung-Joong Yoon, July 3, 1965; children: Andrew, Caroline, Jennifer, Patricia. MD, Seoul Nat. U., 1961. Diplomate Am. Bd. Pediatrics, Am. Bd. Anesthesiology. Intern Seoul Nat. U. Hosp., 1961-62, French Hosp., N.Y.C., 1965-66; pediatric resident Wyckoff Heights Hosp., Bklyn., 1966-68; pediatric clinic fellow Down State Med. Ctr., Bklyn., 1968-69, anesthesia resident, 1969-71; med. staff Phelps Meml. Hosp. Ctr., North Tarrytown, N.Y., 1971-84, dir. anesthesia dept., 1984-91, sr. attending anesthesia dept., 1991—. Med. officer Army of Republic of Korea, 1962-65. Fellow Am. Coll. Anesthesiologists; mem. AMA, Am. Soc. Anesthesiologists, Internat. Soc. Anesthesiologists. Home and Office: 53 Cottonwood Ln Briarcliff Manor NY 10510-2140

KIM, SUK SIK, psychiatrist; b. Book Chung, Korea, May 13, 1937; came to U.S., 1965; s. Eiu Guk and Eun Joo (Park) Kim; m. Yae Kyung, June 17, 1965; children: Mi Kyung (dec.), Mi Hae, Mi Won. MD, Seoul (Korea) Nat. U., 1962, MS, 1964. Diplomate Am. Bd. Psychiatry and Neurology, Am. Inst. for Psychoanalysis. Intern Seoul Nat. U. Hosp., 1962-63, psychiatric resident, 1963-65; intern Somerset Hosp., Somerville, N.J., 1965-66; psychiatric resident Bellevue Hosp., N.Y.C., 1966-70; staff psychiatrist Meyer Psychiatric Hosp., N.Y.C., 1970-73, Coney Island Hosp., Bklyn., 1973—. Contbr. articles to profl. jours. Mem. Am. Psychiatric Assn. Office: Coney Island Hosp 2601 Ocean Pky Brooklyn NY 11235-7791

KIM, SUNG SOON, cardiology educator; b. Seoul, Republic of Korea, Nov. 23, 1945; s. Chong Sung and Chung Hyun (Noh) K.; m. Ghi Su Kim; children: Ge Young, Ge Sun. MD, Yonsei U., Seoul, 1970, MS, 1974, DMS, 1979. Intern, then resident Yonsei U. Coll. Medicine Severance Hosp., 1970-75; instr. Yonsei U. Coll. Medicine, 1975-79, assoc. prof. medicine, 1986-91, prof. medicine, 1991—, chief divsn. cardiology, 1992—; fellow in cardiology St. Louis U. Sch. Medicine, 1979-81, instr., 1979-82; fellow in electrophysiology U. Ill. Hosp., Chgo., 1982-83; instr. Washington U. Sch. Medicine, St. Louis, 1983-84, asst. prof., 1984-86; staff cardiologist Severence Hosp., Seoul, 1975-79, St. Louis U. Hosp., 1981-82; dir. telemetry unit, Jewish Hosp. of St. Louis, 1983-86. Fellow ACP, Am. Coll Cardiology, Council on Clin. Cardiology; mem. Cardiac Electrophysiology Soc., N.Am. Soc. Pacing and Electrophysiology.d. Office: Yonsei Cardiovascular Ctr Cardiology Divsn, Yonsei U Medicine CPO Box 8044, 120-752 Seoul Republic of Korea

KIM, WAYNE WOOYONG, osteopath, family practice physician; b. Dagu, Korea, Nov. 3, 1962; came to the U.S., 1975; s. Srong Soo and Dong Sook (Park) K.; m. Esther Eun Chu Beak, Dec. 3, 1988; children: Daniel, Joseph, Katie. BA, U. Calif., Davis, 1985; DO, Coll. Osteo. Medicine Pacific, 1990. Bd. cert. family practice Am. Coll. Osteo. Bd. Family Practice. Mem. Am. Osteo. Assn., Am. Coll. Osteo. Family Practice, Calif. Med. Assn. Home: 3525 Melgren Ave Modesto CA 95356

KIM, YEE S., pharmacology educator, researcher, consultant; b. Seoul, Korea, Apr. 15, 1928; came to U.S., 1955; s. Ik Yong and Oh Min (Oh) K.; m. Young S. Lee, Apr. 19, 1954; children: Karl E., Ruth E., Grace E., Elizabeth E. MS, Kans. State U., 1960; PhD, St. Louis U., 1965. Rsch. scientist Union Starch/Miles Lab., Granite City, Ill., 1960-64; rsch. assoc. SUNY, Buffalo, 1965-66; asst. prof. Sch. of Medicine St. Louis U., 1966-70, assoc. prof. Sch. of Medicine, 1970-76, prof. Sch. of Medicine, 1976—; cons. Union Starch/Miles Lab., 1966-71; reviewer in field. Author: Diabetic Pregnancy, 1985; contbr. articles to Jour. Biol. Chemistry, Endocrinology. Pres. Korean-Am. Soc., St. Louis, 1971. Lt. Republic of Korea Naval Res., 1950-54. Grantee NIH. Mem. AAAS, Am. Soc. Pharm. Exptl. Therapy (Travel award 1975), Am. Chem. Soc. Office: St Louis U Dept Pharm Physiology 1402 S Grand Blvd Saint Louis MO 63104-1004

KIM, YOON BERM, immunologist, educator; b. Pyongnam, Korea, Apr. 25, 1929; came to U.S., 1959, naturalized, 1975; s. Sang Sun and Yang Rang (Lee) K.; m. Soon Cha Kim, Feb. 23, 1959; children: John, Jean, Paul. M.D., Seoul Nat. U., 1958; Ph.D., U. Minn., 1965. Intern Univ. Hosp. Seoul Nat. U., 1958-59; mem. faculty U. Minn., Mpls., 1960-73; assoc. prof. microbiology U. Minn., 1970-73; mem., head lab. ontogeny of immune system Sloan Kettering Inst. Cancer Research, Rye, N.Y., 1973-83; prof. immunology Cornell U. Grad. Sch. Med. Scis., N.Y.C., 1973-83; chmn. immunology unit Cornell U. Grad. Sch. Med. Scis., 1980-82; prof. microbiology, immumology and medicine, chmn. dept. micorbiology and immunology Finch U. Health Scis., Chgo. Med. Sch., 1983—, acting dean Sch. Grad. and Postdoctoral Studies, 1994-95; mem. Lobund adv. bd. U. Notre Dame, 1977-88. Contbr. numerous articles on immunology to profl. jours. Recipient rsch. career devel. award USPHS, 1968-73, Morris Parker Rsch. award U. Health Scis., Chgo. Med. Sch., 1984. Fellow Am. Acad. Microbiology; mem. AAAS, Assn. Gnotobiotics (pres.), Internat. Assn. for Gnotobiology (founding), Am. Assn. Immunologists, Am. Soc. Microbiology, Am. Assn. Pathologists, Korean-Am. Med. Assn., N.Y. Acad. Scis., Soc. for Leucocyte Biology, Internat. Soc. Devel. Comparative Immunology, Harvey Soc., Internat. Soc. Interferon and Cytokine Rsch., Chgo. Assn. Immunologists (pres.), Assn. Med. Sch. Microbiology and Immunology Chairs, Internat. Endotoxin Soc. (charter), Soc. Natural Immunity (charter), Sigma Xi, Alpha Omega Alpha. Home: 313 Weatherford Ct Lake Bluff IL 60044-1905 Office: Finch U Health Scis Chgo Med Sch 3333 Green Bay Rd North Chicago IL 60064-3037

KIM, YOUNG HO, orthodontist; b. Seoul, Korea, Oct. 17, 1927; came to U.S., 1952, naturalized, 1962; s. Woo Hyun and Doo Keum (Park) K.; m. Mazie Ann Lim, May 19, 1956; children: Stuart K., Jonathan C. D.D.S., Seoul Nat. U., 1949; M.S., U. Rochester, 1958; D.M.D., Tufts U., 1960. Diplomate Am. Bd. Orthodontists. Specialist in orthodontics, Weston, Mass., 1964—; instr. Harvard Dental Sch., 1960-65; assoc. prof. Boston U. Grad. Sch. Dentistry, 1967-70; vis. clin. prof. Yonsei U. Coll. Dentistry, 1972; cons. VA Hosp., West Roxbury, Mass., 1974-83; assoc. clin. prof. Tufts U. Sch. Dental Medicine, 1981-92. Chmn. bd. trustees Myung Hwee Won Found., 1976-86; pres. North Atlantic Component of The Angle Soc. Orthodontists, 1989-90; pres. Multiloop Edgewise Arch-Wire Technic and Rsch. Found., 1991—. Mem. ADA, Am. Assn. Orthodontists, Mass. Dental Soc., Angle Soc. Orthodontists, Omicron Kappa Upsilon. Home: 396 Glen Rd Weston MA 02193-1403 Office: 30 Colpitts Rd Weston MA 02193-1534

KIM, ZAEZEUNG, allergist, immunologist, educator; b. Hamhung, Korea, Feb. 21, 1929; came to U.S., 1967; s. Suh and Suyeo (Hahn) K.; m. Youngju Kim, June 2, 1961; children: Keungsuk, Maria. Student, Hamhung Med. Coll., Korea, 1946-50; MD, Seoul U., Korea, 1960; PhD in Immunology, U. Cologne, Fed. Republic of Germany, 1968. Diplomate Am. Bd. Allergy and Immunology. Intern Seoul Nat. U. Hosp., 1960-61, resident in medicine, 1961-63; resident in medicine Heidelberg U. Hosp., Fed. Republic of Germany, 1963-64; research fellow Max-Planck Inst., Cologne, 1965-67; fellow in hematology U. Tex., Houston, 1967-68; resident in allergy and immunology Temple U. Hosp., Phila., 1968-69; fellow in medicine Ohio State U., Columbus, 1969-71; instr. medicine Med. Coll. Wis., Milw., 1972-75, asst. prof., 1975-78, assoc. clin. prof., 1978—; practice medicine specializing in allergy and immunology Racine, Wis. Contbr. articles to profl. jours. Fellow Am. Acad. Allergy and Immunology, Am. Coll. Allergists; mem. AMA. Home: 461 W Sunnyview Dr # 13 Oak Creek WI 53154 Office: 1300 S Green Bay Rd Racine WI 53406-4469

KIMBALL, ANN MARIE, medical educator. BS, Stanford U., 1972; MD, U. Wash., 1976, MPH, 1981. Fellow Divsn. Infectious Diseases, Seattle, 1980-81; dep. dir. Project SHDS, Abidyan, 1981-82; ind. cons. Min. of Health, Sanaa, Yemen Arab Republic, 1983-85; resident advisor to Senegal rsch. program Columbia U., 1985-88; regional advisor for AIDS WHO, Washington, 1989-91; dir. divsn. AIDS/HIV/ATD State Dept., Seattle and Olympia, Wash., 1991-93; attending physician Madison AIDS Clinic, Seattle, 1991—; assoc. prof. Health Svcs. and Epidemiology, Seattle, 1993—; acting dir. internat. health program U. Wash., Seattle, 1994, 95, chair MPH curriculum force, 1995—, mem. pres. force on internat. edn., 1995—; acting dir. Asian Pacific Alliance Against AIDS, Yokohama, Japan, 1994. Contbr. articles to profl. jours. Fellow Royal Coll. Medicine; mem. APHA, Am. Venereal Disease Assn., Soc. for Epidemiol. Rsch., Wash. Coun. for Internat. Trade, Assn. Students of Stanford U. (pres. 1972), Alpha Omega Alpha. Office: Health Svcs Box 357660 1959 NE Pacific St Seattle WA 98195

KIMBALL, HARRY RAYMOND, medical association executive, educator; b. L.A., 1937. MD, Wash. U., 1962. Intern King County Hosp., Seattle, 1962-63; resident in internal medicine U. Wash. Hosps., Seattle, 1963-64, 67-68; fellow infectious diseases NIH Hosps., Bethesda, Md., 1964-67; pres. Am. Bd. Internal Medicine, Phila. Office: Am Bd Internal Med U City Sci Ctr 3624 Market St Philadelphia PA 19104-2675*

KIMBELL, CHARLES WILLIAM, III, health care executive; b. Utica, N.Y., May 7, 1943; s. Charles William and Florence (Starr) K.; m. Beverly Carol Moore, Nov. 22, 1969. BA in Human Rels., Salem Coll., 1966. Dist. exec. to dir. exploring Nassau County Coun. Boy Scouts Am., Roslyn, N.Y., 1966-73; exec. dir. Five Towns United Way, Woodmere, N.Y., 1973-78; dir. devel. Franklin Gen. Hosp., Valley Stream, N.Y., 1978-84; dir. resource devel./pub. rels. St. John's Episcopal Hosp., Far Rockaway, N.Y., 1984-87; dir. resource devel. Episc. Health Svcs., Inc., 1987-91; pres. Masonic Charity Found., Wallingford, Conn., 1991—. Chmn. bd. dirs. Five Towns United Way, 1978-90; bd. dirs., pres. Rockaway Devel. & Revitalization Corp., 1984-91; mem. vestry Trinity-St. John's Episc. Ch., Hewlett, N.Y., 1983-88, St. Mark's Episcopal Ch., Islip, N.Y.; mem. U.S. Coast Guard Aux. Flotilla; gen. chmn. Episc. Charities of L.I. Appeal, 1991. Recipient Silver Beaver award Boy Scouts Am., 1983, Bishop Cross Disting. to Diocese of L.I., 1991. Nat. Soc. Fund Raising Execs. (past pres. L.I. chpt., Outstanding Fund Raising Exec. 1991, pres. Conn. chpt. 1993-95), Rockaway C. of C. (bd. dirs. 1985-87). Republican. Club: Cedarhurst Yacht, South Bay Cruising. Lodge: Kiwanis (bd. dirs. 1967-87), Trubull Lodge # 22 Masons, 32 Degree Scottish Rite, Sphinx Shrine. Home: 129 S Penataquit Ave Bay Shore NY 11706-8834 Office: Masonic Charity Found Conn PO Box 70 Wallingford CT 06492

KIMBER, WILLIAM JOHN, cardiologist; b. Glen Ridge, N.J., Nov. 10, 1931; s. William Francis and Jean Miriam (Hogg) K.; m. Patricia Mary Moynihan, Aug. 11, 1956 (div. 1981); children: Katherine Anne, James Robert, David Patrick, John Michael; m. M. Ann Chubbuck, Dec. 5, 1981. BA, Cornell U., 1954; MD, U. Pa., 1960. Diplomate Am. Bd. Internal Medicine, Am. Bd. Cardiology. Intern Mountainside Hosp., Montclair, N.J., 1960-61; resident in medicine Mayo Clinic, Rochester, Minn., 1962-65, fellow in cardiology, 1965-67; assoc. in cardiology Geisinger Med. Ctr. Clinic, Danville, Pa., 1968—, dir. cardiac catheterization lab., 1974—, asst. dir. dept. cardiology, 1986—, dir. Cardiovascular Sch. Tech., 1991—; clin. prof. medicine Pa. State U., Hershey, 1984-88, Jefferson Med. Coll., Phila., 1989—. Fellow Am. Coll. Cardiology; mem. Am. Heart Assn. (chpt. pres. 1974-75, v.p. Pa. affiliate 1979, Disting. Svc. award 1975, Merit Svc. medal 1979). Office: Geisinger Med Ctr N Academy Ave Danville PA 17822

KIMBLE, DANIEL PORTER, psychology educator; b. Chgo., Nov. 18, 1934; s. Ralph Archibald and Ruth (Hazen) K.; m. Reeva Jacobson; children: Matthew, Evan, Sara. BA, Knox Coll., 1956; PhD, U. Mich., 1961. Asst. prof. U. Oreg., Eugene, 1963-66, assoc. prof., 1966-69, prof. psychology, 1969—, head dept., 1989-92. Author: Physiological Psychology: A Unit for Introductory Psychology, 1963, Psychology as a Biological Science, 2d rev. edit. 1977; editor: The Anatomy of Memory, 1965, The Organization of Recall, 1967, Experience and Capacity, 1968, Readiness to Remember, 1970, Contrast and Controversy in Modern Psychology, 1977, Biological Psychology, 1988, 2nd edit., 1992; contbr. articles to profl. jours. Recipient Teaching awards, 1967, 90; Woodrow Wilson fellow, 1956-57, Horace Rackham fellow, 1958-59, NIH fellow, 1961-63, NSF fellow, 1969-70. Fellow Am. Assn. Sci.; mem. Am. Psychol. Soc., Neurosci. Soc. Office: U Oreg Inst Neuroscience Dept Psychology Eugene OR 97403

KIMBLE, GLADYS AUGUSTA LEE, nurse, civic worker; b. Niagara Falls, Can., June 28, 1906; d. William and Florence Augusta Baker (Buckton) Lee; naturalized citizen of the U.S.; RN, Christ Hosp., Jersey City, 1929; BS, Columbia U. Tchrs. Coll., 1938, MA, 1948; m. George Edmond Kimble, Jan. 5, 1952. Nurse, Willard Parker Hosp., N.Y.C., 1931; asst. and supervisory relief nurse Margaret Hague Maternity Hosp., Jersey City, 1931-37; staff nurse, relief supr. Manhattan Eye, Ear and Throat Hosp., N.Y.C., 1937-38; sr. staff, asst. nurse supr. Vis. Nurse Svc., N.Y.C., 1938-41; sr. pub. health nurse USPHS, Little Rock, 1941-43; pub. health supr. Providence Dist. Nursing Assn., 1943-46; edn. dir. Jersey City Pub. Health Nursing Svc., 1946-49, also instr. Seton Hall U., South Orange, N.J., 1947-49; pub. health nurse cons. U.S. Inst. Inter-Am. Affairs, Brazil, 1949-51; dir. pub. health dept. Englewood (N.J.) Hosp., 1951-53; nurse coord. exch. visitor nurse program Overlook Hosp., Summit, N.J., 1964-71. Recipient Appreciation award for svc. rendered Providence Hosp., 1944; Woman of Yr. award Essex County Bus. and Profl. Women, 1968. Fellow Am. Pub. Health Assn. (life), mem. Sarasota Geneal. Soc. (charter), Daus. of the Nile, Nyla (charter, Sarasota, Fla.), Ladies Oriental Shrine of N.Am. (SAR-I Ct. 79), Royal Order of Jesterettes, Eillim Ives #18, Sarasota. Episcopalian. Home: 4540 Bee Ridge Rd Apt 12 Sarasota FL 34233-2524

KIMBLE, WANDA VELORIA, medical technologist; b. Shreveport, La., Aug. 15, 1964; d. James C. and Velma Ree (Bradford) Tyler; m. Larry Wayne Kimble, July 22, 1988; children: Kayberlyn O., Larry Wayne. Student, Northwestern State U., Natchitoches, La., 1987-89; AD in Sci., So. U., Shreveport, 1990. Diplomate La. State Bd. Med. Examiners; registered med. technologist. Med. lab. technologist HCA Highland Hosp., Shreveport, 1990-94; chief med. technologist Centenary Family Medicine, Shreveport, 1990—. Mem. choir, youth dept. First Bapt. Ch., Shreveport. Recipient DAR award, 1982. Mem. Assn. Med. Technologists, Am. Soc. Clin. Pathologists. Democrat. Home: 3222 Tower Dr Shreveport LA 71107 Office: Centenary Family Medicine 2020 Centenary Shreveport LA 71104

KIMBRELL, ODELL CULP, JR., physician; b. Spartanburg, S.C., May 2, 1927; s. Odell Culp and Leona (Nicholas) K.; m. Etta Lou; children from former marriage: Odell Culp III, Cynthia Anne. A.B., Duke U., 1947; M.D., U. Pa., 1951. Diplomate: Am. Bd. Internal Medicine, Am. Bd. Life Ins. Medicine. Intern Med. Coll. Va., Richmond, 1951-52, resident in internal medicine, 1954-56; sr. resident in internal medicine VA Hosp., Phila., 1956-57; practice medicine specializing in internal medicine and endocrinology Gallipolis, Ohio, 1957-60; practice medicine specializing in internal medicine and endocrinology Raleigh, N.C., 1960-93, practice ins. medicine, 1967—; mem. staff Wake Med. Ctr., Raleigh Community Hosp.; clin. prof. medicine U.N.C. Med. Sch., 1970-90; med. dir. Pa. Life Ins. Co. and Occidental Life Ins. Co. N.C., Integon Life Ins. Co. Contbr. articles to med. jours. Bd. dirs. Wake County Hosp. System Inc., Raleigh, 1971-81, sec., 1973-74, chmn., 1974-76; bd. dirs. Wake Health Facilities and Service Inc., 1975-81, pres., 1975-76; chmn. Wake County Heart Fund, 1961; deacon Hudson Meml. Presbyn. Ch., Raleigh, 1971-73. Served with USAF, 1952-54. Fellow ACP; mem. AMA, N.C. Med. Soc., Wake County Med Soc., Am. Soc. Internal Medicine, N.C. Soc. Internal Medicine, Am. Acad. Ins. Med., Mid-Atlantic Med. Dirs. Club (pres. 1979-80, 92). Democrat. Lodge: Lions. Home: 1905 Hunting Ridge Rd Raleigh NC 27615-5515 Office: 2610 Wycliff Rd Raleigh NC 27607

KIMBROUGH, ROBERT COOKE, III, infectious diseases physician; b. Washington, Nov. 26, 1941; s. Robert Cooke Jr. and Victoria Walton (Fitz Gerald) K.; m. Susan Jane Brackney (div.); children: Susan Fitz Gerald Kimbrough Gilson, Robert Cooke IV; m. Susan Kay Utterback, Apr. 11, 1974; children: John Williams, Bradley Warren. BS, U. Kans., 1963; MD, U. Kans., 1969. Diplomate Am. Bd. Internal Medicine. Intern, resident Baylor Coll. Medicine, Houston, 1969-73; chief resident St. Luke's Episcopal Hosp., Houston, 1972; fellow in infectious disease Baylor Coll. Medicine, 1972-74, U. Oreg. Med. Sch., Portland, 1974-75; instr. infectious diseases U. Oreg. Health Scis. Ctr., Portland, 1975-79; from asst. prof. to assoc. prof. infectious diseases Oreg. Health Scis. U., Portland, 1979-89; pvt. practice The Ferrell-Duncan Clinic, Inc., Springfield, Mo., 1989-93; prof. infectious diseases Tex. Tech. U. Health Scis. Ctr., Lubbock, 1993—. Reviewer Archives Internal Medicine, Jour. Infectious Diseases, Clin. Infectious Diseases, Annals Internal Medicine. Fellow ACP (chmn. assoc. com. 1984, 85, v.p. Oreg. chpt. 1986, pres. 1987-89, Howard P. Lewis tchg. award 1988), Infectious Diseases Soc. Am.; mem. AMA, Am. Fedn. Clin. Rsch., Am. Soc. Microbiology, Am. Assn. History of Medicine, Am. Osler Soc., Oreg. Med. Assn. (chmn. nominating com. 1985, chmn. pharmacy liaison com. 1986-89, trustee 1987-89, profl. cons. com. 1987-89), Multnomah County Med. Soc. (chmn. strategic planning com. 1985, sec. 1986, v.p. 1987, pres.-elect 1988), Tex. Med. Assn., Lubbock Med. Soc., Garza Med. Soc., Crosby County Med. Soc.. Home: 3109 80th St Lubbock TX 79423 Office: TTUHSC Dept Medicine 3601 4th St Lubbock TX 79430

KIMBROUGH, WILLIAM WALTER, III, psychiatrist; b. Cleve., Sept. 26, 1928; s. William Walter and Wilhelmina Grace (Champion) K.; student Cornell U., 1945-46; BS, U. Mich., 1948, MD, 1952; m. Jo Ann Greiner, July 6, 1953; children: Elizabeth, Douglas. Intern, Ohio State U. Health Ctr., Columbus, 1952-53; resident U. Chgo. Clinics, 1955-56, Ypsilanti (Mich.) State Hosp., 1956-59; assoc. psychiatrist U. Mich. Health Ctr., Ann Arbor, 1959-61; practice medicine specializing in psychoanalytic psychiatry, Ann Arbor, 1961—; cons. atty. gen. U.S., 1974—, Ctr. for Forensic Psychiatry, 1958—, Brighton Found. for Alcoholism, 1961—, Washtenaw County (Mich.) Community Mental Health Svcs., 1978—, Mich. Dept. Social Svcs., 1978—, Mich Dept. Mental Health, 1989—; reviewer Mich. Peer Rev. Orgn.; clin. dir. Livingston County (Mich.) Community Mental Health Svcs., 1983-85, Mich. Dept. Corrections, 1985-88; exec. com. Northville Regional Psychiatric Hosp.; pres. Northville (Mich.) Psychiat. Assn., 1991-93; pres. Physicians for Mercy, 1995—. Capt. USPHSR, 1953-96. Recipient Physicians Recognition awards AMA, 1972-96. Fellow Am. Acad. Psychiatry and Law, Am. Soc. Psychoanalytic Physicians; mem. AAAS, Am. Acad. Psychotherapists, Am. Psychiat. Assn. (life), Ann Arbor Psychiat. Assn., Northville Psychiat. Assn. (pres. 1991-93), Am. Acad. Psychiatrists in Alcoholism and Addiction (founding mem.), Mich. Psychiat. Soc. (com. on legislation and govt. affairs), N.Y. Acad. Sci., Hon. Order Ky. Cols., Sigma Alpha Epsilon, Phi Rho Sigma. Clubs: Ann Arbor Town, Ann Arbor Racquet, Univ., Travis Pointe Country (Ann Arbor); Little Harbor (Harbor Springs, Mich.), Round Table (Plymouth, Mich.). Home: 1903 Boulder Dr Ann Arbor MI 48104-4165 Office: 400 Maynard St Ann Arbor MI 48104-2440

KIMELBERG, HAROLD KEITH, neuroscience researcher, educator; b. London, Dec. 5, 1941; came to U.S., 1963; s. Maurice and Sarah (Cohen) K. BSc in Zoology, U. London, 1963; PhD in Biochemistry, SUNY, Buffalo, 1968. Sr. cancer rsch. scientist dept. neurosurgery Roswell Park Meml. Inst., Albany, N.Y., 1970-74; asst. rsch. prof. dept. biochemistry Roswell Park Div. SUNY, Albany, 1973-74; assoc. prof. biochemistry, rsch. assoc. prof. neurosurgery Albany Med. Coll., 1974-80; rsch. prof. neurosurgery, prof. pharmacology, neurosci. and biochemistry Albany Med. Coll., 1980—; prof. Sch. Pub. Health Scis. SUNY, Albany, 1988—; adj. prof. biology SUNY, Albany, 1980—; mem. neurol. scis. study sect. NIH, Bethesda, Md., 1991-94. Editorial bd.: Glia, Jour. Neurochemistry, Jour. Cerebral Blood Flow & Metabolism; contbr. articles to Scientific American, Science, Nature, Jour. Neurosci. Fulbright fellow; grantee NIH. Office: Albany Med Coll Divsn Neurosurgery A-60 47 New Scotland Ave Albany NY 12208-3412

KIMMEL, HOWARD MYLES, podiatrist; b. Bklyn., Apr. 9, 1965; s. Richard and Delane Salli (Rein) K.; m. Lisa Marie Cerveti, May 8, 1993. BA, U. South Fla., 1986; DPM, Ohio Coll. Podiatric Medicine, 1990. Resident Hawthorne (Calif.) Hosp., Baja Project for Crippled Children, 1990-92; podiatrist Buckeye Foot Care, Brook Park, Ohio, 1993—; faculty surg. Ohio Coll. Podiatric Medicine, Cleve., 1994—; spkr. panel Pfizer Labs., 1995—. Author: Clinics in Podiatric Medicine and Surgery, 1996. Vol. Free Clinic Cleve., 1993—; bd. dirs. Jewish Big Bros., Cleve. Mem. Am. Podiatric Med. Assn., Am. Coll. Foot and Ankle Surgeons (assoc.), Am. Coll. Podiatric Orthop. (assoc.). Home and Office: Buckeye Foot Care 14401 Snow Rd #102 Brook Park OH 44142

KIMURA, KIMI TAKEUCHI, social worker, educator; b. Kyoto, Japan, Apr. 13, 1926; came to U.S., 1954; d. Kinzo Fujiwara and Miyo Takeuchi; divorced; 1 child, Fumi Kimura Inouye. BA, Doshisha Women's Coll., Kyoto, 1938; postgrad., Columbia U., 1955-56; MFA, Boston U., 1957. Cert. secondary English tchr., interpreter, Japan. Rsch. assco. South Manchurian RR Rsch., Toyko, 1936-41; travel cons. SITA Internat. Travel, N.Y.C., 1957-58; vis. prof. Howard U., Washington, 1958-59; overseas adv. Japan Pubs. Assn., Tokyo, 1959-68; asst. cultural attache Embassy of Japan, Washington, 1962-66; sr. rsch. assoc. Columbia U., N.Y.C., 1973-76; case worker Lenox Hill Neighborhood Assn., N.Y.C., 1977-78; ret., 1978; trade negotiator, various bus. firms, Tokyo, N.Y.C., 1945—; dir. social work Japan/Am. Assn., N.Y.C., 1983-84; cons. Nat. Theatre of Japan, Tokyo, 1966-73; fundraiser The Vol. Coun. of Philharmonic- Symphony Soc. N.Y. Inc., 1986—, N.Y.C. Opera Guild (vol. 1994—). Contbr. numerous features articles to jours.; producer various plays, 1957. Campaign worker Dem. Party, n.Y.C., 1976-78; vol. Lincoln Ctr. Performing Arts, Inc.; fundraiser Consol. Corp. Fund, 1992—. Recipient Translation award, Nat. Sci. Found., Washington, 1973-76, Older Am. Act, Title III, Washington, 1977—. Mem. Am. Ednl. Theatre (officer 1972-73, Citation 1973), N.Y. Philharmonic (assoc. mem., Citation 1989). Home: 350 65th St Apt 12A Brooklyn NY 11220-4942

KIMURA, KUNIHIKO, anatomy educator; b. Tokyo, May 25, 1927; s. Jiro and Shizu (Kawamura) K.; m. Kazuko Natsuaki, Apr. 8, 1956; 1 child, Kotohiko. BSc, U. Tokyo, 1951; PhD, Osaka (Japan) City Med. Sch., 1957; DSc, U. Tokyo, 1962. Asst. Sch. of Medicine, Osaka City U., 1951-56; lectr. Sch. of Medicine Toho U., Tokyo, 1956-57, asst. prof. Sch. of Medicine, 1957-61; lectr. faculty of medicine U. Tokyo, 1961-64; prof. Kanagawa Dental Coll., Yokosuka, Japan, 1964-65; prof. faculty of phys. edn. Tokyo U. Edn., 1965-76; prof. Nat. Def. Med. Coll., Tokorozawa, Saitama, 1976-93, prof. emeritus, 1993—; councilor Rsch. Inst. Human Posture, Tokyo, 1966-81, dir., 1981—. Author: Human Anatomy, 1969, Growth, 1979; translator: Gray-Goss: Anatomy of Human Body, 1981, Zihlman: The Human Evolution, 1987. Mem. Am. Assn. Phys. Anthropologists, Am. Assn. Anatomists, Anthropol. Soc. Nippon, Soc. for Study of Human Biology, Japanese Assn. Anatomists. Home: 1-1-36, Sekimachi-higashi,, Nerima-ku, Tokyo 177, Japan Office: Kimura Auxological Inst, Dept of Anatomy, 1315-71 Irumagawa Sayama, Saitama 350-13, Japan

KIMURA, TAKANORI, health facility administrator, family physician; b. Yawatahama, Ehime, Japan, Dec. 27, 1930; s. Masao and Shizako (Koizumi) K.; m. Tomoko Inoh, Oct. 24, 1961; children: Takashi, Yoshiye, Hiromi. MD, Kyushu U., 1955. Diplomate Am. Bd. Family Practice. Resident in contagious disease Cook County Hosp., Chgo., 1958-59; resident in tuberculosis Sea View Hosp., S.I., N.Y., 1959-60; resident in gen. practice Louise Obici Meml. Hosp., Suffolk, Va., 1964-66; chief examiner Ministry of Health and Welfare, Tokyo, 1962-63; dep. dir. Nakamura (Japan)-shimin Hosp., 1972-73; chief family practice, dir. Benda Hosp., Pineland Center, Maine, 1976-77; dep. dir. Iyo (Japan) Hosp., 1982-83, Matsuyama (Japan) Bethel Hosp., 1983-86; dir. Tojima Clinic, Uwajima, Japan, 1987—. Coauthor: Handbook of Everyday Practice, 1987; author: (mag.) The Den-den jidai, 1979; contbr. articles to profl. jours. Recipient Disting. Svc. cert. Japan Primary Care Assn., 1987, Disting. Svc. cert. Nat. Health Ins. Groups, 1993. Fellow Am. Acad. Family Physicians; mem. Japan Med. Assn. (cert. specialist in occupational health 1991). Buddhist. Home: 1983 Tojima, Uwajima Ehime, Japan Office: Tojima Clinic, 2014 Tojima, Uwajima Ehime, Japan

KINATEDER, RONALD JOSEPH, surgeon; b. Kansas City, Mo., June 28, 1941; m. Mary M. Geng, June 11, 1966. AB, Rockhurst Coll., Kansas City, 1962; MD, U. Mo., 1966. Diplomate Am. Bd. Surgery. Intern U. Calif., San Diego, 1966-67; resident in gen. surgery Middlesex Gen. Hosp., New Brunswick, N.J., 1969-73; instr. in surgery Robert Wood Johnson Med. Sch., New Brunswick, 1973-75; pvt. practice surgery New Brunswick, 1975-86, Keokuk, Iowa, 1986—; surgery sect. chief Keokuk Area Hosp., 1989-95; clin. instr. surgery Washington U., St. Louis. Capt. U.S. Army, 1967-69. Fellow ACS. Office: 1603 Morgan Keokuk IA 52632

KINCAID, CARL HENRY, marketing professional; b. Biloxi, Miss., Nov. 26, 1963; s. Lawrence Henry and Frances Carlene (Morgan) K.; m. Jackie Diane Davis, Dec. 29, 1984; children: Seth Corbin, Andie Blair, Jaxon Reed. BA in Liberal Arts, Mid-Am. Nazarene, Olathe, Kans., 1985. Pharm. sales specialist Miles, Inc. (now Bayer), Olathe, 1990-91, hosp. sales specialist, 1991-92; hematopoietic product specialist Ortho Biotech Inc., Olathe, 1992-95, immunobiology product specialist, 1994-95; immunobiology product mgr. Ortho Biotech Inc., Raritan, N.J., 1995—. Office: Ortho Biotech Inc 700 Route 202 S Raritan NJ 08869

KINCAID, ELSIE ELIZABETH, educational therapist; b. Vernon, Tex., Nov. 29, 1929; d. Richard Oscar Paul and Bertha Rosanna (Quast) Schuetze; m. Richard Warren Kincaid, June 1, 1949; children: Carol Jean, Richard Warren, Sandra Elizabeth, Robert Rendall. AA, Del Mar Coll., 1949; BS magna cum laude, Tex. Agrl. and Industry U., 1976; MS, Corpus Christi (Tex.) State U., 1978; PhD, Columbia Pacific U., 1985. Dir., diagnostician, edn. therapist Corpus Christi Acad. Devel. Services, 1979-80; dir., diagnostician, ednl. therapist Corpus Christi Acad. Devel. Svcs., Corpus Christi, 1980-86; diagnotician, ednl. therapist Acad. Devel. Svcs., Corpus Christi, 1987; ednl. therapist Clinic for Learning Disabilities, Dallas, 1989; pvt. practice McKinney and Dallas, Tex., 1990-92, Plano, Tex., 1992—; spl. edn. substitute tchr. Corpus Christi Ind. Sch. Dist., 1986-88. Author: Reasoning Process As Early Intervention for Reading Disability, 1985, The Preschool Diagnostic Development Screening Test, 1987. V.p. Symphony Guild Corpus Christi, 1973; bd. dirs. Ada Wilson Hosp. for Children, Corpus Christi, 1986-89, Samaritan Counseling Ctr. of Coastal Bend, 1987-89 (v.p. 1988), Holy Family Sch., McKinney, 1990-92; mem. adv. bd. "Any Baby Can" Project, Corpus Christi, 1988-89; mem. High Risk Infant Task Force, Art Mus. So. Tex. and Corpus Christi, 1988-89; vol. Collin County Community Food Pantry, 1990-91. Mem. Jennete Hammer Guild (pres. 1984-85), CPA Wives (pres. 1970), Mental Health Assn. Collin County, Estate Garden Club (pres. 1981), Daus. of King (v.p. 1986-88), Plano Rep. Womens Club, Plano Chamber Orch. Encore, Kappa Delta Pi (Xi Omicron chpt.), Beta Sigma Phi (Xi Chi Pi chpt.), Heard Natural Sci. Mus. and Wildlife Sanctuary of McKinney Guild. Republican. Episcopalian. Home and Office: 1820 Azurite Trl Plano TX 75075-2106

KING, ALAN J., optometrist; b. Grand Forks, N.D., Mar. 13, 1947; s. Earle J. and Dorothy M. (Brown) K.; m. Maria K. Mowger, Mar. 2, 1979; children: Angela, Chad, Ryan, Sara, Casey. OD, Ill. Coll. Optometry, 1976. Pvt. practice Langdon, N.D., 1976-79, Western Eye Clinic, Ltd., Dickinson, N.D., 1979—. Commr. Parks and Recreation Dept. Dickinson, 1990—; bd. dirs. Cavaba County Meml. Hosp., Langdon, 1977-79. Mem. Am. Optometric Assn., N.D. Optometric Assn., Elks Lodge. Home: 586 Park St Dickinson SD 58601 Office: Western Eye Clinic 45 W 8th St Dickinson SD 58601

KING, BARBARA JEAN, nurse; b. Cape Girardeau, Mo., June 28, 1941; d. Otto Samuel and Goldie Elizabeth (Clover) Fowler; student Weatherford Jr. Coll., 1965; RN, John Peter Smith Hosp. Sch. Profl. Nursing, 1969. Cert. advanced cardiac life support; m. Charles Basil King, Jr., Sept. 4, 1972; children—Otto Samuel, Christopher Lee. Head nurse pediatrics and isolation County Hosp., also intensive care and coronary care units Small Gen. Hosp., Ft. Worth, 1969-72; dir. nursing service Jarvis Heights Nursing Center, Ft. Worth, 1976-77; dir. nursing services Ft. Worth Rehab. Farm, 1978-80; staff nurse, asst. supr. shift Decatur Community Hosp. (Tex.), 1983-85; staff nurse and supr. Burdgeport Hosp., Tex., 1986—; clin. supr., patient care coord. Hospice of Tejas; instr. vocat. nursing Cooke County Coll., Gainesville, Tex., 1981; clin. care supr. home health dept. Faith Community Hosp., 1992, assoc. dir. 1993—; patient care coord. Family Svcs. Home Health Svcs., Inc., 1994, adminstrn, for choice, 1995; cons. convalescent centers and hosps. Chmn. child care com. Women of Moose, 1977—; ch. organist Bethel Baptist Ch., assoc. pianist, 1996. Served with M.C., USN, 1962-65. Mem. Dirs. Nursing Homes Assn. Tarrant County (v.p.). Democrat. Home: Route 1 RR 1 Box 198 Alvord TX 76225-9735

KING, BERNARD DAVID, cardiologist, pharmaceutical company executive; b. Lima, Ohio, Feb. 4, 1949; s. David Bernard and Edith Hedwig (Schimmens) K.; m. Kathleen Marek, Nov. 11, 1984; children: Matthew, Meaghan, Hillary, Michael. BS cum laude, U. Notre Dame, Ind., 1970; MD cum laude, Ohio State U., Columbus, 1973; MBA, U. Pa., 1992. Intern in medicine Riverside Meth. Hosp., Columbus, Ohio, 1973-74, sr. resident in medicine, 1978-79; resident in pathology The Ohio State Univ. Hosps., Columbus, 1977-78; fellow in cardiology Mt. Sinai Med. Ctr., N.Y.C., 1979-81; asst. prof. medicine N.Y. Med. Coll., Valhalla, 1981-86, asst. prof. physiology, 1984-89; dir. cardiology tng. program Westchester County Med. Ctr., Valhalla, 1983-86; dir. clin. cardiovascular investigation Smith Kline & French Labs., Phila., 1986-89; med. dir. ConvaTec div. Squibb Co., Princeton, N.J., 1989-90; v.p. med. and regulatory affairs Worldwide Convatec div. Bristol-Myers Squibb, Princeton, N.J., 1990-92; sr. v.p. rsch. and clin. devel. Advanced Tissue Scis., LaJolla, Calif., 1992-93; pres. Segenix, Inc., La Jolla, Calif., 1993-94; exec. v.p. med. & reg. affairs & strategic technical devel. Houghten Pharms., Inc., San Diego, Calif., 1995-96; exec. v.p. biol. scis. and devel. Houghten Pharms., San Diego, 1996—; mem. com. for protection of human subjects, N.Y. Med. Coll., Valhalla, 1982-86, faculty senate, 1984-86. Contbr. articles to sci. jours. Served as capt. USAF, 1974-77. Grantee Am. Heart Assn., 1985-87. Fellow ACP, Am. Coll. Cardiology, N.Y. Cardiol. Soc., Soc. For Cardiac Angiography; mem. Am. Fedn. Clin. Research. Roman Catholic. Home: 4574 Mercurio St San Diego CA 92130-2731 Office: Houghten Pharms Inc 3550 Gen Atomics Ct San Diego CA 92121

KING, BERT THOMAS, research administrator; b. N.Y.C., Mar. 28, 1927; s. Norbert T. King and Rose J. (Kacin) King Elwell; m. Margaret MacKinnon, Aug. 26, 1950 (div. 1982); children—Cheryl, Douglas, Jeffrey. B.S., Rutgers U., 1950; M.S., Yale U., 1952, Ph.D., 1955. Lic. psychologist, Conn. Research psychologist U.S. Navy Submarine Base, New London, Conn., 1956-58; dir. tng. div. U.S. Navy Personnel Research, Washington, 1958-60; social sci. analyst USIA, Washington, 1960-63; dir. psychology dept. USN Personnel Research, Washington, 1963-65; program mgr. Office of Naval Research, Washington, 1965—; lectr. various colls. and univs. Editor: Attitudes, Conflict and Social Change, 1972; Managerial Control and Industrial Democracy, 1977. Contbr. articles to profl. jours. Served with USN, 1945-46. Woodrow Wilson fellow, 1950-52. Fellow Am. Psychol. Assn. (com. head 1980-83); mem. D.C. Psychol. Assn. (com. head 1985—), Phi Beta Kappa, Sigma Xi. Unitarian. Avocations: music; dancing. Home: 111 S Atlantic Ave Apt 805 Ormond Beach FL 32176 Office: Office of Naval Research 800 N Quincy St Arlington VA 22217

KING, BRYAN HARRY, neuropsychiatrist, medical educator and researcher; b. Fullerton, Calif., May 18, 1957; s. Raymond Ward and Marian Joan King; m. Jacquelyn G. Lund, June 4, 1983; children: Annalise Louise, Harrison Raymond. BS magna cum laude, U. Calif., Irvine, 1979; MD, Med. Coll. of Wis., 1983. Diplomate Am. Bd. Psychiatry, Am. Bd. Psychiatry and Neurology, Am. Bd. Child and Adolescent Psychiatry. Intern in internal medicine UCLA Ctr. for Health Sci., 1983-84; resident in psychiatry UCLA Neuropsychiat. Inst., 1985-87, fellow in child psychiatry, 1987-90; asst. prof. UCLA Sch. Medicine, 1990-95, assoc. prof., 1996—; psychiatry cons. Lanterman State Developmental Ctr., Pomona, Calif., 1989— (behavior mgmt. com. 1990—, pharmacy and therapeutics com. 1994—), Fairview State Devel. Ctr., Costa Mesa, Calif., 1993—, People Assisting the Homeless, L.A., 1994-95; psychopharmacology cons. UCLA Neuropsychiat. Hosp., 1991—; psychiatry expert cons. U.S. Dept. Justice, 1993, Calif. Dept. Devel. Svcs. and Office of Atty. Gen., 1995—; profl. adv. bd. Nat. Tuberous Sclerosis Assn., 1993—; bd. mem. Child SHARE, Glendale, Calif., 1994—. Cons. editor Am. Jour. Mental Retardation, 1993—; ad hoc reviewer

Archives of Gen. Psychiatry, Brit. Jour. Pharmacology, Gen. Hosp. Psychiatry, Brain Dysfunction, Life Sciences; co-editor: A Curriculum Guide to Psychiatry and Mental Retardation, 1995; contbr. articles to profl. jours., chpts. to books. Laughlin fellow Am. Coll. Psychiatrists, 1988, Gertrude Rogers Greenblatt fellow UCLA Divsn. Child Psychiatry, 1988; recipient NIMH Individual Rsch. Svc. award, 1988-89, NIMH Scientist Development award, 1991-96, George Tarjan award for achievement in mental retardation, Am. Acad. Child and Adolescent Psychiatry, 1995. Mem. Am. Psychiat. Assn. (com. mental retardation and devel. disabilities 1990—, workgroup on rsch. 1992-95), Am. Assn. on Mental Retardation, Acad. on Mental Retardation, Soc. for Rsch. in Child and Adolescent Psychiatry, Soc. for Neurosci., Group for the Advancement of Psychiatry, So. Calif. Psychiat. Soc. Presbyterian. Office: UCLA Neuropsychiatric Inst 760 Westwood Plaza Los Angeles CA 90024

KING, CHARLES MARK, dentist, educator; b. Ft. Benning, Ga., Mar. 15, 1952; s. Charles Ray and Marilyn Anita (Alexander) K.; children: Kelley Michelle, Kevin Marcus, Mark Alexander. BS, U. Ala., 1973, MS, 1977, DMD, 1981, postgrad. Birmingham Sch. Law, 1989—. cert. Pain Management Practitioner, 1992. Lab. technician Med. Lab. Assn., Birmingham, Ala., 1973-74; rsch. asst. dept. surgery Univ. Hosp., Birmingham, 1974-76, dept. anesthesiology, 1976-78; gen. practice dentistry, Birmingham, 1981—; clin. instr. U. Ala. Sch. Dentistry, Birmingham, 1982-89; mem. bd. advisors Dist. Dental Assts. Soc., 1984-90. Contbr. articles to profl. jours. Lt. col. Ala. Army NG. Named Best Clin. Instr., Student Body U. Ala. Sch. Dentistry 1985. Mem. Acad. Pain Management, 7th Dist. Dental Soc., Acad. Gen. Dentistry, Assn. Mil. Surgeons U.S., Nat. Assn. Doctors, Scottish Rite, Shriners, Masons, Delta Sigma Delta. Republican. Baptist. Avocations: archery, martial arts, hunting, water sports, flying. Masons, Shriners. Office: 5620 Chalkville Rd Birmingham AL 35235-2149

KING, CLARENCE CARLETON, managed care executive; b. Asheville, N.C., June 12, 1956; s. Clarence Carleton K. and Betty Ann (Barker) Haddon; m. Janet Susan Kerley, Aug. 20, 1981; 1 child, Douglas Carleton. BBA, Ga. State U., 1978; M of Health Adminstrn., Duke U., 1980. Diplomate Am. Coll. Health Execs. Adminstr. Hosp. Affiliates Internat., Nashville, 1980-81, Hosp. Corp. Am., Nashville, 1981-86; v.p. devel. Carle Care HMO, URbana, Ill., 1986-88; COO Health Alliance Med. Plans, URbana, Ill., 1988-90, CEO, 1990-95; exec. dir. North Tex. ops. Prudential Healthcare Group, Dallas, 1995—. Mem. Med. Group Mgmt. Assn. Home: 521 Laredo Cir Allen TX 75013 Office: Prudential Healthcare Group 4100 Alpha Rd Ste 400 Dallas TX 75244

KING, EDWARD JOSEPH, clinical chemist, laboratory administrator; b. Bronx, N.Y., Nov. 17, 1955; s. Edward Paul and May Frances (Kern) K. BS, Manhattan Coll., Riverdale, N.Y., 1978. Cert. specialist in chemistry Nat. Registry Clin. Chemistry. Sr. technologist MetPath, Teterboro, N.J., 1979-91, MetLife Lab., Elmsford, N.Y., 1991-93; lab. mgr. East Side Physicians P.C., N.Y.C., 1993—. Mem. Am. Assn. Clin. Chemistry, Am. Soc. Clin. Pathologists (cert.), Am. Chem. Soc., Clin. Lab. Mgmt. Assn. Home: 7 Balint Dr Yonkers NY 10710 Office: East Side Physicians PC 55 E 86th St New York NY 10128

KING, EDWARD LESLIE, medical group administrator; b. Somerville, Mass., Apr. 16, 1946; s. Leslie Reginald and Gertrude Druscilla K.; BS magna cum laude, Suffolk U., 1976; children: Christopher, Deborah. Asst. mgr. Legal Stock Transfer dept. Investment Cos. Services Corp., Boston, 1969-77; prin. King & Assocs., Bangor, Maine, 1979—. Trustee Maine DeMolay and Pine Tree Youth Found. Served with USN, 1967-69; mem. Res. (ret.). Fellow Am. Coll. Med. Practice Execs., Philalethes Soc. (life), Navy Cryptologic Vets. Assn.; mem. Med. Group Mgmt. Assn. (past pres. anesthesia adminstrn. assembly), Maine Med. Group Mgmt. Assn. Maine (pres., founder), Naval Enlisted Res. Assn., Am. Topical Assn., Masonic Stamp Club N.Y., NRA (life). Lodges: Masons (past master, brotherhood blue forget-me-not), Shriners, Order of DeMolay (Degree of Chevalier, Cross of Honor, past comdr. Ct. Chevaliers, trustee DeMolay Pine Tree Youth Found.), CompuServe Trainers' and Tng. Forum, CompuServe Office Automation Forum.

KING, FRED LEE, radiologist, author; b. Queen City, Mo., Aug. 9, 1931; s. Fred and Lillian D. (Campbell) K.; m. Anita Marie White, Aug. 12, 1956; children—Vincent, Christopher, Phyllis. B.S., N.E. Mo. State U., 1959; D.O., Kirksville Coll. Osteo. and Surgery; LL.B., LaSalle Extension U., Chgo., 1967. Cert. Roentgenology Am. Osteo Coll. Radiology. Practice gen. medicine and radiology Laughlin Hosp., Kirksville, Mo., 1961-83, Samaritan Meml. Hosp., Macon, Mo., 1983-86; practice medicine specializing in radiology Mo. State Prison System, 1986-92; prison physician and radiologist Iowa State Prison Sys., Iowa Med. & Classification Ctr., Oakdale, Iowa, 1992—. Author: weekly newspaper column" Nostalgia", 1983-86; contbr. articles to med. jours. Served with USN, 1951-55; Mem. Am. Osteo. Assn., Mo. Osteo. Assn., Am. Osteo. Coll. Radiology, Northeast Mo. Osteo. Assn., Republican. Lodge: Masons. Avocations: writing; antique collecting; history; old radio tapes. Home: Golf View MCH # 140 North Liberty IA 52317-9631 Office: Iowa Med & Classification Ctr Oakdale IA 52319

KING, JANET CARLSON, nutrition educator, researcher; b. Red Oak, Iowa, Oct. 3, 1941; d. Paul Emil and Norma Carolina (Anderson) Carlson; m. Charles Talmadge King, Dec. 25, 1967; children: Matthew, Samuel. BS, Iowa State U., 1963; PhD, U. Calif., Berkeley, 1972. Dietitian Fitzsimmons Gen. Hosp., Denver, 1964-67; NIH postdoctoral fellow dept. nutrition sci. U. Calif., Berkeley, 1972-73, asst. prof. nutrition dept. nutrition sci., 1973-78, assoc. prof. nutrition dept. nutrition sci., 1978-83, prof. nutrition dept. nutrition sci., 1983—, chair dept. nutrition sci., 1988-94; dir. USDA Western Human Nutrition Rsch.Ctr., San Francisco, 1995—; Frances E. Fischer Meml. nutrition lectr. Am. Dietetic Assn. Found., 1985, Lotte Arnrich Nutrition lectr. Iowa State U., 1985; Massee lectr. N.D., 1991, Lydia J. Roberts lectr. U. Chgo., 1995. Contbr. articles to Jour. Am. Diet. Assn., Am. Jour. Clin. Nutrition, Jour. Nutrition, Nutrition Rsch., Obstetrics and Gynecology, Brit. Jour. Obstetrics and Gynaecology. Recipient Lederle Labs. award in human nutrition Am. Inst. Nutrition, 1989. Mem. NAS, AAAS, Am. Dietetic Assn., Inst. Medicine, Am. Inst. Nutrition, Am. Soc. Clin. Nutrition. Office: USDA Western Human Nutrition Rsch Ctr PO Box 29997 San Francisco CA 94129

KING, JERRY N., surgeon; b. Mitchell, Ind., Dec. 25, 1939; m. Donna J. King; children. MS, Ind. Univ., 1961, MD, 1965. Diplomate Am. Bd. Surgery, Am. Bd. Thoracic Surgery. Internship Allentown (Pa.) Hosp., 1965-66, residency gen. surgery, 1968-72; residency thoracic and cardiovascular surgery Temple Univ. Hosp., Phila., 1972-74; externship St. Vincent's Hosp., Indpls., 1963-65; dir. Aerospace Medicine Malmstrom Air Force Base, Great Falls, Mont., 1966-67; chief aerospace medicine NHA Trang Air Force Base, Republic of Vietnam, 1967-68; assoc. staff Allentown Sacred Heart Hosp. Ctr., Allentown, 1974-75, Sacred Heart Hosp., Allentown, 1974-75; gen. thoracic and cardiovascular surgeon Wright Patterson Air Force Base Medical Ctr., Dayton, Ohio, 1975; dir. gen. surgery clinic Wright Patterson Air Force Base, Dayton, 1975; cardiovascular surgeon Christ Hosp. & Medical Ctr., Oak Lawn, Ill., 1975—; medical staff rep. to governing coun. Christ Hosp. & Medical Ctr., 1992—, corp. com to find system v.p. medical affairs, 1992, clinical equipment adv. com., 1993—, mem. steering com. ops. improvement, 1993, mem. exec. com., 1986—, pres. medical staff, 1990-92, pres-elect, 1988-90, chmn. credentials com., 1988-90, chmn. quality assurance com. dept. surgery, 1984-88, mem. surgical adv. & edn. com., 1984-90, chmn. cardiovascular divsn. dept. surgeon, 1987—, mem. emergency medical care com., 1983, mem. dir. surgery, 1976—; lectr. in field. Contbr. articles to profl. jours. Decorated Disting. Flying Cross medal, Bronze Star medal, Air Medal with two oak leaf clusters, Nat. Def. medal, Vietnam Svc. medal with two stars. Mem. Am. Coll. Surgeons, Soc. Thoracic Surgeons, Soc. Clinical Vascular Surgery, Am. Coll. Chest Physicians, AMA, Ill. State Medical Soc., Chgo. Medical Soc., Pan Pacific Surgical Assn. Office: Physician's Pavilion 4400 West 95th St Ste 403 Oak Lawn IL 60453

KING, JOAN CALUDA, medical educator, neuroscientist; b. New Orleans, Mar. 6, 1938. BS, St. Mary's Dominican Coll., 1961; MS, U. New Orleans, 1970; PhD, Tulane U., 1973. Rsch. assoc. in neuroanatomy U. Iowa Coll. Medicine, Iowa City, 1973-74; NIH postdoctoral fellow (neuroscis.) Tulane U., New Orleans, 1974-76, rsch. assoc., vis. asst. prof. neurosci., 1976-79; asst. prof. anatomy Tufts U. Sch. Medicine, Boston, 1979-85, assoc. prof. anatomy and cellular biology, 1985-92, prof., chmn. anatomy and cellular biology, 1992—, dir. reproductive ctr., 1992—; mem. many nat. rev. coms., NSF, NIH, NICHD, 1979—. Co-author: Exploring the Basic Structures of the Brain, 1991, A Responsive Learning Environment for Medical Neurosciences: Sensory and Motor Pathways in the Spinal Cord, 1991; contbr. articles to profl. jours., chpts. to books; presenter in field; invited participant in numerous rsch. seminars and symposia; editl. bd. Biotechniques; ad hoc reviewer Science, Nature, Biology of Reproduction, Brain Rsch., Brain Rsch. Bull., Endocrinology, Jour. Histochemistry Cytochemistry, Jour. Neurosci., Neuroendocrinology, Neurosci., Peptides. Recipient Career Devel. award USPHS, 1979-84. Mem. Am. Assn. Anatomists, Internat. Soc. Psychoneuroendocrinology, Soc. Neurosci., Endocrine Soc. (animal welfare subcom. 1989), Kappa Delta Pi. Office: Tufts Univ Sch Medicine Dept Anatomy & Cellular Bio 136 Harrison Ave Boston MA 02111

KING, JOSEPH CLEMENT, physician; b. Colorado Springs, Colo., Aug. 20, 1922; s. Charles Clement and Gladys (Ascher) K.; BS Tulane U., 1944, MD, 1946; m. Margie Freudenthal Leopold, Apr. 2, 1947; children: Leopold Ascher, Jocelyn King Tobias. Instr. zoology Tulane U., 1941-42; rotating intern Michael Reese Hosp., Chgo., 1946-47, resident in internal medicine, 1947-50; assoc. with Dr. Sidney Portis, Chgo., 1950-51; practice medicine specializing in internal medicine, Chgo., 1953-77, Palm Springs, Calif., 1977-79, 89—; attending staff Louis A. Weiss Hosp., Chgo., 1953-77, hon. staff, 1979-90; attending staff Desert Hosp., 1977-79, 89-92; med. dir. Life Extension Inst., Chgo., 1979-80; dir. employee health svcs. Continental Ill. Nat. Bank, Chgo., 1980-87; exec. cons. health care mgmt. Coopers & Lybrand, Chgo., 1987-88; asst. to assoc. clin. prof. internal medicine Northwestern U. Med. Sch., Chgo., 1954-67; clin. asst. prof. medicine Abraham Lincoln Sch. Medicine U. Ill., 1973-77; clin. asst. prof. preventive medicine and community health Northwestern U. Med. Sch., 1980-88 ; asst. prof. preventive medicine Rush Med. Coll., 1986-88. Capt. M.C., AUS, 1944-46, 1951-53. Diplomate Am. Bd. Internal Medicine. Fellow ACP, Am. Coll. Occupl. and Environ. Med.; mem. Chgo. Soc. Internal Medicine, Chgo. Med. Soc , AMA, Ill. Med. Assn., Riverside County Med. Assn., Calif. Med. Assn., Am. Heart Assn., Chgo. Heart Assn. (past bd. govs.), Am. Rheumatism Assn., Assn. Bank Med. Dirs., Am. Cancer Soc. (past v.p. Chgo. unit), Western States Assn. Occupl. Medicine, Tulane Med. Alumni Assn. (past dir.), Medic Alert (past mem. midwest adv. bd.), Chgo. Assn. Commerce and Industry (past mem. occupational medicine com.), Med. Dirs. Club Chgo. (past pres.), Phi Beta Kappa, Beta Mu, Alpha Omega Alpha. Contbr. numerous articles in field to med. jours. Office: 275 N El Cielo Rd Palm Springs CA 92262-6914

KING, JOSEPH WILLET, child psychiatrist; b. Springfield, Mo., Aug. 26, 1934; m. Doris Ann Toby; children: Pamela Renee, Timothy Wells, Michael Brian, Bradley Christopher. BA, So. Meth. U., 1956; MD, U. Tex. Southwestern, 1962. Diplomate Am. Bd. Psychiatry and Neurology; ordained deacon Episcopal Ch., 1996. Intern Baylor U. Med. Ctr., Dallas, 1962-63; resident in gen. psychiatry Timberlawn Psychiat. Hosp., 1963-64, Lisbon VA Hosp., 1965; fellow in child psychiatry U. Tex. Southwestern Med. Sch., 1965-67, Hillside Hosp., Glen Oaks, N.Y., 1967; staff child psychiatrist, dir. child and adolescent svcs. Timberlawn Psychiat. Ctr., Inc., Dallas, 1967-78; assoc. attending child psychiatrist dept. psychiatry Baylor U. Med. Ctr., Dallas, 1967-78; active attending child psychiatrist Children's Med. Ctr., Dallas, 1967-78; attenting staff Dallas County Hosp. Dist./Parkland Meml. Hosp., 1967-78; cons. child psychiatry Girls Day Care Rehab. Ctr. Dallas County, Dallas, 1970-73; cons. child psychiatry and adminstrn. Meridell Achievement Ctr., Austin, Tex., 1971-73; dir. adolescent svcs. Portsmouth (Va.) Psychiat. Ctr., 1978-79; active attending child psychiatrist Maryview Hosp., Portsmouth, 1978-80; med. dir., chief exec. officer Psychiat. Inst. Richmond, Va., 1980-86; chief exec. officer, psychiatrist-in-chief Shadow Mountain Inst., Tulsa, 1987-90; v.p. Century Healthcare, Tulsa, 1987-90; assoc. clin. prof. Med. Coll. Va., Va. Commonwealth U., 1980-90, Med. Sch. U. Okla., Tulsa, 1987—. Contbr. articles to profl. jours. Fellow Am. Psychiat. Assn. (Okla. dist. br.), Am. Soc. Adolescent Psychiatry (nat. pres. 1975-76), Am. Orthopsychiat. Assn., Am. Coll. Psychiatrists; mem. AMA, Tex. Med. Assn. (various coms.), Dallas County Med. Soc. (various coms.), Am. Acad. Child and Adolescent Psychiatry (ins. com. 1981-86, pres. Okla. coun. 1991-92, state del. to nat. coun.), Tex. Soc. Child Psychiatry (past officer), Nat. Assn. Pvt. Psychiat. Hosps. (chmn. adolescent care com. 1971-81, multiple com./task force functions, pres. ind. for profit sect. 1991-92, trustee 1992-95), Okla. Med. Soc., Tulsa County Med. Soc., Tulsa Psychiat. Assn., Alumni Assn. U. Tex. Southwestern Med. Sch. (pres. 1991-94). Office: 7146 S Braden Ave Tulsa OK 74136-6371

KING, KATHERINE CHUNGHO, pediatrician; b. Beijing, People's Republic of China, Aug. 27, 1937; came to U.S., 1955; d. Ginpoh Yeh and Wen Ying (Hsu) King; m. Peter A.J. Adam (wid. June 1980); m. Louis H. Li, June 8, 1985. BA, Meredith Coll., 1957; MD, Bowman Gray Sch. Medicine, 1962. Diplomate Nat. Bd. Med. Examiners, Am. Bd. Pediatrics, Am. Bd. Neonatal-Perinatal Medicine. Resident in pediatrics Cleve. Metro Gen. Hosp./Case Western Res. U., 1962-66; instr. of pediatrics Case Western Res. U., Cleve., 1969-71, asst. prof. to assoc. prof. pediatrics, 1971-85, assoc. prof. reproductive biology, 1979-85; assoc. prof. pediatrics Albert Einstein Coll. of Medicine, N.Y.C., 1989—; co-dir. Perinatal Clin. Rsch. Ctr. Cleve. Metro Gen. Hosp., 1969-85, dir. div. neonatology, 1981-85; staff neonatologist Schneider Children's Hosp., New Hyde Park, N.Y., 1985—. Contbr. articles to profl. jours. Recipient grants for Devel. of Glucose Control, Diabetics Assn. of Greater Cleve., 1968-70, Disordered Fetal Metabolism, NIH, 1983-88, GIP Responses of Newborns, Ross Labs., 1983, Perinatal Outreach, Fan Fox and Leslie R. Samuel Found., N.Y., 1990. Fellow Am. Acad. Pediatrics, Am. Coll. Nutrition; mem. Am. Fedn. Clin. Rsch., Soc. Pediatric Rsch., Ea. Soc. Pediatric Rsch., Am. Diabetes Assn. Home: 19 Gramatan Ct Bronxville NY 10708-3015 Office: Schnieder Children's Hosp New Hyde Park NY 11042

KING, KENNETH VERNON, JR., pharmacist; b. Lexington, Miss., Dec. 17, 1950; s. Kenneth Vernon Sr. and Louise (Jordan) K.; m. Janis Marie Guynes, June 12, 1976; children: Kenneth V. King III, Nanette Marie King, Jason Guynes King. AA, Holmes Jr. Coll., 1971; BS in Pharmacy, U. Miss., 1973; cert. sterile compounding dosage units, Profl. Compounding Ctrs. Am., Houston, 1993. Registered pharmacist, Miss., Pa.; cert. in sterile aseptic compounding medicinal units. Pharmacist Barretts Drug Store, Greenwood, Miss., 1973-74; registered pharmacist Eckerd Drugs, Greenwood, 1974-76, 77-88, Medi-Save Drugs Ellis Isle, Jackson, Miss., 1976; registered pharmacist Eckerd Drugs, Pearl, Miss., 1988-90, Jackson, 1990-92; compounding pharmacist Marty's Discount Drugs, Flowood, Miss., 1992-96, co-owner, 1996—; cons. Sta-Home Hospice care of Miss., Grace House of Jackson, 1992—, Hospice Care Fund., Vicksburg, Miss., 1993-94; cons. Whispering Pines Hospice (inpatient), 1992—, Hospice of Ctrl. Miss. (outpatient), 1993—; owner, contractor, rschr., cons. Profl. Pharm. Svcs. in Miss., Jackson; owner Pharmakan Inc., Pharmakeus Inc.; presenter regional seminars Profl. Compounding Ctrs. of Am., Birmingham, Ala., 1993, 94, Charlotte, N.C., 1994, Symposium on Man and His Environment, Am. Acad. Environ. Medicine, 1995; clin. pharmacy instr. U. Miss. Sch. Pharmacy, Oxford, 1985-92, 95—; tchr. environ. illness VA Hosp.; hospice pharmacist, cons., 1992—; mem. Profl. Compounding Corp. Am., Houston, P2C2 Profl. Care, Inc., Houston; co-writer compounding criteria Miss. State Bd. Pharmacy, Pharmacy Practice Act, 1993, co-investigator prescribing protocols, 1994; participant AIDS Update '96 for Delta Region (Miss., Ark. and La.), Jackson, 1996. Advisor Leflore County 4-H, Greenwood, 1974-76; aux. patrolman Greenwood Police Dept., 1982-86; drug identification specialist Greenwood Aux. Police Dept., 1984-85; pres., founder Human Ecology Action League Miss., Inc., 1988—, bd. dirs. 1991—, advt. coord., Atlanta, 1989%, sec., 1984—; coord. Environ. Assocs. Jack Eckerd, Inc., 1990-92; mem. Rainbow Whole Food Coop., 1989—; coord. regional support svcs. HEAL Inc., 1989—. Mem. Environ. Coalition of Miss. (co-founder), Environ. Assocs. of Jack Eckerd Inc. (coord.), Miss. Soc. Cons. Pharmacists. Mem. Word of Life Ch. Office: Profl Pharm Svcs 1050C 3 N Flowood Dr Jackson MS 39208

KING, LOWELL RESTELL, pediatric urologist; b. Salem, Ohio, Feb. 28, 1932; s. Lowell Waldo and Vesta Ethylwin (Snyder) K.; m. Mary Elizabeth Hill, July 9, 1960 (div. 1991); children—Andrew Restell, Erika Lillie. BA, Johns Hopkins U., 1953, MD, 1956. Intern Johns Hopkins Hosp., Balt., 1956-57; resident in urology Johns Hopkins Hosp., 1957-62; asst. prof. urology Johns Hopkins U., 1962-63; asst. prof. urology Northwestern U., 1963-67, assoc. prof., 1967-70, prof., 1970-81, prof. surgery, 1974-81; prof. urology and pediatrics Duke U., Durham, N.C., 1981—; prof., chmn. dept. urology Presbyn.-St. Luke's Hosp., 1968-70; surgeon-in-chief Children's Meml. Hosp., Chgo., 1974-80. Author: (with P.P. Kelalis) Clinical Pediatric Urology, 1976, 3d edit., 1992, Bladder Replacement and Continent Urology Diversion, 1986, 2d edit., 1991, Urologic Surgery in the Neonate and Young Infant, 1992, Reconstructive Urology, 1992, Urologic Surgery in Infants and Children, 1996; assoc. editor Urology; editor profl. jours.; contbr. articles to sci. jours. Vestryman, sr. warden Ch. of Our Savior, 1974-80; bd. dirs. Gads Hill Settlement House, 1969-73. Recipient Gold medal All India Urologic Congress, 1996. Mem. AMA, Am. Urol. Assn., Am. Acad. Pediats. (chmn. sect. urology 1969-72, sec. 1972-76, Gold meda Mex. 1991, Urology medal 1992), Soc. Pediat. Urology (pres. 1983), Soc. U. Urologists, Am. Assn. Genitourinary Surgeons, Clin. Soc. Genitourinary Surgeons (pres. 1996). Republican. Episcopalian. Home: 1720 Tisdale St Durham NC 27705-5632 Office: Duke U Med Ctr PO Box 3831 Durham NC 27702-3831

KING, MARK ALLEN, osteopathic family physician; b. Winterset, Fla., Dec. 20, 1955; s. Charles William and Barbara Jo (Dowler) K.; m. Jamie Leigh Momper, Nov. 24, 1978; children: Rachel, Michelle, Megan. BA in Biology and Bus., Simpson Coll., 1978; DO, U. Medicine and Health Scis., Des Moines, 1987. Diplomate Am. Bd. Family Practice Physicians. Resident Ind. U., Ft. Wayne, 1990; family physician BMA PC, Ft. Wayne, Ind., 1990—; asst, dir. family practice residency Ft. Wayne Med. Edn. Program, 1990—; profl. team physician Ft. Wayne Wizards basketball team, 1992—, Ft. Wayne Fury baseball team, 1992—; dir. exec. com. Bklyn. Med. Assn., Ft. Wayne, 1990—; assoc. prof. family medicine U. Ind. Med. Sch., Ft. Wayne, 1992—; chmn. bd. Luth. Hosp., Ft. Wayne, 1995—. Bd. dirs. Duke's Day Med. Scholarships, Ft. Wayne, Ind., 1992—. Mem. AMA, Am. Osteo. Assn., Am. Acad. Family Physicians, Ind. State Med. Assn., Ft. Wayne Med. Soc. Republican. Roman Catholic. Home: 4430 Old Mill Rd Fort Wayne IN 46809 Office: BMA PC 3610 Brooklyn Ave Fort Wayne IN 46807

KING, MELISSA BUFFINGTON, internist, educator; b. Phila., Aug. 9, 1959. AB magna cum laude, Franklin and Marshall Coll., 1981; MD, Johns Hopkins U., 1985. Diplomate Am. Bd. Internal Medicine, Pulmonary Diseases, Critical Care; lic. dr. Minn. Resident U. Minn., Mpls., 1985-89; fellow pulmonary and critical care medicine Thomas Jefferson U. Hosp., Phila., 1989-90; fellow rsch. pulmonary and critical care medicine U. Minn., Mpls., 1990-92, instr. pulmonary medicine and critical care, 1992—. Contbr. articles to profl. jours. Recipient Southeastern Pa. Chem. Soc. award, 1979, 1st pl. ann. Fellows' Case Presentation Laennec Soc. Phila., 1990, Pulmonary Fellowship award Allen and Hanburys Respiratory Inst., 1992, Dept. Medicine Rsch. award, 1993. Mem. Am. Coll. Chest Physicians (Physician Scientist award 1993-95), Minn. Thoracic Soc. Office: Pulmonology & Critical Care Med PO Box 276 UMHC 420 Delaware St SE Minneapolis MN 55455-0374

KING, MICHAEL JAMES, podiatric surgeon; b. Sandusky, Ohio, Oct. 17, 1957; s. James Everett and Nola Jean (potts) K.; m. Laura Ann Novak, June 4, 1983; children: Lindsay, Christopher. BS, Baldwin-Wallace Coll., 1979; D of Podiatric Medicine, Ohio Coll. Podiatric Medicine, 1983. Diplomate Am. Bd. Podiatric Surgery. Surg. resident Toledo Riverside Hosp., 1983-85; podiatric surgeon pvt. practice Howell, N.J., 1985-87; podiatric surgeon Foot Care Assocs., Inc., Fall River, Mass., 1987—; trustee Fund for Podiatric Med. Edn., 1994—. Author: (book chpts.) Infectious Diseases of the Lower Extremity, 1990. Fellow Am. Coll. Foot Surgeons (1st Pl. for papers written 1985), Mass. Podiatric Med. Soc. (1st v.p. 1992-94, pres. 1995—, trustee fund for podiatric med. edn.). Office: 222 Milliken Blvd Fall River MA 02721-1623

KING, PATRICIA A., medical researcher. PhD in Physiology, Brown U., 1982. Rsch. assoc. physiology Emory U. Sch. Medicine, 1984-87; rsch. assoc. U. Vt. Coll. Medicine, 1987—. Mem. Inst. Med.-Nat. Acad. Sci. Office: U Vt Coll Medicine Given Bldg Burlington VT 05405*

KING, PETER TIAN-LUNG, physician; b. Shanghai, Republic of China, May 9, 1947; arrived in Hong Kong, 1958.; s. Gordon S. and Sunny (Moh) K. BS, Fordham U., N.Y.C., 1970; MD, Temple U., Phila., 1974. Diplomate Am. Bd. Internal Med., Am. Bd. Internal Med. subspecialty Cardiovascular Diseases. Intern Pacific Med. Ctr., San Francisco, 1974-75; resident UCLA and VA Med. Ctr., Sepulveda, Calif., 1975-78; fellow in cardiology UCLA and VA Med. Ctr., 1978-80; attending cardiologist and dir. Hong Kong Adventist Hosp. Heart Ctr., 1980—, dir. intensive care unit, cardiac rehab. program, cardiopulmonary lab., 1981-83. Author, editor: Cardiac Rehabilitation for Nurses, 1982. Fellow ACP, Am. Coll. of Chest Physicians. Club: Rotary. Office: Prince's Bldg Suite 1508, 10 Chater Rd, Hong Kong Hong Kong

KING, ROBERT EDWARD, retired pharmacy educator; b. Zanesville, Ohio, Dec. 27, 1923; s. Ray Harrison and Edna Elizabeth (Bowman) K.; m. Jane Wanner Klein, Aug. 12, 1950; children: Susan J., Timothy P., Peter R., Christina A., Jonathan D. BS in Pharmacy, Ohio State U., 1944; PhD in Pharmaceutical Chemistry, U. Minn., 1948. Rsch. assoc. Merck Sharp & Dohme, West Point, Pa., 1948-61; prof. pharmacy Phila. Coll. Pharmacy and Sci., 1961-86, prof. emeritus, 1986—; Author: Remington's Pharmaceutical Sciences, 1965-85; editor: (jour.) Parenteral Drug Assn., 1966-78. Republican. Episcopalian. Home: 3475 Aquetong Rd Doylestown PA 18901

KING, ROGER DUANE, II, medical, surgical and geriatrics nurse; b. Lancaster, Calif., Jan. 20, 1966; s. Roger Duane King and Roxie Ann (Frazier) Larsen; m. Sandra Faye Cunningham, Feb. 29, 1992; 1 child, Roger Duane III. Grad., Barton County Coll., Hays, Kans. LPN, Kans. Nurse Hays Med. Ctr., 1991-93, Wheatland Nursing, Russell, Kans., 1993—. Home: PO Box 272 Hays KS 67601-0272

KING, RONOLD WYETH PERCIVAL, physics educator; b. Williamstown, Mass., Sept. 19, 1905; s. James Percival and Edith Marianne Beate (Seyerlen) K.; m. Justine Merrell, June 22, 1937 (dec. Aug. 1990); 1 son, Christopher Merrell; m. Mary M. Govoni, June 1, 1991. A.B., U. Rochester, 1927, S.M., 1929; Ph.D., U. Wis., 1932; student, U. Munich, Germany, 1928-29, Cornell U., 1929-30. Asst. in physics U. Rochester, 1927-28; Am.-German exchange student, 1929-30; White fellow in physics Cornell U., 1929-30; U. fellow in elec. engring. U. Wis., 1930-32, research asst., 1932-34; instr. physics Lafayette Coll., 1934-36, asst. prof., 1936-37; Guggenheim fellow Berlin, Germany, 1937-38; with Harvard U., 1938—, successively instr., asst. prof., assoc. prof., 1938-46, prof. applied physics, 1946-72, prof. emeritus, 1972—; cons. electromagnetics and antennas, 1972—. Author: Electromagnetic Engineering, Vol. 1, 1945, 2d edit, Fundamental Electromagnetic Theory, 1963, Transmission Lines, Antennas and Wave Guides, (with A.H. Wing and H.R. Mimmo), 1945, 2d edit., 1965, Transmission-Line Theory, 1955, 2d edit., 1965, Theory of Linear Antennas, 1956, (with T.T. Wu) Scattering and Diffraction of Waves, 1959, (with R.B. Mack and S.S. Sandler) Arrays of Cylindrical Dipoles, 1968, (with C.W. Harrison, Jr.) Antennas and Waves: A Modern Approach, 1969, Tables of Antenna Characteristics, 1971, (with G.S. Smith et al) Antennas in Matter, 1981 (with S. Prasad) Fundamental Electromagnetic Theory and Applications, 1986, (with M. Owens and T.T. Wu) Lateral Electromagnetic Waves Theory and Applications to Communications, Geophysical Exploration and Remote Sensing, 1992; also articles in field. Guggenheim fellow Europe, 1937, 58, IBM scholar Northeastern U., 1985; recipient Disting. Service citation U. Wis., 1973, Pender award U. Pa., 1986. Fellow IEEE (Centennial medal 1984), AAAS, Am. Acad. Arts and Scis., Am. Phys. Soc.; mem. IEEE Antennas and Propagation Soc. (Disting. Achievement award 1991), AAUP, Internat. Sci. Radio Union, Bavarian Acad. Sci. (contbg. mem.), Phi Beta Kappa, Sigma Xi. Home: 92 Hillcrest Pky Winchester MA 01890-1440 Office: Gordon McKay Lab 9 Oxford St Cambridge MA 02138-2901

KING, STEPHEN, pediatrician; b. N.Y.C., May 5, 1944; s. Harry and Grace (Fruchter) K.; m. Joan Fay Eden; children: Traci, Lisa. BA, NYU, 1965; JD, MD, SUNY, Bklyn., 1969; postgrad., Kennesaw State Coll. Intern U. Hosp. of Cleve., 1969-70, resident, 1970-71; resident Yale U. Hosp., New Haven, 1971-72; pvt. practice, pres. Pediatrics and Adolescent Medicine, Atlanta, 1974—; clin. assoc. prof. Emory U., Atlanta, 1974—;

asst. prof. Ga. Bapt. Sch. Nursing, Atlanta, 1974—; chmn. pediatrics Northside Hosp., Atlanta, Scottish Rite Hosp. for Children, Atlanta; mem. med. adv. bd. MetLife, Scottish Rite Pediatric Ptnrs., Morgan Health Care Group. Contbr. articles to profl. jours. Founder, pres. Congregation Etz Chaim, Marietta, Ga., 1975-78; bd. dirs. United Way of Cobb County, Marietta, 1980-81, Atlanta Jewish Community Ctr., Jewish Family and Children's Svcs., Atlanta. Maj. USAF, 1972-74. Fellow Am. Acad. Pediatrics; mem. AMA, Med. Assn. Ga., Med. Assn. Atlanta, Alpha Omega Alpha Honor Soc. Republican. Home: 970 Riverside Trce NW Atlanta GA 30328-3640 Office: Pediatrics & Adolescent Med 6667 Vernon Woods Dr NE Atlanta GA 30328-3215 also: 2155 Post Oak Marietta GA 30062

KING, SUSAN LOUISE SEDDON, geriatrics nurse; b. Natick, Mass., Dec. 27, 1956; m. Thomas P. King, Jan. 1, 1975; children: Michael, Matthew. AD, Quinsigamond C.C., Worcester, Mass., 1991. RN, Mass.; cert. intravenous nurse, CPR. Staff nurse Luth. Nursing Home, Worcester, 1991-94, Holy Trinity Nursing Home, 1994—. Vol. hospice nuse Vis. Nurse Assn., Worcester, 1991-95. Home: 46 Parker Ave Holden MA 01520

KING, VICTORIA VAN BEUREN, otolaryngologist; b. St. Louis, Jan. 16, 1953; d. Willard Van Beuren and Frances Howell (Lewis) K. BA in Human Biology with honors, Stanford U., 1975; MD, U. Mo., Columbia, 1979. Diplomate Am. Bd. Otolaryngology. Resident in otolaryngology Stanford U. Hosp., 1980-83, pvt. practice medicine specializing in otolaryngology surgery, Palo Alto, Calif., 1983-95, Canon City, Colo., 1995—. Mem. U.S. Olympic Swimming Team, 1968, U.S. Swimming Teams to Australia, Tahiti, Can. and Eng., 1969-72. Lt. Calif. Air N.G., 1986-95. U.S. Nat. Swimming Champion, 1969; recipient award for scholastic achievement Am. Med. Women's Assn. Fellow ACS; mem. AMA, Am. Acad. Facial Plastic and Reconstructive Surgery, Am. Acad. Otolaryngology/Head and Neck Surgery, Alpha Omega Alpha. Office: 1439 Main St Ste C Canon City CO 81212

KING, VIVIAN KAY, psychotherapist, writer, educator; b. Hutchinson, Kans., Feb. 18, 1946; d. Allen Erb and Fannie (Yutzy) K.; m. John Adams, Dec. 28, 1965 (div. 1978); m. Will Solenthaler, June 15, 1980 (div. 1983); 1 child, Mark. BSN, Goshen (Ind.) Coll., 1968; MA in Counseling Psychology, Goddard Coll., 1978; PhD in Psychology, Sierra U., 1988. Nurse Goshen Gen. Hosp., 1968-69; psychiat. nurse Elkhard (Ind.) Gen. Hosp., 1969-71, Howard Community Hosp., Kokomo, Ind., 1972-75, Pomona (Calif.) Psychiat. Hosp., 1975-79; counselor, educator Pasadena (Calif.) Psychosynthesis Ctr., 1978-80, Synthesis, Hutchinson, 1980-83; dir., ednl. counselor Psychosynthesis Ctr., Pasadena, 1983-90; founder, dir. Inner Theatre, Inc., 1990—. Contbr. articles to profl. jours. Fellow Internat. Found. Internal Psychology, Assn. for Transpersonal Psychology, Assn. for Humanistic Psychology. Home and Office: 101 Spirit Mountain Santa Fe NM 87505-9510

KING, WALTER WING-KEUNG, surgeon, head and neck surgery consultant; b. Hong Kong, Jan. 27, 1950; s. Albert Cheng and Josephine Shou-Fan (Chao) K.; m. May Kam-Wei Poon, June 8, 1985; children: Kenneth S. F., Spencer S. W. BA with honors, U. Wis., 1971; MD, Vanderbilt U., 1975. Diplomate Am. Bd. Surgery. Intern Vanderbilt U. Hosp., Nashville, 1975-76; resident surgeon SUNY, Stony Brook, 1976-80; clin. asst. in surgery Mass. Gen. Hosp., Boston, 1980-82; clin. fellow in surgery Harvard U., Boston, 1980-82; fellow, head and neck svc. Meml. Sloan-Kettering Cancer Ctr., N.Y.C., 1982-83; asst. prof. surgery SUNY, Stony Brook, 1983-84; vis. fellow otolaryngology Stanford (Calif.) U. Med. Ctr., 1984; lectr. head and neck surgery Chinese U., Hong Kong, 1984-88, sr. lectr. surgery, 1988-93, reader surgery, 1993-95, prof. surgery, 1995—; asst. dir. Nutritional Support Unit, Mass. Gen. Hosp., Boston, 1981-82; cons. surgeon head and neck-plastic surgery Prince of Wales Hosp., Sha Tin, Hong Kong, 1988—. Contbr. articles to profl. jours. Shriners Burn Inst. rsch. fellow, 1980-82; Am. Soc. for Head and Neck Surgery fellow, 1984, Royal Coll. Surgeons Edinburgh fellow, 1991. Fellow Am. Coll. Surgeons, Royal Coll. Surgeons Can.; mem. Soc. Head and Neck Surgeons, Am. Burn Assn., Am. Soc. for Head and Neck Surgery, Internat. Assn. Endocrine Surgeons, Am. Acad. Facial Plastic and Reconstructive Surgery, Coll. Surgeons Hong Kong. Office: Prince of Wales Hosp, Dept Surgery, Sha Tin Hong Kong

KING CALKINS, CAROL COLEMAN, health science association administrator; b. L.A., May 31, 1949; d. Harold S. and Gladys (Blumenthal) Coleman; 1 child, Katrina Elizabeth King; m. Michael Steven Calkins, Oct. 10, 1987. BA in Psychology, U. Colo., 1972; MBA, U. No. Colo., 1982. Dir. group living Nat. Jewish Ctr. Immunology and Respiratory Medicine, Denver, 1980-82; dir. clin. support svcs. Nat. Jewish Ctr. Immunology and Respiratory Medicine, 1982-83, dir. spl. projects, 1983-84, asst. dir. adminstrv. svcs., 1984, dir. adminstrv. svcs., 1984-95; dir. facilities svcs. U. Colo. Health Scis. Ctr., Denver, 1995—; chair purchasing and contract subcom. Denver Health and Hosps. New Authority, 1994-96; speaker in field. Recorder improvement process coun. Jefferson County (Colo.) Schs., 1989. Mem. Colo. Hosp. Assn. Risk Mgrs., Am. Coll. Healthcare Execs., Assn. Commuter Transp. (v.p. Rocky Mountain chpt. 1992). Office: 1400 Jackson St Denver CO 80206-2761

KINGHORN, ALAN DOUGLAS, pharmacy educator; b. Newcastle-upon-Tyne, U.K., Aug. 31, 1947; came to the U.S., 1975; s. Alan Douglas and Lilian Isabel (Henderson) K.; m. Helen Maria Bermudez, July 17, 1976. B in Pharmacy with honors, U. Bradford, U.K., 1969; MSc, U. Strathclyde, Glasgow, U.K., 1970; PhD, U. London, Eng., 1975, DSc, 1990. Cert. pharmacy Great Britain, No. Ireland. Analytical chemist Burroughs Wellcome Co., Dartford, Kent, U.K., 1970-71; tchg. fellow U. London (Eng.) Sch. Pharmacy, 1971-75; postdoctoral fellow U. Miss., Oxford, 1975-76; rsch. assoc. U. Ill. Med. Ctr., Chgo., 1976-77, asst. prof., 1977-81, assoc. prof., 1981-86, prof., 1986—, assoc. dir. program for collaborative rsch. in pharm. scis., 1992—; asst. head dept. medicinal chemistry and pharmacognosy, 1995—; guest prof. Swiss Fed. Inst. Tech., Zurich, 1990; chmn. internat. adv. com. Internat. Symposium on Sweeteners, Jerusalem, 1996. Editor: Toxic Plants, 1979; co-editor: Human Medicinal Agents from Plants, 1993; editor-in-chief Jour. Natural Products, 1994—; contbr. articles to profl. jours. B. Kenneth West U. scholar U. Ill. Alumni Found., 1993. Fellow Linnean Soc. London, Royal Pharm. Soc. Great Britain; mem. Am. Soc. Pharmacognosy (pres. 1990-91), Soc. for Econ. Botany (pres. 1991-92). Office: Univ Ill Coll Pharmacy 833 S Wood St Chicago IL 60612

KINGHORN, CAROL ANN, school psychologist. BA in English, Libr. Sci., SUNY, Albany, 1957, MA in English, Secondary Edn., 1958; MA in Sch. Psychology, Hofstra U., 1969, PhD in Psychology, 1973. Various positions, 1953-71; assoc. prof. dept. behavioral scis. N.Y. Inst. Tech., 1971-72, 74; instr. dept. social scis. SUNY, Farmingdale, 1972-73; sch. psychologist Kings Point Sch., Great Neck, N.Y., 1972-74; lectr. grad. dept. psychology Hofstra U., 1973-74; assoc. prof. grad. dept. counselor edn. C.W. Post Coll., 1974-77; psychologist Hofstra U. Counseling Ctr., 1973-77; pvt. practice psychotherapy Hempstead and Roslyn, N.Y., 1974—; psychologist South Shore Ctr. for Psychotherapy, 1974-83; sch. psychologist Garden City (N.Y.) Pub. Schs., 1978—. Mem. Am. Psychol. Assn., Nassau County Psychol. Assn., Nassau County Psychol. Svcs. Inst. (bd. dirs. 1989—). Home: 14 St James Pl Hempstead NY 11550-1118 Office: 1405 Old Northern Blvd Roslyn NY 11576-2146 Also: 131 Fulton Ave Hempstead NY 11550-3701

KINGORE, EDITH LOUISE, retired geriatrics and rehabilitation nurse; b. Parsons, Kans., Nov. 18, 1922; d. George Richard and Josephine (Martin) K. Diploma, Mo. Meth. Hosp., St. Joseph, 1955. RN. Staff nurse El Cerrito Hosp., Long Beach, Calif., 1966-69; nurse Alamitos-Belmont Convalescent Hosp., Long Beach, 1973-75; staff nurse Freeman Hosp., Joplin, Mo., 1975-76, Oak Hill Osteo. Hosp., Joplin, 1976-77; surg. care and rehab. nurse St. Francis Med. Ctr., Cape Guiardo, Mo., 1977-78; psychiat. nurse Western Mo. Mental Health Ctr., Kansas City, Mo., 1978; pvt. duty nurse, 1978-83. Historian South Coast Ecumenical Coun., 1993-94. Home: 3333 Pacific Pl Apt 108 Long Beach CA 90806-1261

KINGSLEY, BENEDICT, medical foundation administrator; b. Vienna, Austria, Apr. 12, 1923; came to U.S., 1938; s. Naum and Olga (Reiskin) Koenigfest; m. Martha Simche, Jan. 26, 1947; children: Ronald Mark, Leonard Evan, Jeffrey David. BSEE, CUNY, 1947; MSc in Math., NYU, 1950; ScD, Ind. No. U., 1972. Physicist Bklyn. Navy Yard, 1947-48; design engr. Espey Radio, N.Y.C., 1948-50; Univac sys. engr. Remington Rand, Phila., 1950-54; supervisory engr. Applied Sci. Corp. Princeton, N.J., 1954-56; radar and sonar sys. engr. RCA, Moorestown, N.J., 1956-63; adj. assoc. prof. cardiology, asst. prof. radiology Hahnemann Med. U., Phila., 1963-79; ptnr. Echelon Noninvasive Diagnostic Lab., Voorhees, N.J., 1978-81; pres., program dir. Nat. Found. for Noninvasive Diagnostics, Princeton, 1978—; cons. in diagnostic ultrasound West Jersey Hosp. Sys., Camden and Voorhees, 1964-81, Met. Hosp., Phila., 1978-81. Author: Advances in Noninvasive Diagnostic Cardiology, 1976; editor, author Noninvasive Diagnostics Newsletter, 1972-79; contbg. editor, author, cons. editor Med. Elctronics and Data Jour., 1973—; contbr. articles to med. and biomed. jours. Guide walking tour Hist. Soc. Princeton, 1991—. With USN, 1944-46, PTO. Mem. IEEE (sr.). Democrat. Jewish. Home and Office: 163 Loomis Ct Princeton NJ 08540

KINGSMORE, STEPHEN F., physician, scientist; b. Motherwell, Scotland, Sept. 3, 1960; came to U.S., 1988; s. Brian and Rona K. (Ritson) K.; m. Fiona J. McQuaid, Nov. 7, 1988; children: Daniel R., Rebekah F.P. BS with honors, Queen's U., Belfast, Ireland, 1982; MB, ChB, BAO, Queen's U., Belfast, No. Ireland, 1985. Diplomate Am. Bd. Internal Medicine. Intern Craigavon Hosp., Portadown, No. Ireland, 1985-86; resident Queen's U., Belfast, 1986-88; fellow Duke U., Durham, N.C., 1988-89, intern, 1989-90, resident, 1990-91, fellow, 1991-93, assoc. in medicine, 1993-94; asst. prof. U. Fla., Gainesville, 1994—. Contbr. articles to profl. jours. Recipient Sr. scholar award Am. Coll. Rheumatology, 1994, Arthritis Investigator award Arthritis Found., 1995. Mem. Am. Fedn. Clin. Rsch. (Trainee Investigator award 1994, Jr. Faculty award 1996), Internat. Mammalian Genome Soc. Office: U Fla PO Box 100221 Gainesville FL 32610

KINGSNORTH, ANDREW NORMAN, surgery educator; b. Dartford, Kent, U.K., Nov. 20, 1948; s. John Norman and Kathleen Dorothy Bassett K.; m. Jane Mary Poulter, June 1, 1974; children: Edward Anthony, Bryony Jane, Peter John. BS with honors, U. London, 1970, MBBS, 1973, MS, 1982. Registrar in surgery John Radcliffe Hosp., Oxford, U.K., 1977-80; rsch. fellow Harvard U., Boston, 1980-81; lectr. in surgery U. Edinburgh, U.K., 1982-86; jr. cons. Groote Schuur Hosp., Cape Town, South Africa, 1986-87; sr. lectr. in surgery U. Liverpool, U.K., 1987-95; reader in surgery U. Liverpool, 1995-96; prof. surgery Derriford Hosp., Plymouth, Eng., 1996—; sec. Oesophageal sect. Brit. Soc. Gastroenterology, 1992—; mem. com. Surg. Rsch.Soc., U.K., 1995—. Co-editor: Management of Gastrointestinal Cancer, 1996, Management of Abdominal Hernias, 2d edit. 1996; editl. bd. Surg. Rsch. Comms. Fellow Assn. Surgeons of Gt. Britain and Ireland, Royal Coll. Surgeons (mem. ct. of examiners 1994—); mem. Formby Bridge Club. Office: Plymouth Postgrad Med Sch, Med Ctr Derriford Hosp, Plymouth Devon PL6 8DH, England

KINGSTON, DAVID GEORGE IAN, chemistry educator; b. London, Nov. 9, 1938; came to U.S., 1966, naturalized, 1993; s. Charles John Ewart and Norah Blanche (Holcroft) K.; m. Beverly Hazel Mark, June 18, 1966; children: Joy Ellen, Christina Anne, Jonathan David. BA in Natural Sci., Cambridge U., 1960; diploma in Theology, London U., 1962; PhD in Chemistry, Cambridge U., 1963. Rsch. chemist Vinyl Products, Carshalton, Eng., 1957; rsch. assoc. MIT, Cambridge, Mass., 1963-64; asst. prof. chemistry SUNY, Albany, 1966-71; assoc. prof. Va. Poly. Inst. and State U., Blacksburg, 1971-77, prof., 1977—; chmn. contracts review com. Devel. Therapeutics Program, Nat. Cancer Inst., 1988-91; assoc. editor Jour. Natural Products, Columbus, Ohio, 1984—. Contbr. articles to profl. jours.; patentee in field. Elder, Blacksburg Christian Fellowship, 1971—. NATO fellow Cambridge U., 1964-66, Rsch. fellow Queen's Coll., Cambridge, 1962-66; Rsch. grantee NIH, 1971—, NSF, 1981-84, Am. Cancer Soc., 1983-88, Bristol-Myers Squibb, 1991—, SmithKline Animal Health Products, 1980-86. Mem. Am. Soc. Pharmacognosy (v.p. 1987-88, pres. 1988-89, chmn. rsch. award com. 1987-90), Am. Chem. Soc., Royal Soc. Chemistry. Office: Va Poly Inst and State U Dept Chemistry Blacksburg VA 24061-0212

KING-WRIGHT, HELEN L., medical records administrator; b. Atlanta, Mar. 23, 1955; d. John Lewis Jr. and Evelyn (Davis) Battle; m. Lynn Cyrus King, Mar. 27, 1977 (div.); children: Lynn T., Valencia M.; m. Paul R. Wright, Oct. 16, 1987. BMS, Emory U.; student, Clark Coll., Atlanta. Registered records adminstr. Mgr. Grady Meml. Hosp., Atlanta. Office: Grady Memorial Hospital 80 Butler St SE Atlanta GA 30000

KINLEY, DAVID, physical therapist, acupuncturist; b. Newark, Dec. 16, 1935; m. Helen Sandra Wehrle, Mar. 14, 1958; children: Sandra, Deborah, Denise. D Mechanotherapy, Easton Coll., 1970; postgrad in trad. Chinese acupuncture, Tri State Inst., 1979-82. Lic. in acupuncture, phys. therapy and massage; cert. in hypnosis, biofeedback, touch for health. Pvt. massage practice Newark, 1957-60; pvt. phys. therapy practice Cranford, N.J., 1960-63; founder, massage instr., phys. therapist, acupuncturist, hypnotherapist Kinley Comprehensive Ctr. for Acupuncture and Phys. Therapy, Clark, N.J., 1963—; cons. in phys. therapy Vis. Nurse Assn., 1970; practice in biofeedback, 1972; established ctr. for phys. therapy and rehab., Elizabeth, N.J.; clin. affiliate N.Y. State Phys. Therapy Coll., 1982; cons. in acupuncture and phys. therapy Sunny Isles Med. Ctr., Miami Beach, Fla., 1982, pain mgmt. No. Miami Inst. Fla.; founder Kinley Comprehensive Ctr. for Acupuncture/Phys. Therapy, Fla.; asst. in preparation of licensing legis. for N.J. Acupuncture; mem. acupuncture examining bd. N.J. Bd. Med. Examiners. Recipient Lydia Hayes achievement award, 1957. Mem. N.J. State Phys. Therapy Assn. (officer 1959—, pres. 1993, exec. dir., bd.dirs., sr. advisor), Am. Acupuncture Assn. and Oriental Medicine (pres. Acupuncture and Moxibustion Assn. 1973-87), Assn. Applied Psycho Physiology and Biofeedback, Internat. Soc. Profl. Hypnotist, Internat. Soc. Myomassethics, Fla. State Massage Assn., Fla. State Acupuncture Assn., Am. Acad. Environ. Medicine, N.J. Acupuncture Assn. (pres. 1991-93). Home and Office: Kinley Inst 668 Raritan Rd Clark NJ 07066-2232

KINN, ROBERT MARK, physician; b. Chgo., May 28, 1959; s. Arthur William and Florence Louise (Sweica) K.; m. Elizabeth Ann Serviss, May 4, 1985; children: Patrick Michael, Daniel Joseph, Eric Alexander. BS, U. Ill., Urbana, 1981; MD, U. Ill., Chgo., 1985. Diplomate Am. Bd. Internal Medicine in internal medicine, cardiology and electrophysiology. Resident internal medicine U. Ill., Chgo., 1985-88; fellow cardiology U. Pitts., 1988-91, instr. medicine, 1991-92; asst. prof. medicine Rush-Presbyn.-St. Lukes Med. Ctr., Chgo., 1992-93; staff physician Edward Hosp., Naperville, Ill., 1994—, Good Samaritan Hosp., Downers Grove, Ill., 1996—. Contbr. articles to profl. jours., chpts. to books. Aux. min. Chgo. Archdiocese Roman Cath. Ch., 1982. Fellow Am. Coll. Cardiology; mem. ACP, Am. Fedn. Clin. Rsch., Am. Med. Soc., Ill. State Med. Soc., DuPage County Med. Soc. Office: Midwest Heart Specialists 3825 Highland Ave Ste 400 Downers Grove IL 60515

KINNARD, WILLIAM JAMES, JR., pharmacy educator; b. Wilmington, Del., Apr. 18, 1932; s. William J. and Helen F. (Ossenkemper) K.; m. Dolores F. Malia, July 18, 1959. B.S., U. Pitts., 1953, M.S., 1955; Ph.D., Purdue U., 1957. From instr. to prof. U. Pitts., 1957-68; prof. pharmacology, dean Sch. Pharmacy U. Md., Balt., 1968-89, dean Grad. Sch., acting vice chancellor grad. studies and research, 1985, acting pres., 1989-90; acting asst. chancellor U. Md. System, 1991, prof. pharm. practice and sci., 1992—; chmn. bd. U.S. Pharmacopeial Conv., 1975-85; nat. pharm. cons. surgeon gen. USAF, 1983-89; mem. Am. Coun. Pharm. Edn., 1986-92, v.p., 1990-92. Contbr. jours. in field. Fellow Am. Found. Pharm. Edn., 1954-57; recipient Honors Achievement award Angiology Research Fedn., 1960-65; Disting. Alumnus award U. Pitts. Sch. Pharmacy, 1973, Purdue U. Sch. Pharmacy, 1985. Fellow Am. Coll. Clin. Pharmacology, AAAS, Acad. Pharm. Sci.; mem. Am. Pharm. Assn., Inst. Medicine of Nat. Acad. Scis., Am. Assn. Coll. of Pharmacy (pres. 1976-77), Rho Chi. Lutheran. Home: 4000 N Charles St Baltimore MD 21218-1756

KINOSHITA, SHIGERU, ophthalmologist; b. Osaka, Japan, Mar. 14, 1950; s. Kanezo and Masako K.; m. Junko Mikawa, Apr. 29, 1974; children: Manabu, Makoto. MD, Osaka U., 1974, DSc, 1983. Resident Osaka U. Hosp., 1974-79; rsch. fellow Harvard Med. Sch., Boston, 1979-82; instr. Med. Sch. Osaka U., 1982-84, asst. prof., 1984-92; dir. eye div. Osaka Rosai Hosp., 1984-88; dir. cornea svc. Osaka U. Hosp., 1988-92; assoc. chief ophthalmology Osaka U., 1991-92; prof., chmn. ophthalmology Kyoto Pref. Univ. Medicine, 1992—. Home: 1-3-11 Kitabatake Abenoku, Osaka 545, Japan

KINOSHITA, SHINJI, cardiologist, educator; b. Otaru, Hokkaido, Japan, Jan. 7, 1931; s. Sakuzo and Torayo (Takahashi) K.; m. Hitomi Sano, Oct. 2, 1962; children—Yorko, Makoto. M.D., Hokkaido U., 1955, D.M.S., 1959. Intern, City of Otaru Hosp., Japan, 1954-55; research assoc. 2d dept. medicine, Sch. Medicine, Hokkaido U., Sapporo, Japan, 1955-68, instr., 1968-76, assoc. prof., 1976-83; prof. Health Adminstrn. Center, Hokkaido U., 1983-94, dir., 1986-94, prof. emeritus Hokkaido U., 1994—. Inventor color-vectorcardiograph; contbr. articles to profl. jours. in field including: Circulation, Am. Jour. Cardiology. Fellow Hokkaido Br. Japanese Circulation Soc.; mem. Japanese Circulation Soc., N.Y. Acad. Scis., Am. Heart Assn. (reviewer 1978-81). Home: 4-Jo 3-Chome 3-27, Tonden, Kita-ku, Sapporo Hokkaido 001, Japan Office: Health Adminstrn Ctr, Hokkaido Univ, Kita-8 Nishi-5 Kita-Ku, Sapporo Hokkaido 060, Japan

KINSELLA, RALPH ALOYSIUS, JR., physician; b. St. Louis, June 4, 1919; s. Ralph A. and Mabel Lamb (Downey) K.; m. Margaret Neville Boyle, Aug. 9, 1947; children: Ralph Aloysius, III, Mary, John, Eileen, Michael, Margaret, Matthew, Charles. AB, St. Louis U., 1939, MD, 1943. Diplomate: Am. Bd. Internal Medicine. Intern Presbyn. Hosp., N.Y.C., 1943; postgrad. St. Louis U., 1946-47, mem. faculty, 1948-95, prof. medicine, 1972-95, emeritus prof., 1995—; chief unit II St. Louis U. Med. Service, St. Louis City Hosp., 1958-80, med. dir., 1980-85; med. dir. St. Louis Univ. Hosp., 1985-95; pres. Inst. Med. Edn. and Rsch., St. Louis, 1972-95. Served with U.S. Army, 1944-46. Charles H. Nielson fellow, 1947-48; John and Mary Markle scholar, 1948-53. Fellow A.C.P.; mem. St. Louis Soc. Internal Medicine, St. Louis Med. Soc., Mo. Med. Soc., Endocrine Soc., Soc. Exptl. Biology and Medicine, Central Soc. Clin. Research, AMA, Am. Chem. Soc., N.Y. Acad. Scis., AAAS, Sigma Xi. Roman Catholic. Club: Univ. Home: 53 Hanley Downs Saint Louis MO 63117-1366

KINSEY, JULIA CATHERINE, medical records coding specialist; b. Midland, Tex., Jan. 12, 1957; d. Hershel H. and Julia Blackford (Jette) K.; m. Bryce Douglas Welch, Apr. 3, 1993. Student Plan II honors Program, U. Tex., 1975-77. Cert. coding specialist. Instr. English conversation Lang. House, Inc., Takamatsu, Japan, 1978; med. transcriptionist Brackenridge Hosp., Austin, Tex., 1979-82, St. David's Hosp., Austin, 1982-84; coding technician St. David's Health Care Sys., Austin, 1984-94, Health Info. Assocs. LLC, Richardson, Tex., 1995—. Mem. Am. Assn. Med. Transcription (organizer, 1st pres. local chpt. 1983-84), Am. Health Info. Mgmt. Assn., Soc. Clin. Coding, Tex. Health Info. Mgmt. Assn., Am. Acad. Procedural Coders, Am. Hosp. Assn., Soto Zen. Office: Austin Coding Coop PO Box 4540 Lago Vista TX 78645

KINSINGER, JACK BURL, chemist, educator; b. Akron, Ohio, June 23, 1925; s. William Franklin and Idelle (Althaus) K.; m. Addie Jean Parker, Sept. 2, 1946 (div. 1987); children: Paul Craig, Amy Jo. BA, Hiram Coll., 1948; MS, Cornell U., 1951; PhD, U. Pa., 1958. Group leader rsch. Rohm & Haas Co., Phila., 1951-56; asst. prof. Mich. State U., East Lansing, 1957-61, assoc. prof., 1961-66, prof. chemistry, 1966-82, assoc. chmn. dept. chemistry, 1965-69, chmn. dept., 1969-75, asst. v.p. rsch. and devel., 1977, assoc. provost, 1977-82; prof. chemistry Ariz. State U., Tempe, 1982-87, v.p. acad. affairs, 1982-87; pres., CEO, Chgo. Osteo. Health Systems and Midwestern U., 1987-96; ret.; cons. Union Carbide Co., 1958-80, vice chmn. div. polymer chemistry, 1966-68, chmn., 1969; dir. chemistry div. NSF, 1975-77; trustee Kirksville Osteo. Med. Coll., 1984-87, Ariz. State U. Res. Park; exec. com. Fed. Independent Ill. Colls. and Univs., 1993-95. Editor computer symposium Jour. Polymer Sci., 1968. 2nd lt. USAAF, 1943-45. Recipient Disting. Alumnus award Hiram Coll., 1984. Fellow AAAS; mem. Am. Chem. Soc., Coun. Chem. Rsch. (vice chair exec. com. 1980-81). Home: 680 N Lake Shore Dr Apt 1118 Chicago IL 60611

KINSMAN, ROBERT PRESTON, biomedical plastics engineer; b. Cambridge, Mass., July 25, 1949; s. Fred Nelson and Myra Roxanne (Preston) K. BS in Plastics Engring., U. Mass., Lowell, 1971; MBA, Pepperdine U., Malibu, Calif., 1982. Cert. biomed. engr., Calif.; lic. real estate sales person, Calif. Product devel. engr., plastics divsn. Gen. Tire Corp., Lawrence, Mass., 1976-77; mfg. engr. Am. Edwards Labs. divsn. Am. Hosp. Supply Corp., Irvine, Calif., 1978-80, sr. engr., 1981-82; mfg. engring. mgr. Edwards Labs., Inc. subs. Am. Hosp. Supply Corp., Añasco, P.R., 1983; project mgr. Baxter Edwards Critical Care divsn. Baxter Healthcare Corp., Irvine, 1984-87, engring. and prodn. mgr., 1987-93; pres. Kinsman & Assocs., Irvine, Calif., 1993—; mem. mgmt. adv. panel Modern Plastics mag., N.Y.C., 1979-80. Vol. worker VA, Bedford, Mass., 1967-71; instr. first aid ARC, N.D., Mass., Calif., 1971-82; pres., bd. dirs. Lakes Homeowners Assn., Irvine, 1985-91; bd. dirs., newsletter editor Paradise Park Owners Assn., Las Vegas, Nev., 1988—; bd. dirs. Orange County (Calif.) divsn. Am. Heart Assn., 1991—, chmn. devel. com., 1993-95, v.p. bd. dirs., 1993-94, chmn.-elect bd. dirs., 1994-95, chmn. bd. dirs., 1995-96, adv. coun. rep., 1994—; mem. steering com. Heart and Sole Classic fundraiser, 1988—, chmn. subcom., 1989, vice-chmn., 1990, event chmn., 1991-92, mem. devel. com. Calif. affiliate, 1993-95. Capt. USAF, 1971-75, USAFR, 1975-81. Recipient Cert. of Appreciation, VA, 1971, Am. Heart Assn., 1991, 92, 93; selected Comty. Hero Torchbearer 1996 Olympic Games, United Way Am. and Atlanta Com. for Olympic Games. Baxter Found. grantee, Deerfield, Ill., 1992, 93. Mem. Soc. Plastics Engrs. (sr., Mem. of Month So. Calif. sect. 1989), Am. Mgmt. Assn., Arnold Air Soc. (comptr. 1969, pledge tng. officer 1970), Plastics Acad., Demolay, Profl. Ski Instrs. Am., Mensa, Am. Legion, Elks, Phi Gamma Psi. Office: Kinsman & Assocs 4790 Irvine Blvd Ste 105-289 Irvine CA 92720-1973

KIPNIS, DAVID MORRIS, physician, educator; b. Balt., May 23, 1927; s. Rubin and Anna (Mizen) K.; m. Paula Jane Levin, Aug. 16, 1953; children—Lynne, Laura, Robert. A.B., Johns Hopkins U., 1945, M.A., 1949; M.D., U. Md., 1951. Intern Johns Hopkins Hosp., 1951-52; resident Duke Hosp., Durham, N.C., 1952-54, U. Md. Hosp., 1954-55; asst. prof. medicine Washington U. Sch. Medicine, St. Louis, 1958-63; assoc. prof. Washington U. Sch. Medicine, 1963-65, prof., 1965—, Busch prof., chmn. dept. medicine, 1973-92; disting. univ. prof. of medicine Washington U. Sch. of Medicine, St. Louis, 1992—; asst. physician Barnes Hosp., asso. physician, 1963-72, physician-in-chief, 1973-93, distinguished Univ Prof; Chmn. endocrine study sect. NIH, 1963-64, mem. diabetes tng. program com., 1970—; chmn. Nat. Diabetes Adv. Bd. Editor: Diabetes, 1973; Asso. editor: Am. Jour. Medicine, 1973; Editorial bd.: Am. Jour. Med. Scis; Contbr. articles to profl. jours. Served with AUS, 1945-46. Markle scholar in med. scis., 1957-62; Banting lectr. Brit. Diabetes Assn., 1972. Mem. NAS, Am. Soc. Clin. Investigation, Assn. Am. Physicians (Kober medal 1994), Am. Fedn. Clin. Rsch., Am. Diabetes Assn. (Lilly award 1965, Banting medal 1977, Best medal 1981), Endocrine Soc. (Oppenheimer award 1965), Am. Soc. Biol. Chemists, Am. Acad. Arts and Scis., Inst. Medicine of NAS. Home: 7200 Wydown Blvd Saint Louis MO 63105-3023 Office: Barnes Hosp Dept Medicine PO Box 8212 660 S Euclid St Saint Louis MO 63110*

KIPPEL, GARY M., psychologist; b. Bklyn.; s. Philip and Florence (Wiederlight) K.; m. Ronnie G. Spilka, July 27, 1977. BA, Bklyn. Coll., 1963; MA, Queens Coll., 1964; PhD, NYU, 1973. Cert. psychologist, N.Y.; lic. tchr.; cert. adminstr. and supr. Research asst. Ctr. for Urban Edn., Inst. Child Devel. and Exptl. Edn., N.Y.C., 1965-67; tchr. P.S. 219, Bklyn., 1967-69; research asst. Hdqrs. N.Y.C. Bd. Edn., Bklyn., 1969-73, research assoc., 1974-77, asst. dir. edn. research, 1978-90; chief adminstr. for test devel. and tech. support Office of Recruitment, Pers. Assessment and Licensing, 1990—; adj. assoc. prof. ednl. psychology NYU, N.Y.C., 1971, 80; adj. assoc. prof. mgmt. Pace U., N.Y.C., 1978—. Contbr. articles to profl. jours., chpts. to books. V.p. E. Midwood Jewish Ctr., Bklyn., 1989-94, pres. 1994—; chmn. bd. edn. Rabbi Harry Halpern Day Sch., Bklyn., 1987-90. Univ. Scholar Queens Coll., 1964. Mem. Am. Psychological Assn., Nat. Coun. Measurement in Edn., Am. Ednl. Research Assn., Soc. Indsl. and Organizational Psychology. Office: NYC Bd Edn 65 Court St Brooklyn NY 11201-4954

KIPPING, HANS F., dermatologist; b. Chgo., Jan. 8, 1924; s. Johaanes and Johannah (Rauch) K.; m. Rosemary New, Jan. 3, 1928 (dec.); children: Susan, John, David. MD, U. Buffalo, 1947. Intern, Buffalo Gen. Hosp., N.Y., 1947-48, resident in indsl. medicine, Millard Fillmore Hosp., Buffalo,

1948-49; resident in dermatology E.J. Meyer Meml. Hosp., Buffalo, 1953-56; practice medicine specializing in dermatology, Buffalo, 1956—; clin. prof. dermatology SUNY-Buffalo; attending dermatologist Erie County Health Care Ctr., 1979; dermatologist Buffalo Gen. Hosp., cons. dermatology Roswell Park Meml. Inst., 1980—; cons., lectr. in field. Contbr. articles, research studies to profl. jours. Served to capt. USAF, 1950-52. Fellow Am. Soc. Dermatopathology; mem. Assn. Profs. Dermatology, AMA, Soc. Investigative Dermatology, Am. Acad. Dermatology, Dermatology Found., Toronto Dermatology Soc., Buffalo-Rochester Dermatology Soc. (pres. 1962-63), N.Y. State Dermatology Soc. (pres. 1974-75). Republican. Methodist. Club: Youngstown Yacht. Home: 192 Castlebrook Ln Buffalo NY 14221-4475 Office: 4444 Main St Buffalo NY 14226-4420

KIRACOFE, GREGORY ALBERT, optometrist; b. Hamilton, Ohio, Jan. 12, 1955; s. Henry Albert and Hester Juanita (Messinger) K.; m. Karen Lynn Jones, Sept. 2, 1978; children: Allyson, Lauren, Spencer. BS, Ea. Ky. U., 1977; OD, Ohio State U., 1981. Lic. optometrist, Ohio, N.Y.; cert. low vision specialist, N.Y. State Optometric Assn. Resident optometry VA Med. Ctr., Chillicothe, Ohio, 1981-82; staff optometrist VA Med. Ctr., Montrose, N.Y., 1982-88; chief optometry sect. VA Med. Ctr., Dayton, Ohio, 1988—; adj. asst. prof. Coll. Optometry Ohio State U., Columbus, 1990—; examiner Nat. Bd. Examiners in Optometry, Bethesda, Md., 1990—. Referee profl. manuscripts Clin. Eye and Vision Care Jour., Balt., 1994—; sect. editor newsletter Multidisciplinary Practice-Horizon; contbr. articles to profl. jours. Fellow Am. Acad. Optometry; mem. APHA, Am. Optometric Assn., Nat. Assn. VA Optometrists, Assn. Mil. Surgeons of U.S. Home: 6824 St Laurent Cir Dayton OH 45459 Office: VA Med Ctr Optometry Sect 112E 4100 W 3d St Dayton OH 45428

KIRBENS, CHERYL ANN, medical, surgical nurse; b. Wilmington, Del., Aug. 8, 1956; m. Drew Joseph Kirbens, July 6, 1985; children: Kristy A., Joshua David. Nursing diploma, Lankenau Hosp. Sch. Nursing, Phila., 1977; BSN, U. Wyo., 1993. Cert. ACLS. Surg. nurse Vets. Hosp., Wilmington, 1977-81; ICU nurse Vets. Hosp., Grand Juction, Colo., 1981-84, 85-87, Phila., 1984-85, Peterborough, N.H., 1988-90; med., surg. nurse Vets. Hosp., Cheyenne, Wyo., 1991—; office mgr. Drew J. Kirbens, MD, Peterborough, 1987-89, Laramie, Wyo., 1990-91. Vol. ARC, 1992-94; mem. ladies auxiliary Monadnock Cmty. Hosp., Peterborough, 1987-91. Recipient Outstanding Scholastic Achievement and Excellence award Golden Key, 1993. Mem. Sigma Theta Tau, Beta Sigma Phi. Home: 208 W 4th Ave Cheyenne WY 82001

KIRBY, BRIAN JOHN, physician, academic administrator, educator; b. Southend-on-Sea, Eng., Aug. 25, 1936; s. George and Lily Ann (Deighton) K.; m. Rachel Mary Pawson; children: Timothy Pawson, Juliet Clare. MB, Ch.B, U. Leeds, Eng., 1960. House appts. St. James's Univ. Hosp., Leeds, 1960-63; registrar in medicine Cen. Middlesex Hosp., London, 1963-65, rsch. fellow, 1965-67; instr. medicine Med. Coll. Va., Richmond, 1967-68; registrar in cardiology Royal Postgrad. Med. Sch., London, 1968-69; lectr. medicine U. Edinburgh, Scotland, 1969-74; sr. lectr., dept. dir. postgrad. med. sch., cons. physician U. Exeter (Eng.), Royal Devon and Exeter Hosp., 1974—; chmn. adv. bd. on the Registration of Homeopathic Products, S.W. Action on Smoking and Health, Exeter; mem. Com. on Safety of Medicines; mem. Safety Efficacy and Adverse Reactions Com., London; vice chmn. Com. on the Rev. of Medicine; chmn. Coronary Prevention Group, London. Contbr. articles to profl. jours. Rsch. grantee MRC, 1965-67, Brit. Heart Found., Northcott Devon Rsch. Found., Southwestern Regional Health Authority, 1987-90, Nat. Hosp. Trust, 1991—, Healthy Heart Rsch. Trust, 1990, others. Royal Coll. Physicians London, Royal Coll. Physicians Edinburgh, Royal Soc. Medicine. Office: Postgrad Med Sch, Barrack Rd, Exeter EX2 5DW, England

KIRBY, DEBORAH MACDONALD, rehabilitation psychologist; b. Washington, May 19, 1948; d. Robert Angus and Margarett Mary (Harrison) MacDonald; m. Stephen Edward Kirby, Sept. 6, 1980; 1 child, Jessica Lynn. B.A., George Washington U., 1970; M.Ed., Am. U., 1972. Psychiat. asst. Chestnut Lodge Psychiat. Hosp., Rockville, Md., 1969-70; rsch. psychologist Dept. Army, 1970; clin. intern Am. U., Counseling Ctr., 1972; clin. psychologist Bay County Guidance Clinic, Panama City, Fla., 1972-73; rehab. counselor State of Fla., Panama City, 1974; rehab. psychologist Woodrow Wilson Rehab. Center, Fisherville, Va., 1975-84; dir. Shenandoah Counseling Assocs., P.C., 1981-88, pres., 1989—; mem. med. staff Augusta Med. Ctr., Fisherville, Va. 1982—. Author papers in field. Fellow Am. Bd. Med. Psychotherapists (diplomate); mem. Am. Psychol. Assn., Va. Assn. Clin. Counselors (bd. dirs., chairperson profl. advocacy coms. 1994—, Leadership award 1995), Va. Psychol. Assn., Va. Counselors Assn., Charlottesville-Albemarle Kennel Club (past bd. dir.), Kappa Alpha Theta. Democrat. Office: Shenandoah Counseling Assocs PC PO Box 696 1048 W Beverley St Staunton VA 24402-0696

KIRBY, DOROTHY MANVILLE, social worker; b. Burke, S.D., Oct. 23, 1917; d. Charles Vietz and Gail Lorena (Coonen) Manville; m. Sigmund Kirby, July 11, 1941 (div. 1969); children; Paul Howard, Robert Charles. BA, Wayne State U., 1970, MSW, 1972. Cert. social worker, Mich.; lic. marriage and family therapist, Mich. Pvt. practice social work Allen Park, Mich., 1973—; conduct seminars on stress, personal effectiveness and communication for various orgns., hosps. and bus. Pres. Allen Park Symphony Orch., 1990-92. Mem. AAUW, Am. Group Psychotherapy Assn., Nat. Assn. Social Workers (clin.), Nat. Assn. Marriage and Family Counseling, Mich. Assn. Marriage and Family Counseling (sec. 1982), LWV (pres. Allen Park 1965-66). Presbyterian. Lodge: Soroptimists. Home and Office: 15720 Wick Rd Allen Park MI 48101-1535

KIRBY, THOMAS RANDALL, optometrist; b. Greenville, N.C., June 11, 1967; s. Kenneth Nathaniel and Lannie Ruth (Ross) K.;. BA in Biology, Psychology, U. N.C., Chapel Hill, 1989; OD, U. Houston, 1994. Cert. N.C. State Bd. Optometry. Pvt. practice Wilmington, N.C. Capt. U.S. Army Nat. Guard. Mem. Am. Optometric Assn., N.C. Optometric Soc., Armed Forces Optometric Soc., Kappa Sigma, Omicron Delta Kappa. Republican. Baptist. Office: 33 S Kerr Ave Wilmington NC 28403

KIRCH, DARRELL G., dean; b. Denver, May 3, 1949; m. Deborah M. Kirch; children: Samantha M., Madeline A. BA in Philosophy, U. Colo., 1973, MD magna cum laude, 1977. Diplomate Am. Bd. Psychiatry and Neurology, Nat. Bd. Med. Examiners. Resident in psychiatry U. Colo. Health Scis. Ctr., Denver, 1977-82; med. staff fellow adult psychiatry br. NIMH, Washington, 1982-84, sr. staff fellow neuropsychiatry br., 1984-87, med. dir. neuropsychiat. Rsch. Hosp., 1987-89, chief unit on neurobehavioral studies, 1989-92; dep. scientific dir. NIMH, Bethesda, Md., 1992-93; prof. sch. grad. studies, prof. dept. psychiatry Med. Coll. Ga., Augusta, 1994—, dean sch. medicine, 1994—; dir. Robert Wood Johnson Found. Generalist Initiative Implementation Grant Med. Coll. Ga., 1994—, chair VA Med. Ctr. Dean's Com., 1994—; chair adv. bd. Ga. Radiation Therapy Ctr., Augusta, 1994—; mem. clin. enterprise exec. com. Med. Coll. Ga., 1994—, chair clin. enterprise coun., 1994—, mem. exec. com., bd. trustees physicians practice group, 1994—, mem. exec. com. med. and dental staff, 1994—; merit reviewer rsch. svc. U.S. Dept. VA, Washington, 1989—; examiner Am. Bd. Psychiatry and Neurology, Deerfield, Ill., 1985—; many others. Reviewer numerous profl. jours.; assoc. editor: Psychopharmacology Bull., 1990—, Schizophrenia Bull., 1989—. Capt. USPHS, 1986-94. Decorated Commendation medal. Mem. AAAS, AMA, Am. Psychiat. Assn., Am. Soc. Clin. Psychopharmacology, Assn. for Acad. Psychiatry, Ga. Psychiat. Physicians Assn., Internat. Soc. for Psychiatric Genetics, Med. Assn. Ga., Richmond County Med. Soc., Soc. for Neurosci., SOc. Biol. Psychiatry. Home: 8 Winged Foot Dr Augusta GA 30907 Office: Med Coll Ga Sch Medicine Office of Dean Augusta GA 30912*

KIRCH, WILHELM, educator, internist, nephrologist, pharmacologist; b. Cologne, Germany, July 4, 1947; s. Johannes Kirch and Rosemarie Schroeder; m. Gabriele Jacubasch, Nov. 17, 1978; children: Vanessa, Anne. Degree in Dentistry, U. Mainz, 1972, DD, 1974, MD, 1975. Intern Univ. Hosp. Mainz, 1975-81; sr. registrar Univ. Hosp., Essen, 1982-86; physician U. Berne, Switzerland, 1985; sr. registrar Univ. Hosp., Kiel, 1987-93, prin. physician, lectr. internal medicine, prof., 1993—; med. dir., clin. pharmacology and therapeutics, vice dean med. faculty Tech. U., Dresden, Germany, 1993—; pres. Saxonian Pub. Health Rsch. Found. Author: Internal Medicine and Dentistry, 1987, 2d edit., 1994; editor: Misdiagnoses in Internal Medicine, 1992, Practical Drug Therapy, 1996; contbr. articles to Lancet, Gastroenterology, Gut, Cin. Pharm. Therapeutics, Brit. Jour. Cin. Pharmacology, Am. Heart Jour. Recipient Ludolf Krehl prize S.W. German Soc. Internal Medicine, Homburg prize Regensburg Acad. Med. Sci. Mem. German Soc. Clin. Pharmacol. Therapy (v.p.), Profl. Soc. German Clin. Pharmacologists (bd. dirs. 1989—), German Soc. Internal Medicine, Brit. Pharm. Soc., Am. Soc. Clin. Pharmacology, European Soc. Clin. Investigation, Am. Coll. Clin. Pharmacology. Office: Clin Pharmacology & Therapeutics, Med Hosp Tech Univ Fiedlerstr 27, D-01307 Dresden Germany

KIRCHER, JOHN RAYMOND, physician assistant, educator; b. Detroit, Apr. 15, 1947; s. Fred Earnest Kircher and Virginia Lee (Fleek) Benson; m. Mary Theresa Kearns, Nov. 17, 1967; children: Lisa Marie, Amy Elizabeth. BS cum laude in Medicine, Western Mich. U., 1974; cert. in entrepreneurial program, Saginaw Valley State U., 1994. Cert. med. staff recruiter. Physician asst. Doctor's Moeller & Loan, Essexville, Mich., 1974-81, Blue Care Network, Essexville, 1981-94; asst. prof. U. Detroit, 1992—; CEO PA Search, Bay City, Mich., 1992—; instr. EMT program Delta Coll., University Center, Mich., 1975-76; mem. compensation com. City of Bay City, 1992—; bd. dirs. Physician Asst. Taqsk Force of Mich., 1985-94, Mich. Osteo. Bd. Medicine, 1987-89. Contbr. articles to profl. jours. Bd. dirs. Child and Family Svc. of Bay County, 1978-87, pres., 1982-84. Capt. Mich. Army N.G., 1978—. Recipient Bronze Star U.S. Army, 1969. Fellow Mich. Acad. Physician Assts. (founder, pres., treas. 1974—), Am. Acad. Physician Assts. (chief del. 1974-84), Mich. Physician Asst. Found. (trustee, sec. founder, 1991—), Vietnam Vets. Am. Home and Office: 2135 Seventh St Bay City MI 48708

KIRCHHEIM, DIETER, urologist, educator. Student, Goethe U., Frankfurt, Germany, 1946-48, U. Zurich, 1948-50; MD, Goethe U., 1951. Bd. cert. urology. Intern Ottawa (Can.) Civic Hosp., 1951-52; resident All Saints Hosp., Fort Worth, Tex., 1952-53; urology fellow Mayo Clinic, Rochester, Minn., 1954-56; chief resident urology John Gaston Hosp., U. Tenn., Memphis, 1956-57; urologist Med. Arts Clinic, Regina, Sask., Can., 1957-58; staff urologist Regina (Sask.) Gen. Hosp. and Grey Nuns Hosp., 1957-58; sr. resident gen. surgery U. Ottawa, Ottawa Civic Hosp., 1958-59; urologist Des Moines, 1960-62; rsch. fellow Brady Inst. Urology Johns Hopkins Hosp., Balt., 1962-68; asst. prof. urology U. Oreg. Med. Sch., Portland, 1968—; pvt. practice urology Olympia, Wash., 1968—; clin. assoc. prof. dept. urology U. Wash., Seattle, 1968—. Contbr. chpts. to textbooks and articles to profl. jours. Fellow Royal Coll. Surgeons Can. Office: FACS Black Hills Ln SW Olympia WA 98502

KIRCHNER, JEFFREY THOMAS, physician; b. Lancaster, Pa., Aug. 5, 1959; s. Thomas John and Geraldine Grace (Huegel) K.; m. Tracy Elizabeth Johnston, Apr. 21, 1990; children: Joseph Thomas, Grace Joann, Rose Elizabeth. BS in Biology, Villanova U., 1981; DO, Phila. Coll. Osteo. Medicine, 1985. Diplomate Am. Bd. Family Practice. Resident family practice Abington (Pa.) Meml. Hosp., 1986-89; staff physician Healthcare for Homeless Project, Washington, 1989-90; clin. instr. Georgetown U. Sch. Medicine, Washington, 1990-91; assoc. residency dir. family and cmty. medicine Lancaster Gen. Hosp., 1991—; asst. clin. prof. Pa. State Coll. Medicine, Hershey, 1994—. Mem. editl. bd. Family Practice Recertification Jour., 1992—, Postgrad. Medicine Jour., 1993—; contbr. articles to profl. jours. Fellow Am. Acad. Family Physicians; mem. AMA (Physician Recognition award 1990-93, 93-96), Soc. Tchrs. of Family Medicine, Physicians for Social Responsibility, Pa. Med. Soc., Pa. Acad. Family Physicians, Lancaster County Med. Soc., Lancaster City Med. Soc., Am. Med. Writers Assn. Home: 585 N School Ln Lancaster PA 17603 Office: Lancaster Gen Hosp Dept Family & Cmty Medicine Lancaster PA 17604

KIRCHNER, PETER THOMAS, physician nuclear medicine, educator, consultant; b. July 2, 1939; s. Elek and Julia (Kossy) K.; m. Mary Coleman Kirchner, Dec. 18, 1965; children: David, Annette, Julie. BA Physics, Yale U., 1960; MD, Columbia U., 1964. Diplomate Am. Bd. Internal Medicine, Am. Bd. Nuclear Medicine. Intern, then resident, chief resident in internal medicine Nat. Naval Med. Ctr., Bethesda, Md., 1964-70; fellow in nuclear medicine Johns Hopkins U., Balt., 1970-72; head nuclear medicine Nat. Naval Med. Ctr., Bethesda, Md., 1972-77; asst. prof. radiology George Washington U., Washington, 1974-77; assoc. dir. nuclear medicine U. Chgo., 1978-81, assoc. prof. radiology, 1977-81; assoc. prof. radiology U Iowa, Iowa City, 1981-84, prof. radiology, 1984—, prof. medicine, 1989—; dir. nuclear medicine U. Iowa Hosps. and Clinics, Iowa City, 1981—; mem. radiology study sect. NIH, 1995—. Editor Nuclear Medicine Review Syllabus, 1980; co-editor Nuclear Medicine Self Study I, 1988; author more than 80 sci. articles, 12 book chpts. Ea. Iowa alumni schs.com. chair Yale U., 1989-94. Capt. USNR, 1963-92. Out Svc. Tng. grantee USN 1970; recipient Von Hevessy award Hungarian Soc. Nuclear Medicine, 1993. Fellow ACP, Am. Coll. Nuclear Physicians (chair quality assurance and practice cert. com. 1993-95, bd. regents 1993—); mem. Am. Bd. Nuclear Medicine (sec. 1992-94, chair exam. com. 1991-94, vice chair 1994, 95), Radiol. Soc. N.Am. (sci. program com. 1992—), Inst. Clin. Positron Emission Tomography (bd. dirs., pres. 1993-94). Office: U Iowa Dept Radiology Iowa City IA 52242

KIRIAKOPOULOS, GEORGE CONSTANTINE, dentist; b. Derby, Conn., June 3, 1926; s. Constantine Elias and Rose (Yerontakis) K.; AA, U. Paris (France), 1947; AB, Bklyn. Coll., 1950; DDS, Columbia, 1954; m. Virginia Demos, June 3, 1956; 1 dau., Stephanie. Pvt. practice gen. dentistry, Fort Lee, N.J., 1955—; assoc. dir. dept. dentistry St. Giles Hosp., Bklyn., 1955-60; attending dept. oral surgery Lenox Hill Hosp., N.Y.C., 1956-60, adj. oral surgeon, 1960-64; assoc. prof., then prof. dept. pedodontics Columbia, 1956—; attending in dentistry Presbyn. Hosp., 1986—; mem. adv. com. Columbia Presbyn. Hosp. Med. Ctr.; mem. adv. com. to dean Sch. Dental and Oral Surgery Columbia U. Served with AUS, 1943-46. Decorated Bronze Star, Silver Star, D.S.M.; recipient Medal of Meritorious Service, Lenox Hill Hosp., 1964. Fellow Royal Soc. Health; mem. ADA, Am. Assn. Hosp. Dentists, N.Y. State Dental Soc., Columbia U. Alumni Assn., Psi Omega. Greek Orthodox (pres. Parish Coun., Cathedral St. John, Tenafly, 1980-83). Author: Your Child's Teeth - the Layman's View, 1966; Who Wants to Be a Dentist?, 1968; The Modern Thermopylae—Battle of Crete, May 1941, 1978; Portrait of a Cretan Hero, 1978; Cyprus and the Polish Connection, 1980; Ten Days to Destiny, 1985, Paperback edit., 1985, The Nazi Occupation of Crete: 1941-45, 1995, others. Home: 2205 Mackay Ave Fort Lee NJ 07024-5034 Office: 415 West St Fort Lee NJ 07024-5010

KIRK, GERALD ARTHUR, nuclear radiologist; b. L.A., Jan. 20, 1940; s. Arthur H. and Aural (Roderick) K.; m. Cherie J. Hutson, Dec. 27, 1965; children: Shannon Richard, Joel Daryn. BA in Physics, La Sierra Coll., 1962; MD, Loma Linda U., 1967. Intern Deaconess Hosp., Spokane, Wash., 1967-68; staff physician Empress Zandith Meml. Hosp., Addis Ababa, Ethiopia, 1968-69; pvt. practice Simi Valley, Calif., 1969-70; resident in radiology Loma Linda (Calif.) Med. Ctr., 1972-75, dir. sect. nuclear radiology, 1975—. Maj. USPHS, 1970-72. Home: 1341 Pine Knolls Cres Redlands CA 92373-6545 Office: Loma Linda U Sch Medicine Dept Nuclear Radiology Loma Linda CA 92354*

KIRK, KARLA Y., optometrist; b. Carbondale, Ill., June 29, 1956; d. Carl B. and Wanda L. (Butts) K.; m. Richard L. Perrin, Sept. 22, 1985; children: Ryan K., Matthew K. BS in Visual Sci., Ill. Coll. Optometry, 1979; BA, So. Ill. U., Carbondale, 1978; OD, Ill. Coll. Optometry, 1981. Pvt. practice, Du Quoin, Ill., 1981—, Murphysboro, Ill., 1985—. Treas. Murphysboro Jr. Women's Club. Mem. Am. Optometric Assn., Ill. Optometric Assn., So. Ill. Optometric Soc. (sec.-treas.), Murphysboro C. of C. Home: RR 1 Box 705 Du Quoin IL 62832 Office: PO Box 129 1008 N 14th St Murphysboro IL 62966

KIRK, WILLIAM SMITH, dentist; b. Salisbury, N.C., Apr. 22, 1928; s. Frank Walter and Suzanne Sovereign (Smith) K.; m. Lois Jean Smith, Feb. 5, 1951; children: William Smith, Margaret Suzanne, Timothy Davis. Student, U. N.C., 1944-45, postgrad., 1957-58; DDS, Northwestern U., 1949. Pvt. practice Salisbury, 1952-57, pvt. practice specializing in orthodontics, 1958—. Bd. dirs. North Hills Christian Sch., 1966-73; adv. bd. Salvation Army, 1966-87, chmn., 1984-86. With USAF, 1949-52. Mem. ADA, Am. Assn. Orthodontists, So. Soc. Orthodontists, N.C. Orthodontic Soc. (pres. 1973-74), N.C. Dental Soc., Flying Dentists Assn., World Radio Missionary Fellowship (spl. rep. 1964), 2d Dist. Dental Soc. N.C. (pres. 1969), Rotary (dist. gov. 1989-90). Presbyterian. Home: 176 Broadbill Dr Mooresville NC 28115-9196 Office: 1819 Brenner Ave Salisbury NC 28144-2519

KIRKHAM, JOHN SQUIRE, surgeon; b. Bedfordshire, Eng., Sept. 20, 1936; s. Squire Wilfred and Una Mary (Baker) K.; m. Charlotte Giersing, Sept. 19, 1969; children: Alexander Paul Squire, Sophie. BA, Cambridge (Eng.) U., 1957, BChir, 1960, MB MA, 1961, MChir, 1966. House surgeon, physician Westminster Hosp., 1960-61; sr. house surgeon Birmingham Accident Hosp., 1961-62; ship's surgeon Union Castle Line, 1962-63; sr. house officer and registrar Hosp. for Sick Children, London, 1963-64; surg. registrar Aberdeen Royal Infirmary, 1964-66; sr. surg. registrar Charing Cross Hosp, London, 1967-70; cons. surgeon St. Georges Hosp., London, 1971-90, Queen Mary's Univ. Hosp., London, 1991—; vis. prof. U. Monash, Sydney, Australia, U. Basrah, Iraq, U. Cairo, Gordon U., khartoum; examiner Royal Coll. Surgeons of Edinburgh, U. London, Khartoum, Basta. Author: (with others) Abdominal Operations, 1984, Surgery of Obesity, 1986, Current Surgical Practice 5, 1990; contbr. articles to profl. jours. Vol. work in Kenya, St. Vincent, Brit. V.I. Named Baron, Holy Roman Empire. Fellow Royal Coll. Surgeons (Eng., Edinburgh), Royal Soc. Medicine, Pancreatic Soc. Great Britain and Ireland, Assn. Surgeons Great Britain and Ireland, Brit. Assn. Clin. Anatomists; mem. Brit. Med. Assn., Brit. Soc. Gastroenterology, The Athenaeum Club, The Naval and Military Club. Mem. Conservative Party. Anglican. Home: 3 The Little Boltons, Kensington London SW10 9LJ, England Also: Garden Cottage, Drayton St Leonard, Oxfordshire England Office: 149 Harley St, London W1N 2DH, England

KIRKLAND, KIRBY CALVIN, surgeon; b. Brewer, Maine, Nov. 3, 1932; s. Theo Calvin and Henrietta Marion (Marsh) K.; m. Merry Ann Carlberg, Jan. 5, 1991. BH, U. Maine, 1954; MD, Tufts U., 1958. Diplomate Am. Bd. Surgery. Mem. med. staff Worcester (Mass.) Hahneman Hosp., 1966-81, Worcester City Hosp., 1966-81, Fairlawn Hosp., 1966-81; asst. prof. surgery U. Mass., Worcester, 1972-81. Capt. USAF, 1963-66. Fellow ACS; mem. Masons. Home: 1003 Durango Dr Douglas WY 82633 Office: 111S 5th Ste 1 Douglas WY 82633

KIRKLIN, JAMES K., cardiac surgeon; b. Rochester, Minn., Jan. 20, 1947; s. John Webster K.; children: Kimberly, Adam. MD, Harvard Med. Sch., 1973. Prof. surgery, dir. cardiothoracic transplantation U. Ala., Birmingham, 1981—. Mem. Am. Assn. Thoracic Surgery, Am. Soc. Transplant Physicians, Internat. Soc. Heart Transplantation (sec. treas. 1991-93). Office: U Ala at Birmingham 739 Zeigler Bldg Birmingham AL 35294

KIRKLIN, JOHN WEBSTER, surgeon; b. Muncie, Ind., Aug. 5, 1917; m. Margaret Katherine; 3 children. BA summa cum laude, U. Minn., 1938; MD magna cum laude, Harvard U., 1942; MD (hon.), U. Munich, 1961; DSc (hon.), Hamline U., 1966, U. Ala., Birmingham, 1978, Ind. U., Bloomington, 1983; hon. degree, U. Bordeaux, France, 1982, Universidad de la República, Uruguay, 1982. Diplomate: Am. Bd. Surgery, Am. Bd. Thoracic Surgery (mem. exam. and tng. programs coms.). Intern Hosp. U. Pa., 1942-43; resident in surgery Mayo Clinic and Mayo Grad. Sch. Medicine, Rochester, Minn., 1943-44, 46-48, first asst. in surgery, 1949-50, chmn. dept. surgery, 1964-66; asst. resident in surgery Children's Hosp., Boston, 1948-49; surgeon Mayo Clinic, 1950-66, instr. surgery, 1951-53, asst. prof., 1953-57, asso. prof., 1957-60, prof., 1960-66, bd. govs., 1965-66; surgeon-in-chief U. Ala., Birmingham, 1966-82; Fay Fletcher Kerner prof. surgery U. Ala.-Birmingham Sch. Medicine and Med. Ctr., 1966—; assoc. chief staffy U. Ala.-Birmingham Hosps., 1966—; chmn. dept. surgery U. Ala.-Birmingham Sch. Medicine and Med. Ctr., 1966-82, dir. div. cardiothoracic surgery, dir. Congenital Heart Disease Research and Tng. Ctr., 1982-84, prof. surgery, 1990; mem. task force on prevention and treatment of cardiovascular disease in the young Nat. Heart, Lung and Blood Inst., 1977-78; mem. policy adv. bd. for coronary artery surgery, mem. adv. com. crippled children services regional program NIH. Author: (with R.B. Karp) The Tetralogy of Fallot from a Surgical Viewpoint, 1970, (with others) Cardiac Surgery and the Conduction System, 1983; contbr. articles to profl. publs.; editorial bd.: Am. Heart Jour, 1964-76, Am. Jour. Cardiology, 1974-80, Circulation, 1967-78, Jour. Thoracic and Cardiovascular Surgery, 1971-83, Year Book Cardiovascular Medicine and Surgery; corr. mem. editorial bd.: European Jour. Intensive Care Medicine, 1974—; former editorial bd.: Jour. French Soc. Thoracic Surgery. Served to capt. U.S. Army, 1944-46. Fellow Royal Australasian Coll. Surgeons (hon.), Royal Coll. Surgeons Ireland (hon.), Royal Coll. Surgeons Edinburgh (hon.), Royal Coll. Surgeons Eng. (hon.), Assn. Surgeons Gt. Britain and Ireland (hon.); mem. AAUP, AMA, ACS, Ala. Acad. Sci., Ala. Heart Assn., Am. Acad. Pediatrics, Am. Assn. Thoracic Surgery (pres. 1978-79), Am. Coll. Cardiology (v.p. bd. govs. 1973-74), Am. Heart Assn., Am. Soc. Artificial Internal Organs, Am. Soc. Critical Care Medicine, Am. Surg. Assn. (recorder 1967-71), Birmingham Surg. Soc., Cardiac Soc. Australia and N.Z. (corr.), Deutsche Gesellschaft Fur Chirurgie, Harvard Med. Alumni Assn., Internat. Surg. Group, Jefferson County Med. Soc., Mayo Found. Alumni Assn., Nat. Acad. Scis., N.Y. Acad. Scis., Royal Soc. Medicine (affiliate), Soc. Clin. Surgery, Soc. Critical Care Medicine, Soc. Surg. Chairmen, Soc. Thoracic Surgeons, Soc. Univ. Surgeons, Soc. Vascular Surgery, So. Soc. Clin. Investigation, So. Surg. Assn., Surg. Biology Club, European Soc. Cardiovascular Surgery (hon.), Mexican Soc. Cardiology (hon.), N.Y. Soc. Thoracic Surgery (hon.). Office: U Ala Sch Medicine & Med Ctr Dept Surgery Birmingham AL 35294*

KIRKPATRICK, RICHARD ALAN, internist; b. Rochester, Minn., Jan. 17, 1947; s. Neal R. and Ethel C. (Hull) K.; m. Susan Baxter; children: James N., Ronald S., David B., Mary J., Scott B., Christina Marie. BA in Chemistry with honors, U. Wash., 1968, BS in Psychology, 1968, MD, 1972. Diplomate Am. Bd. Internal Medicine. Intern, resident in internal medicine Mayo Grad. Sch., Rochester, 1972-76, spl. resident in biomed. communications, 1974-75; pvt. practice specializing in internal medicine Longview, Wash., 1976—; founding ptnr. Internal Medicine Clinic of Longview; mem. clin. faculty U. Wash.; dir. cardiac rehab. program St. John's Hosp.; sec. The Physicians Alliance. Editor: Drug Therapy Abstracts, Wash. Internists; mem. editorial adv. bd. Your Patient and Cancer, Primary Care and Cancer; weekly med. TV talk show host, 1978—; contbr. articles to med. jours. Bd. dirs., v.p. Columbia Theatre for Performing Arts; mem. City Coun., Longview; mem. S.W. Wash. Symphony; bd. dirs. S.W. Wash. Youth Symphony; pres., bd. dirs. Sta. KLTV. Fellow ACP (gov.'s coun., sec. Washington chpt.); mem. Wash. State Soc. Internal Medicine (trustee, past pres.), Am. Geriatrics Soc., Am. Soc. Echocardiography, Am. Soc. Internal Medicine, Wash. Med. Assn. (coun. med. svc.), Am. Cancer Soc. (local bd. dirs.), Am. Soc. Clin. Oncology, AMA, Am. Med. Writers Assn. Office: Washington Way at Civic Ctr Longview WA 98632

KIRKPATRICK, WILLIAM HUNTER, orthopedic surgeon; b. Pitts., July 19, 1955; s. Wallace and Nancy (Stephens) K.; m. Kimberly Kirkpatrick; 3 children. BA, Harvard U., 1977; MD, U. Cin., 1982. Resident orthop. surgery U. Pitts., 1987; fellow Thomas Jefferson U. Hosp., Phila., 1988; surgeon Hand Rehab. Ctr., Phila., 1988-93, Hand Surg. Assocs., Bryn Mawr, Pa., 1993—; clin. assoc. prof. Thomas Jefferson U. Hosp., Phila., 1996—. Author: (with others) Rehabilitation of the Hand, 1992; contbr. articles to profl. jours. Fellow Am. Acad. Orthop. Surgeons; mem. AMA, Am. Soc. for Surgery of Hand, Pa. Med. Soc., Jefferson Orthop. Soc., Jefferson Hand Soc. Office: Hand Surg Assocs 830 Old Lancaster Rd # 301 Bryn Mawr PA 19010

KIRKWOOD, JAMES MACE, pharmaceutical benefit management company executive; b. Chgo., Sept. 19, 1942; s. Robert Charles and Helen Maxine (Butler) K.; m. Anne Naylor, June 21, 1965 (div. Oct. 1972); m. Nancy Lynne Siessman, Oct. 4, 1986; 1 child, Jocelyn Anne. BS in Pharmacy, U. Pitts., 1965; D in Pharmacy (hon.), U. Md., 1981. Lic. pharmacist Pa., Md., Del., Va., N.J., W.Va., Maine, Ohio; cert. analyst Walter V. Clarke Activity Vector Analysis. Pharmacy, store mgr. Sun Drug Co., Greensburg, Pa., 1966-72; owner Profl. Bldg. Pharmacy, Greensburg, 1972-74; pharmacy area supr. Keystone Stores, Lebanon, Pa., 1974-76; dir. profl. placement Rite Aid, Balt., 1976-80; pharmacy dist. mgr. Grand Union Corp., Elwood Park, N.J., 1980-81; dir. pharmacy ops. White Shield Stores, Camp Hill, Pa., 1981-85; mgr. loss prevention White Shield Stores, Camp Hill, 1981-85; from pharmacy supr. to corp. supr. 3d party ops. Rite Aid, N.J., Pa., 1985-89; dir. profl. pers. Rite Aid Corp., Harrisburg, Pa., 1989-93;

mgr. bus. re-engring. Rite Aid Corp., Harrisburg, 1993-94; mgr. Strategic Bus. Solutions, 1994-95; v.p. profl. svcs. MediClaim Inc., Lemoyne, Pa., 1995—; adj. instr. U. Pitts. Sch. Pharmacy, 1989—; founder, v.p. Ednl. Horizons, Hershey, Pa., 1995—; cons. Rivercrest Ctr., Mont Clar, Pa., 1982—, Hanover Surgicenter, 1991—, ASA Cons., Lemoyne, Pa., 1995—, Managed Care Rx, Camp Hill, 1996. Recipient U. Pitts. Sch. Pharmacy Disting. Alumni award, 1994, named Vol. of Yr., 1995. Mem. Am. Soc. Cons. Pharmacists, Ctrl. Pa. Pitts. Club (pres. 1990-92), U. Pa. Alumni Assn. (mem. strategic planning com., bd. dirs.), Pitts. Band Alumni Assn. (pres. 1992-93), U. Pitts. Alumni Coun., Pa. Pharmacy Assn., U. Pitts. 1787 Soc., N.Y. Skyliners, Reading Buccaneer Alumni Assn., Capitol Area Pharmacy Assn., Lions, Rotary, Westshoremen Alumni Assn., U. Club of Pitts., Brandermill Country Club. Republican. Lutheran. Home: 394 Rising Sun Ln Millersburg PA 17061-1456 Office: Medi-Claim Inc 20 Erford Rd Lemoyne PA 17043

KIRN, DANIEL PATRICK, optometrist; b. Reading, Pa., May 16, 1968; s. Louis Michael Jr. and Janice Young (Rothenberger) K. BS in Biology, Albright Coll., 1990; D in Optometry, Pa. Coll. Optometry, 1994, primary care residency cert., 1995. Primary care resident Pa. Coll. Optometry, Phila., 1994-95; ptnr., optometrist Dr. Daniel P. Kir, Dr. Katherine M. White, Residency-Trained, Harrisburg, Pa., 1995—; optometrist Resident Eye Care Assocs., York, Pa., 1995—; lectr., lab. instr. Pa. Coll. Optometry, Phila., 1994-95. Mem. Am. Optometric Assn., Pa. Optometric Assn., Ctrl. Pa. Optometric Soc., Jaycees. Home: Apt A-2 2121 Sir Lancelot Dr Harrisburg PA 17110 Office: East Shore Med Ctr 2405 Lingleston Rd Harrisburg PA 17110

KIRRER, ERNEST DOUGLAS, physician; b. Passaic, N.J., Dec. 28, 1948. BA, NYU, 1971; MD, U. Antwerp, 1982. Diplomat Am. Bd. Family Practice. Resident in family practice St. Mary Hosp., Hoboken, N.J., 1982-85; attending physician Gen. Hosp. Ctr. Passaic, N.J., 1985—. Fellow Am. Acad. Family PRactice; mem. Med. Soc. N.J., PAssaic County Med. Soc. Office: 40 Union Ave Clifton NJ 07015

KIRSCHNER, ERIC, cardiologist; b. East Orange, N.J., Mar. 10, 1956; s. Francis and Lillian (Zentkowski) K.; m. Gail Shulman, July 3, 1986; children: Rebecca, Anne. BA, Clark U., 1974-78; MD, Mount Sinai Sch. Medicine, 1982-85. Diplomate Am. Bd. Internal Medicine. Intern internal medicine Beth Israel Med. Ctr., N.Y.C., 1985-86, resident internal medicine, 1986-88, fellow in cardiology, 1988-91, cardiologist, 1991-94; pvt. practice N.Y.C., 1994—. Contbr. articles to profl. jours. Fellow Am. Coll. Cardiology. Office: 41 Park Ave New York NY 10016

KIRSCHNER, MARC WALLACE, biochemist, cell biologist; b. Chgo., Feb. 28, 1945. BA, Northwestern U., 1966; PhD in Biochemistry, U. Calif., Berkeley, 1971. Asst. prof. Princeton U., 1972-77, prof. biochemistry, 1977-78; prof. dept. biochemistry and biophysics U. Calif., San Francisco, 1978—. Recipient Rsch. Career Devel. award NIH, 1975-80; NSF fellow U Calif., 1971-72. Mem. NAS (Richard Lounsberg award 1991), Am. Soc. Biol. Chemists, Am. Soc. Cell Biology, Am. Acad. Arts and Sci. Office: Harvard Medical Sch Dept Cell Biology 25 Shattuck St Boston MA 02115-6027

KIRSCHNER, RICHARD MICHAEL, naturopathic physician, speaker, author; b. Cin., Sept. 27, 1949; s. Alan George and Lois (Dickey) K.; 1 child, Aden Netanya; m. Lindea Bowe. BS in Human Biology, Kans. Newman Coll., 1979; D in Naturopathic Medicine, Nat. Coll. Naturopathic Medicine, 1981. Vice pres. D. Kirschner & Son, Inc., Newport, Ky., 1974-77; co-owner, mgr. Sunshine Ranch Arabian Horses, Melbourne, Ky., 1975-77; pvt. practice Portland, Oreg., 1981-83, Ashland, Oreg., 1983—; seminar leader, trainer Inst. for Meta-Linguistics, Portland, 1981-84; cons. Nat. Elec. Contractors Assn., So. Oreg., 1985-86, United Telephone N.W., 1986; spkr. Ford Motor Co., Blue Cross-Blue Shield, Balfour Corp., NEA, AT&T, Triad Sys., Supercuts, 1986-89, Hewlett-Packard, Pepsi Co., George Bush Co., 1990-91, Goodwill Industries Am., Motorola, 1992, The Homestead T.V.A., Federated Ambulatory Surg. Assn., V.H.A. Satellite Broadcast, 1993, Oreg. Dept. Edn., Anaheim Meml. Hosp., 1994, Inc. 500 Conf., U.S. C. of C., Inst. Indsl. Engrs., 1995, EDS, ASFSA, Safeco Ins., Fairfax County, Va.; spkr., trainer Careertrack Seminars, Boulder, Colo., 1986-93; owner, spkr., trainer R & R Prodns., Ashland, Oreg., 1984—. Co-author: audio tape seminar How to Deal with Difficult People, 1987, video tape seminar, 1988; author: (audio tape seminar) How to Find and Keep a Mate, 1988, (videotape seminar) How to Find a Mate, 1990, The Happiness of Pursuit, 1994, (videotape seminar) How to Deal with Difficult People, Vol. II, 1992, (book) Dealing With People You Can't Stand, 1994, Digital Publishing on e World, Discussions of Problem People and Happiness, 1995. Spokesman Rogue Valley PBS, 1986, 87. Mem. Am. Assn. Naturopathic Physicians (bd. dirs., chmn. pub. affairs 1989-93), Wilderness Soc., Internat. Platform Assn. Republican. Office: R&R Prodns PO Box 896 Ashland OR 97520-0030

KIRSCHNER, RONALD ALLEN, osteopathic plastic surgeon, otolaryngologist, educator; b. N.Y.C., Jan. 18, 1942; s. Hyman C. and Eleanor (Pinkus) K.; m. Olivia Barbara Schlesinger, June 27, 1964; children: Andrew Scott, Julie Renee. AB, NYU, 1962; DO, Phila. Coll. Osteo. Medicine, 1966, MS in Otolaryngology, 1972. Diplomate Am. Osteo. Bd. Otolaryngology. Intern Le Roy Hosp., N.Y.C., 1966-67; resident Grandview Hosp., Dayton, Ohio, 1967-68; resident Phila. Coll. Osteo. Medicine, 1970-72, asst. prof., 1972-74, assoc. prof., 1974-76, clin. assoc. prof., 1976-85, clin. prof., 1985-90, prof., chmn. dept. otolaryngology, bronchoesophagology and facial plastic surgery, 1990-92, dir. emerging tech., 1992—; dir. neurosensory unit, 1973-76; chmn. laser surgery City Ave Hosp., Grad. Health System, 1994—; NIH fellow Armed Forces Inst. Pathology, Washington, 1971; practice medicine specializing in plastic, otolaryngology and laser surgery, Bala Cynwyd, Pa., 1976—; attending physician Grad. Hosp., 1991—; attending physician, cons. Presbyn.-U. Pa. Med. Ctr., 1987—, Hosp. of Phila. Coll. Osteo. Medicine, chmn. laser and endoscopy com., 1987-89, 91—, mem. exec. com., 1990-92; attending physician Suburban Gen. Hosp., chief ear, nose and throat and plastic surgery, 1976—, chmn. divsn. surgery, 1983-89, exec. com., 1983-89; attending physician, cons. Del. Valley Med. Ctr., 1985-92; v.p., chief med. adv. Courtlandt Group, 1979-85, exec. v.p., 1985-86, also dir. rsch. and edn., 1986; otolaryngologist Pa. Hearing Assn., 1986—; preceptor Xanar Laser Divsn., Johnson & Johnson, 1982; design cons. Pilling, Inc., 1982-87, Inframed Inc., 1985—, Sigma Dynamics Inc., Rhein Med., Inc., 1988—; otologic cons. Nat. Childrens' Hearing Aid Bank; pres. Kirschner Design Group, Inc., 1987—; bd. dirs. KDG-Rotem U.S.A., Pa. Acad. Cosmetic Surgery; dir. head and neck YAG laser protocol Cooper Lasersonics, 1983-88; chmn. med. symposium Internat. Conf. on Applied Laser Electro Optics, 1986, 87, 91; session chair Medtech '89, Free Univ., Berlin, 1989; vis. prof. internat. sch. for quantam electronics Etore Majorana Nato, Erice, Sicily, 1990; cons. Bur. Vocat. Rehab., Imunodiagnostics Lab., Allergy Mgmt. Systems Inc.; dir. 1st World Congress on Cosmetic Laser Surgery, 1992; workshop dir. Internat. Conf. on Occuloplastic Surgery, 1995. Served with M.C., USN, 1968-70; lt. comdr. Res. Recipient award for disting. teaching Lindbach Found., 1973, Legion of Honor, Chapel of Four Chaplains, 1982; Survivor of Yr. award, 1984; named Disting. Practitioner Am. Acads. of Practice. Fellow Pan Am. Allergy Assn., Phila. Acad. Facial Plastic Surgery, Phila. Laryngologic Soc., Phila. Coll. Physicians, Am. Soc. Lasers in Medicine and Surgery, Am. Auditory Soc., Am. Acad. Otolaryngology-Head and Neck Surgery, Soc. Ear, Nose, and Throat Advances in Children, Am. Acad. Facial Plastic Surgery (assoc.), Soc. Photo Optical Engrs., Osteo. Coll. Ophthalmology and Otorhinolaryngology, Am. Acad. Cosmetic Surgery; mem. AMA, Am. Osteo. Assn. (editorial cons. Jour. 1977—, editorial referee 1980—), Am. Soc. Esthetic and Reconstructive Surgery, Pa. Med. Soc., Pa. Acad. Otolaryngology, Pa. Acad. Cosmetic Surgery (bd. dirs. 1990—), Internat. Soc. Cosmetic Plastic Surgeons (bd. dirs.), Philadelphia County Osteo. Med. Assn. (chair laser com.), Centurian Club of Deafness Rsch. Found., Internat. Assn. Logopedics and Phoniatrics, Midwestern Biolaser Inst., Inst. for Applied Laser Surgery (pres.), Pa. Osteo. Med. Assn. (chmn. com. otolaryngology 1984-88, 90—, chmn. com. promotion of rsch. 1985-88), Am. Acad. Osteopathy, Survivors Club of Phila. Coll. Osteo. Medicine (pres. 1981-82), Internat. Soc. for Optical Engring., AAAS, AMA, Acad. Surgical Rsch., N.Y. Acad. Scis., Am. Soc. Liposuction Surgery, Laser Assn. Am. (sec. 1985-88), Laser and Electro Optics Mfrs. Assn., Am. Assn. Advancement Med. Instrumentation, Am. Soc. Cosmetic Surgeons, Pa. Hearing Aid Soc. (otologist), Pan Am. Assn. Otolaryngology and Bronchoesophagology, Pmology and Otolaryngology, Pa. Osteo. Med. Soc., Del Valley Tinnitus Assn. (chmn. com. otolarynology 1984-88, 90—, chmn. med. adv. bd.), Laser Inst. Am. (sr. Outstanding Svc. award 1986, chmn. lasers 1987-89, bd. dirs. 1989—, dir., chmn. com. on biology and medicine 1989—), Pa. Acad. Cosmetic Surgery (bd. dir.), Am. Acad. Cosmetic Laser Surgery (bd. dirs. 1991—), Pa. Med. Soc., Montgomery County Med. Soc., Sigma Xi, Sigma Chi, Lambda Omicron Gamma (pres. 1981-82, Disting. Service award Caduceus chpt. 1982), Variety Club, NYU Club, Vesper Club, Pickwick Club of Phila., Masons, Shriners. Jewish. Med. editor Med. Portfolio, 1980-85; guest editor Surg. Clinics of N.Am., 1984; monthly columnist Photonics Spectra, 1987-91; contbg. editor Photonics Spectra, 1988—; mem. editorial bd. Pa. Osteo. Med. Jour., Laurin Publs., 1987—, Laser Applications; contbr. articles to med. jours., chpts. in med. texts; developer various med. instruments. Office: 2 Bala Cynwyd Plz Ste 17il Bala Cynwyd PA 19004

KIRSCHNER, SIDNEY, hospital administrator. Pres., CEO Northside Hosp., Atlanta, 1995—. Office: Northside Hospital 1000 Johnson Ferry Rd NE Atlanta GA 30342-1611*

KIRSCHNER-BROMLEY, VICTORIA ANN, clinical counselor; b. Detroit, May 21, 1960; d. Isadore Ann and Leah (Goodman) Kirschner; m. Howard Russ Bromley, June 24, 1984. BA in Communications, U. Mich., 1983; MEd in Clin. Counseling, The Citadel, Charleston, S.C., 1990. Lic. profl. counselor; credentialed clin. counselor for alcohol and other drugs. Vol. for sexually and emotionally abused children Carolina Youth Devel. Ctr., North Charleston, 1988-89; intern in psychology VA Med. Ctr., Charleston, 1990; clin. counselor Trident Med. Ctr., 1990-92; pvt. practice specializing in couples therapy and eating disorders, 1990-92; case mgr. for chronically mentally ill Berkeley Cmty. Mental Health Ctr., 1992-93; counselor dept. alcohol and other drug abuse svcs., 1994—. Mem. Internat. Assn. Eatiing Disorder Profls. Home: 966 Kushiwah Creek Dr Charleston SC 29412-4405

KIRSCHSTEIN, RUTH LILLIAN, physician; b. Bklyn., Oct. 12, 1926; d. Julius and Elizabeth (Berm) K.; m. Alan S. Rabson, June 11, 1950; 1 child, Arnold. B.A. magna cum laude, L.I. U., 1947; M.D., Tulane U., 1951; D.Sc. (hon.), Mt. Sinai Sch. Medicine, 1984; LL.D. (hon.), Atlanta U., 1985; DSc (hon.), Med. Coll. Ohio, 1986; LHD (hon.), L.I. U., 1991. Intern Kings County Hosp., Bklyn., 1951-52; resident pathology VA Hosp., Atlanta, Providence Hosp., Detroit, Clin. Ctr., NIH, Bethesda, Md., 1952-57; fellow Nat. Heart Inst. Tulane U., 1953-54; asst. dir. div. biologics standards NIH, 1971-72; dep. dir. Bur. Biologics, FDA, 1972-73, dep. assoc. commr. sci., 1973-74; dir. Nat. Inst. Gen. Med. Scis., 1974-93; acting assoc. dir. woman's health NIH, Bethesda, 1974-93; acting dir. NIH, 1993, dep. dir., 1993—; mem. Found. Advanced Edn. Scis.; chmn. grants peer rev. study team NIH; mem. Inst. Medicine, NAS, 1982—; co-chair, sec. Spl. Emphasis Oversight Com. on Sci. and Tech., 1989—; co-chair PHS Coordinating Com. on Women's Health Issues, 1990—; mem. Office of Tech. Assessment Adv. Com. on Basic Rsch., 1989—. Recipient Superior Svc. award, 1980, Presdl. Disting. Exec. Rank award, 1985, 95, Pub. Svc. award Fedn. Am. Socs. for Exptl. Biology, 1993, Nat. Pub. Svc. award Am. Soc. Pub. Adminstrn./Nat. Acad. Pub. Adminstrn., 1994, Roger W. Jones award for exec. leadership Am. U., 1994, Georgeanna Seegar Jones Women's Health Lifetime Achievement award, 1995. Mem. AMA (Dr. Nathan Davis award 1990), NAS-IOM, Am. Assn. Immunologists, Am. Assn. Pathologists, Am. Soc. Microbiology, Am. Acad. Arts and Scis., Inst. Medicine. Home: 6 West Dr Bethesda MD 20814-1510 Office: NIH Shannon Bldg 1 Rm 126 1 Center Dr MSC 0148 Bethesda MD 20892-0148

KIRSHENBAUM, ABRAHAM HYMAN, neurosurgeon; b. Owen Sound, Ontario, Can., Dec. 31, 1924; came to U.S., 1952; s. David and Pearl Malka (Rozenson) K.; m. Judith Harriet Iseson, Apr. 20, 1935; children: Wendy Bella, Barry Andrew. BSc. with honors, U. Western Ontario, 1948, MD, 1951. Diplomate Am. Bd. Neurosurgery. Rotating internship Victoria Hosp., London, Ontario, Can., 1951-52; asst. resident gen. surgery Michael Reese Hosp., Chgo., 1952-53; resident in neurosurgery Beth Israel Hosp., N.Y.C., 1953; asst. resident in neurosurgery Mt. Sinai Hosp., N.Y.C., 1954, chief resident in neurosurgery, 1955, 56; attending neurosurgeon Beth Israel Med. Ctr., N.Y.C., 1957-85; dir. neurosurgery Astoria Gen. Hosp., Long Island, N.Y., 1970-85, Hillcrest Gen. Hosp., Flushing, N.Y., 1970-85; from asst. to assoc. clin. prof. dept. neurol. surgery N.Y.U. Faculty of Medicine, 1973-86; chairman, CEO U.S. Neurosurgical, Inc., Automated Med. Products, Inc., Internat. Neurosurgical, Inc. Mem. Nat. Rep. Senatorial Com., N.Y., 1995-96. Mem. Am. Assn. Neurol. Scis., Neurosurg. Assn. City of N.Y., N.Y. State Neurosurg. Assn., Am. Assn. for the Advancement of Sci. Jewish. Home and Office: 115 Central Park W Apt 14H New York NY 10023

KIRSHENBAUM, JAMES M., cardiologist; b. Omaha, Nov. 27, 1952; s. Kevee and Myrna (Samuelson) K.; m. Susan T. Nemetz; children: Andrew, Sarah, Ariel. BA, Harvard U., 1975, MD, 1979. Dir. acute interventional cardiology program Brigham and Women's Hosp., Boston, 1987—, co-dir. clin. cardiology svc., 1995—; asst. prof. medicine Harvard Med. Sch., Boston, 1992—. Fellow Am. Coll. Cardiology; mem. Am. Heart Assn., Coun. Clin. Cardiology, Am. Coll. Physicians. Office: Brigham and Womens Hosp 75 Francis St Boston MA 02115

KIRSHENBAUM, RICHARD IRVING, public health physician; b. Bklyn., Aug. 19, 1933; s. Joseph and Anne (Hantman) K.; m. Jean Shicher, Aug. 17, 1957; children: Miriam, Susan, Rachel. AB, Temple U., 1955; DO, Phila. Coll. Osteo. Medicine, 1959; MPH, Columbia U., 1971. Diplomate Am. Bd. Preventive Medicine. Resident intern Met. Hosp., Phila., 1959-60; pvt. practice medicine Bklyn., 1960-70; resident in pub. health N.Y.C. Dept. Health, 1970-73, pub. health physician, 1973-81, regional health dir. for Queens County, 1977-80, chief epidemiologist for Manhattan Borough, 1980-81; pub. health physician N.Y. State Dept. Health, N.Y.C., 1981—. Contbr. articles to profl. jours. Lt. col. Med. Corps N.Y. Army NG, 1981-91, USAR, 1991-93. Recipient Physician's Recognition award AMA 1973, 76, 79, 82, 85, 88, 90, 93. Fellow Am. Coll. Preventive Medicine; mem. APHA, N.Y. Acad. Scis. Home: 313 Whitman Dr Brooklyn NY 11234-6935 Office: NY State Dept Health 5 Penn Plz Fl 5 New York NY 10001-1810

KIRSHNER, JACOB, physician; b. N.Y.C., Jan. 9, 1927; s. Philip and Irene (Walzer) K.; m. Sylvia Ann Shyken, Aug. 19, 1956; children: Daniel, Miriam, Eli, Ruth. BS magna cum laude, CCNY, 1945; AM, Columbia U., 1947; MD, SUNY, 1951. Diplomate Am. Bd. Internal Medicine. Rotating inter Mt. Sinai Hosp., N.Y.C., 1951-52, asst. resident internal medicine, 1953-54; jr. asst. resident Montefiore Hosp., Bronx, N.Y., 1952-53; sr. resident VA Hosp., Bronx, 1954-55, fellow cardiology, asst. chief cardiac sect. dept. medicine, 1955-57; cons. medicine dept. medicine South Amboy (N.J.) Meml. Hosp., 1957-94; sr. attending physician dept. medicine St. Peter's Med. Ctr., New Brunswick, N.J., 1957-94; clin. asst. prof. Coll. Medicine & Dentistry N.J. Robert Wood Johnson Med. Sch, New Brunswick, 1971-82, clin. assoc. prof., 1982-93, prof., 1993-94; mem. exec. com. med. dental staff St. Peters Med. Ctr., New Brunswick, 1962-94, sec.-treas., 1985-86, v.p., 1987-88, pres., 1989-90. V.p. Congregation Anshe Emeth of South River, 1971-72, pres., 1972-75; v.p. Jewish Fedn. Raritan Valley, 1976-78, pres., 1978-80; life mem. bd. dirs. Jewish Fedn. Greater Middlesex County, 1985—; chmn. local com. State of Israel Bonds; mem. State Bd. Jewish Nat. Fund; co-chmn. Jewish Community Rels. Coun. Middlesex County, 1985-87; mem. exec. com. Nat. Jewish Community Rels. Adv. Coun., 1986-89, 90—, co-chmn. strategy com. World Jewry and Internat. Human Rights, 1990—, vice chmn., 1993—. With USN, 1945-46. Recipient David Ben Gurion award State of Israel Bonds, 1976, Samuel I. Hoddeson Humanitarian award Jewish Fedn. Raritan Valley, 1981, Presdl. award Jewish Fedn. Greater Middlesex County, 1988. Mem. Med. Soc. N.J., Middlesex County Med. Soc., Alpha Omega Alpha, Phi Beta Kappa. Home: 53 Ferris St South River NJ 08882-1829 Office: Old-Bridge-Sayreville Med Group 53 Main St Sayreville NJ 08872-1559

KIRSNERS, ERICA, social worker. MSW, Smith Coll., 1976. Lic. ind. clin. social worker; diplomate Am. Bd. Examiners in Clin. Social Work, ACSW. Program dir. Adolescent Day Program, Worcester, Mass., 1977-81; clin. social work supr. in-patient psychiatry Faulkner Hosp., Boston, 1981-87; pvt. practice Brookline and Cambridge, Mass., 1978—. Mem. NASW, Nat. Fedn. Socs. for Clin. Social Work. Office: 344 Harvard St Brookline MA 02146

KIRST, HERBERT ANDREW, chemist; b. St. Paul, Sept. 22, 1944; s. Gilbert Thomas and Florence Ingrid (Jensen) K.; m. Peggy A. Hillman, Jan. 1988. BChem, U. Minn., 1966; PhD in Chemistry, Harvard U., 1971. Postdoctoral fellow Calif. Inst. Tech., Pasadena, 1971-73; sr. chemist Eli Lilly & Co., Indpls., 1973-77, rsch. scientist, 1977-83, sr. rsch. scientist, 1984-91, rsch. advisor, 1992—; organizer symposia at sci. mtgs.; lectr. in field. Editor: Antimicrobial Agents & Chemotherapy, jour. ASM, 1991-96; referee sci. jours.; contbr articles to profl. jours., chpts. to books. Mem. AAAS, Am. Chem. Soc., Am. Soc. Microbiology, N.Y. Acad. Sci., Ind. Acad. Sci. Office: Eli Lilly & Co PO Box 708 2001 W Main St Greenfield IN 46140-0708

KIRSTEIN, DAVID PETER, research administrator; b. Newark, Sept. 28, 1948; s. Albert Ferdinand and Barbara Jean (Brunning) K.; m. Linda Lee Wheeler, Aug. 15, 1970; children: Kathryn Jane, Aura Rosario, Andrew Peter. BS in Biology, Bates Coll., Lewiston, Maine, 1969; MS in Biology, Villanova U., 1971. Rsch. asst. Harvard Med. Sch., Boston, 1971-73; sr. rsch. asst. Trudeau Inst. Inc., Saranac Lake, N.Y., 1973-80, adminstrv. asst. to dir., 1980-91, asst. dir. ops., 1991—. Bd. dirs. Gen.Hosp. Saranac Lake, 1978-81, 88-91, Adirondack Med. Ctr., Sranac Lake, 1991—, chmn. bd., 1993—; treas. Paul Smiths-Gabriels (N.Y.) Vol. Fire Dept., 1984—. Republican. Office: Trudeau Inst Inc PO Box 59 Saranac Lake NY 12983-0059

KIRTON, ORLANDO CECILIO, surgeon, educator; b. Gamboa, Panama, Sept. 14, 1958; s. Leafton and Ruth Isabel (Atkinson) K.; m. Jillian Euphemia, July 4, 1987; 1 child, Phillip. BA in Biochemistry, Brown U., 1978; MD cum laude, Harvard U., 1983. Diplomate Am. Bd. Surgery. Intern surgery Health Sci. Ctr. SUNY, Bklyn., 1983-84, resident surgery, 1984-85, 1987-89, chief resident surgery, 1989-90; clin. instr., rsch. fellow dept. pathology Children's Hosp., Boston, 1985-87; fellow surg. critical care dept. surgery Sch. Medicine Jackson Meml. Hosp./ U. Miami, 1990-91, fellow surgery trauma, 1991-92, med. dir. advanced trauma life support, 1996—; asst. prof. clin. surgery dept. surgery U. Miami, 1992—; assoc. dir. surg. intensive care Jackson Meml. Med. Ctr., 1992—; attending physician trauma & surg. care Jackson Meml. Hosp., 1992—, mem. faculgy gen. surg. & trauma critical care, 1992—, mem. faculty anesthesia critical care, 1992—, attending nutritional and metabolic support svcs., 1993—, attending physician dept. hyperbaric medicine, 1995—; attending surgeon VA Hosp., Miami, 1995—. Cons. editor Chest, 1996—; contbr. articles to profl. jours. Spkr. 4th Ann. Black History Month program Miami Arena, 1995; mem. Dade County Trauma adv. com., 1996—. Maj. U.S. Army Res., 1992—. Recipient H. Quillian Jones award Fla. Com. Trauma, 1991, Disting. Svc. award South Fla. Coalition Black Trade Unionists, 1993, DuPont Critical Care Rsch. award Am. Coll. Chest Physicians, 1995, Young Investigator award, 1993; grantee Nat. Rsch. Svc., 1985-87, Merck & Co., 1993, Zeneca Pharms., 1995—; rsch. fellow N.Y. Dept. Health, 1979. Fellow ACS (candidate group 1984-92); mem. AMA, Nat. Med. Assn., Am. Trauma Soc., Am. Assn. Surgery Trauma, Assn. Acad. Surgeons, Soc. Critical Care Medicine (abstract reviewer 1994-96, editor surg. sect. newsletter 1995—), So. Med. Assn., Eastern Assn. Surgery Trauma, Assn. Surg. Edn., Alpha Omega Alpha. Office: U Miami Dept Surgery PO Box 016960 (D-40) Miami FL 33101

KIRYCHUK, DARLENE, psychiatric clinical nurse; b. Meriden, Conn.; d. Nicholas Gregory and Josephine J. (LaRosa) K. Degree, Middlesex Tech. C.C., 1989, Ona M. Wilcox Coll. Nursing, 1989. Cert. psychiatric and mental health nurse ANA. Cert. nursing asst. Bradley Home for Aged, Meriden, 1985-89; clin. nurse Altobello Youth Ctr., Meriden, 1989-93; clin. nurse instr. Wallingford (Conn.) Adult Edn., 1992—; clin. nurse coord. Riverview Hosp., Middletown, Conn., 1993—; infection control pharmacy coord. Riverview Hosp., Middletown, 1993—; patient and family edn. coord. Riverview Hosp., 1995—. Roman Catholic. Office: Riverview Hosp 915 River Rd Middletown CT 06457

KISABETH, TIM CHARLES, obstetrician, gynecologist; b. Fostoria, Ohio, Oct. 29, 1957; s. Donald C. and Doris J. (Smith) K. BA in Chemistry, Capital U., 1979; MD, Ohio State U., 1982. Diplomate Nat. Bd. Med. Examiners, Am. Bd. Obstetrics and Gynecology. Resident in ob-gyn Oakwood Hosp., Dearborn, Mich., 1982-86; chief resident Oakwood Hosp., Dearborn, 1985-86; pvt. practice Alton, Ill., 1986—; lab. dir. Alton Multispecialists, 1995—; also bd. dirs.; chmn. ob-gyn. dept. Alton (Ill.) Meml. Hosp., 1991-93, 95—. Mem. Greater Alton-Twin River Growth Assn., 1987—; bd. dirs. Pride, Inc., 1992—, chmn. Alton Lake com., 1993-95. Fellow Am. Coll. Ob-Gyn.; mem. AMA (del. resident sect. 1984-86, del. yhoung physicians sect. 1990-92), Ill. Med. Soc. (ho. of dels. 1987—, young physicians com. 1987-92, com. on pub. rels. and membership 1992—), Madison County Med. Soc. (pres. 1994-95), Am. Fertility Soc., Masons DeMolay (Legion of Honor award 1988), Alton Waterski Club. Lutheran. Home: 3312 Rosenberg Ln Godfrey IL 62035-1172 Office: Alton Multispecialists Ltd 2 Saint Anthonys Way Ste 111 Alton IL 62002-4569

KISER, GLENN AUGUSTUS, retired pediatrician, philanthropist, investor; b. Bessemer City, N.C., July 13, 1917; s. Augustus B. and May (Carpenter) K.; m. Katherine Parham, June 13, 1941 (dec. 1972); m. Muriel Coykendall, Feb. 4, 1973. BS, Duke U., 1941, MD, 1941. Diplomate Nat. Bd. Med. Examiners. Resident physician Duke Hosp., Durham, N.C., 1946-48; resident Johns Hopkins U., Balt., 1946; pvt. practice Salisbury, N.C., 1947-55; ret. Salisbury, 1955—; founder stockholder Food Lion, Inc.; med. cons. State of N.C., Raleigh, 1961-64, 75-76, New River Mental Health Ctr., Boone, N.C., 1976-77; chief pediatric dept. Rowan Meml. Hosp., Salisbury, 1947-55, chief of staff, 1951-52. Bd. advisors Chowan Coll., Murfreesboro, N.C., 1977-78; trustee Rowan Regional Med. Ctr. Found., Salisbury. With USPHS, 1941-46, surgeon, 1991-96. Recipient Exemplary Life Svc. award Catawba Coll., 1995. Mem. Pinnacle Club Duke Med. Ctr. (charter), Duke Med. Ctr. Alumni Assn. (coun. 1988), Duke U. Founders Soc., Lions (dep. dist. gov. N.C. chpt. 1959, pres. Milford Hills chpt. 1959, zone chmn. 1959, dep. dist. gov. 1960, internat. amb. 1961), Salisbury Country Club. Republican. Presbyterian. Home: 728 Klumac Rd Apt 138C Salisbury NC 28144-5716

KISER, KAREN MAUREEN, medical technologist, educator; b. St. Louis, Sept. 28, 1951; d. Arthur John and Elizabeth M. (Boyer) Meier; m. Winston Kiser, July 21, 1973; children: Cynthia Kay, Jessica Lea. BS in Med. Tech., S.E. Mo. State U., 1973; MA in Health Care Edn., Cen. Mich. U., 1984. Part-time lab. asst. Luth. Med. Ctr., St. Louis, 1970-71; part-time lab. technician Jewish Hosp., St. Louis, 1972-73, med. technologist, 1973-77; assoc. prof., edn. coord. St. Louis C.C. at Forest Park, 1977—; on-site surveyor Nat. Accrediting Agy. for Clin. Lab. Sci., Chgo., 1986, 94; self-study reviewer, 1994, 95; reviewer F.A. Davis, 1995, W.B. Saunders Co., Phila., 1986-91; spkr. in field. Leader Girl Scouts U.S., 1986-90, 91-92, co-leader, 1990—; assoc. advisor Explorer Scouts, 1978-81; capt. United Way, St. Louis, 1989, 90, 93. Recipient Emerson Electric award for Teaching Excellence, 1993, Gov.'s award for Excellence in Teaching, 1993. Mem. NEA, Am. Soc. for Clin. Lab. Sci., Mo. Soc. for Clin. Lab. Sci., Am. Soc. for Microbiology, Mo. Edn. Assn., Mo. Assn. Cmty. and Jr. Colls., Am. Soc. Clin. Pathologists. Office: Saint Louis CC 5600 Oakland Ave Saint Louis MO 63110-1316

KISER, ROBERTA KATHERINE, medical administrator, education educator; b. Alton, Ill., Aug. 13, 1938; d. Stephen Robert and Virginia Elizabeth (Lasher) Golden; m. James Robert Crisman, sept. 6, 1958 (div. May 1971); 1 child, Robert Glenn; m. James Earl Kiser, Dec. 19, 1971; 1 child, James Jacob. BEd, So. Ill. U., 1960. Cert. tchr., Ill., Calif. Librarian Oaklawn (Ill.) Elem. Sch., 1960-62, Alsip (Ill.) Elem. Sch., 1966-69; tchr. Desert Sands Unified Sch. Dist., Indio, Calif., 1969-79; prin. Mothercare Infant Sch., Rancho Mirage, Calif., 1980-89; substitute tchr. Greater Coachella Valley Sch., Calif., 1989-91; med. acct. Desert Health Care, Bermuda Dunes, Calif., 1990-92; mentor tchr., computing, typing skils Wilde Woode Children's Ctr., Palm Springs, Calif., 1990-92; chiropractic asst. Rapp Chiropractic Health Ctr, Palm Desert, Calif., 1992-93; sr. med. records clk. Eisenhower Med. Ctr., Rancho Mirage, 1993—. V.p. Palm Desert (Calif.) Community Ch. Montessori Sch. Bd., 1982-85. Republican. Presbyterian. Home: 39-575

Keenan Dr Rancho Mirage CA 92270-3610 Office: Eisenhower Med Ctr 39000 Bob Hope Dr Rancho Mirage CA 92270-3221

KISER, SHARON ANN, health facility professional; b. Dayton, Ohio, Aug. 2, 1945; d. Charles Russell and Louise Matilda (Baer) Warner; m. Peter Joseph D'Onofrio, Oct. 16, 1971 (div. June 1976); m. Ronald Eugene Kiser, June 14, 1986; 1 stepchild, Rebecca Erin. Degree in secretarial sci., Miami Jacobs Jr. Coll., 1971; AS in Bus. Adminstrn., Sinclair Community Coll., 1986; BA in Mgmt., Antioch U., 1990. Cert. dir. volunteer services, Ohio. Exec. sec. NCR Corp., Dayton, 1963-78; dir. vol. services Grandview Hosp. and Med. Ctr., Southview Hosp. and Family Health Ctr., Dayton, 1978—; speaker Nat. Osteo. Guild Assn., Dayton, 1981; nat. speaker Am. Soc. Dirs. Vol. Services Ednl. Conf., Houston, 1983, Cin., 1984, Phila., 1986; mem. tng. com., human resources com. Voluntary Action Ctr. United Way, Dayton, 1983, 86. Contbr. articles to profl. jours. V.p. Sulphur Grove United Meth. Women, 1993-95. Mem. Am. Soc. Dirs. Vol. Svcs. (innovative programming com. 1987, Creative Achievement award 1983, 84, 86), Ohio Soc. Dirs. Vol. Svcs. (bylaws com. 1980-81, mentor membership com. S.W. Ohio chpt. 1981-85, newspaper rep. 1982-84, co-chmn. award for creative achievement 1991-92). Home: 7201 Claircrest Dr Huber Heights OH 45424-2912 Office: Grandview Hosp and Med Ctr 405 W Grand Ave Dayton OH 45405-4720

KISH, GEORGE FRANKLIN, thoracic and cardiovascular surgeon; b. Toledo, Ohio, Mar. 30, 1944; s. George F. and Ann (Kucharski) K.; m. Joann Mata Kish, Mar. 16, 1968; children: Jeremy, Nathan. BS, Ohio State U., 1966, MD, 1970. Surg. intern George Washington U. Med. Ctr., 1970-71, surg. resident, 1971-74, surg. rsch. fellow, 1974-75, chief surg. resident, 1975-76, thoracic and cardiovascular surgery resident, 1976-78; asst. prof. surgery W.Va. U. Med. Ctr., Morgantown, 1978-80; cardiovascular surgeon D'Angelo Clinic, Erie, Pa., 1980—; chief cardiovascular surgery Hamot Med. Ctr., Erie, 1982-93. Contbg. author International Trends in General Thoracic Surgery, Vol. 7, 1991; contbr. articles to profl. jours. Dr. I.S. Grisoff fellow cardiovascular surgery George Washington U., 1974-75; affiliate rsch. grantee Am. Heart Assn., W.Va. Med. Ctr., 1979. Fellow ACS, Internat. Soc. Cardiovascular Surgeons, Soc. Thoracic Surgeons, Am. Coll. Cardiology, Am. Coll. Chest Physicians, Southeastern Surg. Congress, Internat. Coll. Angiology. Home: 218 Frontier Dr Erie PA 16505-2506 Office: D'Angelo Clinic 104 E 2nd St Erie PA 16507-1532

KISHABA, TOMOKAZU, physician; b. Naha, Okinawa, Feb. 16, 1942; s. Chorei and Kayo Kishaba; M.D., Kyoto (Japan) U., 1966; m. Ayako Nakamoto, Apr. 19, 1969; children: Waka, Yuka, Chika, Taka. Intern, Phila. Gen. Hosp., 1970-71; resident in medicine D.C. Gen. Hosp., 1971-74; fellow in infectious diseases U. Louisville Med. Sch., 1974-76; asst. chief sect. internal medicine Okinawa Chubu Hosp., 1976—. Diplomate Am. Bd. Internal Medicine, Am. Bd. Infectious Diseases. Mem. Japanese Soc. Internal Medicine, Japanese Soc. Infectious Diseases, Japanese Soc. Chemotherapy. Author articles in field. Home: 1944 Hiyane, Okinawa City, Okinawa 904-21, Japan Office: Okinawa Chubu Hosp, 208-3 Miyasato Gushikawa City, Okinawa 904-22, Japan

KISHI, SHOJI, ophthalmologist, educator; b. Tokyo, Dec. 31, 1950; m. Yasuko Yoshida, Mar. 4, 1979; children: Maiko, Takahisa. MD, Gunma U., 1976, PhD, 1987. Resident Gunma U. Hosp., Maebashi, Japan, 1976-79; fellow U. Ill., Chgo., 1981-83; instr. Gunma U. Hosp., Maebashi, 1984-9, asst. prof., 1992—. Home: 19-4 Midorigaoka, Maebashi Gunma 371, Japan Office: Dept Ophthalmology, Gunma Univ Hosp, 3 Maebashi Gunma 371, Japan

KISKER, CARL THOMAS, physician, medical educator; B.A., Johns Hopkins U., 1958; M.D., U. Cin. Coll. Medicine, 1962. Diplomate Am. Bd. Pediatrics, Am. Bd. Pediatric Hematology-Oncology. Licensed physician Ohio, Iowa. Intern, U. Oreg. Coll. Medicine, 1962-63; sr. asst. surgeon NIH, 1963-65; jr. resident pediatrics Children's Hosp., Cin., 1965-66, sr. resident pediatrics, 1966-67; fellow pediatric hematology, 1967-69; asst. attending pediatrician, 1968-69, attending pediatrician, 1969-73; dir. hemophilia project, 1971-73, dir. clin. hematology lab., 1972-73; asst. prof. pediatrics U. Cin., 1969-72, assoc. profl pediatrics, 1972-73; assoc. prof. pediatrics U. Iowa, Iowa City, 1973-79, dir. div. pediatric hematology-oncology, 1973—, prof. pediatrics, 1979—; med. lectr. various student and profl. groups; active mem. Pediatric Hematology-Oncology Group, Cin., Children's Cancer Study Group, Los Angeles; pres. Midwest Blood Club; mem. editorial bd. Pediatrics Today; mem. adv. council Nat. Hemophilia Ctrs., 1979—. Contbr. numerous sci. papers to profl. jours. and chpts. to books. Mem. Iowa Found. Fund Raising Com. Lederle Med. Student Research fellow, 1959; recipient state and fed. grants. Mem. Am. Soc. Hematology, Mid-west Soc. for Pediatric Research, Am. Fedn. for Clin. Research, Am. Heart Assn., Internat. Soc. Thrombosis and Haemostasis (sub-com. on neonatal hemostasis), Central Soc. for Pediatric Research, Soc. for Pediatric Research, Johnson County Med. Soc., Prairie Region Affiliated Blood Services, Am. Pediatric Soc. Office: Univ of Iowa Hosp 2520 Jcp Iowa City IA 52242

KISSINGER, JOHN CALVIN, retired microbiologist; b. Shamokin, Pa., June 8, 1925; s. Claude Calvin and Flora (Smith) K.; m. Nancy Louise Wagner, Sept. 30, 1950 (dec. Jan. 1985); children: John A., George B.; m. Nancy Reamer, June 23, 1987. BS, Bucknell U., 1949, MS, 1950. Chemist Campbell's Soup, Camden, N.J., 1950-51; microbiologist Merck Sharpe & Dohme, Glenolden, Pa., 1951-53, Merck Sharge & Dohme, Danville, Pa., 1953-55; supr. Grain Processing Corp., Muscatine, Iowa, 1955-57; rsch. microbiologist USDA, Phila., 1957-83; tech. cons. N.Am. Maple Producers Coun., Bainbridge, N.Y., 1964-73. Contbr. articles to profl. jours. Prin. cellist North Penn Symphony Orch., Lansdale, Pa., 1971-89. With U.S. Army, 1943-46. Assn. of Ofcl. Analytical Chemists fellow, 1976; recipient Cert. of Merit U.S. Dept. Agr., 1969, Indsl. Wastes medal Fedn. Sewage and Indsl. Wastes Assns., 1957. Republican. United Ch. of Christ. Home: 1018 S 10th St Emmaus PA 18049-3619

KISSINGER, KERRY W., health care consultant; b. Reading, Pa., Dec. 14, 1940; s. Harvey Adam and Helen Elizabeth (Heffner) K.; m. Janice Kissinger, Aug. 28, 1962; children: Kevin, Drew, Ben. BS in Indsl. Engring., Pa. State U.; MS, Frostburg State U. Sales rep. data processing divsn. IBM, Youngstown, Ohio, 1962-68; mktg. mgr. IBM, Pitts., 1968-72; health industry mktg. mgr. IBM, Bethesda, Md., 1972-74; br. mgr. IBM, Hagerstown, Md., 1974-78; mgr. advanced tech. IBM Biomed. Systems, Mt. Kisko, N.Y., 1978-80; mktg. dir. IBM Biomed. Systems, Cranberry, N.J., 1980-84; v.p. sales and mktg. Health Systems Internat., New Haven, Conn., 1984-86; cons. Princeton, N.J., 1986-87; area dir., ptnr. Ernst & Young LLP, Boston, 1987—. Author, editor: Information Technology for Integrated Health Systems, 1995. Pres. Washington County Loan Closet, Hagerstown, 1977-78. Mem. HIMSS, HFMA. Home: 207 Elizabeth Ridge Rd Carlisle MA 01741 Office: Ernst & Young LLP 200 Clarendon St Boston MA 02116

KISSMEYER-NIELSEN, PERLA M.S., psychiatrist; b. Pasay City, Philippines, Jan. 16, 1931; came to U.S., 1955; d. Teodorico B. and Fidela Santos; m. Erik Kissmeyer-Nielsen; children: Paul Erik, Kirsten Yvette. MD, U. Philippines, 1955. Intern So. Balt. Gen. Hosp., 1955-56; resident in pediatrics North Shore Hosp., Manhasset, L.I., 1956-58; resident in pediatric cardiology St. Francis Hosp. and Sanatorium, Roslyn, L.I., 1958-59; fellow in cardiology Johns Hopkins Hosp., Balt., 1960-61; staff psychiatrist Del. State Hosp., New Castle, 1965-68; staff psychiatrist VA Med. Ctr., Bedford, Mass., 1968-75, Manchester, N.H., 1975—. Mem. Holocaust Meml. Mus., Washington. Recipient Svc. award Dept. Vet. Affairs., Manchester, N.H., 1993; cert. of Appreciation Am. Legion, 1993. Mem. Am. Psychiatric Assn., Mass. Psychiat. Soc., Mass. Med. Soc., Acad. Psychomatic Medicine, Physicians for Human Rights, Amnesty Internat., Habitat Internat., Colonial Williamsburg Found. Home: 65 Crabtree Rd Concord MA 01742-2011 Office: VA Med Ctr 718 Smyth Rd Manchester NH 03104-7004

KITAGAWA, TOKUJIRO, pharmaceutical science educator; b. Osaka, Japan, Nov. 8, 1942; s. Manji and Chieko (Nukata) K.; m. Kuniko Murakami, Sept. 15, 1974; children: Tomoyasu, Wakako. B in Pharmacy, Kyoto (Japan) Coll. Pharmacy, 1966; MS, Kyushu U., Fukuoka, Japan, 1970, DSc, 1975. Asst. Kyoto Coll. Pharmacy, 1967-68; asst. Kobe (Japan) Gakuin U., 1973-76, instr., 1977-79, asst. prof., 1980-83, prof. pharm. sci., 1984—. Mem. Am. Chem. Soc., Pharm. Soc. Japan, Soc. Synthetic Organic Chemistry Japan. Home: 7-11 Tsutsujigaoka 1-Chome, Tarumi-Ku, Kobe 655, Japan Office: Kobe Gakuin U, Faculty Pharm Scis, Ikawadani-Cho, Nishi-Ku, Kobe 651-21, Japan

KITAMURA, TOSHINORI, psychiatrist; b. Yokohama, Kanagawa, Japan, Oct. 16, 1947; s. Masanori and Kikuko (Matsumoto) K.; m. Fusako Oami, Mar. 17, 1973. M.D., Keio Gijuku U. Sch. Medicine, Tokyo, 1972. Psychiatrist, Inst. Psychiatry, Tokyo, 1973-76; hon research fellow U. Birmingham (U.K.), 1976-80; clin. instr. Keio Gijuku U., Tokyo, 1980-83, lectr., 1983; chief sect. mental health for elderly NIMH, Ichikawa, Japan, 1983-91, dir. dept. sociocultural environ. rsch., 1991—; vis. lectr. Keio Gijuku U., 1986—; head Group for Research Assessment in Psychiatry, Tokyo, 1981—; mem. com. Med. Selection Japanese Astronauts, 1987-88, 95-96, com. Psychiatric Diagnostic Criteria Japan, 1987-89, com. Guideline for Psychiatric Treatment, 1987-88. Editor-in-chief Archives of Psychiat. Diagnostics and Clin. Evaluation, Tokyo, 1989-91; editor Brit. Jour. Psychiatry, 1994—, Internat. Jour. Behavioral Medicine, 1994—; contbr articles to profl. jours. Fellow Royal Coll. Psychiatrists, British Council Japan Assn., Japanese Assn. Psychiatry and Neurology (coun. 1991-94). Home: 8-12-4-305 Akasaka, Minato-ku, Tokyo 170, Japan Office: NIMH, 1-7-3 Konodai, Ichikawa, Chiba 272, Japan

KITAZAWA, YOSHIAKI, medical educator; b. Tokyo, Apr. 1, 1937; s. Katsuro and Suzu (Miyakoshi) K.; m. Mariko Ishikawa, Mar. 4, 1991. MD, Chiba U., Japan, 1961; PhD, Chiba U., 1967. Diplomate Japanese Bd. Ophthalmology. Instr. ophthalmology, asst. prof. Chiba U., Japan, 1967-76; assoc. prof. ophthalmology U. Tokyo, 1976-84; prof. ophthalmology, chmn. dept. Gifu U., Japan, 1985—. Author: Clinical Glaucoma, 1985, The Atlas of Gonioscopy, 1995. Recipient Alcon award Alcon Rsch. Inst., 1994. Mem. Internat. Glaucoma Soc. (pres. 1994, sec. 1990-94), Internat. Perimetric Soc. (v.p. 1994—), Asea-Oceanic Glaucoma Soc. (pres. 1996—), Assn. Rsch. for Vision and Ophthalmology, Am. Acad. Ophthalmology. Home: 8-17-3 Hino-minami, Gifu 500, Japan Office: Gifu Univ Dept Ophthalmol, 40 Tsukasa-machi, Gifu 500, Japan

KITCHELL, ROBERT W., internist; b. Seattle, Jan. 5, 1955; s. Frank Robert and Virginia (Price) K.; m. Carolyn Rives Claar, June 25, 1983; children: Virginia Rives, Sarah, William. BA, Amherst Coll., 1978; MD, U. Va., 1982. Resident Mt. Auburn Hosp. Harvard Med. Sch., Boston, 1982-86; internist Polyclinic, Seattle, 1986—; mem. exec. com. Polyclinic, Seattle, 1988, mem. physician pers. com., 1990—. Active alumni bd. Lakeside High Sch., Seattle, 1990-93, pres., 1993, trustee, 1993. Mem. King County Med. Soc., Wash. State Med. Soc. Home: 233 36th Ave E Seattle WA 98112 Office: Polyclinic 1145 Broadway Seattle WA 98122

KITE, JOSEPH HIRAM, JR., microbiologist, educator; b. Decatur, Ga., Nov. 11, 1926; s. Joseph Hiram and Lulie (Hatch) K.; m. Jane Pascale, Aug. 6, 1970. AB, Emory U., 1948; MS, U. Tenn., 1954; PhD, U. Mich., 1959. Med. technician in bacteriology Communicable Disease Ctr., Atlanta, 1950-51, VA Hosp., 1951-52; rsch. assoc. U. Buffalo, 1958-59, instr., 1959-63; asst. prof. bacteriology and immunology SUNY-Buffalo, 1963-68, assoc. prof. microbiology, 1968-72, prof. microbiology, 1972—. Contbr. articles to med. jours., chpts. to med. textbooks. Served with AUS, 1945-46. Mem. Am. Assn. Immunologists, Am. Soc. Microbiology, Tissue Culture Assn., AAAS, N.Y. Acad. Scis. Methodist. Subspecialties: Immunology (medicine); Microbiology (medicine). Current work: tuberculosis and autoimmune diseases; teaching medical, dental and graduate students; research on mechanisms of protective immunity to Mycobacterium tuberculosis, and autoimmune regulation in thyroiditis. Home: 108 Chasewood Ln East Amherst NY 14051-1888 Office: Med Sch SUNY Dept Microbiology Buffalo NY 14214

KITO, SHOZO, pharmacology and neurology educator; b. Nagoya, Japan, Jan. 29, 1927; s. Chiyoju and Tane (Goshima) K.; m. Sachiko Wada, May 16, 1955; 1 child, Tatsuo. MD, Tokyo U., 1951, PhD, 1959. Instr. Tokyo U. Sch. Medicine, 1959-67, 68-71; asst. prof. Tokyo Women's Med. Coll., 1971-73; prof. Hiroshima (Japan) U. Sch. Medicine, 1973-90; emeritus prof. Hiroshima (Japan) U., 1995—; prof. U. of Air Japan, Chiba, 1990; vis. prof. U. Ariz., 1982, U. B.C., Vancouver, Can., 1989-94; mng. dir. cmty. med. care rsch. com. Hiroshima Prefecture, 1973-90, mem. intractable diseases rsch. com., 1973-90. Editor sci. jours. Mem. Soc. Neuroscience (emeritus), Internat. Brain Rsch. Orgn., Internat. Soc. Devel. Neurosci., Internat. Basal Ganglia Soc., Internat. Soc. Neurochemistry, Japanese Med. Assn. (award 1976), N.Y. Acad. Scis., numerous other sci. orgns. Office: U of Air Japan, 2-11 Wakaba Mihamaku, Chiba 261, Japan

KITT, WALTER, psychiatrist; b. N.Y.C., Dec. 18, 1925; s. Elias and Mary (Opiela) K.; m. Terry Escorcia, May 15, 1955 (dec. 1974); 1 child, Gregory; m. Sally Anderson Chappell, June 22, 1977. Student, CCNY, 1942-44; AB magna cum laude, Syracuse (N.Y.) U., 1948; MD, Chgo. Med. Sch., 1952. Diplomate Am. Bd. Psychiatry and Neurology. Resident Neuropsychiat. Inst., Chgo., 1953-56; practice medicine specializing in psychiatry Chgo., 1956-64, Munster, Ind., 1963-80; psychiatrist Lakeside VA Med. Ctr., Chgo., 1981-92; practice medicine specializing in psychiatry Park Ridge, Ill., 1992—; acting chief psychiat. services Lakeside VA Med. Ctr., Chgo., 1985-87; asst. prof. clin. psychiatry U. Ill. Med. Ctr., Chgo., 1958-64, Northwestern U., Chgo., 1974-96; chmn. divsn. psychiatry Our Lady of Mercy Hosp., Dyer, Ind., 1970-72. Mem. Am. Psychiat. Assn. Home: 3750 N Lake Shore Dr Chicago IL 60613-4238 Office: 1460 Renaissance Dr # 209 Park Ridge IL 60068

KITTLE, CHARLES FREDERICK, surgeon; b. Athens, Ohio, Oct. 24, 1921; s. Frederick F. and Ida (Falls) K.; m. Jeane Mignon Groenier, 1945 (div. 1973); children: Candace Mignon, Bradley Dean, Leslie Jeane, Brian David; m. Ann Catherine Bates, 1981. AB with honors, Ohio U., Athens, 1942, LLD, 1967; MD with honors, U. Chgo., 1945; MS in Surgery, U. Kans., 1950. Diplomate Am. Bd. Surgery, Am. Bd. Thoracic Surgery (mem. bd. 1967-75, chmn. 1973-75). Intern U. Chgo. Clinics, 1945-46; resident gen. and thoracic surgery U. Kans. Med. Center, 1948-52; spl. tng. radio-isotopes for med. use Oak Ridge Inst. Nuclear Studies, 1950, cons. med. div., 1950-55; mem. faculty U. Kans. Sch. Medicine, 1950-66; assoc. prof. surgery, lectr. history medicine, 1959-66; cons. thoracic surgery VA Hosp., Wadsworth, Kans., 1954-57; cons. gen. surgery VA Hosp., 1957-60; attending gen. surgery VA Hosp. Kansas City, Mo., 1954-66, Wichita, Kans., 1955-62; prof. surgery, head sect. thoracic and cardiovascular surgery U. Chgo. Clinics, 1966-72; prof. surgery, dir. thoracic surgery sect. Rush Med. Coll. and Presbyn.-St. Luke's Hosp., 1973-92, prof. emeritus, 1992—; dir. Rush Cancer Ctr., 1978-86; mem. staff McNeal Hosp., Berwyn, Ill., 1986-92; cons. Mcpl. TB Sanatorium, Chgo., 1968-74, Hines VA Hosp., Maywood, Ill., 1973-92; spl. rsch. cardiovascular surgery, control of blood flow. Served as lt. (j.g.) USNR, 1946-48. Clin. fellow Am. Cancer Soc., 1950-52; Markle scholar med. scis., 1952-58. Mem. AAAS, ACS (bd. dirs. Kans. 1965-68), Am. Assn. History Medicine, Am. Assn. Thoracic Surgery, Am. Coll. Cardiology (bd. dirs. Kans. 1963-66), Chgo. Surg. Soc. (pres. 1972-73), Am. Heart Assn. (chmn. program com. cardiovasc. surgery 1965-88, exec. com. cardiovasc. surgery coun. 1962-74, chmn. coun. 1972-74), Am. Physiol. Assn., Cen. Surg. Soc., Chgo. Med. Soc., Am. Surg. Assn., Internat. Cardiovasc. Soc. (sec. 1965-71), Internat. Soc. Surgery, Soc. Med. Hist. (pres. Chgo. 1983-85), N.J. Thoracic Surgery Soc., Ill. Thoracic Surgery Soc. (pres. 1983-84), Soc. Clin. Surgery, Soc. Surg. Oncology, Soc. Vascular Surgery, Soc. Univ. Surgeons (pres. 1966-67), Soc. Thoracic Surgery, Univ. Village Assn. (bd. dirs. 1986-89, pres. 1989), Arthur Conan Doyle Soc., Caxton Club, Hounds of Baskerville, Chgo. Lit. Club, Phi Beta Kappa, Sigma Xi, Alpha Omega Alpha. Home: 856 S Laflin St Chicago IL 60607-4026

KITTS, JAMES JOSEPH, pharmacist; b. Cooperstown, N.Y.. Feb. 18, 1943; s. Edward A. and Mildred (Filkins) K.; m. Janet Marx, June 17, 1967; children: Lisa Renee, Wendy Lee. BS in Pharmacy, Union U., Albany, N.Y., 1966. Pharmacy supr. C.U.S. Pharmacy, Albany, 1977—. Mem. Pharm. Soc. of N.Y. State, Chain Pharmacy Assn. of N.Y. State (v.p. 1977-89, pres. 1989-92). Office: CUS Pharmacy PO Box 2011 Clifton Park NY 12065-9011

KITZ, RICHARD JOHN, anesthesiologist, educator; b. Oshkosh, Wis., Mar. 25, 1929; s. Edward G. and Lona M. (Schneider) K.; m. Jeanne Hogan, Feb. 27, 1954; 1 child, Anne Marie. B.S., Marquette U., 1951, M.D., 1954; M.A. (hon.), Harvard U. Med. Sch., 1969. Diplomate: Am. Bd. Anesthesiology (dir.). Intern in surgery Columbia U., 1954-55; resident in surgery, 1956-57, resident in anesthesiology, 1958-60, instr. in anesthesiology, 1960-61, NIH spl. research fellow, 1961-62, asst. prof. anesthesiology, 1962-66, assoc. prof., 1966-69; prof. Harvard U. Med. Sch., 1969—, Henry Isaiah Dorr prof. anaesthesia, 1970—; prof. research and teaching in anesthesia Harvard U.-MIT, co-dir. div. health scis. tech., 1985-91; anaesthetist-in-chief Mass. Gen. Hosp., Boston, 1969-94; faculty dean clinical affairs Harvard Med. Sch., 1994—; cons. FDA; prin. investigator Harvard Anaesthesia Rsch. and Rsch. Tng. Ctr., 1969-93. Contbr. numerous articles, rev. to profl. publs.; editor: (with E.M. Papper) Uptake and Distribution of Anesthetic Agents, 1963, (with M.B. Laver) Scientific Basis of Anesthesia; editor-in-chief Jour. Clin. Anesthesia, 1987-95. Served with M.C. USN, 1955-57. Fellow Coll. Anesthesiologists; mem. NAS, Inst. Medicine, AMA, Assn. Univ. Anesthetists, Am. Soc. Anesthesiologists, Mass. Soc. Anesthesiologists, Royal Coll. Surgeons Ireland (hon. mem. faculty anesthetists), Royal Coll. Anesthetists Eng. (hon.), Harvard Club (Boston), Beverly Yacht Club, Blue Water Sailing Club. Roman Catholic. Home: 6 Pond St Dover MA 02030-2432 Office: Mass Gen Hosp Dept Anesthesia Boston MA 02114

KITZKE, EUGENE DAVID, research management executive; b. Milw., Sept. 2, 1923; s. Leo R. and Regina R. (Tomczyk) K.; m. Lorraine Grace Shummon, Sept. 2, 1946; children: Mary Victoria, Paul Simon, Patrice Lynn, Jerome Peter. B.S., Marquette U., 1945, M.S., 1947. Instr. microbiology St. Mary's Sch. Nursing, Grand Rapids, Mich., 1946-47; assoc. prof. Aquinas Coll., 1947-51; lab researcher S.C. Johnson & Son, Inc., Racine, Wis., 1951-57, research mgr., 1957-76, v.p. corp. research and devel., 1976-81; pres. Oak Crete Block Corp., South Milwaukee, Wis., 1980—; developer Wind Crest Subdiv., Wind Lake, Wis., 1993; asst. clin. prof. dept. environ. medicine Med. Coll. Wis., Milw., 1973-81; owner Danel Enterprise, South Milwaukee; bd. dirs. Songcards, Inc.; judge marquette U. Sci. Fair. Author: For the Next Generation, 1986; patentee (in field); contbr. articles to tech. jours., fiction and poetry to mags. Mem. Pres.' Council Alverno Coll., 1979-87. Mem. Palm Soc. (exec. bd., past pres.), AAAS, History of Sci. Soc., Sigma Xi, Phi Sigma, Sigma Tau Delta. Roman Catholic. Home: 616 Aspen St South Milwaukee WI 53172-1702 Office: PO Box 413 South Milwaukee WI 53172-0413 Office: 7101 S Pennsylvania Ave Oak Creek WI 53154-2439

KIVEL, MICKIE KESSLER (MAXINE KIVEL), public health advisor; b. Sebewaing, Mich., Aug. 8, 1934; d. Morris Bernard Kessler and Irene Nass; m. Joseph Kivel, June 16, 1956 (div. 1982); children: Karen Sue, Patricia Lynn. BA, U. Mich., 1956. Tech. writer, editor Atlantic Rsch. Corp., Alexandria, Va., 1965-68, Bell Tel. Labs., Whippany, N.J., 1968-69, U.S. FDA, Rockville, Md., 1970—. Editor: (tech. newsletter) Radiol. Health Bull., 1975-93, Med. Devices Bull., 1992-93, Mammography Matters, 1993—. Represented U.S. in World Bridge Olympiad, 1978, 86, 90. Recipient N.Am. Bridge Championship (Women's Pairs), 1986. Mem. Am. Contract Bridge League (life).

KIVISTO, ERIC ALFRED, surgeon; b. Berwyn, Ill., Oct. 30, 1956; s. Lauri John and Carol Rita (Opsahl) K.; m. Sharon Lynn Sarges, June 15, 1986. AS, Coll. of DuPage, Glen Ellyn, Ill., 1980; BS in Biology, Mich. Tech. U., Houghton; DO, Chgo. Coll. Osteo. Medicine, 1989. Diplomate Am. Bd. Surgery. Intern Chgo. Coll. Osteo. Medicine, 1989-90; resident in gen. surgery Pontiac (Mich.) Osteo. Hosp., 1990-94; gen. surgeon Gibson (Ill.) Cmty. Hosp., 1995—. Mem. AMA (student rep.), Ill. Med. Assn., Chgo. Med. Assn., Am. Osteo. Assn. Home: 814 E LE Fevre Ave Gibson City IL 60936-2113

KIYOTA, HEIDE PAULINE, clinical psychologist; b. Bamberg, Fed. Republic Germany, July 6, 1942; came to U.S., 1970; d. Fritz and Marcella (Schropfer) S.; m. Ronald Masaki Kiyota, Dec. 26, 1982; children: Heather E., Catherine M., Michelle H. BS, U. Md., 1975, MA, 1979; PhD, U. Hawaii, 1986. Lic. psychologist, Hawaii. Counselor-trainee Regional Inst. for Children & Adolescents, Balt., 1976-77; supr.-counselor Multiple Offender Alcoholism Program, Balt., 1977-80; therapist-intern VA, Honolulu, 1983-84; clin. psychologist Kalihi-Palama Counseling Svcs., Honolulu, 1987-89; pvt. practice psychologist Honolulu, 1988—; presenter in field. Contbr. articles to profl. jours. Mem. Am. Psychol. Assn., Hawaii Psychol. Assn., Phi Kappa Phi. Home: 1812 Nahenahe Pl Wahiawa HI 96786 Office: Heritage Counseling Clinic 95-390 Kuahelani Ave Ste 2F Mililani HI 96789-1182

KIZER, KENNETH WAYNE, physician, educator; b. Decatur, Ind., May 28, 1951; s. Homer Martin Kizer and Ellen Hope Howland; m. Suzanne A. Stoddard, Aug. 26, 1972; children: Kelli Christina, Kimberly Casey. BS with honors, Stanford U., 1972; MD with honors, MPH in Epidemiology, UCLA, 1976. Rotating internship Naval Regional Med. Ctr., Portsmouth, Va., 1977; undersea medicine fellowship Naval Undersea Med. Inst., Groton, Conn., 1977; resident in diagnostic radiology U. Calif, San Francisco, 1980-81, resident in occupational medicine, 1982-83; firefighter, physician; dir. Emergency Med. Svcs. Authority State of Calif., 1983-84; chief dep. dir. and chief of pub. health Calif. Dept. Health Svcs., Sacramento, 1984-85, dir., 1985-91; prof., chmn. dept. community and internat. health U. Calif., Davis, 1991—; educator, researcher, consultant in field. Contbr. numerous articles to profl. jours., chpts. to books. Chair Black Infant Health Leadership Com., Calif., 1989-91, Lyme Disease Steering Group, AIDS Vaccine Rsch. and Devel. Adv. Com., 1986-91, Calif. Radiation Emergency Screening Team, 1988-91, Interagency Task Force for Oversight of Dept. of Energy Facilities in Calif., 1989-90, Hazardous Waste Appeal Bd., 1990; co-chair Calif. AIDS Leadership Com.; mem. Diving Control Bd. U. Calif., 1980-91, Gov.'s Emergency Ops. Exec. Coun., 1984-91, Governing Bd. Calif YMCA Model Legislature Program, 1986-90, Chem. Emergency Planning and Response Commn., 1989-90; chair S.W. Low Level Radioactive Waste Compact Commn., 1990-91, tobacco edn. oversight com. State Calif., 1990-91, exec. com. San Francisco Bay Area Youth Excellence Initiative, 1989-90, mgmt. com. Santa Monica Bay Restoration Project, 1987-91; former mem. Gov's Task Force on Toxics, Waste and Tech., 1985-86; former sec. commn. emergency med. svcs. State of Calif., 1984; bd. dirs. Calif. Wellness Found., 1992—, Matthews Found., 1991—, Ctr. for AIDS Rsch., Edn. and Svcs., 1992—, Infection Control Coun., 1991—; mem. adv. bd. Preventive Sports Medicine Inst., 1991—. Lt. USN, 1976-80. Recipient Humanitarian Svc. medal Dept. of Def., 1979, Spl. Recognition award No. Calif. Emergency Med. Care Coun., 1984, Golden State Med. Assn., 1986, Calif. Div. Am. Lung Assn.,1988, Calif. Health Fedn., 1988, cert. of Recognition Calif. Asian Pacific Health Coalition, 1989, Spl. Achievement award Calif. Emergency Physician Med. Group, 1989, Jean Spencer Felton award for Excellence in Scientific Writing, 1989, spl. awards from March of Dimes, Am. Cancer Soc., Calif. State Senate, Calif. Conf. Local Health Officers, others, 1991—; named Toll fellow Coun. State Govts., 1987. Fellow Am. Coll. Preventive Medicine, Am. Coll. Emergency Physicians, Am. Coll. Occupational Medicine, Am. Acad. Clin. Toxicology, Royal Soc. Health, Royal Soc. Medicine; mem. APHA, Internat. Soc. Toxinology, Am. Coll. Physician Execs., Am. Coll. Sports Medicine, South Pacific Underwater Med. Soc., Wilderness Med. Soc., Undersea and Hyperbaric Med. Soc., Nat. Soc. YMCA Youth Govs., Nat. Assn. Underwater Instrs. (Outstanding Contribution to Diving award 1984), Delta Tau Delta (Beta Rho chpt. Hall of Fame 1987), Alpha Omega Alpha, Delta Omega. Republican. Office: U Calif Sch Medicine TB-168 Dept Community And He Davis CA 95616

KLABUNDE, RICHARD EDWIN, physiologist; b. Pasadena, Calif., Oct. 7, 1948; s. Robert Frank and Sally Ann (Sprunk) K.; m. Karen Marie Hamm, Aug. 16, 1968; children: Ronald, Kenneth, Aaron, Timothy. BS, Pepperdine U., L.A., 1970; PhD, U. Ariz., 1975. Postdoctoral fellow U. Ariz., Tucson, 1975-76, U. Calif., San Diego, 1976-78; asst. to assoc. prof. W.Va. U., Morgantown, 1978-85; sr. pharmacologist Abbott Labs., Abbott Park, Ill., 1985-93; assoc. dir. to dir. Deborah Rsch. Inst., Browns Mills, N.J., 1993—; rsch. com. W.Va. Heart Assn., Ill., N.J., 1979-96. Contbr. articles to profl. jours. including Am. Jour. Physiology, European Jour. Pharmacology, others. Mem. Am. Physiol. Soc., Microcirculatory Soc. Office: Deborah Rsch Inst Dept Pharmacology D46R 20 Pine Mill Rd Browns Mills NJ 08015

KLAFTER, GEORGE, urologist; b. Malmo, Sweden, Apr. 7, 1948; came to U.S., 1954; s. Abraham and Rachel K.; m. Roberta Teller, Oct. 26, 1980; children Farrah Elyse, Carly Samantha. BA, Yeshiva U., 1970; MD, N.Y. Med. Coll., 1974. Diplomate Am. Bd. Urology. Resident in surgery

Montefiore Hosp. & Med. Ctr., Bronx, 1974-76; resident in urology N.Y. Med. Coll., N.Y.C., 1976-78, NYU Med. Ctr., N.Y.C., 1978-80; urologic oncology fellow Roswell Park Meml. Cancer Inst., Buffalo, 1977, Meml. Sloan Kettering Hosps., N.Y.C., 1979; urologic surgeon Ross Loos Med. Group, L.A., 1980-81, Health Ins. Plan of Greater N.Y., Bronx, 1981-83, George Klafter, M.D., P.C., Cliffside Park, N.J., 1981—; chief dept. urology St. Barnabas-Union Hosps., Bronx, 1987—. Exec. bd. Israel Bonds, 1993—. Recipient Leonard Wershub Meml. Prize in urology N.Y. Med. Coll., 1974; Mosby Books scholar, 1974. Office: 663 Palisade Ave Ste 301 Cliffside Park NJ 07010 also: 2371 Arthur Ave Bronx NY 10458

KLAGSBRUN, SAMUEL C., psychiatrist, medical director; b. Antwerp, Belgium, Sept. 23, 1932; came to U.S., 1941; s. Solomon and Rachel (Bodner) K.; m. Francine Lifton, Jan. 21, 1955; 1 child, Sarah Devora. BA, CCNY, 1955; BRE, Jewish Theol. Sem., 1954; MD, Chgo. Med. Sch., 1962. Resident in psychiatry Yale U. Sch. Medicine, 1963-66; chief of psychiatry New London (Conn.) Submarine Base, 1966-68; clin. instr. Yale U. Sch. of Medicine, New Haven, 1966-68; staff psychiatrist New London Child Guidance Clinic, 1966-68; psychiatrist pvt. practice, N.Y.C., 1968-80; assoc. dir. St. Lukes Hosp. Psychiatric Walk-in-Clinic, N.Y.C., 1968-69; dir. St. Lukes Psychiatric Day Hosp., N.Y.C., 1969-71, St. Lukes Psychiatric Consultation Svc., N.Y.C., 1971-74; assoc. clin. prof. Columbia U., N.Y.C., 1971-88; exec. med. dir. Four Winds Hosp., Katonah, N.Y., 1977—; mem. faculty Columbia U. Coll. Psychiatric Surgery, 1971-88; visitor St. Christopher's Hosp., London, Eng., 1975—; faculty mem. Mt. Sinai Hosp., Sch. of Medicine, N.Y.C., 1988-93; vis. prof., chmn. in pastoral psychiatry Jewish Theol. Sem., N.Y.C., 1973—; lectr. in field. Contbr. numerous articles to profl. jours. Recipient Gittleson Scholarship award Jewish Theol. Sem., 1954. Fellow Am. Psychiatric Assn.; mem. AMA, Westchester County Mental Health Assn. Jewish. Office: Four Winds Hosp 800 Cross River Rd Katonah NY 10536-9694

KLAHR, ARYEH LESLIE, psychiatrist; b. Bklyn., July 25, 1952; s. Robert and Eva (Richtman) K. BA, Yeshiva U., 1973; MD, U. Guadalajara, Mexico, 1977. Diplomate Am. Bd. Neurology and Psychiatry. Intern SUNY Sch. Medicine, Buffalo, N.Y., 1978; staff physician Bklyn., 1979-80; employee health physician Union Carbide Corp., N.Y.C., 1981; dir. employee health Gracie Sq. Hosp., N.Y.C., 1982-83; resident in psychiatry Hillside Hosp. Div. Jewish Med. Ctr., Glen Oaks, N.Y., 1984-87; fellow in Addictionology Fair Oaks Hosp., Summit, N.J., 1987-88; dir. alchoholism treatment svcs. Fair Oaks Hosp., Summit, 1988-90; med. dir. Indsl. Medicine Assocs., White Plains, N.Y., 1990—; clin. asst. prof. N.Y. Med. Coll. Dept. Psychiatry, 1991—. Contbr. articles to profl. jours. and chpts. to med. books. Recipient Regents scholarship State of N.Y. Bd. Regents, Albany, 1969-73. Fellow Am. Psychiat. Assn.; mem. AMA, Med. Soc. State of N.Y., Am. Soc. Addiction Medicine, Am. Acad. Clin. Psychiatrists. Jewish. Home: 50 W 75th St New York NY 10023-2024

KLAHR, SAULO, physician, educator; b. Santander, Colombia, June 8, 1935; came to U.S., 1961, naturalized, 1970; s. Herman and Raquel (Konigsberg) K.; m. Carol Declue, Dec. 29, 1965; children: James Herman, Robert David. B.A., Colegio Santa Librada, Cali, Colombia, 1954; M.D., U. Nat., Bogota, Colombia, 1959. Intern Hosp. San Juan de Dios, Bogota, 1958-59; resident U. Hosp., Cali, 1959-61; mem. faculty Washington U. Sch. Medicine, St. Louis, 1966—, prof. medicine, 1972-86, Joseph Friedman prof. renal disease, 1986-91, Simon prof. medicine, co-chmn. dept., 1991—, dir. renal div., 1972-91; physician in chief Jewish Hosp., St. Louis, 1991-96; assoc. physician Barnes Hosp., 1972-75, physician, 1975—; established investigator Am. Heart Assn., 1968-73; mem. adv. com. artificial kidney chronic uremia program USPHS, 1971—; bd. dirs. Eastern Mo. Kidney Found., 1973-75, chmn. med. adv. bd., 1973-74; rsch. com. Mo. Heart Assn., 1973-80, chmn., 1980-81; sci. adv. bd. Nat. Kidney Found., 1978, chmn., 1983-84, chmn. rsch. and fellowship com., 1979-81, v.p., 1986-88, pres., 1988-90; mem. gen. medicine B study sect. USPHS, 1979-83, chmn. gen. medicine B study sect., 1981-83; mem. cardiovascular and renal rev. group FDA, mem. VA Merit Rev. Bd. Nephrology, 1984-87, chmn., 1986-87; chmn. rsch. com. adv. bd. kidney, urology Nat. Inst. Diabetes and Digestive and Kidney Diseases, 1991-92, chmn. adv. bd., 1992-93; mem. adv. coun. Inst. Diabetes, Digestive Diseases and Kidney Diseases, 1995—. Editor: Contemporary Nephrology, Chronic Renal Disease, Nutrition and the Kidney; editor in chief Am. Jour. Kidney Diseases; mem. editorial bd. Am. Jour. Nephrology, Am. Jour. Physiology and Renal and Electrolyte, Kidney and Body Fluids in Health and Disease, Internat. Jour. Pediatric Nephrology; assoc. editor Jour. Clin. Investigation; contbr. articles to profl. jours., book chpts. USPHS postdoctoral fellow, 1961-63; recipient David M. Hume award Nat. Kidney Found., 1992, Thomas Addis medal Internat. Soc. Nutrition and Renal Metabolism, 1996. Fellow ACP, AAAS, Australian, Chilean, Colombian and Italian Socs. Nephrology (hon.); mem. Am. Soc. Nephrology (councillor 1980-81, sec.-treas. 1981-84, pres. 1985-86), Am. Soc. Clin. Investigation, Am. Physiol. Soc., Biophys. Soc., N.Y. Acad. Scis., Am. Soc. Renal Biochemistry and Metabolism (pres. 1982-84), Ctrl. Soc. Clin. Rsch., Soc. Exptl. Biology and Medicine, Assn. Am. Physicians, Soc. Gen. Physiologists, Internat. Soc. Nephrology (councillor 1987-95, mem. mgmt. com. 1987-95, chmn. program com. Sydney meeting 1997), Sigma Xi, Alpha Omega Alpha. Home: 11544 Ladue Rd Saint Louis MO 63141-8341

KLAICH, DOLORES, health educator; b. Cleve., Aug. 9, 1936; d. Jacob and Caroline (Stampar) K. BA, Case Western Res U., 1958; postgrad., SUNY Stony Brook, 1994—. Reporter Life mag., N.Y.C., 1962-67; freelance writer, editor, lectr., 1967—; edn. coord. L.I. Assn. for AIDS Care, Huntington, N.Y., 1987-89; lectr. SUNY Sch. Health, Tech. and Mgmt., 1989—; judge Ferro-Grumley Lit. Awards, N.Y.C., 1989, 90. Author: Woman Plus Woman: Attitudes toward Lesbianism, 1974, Heavy Gilt, 1988. Co-chmn. East End Lesbian and Gay Orgn., Southampton, N.Y., 1977-85; del. Nat. Women's Conf., Houston, 1977. Mem. Suffolk County Women and AIDS Coalition. Democrat. Home: 407 W Main St Huntington NY 11743 Office: SUNY R07551 L-2 075 AIDS Resource Ctr Stony Brook NY 11794

KLAINBERG, MARILYN BLAU, community health educator; b. N.Y.C., Jan. 6, 1942; d. George Blau and Etta (Nagel) Konrad; m. Bernard Klainberg, June 3, 1961; children: Dennis, Danielle, Gregory, Joshua. BS, Adelphi Coll., 1963; MS, Adelphi U., 1977; EdD, Columbia U., 1994. RN, N.Y. Mem. adj. faculty Adelphi U., Garden City, N.Y., 1977-86, mem. vis. faculty, 1986-87, mem. adj. faculty, 1987-89; asst. prof., dir. continuing edn. SUNY Health Sci. Ctr., Bklyn., 1989—, faculty officer, 1992-93, dir. continuing edn., asst. prof. Coll. Nursing, 1995—; summer program nurse, dir. Manhasset (N.Y.) Pub. Schs., 1974-88, cons. health promotion programs, 1991-92, chmn. substance abuse com., 1991; edn. dir. Friends of Hospice, Manhasset, 1990—, chmn. rsch. grant com.; cons. on drugs and alcohol Manhasset Youth Coun.; presenter in field. Newspaper columnist Manhasset Press, 1980-84; co-author: A Guidebook for the Prevention of Substance Abuse, 1990; mem. editl. bd. NACLI. Mem. Manhasset Student Com., 1989—; mem. exec. bd. Manhasset Student Aid Assn., 1990-95, Manhasset Schs. Parent Coun.; chmn. Safe Homes, 1988; edn. chair exec. bd. Friends of Hospice, 1993—, rsch. grant chairperson, 1994-95. Recipient Ruth W. Harper Disting. Svc. award Nurses Assn. of Counties of L.I., 1995; New Faculty rsch. grantee SUNY, 1991. Mem. ANA, Am. Assn. Higher Edn., Assn. Counties of L.I. (membership com., exec. bd. 1992-93), Kappa Delta Pi, Sigma Theta Tau (exec. bd. by-laws com. 1990-93, chmn. fundraising com. 1989, nominating com. 1994, dist 14 editl. bd. 1993-94, co-chmn. spring conf. and 1995 25th anniversary celebration, co-chmn. by-laws com., pres. Alpha Omega chpt. 1996—). Home: 14 Short Dr Manhasset NY 11030-3421 Office: SUNY Health Sci Ctr 450 Clarkson Ave Brooklyn NY 11203-2012

KLAKEG, CLAYTON HAROLD, cardiologist; b. Big Woods, Minn., Mar. 31, 1920; s. Knute O. and Agnes (Folvik) K.; student Concordia Coll., Moorhead, Minn., 1938-40; BS, N.D. State U., 1942; BS in Medicine, N.D. U., 1943; M.D., Temple U., 1945; MS in Medicine and Physiology, U. Minn.-Mayo Found., 1954; children: Julie Ann, Robert Clayton, Richard Scott. Intern, Med. Ctr., Jersey City, 1945-46; mem. staff VA Hosp., Fargo, N.D., 1948-51; fellow in medicine and cardiology Mayo Found., Rochester, Minn., 1951-55; internist, cardiologist Sansum Med. Clinic Inc., Santa Barbara, Calif., 1955—; mem. staff Cottage Hosp., St. Francis Hosp. Bd. dirs. Sansum Med. Rsch. Found., pres., 1990. Served to capt. M.C., USAF, 1946-48. Diplomate Am. Bd. Internal Medicine. Fellow ACP, Am. Coll. Cardiology, Am. Coll. Chest Physicians, Am. Heart Assn. (mem. council on clin. cardiology); mem. Calif. Heart Assn. (pres. 1971-72, Meritorious Service award 1968, Disting. Service award 1972, Disting. Achievement award 1975), Santa Barbara County Heart Assn. (pres. 1959-60, Disting. Service award 1958, Disting. Achievement award 1971), Calif. Med. Assn., Los Angeles Acad. Medicine, Santa Barbara County Med. Assn., Mayo Clinic Alumni Assn., Santa Barbara Soc. Internal Medicine (pres. 1963), Sigma Xi, Phi Beta Pi. Republican. Lutheran. Club: Channel City. Contbr. articles to profl. jours. Home: 5956 Trudi Dr Santa Barbara CA 93117-2175 Office: Sansum Med Clinic Inc PO Box 1239 Santa Barbara CA 93102-1239

KLAMERUS, KAREN JEAN, pharmacist, researcher; b. Chgo., Aug. 10, 1957; d. Robert Edward and Jane Mary (Nawoj) K.; m. Frederick P. Zeller. BS in Pharmacy, U. Ill., 1980; PharmD, U. Ky., 1981. Registered pharmacist Ky., Ill., Pa. Staff pharmacist Haggin Meml. Hosp., Harrodsburg, Ky., 1980-81, Regional Med. Ctr., Madisonville, Ky., 1982; critical care liasion Regional Med. Ctr., Madisonville, 1982; clin. pharmacist resident U. Nebr., Omaha, 1983; clin. pharmacist cardiothoracic surgery U. Ill., Chgo., 1983-88, clin asst. prof. dept. pharmacy practice, 1983-86, asst. prof., 1986-88, departmental affiliate dept. pharmaceutics, 1986-88; sr. pharmacokineticist Wyeth-Ayerst Rsch., Phila., 1988-91, asst. dir. clin. pharmacology, 1991-95, assoc. dir. clin. pharmacology, 1995—; cons. Dimensional Mktg. Inst., Chgo., 1983-88, Channing Weinbergs' Co., Inc., N.Y.C., 1983-88. Fellow Am. Coll. Clin. Pharmacy (mem. indsl. rels. com. 1995); mem. Am. Soc. Clin. Pharmacol. and Therapeutics, Mid-Atlantic Coll. Clin. Pharmacy (sec. 1991, pres. 1992-94). Office: Wyeth-Ayerst Rsch PO Box 8299 Philadelphia PA 19101-0082

KLARMAN, HERBERT ELIAS, economist, educator; b. Chmielnik, Poland, Dec. 21, 1916; came to U.S., 1929, naturalized, 1929; s. Joseph Louis and Helen (Klarman) K.; m. Mary A. Monk, 1967; children: Seth Andrew, Michael Joseph. A.B., Columbia U., 1939; M.A., U. Wis., 1941, Ph.D., 1946. Economist nat. income dept. Dept. Commerce, 1946-47; asst. prof. econs. Bklyn. Coll., 1948-49; Asst., then assoc. dir. Hosp. Council Greater N.Y., 1949-51, 52-62; asst. dir. N.Y. State Hosp. Study, Columbia U., 1948-49; med. economist Nat. Security Resources Bd., 1951-52; mem. faculty Johns Hopkins U., 1962-69, prof. public health adminstrn. and polit. economy, 1965-69; prof. environ. medicine and community health Downstate Med. Center, SUNY, 1969-70; prof. econs. NYU Grad. Sch. Public Adminstrn., N.Y.C., 1970-82; sr. assoc. Johns Hopkins U. Sch. Hygiene and Pub. Health, 1982—; mem. health services rsch. study sect. NIH, 1962-66; chmn. planning com. 2d Conf. on Econs. Health, 1967-69; mem. U.S. Nat. Com. on Vital and Health Stats., 1967-71, N.Y. State Health Adv. Council, 1976-83; mem. spl. med. adv. group VA, 1977-81; mem. Inst. Medicine, Nat. Acad. Scis., 1971. Author: Hospital Care in New York City, 1963, Economics of Health, 1965; also articles, chpts. in books.; editor: Empirical Studies in Health Economics, 1970. Served to capt. AUS, 1942-46. Recipient 1st Norman A. Welch Meml. award, 1965, Disting. Career award in health svcs. rsch. Assn. for Health Svcs. Rsch., 1989; Guggenheim fellow, 1976-77. Fellow AAAS, Am. Public Health Assn.; mem. Am. Econ. Assn., Am. Statis. Assn., Royal Econ. Soc., Phi Beta Kappa. Home: 1 E University Pky Baltimore MD 21218-2451

KLASSEK, CHRISTINE PAULETTE, behavioral scientist; b. Chgo., Dec. 28, 1947; d. Walter and Pauline (Bogolin) Strom; m. Alexander George Klassek, June 14, 1969; 1 child, Margaret Mary. BA in Applied Behavioral Sci., Nat. Louis U., 1989, cert. in leadership, 1993. Asst. juvenile libr. Bolingbrook (Ill.) Fountaindale Libr., 1974-79; behavior modification counselor J.P. Kennedy Sch. for Exceptional Children, Palos Park, Ill., 1982-86; tchr. spl. edn. Little Friends Orgn., Downers Grove, Ill., 1986-89; program dir. Carmelite Carefree Village, Darien, Ill., 1989—; bd. mem. Benedictine Univ. Adv. Bd. for Sr. Programs and Issues, 1996. Treas. Young Democrats Will County, 1972; chmn., pres. bd. dirs. Dem. Women's Com. DuPage Twp., Ill., 1973-76; leader Campfire Girls Assn.; mem. adv. coun. case mgmt. Little Friends Assn., 1988; cert. pastoral min. care St. Charles Borromeo Pastoral Ctr.; vol. Pub. Action to Deliver Svc., Helping Hands Rehab. Ctr., Ray Graham; active Cath. Coun. Women; bd. dirs., mem. human rels. com. J.P. Kennedy Sch. Exceptional Children, 1985-86. Recipient Cert. of Appreciation, Am. Cancer Soc., 1991, Achievement award Life Svcs. Network Ill., 1995, DuPage County Consortium Intergenerational Task Force, 1996. Mem. LWV, Assn. Sr. Svc. Providers, Ill. Activity Profl. Assn., Surburban Activity Therapists Assn., Jaycees. Roman Catholic. Home: 240 Davis Ln Bolingbrook IL 60440-2369 Office: Carmelite Carefree Village 8419 Bailey Rd Darien IL 60561-5361

KLASSEN, OTTO DYCK, psychiatrist; b. Bluffton, Ohio, May 10, 1927; s. John Peter and Anna (Dyck) K.; m. Helen Bohn, Dec. 18, 1948 (dec. Mar. 1969); children: Ruth Klassen Andrews, Frieda Klassen McCrae, Beth Klassen Landis, Olivia Klassen Elliott; m. Jerrie May, July 7, 1973; 1 child, Michelle Antioho. BS, Bluffton Coll., 1949; MD, U. Ill., Chgo., 1953. Rotating intern Wayne County Gen. Hosp., Plymouth, Mich., 1953-54; resident in psychiatry Karl Menninger Sch. Psychiatry, Topeka, 1954-57, resident in child psychiatry, 1957-59; pvt. practice child psychiatry Adams Newsom & Morrow, Wichita, Kans., 1959-62; founding med. dir. Oaklawn Psychiat. Ctr., Elkhart, Ind., 1962-87; sr. psychiatrist Oaklawn Psychiat. Ctr., Goshen, Ind., 1987-91; pvt. practice child psychiatry Goshen, 1991—. Bd. dirs. Elkhart County Bd. Health, Goshen, 1994—, Boys' and Girls' Clubs, Goshen, 1995—. Fellow Am. Orthopsychiat. Soc. (life), Am. Psychiat. Assn. (life, dist. br. pres.), Am. Acad. Child and Adolescent Psychiatry (life), Assn. of Social Psychiatry; mem. AMA, Rotary, Alpha Omega Alpha. Mennonite Ch. Home: 1405-1 Pembroke Cir Goshen IN 46526

KLAUBER, GEORGE THOMAS, pediatric urologist; came to U.S., 1971; s. Walter and Eva E. (Strass) K.; children: Adam, Benjamin, Blake, Rachel. MB, BS, U. London, 1964. Diplomate Am. Bd. Urology. Resident Hosp. for Sick Children, London, 1965-66; resident in surgery McGill U., Montreal, Can., 1967-68, resident in urology, 1967-71; fellow in pediatric urology Alderhey Hosp., Liverpool, U.K., 1971-72; assoc. prof., chief pediatric urology U. Conn., Farmington, 1972-79; dir. pediatric urology Newington Childrens Hosp., Conn., 1972-79; prof. urology and pediatrics, chief pediatric urology Tufts U., Boston, 1979—. Contbr. articles to profl. jours. Mem. adv. bd. R.I. Spina Bifida Assn., 1981—, Tuberous Sclerosis Assn. Am., 1984—, Nat. Kidney Found. Mass. Chpt. Fellow ACS, Am. Acad. Pediatrics, Royal Coll. Physicians and Surgeons Can.; mem. Am. Urologic Assn., Soc. Pediatric Urology, British Assn. Urologic Surgeons, Soc. Geritourinary Reconstructive Surgery, Mass. Soc. Practicing Urologists, (past pres.), Ea. Pediatric Urology Soc. (past pres.), Fetal Urology Urodynamic Soc. Office: New Eng Med Ctr 750 Washington St # 92 Boston MA 02111-1533

KLAUS, RICHARD MENDEL, orthopedist; b. Phila., June 26, 1938; s. Irving Goncer and Ruth Rosalia (Mendel) K.; m. Barbara Ann Tuckerman, Dec. 23, 1962; children: David Taylor-Klaus, Karen Jill. BA, Muhlenberg Coll., 1960; MD, U. Pa., 1964. Intern Albert Einstein Med. Ctr., Phila., 1965, resident in orthopedics, 1971; chief of orthopedics Cobb Hosp. and Med. Ctr., Ausbell, Ga.; chief of orthopedics Promina Hosp., Marietta, Ga., chief of staff, 1995-96; practice orthopaedic surgery, 1996—. Capt. U.S. Army, 1965-67, Vietnam. Fellow ACS, Am. Acad. Orthopaedic Surgeons; mem. Rotary (bd. dirs. 1992-96). Republican. Jewish. Office: Ga Orthopedics Sports Medi 1620 Mulkey Rd Metairie LA 30001

KLAVINS, JANIS VILIBERTS, oncologist, vocalist; b. Rugaji, Abrene, Latvia, May 6, 1921; came to U.S., 1951; s. Janis and Ida Aline K.; m. Ilga Minjona Krumins, July 4, 1950; children: Ilze Mara, Lize Kristine, Janis Peteris, Filips Klavs. MD, U. Kiel, Fed. Republic of Germany, 1948, PhD, 1959; D in Biology (hon.), U. Latvia, 1991. Prof. pathology Duke U., Durham, N.C., 1963-65, Columbia U. Coll. Physicians & Surgeons, N.Y.C., 1967-70, Downstate Med. Ctr., Bklyn., N.Y., 1965-85, SUNY, Stony Brook, 1970-85; dir. dept. labs. Queens Hosp. Ctr. Long Island Jewish Ctr. Affiliate, Queens, N.Y., 1970-77; prof. pathology Cornell U. Med. Coll., N.Y.C., 1985—; chmn. dept. pathology Cath. Med. Ctr. Bklyn & Queens, Jamaica, N.Y., 1977—. Author: (with others) Human Tumor Markers, Biological Basis and Nieburgs, 1983, Tumor Markers, Clinical and Laboratory Studies, 1985, Human Tumor Markers. Biology and Clinical Application, 1987; contbr. 160 articles to profl. jours.; editor-in-chief Jour. Tumor Marker Oncology, 1987—; singer Latvian songs in numerous recs., 1965—. V.p. Latvian Cultural Inst., N.Y.C., 1974-78; chmn. music sect. Latvian Cultural Found., Washington, 1988—; chmn., bd. dirs. Flushing Meadow Community Devel. Corp., Jamaica, N.Y., 1986-88; bd. dirs. N.C. State Ballet Co., 1963-65. Recipient Gt. Gold medal in music, Schubertbund, Vienna, Austria, 1984; named Laureate Musician Beaux Arts Internat., Inc., N.Y.C., 1980. Mem. Soc. Urban Physicians (sec.-treas. 1970-75), Assn. Clin. Scientists (pres. 1980-81, chmn. sci. sect. 1982-88, Scientist of Yr. award 1983), Egyptian Soc. Tumor Mark Oncologists (hon.), Latvian Acad. Sci. (fgn.), Internat. Acad. Tumor Mark Oncology (pres. 1984—), Latvian-Am. Assn. Univ. Profs. and Scientists (pres. 1985—), Nat. Acad. Medicine Venezuela (corr.). Home: 5 Broadmoor Rd Scarsdale NY 10583-7649

KLEBANOFF, SEYMOUR JOSEPH, medical educator; b. Toronto, Feb. 3, 1927; s. Eli Samuel and Ann Klebanoff; m. Evelyn Norma Silver, June 3, 1951; children: Carolyn, Mark. MD, U. Toronto, 1951; PhD in Biochemistry, U. London, 1954. Intern Toronto Gen. Hosp., 1951-52; postdoctoral fellow Dept. Path. Chemistry, U. Toronto, 1954-57, Rockefeller U., N.Y.C., 1957-62; assoc. prof. medicine U. Washington, Seattle, 1962-68, prof., 1968—; mem. adv. coun. Nat. Inst. Allergy and Infectious Diseases, NIH, 1987-90. Author: The Neutrophil, 1978; contbr. over 200 articles to profl. jours. Recipient Merit award NIH, 1988, Mayo Soley award Western Soc. for Clin. Investigation, 1991, Bristol-Myers Squibb award for Disting. Achievement in Infectious Disease Rsch., 1995. Fellow AAAS; mem. NAS, Am. Soc. Clin. Investigation, Am. Soc. Biol. Chemists, Assn. Am. Physicians, Infectious Diseases Soc. Am. (Bristol award 1993), Endocrine Soc., Reticuloendothelial Soc. (Marie T. Bonazinga rsch. award 1985), Inst. of Medicine. Home: 509 Mcgilvra Blvd E Seattle WA 98112-5047 Office: U Wash Dept Medicine Div Al & Infectious Disease Box 357185 Seattle WA 98195-7185

KLECK, ROBERT ELDON, psychology educator; b. Archbold, Ohio, Aug. 3, 1937. AB in Philosophy, Denison U., 1959; PhD in Social Psychology, Stanford (Calif.) U., 1963. Postdoctoral fellow Stanford U., 1963-64; asst. prof. Williams Coll., Williamstown, Mass., 1964-66; asst. to assoc. prof. Dartmouth Coll., Hanover, N.H., 1966-75, prof. psychology, 1975—, John Sloan Dickey Third Century Prof. of Social Scis., 1985-90, chmn. dept. psychology, 1993—; vis. rsch. prof. Boy's Town Ctr. Study of Youth Devel., Stanford U., 1974-75; cons. VA Stroke Project, 1983—, Disadvantaged Children in N.H., 1974, Bur. Devel. Disabilities, Concord, N.H., 1975-80, Crotchet Mountain Rehab. Ctr., 1973, Abilities, Inc., Albertson, N.Y., 1979-81, Can. Rsch. Coun., NSF, USPHS; faculty sponsore USPHS Post-doctoral fellowship, 1977-78. Cons. editor Jour. Personality and Social Psychology, 1974-78, assoc. editor 1971-72; mem. editorial bd. Jour. Nonverbal Behavior, 1990-93; mem. editorial adv. bd. Action for Children's TV, 1975-79; editorial cons.various jours.; contbr. articles to profl. jours. Danforth fellow, 1959-63; Gen. Motors scholar, 1955-59. Mem. Am. Psychol. Soc., Internat. Soc. Rsch. on Emotion, Soc. Experimental Social Psychology, New Eng. Psychol. Assn., New Eng. Soc. Psychol. Assn., Soc. Kent and Danfoth Fellows, Sigma Xi, Phi Beta kappa. Home: 28 Low Rd Hanover NH 03755-2207 Office: Dartmouth Coll Dept Of Psychology Hanover NH 03755

KLEE, GERALD D'ARCY, psychiatrist; b. N.Y.C., Jan. 29, 1927; s. Bertel Bernard and Eleanor (D'Arcy) K.; children: Brian, Kenneth, Sheila, Susan, Louise. MD, Harvard U., 1952. Intern USPHS Hosp., S.I., N.Y., 1952-53; surgeon USPHS Med. Ctr. Fed. Prisoners, 1953-54; resident in psychiatry VA Hosp. - Johns Hopkins U., Perry Point, Md., 1954-56; rsch. assoc. Psychiat. Inst. U. Md., 1956-58; assoc. prof. psychiatry Med. Sch. U. Md., Balt., 1960-67; prof. psychiatry Temple U., Phila., 1967-70; lectr. psychiatry Johns Hopkins U., Balt., 1976—; pvt. practice psychiatry Towson, Md., 1970—; cons. NIMH, 1959-68. Contbr. articles to profl. jours. With U.S. Army, 1945-46; med. dir. USPHS Res. Fellow Am. Psychiat. Assn. (life); mem. Md. Psychiat. Assn. (pres. 1962-63).

KLEEMAN, FRANCIS JULIAN, physician, urologist; b. N.Y.C., May 18, 1935; s. Francis Julian Kleeman and Dorothy Frances (Eising) Souza; m. Susan Emily Thurman Solomon, June 10, 1957 (div. June 1968); children: Jeffrey, Michael, Christopher, Julie; m. Alphine Louise Carnes, June 16, 1969. BA, Yale U., 1956, MD, 1960; DSc, U. New Eng., Biddeford, Maine, 1995. Diplomate Am. Bd. Urology. Intern, resident in surgery New Eng. Ctr. Hosp., Boston, 1960-63; resident in urology Boston VA Hosp., 1963-66; asst. chief urology U.S. Naval Hosp., Oakland, Calif., 1966-68; pvt. practice urology Newton-Wellesley Hosp., Newton Lower Falls, Mass., 1968-86, various other hosps., Boston area, 1968-86, So. Maine Med. Ctr., Biddeford, 1986—; founder, pres. Biddeford Free Clinic, 1993—. Various positions Med. Explorer program Boy Scouts Am., Newton Lower Falls, 1976-86. Lt. comdr. USN, 1966-68. Recipient Jefferson award Am. Inst. for Pub. Svc., 1994, Humanitarian award Biddeford-Saco Rotary, 1994, Vol. of Yr. award City of Biddeford, 1994. Fellow ACS; mem. Boston Surg. Soc., Maine Med. Assn., Mass. Med. Soc. Home: 222 Sea Rd Kennebunk ME 04043 Office: 24 W Cole Rd Ste 4 Biddeford ME 04005

KLEER, NORMA VESTA, critical care nurse; b. London, Apr. 23, 1933; d. Harold N. and Julia Bonanova (Ball-Dale) Wragg; divorced; children: Valerie Mainguy, David. Diploma, Torbay (South Devon, Eng.) Hosp., 1954, St. Francis Hosp., Trenton, N.J., 1964. Critical care nursing mgr. Bayfront Med. Ctr., St. Petersburg, Fla.; dir. nursing PRN Inc., St. Petersburg, Am. Healthcare Mgmt., St. Petersburg; nursing coord. Care Plus Inc. Hi-Tech. Home Infusion Co., Fla.; case mgr., DON Bayada Nurses Home Care Specialists, St. Petersburg, Fla.; dir. nurses PRN, Tampa Bay, Fla.; pioneer in devel. of EMS Sys., Pinellas Co. Mem. Fla. Emergency Nurses Assn. (founder, 1st pres.).

KLEES, DAVID ALAN, osteopathic general practitioner; b. Danville, Pa., Mar. 1, 1957; s. Jack D. and Mary E. (Stahl) Klees Albert; children: Ashley E., Kyleigh M. BS, Muhlenberg Coll., 1979; DO, Phila. Coll. Osteo. Medicine, 1985. Intern Metro Health Ctr., Erie, Pa., 1985-86; pvt. practice, Erie, 1986—. Mem. AMA, Am. Osteo. Assn., Pa. Med. Soc., Erie County Med. Soc., Christian Med. and Dental Soc., Am. Coll. Osteo. Family Practc. Republican. Pentecostal. Office: 217 W 11th St Erie PA 16501

KLEES, JULIA ELENA, physician; b. Phila., Jan. 7, 1961; d. Athanasius C. and Katherine E. (Kokines) K. BA, Lehigh U., Bethlehem, Pa., 1982; MD, Hahnemann U., Phila., 1984; MPH, U. Calif., Berkeley, 1989. Diplomate Am. Bd. Internal Medicine, Am. Bd. Occupl. Medicine. Resident Mayo Grad. Sch. Medicine, Rochester, Minn., 1984-87; fellow U. Calif., San Francisco, 1987-89; med. dir. occupl. health svc. Albert Einstein Med. Ctr., Phila., 1989-91; asst. prof. medicine Jefferson Med. Coll., Phila., 1991-95; asst. corp. med. dir. BASF Corp., Mount Olive, N.J., 1995—; adj. asst. prof. Jefferson Med. Coll., Phila., 1995—. Contbr. articles to profl. jours. Fellow Am. Coll. Occupl. and Environ. Medicine (del. 1993-95); mem. AMA, APHA, Am. Coll. Physicians, Am. Med. Women's Assn. Office: BASF Corp 3000 Continental Dr N Mount Olive NJ 07828

KLEGERMAN, MELVIN EARL, microbiologist, educator; b. Chgo., Aug. 30, 1945; s. Hyman Joseph and Esther Elizabeth (Tartas) K.; m. Marjorie Sherwood Amsbary, Dec. 19, 1968 (div. 1973); children: Robin Howard Allen, Joshua Sherwood Allen; m. Wanda Ann Budzynski, Sept. 13, 1973; children: Melanie Esther, Jessica Ann. BA, U. Ill., Chgo., 1967; PhD, Loyola U., Chgo., 1984. Asst. editor Ency. Britannica, Chgo., 1970-73; rsch. assoc. Loyola U. Med. Ctr., Maywood, 1973-78, Evanston (Ill.) Hosp., 1979; rsch. investigator Michael Reese Hosp. and Med. Ctr., Chgo., 1980-86; rsch. assoc. Rush-Presbyn. St. Luke's Med. Ctr., Chgo., 1986-87; assoc. dir. Inst. Tuberculosis Rsch. U. Ill., Chgo., 1987—, asst. prof. pharms., 1988-95, adj. asst. prof. pharms., 1995—. Editor: Pharmaceutical Biotechnology: Fundamentals and Essentials, 1992; contbr. articles to Jour. Lab. Clin. Medicine, Jour. Infectious Disease, Cancer Letters, others. Grantee Organon Teknika, 1988, 93, WHO, 1989. Mem. AAAS, Am. Soc. Microbiology, Am. Assn. Pharm. Scientists, N.Y. Acad. Scis. Home: 1211 W Elmdale Ave Chicago IL 60660-2525 Office: Inst for Tuberculosis Rsch M/C 964 950 S Halsted St Chicago IL 60607

KLEIN, ARNOLD WILLIAM, dermatologist; b. Mt. Clemens, Mich., Feb. 27, 1945; s. David Klein; m. Malvina Kraemer. BA, U. Pa., 1967, MD, 1971. Intern Cedars-Sinai Med. Ctr., Los Angeles, 1971-72; resident in dermatology Hosp. U. Pa., Phila., 1972-73, U. Calif., Los Angeles, 1973-75; pvt. practice dermatology Beverly Hills, Calif., 1975—; assoc. clin. prof.

dermatology/medicine U. Calif. Ctr. for Health Scis; mem. med. staff Cedars-Sinai Med. Ctr.; asst. clin. prof. dermatology Stanford U., 1982-89; asst. clin. prof. to assoc. clin. prof. dermatology/medicine, UCLA; Calif. state commr., 1983-89; med. adv. bd. Skin Cancer Found., Lupus Found. Am., Collagen Corp.; presenter seminars in field. Reviewer Jour. Dermatologic Surgery and Oncology, Jour. Sexually Transmitted Diseases, Jour. Am. Acad. Dermatology; mem. editorial bd. Men's Fitness mag., Shape mag., Jour. Dermatologic Surgery and Oncology; contbr. numerous articles to med. jours. Mem. AMA, Calif. Med. Assn., Am. Soc. Dermatologic Surgery, Internat. Soc. Dermatologic Surgery, Calif. Soc. Specialty Plastic Surgery, Am. Assn. Cosmetic Surgeons, Assn. Sci. Advosors, Los Angeles Med. Assn., Am. Coll. Chemosurgery, Met. Dermatology Soc., Am. Acad. Dermatology, Dermatology Found., Scleroderma Found., Internat. Psoriasis Found., Lupus Found., Am. Venereal Disease Assn., Soc. Cosmetic Chemists, AFTRA, Los Angeles Mus. Contemporary Art (founder), Dance Gallery Los Angeles (founder), Am. Found. AIDS Research (founder, dir.), Friars Club, Phi Beta Kappa, Sigma Tau Sigma, Delphos. Office: 435 N Roxbury Dr Ste 204 Beverly Hills CA 90210-5004

KLEIN, BERNARD ROBERT, ophthalmologist, surgeon; b. N.Y.C., Aug. 21, 1941; s. Leonard and Evelyn (Rotkowitz) K.; m. Jean Ann Hunt, Oct. 17, 1981; children: Ian David and Leah Renée (twins). BA, NYU, Bronx, 1962; MD, Dalhousie U., Halifax, N.S., Can., 1968. Diplomate Am. Bd. Ophthalmology, Am. Bd. Med. Examiners. Rotating intern Dalhousie U., 1967-68; resident in ophthalmology SUNY, Bklyn., 1968-71, chief resident in ophthalmology, 1971-72, clin. instr. in ophthalmology, 1972-73; clin. instr., ophthalmologist Albert Einstein Coll. Medicine, Bronx, 1972-85; chief of ophthalmology, dir. La Guardia Hosp., Forest Hills, N.Y., 1974—; assoc. ophthalmologist Beth-Israel Hosp., N.Y.C., 1986—. Lt. comdr. USNR, 1963-77. Fellow ACS, Am. Acad. Ophthalmology; mem. Am. Soc. Contemporary Ophthalmology (internat. glaucoma congress 1978—). Office: 66-07 102nd St Flushing NY 11374-4522

KLEIN, DONALD CHARLES, psychologist; b. Worcester, Mass., Aug. 10, 1923; s. Abraham Albert and Anne (Shapero) K.; m. Lola Perl, Mar. 31, 1946; children: Stefan, Jonathan, Alan, Jeremy. AB, Roosevelt U., Chgo., 1947; PhD, U. Calif., Berkeley, 1952. Cert. psychologist, Md. Sr. psychologist Berkeley (Calif.) State Mental Hygiene Clinic, 1950-53; exec. dir. Human Rels. Svc., Wellesley, Mass., 1953-63; dir. Human Rels. Ctr. Boston U., 1963-67, assoc. prof. dept. psychology, 1963-67; program dir. NTL Inst. for Applied Behavioral Sci., Washington, 1967-72; adj. prof. Johns Hopkins U. Evening Coll., Balt., 1972-81; core faculty mem. The Union Inst., Cin., 1981—; tng. cons. The Race Inst., Washington, 1970. Author: Community Dynamics and Mental Health, 1968, (with M. Broom) Power: The Infinite Game; editor: Psychology of the Planned Community, 1978, Community Research, 1985. Bd. mem. NTL Inst. Applied Behavioral Sci., Washington, 1960, Black Family Life Ctr., Columbia, Md., 1975. With U.S. Army, 1943-46. Fellow Am. Psychol. Assn. (disting. practice award div. community psychology 1987), Am. Pub. Health Assn., Am. Orthopsychiat. Assn., OD Network. Home: 4730 Sheppard Ln Ellicott City MD 21042-1441 Office: Union Inst 440 E Mcmillan St Cincinnati OH 45206-1925

KLEIN, DONALD FRANKLIN, psychiatrist, scientist, educator; b. N.Y.C., Sept. 4, 1928; s. Jesse and Rose K.; m. Rachel Gittelman, Dec. 29, 1968; children: Beth, Geri, Hilary, Michelle, Erika. B.A. magna cum laude, Colby Coll., Waterville, Maine, 1947; M.D., SUNY-Bklyn., 1952. Rotating intern USPHS Hosp., S.I., N.Y., 1952-53; resident in psychiatry Creedmoor State Hosp., 1953-54, 56-58; dir. research and evaluation, dept. psychiatry L.I. Jewish-Hillside Med. Center, 1972-76; prof. psychiatry SUNY Med. Sch., Stony Brook, 1972-76; dir. research and therapeutics N.Y. State Psychiat. Inst., N.Y.C., 1976—; attending psychiatrist Presbyn. Hosp., N.Y.C., 1977—; prof. psychiatry Columbia U. Coll. Physicians and Surgeons, N.Y.C., 1978—; chmn. clin. psychopharmacology study sect. NIMH, 1973-75; sr. sci. advisor Alcohol Drug Abuse Mental Health Adminstrn., 1989-91; cons. Nat. Inst. Drug Abuse, 1991—. Co-author: Diagnosis and Drug Treatment of Psychiatric Disorders: Adults and Children, 2d edit., 1980, Mind, Mood and Medicine, 1981, Understanding Depression, 1993; co-editor: Critical Issues in Psychiatric Diagnosis, 1978, Anxiety: New Research and Changing Concepts, 1980; contbr. articles to med. jours. Sr. asst. surgeon USPHS, 1954-56. Recipient A.E. Bennett Neuropsychiat. Rsch. award, 1964, Found.'s Fund prize for rsch. in psychiatry Am. Psychiat. Assn., 1988, Gold medal Soc. Biol. Psychiatry, 1990, Heinz Lehmann award N.Y. State Office of Mental Health, 1991, Thomas W. Salmon award, 1993. Fellow Psychiat. Rsch. Soc., Am. Psychopathol. Assn. (past pres., Hamilton award 1980), Am. Coll. Neuropsychopharmacology (life, past pres., Paul Hoch award 1991), Royal Coll. Psychiatry (founding); mem. Am. Soc. Clin. Psychopharmacology (pres. 1993—). Home: 1016 Fifth Ave # 14D New York NY 10028-0132 Office: NY State Psychiat Inst 722 W 168th St New York NY 10032-2603 also: 182 E 79th St Ste E New York NY 10021-0422

KLEIN, (MARY) ELEANOR, retired clinical social worker; b. Luzon, Philippines, Dec. 13, 1919; came to U.S., 1921; (parents Am. citizens); d. Roy Edgar and Edith Lillian Hay; m. Edward George Klein, June 24, 1955. BA, Pacific Union Coll., 1946; MSW, U. So. Calif., 1953. Lic. clin. social worker. Social worker White Meml. Hosp., Los Angeles, 1948-56; clin. social worker UCLA Hosp. Clinics, 1956-65, supr. social worker, 1965-67, assoc. dir., 1967-73, dir., 1973-82. Bd. dirs., treas. Los Amigos de la Humanidad, U. So. Calif. Sch. Social Work; hon. life mem. bd. dirs. Calif. div. Am. Cancer Soc., mem. vol. bd. Calif. div., 1964—, del. nat. dir., 1980-84, chmn. residential crusade for Orange County (Calif.) unit, 1985-86; bd. dirs. Vol. Exchange, 1988—, sec., 1991—. Recipient Disting. Alumni award Los Amigos de la Humanidad, 1984, Outstanding Performance award UCLA Hosp., 1968, various service awards Am. Cancer Soc., 1972-88. Fellow Soc. Clin. Social Work; mem. Nat. Assn. Social Workers (charter), Am. Hosp. Assn., Soc. Social Work Administrs. in Health Care (formerly Soc. Hosp. Social Work Dirs.) (nat. pres. 1981, bd. dirs. 1978-82, life mem. local chpt.), Am. Pub. Health Assn. Democrat. Adventist. Home: 1661 Texas Cir Costa Mesa CA 92626-2238

KLEIN, FAY MAGID, health administrator; b. Chgo., Jan. 12, 1929; d. Victor and Rose (Begun) Magid; m. Jerome G. Klein, June 27, 1948 (div. 1970); children: Leslie Susan Janik, Debra Lynne Maslov; m. Manuel Chait, Aug. 28, 1994. BA in English, UCLA, 1961; MA in Pub. Adminstrn., U. So. Calif., 1971. Cert. health adminstrn. Supr. social workers L.A. County, 1961-65; program specialist Econ. and Youth Opportunity Agy., L.A., 1965-69; sr. health planner Model Cities, L.A., 1971-72; dir. prepaid health plan Westland Health Svcs., L.A., 1972-74; exec. dir. Coastal Region Health Consortium, L.A., 1974-76; grants and legis. cons. Jewish Fed. Council of L.A., 1976-79; planning council Jewish Fed. Councils of So. Fla., Palm Beach to Miami, 1979-82; adminstrv. dir. program in kidney diseases Dept. Medicine UCLA, 1982-84; exec. dir. west coast Israel Cancer Rsch. Fund, L.A., 1984-94; cons. to non-profit orgns. Santa Monica, 1994—; cons. Arthritis Found., Los Angeles, 1984, Bus. Action Ctr., Los Angeles, 1982, Vis. Nurses Assn., Los Angeles, 1982. Charter mem. Los Angeles County Mus. of Art, Mus. of Contemporary Art, Los Angeles; cons. Los Angeles Mcpl. Art Gallery, 1979; mem. Art Council Wight Gallery, UCLA. Fellow U.S. Pub. Health, U. So. Calif., 1970-71. Mem. Am. Pub. Health, UCLA Alumni Assn. (life), U. So. Calif. Alumni Assn. (life).

KLEIN, GLORIA RITTERBAND, social worker; b. N.Y.C., Sept. 26, 1928; d. Max and Sara (Abelson) Ritterband; m. Morton Klein, July 31, 1949; children: Lisa, Melanie. MSW, Adelphi U., 1976. Lic. clin. social worker, sch. social worker; cert. social worker Acad. Cert. Social Workers. Social worker St. Mary's Hosp., Hoboken, N.J., 1976-85; supr. family therapy, psychiat. social worker St. Joseph's Hosp., Paterson, N.J., 1985—; clin. project assoc. Ackerman Inst. for Family Therapy, N.Y.C., 1993—. Mem. Nat. Assn. Social Workers. Office: St Joseph's Hosp 703 Main St Paterson NJ 07503-2621

KLEIN, GORDON LESLIE, pediatrician, educator; b. N.Y.C., Aug. 26, 1946; s. Hyman David and Ruth Harriet (Katz) K.; m. Joann Pamela Schulz, July 1, 1973; 1 child, Adrienne Lindsay. BA, Columbia U., 1967; postgrad., Cambridge U., 1970-71; MD, Albert Einstein Coll. Medicine, 1971; MPH, UCLA, 1980. Intern, resident in pediatrics Stanford (Calif.) U. Med. Ctr., 1971-74; postdoctoral fellow Johns Hopkins U. Med. Sch., Balt., 1976-78; postdoctoral fellow in pediatric gastroenterology UCLA, 1978-80, adj. asst. prof. pediatrics, 1980-82; asst. prof. pediatrics Tulane U. Med. Sch., New Orleans, 1982-84; pediatric gastroenterologist City of Hope Med. Ctr., Duarte, Calif., 1984-86; assoc. prof. pediatrics U. Tex. Med. Br., Galveston, 1986-95, prof. pediatrics, 1995—; mem. com. revision U.S. Pharmacopeia, Rockville, Md., 1990—, chmn. gastroenterology adv. panel, 1990—; cons. to Nicaraguan Ministry of Health, 1992. Editor: Metabolic Bone Disease in Total Parenteral Nutrition, 1985; contbr. articles to profl. jours. Lt. comdr. USN, 1974-76. Named Clin. Assoc. Physician NIH, 1980-82; recipient Nat. Rsch. Svc. award, 1979-80, Nutrition Program fellow Project HOPE Nicaragua, 1992. Fellow Am. Acad. Pediatrics; mem. North Am. Pediatric Bone and Mineral Working Group (founder, sec.-treas. 1984-85), Soc. for Pediatric Rsch., Am. Soc. for Bone and Mineral Rsch., Am. Soc. for Clin. Nutrition, Am. Gastroent. Assn., Am. Soc. for Parenteral and Enteral Nutrition (tech. adv. group 1990—), Princeton Club N.Y. Office: U Tex Med Br Dept Pediatric 301 University Blvd Galveston TX 77555-0352

KLEIN, HERBERT ALAN, nuclear physician; b. Milw., Mar. 28, 1936; s. David Xavier and Sophie (Posner) K.; m. Inara Berzins, Jan. 5, 1973; children: Benjamin C., Alexandra E. AB, Columbia U., 1956, MD, 1960; MA in Biochemistry, Harvard U., 1968, PhD in Biochemistry, 1975. Diplomate Am. Bd. Nuclear Medicine; lic. physician. Staff physician Wilford Hall USAF Hosp., Lackland AFB, Tex., 1962-64; teaching fellow Harvard Med. Sch., Boston, 1966-67; instr. NYU, 1970-72; summer faculty Manhattanville Coll., Purchase, N.Y., 1973; faculty SUNY Coll. Medicine, Bklyn., 1975-80; co-dir. nuclear medicine L.I. Coll. Hosp., Bklyn., 1975-76, dir. nuclear medicine, 1976-80; faculty U. Pitts. Sch. Medicine, 1980—; chief nuclear medicine VA Med. Ctr., Pitts., 1991—; med. staff Presbyn.-Univ. Hosp., Pitts., 1980—, Montefiore U. Hosp., Pitts., 1990—; assoc. dir. nuclear medicine dept. radiology U. Pitts., 1980-96. Contbr. articles to profl. jours. Capt. USAF, 1960-62. Am. Cancer Soc. postdoctoral scholar, 1964; NIH spl. rsch. fellow, 1968; Wechsler Rsch. Found. grantee, 1984, Health Rsch. and Svc. Found. grantee, 1986. Mem. Soc. Nuclear Medicine (mem. brain imaging coun., computer coun., acad. coun.), Harvey Soc., Assn. Univ. Radiologists, Phi Beta Kappa. Home: 102 Pheasant Dr Pittsburgh PA 15238-2208 Office: VA Med Ctr University Dr # C Pittsburgh PA 15240

KLEIN, JEAN-MARC YVES, dermatologist; b. Paris, Mar. 17, 1941; s. Bernard Paul Klein and Suzanne Sarazin; children: Marc, Karina. DMS, Paris U., 1967; laureate faculty medicine (hon.). Diplomate Am. Bd. Dermatology; lic. by Med. Coun. Can. Monitor asst. faculty Faculty Medicine, Paris, 1965; physician Ctr. Rsch. on Leprosy, Bamako, Mali, 1965-67; expert leprologist KHMER Govt., Cambodia, 1968; chief cons. dermatology Queen Elizabeth Hosp., Charlottetown, Can., 1986-89; cons. St. Joseph Hosp., Ontario, Can., 1973-85. Author: (textbook) Theory of Missing Link, 1978, Neurotransference Theory, 1979, What you should know About Skin Infections, 1981; contbr. articles to profl. jours. Capt. Can. Army. Fellow Am. Acad. Dermatology, Royal Coll. Physicians and Surgeons of Can., Atlantic Province Dermatology Assn. Office: 182 Belvedere Ave, Charlottetown, PE Canada CA1 2Z1

KLEIN, JEFFREY B., orthopedic surgeon; b. Passaic, N.J., Nov. 5, 1950; s. Arnold R. and Lorraine (Hertz) K.; m. Sherrie M. Bubis, May 30, 1976; children: Heather Alyse, Jason Scott. BS, Hobart Coll., 1972; MD, Chgo. Med. Sch., 1976. Diplomate Am. Bd. Orthopedic Surgeon. Pvt. practice Garland, Tex., 1981—; chief surgeon Baylor Med. Ctr. of Garland, 1989-93. Team physician Garland Ind. Sch. Dist., 1981—. Fellow Am Acad. of Orthopedic Surgery. Office: Orthopedic and Sports Medicine of Garland 2241 Pressy Lane A Garland TX 75042

KLEIN, JEFFREY HOWARD, oncologist, internist; b. Cleve., Jan. 24, 1943; s. Joseph Bart and Tillie Alice Klein; m. Nancy Klein, June 5, 1971; 1 child, Bart Edward. BS in Medicine, Northwestern U., 1966, MD, 1968. Diplomate Am. Bd. Internal Medicine, Am. Bd. Med. Oncology. Intern Cleve. Met. Gen. Hosp., 1968-69, resident, 1969-70; resident Rush-Presbyn. St. Luke's Med. Ctr., Chgo., 1970-71, Am. Cancer Soc. clin. fellow, 1971-72; pvt. practice internist, oncologist Lombard Med. Group, Thousand Oaks, Calif., 1974—; also bd. dirs. Lombard Med. Group, Thousand Oaks; chief of medicine Los Robles Regional Med. Ctr., Thousand Oaks, 1976-77, chief of staff, 1979-81; trustee Columbia/Los Robles Med. Ctr., Thousand Oaks, 1995—. Maj. USAF, 1972-74. Mem. Am. Soc. Clin. Oncology, So. Calif. Acad. Clin. Oncology (charter), Phi Beta Kappa, Pi Kappa Epsilon, Alpha Omega Alpha. Office: Lombard Med Group Inc 2230 Lynn Rd Thousand Oaks CA 91360

KLEIN, JEROME OSIAS, pediatrician, educator; b. N.Y.C., Feb. 10, 1931; s. Max N. and Elizabeth (Schlanger) K.; m. Linda Sue Breskin, June 19, 1955; children—Andrea, Bennett, Adam. A.B., Union Coll., 1952; M.D., Yale U., 1956. Diplomate Am. Bd. Pediatrics. Intern, U. Minn. Hosps., Mpls., 1956-57; resident in pediatrics Boston City Hosp., 1959-61; assoc. dir. pediatrics 1967-72; dir. pediatric infectious diseases, 1973—; assoc. prof. pediatrics Harvard Med. Sch., Boston, 1967-74; prof. Boston U. Sch. Medicine, 1974; lectr. Harvard U. Med. Sch., 1974—; cons. dept. pediatrics Mass. Gen. Hosp., 1970-74; cons. adv. com. on vaccines and biologics FDA, 1983-85. Author/editor: (with J. S. Remington) Infectious Diseases of the Fetus and Newborn Infant, 1976, 2d edit., 1983, 3d edit., 1990, 4th edit., 1995; author: (with C.D. Bluestone) Otitis Media in Infants and Children, 1987, 2d edit. 1995. Editor: (text) Report of the Committee on Infectious Diseases, Am. Acad. Pediatrics, 19th edit.; assoc. editor Reviews of Infectious Diseases, 1978-89; Pediatric Infectious Diseases Jour., 1982-92. Contbr. numerous articles on rsch. in infectious diseases of children to profl. jours. Asst. surgon USPHS, 1957-79. Peabody fellow Harvard U., 1963-64; grantee Nat. Inst. Allergy and Infectious Diseases. Mem. Am. Acad. Pediatrics (com. on infectious diseases 1974-82), Infectious Diseases Soc. Am. (councellor 1980-83, treas. 1987-92, disting. physician award, 1995, Bristol award, 1995), Phi Beta Kappa, Alpha Omega Alpha. Office: Boston City Hosp Maxwell Finland Lab Infect Dis Boston MA 02118

KLEIN, JEROME ROBERT, plastic surgeon; b. N.Y.C., Feb. 27, 1954; s. Jerome Comet and Elaine Joy (Levy) K. BA cum laude, U. Pa., 1975; MD, NYU, 1979. Diplomate Am. Bd. Ophthalmology. Resident, vis. clin. instr. Columbia Presbyn. Med. Ctr., N.Y.C., 1979-80; resident, chief resident NYU Med. Ctr., 1981-84; clin. instr. NYU Bellevue Med. Ctr., 1984-87; pvt. practice Beverly Hills, Calif., 1984—; asst. clin. prof. Jules Stein Eye Inst., UCLA Med. Ctr., 1984—, UCLA Med. Ctr., 1984—. Contbr. articles to profl. jours.; skpr., lectr. in field. Fellow ACS, Am. Acad. Ophthalmology, Am. Acad. Cosmetic Surgery, Am. Acad. Facial Plastic & Reconstructive Surgery; mem. AMA, NYU Sch. Medicine Alumni Assn. (bd. govs.), Kerato-Refractive Surgery Soc., Harmonie Club (N.Y.C.). Office: 9454 Wilshire Blvd Ste M1 Beverly Hills CA 90212-2925 also: 465 Park Ave New York NY 10022

KLEIN, JOEL TIBOR, psychotherapist; b. Megyaszo, Hungary, Jan. 1, 1923; came to U.S., 1957; s. Jeno and Serena (Reich) K.; m. Anna Berkovits, June 28, 1949; children: Leslie M., Judy K. PhD, U. Sci., Budapest, Hungary, 1947. Cert. pastoral counselor, N.H.; cert. marriage and family therapist; cert. sex counselor. Psychiatric chaplain VA, Downey, Ill., 1962-64, White River, Vt., 1964-77; assoc. Silverman and Assocs., Haverhill, Mass., 1973-77; pvt. practice Manchester and Bedford, N.H., 1977—; bd. examiners N.H., 1979-83; mem. Interdisciplinary Team on Child Abuse and Neglect Divsn. Children and Youth, Manchester, 1983; adj. prof. psychology Notre Dame Coll., Manchester, N.H. Fellow APA, Am. Assn. Pastoral Counselors (regional membership com., legis. com.), Am. Assn. Marriage and Family Therapy (approved supr., pres. N.H. unit 1984-86), Am. Assn. Sex Educators, Counselors, and Therapists; mem. N.H. Psychol. Assn. (exec. bd., treas. 1993-96). Home: 562 Fairfield St Manchester NH 03104-2857 Office: 700 Lala Ave Manchester NH 03103-2734

KLEIN, KIMBERLY ANN, family nurse practitioner; b. Sharon, Pa., Feb. 27, 1959; d. Charles Andrew and Veronica Dorothy (Thomas) Kohut; m. Michael John Klein, Sept. 20, 1991. BS, Duquesne U., Pitts., 1981; MS, Tex. Woman's U., Denton, 1991; cert. family nurse practitioner, U. Tex., Arlington, 1995. RN, Tex; cert. family nurse practitioner, Tex. Critical care nurse St. Luke's Episcopal Hosp., Houston, 1981-82; office staff nurse Houston Cardiovascular Assocs., 1982-83; critical care nurse Med. City Dallas Hosp., 1983—; family nurse practitioner David A. Haymes, M.D., 1996—; instr. ACLS Am. Heart Assn.,Dallas, 1993—. Supporter Tex. Citizen's Action, Austin, Tex., 1995—. Recipient Cert. of Honor and Dedication, Denton Cooley, MD and St. Luke's Episcopal Hosp., Houston, 1981. Mem. AACCN, Am. Acad. Nurse Practitioners, Am. Heart Assn., Tex. Nurse Practitioners, North Tex. Nurse Practitioners, Dallas County Assn. Critical Care Nurses. Office: 7777 Forest Ln Ste B-412 Dallas TX 75230

KLEIN, MICHAEL ELIHU, physician; b. N.Y.C., Apr. 6, 1946; s. Leo and Edith (Rigrod) K.; m. Elizabeth Angela McGehee, Oct. 8, 1988; children: Michael, Debra, Daniel. BA, Wesleyan U., Middletown, Conn., 1967; MD, Yale U., 1972, MPH, 1972. Diplomate Am. Bd. Internal Medicine. Asst. dir. hematology U. Md., Balt., 1979-83; sr. investigator U. Md. Cancer Ctr., Balt., 1979-83; pvt. practice specializing in hematology/oncology Cowley Assocs., Camp Hill, Pa., 1983—; cons. in hematology and oncology Polyclinic Hosp., Harrisburg, Pa., 1983—, Holy Spirit Hosp., Camp Hill, 1983—. Author: Political Dynamics National Health Insurance in New York, 1972; contbr. articles to profl. jours., chpts. to books. Founder, bd. dirs. Number Nine, New Haven, 1971. Comdr. lt. USPHS, 1974-77. Mem. AMA, Am. Soc. Clin. Research, Am. Soc. Clin. Oncology, Am. Soc. Hematology, Am. Legion, Masons, Balt. Blood Club (pres. 1979-83). Office: Cowley Associates 425 N 21st St Camp Hill PA 17011-2223

KLEIN, MURRAY, physician; b. Phila., Feb. 10, 1950; s. Louis and Eva (Nowak) K.; m. Claudia Marie Petruncio, Nov. 27, 1983; Louis, Daniel, Eric. BS, Del. Valley Coll., 1976; DO, Phila. Coll. Osteo. Medicine, 1977. Diplomate Am. Bd. Phys. Medicine and Rehab., Am. Osteo. Bd. Rehab. Medicine. Resident in physical medicine and rehab. Jefferson U. Hosp., Phila., 1978-81; chmn. dept. phys. medicine and rehab. Brandywine Hosp., Caln, Pa., 1981-82; asst. prof. Phila. Coll. of Osteo. Medicine, 1982-84; prof. rehab. medicine Phila. Coll., 1995—; chmn. dept. phys. medicine and rehab. Met. Hosp., Phila., 1984-92; pvt. practice JFK Monoria Hosp., Cherry Hill, N.J., 1989—, chmn. phys. medicine and rehab., 1994—. Fellow Am. Acad. Phys. Med. and Rehab., Am. Osteo. Coll. Rehab. Medicine. Home: 125 East Beechwood Ave Oaklyn NJ 08107 Office: 2201 Chapel Ave West Cherry Hill NJ 08002

KLEIN, NEIL CHARLES, physician; b. N.Y.C., Jan. 6, 1935; s. Martin and Jeannette F. (Pazow) K.; divorced; children: Lisa, Susie, David; m. Phyllis Klein, Nov. 26, 1989. AB, Columbia U., 1956; MD, Cornell U., 1960. Diplomate Am. Bd. Internal Medicine, Am. Bd. Gastroenterology, Nat. Bd. Med. Examiners. Intern N.Y. Hosp., 1960-61, resident, 1964-67; fellow in medicine Cornell Med. Coll., 1965-67, clin. instr. in medicine, 1967-70, asst. clin. prof. medicine, 1970-77; assoc. clin. prof. medicine N.Y. Med. Coll., 1977-84; clin. prof. medicine N.Y. Med. Coll., 1984—; asst. clin. attending physician N.Y. Hosp., 1970-77, St. Joseph's Hosp., Stamford, Conn., 1967-72; from asst. to assoc. attending physician Stamford (Conn.) Hosp., 1967—, assoc. chief medicine, 1972-75, chief divsn. gastroenterology, 1978-84. Bd. dirs. Conn. Med. Ins. Co., 1988—, fin. com., 1988—, sec., 1990—; bd. dirs. Stamford Health Network, 1987-93, chmn. fin. com., 1994—; mem. sci. adv. coun. Fairfield-Westchester Ileitis-Colitis Found., 1982—; mem. Commn. of Aging, Stamford, 1971-82. Fellow ACP, Am. Coll. Gastroenterology, Royal Soc. Tropical Medicine and Hygiene; mem. Fairfield County Med. Assn. (trustee 1980-87, chmn. bd. trustees 1984-85, pres. 1985-86), Conn. State Med. Assn., Am. Soc. Gastrointestinal Endoscopy, Am. Fedn. Clin. Rsch., Am. Gastrointestinal Assn., Cornell Med. Coll. Alumni Assn. (pres. 1976-78, sr. advisor 1978—), Stamford Med. Soc. (pres. 1990-91). Office: Stamford Med Group 1450 Washington Blvd Stamford CT 06902-2451

KLEIN, PAUL, optometrist, managed vision care consultant; b. Buenos Aires, Aug. 12, 1948; came to U.S., 1957; s. Earl and Sara (Mendelsohn) K.; m. Regina Gurfinkiel, Nov. 6, 1971; children: Monica, Karen. BA, Bklyn. Coll., 1971; OD, New Eng. Coll. Optometry, 1979. CEO Broward Eyecare Assocs., Ft. Lauderdale, Fla., 1979—; mem. adj. faculty Pa. Coll. Optometry, Phila., 1979—; mem. adv. bd. Better Vision Inst., Roslyn, Va., 1991-94; nat. optometric cons. Block Vision Care, Boca Raton, Fla., 1994—. Founding editor Optometry Today, 1992—; professional columnist Vision Monday, 1994—; contbr. articles to Rev. Optometry, Jour. Am. Optometry Assn., Contact Lens Forum, Optometry & Vision Sci. Mem. fundraising com. Broward Performing Arts Ctr., Ft. Lauderdale, 1995. Fellow Am. Acad. Optometry; mem. Nat. Eye Rsch. Found. (cert. contact lenses). Office: Broward Eyecare Assocs 2502 E Oakland Pk Blvd Fort Lauderdale FL 33306

KLEIN, RAYMOND SIMON, psychologist; b. L.A., Jan. 24, 1934; s. Samuel J. and Cornelia (Korbel) K.; m. Linda M. Sepkowitz, Jan. 22, 1957 (div. 1990); children: Steven M., Susan T. BS, CCNY, 1957, MS, 1959; EdD, SUNY, Buffalo, 1964. Lic. psychologist, Pa. With Children's Ctr., N.Y.C., 1954-57; tchr. N.Y.C. pub. schs., 1957-59; asst. prof. SUNY, Buffalo, 159-63; prof. tng. N.Y.State Health Dept., Albany, 1963-64; manpower researcher N.Y. State Dept. Labor, Albany, 1964-66; research dir. Master Plan/Voc. Rehab., State N.Y., Albany, 1966-69; assoc. prof. Pa. State U., Middleton, 1970-74; psychol. cons. Albany, 1974-86; owner Psychol. Testing Svcs., Mechanicsburg, Pa., 1986—; pres. Geriatric Psychol. Svcs. Pa., Lemoyne, Pa., 1994, Behavioral Health P.C., Camp Hill, Pa., 1995; cons. in field. Chmn. Mayors campaign, Lemoyne, Pa., 1989. With USN, 1952-54. Mem. Am. Psychol. Assn., Am. Bd. Adminstrv. Psychology, Pa. Psychol. Assn., Rotary (pres. 1991-92). Office: Psychol Testing Svcs 1229 Scenery Dr Mechanicsburg PA 17055-1942

KLEIN, RICHARD MAXWELL, ophthalmologist; b. Waltham, Mass., Dec. 1, 1944; s. Arthur and Beatrice Dean (Temko) K.; B.A., Amherst Coll., 1966; M.D., Johns Hopkins U., 1970; m. Ronnie Reece Boriskin, Feb. 21, 1970; children—Michael Andrew, Kathryn Suzanne, Douglas Joseph. Intern, N.Y. Hosp./Cornell U., N.Y.C., 1970-71; resident in ophthalmology, fellow in retinal disease Manhattan Eye, Ear and Throat Hosp., N.Y.C., 1971-75, asst., then asso. attending surgeon, 1975—, coordinator resident tng. ophthalmology dept., 1978-80; practice medicine specializing in vitreous and retina surgery, N.Y.C. and Teaneck, N.J., 1975—; attending surgeon Hackensack (N.J.) Hosp., Englewood (N.J.) Hosp., Holy Name Hosp., Teaneck; asst. clin. prof. dept. ophthalmology Mt. Sinai Med. Sch., 1979—, N.J. Coll. Medicine, 1981—. Served with USNR, 1970-74. Diplomate Am. Bd. Ophthalmology. Fellow ACS; mem. Am. Acad. Ophthalmology, AMA, Am. Assn. Ophthalmology. Author: Microsurgery of the Vitreous, 1978; also articles. Office: 628 Cedar Ln Teaneck NJ 07666-1704

KLEIN, RICHARD STEPHEN, internist; b. N.Y.C., Nov. 20, 1938; s. Sydney G. and Rosalind (Paul) K.; B.S., Queens Coll., 1962; M.D., N.Y. Med. Coll., 1967; m. Susan Lois Teller, Dec. 29, 1963 (dec. June 11, 1978); children—Brian Seth, Elyse Lynn; m. 2d, Barbara Greenebaum, June 22, 1980; 1 dau., Jessica Sydney; step children—Mark, Craig, Peter. Intern, N.Y. Med. Coll., 1967-68, resident, 1968-69; resident Montefiore Hosp., Bronx, 1969-70, clin. fellow infectious diseases, also Einstein Hosp., 1970-71; practice medicine specializing in internal medicine, Yorktown, N.Y., 1970—; chief infectious disease clinic N.Y. Med. Coll., 1971-72, clin. asso. prof. medicine, attending physician, 1971—; chief infectious disease dept. Fordham & Misericordia Hosp., Bronx, 1971-72; attending physician, cons. in infectious diseases No. Westchester Hosp. Center, Mt. Kisco, N.Y., 1971—, chmn. infection control com., 1973—; pres., chief exec. officer Doctor's Fast; med. bd. dirs. Tech. Exchange Corp., N.J., 1971—, Planned Parenthood, Guiding Eyes; cons. Peekskill Community Hosp., 1974—; faculty medicine and surgery U. Rome (Italy), 1962-65. Bd. dirs. Yorktown High Sch. Scholarship Found., 1973—, United Jewish Appeal of Greater N.Y. Area; trustee Yorktown Jewish Center, 1973—; campaign chmn. United Jewish Appeal, Yorktown and Mt. Kisco, 1974—, co-chmn. No. Westchester div., chmn. Westchester fedn., 1977—; chmn. N. Westchester/Putnam Jewish Community Relations Council; mem. med. bd. dirs. Planned Parenthood Westchester; co-chmn. Israel Bonds of Westchester; chmn. 1988—; vol. physician Yom Kippur-Arab-Israeli War, 1973; dem. candidate U.S. 19th Congl. Dist. of N.Y., 1996. Served with USNR, 1957-59. ACP scholar, 1969-70, 70-71; recipient E. Spiegle award for distinction in allergy, 1967. Mem. Am. Soc. Microbiology, Am. Physicians Fellowship, Med. Soc. N.Y., Med. Soc. Westchester County (N.Y.), Internat. Assn. Study of Pain, Am. Pain Soc., Eastern Pain Soc., Flying Physicians Assn. Am. Clubs: Men's (Yorktown); Shorin-Ryu Karate Do-Philapine Karate Assn. Author: Wine Tasters Album. Contbr. articles to profl. jours. Home: 46 Annandale Rd Chappaqua

NY 10514-1812 Office: 1872 Commerce St Yorktown Heights NY 10598-4430

KLEIN, ROBERT WARD, ophthalmologist, educator; b. N.Y.C., Jan. 10, 1949; s. Emanuel Wirth and Judith Hope (Silverman) K. BA, NYU, 1970, MD, 1974. Diplomate Am. Bd. Ophthalmology. Med. intern NYU Med. Ctr., 1974-75, resident in ophthalmology, 1975-78, fellow in med. retina, 1978-79; pvt. practice, N.Y.C., 1979—; dir. ophthalmology Goldwater Meml. Hosp., Roosevelt Island, N.Y., 1979—; clin. asst. prof. NYU Sch. Medicine, NY.C., 1983—; mem. courtesy staff Manhattan Eye, Ear and Throat Hosp., N.Y.C., 1987-95; asst. attending ophthalmologist Bellevue Hosp., N.Y.C., 1995—; book cons. FYI-Unexpected Answers to Everyday Questions, 1982. Fellow Internat. Coll. Surgeons; mem. Alpha Omega Alpha. Office: Vitreous Retina Macula Cons NY 519 E 72d St Ste 203 New York NY 10021

KLEIN, SANDER PAUL, retired endocrinologist; b. Detroit, Feb. 24, 1918; s. Simon and May (Rosen) K.; m. Margot Ferne Staub; children: Marshall, Gary, Rodney. BS, Wayne State U., 1938, BS in Medicine, 1941, MD, 1942. Diplomate Am. Bd. Internal Medicine, Am. Bd. Endocrinology. Intern Detroit Receiving Hosp., 1941-42; resident Boston City Hosp., 1946-48; fellow in endocrinology Michael Reese Hosp., Chgo., 1948-49; pvt. practice medicine, Detroit, 1949-91; asst. prof. clin. medicine Wayne State U. Coll. Medicine, Detroit, 1949-92; chief endocrinology Mt. Carmel Mercy Hosp., Detroit, 1949-90, Sinai Hosp., Detroit, 1951-90; endocrinologist Beaumont Hosp., Royal Oak, Mich., 1989-91. Contbr. articles to med. jours. Capt. M.C., U.S. Army, 1942-46, ETO. Fellow ACP, Am. Coll. Endocrinology; mem. AMA, Alpha Omega Alpha. Jewish. Home: 216 Coral Cay Ter Palm Beach Terrace FL 33418

KLEIN, STEVEN PAUL, clinical psychologist; b. N.Y.C., Feb. 27, 1959; s. Arthur Steven and Dorothy (Saltzberg) K.; m. Debra Lynn Lanaghan, June 23, 1989. BA, SUNY, Binghamton, 1980; MS, U. Idaho, 1982; PhD, Wash. State U., 1986. Lic. psychologist, Wis. Psychology intern U. Wis. Med. Sch., Madison, 1985-86; staff psychologist Theda Clark Regional Med. Ctr., Neenah, Wis., 1986-88; pvt. practice psychology Appleton, Wis., 1988—; cons. in field; clin. dir. I'ACT Emotional Wellness Ctr., Appleton, 1989—; supr. Luth. Social Svcs., Oshkosh, Wis., 1990—. Contbr. articles to profl. jours. NIMH fellow, 1982. Mem. Am. Psychol. Assn., Midwest Psychol. Assn., Fox Valley Psychol. Assn. (founder), Wis. Psychol. Assn. (bd. govs. 1991—).

KLEIN, SUSAN ELIZABETH, medical technologist; b. Brunswick, Md., Mar. 5, 1952; d. Franklin Joseph and Verna Charlotte (Hartman) K. AD, Luzerne C.C., 1986. Med. technologist microbiology Mercy Hosp., Wilkes-Barre, Pa., 1972—. Vol. Hospice St. John, Wilkes-Barre, 1992—. Mem. Am. Med. Technologists Assn., Assn. Clin. Pathologists. Republican. Home: 664 E Main St Naticoke PA 18634 Office: Mercy Hosp 25 Church St Wilkes Barre PA 18765

KLEIN, SUSAN KERINS, pediatrician, psychologist, educator; b. Pitts., Feb. 5, 1955; d. John Lamson and Ursula (Fey) Kerins; m. Eric Alan Klein, Dec. 27, 1980. AB, Smith Coll., Northampton, Mass., 1977; MD, U. Pitts., 1981; MA in Psychology, Case Western Res. U., Cleve., 1994, PhD in Psychology, 1996. Diplomate Am. Bd. Pediatrics, Am. Bd. Psychiatry and Neurology, Nat. Bd. Med. Examiners. Intern pediatrics Rainbow Babies & Childrens, Cleve., 1981-82, resident, 1982-83, fellow child neurology, 1983-86; postdoctoral fellow rsch.-child neurology Albert Einstein Coll. Medicine, Bronx, N.Y., 1986-89; asst. prof. pediatrics and neurology Case Western Res. U., Cleve., 1989-92, grad. asst. psychology, 1992-96, clin. asst. prof. pediatrics, 1996—, lectr. dept. psychology, 1995-96. Recipient Individual Nat. Rsch. Svc. award Nat. Inst. Child Health and Devel., 1988-89. Fellow Am. Acad. Pediatrics; mem. Am. Acad. Neurology, Child Neurology Soc., Behavior Genetics Assn., Am. Psychol. Soc., Internat. Neuropsychol. Soc. Office: Case Western Res U Dept Psychology 10900 Euclid Ave Cleveland OH 44106-7123

KLEIN, THOMAS W., urologist; b. Stockton, Calif., June 10, 1940; s. Francis W. and Helen W. (Wilcox) K.; m. Virginia Lee Salo, June 29, 1963; children: Karl Thomas, Eric William. BA, U. Calif., 1963; MD, Tulane U., 1967. Diplomate Am. Bd. Urology. Resident in surgery/urology U. Calif. Med. Ctr., San Diego, 1967-75; gen. and pediatric practice Idaho Urology Clinic, Caldwell, 1975-89; chief urology sect. Lake City (Fla.) V.A. Med. Ctr., 1991-92, Portland (Oreg.) V.A. Med. Ctr., 1992—; asst. prof. surgery Oreg. Health Scis. U., Portland, 1992—. Mem. Am. Urol. Assn., Northwest Urol. Soc., Oreg. Urol. Assn., Lepidopterists Soc., Sigma Xi, Rotary. Office: Portland VAMC Urology Sect 3710 SW Veterans Hosp Rd Portland OR 97207

KLEIN, VIRGINIA SUE, psychotherapist; b. Liberty, N.Y., Dec. 30, 1936; d. Abe and Lillian (Malin) Levine; m. Andrew Klein, Mar. 29, 1959; children: Earl Saul, Holly Jo. BS, Rutgers U., 1972, MSW, 1974, PhD, 1978. Lic. psychotherapist, clin. social worker, N.J. Psychotherapist N.J. Correctional Inst. for Women, Clinton, 1973-75; pvt. practice Somerville, N.J., 1974—; prodr., host cable TV shows and series, including Growing Up in the 80's, 1986-88; radio show host Through the Looking Glass, 1988—; presenter seminars and tng. programs; lectr., cons. in field; co-founder., chmn. internat. confs. on incest and related problems; co-founder Internat. Network Against Incest and Child Secual Abuse; co-dir. The Tng. Inst., Switzerland, 1989, 90. Author: How to Get Free!, 1985, Bad Mad Boy, Honey Bear, and the Magic, Waterfall (A Continuing Family Story), 1986, I-am, Pa-pah and Ma-me, 1986. Mem. NASW, Acad. Cert. Social Workers, Am. Inst. Counseling and Psychotherapy (diplomate). Home and Office: 18 S Cadillac Dr Somerville NJ 08876-1732

KLEINELP, WILLIAM CHARLES, III, biology educator, editor; b. Yonkers, N.Y., Apr. 4, 1948; s. William Charles II and Lillian (Chytraus) K.; m. Mary Collins. BA, Fairleigh Dickinson U., 1970, MS, 1972; postgrad., William Paterson Coll., 1984-88. Tchr. sci. Dwight Morrow High Sch., Englewood, N.J., 1969-70; grad. fellow Fairleigh Dickinson U., Teaneck, N.J., 1970-72; assoc. prof. biology, dir. biotech. Middlesex County Coll., Edison, N.J., 1972&; critical editor W.C. Brown Publs., Dubuque, Iowa, 1981-87, HarperCollins Pubs., N.Y.C., 1985-88, Benjamin Cummings, Boston, 1986; editor Wood River Publs., Rumson, N.J., 1988—. Author: Investigations in Science, 1986, Experiments in Vertebrate Physiology, 1986, Experiments in Physiology, 1988; author computer module Anatomy and Physiology, 1987. Advisor Dept. Health, Piscataway, N.J., 1982; mem. Speakers Bur. Middlesex, Edison, 1986—. Recipient award N.J. Leukemia Soc., 1983. Mem. Am. Inst. Biol. Sci., AAAS, News in Physiologic Sci. Office: Middlesex County Coll 155 Mll Rd PO Box 3050 Edison NJ 08818-3050

KLEINER, KATHLEEN ALLEN, psychology educator; b. Phila., Nov. 12, 1958; d. William Anton and Marjorie Anne (Fine) K.; m. Roy Owen Gathercoal, Aug. 9, 1988; 1 child, Glen William Gathercoal. AB, Franklin & Marshall Coll., Lancaster, Pa., 1981; MA, PhD, Case Western Res. U., 1985. Teaching asst. Franklin & Marshall Coll., 1980-81; rsch. asst. Case Western Res. U., Cleve., 1981-85; researcher U. Calif., Berkeley, 1985-87; asst. prof. psychology Ind. U.-Purdue U., Indpls., 1987-93; assoc. prof. psychology, chair dept. psychology George Fox Coll., Newberg, Oreg., 1993—; summer faculty fellow Ind. U., Bloomington, 1988. Contbr. articles to profl. jours. Evaluation mem. Campaign for Healthy Babies, Indpls., 1990-92; active Yamhill County Commn. on Children and Families. Nat. Inst. Child Health and Human Devel. predoctoral fellow, 1981-85; Case Western Res. U. grad. alumni grantee, 1984, Project Devel. Program Interdisciplinary grantee Ind. U.-Purdue U., 1990, Intercampus Rsch. Funds, Ind. U., 1991. Mem. Mem. APA, Western Psychol. Assn., Soc. Rsch. in Child Devel., Internat. Soc. Infant Studies, Psi Chi. Mem. Soc. of Friends. Home: 2504 Haworth Ave Newberg OR 97132-1951 Office: George Fox Coll 414 N Meridian St Newberg OR 97132-2625

KLEINMAN, ARTHUR MICHAEL, medical anthropologist, psychiatrist, educator; b. N.Y.C., Mar. 11, 1941; s. Marcia F. (Kaplan) K.; m. Joan Andrea Ryman, Mar. 20, 1965; children: Peter John, Anna Simone. A.B., Stanford U., 1962, M.D., 1967; M.A., Harvard U., 1974. Diplomate: Nat. Bd. Med. Examiners, Am. Bd. Neurology and Psychiatry. Med. intern Yale-New Haven Hosp., 1967-68; surgeon USPHS, Bethesda, Md., Taiwan, 1968-70; resident in psychiatry Mass. Gen. Hosp., Boston, 1972-75; assoc. prof. U. Wash., Seattle, 1976-79, prof. psychiatry and anthropology, 1979-82; prof. med. anthropology and psychiatry Harvard U., Cambridge, Mass., 1982—, chmn. dept. social medicine, dir. Ctr. for Study Culture and Medicine, 1991—, Maude and Lillian Presley prof. med. anthropology, 1993—; co-chair com. on culture, health and devel. Social Sci. Rsch. Coun. Author: Patients and Healers in the Context of Culture, 1980 (Wellcome medal Royal Anthrop. Inst.), Social Origins of Distress and Disease, 1986, The Illness Narratives, 1988, Rethinking Psychiatry, 1988; co-editor: Relevance of Social Science for Medicine, 1981, Culture and Depression, 1985, Pain as Human Experience, 1992; editor-in-chief: Culture, Medicine and Psychiatry: A Jour. of Internat. Cross-Cultural Rsch., 1976-86. Recipient Rsch. award NIMH, 1977-79, Rockefeller Found., 1983-86, 88-89, NSF,1983-86, R.W. Johnson Found., 1988-89; grantee NIMH, 1984—, Carnegie Corp., 1990-92, MacArthur Found., 1992-94, Rockefeller Found., 1992-94; Guggenheim fellow, 1992. Fellow AAAS, Am. Psychiat. Assn., Am. Anthrop. Assn., Inst. Medicine of Nat. Acad. Scis. (chmn. com. on chronic pain, illness behavior and disability), Royal Anthrop. Inst., Am. Acad. Arts and Scis. *

KLEINMAN, CHARLES STEPHAN, physician, medical educator; b. N.Y.C., Mar. 12, 1947; s. Meyer and Dora (Levine) K.; m. Jessica Sue Pollack, June 14, 1969; children: Ari David, Joshua Michael. BA, NYU, 1967; MA, Rutgers U., 1968; MD, N.Y. Med. Coll., 1972; MA (hon.), Yale U., 1986. Diplomate Am. Bd. Pediatrics. Instr. pediatrics Cornell U. Med. Coll., N.Y.C., 1974-76; asst. prof. pediatrics Yale U., New Haven, 1977-81, assoc. prof., 1981-86, prof. pediatrics, diagnostic imaging and ob-gyn., 1986—; chief pediatric cardiology Yale U./Yale-New Haven Med. Ctr., New Haven, 1986—. Office: Yale Sch Medicine Sect Pediatric Cardiology 333 Cedar St New Haven CT 06510-3206*

KLEINMAN, STUART BRUCE, physician; b. N.Y.C., June 21, 1959; s. Gerald and Sally (Lebenson) K. BA, Lehigh U., 1981; MD, Med. Coll. of Phila., 1983. Diplomate Am. Bd. Psychiatry and Neurology. Intern in psychiatry and medicine Pa. Hosp., Phila., 1983-84; residency in psychiatry Inst. of Pa. Hos., Phila., 1984-87; fellow in forensic psychiatry Ctr. for Social Legal Studies U. Pa., Phila., 1986-87; fellow in psychiatry and law NYU Med. Ctr., Bellevue Hosp., N.Y.C., 1987-88; med. dir. Crime Victims Ctr./Victim Svcs. Agy., Bklyn., 1988—; attending psychiatrist Forensic Psychiatry Clinic Criminal/Supreme Cts. Manhattan, N.Y.C., 1988—; instr. in clin. psychiatry Columbia U. Coll. Physicians and Surgeons, N.Y.C., 1988-90, asst. prof. clin. psychiatry, 1990—; clin. instr. in psychiatry NYU Sch. Medicine, 1989-94, asst. clin. prof. psychiatry, 1994—. Recipient Therman award Pa. Hosp., 1987, Kenneth Appel award Phila. County Med. Soc., 1987, Menninger award Cen. Neuropsychiat. Assn., 1987; named Outstanding Alumnus U. Pa. Ctr. for Social and Legal Studies, 1990. Mem. Am. Acad. Psychiatry and Law (chmn. com. on victimology, pres. Tri-state chpt.), Soc. for Traumatic Stress Studies (pres. N.Y. chpt. 1993-95), Am. Psychiat. Assn., Phi Beta Kappa, Alpha Omega Alpha, Sigma Tau Delta. Jewish. Office: 420 E 64th St New York NY 10021-7853

KLEINROCK, ROBERT ALLEN, physician; b. Bronx, N.Y., July 25, 1950; s. Morris and Pearl (Levine) K.; m. Marie Louise Swinehart, Aug. 13, 1979. BS, CCNY, 1970; MD, NYU, 1974. Diplomate Am. Bd. Pediats. Pediatrician Permanente Med. Group, Vallejo, Calif., 1977—. Office: Permanente Med Group 975 Sereno Dr Vallejo CA 94705

KLEIN-SZANTO, ANDRES J. P., pathologist; b. Buenos Aires, Apr. 25, 1943; s. Geza and Madeleine K.-Z.; m. Maria U. Weyrauch, Dec. 30, 1972; children: Walter, Matias, Julian. MD, U. Buenos Aires, 1965, D.Med.Sci., 1970. Chief instr. dept. pathology U. Buenos Aires, 1967-73; staff scientist Argentine AEC, Buenos Aires, 1970-77; sr. med. scientist Oak Ridge (Tenn.) Nat. Lab., 1978-82; prof. U. Tex., Smithville, Houston, 1982-86; sr. pathologist and head exptl. histopathology service Fox Chase Cancer Ctr., Phila., 1986—; chief asst. dept. oral structural biology U. Zurich, 1974-76; mem. com. on role of tumor promoters, hormones, and other cofactors in human cancer causation Nat. Cancer Inst., Bethesda, Md., 1980, chem pathology study sect., 1986, 87-91; mem. environ. health scis. com. NIH, 1993-96. Assoc. editor: Acta Odontologica Latonoamericana, 1984—, Molecular-Carcinogenesis, 1995—; assoc. editor Jour. of Cutaneous Pathology, 1981, editor-in-chief, 1981-83; editor 4 books in field; contbr. numerous articles to profl. jours., chpts. to books. Mem. AAAS, Am. Assn. Cancer Rsch., Radiation Rsch. Soc., Internat. Acad. Pathology (divsn. sec. 1978), European Soc. Pathology, Am. Assn. Pathologists. Office: Fox Chase Cancer Ctr 7701 Burholme Ave Philadelphia PA 19111-2412

KLEIT, STUART ALLEN, nephrologist, physician, educator, dean; b. Passaic, N.J., July 29, 1933; s. Morris W. and Ruth (Gelman) K.; m. Cynthia A. Levenson, Aug. 31, 1958; children: Andrew N., David H. Student, Williams Coll., Williamstown, Mass., 1951-53; DDS, U. Pa., 1957; MD, U. Fla., 1961. Intern Ind. U. Hosps., Indpls., 1961-62; chief resident Ind. U. Hosps., 1964-65; resident physician Shands Teaching Hosp., Gainesville, Fla., 1962-63; fellow in renal medicine Shands Teaching Hosp., Gainesville, 1963-64; asst. prof. medicine, chief renal sect. Ind. U. Sch. Medicine, Indpls., 1967-71, assoc. prof. medicine, chief renal sect., 1971-74, prof. medicine, chief renal sect., 1974-88, acting dir. univ. hosp., 1984-85, prof. medicine, assoc. dean clin. affairs, 1985—; chmn. Edn Stage Renal Disease Network, Ind., 1978-79. Contbr. articles to profl. jours. Trustee Nat. Kidney Found., N.Y.C., 1972-88, pres., 1978-80; chmn. Nat. Kidney and Urologic Disease Adv. Bd., NIH, 1987-90; bd. dirs., treas. Am. Blood Commn., Washington, 1974-78. Recipient Cert. of Merit, Am. Acad. Dental Medicine, 1961, Martin K. Wagner award Nat. Kidney Found., 1984, Legion of Merit award Ind. Kidney Found., Disting. Contbns. award Am. Urologic Assn., 1990; NIH fellow, 1963-64. Fellow ACP (coun. subspecialties 1981-82); mem. AMA, Internat. Soc. Nephrology, Am. Soc. Nephrology (Disting. Svc. award 1990), Soc. Artificial Internal Organs. Office: Ind U Sch Medicine 1120 South Dr Indianapolis IN 46202-5114

KLENK, ROSEMARY ELLEN, pediatrician; b. Pitts., June 16, 1948; d. Joseph Albert and Frieda (Roppolo) Meisner; m. Kenneth Klenk, June 26, 1977; children: Kara, Jacob, Caitlin, David, Colin, Kevin. BA in History, U. Rochester, 1970; BSN, Columbia U., 1972; MD, Cornell U., 1980. Diplomate Nat. Bd. Med. Examiners, Am. Bd. Pediat.; RN. Ptnr., pvt. practice New England Pediat., Stamford, Conn., 1983—; bd. dirs. So. Conn. Child Guidance Ctr.; med. bd. Stamford (Conn.) Hosp.; part-time instr. Coll. Physicians & Surgeons Columbia U., 1983—. Contbr. articles to profl. jours. Fellow Am. Acad. Pediat.; mem. Conn. State Med. Soc., Fairfield County Med. Soc. Office: New England Pediatrics 166 W Broad St Ste 103 Stamford CT 06902

KLENOFF, BRUCE HOWARD, otolaryngologist; b. N.Y.C., May 6, 1944; s. Harry and Anne (Sager) K.; m. Joyce Ellen Potash, Nov. 30, 1968; children: Heather, Jason, Mindy. BS, Rensselaer Poly. Inst., 1965; MD, Tufts U., 1969. Diplomate Am. Bd. Otolaryngology. Resident in gen. surgery Albert Einstein Hosp., Bronx, N.Y., 1969-70, St. Elizabeth's Hosp., Boston, 1972-73; resident in otolaryngology, head and neck surgery Harvard U., Boston, 1973-76; dir. dept. eye, ear, nose and throat St. Joseph Hosp., Stamford, Conn., 1990—; dir. divsn. ear, nose and throat Stamford Hosp. Inventor swim radio, 1987. Lt. comdr. USCG, USPHS, 1970-72. Fellow ACS, Am. Acad. Otolaryngology; mem. AMA, Conn. Med. Assn., Fairfield County Med. Soc. Office: 188 North St Stamford CT 06901-1110

KLEPNER, JERRY D., federal agency administrator; b. St. Louis, Dec. 4, 1944; s. Philip and Theresa (Smith) K.; m. Bonnie Klepner, July 1, 1966 (div. 1980); children: Robert, Melissa; m. Karetta Hubbard, June 6, 1981. BA, Washington U., 1967. Nat. exec. v.p., dir. legislation Nat. Treasury Employees Union, Washington, 1971-84; ptnr. Anderson, Benjamin, Read & Haney, Washington, 1986-87; staff dir. U.S. Ho. of Reps. Subcom. on Compensation and Employee Benefits, Washington, 1984-86; dir. legislation Am. Fedn. State, County and Mcpl. Employees, Washington, 1987-93; asst. sec. legislation Dept. Health and Human Svcs., Washington, 1993—; commr. Va. Statewide Health Coordinating Coun., Richmond, 1986-87; dir. No. Va. Health Systems Agy., Fairfax, 1984-87. Active YMCA. Democrat. Jewish. Office: Dept Health & Human Svcs 200 Independence Ave SW Washington DC 20201-0004*

KLEPONIS, JEROME ALBERT, dentist; b. Ashland, Pa., July 26, 1955; s. Albert Francis and Anna Mae Catherine (Burns) K. BS in Biology summa cum laude, Allentown Coll. St. Francis de Sales, 1977; DMD, U. Pa., 1981. Resident in gen. dentistry Geisinger Med. Ctr., Danville, Pa., 1981-82; assoc. Office of Dr. Stephen D. Eingorn, Bethlehem, Pa., 1982-83; dir. dental svcs. Lock Haven (Pa.) Hosp., 1983-86; sr. staff dentist Tri-Town Med. Ctr., Williamstown, Pa., 1986-87; dir. dental svcs. Embreeville Ctr., Coatesville, Pa., 1987-92, Danville (Pa.) State Hosp., 1992—. Vol. Chester County Buddies, West Chester, Pa., 1990-92; CPR instr. Am. Heart Assn., 1989—; mem. leadership com. Cardinal Brennan Jr./Sr. H.S., 1994—. Recipient Alumni Svc. award Allentown Coll., 1993; named to Outstanding Young Men of Am., 1988, 89. Fellow Am. Assn. Hosp. Dentists, Acad. Gen. Dentistry, Acad. Dentistry for Persons with Disabilities (chairperson ad hoc com. on mental health 1995—); mem. ADA (vol. PEERS network on mental illness 1995—), Am. Soc. Geriatric Dentistry, Pa. Dental Assn., Tri-County Dental Soc., Am. Soc. Dentistry for Children, Am. Soc. Forensic Odontology, Am. Assn. Mental Retardation, Elks, Am. Hose Co., Am. Legion Sons of Vets., Allentown Coll. Alumni Assn. (bd. dirs. 1983-94, sec. bd. dirs. 1985-87, pres. bd. dirs. 1991-94), Psi Omega (editor Zeta chpt. 1979-81). Roman Catholic. Home: 1201 Arch St Ashland PA 17921-1213 Office: Danville State Hosp PO Box 700 Danville PA 17821-0700

KLEPPER, CAROL JEAN, mental health therapist; b. Wagner, S.D., July 17, 1933; d. Forrest Glenwood and Augusta Wilhamina (Mills) Herdman; m. Albert Raymond Klepper, May 14, 1955; children: James David, Leesa Lynn, Krista Patrice. BS in Psychology cum laude, S. Oreg. State Coll., 1987; MS in Counseling, Oreg. State U., 1989. Nat. cert. counselor, lic. profl. counselor. Dir. counseling Klamath Hospice, Klamath Falls, Oreg., 1990-91; staff therapist Klamath Mental Health Ctr., 1991-94; in-house counselor Wednesday's Child, 1995—, title 19 adminstr., 1996—; data rschr. Rich Pickett and Co., Klamath Falls, 1986-90; pre-commitment investigator Klamath Mental Health Ctr., 1991-94; EPSDT coord. County of Klamath, 1991-94. Mem. youth svcs. team local mid-schs., Klamath Falls, 1992-94; juv. fire-setters network Klamath Falls Fire Dist. # 1, 1992—; head start health bd., Klamath Falls, 1991—, RAPP Team Mem., 1995—. Mem. Psi Chi. Home: 8926 Highway 66 Klamath Falls OR 97601-9538 Office: 8926 Hwy 66 Klamath Falls OR 97601-9638

KLERIGA-GROSSGERGE, ENRIQUE, neurosurgeon; b. Mexico City, Oct. 26, 1946; s. Efrain Kleriga-Vera and Marcela Grossgerge-Rangel; m. Maria de Lourdes Alomia-Bosada, June 20, 1983; children: Luis, Maria de Lourdes, Carolina. MD, U. Nat. Autonoma de Mex., 1971; postgrad., SUNY, Bklyn., 1975. Diplomate Am. Bd. Neurol. Surgeons. Asst. instr. neurosurgery SUNY, Bklyn., 1975; medic Centro Medico Nac. IMSS, Mexico City, 1979-85; mem. staff ABC Hosp., Mexico City, 1984—, chief of surgery, 1989-92, sec., 1991-92; mem. staff Angeles del Ped. Hosp., Mexico City, 1984—. Mem. ACS, Congress Neurol. Surgeons, Internat. Microsurg. Soc., N.Y. Acad. Scis., Soc. Mexicana de Cirugia Neurologica. Roman Catholic. Office: Cirugia Neurologica SC, Sur 136 esp Observatorio-411, 01120 Mexico City Mexico

KLESGES, ROBERT C., medical educator, clinical psychology researcher; b. May 26, 1953; married; 2 children. AA in Biology, Glendale (Calif.) Cmty. Coll., 1974; BA in Psychology, Pepperdine U., 1976; MS in Clin. Psychology, U. Wyo., 1978, PhD in Clin. Psychology, 1980. Psychology intern, dept. psychiatry and behavioral scis. U. So. Calif. Sch. Medicine, L.A., 1979-80; asst. prof. clin. psychology N.D. State U., Fargo, 1980-84, assoc. prof., dir. clin. tng., 1984-85; prof. psychology U. Memphis, 1985—, program coord., behavioral medicine subsplty., 1986—; adj. assoc. prof. biostats. and epidemiology U. Tenn., Memphis, 1987—, rsch. prof. pediat. 1986—, adj. prof. preventive medicine 1992—, special asst. dept. athletics, 1994—. Contbr. articles to profl. jours. Office: U Memphis Dept Psychology Univs Prevention Ctr Memphis TN 38152*

KLIEFOTH, A(RTHUR) BERNHARD, III, neurosurgeon; b. San Antonio, Nov. 26, 1942; s. Arthur Bernhard, Jr. and Pauline (Grey) K.; m. Ingrid R. Kunde, Apr. 22, 1968; children: Karena, Tanya. AB in Chemistry, Princeton U., 1965; M.D. U. Tex., 1970. Diplomate Am. Bd. Neurol. Surgery. Intern, Naval Hosp., Oakland, Calif., 1970-71; resident gen. surgery Naval Hosp., San Diego, 1972-73; neurosurg. tng. Washington U., St. Louis, 1973-78; research fellow dept. radiation scis. Washington U., 1977-78; commd. ensign U.S. Navy, 1969, advanced through grades to comdr., 1977; staff neurosurgeon Naval Regional Med. Ctr., Oakland, 1978-81; resigned, 1981; capt. USNR, 1985; practice medicine specializing in neurosurgery, Knoxville, Tenn., 1981—; mem. staff U. Tenn. Hosp., St. Mary's Hosp., chmn. dept. surgery, 1989-90; clin. assoc. prof. surgery, U. Tenn.; bd. dirs. Tenn. Donor Svcs. Bd. dirs. Cole Neurosci. Found., Knoxville Donor Svcs.; pres. Princeton Alumni Assn. Knoxville and Eastern Tenn. Fellow ACS, Stroke Council Am. Heart Assn.; mem. AMA, Am. Assn. Neurol. Surgeons, Am. Soc. Stereotactic and Functional Neurosurgery, Tenn. Neurosurg. Soc., World Soc. Stereotactic, and Functional Neurosurgery, Congress Neurol. Surgeons, So. Neurosurgical Soc., So. Med. Assn., Tenn. Med. Assn., Knoxville Acad. Medicine, San Francisco Neurol. Soc., Soc. Med. Cons. to Armed Forces, Assn. Mil. Surgeons U.S., Soc. for Neurosci. Office: 939 Emerald Ave Ste 905 Knoxville TN 37917

KLIESCH, WILLIAM FRANK, physician; b. Franklinton, La., Nov. 4, 1928; s. Edward Granville and Elsie Jeni (Sylvest) K.; m. May Virginia Reid, Dec. 17, 1955; children: Thomas Karl, William August, John Francis. BS, La. State U., 1949, MD, 1953. Intern Valley Forge Hosp., Phoenixville, Pa., 1953-54; intern in med. rsch. Charity Hosp., New Orleans, 1956-57; resident, fellow in internal medicine Ochsner Found. Hosp., New Orleans, 1957-59; pvt. practice New Orleans, 1959-69, Jackson, Miss., 1969—; dir. spinal injury svc. Miss. Meth. Rehab. Ctr., Jackson, 1980—. Capt. U.S Air Force, 1953-56. Fellow Am. Coll. Emergency Physicians; mem. Am. Spinal Injury Assn., Internat. Paraplegia Soc. Episcopalian. Home: 8892 Gay Rd Jackson MS 39212-9732 Office: Miss State Hosp Whitfield MS 39193

KLIMA, ROGER R., physiatrist; b. Prague, Czechoslovakia; came to U.S., 1982, naturalized, 1988; s. Josef and Radka Klima. BA, Zatlanka Coll., Prague, 1971; MD, Charles U., Prague, 1978. Diplomate Am. Bd. Phys. Medicine and Rehab., Am. Bd. Electrodiagnostic Medicine. Resident in surgery Charles U., 1978-79, resident in orthopedic surgery, 1979-81; fellow, clin. clk. Beverly Hills Med. Ctr. and Cedars-Sinai Med. Ctr., L.A., 1984-86; resident in surgery U. Medicine and Dentistry-N.J. Med. Sch., Newark, 1986-87; resident in phys. medicine and rehab. U. Medicine and Dentistry-N.J. Med. Sch./Kessler Inst., Newark and West Orange, 1987-90; mem. phys. medicine and rehab. faculty Stanford (Calif.) U. and affiliated hosps., 1990—; dir. phys. medicine and rehab. outpatient svcs. Palo Alto (Calif.) VA Health Care Sys., 1992—, also co-dir. comprehensive pain mgmt.; clin. instr. in phys. medicine and rehab. U. Medicine and Dentistry-N.J.Med. Sch., 1989-90; clin. instr. in phys., medicine and rehab. Stanford U. Sch. Medicine, 1990-96, asst. prof., 1996—. Contbr. articles to profl. jours. Recipient first ann. Thompson Humanitarian award Stanford U. Phys. Medicine and Rehab., 1994. Mem. Am. Acad. Phys. Medicine and Rehab. (liaison resident physician coun. 1989-90), Assn. Acad. Physiatrists, Am. Assn. Electrodiagnostic Medicine. Office: Stanford U Med Ctr Divsn Phys Medicine and Rehab Rm NC 104 Stanford CA 94305

KLIMEK, JOSEPH JOHN, physician; b. Wilkes Barre, Pa., Sept. 14, 1946; s. Joseph John and Frances Carol (Pavloski) K.; m. Jane Marie Stout, June 26, 1971 (div.); 1 child, Adam. AB cum laude, Princeton U., 1968; MD, Pa. State U., 1972. Diplomate Am. Bd. Internal Medicine, Am. Bd. Infectious Diseases. Intern, resident in internal medicine, fellow in infectious disease Hartford Hosp., Conn., 1972-76, chief epidemiology 1976-87, dir. subspecialty medicine, 1985-87, assoc. dir. medicine, 1987-90; assoc. dir. dept. medicine and chmn. AIDS program Hartford Hosp., 1987-90, dir. Dept. of Medicine, 1990—, chmn. AIDS task forc, 1985-90; asst. prof. medicine U. Conn., Farmington, 1977-84, assoc. prof. 1984-90, prof. medicine, 1990—. Conn. mem. numerous faculties pharm. industry. Sr. assoc. editor: Am. Jour. Infection Control, 1980—; med. editor Asepsis, The Infection Control Forum; also mem. numerous editorial bds. in field; contbr. articles to profl. jours.; integrated internal medicine residency of Hartford Hosp. with U. Conn. sch. medicine; developed hosp. community linkage network for aids care in greater Hartford. Recipient Lange award Hershey Med. Sch., 1972, Disting. Alumnus award, 1978, ARC award, 1986. Fellow ACP, Infectious

Disease Soc. Am.; mem. Assn. Practitioners in Infection Control, Am. Soc. Microbiology, N.Y. Acad. Sci., Am. Pub. Health Assn., Am. Fedn. Clin. Research, Soc. Hosp. Epidemiologists Am., Am. Venereal Disease Assn., AAAS, Am. Med. Writers Assn. Avocations: painting; sketching; woodwork; photography; skiing. Home: 10 Mathers Crossing Simsbury CT 06070 Office: Hartford Hosp 80 Seymour St Hartford CT 06115

KLIMEK, RUDOLF, obstetrics and gynecology educator; b. Kraków, Poland, Dec. 12, 1932; s. Sylwester and Józefa Klimek; m. Ewa Kownacka, Apr. 21, 1961; 1 child, Marek. Physician diploma, Copernicus U., Kraków, 1955, MD, 1961; MD habilitation Ob-gyn., Copernicus U., 1964. Cert. obstetrician and gynecologist, neuroendocrinologist. Clin. investigator Copernicus U. Sch. Medicine, Kraków, 1957-65, head cen. endocrine lab., 1965-69, head dept. encocrinology Inst. Ob-gyn., 1969—, dean Sch. Nursing, 1975-81; cons. in field; mem. sci. bd. Polish Ministry Health and Social Welfare, 1981-86; sci. bd., exec. bd. FIGO, 1982—; exec. bd. EAGO, 1986-91. Recipient Bachelor's Cross Polonia Restituta, 1975, 1st Grade Ednl. award Polish Health and Social Welfare Ministry, 1976, 77, Gold medal City of Cracow, 1978, medal World Polonia, 1987. Mem. Polish Gynecol. Soc. (hon., pres.), Internat. Soc. Endocrinology, French Endocrine Soc., All-Union Sci. Soc. Ob-gyn. (hon.), Am. Fertility Soc., Polish Gynecologists' World Club (pres. 1988), Hungarian Gynecology Soc., German Gynecology Soc., Israeli Gynecology Soc., N.Y. Acad. Scis., Internat. Soc. Prenatal and Perinatal Psychology and Medicine (pres. 1991). Home: Sebastiana 10/3, 31-049 Kraków Poland Office: Inst Ob-gyn, Kopernika 23, 31-501 Kraków Poland

KLINCEWICZ, STEPHEN LOUIS, preventive medicine physician; b. Jersey City, Aug. 18, 1956; s. Watson L. and Gisele H. (Luipersbeck) K.; m. Leslie A. Devine, Jan. 12, 1985. BA with honors, McGill U., Montreal, Can., 1977; DO, U. Osteopathic Medicine, Des Moines, 1983; MPH, Med. Coll. Wis., Milw., 1991; JD, Widener U., 1996. Diplomate Am. Bd. Preventive Medicine (occupl.), Am. Osteo. Bd. Preventive Medicine (occupl. and environ. medicine). Asst. dir. emergency svcs. USAF Hosp., Homestead, Fla., 1984-87; med. officer Ctr. Disease Control/ Nat. Inst. Occupl. Safety & Health, Cin., 1987-89; dir. occupational and environ. medicine Sacred Heart Hosp., Allentown, Pa., 1989-91; dir. occupational health Brandywine Hosp., Exton, Pa., 1991-95; asst. dir. drug safety/pharmacoepidemiology Zeneca Pharms., Wilmington, Del., 1995—. With U.S. Pub. Health Svc., 1987—, USAFR, 1979-87. Mem. ABA, Am. Acad. Pharm. Physicians, Am. Osteo. Assn. Am. Coll. Occupational Environ. Medicine. Home: 462 Creekside Dr Downingtown PA 19335 Office: Zeneca Pharms. 1800 Concord Pk Wilmington DE 19850

KLINE, BARBARA A., nursing case manager; b. Pitts., July 11, 1958; d. Robert T. and Janet (Falkenstein) K. BSN, Cedar Crest Coll., Allentown, Pa., 1982; MSA in Health Adminstrn., West Chester U., 1988; postgrad., U. Pa., 1995—, U. Pa. Cert. med.-surg. nurse, ACLS. Staff nurse Crozer-Chester Med. Ctr., Upland, Pa.; primary nurse Paoli (Pa.) Meml. Hosp.; mktg. dept. liaison U. Pa. Med. Ctr.; clin. resource mgr. adminstrn. Hosp. of U. Pa., Phila., 1994—. Named Nurse of Hope, Am. Cancer Soc., 1984.

KLINE, FRANK MENEFEE, psychiatrist; b. Cumberland, Md., May 14, 1928; s. Frank Huber and Margaret (Menefee) K.; m. Shirley Steinmetz, June 27, 1953; children: Frank F., Margaret L. BS, U. Md., 1950, MD, 1952; PhD, So. Calif. Psychoanalytic Ins., 1977. Diplomate Am. Bd. Psychiatry and Neurology (examiner 1970-96). Intern Cin. Gen. Hosp., 1952-53; resident Brentwood VA Med. Ctr., West L.A., 1955-58; Regional chief West Cen. Mental Svc., L.A. County Dept. Mental Health, L.A., 1967-68; assoc. dir. adult psychiatry out-patient dept. L.A. County, U. So. Calif. Med. Ctr., 1968-77, acting dir. adult psychiatric dept., 1977-78; chief psychiatry VA Med. Ctr., Long Beach, Calif., 1977-91; assoc. prof. U. So. Calif., clin. prof.; clin. prof., vice-chair U. Calif.-Irvine, 1978-91; clin. prof. Drew King, 1992—, MS; reviewer Hosp. Comty. Psychiatry, 1978—, Am. Jour. Psychiatry, 1978—, Readings, 1995—. Editor: A Handbook of Group Psychotherapy, 1983. 1st lt. M.C., U.S. Army, 1953-55. Office: 24 Sorrel Ln Rolling Hills Estates CA 90274

KLINE, JACOB, biomedical engineering educator; b. Boston, Aug. 3, 1917; s. Joseph and Jennie (Goldman) K.; m. Barbara Fine, Dec. 22, 1957; children: David, Jonathan, Pamela. B.S., MIT, 1942, M.S., 1951; Ph.D. (NSF fellow), Iowa State U., 1962. Cert. clin. engr. Electronics engr. Internat. Tel. & Tel. Co., Newark, 1942-46; chief video sect. optical rsch. lab. Boston U., 1946-48; rsch. asst. MIT, 1948-51, rsch. engr., 1951-52; mem. faculty U. R.I., Kingston, 1952-66; assoc. prof. engring. U. R.I., 1956-60, dir. bio-med. engring. program, 1962-66; prof. biomed. engring., dir. biomed. engring. program U. Miami, Coral Gables, Fla., 1966-79; chmn. dept. biomed. engring. U. Miami, 1979—; cons. lab. for criminal investigation U. R.I., 1952-66; cons., tech. advisor to attys. on elec. and biomed. problems, 1952—; cons. on relaxation therapy Lab. for Clin. Physiology, Chgo., 1949-53, on lab. rsch. Boston Psychopathol. Hosp., 1949-53, on orthodontic rsch. Tufts U. Dental Sch., 1951-53; cons. Venice (Fla.) Hosp., St. Francis Hosp., Miami Beach, Fla., Children's Hosp., Miami, Miami Heart Hosp., Miami Beach, Tex. Tech. U. Med. Sci. Ctr., Odessa; cons. Lab. for Clin. Physiology, Chgo., 1949-53, Boston Psychiatric Hosp., 1949-53, Venice Hosp., Fla., St. Francis Hosp., Miami, Childrens Hosp., Miami, Miami Heart Hosp., Jackson Meml. Hosp., Miami, 1966—, Tex. Tech. Med. Sci. Ctr., Odessa, 1996—. Author: Biomedical Foundation for Biomedical Engineers, 1976, Handbook for Biomedical Engineers, 1987 (translated into Chinese 1991); contbr. articles to profl. jours.; patentee hydrogel surface of urol. prosethesis. NASA/Am. Soc. Engring. Edn. fellow, summers, 1965, 66. Fellow Am. Acad. Dental Electrosurgery, AAAS; mem. IEEE (dir. 1943—), Am. Soc. Artificial Organs, Am. Assn. Advancement Med. Instrumentation (chmn. bd. trustees AAMI Found. 1982-85). Office: U Miami Coll Engring Coral Gables FL 33124

KLINE, MARTIN SCOTT, hospital administrator; b. Winchester, Va., May 22, 1948; s. Ivan Philip and Vivian Louise (Sanford) K.; m. Patricia Noel Weaver, June 5, 1971; children: Stacy Erin, Brian Scott. Postgrad. in Pub. Adminstrn., Coll. William and Mary, 1973; MPA, Va. Commonwealth U., 1997. Lic. nursing home adminstr.; cert. tng. preceptor. Acct. Ea. State Hosp., Williamsburg, Va., 1971-75, dir. fin., 1975-87, hosp. adminstr., 1987—. Coach boys basketball Williamsburg Dept. Recreation, 1987-92, girls softball, 1988-90, boys baseball, 1991-92; agy. chmn. Greater Williamsburg United Way, 1980-91, chmn. pub. sector divsn., 1982-85; treas., bd. dirs. Williamsburg Pastoral Counseling Ctr., 1991-92, Sunday sch. tchr. Williamsburg United Meth. Ch. Methodist. Home: 118 Ware Rd Williamsburg VA 23185-3144 Office: Ea State Hosp PO Box 8791 4601 Ironbound Rd Williamsburg VA 23187-8791

KLINE, PRISCILLA MACKENZIE, nursing educator; b. Elgin, Ill., Sept. 25, 1944; d. Gordon Innes and Esther May (Brooks) Mackenzie; m. Ellis Lee Kline, June 12, 1965; children: Heather, Heidi. BSN, U. Ill., 1965, MSN, 1969; EdD, Clemson (S.C.) U., 1987. RN, S.C. Project dir. Alzheimer's Community Edn. Project; pvt. practice Clemson; psychiat. nurse transitional care program Elgin State Hosp., 1967-68; lectr. psychiat. nursing Sacramento State Coll., 1968-69; in-svc. coord. Woodland (Calif.) Meml. Hosp., 1969-71; asst. prof. psychiat. nursing Edinboro (Pa.) State Coll., 1974-78; assoc. prof. Clemson U. Coll. Nursing, 1988—, assoc. dean, 1988-93, acting head dept. profl. svcs., 1991-93; nurse psychotherapist Clemson U. Coll. Nursing. Contbr. numerous articles to profl. jours. Vol. nurse Hospice of Anderson, S.C.; leader Girl Scouts U.S., 1976-89; mem. Alzheimer's adv. com. S.C. Commn. on Aging, 1987—, chair, 1989—. Recipient merit award AAUP, 1984, Centennial Outstanding Grad. award Clemson U. Coll. Edn., 1989, Award of Excellence S.C. League for Nursing, 1996. Mem. ANA (Pres.'s award S.C. chpt. 1993), Nat. League Nursing, S.C. League Nursing (Excellence award 1996), So. Nursing Rsch. Soc., S.C. Gerontol. Soc., Sigma Theta Tau (internat. treas. 1991-93, 93-95, Excellence in Nursing award 1993), Sigma Theta Tau Found. (chair, bd. dirs. 1994-95, treas. 1995—, 75th Anniversary Dising. Lectr. 1995—). Home: 203 N Elm St Pendleton SC 29670-1731 Office: Clemson U Coll Nursing Clemson SC 29634

KLINE, ROBERT JOSEPH, psychologist; b. Spangler, Pa., May 31, 1944; s. Robert Henry and Louise (Duman) K.; m. Marilyn Maloy, June 5, 1970; 1 child, Julie. BA, St. Vincent Coll., 1966, MDiv, 1970; MA, Ind. U. Pa., 1971; PhD, Brigham Young U., 1974. Lic. psychologist, counselor. Dir. Auburn (Ala.) U., 1973-74; clin. dir. Cheaha Mental Health, Sylacauga, Ala., 1974-86; pvt. practice Sylacauga, 1986-88; psychologist Ala. Inst. for the Deaf and Blind, Talladega, Ala., 1988—. Grantee Ala. Inst. for Deaf and Blind, 1990. Mem. APA, Am. Soc. Clin. Hypnosis. Home: 204 Edgewood Dr Childersburg AL 35044-1326 Office: ACTS 204 S Broadway Ave # A Sylacauga AL 35150-3003

KLINE, SUSAN ANDERSON, medical school administrator, internist; b. Dallas, June 4, 1937; d. Kenneth Kirby and Frances Annette (Demorest) Anderson; m. Edward Mahon Kline, Dec. 26, 1964 (dec. July 1990). BA, Ohio U., 1959; MD, Northwestern U., 1963. Diplomate Am. Bd Internal Medicine, Nat. Bd. Med. Examiners (bd. dirs. 1977-81). Dir. cardiac catheterization lab. The New York Hosp., 1971-80; assoc. dean student affairs Cornell Med. Sch., Ithaca, N.Y., 1974-78, assoc. dean admissions and student affairs, 1978-80; mgr. occupl. med. programs GE Co., 1980-84; sr. assoc. dean student affairs N.Y. Med. Coll., Valhalla, 1984-94, interim dean, v.p. med. affairs, 1994—, exec. vice dean acad. affairs, vice provost student svcs., 1996—; bd. dirs. Nat. Residency Matching Program, 1996—. Bd. visitors Coll. of Arts, Ohio U., Athens, 1981-91; mem. test com. ECFMG, Phila., 1985-92, USMLE tests accommodations com. NBMZ, Phila., 1992—. Recipient Leaders of the Future award Nat. Coun. Women, N.Y.C., 1978, Cert. of Appreciation, Ohio U., 1978. Fellow Am. Coll. Cardiology, Coun. on Clin. Cardiology of Am. Heart Assn. N.Y. Cardiologists Soc.; mem. AAMC (N.E. group on student affairs vice chair, chair 1989-93). Cruising Club of Am., Alpha Omega Alpha (Roache award 1963). Home: 551 Pequot Ave Southport CT 06490 Office: New York Medical College Sunshine Cottage Valhalla NY 10595

KLING, MICHAEL ANTHONY, optometrist; b. Wabash, Ind., June 30, 1967; s. Verlin Rex and Clarice Ellen (Mast) K. BS in Biology, Southern Coll. Optometry, Memphis, 1993, OD cum laude, 1993. Resident in ocular disease Omega Eye Care Ctr., Jackson, Tenn., 1993-94; clin. optometrist Alvarado Eye Assocs., San Diego, 1994—. Recipient Fison's Award for Clin. Excellence, So. Coll. Optometry, 1993, X-Cel Contact Lens award, 1993. Mem. Am. Optometric Assn., Calif. Optometric Assn., San Diego County Optometric Soc. (sec. 1996—). Repbulican. Office: 5555 Reservoir Dr Ste 300 San Diego CA 92120

KLINGEL, PATTI JEAN, health facility administrator; b. Marion, Ohio, Dec. 28, 1955; d. Elmer N. and Reba J. (Freeman) Noe; m. Jeffrey J. Klingel, Aug. 16, 1974; children: Shane, Seth, Bethann. Lic. practical nurse, Marion Gen. Hosp. Sch. Nursing, 1975; student, Ohio State U., 1984-85; AD in Bus. Adminstrn. magna cum laude, Marion Tech. Coll., 1993; grad. summa cum laude Sch. Bus., Spring Arbor Coll., 1996. Assembler Whirlpool Corp., Marion, 1974; nurse Marion Gen. Hosp., 1975-79; childbirth educator, 1977-92; nurse Community Med. Ctr., Marion, 1981-83; instr., cons. Tri-Rivers Joint Vocat. Sch., Marion, 1996; office mgr., adminstrv. asst. J.T. Spare M.D., Inc., Marion, 1986-94; quality improvement coord. MedCtr. Hosp., Marion, 1994—; cons. Marion Tech. Coll., 1991. Spokesperson Nurse Hope-Am. Cancer Soc., Marion, 1982; advisor 4-H, Marion, 1986-93; bus. adminstr. United Way, Marion, 1989. Recipient scholarship Ohio State U., Columbus, 1985, Marion (Ohio) Tech. Coll., 1991, Walters scholarship, 1992-93, Wall St. Jour. award. Mem. NAFE, Nat. Assn. for Healthcare Quality, Ohio Assn. Healthcare Quality, Parents Assn. Childbirth Edn. (pres., instr. rep. 1976-92, top instr. 1989), Internat. Childbirth Edn. Assn., Am. Assn. Office Nurses, Lic. Practical Nurses Assn. (sec. 1975-76), Marion County Jr. Fair Bd. (advisor 1987-92). Mem. Assembly of God Church. Home: 3966 Cardington Rd Marion OH 43302 Office: 1050 Delaware Ave Marion OH 43302-6416

KLINGENSTEIN, R. JAMES, physician; b. N.Y.C., Oct. 30, 1948; s. Paul and Selma (Feldman) K. AB magna cum laude, Case Western Res. U., 1970; MD with honors, NYU, 1974; JD, Boston Coll., 1989; student, Harvard Sch Pub. Health, 1988. Intern Mt. Sinai Hosp., N.Y.C., 1974-75, resident, 1975-76; resident Bellevue Hosp., N.Y.C., 1976-77; clin. assoc. immunology br. Nat. Cancer Inst. NIH, HEW, Bethesda, Md., 1977-79; fellow in gastroenterology Mass. Gen Hosp., Boston, 1979—; clin. research fellow Harvard U., Boston, 1979-82; clin. assoc. medicine Mass. Gen. Hosp., 1982—; instr. in medicine Harvard Med. Sch., 1982-83, Tufts U. Sch. Medicine, 1983-87; asst. prof. Tufts U., 1987—. Assoc. editor: Internat. Jour. of Risk and Safety in Medicine; contbr. articles to profl. jours. Fellow ACP; mem. Am. Gastroenterol. Assn., Phi Bbeta Kappa. Home: 2000 Washington St # 543 Newton MA 02162 Office: Mass Gen Hosp Gi Unit Boston MA 02114

KLINGER, GEORGE M., health administrator; b. St. Louis, June 15, 1937; s. George Malcolm and Kathryn Ursalee (Neil) K.; m. Sharon Leslie Elliott, June 17, 1967; children: Katherine Cherisse, Joseph Michael, Mary Beth. BS in Chemistry and Biology, Drury Coll., 1959; MD, U. Mo., 1963. Bd. cert. Nat. Bd. Med. Examiners, Am. Bd. Family Practice. Chief of health programs, chief med. officer U.S. Med. Ctr. for Fed. Prisoners, Springfield, Mo. Fellow Am. Acad. Family Physicians; mem. Am. Coll. Health Care Execs., Sertoma Club. Office: US Med Ctr Fed Prisoners 1900 W Sunshine Springfield MO 65808

KLINGER, LYNNETTE ANN, social worker, therapist; b. Allentown, Pa., July 25, 1961; d. Marvyn LeRoy and Darlene Jean (Snyder) Souders; m. Karl Eugene Klinger, Aug. 23, 1986. BA in Psychology and Social Work, Moravian Coll., 1983; MA in Counseling Psychology, Kutztown (Pa.) State U., 1989. Coord. victim's svcs. Rape Crisis Coun., Allentown, 1983-84; vocat. counselor Hoover Rehab. Svcs., Allentown, 1984-85, vocat. counselor supr., 1986-87; sr. caseworker Lehigh County Children & Youth, Allentown, 1987-96, casework supr., 1996—; therapist Florence Child Guidance Ctr., Allentown, 1989—. Mem. AACD, Assn. of Play Therapy. Office: Florence Child Guidance Ctr 1812 W Allen St Allentown PA 18104-5025

KLINGER, RONALD FRED, neurologist; b. Bklyn., June 14, 1958; s. Erwin and Roberta May (Haagman) K.; m. Ruth Ann Gargan, Jan. 18, 1986; children: Sarah, Jessica, Joshua. BS in Chemistry, Pace U, 1978; MD, Bowman Gray-Wake Forest U., 1982. Diplomate Am. Bd. Neurology. Intern Brookdale Hosp., Bklyn., 1982-83; resident in neurology North Shore Hosp., Manhasset, N.Y., 1983-86; pvt. practice in neurology L.I., 1986—; clin. instr., N.Y. Hosp. Mem. Am. Acad. Neurology. Republican. Jewish.

KLINT, KENNETH, physician; b. Seattle, Dec. 13, 1936; s. Clarence Walter and Eva Mary (Hollier) K.; m. Sharleen Joann Dawson, June 17, 1960; children: Randall David, Carol Ann, Gary Steven. Student, U. Puget Sound, 1955-56; BA, Whitworth Coll., 1959; postgrad., Cen. Wash. Coll., 1959-60; MD, U. Wash., Seattle, 1964; MPH, U. Tex., Houston, 1980. Diplomate Nat. Med. Examiners. Staff psychiatrist No. State Hosp., Sedro-Woolley, Wash., 1970-71, Ariz. State Hosp., Phoenix, 1971-72; clin. dir. Maricopa County Mental Health Clinic, Phoenix, 1972-76; commd. lt. col. USAF, 1976, advanced through grades to col.; chief flight medicine Sheppard AFB (Tex.) Hosp., 1976-79; dir. aeromed. svcs. Wright-Patterson AFB (Ohio) Hosp., 1981-87; comdr., staff psychiatrist Hill AFB (Utah) Hosp., 1987-91; comdr. staff psychiatrist 24th med. group Howard AFB, Panama, 1991-95; staff psychiatrist Bluegrass Regional Mental Health Bd., Lexington, Ky., 1995—; cons. to surgeon Air Force Logistics Command. Wright-Patterson, 1985-91; clin. instr. in psychiatry Maricopa County Residency Program, Phoenix, 1971-76; asst. clin. prof. com. medicine Wright State U., Dayton, Ohio, 1982-87. Named Air Tng. Command Flight Surgeon of Yr., Soc. USAF Flight Surgeons, 1977. Mem. Assn. Mil. Surgeons of U.S. Republican. Presbyterian.

KLITZMAN, ROBERT LLOYD, physician, author; b. N.Y.C., July 1, 1958; s. Joseph Arthur and Joan Marilyn (Kahn) K. AB, Princeton U., 1980; MD, Yale U., 1985. Diplomate Am. Bd. Psychiatry and Neurology. Rsch. asst. Nat. Inst. Health, Bethesda, Md., 1980-81; researcher Papua New Guinea Inst. Med. Rsch., 1980-81; intern The N.Y. Hosp. Cornell U. Med. Ctr., N.Y.C., 1985-86, resident, 1986-89; fellow Columbia Presbyn. Med. Ctr., N.Y.C., 1989—. Author: A Year-long Night, 1989, In a House of Dreams and Glass, 1995; contbr. articles to profl. jours., chpts. to books. Recipient Keese prize Yale U., 1985; Robert Wood Johnson Found. clin. scholar U. Pa., 1991-93, MacDowell Colony fellow, 1991, DuPont fellow, 1982, Burroughs-Wellcome fellow Am. Psychiat. Assn., 1987, Aaron Diamond Found. fellow, 1993-96, Merck Co. Found. fellow Corp. of Yaddo, 1994, Picker-Commonwealth fellow, 1996—. Mem. PEN, Am. Psychiat. Assn. (mem. N.Y. County dist. br. com. on AIDS 1989—, commn. on AIDS 1988-89, steering com. of AIDS edn. project 1987-88).

KLIVINGTON, KENNETH ALBERT, research administrator; b. Cleve., Sept. 23, 1940; s. Albert Cecil and Evelyn Louise (Groom) K.; m. Karen Jensen, Jan. 4, 1968 (div. Sept. 1975); 1 child, Jason; m. Marie Rose Lopez, Nov. 17, 1975. SB, MIT, 1962; MS, Columbia U., 1964; PhD, Yale U., 1967. Asst. rsch. neuroscientist U. Calif., San Diego, 1967-68; dir. R & D Fisher/Jackson Assocs., N.Y.C., 1968-69; vis. rsch. scientist U. Calif., San Diego, 1973; sr. staff officer Nat. Acad. Scis., Washington, 1975-76; program officer & adminstr. Alfred P. Sloan Found., N.Y.C., 1969-31; v.p. R & D, dir. rsch. Electro-Biology, Inc., Fairfield, N.J., 1981-84; asst. to pres. Salk Inst., San Diego, 1984-93; v.p. sci. Fetzer Inst., Kalamazoo, Mich., 1993—; cons. in field; fellow, chmn. rsch. adv. com. Fetzer Inst., Kalamazoo, 1990-93. Author: Science of Mind, 1989, The Brain, Cognition and Education, 1986; contbr. articles to profl. jours. Mem. Soc. for Neurosci., Cognitive Sci. Soc., Bioelectromagnetic Soc., Internat. Brain Rsch. Orgn.

KLOEHN, RALPH ANTHONY, plastic surgeon; b. Milw., Dec. 18, 1932; s. Ralph Charles and Virginia Mary (Kosak) K.; m. Mary Theresa Landers, Nov. 4, 1961; Children: Colleen, Gregory, Kristine, Patricia, Timothy, Philip, Michelle. BS, Marquette U., 1954, MD, 1958. Diplomate Am. Bd. Plastic Surgery. Rotating intern Charity Hosp. La., New Orleans, 1958-59; gen. surgery resident Marquette U. Hosps., Milw., 1961-65; resident in plastic and maxillofacial surgery U. Tex. Med. Br., Galveston, 1965-68; fellowship in plastic and reconstructive surgery African Med. Rsch. Found., Nairobi, Kenya, 1968-69; pvt. practice medicine specializing in plastic surgery Milw., 1969—; med. cons. Mentor/Sonique Surg. Sys., Santa Barbara, Calif. Contbr. articles to profl. jours. Lt. USNR, 1959-61. Fellow ACS, Internat. Coll. Surgeons; mem. AMA, Am. Soc. Aesthetic Plastic Surgery, Am. Soc. Plastic and Reconstructive Surgery, Singleton Surgical Soc., Am. Soc. Maxillofacial Surgeons, Can. Soc. Aesthetic for (Cosmetic) Plastic Surgery. Republican. Roman Catholic. Home: N14 W 30082 High Ridge Rd # 5 Pewaukee WI 53072 Office: Affiliated Cosmetic and Plastic Surgeons 2323 N Mayfair Rd Ste 503 Milwaukee WI 53226-1507

KLOESEL, GREGORY BERNARD, optometrist; b. Baytown, Tex., Feb. 22, 1964; s. Bernard Edward and Velma Barbara (Kowis) K. BS in Optometry, U. Houston, 1986, OD, 1989. Optometrist 1st Eye Care, Arlington, Tex., North Richland Hills, Tex., Hurst, Tex., 1989—. Mem. Tex. Optometric Assn. (polit. action com. 1988—), Am. Optometric Assn. (contact lens sect., polit. action com. 1988—), Phi Kappa Phi. Home: Ste C 833 W Harwood Rd Apt C Hurst TX 76054-3271 Office: 1st Eye Care 620 W Harwood Rd Hurst TX 76054-3162

KLOETZEL, JOHN ARTHUR, biology educator, cell biology researcher; b. Cambridge, Mass., Mar. 21, 1941; s. Milton Carl and Elizabeth (Gorder) K.; m. Judith Ann Nattress, Aug. 17, 1962; children: Jeffrey, Steven, Jennifer, Melanie. AB, U. So. Calif., 1962; PhD, Johns Hopkins U., 1967. NIH postdoctoral rsch. fellow U. Colo., Boulder, 1967-70; asst. prof. U. Md., Catonsville, 1970-76, assoc. prof., 1976—; vis. assoc. prof. Johns Hopkins Sch. Medicine, Balt., 1987-88. Contbr. rsch. articles to profl. jours. Host family Am. Field Svc., Catonsville, Md., 1987. Alexander von Humboldt Found. rsch. fellow, U. Tübingen, Fed. Republic Germany, 1978; Rsch. grantee NIH, NSF, Am. Cancer Soc. Mem. Am. Soc. Cell Biology, Soc. Protozoologists (exec. com. 1993—), Microscopy Soc. Am., Chesapeake Soc. Microscopy (pres. 1981-82). Office: Univ of Maryland Balt Co Dept Biological Sci Catonsville MD 21250

KLOIN, JAY ELLIOT, physician; b. Bklyn., Feb. 27, 1947; s. Leo H. and Beatrice (Baram) K.; div. May 1995; children: Jennifer, Jacquelyn. MD, U. Paris, 1975. Physician Med. Assoc. of Lehigh Valley, Emmaus, Pa., 1978—; internist Dept. Vets. Affairs, Allentown, Pa., 1979—; staff physician Lehigh Valley Hosp., Allentown, Pa., 1979—, Allentown Osteo. Hosp., 1979—; coord. quality assurance care N.Y. Life, Emmaus, 1995—; asst. clin. prof. medicine Hahnemann U., Phila., 1980—; clin. asst. prof. medicine Pa. State U., Hershey, 1995—; med. dir. Nursefinders, Allentown, 1995—; mem. infectious disease com. Lehigh Valley Hosp. Ctr., mem. geriatrics adv. com., dept. medicine divsn. internal medicine & geriatrics. Physician Parkland High Sch. Sys. Fellow Am. Coll. Physicians; mem. AMA, Am. Soc. Internal Medicine, Pa. Med. Soc. (alt. del.), Lehigh County Med. Soc., Maimonides Soc. (charter). Office: 431 Chestnut St Emmaus PA 18049

KLONOFF, HARRY, psychologist; b. Winnipeg, Man., Can., July 29, 1924; s. Abraham and Ida (Aronovitch) K.; m. Mary Plosker, Aug. 16, 1948; children: Hillary, Pamela, Melanie. BA, U. Man., 1949; MA, U. Toronto, 1951; PhD, U. Wash., 1954. Head dept. psychology Shaughnessy Vets. Hosp., Vancouver, B.C., Can., 1955-61, Shaughnessy Hosp., 1961-77; head divsn. psychology, dept. psychiatry U. B.C., Vancouver, 1961-82, prof., 1970-90, prof. emeritus, 1990—; head dept. psychology Health Scis. Ctr. Hosp., 1981-82; head sect. psychology Vancouver Gen. Hosp., 1970-78. Contbr. articles on psychology and psychiatry to sci. publs., chpts. in books. Served with AUS, 1944-46. Nat. Health Med. Rsch. Coun. grantee, 1968—. Mem. AAAS, APA, Can. Psychol. Assn., Western Psychol. Assn., B.C. Psychol. Assn. (pres. 1957-58), Internat. Neuropsychology Soc., Gerontol. Soc., Assn. Am. Med. Colls., Can. Mental Health Assn. Home: 4533 Belmont Ave, Vancouver, BC Canada V6R 1C5 Office: Fairmont Med Ctr, 807-750 W Broadway, Vancouver, BC Canada V5Z 1H7

KLOOSTER, JUDSON, academic administrator, dentistry educator; b. La Combe, Alta., Can., Dec. 24, 1925; s. Henry J. and Evelyn Mae (Eglin) K.; m. Arlene Jean Madsen, Nov. 28, 1948; children: Cherylin Klooster Peach, Lynette Carol Tibbetts, Terrill Ann Klooster McClanahan Hannum. Student, Andrews U., 1942-43, Pacific Union Coll., 1943-44; DDS, U. Pacific, 1947; MMS, Tulane U., 1968. Pvt. practice dentistry San Francisco, 1947-49, Escondido, Calif., 1949-67; part-time mem. faculty Loma Linda (Calif.) U. Sch. Dentistry, 1956-67, full-time prof. restorative dentistry, 1967—, dir. continuing edn., 1968-72, dean, 1971-94, dean emeritus, 1994—; mem. faculty U. Pacific Sch. Dentistry, 1947-49; cons. USPHS, VA. Treas. Am. Fund for Dental Health, 1987-89, v.p. 1990-91, pres., 1992-93. Lt. Dental Corps USNR, 1953-55. Fellow Am. Coll. Dentists, Internat. Coll. Dentists (councillor); mem. ADA, Calif. Dental Assn. (chmn. coun. dental edn. 1972-75), Tri-County Dental Soc. (ex officio dir. 1971-94, pres.-elect 1978-79, pres. 1979-80), Rotary (pres. San Bernardino S. club 1977-78), Xi Psi Phi. Republican. Mem. Seventh Day Adventist Ch. (elder 1969—). Home: 25131 Crestview Dr Loma Linda CA 92354-3508 Office: Loma Linda U Sch Dentistry Prince Hall Rm 1200 Loma Linda CA 92350

KLOPOTT, ZVI SIMCHA, psychiatrist; b. Petah-Tikva, Israel, Nov. 6, 1948; d. Ludwig Eliezer and Sarah (Czerczewski) K. BA, SUNY, Binghamton, 1970; MD, Albany Med. Coll., 1974. Diplomate Am. Bd. Psychiatry and Neurology, Am. Bd. Child Psychiatry. Consulting psychiatrist Samaritan Hosp., Troy, N.Y., 1978; attending psychiatrist Capital Dist. Psychiatric Ctr., Albany, N.Y., 1977-78; fellow in child psychiatry Albany Med. Coll., 1978-81; co-med. dir. Unified Svcs. for Children and Adolescents of Rensselaer Co., Troy, 1981-86, med. dir., 1986—; cons. child psychiatrist Project Strive, Albany, 1981—, Jewish Family Svcs., Albany, 1986-91; pvt. practice Albany, N.Y., 1981—; assoc. clin. prof. Albany Med. Coll., 1977; cons. child psychiatrist Wildwood Sch., Niskayuna, N.Y., 1986—, Cmty. Maternity Svcs., 1991—; cons. Psych.-Residential Opportunities, Inc., 1992—; lectr. local and nat. confs. on childhood psychopathology, dual diagnosis and emotional disturbance. Named Disting. Tchr. Psychiatry Dept. Albany Med. Coll., 1977. Mem. Capital Dist. Council for Child and Adolescent Psychiatry (pres. 1987-89), Am. Psychiatric Assn., Am. Acad. Psychiatry and Law, Am. Acad. of Child and Adolescent Psychiatry. Office: Bldg 5 Pine West Plaza Ste 508 Albany NY 12205

KLÖPPEL, GÜNTER KARL PAUL, pathology educator, hospital administrator; b. Darmstadt, Hessen, Germany, Apr. 22, 1943; s. Kurt and Elsbeth (Krönke) K.; m. Rita Häge, May 2, 1970; children: Ulrike, Renate, Cordelia. Grad. in medicine, U. Hamburg, Fed. Republic of Germany, 1967, MD, 1970, PhD, 1976. Resident in pathology Inst. Pathology, U. Hamburg, 1970-75, specialist, 1975, lectr., 1976-81, prof., 1981-87; prof., head dept. pathology Acad. Hosp. Jette Free U. Brussels, 1987-95; with dept. pathology Univ. Hosp., Kiel, Germany, 1995—. Editor, author: Pancreatic Pathology, 1984, Atlas of Exocrine Pancreatic Tumors, 1991; co-author:

Diabetic Pancreas, 1985, Functional Endocrine Pathology, 1991, Textbook of Diabetes, 1992, The Pancreas, 1993, Histopatholoy of Endocrine Tumors, 1993, Acute Pancreatitis, 1994, Radiology of the Pancreas, 1994, WHO Classification of Tumors of the Exocrine Pancreas, 1996; mem. editl. bd. Ultrastructural Pathology, Jour. Pathology, Leber-Magen-Darm, Pathology Rsch. and Practice, Endocrine Pathology, Pancreas; mng. editor Virchows Archiv. Recipient Martini prize U. Hamburg, 1972, 81, Voss prize Werner Otto Stiftung, 1982, Ferdinand Bertram prize German Diabetes Orgn., 1983, Konjetzny prize Hamburger Krebsgesellschaft, 1983, Bard Urology award, 1987, Nizze prize German Soc. Urology, 1986, prize Hoechst Aktiengesellschaft Found., Graz, 1987. Mem. German Soc. Pathology, German Diabetes Soc., European Assn. Study Diabetes, European Pancreatic Club, Soc. Histochemistry, Am. Pancreatic Assn., Internat. Acad. Pathology, Pathology Soc. Gt. Britain and Ireland, Internat. Assn. Pancreatology. Office: U Kiel U Hosp Dept Pathology, Michaelisstrasse 11, D-24105 Kiel Germany

KLOSINSKI, DEANNA DUPREE, medical laboratory sciences educator; b. Goshen, Ind., Dec. 28, 1941; d. George C. and Gertrude (Todd) Dupree (dec.); m. Michael A. Klosinski, Jan. 30, 1965; children: Elizabeth, John, Robert, Lara. BS, Ind. State U., 1964; MS, Purdue U., 1972; PhD, Wayne State U., 1990. Diplomate in lab. mgmt. Am. Soc. Clin. Pathologists; cert. med. technologist. Med. technologist South Bend (Ind.) Med. Found., 1959-68; lab. specialist Home Hosp., Lafayette, Ind., 1968-74; program dir. Ind. Vocat. Tech. Coll., Lafayette, 1968-75; clin. asst. prof. Oakland U., Rochester, Mich., 1985—; adj. asst. prof. Wayne State U., Detroit, 1991—, Mich. State U., Lansing, 1991—, chair adv. com. Schs. Allied Health; program dir., asst. adminstr. William Beaumont Hosp., Royal Oak, Mich., 1979—. Author: (videotape, monograph) Blood Collection: The Difficult Draw, 1992; co-author: (videotape, monograph) Blood Collection: The Routine Venipuncture, 1989 (chpt.) Molecular Biology and Pathology, 1993. Mem. pastoral coun. St. Hugo Cath. Ch., Bloomfield Hills, Mich., 1991-94. Named Outstanding Bus. Person Mich. Coun. on Vocat., 1992, Mich. Clin. Lab. Scientist, 1993; rsch. grantee William Beaumont Hosp., 1989-90. Mem. Am. Soc. Clin. Pathologists (chmn. Tech. Sample 1984-93, mem. editl. bd. Lab. Medicine 1993-96, editor Profl. Perspectives 1993-95, Technologist of Yr. 1994), Am. Assn. for Clin. Chemistry (mem. continuing edn. com. 1995-97), Am. Soc. for Clin. Lab. Sci. (mem. edn. sci. assembly, co-chairperson clin. lab. edn. conf. 1991, bd. dirs. edn. and rsch. fund 1996—), Internat. Fed. Clin. Chemistry (edn. & mgmt. divsn. com. programmes & courses 1996—), Assn. Women in Sci., Mich. Soc. for Clin. Lab. Sci. (treas. 1984-86, 88-92, pres. 1995-96, past pres., ann. meeting gen. chair 1996—), Sigma Xi (sec. Oakland U. chpt. 1994-96), Alpha Mu Tau (Scholarship award 1985, 87, 90), Delta Gamma Alumnae (treas. 1978-81, v.p. 1991-93, pres. 1993-95). Home: 90 Devon Rd Bloomfield Hills MI 48302-1119 Office: William Beaumont Hosp 3601 W Thirteen Mile Rd Royal Oak MI 48073-6769

KLOSS, REBECCA KAY, nurse technician; b. Tulsa, Okla., Feb. 16, 1959; d. Bill Dale and Virginia Lee (Benton) Dobbs; m. Robert John Kloss, May 17, 1980; 1 child, Donal. BS magna cum laude, Tex. Woman's U., 1994. RN. Nurse technician Irving (Tex.) Healthcare Sys., 1993-94; school nurse T.A. Howard Intermediate Sch., Mansfield, Tex., 1996—. Bd. dirs., Mayor's Com. for People with Disabilities, Irving, Tex., 1994— (pub. rels. chair, 1994—). Mem. Gamma Beta Phi, Sigma Theta Tau, Phi Theta Phi, Phi Theta Kappa. Home: 900 Branch Creek Mansfield TX 76063

KLOTH, RACHELL DARDEN, herbalist; b. Kinston, N.C., May 7, 1939; d. Johnnie White and Susan Winnifred (Stroud) Spychalla; m. N. Rollie Kloth; children: Jonathan, Janine. D. of Reflexology, Bernadean U., 1982; M. Herbalist, Emerson Coll., Canada, 1984. Cert. reflexologist, iripologist, nutritional cons. cons. in field. Home: 2210 S 57th St Milwaukee WI 53219 Home and Office: Kloth Health House 2210 S 57th St Milwaukee WI 53219-2205 Office: Kloth's Root Cellar 400 S Linwood Ave Appleton WI 54914

KLOTZ, LINDA KATHERINE, nursing educator; b. Carlsbad, N.Mex., June 26, 1948; d. Robert Inzer and Steva L. (Krensavage) Naylor. BSN, U. N.Mex., 1970; MSN, U. Ariz., 1978; PhD, U. Tex., 1986. Asst. head nurse Alaska Native Med. Ctr., Anchorage, 1970-73; charge nurse Harper Hosp., Detroit, 1973; edn. coordinator United Hosps., Detroit, 1974-76; instr. Pima Community Coll., Tucson, 1978-82, U. Ariz., Tucson, 1980-82; assoc. prof. U. Tex., Tyler, 1982—, dir. divsn. of nursing, 1993—; med. coord. Alaska Coun. on Drug Aid, Anchorage, 1970-73; edn. coord. Hospice of East Tex., Tyler, 1984—, mem. edn. com., 1986—; rsch. cons. Cmty. Group Oncology Program, 1986—; mem. program com. Am. Heart Assn., 1986-94. Bd. dirs. Am. Cancer Soc., Tyler, 1984—; bd. trustees Columbia-Longview (Tex.) Regional Med. Ctr., 1996—. Noyes Found. scholar, 1966-70; Univ. fellow, U. Tex., 1985. Mem. Nat. League Nursing, Tex. Nurses Assn. (pres. 1984-85), Oncology Nurses Soc. (membership chairperson 1986-87), Nature Conservancy. Roman Catholic.

KLOTZ, RICHARD DAVID, ophthalmologist; b. N.Y.C., Sept. 6, 1942; m. Barbara Joan Caplin, Feb. 19, 1972; children: Alison, Evan, Julie. BA, Grinnell Coll., 1964; MD, SUNY, Syracuse, 1968. Diplomate Am. Bd. Ophthalmology. Intern USPHS Hosp., San Francisco, 1968-69; resident North Shore Univ. Hosp., Cornell Univ. Med. Sch., 1970-73; pvt. practice, owner Pacifica Laser Eye Ctr., Huntington Beach, Calif., 1981—; chief of surgery Pacifica Hosp., Huntington Beach, 1992, 93. Bd. dirs. MD EyePac of Calif., San Francisco, 1984-95. With USPHS, 1968-70. Fellow Am. Acad. Ophthalmology; mem. AMA (Physician Recognition award 1973—), Calif. Assn. Ophthalmology (bd. dirs. 1984—). Office: Pacifica Laser Eye Ctr 18800 Main St #101 Huntington Beach CA 92648

KLOVE, HALLGRIM, psychologist, educator; b. Moss, Norway, June 22, 1927; s. Olav and Gudrun (Skram) K.; widowed; children: Brynjulf, Kari, Erik. PhD, U. Oslo, Norway, 1952. Intern in psychology Nat. Hosp., Oslo, 1950-51, staff psychologist, 1952-54; Smith-Mundt, Fullbright fellow Ind. U., Bloomington, 1954-55; rsch. fellow, asst. prof. Med. Sch. Ind. U., Indpls., 1955-62; from assoc. prof. to prof. Med. sch. U. Wis., Madison, 1962-71; prof. psychology U. Bergen, Norway, 1971—; assoc. dean U. Bergen, 1974-76, dean, 1977-85; Editor, cons., contbr. articles to sci. jours. Editor: International Jour. Experimental and Clinical Neuropsychology. Fellow Am. Psychol. Assn.; mem. Am. Acad. Neurology, Norwegian Psychol. Assn. (diplomate), Internat. Neuropsychol. Soc. (pres. 1985-86). Home: Fantoftassen 21A, N-5032 Bergen-Minde Norway Office: U Bergen, Dept Neuropsychology, Aarstadv 21, N-5009 Bergen Norway

KLUCK, CLARENCE JOSEPH, physician; b. Stevens Point, Wis., June 20, 1929; s. Joseph Bernard and Mildred Lorraine (Helminiak) K.; divorced; children: Paul Bernard, Annette Louise Kluck Winston, David John, Maureen Ellen. BS in Med. Sci., U. Wis., 1951, MD, 1954. Resident San Joaquin Hosp., French Camp, Calif., 1955-56; asst. instr. medicine Ohio State U., Columbus, 1958-60; physician, chief of medicine Redford Med. Ctr., Detroit, 1960-69; practice medicine specializing in internal medicine Denver, 1969-83; med. dir. Atlantic Richfield Co., Denver, 1983-85; corp. med. dir. Cyprus Minerals Co., Englewood, Colo., 1985-92; pres. Kluck Med. Assocs., Englewood, 1992—; bd. dirs. Climbo Catering, Detroit, 1967-69, Met. Labs., Denver, 1970-81, Provost, Inc., Denver, 1985-92; pres., CEO, chmn. bd. Corpcare, Inc., Englewood, 1992—; CEO, pres. Corpcare Med. Assocs., P.C., 1992—; pres. Denver Occupational and Aviation Medicine Clinic, P.C., 1995—. Contbr. articles to profl. jours. Served to capt. U.S. Army, 1956-58. Recipient Century Club award Boy Scouts Am., 1972. Fellow Am. Occupational Med. Assn., Am. Coll. Occupational and Environ. Medicine, Am. Coll. Occupational Medicine; mem. Am. Acad. Occupational Medicine, Rocky Mountain Acad. Occupational Medicine (bd. dirs. 1985-88), Arapahoe County Med. Soc., Denver Med. Soc. (del. 1973-74, council mem. 1981-87), Colo. Med. Soc. (del. 1973-74, 81-87), Am. Mining Congress Health Commn., Am. Soc. Internal Medicine, Colo. Soc. Internal Medicine. Roman Catholic. Clubs: Flatirons (Boulder, Colo.); Metropolitan. Office: Ste 200 3700 Havana St Denver CO 80239

KLUCKA, CHARLES VINCENT, osteopath; b. Detroit, Sept. 2, 1960; s. A. Robert and Shirley A. (Brothers) K. BArch, U. Notre Dame, 1983, BS, 1984; DO, Tex. Coll. Osteo. Medicine, Ft. Worth, 1988. Diplomate Am. Bd. Internal Medicine. Intern Grandview Hosp., Dayton, Ohio, 1988-89; resident in internal medicine Henry Ford Hosp., Detroit, 1989-92, allergy and clin. immunology fellow, 1992-94; pvt. practice Ft. Meyers, Fla., 1994—. Named Allergy Fellow of Yr., Mich. Allergy Soc., 1994. Mem. Am. Acad. Allergy, Asthma, and Immunology, Am. Coll. Allergy, Asthma, and Immunology, Am. Osteo. Assn., Fla. Osteo. Med. Assn. Office: 2684 Swamp Cabbage Ct Fort Myers FL 33901-9332

KLUFT, GERALD MCELROY, periodontist; b. Glen Ridge, N.J., Apr. 20, 1947; s. Ernest Joseph and Dorothy (McElroy) K.; m. Dana Kay Baumgardner, Aug. 15, 1970; children: Ryan, Troy, Jonathon. BS in Chemistry, U. Fla., 1969; DDS, Med. Coll. Va., Richmond, 1973; Cert. in Periodontics, U. Ky., 1975. Pvt. practice, Periodontal Assocs., Tampa, Fla., 1975—; bd. dirs. The Terrace Bank Fla., Tampa; treas. Pilot Bancshares, 1995—. Pres. Corpus Christi Sch. Bd., Tampa, 1984-85; mem. governing bd. Acad. Holy Names, Tampa, 1989. Pres. Corpus Christi Sch. Bd., Tampa, 1984-85; mem. governing bd. Acad. Holy Names, Tampa. Fellow Internat. Coll. Dentists; mem. ADA, Am. Acad. Periodontology, So. Acad. Periodontology, Fla. Soc. Periodontists (pres. 1984-85), U. South Fla. Green Jacket Club (bd. dirs. 1986-91). Republican. Roman Catholic. Home: 16408 Avila Blvd Tampa FL 33613-1033 Office: Periodontal Assocs 5208 E Fowler Ave Ste F Tampa FL 33617-2152

KLUIBER, RUDOLPH MARK, colon and rectal surgeon; b. Hackensack, N.J., Oct. 18, 1961; s. Rudolph Ward and Mary Ann Kluiber. BA, Northwestern U., 1982, MD, 1986. Diplomate Am. Bd. Surgery, Am. Bd. Colon and Rectal Surgery. Resident Rush Presbyn. St. Luke's Med. Ctr., Chgo., 1986-91, Mayo Clinic, Rochester, Minn., 1991-92; asst. clin. prof. Med. Coll. Wis., Milw., 1993—; surgeon Milw. Med. Clinic, 1992—. Bd. dirs. Crohn's Colitis Found., Milw., 1992-93, med. advisor, 1994—. Fellow ACS; mem. Am. Soc. Colon and Rectal Surgeons, Milw. Acad. Surgery. Office: Milw Med Clinic 3003 W Good Hope Rd Milwaukee WI 53217

KLUMP, RICHARD, urologist; b. Cleve., Dec. 16, 1958; s. George and Magdalena (Gass) K. BS, Ohio State U., 1981; MD, Med. Coll. Ohio, 1985. Diplomate Am. Bd. Urology. Resident Ohio State U., Columbus, 1986-90; staff Olathe (Kans.) Med. Ctr., 1990-92; pvt. practice Mid-Ohio Urology, Inc., Columbus, 1992—. Author original rsch. in vivo, 1990. Fellow ACS. Office: Mid Ohio Urology Inc 5965 E Broad St Columbus OH 43213

KLUSMEYER, PAUL WADE, microbiologist; b. Americus, Mo., Dec. 10, 1919; s. Oscar Charles and Mabel Clare (Cundiff) K.; m. Shirley Maxine Thomas, Sept. 3, 1950; 1 child, Paula Sue. BS, U. Mo., 1949, MS, 1950. Milk insp. City of St. Joseph (Mo.), 1950-53; county sanitarian, Jefferson County, Mo., 1953-54; bacteriology lab. technician Mo. Div. Health, Jefferson City, 1954-58; bacteriologist Henningsen Foods, Springfield, Mo., 1958-69; microbiologist Wilson Foods Corp., Oklahoma City, 1969-89; pres. OKLABS, Inc., Oklahoma City, 1989-96, ret. 1996. Served with AUS, 1942-45. Decorated Purple Heart, Combat ribbon with three stars. Mem. Am. Public Health Assn., Am. Soc. Microbiology, Internat. Assn. Milk, Food and Environ. Sanitarians, Inst. Food Technologist (treas. Okla. sect. 1979-90). Republican. Methodist. Home: 1808 Guilford Ln Oklahoma City OK 73120-4731

KLUTZOW, FRIEDRICH WILHELM, neuropathologist; b. Bandoeng, Preanger, Indonesia, Aug. 6, 1923; came to U.S., 1953; s. Rudolph F.W. and Pauline (Van Thiel) K.; m. Apr. 2, 1954; children: Judith A., Michael J. MD, U. Utrecht, Netherlands, 1951. Diplomate Am. Bd. Neuropathology and Anatomic Pathology. Chief staff Community Meml. Hosp., Oconto Falls, Wis., 1965-68; pathology resident U. Wis., Madison, 1968-72; neuropathologist VA Hosp., Mpls., 1972-75; dir. pathology dept. VA Hosp., Brockton, Mass., 1975-83, Wichita, Kans., 1983-87; chief staff VA Hosp., Bath, N.Y., 1987-90; neuropathologist VA Hosp., Bay Pines, Fla., 1991—; clin. assoc. prof. pathology U. Rochester (N.Y.) Sch. Medicine, U. South Fla., Tampa. Prin. author: Neuropathology Manual: The Practical Approach, 1996; contbr. articles to profl. jours. Col. USAR, 1979-85. Paul Harris fellow Rotary Internat., Bath, 1990; recipient Outstanding Career award Dept. Vet. Affairs, Bath, 1990. Fellow Coll. Am. Pathologists; mem. Am. Assn. Neuropathologists. Republican. Home: PO Box 7846 Sarasota FL 34278-7846

KLYMAN, FRED IRWIN, managed healthcare executive; b. Memphis, Feb. 23, 1946; s. Joseph and Lena (O'Mell) K.; m. Suzanne Bowman; children: Marnie O'Mell, Alicia Catherine. AA, Memphis State U., 1966, BS, 1967, MEd, 1970; EdD, Okla. State U., 1973. Instr. dept. sociology Memphis State U., 1970-71; asst. prof. dept. adminstrn. of justice Wichita (Kans.) State U., 1971-75; assoc. prof. crime study ctr. So. Ill. U., Carbondale, 1976-78; tng. comdr. police acad. Memphis Police Dept., 1978-86; asst. program dir., prof. Health Care Adminstrn. Baccalaureate program Tusculum Coll., Memphis, 1986-89; dir. provider rels. CIGNA Health Plan, Memphis, 1989-92; regional dir. provider rels. Healthsource Tenn., Inc., Memphis, 1993—; cons. police tng. Kans. Atty. Gen., Topeka, 1973-76; cons. Wichita Police Dept., 1974-76; lectr. Nat. Acad. FBI, Quantico, Va., 1975-76; adj. lectr. Shelby County Sheriff's Acad., Memphis, 1988—. Editor: POlice Roles in a Changing Community, 1972, Accountability and the Criminal Justice Instructor, 1973, Introduction to Law Enforcement, 1975, Introduction to Police Administration, 1978. Tng. officer res. bur. Shelby County Sheriff's Dept., Memphis, 1987—. Recipient Police Neighborhood Svc. Ctr. award U.S. Dept. Justice, 1973, Police Community Rels. Inst. award U.S. Dept. Justice, 1974, Community-Centered Crime Prevention award U.S. HUD, 1978, Police Roles in Sch. Crime Prevention award U.S. Dept. Justice, 1975, Crime Prevention Tng. award U.S. Dept. Justice, 1985. Mem. Mid-South Med. Mgmt. Assn. Jewish. Home: 1728 Maiden Cv Memphis TN 38139-3253 Office: Healthsource Tenn Inc 1790 Kirby Pky Memphis TN 38138-7420

KMETZ, DONALD R., academic administrator. Dean Sch. Medicine U. Louisville, 1981—, v.p. health affairs, 1992—. Office: U Louisville Sch Medicine Health Scis Ctr Louisville KY 40292

KMUCHA, STEVEN THOMAS, physician, surgeon; b. Wis., June 23, 1958; s. Thomas Vernon and Lenore Eleanor (Hirst) K. BA in German Lit., U. Ill., Urbana, 1979, BS in Biochemistry, 1980, MS in Physiology, 1980; MD, U. Ill., Chgo., 1984. Diplomate Am. Bd. Otolaryngology. Intern in gen. surgery Yale-New Haven Hosp., New Haven, Conn., 1984-85; resident Yale U., 1984-88, chief resident, 1988-89, clin. instr. surgery, 1988-89; pvt. practice San Francisco & Daly City, Calif., 1990—; clin. isntr. surgery Stanford U., 1989-94; med. dir. Preferred Benefits Adminstrs., San Mateo, Calif., 1995—; vis. prof. Boehringer-Ingelheim Pharm., Ridgefield, Conn., 1995—. Author: (with others) Essential Otolaryngology, 5th edit., 1991, 6th edit., 1995; cons. editor Krames med. Pub., 1994—; contbr. articles to profl. jours. Recipient Silver medal XIV World Congress Otorhinolaryngology, 1989; named Best Drs. in Bay Area, San Francisco Focus, 1994. Fellow ACS, Am. Bd. Otolaryngology, Am. Acad. Otolaryngic Allergy, Am. Acad. Otolaryngology; mem. Calif. Med. Assn., San Mateo County Med. Assn. (bd. dirs., bioethics com., legis. com.), Hearing Soc. Bay Area, Physicians for Human Rights, Alpha Phi Omega (life), Alpha Omega Alpha. Office: 490 Post St # 500 San Francisco CA 94102 also: 1800 Sullivan Ave # 604 Daly City CA 94015

KNABE, GEORGE WILLIAM, JR., pathologist, educator; b. Grand Rapids, Mich., June 29, 1924; s. George William and Dorothy Emma (Fischofer) K.; m. Lorine Jeanette Moffit, Jan. 16, 1954; children: Katharine J., Elizabeth J., Ann C., Dorothy M. Student, Mich. State U., 1942-43, The Citadel, Charleston, SC, 1943-44, Johns Hopkins U., 1944-45; MD, U. Md., 1949. Diplomate Am. Bd. Pathology. Intern Balt. City Hosp., 1949-50; resident pathology Cleve. Clin. Found., 1950-51, Henry Ford Hosp., Detroit, 1953-54; chief lab. svc. VA Ctr., Dayton, Ohio, 1955-57; vis. prof. pathology U. El Salvador Sch. Medicine, 1957-59; asst. prof. pathology U. P.R. Sch. Medicine, 1959-60; prof., chmn. dept. pathology Sch. Medicine, U. S.D., 1960-68, dean., 1967-72; dir. med. edn. St. Luke's Hosp., Duluth, 1972-78; prof. pathology U. Minn.-Duluth Sch. Medicine, 1972—, assoc. dean clin. affairs., 1972-76; chief. dept. pathology Virginia (Minn.) Regional Med. Ctr., 1978—; bd. dirs Health Systems Agy. of Western Lake Superior, Duluth 1975-82, Northern Lakes Health Care Consortium, 1984—, U. Minn. Health & Med. Sch. Adv. Groups 1972—. 1st lt. to capt. M.C., USAF, 1951-53; surgeon to capt., USPHS Res., 1957—. Mem. AMA, U.S. and Can. Acad. Pathology, Am. Soc. Clin. Pathologists, Coll. Am. Pathologists. Home: 1008 S 7th Ave Virginia MN 55792-3151 Office: Va Regional Med Ctr 901 9th St N Virginia MN 55792-2325

KNAFO, DANIELLE SYLVIA, clinical psychologist; b. Morocco, Mar. 18, 1953; d. Maurice and Rosine (Cohen) Knafo. BA magna cum laude, Tel Aviv U., Israel, 1977, MA magna cum laude, 1979; PhD, CUNY, 1987; cert. in psychoanalysis, NYU, 1992; postgrad., Inst. Psychoanalytic Tng., 1994. Clin. psychology intern Bronx (N.Y.) Psychiatric Ctr., 1984-85; dir. psychol. svcs. St. Barnabas Hosp., Bronx, 1986-88; pvt. practice N.Y.C., 1987—; psychodiagnostician Holliswood (N.Y.) Hosp., 1988-89; supervising psychologist Bronx-Lebanon Hosp. Ctr., 1988-90; adj. lectr. CCNY, Bklyn. Coll., 1982-83, New Sch. Social Rsch., 1983-84; mem. faculty Eugene Lang Coll., 1989—, Tel-Aviv U., 1995—; clin. supr. grad. psychology program Pace U., 1988—; program content cons. telecourse on abnormal psychology, PBS; clin. adj. CUNY PhD Clin. Psych. Program, 1996. Author: Egon Schiele: A Self in Creation, 1993; reviewer jours. Hosp. and Cmty. Psychiatry, 1988—, Psychoanalytic Books, Contemporary Psychology. Counselor St. Vincent's Hosp. Rape Crisis Program, 1981-84; dir. Suicide Prevention Program, Bronx, 1986-88. Fellow NIMH, 1981, BRA Found. fellow, 1987, Faculty Devel. Fund fellow, 1991. Mem. Am. Psychol. Assn., Internat. Psychoanalytic Assn., N.Y. Acad. Scis., World Fed. for Mental Health, Internat. Psychohistory Assn. (rsch. assoc.), Israel Psychol. Assn., Women Psychoanalysts (study group). Office: 2166 Broadway Apt 14F New York NY 10024-6671

KNAPP, DAVID ALLAN, pharmaceutical educator, researcher; b. Cleve., Feb. 25, 1938; s. Frederick Allan and Ethel R. (Ogden) K.; m. Deanne Evander, June 2, 1962; 1 child, Wendy Kay Knapp Steagall. BS, Purdue U., 1960, MS, 1962, PhD, 1965. Lic. pharmacist. Asst. prof. Coll. Pharmacy Ohio State U., Columbus, 1964-67, assoc. prof., 1967-71; assoc. prof., now prof. Sch. Pharmacy U. Md., Balt., 1971—, assoc. dean grad. edn. and rsch., 1981-83, chmn. dept. pharm. practice and adminstrn. sci., 1987-91, dir. Ctr. on Drugs and Pub. Policy, 1987—, acting dean Sch. Pharmacy, 1989-91, dean, 1991—; vis. scholar U. Mich. Sch. Pub. Health, 1970-71; intramural researcher Nat. Ctr. for Health Svc. Rsch., Dept. HHS, Hyattsville, Md., 1978; scholar in residence Am. Assn. Colls. Pharmacy, Alexandria, Va., 1986-87. Author: Pharmacy Drugs and Medical Care, 5 edits., 1972-92; contbr. articles to profl. jours. Recipient numerous grants and contracts. Fellow AAAS, APHA, Am. Assn. Pharm. Scientists, Am. Found. Pharm. Edn. (bd. dirs. 1994—, exec. com. 1995—); mem. Am. Assn. Colls. Pharmacy (bd. dirs. 1986-89, 93—, Volwiler Rsch. Gold medal 1986, pres. 1994-95), Am. Pharm. Assn. (rsch. achievement award 1984), Am. Soc. Hosp. Pharmacists (commn. on goals 1996), Sigma Xi, Rho Chi. Unitarian. Office: Sch Pharmacy U Md at Balt 20 N Pine St Baltimore MD 21201-1142

KNAPP, DON BRODERICK, II, physician; b. Pitts., July 18, 1938; s. Don Broderick and Sara Elizabeth (Wallace) K. AB, Dartmouth Coll., 1960; MD, Jefferson Med. Coll., 1964. Diplomate Am. Bd. Ophthalmology. Rotating intern Mound Park Hosp., St. Petersburg, Fla., 1964-65, gen. surgery resident, 1965-66; ophthalmology residency McGuire VA Hosp./MCV, Richmond, Va., 1966-69; ophthalmologist U.S. Army, Tokyo, 1969-71; asst. chief ophthalmology U.S. Army Hosp./Tripler, Honolulu, 1971-72; pvt. practice ophthalmology St. Petersburg, 1972—. Maj. U.S. Army, 1969-72. Office: 6499 30th Ave N B-1 Saint Petersburg FL 33710

KNAPP, HOWARD RAYMOND, internist, clinical pharmacologist; b. Red Bank, N.J., Oct. 5, 1949; s. Howard Raymond and Jane Marie (Ray) K.; m. Brenda Louise Carr, 1984; 1 child, Matthew. AB in Biology, Washington U., St. Louis, 1971; MD, Vanderbilt U., 1977, PhD in Pharmacology, 1984. Diplomate Am. Bd. Internal Medicine; lic., Iowa, Tenn. Asst. prof. medicine and pharmacology Vanderbilt U., Nashville, 1984-89, assoc. prof., 1990; assoc. prof. internal medicine and pharmacology U. Iowa, Iowa city, 1990—, assoc. dir. NIH Clin. Rsch. Ctr., 1991—; mem. NIH Nutrition Study Sect., Bethesda, Md., 1994—cons. pharm. firms, grant orgns. and govtl. entities. Editor-in-chief Lipids, 1995—; contbr. numerous articles to profl. jours., chpts. to books. Grantee NIH, Am. Heart Assn., others. Fellow ACP, Am. Heart Assn. (vascular biol. rsch. rev. com. 1993-95, arteriosclerosis coun.); mem. Ctrl. Soc. for Clin. Rsch. (chair clin. pharmacol. sect. 1992-95), Am. Soc. for Clin. Pharmacology and Therapeutics. Office: U Iowa Div Clin Pharm Dept Int Med C31-P Gen Hosp Iowa City IA 52242

KNAPP, LOIS ESTELLE, occupational medicine physician; b. Washington, July 8, 1938; d. Doris (Carlton) K. MD, George Washington U., 1961. Cert. in occupl. medicine, pub. health & preventive medicine, pediat. Commd. USN, 1960, advanced through ranks to lt. col., 1981; intern George Washington U. Hosp., 1962; jr. asst. pediatric resident N.C. Bapt. Hosp., Winston-Salem, N.C., 1963; sr. pediatric resident Charleston (W.Va.) Area Med. Ctr., 1964; dir. vaccination asst. project W.Va. Health Dept., Charleston, 1964-66; surgeon, commd. pediatrician USPHS, Shiprock, N.Mex., 1966-68; pediatrician W.Va. Health Dept., Charleston, 1968-81; chief occupl. medicine Darnell Army Cmty. Hosp., Fort Hood, Tex., 1981-87, Wm. Beaumont Army Med. Ctr., El Paso, Tex., 1987-89, U.S. Army Med. Clinic, Toole, Utah, 1991-93, U.S. Army Hosp., Ft. Huachuca, Ariz., 1993-95; med. dir. Mine Safety Health Adminstrn., Arlington, Va., 1995—. Contbr. articles to profl. jours. Mem. adv. bd. City of South Charleston, W.Va., 1980; Tex. state dir. Am. Med. Women's Assn., 1983-85. Master Am. Coll. Occupl. Medicine; fellow Am. Coll. Preventive Medicine, Am. Assn. Pediatricians; mem. Acad. Medicine, Tchrs. Preventive Medicine and Pub. Health, W.Va. State Med. Assn., Kanawha County Med. Soc. Home: 5300 Columbia Pike # 807 Arlington VA 22204

KNAPP, MICHAEL EDWARD, clinical psychologist; b. Portland, Oreg., June 25, 1949; s. Winchell Elwood and Corabelle (Edes) K.; m. Patricia Ann Knapp, Aug. 18, 1992; 1 child, Nathan Michael. BS in Psychology, So. Oreg. State Coll., Ashland, 1971; MS in Psychology, N.Mex. Highlands U., Las Vegas, 1972; PhD in Clin. Psychology, U. Mont., 1982. Lic. clin. psychologist, Oreg. Children's specialist Cumberland River Mental Health Clnic, Corbin, Ky., 1972-73; staff psychologist Baker County Mental Health Clinic, Baker City, Oreg., 1973-74; children's behavior specialist JacksonCounty Edn. Svc. Dist., Medford, Oreg., 1974-76, sch. psychologist, 1976-78; pvt. practice psychologist assoc. Ashland, Oreg., 1976-78; psychologist trainee Mont. State Prison, Deer Lodge, 1978-79; testing cons. Missoula (Mont.) Sch. Dist. #1, 1980-81; psychologist intern Atascadero (Calif.) State Hosp., 1981-82, psychologist resident, 1982-83; pvt. practice Ashland, 1983—. Mem. APA, Assn. for Treatment of Sex Abusers, Oreg. Psychol. Assn. Office: 1875 Hwy 99N # 1 Ashland OR 97520

KNAPP, MILDRED FLORENCE, social worker; b. Detroit, Apr. 15, 1932; d. Edwin Frederick and Florence Josephine (Antaya) K.; BBA, U. Mich., 1954, MA in Cmty. and Adult Edn. (Mott Found. fellow 1964), 1964, MSW (HEW grantee 1966), 1967. Dist. dir. Girl Scouts Met. Detroit, 1954-63; planning asst. Coun. Social Agys. Flint and Genessee County, 1965; sch. social worker Detroit public schs., 1967—; field instr. grad. social workers. Mem. alumnae bd. govs. U. Mich., 1972-75, scholarship chmn., 1969-70, 76-80, chmn. spl. com. women's athletics, 1972-75, class agt. fund raising Sch. Bus. Adminstrn., 1978-79; mem. Founders Soc. Detroit Inst. Art, 1969—, Friends Children's Mus. Detroit, 1978—, Women's Assn., Detroit Symphony Orch., 1982-89, Mich. Humane Soc., 1991—; vol. Coun. Detroit Symphony Orch., 1990—; trustee, fin. chmn. Children's Mus. Recipient various certs. appreciation. Mem. Nat. Assn. Social Workers, Acad. Cert. Social Workers, Nat. Cmty. Edn. Assn. (charter), Sch. Social Work Assn. Am. (charter), Outdoor Edn. and Camping Coun. (charter), Mich. Sch. Social Workers Assn. (pres. 1980-81), Detroit Sch. Social Workers Assn. (past pres.), Detroit Assn. U. Mich. Women (pres. 1980-82), Detroit Fedn. Tchrs. Methodist. Home: 702 Lakepointe St Grosse Pointe MI 48230-1706 Office: Longfellow Annex Rm 247 13141 Rosa Parks Blvd Detroit MI 48238

KNAPP, NANCY HAY, mental health administrator; b. Cleve., June 2, 1922; d. Henry Homer and Aurore Louise (LaCroix) Hay; m. Richard Dominick Knapp, Sept. 11, 1955; 1 child, Pamela Hay. BA, Hunter Coll., 1957; MSEd in Counseling Psychology, U. Pa., 1971, EdD in Counseling Psychology, 1987. Nat. cert. counselor; clin. assoc. Am. Bd. Med. Psychotherapists. Career and edn. counselor Johnson O'Connor Rsch. Found., N.Y.C., 1950-53; counselor, report writer The Pers. Lab., N.Y.C., 1953-63; cons. Chapel Hill, N.C., 1963-65; cons., Phila., 1965-69; counseling dir. Resources for Women U. Pa., Phila., 1972-78; dir. profl. svcs. Crossroads Career Planning Corp., Phila., 1978-80; dir. consultation and edn. Crozer-Chester Med. Ctr., Upland, Pa., 1980-90, chmn. staff tng. com., 1985-90; pvt. practice counseling, couples and family therapy, 1971—; mem.

faculty Main Line Sch. Night, Ardmore, Pa., 1978-80; trainer Pa. Dept. Health, Harrisburg, 1982-85. Author: (tng. manuals) Prevention: Drug Misuse, 1983, Growing, Together, 1985. Bd. dirs. Resources for Women, U. Pa., Phila., 1976-80; mem. steering com. Coalition for Edn./Placement of Women, Phila., 1976-78, coord., 1978-80; mem. Chester (Pa.) Vocat./Ednl. Outreach, 1980-82, dir., 1982-84. Recipient Community Devel. award Pa. Cons. Edn. Coun., 1981; grantee Pa. Dept. Health, 1981, 83. Mem. Am. Counseling Assn., APA (assoc.), Cons. Assn. Greater Phila., Phi Delta Kappa. Home: 326 Sprague Rd Narberth PA 19072-1124

KNAPP, PETER M., JR., urologist; b. Patterson, N.J., Nov. 11, 1954; m. Barbara Brinkman, May 3, 1978; children: Laura, Michael, Emily. MD, Ind. U., 1980. Intern U. Mich. Hosps., Ann Arbor, 1980-81, resident, 1981-85; pvt. practice GU Surgeons of Ind., Indpls., 1985—; clin. asst. prof. urology Ind. U. Sch. Medicine, Indpls., 1987—. Office: GU Surgeons of Ind 1801 N Senate Blvd Indianapolis IN 46202

KNAPP, WILLIAM ARNOLD, JR., veterinarian; b. Atlanta, Oct. 4, 1925; s. William Arnold and Nella (Bricken) K.; m. Mary Agnes Reed, Aug. 11, 1950; children: Ellen, Sharon, Carol. DVM, U. Ga., 1951, MS, 1964. Pvt. practice Decatur, Ala., 1952-54; asst. prof. coll. vet. medicine U. Ga., Athens, 1954-62; dir. research Morris Rsch. Labs., Topeka, Kans., 1962-65; assoc. dir. toxicology div. Hazleton Labs, Inc., Vienna, Va., 1965-67; pres. Hazleton Research Animals, Inc., Vienna, 1967-71; dir. animal sci. products div. Flow Labs., Inc., McLean, Va., 1971-75; v.p. Flow Labs., Inc., McLean, 1975-83; cons. indsl. vet. W.A. Knapp Assocs., Raleigh, N.C., 1983—; vis. prof. pharmacology N.C. State U. Coll. Vet. Medicine, 1983-87, adj. prof., 1987-89. Tech. sgt. U.S. Army, 1943-46. Mem. Am. Assn. Indsl. Vets. (Indsl. Vet. of Yr. 1977), Am. Vet. Med. Assn., U.S. Animal Health Assn., Rotary. Methodist. Office: WA Knapp Assocs 3212 Queens Rd Raleigh NC 27612-6233

KNAPTON, PAUL MICHAEL, general practitioner; b. Leeds, Yorkshire, Eng., Aug. 16, 1958; s. John Kenneth and Barbara (Knipe) K. MB, Cambridge (Eng.) U., 1982, BChir, 1982, MA, 1983. Diplomate Royal Coll. of Obs-Gyns. Gen. practitioner Cambridge, 1987-95, locum gen. practitioner, 1995—; supr. physiology Corpus Christie Coll., Cambridge, 1988—; lectr. clin. medicine Cambridge U., 1989-95, trainer in gen. practice, 1991-95; gen. practice tutor Addenbrooks Postgrad. Ctr., 1994—. Mem. Royal Coll. Gen. Practitioners. Anglican. Home: 94 Shelford Rd, Cambridge CB2 2NF, England

KNAUER, WILLIAM JEROME, JR., ophthalmologist, educator; b. Jacksonville, Fla., Aug. 7, 1924. Student U. Fla., 1942-44; M.D., George Washington U., 1948. Diplomate Am. Bd. Ophthalmology, 1953. Intern Emory U., Atlanta, 1948-49; resident Johns Hopkins Hosp. Wilmer Eye Inst., Balt., 1949-52, 54-56; pvt. practice ophthalmology, Jacksonville, Fla., 1956—, chief dept. ophthalmology St. Vincent's Med. Ctr., Jacksonville, 1961-75, chief med. and dental staff, 1975-76, presently mem. staff; mem. staff Riverside Hosp., Jacksonville; mem. courtesy staff Bapt. Meml., St. Luke's, Univ. hosps., Jacksonville; instr. ophthalmology U. Fla., Gainesville. Bd. dirs. Young Life, 1969-71; vestryman St. Mark's Episcopal Ch., 1957-70; bd. dirs. Mental Health Assn., 1959-62; trustee Bartram Sch., 1972-74; exec. com. United Fund; mem. Com. 100 and 2 per cent Club, Jacksonville. Fellow Am. Bd. Ophthalmology, Am. Acad. Ophthalmology and Otolaryngology, ACS, Soc. Eye Surgeons; mem. Am. Soc. Contemporary Ophthalmology, Duval County Med. Soc. (sec. 1958), Fla. Med. Assn., AMA, So. Med. Assn., Internat. Glaucoma Congress, Duval County Soc. Ophthalmology (pres. 1958), Fla. Soc. Ophthalmology, Found. for Sight (chmn., bd. dirs.), Assn. Cryosurgery, Am. Intraocular Lens Implant Soc., U.S. Eye Study Club (pres. 1973), Soc. Cons. Clin. Ophthalmologists, Contact Lens Assn. Am., Smith-Reed Russell Soc., William Beaumont Soc., Sigma Alpha Epsilon. Clubs: Rotary (bd. dirs. 1982-84), Ye Mystic Revelers (capt. 1974, king 1980), Fla. Yacht, Timuquana Country (bd. govs. 1967-69), Ponte Vedra, River, Tournament Players Championship Assn. Contbr. articles to med. jours. Office: 2535 Riverside Ave Jacksonville FL 32204-4710

KNAUFF, HANS GEORG, physician, educator; b. Bad Hersfeld, Germany, July 8, 1927; s. Friedrich and Sophie (Sauer) K.; student U. Erlangen, 1947-49, U. Freiburg, 1949, U. Basel, 1949-51, U. Heidelberg, 1951-52; Dr. Med., U. Heidelberg, 1953; m. Sigrid W. Keppner, Aug. 28, 1956; children—Ursula v. Wrangel, Barbara K. Asst., pharmacology dept. Heidelberg (W. Ger.) U., 1953; with pharmacology dept. Univ. Coll., London, 1953, Royal Coll. Surgeons, London, 1954; with Pathol. Inst., Heidelberg U., 1955, Med. Clinic, U. Munchen, 1955-63; privat dozent for internal medizin München and Marburg, 1961-67; prof. internal medizin, 1967; prof. Med. Clinic, U. Marburg (W. Ger.), 1967-83. Served with German Air Force, 1943-45. Mem. Deutsche Gesellschaft für Innere Medizin, Gesellschaft für Verdauungs und Stoffwechselkrankheiten. Mem. Luth. Ch. Contbr. articles to sci. jours. Home: 2155 Westhill Wynd, West Vancouver, BC Canada V7S 2Z3

KNAUSS, THOMAS ALVIN, pediatric neurologist; b. Buffalo, Nov. 24, 1940; s. Alvin C. and Dolores E. Knauss; children: Pam, Janet. BA, Knox Coll., 1961; PhD, UCLA, 1966, MD, 1969. Diplomate Am. Bd. Neurology, Am. Bd. Child Neurology. Med. intern UCLA, 1969-70; resident in pediatrics U. Wash., Seattle, 1970-71, resident in neurology, 1971-74, asst. prof. pediatrics, 1974-77, asst. clin. prof. pediatrics, 1977-85, assoc. clin. prof. pediatrics, 1985—; neurologist Group Health of Puget Sound, Seattle, 1977—.

KNECHT, RICHARD ARDEN, family practitioner; b. Grand Rapids, Mar. 7, 1929; s. Fredrick William and Eva Rae (Blakley) K.; m. Joan Matson, Dec. 26, 1951 (div. 1975); children: Richard Arden, Karrie Jo, Jeffrey Paul; m. Patricia Irene Gilmore, Aug. 14, 1976; 1 child, Kimberly Kahler. BS, U. Mich., 1951, MD, 1955. Diplomate Am. Bd. Family Practice, Am. Bd. Geriatric Medicine; cert. med. dir. Intern St. Mary Hosp., Grand Rapids, Mich., 1955-56; pvt. practice, Indian River, Mich., 1956—. Fellow Am. Acad. Family Physicians, Am. Geriatric Soc., Royal Soc. Medicine; mem. Mich. Med. Soc. (com. on aging 1988—), Mich. Acad. Family Practice (chmn. com. on aging 1986-88, pub.'s award 1988), Mich. Med. Dirs. Assn. (pres. 1996—). Home and Office: PO Box 2190 Indian River MI 49749

KNECHTLE, STUART JOHNSTON, medical educator, transplant immunologist; b. N.Y.C., May 17, 1956; s. Emilio Beato and Ann (Johnston) K.; m. Mary Banks Anderson, Aug. 18, 1984; children: William Stuart, David Anderson, Ann Walker, Peter Johnston. AB, Princeton U., 1978; MD, Cornell U., 1982. Diplomate Am. Bd. Surgery, Am. Bd. Surgery and Surg. Critical Care. Resident in surgery Duke U. Med. Ctr., Durham, N.C., 1982-89; fellow in transplant surgery U. Wis., Madison, 1989-91; asst. prof. surgery U. Wis., 1991-96, assoc. prof. surgery, 1996—. Author, editor: Portal Hypertension: Current Management, 1996. Fellow ACS (Faculty fellow 1992-94); mem. Am. Soc. Transplant Surgeons, The Transplantation Soc., Soc. Univ. Surgeons, Assn. Acad. Surgeons, Soc. Surgery of Alimentary Tract. Office: U Wis Hosp 600 Highland Ave Madison WI 53792

KNEEN, JAMES RUSSELL, health care administrator; b. Kalamazoo, Dec. 16, 1955; s. Russell Packard and Joyce Elaine (Knapper) K.; m. Peggy Jo Howard, Aug. 4, 1979; children: Benjamin Russell, Katherine Elaine. BA, Alma Coll., 1978; MHA, U. Mo., 1982. Systems analyst Bronson Meth. Hosp., Kalamazoo, 1976-79; cons. U. Mo., Columbia, 1979-81; adminstrv. resident Meth. Hosp. Ind., Indpls., 1981-82; div. dir. psychiat. care svcs. Parkview Meml. Hosp., Ft. Wayne, Ind., 1982-88; exec. v.p. Meml. Hosp., Ocomonowoc, Wis., 1988-90; exec. dir. Meml. Hosp. Found., Oconomowoc, 1988-90; pres., CEO Fostoria (Ohio) Community Hosp., 1990-94; pres. United Health Partnership, Toledo, 1995—. Bd. dirs. Washington House Alcoholism Treatment Ctr., 1983-88; bd. dirs., sec.-treas. Parkview Regional Outreach, 1985-88; bd. dirs., pres. Seneca County chpt. Am. Cancer Soc. Fellow Am. Coll. Healthcare Execs.; mem. Am. Hosp. Assn., Wis. Hosp. Assn. (coun. on health care delivery systems), Regent's Adv. Coun. Wis. (bd. dirs.), Ohio Hosp. Assn. (various coms.), Rotary (bd. dirs. Fostoria chpt). Office: United Health Ptrn 104 N Summit St Toledo OH 43604-1034

KNEPPER, JOHN ALLEN, physician; b. Chicago Heights, Ill., Feb. 2, 1962; s. Dwain LaVerne and Shirley M. (Meltzer) K.; m. Helen Katrina Hicks, Apr. 6, 1991. BS in Biology with honors, U. Ill., 1984; DO, Phila. Coll. Osteo. Medicine, 1988. Diplomate Am. Bd. Family Practice. Family practitioner Carolina Primary Care, N. Charleston, S.C., 1994-96. Lt. comdr. USN, 1988-94. Mem. Am. Acad. Family Practice, Am. Coll. Osteo. Family Physicians, Am. Osteo. Assn., S.C. Med. Assn. Office: Carolina Primary Care 5290 Rivers Ave Ste 101E North Charleston SC 29406

KNEPPER, LAURIE ELIZABETH, neurologist, educator; b. Pitts., July 15, 1959; d. James Wallace and Janet Ruth (Drummond) K.; m. Jerry Lee Carter, Dec. 12, 1987; children: Sara Ann, Mary Elizabeth. BA in Chemistry, Franklin and Marshall U., 1981; MD, U. Pitts., 1985. Intern Allegheny Gen. Hosp., Pitts., 1985-86; resident U. Iowa Hosp., Iowa City, 1986-89; stroke fellow U. Pitts. Med. Ctr., 1989-90, asst. prof. neurology, 1990—. Mem. AMA, Am. Acad. Neurology, Pa. Med. Soc., Allegheny County Med. Soc., Phi Beta Kappa. Office: U Pitts Med Ctr 3471 5th Ave Pittsburgh PA 15213

KNESEL, ERNEST ARTHUR, JR., diagnostic company executive; b. New Orleans, Dec. 11, 1945; s. Ernest Arthur and Catherine Charlotte (Maier) K.; m. Lavina Lynn Menge, June 2, 1968; children: Eric Ernest, Tami Lynn, Bradley William. Student, Armstrong Coll., 1963-64; BS, Fairleigh Dickinson U., 1968, MS, 1970. Cert. clin. chemist. Technologist Am. Biol. Control Lab., Tenefly, N.J., 1966-68; sr. technologist Englewood (N.J.) Hosp., 1968-69; founder, v.p. Biomed. Reference Labs., Inc., Burlington, N.C., 1969-82; sr. v.p. Roche Biomed. Labs., Inc., Burlington, 1982-95; pres., founder Roche Image Analysis Systems, Inc., Elon College, N.C., 1989—. Inventor serum filter/dispenser vial, automated aliquoting system, cyto-rich automated cytology preparation system and simultaneous machine and human interactive cytology evaluation system. Mem. Am. Assn. Clin. Chemistry, Am. Soc. Clin. Pathologists (assoc.). Roman Catholic. Office: Roche Image Analysis Systems Inc 112 Orange Dr Elon College NC 27244-9230

KNIERIM, RUPERT WILLIAM, orthodontist; b. Indpls., Jan. 13, 1943; s. Rupert Louis and Lillian Margaret (Heck) K.; m. Pamela Lee Watson, Aug. 11, 1969; children: Angela, Grace, Kristin. BS in Pharmacy, Purdue U., 1965; DDS, Ind. U. Indpls., 1970, MS in Orthodontistry, 1972. Diplomate Am. Bd. Orthodontics. Pharmacist various, Ind., 1965-70, dentist, 1970-72; pvt. practice Knoxville, Tenn., 1972—. Inventor in field; contbr. articles to profl. jours. Mem. ADA, Am. Orthodontic Assn., Multi-loop Edgewire Found. Home: 6106 Top O' Knox Knoxville TN 37918 Office: 2606 Greenway Dr Knoxville TN 37918

KNIES, ROBERT CARL, JR., critical care nurse; b. Wilkes-Barre, Pa., Sept. 7, 1960; s. Robert Carl and Alice Ann (Swartman) K.; m. Lisa Ann Stumhofer, May 17, 1986. Diploma, St. Joseph Hosp. Sch. Nursing, Reading, Pa., 1983; BSN, Pa. State U., 1990; MSN, Villanova U., 1996. Cert. emergency nurse, CPR instr., emergency med. technician, ACLS. Staff nurse St. Joseph Hosp., Reading, 1983-84; clin. nurse Community Gen. Hosp., Reading, 1984-89; nurse Med. Pers. Pool, Allentown, Pa., 1989-91, Pottstown (Pa.) Meml. Med. Ctr., 1990-96; clin. nurse specialist emergency svcs. Health Sys. Minn., 1996—; adj. faculty Reading Area C.C., 1991-95. Mem. Emergency Nurses Assn., Sigma Theta Tau, Alpha Sigma Lambda.

KNIGHT, CHARLES DANIEL, JR., surgeon, educator; b. Rochester, Minn., June 13, 1953; s. Charles Daniel and Dorothy Corinne (Willius) K.; m. Anne Brevard Hall Knight, Jan. 24, 1995; children: Kathryn Anne, Emily Elizabeth, Alice Brevard. BA summa cum laude, Vanderbilt U., 1975, MD, 1979. Diplomate Am. Bd. Surgery; lic. physician, Minn., La. Resident Mayo Clinic, Rochester, Minn., 1979-84, fellow, 1984-85; gen. and vascular surgeon Highland Clinic, Shreveport, La., 1985—; clin. assoc. prof. surgery La. State U. Med. Ctr., Shreveport, 1985—. Contbr. articles to profl. jours. Mem. nat. heart, lung, blood adv. coun. NIH, 1984-86. Justin Potter scholar, 1975-79; Howard Kramer Gray grantee, 1982. Fellow ACS (v.p. La. chpt. 1996); mem. AMA, La. Med. Soc., Shreveport Med. Soc., Southeastern Surg. Congress, Gulf Coast Vascular Soc., Perpheral Vascular Surgery Soc., Priestley Soc., Mayo Clinic Alumni Assn., Vanderbilt U. Alumni Assn., Pierremont Oaks Tennis Club, Shreveport Country, Phi Delta Theta, Phi Beta Kappa, Phi Eta Sigma, Alpha Omega Alpha. Methodist. Home: 608 Longleaf Rd Shreveport LA 71106 Office: Highland Clinic 1455 E Bert Kouns Shreveport LA 71106

KNIGHT, DAVID CLOUGH, physician; b. Worcester, Mass., Mar. 28, 1950; s. Carleton and Mary (Burnett) K.; m. Francine Charles, Aug. 23, 1975; children: Jessica, Emily, Abigail, Charles. BA, Harvard U., 1972; MBBch, Royal Coll. of Surgeons, Dublin, Ireland, 1981. FACS. Physician Surg. Assocs. of Waterbury, P.C., Conn., 1986—; pres. GWHN and Physicians, Inc., Waterbury, 1994—; trustee Waterbury Hosp., 1995—. Fellow Am. Coll. Surgeons. Office: Surg Assocs of Waterbury PC 1211 W Main St Waterbury CT 06708

KNIGHT, EDWARD HOWDEN, retired hospital administrator; b. Vancouver, B.C., Can., Apr. 13, 1933; s. Edward Allen and Helen Blackley (Howden) K.; m. Glenda Carol Wiggins, Mar. 6, 1964; children: Carolyn, Patricia, Brett. B of Commerce, diploma in hosp. adminstrn., U. B.C., 1956. Adminstrv. asst. Vancouver Gen. Hosp., 1956-57; adminstr. Prince Rupert Gen. Hosp., 1957-61, Red Deer Gen. Hosp., 1961-72, Dr. Richard Parsons Aux. Hosp., 1963-72, Valley Park Manor Nursing Home, 1969-72; dep. exec. dir. Calgary (Alta.) Gen. Hosp., 1972-74, exec. dir., 1974-83, pres., 1983-88; pres. E.H. Knight & Assocs. Inc., Calgary, 1988-92; lectr. Red Deer Coll., 1968-72; adj. asst. prof. faculty medicine U. Calgary, 1978-91; trustee Alta. Blue Cross Plan, 1963-68; mem. Fed. Task Force on Cost of Health Services in Can., 1969. Recipient Queen's Silver Jubilee medal, 1977. Fellow Can. Coll. of Health Service Execs. (dir. 1972-74, founding charter mem.), Am. Coll. Healthcare Execs. (regent for Alta. 1973-76, 79-82); mem. Can. Hosp. Assn (dir. 1981-83), Alta. Hosp. Assn. (dir. 1977-84, pres. 1983), Assn. Can. Teaching Hosps. (pres. 1986-87), Phi Delta Theta. Clubs: Red Deer, Kinsmen (pres. 1971-72), Glencoe. Lodge: Rotary. Home: 820 Windridge Cir San Marcos CA 92069-7917

KNIGHT, FRANK JAMES, pharmaceutical marketing professional; b. L.A., July 17, 1947; s. George Orlando Jr. and Virginia Clarabelle (Seig) K.; m. Mary Jane Vargo, Aug. 7, 1977 (div. July 1989); children: Cheryl Lynne, Michael Scott; m. Barbara Lorrene Garlick, June 19, 1993. BS, Okla. State U., 1970. Mktg. rep. Mobil Oil Corp., N.Y.C., 1971-73; sales rep. Monarch Crown Corp., N.Y.C., 1974-78; territory mgr. V.H. Monette, Inc., Smithfield, Va., 1978-81; profl. rep. Dermik Labs., Blue Bell, Pa., 1981-83; spl. markets assoc. Sandoz Pharms., East Hanover, N.J., 1983—. Capt. U.S. Army, 1970. Mem. Harley Owners Group. Home: 14807 Velvet St Chino Hills CA 91709-2070 Office: Sandoz Pharms Corp 59 State Route 10 East Hanover NJ 07936-1011

KNIGHT, JAMES ALLEN, psychiatrist, educator; b. St. George, S.C., Oct. 20, 1918; s. Thomas Samuel and Carolyn (Carn) K.; m. Sally Templeman, June 8, 1963; 1 child, Steven Allen. A.B., Wofford Coll., 1941; B.D., Duke U., 1944; M.D., Vanderbilt U., 1952; M.P.H., Tulane U., 1962. Intern Grady Meml. Hosp., Atlanta, 1952-53; asst. resident pediatrics Duke U. Hosp., 1953-54; resident psychiatry Tulane U. Service Charity Hosp., 1955-58; mem. faculty Baylor U. Coll. Medicine, 1958-61, assoc. prof. psychiatry, 1961, asst. dean, 1960-61; assoc. prof. psychiatry, dir. sect. community psychiatry Tulane U. Sch. Medicine, 1961-63, prof. psychiatry, assoc. dean, 1964-74; dean Tex. A & M Coll. Medicine, College Station, 1974-77; prof. psychiatry and humanities in medicine Tex. A & M Coll. Medicine, College Station, Tex., 1992—; prof. psychiatry and med. ethics La. State U. Sch. Medicine, New Orleans, 1978-91; Harkness prof. psychiatry and religion, dir. program psychiatry and religion Union Theol. Sem., N.Y.C., 1963-64. Author: Counselling the Dying, 1964, A Manual for the Comprehensive Community Mental Health Clinic, 1964, A Psychiatrist Looks at Religion and Health, 1964, Allergy and Human Emotions, 1967, Motivations in Play, Games and Sports, 1967, For the Love of Money, 1968, Conscience and Guilt, 1969, Medical Student: Doctor in the Making, 1973, Doctor-To-Be: Coping with the Trials and Triumphs of Medical School, 1981. Served as chaplain USNR, 1944-46. Travelling fellow WHO at C.G. Jung Inst., Zurich, Switzerland, 1961. Mem. Am. Psychiat. Assn., Am. Acad. Psychoanalysis, Group Advancement Psychiatry, Am. Osler Soc., Soc. Health and Human Values (pres. 1983-84), Phi Beta Kappa. Home: 2110 Chippendale St College Station TX 77845-5581

KNIGHT, JAMES HARRY, technical services manager; b. Enterprise, Ala., Jan. 21; s. James Harry and Sybil (McDonald) K.; m. Judy Lynne Upchurch, Dec. 11, 1971; children: Laura Lynne, James H. III, Emily Catherine. BS, Auburn U., 1971, MS, 1973. Mgr. Baxter Travenol, Kingstree, S.C., 1973-77, Gist Brocades, Kingstree, S.C., 1977-86, Schering Plough HealthCare, Memphis, 1986—; isntr. Williamsburg Tech. Coll., Kingstree, 1979-86. Methodist. Home: 2866 Flowerwood Rd Memphis TN 38134 Office: Schering Plough HelathCare 3030 Jackson Ave Memphis TN 38151

KNIGHT, JOSEPH ADAMS, pathologist; b. Provo, Utah, Dec. 22, 1930; s. John Clarence and Martha Maude (Adams) K.; m. Pauline Brown, Oct. 18, 1949; children: David Paul, Leigh Knight Smith. BS in Chemistry, Brigham Young U., 1955, MS in Organic Chemistry, 1957; MD, U. Utah, 1963. Diplomate Am. Bd. pathology; lic. Utah, Calif., Nev., Wyo. Intern U. Utah Hosp., Salt Lake City, 1963-64, residency in pathology, 1964-67; instr. pathology Sch. Medicine U. Utah, Salt Lake City, 1966-67, clin. instr. pathology, 1967-70; assoc. pathologist Holy Cross Hosp., Salt Lake City, 1967-70; asst. clin. prof. pathology Sch. Medicine U. Utah., Salt Lake City, 1970-75; assoc. Health Svcs. Corp., Salt Lake City, 1969-75; assoc. pathologist Santa Rosa Med. Ctr., San Antonio, 1975-76; assoc. clin. prof. pathology Sch. Medicine U. Tex., San Antonio, 1975-76; dir. clin. labs. Primary Children's Med. Ctr., Salt Lake City, 1976-79; assoc. clin. prof. Sch. Medicine U. Utah, Salt Lake City, 1977-79, assoc. prof. pathology, 1979-88, prof. pathology, 1988—; assoc. chmn. pathology, head div. edn. VA Med. Ctr., Salt Lake City, 1986—, chief lab. svc., 1990—; vis. prof. pathology Sch. Medicine U. Conn., Farmington, 1985-86; mem. admissions com. Sch. Medicine U. Utah, 1981-82, chmn. pathology residency com., 1980-85, co-chmn. pathology residency com., 1987-90, mem. grad. sch. com. Sch. Med. Technologists U. Utah, 1981-85. Author: (with others) Laboratory Examination of Cerebrospinal, Synovial and Serous Fluids: A Textbook Atlas, 1982, Body Fluids: A Textbook Atlas, 2nd edit., 1986, 3d edit., 1993; author: Laboratory Medicine and the Aging Process, 1996; reviewer Clin. Chemistry, 1971, 77, 84, 86—; contbr. articles to profl. jours. Served with U.S. Navy, 1948-52, Korea. Fellow Am. Soc. Clin. Pathologists, Coll. Am. Pathologists, Nat. Acad. Clin. Biochem.; mem. AMA, Am. Assn. Clin. Chemists, Utah Soc. Pathologists (pres. 1968-70, 79-80), Am. Bd. Pathology (test com. 1987-92), Am. Soc. Clin. Pathology (editl. rev. bd. 1987—, numerous other coms.), Assn. Clin. Scientists (mem. com. 1985—, v.p. 1995, pres. 1996), Coll. Am. Pathologists (inspector 1978—), Alpha Omega Alpha. Republican. Mormon. Office: U Utah Sch Medicine Dept Pathology 50 N Medical Dr Salt Lake City UT 84132-0001

KNISELY, RALPH FRANKLIN, retired microbiologist; b. Altoona, Pa., Mar. 30, 1927; s. Calvin Ross and Frieda Pauline (Neher) K.; m. Joan Marie Fitzgerald, Jan. 29, 1949 (div. 1955); 1 child, Patricia Ann; m. Ann Martin, May 21, 1960. BS, Pa. State U., 1953, postgrad., 1953. Bacteriologist Altoona Hosp., 1953-56, adminstrv. asst. to pathologist, 1957-59; microbiologist Chem. Corps Dept. Army, Ft. Detrick, Md., 1959-72; rsch. microbiologist Edgewood Arsenal, Aberdeen Proving Ground, Md., 1972-86. Contbg. author: Rapid Identification of Biological Agents, 1966; contbr. articles to Jour. Bacteriology, European Jour. Microbiology. Pres. Eastview Civic Assn., Frederick, Md., 1968-69. With USN, 1945-46, 50-51; capt. Res. ret., 1945-87. Mem. Am. Soc. for Microbiology (emeritus), Rsch. Soc. Am. (emeritus), Assn. Mil. Surgeons U.S. (life), N.Y. Acad. Sci. (emeritus), Ret. Officer's Assn. (chpt. v.p. 1969-70), AARP (bd. dirs. chpt. 636 1989-90, chpt. pres. 1995—), Fleet Res. Assn., Nat. Assn. Ret. Fed. Employees (pres. chpt. 409 1995—), Internat. Platform Assn., Nat. Sojourners (pres. chpt. 354 1965, 81, sec. 1986—), George Washington Masonic Stamp Club (pres. 1978-80, sec. 1988—), Knisely Reunion Assn. (pres., historian 1994-95), Am. Legion, Elks, Masons, Scottish Rite, Jaffa Shrine Temple, Legion of Honor, Am. Philatelic Soc. (life), Masonic Rsch. Soc., Philalethes Soc., Quatour Coronati Corr. Cir. (London), Sampson WWII Vets. (Md. state dir., exec. trustee). Republican. Lutheran. Home: 7400 Skyline Dr Frederick MD 21702-3652

KNISELY, WILLIAM HAGERMAN, anatomical sciences educator emeritus, retired university dean; b. Houghton, Mich., Feb. 3, 1922; s. Samuel Henry and Flora Belle (Hagerman) K.; m. Marguerite Marie Labasse, Jan. 18, 1947; children: Chantal Patton, Marc, Paul, Colette, Philip. PhB, U. Chgo., 1947, BS, 1950; MS, Med. Coll. S.C., 1952, PhD, 1954; LittD (hon.), Coll. of Charleston, 1977; LHD (hon.), Lander Coll., 1982. Orderly, night clk. U. Chgo. Hosp., 1946-49; research asst. Med. Coll. S.C., Charleston, 1949-54; from instr. to assoc. prof. Duke U., Durham, N.C., 1954-59; prof., chmn. dept. anatomy U. Ky., Lexington, 1959-63; prof., dir. Inst. Biology and Medicine Mich. State U., East Lansing, 1963-70; prof., vice chancellor for health affairs U. Tex. System, Austin, 1970-75; pres. Med. U. S.C., Charleston, 1975-82; exec. assoc. dean Coll. Medicine U. Okla., Oklahoma City, 1982-87; assoc. dean rsch. affairs, 1987-89; assoc. dean Coll. Grad. Studies U. Okla., Oklahoma City, 1982-89; prof. anat. scis. emeritus, 1989—; sr. program assoc. biomed. and health care ethics program U. Okla. Health Sci. Ctr., 1989-93; Chmn. program planning com. Physician Manpower div. Nat. Adv. Council on Edn. for Health Professions, 1970-72; mem. steering com. for edn. devel. Mass. Gen. Hosp., 1978-80; cons. Dept. Medicine and Surgery VA, 1974. Commr. Navajo Health Authority, 1972-76; chmn. Tex. coordinating bd. Higher Edn. Task Force on Med. and Dental Edn., 1972-74. Served with U.S. Army, 1943-46, ETO. Recipient Sesquicentennial Disting. Alumnus award Med. U. S.C., 1974, Honors of the Soc. award Am. Soc. Allied Health Professions, 1984, Amicus Medicinae award U. Okla. Med. Alumni Assn., 1992; William Knisely award named in his honor U. Ky., 1981; Am. Heart Assn. rsch. fellow, 1955-57; USPHS sr. rsch. fellow, 1957-59. Fellow Royal Microscopical Soc. London; mem. Am. Assn. Anatomists, Am. Assn. for History of Medicine, AMA (affiliate), So. Hist. Assn., Am. Dietetic Assn. (hon. 1976—).

KNOBLER, ROBERT MARTIN, dermatologist, educator, research scientist; b. Sucre, Bolivia, Dec. 6, 1945; s. Richard R. and Lily E. (Mayer) K. BA, Columbia U., 1967, BS, 1969; MD, U. Vienna, Austria, 1977. Cert. educator, 1979. Intern Mistelbach Hosp., Austria, 1977-79; vis. scientist coll. of physicians and surgeons Columbia U., N.Y.C., 1984-85; intern Mistelbach (Austria) Hosp., 1977-79; head photopheresis unit dept. dermatology U. Vienna (Austria), 1985—, head chem. lab., 1988-91, head of cell biology lab., 1991-93; fellow dept. dermatology Columbia U., N.Y.C., 1983-85; asst. prof. dermatology Med. Sch., U. Vienna, Austria, 1993, assoc. prof. dermatology, 1993—; lectr. dermatology Columbia U., N.Y.C., 1983—. Contbr. articles to profl. jours. Recipient Gold medal Am. Acad. Dermatology, 1992, Rsch. award AESCA & Co., 1993. Mem. European Soc. Extracorporeal Photochemotherapy (pres. 1992—), European Orgn. Rsch. & Treatment of Cancer (mem. cutaneous lymphoma group, sec. 1992—). Office: U Vienna Gen Hosp Dept Dermatology, Wahringergürtel 18-20, A-1090 Vienna Austria

KNOLLE, PETER, consultant; b. Gadderbaum, Fed. Republic Germany, July 5, 1931; s. Martin and Maria (Wilmanns) K.; m. Gisela Bartelt, Dec. 1962; 1 child, Oliver-Michael. BS, Purdue U., 1953, PhD, 1960; Physikum, FU, Fed. Republic Germany, 1954. Postdoctoral Ind. U., Bloomington, 1960; asst. Max-Planck Inst. for Hereditary Biology, West Berlin, 1961-65; rsch. asst. NYU Sch. Medicine, 1966-67, rsch. asst. prof., 1968-69; guest prof. Northwestern U. Dept. Biology, Evanston, Ill., 1969-70; head chemotherapy Hoffmann-LaRoche Inc., Basel, Switzerland, 1970-71; head virusgenetics U. Giessen, Fed. Republic Germany, 1971-74; med. R&D dir. Mundipharma GmbH, Limburg, Fed. Republic Germany, 1974-78; pres. Inst. for Med. Rsch., Saint-Sulpice, 1982—, Cappamed S.á.r.l., Luxembourg, 1987—; cons. Cappacon AG, Zug, Switzerland, 1975—, Medi Aid Ag, Zug, Switzerland, 1981—; coord. Medi Aid GmbH, Wiesbaden, Fed. Republic Germany, 1983—. Contbr. articles to profl. jours. Fulbright fellowship Purdue U., 1952-53; rsch. fellowship Elks Cancer Fund, Purdue U., 1955-57; habil. grant Deutsche Forschungsgemeinschaft, 1965-66, rsch. grant Schering Corp., 1966-69. Mem. Soc. for Applied Medicine (pres. 1984—), Swiss Health Counsel Club (founding mem.), German Health Club, Green Ring (pres. 1984—). Home: Paqueret, CH-1025 Saint-Sulpice Switzerland Office: Inst Med Rsch, Paqueret, Ch-1025 Saint-Sulpofrice Switzerland also: Deutscher Gesundheitsclub, Kapellenstr 78, D-65193 Wiesbaden Germany

KNOOP, FLOYD C., medical microbiologist, educator; b. Dayton, Ohio, Nov. 11, 1944; s. Floyd C. Sr. and Pearl E. (Reiffenstein) K.; m. Pamela Kay Johnson, June 3, 1967; 1 child, Tiffany N. BS, Defiance (Ohio) Coll., 1966; MS, U. Dayton, 1969; PhD, U. Tenn., 1974. Instr. U. Tenn. Med. Ctr., Memphis, 1974-75; prof. med. microbiology Sch. Medicine Creighton U., Omaha, 1975—; cons. microbiology lab. St. Joseph Hosp., Omaha; cons. Omaha-Douglas County Health Dept., 1978—, Burns-Biotec Labs., Omaha, 1978-82, Dellen Labs., Omaha, 1980-83, Norden Labs., 1982-85, Fermenta Animal Health, Omaha, 1985—. Reviewer Jour. of Infection and Immunity, 1980—, Jour. Current Microbiology, 1981—, NSF, 1984—, Am. Jour. Epidemiology, 1984—, VA Merit Rev. Bd., 1988—, USDA, 1995—; contbr. numerous jours. including Biochem. Exptl. Biology, Can. Jour. Microbiology, Jour. Clin. Microbiology, Current Microbiology, Clin. Rsch., Nebr. Med. Jour., Jour. Infection and Immunity, Internat. Jour. Biochemistry, Jour. Infectious Diseases. Mem. AAAS, Am. Soc. for Microbiology, Mo. Valley chpt. Am. Soc. for Microbiology, Am. Soc. for Biochemistry and Molecular Biology, Internat. Ctr. for Diarrheal Diseases, Internat. Soc. on Toxinology, N.Y. Acad. Scis., Sigma Xi. Home: 208 S Bellevue Blvd Bellevue NE 68005-2443 Office: Creighton U Sch Medicine 2500 California Pla Omaha NE 68178-0001

KNOPF, IRWIN JAY, psychology educator; b. N.Y.C., June 14, 1924; s. Joseph and Esther (Inselman) K.; m. Roberta Iris Olin, Dec. 29, 1951; children: William Douglas, David Richard, Judith Ann. A.B., N.Y.U., 1948; M.A., Northwestern U., 1949, Ph.D., 1952. Diplomate: clin. psychology Am. Bd. Examiners Profl. Psychology. Asst. prof. clin. psychology, then asso. prof. clin. psychology, then asso. prof., head div. psychology, dept. psychiatry State U. Iowa, 1952-58; prof., chmn. div. psychology U. Tex. Southwestern Med. Sch., 1958-64; prof. psychology, chmn. dept. Emory U., 1964-83, Disting. prof. psychology, 1980-92, Disting. prof. emeritus, 1992—; cons. in field. Field selection officer Peace Corps; chmn. com. teaching awards Am. Psychol. Found. Author: Childhood Psychopathology: A Developmental Approach, 1979, 2d edit., 1984; mem. editl. bd. Jour. Psychoednl. Assessment, 1982-93; contbr. articles to profl. jours.; cons. editor: Contemporary Psychology, 1961-73. Served with inf. AUS, 1944-45. Decorated Purple Heart. Fellow APA, Am. Orthopsychiat. Assn., Am. Psychol. Soc., Southeastern Psychol. Assn. (pres. 1979-80), Phi Beta Kappa, Sigma Xi. Home: 1091 Tennyson Pl NE Atlanta GA 30319-1924

KNOPP, REINHOLD, medical educator; b. Koblenz, Rhine, Germany, Mar. 10, 1938; s. Johannes and Magdalena (Moeren) K.; m. Renate Schuetz, Aug. 19, 1966; children: Monika, Birgitta, Susanne. Dipl. physics, Tech. U. Aachen, 1963, dr. rer. nat., 1966. Sci. asst. Tech. U. Aachen, Germany, 1963-66, U. Bonn, Germany, 1966-75; lectr. U. Bonn, 1975-78, prof., 1978—. Mem. Deutsche Gesellschaft Nuklear Medizin, Deutsche Gesellschaft Medizininche Physik, European Assn. Nuc. Medicine, Soc. Nuc. Medicine. Office: Klinik J Nuklearmedizin, Sigmund Freud Str 25, D-53127 Bonn Germany

KNOTT, LARRY HARDING, surgeon; b. Durham, N.C., Dec. 19, 1946; s. Lawrence Harding and Melba (Roberts) K.; m. Patricia Ann Knott, Apr. 2, 1972; children: Renee, Derek. AB, U. N.C., 1968; MD, Bowman Gray Sch. Medicine, 1972. Diplomate Am. Bd. Surgery. Intern Parkland Meml. Hosp., Dallas, 1972-73; resident in gen. surgery U. Minn. Med. Ctr., Jackson, 1975-79; fellow in vascular surgery U. Fla., Gainesville, 1979-80; surgeon New Hanover Regional Med. Ctr., Wilmington, N.C., 1989—, Lenoir Meml. Hosp., Kinston, N.C., 1980-89. Capt. USAF, 1973-75. Fellow ACS. Office: 1922 Tradd Ct Wilmington NC 28401

KNOUSE, JOHN DOYLE, optometrist; b. Waverly, N.Y., May 29, 1962; s. Jack Bruce and Betty Marge (Lehman) K.; m. Maureen Joan McDonough, Oct. 21, 1989; children: Ryan John, Allison Beth. BS in Biology, Pa. State U., 1984; OD, Pa. Coll. Optometry, Phila., 1988. Diplomate Am. Bd. Optometry. Optometrist Montgomeryville (Pa.) Eye Assocs., 1988-90; optometrist, dir. optometry Total Vision Care, Whitehall, Pa., 1990-92; optometrist, clin. dir. Trachtenberg/Moran Eye Assocs., Allentown, Pa., 1992—; optometrist, owner Pennridge Family Eye Care, Dublin, Pa., 1995—; preceptor, externship program Pa. Coll. Optometry, Phila., 1993—, adj. faculty, 1994—. Mem. Hilltown Civic Assn., Hilltown Twp., Pa., 1992—. Mem. Am. Optometric Assn., Pa. Optometric Assn., Lehigh Valley Optometric Soc., Pa. State Alumni Assn. Lutheran. Office: Pennridge Family Eye Care 174 N Main St PO Box 1149 Dublin PA 18917

KNOWLES, CHRISTOPHER ALLAN, healthcare executive; b. Washington, Oct. 24, 1949; s. Charles Edward and Eleanor Patricia (Murphy) K.; m. Mary Margaret O'Loughlin, Feb. 14, 1988; children: Sean Christopher, James Charles, Thomas Patrick. BA, U. Nebr., 1975; MPA, Drake U., Des Moines, 1982; postgrad., Fordham U., 1987-91. Adminstrv. asst. to dir. Nebr. Dept. Water Resources, Lincoln, 1976-78; environ. planner Iowa Natural Resources Council, Des Moines, 1978-81, Md. Environ. Trust, Balt., 1982; fin. analyst Norwest Corp., Des Moines, 1982-83; asst. dir., dir. fin. Hospice of Cen. Iowa, Des Moines, 1983-85; assoc. dir. home health svcs. dept. Hackensack Med. Ctr., N.J., 1985-86; fiscal mgr. Family Health Ctr. Montefiore Med. Ctr., N.Y.C., 1986-87; assoc. dir. and adminstr. Comprehensive Family Care Ctr., Albert Einstein Coll., N.Y.C., 1987-88; exec. dir. Hospice Care of L.I., 1988; assoc. dir. Bronx-Lebanon Hosp., N.Y.C., 1989; chmn., chief exec. officer Knowles Econometrics, Inc., Pelham Manor, N.Y., 1990-91; asst. controller N.Y.C. Health & Hosps. Corp., 1990; dep. dir. Coalition Vol. Mental Health Agys., N.Y.C., 1990-91; dir. Vis. Nurse Svc., Martha's Vineyard Cmty. Svcs., Oak Bluffs, Mass., 1991—; chief economist Knowles Econometrics, Vineyard Haven, Mass., 1994—; pres. The Wintertide Coffeehouse, Inc., Vineyard Haven, Mass., 1993-94; treas. AIDS Alliance of Martha's Vineyard (Mass.), Inc., 1992-93; chmn. Dukes County (Mass.) Health and Human Svcs. Adv. Com., 1995-96. U.S. Dept. Edn. grantee, 1981-82. Mem. Pi Sigma Alpha, Pi Alpha Alpha. Democrat. Episcopalian. Office: PO Box 369 Vineyard Haven MA 02568-0369

KNOWLES, MARGARET ANNE, medical researcher; b. Canterbury, Kent, Eng., July 11, 1952; d. Norman Gaze and Joan Margaret (Osborn) Pace; m. David Justin Charles, June 15, 1974; children: Timothy, Sarah, Lucy, Benjamin. BSc in Microbiology, U. Bristol, Eng., 1973; PhD in Zoology, U. London, 1977. Rsch. asst. dept. oncology Middlesex Hosp. Med. Sch., 1977-81, rsch. assoc., 1981-82; group leader Molecular Genetics Lab., Marie Curie Rsch. Inst., 1983—. Mem. Ch. of England. Office: Marie Curie Rsch Inst Molecular Genetics Lab, The Chart, Surrey RH8 0TL, England

KNOX, GLENDA JANE, retired health and safety specialist, educator; b. Abernathy, Tex., Mar. 8, 1939; d. Raymond Arnold and Viola Jane (Melton) Boykin; m. William Gene Bright, Mar. 2, 1954 (dec. July 1974); children: Rocky Dwain, Jeannie Ann, Mary Jane, Tommy Lynn; m. Arthur Richard Knox, May 1, 1978; step-sons: Ricky Lynn Stinson, Tony Ray Knox; foster son, Roy David Haney. Grad., Comml. Coll., Baton Rouge, 1985; student, Odessa Coll., 1986-89. Cert. water safety instrn. trainer, health and safety specialist, infant, presch. and parent swimming instr. specialist. Sales clk. Flying B Western Wear, Odessa, Tex., 1975-76; mgr. Redondo Western Wear, Odessa, Tex., 1976-78, Andy's Western Wear, Odessa, Tex., 1978-79; owner Classy Original's Western Wear, Odessa, Tex., 1979-81; water safety instr. Odessa Family YMCA, 1979-82; water safety instr. Odessa Coll., 1981-83, water safety coord., 1983-96, health and safety instr., 1987-96, aquatics coord. continuing edn., 1983-92; ret., 1996; instr. Arthritis Found. YMCA Aquatics Program, Odessa, 1990—, Aquatic Exercise Assn., Odessa, 1987—; instr. specialist ARC Adapted Aquatics, Midland, Tex., 1986—; lifeguard instr. trainer ARC, Odessa, 1979—, CPR instr. trainer, 1981—, 1st aid instr. trainer, 1981—, canoeing instr., 1988-91; water safety specialist Boy Scouts and Girl Scouts Am., Odessa, 1980—; 1st aid instr. Medic First Aid, Odessa, 1990—. Author, editor, artist: Water Aerobics, 1986; author, editor: Food Safety Svc., 1992; designer logo and pin West Tex. Ter. Am. Red Cross, 1988. Vol. Salvation Army, Odessa, 1979-83; mem. exec. bd. ARC, Odessa, 1992, nat. awards chmn., 1992-95, health and safety chmn. region III, terr. 3, 1987-95. Recipient Outstanding Vol. Svc. award Commodore Longfellow Soc., 1994, 95, ARC, 1994, others. Mem. NAFE, Commodore Longfellow Soc. (Outstanding Svc. award 1990, 94), Smithsonian Inst., Nat. Trust for Hist. Preservation, Northshore Animal League (Benefactor award 1988, 89). Baptist. Home: 10177 W 26th St Odessa TX 79763-6333

KNOX, MARK ALLAN, physician, educator; b. Ft. Sill, Okla., May 25, 1954; s. Bruce Elwin and Susan (Marshall) K.; m. Miriam Poorman, June 12, 1976; children: Jennifer Susan, Jeffrey Bruce. BA magna cu. laude, Macalester Coll., 1975; MD, Pa. State U., 1979. Diplomate Am. Bd. Family Practice. Resident in family practice Conemaugh Valley Meml. Hosp., Johnstown, Pa., 1979-82; pvt. practice Bellefonte, Pa., 1982-88; med. dir., attending physician Centre Crest Nursing Home, Bellefonte, Pa., 1987-88; med. treatment supr. William L. Clark and Assocs., Bellefonte, Pa., 1984-88; consulting physician Rehab. Hosp. for Spl. Svcs., Pleasant Gap, Pa., 1983-88; active staff Luther Hosp., Eau Claire, Wis., 1993—, Sacred Heart Hosp., Eau Claire, Wis., 1993—; asst. prof. dept. family medicine U. Wis. Sch. Medicine, 1988-94, assoc. prof., 1994—; presenter in field. Contbr. articles to profl. jours. Recipient prize Am. Cyanamid, 1975. Fellow Am. Acad. Family Physicians; mem. Soc. Tchrs. of Family Medicine, Wis. Academy of Family Physicians, Pa. Med. Soc., Centre County Med. Soc., Phi Beta Kappa. Presbyterian. Home: 1412 Rust St Eau Claire WI 54701 Office: Eau Claire Family Practice Residency 807 S Farwell St Eau Claire WI 54701

KNOX, MICHAEL DENNIS, medical educator, research center administrator; b. Wyandotte, Mich., May 9, 1946; s. Harold L. and Mary (Latta) K.; m. Lucinda Carol Page, May 6, 1972; children: John M.P., James R. S. BA, Ea. Mich. U., 1968; MSW, U. Mich., 1971, MA in Psychology, 1973, PhD in Psychology, 1974. Lic. psychologist, Fla., Va., W.Va. Dir. Applied Sci., Inc., Ann Arbor, Mich., 1974-76; clin. dir. Community Mental Health Ctr., Inc., Huntington, W.Va., 1976-78; clin. instr. Sch. of Medicine Marshall U., Huntington, 1977-78; dir. Western Tidewater Mental Health Ctr., Suffolk, Va., 1978-86; asst. prof. Eastern Va. Med. Sch., Norfolk, 1979-86; assoc.prof., chmn. dept. community mental health U. South Fla., Tampa, 1986-91, prof., chmn. dept. community mental health, 1991-95, prof. dept. cmty. mental health, 1991—, dir. Ctr. for HIV Edn. and Rsch., 1988—; prof. medicine Dept. Internal Medicine, U. South Fla. Coll. Medicine, 1994—; adj. prof. psychology Marshall U., 1977-78, U. South Fla., 1988—, mem. faculty senate, exec. com. mem., 1992—, pres. faculty senate, 1995—; chmn. adv. coun. faculty senate Fla. State U. Sys., 1996—; cons. USPHS, Bethesda, Md., 1990—, NIMH, Rockville, Md., 1990—; lectr. in field, 1980—; tech. advisor state and local govts. Author books including: Last Wishes: A Handbook to Guide Your Survivors, 1995, HIV and Community Mental Healthcare, 1996; contbr. articles on AIDS and psychology; invited reviewer 5 acad. jours., 1982—. Advisor Joint Commn. on Accreditation of Hosps., Chgo., 1982-84; bd. dirs. U.S. Power Squadron, Raleigh, N.C., 1983-84. Emory U. grantee, 1988-91, NIMH grantee, 1991-93, U. Miami grantee, 1991—; recipient Disting. Svc. award Nat. Coun. Community Mental Health Ctrs., 1984, Resolution of Appreciation, 1993. Fellow APA, Am. Assn. Applied and Preventive Psychology, Am. Psychol. Soc.; mem. Internat. AIDS Soc., Fla. Coun. for Cmty. Mental Health, Internat. Soc. AIDS Edn., U. Mich. Alumni ASsn. Home: 11917 Riverhills Dr Temple Terrace FL 33617-1819 Office: U South Fla MHC-7-214 MHC 4-119 13301 Bruce B Downs Blvd Tampa FL 33612-3899

KNUDSEN, GITTE MOOS, neurologist, researcher; b. Copenhagen, Feb. 15, 1959; d. Kjeld Ejner and Karen Margrethe (Moos) K.; m. Tore Vulpius, Nov. 4, 1989; children: Rune, Gunild Margrethe, Siri Amalie. MD, U. Copenhagen, 1984, DMSc, 1994. Diplomate Danish Med. Bd. Intern Rigshospitalet, Copenhagen, 1984-85, jr. rschr., 1986-89, resident, 1990-92; sr. resident Rigshospitalet, Hillerod and Copenhagen, 1992-95; specialist, rsch. neurology U. Hosp. Rigshospitalet, Copenhagen, 1995—, dir. clinic, cons. Contbr. numerous articles to profl. jours. Mem. Internat. Soc. Cerebral Blood Flow and Metabolism, Danish Soc. Neurology (Mogens Fog prize 1993, Synthelabo prize 1994). Office: U Hosp Rigshospitalet, Dept Neurology N2082, 9 Blegdamsvej, DK 2100 Copenhagen Denmark

KNUDSEN, THOR ANDERSEN, surgeon; b. Breum, Denmark, July 10, 1947; s. Harald and Jenny (Andersen) K.; m. Gitte Islev, Oct. 22, 1988; children: Dine, Jan, Markus, Mette. MD, U. Copenhagen, 1978. Specialist in surgery U. Sweden, Ostersund, 1986—, U. Denmark, Copenhagen, 1986—. Home: Olgajev 50, 7800 Skive Denmark

KNUDSON, ALFRED GEORGE, JR., medical geneticist; b. Los Angeles, Aug. 9, 1922; s. Alfred George and Mary Gladys (Galvin) K.; m. Anna T. Meadows, June 20, 1977; children by previous marriage: Linda, Nancy, Dorene. B.S., Calif. Inst. Tech., 1944, Ph.D., 1956; M.D., Columbia U., 1947. Chmn. dept. pediatrics City of Hope Med. Center, Duarte, Calif., 1956-62; chmn. dept. biology City of Hope Med. Center, 1962-66; assoc. dean Health Sci. Center, SUNY, Stony Brook, 1966-69; dean Grad. Sch. Biomed. Scis., U. Tex. Health Sci. Center, Houston, 1970-76; dir. Inst. Cancer Research, Fox Chase Cancer Center, Phila., 1976-83, sr. mem., 1976—, disting. sci., 1992—, pres., 1980-82; mem. Assembly Life Scis., NRC, 1975-81. Author: Genetics and Disease, 1965; contbr. articles to profl. jours. Recipient Charles S. Mott prize GM Cancer Rsch. Found., 1988, medal of honor Am. Cancr Soc. 1989, Charles Rodolphe Brupbacher Found. prize, 1995. Fellow AAAS; mem. NAS, Am. Philos. Soc., Am. Acad. Arts and Scis., Internat. Soc. Pediatric Oncology, Am. Soc. Human Genetics (pres. 1978, Allan award 1991), Assn. Am. Physicians, Am. Pediatrics Soc., Am. Assn. Cancer Rsch. Office: Inst Cancer Rsch 7701 Burholme Ave Philadelphia PA 19111-2412

KNUDSON, DONALD HENRY, surgeon; b. Yankton, S.D., May 20, 1947; s. Donald Lee and Laurel June (Lund) K.; m. Dorene E. Weinstein, Apr. 18, 1980 (div. June 1986); children: Ann, Kathryn, Brooke. BS, Iowa State U., 1969; MD, Washington U., St. Louis, 1973. Diplomate Am. Bd. Surgery. Intern U. Mo. Med. Ctr., 1973-74; asst. clin. prof. surgery U. S.D. Med. Sch., Sioux Falls, 1978—; resident U. S.D. Med. Sch., 1974-78; active med. staff McKennan Hosp., Sioux Falls, 1978—, Sioux Valley Hosp., Sioux Falls, 1978—. Fellow ACS; mem. DeWeese Surg. Soc. Republican. Lutheran. Home: 701 Plum Creek Rd Sioux Falls SD 57105 Office: Ctrl Plains Clinic 1100 E 21st St Sioux Falls SD 57105

KNUDSON, MARK BRADLEY, medical corporation executive; b. Libby, Mont., Sept. 24, 1948; s. Melvin R. and Melba Irene (Joice) K.; m. Susan Jean Voorhees, Sept. 12, 1970; children: Kirstin Sue, Amy Lynn. BS, Pacific Luth. U., 1970; PhD, Wash. State U., 1974. Lectr. Wash. State U., Pullman, 1973-75; research assoc., U. Wash., Seattle, 1976-78, asst. prof., 1976-79; physiologist Cardiac Pacemakers, Inc., St. Paul, 1979-80, mgr. research, 1980-82, dir. applied research, 1982-83; pres., chmn. bd. SenTech Med. Corp., St. Paul, 1983-86; pres. Arden Med. Systems Inc. subs. Johnson & Johnson, 1986-89, pres., dir. Johnson and Johnson Profl. Diagnostics, Inc., Raritan, N.J., 1988-89; ptnr. Med. Innovation Ptnrs., 1989—; mng. ptnr. Med. Innovation Funds; lectr. in field. Bd. dirs. Diametrics Med. Inc., In Control, Inc., Heartstream, Inc., Integ, Inc., Luther Sem.; active Am. Heart Assn. NIH fellow Wash. State U., 1974-75, U. Wash. 1975-76. Mem. AAAS, Sigma Xi. Republican. Lutheran. Contbr. articles to profl. jours.; patentee in field. Office: Med Innovation Ptnrs 9900 Bren Rd E Ste 421 Hopkins MN 55343-9667

KNUDTSON, NANCY ANN, family nurse practitioner; b. Spencer, Iowa, Nov. 29, 1962; d. Ronald Arthur and Willa May (Nagel) Moeller; m. Donald Wayne Knudtson, Sept. 6, 1987. BSN, U. Iowa, 1986; MS, S.D. State U., 1995. RN, Iowa, Minn.; cert. family nurse practitioner ANCC; cert. instr. BCLS, Am. Heart Assn. Nurse orthopedic, surg. St. Mary's Hosp., Rochester, Minn., 1986-87; nurse med./surg. North Iowa Med. Ctr., Mason City, 1987-88; nurse ICU, critical care unit Naeve Hosp., Albert Lea, Minn., 1988-90, St. Joseph Mercy Hosp., Mason City, 1990-91; clinic supr. Lake Mills and Northwood, Iowa, 1991-93; office nurse Lake Mills and Northwood, Iowa, 1991-95; family nurse practitioner Lake Mills (Iowa) Clinic Mayo Health Sys., 1995—. Mem. Am. Acad. Nurse Practitioners, Am. Coll. Nurse Practitioners, Iowa Assn. Nurse Practitioners, Sigma Theta Tau. Home: 222 482nd St Lake Mills IA 50450-8032

KNUTSEN, ALAN PAUL, pediatrician, allergist, immunologist; b. Mpls., July 21, 1948; s. Donald Richard and Shirley Marie (Erickson) K.; m. Patricia Gaye Low, Dec. 21, 1974; children: Laura Joelle, Brian A., Benjamin C., Elizabeth G., Katherine M., Amy S. BA, U. Calif., Riverside, 1971; MD, St. Louis U., 1975. Resident pediatrics St. Louis U. Med. Ctr., 1975-78; fellow allergy Duke U. Med. Ctr., Durham, N.C., 1978-80;, 1980-93; dir. St. Louis U. Med. Ctr., 1985—; prof. St. Louis U., 1993—, 1993—; mem. credentials com. St. Louis U. Med. Ctr., 1980—, infectious disease com., 1980—; dir. diagnostic pediatric immunology lab, 1983—; cons. NIOSH, 1984. Contbr. articles to profl. jours. Mem. Am. Acad. Allergy/Immunology, Southwestern Allergy Assn., Mo. State Allergy Assn., So. Pediatric Rsch., Phi Beta Kappa, Alpha Omega Alpha. Democrat. Presbyterian. Home: 234 W Jackson Rd Saint Louis MO 63119-3651 Office: St Louis U Pediatric Rsch Inst 1465 S Grand Blvd Saint Louis MO 63104-1003

KNUTSSON, ANDERS, occupational epidemiologist; b. Burtrask, Sweden, Aug. 15, 1942; s. Knut and Miriam (Lindahl) Pettersson; m. Ingrid Marklund, Aug. 1, 1970; children: Bjorn, Ylva, Dag, Karin. MD, U. Umeå; Dr.med.sci., Karolinska Inst.; MPH, U. Minn., 1991. Occupational health physician SCA, Sundsvall, Sweden, 1973-94; assoc. prof. U. Umeå, 1995—. Author: Lancet, 1986, (with others) Occupational Health; contbr. articles to profl. jours. Office: Dept Occupational Environ Med, Umea Univ Hosp, 90185 Umea Sweden

KO, ALLEN HIU-CHING, orthodontist; b. Hanzhow, Chekiang, China, Jan. 27, 1953; came to U.S., 1972; s. Ki Chung and Yu Chung (Lee) K.; m. Annie Sze-han Yang, Dec. 20, 1982; children: Christopher, Elizabeth. DDS, Loyola U. Sch. of Dentistry, Maywood, Ill., 1979, cert. of specialty, 1981. Cert. Am. Bd. Orthodontists, dentist, orthodontist, Ill. Orthodontist Old Town Dental Ctr., Chgo., 1980-87; pvt. practice orthodontics Glendale, Galif., 1990-94; commodity trading advisor, Chgo., 1984—. Mem. Calif. Dental Assn., Rotary, Phi Kappa Phi.

KOBAK, ALFRED JULIAN, JR., obstetrician, gynecologist; b. Chgo., Feb. 10, 1935; s. Alfred J., and Rose B. (Baron) K.; m. Sue B. Stein, May 3, 1959; children—William, Steven, Jane, Deborah. B.S., U. Ill., 1957, M.D., 1959. Diplomate Am. Bd. Ob-Gyn. Intern Michael Reese Hosp., Chgo., 1959-60; resident Cook County Hosp., 1960-62, 64-65; practice medicine specializing in ob-gyn., Valparaiso, Ind., 1965—; mem. med. staff Porter Meml. Hosp., Valparaiso, 1965—, pres., 1981-82; asst. clin. prof. ob-gyn Ind. U.; clin. instr. ob-gyn Rush Med. Sch., Chgo.; pres. Ob-Gyn Assocs., Valparaiso, 1970—. Bd. dirs. Northwest Ind. Jewish Fedn., 1970-84, Porter County Bd. Health, 1991—. Served to capt. USAF, 1962-64. Fellow ACS, Internat. Coll. Surgeons, Am. Coll. Ob-Gyn.; mem. AMA, Am. Fertility Soc., Ind. Med. Assn., Cen. Assn. Obstetricians and Gynecologists, Porter County Med. Soc. (pres. 1979, 86), Chgo. Gynelogical Soc., Physicians Med. Alliance Ind. (bd. dirs.), Valparaiso Country Club. Republican. Contbr. articles to med. jours. Office: 1101 Glendale Blvd Valparaiso IN 46383-3724

KOBATA, AKIRA, health facility director; b. Nemuro, Hokkaido, Japan, Mar. 17, 1933; s. Kyozo and Kotoko K.; m. Misako Ohshima, Oct. 9, 1960; children: Etsuko Adelman, Kenichiro, Makoto. BA, U. Tokyo, 1956, MS, 1958, PhD, 1962. Staff mem. Rsch. Inst./Takeda Chem. Co., Osaka, 1958-67; prof., chmn. Kobe U. Sch. Medicine, Japan, 1971-83; prof., chmn. IMS/U. Tokyo, 1982-93, dir., 1990-92; dir. Tokyo Met. Inst. Gerontology, 1993—; vis. assoc. LBP, NIAMD, NIH, Bethesda, Md., 1967-69, vis. scientist, 1970-71. Author: Biology of Carbohydrate, 1984 (Toray Sci. Tech. prize 1985, Claude S. Hudson award 1992, Soc. award Pharm. Soc. Japan 1992, Japan Acad. prize 1992); contbr. articles to profl. jours. Fogarty Scholar-in-Residence, Fogarty Internat. Ctr., Bethesda, 1985-87. Mem. Japanese Biochem. Soc. (bd. dirs. Tokyo chpt. 1989-91), Japanese Soc. Protein Engring. (bd. dirs. 1988-93), Japanese Cancer Assn. (councilor 1984—), Internat. Glycoconjugate Orgn. (nat. rep. 1987—). Mem. Christian Ch. Office: Tokyo Met Inst Gerontology, 35-2 Sakaecho, Itabashi-ku, 173 Tokyo Japan

KOBAYASHI, ROGER HIDEO, allergy and immunology educator; b. Honolulu, May 21, 1947; s. Roy T. and Setsuko (Ebesugawa) K.; m. Ai Lan Doan, May 21, 1974; children: Lisa, Timothy. MS in Physiology, U. Hawaii, 1975; MD, U. Nebr., 1975. Diplomate Am. Bd. Allergy and Immunology, Am. Bd. Pediatrics, Nat. Bd. Med. Examiners. Asst. prof. pediatrics U. Nebr. Med. Ctr., Omaha, 1980-84, asst. prof. medical microbiology, 1980-85, dir. pediatric allergy and immunology, 1980-88, assoc. prof. pediatrics, 1984-88, assoc. prof. pathology and microbiology, 1985-88; assoc. prof. pediatrics UCLA, 1988-90, assoc. clin. prof. pediatrics, 1990-95, clin. prof. pediatrics, 1995—; bd. dirs. Am. Lung Assn. Nebr., Asthma and Allergy Found. Am., Am. Lung Assn. Nebr.; cons. physician Children's Hosp., 1980—, Rare Antibody and Antigen Corp., Shanghai; mem. U. Nebr. Chancellor's Com. on Rural Health, 1982-88. Grantee: Enzon Inc., 1986-88, Sandoz, Inc. 1986-87, 88-92, Schering Co. 1987-88, 90-93, NIH 1982, Mead-Johnson 1983-84, Fisons, Inc. 1990-92, Pfizer 1990-91, Rorer Pharm. 1993-96, Glaxo Inc., 1993-96, Genentech, 1994-96, Smith Kline Beecham, 1994-96, Miles Labs., 1995, Hoechst, 1995-96, McNiel, 1995, Muro, 1996—, Zeneca, 1996—, Bayer Pharm., 1996—. Fellow Am. Acad. Pediatrics (sec.-treas. Nebr. chpt. 1985-88), Am. Acad. Allergy and Immunology; mem. Nebr. Allergy Soc. (pres. 1981-84), Am. Fedn. Clin. Rsch., Am. Soc. Microbiology, Clin. Immunol. Soc. Home: 9942 Lafayette Ave Omaha NE 68114-2132

KOBAYASI, TAKASI, dermatologist, researcher; b. Osaka, Japan, Aug. 7, 1927; arrived in Denmark, 1965; s. Yosabro and Shikae (Yoshida) K.; m. Aiko Kumazawa, 1952; children: Chiyuki, Kazuhide. MD, U. Osaka, 1960. Trainee, intern Teishin Hosp., Osaka, 1950-51; asst. physician U. Hosp., Kyoto, 1951-57; rsch. fellow U. Osaka, 1957-60; chief physician City Hosp., Kurobe, 1960-63; assoc. prof. U. Yamaguchi, Ube, 1963-66; rsch. fellow Rigshospital, U. Copenhagen, 1965-70, assoc. prof., 1970-92, rschr., 1993—. Author: Electron Microscopy in Clinical Dermatology, 1989, Electron Microscopy in Dermatology, 1994, Pathogenesis and Management of Scleroderma and Connective Tissue Diseases, 1994; contbr. articles to profl. jours. including Acta Dermatovenereologica. Recipient Honor award Internat. Congress Dermatology, 1982; grantee Danish Rheumatism Assn., 1989. Mem. Danish Dermatol. Assn., Japanese Dermatol. Assn. (honor award 1990), Soc. for Cutaneous Ultrastructure Rsch., Scandinavian Soc. Electron Microscopy. Office: Bispebjerg Hosp Dermatology Dept D, Bispebjerg Bakke 23, DK-2400 Copenhagen NV, Denmark

KOBER, PHILIP MASON, physiologist, physician; b. Chgo., June 20, 1952; s. Philip James and Margaret (Mason) K. BS, DePaul U., Chgo., 1975; MS, Northwestern U., Evanston, 1977; PhD, Loyola U., Chgo., 1983; MD, Rush Med. Coll., 1994. Rsch. assoc. U. Calif., LaJolla, 1982-83; rsch. assoc. Loyola U., Maywood, Ill., 1983-87, asst. prof. med. ctr., 1987-89, 89-90; freelance computer cons., 1989-90; intern in internal medicine U. Wis., 1994-95; cons. Jandel Sci. Corp., Calif., 1986, Crunch Software Corp., Oakland, Calif., 1988. Contbr. articles to profl. jours. Active Anti-Handgun Lobby; mem. basic sci. coun. Am. Heart Assn. Contbr. articles to profl. jours. Mem. Am. Heart Assn., Am. Physiol. Soc., Nat. Parks and Conservation Assn., Am. Soc. Hypertension, Am. Med. Informatics Assn., Internat. Endotoxin Soc., Shock Soc., N.Y. Acad. Scis. Republican. Lutheran. Home: 2527 Targhee St Fitchburg WI 53711

KOBIRI, ALFRED, anesthetist; b. Jirapa, Upper West, Ghana, June 30, 1956; s. Gongol Fabian and Anso Agartha; separated; 1 child, Isaac. RN; cert. nurse anaesthetist. RN Agogo (Ghana) Hosp., 1982-86, anaesthetist, 1988-95; anaesthetist U. Hosp., Kumasi, Ghana, 1995—; lectr. Nurses' Tng. Coll., Agogo, 1982-94. Mem. Anaesthetist Assn. Roman Catholic. Office: U Hosp, U Sci and Tech, Kumasi Ghana

KOBOS, JOSEPH CASIMER, psychology educator; b. Chgo., Nov. 23, 1942; s. Casimer and Josephine (Lucarz) K.; m. Carolyn June Fetko, Aug. 28, 1965; children: Philip, Paul, Adam. BA, St. Benedict's Coll., Atchison, Kans., 1964; MS, Ohio U., 1967, PhD, 1970. Diplomate Am. Bd. Profl. Psychology. Asst. prof. psychiatry U. Tex. Health Sci. Ctr., San Antonio, 1970-76; dir. counseling svc. U. Tex. Health Sci. Ctr., 1976—, assoc. prof. psychology, 1984-90, prof., 1990—; lectr. in field; cons. in field. Author: (with G. Bauer) Brief Therapy: Short-Term Psychodynamic Intervention, 1987; prodr., dir. videotapes Psychology of the Heart, 1987, Mock Oral Exam, 1987, Money Matters, 1988, Brief Dynamic Psychotherapy, A Demonstration, 1991; editor Tex. Psychologist, 1981, Psychol Reports, 1985; mem. editl. bd. Psychotherapy theory, 1989—, Profl. Psychology: Rsch. and Practise, 1994—, Group Dynamics: Theory, Research and Application, 1996—. Bd. dirs. Leon Valley Pub. Libr., 1988-91. U.S. Dept. Edn. grantee, 1989-90, 91-93. Fellow APA (coun. reps. 1989-91, pres. divsn. 49 group psychology and group psychotherapy 1991-93, bd. profl. affairs 1992-94, chair 1994, com. on accreditation 1996—), Am. Group Psychotherapy Assn.; mem. Am. Bd. Profl. Psychology (intermountain regional bd. 1989-93), Tex.

Psychol. Assn. (pres. 1978-79), Bexar County Psychol. Assn. (pres. 1975, 77), Southwestern Psychol. Assn., Southwestern Group Therapy Soc. (treas. 1983-85), San Antonio Group Psychotherapy Soc. (exec. com. 1975-77, 83, 90-91). Roman Catholic. Office: U Tex Health Sci Ctr 7703 Floyd Curl Dr San Antonio TX 78284-7202

KOBRICK, JOHN LEO, research psychologist, educator; b. Hazleton, Pa., Sept. 11, 1925; s. John and Theresa (Demcik) K.; m. Alice Charlotte Lindsay, Aug. 28, 1954; children: John Douglas, Christopher Stuart. BS, Pa. State U., 1948, MS, 1950, PhD, 1953. Lic. psychologist, Mass. Grad. asst. dept. psycyhology Pa. State U., State College, 1948-53; rsch. psychologist U.S. Army Q.M. Climatic Rsch. Lab., Lawrence, Mass., 1953, U.S. Army R & D Command, Natick, Mass., 1953-64; rsch. psychologist U.S. Army Rsch. Inst. Environ. Medicine, Natick, 1964—, acting dir. Behavioral Scis. Lab., 1971-72, acting dir. health and performance div., 1981-83; sr. lectr. Northeastern U. Univ. Coll., Boston, 1962—; U.S. Army rep. com. on vision NAS-NRC, bioeffects adv. group U.S. Army Med. R & D Command; mem. Tri-Svc. Joint Working Group for Assessment Drug-Dependent Degradation Mil. Performance; mem. Nat. Rsch. Coun. Com. on Toxicology, 1986; presenter to numerous confs. and profl. meetings. Contbr. over 75 articles to profl. jours., chpts. to books. Fellow APA, Am. Psychol. Soc.; mem. Psychonomic Soc., Human Factors Soc. (v.p., treas. New Eng. chpt. 1962-64), Aerospace Med. Assn., N.Y. Acad. Scis., Ea. Psychol. Assn., New Eng. Psychol. Assn., Mass. Psychol. Assn., Nat. Rsch. Coun. (com. on toxicology), Sigma Xi (pres.-elect Natick chpt. 1989-90). Home: 16 Hemlock Dr # 5839 Holliston MA 01746-1506 Office: US Army Rsch Inst Environ Medicine Kansas St Natick MA 01760-2612

KOCH, BARBARA LOUISE, foreign service family nurse; b. Harrisburg, Pa., July 16, 1946; d. Robert A. and Miriam Irene (Shaffer) K.; m. Magdy El Shereiy, April 8, 1988. Diploma in nursing, Washington Hosp. Ctr. Nursing, 1970; cert., U. N.D., Grand Forks, 1991. RN N.Y., cert. P.A., Gerontological NP, ANCC, physician asst., Family Nurse Practitioner. Staff nurse Wash. Hosp. Ctr., 1970-71; grant student U. Rochester (N.Y.), 1971-72; pvt. practice with gen. surgeon and family practitioner Victor M. Breen, M.D., Roy Robinson, M.D., Dansville, Wayland, N.Y., 1972-78; foreign svc. U.S. Dept. State, Wahington, D.C., 1978—. Democrat. Episcopalian. Home and Office: Am Embassy Kiev C/O Dept State Washington DC 20521-5850

KOCH, DOUGLAS DONALD, ophthalmologist; b. Port Huron, Mich., May 28, 1951; s. Donald Allen and Helen Baptie (Webster) K. BA, Amherst Coll., 1973; MD, Harvard U., 1977. Diplomate Am. Bd. Ophthalmology. Intern St. Luke's Episcopal Hosp., Houston, 1977-78; resident in ophthalmology Baylor Coll. Medicine, Houston, 1978-81, assoc. prof. ophthalmology, 1982—; ophthalmologist Cullen Eye Inst., Houston. Mem. University Club, River Oaks Breakfast Club, Phi Beta Kappa, Alpha Omega Alpha. Office: Cullen Eye Inst 6501 Fannin St #NC200 Houston TX 77030-2703

KOCH, JO ANNE, medical technologist, educator; b. Jackson Heights, N.Y., Dec. 6, 1940; d. Francis August Emanuele and Tulia Emily (Quattrochi) Boesen; m. Anton Peter Koch, May 12, 1962; children: Tulia Emily, Christopher Francis. Degree in med. tech., Fla. Coll., Miami, 1960; BS, Nova Southeastern U., Davie, Fla., 1985; postgrad., Barry U., Miami Shores, Fla. Cert. clin. lab. scientist, med. technologist. Clin. lab. supr. Hollywood (Fla.) Med. Lab., 1960-68; med. technologist, hematology supr. Broward Gen. Med. Ctr., Ft. Lauderdale, Fla., 1968-83; lab. supr. Holy Cross Hosp., Ft. Lauderdale, 1984-86; asst. chief technologist Meml. Hosp., Hollywood, 1985-87; lab. mgr. North Miami Med. Ctr., 1987-89; faculty Miami Dade C.C., Miami, 1987—; med. technologist, mgr. Empapper Clin. Immunology Lab. U. Miami, 1991—; faculty Broward C.C., Davie, 1991, Barry U., Miami Shores, 1991; accreditation team mem. So. Assn. Colls. and Schs., Decatur, Ga. Editl. bd. Jour. Clin. Lab. Sci.; editor Fla. Jour. Med. Tech.; co-editor: The Flor Occular. Spkr. Babies and You, March of Dimes, South Fla., Dade County pub. schs. Mem. Am. Med. Technologists (pres. Fla. chpt., Mem. of Yr. 1974, Exceptional Merit 1977, Leona Lyons Carter award 1974, 76), Am. Soc. Clin. Lab. Sci., Nat. Cert. Agy. for Lab. Pers., Clin. Lab. Mgmt. Assn., Nat. Soc. Histotech., N.Y. Acad. Scis., Am. Assn. Clin. Chemistry. Democrat. Roman Catholic. Home: 6301 Mayo St Hollywood FL 33023-2250 Office: U Miami Sch Medicine Dept Medicine R-42 Immunol Lab PO Box 016960 Miami FL 33101

KOCH, JOHN HENRY, JR., physician assistant; b. Poughkeepsie, N.Y., May 28, 1943; s. John Henry Sr. and Muriel Beatrice (Ingraham) K.; m. Deborah K. Carron, June 11, 1983; children: Amy Ruth, Keri Leah, Brandon Ardon. Mortuary Sci., Simmons Sch., 1968-69; AAS, Albany Physician Asst. Program, 1975, Physician Asst. Cert., 1975. Registered physician asst. Physician asst. VA Med. Ctr., Canandaigua, N.Y., 1976-82, Syracuse, N.Y., 1982-89; physician asst. Health Sci. Ctr., Syracuse, N.Y., 1989-90, Williamson (N.Y.) Med. Ctr., 1990-93, Wayne Med. Group, Newark, 1993—; clin. cons. LeMoyne Coll. Physician Asst. Program, Syracuse, 1994, adv. com., 1995, admissions com., 1995, adj. faculty, 1995. Editor PACNY News Letter Quar., 1985—; contbr. articles to profl. jours. Corpsman USN, 1961-64. Named Ctrl. N.Y. Physician Asst. of Yr. award PACNY, 1993. Mem. Physician Assts. of Ctrl. N.Y. (coord. 1985-92), Physician Assts. of Ctrl. N.Y. (regional coord. 1992—), N.Y. State Soc. Physician Assts. (N.Y. State Physician Asst. of the Yr. 1993). Home: RD #6 Box 264 Auburn NY 13021 Office: Wayne Med Group 1200 Driving Park Ave Newark NY 14513

KOCH, KATHRYN ANN, physician, medical ethicist; b. Chgo., Jan. 31, 1951; d. Arthur Louis and Ruth Emma (Kunst) K. Student, Ind. U., 1967-70; BA, Johns Hopkins U., 1972, MD, 1975. Diplomate in internal medicine and critical care medicine Am. Bd. Internal Medicine. Intern Med. U. S.C., Charleston, 1975-76, resident in internal medicine, 1976-77, chief med. resident, 1979-80; fellow in critical care medicine and clin. pharmacology Univ. Hosps. of Cleve., 1977-79; dir. med. ICU, asst. prof. Univ. Hosps. of Cleve./Case We. Res. U., 1980-82; pvt. practice critical care medicine Meml. Med. Ctr., Jacksonville, Fla., 1982-84; dir. med. ICU, asst. prof. U. Fla. Health Sci. Ctr., Jacksonville, 1984-93, dir. critical care svcs., chief div. critical care, 1985—, assoc. prof.dept.medicine, 1993—; pres. Fla. Bioethics Network, 1994-95; physican dir. medicine, patient care group Univ. Med. Ctr., 1995—. Contbr. articles to profl. jours. Fellow ACP, Am. Coll. Chest Physicians, Coll. Critical Care Medicine; mem. Soc. Critical Care Medicine, Fla. Med. Assn., Am. Soc. Law Medicine and Ethics, Duval County Med. Soc., Soc. Bioethics Cons., Fla. Hosp. Assn., Soc. for Health and Human Values. Office: Univ Med Ctr Dept Internal Medicine 655 W 8th St Jacksonville FL 32209

KOCH, PEGGY JEAN, medical surgical nurse; b. Fargo, N.D., June 14, 1955; d. Francis Eugene and Doris Mae (Wical) Burdick; m. Randall Lynn Koch, June 30, 1973; children: Naomi Lynn, Natalie Jean, Joseph Randall. BA, Jamestown Coll., 1993. RN, N.D. Med. surg. nurse Mercy Hosp., Valley City, N.D., 1993—. Congregationalist. Home: 12039 18th R St SE Laverne ND 58056

KOCH, THERESE, nun, eucharistic minister, administrator healthcare facility; b. Petersburg, Nebr., Oct. 28, 1924; d. Frank Joseph and Elizabeth 9Brachle) K. Student, Chadron State Tchrs. Coll., 1942, Creighton U., 1944, St. Mary's Coll., 1944-45, St. Louis U., 1957, Columbia U., 1960-61. Joined Religious Fedn. St. Scholastica, Roman Cath. Ch., 1977. Mem. Missionary Benedictine Sisters, Norfolk, Nebr., 1944-77; sec.-treas. Benedictine Sisters, Liberty, Mo., 1977—; transferred vows Fedn. St. Scholastica Priory, Tulsa, 1980-89, Queen of Angels Monastery, Liberty, 1989—; adminstr. Immacolata Manor, Liberty 1981—, pres. bd. 1981-84, treas. 1981-96, spiritual leader aux., 1982—; editor Immacolata newsletter; pres. Immacolata Manor Found., 1995—. Recipient Charles Pfizer Co. award U.S. Civil Def., 1970, award of merit, Mid.-Am. Coun. Boy Scouts Am., 1975, Women Helping Women award Soroptimist Internat., 1984, William E. Yates Disting. Svc. medallion William Jewell Coll., 1992, Spirit Kansas City award, 1995. Home and Office: 717 King's Hwy Liberty MO 64068

KOCHANSKI, ADRIAN JOSEPH, human services educator; b. Milw., July 29, 1918; s. Alois S. and Antionette (Czerwinski) K.; m. Marianne Schaaf. A.B., St. Louis U., 1941, M.A., 1942, Ph.L., 1943, S.T.L., 1949; Ph.D., U. Chgo., 1955. Tchr., head prefect Campion High Sch., Prairie du Chien, Wis., 1942-46; asst. prof. edn. Marquette U., 1954-60; dean Marquette U. (Coll. Liberal Arts), 1954-60; regional dir. edn. Wis. Province Soc. of Jesus, 1960-68; founder Sogang U., Seoul, Korea, 1960, The Cath. U. of Salta, Argentina, 1964; vis. scholar Stanford, 1968-69; exec. asst. v.p. acad. affairs San Diego State U., 1969, dean acad. planning, prof. pub. adminstrn., 1970-79; assoc. dean San Diego State U. Coll. Human Services, 1979-83, prof. emeritus, 1983—; initiator, overseer Grad. Sch. Pub. Health, San Diego State U., 1970-79. Past vice chmn. Coordinating Council for Edn. in Health Scis., San Diego and Imperial Counties. Address: 2884 Ariane Dr San Diego CA 92117-2428

KOCHEN, MICHAEL MOSZE, physician; b. Munich, Oct. 2, 1950. MD, Free U. Berlin, 1976; MPH, U. Calif., Berkeley, 1979; PhD, U. Munich, 1988. Resident German Cancer Rsch. Ctr., Heidelberg, 1976-77; rsch. fellow Stanford U. Med. Ctr., Palo Alto, Calif., 1977-78; with U. Calif. Sch. Pub. Health, Program in Epidemiology, Berkeley, 1978-79; resident Free U. Berlin, 1979-82, Med. Poliklinik U. Munich, 1982-85; gen. practitioner and lectr. gen. practice family medicine Munich, 1985-89; prof. and head dept. gen. practice family medicine U. Göttingen, 1989—. Fellow Royal Coll. Gen. Practitioners. Office: U Göttingen, Abt Allgemeinmedizin, D-37075 Göttingen Germany

KOCHERIL, ABRAHAM GEORGE, physician, educator; b. Alwaye, Kerala, India, Feb. 20, 1962; came to U.S., 1970; s. George Paul and Mary G. (Kallappara) K.; m. Elizabeth Kuruvilla, Jan. 3, 1988; 1 child, George Stephen. AB, N.Y.U., 1982, MD, 1986. Diplomate Am. Bd. Internal Medicine, Am. Bd. Cardiovascular Disease, Am. Bd. Clin. Cardiac Electrophysiology. Intern, resident, chief resident Miriam Hosp. Brown U., Providence, R.I., 1986-90; fellow Yale U., New Haven, Conn., 1990-93; dir. clin. electrophysiology, asst. prof. medicine Med. Coll. Ga., Augusta, 1993-95; cardiac electrophysiologist Carle Clinic Assn., Urbana, Ill., 1995—; clin. asst. prof. medicine U. Ill., Urbana, 1995—. Contbr. articles to profl. jours.; various TV appearances. Presdl. scholar N.Y.U., 1979-82. Fellow Am. Coll. Cardiology; mem. ACP, AMA, N.Am. Soc. Pacing and Electrophysiology, Phi Beta Kappa. Office: Carle Heart Ctr 602 W University Ave Urbana IL 61801

KOCHMAN, JENNIFER LYNN, physician; b. Flushing, N.Y., May 9, 1970; d. Emil Joseph and Mary Ann (Cicack) K. BA, Binghamton U., 1992; MS, Boston U., 1996; postgrad., N.Y. Coll. Osteopathic Med., 1994—. Mem. Am. Med. Student Assn., Assn. Military Physicians and Surgeons, Assn. Military Surgeons of the U.S., Emergency Med. Osteopathic Physician Assn. Home: 98 Calvert Ave Ronkonkoma NY 11779

KOCH-SHERAS, PHYLLIS REBECCA, clinical psychologist, psychotherapist; b. Chgo., June 9, 1944; d. Morton Irving and Delores Edith (Lasser) Koch; m. Alan M. Sager, May 30, 1965 (div. 1973); m. Peter Loren Sheras, Jan. 1, 1977; children: Daniel, Sarah. BA, Roosevelt U., 1966; MA, Northwestern U., 1967; PhD, U. Tex., 1975. English tchr. Locust Jr. High Sch., Wilmette, Ill., 1967-69; dir. staff devel. children's psychiat. unit Austin (Tex.) State Hosp., 1969-72; psychology intern VA Hosp., Palo Alto, Calif., 1974-75; dir. tng. U. Va. Counseling Ctr., Charlottesville, 1975-80; pvt. practice Charlottesville, 1980—; adj. asst. prof. dept. psychology U. Va., Charlottesville, 1975-80, clin. sch. psychology program, 1981—; pres. Va. Applied Psychology Acad., Richmond, 1987-89, Creative and Healing Arts Inst., Charlottesville, 1990—. Co-author: Dream On: A Dream Interpretation and Exploration Guide for Women, 1983, The Dream Sourcebook: A Guide to the History, Theory and Interpretation of Dreams, 1995, The Dream Sourcebook Journal, 1996. Performer U. Va. Opera Workshop, 1989—, First Night Va., Charlottesville, 1986, 88, Four County Players, Act One, Light Opera Co., benefit recitals for U. Va. Art Mus., Psychology programs, Hillel Found., Med. Ctr., 1986—. NIMH grantee, 1970-72; fellow Inst. for Psychoanalysis, 1968-69. Mem. Am. Psychol. Assn., Va. Psychol. Assn. Va. Acad. Clin. Psychology, Va. Applied Psychology Acad.. Democrat. Jewish. Office: 211 W Main St Charlottesville VA 22902-5033

KOCHUPILLAI, VINOD, medical oncologist; b. Ludhiana, Punjab, India, Apr. 4, 1945; d. Siri Ram and Savitri Devi (Kansal) K.; m. Narayanan Panicker Kochupillai, June 22, 1978; children: Malini, Mrinalini. MBBS, Med. Sch., Jabalpur, India, 1968. Resident in medicine Med. Sch., Jabalpur, India, 1968, Hosps., U.K., 1968-73; fellow hemato-oncology U. Hosp., Birmingham, Ala., 1973-75; pool officer medicine All India Inst. Med. Scis., New Delhi, 1975-76, faculty dept. medicine. 1976-84, faculty med. oncology, 1984—; prof., head med. oncology All India Inst. Med. Scis., New Delhi, SD, 1986—, chief, 1992—; prof., head med. oncology Inst. Rotary Cancer Hosp., New Delhi, 1984-87; tech. expert Ministry of Health, Govt. of India, New Delhi, 1995—; vis. scientist Ind. Coun. Med. Rsch., 1988, WHO, 1991. Contbr. articles to profl. jours. Organizer Cancer Detection Camps Rural North India; mem. exec. com. Cancer Found., New Delhi, 1992—. Recipient Mahila Shiromani award Shiromani Inst., 1995; WHO fellow. Fellow Royal Coll. Physicians; mem. Internat. Planetary Soc., Indian Soc. Med. and Pediatric Oncology (pres. 1995—), Internat. Soc. Nutrition and Cancer (sci. councillor 1994—), Internat. Bone Marrow Transplant Registry (co-rep. from India), N.Y. Acad. Sci. Home: C1/19 Ansari Nagar, New Delhi 110 029, India Office: IRCH AIIMS, Ansari Nagar, New Delhi 110 029, India

KOCIS, KEITH CHRISTOPHER, pediatrician; b. Bklyn., Sept. 4, 1962; s. Daniel Joseph and Norma Patricia K. BS, SUNY, 1983, MD, 1987; MSc, U. Mich., 1993. Diplomate Nat. Bd. Med. Examiners, Am. Acad. Pediatrics. Resident in pediatrics Children's Nat. Med. Ctr., Washington, 1987-90; fellow in pediatric cardiology U. Mich., Ann Arbor, 1990-93; fellow in pediatric critical care The Johns Hopkins Med. Instns., Balt., 1994-96; with Children's Hosp., L.A., 1996—. Fellow Am. Acad. Pediatrics, Am. Coll. Cardiology.; mem. Soc. Critical Care Medicine. Roman Catholic. Office: Children's Hosp LA 5650 Sunset Blvd Los Angeles CA 90027

KOCKS, C. STEVEN, optometrist; b. Saginaw, Mich., Oct. 27, 1961; s. Carl Francis and Lillian Lorraine (Woolgar) K.; m. Lisa Anne Gray, Sept. 9, 1989; children: Carley Elizabeth, Andrew Steven. AAS, Ferris State U., 1981, DO, 1986. Lic. optometrist, Mich. Ptnr. Drs. Hilligan & Kocks, Saginaw, 1986-95, Andersen Eye Assocs., Saginaw, 1995—; asst. prof. Ferris State U., Big Rapids, Mich., 1987—. Mem. Am. Optometric Assn., Mich. Optometric Assn., Saginaw Valley Optometric Soc. (pres. 1989), Coll. Optometrists in Visual Devel., Optometric Extension Program, Saginaw Jaycees (v.p. 1988-90, pres. 1990-91, Jaycee of Yr. award 1989). Office: Andersen Eye Assocs 4344 State St Saginaw MI 48603

KOCOLOSKI, PHILIP WALTER, anesthesiologist; b. Pitts., May 13, 1958; s. Blaine Lawrence and Josephine (Filus) K.; m. Joan Frances Nedimyer, June 27, 1981; children: Adam, Matthew, Amanda, Brian, Mark, Genevieve. BS in Biology, St.Francis Coll., Loretto, Pa., 1980; DO, Phila. Coll. Osteo. Medicine, 1984. Diplomate Am. Bd. Anesthesiology. Intern Met. Hosp., Phila., 1984-85; resident in anesthesiology Wilford Hall USAF Med. Ctr., San Antonio, 1987-90; staff anesthesiologist Good Samaritan Med. Ctr., Zanesville, Ohio, 1992-93, chmn. dept., med. dir. ACLS, 1993—, spkr. continuing med. edn., 1994; pres. Anesthesia Cons. Zanesville, Inc., 1993—. Spkr. Cmty. Healthsource, Zanesville, 1996. Maj. M.C., USAF, 1985-92. Mem. Am. Soc. Anesthesiologists, Am. Soc. Regional Anesthesia, Internat. Anesthesia Rsch. Soc., Ohio Soc. Anesthesiologists. Office: Good Samaritan Med Ctr Anesthesia Dept 800 Forest Ave Zanesville OH 43000

KOCSIS, JAMES HOWARD, psychiatrist; b. Torrington, Conn., June 20, 1942; s. Frank and Barbara Jean (Kellogg) K.; m. Andrea Freeburg, May 27, 1967 (div. 1980); children: Alison, James A.; m. Randy Lehrer, May 12, 1984. BA, Amherst Coll., 1964; MD, Cornell U., 1968. Diplomate Am. Bd. Psychiatry and Neurology. Instr. dept. psychiatry Cornell U. Med. Coll., N.Y.C., 1975-77, asst. prof., 1977-83, assoc. prof., 1983-91, prof., 1992—; intern Cornell North Shore Meml. Hosp., N.Y.C., 1968-69; resident N.Y. Hosp., 1969-70, 72-75, chief resident, 1974-75; pvt. practice Payne Whitney Clinic, N.Y.C., 1975—. Contbr. articles to profl. publs., chpts. to books. Lt. comdr. USN, 1970-72. Fellow Am. Psychiatric Assn.; mem. Am. Coll. Neuropsychopharmacology, Washington Club. Office: Payne Whitney Clinic 525 E 68th St New York NY 10021-4873

KODSI, SYLVIA ROSE, ophthalmologist; b. Boston, Nov. 13, 1962; d. Baroukh and Marie Kodsi; m. Michael Evan Rettig, May 13, 1990; children: Stephanie, Samantha. BS, Stanford U., 1983; MD, NYU, 1987. Intern in internal medicine Beth Israel Med. Ctr., N.Y.C., 1987-88; resident in ophthalmology St. Vincent's Med. Ctr., N.Y.C., 1988-91; neuro-ophthalmology fellow Mayo Clinic, Rochester, Minn., 1991-92; pediatric ophthalmology fellow U. Minn., Mpls., 1992-93; attending physician in-charge pediatric ophthalmology L.I. Jewish Med. Ctr., New Hyde Park, N.Y., 1994—. Fellow Am. Acad. Ophthalmology; mem. Assn. Pediatric Ophthalmology and Strabismus, N.Y. Soc. Pediatric Ophthalmology and Strabismis. Office: Long Island Jewish Med Ctr 270-05 76th Ave New Hyde Park NY 11040

KOEHN, JAN, industrial hygienist; b. Houston, June 11, 1957; d. Wilbert A. and Lorene C. Koehn. BS, Tex. A&M U., 1979; MS, U. Tex., Houston, 1983. Cert. indsl. hygienist. Rsch. asst. I U. Tex. Med. Sch., Houston, 1979-81; rsch. asst. II U. Tex. Sch. Pub. Health, Houston, 1981-82, grad. rsch. asst., 1982-83; biohazard safety specialist U. Tex. Health Sci. Ctr., Houston, 1983-86, dir. chem. and biol. safety, 1986-87; pres. Jan Koehn, M.S., CIH, Inc., Houston, 1987—. Mem. Am. Soc. Safety Engrs., Environ. Info. Assn., Am. Indsl. Hygiene Assn., Gulf Coast Indsl. Hygiene Assn. (sec. 1987-88, bd. dirs. 1988-90, pres.-elect 1993, pres. 1994, past pres. 1995), Am. Bus. Women's Assn. Office: 8926 Kirby Dr Houston TX 77054-2810

KOEHNKE, JANET DEL, audiology educator, researcher; b. Newark, Aug. 26, 1954; d. George and Lotte (Heuman) Blustein. BS in Comm. Disorders, U. Mass., 1976; MA in Audiology, SUNY, Geneseo, 1977; PhD in Comm. Scis., U. Conn., 1983. Audiologist Waltham (Mass.) Pub. Schs., 1978-79, VA Med. Ctr., Newington, Conn., 1979-80; postdoctoral fellow MIT Rsch. Lab. Electronics, Cambridge, 1983-86; rsch. asst. prof. dept. communication disorders Boston U., 1985-90, sr. rsch. assoc. dept. biomed. engring., 1990—; asst. prof. dept. communication scis. U. Conn., Storrs, 1990-92; asst. prof. dept. comm. scis. and disorders La. State U., Baton Rouge, 1992-94, assoc. prof., 1994-95; assoc. prof. dept. speech pathology and audiology U. South Ala., Mobile, 1995—; vis. scientist MIT Rsch. Lab. Electronics, Cambridge, 1986-92. Editor book/software rev. sect., editor-at-large Ear and Hearing Jour.; contbr. articles to profl. jours. Recipient First Ind. Rsch. and Transition award NIH, 1987-94, Deafness Rsch. Found. award, 1989-90, 90-91, 91-92, 94, 95, 96; grantee Am. Hearing Rsch. Found., 1996. Mem. Am. Speech-Lang.-Hearing Assn. (cert. clin. competence), Acoustical Soc. Am., Assn. Rsch. Otolaryngology, Am. Auditory Soc. Office: Univ South Ala Speech Pathology/Audiology 2000 University Commons Mobile AL 36688

KOELLE, GEORGE BRAMPTON, university pharmacologist, educator; b. Phila., Oct. 8, 1918; s. Frederick Christian and Emily Mary (Brampton) K.; m. Winifred Jean Angenent, Feb. 6, 1954; children: Peter Brampton, William Angenent, Jonathan Stuart. BS, Phila. Coll. Pharmacy and Sci., 1939, DS (hon.), 1965; PhD, U. Pa., 1946; MD, Johns Hopkins U., 1950; Dr. Med. (hon.), U. Zurich, Switzerland, 1972. Bio-assayist LaWall & Harrisson, 1939-42; asst. prof. pharmacology Coll. Phys. and Surg., Columbia U., 1950-52; prof. pharmacology Grad. Sch. Medicine, U. Pa., 1952-59; chmn. dept. physiology and pharmacology, dean Grad. Sch. Medicine U. Pa., 1957-59, chmn. dept. pharmacology Med. Sch., 1959-81, disting. prof., 1981—; spl. lectr. U. London, 1961; vis. lectr. U. Brazil, 1962, Polish Acad. Scis., 1979; vis. prof., Guggenheim fellow U. Lausanne, 1963-64; vis. prof. pharmacology, chmn. dept. Pahlavi U., Shiraz, Iran, 1969-70; cons. McNeil Labs., 1951-66, Phila. Gen. Hosp., 1953-65, Valley Forge Army Hosp., 1954-71, Army Chem. Corps, 1956-60, Phila. Naval Hosp., 1957-65; vis. lectr. pharmacology Phila. Coll. Pharmacy and Sci., 1955-57; vis. prof. Mahidol U., Bangkok, Thailand, 1978; mem. pharmacology study sect. USPHS, 1958-62, chmn. pharmacology study sect., 1965-68; sec. gen. Internat. Union of Pharmacology, 1966-69, v.p., 1969-72; mem. bd. sci. Counselors Nat. Heart Inst., NIH, USPHS, 1960-64, mem. nat. adv. neurol. diseases and stroke council, 1970-75. Assoc. editor: Remington's Practice of Pharmacy, 1951; mem. editorial bd. Pharmacol. Revs, 1955-63; chmn., 1959-62; hon. editorial adv. bd. Biochem. Pharmacology, 1958-72; editorial adv. bd. Internat. Jour. Neurosci, 1970-75; editorial com. Ann. Rev. Pharmacology, 1959-65; editorial bd. Internat. Ency. Pharmacology and Therapeutics; editor: Cholinesterases and Anticholinestrerase Agents, 1963; contbr. articles on pharmacology to profl. jours. Trustee Phila. Coll. Pharmacy and Sci., Found. for Vascular-Hypertension Research; mem. bd. mgrs. Wistar Inst. Served to 1st lt. Med. Adminstrn. Corps AUS, 1942-46. Recipient Abel prize in pharmacology Am. Soc. Pharmacology and Exptl. Therapeutics, 1950; Travel award XVIIIth Internat. Physiol. Congress, Copenhagen; Borden undergrad. research award, 1950; U. Turku Meml. medal, 1972; U. Helsinki Meml. medal, 1984; Sr. Internat. fellow CNRS, Ecole Normale Superieure, Paris, 1986-87. Fellow AAAS (v.p. 1971), N.Y. Acad. Scis., Am. Coll. Clin. Pharmacology (hon.); mem. NAS (del. to USSR 1989), Am. Soc. Pharmacology and Exptl. Therapeutics (pres. 1965-66, plenary lectr. 1981, Torald Sollmann award 1990), Histochem. Soc., Harvey Soc., Soc. Biol. Psychiatry, John Morgan Soc., Sydenham Coterie, Sons Copper Beeches, Brit. Pharmacol. Soc., Biol. Soc. Chile (hon.), Internat. Neurochem. Soc., Soc. for Neurosci., Pharmacol. Soc. Peru (hon.), Pharmacol. Soc. Japan (hon.), Shakespeare Soc. Phila., Sigma Xi, Alpha Omega Alpha. Home: 205 College Ave Swarthmore PA 19081-1408 Office: Sch Medicine Univ Pa. Philadelphia PA 19104-6084

KOENIG, GINA LEE, microbiologist; b. Scranton, Pa., July 3, 1962; d. Leon Henry Koenig and Carmela Ann (Romolo) Koenigsberg; m. John Henry Carter III, Feb. 11, 1989 (div. 1995). BS, Pa. State U., 1984; MA with honors, San Francisco State U., 1993. Rsch. asst. Ctr. for Air Environ. Studies, State College, Pa., 1983-84; fisheries biologist Nat. Marine Fisheries Service, Seattle, 1984-85; rsch. asst. Monterey Mushrooms, Watsonville, Calif., 1985-87; microbiologist Genencor, Internat., South San Francisco, 1987-92; rsch. scientist, curator culture collection dept. Roche Molecular Systems, Alameda, Calif., 1992-96, mem. instnl. biol. safety com., 1992—, sr. scientist, 1996—. Contbr. articles to profl. jours. Recipient 1st pl. award Calif. State U. Biology Student Rsch. Competition, 1992. Mem. Am. Soc. Microbiology (com. for culture collections 1994—), Soc. for Cryobiology, U.S. Fedn. Culture Collections (program com. 1992, chmn. publicity com. 1992-94, exec. bd. dirs.-at-large 1993-96), World Fedn. Culture Collections (program com. 1996), Toastmasters Internat. (v.p. edn. 1996, Competent Toastmaster 1996), Mycological Soc. Am., Mycological Soc. San Francisco, Pa. State U. Alumni Assn., Soc. for Indsl. Microbiology. Democrat. Mem. Christian Ch. Office: Roche Molecular Systems Inc 1145 Atlantic Ave Alameda CA 94501-1145

KOENIGSBERG, JUDITH Z. NULMAN, clinical psychologist; b. Bklyn., Apr. 21, 1951; d. Macy and Sarah (Rosenberg) Nulman; m. David I. Koenigsberg, June 18, 1972; children: Benjamin, Rachel. Grad. summa cum laude, Yeshiva U. Tchrs. Inst., New York City, 1971; BA with honors, Bklyn. Coll., 1972; MA, Northeastern Ill. U., 1980; postgrad., U. Chgo., 1980-82; MEd, Loyola U., Chgo., 1985; PhD in Psychology, Northwestern U., 1990. Lic. and reg. clin. psychologist, Ill.; Nat. Register of Health Service Providers in Psychology. Clin. specialist Charter Barclay Hosp., Chgo., 1985-86; psychology extern Luth. Gen. Hosp., Park Ridge, Ill., 1987-88; psychol. testing extern Evanston (Ill.) Hosp., 1988-89, psychology intern, 1989-90; psychology postdoctoral resident Loyola U. Chgo., 1991-92; clin. psychologist U. Chgo., 1993-94; cons. Tutors Unltd., Inc., 1995—; co-investigator rsch. project U. Chgo., 1995—. Contbr. articles to profl. jours. Recipient Outstanding Achievement award Nat. Culture Coun., 1972; scholarship award dept. modern langs. Bklyn. Coll., 1972, Kappa Delta Pi, 1972. Fellow Prescribing Psychologists' Register (cand.); mem. APA, Ill. Psychol.

Assn., Northwestern U. Alumni Assn. Sch. Edn. and Social Policy (dir. bd. 1993-94), Early Career Preventionists Network (steering com. 1995). Office: 708 Church St Ste 243 Evanston IL 60201 also: 166 E Superior St Ste 311 Chicago IL 60611-2920 also: Tutors Unltd Inc 7366 N Lincoln Ave Ste 404 Lincolnwood IL 60646

KOENIGSBERG, ROBERT ALAN, neuroradiologist; b. Phila., Sept. 10, 1956; s. Abraham and Eleanor Marilyn (Teacher) K.; m. Bess Shira, Aug. 18, 1985; children: David Louis, Sarah Michelle. BA, Brandeis U., 1978; DO, Phila. Coll. Osteo. Medicine, 1982, MS, 1988. Diplomate Nat. Bd. Examiners for Osteo. Physicians, Am. Osteo. Bd. Radiology. Intern Met. Hosp., Phila., 1982-83; resident in diagnostic radiology Phila. Coll. Osteo. Medicine, 1984-87; resident in neurology Hahnemann U., Phila., 1983-84; fellow in neuroradiology L.I. Jewish Med. Ctr., New Hyde Park, N.Y., 1987-89; fellow interventional neuroradiology U. Ill., Chgo., 1994-95; asst. prof. radiology L.I. Jewish Med. Ctr., New Hyde Park, 1989-90; asst. prof. radiology Med. Coll. Pa., Phila., 1990—, dir. neuroradiology, 1992—, mem. stroke task force, 1992-93, mem. trauma com., 1992-93; fellow in interventional neuroradiology U. Ill., Chgo., 1994-95; mem. edtl. rev. com. Am. Osteo. Coll. Radiology, 1990-92, Am. Coll. Radiology, 1992; presenter Am. Soc. Neuroradiology, 1990, Radiol. Soc. N.Am., Chgo., 1990, others. Contbr. articles to profl. jours. Mem. Brandeis Alumni Admissions Coun., Phila., 1992—. Mem. Am. Soc. Neuroradiology, Am. Osteo. Coll. Radiology, Am. Osteo. Assn., Am. Coll. Radiology, Pa. State Radiol. Soc., Radiol. Soc. N.Am., Am. Roentgen Ray Soc., Brandeis U. Alumni Assn. Office: Med Coll Pa 3300 Henry Ave Philadelphia PA 19129-1121

KOEP, LAWRENCE JAMES, surgeon; b. Pasadena, Calif., May 6, 1944; s. Ambrose Urban and Loma Mary (Riordan) K.; m. Jennifer Leigh James, FEb. 4, 1982 (div. Jan. 1992); children: Alexander, Erik, Lauren. BS, Johns Hopkins U., 1966, MD, 1970. Diplomate Am. Bd. Surgery. Intern Johns Hopkins Hosp., Balt., 1970-71, resident, 1971-76; assoc. prof. U. Colo., Denver, 1976-81; pvt. practice Phoenix, 1981—; bd. dirs. Donor Network Ariz. Mem. ACS, Am. Soc. Transplant Surgeons, Western Surg. Assn. Home: 3729 E Rancho Dr Paradise Vly AZ 85253-5022 Office: 1410 N 3rd St Phoenix AZ 85004-1608

KOEPKE, RONALD PAUL, cardiologist; b. Madras, India, Nov. 21, 1948; s. Robert Theodore and Lorene Mildred Koepke; m. Marilyn Ann Schleicher, June 24, 1978; children: Katherine Ann, Laura Elizabeth, Paul Theodore. BSc, Valparaiso U., 1970; MD, St. Louis U., 1974. Internship and residency in internal medicine Charity Hosp., New Orleans, 1974-77; fellowship in cardiovascular diseases Tulane Affiliated Hosps., 1977-79; asst. prof. internal medicine dept. cardiology Tulane U., New Orleans, 1979-83; pvt. practice West Monroe, La., 1983—; med. dir. coronary care unit, cardiac catheterization lab. St. Francis Med. Ctr., Monroe, La., 1987—, Glenwood Regional Med. Ctr., W. Monroe, La., 1992—. Fellow Am. Coll. Cardiology, Am. Coll. Chest Physicians; mem. AMA, ACP, So. Med. Assn., Ouachita Med. Soc. (v.p. 1992, pres.-elect 1993). Lutheran. Office: 200 Professional Dr West Monroe LA 71291-5359

KOEPPE, PATSY PODUSKA, internist, educator; b. Memphis, Nov. 18, 1932; d. Ben F. and Lily Mae (Reid) Poduska; m. Douglas F. Koeppe Sr., Sept. 8, 1967; 1 child, Douglas F. Jr. BA, Tex. Woman's U., 1954; MD, U. Tenn., 1957. Intern Roanoke (Va.) Meml. Hosp., 1960-61; resident in internal medicine VA Teaching Group Hosp., Memphis, 1961-62, Lahey Clinic, Boston, 1962-63; fellow in endocrinology and metabolism U. Tex. Med. Br., Galveston, 1963-65; pvt. practice Kingsville, Tex., 1972-73; dir. Women's Health Care Ctr., College Park, Md., 1974-77; instr. internal medicine and endocrinology U. Tex., Galveston, 1965-69; asst. prof. endocrinology Med. Br., U. Tex., Galveston, 1969-72, asst. prof. internal medicine, 1969-72, 78-87; assoc. prof. U. Tex., Galveston, 1987-93, prof., 1994—; mem. grad. faculty biomed. sci. Med. Br., U. Tex., Galveston, 1983—, acting dir. div. geriatrics, 1991-92. Mem. Am. Geriatric Soc., Tex. Med. Assn., Tex. Med. Found., Galveston County Med. Soc. Presbyterian. Home: 323 Brookdale Dr League City TX 77573-1668 Office: Univ Tex Med Br 30325 Jennie Sealy Hosp D60 Galveston TX 77555-0460

KOERNER, JO ELLEN, hospital executive; b. Sioux Falls, S.D., Aug. 13, 1946; d. Reuben and Florence Carolyn (Gering) Goertz; m. Dennis J. Koerner, Feb. 17, 1967; children: Kristi Jo, Christopher John. Diploma, Sioux Valley Hosp. Sch. Nursing, Sioux Falls, 1967; BS, Mt. Marty Coll., 1980; MS, S.D. State U., 1982; PhD, Fielding Inst., 1993. RN, S.D. Nurse mgr. Sioux Valley Hosp., Sioux Falls, 1968-70; physicians asst. Rural Med. Clinics, Freeman, S.D., 1973-75; dir. nursing dept. Freeman Jr. Coll., 1975-82; exec. sec. S.D. Bd. of Nursing, Sioux Falls, 1982-84; v.p. patient svcs. Sioux Valley Hosp., Sioux Falls, 1984—; preceptor U. Minn., Mpls., 1985—; cons., New Zealand, Czechoslovakia; mem. PEW Health Professions Commn.; faculty Ctr. for Nursing Leadership and Inst. Health Care Execs. Co-author: for F.A. Davis Book Co., 1983; mem. editl. bd. Jour. Nursing Adminstrn., Nursing Outlook, Jour. Profl. Nursing, Nursing Adminstrn. Quarterly; editor book in field, 1994; contbr. articles to profl. jours. Task force mem. Nat. Commn. on Nursing, 1987—; v.p. S.D. Bd. Nursing, Sioux Falls, 1980-82; nursing rep. Gov.'s Task Force; treas., bd. dirs. Family Svcs., Sioux Falls, 1987—; mem. S.D. Women's Advocacy Network, Sioux Falls, 1985—; sec., bd. dirs. Freeman Hosp., 1980-86. Named S.D. Woman of Yr., Am. Adv. Bd., 1980; Top 10 Businesswoman of S.D., 1994; recipient Golden Heart award, 1985, Profl. Leader of Yr. award YWCA, 1992, Disting. Alumni award profl. divsn. S.D. State U., 1993; fellow U. Pa. Wharton Sch., 1986. Fellow Am. Acad. Nursing; mem. S.D. Nurses Assn. (bd. dirs. 1985-87, Pres.'s award 1987), S.D. Orgn. Nurse Execs. (nat. bd. dirs. 1991, coun. rep. 1985—), Sioux Falls C. of C. (bd. dirs., treas. 1993), Profl. and Bus. Women's Assn., Am. Orgn. Nurse Execs. (pres. 1996—), Dorcas Soc., Phi Kappa Gamma, Sigma Theta Tau (disting. lectr. award). Republican. Office: Sioux Valley Hosp 1100 S Euclid Ave Sioux Falls SD 57105-0411

KOERNER, MICHAEL K., neurologist; b. Hamburg, Germany, Aug. 30, 1950; came to the U.S., 1956; s. Karl and Gerlind B. (Kump) K. MD, U. Mich., 1977. Intern Miriam Hosp., Providence, R.I., 1977-78; resident U. N.Mex., Albuquerque, 1978-81; pvt. practice Marquette, Mich., 1982-85; fellow in epilepsy Good Samaritan Hosp., Portland, Oreg., 1985-87, U. Wash., Seattle, 1987-88; pvt. practice Everett, Wash., 1988—. Mem. Am. Acad. Neurology, Am. Epilepsy Soc., Epilepsy Assn. Western Wash., Wash. Med. Assn. Office: 2320 Rucker Ave Everett WA 98201

KOESTERER, LARRY J., pharmacist; b. Belleville, Ill.. Dec. 13, 1956; s. Edward John and Antionette Catherine (Meister) K.; m. Sandra J. Meyers, Jan. 5, 1991. BS in Pharmacy, St. Louis Coll. Pharmacy, 1974; MBA, Webster U., St. Louis, 1989. Registered pharmacist, Mo., Ill. Pharmacy intern Meml. Hosp., Belleville, 1976-79; staff pharmacist St. Elizabeth's Hosp., Belleville, 1979-88, ops. coord., 1988-89; dir. pharmacy St. Louis Children's Hosp., 1989-94; dist. mgr. Owen Healthcare, St. Louis, 1994—; bd. dirs. Child Health Corp., pharmacy com. 1994; mem. Pediat. Pharmacy Advocacy Group, 1994. Bd. dirs. Second Generation Swing, Belleville, 1979—. Mem. Rho Chi. Roman Catholic. Office: Owen Healthcare One City Pl Ste 290 Saint Louis MO 63141

KOFFLER, HERBERT, health facility administrator, educator; b. Columbus, Ohio, July 7, 1940; s. Joseph and Esther Koffler; m. Michelle Ann Koffler, Dec. 29, 1965; children: evan Douglas, Joshua Adam. BS in Zoology, U. Cin., 1962, MD, 1966; postgrad., Ariz. State U., 1989-91; MS in Adminstrv. Medicine, U. Wis., 1993. Diplomate Am. Bd. Pediatrics, Am. Bd. Neonatology. Instr. in pediatrics U. Cin., 1969-70, 72-74, U. Calif., Davis, 1971-72; assoc. prof. pediatrics U. N.Mex., Albuquerque, 1974-78, dir. newborn svcs. divsn. neonatology, 1976-88, assoc. prof. pediatrics and ob-gyn., 1978-88, prof. pediatrics and ob-gyn., 1988-95, prof. emeritus, 1995, clin. prof. family and cmty. medicine, 1995—; asst. dir. managed care svcs. U. N.Mex. Hosp., Albuquerque, 1992-95; med. dir. Prudential HealthCare, Albuquerque, 1995—; mem. cons. staff pediatrics Presbyn. Hosp., Albuquerque, 1974-95, Lovelace Hosp., Albuquerque, 1974-95. Author: (with R. Coen) Primary Care of the Newborn, 1987. Bd. dirs. Chaparral Home and Adoption Svcs., Family and Children Svcs., Albuquerque, 1984, Ronald McDonald Charities, Albuquerque, 1987—. Maj. USAF, 1970-72. Herb Koffler Day proclaimed in his honor State of N.Mex. and U. N.Mex., 1995. Mem. Am. Acad. Pediatrics, Am. Coll. Physician Execs., Western Soc. for Pediatrics Rsch., Greater Albuquerque Med. Assn. (alternate del., del. 1992—), Phi Delta Epsilon. Home: 4701 Larchmont Dr NE Albuquerque NM 87111 Office: Prudential Health Care 1700A Louisiana Blvd 230 Albuquerque NM 87110

KOFFSKY, ROBERT MICHAEL, biomedical engineering company executive; b. Albany, N.Y., Apr. 27, 1937; s. Samuel Koffsky and Nancy (Bittman) Raphael; m. Barbara Schwartz, Apr. 2, 1961. BS in Indsl. Engring., Calif. State Poly. Coll., 1965; MS in Indsl. Engring., Columbia U., 1966. Design engr. Achievement House, San Luis Obispo, Calif., 1963-64; systems analyst Gen. Foods Corp., White Plains, N.Y., 1965-66; sr. research assoc. Columbia U., N.Y.C., 1966-73; project leader ALZA Research Inc., Palo Alto, Calif., 1973-76; sr. bioengr. Mt. Sinai Med. Ctr., N.Y.C., 1985-96; cons. Miller Hill Ltd., Hopewell Junction, 1977—. Contbr. articles to profl. jours. Served with U.S. Army, 1956-59. Recipient Cert. Achievement Soc. Mfg. Engrs., 1965. Fellow Am. Inst. Indsl. Engring., N.Y. Acad. Medicine; mem. Am. Heart Assn., Am. Soc. Artificial Internal Organs, Phi Kappa Phi, Tau Sigma.

KOFKE, WILLIAM ANDREW, anesthesiologist, medical administrator; b. Drexel Hill, Pa., Feb. 4, 1952; s. William Albert Jr. and Joan (Healey) K.; m. Marianne Lydia Maniet, July 24, 1976; children: Lauren Marie, Matthew Joseph, Marisa Anne, Elise Christine. BS in Chemistry, Bucknell U., 1974; MD, U. Pitts., 1978. Diplomate Am. Bd. Anesthesiology, Am. Bd. Critical Care Medicine. Intern Mercy Hosp., Pitts., 1978-79; resident Mass. Gen. Hosp., Boston, 1979-81; instr. in anesthesiology Harvard Med. Sch., Boston, 1981-82, resident, 1982-83; asst. prof. anesthesiology Pa. State U., Hershey, 1983-88; assoc. prof. anesthesiology U. Pitts., 1988-96, prof., 1996—; dir. neurointensive care unit U. Pitts. Med. Ctr. Editor: Postoperative Critical Care Procedures of the Massachusetts General Hospital, 1986; contbr. articles to profl. jours. Named Parker B. Francis Investigator in Anesthesiology, Am. Soc. Anesthesiologists, 1984-86. Fellow Am. Coll. Critical Care Medicine; mem. Assn. Univ. Anesthesiologists, Pa. Soc. Critical Care Medicine (pres. 1990-92). Office: U Pitts Dept Anesthesia A1305 Scaife Hall Pittsburgh PA 15261-2013

KOFSKY, PHILLIP MARK, surgeon; b. Bklyn., June 12, 1956; m. Pamela Dana Furman. BS, Muhlenberg Coll., 1978; MD, Temple U., 1984. Diplomate Am. Bd. Surgery, Am. Bd. Colon and Rectal Surgery. Resident in gen. surgery Albert Einstein Med. Ctr., Phila., 1984-89; fellow in colon-rectal surgery Lehigh Valley Hosp. Ctr., Allentown, Pa., 1989-90; ptnr. Associated Surgeons, Norristown, Pa., 1990—; attending surgeon Montgomery Hosp., Norristown, Pa., 1990—, Suburban Gen. Hosp., Norristown, Pa., 1994—. Contbr. articles to profl. jours. Fellow Am. Coll. Surgeons, Pa. Soc. Colon and Rectal Surgeons; mem. Am. Soc. Colon and Rectal Surgeons, Soc. Am. Gastrointestinal Endoscopic Surgeons, Pa. Med. Soc., Montgomery County Med. Soc. Office: Associated Surgeons 21 W Fornance St Norristown PA 19401

KOGAN, RICHARD JAY, pharmaceutical company executive; b. N.Y.C., June 6, 1941; s. Benjamin and Ida K.; m. Susan Linda Scher, Aug. 29, 1965. BA, CCNY, 1963; MBA, NYU, 1968. Dir. planning and adminstrn. Ciba Corp., Summit, N.J., 1968-69; v.p. planning, pharm. div. Ciba-Geigy Corp., Summit, 1970-76; pres. Can. pharm. div. Ciba-Geigy Corp., Can., 1976-79; pres. U.S. pharm. div. Ciba-Geigy Corp., Summit, 1979-82; exec. v.p. pharm. ops. Schering-Plough Corp., Madison, N.J., 1982-86; pres., chief oper. officer Schering-Plough Corp., Kenilworth, N.J., 1986—; bd. dir. Schering-Plough Corp., Kenilworth; bd. dirs. Nat. Westminster Bancorp, Rite Aid Corp., Gen. Signal Corp. Trustee St. Barnabas Med. Ctr.; bd. overseers Sch. Bus. NYU. Office: Schering-Plough Corp PO Box 1000 Madison NJ 07940-1027*

KOHLER, F. PETER, urologic surgeon; b. Germany, Dec. 22, 1928; came to U.S., 1949; m. Marjorie M. Mulder, June 15, 1956; children: Karen, Susan, Ellen. BS, Haverford Coll., 1952; MD, U. Pa., 1956. Diplomate Am. Bd. Urology. Chief divsn. urology Lankenau Hosp., Wynnewood, Pa., 1976-87; assoc. clin. prof. urology Jefferson U., Phila.; pediatric urologist MacKinney, Kohler, Kelsey P.C., Wynnewood; pres. Lankenau Hosp. Contbr. over 60 articles to med. jours. Hon. consul gen. Fed. Republic of Germany, Phila., 1987-95. Capt. USAF, 1959-61. Decorated DSC; NSF fellow. Mem. Am. Urology Assn., Delaware County Med. Soc. (pres.), German Soc. of Pa., Franklin Inn Club, Med. Club Phila. (pres.), Phi Beta Kappa. Office: MacKinney Kohler Kelsey PC 361 Medical Blvd E Wynnewood PA 19096

KOHLER, FREDERICK WILLIAM, JR., pharmacist; b. Passaic, N.J., Apr. 28, 1955. Student, U. Toledo, U. Md.; BS in Pharmacy, Temple U., 1981, MS in Pharmacology, 1985, PhD in Pharmacology, 1990. Registered pharmacist, N.J., Pa. Instr. pharmacology Temple U. Sch. Dental Hygiene, Phila., 1982-87; teaching asst. anatomy, pharmacy, pharmacology labs. Temple U. Sch. Pharmacy, Phila., 1982-87, teaching assoc. pharmacology, 1987-90; dir. Michael and Charles Barnett Meml. Lab. Lab. Mitochondrial Disease Biochemistry, 1991-95; lectr. Gwynedd-Mercy Coll., Gwynedd Valley, Pa., 1995—; med. info. projects mgr. Zeneca Pharmaceuticals, Wilmington, Del., 1996—; pharmacist RXD PHarmacies, Inc., Collingswood, N.J., 1994—; dir. undergrad. pharmacology lab. Temple U. Sch. Pharmacy, 1986-95, admissions com. mem., 1987-95, coord. grad. seminar, 1989-93, grad. rsch. com. for PhD candidate, 1990-95, dir. pharmacology grad. rsch. data analysis and computer programming, 1990-95, chmn. tchg. evaluation and recognition com., 1991-93, disciplinary com. mem., 1992, grad. thesis reading com. for MS candidate, 1993; collection devel. cons. Temple U. Health Sci. Libr., 1990-95; cons. Law Offices Reuss, Cavaglarao & Kaspar, 1995; ind. contractor Target Rsch. Assocs., Scotch Plains, N.J., 1995; cons. Dept. Atty. Gen. of Commonwealth of Pa., 1995—. Recipient Furst award Am. Coll. Toxicology, 1987, Upjohn Pharmacy Rsch. award, 1990. Mem. AAAS, Am. Assn. Coll. Pharmacy, Am. Pharm. Assn., Mid-Atlantic Pharmacology Soc., Mid. Atlantic Reprodn. and Teratology Assn., Mid. Atlantic Soc. Toxicology, Montgomery County Pharm. Assn., Rotary, Sigma Xi, Rho Chi, Kappa Psi (faculty advisor 1991-95). Office: Zeneca Pharmaceuticals 1800 Concord Pike PO Box 15437 Wilmington DE 19850-5437

KOHLER, PETER OGDEN, physician, educator, university president; b. Bklyn., July 18, 1938; s. Dayton McCue and Jean Stewart (Ogden) K.; m. Judy Lynn Baker, Dec. 26, 1959; children: Brooke Culp, Stephen Edwin, Todd Randolph, Adam Stewart. BA, U. Va., 1959; MD, Duke U., 1963. Diplomate Am. Bd. Internal Medicine and Endocrinology. Intern Duke U. Hosp., Durham, N.C., 1963-64, fellow, 1964-65; clin. assoc. Nat Cancer Inst., Nat Inst. Child Health and Human Devel., NIH, Bethesda, Md., 1965-67, sr. investigator, 1968-73, head endocrinology service, 1972-73; resident in medicine Georgetown U. Hosp., Washington, 1969-70; prof. medicine and cell biology, chief endocrinology divsn. Baylor Coll. Medicine, Houston, 1973-77; prof., chmn. dept. medicine U. Ark., 1977-86, interim dean, 1985-86; chmn. Hosp. Med. Bd., 1980-82, chmn. council dept. chmn., 1979-80; prof., dean Sch. Medicine, U. Tex., San Antonio, 1986-88; pres. Oreg. Health Scis. U., Portland, 1988—; cons. endocrinology merit rev. bd. VA, 1985-86; mem. endocrinology study sect. NIH, 1981-85, chmn., 1984-85; mem. bd. sci. counselors NICHD, 1987-92, chair, 1990-92; chair task force on health care delivery AAHC, 1991-92; bd. dirs. Standard Ins. Co., First Interstate Bank-Oreg., HealthChoice, Assn. Acad. Health Ctrs., OHSU; mem. adv. bd. Loaves and Fishes, 1989; mem. Gov.'s adv. com. Commn. on Tech. Edn., 1989—; chair Oreg. Health Coun., 1993-95; mem. bd. govs. Am. Bd. Internal Medicine, 1987-93, mem. endocrinology bd., 1983-91, chmn., 1987-91. Editor: Current Opinion in Endocrinology and Diabetes, 1994—, Diagnosis and Treatment of Pituitary Tumors, (with G. T. Ross), 1973, Clinical Endocrinology, 1986; assoc. editor: Internal Medicine, 1983, 87, 90, 94; contbr. articles to profl. jours. With USPHS, 1965-68. NIH grantee, 1973—; Howard Hughes Med. Investigator, 1976-77; recipient NIH Quality awrds, 1969, 71, Disting. Alumnus awrad Duke Med. Sch., 1992, MRF Mentor award, Med. Rsch. Found., 1994, Humanitarian award Am. Lung Assn., 1996. Fellow ACP; mem. AMA (William Beaumont award 1988), Inst. Medicine, Am. Soc. Clin. Investigation, Am. Fedn. Clin. Rsch. (nat. coun. 1977-78, pres. so. sect. 1976), So. Soc. Clin. Investigation (coun. 1979-82, pres. 1983, Founder's medal 1987), Am. Soc. Cell Biology, Assn. Am. Physicians, Am. Diabetes Assn., Endocrine Soc. (coun. 1990-93), Raven Soc., Phi Beta Kappa, Sigma Xi, Alpha Omega Alpha, Omicron Delta Kappa, Phi Eta Sigma. Methodist. Office: Oreg Health Scis U Office of Pres 3181 SW Sam Jackson Park Rd Portland OR 97201-3098

KOHLER, REGIS CHARLES, radiographer, educator; b. Johnstown, Pa., Feb. 26, 1961; s. John Francis and Patrica Mae (Neal) K.; m. Ida June MacIntyre, Apr. 29, 1989; children: Olivia June, Alexander John. Radiography cert., Conemangh Valley Meml. Hosp., Johnstown, Pa., 1982; BS, U. Pitts., Johnstown, 1985; MS, Bloomsburg U., 1991. Radiographer Windber (Pa.) Hosp., 1982-83, 84-85, Broad Top (Pa.) Area Med. Ctr., 1983-84, Conemaugh Valley Meml. Hosp., Johnstown, 1986-87; assoc. prof. Pa. Coll. Tech., Williamsport, Pa., 1987—; mem. adv. bd. Pa. Coll. Tech., Williamsport, 1987—. Author: (computer program) Interactive Skeletal Anatomy, 1991. Mem. Am. Soc. Radiologic Technologists, Pa. Soc. Radiologic Technologists (bd. dirs. 1993-97, edn. rep. 1987—). Roman Catholic. Office: Pa Coll Tech 1 College Ave Williamsport PA 17701

KOHLER, WILLIAM CURTIS, sleep specialist, neurologist; b. Wharton, N.J., May 22, 1942; s. Walter Henry and Elizabeth (Curtis) K.; m. Barbara Bauman, Sept. 1, 1962; children: Jonathan, Kristina, Elizabeth. AB, Oberlin Coll., 1964; MD, U. Fla., 1968. Diplomate Am. Bd. Pediats., Am. Bd. Neurology, Am. Bd. Electroencephalography and Neurophysiology, Am. Bd. Sleep Medicine. Asst. prof. pediatrics U. Fla., Gainesville, 1973-76; neurologist Tallahassee Neurol. Clinic, 1976-94, Billings (Mont.) Clinic, 1994—; staff neurologist Wilford Hall Med. Ctr., USAF, San Antonio, 1973-75; from asst. to assoc. prof. neurology U. Tex., San Antonio, 1973-75; cons. child neurology Divsn. Children's Med. Svcs. Fla., Tallahassee, 1973-94; med. dir. Lancaster Youth Devel. Ctr., Trenton, Fla., 1975-76. Bd. dirs. United Cerebral Palsy Assn., 1977-84, Big Bend Epilepsy Assn., 1977-92. Recipient Humanitarian Svc. award United Cerebral Palsy Assn. Fellow Am. Acad. Pediatrics, Am. Acad. Neurology, Am. Sleep Disorders Assn.; mem. Am. Med. EEG Assn., Am. Epilepsy Soc., AMA (physician's recognition award). Office: The Sleep Ctr 2900 12th Ave North Box 34 Billings MT 59101

KOHN, ALAN NORMAN, ophthalmologist; b. N.Y.C., Apr. 4, 1943; children: Jill Caroline, Gregory Troy. BS, Cornell U., 1965, MS, 1967; MD, Washington U., 1973. Diplomate Am. Bd. Opthalmology. Intern St. John's Med. Ctr., St. Louis, 1973-74; resident Mt. Sinai Med. Ctr., N.Y.C., 1974-77, fellow in glaucoma, 1977-78; pvt. practice West Palm Beach, Fla., 1978—; chief opthalmology St. Mary's Hosp., West Palm Beach, 1987-96. Fellow Heed Ophthal. Found., 1977-78. Fellow ACS, Am. Acad. Ophthalmology; mem. Fla. Soc. Ophthalmology, Palm Beach Cmty. Ophthalmologic Soc. (v.p. 1991-93, pres. 1993-95), Surg. Eye Expeditions (Ghana 1996). Office: Eye Surgeons Palm Beaches 2121 N Flagler Dr West Palm Beach FL 33407

KOHN, GERHARD, psychologist, educator; b. Neisse, Germany, Nov. 18, 1921; s. Erich and Marie (Prager) K.; m. Irene M. Billinger, Feb. 9, 1947; children: Mary, Eric. B.S., Northwestern U., 1948, M.A., 1949, Ph.D., 1952; postgrad. U. So. Calif., 1960. Diplomate Am. Bd. Forensic Examiners (fellow). Instr., Northwestern U., 1947-49; instr., counselor, dir. pub. relations Kendall Coll., Evanston, Ill., 1947-51; psychologist, counselor Jewish Vocat. Services, Los Angeles, 1951-53, Long Beach Unified Sch. Dist., Calif., 1953-61; instr. Long Beach City Coll., 1955-61; asst. prof. psychology Long Beach State U., 1955-56; counselor, instr. Santa Ana Coll., Calif., 1961-65; prof. Calif. State U., Fullerton, 1971-72; lectr. Orange Coast Coll., 1972-75; asst. clin. prof. psychiatry U. Calif.-Irvine; dir. Reading Devel. Ctr., Long Beach, 1958-88, Gerhard Kohn Sch. Ednl. Therapy, 1967-85; exec. dir. Young Horizons; pvt. practice psychology, 1958—; for juvenile diversion program Long Beach Area, 1982—; cons. HEW, Bur. Hearing and Appeals, Social Security Adminstrn., Long Beach/Orange County B'nai B'rith Career and Counseling Svcs. (cons. to Long Beach Coun.), Long Beach Coun. of Parent Coop. Nursery Sch., Orange County Headstart, Orange County Coop. Pre-Schs. With AUS, 1942-47. Mem. NEA, Am. Pers. and Guidance Assn., Nat. Vocat. Guidance Assn., Am. Psychol. Assn., Calif. Psychol. Assn. (dir. 1976-79, 91-94, sec. 1980-81), Orange County Psychol. Assn. (dir., pres. 1974), Long Beach Psychol. Assn. (pres. 1985, 86, 93, 94, 95, sec. 1989, treas. 1991, chmn. govtl. affairs com., dir. 1996), L.A. County Psychol. Assn. (treas., sec.), Calif. Assn. Sch. Psychologists, Elks, Kiwanis, Phi Delta Kappa, Psi Chi. Office: 320 Pine Ave Ste 308 Long Beach CA 90802-2307

KOHN, JOHN CLEMENT, JR., anesthesiologist; b. Teaneck, N.J., June 19, 1955; s. John Clement and Margaret (Lynch) K.; m. Barbara Sue Brochu, July 9, 1983; children: John Clement III, William Patrick, Peter Joseph, Kristina Margaret. BS, Rockhurst Coll., 1977; DO, U. Health Scis., 1981. Bd. cert. diplomate Am. Osteo. Bd. Anesthesiology. Intern Flint (Mich.) Osteo. Hosp., 1981-82, internal medicine resident, 1982-83, anesthesiology resident, 1986-89; attending anesthesiologist Genesys Regional Med. Ctr. Flint (Mich.) Osteo., 1989—, chmn. dept. anethesiology, 1994—; asst. clin. prof. Mich. State U. Coll. Osteo. Medicine, East Lansing, 1990—. Lt. comdr. USN, 1983-86. Mem. Am. Osteo. Assn., Am. Soc. Anesthesiologists, Internat. Anesthesia Rsch. Soc., Mich. Soc. Anesthesiologists, KC. Roman Catholic. Home: 5216 S Genesee Rd Grand Blanc MI 48439 Office: Flint Anesthesia Assocs PO Box 4009 Flint MI 48504

KOHN, MARY LOUISE BEATRICE, nurse; b. Yellow Springs, Ohio, Jan. 13, 1920; d. Theophilus John and Mary Katharine (Schmitkons) Gaehr; m. Howard D. Kohn, 1944; children: Marcia R., Marcia K. Epstein. AB, Coll. Wooster, 1940; M.Nursing, Case Western Res. U., 1943. Nurse, 1943-44, Atlantic City Hosp., 1944, Thomas M. England Gen. Hosp., U.S. Army, Atlantic City, 1945-46, Peter Bent Brigham Hosp., Boston, 1947, Univ. Hosps., Cleve., 1946-48; mem. faculty Frances Payne Bolton Sch. Nursing Case Western Res. U., 1948-52; vol. nurse Blood Svc., ARC, 1952-55; office nurse, Cleve., part time 1955-94; free-lance writer. Author: (with Atkinson) Berry and Kohn's Operating Room Technique, 5th edit., 1978, 6th edit., 1986, 7th edit., 1992; asst. editor Cleve Physician Acad. Medicine, 1966-71. Bd. dirs. Aux. Acad. Medicine Cleve., 1970-72, officer, 1976; mem. Cleve. Health Mus. Aux., Am. Cancer Soc. vol.; mem. women's com. Cleve. Orch., 1970; mem. women's coun. WVIZ-TV. Mem. ANA, Ohio, Greater Cleve. Nurses Assn., alumni assns. Wooster Coll., Frances P. Bolton Sch. Nursing (pres. 1974-75), Assn. Oper. Rm. Nurses, Assn. Oper. Rm. Nurses of Greater Cleve., Antique Automobile Assn. Am., Western Res. Hist. Soc., Am. Heart Assn., Cleve. Playhouse, Internat. Fund for Animal Welfare, Cleve. Animal Protective League, U.S. Humane Soc., Friends of Cleve. Ballet, Smithsonian Instn., Council World Affairs, Orange Cmty. Arts Coun., Cleve. Art Mus., Cleve. Children's Mus., Cleve. Zool. Soc., Cleve. Racquet Club, Women's City Club (Jewel award 1992). Home: 28099 Belcourt Rd Cleveland OH 44124-5615

KOHN, ROGER ALAN, surgeon; b. Chgo., May 1, 1946; s. Arthur Jerome and Sylvia Lee (Karlen) K.; m. Barbara Helene, Mar. 30, 1974; children: Bradley, Allison. BA, U. Ill., 1967; MD, Northwestern U., 1971. Diplomate Am. Bd. Opthalmology. Internship UCLA, 1971-72; residency Northwestern U., Chgo., 1972-75; fellowship U. Ala., Birmingham, 1975, Harvard Med. Sch., Boston, 1975-76; chmn. dept. ophthalmology Kern Med. Ctr., Bakersfield, Calif., 1978-87; asst. prof. UCLA Med. Sch., 1978-82, assoc. prof., 1982-86, prof., 1986—. Author: Textbook of Ophthalmic Plastic and Reconstructive Surgery, 1988; contbr. numerous articles to profl. jours.; author chpts. in 15 additional textbooks; patentee in field. Bd. dirs. Santa Barbara (Calif.) Symphony, 1990—. Capt. USAR, 1971-77. Named applied to med. syndrome Kohn-Romano Syndrome. Mem. Am. Soc. Ophthalmic Plastic and Reconstuctive Surgery (cert.), Pacific Coast Ophthal. Soc. (bd. dirs. 1986—, 1st v.p. 1990). Jewish. Office: 525 E Micheltorena St Ste 201 Santa Barbara CA 93103-2254

KOHR, ROLAND ELLSWORTH, retired hospital administrator; b. Middletown, Ohio, Dec. 22, 1931; s. Roland Meredith and Mildred (Brandeberry) K.; m. Hilda Scherz, Sept. 6, 1952; children: Linda Kohr Harper, Roland Meredith, Jeffrey Stuart. BS, U. Cin., 1954; MS in Health Adminstrn., Northwestern U., 1959. Resident and adminstrv. asst. Bethesda Hosp., Cin., 1958-60; adminstr. William S. Major Hosp., Shelbyville, Ind., 1961-66; pres. Bloomington (Ind.) Hosp., 1966-95; past chmn. bd. dirs. So. Ind. Med. Group, Inc., Bloomington Convalescent Ctr., Inc.; asst. prof., vis. lectr. Sch. Pub. and Environ. Affairs, Ind. U.; bd. dirs. Precision Healthcare, Inc., Bank One, Bloomington, VHA-Tri-State Inc., Indpls. Contbr. hosp. adminstrn. articles to profl. jours.; mem. editl. bd. Trustee mag. Past pres. United Way of Bloomington and Monroe County; mem. bd. dirs. Bloomingotn Cmty. Found., Inc. Named for disting. svc. Shelbyville C. of C., 1966, Ind. Hosp. Assn., 1987, Sagamore of the Wabash, Gov. of State of Ind.; Paul Harris fellow Rotary Internat.; hon. Ky. col. Fellow Am. Coll.

Healthcare Execs.; mem. Bloomington and Monroe County C. of C. (bd. dirs.), Rotary (Bloomington chpt. pres. 1987-88, bd. dirs. Bloomington Rotary Found. 1988—), Ind. Hosp. Assn. (past chmn. bd. dirs.), Masons, Am. Hosp. Assn. (coun. on governance). Home: 2989 N Bankers Dr Bloomington IN 47408-1021 Office: Bloomington Hosp PO Box 1149 625 W 2d St Bloomington IN 47402

KOHRMAN, ARTHUR FISHER, pediatric educator; b. Cleve., Dec. 19, 1934; s. Benjamin Myron and Leah (Fisher) K.; m. Claire Hoffenberg, Nov. 10, 1955; children: Deborah, Benjamin, Ellen, Rachel. BA, BS, U. Chgo., 1955; MD, Western Res. U., 1959. Diplomate Am. Bd. Pediatrics. Lic. MD, Ill., Mich. Calif., Ind. Intern Cleve. Met. Gen. Hosp., 1959-60; resident in pediatrics Western Res. U., Cleve., 1960-62; post doctoral fellow Stanford U., Palo Alto, Calif., 1965-68; asst. prof. to prof. Mich. State U., East Lansing, 1968-81, assoc. chmn. dept. human devel., 1968-78, assoc. dean Coll. Human Medicine, 1977-81; prof., assoc. chmn. dept. pediatrics U. Chgo., 1981-96; pres. La Rabida Children's Hosp. and Research Ctr., Chgo., 1981-96; Congl. fellow Office Tech. Assessment, U.S. Congress, 1980-81; pres. Children's Hospice Internat., Alexandria, Va., 1983-86; chmn. instl. rev. bd. U. Chgo., 1986—. Contbr. numerous scholarly articles to profl. jours. Served to capt. USAF, 1962-65. Recipient Outstanding Service award Am. Diabetes Assn. Mich. chpt., 1977. Fellow Am. Acad. Pediatrics (chmn. com. on bioethics 1990-94); mem. Am. Pediatric Soc., Ambulatory Pediatric Assn., Soc. Pediatric Rsch., Soc. Health and Human Values, Lawson Wilkins Pediatric Endocrine Soc., Alpha Omega Alpha. Office: La Rabida Children's Hosp E 65th St At Lake Mich Chicago IL 60649

KOHRMAN, BRUCE D., neurologist; b. Anniston, Ala., June 27, 1954; s. S. Lee and Margery (Smith) K.; m. Diane Krieger; 3 children. BS, Stanford U., 1977; MD, Case Western Res. U., 1982. Neurologist Neurol. Cons., Miami, Fla., 1989—. Mem. Am. Acad. Neurology, Am. Soc. Neuroimaging, N.Am. Neuro-Ophthalmology Soc., Phi Beta Kappa, Alpha Omega Alpha. Office: 7330 SW 62d Pl PO Box 432250 South Miami FL 33243-2250

KOHUT, ROBERT I., physician; b. Chgo., Oct. 29, 1932; s. Emil and Ruth Irene (Searls) K.; widowed; children: James Robert, Paul Andrew, Robert John, John Emil; m. Frances Irene Speas, June 6, 1983. AB, Wittenburg Coll., 1956; MD, U. Chgo., 1960. Student instr. U. Chgo., 1959, instr. surgery, 1964; asst. prof. surgery U. Fla., Gainesville, 1966-68, assoc. prof. otol., 1968-71, assoc. prof., acting chmn., 1971-72; prof., chief U. Calif. - Irvine, 1972-79; prof., chmn. Bowman Gray Sch. of Medicine, Winston-Salem, N.C., 1979—; bd. dirs. Am. Bd. Otol.; adv. bd. liaison Nat. Inst. of Deafness and Other Comm. Disorders, 1993—; guest speaker Japanese Equilibrium Soc., Japan; guest of honor 125th Ann. Sun-Yetsen U., Japan, Triological Soc., Naples, Fla., 1996. Editor/author: (book) Head and Neck Surgery-Otolaryngology, 1993; editl. bd. Archives of Otolaryngology, 1992—. With USAF, 1950-53, Japan. Rsch. grantee NIH/NINDS, Fla., NIH/NIDCK, N.C., Deafness Rsch. Found., N.C., Am. Otol. Soc., N.C. Mem. Am. Otol. Soc. (pres. 1993-94), Soc. of Univ. Otolaryngologists (pres.). Lutheran. Home: 2729 Bartram Rd Winston Salem NC 27106 Office: Bowman Gray Sch of Medicine Medical Ctr Blvd Winston Salem NC 27157

KOHUT, ROBERT IRWIN, otolaryngologist, educator; b. Chgo., Nov. 29, 1932; s. Emil and Ruth Irene Kohut; m. Joanne Kay Hughes, Dec. 26, 1953 (dec. Oct. 1982); children: James, Paul, Robert, John; m. Frances Irene Speas, June 6, 1983. BA, Wittenburg Coll., 1956; MD, U. Chgo., 1960. Diplomate Am. Bd. Otolaryngology (bd. dirs. 1979). Intern U. Chgo., 1961-62, resident in otolaryngology, 1962-65, NIH fellow, 1965-66, instr. in otolaryngology, 1965-66; assoc. prof. U. Fla., Gainesville, 1966-68, 1968-71, assoc. prof., acting chmn., 1971-72; prof., chief otolaryngology U. Calif., Irvine, 1972-79; prof., chmn. otolaryngology Bowman Gray Sch. Medicine, Winston-Salem, 1979—; mem. study sect. Nat. Insts. Neurol. and Communicative Disorders and STroke, NIH, Bethesda, Md., 1981-86; cons. NASA, 1982-84; mem. adv. bd. Nat. Inst. Deafness and Other Comm. Disorders, 1991-94. Contbr. numerous chpts. to books and articles to profl. jours.; editor otology divsn. Head and Neck Surgery-Otolaryngology; mem. editorial bd. Am. Jour. Otology, 1992—, Am. Jour. Otolaryngology, 1982—, Archives of Otolaryngology, 1980—, Laryngoscope, 1976—. With USAF, 1950-53. Recipient Norvel Pierce award Chgo. Laryngological Soc., 1965, Basic Rsch. award Acad. Ophthalmology and Otolaryngology, 1968. Mem. ACS, Soc. Univ. Otolaryngologists (pres. 1978-79), Barany Soc., Am. Laryngological Soc., Rhinological and Otological Soc. (exec. coun. 1987-90, Edmund Fowler award 1974, Guest of Honor, So. sect. 1996), Am. Broncho-Esophagological Assn., Am. Neurotology Assn., Otosclerosis Study Group, Am. Otological Soc. (sec.-treas. 1987-92, pres.-elect 1992-93, pres. 1993-94), Assn. Acad. Depts. Otolaryngology, Pacific Coast Oto-Ophthalmol. Soc., Forsyth County Med. Soc., N.C. Med. Soc., N.C. Soc. Otolaryngology Head and Neck Surgery (v.p. 1985, pres. 1986-87), Assn. for Rsch. in Otolaryngology, Am. Acad. Otolaryngology-Head and Neck Surgery, Am. Soc. Head and Neck Surgery, Internat. Fedn. Oto-Rhino-Laryngological Soc. (chmn. standing com. edn.), others. Office: Bowman Gray Sch Med Dept Otolaryngology Wake Forest U Med Ctr Blvd Winston Salem NC 27157-1034

KOHUTIAK, VSEVOLOD, physician; b. Ukraine, July 22, 1938; came to U.S., 1950; s. Vladimir and Maria (Tokarsky) K.; m. Lidia M. Hoszowsky, June 15, 1963; children: Roma, George. BA, Syracuse U.; MD, SUNY, Syracuse. Resident in internal medicine St. Michael Hosp., Alcron City Hosp.; pvt. practice internal medicine and cardiology Media, Pa., 1971—; dir. vascular lab. Riddle Meml. Hosp. Capt. U.S. Army, 1966-68, Vietnam. Fellow Am. Coll. Physicians, Am. Coll. Angiology; mem. AMA, Pa. Med. Soc., Media Med. Soc. Office: Broy-Kohutiak-Jamali Ltd 1098 W Baltimore Pike Media PA 19063

KOITHAN, MARY SUSAN, nursing educator; b. Cin., Feb. 25, 1956; d. Norman J. and Dorothy B. (Harrell) Zemites; m. Ronald Koithan, Sept. 17, 1980; children: Andrea, Matthew. BSN, U. Cin., 1978; MSN, U. Nev., 1986; PhD in Nursing, U. Colo., 1994. Charge nurse, supr. Desert Springs Hosp., Las Vegas, Nev., 1981-84; instr. nursing Clark County C.C., Las Vegas, 1984-90; home healthcare educator Las Vegas, 1987—, ind. home healthcare educator, 1985-92, ind. cons., 1986—. Bd. dirs. ARC, 1989-94, co-chair nursing com., 1984-94, nurse educator, mem. disaster team Clark County chpt.; bd. dirs. cmty. edn. Clark County chpt. Am. Cancer Soc., 1993. U.S. Dept. HEW grantee, 1979; Barrick fellow, 1986; recipient Intramural Rsch. fellow award, 1995. Mem. ANCC (commn. on accreditation 1993-96), ANA (del. 1989-96, constituent assembly 1989-93, Congress on Nursing Practice 1992-96, edn. com. 1993-94, chair disaster task force 1993), Nev. Nurses Assn. (pres. 1989-93), Western Inst. Nursing, Western Soc. for Nursing Rsch., Am. Nurses Found., Phi Kappa Phi, Sigma Theta Tau. Home: 7825 Bermuda Rd Las Vegas NV 89123-1815

KOITHAN, THOMAS K., psychiatrist; b. Battle Creek, Iowa, Oct. 14, 1962; s. George C. and Evelyn J. (Justi) K.; m. Wanda Sue Lewis, June 3, 1989; children: Mary Katherine Elizabeth, Mogran Audrey. BS in Psychology, Iowa State U.; DO, U. Osteo Medicine/Health Scis. Psychiatry resident Menninger, Topeka, Kans., 1989-93; psychiatrist Wadle & Assocs., Des Moines, 1993—. Mem. Alpha Lambda Delta. Lutheran. Office: Wadle & Assocs 2327 70th St Des Moines IA 50321

KOIVISTO, ERKKI LAURI MATIAS, radiologist, educator; b. Seinäjoki, Finland, Jan. 19, 1927; s. Lauri Eemil and Oili Siviä (Jatkola) K.; m. Helena Kaasila, Mar. 25, 1954; children: Inkeri, Anna-Leena, Kaisu, Maria. BSc in Bus. Adminstrn., U. So. Calif., L.A., 1951; B Medicine, U. Helsinki, Finland, 1955; MD, U. Turku, Finland, 1959; ScD in Medicine, U. Oulu, Finland, 1969. Cert. radiologist, Finland. Rsch. asst. Wenner-Gren Cardiovascular Rsch. Lab., Stockholm, 1959; resident in radiology Turku U. Hosp., 1960-61; sales mgr. L. Koiviston Autoliike Oy, Seinäjoki, 1964-66; dir. Med. Office of Health Ins. Dist. Western Finland, Seinäjoki, 1964-66; asst. instr. in radiology U. Oulu, 1967, assoc. prof. roentgenology, 1967-70, 72-78; prof. diagnostic radiology U. Tampere, Finland, 1978-90, asst. prof. diagnostic radiology, 1990—; chief dept. diagnostic radiology Tampere U. Cen. Hosp., 1978-90; mem. adv. bd. on radiation safety of patients, Med. Bd. Finland, 1975-84; mem. Finnish Bd. Examiners in Radiology, 1979-90; mem. editorial bd., Diagnostic Imaging in Clin. Medicine, 1976-86, Frontiers in European Radiology, 1982-89, Acta Radiologica Portuguesa, 1989—; mem. adv. bd., Product Comparison System, McGraw-Hill, 1984—; mem. organizing com., World Med. Assn. Congress, Helsinki, 1964; trustee, Union Bank of Finland, Tampere. Author books and articles on diagnostic radiology. Chmn. Seinäjoki City Tourist Bd., 1962-65; bd. dirs., Seinäjoki Bus. Coll., 1966-68, Tampere U. Lang. Ctr., 1986-88. Recipient Silver medal, Turku U. Heart Ctr., 1987. Mem. Radiol. Soc. Finland (Sakari Mustakallio medal 1987), European Assn. Radiology (Boris Rajewski medal 1989), Deutsche Acad. Naturforscher Leopoldina, Finnish Med. Assn., Swedish Soc. Med. Radiology, Deutsche Röntgengescellschaft, Polish Soc. Med. Radiology, Gesellschaft Medizinische Radiologie German Dem. Republic, Finnish Soc. Tech. Assessment in Health Care, Med. Info. Soc. Finland, Union Internat. Cinema d'Amateurs (Gold medal 1979), Radiological Soc. Finland Scandinavian Assn. of Radiology (hon.), Polish Soc. Radiology, German Soc. Radiology, Soviet Union Soc. Radiology. Lutheran. Home: Hukankatu 4 B, FIN33530 Tampere Finland Office: U Tampere, Teiskontie 35, FIN33530 Tampere Finland

KOIZUMI, SHUNZO, surgeon; b. Kyoto, Japan, Mar. 14, 1946; s. Haruo and Chieko (Ushioda) K.; m. Yoko Yokoe, Aug. 19, 1971; children: Miyuu (dec.), Mitsuteru, Arei. MD, Kyoto U., 1971. Diplomate Am. Bd. Surgery. House staff in medicine Yamagami (Japan) Hosp., Yamato-Takada (Japan) City Hosp.; house staff in anesthesiology Osaka (Japan) Red Cross Hosp., 1972-74; resident Youngstown (Ohio) Hosp. Assn., 1975-76; gen. surg. resident St. Vincent's Med. Ctr., Bridgeport. Conn., 1976-80, chief surg. resident, 1979-80; staff first surg. dept. Kyoto U. Hosp., 1980; surg. cons. for residency dept. abdominal surgery Tenri (Japan) Hosp., 1980-94; dir. Ichijoji Ctr. Meta-Med. Studies and Transnat. Lodge, Sayko-ku, Kyoto, 1991—; prof., chmn. dept. gen. medicine Saga (Japan) Med. Sch., 1994—. Editor resident's manual, 1995. Mem. ACS, Japan Surg. Soc., Japan Soc. Med. Edn. Home: 16-1 Ichijoji-Iorino-cho, Sakyo-ku Kyoto 606, Japan Office: Saga Med Sch, 5-1-1 Nabeshima, Saga 849, Japan

KOKASKA, CHARLES JAMES, educational psychologist; b. Chgo., Apr. 29, 1937; s. Charles August and Francene (Larva) K.; m. Sharen Elizabeth Metz, June 26, 1970; 1 child, Laurel Ann. B.A., Valparaiso U., 1958; M.A., Northwestern U., 1961; Ed.D., Boston U., 1968. Tchr. children with emotional problems The Day Sch., Chgo., 1959-60; tchr., head dept. spl. edn. North Phoenix High Sch., 1961-64; asst. prof. spl. edn. Eastern Mich. U., 1967-69; prof. ednl. psychology Calif. State U., Long Beach, 1969—, coord. spl. edn. grad. program, 1979—; project dir. intern program L.A. County Office of Edn., 1993—; bd. dirs. computer applications in spl. edn. Chancellor's Office, Calif. State U., several workshops, study insts. and funded tng. grants in edn. of exceptional children. Author: (with J. Gowan, G. Demos) The Guidance of Exceptional Children, 1972, (with D. Brolin) Career Education for Handicapped Children and Youth, 1979, Career Education for Handicapped Individuals, 1985; (with L. Miller and L. Glascoe) Life Centered Career Education Activity, Book 1 and 2, 1986; (with G. Greene, L. Albright and C. Beacham-Greene) Instructional Strategies for Special Education Students in Regular Vocational Classes, 1987, (with others) The Transition of Youth with Disabilities to Adult Life, 1988; exec. editor: Career Devel. for Exceptional Individuals, 1977-82; contbr. articles and cons. editor to profl. jours. Mem. community edn. council on spl. edn. Long Beach Unified Sch. Dist., 1971-72. Office of Edn. fellow mental retardation, 1964-67. Fellow Am. Assn. Mental Deficiency; mem. Council for Exceptional Children (pres. div. on career devel. 1985-86), Tau Kappa Epsilon. Home: 618 Havana Ave Long Beach CA 90814-1931

KOKOT, FRANCISZEK JÓZEF, physician; b. Olesno, Silesia, Poland, Nov. 24, 1929; s. Franciszek and Franciszka (Kostka) K.; m. Malgorzata Skrzypczyk, Dec. 26, 1955; children: Stefan, Klaudiusz, Jan, Tomasz. Physician diploma summa cum laude, Silesian Sch. Medicine, Katowice, Poland, 1953, MD, 1957; Dr. h.c. (hon.), Med. Acad. Wroclaw, 1990, Med. Acad. Katowice, 1993, Pomeranian Med. Acad., Szczecin, 1995. Technician dept. chemistry Silesian Sch. Medicine, Katowice, 1949-50, asst. and sr. asst. dept. pharmacology, 1950-57, asst. prof. dept. internal medicine, 1957-62, assoc. prof. dept. internal medicine, 1962-69, extraordinary prof. dept. internal medicine, 1969-74, extraordinary prof. dept. nephrology, 1974-82, ordinary prof. dept. nephrology, 1982—; rsch. fellow Clinique Therapeutique, Geneva, 1958-59; WHO fellow Middlesex Hosp., London, 1970. Mem. European Dialysis and Transplant Assn., Polish Acad. Scis., Polish Acad. Arts and Scis.; hon. mem. Bulgarian Soc. Nephrology, German Soc. Nephrology, Yugoslavian Soc. Nephrology, Hungarian Soc. Nephrology, Macedonian Soc. Nephrology, Italian Soc. Nephrology, Czechoslovakia Soc. Nephrology. Roman Catholic. Home: Korfanty 8/162, 40-008 Katowice Poland Office: Dept Nephrology, Franciszka 20, 40-027 Katowice Poland

KOLANSKY, HAROLD, physician, psychiatrist, psychoanalyst; b. Carbondale, Pa., Aug. 15, 1924; s. Abe and Miriam (Raker) K.; m. Elsa Harwitz, June 8, 1948; children: Jeffrey, Betta, Daniel. Student, U. Scranton, 1942-44; MD cum laude, Georgetown U., 1948. Rotating intern Walter Reed Army Hosp., Washington, 1948-49; resident Coatesville (Pa.) VA Hosp. and Deans' Com. Program, Phila., 1949-52; practice medicine specializing in psychiatry and psychoanalysis Phila., 1952—, Elkins Park, Pa., 1959—; clin. assoc. prof. psychiatry U. Pa. Sch. Medicine, 1972-77, clin. prof., 1977, 91—; mem. steering com. Psychoanalytic Cluster, 1991—; prof. psychiatry and human behavior Jefferson Med. Coll., Thomas Jefferson U., Phila., 1977-91, dir. sect. child and adolescent psychoanalysis, 1980-90, dir. sect. psychoanalysis, 1982-90; mem. psychiatry staff Albert Einstein Med. Ctr., 1952-69, 82—, sr. attending, 1983—, dir. divsn. child psychiatry, 1955-69, acting chmn. dept. psychiatry, 1968-69, dir. child psychiatry fellowship, 1960-69, dir. ctr. for psychoanalysis, 1991—, mem. exec. com., tng. com. and curriculum com., 1991—; mem. faculty Inst. Phila. Assn. Psychoanalysis, 1960—, chmn. administrv. bd., 1966-69, dir. divsn. childrn and adolescent psychoanalysis, 1975-84, tng. and supervisory analyst, 1976—, chmn. tng. analyst com., 1982-83, 93-94, 95—, chmn. curriculum com., 1982-88, dir. consultation and evaluation divsn., 1988-89, mem. ednl. com., 1989-94, chmn., liaison com. med. edn., 1994—; mem. staff psychiatry Phila. Psychiat. Ctr., 1952-81; pres. Regional Coun. Child Psychiatry, Pa., S.E. N.J., Del., 1967-68, 72-73, chmn. exec. com., 1970-73; chmn. med. bd. Es. State Sch. and Hosp., Trevose, Pa., 1966-69; asst. prof. psychiatry Hahnemann Med. Coll. and Hosp., Phila., 1952-60; mem. Pa. Task Force on Mental Health Children, 1971-74; vis. prof. psychiatry U. P.R. Sch. Medicine, 1982—; mem. steering com. psychoanalytic cluster U. Pa. Sch. Med., 1991—. Contbg. author to numerous texts on psychoanalysis and psychiatry including: A Handbook of Child Psychoanalysis, 1968, Behavior Pathology of Childhood and Adolescence, 1973, Controversy in Psychiatry, 1978, Prognosis, 1981; contbr. numerous articles on child and adult psychiatry and psychoanalysis to profl. jours. Capt. M.C., U.S. Army, 1950-51, Korea. Recipient 1st prize biochemistry Georgetown U., 1945, Robert Waelder award for Teaching Excellence in Psychiatry Thomas Jefferson Med. Coll., 1987, Dedication to Edn. award, 1990, award for teaching excellence dept. psychiatry Albert Einstein Med. Ctr., 1993; 1st pl. U.S. in Surgery Nat. Bd. Med. Examiners, 1948. Fellow Am. Psychiat. Assn., Am. Acad. Child Psychiatry (chmn. com. continuing med. edn. 1974-82, citation for developing continuing med. edn. program 1976, councillor), Phila. Coll. Physicians; mem. AMA, Phila. Assn. Psychoanalysis (bd. dirs. 1984-86, pres. 1984-86, Gerald Pearson Prize award 1960), Assn. Child Psychoanalysis, Phila. Psychiat. Soc., Internat. Psychoanalytic Assn., Am. Psychoanalytic Assn. (exec. counselor 1969-73, 77-82, fellow bd. profl. standards 1983-89, 1992—, mem. com. on child and adolescent analysis 1984-90, acting fellow bd. on prof. standards 1989), Pa. Med. Soc., Phila. County Med. Soc. Home: 8365 Fisher Rd Elkins Park PA 19027-1502

KOLB, DAVID ALLEN, chiropractor, homeopath, herbalist, nutrition consultant, acupuncturist; b. El Paso, Tex., May 14, 1946; s. David Crocket Kolb and Ann Laura (Thrash) Kolb Swingle; m. Barbara Paul Carey, May 3, 1980; children: Aaron Scott, Samantha Tapri. AAS, U. Odessa, 1967; BA, U. Tex., 1971; DChiropractic magna cum laude, Palmer Coll. Chiropractic, 1979; postgrad. in homeopathy Occidental Inst. Rsch. Found., Bellingham, Wash., 1980; postgrad. in acupuncture Nat. Coll. Chiropractic, Lombard, Ill., 1983, 84, Peoples Republic China, 1984. Computer operator Dallas Bank Commerce, 1969; computer operator Tex. Instruments, Austin and Dallas, Tex., 1970-72, computer programmer, 1972-73; researcher on meditation Maharishi U., Santa Barbara, Calif., 1973-74; computer operator Austin Nat. Bank, Tex., 1974; computer programmer Tex. Water Resources, Austin, 1974-75; chiropractor, bd. dirs. Profl. Healthcare Services, Inc., Austin, 1979—; bd. dirs. Biol. Products, Inc. Asst. scoutmaster Capital Area Coun. Boy Scouts Am. Mem. Am. Chiropractic Assn., Tex. Chiropractic Assn., Travis County Chiropractic Soc., Internat. Found. Homeopathy, Occidental Inst. Rsch. Found. (rsch. assoc.), Pi Tau Delta. Avocations: hiking; camping; jogging; swimming; science fiction. Office: Profl Healthcare Svcs Inc Ste 1029 4501 Spicewood Springs Rd Austin TX 78759-8538

KOLB, FREDERICK JOHN, JR., retired technical specialist; b. Rochester, N.Y., May 7, 1917; s. Frederick John Sr. and Emilie Ann (Haefele) K.; m. Priscilla Packard Pollock, Oct. 10, 1942 (dec. Oct. 1987); children: Carolyn, Katharine, Frederick John III, Merribeth. SB, MIT, 1938, SM, 1939, ScD, 1947. From project group leader to coord. project devel. mfg. Eastman Kodak, Rochester, 1942-83, tech. assoc. rsch. labs., 1983-86; ret., 1986; cons. imaging sci. Magnetic Records, 1986—; tech. specialist Internat. Standards Orgn./TC 36, 1970—. Patentee magnetic heads; contbr. articles to profl. jours. Chmn. ednl. coun. MIT, Rochester, 1950—; elder Summerville Presbyn. Ch., Rochester, 1959—. Fellow Tau Beta Pi 1938-39, Fedn. Paint and Varnish Prodn. Clubs 1940-42. Fellow SMPTE (Warner medal sound on film 1988, Kalmus medal contbns. to color films 1995); mem. IEEE, AAAS, BKSTS, AIChE, Am. Chem. Soc., Soc. Imaging Sci. and Tech., Sigma Xi. Republican. Home and Office: 211 Oakridge Dr Rochester NY 14617-2511

KOLB, GARY E., physician; b. Beaver Falls, Pa., Apr. 6, 1949; s. James E. and Frances M. (Majors) K.; m. Kathleen Ann (Baker) Kolb, Aug. 21, 1971; children: Kirsten Lynn, Gary E. Jr., Jeremiah J., Kiley E. BA, Washington & Jefferson Coll., 1971; DO, Chgo. Coll. Osteo. Medicine, 1975. Bd. cert. Am. Osteo. Bd. Family Practice. Lt. col. USAR, Mobile, Ala., 1989—. Active Com. 2000, Bay Minette, Ala., 1982-84; bd. dirs. Am. Lung Assn., Mobile, 1987, bd. dirs. Am. Diabetes Assn.; pres. elect Baldwin County Med. Assn.; mem. USAR, active rank lt. col. Mem. Am. Diabetes Assn., Ala. Osteo. Assn., Ala. State Med. Assn., KC. Republican. Roman Catholic. Office: 2101 Hand Ave Bay Minette AL 36507

KOLB, LAWRENCE COLEMAN, psychiatrist; b. Balt., June 16, 1911; s. Lawrence and Lillian Hess (Coleman) K.; m. Madeleine Currie, July 3, 1937; children: Pamela Currie Leadbitter, Mary Clark Estes, Richard Jennings. BA, Trinity Coll., Dublin U., Ireland, 1932; MD, Johns Hopkins U., 1934; DSc (hon.), Albany Med. Coll., 1994. Diplomate: Am. Bd. Psychiatry and Neurology (dir. 1960-68, pres. 1968). Intern medicine, surgery Strong Meml. Hosp., Rochester, N.Y., 1934-36; fellow neurology Johns Hopkins U., 1936-38, instr., 1939-40; Markle fellow neurology Nat. Hosp. Queens Sq., Eng., 1938-39; psychiatrist Milw. Sanitorium, 1941; dir. research projects NIMH, also pvt. practice psychiatry, 1946-49; research assoc. Washington Sch. Psychiatry, 1946-49; cons. Mayo Clinic; also assoc. prof. psychiatry U. Minn., 1949-54; dir. N.Y. State Psychiat. Inst.; prof., chmn. dept. psychiatry Columbia U., 1954-75, prof. emeritus, 1975—, Lawrence C. Kolb prof. psychiatry Coll. Physicians and Surgeons, 1977; prof. Albany Med. Coll., 1978; dir. psychiat. service Presbyn. Hosp., N.Y.C., 1954-75; commr. N.Y. State Dept. Mental Hygiene, 1975-78; Disting. physician in psychiatry U.S. VA, 1978-88; pres. med. bd. Presbyn. Hosp., N.Y.C., 1962-64, trustee, 1971-73, hon. trustee, 1974—; prof. psychiatry Albany Med. Coll., 1978—; cons. nat. adv. council USPHS, HEW; mem. panel med. scis. to asst. sec. of def., 1954-60; mem. career investigator com. NIMH, 1956-60, chmn., 1962, mem. bd. sci. counsellors, 1959-62, chmn., 1962; mem. spl. adv. com. to commr. hosps., N.Y.C., 1961; mem. Salmon Com. Mental Hygiene; adv. bd. P.R. Inst. Psychiatry, 1972—. Author: (with O.R. Langworthy and L.G. Lewis) Physiology of Micturition, 1940, The Painful Phantom, 1954, Modern Clinical Psychiatry, 10th edit, 1982, (with L. Ruizin) The First Psychiatric Institute, 1993. Bd. dirs. Founds. Fund for Research in Psychiatry, 1959-61; bd. dirs., pres., chmn. bd. Research Found. for Mental Hygiene, 1960-76; trustee Austin Riggs Center, pres. 1983-85; trustee Silver Hill Found., 1967-74. Recipient Henry Wisner Meml. award, 1962; Oscar K. Diamond award, 1971; Joan Plehn award for human service Mental Health Assn. N.Y. and Bronx Counties, 1972; Richard H. Hutchings award N.Y. State Hosps. Alumni Assn., 1975; Dedication of Lawrence C. Kolb Research Lab. N.Y. State Psychiat. Inst., 1983, Paul H. Hoch Disting. Svc. award Office Mental Health, N.Y. State, 1990, Pioneer award Internat. Soc. Traumatic Stress, 1991. Fellow Am. Psychiat. Assn. (pres. 1968, Disting. Service award 1983), Am. Acad. Neurology, N.Y. Acad. Sci.; mem. Am. Coll. Psychiatry (Bowis award 1977), Am. Neurol. Assn., Am. Psychoanalytic Assn., Assn. Research Nervous and Mental Diseases (pres. 1969), Johns Hopkins Soc. Scholars, Sigma Xi, Alpha Omega Alpha. Clubs: Century Assn. (N.Y.C.), University (N.Y.C.); Vidonia Practioners. Home: Van Wies Pt Glenmont NY 12077

KOLBE, LLOYD JOSEPH, federal agency administrator; b. Balt., Oct. 13, 1948; s. Lloyd Arthur and Blanche (Cossentino) K. BS, Towson State U., 1973; MEd, U. Toledo, 1975, PhD, 1978. Asst. prof. U. No. Colo., Greeley, 1976-77; dir. evaluation Nat. Ctr. for Health Edn., San Francisco, 1978-79, dir., sch. health edn., 1980-81; chief, evaluation section U.S. Office Disease Prevention, Washington, 1982; assoc. dir. Ctr. Health Promotion Rsch. U. Tex., Houston, 1983-85, assoc. prof. Sch. Pub. Health, 1983-85; chief Sch. Health Ctr. U.S. Ctr. for Disease Control, Atlanta, 1986-87, dir., Div. Adolescent and Sch. Health, 1988—; dir. Ctr. for Sch. Health WHO, Atlanta, 1990—. Co-author: (book) School Health in America, 1988. Recipient Superior Svc. award USPHS, Washington, 1989, Disting. Svc. award State Dirs. of Health Edn., Washington, 1988, Honor award Eta Sigma Gamma, Muncie, Ind., 1989; named Outstanding Alumnus, U. Toledo, 1985. Fellow Am. Sch. Health Assn. (pres. 1989-90); mem. Assn. Advancement of Health Edn. (Scholar award 1989), APHA, Soc. for Pub. Health Edn., Internat. Union for Health Edn. (trustee 1986—). Home: 4411 Hidden Bluff Way Lithonia GA 30058-7078 Office: US Ctr Disease Control 1600 Clifton Rd NE Atlanta GA 30329-4018

KOLBECK, RALPH CARL, physiology and pulmonary educator; b. Wausau, Wis., Sept. 2, 1944; s. John and Elma L. (Kersten) K.; m. Donna Jean Belling, July 16, 1966; children—Lisa Jean, John Carl. B.A. in Physiology, U. Minn., 1966, Ph.D. in Physiology, 1970. Teaching asst. physiology U. Minn., Mpls., 1966-67, lectr., 1968-73, postdoctoral fellow, 1970-73; instr. medicine Med. Coll. Ga., Augusta, 1973-76, asst. prof., 1976-80, assoc. prof. depts. of medicine, physiology and endocrinology, 1980—, dir. pulmonary research lab., Med. Coll. of Ga.; bd. dirs. Sci. Fair Am.; active Am. Heart Assn. Recipient Investigatorship award Am. Heart Assn., 1977-82; grantee NIH, Ga. Heart Assn., Am. Heart Assn., Am. Lung Assn. Mem. AAAS, Am. Assn. Lab. Animal Sci., Am. Physiol. Soc., So. Soc. Clin. Investigation, Biophysics Soc., Sigma Xi. Contbr. numerous articles to profl. jours. Home: 3235 Winding Wood Pl Augusta GA 30907-3762 Office: Med Coll Ga Dept Medicine Augusta GA 30912

KOLF, JAMES, home healthcare executive; b. Detroit, July 22, 1948; s. John A. and Mary M. (Whalen) K.; m. Sara Jo Klein, Oct. 1994; children: Heather Anne, Rebecca Lynn, Kelly Marie. BS, Wayne State U., 1970, postgrad., 1972-73. Cert. tchr., Mich. Tchr. St. Raymond Sch., Detroit, 1970-73; pharm. sales Eaton Labs., Norwich, N.Y., 1973-74; ter. mgr. Baxter Travenol Labs., Deerfield, Ill., 1974-75, field tng., 1976-81; med. edn. coord. Mt. Carmel Hosp., Detroit, 1975-76; gen. mgr./antibiotic/TPN specialist Home Health Care Am., Newport Beach, Calif., 1981—; gen. mgr. New Eng. Critical Care, 1987—, mgr. tng. and devel., 1989-90, dir. nat. accounts, 1990, dir. bus. devel. Nat. Med. Care-Homecare Ventures, Inc., 1990-91, v.p., 1991—, regional dir., 1992—; nat. dir. sales/bus. devel. Kelly Assisted Living Svcs., 1994—; mem. Home Therapy Task Force, Grand Rapids, Mich., 1987. Co-author: (textbook) Principles and Practices of Home Health Care, 1996. Mem. adminstrn. com. St. Paul of Tarsus, 1988—, Negotiating Skills, Boston Coll., 1988, Leadership Devel. Conf., Eckerd Coll., 1988, Mgmt. Devel. Program Sterling Inst., 1989. PTO grantee, 1971. Mem. Assn. Hosp. Med. Edn., Sigma Pi (sec. 1967-68), 200 Club, 400 Club. Republican. Roman Catholic.

KOLFF, WILLEM JOHAN, internist, educator; b. Leiden, Holland, Feb. 14, 1911; came to U.S., 1950, naturalized, 1956; s. Jacob and Adriana (de Jonge) K.; m. Janke C. Huidekoper, Sept 4, 1937; children: Jacob, Adriana P., Albert C., Cornelis A., Gualtherus C.M. Student, U. Leiden Med. Sch., 1930-38; M.D. summa cum laude, U. Groningen, 1946; M.D. (hon.), U. Turin, Italy, 1969, Rostock (Germany) U., 1975, U. Bologna, Italy, 1983; D.Sc. (hon.), Allegheny Coll., Meadville, Pa., 1960, Tulane U., 1975, CUNY, 1982, Temple U., 1983, U. Utah, 1983; D. of Tech. Scis. (hon.), Tech. U. Twente, Enschede, The Netherlands, 1986; D.Sc. (hon.), U. Athens, 1988, Aix-Marseille II, 1993. Internist, head med. dept. Mcpl. Hosp., Kampen,

Holland; dir. div. artificial organs Cleve. Clinic Found., 1950-67; privaat docent, dept. medicine U. Leiden, 1950-67; prof. surgery U. Utah Coll. Medicine, Salt Lake City, 1967—, Disting. prof. medicine and surgery, 1979—; prof. internal medicine U. Utah Coll. Medicine, 1981—, dir. Kolff's Lab., 1986—, dir. Inst. for Biomed. Engring., dir. div. artificial organs, 1967-86. Patent for ventricular assist device and method of manufacturing, collapsible artificial ventricle and pumping shell, ventricular assist device with volumne displacement chamber, electrohydraulic heart with septum mounted pump, muscle and air powered left ventricular assist device. Decorated commandeur Orde Van Oranje Netherlands, 1970; Orden de Mayo al Merito en el Grade de Gran Official Argentina, 1974; recipient Landsteiner medal for establishing blood banks during German occupation in Holland, Netherlands Red Cross, 1942, Cameron prize U. Edinburgh (Scotland), 1964, Gairdner prize Gairdner Found., 1966, Valentine award N.Y. Acad. Medicine, 1969, 1st Gold medal Netherlands Surg. Soc., 1970, Leo Harvey prize Technion, Israel, 1972, Sr. U.S. Scientist award Alexander Von Humboldt Found., 1978, Austrian Gewerbeverein's Wilhelm-Exner award, 1980, John Scott medal City of Phila., 1984, Japan prize Japan Found. Sci. and Tech., 1986, Rsch. prize Netherlands Royal Inst. Engrs., 1986, 1st Jean Hamburger award Internat. Soc. Nephrology, 1987, 1st Edwin Cohn-De Laval award World Apheresis Assn, 1990, Fed. prize Fedn. Sci. Med. Assn., 1990, Father of Artificial Organs award and medal Internat. Soc. Artificial Organs, 1992, Christopher Columbus Discovery award in biomed. rsch. NIH, 1992, Legacy of Life award LDS Deseret Found., 1995; named to Nat. Inventors Hall of Fame, 1985, named to On the Shoulders of Giants Hall of Fame, Cleve., 1989. Mem. AMA (Sci. Achievement award 1982), AAUP, Am. Physiol. Soc., Soc. Exptl. Biology and Medicine, AAAS, Nat. Acad. Engring. (City of Medicine award 1989), N.Y. Acad. Scis., Am. Soc. Artificial Internal Organs, Nat. Kidney Found., European Dialysis and Transplant Assn., ACP, Austrian Soc. Nephrology (hon.), Academia Nacional de Medicine (Colombia, hon.), NAE. Lodge: Rotary. Office: U Utah Coll of Engring Dept Biomed Engring 2460-A Merrill Engring Bldg Salt Lake City UT 84112

KOLHE, PRALHAD SHIVARAM, plastic surgeon, consultant; b. Bamnod, India, Sept. 17, 1945; arrived in Scotland, 1974; s. Shivaram Raoji and Bhagirathi Kolhe. MB BChir, BJMC, Poona, India, 1967, MS in Gen. Surgery, 1971, MS in Anatomy, 1974; MCh in Plastic Surgery, Bombay U., 1981. Cons. plastic surgeon NHS, Aberdeen, Scotland, 1991—. Fellow Royal Coll. Surgeons (Edinburgh). Home: 16 Colsea Rd, Aberdeen AB1 4NP, Scotland Office: Aberdeen Royal Infirmary, Plastic Surg Dept Ward 39, Aberdeen AB9 2ZB, Scotland

KOLINSKY, MICHAEL ALLEN, emergency physician; b. Phila., Dec. 23, 1947; s. Maurice and Lenore (Rose) K.; m. Barbara Victorine, June 20, 1981; children: Nicole, Daniel, Samuel. BA, U. Wis., 1970; MD, Rush U., 1979. Diplomate Am. Bd. Emergency Medicine. Staff physician emergency dept. River Parishes Hosp., LaPlace, La., 1982-85; co-med. dir. emergency dept. Meadowcrest Hosp., Gretna, La., 1985-92; co-med. dir. City of New Orleans Emergency Med. Svcs., 1987—; med. dir. emergency dept. Tulane U. Med. Ctr., New Orleans, 1992—. Fellow Am. Acad. Emergency Medicine, Am. Coll. Emergency Physicians. Office: Tulane Med Ctr Emergency Dept 1415 Tulane Ave New Orleans LA 70112

KOLISEK, FRANK R., orthopedist, educator; b. Benton, Ill., July 23, 1960; s. John and Janet Anne (Simkovich) K.; m. Lisa Ann Kolisek, May 3, 1986; children: Jacob, Charles, Kelsie. BA, Wabash Coll., 1982; MD, U. Ill., 1986. Diplomate Am. Bd. Orthopedic Surgery; lic. Ind. Intern Univ. Med. Ctr., Jacksonville, Fla., 1986-87; resident orthopedic surgery U. Fla. Health Sci. Ctr., Jacksonville, 1987-91; fellow arthritic reconstructive surgery of hip and knee Emory U., Peachtree Orthopedic Clinic, Piedmont Hosp., Atlanta, 1991-92; orthopedist Specialty Ctrs. for Orthopedic and Rehab. Excellence, Indpls., 1992—; asst. clin. prof. Dept. Orthopedic Surgery Emory U., Atlanta, 1991-92, Ind. U. Sch. Medicine, Indpls., 1992—. Presenter in field; contbr. articles to profl. jours. Mem. AMA, Am. Acad. Orthopedic Surgeons, Mid-Am. Orthopedic Assn., Ind. Orthopedic Soc., Ind. State Med. Soc., Indpls. Med. Soc., Indpls. Orthopedic Club. Office: S C O R E 1550 E County Line Rd S 200 Indianapolis IN 46227

KOLKER, ALLAN ERWIN, ophthalmologist; b. St. Louis, Nov. 2, 1933; s. Paul P. and Jean K.; m. Jacquelyn Krupin, Dec. 8, 1957; children: Robin, Marci, David, Scott. AB, Washington U., St. Louis, 1953, MD, 1957. Diplomate Am. Bd. Ophthalmology (bd. dirs. 1994—). Intern St. Louis Children's Hosp., 1957-58; resident in ophthalmology Washington U./Barnes Hosp., 1960-65; staff, faculty Washington U., 1964—, prof. ophthalmology, 1974—; mem. glaucoma com. Prevent Blindness Am.; bd. dirs. Am. Bd. Ophthalmology, 1994—. Author: (with J. Hetherington) Becker and Shaffer's Diagnosis and Therapy of the Glaucomas, 3d, 4th. 5th edit., 1983; contbr. numerous articles to profl. jours. Served with USPHS, 1958-60. NIH spl. fellow, 1963-65; grantee, 1969-80; Disting. Alumni award Washington U., 1990; glaucoma fellow Washington U., 1963-64. Mem. AMA, Assn. Rsch. in Vision and Ophthalmology, Am. Acad. Ophthalmology (mem. coun. 1986-92, mem. bd. trustees 1994—), Am. Ophthal. Soc., Am. Glaucoma Soc. (founding, pres. 1992-94), Mo. Ophthal. Soc. (pres. 1986-87), St. Louis Med. Soc. Home: 176 Plantation Dr Saint Louis MO 63141-8352 Office: 660 S Euclid Ave Saint Louis MO 63110-1010

KOLLARITS, CAROL ROTH, ophthalmologist; b. Cleve., Jan. 30, 1946; d. Jay Marshall and Edna Winifred (Work) Roth; m. Frank J. Kollarits, July 5, 1969; children: Edna M., Matthew D. BA, MD, Ohio State U., 1970, MSc, 1974. Diplomate Am. Bd. Ophthalmology, 1975. Intern Columbus Children's Hosp., 1970-71; resident in ophthalmology Ohio State U., 1971-74; staff fellow Nat. Eye Inst., NIH, Bethesda, Md., 1974-76; dir. div. ophthalmology Med. Coll. Ohio, Toledo, 1976-84; med. dir. Eye Inst. Northwestern Ohio, Toledo, 1984—. Fellow Am. Acad. Ophthalmology; mem. Ohio Ophthalmologic Soc., N.W. Ohio Ophthalmologic Soc., Ohio State Med. Assn., Outpatient Ophthal. Surg. Soc. Office: Eye Inst NW Ohio 5555 Airport Hwy Ste 110 Toledo OH 43615

KOLLEGGER, HARALD DONAT, neurologist, researcher; b. Bruck, Styria, Austria, Mar. 14, 1955; s. Ernst and Gertrude (Tuller) K.; m. Gudrun Isolde Wildpanner, Oct. 23, 1983; children: Vitus Sebastian, Liane Maria, Xaver Emil. MD, U. Graz, Austria, 1981. Cert. specialist for neurology and psychiatry. Resident LKH Leoben, Austria, 1982-84; resident in neurology Univ. Clinic, Vienna, 1984-90; rsch. fellow in biochemistry Trinity Coll., Dublin, Ireland, 1990-91; head of rsch. lab. U. Clinic Vienna, 1993—; neurol. cons. KH Stockerau, Austria, 1992-96. Author, editor: Neurologische und Psychiatrische Akutmassnahmen, 1993; author: Excitatory Amino Acids and Brain Damage, 1993; contbr. articles to profl. jours. Erwin Schrödinger scholar Fonds zur Förderung der Wissenschaftlichen Forschung, 1990. Mem. European Soc. Neurochemistry, Österreichische Gesellschaft Akupunktur. Home: Belvederegasse 11, A-1040 Vienna Austria Office: Univ Clinic Neurology, Währinger Gürtel 18-20, A-1090 Vienna Austria

KOLLER, LOREN D., veterinary medicine educator; b. Pomeroy, Wash., June 16, 1940; s. Edwin C. and Doris K. (Shelton) K.; m. Kathleen Noel Ringness, Sept. 7, 1963; children: Susan E., Michael D., Christopher L. DVM, Wash. State U., 1965; MS, U. Wis., 1969, PhD, 1971. Head diagnostic and comparative pathology Nat. Inst. Environ. Health Scis., Research Triangle Park, N.C., 1971-72; rsch. assoc. dept. vet. medicine Oreg. State U., Corvallis, 1972-76, assoc. prof., 1976-78, prof., 1995—, dean Coll. Vet. Medicine, 1985-95; assoc. prof., asst. dean Dept. Vet. Medicine, U. Idaho, Moscow, 1978-81, assoc. prof., assoc. dean, 1981-82, prof., assoc. dean, 1982-85; research asst. Dept. Vet. Sci. U. Wis., Madison, 1968-71; assoc. veterinarian Blue Cross Vet. Clinic, Corvallis, 1965-66. Contbr. articles to profl. jours., chpts. to books. Served to capt. M.C., U.S. Army, 1966-68. Grantee NIH, USDA, Dow Chem. Co., EPA, FDA, Merck Sharp & Dohme, Warner-Lambert, Pew Found. Mem. AVMA, NAS (mem. com. toxicology), Am. Assn. Vet. Immunologists, Soc. Toxicology, Soc. Toxicologic Pathologists, Assn. Vet. Med. Colls., Oreg. Vet. Med. Assn.

KOLLMEYER, KENNETH ROBERT, surgeon; b. Berwyn, Ill., Feb. 1, 1947. BS in Biology-Chemistry, Randolph-Macon Coll., 1969; PhD in Physiology, U. Cin., 1973; MD cum laude, U. Colo., 1977. Diplomate Am. Bd. Surgery, Am. Bd. Gen. Vascular Surgery. Rsch. asst. Cardiac Rsch. Lab., Sch. Medicine U. So. Calif., L.A., 1967; head lab divsn. thoracic and cardiovascular surgery Med. Ctr. Va., Richmond, 1968-69; NIH rsch. fellow dept. clin. physiology Nat. Asthma Ctr., Denver, 1973-74; intern in surgery Parkland Meml. Hosp., Dallas, 1977-78, resident in surgery, 1978-80, chief resident in surgery, 1980-81; fellow in vascular surgery, instr. dept. surgery U. Tex. Southwestern Med. Sch., Dallas, 1981-82, clin. asst. prof. surgery, 1982—; dir. S.W. Vascular Lab., Dallas, 1982—; attending vascular surgeon Meth. Med. Ctr., Dallas, 1982—; mem. staff Charlton Meth. Hosp., St. Paul Med. Ctr., Parkland Meml. Hosp., Med. City Hosp.; teaching asst. dept. physiology U. Cin. Coll. Medicine, 1972-73; chmn. Doctors Care PA, Dallas; presenter in field. Contbr. articles to profl. publs. Fellow ACS; mem. AMA, Tex. Med. Assn., Tex. Surg. Soc., Dallas County Med. Soc., Dallas Soc. Gen. Surgeons, Soc. for Non-Invasive Vascular Tech., Nat. Hon. Biol. Soc., Parkland Surg. Soc., Alpha Omega Alpha. Office: SW Vascular and Surg Group Meth Med Ctr Pavilion II 221 W Colorado Blvd Ste 625 Dallas TX 75208-2345

KOLMEN, SAMUEL NORMAN, consultant; b. Brownsville, Tex., Mar. 20, 1930; s. Joseph and Cyla (Gerson) K.; m. Barbara Kass, June 13, 1954; children: Benita Kolmen Solomon, Jeannette Kolmen Rosato. BA, U. Tex., Austin, 1954; PhD in Physiology, U. Tex. Med. Br., Galveston, 1957. James W. McLaughlin fellow in infection and immunology U. Tex. Med. Br., Galveston, 1955-57; Jeane B. Kempner postdoctoral fellow in medicine, London, 1957-58; asst. prof., assoc. prof., prof. U. Tex. Med. Br., Galveston, 1958-75; prof. physiology, chmn. dept. Coll. Sci. and Engring., Sch. Medicine Wright State U., Dayton, Ohio, 1975-84, prof., asst. dean Sch. Medicine, 1980-84; asst. to pres. in rsch. Wright State U., Dayton, 1979-84; prof., assoc. dean, co-founder liaison com. for computing Hahnemann U. Sch. Medicine, Phila., 1984-89; dir. med. edn. and rsch. Mercy Hosp. Pitts., 1989-94; pres. Kolmen & Assocs., 1994—; rsch. coord. Shriners Burns Inst., Galveston, 1970-75; cons. Nat. Bd. Med. Examiners, Phila., 1989. Contbr. over 35 articles to sci. jours. Pres. Congregation Beth Jacob, Galveston, 1970-72; bd. dirs. Jewish Assn. South Dayton, 1976-83; mem. sci. rev. coun. Miami Valley chpt. and Ohio Regional coun. Am. Heart Assn., 1981-83; vol. cons. Allegheny Policy Coun., Coalition on Math. and Sci. (K-12); vol. Career and Passport Commn. Operation Safety Net. Recipient Disting. Alumnus award U. Tex. Med. Br., 1981. Democrat. Office: Kolmen & Assocs. 256 Sweet Gum Rd Pittsburgh PA 15238

KOLMOS, HANS JORN JEPSEN, clinical microbiologist, physician; b. Sonderborg, Denmark, June 10, 1948; s. Jes Jessen and Anne Marie (Jepsen) K.; m. Lisbet Stokkebye Christiansen, June 10, 1972; children: Niels Bo, Maja, Marie. MD, U. Odense, 1974, D of Med. Scis., 1985. Cert. specialist in med. microbiology. Registrar U. Hosp., Odense, 1974-83, State Serum Inst., Copenhagen, 1984-86; cons. U. Hosp., Copenhagen, 1986-87; chief physician Copenhagen U. Hosp., Hvidovre, Denmark, 1987; assoc. prof. Copenhagen U., 1990—; bd. dirs. Internat. Fedn. Infection Control. Contbr. articles to profl. jours. Lt. Med. Svcs., 1976-77. Mem. Danish Med. Assn., Danish Soc. for Clin. Microbiology (bd. dirs. 1984-90, pres. 1995—), Danish Soc. for Infectious Diseases, Danish Club for Ctrl. Sterilization and Hosp. Hygiene (chmn. 1989-95). Office: Hvidovre Hosp, Dept Clin Microbiology 445, Kettegaard alle 30, DK 2650 Hvidovre Denmark

KOLODNER, ELLEN L., occupational therapy manager and educator; b. Phila., Dec. 26, 1947; d. Oscar S. and Anita (Dorfman) Lichtenstein; m. Bernard B. Kolodner, Dec. 29, 1968; children: Michael, Louis. BS, U. Pa., 1969; MSS, Bryn Mawr Coll., 1980. Lic. occupational therapist, Pa. Dir. therapeutic activities dept. Phila. Psychiat. Ctr., 1981-82; asst. prof. occup. therapy, asst. to dean, coord. fieldwork Thomas Jefferson U., Phila., 1982-92; dir. occupl. therapy dept. Magee Rehab. Hosp., 1992-94; neurorehab. program mgr. U. Pa. Health Sys., 1994-95; dir. clin. profl. devel. NovaCare, Inc., 1995—; adj. asst. prof. Thomas Jefferson U., 1992—. Contbr. chpts. to books, articles to profl. jours. Fellow Am. Occupl. Therapy Assn. (cert., exec. bd. 1992, Outstanding Svc. award 1992); mem. NASW, Pa. Occupl. Therapy Assn. (Outstanding Achievement award 1985), World Fedn. Occupl. Therapy, Day Care Assn. Montgomery County, Fedn. Day Care Svcs., Alpha Eta. Address: 918 Frazier Rd Rydal PA 19046-2408

KOLODNER, RICHARD DAVID, biochemist, educator; b. Morristown, N.J., Apr. 3, 1951; s. Ignace Izack and Ethel (Zelnick) K.; m. Karin Ann Gregory, Aug. 6, 1983 (div. May 1991). BS, U. Calif., Irvine, 1971, PhD, 1975; MS (hon.), Harvard U., 1988. Rsch. fellow Harvard U. Med. Sch., Boston, 1975-78; asst. prof. Dana Farber Cancer Inst. and Harvard U. Med. Sch., Boston, 1978-83, assoc. prof., 1983-88, prof. biochemistry, 1988—; chmn. divsn. cellular molecular biology Dana-Farber Cancer Inst., Boston, 1991-94, head x-ray crystallography lab., 1991—, chmn. divsn. of human cancer genetics. Editor PLASMID jour., 1986-95; assoc. editor Cancer Rsch., Cell; contbr. articles to sci. jours. Recipient Jr. Faculty Rsch. award Am. Cancer Soc., 1981, Faculty Rsch. award, 1984, Merit award NIH, 1993, Charles S. Mott medal GM, 1996; rsch. grantee Am. Cancer Soc., 1980, 16 grants NIH, 1978-95. Mem. Am. Soc. for Biochemistry and Molecular Biology, Am. Soc. for Microbiology, Genetics Soc. Am. Home: 241 Perkins St Apt 602A Jamaica Plain MA 02130-4002 Office: Dana Farber Cancer Inst 44 Binney St Boston MA 02115-6013

KOLODNY, ABRAHAM LEWIS, physician; b. Norfolk, Va., July 2, 1917; s. William and Jennie (Eisenberg) K.; m. Mildred Fiske, Aug. 10, 1942; children: William (dec.), David Greene, Suki, Douglas Merrill, Peggy Lee. Grad., U. Va., 1941. Intern South Balt. Gen. Hosp., 1941-42; residency Ashburn Army Arthritis Ctr., McKinney, Tex., 1944-46; with Arthritis Clinic/Sinai Hosp., Balt., 1948-70; chief, rheumatology N. Charles Hosp., Balt., 1951-90; co-chief, rheumatology Franklin Square Hosp., Balt., 1970-95; commr. Md. Commn. Rheumatic Diseases, 1987-91; pres. North Charles Gen. Hosp., 1963-67; staff mem. Franklin Sq. Hosp., 1970-95; state commr. Arthritis and Related Diseases, 1986-91; ret. chief rheumatology Homewood Hosp. Ctr.; formerly active Johns Hopkins Med. Health Systems. Contbg. author textbooks in field, articles to profl. jours. Maj. U.S. Army, 1942-47, CBI. Decorated Bronze Star, Combat Med. badge, Presdl. Unit citation, Victory medal, Chinese Victory medal, others. Fellow Am. Coll. Rheumatology, N.Y. Acad. Scis.; mem. AMA, Am. Soc. Clin. Pharmacology, Md. Arthritis Found. (bd. dirs. 1975-91), Md. Soc. for Rheumatic Diseases (co-founder), So. Med. Assn. Office: 9101 Franklin Square Dr #321 Baltimore MD 21237-3930

KOLODNY, EDWIN HILLEL, neurologist, geneticist, medical administrator; b. Boston, Mar. 15, 1936; s. Myer Zeman and Naomi Lillian (Zalkind) K.; m. Roselyn Leinwand, May 31, 1958; children: Nancy, Leonard Benjamin, Robin, Noah Jacob. AB cum laude in Econs., Harvard Coll., 1957; MD with honors, NYU, 1962. Diplomate Am. Bd. Psychiatry and Neurology, Am. Bd. Med. Genetics. Intern, resident in internal medicine Bellevue Hosp., N.Y.C., 1962-64; resident in neurology Mass. Gen. Hosp., Boston, 1964-67; spl. fellow lab. neurochemistry Nat. Inst. Neurol. Diseases, Bethesda, Md., 1967-70; asst. prof. neurology Harvard Med. Sch., Boston, 1970-76, assoc. prof. 1976-85, prof., 1985-91; Bernard and Charlotte Marden prof., chmn. dept. neurology NYU Med. Ctr., N.Y.C., 1991—; vice chmn., exec. com. Med. Bd. Tisch Hosp., N.Y., 1993—; vis. prof. Weizmann Inst. Sci., Rehovot, Israel, 1988, 1990; assoc. dir. Eunice Kennedy Shriver Ctr. Mental Retardation, Inc., Waltham, Mass., 1976-83, acting dir., 1983-84, dir., 1984-90; assoc. neurologist Mass. Gen. Hosp., Boston, 1976-87, neurologist, 1988-91; chmn. com. Research Ctrs. Forward Planning Mental Retardation, Nat. Inst. Child Health and Human Devel., 1983-84; cons. pres.' com. Mental Retardation, 1982; adv. genetic services Dept. Pub. Health Mass., 1977-80; mem. Mass. Nat. Inst. Health Centennial Com., 1987-88, profl. adv. bd. Internat. Rett Syndrome Assn., 1986-94, sci. adv. bd. United Leukodystrophy Found., 1986-94, sci. med. adv. com. Canavan Found, 1994—. Mem. editorial bd. Annals of Neurology, 1984-89. Contbr. articles to profl. jours. Mem. sci. adv. bd. Nat. Tay Sachs and Allied Diseases Assn., 1970—; v.p., trustee Temple Emanuel, Newton, Mass., 1983-89; trustee Hebrew Coll., Brookline, Mass. Recipient Solomon A. Berson Medical Alumni Achievement award clin. sci. NYU Sch. Med., 1993. Fellow Am. Acad. Neurology (S. Wier Mitchell award 1970); mem. Am. Assn. Neuropathology (Moore award 1975), Am. Neurol. Assn., Am. Soc. Human Genetics, Am. Soc. Neurochemistry, Child Neurology Soc., Harvard Varsity Club (Cambridge), NYU, Alpha Omega Alpha. Avocations: Judaica, photography. Home: 110 Bleecker St Apt 24D New York NY 10012-2106 Office: NYU Med Ctr 550 1st Ave New York NY 10016-6481

KOLONAY, BARBARA A., management consultant; b. Pitts., Apr. 23, 1959; d. Joseph and Marie T. (Farina) Murphy; m. Ronald J. Kolonay, Oct. 23, 1982; children: Bradley M., Kelly M. BSN, Duquesne U., 1981; MS in Human Resource Mgmt., La Roche Coll., 1992. RN, Pa. Staff nurse Presbyn. U., Pitts., 1981-82; telemetry nurse St. Margaret's Hosp., Pitts., 1982-85; vis. nurse St. Francis Hosp., Pitts., 1984-85; tng. and devel./quality assurance coord. Cignal (formerly Equicor), Pitts., 1985-91; cons. managed care, human resource mgmt. Pitts., 1991—; part-time prof. Robert Morris Coll., Pitts., 1995—; managed care consulting case mgr. Alpha Health Network, Pitts., 1991-94; med. billing/re-engring. cons. Transact, Pitts., 1992-94. Den leader Boy Scouts Am., Pitts.; asst. leader Daisies, Girl Scouts U.S., Pitts. Home: 4876 Ottawa Ct Gibsonia PA 15044

KOLOWICH, PATRICIA ANN, orthopedic surgeon; b. Mt. Clemens, Mich., Mar. 17, 1958; m. Jared Pratt Buckley, Sept. 18, 1983; children: Patrick, Jessica, Jacqueline. BS, U. Mich., 1980, MD, 1982. Intern U. Mich., Ann Arbor, 1982-83, resident, 1983-87; sr. staff Henry Ford Hosp., Detroit, 1988—; team physician Detroit Red Wings Hockey Team, 1988—; cons. Detroit Tigers Baseball Team, 1988-95, Detroit Drive Arena Football, 1990-91, Detroit Rockers Soccer Team, 1990-95, Performing Artists Ctr., Detroit, 1989—; fellow in sports medicine, Salt Lake City. Contbr. articles to profl. jours. and chpts. to books. Mem. AMA (vice chairperson resident physician sect. governing coun. 1986-87, sec. 1985-86, Mich. del. 1984-85, task force on long range planning 1984), Am. Orthopedic Soc. Sports Medicine, Arthroscopy Assn. N.Am., Am. Acad. Orthopedic Surg eons, Detroit Acad. Orthopaedic Surgery,. Office: Henry Ford Hosp 2799 W Grand Blvd Detroit MI 48202-2608

KOLSRUD, HENRY GERALD, dentist; b. Minnewaukan, N.D., Aug. 12, 1923; s. Henry G. and Anna Naomi (Moen) K.; m. Loretta Dorothy Cooper, Sept. 3, 1945; children—Gerald Roger, Charles Cooper. Student Concordia Coll., 1941-44; DDS, U. Minn., 1947. Gen. practice dentistry, Spokane, Wash., 1953—. Bd. dirs. Spokane County Rep. Com., United Crusade, Spokane; at-large-del. Republican Planning Com.; mem. Republican Presdl. Task Force. Capt. USAF, 1950-52. Recipient Employer of the Yr. award Lilac City Bus. and Profl. Women, 1994. Mem. ADA, Wash. State Dental Assn., Spokane Dist. Dental Soc. Lutheran. Clubs: Spokane Country, Spokane, Empire. Lodges: Masons, Shriners. Home: 2107 W Waikiki Rd Spokane WA 99218-2780 Office: 3718 N Monroe St Spokane WA 99205-2850

KOLTER, JOSEPH PAUL, JR., surgeon; b. New Brighton, Pa., Sept. 24, 1949; s. Joseph Paul and Dorothy Marie (Gray) K.; m. Rebecca Louise Smith, Aug. 29, 1971; children: Jason, Richard. BS in Biology, U. Pitts., 1971, MD, 1975. Diplomate Am. Bd. Surgery. Intern, Hosps. of Univ. Health Ctr. Pitts., 1975-76, resident, 1976-81; practice medicine specializing in surgery, Pitts., 1981—; mem. staff St. Clair Meml. Hosp. Mem. A.C.S., AMA, Pa. Med. Soc., Allegheny Med. Soc., Pitts. Surg. Soc., Phi Beta Kappa. Democrat. Roman Catholic. Avocations: reading, chess, racquetball, creative writing, golf. Office: Bldg 2400 Suite 3 The Bourse at Virginia Manor 2275 Swallow Hill Rd Pittsburgh PA 15220-1656

KOMINEK, LEO ALOYSIUS, psychologist; b. Chgo., Apr. 11, 1937; s. Leo Anton and Sylvia Helen (Klarkowski) K.; m. Anita Joan Mars, Sept. 5, 1959; children: Stephen, Laura, Mary, Leo. BS, St. Joseph's Coll., 1959; PhD, U. Ill., 1964; MA, Western Mich. U., 1995. Rsch. scientist Upjohn, Kalamazoo, Mich., 1964-70, sr. rsch. scientist, 1970-73, sr. scientist, 1973-78, 79-96, ret., 1996; psychologist Borgess Behavioral Medicine, Kalamazoo, Mich., 1996—. Contbr. articles to profl. jours., including Antimicrobial Agents and Chemotherapy, Biochem. Biophys. Acta, Ann. N.Y. Acad. Sci. Fellow Am. Acad. Microbiology, Sigma Xi; mem. Am. Soc. Microbiology, N.Y. Acad. Scis., Am. Chem. Soc. Roman Catholic. Home: 2209 Hickory Point Dr Kalamazoo MI 49024 Office: Borgess Behavioral Medicine Delano Outpatient Clinic 1722 Shaffer St Kalamazoo MI 49001-1643

KOMISAR, ARNOLD, otolaryngologist, educator; b. N.Y.C., Nov. 27, 1947; s. Samuel and Sonia (Schwartz) K.; m. Lenora I. Felderman, Dec. 23, 1984; children: Alexandra Danielle, Jonathan Reed. BS, Bradley U., 1968; DDS, NYU, 1972; MD, Hahnemann Med. Coll., 1975. Diplomate Am. Bd. Otolaryngology. Resident in surgery Beth Israel Med. Ctr., N.Y.C., 1975-76; resident in Otolaryngology Mt. Sinai Med. Sch., N.Y.C., 1976-79; asst. prof. otolaryngology Albert Einstein Coll. Medicine, N.Y.C., 1979-85, assoc. prof., 1985-86, assoc. clin. prof., 1986-90; assoc. dir. head and neck surgery Albert Einstein Affiliated Hosps., N.Y.C., 1982-86; attending otolaryngologist Montefiore Hosp. and Med. Ctr., N.Y.C., 1979-90, Bronx Mcpl. Hosp. Ctr., N.Y.C., 1979-90, N. Cen. Bronx Hosp., N.Y.C., 1979-90; clin. assoc. prof. otolaryngology Cornell U. Med. Coll., N.Y.C., 1990-94; clin. prof. otolaryngology Cornell U. Med. Coll., Ithaca, N.Y., 1994—; otolaryngologist Lenox Hill Hosp., N.Y.C., 1986—, asst to dir. resident edn. dept. otolaryngology, 1986—, adj. otolaryngologist, 1987—, attending otolaryngologist, 1989—, assoc. dir. otolaryngology, 1990—; cons. otolaryngology N.Y. Eye and Ear Infirmary, N.Y.C., 1986-89; courtesy staff surgery-otolaryngology Drs. Hosp., N.Y.C., 1986-90; attending staff Manhattan Eye Ear and Throat Hosp., 1995—; presenter in field. Contbr. articles to profl. jours. Fellow Am. Coll. Surgeons, Am. Soc. Head and Neck Surgery, Am. Acad. Facial Plastic and Reconstructive Surgery, Am. Acad. Otolaryngology/Head and Neck Surgery (Honor award), Triological Soc. (Mosher award), Am. Bronchoesophalogical Soc., N.Y. Acad. Medicine, Am. Laryngol. Assn.; mem. AMA, Pan-Am. Soc. Brocho-esophagology, Soc. Univ. Otolaryngologists, N.Y. Head and Neck Soc., Med. Soc., N.Y., N.Y. County Med. Soc. Office: 1317 3rd Ave New York NY 10021-2995

KOMORN, ROBERT MELVIN, head and neck surgeon; b. Detroit, June 24, 1939; s. William and Gertrude (Katzman) K.; M.D., U. Mich., 1964, MS in Otolaryngology-Head and Neck Surgery, 1970; m. Judith Gail Katz, Aug. 21, 1961; children: Sherri Lynne, Deborah Susan, Janet Elizabeth. Intern, Sinai Hosp., Detroit, 1964-65, resident in gen. surgery, 1965-66; resident in otolaryngology U. Mich. Hosp., Ann Arbor, 1966-70; chief otolaryngology sect. VA Hosp., Houston, 1970-74; practice medicine specializing in head and neck surgery-otolaryngology, Houston; mem. staff Methodist, St. Joseph, St. Luke's, Tex. Children's hosps.; chief otolaryngology, head and neck surgery St. Joseph Hosp., 1976-87; asst. prof. otolaryngology Baylor U. Coll. Medicine, 1970-74, clin. asst. prof., 1974—. Diplomate Am. Bd. Otolaryngology-Head and Neck Surgery. Fellow A.C.S., Am. Acad. Otolaryngology, Soc. Univ. Otolaryngologists, Am. Soc. Head and Neck Surgery, Am. Acad. Facial Plastic and Reconstructive Surgery; mem. AMA, Tex. Med. Assn., Harris County Med. Soc., Tex. Otolaryn. Assn., Houston Otolaryn. Soc. (pres. 1976-77), Alpha Omega Alpha, Phi Kappa Phi. Contbr. chpts. to books, articles to med. jours. Home: 5219 Loch Lomond Dr Houston TX 77096-2510 Office: 6560 Fannin St Suite 1228 Houston TX 77030

KONDO, MASATOSHI S., pharmaceutical executive, educator; b. Asahikawa, Hokkaido, Japan, Feb. 8, 1940; came to U.S, 1984; s. Saburo Mikame and Hanae Kondo; m. Yumiko Iijima. June 19, 1992; 1 child, Mika Naomi. BS, Tokyo U., 1962; PhD, U. Ill., Urbana, 1967; DSc, U. Antwerp, Belgium, 1976. Asst. prof. U. Zurich, Switzerland, 1970-72; prof. U. Antwerp, 1972-82; dir. Yamanouchi Pharm. Co., Tokyo, 1982-84, Bristol-Myers Co., Wallingford, Conn., 1984-88; mng. ptnr. Strategic Informatica Internat., North Haven, Conn., 1988—; adviser C. Itoh & Co., Ltd., Tokyo, 1989-94; pres. Lifegene Corp., Hamamatsu, Japan, 1995—; bd. dirs. SII Med. Info., Inc.; prof. Yale U., New Haven, 1985—, U. Conn., Storrs, 1986—. Author: Microbiology (in Dutch), 1975. Policy advisor Sakigake Polit. Party, Tokyo, 1994—. Fellow Internat. Agy. for Research on Cancer, WHO, 1976, sr. NATO, 1981; named Leopold II Knight , Kingdom of Belgium, 1980. Mem. AAAS, German Biochem. Soc., Belgian Biochem. Soc., Austrian Biochem. Soc., N.Y. Acad. Scis.

KONDZIELA, JOSEPH RICHARD, psychiatrist; b. Stamford, Conn., Oct. 27, 1954; s. Frank Joseph and Rose Dianne (Calitri) K. BS magna cum laude, Fairfield Coll., 1976; MD, St. Louis U., 1980. Diplomate Am. Bd. Psychiatry and Neurology. Resident in psychiatry Fairfield Hills Hosp., Newtown, Conn., 1980-83; chief resident in psychiatry N.Y. Med. Coll., Valhalla, N.Y., 1983-84; staff psychiatrist Dept. of Psychiatry Danbury (Conn.) Hosp., 1984-87; pvt. practice Fairfield, Conn., 1984—; cons. Danbury Hosp. Mental Health Clin., 1984-87; sec. Dept. of Psychiatry Danbury

Hosp., 1984-85. Contbr. articles profl. jours. Vol. Spl. Olympics Found. for the Mentally Retarded, Fairfield, 1979-80; vol. med. faculty N.Y. Med. Coll., 1984—. Mem. Am. Psychiat. Assn., Conn. Psychiat. Soc., St. Louis U. Med. Alumni Club. Republican. Roman Catholic. Home: 953 Old Post Rd Fairfield CT 06430-5906 Office: 1583 Post Rd Fairfield CT 06430-5932

KONG, BOBBY KIPAK, surgeon; b. Hong Kong, Aug. 19, 1956; came to U.S., 1975; s. Claire Chang Kong; m. Barbara Kong; children: Michael, Sarah, Julia. BS in Mech. Engring., Washington U., St. Louis, 1979; MD, St. Louis U., 1983. Diplomate Am. Bd. Gen. Surgery, Am. Bd. Thoracic Surgery. Resident gent surgery Presbyn. U. Pa., Phila.; resident thoracic surgery St. Louis U.; thoracic surgeon St. Joseph Mercy Hosp., Ann Arbor, Mich., 1991—. Fellow ACS, Am. Coll. Cardiology, Internat. Coll. Surgeons; mem. Soc. Thoracic Surgeons. Home: 18 Regent Dr Ann Arbor MI 48104 Office: Mich Heart & Vascular Inst PO Box 972 Ste 102 Ann Arbor MI 48106-0972

KONG, ERIC SIU-WAI, research scientist; b. Hong Kong, Jan. 14, 1953; s. Woon-Man and Chau-Mui Kong; m. Susanna May-Man Lee, June 24, 1974; children: Myron Hok-Ben, Julian Hok-Koon. AB in Biochemistry, U. Calif., Berkeley, 1974; MSc in Chemistry, Rensselaer Poly. Inst., 1976, PhD in Chemistry, 1978. Research fellow Va. Poly. Inst., Blacksburg, 1978-79; research scientist NASA-Ames/Stanford U. Joint Inst., Moffett-Field, Calif., 1979-83; mem. tech. staff Sandia Nat. Labs., Livermore, Calif., 1983-84, Hewlett-Packard Labs., Palo Alto, Calif., 1984-86; biomaterials tech. advisor Mentor Corp., Santa Barbara, Calif., 1986-89; mem. faculty of medicinal chemistry U. Calif., San Francisco, 1989-90; sr. rsch. chemist Becton Dickinson, Los Gatos, Calif., 1990-92; dir. rsch. & devel. Materials Sci. & Tech. Inst., Palo Alto, Calif., 1992—. Contbr. articles to profl. jours. Fellow N.Y. Acad. Scis., Am. Inst. Chemists; mem. Materials Research Soc., Soc. Polymer Sci. of Japan, Soc. Plastics Engrs. (chmn. Golden Gate Plastics Analysis div. 1983-84). Home: 4250 El Camino Real Ste A206 Palo Alto CA 94306 Office: Materials Sci & Tech Inst Palo Alto CA 94306

KONIECZNY, STEPHEN FRANCIS, medical educator; b. Pawtucket, R.I., Oct. 26, 1954. BS in Zoology, U. Mass., 1977; PhD in Biology, Brown U., 1982. Postdoctoral fellow biology U. Va., charlottesville, 1982-86; from asst. prof. to prof. biological scis. Purdue U., West Lafayette, Ind., 1986-96, prof. biol. scis., 1996—. Contbr. numerous articles to profl. jours. NIH fellow, 1980-83, Muscular Dystrophy Assn. fellow, 1983-85; grantee Am. Cancer Soc., 1978-79, Am. Heart Assn., 1991-96, Lafayette Lions Club, 1994; Am. Heart Assn. grantee-in-aid, 1995-96. Mem. Am. Soc. Microbiology, Am. Soc. Cell Biology, Soc. Devel. Biology. Office: Purdue U Dept Biol Scis West Lafayette IN 47907

KONIETZKO, KURT O., psychologist; b. Free City of Danzig, Germany, Sept. 25, 1924; came to U.S., 1939; s. Hermann and Anna (Baenfer) K.; m. Ruth Rittenhouse, 1949 (div. 1976); 1 child, Debra; m. Myrna DeVoren, 1982. BA, U. Chgo., 1951; MA, Temple U., 1953, PhD, 1959. Lic. clin. psychologist, Pa. Dist. supr. Commonwealth of Pa. Bd. of Parole, Phila., 1963-66; dir. Inst. for Rational Living, Phila., 1966-69, Inst. for Living, Inc., Phila., 1969-76; cons. Dept. of Edn., V.I., 1976-79; coord. Community Mental Health Svcs., V.I., 1976-77; dir. children's svcs. Mental Health Div., V.I., 1977-79; acting adminstr. Community Mental Health Ctr., V.I., 1976-77; pres. Self Mgmt. for Successful Living, Inc., Phila., 1979-91; pvt. practice Contractors for Managed Care. Contbr. articles to profl. jours. Past pres. World Federalists Assn. (Phila. chpt.), Brynford Civic Assn., Haverford, Pa., Delaware County Dem. Orgn., Phila.; candidate Haverford Twp. Commr., Phila. area, 1991; vol. House of Corrections SMART Recovery Program. With USN, 1942-48. Mem. APA, Pa. Psychol. Assn., Phila. Soc. Clin. Psychologists, Delaware Valley Group Psychotherapy Soc.

KONIGSBERG, STEPHEN FEUER, surgeon; b. N.Y.C., Apr. 26, 1938; s. Louis and Edith (Feuer) K.; m. Rhoda Rachap, Sept. 3, 1966; children: David Eric, Paul Benjamin. AB, Columbia U., 1958; MD, Harvard U., 1962. Diplomate Am. Bd. Surgery with subspecialty in general vascular surgery. Intern Yale-New Haven Med. Ctr., 1962-63; resident Peter Bent Brigham Hosp., Boston, 1963-66; chief resident/sr. resident Albert Einstein Hosp., N.Y.C., 1966-68; pvt. practice surgery New Brunswick, N.J., 1970—; pres. med. staff RWJ Hosp. New Brunswick, 1980-88. Ltd. comdr. USN, 1968-70. Mem. AMA, N.J. State Med. Soc., Middlesex County Med. Soc. (pres. 1993-94, bd. trustees 1990-95), N.J. Vascular Soc., N.J. Oncology Soc., Internat. Soc. Cardo-Vascular Surgery. Office: Highland Park Surg Assocs 31 River Rd Highland Park NJ 08904

KONIKIEWICZ, LEONARD WIESLAW, biomedical communications educator; b. Lvow, Poland, July 24, 1928; came to U.S., 1959; s. Lubin Adolph and Melania (Rogozinska) K.; m. Antonina Kazimiera Grodowska; 1 child, Annette Melany. BS in Liberal Arts, SUNY, 1981; PhD in Natural Sci., Universitatis Polonorum, London, 1985. Registered biomedical photographer, illustrator. Med. photographer Cornell U., N.Y.C., 1960-67; dir. visual communications Poly. Med. Ctr., Harrisburg, Pa., 1967-85; dir., clinics asst. prof. biomed. communications James H. Quillen Coll. of Medicine, East Tenn. State U., Johnson City, Tenn., 1985—; export cons. in U.S.-Eastern Europe; cons. NASA Plant Space Biology Lab. Author: Bioelectrography, 1984, Career of Joanna Kurtz, 1995; contbr. articles to profl. jours. and books; patentee in field. Vol. interpreter ARC, Harrisburg, 1979-85; mem. refugee com. Polish Cultural Assn., Harrisburg, 1982, v.p. 1978-79; vol. organist Our Lady Cath. Ch., Harrisburg, 1970-85; rschr. Cystic-Fibrosis, Cancer, Harrisburg, 1975-85; v.p. Polish Cultural Assn., 1978-79. Decorated Medal of Home Army; recipient 2d prize Pa. Arts Coun., 1972, best cover award Lab World, 1975, best med. picture award Med. World News, 1977; rsch. grantee Pa. March of Dimes, 1976-78, Pa. Cystic Fibrosis Found., 1978-81, Betatron Corp., 1983-84. Mem. Biol. Photog. Assn., Assn. Biomed. Communications Dirs., Internat. Assn. Polish Combat Vets. Home: 2023 Sundale Rd Johnson City TN 37604-3027 Office: East Tenn State U James H Quillen Coll Med PO Box 70583 Johnson City TN 37614

KONOPINSKI, VIRGIL JAMES, industrial hygienist; b. Toledo, Ohio, July 11, 1935; s. Mack and Mary Veronica (Jankowski) K.; m. Joan Mary Wielinski, June 27, 1964; children—Ann Marie, Carol Sue, Peter James. BS in Chem. Engring., U. Toledo, 1956; MS in Chem. Engring., Pratt Inst., 1960; MBA, Bowling Green State U., 1971. Registered profl. engr., Ohio, Ind., Calif.; cert. indsl. hygienist; cert. safety profl. Assoc. engr. Owens Illinois, Toledo, 1956, 60; real estate developer, Grand Rapids, Ohio, 1961; chem. engr. USPHS, Cin., 1961-64; sr. environ. engr. Vistron Corp., Lima, Ohio, 1964-67; environ. specialist, asst. to dir. environ. control Owens Corning Fiberglas, Toledo, 1967-72; gen. mgr. Midwest Environ. Mgmt., Maumee, Ohio, 1972-73; staff specialist, indsl. hygienist Williams Bros. Waste Control., Tulsa, Okla., 1973-75; dir. div. indsl. hygiene and radiol. health Ind. State Bd. Health, Indpls., 1975-87, exec. v.p. ACT of Ind., Indpls., 1987-89; sr. cons. Occusafe, 1990-91; regional safety engr., human resources analyst/safety U.S. Postal Svc., 1991— ; bd. dir. IOSHA indsl. hygiene, 1975-83; cons. indoor air, radon, occupational health, Zionsville, 1987-91, Cary, 1991—, ; lectr. With USNR, 1956-59. Mem. Am. Indsl. Hygiene Assn., Am. Conf. Govtl. Indsl. Hygienists, Am. Soc. Safety Engrs., Naval Res. Assn., Ret. Officers Assn. Republican. Roman Catholic. Contbr. articles to profl. jours. Home: 14 Fairfield Ln Cary IL 60013-1946 Office: 433 W Van Buren St Chicago IL 60699-0842

KONSTANS, DOROTHY JANICE, school psychologist, special educaion coordinator; b. Chgo., Apr. 21, 1936; d. James T. and Winifred M. (Hayhurst) Hume; m. Constantine Kontans, Feb. 28, 1959; children: Chris T., Randall J., Russell D. AB, Ripon (Wis.) Coll., 1958; MA, U. Chgo., 1961. Registered psychologist, Ill. Psychologist Silver Cross Hosp., Joliet, Ill., 1961-62; sch. psychologist Dist. 303, St. Charles, Ill., 1963-73; sch. psychologist, spl. edn. coordinator Dist. 301, Burlington, Ill., 1973—. Mem. Nat. Assn. Sch. Psychologists, Nat. Health Service Providers, Ill Sch. Psychologists Assn., Phi Beta Kappa. Methodist. Home: PO Box 527 Saint Charles IL 60174-0527 Office: Dist 301 PO Box 396 Burlington IL 60109-0396

KOO, KIM ENG, neurological surgeon; b. Kamunting, Perak, Malaysia, Sept. 2, 1951; came to the U.S., 1970; d. Seow Hean Koo and Gim Hiok Kua; m. Richard Thomas Smith Jr.; children: Nathan J., Nicholas J. AB, Bryn Mawr Coll., 1973; MD, Temple U., 1982. Diplomate Am. Bd. Neurol. Surgery. Intern Presbyn. U. Pa. Med. Ctr., Phila., 1982-83; resident Thomas Jefferson U. Hosp., Phila., 1983-88; pvt. practice Phila., 1988—. Mem. Am. Assn. Neurol. Surgeons, Pa. Neurosurg. Soc., Congress Neurol. Surgeons, Alpha Omega Alpha. Office: 3300 A Ryan Ave Philadelphia PA 19136

KOOCHER, GERALD PAUL, psychologist; b. Cambridge, Mass., Mar. 13, 1947; s. David and Marion (Cohen) K.; m. Robin Carol Greenwald, July 1, 1973; 1 child, Abby Greenwald Koocher. AB in Psychology, Boston U., 1968; AM in Psychology, U. Mo., 1970, PhD in Psychology, 1972. Diplomate Am. Bd. Clin., Forensic, & Health Psychology. Intern Children's Hosp., Boston, 1971-72, sr. assoc., 1980-83; chief psychologist Children's Hosp., 1988—; assoc. prof. psychology Harvard Med. Sch., Boston, 1984—; exec. dir. Linda Pollin Inst., Harvard Med. Sch., 1994—. Author: The Damocles Syndrome, 1981, Children's Competence to Consent, 1983, Ethics in Psychology, 1985, Children, Ethics and the Law, 1990; editor: Ethics and Behavior, 1989—, Jour. of Pediatric Psychology, 1982-87, The Clin. Psychologist, 1986-89. Recipient Disting. Profl. Contribution award Soc. Pediatric Psychology, 1988. Fellow AAAS, APA (Jack D. Krasner award 1981, Nicholas Hobbs award 1988), Am. Orthopsychiatric Assn. Office: Children's Hosp 300 Longwood Ave Boston MA 02115-5724

KOOISTRA, WILLIAM HENRY, clinical psychologist; b. Grand Rapids, Mich., May 20, 1936; s. Henry P. and Marguerite (Brinks) K.; m. Jean Heynen, Aug. 24, 1957 (div. Dec. 1984); children: Kimberly Lynn, William Peter, Kristin Jean, Allison Carol; m. Carol Sue Smitter, Mar. 9, 1985. BA, Calvin Coll., 1957; PhD, Wayne (Mich.) State U., 1963. Diplomate Am. Bd. Profl. Psychology. Intern psychology Lafayette Clinic, Detroit, 1961-62; chief psychologist Pine Rest Christian Hosp., Grand Rapids, Mich., 1964-67; clin. psychologist Kooistra, Jansma, Elders, Teitsma & DiNallo, Grand Rapids, 1967—; instr. Wayne State U., 1959-63, Hope Coll., Holland, Mich., 1964, Calvin Coll., Grand Rapids, 1964-81, Grand Valley State U., 1987-92. Founder Project Rehab., Grand Rapids, 1968, bd. dirs., 1969—, pres., 1972-74; mem. Kent County Dem. Exec. Com., 1969-73, 79-82, 86—, mem. governing bd. Fountain Street Ch., 1989-95, pres. 1994; rep. 3d dist. Presl. Electoral Coll., 1992. Mem. Am. Psychol. Assn. (council rep. 1982-85), Am. Soc. Psychologists in Pvt. Practice (sec. 1973-75), Mich. Psychol. Assn.(pres. 1979), Mich. Soc. Forensic Psychology, Grand Rapids Area Psychol. Assn (pres. 1968). Home: 2946 Cascade Rd SE Grand Rapids MI 49506-1965 Office: 3330 Claystone St SE Grand Rapids MI 49546-7716

KOONTZ, EVA ISABELLE, medical technologist; b. Jetmore, Kans., Feb. 3, 1935; d. Vernon Ward and Lillian Mae (Bell) K. BS in Natural Scis., Sterling (Kans.) Coll., 1957; cert. in med. tech., U. Kans. Med. Ctr., 1958. Office technologist Group Practice, Mission, Kans., 1958-60; chemistry supr. Bethany Hosp., Kansas City, Kans., 1960-64; rsch. asst. pediatric hematology and metabolic rsch. U. Kans. Med. Ctr., Kansas City, Kans., 1964-72, R&D Tech., Providence-St. Margaret's Health Care Ctr., Kansas City, Kans., 1972-74; staff technologist St. Lukes Hosp., Kansas City, Mo., 1974-79; clin. lab. mgr. and supr. Quincy Rsch. Ctr., Kansas City, Mo., 1979-80; staff technologist Lakeside Hosp., Kansas City, Mo., 1980-82; med. technologist supr. Midwest Rsch. Inst., Kansas City, Mo., 1982-88; cert. toxicology scientist Clin. Reference Labs., Inc., Lenexa, Kans., 1988—. Mem. Am. Soc. for Med. Tech., Am. Assn. for Clin. Chemistry, Mo. Soc. Med. Technologists. Republican. Presbyterian. Home: 10251 Cedarbrooke Ln Kansas City MO 64131-4209 Office: Clin Reference Labs Inc 8433 Quivira Rd Lenexa KS 66215

KOOP, CHARLES EVERETT, surgeon, educator, former surgeon general; b. Bklyn., Oct. 14, 1916; s. John Everett and Helen (Apel) K.; m. Elizabeth Flanagan, Sept. 19, 1938; children: Allen van Benschoten, Norman Apel, David Charles Everett, Elizabeth. AB, Dartmouth Coll., 1937, DSc (hon.), 1989; MD, Cornell U., 1941; DSc in Medicine, U. Pa., 1947, DSc (hon.), 1990; LLD (hon.), Ea. Bapt. Coll., 1960, Phila. Coll. Osteo. Medicine, 1979, LaSalle Coll., 1983, Colby-Sawyer Coll., 1988, Princeton U., 1989, Hahnemann U., 1989, U. Miami, 1991, U. Cin., 1991; MD (hon.), U. Liverpool, Eng., 1968; LHD (hon.), Wheaton Coll., 1973, Phila. Theol. Sem., 1980, Chgo. Med. Sch., 1988, Brown U., 1990; DSc (hon.), Gwynedd Mercy Coll., 1978, Washington and Jefferson Coll., 1979, Marquette U., 1983, Ea. Mich. U., 1985, N.Y. Med. Coll., 1985, Ball State U., 1987, Kirskville Coll. Osteo. Med., 1988, Albany Med. Coll., 1988, Colby Coll., 1988, Yeshiva U., 1988, Phila. Coll. Pharmacy and Sci., 1988, Baylor Coll. Medicine, 1988, U. Mass., Boston, 1989, Brandeis U., 1990, Northwestern U., 1990; D. Pub. Svc. (hon.), George Washington U., 1991. Diplomate Am. Bd. Surgery, Nat. Bd. Med. Examiners. Intern Pa. Hosp., Phila., 1941-42; fellow in surgery U. Pa. Hosp., Phila., 1942-47; fellow in pediat. surgery Children's Hosp., Boston, 1946; surgeon-in-chief Children's Hosp. of Phila., 1948-81; with U. Pa. Sch. Medicine, 1942-85, prof., 1959-85; former dep. asst. sec. for health HHS; surg. gen. of U.S., 1981-89; former dir. internat. health USPHS, from 1982; chair Safe Kids Nat. Campaign, Washington; dir. Elizabeth De Camp McInery prof. surgery C. Everett Koop Inst. Dartmouth-Hitchcock Med. Ctr., Hanover, N.H., 1993—; cons. USN, 1964-81; sr. scholar the C. Everett Koop Inst. at Dartmouth; dir. Room to Learn Program Carnegie Found., 1993. Author: Visible and Palpable Lesions in Children, 1976, The Right to Live, The Right to Die, 1976, rev. edit., 1980, Smoking: The New Book of Knowledge, 1989; (with E. Koop) Sometimes Mountains Move, 1979; (with F. A. Schaeffer) Whatever Happened to the Human Race?, 1979, (with T. Johnson) Koop: The Memoirs of America's Family Doctor, 1991, Let's Talk, 1992; editor surgery sect. Jour. Clin. Pediatrics, 1961-64; mem. editorial bd. Zeitschrift fur Kinderchirurgie and Grenzgebiete, 1964-81; editor in chief: Jour. Pediatric Surgery, 1965-77; editorial cons. Japanese Jour. Pediatric Surgery and Medicine, 1970-81; chmn. editorial bd. PHS Reports, 1982-89; mem. editorial adv. bd. Tobacco Control: An Internat. Jour.; contbr. publs. in surg. physiology, biomed. ethics, physiology of surg. neonate, tech. advances in pediatric surgery. Bd. dirs. Med. Assistance Programs, Inc., Brunswick, Ga., Friends Nat. Libr. of Medicine, Nat. Mus. of Health and Medicine Found. Inc. (pres.). Decorated chevalier Legion of Honor (France); Order Duarte, Sanchez and Mella (Dominican Republic); recipient medal City of Marseille, Presbyn. Man of Yr. award Presbyn. Social Union Phila., 1975, Super Achiever of Yr. award Phila. chpt. Juvenile Diabetes Found., 1975, Man of Yr. award Jewish Community Chaplaincy Svc. Phila., 1975, Copernicus medal Polish Surg. Soc., 1977, Gold medal Children's Hosp. Phila., 1981, Sec. of Health of Commonwealth of Pa. award, 1981, Thomas Linacre award Nat. Fedn. Cath. Physicians Guild, 1981, Key to City of St. Louis, 1985, Award of Distinction Alumni Assn. Cornell U. Med. Coll., 1988, Humanitarian Svc. award City of Boston, 1989, Harry S. Truman award City of Independence, Mo., 1990, Daniel Webster award Dartmouth Coll., 1990, John Wiley Jones Disting. Lectr. award Rochester Inst. Tech., 1990, NAS Public Welfare medal, 1990, Tyler prize U. So. Calif., 1991, Albert Schweitzer prize Johns Hopkins U., 1991, Person of Yr. award Nat. Hosp. Orgn., 1991, others; named Hon. Citizen, City of Balt., 1985; C. Everett Koop Hon. Lectr. medal named in his honor Anchor & Caduceus Soc., 1991, C. Everett Koop Health Adv. award named in his honor Am. Soc. for Health Care ktg. and Pub. Rels, Gustav O. Lienhard award Inst. Medicine, 1992, Presdl. medal of Freedom, 1995, Heinz Found. award, 1995; Disting. scholar to Carnegie Found. for advancement of teaching. Fellow ACS, Am. Acad. Pediatrics (William E. Ladd Gold medal), Royal Coll. Surgeons Eng. (hon.), Royal Coll. Physicians and Surgeons of Glasgow (hon.); mem. AMA, Am. Surg. Assn., Soc. U. Surgeons, Brit. Assn. Pediatric Surgeons (Dennis Browne Gold medal), Internat. Soc. Surgery, Assn. Mil. Surgeons U.S. (pres. 1982, 87, Founders medal), Societé Française de Chirurgie Infantile, Deutschen Gesselschaft für Kinderchirugi, Societé Suisse De Chirurgie Infantile, Sigma Xi. Office: Dartmouth Coll Dartmouth-Hitchkock Med Ctr C Everett Koop Inst Hanover NH 03755 also: 6707 Democracy Blvd Ste 107 Bethesda MD 20817-1129

KOOP, TOBEY KENT, research consultant, educational psychologist; b. Victoria, Tex., Jan. 3, 1955; s. Francis Dietrich and Jewel Virginia (Williams) K. BA, U. Houston, 1978; PhD, U. Tex., 1985. Rsch. cons. Austin, 1985—; owner statis. and psychometric software PsychStat, Austin, 1991—. Author: (chpt.) Facet Theory Approaches to Social Research, 1985; author (software and manual) PsychStat MAX 2.1, 1991, PsychStat MAX 2.2, 1993. Mem. U. Tex. Ex-students Assn., Phi Kappa Phi. Office: PsychStat 2605 Goldfinch Dr Cedar Park TX 78613-5113

KOOPMAN, CHERYL ANN, social psychologist; b. Red Bluff, Calif., June 14, 1950; d. William Warren and Norma Jean (Long) K.; m. Thomas K. Dawes, Aug. 22, 1982 (div. Oct. 1986). BA in Psychology, U. California, Berkeley, 1972; MA in Ednl. Psychology, UCLA, 1974; PhD in Ednl. Psychology, U. Va., 1979. Intern U.S. Office of Edn., Washington, 1977; lectr. U. Wis., Milw., 1978-79; post-doctoral fellow Harvard U., Boston, 1979-82, Columbia U., N.Y.C., 1982-87; sr. rsch. fellow Pub. Agenda Found., N.Y.C., 1987-88; rsch. scientist N.Y. State Psychiat. Inst., N.Y.C., 1988-91; asst. prof. clin. psychology Columbia U., N.Y.C., 1989-92; sr. rsch. scientist dept. psychiatry Stanford U., Palo Alto, Calif., 1993-95, acting assoc. prof. psychiatry, 1995—; cons. Harvard Med. Sch., Boston, 1980-82. Author: Adolescents and AIDS, 1992, Children and AIDS, 1991, Ethics of Research on Children and Adolescents, 1991, Adolescent Stress: Causes and Consequences, 1991, Encyclopedia of Adolescence, 1991, Adolescents and AIDS, 1992, Troubled Adolescents and HIV Infection, 1989, Handbook of Dissociation, 1996. Mem. N.Y. Psychologists for Social Responsibility, N.Y.C., 1982-91; co-founder Mass. Psychologist for Social Reponsibility, Boston, 1981-82; mem. staff Pub. Citizen Health Rsch. Group, Washington, 1976; vol. Mo Udall's nat. campaign for Pres., Washington, 1975. Recipient Viola Bernard award Columbia U. Dept. Psychiatry, N.Y.C., 1988-89; NIMH grantee Columbia Tchrs. Coll., N.Y.C., 1982-84, Harvard Med. Sch., Boston, 1979-81; Carnegie and Ford Found. fellow Columbia U. Sch. Internat. Affairs, 1984-86. Mem. Am. Psychol. Assn., Internat. Soc. Polit. Psychology, Soc. for Psychol. Study of Social Issues, Soc. for Personality and Social Psychology. Mem. Green Party. Home: 1026 Middle Ave # B Menlo Park CA 94025-5166 Office: Stanford U Dept Psychiatry MC:5544 Stanford CA 94305

KOOYMAN, MELBA MAE, nursing educator; b. Ogden, Utah, July 28, 1936; d. Ronald Carl and Louise Marian (Agee) Bingham; m. Gerald L. Kooyman, July 6, 1962; children: Carsten Agee, Tory Gordon. Diploma in nursing, San Jose (Calif.) Hosp., 1957; BS magna cum laude, U. Utah, 1959; MS, U. Calif., San Francisco, 1964. RN, Calif., RNC, med.-surg. Stewardess United Air Lines, San Francisco; instr. San Jose (Calif.) Hosp. Sch. Nursing, 1961-62; asst. prof. U. Ariz., Tucson, 1962-66; assoc. prof. Palomar Coll., San Marcos, Calif., 1968-69, 74-75, 1985—; med., geriatrics nurse. Rsch. on Strategies to Promote Critical Thinking. Named Coll. Tchr. of 1989-90, Escondido C. of C. Mem. Calif. Nurses Assn.

KOPCZYNSKI, HELEN DOROTHY, nursing educator; b. Bklyn., July 4, 1927; d. Walter and Sadie E. (Kazmierczak) K. Diploma, Kings County Hosp. Ctr., 1948; BS in Nursing, St. John's U., 1955, MS in Nursing, 1958. Cert. nurse adminstr.; cert. med.-surg. nurse clin. specialist. Nurse adminstr. USAF, Kirtland AFB, N.Mex.; asst. chief nurse VA Med. Ctr., Albuquerque; nurse faculty Albuquerque Tech. Vocat. Inst.; instr. U. N.Mex., Air C.C., 1971; educator N.Mex. AIDS program. Contbr. articles to profl. jours. Col. USAF. Named Flight Nurse of the Yr., 1969. Mem. ANA, Nat. League Nursing, Am. Bus. Women's Assn., N.Am. Nursing Diagnosis Assn., Am. Nurses Assn. for AIDS Care, N.Mex. League Nursing (pres.), Aerospace Med. Assn., Assn. of Christian Therapists, Sigma Theta Tau. Home: 5124 Justin Ave NW Albuquerque NM 87114-4315

KOPEČEK, JINDŘICH, biomedical scientist, biomaterials and pharmaceutics educator; b. Strakonice, Bohemia, Czechoslovakia, Jan. 27, 1940; came to U.S., 1986; s. Jan and Herta Zita (Krombholz) K.; m. Marie Porcari, Aug. 11, 1962 (Div. 1984); 1 child, Jana; m. Pavla Hrušková, Apr. 27, 1985. MS in Polymer Chemistry, Inst. Chem. Tech., Prague, Czechoslovakia, 1961; PhD in Polymer Chemistry, Inst. Macromolecular Chemistry, Prague, 1965; DSc in Chemistry, Czechoslovak Acad. Scis., Prague, 1990. Rsch. sci. officer Inst. Macromolecular Chemistry, Prague, 1965-67, 68-72, head lab. of med. polymers, 1972-80; postdoctoral fellow NRC, Ottawa, Can., 1967-68; head lab. of biodegradable polymers Inst. Macromolecular Chemistry Czechoslovak Acad. of Scis., Prague, 1980-88; co-dir. Ctr. Controlled Chem. Delivery U. Utah, Salt Lake City, 1986—, prof. bioengring., pharmaceutics and phamaceutical chemistry, 1989—; vis. prof. Université Paris-Nord, Paris-Villetaneuse, 1983, U. Utah, 1986-88; adj. prof. material sci. U. Utah, 1987—; invited lectr. internat. meetings, univs. Editorial bd. mem. 12 sci. jours., U.S., U.K., The Netherlands, Poland, 1973—; contbr. over 230 articles to sci. publs. Recipient best sci. papers award Praesidiums of the Czechoslovak and USSR Acads. of Sci., 1977, awards Chem. Sec. of Czechoslovak Acad. Scis., 1972, 75, 77, 78, 85; rsch. grantee NIH, U. Utah, industry, 1986—, Czechoslovak Acad. of Sci., 1970-88. Fellow Am. Assn. Pharm. Sci., Am. Inst. Med. and Biol. Engring.; mem. AAAS, Am. Chem. Soc., Am. Assn. Cancer Rsch., Soc. Biomaterials (Clemson award for basic rsch. 1995), Soc. for Molecular Recognition, Controlled Release Soc. (bd. govs. 1988-91, v.p. 1993-94, pres.-elect 1994-95, pres. 1995-96). Office: U Utah Dept Bioengring 205 Biomed Polymer Rsch Bldg Salt Lake City UT 84112-1180

KOPEL, KENNETH FRED, clinical psychologist, educator; b. Austin, Tex., July 29, 1947; s. Jim and Helen (Eshman) K.; m. Sandra Marks, Aug. 25, 1968; children: Gregory, Andrew, Deborah. BA, U. Tex., 1968, PhD, 1972. Lic. psychologist, Tex.; cert. nat. Register Human Svc. Providers in Psychology. Dir. tng. VA Med. Ctr., Houston, 1972-95; pvt. practice Psychol. Assocs. Tex., Houston, 1986—; clin. assoc. prof. Baylor Coll. Medicine, Houston, 1975—; adj. asst. prof. U. Houston, 1975—; mem. Tex. Bd. Examiners Psychologists, 1989-95. Recipient Nat. Profl. Svc. award VA, 1990. Mem. APA, Tex. Psychol. Assn. (exec. com. 1988-89), Houston Psychol. Assn. (pres. 1981-82).

KOPENHAVER, PATRICIA ELLSWORTH, podiatrist. Student, Columbia U., 1950-53; BA, George Washington U., 1954; MA, Columbia U., 1956; Dr. Podiatric Medicine, N.Y. Coll. of Podiatric Medicine, 1963; postgrad., N.Y. Coll. Podiatric Medicine, 1980. Diplomate Nat. Bd. Podiatry Examiners. Pvt. practice podiatry Greenwich, Conn., 1964—; mem. staff Laurelton Convalescent Hosp., Greenwich. Bd. dirs. Monmouth Opera Guild, 1965; trustee Monmouth Opera Festival, 1966, v.p., 1964; mem. Greenwich Arts Coun.; program chmn. Greenwich Women's Rep. Club, 1983-84, 4th dist. rep., 1984-85, 87—. Recipient Hosp. Fund award for med. research translations ARC. Mem. AAUW (v.p. 1991, pres. Greenwich br. 1992-94, bd. dirs. 1996), NOW, Conn. Podiatric Med. Assn., Hist. Soc., Asian Soc., Fairfield Podiatry Assn., Am. Assn. Women Podiatrists (charter pres. 1969-78), Acad. Podiatry, Am. Podiatry Coun., UN Assn. U.S.A., Acad. Podiatric Medicine (chmn. nominating com. 1981, 1st v.p. 1983-84, chmn. fundraising 1984-85, chmn. women's issues 1985, chmn. cmty. edn. 1989), Am. Acad. Sports Medicine, Am. Acad. Podiatric Sports Medicine (assoc. 1989), George Washington U. Alumni Assn., Columbia Alumni Assn., Fairfield County Alumni Assn. Columbia U., Nat. Fedn. Rep. Women, Bruce Mus., Nature Conservancy, Federated Garden Clubs Conn., St. Mary Ladies Guild, Greenwich Gardeners, Womans' Club (ways and means com. 1989, pres.), English Speaking Union, Soroptimists Internat. Am. (pres. Greenwich br. 1990—, bd. dirs. 1995-96), Inc. (vice chmn. program com. 1985—, regional med. scholarship chmn. 1987, med. scholarship chmn. N.E. region 1988, program dir. 1988—, pres. Greenwich br. 1990-92), Toastmasters, Travel Club (program com. 1984—), Pi Epsilon Chi. Home: 2 Sutton Pl S New York NY 10022-3070 Office: 8 Dearfield Dr Greenwich CT 06831-5348

KOPERSKI, NANCI CAROL, women's health nurse; b. Omaha, Sept. 14, 1962; d. William S. Jr. and Ethel A. (Friday) Koperski; divorced. Student, Marquette U.; BSN cum laude, Creighton U., 1984; MBA, MHSA, Ariz. State U. RN, Ariz.; cert. women's health nurse. Staff nurse Phoenix Meml. Hosp., Phoenix Gen. Hosp., Community Hosp., Phoenix, Phoenix Indian Med. Ctr.; clin. care coord. Ahwatakee Foothills Samaritan Health Ctr., 1992—. Mem. NAACOG, Ariz. Nurse's Assn., Sigma Theta Tau. Home: 11230 N 49th Dr Glendale AZ 85304-4002

KOPFLER, WILLIAM, internist; b. 1962. MD, Tulane U., 1988. Postdoctoral fellow U. Tex. Southwestern Med. Ctr. Recipient Clinician-Scientist award Am. Heart Assn., 1995-96. Office: 5929 Norway Rd Dallas TX 75230-4003*

KOPILOFF, GEORGE, psychiatrist; b. Buenos Aires, Argentina, Jan. 20, 1939; came to U.S., 1975; s. Gregorio and Matilde (Garcia) K.; m. Nelly Caceres, Apr. 19, 1964; children: Araceli, George. BA, Vasquez Acevedo Inst., Montevideo, Uruguay, 1958; MD, Facultad de Medicina, Montevideo,

Uruguay, 1969. Diplomate Internal Medicine Acad. Uruguay, diplomate Am. Bd. Psychiatry and Neurology. Intern and resident in internal medicine Montevideo, 1969-74; resident in internal medicine Northeastern Ohio U. and Youngstown (Ohio) Hosp. Assn., 1975-76; resident in psychiatry Temple U. and Ancora Psychiat. Hosp., Phila., 1976-77; resident in psychiatry Loma Linda (Calif.) U. Sch. Medicine, 1978-79, asst. prof. psychiatry, 1979—; pvt. practice specializing in internal medicine Uruguay, 1969-75; staff psychiatrist Hemet (Calif.) Valley Health System, 1978—; med. dir. behavioral health svcs. Hemet (Calif.) Valley Hosp., 1986-88, 90—; chief Triage Psychiat. Clinic Jerry L. Pettis Meml. VA Hosp., Loma Linda. 1979-83, chief day treatment ctr., 1983-89, staff psychiatrist, 1989—; staff psychiatrist Kellogg Psychiat. Hosp., Corona, Calif., 1979-83, Riverside (Calif.) Gen. Hosp., 1979-87; psychiatrist Continuing Community Care Program, Riverside, 1979-87. Recipient Exemplary Psychiatrist award Nat. Alliance for the Mentally Ill, 1993. Fellow Am. Psychiat. Assn., Interam. Coll. Physicians and Surgeons; mem. AMA, Rivers County Med. Assn., APA, So. Calif. Psych. Soc., Nat. Assn. VA Physicians, Am. Assn. Geriatric Psychiatry, World Fedn. Mental Health, So. Calif. Psychiat. Soc. (sec. Inland region 1982-83, pres. 1984-85), Am. Psychiatric Assn., Union Am. Physicians and Dentists Alumni Assn., Am. Acad. Clin. Psychiatrists. Seventh Day Adventist. Home: 678 Chaucer Ct Redlands CA 92374-6351 Office: 1117 E Devonshire Ave Hemet CA 92543-3084

KOPLEWICZ, HAROLD SAMUEL, child and adolescent psychiatrist; b. Bklyn., Jan. 12, 1953; s. Joseph and Romana (Magid) K.; m. Linda Jane Sirow, June 22, 1980; children: Joshua, Adam, Sam. BS, U. Md., 1973; MD, Albert Einstein Coll. of Medicine, 1978. Diplomate Am. Bd. Psychiatry and Neurology, Am. Bd. Child Psychiatry. Med. dir. preschool hyperactivity program N.Y. State Psychiat. Inst., N.Y.C., 1982-85, med. dir. children's anxiety clinic, 1983-86; dir. gen. residency tng. child psychiatry Columbia Coll. Physicians and Surgeons, N.Y.C., 1985-86; chief divsn. child and adolescent psychiatry Schneider Children's Hosp. and Hillside Hosp. of L.I. Jewish Med. Ctr., N.Y.C., 1986-96; editor Youth Mental Health Update, 1989—; assoc. prof. psychiatry Albert Einstein Coll. Medicine, N.Y.C., 1991-96; prof. clin. psychiatry N.Y. Sch. Medicine, 1996—; vice chmn. psychiatry, chief for child and adolescent psychiatry NYU Med. Ctr./Bellevue Hosp. Ctr., 1996—; cons. Riverdale Cmty. Ctr., 1981-86, The Dalton Sch., 1991—, The N.Y. Infirmary, 1991, The Family Acad., 1991-96, Jewish Child Care Assn., 1992-96, Health Edn. Task Force, Roslyn Sch. Dist., 1993—. Bd. dirs. Raoul Wallenberg New Leadership Soc., 1983-87, Cmty. Mainstreaming Assocs., 1990; chmn. Simon Wiesenthal Ctr., 1984-86; commr. N.Y. State Commn. for Study of Youth Crime and Violence and Reform of the Juvenile Justice Sys., 1993-96; prin. investigator Developing Innovative Mental Health Care Delivery for Adolescents, Hewlett-Woodmere Sch. Dist., 1992; adv. bd. Our Children's Found., 1996—. Recipient award Lowenstein Found., 1986, Hulse award N.Y. Coun. Child and Adolescent Psychiatry, 1995. Fellow Am. Acad. Child and Adolescent Psychiatry; mem. Am. Psychiat. Assn., Soc. Profs. Child and Adolescent Psychiatry, Am. Bd. Psychiatry and Neurology (examiner 1988—), Nat. Bd. Med. Examiners (mem. psychiatry com. 1993-96), Nat. Found. Depressive Illness (nat. bd. dirs. 1992—). Office: NYU Med Ctred Ctr (NB21E7) 550 First Ave New York NY 10016

KOPLIN, WILLIAM ROBERT, orthodontist; b. Cleve., Aug. 12, 1943; s. Elmer William and Eveline E. (Feidler) K.; m. Linda Mary Fatibeno, Mar. 23, 1968; 1 child, Derek. AB, Western Res. U., 1964; DDS, Case Western Res. U., 1968; MScD, Boston U., 1970. Pvt. practice orthodontics Franklin, Mass., 1970—. Recipient Presdl. award Mass. Jaycees, 1976-77; named Jaycee of Yr., Franklin Jaycees, 1974, 77. Mem. Mass. Assn. Orthodontists, R.I. Assn. Orthodontists (assoc.), United C. of C., Franklin Rotary Club (pres. 1980-81, past bd. dirs., mem. dist. gov.'s com. 1982). Methodist. Office: 76 Emmons St PO Box 451 Franklin MA 02038

KOPMAN, ELIZABETH SUZANNE, health center operations manager; b. Phila., Aug. 27, 1950; d. Frederick and Beatrice (Gans) Perlitch; m. Arthur Kopman, June 21, 1970 (div. June 1986); children: Brad, Jaime. Diploma in Nursing, Temple U., 1971; AA, LaSalle Extension U., 1974; student in Health Care Asministrn., St. Joseph's Coll., 1989. Head nurse Phila. Geriatric Ctr., 1971-73; supr. St. Mary's Hosp., Phila., 1974-75; nursing supr. Ashton Hall Rehab. Ctr., Phila., 1975-78; dir. nursing Northwood Nursing Home, Phila., 1978-80, adminstr., 1980-82; asst. dir. Mayo Nursing Ctr., Phila., 1982-84, adminstr., 1986-88; owner Popcorn Video, Phila., 1984-86; mem. products com. GERI-Med., Phila., 1987—, regional contr., 1988-89, regional adminstr., 1989-91, v.p. ops., 1991-93, dir. med. svcs., 1993—; instr. first aid Loesche Sch., Phila., 1982; buyer movies Popcorn Video, Phila., 1984—. Contbr. articles to profl. jours. Coach Max Meyers Athletic Club, Phila., 1985—. Mem. Nat. Assn. of Female Execs., Long Term Nursing Adminstrs., Am. Mgmt. Assn. Democrat. Jewish. Home: 891 Mallard Rd Feasterville PA 19053 Office: Wood River Village 3200 Bensalem Blvd Bensalem PA 19020

KOPPULA, MOREEN, physician; b. Kurnool, India; came to U.S. 1977; d. James and Kamala (Kandukuri) R; m. Sampurnarao Koppula, Dec. 29, 1973; children: Patrick, Anthony. MBBS, Guntur Med. Coll., India, 1973. Diplomate Am. Bd. of Anesthesiology. Intership Govt. Gen. Hosp., Guntur, 1973-75; sr. house officer in anesthesia East Birmingham (U.K.) Hosp., 1976-77, Worthing (U.K.) Hosp., 1977; resident Hahnemann Med. Coll. and Hosp., Phlia., 1978-79, Children's Hosp. of Phila., 1979; resident in pediatrics Cooper Med. Ctr., Camden, N.J., 1979-80; chief resident in anesthesia Hahnemann Med. Coll. and Hosp., Phila., 1980-81; fellow in anesthesia Childrens Hosp. of Phila., 1981; mem. staff anesthesiologist Our Lady Of Lourdes Hosp., Camden, 1981-82; mem. staff in anesthesiologist Maricopa Med. Ctr., Phoenix, 1982—, Good Samaritan Med. Ctr., Phoenix, 1983—, St. Joseph's Hosp., Phoenix, 1983—, Thuderbird Samaritan Hosp., Glendale, Ariz., 1983—, St. Luke's Hosp., Phoenix, 1983—, Tempe (Ariz.) St. Luke's Hosp., 1983—; dir. of obstetrical anesthesia Desert Samaritan Hosp., Mesa, Ariz., 1988—. Mem. Am. Soc. of Anesthesiologist, Ariz. Soc. of Anesthesiologist, Maricopa County Soc. of Anesthesiologist. Republican. Lutheran. Home: 6997 E Paradise Ranch Rd Paradise Vly AZ 85253-3152 Office: Canyon State Anesthesiologists PC 4820 E McDowell Rd Ste 101 Phoenix AZ 85008

KOPROWSKA, IRENA, cytopathologist, cancer researcher; b. Warsaw, Poland, May 12, 1917; came to U.S., 1944; d. Henryk and Eugenia Grasberg; m. Hilary Koprowski, July 14, 1938; children: Claude, Christopher. BA, Popielewska/Roszkowska, Warsaw, 1934; MD, Warsaw U., 1939. Cert. Am. Bd. Pathology, Internat. Bd. Cytology. Intern in medicine Villejuif Lunatic Asylum, Seine, France, 1940; asst. pathologist Rio De Janeiro City Hosp., Miguel Couto, Brazil, 1942-44; rsch. fellow dept. pathology Cornell U. Med. Coll., N.Y.C., 1945-46, rsch. asst. dept. pharmacology, 1949-50, rsch. fellow dept. of anatomy, 1949-54; rsch. fellow applied immunology Pub. Health Rsch. Inst. of The City of N.Y., 1946-47; asst. pathologist N.Y. Infirmary for Women and Children, N.Y.C., 1947-49; asst. prof. dept. pathology SUNY Downstate Med. Ctr., N.Y.C., 1954-57; assoc. prof. pathology, dir. cytology lab./Sch. Cytotech. Hahnemann Med. Coll., Phila., 1957-64, prof. pathology dir. cytology lab., sch. cytotechnology, 1964-70; prof. pathology, dir. cytology lab. Temple U. Sch. Med., Phila., 1970-87, prof. emerita, 1987—; cons. WHO, Switzerland, Egypt, Iran, Latin Am., India, 1960-85, Armed Forces Inst. Pathology, Air Force Cytology Rescreen Project, 1979-80. Author: Woman Wanders Through Life and Science, 1996; contbr. articles on cancer rsch. to profl. and sci. jours. Named Woman Physician of Yr., Polish Am. Med. Assn., 1977; grantee USPHS-Nat. Cancer Insts., 1954-75, rsch. grantee Bender Co., Vienna, Austria, 1983-89. Fellow Am. Soc. Clin. Pathologists (emeritus), Coll. Am. Pathologists (emeritus), Coll. Physicians of Phila., Internat. Acad. Cytology (hon.), Internat. Acad. Pathology (emeritus); mem. Am. Assn. for Cancer Rsch. Inc. (emeritus), Am. Assn. Pathologists Inc. (emeritus), Am. Med. Women's Assn., Am. Soc. Cytology (life, Papanicolaou award 1985), Am. Soc. Exptl. Pathology, Argentinian Soc. Cytology (hon.), Path. Soc. Phila. Home: 334 Fairhill Rd Wynnewood PA 19096-1804

KOPROWSKI, HILARY, microbiologist, educator; b. Warsaw, Poland; s. Pawel and Sarah (Berland) K.; m. Irena Grasberg; children: Claude Eugene, Christopher Dorian. BA, Nikolaj Rej Gymnasium of Luth. Congregation, Warsaw; MD, U. Warsaw; grad., Warsaw Conservatory Music and Santa Cecilia Acad., Rome; DSc (hon.), Ludwig-Maximilian U., Munich, Widener Coll.; D of Medicine and Surgery, U. Helsinki, Finland; MD (hon.), U. Uppsala, Sweden; LittD (hon.), Thomas Jefferson U.; DMS (hon.), U. Lublin, Poland. Rsch. asst. dept. exptl. and gen. pathology U. Warsaw, 1936-39; staff Yellow Fever Rsch. Svc., Rio de Janeiro, 1940-44; staff rsch. divsn. Am. Cyanamid Co., 1944-46; asst. dir. viral and rickettsial rsch. Lederle Lab., Pearl River, N.Y., 1946-57; dir. Wistar Inst., Phila., 1957-91, prof., 1957-93, prof. laureate, 1993—; Wistar Inst. prof. of rsch. medicine U. Pa., 1957—; prof. microbiology and immunology Thomas Jefferson U., Phila., 1992—; dir. Ctr. Neurovirology, Inst. of Biotechnology and Advanced Molecular Medicine, 1992—; cons. WHO, 1950—; mem. microbiology study sect. NIH, 1956-60; mem. PAHO; mem. adv. com. Nat. Multiple Sclerosis Soc., 1970-78; mem. immunobiology adv. com. NIH, USPHS, 1975-76; mem. bd. sci. counselors div. cancer etiology Nat. Cancer Inst., 1982-86, chmn., 1987-90; mem. biol. response modifiers program decision network com. NIH, 1985-87; mem. immunobiol. adv. com. NIH, USPHS, 1975-76. Co-editor: Methods in Virology, Viruses and Immunity, Current Topics in Microbiology and Immunology, 1965—. Hon. trustee Kosciuszko Found., 1993—. Decorated commandeur Order du Mèrite pour la Recherche et l'Invention, chevalier Order Royal De Lion Belgium, comdr. Order of The Lion of Finland, 1995, officer Order of the Polish Republic; recipient Alvarenga prize Coll. Physicians Phila., 1959, Alfred Jurzykowski Found. Polish Millenium prize, 1966, Felix Wankel Tierschutz prize, 1979, Alexander Von Humboldt Sr. U.S. Scientist award, Phila. Cancer Rsch. award Phila. Cancer Club, 1989, San Marino award, 1989, John Scott award, Nicolaus Copernicus medal Polish Acad. Scis., 1989, The Phila. award, 1990, John Scott award, 1990; Hon. trustee Kosciuszko Found., 1993; Fulbright scholar Max Planck Inst. für Verhaltensphysiologie, Seewiesen, Fed. Republic Germany, 1971. Fellow AAAS, N.Y. Acad. Medicine, Phila. Coll. Physicians; mem. Nat. Acad. Arts and Scis., Yugoslavian Acad. Scis., Polish Acad. Scis., Russian Acad. Med. Scis., Finnish Acad. Arts and Scis., N.Y. Acad. Scis. (pres. 1959, trustee 1960-72). Office: The Wistar Inst 3601 Spruce St Philadelphia PA 19104-4205 also: Thomas Jefferson U M-85 Jefferson Alumni Hall 1020 Locust St Philadelphia PA 19107-6731

KOPSCO, CAROL JEAN, social worker, mental health psychotherapist, counselor; b. Amherst, Ohio, Sept. 2, 1947; d. John and Elizabeth G. (Horvath) K. BA, Baldwin-Wallace Coll., 1970; MA, U. Miami, 1973; MSW, Ariz. State U., 1990. Cert. substance abuse counselor. Social worker Fla. State Health and Rehabilitative Svc., Miami, 1974-76, pub. assistance eligibility specialist II, 1976-82; eligibility specialist II Ariz. Dept. Econ. Security, Tucson, 1985-86; crisis counselor supr. Info. and Referral Svc. of Tucson, 1987-90; child and family therapist Ariz. Children's Home Assn., Tucson, 1990—; mental health psychotherapist Ariz. State Dept. Health Svcs., Tucson, 1990-91; med. social worker Samaritan Nursing Svcs., Tucson, 1991—; team leader student group producing quick reference for cmty. crisis orgn. Ariz. State U. Sch. Social Work, Tucson, 1989; med. social worker Olsten-Kimberly Vis. Nurse Svc., 1992-94; Indian health svc. med. social worker and discharge planner area hosps., 1994-95. Vol. Casa San Juan Bosco Shelter, Nogales, Sonora, Mexico, 1985-87, Help-On-Call Crisis Hotline, Tucson, 1987-90. Mem. NASW (student rep. 1989), Phi Kappa Phi. Democrat. Home: 4825 S Lincoln Ridge Dr Tucson AZ 85730-4818

KORACH, KENNETH STEVEN, endocrinologist, researcher; b. Buffalo, Nov. 26, 1946; s. Samuel and Mildred (Protich) K.; m. Karen Lazar, June 6, 1970; children: Chad Steven, Kendal Anne. BS, Augusta Coll., 1969; PhD, Med. Coll. Ga., 1974. Rsch. fellow Harvard Med. Sch., Boston, 1974-76; staff fellow Nat. Inst. Environ. Health-NIH, Research Triangle Park, N.C., 1976-78, sr. staff fellow, 1978-80, rsch. endocrinologist, 1980-85, sr. rsch. endocrinologist, 1985—, chief receptor biol. sect., acting chief lab. reprod. devel., 1987—; acting chief lab. of reproductive devel. Nat. Inst. Environ. Health-NIH, Research Triangle Park, 1992—; adj. prof. pharmacology U. N.C. Med. Sch., Chapel Hill, 1989—, adj. mem. pediat. endocrinology, lab. reproductive biology; adj. prof. biochemistry N.C. State U., Raleigh, 1990—; cons. Glaxo, Inc., Research Triangle Park, 1990-93, Berlex Rsch. Lab., Richmond, Calif.; William Sadler lectr. NICHD, 1995; Levitt lectr. U. Fla., 1995; Muldoon Meml. lectr. Med. Coll. Ga., 1996. Author: (with others) Receptor Purification, 1990; author, editor: (book) Endocrin Toxicology, 1984; contbr. articles to sci. pubis. Rsch. fellow Ford Found., Harvard Med. Sch., 1975-76; recipient Disting. Alumnus award Med. Coll. Ga., 1992. Mem. Endocrine Soc. (editl. bd. 1989-92, editor 1993—, Edwin B. Astwood award 1995), Soc. Toxicology (trans-Atlantic lectr. 1984), Sigma Xi. Office: Nat Inst Environ Health NIH PO Box 12233 104 Alexander Ave Durham NC 27705

KORAN, LORRIN MICHAEL, psychiatrist, educator; b. Los Angeles, Apr. 4, 1940; s. Aaron Baer and Shirley Mildred (Kassan) K.; m. Stephanie Miller, Jan. 11, 1967; children—Joshua, Jessica. B.A. magna cum laude, Harvard U., 1962, M.D. cum laude, 1966. Diplomate Am. Bd. Psychiatry and Neurology. Intern UCLA Med. Ctr., 1966-67; resident Stanford Med. Ctr., Calif., 1967-70; spl. asst. to dir. NIMH, Bethesda, Md., 1970-72; asst. prof. SUNY-Stony Brook, 1972-76, assoc. prof., 1976-77, assoc. prof. Med. Ctr., Stanford U., 1979-84, prof., 1984—, dir. residency tng., 1979-81; chief psychiat. cons./liaison service, Santa Clara Valley Med. Ctr., San Jose, Calif., 1977-80; med. dir. comprehensive medicine unit Stanford Hosp., 1980-88. dir. Obsessive-Comprehensive Disorders clin. 1989—. Author articles in book and jours. Served to lt. comdr. USPHS, 1970-72. Fellow Am. Psychiat. Assn.; mem. Calif. Med. Assn., No. Calif. Psychiat. Soc. Jewish. Office: Stanford Univ Med Ctr Dept Psychiatry OCD Clinic Stanford CA 94305

KORANT, BRUCE DAVID, virologist, molecular biologist; b. Bklyn., Aug. 9, 1943; s. Samuel and Rose (Greissman) K.; m. Mary Anne Tilmont, May 14, 1969; 1 child, Deborah Susan. BS in Biology, CUNY, 1965; MS, Pa. State U., 1967, PhD in Microbiology, 1969. Postdoctoral rsch. fellow DuPont Co., Wilmington, Del., 1969-70, mem. rsch. staff, 1970-79, group leader virology dept., 1979-81, rsch. supr., 1981-90; rsch. supr. DuPont-Merck Pharm. Co., Wilmington, 1991—; mem. faculty NATO, summers 1978, 82, 84; mem. adv. com. Nat. Coop. Drug Discovery (AIDS), NIH, Bethesda, Md., 1986-89; bd. govs. Pa. State U. Coll. of Sci., University Park, 1981-84. Mem. Am. Soc. Virology, Am. Soc. Microbiology. Office: DuPont Merck Pharm Co Experimental Sta Bldg 336 Wilmington DE 19880-0336

KORBEN, DONALD LEE, psychologist; b. Bklyn., Apr. 4, 1948; s. Abraham and Betty K.; BA, Butler U., 1972; MS, Ind. U., 1973, EdD, 1976; postdoctorate Duke U., 1982-84. Intern counseling and psychol. services Ind. U., 1974-76; counseling psychologist Counseling Ctr., St. Bonaventure U., 1976—, dir., 1993—, counselor, 1993—, chmn. univ. scholastic evaluation com., 1976—, instl. rev. bd., 1980—, mem. adj. faculty Grad. Sch., 1977-80, chairperson pres.'s council alcohol and drug awareness program, 1982-89, dir., counselor, adminstr., dir. Drinking Driver Rehab. Program, 1976—; psychologist St. Bonaventure U. Men's Basketball Team, 1989—; cons. Proprietory Home Assn. Western N.Y., 1976-80, Alpha Phi Omega; cons., mem. Cattaraugus County Council Alcohol and Substance Abuse, 1980; cons. select com. alcohol and alcohol abuse N.Y. State Senate, 1980; advisor Alpha Phi Omega Nat. Service Orgn., 1984—, Students Against Drunk Driving, 1986—; bd. dirs. Pres.'s Council on Alcohol and Drug Abuse St. Bonaventure Univ., 1981—, Cattaraugus County Mental Health Assn. Adv. Com., 1988—; instr. Wyo. Sem. Inst. for drug and alcohol abuse, 1984—. Vol. Salvation Army, 1966-76, 1984—, Boy Scouts Am., 1966-72, Mental Health Assn. Ind., 1967-70, Nat. Epilepsy Found., 1973-76, 1985—; mem. host com. N.Y. State Spl. Olympics, 1979. Named Outstanding Young Man of Am., Jaycees, 1978; NSF grantee, 1970-71; Ind. U. grantee, 1976. Mem. Am. Psychol. Assn. (mem. div. psychotherapy), Am. Counseling Assn., Am. Mental Health Counselors Assn., Phi Delta Kappa. Jewish. Achievements include research on the biophysics of neurological effects of hibernation monitoring regional cerebal circulation, factors in assertive tng. with females, construct validity of the strong-vocat. interest inventory, psychophysical effects on physiological optics, others. Home: 757 Main St Olean NY 14760-1550

KORBET, STEPHEN MICHAEL, physician, nephrologist; b. Alton, Ill., June 13, 1953; s. Thomas John and Eva Mae (Matthews) K.; m. Barbara I. Korbet, July 4, 1981. BA summa cum laude, Millikin U., 1975; MD, Rush Med. Coll., 1979. Diplomate in internal medicine and nephrology Am. Bd. Internal Medicine; diplomate Nat. Bd. Med. Examiners. Intern Rush-Presbyn. St. Luke's Med. Ctr., Chgo., 1979-80, resdient, 1980-82, fellow in nephrology, 1982-84, adj. attending dept. internal medicine, 1983-84, asst. attending sect. nephrology, 1984-88, assoc. attending, 1988—; from asst. to prof. internal medicine Rush Med. Coll., Chgo., 1979—. Mem. editorial bd. Am. Jour. Kidney Diseases; contbr. articles to profl. jours.; patentee in field. Recipient rsch. grants. Fellow ACP; mem. AMA, Internat. Soc. Nephrology, Ill. State Med. Soc., Chgo. Med. Soc. (Robert M. Kark prize for rsch. 1985), N.Y. Acad. Scis., Am. Soc. Nephrology, Chgo. Soc. Internal Medicine, Nat. Kidney Found., Renal Physicians Assn., Am. Soc. Internal Medicine, Am. Soc. for Artificial Internal Organs, Alpha Omega Alpha, Phi Kappa Phi, Alpha Epsilon Delta, Sigma Zeta. Greek Orthodox. Office: 1653 W Congress Pkwy Chicago IL 60612

KORBITZ, BERNARD CARL, retired oncologist, hematologist, educator, consultant; b. Lewistown, Mont., Feb. 18, 1935; s. Fredrick William and Rose Eleanore (Ackmann) K.; m. Constance Kay Bolz, June 22, 1957; children: Paul Bernard, Guy Karl. B.S. in Med. Sci., U. Wis.-Madison, 1957, M.D., 1960, M.S. in Oncology, 1962; LL.B., LaSalle U., 1972. Asst. prof. medicine and clin. oncology, U. Wis. Med. Sch., Madison, 1967-71; dir. medicine Presbyn. Med. Ctr., Denver, 1971-73; practice medicine specializing in oncology, hematology, Madison, 1973-76; med. oncologist, hematologist Radiologic Ctr. Meth. Hosp., Omaha, 1976-82; practice medicine specializing in oncology, hematology, Omaha, 1982-95, ret., 1995; sci. advisor Citizen's Environ. Com., Denver, 1972-73; mem. Meth. Hosp., Omaha, 1977—; dir. Bernard C. Korbitz, P.C., Omaha, 1983—; bd. dirs., pres. B.C. Korbitz P.C., ret., 1996. Contbr. articles to profl. jours. Webelos leader Denver area Council, Mid. Am. Council of Nebr. Boy Scouts Am.; bd. elders King of Kings Luth. Ch., Omaha, 1979-80; bd. elders St. Mark Luth. Ch., Omaha, 1993—; mem. People to People Del. Cancer Update to People's Republic China, 1986, Eastern Europe and USSR, 1987; mem. U.S. Senatorial Club, 1984, Republican Presdl. Task Force, 1984. Served to capt. USAF, 1962-64. Fellow ACP, Royal Soc. Health; mem. Am. Soc. Clin. Oncology, Am. Coll. Legal-Medicine, Am. Soc. Internal Medicine, AMA, Nebr. Med. Assn., Omaha Med. Society, Omaha Clin. Soc., Phi Eta Sigma, Phi Beta Kappa, Phi Kappa Phi, Alpha Omega Alpha. Avocations: photography, fishing, travel. Home: 9024 Leavenworth St Omaha NE 68114-5150

KORC, MURRAY, endocrinologist; b. Gunsburg, Fed. Republic of Germany, Apr. 3, 1947; came to U.S., 1960; m. Antoinette Korc. BA, Bklyn. Coll., 1968; MD, Albany (N.Y.) Med. Coll., 1974. Intern, then resident Albany Med. Ctr. Hosp., 1974-77; endocrinology fellow U. Calif., San Francisco, 1977-79; from prof. to chief divsn. endocrinology, diabetes and metab U. Calif., Irvine, 1989—. Office: U Calif Div Endocrinology Med Sci I # C240 Irvine CA 92717

KORDECKI, HUBERT JULIUSZ, gastroenterologist, hematologist; b. Szczecin, Pomerania, Poland, Apr. 12, 1948; s. Wladyslaw and Felicja (Wilczek) K.; m. Elzbieta Glab, Oct. 13, 1980 (dec. Mar. 1993); children: Agnieszka, Joanna. Physician, Med. Acad., Szczecin, Poland, 1972, MD, PhD, 1980. Med. Diplomate in Gastroenterology and Internal Medicine. Jr. asst. Inst. Internal Medicine, Szczecin, Poland, 1972-74; asst. Clinic of Haematology, Szczecin, Poland, 1974-75, sr. asst., 1975-78; lectr. Inst. Internal Medicine, Szczecin, Poland, 1978-81, first asst., 1981-87; head dept. Pomeranian Provincial Hosp., Szczecin, Poland, 1987—; cons. Pomeranian Med. Acad., Szczecin, 1975-87, Pomeranian Province Hosp., 1987—. Contbr. articles to profl. jours. Recipient prizes Pomeranian Med. Acad., 1976, 78, 79, 83. Mem. Polish Assn. Gastroenterology (Pomeranian divsn. pres. 1995—), Pomeranian Rheumatic Assn. (v.p. 1986-95), Polish Assn. Internal Medicine (local bd. dirs. 1987-95), Polish Assn. Haematology. Roman Catholic. Home: Jagiellonska 74/11, 70-465 Szczecin Poland Office: Pomeranian Province Hosp Dept Gastroenterology, Arkońskastr 4, 71-455 Szczecin Poland

KORDENBROCK, DOUGLAS WILLIAM, biomedical electronics technician; b. Covington, Ky., June 8, 1964; s. Richard George and Mary Joyce K. A in Biomed. Electronics Tech. cum laude, Cin. Tech. Coll., 1983; BA in Adminstrn. Mgmt., Ohio U., 1994. Cert. biomed. electronics technician. Driver Esterkamps Auto Parts, Cin., 1980-84; biomed. electronics technician II Mercy Hosp., Hamilton, Ohio, 1982-86; biomed. electronics technician I Novare Biomed. Svcs., Cin., 1986-89, lead biomed. electronics technician, 1989-92, sr. biomed. electronics technician, account mgr., 1993—. Mem. Delta Mu Delta. Republican. Office: Novare Biomed Svcs 345 Neeb Rd Cincinnati OH 45233

KORDISH, THERESA ANN, family practice physician; b. Lansing, Mich., May 13, 1954; d. Burton Anthony and Shirley Ann Helen (Colby) Woldecker; m. Dennis Errol Kordish, Jan. 31, 1976. BS, Western Mich. U., 1983; DO, UOMHS, Des Moines, 1988. Diplomate Am. Bd. Family Practice. Asst. clin. prof. Mich. State U., Kalamazoo, 1991—; regional med. dir. Blue Core Network, Kalamazoo, 1995—; chmn., pres. Health Care Assocs., Kalamazoo, 1995—. Office: Health Care Associates 820 John St Ste 201 Kalamazoo MI 49001

KORENGOLD, GEORGE MATTHEW, physician; b. N.Y.C., Dec. 16, 1946; s. Marvin Curtis and Edna (Gerler) K.; m. Barbara Lynn Korengold, Aug. 23, 1970; children: Adam Stuart, Erin Carol. BA, U. Pa., Phila., 1968; MD, George Washington U., 1992. Diplomate Am. Acad. Pediatrics. Pediatric resident Children's Nat. Med. Ctr., Washington, 1972-75; pediatrician Wiczer, Korengold, Mayol, Deutsh & Walters, MD's., Bethesda, Md., 1975—. Mem. Montgomery County Med. Soc., Montgomery-Prince George's Pediatric Soc. (pres. 1990). Office: 6410 Rockledge Dr Bethesda MD 20817

KORENMAN, GARY, neurologist; b. N.Y.C., Sept. 29, 1937; s. Irving and Minnie (Klein) K.; m. Ella Mary Kopelman, June 4, 1961; children: Eric, Jeffrey. AB, Dartmouth Coll., 1959, 2-yr. diploma in medicine, 1960; MD, Cornell U., 1962. Staff, neurology St. Luke's-Roosevelt Hosp., N.Y.C., 1968—, Mt. Sinai Hosp., N.Y.C., 1968—; cons., neurology Isabella Geriatric Ctr., N.Y.C., 1968—. To Capt., U.S. Army Med. Corps, 1963-65. Am. Acad. Neurology, Dartmouth Med. Sch. Alumni Coun. (pres. 1995—, chmn. ann. fund 1993-95), Marshall Chess Club, Alpha Omega Alpha. Republican. Jewish. Office: 950 Park Ave New York NY 10028

KORETZ, E. BARBARA PEARLMAN, social worker; b. L.A., Mar. 6, 1952; d. Ralph and Dorothy Madelaine (Krauss) Pearlman; m. Elliott Lewis Koretz, NOv. 2, 1986; children: Zachary Aaron, Tamara Lynne. BA, Calif. State U., Northridge, 1977; MSW, Calif. State U., Sacramento, 1980. Lic. clin. social worker, 1986; diplomate Am. Bd. Examiners in Clin. Social Work, 1989. Counselor WEAVE A Battered Women's Shelter, Sacramento, 1979-80; clin. social worker Soc. for Crippled Children, Maui, Hawaii, 1981-82; psychiatric social worker Braille Inst., L.A., 1982-85; clin. social worker UCLA Med. Ctr, 1985-87, Affiliated Psychiatric Med. Group, Rosemead, Calif., 1987-88; pvt. practice clin. social worker North Hollywood, Calif., 1988—; concons. St. Luke's Hosp., Pasadena, Calif., 1987-88; liason Affiliated Psychiatric Med. Group and EAP, Rosemead, 1987-88. Fellow Nat. Assn. Clin. Social Work, Calif. Soc. for Clin. Social Work. Office: 4731 Laurel Canyon Blvd Ste 1 North Hollywood CA 91607-3962

KORITZ, TIMOTHY NEAL, anesthesiologist; b. Rochelle, Ill., Mar. 3, 1956; s. Lloyd Thomas and Mary (Flagg) K.; m. Julie P. Oliver, Mar. 17, 1989; children: Katherine M., Sarah J., Jennifer M. BS, U. Ill., 1978; PhD, U. Cambridge, Eng., 1982; MD, Harvard U., 1987. Lic. physician, Ill., Iowa, N.Mex.; diplomate Am. Bd. Anesthesiology, Am. Bd. Med. Examiners. Intern internal medicine U. Wash., Seattle, 1987-88; resident anesthesiologist U. Iowa, Iowa City, 1992-94; staff anesthesiologist Rockford (Ill.) Meml. Hosp., 1994—; clin. assoc. U. Ill. Coll. Medicine, Rockford, 1995—. Contbr. articles to profl. jours. Scoutmaster Boy Scouts Am., Alamogordo, N.Mex., 1990-91. Maj. USAF, 1988-91. Recipient Marshall scholarship Marshall Aid Commemoration Commn., London, 1978. Mem. Am. Soc. Anesthesiology, Internat. Anesthesia Rsch. Soc. Presbyterian. Office: 3722 N Main St Rockford IL 61103

KORMAN, LOUIS YVES, physician, educator; b. Paris, Apr. 2, 1947; came to U.S., 1951; s. Israel and Ester (England) K.; m. Iris Bernice Stein; children: Jessica, Zachary. BA, CUNY, 1967; B in Med. Sci., Free U., Brussels, 1973; MD, SUNY, Syracuse, 1975. Intern SUNY, Syracuse, 1975-76, resident, 1976-77, fellowship in gastrointestinology, 1977-78; clin. assoc. NIH,

Bethesda, Md., 1978-81; chief gastrointestinal rsch. VA Med. Ctr., Washington, 1981—; prof. med. sch. Georgetown U., Washington, 1981—; cons. Glaxo Rsch., Research Triangle Park, N.C., 1986-88, Parke Davis, Ann Arbor, Mich., 1990-92, Fujinon Inc., Wayne, N.J., 1985-87, NCRIC Ins., Washington, 1990—. Contbr. articles to profl. jours. Bd. dirs. Generation After, Washington, 1988-90; with Jewish Social Svcs. Agy., 1993—. Lt. Comdr. USPHS, 1978-81. Rsch. grantee VA, 1981—. Fellow Am. Coll. Gastroenterology; mem. AMA, AAAS, Am. Gastroent. Assn., Am. Soc. Gastrointestinal Endoscopy (chmn. informatics com. 1992—). Office: VA Med Ctr 50 Irving St NW Washington DC 20422-0001

KORN, DAVID, educator, pathologist; b. Providence, Mar. 5, 1933; s. Solomon and Claire (Liebman) K.; m. PhoebeRichter, June 9, 1955 (div. Dec. 1993); children: Michael Philip, Stephen James, Daniel Clair. B.A., Harvard U., 1954, M.D., 1959. Intern Mass. Gen. Hosp., Boston, 1959-60; resident in Pathology Mass. Gen. Hosp., 1960-61; research asso. NIH, 1961-63; mem. staff Lab. Biochem. Pharmacology; also asst. pathologist NIH, 1963-68; prof. pathology Sch. Medicine Stanford (Calif.) U., 1968—, chmn. dept. pathology Sch. Medicine, 1968-84; physician-in-chief pathology Stanford Hosp., 1968-84, dean Sch. Medicine, 1984-95, v.p., dean, 1986-95; cons. pathology Palo Alto VA Hosp., 1968-84; sr. surgeon USPHS, 1961-66; mem. cell biology study sect. NIH, 1973-77, chmn., 1976-77; mem. bd. sci. counselors, divsn. cancer biology and diagnosis Nat. Cancer Inst., 1977-82, chmn., 1980-82; chmn. Nat. Cancer Adv. Bd., 1984-91; disting. scholar in residence Assn. Am. Med. Colls., 1995—; sr. fellow sci. and health policy Assn. Acad. Health Ctrs., 1995—. Mem. editorial bd. Human Pathology, 1969-74; assoc. editor, 1974-88; mem. editorial bd. Jour. Biol. Chemistry, 1973-79. Recipient Young Scientist award Md. Acad. Sci., 1967. Mem. Am. Soc. Biol. Chemists, Am. Assn. Pathologists, Am. Soc. Cell Biology, Am. Soc. Microbiology, Fedn. Am. Soc. Exptl. Biology (bd. dirs., mem. exec. com.), Inst. of Medicine. Home: 2727 29th St NW Apt 312 Washington DC 20008 Office: Stanford U Sch Medicine MSOB X226 Stanford CA 94305

KORN, ROY JOSEPH, SR., educator, physician; b. Chgo., July 25, 1920; s. Isaac Emanuel and Anna Amanda (Andersson) K.; m. Elsie Ann Kral, Jan. 15, 1955; children: Steven Arthur, Roy Joseph Jr., Michael R., Patricia Ann. B.S., Northwestern U., 1942, M.D., 1946. Diplomate: Am. Bd. Internal Medicine. Intern Wesley Meml. Hosp., Chgo., 1945-46; resident VA Hosp., Hines, Ill., 1949-51; chief med. service VA West Side Hosp., Chgo., 1958-62; chief staff VA West Side Hosp., 1972-86; adv. prof. faculty medicine Chiengmai (Thailand) U., 1962-64; asso. prof. U. Ill. Med. Sch., Chgo., 1959-64; prof. Chgo. Med. Sch., 1964; prof. medicine U. Ind. Med. Sch., 1965-72; chief staff VA Hosp., Indpls., 1965-72; prof. medicine U. Ill. Coll. Medicine, Chgo., 1972-86, prof. emeritus, 1986—. Served to capt. M.C. AUS, 1946-48. Fellow A.C.P.; mem. Inst. Medicine Chgo., Chgo. Soc. Internal Medicine. Home: 516 N Lincoln St Hinsdale IL 60521-3447

KORNADT, HANS-JOACHIM KURT, psychologist, researcher; b. Stargard, Ger., June 16, 1927; s. Kurt Karl and Katharina (Bodenburg) K.; m. Gisela Trommsdorff; children from previous marriage: Claus-Ulrich, Tilmann, Nikola, Oliver. Diplom Psychol., U. Marburg, 1952, Ph.D., 1956. Research asst. U. Marburg, 1957; wissenschaftlicher asst. Wü rzburg, 1957-61; dozent Tchr. Tng. Coll., Saarbrü cken, 1961-64, prof., 1964-68; prof. ednl. psychology U. Saar, Saarbrucken, 1968—, dep. dir. Social-Psychol. Research Centre Devel. Planning, 1968-88; research in E. Africa, 1965; lectr. Ruhr-U. Bochum, 1968. Mem. wissenschaflicher beirat Fed. Ministry Econ. Coop. and Devel., 1968—; exec. com. Wissenschaftsrat, 1975-81; chmn. Beirat Hochschulzugangstest der Kultus Minister Konferenz, 1976-86, mem. Kuratorium, 1976—, chmn., 1992—, Beirat Deutsches Inst. Japan-Studien, Tokyo, 1988-95, vice chmn., 1991-95; chmn. Landes-Hochschulstruktur-Kommission Sachsen-Anhalt, 1991-92; chmn. Commn. Reform Lehrer-Ausbildung in Schleswig-Holstein, 1993. Author: Thematische Apperzeptions Verfahren, 2d edit., 1979; Situation und Entwicklungsprobleme des Schulsystems in Kenya, vol. 1, 1968, vol. 2, 1970; Toward a Motivation Theory of Aggression and Aggression Inhibition, 1974; Lehrziele, Schulleistung und Leistungs beurteilung, 1975; Cross-cultural Research on Motivation, 1980; Aggression and Frustration, Vol 1, 1981, Vol. 2, 1991; Aggressionsmotiv und Aggressions-Hemmung, 1982; Zur Lage Der Psychologie, 1985, Developmental Conditions of Aggression in Eastern and Western Cultures, 1991, Deutsch-Japanische Begegnungen in den Sozial Wissenschaften, 1993, Sprache und Kognition, 1994. Acad. stipende VW Found., 1977-78; research fellow Japan Soc. Promotion Sci., 1979, Japanese-German Research award, 1988, Saarland Verdienst-Orden, 1995. Mem. German Assn. Psychology (pres. 1982-84), Internat. Council Psychologists, Internat. Soc. Research on Aggression, Internat. Assn. Cross Cultural Psychology, Japanese-German Soc. for Social Scis. (pres. 1989—). Mem. Free Democratic Party. Home: PO Box 129, D-67142 Deidesheim Germany Office: U Saar, PO Box 151150, D-66041 Saarbrücken Germany

KORNBERG, ARTHUR, biochemist; b. N.Y.C., N.Y., Mar. 3, 1918; s. Joseph and Lena (Katz) K.; m. Sylvy R. Levy, Nov. 21, 1943 (dec. 1986); children: Roger, Thomas Bill, Kenneth Andrew; m. Charlene Walsh Levering, 1988 (dec. 1995). BS, CCNY, 1937, LLD (hon.), 1960; MD, U. Rochester, 1941, DSc (hon.), 1962; DSc (hon.), U. Pa., U. Notre Dame, 1965, Washington U., 1968, Princeton U., 1970, Colby Coll., 1970; LHD (hon.), Yeshiva U., 1963; MD honoris causa, U. Barcelona, Spain, 1970. Intern in medicine Strong Meml. Hosp., Rochester, N.Y., 1941-42; commd. officer USPHS, 1942, advanced through grades to med. dir., 1951; mem. staff NIH, Bethesda, Md., 1942-52, nutrition sect., div. physiology, 1942-45; chief sect. enzymes and metabolism Nat. Inst. Arthritis and Metabolic Diseases, 1947-52; guest research worker depts. chemistry and pharmacology coll. medicine NYU, 1946; dept. biol. chemistry med. sch. Washington U., 1947; dept. plant biochemistry U. Calif., 1951; prof., head dept. microbiology, med. sch. Washington U., St. Louis, 1953-59; prof. biochemistry Stanford U. Sch. Medicine, 1959—, chmn. dept., 1959-69, prof. emeritus dept. biochemistry, 1988—; Mem. sci. adv. bd. Mass. Gen. Hosp., 1964-67; bd. govs. Weizmann Inst., Israel. Author: For the Love of Enzymes, 1989; contbr. sci. articles to profl. jours. Served lt. (j.g.), med. officer USCGR, 1942. Recipient Paul-Lewis award in enzyme chemistry, 1951; co-recipient of Nobel prize in medicine, 1959; recipient Max Berg award prolonging human life, 1968, Sci. Achievement award AMA, 1968, Lucy Wortham James award James Ewing Soc., 1968, Borden award Am. Assn. Med. Colls., 1968, Nat. medal of sci., 1979. Gairdner Foundation International Awards, 1995. Mem. Am. Soc. Biol. Chemists (pres. 1965), Am. Chem. Soc., Harvey Soc., Am. Acad. Arts and Scis., Royal Soc., Nat. Acad. Scis. (mem. council 1963-66), Am. Philos. Soc., Phi Beta Kappa, Sigma Xi, Alpha Omega Alpha. Office: Stanford U Med Ctr Dept Biochemistry Stanford CA 94305-5307

KORNBERG, JOEL BARRY, lawyer, emergency physician; b. Bklyn., June 17, 1953; s. Bernard Fred and Ada (Ritterstein) K.; m. Mira Lee Miller, Dec. 26, 1976; children: Dana Nicole, Jordan Reid. AB, Boston U., 1975; MD, N.Y. Med. Coll., 1980; JD, Nova U., 1989. Bar: Fla. 1989, D.C. 1990, U.S. Dist. Ct. (so. dist.) Fla. 1989, U.S. Supreme Ct. 1994; cert. mediator, Fla. 1995; cert. Am. Bd. Emergency Medicine, healthcare risk mgr., Fla. Resident Long Island Jewish-Hillside Med. Ctr., New Hyde Park, N.Y., 1980-81; emergency physician Emergency Med. Svcs. Assocs., Inc., Plantation, Fla., 1981-83, Joel B. Kornberg, M.D. P.A., Coral Springs, Fla., 1983-90, EMSA Ltd. Partnership, Plantation, 1990—; med. dir. Dept. Emergency Svcs. Humana Hosp., Pompano Beach, Fla., 1985-92, regional med. dir., 1992-94; pvt. practice Joel Kornberg, M.D., J.D., Boca Raton, Fla., 1989-94; med. dir. dept. emergency medicine Cedars Med. Ctr., Miami, ., 1993-94; pvt. practice Joel Kornberg MD, JD, Boca Raton, Fla., 1994—; mem. exec. com. Humana Hosp. Cypress, Pompano Beach, 1985-92, corp. counsel med. affairs; risk mgmt. cons. EMSA Ltd. Partnership, Plantation, 1989-94; dir. edn. Voice Billstat, Plantation, 1992-94. Head coach Coral Springs Youth Soccer Assn., 1989—, mgr. Worth Springs Little League, 1995—. Fellow Am. Coll. Legal Medicine, Am. Coll. Emergency Physician; mem. ABA, Nat. Health Lawyers Assn., Am. Soc. Law and Medicine, Nat. Bd. Med. Examiners. Office: Joel Kornberg MD JD Ste 305C 7301 A W Palmetto Park Rd Boca Raton FL 33433

KORNBLUTH, RALPH ROSS, physician; b. Montreal, Que., Can., Apr. 18, 1938; came to U.S., 1965.; s. Max and Sarah (Tieger) K.; m. Anita DuBow, Apr. 2, 1966; children: Deborah Rochelle Berger, Ira David, Michael Ari. BS, McGill U., 1962, MD, 1964. Diplomate Nat. Bd. Med. Examiners. Rotating intern Jewish Gen. Hosp., Montreal, 1964-65; cons. Douglas Hosp., Verdun, Can., 1965; resident psychiatrist Michael Reese Hosp., Chgo., 1965-68; cons. Ill. State Hosp. System, Chgo., 1968; staff psychiatrist Portsmouth (Va.) Psychiat. Ctr., 1970-71; attending physician Fairfax (Va.) Hosp., 1971-74; pvt. practice Fairfax, 1971—; supr. of psychologists, Fairfax, 1971—. Mem. com. B'nai Israel Congregation, Rockville, Md., 1978—; vice chmn. med. div. United Jewish Appeal, Washington, 1980. Lt. comdr. USN, 1968-71. Recipient Physician's Recognition award AMA, 1979—, Resident's award Ill. Psychiatry Soc., 1968, Rsch. award 1st place Psychosomatic and Psychiat. Inst., 1968. Mem. Am. Physicians Fellowship, Fairfax County Med. Soc. (credentials com. 1987—, mental health com. 1992, profl. affairs com. 1995—), Am. Psychiat. Assn. (internat. affairs com. 1991—, pvt. practice com. 1991—), Washington Psychiat. Soc. Jewish. Home: 9812 Woodford Rd Potomac MD 20854-5034 Office: 8303 Arlington Blvd Ste 207 Fairfax VA 22031-2903

KORNEL, LUDWIG, medical educator, physician, scientist; b. Jaslo, Poland, Feb. 27, 1923; came to U.S., 1958, naturalized, 1970; s. Eziel Edward and Ernestine (Karpf) K.; m. Esther Muller, May 27, 1952; children: Ezriel Edward, Amiel Mark. Student, U. Kazan Med. Inst., USSR, 1943-45; M.D., Wroclaw (Poland) Med. Acad., 1950; Ph.D., U. Birmingham, Eng., 1958. Intern Univ. Hosp., Wroclaw, 1949-50, Hadassah-Hebrew U. Hosp., Jerusalem, 1950-51; resident medicine Hadassah-Hebrew U. Hosp., 1952-55; Brit. Council scholar, Univ. research fellow endocrinology U. Birmingham, 1955-57, lectr. medicine, 1956-57; fellow endocrinology U. Ala. Med. Ctr., 1958-59, successively asst. prof., assoc. prof. prof. medicine, 1961-67; dir. steroid sect. U. Ala. Med. Center, 1962-67, assoc. prof. biochemistry, 1965-67; postdoctoral trainee in steroid biochemistry U. Utah, 1959-61; prof. medicine U. Ill. Coll. Medicine, Chgo., 1967-71; dir. steroid unit Presbyn.-St. Lukes Hosp., Chgo., 1967-93; assoc. biochemist Presbyn.-St. Lukes Hosp., 1967-70, sr. biochemist on sci. staff, 1970-71, attending physician, 1967-71; prof. medicine and biochemistry Rush Med. Coll., 1970-93, prof. emeritus of internal medicine and biochemistry, 1993—; sr. attending physician, sr. scientist Rush-Presbyn.-St. Lukes Med. Ctr., 1971—, dir. steroid hypertension rsch. lab., 1971—; hon. guest lectr. Polish Acad. Sci., Warsaw, 1965; vis. prof. Kanazawa (Japan) U., 1973, 82, 88, 93. Mem. editl. bd. Clin. Physiol. Biochemistry, 1975-94, Endocrinology, 1994—; co-editor: Yearbook of Endocrinology, 1986-90; co-author: Ency. of Human Biology, 1991, 96; contbr. articles on endocrinology and steroid biochemistry to profl.jours.; contbr. chpts to textbooks. Recipient Physicians Recognition award AMA, 1969, 73, 76, 81, 86, Outstanding New Citizen award Citzenship Council Met. Chgo., 1970. Fellow Am. Coll. Clin. Pharmacology and Chemotherapy, Nat. Acad. Clin. Biochemistry (bd. dirs. 1982-86), Royal Soc. health; mem. AMA, AAAS, AAUP, Endocrine Soc., Am. Fedn. Clin. Rsch., N.Y. Acad. Scis., Am. Physiol. Soc., Cen. Soc. Clin. Rsch., Israel Soc. for Biochemistry and Molecular Biology, Am. Acad. Polit. and Social Scis., Fedn. Am. Socs. for Exptl. Biology (nat. corr. 1975—), Fedn. Israel Socs. for Exptl. Biology, Sigma Xi. Home: 3950 N Lake Shore Dr Chicago IL 60613-3434 Office: Rush Presbyn St Lukes M C 1653 W Congress Pky Chicago IL 60612-3833

KORNFELD, STUART A., hematology educator; b. St. Louis, Mo., Oct. 4, 1936. AB, Dartmouth Coll., 1958; MD, Washington U., 1962. Rsch. asst. biochemistry dept. sch. medicine Washington U., St. Louis, 1958-62, from instr. to asst. prof. medicine, 1966-70, from asst. to assoc. prof. biochemistry, 1968-72, prof. medicine dept. internal medicine, 1972—, prof. biochemistry, co-dir. divsn. hematology and oncology, 1976—, dir. divsn. oncology, 1973-76; intern med. ward Barnes Hosp., 1962-63, asst. resident, 1965-66; rsch. assoc. nat. inst. arthritis and metabolic disease NIH, 1963-65; faculty rsch. assoc. Am. Cancer Soc., 1966-71; mem. cell biology study sect. NIH, 1974-77; mem. bd. sci. counselors Nat. Inst. Arthritis, Diabetes & Digestive & Kidney Disease, 1983-87; mem. sci. rev. bd. Howard Hughes Med. Inst., 1986—; mem. bd. sci. advisers Jane Coffin Childs Meml. Fund. Res., 1987—; Jubilee lectr. Biochemistry Soc., 1989. Assoc. editor Jour. Clin. Investigation, 1977-81, editor, 1981-82; assoc. editor Jour. Biol. Chemistry, 1982-87; author 145 publs. Recipient Borden award, 1962, Rsch. Career Devel. award NIH, 1971-76; named Harden Medallist, Biochemistry Soc., 1989, Passano Found. laureate, 1991. Mem. NAS (mem. inst. medicine), Am. Soc. Clin. Investigation (counselor 1972-75), Am. Soc. Hematology, Am. Soc. Biol. Chemists, Assn. Am. Physicians (sec. 1986—), Am. Acad. Arts and Sci., Am. Chem. Soc., Sigma Xi. Office: Washington U Sch Med Dept Internal Medicine 660 S Euclid Ave Saint Louis MO 63110-1010*

KORNREICH, MARTIN ALLEN, orthopedic surgeon; b. N.Y.C., Oct. 1, 1938; s. Lawrenc E. and Rose (McKibbie) K.; m. Rosemary Southward, Jan. 8, 1965; children: Larry, Mark, Michael. BA, NYU, 1959; MD, U. Fla., 1965. Diplomate Am. Bd. Orthop. Surgery. Intern in pediat. N.C. Bapt. Hosp.; resident in orthops. N.C. Bapt. Hosp.-Bowman Gray, Winston Salem, 1970; team physician, orthop. cons. Toronto (Can.) Blue Jays Baseball Club, 1977-92; chief dept. surgery Mease Hosp., Dunedin, Fla., 1979, med. staff sec., 1980, med. staff v.p., 1981, med. staff pres., 1982. Maj. U.S. Army Med. Corps, 1970-72. Mem. ACS, Am. Acad. Orthop. Surgeons. Office: 601 Main St Dunedin FL 34698

KORNRICH, RHODA, psychologist; b. N.Y.C., Nov. 17, 1930; d. Irving and Celia (Edlin) Adelstein; m. Seymour Warshaw (div. 1973); children: Lynne Gilman, Sheryl Kraft, Michael Warshaw; m. Milton Kornrich, 1985. BA, CUNY-Hunter Coll., 1951; MS, Queens Coll., Flushing N.Y., 1971; PhD, Fordham U., 1978. Tchr. Long Beach (N.Y.) Pub. Schs., 1951-52, 56-71; psychologist Yonkers (N.Y.) Pub. Schs., 1971-72; psychotherapist North Suffolk Mental Health Ctr., Smithtown, N.Y., 1974-79, Commack (N.Y.) Consultation Ctr., 1979-85; psychologist Behavioral Stress Ctr., Levittown, N.Y., 1983-86, Smithtown Pub. Schs., 1975-93; pvt. practice Smithtown, 1993—; psychotherapist Inst. for Rational Counseling, Bohemia, N.Y., 1995—. Mem. APA, Nassau County Psychol. Assn., N.Y. State United Tchrs.

KORNYLAK, HAROLD JOHN, osteopathic physician; b. Jersey City, Feb. 16, 1950; s. Andrew Thomas and Lucille Bertha (Reilly) K.; children: Laura, Michael. BS in Physics with honors, Stevens Inst. Tech., 1971; MA, Maharishi Internat. U., 1977; MS, Maharishi European Rsch. U., 1977; DO, U. New Eng., 1983. Mem. indsl. R & D staff Kornylak Corp., Hamilton, Ohio, 1971-73, mgr. data processing, 1974-79; researcher Maharishi European Rsch. U., Weggis, Switzerland, 1973-74; intern Mich. Osteo. Med. Ctr., Detroit, 1983-84; staff physician Indian Health Svc., USPHS, San Carlos, Ariz., 1984-87, St. Louis Orthopedic Sports Medicine Clinic, 1987-88; pvt. practice Virginia Beach, Va., 1989—; cons. in systems analysis; instr. Atlantic U., Virginia Beach, 1989—, Harold J. Reilly Sch. Massotherapy, Virginia Beach, 1989—. Mem. Am. Osteo. Assn., Am. Acad. Osteopathy, Am. Acad. Med. Acupuncture, Cranial Acad., Va. Osteo. Med. Assn. Home and Office: 1432 E Bay Shore Dr Virginia Beach VA 23451-3760

KORR, IRVIN MORRIS, physiologist, medical educator; b. Phila., Aug. 24, 1909; s. Samuel Pincus and Anna (Goldberg) K.; m. Margot Lindsay, June 13, 1939 (dec. Jan. 1975); 1 child, David L.; m. Janet R. Meneley, June 6, 1986. BA., U. Pa., 1930, MA, 1931; PhD, Princeton U., 1935; DSc (hon.), Kirksville Coll. Osteo. Medicine, 1976; DO Edn. (hon.) Coll. Osteopathy Medicine of Pacific, 1981; Instr. physiology NYU Coll. Medicine, N.Y.C., 1936-42; sr. physiologist U.S. War Dept., 1942-45; prof. physiology Kirksville Coll. Osteo. Medicine, Mo., 1945-75; prof. biomechanics Mich. State U., East Lansing, 1975-78; prof. med. edn. Tex. Coll. Osteo. Medicine, Ft. Worth, 1978-89; ret. Author: (with E.L. Hix and K.A. Buzzell) Physiological Basis of Osteopathic Medicine, 1970; Collected Papers of I.M. Korr, 1979, Vol. 2, 1996. Editor: Neurobiologic Mechanisms in Manipulative Therapy, 1978. Contbr. articles to profl. jours. Recipient Founder's medal Tex. Coll. Osteo. Medicine, 1982, Kistner award Am. Assn. Colls. Osteo. Medicine, 1983, Gutensohn/Denslow Laureate award, 1987. Fellow AAAS; mem. Am. Physiol. Soc., Soc. Neurosci., Am. Soc. Neurochemistry, Harvey Soc. (life), ACLU, Common Cause, Sierra Club. Home: 911 9th St Boulder CO 80302-7225

KORSCH, BARBARA M., pediatrician; b. Jena, Germany, Mar. 30, 1921; widowed; 1 child. BA, Smith Coll., 1941; MD, Johns Hopkins U., 1944. Cert. Am. Bd. Pediats. Asst. resident Bellevue Hosp., 1945, Mary Imogene Basset Hosp., 1946; asst. resident N.Y. Hosp., 1947, fellow Inst. Child Devel., 1948-49; asst. pediats. Med. Coll. Cornell U., 1949-50, from instr. to assoc. prof., 1950-61; assoc. clin. prof. preventive medicine Sch. Medicine UCLA, 1961-64; assoc. prof. U. So. Calif., L.A., 1964-69, prof. pediats. Sch. Medicine, 1969—; George Armstrong lectr. Ambulatory Pediat. Assn., 1973; Katherine D. McCormick Disting. lectr. Stanford U., 1977; Kathy Newman Meml. lectr. Tulane U., 1987; asst. outpatient pediatrician N.Y. Hosps., 1949-50, asst. attending pediatrician, 1950-55, clin. dir. pediat. outpatient dept., 1950-61, assoc. attending pediatrician, 1955-61; pediat. cons. Dept. Health, N.Y., 1949-51, Hosp. Spl. Surgery, 1955-61, Gen. Pediat. Childrens Hosp., L.A., 1961-65, Med. Ctr., U. So. Calif., 1969-74; coord. pediat. rehab. program Nat. Found. Infantile Paralysis, 1953-61; pediat. dir. Obs. Clinic Children L.A., 1961-64; assoc. attending pediatrician Cedars Lebanon Hosp., 1961—; vis. prof. numerous U.S. and fgn. univs., 1973-89; hon. staff mem. dept. pediats. Cedars-Sinai Med. Ctr., 1976—. Mem. Inst. Medicine-NAS, Am. Acad. Pediats. (C. Anderson Aldrich award 1988), Am. Pediat. Soc., Soc. Behavioral Pediats. (pres. 1985), Soc. Pediat. Rsch., Sigma Xi. Office: Childrens Hosp Divsn Gen Pediats 4650 Sunset Blvd Los Angeles CA 90027*

KORSON, ROY, retired pathology educator; b. Phila., Oct. 24, 1922; s. David and Sarah (Gross) K.; m. Lorraine Bagdon, Sept. 8, 1946. AB, U. Pa., 1943; MD, Jefferson Med. Coll., Phila., 1947. Diplomate Am. Bd. Pathology. Intern Einstein Med. Ctr., Phila., 1947-48; postdoctoral fellow Columbia U., N.Y.C., 1948-49; postdoctoral fellow U. Vt., Burlington, 1949-50, resident pathology, 1949-52, asst. prof., 1951-57, assoc. prof., 1957-67, prof., 1967-92, prof. emeritus, 1992—; vis. scientist Middlesex Hosp. Med. Sch., London, 1961-62; dir. surg. pathology and cytology Med. Ctr. Hosp. of Vt., Burlington, 1974-89. Contbr. articles to profl. publs. Bd. dirs. Am. Cancer Soc., Atlanta, 1982-92, pres. Vt. div., Burlington, 1976-78, 84-86. Capt. M.C., U.S. Army, 1952-54. Recipient practice prize in medicine Jefferson Med. Coll., Phila., 1947, Career Devel. award, USPHS, 1958-63; named Buttles prof. of pathology, U. Vt., 1984-89. Fellow Coll. Am. Pathologists; mem. AAAS, AMA, Internat. Acad. Pathology, Am. Soc. Cytology, N.Y. Acad. Scis., Alpha Omega Alpha, Sigma Xi.

KORSTAD, JOHN EDWARD, biology educator; b. Woodland, Calif., July 4, 1949; s. Vernon E. and Jeanette (Beard) K.; m. Sally Diane Steffen, July 29, 1972; children: Shauna, Sarah, Joya, Janna. BA, BS, Calif. Luth. U., Thousand Oaks, 1972; MS, Calif. State U., Hayward, 1979, U. Mich., 1979; PhD, U. Mich., 1980. Postdoctoral fellow SINTEF, Trondheim, Norway, 1987-88; prof. biology Oral Roberts U., Tulsa, 1980—; asst. dir., dir. collegiate acad. Okla. Acad. Sci., 1984-89. Bd. dirs. MEND Pregnancy Crisis Ctr., Broken Arrow, Okla., 1991—. Fulbright fellow in aquaculture rsch., Norway, 1993-94. Mem. Am. Soc. Limnology and Oceanography, World Aquaculture Soc., Catfish Farmers of Okla., Am. Assn. of Zool. Parks and Aquariums (advisor marine fishes adv. com. 1991—), Beta Beta Beta (advisor), Sigma Xi. Republican. Office: Oral Roberts U Dept Biology Tulsa OK 74171

KORSUN, ANGELINA, hospital administrator, critical care nurse; b. Bronx, N.Y., Nov. 10, 1952; d. Benjamin and Vera (Kubit) K. BSN, Hunter Coll.-CUNY, 1974, MSN, 1980; MPA, Baruch U., N.Y., 1987. RN, N.Y. Perdiem RN Bellevue Hosp. Ctr., N.Y.C., 1973-74, staff RN emergency ward, 1974-75; team leader SICU, VA Med. Ctr. Manhattan, N.Y.C., 1975-80, critical care instr., 1980; clin. supr. Mt. Sinai Med. Ctr., N.Y.C., 1980-87, adminstrn. coord., 1987-88, adminstrn. dir. transplant, 1988—; adj. prof. CUNY, 1985-88; chairperson Transplant Adminstrn. Forum, United Network Organ Sharing, 1992-95. Office: Mt. Sinai Med. Ctr. One Gustave Levy Pl No 1104 New York NY 10029

KORTEBEIN, STUART ROWLAND, orthopedic surgeon; b. Evanston, Ill., Apr. 17, 1930; s. Rowland J. and Grace K.; m. Alice C. Johnson, July 10, 1954; children: William, David. AA, North Park Coll., 1950; BS, Wheaton Coll., 1952; postgrad., North Park Theol. Sem., 1952-53; MD, Loyola U., 1957; JD, Jefferson Coll. Law, 1983. Diplomate Nat. Bd. Med. Examiners, Am. Bd. Orthopaedic Surgery. Intern Akron (Ohio) Gen. Hosp., 1957-58, resident, 1961-64; resident Hines (Ill.) VA Hosp., 1960, Northwestern U., Chgo., 1964; pvt. practice medicine specializing in orthopedic surgery Arlington Heights, Ill., 1965-88; mem. orthopaedic surgeon staff U.S. Naval Regional Med. Ctr., Memphis, 1986—; pvt. practice medicine specializing in orthopedic surgery Milw., 1988—; chief dept. orthopedic surgery U.S. Naval Hosp., Great Lakes, Ill., 1987; mem. orthopaedic surgeon staff Sinai-Samaritan Med. Ctr., Milw., 1988—; attending surgeon N.W. Cmty. Hosp., Arlington Heights, 1965-90, chief orthopedics, 1976; v.p. Magnetrans Rsch. and Devel. Corp., 1972-84, Window Well Protectors, Inc., McHenry, Ill., 1983-86; coord. med. cons. Compusoft Corp., Darien, Ill., 1984—, Pomsoft Corp., Willowbrook, Ill.; instr. emergency medicine technician course Haper Coll., 1973-84; vis. instr. police self-def. tactics Oakton Cmty. Coll., 1984-88. Water safety instr. ARC, 1949-54; aux. police officer City of Rolling Meadows, Ill., 1984-89; bd. dirs. Chicagoland Drug Prevention Program, 1971-84; choir dir. First Bapt Ch., Twenty Nine Palms, Calif., 1959-60, tech. advisor Jubo-Kai Internat., 1977—. Lt. M.C., USNR, 1958-60. Mem. Am. Acad. Orthopaedic Surgeons, Physicians Martial Arts Assn., Soc. Black Belts Am., Christian Med. Soc., Wis. Orthopaedic Soc., Milw. Orthopaedic Soc., Hakko-Ryu Jitsu Fed., Jiu Jitsu Black Belt Fedn. Am. (pres. Ill., rep. 1971-74), Oikiru-Ryu Jitsu (Sandan instr. 1977-35), U.S. Judo Assn. (Sho Dan life mem.). Office: 500 N 19th St Milwaukee WI 53233-2123

KORTTILA, KARI, anesthesiologist, educator; b. Turku, Finland, Jan. 11, 1948. MB, U. Helsinki, Finland, 1968, MD, 1972, PhD, 1975. Rsch. assoc. Acad. Finland U. Helsinki, 1973-76, acting lectr. anesthesia, 1977-78; house officer, acting lectr. U. Helsinki/ Helsinki U. Ctrl. Hosp., 1978-79; housestaff, faculty mem. U. Iowa, Iowa City, 1979-81; lectr. anestesia U. Helsinki/ Helsinki U. Ctrl. Hosp., 1981-84; docent exptl. anesthesiology U. Helsinki, 1977-83, docent anaesthesiology, 1983—, sr. physician, chief dept. anaesthesia Women's Hosp., 1984—; prof. anesthesia and critical care U. Chgo., 1986-88, vis. prof. dept. anesthesia & critical care, 1995—; presenter in field. Reviewer Annals Clin. Rsch., 1979—, Acta Anaesthesiologica Scandinavica, 1979—, Drugs, European Jour. Anaesthesiology, 1984, Acta Obstetrica et Gynecologica Scandinavica, 1991—, Jour. Clin. Anesthesia, 1993—, Anesthesia & Analgesia, 1995—, Pharmacoeconomics, 1995—; assoc. editor Acta Anesthesiologica Scandinavica, 1991—. Grantee Finnish Acad., 1973-91, NIH, 1984-91. Mem. Am. Soc. Anesthesiologists, Internat. Anesthesia Rsch. Soc., European Anesthesia Acad. (senator 1991—), European Soc. Anesthesia (chair subcom. outpatient anesthesia 1991-95), Finnish Soc. Anaesthesiologists, Finnish Pharmacol. Soc., Scandanavian Soc. Anaesthesiologists, Assn. Anesthetists Gt. Britain & Ireland, Soc. Ambulatory Anesthesia (grant evaluation com. 1992—). Office: U Helsinki Dept Ob-Gyn, Haartmaninkatu 2, Helsinki Finland

KORTVÉLYESSY, GYULA, scientific director; b. Budapest, Hungary, Nov. 6, 1944; s. Antal and Ilona (Schodl) K.; m. Gyuláné Nagy, Aug. 5, 1967; children: Csilla, Eszter, Gábor. MS, L. Eötvös U., Budapest, 1967, PhD, 1973. Rsch. fellow Szeviki, Budapest, 1967-83, head dept., 1983-85, sci. dir., 1985—; postdoctoral rschr. Tech. U., Budapest, 1974; patent examiner Hungarian Patent Office, 1970-81; mem. supervisory com. First chem. Industria, 1994—. Contbr. articles to profl. jours.; patentee in field; mem. bd. Hungarian Chemists Jour., 1985—. Recipient Award for Chem. Engrs., Hungarian Ministry of Industry, 1989, Dénes Gábor's prize, Budapest, 1992. Mem. Hungarian Chem. Soc. (bd. dirs. 1985—, dep. sec.-gen. 1990—), Hungarian Acad. Sci. (mem. com. 1985—). Home: Bimbó 30, 1022 Budapest Hungary Office: Szeviki, Stáhly 13, 1085 Budapest Hungary

KORYTKOWKSI, MARY T., physician; b. Buffalo, Nov. 15, 1949. BSN, D'Youville Coll., 1971; MN, Emory Univ., 1976; MD, Univ. N.C., 1982. Diplomate Am. Bd. Internal Medicine, Diplomate Am. Bd. Endocrinology and Metabolism. Internship, residency Francis Scott Key Medical Ctr., Balt., 1982-85; fellow Sinai Hosp. Balt., Johns Hopkins Hosp., Balt., 1986-88; head nurse St. Joseph's Hosp., Asheville, N.C., 1972-74; staff nurse Clinic for Migrant Health Workers, Hendersonville, N.C., 1972; instr. dept. nursing Western Carolina Univ., Cullowhee, N.C., 1974-75, asst. prof. nursing, 1976-78; instr. dept. medicine John Hopkins Hosp. Sch. Medicine, Balt., 1988-89; asst. prof. medicine, dir. ambulatory care divsn. endocrinology Univ. Pitts., 1989—; staff physician Wyman Park Hosp., Balt., 1985; staff physician endocrine cons. Chesapeake Physician's Profl. Assn., Balt., 1988-89; speaker at various conf., lectr. in field; co-dir., speaker Women's Health Issues Conf., 1993; mem. planning com., speaker Women and Children with DM, 1994; task force for DKA, 1994; reviewer Jour. Am. Medical Assn. Contbr. numerous articles to profl. jours. Planning com. Am. Diabetes Assn. meeting. Recipient Mother D'Youville award, 1967, Rathburn award Francis Scott Key Medical Ctr., 1983; numerous rsch. grants. Mem. Am. Coll. Physicians, Am. Diabetes Assn., Am. Fedn. Clinical Rsch., The Endocrine Soc., Sigma Theta Tau. Home: 1320 Macon Ave Pittsburgh PA 15218 Office: Univ Pitts Medical Ctr 3601 Fifth Ave Falk Rm 588 Pittsburgh PA 15213

KOSANOVIC, NIKOLA, surgeon; b. Rijeka, Croatia, Jan. 25, 1947; arrived in New Zealand, 1994; s. Ilija and Angela (Ivosevic) K.; m. Ljubica Vicic, Dec. 31, 1970; children: Nika, Gorana-Montana. MD, U. Zagreb, Croatia, 1971, Postgrad. Diploma Sports Physician, 1976; Postgrad. Diploma in Gen. Surgery, Mil. Med. Acad., Belgrade, Yugoslavia, 1982. Registered physician, Australia. Gen. practice Gen. Practice Svc., D. Selo, Croatia, 1972-78; resident in gen. surgery Mil. Hosp., Zagreb, 1978-81; sr. resident in gen. surgery Mil. Med. Acad., Belgrade, 1981-82; state specialist/surgeon Gen. Hosp., Zagreb, 1982-84, cons. surgeon, 1984-94, vascular team coord., 1982-88, coord. kidney and pancreas transplantation, 1988-94; pvt. practice surgery Charlton Bush Nursing Hosp., Charlton, Victoria, Australia, 1995—. Col. M.C. Croatian Army, 1991-92. Recipient Prize for Exemplary Work, Yugoslav Govt., 1980, Mil. Merit Decoration, 1987. Fellow Croatian Med. Assn., Croatian Soc. Surgery; mem. Rotary. Mem. Social Democrat Party. Roman Catholic. Home: 16 Rutherford St, Charlton Vic 3525, Australia Office: Charlton Bush Nursing Hosp, 6 Menzies St, Charlton Vic 3525, Australia

KOSASKY, HAROLD JACK, gynecologist; b. Winnipeg, Man., Can., Oct. 19, 1927; s. Jack and Lillian (Resnick) K.; m. Shirley Anne Johnston, Sept. 3, 1955; children: Julia, Leah, Robert. BA, U. Manitoba, Can., 1948; MD, U. Manitoba, 1953. Diplomate Am. Bd. Ob-gyn.; lic. Coll Physicians and Surgeons Can., Med. Coun. Can., Ky. State Bd. Health, Idaho State Bd. Health, Mass. Bd. Registration in Medicine. Intern Deer Lodge VA and Grace Hosps., Winnipeg, Man., Can., 1952-53; resident in gen. surgery Col. Belcher Hosp., Calgary, Alta., Can., 1953-54; resident in psychiatry Warren (Pa.) State Hosp., 1955-56; jr. asst. resident, asst. resident, sr. resident in ob-gyn. Chgo. Lying-In Hosp., 1956-59; asst. and assoc. prof. U. Louisville Sch. Med., 1961-65; asst. and assoc. in ob-gyn. various hosps., Boston, 1966-81; gynecologist and obstetrician Boston Hosp. for Women, 1965-81; gynecologist Brigham & Women's Hosp., Boston, 1981—; instr. ob-gyn. Harvard U., 1965—; cons. Jordan Hosp., Plymouth, Mass., 1969—, Ovutime, Boston, 1972—; pres. Saltime Co., 1994—; asst. vis. surgeon Boston City Hosp., 1967-69; mem. Ky. Govs. Task Force on Mental Retardation, 1964-65, Com. on Malignancy, chmn., 1963-65. Contbr. numerous articles to profl. jours.; co-inventor Ovutime and Saltime Ovulation group of instruments. Fellow ACS, Royal Coll. Surgeons of Can. (cert.), Royal Soc. Health, Boston Obstetric Soc. (emeritus); mem. AAAS, Gen. Med. Coun. Gt. Britain (lic.), Royal Coll. Obstetricans and Gynecologists, Assn. Prof. Ob-gyn., Louisville Obstet. and Gynecol. Soc. (sec., treas. 1962-65), Louisville Med. Forum (v.p.). Episcopalian. Club: Harvard. Office: 25 Boylston St Chestnut Hill MA 02167-1710

KOSCO, PAMELA JEAN, oncology nurse; b. Pitts., May 7, 1970; d. John and Stella Barbara (Rycyk) K. BSN, U. Pitts., 1992, postgrad., 1992-95. Clin. nurse III U. Pitts. Med. Ctr., 1993—. Mem. APHA, Oncology Nursing Soc., Pa. Pub. Health Assn.

KOSIK, JOANN GRACE, physician assistant; b. Pittston, Pa., Nov. 20, 1964; d. Joseph Francis and Mary Josephine (Bufalino) Dileo; m. James John Kosik, Sept. 30, 1989; 1 child, Julie. BS Physician Asst., Norwalk Hosp./Yale U., 1986; MHA, U. Scranton, 1995. Cert. physician asst. Cardiothoracic surg. physician asst. Temple U. Hosp., Phila., 1987-89, Bryn Mawr (Pa.) Hosp., 1989-94; part-time clin. physician asst. Student Health Clinic King's Coll., Wilkes-Barre, Pa., 1993—, program curriculum coord., 1992—. Pres. Seton Cath. H.S. Alumni Assn., Pittston, 1991—. Fellow Am. Acad. Physician Assts.; mem. Pa. Soc. Physician Assts., Acad. Physician Asst. Programs. Democrat. Roman Catholic. Office: Kings College Physician Asst Program 133 N River St Wilkes Barre PA 18711

KOSOWSKY, DAVID I., retired biotechnical company executive; b. N.Y.C., Feb. 27, 1930; m. Ingrid M. Mehlstaeubl; children: Michael, Richard P., Steven A. BEE summa cum laude, CUNY, 1951; SM, MIT, 1952, ScD, 1955. Chmn. emeritus Damon Corp., Needham Heights, Mass.; speaker, lectr. on policy developments and trends in the health care industry. Patentee in field. Mem. Corp. MIT, mem. vis. com. dept. biology; trustees Beth Israel Hosp., U. Hosp., New Eng. Aquarium, Children's Hosp.; mem. exec. group Harvard Med. Ctr. bd. trustees; mem. Corp. Joslin Diabetes Ctr., Inc., Corp. Mus. Sci.; mem. Commn. on Acad. Health Ctrs., Economy of New Eng. for the New Eng. Bd. of Higher Edn. Mem. N.Y. Acad. of Scis., IEEE, Sigma Xi, Tau Beta Pi, Eta Kappa Nu, Order of St. John, Knights of Malta. Home: 403D Dedham St Newton MA 02159-3300

KOSS, LEOPOLD G., physician, pathologist, educator; b. Gdansk, Poland, Oct. 2, 1920; came to U.S., 1947, naturalized, 1952; s. Abram and Rose (Merenholc) Kon; m. Lydia Palla; children: Michael S., Andrew C., Richard P. M.D., U. Berne, Switzerland, 1946. Intern, Lincoln Hosp., N.Y.C., 1947-48; tng. pathology St. Gallen, Switzerland, 1946-47, Kings County Hosp., Bklyn., 1949-52; instr. pathology L.I. (N.Y.) U. Coll. Medicine, 1949-52; mem. staff Meml. Hosp. Cancer and Allied Diseases, N.Y.C., 1952-70, attending pathologist, 1961-70, chief cytology service, 1961-70; pathologist-in-chief Sinai Hosp. Balt., 1970-73; prof., chmn. dept. pathology Montefiore Hosp., Med. Ctr. Albert Einstein Coll. Medicine, Bronx, N.Y., 1973-92, prof., chair emeritus, 1993—; hon. prof. pathology Severance Med. Coll., Seoul, Korea, 1956; assoc. mem. Sloan-Kettering Inst. Cancer Research, N.Y.C., 1957-70; assoc. prof. pathology Sloan-Kettering div. Postgrad. Sch. Med. Scis., Cornell U., 1957-70; prof. pathology Jefferson Med. Coll., Phila., 1970-73; clin. prof. pathology U. Md. Med. Sch., 1971-73; vis. pathologist James Ewing Hosp., N.Y.C., 1952-60; former cons. pathologist N.Y. State Dept. Health, Hosp. Spl. Surgery, N.Y.C.; cons. pathologist Walter Reed Army Med. Ctr., Nassau County Med. Ctr. Author: Diagnostic Cytology and Its Histopathologic Bases, 4th rev. edit. 1992, Tumors of the Urinary Bladder, 1975, Supplement, 1984, Aspiration Biopsy: Cytologic Interpretation and Histologic Bases, 2nd rev. edit. 1992; editor: Advances in Clinical Cytology, Vol. I, 1981, Vol. II, 1984, Papillomaviruses and Human Diseases, 1987; contbr. articles to profl. jours. and chpts. to books also monographs. Served to maj. M.C., AUS, 1955-57. Recipient Wien award Papanicolaou Cancer Inst., 1963, Alfred P. Sloan award cancer rsch., 1964, Fred Stewart award, 1984, Vandenbergne-Hill award, 1984, Meritorious medal U. Brussels, 1987, Jurzykowski award, 1991. Fellow Am. Soc. Clin. Pathology, Coll. Am. Pathologists, Internat. Acad. Cytology (Goldblatt award 1962, Kazumasa Masubuchi Life-Time Achievement award in clin. cytology, 1995); mem. AMA, Am. Soc. Exptl. Path. (Gold Cane award 1993), James Ewing Soc., Am. Soc. Cytology (pres. 1962, Papanicolaou award 1966), Internat. Acad. Pathology (Maude Abbott lectr. 1989), N.Y. Pathology Soc. (pres. 1985-87, Middleton-Goldsmith lectr. 1992), N.Y. State Soc. Pathology (Lansky-Ratner award 1989), Royal Acad. Medicine Spain (corr.), Brit. Soc. Clin. Cytology (hon.), Korean Med. Assn., Mex. Soc. Cytology, Argentinian Soc. Cytology, Japanese Soc. Pathology, Polish Soc. Pathology, Peruvian Soc. Ob-Gyn., German Acad. Sci. (Leopoldina), Internat. Soc. of Urol. Pathology (F.K. Mostofi Disting. Svc. award 1995), Am. Soc. for Colposcopy and Cervical Pathology (Disting. Svc. award 1996). Office: Montefiore Medical Ctr 111 E 210th St Bronx NY 10467-2490

KOSSOR, STEVEN ALBERT, psychologist; b. Plainfield, N.J., Nov. 29, 1954; s. Albert Aloyissus and Lieselotte Margot (Zierman) K.; m. Kathleen Zampana, Nov. 8, 1980. BA, Montclair (N.J.) State Coll., 1975; MA, Fairleigh Dickinson U., Madison, N.J., 1977. Lic. psychologist, Pa.; cert. sch. psychologist, Pa. Pvt. practice Coatesville, Pa., 1981—; dir. psych. svcs. TEHST, Inc. Cmty. Mental Health Agy., Reading, Pa.; dir., sec.-treas. Brandywine Judo Sch., Thorndale, Pa., 1992—; lectr. in field; mem. med. staff Brandywine Hosp. and Trauma Ctr., Brandywine Valley Pain Control Ctr. Author, editor: The Kossor Edn. Newsletter, 1992—. Mem. N.Am. Assn. Masters in Psychology (charter), Greater Phila. Pain Soc., Greater Phila. Assn. Clin. Hypnosis. Home and Office: 848 W King's Hwy Coatesville PA 19320

KOST, GERALD JOSEPH, physician, scientist; b. Sacramento, July 12, 1945; s. Edward William and Ora Imogene K.; m. Angela Louise Baldo, Sept. 9, 1972; children: Christopher Murray, Laurie Elizabeth. BS in Engring., Stanford U., 1967, MS in Engring.-Econ. Systems, 1968; PhD in Bioengring., U. Calif., San Diego, 1977; MD, U. Calif., San Francisco, 1978. Diplomate Nat. Bd. Med. Examiners, Am. Bd. Pathology. Resident dept. medicine UCLA, 1978-79, resident dept. neurology, 1979-80; resident dept. lab. medicine U. Wash., Seattle, 1980-81, chief resident dept. lab. medicine, 1981-82, cardiopulmonary-bioengring. and clin. chemistry researcher, 1982-83; asst. prof. pathology U. Calif., Davis, 1983-87, assoc. prof., 1987-93, prof., dir. clin. chemistry, faculty biomed. engring., 1993—; vis. prof. and Lilly scholar, 1990; numerous sci. cons., nat. and internat. speaker, invited lectr. Contbr. numerous articles to profl. and sci. jours.; editor, author various monographs, video and audio prodns. Recipient awards, honors and rsch. grants including Bank Am. Fine Arts award, 1963, Millberry Art award, 1970, Nat. Rsch. Svc. award Nat. Heart, Lung and Blood Inst., 1972-77, Young Investigator award Acad. Clin. Lab. Physicians and Scientists, 1982, 83, Nuclear Magnetic Resonance award U. Calif., Davis, 1984-88; S.A. Pepper Collegiate scholar, 1963; fellow Stanford U., 1967-68, Internat. scholar MOP, Venezuela, 1967, NIH, 1970, Highest Honor Calif. Scholarship Fedn.; grantee Am. Heart Assn., U. Calif., Davis, Lawrence Livermore Nat. Lab., others. Mem. Sigma Xi, Phi Kappa Phi, Mu Alpha Theta.

KOSTER, ANDRIES SJOERD, pharmacologist; b. Apeldoorn, Veluwe, The Netherlands, July 1, 1952; s. Sjoerd and Maria (Van Werven) K. BS in Biology, U. Utrecht, 1973, MS in Exptl. Devel. Biology, 1979, PhD in Pharmacology, 1985. Registered pharmacologist, The Netherlands. Teaching asst. Fac. of Pharmacy U. Utrecht, 1979-81, researcher Fac. of Pharmacy, 1981-85, asst. prof. pharmacology Fac. Pharmacy, 1985—. Author 24 sci. publs.; co-author 28 sci. publs.; editor: Intestinal Metabolism of Xenobiotics, 1989. Fellow Dutch Inst. Biologists; mem. Dutch Soc. Pharmacology, Dutch Soc. Lab. Animal Sci., Dutch Soc. Pharm. Scis., Dutch Soc. Immunology, European Soc. Biochem. Pharmacology. Office: Dept Pharmacology Fac Pharmacy, PO Box 80082, 3508 TB Utrecht The Netherlands

KOSTER, KAREN ANN, operating room nurse; b. Corinth, N.Y., Sept. 1, 1960; 1 child, Danielle Marie. AAS in Nursing, Adirondack C.C., 1982; Flight Nurse, Sch. of Aerospace Medicine, San Antonio, 1986. Cert. ACLS. Staff nurse ICU Ellis Hosp., Schenectady, N.Y., 1982-87; staff nurse open heart recovery Albany (N.Y.) Med. Ctr. Hosp., 1987-89; staff nurse oper. rm./post anesthesia care unit Glens Falls (N.Y.) Hosp., 1989-93, staff nurse day surg. unit, outpatient orthopedics/ophthaml., 1993—. Mem. AORN, Am. Soc. Ophthalmic Registered Nurses, Rotary (pres. 1996—). Roman Catholic. Home: 214 Walnut St Corinth NY 12822-1224

KOSTERE, KIM MARTIN, psychologist; b. Detroit, Jan. 22, 1954; d. Walter Thomas and Shirley Marian (Goebel) K. BA, Mercy Coll., 1977; MA, Ctr. Humanistic Studies, Detroit, 1983; PsyS, Ctr. Humanistic Studies, 1986; PhD, Union Inst., Cin., 1989. Therapist Metro T.A.G., Livonia, Mich., 1978-81, Highland Waterford Ctr., Waterford, Mich., 1981-83; psychologist, v.p. substance abuse svcs. Square Lake Counseling Ctr., Bloomfield Hills, Mich., 1983-90; psychologist, co-dir. Counseling Ctr., P. C., Bloomfield Hills, Mich., 1991—; co-founder, dir. Ont. (Can.) NLP Inst., 1979-80. Author: A Brief Account of the Center for Humanistic Studies, 1987; co-author: Get the Results You Want, 1987, Maps, Models and the Structure of Reality, 1989, Utilizing the Metaphor: An Ericksonian/NLP Approach, 1992. Democrat. Roman Catholic.

KOSTICH, SHIRLEY ANN, health services administrator; b. Milw., June 3, 1944; d. Ferdinand and Vetial (Burbey) Homan; m. Nikola Peter Kostich, May 28, 1969; children: Natasha and Aleksandar. BS, U. Wis., 1967. Case worker social svcs. Unicare, Milw., 1967-69; cons. residential care Unicare, Madison, Wis., 1969-70; with after care team Med. Coll. Wis./Milw. County, 1979-80; administrv. coord. med. svcs. Milw. County Mental Health Complex, 1981—; coordinator Am. Bd. Psychiat. and Neurology Oral Exams, Milw. 1986; cons. seminar Alliance Mentally Ill, Milw. 1985-86. Editor Newsletter Mental Health Complex, 1986—. Chmn. Shorewood (Wis.) High Sch. Post Prom Com., 1986; pres. adv. coun. sexual assault treatment ctr. Good Samaritan Med. Ctr., 1987—; coord. Milwaukee County Mental Health Complex campaign United Way, 1986-89. Recipient Silver award, Chmn.'s award, Leadership award, Gold award, Lifetime Achievement award United Way, 1996. Mem. NAFE, NOW, Eidotr's Forum (Nat. Competition award), Nat. Assn. Med. Staff Svcs. Serbian Orthodox. Home: 3715 N Lake Dr Milwaukee WI 53211-2647 Office: Milw County Mental Health Complex 9455 W Watertown Plank Rd Milwaukee WI 53226-3559

KOSTICK, RICHARD JOHNSON, radiologist; b. Mpls., Jan. 14, 1944; s. Raymond Francis and Ruby Gunila (Johnson) K.; m. Barbara Blake Hughes, Sept. 8, 1972; children: Karen Elizabeth, Richard Hughes. BA, U. Minn., 1964, MD, 1968. Diplomate Am. Bd. Radiology, Am. Bd. Nuclear Medicine. Intern Harbor Gen. Hosp., Torrance, Calif., 1968-69; resident in radiology U. Minn. Hosp., Mpls., 1969-72; radiologist Washington Radiologists Med. Group, Inc., Fremont, Calif., 1975—. Maj. U.S. Army, 1973-74, Okinawa, Japan. Mem. Am. Coll. Radiology, Radiological Soc. N.Am., Soc. Nuclear Medicine, Calif. Med. Assn., Calif. Radiological Soc., Alameda-Contra Costa Med. Assn., Alpha Omega Alpha. Republican. Episcopalian. Office: Washington Radiologists Med 2000 Mowry Ave Fremont CA 94538

KOSTIS, JOHN BASIL, cardiologist; b. Yannina, Greece, June 14, 1936; came to U.S., 1964; s. Basil John and Vasiliki Ilia (Masouras) K.; m. Barbara Charleston, June, 1969; children: William Jason, Steven Lawrence. MD, U. Salonica, Greece, 1960; student, USAF Sch. Aerospace Medicine, 1963, U. Pa., 1967-68. Diplomate Am. Bd. Internal Medicine, subspecialty cardiovascular disease. Resident internal medicine Evangelismos Hosp., 404 Gen. Hosp., Athens and Larissa, Greece, 1963-64; intern Bklyn.-Cumberland Med. Ctr., 1964-65, med. resident, 1965-67; fellow cardiology Phila. Gen. Hosp., 1967-69; instr. physiology and aviation medicine Sch. Aviation Medicine, Athens, 1969-70; assoc. clin. medicine, asst. prof. medicine U. Pa., Phila., 1971-72; assoc. prof. Coll. Medicine and Dentistry N.J.-Rutgers Med. Sch., New Brunswick, 1972-76; chief cardiology Robert Wood Johnson U. Hosp., New Brunswick, 1980—; adj. prof. biomed. engring. Rutgers U. Coll. Engring., Piscataway, N.J., 1975—, Grad. Sch. Biomed. Engring., 1976—; prof. medicine U. Medicine and Dentistry N.J.-Robert Wood Johnson Med. Sch., New Brunswick, 1976—, chief div. cardiovascular disease, 1982-84, chief div. cardiovascular disease and hypertension, 1984—, prof. pharmacology, 1986—, John G. Detwiler prof. cardiology, 1987—, chmn. dept. medicine, 1990—; cons. pharm. industry. Co-editor: Essentials of Cardiovascular Diagnosis, 1984, Beta Blockers in the Treatment of Cardiovascular Disease, 1984, The Pharmacological Treatment of Cardiovascular Diseases, 1986, Angiotensin Converting Enzyme Inhibitors, 1987, The Prevention of Sudden Cardiac Death, 1990; mem. editorial bds. Am. Jour. Cardiology, Am. Jour. Noninvasive Cardiology, Am. Jour. Cardiology, Clin. Therapeutics, Cardiovascular Drug Reviews, others; co-inventor device noninvasive diagnostic system for coronary artery disease. Grantee pharm. industry, NHLBI, NIH, NIA. Fellow ACP, Am. Coll. Cardiology; mem. Am. Heart Assn. (disting. leadership in rsch. award 1986), Assn. U. Cardiologists, Am. Coll. Angiology, Am. Coll. Chest Physicians, Am. Soc. Hypertension, Internat. Soc. Hypertension, Assn. Profs. of Medicine, Assn. Profs. Cardiology. Office: U Med and Dentistry Robt Wood Johnson Med Sch 1 Robert Wood Johnson Pl # 19 New Brunswick NJ 08901-1928

KOSTRZEWA, RICHARD MICHAEL, pharmacology educator; b. Trenton, N.J., July 22, 1943; s. John Walter and Wladyslosa (Wnuk) K.; m. Florence Agnes Palmer, Sept. 4, 1965; children: Theresa, Richard, Joseph, Maria, Krystyna, Thomas, John Palmer, Francis, Roseanna, Monica. BS, Phila. Coll. Pharmacy and Sci., 1965, MS, 1967; PhD, U. Pa., 1971. Rsch. pharmacologist VA Hosp., New Orleans, 1971-75; asst. prof. pharmacology Tulane Med. Ctr.-New Orleans, 1972-76; asst. prof. physiology La. State U. Med. Center-New Orleans, 1975-78; assoc. prof., then prof. pharmacology East Tenn. State U. Med. Sch.-Johnson City, 1978—. Mem. exec. com. Appalachian March of Dimes, Johnson City, Tenn., 1980-88. Recipient Research award East Tenn. State U. Found., 1981. Mem. Am. Soc. Pharmacology, Soc. Neurosci., Internat. Brain Rsch. Orgn. Roman Catholic. Author: Pharmacology, 1995; mem. editorial adv. bd.: Peptides, 1980—; contbr. sci. articles to profl. publs. Achievements include NIMH project on tardive dyskinesia, Scottish Rite project on schizophrenia. Office: East Tenn State Univ P O Box 70577 Johnson City TN 37614

KOSTY, MICHAEL PAUL, oncologist, educator; b. South Bend, Ind., Sept. 17, 1950; s. Michael Peter and Irene Wanda (Czaskowski) K.; m. Antonette Christine Leone, May 18, 1980; children: Michael Phillip, Allison Elizabeth. BS, U. Calif., Berkeley, 1972, MA, 1975; MD, George Washington U., 1979. Commd. ensign USN, 1979, advanced through grades to comdr., 1988, resigned, 1989; intern U.S. Naval Hosp., San Diego, 1979-80, resident in internal medicine, 1981-83, fellow divsn. hematology/oncology, 1983-86, asst. head divsn. hematology/oncology, 1986-89; med. officer USS Belleau Wood, 1980-81; resigned USN, 1989; staff oncologist divsn. hematology and oncology Scripps Clinic and Rsch. Found., La Jolla, Calif., 1989—, assoc. dir. edn./tng. Ida M. & Cecil H. Green Cancer Ctr., 1992—; clin. investigator Cancer and Leukemia Group B, 1988—, clin. asst. prof. U. dept. internal medicine U. Calif., San Diego, 1986—. Contbr. articles to profl. jours. Capt. USNR. Mem. ACP, Am. Soc. Hematology, Am. Soc. Clin. Oncology, Phi Beta Kapa, Tau Beta Pi. Democrat. Office: Scripps Clinic and Rsch Found Divsn Hematology Oncology 10666 N Torrey Pines Rd La Jolla CA 92037-1027

KOSZEWSKI, BOHDAN JULIUS, internist, medical educator; b. Warsaw, Poland, Dec. 17, 1918; Came to U.S., 1952; s. Mikolaj and Helen (Lubienski) K.; children Mikolaj, Joseph, Wanda Marie, Andrzej Bohdan. MD, U. Zurich, Switzerland, 1946; MS, Creighton U., 1956. Resident in pathology U. Zurich, 1944-46, resident in internal medicine, 1946-50, assoc. in medicine, 1950-52; intern St. Mary's Hosp., Hoboken, N.J., 1953; practice medicine specializing in internal medicine Omaha, 1956-90; mem. staff St. Joseph's Hosp., Mercy and Meth. Hosps.; instr. internal medicine Creighton U., 1956-57, asst. prof., 1957-65, assoc. prof. internal medicine, 1965-90; cons. hematology Omaha VA Hosp., 1957-90. Author: Prognosis in Diabetic Coma, 1952; contbr. numerous articles to profl. jours. Served with Polish Army, 1940-45. Fellow ACP, Am. Coll. Angiology; mem. AAAS, Am. Fedn. Clin. Research, Internat. Soc. Hematology, Polish-Am. Congress Nebr. (pres. 1960-68, 82-92). Home: 2901 Park Place Dr Lincoln NE 68506-2818 Office: Lincoln Ctr Bldg Lincoln NE 68542

KOTB, MAMDOUH MOHAMED, surgeon, consultant; b. Damanhour, Egypt, Oct. 19, 1952; s. Mohamed Kotb and Soad Ahmed Abdelgaphar; m. Salwa Mahmoud Ashour; children: Ahmed, Mohamed, Aiyl. MBChB, Faculty Medicine, Alexandria, Egypt, 1976, MS in Surgery, 1980, MD in Surgery, 1989. House officer Alexandria U., 1977-78, resident surgery, 1978-81, asst. lectr. surgery, 1981-89, lectr. surgery, 1989-95, asst. prof. surgery, 1995—; fellow vascular surgery NCMH, Chapel Hill, N.C., 1983-85; cons. vascular surgeon health ins. Damanhour, Egyp, 1990—, Mebara Hosp., Damanhour, 1990—. Office: Faculty Medicine, Alazza Ritta, Alexandria Egypt

KOTESKEY, RONALD LYNN, psychology educator; b. Petoskey, Mich., Mar. 15, 1942; s. Ronald Edward and Bessie Elizabeth (Belknap) K.; m. Bonita Rose Gill, June 22, 1964; children: Keith, Cheryl, Kent. BA, Asbury Coll., 1963; MA, Wayne State U., 1966, PhD, 1967. Asst. prof. Greenville (Ill.) Coll., 1967-70; assoc. prof. Asbury Coll., Wilmore, Ky., 1970-77, prof., 1977—. Author: Psychology from a Christian Perspective, 1980, General Psychology for Christian Counselors, 1983, Understanding Adolescence, 1987, The Love Triangle, 1989, Psychology from a Christian Perspective, 1991. Vice pres., pres. Jessamine County 4-H Coun., Nicholasville, Ky., 1978-82; mem. adminstrv. bd. United Meth. Ch., Wilmore, 1980-92. Fellow Am. Sci. Affiliation; mem. APA, Midwestern Psychol. Assn., Ky. Psychol. Assn., Christian Assn. for Psychol. Studies, Soc. for Sci. Study of Religion, Ky. Assn. Profl. Educators. Republican. Office: Asbury Coll 1 Macklem Dr Wilmore KY 40390-1152

KOTHERA, LYNNE MAXINE, clinical psychologist; b. Cleve., Dec. 18, 1938; d. Leonard Frank and Lillian (Shackleton) K.; m. Richard Litwin, Oct. 24, 1965 (dec.). BA with hons., Denison U., Granville, Ohio, 1960; MA, NYU, 1983; PhD, L.I. U., Bklyn., 1989; postgrad. psychotherapy/psychoanalysis, NYU, 1992—. Dancer Martha Graham Dance Co., N.Y.C., 1961-62, Carmen DeLavallade Dance Co., N.Y.C., 1965-68, Glen Tetley Dance Co., N.Y.C., 1965-69; prin. dancer John Butler's, N.Y.C., 1971; artist-in-residence Boston High Schs. - Title III, 1969-71, Hobart-Smith Coll./Denison U., 1973; auditor N.Y. State Council of the Arts, N.Y.C., 1974-78; predoctoral fellow clin. psychology Yale-New Haven Hosp., 1987-88; postdoctoral fellow neuropsychology Inst. of Living, Hartford, Conn., 1989-91; with dept. rehab. medicine Mt. Sinai Med. Ctr., N.Y.C., 1991—, co-dir. tng. in-patient, 1995—. Mem. APA (divsn. 39, 40, 42 and 49), Internat. Neuropsychol. Soc. Democrat. Home: 23 E 11th St New York NY 10003-4450 Office: Mt Sinai Med Ctr Rehab Med KCC-365-G PO Box 1674 1 Gustave Levy Pl New York NY 10029

KOTILAINEN, HELEN JEAN ROSEN, infection control epidemmiologist, researcher; b. Boston, July 1, 1954; d. Theodore Paul and Dorothy Mary (Alex) Rosen; m. Peter Wayne Kotilainen, June 22, 1975; children: Aaron, Hillary. BS, Worcester Poly. Inst., 1975; MA, Clark U., 1978. Cert. in infection control Bd. Infection Control; cert. med. tech. Am. Soc. Clin. Pathology; cert. clin. lab. scientist Nat. Cert. Agy. Med. Lab. Profls. Sr. rsch. assoc. U. Mass. Med. Ctr., Worcester, 1976-80, epidemiologist, infection control, 1980-88, clin. coord./lab. dir. infection control, 1988-92; mgr., infection control Med. Ctr. Ctrl. Mass., Worcester, 1992-96, dir. measurement, clin. process improvement, 1996—; cons. 3M Co, Calgon, Mass. Dept. Pub. Health, FDA, 1984—; mem. guidelines com. Assn. Profs. Infection Control, Washington, 1992. Editl. bd. Am. Jour. Infection Control, 1987—; editor APIC News, 1995-96. Sec., parents' adv. coun., Nashoba Sch. Dist., Bolton, Mass., 1994-95. Recipient grants Program Healthcare Innovation, 1992, FDA, 1989. Mem. Am. Soc. Microbiology, Assn. Infection Control Dirs., Assn. Advancement Med. Instruments, Soc. Healthcare Epidemiol. of Am., Mass. Pub. Health Assn. Office: Med Ctr Ctrl Mass Clin Process Improvement 119 Belmont St Worcester MA 01605-2903

KOTIN, PAUL, pathologist; b. Chgo., Aug. 13, 1916; s. Elias and Rose (Spunt) K.; m. Pauline H. Stephan, Dec. 12, 1970; children: Joel Tepper, David Bernard. B.S., U. Ill., 1937, M.D., 1940. Intern Deaconess Hosp., Chgo., 1939-40; resident pathology Deaconess Hosp., 1940-41; pvt. practice pathology and internal medicine San Luis Obispo, Calif., 1946-48; researcher pathology U. So. Calif., 1949-50; med. microbiologist Los Angeles County Hosp., 1950-51, attending staff pathologist, 1951-62; mem. faculty U. So. Calif., 1951-62, prof. pathology, 1959-60, Paul Pierce prof. pathology, 1960-62; chief carcinogenesis studies br. Nat. Cancer Inst., 1962-63, asso. dir. for field studies, 1963-64, sci. dir. for etiology, 1964-66; dir. div. environ. health scis. NIH, 1966-69; dir. Nat. Inst. Environ. Health Scis., 1969-71; v.p. for health scis., dean Sch. Medicine, Temple U., Phila., 1971-74; sr. v.p. health, safety and environment Johns-Manville Corp., 1974-81; Edgar Allen Meml. lectr. Yale Sch. Medicine, 1957; vis. prof. oncology U. Wis., 1959-60; vis. prof. pathology U. N.C., also Duke U., 1967-71; Harry Shay Meml. lectr. Temple U., 1964; Sappington Meml. lectr. Am. Occupational Medicine Assn., Anaheim, Calif., 1979, Gehrmann lectr., Nashville, 1981; chmn. Gordon Research Conf. Cancer, 1965; adj. prof. pathology U. Colo., 1974—; Cons. air pollution med. program, div. spl. health service USPHS, 1958-62; mem. sci. adv. bd. Council Tobacco Research-U.S.A., 1952-65; adv. com. r.r. diesel gases and dust Calif. Pub. Utilities Commn., 1956-62; adv. com. research pathogenesis cancer Am. Cancer Soc., 1962-65; pathology study sect. NIH, 1962-66, lung cancer task force, 1967-68; corr. mem. permanent European com. Research Chronic Hazards, 1960—; cancer prevention com. UICC, 1962-66, com. on exptl. design and methodology in carcinogenesis, 1967-70; sci. com. Inst. Occupational and Environ. Health, Quebec. Asbestos Mining Assn., 1966-75; mem. Fed. Com. Pest Control, 1964-71; program com. Tenth Internat. Congress, 1967-70; mem. Expert Panel on Carcinogenicity, 1962-70, Nat. Environ. Health Scis. Center, 1965, Nat. Adv. Com. Occupational Safety and Health, 1975-78, Armed Forces Epidemiol. Bd., 1976-80. Editorial adv. bd.: Cancer Research, 1957-61, Internat. Rev. Exptl. Pathology, 1968—; editorial bd.: AMA Archives Pathology, 1965-71, Environ. Research, 1966—, Am. Jour. Pathology, 1971-82; Contbr. articles to med. jours. Served with AUS, 1941-46. Recipient Superior Service award HEW, 1966, Disting. Service award, 1969; Sr. postdoctoral fellow NSF, 1959-60; named Alumnus of Yr. U. Ill. Coll. of Medicine, 1990. Fellow Coll. Am. Pathologists, N.Y. Acad. Scis., Am. Acad. Occupational Medicine; mem. AMA (com. research on tobacco and health 1966-78), Am. Assn. Cancer Research (dir.), Am. Assn. Pathologists and Bacteriologists, AAAS, Am. Indsl. Hygiene Assn. (hon.), Am. Occupational Medicine Assn.

(Knudsen award 1981), Sigma Xi, Alpha Omega Alpha. Home: 2304 E Sausalito Trail Tucson AZ 85737

KOTIS, ANDREW, surgeon; b. Chgo., May 11, 1958; s. Nick and Athanasia (Rizopoulous) K. BA, Northeastern Ill. U., 1980, MS, 1982; DO, Chgo. Coll. Osteo. Medicine, 1991. Exercise physiologist Cook County Hosp., Chgo., 1982-83; coord. sports medicine dept. Olympia Fields (Ill.) Osteo. Hosp., 1983-87; intern Chgo. Osteo. Hosps., 1987-94, cardiology fellow, 1994—. Mem. Am. Osteo. Assn., Am. Coll. Osteo. Internists, Am. Coll. Cardiology (affiliate), Am. Coll. Chest Physicians. Office: Midwestern U 555 31st St Downers Grove IL

KOTKOV, BENJAMIN, clinical psychologist; b. Boston, Apr. 8, 1910; s. Moses and Annie (Hopner) K.; m. Sally B., Jan. 28, 1941; children: Ralph, Frank. AB, Cornell U., 1929; MA, Harvard U., 1934; PhD, Ottawa U., Ont., Can., 1954. Diplomate Am. Bd. Clin. Psychology, Am. Bd. Med. Psychotherapists, Am. Bd. Disability Cons.; cert. clin. hypnosis Am. Soc. Clin. Hypnosis. Staff to chief Nerve Clinic, New Eng. Med. Ctr., Boston, 1934-42, VA Mental Hygiene Unit, Boston, 1946-52; chief psychologist Mental Hygiene Clinics, State of Del., 1952-53; clin. exec. Child Guidance Ctr., Brattleboro, Vt., 1954-64; staff to prof. and faculty head Windham Coll., Putney, Vt., 1964-76; pvt. practice psychology, Brattleboro, 1976—; internat. adv. bd. Acad. of Psychoanalysis, Germany, 1969—. Contbr. numerous articles to profl. jours. Lt. U.S. Army, 1942-46. NSF grantee, 1956, 57; recipient Editor's award Internat. Jour. Profl. Hypnosis, 1977, medallion Acad. Psychosmatic Medicine, 1979, Membership Leader award Vt. Lions, 1993-94. Fellow Am. Psychol. Soc., Internat. Soc. Profl. Hypnosis, Acad. Sci. Hypnotherapy, Am. Assn. Applied and Prevention Psychology, Acad. Clin. Psychology; mem. AAUP (emeritus), APA (life), Soc. Personality Assessment (life), Vt. Psychol. Assn. (pres. 1968-69, chmn. cert. bd. 1974-76), New Eng. Soc. Clin. Hypnosis (pres. 1988), DAV (life), Lions (pres. 1973-74, 84-85, 94—), Elks. Home and Office: 8 Orchard St Box 70 Brattleboro VT 05301

KOTLER, JOHN MICHAEL, psychologist; b. L.A., July 28, 1957; s. Howard Norman Kotler and Lois Jane (Arkush) Spector; m. Debra Lynn Hurt, June 17, 1988; children: Kathryn Rose. BA, U. Calif., 1979; MA, Calif. Sch. Profl. Psychology, 1983, PhD, 1989. Lic. psychologist. Psychologist Ctrl. Valley Regional Ctr., Visalia, Calif., 1988-90; clin. psychologist Calif. Dept. Edn., Fresno, 1990-95; adj. prof. Fresno City Coll., 1989-95. Mem. Am. Autism Soc. (v.p. ctrl. Calif. chpt. 1993-95, disting. svc. award 1994). Office: Diagnostic Ctr 1818 W Ashlan Ave Fresno CA 93705

KOTLER, JON ALLEN, physician, researcher; b. Bridgeton, N.J., Dec. 16, 1949; s. Herbert and Idella Kotler; m. Anita Paoli; children: Jillian, Joshua. BA, U. Pa., 1972; MD, Emory U., 1976. Diplomate Am. Bd. Internal Medicine, Am. Bd. Nuclear Medicine. Intern Tufts U. Affiliated Hosps., Boston, 1976-77; resident U. Hawaii, 1977-79; nuclear medicine resident U. Wash., 1980-82; instr. radiology U. Ariz., Tucson, 1982-84, asst. prof., 1984-85, asst.prof. medicine, 1984-85; asst. chief nuclear medicine VA Med. Ctr., Tucson, 1983-85, attending physician internal medicine, 1983-85; dir. nuc. medicine Cleveland Clin. Fla., 1988-90, dir. internal medicine, 1989-90; clin. asst. prof. radiology U. Miami Jackson Meml. Hosp., 1985—; dir. nuclear medicine Holy Cross Hosp., Ft. Lauderdale, 1990—; spkr. in field. Contbr. articles to profl. jours. Mem. AMA, Am. Coll. Nuclear Physicians, Am. Coll. Physicians, Fla. Med. Assn. Ariz. Nuclear Medicine Physicians (sec.-treas. 1984-85, program chmn. ann. mtg. 1985), Broward County Med. Assn., Soc. Nuclear Medicine (mem. sci. exhibits subcom. 1984). Office: Holy Cross Hosp 4725 N Federal Hwy Fort Lauderdale FL 33308

KOTLER, RONALD LEE, physician, educator; b. Pitts., June 10, 1956; s. Milton and Marion (Oppenheimer) K.; m. Jane Ellyn Cobin, Feb. 20, 1982; children: Jennifer, Rachel, Drew. BA, Emory U., 1978; MD, U. Pa., 1982. Diplomate Am. Bd. Internal Medicine, Am. Bd. Pulmonary Disease, Am. Bd. Critical Care Medicine. Intern Pa. Hosp., Phila., 1982-83, resident, 1983-85; fellow pulmonary disease Hosp. U. Pa, Phila., 1985-87; clin. assoc. in medicine U. Pa. Sch. Medicine, Phila., 1987-88, clin. asst. prof., 1988-95; clin. asst. prof. Thomas Jefferson U., Phila., 1994—; co-dir. hosp. sleep lab. Pa. Hosp., Phila., 1991—. Contbr. articles to profl. jours. Lectr. City Phila. Dept. Health, Phila., 1988, 89, Pa. Hosp., 1995. Fellow ACP, Am. Coll. Chest Physicians; mem. Am. Thoracic Soc., Phi Beta Kappa, Omicron Delta Kapp, Alpha Omega Alpha. Office: Casey Lugano Kotler Assocs 700 Spruce St Ste 500 Philadelphia PA 19106

KOTTAMASU, MOHAN RAO, physician; b. Gudivada, India, Jan. 13, 1947; came to U.S., 1973; s. Janardana Rao and Kantharatnamma (Maddi) K.; m. Sarada Devi Vusirikala, Dec. 20, 1992; 1 child, Pallavi. MBBS, Gulbarga Med. Coll., 1972. House surgeon Govt. Gen. Hosp., Gulbarga, India, 1971-72; intern St. Vincent's Med. Ctr. of Richmond, S.I., N.Y., 1973-74, resident, 1974-76, chief resident, 1976-77; pulmonary diseases fellow Deaconess Hosp., Boston, 1977-79; clin. fellow Harvard Med. Sch., Boston, 1978-79; assoc. Valley Pulmonary and Med. Assocs., Springfield, Mass., 1979-81, ptnr., v.p., 1981—; adj. asst. prof. clin. pharmacy Mass. Coll. Pharmacy and Allied Health Scis., 1984—. Pres. house staff St. Vincent's Med. Ctr., 1976; founding pres. Indian Assn. Greater Springfield, 1985-86; pres. med. staff Mercy Hosp., Springfield, 1989-91. Fellow Am. Coll. Physicians, Am. Coll. Chest Physicians; mem. Am. Thoracic Soc., Mass. Med. Soc. Hindu. Home: 112 Twin Hills Dr Longmeadow MA 01106-2952 Office: Valley Pulmonary Med Assocs 222 Carew St Springfield MA 01104-4103

KOTTLER, RONALD, psychotherapist, social worker; b. Pitts., Oct. 17, 1934; s. I.B. and Ethel (Caplan) K.; m. Jean Elaine Rosenbloom, Mar. 30, 1958; 1 child, Bruce S. AB, U. Pitts., 1958, MSW, 1960. Lic. social worker, Pa. Sr. clin. social worker VA, Erie, Pa., 1960-62, Bay Pines, Fla., 1962-65; dir. Protestant Home for Children/Pressley Ridge Sch., Pitts., 1965-70; adminstr. Staunton Clinic Sewickley (Pa.) Valley Hosp., 1970-82; exec. dir. Jewish Family and Children's Svc., Pitts., 1982-90; pvt. practice Sewickley, 1990—; pres. Bickur Cholim Convalescent & Nursing Home Found., Pitts., 1982—; lectr. Internat. Conf. of Jewish Communal Workers, 1988. Prog. dir. Nat. Assn. Jewish Family and Children's Agys., 1987-88; bd. dirs. U.S. Jewish Family & Children Agys., 1987-90. With U.S. Army, 1954-56. Fellow Am. Orthopsychiat. Assn.; mem. NASW (sec., v.p. 1956-60), United Jewish Fedn., U. Pitts. Sch. of Work Alumni Assn. (pres. 1986-88), U. Pitts. Gen. Alumni Assn. (sec. 1987-88). Democrat. Home: 989 Balmoral Dr Pittsburgh PA 15237-6245

KOTWALL, CYRUS ASPI, surgical oncologist; b. Sept. 1, 1955; came to U.S., 1993; m. Lorna Marie Bell, Apr. 26, 1986; children: Joleen, Benjamin, Ashley. MD, U. Saskatchewan, Can., 1978; MSc, U. Alberta, Can., 1983. Diplomate Am. Bd. Surgery. Tchg. fellow U. Alberta Hosps., 1984-85; fellow head and neck surgery Roswell Park Meml. Inst., Buffalo, 1985-86, fellow surg. oncology, 1986-87; clin. fellow gen. surgery U. Toronto, Can., 1987-88; lectr. in surgery U. Toronto, 1988-91, asst. prof. surgery, 1991-93; attending surgeon St. Michael's Hosp., Toronto, 1988-93; asst. prof. surgery U. N.C., Chapel Hill, 1993—; attending surgeon New Hanover Regional Med. Ctr., Wilmington, N.C., 1993—; cons. dept. surgery Princess Margaret Hosp., Toronto, 1989-93; mem. instl. review bd. New Hanover Regional Med. Ctr., 1994—, oncology adv. com., 1993—, prin. investigator oncology clin. trials, 1995—. Contbr. articles to profl. jours. Recipient Residents Rsch. 1st prize Med. Coll. Ohio, 1980; Med. Rsch. scholar Alberta Heritage Found., 1982-83, Best Clin. Rsch. paper Roswell Park Meml. Inst., 1986. Fellow Royal Coll. Physicians and Surgeons Can., Am. Coll. Surgeons; Am. Soc. Clin. Oncology, Soc. Surg. Oncology, N.C. Am. Coll. Surgeons (com. on cancer), Roswell Park Surg. Soc. Zoroastrian. Office: Coastal Area Health Edn Ctr 2131 S 17th St PO Box 9025 Wilmington NC 28402-9025

KOUBA, STEPHEN HOWARD, orthopedic surgeon; b. Morristown, N.J., Mar. 24, 1954; s. Clarence Vincent and Inez Nadine (Acosta) K.; m. Marsha Lynn, May 23, 1981; children: Jessica, Stephen Jr. BA, Rutgers Coll., 1976; MD, Georgetown U., 1980. Diplomate Am. Bd. Orthopedic Surgery. Intern Walter Reed Med. Ctr., Washington, 1980-81; resident Brooke Army Med. Ctr., San Antonio, 1981-85; orthop. surgeon Cape Fear Valley Med. Ctr., Fayetteville, N.C., 1987—; chmn. orthop. surgery physician asst. program Meth. Coll., Fayetteville, 1996—. Maj. U.S. Army, 1980-87. Mem. AMA, Am. Acad. Orthop. Surgeons, Soc. Mil. Orthop. Surgeons, Cumberland County Med. Soc. Republican. Roman Catholic. Office: Cape Fear Orthop Clinic 1300 Medical Dr Fayetteville NC 28304

KOUCHOUKOS, NICHOLAS THOMAS, surgeon; b. Grand Rapids, Mich., Dec. 26, 1936; s. Thomas Paul and Antoinette (Karver) K.; m. Judith Buell, Aug. 24, 1966; children—Nicholas Thomas, Robert Buell, Thomas Paul. Student (James B. Angell scholar), U. Mich., 1954-57; M.D. cum laude, Washington U., 1961. Diplomat Am. Bd. Thoracic Surgery (bd. dirs. 1989—). Intern Barnes Hosp., Washington U. Med. Ctr., St. Louis, 1961-62; asst. resident in surgery Barnes Hosp., Washington U. Med. Ctr., 1962-65, chief adminstrv. resident, 1965-66; sr. clin. trainee in surgery USPHS, 1966-67; asst. in surgery Sch. Medicine Washington U., St. Louis, 1961-65; instr. surgery Sch. Medicine Washington U., 1965-67, John M. Shoenberg prof. cardiovascular surgery, 1984—, vice chmn. dept. surgery, 1993—; research fellow surgery Sch. Medicine, U. Ala., Birmingham, 1967-68; instr. surgery Sch. Medicine, U. Ala., 1967-69, advanced trainee thoracic and cardiovascular surgery, 1968-70, asst. prof. surgery, 1969-71, assoc. prof., 1971-74, prof., vice-dir. div. thoracic and cardiovascular surgery, 1974-81, clin. prof., 1981-84; cardiovascular surgeon-in-chief Jewish Hosp. of St. Louis, 1984—, surgeon in chief, 1988—; mem. cardiovascular research study com. Am. Heart Assn., 1977-79; surgery study sect. USPHS, Bethesda, Md., 1977-80; vice chmn. dept. surgery Washington U. Sch. Medicine, St. Louis, 1991—; ad hoc cons. Specialized Centers in Research Arteriosclerosis, Nat. Heart and Lung Inst., Bethesda, 1971-72, mem. ad hoc rev. com. for collaborative studies on coronary artery surgery, 1973-75, surgery A study sect., 1976-77; mem. merit rev. bd. in cardiovascular studies VA, Washington, 1976-78. Editorial bd. Jour. Cardiac Rehab., 1979-84, Current Topics in Cardiology, 1977-92, Circulation, 1978-81, 86-88, Cardiology Update, 1979-92, Annals Thoracic Surgery, 1980-89, Cardiosat, 1984-92. Fellow ACS, Southeastern Surg. Congress, Am. Coll. Cardiology (finalist Young Investigators award 1962); mem. AMA, AAUP, Am. Assn Thoracic Surgery, Am. Surg. Assn., Assn. Clin. Cardiac Surgeons, Assn. Acad. Surgery, Internat. Surg. Soc., St. Louis Met. Med. Soc., John Kirklin Soc., Soc. Thoracic Surgeons (sec. 1992—), St. Louis Thoracic Surg. Soc. (pres. 1993—), So. Thoracic Surg. Assn., So. Surg. Assn., Soc. Univ. Surgeons, Soc. Vascular Surgery, Internat. Cardiovascular Soc., Phi Beta Kappa, Alpha Omega Alpha. Home: 25 Picardy Ln Saint Louis MO 63124-1606 Office: Jewish Hosp 216 S Kingshighway Blvd Saint Louis MO 63110-1026

KOURI, GUSTAVO PEDRO, virologist; b. Havana, Cuba, Jan. 11, 1936; s. Pedro and Mercedes (Flores) K.; m. Lidia Cardella (div. 1979); children: Lilliam, Vivian, Gustavo; m. Maria G. Guzman, Nov. 25, 1980; 1 child, Pedro. MD, Havana U., 1962; PhD, Nat. Ctr. Sci. Rsch., Havana, 1973; ScD, Charles U., Prague, Czechoslovakia, 1990. Chief virology dept. Nat. Ctr. for Sci. Rsch., Havana, 1965-70, dep. dir., 1965-70; vice-dean med. faculty Havana U., 1970-73, vice rector, 1973-76; nat. dir. for sci. Ministry of Higher Edn., Havana, 1976-78; dir. gen. Tropical Medicine Inst. "Pedro Kouri", Havana, 1979—; dir. WHO Collaborating Ctr. for Biol. Vector Control, Havana, 1990—; temp. advisor Pan Am. and WHO to present; lectr. in field; cons. in field. Contbr. numerous articles to profl. jours. Grantee TDR, 1979, 81, 82, 83, 84, 85, 86, IDRC, 1983, 86, French Govt., 1989; recipient Carlos Finlay Nat. Order and medal Cuban State Coun., 1990, Silver medal Charles U., 1988, Cesar Uribe medal NIH, Colombia, 1991. Fellow Third World Acad. Scis.; mem. AAAS, N.Y. Acad. Sci., Cuban Acad. Sci. (presidium mem. 1978), Real Academia de Medicina y Cirujia de Galicia, Royal Soc. Tropical Medicine Hygiene, Latin Am. Soc. Tropical Medicine (pres.), Cuban Soc. Microbiology and Parasitology (pres. 1980), Latin Am. Soc. Parasitology (pres.), others. Office: Inst Medicina Tropical, Autopista Novia del Mediod, Havana Cuba

KOURY, THOMAS LEO, plastic and reconstructive surgeon, educator; b. Upland, Pa., Nov. 15, 1923; m. Elizabeth Koury; children: Carol Anne, Thomas Edwin, Virginia Lee, Jennifer Elaine. Student, Swarthmore Coll.; DDS magna cum laude, Temple U., 1948, MD, 1952. Diplomate Am. Bd. Plastic Surgery. Intern Temple U. Hosp., Phila., 1952-53; gen. surg. resident Vets. Hosp., Phila., 1953-54; gen. surg. resident Kansas U. Med. Ctr., Kansas City, 1956-57, plastic surg. resident, 1957-59; pvt. practice plastic and reconstructive surgery Silver Spring, Md., 1959—; chief attending plastic surgeon D.C. Maternal Health-Children With Special Needs, Washington, 1963-94; asst. prof. plastic surgery Georgetown U., Washington, 1963—; pres. I Care-Children of The Andes Found., Silver Spring, 1990—; chief plastic surgery Holy Cross Hosp., Silver Spring, 1990-94; lectr. cleft lip and palate and orthognathic surgery Howard U. Orthodontic Sch., Washington, 1982—; lectr. surg. procedures dept. plastic surgery Georgetown U. Med. Sch., Washington, 1963—; surgery tchr., contbr. Naval Hosp. and Hosp. del Ninos, Lima, Peru, 1989—, Hosp. Militar # 3 Cuenca, Ecuador, 1994—. Mem. Woodside Pk. Civic Assn., Silver Spring, 1991. Lt., M.C., USN, 1954-56. Mem. Am. Soc. Plastic and Reconstructive Surgeons, Am. Soc. Maxillo-Facial Surgeons, Am. Cleft Palate-Cranofacial Assn. Office: 9801 Georgia Ave Ste 2-29 Silver Spring MD 20902-5276

KOUSSEFF, BORIS GEORGIEV, geneticist, pediatrician; b. Berlin, Mar. 15, 1935; came to U.S., 1970; s. George Vladimirov and Theodora (Friedrichs) K. MD, Higher Inst. Medicine, Sofia, Bulgaria, 1959. Diplomate Am. Bd. Pediatrics, Am. Bd. Clin. Genetics. Pediatrician Mcp. Hosp., Ichtiman, Bulgaria, 1962-65, Children's Hosp., Bankja, Bulgaria, 1965-68; registrar in neonatology Royal Maternity Hosp., Glasgow, 1968-69; registrar in pediatrics County Hosp., York, Eng., 1970; resident in pediatrics U. Iowa, Iowa City, 1970-71, Albert Einstein Med. Ctr., Phila., 1971-72; fellow in genetics Mt. Sinai Hosp., N.Y.C., 1972-74; dir. Ctr. for Developmentally Disabled Children Queens Hosp., Jamaica, N.Y., 1974-77; dir. genetics So. Ill. U., Springfield, 1978-81, U. South Fla., Tampa, 1981—. Contbr. numerous articles to sci. and profl. jours. Fellow Am. Acad. Pediatrics; mem. AMA, Am. Pediatric Soc., Am. Soc. Human Genetics, Birth Defect and Glin. Genetics. Office: U South Fla Regional Genetics 10770 N 46th St Ste C-900 Tampa FL 33617-3442

KOUW, WILLY ALEXANDER, clinical psychologist; b. Leiden, Netherlands, Dec. 20, 1932; married. Student, U. Leiden, 1956-58; BA in Psychology, McMaster U., Can., 1961; PhD in Psychology, U. Tex., 1965; tng. in transactional analysis with John Gladfelter, 1974-77, tng. in Gestalt therapy with Jim Norwood, 1975-76. Fellow, diplomate Am. Bd. Med. Psychotherapists. Social sci. research assoc. I, II U. Tex., 1961-64, teaching asst., child psychology, 1962-64, spl. instr. in psychology, summer 1963, social sci. research assoc. III, 1964-65; postdoctoral fellow, clin. child psychology, div. child psychiatry U. Tex. Med. Br., 1965-66, asst. prof., dept. neurology and psychiatry, div. child psychiatry, 1966-67; clin. asst. prof. psychology U. Houston, 1966-67; pvt. practice clin. psychology, San Antonio, 1967—; cons. Tex. Dept. Mental Health and Mental Retardation, 1968, San Antonio State Hosp., 1969; clin. asst. prof., dept. psychiatry U. Tex. Med. Sch., San Antonio; workshop cons. multiple impact therapy William Roper Hull Home, Calgary, Alta., Can., 1971; faculty coord. Fielding Inst., Santa Barbara, Calif., 1976—, trustee, 1990-93; bd. dirs. Project MEND, San Antonio, 1993—. Contbr. numerous articles to profl. jours.; also book revs., study guides, abstracts. Fellow Bexar County Psychol. Assn.; mem. Am. Psychol. Assn., Bexar County Psychology Assn. (pres. 1970-72), Acad. of Psychologists in Marital, Sex and Family Therapy (clin. mem. 1979—), Team-Family Methods Assn., Acad. Family Mediators (assoc.), Am. Group Psychotherapy Assn. Inc., Internat. Assn. Group Psychotherapy, World Fedn. for Mental Health.

KOVACH, BARBARA ELLEN, management and psychology educator; b. Ann Arbor, Mich., Dec. 28, 1941; d. Harry Arnold and Margaret Mayne (Buell) Lusk; m. Craig Randall Duncan, Dec. 28, 1963 (div. 1973); children: Deborah Louise, Mark Randall; m. Randall Louis Kovach, May 2, 1981; 1 child, Jennifer Elizabeth. BA magna cum laude, Stanford U., 1963, MA, 1964; PhD, U. Md., 1973. Asst. prof. psychology U. Mich., Dearborn, 1973-77, assoc. prof., 1977-82, prof., 1982-84, chair Dept. Behavioral Scis., 1980-83; dean Univ. Coll. Rutgers U., New Brunswick, N.J., 1984-88, prof. mgmt. and psychology, 1984—, dir. leadership devel. program, 1988—; pres. Leadership Devel. Inst., Princeton, N.J., 1990—; cons. Rochester (N.Y.) Products-GM, Grand Rapids, Mich., 1982-87, Ford Motor Co., Dearborn, 1981-82, Mich. Bell Telephone, 1980-81, Rockwell Internat., Troy, Mich, 1993—, Johnson & Johnson, 1995—. Author: Sex Roles and Personal Awareness, 1978, 90, Power and Love, 1982, Organizational Synch, 1983, Adolescent Experience, 1983, The Flexible Organization, 1984, Survival on the Fast Track, 1988, 93, Organization Gameboard, 1989, Leaders in Place, 1994, More About Survival on the Fast Track, 1996; producer (videotape series) Keys to Leadership I, 1991-93, II, 1993-94, III, 1995-96; contbr. articles to profl. jours.. Daniel E. Prescott fellow U. Md., 1972; recipient Susan B. Anthony and Faculty Recognition awards U. Mich., 1980. Mem. Am. Psychol. Assn., Acad. Mgmt., Organizational Devel. Network, Phi Beta Kappa. Republican. Episcopalian. Home: 95 Cuyler Rd Princeton NJ 08540-3460 Office: Rutgers U Sch of Bus New Brunswick NJ 08903

KOVACHY, EDWARD MIKLOS, JR., psychiatrist; b. Cleve., Dec. 3, 1946; s. Edward Miklos and Evelyn Amelia (Palenscar) K.; m. Susan Eileen Light, June 21, 1981; children: Timothy Light, Benjamin Light. BA, Harvard U., 1968, JD, 1972, MBA, 1972; MD, Case Western Reserve U., 1977. Diplomate Nat. Bd. Med. Examiners. Resident in psychiatry Stanford U. Med. Ctr., Stanford, Calif., 1977-81; pvt. practice psychiatry mediator mgmt. cons. Menlo Park, Calif., 1981—; mediator, mgmt. cons. Columnist The Peninsula Times Tribune, 1983-85. Bd. trustees Mid Peninsula H.S., Palo Alto, Calif., 1990—; mem. gift com. Harvard Coll. Class of 1968, 25th reunion chmn. participation, San Francisco, 1993. Mem. Am. Psychiat. Assn., Physicians for Social Responsibility, Assn. Family and Conciliation Cts., No. Calif. Psychiat. Soc., San Francisco Acad. Hypnosis. Presbyterian. Office: 1187 University Dr Menlo Park CA 94025-4423

KOVACS, COLLEEN RAE, speech pathologist; b. Ravenna, Ohio, June 16, 1951; d. Ray W. and Helen M. (Benich) Braden; m. John Stephen Kovacs, June 19, 1976. BS, Ohio State U., 1973, MA, 1982; cert. in supervision, Millersville U., 1988; postgrad., Widener U., 1989-90. Cert. clin. competence-speech pathology, Pa., Md. Speech-lang. pathologist Loudonville (Ohio) Perrysville Schs., 1973-76, Pickaway County MR-DD Program, Circleville, Ohio, 1976-83, Lancaster-Lebanon Intermediate Unit 13, East Petersburg, Pa., 1983-90; supr. speech pathology RICA, Balt., 1990-91; speech pathologist Hartford County Pub. Schs., 1991—. Mem. ASCD, Am. Speech and Hearing Assn., Md. Speech and Hearing Assn., Speech Pathologists of Harford County, Phi Kappa Phi. Address: 1716 Sable Ct Bel Air MD 21014-6217

KOVACS, GAIL LOUISE PATEK, business administrator, consultant, nurse, biologist; b. Cleve., Feb. 17, 1949; d. Louis Cornelius and Veronica Rose (Skerl) Patek; m. John Joseph Kovacs, June 24, 1972 (div.); 1 child, Jeffrey Joseph. BA in Biology cum laude, Ursuline Coll., 1971; RN, Cleve. Met. Sch. Nursing, 1975; MBA magna cum laude, Cleve. State U., 1982. Med. technologist Cleve. Clinic Found., 1971-72; immunology rsch. asst. Case Western Res. U., Cleve., 1972-73; staff nurse Mt. Sinai Hosp., Cleve., 1975-76; staff nurse Cleve. Met. Gen. Hosp., 1976, infectious disease nurse, 1976-78; assoc. dir. supply services Univ. Hosps of Cleve., 1978-79, asst. dir. material mgmt., 1979, adminstrv. assoc., 1979-80, assoc. dir. material mgmt., 1980-84, asst. gen. mgr. adminstrn., 1984-87; dir. ops. Meridia Health Ventures, Inc., 1988-91; v.p. Meridia Euclid Hosp., Euclid, Ohio, 1991-95, corporate dir., 1995-96; mgr. healthcare consulting Ernst & Young, Cleve., 1996—; lectr. mgmt., epidemiology and material mgmt.; mem. (4) bd. dirs. Mem. rsch. bd. advisors Am. Biog. Inst. Recipient Paul Widman Meml. award Ctr. Health Affairs/Greater Cleve. Hosp. Assn., 1985; Cleve. Found. grantee, 1980-81. Mem. Am. Coll. Health Care Execs. (diplomate), Health Care Adminstrs. Assn. N.E. Ohio, Healthcare Fin. Assn., Lake Erie Orgn. Nurse Execs. (bd. dirs. 1995), Greater Cleve. Hosp. Assn. Nurse Exec. Com., Ohio Nurses Assn., Greater Cleve. Nurses Assn.,Transplantation Soc. of N.E. Ohio, Health Care Fin. Mgmt. Soc., Health Care Material Mgmt. Soc. (v.p.; Presdl. citation 1985), Internat. Material Mgmt. Soc., Soc. for Hosp. Purchasing and Material Mgmt., N.E. Ohio Soc. for Health Care Material Mgmt., Health Action Council, Beta Gamma Sigma. Roman Catholic. Home: 1450 Blossom Park Ave Cleveland OH 44107-4402 Office: Ernst & Young 1300 Huntington Blvd 925 Euclid Ave Cleveland OH 44115

KOVAR, MICHAEL DAVID, psychologist; b. L.A., Apr. 12, 1950; s. David and June Claire (Rosslyn) K.; m. Fay Lee Nienhaus, May 25, 1986; 1 child, Julie. AA, L.A. Valley Coll., 1969; BA, U. Calif. Berkeley, 1971; MA, U. Chgo., 1973; PhD, Loyola U., Chgo., 1983. Lic. clin. psychologist, Ill., lic. psychologist, Wis. Psychologist Ill. Dept. Mental Health, Manteno (Ill.) Mental Health Ctr., 1984-85, Inst. for Juvenile Rsch., Chgo., 1985-90; cons. psychologist Assocs. in Adolescent Psychiatry, Riveredge Hosp., Forest Park, Ill., 1987-92; regional psychologist cons. Social Security Adminstrn, Region V, Chgo., 1988—; pvt. practice in forensic consultation, 1988—. Mem. civil rights com. Anti-Defamation League of Binai B'rith, Chgo., 1986-91. Mem. APA, Am. Coll. Forensic Psychology, Am. Orthopsychiat. Assn. Jewish. Office: 30 N Michigan Ave Ste 1126 Chicago IL 60602

KOWAL, KAREN, physician's assistant; b. N.Y.C., Aug. 5, 1956. BS, Rutgers U., 1979. Cert. physician asst., Pa., Conn. Physician's asst. St. Mary's Hosp., Waterbury, Conn., 1979-85, Children's Seashore House, Phila., 1985-87, Maxicare HMO, Phila., 1985-92, Ches Penn Health Svcs., 1987-92, Judith L. Ross MD, Phila., 1989—; clin. asst. instr. Hahnemann Physician's Assn. Program, Phila., 1987—. Mem. Tristate Diabetic Educators Assn. Home: 88 Manor Ave Oaklyn NJ 08107 Office: Thomas Jefferson U 1025 Walnut St Ste 727 Philadelphia PA 19107

KOWALCZYK, MACIEJ STANISLAW, obstetrician, gynecologist; b. Kraków, Poland, June 8, 1956; s. Bogumil Wieslaw and Teresa Maria (Matowska) K. MD, Med. Acad., Kraków, 1984; postgrad., Polish Acad. Sci., Kraków, 1984, Inst. Gyn.-Ob, 1988-91, Instn. Sexology and Pathology, Warsaw, 1992-96. Intern Narutowicz Hosp., Kraków, 1984-85; gen. practice medicine ambulatory Kraków-Srödmiescie, Kraków, 1984-85; gen. practice ambulatory medicine First Aid Svc., 1985-87; asst. in ob-gyn Szpital Polozniczy, Kraków, 1986—, Maternity Amb. for Sch. Tchrs., Kraków, 1987-92; tchr. Cathedral Normal Anatomy, Med. Acad., Krakow, 1984-86; prof. Med. Coll. for Midwives, 1991; mem. commn. in Soc. Ins. Instn., 1986-88. Contbr. articles to profl. jours. Recipient Organon Poster award, Japan, 1995. Mem. Polish Gynecol. Soc., Vol. Life Saver's Assn., Polish Androl. Soc., Polish Sexology Soc., Polish Radiol. Soc. (ultrasound sect.), Am. Soc. Colposcopy and Cervical Pathology, N.Y. Acad. Sci., Polish Sonographic Soc., Internat. Soc. Ultrasound in Ob-Gyn., European Soc. Contraception, European Soc. Human Reprodn. and Embriology, European Tourist Club; gen. mem. Am. Inst. Ultrasound in Medicine. Roman Catholic. Home: Odroważa 22/7, Cracow 30009, Poland Office: Szpital Polozniczo-Ginekologiczny, ul Siemiradzkiego 1, Cracow 31 137, Poland

KOWALEWSKI, JAN KAZIMIERZ, hematology educator; b. Chełm, Poland, Mar. 30, 1921; s. Kazimierz and Stanisława (Nestorowicz) K.; m. Jadwiga Grabowska, Dec. 31, 1948; children: Magdalena, Piotr. Grad. medicine, Med. Acad. Lublin (Poland), 1950, MD, 1961. Asst. dept. internal medicine Med. Acad. Lublin, 1951-67, asst. prof., 1967-70, head dept. hematology, 1971-91; cons. Rwy. Health Svc., Lublin, 1973-91. Co-author: Phytotherapy, 1980, Intensive Therapy, 1984. Lt. Polish Army, 1942-44. Recipient Partisan Cross, State Coun., 1972. Mem. Polish Soc. Hematologists and Transfusiologists (v.p. 1983-91). Roman Catholic. Home: Belinikow 3, 20-045 Lublin Poland Office: Dept Hematology, Jaczewskiego 8, 20-950 Lublin Poland

KOWALSKI, LUIZ PAULO, head and neck surgeon, educator; b. Curitiba, Brazil, Aug. 16, 1956; s. Paulo and Ibra da Luz Kowalski; m. Ivonete Sanches Giacometti, June 13, 1992; 1 child, Carolina Giacometti. MD, U. Fed. Paraná, Curitiba, 1979; MS, Escola Paulista de Medicina, São Paulo, Brazil, 1986, PhD, 1989. Med. resident Fundação Antonio Prudente, São Paulo, 1980-83; dir. head and neck surgery A. C. Camargo Hosp., São Paulo, 1990—; attending surgeon Hosp. Heliópolis, São Paulo, 1984-90; chief epidemiology unit Fundação Oncocentro de São Paulo, 1990; prof. epidemiology dept. oncology U. São Paulo, 1991—; pres. head and neck dept. Paulista Med. Assn., São Paulo, 1994—. Editor Acta Oncológica Brasilian, 1993—; contbr. articles to profl. jours. Recipient grants for study. Mem. Soc. Head and Neck Surgeons, Brasilian Soc. Head and Neck Surgery, N.Y. Acad. Scis. Office: Fundação Antonio Prudente, R Prof Antonio Prudente 211, 01509-010 São Paulo Brazil

KOWALSKI, TIMOTHY JOSEPH, child and adolescent psychiatrist, educator; b. Detroit, Apr. 14, 1956; s. Alfred Stanley and Mary Ann (O'Neil) K.; m. Robin E. Daum, Mar. 5, 1988; 1 child, Allison Marie. BA in Biology, Wayne State U., 1979; DO, Mich. State U., 1983. Transitional internship Tripler Army Med. Ctr., Honolulu, 1983-84, gen. psychiatry resident, 1986-89, child psychiatry fellowship, 1989-91; gen. med. officer 3rd Gen. Dispensary, Karlsruhe, West Germany, 1984-85; comdr. 19th Med. Detachment, Germersheim, West Germany, 1985-86; divsn. psychiatrist 25th Light Inf. Divsn., Schofield Bamacks, Hawaii, 1991-93; chief adolescent high mgmt. svc. William S. Hall Psychiatric Inst., Columbia, S.C., 1993-96; sr. psychiatrist Columbia Area Mental Health Ctr., 1996—; asst. prof. psychiatry and behavioral scis. U. S.C. Sch. Medicine, 1993—. Maj. USAR. Mem. APA (cons. corr. task force on rural psychiatry 1995—), Am. Osteopathic Assn., Am. Osteopathic Coll. Neurologists and Psychiatrists (bd. govs. 1995—), Am. Acad. Child and Adolscent Psychiatrists, S.C. Psychiatric Assn. (rural psychiatry liasion 1995—). Home: 421 Persimmon Fork Rd Blythewood SC 29016 Office: Columbia Area Mental Health Ctr 1801 Sunset Dr Columbia SC 29202

KOWALSKY, STEVEN WAYNE, urologist; b. Detroit, Apr. 29, 1953; s. Larry and Edith B. (Stein) K.; m. Ilene L. burk, Nov. 22, 1979; children: Marisa, Daniel. BGS, U. Mich., 1974, MD, 1979. Diplomate Am. Bd. Urology. Resident U. Mich., Ann Arbor, 1979-84; urologist Met. Urology, Allen Park, Mich., 1984—. Office: Metropolitan Urology 14801 Southfield Rd Allen Park MI 48101

KOWALYSHYN, THEODORE JACOB, physician; b. Northampton, Pa., Dec. 12, 1935; s. Stephen and Anna (Kuzyk) K.; m. Mary Ann West, Aug. 19, 1967; children: Alexander West, Andrew Jacob. BS, Lehigh U., 1957; MD, Hahnemann U., 1966. Diplomate Am. Bd. Internal Medicine in Internal Medicine and Hematology. Intern St. Lukes Hosp., Bethlehem, Pa., 1966-67, resident, 1967-70; fellow in hematology U. Cin. Med. Ctr., 1970-72; pvt. practice East Stroudsburg, Pa., 1972-93; staff physician Pocono Hosp., East Stroudsburg, Pa., 1972-84, cons. physician, 1985-93; staff physician Bethlehem Steel Family Health Ctr., 1993—; designated sr. med. examiner FAA, 1975-93; affiliate staff St. Luke's Hosp., Bethlehem, 1994—, Muhlenberg Hosp. Ctr., Bethlehem, 1994—; clin. asst. prof. medicine Med. Coll. Pa., Phila., 1980-84; adj. clin. prof. Sch. Nursing U. Pa., Phila., 1984-85. Contbr. articles to profl. jours. Bd. dirs. Am. Cancer Soc. of Monroe County, Pa., 1975-83, Pocono Hosp., 1978-81, Ea. Pa. Health Care Found., Allentown, Pa., 1977-82. With U.S. Army, 1958-60. Mem. ACP, Am. Soc. Internal Medicine, Pa. Soc. Hematology and Oncology, Alpha Omega Alpha. Ukrainian Orthodox. Home: 714 Sarah St Stroudsburg PA 18360-2122 Office: Health Ctr 1665 Valley Center Pky Bethlehem PA 18017-2269

KOWARSKI, ALLEN AVINOAM, endocrinologist, educator; b. Tel Aviv, Dec. 30, 1927; s. Hanoch and Sima (Tkazh) K.; m. Hanna Rose Zas, Mar. 24, 1950; children: David, Ruth. Student, Hebrew U., Jerusalem, 1946-47, MD, 1955; student, U. Lausanne (Switzerland) Med. Sch., 1949-52. Academic physician Hebrew U., 1955-62; instr., fellow Johns Hopkins U., Balt., 1962-68, asst. prof., 1968-72, assoc. prof., 1972-81; prof. U. Md., Balt., 1981—. Patentee in field; contbr. over 170 articles to profl. jours.; inventor: Nonthrombogenic Blood Withdrawal System, Nonthrombogenic Glucose Monitor; discovered the Dawn Phenomenon in diabetes and the bioinactive Growth Hormone, the Integrated Concentration of Growth Hormone for diagnosis of Growth Hormone Deficiency. Grantee NIH, 1979-84, 83-85, 85-94, 94-96, 96—, McNeil Pharm., 1984-86, DuPont Critical Care, 1985-90, Genentech Found. for Growth & Devel., 1994-95, Lilly Rsch. Lab. 1996—. Mem. Am. Pediatric Soc., Soc. Pediatric Research, Lawson-Wilkins Pediatric Endocrine Soc., The Endocrine Soc., Am. Fedn. Clin. Research, Am. Diabetes Assn. (diabetes research award 1983, Charles H. Best medal for disting. svc. 1994). Office: U Md Med Ctr 22 S Greene St Baltimore MD 21201-1544

KOWLESSAR, MURIEL, retired pediatric educator; b. Bklyn., Jan. 2, 1926; d. John Henry and Arene (Driver) Chevious; m. O. Dhodanand Kowlessar, Dec. 27, 1952; 1 child, Indrani. AB, Barnard Coll., 1947; MD, Columbia U., 1951. Diplomate Am. Bd. Pediatrics. Instr. Downstate Med. Ctr., Bklyn., 1958-64, asst. prof., 1965-66; asst. prof. clin. pediatrics Temple U., Phila., 1967-70; assoc. prof. Med. Coll. Pa., Phila., 1971-83, dir. pediatric group svcs., 1975-90, acting chmn. pediatrics dept., 1981-83, vice chair pediatrics dept., 1982-91, prof., 1983-91, prof. emeritus, 1991—. Contbr. articles to med. jours. Mem. Pa. Gov.'s Task Force on Spl. Supplemental Food Program for Women, Infants and Children, Harrisburg, 1981-83, Phila. Bd. Health, 1982-86; vol. Phila. Com. for Homeless, 1991-92, Gateway Literacy Program, YMCA, Germantown Bridge, Pa., 1992-93. Fellow Am. Acad. Pediatrics (emeritus); mem. Phila. Pediatric Soc., Cosmopolitan Club Phila., Phi Beta Kappa. Democrat.

KOWNACKI, JOHN J., ophthalmologist; b. Bitburg AFB, Germany, Apr. 18, 1963; s. Roman J. and Mary J. Kownacki; children: Cody, Jordan. BA in Chemistry, U. San Diego, 1985; MD, St. Louis U., 1989. Diplomate Am. Bd. Ophthalmology. Resident in ophthalmology St. Louis U., 1990-93; commd. maj. USAF, 1993—; dep. chief ophthalmologist Vandenburg AFB Hosp., Lompoc, Calif., 1993-95; chief ophthalmologist Davis-Monthan AFB Hosp., Tucson, 1995—. Contbr. articles and abstracts to profl. jours. Am. Heart Assn. Rsch. fellow, 1985. Fellow Am. Acad. Ophthalmology; mem. Am. Soc. Cataract and Refractive Surgery. Republican. Office: Ophthalmology Clinic Davis Monthan AFB 4175 S Alamo Ave Tucson AZ 85707

KOYFMAN, SIMON, osteopath; b. Beltsy, Moldova, Oct. 19, 1947; s. Samuel and Anna (Shmuner) K.; m. Frieda Vinzfeld, Aug. 10, 1968; children: Isaac, Sander. MD, Moscow Med. Sch., 1971; DO, N.Y. Coll. Osteo. Medicine, 1995. ENT dept. attending City Hosp., Penza, Russia, 1972-79, Beltsy, 1979-91; FP resident St. Barnabas Hosp., Bronx, N.Y., 1995—. Mem. Am. Osteo. Assn., Am. Coll. of Osteo. Family Physicians. Home: 6413 24th Ave Apt 1R Brooklyn NY 11204 Office: St Barnabas Hosp 183rd St 3rd Ave Bronx NY 10457

KOYL, PATTY ANN, critical care nurse, educator; b. Oberlin, Ohio, Sept. 14, 1954; d. Earl and Billie Mae (Little) Young; m. Glenn Arthur Koyl, May 6, 1989; 1 child, Travis. ADN, Lorain County C.C., 1980; BSN, Bowling Green State U., 1988; postgrad., Case Western Res. U., 1993—. RN, Ohio; cert. adult nurse practitioner, cert. critical care nurse. Staff nurse surg. ICU/cardiac surgery Fairview Gen. Hosp., Fairview Park, Ohio, 1980-90; clin. nurse specialist for cardiothoracic surgery Elyria (Ohio) Hosp., 1989-90; adult nurse practitioner corp. primary care Progressive Ins. Co., Mayfield, Ohio, 1990—; assoc. clin. faculty Case Western Res. U.; camp nurse Ch. of God of Prophecy, Cambridge, Ohio, 1981-85. Mem. ANA, Ohio Nurses Assn., Greater Cleve. Nurses Assn., Am. Acad. Nurse Practitioners, Ohio Coalition of Nurses with Splty. Cert., N.E. Ohio Nurse Practitioner Group. Home: 4096 W 229th St Fairview Park OH 44126 Office: The Progressive Co 6300 Wilson Mills Rd Highland Heights OH 44143

KOZAK, KIMBERLY ANN, plastic surgeon; b. Hazard, Ky., Mar. 12, 1964; d. Donald George and Ruth Ann (Gearhart) Spencer; m. Ralph Bradley Kozak, Oct. 21, 1995. BS in Biophysiology, Ea. Mich. U., 1987; DO, Mich. State U., 1992; postgrad., Iowa State U., 1994-95, Wayne State U., Detroit, 1994. Intern Oakland Gen. Hosp., Madison Heights, Mich., 1992-93, resident in gen. surgery, 1993-94, resident in otorhinolaryngology, oro-facial plastic surgery, 1994—. Pres. Med. Scribe Svc., Mich. State U., Lansing, 1988-90. Scholar March of Dimes, 1982-83, Ea. Mich. U., 1982. Mem. AMA, Am. Osteo. Assn., Am. Acad. Otolaryngology, Head and Neck Surgery, Mich. Assn. Osteopathic Physicians and Surgeons. Baptist. Office: ENT Surg and Assocs 27483 Dequindre Madison Heights MI 48071

KOZAK, MICHAEL JOSEPH, clinical psychologist; b. Phila., May 17, 1952; s. Michael Longin and Hannah Elizabeth (Creely) K. AB in Psychology, U. Pa., 1974; MS in Psychology, U. Wis., 1978, PhD in Clin. Psychology, 1982. Instr., psychology intern Rush Presbyn. St. Luke's Hosp., Chgo., 1980-81; asst. prof. psychology U. Brit. Columbia, Vancouver, B.C., Can., 1981-82; rsch. assoc. psychiatry Temple U. Sch. Medicine, Phila., 1982-84, asst. prof. psychiatry, 1984-86; asst. prof. psychiatry Med. Coll. Pa., Phila., 1986-89, assoc. prof. psychiatry, 1989—; clin. dir. Ctr. for Treatment & Study of Anxiety, 1995—; editorial cons. Clin. Psychology Review, Cognitive Therapy and Rsch., Jour. Abnormal Psychology, Jour. Behavior Therapy and Exptl. Psychiatry, Jour. Clin. and Exptl. Hypnosis, NSF, Psychosomatic Medicine, VA. Contbr. numerous articles to profl. jours; presenter at numerous sci. meetings. Vol. U. Wis. Crisis Line, Madison, 1978-79; mem. Women Organized Against Rape, Phila., 1990—, OCD Found., 1991—. Grantee NIMH, 1986-88, 1986-89, 89-94, Ciba-Geigy Corp., 1986-88, Kali-Duphar Labs., 1987-89, Smith, Kline, Beecham, 1991-92, others. Mem. Soc. for Psychophysiol. Rsch. (program com. 1985, 95), APA, Assn. for Advancement of Behavior Therapy (program com. 1990), Phila. Behavior Therapy Assn. (bd. dirs. 1986-87, 89-90), Behavior Therapy and Rsch. Soc. Office: Med Coll of Pa Psychiatry 3200 Henry Ave Philadelphia PA 19129-1137

KOZBERG, DONNA WALTERS, rehabilitation administration executive; b. Milford, Del., Jan. 1, 1952; d. Robert Glyndwr and Gailey Ruth (Bedorf) Walters; m. Ronald Paul Kozberg, June 8, 1974. BA, U. Fla., 1973, M in Rehab. Counseling, 1974; MFA, CUNY, 1979; MBA, Rutgers U., 1986. Cert. rehab. counselor. Rehab. counselor Office Vocat. Rehab., N.Y.C., 1975-81; area dir. Lift, Inc., Staten Island, N.Y., 1981-83; ea. region dir. pub. relations, advt. Lift, Inc., Mountainside, N.J., 1983-85, v.p., 1985—, v.p., chief fin. officer, 1988, exec. v.p., 1991-93, pres., 1993; co-founder, mng. dir. Expert Strategies, Inc., Mountainside, N.J., 1992—; self-employed writer, editor, 1975—; adv. bd. Rutgers Exec. Master Bus. Adminstrn. Contbr. articles to profl. jours.; assoc. editor Parachute mag., 1978; editor-in-chief (newsletter) Counselor Adv, 1980. Pres. Com. on Employment of People with Disabilities; trustee Ctr. for Creative Living; bd. dirs. N.J. Adv. Coun. for Independent Living, adv. panel NYU. Mem. Nat. Rehab. Assn. (Spl. citation 1974, grantee 1973), Nat. Rehab. Adminstrs. Assn., Nat. Rehab. Counselors Assn., N.J. Rehab. Counselors Assn. (pres. 1996), Poets and Writers. Home: 45 Dug Way Watchung NJ 07060-6011 Office: Lift Inc PO Box 1072 Mountainside NJ 07092-0072

KOZBERG, STEVEN FREED, psychologist; b. Mpls., Apr. 30, 1953; s. Martin L. and Lois (Bix) K. BA, Macalester Coll., 1975; MA, U. Minn.-Duluth, 1978; PhD, U. Wis.-Madison, 1981. Lic. psychologist, Minn. Research asst. dept. counseling and guidance U. Wis.-Madison, 1978-79, teaching asst., 1980-81, research asst. Guidance Inst. for Talented Students, 1979-80; counseling psychologist, asst. prof. psychology Carleton Coll., Northfield, Minn., 1981-88, counseling psychologist, lectr. psychology, 1988-92, counseling psychologist, sr. lectr. psychology, 1992-95, sr. lectr. psychology, 1995—, pvt. practice, Mpls., 1995—. Mem. APA, Minn. Psychol. Assn., Soc. Rsch. on Adolescence, Midwestern Psychol. Assn., Assn. Advancement of Psychology, Phi Kappa Phi. Home: 5121 Tifton Dr Minneapolis MN 55439-1464 Office: Lake Pointe Corporate Ctr 3100 West Lake St Ste 465 Minneapolis MN 55416

KOZICKI, DANIEL RAYMOND, dentist; b. Chgo., May 15, 1951; s. Raymond Joseph Kozicki and Sabina Elaine (Zielinski) Wolski; m. Vivian Linda Lamastus, June 22, 1974; children: Daniel Raymond, William Robert, Raymond Joseph. BS in Biology with honors, U. Ill., Chgo., 1973, BS in Dentistry with honors, 1976, DDS with honors, 1978. Sr. comprehensive instr. U. Ill. Coll. Dentistry, Chgo., 1978-79; gen. practice dentistry Chgo., 1978—. Cubmaster Chgo. area coun. Boy Scouts Am., 1986-89. James scholar U. Ill., Chgo., 1969. Mem. ADA, Ill. Dental Soc., Chgo. Dental Soc., Acad. Gen. Dentistry, Acad. Laser Dentistry, Omicron Kappa Upsilon, Phi Eta Sigma. Republican. Roman Catholic. Club: Dental Arts (Chgo.). Office: 4114 W 63rd St Chicago IL 60629-5008

KOZIN, FRANKLIN, physician; b. Detroit, Feb. 12, 1943; s. Louis and Adele (Leavitt) K.; m. Linda Maree Poznanski, June 8, 1969; children: Simon Edward, Eliana Lois, Arielle Susan. BS, U. Ill., 1965; MD, U. Chgo., 1969. Asst. prof. Med. Coll. Wis., Milw., 1974-77, assoc. prof., 1977-80; vis. investigator Scripps Rsch. Inst., La Jolla, Calif., 1980, asst. mem., 1981-85, clin. assoc. mem., 1985-96; staff physician Scripps Clinic Med. Group, La Jolla, Calif., 1983-96; med. dir. Scripps Health Pain Ctr., La Jolla, Calif., 1994—. Office: Scripps Clinic & Rsch Found 10666 N Torrey Pines Rd La Jolla CA 92037

KRAATZ, DAVID CHARLES, podiatrist, consultant; b. Newark, Apr. 25, 1954; s. Charles Joseph and Eva Minerva (Pilla) K.; m. Carolyn Jane Carpenter, June 28, 1986; children: Alessandra, Kara. AAS, Middlesex County Coll., 1976; BS, Monmouth Coll., 1979; D of Podiatric Medicine, Ohio Coll. Podiatric Medicine, 1983. Diplomate Am. Bd. Podiatric Surgery. Resident in podiatric surgery Met. Hosp., Phila., 1983-84; podiatrist Collingswood, N.J., 1984—; staff cons. Cooper River Convalescent Ctr., Pennsauren, N.J., 1988-93; dir. residency edn. JFK Hosp., Cherry Hill, N.J., 1986—, sec. dept. podiatry, 1994—; lectr. Gerimed Nursing Staff, Pannsauken, 1988-91, Eldermed St. Citizen Orgn., Stratford, N.J., 1986-91, N.J. Diabetic Assn., Am. Diabetic Assn., Cherry Hill, 1990-94, Kennedy Hosp., 1990-94.; lectr. region III Am. Podiatry Assn., 1995, Ohio Coll. Podiatric Medicine, 1995. Fellow Am. Coll. Foot and Ankle Surgeons; mem. Am. Podiatric Med. Assn., N.J. Podiatric Med. Assn. (del. N.J. State Assn. 1991). Home: 10 Burgundy Dr Marlton NJ 08053-3809 Office: 570 Haddon Ave Collingswood NJ 08108-1443

KRABATSCH, THOMAS, physician; b. Prenzlau, Germany, Aug. 3, 1965; s. Ernst Franz and Margit Ida (Kurz) K.; m. Kerstin Kipka, Febr. 4, 1988; children: Alexandra, Clara. Med. Diploma, Humboldt U., Berlin, 1991; MD, Charité Hosp., Berlin, 1992. Staff laser medicine Deutsches Herzzentrum, Berlin, 1991—. Author: (book) Transmyocardial Laser R., 1995. Sponsor German Red Cross, Berlin, 1994—. Mem. German Cardiothoracic Soc. Office: Deutsches Herzzentrum Berlin, Augustenburger Platz 1, D-13353 Berlin Germany

KRABILL, ROBERT ELMER, osteopathic physician; b. Wayland, Iowa, June 4, 1934; s. Robert H. and Amanda (Wyse) K.; m. Ellen Savage, Sept. 1, 1963; children: Keith Andrew, Angela Kay, Valerie Ann, Kelly Dawn. BS, Iowa Wesleyan Coll., 1961; DO, Kirkville (Mo.) Coll. Osteo. Medicine, 1966. Diplomate Am. Bd. Family Practice. Intern Cuyahoga Falls (Ohio) Gen. Hosp., 1966-67, mem. staff, 1967—; gen. practice osteo. medicine Uniontown, Ohio, 1967—; sec., treas. gen. practice dept. Cuyahoga Falls Gen. Hosp., 1985-86. Named one of Outstanding Young Men of Am., U.S. Jaycees, 1969. Mem. Am. Osteo. Assn., Ohio Osteo. Assn., Am. Coll. Gen. Practitioners Osteo. Medicine and Surgery. Mennonite. Home: 3733 N Vista St NW Uniontown OH 44685-8496 Office: 13017 Cleveland Ave NW Box 399 Uniontown OH 44685

KRACHMAN, DONALD A., osteopath; b. Phila., Jan. 23, 1947; s. Louis and Nettie Krachman; m. Barbara Steinberg, Dec. 25, 1969; children: Army, Caren. BS, Temple U., 1968; DO, Phila. Coll. Osteo. Medicine, 1973. Diplomate Am. Osteo. Bd. Family Medicine, Nat. Bd. Osteo. Examiners. Clin. asst. prof. dept. family practice UMDNJ, 1977—; pres., CEO Atrium Med. Assocs., Cherry Hill and Camden, N.J.; med. inspector Cherry Hill Pub. Schs., 1974-94; disability determination physician State of N.J.; med. exec. com. Cherry Hill Med. Ctr., JFK Meml. Hosp., 1976-81, chmn. credentials com., 1979-81, vice chmn. sect. of family practice, 1979-81, chmn. med. exec. com., 1980-82; med. dir. My Bros.' Keeeper, Camden; clin. asst. prof. N.Y. Coll. Osteo. Medicine; preceptor for clin. tng. W.Va. Coll. Osteo. Medicine, Phila. Coll. Osteo. Medicine. Mem. Am. Coll. Family Practice, Am. Osteo. Assn., N.J. Assn. Osteo. Physicians and Surgeons, Camden County Soc. Osteo. Physicians and Surgeons, Alpha Epsilon Pi (life), Lambda Omicron Gamma. Home: 18 N Woodleigh Dr Cherry Hill NJ 08003 Office: Atrium Med Ctr 1910 Rt 20 E Ste 6 Cherry Hill NJ 08003 also: North Camden Med Ctr 801 State St Camden NJ 08102

KRACKOW, KENNETH ALAN, orthopaedic surgeon, educator, inventor; b. Balt., Sept. 6, 1944; s. Eugene Howard and Audrey Ruth (Goldstein) K.; children: Sidney E., Andrea G.; m. Joan Nicole Darmstaedter, July 25, 1993. AB in Math. with honors, Johns Hopkins U., 1966; postgrad., Duke U., 1968-69, MD, 1971. Diplomate Am. Bd. Med. Examiners, Am. Bd. Orthopaedic Surgeries. Intern in gen. surgery Johns Hopkins Hosp., Balt., 1971-72, asst. resident in gen. surgery, 1972-73, successively asst. resident, sr. asst. resident, chief resident in orthopaedic surgery, 1973-76, mem. staff in orthopaedic surgery; mem. staff in orthopaedic surgery Good Samaritan Hosp., Balt., 1976-92, Children's Hosp., Balt., 1976-92; mem. staff Union Meml. Hosp., Balt., 1986-92; pvt. practice Drs. Filtzer, Reichmister & Becker, P.A., Balt., 1976-78; instr. orthopaedic surgery Johns Hopkins U., Balt., 1976-78, asst. prof., 1978-84, assoc. prof., 1984-90, prof., 1990-92, acting chief div. arthritis surgery dept. orthopaedic surgery, 1986; chief dept. orthopaedic surgery Buffalo Gen. Hosp., 1992—; prof. orthopaedic surgery SUNY at Buffalo, 1992—; pres. med. staff Good Samaritan Hosp., Balt., 1985-88, v.p. med. staff, 1984-85, sec. med. staff, 1980-83, med. exec. com., 1980-87, utilization rev. com. orthopaedic sect., 1976-81, ethics com., 1978-79; chmn. tissue com. Balt. County Gen. Hosp., 1977-78, by-laws com., 1977-78; chief divsn. orthopaedic surgery VA Hosp., Balt., 1980-87, vis. prof. U. Buffalo, 1983; bd. examiner Am. Bd. Orthopaedic Surgery, Chgo., 1989—; cons. Johns Hopkins Hosp., 1976-78, lectr., presenter in field. Author: Technique of Total Knee Arthroplasty, 1990, (with others) Total Knee Arthroplasty: A Comprehensive Approach, 1983, Non-Cemented Total Hip Arthroplasty, 1988, Total Joint Replacement, 1991; editor Advances in Orthopaedic Surgery, 1982—; asst. chief editor Jour. Arthroplasty, 1988—; mem. editorial bd. Am. Jour. Knee Surgery, 1988-92, Sports Medicine News, 1991—; founding editor Jour. Orthopaedic Techniques; contbr. articles and abstracts to profl. jours. Active Md. br. Arthritis Found., 1977-92, Md. Soc. Rheumatic Diseases, 1977-92. Recipient Peer Rev. award Genucom, 1986-88; Instl. grantee Johns Hopkins U., 1980-81; grantee O'Neil Found., 1979-80, Orthopaedic Rsch. and Edn. Found., 1980-81, Howmedica, Inc., 1988-90. Mem. AMA, Am. Orthopaedic Assn., Am. Acad. Orthopaedic Surgery, Am. Knee Soc., Md. Orthopaedic Soc., Md. Soc. Med. Rsch., Johns Hopkins Med. Surg. Soc., Acad. Orthopaedic Soc., Orthopaedic Rsch. Soc., Assn. Arthritic Hip and Knee Surgeons, Phi Beta Kappa. Home: 58 N Woodside Ln Williamsville NY 14221-5953 Office: Buffalo Gen Hosp 100 High St Ste B203 Buffalo NY 14203-1126

KRAELING, ROBERT RUSSELL, research animal physiologist; b. Pitts., Aug. 22, 1942; s. William Dolphe and Mary Jane (Lowry) K.; m. Lois Claire Sunderland, Sept. 29, 1962; children: David Joseph, William Allen, Michael Andrew, James Edward, Margaret Elizabeth. BS, U. Md., 1964, MS, 1967; PhD, Iowa State U., 1970. Rsch. physiologist USDA-ARS, Beltsville (Md.) Agrl. Rsch. Ctr., 1970-74, USDA-ARS, Richard Russel Agrl. Rsch. Ctr., Athens, Ga., 1974-81; rsch. leader USDA-ARS, Richard Russel Agrl. Rsch. Ctr., Athens, 1981—. Mem. editl. bd. Jour. Animal Sci., 1980-83, 87-90, Biology of Reprodn., 1990-95, Domestic Animal Endocrinology, 1987-90. Contbr. sci. manuscripts to field. Recipient Predoctoral fellowship NIH, 1968-70, Physiology and Endocrinology Rsch. award Am. Soc. Animal Sci., 1990. Mem. Am. Soc. of Animal Sci., Soc. for Study of Reproduction. Office: USDA ARS Russell Rsch Ctr PO Box 5677 Athens GA 30604-5677

KRAFT, DAVID PETERSON, psychiatrist, consultant; b. Waterbury, Conn., Mar. 23, 1942; s. Howard Russell and Marian Augusta (Northrop) K.; m. Stephanie Elizabeth Barlett, June 13, 1966; children: Claire Elizabeth, Paul David. AB, Wheaton (Ill.) Coll., 1964; MD, Northwestern U., 1968; MPH, Harvard U., 1994. Diplomate Am. Bd. Psychiatry and Neurology. Mental health officer Job Corps Health Staff U.S. Dept. Labor, Washington, 1972-73, prin. med. officer, 1973-74, regional mental health cons., 1978—; mental health dir. Univ. Health Svcs. U. Mass., 1978-83, exec. dir. Univ. Health Svcs., 1984-94; med. dir., psychiatrist ServiceNet Clinic, Northampton, Mass., 1994—; accreditation surveyor Accreditation Assn. for Ambulatory Health Care, Skokie, Ill., 1984-94. Contbr. 10 articles to Jour. Am. Coll. Health, 1977-94. Surgeon USPHS, 1972-74. Fellow Am. Psychiatric Assn., Am. Coll. Health Assn. (pres. 1992-93). Home: 35 Mount Pleasant St Amherst MA 01002 Office: ServiceNet Medication Clin 50 Pleasant St Northampton MA 01060

KRAFT, GEORGE HOWARD, physician, educator; b. Columbus, Ohio, Sept. 27, 1936; s. Glen Homer and Helen Winner (Howard) K.; children: Jonathan Ashbrook, Susannah Mary. AB, Harvard U., 1958; MD, Ohio State U., 1963, MS, 1967. Cert. Am. Bd. Phys. Medicine and Rehab., Am. Bd. Electrodiagnostic Medicine. Intern U. Calif. Hosp., San Francisco, 1963-64, resident, 1964-65; resident Ohio State U., Columbus, 1965-67; assoc. U. Pa. Med. Sch., Phila., 1968-69; asst. prof. U. Wash., Seattle, 1969-72, assoc. prof., 1972-76, prof., 1976—, chief of staff Med. Ctr., 1993-95; dir. electrodiagnostic medicine U. Wash. Hosp., 1987—, dir. Multiple Sclerosis Clin. Ctr., 1982—; co-dir. Muscular Dystrophy Clinic, 1974—; assoc. dir. rehab. medicine Overlake Hosp., Bellevue, Wash., 1989—; bd. dirs. Am. Bd. Electrodiagnostic Medicine, 1993—, chmn., 1996—. Co-author: Chronic Disease and Disability, 1994, Living with Multiple Sclerosis: A Wellness Approach, 1996; cons. editor: Phys. Medicine and Rehab. Clinics, 1990—, EEG and Clin. Neurophysiology, 1992—; assoc. editor Jour. Neurol. Rehab., 1988—; contbr. articles to profl. jours. Adv. com. World Rehab. Fund, N.Y.C., 1988—; sci. peer rev. com. C Nat. Multiple Sclerosis Soc., N.Y.C., 1990—, chmn., 1993—, med. adv. bd., exec. com. med. adv. bd., 1991—; bd. sponsors Wash. Physicians for Social Responsibility, Seattle, 1986—. Rsch. grantee Rehab. Svcs. Adminstrn., 1978-81, NEW, 1976-79, Nat. Inst. Handicapped Rsch., 1984-88, Nat. Multiple Sclerosis Soc., 1990-92, 94-95. Fellow Am. Acad. Phys. Medicine and Rehab. (pres. 1984-85, Zeiter award 1991); mem. Am. Assn. Electrodiagnostic Medicine (cert., pres. 1982-83), Assn. Acad. Physiatrists (pres. 1980-81), Am. Acad. Clin. Neurophysiology (pres. 1995—), Am. Acad. Neurology, Internat. Rehab. Medicine Assn. Episcopalian. Office: U Wash Dept Rehab Dept Rehab PO Box 356490 Seattle WA 98195-0004

KRAFT, IRVIN ALAN, psychiatrist; b. Huntington, W.Va., Nov. 20, 1921; m. Shirley Goldin, July 4, 1951; children: Karen Kraft Pennebaker, Joanna Kraft Katz, Elizabeth Kraft Schmachtenberger, Mark. BS, NYU, 1943, MD, 1949. Diplomate Am. Bd. Psychiatry and Neurology, Am. Bd. Child Psychiatry. Chief psychiatry Tex. Children's Hosp., Houston, 1958-65; prof. mental health U. Tex., Houston, 1975-91, emeritus prof. mental health, 1991—; assoc. clin. prof. pediatrics Baylor Coll. Medicine, Houston, 1977—, clin. prof. psychiatry, 1977—; med. dir. Tex. Inst. Family Psychiatry, Houston, 1964-79; dir. Houston Heart Assn., 1969-70; med. dir. Adult Adolescent Rehab. Ctr., Houston, 1982-85; chmn. subcom. Mental Health Needs Coun., Houston, 1988-89. Author: Adolescent Group Psychotherapy, 1989, Bibliography of Child and Adolescent Psychiatry, 1990; co-editor: Child Group Psychotherapy: Future Tense, 1986; mem. editorial bd. Jour. Child and Adolescent Group Therapy, 1989—. Mem. drug prevention com. High Sch. for Health Professions, Houston, 1989-90; mem. Tex. House Rep. Com. on Edn., 1974. N.Y. Acad. Scis. fellow, 1971—; recipient Gold award Am. Acad. Pediatrics, 1969, cert. of award Am. Group Psychotheraphy Assn., 1970. Fellow Am. Acad. Child and Adolescent Psychiatry (life), Am. Acad. Psychoanalysis, Am. Psychiat. Assn., Houston Group Psychotherapy Soc., Southwestern Group Psychotherapy Soc., Houston Psychiat. Soc., Tex. Soc. Psychiat. Physicians, Tex. Soc. of Child and Adolescent Psychiatry, Am. Orthopsychiatry Assn. Home: 2423 Gramercy St Houston TX 77030-3105 Office: 3100 Weslayan St Ste 260 Houston TX 77027-5752

KRAFT, WILLIAM FREDERICK, clinical psychologist, educator; b. Pitts., July 8, 1938; s. William F. and Margaret A. (Seman) K.; m. Patricia A. O'Brien, June 17, 1967; children: William P., Jennifer A. BA, Duquesne U., 1960, MA, 1962, PhD, 1965. Trainee Woodville Psychiat. Hosp., Pitts., 1961-63; dir. psychol. svcs. Somerset (Pa.) Psychiat. Hosp., 1965-68, Dixmont Psychiat. Hosp., Glenfield, Pa., 1968-70; pvt. practice, Pitts., 1965—; assoc. prof. Carlow Coll., Pitts., 1965-68, prof., 1969—; instr. Duquesne U., Pitts., 1965-69, adj. prof., 1985—; lectr. to various groups in U.S. and Italy, 1965—; psychologist to religious communities, Pitts., 1967—. Author: The Search for the Holy, 1971, A Psychology of Nothingness, 1974, Normal Modes of Madness, 1978, Sexual Dimensions of the Celibate Life, 1979, Achieving Promises: A Spiritual Guide for the Transitions of Life, 1981, Whole and Holy Sexuality, 1989; also numerous articles. Mem. APA, Pa. Psychol. Assn., Psychologists in Ind. Practice, Psychology and Religion. Democrat. Roman Catholic. Home: 8072 Brittany Pl Pittsburgh PA 15237-6357 Office: Carlow Coll 3333 5th Ave Pittsburgh PA 15213-3109

KRAH, JOHN GUEST NEALE, medical association executive; b. Pittsburgh, Nov. 10, 1953; s. Elwood Walter and Luella Carol (Neale) K.; m. Nancy Elizabeth Kerr, Jan. 2, 1981; children: Susan Alexandra, Elizabeth Ann. BA in Econs., Lafayette Coll., 1975; MBA, U. of Pitts., 1981. Exec. asst. Allegheny County Med. Soc., Pitts., 1975-79, asst. exec. dir., 1979-88, exec. dir., 1989—; exec. v.p. Allegheny Physicians Svc. Corp., Pitts., 1979-89, Allegheny MedCare, Pitts., 1984-89; exec. dir. Allegheny County Med. Soc. Found., Pitts., 1989—. Contbr. articles to med. bull. Dir. North Side Civic Devel. Coun., Pitts., 1991—, Consumer Credit Counseling Svc., Pitts., 1991—; sec., treas. Pitts. Soc. Assn. Execs., 1988-89, v.p., 1989-90, pres., 1990-91, dir., 1991-92; bd. dirs. Allegheny County Alliance on Aging. Mem. BBB (bd. dirs. 1994—), Am. Soc. Assn. Execs., Am. Assn. Med. Soc. Execs., Pitts. Soc. Assn. Execs., Allegheny Club, Univ. Club. Republican.

Presbyterian. Office: Allegheny County Med Soc 713 Ridge Ave Pittsburgh PA 15212-6002

KRAHNERT, JOHN FREDERICK, surgeon; b. Elizabeth, N.J., Apr. 13, 1957; s. John Frederick and Dianne Evelyn (Brock) K.; m. Anne Cameron Beard, Dec. 19, 1981; children: John, Lauren. BA in Biology, Wake Forest U., 1979; MD, Bowman Gray Sch. of Medicine, 1982. Diplomate Am. Bd. Surgery, Am. Bd. Thoracic Surgery, Am. Coll. Cardiology, Am. Coll. Surgery. Intern in gen. surgery U. Ky. Med. Ctr., Lexington, 1983-84, resident in gen. surgery, 1984-88, resident in cardiovascular and thoracic surgery, 1988-90; dir. cardiac surgery Moore Regional Hosp., Pinehurst, N.C., 1990—; cons. staff cardiothoracic surgery Pitt Regional Med. Ctr., Greenville, N.C., 1990—; sec., treas. Pinehurst Surg. Clinic; chmn. sect. of gen. thoracic surgery Moore Regional Hosp., chmn. cardiology svc. line. Mem. Alpha Omega Alpha. Republican. Presbyterian. Office: Pinehurst Surg Clin One Memorial Dr Pinehurst NC 28374

KRAIKIT, SOMPONG, nephrologist; b. Nakornsawan, Thailand, Oct. 4, 1942; came to U.S., 1968; s. Kraikit and Tieng Kraikit; m. Suwanee Karikit, May 11, 1972; children: Tom, Wanda. MD, Chieng Mai U., 1967. Diplomate Am. Bd. Internal Medicine, Nephrology. Asst. prof. internal medicine U. Okla., Oklahoma City, 1974-76; pvt. practice Florence, S.C., 1976—; clin. asst. prof. internal medicine Med. Univ. S.C., Charleston, 1976—. Fellow ACP. Home: 1120 Dunvegan Florence SC 29501 Office: 255 S Warley St Florence SC 29501

KRAINES, JEFFREY L., managed care company physician executive; b. N.Y.C., Dec. 9, 1950; k; s. Sidney and Evelyn (Korn) K.; m. Linda Kaplan; children: Kirkland, Morganne. BA, Wesleyan U., 1971; MD, U. Chgo., 1975. Pvt. practice medicine Concord, N.H., 1981-85, Boston, 1985-92; med. dir. Pvt. Healthcare Sys., Waltham, Mass., 1989-94, Blue Cross, Blue Shield, Cambridge, Mass., 1995—. Bd. dirs. ACLU Mass., Boston, 1987-93. Mem. AMA, ACP, Am. Coll. Physician Execs., Am. Arthritis Assn., Mass. Med. Soc. Democrat. Office: Blue Cross Blue Shield Mass 101 Main St 03/09 Cambridge MA 02142-1519

KRAININ, JAMES MARK, psychiatrist; b. N.Y.C., July 24, 1940; s. Philip and Stella (Ornstein) K.; m. Jane Elizabeth McLaughlin, May 27, 1966 (div. Mar. 1978); 1 child, Penelope Ann; m. Beverly Ruth Johnson, May 1, 1982; children: Benjamin Matthew, Michael Spencer. BA magna cum laude, Harvard U., 1962, MD, 1966. Diplomate Am. Bd. Psychiatry and Neurology with added qualifications in geriatric psychiatry. Intern in medicine Jewish Hosp. of St. Louis, 1966-67; resident in psychiatry Bronx Mcpl. Hosp. Ctr., N.Y.C., 1967-70; pvt. practice Newton, Mass., 1972-74, Norwood, Mass., 1974—; cons. Albert Danielsen Pastoral Counseling Ctr., Boston U., 1973-78; clin. instr. Boston U. Sch. Medicine, 1987—; pres. Soc. for Family Therapy and Rsch., Boston, 1976-78. Contbr. articles to profl. jours. Maj. M.C. USAF, 1970-72. Mem. Am. Psychiatric Assn., Mass. Med. Soc. Democrat. Jewish. Office: 470 Washington St Norwood MA 02062-2337

KRAIZER, SHERRYLL A., health services and interpersonal violence protection educator; b. San Antonio, June 12, 1948; d. Faye Burton and Phyllis Anne (Ringer) Graves; m. Alvin T. Kraizer, July 30, 1978; children: Charles, Ben. BS in Edn./Spl. Edn., Emporia State U., 1969, MS in Edn./Psychology, 1970; postgrad., U. Minn., 1973; PhD in Edn., The Union Inst., 1991. Pres., exec. dir. Coalition for Children, 1983—; presenter confs. in field; expert witness on child abuse, instnl. abuse, stds. and practices. Author: The Safe Child Book, 1995; author (tng. programs) The Safe Child, 1989, 2d edit., 1994, Dating Violence: Prevention and Intervention, 1991, Domestic Violence Prevention and Intervention, 1991, Reach, 1992, Challenge, 1992, Recovery, 1992. Recipient Nat. Prog. award Child Abuse Prevention Coun., Houston, 1989, rsch. grant Nat. Ctr. on Child Abuse and Neglect, 1987, prog. devel. grant Small Bus. Adminstrn., 1988. Mem. Internat. Soc. Prevention of Child Abuse and Neglect, Nat. Assn. Prevention of Child Abuse and Neglect, Nat. Assn. Edn. of Young Children, Am. Profl. Soc. on Abuse of Children. Office: Coalition for Children PO Box 6304 Denver CO 80206-0304

KRAKAUER, RANDALL SHELDON, physician; b. N.Y.C., Apr. 25, 1949; s. Henry and Violet T. K.; m. Marcia Sue Katcher, June 15, 1969; children: Meryl, Ari, Barak. BS, Rensselaer Poly. Inst., Troy, N.Y., 1972; MD, Albany Med. Coll., 1972. Intern Univ. Hosps., Mpls., 1972-73; med. resident Univ. Hosps., 1973-74; clin. assoc. NIH, 1974-76; rheumatology fellow Mass. Gen. Hosp., Harvard Med. Sch., Boston, 1976-77; dir. clin. immunology Cleve. Clini, 1977-83; prof., chmn. dept. rheumatology med. sch. Seton Hall U., South Orange, N.J., 1983—; pres. Freehold (N.J.) Area Physicians, PA, 1993-96; medical dir. Old Bridge Medical Group, 1995-96; regional med. dir. N.J. Prime Care Internat., 1996—. Contbr. articles to profl. jours.; editor: Immunopharmacology, 1977-86, Drug Information Bull., 1983—; author books. Med. dir. Ohio Lupus Found., Cleve., 1978-81; v.p. Freehold Area Physicians, P.A., 1989—. Lt. comdr. USPHS, 1974-76. Fellow ACP, Am. Coll. Rheumatologists; mem. Nat. Assn. Managed Care Physicians (co-chmn. med. dirs. coun.). Republican. Jewish. Office: Arthritis Assocs 4247 Us Highway 9 Freehold NJ 07728-8348

KRAMER, ALBRECHT HELMUTH, surgeon, educator; b. Santiago, Chile, Mar. 24, 1946; s. Hermann and Lisa Mercedes (Schumacher) K.; m. virginia Silva Karmy, June 5, 1971; children: Walter, Christiane, Veronica. MD, U. Chile, 1971. Diplomate Am. Bd. Surgery with subspecialty in gen. vascular surgery. Surg. intern St. Thomas Hosp., Akron, Ohio, 1971-72; resident in surgery Cleve. Clinic, 1972-76, fellow in vascular surgery, 1976-77; asst. prof. surgery Cath. U., Santiago, 1977-83, assoc. prof., 1984-94, prof. surgery, 1995—, chief sect. vascular surgery, 1979—. Internat. Guest scholar ACS, 1985. Fellow ACS; mem. Colegio Cirujanos Vasculares Habla Hispana (founding mem.), Deutsche G. für Gefässchirurgie (corr.). Lutheran. Home: Casilla 9677, Santiago Chile Office: Instituto Vascular Santiago, Apoquindo 3990 #601, Santiago Chile

KRAMER, ALEX JOHN, dentist; b. Aurora, Ill., Dec. 21, 1939; s. Roy Edward and Frances (Astromskis) K.; m. Phyllis Rose Gonsky, July 15, 1967 (div. Sept. 1978); m. Brenda Jean Schillinger, Sept. 12, 1981; children: Ian Alexander, Elizabeth Katherine. Student, Marquette U., 1957-60; DDS, U. Ill., Chgo., 1964. Gen. practice dentistry Montgomery, Ill., 1966-88, Ashland, Wis., 1988-91; priv. practice craniofacial pain Duluth, Minn., 1991-94; gen. dental practice Duluth, 1994—. Mem. exec. bd. Two Rivers Boy Scouts Am., St. Charles, Ill., 1969-79. Lt. Dental Corps USNR, 1964-66. Master Internat. Coll. Craniomandibular Orthopedics; mem. ADA, Am. Assn. Maxillofacial Orthopedics, Ill. State Dental Assn., Chgo. Dental Soc., Wis. State Dental Assn., No. Wis. Dental Assn., Am. Acad. Gnathological Orthopedics, Am. Soc. Gen. Dentistry, Dentafacial Orthopedics Study Club Mo., Am. Assn. Functional Orthodontics, Internat. Acad. Orthomolecular and Preventive Medicine, Am. Acad. Pain Mgmt. (diplomate), Minn. State Dental Assn., U. Ill. Alumni Assn. (life), Pershing Rifles Hon. Mil. Frat., Psi Omega. Republican. Methodist. Club: Aurora (Ill.) Country. Lodge: Optimists. Home: 54 E Kent Rd Duluth MN 55812-1420 Office: 1601 Woodland Ave Duluth MN 55803-2629

KRAMER, BARNETT SHELDON, oncologist; b. Balt., July 29, 1948; s. Mervin and Muriel Hannah (Woolf) K.; m. Ruth Solomon, June 25, 1972; 1 child, Jeremy. Student, Johns Hopkins U., 1966-69, MPH, 1991; MD, U. Md., 1973. Intern Washington U., St. Louis, 1973-74, med. resident, 1974-75; fellow Nat. Cancer Inst., Bethesda, Md., 1975-78, sr. investigator, 1986-90, assoc. dir., 1990-96, dep. dir. Divsn. Cancer Prevention and Control, 1996—; assoc. prof. U. Fla., Gainesville, 1978-83, 1983-86; prof. medicine Uniformed Svcs. U. Health Scis., Bethesda, Md., 1989-90, clin. prof. medicine, 1990—. Assoc. editor Jour. Nat. Cancer Inst., 1988-94, editor-in-chief, 1994; mem. editl. bd. Physicians Data Query, 1988—, chairperson cancer prevention com., 1992—; contbr. articles to profl. publs., chpts. to books. With USPHS, 1975-78. Fellow ACP; mem. Am. Soc. Clin. Oncologists, Am. Assn. Cancer Rsch., Alpha Omega Alpha, Delta Omega. Office: Nat Cancer Inst DCPC Bldg 31 Rm 1049 9000 Rockville Pike Bethesda MD 20892-2580

KRAMER, BARRY ALAN, psychiatrist; b. Phila., Sept. 9, 1948; s. Morris and Harriet (Greenberg) K.; m. Paulie Hoffman, June 9, 1974; children—Daniel Mark, Steven Philip. B.A. in Chemistry, NYU, 1970; M.D., Hahnemann Med. Coll., 1974. Resident in psychiatry Montefiore Hosp. and Med. Ctr., Bronx, N.Y., 1974-77; practice medicine specializing in psychiatry, N.Y.C., 1977-82; staff psychiatrist L.I. Jewish-Hillside Med. Ctr., Glen Oaks, N.Y., 1977-82; asst. prof. SUNY, Stony Brook, 1978-82; practice medicine specializing in psychiatry, L.A., 1982—; asst. prof. psychiatry U. So. Calif., 1982-89, assoc. prof. clin. psychiatry, 1989-94, prof. clin. psychiatry U. So. Calif. U. Hosp., 1994—; ward chief Los Angeles County/U. So. Calif. Med. Ctr., 1982—; mem. med. staff USC U. Hosp., Cedars Sinai Hosp.; cons. Little Neck Nursing Home (N.Y.), 1979-82, L.I. Nursing Home, 1980-82; dir. ECT U. So. Calif. Sch. Medicine, 1990. Reviewer: Am. Jour. Psychiatry, Hospital and Community Psychiatry; mem. editorial bd. Convulsive Therapy; contbr. articles to profl. jours., papers to sci. meetings. NIMH grantee, 1979-80; fellow UCLA/U. So. Calif. Long-Term Gerontology Ctr., 1985-86. Fellow Am. Psychiat. Assoc.; mem. AMA, Assn. Convulsive Therapy (editorial bd.), Soc. Biol. Psychiatry, Calif. Med. Assn., L.A. Med. Assn., Am. Assn. Geriatric Psychiatry, Gerontol. Soc. Am., So. Calif. Psychiat. Soc. (chair ETC com.). Jewish. Office: U So Calif U Hosp 1510 San Pablo St Ste 600 Los Angeles CA 90033-4508 also: PO Box 5792 Beverly Hills CA 90209-5792

KRAMER, CAROL GERTRUDE, marriage and family counselor; b. Grand Rapids, Mich., Jan. 14, 1939; d. Wilson John and Katherine Joanne (Wasdyke) Rottschafer; m. Peter William Kramer, July 1, 1960; children: Connie R. Kramer Sattler, Paul Wilson Kramer. AB, Calvin Coll., 1960 MA, U. Mich., 1969; PhD, Holy Cross Coll., 1972; MSW, Grand Valley State U., 1985. Diplomate Internat. Acad. Behavioral Medicine, Counseling and Psychotherapy; cert. addictions/substance abuse counselor, Mich.; cert. hypnotist/psychotherapist. Elem. tchr. Jenison (Mich.) Pub. Sch. 1960-64; sch. social worker Grand Rapids Pub. Sch., 1964-81; pvt. practice marriage and family counselor Grand Rapids, 1973—; v.p. Human Resource Assocs., Grand Rapids, 1983-88; pres. Telecounseling, 1996—; guest lectr. Calvin Coll., Mich. State U., Grand Valley State U., 1975-85. Co-author: Parent Involvement Program, 1993, Stop Sexual Abuse for Everyone, 1995. Ruling elder 1st Presbyn. Ch., Grand Rapids, 1975-78; mem. Gerald R. Ford Rep. Women, Grand Rapids, 1980-87; mem. Mich. Bd. of Licensing Marriage Counselors, 1985-88, co-chair pastoral rels. com. Gun Lake Community Ch., 1989-91, v.p. consistory, 1991-93. Named one of Outstanding Young Women in Am., 1974; recipient Meritorious Svc. award Kent County Family Life Coun., 1983. Fellow Am. Assn. Marriage and Family Therapists; mem. NASW, Mich. Assn. Marriage Counselors (awards com. 1988, chmn. 1991, nominations com. 1992—), Kent County Family Life Coun. (pres. 1975), Voters Against Sexual Abuse (pres., bd. dirs. 1992—). Home: 12622 Park Dr Wayland MI 49348-9322 Office: Psychology Ctr 2059 Lake Michigan Dr NW Grand Rapids MI 49504-4742

KRAMER, JAY HARLAN, physiologist. researcher, educator; b. Bklyn., Dec. 26, 1952; s. Albert and Blossom K.; m. Aisar Atrakchi, Apr. 18, 1993. BA with honors, Northeastern U., 1976; MS, Lehigh U., 1979, PhD, 1982. Clin. lab. technician Boston Med. Lab., Waltham, Mass., 1974-75; rsch. asst. Lehigh U., Bethlehem, Pa., 1979-81; rsch. assoc. Med. Coll. Va., Richmond, 1982-83; sr. rsch. assoc. Okla. Med. Rsch. Found., Oklahoma City, 1983-85; rsch. assoc. George Washington U., Washington, 1985-86, asst. rsch. prof. medicine, 1986-90, assoc. rsch. prof., 1990—, adj. assoc. prof. physiology, 1991—; lectr. physiology George Washington U., Washington, 1987-89; cons. Squibb & Sons, Princeton, N.J., 1989, mem. George Washington U. Instl. Animal Care and Use Com., 1988—. Contbr. more than 40 articles to profl. jours.; article referee profl. jours. Mem. basic sci. faculty assembly coun. George Washington U., 1992-94. Grad. sch. scholar Lehigh U., 1980; named one of Outstanding Young Men of Am., Jaycees, 1981, 82. Mem. Am. Heart Assn., Am. Physiol. Soc., N.Y. Acad. Scis. (invited speaker 1993, presenter various nat. scientific meetings), Internat. Soc. for Heart Rsch., Internat. Soc. for Free Radical Rsch., Soc. for Exptl. Biology and Medicine, Acad. Honor Soc., Phi Sigma. Office: George Washington U Dept Medicine 2300 I St NW Washington DC 20037-2337

KRAMER, JEFFREY BRUCE, surgeon; b. Kansas City, Mo., Feb. 26, 1954. BA, Haverford Coll., 1976; MD, Washington U., 1980. Intern, resident Washington U., St. Louis, 1980-90; pvt. practice as cardiothoracic surgeon Prairie Village, Kans., 1990—. Office: Thoracic and Vascular Surge 4121 W 83d St # 132 Prairie Village KS 66208

KRAMER, JOHN ROBERT, JR., cardiologist, researcher; b. Cleve., July 29, 1942; s. John Robert and Janice Marion (Dye) K.; m. Joanne Soderquist, Dec. 28, 1966 (div. Apr. 1976); children: William Pearson, Charles Guy; m. Christine Elizabeth Wilber, Sept. 3, 1976; children: Mark Alan, Katherine Lindsey. BA in Biology with honors, Oberlin Coll., 1964; MD, U. Va., 1969. Med. intern Cleve. Clinic Found., 1969-70, resident, 1970-71, fellow in cardiology, 1971-73, staff invasive cardiologist, 1975—; vis. scientist MIT, Cambridge, 1983—, core investigator Laser Biomed. Rsch. Ctr., 1989—, Am. Internat. Health Alliance Cleve.-Ashgabat Ptnrs.; lectr. in Japan, The Netherlands, Fed. Republic Germany, Chile, Argentina, Turkey, Morocco, Egypt, Eng., France, Brazil, Can., Norway, Russia, Switzerland, Austria, Turkmenistan; referee Am. Heart Jour., Circulation, Cleve. Clinic Jour. Medicine, Jour. Am. Coll. Cardiology, Archives Internal Medicine, Catheterization and Cardiovascular Diagnosis. Contbr. 81 articles to sci. jours., chpts. to books. Maj. M.C., USAF, 1973-75. Fellow Am. Coll. Cardiology, Soc. for Cardiac Angiography and Interventions, Am. Coll. Angiology; mem. Chilean Soc. Cardiology and Cardiovascular Surgery (corr.), IEEE Lasers and Electro-optics Soc. Republican. Home: 530 Riverview Rd Gates Mills OH 44040-9649 Office: Cleve Clinic Found 9500 Euclid Ave Cleveland OH 44195-5066

KRAMER, KAREN SUE, mind-body psychologist; b. L.A., Sept. 6, 1942; d. Frank Pacheco Kramer and Velma Eileen (Devlin) Moore; m. Stewart A. Sterling, Dec. 30, 1965 (div. 1974); 1 child, Scott Kramer Sterling. BA, U. Calif., Berkeley, 1966; MA, U.S. Internat. U., 1976; PhD, Profl. Sch. Psychology, 1980. Psychometrist U. Calif. Counseling Ctr., Berkeley, 1966-67; social worker Alameda County Welfare Dept., Oakland, Calif., 1967-69; vol. coord. San. Diego County Probation Dept., 1971-73; officer San Diego County Probation Dept., 1973-76; counselor and coord. clin. and outreach programs Western Inst., San Diego, 1976-77; program coord. and counselor Women's Resource Ctr., Oceanside, Calif., 1977-78; pvt. practice psychology San Diego, 1978-81; planner/analyst San Diego County Dept. Health Svcs., 1979-81; social svcs. program cons. Calif. Dept. Social Svcs., Emeryville, 1981-83; affirmative action officer State Compensation Ins. Fund, San Francisco, 1983-87; regional property mgr. Compensation Ins. Fund, San Francisco, 1991—; community psychologist Calif. Dept. Mental Health, 1987-89; pvt. practice psychology Berkeley, 1990—; cons. psychologist Calif. Dept. Mental Health, 1987-89; personal analyst State Comp. Ins. Fund, 1989-91; regional property mgr. State Compensation Ins. Fund, San Francisco, 1991-95; prof. Nat. U. San Diego, 1979-81; pres. North County Coun. Social Concerns, Vista, Calif., 1977-78; advisor USMC Camp Pendleton Human Svcs., 1978-87; mem. adv. bd. Chinatown Resources Devel. Ctr., San Francisco, 1984-87, San Francisco Rehab., 1984-37; bd. dirs. Network Cons. Svcs., Napa, Calif.; founder Qi Gong in China-Ednl. Svcs., 1994. Mem. Peer Counselors Assn. (adv. bd. 1987-90), Calif. Prevention Network (bd. dirs. 1989-93, editorial advisor jour. 1992-93).

KRAMER, LESLIE, dermatologist; b. Bklyn., Mar. 5, 1953; d. Joseph and Doris Kramer.; m. Miles Weinberger, Aug. 22, 1992. BS, Bklyn. Coll., 1976; MS, L.I. U., 1979; D of Osteopathy, U. Osteopathic Medicine and Health Scis., 1990. Tchr. N.Y.C. Bd. Edn., Bklyn., 1976-79; physician asst. HIP, USN, N.Y.C. Dept. Health, 1981-86; physician UMDNJ/Union (N.J.) Hosp., 1990-91; resident dermatology Kirksville (Mo.) Coll. Osteo. Medicine, 1994; dermatologist pvt. practice, Cedar Rapids, Iowa, 1995—. Recipient Fisons Resident award Fisons Pharm., 1994-95. Mem. Am. Osteo. Assn., Am. Osteo. Coll. Dermatology (trustee 1992), Am. Soc. Dermatology, Iowa Med. Soc., Soc. Pediatric Dermatology, Women's Dermatological Soc. Office: Cedar Rapids Dermatology 411 10th St SE Cedar Rapids IA 52403

KRAMER, MARC B., forensic audiologist; b. N.Y.C., Mar 25, 1944; s. William C. and Rose G. (Bernstein) K. m. Diane Leslie Haas, Sept. 13, 1970; 1 child, Penny Colette. B.A., Temple U., 1965, M.A., 1967; Ph.D., City U. N.Y., 1972. Pvt. practice audiology; chief dept. audiology Lutheran Med. Ctr., 1969-73; asst. prof. speech scis. Hofstra U., 1972-77; dir. div. audiology, dir. auditory rsch. lab. L.I. (N.Y.) Coll. Hosp., 1973-81; prin. cons. Noise & Hearing Cons., N.Y.C., 1969—; assoc. Forensic Audiology Assocs., N.Y.C., 1978—; cons. in audiology Med. Div. Fire Dept., N.Y.C., 1972—, also hon. dep. chief; cons. in audiology Police dept., City of N.Y., hon. police surgeon; cons. med. dept. Port Authority N.Y./N.J., 1984—, Meml. Sloan Kettering Cancer Ctr., 1985—; adj. asst. prof., dir. hearing & speech svc. N.Y. Hosp. and Cornell U. Med. Coll., N.Y.C., 1982—; adj. assoc. prof. audiology Pace U., N.Y.C., 1981-83; med. cons. and expert witness in forensic audiology, occupational noise exposure and effects of noise on man; noise specialist and citizen mem. of N.Y.C. Environ. Control Board (appointed by Mayor Edward I. Koch), 1988-92. Author chpts. to books; co-editor: Forensic Audiology, 1982; editor: Hearing Conservation, A Guide to Preventing Hearing Loss, 1983; contbr. articles to profl. jours. Trustee The Floating Hosp. Fellow Am. Speech and Hearing Assn. (chmn. com. on hearing conservation and indsl. audiology, spl. course faculty 1982—, chmn. com. on profl. liability and risk mgmt.), Am. Acad. Audiology (mem. ethical practices bd.); mem. Am. Acad. Otolaryngology (instructional course faculty 1979—, Cert. of honor 1989), Internat. Soc. Audiology, Am. Auditory Soc., Acoustical Soc. Am. Jewish. Office: 329 E 68th St New York NY 10021-5606

KRAMER, MARY ALISON, medical and surgical nurse; b. Suffolk, Eng., Mar. 7, 1951; came to U.S., 1988; d. Noble Harding Percival Charles and Violet Alice Mary (Symonds) English; m. Malcolm James Wilder, June 28, 1969 (div. Nov. 1987); m. William Ralph Kramer, Jan. 23, 1988. ADN with honors, MGCCC Jeff Davis Campus, Gulfport, Miss., 1993. RN, Miss; cert. BLS, Miss. Clk., tax officer Her Majesty's Insp. of Taxes, Ipswich, Suffolk, Eng., 1967-88; tax preparer H & R Block, Gulfport, Miss., 1989-92; RN Meml. Hosp., Gulfport, 1993—. Mem. Phi Theta Kappa.

KRAMER, MILTON, psychiatrist; b. Chgo., Nov. 11, 1929; s. Abe and Rose Kramer; m. Aug. 28, 1955; children: Ruth, Daniel, Mary, Samuel. BS in Zoology, U. Ill., 1950, MD, 1954. Diplomate Am. Bd. Psychiatry and Neurology, Nat. Bd. Med. Examiners; lic. psychiatrist, Ill., Calif., Ohio; accredited clin. polysomnographer. Rotating intern Cin. Gen. Hosp., 1954-55, resident in psychiatry, 1955-58; instr. U. Cin., 1960-64, asst. prof., 1964-68, assoc. prof., 1968-72, prof., 1972-82, vol. prof., 1989—; pvt. practice Cin., 1960—; clin. prof. psychiatry Wright STate U., Dayton; examiner Am. Bd. Psychiatry and Neurology, Cin., 1962—; adj. prof. psychology U. Cin., 1979-82, 92—, lectr., 1986-87; dir. div. of somnology U. Miss., 1982-84; staff psychiatrist VA Hosp., Cin., 1960-64, asst. chief dept. psychiatry, 1964-82, acting assoc. chief of staff for rsch., 1976-78; staff psychiatrist VA Med. Ctr., Jackson, Miss., 1982-84; clinician in psychiatry outpatient dept. Cin. Gen. Hosp., asst. attending psychiatrist, 1961-64, attending psychiatrist on staff, 1965-76, dir. med. staff, 1976-82; cons. Rollman Psych. Inst., Cin., 1965-70, Peace Corps Tng. Group Ohio U., Athens, 1962-64, Indian Health Svc., 1985-90, Social Security Adminstrn., 1986—, AMA Coun. on Drugs, 1982; attending physician U. Miss. Med. Ctr., Jackson, 1982-84; mem. staff Cin. hosps. including Jewish Hosp., Christ Hosp., Bethesda Hosp.; investigator sleep/dreams NIMH, 1960-67, VA Hosp., 1961-70, 1970-84, others; dir. Dream Sleep Lab. VA Hosp., Cin., 1960-82, Jackson, 1982-84, dir. psychiatric rsch., Cin., 1963-82; liaison rep. APA-UAW Ins. Plan, Cin., 1966-67; dir. Sleep Disorders Ctr. U. Cin., 1976-82, Sleep Disorders Ctr. U. Miss., 1982-84, Sleep Disorders Ctr. Greater Cin. Bethesda Oak Hosp., 1984—; mem. Better Sleep Coun., 1979-80; mem. policy com. Continuing Edn. Program in Community Mental Health, 1966-70, chmn., 1968-69; mem. rsch. adv. com. Div. Mental Health and Retardation State of Ohio, 1969-70; mem. Gov.'s Task Force on Mental Health and Retardation, 1975-76; mem. mental health and mental retardation adv. bd. Dept. Mental Health State of Ohio, 1974-76, chmn., 1975-76; vice-chmn. Joint Mental Health and Mental Retardation Adv. and Rev. Commn., 1976-78; mem. adv. bd. Neuroscis. Info. Ctr., 1980-85. Author: Dream Psychology and The New Biology of Dreaming, 1969, Dimensions of The Dream, 1979; reviewer Am. Jour. Psychiatry, 1966—, Diabetes, 1970-72, Jour. of Abnormal Psychology, 1975—, Sleep, 1978—, Psychopharmocology, 1981—, Archives of Gen. Psychiatry, 1960—, Jour. Nervous and Mental Disease, 1975—; editor: (book) Comprehensive Psychiatry, 1968-70; contbr. articles to Am. Jour. Psychiatry, Jour. Nervous Mental Disorders, Internat. Jour. Group Psychotherapy, Sleep Rsch., Jour. Clin. Psychiatry, Jour. AMA, Jour. Am. Acad. Psychoanalysis, numerous others. Capt. U.S. Army, 1958-60. Fellow Am. Psychiat. Assn. (Hofheimer Prize bd. 1976-79), Am. Coll. Psychiatry (publs. com. 1983-87, budget com. 1988-90); mem. AMA, Am. Acad. Psychoanalysis (sci. assoc. 1975—), Am. Coll. Neuropsychopharmacology, Assn.. for the Psychophysiol. Study of Sleep (exec. com. 1975-77, subcom. on the evaluation of the pharmacology of sleep 1976), Assn. Sleep Disorders Ctrs. (cert. com. 1976-79, chmn. cert. com. 1976-78), Assn. for Study of Dreams (pres. elect 1985-86, pres. 1986-87), Cin. Soc. Neurology and Psychiatry (sec.-treas. 1967-69, pres. Cin. Psychiatric. Soc. 1977-78), Group for Advancement of Psychiatry (therapeutic care com. 1970—, chmn. therapeutic care com. 1984-87, Ginsberg fellowship com. 1979-81, publs. com. 1985-90, Ohio Psychiatric Assn. (mem. program com. 1962-65, chmn. program com. 1964-65, co-chmn. membership com. 1965-67, sec. 1968-69, pres. elect 1970-71, pres. 1972-73, sec. rsch. and edn. found. 1969-70, pres. rsch. and edn. found. 1973-74), Sigma Xi. Democrat. Jewish. Office: Bethesda Sleep Disorders 619 Oak St Cincinnati OH 45206-1613

KRAMER, MORTON, biostatistician, epidemiologist; b. Balt., Mar. 21, 1914; s. David and Sarah (Valenstein) K.; m. Pauline Weinstein, Sept. 24, 1939; children: Barry Kenneth, James Lawrence, Nancy, Richard. AB, Johns Hopkins U., 1934, postgrad. Sch. Chemistry, 1934-35, ScD, Sch. of Hygiene and Pub. Health, 1939. Student asst. biostatistics Johns Hopkins Sch. Hygiene and Pub. Health, 1937-38; instr. preventive medicine N.Y.U. Med. Sch., 1938; statistician N.Y. State Dept. Health, Albany, 1939-40; asst. prof. biostatistics Sch. Tropical Medicine; also statistician Insular Dept. Health, San Juan, P.R., 1940-42; econ. analyst Treasury Dept., Washington, 1942-43; Tb statistician Cleve. and Cuyahoga County, 1943-46; assoc. in biostatistics Western Res. U. Sch. Medicine, 1943-46; chief info. and research Office Internat. Health Relations, USPHS, 1946-49; chief biometry br. NIMH, 1949-75; dir. div. biometry and epidemiology NIMH, Alcohol, Drug Abuse, and Mental Health Adminstrn., 1975-76; prof. dept. mental hygiene, also joint appointment in biostatistics Johns Hopkins Sch. Hygiene and Pub. Health, 1976-84, prof. emeritus, 1984, prin. investigator Balt. Epidemiol. Catchment Area Program, 1979-85; commd. sr. scientist (res.) USPHS, 1949; cons. mental health WHO, 1959—, mem. expert panel health statistics, 1961-84; adv. U.S. del. 5th Session Interim Commn. WHO, Geneva, 1948, 6th Session, 1948, 1st World Health Assembly, Geneva, 1948; vis. scientist dept. pub. health London (Eng.) Sch. Hygiene and Tropical Medicine and Social Medicine Research Unit of Med. Research Council, 1968-69; mem. task panel Pres.'s Commn. on Mental Health, 1977-78; mem. adv. panel on health research studies Three Mile Island, Harrisburg, Pa., 1979-85; mem. selection panel for multidisciplinary dept. geriatrics and gerontology Govt. Ont., Can., 1987. Contbr. articles to sci. publs. Recipient Superior Svc. award HEW, 1962, Disting. Svc. award HEW, 1974, Abbot S. Weinstein Meml. award N.Y. State Office Mental Health, 1986, Health for All medal WHO, 1987, Cert. of Recognition for contbns. to psychiat. epidemiology and biostats. Harvard Inst. Psychiat. Epidemiology and Genetics, 1995; named to Hall of Fame, Balt. City Coll., 1994. Fellow Am. Statis. Assn., Am. Pub. Health Assn. (Rema Lapouse award 1973, honor award for contbns. to epidemiology of mental health 1986), Am. Psychiat. Assn. (hon.), Am. Orthopsychiat. Assn., Am. Epidemiol. Soc.; mem. Am. Coll. Epidemiology, NAS-Inst. Medicine (sr.), Cosmos Club (Washington), Phi Beta Kappa, Phi Lambda Upsilon, Delta Omega (pres. Alpha chpt. 1988-89, Nat. Merit award 1985). Home: 725 Mount Wilson Ln Apt 500 Baltimore MD 21208-1123 Office: Johns Hopkins U Sch Hygiene and Pub Health Hampton House 624 N Br Baltimore MD 21205

KRAMER, PETER DAVID, psychiatrist; b. N.Y.C., Oct. 22, 1948; s. Eric M. and Lore E. (Sanger) K.; m. Rachel M. Schwartz, June 29, 1980; children: Sarah Elizabeth, Jacob Aaron, Matthew Charles. AB, Harvard Coll., 1970; postgrad., University Coll., London, 1970-72; MD, Harvard Med. Sch., 1976. Diplomate Am. Bd. Psychiatry & Neurology. Med. resident U. Wis. Hospitals, Madison, 1976-77; psychiatry resident Yale U., New Haven, 1977-80; acting dir. div. sci. Alcohol, Drug Abuse, Mental Health Adminstrn., Rockville, Md., 1980-82; outpatient dir. R.I. Hosp., Providence, 1982-84; asst. prof. dept. psychiatry Brown U., Providence, 1982-91, assoc. prof., 1991-95, prof., 1995—; asst. prof. psychiatry George Washington U., 1981-82. Author: Moments of Engagement, 1989, Listening to Prozac, 1993;

mem. editl. bd. Psychiat. Times, 1985—, The Psychodynamic Letter, 1990-92, Am. Jour. Psychotherapy, 1996—; contbr. articles to profl. jours. Mem. Am. Psychiat. Assn. (pvt. practice com. 1988—, chmn. 1992-94), R.I. Med. Soc., R.I. Psychiat. Soc. (pres. 1990-91). Office: 236 Hope St Providence RI 02906-2212

KRAMER, SHELDON ZACHARY, psychologist, educator; b. Phila., Mar. 15, 1951; s. Bernard Herman and Reba Rose (Feinman) K. BA in Psychology, Religion, Pa. State U., 1972; MEd in Counseling, Antioch U., 1976; PhD in Clin. Psychology, Calif. Sch. Profl. Psychology, San Diego, 1983. Lic. psychologist, Calif.; lic. marriage and family therapist, Calif. Staff psychologist Phila. Psychiat. Ctr., 1978, sr. psychologist Westpark program, 1978; psychologist B'Nai B'Rith Career and Counseling Service, Phila., 1978-80; pvt. practice clin. psychology, marriage and family therapy, San Diego, 1976—; instr. Palomar Coll., San Marcos, Calif., 1981-84; asst. prof. psychology U.S. Internat. U., San Diego, 1983-90; pvt. instr. family therapists, San Diego, 1984—, acting dir. marriage-family therapy program USN, San Diego, 1986-88, asst. tng. dir. psychology, 1987-88; med. cons. Balboa Manor Hosp.; assoc. psych. ctrs. San Diego; dir. Inst. Transformations Workshop Mind-Body Medicine; lectr. in field. Mem. Am. Family Therapy Assn., Am. Assn. Marital and Family Therapists, Calif. Psychol. Assn., Assn. Transpersonal Psychology, Acad. San Diego Psychologists (assoc.), Assn. Humanistic Psychologists. Address: 2615 Camino Del Rio S Ste 300 San Diego CA 92108-3713

KRAMER, STEVEN G., ophthalmologist; b. Chgo., Feb. 28, 1941; s. Paul and Maria Kramer; m. Anne Crystal Kramer, Dec. 26, 1961 (div.); children: Janice Lynn, Kenneth David; m. Bernadette E. Coatar, June 30, 1974; children: Daniel Steven, Susan Mary. BA in Biology, U. Chgo., 1967; MD, Case Western Res. U., 1965; PhD, U. Chgo., 1971. Cert. assoc. examiner Am. Bd. Ophthalmology; lic. ophthalmologist, Calif., Wash. Instr. ophthalmology U. Chgo., 1968-71; chief of ophthalmology Madigan Army Med. Ctr., Tacoma, 1971-73; chief of ophathlmology VA Med. Ctr., San Francisco, 1973-75; prof. ophthalmology, chmn. U. Calif., San Francisco, 1975—, dir. Beckman Vision Ctr., 1988—; mem. various coms. VA Hosp., San Francisco, 1973—; mem. exec. med. bd. sch. medicine U. Calif., 1975—, mem./chmn. various coms., 1975—, mem. clin. dept. chmn. group, 1975—, mem. governing bd. continuing med. edn. program, 1984-85, mem. clin. rev. working group, 1985-86, pres.-elect med. staff, 1985, pres., 1986-88, mem. chancellor's governance group, 1986—, mem. adv. group devel. spine svcs., 1992—; v.p. That Man May See, Inc., 1975—, bd. trustees, 1975—, campaign cabinet mem. for Vision Rsch. Ctr., 1983—; sec., bd. govs. Francis Proctor Found. for Rsch. in Opthalmology, 1975—; mem. Rsch. to Prevent Blindness, Inc., N.Y., 1976—, ad hoc adv. com., 1976-77; NIH mem. vision rsch. program com. NEI, 1978-82, chmn., 1980-82; site visit chmn. U. Wash., Seattle, 1979, Mass. Eye and Ear Infirmary, Boston, 1980, dept. neurobiology Harvard Med. Sch., Boston, 1980; mem. joint program and planning bd. sch. medicine U. Calif./Mt. Zion, 1985-88; mem. courtesy staff San Francisco Gen. Hosp.; lectr. in field. Editor, editl. bd. therapeutics rev. sect. Survey of Ophthalmology, 1977-84, diagnostic and surg. techniques sect., 1984—; sci. referee Am. Jour. Ophthalmology, 1967-81, editl. bd., 1981—; editl. bd. Ophthalmic Soc.; sci. referee Life Scis.; editor CMA Ophthalmology Epitomes, Western Jour. Medicine, 1976-77; med. adv. bd. Nat. Soc. to Prevent Blindness, 1979—; editor sect. cornea and sclera Yearbook of Ophthalmology, 1982. Mem. legis. com. for State of Calif., 1977; bd. dirs. Found. for Glaucoma Rsch., 1980—. Maj. U.S. Army, 1971-73. USPHS Spl. fellow in ophthalmologic rsch., 1970; VA Hosp. Rsch. Program grantee; NIH grantee, That Man May See grantee. Mem. AMA, ACS, Am. Acad. Ophthalmology, Am. Intra-Ocular Implant Soc., Assn. for Rsch. in Vision and Ophthalmology, Pacific Coast Oto-Ophthalmology Soc., Frederick C. Cordes Eye Soc., Calif. Med. Assn. (sci. adv. panel 1974—, adv. panel on ophthalmology subcom. for accreditation 1976-77, 78), Calif. Assn. Ophthalmology (adv. cons.), Assn. Univ. Profs. of Ophthalmology (chmn. resident placement svc. com., mem. ophthalmology resident and fellowship edn. com.), No. Calif. Soc. to Prevent Blindness (med. adv. bd.), Pan Am. Assn. Ophthalmology, Am. Congress, San Francisco Ophthal. Round Table, Rsch. to Prevent Blindness, Inc., Retinitis Pigmentosa Internat. Soc. (founding mem., sci. adv. bd.), Castroviejo Corneal Soc., Internat. Cornea Soc., Internat. Soc. Refractive Keratoplasty, Calif. Cornea Club, Ophthalmologic Hon. Soc. of Am. Ophthal. Soc., Phi Beta Kappa, Alpha Omega Alpha, Sigma Xi. Office: U Calif 10 Kirkham St # K-301 San Francisco CA 94122-3815*

KRANE, STEPHEN MARTIN, physician, educator; b. N.Y.C., July 15, 1927; s. Daniel Golden and Bessie (Berman) K.; m. Cynthia Ramin, June 28, 1952; children: David Alan, Peter Jay, Ian Matthew, Adam. A.B., Columbia U., 1946, M.D., 1951; A.M. (hon.), Harvard U., 1968; M.D. (hon.), U. Geneva, 1989. Intern to chief resident in medicine Mass. Gen. Hosp., Boston, 1951-57, chief arthritis unit, 1961, physician, 1969; research fellow Washington U., St. Louis, 1956; asst. in medicine Harvard U. Med. Sch., Boston, 1958, prof., 1972-87, Persis, Cyrus and Marlow B. Harrison prof. clin. medicine, 1987—. Contbr. articles to profl. jours. Served with USNR, 1945-46. Recipient Kappa Delta award Orthopedic Rsch. Soc., 1977, Herberden medal Herberden Soc., London, 1980; named Guggenheim fellow Oxford U., 1973-74. Fellow ACP, AAAS, Am. Acad. Arts and Scis., Am. Coll. Rheumatology (master, Disting. Investigator award 1995); mem. Am. Soc. Clin. Investigation, Assn. Am. Physicians, Am. Fedn. Clin. Rsch., Am. Soc. Biol. Chemistry, Molecular Biology, Soc. Bone Mineral Rsch., Endocrine Soc. Home: 101 Windsor Rd Newton MA 02168-1121 Office: Mass Gen Hosp Boston MA 02114

KRANTZ, KERMIT EDWARD, physician, educator; b. Oak Park, Ill., June 4, 1923; s. Andrew Stanley and Beatrice H. (Cibrowski) K.; m. Doris Cole Krantz, Sept. 7, 1946; children: Pamela (Mrs. Richard Huffstutter), Sarah Elizabeth, Kermit Tripler. BS, Northwestern U., 1945, BM, 1947, MS in Anatomy, 1947, MD, 1948; LittD (hon.), William Woods Coll., 1971. Diplomate Am. Bd. Ob-Gyn. Intern ob-gyn. N.Y. Lying-In Hosp., 1947-48; asst. resident, asst. ob-gyn. Cornell U. Med. Coll., N.Y. Lying-In Hosp., N.Y. Hosp., 1948-50; fellow, resident in ob-gyn Mary Fletcher Hosp., Burlington, Vt., 1950-51; dir. Durfee Clinic, 1952-55; instr., then asst. prof. U. Vt. Coll. Medicine, 1951-55; asst. prof. U. Ark. Med. Sch., 1955-59; prof., chmn. dept. ob-gyn. U. Kans. Med. Ctr., 1959-90, Univ. Disting. prof., 1990-94, prof. anatomy, 1963—, lectr. history medicine, 1959—, dean clin. affairs, 1972-74, chief staff, 1972-74, obstetrician and gynecologist in chief, 1959-90, assoc. to exec. vice chancellor for facilities devel., 1974-83; univ. disting. prof. emeritus ob/gyn. and anatomy U. Kans., 1994—; cons. in field. Author numerous articles in field. Mem. Nat. Adv. Child Health and Human Devel. Council, NIH, 1974-76. Bowen-Brooks fellow N.Y. Acad. Medicine, 1948-50; recipient Found. award South Atlantic Assn. Obstetricians and Gynecologists, 1950, Found. award Am. Assn. Obstetricians and Gynecologists, 1950, Wyeth-Ayerst Pub. Recognition award 1st Am. Assn. Prof. of Gynecology and Obstetrics, 1988; named Outstanding Prof. in Coll. of Medicine Nu Sigma Nu, 1955; Robert A. Ross lectureship award Armed Forces Dist. meeting Am. Coll. Obstetricians and Gynecologists, 1972, Outstanding Civilian Service medal U.S. Army-Dept. Def., 1985; Charles A. Durham Meml. lectr. Ann. Session Tex. Med. Assn., 1978; Markle scholar med. sci., 1957-62; Kermit E. Krantz Soc. established at U. Kans. Med. Ctr., 1982. Founding fellow Am. Coll. Obstetricians and Gynecologists (Kermit E. Krantz Lectureship award established 1973, Outstanding Dist. Services award 1978, 82); fellow ACS, Am. Coll. Ob-Gyn (life); mem. Am. Assn. Anatomists, Am. Fedn. Clin. Research, AMA, Am. Med. Writers Assn., Am. Fertility Soc., AAUP, Soc. Exptl. Biology and Medicine, Aerospace Med. Assn., Endocrine Soc., Soc. Gynecologic Investigation, Central Assn. Obstetricians and Gynecologists, N.Y. Acad. Medicine, N.Y. Acad. Sci., Kans. Med. Soc., Assn. Mil. Surgeons U.S. (sustaining), Kans. Obstet. Soc., Sigma Xi, Alpha Omega Alpha. Home: 6711 Overhill Rd Shawnee Mission KS 66208-2263 Office: U Kans Med Ctr Kansas City KS 66160-7316

KRANTZ, SANFORD BURTON, physician; b. Chgo., Feb. 6, 1934; s. Max and Fannie (Orenstein) K.; m. Sandra R. Goldstein, Dec. 28, 1958; children—Michael David, Marcy Sharon, Alan Thomas, Sarah Ann. A.B., U. Chgo., 1954, B.S., 1955, M.D., 1959. Intern U. Chgo. Hosps., 1959-60; asst. resident medicine, 1960-63; NATO postdoctoral fellow biochemistry U. Glasgow, 1964-65; asst. prof. medicine U. Chgo. Hosps. and Argonne Cancer Research Hosp., Chgo., 1965-68; asst. chief hematology service clin. center NIH, Bethesda, Md., 1968-70; chief hematology VA Hosp., Vanderbilt Med. Sch., Nashville, 1970—; asso. prof. medicine Vanderbilt U., 1970-74, prof. medicine, chief hematology, 1974—. Author: (with L.O. Jacobson) Erythopoietin and the Regulation of Erythropoiesis, 1970. Recipient Joseph A. Capps prize for med. research, 1964; USPHS postdoctoral fellow, 1962-64; NATO postdoctoral fellow, 1964; Leukemia Soc. scholar, 1965-68; NIH grantee, 1971—. Fellow A.C.P.; mem. Am. Fedn. Clin. Research, Am. Soc. Clin. Investigation, Assn. Am. Physicians, AAAS, Am. Soc. Hematology, Internat. Soc. Exptl. Hematology, Central Soc. Clin. Research, Am. Soc. Exptl. Pathology, So. Soc. Clin. Investigation (pres. 1985-86), Sigma Xi. Home: 300 Estbury Ct Nashville TN 37215-5801

KRASNER, JAY B., internist; b. Providence, R.I., Jan. 25, 1954; s. Harold N. and Claire S. (Gorenstein) K.; m. Sharon L. Bell, June 27, 1981; children: Elliott, Laurel. BS, MIT, 1976; MD, Brown U., 1980. Diplomate Nat. Bd. Med. Examiners (task force on computer based examination 1983), Am. Bd. Internal Medicine; lic. Ky., Mass., Pa. Resident in internal medicine Grad. Hosp. U. Pa., Phila., 1980-83, chief resident, 1983-84; attending physician emergency depts. various local hosps., Phila., 1981-93; attending physician sect. of internal medicine Albert Einstein Med. Ctr. no. divsn., Phila., 1984-87; med. officer Fed. Correctional Instn., Lexington, Ky., 1987-90; pvt. practice internal medicine Sudbury, Mass., 1990—; clin. instr. internal medicine U. Pa. Sch. Medicine, Phila., 1980-84, asst. prof. internal medicine Temple U. Sch. Medicine, Phila., 1985-87, clin. asst. prof. internal medicine, U. Ky. Sch. Medicine, Lexington, 1988-90; mem. med. staff Emerson Hosp., Concord, Mass., 1990—, Newton Wellesley Hosp., Newton, Mass., 1993—; courtesy med. staff MetroWest Med. Ctr. Framingham, Mass., 1991—; med. dir. Parmener Health Svcs., 1991—; impartial med. examiner Commonwealth Mass. dept. indsl. accidents, 1993—; clin. reactor IM Internal Medicine, 1994—; course dir. Tufts U. Sch. of Medicine, 1992—; assoc. med. dir. for quality assurance and utilization rev. Ctrl. Mass. Region HMO Blue, 1992-94; reviewer Computer News for Physicians, 1987-90, Med. Software Revs., 1991—, Annals of Internal Medicine, 1985-87. Contbr. articles and reviews to profl. jours., chpt. to Medicine: Future Practice Alternatives, 1993; creator software programs in internal medicine. Cmmdr. Pub. Health Svc., 1987-90. Mem. Am. Soc. Internal Medicine, Mass. Med. Soc., Soc. for Gen. Internal Medicine, Am. Coll. Physicians, Am. Med. Joggers Assn., Alpha Omega Alpha, Eta Kappa Nu, Sigma Xi. Office: Jay B Krasner MD 111 Boston Post Rd Sudbury MA 01776

KRASNER, PAUL R., psychologist; b. N.Y.C., May 10, 1951; s. Ernest and Elisa A. (Abrams) K.; m. Trudi Robin Klarman, June 17, 1973; children: Lori Alison, Ami Aileen, Michelle Jamie. MA, Adelphi U., 1976, PhD, 1979. Staff psychologist N.C. Dept. Human Resources, Butner, 1978-81; dir. psychology Thoms Hosp., Ashville, N.C., 1981-85; clin. dir. Cary (N.C.) Psychology, 1985-95; psychologist Psychol. Health Assoc., Cary, N.C., 1995—. Contbr. articles to profl. jours. Pres. Am. Diabetes Assn. N.C., Raleigh, 1985; bd. dirs. Beth Shalom, 1987-95. Office: 1145A Executive Cir Cary NC 27511-4526

KRASNER, SCOTT ALLAN, physician, health facility administrator; b. Chgo., Mar. 29, 1956; s. Oscar J. and Bella (Kidder) K.; m. Terri Lee Henderson, Aut. 19, 1979; children: Jennifer Alyse, Lauren Michelle, David Andrew. BS with honors, UCLA, 1978; MD, Med. Coll. Wis., 1983; MPH, U. Ariz., 1993. Diplomate Nat. Bd. Med. Examiners, Am. Bd. Preventive Med., Am. Bd. Independent Med. Examiners. Resident Union Meml. Hosp., Balt., 1983-86, U. Ariz., Tucson, 1986-88; med. dir. clin. svcs. Helian Occupl., Tucson, 1988—; asst. med. dir. Planned Parenthood Ariz., Tucson, 1986—; clin. assoc. prof. Univ. Ariz., Tucson., 1989—; profl. adv. com. Judy's Nurses, Tucson, 1992—; chair peer rev. com. Helian Occupl., Tucson, 1995—. Chair fin. com. Stone Ave. Temple Restoration, Tucson, 1995—. Recipient Wagner award Med. Coll. Wis., 1983. Mem. Am. Coll. Occupl. and Environ. Med., Western Occupl. Med. Assn., Pima County Med. Soc., Ariz. Med. Assn. Jewish. Home: 5901 W Broomtail Pl Tucson AZ 85743 Office: Helian Occupl 2545 E Adams Tucson AZ 85716

KRASNOFF, SIDNEY OURIN, internist, educator, cardiologist, administrator, writer; b. Phila., July 11, 1918; s. Abraham Max and Sophia (Ourin) K.; m. Ruth B. Bernstein, June 11, 1946 (dec. 1982); children: Stuart B., Jonathan R., Robert M. (dec.); m. Suzanne Stern, May 22, 1983 (dec. 1993); children: Jeffrey P., Peter M. BA, U. Pa., 1938, MD, 1942. Diplomate Am. Bd. Internal Medicine. Intern, Jewish Hosp., Phila., 1942-43, resident in internal medicine, 1946-47; sr. attending physician Albert Einstein Med. Ctr., Phila., 1967—; clin. prof. medicine Temple U. Sch. Medicine, Phila., 1973-88; chmn. dept. medicine Rolling Hill Hosp., Elkins Park, Pa., 1970-78, med. dir., mem. governing bd., 1983-86; pres. Pa. Med. Care Found., Harrisburg, 1976-78, Pa. Statewide Profession Standards Rev. Council, Harrisburg, 1977-78. Author: Computers in Medicine, 1967. Contbr. articles to profl. publs. Bd. dirs. Care-Medico, Phila., 1966-80, overseas service, Afghanistan, 1968; election judge Cheltenham Twp., Pa., 1977-80. Capt. U.S. Army, 1943-46, ETO. Recipient Maimonides award State of Israel Bonds, 1943-45; rsch. grantee Truman Libr., 1990. Fellow ACP, Am. Coll. Cardiology, Phila. Coll. Physicians, Phila. Acad. Cardiology; mem. Am. Heart Assn., AMA, Pa. Med. Soc., Philadelphia County Med. Soc. (sec. 1972-73, v.p. 1978, pres. 1980, chmn. bd. censors 1983-88), Pa. Soc. Internal Medicine (pres. 1960). Republican. Jewish. Avocations: photography; fishing; sailing; tennis. Home: 1801 S Flagler Dr Apt 1806 West Palm Beach FL 33401

KRASNOW, MICHAEL ARTHUR, ophthalmologist; b. Worcester, Mass., Mar. 26, 1945. BA, PhD, U. Mass., 1967, 73; AM, U. Cin., 1969; OD, New Eng. Coll. Optometry, 1978, Coll. Osteo. Medicine, Pomona, Calif., 1985. Staff optometrist Nat. Valley Eye Group, Mission Hills, Calif., 1979-82; intern Chgo. Osteo. Hosp., 1985-86; resident Tulsa Regional Med. Ctr., 1986-89; fellow U. Iowa, 1986-89; ophthalmologist, glaucoma specialist Huntington (W.Va.) Eye Assocs., 1990-94, Univ. Eye Surgeons, 1994—; vis. adj. prof. ophthalmology W.Va. Osteo. Med. Sch., 1991—; assoc. prof. family medicine and cmty. health Marshall U. Sch. Medicine, 1992—; assoc. prof. dept. surgery, 1992—. Contbr. articles to profl. publs. Mem. Am. Osteo. Assn., Am. Acad. Ophthalmology, Osteo. Acad. Ophthalmology and Otolaryngology, Am. Glaucoma Soc., W.Va. Osteo. Assn., W.Va. State Med. Soc., Iowa Eye Assocs., Sigma Xi, Phi Kappa Phi. Office: 1320 12th St # 6 Huntington WV 25701-4048

KRASSAS, GERASIMOS EFTHIMIOS, endocrinologist; b. Athens, Greece, May 5, 1943; s. Efthimios G. and Danai L. (Petichaki) K.; m. Evagelia Karamichou M., Dec. 13, 1967 (div. June 1988); children: Efthimios, Afroditi; m. Chariklia Gkiati G., Mar. 6, 1990. MD, Thessaloniki (Greece) U., 1973. Asst. U. Thessaloniki, 1970-72; clin. asst. Cen. Middlesex Hosp., London, 1972-73; rsch. registrar North Middlesex Hosp., London, 1973-76; lectr. Thessaloniki U., 1976-78; cons. Panagia Hosp., Thessaloniki, 1978-96; lectr. Athens U. Med. Sch., 1987; vis. prof. U. Mass. Med. Sch., Boston, 1981. Author: The Male Climacteric, 1987; contbr. articles to profl. jours. Recipient Clin. award Brent and Harrow Health Authority, London, 1973, Organon award 15th World Congress Fertility and Sterility, 1995. Mem. Hellenic Endocrine Soc. (v.p. 1988), Hellenic Diabetic Soc., Med. Soc. Thessaloniki, Endocrine Soc. Great Britain. Home: Tsimiski 92, 54622 Thessaloniki Greece

KRAUS, HENRY, retired physician, educator; b. Akron, Ohio, Apr. 12, 1923; s. Charles Morton and Gertrude (Gibans) K.; m. Esther Elizabeth Mackey, July 7, 1946; children: Charles Thomas, Thomas Henry, Anne Elizabeth, James Douglas. Cert., Harvard U., 1943; MD, Case Western Res. U., 1947. Diplomate Am. Bd. Internal Medicine. Intern in medicine Univ. Hosps. Cleve., 1947-48, asst. resident in medicine, 1948-49; fellow in cardiology Thorndike lab. Boston City Hosp., 1949-50; sr. resident in medicine West Roxbury Vets. Hosp., Boston, 1950-51; sr. attending physician Akron Gen. Med. Ctr., 1956-91, chief of medicine, 1958-62; assoc. clin. prof. medicine Northeastern Ohio U. Coll. of Medicine, Rootstown, 1980-91; ret., 1991; bd. of trustees Akron Gen. Med. Ctr., 1972—, mem. exec. com., 1972-88; bd. dirs. PIE Ins. Co., Cleve. Bd. dirs. Pioneer Western Life Ins. Co., 1959-76. 1st lt. USMC, 1953. Mem. ACP, Mayflower Club (Akron), Alpha Omega Alpha. Republican. Home: 395 Delaware Ave Akron OH 44303-1233

KRAUS, MICHAEL ALAN, nephrologist; b. Hammond, Ind., Oct. 10, 1959; s. Clifford Emil and Regina Ruth (Inwald) K.; m. Molly Leigh Ahlgrim, May 21, 1983; children: Whitney, Ryan, Charles, Carolyn. AB, Wabash Coll., 1981; MD, Ind. U., Indpls., 1985. Diplomate Am. Bd. Internal Medicine, Am. Bd. Nephrology. Resident in internal medicine Ind. U. Indpls., 1985-88; fellow in neurology U. Iowa, Iowa City, 1990-91, assoc., 1991-92; clin. dir. nephrology Wishard Meml. Hosp., Indpls., 1992-94; from asst. to assoc. prof. medicine Ind. U., Indpls., 1992—, med. dir. acute dialysis unit, 1994—, med. dir. peritoneal dialysis unit, 1994—; med. dir. dialysis Vencor Hosp., Indpls., 1993-94; mem. med. adv. bd. Ind. chpt. Nat. Kidney Found., Indpls., 1995—, physician mem. patient activities Iowa chpt., Cedar Rapids, 1990-92; cons. Baxter, Chgo., 1995. Office: Ind U UH1115 550 University Blvd Indianapolis IN 46202

KRAUSE, CHARLES JOSEPH, otolaryngologist; b. Des Moines, Apr. 21, 1937; s. William H. and Ruby I. (Hitz) K.; m. Barbara Ann Steelman, June 14, 1962; children—Sharon, John, Ann. B.A., State U. Iowa, 1959, M.D., 1962. Diplomate: Am. Bd. Otolaryngology. Intern Phila. Gen. Hosp., 1962-63; resident in surgery U. Iowa, 1965-66, resident in otolaryngology, 1966-69; fellow dept. plastic surgery Marien Hosp., Stuttgart, W. Ger., 1970; asst. prof. otolaryngology U. Iowa, 1969-72, asso. prof., 1972-75, vice chmn. dept. otolaryngology, 1973-77, prof., 1975-77; prof., chmn. dept. otolaryngology U. Mich. Med. Sch., Ann Arbor, 1977-92; chief clin. affairs U. Mich. Hosps., Ann Arbor, 1986-89; asst. dean for clin. affairs U. Mich., 1986-89, sr. assoc. dean U. Mich. Med. Sch., 1991-95, chief clin. affairs, 1991-95, sr. assoc. hosp. dir., 1995-96. Author book in field; contbr. chpts. to books, articles to profl. jours. Served to capt. USAF, 1963-65. Fellow Am. Soc. Head and Neck Surgery (coun. 1980-83, chmn. rsch. com. 1980-83, pres. 1987-88); mem. AMA, Am. Acad. Otolaryngology Head and Neck Surgery (bd. dirs. 1987-93, sec.-treas. 1987-93, pres.-elect. 1995, pres. 1996), Am. Acad. Facial Plastic and Reconstructive Surgery (regional v.p.1977-80, chmn. rsch. com. 1977-80, pres. 1981-82), A.C.S. (adv. coun. otolaryngology 1979-83), Assn. Head and Neck Oncologists Gt. Britain (corr. mem.), Am. Assn. Cosmetic Surgeons, Assn. rsch. in Otolaryngology, Washtenaw County Med. Soc. (exec. com. 1979-82), Mich. State Med. Soc., Mich. Otolaryngol. Soc., Am. Acad. Depts. Otolaryngology, Soc. Unit. Otolaryngologists, Walter P. Work Soc. (pres. 1987), Am. Cancer Soc. (med. adv. com. Washtenaw County unit), Am. Laryngol., Rhinol. and Otol. Soc., Am. Laryngol. Assn., Centurions of Deafness Rsch. Found., Am. Bd. Otolaryngology (bd. dirs 1984—, exam. com. chair 1993—, pres.elect 1996—). Republican. Presbyterian. Home: 3100 Hunting Valley Dr Ann Arbor MI 48104-2845 Office: U Mich 1904 Taubman Ctr 15005 E Medical Ctr Dr Ann Arbor MI 48109-0600

KRAUSE, JOHN LAWRENCE, plastic surgeon; b. Queens, N.Y., Mar. 5, 1936; s. John L. and Grace Rose (Wagner) K.; m. Andrea Van Nostrand, Apr. 20, 1963 (dec. Sept. 1994); m. Irene Krause, Dec. 23, 1995. BS, Queens (N.Y.) Coll., 1957; MD, Cornell U., 1961. Diplomate Am. Bd. Surgery.; lic. surgeon, N.J., N.Y. Intern Strong Meml. Hosp., Rochester, N.Y., 1961-62; resident Mary Imogene Bassett Hosp., Cooperstown, N.Y., 1962-66; plastic surgeon Columbia U. Presbyn. med. Ctr., N.Y.C., 1968-70; pvt. practice Cherry Hill, N.J., 1970—; mem. staff West Jersey Hosp., Camden, N.J., Voorhees, N.J., Berlin, N.J., West Jersy Health Sys., John F. Kennedy Meml. Hosp., Stratford, N.J., Garden State Hosp., Marlton, N.J., Our Lady of Lourdes Hosp., Camden. Contbr. articles to profl. jours. Mem. exec. com. Am. Cancer Soc., Camden County; commr. Bd. of Health, Haddonfield, N.J., 1983-92, pres., 1992—. Fellow ACS (v.p. 1989-91, pres. 1992-93); mem. AMA, Am. Soc. Plastic and Reocnstructive Surgeons, Am. Burn Assn., Am. Soc. Aesthetic Plastic Surgery, N.J. Soc. Plastic and Reconstructive Surgeons (sec.-treas. 1974-81, v.p. 1981-82, pres. 1982-83), Med. Soc. N.J., Camden County Med. Soc., Cleft Palat Soc., Robert H. Ivy Soc. Office: South Jersey Med Ctr 1401 Rte 70 E Ste 22 Cherry Hill NJ 08034

KRAUSE, JUSTIN GARDNER, osteopath; b. Cin., May 29, 1923; s. Albert Paul and Vadna (Gardner) K.; m. Glenna Bonita (dec.); children: Justin G., Paula K., Cecelia Sue, Elizabeth Jane, Patti Ann; m. Lois Jackquelin Fowler, Dec. 17, 1969; 1 child, Matthew Fowler. Student, Carnegie Tech., 1941-42, Miami U., Oxford, Ohio, 1942, U. Cin., 1945-46; DO, Kansas City Coll. Osteo. Medicine, 1950. Diplomate Am. Bd. Family Practice, Am. Bd. Gen. Practice. Intern Grandview Hosp., Dayton, Ohio; fellow in geriatrics St. Margaret Hosp., Pitts.; gen. practice osteo. medicine Kansas City, 1950—; coroner Greene County, Ohio, 1964—. Served to sgt. U.S. Army, 1942-45, ETO. Decorated Bronze Star. Fellow Am. Acad. Family Practice, Amer. Acad. Forensic Sci. Democrat. Methodist. Home: 7069 Russell Ct Arvada CO 80007

KRAUSE, LAWRENCE M., general surgeon; b. Chgo., Sept. 8, 1953. BS, U. Ill., 1975, MD, 1979. Diplomate Am. Bd. Surgery. Clin. asst. prof. U. Chgo., 1985-90, U. Ill., 1990—; attending surgeon Michael Reese Hosp., Chgo., 1987—. Fellow Am. Coll. Surgeons; mem. AMA, AAAS, Chgo. Surg. Soc. Office: Lake Shore Surg Assn 111 N Wabash Ste 1501 Chicago IL 60601

KRAUSE, RICHARD MICHAEL, medical scientist, government official, educator; b. Marietta, Ohio, Jan. 4, 1925; s. Ellis L. and Jennie Mae (Waterman) K. B.A., Marietta Coll., 1947, D.Sc. (hon.), 1978; M.D., Case Western Res. U., 1952; D.Sc. (hon.), U. Rochester, 1979, Med. Coll. Ohio, Toledo, 1981, Hahnemann Med. Coll. and Hosp., 1982; LLD (hon.), Thomas Jefferson U., 1982. Rsch. fellow dept. preventive medicine Case Western Res. U., 1950-51; intern Ward Med. Service, Barnes Hosp., St. Louis, 1952-53; asst. resident Ward Med. Service, Barnes Hosp., 1953-54; asst. physician to hosp. Rockefeller Inst., 1954-57, asst. prof., assoc. physician to hosp., 1957-61; prof. epidemiology Sch. Medicine, Washington U., St. Louis, 1962-66; assoc. prof. medicine Sch. Medicine, Washington U., 1962-65, prof. medicine, 1965-66; assoc. prof., physician to hosp. Rockefeller U., 1966-68, prof., sr. physician, 1968-75; dir. Rockefeller U. (Animal Rsch. Ctr.), 1974-75, Nat. Inst. Allergy and Infectious Diseases, NIH, HEW, Bethesda, Md., 1975-84; USPHS surgeon, 1975-77, asst. surgeon gen., 1977-84; dean Emory U. Sch. Medicine, Atlanta, 1984-89, Robert W. Woodruff prof. medicine, 1984-89; mem. program com. Inst. Medicine, 1986-87; sr. sci. adv. Fogarty Internat. Ctr. NIH, Bethesda, 1989—; Bd. dirs. Mo.-St. Louis Heart Assn., 1962-66, mem. research com., 1963-66; mem. exec. com. council on rheumatic fever and congenital heart disease Am. Heart Assn., 1963-66, chmn. council research study com., 1963-66, mem. assn. research com., 1963-66, mem. policy com., 1966-70; mem. commn. streptococcal and staphylococcal diseases U.S. Armed Forces Epidemiol. Bd., 1963-72, dep. dir., 1968-72; bd. dirs. N.Y. Heart Assn., 1967-73, chmn. adv. council on research, 1969-71, mem. dirs. council, 1973-75; cons., mem. coccal expert com. WHO, 1967—; mem. steering com. Biomed. Sci. Scientific Working Group, WHO, 1978; mem. infectious disease adv. com. Nat. Inst. Allergy and Infectious Disease, NIH, 1970-74; bd. dirs. Royal Soc. Medicine Found., Inc., 1971-77, treas., 1973-75; bd. dirs. Allergy and Asthma Found. Am., 1976-77, Lupus Found. Am., 1977-79. Assoc. editor: Jour. Immunology, 1963-71; sect. editor: Viral and Microbial Immunology, 1974-75; editor: Jour. Exptl. Medicine, 1973-75; adv. editor, 1976-84; mem. editorial bd. Bacteriological Revs, 1969-73, Infection and Immunity, 1970-78, Immunochemistry, 1973-80, Clin. Immunology and Immunopathology, 1976-78; contbr. numerous articles to profl. jours. Served with U.S. Army, 1944-46. Decorated Gumhuria medal Egypt; recipient Disting. Service medal HEW, 1979; C. William O'Neal Disting. Am. Service award; Robert Koch Medal in Gold, Berlin, 1985; Sr. U.S. Scientist award Alexander Von Humboldt Found., Fed. Republic Germany, 1986. Mem. U.S. Nat. Acad. Scis., Inst. Medicine, Assn. Am. Physicians, Am. Acad. Allergy, Am. Soc. Biol. Chemists, Am. Soc. Clin. Investigation, Am. Assn. Immunologists, Am. Soc. Microbiology, Harvey Soc., Am. Coll. Allergists, AAAS, Infectious Diseases Soc. Am., Royal Soc. Medicine, Practitioner's Soc. N.Y., Am. Epidemiol. Soc. Clubs: Century Assn. (N.Y.C.); Cosmos (Washington). Home: 4000 Cathedral Ave NW Apt 413B Washington DC 20016-5249 Office: NIH Fogarty Internat Ctr 16 Ctr Dr MSC 6705 Bethesda MD 20892-6705

KRAUSEN, ANTHONY SHARNIK, surgeon; b. Phila., Feb. 22, 1944; s. B.M. and Kay S. (Sharnik) K.; m. Susan Elizabeth Park, Sept. 6, 1970; children: Nicole, Allison. Student Germantown Acad., 1949-61; B.A., Princeton U., 1965; M.D., U. Mich., 1969. Intern, Presbyn. Med. Center, Denver, 1969-70; resident St. Joseph Hosp., Denver, 1970-71, Barnes Hosp., St. Louis, 1972-76; with Milw. Med. Clinic, 1976—, head dept. facial plastic surgery, 1984—; mem. staffs Columbia, St. Michael, Children's, St. Mary Hosp., Oankee. Pres. Contemporary Art Soc., Milw. Art Mus., 1983, bd. dirs. Friends of Art. Served with U.S. Army Nat. Guard, 1970-76. Fellow ACS, Am. Acad. Cosmetic Surgery, Am. Acad. Facial Plastic and Reconstructive Surgery, Am. Acad. Otolaryngology; mem. Nat. Neurofibromatosis Soc. (med. advisor Wis. chpt. 1985-92), Wis. Otolaryngological Soc. Clubs: Ivy (Princeton, N.J.), Town Club (Milw.). Office: 3003 W Good Hope Rd Milwaukee WI 53209-2042

KRAUSKOPF, CHARLES JOSEPH, psychology educator; b. Evanston, Ill., Oct. 18, 1931; s. Karl Hort and Edna Alice (Fleming) K.; m. Joan Miday, July 4, 1954; children: Timothy Karl, David Andrew. AB, Ohio U., 1953; PhD, Ohio State U., 1960. Lic. psychologist, Ohio. Counselor U. Colo., Boulder, 1960-62; asst. prof., assoc. prof., then prof. U. Mo., Columbia, 1962-87; prof. psychology Ohio State U., Columbus, 1987—; cons. Head Start, Community Clinic, others; bd. dirs. Personality Assessment System Found. Author Mo. Math. Placement Test, 1967; author: (with D.R. Saunders) Personality and Ability, 1994. Lt. USNR, 1953-55, Korea. Grantee U.S. Office of Edn., 1964, Social-Rehab. Svcs., 1969, Psychol. Assessment Assocs., 1973, 76. Fellow Am. Psychol. Assn., Soc. Personality Assn.; mem. Sigma Xi. Office: Ohio State Univ 1885 Neil Ave Columbus OH 43210-1222

KRAUSS, BEATRICE JOY, psychology researcher, educator; b. Portland, Oreg., Dec. 26, 1943; d. Edwin Eugene and Mable Maru (Wilhelm) Osgood; m. Herbert Harris Krauss, Aug. 28, 1965; children: Michael Conal, Daniel Avram. MusB, Northwestern U., 1965; MA, U. Kans., 1967; PhD, CUNY, 1979. Dir. rsch. Community Sch. Dist. 18, Bklyn., 1978-79; asst. prof. Coll. of New Rochelle, N.Y., 1979-87, assoc. prof., 1987-90, dir. coll. ctr., dir. women's studies, 1989-90; mgr. rsch. group Eric Marder Assocs., N.Y.C., 1986-89; sr. rsch. assoc. Meml. Sloan Kettering Cancer Ctr., N.Y.C., 1990-93; sr. project dir., prin. investigator Nat. Devel. and Rsch. Inst., Inc., N.Y.C., 1993—; treas. Internat. Orgn. for Study Group Tensions, N.Y.C., 1987—; mem. Jacob's Inst. for Women's Health. Reviewer Jour. Health and Social Behavior, Psycho-Social Oncology, AIDS Education and Prevention, (with others) Living with Anxiety and Depression, 1974; contbr. articles to profl. jours. Cons. Com. on Alcohol and Drug Abuse, Irvington, N.Y., 1983-84; pres. Sleepy Hollow Concert Assn., Tarrytown, N.Y., 1983-85, 90-92. Grantee Coll. of New Rochelle, 1985, NIMH, 1990, 94, SPSSI, 1992, N.Y. State Legis., 1993, N.Y. State AIDS Inst., 1993, 95. Mem. AAAS, APA (task force on teaching psychology of women 1982-84), Am. Evaluation Assn., Assn. for Women in Psychology (assoc. editor newsletter 1988), N.Y. Acad. Scis., Sigma Xi, Psi Chi. Home: 6 Downing Ct Irvington NY 10533-2330

KRAUSS, HENRY FREDERICK, JR., optometrist; b. Sewickley, Pa., Apr. 10, 1952; s. Henry Frederick and Mirella Anna (Guerrieri) K.; m. Sally Winston Miller, July 5, 1975; children: Molly Anne, Henry Neil, Malinda Paige, Michael Winston. BS, Centre Coll. Ky., 1976; OD, U. Houston, 1980. Optometrist, owner Eye Care Assocs., Richardson, Tex., 1980—; v.p. ProComp Systems Inc., Albuquerque, 1983-86; ptnr. K-W Distbrs., Dallas, 1983-86, Summit Seminars, Richardson, 1985—. Bd. dirs. Found. for Edn. and Research in Vision, 1988-89, Southwest Vision Service Plan, 1982-84. Fellow Am. Acad. Optometry; mem. Am. Optometric Assn., Tex. Optometric Assn. (Young Optometrist of Yr. award 1985), North Tex. Optometric Assn. (pres. 1983-84), Am. Pub. Health Assn. (vision care sect.). Republican. Mormon. Avocations: golf, tennis, photography, horsemanship, sailing. Office: Eye Care Assocs 660 W Campbell Rd Richardson TX 75080-3301

KRAUSS, HERBERT HARRIS, psychologist; b. Phila., June 13, 1940; s. Leon and Ethel Sarah (Cohen) K.; m. Beatrice Joy Osgood, Aug. 26, 1965; children: Michael Conal, Daniel Avram. BS, Pa. State U., 1961, MS, 1962; PhD, Northwestern U., 1966. Lic. psychologist, N.Y. Intern in med. psychology U. Oreg. Med. Sch., 1962-63; asst. prof. psychiatry, psychology U. Kans. Med. Sch., Kansas City, Kans., 1966-67; asst. prof. psychiatry, psychology, chief psychologist in child psychiatry Ohio State U. Coll. Medicine, Columbus, 1967-69; assoc. prof. psychology U. Ga., Athens, 1969-71; prof. psychology Hunter Coll., CUNY, N.Y.C., 1971—, chair dept. psychology, 1992—; dir. rehab. rsch. Internat. Ctr. for the Disabled, N.Y.C., 1984—; cons. Managed Health Network, N.Y.C., 1979-90, PhD Program, NYU, rehab. counselling, 1991—; adj. assoc. prof. psychiatry Cornell Med. Sch., N.Y.C., 1978—; assoc. attending psychologist Payne Whitney Clinic, N.Y. Hosp., 1978—; ptnr. Health Resources Mgmt. Co-author: Living with Anxiety and Depression, 1974; co-editor: Between Survival and Suicide, 1976, A Provider's Guide to Psychiatric Services in the General Hospital, 1986, The Aging Workforce: A Guide for University Administrators, 1992; co-editor Internat. Jour. Group Tensions, 1995—; cons. editor Jour. Individual Psychology, 1996—. Cons. Irvington, N.Y. Drug Coun., 1983; coach football and wrestling Irvington Sunnysiders, 1978-83, soccer Am. Youth Soccer Orgn., Houston, 1976-78. Named Outstanding Teacher Psychology, N.Y. Psychol. Assn., 1972. Mem. APA, N.Y. Acad. Scis., Ea. Psychol. Assn., Internat. Organ for Study of Group Tensions (v.p.), Congress of Rehab. Medicine, Am. Evaluation Assn., Ardsley Curling Club, Cornell Club, Sigma Xi. Home: 6 Downing Ct Irvington NY 10533-2330 Office: Hunter Coll 695 Park Ave New York NY 10021-5024

KRAUSS, JUDITH BELLIVEAU, nursing educator; b. Malden, Mass., Apr. 11, 1947; d. Leo F. and Dorothy (Conners) Belliveau; m. Ronald L. Krauss, Sept. 5, 1970; children: Jennifer Leigh, Sarah Elizabeth. BS, Boston Coll., 1968; MSN, Yale U., 1970. RN, Conn. Clinical specialist Conn. Mental Health Ctr., New Haven, 1971-73; clin. specialist Yale Sch. Nursing, New Haven, 1971-73; asst. prof. rsch. Yale U. Sch. Nursing, New Haven, 1973-78, assoc. dean, 1978-85; prof., dean Yale U. Sch. Nursing, New Haven, Conn., 1985—; cons. pharm. and pub. cons., sch., govt. agys. Author: The Chronically Ill Psychiatric Patient and the Community, 1982 (Am. Jour. Nursing Book of Yr. 1982); editor Archives of Psychiat. Nursing, 1986—; mem. editorial bd. Issues in Mental Health Nursing, Psychosocial Rehab., Psychiat. Nursing Forum, Psychiat. Svcs.; contbr. articles to profl. jours. Am. Nurses Found. scholar, 1978; recipient Chamberlain award Soc. Edn. and Rsch. in Nursing, 1994; named Disting. Alumna Yale Sch. Nursing, 1984. Mem. ANA (Disting. Contbn. to Psychiat. Nursing award 1992), Am. Acad. Nursing, Conn. Nurses Assn. (mem. cabinet on edn. 1987-89, bd. dirs. 1988-91, rep. to ANA house of dels. 1988-91, Josephine Dolan award 1989), Sigma Theta Tau (Disting. Lectr. award 1987), Delta Mu (Founders award 1987). Office: Yale U Sch Nursing PO Box 9740 New Haven CT 06536-0740

KRAUSS, LEO, urologist, educator; b. N.Y.C., Nov. 5, 1928; s. Moe and Marie (Shapiro) K.; m. Harriet Powell, Dec. 4, 1955; children: Robert, Jennifer. BA summa cum laude, Syracuse U., 1948; MD, NYU, 1953. Diplomate Am. Bd. of Urology. Attending urologist N. Shore U. Hosp., Plainview, N.Y., 1963—, Manhasset, N.Y., 1987—; chief of urology Syosset (N.Y.) Comty. Hosp., 1963-78; urologist pvt. practice, Plainview, 1963—; consulting urologist USAF, Plattsburgh, N.Y., 1961-63, VA Hosp., Tupper Lake, N.Y., 1961-63; asst. prof. urology SUNY, Stony Brook, 1976—. Contbr. articles and abstracts to profl. jours. Bd. dirs. Long Island Cancer Coun., Huntington, N.Y., 1977-79. Capt. USAF, 1954-56, Korea. Named Attending Urologist of Yr., Nassau County Med. Ctr., E. Meadow, N.Y., 1981. Fellow ACS; mem. AMA, N.Y. State Urol. Soc., Am. Assn. Clin. Urologists, Am. Fedn. for Clin. Rsch., Am. Urol. Assn., Alpha Omega Alpha. Home: 33 Orchard Dr Woodbury NY 11797 Office: 875 Old Country Rd Plainview NY 11803

KRAUT, JOEL ARTHUR, ophthalmologist; b. Jersey City, July 21, 1937; s. Alan and Lillian Betty (Kravitz) K.; m. Cathy Jane Kleven, June 30, 1963; children: David Terence, Amy Melissa. AB cum laude, Princeton U., 1958; MD, Columbia U., 1962. Diplomate Am. Bd. Ophthalmology. Intern Boston U. Med. Ctr., 1962-63; resident in ophthalmology NYU-Bellevue Med. Ctr., N.Y.C., 1963-66; chief ophthalmology USAF Hosp., Tachikawa, Japan, 1966-68; pvt. practice specializing in ophthalmology Brookline, Mass., 1968-96; asst. prof. Ophthalmology Harvard Med. Sch., 1996—; clin. assoc., clin. instr. ophthalmology Harvard U. Med. Sch.; clin. instr. ophthalmology Tufts U. Sch. Medicine, 1968-91, clin. assoc. prof. ophthalmology, 1991—, assoc. surgeon ophthalmology, 1981-91, surgeon in ophthalmology, 1991—; dir. Low Vision Ctr., Mass. Eye & Ear Infirmary, 1968—, med. dir. Rehab. Ctr., bd. surgeons, 1993—, pres. eye staff, 1994-96, pres. med. staff, 1995-96, bd. dirs.; mem. med. staff Beth Israel Hosp., 1991—; bd. dirs. physiol. optics dept. ophthalmology Tufts-New Eng. Med. Ctr., 1968-73; cons. U.S. 5th Air Force, Japan, 1966-68. Contbr. articles to med. and profl. jours. Chmn. United Way campaign, 1973; bd. dirs. Boston Aid to Blind, 1987— (Man of Vision award 1996); mem. adv. bd. Mass. Commn. for Blind, 1988-94; mem. adv. bd. Nat. Assn. of Visually Handicapped, 1991—. Cane scholar, 1954-58, St. John-Princeton scholar, 1958-62; U. Calif. Rsch. fellow, 1960. Fellow ACS; mem. Royal Soc. Medicine, Am. Acad. Ophthalmology (honor award 1991), New Eng. Ophthal. Soc., Mass. Ophthal. Soc., Soc. Geriatric Ophthalmology, Intraocular Lens Soc., New Eng. Implant Soc. (sec. 1979-81, pres. 1981-83), Mass. Med. Soc. Greater Boston, Med. Soc., Mass. Soc. Eye Physicians and Surgeons (exec. bd. 1988—, recorder 1991-94, treas. 1995-96, pres.-elect 1996—), Hazel Hotchkiss Wightman Tennis Club, du Bailliage de la Chaine des Rotissurs, Princeton U. Club (spl. gifts com. 1992-93), Phi Beta Kappa, Sigma Xi. Office: 16 Webster St Brookline MA 02146-4938

KRAVATH, RICHARD ELLIOT, pediatrician, educator; b. N.Y.C., May 25, 1935; s. Reuben and Fannie Kravath; m. Pauline Sara Hauser, Aug. 27, 1960; children: Robert, Peter, Caroline. AB, Columbia U., 1956; MD, SUNY, Bklyn., 1960. Diplomate Am. Bd. Pediatrics. Intern Montefiore Med. Ctr., 1960-61, pediatric resident, chief resident, 1964-66, pediatric pulmonary fellowship, 1966-68; dir. div. intensive care pediatrics Albert Einstein Coll. Medicine, Bronx, 1981-82, prof. pediatrics, 1982; dir. in-patient pediatrics King's County Hosp. Ctr., Bklyn., 1982—; prof. clin. pediatrics SUNY, Bklyn., 1982—. Author, co-author Pediatrics: Pretest, 1987, 89, 92, 95; co-author: Water and Electrolytes in Pediatrics, 1982, 2d edit., 1993; contbr. articles to profl. jours. Capt. USAF, 1961-64. Mem. Alumni Assn. SUNY-Bklyn. (pres. 1992). Home: 6 Scott St Dobbs Ferry NY 10522-2614 Office: SUNY Bklyn Dept Pediatrics 450 Clarkson Ave Brooklyn NY 11203-2012

KRAVEC, CYNTHIA VALLEN, microbiologist; b. Newark, Sept. 8, 1951; d. William George and Elizabeth Irene (VanAllen) K. BS, Syracuse (N.Y.) U., 1974; MS, Seton Hall U., S. Orange, N.J., 1980; MBA, Monmouth Coll., W. Long Branch, N.J., 1986. Registered microbiologist. Sr. technician GIBCO/Invenex, Millburn, N.J., 1974-79; rsch. scientist Wampole Labs. div. Carter-Wallace Inc., East Windsor, N.J., 1979-90; scientist Roche Diagnostic Systems subsidiary Hoffmann-LaRoche, Inc., Nutley, N.J., 1990—. Contbr. articles to profl. jours. Mem. Am. Soc. Microbiology, Tissue Culture Assn., Soc. of Indsl. Microbiology. Home: 1006 Coolidge St Westfield NJ 07090-1215 Office: Roche Diagnostic Systems 1080 US Highway 202 S North Branch NJ 08876-3733

KRAVETS, BARBARA ZEITLIN, clinical nutritionist; b. Chgo., Apr. 22, 1935; d. Nathaniel S. and Rosalyn R. Zeitlin; m. Leonard Kravets, July 7, 1957 (div. 1976); children: Laura Kravets-Gautier, Linda K., James Z. BS magna cum laude, Northwestern U., 1957. Cert. clin. nutritionist; lic. nutrition cons. Dir. nutrition Am. Heart Assn. Health and Fitness Program, Northbrook, Ill., 1976-78; project mgr. Dorenfest and Assocs., Northbrook, 1978-79; dir. nutrition Nutri-Dyn Products, Inc., Niles, Ill., 1979-84; dir. nutrition outreach svcs., dir. nutrition reference svc. Am. Internat. Hosp., Zion, Ill., 1985-86; cons. in field Highland Park, Ill., 1986—; mem. complementary health therapies com. Chgo. Dept. Pub. Health, 1991—; mem. dept. metabolism, endocrinology and diabetes colloquium Northwestern U. Med. Sch., 1984—; drafter Ill. Pub. Law Dietetic and Nutrition Svcs. Practice Act, 1992; mem. Ill. Dietetic and Nutrition Svcs. Practice Bd., 1996—; dir. nutrition The Claremont Rehab. and Living Ctr., 1995—. Sci. editor: Whole Foods, Conscious Choice; author: Why Eat Your Heart Out, A Fourth Horse for Doctor Elliott Joslin, Nutrition Reference Manual. Named Am. Biog. Inst. Woman of the Yr., 1992. Mem. Nutrition for Optimal Health Assn., Am. Diabetes Assn. (com. on edn. 1980-81), U. Ill. Med. Sch. Nutrition Group, Nat. Nutritional Foods Assn. (acad. establishment com. 1982), Internat. and Am. Assns. Clin. Nutritionists (nat. competency examination com. 1991—), Phi Beta Kappa. Office: 1437 Toulon Ct Highland Park IL 60035-3940

KRAVIS, NATHAN MARK, psychiatrist; b. Phila., Nov. 21, 1957; s. Irving Bernard and Lillian Beatrice (Panzer) K.; m. Leora Kahn, Mar. 12, 1983; children: Samuel, Talia. BA, U. Pa., 1979, MD, 1983; cert. in psychoanalytic medicine, Columbia U., 1993. Diplomate Am. Bd. Psychiatry & Neurology. Intern The N.Y. Hosp., N.Y.C., 1983-84; resident in psychiatry Payne Whitney Clinic, N.Y.C., 1984-87, research fellow, 1987-89, instr. of psychiatry, 1987-89; asst. dir. Cornell Med. Ctr. AIDS Tng. Program, N.Y.C., 1988-89; pvt. practice of psychiatry N.Y.C., 1987—; clin. instr. psychiatry Payne Whitney Clinic, N.Y.C., 1989-93, clin. asst. prof. psychiatry, 1993—; faculty Columbia U. Ctr. Psychoanalytic Tng. and Rsch., 1993—. Recipient Kenneth E. Appel Psychiatry prize U. Pa. Sch. Medicine, 1983, History of Medicine prize, 1983; William T. Lhamon Rsch. prize Payne Whitney Clinic, 1987; Alexander Beller award Columbia U. Ctr. Psychoanalytic Tng. and Rsch., 1992. Mem. AAAS, Am. Psychiat. Assn., Assn. Psychoanalytic Medicine, N.Y. Acad. Sci., Am. Psychoanalytic Assn., Am. Assn. History of Medicine. Office: 141 E 55th St Apt 2F New York NY 10022-4037

KRAVITZ, HENRY, psychiatrist, psychoanalyst; b. Poland, Oct. 18, 1918; came to Can., 1929, naturalized, 1929; s. Julius and Erna (Hops) K.; B.A., McGill U., 1946, M.D.C.M., 1949, D.P.M., 1954; m. Mona Brenda Samuels, July 1, 1971; 1 child, Susan. Intern, Montreal (Que., Can.) Gen. Hosp., 1949-50, resident, 1950-54; chief dept. psychiatry Jewish Gen. Hosp., Montreal, Que., Can., 1967-88; emeritus chief, 1988—; prof. psychiatry McGill U., 1970—, chmn. med. exec., 1970-85; sec. Inst. Psychoanalysis, 1987-89, 89-91; dir. Inst. of Psychoanalysis, Can., 1981-83, 89-91. With RCAF, 1940-45. Fellow Royal Coll. Physicians and Surgeons Can. (chmn. sect. of psychiatry 1979-85, life), Am. Coll. Psychiatrists, Am. Coll. Psychoanalysts (life), Am. Psychiat. Assn. (life); mem. Can. Psychiatry Assn. (editor book rev., life), Jour. of Psychiatry. Jewish. Club: Montefiore. Editor Psychiatry Issue, Medicine N.A., 1983; contbr. writings to profl. jours., films. Home: 4994 Circle Rd, Montreal, PQ Canada H3W 1Z7 Office: 4333 Ch Cote, Ste Catherine, Montreal, PQ Canada H3T 1E2

KRAVITZ, HILARD L(EONARD), physician; b. Dayton, Ohio, June 26, 1917; s. Philip and Elizabeth (Charek) K.; divorced; children: Kent C., Kerry, Jay; m. Ellen King, Jan. 9, 1972; 1 child, Julie Frances. BA, U. Cin., 1939, MD, 1943. Lic. physician, Calif., Ohio. Resident in internal medicine Miami Valley Hosp., VA Hosp., Dayton, 1946-49; practice medicine specializing in internal medicine Dayton, 1950-54, Beverly Hills and Los Angeles, Calif., 1955—; practice medicine specializing in internal medicine and cardiology Los Angeles, 1955—; attending physician Cedars-Sinai Med. Ctr., 1955—; cons., med. dir. Adolph's Ltd., Los Angeles, 1955-74; mem. exec. com. Reiss-Davis Clinic, Los Angeles, 1966-70; chmn. pharmacy and therapeutic com. Cent City Hosp., Los Angeles, 1974-79; mem. pain commn. service Dept. Health and Human Services, Washington, 1985-86. Patentee sugar substitute, 1959, mineral-based salt, 1978. V.p. Friends of Music Calif. State U., Los Angeles, 1979-81. Served to capt. U.S. Army, 1944-46, ETO. Decorated Bronze Star with oak leaf cluster; Fourragere (France). Mem. AMA, Calif. Med. Assn., Los Angeles County Med. Assn., Am. Soc. Internal Medicine, Calif. Soc. Internal Medicine (del. 1974). Jewish. Office: 436 N Bedford Dr Ste 211 Beverly Hills CA 90210-4312

KRAWCHUK, MYRON EUGENE, chiropractor; b. Columbia, S.C., Apr. 13, 1955; s. Myron and Olga (Romaniuk) K.; m. Rosalinda Holguin, Mar. 8, 1983; children: Larissa, Ariadna. BS, Columbia U., 1977; MD, U. Autonoma de Cd. Juarez, Mex., 1985; DC, Tex. Chiropractic Coll., Pasadena, 1992. Diplomate Nat. Bd. Chiropractic Examiners. Pvt. practice Back and Neck Pain Ctr., Santa Maria, Calif., 1993-95, Advanced Family Chiropractic, Manhattan Beach, Calif., 1995—. Recipient Chiropractic Spinography Achievement award Parker Chiropractic Resource Found., 1992. Mem. Found. for Chiropractic Edn. and Rsch., Internat. Acad. Chiropractic Occupational Health Cons. Republican. Roman Catholic. Office: Advance Family Chiropractic 505 N Sepulveda Blvd # 9 Manhattan Beach CA 90266

KRAWETZ, STEPHEN ANDREW, molecular biology and genetics educator; b. Fort Frances, Ont., Can., Sept. 17, 1955; s. Stephen and Michaelene (Medynski) K.; m. Lorraine Ruth St. John, Aug. 19, 1977; children: Rhochelle Tairaesa, Alexandra Renée. BS, U. Toronto, Ont., 1977, PhD, 1983. Tchr. Scarborough Bd. Edn., Ont., 1976-77; Alberta Heritage Found. Med. Rsch. postdoc. fellow U. Calgary, Alta., Can., 1983-89; asst. prof. rsch. Ctr. for Molecular Biology Wayne State U., Detroit, 1989, asst. prof. molecular biology and genetics, 1989-92, asst. prof. obstetrics and gynecology and molecular biology and genetics, 1992-94, assoc. prof. ob/gyn. and molecular medicine and genetics, 1994—; biotech. cons., Calgary, 1985-89, Grosse Pointe Woods, Mich., 1989—; co-founder Genetic Imaging, Inc., 1988; mem. fetal therapy group Hutzel Hosp., Detroit, 1994—. Mem. editl. bd. BioTechniques, Ag Biotech News and Info., Gene-Combis; contbr. numerous articles to scholarly jours. Recipient B.C. Childrens Hosp. Rsch. award, Vancouver, 1984, Computer Applications in Molecular Biology award, IntelliGenetics Inc., Mountain View, Calif., 1988; Alta. Heritage Found. Med. Rsch. fellow, 1985-88. Mem. AAAS, Can. Biochem. Soc., Am. Soc. Human Genetics. Home: 805 Canterbury Rd Grosse Pointe MI 48236-1285 Office: Dept Ob-Gyn Ctr Molecular Med Genetics Detroit MI 48201

KRAWINKEL, MICHAEL BERNHARDT, pediatrician; b. Frankfurt, Fed. Republic Germany, June 18, 1950; s. Guenther Herrmann and Margarete Elise (Maskus) K.; m. Barbara Eichler, Apr. 11, 1980; children: Moritz Helge, Niklas Marian. Staatsexamen, U. Frankfurt, 1976. Approbation as med. doctor, 1977, pediatrician, 1989, asst. prof. for pediatrics, 1992. Registrar dept. surgery Univ., Bonn, Germany, 1978; registrar dept. pediatrics Univ., Bonn, Fed. Republic Germany, 1979-80, 83—; med. officer Ministry Health, Juba, Sudan, 1981-83; cons. Kreditanstalt fuer Wiederaufbau, Frankfurt, 1987; guest lectr. Inst. Tropical Hygiene, Heidelberg, Germany, 1984-91, Bernhard-Nocht Inst., Hamburg, 1986-92. Contbr. articles to profl. jours. Mem. Deutsche Gesellschaft fuer Kinderheilkunde, Deutsche Tropenmedizinische Gesellschaft, Deutsche Gesellschaft fuer Sozialpaediatrie, Deutsche Gesellschaft fuer Ernaehrung, German Assn. Tropical Paediatrics (sec. 1986—), European Intestinal Transplantation Study Group. Democrat. Office: Universitaetskinderklinik, Schwanenweg 20, D-230001 Kiel Germany

KRAWITT, EDWARD LEN, gastroenterologist, educator; b. N.Y.C.; s. David and Elizabeth K.; m. Laura Prange, June 9, 1959; children—Anne Marie, Edward Prange, John David, Andrew Lawrence, Carl Anthony, Eric Prange, B. Justin. A.B., Cornell U., 1955, M.D., 1959. Intern Univ. of Utah, Salt Lake City, 1959-60, resident in internal medicine, 1963-65; fellow in gastroenterology Univ. Iowa, Iowa City, 1965-67; fellow McArdle Lab., U. Wis., Madison, 1967-69; practice medicine specializing in gastroenterology Burlington, Vt., 1969—; mem. faculty Med. Sch. U. Vt., Burlington, 1969—, prof. medicine, 1978—, dir. gastroenterology unit, 1978-95. Contbr. articles to profl. jours. Served to capt. USAF, 1960-62; Turkey. USPHS career devel. awardee 1972-76. Mem. Am. Assn. Study Liver Disease, Am. Gastroenterol. Assn. Home: Bishop Rd Shelburne VT 05482 Office: Med Sch U Vt Burlington VT 05405

KREATSOULAS, NICHOLAS CHRIS, emergency medicine physician; b. Warren, Ohio, Sept. 2, 1964; s. Chris Michael and Maria J. (Mavrogianis) K.; m. Deborah Ann Evan, Sept. 15, 1964; children: Daniel Christopher, David John. AS in Gen. Scis., Kent State U., 1984, BBA in Computer Sci., 1986, BBA in Bus. Mgmt., 1986; DO, Ohio U., 1990. Diplomate Am. Bd. Emergency Medicine. Rotating intern Youngstown (Ohio) Osteo. Hosp., 1990-91; emergency medicine resident Allegheny Gen. Hosp., Pitts., 1991-94, chief resident emergency medicine, 1993-94; emergency medicine attending physician Trumbull Meml. Hosp., Warren, Ohio, 1994—; ACLS, ATLS instr., tchg. appointment N.E. Ohio U. Coll. Medicine. Mem. Am. Coll. Emergency Physicians, Alpha Beta Gamma, Omicron Delta Kappa. Greek Orthodox. Office: Trumbull Meml Hosp 1350 E Market St Warren OH 44482

KREB, ROBERT JOSEPH, III, physiatrist; b. Phila., Apr. 30, 1945; s. Wellington D. and Elia (di Medici) K.; m. Patricia Napp Holstin, July 19, 1979 (div. July 1989); children: Ashley C., Whitney H., Amanda L., Hilary A.; m. Eileen Eagan, Oct. 6, 1990. BS, St. Joseph's U., Phila., 1967; MD, U. Pa., 1971; MPH, Harvard U., 1973. Pvt. practice Phila., 1986—; chmn. phys. medicine and rehab. Chester County Hosp., Pa., 1986—, DCMH and Brandywine Hosp.; assoc. prof. U. Pa., Phila., 1980-90; cons. Johnson & Johnson, N.J., 1983-86, Merck, N.J., 1976-78, Becton-Dickinson, N.J., 1979-82. Inventor in field. With DCM Hosp. Found., Drexel Hill, Pa., 1990—, Brandywine Hosp. found., Calan, Pa., 1992—. Comdr. USPHS, 1972-73. NIH fellow, 1973-74. Fellow NIH, 1973-74. Fellow Am. Acad. Phys. Medicine and Rehab., Am. Soc. Clin. Evaluation, Am. Acad. Pain Mgmt., Am. Assn. Neurophysiology, Pa. Acad. Phys. Medicine and Rehab., Phila. Coll. Physicians; mem. Phila. Soc. Phys. Medicine and Rehab. Republican. Episcopalian.

KREBS, EDWIN GERHARD, biochemistry educator; b. Lansing, Iowa, June 6, 1918; s. William Carl and Louise Helena (Stegeman) K.; m. Virginia Frech, Mar. 10, 1945; children: Sally, Robert, Martha. AB in Chemistry, U. Ill., 1940; MD, Washington U., St. Louis, 1943, DSc (hon.), 1995; DSc honoris causa, U. Geneva, 1979; hon. degree, Med. Coll. Ohio, 1993; DSc (hon.), U. Ind., 1993, U. Ill., 1995; D honoris causa, Universidad Nacional De Cuyo, 1993. Intern, asst. resident Barnes Hosp., St. Louis, 1944-45; rsch. fellow biol. chemistry Wash. U., St. Louis, 1946-48; prof., chmn. dept. biol. chemistry Sch. Medicine U. Calif., Davis, 1968-76; asst. prof. biochemistry U. Wash., Seattle, 1948-52, assoc. prof. biochemistry, 1952-57, prof. biochemistry, 1957-66, prof., chmn. dept. pharmacology, 1977-83, prof. biochemistry and pharmacology, 1984-91; investigator, sr. investigator Howard Hughes Med. Inst., Seattle, 1983-90, sr. investigator emeritus, 1991—; mem. Phys. Chemistry Study Sect. NIH, 1963-68, Biochemistry Test Com. Nat. Bd. Med. Examiners, 1968-71, rsch. com. Am. Heart Assn., 1970-74, bd. sci. counselors Nat. Inst. Arthritis, Metabolism and Digestive Diseases, NIH, 1979-84, Internat. Bd. Rev., Alberta Heritage Found. for Med. Rsch., 1986, External Adv. Com. Weis Ctr. for Rsch., 1987-91; mem. subgroup interconvertible enzymes IUB Spl. Interest Group Metabolic Regulation; mem. internat. adv. bd. Advances in Second Messenger Phosphoprotein Rsch.; adv. com., Rowe chair U. Calif., Davis; adv. bd. Sam and Rose Stein Inst. Rsch. on Aging U. Calif., San Diego; external adv. com. Cell Therapeutics Inc., Seattle; adv. bd. Vollum Inst., Portland, Oreg. Mem. editorial bd. Jour. Biol. Chemistry, 1965-70; mem. editorial adv. bd. Biochemistry, 1971-76; mem. editorial and adv. bd. Molecular Pharmacology, 1972-77; assoc. editor Jour. Biol. Chemistry, 1971-93; mem. internat. adv. bd. Advances in Cyclic Nucleotide Rsch., 1972—; editorial advisor Molecular and Cellular Biochemistry, 1987—. Recipient Nobel Prize in Medicine or Physiology, 1992, Disting. lectureship award Internat. Soc. Endocrinology, 1972, Gairdner Found. award, Toronto, Ont., Can., 1978, J.J. Berzelius lectureship, Karolinska Institutet, 1982, George W. Thorn award for sci. excellence, 1983, Sir Frederick Hopkins Meml. lectureship, London, 1984, Rsch. Achievement award Am. Heart Assn., Anaheim, Calif., 1987, 3M Life Scis. award FASEB, New Orleans, 1989, Albert Lasker Basic Med. Rsch. award, 1989, CIBA-GEIGY-Drew award Drew U., 1991, Steven C. Beering award, Ind. U., 1991, Welch award in chemistry Welch Found., 1991, Louisa Gross Horwitz award Columbia U., 1989, Alumni Achievement award Coll. Liberal Arts & Scis. U. Ill., 1992; John Simon Guggenheim fellow, 1959, 66. Mem. NAS, Am. Soc. Biol. Chemists (pres. 1986, ednl. affairs com. 1965-68, councillor 1975-78), Am. Acad. Arts and Scis., Am. Soc. Pharmacology and Exptl. Therapeutics. Office: U Wash Dept Pharmacology Box 357370 Seattle WA 98195

KREBS, JAMES ARTHUR, JR., internist; b. Pitts., Aug. 23, 1948; s. James Arthur and Helen M. (McGrogan) K.; m. Cathy Ann Morrow, Aug. 5, 1988. BS, Pa. State U., 1970; MD, U. Pitts., 1974. Diplomate Am. Bd. Internal Med.; cert. geriatrics ACP, Am. Acad. Family Practice. Intern Mercy Hosp., Pitts., 1974-75; resident St. Francis Gen. Hosp., Pitts., 1975-77; assoc. mem. staff Washington (Pa.) Hosp., 1977-80, active mem. staff, 1981—; co-med. dir. Presbyn. Med. Ctr., Washington, Pa., 1992—. Mem. AMA, Pa. Med. Soc., Allegheny County Med. Soc. Democrat. Roman Catholic. Home: 6 Conklin Rd Washington PA 15301-9999 Office: Internal Med & Geriatrics Southminster Pl 825 S Main St Washington PA 15301-6267

KREBS, WILLIAM HOYT, company executive, industrial hygienist; b. Detroit, Apr. 6, 1938; s. William Thomas and Mary Louise (Hoyt) K.; m. Susan Kathryn Bartholomew, Aug. 8, 1964 (div. July 1976); children: Elizabeth Louise, William Thomas II; m. Jane Germer Meikle, June 18, 1983; stepchildren: David Andrew, Sarah Elizabeth. BS, U. Mich., 1960, MPH (IH), 1963, MS, 1965, PhD, 1970. Rsch. asst. U. Mich., Ann Arbor, 1962-63; indsl. hygienist Lumbermens Mut. Casualty Co., Chgo., 1963-64;

indsl. hygienist GM Corp., Detroit, 1970-77, mgr. toxic materials control activity, 1977-81, dir. toxic materials control activity, 1981-90, dir. indsl. hygiene activity, 1990-93; v.p. Indsl. Health Scis., Inc., Grosse Pointe Park, Mich., 1993—; mem. asbestos adv. com. Mich. Occupational Health Standards Commn., Lansing, 1984—. Contbr. articles to profl. jours. Mem. Grosse Pointe Meml. Ch., Grosse Pointe Farms, 1954; mem. health and safety com. Detroit Area coun. Boy Scouts Am., 1980. Fellow Am. Indsl. Hygiene Assn. (hon. mem.; bd. dirs. 1976-79, v.p. 1985-87, pres. 1988-89); mem. AAAS, APHA, Mich. Indsl. Hygiene Soc. (pres. 1980-81), Brit. Occupational Hygiene Soc., Internat. Occupational Hygiene Assn. (v.p. 1990-91, pres. 1992-93). Republican. Presbyterian. Home: 1014 Bishop Rd Grosse Pointe MI 48230-1421 Office: Indsl Health Scis Inc 1014 Bishop Rd Grosse Pointe MI 48230-1421

KREEK, MARY JEANNE, physician; b. Washington; d. Louis Francis and Esperance (Agee) Kreek; BA, Wellesley Coll., 1958; MD, Columbia, 1962; m. Robert A. Schaefer, Jan. 24, 1970; children: Robert A., Esperance Anne. Med. researcher NIH, Bethesda, Md., 1957-62; intern, resident Cornell N.Y. Hosp. Med. Ctr., N.Y.C., 1962-65, fellow, 1965-67; instr. medicine Cornell Med. Coll., 1966-67; acad. medicine specializing in internal medicine, endocrinology, gastroenterology, clin. pharmacology, N.Y.C., 1966—; mem. staff N.Y. Hosp.-Cornell U., 1968-77, clin. asst. prof., asst. attending physician, now assoc. attending physician, adj. assoc. prof.; asst. prof. Rockefeller U., 1967-72, sr. rsch. assoc., physician, 1972-83, assoc. prof., physician, 1983-94, prof., sr. physician, head of lab., 1994—; head Ind. Lab. on Biology of Addictive Diseases, 1975-94, head Lab., 1994—; sr. physician Rockefeller U. Hosp., 1994—; mem. gen. medicine study sect. NIH, 1973-77; co-chmn. John E. Fogarty (NIH) Internat. Conf. Hepatotoxicity Due to Drugs and Chems., 1977; vis. prof. Pahlavi U., Shiraz, Iran, summer 1977; spl. adv. Nat. Inst. Drug Abuse, 1976-86, mem. Nat. Adv. Coun., 1991-95, prin. investigator Rsch. Ctr. Biol. Bass Addictive Diseases, 1987—; mem. gastroenterology adv. com. FDA, 1975-79, 92-96, NIH Gen. Clin. Recipient Borden Rsch. award, 1962; Career Scientist award Health Rsch. Council City N.Y., 1974-75; Dole/Nyswander award; Rsch. Scientist award, NIH Gen. Clin. sect., 1978—. NIH Gen. Rsch. Ctr. Study Sect., 1979-83, chmn., 1982-83; mem. exec. com. Coll. Problems Drug Dependence, 1982-87, 89-94, chmn. exec. com., 1985-87, chair sci. program com., 1991-95; fellow CPDD 1992—; dir. NIH-NIDA Rsch. Ctr., 1987—. Soc Fellow ACP, Am. Coll. Neuropsychopharmacology, Am. Fedn. for Clin. Rsch.; mem. Shakespeare Soc. of Wellesley, Am. Gastroent. Assn., N.Y. Gastroent. Assn. (pres. 1987), Endocrine Soc., Am. Assn. Study Liver Diseases, Internat. Assn. Study Liver, Internat. Narcotic Research Conf. Group (exec. com. 1993—), Research Soc. on Alcoholism, Soc. on Neurosciences, Phi Beta Kappa, Sigma Xi. Home: 1175 York Ave New York NY 10021-7169 Office: Rockefeller U New York NY 10021

KREFT, ITA GRETA GERDA, statistics educator; b. The Hague, The Netherlands, Jan. 21, 1940; came to U.S., 1987; d. Leonardus Appollonius and Johanna (Van Der Meij) K.; m. Simon Oppe, Dec. 21, 1962 (div. Aug. 1969); 1 child, Simone; m. Jan De Leeuv, Dec. 14, 1971; 1 child, Tony. BA in Edn., Coll. Edn., Leiden, The Netherlands, 1962; BS in Psychology, U. Leiden, 1978, MA in Psychology, 1981; PhD in Edn., U. Amsterdam, 1987. Tchr. primary sch. City of Leiden, 1962-75; asst. prof. U. Amsterdam, 1984-87; rsch. assoc. U. Calif., L.A., 1988-91; assoc. prof. Calif. State U., L.A., 1991-96, prof., 1996—; dir. Program Evaluation and Rsch. Collaborative, L.A., 1995—. Author: Multilevel Analysis, 1987, Multilevel Models for Regression, 1996; editor profl. jours. in field. Rsch. grantee Nat. Inst. on Drug Abuse, L.A., 1994. Mem. Am. Ednl. Rsch. Assn., Am. Statis. Assn., Western Am. Psychol. Assn. Home: 130 Vista Pl Venice CA 90291 Office: Calif State U L A Sch Edn 5151 State University Dr Los Angeles CA 90032

KREGER, DAVID LAWRENCE, gastroenterologist; b. Portsmouth, Va., Feb. 8, 1946; s. H. Sol and Ruth S. (Silverman) K.; m. Ruth H., Mar. 31, 1974; children: Seth Adam, Anita Lauren. BA, Duke U., 1968; MD, Med. Coll. Va. Intern Med. Coll. Va. Hosp., Richmond, 1972-73, resident, 1973-75; gastroenterologist Gastroen. Assocs. Tidewater, Norfolk, Va., 1978—. Gastroenterology fellow Duke U. Med. Ctr., Dugham, N.C., 1975-77. Office: Gastroen Assocs Tidewater 160 Kingsley Ln Ste 200 Norfolk VA 23005

KREGER, DON WAYNE, industrial designer; b. San Antonio, Feb. 26, 1959; s. Arthur Eveitt and Dorothy Christine (Knopp) K. AA, Pasadena (Calif.) City Coll., 1981; BS, Calif. State U., Long Beach, 1984; MA, U.S. Internat. U., San Diego, 1989. Design dir. Golden Rain Found., Seal Beach, Calif., 1982-84; v.p. design Foam Fabricators, Compton, Calif., 1984-85; pres., chief exec. officer Kreger Design Corp., Santa Fe Springs, Calif., 1985-90; creative dir. Epic Products Corp., Fountain Valley, Calif., 1990—; cons. A.C. Internat., Santa Fe Springs, 1986-89, Nat. Sales Hdqrs., Santa Fe Springs, 1986-89, Empire Container, Compton, 1985-86. Patentee in field. Counselor Ctr. for Creative Alternatives, Huntington Beach, Calif., 1987-88; vol. Dem. party, Long Beach, 1988; sponsor World Vision, Anaheim, Calif., 1986-89. Mem. Indsl. Designers Soc. Am., Psi Chi.

KREIDER, CAROLE COMPTON, professional counselor, consultant; b. Boston, Mar. 3, 1939; d. Lemuel Cliff and Dorothy Bell (Leister) Compton; m. Kenneth Gruber Kreider, Dec. 2, 1961; children: Cynthia Louise, Kenneth Brett, Christopher Lee. BS, Simmons Coll., 1960; MA, cert. in family counseling, Bowie U., 1985. Cert. profl. counselor, Md. Mental health counselor Affiliated Community Counselors, Inc., Rockville, Md., 1985—, intake coord., 1990-96, adminstrv. dir., 1990-96; seminar leader Adlerian Parenting Workshops, Md., 1984-86. Vol. election precinct, Rockville, 1984, Stepping Stones Shelter, Rockville, Community Block Grants, Rockville, 1989—; group piano coord. Cold Spring Elem. Sch., Rockville. Mem. Am. Assn. for Counseling and Devel., Md. Assn. Counseling and Devel. Democrat. Home: 9232 Copenhaver Dr Rockville MD 20854-3018 Office: Affiliated Community 50 W Montgomery Ave # 110 Rockville MD 20850-4216

KREIDER, JOHN WESLEY, medical educator; b. Phila., Mar. 24, 1937; s. Wesley Johnson and Angeline (Scafidi) K.; m. Kathleen Anne Porter, June 1, 1963; children: Eric, Ted. AB, LaSalle U., 1959; MD, U. Pa., 1963. Resident Yale U., New Haven, 1963-64; resident, postdoctoral fellow U. Pa., 1964-68; from asst. prof. to prof. Pa. State U., Hershey, 1968—; chief divsn. exptl. pathology, dir. Jake Gittlen Cancer Rsch. Inst. Hershey Med. Ctr.; cons. biotech. firms. Mem. AMA, Pa. Med. Soc. Home: 600 Pine Rd Palmyra PA 17078 Office: Hershey Med Ctr Exptl Pathology PO Box 850 Hershey PA 17033

KREISBERG, JEFFREY I., medical educator, researcher. BS in Biology, SUNY, Albany, 1971; PhD in Exptl. Pathology, U. Md., 1975. Instr. dept. pathology Harvard Med. Sch., Boston, 1977-78, asst. prof. dept. pathology, 1978-80; asst. biologist dept. medicine Mass. Gen. Hosp., Boston, 1979-80; asst. prof. dept. pathology U. Tex. Health Sci. Ctr., San Antonio, 1980-83, assoc. prof. dept. medicine, 1983—, assoc. prof. dept. pathology, 1983-89, prof. dept. medicine, prof. dept. pathology, 1989—, career scientist dept. VA dept. pathology, 1989—. Contbr. articles to profl. jours., chpts. to books. Recipient Rsch. award Am. Diabetes Assn., 1996. Office: U Tex Health Sci Ctr Dept Pathology 7703 Floyd Curl Dr San Antonio TX 78284*

KREITZER, STEPHEN M., physician, consultant; b. N.Y.C., Feb. 7, 1946; s. Herman Joel and Hazel (Green) K.; m. Laura Drina Hershman; children: Joshua, Jason, Ethan. BA, CUNY, 1967; MD, Albert Einstein Coll. Medicine, 1971. Diplomate Am. Bd. Internal Medicine, Am. Bd. Pulmonary Disease. Intern, resident Albert Einstein-Bronx Mcpl. Hosp., N.Y.C., 1971-73, chief med. resident, 1973-74; pulmonary rsch. fellow Harvard Med. Sch., Boston, 1976-78; pvt. practice Pulmonary Assocs. Tampa, Fla., 1976—; med. cons. Apria Health Care, Fountain Valley, Calif., 1993—; CEO Tampa Med. Rsch. Assocs., Tampa, 1994—; chmn. med. ethics com. Meml. Hosp., 1986—, chief of medicine, 1982-86. Contbr. articles to profl. jours. V.p. B'nai B'rith, Tampa, 1980-82. Maj. USAF, 1974-76. Recipient Vol. of Yr. award United Way of Tampa, 1988, 89. Mem. Hillsborough County Med. Assn. (chmn. bd. censors 1993—). Judism. Office: Pulmonary Assocs Tampa 2919 Swann Ave Ste 202 Tampa FL 33609

KREMBERG, MARVIN ROY, psychiatrist; b. N.Y.C., Mar. 19, 1951; s. Rubin and Rose (Kaplan) K. BA, Bklyn. Coll., 1972; MD, Columbia Coll., 1976. Diplomate Am. Bd. Psychiatry & Neurology, Nat. Bd. of Med. Examiners. Resident in psychiatry St. Luke's Hosp., 1976-78, fellowship, 1978-80; pvt. practice N.Y.C., 1980—; chief psychiatrist Cath. Charities Family and Children's Svcs., Inwood Br., N.Y., 1981-88; asst. attending physician Dept. of Psychiatry St. Luke's-Roosevelt Hosp., N.Y.C., 1983—; instr. clin. psychiatry Columbia U., N.Y.C., 1981—. Recipient Physicians Recognition award AMA, 1980, 83, 86, 89. Mem. Am. Psychiat. Assn. (com. alcoholism and drug abuse N.Y. County dist. br. 1986—, com. impaired physicians 1982—, Physicians Recognition award 1980-, 83, 86, 89), Am. Acad. Child Psychiatry, Med. Soc. State N.Y. (impaired physicians programs 1982—), N.Y. County Med. Soc. (com. pub. relations 1982-87, maternal and child welfare com. 1988—), N.Y. Coun. on Child Psychiatry, Nat. Arts Club, Phi Beta Kappa. Office: 315 W 57th St Apt 9H New York NY 10019-3141

KREMENTZ, EDWARD THOMAS, surgeon; b. Newark, Apr. 30, 1917; s. Albert Martin and Agnes Templeton (Aiguier) K.; m. Carolyn Butler, Oct. 5, 1946; children: Edward T. (dec. 1983), Anne Butler Bigliani, Cynthia Aiguier Geoghegan, David George, Elizabeth Avery Guice. AB, Wesleyan U., 1939; MD, U. Rochester, 1943. Asst. in surgery Yale U., 1943-48, Jane Coffin Childs Meml. Fund fellow, 1948-49, instr. surgery, 1948-50; instr. surgery Tulane U., 1950-53, asst. prof., 1953-57, assoc. prof., 1957-61, prof., 1961-88, prof. emeritus, 1988—, acting chmn. dept., 1967-68, 77-78, cancer teaching coord., 1953-82; dir. Tulane Cancer Clin. Rsch. Ctr., Charity Hosp., 1961-75, Am. Cancer Soc. prof. clin. oncology, 1977-83; cons. Charity Hosp.; hon. cons. Touro Infirmary, New Orleans, 1963—; cons. Hotel Dieu, New Orleans, 1959-87; chmn. bd. dirs. La. Cancer Consortium, 1985—; surg. cons. several hosps.; chmn. N.Am. Perfusion Group, 1983—. Mem. editl. bd. Jour. Soviet Oncology, 1980-85; mng. editor Reg. Cancer Treatment, 1988-93; assoc. editor Jour. Exptl. Therapeutics and Oncology, 1995—. Chmn. bd. dirs. La. Tumor Registry, 1974-81; chmn. bd. dirs. Charity Hosp. Tumor Registry, La., 1955-87; elder St. Charles Ave. Presbyn. Ch., 1980-87. Recipient Rsch. Career award Nat. Cancer Inst NIH, 1962-67. Mem. AAAS, ACS, AMA (co-recipient Hektoen Gold medal 1959), Am. Assn. Cancer Edn. (Margaret Hays Edward medal 1989), Am. Assn. Cancer Rsch., La. divsn. Am. Cancer Soc. (Aesculpian award 1988), Am. Soc. Clin. Oncology, Soc. Surg. Oncology (Lucy Wortham James Clin. Cancer Rsch. award 1985), Am. Surg. Assn., Conn. Tissue Oncology Soc., La. State and Orleans Parish Med. Svcs. (Outstanding Physician award 1988), New Orleans Surg. Soc. (pres. 1970), So. Surg. Assn. (Shipley Gold medal 1964), Soc. Exptl. Biology and Medicine, Societe Internat. de Chirurgie, Soc. Univ. Surgeons, Southeastern Surg. Congress, So. Med. Assn. (Disting. Svc. award 1993), S.W. Oncology Group, Surg. Assn. La., WHO Internat. Group clin. Study Melanoma, So. Assn. for Oncology, Tulane Surg. Soc. (pres. 1993), New Orleans Country Club, Round Table Club, Sigma Xi, Alpha Omega Alpha. Home: 500 Walnut St New Orleans LA 70118-4930 also: 3839 Ulloa St New Orleans LA 70119

KRÉMER, RENÉ EDMOND, cardiologist; b. Arlon, Luxembourg, Belgium, July 25, 1926; s. León and Aline (Bricart) K.; m. Angelè Hans; children: Françoise, Marie-Anne. MD, Cath. U. Louvain, Belgium, 1951; Agregation de Lénseignement Superieur, 1969. Prof. U. Louvain-Mont Godinne, Belgium, 1972; chief dept. cardiology U. Louvain-Mont Godinne, 1975-91, med. dir., 1989-91, cons. cardiology, 1991—; pres. Assn. Physicians Cath. U. Louvain, 1993; med. dir. Clinique St. Joseph, Lobbes, 1992—; sec. Louvain Med., 1993—. Editor Acta Cardiologica, 1980—; contbr. articles to med. jours. Mem. Belgian Soc. Cardiology (chmn. 1975-77), European Soc. Cardiology (chmn. working group valvular disease 1994-96). Roman Catholic. Home: Rue W Ernst 11/17, 6000 Charleroi Belgium Office: Assn Anciens Etudiants, Ave Mounier 52 Box 5265, 1200 Brussels Belgium

KRESHON, MARTIN JOHN, SR., ophthamologist; b. East Liverpool, Ohio, Nov. 11, 1929; s. James I. and Elizabeth (Maroni) K.; m. Jerri May Jerome, Aug. 31, 1952; children—Kathy, Susan, Karol, Martin John, Michael, Amy Lou, Elizabeth, John. B.S. cum laude, Geneva Coll., 1950; M.D., Marquette U., 1954. Diplomate Am. Bd. Ophthalmology. Rotating intern Hamot Hosp., Erie, Pa., 1954-55; resident in ophthalmology Duke U. Hosp., Durham, N.C., 1957-60; practice medicine specializing in ophthamology, Charlotte, N.C., 1961; mem. staff Charlotte Eye, Ear, Nose and Throat Hosp., Meml. Hosp., Mercy Hosp.; assoc. clin. prof. Duke U., 1961—; dir. Piedmont Eye Clinic, Charlotte. Bd. dirs. N.C. Cancer Soc., Mecklenburg Assn. for Blind, Piedmont Sci. Fair, N.C. Eye Bank. Served to capt. U.S. Army, 1955-57. Mem. Am. Acad. Ophthamology and Otolaryngology, N.C. Med. Soc., Mecklenburg County Med. Soc., Am. Assn. Ophthamology, So. Med. Soc., N.C. Soc. Ophthamology (pres. 1977-78). Lodge: Lions. Contbr. articles to med. jours. Home: 6616 Bevington Brook Ln Charlotte NC 28277 Office: Charlotte Eye Ear Nose & Throat Hosp 1600 E 3rd St Charlotte NC 28204-3202

KRESIC, EVA, pediatrician; b. Zagreb, Croatia, July 20, 1935; came to U.S., 1969; d. Ignatz and Marta (Neumann) Klein; m. Mark Miljenko Kresic, July 26, 1956; children: Mladen, Daniela. MD, U. Zagreb, 1960. Resident in pediats. Mt. Sinai Hosp., Elmhurst, N.Y., 1970-72; fellow L.I. Jewish Hosp., New Hyde Park, N.Y., 1972-74; attending, clin. instr. Mt. Sinai, Elmhurst, 1972-77; pediatrician HIP-Queens/L.I. Med. Group, Flushing, N.Y., 1972—; Bd. cert. Am. Acad. Pediats. Fellow Am. Acad. Pediats. (bd. cert.); mem. N.Y. State Med. Soc., Queens Med. Soc., Queens Pediat. Soc. Republican. Jewish. Office: HIP-Queens LI Med Group 140-15 Sanford Ave Flushing NY 11355

KRESLOFF, RICHARD STEPHEN, ophthalmologist; b. Englewood, N.J., May 9, 1944; s. Morris and Sadie (Silver) K.; m. Judith Ina Rosenkranz, Dec. 17, 1966; children: Michael, Lisa, Lauren. BS, Muhlenberg Coll., 1966; MD, U. Pa., Phila., 1970. Diplomate Am. Bd. Ophthalmology. Rotating intern II Abington (Pa.) Meml. Hosp., 1970-71; resident Scheie Eye Inst., Phila., 1975-78; pvt. practice Collingswood, N.J., 1978—. Lt. comdr. USPHS, 1971-73. Fellow Am. Acad. Ophtholmology, Am. Coll. Surgeons. Office: Richard S Kresloff MD 900 Haddon Ave Collingswood NJ 08108-2101

KRESSEL, HERBERT YEHUDE, medical educator; b. Bklyn., Nov. 20, 1947. BA, Brandeis U., Waltham, Mass., 1968; MD, U. So. Calif., L.A., 1972. Diplomate Am. Bd. Radiology in diagnostic radiology; lic. physician, Calif., Pa., Wis., N.Y., N.J., Mass. Intern in medicine U. Wash. Hosp., Seattle, 1972-73; resident in radiology U. Calif., San Francisco, 1973-74, NIH fellow in diagnostic radiology, 1974-76, clin. instr. radiology, 1976-77, asst. prof., 1977-80, assoc. prof., 1980-85, prof., 1985-93; Miriam H. Stoneman prof. radiology Harvard Med. Sch., Boston, 1993—; attending physician GI radiology sect. dept. radiology Hosp. of U. Pa., 1977-82, dir. continung edn., 1979-93, attending physician, chief MRI sect., 1982-93; radiologist-in-chief dept. radiology Beth Israel Hosp., Boston, 1993—; mem. plan devel. adv. task force on magnetic resonance for 1986 HealthSystems Plan-Health Systems Agy. Southeastern Pa., Inc., 1985-87; dir. R.I. Magnetic Resonance Imaging Network, Providence, 1988-93; mem. sci. adv. com. for rsch. grants Am. Cancer Soc., 1990-93; task force chmn. Com. on Studies Involving Human Beings, U. Pa., 1985-92; mem. coun. for continuing med. edn. U. Pa., 1990-93. Mem. editl. bds. Radiology, 1985-91, Magnetic Resonance in Medicine, 1987—; editor Magnetic Resonance Ann., 1985-88, Magnetic Resonance Quar., 1988-94; patentee in field. Recipient Sylvia Sorkin Greenfield award Am. Assn. Physicists in Medicine, 1993. Fellow Am. Coll. Radiology (Commn. on Magnetic Resonance 1987-90, com. on pub. rels. 1987—, com. MR stds. and accreditation 1987—, chmn. com. on MR clin. applications 1987, Commn. on Govt. Rels. 1992—), Soc. Magnetic Resonance in Medicine (trustee 1987, sci. program com. chmn. 1989-90, pres.-elect 1990-91, pres. 1991-92, Crues Kressel award sect. magnetic resonance technologists 1991, Silver medal 1994), Radiol. Soc. N.Am. (refresher course com. 1992-93), Am. Roentgen Ray Soc., Soc. Gastrointestinal Radiologists, Soc. Computed Body Tomography (rsch. com. 1990-93), Mass. Radiol. Soc., New Eng. Roentgen Ray Soc. Office: Beth Israel Hosp Dept Radiology 330 Brookline Ave Boston MA 02215*

KRETCHMER, KENNETH RONALD, physician; b. New Orleans, June 24, 1949; s. Henry Edmund and Joan Ronald (Gordon) K.; m. Janet Spitz, Aug. 19, 1973; children: Emily, Lisa, Daniel. BA magna cum laude, U. Rochester, 1971; MD, Case Western Res. U., 1975. Diplomate Nat. Bd. Med. Examiners, Am. Bd. Internal Medicine, with specialty in pulmonary diseases; cert. ALS Am. Heart Assn. Summer rsch. fellow divsn. pulmonary pathology St. Luke's Hosp., Cleve., 1969; summer rsch. asst. divsn. surg. rsch. Met. Gen. Hosp., Cleve., 1970; clin. fellow Am. Soc. Anesthesiologists/Univ. Hosps., Cleve., 1973; intern in internal medicine Cleve. Met. Gen. Hosp., 1975-76, asst. resident in medicine, 1976-77, sr. resident in medicine, 1977-78, fellow in pulmonary medicine, 1978-80; preceptor in clin. medicine Case Western Res. U., Cleve., 1976-79, tchg. fellow dept. internal medicine, 1978; chief pulmonary svcs. Akron (Ohio) City Hosp., 1980-93, med. dir. respiratory therapy, 1980—; asst. prof. dept. internal medicine Coll. Medicine Northeastern Ohio U., Rootstown, 1980; ednl. coord. pulmonary svc. Akron (Ohio) City Hosp., 1993—; med. dir. respiratory therapy Edwin Shaw Hosp., Akron, 1993—; mem. staff dept. internal medicine Akron City Hosp., 1980-92, Summa Health Sys., Akron, 1992—; cons. staff dept. internal medicine Edwin Shaw Hosp., 1984—; mem. courtesy staff Children's Hosp. Med. Ctr., Akron, 1988-90, St. Thomas Med. Ctr., Akron, 1991-92, Akron Gen. Med. Ctr., 1992—; mem. subcoun. pulmonary disease Northeastern Ohio U. Coll. Medicine, 1980—; prin. investigator study in field; presenter in field. Fellow , AMA, Am. Coll. Chest Physicians; mem. ACP, Ohio Thoracic Soc. (chmn. practice and edn. com. 1987, v.p. 1988, pres.-elect 1989, pres. 1990) Ohio State Med. Assn., Summit County Med. Soc. Office: Akron Pulmonary Assocs Inc 75 Arch St Ste 104 Akron OH 44304

KREUTER, JÖRG WILHELM RUDOLF, medical educator; b. Gelnhausen, Hessen, Fed. Republic Germany, Jan. 4, 1948; s. Philipp and Ursula (Henke) K.; m. Susan Hildegard Szabo, Dec. 16, 1971; children: Simone, Julian. D Pharmacy, Philipps U., Marburg, Fed. Republic Germany, 1971; PhD, Swiss Fed. Inst. Tech., Zurich, 1974, Habilitation diploma, 1982. Asst. Swiss Fed. Inst. Tech., 1975, chief asst., 1976-82; postdoctoral position U. Kans., Lawrence, U.S., 1977, U. Mich., Ann Arbor, U.S., 1979; lectr. Swiss Fed. Inst. Tech., 1982-84; prof. J.W. Goethe U., Frankfurt, Fed. Republic Germany, 1984—; vis. assoc. prof., U. Wis., Madison, 1983; dean, Dept. Pharmacy, U. Frankfurt, 1988-89; sci. adv. bd. Siegfried AG, Zofingen, Switzerland, 1987—. Patentee in field; contbr. articles to profl. jours. Recipient medal Swiss Fed. Inst. Tech., 1975. Fellow Am. Assn. Pharm. Scientists; mem. Controlled Swiss Release Soc. (bd. govs. 1988-90), Arbeitsgemeinschaft für Pharmazeutische Verfahrenstechnik (prize 1981), German Pharm. Soc., Internat. Fedn. Pharmaceutics, Reticulendothelial Soc. Home: Georg-August-Zinn-Str 13, D-61350 Bad Homburg Hessen Germany Office: J W Goethe U Bioctr, Marie-Curie Str 9, D-60439 Frankfurt Hessen Germany

KREVANS, JULIUS RICHARD, university administrator, physician; b. N.Y.C., May 1, 1924; s. Sol and Anita (Makovetsky) K.; m. Patricia N. Abrams, May 28, 1950; children: Nita, Julius R., Rachel, Sarah, Nora Kate. B.S. Arts and Scis, N.Y. U., 1943, M.D., 1946. Diplomate: Am. Bd. Internal Med. Intern, then resident Johns Hopkins Med. Sch. Hosp., mem. faculty, until 1970, dean acad. affairs, 1969-70; physician in chief Balt. City Hosp., 1963-69; prof. medicine U. Calif., San Francisco, 1970—, dean Sch. Medicine, 1971-82, chancellor, 1982-93, chancellor emeritus, 1993—. Contbr. articles on hematology, internal med. profl. jours. Served with M.C. AUS, 1948-50. Mem. A.C.P., Assn. Am. Physicians. Office: U Calif San Francisco Sch Medicine San Francisco CA 94143-0296

KREVSKY, BENJAMIN, medical educator; b. Elizabeth, N.J., May 11, 1952; s. Harold and Eleanor (Butt) K.; m. Abby Binder, Mar. 28, 1981; children: Sarah, Elizabeth. BS, Yale U., 1974, MPH, 1979; MD, U. Cin., 1979. Diplomate Am. Bd. Internal Medicine. Resident Montefiore Med. Ctr., Bronx, N.Y., 1979-82; clin. instr. Temple U. Sch. Medicine, gastroenterology sect., med. dept., Phila., 1982-84, asst. prof. medicine, 1984-90, assoc. dir. fellowship tng., 1986—, dir. endoscopy, 1987-89, assoc. chmn., 1989—; assoc. prof. Temple U. Sch. Medicine, Phila., 1990—. NIH grantee, 1986-89, 91-96. Fellow ACP, Am. Coll. Gastroenterology, Am. Soc. Laser Surgery and Medicine; mem. Am. Gastroenterol. Assn., Am. Fedn. Clin. Rsch., Am. Soc. for Gastrointestinal Endoscopy. Republican. Jewish. Office: Temple U Hosp GI Sect 3401 N Broad St Philadelphia PA 19140-5189

KRICK, JAMES MICHAEL, urologist; b. Portsmouth, Ohio, Oct. 31, 1957; s. Howard Thomas and Herma (Frazier) K.; m. Kristin Moore, Sept. 1988; children: Emily, Aaron. BS, Ohio U., 1980, DO, 1985. Diplomate Am. Bd. Osteo. Medicine. Intern Cuyahoga Falls (Ohio) Gen. Hosp., 1985-86, resident in family practice, 1986-87, resident in gen. surgery, 1990-91; emergency staff physician Meml. Hosp. Union County, Marysville, Ohio, 1987-88, Grady Meml. Hosp., Delaware, Ohio, 1988-90; resident in urologic surgery Botsford Gen. Hosp., Farmington Hills, Mich., 1991-95; mem. curriculum adv. com. Ohio U., Athens, 1982-84, assoc. instr. coll. osteo. medicine, Athens, 1988—. Cmty. bd., vol. outreach coord. Care Line Crisis Intervention Ctr., Athens, 1978-80. Mem. Am. Coll. Osteo. Surgeons (Best of Show nat. conf. 1992), Am. Osteo. Assn., Ohio State Med. Assn., Knights of Columbus. Office: James M Krick DO 1835 Oakland Ave Portsmouth OH 45662

KRIEGER, DERK WOLFGANG, neurologist, researcher; b. Nordhorn, Germany, Apr. 26, 1960; s. Knut Helmut and Inge Anni (Kuff) K.; m. Silke Herrmann, July 15, 1995; 1 child, Jonathan. MD, RWTH, Aachen, Germany, 1985; PhD in Neurophysiology, RKU, Heidelberg, Germany, 1993. Resident dept. neurology U. Heidelberg, 1987-91, attending neurologist, 1991-95; dir. dept. neurology U. Tex., Houston, 1996—; rsch. fellow Tufts U., Boston, 1992-93, vis. lectr., 1995. Editor: Neuro Critical Care, 1996; contbr. articles to profl. jours. Recipient Erb Family prize, 1995, ANIM award German Soc. Neurology, 1992-93. Mem. Am. Assn. Neurologists, European State coun., N.Am. Consortium of Acute Brain Injury, World Wildlife Found. Lutheran. Office: Univ of Texas Dept Neurology 6431 Fannin Houston TX 77030

KRIEGER, JOHN NEWTON, urology educator; b. Phila., May 3, 1948; s. Rivan and Leah (Moses) K.; m. Monica Schoelch, July 22, 1972. AB, Princeton U., 1970; MD, Cornell U., 1974. Diplomate Am. Bd. Urology. Resident in surgery N.Y. Hosp., N.Y.C., 1974-76, resident in urology, 1976-80; fellow in urology U. Va., Charlottesville, 1980-82; asst. prof. urology U. Wash., Seattle, 1982-86, assoc. prof., 1986-90, prof., 1990—. Author 2 books; contbr. more than 200 articles to profl. jours. Mem. Am. Urol. Assn. (F.C. Valentine prize, N.Y.C. sect. 1977, Scholar award, Balt. 1980), ACS, Am. Soc. Microbiology, Am. Venereal Disease Assn., Infectious Disease Soc. Am. Office: U Wash Dept Urology RL-10 Pacific St NE Seattle WA 98195

KRIEGER, LESLIE HERBERT, psychologist; b. Newark, Nov. 21, 1938; s. Ben L. and Esther (Reingold) K. AB in Psychology, Rutgers U., Newark, 1960; MS in Psychology, Rutgers U., New Brunswick, 1963; PhD in Psychology, Rutgers U., 1966. Lic. psychologist, Fla., Pa. Asst. prof. psychology Rutgers U., Newark, 1966-67, Duquesne U., Pitts., 1967-69; assoc. prof. psychology Point Park Coll., Pitts., 1969-72; cons. psychologist Psych Cons. to Industry, Pitts., 1968-73; prof. psychology U. North Fla., Jacksonville, 1972-86; pres./cons. psychologist Humanalysis Sys., Jacksonville, 1980-89; sr. ptnr., cons. psychologist Human Resource Ctr., Jacksonville, 1990-92; v.p., cons. psychologist People Devel. Techs., Jacksonville, 1992-95; sr. psychologist Saville & Holdsworth Ltd., Jacksonville, 1995—; v.p. human resources Paul W. Davis Systems, 1992-95. Contbr. articles to profl. jours. Pres. River Region Human Svcs., Jacksonville, 1989-91, bd. dirs., 1983—, Big Bros./Big Sisters, Jacksonville, 1986-92. Mem. APA, ASTD, Soc. Human Resource Mgmt., Met. N.Y. Assn. Applied Psychology. Office: Saville & Holdsworth Ltd Ste 108 10991-55 San Jose Blvd Jacksonville FL 32223

KRINSKY, MARY MCINERNEY, lawyer; b. Oklahoma City, l, Dec. 12, 1946; d. Henry B. and Lucille L. (Walker) McInerney; m. William L. Krinsky, Oct. 3l, 1970; children: David M., Benjamin H. BS, Iowa State U., 1967; MPh, PhD, Yale U., 197l; JD, U. Mont., 1977. Bar: Conn. 1978, U.S. Patent Office 1986. Rsch. assoc. Cornell U., Ithaca, N.Y., 1971-74; researcher hist. legal documents North Haven (Conn.) Hist. Soc., 1979-88; assoc. St. Onge, Steward, Johnston & Reens, Stamford, Conn., 1988-94, ptnr., 1994—. Contbr. articles to sci. jours. Mem. Am. Intellectual Property Law Assn., Conn. Patent Law Assn. Office: 986 Bedford St Stamford CT 06905-5621

KRIPPNER, STANLEY CURTIS, psychologist; b. Edgerton, Wis., Oct. 4, 1932; s. Carroll Porter and Ruth Genevieve (Volenberg) K.; m. Lelie Anne Harris, June 25, 1966; stepchildren: Caron, Robert. BS, U. Wis., 1954; MA,

Northwestern U., 1957, PhD, 1961; PhD (hon.), U. Humanistic Studies, San Diego, 1982. Diplomate Am. Bd. Sexology. Speech therapist Warren Pub. Schs. (Ill.), 1954-55, Richmond Pub. Schs. (Va.), 1955-56; dir. Child Study Ctr. Kent (Ohio) State U., 1961-64; dir. dream lab. Maimonides Med. Ctr., Bklyn., 1964-73; prof. of psychology Saybrook Inst., San Francisco, 1973—; adj. prof. psychology Calif. Inst. Human Sci., 1994—; vis. prof. U. P.R., 1972, Sonoma State U., 1972-73, U. Life Scis., Bogota, Colombia, 1974, Inst. for Psychodrama and Humanistic Psychology, Caracas, Venezuela, 1975, West Ga. Coll., 1976, John F. Kennedy U., 1980-82, Inst. for Rsch. in Biopsychophysics, Curitiba, Brazil, 1990, Calif. Inst. Integral Studies, 1991—; lectr. Acad. Pedagogical Scis., Moscow, 1971, Acad. Scis., Beijing, 1981, Minas Gerais U., Belo Horizonte, Brazil, 1986-87. Author: (with Montague Ullman) Dream Telepathy, 1973, rev. edit., 1989, Song of the Siren: A Parapsychological Odyssey, 1975; (with Alberto Villoldo) The Realms of Healing, 1976, rev. edit., 1987, Human Possibilities, 1980, (with Alberto Villoldo) Healing States, 1987; (with Jerry Solfvin) La Science et les Pouvoirs Psychiques de l'Homme, 1986, (with Joseph Dillard) Dreamworking, 1988, (with David Feinstein) Personal Mythology, 1988, (with Patrick Welch) Spiritual Dimensions of Healing, 1992, (with Dennis Thong and Bruce Carpenter) A Psychiatrist in Paradise, 1993; editor: Advances in Parapsychological Research, Vol. 1, 1977, Vol. 2, 1978, Vol. 3, 1982, Vol. 4, 1984, Vol. 5, 1987, Vol. 6, 1990, Vol. 7, 1994, Psychoenergetic Systems, 1979; co-editor: Galaxies of Life, 1973, The Kirlian Aura, 1974, The Energies of Consciousness, 1975, Future Science, 1977, Dreamtime and Dreamwork, 1990; mem. editl. bd. Alternative Therapies in Health and Medicine, Jour. Humanistic Psychology, Jour. Transpersonal Psychology, Jour. Indian Psychology, Dream Network, Humanistic Psychologist, Transpersonal Rev., Jour. Creative Children and Adults; contbr. 500 articles to profl. jours. Bd. dirs., adv. bd. Acad. Religion and Phys. Rsch., Survival Rsch. Found., Hartley Film Found., Inst. for Multilevel Learning, Humanistic Psychology Ctr. N.Y., Life Action Found. Recipient Svc. to Youth award YMCA, 1959, Citation of Merit Nat. Assn. Creative Children and Adults, 1975, Cert. Recognition Office Gifted and Talented, U.S. Office Edn., 1976, Volker medal South Africa Soc. Psychical Rsch., 1980, Bicentennial medal U. Ga., 1985, Charlotte and Karl Bühler award, 1992, Dan Overlade Meml. award, 1994. Fellow Am. Soc. Clin. Hypnosis, Am. Psychol. Assn., Am. Psychol. Soc., Soc. Sci. Study Religion, Soc. Sci. Study Sexuality, Western Psychol. Assn.; mem. AAAS, Am. Soc. Psychical Rsch., Am. Ednl. Rsch. Assn., Am. Counseling Assn., Internat. Council Psychologists, Assn. for Study of Dreams (pres. 1993-94), Soc. for the Anthropology Consciousness, Com. for Study Anomalistic Rsch., Inter-Am. Psychol. Assn., Assn. Humanistic Psychology (pres. 1974-75), Assn. Transpersonal Psychology, Internat. Soc. Hypnosis, Internat. Soc. for Study of Dissociation, Nat. Assn. for Gifted Children, Sleep Rsch. Soc., Soc. Sci. Exploration, Biofeedback Soc. Am., Coun. Exceptional Children, Soc. Accelerative Learning and Tchg., Soc. Gen. Sys. Rsch., Swedish Soc. Clin. and Exptl. Hypnosis, Western Psychol. Assn., World Coun. for Gifted and Talented Children, Internat. Soc. Gen. Semantics, Menninger Found., Nat. Soc. Study of Edn., Parapsychol. Assn. (pres. 1983), Soc. Clin. and Exptl. Hypnosis, World Future Soc. Home: 79 Woodland Rd Fairfax CA 94930-2153 Office: Saybrook Inst 450 Pacific Ave # 300 San Francisco CA 94133-4640

KRISHER, THOMAS JOHN, psychologist; b. Buffalo, Aug. 26, 1955; s. John F. and Doris M. (Schmidt) K.; m. Judy A. Cecere, June 2, 1979; children: Jesse T., Emma C. Student, William Rainey Harper Coll., 1973-74; BS in Human Devel. magna cum laude, Syracuse U., 1977; D in Psychology, Hahnemann U., 1986. Lic. psychologist, N.Y. Dir. human devel. St. Margaret's Parish, Mattydale, N.Y., 1977-79; emergency psychiatric observation svc. Crouse Irving Meml. Hosp., Syracuse, N.Y., 1979-81; adult inpatient svcs. Phila. Psychiatric Ctr., Phila., 1981-82; outpatient adult, child and family psychotherapy Guidance Ctr. Camden County, Cherry Hill, N.J., 1982-83; outpatient child and adolescent psychotherapist Ctr. City Child Outpatient Svcs. JFK Community Mental Health Ctr., Phila.; intern in neuropsychology lab. U. Pa. Hosp., Phila., 1984-85; intern Student Counseling Ctr. Hahnemann U., 1985-86; assoc. psychologist outpatient Madison County Mental Health Dept., 1986-88; psychologist James St. Outpatient Clinic Hutchings Psychiat. Ctr., Syracuse, N.Y., 1988-93, unit psychologist inpatient residential rehab. svc., 1993—, psychologist Irving Ave. Outpatient Clinic, 1995—; pvt. practice psychotherapy consultation and assessment Syracuse, 1991—; adj. prof. grad. program psychology Chapman Coll. Mem. APA, N.Y. State Psychol. Assn., Ctrl. N.Y. Psychol. Assn., Omicron Nu, Theta Chi Beta, Phi Kappa Phi. Home: 221 Hunt Dr Fayetteville NY 13066 Office: 6836 E Genesee St Fayetteville NY 13066

KRISHNAN, KRISHNASWAMY RANGA RAMA, psychiatrist; b. Madras, India, Apr. 22, 1956; came to U.S., 1981; s. N. Krishnaswamy and Sulochana (Govinda) Reddy; m. Sripriya Chithamoor, May 21, 1987; 1 child, Vaishnavi. MBBS, U. MAdras, 1978. Sr. house officer Queen Elizabeth Hosp., Barbados, West Indies, 1980-81; asst. prof. Duke U., Durham, N.C., 1984-89, assoc. prof., 1989-95, head divsn. biol. psychiatry, 1989—, dir. program, 1989—, prof. psychiatry, 1995—; mem. NIMH Review Com., Washington, 1990—. Author: Chronic Pain, 1988; contbr. articles to profl. jours. Recipient Laughlin award Am. Coll. Psychiatry, 1984, Rafaelsen award CINP, 1988, Doreman award Psychosmatics, 1990. Mem. Am. Psychiat. Assn., Am. Coll. Neuropsychopharmacology, Nat. Bd. Med. Examiners. Office: Duke U Med Ctr Box 3018 Durham NC 27710

KRISSOFF, WILLIAM BRUCE, orthopaedic surgeon; b. Grand Rapids, Mich., Oct. 16, 1946; s. Abraham and Sylvia (Gittlen) K.; m. Christine McGee, Sept. 16, 1978; children: Nathan Michael, Austin Price. BA cum laude, Oberlin Coll., 1968. Diplomate Am. Bd. Orthopaedic Surgery. Intern San Francisco Gen., 1972-73; resident surgery U. Colo., Denver, 1973-74; resident orthopaedic surgery U. Calif., Davis, 1975-79; pvt. practice orthopaedic surgery Truckee, Calif., 1979—; emergency room physician St. Anthony Hosp., Denver, 1974-75; vice chief of staff Tahoe Forest Hosp., Truckee, 1985-86, chief of surgery, 1987-88, 93; clin. asst. prof. orthopaedics U. Calif. Davis, Sacramento, 1981-94; clin. assoc. prof. surgery Stanford (Calif.) U., 1995—; clin. asst. prof. U. Nev., Reno, 1994—. Contbr. articles to profl. jours. Mem. Am. Acad. Orthopaedic Surgeons, Am. Soc. Sports Medicine.

KRISTAN, RONALD WAYNE, physician, consultant; b. Yonkers, N.Y., Nov. 22, 1954; s. John Vincent and Gilda MAry (Gemma) K.; m. Connie B. Batlow, Apr. 27, 1980; children: Jonathan, Stephen, Joseph. BA in Chemistry summa cum laude, NYU, 1976, MD, 1980. Diplomate Am. Bd. Ophthamology. Mng. ptnr. Atlantic Eye Physicians, Long Branch, N.J., 1985—; chmn. Motor Vehicle Vision Panel N.J. Dept. Motor Vehicles, 1996; spkr. in field. Contbr. articles to profl. jours. Fellow Am. Soc. Ophthalmic Plastic and Reconstructive Surgery; mem. Am. Acad. Ophthamology, Am. Coll. Surgeons, N.J. Acad. Ophthamology (pres. 1996—, officer, bd. govs. 1985—, chmn. 3d party liaison), Phi Beta Kappa. Office: Atlantic Eye Physicians 279 3d Ave Long Branch NJ 07740

KRISTMUNDSDÓTTIR, THÓRDÍS, pharmacy educator; b. Reykjavík, Iceland, Nov. 13, 1948; s. Kristmundur and Ástdis (Gisladóttir) Jakobsson; m. Eirikur Örn Arnarson, Dec. 12, 1971; children: Hildur, Kristin Björk. Exam. Pharm., U. Iceland, Reykjavík, 1971; MSc, U. Manchester, Eng., 1974, PhD, 1976. Cert. in pharmaceutics, 1977. Rsch. fellow dept. pharmacy U. Manchester, 1977-79; rschr. dept. pharmacy U. Iceland, Reykjavík, 1979-86, prof., 1986—, head dept. pharmacy, 1993—; vice chmn. biomed. sci. sect. Icelandic Coun. of Sci., 1987-94; vice chmn. Cancer Soc. Sci. Coun., Iceland, 1990-91, chmn., 1991-92; governing bd. Nordic Rsch. Courses, 1990-91, Nordic Acad. for Advanced Study, 1991—. Editor The Icelandic Pharm. Jour., 1980-84; contbr.: (book) Polymeric Delivery Systems, 1993; contbr. articles to profl. jours. I.C.I. Rsch. grantee, Eng., 1974-76, U. Iceland Rsch. Fund./Icelandic Coun. Sic. Rsch. grantee, 1981—; NATO Sci. scholar, 1974. Mem. Icelandic Acad. Sci., Internat. Pharm. Fedn., N.Y. Acad. Sci. Home: Granaskjól 48, 107 Reykjavík Iceland Office: Univ of Iceland, Dept Pharmacy, Hagi Hofsvallagata 53, 107 Reykjavík Iceland

KRIVACSKA, JAMES JOSEPH, psychologist; b. Montreal, Dec. 19, 1957; came to U.S., 1959; BA, Rutgers Coll., 1979, D in Psychology, 1984. Cert., lic. psychologist, N.J. Sch. psychologist, dir. pupil personnel svcs. Boonton (N.J.) Pub. Schs., 1982-83; sch. psychologist South River (N.J.) Pub. Schs., 1983-86; pvt. cons. Ednl. Program Cons., Milltown, N.J., 1985—; sch. psychologist Middletown (N.J.) Pub. Schs., 1987-90; clin. dir. Children's Ctr. Monmouth County, Neptune, N.J., 1990-94; cons. Profl. Evaluation Svcs., Milltown, 1992—; pvt. practice N.J., 1990—; cons. psychologist N.J. YM-YWHA Camp for Learning Disabled, Fairfield, 1982-85; field supr. Rutgers U., New Brunswick, N.J., 1985—. Author: IEP Planner System, 1987, Designing Child Sexual Abuse Prevention Programs, 1990, The IEP Process, 1994; co-author: Compendium of Goals and Objectives, 1986; co-editor: Handbook of Forensic Sexology, 1994; software rev. editor Spl. Svcs. in Schs., 1985-89; contbr. articles to profl. jours., 5 chpts. to books; assoc. editor: Jour. Ednl. and Psychol. Consultation, 1993—. Mem. Milltown Drug/Alcohol Abuse Commn., 1987-90; mem. Milltown Bd. Edn., 1978-94, v.p., 1991, pres., 1994; trustee Milltown Libr., 1977-78. Recipient Recognition of Svc. award Milltown Bd. Edn., 1981, 91, 94, Assembly commendation N.J. State Assembly, 1993. Mem. APA, Nat. Assn. Sch. Psychologists (cert., co-chair children's svcs. com. 1991-92, Legis. award 1993), N.J. Assn. Sch. Psychologists (chmn. rsch. com. 1987-88, chmn. legis. com. 1988-89, 93-94, pres. 1990, Pres.'s award 1992), N.J. Edn. Assn., N.J. Sch. Bds. Assn. (spl. edn. com., county exec. com. 1981-91, v.p. 1989), Am. Orthpsychiatric Assn., Soc. for the Scientific Study of Sex, Sexuality Info. and Edn. Coun. of U.S. Home: 29 Elm Pl Milltown NJ 08850-1145 Office: Profl Evaluation Svcs 29 Elm Pl Milltown NJ 08850-1145

KRIZAN, KELLY JOE, physician, leather craftsman; b. Winner, S.D., Jan. 16, 1951; s. Miles Woodrow and Sadie Mae (DeSmet) K.; m. Susan Barker, Aug. 21, 1971 (div. Aug. 1983); children: Jennifer Rebecca, Nicholas Miles; m. Cynthia Lydia Obras, Aug. 6, 1983. BS, S.D. State U., 1973; BS in Medicine, U. S.D., 1976; MD, Tufts U., 1978. Diplomate Am. Bd. Family Practice. Commd., Am. Bd. Radiology. (first active duty capt. U.S. Air Force, 1978, advanced through grades to lt. col., 1984. Intern USAF Med. Ctr., Scott AFB, Ill., 1978-79, resident, 1979-81; staff physicain USAF Hosp., Hill AFB, Utah, 1981-83; chief emergency svcs., chief family practice USAF Hosp., Hill AFB, Utah, Incirlik AB, Turkey, 1983-84, chmn. dept. family practice, 1985-86; resident radiology U. Wash., 1986-90, clin. asst. prof., 1990—; chmn. dept. radiology 13th AF Med. Ctr., Clark AB, Philippines, 1990-91, St. Mary's Health Care Ctr., Pierre, S.D., 1993—. Artist leather goods, winner various awards. U. S.D. Presdl. scholar, 1969. Fellow Am. Acad. Family Physicians; mem. Am. Coll. Radiology, Am. Roentgen Ray Soc., Radiological Soc. N.Am., Phi Kappa Phi. Roman Catholic.

KROBATH, KRISTA ANN, pharmacist; b. Pottsville, Pa., July 8, 1962; d. James Joseph and Gaye Diane (Anderson) E.; m. Gilbert Krobath. BS in Pharmacy, Temple U., 1985. Registered pharmacist. Pharmacist People's Drug, Harrisburg, Pa., 1985-86; pharmacist, mgr. Amcare Health Svcs., Harrisburg, 1986-96; pharmacist Pharmacy Corp. Am., Harrisburg, 1996—. Mem. Pa. Pharm. Assn., Capital Area Pharm. Assn. Office: Pharmacy Corp Am 440 Lewis Rd Harrisburg PA 17111

KROGH-JENSEN, MOGENS, hospital administrator, consultant; b. Viborg, Denmark, Feb. 12, 1935; s. Viggo and Gurli (Justesen) Jensen;m. Kirsten Nyvang Mariussen, Oct. 14, 1961; children: Morten, Marianne, Marie-Louise. MD, U. Aarhus (Denmark), 1961; PhD, U. Copenhagen, 1967. Cert. internal medicine and haematology. Registrar Univ. Hosp., Copenhagen, 1962-67, sr. registrar, 1967-73; cons., head dept. haematology Regional Hosp., Aalborg, Denmark, 1973—; pres. Consultants of Aalborg Hosp., 1976-78. Author: Chromosome Studies in Acute Leukemia. 1967; co-author: Danish Text Book Haematology, 1988, 93; contbr. numerous articles on haematology and internal medicine to profl. jours. Mem. of the com. Conservative Party, Aalborg, 1982-87, pres., 1987-91. Fellow Danish Soc. Internal Medicine, Danish Soc. Cancer Rsch., Physicians of No. Jutland (pres. 1987-92), Danish Soc. Med. Priority (bd. dirs. 1989-94), Rotary (pres. 1984-85), Danish Soc. Bus. Adminstrn. Mem. Ch. of Denmark. Home: Rosenlunden 15 Hasseris, DK Aalborg Denmark Office: Aalborg Hosp, Dept of Medicine B, DK 9000 Aalborg Denmark

KROHN, KENNETH ALBERT, radiology educator; b. Stevens Point, Wis., June 19, 1945; s. Albert William and Erma Belle (Cornwell) K.; 1 child, Galen. BA in Chemistry, Andrews U., 1966; PhD in Chemistry, U. Calif., 1971. Acting assoc. prof. U. Wash., Seattle, 1981-84, assoc. prof. radiology, 1984-86, prof. radiology and radiation oncology, 1986—, adj. prof. chemistry, 1986—; guest scientist Donner Lab. Lawrence Berkeley (Calif.) Lab., 1980-81; radiochemist, VA Med. Ctr., Seattle, 1982—. Contbr. numerous articles to profl. jours.; patentee in field. NDEA fellow. Fellow AAAS; mem. Am. Chem. Soc., Radiation Rsch. Soc., Soc. Nuclear Medicine, Acad. Coun., Sigma Xi. Home: NE550 Lake Ridge Dr Belfair WA 98528 Office: U Washington Imaging Rsch Lab Box 356004 Seattle WA 98195-6004

KROKEN, PATRICIA ANN, health science association administrator; b. Sturgis, Mich., June 26, 1947; d. Jesse W. and Dorothy Beth (Hollister) Penn; m. Bruce Edward Kroken, Jan. 28, 1967; children: Christina, Jennifer. BS in English cum laude, No. Mich. U., 1970. Reporter Marinette (Wis.) Eagle-Star, 1973-77; account exec. Sta. KGRT/KGRD, Las Cruces, N. Mex., 1977-78, Sta. KRZY, Albuquerque, 1978-80, Sta. KGGM-TV, Albuquerque, 1980-81; v.p., acctg. supr. Rick Johnson & Co., Albuquerque, 1984-87; expansion sales mgr. Bueno Foods, 1987-89; bus. devel. dir. Radiology Assocs., Albuquerque, 1990-93, exec. dir., 1993—; adj. prof. U. N. Mex, Albuquerque, 1983-94. Contbr. articles to various jours. Lectr. N. Mex. Womens Polit. Caucus, Albuquerque, 1986. Mem. Radiology Bus. Mgmt. Assn. (Calhoun award 1996), N.Mex. Med. Group Mgmt. Assn. (pres. 1995). Home: 12501 Oakland Ave NE Albuquerque NM 87122-2274 Office: Radiology Assocs 8307 Constitution NE Albuquerque NM 87110

KROLL, MARTIN HARRIS, pathologist; b. Washington, June 19, 1952; s. Bernard Hilton and Doris (Weinblum) K.; m. Ellen Linda Coonin, June 22, 1975; children: Allison, Jonathan, Lauren. BS, U. Md., 1974, MD, 1978. Resident in pathology U. Md. Hosp., Balt., 1978-82, chief resident in pathology, 1981; fellow in clin. chemistry NIH, Bethesda, Md., 1982-84, med. staff, 1984-93; assoc. dir. clin. chemistry divsn. and ctrl. svcs. Johns Hopkins Hosp., Balt., 1994-95, dir. ctrl. svcs. divsn., 1994—, dir. ctrl. svcs. divsn., Green Spring Sta Lab., 1995—; cons. Baxter Travenol, Irvine, Calif., 1988, Abbot Labs., Diagnostics Divsn., Chgo., 1994-95. Contbr. articles to profl. jours. Chmn. libr. com. North Potomac (Md.) Citizens Assn., 1988-93, edn. com., 1991, Quince Orchard/Rt. 28 ad hoc Libr. Adv. Com., Montgomery County, Md., 1991. NSF fellow, 1973. Mem. Am. Chem. Soc., Acad. Clin. Lab. Physicians and Scientists (Young Investigator award 1983), Am. Assn. for Clin. Chemistry (sec. Capitol sect. 1988, chmn. 1990, adv. bd. Clin. Chemistry News, A.O. Beckman Conf. Com. 1995-96, Chmn. award 1990, Roe award, 1995), NIH Internist Chaos Coun. (steering com. 1990-91), Coll. Am. Pathologists (instrumentation com., program com. 1994-95, chmn. 1996—, chemistry resource comm., 1996—), Nat. Com. for Clin. Lab. Standards (sub com. on stats., area com. on evaluation). Democrat. Jewish. Home: 7 Latimore Way Owings Mills MD 21117 Office: Johns Hopkins Hosp Dept Path Clin Chem Divsn 600 N Wolfe St Meyer B-125 Baltimore MD 21287-7065

KROMHOLZ, W. NOAH, endocrinologist; b. Bronx, Aug. 25, 1945. BA, Columbia Coll., 1967; MD, SUNY, 1971. Diplomate Am. Bd. Internal Medicine, Am. Bd. Endocrinology & Metabolism. Intern Kings County Hosp. Ctr., 1971-72; resident in internal medicine US PHS, Balt., 1972-74; fellow in endrocrinology and metabolism Nassau County Med. Ctr., East Meadow, N.Y., 1974-76, attending physician, 1976—; asst. prof. medicine SUNY, Stonybrook, 1976—. Mem. Am. Coll. Physicians, Am. Diabetes Assn., Endocrine Soc. Office: Nassau County Med Ctr 2201 Hempstead Tpke East Meadow NY 11554

KRON, LEO, psychiatrist, educator; b. Aug. 1, 1946; m. Jill Rubin, Dec. 31, 1979; children: Joshua, Emily. MD, U. B.C., Vancouver, Can., 1971. Diplomate Am. Bd. Psychiatry and Neurology, Am. Bd. Child Psychiatry. Intern Queens Med. Ctr., Honolulu, 1971-72; resident in psychiatry Albert Einstein Coll. Medicine, N.Y.C., 1973-76; resident in child psychiatry Columbia U. Coll. Physicians and Surgeons, N.Y.C., 1976-78, asst. clin. prof. psychiatry, 1986—; tng. in psychoanalysis N.Y. Psychoanalytic Inst., N.Y.C.; pvt. practice, N.Y.C., 1976—; dir. div. child and adolescent psychiatry St. Luke's Hosp. Ctr., N.Y.C., 1986-90; corp. dir. divsn. child and adolescent psychiatry St. Luke's-Roosevelt Hosp. Ctr., N.Y.C., 1990-93, dir. consultation and liaison, 1994—; psychiat. cons. Assn. To Benefit Children, N.Y.C., 1995—, Hunter Coll., CUNY, 1989—. Contbr. numerous articles to med. jours., chpts. to books. Fellow Royal Coll. Physicians Canada; mem. Am. Psychiat. Assn., Am. Acad. Child and Adolescent Psychiatry, Am. Soc. Clin. Psychopharmacology, Can. Med. Assn., N.Y. Psychoanalytic Soc. Office: 30 E 76th St Ste 3A New York NY 10021

KRONEN, JERILYN, psychologist; b. N.Y.C., July 17, 1947; d. Morris and Hester (Engel) Levy; m. Kenneth Kronen, Apr. 11, 1976; children: Ari, Joshua. PhD, Yeshiva U., 1982; cert. in psychotherapy & psychoanalysis, N.Y.U., 1988. Lic. psychologist, N.Y. Tchr. Pub. Sch. 119, N.Y.C., 1969-72; sch. psychologist Bd. Coop. Edn. Svc., N.Y.C., 1972-82; pvt. practice N.Y.C., 1982—; mem. faculty Resolve, N.Y.C., 1989—; adj. clin. supr. Ferkauf-Yeshiva U., N.Y.C., 1989—; lectr. in field. Bd. dirs. Couples Club Kehilat Jeshurun Synagogue, N.Y.C., 1989-91, adoption resource person, 1990—; liaison mem. Lower Sch. Ramaz, N.Y.C., 1990-92. Mem. APA, Div. 39 Psychoanalysis. Home and Office: 137 E 36th St Ste 14 New York NY 10016-3528

KRONENBERG, RICHARD SAMUEL, physician, educator; b. Chgo., Aug. 7, 1938; s. Frank Paul and Ruth Ida (Zaretzsky) K.; m. Carole Marie Hurd, Oct. 13, 1963; children: Karen, Marilyn, Brenda. BA, Northwestern U., 1960, MD, 1963. Intern Parkland Meml. Hosp., Mpls., 1967-68, resident in internal medicine, 1968; rsch. fellow Cardiovascular Rsch. Inst. U. Calif., San Franciso, 1968-70; asst. prof. medicine U. Minn., 1970-74, assoc. prof., 1974-79, prof., dir. pulmonary div., 1979-84; prof. U. Tex. Health Sci. Ctr., Houston, 1984—; prof. medicine, exec. assoc. dir. clin. affairs U. Tex. Health Ctr., Tyler, 1984—; reviewer subsplty. programs in internal medicineAccreditation Coun. Grad. Med. Edn., Chgo., 1985—. Mem. editorial rev. bd. The Asbestos Monitor, Nat. Asbestos Coun. Jour., 1990—; contbr. chpts. to books. Capt. USAF, 1965-67. Recipient Rsch. Career Devel. award NIH, 1973-78. Fellow ACP, Am. Coll. Chest Physicians; mem. Nat. Asbestos Coun. (bd. dirs. 1990—), Asbestos Disease Assn. (pres. 1990-93), Ctrl. Soc. Clin. Rsch. Home: 5615 Cedar Hill Cir Tyler TX 75703-3895 Office: U Tex Health Ctr PO Box 2003 Tyler TX 75710-2003

KRONENFELD, JENNIE JACOBS, medical sociologist; b. Hampton, Va., Aug. 11, 1949; d. Harry and Bessie (Pear) J.; m. Michael Reed Kronenfeld, Sept. 8, 1970; children: Shaun Jacobs, Jeffrey Brian, Aaron Benjamin. B.A., U. N.C., 1971; M.A., Brown U., 1972, Ph.D., 1976. Asst. prof. U. Ala., 1975-80; assoc. prof. Sch. of Pub. Health, U. S.C., Columbia, 1980-85, prof., 1985-90; prof. sch. health adminstrn and policy Ariz. State U., 1990—; scientist Multi-purpose Arthritis Ctr. & Diabetes Research & Tng. Ctr., 1978-80; vis. faculty Princeton U., 1982. Co-editor: Social and Economic Impact of Coronary Artery Disease, 1980; U.S. Health Policy, 1984; Sex Role Changes, 1986, Captive Populations, 1990, Controversial Issues In Health Care Policy, 1993, Research in the Sociology of Health Care, Vol. 10, 1993, Vol. 11, 1994; editor: Research in the Sociology of Health Care, Vol. 11, 1995; co-author: Getting Tenure, 1993, Dealing with Ethical Dilemmas on Campus, 1994. Assoc. editor Jour. Health and Social Behavior, 1983-85. Mem. Am. Sociol. Assn. (sec., treas., chair med. sociol. sect. 1990-91), Assn. Social Scientists in Health (council mem. 1979-84, 89-91), Southern Sociol. Soc. (com. mem., v.p. 1989-90), NOW. Democrat. Jewish. Avocation: gardening. Office: Ariz State U Coll Bus Sch Health Adminstrn and Policy Box 874506 Tempe AZ 85287-4506

KRONER, DAVID ROBERT, surgeon; b. Tokyo, Nov. 30, 1948; s. Arthur Frank and Gertrude Claudia (Katz) K.; m. Rebecca Elgin (div. 1985); children: Paige, Christopher; m. Constance Rodney, June 12, 1985; 1 child, Bobbi. BA, U. Va., 1970; MD, Med. Coll. Va., 1974. Diplomate Am. Bd. Surgery. Chief surgery, med.dir. Alice Peck Day Hosp., Lebanon, N.H., 1985—. Lt. col. USAF, 1973-85. Paul Harris fellow Rotary Internat., 1995. Fellow ACS; mem. Am. Soc. Gen. Surgeons, Soc. Laporoendoscopic Surgery, N.H. Med. Soc. Office: Alice Peck Day Hosp 129 A Mascoma St Lebanon NH 03766

KRONFOL, ZIAD ANIS, psychiatrist, educator; b. Beirut, Mar. 29, 1949; came to U.S., 1974; s. Anis and Inam (Ardati) K.; m. Rima Naja, Mar. 26, 1983; children: Zeina, Sara. BS, Am. U. Beirut, 1970, MD, 1974. Diplomate Am. Bd. Psychiatry and Neurology. Intern Am. U. Beirut, 1973-74, instr. psychiatry, 1977-79; resident in psychiatry U. Iowa, Iowa City, 1974-77, asst. prof., 1982-85; rsch. fellow U. Mich., Ann Arbor, 1979-82, assoc. prof. psychiatry, dir. psychoimmunology, 1986—; staff psychiatrist, rsch. dir. adult inpatient psychiatry U. Mich. Med. Ctr., Ann Arbor, 1986—; chief consultation/liaison psychiatry VA Med. Ctr., Iowa City, 1984-85; cons. intensive psychiat. cmty. care VA Med. Ctr., Ann Arbor, 1995—; presenter at profl. confs. Contbr. to profl. publs. Grantee NIMH, 1987-90, NIAAA, 1988. Mem. AAAS, Am. Psychiat. Assn., Soc. Biol. Psychiatry, N.Y. Acad. Scis., Am. Psychosomatic Soc., Soc. Neurosci., Internat. Soc. Neuroimmunomodulation (charter). Home: 1220 Severn Ct Ann Arbor MI 48105-2863 Office: Univ Mich Med Ctr 1500 E Medical Center Dr Ann Arbor MI 48109-0118

KRONKE, DORENE EMMA, pharmaceutical executive; b. Tyler, Minn., May 20, 1950; d. Arthur John and Elaine Irene (Wendorff) K.; m. Jonathan Krim, June 21, 1980 (div. Oct. 1983); m. Michael William Rossi, Nov. 19, 1983 (separated). BA in Bus. Adminstrn., SW State U., 1973; MBA, Ariz. State U., 1981. Unit mgr. Good Samaritan Hosp., Phoenix, 1973-75; waitress Phoenix Country Club, 1976-77; sales rep. Treasure Chem. Co., Billings, Mont., 1977; profl. rep. Merck Sharp & Dohme, Missoula, Mont., 1978-80; program coord. Merck Sharp & Dohme, West Point, Pa., 1981-83; dist. mgr. Merck Sharp & Dohme, San Diego, 1983-86; product mgr. Merck Sharp & Dohme, West Point, 1986-88; region dir. Merck Sharp & Dohme, Mpls., 1988-91; v.p. sales and mktg. MGI Pharma, Inc., Mpls., 1991-92; exec. dir. info. edn. and svcs. Astra Merck, Inc., Wayne, Pa., 1992-95, exec. dir. field sales, 1995—. Bd. dirs. Nat. Soc. for Prevention of Blindness, Orange, Calif., 1986; trustee First Unitarian Soc., Mpls., 1990; mem. St. David's Episcopal Ch., Phila. Mus. Art, Nat. Parks & Conservation Assn., Washington, Nature Conservancy, Nat. Mus. of Women in the Arts, Washington. Mem. NOW, Ariz. State U. Alumni Assn., S.W. State U. Alumni Assn. (Childreach sponsor). Office: 725 Chesterbrook Blvd Wayne PA 19087-5637

KROOP, MERLE SONDRA, psychiatrist; b. Phila., Jan. 24, 1939; d. Morris and Jerrie (Yentis) K.; 1 child, Steven Kroop. BS, U. Fla., 1959; MD, U. Miami, 1970. Diplomate Am. Bd. Sexology (coin supr.). Resident in psychiatry Beth Israel Med. Ctr., N.Y.C., 1970-73; pvt. practice N.Y.C., 1973—; psychiat. cons. Family Ct., Bklyn., 1973-74; co-dir. sex therapy program Jewish Bd. of Family and Children's Svcs., N.Y.C., 1974-84; clin. asst. prof. psychiatry N.Y. Hosp., Cornell Med. Ctr., N.Y.C., 1973-88, assoc. dir. human sexuality tchg. program, 1973-88. Contbr. articles to profl. jours. Mem. Am. Psychiat. Assn., Med. Soc. N.Y., Women's Med. Assn. N.Y., Soc. for Sex Therapy and Rsch.

KROPP, KENNETH A., urologist; b. Lakewood, Ohio, 1935. MD, Northwestern U., 1961. Diplomate Am. Bd. Urologists. Intern U. Northwestern Hosps., Chgo., 1962, resident, 1965; urologist Med. Coll. Hosp., Toledo, Ohio; prof. urology Med. Coll. Ohio, Toledo. Mem. ACS, AMA, Am. Urology Assn., Am. Assn. Pediatricians, ASTS. Office: Med Coll Ohio Urology Dept 3000 Arlington Ave Toledo OH 43614-2595*

KROPP, THOMAS M., ophthalmologist, plastic surgeon; b. Milw., June 19, 1954; m. Marcia Rice, May 8, 1982; children: Jeffrey, Lauren. BS, Fla. State U., 1977; MD, U. Fla., 1980. Diplomate Am. Bd. Ophthalmology. Intern in ophthalmology U. Tex. Med. Br., 1981-84; resident in oculoplastic and reconstructive surgery Children's Hosp. Phila., Scheie Eye Inst., 1984-85; physician Randolph Carter, MD, Deland, Fla., 1985-87; ptnr. Carter and Kropp Ophthalmology, Deland, Fla., 1986-92, Kropp and Cordero Ophthalmology, Deland, Fla., 1993—; bd. dirs. Eye Specialists Network, Fla., 1995—. Co-author book chpts. Ocluloplastic, Orbital and Reconstructive Surgery, vol. II, 1990. Mem. AMA, Am. Acad Ophthalomology, Am. Soc. Ophthalmic, Plastic and Reconstructive Surgery, Fla. Med. Assn., Ctrl. Fla. Soc. Ophthalmology. Office: Kropp and Cordero Ophthalm 305 E New York Ave Deland FL 32724

KROSSNER, RHONDA PARRELLA, psychologist; b. Mt. Vernon, N.Y., Dec. 29, 1951; d. Joseph and Ida (Cornacchia) Parrella; m. William J.

Krossner Jr., Sept. 4, 1977; children: Steven, Laura. BS summa cum laude, Fordham U., 1973, MA, 1975, PhD, 1983. V.p. Psy. Minn. Corp., Duluth, 1977—; head neuropsychology div. Neurosci. Inst., Duluth, 1984-88; staff psychologist The Duluth Clinic, Ltd., 1988—. NIMH fellow, 1975. Mem. Nat. Acad. Neuropsychology, Am. Psychol. Assn., Phi Beta Kappa. Home: PO Box 3047 Duluth MN 55803-3047 Office: The Duluth Clinic 400 E 3rd St Duluth MN 55805-1951

KROSTAG, DIANE THERESA MICHAELS, clinical informatics analyst; b. Wilkes-Barre, Pa., Apr. 13, 1959; d. William Adam Michaels and Theresa J. Zielinski Stauber; m. William Joseph Krostag, Oct. 20, 1979. AAS in Nursing, Luzerne County Community Coll., Nanticoke, Pa., 1979; postgrad., U. N.Mex., Albuquerque. Staff nurse pediatrics U. Hosp., Albuquerque, 1979-80, staff nurse newborn nursery, 1980-81, asst. head nurse newborn nursery, 1981-85; charge nurse pediatric clinic U. Hosp.-Children's Hosp. N.Mex., Albuquerque, 1985-92; clin. info. specialist Shared Med. Systems Action System Univ. Hosp., Albuquerque, N. Mex., 1992-95; clin. informatics analyst Cerner Pronet System Univ. Hosp., Albuquerque, 1995—. Recipient Disting. Nurse award Univ. Hosp., 1989. Mem. ANA, Am. Nursing Informatics Assn., N. Mex. Nurses Assn., Balloon Fedn. Am., Albuquerque Aerostat Ascension Assn. Home: 77 Arizona Sunset Rd NE Albuquerque NM 87124-2538

KROTH, JEANNIE MAE, pediatrics nurse; b. Waverly, Ohio, May 3, 1944; d. Reginald Henry and Marjorie Ellen (Stephens) K.; 1 child, Regina Ellen. LPN, Shawnee State C.C., Portsmouth, Ohio, 1980; student, Ohio U. RN, Ohio, Ky. Staff nurse Mercy Hosp., Portsmouth, Ross County Med. Ctr., Chillicothe, Ohio, Am. Nursing Care Children's Hosp., Columbus, Ohio; staff nurse, supr. Pike Cmty. Hosp., Waverly, Western Med. Svcs., Columbus, Tri State Infusion, Portsmouth, Ohio. Mem. Phi Theta Kappa. Home: 98 Fish Game Rd Waverly OH 45690

KROTOSKI, WOJCIECH ANTONI, research physician, educator; b. Riga, Latvia, June 20, 1937; came to U.S., 1949; naturalized U.S. citizen, 1955.; s. Ludwik Jozef and Leokadia Jozefina (Pawlowska) K.; m. Danuta Mary Gwozdziowski (annulled); 1 child, Aleksandra Krystyna; m. Judith Ann Goins, Aug. 2, 1985; 1 stepchild, John Alfred Bell IV. BA, UCLA, 1960, PhD, MD, 1968; MPH, U. Calif., Berkeley, 1974. Diplomate Calif. State Bd. Med. Examiners. Commd. med. officer USPHS, 1969, advanced through grades to med. dir., 1984; staff assoc. unit human malaria NIH, Atlanta, 1969-70, med. officer in charge unit human malaria, 1970-71; rsch. assoc. unit primate malaria NIH, Chamblee, Ga., 1971-72; clin. fellow tropical medicine Sch. Medicine U. Calif., San Francisco, 1972-74; resident internal and preventive medicine USPHS Hosp., San Francisco, 1972-74; asst. chief medicine, asst. chief clin. rsch. USPHS Hosp., New Orleans, 1975-78, chief tropical infectious disease rsch. program, 1975-81, chief clin. rsch., 1978-81; clin. assoc. prof. dept. tropical medicine Sch. Pub. Health and Tropical Medicine Tulane U., 1975-86; clin. assoc. prof. dept. tropical medicine and med. parasitology Sch. Medicine La. State U., New Orleans, 1978-84, clin. assoc. prof. infectious diseases Sch. Medicine, 1978—, assoc. mem. faculty Sch. Grad. Studies Med. Ctr., 1980—, clin. assoc. prof. internat. and tropical medicine Sch. Medicine, clin. assoc. prof. med. parasitology, 1984—; rsch. physician Gillis W. Long Hansen's Disease Ctr. La. State U., Baton Rouge, 1993-95; dir. Nat. Ambulatory Hansen's Disease Program, Bureau Health Care Delivery and Assistance USPHS, 1990-91; physician microbiologist, immunologist Nat. Hansen's Disease Ctr., Carville, La., 1981-83, dep. chief lab. rsch. br., 1983-85; rsch. physician lab. rsch. br. GWL Hansen's Disease Ctr., Carville, 1985-90, acting chief pathology rsch. dept. lab. rsch. br., 1992-93; ret. USPHS, 1995; adj. prof. tropical medicine Sch. Vet. Medicine La. State U., Baton Rouge, 1987-94, adj. prof. pathology, 1993—; mem. Marshall Islands health survey team Brookhaven (N.Y.) Nat. Lab., 1977-82, ctrl. clin. investigations com. Bureau Med. Svcs. USPHS, 1978-81; peer rev. panelist cholera rsch. devel. program Bd. Regents, State of La., 1980-81; cons. leprosy vaccine immunology leprosy sci. working group World Health Orgn., Geneva, Switzerland, 1982, 85; mem. Hansen's disease rsch. adv. com. bur. health care delivery and assistance USPHS, 1983-89; rsch. affiliate Delta Regional Primate Rsch. Ctr., Tulane U., Covington, La., 1984-87; participant New Orleans Infectious Disease Conf., 1984—; presenter in field. Contbr. numerous articles to med. and sci. jours. Recipient Cert. Merit, State of La. Bd. Regents Rsch. and Devel. Program, 1980; nominee Nobel Prize in physiology and medicine, 1989. Fellow Royal Soc. Tropical Medicine and Hygiene; mem. Am. Soc. Tropical Medicine and Hygiene (sci. program com. 1978-79), USPHS Profl. Assn. (sci. program chmn. 1989), Assn. Mil. Surgeons U.S., La.-Miss. Infectious Diseases Soc., La. Soc. Electron Microscopy, Internat. Leprosy Assn., Nat. Right-to-Life, Baton Rouge Right-to-Life, Southeastern Soc. Parasitologists. Roman Catholic.

KRUC, ANTOINETTE CAMPION, family physician; b. Scranton, Pa., May 9, 1939; d. Robert Francis and Mary Elizabeth (Boyle) Campion; m. Peter John Kruc, Mar. 2, 1962 (div. Sept. 1973); children: Kathryn Anne, David Campion. BS, Phila. Coll. Pharmacy & Sci., 1961; DO, Phila. Coll. Osteo. Medicine, 1977. Physician/owner Spruce Hill Med. Assocs., Phila., 1978-95, Kruc/Palmerio Part, Phila., 1982-94; physician AHERF, Phila., 1995—; corp. mem. Pa. sBlue Shield, Harrisburg, 1995—. Bd. dirs. West Cath. H.S., Phila., 1994—; spkr. Optimists-Overbrook, Phila., 1985—. Recipient Cmty. Svc. award Pa. House of Reps., 1983, Optimists Internat., 1993. Mem. PAMA, POFPS, AC of GP, PCOS, Alpha Omega Alpha. Office: Spruce Hill Family Practice 537 S 46th St Philadelphia PA 19143

KRUCKENBERG, WAYNE LEONARD, biologist; b. Minot, N.D., Mar. 11, 1950; s. Leonard Armine and Helen Ruth (Spong) K. Student, S.D. State U., 1970-71; BS, Westmar Coll., 1972; postgrad., S.D. State U., 1972-73, 77-78. Biologist U.S. Fish & Wildlife Svc., Madison, S.D., summer 1970-71; with aquaculture extension Bur. of Fisheries/Aquatic Resources, Bohol, Philippines, 1973-75; aquaculture rsch. Brackish Water Aquaculture Ctr., Iloilo, Philippines, 1975-76; biol. technician S.D. State U., Brookings, 1977-78; aquaculture biologist Aqua Farms Internat., Mecca, Calif., 1978-79; fish biologist aquaculture Valley Fish Farms, Brawley, Calif., 1979; fish biologist, comml. fisheries and sport fish devel. Guam Div. Aquatic and Wildlife Resources, Agana, 1979—; with seafood sales dept. Safeway Supermarket, Dededo, Guam, 1988-89. Member Guam chpt. Nat. Audubon Soc., 1991—. Mem. Am. Fisheries Soc., World Aquaculture Soc., Nat. Audubon Soc. Mem. United Methodist. Home: PO Box 1771, Agana 96910, Guam Office: Aquatic Wildlife Resources Dept Agr, PO Box 2950, Agana 96910, Guam

KRUEGER, GERALD PETER, psychologist; b. Evanston, Ill., Apr. 3, 1944; s. Albert August and Pauline Mary (Didier) K.; m. Jessica Ann Prendergast, Aug. 26, 1967; children: Michael G., Deborah L., Kevin A. BA in Psychology, U. Dayton, 1966; MA in Exptl. & Engring. Psychology, Johns Hopkins U., 1975, PhD in Exptl. Psychology, 1977; Grad., U.S. Army Command and Gen. Staff Coll., 1980, U.S. Army War Coll., 1988. Cert. profl. ergonomist. Engring. psychology researcher Bunker-Ramo Corp., Wright-Patterson AFB, Ohio, 1966-69; human factors rsch. psychologist U.S. Army Human Engring. Lab., Aberdeen, Md., 1969-71; R&D coord. Def. Advanced Rsch. Projects Agy., Saigon, Vietnam, 1971-72; mil. police ops. officer U.S. Army, Ft. Meade, Md., 1972; aviation psychologist aeromed. rsch. lab. U.S. Army, Ft. Rucker, Ala., 1976-80; rsch. & devel. programs staff officer headquarters USA Med. Rsch. & Devel. Command, Ft. Detrick, Md., 1980-84; dep. chief dept. behavioral biology Walter Reed Army Inst. Rsch., Washington, 1984-88; dir. biomed. applications rsch. div. U.S. Army Aeromed. Rsch. Lab., Ft. Rucker, 1988-90; comdr., scientific tech. dir. U.S. Army Rsch. Inst. Environ. Medicine, Natick, Mass., 1990-94; ret., 1994; v.p. ergonomics R & D svcs. Biomechanics Corp. Am., Melville, N.Y., 1994-95; prin. rsch. scientist Star Mountain, Inc., Alexandria, Va., 1995—; tchr. U.S. Armed Forces Inst., Saigon, 1971, Johns Hopkins U., 1974-75, U. So. Calif., 1977-80. Assoc. editor Military Psychology, 1991—; guest editor jours. in field; contbr. numerous articles to profl. publs. Recipient Richard M. Griffith Meml. award So. Soc. Philosophy & Psychology, 1978, order of military med. merit for career contbns. army med. dept., 1992, Legion of Merit, 1994, Bronze Star U.S. Army, 1972, meritorious svc. medals (2 oak leaf clusters), 1980, 84, 89, commendation medals, 1971, 90, achievement medal, 1988, nat. def. svc. medal, 1969, 91, Vietnam svc. medal (2 battle campaign stars), 1972, armed forces svc. medal, 1976, Rep. Vietnam staff svc. medal, 1972, Rep. Vietnam cross of gallantry, 1972. Fellow APA (pres. divsn. mil. psychology 1995-96, divsn. engring. psychologists), Soc. for Indsl. Orgnl. Psychologists; mem. AAAS, Am. Indsl. Hygiene Assn., Internat. Assn. Applied Psychology, Am. Psychol. Soc., Assn. U.S. Army, Am. Def. Preparedness Assn., Internat. Assn. for Stress Mgmt., Human Factors and Ergonomics Soc., Ergonomics Soc., Aerospace Med. Assn., Aerospace Human Factors Assn., Applied Ergonomics (Moscow), Army War Coll. Alumni Assn., VFW, Am. Legion. Roman Catholic. Office: Star Mountain Inc 3601 Eisenhower Ave Alexandria VA 22304-6496

KRUEGER, GERHARD RICHARD FRANZ, pathologist; b. Berlin, Nov. 21, 1936; s. Richard F. H. and Irmgard E. M. (Dieke) K.; m. Maria-Barbara Philipp, June 2, 1960; children: Rolf, Claudia S., Elke. MD, Free U., Berlin, 1962. Diplomate pathologist. Internship Free U. Berlin, Germany, 1962-64; pathologist Mcpl. Hosp. Spandau, Berlin, Germany, 1964-65; rsch. scientist Nat. Cancer Inst., Bethesda, Md., 1965-67; rsch. pathologist Nat. Cancer Inst., Bethesda, 1968-72; pathologist Dept. Pathology, Free U., Berlin, 1967-68; prof. pathology, sect. head Immunopathology Lab., Dept. Pathology, U. Cologne, Germany, 1972-91; prof. dept. pathology U. Cologne, vice dean med. faculty, 1996; prof. pathology and lab. medicine Dept. Pathology Lab. Medicine, U. Tex. Med. Sch., Houston, 1991-92; chmn. Internat. Inst. Immunopath., Inc., Houston, 1989—. Author: Immunopathology, 1986; coauthor: Human Herpesvirus-6, 1992; contbr. articles to profl. jours. Med. examiner U. Cologne, State of Northrine-Westfalia, Germany, 1974-96.

KRUEGER, NANCY ASTA, physical therapist; b. Manhattan Beach, Calif., Jan. 8, 1947; d. Henry Adolph and Asta Ida (Harrison) Graef; m. Gary Patrick Krueger, June 14, 1969. Student, Lewis & Clark Coll., 1964-66; BS, U. So. Calif., L.A., 1969; postgrad., U. So. Calif., Downey, 1980-81. Staff phys. therapist Los Angeles County-U. So. Calif. Med. Ctr., L.A., 1969-71, Stockton (Calif.) State Hosp., 1971; pediatric phys. therapist Calif. Childrens Svcs.-San Joaquin County, Stockton, 1972-73; sr. phys. therapist Calif. Childrens Svcs.-San Diego County, San Diego, 1974-80; mng. dir. therapy svcs. Sharp-Cabrillo Hosp., San Diego, 1981-83; sr. phys. therapist El Cajon (Calif.) Valley Hosp., 1983-84; prin. El Cajon Therapy Assocs., 1984—; cons. Teledyne Ryan Aero., San Diego County, 1984—, San Diego Marriott Hotel, 1995—; speaker in field. Singer Old Globe Madrigal Singers, 1983; vice chair adv. com. Maternal, Child and Adolescent Health, San Diego County, 1987-89; active local polit. campaigns; advisor Mesa Coll., 1985—; mem. edn. and sci. com. Arthritis Found., 1986-87; chairperson adv. com. Mesa Coll., 1994-96. Fellow Am. Acad. Sports Medicine, Orthopedic Soc.; mem. Am. Phys. Therapy Assn. (chmn. San Diego dist. 1977-78, bd. dirs. Calif. chpt. 1983-84, mem. nominating com. 1989-91, chmn. 1991, v.p. 1994—, fin. com. Orthopedic sect. 1993—), Aux. Am. Optometric Assn., Arthritis Health Profls. Assn. (v.p. 1991-93), Jrs. of Social Svc. (treas. 1991-93), Soroptimists (sec. El Cajon chpt. 1982, chmn. 1994), Rotary Internat. Republican. Episcopalian. Home: 4657 Rancho Park Ave San Diego CA 92120 Office: El Cajon Therapy Assocs 590 S Magnolia Ave El Cajon CA 92020-6011

KRUG, DOUGLAS EDWARD, emergency physician; b. Chelsea, Md., June 8, 1953; s. Edward Thatcher and Joan Marie (Gettell) K.; m. Lorraine Anne Schmidt, June 22, 1980; children: Ryan, Courtney, Kaitlin. AB, Colgate U., 1975; MS, Georgetown U., 1976, MD, 1980. Physician Promina Kennestone Hosp., Marietta, Ga., 1985—. Fellow Am. Coll. Emergency Physicians. Office: Kennestone Emergency Group 677 Church St Marietta GA 30060

KRUGER, BARBARA, audiologist, speech and language pathologist; b. Corpus Christi, Tex., Aug. 16, 1944. BA in Psychology cum laude, CUNY, 1967, MA in Speech Pathology, 1970, PhD in Audiology and Hearing Sci., 1975. Asst. prof. audiology, dir. hearing research lab. Columbia U., N.Y.C., 1975-78; asst. prof. otolaryngology, dir. audiology and speech lang. pathology Albert Einstein Coll. Medicine, Montefiore Med. Ctr. Yeshiva U., Bronx, N.Y., 1978-87; cons. Kruger Assocs., Commack, N.Y., 1987—; dir. Audiology and Communicaton Services, 1987—; adj. prof. Columbia U., 1979-82; chmn. earphone calibration Internat. Electrotech. Commn., Am. Nat. Standards Inst.; cons. Albert Einstein Coll. of Medicine, Kennedy Ctr., 1987-90. Spencer Found. grantee, 1976-78, Am. Otological Soc. grantee, 1978-79, Rose M. Badgeley Residuary Charitable Trust grantee, 1981-84; recipient Program Project award NIH, 1984-86. Fellow Am. Speech-Lang. Hearing Assn. Home and Office: 37 Somerset Dr Commack NY 11725-1636

KRUGER, GUSTAV OTTO, JR., oral surgeon, educator; b. N.Y.C., Sept. 28, 1916; s. Gustav Otto and Anna Charlotte (Mellquist) K.; m. Helyn E. Hollingsworth, Apr. 12, 1947; children: Deborah Ann (Mrs. M. Henry King III), Tristram Coffin, Abigail Hollingsworth Imus. B.S., George Washington U., 1938, A.M., 1939; D.D.S., Georgetown U., 1939, Sc.D. (hon.), 1977. Diplomate: Am. Bd. Oral and Maxillofacial Surgery (pres. 1964). Intern Johns Hopkins Hosp., 1939-40; fellow Mayo Found., 1940-42, 45-48; mem. faculty Georgetown U. Sch. Dentistry and Grad. Sch., 1948-87, prof. oral surgery, chmn. dept., 1948-87, prof. emeritus, 1987—, asso. dean, 1966-82; chief dental dept. Georgetown U. Hosp., Washington, 1948-82; cons. VA hosps., Martinsburg, W.Va. and Washington, U.S. Naval Hosp., Bethesda, D.C. Gen. Hosp., Washington; cons. to Pres.'s physician, 1960-64; cons. Walter Reed Army Med. Ctr.; mem. cancer tng. com. Nat. Cancer Inst., USPHS, 1967-71, chmn., 1969-71. Author: Textbook of Oral and Maxillofacial Surgery, 1959, 6th edit., 1984; contbr. articles to profl. jours. Served to capt. Dental Corps AUS, 1942-45, CBI, PTO. Recipient Arnold K. Maislen award N.Y. U., 1970; Simon P. Hullihen award W.Va. Soc. Oral Surgeons and W.Va. Med. Center, 1980; named Man of Year Georgetown U. Alumni Assn., 1961, Disting. Svc. award, 1992. Fellow AAAS, Am. Coll. Dentists (chmn. D.C. sect. 1969-71), Internat. Coll. Dentists (chmn. D.C. sect. 1967-70); mem. ADA (chmn. oral surgery sect. 1961, mem. rev. commn. on advanced edn. in oral surgery 1965-71, chmn. commn. 1969-71), D.C. Dental Soc. (pres. 1960, Sterling V. Mead award 1989), Am. Assn. Oral and Maxillofacial Surgeons (program chmn. 1961), Middle Atlantic Soc. Oral and Maxillofacial Surgeons (pres. 1952), Am. Acad. Oral Pathology, Am. Acad. Oral and Maxillofacial Radiology, Internat. Assn. Dental Research, Am. Coll. Oral and Maxillofacial Surgeons (Harry Archer award 1992), Wash. Dental Study Club (pres. 1993), Xi Psi Phi, Sigma Gamma Epsilon, Omicron Kappa Upsilon. Lodge: Kiwanis (co-chmn. orthopedic com. 1971-86). Home: 6806 Bradgrove Cir Bethesda MD 20817-3001

KRUGMAN, RICHARD DAVID, physician, university administrator, educator; b. N.Y.C., Nov. 28, 1942; s. Saul and Sylvia (Stern) K.; m. Mary Elizabeth Kerber, July 9, 1966; children: Scott, Joshua, Todd, Jordan. AB, Princeton U., 1963; MD, NYU, 1968. Resident U. Colo. Sch. Medicine, Denver, 1968-71; staff assoc. Nat. Inst. Health, Bethesda, Md., 1971-73; asst. prof. U. Colo. Sch. Medicine, 1973-78, assoc. prof., 1978-87, prof. of pediatrics, 1988—, dean, 1992—. Author: Review of Pediatrics, 4th edit., 1992; editor: (jour.) Child Abuse/Neglect, 1986. Chmn. U.S. Adv. Bd. Child Abuse and Neglect, Washington, 1989-91; dir. Kempe Nat. Ctr. for Prevention and Treatment of Child Abuse and Neglect, Denver, 1981-92. Recipient C. Henry Kempe award Nat. Conf. on Child Abuse, 1989, St. Geme award U. Colo. Sch. Medicine, 1992; Paul Harris fellow Rotary Internat., Sydney, Australia, 1992. Mem. Internat. Soc. Prevention of Child Abuse and Neglect (pres. 1992-94), Am. Acad. Pediatrics (Ray Helfer award 1995, Brandt Steele award 1996), Am. Pediatric Soc. Office: U Colo Sch Medicine 4200 E 9th Ave Denver CO 80262

KRULEWITCH, CARA J., epidemiologist; b. Chgo., Aug. 20, 1954; d. Paul Hershel and Arline (Berman) K. BS in Biology, U. Ill., 1976; diploma in nursing, Evanston Hosp. Sch. Nursing, 1978; BSN, U. Ill., Chgo., 1982, MS in Nursing Scis., 1984; PhD, U. Md., Balt., 1992. RN, Md., W.Va., Ill. Staff nurse obstetrics unit Mercy Ctr. Svcs., Aurora, Ill., 1979-81; clin. nurse labor and delivery U. Ill. Hosp., Chgo., 1981-87; clin. instr. Sch. Nursing St. Anne's Hosp., Chgo., 1985-86; asst. clin. dir. maternal child health St. Francis Cabrini Hosp., Chgo., 1986-87; instr. Sch. Nursing W.Va. U., Morgantown, 1987-88; grad. rsch. asst. patient intensity for nursing index study U. Md., Balt., 1988-89; clin. rsch. assoc. Biospherics Inc., Laurel, Md., 1988-89; registry nurse Med-Force Inc., Arlington, Va., 1988-93; statistician Nat. Ctr. for Health Stats Ctr. for Disease Control and Prevention, Hyattsville, Md., 1991-93; epidemiologist divsn. reproductive health Ctr. for Disease Control and Prevention, Washington, 1993—; adj. instr. Columbia Union Coll., Takoma Park, Md., 1990—; NIH summer intramural fellow divsn. prevention rsch. Nat. Inst. Child Health and Devel., USPHS, Bethesda, 1990, epidemiol. rsch. asst., 1990-91; presenter in field. Contbr. articles to profl. publs.; developer computer program in field. Mem. adv. com. Chgo. Dist., past chmn. health profls. Mid-Am. chpt. ARC, past-chmn. health edn. subcom., past mem. safety and health edn. com. DuPage dist., past mem. Chess com. Chgo. dist., instr. various courses; past treas., past mem. planning com. dist. 5 W.Va. Nurses Assn. Mem. APHA, Am. Coll. Nurse-Midwives (assoc., adv. bd. divsn. rsch.), Nat. Perinatal Assn., Sigma Theta Tau.

KRULL, JOY DENISE, physical therapist; b. Waverly, Iowa, Jan. 13, 1950; d. Harry Emmot and Darlene Marie (Wilmot) Jungling; m. Carey Gene Krull, June 19, 1970; children: Lynde Renee, Christian Carey. AS, Cottey Jr. Coll., 1970; BGS, U. Iowa, 1981. Cert. phys. therapist, Iowa. Ward sec. Mercy Hosp., Cedar Rapids, Iowa, 1971-73, ins. specialist, 1973-78; phys. therapist Grant Wood Area Edn. Agy., Cedar Rapids, 1983-90, U. Iowa Hosp. Sch., Iowa City, 1990—; part time phys. therapist Mercy Hosp., Cedar Rapids, 1983-88. Libr. 1st Presbyn. Ch., Marion, 1989—, children's music dir., 1990—. Mem. Am. Phys. Therapy Assn., Iowa Phys. Therapy Assn. (pediatric sect.), PEO Sisterhood (chaplain 1985-86, v.p. 1986-88, pres. 1988-91, reciprocity pres. 1991-93). Home: 1040 Hillview Dr Marion IA 52302-4615 Office: U Hosp Schs Div Devel Disabilities Iowa City IA 52242

KRUMHOLZ, ALLAN, medical educator; b. Lodz, Poland, Jan. 1, 1945; came to U.S., 1949; s. Jacob and Mera (Rosen) K.; m. Francine Iris Herzog, Aug. 20, 1967; children: Matthew, Andrea. BA, Queens Coll., 1966; MD, Chgo. Med. Sch., 1970. Intern, med. resident Balt. City Hosp., 1970-72; neurology resident Johns Hopkins Hosp., Balt., 1972-76; asst prof. neurology Johns Hopkins Hosp., 1978-85, EEG fellowship, 1979, assoc. prof. neurology, 1985-90; asst. prof. neurology SUNY (Stony Brook) Med. Sch., 1976-77; prof. neurology U. Md., Balt., 1989—; chmn. profl. adv. bd. Epilepsy Found. Am., Landover, Md., 1995-97. Capt. Md. NG, 1970-76. Named Physician of Yr. Gov.'s Com. (Md.), 1987; recipient Outstanding Tchr. award U. Md. neurology residents, 1991. Fellow Am. Acad. Neurology, Am. Neurol. Assn., Am. Epilepsy Soc. Home: 5404 Springlake Way Baltimore MD 21212 Office: U MD Hosp Dept Neurology 22 S Greene St Baltimore MD 21201-1544

KRUPATKIN, ALEXANDER ILYICH, physiology educator; b. Moscow, Feb. 17, 1961; s. Ilya Lvovich and Eva Naumovna (Roytberg) K. MD, Med. Inst. Tver, Russia, 1983; PhD, Ctrl. Inst. Traumatology, Moscow, 1989. Physician Regional Hosp., Tver, 1983-84; from jr. rschr. to sr. rschr. Ctrl. Inst. of Traumatology and Orthops., Moscow, 1984—. Author: Polarographic Method in Traumatology and Orthopaedics, 1986; contbr. articles to profl. jours. Mem. Russian Assn. Functional Diagnosis, N.Y. Acad. Scis. Home: Voljsky bulvar, Kvartal 95 corpus 3 kv 4, 109125 Moscow Russia

KRUPKO, THOMAS ANDREW, orthopaedic surgeon; b. Youngstown, Ohio, Oct. 27, 1954; s. Paul Edward and Emma Marie (Burkey) K.; m. Cathy Louise Suitca, Oct. 23, 1982; children: Catherine, Thomas, Amy, Allison, James, Daniel. BS in Microbiology, Ohio State U., 1977, MD, 1980. Diplomate Am. Bd. Orthopaedic Surgeons; lic. physician, Ohio. Intern Akron (Ohio) City Hosp., 1980-81, orthopaedic surgery resident, 1981-85; fellow in foot/ankle surgery G.J. Sammarco, M.D., Cin., 1985; pvt. practice Cuyahoga Falls, Ohio, 1986-91, Alliance, Ohio, 1991—; clin. instr. N.E. Ohio Coll. Medicine, Rootstown, 1986—. Fellow Am. Acad. Orthop. Surgeons; mem. AMA, Clin. Orthop. Soc., Foot and Ankle Soc.,Am. Orthop. Foot and Ankle Soc. Trauma Com., Ohio State Med. Assn., Stark County Med. Soc. (bd. trustees, bd. censors 1994-96), Ohio State U. Med. Alumni Assn. Office: 1207 W State St Ste C Alliance OH 44601

KRUPNICK, JANICE LEE, psychologist, psychotherapist, educator; b. Newark, Mar. 7, 1950; d. Jacob and Betty (Katz) K.; m. Richard Michael Suzman, July 21, 1976; children: Daniel, Jessica. AB, Oberlin Coll., 1972; MSW, U. Mich., 1974; MA, U. Calif., Berkeley, 1985, PhD, 1988. Lic. psychologist, Md., D.C. Social worker Long Beach (Calif.) Neuropsychol. Inst., 1974-75; fellow Mt. Zion Hosp./Med. Ctr., San Francisco, 1975-77; program analyst NIMH, Rockville, Md., 1980-81; asst. clin. prof. U. Calif., San Francisco, 1977-83; cons. NAS, Washington, 1983-84; asst. clin. prof. Georgetown U., Washington, 1984-90; asst. rsch. prof. George Washington U., Washington, 1988-91; assoc. clin. prof. Georgetown U., Washington, 1990-94, clin. prof., 1994—; cons. NIMH, Bethesda, Md., 1990-91, Am. Psychiat. Assn., 1990-91; tchr. dynamic psychotherapy seminar for advanced psychiat. residents Georgetown U., lectr. interpersonal psychotherapy course. Co-author: Personality Styles and Brief Psychotherapy, 1984; contbr. articles to psychiat. and psychol. jours. Participant rallies for women's rights, Washington, 1986—. Clin. fellow NIMH, 1975-77, rsch. fellow NIMH, 1986-88. Mem. Am. Psychol. Assn., Soc. for Clin. Social Work, Soc. for Psychotherapy Rsch. Jewish. Home: 4100 Oliver St Chevy Chase MD 20815-7120 Office: 5480 Wisconsin Ave Ste 220 Chevy Chase MD 20815-3503

KRYJAK, MICHAEL ANTHONY, counselor; b. Shenandoah, Pa., Feb. 7, 1955; s. Paul Frank and Sylvia Theresa K. BA with honors in Sociology, Schiller U., Heidelberg, West Germany, 1976; postgrad., Harvard U., 1988; cert. clin. inverview in psychiatry, Yale U., 1989; cert. fundamental econs., Henry George Inst., N.Y.C.; postgrad., Audio Digest Found., 1988—. Security aide Bloomsburg (Pa.) U., 1974-75; libr. staff Schiller U., Heidelberg, Germany, 1975-76; ind. edn1. cons. Shenandoah, Pa., 1978-81; sec.-treas. Shenandoah Mchts. Assn., 1979-81; com. mem. Shenandoah Downtown Task Force, 1979-81; rsch. asst., lectr. Pa. State U., Hazleton, 1981-83; residential advisor Keystone Job Corps Ctr., Drums, Pa., 1985-86; sr. counselor Schuylkill County Prison, Pottsville, Pa., 1986—; psychiat. caseworker St. Joseph's Med. Ctr., Reading, Pa., 1995—; facilitator Dept. Accelerated Degrees & Cont. Studies Rosemont (Pa.) Coll., 1995—; mem. adj. faculty Reading (Pa.) Area C.C., 1988—; mental health counselor Brandywine Hosp. and Trauma Ctr., Coatsville, Pa., 1988; guest lectr. King's Coll., Wilkes-Barre, Pa., 1981, Kutztown (Pa.) State Coll., 1982, Pa. State U., 1982; guest lectr. Pa. State U., Bloomsburg (Pa.) State Coll., Pa. State U., Hazleton, 1982, 83; co-dir. support group Family Svc. Agy., Pottsville, Pa., 1989—; presenter in field. Rsch. asst.: The Disaster is Above Ground, 1990. Mem. Am. Sociol. Assn., Am. Orchid Soc., Colonial Williamsburg Found., The Cymbidium Soc. Am., British Broadcasting Corp. World Svc. Radio Club, Health Systems Agy. Northeastern Pa. Home: 32 N Catherine St Shenandoah PA 17976-1505 Office: Schuylkill County Prison 2D And Sanderson St Pottsville PA 17901

KRYSTAL, JOHN HARRISON, psychiatrist, educator; b. Detroit, Feb. 27, 1958; s. Henry and Esther (Reichstein) K.; m. Bonnie Becker; children: Samuel Ethan and Hannah Lauren. BA, U. Chgo., 1980; MD, Yale U., 1984. Resident in psychiatry Yale U., New Haven, 1984-88, assoc. inpatient chief clin. neurosci. rsch. unit, 1988-89, asst. prof., 1989-93, assoc. prof., 1993-96, dir. divsn. cognitive and clin. neurosci., dept. psychiatry, 1996—; dir. clin. rsch. psychiat. svc. West Haven (Conn.) VA Med. Ctr.-Yale U., 1988—. Contbr. over 160 articles to med. jours., chpts. to books. Bourroughs-Welcome fellow, 1986-88. Mem. Am. Psychiat. Assn. (com. on rsch. tng. 1989—, Penwait award 1988), Am. Coll. Neuropsychopharmacology (assoc.), Soc. Nuclear Medicine, Soc. for Neurosci., Internat. Soc. for Traumatic Stress Studies (bd. dirs. 1988—, Chaim Danielli award 1989), Phi Beta Kappa. Home: 119 Maplevale Dr Woodbridge CT 06525-1142 Office: West Haven VA Med Ctr Psychiat Svc West Haven CT 06516

KRYSZTOFORSKI, JOSEPH THEODORE, diversified healthcare services company executive; b. Bklyn., Sept. 30, 1953; s. Theodore and Theresa Constance Krysztoforski; m. Stavreoula Psihogous, Aug. 24, 1974 (div. Oct. 1982). Student, Bklyn. Coll., 1972-73; BA, MA in Psychology, SUNY, Stony Brook, 1977. Cert. secondary educator, N.Y. Programmer Carulli & Sons Produce, Bklyn., 1973-76; cons., owner SCDPI, Smithtown, N.Y., 1976-78; cons., pres. Stavjo Data Processing, Smithtown, 1977-79; sr. systems analyst Citicorp Credit Svcs., Inc., Melville, N.Y., 1978-79, project leader, 1979-80, ops. head, 1982-84; mgr. systems software Citicorp Sales Mgmt., Melville, 1980-82; dir. info. svc. Citicorp Card Acceptance Svcs., Melville, 1984-88; v.p. planning and acquisitions Citicorp Establishment Svcs., Huntington, N.Y., 1988-92; dir. R&D CARD Establishment Svcs., Melville, N.Y., 1992-93; founding dir., exec. dir. SmartCard Forum, 1993-95; dir., founder Health Info. and Adminstrv. Tech. Assocs., 1993-95, PDS Healthcare Informatics, 1994—; sr. v.p., dir. strategic planning CES Healthcare Info. Svcs., Melville, N.Y., 1994-95; sr. v.p. MEDE Am. Corp., 1995—;

chmn. Healthcare Workgroup, 1992-95; cons. Smithtown Ctrl. Schs., 1977-78; rsch. analyst Ctrl. Islip (N.Y.) State Hosp., 1973-74. Photographer: American History, 1976; designer, developer: (computer software) Dental/Medicine Office Management, 1980, Batch Authorization/POS, 1982, Abode, 1992 (Best in Category award 1992). Organizer Lake Grove (N.Y.) Civic Soc., 1987; organizer, tchr. First Steps Stony Brook, 1976; mem., organizer Green Party, Lake Grove, 1987. Recipient Best in Show award Inst. Cert. PHotographers, 1977-80. Mem. Data Processing Mgmt. Assn., Am. Mgmt. Assn. Home: PO Box 1311 Lake Grove NY 11755-0611 Office: CES Healthcare Info Svcs 265 Broadhollow Rd Melville NY 11747-4802

KRZANOWSKI, JOSEPH JOHN, JR., pharmacology educator; b. Hartford, Conn., Feb. 4, 1940; s. Joseph John and Anna (Szydlo) K.; m. Patricia Eugenia Teper, June 22, 1963; children: Karen Marie, Jenifer Ann. BS in Pharmacy, U. Conn., 1962; MS in Pharmacology, U. Tenn., Memphis, 1965, PhD in Pharmacology, 1968; MA in Religious Studies, Barry U., 1987. Lic. pharmacist, Maine, Conn.; ordained deacon Roman Cath. Ch., 1987. Postdoctoral fellow dept. pharmacology Washington U., St. Louis, 1968-71; asst. prof. dept. pharmacology and therapeutics U. So. Fla. Coll. Medicine, Tampa, 1971-75, assoc. prof. dept. pharmacology and therapeutics, 1975-83, prof., 1983—, vice chmn. dept., 1981—, acting chmn. dept., 1986-88, 89-91, assoc. dean rsch. and grad. affairs, 1991—; presenter in field, 1965—. Author: (with Woodbury and Sticht) Medical Examination Review: Pharmacology, 6th edit., 1987, (with Woodbury, Hanna and Cantrell) 7th edit., 1991, (with Woodbury and Polson) 8th edit., 1995; field editor Basic Sci., Jour. Fla. Med. Assn.; contbr. numerous articles and abstracts to profl. jours., 11 chpts. to books; ad hoc reviewer Jour. Allergy and Clin. Immunology. Bd. dirs. Cath. Social Svcs., Tampa, 1983-88, pres., 1989; bd. dirs. Inst. Environ. Studies, 1989—. Fla. Heart Assn. grantee, 1974-77, NIH grantee, 1974-76, 79-83, Sandoz Inc. grantee, 1980-87. Mem. Am. Soc. for Pharmacology and Exptl. Therapeutics, AAAS, Am. Acad. Allergy and Immunology, S.E. Pharmacology Soc., N.Y. Acad. Scis., Mortar and Pestle, Sigma Xi, Rho Chi. Republican. Office: U South Fla Coll Medicine 12901 Bruce B Downs Blvd Tampa FL 33612

KRZEMINSKA-PAKULA, MARIA, cardiologist, researcher; b. Wtoctawek, Poland, Aug. 28, 1938; d. Kazimierz and Helena (Ziotkowska) Krzeminski; m. Jan Pakula, 1965. Diploma with distinction, U. Lódz, Poland, 1963, MD, 1969. Resident dept. internal medicine, surgery and gynecology U. Lódz, 1963-64; asst. in cardiology U. Lódź, 1965-69, cons., 1970-76, asst. prof., 1977-83, prof., 1984—; head dept. cardiology, head cardiology svc. Med. U. Lódz, 1978—. Author: Non Invasive Methods in the Diagnosis of Cardiovascular Diseases, 1982, Cardiac Emergencies, 1986, 3d edit., 1992, Cardiac Imaging, 1991; contbr. more than 200 articles to profl. jours. Fellow European Soc. Cardiology; mem. FESC, Polish Soc. Cardiology. Home: Zamenhofa 5 M 11, Lódź 90-431, Poland Office: Med U, Milionowa 14, Lódź 93-113, Poland

KRZESINSKI, MARIBETH, dentist, maxillofacial prosthodontist; b. Elmira, N.Y., Feb. 22, 1960; d. Edwin Paul and Emily Alice (Brzeski); m. Gregory M. Semashko, June 7, 1986. BA, Coll. of the Holy Cross, 1982; DDS, Georgetown U., 1986; cert. in prosthodontics, U. Medicine & Dentistry N.J., 1992; cert. in maxillofacial prosthetics, U. Pitts., 1994. Resident in gen. practice Jersey City Med. Ctr., 1986-87; gen. dentist U.S.A. DENTAC, Ft. Benning, Ga., 1987-90; prosthodontist Howard Charlebois Corp., Monroeville, Pa., 1993-96; asst. prof. dept. maxillofacial prosthetics U. Pitts. Sch. Dental Medicine, 1995—. Recipient Commdr.'s award for Pub. Svc., U.S. Dental Corps, 1990. Mem. Am. Coll. Prosthodontics, Nat. Med. Dental Assn., Acad. Maxillofacial Prosthetics (award 1995), Delta Sigma Delta. Roman Catholic. Home: 202 Hillside Dr Zelienople PA 16063

KUBACKI, JOSEPH JOHN, ophthalmologist; b. Reading, Pa., Apr. 7, 1949; s. John C. and Mary E. (Stockler) K. BA with distinction, U. Va., 1971; MD, Temple U., 1975. Diplomate Am. Bd. Ophthalmology. Resident in ophthalmology Temple U. Hosp., Phila., 1976-79; fellow in pediatric ophthalmology Wills Eye Hosp., Phila., 1979-80; clin. instr. in ophthalmology Temple U. Sch. Medicine, Phila., 1979-80, asst. prof. ophthalmology, 1980-90, assoc. prof. ophthalmology, 1990-96, chmn. ophthalmology, 1995—, prof. ophthalmology, 1996—; chief pediatric ophthalmology St. Christopher's Hosp., Phila., 1982—; rsch. study investigator in field. Mem. sci. adv. bd. Fight for Sight of Greater Phila., 1992. Recipient 1st Humanitarian award Lions Internat. Dist. 14A, 1986. Mem. AMA (mem. physician recognition award 1994), ACS, Am. Acad. Ophthalmology, Pa. Med. Soc., Phila. Coll. Physicians, Delaware Valley Pediatric Ophthalmology Assn., Assn. Univ. Profs. in Ophthalmology, Polish Am. Congress, U. Va. Alumni Assn., Temple U. Sch. Medicine Alumni Assn. Office: Temple Ophthalmology Dept 3401 N Broad St Philadelphia PA 19144

KUBIK, CRAIG MICHAEL, physician; b. Buffalo, N.Y., Mar. 23, 1958; s. Donald M. and Joanne B. K.; m. Sandra C. Kubik, Aug. 12, 1989; children: Molly E., Michael J.. Emily E. BS in Biology, St. John Fisher Coll., 1980; DO, N.Y. Coll. Osteo. Medicine, 1985. Diplomate Am. Bd. Internal Medicine, Am. Bd. Gastroenterology. Intern Delaware Valley Med. Ctr., Langhorne, Pa., 1985-86; resident internal medicine Mercy Hosp., Buffalo, N.Y., 1986-89; internist 833rd Med. Group, Holloman AFB, N.Mex., 1989-92; gastroenterology fellow Wilford Hall Med. Ctr., Lackland AFB, Tex., 1992-94; gastroenterologist Wright-Patterson Med. Ctr., Wright-Patterson AFB, Ohio, 1994-96; with Clinch Valley Physicians, Inc., Richlands, Va., 1996—. Maj. USAF, 1989-96. Mem. Am. Coll. Gastroenterology, Am. Coll. Physicians, Am. Soc. Gastrointestinal Endoscopy. Office: The Clinic PO Box CVPI Richlands VA 24641

KÜBLER-ROSS, ELISABETH, physician; b. Zurich, Switzerland, July 8, 1926; came to U.S., 1958, naturalized, 1961; d. Ernst and Emma (Villiger) K.; m. Emanuel Robert Ross, Feb. 7, 1958; children: Kenneth Lawrence, Barbara Lee. M.D., U. Zurich, 1957; D.Sc. (hon.), Albany (N.Y.) Med. Coll., 1974, Smith Coll., 1975, Molloy Coll., Rockville Centre, N.Y., 1976, Regis Coll., Weston, Mass., 1977, Fairleigh Dickinson U., 1979; LL.D., U. Notre Dame, 1974, Hamline U., 1975; hon. degree, Med. Coll. Pa., 1975, Anna Maria Coll., Paxton, Mass., 1978; Litt.D. (hon.), St. Mary's Coll., Notre Dame, Ind., 1975, Hood Coll., 1976, Rosary Coll., River Forest, Ill., 1976; L.H.D. (hon.), Amherst Coll., 1975, Loyola U., Chgo., 1975, Bard Coll., Annandale-on-Hudson, N.Y., 1977, Union Coll., Schenectady, 1978, D'Youville Coll., Buffalo, 1979, U. Miami, Fla., 1976; D.Pedagogy, Keuka Coll., Keuka Park, N.Y., 1976. Rotating intern Community Hosp., Glen Cove, N.Y., 1958-59; rsch. fellow Manhattan State Hosp., 1959-62; resident Montefiore Hosp., N.Y.C., 1961-62; fellow psychiatry Psychopathic Hosp., U. Colo. Med. Sch., 1962-63; instr. psychiatry Colo. Gen. Hosp., U. Colo. Med. Sch., 1962-65; mem. staff LaRabida Children's Hosp. and Rsch. Ctr., Chgo., 1965-70; asst. prof. psychiatry, asst. dir. psychiatric consultation and liaison service Billings Hosp., U. Chgo., 1965-71; chief cons. and rsch. liaison sect. LaRabida Children's Hosp. and Rsch. Ctr., 1969-70; med. dir. Family Service and Mental Health Ctr. S. Cook County, Chicago Heights, Ill., 1970-73; pres. Ross Med. Assos. (S.C.), Flossmoor, Ill., 1973-77; pres., chmn. bd. Shanti Nilaya Growth and Health Ctr., Escondido, Calif., 1977—; consulting psychiatrist Chicago Lighthouse for the Blind, 1965-71; consultant Peace Corps, 1965-71, Illinois State Psychiatric Inst., 1965-71; mem. numerous adv., cons. bds. in field. Author: On Death and Dying, 1969, Questions and Answers on Death and Dying, 1972, Death: The Final Stage, 1974, To Live Until We Say Goodbye, 1978, Working It Through, 1981, Living With Death and Dying, 1981, Remember The Secret, 1981, On Children and Death, 1985, AIDS: The Ultimate Challenge, 1988, On Life After Death, 1991, Death is of Vital Inportance: On Life, Death and Life After Death, 1994; contbr. chpts. to books, articles to profl. jours. Recipient Teilhard prize Teilhard Found., 1981; Golden Plate award Am. Acad. Achievement, 1980; Modern Samaritan award Elk Grove Village, Ill., 1976; named Woman of the Decade Ladies Home Jour., 1979; numerous others. Mem. AAAS, Am. Holistic Med. Assn. (founder), Am. Med. Women's Assn., Am. Psychiat. Assn., Am. Psychosomatic Soc., Assn. Cancer Victims and Friends, Ill. Psychiat. Soc., Soc. Swiss Physicians, Soc. Psychophysiol. Research, Second Attempt at Living. Address: PO Box 6168 Scottsdale AZ 85261

KUBSKI, GEORGE MARIAN, psychiatrist, neurologist; b. Erlangen, Germany, Oct. 2, 1947; came to U.S., 1952, naturalized, 1957; s. Lester Augustine and Louise Helen (Lanca) K.; m. Nayda Lavinia Gonzalez, May 27, 1977; children: Tania, Jessika. BS in Psychology, Georgetown U., 1969; MD, U. Autonoma de Guadalahara, Mex., 1974. Diplomate Am. Bd. Quality Assurance, Utilization Review Physicians, 1987, Am. Bd. Psychiatry and Neurology. Resident L.I. Jewish-Hillside Med. Ctr., New Hyde Park, N.Y., 1974-78, med. dir., 1978-79; med. dir. Rockaway N.Y. Mental Health Ctr., 1979-81, Palm Beach Comprehensive Mental Health, West Palm Beach, Fla., 1981-83; pres. Kubski & Kubski, West Palm Beach, 1981—; chmn. dept. psychiatry Good Samaritan Hosp., West Palm Beach, 1989-93; chief dept. psychiatry Humana Hosp. Palm Beaches, West Palm Beach, 1990-92; med. dir. St. Mary's Hosp. Inst. Mental Health, 1991—; fellow in psychiatry Duke U. Med. Ctr., Durham, N.C., 1995; cons. Hazelden Found., 1987—. Mem. Am. Psychiat. Assn., Fla. Med. Assn. Palm Beach County Med. Soc., Palm Beach County Psychiat. Soc. (pres. 1996—). Office: 927 45th St Ste 302 West Palm Beach FL 33407-2450

KUCHERA, MICHAEL LOUIS, osteopathic educator; b. Kirksville, Mo., June 25, 1955; s. William Arthur and Natalie Ione (Zange) K.; m. Eva Maria Stahl, Nov. 18, 1978; children: Katherine, Jennifer, Tiffany, David. BA History, BS in Zoology, Iowa State U., 1976; DO, Kirksville Coll. Osteo. Medicine, 1980. Diplomate Nat. Bd. Osteo. Examiners; cert. in osteo. manipulative medicine. Intern Richmond Heights (Ohio) Gen. Hosp., 1980-81; fellow in electromyography Cleve. Clin. Found., 1981; asst. prof. Kirksville Coll. Osteo. Medicine, 1981-87, assoc. prof. 1987-92, prof., 1992—, chmn. dept. osteo. manipulative medicine, 1987—; co-dir. osteo. manipulative medicine residence program Kirkville Coll. Osteo. Medicine, 1989—; dir. Nat. Levitor Ctr., Kirksville, 1983—; cons. Inst. for Gravitational Strain Pathology, Inc., Rangeley, Maine, 1982—; vice chmn. bd., chmn. long range com. Mo. Arthritis Adv. Bd., Jefferson City, 1983-94, chmn., 1994—; chmn. Job Raising Task Force Mo., 1992-93; cons. Nat. Osteo. Bd. Examiners, 1985—, chmn., 1990—; nat. faculty sponsor Undergrad. Acads. Osteopathy, Indpls., 1987-93; editl. cons. Jour. Am. Osteo. Assn., 1992—. Co-author: Osteopathic Considerations in Systematic Dysfunction, 1990, 2d edit., 1991, Osteopathic Principles in Practice, 2d edit., 1991; section editor, chpt. author: Foundations for Osteopathic Medicine, 1996; editor Levitor Networker Quar.; editl. cons. Jour. Am. Osteo. Assn.; contbr. articles to profl. jours. Clk. of vestry Trinity Episcopal Ch., Kirksville, 1982-87, 91-93; bd. dirs., mem. ednl. com. N.E. Mo. Regional Arthritis Ctr., Kirksville, 1984—. Fellow Am. Acad. Disability Evaluating Physicians, Am. Acad. Osteopathy (chmn. undergrad. acads. 1987-93, bd. govs. 1990—, bd trustees 1993—, chmn. postgrad. stds. and evaluation com. 1992—, Louisa Burns rsch. com., vis. clinician ednl. spkr., pres.-elect 1995, pres. 1996); mem. Am. Osteo. Assn. (vice chmn. bur. rsch. 1991-93, chmn. outsomes rsch. 1993—, pres.'s task force on enhancing osteo. principles and practice/osteo. manipulative treatment 1994-95, faculty Osteo. Med. Edn. Leadership Conf. 1994—), N.Am. Acad. Musculoskeletal Medicine (mem. bd. counsillors 1991-92), Am. Assn. Orthop. Medicine (bd. dirs. 1993—, chmn. edn. com.), Am. Assn. Electrodiagnostic Medicine, Internat. Back Pain Soc., Mo. Assn. Osteo. Physicians and Surgeons (bd. dels. 1990-93, 96, Mo. medallion of honor 1995), Thousand Hills Physicians Network (v.p. 1991-92), N.E. Mo. Osteo. Assn. (pres. 1985-86), Sigma Xi. Republican. Home: 2 Fairlane Kirksville MO 63501-1926 Office: Kirksville Coll Osteo Medicine 800 W Jefferson St Kirksville MO 63501-1443

KUCHNER, EUGENE FREDERICK, neurosurgeon, educator; b. N.Y.C., Nov. 19, 1945; s. Morton H. and Edna Estelle (Marks) K. m. Joan Ruth Freedman, Sept. 2, 1968; children: Marc Jason, Eric Benjamin. AB, Johns Hopkins U., 1967; MD, U. Chgo., 1971. Diplomate Am. Bd. Neurol. Surgery. Resident in surgery Yale U. Sch. Medicine, New Haven, 1971-72; resident in neurosurgery Montreal (Que., Can.) Neurol. Inst., McGill U., 1972-76, spine fellow, 1976; neurosurgeon Sch. Medicine, SUNY, Downstate, 1976-79, Stony Brook, 1979—; mem. staff North Shore U. Hosp.-Cornell U. Med. Ctr., Univ. Hosp., Stony Brook, Nassau County Med. Ctr., St. John's Hosp.; cons. in field. Contbr. articles to profl. publs.; specialist in microsurgery, magnetic resonance imaging, spinal trauma, pituitary surgery. Recipient K.G. McKenzie Meml. award Royal Coll. Physicians and Surgeons Can., 1976, Open Scholarship award Johns Hopkins U., yearly, 1963-66, Scholarship award U. Chgo., yearly, 1967-70; NSF fellow, 1968, Blackman-Hoffman Found. fellow, 1969-70, USPHS fellow, 1969. Mem. ACS, AMA, Am. Assn. Neurol. Surgeons, Congress Neurol. Surgeons, N.Y. Acad. Scis., L.I. Neurosci. Acad., Suffolk Acad. Medicine, Montreal Neurol. Ins. Fellows Soc., N.Y. State Neurosurg. Soc., N.Y. State Med. Soc., N.Y. State Soc. Surgeons, Am. Epilepsy Soc., Am. Soc. Neuroimaging (cert. neuroimager and computerized tomography, magnetic resonance imaging), Internat. Platform Assn., Nat. Alumni Schs. (chmn. com. Johns Hopkins U.), Assn. Yale Alumni in Medicine, Sterling Assn. Yale U. Alumni, Princeton Club N.Y., Johns Hopkins Club, Sigma Xi. Office: Stony Brook Med Ctr PO Box 721 Stony Brook NY 11790-0721

KUCK, MARIE ELIZABETH BUKOVSKY, retired pharmacist; b. Milw., Aug. 3, 1910; d. Frank Joseph and Marie (Nozina) Bukovsky; Ph.C, U. Ill., 1933; m. John A. Kuck, Sept. 20, 1945 (div. Nov. 1954). Pharmacist, tchr. Am. Hosp., Chgo., 1936-38, St. Joseph Hosp., Chgo., 1938-40, Ill. Masonic Hosp., Chgo., 1940-45; chief pharmacist St. Vincent Hosp., Los Angeles, 1946-48, St. Joseph Hosp., Santa Fe, 1949-51; dir. pharm. services St. Luke's Hosp., San Francisco, 1951-76; pharmacist Mission Neighborhood Health Center, San Francisco, 1968-72; docent Calif. Acad. Sci., 1977—, DeYoung Mus., 1989—; mem. peer rev. com. Drug Utilization Com., Blue Shield Calif. and Pharm. Soc. San Francisco. Recipient Bowl of Hygeia award Calif. Pharm. Assn., 1966. Mem. No., Calif. (legis. chmn. aux. 1967-69, chmn. fund raising luncheon 1953-71, pres. San Francisco aux. 1974), Nat., Am., No. Calif. (pres. 1955-56, pres. San Francisco aux. 1965-66, editor ofcl. publ. 1967-70), San Francisco (sec. 1977-79, treas. 1979-80, pres. 1982-83; Pharmacist of Yr. award 1978) pharm. socs., Am. Pharm. Assn. (pres. No. Calif. br. 1956-57, nat. sec. women's aux. 1970-72, hon. pres. aux. 1975—), Calif. Council Hosp. Pharmacists (organizer 1962, sec.-treas. 1962-66), Am. Soc. Hosp. Pharmacists, Assn. Western Hosps. (gen. chmn. hosp. pharmacy sect. conv. San Francisco 1958), Internat. Pharmacy Congress (U.S. del. Brussels 1958, Copenhagen 1960), Fedn. Internationale Pharmaceutique, Lambda Kappa Sigma. Home: 2261 33rd Ave San Francisco CA 94116-1606

KUDRLE, VENETIA HILARY MARY, health services administrator; b. Bideford, Eng.; d. David Anthony Howell and Jill Marriott (Bishop) Thomas; m. Robert T. Kudrle; children: Paul, Tom. BA, Oxford U., 1969. Asst. adminstr. Abbott Northwestern Hosp., Mpls., 1981, adminstr., 1984, sr. adminstr., 1986, ops. v.p., bd. chair, 1993; pres. St. Francis Regional Med. Ctr., Shakopee, Minn., 1996; bd. chair Meml. Blood Ctrs., Mpls., exec. com., Mpls.; site coord. Healthcare Forum Transforming Health Care Project, San Francisco. Office: St Frances Regional Med Ctr Allina Health Sys 325 W 5th Ave Shakopee MN 55379

KUDRLE, VENETIA H.M., health facility administrator; b. Bideford, England; d. David Anthony Howell and Jill Marriott (Bishop) Thomas; m. Robert T. Kudrle; children: Paul, Tom. BA, Oxford U., 1969. Asst. adminstr. Abbott Northwestern Hosp., Mpls., 1981, adminstr., sr. adminstr., 1986, ops. v.p., 1992; pres. St. Francis Regional Med. Ctr., Shakopee, 1996; chair bd. Meml. Blood Ctrs., Mpls., 1994 mem. exec. com.; site coord. transforming healthcare delivery Healthcare Forum, San Francisco, site coord. learning lab I, learning lab II. Office: St Francis Regional Med Ctr 1455 St Francis Ave Shakopee MN 55379-3380

KUDRLE, WILLIAM ALAN, biomedical engineer; b. Casper, Wyo., Feb. 4, 1954; s. Robert Earl and Joyce Marian (MacMurphy) K. BS in Elec. Engring., Rice U., 1980; MS in Elec. Engring., Southern Meth. U., 1983; PhD of Biomed. Engring., U. Tex., Austin, 1994. Product engr. Tex. Instruments, Houston, 1980-83; rsch. asst. U. Tex., Austin, 1983-85; tech. adminstr. Tex. Dept. of Highways, Austin, 1985-86; systems analyst U. Tex. Med. Sch., Houston, 1986-95; v.p. R&D AWAKE Software, Pearland, Tex., 1995—. Recipient Univ. fellowship, U. Tex., Austin, 1983. Mem. IEEE, Soc. Magnetic Resonance in Medicine, Soc. Magnetic Resonance Imaging Office: AWAKE Software 2308 Cunningham Pearland TX 77581-3808

KUDZMA, ELIZABETH ANNE CONNELLY, nursing educator; b. N.Y.C., Jan. 31, 1946; d. Sherman T. and Irene (Fechhelm) Connelly; m. Daniel Edward Kudzma, Oct. 11, 1969; 1 child, Katherine Elizabeth. BS cum laude, Boston Coll., 1967, MS, 1969; D in Nursing Sci., Boston U., 1980; MPH, Harvard U., 1989. Cert. ob-gyn. nurse practitioner, NCC. Instr. Boston (Mass.) Coll. Sch. Nursing, 1969-73; asst. prof. Laboure Coll., Boston, 1973-76, Curry Coll. Div. Nursing Studies, Milton, Mass., 1977-79; assoc. prof. Curry Coll. Div. Nursing Studies, Milton, 1979-84, prof., 1984—, chairperson, 1982—; adj. asst. prof. Boston Coll. Sch. Nursing, Chestnut Hill, Mass., 1976-77; adj. assoc. prof. Boston U. Sch. Nursing, 1980-82; cons. WHO, Indonesia, India, 1982, WHO, U. Ljubljiana, Yugoslavia, 1985, 86; mem. corp. bd., trustee Hahnemann Hosp., Boston, 1985-94, others. Contbr. articles to profl. jours. Mem. AAUP, ANA, Mass. Nurses' Assn. (cabinet on nursing ethics 1984-90, adv. com. on Mass. med. malpractice legis. 1986), Am. Assn. Colls. Nursing (coll. rep. 1982—), Mass. Assn. Colls. Nursing (deans and dirs. assn. Mass., coll. rep. 1981—, sec. 1984—, vice-chair 1994—, chair faculty devel. conf. 1989—), NLN (program evaluator), Sigma Theta Tau (charter mem. Alpha Chi chpt., Theta-at-large), others. Home: 195 Holly Rd Marshfield MA 02050-1725 Office: Curry Coll Divsn Nursing 1071 Blue Hill Ave Milton MA 02186-2302

KUEHN, KLAUS KARL ALBERT, ophthalmologist; b. Breslau, Germany, Apr. 1, 1938; came to U.S., 1956, naturalized, 1971; s. Max and Anneliese (Hecht) K.; m. Eileen L. Nordgaard, June 22, 1961 (div. 1972); children: Stephan Eric, Kristina Annette; m. Lynda O. Hubbs, Oct. 2, 1974. Student, St. Olaf Coll., 1956-57; BA, BS, U. Minn., 1961; MD, 1963. Diplomate Am. Bd. Ophthalmology. Resident in ophthalmology UCLA Affiliated Hosps., 1968-71; practice medicine specializing in ophthalmology, San Bernardino, Calif., 1971—; chief ophthalmology dept. San Bernardino County Med. Ctr., 1979-80; assoc. clin. prof. ophthalmology Jules Stein Eye Inst. and UCLA Med. Ctr., 1978-81. Served to capt. U.S. Army, 1963-64. Fellow Am. Acad. Ophthalmology; mem. AMA, Calif. Med. Assn., Calif. Assn. Ophthalmology (bd. dirs.). Office: 902 E Highland Ave San Bernardino CA 92404-4007

KUEHNER, MARVIN ERNEST, surgeon; b. Pflugerville, Tex., Oct. 12, 1934; s. Ernest Frank and Blanche Annie (Kilian) K.; m. Hope Stephanie Maki, Mar. 31, 1990; children: Mark, Jon, Daryl, Kathryn, Michael, David, Steven, Karolyn, Daniel. BS in Pharmacy, U. Tex., 1957; MD, Washington U., 1961. Diplomate Am. Bd. Surgery. Resident surgery Jewish Hosp., St. Louis, 1961-66; staff surgeon Interstate Med. Ctr., Red Wing, Minn., 1969-74; staff surgeon Marshfield (Wis.) Clinic, 1974—, chmn. salary com, 1983-93; mem. salary com., 1994—. Contbr. articles to profl. jours. With AUS, 1966-69. Fellow ACS; mem. AMA, Internat. Soc. Cardiovascular Surgery, Midwestern Vascular Surgery Soc., Midwest Surgical Assn. Lutheran. Office: Marshfield Clinic 1000 N Oak Ave Marshfield WI 54449-5703

KUEHNERT, DEBORAH ANNE, medical center administrator; b. Raleigh, N.C., Nov. 21, 1949; d. Eldor Paul and Lila Catherine (Gilbert) K. Student, Valparaiso (Ind.) U., 1967-69; BS in Biology, Lenior Rhyne Coll., Hickory, N.C., 1977. Cert. med. technologist. Rsch. asst. Strong Meml. Hosp., Rochester, N.Y., 1967-68; lab. technician Richard Baker Hosp., Hickory, N.C., 1969-76; med. technician, shift supr. Glenn R. Frye Hosp., Hickory, 1977-83; lab. tech. dir. Frye Regional Med. Ctr., Hickory, 1983-85, adminstrv. dir. lab. svcs., 1986-92; sr. tech. dir. lab. svcs. Al-Fanateer Hosp., Jubail, Saudia Arabia, 1993; med. technologist lab. Chinle (Ariz.) Health Care Facility, Navajo Indian Reservation USPHS Hosp., 1993; instr. microbiology Catawba Valley Tech. Coll., Hickory, 1977-94, Lenoir Rhyne Coll., Hickory, 1978-94; chief tech. lab. No. Area Armed Forces Hosp., Hafr Al Batin, Saudi Arabia, 1994—; cons. Frye Physicians, Hickory, 1985—; lab. cons. Am. Med. Internat., New Orleans, 1986, Lake City, Fla., 1984-85; cons. Med. Lab. Observer, Chgo., 1989; spkr. in field. Recipient Svc. of Appreciation award Govt. Saudi Arabia, 1996. Mem. Am. Soc. Clin. Pathologists, N.C. Soc. Blood Bankers. Lutheran. Home: 58 Penny Ln Hickory NC 28601-9341

KUFFNER, GEORGE HENRY, dermatologist; b. S.I., N.Y., Aug. 22, 1949; s. George Henry and Wilmuth Anne (Clendenin) K.; m. Lynne Diane Blakeslee, May 17, 1975; children: Kevin, Todd A. BA, Johns Hopkins U., 1971, MD, 1975. Intern U. Hosps. Cleve., 1975-78, resident, 1978-81; staff dermatologist Wooster (Ohio) Clin., Inc., 1981—; asst. clin. prof. dermatology U. Hosps. Cleve., 1981—. Contbr. articles to profl. jours. Fellow Am. Acad. Dermatology; mem. AMA, Ohio State Med. Assn., Ohio Dermatology Assn., Cleve. Dermatology Soc. Methodist. Office: Wooster Clin Inc 1740 Cleveland Rd Wooster OH 44691

KUGLER, GARY, podiatrist; b. Queens, N.Y., Nov. 24, 1964; s. Martin and Linda Kugler; m. Ellen Joyce Finkelstein, July 3, 1994. Student, San Diego State U., 1982-86; DPM, BS, Scholl Coll. Podiatric Medicine, 1990. Diplomate Am. Bd. Podiatric Surgery. Resident VA Med. Ctr., Tucson, 1990-91; pvt. practice Countryside Foot and Ankle Ctr., Sterling, Va., 1994—. Contbr. articles to profl. jours. Capt. USAF, 1991-94. Fellow Am. Coll. Foot and Ankle Surgeons; mem. Am. Podiatric Med. Assn., Soc. Armed Forces Podiatrists, Va. Podiatric Med. Assn., Rotary Internat. Office: Countryside Foot & Ankle 20 Pidgeon Hill Dr Ste 103 Sterling VA 20165

KUHL, DAVID EDMUND, physician, nuclear medicine educator; b. St. Louis, Oct. 27, 1929; s. Robert Joseph and Caroline Bertha (Waldemar) K.; m. Eleanor Dell Kasales, Aug. 7, 1954; 1 son, David Stephen. AB, Temple U., Phila., 1951; MD, U. Pa., 1955; LHD (hon.), Loyola U. Chgo., 1992. Diplomate: Am. Bd. Radiology, Am. Bd. Nuclear Medicine (a founder; life trustee 1977—). Intern, then resident in radiology Sch. Medicine and Hosp. U. Pa., 1955-56, 58-63, mem. faculty, 1963-76, prof. radiology, 1970-76, vice chmn. dept., 1975-76, chief div. nuclear medicine, 1963-76; prof. radiol. scis. UCLA Sch. Medicine and Hosp., 1976-86, chief div. nuclear medicine, 1976-84, vice-chmn. dept., 1977-86; prof. internal medicine and radiology, chief div. nuclear medicine U. Mich. Sch. Medicine, Ann Arbor, 1986—; Disting. Faculty lectr. in biomed. rsch. U. Mich. Med. Sch., 1992; mem. adv. com. Dept.Energy, NIH, Internat. Commn. on Radiation Units and Measures; mem. sci. adv. bd. Max Planck Inst., Cologne. Mem. editorial bd. various jours.; contbr. articles to med. jours. Served as officer M.C. USNR, 1956-58. Recipient Research Career Devel. award USPHS, 1961-71, Ernst Jung prize for medicine Jung Found., Hamburg, 1981, Emil H. Grubbe gold medal Chgo. Med. Soc., 1983, Berman Found. award peaceful uses atomic energy, 1985, Steven C. Beering award for advancement med. sci. Ind. U., 1987, Disting. Grad. award U. Pa. Sch. Medicine, 1988, William C. Menninger Meml. award ACP, 1989, Javits Neuroscience Investigator award NIH, 1989. Fellow Am. Coll. Radiology, Am. Coll. Nuclear Physicians, Nat. Inst. for Med. and Biol. Engring.; mem. Assn. Am. Physicians, Am. Epilepsy Soc., Assn. Univ. Radiologists, Radiol. Soc. N.Am., Soc. Nuclear Medicine (Nuclear Pioneer citation 1976, Herman L. Blumgart, M.D. Pioneer award 1979, Disting. Scientist award 1981, ann. lectr. 1991, George Charles de Hevesy Nuclear Medicine Pioneer award 1995, Benedict Cassen Prize for Rsch. 1996), Am. Heart Assn. (fellow coun. circulation), Am. Neurol. Assn., Rocky Mountain Radiol. Soc., Soc. Neurosci., Inst. Medicine Nat. Acad. Scis., Sigma Xi, Alpha Omega Alpha. Office: U Mich Hosp Divsn Nuc Medicine 1500 E Medical Center Dr Ann Arbor MI 48109-0999

KUHL, STEVEN ALLEN, pathogenic microbiology and molecular biology educator; b. Des Moines, Mar. 4, 1951; s. Eldred Francis and Audrey Mae (Sandon) K.; m. Claire Fields, Aug. 6, 1983. BS, Purdue U., 1973; MS, Iowa State U., 1977; PhD, U. S.C., 1983. Rsch. asst. dept. biochemistry U. Minn., St. Paul, 1978-79; rsch. asst. dept. biology U. S.C., Columbia, 1979-83; postdoctoral rsch. assoc. dept. microbiology U. Ill., Urbana-Champaign, 1983-86; postdoctoral rsch. assoc. dept. molecular genetics Ohio State U., Columbus, 1986-88; postdoctoral rsch. assoc. U. Ariz., Tucson, 1988, rsch. asst. prof., 1989-90; asst. prof. dept. biol. scis. No. Ill. U., De Kalb, 1990—. Contbr. articles to profl. jours. Young Investigator Matching grantee Nat. Found. Infectious Diseases, 1989-90, NIH Biomed. Rsch. Support grantee U. Ariz., 1989-90, Local Rsch. Starter grantee Am. Lung Assn. Ill., 1992—. Mem. AAAS, Am. Soc. for Microbiology, Sigma Xi. Office: Northern Ill U Dept Biol Scis De Kalb IL 60115

KUHLMAN, KIMBERLY ANN, clinical dietician; b. Toledo, June 30, 1954; d. James Gilbert and Jane Marie (Konczal) Schramm; m. Carl Edwin Kuhlman Jr., May 23, 1981; children: Eric, Christopher. BS in Pub. Health, U. Toledo, 1977; BS in Dietetics, Bowling Green State U., 1978; MEd in Health Edn., U. Toledo, 1988. Cert. diabetes educator. Dietetic intern Good Samaritan Hosp., Cin., 1979; dietitian, tchr. The Toledo Hosp., 1980, clinical dietitian, 1981-83, nutrition support dietitian, 1983-86; dietitian Alcohol Treatment Ctr., Toledo, 1986-87; clin. dietitian Coop. Care Unit, Toledo Hosp., 1987-88; mem. faculty W.W. Knight Family Practice, Toledo,

1988-94, Mercy Coll. N.W. Ohio, 1995—; chief clin. dietitian Mercy/St. Charles Hosp., 1995—; guest lectr. Toledo Pub. Schs., 1983-84, guest speaker pvt. industry coun., 1989—; instr. Health Aware program Toledo Hosp. Community Health Project, 1980-83. Author: (fact sheet) Home Prental Nutrition; (booklet) Pediatric Nutrition, A Guide to Sensible Eating; reviewer (nutrition pieces) Am. Acad. of Family Physicians Found., 1996—. Mem. Toledo Art Mus., Toledo Zoo, Toledo Bot. Garden; treas. Presch. Nutrition Coun. N.W. Ohio, Toledo, 1986-89, Am. Cancer Soc. Babe Zaharias Classic; Cub Scout leader Boy Scouts Am. Recipient Patient Care award Am. Acad. Family Physicians, Soc. Tchrs. Family Medicine, Patient Care Mag., 1994. Mem. Nutrition Educators of Health Profls. Practice Group, Sports and Cardiovascular Nutritionists Practice Group of Am. Dietetics Assn., Toledo Dietetic Assn. (chmn. regulations com. 1986-88, co-chmn. membership com. 1983-84, chmn. 1984-85), Toledo Hosp. Corp. Wellness Planning Com., Ann. Conf. on Patient Edn. for AAFP (planning com.), Soc. Tchrs. of Family Medicine. Lutheran. Home: 4264 River Rd Toledo OH 43614-5528

KUHN, IRVIN NELSON, hematologist, oncologist; b. Winnipeg, Man., Can., Aug. 18, 1928; s. Gottfred and Wanda Lena Kuhn; m. Doreen Mary L. Elvedahl, July 3, 1956; children: Jill A., Erin R., Jay N. BA in Chemistry, Loma Linda U., 1950; MD, Loma Linda (Calif.) U., 1955. Diplomate Nat. Bd. Med. Examiners, Am. Bd. Internal Medicine; cert. Thai Med. Bd., Advanced Internal Medicine, Hematology and Med. Oncology; lic. physician, Calif. Rotating intern then resident gen. internal medicine White Meml. Med. Ctr., L.A., 1955-59; resident gen. pathology U. B.C. at Vancouver Gen. Hosp., Can., 1959-60; instr. med. Loma Linda (Calif.) U., 1961-65, asst. prof., 1965-72, assoc. prof., 1972-78, prof., 1978—, cons. in clin. hematology and oncology, 1966—; dir. Adult Hemophilia Treatment Ctr., 1974-85; chief med. svc. Jerry L. Pettis Meml. VA Hosp., Loma Linda, 1977-80, assoc. chief staff edn., 1980—, active staff, 1977—; ind. investigator Nat. Cancer Inst. Leukemia and Chemotherapy, 1970-85; assoc. investigator Western Cancer Study Group, subcom. Lymphoma and Leukemia, 1972-76; mem. Loma Linda Med. Oncology rsch. team Coop. Group Outreach program/Puget Sound Oncology Consortium S.W. Oncology Group, 1985-88; com. grad. med. edn. Loma Linda U. Sch. Medicine, 1980—, health adv. com. 1980-83, chmn. rsch. funding adv. com. 1982-86, acad. com. 1977—, resident tng. com. 1979—, adv. com. Med. Record adminstrn. 1976-78, quality assurance com. 1972-76, transfusion com. 1972-80, risk mgmt. com. 1973-75; mem. Jerry L. Pettis Meml. VA Hosp., 1977—, radiosotope and nuclear medicine com. 1977-89, clin. exec. bd. 1977—, pharmacy adn therapeutics com. 1977-80, rsch. devel. com. 1977-84, dean's com. 1980—, chmn. hosp. edn. com. 1980-94, chmn. travel and tuition funds cons. 1980-84, joint conf. coun., 1982-85, chmn. Case Mix Mgmt. steering com. 1984-88; presenter numerous symposia, seminars and confs. to various agys., schs. and health orgns., 1970—; cons. in field. Contbr. articles to profl. jours. Blood Coagulation Rsch. Lab. fellow Churchill Hosp., 1964, Laboratorie d' Hemostase fellow St. Louis Hosp., 1964, clin. and rsch. fellow U. Wash., 1965-66. Fellow ACP (gov.'s adv. com. 1980-88); mem. AAAS, Walter E. MacPherson Soc. (charter, bd. dirs. 1993—), AMA, Calif. Med. Assn. (legis. com. 1987, dist. II del. 1983-87, alt. del. 1974-83, comprehensive health planning commn. 1974-76, CALS surveyor 1990—), San Bernardino County Med. Assn., Loma Linda U. Sch. Medicine Alumni Assn. (life, med. evangelism coun. 1975-76, conv. governing bd. dirs. 1983-92, pres. 1989-90), Am. Soc. Internal Medicine, Calif. Soc. Internal Medicine, Inland Soc. Internal Medicine, Am. Soc. Hematology, Nat. Assn. VA Physicians, Am. Coll. Physic Exec. San Bernardino County Med. Soc. (numerous offices and com. mems. found. med. care 1970—), Loma Linda Physicians Med. Group, Inc. (bd. dirs. 1969-73), Sigma Xi (life), Alpha Omega Alpha. Office: Jerry L Pettis Meml VA Hosp Office Assoc Chief Staff Edn 11201 Benton St Loma Linda CA 92357-1000

KUHN, RICHARD JOHN ALOIS, pharmacist; b. Johnson City, N.Y., Feb. 9, 1936; s. Frank Alois and Maria Antonia (Fuhr) K.; m. Margarete Hildegarde Nitschke, July 14, 1962; children: Martin Richard, Michele Luise. BS in Pharmacy, Albany Coll. Pharmacy, 1958. Lic. pharmacist, N.Y., Calif., Vt. Intern pharmacist E-J Med. Dept., Johnson City, 1956-58, pharmacist, 1960-63; pharmacist L-F Hamlin Inc., Binghamton, N.Y., 1958-60, Geroulds Pharmacy, Elmira, N.Y., 1964—. Mem. Am. Pharm. Assn., Nat. Assn. Retail Druggists, N.Y. State Pharm. Soc., Am. Soc. History of Pharmacy, Calif. Pharm. Assn., Nat. Rifle Assn., Internat. Platform Assn., N.Y. State Rifel and Pistol Assn. (life), Assn. Rsch. and Elightenment, Elks. Republican. Lutheran. Home: 933 Palisades Blvd 17 Palisades Blvd Elmira NY 14903 Office: Geroulds Pharmacy 130 S Main St Elmira NY 14904-1309

KUHNERT, HELEN LAVON, clinical research nurse; b. Wichita Falls, Tex., Sept. 25, 1940; d. Cecil Vaughn and Helen Maurine (Castlebury) Graves; divorced; children: Alison, Amy, Laurie, Warren; m. Robert Morris Kuhnert, July 23, 1976. Diploma in nursing, Lillie Jolly Sch. Nursing, Houston, 1961; BSN, Tex. Woman's U., 1974. RN, Tex. Staff nurse ICU Presbyn Hosp., Dallas, 1974-75, rsch. nurse U. Tex. Southwestern Med. Ctr., 1977-80, clin. coord., 1981-87, sr. clin. rsch. assoc. Bristol-Myers Squibb, 1988—. Contbr. articles to profl. jours. Mem. Assn. clin. Pharmacology, Drug Info. Assn., Sigma Theta Tau. Home and Office: 2019 Springcress Dr Mc Kinney TX 75070-5283

KUHNLEIN, URS, molecular biologist, educator, researcher; b. Zurich, Switzerland, Sept. 17, 1940; s. Viktor and Hedwig (Gohner) K.; m. Harriet Veronica Kling, July 29, 1972; children—Letitia, Matthew, Peter. B.Sc. in Exptl. Physics, Fed. Inst. Tech., 1965; Ph.D. in Biology, U. Geneva, 1970. Postdoctoral fellow Stanford Med. Sch., Calif., 1970-72; research biochemist U. Calif., Berkeley, 1972-76; research scholar, sr. scientist B.C. Cancer Research Ctr., Vancouver, 1976-84; assoc. prof. animal sci. McGill U., Montreal, Que., 1985—. Contbr. articles to profl. jours. Nat. Cancer Inst. Can., grantee, 1976-83; Med. Research Council Can. grantee, 1981—; Nat. Sci. and Engring. Research Council Can. grantee, 1985—. Mem. Can. Soc. Animal Sci., Agrl. Inst. Can. Avocations: skiing; mountaineering. Office: Macdonald Coll of McGill Univ, 21 111 Lakeshore Rd, Sainte Anne de Bellevue, PQ Canada H9X 1C0

KUHNS, DAVID WALLACE, emergency physician; b. Indiana, Pa., May 12, 1958; s. Jack Wallace and Rachel Louise (Stineman) K.; m. Catherine Marie Couch, Sept. 2, 1992 (dec. June 1994). BA in Physics, Indiana U. of Pa., 1980; MD, Temple U., 1985. Diplomate Am. Bd. Emergency Medicine. Resident in emergency medicine Darnell Army Hosp., Ft. Hood, Tex., 1985-88; emergency physician Womack Army Med. Ctr., Ft. Bragg, N.C., 1988-92, dir. pre-hosp. care, 1988-90, dir. emergency svcs., 1990-92; emergency physician Bannock Regional Med. Ctr., Pocatello, Idaho, 1992; emergency physician Boundary County Hosp., Bonners Ferry, Idaho, 1992—, dir. emergency svcs., 1993—, chief of staff, 1995—. Contbr. articles to profl. jours. Maj. U.S. Army, 1985-92. Fellow Am. Coll. Emergency Physicians, Am. Acad. Emergency Medicine. Home: HCR 85 Box 349 Bonners Ferry ID 83805 Office: Boundary County Hosp HCR 61 Box 61-A Bonners Ferry ID 83804

KUHRT, SHARON LEE, nursing administrator; b. Denver, July 20, 1957; d. John Wilfred and Yoshiko (Ueda) K. BSN, Loretto Heights Coll., 1982; MSN, Regis U., 1992. RN, Colo., Hawaii, Mass., Maine. RN level III Porter Meml. Hosp., Denver, 1981-87; transport supr. Kapiolani Med. Ctr. for Women & Children, Honolulu, 1987-89; dir. patient care unit Aspen Valley Hosp., Colo., 1989-91; dir. clin. practice Ctrl. Maine Med. Ctr., Lewiston, 1991—. Mem. ANA (cert. in pediat. nursing and nursing adminstrn.). Home: 27 Chandler Mill Rd New Gloucester ME 04260-9999

KULA, KATHERINE SUE, dentist; b. Dayton, Ohio, Oct. 5, 1945; d. James Adam and Adelaide Charlotte (Thaler) Miller; m. Theodore John Kula Jr., Aug. 2, 1969; children: Stacy Charlotte, Theodore John III. BS, U. Dayton, 1966, MS, 1972; DMD, U. Ky., 1977; MS, U. Iowa, 1979; cert. in orthodontics, U. Md., 1992. Sci. tchr. Lexington (Ky.) Cath. High Sch., 1969-71, chem. sci. dept., 1971-73; resident U. Iowa Dental Sch., Iowa City, 1973-77; asst. prof. U. Md. Dental Sch., Balt., 1979-84, assoc. prof., 1984-92; assoc. prof. depts. orthodontics and pediatric dentistry U. N.C. Dental Sch., Chapel Hill, 1992—; mem. staff U. N.C. Hosp., Chapel Hill, 1992—, dental faculty practice, 1992—; outside grant reviewer NIH-NIDR, Washington, 1993-94; manuscript reviewer Pediatric Dentistry Jour., Chgo., 1962—. Contbr. articles to profl. jours. and chpts. to books. Bd. dirs. Bridges-Leadership for Women, Chapel Hill, 1995—. Grantee NIH-NIDR, 1994. Fellow Am. Coll. Dentists, Am. Acad. Pediatric Dentists (First place award table clinic ednl. rsch. found. 1994, rsch. award 1980); mem. Md. Soc. Dentistry for Children (pres., sec.-treas. 1979-92), Am. Assn. Dental Rsch. (sec.-treas. Balt. sect. 1979—), Am. Assn. Dental Schs. (sec., chair elect orthodontics sect. 1989—), Am. Assn. Orthodontists. Office: U NC Dental Sch CB # 7450 Braver Hall Chapel Hill NC 27599-7450

KULB, THOMAS BAYARD, physician; b. Indpls., Oct. 31, 1952; s. Bayard A. and Nancy A. (Bell) K.; m. Debra L. Eckerd, Aug. 21, 1972 (div. Nov. 1984); children: Samuel, Steven; m. Theresa S. Kindt, Sept. 4, 1985; children: David, Athena. AB in Biology, Ind. U., 1974, MD, 1977. Diplomate Am. Bd. Urology. Commd. ensign USN, 1974, advanced through grades to lt. comdr., 1982; med. officer USS AJAR AR-6, FPO San Diego, 1978-79, NRMC San Diego, 1979-82; resident in surgery Maricopa Med. Ctr., Phoenix, 1982-83; resident in urology Ind. U., Indpls., 1983-87; pvt. practice Fransen-Kulb Urology, Bloomington, Ill., 1987—; asst. prof. medicine George Washington U., 1980-82. Author: Urologic Emergencies, 1986; contbr. articles to profl. jours. Fellow Am. Coll. Surgeons; mem. AMA, Soc. Clin. Urologists, Soc. Endourology, Phi Eta Sigma. Republican. Roman Catholic. Office: Fransen Kulb Urology Ltd 332 Fairway Dr Bloomington IL 61701

KULIK, JANICE E., internist; b. Niagara Falls, N.Y., Oct. 21, 1950; d. Paul Benjamin and Marcia Berneice (Printup) K.; m. John Schmidt, Jan. 29, 1977; children: Alan P. Schmidt, Karen P. Schmidt. BS, Cornell U., 1972; MD, Harvard Med. Sch., 1976. Internist Indian Health Svc., Tuba City, Ariz., 1979-81; student health internist U. Pa., Phila., 1981-84; pvt. practice Internal Medicine Assocs., Pueblo, Colo., 1984—. Mem. Am. Coll. Physicians, Am. Soc. Internal Medicine, Colo. Med. Soc., Pueblo County Med. Soc. Republican. Baptist. Office: Internal Medicine Pueblo 1619 N Greenwood Pueblo CO 81003

KULIK, LEWIS TASHRAK, dentist; b. N.Y.C., Mar. 5, 1946; s. Arthur and Miriam (Zevin) K.; m. Loretta Margaret Smyth, Sept. 17, 1978; children: Jeanneil, Nicole Loretta. Student, Bklyn. Coll., 1963-66; DDS Coll. of Dentistry, NYU, 1970. Intern Bronx-Lebanon Hosp. Ctr., N.Y., 1970-71; clin. asst. prof. Coll. of Dentistry NYU, 1981-86; pvt. practice N.Y.C., 1971—; cons. N.Y. State Office of Profl. Discipline, 1981-84; chmn. profl. discipline com. N.Y. State Bd. for Dentistry, 1988-91; steering com. North East Reg. Bd. Dental Examiners, Washington, 1992-95; mem. N.Y. State Bd. for Dental Lic. & Discipline panel, 1994—. Mem. editorial bd. N.Y. Jour. Dentistry, 1981-83, Ea. Dental Soc. Jour., 1981-83. Vice-chmn. Trees for Rye, N.Y., 1991-92; mem. N.Y. State Bd. for Dentistry, 1984-94, mem. lic. and discipline panel, 1994—. Fellow Acad. Gen. Dentistry, Internat. Coll. Dentists, Am. Coll. Dentists, Royal Soc. Medicine, Pierre Fauchard Acad.; mem. ADA, Dental Soc. State N.Y., Ea. Dental Soc., Am. Prosthodontic Soc., Am. Assn. Dental Examiners, North East Regional Bd. Dental Examiners, Rotary Club of N.Y. (bd. dirs. 1990-96, 1st v.p. 1996-97). Republican. Jewish. Office: 30 Central Park S Rm 12B New York NY 10019-1628

KULIKOWSKI, CASIMIR ALEXANDER, computer science educator, medical informatics researcher; b. Hertford, Herts, Eng., May 4, 1944; came to U.S., 1961; s. Victor A. and Isabel S. (Tuckett) K.; m. Christine A. Wilk, May 31, 1969; children: Michael Edward, Victoria Anne. BE with honors, Yale U., 1965, MS, 1966; PhD, U. Hawaii, 1970. From asst. prof. to assoc. prof. Rutgers U., New Brunswick, N.J., 1970-77, prof., 1977—, chmn. dept. computer sci., 1984-90, dir. Lab. Computer Sci. Rsch., 1985-96; Editl. bd. Jour. Am. Med. Informatics Assn., Bethesda, Md., 1993—, Computers in Biology and Medicine, Washington, 1980—; mem. bd. sci. counselors Nat. Libr. Medicine, Bethesda, 1984-87. Author: A Practical Guide to Designing Expert Systems, 1984, Computer Systems that Learn, 1992; editor: Artificial Intelligence Expert Systems and Languages in Modeling & Simulation, 1988. Pres. Highland Park (N.J.) Residents Assn., 1983-88. Fellow AAAS, IEEE, Am. Assn. Artificial Intelligence, Am. Coll. Med. Informatics; mem. NAS Inst. Medicine. Office: Rutgers U Dept Computer Sci Hill Ctr Busch Campus New Brunswick NJ 08903

KULILD, JAMES CLINTON, dentist, army officer; b. Sioux City, Iowa, Apr. 6, 1947; s. James Clinton and Maxine Gertrude (Croy) K.; m. Janice Ellen Morgan, June 24, 1972; children: Ana K., Emily B., Jamie E. BA, U. Mo., Columbia, 1969; DDS, U. Mo., Kansas City, 1973; MS in Oral Biology, George Washington U., 1982. Diplomate Am. Bd. Endodontics. Pvt. practice, Nevada, Mo., 1975; pvt. practice Ogden, Iowa, 1976; commd. ensign U.S. Army, 1970, advanced through grades to Col., 1989; co. comdr., asst. clinic chief U.S. Army Dental Activity, Ft. Sill, Okla., 1976-80; resident in endodontics U.S. Army Inst. Dental Rsch., Washington, 1981-82, Madigan Army Med. Ctr., Ft. Lewis, Wash., 1982-83; chief endodontics U.S. Army Dental Activity, Heidelberg, Fed. Republic Germany, 1983-86; dental insp. gen. 7th Med. Command, Heidelberg, 1986-87; asst. dir. endodontic residency program U.S. Army Dental Activity, Ft. Gordon, Ga., 1987-90, dir., 1990-92; commdr. U.S. Army Dental Activity, Ft. Sam Houston, Tex., 1992-93, chief dept. dental sci., 1993-95; dean and commandant acad. health scis. U.S. Army Med. Dept. Ctr. and Sch., Ft. Sam Houston, 1994, U.S. Army War Coll., Carlisle, Pa., 1995-96; chief dept. health edn. and tng. Acad. Health Scis. AMEDDC & S, Fort Sam Houston, Tex.; endodontic cons. Heidelberg Army Hosp., 1983-86; vis. endodontic cons. U.S. Army Dental Activity, Ft. Riley, Kans., 1989-92, Ft. Benning, Ga., 1990-92; asst. clin. prof. oral biology and endodontics Sch. of Dentistry and Sch. Grad. Studies, Med. Coll. of Ga., 1988-92. Contbr. articles to dental jours. Deacon Richmond Hill Road Ch. of Christ, Augusta, Ga., 1989-92. Officer USN, 1973-75. Recipient Fairbank medal Health Svcs. Command, Ft. Sam Houston, Tex., 1981, order of Mil. Med. Merit, legion of Merit. Fellow Internat. Coll. Dentists; mem. ADA, Am. Assn. Endodontists, U.S. Army Assn. Endodontists (v.p. 1989-90, pres.-elect 1990-91, pres. 1991). Republican. Home: 454 Graham Rd Fort Sam Houston TX 78234

KULKA, J(OHANNES) PETER, retired physician, pathologist; b. Vienna, Austria, Feb. 7, 1921; came to U.S., 1933; s. Ernest Walter and Anna Maria (Jolles) K. AB, Cornell U., 1941; MD, Johns Hopkins U., 1944. Diplomate Am. Bd. Pathology. Intern in pathology Strong Meml. Hosp., Rochester, N.Y., 1944-45; asst. resident in pathology Mass. Gen. Hosp., Boston, 1945-47; instr. anatomy Harvard U. Med. Sch., Boston, 1947-49, instr. pathology, 1949-52, assoc. clin. prof. pathology, 1967-70, clin. fellow in psychiatry, 1970-73; pathologist Robert B. Brigham Hosp., Boston, 1955-58, 61-70, assoc. dir. grad. tng. grant, 1961-68; chmn. med. staff Robert B. Brigham Hosp., Boston, Mass., 1965-67; assoc. in pathology Peter Bent Brigham Hosp., Boston, 1955-58, asst. in medicine, 1958-61; clin. instr. medicine, gen. physician Health Svc., Tufts U., Medford, Mass. Mem. editl. bd. Arthritis and Rheumatism, 1960-68; contbr. articles to med. jours. Capt. M.C., U.S. Army, 1953-55. Home: PO Box 316 Lincoln MA 01773

KULKOSKY, PAUL JOSEPH, psychology educator; b. Newark, N.J., Mar. 3, 1949; s. Peter Francis and Rose Mary (Leonetti) K.; m. Tanya Marie Weightman, Sept. 16, 1978. BA, Columbia U., N.Y.C., 1971, MA, 1972; PhD, U. Wash., 1975. Research assoc. Cornell U., White Plains, N.Y., 1980-81, instr. psychiatry, 1981-82; asst. prof. psychology U. So. Colo., Pueblo, 1982-86, assoc. prof., 1986-89, chmn. dept. psychology, 1988-91, prof., 1989—; bd. advisors Pueblo Zool. Soc., 1984-85, 1988-91, bd. dirs., 1985-88; editorial cons. to pubs. Contbr. chpts. to books, articles to profl. jours.; referee psychol. jours. Liaison Rocky Mountain region Coun. Undergrad. Psychology Programs, 1990-91. Named Hon. Affiliate Prof. Am. U., Washington, 1977; rsch. grantee NIH, 1984—; staff fellow Nat. Inst. Alcohol Abuse and Alcoholism, 1976-80. Mem. AAAS (vice chmn. psychol. scis. sect. Southwestern and Rocky Mountain divsn. 1990-91, chmn. 1991-92, exec. com. Colo. rep. 1991-94, pres.-elect 1994-95, pres. 1995—), Consortium Aquariums, Univs. and Zoos, N.Y. Acad. Scis., Internat. Brain Rsch. Orgn., Soc. for Neurosci., Internat. Soc. Biomed. Rsch. on Alcoholism (charter), Psychonomic Soc., Soc. for Study Ingestive Behavior (charter), Colo.-Wyo. Acad. Sci., U. So. Colo. Club, Sigma Xi (treas. 1986—), Phi Kappa Phi, also others. Home: 417 Tyler St Pueblo CO 81004-1405 Office: U So Colo 2200 Bonforte Blvd Pueblo CO 81001-4901

KULP, EILEEN BODNAR, social worker; b. Glens Falls, N.Y., Sept. 25, 1941; d. Joseph and Bertha (Choquette) Bodnar; m. Randolph Heath Kulp, June 5, 1961; children: Kimberly, Randolph Heath II, Kevin Joseph. B in Sociology, Hampton U., 1978; MSW, Norfolk State U., 1981. Lic. clin. social worker, Va.; diplomate in clin. social work Nat. Bd. Examiners; cert. addictions specialist. Social worker II adult chem. dependency Peninsula Hosp., Hampton, 1981-82, leader treatment team adolescent chem. dependency unit, 1982-84, sr. clinician adult chem. dependency unit, 1984-86, program coord. adult chem. dependency unit, 1986-88, dir. adult treatment programs, 1988-92; pvt. practice Newport News, Va., 1986-93; dir. new founds drug and alcohol programs Riverside Regional Med. Ctr., Newport News, 1994—; dir. New Founds., Newport News; mem. addictions profls. team People Exch. Program, Norway, Sweden, Germany, 1989—; dir. intensive outpatient treatment programs Chesseh & Assocs., 1993-94. Bd. dirs Hampton Count PTA's, pres., 1979-80; bd. dirs. Hampton City Schs. Bd. Edn., 1981-85, Safe Haven Home for Abused Children, 1993—, Commonwealth Va. Citizens Adv. Bd. Youth and Family Svcs., Dept. Corrections, 1989—; chmn. adv. bd. Hampton Juvenile and Domestic Rels. Ct., bd. dirs., 1984—. Mem. Va. Coun. Social Welfare (pres. Tidewater chpt. 1987-88), Nat. Assn. Social Workers, Va. Assn. Alcoholism and Drug Abuse Counselors, Am. Coun. Alcoholism, Hampton Mental Health Bd. (pres. 1988-89), Va. Soc. Clin. Social Workers, Va. Coun. PTA's (life), Acad. Cert. Social Workers (cert.), Alpha Kappa Mu. Roman Catholic. Home: 26 Sarfan Dr Hampton VA 23664-1760

KUMAR, HARINATH V., urologist, surgeon; b. Hyderabad, Andhra Pradesh, India, Sept. 2, 1938; came to U.S., 1964; s. Ramchander and Seetha Rao; m. Leela Murthy, Mar. 13, 1967; children: Vivek, Naveen, Veena. MB BS, Gandhi Med. Coll., Hyderabad, 1963. Diplomate Am. Bd. Urology. Intern Lawrence and Meml. Hosp., New London, Conn., 1965; resident in surgery Norwalk (Conn.) Hosp., 1966-67; resident in urology Bellevue Hosp., N.Y.C.; resident in urology Montefiore Hosp. and Med. Ctr., Bronx, N.Y., fellow in urology, 1970-72; attending urologist Morrisania City Hosp., Bronx, 1972-74; attending urologist Northwestern Med Ctr., Oil City, Pa., 1975—, Franklin, Pa., 1980—; attending urologist Titusville (Pa.) Area Hosp., 1976—. Fellow ACS, Internat. Coll. Surgeons; mem. AMA, Am. Assn. Clin. Urologists, Pa. Med. Assn., Urol. Assn. Pa. Inc. Home: 3 Crestview Dr Oil City PA 16301-2009 Office: 32 Seneca St Oil City PA 16301-1314 also: 422 N Monroe St Titusville PA 16354 also: 621 Elm St Tionesta PA 16353

KUMAR, SUBHASH, nephrologist; b. Bhawanigarh, Punjab, India, Dec. 20, 1948; came to U.S., 1977.; s. Roshan Lal and Lajwanthi Singla; m. Rashmi Kumar, Jan. 28, 1979; children: Sameera, Surina. MB BChir, Punjab U., Chandigarh, India, 1995. Diplomate Am. Bd. Internal Medicine, Am. Bd. Nephrology. Resident in internal medicine Med. Coll. Hosp., Rohtak, India, 1972-74, Sunderland (Eng.) Gen. Hosp., 1974-76, Jewish Hosp. Med. Ctr., Bklyn., N.Y., 1977-78; clin. fellow renal medicine U. Mass. Med. Ctr., Worcester, 1978-80; pvt. practice Huntington, W.Va., 1981—; assoc. prof. medicine Marshal U., Huntington. Contbr. articles to profl. jours. Mem. Royal Coll. Physicians, Am. Soc. Nephrology, Am. Soc. Hypertension, Internat. Soc. Nephrology. Office: 1656 13th Ave Huntington WV 25701-3829

KUMATE, RODRIGUEZ JESUS, physician; b. Mazatlan, Sinaloa, Mex., Nov. 11, 1924; s. Efren Kumate and Josefina Rodriguez; m. Bertha Guerra Rovelo, Mar. 2, 1957. BSc, Escuela Preparatoria, Mazatlan, Mex., 1940; MD, Med. Militar, Mexico City, 1946; PhD, Escuela Nal. Cienc. Biol., Mexico City, 1963; DSc (hon.), U. de Nuevo Leon, Monterrey, Mex., 1990, U. de Sinaloa, Mex., 1995. Diplomate Bd. Infectious Diseases. Asst. prof. Escuela Med. Militar, Mexico City, 1949-54; physician Hosp. Infantil, Mexico City, 1953-80; assoc. prof. Facultad de Medicina, Mexico City, 1960-70, prof., 1970-80; lectr. Polytechnic Inst., Mexico City, 1974-80; investigator Instituto Mexicano Seguro Social, Mexico City, 1981—; dir. Hosp. Infantil, 1979-80; coord. Nat. Insts. Health, Mexico City, 1983-84; undersec. Health Svcs., Mexico City, 1985-88, sec., 1988-94. Author: Manual de Infectologia. Maj. Mex. Army, 1940-54. Recipient Legion of Honor, Govt. of France, 1978-88, Disting. Svcs. award Def. Sec. Mex., 1988, Oswaldo Robles award Govt. Guatemala, 1993. Roman Catholic. Home: Corot 15-81, 03720 Mexico City Mexico Office: Instituto Mexicano Seguro Social, Cuauhtemoc 330, 06725 Mexico City Mexico

KUMIN, LIBBY BARBARA, speech language pathologist, educator; b. Bklyn., Nov. 11, 1945; d. Herbert H. and Berniece (Shuch) K.; m. Martin J. Lazar, Jan. 18, 1969; 1 child, Jonathan Kumin. BA summa cum laude, LIU, 1965; MA, NYU, 1966, PhD, 1969. Lic. speech pathologist, Md.; cert. clin. competence in speech-lang. pathology. Asst. prof. speech pathology U. Md., College Park, 1972-76; cons., 1976-80; adj. prof. Loyola Coll., Balt., 1976-80, assoc. prof., 1980-88, chmn. dept. speech and lang. pathology, 1983—, prof., 1988—; specialist in speech and language in Down Syndrome; mem. profl. adv. bd. Nat. Down Syndrome Cong; mem. Down Syndrome Med. Interest Group. Author: Aphasia, 1978, Communication Skills in Children with Down Syndrom, 1994; therapies editor: Down Syndrome Qtrly.; chief editor: Communicating Together; contbr. articles on Down Syndrome, others. Vol. cons. Howard County Office on Aging, 1977-83. Recipient Outstanding Individual of Year award Howard County Assn. Retarded Citizens, Nat. Meritorious Service award Nat. Down Syndrome Congress, 1987, Svc. Learning award Shriver Ctr., 1996. Aaron and Lillie Straus Found. grantee, 1983-89; Columbia Found. grantee, Joseph P. Kennedy Found. Faculty Innovation grantee, 1995; recipient summer research award Loyola Coll., 1983, 91. Mem. Am. Speech/Lang./Hearing Assn. (cert.), Md. Speech and Hearing Assn., ARC, Sigma Tau Delta, Pi Lambda Theta. Office: Loyola Coll Dept Speech Pathology 4501 N Charles St Baltimore MD 21210-2601

KUMMEL, BERTRAM M., orthopedic surgeon; b. East Newark, Conn., Apr. 27, 1926; s. Max and Florence (Makowsky) K.; m. Jane Stillman, Dec. 22, 1979 (div.); children: Polly, Patricia, Eve, Andrea. AB, Haverford Coll., 1948; MD, U. Pa., 1848. Diplomate Am. Bd. Orthopedic Surgery, Am. Bd. Ind. Med. Examiners. Pvt. practice orthopedic surgery Morristown, N.J., 1956—; cons. Liberty Mut. Ins. co., 1981—, Prudential Ins. Co., 1995—. 1st lt. USAMC, 1951-53, Korea. Mem. Acad. Orthopedic Surgeons, N.Am. Spinal Soc., Am. Coll. Occupl. & Environ. Medicine, Am. Orthopedic Soc. for Sports Medicine. Office: 290 Madison Ave Morristown NJ 07960

KUNCE, AVON ESTES, vocational rehabilitation counselor; b. Sarasota, Fla., Apr. 20, 1927; d. William Breckinridge and Avon Mary (Zahlten) Estes; m. Henry Warren Kunce, May 26, 1948; children: Catherine Avon Hilton, Nancy Lynn Evers, Christopher Warren, Cynthia Tyree Kent, James Breckinridge. BEd in Secondary Edn., U. Miami, 1972; MS in Mgmt., Fla. Internat. U., 1977. Social worker State of Fla. Health & Rehab. Svcs., Miami, 1972-76; social and rehab. svcs. supr. State Disabled Adult Abuse Investigation Unit Adult Congregate Living Lic., Miami, 1976-82; med. disability specialist State of Fla. Health & Rehab. Svcs., Miami, 1982-89; sr. vocat. rehab. counselor State of Fla. Dept. of Labor, Miami, 1989—. Pres. LWV, Rockhill, Mo., 1955, mem., Miami, 1965-69; mem. South Dade Dem. Women's Club, Miami, 1967-69. Mem. ASPA, Nat. Assn. Disability Examiners, Nat. Rehab. Assn., Phi Lambda Pi, Gamma Theta Upsilon, Epsilon Tau Lambda, Pi Alpha Alpha. Democrat. Quaker. Home: 5025 SW 74th Ter Miami FL 33143-6003 Office: State of Fla Vocat Rehabilitation 5040 NW 7th St Ste 330 Miami FL 33126-3422

KUNDEL, HAROLD LOUIS, radiologist, educator; b. N.Y.C., Aug. 15, 1933; s. John A. and Emma E. (Tolle) K.; m. Alice Marie Pape, Mar. 28, 1958; children—Jean, Catherine, Peter. A.B., Columbia U., 1955, M.D., 1959; M.S., Temple U., 1963; M.A. (hon.), U. Pa., 1980. Diplomate Am. Bd. Radiology. Asst. to assoc. prof. Temple U., Phila., 1967-73, prof. radiology, 1973-80; Matthew J. Wilson prof. research radiology U. Pa., Phila., 1980—; dir. Pendergrass Diagnostic Imaging Labs., U. Pa., Phila., 1980—. Contbr. articles to profl. jours. Com. mem. Nat. Council Radiation Protection and Measurements. Served to capt. USAF, 1963-65. Fellow Am. Coll. Radiology; mem. Assn. Univ. Radiologists (Meml. award 1963, Stauffer award 1982), Radiol. Soc. N.Am. Honor award 1978), Am. Roentgen Ray Soc., Soc. Med. Decision Making, Soc. Thoracic Radiology, Alpha Omega Alpha. Lutheran. Office: U Pa Hosp 3400 Spruce St Philadelphia PA 19104

KUNEN, SETH, psychology educator; b. Washington, June 5, 1949. BA in Psychology, Beloit Coll., 1971; MS in Ednl. Psychology, U. Wis., 1974, PhD in Ednl. Psychology, 1976. Lic. psychologist, La.; diplomate Profl. Acad.

Custody Evaluators. Rsch. asst. Washington Sch. Psychiatry, 1970, Nat. Children's Ctr., Washington, 1972; teaching asst. dept. ednl. psychology U. Wis., Madison, 1972-76; instr. U. Wis. Extension, 1973; cons., researcher Tricycle Years Project, Madison, 1973-74; asst. prof. dept. psychology U. New Orleans, 1977-81, assoc. prof. dept. psychology, 1982-90, prof., 1991—; group leader New Orleans Multiple Sclerosis Soc., 1977-81; clin. assoc. prof. medicine La. State U. Sch. Medicine, 1984-85; psychol. cons. Assoc. Cath. Charities Group Homes for Mentally Retarded Citizens, 1987—, Padua Community Svcs., 1988—, Yellowstone Group Homes for Mentally Retarded Adults, 1989—, Allied Health Corp. Group Homes for Mentally Retarded, 1990—, New Orleans Office of Child Protection, 1992—; expert witness in child abuse, parental competency and child custody cases; various presentations at confs. throughout U.S. Reviewer Jour. Nervous and Mental Disease, Child Devel., Jour. Ednl. Psychology, Jour. Exptl. Child Psychology; columnist for Health and Home mag., 1992-95; contbr. articles to profl. jours. Rsch. grantee U. New Orleans Grad. Sch., 1979-80, 81-82; fellow Profl. Acad. Custody Evaluation, 1994-96. Mem. APA, Am. Profl. Soc. on the Abuse of Children, Profl. Acad. Custody Evaluators, Am. Coll. Forensic Examiners. Home: 5362 Chatham Dr New Orleans LA 70122

KUNG, PATRICK CHUNG-SHU, biotechnology executive; b. Nanjing, China, July 10, 1947; came to U.S., 1969; s. Tao and Yuing (Li) K.; m. Rita Wu, Feb. 11, 1980; children: Julia, Calvin. BS, FuJen U., Taiwan, 1968; PhD, U. Calif., Berkeley, 1974. Rsch. fellow MIT, Cambridge, 1974-77; sr. rsch. fellow Ortho Pharm. Co., Raritan, N.J., 1978-81; v.p. rsch. Centocor Inc., Malvern, Pa., 1982-83; co-founder, exec. v.p. T Cell Scis., Inc., Cambridge, 1984-88, vice chmn. bd., 1989—; mem. exec. bd. Coll. Letters and Scis. U. Calif., Berkeley, 1989-91; chmn., pres. Global Pharm. Ltd., 1994—; bd. dirs. Asian Am. Bank and Trust Co., Boston, 1994—. Contbr. articles to profl. jours. Trsute Park Sch., Brookline, Mass., 1992-95. Recipient Philip Hoffman award Johnson & Johnson Co., 1979, Achievement award Chinese Inst. Engrs., 1988, Discoverers award Pharm. Mfrs. Assn., 1991, Thomas Alva Edison award N.J. Rsch. Coun., 1991. Mem. Am. Assn. Immunologists, N.Y. Acad. Scis., Soc. Chinese Bioscientists in Am. (pres. bio/pharm. scis. divsn. 1995), Sigma Xi. Office: T Cell Scis Inc 119 4th Ave Needham MA 02194-2725

KUNG, SHAIN-DOW, molecular biologist, academic administrator, educator; b. China, Mar. 14, 1935, came to U.S., 1971, naturalized, 1977; s. Chao-tzen and Chih (Zhu) K.; grad. Chung-Hsing U., Taiwan, China, 1958; Ph.D., U. Toronto, Can., 1968; m. Helen C.C. Kung, Sept. 5, 1964; children: Grace, David, Andrew. Research fellow Hosp. for Sick Children, Toronto, 1968-70; biologist UCLA, 1971-74; asst. prof. biology U. Md., Baltimore County, 1974-77, assoc. prof., 1977-82, prof., 1982-86, acting chmn. dept., 1982-84, assoc. dean arts and sci., 1985-86, prof. botany U. Md., College Park, 1986-93; hon. prof. Fudan U., 1986, Beijing Agrl. U., 1987; acting dir. U. Md. Ctr. for Agrl. Biotech, 1986-88, dir. 1988-93, acting provost Md. Biotech. Inst., 1989-91; dean Sch. Sci. Hong Kong U. Sci. and Tech., 1991-92, v.p. for acad. affairs, 1992—. Author 1 book; editor 12 books; contbr. chpts. to books, articles to profl. jours. Recipient Philip Morris award for disting. achievement in tobacco sci., 1979, Outstanding Alumni award, 1990, Outstanding Svc. award, 1990; named Disting. Scholar, Nat. Acad. Sci., 1981; Fulbright grantee, 1982-83, grantee NSF, NIH. Mem. Am. Soc. Plant Physiologists, AAAS. Office: Hong Kong U Sci and Tech, Clear Water Bay, Kowloon Hong Kong

KUNNU, ELIZABETH IDOWU, health information administrator; b. Ebute-Meta, Lagos, Nigeria, Jan. 2, 1947; d. Olatunji and Ogunwumi Ajoke (Ogedemgbe) Subair. AAS in Med. Record Tech., Essex County Coll., Newark, 1972; BS in Health Record Adminstrn., Ea. Ky. U., Richmond, 1978; MEd in Ednl. Adminstrn. and Supervision, Tenn. State U., 1991. Cert. and registered RRA, Am. Health Info. Mgmt. Assn. Dir. med. record dept. Lyons Health Ctr., Newark, 1974-75; dir. med. record adminstrn. Matthew Walker Comprehensive Health Ctr., Nashville, 1978-85; program dir. health info. mgmt. Tenn. State U., Nashville, 1985—; conf. site coord. Health Occupations Students of Am., Nashville, 1993—. Faculty adv. team mem. Cath. Assn., Nashville, 1994—; team mother SVS Jr. Varsity Basketball Team, Nashville, 1994-96. Recipient Significant Contbn. award Health Occupations Students Am., Nashville, 1993, 94. Mem. Am. Health Info. Mgmt. Assn., Tenn. Health Info. Mgmt. Assn. Home: 282 Richbriar Rd Nashville TN 37211 Office: Tenn State U 3500 John Merritt Blvd Nashville TN 37209

KUNSMAN, CYNTHIA LOUISE MULLEN, critical care nurse; b. Allentown, Pa., Sept. 29, 1966; d. Donald Lee and Phyllis Ann (Herbert) Mullen; m. Gary Wayne Kunsman, May 5, 1990. ASN, Gwynedd-Mercy Coll., 1986, BSN, 1987; MMin, Chesapeake Bible Seminary, 1994; D of Naturopathy, Clayton Sch. Natural Healing, 1995. CCRN. Staff nurse oncology/urology med./surg. Lehigh Valley Hosp. Ctr., Allentown, 1986; staff nurse PCCU Lehigh Valley Hosp. Ctr., 1987-88, staff nurse ICU, 1989; staff nurse MICU La. State U., Shreveport, La., 1990-91; asst. head nurse cardiovascular svcs. HCA Presbyn. Hosp., Oklahoma City, 1992-93; staff nurse cardiothoracic ICU U. Md. Med. Sys., Balt., 1993-95; dir. R & D, prof. biol. sci. Chesapeake Bible Coll., 1993—; sole proprietor Gilead Health Assocs., Pasadena, Md., 1995—; staff nurse Hospice of the Chesapeake, Millersville, Md., 1995—. Author: (book) Arrhythmia Interpretation: A Guide for Nurses, 1991; contbr. articles to profl. jours. Mem. AACN, Pa. Nurses Assn. (chair nominations com. local dist. 1988-90), Orgn. for the Advancement of ASN, Ctr. for Bioethics and Human Dignity. Office: Gilead Health Assocs 672 Old Mill Rd # 169 Millersville MD 21108

KUNSTADT, DOROTHY, cardiologist; b. Mar. 16, 1936; came to U.S., 1966; d. Samuel and Hana (Grizer) Rubinstein; m. Herbert Kunstadt. MB, BS, U. Melbourne, 1959, MD, 1965. Resident jr. house officer The Royal Melbourne Hosp., 1960-61; med. house officer Royal Children's Hosp., 1961-62; med. registrar Royal Melbourne Hosp., 1963-65; med. officer, jr. specialist Repatriation Gen. Hosp., Melbourne, 1963-65; jr. assoc. in medicine Peter Bent Brigham Hosp., Boston, 1965-66; instr. in medicine Harvard Med. Sch., Boston, 1966-68; asst. cardiologist Flowers & Fifth Ave Hosp., N.Y.C., 1966-70; asst. prof. medicine N.Y. Med. Coll., 1968-74, clin. assoc. prof. of medicine, 1974—; chief of cardiology Met. Hosp., 1970-72; adj. physician Lenox Hill Hosp.; assoc. attending physician Beth Israel Med. Ctr. Office: 927 Park Ave New York NY 10028

KUNTZMAN, RONALD, pharmacology research executive; b. Bklyn., Sept. 17, 1933; s. Herman and Fanny Kuntzman; m. Bernice Russman, May 29, 1955; children: Fred, Gary. B.S., Bklyn. Coll., 1955; M.S., George Washington U., 1957, Ph.D. in Biochemistry, 1962. Biochemist lab. chem. pharmacology Nat. Heart Inst., NIH, Bethesda, Md., 1955-62; sr. biochemist Wellcome Research Labs.-Burroughs Wellcome & Co. U.S.A. Inc., Tuckahoe, N.Y., 1962-66, dep. head biochem. pharmacology dept., 1967-70; assoc. dir. dept. biochemistry and drug metabolism Hoffmann-La Roche Inc., Nutley, N.J., 1970-71, assoc. dir. biol. research, 1972-73, dir. therapeutics research, 1973-79, asst. v.p., 1974-81, dir. pharm. R & D, 1980-81, v.p. pharm. R&D, 1981-84, v.p. R&D, 1984-92; adj. prof. dept. chem. biology and pharmacognosy Rutgers U. Coll. Pharmacy, Piscataway, N.J., 1990—; adj. mem. Roche Inst. Molecular Biology, Nutley, N.J., 1992—; mem. adv. coun. Nat. Orgn. for Rare Disorders, 1987-91. Mem. editl. bd. Biochem. Pharmacology, 1966-68, Neuropharmacology, 1970-78, Xenobiotica, 1970-84, Archives of Biochemistry and Biophysics, 1971-78, Life Scis., 1973-78; contbr. numerous articles to profl. jours. Mem. AAAS, Am. Soc. Pharmacology and Exptl. Therapeutics (editorial bd. jour. 1968-75, nominating com. 1972, chmn. div. nominating com. 1977, chmn. div. drug metabolism 1978-81, sec.-treas. 1981-83, coun. 1981-83, chmn. long-range planning com. 1987-92, exec. com. div. drug metabolism 1973-76, John Jacob Abel award 1969), Am. Soc. Biol. Chemists, Am. Coll. Neuropsychopharmacology, Soc. Toxicology, George Washington U. Alumni Assn. (Dist. Alumni Achievement award 1988), Roche Inst. of Molecular Biology (adj. 1992—), Sigma Xi. Address: 12 Augustine Ave Ardsley NY 10502

KUNZ-RAMSAY, YVETTE W., scientist; b. Basel, Switzerland, Feb. 19, 1928; arrived in Ireland, 1963; d. Hans Karl Viktor and Yvonne Camilla (Staub) K.; m. William John Ramsay, Feb. 11, 1966; children: Oengus Niall, Ciaran Oisin. MA, PhD, U. Basel, 1963; DSc, Nat. U. Ireland, 1992. Grad. rsch. asst. Cornell U., Ithaca, N.Y., 1957-58; postdoctoral rsch. assoc. U. Dublin, Trinity Coll., Ireland, 1963-64; coll. lectr. U. Coll. Dublin, The Nat. U. Ireland, 1964-70, lectr., 1970-81, statutory lectr., 1981-93; emeritus scientist Nat. U. Ireland, Dublin, 1993—; cons. The Marine Biol. Lab. Woods Hole, Mass., 1978, 79, Cornell U., 1988-93, Harvard U., 1993-94. Contbr. articles to profl. jours. Rsch. grantee Wellcome Trust, London, 1991-93; Med. Rsch. Coun. grantee, Dublin, 1986-89; recipient Janggen-Poehn Found. award, St. Gall, Switzerland, 1963. Fellow Royal Irish Acad. Medicine, Fellowship Cath. Scholars; mem. Internat. Soc. Devel. Biology, Assn. Rsch. Vision and Ophthalmology, European Soc. Photobiology. Roman Catholic. Office: Nat U Ireland U Coll, Belfield, Dublin Ireland

KUO, LIH, medical educator; b. Taipei, Taiwan, Aug. 28, 1957. BS in Biology, Tunghai Univ., Taichung, Taiwan, 1979; MS in Physiology, Nat. Taiwan U., 1983; DPhil, Med. Coll. Va., 1987. Rsch. asst. Dept. Physiology & Biophysics Nat. Def. Med. Ctr., 1979-81; tchg. asst. Dept. Physiology Nat. Taiwan U., 1981-83, Med. Coll. Va., Richmond, 1985-87; postdoctoral rsch. assoc. Dept. Med. Physiology Tex. A&M U., 1990-91; asst. prof. Tex. A&M U. Health Ctr., 1992—; mem. exptl. cardiovascular scis. study sect. NIH, 1994—; spkr. in field. Contbr. articles to profl. jours. Dr. Sun Yet Sen Sci. scholar Tunghai U., 1977-79, Ministry Edn. scholar Outstanding Student Coll. Medicine Nat. Taiwan U., 1981-83; A.D. Williams award Postdoctoral fellow Med. Coll. Va., 1983-85. Med. Coll. Va. Grad. fellow, 1985-87. Fellow Am. Heart Assn. (coun. circulation), Am. Physiol. Soc. (cardiovascular sect.); mem. Chinese Physiol. Soc., Microcirculatory Soc. (Grega-Zacharkow Young Investigator award 1990), Phi Kappa Phi. Office: Tex A&M U Dept Med Physiology College Station TX 77843-1114

KUO, PAUL C., transplant surgeon; b. Taiwan, Sept. 15, 1961; s. Sun-Luin and Helen (Huang) K.; m. Rebecca Ann Schroeder, June 20, 1992; children: Andrew, Marissa. BA, Johns Hopkins U., 1982, MD, 1985. Diplomate Am. Bd. Surgery. Now transplant surgeon U. Md. Med. Ctr., Balt. Office: U Md Med Ctr 29 S Greene St # 200 Baltimore MD 21201

KUPERS, TERRY ALLEN, psychiatrist, educator; b. Phila., Oct. 14, 1943; s. Edward Carlton and Frances Shirley (Praissman) K.; m. Ruth Kupers, June 1968,(div. 1978); children: Eric, Jesse; m. Arlene Marilyn Shmaeff, Jan. 16, 1983; 1 child, Jake (adopted). BA, Stanford U., 1964; MD, UCLA, 1968, M in social psychiatry, 1974. Diplomate Am. Bd. Psychiatry and Neurology, 1974. Intern Kings County Hosp., Brooklyn, 1968-69; resident in psychiatry UCLA, 1969-72, fellow in social & community psychiatry, 1972-74; asst. prof. Martin L. King, Jr. Hosp., L.A., 1974-77; staff psychiatrist Richmond (Calif.) Community Mental Health Ctr., 1977-81; pvt. practice Oakland, Ca., 1977—; psychology prof. Wright Inst., Berkeley, Ca., 1980—. Author: Public Therapy: The Practice of Psychotherapy in the Public Mental Health Clinic, 1981, Ending Therapy: The Meaning of Termination, 1988, Revisioning Men's Lives: Gender, Intimacy and Power, 1993; editor: Using Psychodynamic Principles in Public Mental Health, 1990; contbr. articles to profl. jours. Fellow. Am. Psychiatric Assn., Am. Orthopsychiatric Assn.; mem. Physicians Social Responsibility, Alpha Omega Alpha. Democrat. Jewish. Office: 8 Wildwood Ave Oakland CA 94610-1044

KUPFER, CARL, ophthalmologist, science administrator; b. N.Y.C., Feb. 9, 1928; s. James and Hannah Kupfer; m. Muriel I. Kaiser, Dec. 9, 1969; children: Charles, Sarah. AB, Yale U., 1948; MD, Johns Hopkins U., 1952; DSc (hon.), U. Pa., 1982, SUNY, 1992. Diplomate Am. Bd. Ophthalmology. Intern, then resident Johns Hopkins U., 1952-55, 57-58; asst. prof. Harvard U. Med. Sch., Boston, 1960-66; prof., chmn. dept. ophthalmology U. Wash. Sch. Med., Seattle, 1966-69; dir. Nat. Eye Inst. NIH, Bethesda, Md, 1970—. Recipient Migel award Am. Found. for Blind, 1976, Pisart award Lighthouse for Blind, N.Y.C., 1984, Presdl. Rank award, 1991, Humanitarian award Lions Club Internat., 1992. Mem. NAS, Johns Hopkins Soc. Scholars, Insts. Medicine. Office: NEI/NIH Bldg 31 Rm 6A03 31 Center DR MSC 2510 Bethesda MD 20892-2510

KUPFER, DAVID J., psychiatry educator; b. N.Y.C., Feb. 14, 1941; s. Alex and Muriel (Greenfield) Kupferstein; m. Barbara Stern Burstin, June 1963 (div. Mar. 1975); m. Ellen Frank, June 1975; children: Andrea, Jeffrey, Deborah, Nancy, Erica, Tonia. BA magna cum laude, Yale U., 1961, MD, 1965. Diplomate Am. Bd. Psychiatry and Neurology. Med. intern Montefiore Hosp. Ctr., N.Y.C., 1965-66; clin. fellow in psychiatry Yale U. Sch. Medicine, New Haven, 1966-67; postdoctoral fellow, chief resident in psychiatry Dana Psychiat. Clinic, Yale-New Haven Hosp., 1969-70; asst. prof. Yale U. Sch. Medicine, New Haven, 1970-73; assoc. prof. psychiatry U. Pitts., 1973-75, prof., 1975—, chmn. dept., 1983—; dir. rsch. Western Psychiat. Inst. and Clinic Western Psychiat. Inst. and Clinic, Pitts., 1973—, Thomas Detre prof., chmn. dept. psychiatry, 1994—. Office: U Pitts Western Psychiat Inst & Clinic 3811 Ohara St Pittsburgh PA 15213-2593

KUPPUSAMY, PERIANNAN, medical educator, medical researcher; b. Apr. 4, 1954; m. Lakshmi Kuppusamy; 2 children. BSc in Math., Physics and Chemistry, U. Madras, India, 1975, MSc in Chemistry, 1977; PhD in Electron Paramagnetic Resonance Spectroscopy, Indian Inst. of Tech. 1985. Lectr. dept. chemistry Pachaiyappa's Coll., Madras, India, 1978-80, asst. prof. dept. chemistry, 1985-86; tchr. fellow dept. chemistry Indian Inst. of Tech., Madras, 1980-85; rsch. fellow divsn. cardiology Johns Hopkins U. Sch. of Medicine, Balt., 1987-90, instr. medicine, 1990-92, asst. prof., 1992—. Mem. editl. rev. Shock, Stroke, Magnetic Resonance in Medicine; contbr. articles to profl. jours, chpts. to books. Tchr. fellow Univs. Grants Commn., Govt. of India, 1984, Fogarty fellow NIH, 1987; recipient Rsch. award Chesapeake Ednl. & Rsch. Trust, 1991. Mem. Am. Heart Assn. (Established Investigator award 1996), Am. Chem. Soc., N.Y. Acad. Scis., Biophys. Soc., Oxygen Soc. Home: 2910 Brightwater Ln Abingdon MD 21009 Office: Johns Hopkins U Sch Medicine EPR Labs Divsn Cardiology 5501 Hopkins Bayview Cir LA-14 Baltimore MD 21224

KURAMOTO, KIZUKU, hospital executive; b. Hiroshima, Japan, Sept. 5, 1927; s. Mitsugi and Shizuko (Hamada) K.; m, Haruko Miwa, May 1, 1960; children: Akiko, Michiko. MD, U. Tokyo, 1952, D of Med. Sci., 1959. Physician Dept. Med. U. Tokyo Hosp., 1953-72; chief dept. clin. rsch. Tokyo Metro. Geriat. Hosp., 1972-75, vice dir., 1975-90, dir., 1990-93 cons. physician, 1993—. Bd. dirs. Tokyo Metro Inst. Gerontology, 1980-93. Mem. Japan Assn. Internal Medicine, Japan Circulation Soc., Japan Geriatric Soc., Japan Hypertension Soc., Japan Coll. Angiology. Home: 3-43-19 Fujimidai, Nerima-Ku, Tokyo Japan Office: Tokyo Metr Geriat Hosp, 35-2 Sakae-cho, Itabashi-ku, Tokyo 173, Japan

KURIAN, PIUS, physician; b. Arpookara, Kerala, India, May 9, 1959; s. Pylo and Mariamma Kurian; m. Sally Kurian, May 11, 1986; children: Michelle Maria, Matthew Paul, Catherine Tresa. BSc, Kuriakose (India) Elias Coll., 1979; MB, BS, Kottayam (India) Med. Coll., India, 1986. Diplomate Am. Bd. Internal Medicine, Am. Bd. Nephrology. Sr. staff physician Sacred Heart Med. Ctr., Kottayam, 1986; resident physician Nassau County Med. Ctr., East Meadow, N.Y., 1988-91; fellow in nephrology Nassau County Med. Ctr., East Meadow, 1991-94; attending physician in nephrology Mercy Med. Ctr. and Cmty. Hosp., Springfield, Ohio, 1994—. Mem. ACP, AAAS, AMA, Am. Soc. Hypertension, Am. Soc. Nephrology, Am. Coll. Physicians Execs. Roman Catholic. Office: 247 S Burnett Springfield OH 45505

KURIATA, MARK A., physician; b. Paw Paw, Mich., Oct. 21, 1965; s. Walter H. and Dolores A. (Jones) K.; m. Shelley L. Long, Dec. 27, 1986; children: Elyse M., Christopher M. AAS, Lake Mich. Coll., 1986; BS in Medicine, Western Mich. U., 1989; DO, U. Osteo. Med. & Health Scis., Des Moines, 1994. Diplomate Am. Bd. Osteo. Med. Examiners. Dermatology physician asst. Stephen Presser, M.D., Rochester, N.Y., 1989-90; intern Cmty. Health Ctr. Br. County, Coldwater, Mich., 1994-95; resident in dermatology Kirksville (Mo.) Coll. Osteo. Medicine, 1996—. Contbr. articles to profl. jours. Recipient Ella and Clifford Chapman Distinc. Svc. scholarship Western Mich. U., 1989, acad. scholarship, 1987-89, Health Scis. Divsnl. scholarship Lake Mich. Coll., 1985-86. Fellow Am. Acad. Physician Assts.; mem. Christian Med. and Dental Soc., Am. Osteo. Coll. Dermatology, Am. Osteo. Assn., Am. Soc. Clin. Pathologists, Am. Soc. for Med. Tech., Internal Medicine Club, Phi Theta Kappa. Home: 9 Quail Dr Kirksville MO 63501 Office: Kirksville Coll Osteo Med Dept Dermatology 700 W Jefferson St Kirksville MO 63501

KURIEN, SANTHA T., psychiatrist; b. Perumpavoor, Kerala, India, June 15, 1945; came to U.S., 1973; d. Varghese and Mary (Thomas) Koshy; m. Thomas K. Kurien; children: Susan, Miriam. MD, Calicut Med. Coll., Kerala, India, 1970. Diplomate Am. Bd. Psychiatry and Neurology; cert. geriatric psychiatry. Sr. house surgeoncy Vellore (Madras) Med. Coll., 1970-71; gen. med. practice St. Thomas Memorial Hosp., Vadasserikara, Kerala, India, 1971-72; psychiat. residency Fairfield Hills Hosp., Newtown, Conn., 1973-76; staff psychiatrist Fairfield Hills Hosp., Newtown, 1976-77, Danbury (Conn.) Hosp., 1977-82; psychiatrist pvt. practice, Danbury, 1982—; consulting psychiatrist Pope John Paul Ctr., Danbury, Conn., 1991—. Mem. Am. Psychiat. Assn., Am. Assn. Geriatric Psychiatry, New Haven County Med. Assn., Danbury Med. Soc., Assn. Kerala Med. Grads., Internat. Psychogeriatric Assn., Am. Soc. Clin. Psychopharmacology. Office: Santha T Kurien MD PC 27 Hospital Ave Ste 304 Danbury CT 06810-5954

KURIGA, STEVEN MICHAEL, medical group administrator; b. Milw., June 3, 1958; s. Edward Thomas and Ellen Odessa (Long) K. BS, Gannon U., 1981; MS, Cardinal Stritch Coll., 1986; cert. travel agt., San Diego County, 1988; crt. meeting planning, San Diego State U., 1990. Physician asst. Mt. Sinai Med. Ctr., Milw., 1981-85, Kaiser Permanente Med. Group, L.A., 1985-87, Smith-Hanna Med. Group, San Diego, 1987-89; adminstr Mission Hills Med. Group, San Diego, 1989—; speaker on med.-legal issues, health care billing and collections. Fellow Am. Acad. Physician Assts.; mem. Calif. Acad. Physician Assts., Caucus of Adminstrv. Exec. Physician Assts. (v.p. 1990-92), San Diego County Physician Asst. Soc. (pres. 1991-92). Office: 2017 1st Ave Ste 200 San Diego CA 92101-2033

KURIMOTO, SOJI, anesthesiologist; b. Obama Fukui, Japan, June 4, 1930; s. Koji and Toku (Akita) Kurimoto; m. Yoko Akedo, Dec. 3, 1967; children: Akedo, Akiko. MD, Osaka Med. Sch., 1954, Osaka Med. Sch., 1965; LLB, Kobe U., 1990. Intern Nat. Hosp., Kyoto, Japan, 1954-55; resident, asst. St. Luke's Internat. Hosp., Tokyo, 1955-62; asst., lectr. Osaka Med. Sch., Takatsuki, Japan, 1962-67, prof. clin. anesthesiology, 1967—. Scholar Brit. Coun., 1961-62, Fulbright scholar, 1965-67. Mem. Japan Soc. Anesthesiology, Am. Soc. Anesthesiologists, Assn. Anesthesiologists, Royal Soc. Medicine, Japan-Am. Soc., Japan-Brit. Soc., Brit. Coun. Japan Assn., Fulbright Assn. Home: 6-50-353 Koyoen Honjocho, Nishinomiya 662, Japan Office: Osaka Med Sch, 2-7 Daigakucho, Takatsuki 569, Japan

KURIYAMA, KINYA, pharmacology educator; b. Kyoto, Japan, July 11, 1932; s. Haruya and Kouko Kuriyama; m. Chieko Imamura, Dec. 8, 1958; children: Takuya, Nagato. MD, Kyoto Prefecture U. Medicine, 1957, PhD, 1963. Rsch. assoc. Johns Hopkins Sch. Medicine, Balt., 1963-64; sr. rsch. scientist City of Hope Med. Ctr., Duarte, Calif., 1964-67; assoc. prof. Loma Linda (Calif.) U. Sch. Medicine, 1967-69; from assoc. prof. to prof. SUNY, Bklyn., 1969-72; prof., chmn. Kyoto Prefecture U. Medicine, 1971-96, pres., 1994—. Exec. editor: Neurochemistry Internat., 1983—; editor: Med. Pharmacology, 1985, Neurotransmitters, 1986, Neurotransmitter Receptors and Signal Trans., 1988. Recipient Med. award Japan Med. Assn., 1980, Miyata Meml. award Miyata Found., 1993, Uehara Rsch. award Uehara meml. Found., 1985; Naito rsch. grantee Naito Found., 1988. Disting. Cultural award, Kyato Press, 1995. Mem. Japanese Pharmacol. Soc. (coun. mem. 1987-93), Japanese Neurochem. Soc. (coun. mem. 1989-93, pres. 1977-78), Sci. Coun. Japan (coun. mem. 1989-93), Japanese Neirosci. Soc. (coun. mem. 1989-93), Japanese Neurosci. Soc. (coun. mem. 1990-92), Japan Soc. Alcohol Studies (pres. 1986-90, 95), Internat. Soc. Biomed. Rsch. on Alcohol (v.p. 1990-94, pres. 1994—), Internat. Soc. Neurochemistry (pres. 1993—). Buddhist. Home: 69-1 Iwagakakiuchi-cho, Kita-ku Kyoto 603, Japan Office: Kyoto Pref U Med, Kawaramachi-Hirokoji, Kamikyo Kyoto 602, Japan

KURK, MITCHELL, physician; b. N.Y.C., Aug. 25, 1931; s. Benjamin and Frieda (Steinbaum) K.; m. Marcia Carol Leon (dec. 1981); children: Hope, Nancy, Cindy. BS, MS, Columbia U., 1954; OD, Mass. Coll. Optometry, 1955; DO, Phila. Coll. Osteopathic, 1960; MD, U. Calif., 1962. Diplomate Am. Bd. Gen. Practice. Clin. asst. Queens (N.Y.) Gen. Hosp.; pvt. practice N.Y.C., 1962—; dir. Biomed. Revitalization Ctr., Lawrence, N.Y., 1980-85; attending physician Peninsula Hosp. Ctr.; mem. alcohol adv. bd. Southshore Hosp., Quens, 1978-80. Author: Kurkian Way To Hold Back the Aging Process, 1989. Fellow Internat. Coll. Applied Nutrition; mem. Internat. Acad. Preventive Medicine, Am. Holistic Med. Assn., AMA, N.Y. State Med. Soc., Nassau County Med. Soc., Nassau Acad. Medicine. Republican.

KURLAN, MARVIN ZEFT, surgeon, educator; b. Wilkes-Barre, Pa., Feb. 20, 1934; s. Ephraigm Joseph and Fannye Lillian (Rosenbluth) Kurlancheek; m. Eleanor Frank, June 21, 1964; 1 child, Todd. BA, Wilkes Coll., 1957; MS, U. Ill., 1958; MD, SUNY, Buffalo, 1964. Diplomate Nat. Bd. Med. Examiners, Am. Bd. Surgery. Intern then resident in surgery Millard Fillmore Hosp., Buffalo, 1964-69, dir. trauma svcs., 1974-82, sr. attending surgeon, 1984-95; surgeon emeritus, 1995—; plant surgeon Bethlehem (Pa.) Steel Corp., 1969-74; med. dir. Bros. of Mercy Health Facilities, Clarence, N.Y., 1974-82; assoc. examiner Am. Bd. Surgery, Phila., 1987-95; chmn. James Platt White Soc., Sch. Medicine and Biomed. Scis., SUNY, Buffalo, 1992-94 (Dean's adv. coun., 1995—); cons. in surgery Walter Reed Army Med. Ctr., Washington. Contbr. articles to profl. jours. Vol. Empire State Games, Buffalo, 1986; mem. Jack Kemp Forum, Buffalo, 1985-91; bd. dirs. Jewish Fedn. Allentown, Pa., 1972-74. Served AUS (res.) to lt. col. Med. Corps, 1965-91, active duty operation Desert Shield and Desert Storm. Recipient Army Svc. medal with Oak Leaf Cluster. Fellow Am. Coll. Gastroenterology, Am. Trauma Soc. (founder), N.Y. Acad. Scis.; mem. ACS (life fellow leadership soc.), Assn. Mil. Surgeons U.S., Hastings on Hudson Bioethics Ctr., Buffalo Surg. Soc. (sec. 1986-88, v.p. 1988-89, pres. 1989-90), SUNY at Buffalo Found. (pres.'s assoc.), Grand Coun. World Parliament, Confedn. Chivalry, Knight of Humanity, Order White Cross Internat. (dist. comdr. N.Y., U.S.), Chevalier Grand Cross, Ordre Soverain et Militaire de Milice du St. Sepulcre, Phi Lambda Kappa (nat. pres. 1993), Nu Sigma Nu. Republican. Club: Sci. Progress Research (Buffalo) (v.p. 1983-84). Lodges: Masons, Shriners. Home and Office: 413 Dan Troy Dr Buffalo NY 14221-3558

KURLINSKI, JOHN PARKER, physician; b. Buchanon, W.Va., Jan. 17, 1948; s. John Peter and Jean (Holloway) K.; m. Claire Sawyer, June 12, 1971; children: Joshua John, Ryan Edward, Seth Parker. AB cum laude, Williams Coll., 1970; MD, Johns Hopkins Sch. Medicine, 1974. Intern, then resident Johns Hopkins Hosp., Baltimore, 1974-77; fellowship neonatal/perinatal medicine U. Calif., San Diego, 1977-79; chief resident pediatrician Johns Hopkins Hosp., 1979-80; clin. assoc. prof. pediatrics U. Nev. Sch. Medicine, Reno, 1994—; vice chief of staff Sunrise Children's Hosp., Las Vegas, 1989-90, chief of staff, 1990-95; pediatrician, co-dir. neonatology S.W. Regional Neonatal Ctr. at Sunrise Hosp. and Med. Ctr., Las Vegas, 1980-93; vice chief pediatrics Sunrise Hosp., Las Vegas, 1983-90; dir. NICU Sunrise Children's Hosp., 1994—; bd. dirs. S.W. Regional Neonatal Ctr. Edn. Found.; chmn. bd. dirs. Sunrise Children's Hosp. Found.; mem. Med.-Legal Screening Panel, Nev., 1986—; many hosp. coms., 1980—. Bd dirs. So Nev. chpt. March of Dimes, Las Vegas, 1984—. Mem. AMA, Am Acad. Pediatrics (v.p. Nev. chpt. 1987-90, pres. 1990-93, coun. mem. dist. VIII sect. on perinatal pediatrics), Clark County Med. Soc., Las Vegas Pediatric Soc. (founding), Phi Beta Kappa. Home: 3322 Beam Dr Las Vegas NV 89139-5902 Office: Sunrise Childrens Hosp 3186 S Maryland Pky Las Vegas NV 89109-2317

KURNICK, JOHN EDMUND, hematologist, educator; b. N.Y.C., Feb. 9, 1942; s. Nathaniel B. and Dorothy (Manheimer) K.; m. Luann Fogliani, July 9, 1969; children: David, Katherine. BA, Harvard U., 1962; MD, U. Chgo., 1966. Diplomate Am. Bd. Internal Medicine, Am. Bd. Oncology, Am. Bd. Hematology. Intern U. Wash., Seattle, 1966-67; resident Stanford U., Palo Alto, Calif., 1967-68; asst. prof. medicine U. Colo. Med. Ctr., Denver, 1973-78; chief hematology VA Hosp., Denver, 1973-78; pvt. pracice Downey, Calif., 1979—; assoc. clin. prof. medicine U. Calif., Irvine, 1979—; lectr., expert witness in field. Contbr. articles to med. jours. Maj. Med. Corps., USAR, 1970-73. Fellow U. Colo., 1968-70. Fellow ACP; mem. Am. Soc. Hematology, Am. Soc. Clin. Oncology, Western Soc. Clin. Rsch., Internat. Soc. Hematology, Am. Fedn. Clin. Rsch., Am. Assn. Cancer Edn. Democrat. Office: 11411 Brookshire Ave Downey CA 90241-5003

KURNICK, NATHANIEL BERTRAND, oncologist-hematologist, educator, researcher; b. N.Y.C., Nov. 8, 1917; s. Jacob Kurnick and Celia

(Levine) Zackheim; m. Dorothy Manheimer, Oct. 4, 1940 (dec. Dec. 1985); children: John E., Katherine (dec.), James T.; m. Sally Ann Kreeger, June 23, 1989. BA, Harvard U., 1936, MD, 1940. Diplomate Am. Bd. Internal Medicine, Am. Bd. Med. Oncology, Am. Bd. Hematology, Am. Bd. Med. Examiners. Intern Mt. Sinai Hosp., N.Y.C., 1941-42, chief resident internal medicine, 1946; asst. prof. medicine Tulane U. Med. Sch., New Orleans, 1949-54; chief hematology svc. VA Hosp., Long Beach, Calif., 1954-59, cons., 1954—; assoc. clin. prof. medicine U. Calif., L.A., 1954-64; clin. prof. medicine U. Calif., Irvine, 1964—; pvt. practice Long Beach, 1959-83; Bixby Hematology-Oncology Lab.; dir. Bixby Lab. Long Beach Cmty. Med. Ctr., 1982—; chmn. cancer activities, 1968-90, chmn. dept. medicine, 1966-68, chmn. dept. med. oncology and hematology, 1982-87; pres. Long Beach Soc. Internal Medicine, 1971; chmn. Franklin Thrift & Loan, Orange, Calif., 1988—. Contbr. articles to jours. in field. Trustee Garden Grove, Calif. Union High Sch.Dist., 1960-64. Capt. M.C., U.S. Army, 1942-46. Am. Cancer Soc./NRC fellow, 1946-47, Rockefeller Inst., 1946-47, Nobel Inst., 1947-49; NIH/Am. Cancer Soc. grantee, 1949-1972; Henry Hunter Workman rsch. fellow Harvard Med. Sch./Mass. Gen. Hosp., 1940-41. Fellow ACP; mem. Intern. Soc. Exptl. Hematology, Am. Soc. Hematology, Western Soc. Clin. Rsch., Cen. Soc. Clin. Rsch., Sigma Xi (fellow 1951). Democrat. Jewish. Office: Long Beach Cmty Hosp Bixby Hematology-Oncology Lab 1760 Termino Ave G-20 Long Beach CA 90804-2105

KURSTIN, RONALD DALE, general and oncologic surgeon, educator; b. Washington, July 6, 1945; s. William and Sally (Greenbaum) K.; m. Coralie Bendheim, June 6, 1971; children: Randy, Todd, Joshua, Melanie. BA in Pre-med., Tulane U., 1967; MD, George Washington U., 1971. Diplomate Am. Bd. Surgery. Intern U. Minn., 1971-72; resident surgery George Washington U., Washington, 1972-75, chief resident, instr. surgery, 1975-76, asst. clin. prof., 1979—; surg. attending physician Landstuhl (Germany) Army Med. Ctr., 1976-79; house physician Wolf Trap Park for Performing Arts, Fairfax, Va., 1988—; cons. Nat. Capital Reciprocal Ins. Co., Washington, 1990-93. Presenter in field; contbr. artilces to profl. jours. Guardian Washington Hebrew Home, Rockville, Md., 1994. Major U.S. Army, 1976-79. Recipient Physicians Recognition award AMA. Fellow Southeastern Surg. Congress; mem. Jacobi Med. Soc., D.C. Med. Soc., Chesapeak Colo-rectal Soc., Woodmount Country Club. Jewish.

KURTH, MATTHIAS C., neurologist; b. Leipzig, Germany, Mar. 16, 1955; m. Janice Hall, May 23, 1987; children: Carol, Susan. BA, Rice U., 1977; PhD, Baylor U., 1986, MD, 1986. Asst. prof. dept. neurology Tex. Tech. U., Lubbock, 1991-93; med. dir. Young Parkinson Referral Ctr., Santa Maria, Calif., 1993-95; asst. clin. dir. Nat. Parkinson Found., Miami, Fla., 1995—; assoc. dir. movement disorders Barrow Neurol. Inst., Phoenix, 1993-96, co-dir. movement disorders, 1996—. Recipient Cohen scholarship, Houston, 1973; grantee Welch Found., 1976; predoctoral fellow NIH, 1977. Office: St Josephs Hosp & Med Ctr Barrow Neurol Inst 222 W Thomas Rd Ste 401 Phoenix AZ 85013

KURTZ, ALFRED BERNARD, radiologist; b. Albany, N.Y., May 1, 1944; s. Leonard David and Esther (Lederman) K.; m. Barbara Ellen, July 3, 1973; children: Dana, Liza, Amy. BA, NYU, 1966; MD, Stanford U., 1972. Diplomate Am. Bd. Radiology. Internal medicine intern Montefiore Hosp. and Med. Ctr., Bronx, N.Y., 1972-73, resident in internal medicine, 1973-74, resident in diagnostic radiology, 1974-77; fellow in ultrasound and body CT Jefferson Med. Coll., Thomas Jefferson Univ. Hosp., Phila., 1977-78, assoc. prof. ob/gyn, 1982-85; assoc. dir. Div. of U.S. and Radiol. Imaging, Phila., 1982-86, Body Computed Tomography, Thomas Jefferson U. Hosp., Phila., 1986-89, Div. Diagnostic U.S., Thomas Jefferson U. Hosp., Phila., 1986-89; prof. radiology Jefferson Med. Coll., Thomas Jefferson U. Hosp., Phila., 1983—, prof. ob/gyn., 1985—, vice chmn. dept. radiology, 1989—; fellowship ultrasound and body ct. Montefiore Hosp. and Med. Ctr., Bronx, N.Y., 1977-78; examiner oral bds. in ultrasound category Am. Bd. Radiology, 1985—; med. advisor Blue Shield of Pa., Phila., 1983—; mem. adv. com. Ctr. of Excellence in Biomed. Imaging, Phila., 1987—. Author: Ultrasound: The Requisites, 1995, Obstetrical Measurements in Ultrasound: A Reference Manual, 1988; editor: Atlas of Ultrasound Measurements, 1990; contbr. articles to profl. jours. Grantee Nat. Cancer Inst., NIH, 1993-96. Fellow Am. Inst. Ultrasound in Medicine (bd. govs. 1990-92, sec. 2993-97), Am. Coll. Radiology (chmn. com. on edn. and tng. of commn. 1987-93, commn. on ultrasound 1987-93), Soc. Radiologists in Ultrasound (pres. 1991-93), Coll. Physicians Phila. Home: 1050 Indian Creek Rd Wynnewood PA 19096-3407 Office: Thomas Jefferson U Hosp 111 S 11th St Philadelphia PA 19107-4824

KURTZ, KENNETH JOHN, internist, educator; b. Pitts., Feb. 20, 1944; s. John Edmund and Elizabeth (Weimer) K.; m. Patricia Mae Albright, Dec. 17, 1972; 1 child, Roger. BA in Biology with honors, Williams Coll., 1966; MD, Cornell U., 1970; postgrad., Naval Aerospace Med. Inst., 1972. Diplomate Nat. Bd. Med. Examiners; diplomate in internal medicine and geriatric medicine Am. Bd. Internal Medicine. Fellow in Endocrinology U. Wash., Seattle, 1970-71; intern U. Calif., San Diego, 1971-72; resident II, III in internal medicine U. Calif., San Francisco, 1976-78; clin. prof. internal medicine U. Nev. Sch. Medicine, Reno, 1990—; mem. active staff VA Med. Ctr., Reno, 1978—. Contbr. chpts. to books, articles to med. jours. Served as flight surgeon USN, 1973-76. Recipient Dwight Bot. prize, 1966, Seligman award, 1970, citation for Outstanding Advocacy and Teaching, U. Nev. Med. Sch., 1992. Fellow ACP. Home: 3235 Markridge Dr Reno NV 89509-3837 Office: VA Med Ctr 1000 Locust St Reno NV 89520-0111

KURTZ, PERRY JAMES, toxicologist; b. Staten Island, N.Y., Aug. 13, 1948; s. Arthur Joseph and Isabel Tiffany (Perry) K.; m. Adore Marie Flynn, Aug. 28, 1971; children—Robert, Brian. B.S., Fordham U., 1970; M.S., Syracuse U., 1973, Ph.D., 1975. Instr. Syracuse U., N.Y., 1974; prin. research toxicologist Battelle Meml. Inst., Columbus, Ohio, 1978-79, assoc. mgr. toxicology and pharmacology sect., 1979-80, sr. research toxicologist, 1981-84; rsch. assoc. Stauffer Chem. Co. Environ. Health Ctr., Farmington, Conn., 1984-88, program mgr. Battelle Meml. Inst., 1988-90, sr. program mgr., 1991-94; assoc. dir. Regulatory Toxicology, Wyeth-Ayerst Res., Chazy, N.Y., 1994-96, dir. regulatory toxicology, 1996—; adj. asst. prof. Ohio State U., 1979-84; lectr. Wayne State U., Detroit, 1979-86. Mem. editorial bd. Drug and Chem. Toxicology, Jour. of Am., Coll. Toxicology. Named Prin. Investigator, Nat. Cancer Inst., 1978-84, Nat. Inst. Environ. Health Sci., 1978-84. Capt. U.S. Army, 1975-78. Mem. AAAS, Soc. Toxicology, Am. Coll. Toxicology, Am. Indsl. Health Coun. Coms., Chem. Mfrs. Assn., Sigma Xi. Office: Wyent Ayerst Rsch PO Box 150 Chazy NY 12921

KURTZ, SUZANNE MARIE, gerontology nurse, educator; b. Buffalo, Feb. 3, 1954; d. Ronald and Mary (Manns) K. BSN, D'Youville Coll., Buffalo, 1975; MS in Nursing, SUNY, Buffalo, 1980. Diabetes teaching nurse Buffalo Gen. Hosp., 1982-83; instr. Sisters Hosp. Sch. Nursing, Buffalo, 1983-87; insvc./infection control coord. Amherst Presbyn. Nursing Ctr., Williamsville, N.Y., 1987-89; clin. coord. skilled nursing facility DeGraff Meml. Hosp., North Tonawanda, N.Y., 1989-90; DON skilled nursing facility De Graff Meml. Hosp., 1990-91; mem. DNS Niagara Luth. Delaware Home, Inc., 1991-92; nurse mgr. St. Catherine Laboure Health Care Ctr., Buffalo, 1993; ret. Mem. Am. Diabetes Assn. (vol.), Juvenile Diabetes Found., Profl. Nurses Assn. We. N.Y., N.Y. State Nurses Assn. Home: 8 Christopher Dr Buffalo NY 14224-4002

KURTZ, THEODORE STEPHEN, psychoanalyst, educator; b. N.Y.C., Apr. 25, 1944; s. Maxwell Arthur and Evelyn R. (Rosenberg) K.; A.B., Boston U., 1964; M.A., N.Y. U., 1965; postgrad. N.Y. Soc. Freudian Psychologists, 1968-74; m. Maritza J. Zurita, Sept. 12, 1975. Caseworker, N.Y.C. Dept. Social Services, 1965-66; tchr., coordinator classes for emotionally disturbed Northport (N.Y.) Pub. Schs., 1966-70; pvt. practice psychoanalytic psychotherapy, 1968—; prin. Luther E. Woodward Sch. for Emotionally Disturbed Children, Freeport, N.Y., 1970-74; asst. prof. edn. C.W. Post Coll., L.I. U., Greenvale, N.Y., 1974-81; psychol. cons. to pvt. industry, 1971—. Diplomate Am. Inst. Counseling and Psychotherapy; cert. Soc. for Psychoanalytic Psychotherapy. Fellow Am. Orthopsychiat. Assn.; mem. Am. Assn. Marriage and Family Counselors (clin. mem.), Am. Acad. Psychotherapists, Am. Group Psychotherapy Assn., Am. (asso.), Nassau County (exec. bd. 1977-78, chmn. com. on acad. psychology 1977-78) psychol. assns., N.Y. Soc. Clin. Psychologists (asso.), Am. Inst. Profl. Con-s.'s (sr.), Am. Soc. Tng. and Devel., Acad. Psychologists in Marital, Sex and Family Therapy, Council Advancement of Psychol. Professions and Scis. Jewish. Contbr. articles to profl. jours. Home: Willow Brook Rd PO Box 529 Cold Spring Harbor NY 11724-0529

KURTZKE, JOHN FRANCIS, SR., neurologist, epidemiologist; b. Bklyn., Sept. 14, 1926; s. John Ambrose and Teresa Rose (Knipper) K.; m. Margaret Mary Nevin, June 30, 1950; children: John Francis Jr., Catherine Kurtzke Brown, Elizabeth Kurtzke Siebert, Joan Kurtzke Brennan, Robert, James, Christine Kurtzke Hughes. B.S. summa cum laude, St. John's U., 1948; M.D., Cornell U., 1952. Diplomate in neurology Am. Bd. Psychiatry and Neurology (asst. examiner, then examiner and sr. examiner in neurology 1964—, cert. appreciation 1990). Intern Kings County Hosp., Bklyn., 1952-53; resident in neurology VA Hosp., Bronx, N.Y., 1953-56; chief neurology service VA hosps. Coatesville, Pa., 1956-63, Washington, 1963-95; chief neuroepidemiology sect. VA Med. Ctr., Washington, 1995—; mem. faculty Jefferson Med. Coll., Phila., 1958-63, asst. prof. clin. neurology, 1963; mem. faculty Georgetown Med. Sch., Washington, 1963—, prof. neurology, 1968—, vice chmn. dept. neurology, 1976-95, prof. cmty. and family medicine, 1968-95; Disting. prof. neurology uniformed svcs. U. Health Scis., Bethesda, 1992—, USN med. student liaison officer, 1979-85; vis. prof. neurology and neuroepidemiology Temple U. Sch. Medicine, 1984-89; cons. neurology Nat. Naval Med. Ctr., Bethesda, 1966—, Surgeon Gen. Navy, 1970—; mem. med. adv. bd. Nat. Multiple Sclerosis Soc., 1966-94, hon. mem., 1995—, mem. working group on design of clin. studies in multiple sclerosis, 1976-84, mem. exec. com., 1981-83; med. adv. bd. Internat. Fedn. Multiple Sclerosis Socs., 1972—, mem. specialist adv. group, 1991—; mem. com. multiple sclerosis World Fedn. Neurology, 1967—, com. neuroepidemiology, 1977—; chmn. epidemiology sect. NIH Epilepsy Adv. Com., 1973-76; med. rsch. program specialist for neurology and neurobiology VA Rsch. Svc., 1977-80; chmn. work group epidemiology HEW Commn. Control of Huntington's Disease, 1976-78; mem. naval exam. bd. Naval Med. Command, 1980-83; mem. Residency Rev. Com. Neurology, 1983-88, vice chmn., 1985-86, chmn., 1987-88; chmn. U.S. Naval Res. Med. Flag Coun., 1985-86; mem. instnl. rev. bd. Nat. Inst. Neurol. Diseases and Stroke, 1989—; established investigator Nat. Multiple Sclerosis Soc., 1987—; mem. spl. panel Inst. Medicine, 1990. Author, co-author: Epidemiology of Multiple Sclerosis, 1968, Epidemiology of Cerebrovascular Disease, 1969, Epidemiology of Neurologic and Sense Organ Disorders, 1973; mem. editorial bd. Neuroepidemiology, 1980—, Neurology, 1984-92, Stroke, 1986—, Jour. Clin. Epidemiology, 1988—, Jour. Neurol. Sci., 1990-96, Acta Neurologica Scandinavica, 1990—; contbr. more than 400 articles to profl. jours., chpts. to books. Served with USN, 1944-46; rear adm. M.C., USNR, ret. 1986. Decorated Legion of Merit, Navy Commendation medal, Armed Forces Res. medal; recipient cert. of merit Surgeon Gen. of Navy, 1969, Gold Vicennial medal Georgetown U., 1982, others. Fellow AAAS, ACP, Am. Acad. Neurology (chmn. sect. on neuro-epidemiology 1971-75, chmn. com. nat. needs in neurology 1981-85, subcom. nat. needs in neurology 1985-86), Am. Coll. Epidemiology, N.Y. Acad. Sci., Am. Coll. Preventive Medicine, Pan Am. Med. Assn. (coun. neurology sect.), Am. Heart Assn. (stroke coun. 1991—); mem. AAUP, AMA, So. Med. Assn., Assn. Mil. Surgeons (life), Am. Neurol. Assn. (chmn. bylaws ad hoc com. 1990-91), Am. Epidemiol. Soc., Internat. Epidemiol. Assn., Assn. Rsch. in Nervous and Mental Disease, Am. Public Health Assn., Soc. Epidemiol. Rsch., Am. Epilepsy Soc., Am. Soc. Microbiology, Internat. Stroke Soc., Senior Stroke Soc., Danish Neurol. Soc. (hon.), French Soc. Neurology (hon., fgn.), Soc. Med. Cons. to Armed Forces (com. on res. affairs 1980-83, com. on manpower 1984—), German Soc. Neurology (hon.), Naval Res. Assn. (life), Naval Order U.S. (life), Res. Officers Assn. (life), Naval Inst. (life), Fleet Res. Assn. (life), Navy League (life), The Ret. Officers Assn. (life). Home: 7509 Salem Rd Falls Church VA 22043-3240 Office: VA Med Ctr 50 Irving St NW Washington D

KURTZMAN, NEIL A., medical educator; b. Bklyn., June 18, 1936; s. Louis S. and Roselie (Yegla) K.; m. Sandra Sabatini, Feb. 14, 1976; children from previous marriage: Jonathan, Laura. BA with honors, Williams Coll., 1957; MD, N.Y. Med. Coll., 1961. Intern Robert Packer Hosp., Sayre, Pa., 1961-62; resident Ohio State U. Hosp., Columbus, 1962-63; asst. chief med. services Nobel Army Hosp., Ft. McClellan, Ala., 1963-64; med. resident William Beaumont Gen. Hosp., El Paso, Tex., 1964-65, chief med. resident, 1965-66; fellow in nephrology U. Tex. Southwestern Med. Sch., Dallas, 1966-68; chief renal div. Brooke Army Med. Ctr., Ft. Sam Houston, Tex., 1969-72; prof., chief nephrology sect. U. Ill. Coll. Medicine, Chgo., 1972-84; Arnett prof., chmn. dept. internal medicine, chief nephrology div. Tex. Tech U. Health Scis. Ctr., Lubbock, 1985—, chief of staff univ. med. ctr., 1990-92; mem. gen. medicine B study sect. Nat. Inst. Arthritis, Metabolic and Digestive Diseases, Bethesda, Md., 1978-83; mem. merit rev. bd. VA, Washington, 1979-82, chmn., 1981-82; mem. sci. adv. bd. Nat. Kidney Found., N.Y.C., 1981-92, chmn., 1988-90, v.p., 1990-92, pres., 1992-94; prin. investigator regulation urinary acidification NIH, Bethesda, 1978—. Author: Handbook of Urinalysis and Urinary Sediment, 1974, Pathophysiology of the Kidney, 1977; also more than 270 sci. papers, more than 600 sci. presentations; editor-in-chief Seminars in Nephrology, 1981—; assoc. editor Am. Jour. Nephrology; mem. editorial bd. 7 sci. jours.; referee 16 sci. jours. Faculty advisor Alpha Omega Alpha, U. Ill., 1977-84, Tex. Tech U. Health Sci. Ctr., 1985—. Served to lt. col. U.S. Army, 1963-72. Decorated U.S. Army Meritorious Svc. award; recipient Pres.'s award Nat. Kidney Found., 1990, Outstanding Acad. Achievement award N.Y. Med. Coll., 1992, So. Soc. for Clin. Investigation's Founder's award, 1996. Mem. Am. Physiol. Soc., Am. Soc. Clin. Investigation, Assn. Am. Physicians, Cen. Soc. Clin. Research, So. Soc. Clin. Investigation, Alpha Omega Alpha. Office: Tex Tech U Health Scis Ctr Sch of Medicine Lubbock TX 79430

KURZ, FRANK JOSEPH, physician; b. Oakland, Calif., Jan. 17, 1952; s. Stan G. and Anne E. (Jarboe) K.; m. Mary Catherine, Apr. 6, 1974; children: Catherine, Michael. BS in Engring., U. Calif., Berkeley; MD, Baylor Coll. Medicine. Intern U. Oreg. Health Scis. Ctr., Portland, 1978-79, resident, 1979-81; physician Cascade Physicians, Portland, 1981—, pres., 1992—; pres. Cascade Med. Group, Portland, 1992—; chmn. bd. dirs. Managed Health Care N.W., Portland, 1989-95. Mem. Northwest Proup Practices Assn. (pres. 1995—), Assn. Northwest Physicians (pres. 1987-92). Mem. Soc. of Friends. Office: Cascase Med Group 2222 NW Lovejoy #505 Portland OR 97210

KURZENBERGER, DICK, health services executive; b. Ind., Nov. 26, 1949; children: Jon Ross, Blake Mead. BBA, Ft. Lauderdale U., 1970; MBA, U. Palm Beach, 1971. Asst. dir. St. Mary's Hosp., West Palm Beach, Fla., 1972-75; adminstr. The Hauser Clinic, Houston, 1975-79, Post Oak Psychiatry, Houston, 1979-86; asst. adminstr. Green Oaks Hosp., Dallas, 1986-88; div. adminstr. St. Joseph Hosp., Houston, 1988-90; exec. dir., chief exec. officer Greenwood Group, Houston, 1990-92; div. mgr. Kelsey Seybold Clinic, Houston, 1992—; pres., bd. dirs. Mental Health Assn. of Houston and Harris County, 1989-90; chmn. psychiat. sect. Greater Houston Hosp., 1988-90; del. dir. State Mental Health Bd., Austin, 1987-92. V.p. MHA Houston, 1982-86, Dallas, 1987; del. Mental Health Needs Coun., Houston, 1989-90. Recipient Vol. of Yr. award United Way, 1986, MM award M.M. Anderson, 1978, John Z. Rasco award, 1993, BBH Adminstr. of Yr. award, 1994. Mem. Tex. Hosp. Assn., Med. Group Mgmt. Assn. Home: 8803 Ashridge Park Dr Spring TX 77379 Office: Kelsey Seybold Clinic 5757 Woodway Dr Houston TX 77057-1506

KURZER, ANN ROBIN, optometrist; b. Dayton, Ohio, Aug. 13, 1961; d. Michael Kurzer and Fern (Seidenstein) Archer; m. Steven Charles Sherbet, June 11, 1989; children: Michael Charles, Evan Harris. OD, Ohio State U., 1985. Staff optometrist, rschr. Vistech Cons., Inc., Dayton, Ohio, 1984-88; staff optometrist HMO, Dayton, 1985-89, B.C. Vision, Inc., Dayton, 1987—. Contbr. articles to profl. jours. Bd. dirs. Young Women's Divsn. Jewish Fedn., Dayton, 1995-96. Mem. Am. Optometric Assn., Miami Valley Optometric Soc., Ohio Optometric Assn., Ohio State Alumni Assn., Epsilon Psi Epsilon. Republican. Home: 3758 Greenbay Dr Dayton OH 45415 Office: Spectacle Shop 2762 Wilmington Pike Dayton OH 45419

KURZWEIL, ALAN DENNIS, social worker, marriage and family therapist, consultant; b. N.Y.C., May 27, 1950; s. Raffael and Hilda Molly (Meisel) K.; m. Paula Lee Backstrom, Oct. 24, 1971; children: Jeffrey Michael, Justin Henry. BA in Psychology, Allegheny Coll., 1971; MSSA, Case Western Reserve, 1976. Diplomate Clin. Social Work; lic. ind. social worker, Ohio. Theraeputic activities worker Polk (Pa.) State Sch., 1972-74; planning intern Geauga County Mental Health Bd., Chardon, Ohio, 1974-75; clin. social worker intern Akron Child Guidance Ctr., Barberton, Ohio, 1975-76; clin. social worker Western Reserve Human Services, Akron, Ohio, 1976-88; psychiatric social worker Kaiser-Permanente, Akron, 1988-91, regional coord. of psychiatric social work, Ohio region, 1991—; pvt. practice marriage and family therapist Fairlawn, Ohio, 1983—; co-dir. Stages, Fairlawn, 1984—. Coach N.W. Akron Indoor Soccer, 1986-87; asst. coach Revere Soccer Club, 1991-94; team capt. Summit County Slow Pitch Club, 1984-94. Mem. NASW (dist. sec. 1980-82, dist. treas. 1982-86, mental health chairperson 1980-91, dist. v.p. 1986-89, Social Worker of Yr. 1988), Registry Clin. Social Workers. Democrat. Jewish. Home: 4601 Pinewood Path Akron OH 44321-1246 Office: Fairlawn Med Bldg 3094 W Market St Ste 120 Fairlawn OH 44333

KUSHNER, MARLA DIANE, physician; b. Des Moines, Apr. 12, 1960; d. Sander Allen and Elinor Sue (Prady) K.; m. Robert Marvin Sawyer, Jr., May 26, 1991; children: Jordan Daniel, Noah Evan. Student, Mich. State U., 1978-81, DO, 1985. Diplomate Am. Osteo Bd. Family Physicians. Rotating internship Botsford Gen. Hosp., Farmington Hills, Mich., 1985-86, resident in gen. practice, 1986-87; resident in gen. practice and adolescent medicine Chgo. Osteopathic Med. Ctr., 1987-89; resident in adolescent and young adult medicine Rush-Presbyn. St. Luke's, Chgo., 1987-89; assoc. med. dir. youth program Parkside Lodge of DuPage, Downers Grove, Ill., 1989-90; staff physician Chgo. Osteopathic Acad. Med. Practice Plan, 1989-92; med. dir. inpatient/outpatient programs Parkside Recovery Ctr. at Little Company of Mary Hosp., Evergreen Park, Ill., 1990-94; pvt. practice Evergreen Park, Ill., 1992-94; assoc. med. dir. outpatient program Luth. Gen. Recovery Ctr. of Mundelein, Vernon Hills, Ill., 1995—; dir. adolescent medicine Mercy Hosp., Chgo., 1996; affiliate clin. asst. prof. Midwestern U., Downers Grove, Ill.; lectr. in field; mem. med. staff Am. Diabetic Assn. Teen Camp, Iron River, Mich., 1987, 88, attending med. dir., 1989, mem. med. staff, Lake Geneva, Wis., 1988; team physician Kenwood Acad. Football Team, Chgo., 1988; rsch. assoc., clin. interviewer AMA Adolescent suicide study, 1988-89. Recipient Mead Johnson grant Nat. Osteopathic Found., 1988. Mem. Am. Osteopathic Assn., Am. Coll. Osteopathic Family Physicians, Am. Soc. Addiction Medicine (cert.), Soc. for Adolescent Medicine, Ill. Assn. Osteopathic Physicians and Surgeons. Jewish. Office: Mercy Hosp 2525 S Michigan Ave Chicago IL 60616-2477

KUSHNER, RICHARD MICHAEL, podiatrist; b. Bronx, Feb. 27, 1946; s. David and Miriam (Reitman) K.; m. Michaele Rose Lebenbaum, Aug. 27, 1967; children: Bradley Daniel, Alexandre Stephan, Elizabeth Sarah. BA, NYU, 1966; DPM, N.Y. Coll. Podiatric Medicine, 1970. Chief podiatry New Rochelle (N.Y.) Hosp., 1970-77, New Brighton Hosp. and New Vanderbilt Hosp., S.I., N.Y., 1971-77; attending podiatrist Workmen's Cir. Clinic, N.Y.C., 1971-73. Mem. Navy League.

KUSY, ROBERT PETER, biomedical engineering and orthodontics educator; b. Worcester, Mass., Oct. 19, 1947; s. Stanley J. and Mary B. (Rutkiewicz) K.; m. Gisela Bauer, June 27, 1969; children: Kimberly, Kevin. BSME, Worcester (Mass.) Poly. Inst., 1969; MSMetE, Drexel U., 1971, PhD in Materials Sci., 1973. Rubber rsch. technician Vellumoid Gasket Corp. divsn. Fed.-Mogul Corp., Worcester, 1966-69; rsch. asst. dept. metall. engring. Drexel U., Phila., 1969-72; rsch. assoc. Dental Rsch. Ctr., U. N.C., Chapel Hill, 1972-74, asst. prof. oral biology dept. orthodontics, Dental Rsch., 1974-79, assoc. prof. orthodontics dept. orthodontics, Dental Rsch., 1979-89, assoc. prof. biomed. engring. Sch. Medicine, 1985-89; prof. orthodontics, prof. biomed. engring. Schs. Dentistry and Medicine, U. N.C., Chapel Hill, 1989—, adj. prof. curriculum applied scis., 1990—; mem. adminstrv. bd. Grad. Sch. U. N.C., Chapel Hill, 1989-95; cons. Internat. Nickel, Structure-Probe, DuPont, Kodak, CTL Tech., Rising Star, Smiling Faces, Epolin, Dental Rsch. Corp., Tracor Aerospace, Enron Chem., Unitek, 3M, Ormco Corp., Flexmedics Corp., Lancer Orthodontics, Aristech, Orthodontic Ptnrs., Hutchinson Tech., Wyeth-Ayerst Rsch., Composite Products, A-Company, Ortho Organizers, U. N.C.; reviewer small projects grants NIH, 1985—, project site visitor, 1986—; mem. bd. sci. adv. com. Epolin Corp., 1986-89. Mem. rev. staff Am. Jour. Orthodontics, 1982—, Polymer, 1985—, Jour. Applied Polymer Sci., 1985—, Dental Materials, 1986—, Jour. Polymer Sci., 1987—, Jour. Biomed. Materials Rsch.-Applied Biomaterials, 1989—; mem. adv. bd. Jour. Materials Sci., Materials in Medicine; contbr. over 150 articles to profl. jours. Pres. Hills of the Haw Home Owners' Assn., 1986-88; mem. pastoral coun. Newman Ctr., 1986-87; organizer Sr. Basketball Club, Chapel Hill Cmty. Ctr., 1985-88; coach Children's Basketball League, Chapel Hill, Carrboro, 1981-82, 83-86; mem. ch. choir, 1987-89, 92—. Capt. U.S. Army, 1969-77. Recipient Johnson & Johnson Focused Giving award, 1993-96, B.F. Dewel Hon. Rsch. award, 1995, Orthodontics Tchg. award, 1996. Mem. N.Am. Thermal Analysis Soc., Am. Soc. Materials, Am. Chem. Soc. (divsn. polymer chemistry divsn. phys. chemistry), Internat. Assn. Dental Rsch., Am. Assn. Dental Rsch., Internat. Metallographic Soc., Soc. Biomaterials, Soc. Plastics Engrs. Roman Catholic. Office: U NC Bldg 210H Rm 313 CB # 7455 Chapel Hill NC 27599

KUTROVATZ, MARIA I., medical technologist; b. Ercsi, Hungary, Dec. 3, 1937; arrived in U.S., 1969; d. John and Maria (Laczkovics) K. Medical tech. degree, Hungary, 1959. Medical tech. Children's Meml. Hosp., Chgo., 1985-89, St. Joseph Hosp., Chgo., 1980-85, Talcott Int. Medicine, Chgo., 1989-92, Chgo., 1993-95, CNA, Chgo., 1995—; medical tech. in hosps., Austria, 1964-69. Office: AMT Park Ridge IL 60056

KUTSCHER, KATHLEEN ANN, social welfare administrator, social worker; b. Springfield, Mass., Dec. 1, 1955; d. Henry W. and Gloria R. (Gallegos) Stepanik; m. William Lee Kutscher, Dec. 15, 1979 (div. Dec. 1987). BA in Sociology, U. Colo., 1983; MSW, U. Denver, 1985. Dir. ret. sr. vol. program Vols. of Am., Denver, 1985-86; coord. exceptional family mem. program U.S. Army/Fitzsimons Med. Ctr., Aurora, Colo., 1986-87; coord. state family program Colo. Army N.G., Denver, 1987-89; mgr. family advocacy program U.S. Army, Wildflecken, Germany, 1989-91, dir. army community svc., 1990-91; supervising social worker U.S. Army, Vilseck, Germany, 1991-94; mental health utilization mgr. managed care divsn. Madigan Army Med. Ctr., Tacoma, Wash., 1994—. Mem. allocation com. Mile High United Way, Denver, 1986-87. Sgt. U.S. Army, 1976-82, ETO. Mem. NASW. Democrat. Roman Catholic. Home: 10907 62nd St E Puyallup WA 98372-2738

KUURE, BOJAN MARLENA, operating room nurse; b. Jakobstad, Finland, Nov. 14, 1942; d. Anders Arne and Aina Viktoria (Back) Sundqvist; m. Arvo Antero Kuure, Nov. 3, 1965; 1 child, Saara Bojan. Diploma, Helsingfors Svenska Sjukvardsinstitut, Helsinki, Finland, 1964; specialty nursing in anesthia & surgery, Helsingfors Svenska Sjukvards, Helsinki, Finland, 1967-68; Aprubatur in Edn., U. Helsinki, 1972. Staff nurse U. Finland Hosp., 1964-67, specialty nurse, 1968-70; tchr. dir. Nursing Inst., Helsinki, 1970-72; oper. rm. nurse Island Hosp., Anacortes, Wash., 1972-83, surg. dir., 1983. Vol. Interplast, Inc., Healing the Children. Mem. Am. Assn. Oper. Rm. Nurses, Oper. Rm. Mgrs. Wash., Wash. State Coun. Peri-op Nursing, Wash. Orgn. Nurse Execs. Home: 1201 5th St Anacortes WA 98221-1709

KUVIN, SEYMOUR FLEISHFARB, psychiatrist; b. Newark, Nov. 30, 1924; s. Jacob Fleishfarb and Frieda Kuvin; m. Judith Kate Saxe (dec.); children: June Volk, Joshua. BS, Pa. State U., 1948, MS, 1949; MB, Chgo. Med. Sch., 1953, MD, 1954. Diplomate Am. Bd. Pediatrics. Intern Morristown (N.J.) Meml. Hosp., 1953-54; resident in pediatrics St. Michael's Med. Ctr., Newark, 1954-56; resident in psychiatry Greystone Park Psychiat. Hosp., 1967-70; dir. psychiat. inst. Psychiat. Inst., Newark, 1970-90; sr. attending psychiatrist St. Michael's Med. Ctr., Newark, 1971-90, psychiatrist emeritus, 1990—; pvt. practice pediatrics Morristown, 1956-70; med. dir. Morris County Sch. Emotionally Disabled, Morris Plains, N.J., 1961-67; clin. asst. prof. psychiatry U. Medicine and Dentistry of N.J., Newark, 1970-90; assoc. prof. psychiatry Seton Hall Grad. Sch. Medicine, 1988—; prin. psychiatrist N.J. Bell, Newark, 1971-90. Contbr. articles to profl. jours. Active Bd. Health, Morristown, 1965-69; docent Turtle Back Zoo, West Orange, 1982-90; post surgeon VFW, Livingston, N.J., 1986-90, sr. vice comdr., 1990-92, comdr., 1993-94. Cpl. U.S. Army, 1941-46. Fellow Am. Acad. Pediatrics, Am. Coll. Physicians, Falk fellow Am. Psychiat. Assn. Jewish. Office: 1735 Hooper Ave Toms River NJ 08753

KUWABARA, DENNIS MATSUICHI, optometrist; b. Honolulu, July 20, 1945; s. Robert Tokuichi and Toshiko (Nakashima) K.; m. Judith Naomi Tokumaru, June 28, 1970; children: Jennifer Tomiko, Susan Kazuko. BS, So. Calif. Coll. Optometry, 1968, OD cum laude, 1970. Pvt. practice optometry Waipahu, Honolulu, Hawaii, 1972—; pres. 1st Study Club for Optometrists, Honolulu, 1982-83; chmn. Bd. Examiners in Optometry, Honolulu, 1982-90; state dir. Optometric Extension Found., Honolulu, 1980-88. Served to lt. Med. Service Corps, USN, 1970-72. Named Outstanding Young Person of Hawaii, Hawaii State Jaycees, 1979. Fellow Am. Acad. Optometry (diplomate cornea and contract lens sect. 1991); mem. Hawaii Optometric Assn. (pres. 1979-80, Man of Yr. award 1976, Optometrist of Yr. 1983), Am. Optometric Assn., Armed Forces Optometric Soc. Home: 94-447 Holaniku St Mililani HI 96789-1710 Office: 94-748 Hikimoe St Waipahu HI 96797-3350 also: 1441 Kapiolani Blvd Ste 710 Honolulu HI 96814-4404

KUWAMOTO, RODERICK DEAN, JR., physician assistant, perfusionist, educator; b. Ft. Dix, N.J., Mar. 9, 1949; s. Roderick Dean Kuwamoto and Albertina Carolina (Gasser) Niest; m. Constance Marie Elslander, July 9, 1988; children: Michael, Brett, Matthew. AAS, Ft. Steilacoom C.C., Steilacoom, Wash., 1977; student, U.S. Army Acad. Health Sci., Ft. Sam Houston, Tex., 1980-82; BS in Applied Health Care Sci., Creighton U., 1989; M Med. Sci., St. Francis Coll., Loretto, Pa., 1994. Cert. Nat. Commn. Cert. Physician Assts.; nat. cert. clin. perfusionist. Enlisted man U.S. Army, 1968, advanced through grades to maj., 1995; medic 10th U.S. Army 10th Spl. Forces, Ft. Devens, Mass., 1970-80; family practice physician asst. 197th Mechanized Inf. Brigade, Ft. Benning, Ga., 1982-87; troop med. clinic physician asst. Martin Army Cmty. Hosp., Ft. Benning, 1987-88; physician asst. clinic chief 122d Main Support Bn., 3d Armored Divsn., Hanau, Germany, 1988-90; aviation medicine physician asst. 3d Bn., 227th Aviation Brigade, Hanau, 1990-91; cardiovasc. surg. physician asst. Walter Reed Army Med. Ctr., Washington, 1991-92, clin. perfusionist, physician asst., 1992-93, chief perfusionist, 1993—, program dir. Sch. Cardiovasc. Perfusion Tech., 1992-95; officer in chg. Troop Med. Clinic, Aberdeen Proving Ground, Md., 1996—; cons., clin. perfusionist NIH, Bethesda, Md., 1990-93. Soccer coach, editor newsletter Columbus (Ga.) Youth Soccer, 1986-88; organizer, dir. Spl. Olympics, Hanua, 1989; sports medicine trainer U.S. Army European Champion All Star Soccer Team, Hanua, 1989-91. Decorated Bronze Star; named Physician Asst. of Yr. European Surgeon Gen., 1991. Fellow Am. Acad. Physician Assts.; mem. Am. Acad. Cardiovasc. Perfusion, Soc. Army Physician Assts., Perfusion Program Dirs. Coun. Home: 6215 Manchester Way Baltimore MD 21227 Office: Kirk Army Clinic Sch Cardio Perfusion Tech Aberdeen Proving Ground MD 21005

KUWAYAMA, S. PAUL, physician, allergist, immunologist; b. Sapporo, Hokkaido, Japan, Nov. 8, 1932; s. Satoru and Chiyoho (Nishikawa) Kuwayama; m. Barbara Ann Dresback, June 29, 1974; chidlren: David, Steven, Jason. BS, Hokkaido U., Sapporo, 1955, MD, 1959. Diplomate Am. Bd. Pediatrics, 1965, Am. Bd. Allergy & Immunology, 1972, Am. Bd. Pediatric Allergy, 1970; lic. Nat. Bd. Med. Examiners of Japan, 1959, Wis. State Bd. Med. Examiners, 1968, Ariz. State Bd. Med. Examiners, 1987, N.Mex. State Bd. Med. Examiners, 1987, Tenn. State Bd. Med. Examiners, 1992; cert. Am. Med. Qualification Examination. Intern U.S. Naval Hosp., Seattle, 1959-60, St. Mary's Hosp., Milw., 1960-61; jr. pediatric resident dept. pediatrics Temple U. Sch. of Medicine, Kansas City, 1961-62; chief pediatric resident dept. pediatrics W.Va. U. Sch. of Medicine, Morgantown, 1962-63; postdoctoral fellow in immunology, sr. fellow in pediatric allergy U. Kansas Sch. Medicine and The Children's Mercy Hosp., Kansas City, 1964-65; staff pediatrician atomic bomb casualty commn. in Hiroshima, U.S. Nat. Acad. of Scis. and U.S. Atomic Energy Commn., 1966-67; Dept. Immunobiology, U. Kansas Sch. Medicine, 1967-68; asst. clin. prof. pediatric allergy & immunology The Med. Coll. Wis., Milw., 1970—. Contbg. author chpt. and forward to books. Fulbright scholar, 1960-63. Fellow Am. Acad. Pediatrics (sect. on allergy & immunology), Am. Coll. Allergy & Immunology, Am. Assn. Cert. Allergists, Am. Acad. Allergy, Asthma and Immunology, Am. Assn. Clin. Immunology and Allergy; mem. AMA, Fulbright Scholarship Grantee Alumni Assn., State Med. Soc. of Wis., Milw. Pediatric Soc. Office: 11035 W Forest Home Ave Hales Corners WI 53130

KUYT, STEPHENIE LYNN, legal assistant, nurse; b. Grand Rapids, Mich., Nov. 13, 1952; d. Curtis Russell Broski and Virginia Ruth (Rudnick) Broski-Kuzins; div.; 1 child, Chad Hesselink. Grad. in nursing, Mercy Hosp., Cadillac, Mich., 1971; grad. with high honors, Para-Legal Inst., Phoenix, 1981. Lic. practical nurse, Mich. Nurse Osteo. Hosp., Grand Rapids, 1971-73, Mercy Hosp., 1972, Drs. Sentkeresty and Dark, Grand Rapids, 1974-79; legal asst. Norris, Keyser & Marshall, Grand Rapids, 1979-81, Baxter & Hammond, Grand Rapids, 1981-83; collections and legal asst. R & S Repossession and Collection Agy. Legal Asst. Svcs., Wyoming, Mich., 1984-85; med.-legal asst. Smith, Haughey, Rice & Roegge, Grand Rapids, 1985—; legal asst. Seminar on Investigation and Legal Assisting, 1985; presenter legal asst. employment Davenport Coll., 1991. Osteo Hosp. grantee, 1970. Mem. Mich. Bar Assn. (affiliate), Legal Assts. Assn. Mich., Kent County Legal Assts. Assn., Mich. Nurses Assn. Republican. Lutheran. Home: 3954 Monte Carlo Ct SE Kentwood MI 49512-1831 Office: Smith Haughey Rice & Roegge 200 Calder Plz Bldg Grand Rapids MI 49503

KUZMAK, LUBOMYR IHOR, surgeon; b. Balyhorod, Ukraine, Aug. 2, 1931; s. Wolodymyr and Lidia (Litynsky) K.; came to U.S., 1965, naturalized, 1968; MD, Med. Acad., Lodz, Poland, 1953; DSc, Silesian Acad. Medicine, Katowice, Poland, 1965. Diplomate Am. Bd. Surgery. m. Roxana A. Smishkewych, Jan. 22, 1966; 1 dau., Roxolana. Resident, chief resident in gen. surgery Silesian Acad. Medicine, III Surg. Clinic, Bytom, Poland, 1954-61, gen. surgeon head div., asso. prof., 1961-65; resident, chief resident in gen. surgery St. Barnabas Med. Ctr., Livingston, N.J., 1966-71; practice medicine specializing in gen. vascular and obesity surgery, Newark, 1971—; former chief of surgery Irvington (N.J.) Gen. Hosp.; mem. teaching staff St. Barnabas Med. Center, Livingston; lectr. in field; vis. surgeon obesity surgery Padua Univ., Italy, 1990—. Fellow Internat. Coll. Surgeons, Am. Soc. Abdominal Surgeons; mem. AMA (Physician's Recognition award 1970-79, 76-79, 79-82, 82-85, 85-88, 88-91, 91—), Am. Soc. Bariatric Surgery, Ukrainian Med. Assn. N.Am., Am. Soc. Contemporary Medicine and Surgery, Internat. Platform Assn. Contbr. articles to profl. jours., chpts. to books; patentee in field. Achievements include development of novel surgical procedure in the management of sever obesity: Stoma Adjustable Silicone Gastric Banding method. Office: 340 E Northfield Rd Ste 1 D Livingston NJ 07039-4812

KVEDAR, VICKI SHANGRAW, ophthalmologist; b. Hartford, Conn., Jan. 23, 1959; d. Robert Dixon and Mary Janice (Bonacker) Shangraw; m. Joseph Charles Kvedar, June 11, 1983; children: Derek, Julie, Megan. BS, U. Vt., 1981; student, U. Conn., 1981-82; MD, Boston U., 1987. Diplomate Am. Bd. Ophthalmology. Intern Boston U. Hosp., 1987-88; resident in ophthalmology Boston U. Affil. Hosps., 1988-91; clin. rsch. asst. in ocuplastics and botulinum toxin Mass. Eye and Ear Infirmary, Boston, 1991-92, gen. ophthalmologist Biopure-clin. trials on botulinum toxin, 1993-94; gen. ophthalmologist New Eng. Med. Ctr., Boston, 1991-92, Robert Freedman, MD, Swampscott, Mass., 1992-93, Eye Care Cons., Inc., Malden, Mass., 1994—. Fellow Am. Acad. Ophthalmology. Roman Catholic. Office: Eye Care Cons Inc 578 Main St Malden MA 02148

KWA, ANTHONY KIN-HO, orthopaedic surgeon; b. Hong Kong, Oct. 13, 1957; arrived in Australia, 1968; MBBS with honors, U. Sydney, Australia, 1983. Registered specialist med. practitioner N.S.W. Med. Bd. Intern Royal North Shore Hosp., Sydney, 1983-84, resident, 1984-85, sr. resident, 1985-86; surg. registrar Prince Wales Hosp./Prince Henry Hosp., Sydney, 1986-88; advanced surg. trainee Royal Australasian Coll. Surgeons, 1988-91; orthopaedic surgeon, cons., 1991—; cons. Royal Australian Air Force, 1991—; vis. orthopaedic surgeon Western Area Health, Sydney, 1992—; hon. orthopaedic surgeon No. Area Health, Sydney, 1994—. Fellow Royal Australasian Coll. Surgeons; mem. Internat. Soc. Orthopaedic Surgery and Traumatology, Australian Orthopaedic Assn., Australian Med. Assn. Office: Specialist Med Rms, 44 Denistone Rd Eastwood, Sydney NSW 2122, Australia

KWAAN, JACK HAU MING, retired physician; b. Hong Kong, Apr. 9, 1928; came to U.S., 1953; s. Y.K. and Rose W. Kwaan; m. Min K. Ho, Feb. 11, 1973; children: Mary, Peter, Rebecca, Nicholas. MD, U. Hong Kong, 1952. Diplomate Am. Bd. Radiology, Am. Bd. Surgery, Am. Bd. Thoracic Surgery. Resident in radiology Roswell Park Meml. Inst., 1955-56; chief resident Peter Bent Brigham Hosp., 1956-57; rsch. fellow in radiology Harvard Med. Sch., Boston, 1956-57; sr. cancer rsch. radiol. therapist Roswell Park Meml. Inst., Buffalo, 1958-59; asst. prof. radiology U. Ky., Lexington, 1963-65; resident in surgery U. Calif., Irvine, 1965-68; rsch. fellow oncologic surgery M.D. Anderson Hosp., Houston, 1968-69; resident in thoracic U. Calif., Irvine, 1969-71, chief resident thoracic surgery, 1970, asst. prof. surgery, 1972-73; chief vascular surgery sect., co-dir. vascular surgery tng. program U. Calif. Irvine/Long Beach VA Med. Ctr., 1974-87; prof. surgery U. Calif., Irvine, 1983-87; sr. resident in thoracic surgery U. So. Calif./L.A. County Med. Ctr., 1971; staff thoracic cardiovasc. surgeon Long Beach VA Hosp., 1972-73; asst. chief dept. surgery Valley Med. Ctr., Fresno, Calif., 1973-74; prof. surgery U. Okla., Tulsa, 1987-93; ret., 1993; chief dept. surgery Valley Med. Ctr., Fresno, Calif., 1973-74; chief vascular surgery sect. Long Beach VA Med. Ctr., 1974-87; surgical cons. Kaiser Permanente Hosp. Contbr. articles to profl. jours. Fellow Am. Coll. Surgeons; mem. Brit. Med. Assn., Gen. Med. Coun. London (registrant), Assn. Mil. Surgeons of U.S. (life), Assn. VA Surgeons, Internat. Cardiovascular Soc. Home: 2141 Ocana Ave Long Beach CA 90815

KWALICK, DONALD S., human services manager. BA, Rutgers U., 1960; MD, NYU, 1964; MPH, Columbia U., 1969. Diplomate Am. Bd. Med. Mgmt.; cert. pub. health Am. Bd. Preventive Medicine. Rotating intern U.S. Army Tripler Gen. Hosp., Hawaii, 1964-65; preventive medicine officer U.S. Army, Ft. Bliss, Tex., 1965-67; pub. health resident N.J. State Health Dept., 1967-70, dir. cmty. study of pesticides, 1969-71, asst. state health commr. cmty. health svcs., 1973-80, dir. pub. health residency program, 1975-80; med. dir. Trenton Neighborhood Health Ctr., 1971-73; clin. assoc. prof. cmty. medicine Rutgers Med. Sch., 1976-81; dir., county health officer Hillsborough County Health Dept., Tampa, Fla., 1980-90; clin. assoc. prof. U. So. Fla. Sch. Medicine, 1980-90, U. So. Fla. Coll. Pub. Health, 1983-90; prof. family cmty. medicine U. Nev. Sch. Medicine, 1990—; state health officer Nev. Health Divsn., 1990—; chmn. Nev. AIDS Task Force, 1993—, Nev. Medicaid Med. Adv. Com., 1993—; food and drug commr. Nev. FDA Commn., 1990—. Mem. manuscript rev. bd. Jour. of the Med. Soc. of N.J., 1978-80; mem. editl. bd. Fla. Jour. Pub. Health, consulting editor, 1986-90, mng. editor, 1988-90; contbr. articles to profl. jours.; presenter in field. Mem. exec. com. N.J. Devel. Disabilities Coun., 1973-80; chmn. N.J. Pub. Health Examining Bd., 1976-80; mem. Hillsborough County Anti-Drug Abuse Adv. Coun., 1990; founding mem., bd. dirs. Tampa Bay Planned Parenthood, 1984-88, Nev. Tobacco Prevention and Control Coalition, 1994, Nev. Pub. Health Found., Inc., 1996; bd. dirs. ARC, Tampa chpt., 1985-90, Tampa Cmty. Health Ctr., 1984-88, Boys and Girls Clubs Tampa, 1985-90, Ruskin Cmty. and Migrant Health Ctr., 1984-88, chmn. 1986; mem. Gulf Coast Health Sys. Agy., 1980-83, Health Insight Nev. State Coun., 1994—; mem. profl. edn. com. Am. Cancer Soc. Nev. chpt., 1991; mem. plan devel. com. Nev. State Health Coordinating Coun., chmn. prevention subcom., 1991-93, others. Trustee scholar Rutgers U., 1956-60, scholar Pub. Health Leadership Inst., 1991-92; Robert Wood Johnson Found. fellow, 1960-64; recipient Physician Recognition award AMA, 1966—. Fellow APHA (region VI affiliate rep. com. of affiliates 1988-90, chmn. reference com. 1991, mem. joint policy com. 1991), Am. Coll. Preventive Medicine; mem. am. coll. Physician Execs., Am. Assn. Pub. Health Physicians, Assn. of State and Territorial Health Ofcls. (mem. tobacco or health com. 1991, chmn. 1992-95, rep. to Am. Coll. Preventive Medicine task force 1992-93, mem. exec. com. 1995—), N.J. Health Officers Assn. (hon.), Nev. State Med. Soc. (mem. spl. com. on AIDS 1990-93, mem. com. on pub health 1993—, mem. task force on health and fitness 1993-95), Nev. Pub. Health Assn. (mem.-at-large 1991, mem. exec. bd., chmn. newsletter com.). Office: Dept Human Resources Health Divsn 505 E King St Rm 201 Carson City NV 89710

KWAN, GRACE, nurse, educator; b. Taipei, Taiwan, Feb. 12, 1963; came to U.S., 1977; d. Joshua and Esther (Tsai) Peng; m. Sik Chung Kwan, Dec. 3, 1981 (div. Mar. 1990); children: Wesley Jeffrey, Timothy Justin, Anthony James. BSN, Dominican Coll., 1993; FNP, MS, Pace U., 1996. RN, N.Y.; cert. med. surg. nurse. Sales mgr. Esther's Jewelry, Bronx, N.Y., 1985-91; RN N.Y. Hosp., N.Y.C., 1993—; adj. prof. nursing Pace U., Pleasantville, N.Y., 1995—; pres. Nursing Jour. Club N.Y. Hosp., 1995. Mem. Sigma Theta Tau. Home: 1 Queens Ct Orangeburg NY 10962

KWAN, MARCUS R., surgeon; b. L.A., Dec. 14, 1941. BS in Mec. Sci., U. Calif., San Francisco, 1963, MD, 1967. Diplomate Am. Bd. Surgery. Intern Bronx (N.Y.) Mcpl. Hosp. Ctr., 1967-68; resident in surgery Albert Einstein Coll. Medicine, Bronx, 1968-70, Ariz. Med. Ctr./U. Ariz., Tucson, 1972-74; NIH fellow in acad. surgery U. Calif., Berkeley, 1970-72; pvt. practice surgery Santa Cruz, Calif., 1977—; mem. staff Watsonville (Calif.) Cmty. Hosp., Dominican-Santa Cruz Hosp., Santa Cruz Surgery Ctr. Commr. Bd. Parks and Recreation, Santa Cruz County, 1990-94. Lt. comdr. U.S. Army, 1973-77. Fellow ACS; mem. Santa Cruz County Med. Assn., Calif. Med. Assn. Office: 1595 Soquel Dr # 340 Santa Cruz CA 95065

KWETKAUSKIE, JOHN A., medical technologist; b. Elizabeth, N.J., June 25, 1947; s. Albert and Genevieve (Loutinsky) K.; m. Patricia Manning, May 13, 1972; children: Brian R., Lara A. BS in Life Scis., N.Y. Inst. Tech., 1970. Cert. med. technologist, Pa. Med. technologist Geisinger Wyoming Valley Med. Ctr., Wilkes-Barre, Pa., 1974—; part-time EMT, edn. coord. & designated officerMed. Transport, Inc., Hazleton, Pa., 1988—; EMT instr. Pa. Dept. Health, Harrisburg, 1990—; adj. faculty Luzerne County C.C., 1994—, Lehigh Carbon County C.C., 1992—. Author: (instr. manuel) Prevention of Infectious Diseases - for EMS-Fire Fighter and Law Enforcement Personnel, 1996. With U.S. Army, 1970-74. Mem. Nat. Assn. EMS Educators. Office: Geisinger Wyoming Med Ctr 1000 E Mountain Dr Wilkes Barre PA 18711

KWIK-KOSTEK, CHRISTINE IRENE, physician, air force officer; b. Lvov, Poland, Sept. 12, 1939; d. Karol Stanislaus and Leonarda Fryderica (Seniuk) Kostek; widowed; children: Christine, Catherine. Grad. summa cum laude, Med. Acad. Cracow, Poland, 1956-62; student primary aerospace medicine course, Brooks AFB, Tex., 1985; student chief of profl. staff course, Sheppard AFB, Tex., 1988. Diplomate Am. Bd. Emergency Medicine; cert. Bd. Internal Medicine, Poland; cert. Ednl. Coun. Fgn. Med. Grads.; recert. Extended Allergy Care Provider. Intern. Med. Acad. Cracow, Poland, 1962-63; residency in internal medicine II-Clinic of Internal Diseases, Cracow, Poland, 1963-66, staff mem., 1966-69; gen. med. officer Gen. Hosp., Sokoto, Nigeria, 1969-72; intern. Frankford Hosp., Phila., 1972-73; house physician Holy Redeemer Hosp., Meadowbrook, Pa., 1973-74; emergency room physician John F. Kennedy Hosp., Phila., 1974-76, emergency room dir., 1976-78; commd. capt. USAF Med. Corps, 1978, advanced through grades to col., 1993; emergency rm. and primary care physician USAF Clinic, Ramstein, West Germany, 1978-81; officer in charge Emergency Room and Gen. Practice Clinic, Peterson Field, Colo., 1981-84; primary care physician Malcolm Grow Med. Ctr., Andrews AFB, Md., 1984-88; chief clinic svcs. 63d Med. Group/SGH, Norton AFB, Calif., 1988-93; staff physician 60th Med. Group, Travis AFB, Calif., 1993—; asst. tchr., sr. asst. tchr. Inst. Descriptive Anatomy, Cracow, 1963-69; emergency physician on call First Aid Sta., Cracow, 1966-69. Fellow Am. Coll. Emergency Physicians; mem. AMA, Am. Coll. Emergency Physicians, World Med. Assn., Am. Coll. Physician Execs. Office: 694 Inteligence Group AIA Ft G Meade MD 20755

KWITEROVICH, PETER OSCAR, JR., medical science educator, researcher, physician; b. Danville, Pa., June 24, 1940; s. Peter O. Sr. and Mary E. (Marks) K.; m. Kathleen Ann Justin, Aug. 14, 1965; children: Kris Ann, Peter III, Karen Ann. AB, Holy Cross Coll., Worcester, Mass., 1962; B in Med. Sci., Dartmouth Coll., 1964; MD, Johns Hopkins U., 1966. Intern Boston Children's Meml. Hosp., 1966-67; staff assoc. NIH, Bethesda, Md., 1967-70; resident Johns Hopkins Hosp., Balt., 1970-72; from asst. prof. to assoc. prof. in med. sci. Johns Hopkins U., Balt., 1972-84, prof. in med. sci., 1984—; dir. Specialized Ctr. Rsch. Arteriosclerosis, 1991—; bd. dirs. various clinics Johns Hopkins Hosp., 1971—; chmn. steering com. prin. investigation Nat. Dietary Investigation Study in Children, 1987—. Author: Beyond Cholesterol, 1989 (Blakeslee award 1991, Helen B. Taussig award 1992); contbr. articles to profl. jours. Platt rep., Roland Park Civic League, Balt., 1986-88, v.p., 1988-89, pres., 1989-91. Surgeon USPHS, 1967-70. Fellow Coun. Arteriosclerosis; mem. Soc. Pediatrics Rsch., Am. Soc. Clin. Investigation. Republican. Roman Catholic. Office: Johns Hopkins Hosp 600 N Wolfe St Baltimore MD 21205-2110

KWON, BYOUNG SE, geneticist, educator; b. Songak, Dangjin, Korea, Dec. 17, 1947; came to U.S., 1978; s. Won S. and Hyung Gap (Lee) K.; m. Myung Hee Han, Feb. 24, 1973; children: David Hyungjoong, Edwin Eujoong, Patrick Myungjoong. PhD in Cell and Molecular Biology, Med. Coll. Ga., Augusta, 1981; postgrad., Yale U., 1981-83. Assoc. scientist dept. human genetics Yale U., New Haven, 1983-84; scientist Guthrie Rsch. Inst., Sayre, Pa., 1984-88, Walther Oncology Ctr., Indpls., 1988—; assoc. prof. dept. microbiology and immunology Sch. Medicine Ind. U., Indpls., 1988-93, prof., 1993—. Contbr. articles to profl. jours. Capt. Korean Army, 1974-77. Grantee NIH, March of Dimes Birth Defects Found., Am. Heart Assn. Mem. AAAS, AAI, Nat. Orgn. Albinism (bd. dirs.), Gene Cloning and Expression (bd. dirs.), Am. Soc. Microbiology, Sigma Xi. Office: Ind U Sch of Medicine 635 Barnhill Dr # 255 Indianapolis IN 46202-5126

KWON, IK HYUN, internist; b. Korea, Aug. 22, 1937; s. Soo Myong and Jin Joo (Rhim) K.; m. Sook Ja Kwon, 1986; children: Esther, James. M.D., Seoul Nat. U., 1962; Ph.D., Rugers U., 1974. Intern, Martland Med. Center, Newark, 1966-67; resident in internal medicine Bklyn.-Cumberland Med. Center, 1967; practice medicine specializing in internal medicine, South Plainfield, N.J., 1976—; mem. staff John F. Kennedy Med. Ctr., Edison, N.J., Muhlenberg Regional Med. Ctr., Plainfield, N.J. Served with Korean Army, 1963-66. Mem. ACP, AAAS, AMA, N.Y. Acad. Scis. Home and Office: 1526 New Durham Rd South Plainfield NJ 07080-2317

KYLE, ANDREW CROCKETT, III, biomedical electronics engineer; b. Ft. Worth, Tex., Nov. 3, 1945; s. Andrew Crockett and Betty Magdelano K.; m. Regina Anne Walker, Apr. 26, 1975. BSEE with honors, U. Tex., 1968. Design engr. Tracor, Austin, Tex., 1967, Tex. Instruments, Austin, 1967-68; rsch. asst. Baylor Coll. of Medicine, Houston, 1968-69, biomedical and electronic engr., 1969-74; exec. v.p. Life-Tech., Inc., Houston, 1974—; bd. dirs., sec. Life-Tech, Inc., Houston, 1978—. Recipient H.A. Lott scholarship, 1964-68. Mem. Internat. Continence Soc., Soc. for Urology and Engring. Office: Life-Tech Inc PO Box 36221 Houston TX 77236-6221

KYMAN, WENDY, sex therapist, health educator; b. N.Y.C., Mar. 29, 1947; d. Jack and Tess (Starman) K.; l child, Jesse. BS, CCNY, 1968; MS, Bklyn. Coll., 1971; PhD, NYU, 1984. Diplomate, cert. sex therapist and educator Am. Bd. Sexology. Tchr. N.Y.C. Bd. Edn., 1968-74; coord., supr. YWCA Women's Ctr., 1977-78; instr. health edn. SUNY, Old Westbury, 1980-81; instr. allied health SUNY, Nanuet, 1982; family planning counselor NYU Health Svc., N.Y.C., 1984; asst. prof. health edn. CUNY Hunter Coll., 1984-85; sr. pub. health educator Gouverneur Hosp., 1984-87; asst. prof. health edn. CUNY Baruch Coll., 1985—; pvt. practice sex therapy and sex educator, cons., N.Y.C.; teaching fellow NYU, 1980. Contbr. articles to profl. jours. Profl. Staff Congress of CUNY rsch. grantee, 1988-89. Mem. Am. Assn. Sex Educators, Counselors and Therapists (cert. sex educator), Nat. Coun. Women in Medicine, Am. Pub. Health Assn., Nat. Women's Health Network. Home: 272 6th Ave Brooklyn NY 11215-2147 Office: CUNY Baruch Coll 17 Lexington Ave New York NY 10010-5526

KYNCL, JOHN JAROSLAV, pharmacologist; b. Prague, Czechoslovakia, Aug. 16, 1936; came to U.S. 1971; s. Jan Petr and Marie (Mikesova) K.; m. Mila Marie Tomaides, Mar. 4, 1961; children: Marketa Kyncl Leisure, John Anthony. PhD, Komensky U., Bratislava, 1963; ScC, Czech. Acad. Sci., 1967. Pharmacologist Rsch. Inst. for Biochemistry & Pharmacy, Prague, 1963-68; A. von. Humboldt fellow U. Heidelberg, Ger., 1968-71; rsch. fellow Cleveland Clinic Found., 1971-72; E. Volwiler rsch. fellow Abbott Labs., North Chicago, Ill., 1972—. Contbr. over 100 articles to profl. jours. Fellow Coun. for High Blood Pressure Rsch. Am. Heart Assn.; mem. Am. Hypertension Soc., Am. Endocrine Soc., Internat. Hypertension Soc. (Paris), FASEB. Home: 800 Green Bay Rd Lake Bluff IL 60044-1807 Office: Abbott Labs Abbott Park Rd North Chicago IL 60064

KYSOR, DANIEL FRANCIS, psychologist; b. Corry, Pa., Aug. 3, 1956; s. Darrell Francis and Louise Mary (Caglio) K.; m. Kate Galbraith Morrison, Sept. 7, 1991; children: Kenneth Jon Kron, Samuel Morrison. BS, Edinboro U., 1980; MS in Ednl. Psychology, Edinboro U., Pa., 1988; MEd in Secondary Sch. Adminstrn., Edinboro U., 1994; postgrad., Miss. State U., 1991—. Cert. elem. edn., guidance, elem. and secondary adminstr., sch. psychologist; lic. psychologist, Pa. House parent Assn. for Retarded Citizens, Meadville, Pa., 1980-81; tchr. Calhoun County Schs., Grantsville, W.Va., 1982; counselor, tchr. Bradford Children's Home, Bradford, Pa., 1983; residential program counselor Assn. for Retarded Citizens, Meadville, Pa., 1984-86; resident hall dir. Edinboro U., Edinboro, Pa., 1984-86, counselor Edinboro Summer Acad. for the Gifted, 1985—; guidance counselor Cranberry Sch. Dist., Seneca, Pa., 1986; student Edinboro U., Edinboro, Pa., 1987; dropout prevention counselor Erie Sch. Dist., Erie, Pa., 1988; sch. psychologist Seneca Highlands IU #9, Coudersport, Pa., 1989—; pvt. practice Addis & Assocs., Bradford, Pa., 1994—; CEO, dir. psychol. svc. Port Psychol. Svcs., 1996—. Pa. Rural Leadership Program scholar Pa. State U., 1989; Rsch. grantee St. Bonaventure (N.Y.) U.; recipient citations Pa. House of Reps., 1991, 93, 95. Mem. Am. Counseling Assn. (life), Nat. Assn. Sch. Psychologists, Am. Sch. Counselor Assn., Nat. Fedn. Interscholastic Ofls. Assns., Pa. Interscholastic Athletic Assn., N.Y. State High Sch. Officials Assn., Eastern Wrestling League, Eastern Ind. Officials Wrestling Assn., Nat. Wrestling Officials Assn., Clowns of Am. Internat., Inc./POCO Clowns. Democrat. Episcopalian. Home: 409 Arnold Ave Port Allegany PA 16743-1207 Office: Seneca Highlands IU #9 306 N Main St Coudersport PA 16915-1626

LAANO, ARCHIE BIENVENIDO MAAÑO, cardiologist; b. Tayabas, Quezon, Philippines, Aug. 10, 1939; naturalized U.S. citizen; s. Francisco M. and Iluminada (Maaño) L.; m. Maria Esmeralda Eleazar, May 2, 1964; 1 child, Sylvia Marie. A.A., U. Philippines, 1958, B.S., 1959, M.D., 1963; postgrad. Command and Gen. Staff Sch., Ft. Totten, N.Y., Ft. Leavenworth, Kans., 1978-79, Oxford (Eng.) U., 1985-86, Cambridge (Eng.) U., 1986-87. Diplomate Am. Bd. Internal Medicine. Rotating intern Hosp. St. Raphael, New Haven, 1963-64; resident internal medicine, 1964-65; rotating resident pulmonary diseases Laurel Heights Hosp., Shelton, Conn., 1965; affiliated rotating resident Yale-New Haven Med. Ctr., 1965; resident internal medicine Westchester County Med. Ctr., Valhalla, N.Y., 1965-66, resident cardiology, 1966-67; resident fellow cardiology Maimonides Med. Ctr., Bklyn., 1967-68; rotating sr. resident cardiology Coney Island Hosp., Bklyn., 1967-68; fellow internal medicine Mercy Hosp., Rockville Centre, N.Y., 1968-70; med. dir. 54 Main St. Med. Ctr., Hempstead, N.Y., 1971-76, Bloomingdale's, Garden City, N.Y., 1972—, Esselte Pendaflex Corp., Garden City, 1976—; attending staff Nassau County (N.Y.) Med. Ctr., Hempstead Gen. Hosp.; practice medicine specializing in cardiology, internal medicine, Nassau County, 1971—; chief med. svcs., chief profl. svcs. U.S. Army 808th Sta. Hosp., Hempstead, N.Y., 1979—; brig. gen. 1st U.S. Army AMEDD Augmentation Detachment, Ft. Meade, Md., 1989—, M.C., chief of staff, chief profl. svcs. U.S. Army Meddac Hosp., Ft. Dix., N.J., 1990—; med. dir. Cities Svc. Oil Co. (CITGO), L.I. div., 1972— ; mem. adv. bd. Guardian Bank, Hempstead, chmn. adv. coun., 1973-89; clin. prof. medicine SUNY at Stony Brook, 1979—; professorial lectr. medicine (cardiology) U.S. Mil. Acad.-Keller Army Med. Ctr., West Point, N.Y., 1979; affiliated teaching hosp. Harvard Med. Sch, 1979; vis. prof. Harvard U., 1979—; cons. physician ICC, Citgo, Liberty Mut. Ins. Co. Boston, 1972—, U.S. Dept. Transp.; post-doctoral in medicine-cardiovasc. diseases Brasenose Coll., Oxford U., U.K., 1985-65, post-doctoral in medicine-cardiology Corpus Christi Coll., Cambridge U., U.K., 1986-87; counsel White House Commn. on Mil. Medicine, 1988—. Perpetual benefactor endowed Dr. Archie B.M. Laano Professorial Chair in Cardiology, U.P. Coll. of Medicine, U.P.-P.G.H. Med. Ctr., Manila, 1983—, Permanent Endowment Fund, U. Philippines Coll. of Medicine, Manila, 1987—, Dr. Archie B.M. Laano Scholarship Fund, U. Philippines, Diliman, Quezon City, 1987—. Decorated Silver Star, Bronze Star, Legion of Merit, Soldiers medal, Joint Svc. Command medal, Army Meritorious Svc. medal, Dept. Def. Joint Svc. Achievement award, Southwest Asia Svc. award-Desert Storm, others. Fellow Internat. Coll. Angiology, Am. Coll. Angiology, Am. Coll. Internat. Physicians, Internat. Coll. Applied Nutrition, Am. Soc. Contemporary Medicine and Surgery, Acad. Preventive Medicine, Internat. Acad. Med.

Preventives, Philippine Coll. Physicians, Am. Coll. Acupuncture, N.Y. Acad. of Sci.; mem. AMA, Am. Coll. Cardiology, N.Y. Med. Soc., Nassau County Med. Soc., Am. Heart Assn., N.Y. Cardiol. Soc., World Med. Assn., Royal Soc. Medicine (overseas, London), Nassau Acad. Medicine, Am., N.Y. State, Nassau Soc. Internal Medicine, N.Y. Soc. Acupuncture for Physicians, Am. Geriatrics Soc., Nassau Physicians Guild, Res. Officers Assn. U.S., Assn. Mil. Surgeons, Assn. Philippine Physicians Am. (bd. govs. rep. N.Y. State 1984-86, v.p. 1988-89, chmn. com. nominations and election 1987-88. spl. counsel to pres. 1986-87), Philippine Med. Assn. Am. (spl. counsel 1988-89, bd. dirs, 1989-90, spl. counsel to pres, 1986—, dir. continuing med. edn. 1990—, chmn. scholarship com. 1989—), Assn. Philippine Physicians of N.Y. (founding v.p., pres. 1985-87, pres. emeritus 1988—, chmn. com. on constitution and by-laws, nominations and election, med. coord. Internat. Games for Disabled Olympics 1984), Soc. Philippine Surgeons Am. (Medallion of.S. Knights of Rizal, U. Philippines Med. Alumni Soc. (pres. class of 1963, 1981—), U. Philippines Med. Alumni Soc. Am. (chmn. bd. 1985—), Royal Soc. Medicine Club, The Oxford Club, Rolls Royce Club L.I., N.Y. Club (chmn. 1987—), West Point Officers Club, Garden City Country Club, Phi Kappa Mu (overseas coord. U. Philippines 1985—), Beta Sigma (coun. advisers Ea. U.S. 1990—, program chmn. 1975—, chmn. bd. 1978—, pres. 1978-79), Lions (Garden City program chmn. 1975—, chmn. bd. 1978—, pres. 1978-79). Republican. Roman Catholic. Home: 80 Stratford Ave Garden City NY 11530-2531 Office: 230 Hilton Ave Ste 106 Hempstead NY 11550-8116

LABANARIS, PANAXIOTIS GEORGE, urologist, educator; b. Pentalophos, Kozani, Greece, Nov. 3, 1945; s. George Nikos and Angeliki Basiliki (Garou) L.; m. Athanasia Kiouptsi, Apr. 27, 1974. MD, U. Thessaloniki, Greece, 1969. Diplomate Am. Bd. Urology, European Bd. Urology. Intern Neoumedical Sch., Youngstown, Ohio, 1975-76, resident in surgery, 1976-77; resident in urology Erie, Pa., 1977-80, Roswal Park Hosp., Buffalo, 1979-80; dir. urology svc. VA Med. Ctr., Ft. Wayne, Ind., 1980-84; dir. urology Galinos Klinic, Thessaloniki, 1984—. Surgeon Greek Army, 1970-72. Fellow ACC; mem. Am. Urol. Assn., Am. Assn. Clin. Urologists. Greek Orthodox. Home: Dalipi 8, Thessaloniki Greece Office: 10 Agias Sophias St, 54622 Thessaloniki Greece

LABARBERA, ANDREW RICHARD, reproductive biologist; b. Teaneck, N.J., Oct. 6, 1948; s. Mario Richard and Georgine E. (Mart) LaB. BS cum laude, Iona Coll., 1970; MA, Columbia U., 1974, MPhil, 1974, PhD, 1975. Predoctoral USPHS NIH, Washington, 1971-75; staff assoc. Columbia U., N.Y.C., 1975-77; rsch. fellow dept. cell biology Mayo Clinic and Found., Rochester, Minn., 1977-80; asst. prof. dept physiology Northwestern U. Med. Sch., Chgo., 1980-86, dir. radioimmunoassay lab. Ctr. for Endocrinology, Metabolism and Nutrition, 1980-85, asst. prof. dept. ob/gyn., 1985-86, assoc. prof. dept. ob/gyn. and physiology, 1986-88; assoc. prof. tenured dept. ob/gyn. U. Cin., 1988-95, prof., 1995—, adj. assoc. prof. dept. physiology and biophysics, 1988—, vice chmn. dept. ob/gyn., 1989-93; dir. andrology lab. and sperm bank U. Cin. Hosp., 1988—; dir. vitro fertilization lab. Northwestern Meml. Hosp., Chgo., 1985-88; mem. Reproductive Toxicology Working Group, Workshop on Effects of Pesticide on Human Health, Nat. Task Force on Environ. Cancer and Heart and Lung Disease, Keystone, 1988; cons. Nat. Inst. Diabetes, Washington, 1989-90, Diseases and Kidney Spl. Contract Rev. Group, Washington, 1989-90, NIH Reviewers Res., Washington, 1990-94, Nat. Inst. Alcoholism and Alcohol Abuse, 1992, Nat. Inst. Child Health and Human Devel., 1990—. Ad Hoc reviewer Am. Jour. Ob/Gyn., Am. Jour. Physiology, Biology of Reproduction, Endocrinology, Fertility and Sterility, Jour. Andrology, Jour., Clin. Endocrinology and Metabolism, Jour. Pharmacology and Exptl. Therapeutics, NSF, USDA; contbr. chpts. to books and 40 articles to profl. jours. Bd. dirs. West Wellington Condominium Assn., Chgo., 1983-85, pres. Sangamon Lofts Condominium Assn., Chgo., 1986-88. Grantee Population Coun. N.Y.C., 1972-75, faculty Northwestern U., 1981, NIH, 1982-86, 94—, USDA, 1986-92. Mem. AAAS, AAUP, Am. Fertility Soc., Am. Inst. Biol. Scis., Am. Physiol. Soc., Am. Soc. Zoologists, Am. Soc. Andrology, Endocrine Soc., Soc. for Study Reproduction (chmn. info. mgmt. com. 1983-85, chmn. mem. com. 1987-92), Soc. Exptl. Biology and Medicine, Soc. Gynecologic Investigation, Tissue Culture Assn., Sigma Beta Beta Beta. Home: 1168 Eversole Rd Cincinnati OH 45230-3547 Office: U Cin Coll Medicine PO Box 670526 Cincinnati OH 45267-0526

LABARBERA, JUDITH J., nuclear medicine physician; b. San Jose, Calif., Mar. 11, 1961; d. Joseph Donald and Paula Jeane (Tousley) Berry; m. Philip Ray LaBarbera, Sept. 15, 1984. BS, U. Calif., San Diego, 1983; MD, U. Calif., Irvine, 1988. Diplomate Am. Bd. Nuc. Medicine. Assoc. North County Medi-Scan, Vista, Calif., 1993—; cons. in field. Mem. Soc. Nuc. Medicine.

LABEL, NORMAN, emergency physician; b. Phila., Feb. 19, 1941; s. Joseph and Claire Lillian (Weisberg) L.; m. Donna Faye Anderson, Aug. 16, 1981; children: Alyssa, Joseph, Jacob. BSc, Phila. Coll. Pharmacy, 1963; MD, Jefferson Med. Coll., 1968. Diplomate Am. Bd. Emergency Medicine, Am. Bd. Family Practice. Pres. Sierra Pacific Emergency Med. Group, Citrus Heights, Calif., 1990-94, v.p., 1994—. Mem. Sacramento Med. Soc. Office: Emergency Phys Med Group 8350 Auburn Blvd Ste 100 Citrus Heights CA 95610

LABELLA, JOHN SEBASTIAN, hospital administrator; b. Middletown, Conn., Aug. 28, 1953; s. Sebastian Salvatore and Grace Josephine (Panebianco) L.; m. Margaret Mary Martin, July 9, 1977; 1 child, Katherine Anne. BS, U.S. Mil. Acad., 1976; MPH, Yale U., 1983. Commd. 2d lt. U.S. Army, 1976, advanced through grades to capt.; exec. officer, co. comdr. med. co. Silas B. Hays Army Hosp., Ft. Ord, Calif., 1976-77; a.d.c. Letterman Army Med. Ctr., San Francisco, 1978-80; pers. counselor Office Surgeon Gen., Washington, 1980-81; resigned, 1981; adminstrv. resident, assoc. Hartford (Conn.) Hosp., 1981-84; asst. adminstr. Bridgeport (Conn.) Hosp., 1984-87; pres., chief exec. officer NovaMed Corp., Bridgeport, Conn., 1987-89; v.p. ops. Bridgeport Hosp., 1989-95; sr. v.p. ops., pres., CEO NovaMed, 1995—. Yale U. Leadership fellow, 1985. Mem. Am. Coll. Healthcare Execs., Am. Hosp. Assn., Conn. Hosp. Assn., Xavier H.S. Alumni Assn. (sec. Middletown 1981-85), Yale U. Program in Health Care (preceptor). Republican. Roman Catholic. Home: 127 Big Horn Rd Shelton CT 06484-1857 Office: Bridgeport Hosp 267 Grant St Bridgeport CT 06610-2870

LABELLE, EDWARD FRANCIS, physiologist; b. Worcester, Mass., Aug. 11, 1948; s. Edward F. and Viola Louise (Trudel) L.; m. Constance Miriam Reichmann, Aug. 19, 1972; children: Devon, Ross. AB, Holy Cross Coll., 1970, MS, 1970; PhD, U. Mich., 1974. Postdoctoral fellow Cornell U., Ithaca, N.Y., 1974-76; asst. prof. Western Ill. U., Macomb, 1976-78; asst. prof. U. Tex. Med. Br., Galveston, 1978-86, assoc. prof., 1986-87; rsch. scientist Grad. Hosp., Phila., 1987—; adj. assoc. prof. U. Pa., Phila., 1988—. Contbr. articles to profl. jours. Grantee NIH, 1978-84, 87—, Am. Heart Assn., 1986, 88. Mem. Am. SOc. Biochemistry and Molecular Biology, Soc. Gen. Physiologists.

LABENZ, JOACHIM, internist; b. Hamm, Germany, Apr. 9, 1956; s. Karl-Heinz and Gertrud (Silberkuhl) L.; m. Gisela Maria Lange, Aug., 24, 1984; 1 child, Christian. MD, U. Mainz, Germany, 1983. Med. asst. Elisabeth Hosp., Essen, Germany, 1983-84, cons., 1985—. Author: (book) Gastroenterologische Notfälle, 1993; contbr. over 70 articles to profl. jours. Mem. European Assn. Gastroenterology and Hepatology, Internat. Gastro-Surg. Club, German Soc. for Internal Medicine, German Gesellschaft für Verdauungs und Stoffwechselkrankheiten, Deutsche Gesellschaft für Endoskopie und Bildgebende Verfahren. Roman Catholic. Home: Plattenweiler 18, 45239 Essen Germany Office: Elisabeth Hosp, Moltkestrasse 61, 45138 Essen Germany

LABINS, DEBORAH LYNNE, maternal women's health nurse; b. Atlanta, Jan. 5, 1957; d. Harold Whitney and Lois Romaine (Moudy) Hampson; m. Steven Thomas Labins, Mar. 18, 1978; children: Jennifer, Christine, Eric. AA in Nursing, Pierce Coll., Woodland Hills, Calif., 1978. RN, Calif. Nurses' aide Motion Picture and TV Hosp., Woodland Hills; staff nurse labor and delivery room, postpartum, nursery Granada Hills (Calif.) Community Hosp.; nurse labor and delivery room West Hills Regional Med. Ctr. (formerly Humana Hosp.), West Hills, Calif.

LABODA, GERALD, oral and maxillofacial surgeon; b. Phila., Aug. 15, 1936; s. Lewis and Rose (Waldman) L.; m. Sheila Lois Plasky, Aug. 2, 1956; children: Amy, Michèle, Alane, Bruce. Student, Temple U., 1954-56, DDS, 1960; postgrad., U. Pa., 1960-61. Diplomate Am. Bd. Oral and Maxillofacial Surgery. Resident physician in oral and maxillofacial surgery Jefferson U. Hosp., Phila., 1961-63; pvt. practice oral and maxillofacial surgery S.W. Fla. Oral Surgery Assocs., Ft. Myers, 1965—; sr. dir. Barnett Bank of Lee County, Ft. Myers; chmn. bd. trustees S.W. Fla. Regional Med. Ctr., Ft. Myers, 1989-94, sec. bd. trustees, 1974—; med. dir. S.W. Fla. divsn. Columbia/HCA Healthcare Corp., 1994—. Contbr. articles to profl. jours. Pres. YMCA of Lee County, 1976; pres. Found. for Lee County Pub. Schs., Ft. Myers, 1991; vice chmn. Downtown Redevel. Agy., Ft. Myers, 1985-93, chmn., 1993—; bd. dirs. United Way of Lee County, 1981. Fellow Am. Assn. Oral and Maxillofacial Surgeons (trustee Dist. III 1984-87, v.p. 1987-88, pres. 1989-90); mem. Fla. Soc. Oral and Maxillofacial Surgeons (pres. 1980-81), Fla. Dental Soc. of Anesthesiology (pres. 1978-79), S.W. Fla. Dental Soc. (pres. 1974), Oral and Maxillofacial Surgery Found. (bd. dirs. 1993—). Republican. Jewish. Office: SW Fla Oral Surg Assocs Summerlin Med Park 5285 Summerlin Rd Fort Myers FL 33919-7602

LABRIE, BARBARA HOERL, nursing educator; b. Milw., Apr. 24, 1947; d. Edward and Delores (Carlson) Hoerl; m. Dan Labrie, Sept. 21, 1985. ADN, Milw. Area Tech. Coll., 1977; BSN, Ariz. State U., 1983; MS in Community Health Nursing and Edn., U. Conn., 1988. Supr. home health Bodimetric Health Svcs., Phoenix, 1983-84; advice nurse coord. Kaiser Permanente Health Ctr., East Hartford, Conn., 1984-86; tng. cons. Aetna Life and Casualty, Hartford, Conn., 1989-91; nurse Vets. Meml. Hosp., Meriden, Conn., 1991-94; instr. nursing Ona Wilcox Sch. Nursing, 1994—; hospice nurse Middlesex VNA, 1995—. Contbr. articles to profl. jours. Mem. ANA, Nat. Assn. Orthopaedic Nursing, Sigma Theta Tau.

LABRUNA, VINCENT FRANCIS, podiatrist; b. Queen, N.Y., Apr. 29, 1958; s. Joseph S. and Lynn R. (Altomare) LaB.; m. Donna Marie Valerio, Dec. 10, 1989; children: John Joseph, Nicholas. BS, Rutgers U., 1980; D in Podiatric Medicine, N.Y. Coll. Podiatric Medicine, 1984. Resident surgery, podiatric surgery Fairlawn, Mass.; pvt. practice Oakland, N.J., 1986—. Mem. N.J. Podiatric Med. Soc. Office: 43 Yawpo Ave # 11 Oakland NJ 07436-2717 Office: 707 S Orange Ave South Orange NJ 07079-2698

LA BRUNA, VINCENT VITO, orthodontist; b. Regalbuto, Italy, Sept. 4, 1933; came to the U.S., 1935; s. Nunzio and Vincenza (Termine) L.B.; m. Nina La Bruna, June 29, 1958; children: Vincent A., Anthony N. BS, St. John's Coll., 1954; DDS, NYU, 1958; cert. of splty. in orthodontics, Columbia U., 1961. Lic. dentist, N.Y. Pvt. practice N.Y.C., 1961—; dir. dentistry Cabrini Med. Ctr., N.Y.C., 1981—; pres. Met. Rsch. Inst., N.Y.C., 1976—. Contbr. articles to profl. jours. Chmn. orthodontists ARC, N.Y.C., 1970-72; vol. oral cancer screening Am. Cancer Soc., N.Y.C., 1981—; nominated by mayor to Environ. Control Bd., N.Y.C., 1971; mem. adv. coun. N.Y. State Planning Commn., 1974-75. Recipient UN Medal, Pope Paul II, 1995, Man of Yr. award State Cmty. Mayors, 1988. Fellow Am. Coll. Dentistry, Internat. Coll. Dentistry; mem. 1st Dist. Dental Soc. (pres. 1995), Eastern Dental Soc. (pres. 1978), Columbia Orthodontic Soc. (pres. 1973), Italian Am. Profl. and Bus. Assn. (pres. 1985—), Equestrian Order of Holy Sepulchre (knight comdr. 1970—), Sovereign Order of Cypress (knight comdr. 1977—). Roman Catholic. Home and Office: 829 Park Ave New York NY 10021

LACAVE, ANGEL JIMENEZ, oncologist, educator; b. Alcanadre, La Rioja, Spain, May 7, 1946; s. Angel Jimenez and Rosalia Lacave; m. Maria Dolores Fonseca, Oct. 2, 1976; children: Paula, Manuel, Cristina. MD, U. Zaragoza, Spain, 1969; PhD, U. Pamplona, Spain, 1989. Intern Hosp. Gen. Asturias, Oviedo, Spain, 1969-70, resident, 1971-74, asst. doctor, 1974-78, head sect., 1978-82, head med. oncology dept., 1982—; asst. prof. U. Oviedo, 1994—; pvt. practice Oviedo, 1993—. Contbr. articles to profl. jours. Pres. Found. for Devel. of Oncology, 1994. Mem. European Orgn. for Rsch. and Treatment of Cancer, Am. Soc. Clin. Oncology, European Soc. Med. Oncology. Roman Catholic. Office: Hosp Gen Asturias Med Oncol, Julián Clavería S/N, 33006 Oviedo Asturias Spain

LA CELLE, PAUL LOUIS, biophysics educator; b. Syracuse, N.Y., July 4, 1929; s. George Clarke and Marguerite Ellen (Waggoner) La C. A.B., Houghton Coll., 1951; M.D., U. Rochester, 1959. Resident U. Rochester Med. Center-Strong Meml. Hosp., 1960-62; asst. prof. medicine U. Rochester, 1967-70, asso. prof., 1970-74, prof., 1974—, chmn. dept. biophysics, 1977—; sr. assoc. dean for acad. affairs and rsch. Sch. Medicine and Dentistry, U. Rochester, 1993—; cons. to govt. Mem. Gates-Chili Sch. Bd., Rochester, 1964-72; trustee Houghton Coll., 1976-95. Served to lt. USNR, 1952-55. NIH spl. fellow, 1965-66; recipient von Humboldt Sr. Scientist award, 1982-83. Mem. Biophys. Soc., Microcirculation Soc., European Microcirculation Soc., Alpha Omega Alpha. Office: U Rochester Dept Biophysics 601 Elmwood Ave Rochester NY 14642-8408

LACEY, PEELER GRAYSON, diagnostic radiologist; b. Kosciusko, Miss., June 16, 1954; s. Dick Grayson and Beatrice (Peeler) L.; m. Holley Anne Westbrook, July 8, 1978; children: Peeler Grayson Jr., Lauren Elizabeth. BA in Chemistry, Emory U., 1975; MD, U. Miss., 1979. Diplomate Am. Bd. Radiology. Intern U. Miss Med. Ctr., Jackson, 1979-80, resident in diagnostic radiology, 1980-83; diagnostic radiologist South Cen. Regional Med. Ctr., Laurel, Miss., 1983—, Jasper Gen. Hosp., Bay Springs, Miss., 1983—; v.p. Radiology Assocs., Laurel, 1983—. Asst. scoutmaster Troop 32; exec. bd. mem. Pine Burr Area Coun. Boy Scouts Am., chmn. Nat. Eagle Scout Assn.; life mem. Nat. Eagle Scout Assn. Pine Burr Area Coun.; Sun. sch. tchr., deacon. First Bapt. Ch., Laurel. Named one of Outstanding Young Men of Am., 1987. Mem. AMA, NRA (life), Radiol. Soc. N.Am., So. Radiology Soc., Am. Coll. Radiology, Am. Heart Assn., Miss. State Med. Assn., Miss. Radiol. Soc., South Miss. Med. Soc. (past pres.), South Cen. Regional Med. Ctr. (pres. 1994), Roentgen Ray Soc., Cum Laude Soc., Safari Club Internat., Sigma Chi (life loyal Sig.). Home: 2432 Ridgewood Dr Laurel MS 39440-2147 Office: Radiology Assocs 235 S 12th Ave # 2427 Laurel MS 39440-4324

LACH, ELLIOT, plastic surgeon; b. Jan. 1, 1956; m. Tammy Harris; children: Jeremy, Rebecca. BS in Edn., Hebrew Coll., 1976; SB, MIT, 1977; MD, Yale U., 1981. Diplomate Am. Bd. Plastic Surgery, Am. Bd. Hand Surgery. Intern Yale-New Haven Hosp., 1981-82, resident, 1982-83; resident Brigham & Women's Hosp., Boston, 1983-87, fellow, 1985-87; resident Children's Hosp., Boston, 1984-87; fellow Harvard Med. Sch., 1983-87; assoc. prof. U. Mass. Med. Sch., 1987—;, 1987—; with dept. plastic surgery U. Mass. Med. Ctr., Worcester, 1987—. Office: U Mass Med Ctr Dept Plastic Surgery 55 Lake Ave N Worcester MA 01655-0002

LACHANCE, PAUL ALBERT, food science educator, clergyman; b. St. Johnsbury, Vt., June 5, 1933; s. Raymond John and Lucienne (Landry) L.; m. Therese Cecile Cote; children: Michael P., Peter A., M.-Andre, Susan A. BS, St. Michael's Coll., 1955; postgrad., U. Vt., 1955-57; PhD, U. Ottawa, 1960; cert. in pastoral counseling, N.Y. Theol. Sem., 1981; DSc (hon.), St. Michael's Coll., 1982. Ordained deacon Roman Cath. Ch., 1977. Assigned to St. Paul's Ch. Princeton, N.J.; aerospace biologist Aeromed. Research Labs., Wright-Patterson AFB, Ohio, 1960-63; lectr. dept. biology U. Dayton, Ohio, 1963; flight food and nutrition coordinator NASA Manned Spacecraft Center, Houston, 1963-67; assoc. prof. dept. food sci. Rutgers U., New Brunswick, N.J., 1967-72, dir. Sch. Feeding effectiveness research project, 1969-72, prof., 1972—, faculty rep. to bd. trustees, 1988-90, dir. grad. program food sci., 1988-91, chmn. food sci. dept., 1991—, chmn. univ. senate, 1990-93; faculty rep. to bd. govs., 1990-94; cons. Nutritional Aspects of Food Processing; mem. nutrition adv. com. Whitehall-Robins/Lederle Consumer Divsn., 1989—; mem. sci. adv. bd. Roche chem. divsn. Hoffmann La Roche Co., 1976-88; mem. nutrition policy com. Beatrice Foods Co., 1979-86; trustee religious ministries com. Princeton Med. Ctr.; bd. dirs. J.R. Short Milling Co., 1990—. Mem. editorial adv. bd., Sch. Food Service Research Rev., 1977-82, Jour. Am. Coll. Nutrition, 1986—, Jour. Med. Consultation, 1985—, Nutrition Reports Internat., 1963-83, Profl. Nutritionist, 1977-80; contbr. articles to profl. jours. Served to capt. USAF, 1960-63. Recipient Endel Karmas award for excellence in teaching food sci., 1988, WilliamCruess award for excellence in teaching Inst. Food Technologists, 1991. Fellow Inst. Food Technologists, Am. Coll. Nutrition; mem. Am. Assn. Cereal Chemists, AAAS, Am. Inst. Nutrition, N.Y. Inst. Food Technologists (chmn. 1977-78), Am. Soc. Clin. Nutrition, N.Y. Acad. Sci., Am. Dietetic Assn., Soc. Nutrition Edn., Am. Public Health Assn., Nat. Assn. Cath. Chaplains, Sociedad Latino Americano de Nutricion, Sigma Xi, Delta Epsilon Sigma. Home: 34 Taylor Rd Princeton NJ 08540-9521 Office: Rutgers U Cook Coll Food Sci New Brunswick NJ 08903-0231

LACHER, MIRIAM BROWNER, neuropsychologist; b. Bronx, N.Y., Dec. 30, 1942; d. Philip and Ruth Frieda (Rabinowitz) Browner; m. Maury Lacher, Aug. 17, 1963. AB, Cornell U., 1963; PhD, U. Mich., 1970; postgrad., Columbia U., 1981. Asst. prof. psychology Carleton Coll., Northfield, Minn., 1970-77; vis. rsch. assoc. U. Calif., Berkeley, 1976-77; vis. lectr. Vassar Coll., Poughkeepsie, N.Y., 1978-79; assoc. neuropsychology Columbia-Presbyn. Med. Ctr., N.Y.C., 1980-81; cons. N.Y. State Psychiat. Inst., N.Y.C., 1981; chief cognitive rehab. Children's Specialized Hosp., Westfield, N.J., 1982-84; cons. Vassar Coll. Counseling Svc., Poughkeepsie, 1984-90, First Step Nursery Sch., Hyde Park, N.Y., 1988; pvt. practice Poughkeepsie, 1984—. Contbr. articles to profl. jours. Sci. advisor on bd. dirs. Mid-Hudson chpt. Children and Adults with Deficit Disorders, 1989—, Mid-Hudson Assn. for the Learning Disabled, 1992—. Woodrow Wilson fellow, U. Mich., 1963-64. Mem. Am. Psychol. Assn., Internat. Neuropsychol. Soc., Eastern Psychol. Assn., Hudson Valley Psychol. Assn. (sec. 1984-85, 86-87, program chair 1985-86), N.Y. State Psychol. Assn., N.Y. Neuropsychol. Group. Office: 47 S Hamilton St 37 Alda Dr Poughkeepsie NY 12603-5217

LACHICA, R(EYNATO) VICTOR, microbiologist; b. Cebu, Philippines, Feb. 24, 1943; came to U.S., 1960; s. Alfredo and Lily P. (Flores) L.; m. Lois Jean Holmes, June 21, 1974. BA, Wartburg Coll., 1963; PhD, Iowa State U., 1967. Rsch. assoc. U. Wis., Madison, 1967-68; asst. rsch. microbiologist U. Calif., Davis, 1969-74; head microbiology br. WHO-Sponsored Food Control Lab., Guatemala, 1974-80; rsch. microbiologist U.S. Army Natick (Mass.) Ctr., 1984—; adj. prof. U. Ariz., Tucson, 1981-83; vis. microbiologist USDA, Phila., 1983-84; mem. edit. bd. Applied & Environ. Microbiology, 1990—, Letters in Applied Microbiology, 1990—. Contbr. articles to sci. jours. Judge J.F. K. Jr. High Sch. Sci. Fair, Natick, 1985, 86, 87, 88, 89, 90. Mem. Am. Soc. Microbiology, AAAS, Inst. Food Techs. Office: US Army RDE Ctr Kansas St Natick MA 01760

LACHIEWICZ, PAUL FRANCIS, orthopedist, surgeon, educator; b. N.Y.C., July 16, 1951; s. Frank and Helen L.; m. Ava Maria Staler, June 24, 1977; children: Jayne, Anne, Mark, John, Mary Claire. BS, Manhattan Coll., 1973; MD, Cornell Univ., 1977. Intern, then resident U. Minn. Hosps., 1977-79; resident in orthopaedics Hosp. For Spl. Surgery, N.Y.C., 1979-82; assoc. prof. orthopaedics U. N.C., Chapel Hill, 1983—. Recipient Phillip D. Wilson award Hosp. for Special Surgery, N.Y.C., 1983. Fellow Am. Acad. Orthopaedic Surgeons; mem. Hip Soc., Knee Soc., So. Orthopaedic Assn. Office: U NC Dept Orthopaedics Chapel Hill NC 27599-7055

LACHOWICZ, TADEUSZ MICHAL, microbiology educator; b. Drohobycz, USSR, Dec. 28, 1930; arrived in Poland, 1946; s. Jozef and Zuzanna (Kozak) L.; m. Ewa Zablocka, July 14, 1956 (dec. 1965); m. Zofia Lusar, Dec. 20, 1966. MS in Microbiology, Wrocław (Poland) U., 1955, D. in Natural Scis., 1960, D. Habilitation, 1965. Tech. asst. UMCS, Lublin, Poland, 1954-55; tech. asst. Wrocław U., 1955-60, tutor, 1960-65, reader, 1965-68; reader Inst. Immunol. Ther. Expl. P.A.S., Wrocław, 1968-71, prof. extraordinary, 1971-74; prof. extraordinary Wrocław U., 1974-78, prof., 1978-96; ordinary prof. Higher Pedagogic Sch., Zielona, Poland, 1996—; head dept. microbiology Wrocław U., 1961-68, dir. Inst., 1978-90; head dept. microbiol. genetics Inst. Immunol. Exptl. Ther., Wrocław, 1968-74. Home: Bujwida 37 m 1, 50-345 Wrocław Poland Office: Inst Microbiol, Przybyszewskiego 63/77, Wrocław Poland

LACHTER, GERALD DAVID, psychologist, educator; b. N.Y.C., May 3, 1941; s. Lazar and Leah (Weisberg) L.; m. Abbie J. Lowenstein, May 19, 1973; children: Katie Mae, Eloise Rebecca. BA, C.W. Post Coll., 1964; MA, Columbia U., 1966; PhD, CUNY, 1970. Cert. psychologist, N.Y. Asst. prof. psychology L.I. U., C.W. Post Coll., Greenvale, N.Y., 1970-74, assoc. prof., 1974-82, prof., 1982—; cons. psychologist Suffolk Child Devel. Ctr., Smithtown, N.Y., 1981-87, Suffolk AHRC, Commack, N.Y., 1976-81; dir. grad. programs in psychology C.W. Post Coll., 1973-80. Author: Behavior Objectives Unit Handbook, 1974, (with others) Stimulus Schedules: The T-Tau Systems, 1972. Contbr. articles to profl. jours. Mem. Am. Psychol. Soc., Psychonomic Soc., Assn. for Behavior Analysis, Eastern Psychol. Assn., Sigma Xi (v.p. C.W. Post Coll. club 1990-91, pres. 1991-92). Democrat. Jewish. Office: LIU-CW Post Campus Psychology Dept Greenvale NY 11548

LACKEY, MARY MICHELE, physician assistant; b. Johnson City, N.Y., Dec. 22, 1955; d. Joseph Charles and Jane Ann (Weston) Reardon; m. Donald V. Lackey Jr., Oct. 27, 1979 (div. Nov., 1995). AAS in Nursing, Broome Community Coll., Binghamton, N.Y., 1978; cert. family nurse practitioner, Albany Med. Coll., 1982; BS in Psychology and Sociology, U. State of N.Y., Albany, 1989. Cert. physician asst., family nurse practitioner, nurse midwife; RN, N.Y., Conn. Physician asst. Streit, Hickey & Lasky MD, P.C., Saratoga Springs, N.Y., 1982-85, Litchfield Hills Ob/Gyn., Sharon, Conn., 1986-89, Foothills Family Health Ctr., Amenia, N.Y., 1991—; physican asst. Vassar Coll. Health Svcs., Poughkeepise, N.Y., 1990—. Leader, instr. Girl Scouts U.S.A., Dutchess County, N.Y., 1990—. Lt. col. U.S. Army, 1975—. Fellow Am. Acad. Physician Assts., Am. Coll. Nurse Midwives; mem. Nat. Guard Assn. U.S., Malitia Assn. N.Y., Phi Theta Kappa. Roman Catholic. Home: RR 1 Box 222 Salt Point NY 12578-9801

LACLAIR, PATRICIA MARIE, physical education director, medical technician; b. East Liverpool, Ohio, Dec. 29, 1958; d. James Herbert and Irene Marie (Ruthledge) LaC. BS in Edn., Youngstown State U. Dir. elem. phys. edn. Trinity (Tex.) Ind. Sch. Dist., 1985—; instr. CPR AHA, Bryan, Tex., 1985, instr. phys. edn., 1989—; emergency med. svcs. program instr., 1994—, emergency med. svcs. program examiner, 1994—, basic critical incident stress mgmt. trainer, 1994—; instr. Trinity Peninsula Ambulance Svc., 1994-95; sec. bd. dirs. Trinity Emergency Med. Svc., 1990-95, mgr. 1986-95; instr., trainer Primecare Emergency Med. Svc., 1996—, Jacksonville Fire Dept. Emergency Med. Svcs., 1996—. Vol. EMT, 1995-95. Home: 206 Valley Ln Crockett TX 75835

LACOMB-WILLIAMS, LINDA LOU, community health nurse; b. Galion, Ohio, Oct. 1, 1948; d. Horace Allen and Roberta May (Black) Braden; m. Robert Earl LaComb, Feb. 1, 1970 (div. Aug. 1984); children: Robin Marie, Patrick Alan; m. Robert Allen Williams, Aug. 30. 1991; children Erin, Megan. BSN, Capital U., 1970. RN, Fla., Ohio. Staff nurse St. Anne's Hosp., Columbus, Ohio, 1970; pub. health nurse Hillsborough County Dept. Health, Tampa, Fla., 1970-80, community health nurse supr., 1980-87; sr. community health nurse Polk County Dept. Health, Lakeland, Fla., 1987-88; sr. RN supr. Children's Med. Svcs., Tampa, 1988-91, Lakeland, 1991—. 1st lt. flight nurse res. USAF, 1971-75. Recipient Boss of Yr. award Stawberry Chpt. of Am. Bus. Women's Assn., 1985. Mem. ANA, ARC, Fla. Nurses Assn. (grievance rep. state employees profl. bargaining unit 1976-87, pres. 1984-87, 1st v.p. 1989-91, Undine Sams award 1987, Nurse of Yr. award Dist. Four 1987), Sigma Theta Tau (Delta Beta chpt.). Republican. Presbyterian. Home: 502 Shamrock Rd Brandon FL 33511-5548 Office: Children's Med Svcs 1417 Lakeland Hills Blvd Lakeland FL 33805-3200

LACY, PAUL ESTON, pathologist; b. Trinway, Ohio, Feb. 7, 1924; s. Benjamin Lemmert and Amy Cass (Cox) L.; m. Emelyn Ellen Talbot, June 7, 1945; children: Paul E. Jr., Steven T. BA cum laude, Ohio State U., 1945, MD cum laude, MSc in Anatomy, 1948; PhD in Pathology, U. Minn.-Mayo Found., 1955; Doctor of Medicine (honoris causa), Uppsala (Sweden) U., 1977. Asst. instr. anatomy Ohio State U., Columbus, 1944-48; intern White Cross Hosp., Columbus, 1948-49; fellow in pathology Mayo Clinic, Rochester, Minn., 1951-55; postdoctoral fellow Washington U. Med. Sch., St. Louis, 1955-56, instr. pathology, 1956-57, asst. prof. pathology, 1957-61, asst. dean, 1959-61, assoc. prof. pathology, 1961, Mallinckrodt prof., chmn. dept. pathology, 1961-85, Robert L. Kroc prof. of pathology, 1985-95, prof. emeritus pathology, 1995—; pathologist-in-chief Barnes & Allied Hosps., St. Louis, 1985-95, pathologist, 1985-95, prof. emeritus pathology, 1995—.

Served to capt. U.S. Army, 1949-51. Recipient Banting award Brit. Diabetes Assn., 1963, Am. Diabetes Assn., 1970, 3M Life Scis. award FASEB, 1981, Rous-Whipple award Am. Assn. Pathologists, 1984. Fellow AAAS, Am. Acad. Arts and Sci.; mem. NAS, Inst. Medicine. Office: Washington Univ Med Sch Dept of Pathology 660 S Euclid Ave Saint Louis MO 63110-1010

LACY, ROBERT TULLOCH, opthalmologist; b. Ogdensburg, N.Y., July 21, 1941; m. Julie B. Lacy; children: Blair, Britton. BA, Yale U., 1963; MD, Cornell U., 1967. Diplomate Am. Bd. Ophthalmology. Intern Univ. Hosp., San Diego, 1967-68; resident Mass. Eye and Ear Infirmary/Harvard Med. Sch., Boston, 1970-74; ophthalmologist Eye Health Svcs., Inc., South Weymouth, Mass., 1971—; pres. New Eng. Eye Surg. Ctr., Weymouth, Mass., 1985—. Served with USAF, 1968-70. Named one of Best of Boston, Boston Mag., 1995. Mem. Mass. Med. Soc., Am. Acad. Ophthalmology, AMA, New England Ophthal. Soc., Norfolk South Dist. Med. Soc. (pres. 1995—). Office: Eye Health Svcs 696 Main St Weymouth MA 02190

LADDARAN, BENITO PUA, radiologist; b. Cagayan, The Philippines, Oct. 1, 1942; came to the U.S., 1969; s. Hermogenes and Fu (Pua) L.; m. Anita T. Chua, June 24, 1972; children: Andrew, Laddaran. MD, U. Santo Thomas, Manila, 1968. Cert. Am. Bd. Radiology, Am. Bd. Nuc. Medicine. Vice chmn. radiology dept. St. Anthony Hosp., Chgo., 1974-83; pvt. practice radiologist Beverly-Alvarado Med. Ctr., L.A., 1983—. Mem. Am. Coll. Radiology, Radiol. Soc. N.Am., L.A. Radiol. Soc., L.A. County Med. Assn. Office: 2105 Beverly Blvd Ste 117 Los Angeles CA 90057

LADENHEIM, JULES CALVIN, neurosurgeon; b. Union Hill, N.J., Apr. 21, 1923; s. Solomon and Miriam (Preminger) L.; m. Janet Bloom, Feb. 15, 1959; children: Eric, Fred (dec.), Karen. AB, Harvard U., 1944; MD, N.Y. Med. Coll., 1947. Diplomate Am. Bd. Surgery, Am. Bd. Neurologic Surgery. Intern Queens Gen. Hosp., N.Y.C., 1947-48; resident in gen. surgery N.Y. Med. Coll., 1948-50, Pitts. Med. Ctr., 1952-53, Mt. Sinai, Cleve., 1953-54; resident in neurosurgery Serafimer Hosp., Stockholm, 1954-56, Med. Coll. Va., 1956-57, Neurology Inst. N.Y., 1957-58, Mary Hitchcock, Hanover, N.H., 1958-60; pvt. practice Hackensack, N.J., 1960—; staff neurosurgeon Hackensack U. Hosp., 1960—, Holy Name Hosp., Teaneck, N.J., 1960—, Meadowland Hosp., Secaucus, N.J., 1987—, St. Mary Hosp., Hoboken, 1987—. Co-author: Arteriovenous Anerysm, 1956; author: Intraventric Meningiomas, 1961, Leoanrd of Bertapaglia, 1991, Firearms and Ballistics, 1996. Lt. USNR, 1950-52. Mem. Abraham Lincoln Soc. (pres. 1993-94). Home: 664 River Rd Teaneck NJ 07666 Office: 74 Central Ave Hackensack NJ 07601

LADOWSKI, JOSEPH STANLEY, cardiovascular and thoracic surgeon; b. Chgo., Nov. 18, 1955; s. Stanley Frank amd Bernice Ladowski; m. Anne Irene Bochucinski, June 28, 1981; children: Sam, Ben, Jack. BA, U. Chgo., 1976, MD, 1980. Diplomate Am. Bd. Thoracic Surgery. Intern U. Pitts., 1980, resident, 1981-88; surgeon Ind./Ohio Heart, Ft. Wayne, Ind., 1988—. Office: 7910 W Jefferson Blvd Ste 102 Fort Wayne IN 46804-4159

LADWIG, HAROLD ALLEN, neurologist; b. Manilla, Iowa, May 11, 1922; s. Ernest and Iva Marie (Allen) L.; m. Marjorie Lois Foster, June 26, 1946; children: Stephen H., Rosemary A. BA, U. Iowa, 1952, MD, 1947. Intern St. Joseph Hosp., Sioux City, Iowa, 1947-48; resident U. Minn., 1949-50; pres. Omaha Neurol. Clinic, 1972-83. Contbr. articles to profl. jours. Bd. dirs. Boys and Girls Club, Wilson, N.C., 1995—, Salvation Army, Wilson, 1996, Country Drs. Mus., Bailey, N.C., 1995—, Mental Health Bd., Wilson, 1995—. Comdr. USNR, 1950-52. Fellow Am. Coll. Physicians, Am. Acad. Neurology; mem. AMA, Am. Assn. Electrodiagnostic Medicine, Am. Soc. Electroencephalography and Neurophysiology, Wilson County Med. Soc. (sec. 1993, v.p. 1994, pres. 1995), Wilson Meml. Hosp. Found. (pres. 1993—), Douglas County Med. Soc. (exec. bd. 1960-63), Kiwanis (pres. Wilson chpt. 1995, Kiwani of Yr. 1992-93), Phi Beta Beta, Phi Beta Kappa. Methodist. Home: PO Box 3049 Wilson NC 27895-3049

LAEMMEL, KLAUS, psychiatrist; b. Zürich, Switzerland, July 20, 1931; s. Rudolf and Louise Dorothea (Frank) L.; m. Margrit Buergisser; children: Esther, Klaus. MD, U. Zürich, 1956. Bd. cert. diplomate U.S., Switzerland. Intern De Paul Hosp., Norfolk, Va., 1957-58; resident in psychiatry Rockland Psychiat. Ctr., Psychiat. Inst., 1958-61; psychiat. cons. MOC, Stoney Point, N.Y., 1963-73, Pearl River Schs., 1965-72; med. dir. St. Agatha Home, Nanuet, N.Y., 1968-76; chief dept. psychiatry Kantonsspital, Luzern, Switzerland, 1976—; ass.t prof. psychiatry N.Y. Med. Coll., 1970-76, N.Y. sch. Psychiatry, 1970-76. Contbr. articles to profl. jours. Fellow Am. Psychiat. Assn. (corr.); mem. Swiss Psychiat. Assn. Office: Kantonsspital, Dept Psychiatry, 6000 Luzern 16, Switzerland

LAESSIG, RONALD HAROLD, pathology educator, state official; b. Marshfield, Wis., Apr. 4, 1940; s. Harold John and Ella Louise (Gumz) L.; m. Joan Margaret Spreda, Jan. 29, 1966; 1 child, Elizabeth Susan. B.S., U. Wis.-Stevens Point, 1962; Ph.D., U. Wis.-Madison, 1965. Jr. faculty Princeton (N.J.) U., 1966; chief clin. chemistry Wis. State Lab. Hygiene, Madison, 1966-80, dir., 1980—; asst. prof. preventive medicine U. Wis.-Madison, 1966-72, assoc. prof., 1972-76, prof., 1976—, prof. pathology, 1980—; cons. Ctr. Disease Control, Atlanta; dir. Nat. Com. for Clin. Lab. Standards, Villanova, Pa., 1977-80; chmn. invitro diagnostic products adv. com. FDA, 1974-75; mem. rev. com. Nat. Bur. Standards, 1983-86. Mem. editorial bd. Med. Electronics, 1970—, Analytical Chemistry, 1970-76, Health Lab. Sci., 1970—; contbr. articles to profl. jours. Mem. State of Wis. Tech. Com. Alcohol and Traffic Safety, 1970-88. Sloan Found. grantee, 1966; recipient numerous grants. Mem. Am. Assn. Clin. Chemistry (chmn. safety com. 1984-86, bd. dirs. 1986-89, Natelson award 1989, Contbns. Svc. to Profession award 1990), Am. Pub. Health Assn. (Difco award 1974), Am. Soc. for Med. Tech., Nat. Com. Clin. Lab. Standards (pres. 1980-82, bd. dirs. 1984-87), Sigma Xi. Office: State Lab Hygiene 465 Henry Mall Madison WI 53706-1501

LAFARGE, LUCY BERGSON, psychoanalyst, educator; b. N.Y.C., Sept. 3, 1948; d. Abram and Rita Salome (Macht) Bergson. BA magna cum laude, Radcliffe Coll., 1969; MD, Albert Einstein Med. Coll., 1976; cert. in psychoanalysis, Columbia U., 1988. Resident in psychiatry Albert Einstein Med. Coll., Bronx, N.Y., 1976-79; clin. instr. in psychiatry Cornell Med. Coll., White Plains, N.Y., 1979; clin. instr. in psychiatry SUNY Downstate Med. Ctr., Bklyn., 1979-81, asst. clin. prof. psychiatry, 1981-85; asst. clin. prof. psychiatry Columbia U. Coll. Physicians and Surgeons, N.Y.C., 1985—; pvt. practice psychoanalysis N.Y.C., 1979—; tng. and supervising analyst Columbia U. Psychoanalytic Ctr. Mem. Am. Psychoanalytic Assn., Assn. for Psychoanalytic Medicine. Office: 239 Central Park W New York NY 10024-6038

LAFERLA, JEFFREY DONALD, optometrist; b. St. Louis, Apr. 17, 1962; s. Donald George and Gloria Jean (King) L.; m. Joni Kay Smith, May 16, 1992. BS in Biology, Mo. So. State Coll., 1984; OD, Ind. U., 1989. Cert. Mo. State Bd. Optometry. Resident in optometry Vet. Affairs Med. Ctr., Tuscaloosa, Ala., 1989-90, U. Mo., St. Louis, 1990-91; optometrist Pearle Vision Ctr., Kansas City, Mo., 1992—. Contbr. articles to profl. jours. Home: 7794 Lynn's Ln Weatherby Lake MO 64152 Office: Pearle Vision Center 5600 E Bannister Rd Ste #127 Kansas City MO 64137

LAFERRIERE, RITA HODGES, nurse; b. Middletown, Conn., Oct. 4, 1948; m. Donald B. Laferriere, Feb. 22, 1969; children: Heidi Ann, Chad Grant. Diploma, Mary Fletcher Hosp. Sch. Nursing, 1969; BS in Profl. Arts, St. Joseph's Coll., 1983; MSN, U. Vt., 1992. RN, Vt.; cert. cmty. health nurse, adult nurse practitioner, clin. nurse specialist. Staff nurse Pawtucket (R.I.) Meml. Hosp., 1969; charge nurse Northeastern Vt. Regional Hosp., St. Johnsbury, 1969-78; presch. health programs Caledonia Home Health, St. Johnsbury, 1978-83, cmty. health staff nurse, 1983-85, insvc. coord., 1985-87, long term care coord., 1987-89, quality assurance coord., 1989-92, clin. nurse specialist, 1992-96, asst. dir. spl. programs, 1996—; bd. dirs. New Move: Adult Day, St. Johnsbury, 1996—; mem. Regional Planning Coun., St. Johnsbury, 1994—; mem. test devel. com. Am. Nurse Credentialing Ctr., 1994—; mem. bd. on certification Cmty. Health Am. Nurse Credentialing Ctr., 1994—; mem. ad. bd. Vt. Dept. Aging and Disability, 1992—. Contbr. articles to profl. jours. 4-H leader East Haven Riverside Rascals. Recipient scholarship Am. Nurses Found., 1992, Sara Thompson Cmty. Health award U. Vt., 1992, Rsch. grant Vt. Folklife Ctr., 1993; named to Am. Nurse Ho. of Dels., Vt. State Nurses, 1994—. Mem. Vt. Sch. Nurse Assn., Vt. State Nurses Assn. (pres. II 1969—, treast dist. II 1969—). Home: PO Box 36 East Haven VT 05837 Office: Caledonia Home Health Care Sherman Dr Saint Johnsbury VT 05819

LAFF, MARJORIE ARONS, social worker; b. Stamford, Conn., Apr. 18, 1937; d. Howard and Ida (Olshansky) Arons; m. Eugene K. Laff, Apr. 19, 1964; children: Geoffrey, Stephanie. BA, Smith Coll., 1958; MSSW, Simmons Coll. Sch. Social Work, 1962. Lic. clin. social worker, Conn. Sch. social worker Arlington (MAss.) Bd. Edn., 1962-63, Greenwich (Conn.) Bd. Edn., 1963-66; dir., officer Jewish Family Svcs. of Greenwich, Conn., 1989—, resettlement worker, therapist, 1990-91; pvt. practice Cos Cob, Conn., 1991—; bd. dirs. Jewish Family Svc., Stamford; clin. social worker Ctr. for Hope, Darien, Conn., 1992—, N.E. Ctr. for Trauma Recovery, Greenwich, 1994—. Bd. dirs. Russian resettlement; past chair Teen Suicide Prevention Task Force; mem. YWCA, Stamford. Recipient Community Svc. award, 1988, Mitzvah award Jewish Family Svc., 1991. Mem. NASW, Acad. Cert. Social Workers (cert.), Greenwich Jewish Fedn. (bd. dirs. 1989-92). Office: 132 E Putnam Ave Cos Cob CT 06807

LAFFER, DENNIS ROSS, physician; b. Detroit, Mar. 12, 1951; s. Allan and Virginia (Ross) L.; m. Ellen Beth Shapiro, June 22, 1986; children: Lauren Abigail, Jenny Elizabeth. BS in Zoology, Mich. State U., 1972; MD, U. Mich., 1976. Physician pvt. practice, Tampa, Fla., 1982—; chief gastroenterology St. Joseph's Hosp., Tampa, 1993—. Bd. dirs. Tampa Bay Holocaust Mus., Madeira Beach, Fla., 1992—. Fellow Am. Coll. Physicians, Am. Coll. Gastroenterology. Office: 4700 N Habana #700 Tampa FL 33614

LAFON, PETER CHRISTIAN, surgeon; b. Ogden, Utah, Sept. 15, 1959; s. Dee J. and Barbara J. (Malan) Lafon; m. Ahniwake Underwood, Nov. 17, 1979; 1 child, Alexandria. BS, East Cen. Okla. U., 1975; DO, Okla. Coll. Osteopathy, 1980. Diplomate Am. Bd. Surgery. Commd. 2d lt. U.S. Army, 1980, advanced through grades to maj., 1986, resigned, 1990; asst. chief surgery Ireland Army Hosp., Ft. Knox, Ky., 1987, chief gen. surgery, 1987-89; chief surgery Cushing (Okla.) Regional Hosp., 1989—. Mem. Rotary. Home: RR 2 Box 2665 Cushing OK 74023-9597 Office: 1030 E Cherry St Cushing OK 74023-4102

LAFRAMBOISE, CAROL ANN, counselor; b. Saginaw, Mich., Apr. 17, 1953; d. Joseph and Eleanor (Piggott) Schmelzer; m. Michael X. LaFramboise, June 14, 1980; 1 child, Megan. BA, Mich. State U., 1977; MA, Cen. Mich. U., 1983. Lic. profl. counselor; cert. social worker, Mich. Ski instr. Apple Mountain, Saginaw, 1969-71; day care worker Salvation Army, Saginaw, 1973-75; tchr. Sheridan Rd. Christian Sch., Saginaw, 1977-78, St. Mary Sch., Saginaw, 1978-81; psychotherapist Jordan Inst., Saginaw, 1985-86; elem. sch. counselor Essexville-Hampton (Mich.) Pub. Schs., 1986—. Mem. NEA, Mich. Counseling Assn., Mich. Sch. Counselors Assn., Mich. Edn. Assn., Bay-Arenac Sch. Counselors Assn. Democrat. Roman Catholic. Home: 821 Plymouth Rd Saginaw MI 48603-7171 Office: Essexville Hampton Pub Schs 805 Langstaff St Essexville MI 48732-1367

LAGA, EDWARD AUGUST, dentist; b. Chgo., Apr. 9, 1959; s. Edward August Sr. and Marianne Gertrude (Irmen) L.; m. Christine Marie Robertsen, Sept. 9, 1995. BA, St. Mary's Coll., 1971; DDS, Loyola Dental Sch., 1985. Oral and maxillofacial surgery resident U. Mo., Kansas City, 1991-95; oral and maxillofacial surgeon Oral Surgeons Inc., Kansas City, Mo., 1995—; instr. U. Mo. Kansas City Med. Sch., 1991—. Vol. Kansas City Free Health Clinic, 1991-94. Lt. comdr. USNR, 1991-95. Recipient Loyola Leadership award Denta Student Congress, 1985. Mem. ADA, Mo. Dental Soc., Midwestern Soc. of Oral and Maxillofacial Surgery, Greater Kansas City Soc. of Oral and Maxillofacial Surgeons, Greater Kansas City Dental Soc. Office: Oral Surgeons Inc 400 E Red Bridge Rd #302 Kansas City MO 64131

LA GAMMA, EDMUND FRANCIS, pediatrician, research scientist; b. N.Y.C., June 28, 1952; s. Armando Monte and Theresa (Carbone) La G.; m. Kalliope Spanondis, June 13, 1976; children: Armando Michael, Nicholas Alexander. BS, CCNY, 1973; MD, N.Y. Med. Coll., 1976. Intern, N.Y. Hosp.-Cornell U., N.Y.C., 1976-77, resident, 1977-78, neonatal fellow, 1978-80; practice medicine specializing in neonatal-perinatal medicine and pediatrics, N.Y.C., 1981—; postdoctoral scholar U. Calif.-San Francisco Cardiovascular Rsch. Inst., 1980-81; asst. prof. pediatrics N.Y. Hosp.-Cornell U., 1980-86, assoc. prof. pediatrics, perinatal medicine in ob-gyn, 1986, instr. neurology, 1983-84, asst. prof. neurology, 1984-86; assoc. prof. pediatrics and neurobiology and behavior SUNY-StonyBrook, 1986-94, prof., 1994; mem. staff SUNY Hosp., N.Y. Hosp., Lenox Hill Hosp., Jamaica Hosp., U. Hosp. StonyBrook. Contbr., investigator Proc. Nat. Acad. Sci., Jour. Sci. Jour. Circulation Rsch., Jour. Pediatric Rsch., Am. Jour. Ob Gyn, Advances in Pediatrics. Recipient Clin. Investigator award NIH, 1980-85; Basil O'Connor award March of Dimes, 1985-87; Am. Heart Assn. grantee, 1985-88, NSF grantee, 1988-91. Fellow Am. Acad. Pediatrics (Young Investigators award 1985); mem. AAAS, N.Y. Acad. Sci., AMA, Med. Soc. State N.Y., Soc. Pediatric Rsch.(council mem. 1992-95), Soc. Neurosci., N.Y. Perinatal Soc. (pres. 1986-89). Roman Catholic. Office: SUNY Dept Pediatrics and Neurobiology Behavior Stony Brook NY 11794-8111

LAGERCRANTZ, CARL HUGO, clinical scientist; b. Stockholm, Apr. 28, 1945; s. Rutger H.C. and Marit A. (Heyman) L.; m. Rose E. Schmidt, Apr. 5, 1968; children: Leo D.A., E.K. Rebecka, E. Samuel D. MB, Karolinska Inst., Stockholm, 1966, PhD, 1971, MD, 1974. Diplomate Swedish Bd. Pediatrics. Instr. Karolinska Inst., 1966-73, acting prof., 1980-81, assoc. prof., 1981-89, prof., 1989—, vice chmn. pediatrics, 1989-93; resident Huddinge Hosp., Stockholm, 1974-78; fellow Karolinska Hosp., Stockholm, 1978-80, dir., 1989—. EditorL Neurobiology of Breathing, 1987, others; assoc. editor Acta Pediatric, 1990-95, European chief editor Pediatric Rsch.; contbr. 180 articles to sci. jours. Mem. Nobel Assembly, Stockholm, 1994. Mem. Swedish Neonatal Soc. (sec. 1985-87, chmn. 1993-95). Home: Grevgahn 9, 11453 Stockholm Sweden Office: Karolinska Hosp, Stockholm 17176, Sweden

LAGERLUND, TERRENCE DANIEL, neurologist; b. Oak Park, Ill., Aug. 14, 1953; s. Harold and Virginia Marie (Wanamaker) L. BA, Elmhurst Coll., 1970; MS, Va. Poly. Inst. and State U., 1972, PhD in Physics, 1975; MD, U. Miami, Fla., 1982. Diplomate Am. Bd. Psychiatry and Neurology, Am. Bd. Clin. Neurophysiology. Postdoctoral rsch. assoc. MIT, Cambridge, Mass., 1975-78; term physicist Fermi Nat. Accelerator Lab., Batavia, Ill., 1978-80; intern in neurology Mayo Grad. Sch. Medicine, Rochester, Minn., 1982-83, resident in neurology, 1983-86, fellow in electroencephalography, 1986-87; sr. assoc. cons. Mayo Clinic, Rochester, 1987-90, cons. in neurology, 1990—; asst. prof. neurology Mayo Med. Sch., 1987-95, assoc. prof. neurology, 1995—. Contbr.: (chpt.) International Reviews of Neurobiology, 1989, Epilepsy Surgery, 1992, Clinical Neurophysiology, 1996; contbr. articles to profl. jours. including Nuclear Instruments and Methods, Computers in Biology and Medicine, Microvascular Rsch., Am. Jour. Physiology, Jour. of Clin. Neurophysiology, Electroencephalography and Clin. Neurophysiology. Recipient Caton award So. EEG Soc., 1987. Mem. ASTM (electrophysiologic waveforms interchange standards com. 1990—), Am. Epilepsy Soc., Am. EEG Soc. (instrumentation com. 1987—), Am. Acad. Neurology, Cen. EEG Assn., Sigma Xi. Republican. Roman Catholic. Home: 5426 Hawthorn Hill Ln NE Rochester MN 55906-8560 Office: Mayo Clinic 200 1st St SW Rochester MN 55905-0001

LAGRUA, JAMES CHRISTIAN, family physician; b. Oklahoma City, July 26, 1962; s. Michael Braddock and Elizabeth (Kennedy) L. BS, Pa. State U., 1984; DO, Kirksville Coll., 1991. Family practice resident U. Calif.-Davis Med. Ctr., Sacramento, 1991-94; family physician Modoc Med. Ctr., Alturas, Calif., 1992-95; emergency physician Colusa (Calif.) Cmty. Hosp., 1992-95; family physician Ft. Defiance (Va.) Med. Ctr., 1996—. Fellow Am. Coll. Osteo. Family Physicians; mem. Am. Acad. Family Physicians. Office: Fort Defiance Med Ctr PO Box 8 Fort Defiance VA 24437

LAGUNOFF, DAVID, physician, educator; b. N.Y.C., Mar. 14, 1932; s. Robert and Cicele (Lipman) L.; m. Susan P. Powers, Mar. 8, 1958; children: Rachel, Liza, Michael. MD, U. Chgo., 1957. Rsch. asst. microbiology U. Miami, Coral Gables, Fla., 1951-53; intern U. Calif. San Francisco Hosp., 1957-58; postdoctoral fellow dept. pathology U. Wash., Seattle, 1958-59, trainee in pathology, 1959-60, instr. pathology, 1960-62, asst. prof., 1962-65, assoc. prof., 1965-69, prof., 1969-79; prof. dept. pathology St. Louis U., 1979—, chmn. dept. pathology, 1979-96, asst. v.p., 1989-93; assoc. dean rsch. St. Louis U. Sch. Medicine, 1989-96. Nat. Heart Inst. fellow Carlsberg Laboratorium, Copenhagen, 1962-64, Nat. Cancer Inst. fellow Sir William Dunn Sch. Pathology, Oxford, Eng., 1970. Mem. AAAS, AAUP, Am. Soc. Cell Biology, Am. Assn. Pathologists, Am. Assn. Immunologists. Office: St Louis Univ Sch Medicine Dept Pathology 1402 S Grand Blvd Saint Louis MO 63104-1004

LA HAISE-LEWIS, SHARON KAY, epidemiologist, nurse, infection control practitioner; b. San Bernardino, Calif., Jan. 22, 1941; d. Raymond Theodore and Arabell Margaret (Greer) Manning; m. Eugene Ernst LaHaise, Feb. 17, 1962 (div. Aug. 1975); children: Curtis Michael, Craig Thomas; m. David Newton Angelo Lewis, Nov. 23, 1988. AS, San Bernardino Valley Coll., 1961, 73; BS in Nursing, Calif. State U., Fullerton, 1978; MS, cert. in edn., U. Calif., Riverside, 1980-82; PhD/MA in Edn. and Health Services Adminstrn., Columbia Pacific U., Mill Valley, Calif., 1985. RN; cert. in pub. health nursing, adult edn., community coll. teaching, mgmt. and supervisory devel., Calif. Microbiology lab. asst. San Bernardino Valley Coll., 1971-73; nursing coordinator critical care Kaiser Hosp., Fontana, Calif., 1973-78; Western region hosp. specialist Merck & Co., Inc., Rahway, N.J., 1978-81; asst. dir. nursing United Health Careers Inst., San Bernardino, 1981-82; patient care supr. Home Health Care Assn., Colton, Calif., 1981-82; dir. infection control, infection surveillance officer Hemet Valley Hosp. Dist., Hemet, Calif., 1982-86; infection control officer Security Forces Hosp., Riyadh, Saudi Arabia, 1986-87; infection control officer, dir. epidemiology Pomona (Calif.) Valley Hosp. Med. Ctr., 1988—; cons. math. and sci. Hdqrs. U.S. Army Armor and Desert Tng. Ctr., Dept. Def., Fort Irwin, Calif., 1963-71; mem. AIDs task force Inland Counties Health Systems Agy.; v.p. exec. bd. Inland AIDs Project; cons. in infection control; lectr. Contbr. poetry to Calif. Anthology (winner 1st place award), 1958; inventor anoxia and model of decompression chamber, winner 1st place in aerospace medicine, 1959; author: Model for Sexuality Counseling, 1978. Precinct clk. Democratic party, Colton, 1958; dir. wildflower festival Barstow (Calif.) C. of C., 1962; art dir. Colton Recreational Dept., 1962; So. Calif. educator coordinator Student Vocat. Nurses Assn., 1981-82, named Outstanding Nursing Educator, 1982. Recipient 1st place award in sci. talent search Westinghouse Corp., 1958; Alpha Gamma Sigma Soc. scholar, 1959, 70-71; named Outstanding Nurse Grad., dept. nursing San Bernardino Valley Coll., 1973. Mem. AAAS, NAFE, N.Y. Acad. Scis., Soc. Health Care Epidemiology Am., Assn. Profls. in Infection Control and Epidemiology. Roman Catholic. Home: 715 Canary St Colton CA 92324-1505 Office: Pomona Valley Hosp Med Ctr 1798 N Garey Ave Pomona CA 91767-2918

LAHANN, THOMAS ROBERT, pharmacology and toxicology educator; b. Dubuque, Iowa; s. Robert James and Marilynn Margaret (Steinhoff) LaH.; m. Prescilla Pascua, Aug. 10, 1974; children: Matthew Thomas, Daniel Dwight. BS in Chemistry, Beloit (Wis.) Coll., 1970; MS in Pharmacology/Toxicology, U. Wash., 1975, PhD in Pharmacology/Toxicology, 1977. Cert. in gen. toxicology, Am. Bd. Toxicology, 1980. Toxicologist/pharmacologist soap/toilet goods Tech. Divsn., Procter & Gamble Co., Cin., 1977-81, group leader toxicology and project leader, 1981-82, group leader toxicology/project leader health/personal care, 1982-85; asst. prof. pharmacology/toxicology grad. program Wash. State U., Pullman, 1985-90, asst. prof. pharmacology/toxicology Coll. Pharmacy, 1985-90; assoc. prof. pharmacology Idaho State U., Pocatello, 1990—, dir. Ctr. Toxicology Rsch., 1992—; cons. on medicolegal issues, risk assessment issues and drug devel. issues for multiple cos.; lectr. in field. Contbr. articles to profl. jours. Mem. sci. coun. Am. Heart Assn. Mem. Internat. Soc. for Neutron Capture Therapy, Soc. for Neuroscis., Am. Assn. Colls. of Pharmacy, Western Pharmacology Soc., Rho Chi. Home: 2717 Clearwater St Pocatello ID 83201-1873 Office: Idaho State Univ College of Pharmacy Pocatello ID 83209-8334

LAHEY, MARION EUGENE, physician, educator; b. Ft. Worth, Dec. 28, 1917; s. Michael James and Mary Margaret (Kane) L.; m. Edna M. Boyd, June 5, 1942; children—Gene, Michael, Kelly, Maureen, Kathleen, Patrick. A.B., U. Tex., 1939; M.D., St. Louis U., 1943. Intern U.S. Naval Hosp., Great Lakes, Ill., 1943-44; resident pediatrics Hermann Hosp., Houston, 1946-47, Children's Hosp., Cin., 1947-48; chief pediatric resident Children's Hosp., 1948-49; NRC fellow med. scis. U. Utah Med. Sch., 1949-51, mem. faculty, 1951-52, 58—, prof., head dept. pediatrics, 1965—; asst. prof., then asso. prof. pediatrics U. Cin., 1952-58; dir. research Bruce Lyon Meml. Research Lab., Children's Hosp. East Bay, Oakland, Calif., 1964-65. Mem. fellowship com. Leukemia Soc., 1958; mem. hematology tng. grant com. NIH, 1959. Mem. Soc. Pediatric Research (v.p. 1963), Am., Intermountain pediatric socs., Am. Acad. Pediatrics, Am. Soc. Clin. Oncology, Am. Hematology Soc., A.M.A., Western Soc. Pediatric Research, Western Soc. Clin. Research, Utah, Salt Lake County med. socs., Phi Beta Kappa, Alpha Omega Alpha, Alpha Sigma Nu. Home: 2114 Fardown Ave Salt Lake City UT 84121-1409

LAHIRI, DEBOMOY KUMAR, molecular neurobiologist, educator; b. Varanasi, Uttar Pradesh, India, Sept. 9, 1955; came to U.S. 1983.; s. Benoy Kumar and Nilima Rani (Moitra) L.; m. Mithu Mukherjee, Dec. 15, 1991; 1 child, Niloy K. MS, Benaras Hindu U., India, 1975, PhD, 1980. Rsch. fellow Benaras Hindu U., Varanasi, 1975-79; jr. scientist Indian Coun. of Agrl. Rsch., New Delhi, India, 1979-81; postdoctoral fellow McMaster U. Sch. Medicine, Hamilton, Ont., Can., 1982; asst. rsch. scientist NYU, N.Y.C., 1983-86; rsch. assoc. N.Y. State Inst. for Basic Rsch., Staten Island, N.Y., 1987; asst. prof. Mt. Sinai Sch. Medicine, N.Y.C., 1988-90; asst. prof., chief molecular neurogenetics lab. Inst. Psychiat. Rsch. Ind. U. Sch. Medicine, Indpls., 1990—, asst. prof. med. & molecular genetics, 1994-96, assoc. prof. med. neurobiology and med. & molecular genetics, 1996—; presenter in field. Contbr. articles to profl. jours. U.P. Govt. Merit scholar, 1970-75; Univ. Grants Commn. New Delhi jr. rsch. fellow, 1975-79; grantee NIH, 1991—. Mem. AAAS, Am. Soc. Cell Biology, Am. Soc. Human Genetics, Am. Soc. for Neurochemistry, Am. Soc. Biochemistry and Molecular Biology, Genetics Soc. Am., Internat. Soc. for Neurochemistry, Soc. Biol. Psychiatry, Soc. for Neurosci., N.Y. Acad. Scis. Democrat. Hindu. Home: 5731 Arabian Run Indianapolis IN 46208-1684 Office: Inst Psychiat Rsch Ind Univ 791 Union Dr Indianapolis IN 46202-2873

LA HOOD, GARY J., health facility administrator, social worker. BSW, U. Detroit, 1984; MSW, Wayne State U., 1985; M of Health Adminstrn., Ctrl. Mich. U., 1995. Lic. social worker, Mich. Social worker Samaritan Hosp., Detroit, 1985-87; supr. social work St. John Hosp., Detroit, 1987-91; dir. social work & EAP Macomb Hosp. Ctr., Warren, Mich., 1991-95; adminstr., CEO Harbor Oaks Hosp., New Baltimore, Mich., 1995—, Pioneer Healthcare Mich. Active Child Protection, Macomb County, Mich., 1996. Office: Harbor Oaks Hosp 35031 23 Mile Rd New Baltimore MI 48047

LAHOWCHIC, NICHOLAS JOHN, healthcare company executive; b. N.Y.C., Apr. 11, 1947; s. Nicholas and Mary Ellen (Dunn) La H.; m. Diane Forrest; children: Tara Anne, Nicole Marie. Student, Marquette U., 1964-66; BS in Acctg., Fairleigh Dickinson U., 1970; MBA, Pace U., 1980. Acct. Okonite Cable Corp., Passaic, N.J., 1966-68; cost analyst Philips Broadcast Equip. Corp., Paramus, N.J., 1968-69; corporate acct. Thomas J. Lipton, Inc., Englewood Cliffs, N.J., 1969-70, fin. systems analyst, 1970-72, mgr. cash mgmt., 1972-73, mgr. hdqrs. distbn. services, 1974-76, mgr. distbn. and sales services, 1976-77, mgr. ops. planning, 1977-79; gen. mgr. McGraw Hill Book Co., N.Y.C., 1979-81; dir. inventory mgmt. Nabisco Brands Inc., Parsippany, N.J., 1981-84, dir. inventory mgmt. and logistics planning, 1984-85, dir. logistics planning, systems & adminstrn., 1985-87; dir. logistics Colgate-Palmolive Inc., N.Y.C., 1987-89, dir. customer svc. and logistics, 1989-91; v.p. corp. logistics Becton Dickinson & Co., Franklin Lakes, N.J., 1991-95; pres. Becton Dickinson Supply Chain Svcs., Franklin Lakes, N.J., 1995—; dir. effecient healthcare consumer response industry com., 1995-96; cons. in field. Editl. adv. bd. Supply Chain Mgmt. Review; contbr. articles to bus. publs. Mem. Nat. Assn. Accts., Am. Mgmt. Assn., Am. Prodn. and Inventory Control Soc. (dir. 1979-80), Nat. Council Phys. Distbn. Mgmt. (v.p. 1982-83), Health Industry Distbr. Assn., Health Industry Mfrs. Assn.,

Health Industry Bar Code Coun., Grocery Mfrs. Assn. (chmn. distbn. ops. steering com.), Council Logistics Mgmt., Internat. Materials Mgmt. Soc. Pace U. Home: 17 Pond Ln Hastings On Hudson NY 10706-3640 Office: Becton Dickinson Supply Chain Svc 1 Becton Dr Franklin Lakes NJ 07417-1815

LAI, ERIC PONG SHING, family physician, educator; b. Kowloon, Hong Kong, May 20, 1946; s. Man Hoi and Lai Ming (Chau) L.; m. Maria Lai Bing Mak, Sept. 11, 1972; children: Gordon, Jennifer. BSc, Acadia U., Wolfville, Nova Scotia, 1971; MB, B CH, LRCS, LLMRCP, U. Ireland, Dublin, 1977; DFM, Chinese U. Hong Kong, 1989. Med. diplomate, Ireland, UK, Hong Kong. Rsch. fellow Med. Sch. McGill U., Montreal, Can., 1971; resident in medicine Chesterton Hosp. Cambridge (Eng.) U., 1977; resident New Addenbrooke Hosp., Cambridge, 1978; resident in gynecology Princess Margaret Hosp., Kowloon, Hong Kong, 1979-81; pvt. practice family physician Hong Kong, 1981-95; bd. dirs. First Med. Mgmt. Ltd., Calgary, Alta., Can., 1989; found. dir. Chinese Recreation Assn., Calgary; lectr. Hong Kong U., 1986-92, Chinese U. Hong Kong, 1986-92; facilitator Hong Kong Coll. Gen. Practitioners, 1986-92; internat. dir. World Orgn. Health Promotion, 1993-95; cons. G-Way Holdings Internat. Inc., 1993-95; health cons. G-Way Health Centre, Can., 1995. Mem. Hong Kong Dem. Found., 1990-92, Hong Kong Bd. Edn. Coll. Gen. Practitioners, 1986-92, chmn., 1991-92, com. chmn. refresher course, 1991-92; vice chmn. found. Kidney Ctr. Precious Blood Hosp., 1991; adviser S.E. Asia Rsch. Inst., 1992; mem. Pub. Edn. Com., 1993-95; med. cons. World Orgn. Health Promotion, Can., 1993-95. Named Henry Burton De Wolfe scholar to McGill U., 1971. Mem. Internat. Lions Club (v.p. Mt. Cameron chpt. 1986-90, pres. 1990-91, zone chmn. Internat. Club 1991-92). Democrat.

LAI, LESLIE, pathologist, consultant, lecturer; b. Malacca, Malaysia, Sept. 26, 1959; s. Philip and Irene (Toh) L. MBBS, Guy's Hosp., London, 1983; MSc, Charing Cross and Westminster Hosps., 1987; MD, London U., 1990. Sr. house officer St. Stephen's Hosp., London, 1984-85, registrar in pathology, 1985-86; lectr. in chem. pathology St. Mary's Hosp., London, 1986-90; cons., sr. lectr. in clin. biochemistry Freeman Hosp., Newcastle upon Tyne, Eng., 1990—; specialty regional adv. Royal Coll. Pathologists, Eng., 1995—; chmn. no. region. biochemistry audit working group, Eng., 1995—, sec. specialist adv. group clin. biochemistry , 1992—. Contbr. articles to profl. jours. Chmn. Tyneside Cancer Trust, Eng., 1994. Mem. Internat. Soc. Preventive Oncology, N.Y. Acad. Scis., Soc. Endocrinology, Assn. Clin. Biochemists, Brit. Med. Assn., Royal Coll. Pathologists. Office: Dept Clin Biochemistry Freeman Hosp, Freeman Rd, Newcastle upon Tyne Tyne and Wear NE7 7DN, England

LAI, PATRICK KINGLUN, immunologist; b. Hong Kong, Oct. 10, 1944; s. Cho Kwai and Sui Man (Cheung) L.; m. Priscilla T.P. Liu; children: Lee James Robert Allum, Chay Antony Paul Allum. BS, U. Western Australia, 1971, PhD, 1978. Microbiologist Pub. Health Dept., Perth, Australia, 1971-75; rsch. fellow U. Ottawa (Can.), 1978-79, Univ. Coll. London, 1979-82; sr. rsch. officer Royal Postgrad. Med. Sch., London, 1982-84; asst. prof. U. Nebr. Med. Ctr., Omaha, 1984-87; asst. mem. Tampa Bay Rsch. Inst., St. Petersburg, Fla., 1987-90, mem., 1990-96; assoc. prof. Salem-Teikyo U., W.Va., 1993—. Contbr. articles to profl. jours.; inventor, patentee in field. Rsch. fellow Imperial Cancer Rsch. Fund, London, 1979-82, WHO, 1976; Short-Term fellow European Molecular Biology Orgn., 1980; Short-Term scholar Internat. Agy. of Rsch. on Cancer, 1975. Mem. N.Y. Acad. Scis., Am. Assn. Immunologists, AAAS. Office: Salem-Teikyo U Salem WV 26426

LAIKIND, DONNA, psychotherapist, consultant; b. N.Y.C., Oct. 29, 1944; d. Charles and Eleanor (Boyarsky) Ressler; m. Jeffrey Laikind, June 29, 1969; children: Rachel Kate, Daniel Aaron. BA, Cornell U., 1965; MS in Counseling, Bank St. Coll. Edn., 1984; cert. in family therapy, Ackerman Inst. Family Therapy, 1990. Behavioral trainer McDermott & Assocs., N.Y.C., 1982-84; dir. orgnl. devel. Altro Health and Rehab., N.Y.C., 1985-86; family therapy cons. Family Dynamics, N.Y.C., 1987-90; psychosocial cons. Food Allergy Ctr., N.Y.C., 1990-91; family therapy cons. SCAN, N.Y.C., 1990—; pvt. practice N.Y.C. and Weston, Conn., 1987—; dir. Family Dynamics Inc., 1985—, chmn., bd. dirs., 1990-94; guest lectr. workshops in field. Contbr. articles to profl. jours. Bd. dirs. U.S. Com. Sports for Israel, Maccabiah Games, N.Y.C., 1990—, mission dir., 1989, Ackerman Inst. Family Therapy, 1991-96, chmn. bd. 1996—. Address: 37 Cedar Hls Weston CT 06883-2948

LAINSON, PHILLIP ARGLES, dental educator; b. Council Bluffs, Iowa, Feb. 11, 1936; s. Donald Wesley and Olive Ione (Stageman) L.; m. Mary Margaret Tangney, June 18, 1960; children—David, Michael, Elizabeth. B.A., U. Iowa, 1960, D.D.S., 1962, M.S., 1968; Dental Intern Cert., USAF Malcom Crow Hosp., 1963. Diplomate Am. Bd. Periodontology. Instr. dept. periodontics U. Iowa, Iowa City, 1965-69, asst. prof., 1969-71, assoc. prof., 1971-75, prof., 1975—, head dept. periodontics, 1976—; cons. in periodontics VA Hosp., Knoxville, Iowa, 1967—, Iowa City, 1976—, Central Regional Dental Testing Service, Topeka, Kans., 1977-81, Commn. on Dental Accreditation, ADA, Chgo., 1985-90. Contbr. articles to profl. jours. Editor newsletter Midwest Soc. Periodontology, 1982-85. Assoc. editor Iowa Dental Jour., 1974-76. Chmn., Bd. in Control of Athletics U. Iowa, 1984-86. Served to capt. USAF, 1962-65, Iowa Army N.G., 1973-91. Am. Coll. Dentists fellow, 1976; Internat. Coll. Dentists fellow, 1991; Pierre Fauchard fellow, 1991. Mem. Iowa Soc. Periodontology (pres. 1976-78), U. Dist. Iowa Dental Assn. (pres. 1979-80), Midwest Soc. Periodontology (pres. 1987-88), Am. Acad. Periodontology, Internat. Assn. Dental Researcrh, Am. Dental Assn. (coun. on govtl. affairs and fed. dental svcs. 1989-93), Test Construction com., Joint Commn. Nat. Dental Exam., 1995—. Am. Assn. Dental Schs., Sigma Xi, Omicron Kappa Upsilon. Republican. Roman Catholic. Lodge: Rotary. Avocations: sailing; fishing; biking; tennis. Home: 16 Ridgewood Ln Iowa City IA 52245-1632 Office: U Iowa Coll Dentistry Iowa City IA 52242

LAIRD, BRADLEY DUANE, social services administrator, psychotherapist; b. Oakland, Calif., Feb. 5, 1956; s. Duane Richard and Eunice Delphine (Glock) L.; m. Elizabeth Lorraine Hughson, Aug. 3, 1985; children: Cameron James, Rhiannon Elizabeth, Quinn Campbell. AA, Concordia Luth. Coll., 1976; BS in Psychology, Valparaiso (Ind.) U., 1978; MSW, Loyola U., 1986; student, Ctr. Psychoanalytic Study, Chgo. Psychiat. technician Porter-Starke Svcs., Inc., Valparaiso, 1978-81; staff therapist II Tri-City Community Mental Health Ctr., East Chicago, Ind., 1981-83, staff therapist IV, 1983-86, program supr., 1986-88, svc. dir., 1988-90; intern U. Chgo. Hosps., 1985-86; pvt. practice psychotherapist Merrillville, Ind., 1989-91; div. dir. Habilitative Systems, Inc., Chgo., 1990-91; assoc. dir. Children's Campus Family and Children's Ctr., Mishawaka, Ind., 1991-95; exec. dir. Family Svc. Assn. LaPorte County, Inc., Michigan City, Ind., 1995—. Gen. mem. Miller and Gary Citizens Corp., 1984-91—, bd. dirs., treas., 1986-88; bd. dirs. Neighborhood Housing Svcs. of South Bend, 1993—; bd. trustees, v.p. First Unitarian Ch. of South Bend, 1994—. Mem. NASW, Nat. Fedn. Socs. for Clin. Social Work, Am. Group Psychotherapy Assn., Am. Soc. Quality Control.

LAISSY, JEAN PIERRE, health facility administrator, radiologist; b. Neuilly-sur-Seine, France, May 10, 1953; s. Michel and Denise (Alleaume) L.; m. Elizabeth Gabrielle Ironde, Jan. 27, 1975; children: Thomas, Matthieu. MD, U. Paris VII, 1982; PhD, U. Paris V, 1993; Habilite a Diriger des Recherches, 1993. Intern Hosp. de Paris, 1978-82, asst. chef de clinique, 1982-86; praticien hospitalier Paris, 1987—; assoc. dir. radiology dept. Hosp. Bichat, Paris, 1991—; assoc. rschr. U. Paris VII, 1994—. Co-author several med. books, 1986-95; co-author and co-editor: (med. book) Imaging Advances, 1995; contbr. articles to profl. jours. Capt. Med. Support to French Army, 1978-79. Mem. Radiol. Soc. N.Am., French Radiol. Soc. Office: Hop Bichat, 46 Rue Henri Huchard, 75018 Paris France

LAKATTA, EDWARD GERARD, biomedical researcher; b. Scranton, Pa., May 10, 1944; s. Edward and Pauline Ann (Lucas) L.; m. Loretta Ellen Cantwell, July 27, 1968; children: Edward A., Christiana, Lucas A. BS in Biology, U. Scranton, 1966; MD, Georgetown U., 1970. Intern Strong Meml. Hosp., Rochester, N.Y., 1970-71, asst. resident, 1971-72; clin. assoc. Gerontology Rsch. Ctr. cardiovascular sect. NIH, Nat. Child Health & Human Devel., Clin. Physiology Br., Balt., 1972-74; asst. in medicine Johns Hopkins Sch. Medicine, Balt., 1973-74; fellow in cardiology Georgetown U. Hosp., Washington, 1974-75; fellow in med. sci. Am. Coll. Physicians for 1975 dept. physiology Univ. Coll., London, 1975-76; fellow in med. sci. dept. cardiac medicine Cardiothoracic Inst., London, 1975-76; chief cardiovascular sect. clin. physiology br. Gerontology Rsch. Ctr., Nat. Inst. Aging NIH, Balt., 1976-85, chief Lab. Cardiovascular Sci., Gerontology Rsch. Ctr., Nat. Inst. Aging, 1985—, acting sci. dir. Nat. Inst. Aging, 1994-95; prof. medicine Johns Hopkins Sch. Medicine, Balt., 1983—; prof. physiology Sch. Medicine U. Md., Balt., 1985—; vis. physician Bayview Med. Ctr., Balt., Md.; mem. ad hoc study sect. on animal model for study of pathogenesis of spl. heart muscle disease NIH, 1981; mem. ad hoc grant proposal reviews and site visit coms. VA and NSF; ad hoc reviewer Am. Jour. Physiology, Can. Jour. Physiology and Pharmacology, Circulation Rsch., Jour. Molecular and Cellular Cardiology, Sci.; mem. search com. for dir. Nat. Heart, Lung and Blood Inst., 1981, Gerontology Rsch. Ctr., 1988; chmn. intramural promotions and tenure review com. Nat. Inst. Aging, 1989-91; cons. in field. Editor for clin. scis. Exptl. Aging Rsch., 1982-89; assoc. editor Jour. Molecular and Cellular Cardiology, 1987—; mem. editorial bd. Jour. Gerontology, Jour. Molecular and Cellular Cardiology, Cardiosci., Current Problems in Geriatrics, Jour. Cardiovascular Electrophysiology; contbr. numerous articles to profl. jours., chpts. to books. Med. dir. USPHS, 1976. Recipient Paul Dudley White award Assn. Mil. Surgeons of U.S., 1992, Achievement in Aging award Allied Signal, 1993; Eli Lilly Med. Sci. fellow Am. Coll. Physicians, 1975. Fellow Am. Physiol. Soc. (cardiovascular sect.), Am. Heart Assn. (coun. basic sci., Cardiovascular B rsch. study com. 1987-89, application task force Mission to Elderly 1989-90, 90-91), Am. Soc. Clin. Investigation, Am. Assn. Physicians, Internat. Soc. for Heart Rsch. (coun.), Biophys. Soc.; mem. Physiol. Soc. (London). Home: 126 Briarcliff Ln Bel Air MD 21014-5553 Office: Nat Inst Aging Lab Cardiovascular Sci Gerontology Rsch Ctr Rm 3D09 Baltimore MD 21224-2780

LAKDAWALA, SHARAD R., psychiatrist; b. Broach, India, Oct. 7, 1949; came to U.S., 1977; s. Ramprasad D. and Kailasben Lakdawala; m. Bhavna B. Khatri, Jan. 2, 1978; children: Viraj, Ravi. BJ, Med. Coll., Ahmedabad, India, 1972. Diplomate Am. Bd. Psychiatry and Neurology. Intern Civil Hosp., Ahmedabad, 1972-73; resident in psychiatry B.J. Med. Coll. and Civil Hosp., Ahmedabad, 1974-75; med. officer in-charge psychiat. unit Kasama (Zambia) Gen. Hosp., 1975-77; rotating intern NYU Med. Ctr., 1977-78, Bellevue Hosp., 1977-78; resident CUNY/Mt. Sinai Svcs., 1978-81; pvt. practice, 1981—; dir. mental health svcs. Tampa Gen. Hosp., 1988-93, chmn. dept. psychiatry, 1990-93; med. dir., svc. dir. adult psychiatry Charter Hosp. Tampa Bay; chmn. dept. psychiatry Tampa Gen. Hosp.; past pres. med. staff Charter Hosp. Tampa Bay, svc. dir. adult psychiatry; mem. St. Joseph's Hosp., U. Community Hosp., Affiliated Svcs. Tampa Gen. Hosp.; cons. in field. Fellow Am. Psychiat. Assn., Fla. Psychiat. Soc., Tampa Psychiat. Assn. (v.p. 1989-90, pres. 1990-91), Fla. Med. Assn., Hillsborough County Med Assn., Am. Assn. Psychiatrist India (pres-elect Fla. chpt.). Office: 3709 W Hamilton Ave # 2 Tampa FL 33614 also: 505 Eichenfeld Dr # 106 Brandon FL 33511-5956

LAKE, CAROL LEE, anesthesiologist, educator; b. Altoona, Pa., July 14, 1944; d. Samuel Lindsay and Edna Winifred (McMahan) L. BS, Juniata Coll., 1966; MD, Med. Coll. Pa., 1970; postgrad., U. Calif., Irvine. Intern Mercy Hosp., Pitts., 1970-71, resident in anesthesiology, 1971-73; staff anesthesiologist Pitts. Anesthesia Assocs., 1973-75; asst. prof. anesthesiology U. Va., Charlottesville, 1975-80, assoc. prof., 1980-89, prof. anesthesiology, 1989-94; prof. anesthesiology, chair U. Calif., Davis, 1994-95, prof. clin. anesthesiology, 1996—; sr. assoc. examiner Am. Bd. Anesthesiology, Hartford, Conn., 1981—. Author: Cardiovascular Anesthesia, 1985; editor: Pediatric Cardiac Anesthesia, 1988, 2d edit., 1993; Clinical Monitoring, 1990, 2d edit., 1994; co-editor: Blood: Hemostasis, Transfusion and Alternatives in the Perioperative Period, 1995; editor Advances in Anesthesia, 1993—. Fellow Am. Coll. Cardiology; mem. Assn. Cardiac Anesthesiologists (pres. 1987-88), Soc. Cardiovascular Anesthesiologists (bd. dirs. 1988-92), Assn. Univ. Anesthesiologists, Alpha Omega Alpha. Presbyterian. Office: Univ Cali, Davis Sch of Med Univ CA Davis Sch of Medicine Davis CA 95616

LAKES, RODERIC STEPHEN, biomedical engineering educator; b. N.Y.C., Aug. 10, 1948; s. Eric A. and Dorothy E. (Hollweg) L.; m. Diana M. Vezzetti, Aug. 14, 1971. Student, Columbia U., 1964, 65, U. Md., 1969-70; BS, Rensselaer Poly. Inst., 1969, PhD, 1975. NIH predoctoral trainee HEW, 1972-75; rsch. assoc. dept. engrng. and applied sci. Yale U., New Haven, 1975-77; asst. prof. physics Tuskegee (Ala.) Inst., 1977-78; asst. prof. biomed. and mech. engrng. U. Iowa, Iowa City, 1978-82, assoc. prof., 1982-86, prof., 1986—, prof. laser sci., 1987—; vis. prof. materials dept. Queen Mary Coll., London, spring 1984; vis. prof. engrng. mechanics U. Wis., Madison, fall 1990; vis. prof. theoretical and applied mechanics Cornell U., fall 1991; reviewer Allyn and Bacon, 1979-80; external reviewer Nat. Inst. Arthritis Metabolism and Digestive Diseases, NIH, 1979; ad hoc reviewer Pritzker Inst. Med. Engrng., Ill. Inst. Tech., Chgo., 1981; workshop participant Am. Acad. Orthop. Surgeons, 1979. Author: (with J.B. Park) Biomaterials, 1992; reviewer, contbr. numerous articles to profl. jours. Recipient Outstanding Faculty award Student Soc. Biomed. Engrng., U. Iowa, 1985, 86, 88, 94, award for faculty achievement Burlington No. Found., 1987, Instrnl. Improvement award U. Iowa, 1989; Rensselaer scholar, 1965-69, Univ. Faculty scholar, 1990-93; Old Gold fellow, 1986. Fellow ASME (joint biomechanics com. 1984—, AAAS; mem. Am. Soc. Metals Internat., Am. Phys. Soc., Soc. Photo-Optical Instrument Engrs., Sigma Xi. Episcopalian. Office: U Iowa Dept Biomed Engrng Iowa City IA 52242

LAKHANPAL, SHARAD, physician; b. Lucknow, India, Oct. 15, 1951; came to U.S., 1980; s. Rajendra Nath and Indra (Kalia) L.; m. Rashmi Sharma, Nov. 17, 1980; children: Akshai, Shuchi, Virad. Student, Colvin Coll., Lucknow, 1969; MB, BS, K.G. Med. Coll., Lucknow, 1974, Dr.med., 1977. Diplomate Am. Bd. Internal Medicine, Am. Bd. Rheumatology. Rotating intern Ghandi Meml. and Assocs. Hosps., King George's Med. Coll., 1974, resident in medicine, 1975-78; sr. house officer in internal medicine Sunderland Hosp., Hemlington Hosp., Poole Hosp., Eng., 1979-80; resident in internal medicine Meml. Hosp., U. Mass. Med. Sch., Worcester, 1980-82; fellow Mayo Clin., Rochester, Minn., 1983-86; attending physician St. Paul Med. Ctr., Dallas, 1987—; asst. prof. of medicine Southwestern Med. Sch., Dallas, 1989—; instr. Southwestern Med. Sch., Dallas, 1987-89; referee to numerous med. jours. Sr. editor Jour. of Biol. and Chem. Rsch., 1987—; contbr. chpt. to book and articles to profl. jours. Bd. dirs. North Tex. chpt. Arthritis Found., 1992—; trustee DFW Hindu Temple, Gallas, 1994-96; bd. dirs. United Way of Met. Dallas, 1995—, mem. exec com., 1995-96. Recipient Platinum Jubilee Gold medal King Georges Med. Coll., 1986; Am. Rheumatism Assn. fellow, 1984, 85, scholar, 1986; Philips Hench scholar, 1986. Fellow ACP, Am. Rheumatism Assn. (founding), Am. Coll. Rheumatology; mem. Indian Rheumatism Assn., Arthritis Found. (sci. com. and chmn. profl. edn. com. North Tex. chpt., also bd. dirs. 1992—), Lupus Found. Am. (med. adv. bd.), Tex. Med. Assn., Dallas County Med. Soc., Tex. Indo-Am. Physicians Soc. (pres. 1994-95), King George Med. Coll. Alumni Assn. in Am. (sec.-treas. 1988-89, v.p. 1991-92, pres. 1993-94), Dallas-Ft. Worth Rheumatology Club (organizing sec.). Hindu. Office: Rheumatology Assocs 5939 Harry Hines Blvd Bldg 400 Dallas TX 75235-6243

LAKIN, JAMES DENNIS, allergist, immunologist, director; b. Harvey, Ill., Oct. 4, 1945; s. Ora Austin and Annie Pitranella (Johnson) L.; m. Sally A. Stuteville, July 22, 1972; children: Margaret K., Matthew A. PhD, Northwestern U., 1968, MD, 1969; MBA in Med. Group Mgmt., U. St. Thomas, 1996. Diplomate Am. Bd. Internal Medicine, Am. Bd. Allergy and Immunology. Dir. allergy rsch. Naval Med. Rsch. Inst., Bethesda, Md., 1974-76; clin. prof. U. Okla., Oklahoma City, 1976-89; dir. lab., chmn. allergy and immunology dept. Oxboro Clinics, Bloomington, Minn., 1989—; dir. Fairview Allergy and Asthma Svcs., Bloomington, 1995—; bd. dirs. Okla. Med. Rsch. Found., Oklahoma City, 1980-89; regional cons. Diver Alert Network, Duke U., Chapel Hill, N.C., 1987—; cert. diving med. officer NOAA, 1988. Co-author: Allergic Diseases, 1971, 3d edit., 1986; contbr. articles, revs. to profl. publs. Councilperson Our Lord's Luth. Ch., Oklahoma City, 1978-88, Faith Luth. Ch., Lakeville, Minn., 1990-91. Lt. comdr. USN, 1970-76. Fellow ACP, Am. Acad. allergy and Immunology, Am. Coll. Chest Physicians; mem. Am. Assn. Immunologists, Med. Group Mgmt. Assn., Am. Coll. Physician Execs. Office: Oxboro Clinic 600 W 98th St Bloomington MN 55420-4773

LAKS, MICHAEL MILTON, medical educator, cardiovascular researcher; b. Cleve., July 25, 1928; s. Alexander and Helen (Klein) L.; m. Sandra Beller, June 13, 1959; children: Helaina Sharon, Alexander Paul. BA, UCLA, 1951; MD, U. So. Calif., 1956. Diplomate Am. Bd. Internal Medicine, Am. Bd. Cardiovascular Diseases. Asst. dir., dept medicine Cedars-Sinai Med. Ctr., Los Angeles, 1961-64, dir. dept. medicine, 1964-65, physician in charge cardiovascular research lab., 1965-71, sr. research scientist, 1969—; dir. cardiovascular research Harbor-UCLA Med. Ctr., Torrance, Calif., 1971-90, dir. heart sta., 1971—; assoc. chief cardiology Harbor UCLA Med. Ctr., Torrance, Calif., 1975—; disting. prof. sch. medicine UCLA, 1992—; cons. cardiovascular care VA Hosp., Los Angeles, 1971—; ECG research cons. Hewlett-Packard Co., McMinnville, Oreg., 1973—. Author: Vectorial Approach to Electrocardiography, 1986; contbr. over 400 papers, abstracts and revs. to profl. jours. Am. Chem. Soc. scholar, 1947. Fellow ACP (rsch. paper award 1961), Am. Coll. Cardiology, Am. Coll. Chest Physicians, Am. Geriatrics Soc. (founder), Royal Soc. Medicine, Coun. Clin. Cardiology; mem. Internat. Soc. Computerized Electrocardiography (pres., chmn. 1984—), Nat. Inst. Health, Gen. Clin. Rsch. Ctr., Phi Beta Kappa, Alpha Omega Alpha, Phi Kappa Phi. Home: 1939 N Edgemont St Los Angeles CA 90027-1805 Office: Harbor UCLA Med Ctr PO Box 2910 Torrance CA 90509-2910

LAL, ANSELM HLAWN, anesthesiologist; b. Falam, Chin, Burma, Mar. 26, 1944; s. Hrang and Sung (Nuam) Voom; m. Anne Sang Cer, Apr. 12, 1966; 5 children. MB BS, Inst. Medicine, Rangoon, Burma, 1969. Med. officer TB Burma Health Ministry, Falam, 1971-76, 78-79, Matupi, 1976-78; anesthesiologist Burma Health Ministry, Rangoon, 1981-89; anesthesiologist Health Ministry, Muar, Malaysia, 1990-94, Segamat, Malaysia, 1995—. Sec. Twp. Redcross Soc., Falam, 1974-76. Mem. Malaysian Med. Coun., Am. Soc. Regional Anesthesia. Roman Catholic.

LA LONDE, LAWRENCE LEE, family practice physician; b. Bay City, Mich., Feb. 8, 1951; s. Raymond Lawrence and Bernice (Trombley) La L.; m. Laura Christine Madison, June 26, 1976; children: Lawrence Christian, Loren Michael, Lindsey David. B in Gen. Studies, U. Mich., 1973; MD, Wayne State U., 1978. Diplomate Am. Bd. of Family Practice. Resident in Family Practice Saginaw (Mich.) Coop. Hosps., Inc., 1981; physician Oscoda (Mich.) Family Physicians, 1981-85, Ctrl. Calif. Faculty Med. Group, Fresno, Calif., 10985, Saginaw (Mich.) Family Physicians, 1986-87, St. Mary's Seton Corp., Saginaw, Mich., 1987-89, pvt. practice, Saginaw, 1989—. adj. asst. dir. Family Practice Resident Program, Saginaw Coop Hosps., 1986—. Office: Lawrence L La Londe MD PC 5421 N Colony Saginaw MI 48603

LAM, CHI MING, surgeon, researcher; b. Hong Kong, China, Jan. 1, 1963; s. Choi and Yin Fong (Lee) L.; m. Sau Shun Lam. MB BChir, U. Hong Kong, 1987, MS, 1996. Med. officer dept. surgery Queen Mary Hosp., Hong Kong, 1988-95; rsch. fellow U. Dundee, 1995-96; sr. med. officer surgery Queen Mary Hosp., Hong Kong, 1996—. Contbr. reports to profl. publs. Recipient Howard Eddey Gold medal Royal Australasian Coll. Surgeons; 1989. Fellow Royal Coll. Surgeons (Edinburgh), Hong Kong Acad. Medicine; mem. European Assn. Endoscopic Surgery. Home: T8 Bonham Rd, 2A Block A Ning Yeung Ter, Hong Kong China Office: U Hong Kong Dept Surgery, 102 Pokfulam Rd, Hong Kong China

LAM, TINA MARIE, surgeon, educator; b. Chicago Heights, Ill., Oct. 14, 1960; d. Daniel Joseph and Gina (Dang) L.; m. Arthur Michael Sharkey, Apr. 13, 1991; children: Jason Scott Sharkey. BA, U. Chgo., 1982; MD, Loyola U., 1987. Diplomate Am. Bd. Surgery. Rsch. asst. dept. medicine U. Chgo., 1980-82; resident in gen. surgery U. Ill., Chgo., 1987-94; asst. prof., rsch. assoc. dept. surgery Loyola U., Maywood, Ill., 1989-91; lectr. U. Louisville Dept. Surgery, 1994-95; asst. prof. dept. surgery U. Fla., Gainesville, Fla., 1995—; adminstrv. chief resident in gen. surgery U. Ill. Hosps. and Clins., 1993-94; presenter in field. Contbr. articles to profl. pubs. Argonne Nat. Lab. scholar U. Chgo., 1978-82; rsch. fellow Systemic Lupus Erythematosus Soc., 1981; rsch. grantee Alliant Found., Louisville, 1995. Mem. Fla. Med. Soc., Alachua Med. Soc., Assn. Women Surgeons. Office: Univ Fla Dept Surgery PO Box 100286 Gainesville FL 32610

LAMAINA, NICHOLAS FRANCIS, surgeon podiatrist; b. Phila., Dec. 9, 1931; s. Nicholas John and Florence Helen (Vellozzi) La Maina; m. Carolyn Joan Kucinski, Sept. 18, 1965; children: Stephanie Nicole, Nicholas Christian. Student, Rutgers U., 1949-50, LaSalle Coll., Phila., 1950-51; DSc, Temple U., Phila., 1951, DPM, 1955. Intern Temple U. Clinics, Phila., 1955-56; commd. U.S. Army, 1957, advanced through grades to capt.; surg. and clin. resident Watson Army Hosp., Ft. Dix, N.J., 1957-59; pvt. practice Westmont, N.J., 1959—; clin. instr. Pa. Coll. Podiatric Medicine,Phila., 1967-74. Organizer 1st Driving Rodeo, 1st Jr. Miss Am. Competition, Camden County Jaycees, 1960-64. Mem. Am. Podiatric Med. Assn. (del.), N.J. Podiatric Med. Soc. (sec. 1981-82, v.p. 1982-84, pres. 1984-85, chmn. so. divsn. 1969-71, 80-81). Home and Office: 55 E Cuthbert Blvd Westmont NJ 08108

LAMALFA, JOACHIM JACK, clinical psychologist; b. Milw., Aug. 10, 1915; s. Salvatore and Josephine (Foti) L.; m. Constance Zarcone, Dec. 27, 1944; children: Constance Joanne, John Cibik, Jacquelyn Grace, Houston Lee Browne. BS, Marquette U., 1938; MS, U. Wis., 1941; PhD, U. Mich., 1949. Lic. psychologist, Wis. Research asst. U. Mich., Ann Arbor, 1946-47; psychol. intern Milw. County Hosp. for Mental Diseases, 1947-49; instr. psychology Marquette U., Milw., 1951-52; pvt. practice psychology Milw., 1949—; founder, chmn. dept. psychology Milw. County Hosp. for Mental Diseases, 1947, Marquette U. Dept. Psychology, 1947, St. Michael's Hosp. Mental Health Clinic, 1952; mem. affiliate staff St. Mary's Hosp., Ozaukee, Wis., 1994—. Author: (with Henry Viet) Psychosis with Cerebral Arteriosclerosis as Affected by Adrenal Cortical Extract. Mem. Am. Psychol. Assn., Wis. Psychol. Assn., Soc. Clin. Psychologists, Milw. Psychol. Assn., Nat. Register Health Service Providers in Psychology, Phi Kappa Phi, Phi Delta Kappa. Republican. Roman Catholic. Home: 7821 N Lake Dr Milwaukee WI 53217-2911 Office: 121 E Silver Spring Dr Milwaukee WI 53217-4702

LAMANNA, JOSEPH CHARLES, physiologist; b. Bronxville, N.Y., July 12, 1949; s. Alfred Carl and Rosaria (Tavolilla) LaM.; m. Margaret Ann Whelan, June 19, 1971; children: Michelle Marie, Kristen Ruth, Julia Carroll. BS in Biology, Georgetown U., 1971; PhD in Physiology/Pharmacology, Duke U., 1975. Rsch. assoc. Dept. Physiology/Pharmacology, Duke U., Durham, N.C., 1975-77; asst. prof. Dept. Neurology, U. Miami (Fla.), 1978-81, assoc. prof., 1981; assoc. prof. neurology Case Western Res. U., Cleve., 1981-90, prof., 1990—, acting chmn. dept. anatomy, 1993—. Mem. Am. Physiol. Soc., Soc. for Neurosci., Optical Soc. Am., Internat. Soc. for Oxygen Transport to Tissues (exec. com. 1985-89), Biomed. Engrng. Soc., Micro-Circulatory Soc. Office: Case Western Res U Sch of Medicine Neurology 10900 Euclid Ave Cleveland OH 44106-4938

LA MAR, JOHN JOSEPH, JR., pediatrician; b. Salem, N.J., Oct. 28, 1936; s. John Joseph and Glendoris (Benner) L.; m. Marilyn Hart, June 18, 1960; children: Jaimie, Stephanie, Danine. BA, Rutgers U., 1959; MD, SUNY, Buffalo, 1963. Diplomate Am. Bd. Pediatrics. Rotating intern Pa. Hosp., 1963-64; pediat. resident Children's Hosp. of Phila., 1964-66. Bd. trustees Pennsville Pub. Library, Pennsville, N.J., 1980—. Fellow Am. Acad. Pediatrics; mem. Salem Co. Med. Soc. (pres. 1976-77), AMA, Med. Soc. N.J., So. Intercounty Med. Assn. (pres. 1980-87). Home: 44 Supwana Rd # 3 Salem NJ 08079-3217

LAMAR, WAYNE TERRY, orthopaedic surgeon, educator; b. New Albany, Miss., Mar. 16, 1939; s. William Thomas and Estelle (Jones) L.; m. Patricia Chadwick; children: William Chadwick, Patricia Leslie, Lucius Mallory. BA and BS in Chemistry, U. Miss., Oxford, 1962; MD, U. Miss., Jackson, 1966. Intern in mixed surgery U. Miss., Jackson, 1967; resident in general surgery Kennedy VA Hosp., Memphis, 1967-68; resident in orthopaedics Campbell Clinic, Memphis, 1968-71; active med. staff Oxford-Lafayette Med. Ctr., 1976—, chmn. dept. surgery, 1986—; clin. instr. dept. orthopaedic surgery, 1981—; dir., spkr. various confs. and seminars, 1976—. Maj. USAF, 1971-73. Office: 2168 South Lamar Oxford MS 38655

LAMARCHE, PAUL HENRI, pediatrician; b. Boston, Sept. 5, 1929; s. Hormisdas LaMarche; m. Genevieve Judge, July 4, 1952 (div. 1995); children: Paul Jr., Marian, Claire, Patricia, Phillip; m. Erlinda Polvorosa, Dec. 21, 1995. BS, Boston Coll., 1956; MD, Boston U., 1960; MS, MIT, 1973; MA, Brown U., 1973. Med. technologist Norwood (Mass.) Hosp., 1951-60; med. dir., assoc. chief of staff R.I. Hosp., Providence, 1963-75; med. dir., chief of staff Ea. Maine Med. Ctr., Bangor, 1975-95; cons. Ea. Maine Healthcare, Bangor, 1996—; clin. prof. pediatrics Tufts U. Sch. Medicine, Boston, 1975—; pres., founder Norumbega Med. Spec., Bangor, 1991-95, Maine Toxicology Inst., Orono, 1990-95. Contbr. articles to profl. jours. Chmn. Child Abuse Prevention, Maine, 1980-85; dir. Rural Health Outreach, Maine, 1975-85. With USN, 1946-50. Decorated Commendation medal; recipient F.D. Roosevelt award Nat. Found. March of Dimes, 1985. Fellow Am. Acad. Pediatrics; mem. Am. Coll. Physician Execs., Maine Med. Assn., Penobscot Med. Soc. Roman Catholic. Home: RR 2 Box 813 Eddington ME 04428 Office: Eastern Maine Healthcare 489 State St Bangor ME 04401

LAMB, IRENE HENDRICKS, medical researcher; b. Ky., May 9, 1940; d. Daily P. and Bertha (Hendricks) Lamb; m. Edward B. Meadows. Diploma in nursing, Ky. Bapt. Hosp., Louisville; student, Berea (Ky.) Coll., Calif. State U., L.A. RN, Ky. Charge nurse, head nurse acute medicine, med. ICU, surgical ICU, emergency room various med. ctrs., 1963-67; staff nurse rsch. CCU U. So. Calif./L.A. County Med. Ctr., 1968; nurse coord. clin. rsch. ctr. U. So. Calif./Los Angeles County Med. Ctr., L.A., 1969-74; sr. rsch. nurse cardiology Stanford (Calif.) U. Sch. Medicine, 1974-85, rsch. coord. pvt. clin., 1988; dir. clin. rsch. San Diego Cardiac Ctr., 1989-92; sr. cmty. health nurse Madison County Health Dept., Berea, 1993—; clin. rsch. cons., 1988—. Co-contbr. numerous articles to med. jours.; contbr. articles to nursing jours., chpts. to med. books. Mem. Am. Heart Assn. (cardiovasc. nursing sect.). Home: 107 Lorraine Ct Berea KY 40403-1317

LAMB, LESTER LEWIS, hospital administrator; b. Winchester, Va., Aug. 11, 1932; s. Lester Lewis and Nina Elizabeth (Higgs) L.; m. Mary Lou Watson, Aug. 11, 1956; children: Melissa, Amy, Elizabeth. BA, Richmond Coll., 1955, postgrad., 1955-56; MHA, Med. Coll. Va., 1958. Asst. dir. admissions, hosp. div. Med. Coll. Va., Richmond, 1956, adminstrv. resident, 1957; adminstrv. resident Shenandoah County Meml. Hosp., Woodstock, Va., 1957, Washington County Hosp., Hagerstown, Md., 1957-58; adminstr. Hampshire Meml. Hosp., Romney, W.Va., 1958-59, Marmet (W.Va.) Hosp., Inc., 1959-60; asst. dir. U. Va. Hosp., Charlottesville, 1961; adminstr. R.J. Reynolds-Patrick County Meml. Hosp., Stuart, Va., 1961-64, Shenandoah County Meml. Hosp., Woodstock, 1965-69, Mary Greely Meml. Hosp., Ames, Iowa, 1969-70; exec. dir. Radford (Va.) Cmty. Hosp., 1970-81, pres., 1981—; vice chmn. First Va. Reinsurance, 1986—; exec. v.p. Carilion Health System, 1989—; guest lectr., adj. asst. prof. Radford U., 1980-81; chmn. Va. Profl. Underwriters, Inc., 1984-87; chmn. Va. Hosp. Shared Svcs., Va. Healthcare Waste Mgmt. Coop., 1995—, Vol. Hosp. Am. Mid-Atlantic, 1988-90. Mem. Va. Gov.'s Health Svcs. Cost Rev. Commn., 1978-84, Va. State Bd. Health, 1992—, vice chmn., 1994, chmn. 1995—. Fellow Am. Coll. Healthcare Execs., Royal Soc. Health; mem. Am. Hosp. Assn. (Va. del.), Va. Hosp. Assn. (pres. 1981-82), Med. Coll. Va. Hosp. Adminstrn. Alumni Assn. (sec., pres.), Roanoke Area Hosp. Council (pres. 1974), Psi Chi, Rotary (past pres.). Home: 116 Greenbriar Dr Radford VA 24141-3854 Office: Radford Community Hosp 700 Randolph St Radford VA 24141-2430

LAMB, PATRICIA GRACE, nurse, counselor; b. N.Y.C., Mar. 17, 1931; d. Edward Vincent and Anna Agnes (Muller) Landecker; R.N., N.Y. Med. Coll.-Flower Fifth Ave. Hosp., 1952; B.A. in Health Edn., Jersey City State Coll., 1975; M.S. in Community Counseling, C. W. Post Coll., L.I.U., 1982; children—Jerilyn Anne Lamb Pagone, Stephen Vincent, Mark Gerard, Melissa Anne. Surg. nurse Flower Fifth Ave. Hosp., N.Y.C., 1952, surg. nurse, relief supr. St. Joseph's Hosp., Augusta, Ga., 1953; staff nurse St. Vincent's Hosp., S.I., 1954-56, S.I. Hosp., 1956-58, obstetrics nurse Richmond Meml. Hosp., S.I., 1958-60; staff nurse Willowbrook State Sch., N.Y. State Dept. Mental Health, S.I., 1960-62, head nurse, 1962-71, supervising nurse, 1971-80; nurse adminstr. health svc. unit S.I. Devel. Ctr., 1976-79, coord. nursing care ambulatory svcs. and health care, 1979-88; nurse cons. to Community Group Homes S.I. area, liaison between local voluntary hosps. S.I. Devel. Ctr. for Facility clients, 1980-88; coord. ambulatory care S.I. (N.Y.) Univ. Hosp. South (formerly Richmond Meml. Hosp.), 1988-96; coord. mental retardation devel. disabilities S.I. U. Hosp. Active, Monsignor Farrell Alumnae Mother's Club, St. Clare Mother's Club, S.I., St. Joseph by the Sea Family Assn. Mem. S.I. MRDD Coun. (boro pres. com. for handicapped), Am. Mental Health Counselors Assn. Republican. Home: 179 Sycamore St Staten Island NY 10312-5613

LAMB, PETER JAMES, psychologist; b. Troy, N.Y., May 15, 1947; s. Peter J. Jr. and Carmel M. (Comis) L.; m. Pamela A. McKenna, Oct. 28, 1989. BA, Duquesne U., 1969; MA, Assumption Coll., Worcester, Mass., 1974; PhD, Fla. Inst. Tech., Melbourne, Fla., 1984. Lic. psychologist, Del., Md. Psychologist N.H. Hosp., Concord, 1975-79, sr. psychologist, 1981-84; psychology intern Albany County Mental Health Clinic, Albany, N.Y., 1984-85; psychologist Eastern Shore Hosp, Cambridge, Md., 1985-92, chief psychologist, 1992—; psychologist in pvt. practice, Seaford, Del., 1989—; adj. prof. Salisbury (Md.) State U., 1994, 96. Author psychol. test 55-EFS, 1994. With U.S. Army, 1969-72, Vietnam, Germany. Mem. APA, Nat. Register for Health Svc. Providers in Psychology. Democrat. Roman Catholic. Office: Eastern Shore Hosp US Rte 50 PO Box 800 Cambridge MD 21613

LAMBERG, ROBERT LOUIS, ophthalmologist; b. St. Louis, Jan. 20, 1950; s. Lester C. and Beverly J. (Fisher) L. BS in Chemistry, U. Mo., St. Louis, 1972; MD, Washington U., 1976. Diplomate Am. Bd. Ophthalmology. Intern in medicine U. So. Calif.-Los Angeles County Gen. Hosp., L.A., 1976-77; resident in ophthalmology Washington U.-Barnes Hosp., St. Louis, 1980; pres. Eye Healthcare of Clayton (Mo.) Inc., 1980-93; med. dir. Clarkson Eye Care, 1993—; asst. prof. clin. ophthalmology and visual scis. Washington U., St. Louis, 1989—. Mem. Am. Acad. Ophthalmology, St. Louis Met. Med. Soc., Am. Soc. Cataract and Refractive Surgery, Washington U. Alumni Assn. (exec. bd., past pres.), U. Mo. Alumni Assn. Office: Clarkson Eyecare 8060 Clayton Rd Saint Louis MO 63117

LAMBERG, STANLEY LAWRENCE, medical technologist, educator; b. Bklyn., Oct. 2, 1933; s. Joseph and Ray C. (Miller) L.; m. Charlotte Frances Rothschild, June 15, 1963; children: Steven Kenneth, Eric Michael. BS, Bklyn. Coll., 1955; MA, Oberlin Coll., 1957; MS, Tufts U., 1962; PhD, NYU, 1968. Chief lab. tech. dept. biochemistry Sch. Medicine Cornell U., N.Y.C., 1957-58; Charleston rsch. and USPHS fellow dept. physiology Tufts U., Boston, 1958-61; NIDR predoctoral trainee NYU, 1961-66; lectr. dept. biology CCNY, 1966-67; instr. to asst. prof. dept. biology Bklyn. Ctr., LIU, 1967-70; part-time asst. rsch. scientist Guggenheim Inst. for Dental Rsch., NYU, 1968-69; asst. prof. dept. biology SUNY, Farmingdale, 1970-71, asst. prof., 1971-73, assoc. prof., 1973-75, prof., 1975-95. Co-author various lab. manuals. Adv. chmn. Boy Scouts Am., Hauppauge, N.Y., 1982—. Recipient Chancellor's award for Excellence in Teaching SUNY, 1976; NSF fellow, 1971, others. Mem. N.Y. State Histotech. Soc., Nat. Soc. Histotech., N.Y. State Soc. Med. Tech. (treas. 1980-93, bd. dirs. 1980-93, 94—), N.Y. Acad. Scis., Sigma Xi.

LAMBERT, CAROL ANN, audiologist; b. Easton, Pa., June 15, 1947; d. Harry and Clara (Miller) L.; BA, U. Tulsa, 1972, MA, 1977; 1 child, Eugene Read. Lic. audiologist. Audiologist, Tulsa Otolaryngology, Inc., and U. Tulsa, 1977-78; speech reading instr. Tulsa Speech and Hearing Assn., 1977-78; audiologist Ear, Nose and Throat Consultants, Inc., Tulsa, 1978-83; audiologist U. Tulsa, 1983-89; pvt. practice audiology, Tulsa, 1987—; cons. audiologist Springer Clinic, 1979-80; cons. Okla. State Dept. Health, Tulsa Scottish Rite Clinic for Childhood Lang. Disorders, 1979-91; cons. audiologist Broken Arrow Med. Ctr., 1988—, Kaiser Rehab. Ctr., 1991-93, Okla. Early Intervention Program, 1991-93; adj. asst. prof. U. Tulsa, 1981-82; bd. advisors coll. nursing and applied health scis., U. Tulsa, 1991-92. Sustaining mem. Jr. League of Tulsa; mem. Philbrook Art Ctr.; bd. dirs. Children With Attention Deficit Disorder, 1991-93. Mem. NAFE, Nat. Assn. Women Bus. Owners, Am. Speech to Speech and Hearing Assn. (cert. in audiology), Acad. Rehabilitative Audiologist, Okla. Speech and Hearing Assn. (past sec.), Okla. Acad. of Audiology (mem. exec. com.), Tulsa Assn. Speech Pathologists and Audiologists (past pres., bd. dirs. 1988), Tulsa Speech and Hearing Assn. (past dir.). Home and Office: 1145 S Utica Ave # 302 Tulsa OK 74104-4013

LAMBERT, JEAN CATHRYN YODER, nursing educator; b. Nappanee, Ind., Dec. 31, 1924; d. Owen J. and Verda C. Yoder; m. Holly A. Echols, Aug. 1948 (dec.); children: Krina, Jeb (dec.), Kurt, Julie, Kenneth, Jana; m. William H. Lambert, Oct. 26, 1976 (dec.). Diploma, Mennonite Hosp. Sch. Nursing, Bloomington, Ill., 1948; BSN, Bluffton (Ohio) Coll., 1943; MS in Nursing, U. Tex., El Paso, 1980. RN, Fla., Tex., Colo. Dir. nursing Adult Mental Health Clinic, St. Petersburg, Fla.; head nurse psychiat. unit St. Joseph Hosp., El Paso; instr. psychiat. nursing Otero Jr. Coll., La Junta, Colo.; adminstrv. supr. Poudre Valley Hosp., Ft. Collins, Colo., until 1989; ret., 1989; part-time instr. Front Range Community Coll., Ft. Collins. Mem. ANA, Colo. Nurses Assn., Mennonite Health Assn., Mennonite Nurses Assn.

LAMBERT, JEAN MARJORIE, health care consultant; b. Bay City, Mich., Mar. 19, 1943; d. Richard William and Fidelis Rena (LeVasseur) L. BA, Madonna U., Livonia, Mich., 1967; MA, Eastern Mich. U., 1975. Dir. religious edn. Archdiocese of Detroit, 1970-75, dir. of evaluation, 1975-77; assoc. dir. programming Intermedia Found., Santa Monica, Calif., 1977-78; acad. dean St. John Provincial Sem., Plymouth, Mich., 1978-84; asst. dir. quality mgmt. Sisters of Mercy Health Corp., Farmington Hills, Mich., 1984-87; sr. cons. Mercy Collaborative, Livonia., Mich., 1987-88; v.p. Mission Mercy Health System, Cin., 1988-91; v.p. Mission Sisters Providence Health System, Springfield, Mass., 1991—; asst. prof. homiletics St. John Sem., Plymouth, Mich., 1978-85, St. Mary of the Woods Coll., Terre Haute, Ind., summer 1985, St. Meinrad Sem., Ind., summer 1984; bd. dirs. Combined Health Appeal of Mass. Editor Religious Edn., 1975-77. Nat. Cath. Edn. Assn.-Assn. Theol. Schs. for U.S. and Can. grantee, 1983. Mem. NAFE, Groundwork, Network, Am. Hosp. Assn., Am. Mgmt. Assn., Mental Health Assn., Cath. Health Assn. (bd. dirs. New Eng. Conf.), Acad. Leadership in Cath. Health Care. Roman Catholic. Avocations: woodcarving, photography, continuing education. Office: Sisters of Providence Health System 146 Chestnut St Springfield MA 01103-1539

LAMBERT, JOSEPH NORMAN, physician; b. N.Y.C., May 9, 1939; s. Philip and Katherine Ruth (Fried) L. BA, Univ. Rochester, 1959; MD, N.Y. Univ., 1963. Diplomate Am. Bd. Ophthalmology. Pvt practice Newport Beach, Calif., 1972—; assoc. prof. ophthalmology Univ. Calif., L.A., 1970—, Irvine, Calif., 1974—; cons. U.S. Vets. Adminstrn., Long Beach, Calif., 1974—; medical monitor Allergan, Inc., 1988—; assoc. examiner Am. Bd. Ophthalmology, Bala Cynwyd, Pa., 1980—. Capt. USAF, 1965-67. Office: Newport Eye Ctr 1401 Avocado Ave # 505 Newport Beach CA 92660

LAMBERT, JOSEPH PARKER, dentist; b. Bronte, Tex., Oct. 6, 1921; s. Joseph P. and Mary Josephine (Robison) L.; m. Jean Molesworth, Dec. 8, 1945; children: Jean Elizabeth, Mary Catherine, Helen Patricia. Thomas Joseph, Charlotte Anne. DDS, Baylor U., 1952. Cert. Tex. State Bd. Dental Examiners, Wyo. State Bd. Dental Examiners, 1952. Instr. Baylor U. Coll. Dentistry, Dallas, 1952-56, from asst. prof. to prof., dept. chmn., 1957-86, prof. emeritus, 1986—; cons. Baylor U. Med. Ctr., Dallas, VA Hosp., Dallas, VA Hosp., Banham, Tex., VA Hosp. Big Spring, Tex. With USN, 1942-45. Fellow Am. Coll. Dentists; mem. ADA, Tex. Dental Assn., Dallas County Dental Assn., Omicron Kappa Upsilon. Republican. Methodist. Office: Private Dental Office 3707 Gaston Ave Dallas TX 75246

LAMBERT, SHARON WHITE WILLIS, microbiologist; b. Greensboro, N.C., Mar. 15, 1964; d. Roy Frank and LaVerne (Gilchrest) White. BS, N.C. State U., 1986. Tech. asst. III CIBA-Geigy, Greensboro, N.C., 1986-87; asst. rsch. microbiologist CIBA Vision, Alpharetta, Ga., 1987-92; rsch. microbiologist Ciba Vision, Alpharetta, Ga., 1992—; Presenter in field. Mem. Am. Soc. Microbiology. Office: CIBA Vision 11460 Johns Creek Duluth GA 30155-1518

LAMBERT, VICKIE ANN, dean; b. Hastings, Nebr., Oct. 28, 1943; d. Victor E. and Edna M. (Hein) Wagner; m. Clinton E. Lambert, Jr., June 30, 1974; 1 child, Alexandra. Diploma, Mary Lanning Sch. Nursing, 1964; BSN, U. Iowa, 1966; MSN, Case Western Res. U., 1973; DNSc, U. Calif., San Francisco, 1981. RN, Ga. Acting chair dept. nursing adminstrn. Med. Coll. Ga., Augusta, 1982-84, coord. doctoral program nursing, 1984-85; coord. doctoral program nursing George Mason U., Fairfax, Va., 1986-88; assoc. dean Case Western Res. U., Cleve., 1989-90; dean Sch. Nursing Med. Coll. Ga., Augusta, 1990—. Contbr. articles to profl. jours. Fellow Am. Acad. Nursing; mem. ANA, Sigma Theta Tau, Sigma Xi. Home: 1421 Waters Edge Dr Augusta GA 30801

LAMBERTSEN, CHRISTIAN JAMES, environmental physiologist, physician, educator; b. Westfield, N.J., May 15, 1917; s. Christian and Ellen (Stevens) L.; m. Naomi Helen Hill, Feb. 5, 1944; children—Christian James, David Lee, Richard Hill, Bradley Stevens. BS, Rutgers U., 1939; MD, U. Pa., 1943. Prof. pharmacology and exptl. therapeutics, prof. medicine U. Pa. Sch. Medicine, 1946-87; founding dir. Inst. for Environ. Medicine, U. Pa. Med. Ctr., 1968—, disting. prof. environ. medicine, 1985—; mem. adv. panel on med. scis. Office of Asst. Sec. Defense, 1954-61; sec. basic scis. Nat. Bd. Med. Examiners, 1955-71; mem. Pres.'s Space Panel, 1967-70; mem. oceanographic adv. bd. Office of Asst. Sec. of Navy for R & D, 1968-77; mem. marine bd. Nat. Acad. Engring., 1973-77; adviser Office of Marine Resources, NOAA, 1972-76; med. adviser Ocean Systems Inc., Houston, 1960-83; med. dir. SubSea Intern, 1984—; chmn. com. Man in Space; Space Sci. Bd., NAS, 1960-62; chmn. life scis. adv. bd. McDonnell-Douglas Aircraft Corp., St. Louis, 1960-67; mem. research adv. bd. Mead-Johnson Corp., Evansville, Ind., 1960-67; sr. life scis. adviser Union Carbide Corp., Buffalo, N.Y., Westinghouse Elec. Corp., Annapolis, Md., 1972-74, Air Products and Chemicals Corp., Allentown, Pa., 1983-87; pres. Ecosystems Inc., Phila., 1972—. Editor: Underwater Physiology Symposium, II, III, IV, V, 1963-76; mem. editorial bd. Marine Tech. Soc. Jour., 1977-85. Contbr. articles to med., sci. jours. Served to maj. AUS, 1944-46. Decorated Legion of Merit; recipient Lindback award for Disting. Teaching, 1967; Aerospace Med. Assn. Tuttle award, 1970; Undersea Med. Behnke award, 1970; Dept. Def. Disting. Pub. Service medal, 1972; Marine Tech. Soc. award in Ocean Sci. and Engring., 1972; Dept. Navy Commendation Adv. Service, 1972; award in environ. scis. N.Y. Acad. Scis., 1974; Disting. Pub. Service award USCG, 1976; NIH, USN, USAF, NASA, NOAA Research grantee. Fellow Aerospace Med. Assn. (v.p. 1968); mem. Am. Coll. Clin. Pharmacology and Chemotherapy, Am. Soc. Pharmacology and Exptl. Therapeutics, Am. Physiol. Soc., Am. Soc. Clin. Investigation, Assn. Am. Med. Colls., Phila. Coll. Physicians, Internat. Acad. Astronautics, Internat. Astronautic Fedn., Internat. Union Physiol. Scis., Nat. Acad. Engring., John Morgan Med. Rsch. Soc., Marine Tech. Soc., Peripatetic Med. Soc., Undersea Med. Soc. (founding pres.), Phila. County Med. Soc., Pa. Med. Soc., Phila. Maritime Mus., Phila. Physiol. Soc., Cosmos Club (Washington), Sigma Xi. Home: 3500 Westchester Pike No 33 Newtown Square PA 19073 Office: U PA Med Ctr Inst Envrion Medicine 1 John Morgan Bldg Philadelphia PA 19104-6068

LAMBERTSON, LARRY HALL, psychiatrist; b. Chgo., June 1, 1950; s. Wingate Augustus and Eileen Helen (Hall) L.; m. Anna Marie Schober, May 31, 1980; 1 child, Cynthia Ann. BA, U. Ky., 1972, MD, 1977; postgrad. in Psychiatry, Loma Linda U. Med. Ctr., 1980; fellowship in Child Psychiatry, U. Cin., 1982. Diplomate Am. Bd. Psychiatry and Neurology. Pvt. practice psychiatry Irvine, Calif., 1982-88; psychiatric med. dir. So. Va. Mental Health Inst., Danville, 1989-92; med. dir. Park Ctr. Inc., Ft. Wayne, Ind., 1992—; cons. in nutrition Tyson & Assocs., Santa Monica, Calif., 1984-88; dir. adult program Santa Ana (Calif.) Psychiat. Hosp., 1987-88; mem. courtesy staff Danville Meml. Hosp., 1989-92; forensic psychiat. evaluator Commonwealth of Va., Danville, 1989-92; psychiat. cons. Catawba (Va.) State Hosp., 1991-92; assoc. clin. prof. medicine U. Va., 1989-92. Instr. in behavioral emergencies Danville Rescue Squad, 1991. Mem. Chief Med. Officers Assn. (pres. 1992), Danville-Pittsylvania County Acad. Medicine, Monroe Inst. (profl. div.). Home: 2001 Kensington Blvd Fort Wayne IN 46805-4609 Office: Park Ctr Inc 409 E State Blvd Fort Wayne IN 46805

LAMBIRD, PERRY ALBERT, pathologist; b. Reno, Nev., Feb. 7, 1939; s. C. David and Florence (Knowlton) L.; m. Mona Sue Salyer, July 30, 1960; children: Allison Thayer Watson, Jennifer Salyer, Elizabeth Gard, Susannah Johnson. BA, Stanford U., 1958; MD, Johns Hopkins U., 1962; MBA, Okla. City U., 1973. Diplomate Am. Bd. Pathology. Fellow in internal medicine Johns Hopkins Hosp., Balt., 1962-63, resident pathologist, 1965-68, chief resident, 1968-69; med. cons. USPHS, Washington, 1963-65; pathologist Med. Arts Lab., Oklahoma City, 1969—, Okla. Meml. Hosp., Southwest Med. Ctr., 1974—, Nat. Cancer Inst., 1974-81; chmn. Pathcor, 1995—; propr. Lambird Mgmt. Cons. Service, Oklahoma City, 1974—; pres. Ind. Pathology Inst., Inc., 1984-88, chmn. bd. dirs., 1988—; assoc. prof. pathology and orthopedic surgery U. Okla. Coll. Medicine, 1980-90, prof., 1990—; chmn. Pathcor, 1994—; cons. in field. Reviewer Jour. Am. Med. Assn, 1983—; contbr. articles to profl. jours. Pres. Okla. Symphony Orch., 1974-75, Ballet Okla., 1978-79; del. Republican Nat. Conv., 1976, alt. del., 1984; bd. regents Uniformed Svcs. U. Health Scis., 1983-88; mem. task force entitlements and human assistance programs U.S. Ho. of Reps., 1983-88; bd. dirs. Commn. on Office Lab. Assessment, 1988—, chmn., 1992-94. Served to lt. comdr. USPHS, 1963-65. Recipient Exec. Leadership award Oklahoma City U., 1976, Physician's Recognition award AMA, 1969-95, Outstanding Pathologist award Am. Pathology Found., 1984; named Disting. Practioner Nat. Acad. of Practice, 1990. Fellow Am. Soc. Clin. Pathologists, Coll. Am. Pathologists, (gov. 1984-92); mem. AMA (ho. of dels., coun. on med. svc.), Okla. Med. Assn. (ho. of dels., trustee, pres.), Okla. County Med. Soc. (pres.), Okla. Soc. Cytopathology (pres.), Am. Pathology Found. (pres.), Okla. Found. for Peer Rev. (dir.), Arthur Purdy Stout Soc. Surg. Pathologists, Am. Assn. Pathologists, Okla. Assn. Pathologists (pres.), So. Med. Assn., N.Y. Acad. Sci., Am. Soc. Cytology, Okla. Soc. Cytopaths (pres.), Osler Soc., Okla. City Clin. Soc., Johns Hopkins Med. and Surg. Assn., Phi Beta Kappa, Alpha Omega Alpha. Republican. Methodist. Home: 419 NW 14th St Oklahoma City OK 73103-3510 Office: Med Arts Lab 100 Pasteur 1111 N Lee Ave Oklahoma City OK 73103-2620

LAMBOTTE, RENÉ EDGARD, gynecology-obstetrics educator; b. Liege, Belgium, July 30, 1931; s. Eugene and Gertrude (Hoffman) L.; m. Lucy Pirotton, July 30, 1957; children: Philippe, Miguel. Candidate biomed., U. Liege, 1953, MD, 1957, PhD, 1969; docteur honoris causa, U. de Lille 2. Assoc. prof. U. Liege, 1971-73, prof. ordinaire, 1971—, dean of faculty, 1977-82; chmn. Univ. Hosp., 1982-84. Author: Immunology of Amniotic Fluid, 1969, Vulvo-vaginitis, 1979. Mem. Fedn. Gyn. Obst. Langue Francaise (hon. pres. 1990), Fedn. Internat. de Gynecologie Obstetrique (dep. sec. French lang. 1979), Nat. Acad. France (corr.), Royal Acad. Belgium (1st v.p. 1996, titulairetitulaire). Home: Rue du Treize Aout 50, 4050 Chaudfontaine Liege, Belgium Office: Hopital de la Citadelle, Bd XIIe de Ligne 1, 4000 Liege Belgium

LAMBRIS, JOHN DIMITRIOS, immunologist; b. Rodavgi, Greece, June 3, 1954; came to U.S., 1979; s. Dimitrios and Agathi (Phyhogios) L.; m. Rodothea Kokkinou, July 7, 1976; children: Agatha, Dimitrios. BS, U. Patras, Greece, 1976, PhD, 1979. Rsch. asst. Hellenic Anticancer Inst., Athens, Greece, 1976-79; postdoctoral fellow U. N.C., Chapel Hill, 1979-80, rsch. assoc., 1980-81, asst. prof. immunology, 1981-82; vis. prof. Inst. Medical Micro., Mainz, Fed. Republic Germany, 1982-83; asst. mem. Scripps Clinic and Rsch. Found., La Jolla, Calif., 1983-86; mem. Basel Inst. for Immunology, 1986-90; prof. Univ. Pa., 1990—; adj. prof. San Diego (Calif.) State U., 1987—. Contbr. articles to profl. pubis. Grantee Am. Cancer Soc., NIH. Fellow European Molecular Biology Orgn.; mem. Am. Soc. Immunologists, Prot. Chem. Soc., Dev. & Comp. Immunology. Current work: Functional and structural characterization of human complement components and complement receptors. Subspecialty: Immunocytochemistry. Home: 36 Haymarket Ln Bryn Mawr PA 19010-1148

LAMMOT, THEODORE RESSIG, III, orthopaedic surgeon; b. Phila., Oct. 11, 1928; s. Theodore Ressig II and Edith Colquhoun (Taylor) L.; m. Adrienne Treene (dec. 1973); children: Alison, Theodore IV, Elizabeth, Anne, James; m. Susanne Elizabeth Meagher, May 31, 1993; children: Kevin, Christina, Thomas, Daniel. BA, Williams Coll., 1950; MD, U. Pa., 1954. Diplomate Am. Bd. Orthopedic Surgery. Intern and resident U. Mich., Ann Arbor, 1954-59; asst. prof. U. Pa., Phila., 1961-66; assoc. surgeon Children's Hosp., Phila., 1961-66; assoc. prof. Temple U., Phila., 1966-71; chief orthopaedic surgery St. Christophers Hosp. for Children, Phila., 1966-71; assoc. surgeon Shriners Hosp., Phila., 1966-71; orthopaedic surgeon Ft. Collins, Colo., 1971-79, Ventura, Calif., 1979—; cons. Polio Found., Pa. and Colo., 1961-71, 71-79, Calif. Crippled Children, Ventura, 1979-91, Childrens Heart Hosp., Phila., 1961-71, Children's Seashore House, Atlantic City, N.J., 1961-71; chief orthopaedics Gateway Ctr., Fort Collins, 1971-79. Author: Textbook of Pediatrics, 9th edit.; contbr. articles to profl. jours. Sch. bd. St. Pauls Sch., Ventura, 1981-84, 93—. Capt. U.S. Army, 1959-61. Mem. Am. Acad. Orthopaedic Surgeons, Calif. Orthopaedic Assn. (bd. dirs.), Eastern Orthopaedic Assn. (founder), Masons. Republican. Episcopalian. Office: Coastal Orthopaedics 3418 Loma Vista Ste B Ventura CA 93003

LAMONT-HAVERS, RONALD WILLIAM, physician, research administrator; b. Wymondham, Norfolk, Eng., Mar. 6, 1920; came to U.S., 1955, naturalized, 1964; s. William Fredrick L.-H.; m. Gabrielson, Oct. 16, 1965; children—Wendy, Melinda, Ian. B.A., U. B.C., 1942; M.D., U. Toronto, 1946; diploma in internal medicine, McGill U., 1953. Intern Vancouver (B.C., Can.) Gen. Hosp., 1946-48; resident in internal medicine Queen Mary Vets. Hosp., Montreal, Que., Can., 1949-51; Canadian Arthritis and Rheumatism Soc. fellow Columbia Presbyterian Hosp., Coll. Physicians and Surgeons, Columbia U., N.Y.C., 1951-53; med. dir. Canadian Arthritis and Rheumatism Soc., B.C. div., Vancouver, 1953-55, Arthritis and Rheumatism Found., N.Y.C., 1955-64; instr. in medicine Coll. Physicians and Surgeons, Columbia U., 1955-64; assoc. dir. extramural programs NIAMD, Bethesda, Md., 1964-68, dep. dir., 1972-74; assoc. dir. extramural programs NIH, Bethesda, 1968-72; acting dir., dep. dir. NIH, Bethesda, Md., 1974-76, acting dir., 1975, dep. dir., 1974-76; dep. to gen. dir. for rsch. policy and adminstrn. Mass. Gen. Hosp., Boston, 1976-87, v.p. rsch. and tech. affairs, 1987-90, sr. cons. for rsch., 1990—; dep. dir. Cutaneous Biology Rsch. Ctr. Mass. Gen. Hosp. and Harvard U., 1990—; del. USSR-Arthritis Exchange Program, 1964; U.S. coordinator U.S.-USSR Coop. Program in Arthritis, 1973-75;. Served with M.C. Royal Canadian Army, 1944-46. Recipient Golden Pen award Jour. Am. Phys. Therapy Assn., 1965; Superior Service award HEW, 1973; Spl. citation Sec. HEW, 1975. Fellow Royal Coll. Physicians (Can.); mem. Am. Coll. Rheumatology (dir. Met. Washington sect. 1964-66), N.Y. Rheumatism Assn. (pres. 1960), Arthritis Found. (dir., governing mem. 1966-80, pres. Mass. chpt. 1987-89), Am. Acad. Orthopaedic Surgeons (hon.), Am. Gastroent. Assn. (affiliate), Alpha Omega Alpha. Office: Mass Gen Hosp 13th St Bldg 149 Charlestown MA 02129-2000

LAMORE, BETTE, rehabilitation counselor, motivational speaker; b. Chgo., Oct. 1, 1948. BA in Polit. Sci., U. Ariz., 1971, MS in Rehab. Counseling, 1974. Cert. rehab. counselor & ins. rehab. specialist. Social worker Pima County Welfare Dept., Tuscon, 1971-72; residential therapist So. Arix. Mental Health Clinic, Tuscon, 1972-73; drug counselor Awareness House Drug Clinics, Tuscon, 1973-74; dir. residential intervention ctr. YWCA, Tuscon, 1974-75; rehab. counselor Calif. State Dept. Rehab., Ventura and Thousand Oaks, 1975-77; job placement specialist, counselor Moorpark (Calif.) C.C., 1977-81; co-owner, rehab. counselor Experienced Rehab. Advisors, Atascadero, Calif., 1981—; breeder Arabian horses Whispering Oaks Arabians, Atascadero, 1987—; cons. for drug abuse programs Ventura (Calif.) County Health Svcs., 1975; expert witness in field. Author: My Friend Joe, 1984; co-author: Injured Workers Guide to California Workers Compensation System, 1988. Scholar NIMH, 1973. Mem. Calif. Assn. Rehab. Profls., Internat. Arabian Horse Assn. (v.p. Los Robles chpt. 1991), Am. Horseshow Assn., Phi Kappa Phi, Phi Beta Kappa, Pi Lambda Theta. Democrat. Home: PO Box 2863 Atascadero CA 93423-2863 Office: Experienced Rehab Advisors PO Box 1521 Paso Robles CA 93446

LA MOTTE, LOUIS COSSITT, JR., medical scientist, consultant; b. Clinton, S.C., Jan. 21, 1928; s. Louis Cossitt Sr. and Sarah (Hunter) La M.; m. Lila Jean Magruder, Dec. 31, 1948; children: Barbara Jones, Robert, Nancy Warren, Diane La Placa, Cynthia Love. AB, Duke U., 1948; MS in Pub. Health, U. N.C., 1951; ScD, Johns Hopkins U., 1958. Bacteriologist N.C. State Lab. Hygiene, Raleigh, 1948-51; virologist U.S. Army Chem. Corps, Ft. Detrick, Md., 1951-58; chief virus investigations unit Communicable Disease Ctr., Greeley, Colo., 1958-66, asst. chief disease ecology sect., 1965-66; chief cmty. studies br. Communicable Disease Ctr., Atlanta, 1966-69; dir. microbiology divsn. Ctr. for Disease Control, Atlanta, 1969-73, dir.

tech. evaluation and assistance divsn., 1973-86; mem. dean's alumni coun. Sch. Hygiene and Pub. Health Johns Hopkins U., Balt., 1995—; cons. Divsn. Pub. Health Ga., Atlanta, 1994; mem. recombinant adv. com. NIH, Bethesda, Md., 1970; mem. exec. com. Am. Com. on Arthropod-borne Viruses, Atlanta, 1964-66. Author: (with others) Federal Legislation & the Clinical Laboratory, 1981; contbr. articles to profl. jours. Trustee Ga. Fed. Mil. Retiree Coalition, Atlanta, 1990-93; coord. Neighborhood Watch Assn., Dunwoody, Ga., 1986—; advisor Sch. Pub. Health, Emory U., Atlanta, 1994—. Recipient Superior Svc. award USPHS, 1981. Republican. Presbyterian. Home: 4820 Leeds Ct Dunwoody GA 30338

LAMOUREUX, GLORIA KATHLEEN, nurse, air force officer; b. Billings, Mont., Nov. 2, 1947; d. Laurits Bungaard and Florence Esther (Nielsen) Nielsen; m. Kenneth Earl Lamoureux, Aug. 31, 1973 (div. Feb. 1979). BS, U. Wyo., 1970; MS, U. Md., 1984. Staff nurse, ob-gyn DePaul Hosp., Cheyenne, Wyo., 1970; enrolled USAF, 1970, advanced through grades to col.; staff nurse ob-gyn dept. 57th Tactical Hosp., Nellis AFB, Nev., 1970-71, USAF Hosp., Clark AB, Republic Philippines, 1971-73; charge nurse ob-gyn dept. USAF Regional Hosp., Sheppard AFB, Tex., 1973-75; staff nurse ob-gyn dept. USAF Regional Hosp., MacDill AFB, Fla., 1976-79; charge nurse ob-gyn dept. USAF Med. Ctr., Andrews AFB, Md., 1979-80, MCH coord., 1980-82; chief nurse USAF Clinic, Eielson AFB, Alaska, 1984-86, Air Force Systems Command Hosp., Edwards AFB, Calif., 1986-90; comdr. 7275th Air Base Group Clinic, Italy, 1990-92, 42d Med. Group, Loring AFB, Maine, 1992-94; 347th Med. Group, Moody AFB, Ga., 1994-96; chief nursing svcs. divsn. Hdqrs. Air Edn. and Tng. Command, Randolph AFB, Tex., 1996—. Mem. Assn. Women's Health, Obstetric, and Neonatal Nurses (sec.-treas. armed forces dist. 1986-88, vice-chmn. armed forces dist. 1989-91), Air Force Assn., Assn. Mil. Surgeons U.S., Bus. and Profl. Women's Assn. (pub. rels. chair Prince George's County chpt. 1981-82), Assn. Healthcare Execs., Sigma Theta Tau. Republican. Lutheran. Home: 13515 ThessalyRd Universal City TX 78148

LAMPARELLO, PATRICK JOHN, surgeon, educator; b. Jersey City, Mar. 22, 1951; s. Patrick John and Julia Josephine (Castro) L.; m. Alexis Jane Rich, July 27, 1974; children: Patrick, Tracy, Emily, Ashley. BA magna cum laude, U. Pa., 1973; MD, Albert Einstein Coll. Medicine, 1976. Diplomate Am. Bd. Gen. and Vascular Surgery. From resident to chief resident Montefiore Med. Ctr., Bronx, 1976-80; fellow vascular surgery NYU Med. Ctr., N.Y.C., 1980-81, attending surgeon, 1981—, assoc. prof. surgery, 1991—; chief vascular surgery Manhattan VA Hosp., N.Y.C., 1985-88; dir. vascular surgery Bellevue Hosp. Ctr., N.Y.C., 1990—. Author: Current Therapy in Vascular Surgery, 1994; author book chpts. Coach Old Tappan (N.J.) Baseball Assn., 1984-93, Old Tappan Soccer League, 1986-90; team physician Northern Valley Jr. Football League, Bergen County, N.J., 1990-91. Fellow Am. Coll. Surgeons: mem. N.Y. Regional Vascular Soc. (coun. 1984—), Internat. Cardiovascular Soc., Ea. Vascular Soc., Perepheral Vascular Soc., N.Y. Cardiovascular Soc. (v.p. 1990—). Roman Catholic. Office: NYU Med Ctr 530 1st Ave # 6F New York NY 10016-6402

LAMPEL, ANITA KAY, psychologist; b. L.A., May 25, 1946; d. Jack Murray and Rose (Maltun) L.; m. Stanley David Mishcok, Dec. 21, 1975; children: Jacob, David. PhD, Stanford U., 1969. Diplomate Am. Bd. Profl. Psychology; lic. psychologist, Calif. Staff psychologist Children's Meml. Hosp., Chgo., 1970-73; mgr. children's program San Bernardino (Calif.) County Dept. of Mental Health, 1973-79; pvt. practice San Bernardino, 1979—; instr. various univs., Calif., 1973—. Author: (with others) Group Psychotherapy with Children and Adolescents, 1987; contbr. articles to profl. jours. Chair Gifted Edn. Adv. Commn., San Bernardino, 1988-90; mem. Family Life Edn. Adv. Commn., San Bernardino, 1988-91. Mem. Am. Psychology Assn., Calif. State Psychology Assn., Inland Counties Psychol. Assn. (sec. 1988-89), Am. Bd. Profl. Psychology (western regional bd. dirs. 1988-93).

LAMPERT, MORRIS H., neurologist, educator; b. San Antonio, Mar. 1, 1929; s. Abraham Esir and Elsa (Eisenstadt) L.; m. Judy Lee Lewis, Oct. 26, 1963; children: Stephanie Carol, Adam Neal. BS in Biology, Trinity U., San Antonio, 1949; MD, U. Tex., Dallas, 1953. Diplomate Am. Bd. Psychiatry and Neurology. Intern in internal medicine U. N.C., Chapel Hill, 1953-54, resident in neurology, 1954-56; fellow in neuropathology Montefiore Hosp., N.Y.C., 1957; neurologist Diagnostic Clinic San Antonio, 1972-93; pvt. practice, San Antonio, 1959-72, 93—; clin. prof. medicine (neurology) U. Tex. Sch. Medicine, San Antonio, 1960—, mem. faculty course in brain and lang., 1972-75, in cognitive neurosci., 1975-96; lectr. in cognitive neurosci., especially langs. Active various polit. campaigns. Lt. comdr. M.C., USNR, 1957-59. Mem. Tex. Neurol. Soc., Tex. Med. Assn., Bexar County Med. Soc., N.Y. Acad. Scis. Office: 2829 Babcock Rd Ste 425 San Antonio TX 78229

LAMPHEAR, VIVIAN SHAW, psychologist, educator; b. Springfield, Ill., Feb. 4, 1954; d. Frank Shaw and Lois Eileen (Ziegler) Smith; m. Kenneth Allen Lamphear, Jan. 6, 1978; children: Ryan Michelle, Dylan Connor. BA in Psychology summa cum laude, Calif. State U., Long Beach, 1979, MA in Clin. Psychology, 1982; PhD in Clin. Psychology, SUNY, Stony Brook, 1987. Clin. intern Juv. Diversion Program U. Calif., Irvine, 1979-80; program coord. Child Care Worker Social Learning Program Children's Village, U.S.A., Beaumont, Calif., 1980-82; adult and child therapist Psychol. Ctr. SUNY, Stony Brook, 1984-85, therapist and prog. dir., 1982-86; neuropsychol. assessment intern State Univ. of N.Y. Med. Sch. and Univ. Hosp., 1985-86; clin. psychology intern Psychol. Ctr. SUNY, Stony Brook, 1985-86; postdoctoral clin. tng. Family Stress Ctr., Juliann Singer Ctr., L.A., 1987-88; clin. psychologist, clin. dir. Child Devel. Clin. Fuller Grad. Sch. Psychology, Pasadena, Calif., 1986-89; clin. psychologist, dir. Lamphear Counseling Ctr., 1989—; pvt. practice Newport Beach, Los Alimitos, Calif., 1989—; lectr. Long Beach City Coll. and Park and Recreation Dept. on Anger-Control-Parent Tng., 1993; adj. asst. prof. psychology Fuller Grad. Sch. of Psychology, Pasadena, 1989—, asst. prof. 1985-89; instr. stats. psychology dept. SUNY, Stony Brook, 1985-86; co-prin. investigator fed. rsch. project in field, 1988—; founder and project dir. Stony Brook Child Abuse Prevention Project, 1982-86, others. Author: Gentle Eating: Permanent Weight Loss, 1993, Gentle Eating Workbook, Anger Control, 1996; co-author: Gentle Eating, 1993; contbr. numerous articles to profl. jours. Lectr., cons. community programs in field, 1986—. Recipient fellowships SUNY, Stony Brook, 1982, 86, Grad. Dean's Award for Outstanding Achievement in Psychology, Calif. State U., Long Beach, 1982, grants, Nat. Inst. Justice, 1988, Nat. Ctr. for Prevention of Child Abuse, 1988-91, others. Mem. Am. Psychol. Assn., Western Psychol. Assn., Assn. for the Advancement of Behavior Therapy, Soc. for Rsch. in Child Devel., Nat. Com. for the Prevention of Child Aubse, Calif. Profl. Soc. on the Abuse of Children, Long Beach Child Trauma Coun. Republican. Mem. Christian Ch. Office: 4388 Katella Ave Los Alamitos CA 90720-3565

LAMPING, KATHRYN G., medical educator, medical researcher. BS in Biology, U. Ill., 1976; MS in Pharmacology, Med. Coll. Wis., 1982, PhD in Pharmacology, 1983. Postdoctoral rsch. fellow Dept. Internal Medicine, U. Iowa, Iowa City, 1983-86, asst. rsch. scientist, 1986-89, adj. asst. prof., 1989-95, asst. prof., 1995—. Contbr. articles to profl. jours. Mem. Am. Heart Assn. (Established Investigator award 1995), Am. Physiol. Soc., Microcirculatory Soc. Office: U Iowa Coll Medicine E 314-4 Iowa City IA 52242*

LAMPKIN, PEGGY ANN, physician; b. New Britain, Conn., June 17, 1953; d. Julian and Nannie (Ellison) L. BS, cert. physician asst., Howard U., 1978; MD, Spartan Health Sci. U., 1988; MPH, Johns Hopkins U., 1991; cert., Balt. Sch. Holistic Massage, 1995; postgrad., Traditional Sch. Chinese Medicine, Bethesda, Md. Cert. mind/body studies, cert. hypnotist Psychology Immunity and Disease Conf. Family practice resident Prince Georges Hosp., Cheverly, Md., 1989; physician asst. cons. Allied Health and Info. Sys., Dunnloring, Va., 1991-95; dir., founder Progressive Health & Cultural Ctr. Group Inc., Washington, 1995—; presenter in field. Mem. Full Gospel AME Zion, Temple Hills, Md. Mem. Ctr. for Sci. Pub. Interest, Am. Holistic Heatlh Assn., Am. Acad. Physician Assts., Inst. Noetic Studies, Monumental City Med. Soc., Elks Club (Daughters award for high achievement 1993). Methodist. Office: 1324 Whittier Pl NW Washington DC 20012

LAMPKIN, STEVEN BRADLEY, hospital administrator; b. Tulsa, Oct. 23, 1952. BA, Okla. State U., 1975; M Health Adminstrn., Washington U., 1978. Various positions Jeferson Regional Med. Ctr., Pine Bluff, Ark., 1972-76, adm. res., 1976-78, adm. asst., 1978-79, asst. adminstr., 1979-81, assoc. adminstr., 1981-82; asst. adminstr. med. svcs. Baptist Med. Ctr., Little Rock, 1982-83, v.p., 1983-86, adm., 1991—; adm. White River Med. Ctr., Batesville, Ark., 1986-90; corp. v.p. Baptist Med. System, Little Rock, 1990-91. Home: 30 Saint Andrews Dr Little Rock AR 72212-2909 Office: Baptist Medical Center 9601 Interstate 630 Exit 7 Little Rock AR 72205-7202*

LAMPREY, PAUL MICHAEL, physician assistant; b. Weymouth, Mass., Jan. 21, 1954; s. Ernest N. and Rita G. (Linnehan) L.; m. Judith Kay Nash, Aug. 13, 1977; children: Karla Jean Quick, Sean C. BS in Allied Health Sci., U. Ala., Birmingham, 1976. Cert. Nat. Commn. on Cert. Physician Assts. Physician asst. Smith Clinic, Marion, Ohio, 1976-77, Harbin Clinic, Rome, Ga., 1977—. Bd. dirs. Young Am. Bowling Alliance, Rome, 1995-96. Fellow Am. Acad. Physician Assts., Ga. Assn. Physician Assts. Home: 110 Sunridge Dr Rome GA 30165 Office: Harbin Clinic 1825 Martha Berry Blvd Rome GA 30165

LANCASTER, B. JEANETTE, dean, nursing educator. BSN, U. Tenn.; MSN, Case Western Res. U.; PhD, U. Okla. Staff nurse U. Tenn.; nurse clinician Univ. Hosps. of Cleve.; assoc. prof. psychiat. nursing Tex. Christian U.; coord. cmty. health nursing U. Ala., Birmingham, chair master's degree program Sch. Nursing; dean, prof. Sch. Nursing Wright State U., Dayton, Ohio; now dean, prof. nursing U. Va., Charlottesville; assoc. dir. patient care svcs. U. Va. Health Scis. Ctr., Charlottesville; assoc. Va. Health Policy Rsch. Ctr.; chmn. bd. dirs. Statewide Area Health Edn. Ctr. Program; mem. study group for nurse practitioners Va. Gen. Assembly; presenter in field. Author 4 books, including Community Health Nursing: Processes and Practices for Promoting Health; editor Family and Cmty. Health; contbr. articles to profl. jours. Recipient Disting. Alumni award Frances Payne Bolton Sch. Nursing-Case Western Res. U., 1984, Outstanding Alumni award U. Tenn. Coll. Nursing, 1985. Fellow Am. Acad. Nursing; mem. Am. Assn. Colls. Nursing (bd. dirs.). Office: U Va Sch Nursing Charlottesville VA 22903*

LANCASTER, JAMIE WALTER, firefighter, paramedic; b. Detroit, Jan. 31, 1964; s. James Andrew and Dorothy Jean (Howington) L.; m. Christina Leann Rogers, Jan. 18, 1968. Cert. paramedic, East Tenn. State U., 1984, BS in Chemistry, 1989, BS in Biology, 1990. Flight paramedic Tri-City Air Ambulance, Blountville, Tenn., 1985-87, U. Tenn., Knoxville, 1987-90; paramedic-firefighter Kingsport Fire & EMS, 1984-93; edn. coord. Network Med. Assn., Virginia Beach, Va., 1993—; tng. mgr. Med-Trans/Mercy Ambulance Svc., Virginia Beach, 1993—; firefighter, paramedic York County Fire and Rescue, Yorktown, 1993—; instr. ACLS Am. Heart Assn., Va., Tenn., 1986—, instr. PALS, 1990—, instr. BTLS ACS, Va., Tenn., 1987—; instr. paramedic TEMS & PEMS of Va., 1993—. Capt. U.S. Army, 1986-90. Mem. Internat. Assn. of Firefighters, Honeybee Country Club, nat. Assn. of Flight Paramedics, Nat. Assn. of Emergency Med. Tech.-Paramed, Tidewater Volleyball Assn. (capt. 1993), Sigma Phi Epsilon. United Methodist.

LANCASTER, SUZANNE CORBIN, medical technician; b. Washington, Oct. 23, 1947; d. William Boggs and Nadine (Kennedy) Corbin; m. James Harrison Lancaster, June 20, 1969 (div. 1973); 1 child, Martha Elizabeth. AA, DeKalb Community Coll., Clarkston, Ga., 1976, AS, 1982. Cert. advanced emergency med. technologist. Police officer Emory U., Atlanta, 1978-82; paramedic, firefighter DeKalb City Fire Dept., Decatur, Ga., 1982-83, Henry City Fire Dept., McDonough, Ga., 1983-84; physical measurements technician Equifax Services, Atlanta, 1984—. Instr., vol. ARC, Atlanta, 1978—; ski patroller Nat. Ski Patrol, Denver, 1980—, instr. winter emergency care, supr. Dixie Region; instr. advanced life support Am. Heart Assn., 1983-84; v.p. program and edn. bd. Parents Without Ptnrs., Jonesboro, Ga., 1984. Mem. Emergency Med. Technologists Assn., Exec. Womens Assn. Republican. Presbyterian. Club: Atlanta Ski. Home: 3581 Rockbridge Rd Stone Mountain GA 30083

LANCE, JAMES WALDO, neurologist; b. Wollongong, Australia, Oct. 29, 1926; s. Waldo Garland and Jessie Forsyth (Stewart) L.; m. Judith Lilian Logan, July 6, 1957; children: Fiona, Sarah, Jennifer, Robert, Sophie. MB, BS, U. of Sydney, Australia, 1950, MD, 1955; DSc (hon.), U. NSW, 1992. Resident med. officer Royal Prince Alfred Hosp., Sydney, Australia, 1950-51; rsch. fellow U. Sydney, 1952-53; house physician Hammersmith Hosp., London, 1954; asst. house physician Nat. Hosp. for Nervous Diseases, London, 1955; supt. Northcott Neurological Ctr., Sydney, Australia, 1956-60; rsch. fellow Mass. Gen. Hosp., Boston, Mass., 1960-61; neurologist The Prince Henry Hosp., Sydney, 1961-91; prof. of neurology U. of New South Wales, Sydney, 1975-91; cons. neurologist Inst. Neurol. Scis., Randwick, Australia, 1991—. Author: Mechanism and Management of Headaches, 1969, 5th edit., 1993, Migraine and Other HEadaches, 1986; co-author: A Physiological Approach to Neurology, 3d edit., 1981, Introductory Neurology, 1983, 3d edit., 1995. Decorated with comdr. Order of the Brit. Empire, 1978, officer Order of Australia, 1991. Fellow Royal Coll. Physicians (London), Royal Australasian Coll. Physicians, Australian Acad. of Sci. (v.p. 1984-85); mem. Australian Assn. of Neurologists (pres. 1978-81), Internat. Headache Soc. (pres. 1987-89), World Fed. of Neurology (v.p. 1989-93). Home: 15 Coolong Rd, Vaucluse 2030, Australia Office: Inst Neurol Scis Prince of Wales Hosp, High St, Randwick 2031, Australia

LAND, LINDA P., nursing educator; b. San Francisco, Mar. 11, 1948; d. Andrew C. and Alma Aline (Bailey) Vireno; m. R. James Land, May 6, 1972 (dec.); children: Ross, Scott. BS in Nursing, Calif. State U., Chico, 1971; MS, U. Calif., San Francisco, 1981. Staff nurse gen. surgery unit Santa Clara Valley Med. Ctr., San Jose, Calif., 1971-72; staff nurse intermediate ICU Stanford U. Hosp., 1972-74, gen. RN orientation insvc., 1974-76, with dept. insvc., 1976-78; staff nurse, relief charge spl. care unit N.T. Enloe Meml. Hosp., Chico, 1979-80, out-patient cardiac rehab. coord., 1980-82, per diem staff nurse critical care, 1982-85; per diem staff nurse critical care Chico Community Hosp., 1989—; prof. Calif. State U. Sch. Nursing, Chico, 1982—; adj. faculty Calif. State U. Sch. Nursing, 1978-82. Contbr. articles to profl. jours. Recipient numerous grants, 1986—.

LAND, REBEKAH RUTH, marriage and family therapist; b. Columbus, Ga., Feb. 5, 1946; d. Roland Irving and Thelma Rebekah (Gibbins) Van Hooser; m. Richard Dale Land, Sr., May 29, 1971; children: Jennifer Rebekah, Richard Dale Jr., Rachel Elisabeth. AB, Samford U., 1967; M in Religious Edn., New Orleans Bapt. Theol. Sem., 1970; MSW, Tulane U., 1971; PhD, Tex. Woman's U., 1988. Cert. profl. counselor; cert. marital and family therapist; diplomate Am. Bd. Sexology. Sch. social worker Chattanooga Pub. Schs., 1967-68; edn. and youth dir. Trinity Bapt. Ch., New Orleans, 1968-69; caseworker Youth Study Ctr., New Orleans, 1972; adj. prof. Criswell Coll., Dallas, 1976-89; counselor First Bapt. Ch., Dallas, 1982-85; psychotherapist Minirth-Meier Clinic, Richardson, Tex., 1985-87; asst. dir. counseling Dallas Theol. Sem., 1987-89; pvt. practice Nashville, 1989—; coord. Trilogy Program Parthenon Pavilion Psychiat. Hosp., Nashville, 1990-94. Mem. ACA, Am. Assn. Marriage and Family Therapy (clin.), Am. Assn. Sex Educators (cert. sex therapist), Counselors and Therapists, Assn. for Religious Values in Counseling. Republican. Baptist. Office: Parkview Towers 210 25th Ave N Ste 1010 Nashville TN 37203-1611

LANDAU, ARTHUR NORMAN, ophthalmologist; b. Bklyn., Mar. 11, 1948; s. Saul and Esther (Wlodinger) L.; m. Carron L. Klein, Feb. 24, 1980; children: Ross, Seth. BS, Rensselaer Polytech., 1968, MS, 1970; MD, Albert Einstein Coll., 1975. Diplomate Am. Bd. Ophthalmology. Pvt. practice N.Y.C., 1979—; attending surgeon Manhattan Eye Ear Throat Hosp., N.Y.C., 1979—, Med. Ctr. Princeton, 1995. Mem. Internat. Soc. Refractive Keratoplasm, Am. Soc. Cataract and Refractive Surgeons, Am. Acad. Ophthalmology, Eta Kappa Nu, Tau Beta Pi. Office: 601 Ewing St # C-15 Princeton NJ 08540

LANDAU, BENJAMIN, neurosurgeon; b. Jersey City, Oct. 3, 1932; m. Miriam Feldman. BA, Yale U., 1954; MD, Columbia U., 1958. Diplomate Am. Bd. Neurol. Surgeons. Asst. clin. prof. neurosurgery UCLA, 1968—. Lt. USN, 1960-62. Mem. Am. Assn. Neurol. Surgeons, Phi Beta Kappa. Office: 3440 Lomita Blvd Torrance CA 90505-4801

LANDAU, DAVID WILLIAM, gastroenterologist; b. St. Louis, Mar. 16, 1951; s. William Milton and Roberta Anne (Hornbein) L.; m. MaryBeth Pereira, Aug. 28, 1976; children: Leslie, Anne. BA, Swarthmore (Pa.) Coll., 1973; MD, Stanford U., 1977. Diplomate Am. Bd. Internal Medicine, subspecialty gastroenterology. Intern, resident Jewish Hosp., St. Louis, 1977-80; fellow Barnes Hosp., St. Louis, 1980-82; pvt. practice Digestive Disease Specialists, St. Louis, 1982—; clin. instr. Washington U. Sch. Medicine, St. Louis, 1982—. Fellow Am. Coll. Gastroenterology; mem. Am. Soc. Gastrointestinal Endoscopy. Office: Digestive Disease Specialists 11125 Dunn Rd Ste 201 Saint Louis MO 63136

LANDAU, EMANUEL, epidemiologist; b. N.Y.C., Nov. 28, 1919; s. Meyer and Annie (Heller) L.; B.A., CCNY, 1939; Ph.D., Am. U., 1966; m. Davetta Goldberg, Sept. 4, 1948; children: Melanie (dec.), Elizabeth. Supervisory analytical statistician Calif. Dept. Public Health, 1957-59, chief biometry sect., div. air pollution, 1959-62; head lab. and clin. trials sect. Nat. Cancer Inst., 1962-65; statis. adviser Nat. Air Pollution Control Adminstrn., 1965-69; epidemiologist Environ. Health Service, 1969-71, chief epidemiologic studies br. Bur. Radiol. Health, 1971-74; project dir., sci. cons. Am. Pub. Health Assn., 1975—; cons., adv. in field. Vol. White House Health Care Reform Corr. With AUS, 1942-46. Decorated Belgian Fourragere; recipient Superior Service award HEW, 1963. Fellow Am. Pub. Health Assn., Royal Soc. Health; mem. Soc. Epidemiologic Research, Am. Statis. Assn. (chmn. com. on stats. and environ.). Democrat. Jewish. Club: Cosmos (Washington). Author, editor articles, reports in field. Home: 4601 N Park Ave Apt 208 Chevy Chase MD 20815-4520 Office: Am Pub Health Assn 1015 15th St NW Washington DC 20005-2605

LANDDECK, PAULA E., critical care nurse; b. Mundeline, Ill., Aug. 25, 1971. BSN summa cum laude, Valparaiso (Ind.) U., 1993. Mem. nursing staff Oakwood Hosp., Dearborn, Mich., 1993-94, Allen Home Health Care, Ann Arbor, Mich., 1993—, St. Joseph Mercy Hosp., Ypsilanti, Mich., 1994—. Mem. Nightingale Soc., Alpha Lambda Delta, Sigma Theta Tau. Home: 2065 Key Blvd El Cerrito CA 94530-1760

LANDEN, SANDRA JOYCE, psychologist, educator; b. L.A., May 8, 1960; m. Bernard B. Reifkind, Aug. 15, 1981. BA, UCLA, 1982, MA, 1984, PhD, 1988. Lic. clin. psychologist, Calif. Rsch. asst. UCLA Autism Clinic, 1980-82, UCLA Teaching Homes for Devel. Disabilities Project, 1981-82; rsch. assoc. UCLA Project for Devel. Disabilities, 1982-87; co-coord. parent tng. program UCI-UCLA Program for ADHD Children, 1984; teaching assoc. psychology dept. UCLA, 1984-87; psychology intern Hathaway Home for Children, Lakeview Terrace, Calif., 1985-86, clin. staff, 1986-87; clin. postdoctoral fellow Childrens Hosp. L.A., 1987-88; adj. faculty Grad. Sch. Edn. and Psychology Pepperdine U., L.A., 1988—; psychologist L.A., 1987—; dir. Westside Parenting Ctr., L.A., 1992—. Contbr. articles to profl. jours. Recipient scholarship UCLA, 1978-82, fellowship UCLA, 1982-85, dissertation rsch. grant UCLA, 1985-87. Mem. APA (div. psychoanalysis), Calif. Psychol. Assn., L.A. Psychol. Assn., Am. Assn. Mental Retardation. Office: 11340 W Olympic Blvd Ste 245 Los Angeles CA 90064-1612

LANDEO, LUIS AMADOR, surgeon; b. Lima, Peru, Apr. 30, 1933; came to U.S., 1960; s. Sergio Landeo and Atanilda Hinojosa; m. Eva Luz Perez, July 17, 1962; children: Luis, Eva. MD, U. Buenos Aires, 1959. Diplomate Am. Bd. Surgery. Intern Aguadila Dist. Hosp., P.R., 1960-61; resident in gen. surgery Fasardo Dist. Hosp., P.R., 1962-65; preceptoship in gen. surgery Alexandria La. VA Hosp., 1965-67; pvt. practice N.Y.C., 1967—; pres. Hispanish Am. Med. Soc. N.Y., 1989. Democrat. Home: 145 W 67th St Apt 26H New York NY 10023-5937 Office: 685 W End Ave New York NY 10025-6819

LANDERS, SUSAN MAE, psychotherapist, professional counselor; b. Houston; d. James Edward and Frances Pauline (Braunagel) L. BS in Advt., U. Tex.; MS in Psychol. Counseling, U. Houston, Clearlake, 1994; cert. in sales, Dale Carnegie Inst. Lic. profl. counselor. Mktg. rep. K.C. Products, Houston, 1981-83; account exec. Williamson County Express, Austin, Tex., 1984; advt. cons. Stas. KMMM/KOKE, Austin, 1985; key account sales rep. GranTree Furniture Rental, Austin, 1986-89; individual habilitation counselor Ctr. for the Retarded Inc., Houston, 1990; case mgr. Mental Health and Mental Retardation Authority Harris County, Houston, 1991-92; primary therapist Riceland Psychiat. Hosp., 1994—. Mem. ACA, Am. Mental Health Counselors Assn., Tex. Counseling Assn., Tex. Mental Health Counselors Assn., Houston LPC Assn., Houston Group Psychotherapy Soc. Home: 4615 N Braeswood Blvd # 311D Houston TX 77096-2841 Office: Riceland Psychiat Hosp 4910 Airport Rosenberg TX 77471

LANDERS, VERNETTE TROSPER, writer, educator, association executive; b. Lawton, Okla., May 3, 1912; d. Fred Gilbert and LaVerne Hamilton (Stevens) Trosper; m. Paul Albert Lum, Aug. 29, 1952 (dec. May 1955); 1 child, William Tappan; m. 2d, Newlin Landers, May 2, 1959 (dec. Apr. 1990); children: Lawrence, Marlin. AB with honors, UCLA, 1933, MA, 1935, EdD, 1953; Cultural doctorate (hon.) Lit. World U., Tucson, 1985. Tchr. secondary schs., Montebello, Calif., 1935-45, 48-50, 51-59; prof. Long Beach City Coll., 1946-47; asst. prof. Los Angeles State Coll., 1950; dean girls Twenty Nine Palms (Calif.) High Sch., 1960-65; dist. counselor Morongo (Calif.) Unified Sch. Dist., 1965-72, coordinator adult edn., 1965-67, guidance project dir., 1967; clk.-in-charge Landers (Calif.) Post Office, 1962-82; ret., 1982. V.p., sec. Landers Assn., 1965—; sec. Landers Vol. Fire Dept., 1972—; life mem. Hi-Desert Playhouse Guild, Hi-Desert Meml. Hosp. Guild; bd. friends Copper Mountain Coll., 1990-91; bd. dirs., sec. Desert Emergency Radio Service; mem. Rep. Senatorial Inner Circle, 1990-92, Regent Nat. Fedn. Rep. Women, 1990-92, Nat. Rep. Congl. Com., 1990-91, Presdl. Task Force, 1990-92; lifetime mem. Girl Scouts U.S., 1991. Recipient internat. diploma of honor for community service, 1973; Creativity award Internat. Personnel Research Assn., 1972, award Goat Mt. Grange No. 818, 1987; cert. of merit for disting. svc. to edn., 1973; Order of Rose, 1978, Order of Pearl, 1989, Alpha Xi Delta; poet laureate Center of Internat. Studies and Exchanges, 1981; diploma of merit in letters U. Arts, Parma, Italy, 1982; Golden Yr. Bruin UCLA, 1983; World Culture prize Nat. Ctr. for Studies and Research, Italian Acad., 1984; Golden Palm Diploma of Honor in poetry Leonardo Da Vinci Acad., 1984; Diploma of Merit and titular mem. internat. com. Internat. Ctr. Studies and Exchanges, Rome, 1984; Recognition award San Gorgonio council Girl Scouts U.S., 1984—; Cert. of appreciation Morongo Unified Sch. Dist., 1984, 89; plaque for contribution to postal service and community U.S. Postal Service, 1984; Biographee of Yr. award for outstanding achievement in the field of edn. and service to community Hist. Preservations of Am.; named Princess of Poetry of Internat. Ctr. Cultural Studies and Exchange, Italy, 1985; community dinner held in her honor for achievement and service to Community, 1984; Star of Contemporary Poetry Masters of Contemporary Poetry, Internat. Ctr. Cultural Studies and Exchanges, Italy, 1984; named to honor list of leaders of contemporary art and lit. and apptd. titular mem. of Internat. High Com. for World Culture & Arts Leonardo Da Vinci Acad., 1987; named to honor list Foremost Women 20th Century for Outstanding Contbn. to Rsch., IBC, 1987; Presdl. Order of Merit Pres. George Bush-Exec. Coun. of Nat. Rep. Senatorial Com., Congl. cert. of Appreciation U.S. Ho. of Reps.; other awards and certs. Life fellow Internat. Acad. Poets, World Lit. Acad.; mem. Am. Personnel and Guidance Assn., Internat. Platform Assn., Nat. Ret. Tchrs. Assn., Calif. and Nat. Assn. for Counseling and Devel., Am. Assn. for Counseling and Devel. (25 yr. membership pin 1991), Nat. Assn. Women Deans and Adminstrs., Montebello Bus. and Profl. Women's Club (pres.), Nat. League Am. Pen Women (sec. 1985-86), Leonardo Da Vinci Acad. Internat. Winged Glory diploma of honor in letters 1982), Landers Area C. of C. (sec. 1985-86, Presdl. award for outstanding service, Internat. Honors Cup 1992-93), Desert Nature Mus., Phi Beta Kappa, Pi Lambda Theta (Mortar Bd., Prytanean UCLA, UCLA Golden Yr. Bruin 1983), Sigma Delta Pi, Pi Delta Phi. Clubs: Whittier Toastmistress (Calif.) (pres. 1957); Homestead Valley Women's (Landers). Lodge: Soroptimists (sec. 29 Palms chpt. 1962, life mem., Soroptimist of Yr. local chpt. 19, Woman of Distinction local chpt. 1987-88). Author: Impy, 1974, Talkie, 1975, Impy's Children, 1975; Nineteen O Four, 1976, Little Brown Bat, 1976; Slo-Go, 1977; Owls Who and Who Who, 1978; Sandy, The Coy, 1979; The Kit Fox and the Walking Stick, 1980; contbr. articles to profl. jours., poems to anthologies. Guest of honor ground breaking ceremony Landers Elem. Sch., 1989, dedication ceremony, 1991. Home: 632 N Landers Ln PO Box 3839 Landers CA 92285

LANDES, ROBERT ALTON, pharmacist, management consultant; b. Inglewood, Calif., Aug. 31, 1942; s. Glen Alton and Edith Irene (Demmon) L.; m. Cara Lou Hutchinson, Aug. 13, 1966 (div. July 1978); m. Angelita Freeman, Aug. 12, 1990. AA, Compton Coll., 1962; PharmD, U. So. Calif., 1966, postgrad., 1974-75, 81-83; MBA, Calif. State U., 1989. Registered pharmacist Calif., Nev. Staff Pharmacist Titus Pharmacy, Santa Ana, CAlif., 1966-69; clin. pharmacist St. Francis Med. Ctr., Lynwood, Calif., 1968-88, Torrance Meml. Hosp. Med. Ctr., Lynwood, 1988-94; owner, pres. Robert's Reports, Torrance, Calif., 1983—; ptnr., cons. Grier, Landes and Assocs, Stone Mountain, Ga., 1987—. Contbr. articles to profl. jours. Tchr. Sunday Sch. Grace Missionary Bapt. Ch., Redondo Beach, Calif., 1983-84. Mem. Orange County Soc. Hosp. Pharmacists (chmn. clin. services com. 1979-80), Am. Mgmt. Assn., Soc. Advancement Mgmt. (pres. 1984, editor newsletter 1985), AAAS, Am. Soc. Hosp. Pharmacists, Los Angeles C. of C. (chmn.), Phi Delta Chi, Rho Chi. Clubs: Bikecentennial (Missoula, Mont.), SportsConnection (Torrance). Home: 4455 Torrance Blvd # 573 Torrance CA 90503-4398 Office: Grier Landes & Assocs 4968 Post Road Pass Stone Mountain GA 30088

LANDESZ, MONIKA AGATHA, ophthalmologist; b. Budapest, Hungary, Dec. 16, 1963; d. Karoly and György (Proder) L. MD, U. Amsterdam, 1991; PhD, U. Groningen, 1995. Rsch. fellow dept. ophthalmology U. Groningen, The Netherlands, 1991-94, resident in ophthalmology, 1994—. Recipient Trouthan Medal ISCRS, 1995. Roman Catholic. Home: Hardewikerstraat 12, 9712 GT Groningen The Netherlands Office: U Hosp, PO Box 30 001, 9700 RB Groningen The Netherlands

LANDGARTEN, HELEN BARBARA, art psychotherapist, educator; b. Detroit, Mar. 4, 1921; d. Samuel and Lena (Lindenbaum) Tapper; m. Nathan Landgarten, Oct. 10, 1942. BFA, UCLA, 1963; cert. in marriage, family, child counseling, Goddard Coll., 1972. Registered art therapist. Coord. art psychotherapy Cedars-Sinai Med. Ctr., L.A., 1967-90; chmn., dir. clin. art therapy Immaculate Heart Coll., L.A., 1972-80; chmn., prof. dept. clin. art therapy Loyola Marymount U., L.A., 1980-88; cons. U.S. Dept. Defense, Germany, 1982-86; pres. Internat. Art Therapy Consultation, L.A., 1989—; staff rsch. assoc. Rsch. and Edn. Inst. Harbor UCLA Med. Ctr. Author: Clinical Art Therapy, 1980, Art Therapy with Families, 1987, Family Art Psychotherapy, 1988; editor: Adult Art Psychotherapy, Photo Collage, 1993; contbr. articles to profl. jours. Founder L.A. County Art Mus., 1983—, L.A. Contemporary Mus., 1983—. Fellow Soc. Psychopathology of Expression; mem. Am. Art Therapy Assn. (hon., life, bd. dirs. 1969-71, 84-86, treas. 1984-86), So. Calif. Art Therapy Assn. (hon., life, pres. 1972-74).

LANDGROFF, NANCY ANN, physical therapist; b. Youngstown, Ohio, Aug. 16, 1960; d. James Mansell and Edwina (Buchanan) Crum. BS, U. Pitts., 1982; MHS, U. Fla., 1988. Phys. therapist Youngstown Phys. Therapists Inc., 1982-83; sr. rehab. phys. therapist Southside Med. Ctr., Youngstown, 1983-85, supr. phys. therapy, 1985-87; grad. teaching asst. phys. therapy dept. U. Fla., Gainesville, 1987-88; assoc. dir. phys. therapy MIEMSS & Montebello Rehab. Hosp., Balt., 1988-90; dir. phys. therapy U. Md. Med. System/Montebello Rehab. Hosp., Balt., 1990-92; clin. dir. Burch, Rhodes and Loomis Physiotherapy Assocs., Balt., 1992-94, Advanced Physical Therapy, Boardman, Ohio, 1994—; instr. continuing edn. course Hillside Rehab. Hosp., Warren, Ohio, 1990. Mem. Am. Phys. Therapy Assn. (orthopaedic and neurologic sects., treas. Md. chpt. 1991, pub. rels. dir. 1992—), Ohio Phys. Assn. (pub. rels. chair), Neurodevel. Treatment Assn. Mem. Assemblies of God Ch. Home: 3828 Mercedes Pl Canfield OH 44406-8142 Office: Advanced Phys Therapy 914 Trailwood Dr Boardman OH 44512

LANDHOLM, WALLACE MARVEN, ophthalmologist; b. N. Platte, Nebr., Sept. 8, 1933; s. Marven K. and Alma L. (Phillips) L.; BA, U. Nebr., 1956, MD, 1959; m. Marcia Greenlee, 1955; children: James, Cheryl. Intern San Bernardino (Calif.) County Hosp., 1959-60; resident in ophthalmology State U. Iowa Hosp., 1963-65; pvt. practice, Newport Beach, Calif., 1967—; mem. staff Hoag Meml. Hosp.; asst. clin. prof. U. Calif. Med. Sch., Irvine. Served to capt. M.C., USAF, 1960-63. Decorated Air medal; diplomate Am. Bd. Ophthalmology, Am. Bd. Eye Surgery. Mem. AMA, Soc. Eye Surgeons, Am. Acad. Ophthalmology, Am. Intraocular Implant Soc., Newport Beach C. of C., Balboa Bay Club, Alpha Omega Alpha. Lutheran. Office: 320 Superior Ave Ste 350 Newport Beach CA 92663-2742

LANDING, BENJAMIN HARRISON, pathologist, educator; b. Buffalo, Sept. 11, 1920; s. Benjamin Harrison Sr. and Margaret Catherine (Crohen) L.; m. Dorothy Jean Hallas; children: Benjamin H., Susan L. Phillips, William M., David A. AB, Harvard U., 1942, MD, 1945. Diplomate Am. Bd. Pathology (anatomic pathology and pediatric pathology). Intern pathology Children's Hosp., Boston, 1945-46, asst. resident, then resident pathology, 1948-49; resident pathology Boston Lying-in Hosp., 1949, Free Hosp. for Women, Brookline, Mass., 1949; pathologist Children's Med. Ctr., Boston, 1950-53, Cin., 1953-61; pathologist-in-chief Children's Hosp., L.A., 1961-88, rsch. pathologist, 1988—; asst. pathologist Harvard U. Med. Sch., Boston, 1950-53; from asst. prof. to assoc. prof. U. Cin. Coll. Medicine, 1953-61; prof. pathology and pediatrics U. So. Calif. Sch. Medicine, L.A., 1961-91, prof. emeritus, 1991—. Author: Butterfly Color/Behavior Patterns, 1984; author chpts. in books; contbr. articles to profl. jours. Chmn. Pacific S.W. Dist. Unitarian-Universalist Assn., 1968-70; pres. Burbank (Calif.) Unitarian Fellowship, 1964-66. Capt. Med. Corps AUS, 1946-48. Mem. Soc. for Pediatric Pathology (pres. 1973-74), Internat. Pediatric Pathology Soc. (pres. 1980). Democrat. Unitarian-Universalist. Home: 4513 Deanwood Dr Woodland Hills CA 91364-5622 Office: Childrens Hosp LA Box 103 4650 W Sunset Blvd Los Angeles CA 90027-6016

LANDINO, COLLEEN DAWN, physician; b. Kirksville, Mo., July 7, 1966; d. Gerald Joseph and Mardalee Dawn (Wright) Brown; m. Timothy Francis Landino, Oct. 19, 1990; 1 child, Emily Dawn. BS, Mich. State U., East Lansing, 1988; D Osteopathic Medicine, Kirksville (Mo.) Coll. Osteopathic Medicine, 1996. Reg. dietitian. Dietetic intern N.Y. Hosp., Cornell Med. Ctr., N.Y., 1988-89; reg. clin. dietitian Hurley Med. Ctr., Flint, Mich., 1989-91; clin. dietitian St. Lawrence Hosp., Lansing, Mich., 1991-92. Recipient scholarship Student Osteopathic Med. Assn., 1996. Mem. Am. Coll. Osteopathic Family Physicians (scholarship 1996), Ob/Gyn Club, Sigma Sigma Phi. Roman Catholic. Home: 2700 6th St # 104-D Wyandotte MI 48192

LANDINO, DANIEL, speech pathologist; b. New Haven, Nov. 11, 1957; s. Albert and Carmel (Pantano) L.; m. Karen Sabino, July 18, 1980; children: DanaMarie, Daniel II. BA, So. Conn. State U., 1979, MS, 1982. Speech and lang. pathologist Bridgeport (Conn.) Pub. Schs., 1982-85, Derby (Conn.) Pub. Schs., 1985—, Novacare, New Haven, 1989-93, Complex Care, 1993—. Mem. Conn. Speech-Lang.-Hearing Assn. Home: 49 McMahon Ln North Branford CT 06471

LANDINO, RITA ANN, psychologist; b. New Haven, May 1, 1942; d. Michael and Rose (Di Meola) L.; 1 child, Michael Joseph. BS in English Edn., So. Conn. State U., 1964; MA in Liberal Studies, Wesleyan U., 1966; postgrad., Fairfield U., 1971; PhD in Ednl. Psychology, U. Conn., 1985. Nat. cert. counselor. English tchr. Hamden (Conn.) Pub. Schs., 1964-65; English instr. So. Conn. State U., New Haven, 1966-69, counselor, 1969-73, counselor, asst. prof., 1973-85, counselor, assoc. prof., 1985-90, counselor, prof., 1990—, adj. prof., 1982—; dir. Greater new Haven YWCA Bd., 1987-90; trainer, cons. in field. Contbr. articles to profl. jours.; patentee in field. Mem. Bd. of Fin., North Haven, 1989-93; trustee Meml. Libr. Bd., North Haven, 1987-89; mem. Dem. Town Com., North Haven, 1986—. Recipient Rsch. fellowship U. Conn. Rsch. Found., 1983. Mem. AAUP, APA, ACA, Am. Coll. Pers. Assn., Conn. Coll. Pers. Assn. (pres. 1988-91), Nat. Assn. for Women in Edn., Conn. Assn. for Women in Edn. Office: So Conn State U 501 Crescent St New Haven CT 06515-1330

LANDIS, GEORGE HARVEY, psychotherapist; b. Newton, Kans., Dec. 12, 1918; s. Melvin D. and Erie Emma (Byler) L.; m. Lois I. Donaldson, Sept. 26, 1943; children: Judy Carol Landis Forsman, Richard G. Student, Baker U., 1937-38; BA, John Fletcher Coll., 1941; MSW, U. Nebr., 1948. Diplomate Registry of Clin. Social Work; cert. clin. social worker, master social worker, Nebr. Caseworker Family Svc. of Omaha, 1948-50; psychotherapist Midwest Clinic, Omaha, 1950-90; pvt. practice Omaha, 1990—. Served with U.S. Army, 1941-46. Mem. Acad. Cert. Social Workers. Home: 4628 Hascall St Omaha NE 68106-4042 Office: 9239 W Center Rd Ste 200 Omaha NE 68124-1900

LANDOLFI, JENNIE LOUISE, nursing administrator; b. Warren, Ohio, Apr. 19, 1955; d. Gregory A. and Antonette (Cervone) L. Diploma, Trumbull Hosp. Sch. Nursing, Warren, 1978; cert., Brentwood Hosp. Paramedic Sch., Cleve., 1982; student, Akron U.; postgrad. RN, Ohio; cert. provider and instr. ACLS, BLS, instr. and coord. pre-hosp. trauma life support. Staff nurse Trumbull Meml. Hosp., Warren, 1978-82, charge nurse, 1982, coord. emergency med. svc. edn., 1986; coord. emergency med. svc. Kettering (Ohio) Med. Ctr., 1982-83; staff nurse Warren Gen. Hosp., 1984-85; home health care nurse Nurses House Call, Warren, 1987-90, emergency med. svcs./emergency dept. edn. coord., 1990—; hosp. rep. Trumbull County Joint Com. for Emergency Med. Svcs.; instr. course coord. pre-hosp. trauma life support Nat. Assn. EMT's. Contbr. articles to profl. jours. Apptd. State of Ohio EMS bd., 1992, 94, chmn. accreditation com., 1995; vice-chair Continuous Quality Improvement Com., Trumbull County Emergency Med. Svc. Com. Mem. Nat. Assn. Emergency Med. Technicians, Emergency Nurses Assn., Ohio Assn. Emergency Med. Svcs., Trumbull County Fire Chiefs Assn., Ohio Fire Fighters Assn., John F. Kennedy High Sch. Alumni Assn. Democrat. Roman Catholic. Home: 114 Morningside Rd Niles OH 44446-2112 Office: 1350 E Market St Warren OH 44483-6608

LANDOLPH, JOSEPH RICHARD, JR., microbiology, pathology and toxicology educator; b. Upper Darby, Pa., Nov. 9, 1948; s. Joseph Richard Sr. and Ada Nolia (Welch) L.; m. Alice Lee Kaufmann, Jan. 19, 1980; children: Joseph Richard III, Louis Samuel. BS in Chemistry, Drexel U., 1971; PhD in Chemistry, U. Calif., Berkeley, 1976. Chem. technician Rohm and Haas Co., Phila., 1968; jr. chem. technician Smith, Kline & French, Upper Marion, Pa., 1969-70; rsch. asst. U. Calif., Berkeley, 1971-76; postdoctoral fellow Cancer Ctr. U. So. Calif., L.A., 1977-80, asst. prof. pathology Sch. Medicine, 1980-82, asst. prof. microbiology and pathology, 1982-87, assoc. prof. pathology, molecular microbiology and immunology, 1987—; pvt. cons. Am. Petroleum Inst., Washington, 1983-85, Am. Assn. Sci. Advisers, 1988—, EPA, 1993-96; cons. MedLaw, Inc., L.A., 1987, Motorola Corp., 1996, and to various pvt attys.; grant reviewer genetics panel NRC, Howard Hughes Doctoral Fellowships Program, 1989-90. Pub. sci., peer-rev. articles in microbiology, carcinogenesis, mutagenesis, genetic toxicology jours.; mem. editorial bd. Environ. and Molecular Mutogens, 1987-93, Cancer Biochemistry and Biophysics, 1987—; ad hoc reviewer NIEHS, Research Triangle Park, N.C., 1985-86, 95; grant reviewer EPA, Washington, 1985-87; contbr. articles to profl. jours. Capt. USAR, 1976-77. Rsch. grantee Am. Cancer Soc., 1982-84, NIH, Research Triangle Park, 1983—, Nat. Cancer Inst., Bethesda, Md., 1986—, Tobacco-Related Disease Rsch. Program, State of Calif., 1990-94. Mem. Am. Assn. Cancer Rsch., Am. Soc. Biochemistry and Molecular Biology, Am. Soc. Cell Biologists, Am. Chem. Soc. (chmn. chem. pathology and toxicology subdiv. 1990-91), Soc. Toxicologists (councillor So. Calif. sect. 1991-93), Environ. Mutagen Soc. Republican. Unitarian. Home: 1009 E Mendocino St Altadena CA 91001-2562 Office: U So Calif Med Ctr Kenneth Norris Jr Comp Cancer Ctr 1441 Eastlake Ave Los Angeles CA 90033-1048

LANDOLT, ALLISON BOOTH, psychiatrist; b. Bklyn., Oct. 29, 1919; s. Percy Edward and Marie (Allison) L.; m. Nancy Cleland Wagner, Nov. 25, 1944 (div. 1985); children: Nancy, Cleland, Peter, Bruce, Matthew, Sarah; m. Susan Alice Fredell, Feb. 14, 1986. AB, Princeton U., 1941; MD, Columbia U., 1944. Diplomate Am. Bd. Psychiatry and Neurology. Intern in internal medicine Roosevelt Hosp., N.Y.C., 1944-45; resident in psychiatry Westchester div. N.Y. Hosp., White Plains, 1947-50; sr. psychiatrist Westchester div. N.Y. Hosp., White Plains, 1950-58; pvt. practice Bronxville, N.Y., 1958—; asst. attending psychiatrist N.Y. Hosp. Cornell U., N.Y.C., 1958—; asst. prof. Cornell U., 1958-80, adj. asst. prof., 1980—; cons. in field; psychiatrist Dept. Corrections Matteawan, Fishkill, N.Y., 1977. Psychiatrist II Office Mental Health, Newburgh, N.Y., 1987-88, Peekskill, N.Y., 1989—. Capt. M.C., AUS, 1945-47. Fellow ACP, N.Y. Acad. Medicine, Am. Psychiat. Assn.; mem. AMA, N.Y. Med. Soc. (pres. 1984-85, med. dirs. physicians' health com. 1988-89, chmn. bd. trustees 1991-92), Westchester County Med. Soc. (pres. 1969-70). Republican. Episcopalian. Office: 44 Pondfield Rd Bronxville NY 10708-3802

LANDRIGAN, PHILIP JOHN, epidemiologist; b. Boston, June 14, 1942; s. John Joseph and Frances Joan (Conlin) L.; m. Mary Florence Magee, Aug. 27, 1966; children: Mary Frances, Christopher Paul, Elizabeth Marie. A.B., Boston Coll., 1963; M.D., Harvard U., 1967; M.S., London Sch. Hygiene and Tropical Medicine, 1977, D.I.H., 1977. Diplomate Am. Bd. Pediatrics, Am. Bd. Preventive Medicine, Am. Bd. Occupational Medicine, Am. Coll. Epidemiology. Intern Cleve. Met. Gen. Hosp., 1967-68; resident in pediatrics Children's Hosp. Med. Ctr., Boston, 1968-70; fellow in pediatrics Harvard U. Med. Sch., Boston, 1969-70; clin. instr. pediatrics Emory U. Sch. Medicine, Atlanta, 1970-71; epidemic intelligence service officer Ctrs. for Disease Control, Atlanta, 1970-73, dir. research and devel. smallpox erradication program, 1973-74, chief environ. hazards activity, 1974-79; dir. div. Surveillance, Hazard Evaluations and Field Studies Nat. Inst. for Occupational Safety and Health, Cin., 1979-85; prof. community medicine and pediatrics Mt. Sinai Sch. Medicine, N.Y.C., 1985—; dir. div. environ. and occupational medicine Mt. Sinai Sch. Medicine, 1985-90; prof., chmn. dept. community medicine, 1990—; mem. bd. on toxicology and environ. health hazards Nat. Acad. Sci., Washington, vice chmn., 1981-86; clin. prof. environ. health Sch. Pub. Health U. Wash., Seattle, 1983—. Contbr. numerous articles on pediatrics, pub. health, epidemiology, occupational medicine and environ. medicine to med. jours.; cons. editor: Archives of Environ. Health, 1982—, Am. Jour. Indsl. Medicine, 1979—; editor-in-chief Environ. Research, 1987—. Recipient Vol. award Dept. HEW, 1973; recipient Pub. Health Service Career Devel. award, 1975, group citation as mem. of Ctr. for Disease Control beryllium rev. panel, 1978, Meritorious Service medal USPHS, 1985. Fellow Royal Soc. Medicine; mem. Inst. of MedicineInternat. Commn. on Occupational Health, Am. Pub. Health Assn., Am. Epidemiol. Soc., Soc. for Epidemiologic Research, AAAS. Home: 915 Stuart Ave Mamaroneck NY 10543-4124 Office: Mt Sinai Sch Medicine Dept Community Medicine 1 Gustave L Levy Pl New York NY 10029-6504

LANDRY, BARRY GERARD, physician; b. Thibodaux, Ala., Oct. 3, 1955; s. Ambroise J. and Althea Marie (Clement) L.; m. Denorah Jean Borwn, Oct. 13, 1984; children: Brigitte Mary, Samantha Althea. BS, Nicholls State U., 1977; MD, La. State U., 1981. Staff physician Thibodaux (La.) Hosp., 1987—. Methodist. Office: 1101 Audubon Ave Thibodaux LA 70301

LANDRY, MARK EDWARD, podiatrist, researcher; b. Washington, May 24, 1950; s. John Edward and Daphne (Fay) L.; m. Mary Ann Kotey, Sept. 7, 1974; children: John Ryan, Christopher John, Jessica Marie. D in Podiatry, Ohio Coll. Podiatric Medicine, 1975; MS in Edn., U. Kans., 1982. Diplomate Am. Bd. Podiatric Surgery, Am. Bd. Podiatric Orthopedics and Primary Podiatric Medicine. Gen. practice podiatry Kansas City, Mo., 1977—, Overland Park, Kans., 1980—; clin. asst. prof. U. Health Scis., Kansas City, 1985—; clin. assoc. prof. Coll. Podiatric Medicine and Surgery U. Osteo. Medicine and Health Scis., Des Moines, 1985-92; clin. instr. Sch. Medicine U. Mo., Kansas City, 1987-95; founder, bd. dirs. Kansas City Podiatric Residency Program, Kansas City, 1982-91; adv. bd. Rockport Shoe Co. Contbr. articles to profl. jours. Cons. Mid-Am. Track and Field Assn., Lenexa, Kans., 1978-88; com. chmn. Boy Scouts Am., Overland Park, Kans.; coach Johnson County Soccer League, 1987-90; head coach 6th grade girls' Cath. Youth Orgn. Basketball, 1995-96; sponsor 8 & 11 Baseball League, 1987-90. 1st lt. USAF, 1975-77. Recipient Pres.'s award Ohio Sch. Podiatric Medicine, 1975; USAF scholar Armed Forces Health Professions, 1973-75. Fellow Am. Coll. Foot Surgeons, Acad. Podiatric Sports Medicine, Am. Coll. Primary Podiatric Medicine & Podiatric Orthopedics; mem. Mid-Am. Masters Field and Track Assn., Brit. Podiatry Assn. (hon.), Am. Bd. Primary Podiatric Medicine (founding dir.), Holy Cross Social Club (pres. 1983-84), Brookridge Country Club, Bally Club (Overland Park). Republican. Roman Catholic. Home: 8120 W 99th St Shawnee Mission KS 66212-3444 Office: 10550 Quivira #260 Overland Park KS 66215

LANDSBERG, LEWIS, endocrinologist, medical researcher; b. N.Y.C., Nov. 23, 1938. AB, Williams Coll., 1960; MD, Yale U., 1964. From instr. to asst. prof. medicine Sch. Medicine Yale U., 1969-72; from asst. prof. to assoc. prof. Harvard Med. Sch., 1972-77, from assoc. prof. to prof., 1977-86; Irving S. Cutter prof., chmn. dept. medicine Med. Sch. Northwestern U. Med. Sch., 1990—; dir. Ctr. Endocrinology, Metabolism & Nutrition Northwestern U., 1990-93; assoc. physician Yale-New Haven Hosp., 1969-71, attending physician, 1971-72, Beth Israel Hosp., 1974-79, physician, 1979-88, sr. physician, 1988-90; attending physician West Haven VA Hosp., 1970-72; assisting physician Boston City Hosp., 1972-73, assoc. vis. physician, 1973-74; physician-in-chief dept. medicine Northwestern Meml. Hosp., 1990—. Fellow ACP; mem. AAAS, Am. Fedn. Clin. Rsch., Endocrine Soc., N.Y. Acad. Scis., AHA, Am. Soc. Pharmacology and Exptl. Therapeutics, Am. Physiology Soc., Am. Soc. Clin. Investigators, Am. Clin. and Climatological Assn., Assn. Am. Physicians. Office: Northwestern Univ Med Sch Wesley Pavilion 296 250 E Superior Chicago IL 60611

LANDSBERGER, BETTY HATCH, human development professional, gerontologist, educator; b. Tampa Aug. 9, 1918; d. Hugh Brenton and Margaret Lauder (Macdonell) Hatch; B.A. in Sociology, Fla. State U., 1939; M.A. Ed., U. Mich., 1940; Ph.D., Cornell U., 1951; m. Henry A. Landsberger, June 10, 1951; children: Margaret Ann Landsberger Thomas, Samuel Ernest, Ruth Elizabeth Landsberger. Mem. faculty edn. dept. Fla. State U., Cornell U., Roosevelt U., Chgo., 1941-54; program asso. evaluation research Learning Inst. N.C., Durham, 1969-71; mem. faculty U. N.C. Sch. Nursing, Chapel Hill, 1976-88, assoc. prof. emeritus, 1988—. Spokesperson AARP Women's Initiative, 1989-95; adv. bd. Area Agy. on Aging, 1985—; adv. com. for adults N.C. Dept. Human Resources Home and Community Care, 1991-95. Mem. N.C. Assn. Research in Edn. (pres. 1975-76), AAUP (chpt. pres. 1983), Phi Beta Kappa, Phi Kappa Phi, Pi Lambda Theta. Democrat. Author: Long Term Care for the Elderly; contbr. articles to profl. jours. and textbooks. Home: 807 Kings Mill Rd Chapel Hill NC 27514

LANDSBERGER, KURT, scientific, medical products executive; b. Prague, Czechoslavakia, Dec. 28, 1920; came to U.S., 1939; s. Ernest and Helen (Hoffman) L.; m. Anny Terkel, July 25, 1943; children: David I., Allen S. Grad. Handelsakademie, Vienna, Austria, 1938. Founder Bel-Art Products Maddak Inc., Author: Holocaust Collection, applied coatings, Pequannock, N.J., 1946—, chmn. bd., 1982—. Patentee in field. Chmn. planning bd. Borough of Verona, N.J., 1982-85; pres. Verona Democratic Com., 1954-58; mem. Bahamas Nat. Trust; trustee Beth Ahm Congregation, 1986—; bd. dirs. West Essex Rehab. Ctr., 1986—; mem. Essex County Handicapped Adv. Bd., 1986—. Served with U.S. Army, 1942-46. Mem. Verona C. of C. (pres. 1962), N.J. Conservation Found., Chmn. Founder "Save the Mountains", Internat. Wilfelife Fedn., N.J. Hist. Soc., Montclair Art Mus., Newark Mus., Nat. Trust Historic Preservation. Jewish. Lodge: Kiwanis (pres. 1962). Office: Bel-Art Products Pequannock NJ 07442

LANDSBOROUGH, RON JAMES, health care executive; b. Jerome, Idaho, Oct. 9, 1955; s. James Ron and Lola Cora (Kinsey) L. BS in Engring., Ariz. State U., 1981, M in Health Service Adminstrn., 1985. Registered profl. engr., Calif. Indsl. mfg. engr. Gen. Instrument Corp., Chandler, Ariz., 1981; systems engr. Samaritan health Service, Phoenix, 1982-85; healthcare systems cons. Shared Med. Systems, Phoenix, 1985-90; healthcare industry specialist Gateway Data Scis., Tempe, Ariz., 1990-91; sr. sales rep. IBAX Healthcare Systems, Orange, Calif., 1991-92; v.p. program devel. Guynes Designs, Inc., Phoenix, 1992—; cons. Ariz. Dept. Transp., Phoenix, 1980; mem. WesTech Info. Mgmt. Think Tank, 1995—; instr. grad. program for health care mgmt. Western Internat. U., 1995—. Author: Proceedings of the Summer Regional Conference of the Hospital Management Systems Society of the American Hospital Association, 1984, Hospital and Health Services Administration, 1985. Mem. Am. Coll. Healthcare Execs. (diplomate), Healthcare Fin. Mgmt. Assn., Health Adminstrs. Forum, Health Info. Mgmt. Sys. Soc. (treas. Ariz. chpt.), Inst. Indsl. Engrs. Republican. Methodist. Home: 3442 E Hazelwood St Phoenix AZ 85018-3434 Office: Guynes Design Inc 1555 E Jackson St Phoenix AZ 85034-2310

LANDSMAN, ELIOT, psychiatrist, psychoanalyst; b. Boston, May 16, 1912; s. Jacob Louis and Augusta (Hoffman) L.; children: Jay, Lee. BS, U. Mass., 1934; MEd, Boston Tchrs. Coll., 1935; MD, Boston U., 1950. Diplomate Am. Bd. Psychiatry. Teaching fellow Boston Psychopathic Hosp., 1951-53; fellow psychotherapy instr. Beth Israel Hosp., Boston, 1953-65; cons. Medfield (Mass.) State Hosp., 1956-64; clin. instr. Tufts Med. Sch., Boston, 1954-62; chief psychiatrist Hebrew Rehab. Ctr., Boston, 1956—; psychiatrist Faulkner Hosp., Boston, 1963—; asst. psychiatrist, cons. Beth Israel Hosp., Boston, 1963—. Maj. U.S. Army Med. Corps, 1941-46. Mem. Am. Psychoanalytic Assn., Am. Psychiatric Assn., Mass. Med. Soc., Boston Soc. Gerontological Psychiatry (bd. dirs. treas.), Boston Psychoanalytic Soc. and Inst. (trustee, treas.). Home: 239 Windsor Rd Newton MA 02168-1119

LANDWEHR, PETER, radiologist; b. Wuppertal, Germany, Dec. 19, 1959; s. Wolfgang and Anne (Krause) L.; m. Susanne Maria Blank, May 31, 1986; children: Leonard, Konstantin. MD, U. Bonn, 1985. Resident in radiology U. Bonn, Germany, 1986-87, U. Würzburg, Germany, 1987-91; staff radiologist U. Cologne, Germany, 1991-93, asst. med. dir., 1994—. Author: Color Duplex Sonography, 1993; contbr. more than 60 articles to profl. jours. Polit. campaign mgr., Remscheid, Germany, 1984. Mem. Radiol. Soc. North Am., German Roentgen Ray Soc. Roman Catholic. Home: Koenigsberger Str 23, D-50259 Pulheim Germany Office: Inst Radiol Diagnostik, Joseph-Stelzmann Str 9, D-50924 Cologne Germany

LANE, ALFRED THOMAS, medical educator; b. Dayton, Ohio, July 17, 1947. BS, U. Dayton, 1969; MD, Ohio State U., 1973. Diplomate Am. Bd. Pediatrics, Am. Bd. Dermatology; lic. physician, Calif. Intern, resident pediatrics Children's Hosp. L.A., 1973-76; pvt. practice Pleasant Valley Pediatric Med. Group, Camarillo, Calif., 1976-79; resident dermatology U. Colo. Sch. Medicine, Denver, 1979-82; asst. prof. dermatology and pediatrics U. Rochester (N.Y.) Med. Ctr., 1982-88; attending physician Strong Meml. Hosp., 1982-90; staff dermatologist Rochester Gen. Hosp., 1985-90; dir. Dermatology Clinic VA, Rochester, 1985-90; assoc. prof. dermatology and pediatrics U. Rochester Med. Ctr., 1988-90; staff physician in dermatology and pediatrics Stanford (Calif.) U. Med. Ctr., Stanford Children's Hosp., 1990—, dir. pediatric dermatology, 1990—; assoc. prof. dermatology and pediatrics Stanford U. Med. Ctr., 1990—, acting chmn. dept. dermatology, 1995—; acting chief dermatology svc. Stanford U. Med. Ctr., Stanford Health Svcs., 1995—. Author: with W.L. Weston) Color Textbook of Pediatric Dermatology, 1991; (with W.L. Weston and J.G. Morelli) Color Textbook of Pediatric Dermatology, 1995; contbr. articles to profl. jours. Recipient Buswell fellowship U. Rochester, 1982-83, Clin. Investigator award NIH, 1983-88. Fellow Am. Acad. Pediatrics, Am. Acad. Dermatology (mem. task force on pediatric dermatology 1987-92, mem. adv. coun. 1988-90, mem. Presdl. Commn. on Melanoma/Skin Cancer 1988-92, mem. task force on youth edn. 1989-94); mem. Soc. Pediatric Dermatology (bd. dirs. 1986-93, pres. elect 1990-91, pres. 1991-92), Soc. Investigative Dermatology (com. on pub. rels. 1990-94, com. on govt. and pub. rels. 1992-94), Soc. Pediatric Rsch., Am. Dermatol. Assn., Am. Soc. Laser Medicine and Surgery. Office: Stanford U Med Ctr Dept Dermatology 900 Blake Wilbur #W0071 Stanford CA 94305-5334

LANE, BERNARD PAUL, medical educator; b. Bklyn., June 27, 1938; s. Jack Robert and Rose L. (Weiss) L.; m. Dorothy Ellen Spiegel, Aug. 2, 1962; children: Erika, Andrew, Matthew. AB, Brown U., 1959; MD, NYU, 1963; MA in Mgmt., SUNY, 1992. Asst. prof. Sch. of Medicine, NYU, N.Y.C., 1965-69, assoc. prof., 1969-71; assoc. prof. Sch. of Medicine, SUNY, Stony Brook, 1971-75, prof., 1975—. Author chpts. in books; contbr. articles to profl. jours. Active L.I. div. Am. Cancer Soc., 1977—. Maj. USAF, 1969-71. Decorated Air Force medal; NIH fellow NYU, 1964-65; NIH grantee SUNY, 1972-78. Fellow Am. Soc. Clin. Pathologists, Coll. Am. Pathologists; mem. Am. Assn. for Investigative Pathology, Am. Soc. Cell Biology, Am. Assn. Study Liver Diseases, Internat. Acad. Pathology, Suffolk Pathologists Soc., N.Y. State Med. Soc., Suffolk County Med. Soc. Office: SUNY-HSC Dept of Pathology Stony Brook NY 11794

LANE, DANIEL MCNEEL, pediatric hematologist, lipidologist; b. Ft. Sam Houston, Tex., Jan. 25, 1936; s. Samuel Hartman and Mary Maverick (McNeel) L.; m. Carolyn Ann Spruiell, Nov. 28, 1958; children: Linda Ann, Daniel M. Jr., Maury S., Oleta K. MD, U. Tex.-Dallas, 1961; MS, U. Tenn., 1967; PhD, U. Okla., 1973. Asst. prof., head pediatric hematology/oncology U. Okla. Med. Ctr., Oklahoma City, 1966-72; rsch. fellow Okla. Med. Rsch. Found., Oklahoma City, 1969-72, adj. assoc. mem., 1986-92, adj. mem.,

1993—; assoc. prof., head pediatric hematology/oncology Tulane Med. Sch., New Orleans, 1972-73; head hematology/oncology Oklahoma City Clinic, 1973-79; pvt. practice, 1979—; head Okla. Lipid Consultation Group, 1993-95; dir. clin. investigation Presbyn. Meml. Hosp., Oklahoma City, 1975-77; med. monitor HELP System project B. Braun Am., 1988-93, B. Braun Melsungen AG, FRG, cons.; assoc. prof. Tex. Tech. U. Health Scis. Ctr., Odessa, 1996—; chmn., bd. dirs. Poplar Pike Realtors, Inc., Memphis, 1973-85; cons. Programa de Prevenciondel Infarto en Argentina, La Plata. Fin. chmn. Dunlap for Congress, 1976; head Physicians for Gov. Nigh, 1978; Dem. candidate for Congress, 5th Dist., 1982. USPHS fellow, 1964-66; spl. rsch. fellow Nat. Heart Lung and Blood Inst., 1969-72. Mem. AMA, Am. Soc. Clin. Oncology, Am. Soc. Hematology, Am. Oil Chemists Soc., Am. Coll. Nutrition. Democrat. Episcopalian. Research on infant lipid nutrition, lipoprotein plasma pheresis, clin. hematology; pediatrics. Home: 5525 N Independence Oklahoma City OK 73112 Office: Dept Pediat-Tex Tech U 800 W 4th St Odessa TX 79763

LANE, DOROTHY SPIEGEL, physician; b. Bklyn., Feb. 17, 1940; d. Milton Barton and Rosalie (Jacobson) Spiegel; m. Bernard Paul Lane, Aug. 5, 1962; children: Erika, Andrew, Matthew. BA, Vassar Coll., 1961; MD, Columbia U., 1965, MPH, 1968. Diplomate Am. Bd. Preventive Medicine, Am. Bd. Family Practice. Resident preventive medicine N.Y.C. Dept. Health Dist., 1966-68; project dir. children and youth project Title V, HHS N.Y.C. Dept. Health Dist., Rockaway, N.Y., 1968-69; med. cons. Maternal and Child Health Svc. HHS, Rockville, Md., 1970-71; asst. prof. preventive medicine Sch. Medicine SUNY, Stony Brook, 1971-76, assoc. prof., 1976-92; prof., 1992—; assoc. dean Sch. Medicine SUNY, Stony Brook, 1986—; chair dept. community medicine, dir. med. edn. Brookhaven Meml. Hosp. Med. Ctr., Patchogue, N.Y., 1972-86. Contbr. numerous articles to profl. jours. Mem. exec. com. Am. Cancer Soc., L.I. divsn., 1975—; mem. nat. bd. dirs. Am. Cancer Soc.; corp. mem. Nassau Suffolk Health Systems Agy., L.I., 1977—; bd. dirs. Community Health Plan Suffolk, Hauppauge, 1986-91. Grantee HHS-USPHS, 1977-85, 83—, Nat. Cancer Inst., 1987—. Fellow APHA, Am. Coll. Preventive Medicine (regent 1988-96, sec.-treas. 1994-96), Am. Acad. Family Physicians, N.Y. Acad. Medicine, Am. Bd. Preventive Medicine (trustee), Assn. Tchrs. Preventive Medicine (pres. 1996—). Office: SUNY at Stony Brook Sch Medicine Health Scis Ctr L-4 Stony Brook NY 11794-8437

LANE, JOHN GERHART, orthopedic surgeon; b. Topeka, Kans., Dec. 31, 1955; s. Robert Gerhart and Mary Elaine (Griffith) L.; m. Allison Elizabeth Sundberg, Nov. 25, 1989; children: Christian, Katherine, Elizabeth. BS, U. So. Calif., 1978; MD, Yale U., 1984. Diplomate Am. Bd. Orthopedic Surgery. Physician San Diego Ctr. Sports Medicine, 1991—; clin. instr. U. Calif., San Diego, 1989—; adj. prof. San Diego State U., 1995—. Fellow Am. Acad. Orthopedic Surgeons; mem. Am. Orthopedic Soc. Sports Medicine, Arthroscopy Assn. N.Am. (grantee 1996). Office: 8010 Frost St # 510 San Diego CA 92123

LANE, LONNIE G(ENE), perioperative nurse; b. Oskaloosa, Iowa, Dec. 6, 1951; s. Kenneth Dean Sr. and Edith Maxine (Courtney) L. ADN, Okla. State U. Tech. Inst., 1979. Asst. supr. post-anesthesia care unit Baylor U. Med. Ctr., Dallas, 1980-85, staff nurse oper. rm./post-anesthesia care unit, 1986-89; head nurse post-anesthesia care unit Charter Suburban Hosp., Dallas, 1985-86; asst. dir. surg. svcs. Zale Lipshy U. Hosp., Dallas, 1989-91; peri-operative nurse Physicians Day Surgery Ctr., Dallas, 1991—; gen. duty nurse Air N.G., Dallas, 1982-86; operating rm. nurse USAF Res., Carswell AFB, Tex., 1991-92; flight nurse USAF Res., Kelly AFB, Tex., 1992-93; staff devel. officer, Sheppard AFB, Tex., 1993—. Capt. USAFR. Mem. ANA, Tex. Nurses Assn., Am. Soc. Post Anesthesia Nurses (bd. dirs. 1986-89, nat. chair of nat. conf. 1988), Tex. Assn. Post-Anesthesia Nurses (pres. 1985-86), Assn. Oper. Rm. Nurses, Am. Assembly of Men in Nursing. Home: 6808 Eastridge Dr Apt 24 Dallas TX 75231-6809 Office: Physicians Day Surgery Ctr 3930 Crutcher St Dallas TX 75246-1700

LANE, MALCOLM DANIEL, biological chemistry educator; b. Chgo., Aug. 10, 1930; s. Malcolm Daniel Lane and Helga Sofia (Nielsen) Wilke; m. Patricia L. Sonquist, Mar. 17, 1951; children: Claudia J. Lane Fioranelli, M. Daniel Jr. BS, Iowa State U., 1951, MS, 1953; PhD, U. Ill., 1956. Assoc. prof. Va. Poly. Inst., Blackburg, 1956-63, prof. biochemistry, 1963-64; assoc. prof. biochemistry Sch. Medicine N.Y.U., 1964-69, prof. biochemistry Sch. Medicine, 1969-70; prof. biochemistry Sch. Medicine Johns Hopkins U., Balt., 1970-78, DeLamar prof., dir. dept. biol. chemistry, 1978—. Mem. editorial bd.: Jour. Biol. Chemistry, 1969-74, 79-84, Biochem. et Biophysica Acta, 1968-70, 75-79, Archives Biochemistry and Biophysics, 1977-80, Ann. Revs. Biochemistry, 1980-84; exec. editor: Biochem./Biophys. Research Com., 1986—; contbr. numerous articles to profl. jours. Fellow Am. Acad. Arts and Sci.; mem. NAS, Am. Soc. Biochem. Molecular Biology (sec. 1987-89, program chmn. 1990-91, pres., William C. Rose award 1981), Am. Soc. Cell Biology, Am. Inst. Nutrition (Mead-Johnson award 1966), Am. Chem. Soc. Home: 5607 Roxbury Pl Baltimore MD 21209-4501 Office: Johns Hopkins U Sch Medicine 725 N Wolfe St Baltimore MD 21205-2105

LANE, MONTAGUE, physician, educator; b. N.Y.C., Aug. 28, 1929; s. George and Ida (Korn) L.; m. Chrsitine Laura; children: Laura Diane, Adam Reuben. B.A., N.Y. U., 1947; M.B., Chgo. Med. Sch., 1952, M.D., 1953; M.S., Georgetown U., 1957. Diplomate: Am. Bd. Internal Medicine (mem. subcom. on med. oncology 1974-80, cons. 1981-83). Clin. assoc. Nat. Cancer Inst., NIH, 1954-56; sr. investigator Clin. Pharmacology and Exptl. Therapeutics Service; attending physician gen. med. br. Nat. Cancer Inst., 1957-60; assoc. in medicine George Washington U., Med. Sch., 1957-60; asst. prof., assoc. prof. depts. pharmacology and medicine Baylor U. Coll. Medicine, Houston, 1960-67; prof. depts. pharm. and medicine Baylor Coll. Medicine, 1967—, head div. clin. oncology dept. pharmacology, 1969-94, head sect. med. oncology dept. medicine, 1961-92; co-dir. cancer control sci. program Meth. Hosp. and Baylor Coll. Medicine, Houston, 1981-94; mem. study sect. Nat. Cancer Inst., 1966-69, mem. cancer clin. investigations rev. com., 1972-75; chmn. new agts. com. S.W. Cancer Chemotherapy study group; cons. drug evaluations AMA; cons. Merck Manual, U.S. Pharmacopeia, 1981-83; cons. interferon program Schering Corp., 1981-82; cons. com. on orphan drugs FDA, 1986—; cons. UNOMED, 1989-91; mem. adv. bd. Cancer Info. Dissemination and Analysis Ctr., Info Ventures, Inc., 1988-93; mem. sci. adv. bd. Health Infusion, Inc., 1991-94. Assoc. editor: Cancer Research, 1970-80. External adv. bd. Howard U. Cancer Center, 1977-83. Named Disting. Alumnus Chgo. Med. Sch., 1971, Disting. Faculty Mem. Baylor Med. Alumni Assn., 1990. Fellow ACP; mem. Am. Inst. Nutrition, Am. Soc. Clin. Oncology (program chmn. 1970), Am. Soc. Clin. Pharmacology and Exptl. Therapeutics (pres. 1971-72), Am. Soc. Pharmacology and Exptl. Therapeutics, Am. Soc. Hematology, Houston Soc. Internal Medicine (v.p. 1973-74, pres. 1984-85), Am. Assn. Cancer Rsch. (program com. 1990), Harris County Med. Soc. Home: 1514 Bissonnet St Houston TX 77005-1814 Office: 6560 Fannin St Ste 1510 Houston TX 77030-2707

LANE, PATRICIA PEYTON, nursing consultant; b. Danville, Ill., Oct. 5, 1929; d. Louis Weldon Sr. and Ruth Jeanette (Meyer) Peyton; m. H.J. Lane, Dec. 23, 1950 (div.); children: Jennifer Lane-Carr, Peter Lane, Amelia Ozog. Diploma, St. Elizabeth Hosp., 1950; BA in Psychology magna cum laude, Rosary Coll., 1974; postgrad., Lakeview Coll. of Nursing, Danville, Ill., 1987-88; student, Triton Jr. Coll., River Grove, Ill., 1969-72. Staff nurse St. Elizabeth Hosp., Danville, Ill., 1950; staff nurse nursery Ill. Rsch. and Ednl. Hosp., Chgo., 1951, charge nurse tumour clinic, 1951-54; res. sch. nurse elem. schs., Oak Park, Ill., 1969-78; sta. mgr. Oak Park-River Infant Welfare, Oak Park, Ill., 1972-76; vision and hearing screener suburban elem. schs., Ill., 1980-82; sch. nurse West Subrban Assn. Spl. Edn., Cicero, 1978-80; caseworker, counselor Vermilion County Mental Health and Devel. Disabilities, Inc., Danville, 1983-86; case coord., nurse cons. Crosspoint Human Svcs., Danville, 1986-88; staff nurse psychiat. acute care unit Community Hosp. of Ottawa, Ill., 1988-89; dir. social svcs. Pleasant View Luther Home, Ottawa, 1989-93; clin. case coord. Access Svcs., Inc., Mendota, Ill., 1993—; cmty. ombudsman LaSalle County Alternatives for the Older Adult, Peru, Ill., 1993—; cons. in field. Mem. ANA, Ill. State Nurses Assn. (cert. psychiat./mental nurse). Office: Alternatives for the Older Adult 2000 Luther Dr Peru IL 61354-1205

LANE, PATRICIA S., nursing home administrator, media specialist; b. Louisville, July 3, 1932; d. Ransom Grady and Jessie Marie (Lee) Snowden; m. Fred Arlo Lane, Jan. 30, 1953; children: Pat, Freda, Cameron. BA, Stetson U., 1953, MA, 1975. Tchr. City High Sch., Chattanooga, 1953; sec. to dean So. Bapt. Theol. Sem., Louisville, 1954; tchr. Waggener Jr. High Sch., Louisville, 1955-56; church sec. Arlington Bapt. Ch., Jacksonville, Fla., 1957; librarian Lumberton (N.C.) High Sch., 1965; media specialist Mainland Sr. High Sch., Daytona Beach, Fla., 1966-72, DeLand High Sch., 1973-81; adminstr. DeLand Convalescent Ctr., 1982-90, Fairview Manor Ltd., Daytona Beach, FL, 1990-96; sec., treas. Coordinated Care, Inc., Deland, Fla., 1996—; chmn. Missions Devel. Coun., 1991-92. Sunday sch. sec. 1st Bapt. Ch., DeLand, Fla., 1989-93, mem. pers. com., 1987-90. Mem. Fla. Health Care Adminstrs. Assn. (sec. local dist. 1986-87). Democrat. Baptist. Home: 231 W Minnesota Ave Deland FL 32720-3477 Office: Coordinated Care Inc 403 S Amelia Ave Deland FL 32724

LANE, RICHARD ALLAN, physician, health sciences educator; b. Camp LeJuene, N.C., Feb. 5, 1956; s. Howard Allan and Elizabeth Jane (Fischer) L.; m. Cynthia Diane Gastineau, Jan. 7, 1978; children: Tiffany Marie, Laurel Christina. BS, U. Md., 1978, MD, 1982; MPH in Tropical Medicine, Tulane U., 1986. Diplomate Am. Bd. Preventive Medicine. Intern Md. Gen. Hosp., Balt., 1982-83; squadron flight surgeon, 363rd Tactical Fighter Wing USAF, Shaw AFB, 1983-85; resident in aerospace medicine USAF, Brooks AFB, 1986-87; advanced through grades to maj. USAF, 1983-87; chief aeromed. svcs. Warner Robins Air Logistics Ctr., Robins AFB, 1987-89; staff physician, microbiology instr. Liberty U., Lynchburg, Va., 1989-91, assoc. prof. health scis., 1991—; cons., spkr. Liberty Godparent Home, Lynchburg, 1989—; mem. residency adv. bd. Meharry Med. Coll., Nashville, Tenn., 1987-89; adj. faculty health sci. Internat. Health Honduras project James Madison U., Harrisonburg, Va., 1993—. Contbr. articles to profl. jours. Bd. dirs. Network for Women in Crisis, Lynchburg, 1990-91; exec. bd. Lynchburg chpt. ARC, 1991-93; founder Emmanuel Bapt. Ch., chpt. AWANA, Warner Robins, Ga., 1987-89. Fellow Am. Coll. Preventive Medicine; mem. Gideons Internat. (camp treas. 1988-89), N.Y. Acad. Scis., Am. Soc. Tropical Medicine and Hygiene, Aerospace Med. Assn. Republican. Baptist. Home: 103 Village Rd Lynchburg VA 24502-2308 Office: Liberty U Health Svc Dept Lynchburg VA 24506

LANE, ROBERT CHESTER, psychologist, psychoanalyst; b. N.Y.C., Apr. 14, 1921; s. Sol Baylis and Rae (Spitzer) L.; m. Jean Betty Gottlieb, Mar. 14, 1943; children: Jo-Ellen, Steven Barry, Lawrence David. BS, CCNY, 1942, MS, 1943; PhD, NYU, 1954; Cert. in Psychoanalysis, Psychoanalytic Tng. Inst., N.Y. Freudian Soc., 1963. Diplomate Am. Bd. Profl. Psychology. Chief psychologist Westchester County Mental Hygiene Clinics, White Plains, N.Y., 1946-47; psychologist-in-charge psychiat. sect., psychology dept. Kingsbridge VA Hosp., N.Y.C., 1948-53; chief psychologist North Shore Neuropsychiatric Ctr., Roslyn, N.Y., 1950-63; exec. dir. Nassau Psychol. Svcs. Inst., Freeport, N.Y., 1966-68; dir. edn. Hempstead (N.Y.) Cons. Svc., 1968-71; coord. tng., dean Huntington (N.Y.) Mental Health Clinic, 1964-66; faculty and control analyst Met. Acad., N.Y.C., 1970-72; dir. tng. L.I. div. N.Y. Ctr. Psychoanalytic Tng., N.Y.C., 1972-92; clin. prof. psychology Derner Inst. Adelphi U., Garden City, 1980-92; dir. postdoctoral inst. Sch. Profl. Psychology Nova U., Ft. Lauderdale, Fla., 1989—. Editor: Psychoanalytic Approaches to Supervision, 1990, (with M. Meisels) A History of the Division of Psychoanalysis of the American Psychological Association; contbr. more than 50 articles to profl. jours. Staff sgt. USAAF, 1942-46. Named Disting. Practitioner, Nat. Acad. Practice in Psychology, 1984. Fellow APA (coun. rep. 1978-81, 84-87, pres. div. 39 and sects. I and IV, Div. Psychoanalysis, Presdl. award 1982, Disting. Svc. to Psychoanalysis award 1989); mem. Soc. Psychoanalytic Tng. (pres. 1975-78, 80-82), N.Y. Ctr. Psychoanalytic Tng. (Disting. Svc. award 1981, writer 1986, psychoanalyst 1989), Nassau County Psychol. Assn. (pres. 1974-75, Presdl. award 1975), N.Y. State Psychol. Assn. (pres. clin. div. 1977-78, cert. of honor 1978). Home and Office: 1931 Sabal Palm Dr Apt 101 Fort Lauderdale FL 33324-5961

LANE, VIVIAN PRYCE, educational counselor; b. Girardville, Pa., May 26, 1938; d. Edward Thomas and Vivian Adelaide (Portz) Davis; m. Franklin L. Lane, Aug. 13, 1960. BS in Edn. cum laude, Kutztown U., 1960; MSW, Temple U., 1981. Lic. social worker, Pa.; cert. counselor, Pa. Counselor Eastern Sch. Dist., Wrightsville, Pa., 1960-62; counselor, tchr. Penn Manor Sch. Dist., Millersville, Pa., 1962-70; adminstrv. asst. Cattell Sch., Lancaster, Pa., 1970-73; counselor Phila. Sch. Dist., 1982—; ednl. cons., Phila., 1987—. Active Food Cupboard program Diocese of Phila., 1985, outreach com. Episcopal Social Svcs., Phila., 1987-88; coord. info. requests Phila. Tourist/Conv. Bur., 1993-94. Mem. NASW, Am. Assn. Counseling and Devel., Am. Sch. Counelors Assn., Kappa Delta Pi. Democrat. Home: PO Box 186 Clifton Heights PA 19018-0186 Office: Phila Sch Dist 21st St And Pky Philadelphia PA 19103

LANE, WILLIAM KENNETH, physician; b. Butte, Mont., Nov. 5, 1922; s. John Patrick and Elizabeth Marie (Murphy) L.; m. Gilda Antoinette Parision, Aug. 21, 1954; children: William S., Francine Deirdre. Student, U. Mont., 1940-41, Mt. St. Charles Coll., 1941-43; MD, Marquette U., 1946. Intern Queen of Angels Hosp., L.A., 1946-47, resident physician, 1954-56; pvt. practice internal medicine San Francisco, 1947-51; resident in urology VA Hosp., Long Beach, Calif., 1956-58; physician VA Hosp., Long Beach, Oakland and Palo Alto, Calif., 1958—; lectr. on psychology of the elderly Foothill Coll., Los Altos, 1972-74; rschr. in field. Bd. dirs., mem. No. Cheyenne Indian Sch.; mem. Josef Meier's Black Hills Theatrical Group, S.D., 1940. With U.S. Army, 1943-46, ETO, lt. USN, 1951-54, Korea. Mem. AMA, Am. Geriatrics Soc., Nat. Assn. VA Physicians, San Francisco County Med. Soc., Woodrow Wilson Ctr. (assoc.), St. Vincent de Paul Soc., Cupertino Landscape Artists (past pres.), Audubon Soc., Stanford Hist. Soc., San Jose Movie/Video Club, San Jose Camera Club. Roman Catholic. Home: 18926 Sara Park Cir Saratoga CA 95070-4164 Office: Stanford VA Med Ctr 3801 Miranda Ave # 171 Palo Alto CA 94304-1207

LANEY, SUSAN KINCAID, nurse, mental health counselor; b. Lenoir, N.C., Nov. 11, 1938; d. Joseph Wade and mary Sue (Mackie) Kincaid; m. Thomas Fedrick Laney, Aug. 17, 1958; children: Sandra, Thomas. BS in Psychology, Appalachian State U., Boone, N.C., 1984, MA in Psychiat. Counseling, 1989; BSN, Winston-Salem State U., 1992; MSN, U. N.C., Greensboro, 1995. RN, N.C.; nat. cert. counselor. Credit mgr. Kincaid Furniture, Hudson, N.C., 1966-76, in inventory mgmt., 1976-83; nurse Catawba Meml. Hosp., Hickory, N.C., 1988—. Mem. ANA, Am. Psychiat. Nurses Assn. Home: PO Drawer D Granite Falls NC 28630 Office: Catawba Meml Hosp 810 Fairgrove Rd Hickory NC 28602

LANG, ENID ASHER, psychiatrist; b. Los Angeles, Calif., Aug. 28, 1944; s. Alvin Melville and Inez (Silverberg) Asher; m. Norton Lang; children: Eugenie, Aaron. BA, Harvard U., 1966; MD, U. So. Calif., 1970; MPH in Pub. Health, Columbia U., N.Y.C., 1975. Intern Beth Israel Hosp., N.Y.C., 1971-72; resident in psychiatry Columbia Psychiat. Inst., N.Y.C., 1972-75; fellow Columbia Health Svc., N.Y.C., 1974-75; clin. prof. psychiatry Mt. Sianai Med. Sch., N.Y.C., 1976—; lectr. psychiatry and lit. for faculty, Mt Sinai Dept. Psychiatry, N.Y.C., 1983—. Co-author (Dr. E. Ackerman) Study of Health in Rural France, 1978; (with D. Halperin) Group Psychotherapy, 1983. Bd. govs. Harvard U., Cambridge, Mass., 1993—. Recipient Milban fellowship, Barrio Health Care, L.A., 1970-71. Mem. Am. Psychiat. Assn., Am. Womens Med. Assn. Jewish. Office: 1158 Fifth Ave New York NY 10029

LANG, GERHARD, psychology educator; b. Germany, Mar. 19, 1925; came to U.S., 1940; s. Bertold and Else Lang; m. Adell Lang, Dec. 27, 1951; children: Kenneth, Judith Lang Knutsen. BS in Psychology, CCNY, 1952, MA in Sch. Psychology, 1954; PhD in Devel. and Ednl. Psychology, Columbia U., 1958. Cert. psychologist, N.Y.; lic. psychology, N.J. Tchg. fellow, rsch. asst., cons., lectr. CCNY, 1954-60; instr., asst. prof. psychology Fairleigh Dickinson U., Rutherford, N.J., 1958-63, assoc. prof., 1963-64; assoc. prof. psychology and edn. Montclair State U., Upper Montclair, N.J., 1966-70, prof., 1970—, chmn. dept. ednl. rsch. and evaluation, 1970-73, team leader, 1973-94; cons. N.Y.C. Bd. Edn., 1966-90, rsch. assoc. bd. examiners, 1964-66; cons. Jewish Edn. Svc. N.Am., N.Y.C., 1960-84, Title I reading project Dist. 29, Queens, N.Y., 1973-77, Twp. of Montclair, 1991; pvt. practice, 1971—. Author: A Practical Guide to Statistics for Research and Measurements, 5th edit., 1995, A Practical Guide to Research Methods, 5th edit., 1994; contbr. articles to profl. jours., also chpts. and pamphlets. Grantee James McKeen Cattel Fund, 1957, U.S. Dept. Edn., 1962-64, 65-67. Mem. APA, Am. Ednl. Rsch. Assn., Nat. Coun. on Measurements in Edn., Northeastern Ednl. Rsch. Assn. Home: 4-39 Lyncrest Ave Fair Lawn NJ 07410-1634 Office: Montclair State U Dept Psychology Montclair NJ 07043

LANG, JEFFREY, plastic surgeon; b. N.Y.C., July 12, 1941. BA, NYU, 1962; MD, SUNY, Bklyn., 1966. Diplomate Nat. Bd. Med. Examiners. Lic. physician, N.Y., Calif., Fla. Intern various hosps., 1966-67, resident in gen. surgery, 1967-70; resident in plastic surgery Montefiore Hosp. and Med. Ctr., 1970-72; pvt. practice specializing in plastic surgery Ft. Myers, Fla., 1972—; plastic surgeon staff Lee Meml. Hosp., Ft.Myers, Fla., Ossining Inst. Correction, Sing Sing Prison; lectr. in field. Contbr. articles to profl. jours. Recipient Physicians Recognition award, AMA, 1969, 72, 86. Mem. AMA, ACS, Am. Soc. Hand Surgery, Am. Soc. Aesthetic Plastic Surgery, Soc. Plastic and Reconstrv. Surgeons, Fla. Med. Assn., Lee County Med. Soc., Fla. Soc. Plastic and Reconstrv. Surgery, S.E. Plastic and Reconstrv. Surg. Soc. Home: 13530 Brynwood Ln Fort Myers FL 33912-1601 Office: 2780 S Cleveland Ave Ste 806 Fort Myers FL 33901-5857

LANG, NORMA M., dean, nursing educator; b. Wausau, Wis., Dec. 27, 1939. BSN, Alverno Coll., 1961; MSN, Marquette U., 1963, PhD, 1974. Staff nurse, asst. instr. St. Joseph's Hosp., 1961-62; instr., coord. med.-surg. nursing St. Mary's Sch. Nursing, 1964-65; instr., asst. prof. Sch. Nursing, U. Wis., Milw., 1965-69, from asst prof. to prof., 1968-92, dean, 1980-92; dean, prof. Sch. Nursing, U. Pa., Phila., 1992—; nursing coord. Wis. Regional Med. Program, 1968-73; rsch. assoc. U. Wis., Milw., 1977, ctr. sci. Urban Rsch. Ctr., 1977-79. Contbr. articles to profl. jours. Fellow Am. Acad. Nursing; mem. ANA, NAS, AAUP, APHA, Am. Heart Assn. Office: U Pa Sch Nursing 420 Guardian Dr Philadelphia PA 19104-6096*

LANG, RICHARD STEPHEN, preventive medicine physician; b. East Cleveland, Ohio, Oct. 18, 1953; s. John S. and Margaret E. (Molnar) L.; m. Lisa R. Kraemer, Dec. 30, 1977; children: Jonathan, Katherine, William, Daniel. AB in Biology, Harvard U., 1975; MD, U. Cin., 1979; MPH, U. Mich., 1985. Diplomate Am. Bd. Internal Medicine, qualified in Geriatric Medicine, Am. Bd. Preventive Medicine, in Occupational Medicine; cert. FAA Med. Examiner. Resident Cleve. Clinic Found., 1979-82; assoc. clerkship dir. Pa. State-Hershey Internal Clerkship Cleve. Clinic Found., 1987-89; staff physician dept. gen. internal medicine Cleve. Clinic Found., 1986—, head sect. occupational medicine, 1986-93, assoc. dir. internal medicine residency tng. program, 1989—, head sect. preventive medicine, dept. gen. internal medicine, 1990—; sr. clin. instr. Case Western Reserve U., Cleve., 1981-82, 84—; asst. prof. Ohio State U. Coll. Medicine, Columbus, 1992—. Fellow Am. Coll. Physicians. Office: Cleve Clinic Found Desk A11 1 Clinic Ctr Cleveland OH 44195

LANG, TAMI R., optometrist; b. Salem, Oreg., Oct. 30, 1960; d. Vernon L. and Mavourn L. (Wooldridge) L. BA, Oreg. State U., 1982; BS, Pacific U., 1982, OD, 1985. Optometrist LensCrafters, Scottsdale, Ariz., 1989—; sec. Ctrl. Ariz. Optometric Assn., Phoenix, 1992. Sec., treas. Newlife Cmty. Ch., Scottsdale, 1994—. Office: Ste 2140 7014 E Camelback Scottsdale AZ 85251

LANGAN, MARIE-NOELLE SUZANNE, cardiologist, educator; b. White Plains, N.Y., Aug. 4, 1960. Grad., U. Toronto, Can., 1980, MD, 1984. Diplomate Am. Bd. Internal Medicine, Am. Bd. Cardiology, Am. Bd. Clin. Electrophysiology. Intern St. Mary's Hosp./ McGill U., Montreal, Can., 1984-95; resident U. Toronto/ St. Michael's Hosp., 1985-87; cardiology fellow Phila. Heart Inst./ U. Pa. Med. Ctr., 1988-90, 1990-91; clin. instr. medicine Sch. Medicine U. Pa., 1988-89, fellow dept. medicine, 1990-91; asst. prof. medicine, dir. electrophysiology lab. George Washington U., Washington, 1991-93. Contbr. chpts. to books and articles to profl. jours. Fellow Am. Coll. Cardiology, Royal Coll. Physicians & Surgeons Can.; mem. N.Am. Soc. Pacing & Electrophysiology, Am. Heart Assn. (Clinician Scientist award 1996), Coll. Physicians & Surgeons Can.; grantee NIH. Office: Mount Sinai Med Ctr 1 Gustave L Levy Pl Box 1054 New York NY 10028

LANGDELL, ROBERT DANA, medical educator; b. Pomona, Cal., Mar. 14, 1924; s. Walter Irving and Florence Delsa (Reichenbach) L.; m. Alice E. Pritt, June 3, 1948; children—Robert Dana, Sara Ellen. Student, Pomona Coll., 1941-43; M.D., George Washington U., 1948. Intern Henry Ford Hosp., Detroit, 1948-49; mem. faculty Sch. Medicine, U. N.C., Chapel Hill, 1949—; assoc. prof. pathology Sch. Medicine, U. N.C., 1959-61, prof., 1961—; mem. hematology study sect. USPHS, 1968-71. Editor-in-chief Transfusion, 1972-82; assoc. editor Archives of Pathology and Laboratory Medicine, 1983—. Served to capt. M.C. AUS, 1955-56. USPHS sr. research fellow, 1957-61; Career Research fellow, 1962-66. Mem. Am. Assn. Blood Banks (pres. 1972-73), Am. Soc. Clin. Pathology, AMA, Coll. Am. Pathology (gov. 1977-83), N.C. Med. Assn. Episcopalian. Home: 707 Williams Cir Chapel Hill NC 27516-1527

LANGE, MICHAEL P., optometrist; b. Metairie, La., Sept. 15, 1961; s. Richard K. and Betty (McFachen) L. BS in Psychology, U. So. Miss., 1984; BS in Physiol. Optics, So. Coll. Optometry, Memphis, 1988; OD, Pa. Coll. Optometry, 1992. Cert. optometrist, Fla. Staff optometrist Eye Surgery Ctr. of La., New Orleans, 1992, St. Charles Vision, New Orleans, 1992-93; pvt. practice Lange Eye Care & Assocs., Ocala, Fla., 1993—; regional dir., area coord. Excel Telecom., Dallas, 1995—; team dr. (basketball) Ctrl. Fla. C.C., Ocala, 1993—; host radio talk show Sound Off Dr. Lange, WMOP-AM, Ocala, 1993—; shadow program dir. various local high sch.'s, Ocala, 1995—. Guest columnist local Ocala papers, 1993—. Mem. Am. Optometric Assn., Fla. Optometric Assn., Ocala C. of C., Psi Chi, Beta Sigma Kappa. Republican. Methodist. Home: 2901 SW 41st St Ocala FL 34474 Office: 2701 SW College Rd Ste 105 Ocala FL 34474

LANGE, PAUL E., dentist; b. Muskegon, Mich., Jan. 31, 1960; s. Emert R. and Doris E. (Larsen) L.; m. Karen E. Frank, Mar. 25, 1987. BS, Hope Coll., Holland, Mich., 1982; DDS, U. Mich., 1986. Teaching asst. Hope Coll., Holland, Mich., 1980-82; umpire (softball) Ann Arbor Park St. Reserve, 1984-86; dentist Utica, N.Y., 1986-87, Flint, Mich., 1987-94, Pontiac, Mich., 1994—. Recipient Chemistry Student Grant, Nat. Sci. Found., Holland Mich., 1981, Approved Degree Am. Chem. Soc., Holland Mich., 1982. Mem. ADA, Mich. Dental Assn., DED Dental Frat., Ann Arbor (Scribe 1980-81).

LANGE, ROBERT DALE, internist, educator, medical researcher; b. Redwood Falls, Minn., Jan. 24, 1920; s. John Christian and Bertha Semelia (Eggen) L.; m. Mary Jane Adams, Sept. 16, 1944; children: Ruth Ann Lange Rehm, John Carl. B.A., Macalester Coll., 1941; M.D., Washington U., 1944. Diplomate: Am. Bd. Internal Medicine. Intern Barnes Hosp., St. Louis, 1944-45; asst. resident medicine U. Minn. Hosps., Mpls., 1945-46; fellow and instr. medicine div. hematology Washington U. Sch. Medicine, St. Louis, 1948-51; practice medicine specializing in internal medicine St. Louis, 1956-62, Knoxville, Tenn., 1964—; scientist Atomic Bomb Casualty Commn., Hiroshima and Nagasaki, Japan, 1951-53; rsch. assoc. VA Hosp., Mpls., 1953-54; mem. staff Eitel Hosp., Mpls., 1953-54; chief hematology Rsch. Lab. VA Hosp., St. Louis, 1956-62; asst. prof. medicine Washington U. Sch. Medicine, St. Louis, 1956-62; assoc. prof. medicine Med. Coll. Ga., Augusta, 1962-64; mem. staff Talmadge Hosp., Augusta, 1962-65, U. Hosp., Augusta, 1964-65, U. Tenn. Meml. Hosp., Knoxville, 1965; research prof. U. Tenn. Meml. Research Center, Knoxville, 1964-78; asst. dir. research U. Tenn. Meml. Research Center, 1966-76, dir. research, 1977-81; prof. medicine U. Tenn. Center for Health Services, Knoxville, 1970—; prof. U. Tenn. Meml. Research Ctr., 1978-85, prof. emeritus, 1985—; chmn. dept. med. biology, 1978-81; cons. to Oak Ridge Associated Univs., 1969-93, Abbott Labs Rev. Bd., 1974. Contbr. chpts. in hematology to med. books; contbr. numerous articles on research in hematology and exptl. medicine to profl. jours.; reviewer various med. jours., 1960—; editorial bd.: Exptl. Hematology, 1974-77. Served to maj., M.C. U.S. Army, 1954-56. Jackson Johnson scholar, 1941-44; recipient Cert. St. Paul Jr. Assn. of Commerce, 1941. Fellow A.C.P., Internat. Soc. Hematology; mem. Am. Soc. Hematology, Internat. Soc. Exptl. Hematology, Soc. of Research Adminstrs., Soc. Exptl. Biology and Medicine, Central Soc. Clin. Research, So. Soc. Clin. Investigation, Knoxville Soc. Internal Medicine, AMA (Cert. of Merit 1954), Tenn. Med. Assn., Knoxville Acad. Medicine, AAAS, AAUP, Sigma Xi,

Alpha Omega Alpha, Pi Phi Epsilon. Methodist. Home: 8116 Bennington Dr Knoxville TN 37909-2301 Office: U Tenn Med Ctr 1924 Alcoa Hwy Knoxville TN 37920-1511

LANGE, STEPHAN CHARLES, neurosurgeon; b. Ogden, Wash., June 4, 1950; s. Charles J. and Christiane R. Lange; m. Elizabeth Ann Lange; children: Christine, Katherine, Jennifer. BS, Loyola U., L.A., 1972; MS, U. Calif., Irvine, 1976, MD, 1976. Asst. clin. prof. surgery U. Conn.; chmn. dept. neurosurgery St. Francis Hosp., Hartford, Conn.; with Neurolsurg. Assocs., Hartford. Maj. U.S. Army Med. Corps, 1980-84. Fellow ACS; mem. Am. Assn. Neurol. Surgeons, Congress of Neurol. Surgeons, Conn. State Med. Soc., Hartford Conn. Med. Soc. Office: Neurosurg Assocs PC 1000 Asylum Ave Hartford CT 06105-1703

LANGE, STEPHEN MARK, school psychologist; b. Phila., Jan. 17, 1957; s. K. Robert and Sylvia (Pollack) L.; m. Christine M. Holmes, June 21, 1981; children: Jonathan David, Emily Marion. BS, Ursinus Coll., Collegeville, Pa., 1979; MEd, Lehigh U., 1983; PhD, Fordham U., 1996. Cert. nat. sch. psychology, 1989. Caseworker, then casework supr. Children's Bur., Stroudsburg, Pa., 1981-83; psychologist N.Y.C. Bd. Edn., 1983-86; sch. psychologist Greystone Park Psychiat. Hosp., Morris Plains, N.J., 1986-88, Regional Child Study Teams, Franklin, N.J., 1988-90; psychologist Montague/Hamburg Pub. Schs., 1990-96; adj. prof. Sussex County C.C., Sparta, N.J., 1986-91, N.J. Dept. Corrections, 1996—; cons. in field. Mem. editl. bd. Jour. Ednl. and Psychol. Consultation; contbr. articles to profl. jours. Mem. Nat. Assn. Sch. Psychologists, Sussex County Psychol. Assn. Democrat. Jewish. Home: 3572 New Hampshire Ave Easton PA 18045-8120 Office: Mountainview Youth Corrections Facility Annandale NJ 08801

LANGEJANS, GORDON D., health services administrator; b. Holland, Mich., Dec. 30, 1938; s. Edward and Henrietta (DeWeerd) L.; m. Doris Ann Boeve, Apr. 1, 1959; children: Linda Joy, Todd Allen, Scott Gordon. BA, Calvin Coll., 1960; MD, U. Mich., 1964. Diplomate Am. Bd. Internal Medicine, Am. Bd. Rheumatology. Rheumatologist Rockford (Ill.) Clinic, 1971-94; v.p. med. affairs and ambulatory care Rockford (Ill.) Health Sys., 1992—. Office: Rockford Health System 2300 N Rockton Ave Rockford IL 61103-3619

LANGENBERG, PATRICIA WARRINGTON, biostatistics educator, consultant; b. Des Moines, Sept. 10, 1931; d. Harold Paris and Rose Marie (Thompson) Warrington; m. Donald Newton Langenberg, June 20, 1953; children—Karen, Julia, John, Amy. B.S. in Math. Stats., Iowa State U., 1953; M.S. in Math., Temple U., 1975, Ph.D. in Math., 1978. Asst. prof. math. LaSalle Coll., Phila., 1977-80; asst. prof. stats. Temple U., Phila., 1980-83; asst. prof. biostats. Sch. Pub. Health, U. Ill., Chgo., 1983-86, assoc. prof., 1986-91; assoc. prof. biostats. dept. epidemiology U. Md., Balt., 1991—, vice chair dept. epidemiology, 1995; treas. Com. of Pres of Statis. Socs., 1981-86. Contbr. articles to biometric and med. jours. Mem. Am. Statis. Assn. (v.p. NE Ill. chpt. 1989-90), Biometric Soc., Inst. Math. Stats., Caucus for Women in Stats. (sec.). Democrat. Home: 3112 Old Court Rd Pikesville MD 21208-3300 Office: U Md at Balt Epidemiology 111 Howard Hall 660 W Redwood St Baltimore MD 21201-1541

LANGENKAMP, SANDRA CARROLL, retired healthcare policy executive; b. St. Joseph, Mo., Feb. 10, 1939; d. William Harry Minger and Beverly (Carroll) Lee; m. R. Hayden Downie, June 1, 1963 (div. Feb. 1979); children: Whitney, Timothy, Allyson. BS, Tex. Women's U., 1960. Adjunctive therapist Menninger Meml. Hosp., Topeka, 1960-66; asst. adminstr. Hillcrest Med. Ctr., Tulsa, 1977-82; dir. Vol. Action Agy., Tulsa, 1982-83; exec. dir. Tulsa Bus. Health Group, 1983—; v.p. Met. Tulsa C. of C., 1985—; exec. dir. Tulsa Program for Affordable Health Care, 1986-96; ret., 1996; cons. mem. Okla. Employment Security Commn., Oklahoma City, 1988—; exec. dir. Tulsa Cmty. Found. for Indigent Health Care, 1986-96; officer State of Okla. Basic Health Benefits Bd., 1985-96, chmn., 1992-93; exec. dir. Tulsa Program for Affordable Health Care, 1989—; mem. health benefit com. State of Okla. Ins. Commn., 1994—; Gov. Com. Health Care, 1993. Author: editorial column Point of View, 1985—, Tulsa mag., 1985—. Count commn. appointee Tulsa Met. Area Planning Commn., 1973-81; mayor's appointee Tulsa Housing Authority, 1985-88; pres. Tulsa Met. Ministry, 1980-83; bd. dirs. ARC, Tulsa, 1971-73, 84-85. Mem. Am. C. of C. (exec. dir. Okla. chpt.), Met. Tulsa C. of C. (v.p. 1983-95), Tulsa Tennis Club. Democrat. Roman Catholic. Office: Met Tulsa C of C 616 S Boston Ave Tulsa OK 74119

LANGER, COREY JAY, oncologist; b. Freeport, N.Y., Apr. 21, 1957; s. Leon Irwin and Rita (Frank) L.; m. Mindy Ruth Slavin, Apr. 5, 1981; children: Adina Jocelyn, Micah Philip. BA, Boston U., 1981, MS, 1981. Intern Grad. Hosp. of U. Pa., Phila., 1981-82; resident U. Pa., Phila., 1982-84; attending physician Fox Chase Cancer Ctr., Phila., 1987—, chair P&T Com., co-dir. thoracic oncology, 1994—. Presbyn. U. of Pa. Med. Ctr. fellow, 1984-86, Fox Chase Cancer Ctr. fellow, 1986-87. Fellow ACP; mem. Am. Assn. for Cancer Rsch., Am. Soc. Clin. Oncology, Am. Soc. Hematology, Ea. Coop. Oncology Group, Radiation Therapy Oncology Group, Delaware Valley Poets, Phi Beta Kappa. Office: FCCC 7701 Burholme Philadelphia PA 19111

LANGER, DENNIS HENRY, pharmaceutical company executive; b. N.Y.C., Sept. 8, 1951; s. Nathan and Mira (Kenig) L.; m. Susan D. Follett, Jan. 21, 1980; children: William, Thomas. BA, Columbia U., 1971; MD, Georgetown U., 1975; JD cum laude, Harvard U., 1983. Diplomate Am. Bd. Psychiatry. Intern, resident, chief resident Yale U. Sch. Medicine, New Haven, 1975-78; clin. assoc. Nat. Inst. Mental Health, Bethesda, Md., 1978-80; clin. fellow Harvard Med. Sch., Boston, 1980-82, instr., 1982-83; assoc. clin. investigator Eli Lilly and Co., Indpls., 1983-84; assoc. med. dir. Abbott Lab., North Chicago, 1984-86; product mgr. Abbott Lab, North Chicago, 1986-87, sr. product mgr., 1987-88; sr. group product dir. G.D. Searle and Co., Skokie, Ill., 1988-89, sr. dir. mktg., 1989-91; pres., CEO, dir. Neose Technols. Inc., Horsham, Pa., 1991-94; v.p. bus. strategy-U.S. SmithKline Beecham Pharm., Phila., 1994-96; v.p. health mgmt. svcs. SmithKline Beecham Healthcare Svcs., Phila., 1996—; cons. Food and Drug Adminstrn., Rockville 1980-82, clin. assoc. prof. Ind. U. Sch. Medicine, Indpls. 1983-84, U. Health Scis. Chgo. Med. Sch., 1984-91. Contbr. articles to profl. jour. Bd. dirs. Epilepsy Svcs. Northeast Ill., 1985-91, v.p., 1986-89. Mem. Am. Acad. Child and Adolescent Psychiatry (Com. On Rights and Legal Matters), Am. Psychiatric Assn., Am. Soc. Law and Medicine.

LANGER, ELLEN JANE, psychologist, educator, writer; b. N.Y.C., Mar. 25, 1947; d. Norman and Sylvia (Tobias) L. BA, NYU, 1970; PhD, Yale U., 1974. Cert. clin. psychologist. Asst. prof. psychology The Grad. Ctr. CUNY, 1974-77; assoc. prof. psychology Harvard U., Cambridge, Mass., 1977-81; prof. Harvard U., 1981—; cons. NAS, 1979-81, NASA; mem. div. on aging Harvard U. Med. Sch., 1979—, mem. psychiat. epidemiology steering com., 1982-90; chair social psychology program Harvard U., 1982—, chair Faculty Arts and Scis. Com. of Women, 1984-88. Author: Personal Politics, 1973, Psychology of Control, 1983, Mindfulness, 1989; editor: (with Charles Alexander) Higher Stages of Human Development, 1990, (with Roger Schank) Beliefs, Reasoning and Decision-Making, 1994); contbr. articles to profl. anc scholarly jours. Guggenheim fellow; grantee NIMH, NSF, Soc. for Psychol. Study of Social Issues, Milton Fund, Sloan Found., 1982; recipient Disting. Contbn. of Basic to Applied Psychology award APS, 1995. Fellow Computers and Soc. Inst., Am. Psychol. Assn. (Disting. Contributions to Psychology in Public Interest award 1988, Disting. Contributions of Basic Sci. to Applied Psychology 1995); mem. Soc. Exptl. Social Psychology, Phi Beta Kappa, Sigma Xi. Democrat. Jewish. Office: Harvard U Dept Psychology 33 Kirkland St Cambridge MA 02138-2044

LANGER, JACOB CHARLES, pediatric surgeon, educator; b. Toronto, Ont., Can., Sept. 27, 1956; came to the U.S., 1992; s. Bernard and Ryna Donna Langer; m. Ferne Sherkin, June 20, 1978; children: Jessica, Benjamin, Alexander. MD, U. Toronto, 1980. Asst. prof. surgery and pediat. McMaster U., Hamilton, Ont., 1989-92; assoc. prof. surgery and pediat. Washington U., St. Louis, 1992—. Contbr. chpts. to textbooks and articles to profl. jours. Bd. dirs. Temple Shaare Emeth, St. Louis, 1995—. Named Innovative Scientist of Yr., St. Louis Acad. Sci., 1995; rsch. grantee Med. Rsch. Coun. Can., 1990-92, Ethicon Endosurg., 1994-95. Fellow Royalo Coll. Surgeons Can.; mem. Am. Pediatric Surg. Assn., Assn. for Acad. Surgery, Am. Acad. Pediatrics, Soc. for Surgery Alimentary Tract, Can. Assn. Pediatric Surgeons, Soc. Univ. Surgeons. Office: St Louis Childrens Hosp 5W-12 One Childrens Pl Saint Louis MO 63110

LANGER, LEONARD O., JR., radiologist, educator; b. Mpls., Oct. 16, 1928; s. Leonard Otto and Louise (Buro) L.; m. Rollie Helen Segal, Sept. 13, 1952; children: Maren, Sara, Elizabeth, Kristen. BA summa cum laude, U. Minn., 1950, BS, 1951, MD, 1953. Diplomate Am. Bd. Radiology. Intern Salt Lake County Hosp., Salt Lake City, 1953-54; resident in radiology U. Mich. Hosp., 1956-59; instr. radiology U. Pitts. Med. Sch., 1959-60; from instr. to assoc. prof. radiology U. Minn. Med. Sch., Mpls., 1961-66; radiologist Suburban Radiologic Cons., Mpls., 1966-78, 84-89; prof. U. Wis. Med. Sch., Madison, 1978-84; clin. assoc. prof. radiology U. Minn. Med. Sch., Mpls., 1966-78; clin. prof. U. Minn., 1984—; cons. clin. genetics divsn. U. Wis. Med. Sch., 1984—, skeletal dysplasia program, U. Minn. Med. Sch., 1984—; mem. com. Internat. Nomenclature of Constl. Diseases of Bone, Paris, 1969—. Author: Bone Dysplasias, 1974; contbr. over 100 articles to profl. med. jours. Served to capt. USAF, 1953-56. Fellow Am. Coll. Radiology; mem. Internat. Skeletal Soc. (cons. editor Skeletal Radiology 1976-89), Soc. Pediatric Radiology, Radiological Soc. N.Am., Bone Dysplasia Soc., Little People Am. (hon. life, med. adv. bd., 1966—). Democrat. Home: 1235 Yale Pl Apt 710 Minneapolis MN 55403-1945

LANGER, PAUL DANIEL, physician; b. Oak Park, Ill., Oct. 23, 1963; s. Paul and Marie (DiBenedetto) L. BA in Biology, Brown U., 1935; MD, Johns Hopkins U., 1989. Resident in ophthalmology U. Calif., San Francisco, 1990-93; fellow in ophthalmic plastic surgery U. Utah, Salt Lake City, 1993-95; asst. prof. ophthalmology U. Medicine and Dentistry of N.J.-N.J. Med. Sch., Newark, 1995—. Recipient Nat. Leadership award Ciba/Geigy, 1988, fellowship Heed Found., 1994-95. Mem. Am. Acad. Ophthalmology, N.J. Acad. Ophthalmology, Alpha Omega Alpha, Phi Beta Kappa. Office: Univ Medicine and Dentistryof NJ Dept Ophthalmology 90 Bergen St 6th Fl DOC Newark NJ 07103

LANGER, ROBERT SAMUEL, chemical, biomedical engineering educator; b. Albany, N.Y., Aug. 29, 1948; s. Robert Samuel Sr. and Mary (Swartz) L.; m. Laura Feigenbaum, July 31, 1988; children: Michael David, Susan Katherine, Samuel Alexander. BS, Cornell U., 1970; ScD, MIT, 1974. Rsch. assoc. Children's Hosp. Med. Ctr., Boston, 1974—; asst. prof. chem. and biomed. engring. MIT, Cambridge, Mass., 1978-81; assoc. prof. MIT, Cambridge, 1981-85, prof., 1985-89, Germeshausen prof., 1989—; bd. dirs. Alkermes, Cambridge, Acusphere, Cambridge, Focal, Lexington; tchr. Group Sch., Cambridge, 1971-73; endowed lectr. U. P.R., 1983, Case Western Res. U., 1986, U. Mich., 1987, U. Wash., 1988, U. Kans., 1989, U. Calif., San Francisco, 1991, U. Wis., 1991, Ga. Inst. Tech., 1991, Ohio State U., 1991, U. Pitts., 1992, Purdue U., 1992, U. Del., 1993, Pa. State U., 1993, Beth Israel Hosp., 1994, Cornell U., 1994, Calif. Inst. Tech., 1995, Ill. Inst. Tech., 1995, Ohio State Med. Sch., 1995, U. Calif., 1996, U. Tenn., 1996; cons. to numerous cos., including Genetech, San Francisco, 1981—, Merck Sharpe and Dohme, 1981-85; sci. advisor Cygnus, Redwood City, Calif., 1987—, Perspetive Biosys., Cambridge, 1991—. Author: (with D. Cincotta and K. Cole) Group School Chemistry Curriculum, 1972, (with W. Thilly) Laboratory in Applied Biology, 1978, Analaytical Practices in Biochemistry, 1979, (with W. Hrusheysky and F. Theeuwes) Temporal Control of Drug Delivery, 1991; editor: (with M. Chasin) Biodegradable Polymers in Drug Deliveryy, 1990, (with D. Wise) Medical Applications on Control Release, Vols. I and II, 1984, (with R. Steiner and P. Weisz) Angiogenesis, 1992; contbr. over 700 articles to sci. jours.; patentee in field. Recipient John W. Hyatt Svc. to Mankind award Soc. Plastics Engrs., 1995, Internat. award, 1996, Ebert Prize, Am. Pharm. Assn., 1995, Rsch. award Am. Diabetes Assn., 1996; Union Oil fellow, 1970-71, Chevron fellow, 1971-72; cited for Outstanding Patent in Mass., Intellectual Property Owners Inc , 1989. Fellow Soc. Biomaterials (Clemson award 1990), Am. Assn. Pharm. Scis. (Disting. Pharm Sci. award 1993); mem. NAS, AIChE (Food, Pharm. and Bioengring. award 1986, Profl. Progress award 1990, Charles M. Stine Materials Sci. and Engring. award1991), Nat. Acad. Engring., Inst. Medicine of NAS, Am. Inst. Med. and Biol. Engrs. (founding fellow), Am. Acad. Arts and Scis., Am. Chem. Soc. (Creative Polymer award 1989, Phillips Applied Polymer Sci. award 1992, Pearlman Meml. Lectr. award 1992), Internat. Soc. Artificial Internal Organs (Organon-Teknika award 1991), Biomed. Engring. Soc. (bd. dirs. 1991-94, Whitaker lectr. 1994), Controlled Release Soc. (bd. govs. 1981-85, chmn. regulatory affairs com. 1985-89, pres. 1991-92, Founders award 1989, Outstanding Pharm. Paper award 1990, 92), Am. Soc. Artificial Internal Organs (mem. program com. 1984-87), Internat. Soc. Artificial Internal Organs. Office: MIT Dept Chem Engring 77 Massachusetts Ave Cambridge MA 02139-4301

LANGFITT, THOMAS WILLIAM, neurosurgeon, foundation administrator; b. Clarksburg, W.Va., Apr. 20, 1927; s. Frank Valentine and Veda (Davis) L.; m. Carolyn Louise Payne, Jan. 31, 1953; children: David Douglas, John Turner, Frank Davis. AB, Princeton U., 1949; MD, Johns Hopkins U., 1953; ScD (hon.), Salem (W.Va.) Coll., 1983, Phila. Coll. Pharmacy and Sci., 1984. Diplomate Am. Bd. Neurol. Surgery (chmn. 1985-86). Intern Johns Hopkins Hosp., Balt., 1953-54, resident, 1957-61; head neurosurgery sect. Pa. Hosp., Phila., 1961-68; asst., prof., assoc. prof. neurosurgery U. Pa., Phila., 1961-87, Charles Harrison Frazier prof. neurosurgery, chmn. dept., 1968-87; pres., chief exec. officer The Glenmede Trust Co., Phila., 1987—; pres. The Pew Charitable Trusts, Phila , 1987—; bd. dirs. The Glenmede Trust Co., Phila., SmithKline Beecham Corp., Phila., The Sun Co., Radnor, Pa., N.Y. Life Ins. Co., N.Y.C.; med. adv. com. Gen. Motors Corp., Detroit, 1985—. Co-author 200 articles, book chpts. and books. bd. trustees Princeton U.; capt. M.C., U.S. Army, 1955-57. Fellow Royal Coll. Surgeons, Edinburgh (hon.); mem. Inst. Medicine, NAS, Am. Philos. Soc., Soc. Neurol. Surgeons (pres. 1987-88, Grass medal 1984), Union League. Office: Glenmede Trust Co 229 S 18th St Philadelphia PA 19103-6144*

LANGFORD, CAROL A., pediatrician; b. Chgo., July 20, 1940; d. Robert Erwin and Beatrice (Hall) Langford; BA, Stanford U., 1962; MD, U. Chgo., 1969; m. Arthur G. Robins, June 14, 1969 (div.); children: Sebastian, Jeremy; m. George B. Wolfenden, Sept. 2, 1989. Vol., Peace Corps, Columbia, 1962-63, pediatrician Roxbury Dental and Med. Group Boston, 1977-32; pediatrician Roxbury Comprehensive Community Health Ctr., 1984-86; instr. psychiat. day hosp., Tufts U, Boston, 1979-81; instr. pediatrics Tufts U., 1979-88, New Eng. Sch. Acupuncture, Boston, 1981-82; cons. Langford Resort Hotel; health book reviewer New Age mag. Den mother Boy Scouts Am.; tour leader, vol. Arnold Arboretum; mem. Duxbury Solid Waste Adv. Com. May C. Willett fellow in child neurology, 1975-77; mem. Congregational Ch. Diplomate Am. Bd. Pediatrics; mem. Am. Acad. of Pediatrics, Mass. Med. Soc., Fla. Native Plant Soc., Boston Mycological Club, Sierra Club, Audubon Soc., Friends of the Farlow, Duxbury Garden Club (conservation chmn.), Duxbury Art Assn. Mem. United Ch. of Christ. Author booklet: Aloe Vera Queen of Medicinal Plants, 1980. Office: Boston Evening Med Ctr 388 Commonwealth Ave Boston MA 02215 also: 110 Long Pond Rd Plymouth MA 02360-2642

LANGHINRICHSEN-ROHLING, JENNIFER, psychologist, educator; b. Detroit, Oct. 31, 1961; d. Richard Alan and Ruth Helen (Imler) Langhinrichs; m. Martin Louis Rohling, May 24, 1992; 1 child, Alanna Marie. BS magna cum laude, Brown U., 1984; MS, U. Oreg., 1986, PhD in Psychology, 1990. Lic. psychologist, Nebr. Psychology intern Dept. Veterans Affairs Med. Ctr., Palo Alto, Calif., 1989-90; therapist Cascade Assocs., Eugene, Oreg., 1990-91; NIMH postdoctoral fellow SUNY, Stony Brook, 1991-93; asst. prof. psychology U. Nebr., Lincoln, 1993—. Editl. adv. bd. Aggression and Violent Behavior, 1995—; textbook reviewer Brown and Benchmark, Allyn and Bacon, 1994—; contbr. articles to profl. jours. Delegate Chancellor's Commn. on Status of Women, Lincoln, 1994—; applicant interviewer Brown U., 1994—; vol. Unitarian Ch., Lincoln, 1995; vol. shelter, Long Island, N.Y., 1992-93. Recipient Radcliffe-Hicks Debate prize Brown U., Providence, 1982, 83; named among People Who Inspire, Mortar Bd. U. Nebr., 1995; recipient Recognition for Contributions to Students, U. Nebr. Parent's Assn., 1995, 96. Mem. APA, Assn. Advancement Behavioral Therapy, Oustanding Young Scientist, Sigma Xi. Democrat. Unitarian. Office: Univ Nebr Psychology Dept 209 Burnett Hall Lincoln NE 68588-0308

LANGHOLZ, BRYAN MARVIN, biostatistician; b. L.A., May 7, 1956; s. Izak and Faye Ellen (Chason) L.; m. Susan Lynn Auerbach, Dec. 21, 1986; children: Ben, Noah. BA in Math., Humboldt State U., Arcata, Calif., 1979; MS in Biomath., U. Wash., 1982, PhD in Biomath., 1984. Assoc. prof. rsch. U. So. Calif., L.A., 1985—. Mem. Agent Orange and Vietnam Vets. Com., Washington, 1995—. Mem. Internat. Biometrics Soc. Office: U So Calif Dept Preventive Medicine 1540 Alcazar St CHP-220 Los Angeles CA 90033

LANGLEY, GEORGE ROSS, medical educator; b. Sydney, N.S., Can., Oct. 6, 1931; s. John George Elmer and Freda Catherine (Ross) L.; m. Jean Marie Ballantyne, June 22, 1957; children: Joanne Marie, Mark Ross, Richard Graham. B.A., Mt. Allison U., 1952; M.D., Dalhousie U., 1957. Intern Victoria Gen. Hosp., Halifax, N.S., 71957; resident Victoria Gen. Hosp., 1958, Toronto (Ont.) Gen. Hosp., 1960, U. Melbourne, Australia, 1961, U. Rochester, N.Y., 1962; John and Mary Markle scholar in acad. medicine Dalhousie U., Halifax, 1963-68; from lectr. to prof. medicine Dalhousie U., 1963-69, prof., chmn. dept. medicine, 1974-82; chief of service medicine Camp Hill Hosp., Halifax, 1969-74; head dept. medicine Victoria Gen. Hosp., 1974-82; chmn. clin. investigation grants com. Med. Research Council, 1976-78; chmn. clin. and epidemiol. research adv. com., bd. dirs. Nat. Cancer Inst. Can., 1978-86. Contbr. articles to sci. jours. Decorated Queen's Jubilee medal, 1977. Fellow Internat. Soc. Hematology, Royal Coll. Physicians and Surgeons (v.p., coun., Wightman vis. prof. 1990), ACP (bd. govs. 1973-78), Royal Coll. Physicians (Edinburgh); mem. Can. Hematology Soc. (pres. 1976-78), Can. Soc. Clin. Investigation, Am. Soc. Hematology, Can. Soc. Oncology, Alpha Omega Alpha. Mem. United Ch. Can. Home: 6025 Oakland Rd, Halifax, NS Canada B3H 1N9 Office: Victoria Gen Hosp, Ste 8-024, Halifax, NS Canada B3H 2Y9

LANGLEY, PATRICIA COFFROTH, psychiatric social worker; b. Pitts., Mar. 1, 1924; d. John Kimmel and Anna (McDonald) Coffroth; m. George J. Langley, May 1, 1946; children: George Julius III, Mary Patricia, Kelly Joan; stepchildren: Robin Spencer, Veronica Bell. BA, Empire State Coll., 1976; MSW, Hunter Coll., 1980. Diplomate Clin. Social Worker; lic. social worker, Conn.; cert. Conn. Psychiat. rehab. worker. Credentialed alcoholism treatment counselor, supervisor, Bronx Mcpl. Hosp. Center, Albert Einstein Med. Coll., 1970-74, case worker, comprehensive alcoholism treatment center, dept. psychiatry, 1974-80; asst. coordinator outpatient psychiat. alcoholism Meridian Ctr., Stamford, Conn., 1980-83; dir. family treatment Meridian Ctr.; pvt. practice and consultation. Vol., DuBois Day Clinic, Stamford, 1966-67, Greenwich Hosp., 1966-67. Mem. NASW, Conn. Soc. for Clin. Social Workers. Home and Office: 50 Lafayette Place Greenwich CT 06830

LANGMAN, RONALD, family physician; b. N.Y.C., Apr. 27, 1968; s. Philip and Rebecca (Shecktizer) L. BS in Biology, CUNY, Bklyn., 1988; DO, U. Osteopathic Medicine and Health Scis., Coll. Osteopathic Medicine and Surgery, Des Moines, 1992. Diplomate Am. Bd. Family Practice. Intern Peninsula Med. Ctr., Far Rockaway, N.Y., 1993, chief family practice resident, 1994-95; prof. family practice N.Y. Coll. Osteopathic Medicine, Far Rockaway, N.Y., 1995—; med. dir. Glendale (N.Y.) Med. Assocs., 1995—. Mem. AMA, Am. Coll. Family Practitioners, Am. Osteo. Assn., Am. Acad. Family Physicians, N.Y.S. Osteo. Med. Soc., N.Y.C. Osteo. Med. Soc., Med. Soc. State N.Y. Republican. Jewish. Home: 415 Grand St #E-1205 New York NY 10002-4722 Office: Glendale Med Assocs PC 74-01 Myrtle Ave Glendale NY 11385

LANGRIDGE, ROBERT, scientist, educator; b. Essex, Eng., Oct. 26, 1933; came to U.S., 1957; naturalized, 1987.; s. Charles and Winifred (Lister) L.; m. Ruth Gottlieb, June 26, 1960; children: Elizabeth, Catherine, Suzanne. B.Sc. in Physics (1st class honours), U. London, Eng., 1954, Ph.D. in Crystallography, 1957. Vis. research fellow biophysics Yale, 1957-59; research assoc. biophysics M.I.T., 1959-61; research assoc. pathology Children's Cancer Research Found., Boston; research assoc. biophysics, lectr. biophysics, also tutor biochem. scis. Harvard, 1961-66; research assoc. Project MAC, Lab. for Computer Sci., M.I.T., 1964-66; prof. biophysics and info. scis. U. Chgo., 1966-68; prof. chemistry and biochem. scis. Princeton, 1968-76; prof. pharm. chemistry, biochemistry and biophysics, dir. Computer Graphics Lab. U. Calif., San Francisco, 1976—; vis. prof. computer sci. Stanford U., 1983-84; mem. computer and biomath. rsch. study sect. NIH, USPHS, 1968-72, chmn., 1975-77, mem. nat. adv. rsch. resources coun., 1992—; mem. vis. com. biology dept. Brookhaven Nat. Lab , 1977-80, mem. adv. com. neutron diffraction, biology dept., 1980-83; mem. sci. and ednl. adv. com. Lawrence Berkeley Labs., 1988-92; chair U. Calif. Berkeley/U. Calif. San Francisco Grad. Group in Bioengring., 1991—; mem. computer sci. and tech. bd. NRC, NAS, 1988-91. Guggenheim fellow, 1983-84. Fellow AAAS; mem. Inst. Medicine of NAS, Am. Soc. Biol. Chemists, Am. Chem. Soc., Am. Cryst. Assn., Biophys. Soc. (editorial bd. 1970-73, council 1971-74), Assn. Computing Machinery. Office: U Calif 926 Med Sci San Francisco CA 94143-0446*

LANGS, ROBERT JOSEPH, psychiatrist; b. Bklyn., June 30, 1928; s. Louis and Estelle (Levy) L.; children: Charles, Bernard, Sandra. AB, U. Pa., 1948; MD, Chgo. Med. Sch., 1953. Diplomate Am. Bd. Psychiatry and Neurology. Intern USPHS Hosp., S.I., N.Y., 1953-54; resident in psychiatry Albert Einstein Coll. Medicine, Bronx Mcpl. Hosp. Ctr., 1956-59; psychoanalytic tng. Downstate Med. Ctr., Bklyn., 1959-68; pvt. practice N.Y.C., 1959-87; chief Ctr. for Communication Research Beth Israel Med. Ctr., N.Y.C., 1986-89; visiting clin. investigator Nathan S. Kline Inst. for Psychiat. Rsch. NYU, Orangeburg, N.Y., 1989—; visiting clin. prof. Mt. Sinai Sch. Medicine, N.Y.C., 1988—. Author: Empowered Psychotherapy, 1993, The Dream Workbook, 1994, The Daydream Workbook, 1995, Clinical Practice and the Architecture of the Mind, 1995, The Cosmic Circle, 1996. Surgeon USPHS, 1953-56. Fellow Am. Psychiat. Assn.; mem. Am. Psychoanalytic Assn., Internat. Psychoanalytic Assn., N.Y. State Med. Soc. Office: 133 West 72d St Rm #304 New York NY 10023

LANGSDON, PHILLIP ROYAL, plastic surgeon; b. Memphis, May 8, 1953; s. Royal B. Langsdon; m. Carol Harper, Aug. 17, 1983; children: Lindsey, Phillip, Lora, Sarah. BS, U. No. Ala., Florence, 1975; MD, Ark. Coll. Medicine, Little Rock, 1980. Diplomate Am. Bd. Facial Plastics, Am. Bd. Otolaryngology. Pvt. practice Memphis, 1986-93; chief facial plastics U. Tenn., Memphis, 1993—; commr. Tenn. State Health Facilities Commn., Nashville, 1995-98; Senate faculty mem. U. Tenn. Coll. Medicine, Memphis, 1994—. Chmn. Shelby County Rep. Com., Memphis, 1991-95; adv. bd. Victory Bank, Germantown, Tenn., 1995—. Fellow ACS; mem. AMA, Tenn. Med. Assn., Am. Acad. Facial Plastics, Am. Bd. Facial Plastics, Shelby County/Memphis Med. Soc. Office: Facial Plastic Surgery Clinic 7499 Poplar Pike Germantown TN 38138-5934

LANGSLEY, PAULINE ROYAL, psychiatrist; b. Lincoln, Nebr., July 2, 1927; d. Paul Ambrose and Dorothy (Sibley) Royal; m. Donald G. Langsley, Sept. 9, 1955; children: Karen Jean, Dorothy Ruth Langsley Runman, Susan Louise. BA, Mills Coll., 1949; MD, U. Nebr., 1953. Cert. psychiatrist, Am. Bd. Psychiatry and Neurology. Intern Mt. Zion Hosp., San Francisco, 1954; resident U. Calif., San Francisco, 1954-57; student health psychiatrist U. Calif., Berkeley, 1957-61, U. Colo., Boulder, 1961-68; assoc. clin. prof. psychiatry U. Calif. Med. Sch., Davis, 1968-76; student health psychiatrist U. Calif., Davis, 1968-76; assoc. clin. prof. psychiatry U. Cin., 1976-82; pvt. practice psychiatry Cin., 1976-82; cons. psychiatrist Federated States of Micronesia, Pohnpei, 1984-87; resident in geriatric psychiatry Rush-Presbyn./St. Luke Hosp., Chgo., 1989-91; mem. accreditation rev. com. Accreditation Coun. for Continuing Med. Edn. Trustee Mills Coll., Oakland, 1974-78; bd. dirs. Evanston Women's Club. Fellow Am. Psychiat. Assn. (chair continuing med. edn. 1990-96); mem. AMA, Am. Med. Womens Assn., Acad. Medicine Cin., Ohio State Med. Assn., Ill. Psychiat. Assn. (sec. 1993-95, pres.-elect 1995-96, pres. 1996—, accreditation coun. 1996—). Home: 9445 Monticello Ave Evanston IL 60203-1117

LANGSTON, NANCY SUE FRIEDRICH, nursing educator, college dean; b. Little Rock, Dec. 14, 1944. BSN cum laude, U. Ark., 1966; M in Surg. Nursing, Emory U., 1972; PhD in Edn., Ga. State U., 1977. RN, Va. Staff RN U. Ark. Med. Ctr., Little Rock, 1966-67, Doctor's Hosp., Shreveport, La., 1967; instr. Confederate Meml. Med. Ctr. Sch. Nursing, Shreveport, La., 1967-70, Northwestern State U. Sch. Nursing, Shreveport, La., 1970-71, Emory U. Sch. Nursing, Atlanta, 1972-73; adminstrv. intern U. Tex. Sys.

Sch. Nursing, Austin, 1974-75, rsch. assoc., 1975-76; assoc. prof., assoc. dean undergrad. programs U. Nebr. Med. Coll. Nursing, Lincoln, 1976-85; prof., dean U. N.C. at Charlotte Coll. Nursing, 1985-91, Med. Coll. of Va. of Va. Commonwealth U. Sch. Nursing, Richmond, 1991—; nurse-cons. Goodwill Industries of Atlanta, Inc., 1973-74; adj. assoc. prof. U. Nebr. at Lincoln Tchrs. Coll., 1983-85. Contbr. articles to profl. jours., chpts. to books; presenter in field. Mem. bd. Fan Free Clinic, strategic planning com., 1994, med. svcs. com, 1994—, chmn. 1995; mem. Richmond Rotary, med. svcs. com. 1993—, chmn. 1994; mem. adv. bd. Here's To Your Health; bd. dirs. Hospice of Charlotte, 1988-91, chair profl. adv. com., 1989-91; mem. Civitan Charlotte, 1989-91, at-large 1991—; bd. dirs. Lincoln Lancaster Commn. on Status of Women, 1983-85, edn. com. 1981-85; bd. dirs. Southeast Nebr. Health Systems Agy., 1981-82; pub. issues com. Nebr. Cancer Soc., 1978-80; adv. bd. geriat. Atlanta Regional Commn., 1973; chair nursing sect., Shreveport chpt. ARC, 1969-71. Recipient award of honor Alumni Assn. Nell Hodgson Woodruff Sch. Nursing, Emory U., 1989; Am. Nurses' Found. scholar 1972, Rockefeller scholar 1962-64. Mem. ANA, Nat. League for Nursing, So. Nursing Rsch. Coun., Phi Kappa Phi, Phi Theta Kappa, Sigma Theta Tau. *

LANKS, KARL WILLIAM, pathologist, educator; b. Phila., Nov. 1, 1942; s. Gustav Wilhelm and Elizabeth Emma (Rentschler) L.; m. Jane Simon, June 3, 1967 (div. June 1976); children: Claire, Belinda; m. Nena Chin, Apr. 16, 1979; children: Paul, Charles, Cristina. BA, Cen. U., Phila., 1960; BS, Pa. State U., 1963; MD, Temple U., 1967; PhD, Columbia U., 1971. Diplomate Am. Bd. Pathology. Intern Columbia P & S, N.Y.C., 1967-68; instr. Columbia U., N.Y.C., 1970-72; rsch. fellow Francis Delafield Hosp., N.Y.C., 1968-70, Harvard U., Boston, 1970-72; asst. prof. SUNY, Bklyn., 1974-78, assoc. prof., 1978-88, prof., 1988—; dir. pathology S.I. (N.Y.) U. Hosp., 1993—, StressGen Biotechs., Victoria, Can., 1991—. Author: Academic Environment, 1995; contbr. articles to profl. jours. Maj. USA, 1972-74. Grantee NIH, Am. Cancer Soc. Mem. Am. Soc. Cell Biology, Am. Soc. Exptl. Pathology, Am. Soc. Biochemistry and Molecular Biology, Am. Assn. Univ. Pathologists. Office: SI Univ Hosp Dept Pathology 475 Seaview Ave Staten Island NY 10305-3436

LANMAN, ROBERT CHARLES, pharmacology and toxicology educator; b. Bemidji, Minn., Oct. 2, 1930; s. Thomas Bradford and Inga Othelia (Engen) L.; m. Dorothy Ann Desnoyers, Nov. 9, 1957; children: Michael Bradford, Dianne Marie, Douglas Robert, Krista Ann. BS in Pharmacy, U. Minn., 1956, PhD in Pharmacology, 1967. Lic. pharmacist Minn. Pharmacologist Nat. Inst. Health, Bethesda, Md., 1961-66; asst. prof. pharmacology, medicine U. Mo., Kansas City, 1966-72; assoc. prof. U. Mo., 1972-81, prof., 1981—, chmn. div. pharmacology, 1987-92, emeritus prof. pharmacology, 1992—; cons. Hoechst Marion Roussel, Inc., Kansas City, 1985—; exec. v.p. Kansas City Analytical Svcs., Shawnee, Kans., 1984—. Contbr. over 20 aricles to profl. jours. With USN, 1948-52. Grantee in field, 1973-90. Mem. Am. Soc. Pharmacology Experimental Therapeutics, Am. Assn. Pharm. Scientists. Republican. Office: Kans City Analytical Svcs 12700 Johnson Dr Shawnee KS 66216-1643

LANSDELL, HERBERT CHARLES, neuropsychologist; b. Montreal, Que., Can., Dec. 22, 1922; came to U.S., 1954, naturalized, 1961; s. Archibald and Emmie M. (Leonard) L.; m. Judith Kenly Purnell, Oct. 5, 1963 (div. Nov. 1984); children—Grant, Bret. B.Sc., Sir George Williams U., 1944; Ph.D., McGill U., 1950. Asst. prof. McGill U., Montreal, 1949-50; def. research sci. officer Def. Research Med. Labs., Toronto, Ont., Can., 1950-54; asst. prof. U. Buffalo, 1954-58; health scis. adminstr. Nat. Inst. Neurol. Disorders and Stroke, NIH, Bethesda, Md., 1958—. Served with Royal Can. Navy, 1944-45. Fellow AAAS, Am. Psychol. Assn., Am. Psychol. Soc.; mem. Acad. Aphasia, Eastern Psychol. Assn., Internat. Brain Research Orgn., Psychometric Soc., Soc. Neurosci., Sigma Xi. Democrat. Unitarian. Office: NIH Fed Bldg Bethesda MD 20892-9170

LANSKA, DOUGLAS JOHN, neurologist; b. Milw., Aug. 8, 1959; s. Orville Emmanuel Lanska and Margaret Mary (Daly) Kenehan; m. Mary Jo Brook, June 26, 1982; children: Joseph, John. BS, U. Wis., 1980, MS, MD, 1984. Nat. Bd. Med. Examiners; Diplomate Am. Bd. Neurology, Am. Bd. Psychiatry. Intern in internal medicine U. Hosps., Cleve., 1984-85; resident in neurology U. Hosps. Cleve., 1985-88, instr. neurology, 1988-89; computer operator C.S.I. Corp., Butler, Wis., 1977-78, computer programmer, 1978, data processing mgr., 1979-82, cons. computer programmer, 1982-84; computer programmer Med. Coll. Wis., Milw., 1982, rsch. asst., 1982-83; assoc. Sanders-Brown Ctr. on Aging, Lexington, Ky., 1989—; asst. prof. U. Ky. Med. Ctr., Lexington, 1989-93, assoc. prof., 1993—; cons. Ky. Med. Rev. Bd., Frankfort, 1989—, Commonwealth Ky. Ctr. for Excellence in Stroke, Lexington, 1989-91, Internal Medicine Ctr. to Advance Rsch. and Edn., Washington, 1991—, AMA, Chgo., 1991—, Health Care Financing Adminstrn., Balt., 1991—, Agy. for Health Care Policy and Rsch., Rockville, Md., 1992—, Am. Bd. Psychiatry and Neurology, Deerfield, Ill., 1992—; staff neurologist VA Med. Ctr., Lexington, 1989—, Fed. Med. Ctr., Lexington, 1995—. Contbr. articles to profl. jours. Mem., participant Ky. Physicians Care Program/Life, 1989—. Recipient Rsch. Svc. award Nat. Inst. on Aging, 1989, Career Investigator Devel. award, Nat. Inst. Neurol. Disease, Stroke, 1991. Mem. Am. Acad. Neurology, Am. Neurol. Assn., Math. Assn. Am., Soc. for Epidemiologic Rsch., World Fedn. Neuroloy, Internat. Soc. for History of Neurology, Ky. Geriatrics Soc., Phi Beta Kappa, Alpha Omega Alpha. Roman Catholic. Office: U Ky Med Ctr 300 Rose St Lexington KY 40508-3027

LANTAY, GEORGE CHARLES (WAGNER), school psychologist, psychotherapist, environmental consultant; b. N.Y.C., Aug. 1, 1942; s. George Sylvester and Geraldine LeMae (Ogline) L.; children by previous marriage: Scott Christopher, Christina, Susan Kimberly, Erica; m. Susannah Hewson, Dec. 31, 1992; 1 child, George Mason; BA, Hope (Mich.) Coll., 1965; MA, U. Ill., 1968; postgrad. in phys. therapy NYU, 1971-72; postgrad. in phys. and recreation therapy L.I. U., 1978-79; student physician asst. program Touro Coll., 1982-83; postgrad. in U.S. customs and law World Trade Inst., 1989—; postgrad. in E. Asian and African Studies St. John's U., 1993—; postgrad in electronics engring. tech. Tech. Career Inst., N.Y.C., 1993; universal HVAC cert. Mainstream Engring. Corp., 1994; postgrad. residential and comml. air conditioning Bergen County Tech. Schs., 1994-96; cert. programs air conditioning and refrigeration York Internat. Corp., 1996. Asst. prof. psychology Westminster Coll., Princeton, N.J., 1969-70; behavioral scientist, dir. Wagner Assocs., Princeton, 1969—; mgmt. tng. assoc. Western Elec. Co., N.Y.C., 1970; phys. therapist asst. Jewish Meml. Hosp., N.Y.C., 1970-72; sch. psychologist St. Agnes Cathedral High Sch., Rockville Centre, 1976—; ednl. cons. Test Preparation Centers, Riverdale, N.Y., 1975-79; intern psychologist N.Y. State Dept. Mental Hygiene, 1973-75; psychologist Odyssey House Parents Program, Wards Island, N.Y., 1973; adj. prof. behavioral scis. N.Y. Inst. Tech., Old Westbury, L.I., 1974-75; bd. dirs. div. field services N.Y. Testing and Guidance Center, Flushing, 1976—; with Adult Edn. Program Bergen County Tech. Schs., 1994-95. bd. dir. Shangri-La Day Camps, N.Y.C., 1976—; seminar instr. Nat. Traffic Safety Inst., N.Y.C., 1988—; asst. dir. afterschool program Pub. Sch. 234, N.Y.C., 1988; founder Separation Encounter; contbr. U.S. Postal Svc., Cit. Stamp Adv. Coun., 1975-80, Pres.'s Commn. Mental Health, 1977-78; cons. Eastern Regional Inst. Edn., N.Y.U. Med. Sch. Dept. Psychiatry, Newark Council Social Agys., N.Y.C. Bd. Edn., Astor Program Intellectually Gifted Children, N.Y.C. Bd. Edn., Evaluation and Placement Unit, 1977-78, N.Y.C. Bd. Edn. Spl. Edn. Div., Queens Region, 1983, Office Contracted Services, 1983-86, Camp Northwood for Learning Disabilities, summer 1977, Esperanza Day Treatment Center, N.Y.C., 1981-82; psychologist United Cerebral Palsy of N.Y. State, 1986; field ops. supr. N.Y. regional office U.S. Census Bur., 1990; presch. sch. psychologist and outreach coord. St. Mark's Inst. for Community Mental Health, N.Y.C., 1990—; preschool psychologist Karen Horney Clinic Therapeutic Nursery Program, N.Y.C., 1992—; contbr. Commrs. Adv. Council on Vocat. Rehab., N.Y. State Edn. Dept., 1978-79; asst. dir. after school program P.S. 234, N.Y.C., 1988; registrar Ind. Order of Forresters USA, 1991; sales coord. NSA wings program, Northeast Region, USA. Named an Outstanding Young Man of Am., 1975; cert. sch. psychologist, cert. emergency med. technician, N.Y. State; qualified mental retardation profl., N.Y. State. Mem. APA (life), AAUP, Am. Ednl. Research Assn., Am. Assn. Sex Educators, Counselors and Therapists, Am. Phys. Therapy Assn. Am. Acad. Physicians Assts., Air Pollution Control Assn, Am. Soc. Heating, Refrigerating and Air Conditioning Engrs. Clubs: St. Bartholomew's Community, Downtown Glee (N.Y.C.). Author: Activities for Learning Disabled Children, 1980, Radon in Homes & What You Can Do to Protect Your Family's Health, 1987, A Nation Bored of Education, 1996; contbr. articles to Ch. Herald mag.; research on underachievement and masculine identification. Home and Office: 28 Greenwich Ave New York NY 10011-8359

LANZA, ROBERT PAUL, medical scientist; b. Boston, Feb. 11, 1956; s. Samuel and Barbara (Corbett) L. BA, U. Pa., 1978, MD, 1983. Sr. scientist Biohybrid Techs., Shrewsbury, Mass., 1990-93, dir. transplantation biology, 1993—; clin. assoc. prof. surgery Tufts U., 1994-95; assoc. surgery Harvard Med. Sch., 1991-93. Editor: Heart Transplantation, 1984, Medical Science and the Advancement of World Health, 1985, Procurement of Pancreatic Islets I, 1994, Immunomodulation of Pancreatic Islets II, 1994, Immunoisolation of Pancreatic Islets III, 1994, One World, 1996, Tissue Engineering/Cellular Medicine Series, 1995—, Yearbook of Cell and Tissue Transplantation, 1996—, Principles of Tissue Engineering, 1996; contbr. articles to profl. jours. Prof. Howe Buck scholar, 1974-75, Benjamin Franklin scholar, 1975-78, Univ. scholar, 1976-83, Fulbright scholar, 1978-79; Hon. Christiaan Barnard fellow, 1982-84, Mry K. Iacocca Transplantion fellow, 1988-90. Home: South Meadow Pond Island 15-35 S Meadow Rd Clinton MA 01510 Office: BioHybrid Techs 910 Boston Turnpike Shrewsbury MA 01545-3303

LAPAN, DAVID IRA, cardiologist; b. Nuremburg, Germany, Mar. 19, 1948; came to U.S., 1949; s. Joseph and Patricia (Wahl) L.; m. Rosanne F. Lapan, Apr. 28, 1974; children: Lisa, Dana. BA, U. Calif., Berkeley, 1970; MD, U. Calif., San Francisco, 1974. Diplomate Am. Bd. Internal Medicine; lic. cardiologist, Ariz. Intern U. Ariz., Tucson, 1974-75, resident, 1975-77, 1977-78, fellow, 1978-80; cardiologist Pima Heart Assocs., Tucson, 1980—, assoc., 1980—; instr. U. Ariz., 1977-78, lectr., 1977-78; clin. exec. bd. VA Med. Ctr., Tucson, 1977-78, cons., 1981-84; chief cardiology St. Mary's Hosp., 1981-83, 84-86, dir. Spalding Diagnostic Ctr., 1983—, exec., com., 1984-85; dir. cardiovascular svcs. Carondelet Hosp., Pima Heat, 1993—; mem. staff N.W. Hosp., Tucson Med. Ctr. Contbr. articles to profl. jours. Fellow Am. Coll. Cardiology; mem. Pima County Med. Soc.pres. Office: 445 N Silverbell Rd Ste 200 Tucson AZ 85745

LAPHAM, LOWELL WINSHIP, physician educator, researcher; b. New Hampton, Iowa, Mar. 20, 1922; s. Percy Charles and Altha Theresa (Dygert) L.; m. Miriam Amanda Sellers, June 22, 1945 (div. 1982); children: Joan, Steven, Judith, Jennifer. BA, Oberlin Coll., 1943; MD cum laude, Harvard U., 1948. Diplomate Am. Bd. Pathology in neuropathology, Am. Bd. Psychiatry and Neurology in neurology. Instr. Case Western Res. U. Sch. Medicine, Cleve., 1955-57, asst. prof., 1957-64, assoc. prof., 1964; assoc. prof. U. Rochester (N.Y.) Sch. Medicine, 1964-69, prof., 1969-92; prof. emeritus, 1992—; cons. neuropathology Cleve. Met. Gen. Hosp., 1957-64, Cleve. VA Hosp., 1957-64, Genesee Hosp., Rochester, 1966-92, Rochester Gen. Hosp., 1966-92. Contbr. numerous articles to profl. jours. 1st lt. USAR, 1951-53. Fellow Nat. Multiple Sclerosis Soc., 1957-59; rsch. grantee NIH, USPHS. Mem. Am. Assn. Neuropathologists. Unitarian. Home: 121 Kendal Dr Oberlin OH 44074-1905

LAPIDUS, HERBERT, medical products executive; b. N.Y.C., Aug. 10, 1931; s. Harry and Fanny L. (Bagdenofsky) L.; m. Iris Belle Felber, Dec. 21, 1952; children: William Scott, Helane Ruth. BS, Columbia U., 1953, MS, 1955; PhD, Rutgers U., 1967. Instr. Columbia U., N.Y.C.; project leader Julius Schmid Co., N.Y.C., 1957-60; group leader Bristol-Myers Co., Hillside, N.J., 1960-63, dept. head, 1963-67, prin. rsch. investigator, 1967-70; tech. dir. Combe, Inc., White Plains, N.Y, 1970-77, v.p. rsch. devel., 1977—. With U.S. Army, 1956-57. Mem. Am. Chem. Soc., Am. Soc. Clin. Pharmacology & Therapeutics, Am. Assn. Pharm. Scientists, Soc. Cosmetic Chemists, N.Y. Acad. Sci., N.Y. Acad. Medicine. Office: Combe Inc 1101 Westchester Ave White Plains NY 10604

LAPORTA, LAUREN DEIDRA, psychiatrist; b. Hackensack, N.J., May 17, 1962; d. Joyce Nanette (Calandro) LaPorta. BA, Rutgers U., 1984; MD, UMDNJ, N.J. Med. Sch., 1988. Diplomate Am. Bd. Psychiatry and Neurology. Resident U. Fla., Gainesville, 1988-92; acting med. dir. Mental Health Svcs., Inc., Gainesville, Fla., 1992-93; attending psychiatrist Bergen Pines County Hosp., Paramus, N.J., 1993—; staff psychiatrist CompCare Clinic, Hackensack, N.J., 1993—. Contbr. articles to profl. jours.; peer reviewer Jour. Clin. Psychopharm., 1993—; book reviewer Hosp. and Cmty. Psychiatry, 1993-95, Psychiatric Svcs., 1996. Am. Assn. of Dirs. of Psychiat. Residency Tng./Ginsberg Charter fellow, 1992; recipient John A. Adams award, Fla. Psychiat. Soc., Tallahassee, 1990. Mem. AMA, Am. Psychiat. Assn., Phi Beta Kappa. Office: Bergen Pines County Hosp 230 E Ridgewood Ave Paramus NJ 07652

LAPP, CHARLES WARREN, internal medicine physician, pediatrician; b. Bklyn., June 10, 1947; s. Warren Anthony and Katherine Emma (Beard) L.; m. Darie Eleanor Conners, Aug. 28, 1971; children: Lauren Michelle, Warren Rutherford. BS, Rensselaer Poly. Inst., 1969, MBME, 1970; MD, Albany Coll. Medicine, 1974. Diplomate Am. Bd. Internal Medicine, Am. Bd. Pediatrics. Intern U. N.C., Chapel Hill, 1974-75, resident, 1975-78; med. dir. Hill Haven and Blue Ridge Nursing, Raleigh, N.C., 1978-91; assoc. clin. prof. U. N.C., Chapel Hill, 1978-91, Duke. U. Med. Ctr., 1982—; founder and pres. Piedmont Med. Assn., Raleigh, N.C., 1978—; med. dir. Cheney Clinic, Charlotte, N.C., 1991-95; pres. Hunter-Holkins Ctr., P.A., Charlotte, 1995—; cons. TASA Tech. Adviser, Phoenix, 1979—; adv. bd. Raleigh Employee Assistance Plan, 1987-89, Health Plus, 1987-89; med. cons. CFIDS Assn. of Am., Charlotte, 1991—. Contbr. articles to profl. jours. including Jour. AMA and Lancet; presenter exhibits to sci. assemblies. Pres. Muscular Dystrophy Assn., 1982-84. Named Richard T. Beebe Scholar in Medicine, Albany (N.Y.) Med. Coll.) 1974; Man of the Yr., Jaycees, Raleigh, N.C., 1983. Fellow Am. Acad. Family Physicians, Am. Acad. Pediatrics, Am. Assn. Disability Evaluating Physicians; mem. AMA, N.C. Med. Soc., Am. Assn. for Chronic Fatigue Syndrome, Am. Pain Soc. Presbyterian. Office: 10724 Park Rd Ste 105 Charlotte NC 28210

LAPP, ROGER JAMES, consulting pharmacist, writer; b. Buffalo, Jan. 29, 1933; s. Roger Vincent and Georgia James (Saemenes) L.; student Mich. State U., 1952-53; BS in Pharmacy, U. Buffalo, 1957; MA, Trinity Theol. Sem., 1993; m. Judith Bure, Mar. 30, 1956; children: Eric Roger, Mark Frederick. Pharmacist intern Nobb Hill Pharmacy, Buffalo, 1956-57; pharm. intern Buffalo Gen. Hosp., 1957, pharm. resident, 1958; pharmacy mgr. Morton Plant Hosp., Clearwater, Fla., 1960-84, dir. profl. svcs., 1984-86; cons. pharmacist Basic Am. Med. Co., 1986-88; pharmacist, Healthcare Prescription Svcs., Gainesville, Fla., 1986-89, mgr., cons., 1986-91; clin. instr. Sch. of Pharmacy U. Fla., 1990—; mem. adv. coun. Am. McG. Hosp. Pharmacy; tchr. profl. seminars.; cons. pharmacist several nursing homes, Ocala., Fla. Mem. Human Rights Advocacy Com. for Pinellas and Pasco Counties (Fla.), 1973-82, chmn., 1973-81; pres. Upper Pinellas Assn. Mental Retardation Assns., 1970-72, bd. dirs., 1969-78; pres. Am. Cancer Soc., Pinellas County, 1979-82, life bd. dirs.; pres. Pinellas Epilepsy Found., 1978-79; v.p. Fla. Assn. Retarded, 1971-78; exec. v.p., sr. v.p.; bd. dirs. Christian Corp Found. for Mentally Disabled, 1983-86, pres., 1985-86; bd. dirs. Bethel Bethany Homes for the Mentally Disabled, 1986-89, Isaiah Found. for the Disabled, 1990—, vice chmn., 1992—. With U.S. Army, 1958-60, with USAR. Named Man of Yr., Upper Pinellas Assn. Retarded, 1970, Fla. Cons. Pharmacist of Yr., 1987; recipient Nat. Bowl of Hygeia, Fla. Pharm. Assn. and A.H. Robins Co., 1975, Smith award for helping retarded Kiwanis Club, Clearwater Beach, 1978, cert. of merit for public edn. Am. Cancer Soc., 1978, Citizen Health award Clearwater Sun, 1981, Pharmacist Exceeding Expectation award Procter & Gamble, 1995. Fellow Am. Soc. Cons. Pharmacists, Fla. Soc. Hosp. Pharmacists (pres. 1972-73, chmn. bd. 1972-74, dir. 1970-78, 79-81; Fla. Hosp. Pharmacist of Yr. 1975, Fla. Cons. Pharmacist of Yr. 1987), Fla. Pham. Assn. (award for public rels. 1981, futuristic com. 1989-94, chmn. 1992-93), Pinellas Soc. Pharmacists (pres. 1982, exec. sec. 1983-86, dir. 1979-86), S.W. Fla. Soc. Hosp. Pharmacists (pres., sec., dir., President's award 1982), Christian Pharmacists Fellowship Internat. (dir. 1984-95, pres. 1989-92), Fla. Assn. Retarded Citizens (v.p. 1971-79, Brotherhood award 1975, Pres.'s award 1978, sr. v.p. 1979-81, exec. v.p. 1982), Upper Pinellas Assn. Retarded Citizens, Gideons Internat. Republican. Baptist. Author: Antibiotics Handbook, 1974, 5th rev. edit., 1984; co-author: (book) Product Standardization and Evaluation (Orville Baxter Profl. Practice award 1995); contbr. articles to profl. jours. Home: 3527 E Lazy River Dr Dunnellon FL 34434-4771 Office: RJL Consulting 3527 E Lazy River Dr Dunnellon FL 34434-4771

LARAJA, RAYMOND DONALD, surgeon; b. Bklyn., June 12, 1937; s. Raymond and Ida (Pierini) LaR.; m. Adriana Rachel Satori, June 8, 1963; children: Raymond Jr., Celeste, Christopher. AB, Columbia Coll., 1959; MD, NYU, 1963. Diplomate Am. Bd. Surgery. Attending surgeon Bellevue Hosp., N.Y.C., 1970—, Met. Hosp., N.Y.C., 1970—; clin. prof. surgery NYU Sch. Medicine, N.Y.C., 1970—; dir. surgery Cabrini Med. Ctr., N.Y.C., 1976—; prof. clin. surgery N.Y. Med. Coll., Valhalla, 1980—; cons. in field. Co-author: (1 chpt.) Surgical Diseases of HIV Aids Patients, 1994; contbr. articles to profl. jours. Mem. N.Y.C. emergency room evaluation com. Emergency Med. Svcs., N.Y.C., 1981. Maj. U.S. Army, 1968-70, Vietnam. Fellow Am. Coll. Surgeons (regional com. on trauma 1984-88); mem. AMA, N.Y. Surg. Soc., N.Y. Met. Breast Cancer Group, N.Y. Acad. Medicine, Morgagni Med. Soc. (pres. 1990-92). Roman Catholic. Home: 8 Edgehill Close Bronxville NY 10708 Office: Cabrini Med Ctr 227 E 19th St New York NY 10003

LARAVIA, DENNIS ALSON, physician, small business owner; b. Houston, Oct. 28, 1946; s. Ellis and Neita C. LaRavia; m. Sharon Heltman, Aug. 3, 1968; children: Stephanie, Danielle, John, Joshua. Student, La. State U., 1968, MD, 1972. Diplomate Am. Bd. Family Practice. Physician, owner Family Clinic, Ferriday, La., 1973-93; asst. clin. prof. La. State U. Sch. Medicine, Shreveport, 1979-89, assoc. clin. prof., 1993—; clin. preceptor E.A. Conway Hosp., Monroe, La., 1984-89. Chmn. City Planning Commn., Ferriday, 1976-79. Lt. col. La. Army N.G., 1984—. Fellow Am. Acad. Family Physicians; mem. La. Acad. Family Physicians (past pres., Family Physician of the Yr. 1984), Omicron Delta Kappa. Republican. Baptist. Home: 7343 Whispering Pines Rd Shreveport LA 71129 Office: La State U Med Sch Dept Family Medicine 1501 Kings Hwy Shreveport LA 71130

LARAYA-CUASAY, LOURDES REDUBLO, pediatric pulmonologist, educator; b. Baguio, Philippines, Dec. 8, 1941; came to U.S., 1966; d. Jose Marquez and Lolita (Redublo) Laraya; m. Ramon Serrano Cuasay, Aug. 7, 1965; children: Raymond Peter, Catherine Anne, Margaret Rose, Joseph Paul. AA, U. Santo Tomas, Manila, Philippines, 1958, MD cum laude, 1963. Diplomate Am. Bd. Pediatrics. Resident in pediatrics U. Santo Tomas Hosp., 1963-65, Children's Hosp. Louisville, 1966-67, Charity Hosp. New Orleans-Tulane U., 1967-68; fellow child growth and devel. Children's Hosp. Phila., 1968-69; fellow pediatric pulmonary and cystic fibrosis programs St. Christopher's Hosp. for Children, Phila., 1969-71, rsch. assoc., 1971-72; clin. instr. Tulane U., New Orleans, 1967-68; asst. prof. pediatrics Temple Health Scis. Ctr., Phila., 1972-77; assoc. prof. pediatrics Thomas Jefferson Med. Sch., Phila., 1977-79; assoc. prof. pediatrics U. Medicine & Dentistry N. J., Robert Wood Johnson Med. Sch., New Brunswick, 1980-85, prof. clin. pediatrics, 1985—; dir. pediatric pulmonary and cystic fibrosis program U. Medicine and Dentistry, Robert Wood Johnson Med. Sch., New Brunswick, 1981—. Co-editor: Interstitial Lung Diseases in Children, 1988. Recipient Pediatric Rsch. award Mead Johnson Pharm. Co., Manila, 1965. Fellow Am. Coll. Chest Physicians (steering com., chmn. cardiopulmonary diseases in children 1976—), Am. Acad. Pediatrics (tobacco free generation rep. 1986-92); mem. Am. Ambulatory Pediatric Soc., Am. Thoracic Soc., Am. Sleep Disorder Assn., N.J. Thoracic Soc. (chmn. pediatric pulmonary com. 1986-91, governing coun. mem. 1981-94), Am. Coll. Physician Execs., European Respiratory Soc., Lung Club. Home: 100 Mercer Ave Spring Lake NJ 07762-1208 Office: UMDNJ Robert Wood Johnson Med Sch CN19 New Brunswick NJ 08903

LARCH, BILLIE BENTLEY, nursing administrator; b. Texarkana, Tex., Aug. 26, 1919; d. William Calvin and Lula Marie (Cowley) Bentley; m. Monroe P. Larch, Mar. 26, 1936; children: James Monroe, Michael B. BSN, U. Ark., Little Rock, 1962; MSN, U. Cen. Ark., Conway, 1971; MA in Gerontology, U. Little Rock, 1987. Cert. gerontol. nurse, psychiat. clin. nurse; registered lobbyist legis. gen. assembly, 1996—. Nurse cons. Ark. Dept. Mental Health, Little Rock, 1978-89; assoc. chief nursing svc. for edn. John L. McClellan VA Hosp., Little Rock, 1972-85; exec. dir. Ark. State Nurses Assn., Little Rock, 1989-92; nurse cons. Larch Cons. Svcs., 1992—; health care specialist Children and Family Divsn. Ark. Dept. Human Svcs., 1993-96; nurse cons., registered lobbyist Ark. Legis., 1995—; mem. nursing faculty Allied Health, U. Ark., 1973-76; med. rschr. for pros. and def. trial lawyers, 1992—. Developer small group work program Chronically and Mentally Ill, Ark., 1966—; organizer Ark. affiliate chpt. Am. Diabetes Assn., 1973, bd. dirs. 1973-79; healthcare specialist Ark. Dept. Human Svcs., Children's and Family Divsn., 1993—. Recipient Gold Star award Atty. Gen.'s Office, 1989; named to Hall of Fame in Nursing, Ark. State Nurses Assn., 1988. Mem. Nat. League for Nursing (Linda Richards award 1969), Ark. Gerontol. Soc. (bd. dirs. 1982-92, 93—).

LARICHIUTA, INEZ SOPHIA, nurse, administrator; b. Coaldale, Pa., Feb. 4, 1936; d. Dominic and Ida (Fortunato) Totani; m. Albert Larichiuta, Dec. 17, 1982; children: Colleen, Bernadette, Nora, Jamie, Iris. Diploma, Sacred Heart Hosp., Allentown, Pa., 1967; BSN, Coll. Notre Dame, Balt., 1984; postgrad., Kutztown U. Asst. dir. nursing Sacred Heart Hosp., Allentown; nurse chmn. U. Md. Med. Ctr. Hosp., Balt.; dir. nursing Coaldale State Gen. Hosp.; sr. v.p. nursing/profl. svcs. Miners Meml. Med. Ctr., Coaldale, Pa. Mem. ANA, AACCN. Home: RR 1 Box 100 New Ringgold PA 17960-9742

LARKAM, BEVERLEY MCCOSHAM, clinical social worker, family therapist; b. Vancouver, Can., Mar. 3, 1928; came to U.S., 1951; d. William Howard and Marjorie Isobel (Jerome) McCosham; children: Elizabeth, Charles, Daphne, Peter, John. Assoc. Royal Conservatory of Mus. of Toronto, U. Toronto, 1948; BA, U. B.C., 1949, BSW, 1950, MSW, 1951. Diplomate, Lic. bd. cert. master social worker, advanced clin. practitioner, marriage and family therapist, chem. dependency counselor, clin. soc. work, Tex. Psychiat. social worker Brackenridge Hosp., 1952-54; chmn. dept. sr. high sch. Univ. Presbyn. Ch., Austin, Tex., 1952-55, mem. Christian edn. com., 1961-67, mem. community orgn. to establish classes for mentally retarded children, 1966-68, bd. dirs. developing and organizing nursery sch., 1967-70; social worker Counseling-Psychol. Svcs. Ctr. U. Tex., 1971-72; psychiat. social worker, chief supr. adult mental health, children's mental health Human Devel. Ctr.-South, Austin, 1972-79; pvt. practice marriage and family therapy, sex therapy and individual and group psychotherapy, Austin, 1975—; field supr. Sch. Social Work U. Tex.; cons. in field. Mem. City of Austin Commn. for Women, 1978—, chmn., 1982-84, emeritus, 1985—; organizer Austin Assn. for Marriage and Family Therapy, 1980-82; bd. dirs. Nat. Assn. Commns. for Women, 1985-87. Mem. Am. Assn. Marriage and Family Therapy (approved supr.), Am. Group Psychotherapy Assn. (cert. group psychotherapist), Southwestern Group Psychotherapy Soc. (sr. faculty), Am. Assn. Sex Educators, Counselors and Therapists (cert. sex therapist, supr.), Acad. Cert. Social Workers, Nat. Assn. Social Workers, Register Clin. Social Workers, Tex. Soc. for Clin. Social Work (bd. dirs. 1990—), PEO Sisterhood. Presbyterian. Home and Office: 2102 Raleigh Ave Austin TX 78703-2128 also: 207 E 9th St Georgetown TX 78626-5908

LARKIN, DONALD W., clinical psychologist; b. Kingsport, Tenn., June 23, 1947; s. Clarence K. and Frankie E. (Fields) L.; m. Sharon Sue Marsh, Oct. 21, 1966 (div. Mar. 1989); 1 child, Doni Suzanne. BS in Psychology and Math., East Tenn. State U., 1980; MS in Clin. Psychology, Nova U., Ft. Lauderdale, Fla., 1982, PhD, 1987. Lic. clin. psychologist, Tenn. Psychology intern Miami VA, 1983-84; electrician, computer technician Tenn. Eastman Co., Kingsport, 1965-80; therapist Clin. Psychology Inst., Ft. Lauderdale, 1984-86; instr. Nova U., 1982-86; clin. psychologist Johnson City (Tenn.) Med. Ctr. Optifast Program, 1989-90; assoc. staff psychologist Woodridge Psychiat. Hosp., Johnson, 1987-93; clin. psychologist Fairview Assocs., Johnson, 1987—, clin. dir., 1989-93; clin. dir. Woodridge Psychiat. Hosp., Johnson City, 1993—; clin. asst. prof. Quillen Coll. Medicine, Johnson City, 1988—; adj. faculty East Tenn. State U., Johnson City, 1987—. Mem. Hawkins County Bd. Edn., Rogersville, Tenn., 1978-80. Mem. Am. Psychol. Assn., Tenn. Psychol. Assn., Inter-Mountain Psychol. Assn., Psi Chi, Kappa Mu Epsilon. Office: Woodridge Hosp 403 N State Of Franklin Rd Johnson City TN 37604-6034

LARKIN, KEVIN TIMOTHY, psychologist; b. Northville, Mich., Jan. 4, 1957; s. Kenneth Dean and Beverley Joann (Geisler) L.; m. Heather Anne

Hookey, July 28, 1979; children: Emily Blair, Meredith Anne. BA, Wittenberg U., 1979; MA, U. Richmond, 1981; PhD, U. Pitts., 1986. Lic. clin. psychologist. Teaching asst. dept. psychology U. Richmond (Va.), 1979-80, psychometric asst. dept. psychology, 1979-80; mental health worker Westbrook Hosp., Richmond, 1980-81, psychol. asst., 1981-82; clinician Western Psychiat. Inst. and Clinic, Pitts., 1982-85; teaching fellow U. Pitts., 1982-85; psychology intern behavioral medicine U. W.Va. Hosps., Morgantown, 1985-86; asst. prof. dept. psychology W.Va. U., Morgantown, 1986-92, assoc. prof. Psychology, 1992—; adj. asst. prof. dept. counseling W.Va. U., Morgantown, 1987—; clin. asst. prof. Chestnut Ridge Hosp., Morgantown, 1986-93; assoc. prof. dept. behavioral medicine and psychiatry Sch. Medicine U. W.Va., 1993—; staff mem. hypertension clin. U. Hosp., Morgantown, 1990—, anxiety disorders clinic, 1991—, mood disorders clinic, 1995—. Mem. APA, Soc. Behavioral Medicine, Assn. Advancement Behavior Therapy, W.Va. Psychol. Assn. (pres. elect 1991, pres. 1992), Soc. Psychophysiol. Rsch., Am. Psychosomatic Soc. Democrat. Presbyterian. Office: W Va Univ Dept Psychology Ogelbay Hall Morgantown WV 26506-6040

LARNER, JOSEPH, pharmacology educator; b. Brest-Litovsk, Poland, Jan. 9, 1921; came to U.S., 1921; s. George and Ida (Sobel) Likovsky; m. Frances Wolpert, Sept.7, 1947; children: Andrew Charles, James Mitchell, Paul Frederick. BS, U. Mich., 1942; MD, Columbia U., 1945; MS in Chemistry, U. Ill., 1949; PhD in Biochemistry, Washington U., St. Louis, 1951; D honoris causa, U. Barcelona, Spain, 1983. Instr. biochemistry dept. Washington U., St. Louis, 1951-53; asst. prof. chemistry dept. U. Ill., Urbana, 1953-57; assoc. prof. Pharmacology Western Res. U., Cleve., 1957-63, prof., 1963-64; Hill prof. metabolic enzymology U. Minn. Med. Sch., Mpls., 1964-69; prof., chmn. pharmacology dept. U. Va. Med. Sch., Charlottesville, 1969-90; Alumni prof. U. Va. Med. Sch., Charlotte, 1974—; dir. neurosci. program U. Va. Med. Sch., 1972-75, diabetes confs., 1974-91; prin. scientist Insmed Co., Charlottesville, 1989-91. Author: Intermediary Metabolism and Its Regulation, 1971; editor: Methods in Diabetes Research, 1985, Human Pharmacology, 1991. Capt. U.S. Army, 1946-48. Recipient Sesquicentennial Disting. Alumnus award U. Mich., 1967, Established Investigator award Am. Diabetes Assn., 1978-83, David Rumbaugh Sci. award Juvenile Diabetes Found., 1980, Banting medal and lecture Am. Diabetes Assn., 1987, Disting. Rsch. award Am. Assn. Med. Colls., 1987, Rsch. award Japan Soc. for Starch Rsch., 1985, Va. Lifetime Achievement award in Sci., 1992, U. Va. President's Report, 1992, Va. Inventor of Yr. award and Prize, 1993. Mem. Am. Soc. Pharmacology and Exptl. Therapeutics, Am. Soc. Biochemistry, Am. Soc. Chmn. Pharmacology Depts., Am. Inst. Chemists. Jewish. Office: U Va Diabetes Rsch Ctr Jefferson Park Ave Charlottesville VA 22901-9133*

LA ROCCA, RENATO V., oncologist, researcher; b. Cin., June 16, 1957; m. Margaret Carolyn Cauthron, Sept. 5, 1987; children: Alessandra, Marcello, Victoria, Chae. MS, Liceo Sci. Statale, Turin, Italy, 1976; postgrad., U. Padua, Italy, 1976-80; MD, Cornell U., 1982. Diplomate Nat. Bd. Med. Examiners, Am. Bd. Internal Medicine, Am. Bd. Oncology. Resident in internal medicine N.Y. Hosp.-Cornell Med. Ctr., N.Y.C., 1982-85; med. oncology fellow medicine br. Nat. Cancer Inst., Bethesda, Md., 1985-88, sr. investigator medicine br., 1988-90; pvt. practice Kentuckiana Med. Oncology Assocs., PSC, Louisville, 1990—; clin. assoc. prof. medicine U. Louisville Sch. Medicine and U. Ky. Coll. Medicine; cons. Jansen Rsch. Found.; rschr. med. br. Nat. Cancer Inst., NIH, Bethesda; mem. steering com. Ky. Cancer Pain Initiative; chmn. cancer com. Jewish Hosp., Louisville. Author: (chpts. in books) Molecular and Cellular Biology of Prostate Cancer, Molecular Foundations Oncology; contbr. articles to profl. jours.; patentee in field. Recipient USPHS Commendation medal, 1990, Leadership award Am. Cancer Soc., 1995. Fellow ACP; mem. Am. Soc. Clin. Oncology, Am. Assn. Cancer Rsch., Am. Cancer Soc. (v.p. Ky. divsn.), Am. Coll. Physician Inventors, Am. Pain Soc., Jefferson County Med. Soc., Ky. Oncology Soc., Ky. Med. Assn., Ind. Med. Assn., Alpha Omega Alpha. Office: Kentuckiana Med Oncology Assn 250 E Liberty St Ste 802 Louisville KY 40202-1537

LA ROCHELLE, PIERRE-LOUIS, civil engineering educator; b. Quebec, Que., Can., Aug. 20, 1928; s. Emile Joseph and Juliette Marie (Coulombe) LaR.; m. Rachel Gratia Bedard, July 11, 1958 (dec. Aug. 1991); children—Judith, Sophie, Anne. B.A., Seminaire De Quebec, Can., 1950; B.Sc. in Civil Engring., U. Laval, Quebec, 1954, M.Sc., 1956; Ph.D., U. London, 1960. Registered profl. engineer, Que. Asst. prof. engring. U. Laval, Quebec, 1960-63, head dept. civil engring., 1963-67, prof. engring., 1968-96, dir. grad. studies civil engring., 1992-94, ret., 1996; adj. prof. U. Laval, 1996—; pres. Les Cons. PLR Inc.; cons. in geotech. engring., dam design and constrn. Hydro-Quebec, SNC, Golder, others, Can. Contbr. articles to profl. jours. Recipient Can. Geotech. Soc. Prize, 1975, R.F. Leggett award, 1977, Queen Elizabeth Jubilee's medal Can. Govt., 1978. Fellow Engring. Inst. Can.; mem. ASCE, ASTM (Hogentogler award 1985), Royal Soc. Can., Can. Acad. Engring., Internat. Com. on Landslides (pres. 1981-89), Yacht Club (Sillery, Que.; comdr. 1982). Home and Office: 2528 Des Hospitalieres, Sillery, PQ Canada G1T 1V7

LARRIMORE, PATSY GADD, nursing administrator; b. Knoxville, Tenn., Feb. 18, 1933; d. Harry Collins and Frances (Irwin) Gadd; m. Walter Eugene Larrimore; children: Patricia J. Titus, Walter Eugene Jr., Beverly Calderon. BS, Johns Hopkins U., 1976, MEd, 1977. RN. Pediatric supr. Johns Hopkins Hosp., Balt., 1960-68; supr. critical care South Balt. Gen. Hosp., 1968-78; DON Hosp. for Sick Children, Washington, 1978-84; field rep. Joint Commn. Accreditation Hosp., Chgo., 1984-95; dir. nursing Bon Secours Hosp., Balt., 1987-88; assoc. dir. clin. affairs Paralyzed Vets. Am., Washington, 1989-92; pres. Diabetes Action Rsch. and Edn. Found., Inc., Washington, 1991-92, Larrimore and Assocs., Inc., Linthicum, Md., 1991-95; clin. auditor Vencor, Inc., Lousville, 1995—; asst. prof. nursing and allied health Catonsville Community Coll., Balt. Contbr. articles to profl. jours. Bd. dirs. Christian Relief Svcs., Alexandria, Va., 1987-92. Recipient Bronze Svc. award Am. Heart Assn., 1981, Md. affiliate Silver Disting. Svc. award, 1980, Cen. Md. chpt. Bronze Svc. Recognition medallion, 1982, Md. chpt. Founder's award Am. Heart Assn., 1978, D.C. Hosp. Svc. award, 1982. Mem. Am. Heart Assn. (bd. dirs. Balt. chpt. 1972-84, Md. chpt. 1978-85, Bronze Service award Md. affiliate 1981, Silver Disting. Service Cen. Md. chpt. 1980, Bronze Service Recognition award, 1979), Am. Assn. Critical Care Nurses, Am. Nurses Assn., Advanced Nursing Adminstrn., Assn. Care Children's Health (bd. dirs. 1981-82), Am. Soc. Nursing Service Adminstrs., Am. Assn. Spinal Cord Injury Nurses, Phi Delta Kappa.

LARSEN, ARVI ILMARI, rheumatologist; b. Sortavala, Karelia, Finland, Sept. 14, 1939; s. Norman Samuel and Sirkka Kaarina (Laurila) L.; m. Sinikka Laitinen, Oct. 4, 1963 (div. Aug. 1974); children: Senja, Petri, Katja; m. Eva Gunilla Nilsson, Mar. 15, 1985; 1 child, Jens. MD, U. Turku, Finland, 1967. Specialist in rheumatology, Finland, 1974. Resident Rheumatism Found. Hosp., Heinola, Finland, 1969-74; chief rheumatologist Spenshuits Rheumatism Hosp., Halmstad, Sweden, 1978-87, Western Hosp., Vaesteras, Sweden, 1987-90; pvt. practice Vaesteras, 1991-93; chief rheumatologist Kongsvinger (Norway) Hosp., 1993—. Home: Drottninggatan 19B, 72464 Vaesterås Sweden Office: Kongssvinger Hospital, Dept Rheumatology, 2200 Kongsvinger Norway

LARSEN, BRYAN, microbiologist, educator; b. Omaha, Jan. 26, 1949; s. Norman Louis and Shirley Lorraine (Bryan) L.; m. Nancy Esther Nettleton, July 19, 1969; children: Erik Bryan, Jeremy Todd. BS, U. Iowa, 1971, MS, 1973, PhD, 1976. Research asst. scientist U. Iowa, Iowa City, 1976-80, assoc. rsch. scientist, 1980-81; asst. prof. obstetrics and gynecology and asst. prof. microbiology Marshall U., Huntington, W.Va., 1981-84, assoc. prof., 1984-89; prof. 1989—; chief analytical svcs. Microbiol. Cons., Inc., Huntington, 1984—; lectr. and cons. in field regarding pharm. products, infectious disease. Author of book; co-editor of book; contbr. articles to books and profl. jours. Served to lt. col. USAR, 1981-94. Freedom's Found. awardee, Freedom's Found. Valley Forge, 1972; Freedom's Found. Award and Bronze medal, 1973, Johnson and Johnson Focused Giving award, 1990-92; NIH fellow, 1978. Mem. Am. Soc. Microbiology, Infectious Disease Soc. for Obstetrics and Gynecology, Assoc. Profs. Gynecology and Obstetrics, Infectious Disease Soc. Am., Soc. Gynecologic Investigation. Republican. Presbyterian.

LARSEN, RALPH S(TANLEY), health care company executive; b. Bklyn., Nov. 19, 1938; s. Andrew and Gurine (Henningsen) L.; m. Dorothy M. Zeitfuss, Aug. 19, 1961; children: Karen, Kristen, Garret. BBA, Hofstra U., 1962. Mfg. trainee, then supr. prodn. and dir. mfg. Johnson & Johnson, New Brunswick, N.J., 1962-77; v.p. ops., v.p. mktg. McNeil Consumer Products Co. div. Johnson & Johnson, Ft. Washington, Pa., 1977-81; pres. Becton Dickenson Consumer Products, Paramus, N.J., 1981-83; pres. Chicopee div. Johnson & Johnson, New Brunswick, 1983-85; co. group chmn. Johnson & Johnson, New Brunswick, N.J., 1985-86, vice chmn., exec. com., bd. dirs., 1986-89, chmn. bd., pres., CEO, 1989—, also bd. dirs., mem. exec. com.; bd. dirs. N.Y. Stock Exch., Xerox Corp., AT&T Corp. Bd. dirs. UNICEF. Mem. Bus. Coun. (vice chmn.), Bus. Roundtable (co-chmn. policy com.). Republican. Office: Johnson & Johnson 1 Johnson Johnson Plz New Brunswick NJ 08933

LARSON, ALLAN BENNETT, pharmacist; b. Chgo., Feb. 9, 1943; s. Nils Ragnar and Mary Frances (Quigley) L.; m. Virginia Louise, Apr. 16, 1971; children: Michael Allan, Jacie Lynn. BS in Pharmacy, Drake U., Des Moines, 1966; MS in Phys. Pharmacy, U. Wis., 1969; PhD in Indsl. and Phys. Pharmacy, Purdue U., 1972. Sr. rsch. pharmacist Dorsey Labs., Lincoln, Nebr., 1972-76; sr. pharm. scientist Vicks Rsch. & Devel., Mt. Vernon, N.Y., 1976-77, group leader skin care/toiletries, 1977-80; mgr. tech. svcs. Vicks Rsch. & Devel., Shelton, Conn., 1980-84; dir. process rsch. & devel. Wyeth-Ayerst Rsch., Rouses Point, N.Y., 1984—. Contbr. articles to profl. jours. Chmn. summer festival Rowayton (Conn.) Civic Assn., 1983; chmn. Peru (N.Y.) Activity Recreation Ctr., 1985-86; chmn. Peru Bicentennial Com. 1990-92; lay leader Peru Comty. Ch., 1991-93. Mem. Am. Pharm. Assn., Am. Assn. Pharm. Scis., Acad. Pharm. Scis., Soc. Cosmetic Chemists, Internat. Soc. Pharm. Engrs., Drug Info. Assn., Phi Lambda Upsilon, Phi Kappa Phi. Republican. United Ch. of Christ. Home: 5 Bouchard Dr Peru NY 12972-5003 Office: Wyeth-Ayerst Rsch 64 Maple St Rouses Point NY 12979-1424

LARSON, DAVID BRUCE, research epidemiologist; b. Glen Ridge, N.J., Mar. 13, 1947; s. John Owen and Peggy June (Asbury) L.; m. Susan Joan Slingerland, Dec. 20, 1975; children: David Chad, Kristen Joan. BS, Drexel U., 1969; MD, Temple U., 1973; MS in Pub. Health, U. N.C., 1983. Diplomate Nat. Bd. Med. Examiners, Am. Bd. Psychiatry. Intern MacNeal Meml. Hosp., Berwyn, Ill., 1973-74; resident in psychiatry Duke U. Med. Ctr., Durham, N.C., 1974-77, psychosomatics teaching fellow, 1975-77, fellow in behavioral scis., 1976-78; chief resident psychiatry Duke U. Med. Ctr. and Durham County Gen. Hosp., 1977-79; fellow in geropsychiatry Duke U. Med. Ctr., Durham, N.C., 1979-81; epidemiology fellow U. N.C., Chapel Hill, 1982-83; epidemiology fellow NIMH, Rockville, Md., 1983-85, rsch. psychiatrist, 1985-91; sr. policy researcher Office of the Sec., HHS, Washington, 1991-93; sr. analyst office of dir. NIH, 1993-94; pres. Nat. Inst. Healthcare Rsch., 1994—. Contbr. chpts. to books, articles to profl. jours. Mem. AAAS, AMA, So. Med. Assn., Christian Med. Soc., Am. Psychiat. Assn., So. Psychiat. Assn., Christian Assn. Psychol. Studies, Am. Assn. Marital and Family Therapy, Soc. for Sci Study of Religion, Sigma Xi. Episcopalian.

LARSON, ELAINE LUCILLE, nurse researcher, epidemiologist, educator; b. Douglas, Ariz., Apr. 27, 1943; d. John Earl and Jerry Lucille (Hunter) Williamson; m. Steven Mark Larson, June 14, 1965; children: Nathan, Justine. BS, U. Wash., 1965, MA, 1969, PhD, 1981. Registered nurse. Nurse specialist, instr. U. Wash. Hosp., Seattle, 1965-69, hosp. epidemiologist, 1967-70, assoc. dir. nursing., asst. prof., 1976-83; postdoctoral fellow U. Pa., Phila., 1983-85; Nutting chmn. in Clin. Nursing Johns Hopkins U. Sch. Nursing, Balt., Md., 1985—; pres. Cert. Bd. for Infection Control. Contbr. numerous articles to profl. jours. Testified in House and Senate for nursing edn. and research, 1984-85; testified in Joint Econ. Com. for testing of disinfectants. Grantee Johnson & Johnson, 1985. Fellow Am. Acad. Nursing, NSF (inst. of medicine 1986). Presbyterian. *

LARSON, MAUREEN INEZ, rehabilitation consultant; b. Madison, Minn., Mar. 10, 1955; d. Alvin John and Leona B. (Bornhorst) L.; m. Michael Earl Klemetsrud, July 7, 1979 (div. Sept. 1988); m. Kenneth Bell, Dec., 1993. BA in Psychology cum laude, U. Minn., 1977; MA in Counseling, U. N.D., 1978. Cert. rehab. counselor, ins. specialist. Employment counselor II, coordinator spl. programs Employment Security div. State of Wyo., Rawlins, 1978-80; employment interviewer Employment Security div. State of Wash., Tacoma, 1980; lead counselor Comprehensive Rehab. Counseling, Tacoma, 1980-81; dir. counseling Cascade Rehab. Counseling, Tacoma, 1981-87, dist. mgr., 1987-90; regional mgr. Rainier Case Mgmt., Tacoma, 1991-92; owner Maureen Larson and Assocs., Tacoma, Wash., 1992—; state capt. legis. div. Provisions Project Am. Personnel and Guidance Assn., 1980. Advocate Grand Forks (N.D.) Rape Crisis Ctr., 1977-78; mem. Pierce County YMCA; bd. dirs. Boys and Girls Clubs of Tacoma, chairperson sustaining drive, 1991, sec.-treas., 1993, pres., 1994, auction com. and spl. events com. State of Minn. scholar, 1973-77; recipient Alice Tweed Tuohy award U. Minn., 1977, Nat. Disting. Svcs. Registry award Libr. of Congress, 1987; named bd. mem. vol. of Yr. Boys and Girls Clubs of Tacoma, 1992. Mem. Nat. Fedn. Bus. and Profl. Women (rec. sec. 1978-80, runner-up Young Careerists' Program 1980), Nat. Rehab. Assn. (bd. dirs. Olympic chpt. 1988—, pres. 1990-91, chairperson state conf. planning com. 1990, 93, 96), Nat. Rehab. Counseling Assn. (bd. dirs. 1993, State of Wash. Counselor of Yr. 1991, Pacific Region Counselor of Yr. 1992), Nat. Rehab. Adminstrs. Assn. (bd. dirs. 1993), Women in Workers Compensation Orgn., Washington Self-Insured Assn., Nat. Assn. rehab. Profls. in Pvt. Sector, Pi Gamma Mu. Office: M Larson & Assocs 13504 82nd Ave NW Gig Harbor WA 98329-8642

LARSON, ROLAND ELMER, health care executive; b. Chgo., Jan. 21, 1939; s. Elmer Gustav and Anna (Alphida) L.; m. Noel Kathleen Brennan, June 28, 1969; children: Eric R., Jennifer L., Melissa K. BA, Augustana Coll., 1961; MHA, U. Iowa, 1963; postgrad., Harvard U., 1978. Adminstrv. asst. U. Vt. Med. Ctr., Burlington, 1962-64; assoc. adminstr. Roger Williams Hosp., Providence, 1964-73; v.p. adminstrn. Norwalk (Conn.) Hosp., 1973-81; pres., chief exec. officer Nashoba Community Hosp., Ayer, Mass., 1981-88; v.p. Charles River Assn., Boston, 1988-90; cons. Charles River Assocs., Boston, 1990-93; ind. healthcare cons. Harvard, Mass., 1990—. Chmn. Harvard (Mass.) Coalition Against Drugs and Alcohol, Opportunities, Inc., Providence, 1966-68, Greater Norwalk Community Coun., 1980; bd. dirs. Nat. Arthritis Found., N.Y.C., 1967-71, Am. Cancer Soc., Stamford, Conn., 1978-81. Fellow Am. Coll. Healthcare Execs.; mem. Cen. Mass. Hosp. Coun. (chmn. 1987-88), Rotary. Home: 28 Candleberry Ln Harvard MA 01451-1641 Office: Larson & Assocs 28 Candleberry Ln Harvard MA 01451-1641

LARSON, STEPHEN WAYNE, oncologist; b. Omaha, Apr. 11, 1948. BA, Macalester Coll., St. Paul, 1970; MD, Baylor Coll., 1973. Diplomate Am. Bd. Internal Medicine and Med. Oncology. Intern internal medicine Baylor Affiliated Hosps., 1973-74, resident internal medicine, 1974-76; fellow med. oncology Baylor Coll. Medicine, 1976-78; pvt. practice med. oncologist Houston, 1978—. Office: 1315 Calhoun Ste 1103 Houston TX 77002

LARSSON, ANDERS LARS, anesthesiologist; b. Motala, Sweden, Dec. 3, 1952; s. Arne Teofil and Ewa Sara (Edsaer) L.; m. Elna-Marie Barup, Aug. 16, 1975; children: Mans, Elisabet, Hanna. MD, U. Lund, Sweden, 1977; PhD, U. Lund, 1988; DEAA, European Acad. Anaesthesiology, Stockholm, 1990. Intern Kalmar (Sweden) Hosp., 1976-78, resident in anesthesia, 1978-81; resident Univ. Hosp. U. Lund, 1981-83, asst. prof., 1983-89, assoc. prof., 1989—, co-dir. Intensive Care Unit, 1990-92, dir. Intensive Care Unit, 1992—; vis. assoc. prof. Dept. Anesthesiology Health Sci. Ctr. U. Tex., San Antonio, 1989-90. Grantee Swedish Nat Bd. Tech. Devel., AGA Co. Mem. Swedish Med. Assn., Swedish Soc. Med. Sci. (grantee), Swedish Soc. Anesthesiology and Intensive Care, Scandinavian Soc. Anesthesiologists, Soc. Critical Care Medicine, European Soc. Intensive Care Medicine. Home: Gilleskroken 3, Lund S-22647, Sweden Office: Univ Hosp Univ Lund, Dept Anesthesia & ICU, Lund S-22185, Sweden

LARSSON, KNUT BERTIL, psychologist, educator; b. Strovelstorp, Sweden, July 22, 1922; s. Valfrid and Hanna (Nilsson) L. PhD, U. Goteborg, Sweden, 1956; D (honoris causa), U. Paris, 1996. From asst. prof. to prof. psychology U. Goteborg, Sweden, 1956-88; prof. emeritus U. Goteborg, 1989—; vis. prof. Rutger U., N.J., 1970; vis. scientist U. Autonoma de Mex., 1971-84. Contbr. articles to profl. jours. Postdoctoral fellow U. Calif., Berkeley, 1959. Mem. Internat. Acad. Sex Rsch., Internat. Soc. Devel. Neurosci., Internat. Soc. Psychoneuroendocrinology, Internat. Soc. Rsch. on Agression, Acad. Rodinensis pro Remediatione, European Behavioral Pharmacology Soc., Soc. for Study of Reproduction, European Neurosci. Assn., European Brain and Behavior Soc., Animal Behavior Soc. Office: U Goteborg Dept Psychology, Haraldsg 1, S-413 14 Goteborg Sweden

LASAGNA, LOUIS CESARE, medical educator; b. N.Y.C., Feb. 22, 1923; s. Joseph and Carmen (Boccignone) L.; m. Helen Chester Gersten; children: Nina, David, Maria, Kristin, Lisa, Peter, Christopher. BS, Rutgers U., 1943; MD, Columbia U., 1947; DSc (hon.), Hahnemann U., 1980, Rutgers U., 1983. Asst. prof. medicine Johns Hopkins U., Balt., 1954-57, asst. prof. pharmacology, 1954-59, assoc. prof. medicine, 1957-70, assoc. prof. pharmacology, 1959-70; prof. pharmacology and toxicology U. Rochester, 1970-86, prof. medicine, 1970-86; dean Sackler Sch. Tufts U., 1984—, prof. pharmacology and psychiatry, 1984—. Author: The Doctors' Dilemmas, 1962, Life, Death and the Doctor, 1968, Phenylpropanolamine, A Review, 1988; editor: Controversies in Therapeutics, 1980. Sr. asst. surgeon USPHS, 1952-54. Recipient Oscar B. Hunter award Am. Soc. Clin. Pharmacology, 1975, ASPET award Am. Soc. Pharmacology and Exptl. Therapeutics, 1976, Lilly prize Brit. Pharmacological Soc., 1985, Rutgers U. award, 1993, J. Allyn Taylor Internat. prize in Medicine, 1993; named Disting. prof. Tufts U., 1994. Mem. Inst. Medicine of NAS, Am. Coll. Neuropsychopharmacology (pres. 1979-80). Republican. Roman Catholic. Home: 256 Woodland Rd Auburndale MA 02166-2707 Office: Tufts U Sackler Sch Grad Biomed Sci 136 Harrison Ave Boston MA 02111-1800

LASDAY, STEPHEN DAVID, surgeon; b. Pitts., Aug. 15, 1965; s. Louis and Linda Ann (Berger) L.; m. Renae Sharon Chait, June 4, 1994. BA, Franklin & Marshall Coll., 1987; DPM, Pa. Coll. Podiatric Medicine, 1991. Resident The Grad. Hosp., Phila., 1991-93; dir. foot & ankle svcs. St. Rita's Med. Ctr. Wound CLinic, Lima, Ohio, 1994—. Bd. dirs. Temple Beth Israel, Lima, 1995—. Mem. Foot-Ankle Pediatric Soc., Phi Kappa Psi. Office: 830 W High St #202 Lima OH 45805

LASH, JAMES WILLIAM (JAY LASH), embryology educator; b. Chgo., Oct. 24, 1929; s. Joseph and Alice (Smith) L.; m. Natalie Novak, Sept. 10, 1954; 1 child, Rebecca. Phd, U. Chgo., 1954; MS (hon.), U. Pa., 1981. Postdoctoral fellow NIH, Phila., 1955-57; sr. rsch. fellow NIH, London, 1986; from asst. prof. to prof. U. Pa., Phila., 1957-95, prof. emeritus, 1995—; Helen Hay Whitney fellow Helen Hay Whitney Found., Phila., 1958-61, Helen Hay Whitney Established Investigator, 1961-66; cons. NSF, Washington, 1967-70; mem. adv. bd., cons. NIH, 1970-83. Co-editor 6 books in field. Fellow Lalor Found., 1957, Paulo Found., 1969, NIH, 1986; recipient rsch. award Wellcome Found., 1960, Lindback award for disting. tchg. Office: RR 2 Box 716 Woodstock VT 05091-9401

LASH, MYLES PERRY, hospital administrator, consultant; b. Detroit, May 31, 1946; s. Irving and Rose (Simkovitz) L.; m. Linda Pauline Borger, June 19, 1968; children: Alissa Beth, David Howard. B.S., Wayne State U., 1968; M.Hosp. Adminstrn., U. Mich., 1970. Asst. to exec. dir. Peoples Community Hosp. Authority, Wayne, Mich., 1970-72; asst. prof. Grad. Program Hosp. Adminstrn., Ohio State U., Columbus, 1970-72; adminstr. Ohio State U. Hosps., Columbus, 1973-79; exec. dir. Med. Coll. Va., Richmond, 1979-85; nat. dir. health care Arthur Young Co., Washington, 1985-86; pres. Lash Group-Health Care Cons., Washington, 1986—. Contbr. articles to profl. jours. Bd. dirs. Univ. Hosp. Consortium, 1980-85, pres., 1985. Mem. U. Mich. Hosp. Adminstrn. Alumni Assn. (pres.), Am. Hosp. Assn., Am. Coll. Hosp. Adminstrs. (Robert S. Hudgens Meml. award 1982). Home: 6708 Bonaventure Ct Bethesda MD 20817-4026 Office: 555 13th St NW Washington DC 20004-1109

LASHLEY, MARK ALAN, physician assistant; b. Balt., Sept. 17, 1959; s. William George and Verna Joan (Buterbaugh) L.; m. Mary Ellen Cadogan, June 21, 1986; children: Christina Marie, Meredith Anne. BA in Biology, U. Md., Balt., 1981; AA in Physician Asst., Essex (Md.) Community Coll., 1984; MBA, Loyola Coll., Balt., 1987. Cert. physician asst., Md. Emergency room registrar Church Hosp., Balt., 1980-84; surg. physician asst. Baltimore County Gen. Hosp., Balt., 1984, South Balt. Gen. Hosp., 1984-85; physician asst. supr. Union Meml. Hosp., 1985-93; asst. prof. Essex C.C., Balt., 1993-95; part-time physician asst. Union Meml. Hosp., 1993—, Good Samaritan Hosp., 1995—, Mercy Hosp., 1995—; guest speaker dept. nursing Towson State U., Balt., 1987—; part-time faculty Essex C.C., 1990—. Deacon Loch Raven Bapt. Ch. U.S. Senate scholar, 1977. Fellow Am. Acad. Physician Assts., Md. Acad. Physician Assts. (pres. 1994). Republican. Baptist. Home: 2513 Tally Ho Rd Fallston MD 21047-1220 Office: Essex CC PA Program 7201 Rossville Blvd Baltimore MD 21237-3855

LASHOF, JOYCE C., public health educator; b. Phila.; d. Harry and Rose (Brodsky) Cohen; m. Richard K. Lashof, June 11, 1950; children: Judith, Carol, Dan. AB, Duke U., 1946; MD, Women's Med. Coll., 1950; DSc (hon.), Med. Coll. Pa., 1983. Dir. Ill. State Dept. Pub. Health, 1973-77; dep. asst. sec. for health programs and population affairs Dept. Health, Edn., and Welfare, Washington, 1977-78; sr. scholar in residence IOM, Washington, 1978; asst. dir. office of tech. assessment U.S. Congress, Washington, 1978-81; dean sch. pub. health U. Calif., Berkeley, 1981-91, prof. pub. health Sch. Pub. Health, 1981-94, prof. emerita, 1994—; co-chair Commn. on Am. after Roe vs. Wade, 1991-92; mem. Sec.'s Coun. Health Promotion and Disease Prevention, 1988-91; pres. APHA, 1992; chair Pres.'s Adv. Com. on Gulf War Vets. Illnesses, 1995-96. Vice chairperson editl. bd. Wellness Letter, 1983—; mem. editl. com. Ann. Rev. of Pub. Health, 1987-90. Recipient Alumni Achievement award Med. Coll. Pa., 1975, Sedgwick Meml. medal APHA, 1995. Home: 601 Euclid Ave Berkeley CA 94708-1331 Office: U Calif-Berkeley Sch Pub Health 140 Earl Warren Hall Berkeley CA 94720

LASKEY, RICHARD ANTHONY, biomedical device executive; b. N.Y.C., Oct. 24, 1936; s. Charles Lewis and Gertrude Ann (Stolzenthaler) L.; m. Frances M. Pollack, June 29, 1975; children: Victoria Ann, Deborah Lea. Student CCNY; BS in Chemistry, Ohio, MS in Organic Chemistry; PhD in Organic Chemistry, Sussex (Eng.) U., 1970; LLB, U. Chgo., 1972; MD (hon.), Med. Coll. S.A., 1975, fellow, Psychiatry 1976; postgrad. in ob-gyn, U. Pa., 1989-94. Diplomate Am. Bd. Examiners in Psychotherapy. Head sec. med. products, lab. mgr. Hydron Labs., North Brunswick, N.J., 1967-73; v.p. biomed. rsch. Datascope Corp., Paramus, N.J., 1973-82; pres. rsch. Millbrook Labs., Inc., Rochelle Park, N.J., 1982—; cons. in field. Recipient Doctor's award Chgo. Med. Coll., 1975; fellow Am. Acad. Behavioral Sci., 1976. Fellow Am. Inst. Chemist; mem. NRA, AAAS, Md. Med. Soc., Idaho Med. Soc., Nat. Med. Soc., Internat. Coll. Physicians and Surgeons, Am. Inst. Chemist, Am. Psychotherapy Assn., Nat. Psychol. Assn., Assn. Advancement Med. Instrumentation, Soc. Rsch. Adminstrs. Biomed. inventor, patentee. Home: PO Box 133 Washington NJ 07882-0133 Office: PO Box 125 Rochelle Park NJ 07662-0125

LASKIN, OSCAR LARRY, clinical pharmacology educator, virologist; b. Phila., Sept. 11, 1951; s. Bernard and Blanche (Friedman) L.; m. Christine Ann Goril, Apr. 4, 1981. Children—Matthew Benjamin, Joshua Christopher, Jennifer Bonnie, Heather Rose. A.B. summa cum laude, Temple U., 1972, M.D. with honors, 1976. Diplomate Am. Bd. Internal Medicine. Intern Johns Hopkins Hosp., Balt., 1976-77, resident in medicine, 1977-79, fellow in medicine, 1979-82, fellow in pharmacology, 1981-82; asst. prof. clin. pharmacology Cornell U. Med. Coll., N.Y.C., 1982-88, asst. prof. pharamacology and medicine, 1982-88; asst. attending physician N.Y. Hosp., 1982-88; adj. assoc. prof. med. and clin. pharmacology, Cornell U. Med. Coll., 1988—; dir. clin. pharmacology, Merck, Sharp, & Dohme Research Labs., 1988-91, Sandoz Rsch. Inst., 1991-92, exec. dir. clin. pharmacology, 1993—, global head clin. pharmacology, 1994—. Contbr. articles to profl. jours. NIH fellow, 1981; clin. scholar Rockefeller Bros. Fund, 1982; Hartford Found. fellow, 1983; recipient research prize Am. Heart Assn., 1975; pharm. Mfrs. Assn. Found. research starter grantee, 1984-86. Fellow ACP, Infectious Disease Soc. Am., Am. Coll. Clin. Pharmacology; mem. Am. Fedn. Clin. Research, Am. Soc. Microbiology, Am. Soc. Pharmacology and Exptl. Therapeutics (Young Investigator award 1987), Am. Soc. for Clin. Pharmacology and Therapeutics, Am. Bd. Clin. Pharmacology, Am. Soc. Clin. Pharmacology (bd. dirs.), Alpha Omega Alpha. Research on clin. pharmacology of antiviral drugs, anti-infective agents, clin. trial design and pharmacokinetics. Home: 40 Gates Ave Chatham NJ 07928-1414 Office: Sandoz Pharm Co 59 State Route 10 East Hanover NJ 07936-1080

LASKIN, STEVEN E., physician, neurologist; b. Rochester, N.Y.. BA, NYU, 1969, MD, 1975, PhD, 1975. Diplomate in neurology Am. Bd. Psychiatry and Neurology. Resident Duke U. Med. Ctr., Durham, N.C., 1975-76, Columbia-Presbyn. Med. Ctr., N.Y.C., 1976-79; attending neurologist Hackensack (N.J.) Med. Ctr., 1980—, chief neurology divsn., 1994—; asst. prof. neurosci. U. Medicine and Dentistry N.J.-N.J. Med. Sch., Newark, 1979—. Office: Hackensack Med Ctr 211 Essex St #202 Hackensack NJ 07601

LASKO, ALLEN HOWARD, pharmacist; b. Chgo., Oct. 27, 1941; s. Sidney P. and Sara (Hoffman) L.; BS (James scholar), U. Ill., 1964; m. Janice Marilynn Chess, Dec. 24, 1968 (div. Aug. 1993); children: Stephanie Paige, Michael Benjamin. Staff pharmacist Michael Reese Hosp. and Med. Center, Chgo., 1964-68; clin. pharmacist City of Hope Med. Center, Duarte, Calif., 1968-73; chief pharmacist Monrovia (Calif.) Cmty. Hosp., 1973-74, Santa Fe Meml. Hosp., L.A., 1974-77; pvt. investor, 1977-93; clin. pharmacist Foothill Presbyn. Hosp., Glendora, Calif., 1993—. Recipient Roche Hosp. Pharmacy Rsch. award, 1972-73. Mem. Magic Castle, Flying Samaritans, Mensa, Rho Pi Phi. Jewish. Author: Diabetes Study Guide, 1972, A Clinical Approach to Lipid Abnormalities Study Guide, 1973, Jet Injection Tested As An Aid in Physiologic Delivery of Insulin, 1973. Home: 376 Hill St Monrovia CA 91016-2340 Office: Foothill Presbyn Hosp 250 S Grand Ave Glendora CA 91741-4218

LASKOWSKI, IRMA WILLIAMS, hospice administrator; b. Chgo., June 4, 1943; d. Charles F. and Catherine (Hurter) Williams; m. Michael B. Laskowski, Jan. 23, 1965; children: Catherine, Marie, Elizabeth, Paul. BS in Biology, Loyola U., Chgo., 1965; BSN, St. Louis U., 1980. RN. Rsch. assoc. U. Okla., Oklahoma City, 1967-70; staff nurse St. Joseph Hosp., St. Louis, 1980-85; field nurse St. Joseph Home Health, St. Louis, 1985-88; patient care coord. Hospice of the Palouse, Moscow, Idaho, 1988-89; dir. Gritman Home Health/Hospice of the Palouse, Moscow, 1989-95, Latah Health Svcs. Hospice, Moscow, 1995—; cons. home health Idaho Hosp. Assn. Mem. AAUW, Idaho Assn. Home Health Agys. (sec. 1990, pres. 1992-94, treas. 1995—), Idaho Nurses Assn., Home Care Soc. Idaho Hosp. Assn. (pres. 1990-92), Idaho Faculty Women's Club (pres. 1989-90), Sigma Theta Tau. Roman Catholic. Home: 3382 Blaine Rd Moscow ID 83843-8448 Office: Latah Health Svcs Hospice 510 W Palouse River Dr Moscow ID 83843

LASS, JONATHAN HERSCHEL, ophthalmologist; b. Orange, N.J., July 14, 1949; s. David and Stella Lass; m. Leah Lass, Aug. 23, 1970; children: Michael, Jessica. BA magna cum laude, Boston U., 1972, MD cum laude, 1973. Diplomate Am. Bd. Ophthalmology. Rotating intern Mount Auburn Hosp., Cambridge, Mass., 1973-74; resident in ophthalmology Boston U. Med. Ctr., 1974-77; clin. fellow in ophthalmology Harvard Med. Sch. Mass. Eye/Ear, Boston, 1977-79; asst. prof. ophthalmology Case Western Res. U., Cleve., 1979-87, assoc. prof. ophthalmology, 1987-93, Charles I Thomas prof. ophthalmology, 1993—, chmn. dept. ophthalmology, 1994—; dir. dept. ophthalmology U. Hosps. of Cleve., 1994—; active staff U. Hosp. of Cleve., 1979—; chmn. adv. com. Ophthalmic Technician Program, Lakeland Cmty. Coll., 1990—; program chmn. World Congress Cornea IV, 1994—. Author: Corneal Surgery, 1986, Advances in Ocular Immunology, 1994; contbr. articles to profl. jours.; reviewer Investigative Ophthalmology and Vis. Sci., 1983—. Mem. Assn. for Rsch. in Vision and Ophthalmology, Am. Acad. of Ophthalmology (Honor award 1987), Internat. Soc. of Refractive Keratoplasty (bd. dirs. 1989-91), Castroviejo Soc. (bd. dirs. 1992-96), Cleve. Ophthalmol. Soc., Cleve. Ophthalmology Soc. (edn. com. 1982—), Phi Beta Kappa. Home: 33176 Woodleigh Rd Pepper Pike OH 44124 Office: U Hosps of Cleve 11100 Euclid Ave Cleveland OH 44106-5068

LASS, NORMAN JAY, speech science educator; b. N.Y.C., Sept. 20, 1943; s. Louis and Fay (Lerner) L.; m. Martha Irene Greenberger, Dec. 17, 1967; children: Laura Sheryl, Jonathan Ethan. BA, CUNY, 1965; MS, Purdue U., 1966, PhD, 1968. Postdoctoral rsch. fellow Bur. Child Rsch. U. Kans. Med. Ctr., Kansas City, 1968-69; asst. prof., assoc. prof., prof. speech pathology/audiology W.Va. U., Morgantown, 1969—. Author: 14 chpts. in books; editor 17 books; contbr. over 130 articles to profl. jours. Recipient Edn. Found. award Amoco, 1972, Outstanding Tchr. of 1987-88 award W.Va. U. chpt. Nat. Student Speech-Lang.-Hearing Assn., 1988, W.Va. U. Found. Award for Outstanding Teaching, 1991. Mem. Am. Speech-Lang.-Hearing Assn., Am. Assn. Phonetic Scis., Am. Cleft Palate-Craniofacial Assn., W.Va. Speech-Lang.-Hearing Assn., Acoustical Soc. Am., Phi Kappa Phi, Phi Delta Kappa (Outstanding Rsch. in Edn. award 1979). Jewish. Home: 1374 Braewick Dr Morgantown WV 26505-2702 Office: WVa U Dept Speech Pathology and Audiology PO Box 6122 Morgantown WV 26506-6122

LASSER, GAIL MARIA, psychologist, educator; b. Saddle River, N.J., Feb. 29, 1956; d. Dominick A. and Genevieve M. Sanzo; children: Michael, Jason, Jonathan. B.A., Seton Hall U., 1971; teaching cert. William Paterson Coll., 1973; M.A., Montclair State Coll., 1975; postgrad. Seton Hall U., 1977; cert. staff psychologist, N.J., 1977; lic. real estate agt., N.J.; notary pub. Public relations rep. European Health Spa, 1970-71; med. asst. Sci. Prevention and Rehab. Assn., 1973; grad. teaching and research asst. Montclair State Coll., 1973-74; clin. asst. Dr. Brower, 1974; instr. psychology Essex County Coll., 1976-77; clin. psychologist intern Community Mental Health Center, Mt. Carmel Guild, Newark, 1976-77; lectr. St. Michaels Med. Center-N.J. Coll. Medicine, 1977-80; instr. psychology Bergen Community Coll., Paramus, N.J., 1977—; asst. to ct. adminstr. Bergen County Cts., 1977-78; cons. telecom., 1994—. Active Am. Heart Assn. Mem. Am. Psychol. Assn., Am. Soc. for Psychical Research, Pi Lambda Theta, Psi Chi. Home: 7 Westwind Ct Saddle River NJ 07458-3211

LASSETER, KENNETH CARLYLE, pharmacologist; b. Jacksonville Fla., Aug. 12, 1942; s. James and Retta (Shad) L.; BS, Stetson U., 1963; MD, U. Fla., 1967; m. Kathy G. Marks, Aug. 6, 1977; children: Kenneth C. III, Susan, Frank L. Diplomate Am. Bd. Clin. Pharmacology. Intern, resident in medicine U. Ky. Med. Ctr., 1967-71; asst. prof., assoc. prof. pharmacology and medicine U. Miami Med. Sch., 1971-81, clin. assoc. prof., 1981—; adj. assoc. prof. pharmacology, Barry U., 1986—; v.p., dir. Clin. Pharmacology Assos., Inc., Miami, 1981—. Served with USAR, 1971-76. Recipient William B. Peck Sci. Rsch. award Interstate Postgrad. Med. Assn., 1976, rsch. award Alpha Omega Alpha, 1967. Fellow Am. Coll. Clin. Pharmacology; mem. ACP, Am. Soc. Pharmacology and Exptl. Therapeutics, Am. Soc. Clin. Pharmacology and Therapeutics, Sigma Xi. Republican. Contbr. articles to profl. jours. Home: 552 Ocean Dr Key Largo FL 33037-4345 Office: Clin Pharmacol Assocs 2060 NW 22nd Ave Miami FL 33142-7338

LASSITER, ANTHONY T., neurology; b. Vallejo, Calif., Apr. 13, 1955; s. Harvery G. and Ruby M. (Freeman) L.; m. Jeri J. Schmidt, Apr. 28, 1989; children: Alexis Nicole, Angela Camille, Amanda Patricia. MD, Howard U., 1977. Diplomate Am. Bd. Psychiatry & Neurology. Rsch. assoc. Lovelace Found., Albuquerque, 1982-88; from fellow to asst. prof. U. Pitts., 1989-92; asst. prof. Med. Coll. Ohio, Toledo, 1992-95; dir. Regional Epilepsy Ctr. Northwest Ohio, Toledo, 1996—; mem. bd. dirs. EFA NW Ohio, Toledo, 1993—. Mem. IEEE, Am. EEG Soc., Am. Acad. Neurology, Am. Epilepsy Soc. Office: Toledo Neurol Assoc 3949 Sunforest Ct Ste 105 Toledo OH 43623

LASSLO, ANDREW, medicinal chemist, educator; b. Mukacevo, Czechoslovakia, Aug. 24, 1922; came to U.S., 1946, naturalized, 1951; s. Vojtech Laszlo and Terezie (Herskovicova) L.; m. Wilma Ellen Reynolds, July 9, 1955; 1 child, Millicent Andrea. MS, U. Ill., 1948, PhD, 1952, MLS, 1961. Rsch. chemist organic chems. div. Monsanto Chem. Co., St. Louis, 1952-54; asst. prof. pharmacology, divsn. basic health scis. Emory U., 1954-60; prof. and chmn. dept. med. chemistry Coll. Pharmacy, U. Tenn. Health Sci. Ctr., 1960-90, Alumni Disting. Svc. prof. and chmn., dept. medicinal chemistry, 1989-90, professor emeritus, 1990—; cons. Geschickter Fund for Med. Research Inc., 1961-62; rsch. contractor U.S. Army Med. R & D Command, 1964-67; dir. postgrad. tng. program sci. librarians USPHS, 1966-72; chmn. edn. com. Drug Info. Assn., 1966-68, bd. dirs., 1968-69; dir. postgrad. tng. program organic medicinal chemistry for chemists FDA, 1971; exec. com. adv. council S.E. Regional Med. Library Program, Nat. Library of Medicine, 1969-71; chmn. regional med. library programs com. Med. Library Assn., 1971-72; mem. pres.'s faculty adv. council U. Tenn. System, 1970-72; chmn. energy authority U. Tenn. Center for Health Scis., 1975-77, chmn. council departmental chmn., 1977, 81; chmn. Internat. Symposium on Contemporary Trends in Tng. Pharmacologists, Helsinki, 1975. Producer, moderator (TV and radio series) Health Care Perspective, 1976-78; editor: Surface Chemistry and Dental Intequments, 1973, Blood Platelet Function and Medicinal Chemistry, 1984; contbr. numerous articles in sci. and profl. jours.; mem. editorial bd. Jour. Medicinal and Pharm. Chemistry, 1961, U. Tenn. Press, 1974-77; composer (work for piano) Synthesis in C Minor, 1968; patentee in field. Trustee 1st Bohemian Meth. Ch., Chgo., 1951-52, mem. bd. stewards, 1950-52; mem. ofcl. bd. Grace Meth. Ch., Atlanta, 1955-60; mem. adminstrv. bd. Christ United Meth. Ch., Memphis, 1964-72, 73-75, 77-79, 81-83, 88-90, chmn. commn. on edn., 1965-67, chmn. bd. Day Sch., 1967-68. 1st lt. USAR, 1953-57, capt., 1957-62. Recipient Research prize U. Ill. Med. Ctr. chpt. Sigma Xi, 1949, Honor Scroll Tenn. Inst. Chemists, 1976, Americanism medal DAR, 1976; U. Ill. fellow, 1950-51; Geschickter Fund Med. Research grantee, 1959-65, USPHS Research and Tng. grantee, 1958-64, 66-72, 82-89, NSF research grantee, 1964-66, Pfeiffer Research Found. grantee, 1981-87. Fellow AAAS, Am. Assn. Pharm. Scientists, Am. Inst. Chemists (nat. councilor for Tenn. 1969-70), Acad. Pharm. Rsch. and Sci.; mem. ALA (life), Am. Chem. Soc. (sr.), Am. Pharm. Assn., Am. Soc. Pharmacology and Exptl. Therapeutics (chmn. subcom. pre and postdoctoral tng. 1974-78, exec. com. ednl. and profl. affairs 1974-78), Sigma Xi (pres. elect U. Tenn. Ctr. for Health Sci. chpt. 1975-76, pres. 1976-77, Excellence in Rsch. award 1989), Beta Phi Mu, Phi Lambda Sigma, Rho Chi. Methodist. Home and Office: 5479 Timmons Ave Memphis TN 38119-6932

LAST, JOHN MURRAY, medical educator; b. Tailem Bend, Australia, Sept. 22, 1926; s. Raymond Jack and Vera Estelle (Judell) L.; m. Janet Margaret Wendelken, Feb. 14, 1957; children: Rebecca, David, Jonathan. MB, BS, U. Adelaide, Australia, 1949, MD, 1967; DPH, U. Sydney, Australia, 1960; MD (hon.), U. Uppsala, Sweden, 1993. Resident various hosps. and ship's dr., 1950-54; pvt. practice gen. medicine Australia, 1954-59; vis. fellow Med. Rsch. Coun., London, 1961-62; lectr. U. Sydney, 1962-63; asst. prof. U. Vt., Burlington, 1964-65; sr. lectr. U. Edinburgh, Scotland, 1965-69; prof. community medicine U. Ottawa, Ont., Can., 1969—, dept. chmn., 1970-78, sec. sch. medicine, 1980-82, prof. emeritus, 1992—; vis. prof. Mt. Sinai Sch. Medicine, N.Y.C., 1978-79, Nat. U. Singapore and Chinese Acad. Med. Scis., Beijing, 1982; past & present mem. various adv. coms. Fed., Ont. and U.S. Govtl. Agys.; cons., temporary advisor WHO, other internat. agys. Author: Public Health and Human Ecology, 1987; editor-in-chief Maxcy-Rosenau Public Health and Preventive Medicine, 11th edit., 1980, 12th edit., 1985, 13th edit., 1991; editor: A Dictionary of Epidemiology, 1983, 2d edit., 1988, 3d edit., 1995; assoc. editor Am. Jour. Preventive Medicine, 1984-92; sci. editor Can. Jur. Pub. Health, 1981-91; editor Annals Royal Coll. Physicians and Surgeons Can., 1990—; contbr. chpts. to 30 books, over 200 sci. and rev. articles to profl. jours. Recipient Tasmania prize Royal Australian Coll. Gen. Practice, 1967, Sch. of Medicine award for teaching excellence, 1988, U. Ottawa award of excellence, 1990. Fellow Am. Coll. Preventive Medicine (disting. svc. award 1984, spl. recognition award 1991), Royal Australian Coll. Physicians, Royal Coll. Physicians (Can.), Royal Coll. Physicians (U.K) (fellow of faculty of community medicine 1984—), Am. Coll. Epidemiology (Found. fellow), others; mem. APHA (Can. v.p. 1988-89), Can. Assn. Tchrs. Soc. Preventive Medicine (pres. 1973-74), Assn. Tchrs. Preventive Medicine (pres. 1983-84), Can. Pub. Health Assn. (bd. dirs. 1981-91), Internat. Epidemiol. Assn. (coun. mem. 1987-90), others. Home: 685 Echo Dr, Ottawa, ON Canada K1S 1P2 Office: 451 Smyth Rd, Ottawa, ON Canada K1H 8M5

LASTER, ATLAS, JR., psychologist; b. Canalou, Mo., Apr. 18, 1948; s. Atlas Sr. and Rose Ella (Brown) L.; m. Janet Lee Rowe, Aug. 22, 1973; Children: Cedric, Marcus, Rosa, Sophia, Leah, Rachel. Student, Wash. U., 1966-69; BD, Union Theology Sem., 1971; MEd, U. Pitts., 1973, PhD, 1976. Staff psychologist Mon-Yough Mental Health Svcs., McKeesport, Penn., 1975-76; cons. psychologist DePaul Health Ctr. Care Unit, Bridgeton, Mo., 1977; program dir. Dept. Corrections, Menard, Ill., 1978; mgmt. cons. Univ. Pk. Group, Palm Beach, Fla., 1980; counseling coord. So. Ill. U., 1981-82; mgr. Comprehensive Counseling and Cons. Svcs., Pitts., 1982-84; dir. of christian edn. Pilgrim Congl. Ch., St. Louis, 1985-86; cons. psychologist Div. of Family Svcs., St. Louis, 1986—; asst. prof. Psychology Mo. Bapt. Coll., St. Louis, 1991—; vocat. rehab. counselor Mo. Divsn. Vocat. Rehab., St. Louis, 1991-93; pvt. practice Clayton, Mo., 1993—; sr. cons. Hanley, Harsche, Roffman and Druch, St. Louis, 1979-80; cons. Dept. Mental Health, St. Louis, 1986—, St. Louis Pub. Schs., 1989—, Ill. Dept. Children and Family Svcs., East St. Louis, 1990—, Health Mgmt. Svcs. Am., East Detroit, Mich., 1990—, Divsn. Children and Family Svcs., Spokane, Wash., 1990—, Decatur, Ga., 1990—. Contbr. articles to profl. jours. Cons. Congress of Racial Equality St. Louis, 1987—. Diplomate Am. Bd. Diability Analysts (sr.); mem. APA, Nat. Assn. Sch. Psychologists, Mo. Psychol. Assn. Baptist. Home: PO Box 16693 Saint Louis MO 63105-1193 Office: Med West Bldg 950 Francis Pl Ste 201 Clayton MO 63105-2465

LASTER, RICHARD, biotechnology executive, consultant; b. Vienna, Austria, Nov. 10, 1923; came to U.S., 1940; naturalized, 1944; s. Alan and Caroline (Harband) L.; m. Liselotte Schneider, Oct. 17, 1948; children: Susan Laster Rubenstein, Thomas. Student U. Wash., 1941-42; BChE cum laude, Poly. Inst. Bklyn., 1943; postgrad. Stevens Inst. Tech., 1945-47. With Gen. Foods Corp., 1944-82, corp. rsch. and devel., Hoboken, N.J., 1944-58, ops. mgr. Franklin Baker divsn., Hoboken, N.J., Atlantic Gelatin divsn., Woburn, Mass., 1958-64, mgr. rsch. devel. Jell-O divsn., White Plains, N.Y., 1958-64, corp. mgr. quality assurance, White Plains, 1964-67, ops. mgr. Maxwell House divsn., White Plains, 1967-68, exec. v.p. Maxwell House divsn., 1968-69, pres. Maxwell House divsn., 1969-71, corp. group v.p., White Plains, 1971-73, exec. v.p. Gen. Foods Corp., 1974-82, also dir., rsch., devel. and food-away-from-home, 1975-82; bd. dirs. DNA Plant Tech. Corp., 1982-94, chmn., 1988-94, CEO, 1982-92, pres. 1982-91; mgmt. cons., 1994—; bd. dirs. RiceTec, Peptor Ltd.; mem. sch. bd. Chappaqua, N.Y., 1971-74, pres., 1973-74; chmn., mem. bd., 1st v.p. United Way of Westchester, 1978; chmn. adv. com. Poly. Inst. Westchester, 1977; trustee Poly. Inst. N.Y.,1978—; mem. coll. coun. SUNY, Purchase, Purchase Coll. Found, 1986—; mem. corp. N.Y. Botanical Garden; mem. subcom. Export Adminstrn. Pres.'s Export Coun., 1995; chmn. Westchester Edn. Coalition, 1992—; dir. Westchester Holocaust Commn., 1994; chmn. Am. Soc. of Plant Physiologists Edn. Found., 1995; mem. New Castle Town Bd. Recipient Disting. Alumnus award. Fellow Poly. Inst. N.Y. Mem. AAAS, N.Y. Acad. Scis., AIChE (Food and Bioengring. award 1972), Am. Chem. Soc., Am. Inst. Chemists, Tau Beta Pi, Phi Lambda Upsilon. Contbr. articles on food sci. to profl. publs. Patentee in field. Home: 23 Round Hill Rd Chappaqua NY 10514-1622 Office: Richard Laster 103 S Bedford Rd Mount Kisco NY 10549-3440

LASTRA, JOSE RAMON, plant virologist, eductor; b. Orense, Spain, May 22, 1939; arrived in Venezuela, 1954, naturalized; s. Ramon and Maria (Rodriguez) L.; m. Ana Maria Mumm, Mar. 3, 1953; children, Ricardo, Daniel, Eduardo, Andres. Degree in Biology, U. Cent. Venezuela, 1966; MSc in Plant Pathology, U. Calif., Berkeley, 1970, PhD in Plant Pathology, 1974. Head plant virus lab IVIC, Caracas, 1974-85; prof. U. Cen. Venezuela, Caracas, 1976-85; head molecular biology lab. CATIE, 1980-87; coord. IPM project CATIE, Turrialba, Costa Rica, 1985-86; dir. ednl. programs CATIE, 1986-94; dir. edn. and capacity bldg. World Wide Fund for Nature-Internat., Gland, Switzerland, 1994—; cons. in field. Mem. Am. Phytopathol. Soc. (pres. Caribbean divsn. 1978), Soc. Latinoamericana de Fitopatologos, Soc. Venezolana de Fitopatologia, N.Am. Assn. Environ. Educators, Phi Beta Kappa. Roman Catholic. Office: WWF-Int, Ave de Montblanc, 1196 Gland Switzerland

LASZLO, IVAN JOZSEF, psychiatrist; b. Budapest, Hungary, Aug. 26, 1924; came to U.S., 1957; s. Sandor and Ilona (Griesz) L.; m. Veronika Eva Steiner, Sept. 26, 1955; children: Ildiko, Victoria. MD, Budapest Med. Sch., 1951. Diplomate Am. Bd. Psychiatry and Neurology. Dir. pre-sch. program E.P. Bradley Hosp., East Providence, R.I., 1961-69, dir. inpatient program, 1969-76; dir. Mental Health Program, Clifton Springs, N.Y., 1976-85; dir. of outpatient Beth Isreal, Newark, 1985-95; clin. asst. prof. Brown U. Med. Sch., Providence, 1970-76; clin. assoc. prof. Rochester Med. Sch., Rochester, N.Y., 1976—; pvt. practice, 1995—. Author: The Choice, 1971, Malmond, 1995; contbr. articles to profl. publs. Fellow Am. Psychiat. Assn., Am. Orthopsychiat. Assn., Am. Humanistic Psychology. Democrat. Office: Beth Israel Med Ctr 2130 Millburn Ave Maplewood NJ 07040

LASZLO, JOSEPH, physician, educator; b. Cuci, Mures, Romania, Feb. 12, 1932; s. Joseph and Anna (Nagy) L.; m. Alla Grigorievna Gridneva, Nov. 20, 1955; children: Joseph, Olga. Cert. physician, 1st Med. Inst., Moscow, 1957; D in Med. Sci., U. Medicine, Bucharest, Romania, 1973. Asst. Dept. Physiology, U. Medicine and Pharmacy, Targu-Mures, Romania, 1957-80, asst. prof., 1980-89, prof., head, 1990—; mem. senate U. Medicine and Pharmacy, Targu-Mures, 1990—, prodean, 1991-93. Author: The Regulatory Mechanisms of The Human Organism, 1981, The Metabolism and Energetics of The Human Organism, 1985; contbr. articles to profl. jours.; inventor in field. Mem. Hungarian Med. Assn. Am., EME-Med. Sci. Soc. (v.p. 1992—), Bolyai Soc. (bd. dirs. 1990—). Mem. Hungarian Dem. Party in Romania. Office: U Medicine and Pharmacy, Str Marinescu 38, 4300 Targu-Mures Romania

LATCHIS, KENNETH SPERO, emergency physician; b. Brattleboro, Vt., July 5, 1935; s. Spero Demetrius and Angelika (Katsimanis) L.; m. Erika Mechthild Daucher, June 25, 1966; children: Mark T., Christine A., Ingrid K. AB, Brown U., 1957; MD, U. Vt., 1961. Diplomate Am. Bd. Surgery, Am. Bd. Emergency Medicine. Intern George Washington U. Hosp. Med. Ctr., Washington, 1961-62, resident in gen. surgery, 1964-69; fellow in gen. surgery Lahey Clinic, Boston, 1969-70; pvt. practice Fairfax, Va., 1970-77; attending emergency physician Newport (R.I.) Hosp., 1977-83, dir. emergency dept., 1979-83; attending emergency physician R.I. Hosp., Providence, 1983-85; attending emergency physician Washington (D.C.) Hosp. Ctr., 1985—, assoc. dir. emergency dept., 1989-95; tumor bd. dirs. Fairfax Hosp., Falls Church, Va., 1970-77; clin. instr. surgery Georgetown U., Washington, 1971-77; clin. instr. surgery Brown U., Providence, 1983-85; instr. mil. medicine Uniformed Svcs. U. for Health Scis., Bethesda, MD., 1989—. Contbr. articles to profl. jours. Capt. USAF, 1962-64. Fellow Am. Coll. Surgeons, Am. Coll. Emergency Physicians, Southeastern Surg. Congress. Lutheran. Office: Washington Hosp Ctr 110 Irving St NW Washington DC 20010-2931

LATHAM, PATRICIA S., physician; b. Annapolis, Md., Aug. 22, 1946. BS, Simmons Coll., 1968; MD, U. So. Calif., 1972. Intern Yale-New Haven Hosp., 1972-73, resident, 1973-75, fellow in hepatology, 1975-78; resident in anatomic pathology U. Toronto (Can.) Hosp., 1978-80; asst. prof. pathology and medicine U. Md., 1981-88, Nat. Cancer Inst., 1988-90; asst. prof. pathology and medicine George Washington U., 1990-92, assoc. prof. pathology and medicine, 1992—. Office: George Wash U 2300 I St NW Washington DC 20001

LATHROP, CAROLINE B., nurse, quality management administrator; b. Toledo, Ohio, Oct. 30, 1957; d. David M. and Basima (Sadaka) Bassett; m. Clifford Lathrop III, Aug. 12, 1989. BSN, U. Toledo, 1979; MSN, Med. Coll. Ohio, Toledo, 1984. RN; cert. health care profl.; cert. adult nurse practitioner. Staff nurse N.C. U. Hosp., Chapel Hill, 1979-80; nurse, dir. nursing Staff Builders, Toledo, 1980-82; instr. Med. Coll. Ohio/Mercy Sch. Nursing, Toledo, 1982-84, Ariz. State U., Tempe, 1985-89; mgr. quality rev. St. Joseph's Hosp., Phoenix, 1989-93; quality dir. Phoenix Bapt. Hosp., 1993—; nurse cons. to legal firms, Phoenix, 1989—. Contbr. articles to profl. jours. Mem. Sigma Theta Tau.

LATIMER, MARGARET PETTA, nutrition and dietetics educator; b. Sacramento, Aug. 17, 1932; d. Rosario and Helen (Sclafani) Petta; m. Westford Ramos Latimer, June 18, 1978. BS, U. Calif., Berkeley, 1954; MA, Calif. State U., Sacramento, 1982. Registered dietitian, Calif.; life teaching credential, Calif. Therapeutic dietitian U. Calif. Med. Ctr., San Francisco, 1955-65; dietitian Roseville (Calif.) Community Hosp., 1966-67, Mercy San Juan Hosp., Carmichael, Calif., 1967-69; substitute tchr. San Juan Unified Sch. Dist., Sacramento, 1970-75, tchr. adult edn., 1971-74; instr. dietetics American River Coll., Sacramento, 1975-77, San Joaquin Delta Coll., Stockton, Calif., 1975-95; cons. dietitian, Sacramento, 1973-78. Mem. Am. Dietetic Assn., Nutrition Today, Calif. Dietetic Assn. (pres. Golden Empire dist. 1974-75), AAUW (gourmet chmn. 1981-82, editor AAUW Book of Favorite Recipes 1982), SOc. Nutrition Edn. Republican. Roman Catholic.

LATMAN, STEPHEN FREDERICK, orthopedic surgeon; b. Phila., Dec. 27, 1942; s. B. Bernard and Sara (Sklaroff) ; m. Carrie B. Capell, June 9, 1968; children: Joshua L., Robyn E. BS, Muhlenberg Coll., 1964; MD, Temple U., 1968. Diplomate Am. Bd. Orthopedic Surgery. Intern Reading (Pa.) Hosp., 1968-69, resident, 1969-70, 72-75; pvt. practice Winter Orthopedic Clinic, Lancaster, Pa., 1975-76, Reading, Pa., 1976-78, Reading Orthopedic Assocs., West Lawn, Pa., 1978—. Maj. USAF, 1968-77. Mem. AMA, Am. Acad. Orthopedic Surgeons, Pa. Med. Soc., Berks County Med. Soc., Phi Delta Epsilon. Office: Reading Orthopedic Assocs 2130 Penn Ave West Lawn PA 19609

LATTA, GEORGE HAWORTH, III, neonatologist; b. Chattanooga, Sept. 4, 1960; s. George Haworth Jr. and Charlotte (Major) L. BS in Physics, Ga. Inst. Tech., 1982; MD in Medicine, East Tenn. State U., 1986. Cert. in pediats., neonatology. Intern, resident in pediats. Dartmouth (N.H.) U., 1986-88; resident in pediats. Stanford (Calif.) U., 1988-89; fellow in neonatology Vanderbilt U., Nashville, 1989-90, U. Tenn., Memphis, 1990-92; attending neonatologist Rose Med. Ctr., Denver, 1992-94, Forrest Gen. Hosp., Hattiesburg, Miss., 1994-95, Meth. Hosps., Memphis, 1995—. NIH pulmonary trainee grantee Vanderbilt U., 1989; March of Dimes scholar East Tenn. State U., 1984, Johnny J. Jones scholar, 1981. Fellow Am. Acad. Pediats.; mem. Memphis Med. Soc., Shelby County Med. Soc., Phi Eta Sigma. Roman Catholic. Home: # 1002 10 N Main St Memphis TN 38103 Office: Meth Hosps of Memphis 1265 Union Ave Memphis TN 38104

LATTA, WILLIAM ATHERTON, medical group administrator; b. Oakland, Calif., Dec. 20, 1941; s. Lynn Meredith and Irva Louise (Dale) L.; m. Janet Garland Wilson, Aug. 10,. 1963; children: Courtney Lynn, Casey Brooke. BA, Whitman Coll., 1963; MBA, U. Pa., 1965. Asst. adminstr. The Portland (Oreg.) Clinic, 1969-72; adminstr. Meml. Clinic Ltd., P.S., Olympia, Wash., 1972—. Pres. North St. Assn., Olympia, Wash., 1980-82. Capt. USAF, 1966-69. Mem. Med. Group Mgmt. Assn., Am. Med. Group Assn., Wash. Med. Group Mgmt. Assn. (pres. 1979-80), Rotary Club (pres. Olympia, Wash., 1990-91). Episcopalian. Office: Meml Clinic Ltd PS 500 Lilly Rd NE Olympia WA 98506-5102

LATTIMER, JOHN KINGSLEY, physician, educator; b. Mt. Clemens, Mich., Oct. 14, 1914; s. Eugene and Gladys Soulier (Lenfestey) L.; m. Jamie Elizabeth Hill, Jan. 1948; children: Evan, Jon, Gary. AB, Columbia U., 1935, MD, 1938, ScD, 1943; student, Balliol Coll., Oxford (Eng.) U., 1944, Med. Field Svc. Sch., Paris, 1945. Diplomate Am. Bd. Urology. Surg. intern Meth.-Episcopal Hosp., N.Y.C., 1938-40; urol. resident Squier Urol. Clinic Presbyn. Hosp., N.Y.C., 1940-43, dir. Squier Urol. Clinic, 1955-80, dir. urol. svc., 1955-80, also dir. urology Sch. Nursing; staff asst., instr. urology Columbia Coll. Physicians and Surgeons, 1940-53, asst. prof. clin. urology, 1953-55, prof. urology, chmn. dept. urology, 1955-80; vis. prof. Med. Coll. S.C., Med. Coll. Va., Mayo Clinic Med. Sch., Rochester, Minn., 1977, Boston U., Tufts U., U. Oreg., Ind. U., UCLA, Leeds Med. Sch. U. Witwatersrand, South Africa; guest lectr. Akron City Hosp., 1977, Reno Surg. Soc., 1977; chief urology Babies Hosp., Vanderbilt Clinic, Frances Delafield Hosp., N.Y.C., 1955; cons. urology VA, N.Y.C., 1947-80, USPHS Hosp., S.I., N.Y.C., Meth. Hosp., Bklyn., Englewood (N.J.), Yonkers (N.Y.) gen. hosps., Harlem, Roosevelt, St. Lukes hosps. (all N.Y.C.); mem. com. surgery in Tb, genito-urinary Tb, VA; med. cons. Time mag.; cons. to com. on therapy Nat. Tb Assn.; mem. expert adv. panel biology human reprodn. WHO; mem. N.Y. Supreme Ct. Med. Arbitration Panel, 1975; Am. Urol. Assn. rep. to NRC-Nat. Acad. Scis.; mem. tng. grants com. NIH, 1968-72. Contbr. over 350 articles on urology and history to various publs., also chpts. in books; guest author New Eng. Jour. Medicine; rschr., writer, speaker on assassinations of Pres. Lincoln and Kennedy, and Nuremberg Trials. Trustee Presbyn. Hosp., 1974-78; mem. vis. com. Ft. Ticonderoga Mus.; mem. vis. com. sect. arms and armour Met. Mus. Art, 1978, Abraham Lincoln U., Harrogate, Tenn.; chmn. book com. Englewood Hist. Soc., 1984—; mem. Dallas Coun. World Affairs, Phila. Coun. World Affairs; ofcl. historian City of Englewood, N.J. Maj. M.C., AUS, 1943-46; med. officer at Nuremberg Trials, 1945-46. Decorated Croix de Guerre (France and Belgium); recipient Joseph Mather Smith prize for kidney disease rsch. Columbia U., 1943, honor award for meritorious work in field Tb, Am. Acad. Tb Physicians, also prizes for sci. exhibits, gold medal Coll. Physicians and

Surgeons Alumni Assn., 1971, Disting. Svc. award, 1993, Hugh Young medal for outstanding work in infectious diseases, 1973, Belfield medal Chgo. Urol. Soc., Burpeau medal N.J. Acad. Medicine, Edward Henderson gold medal Am. Geriat. Soc., 1978, Gt. medal City of Paris, 1979, Normandy Liberation medal Soc. French War Vets., Paris Liberation medal French Govt., medal Nat. Kidney Fedn., 1987, Am. Acad. Pediatric Urology, 1987; Richard Chute lectr., 1973, Stoneburner lectr. Med. Coll. Va., 1973. Fellow ACS (chmn. adv. com. urology 1962-64, gov. 1966-79, com. on undergrad. tng. 1967-80, chmn. nominating com. 1976-77, com. to study size and composition of bd. govs.), AMA (prize rsch. kidney Tb 1953), Am. Acad. Pediatrics (chmn. com. on pediatric urology, pres. sect. urology 1973-79); mem. AAAS, Am. Assn. Clin. Urologists, Assn. Am. Med. Colls., Clin. Soc. Genito-Urinary Surgeons (pres. 1984), N.Y. Acad. Sci. (trustee), N.Y. Acad. Medicine (chmn. genito-urinary surg. sect. 1956-57, trustee 1978-84, v.p. 1986-87, chmn. bldg. com. 1982-87), Am. Assn. Genito-Urinary Surgeons (pres. 1982), Am. Urol. Assn. (pres. 1975-76, chmn. com. on pediatric urology, pres. N.Y. sect. 1966, exec. com. 1967-80, com. on surgery, rev. and long range planning com., editorial bd. Jour. Urology 1965-68, chmn. com. to gather info. about urology, chmn. coordinating coun. for urology, chmn. nominating com. 1976-77, 1st prize for clin. rsch. 1950, 60, Ramon Guiterez medal 1980, Keyes medal 1996), Am. Thoracic Soc., AAUP, Soc. U. Urologists (pres. 1969), Nat. Inst. Social Scis., St. Nicholas Soc., Assn. Mil. Surgeons Harvey Soc., Nat. Tb ssn., N.Y. State Pediatrics Soc., N.Y. Med. Socs., New York County Med. Soc., Soc. Pediatric Urology (pres. 1961-62), Brit. Assn. Urol. Surgeons (corr.), N.Y. Soc. Surgeons, N.Y. Soc. Professions, Internationale Société d'Urology (v.p. 1967-73, pres.1973-79), Assn. Pediatric Urology (pres. 1961), Spanish Urol. Assn. (hon.), Paleopathology Assn., Charles A. Lindbergh Soc. (ofcl. historian City of Englewood 1990), Dallas Surgical Soc., Japanese Urol. Assn. (hon.), Italian Urol. Assn. (hon.), SAR, Assn. Mil. Historians, Soc. War 1812, Mil. Order Fgn. Wars U.S., Order of Founders and Patriots, Arms and Armour Soc. N.Y., Arms and Armour Soc. Eng., Arms and Armour Soc. Gueurnsey, Soc. Colonial Wars, Englewood Hist. Soc., Manuscript Soc., Revolutionary War Round Table of N.Y., Abraham Lincoln Soc., Lincoln Soc. N.Y., Wis., Ill., Fla., Washington, Civil War Surgeons (hon.), Am. Legion, 82d Airborne Div. Assn., 101st Airborne Div. Assn., Res. Officers Assn., Metropolitan Club, Sigma Xi. Office: Columbia U Med Sch New York NY 10032

LAUBSCHER, LEEANN, medical and surgical nurse; b. Monticello, N.Y., Apr. 24, 1962; d. Lee Gregory Baumgardt and Carole Ann (Blume) Nicolis; m. Robert Francis Laubscher, Aug. 16, 1986. BS in Nursing, Mt. St. Mary Coll., Newburgh, N.Y., 1984; MS in Nursing, SUNY, New Paltz, 1996. RN, N.Y.; cert. med.-surg. nurse. Staff nurse Westchester County Med. Ctr., Valhalla, N.Y., 1984-90; staff nurse Castle Point (N.Y.) VA Med. Ctr., 1990—, nurse mgr. ICU, 1992, women vets. coord., 1995—; breast cancer detection awareness educator Am. Cancer Soc., N.Y., 1995—; cmty. educator LENS (Linking Edn., Nursing and Seniors) Project, N.Y. State Nurses Assn., 1995—. Mem. N.Y. State Nurses Assn. Capital Dist. #9. Office: Castle Point VA Med Ctr Castle Point NY 12511

LAUCKS, SAMUEL S., physician; b. York, Pa., June 3, 1955. MD, Jefferson Med. Coll., 1981. Diplomate Am. Bd. Surgery, Am. Bd. Colon and Rectal Surgery. Active staff York (Pa.) Hosp., 1987—; chmn. bd. York Health Plan. Fellow Am. Coll. Surgeons, Am. Soc. Colon and Rectal Surgeon; mem. AMA.

LAUER, RONALD MARTIN, pediatric cardiologist, researcher; b. Winnipeg, Man., Can., Feb. 18, 1930; m. Eileen Pearson, Jan. 12, 1959; children: Geoffrey, Judith Lauer. BS, U. Man., 1953, MD, 1954. Diplomate Am. Bd. Pediatrics. Asst. prof. pediatrics U. Pitts., 1960-61; asst. prof. pediatrics U. Kans., 1961-67, assoc. prof. pediatrics, 1967-68; prof. pediatrics, dir. pediatrics cardiology U. Iowa, 1968—, vice chmn. pediatrics, 1974-82, prof. pediatrics and preventive medicine 1980—. Home: RR 6 Iowa City IA 52240-9806 Office: U Iowa Coll Medicine Div Pediatric Cardiology Iowa City IA 52242

LAUFER, IRA JEROME, physician; b. N.Y.C., Mar. 29, 1928; s. Irving and Evelyn (Weisman) L.; m. Barbara Alfandari, July 10, 1955; children: Tina, David. BA, NYU, 1948; MD, NYU Sch. Medicine, 1953. Diplomate Am. Bd. Internal Medicine. Instr. clin. medicine NYU Sch. Medicine, N.Y.C., 1959-69, asst. prof. clin. medicine, 1969-83, clin. assoc. prof. medicine, 1983—; dir. diabetes svc. Cabrini Med. Ctr., N.Y.C., 1966-89; dir. medicine N.Y. Eye and Ear Infirmary, N.Y.C., 1978-91; med. dir. Diabetes Treatment Ctr., N.Y.C., 1985-92; physician-in-charge Diabetes Treatment Program, N.Y.C., 1992—; attending physician Cabrini Med. Ctr., N.Y.C., 1989—; assoc. attending physician NYU Med. Ctr., 1983—; lectr. and cons. in field. Co-author: Diabetes Explained, 1976. Capt. USAF, 1955-57, Korea. Recipient Svc. award Am. Diabetes Assn., 1990. Fellow Am. Coll. Clin. Pharmacology, Am. Coll. Endocrinology; mem. ACP. Office: 247 3rd Ave New York NY 10010-7457

LAUFER, NATHAN, cardiologist; b. Montreal, Mar. 12, 1953; came to U.S., 1981; s. Jack and Pearl (Brachfeld) L.; m. Judy Franceska Egett, Sept. 2, 1986; 1 child, Andrew. DCS, McGill U., 1972, MD, 1977. Diplomate Nat. Bd. Med. Examiners, Am. Bd. Internal Medicine; cert. Profl. Corp. Physicians Que. Intern, resident U. Toronto, Can., 1977-81; fellow cardiology U. Mich., Ann Arbor, 1981-83, faculty dept. cardiology, 1983-84; cardiologist Affiliated Cardiologists, Phoenix, 1984—; dir. coronary care Good Samaritan Hosp., Phoenix, 1986-92; clin. asst. prof. medicine, U. Ariz., Tucson, 1986—; pres. Cardiovascular Soc., Phoenix, 1986—; vis. prof. Chigasaki Tokushu-kai Med. Ctr., Kanagawa-ken, Japan, 1988, Leningrad Postgrad. Med. Inst., St. Petersburg, Russia, 1991. Contbr. articles to profl. jours. Fellow ACP, Am. Coll. Cardiology, Am. Coll. Chest Physicians, Royal Coll. Physicians and Surgeons Can.; mem. AMA, N.Am. Soc. Pacing and Electrophysiology, Soc. Cardiac Angiography and Intervention, Am. Assn. Nuclear Cardiology, Am. Heart Assn. (pres.-elect Ariz. affiliate), Ariz. Med. Assn., Can. Cardiovascular Soc., Maricopa County Med. Assn., Cardiovascular Soc. Ariz. (founder, pres.). Home: 9100 N 55th St Paradise Valley AZ 85253 Office: Affiliated Cardiologists 370 E Virginia Phoenix AZ 85004

LAUFMAN, HAROLD, surgeon; b. Milw., Jan. 6, 1912; s. Jacob and Sophia (Peters) L.; m. Marilyn Joselit, 1940 (dec. 1963); children: Dionne Joselit Weigert, Laurien Laufman Kogut; m. June Friend Moses, 1980. BS, U. Chgo., 1932; MD, Rush Med. Coll., 1937; MS in Surgery, Northwestern U., Chgo., 1946, PhD, 1948. Diplomate: Am. Bd. Surgery. Intern Michael Reese Hosp., Chgo., 1936-39; resident in gen. surgery St. Marks Hosp., London, Northwestern U. Med. Sch., Cook County Hosp., Hines VA Hosp., 1939-46; mem. faculty Northwestern U., 1941-65; from clin. asst. to prof., attending surgeon Passavant Meml. Hosp., Chgo., 1953-65; prof. surgery, history of medicine Albert Einstein Coll. Medicine, N.Y.C., 1965-82, prof. emeritus, 1982—; dir. Inst. Surg. Studies, Montefiore Hosp. and Med. Center, Bronx, N.Y., 1965-81; pvt. practice gen. and vascular surgery Chgo., 1941-65, N.Y.C., 1965-81; ret. professorial lectr. surgery Mt. Sinai Sch. Medicine, N.Y.C., 1979-83, emeritus, 1983—; attending surgeon Mt. Sinai Hosp., N.Y.C., 1979-83; cons., lectr. in field; chmn. FDA Classification Panel Gen. and Plastic Surgery Devices, 1975-78; pres. Harold Laufman Assocs., Inc., 1977—, sr. ptnr., 1988—; pres. HLA Systems. Author: (with S.W. Banks) Surgical Exposures of the Extremities, 1953, 2d edit., 1986, (with R.B. Erichson) Hematologic Problems in Surgery, 1970, Hospital Special Care Facilities, 1981, The Veins, 1986; chmn. editorial bd.: Diagnostica, 1974-79; mem. editorial bd.: Surgery, Gynecology and Obstetrics, 1974-92, Infection Control, 1980-88, Med. Instrumentation, 1972-83, Med. Rsch. Engring., 1972-79; contbr. articles to sci. publs. Chmn. bd. dirs. N.Y. Chamber Soloists, 1974-80, Chamber Music Conf. and Composers Forum of the East, 1975-91. Maj. AUS, 1942-46. Named Disting. Alumnus Rush Med. Coll., 1993. Fellow ACS; mem. Assn. Advancement Med. Instrumentation (pres. 1974-75, chmn. bd. 1976-77), Am. Assn. Hosp. Cons., Am. Med. Writers Assn. (pres. 1968-69), Am. Surg. Assn., Société Internationale de Chirurgie, Western Surg. Assn., Cen. Surg. Assn., N.Y. Surg. Soc., Soc. Vascular Surgery, Internat. Cardiovascular Soc., Soc. Surgery Alimentary Tract, Surg. Infection Soc. (councillor 1980-84), Sigma Xi, Alpha Omega Alpha, Phi Sigma Delta, Zeta Beta Tau. Jewish. Clubs: Standard (Chgo.); Harmonie (N.Y.C.); Willow Ridge Country (Harrison, N.Y.). Home and Office: 31 E 72nd St New York NY 10021-4146

LAUFMAN, LESLIE RODGERS, hematologist, oncologist; b. Pitts., Dec. 13, 1946; d. Marshall Charles and Ruth Rodgers; m. Harry B. Laufman, Apr. 25, 1970 (div. Apr. 1984); children: Hal, Holly; m. Rodger Mitchell, Oct. 9, 1987. BA in Chemistry, Ohio Wesleyan U., 1968; MD, U. Pitts., 1972. Diplomate Am. Bd. Internal Medicine and Hematology. Intern Montefiore Hosp., Pitts., 1972-73, resident in internal medicine, 1973-74; fellow in hemotology and oncology Ohio State Hosp., Columbus, 1974-76; dir. med. oncology Grant Med. Ctr., Columbus, 1977-92; practice medicine specializing in hematology and oncology Columbus, 1977—; bd. dirs. Columbus Cancer Clinic; prin. investigator Columbus Cmty. Clin. Oncology Program, 1989—. Contbr. articles to profl. jours. Mem. AMA, Am. Women Med. Assn. (sec./treas. 1985-86, pres. 1986-87), Am. Soc. Clin. Oncology, Southwest Oncology Group, Nat. Surg. Adjuvant Project for Breast and Bowel Cancers. Office: 393 E Town St # 109 Columbus OH 43215-4741 also: 8100 Ravine'S Edge Ct Worthington OH 43235

LAUHIO, ANNELI RITVA, physician; b. Turku, Jan. 30, 1959; s. Kosti and Jenny (Friberg) L. MD, U. Helsinki, 1985, PhD, 1995. Jr. and sr. house officer, acting assoc. head Divsn. of Internal Medicine, Aurora Hosp., Helsinki, 1986-89; sr. house officer, acting assoc. head Divsn. of Internal Medicine, Aurora Hosp., 1991-93; lectr. in microbiology, infectious diseases, pub. health U. Helsinki, 1986—; rschr. dept. bacteriology/immunology, cons. in pub. health Acad. of Finland, 1989-91; rsch. fellow, house officer Helsinki U. Ctrl. Hosp., 1993-94; sr. house officer dept. internal medicine Lahti Ctrl. Hosp., 1995; sr. house officer divsn. internal medicine Helsinki U. Ctrl. Hosp., 1996—; rschr. dept. bacteriology and immunology U. Helsinki, U. Ctrl. Hosp. of Helsinki, Aurora Hosp., Helsinki, 1986—, acting cons. in tropical medicine Finland Aurora Hosp., 1986-89, 91-93. Contbr. articles to profl. jours. Recipient Award Finnish Med. Rsch. Found., 1989, Finnish Cultural Assn., 1991, Med. Assn. Duodecim, 1993. Mem. AAAS, Finnish Kennel Club, Finnish Med. Assn., Finnish Med. Assn. Duodecim, Finnish Connective Tissue Rsch. Assn., Infectious Disease Rsch. Assn., Finnish Rheumatism Assn., N.Y. Acad. Scis. Home: Tehtaankatu 6B 17, 00140 Helsinki Finland Office: U Helsinki Dept Bacteriology/Immunol, Haartmaninkatu 3, 00290 Helsinki Finland

LAUMANN, ANNE ELIZABETH, dermatologist; b. Beaconsfield, Bucks, Eng., Jan. 31, 1946; came to U.S. 1976; d. Richard M. and Suzanne Marie (Weisman) Solomon; m. Edward Otto Laumann, June 21, 1980; children: Christopher Richard, Timothy Otto. MB. ChB, Birmingham Med. Sch., Eng., 1968. Diplomate Am. Bd. Dermatology. Resident in dermatology U. Chgo., 1977-79; asst. prof. dermatology U. Ill., Chgo., 1980-85; clin. asst. prof. U. Chgo., 1987-90; clin. practice dermatology Group Practice South Side Chgo., 1979—, Michael Reese Hosp. Health Plan now Humana HMO, 1986—; clin. asst. prof. dermatology U. Ill., Chgo., 1990—; interim divsn. dir. dermatology Michael Reese Hosp., Chgo., 1995—; mem. various coms. Michael Reese Hosp., Humana HMO. Fellow Am. Acad. Dermatology; mem. Royal Coll. Physicians, Brit. Assn. Dermatology, Am. Women's Dermatology Assn., Chgo. Dermatology Soc., Ill. Dermatology Soc., Am. Soc. of Psychocutaneous Medicine. Episcopalian. Home: 6754 S Euclid Ave Chicago IL 60649 Office: Michael Reese Hosp 2816 S Ellis Chicago IL 60649

LAU-PATTERSON, MAYIN, psychotherapist; b. N.Y.C., May 13, 1940; d. Justin S. and Susan (Lee) Lau; m. Oscar H. L. Bing, Dec. 26, 1962 (div. Dec. 1974); children: David C., Michael H.; m. Michael Morrow Patterson, Nov. 8, 1989. BA, Goucher Coll., 1962; MA, George Washington U., 1966; postgrad., Boston Coll., 1977. Lic. psychologist, Mass.; lic. profl. counselor, Tex.; diplomate in managed mental health care; chem. dependency specialist, marriage and family therapist, criminal justice specialist; compulsive gambling counselor, hypnotherapist, Tex.; cert. criminal justice specialist. Psychologist children's unit Met. State Hosp., Waltham, Mass., 1966-67, clin. psychologist, 1967-68, prin. psychologist, 1968-70, chief psychologist, 1970-76; chief psychologist South Cove Community Health Ctr., Boston, 1976-78; pvt. practice Newton, Mass., 1974-78, Gateway Counseling, Framington, Mass., 1975-78, Alamo Mental Health, San Antonio, 1978-92, The Patterson Relationship and Counseling Ctr., San Antonio, 1992—; clin. instr. psychology Dept. Psychiatry Harvard U. Med. Sch., Cambridge, MAss., 1974-76; instr. Tufts New Eng. Med. Ctr. Hosp., Boston, 1975-78; presenter Am. Acad. Child Psychiatry, 1973, 74. Contbr. articles to profl. jours. Office: Ste 200 3510 N St Marys St Ste 200 San Antonio TX 78212-3164

LAURENO, ROBERT, neurologist; b. Cleve., Mar. 2, 1945; s. Raymond Rudolph and Reva (Gelb) L.; m. Karen Jayne Knoller, July 13, 1969; children: Caroline, Rachel, Meredith. AB, Cornell U., 1967, MD, 1971. From asst. prof. to prof. George Washington U., Washington, 1977—; chmn. dept. neurology Washington Hosp. Ctr., 1977—. Contbr. articles to profl. jours. With USPHS, 1972-74. Grantee Medlantic Rsch. Found. Fellow Am. Assn. for Electrodiagnosis, Am. Acad. Neurology; mem. Am. Neurol. Assn. Office: Washington Hosp Ctr 110 Irving St NW Washington DC 20010-2931

LAURY, GABRIEL VERNET, psychiatrist, educator; b. Paris, May 18, 1932; s. Eric and Erna (Steinitz) L.; m. Marjorie Gurfein, Apr. 23, 1963; children: Daniel, Joel, Valerie. BA, Paris Med. Sch., 1956. Diplomate Am. Bd. Psychiatry and Neurology. Assoc. prof. psychiatry N.Y. Sch. Psychiatry, N.Y.C., 1964-69; instr. assoc. clin. psychiatry Columbia U. Physicians and Surgeons Coll., N.Y.C., 1969-72; asst. prof. clin. psychiatry SUNY, Stony Brook, 1970-73, assoc. prof., 1973-83; assoc. prof. clin. psychiatry N.Y. Med. Coll., Valhalla, N.Y., 1983—; chief psychiatrist ICU Franklin D. Roosevelt Hosp., Montrose, N.Y., 1983—; assoc. instr. clin. psychiatry Columbia U. Coll. Physicians and Surgeons. Author: Comment Vivre Sa Sexualite, 1979, Comovivirm 1980; bd. editors Jour. Cahiers Sexualite, 1973—, Jour. Psychiat. Treatment, 1980-83, Medicine and Hygiene, 1968—; contbr. over 250 articles to med. jours. French Alliance, 1964-83. Maj. USMC, 1967-74, with USAR. Fellow Am. Psychiat. Assn. (pres. Suffolk County chpt. 1982-83). Home: 174 Furnace Dock Rd Cortlandt Manor NY 10566-6532

LAUTENSCHLAGER, GARY JOSEPH, psychology educator, consultant; b. Chgo., Mar. 21, 1949; s. George Frederick and Bernadette (Spaeth) L.; m. Karen Kathleen Keszycki, Apr. 1, 1973; children: Erica Rae, Rene Erin, Alison Lynn. Student Bradley U., 1967-68; BA, U. Ill.-Chgo., 1972, PhD, 1982; MS, San Diego State U., 1976. Instr. U. Ill., Chgo., 1979-82; asst. prof. psychology U. Ga., Athens, 1982-88, assoc. prof., 1988-95, assoc. dept. head, 1993—, prof., 1995—; cons. Rehab. Inst., Chgo., 1978-80, Northwestern Med. Sch., Chgo., 1980-81, Organizational Cons., Inc., Chgo., 1981-82, Augusta VA Hosp., Ga., 1984—, Ga. Dept. Edn., 1990—, U. Ga. Gerontology Ctr., 1989—, Inst. Geronotology U. Mich., Ann Arbor, 1995—. Contbr. articles to profl. jours. NIMH fellow, 1976-78. Mem. Am. Psychol. Assn. (divs. 5, 14), Southeast Psychol. Assn., Am. Edni. Rsch. Assn., Am. Psychol. Soc., Am. Statis. Assn., Soc. for Indsl.-Organizational Psychology. Avocations: guitar, reading, running, softball. Home: RR 1 Box 154-b Colbert GA 30628-9801 Office: U Ga Psychology Dept Athens GA 30602

LAUTENSCHLAGER, YETTA ELIZABETH, clinical social worker; b. New Haven, Jan. 23, 1942; d. Theodore Mikolinski and Yetta Christina (Zdanovich) Meehan; m. Charles M. Lautenschlager, Dec. 11, 1982 (div.); children: Yetta Ann Auger, Kristin M. Wetmore. BS, So. Conn. State U., 1964, MS, 1973; MSW, U. Conn., West Hartford, 1983. Lic. clin. social worker. Educator Bd. Edn., Hamden, Conn., 1964-81; cmty. educator Lower Naugatuck Valley Coun. Alcohol and Drug Abuse, Ansonia, Conn., 1983-84; outpatient clinician Shirley Frank Found., New Haven, 1984-85; dir., clinician Personal Growth Ctr., Hamden, 1984—; employment assistance program cons. Johnson & Johnson Med., Southington, Conn., 1995—; cons. Village for Families and Children, Hartford, Conn., 1992—. Participant Mary Mashinsky campaign, Wallingford, Conn., 1984. Mem. Nat. Assn. Social Workers, Acad. Cert. Social Workers, Menninger Found., Internat. Soc. for New Identity Process (tchg. fellow), Conn. Soc. Clin. Social Workers. Office: Personal Growth Ctr 3074 Whitney Ave Bldg 3 Hamden CT 06518

LAUTER, M. DAVID, family physician; b. Wilmington, Del., Jan. 7, 1951; s. Aaron Mordecai and Anne Marguerite (Scondin) L.; m. Diane R. Lauter, Oct. 11, 1980; children: Michael, Sara. BS, Johns Hopkins U., 1973, Ma, 1974, MD, 1978. Diplomate Am. Bd. Family Physicians. Clin. dir. U.S. Pub. Health Svc. Indian Hosp., Red Lake, Minn., 1981-84; pvt. practice as family doctor York, Maine, 1984—. With Pub. Health Svc., 1981-84. Office: 12 Hospital Dr York ME 03909-1011

LAUTERBACH, EDWARD CHARLES, psychiatric educator; b. Chgo., Mar. 21, 1955; s. Edward G. and Virginia C. (Pochelski) L. AB cum laude, Augustana Coll., Rock Island, Ill., 1977; MD, Wake Forest U., 1982. Lic. psychiatrist, Mo., Pa., N.J., N.C., Ga.; diplomate Nat. Bd. Med. Examiners, Am. Bd. Psychiatry and Neurology. Intern Washington U. Sch. Medicine/Barnes Hosp., St. Louis, 1982-83, resident in psychiatry, 1983-86; clin. asst. Washington U. Sch. Medicine/Barnes Hosp., 1982-86, U. Medicine and Dentistry of N.J., New Brunswick, 1986-87, Mercer U. Sch. Medicine, Macon, Ga., 1988; chief div. adult and geriatric psychiatry, dept. psychiatry and behavioral scis. Mercer U. Sch. Medicine, Macon, 1988—, coord. grand rounds dept. psychiatry and behavioral scis., 1989—, assoc. prof., 1992; coord. grand rounds dept. psychiatry and behavioral scis. Mercer U. Sch. Medicine, Macon, N.C., 1989—; assoc. prof. Mercer U. Sch. Medicine, Macon, 1992-96, prof., 1996—; pvt. practice Charlotte, N.C., 1987-88; chair free comm. IVth World Congress Biol. Psychiatry, Phila., 1985; mem. neurology staff Lyons VA Hosp., 1986; active staff privileges in neurology Mercy Hosp., Charlotte, 1987, cons., 1987; active privileges in psychiatry Med. Ctr. Ctrl. Ga., 1994—, Coliseum Psychiat. Hosp., 1994—, dir. med. staff continuing edn., 1994—. Editorial reviewer Neuropsychiatry, Neuropsychology, and Behavioral Neurology, 1990—, Jour. Neuropsychiatry and Clin. Neuroscis., Biological Psychiatry, Movement Disorders; contbr. articles to profl. jours. Rock Sleyster scholar Wake Forest U., 1981. Mem. AMA (panelist DATTA coun. of sci. affairs 1990—), Am. Acad. Neurology, Am. Psychiat. Assn. (course dir. 1990-92, 94-95, symposium chairwoman 1995-96), Am. Neuropsychiat. Assn. (rsch. com.), Ga. Psychiat. Physicians Assn. (state com. on continuing med. edn.), Bibb County Med. Soc., N.C. Psychiat. Assn., Mecklenburg County Med. Soc., Med. Assn. Ga., Movement Disorder Soc., Charlotte Psychiat. Soc.

LAUTERBUR, PAUL C(HRISTIAN), chemistry educator; b. Sidney, Ohio, May 6, 1929. BS, Case Inst. Tech., 1951; PhD, U. Pitts., 1962; PhD (hon.), U. Liege, Belgium, 1984; DSc (hon.), Carnegie Mellon U., 1987; DEng (hon.), Corpernicus Med. Acad., Cracow, Poland, 1988; DSc (hon.), Wesleyan U., 1989, SUNY, Stony Brook, 1990; DEng (hon.), Rensselaer Poly. Inst., 1991, U. Mons., Hainaut, Belgium, 1996. Rsch. asst. and assoc. Mellon Inst., Pitts., 1951-53, fellow, 1955-63; assoc. prof. chemistry SUNY, Stony Brook, 1963-69, prof. chemistry, 1969-84, with, 1963-85, rsch. prof. radiology, 1978-85, univ. prof., 1984-85; prof. (4) depts. U. Ill., Urbana, 1985—; Disting. Univ. prof. Coll. Medicine U. Ill., Chgo., 1990—. Contbr. articles to profl. jours.; mem. editorial bds.; mem. sci. couns. Cpl. U.S. Army, 1953-55. Recipient Clin. Rsch. award Lasker Found., 1984, Nat. Medal of Sci., U.S.A., 1987, Fiuggi Internat. prize Fondazione Fiuggi, 1987, Roentgen medal, 1987, Gold medal Radiol. Soc. N.Am., 1987, Nat. Medal of Tech., 1988, Gold medal Soc. Computed Body Tomography, 1989, The Amsterdam (Alfred Heineken) prize in medicine, 1989, Laufman-Greatbatch award Assn. for Advancement Med. Intrumentation, 1989, Leadership Tech. award Nat. Elec. Mfr. Assn., 1990, Bower award and prize for achievement in sci. Benjamin Franklin Nat. Meml. Commn. of the Franklin Inst., 1990, Internat. Soc. Magnetic Resonance award, 1992, Kyoto prize, Inamori Foundation, 1994. Fellow AAAS, Am. Phys. Soc. (Biol. Physics prize 1983), Am. Inst. Med. and Biol. Engring.; mem. IEEE (sr.), NAS, Am. Chem. Soc., Internat. Soc. Magnetic Resonance in Medicine (Gold medal 1982). Office: U Ill-Urbana-Champaign 1307 W Park St Urbana IL 61801-2332

LAUTERIO, THOMAS JOHN, medicine and physiology educator; b. Paterson, N.J., June 30, 1956; s. Giovanni Alexander and Helena Marie (Waltz) L.; m. Geraldine Josephine Niedbalski, Sept. 26, 1986; 1 stepchild, Monique; children: Joseph Thomas, Gina Rose. BA in Biology, Rutgers Coll., New Brunswick, N.J., 1977; MS in Zoology, Rutgers U., Piscataway, N.J., 1980; PhD in Nutrition Biochemistry, Rutgers U., New Brunswick, 1985. Postdoctoral fellow Washington U. Med. Sch., St. Louis, 1985, rsch. instr., 1985-86, asst. prof., 1986-87; asst. prof. Eastern Va. Med. Sch., Norfolk, 1987-90, assoc. prof., 1990—, dir. EVMS grad. program, 1996—; chief nutrition Dept. Vets. Affairs Med. Ctr., Hampton, Va., 1990—; study sect. mem. NIH, Bethesda, 1990—; reviewer of grants U.S. Dept. Agriculture, Washington, 1990—; cons. Monsanto Co., St. Louis, 1986-88; adj. assoc. prof. dept. human ecology Hampton U., 1989—, dept. biol. scis. Old Dominion U., Norfolk, 1989—. Jour. reviewer Jour. of Nutrition, Am. Jour. of Clin. Nutrition, Internat. Jour. of Obesity, FASEB Jour., Physiology and Behavior; inventor water stable shrimp pellet; contbr. book chpts. and articles to profl. jours. Chair. Va. Coop. Ext. Com., Hampton, 1988—; head judge Tidewater Regional Sci. Fair, 1989—, Newport News (Va.) Sci. Fair, 1988—; bd. dirs. Minority Sci. Edn. Program, Hampton, 1989—. NIH grantee, 1989—; recipient rsch. award NATO, 1992. Mem. Am. Diabetes Assn. (rsch. grant 1989-90, nutrition coun. 1989—), Am. Inst. Nutrition (grad. student award 1984), Soc. Neurosci., Soc. Exptl. Biology and Medicine, Endocrine Soc., Soc. for Study of Ingestive Behavior. Roman Catholic. Home: 22 Phyllis Ln Hampton VA 23666-5544 Office: Diabetes Insts Med Rsch Svc 151 855 W Brambleton Ave Norfolk VA 23510-1005

LAUTERSTEIN, JOSEPH, cardiologist; b. Vienna, Austria, Dec. 1, 1934; came to U.S., 1940; s. Bernard and Hajnalka (Stern) L.; m. Erika Stein, Jan. 24, 1964 (dec. Aug. 1990); children: Deborah Ann, Brenda Rose; m. Elisabeth Spiegl Lazaroff, Nov. 27, 1994. BA, Syracuse U., 1955; MD, U. Vienna, 1964. Lic. physician, N.Y. Intern, then resident in internal medicine The Bklyn. Cumberland Med. Ctr., 1964-66, 68-69, fellow in cardiology, 1969-70; attending physician, cons. internal medicine and cardiology Hamilton Ave. Hosp., Monticello, N.Y., 1970-78; attending physician, cons. internal medicine and cardiology Community Gen. Hosp. Sullivan County, Harris, N.Y., 1970—, chief cardiology, 1971—, chief of staff, 1981-82; mem. courtesy staff dept. internal medicine and cardiology The Bklyn. Hosp. Ctr., 1971-95; clin. asst. dept. internal medicine and cardiology St. Vincent's Hosp. and Med. Ctr. N.Y., 1974-80, asst. attending physician, 1981-86, assoc. attending physician, 1987-94, attending physician, 1995—; with Sullivan Internal Medicine Group, P.C., Monticello, 1970—; dir. ICU Community Gen. Hosp. Sullivan County, 1971-79, dir. CCU, 1978—, dir. spl. diagnostics, 1984—, pres. med. bd., 1981-82; mem. pacemaker task force Empire State Med. Sci. and Ednl. Found., 1985-89; med. dir. Sullivan County EMT-D Program, 1989—; police surgeon Village of Monticello, 1974—, Sullivan County, 1972—; med. advisor Monticello Vol. Ambulance Corps, 1970-80, 89—; mem. Sullivan County Emergency Svcs. Coun., 1990, 91. Co-contbr. articles to Jour. Cardiovascular Surgery, Annals of Thoracic Surgery, Angiology, Chest. Trustee Cmty. Gen. Hosp. Sullivan County, 1981-82, Cmty. Gen. Hosp. Found., 1990—; mem. Nat. Ski Patrol, 1979—, med. advisor So. N.Y. region, 1989-94, med. advisor So. Catskill sect., 1994—; patroller Holiday Mountain Ski Patrol, 1979—. Capt. M.C., USAF, 1966-68. Named Citizen of Yr., SYDA Found. Sullivan County, 1991. Fellow Am. Coll. Cardiology (N.Y. State chpt., del. to N.Y. Med. Soc. Ho. Dels. 1991—, councilor 1991—, com. mem. 1990—), Am. Coll. Chest Physicians (assoc.), Am. Coll. Angiology, Internat. Coll. Angiology, N.Y. Cardiological Soc. (exec. bd. dirs. 1982—, mem. various coms.), N.Y. Acad. Medicine; mem. AMA, Am. Geriatrics Soc., Am. Soc. Internal Medicine, Soc. for Critical Care Medicine, N.Y. Acad. Scis., N.Am. Soc. for Pacing and Electrophysiology, Med. Soc. State of N.Y., others. Office: Sullivan Internal Medicine Group PC 370 Broadway Monticello NY 12701-1104

LAUVEN, PETER MICHAEL, anesthesiologist; b. Leverkusen, Fed. Republic Germany, May 13, 1948; s. Peter Aloysius and Katharina (Oedekoven) L.; m. Anne-Kareen Wetje, Nov. 7, 1970; children: Anne-Laureen, Lars-Peter. Diploma in Chem., U. Bonn, Fed. Republic of Germany, 1970, Dr. rer. nat., 1974, Dr. med., 1979, priv.-dozent, 1985. Teaching asst. Inst. Organic Chem. U. Bonn, Fed. Republic of Germany, 1970-76, scientist Inst. Anaesthesiology, 1976-79, physician, 1979—, anaesthesiologist, 1983—, asst. dir., 1983-85, vice-chmn., 1985-92, prof. of anaesthesia, 1986—, chmn. dept. Anaesthesiology & Surg. ICU, 1993—; mem. German Fed. Drug Admission Com., 1987—. Author, co-editor: Das Zentralanticholinergische Syndrom, 1985, Klinische Pharmakologie und rationale Arzneimitteltherapie, 1992; author, editor: Anasthesie und der Geriatrische Patient, 1989, Postoperative Schmerztherapie, 1991. Recipient scholarship Stipendien Fonds der Chemischen Inst., Frankfurt, 1970, Paul Martini award, Paul Martini Found., Bonn, 1988. Mem. Gesellschaft Deutscher Chemiker, Deutsche Gesellschaft für Anaesthesiologie und Intensiv Medizin, Deutsche Gesellschaft fur experimentelle und klinische Pharmakologie und

Toxikologie, Am. Soc. Anaesthesiology (affiliate), Am. Soc. Regional Anaesthesia, European Acad. Anaesthesiology, European Soc. Regional Anaesthesia, European Soc. Intensive Care Medicine, European Soc. Anaesthesiology, N.Y. Acad. of Scis. Home: Haendelstr 22, D-33604 Bielefeld Germany Office: Clinic Anaesthesiology and Intensive Care, Teutoburger Str 50, D-33604 Bielefeld Germany

LAUVER, ROBERT HOWARD, healthcare executive; b. Lewistown, Pa., Sept. 27, 1946; s. Robert Donald and Lou (Ceille) Howard) L.; m. Patricia Umstead, Aug. 29, 1971 (div.); children: Aaron Scott, Lindsay Ellen; m. Susan Beth Leitzel, Aug. 14, 1979. BA in Biology, Bloomsburg (Pa.) U., 1973, postgrad., 1974-75. Registered respiratory therapist. Staff respiratory therapy technician Bloomsburg Hosp., 1970-75; tech. dir. respiratory therapy Evangelical Community Hosp., Lewisburg, Pa., 1975-83; pres. CPO2, Inc., Mifflinburg, Pa., 1983—; cons. Medox, Inc., Sarasota, Fla., 1983-84; presenter in field. Sgt. U.S. Army, 1966-69, Vietnam. Decorated Purple Heart, Silver Star. Mem. Nat. Assn. Med. Equipment Suppliers, Pa. Assn. Med. Equipment Suppliers (advt. dir. 1977-80, legis. com. 1987—, pvt. ins. com. 1995—), Masons. Republican. Lutheran. Office: CPO2 Inc 150 E Chestnut St Mifflinburg PA 17844-9672

LAUWERS, PHILIP LOUIS, cardiologist; b. Antwerp, Belgium, Oct. 31, 1930; s. Philip L. Lauwers and Francoise N. de Hasque; m. Anne C. de le Court, May 2, 1958; children: Kathleen, Philippe, Christine. MD, U. Louvain, Belgium, 1956. Head dept. cardiology Clinique St. Michel, Brussels, 1962-95; pres. Medici's Group Practice, Brussels, 1975—; chief med. advisor Life Royal Belgium, 1975—. Contbr. sci. articles to profl. jours. Fellow Royal Coll. Physicians; mem. Belgian Soc. Cardiology. Office: Medicis Group Practice, 251 Ave de Tervuren, Brussels 1150, Belgium

LAUWERYNS, JOSEPH MARIE, pathologist, educator; b. Ostend, Belgium, Feb. 27, 1933; s. Joseph Gerard and Jeanne Marie (Ampe) L.; MD, Cath. U. Louvain, 1958, PhD, 1962; D honoris causa, U. Antwerp, 1990; specialist in clin. pathology, 1963; m. Anne Van Campenhout, Feb. 11, 1961; children: Brigitte, Philippe, Isabelle, Benedicte. Mem. faculty Cath. U. Leuven Faculty Medicine, 1962—, prof. pathology, 1967—, chmn. dept. biomed. rsch., 1979-93, head dept. pathology and histology Vesalius Inst., 1963—; dir. lab. pathology Acad. Ziekenhuizen, Leuven, 1963—. Decorated comdr. Belgian Royal Order Crown, comdr. Belgian Royal Order King Leopold; recipient Specia prize, 1958, Schockaert prize, 1962, Aspen prize, 1973, Smith-Kline-R.I.T. prize, 1983-85; Belgian Public Health travel grantee, 1959; fellow Nat. Belgian Research Funds, 1960-63, WHO, 1963. Mem. Belgian Soc. Pathology (pres. 1975-76), Belgian Soc. Electron Microscopy (pres. 1978—), Assn. Belgian Sci. Socs. (dir.), Royal Belgian Acad. Medicine (prize 1970), Internat. Acad. Pathology, European Soc. Pathology, AAAS. Roman Catholic. Chief editor Tijdschrift voor Geneeskunde, 1974—; discoverer intrapulmonary neuro-epithelial bodies. Office: 12 Minderbroedersstraat, B-3000 Leuven Belgium

LAUZÉ, KAREN PRUDENCE, physician, neurologist; b. Rochester, N.H., Mar. 16, 1956; d. Robert Richard and Estelle Teressa (Nedeau) L.; m. Jose Lopez (dec. 1990); m. Louis Piotrowski (div. 1996). BA, Boston U., 1981, MD, 1985. Diplomate in neurology Am. Bd. Psychiatry and Neurology. Intern Wilford Hall USAF Med. Ctr., Lackland AFB, Tex., 1985-86, resident in neurology, 1986-89; attending in neurology USAF Med. Ctr., Wright-Patterson AFB, Ohio, 1989-93; asst. clin. prof. neurology Wright State U. Sch. Medicine, Dayton, Ohio, 1989-93; staff neurologist No. Mich. Hosp., Petoskey, 1993-96, Burns Clinic, Petoskey, 1993-96, Portsmouth (N.H.) Regional Hosp., 1996—. Decorated Army commendation medal; recipient Air Force Meritorious Svcs. award, 1996. Mem. Am. Assn. for Study of Headache, Nat. Headache Found., Am. Acad. Neurology, Order Eastern Star. Buddhist. Office: Adult Neurology & Headache & Craniofac Pain 875 Greenland Ave B-6 Portsmouth NH 03801

LA VAQUE, THEODORE JOSEPH, psychologist; b. Merrill, Wis., June 24, 1940; s. Theodore Joseph and Mildred Rose (Young) La V.; m. Barbara Jean Moody, June 9, 1962; 1 child, Danielle Denyse. BS, U. Wis., 1963; MS, N.Mex. Highlands U., 1965; PhD, Iowa State U., 1972. Asst. prof. psychology U. No. Iowa, Cedar Falls, 1967-72, U. Ill., Chgo., 1972-75; pvt. practice psychology Downers Grove, Ill., Green Bay, Wis., 1975—; coordinator pain/stress clinic Mercy Ctr. for Health Care Services, Aurora, Ill., 1978-84. Contbr. articles to profl. jours. Mem. Brown County Soc. Clin. Cons. Psychologists, Soc. Clin. and Cons. Psychologists, Inc., Wis. Psychol. Assn., Biofeedback Soc. Am. Office: 125 S Jefferson St Ste 302 Green Bay WI 54301-1900

LA VECCHIA, CARLO, epidemiologist, educator; b. Milan, Feb. 27, 1955; s. Aurelio and Maria Margherita (Lerda) La V.; m. Eva Negri, July 24, 1987; children: Irene, Adriano. MD, U. Studies Milan, 1979; MSc, Oxford (Eng.) U., 1983. Rsch. fellow dept. cmty. medicine Oxford U., 1981-83; assoc. prof. epidemiology U. Lausanne, Switzerland, 1987-92; rsch. fellow Inst. Mario Negri, Milan, 1979-81, staff scientist, 1983-86, head Lab. Epidemiology, 1989—; assoc. prof. epidemiology U. Milan, 1992—; tng. fellow EEC, Brussels, 1981-83; temp. advisor WHO, Geneva, 1988—; mem. fellowship com. UICC, Geneva, 1991-95; vis. lectr., adj. assoc. prof. epidemiology Harvard U. Sch. Pub. Health, Cambridge, Mass., 1996—; European vis. prof. Royal Soc. Medicine, London, 1991. Editor European Jour. Pub. Health, 1993—, Jour. Epidemiology Biostatistics, 1996—; contbr. over 800 articles to sci. jours., including Lancet, Brit. Med. Jour., Epidemiology-Medicine Cancer Rsch., Cancer, Am. Jour. Epidemiology, Am. Jour. Ob-Gyn., Internat. Jour. Cancer. Recipient prize for med. publ. Glaxo S.p.A., 1993. Mem. European Soc. for Human Reprodn. (exec. com. 1991-95), Am. Assn. for Cancer Rsch., Ordine dei Medici, Ordine dei Giornalisti. Home: Via Lattanzio 16, 20137 Milan Italy Office: Inst Rsch Pharm Mario Negri, Via Eritrea 62, 20157 Milan Italy

LAVELL, THOMAS EUGENE, surgeon; b. N.Y.C., June 2, 1928; s. Thomas Eugene and Kathleen (MacDonald) L.; m. Anne M. Prosser, July 10, 1954 (div. 1985); children: Thomas III, Christopher, Patrick, Melissa; m. Jeanne P. Taber, Apr. 23, 1988. BA, Cornell U., 1949; MD, NYU, 1953; MS, Russell Sage Coll., 1980. Diplomate Am. Bd. Surgery. Intern St. Vincent's Hosp., N.Y.C., 1953-54; resident in gen. practice U. Colo. Med. Ctr., Denver, 1957-58; resident in surgery U. Vt. Med. Ctr., Burlington, 1958-60, 63-65; practice gen. medicine Hancock, N.Y., 1960-63; practice medicine specializing in surgery, mem. attending staff Delaware Valley Hosp., Walton, N.Y., 1965-94, chief of surgery, 1974-94; attending surgeon Mary Imogene Bassett Hosp., Cooperstown, N.Y., 1994—; adj. instr. health adminstrn. Russell Sage Coll., Albany, 1981—; clin. asst. prof. surgery SUNY Upstate Med. Ctr., Binghamton, 1986—. pres. Cmty. Svcs. Bd., Walton, 1966-73; bd. dirs., past pres. William B. Ogden Libr., Walton, 1973-91; pres. Health Systems Agy. N.E. N.Y., Albany, 1981-83; mem. N.Y. State Hosp. Rev. and Planning Coun., 1992-95; bd. dirs., N.Y. state dir. Am. Cancer Soc., 1994—. Served as lt. USNR, 1954-57. Richard P. Ettinger fellow N.Y. State div. Am. Cancer Soc., 1976. Fellow ACS; mem. Med. Soc. State N.Y. (pres. 6th dist. 1984-86), Delaware County Med. Soc. (pres. 1972-75), Am. Health Planning Assn., Am. Pub. Health Assn. Republican. Office: Bassett Healthcare Andes Rd Delhi NY 13753

LAVELLE, SEÃN MARIUS, clinical informatics researcher; b. County Mayo, Ireland, May 21, 1928; s. John and Eileen Veronica (Dempsey) L.; m. Frances Angela Roche-Kelly, Apr. 6, 1956; children: Sean, Connla, Diarmuid, Eimear, Eilin, Nuala, Malachy, Frances, Maria (dec.). MB, Nat. U. Ireland, Galway, 1952, MD, 1960. Diplomate Am. Bd. Pathology. Resident Cen. Hosp., Galway, 1952-56, Boston City Hosp., 1956-58; fellow U. Pitts., 1958-60; prof. exptl. medicine Univ. Coll., Galway, 1960-94, bd. govs., 1980-86; cons. Regional Hosp., Galway, 1960-78; mem. Med. Rsch. Coun. Ireland, Dublin, 1968-71, 81-85, rsch. fellow, 1953-55; vice chmn. rsch. com. on bioengring. EEC, Brussels, 1984-91; vis. rsch. prof. SUNY, Bklyn., 1966; rsch. fellow Tufts U., Boston, 1957-58. Editor: Clinical Presentation of Jaundice, 1995; mem. editl. bd. Tech. and Health Care; also articles. Rsch. councillor Galway Hospice Movement, 1987-93. Travel fellow Med. Rsch. Coun., 1956-57. Mem. Royal Coll. Physicians (fellow pathology faculty), Irish Med. Orgn., Assn. for Study Med. Edn. (councillor), Irish Assn. for Cancer Rsch. (chmn. 1979-81), European Assn. for Cancer Rsch. (councillor 1987-93), Irish Fedn. Univ. Tchrs. (chmn. 1970-72), Belmullet Golf Club, Galway County Club. Office: Clin Sci Insts, Univ Hosp, Galway Ireland

LAVEN, DAVID LAWRENCE, nuclear and radiologic pharmacist, consultant; b. Detroit, Jan. 31, 1953; s. Harold Sanford and Ada Rae (Blumenthal) L.; m. Maxine Frances Miller, May 14, 1977; children: Ryan Stuart, Cameron Alexander. BA in History, Biology, Albion Coll., 1975; BS in Pharmacy, U. N.Mex., 1981. Rsch. technologist, biodistbn. specialist U. N.Mex. Coll. Pharmacy, Albuquerque, 1978-81; asst. mgr. Syncor, Inc. (formerly Pharmatopes), Miami, Fla., 1981-84; instr. nuclear pharmacy U. Miami, 1982-85; pres., owner Gammascan Cons., Bay Pines, Fla., 1982—; staff pharmacist Hollywood (Fla.) Med. Ctr., 1983-84; asst. mgr. Nuclear Pharmacy, Inc., Sunrise, Fla., 1984-85; dir. nuc. pharmacy program VA Med. Ctr., Bay Pines, 1985-96; exec. dir. Ala. Pharmacy Assn., 1996—; mem. adv. panel on radiopharms. U.S. Pharmacopeial Conv. Inc., Rockville, Md., 1985—; dir. nuclear pharmacy program VA Med. Ctr., Bay Pines, 1985-96; cons. nuclear pharmacy Nat. Assn. Bds. Pharmacy, Chgo., 1987—; adj. asst. clin. prof. U. Fla. Coll. Pharmacy, Gainesville, 1986—, Nova-Southeastern U. Coll. Pharmacy, North Miami Beach, Fla., 1990—, Mercer U. Coll. Pharmacy, 1995—; edn. cons. Nuclear Tech. Rev. Series Rev., Inc., 1988—; mem. splty. coun. on nuclear pharmacy Bd. Pharm. Specialties, 1988-91. Co-author: Pharmacologic Alterations in the Biorouting/Performance of Select Radiopharmaceuticals Used in Cardiac Imaging, 1990, Pharmacologic Alterations with Biorouting/Performance of Radiopharmaceuticals Used in Nuclear Medicine Abscess, Liver/Spleen, and Tumor/Inflammation Imaging Procedures, 1992, Pharmacologic Alterations in the Biorouting of Radiopharmaceuticals Used in Nuclear Medicine Adrenal, Cerebral, Hepatobiliary, Pulmonary, and Renal Scintigraphic Studies, 1993, International Handbook of Drug-Radiopharmaceutical Interactions and Incompatibilities, 1994; Pharmacologic Alterations in the Biorouting/Performance of Radiopharmaceuticals Used in Cistrnography, Ferrokinetic Studies, Gastrointestinal Imaging, Schillings Testing, Thrombus Localization, Thyroid Uptake/Imaging, and Other Nuclear Medicine Procedures, 1994; editor, co-pub. Clini-Scan Monthly, 1982-84; co-guest editor Jour. Pharmacy Practice, Radiologic Pharmacy I, 1989, II, 1989, III, 1994, mem. editorial bd., 1991—; guest editor Fla. Jour. Hosp. Pharmacy, 1990, cons. editor, 1986—; guest author In-Svc. Rev. in Nuclear Medicine, 1990—; mem. editorial bd. New Perspectives in Cancer Diagnosis and Management, 1992—; nat. field editor ASHP Signal Newsletter, 1985-87; contbr. chpt. to book. Mem. Henry Morgan chpt. B'nai B'rith, Southfield, Mich., 1975-77. Fellow Am. Soc. Hosp. Pharmacists (chmn. specialized practice group on radiologic pharmacy 1993-95, edn. program assoc. 1988-95, practice adv. panel 1992-93, mem. continuing edn. 1995—), Acad. Pharmacy Practice and Mgmt. (del. 1986—, edn. cons. 1987—, nuclear pharmacy sec. ednl. affairs com. 1983—, profl. and scientific affairs com. 1988—, regulatory affairs com. 1984—, Practitioner Merit award 1990, Presentation award 1990, 91, 94, Poster award 1990, 91, 94); mem. Am. Pharm. Assn. (chmn.-elect 1988-89, chmn. sect. on specialized pharm. svcs. 1989-90, chmn.-elect 1992-93, chmn. section on nuclear pharmacy 1993-94, edn. adv. com. 1988-89, 92-94, mem. nuc. pharmacy sect., mem. ednl. affairs com. 1983—, mem. profl. and sci. affairs com. 1988—, mem. regulatory affairs com. 1984—), Am. Assn. Colls. Pharmacy (mem. task force on residency programs and support 1990-91, mem. task force on assessment of experimental function 1994-95), Nat. Coun. State Pharmacy Assn. Execs., Am. Soc. Pharmacy Law, Fla. Pharmacy Assn. (chmn. ednl. affairs coun. 1989-90, chmn. nuclear pharmacy section 1987-89, 91-93, chmn. acad. pharmacy practice 1988-90, 93-95, chmn. orgnl. affairs coun. 1992-93, del. 1988—, edn. cons. 1987—, exec. com. 1989—, pres. com. 1989-90, 94-95, budget and fin. com. 1989-90, 94-95, mem. conv. planning com. 1989-93, 95, mem. exec. com. 1989—, region XII ce on mission of pharmacy in Fla. 1989-92, 95, editor numerous proceedings for nuclear pharmacy lecture series 1993-96, Number 1 Club 1990, Disting. Young Pharmacist award 1990, Acad. Pharmacy Practice Practitioner Merit award 1992, Sidney Simkowitz Pharmacy Involvement award 1992, Disting. Svc. award 1993), Acad. Pharmacy Practice (chmn. 1988-90, 93-95, chmn. nuclear pharmacy sect. 1987-89, 91-93, Poster Presentation 1st Pl. award 1995), Fla. Soc. Hosp. Pharmacists, Fla. Nuclear Medicine Technologists (mem. exec. coun. 1992—, editor Proceedings 22nd ann. meeting 1993, 24th ann. meeting 1995, 25th ann. meeting 1996), Internat. Pharm. Fedn. (scientific poster award 1992, vice chmn. nuclear pharmacy subsection, 1994-95, edn. con. Pharmacy World Congress 1992, 93, 95, 96, editor Radioimmunopharm.: Current and Future Considerations), Soc. Nuclear Medicine (mem. S.E. chpt., mem. govt. affairs com. 1985-86, program com. 1988-89, edn. cons. 1989—, chair pharmacy liaison com. 1995—, mem. Brewster Bill task force 1995, mem. NRC com. 1995—), Pinellas Pharmacist Soc. (mem. exec. com. 1989—, pres.-elect 1991-92, pres. 1992-93, newsletter editor, 1992—, Pharmacist of Yr. award 1992, Pres' award 1993, FPA Unit Assn. Recognition award 1993, 95, PPS Merit award 1994, Practice Merit award 1994, life), Pasco-Hernando Pharmacy Assn. (treas. 1990-93, mem. exec. com. 1990-94, Pharmacist of Yr. 1995), Hillsborough County Pharmacy Assn. (mem. exec. com. 1991—, sec. 1991-92, pres.-elect 1993-94, pres. 1994-95, newsletter editor, 1994—, Pres. award 1994-95, Pharmacist of Yr. 1994), Polk County Pharmacy Assn., Internat. Pharmacy Fedn. (Sci. Poster award Sect. Hosp. Pharmacists 1992, editor proceedings spl. session Pharmacy World Congress 1993, vice chmn. nuclear pharmacy group 1994—), Ala. Pharmacy Assn. (exec. dir. 1996—), Kappa Psi, Psi Chi, Phi Alpha Theta, Beta Beta Beta. Home: 5600 Carmichael Rd # 2327 Montgomery AL 36117 Office: Ala Pharmacy Assn 1211 Carmichael Way Montgomery AL 36106-3672

LAVENDER, ANTHONY, psychologist; b. Epsom, Surrey, Eng., Dec. 25, 1953; s. Arthur Anthony and Florence May (White) L.; m. Jane Lucy Allday, July 29, 1984; children: Ellen Grace, Sarah Rebecca. BS with honors, U. Wales, 1975; M in Philosophy, Inst. Psychiatry, London, 1979; PhD, U. London, 1984. Cert. clin. psychologist. Clin. psychologist Bexley (Eng.) Health Dist., 1979-84, Maidstone (Eng.) Health Dist., 1984-89, David Salomons House, Southborough, Kent, Eng., 1989—. Fellow Brit. Psychol. Soc. Office: David Salomons Ctr, Broomhill Rd, Southborough TN30TG Kent, England

LAVENDER, ARDIS RAY, health care company executive; b. Bedford, Ind., July 2, 1927; s. Hayden and Genevieve (Hendricks) L.; m. Andrea M. Sabol, Dec. 7, 1968; children: Michael, Teresa, Curtis, Kara, Marc. Student Purdue U., 1944-45, Ind. U., 1947-48; MD, Ind. U., 1953. Assoc. prof. medicine U. Chgo., 1954-68; prof. medicine Loyola U., Maywood, Ill., 1968-75; chief nephrology Hines VA Hosp., Maywood, 1968-75; dir. Kidney & Hypertension Inst., Scranton, Pa., 1975-80; cons. Revlon Health Care, Tuckahoe, N.Y., 1980-82, v.p. med. devices, 1982-87; cons. med. devices, 1988—; cons., lectr. in field; staff U. Chgo., 1953-68, Loyola U. McGaw Hosp., 1968-75, Martha Washington Hosp., Chgo., 1975, Moses Taylor Hosp., Scranton, Pa., 1975-79, Mercy Hosp., Scranton, 1975-79, Community Med. Ctr., Scranton, 1975-79, Scranton State Hosp., 1975-79, Mid-Valley Hosp., Peckville, Pa., 1977-79, St. Joseph's Hosp., Carbondale, Pa., 1977-79, Carbondale Gen. Hosp., Pa., 1977-79. Contbr. articles to profl. jours. Editor Pakistanian Jour. Medicine, 1972. Reviewer, Jour. Lab. and Clin. Medicine, Jour. of AMA, Archives of Internal Medicine, Kidney Internat., Jour. Applied Physiology. USPHS Research Career Devel. awardee, 1965-68; recipient Presdl. citation White House, 1970. Mem. Am. Fedn. Clin. Research, AAAS, Am. Heart Assn., N.Y. Acad. Scis., Central Soc. Clin. Research, Internat. Soc. Nephrology, Chgo. Soc. Internal Medicine, Am. Soc. Nephrology, Am. Soc. Artificial Internal Organs, European Dialysis and Transplant Assn., Am. Assn. for Advancement of Med. Instrumentation, AMA, Lackawanna Med. Soc., Pa. Med. Soc., Internat. Soc. Artificial Internal Organs, Am. Soc. Inventors, Am. Fedn. Clin. Research (pres. 1965-66), Alpha Omega Alpha. Office: 1073 Limberlost Ct Columbus OH 43235-2168

LAVERNIA, CARLOS JESUS, orthopaedic surgeon; b. Havana, Cuba, Jan. 4, 1957; m. Kristen Kilbourn. BS in Math., Tulane U., 1977, MS in Biomed. Engring., 1979; MD, U. P.R., 1985. Diplomate Am. Bd. Orthopaedic Surgery, Nat. Bd. Examiners. Instr. math. Interamerican U., San Juan, P.R., 1982-85; instr. physiology U. P.R., San Juan, 1982-85; intern U. Calif., San Diego, 1985-86, resident, 1987-91, clin. instr., 1990-91; asst. orthopaedics dept. orthopaedic surgery Johns Hopkins Sch. Medicine, Balt., 1991-92; chief hip fracture svc. Jackson Meml. Hosp., Miami, Fla., 1992—, dir. hip and knee clinic, 1992—; asst. prof. biomed. engring. U. Miami Sch. Engring., 1992—, asst. prof. orthopaedic surgery, 1992—, dir. divsn. arthritis surgery, 1992—; rsch. engr. Tulane U., New Orleans, 1978-81, 83; editing. cons. The Boll. Bd., San Juan, 1982-85; med. adv. bd. Arthritis Found., Ft. Lauderdale, Fla., 1995—; orthopaedic adv. bd. Ortho-Graphics, Inc., Salt Lake City, 1994—; orthopaedic adv. panel Columbua/HCA, Nashville, 1994—; presenter and researcher in field. Contbr. articles to profl. jours., chpts. to books; mem. editorial bd. Jour. Arthroplasty, 1993—, Jour. Orthopaedic Techniques, 1994—. NIH grantee, 1986-87; NIH rsch. fellow, 1986-87. Fellow Am. Acad. Orthopaedic Surgery; mem. AMA, Am. Student Med. Assn., Fla. Med. Assn. (governing coun. young physician sect. 1994-95), Biomed. Engring. Soc., Soc. Biomaterials, Orthopaedic Rsch. Soc., Tay Beta Pi, Phi Eta Sigma. Office: Cedars Med Ctr 1321 NW 14th St Ste 203 Miami FL 33125

LAVI, HANNAH LEVIN, psychotherapist, educator; b. Jerusalem, Israel, Aug. 7, 1946; came to U.S., 1984; d. Aron and Sarah (Moshatzky) Levin; m. Ehud Cohen, Jan. 15, 1972 (div. Apr. 1974); 1 child, Llor Cohen. BA, Hebrew U., Jerusalem, 1972, MA cum laude, 1977; PhD, U. Toronto (Can.), 1982; MSW, Yeshiva U., 1988. Dir. The Virginia Satir Inst., Jerusalem, 1988-90; supr. mediation The Family Therapy Inst., Tel-Aviv, Israel, 1989-90; dir. and founder The Human Development Clinic, Champaign, Ill., 1990—; vis. sr. lectr. Hebrew U., 1981-85, 90; lectr. psychology Danville (Ill.) C.C., 1991—. Author: (book) Carl Rogers: Bio-Bibliography, 1992; contbr. articles to Jour. Social History and other profl. jours. Founder, pres. Levin Found. for Prevention Domestic Violence and Empowerment Survivors Spousal Abuse, 1995—. Recipient Dean fellowship Hebrew U., 1976; recipient Open fellowship U. Toronto, 1978-80; recipient Ben Euever prize Jewish Agy., 1981. Mem. NASW, NAFE, APA, Am. Acad. Family Mediators, Internat. Soc. Polit. Psychology, Am. Assn. Play Therapists, Am. Assn. Suicidology, Israeli Assn. Social Workers. Jewish. Home and Office: 2308 Brookshire E Champaign IL 61821-6446

LAVIE, ELI, cardiologist; b. Haifa, Israel, Jan. 24, 1957; came to U.S., 1986; BSc, Hebrew U., Jerusalem, 1982, MD, 1986. Diplomate Am. Bd. Internal Medicine in internal medicine and cardiovascular diseases. Resident in internal medicine Mt. Sinai Hosp., Chgo., 1986-89; fellow cardiology Chgo. Med. Sch., North Chicago, 1989-92; attending physician Luth. Gen. Hosp., Park Ridge, Ill., 1992—; clin. instr. U. Chgo., 1994—, Finch U. Health Scis., North Chicago, 1993-94. Fellow Am. Coll. Cardiology. Office: Advocate Med Group 1875 Dempster Ste 525 Park Ridge IL 60068

LAVIENA, LUIS R., psychologist, educator, media specialist; b. Humacao, P.R., Mar. 29, 1955; s. Angel and Julia (DeLeon) L. BA in Psychology, U. P.R., Rio Piedras, 1977; MS in Clin. Psychology, Caribbean Ctr. for Advanced Studies, San Juan, P.R., 1981; PhD in Devel. Psychology, Yeshiva U., 1991. Lic. psychologist, sch. psychologist, N.Y.; cert. hypnotherapist, Puerto Rico, neuropsychologist, N.Y. Bilingual psychologist Bd. Edn. City of N.Y., N.Y.C., 1981-85, 90—, supr. project devel. of norms of Spanish WISC-R, 1986-88; clin. psychotherapist Manhattan Children Psychiat. Ctr., Wards Island, N.Y., 1987-88; neuropsychol. trainee Columbia Presbyn. Hosp., N.Y.C., 1987-88; dir. psychol. svcs. for people with AIDS Luth. Med. Ctr., Bklyn., 1988-90; coord. children's bilingual svcs., specialist psychologist Hearing Handicapped and Visually Impaired Unit, N.Y.C., 1991—; dir. psychol. svcs. Manhattan Eye, Ear and Throat Hosp., 1992—; supr. clin. interns psychology program Fordham Univ., 1994; adj. prof. Seton Hall U., South Orange, N.J., 1991—; cons. Caribbean Biofeedback Assn. P.R., 1979—, Latino Issues in Inst. Human Identity, P.R., 1985—, AIDS films, N.Y.C., 1989—, Hispanic Issues in Gay Men's Health Crisis, N.Y.C., 1989—; presented articles to profl. confs., 1989—. Fellow Nat. Coun. LaRaza, Office of Bilingual Edn. and Minority Lang. Affairs, Neuropsychology Dept. Columbia Presbyn. Hosp. Mem. AAAS, NASP, Am. Orthopsychiat. Assn., Assn. Devel. Behavioral Scis., Assn. Hispanic Mental Health Profls., N.Y. State Assn. Sch. Psychologists, Associacion de Psicologos de Puerto RIco. Home: 401 E 64th St Apt 4E New York NY 10021-7540 Office: Seton Hall U Hearing Handicapped and Vision Impaired 400 1st Ave New York NY 10010-4004 Office: Manhattan Eye Ear and Throat Hosp 210 E 64th St New York NY 10021-7480

LAVIN, PATRICK JAMES, neurologist; b. Dublin, Ireland, May 21, 1946. Grad., Univ. Coll. Dublin, 1970, MB BCh, 1970. Diplomate Am. Bd. Neurology and Psychiatry. Intern St. Vincent's Hosp., Dublin, 1970-71, resident in medicine, 1971-73; gen. practice N.S., Can., 1973; registrar in gen. medicine Leicester Gen. Hosp., 1974-75; registrar in neurology St. James U. Hosp. and Chapel Allerton Hosp., Leeds, Eng., 1976-78; rsch. fellow, hon. sr. registrar Charing Cross Hosp., London, 1978; internist James Connolly Meml. Hosp., Dublin, 1979, Our Lady's Hosp., Navan, Ireland, 1979; registrar in neurology Adelaide Hosp. and St. Vincent's Hosp., Dublin, 1980; chief resident in neurology Case Western Res. U., Cleve., 1980-81, fellow in neuro-ophthalmology, 1981-83, mem. faculty medicine, 1982-83, instr. dept. neurology, 1982-83; asst. prof. dept. neurology, appointee dept. ophthalmology Vanderbilt U., Nashville, 1983-89, assoc. prof. dept. neurology, 1989—; dir. Ocular Motility Lab., Vanderbilt U.; cons. neuro-ophthalmologist VA Med. Ctr. Contbr. articles to profl. publs., chpts. to books; reviewer Archives of Neurology, Neurology, So. Med. Jour., N.Y. State Jour. Medicine. Mem. Royal Coll. Physicians of Ireland, Am. Acad. Neurology, Assn. for Rsch. in Vision and Ophthalmology, Nahsville Acad. Ophthalmology, Tenn. Acad. Ophthalmology, Clin. Eye Movement Soc., N.Am. Neuro-Ophthalmology Soc., S.E. Neuro-ophthalmology Soc. Office: Vanderbilt U Dept Neurology 2100 Pierce Ave Ste 351 Nashville TN 37212-3156

LAVIN, PHILIP TODD, biostatistician, consultant; b. Rochester, N.Y., Nov. 21, 1946; s. Albert A. and Mary (Rapkin) L.; m. Mary Ellen Saunders, Aug. 23, 1970; children: Andrew, Abby. AB, U. Rochester, 1968; PhD, Brown U., 1972. Rsch. asst. prof. Brown U., Providence, 1972-74, SUNY at Buffalo, Amerst, 1974-77; asst. prof. sch. pub. health Harvard U., Boston, 1977-83, assoc. prof. surgery, 1983—; pres. Boston Biostatistics, Inc., Framingham, Mass., 1983—, Boston Biostat Rsch. Found., Newton Upper Falls, Mass., 1988—; mem. editorial bd. Drug Info. Assn., Phila., 1986-88, Anti-microbial Agents and Chemotherapy, Boston, 1987—; cons. FDA, 1983-86, 92—. Contbr. articles to on medicine and stats. to scholarly jours. Bd. dirs. William Graves Fund, Boston, 1989—. NSF trainee, 1968-72; grantee Nat. Cancer Inst., 1976-80, 87—, Nat. Heart, Lung, Blood Inst., 1985-89. Mem. Biometric Soc., Am. Statis. Assn., Soc. Clin. Trials, Regulatory Affairs Profl. Soc., Phi Beta Kappa. Home: 3 Cahill Park Dr Framingham MA 01701-6105 Office: Boston Biostat Rsch Fedn 1007 Chestnut St Newton MA 02164-1101

LAVINSON, NORMAN BARRY, psychologist; b. Trenton, N.J., Mar. 1, 1939; s. Abraham and Harriet (Schnur) L.; children: Melissa Ann, Rebecca Bradley. BA, Upsala Coll., 1961; MA, U. Cin., 1967, PhD, 1969. Lic. psychologist, N.J. Pvt. practice Pa., Lawrenceville, N.J. Mem. APA, N.J. Psychbol. Assn., Gen. Psychol. Svcs. Office: 123 Franklin Corner Rd Trenton NJ 08648-2526

LAW, FLORA ELIZABETH (LIBBY LAW), retired community health and pediatrics nurse; b. Biddeford, Maine, Sept. 11, 1935; d. Arthur Parker and Flora Alma (Knutti) Butt; m. Robert F. Law, 1961; children : Susan E., Sarah F., Christian A., Martha F.; m. John F. Brown, Jr., 1982. BA, Davis and Elkins (W.Va.) Coll., 1957; postgrad., Cornell U.-N.Y. Hosp., N.Y.C., 1960; BSN, U. Nev., Las Vegas, 1976, MS in Counseling Edn., 1981. RN, Nev.; cert. sch. nurse. Staff nurse So. Nev. Community Hosp. (now Univ. Med. Ctr.), Las Vegas, 1975-76; relief charge nurse Valley Psychiat. Inst., Las Vegas, 1976; pub. health nurse Clark County Dist. Health Dept., Las Vegas, 1977-78; sch. nurse Clark County Sch. Dist., Las Vegas, 1978-94; ret., 1994. Chair task force on sch. nursing Nev.'s Commn. for Profl. Standards in Edn.; mem. nurse practice act revision com. Nev. State Bd. Nursing. Mem. Nat. Assn. Sch. Nurses (past state dir., sch. nurse liaison Clark County Tchrs. Assn.), NEA, Clark County Assn. Sch. Nurses (past pres.), Sigma Theta Tau. Home: 3420 Clandara Ave Las Vegas NV 89121-3701

LAWFORD, THOMAS CYRPIAN, medical administrator; b. Newport News, Va., Jan. 13, 1940; s. Thomas C. Sr. and Doris Louise (Petty) L. BSEE, MIT, 1961; MD, U. Va., 1969. Diplomate Am. Bd. Preventive Medicine, Am. Bd. Occupational Medicine. Intern Roanoke (Va.) Meml. Hosp., 1969-70; resident in internal medicine Norfolk (Va.) Gen. Hosp., 1970-72; chief resident in internal medicine Georgetown U. at D.C. Gen. Hosp., Washington, 1972-73; employee health physician Chipperham Hosp., Richmond, Va., 1973-75, Richmond Meml. Hosp., 1975-78; asst. med. dir. Con Edison, N.Y.C., 1978-79; asst. med. dir. occupational medicine NIH, Bethesda, Md., 1979-91; corp. med. dir. Washington Gas Light Co., 1991—.

Mem. Mensa. Office: Washington Gas Co 6801 Industrial Rd Springfield VA 22151

LAWLESS, MICHAEL RHODES, pediatrics educator; b. Baytown, Tex., Oct. 13, 1942; s. Wallace Ervin and Amy Ruth (Broussard) L.; m. E. Sandra Johnson, Aug. 27, 1967; children: Melanie Lawless York, Stephanie Lawless Setzer. BA in Zoology, U. Tex., 1964, MD, 1968. Intern City Memphis Hosp., 1968-69; resident in pediatrics U. Tex. Med. Br., Galveston, 1969-71; instr. U. Rochester (N.Y.), Sch. Medicine, 1971-72; staff pediatrician Portsmouth (Va.) Naval Hosp., 1972-74; asst. prof. pediatrics Wake Forest U., Bowman Gray Sch. Medicine., Winston-Salem, N.C., 1974-80; assoc. prof. pediatrics Wake Forest U., Bowman Gray Sch. Medicine., Winston-Salem, 1980—, deputy assoc. dean student affairs, 1988-96. Lt. comdr. USNR, 1972-74. Fellow U. Rochester, 1971-72. Fellow Am. Acad. Pediatrics (legis. liaison 1980—); mem. Am. Bd. Pediatrics, Am. Profl. Soc. on Abuse of Children, N.C. Pediatric Soc. (child advocate 1974—), Coun. Med. Student Edn. in Pediatrics (exec. com.), Ambulatory Pediatric Assn. Office: Wake Forest U Bowman Gray Sch Medicine Med Ctr Blvd Winston Salem NC 27157

LAWRENCE, ARTHUR WAYNE, pediatrician, allergist; b. Christiana, Manchester, Jamaica, Apr. 16, 1942; s. Ivan Wesley and Elizabeth (Webb) L.; m. Jean Rose-Marie Hunter, Dec. 6, 1969; children: Kevin, Remi. MBBS, U. West Indies, Jamaica, 1967. Diplomate Am. Bd. Pediatrics. Cons. pediatrician Cornwall Regional Hosp., Jamaica, 1974-78, chmn. profl. activities com., 1976-78; cons. pediatrician, allergist Kingston, Jamaica, 1978—; mem. Med. Coun. Jamaica, 1990-93. Fellow Royal Coll. Physicians and Surgeons Can.; mem. Med. Assn. Jamaica (pres. Western br. 1977-78), Pediatric Assn. Jamaica (pres. 1980). Office: Med Assocs Hosp, 18 Tangarine Pk, Kingston 20, Jamaica

LAWRENCE, DAVID M., health facility administrator; b. 1940. MD, U. Ky., 1966; MPH, U. Wash., 1973. Intern in internal medicine, pediat.; with Kaiser Found. Health Plan and Hosps., Oakland, Calif., 1981—, now chmn., CEO; various professorships, directorships and fellowships with U. Wash., Johns Hopkins U., U. Ky.; dir. Pacific Gas and Electric Co., Hewlett Packard, Healthcare Forum, Bay Area Coun., Calif. Coll. Arts and Crafts, Colby Coll. Mem. APHA, Am. Hosp. Assn., Am. Coll. Preventive Medicine, Calif. Assn. Hosps. and Healty Sys., Group Health Assn. Am., Western Consortium for Pub. Health, Calif. Bus. Roundtable, The Conf. Bd. (bd. dirs.), Inst. Medicine/NAS (bd. dirs.). Office: Kaiser Found Health Plan & Hosp 1 Kaiser Plz Oakland CA 94612-3610

LAWRENCE, DEBRA CRIDER, podiatrist; b. Chambersburg, Pa., Aug. 6, 1958; d. Fred Wilson and Evelyn (Burkholder) Crider; m. David Michael Lawrence, Sept. 5, 1987; children: Matthew William, Alexandra Diane. BS in Biology, Houghton (N.Y.) Coll., 1980; D of Podiatric Medicine, Pa. Coll., 1985. Diplomate Am. Bd. Podiatric Orthopedics. Resident Brent Gen. Hosp., 1985-86; pvt. practice Drs. Debra and David, Westerly, R.I., 1988—. Mem. 1st Bapt. Ch. Waterford, 1988—. Mem. Am. Podiatric Med. Assn., Conn. Podiatrict Med. Assn. Home: Great Neck Rd Waterford CT 06385 Office: Drs Debra & David Lawrence 85 Beach St Westerly RI 02891

LAWRENCE, HENRY SHERWOOD, physician, educator; b. N.Y.C., Sept. 22, 1916; s. Victor John and Agnes (Whalen) L.; m. Dorothea Wetherbee, Nov. 13, 1943; children: Dorothea, Victor, Geoffrey. AB, NYU, 1938, MD, 1943. Diplomate Am. Bd. Internal Medicine. Mem. faculty NYU, N.Y.C., 1947—; John Wyckoff fellow in medicine NYU, 1948-49, dir. student health, 1950-57, head infectious disease and immunology div., 1959—, prof. medicine, 1961-79, Jeffrey Bergstein prof. medicine, 1979—, co-dir. med. svcs., 1964—, dir. Cancer Ctr., 1974-79; dir. Ctr. for AIDS Rsch., 1989-94; vis. physician Tisch Hosp., Bellevue Hosp., 1964—; cons. medicine Manhattan VA Hosp., 1964—; infectious disease program com. VA Rsch. Svc., 1960-63; cons. allergy and immunology study sect. USPHS, 1960-63, chmn., 1963-65; assoc. mem. commn. on streptococcal and staphylococcal diseases Armed Forces Epidemiol. Bd., Dept. Def., 1956-74; mem. coms. Nat. Acad. Scis.-NRC, 1957-65, chmn. com. transplantation, 1963-65; mem. NRC, 1970-72; mem. allergy and infectious disease panel Health Rsch. Coun., N.Y.C., 1962-75, co-chmn., 1968-75; mem. sci. adv. council Am. Cancer Soc., 1973-75. Editor: Medical Clinics of North America, 1957, Cellular and Humoral Aspects of Hypersensitive States, 1959, (with M. Landy) Mediators of Cellular Immunity, 1969, (with Kirkpatrick and Burger) Immunobiology of Transfer Factor, 1983; mem. editorial bd. Transplantation, Ann. of Internal Medicine; founder, editor in chief: Cellular Immunology, 1970-96. Served to lt. M.C. USNR, World War II. Commonwealth Fund fellow Univ. Coll., London, 1959; recipient Research Career Devel. award USPHS, 1960-65, prize Alpha Omega Alpha, 1943; Meritorious Sci. Achievement award NYU Alumni Assn., 1970, von Pirquet Gold medal Ann. Forum on Allergy, 1972, Award for Disting. Achievement in Sci. of Medicine ACP, 1973, Sci. Achievement award Am. Coll. Allergists, 1974, Sci. medal N.Y. Acad. Medicine, 1974, Bristol Sci. award Infectious Diseases Soc. Am., 1974, Charles V. Chapin medal, 1975, Lila Gruber honor award Am. Acad. Dermatology, 1975, Alumni Achievement award NYU Washington Sq. Coll., 1979. Fellow ACP (Bronze medal 1973), Am. Acad. Allergy (hon.), Royal Coll. Physicians and Surgeons Glasgow (hon.); mem. Nat. Acad. Scis., Assn. Am. Physicians, Am. Soc. for Clin. Investigation, Am. Assn. Immunologists, Soc. for Exptl. Biology and Medicine (editorial bd. procs.), Interurban Clin. Club, Harvey Soc. (sec. 1957-60, lectr. 1973—, councillor 1974-77), Peripatetic Clin. Soc., Infectious Diseases Soc. (charter, councillor 1970-72, Bristol Sci. award 1974), Royal Soc. Medicine (affiliate) (Eng.), Internat. Transplantation Soc. (chmn. constn. com., councillor), Société Française d'Allergie (corr.), Alpha Omega Alpha. Home: 343 E 30th St New York NY 10016-6417

LAWRENCE, JOSEPH JOHN, radiologist; b. Kingston, Pa., Aug. 11, 1956; s. Andrew F. and Margaret E. (Mikitish) L.; m. Debra A. Cahill, Oct. 18, 1980; children: Joseph Ryan, Jamie Marie, Edward Andrew. BS, U. Scranton, 1978; DO, Phila. Coll. Osteo. Medicine, 1982. Diplomate Am. Bd. Radiology. Intern Met. Gen. Hosp., Pinellas Park, Fla., 1982-83; resident in radiology USAF Med. Ctr., Lackland AFB, Tex., 1980-90; staff radiologist Campbell County Meml. Hosp., Gilette, Wyo., 1992—, mem. exec. com., 1994-95. Maj. USAF, 1983-90. Mem. Am. Coll. Radiology, Rocky Mountain Radiol. Soc., Am. Osteopathic Coll. Radiology, Am. Roentgen Ray Soc., Radiol. Soc. N.Am., Rotary. Roman Catholic. Home: 3325 Paintbrush Dr Gillette WY 82718 Office: Campbell County Meml Hosp 501 S Burme Gillette WY 82716

LAWRENCE, KATHY, medical, surgical, and radiology nurse; b. Searcy, Ark., Dec. 9, 1949; d. S.V. and Pearl (Bolden) Smith; children: Ryan, Damon. ADN, Odessa (Tex.) Coll., 1977; BSN, U. Tex., Galveston, 1992, MSN, 1996. Cert. med. asst., diabetes educator, med.-surg. nurse. Head nurse, acting supr. Med. Ctr. Hosp., Odessa, 1978-80; asst. head nurse Meml. Gen. Hosp., Elkins, W.Va., 1980-81; staff nurse United Hosp. Ctr., Clarksburg, W.Va., 1981-83; field supr. Upjohn/Healthcare Svcs., Midland, Tex., 1983-85; primary nurse, physician's office Naidu Clinic, Odessa, 1985-88; nursing supr. U. Tex. Med. Br., Galveston, 1988-95, case mgr. outcomes evaluation and nursing rsch., 1995—. Mem. ANA, TNA, Am. Assn. Diabetes Educators, Am. Assn. Med. Assts. (sec. local chpt.), Am. Assn. Intravenous Therapists, Am. Radiol. Nurses Assn., Am. Assn. Neurosci. Nurses, Am. Med-Surg. Nurses, Case Mgmt. Soc. Am., Intravenous Nurses Soc., Alpha Nu Chi, Sigma Theta Tau. Home: 6315 Central City Blvd Apt 820 Galveston TX 77551-3809

LAWRENCE, MARTHA SANDERS, health information management; b. Kosciusko, Miss., Dec. 11, 1937; d. Alva Meek and Viola (Williams) Sanders; m. Dewey Lavon Lawrence, May 26, 1956; children: Timothy, Pam L. Eads, Steven, Christopher. Student, Wood Cmty. Coll., 1975. With Blue Cross/Blue Shield, Jackson, Miss., 1957-61, Montfort Jones Hosp., Kosciusko, 1962-95; cons. Montfort Jones Hosp., Kosciusko, 1995, dir. med. records, 1972-95; pres. Miss. Health Info. Mgmt., Jackson, 1994-95, pres.-elect, 1993-94, del., 1991-93. 1st v.p. Bus. and Profl. Women's, Kosciusko, 1994-95, pres.-elect, 1995-96, pres., 1996—. Recipient Golden Circle award Am. Health Info. Mgmt. Assn., 1993. Avocations: reading, walking, painting, enjoying grandchildren, traveling. Home: Dogwood Hills PO Box 827 Kosciusko MS 39090 Office: Montfort Jones Meml Hosp PO Box 677 Kosciusko MS 39090

LAWRENCE, PAULA DENISE, physical therapist; b. Ft. Worth, May 21, 1959; d. Roddy Paul and Kay Frances (Spivey) Gillis; m. Mark Jayson Lawrence, Apr. 20, 1985. BS, Tex. Women's U., 1982. Lic. phys. therapist, Tex., Calif. Sales mgr. R. and K Camping Ctr., Garland, Tex., 1977-82; staff physical therapist Longview (Tex.) Regional Hosp., 1982-83, dir. phys. therapy, 1983-87, dir. rehab. svcs., 1987-88; staff phys. therapist MPH Home Health, Longview, Tex., 1983-84; owner, pres. Phys. Rehabil. Ctr., Hemet, Calif., 1988—; mem. adv. com. div. health occupations Kilgore (Tex.) Coll., 1985-88; mem. profl. adv. bd. Hospice Longview, 1985-88. Bd. dirs. V.I.P. Tots. Mem. NAFE, Am. Phys. Therapy Assn., Calif. Phys. Therapy Assn., Am. Bus. Women's Assn. (v.p. 1987, 89, pres. 1990, Woman of Yr. 1988, 91), Assistance League Aux., Soroptomist (corr. sec. 1992, dir. 1993-95, sec. 1995-97), Hemet C. of C. (bd. dirs.), Psi Chi, Omega Rho Alpha. Home: 43725 Mandarin Dr Hemet CA 92544 Office: 901 S State St Ste 500 Hemet CA 92543-7127

LAWRENCE, ROBERT SWAN, physician, educator, academic administrator; b. Phila., Feb. 6, 1938; s. Thomas George and Catherine (Swan) L.; m. Cynthia Starr Cole, July 1, 1960; children: Job Scott, Matthew Swan, Hannah Starr, Jin Sook, Sang Bo. AB magna cum laude, Harvard U., 1960, MD, 1964. Intern, then resident in internal medicine Mass. Gen. Hosp., 1964-66, 69-70; surgeon USPHS, 1966-69; asst. prof., then assoc. prof. medicine, chief div. community medicine Med. Sch. U. N.C., 1970-74; dir. div. primary care Med. Sch. Harvard U., 1974-91, assoc. prof. medicine Med. Sch., 1980-81, Charles S. Davidson assoc. prof. medicine Med. Sch., 1981-91; chmn. dept. medicine Cambridge (Mass.) Hosp., 1980-91; adj. prof. NYU Sch. of MEdicine, 1992-95; prof. health policy & mgmt. Johns Hopkins Sch. Hygiene & Pub. Health, 1995, prof. medicine, Johns Hopkin's Sch. Medicine, 1995—; mem. com. human rights NAS; chmn. bd. health promotion and disease prevention IOM, 1981-86, chmn. com. health and human rights, 1990—; chmn. U.S. Preventive Svc. Task Force, HHS, 1984-89, active mem., 1990—; fellow Ctr. for Advanced Study in Behavioral Scis., 1988-89; dir. health scis. Rockefeller Found., 1991-95; assoc. dean for profl. edn. Johns Hopkins Sch. Hygiene & Pub. Health, 1995—. Editor Am. Jour. Preventive Medicine, 1990-92; contbr. articles and chpts. in books. Bd. dirs. Physicians for Human Rights, 1986-91, Tchrs. Coll., Columbia U., Am.'s Watch. Recipient Maimonides prize, 1964. Fellow ACP, Am. Coll. Preventive Medicine (Spl. Recognition award 1988); mem. Inst. Medicine, Am. Pub. Health Assn., Soc. Gen. Internal Medicine (pres. 1978-79), Soc. Tchrs. Preventive Medicine (Spl. Recognition award 1993), Phi Beta Kappa. Home: Highfield House 1112 4000 N Charles St Baltimore MD 21218-1737 Office: Johns Hopkins Sch Hygiene & Pub Health 615 N Wolfe St Baltimore MD 21205-2179

LAWRENCE, RUTH BECKER, nurse, contractor; b. Bklyn., June 16, 1925; d. Edward F. and Lillian (Davis) Becker; B.S., nursing diploma Simmons Coll., 1947; m. W. Leland Lawrence, Feb. 8, 1948; children—Stoddard, Thomas, Jeffrey, Leland Davis, Leigh Anne, Richard. Instr. nursing, Simmons Coll., Boston, 1947; staff nurse Nassau Hosp., Mineola, N.Y., 1947-48; staff pediatric nurse Hartford (Conn.) Hosp., 1948-49; dir. nursing service Springfield (Vt.) Hosp., 1977-86; now nurse cons. Choir, tchr. Sunday Sch., Congl. Ch.; den mother Boy Scouts Am.; vol. ARC; bd. dirs. Springfield Sch. Bd., 1962-72. Mem. Am. Nurses Assn., Council Nursing Adminstrs., Vt. Hosp. Assn. Dirs. Nursing.

LAWRENCE, SYLVIA YVONNE, critical care nurse; b. Danville, Pa., July 11, 1937; d. John Jacob and Florence Rebecca (Fenstermacher) Tanner; m. Davey Leon House, Oct. 4, 1958 (div. 1980); children: Susan D., Gayle Y. House Troxell; m. William C. Lawrence (div.). Diploma, Thomas Jefferson U., 1958; BSN, Lycoming Coll., 1991. RN, Pa.; cert. emergency nurse. Nurse various med. facilities, Pa., 1958-70; ho. supr. Sycamore Manor Nursing Home, Williamsport, Pa., 1970-71; gen. duty staff nurse Evangelical Community Hosp., Lewisburg, Pa., 1971-82, surg. staff nurse, 1983-87; surg. staff nurse Twelve Oaks Hosp., Houston, 1982-83; staff nurse emergency dept. Muncy Valley Hosp., 1985-91; patient care mgr. asst. Geisinger Med. Ctr., Danville, 1987—. Mem. Sigma Theta Tau. Republican. Home: PO Box 338 Riverside PA 17868-0338

LAWRENCE, WALTER THOMAS, plastic surgeon; b. Balt., Sept. 5, 1950; s. Walter Jr. and Susan (Shryock) L.; m. Marsha Blake, May 30, 1987. BS, Yale U., 1972; MPH, Harvard U., 1976; MD, U. Va., 1976. Diplomate Am. Bd. Surgery. Diplomate Am. Bd. Plastic Surgery. Intern and resident in gen. surgery U. N.C., Chapel Hill, 1976-78; resident gen. surgery Med. Coll. Va., Richmond, 1978-81; resident plastic surgery U. Chgo., 1981-83; expert NIH, Bethesda, Md., 1983-85; asst. prof. U. N.C., Chapel Hill, 1985-92, assoc. prof., div. chmn., 1992-95; prof., divsn. chmn. U. Mass. Med. Ctr., 1995—. Fellow Am. Coll. Surgeons; mem. Am. Assn. Plastic Surgeons, Am. Soc. Plastic and Reconstructive Surgeons, Plastic Surgery Rsch. Coun., Humera Soc., Womack Soc. Office: U Mass Med Ctr Divsn Plastic Surgery 55 Lake Ave N Worcester MA 01655

LAWRIE, GERALD MURRAY, cardiovascular and thoracic surgeon, educator; b. Murwillumbah, N.S.W., Australia, Oct. 15, 1945; came to U.S., 1974; s. Charles Malcolm and Heather (Murray) L.; m. Susan Wagner, Dec. 28, 1978; children: Heather Cristina, Charles Murray, Elizabeth Jane. M.B., B.S., Sydney (Australia) U., 1969. Resident in gen. surgery Prince Henry/Prince of Wales Teaching Hosps., U. NSW, Sydney, Australia, 1969-72, sr. registrar in cardiothoracic surgery, 1973-74; resident in gen. surgery Royal Coll. Surgeons Eng., London, Plymouth Gen. Hosp., U.K., 1972; fellow Baylor Coll. Medicine, Houston, 1974-75, instr., 1975-76, asst. prof., 1976-78, assoc. prof., 1978-84, prof., 1984—, dir. thoracic surgery residency program, 1992-94; attending surgeon The Meth. Hosp., Houston, 1978—, VA Hosp., Houston, 1980—, Ben Taub Hosp., Houston, 1975—; vice chmn. rsch., dept. surgery St. Joseph Hosp./Baylor Coll. Medicine, Houston, 1995-96. Author 225 published sci. articles and book chpts. Decorated Merit Order of Republic of Egypt, 1980. Fellow Royal Coll. Surgeons (Edinburgh), Royal Australasian Coll. Surgeons, Royal Coll. Surgeons Can., Am. Coll. Cardiology (Gov.'s award 1985); mem. ACS, AMA, Am. Heart Assn. (pres. Houston 1985-86, bd. dirs. Tex. chpt. 1986-89, Vol. Recognition award 1986), Am. Coll. Chest Physicians, South Tex. chpt. ACS, DeBakey Internat. Cardiovascular Soc., Harris County Med. Soc., Southwestern Surg. Congress, Tex. Med. Assn., Royal Soc. Medicine (assoc.), Soc. Thoracic Surgeons, Soc. for Vascular Surgery, Internat. Cardiovascular Soc. (N.Am. chpt.), Am. Assn. for Thoracic Surgery, Soc. for Thoracic Surg. Edn., So. Surg. Assn., N.Am. Soc. of Pacing and Electrophysiology. Presbyterian. Office: Baylor Coll Medicine One Baylor Pla Houston TX 77030

LAWRIE, STEPHEN MACGREGOR, psychiatry educator; b. Shrewsbury, Shropshire, Eng., May 26, 1963; s. Duncan Macgregor and Helen Moira (Burns) L.; m. Rachel Euphemia Campbell. MB BChir, Aberdeen (Scotland) U., 1986; MPhil, Edinburgh (Scotland) U., 1993. Sr. house officer Lothian Health Bd., Edinburgh, 1987-90, registrar, 1990-92; lectr. Edinburgh U., 1992—; rsch. adviser M.E. Found., Edinburgh, 1996—. Contbr. papers to profl. jours. Recipient Essay prize McHarg Fund, 1994; grantee Scottish Office, 1995, travel grantee Scottish Hosps. Endowment Rsch. Trust, 1995. Mem. Royal Coll. Psychiatrists, Brit. Assn. Psychopharmacology. Office: Edinburgh U Dept Psychiatry, Morningside Park, Edinburgh EH10 5HF, Scotland

LAWS, JAMES RUSSELL, hospital administrator; b. Bonne Terre, Mo., Mar. 3, 1947; s. Howard Wilson and Lelia Mae (Parks) L.; m. Anne Elizabeth DiMarco, Jan.24, 1970; children: Russell Howard, David Douglas, Janneane Elizabeth. BS in Park Mgmt., U. Mo., 1970; MBA, Boston U., 1978. Asst. adminstr. Meml. Hosp. of Natrona County, Casper, Wyo., 1980-83, Houston Internat. Hosp., 1983-84; adminstr. Grant Ctr. Hosp., Ocala, Fla., 1984-87, Rsch. Psychiat.Ctr., Kansas City, Mo., 1987-89; regional v.p. Sterling Healthcare, Bellevue, Wash., 1989-93; adminstr. Koala Hosp., 1993-94; divsn. v.p. Sterling Health Care, Indpls., 1994—. Lt. col. U.S. Army, 1970-80. Named Overall Outstanding Adminstr. Hosp. Corp. Am., Ocala, 1987. Mem. Hosp. Fin. Mgmt. Assn. (pres. Wyo. chpt. 1980-83), Nat. Assn. Pvt. Healthcare Orgn. (pres. elect Fla. 1987-87). Republican. Presbyterian. Home: 7778 Lincoln Trail Plainfield IN 46168 Office: Sterling Healthcare 1404 S State Ave Indianapolis IN 46203

LAWS, KENNETH L., physics educator, author; b. Pasadena, Calif., May 30, 1935; s. Allen L. and Florence (Windsor) L.; m. Priscilla Watson, June 3, 1965; children: Kevin Allen, Virginia. BS, Calif. Inst. Tech., 1956; MS, U. Pa., 1959; PhD, Bryn Mawr Coll., 1962. Instr. physics Hobart and William Smith Colls., Geneva, N.Y., 1958-59; from asst. prof. to prof. physics Dickinson Coll., Carlisle, Pa., 1962—; assoc. dean, dir. summer sch. Dickinson Coll., Carlisle, 1971-77, adminstrv. dir. summer ballet program, 1977-87; guest faculty Scientific Aspect of the Art of Dance, U. Washington Med. Sch. and Dance Dept., 1982; bd. reviewers Dance: Current Selected Research, 1985—. Author: The Physics of Dance, 1984; (with Cynthia Harvey) Physics, Dance and the Pas de Deux, 1994; contbr. articles on dance, physics to profl. jours. Pres. Ctrl. Pa. Youth Ballet, Carlisle, 1988-93. Office: Dickinson Coll Dept Physics Carlisle PA 17013

LAWSON, EDWARD EARLE, neonatologist; b. Winston-Salem, N.C., Aug. 6, 1946; s. Robert Barrett and Elsie Chatterton (Earle) L.; m. Rebecca Newhall Fitts, June 21, 1969; children: Katherine Tabor, Robert Barrett II. BA magna cum laude, Harvard U., 1968; MD, Northwestern U., 1972. Diplomate Am. Bd. Pediatrics and Neonatal/Perinatal Medicine. Intern then resident pediatrics Children's Hosp., Boston, 1972-75, fellow neonatology, 1975-78; from asst. prof. pediatrics to prof. pediatrics U. N.C., Chapel Hill, 1978—, chief div. neonatal medicine, 1987-95, interim chmn. dept. pediatrics, 1993-95; v. chmn., Dept. Pediatrics, 1995—. Assoc. editor Jour. of Pediatrics, 1985-95; contbr. numerous articles to profl. jours. Recipient Sidney Farber Meml. Rsch. award United Cerbral Palsy, 1982, Rsch. Career Devel. award NIH, 1982-87; fellow E. L. Trudeau, 1978-81, Alexander Von Humboldt, 1985-86; NIH grantee, 1979—. Fellow Am. Acad. Pediatrics; mem. Am. Lung Assn. (sci. adv. com. 1989-91), Am. Thoracic Soc. (bd. dirs. 1988-90), Am. Bd. Pediatrics, Am. Pediatric Soc., Perinatal Rsch. Soc. Office: U NC Dept Pediatrics CB 7220 Chapel Hill NC 27599-7220

LAWSON, JAMES EARL, osteopath; b. Detroit, June 4, 1945; s. Gerald James and Janet Virginia (Owen) L.; m. Lois Ann Levitt, June 29, 1968 (div. 1975); 1 child, Matthew Owen; m. Mary Ann Spencer, June 10, 1978 (div. 1982); 1 child, David James; m. Marian Judith Marcero, May 8, 1986; 1 child, Logan Thomas. BS in Zoology, U. Mich., 1967; DO, Kirksville (Mo.) Coll. Osteo. Medicine, 1971. Cert. Am. Osteo. Bd. Internal Medicine. Chief exec. officer BioMed. Applications of Detroit, 1978-94; med. dir. Inst. for Health Maintenance, Southfield, Mich., 1981-83; pres. Met. Nephrologists, Detroit, 1981—; clin. assoc. prof. Osteo. Medicine Mich. State U. Coll. Osteo. Medicine, East Lansing, 1976—; clin. asst. prof. Dept. Internal Medicine Wayne State U. Sch. Medicine, Detroit, 1983-95. Team mem. Youth at Risk, Detroit, 1986. Mem. Am. Osteo. Assn., Mich. Assn. Osteo. Physicians and Surgeons, Wayne County Osteo. Assn., Am. Coll. Osteo. Internists, Nat. Kidney Found., Am. Soc. Nephrology, Renal Physicians Assn., Am. Heart Assn., Physicians for Social Responsibility, Am. Med. Athletics Assn., Motor City Striders Club, Riverbend Striders. Office: Met Nephrologists PC 101 Hutzel Profl Bldg 11900 Twelve Mile Ste 200 Warren MI 48093

LAWSON, ROBERT BERNARD, psychology educator; b. N.Y.C., June 20, 1940; s. Robert Bernard Sr. and Isabella Theresa (McPeake) L.; children: Christina Megan, Steven Robert, Jennifer Erin. B.A. in Psychology, Monmouth Coll., 1961; M.A. in Psychology, U. Del., 1963, Ph.D. in Psychology, 1965. Mem. faculty U. Vt., Burlington, 1966—; asst. prof. psychology U. Vt., 1966-69, assoc. prof., 1969-74, prof., 1974—, assoc. v.p. acad. affairs, 1978, assoc. v.p. research, dean Grad. Coll., 1978-86, dir. gen. exptl. psychology, 1988-90; chair dept. pub. adminstrn., 1990-95; presenter, worker in People's Republic of China, Russia, and Italy; cons. Mgmt. Sys., 1986—; vis. scholar Stanford U., 1986-87; pres. Alliance Mgmt. Cons. Group, Burlington, 1987—, N.E. Assn. Grad. Schs., Princeton, N.J., 1983-86; bd. dirs. Grad. Record Exams-ETS, Princeton, 1984-88. Author: (with S.G. Goldstein and R.E. Musty) Principles and Methods of Psychology, 1975, (with W.L. Gulick) Human Stereopsis: A Psychophysical Approach, 1976. Bd. govs. Univ. Press New Eng., 1978-86, dir., 1979-80. Recipient numerous grants NIH, NSF, USDA; numerous awards from Nat. Eye Inst. Mem. AAAS, Psychonomic Soc., Council Grad. Schs., N.Y. Acad. Scis., Am. Psychol. Assn., Am. Eastern psychol. assn. Office: U Vt Dept Psychology John Dewey Hall Burlington VT 05405-0134

LAWSON, WILLIAM, otolargyngologist, educator; b. N.Y.C., Nov. 23, 1934; s. Alexander and Sophia (Elkind) L.; m. Miriam Patkin, Nov. 7, 1965; 1 child, Vanessa Ann. BA, NYU, 1956, DDS, 1961, MD, 1965. Diplomate Am. Bd. Otolaryngology, Am. Bd. Cosmetic Surgery, Am. Bd. Facial Plastic Surgery. Intern Mt. Sinai Hosp., N.Y.C., 1965-66, rsch. fellow in otolaryngology, 1969-70, resident in otolaryngology, 1970-73; resident in gen. surgery Bronx (N.Y.) VA Hosp., 1966-67, chief otolaryngology, head and neck surgery, 1984—; prof. Mt. Sinai Sch. Medicine, N.Y.C., 1980—. Author: Paraganguonic Chemoreceptor Systems, 1982, Surgery of the Paranasal Sinuses, 1988, 2nd edit., 1992, External Ear, 1995; contbr. over 190 articles to med. jours., chpts. to books. Capt. M.C., U.S. Army, 1967-69. Fellow ACS, Am. Acad. Facial Plastic and Reconstructive Surgery (svc. awrd), Am. Soc. Head and Neck Surgery, Am. Soc. Maxillofacial Surgeons, Am. Rhilogic, Otologic and Laryngolic Soc., Am. Laryngol. Soc.; mem. Am. Acad. Otolaryngology (svc. award). Office: Mt Sinai Med Ctr 5 E 98th St New York NY 10029

LAWTON, ALEXANDER ROBERT, III, immunologist, educator; b. Savannah, Ga., Nov. 8, 1938; s. Alexander Robert and Elizabeth (Holdrege) L.; m. Frances Ritchie Crockett, Nov. 25, 1960; children: Julia Beckwith, Alexander Robert IV. BA, Yale U., 1960; MD, Vanderbilt U., 1964. Diplomate Am. Bd. Pediatrics. Resident in pediatrics Vanderbilt U., Nashville, 1964-66; fellow dept. pediatrics U. Ala., Birmingham, 1969-71, from asst. prof. to prof. pediatrics and microbiology, 1971-80; prof. microbiology, Edward C. Stahlman prof. pediatric physiology and cell metabolism Vanderbilt U. Sch. Medicine, Nashville, 1980—; mem. cancer spl. programs rev. com. Nat. Cancer Inst., 1981-84; mem. allergy, immunology and transplantation rev. com. Nat. Inst. Allergy and Infectious Diseases, 1985-88. Contbr. over 150 articles, book chpts. to profl. publs. Surgeon USPHS, 1966-69. Grantee NIH, March of Dimes Birth Defects Found. Mem. Soc. Pediatric Rsch., Am. Pediatric Soc., Am. Soc. Clin. Investigation, Am. Assn. Immunologists, Am. Assn. Pathologists. Episcopalian. Office: Vanderbilt U Sch Medicine D3237 Med Ctr N Nashville TN 37232

LAWTON, MARCIA JEAN, psychologist, educator; b. Pawtucket, R.I., May 21, 1937; d. Walter Lincoln and Jean Fraser (Baldwin) L. AB, Brown U., 1959; MA, Northwestern U., 1961, PhD, 1963. Lic. psychologist, Nebr., Colo., Va. In-patient coord. Nebr. Psychiat. Inst., Omaha, 1963-67; clin. psychologist Arapahoe Mental Health Ctr., Englewood, Colo., 1968-72; pvt. practice clin. psychologist Denver, 1972-73; mgr. Women's Halfway House, Arlington, Va., 1974-75; assoc. prof. Va. Commonwealth U., Richmond, 1975-96; owner Paraclete, Midlothian, Va., 1996—; pres., supr. Growth and Recovery Opportunities, Richmond, 1976-93; editor Addiction Letter, Manisses, Providence, 1985-96. Contbr. articles to profl. jours. Founder, chmn. Greater Richmond Coun. on Alcoholism and Drug Abuse, Richmond, 1978-91. Mem. APA, Va. Psychol. Assn., Va. Alcohol and Drug Abuse Counselors Assn., Nat. Alcohol and Drug Abuse Counselors Assn. (Mel Schulstad award 1983), Phi Beta Kappa, Sigma Xi. Office: Box 1961 Midlothian VA 23112

LAYDEN, WILLIAM EDWARD, ophthalmologist; b. Rutland, Vt., Oct. 26, 1937; s. William Henry and Mildred Mary (Batchelder) L.; m. Mary Ellen Doherty, Sept. 12, 1962 (div.); children: Tracey K., William H.; m. Susan J. Rochester, Jan. 18, 1985; children: Matthew E., Caroline A. BA, U. Vt., 1959, MD, 1963. Instr. ophthalmology U. Louisville, 1970-71, asst. prof., 1971-72; Glaucoma fellow U. Calif., San Francisco, 1972-73; asst. prof. ophthalmology U. South Fla., Tampa, 1973-75, assoc. prof., 1979-80, prof. and chmn. ophthalmology, 1980-91, clin. prof. ophthalmology, 1991—; pvt. practice ophthalmology, 1991—; med. adv. com. Found. for Glaucoma Rsch., San Francisco, 1983-85; chmn. JAEB Instl. Rev. Bd. Contbr. articles to profl. jours., chpts. to books. Capt. USAF, 1964-67. Mem. Nat. Soc. to Prevent Blindness (mem. glaucoma com.). Republican. Roman Catholic. Office: Univ Glaucoma Ctr 13601 Bruce B Downs Blvd Tampa FL 33613-4657

LAYISH, DANIEL T., internist. BA magna cum laude, Boston U., 1986, MD magna cum laude, 1990. Diplomate Am. Bd. Internal Medicine, Nat. Bd. Med. Examiners; ACLS, Advanced Trauma Life Support. Intern/resident, dept. internal medicine Barnes Hosp., St. Louis, 1990-93; pulmonary/critical care/sleep medicine fellow Duke U. Med. Ctr., Durham, N.C., 1994—; critical care staff, assoc. med. staff Christian Hosp. Northeast, St. Louis, 1993-94; staff, Urgent Care Clinic Carolina Permanente, Raleigh, N.C., 1994—. Contbr. articles to profl. jours. Recipient Med. Grad. award, Hewlett-Packard Co., 1990, Young Investigator and Alfred Soffer Rsch. awards, Am. Coll. Chest Physicians, 1995. Mem. AMA, ACP, Am. Thoracic Soc. (assoc.), Am. Coll. Chest Physicians (affiliate), Alpha Omega Alpha. Home: 5202-B Penrith Dr Durham NC 27713-1724 Office: Duke Univ Med Ctr Divsn Pulmonary/Crit Care Durham NC 27710

LAYMAN, DALE PIERRE, medical educator, author, researcher; b. Niles, Mich., July 3, 1948; s. Pierre Andre and Delphine Lucille (Lenke) L.; m. Kathleen Ann Jackowiak, Aug. 8, 1970; children: Andrew Michael, Alexis Kathryn, Allison Victoria, Amanda Elizabeth. AS in Life Sci., Lake Mich. Coll., 1968; BS in Anthropology and Zoology, U. Mich., 1971, MS in Physiology, 1974; EdS in Physiology and Health Sci., Ball State U., 1979; PhD in Health and Safety Studies, U. Ill., 1986. Histological technician in neuropathology Med. Sch. U. Mich., Ann Arbor, 1971-72, tchg. fellow in human physiology Med. Sch., 1972-74; instr. in human anatomy, physiology, and histology Lake Superior State U., Sault Ste. Marie, Mich., 1974-75; prof. med. terminology, human anatomy and physiology Joliet (Ill.) Jr. Coll., 1975—. Author: The Terminology of Anatomy and Physiology, 1983, The Medical Language: A Programmed Body-Systems Approach, 1995; contbr. articles to profl. jours. Mem. AAAS, Human Anatomy and Physiology Soc., Ill. Cmty. Coll. Faculty Assn., Phi Kappa Phi, Kappa Delta Pi. Home: 509 Westridge Ln Joliet IL 60431 Office: Joliet Jr Coll 1215 Houbolt Ave Joliet IL 60431

LAYTON, WILLIAM G., medical center administrator; b. Balt., Aug. 1, 1943; s. William H. and Jean Marie (Diener) L.; m. Suszanna E. Layton, Jan. 1, 1980; 1 child, Chrysanna E. Paramedic, Cen. Fla. Community Coll., Ocala, 1980. Lic. EMT. Paramedic Munroe Regional Med. Ctr., Ocala, 1980, supr. ambulance svc., 1981, mgr. ambulance svc., 1984, dir. ambulance svc., 1989—; v.p. Fla. Regional 6 C.I.S.D.; founder, dir., treas. N. Cen. Fla. Trauma Agy., 1990-92. Vice chmn. Marion County Emergency Mgmt. Coun., 1992—; mem. Withlacoochee Regional Local Emergency Planning Com., Dist. 5, 1990—. Recipient Brian G. McKay award for outstanding contbns. to Emergency Med. Svc. in North Cen. Fla., 1987. Mem. Coun. on Rural Emergency Med. Svc. (past pres., sec.), Emergency Med. Svc. Providers Assn. Fla. (dist. rep.), Am. Trauma Soc. (founding dir., sec. Fla. div.), Fla. Assn. County Emergency Med. Svcs. (bd. dirs. 1994-95), Ocala Civic Theater (bd. dirs. 1995—). Home: 8434 SW 69th Court Rd Ocala FL 34476-8157

LAZAR, EDWARD H., obstetrician and gynecologist; b. Memphis, Mar. 25, 1942; s. Max E. and Annie Ruth (Baer) L.; m. Marxann Sherman, June 18, 1967; children: Sherie Jan, Marc Elliot. BA, Vanderbilt U., 1963; MD, U. Tenn., 1967. Intern Sinai Hosp. of Balt. Inc., 1967-68; resident ob-gyn. City of Memphis Hosps. U. of Tenn., Memphis, 1968-71; pres. Ob-Gyn. Physicians of Memphis, 1990—. Maj. USAF, 1971-73. Fellow Am. Coll. Ob-Gyn., Am. Soc. Reproductive Medicine; mem. Am. Assn. Gynecologists and Laparoscopists, Gynecologic Laser Soc., Ctrl. Assn. Ob-Gyn., Am. Soc. for Culposcopy and Cervical Pathology, Am. Coll. of Physician Execs. Office: 6027 Walnut Grove Rd #317 Memphis TN 38120

LAZAR, GEORGE THEODORE, orthopaedic surgeon; b. Bulgaria, Apr. 24, 1931; came to U.S., 1973; s. Theodore Raitcho and Maria George (Ianakieva) Lazarov; m. Christina Pavlova Christova, Dec. 4, 1959; 1 child, Theodore G. MD, I.P. Pavlov Inst., Plovdiv, Bulgaria, 1956. Resident orthopaedic surgery Trauma Ctr. Inst. Specialization Physicians, Children's Hosp., Kotel, Madan and Sofia, Bulgaria, 1956-60; asst. prof. othopaedics I.P. Pavlov Inst., Plovdiv, 1960-71; specialization hand Inst. Specialization Physicians, Sofia, 1963-68; surgeon Benghasi, Libya, 1972-73, Prof. R. Judet, Paris, 1973; intern Westchester County Med. Ctr., N.Y., 1974-75; resident, fellow Union Meml./Children's/Hopkins, Balt., 1975-78; pvt. practice Orthopedic and Hand Surgery Assocs., Balt., 1978—; bd. dirs. Am. U. Bulgaria. Bd. mem. Bulgarian St. George Ch., Washington, 1983. Mem. ACS, Am. Assn. Surgery Hand, Am. Soc. Surgery Hand, Balt. City Med. Soc., Johns Hopkins Club. Republican. Eastern Orthodox. Office: Orthopedic and Hand Surgery 1050 Old North Point Rd Baltimore MD 21224-3329

LAZAR, JILL, publishing company executive; b. Oak Park, Ill., June 15, 1954; d. Norton David and Carol Ellen (Kaufmann) Freyer; m. Bruce Horwich, Aug. 21, 1976 (div. Sept. 1984); 1 child, Mathew Freyer Horwich; m. Neil Lazar, Nov. 23, 1986. BS in Mktg., No. Ill. U., 1975. Mktg. rsch. assoc. McDonald's Corp., Oak Brook, Ill., 1976-80; renewal coord. Time, Inc., Chgo., 1984-87; product mgr. Macmillan Directory Div., Wilmette, Ill., 1987-82; with Dependicare, Broadview, Ill., 1992—. Mem. Direct Mktg. Assn., Chgo. Assn. Direct Mktg. Office: Dependicare 1815 Gardner Rd Broadview IL 60153

LAZAR, RANDE HARRIS, otolaryngologist; b. N.Y.C., Feb. 27, 1951; s. Irving and Dorothy (Tartasky) L.; m. Linda Zishuk, Aug. 11, 1974; 1 child, Lauren K. BA, Bklyn. Coll., 1973; MD, U. Autonoma de Guadalajara, Mexico, 1978; postgrad., N.Y. Med. Coll., 1978-79. Diplomate Am. Bd. Otolaryngology-Head and Neck Surgery; lic. physician, N.Y., Ohio, Tenn. Gen. surgery resident Cornell-North Shore Community Hosp., Manhasset, N.Y., 1979-80; gen. surgery resident Cleve. Clinic Found., 1980-81, otolaryngology-head and neck surgery resident, 1980-84, chief resident dept. otolaryngology & communicative disorder, 1983-84; physician Otolaryngology Cons. Memphis, 1984—; fellow pathology head and neck dept. otolaryngologic pathology Armed Forces Inst. Pathology, Washington, 1983; pediatric otolaryngology fellow Le Bonheur Children's Med. Ctr., Memphis, 1984-85, dir. pediatric otolaryngology fellowship tng., 1989—, chief surgery, 1989, chief staff East Surgery Ctr.; chmn. dept. otolaryngology head and neck surgery Meth. Health Systems, 1990-91; courtesy staff Bapt. Meml. Hosp., Bapt. Meml. Hosp.-East, Eastwood Med. Ctr., Meth. Hosp., Germantown, Tenn.; chief dept. otolaryngology Les Passees Rehab. Ctr., 1988—. Contbr. articles to profl. jours. Bd. dirs. Bklyn. Tech. Found. Recipient award of honor Am. Acad. Otolaryngology-Head and Neck Surgery, 1991. Fellow Internat. Coll. Surgeons; mem. AMA, Am. Acad. Otolaryngology-Head and Neck Surgery, Am. Acad. Facial Plastic and Reconstructive Surgery, Am. Acad. Otolaryngic Allergy, Centurions Deafness Rsch. Found., Am. Auditory Soc., Nat. Hearing Assn., Soc. Ear, Nose Throat Advances in Children, Am. Soc. Laser Medicine and Surgery, So. Med. Assn., N.Y. Acad. Scis., Tenn. Med. Soc., Tenn. Acad. Otolaryngology-Head and Neck Surgery, Memphis and Shelby County Med. Soc., Memphis/Mid South Soc. Pediatrics. Office: Otolaryngology Cons Memphis 777 Washington Ave Ste 240P Memphis TN 38105-4566

LAZAR, RICHARD BECK, physician, medical administrator; b. N.Y.C., Oct. 9, 1954; s. Harold Paul and Molly (Beck) L.; m. Susan Merle Berman, Oct. 1, 1983; children: Spencer Berman, Winston Harold, Grahan Henry Duke. BA in Biology cum laude, Harvard U., 1976; MD, Northwestern U., 1979. Attending physician Northwestern Meml. Hosp., Chgo., 1984-94, Rehab. Inst. Chgo., 1986-92; exec. v.p., med. dir. Schwab Rehab. Hosp., Chgo.; chair dept. phys. medicine & rehab. Mt. Sinai Hosp., Chgo., 1992—; clin. assoc. prof. surgery Pritzker Sch. Medicine U. Chgo., 1994—, program dir., chief subsect. phys. medicine & rehab., 1995—; mem. adv. com. patient mgmt. & tech. Nat. MS Soc., N.Y.C., 1992—; hon. com. Nat. Head Injury Found., Chgo., 1994; profl. adv. com. Nat. Easter Seal Soc., Chgo., 1994—. Co-author: Handbook of Neurorehabilitation, 1994, Spinal Injury: Medical Management and Rehabilitation, 1994. Fellow Am. Acad. Neurology, Am. Acad. Phys. Medicine, Assn. Acad. Physiatrists, Am. Congress Rehab. Medicine, Am. Soc. Neurorehab. (pres.-elect 1995-96, pres. 1996—, Outstanding Svc. & Leadership award 1990-94). Home: 5490 South Shore Dr 4N Chicago IL 60615 Office: Schwab Rehab Hosp & Care Network 1401 S California Blvd Chicago IL 60608

LAZAR, SUSAN GABER, psychiatrist, psychoanalyst, educator; b. Chgo., July 20, 1944; d. Martin and Lita (LeAnce) Gaber; m. Joel Lazar, June 9, 1965; children: Jessica, Joanna. AB, Radcliffe Coll., 1966; MD, Yeshiva U., 1970. Cert. psychiatrist, psychoanalyst. Intern U. Va. Sch. Medicine, 1970-71; resident in psychiatry Tufts U. Sch. Medicine, 1971-74; asst. prof. psychiatry U. Va. Sch. Medicine, Charlottesville, 1974-77, asst. clin. prof., 1977-82; pvt. practice Bethesda, Md., 1977—; supervising and tng. analyst Wash. Psychoanalytic Inst., 1995—; staff psychiatrist Chestnut Lodge, Rockville, Md., 1977-80; mem. faculty ext. divsn. Washington Psychoanalytic Inst., 1978, instr., 1983—, tchg. analyst, 1988; clin. prof. psychiatry George Washington U. Sch. Medicine, Washington, 1989; clin. prof. psychiatry USUHS, Georgetown U. Sch. Medicine; presenter in field. Fellow Am. Psychiat. Assn.; mem. Am. Coll. Psychiatry, Internat. Psychoanalytic Assn., Am. Psychoanalytic Assn., Va. Psychoanalytic Soc. (charter), Washington Psychoanalytic Soc., Group for the Advancement of Psychiatry, Nat. Coun. for Psychoanalytic Self Psychology, Alpha Omega Alpha. Home and Office: 9104 Quintana Dr Bethesda MD 20817

LAZARE, AARON, psychiatrist, academic administrator; b. Newark, Feb. 14, 1936; s. H. Benjamin and Anne (Storfer) L.; m. Louise Cannon; children: Robert, Jacqueline, David, Sam, Sarah, Hien, Thomas, Naomi. AB, Oberlin Coll., 1957; MD, Case Western Reserve U., 1961. Intern in medicine Bronx (N.Y.) Mcpl. Hosp. Ctr., 1961-62; resident in psychiatry Mass. Mental Health Ctr., 1962-65; asst. in psychiatry Mass. Gen. Hosp., Boston, 1967-68; chief day hosp. inpatient unit Yale-New Haven Hosp., 1967-68; assoc. dir. adult outpatient psychiatry Mass. Gen. Hosp., Boston, 1968-70; dir. adult outpatient psychiatry Mass. Gen. Hosp., 1970-75, acting dir. residency tng., 1972, dir. outpatient psychiatry, 1975-82, dep. chief psychiatry, 1976-82, clin. dir. psychiatry, 1978-82; prof., chmn. dept. psychiatry U. Mass. Med. Ctr., Worcester, 1982—, interim dean, 1989-90, dean, 1990, chancellor, 1991; prof. Harvard U., 1982. Editor: Outpatient Psychiatry, 1979, 1989, 2nd edit.; contbr. articles to profl. jours.; co-author of books in field. Capt. U.S. Army, 1965-67. Named for Disting. Pub. Svc. Commonwealth of Mass., honorable mention U. Mass., 1987, Commonwealth of Mass., U. Mass., Boston, 1988, Brotherhood award NCCJ, 1992. Mem. AAAS, AMA, Am. Psychiat. Assn. (Benjamin Rush award 1992), Mass. Psychiat. Soc. Office: U Mass Med Ctr Off Chancellor 55 Lake Ave N Worcester MA 01655-0002*

LAZARUS, ARNOLD ALLAN, psychologist, educator; b. Johannesburg, Republic of South Africa, Jan. 27, 1932; came to U.S., 1963; s. Benjamin and Rachel Leah (Mosselson) L.; m. Daphne Ann Kessel, June 10, 1956; children: Linda Sue, Clifford Neil. BA with honors, U. Witwatersrand, 1956; MA, U. Witwatersrand, Johannesburg, 1957, PhD, 1960. Diplomate: Am. Bd. Profl. Psychology, Am. Bd. Med. Psychotherapists (fellow), Internat. Acad. Behavioral Medicine, Counseling and Psychotherapy. Pvt. practice clin. psychology Johannesburg, 1959-63, 64-66; vis. asst. prof. dept. psychology Stanford (Calif.) U., 1963-64; prof. psychology Temple U. Med. Sch., Phila., 1967-70; dir. clin. tng. Yale U., New Haven, 1970-72; disting. prof. Rutgers U., New Brunswick, N.J., 1972—; mem. adv. bd. Psychologists for Social Responsibility, 1984—; cons. in field. Author: 15 books including Behavior Therapy and Beyond, 1971, Multimodal Behavior Therapy, 1976, The Practice of Multimodal Therapy, 1981, rev. edit., 1989, In the Mind's Eye, 1984, Martial Myths, 1985, Mind Power: Getting What You Want Through Mental Training, 1987, The Essential Arnold Lazarus, 1991, A Dialogue with Arnold Lazarus, 1991, Don't Believe It For A Minute!, 1993, Abnormal Psychology, 1995; editl. bd. sci. jours.; contbr. articles to profl. jours. Recipient Disting. Svc. award Am. Bd. Profl. Psychology, Disting. Career Achievement award Am. Bd. Med. Psychotherapists, Outstanding Contbns. to Mental Health award Psychiat. Outpatient Ctrs. of the Americas, 1991. Fellow APA (Disting. Psychologist award divsn. of psychotherapy 1992), Am. Bd. Profl. Psychology (diplomate), Internat. Acad. Eclectic Psychotherapists, Acad. Clin. Psychology; mem. Am. Acad. Psychotherapy, Assn. for Advancement Psychotherapy, Nat. Acads. Practice in Psychology (disting.), Soc. for Exploration of Psychotherapy Integration. Home: 56 Herrontown Cir Princeton NJ 08540-2924 Office: Rutgers U PO Box 819 Piscataway NJ 08855-0819

LAZARUS, GERALD SYLVAN, physician; b. N.Y.C., Feb. 16, 1939; s. Joseph W. and Marion (Goldstein) L.; m. Sandra Jacob, Sept. 3, 1961 (dec. 1985); children: Mark, Elyse, Lynne, Laura; m. Audrey Fedyszyn Jakubowski, Apr. 7, 1990. B.A., Colby Coll., 1959; M.D., George Washington U., 1963. Intern, then resident U. Mich., Ann Arbor, 1963-64; resident in medicine U. Mich., 1964-65; NIH research asso. NIH, Bethesda, Md., 1965-68; resident in dermatology Harvard U., Cambridge, Mass., 1968-70; research fellow Strangeways Labs., Cambridge, Eng., 1970-72; assoc. prof. medicine, co-dir. dermatology tng. program Albert Einstein Med. Coll., N.Y.C., 1972-75; J. Lamar Callaway prof. Duke U., Durham, N.C., 1977-82; chief dermatology Duke U., 1975-82; Milton B. Hartzell prof. U. Pa. Sch. Medicine, Phila., 1982—, chmn. dept. dermatology, 1982-93; dean Sch. Medicine U. Calif., Davis, 1993—; mem. study sect. NIH, 1976-80. Author: (with L. Goldsmith) Diagnosis of Skin Disease, 1980, (with Herman Beerman) Tradition of Excellance: History of Dermatology at Univ. Pa. Sch. of Medicine; asso. editor: Jour. Investigative Dermatology, 1977-82; contbr. numerous articles to profl. jours. Served with USPHS, 1965-68. Carl Herzog fellow Am. Dermatology Assn., 1970-72; John Simon Guggenheim fellow U. Geneva, 1986; sr. investigator Arthritis Found., 1972-77; grantee NIH. Fellow ACP, Assn. Am. Physicians, Am. Soc. Clin. Investigation; mem. Am. Dermatol. Assn., Soc. Investigative Dermatology (dir., pres. 1996-97, Disting. alumnus award George Washington U. 1996), Biochem. Soc., Am. Acad. Dermatology (Sultzberger award 1986). Republican. Jewish. Office: U Calif Sch Medicine Office Of The Dean Davis CA 95616

LAZARUS, ROCHELLE BRAFF, advertising executive; b. N.Y.C., Sept. 1, 1947; d. Lewis L. and Sylvia Ruth (Eisenberg) Braff; m. George M. Lazarus, Mar. 22, 1970; children: Theodore, Samantha, Benjamin. AB, Smith Coll., 1968; MBA, Columbia U., 1970. Product mgr. Clairol, N.Y.C., 1970-71; account exec. Ogilvy & Mather, N.Y.C., 1971-73, account supr., 1973-77, mgmt. supr., 1977-84, sr. v.p., 1981—, account group dir., 1984-87; gen. mgr. Ogilvy & Mather Direct, N.Y.C., 1987-88, mng. dir., 1988-89, pres., 1989-91; pres. Ogilvy & Mather, N.Y.C., 1991-94, pres. N. Am., 1991-94; pres., COO Ogilvy & Mather Worldwide, N.Y.C., 1995—, CEO, 1996. Bd. dirs. Ann Taylor, Advt. Edn. Found., YMCA, Nat. Women's Law Ctr., World Wildlife Fund; mem. Com. of 200; mem. bus. com. Solomon R. Guggenheim Mus.; mem. bd. overseers Columbus Bus. Sch.; trustee Smith Coll., Columbia Presbyn. Hosp. Recipient YWCA Women Achievers award, 1985, Matrix award, 1995. Mem. Am. Assn. Advt. Agys. (bd. dirs.), Advt. Women N.Y. (Woman of Yr. 1994). Home: 106 E 78th St New York NY 10021-0302 Office: Ogilvy & Mather Worldwide 309 W 49th St New York NY 10019-7316

LAZDUNSKI, MICHEL, pharmacology educator; b. Marseille, France, Apr. 11, 1938; s. Jacques and Genevieve (Fumagalli) L.; m. Catherine Blanche Honorat, Apr. 12, 1974; children: Fleur, Remi. PhD, U. Laval, 1962; DSc, U. Marseille, 1964. Rsch. assoc. CNRS, Marseille, 1962-66; assoc. prof. U. Marseille, 1966-68; chair dept. biochemistry U. Nice, France, 1968-91; prof. Inst. Univ. de France, Nice, 1991—; dir. Inst. Pharm. CNRS, Nice, 1989—; coun. European Molecular Biology Orgn., 1993—; pres. com. life scis. European Econ. Cmty., 1996—. Mem. Academia Europea, French Acad. Scis., Belgian Royal Acad. Medicine. Home: 21 Ave Colombo, 06100 Nice France Office: Inst Pharmacologie, 660 Rte des Lucioles, 06560 Valbonne France

LAZEAR, SUSAN ENGMAN, nursing educator. Student, U. So. Calif., 1972-74; BSN, U. Md., 1976; MSN, U. Wash., 1981. RN, Calif., Wash., Hawaii; ACLS, first aid instr. Staff nurse Seattle and San Mateo, Calif., 1980-81; chief flight nurse, program coord. critical care air svc. Airlift Northwest, Seattle, 1981-86; clin. inst. dept. physiological nursing U. Wash., Seattle, 1983-86; trauma cons. Dept. of Emergency Med. Svcs./State of Washington, 1987-88; faculty cons. Resource Applications, Balt., 1987-89; dir. med. edn., cons. Specialists in Med. Edn., Seattle, 1986—; presenter workshops in field. Co-editor: Critical Care Nursing, 2nd edit., 1992; contbr. articles to profl. jours., books. Capt. U.S. Army Nurse Corps, 1972-79. Home: 15830 NE 165th St Woodinville WA 98072-8118

LAZERSON, JACK, pediatrician, educator; b. Bronx, Jan. 9, 1936; s. Mayer and Jennie (Gerson) L.; (div.); children: David, Deborah, Darlene, Donna; (div.); 1 child, Samuel. AB, NYU, 1957; MD, U. Chgo., 1961. Diplomate Am. Bd. Pediatrics. Rotating internship L.A. County Gen. Hosp., 1961-62; resident in pediatrics Stanford-Palo Alto (Calif.) Hosp., 1962-64; chief resident in pediatrics, instr. U. Wash. Hosp., Seattle, 1966-67; asst. prof. dept. pediatrics Sch. of Medicine Stanford U., 1969-72; from asst. to assoc. prof. dept. pediatrics U. So. Calif., L.A., 1972-76; assoc. prof. dept. pediatrics U. Wis., Milw., 1976-79; prof. dept. pediatrics Sch. of Medicine U. Calif., Davis, 1979-86, prof. dept. pathology, 1980-86; prof., chmn. dept. pediatrics Sch. of Medicine U. Nev., 1986-94, prof. dept. pediatrics Sch. Medicine, 1986—; chief hemophilia svc. Children's Hosp. Stanford U. Sch. of Medicine, 1969-72; assoc. hematologist div. hematology and oncology Children's Hosp. L.A., 1972-76. Contbr. numerous articles to profl. jours. Bd. dirs. hemostasis program Milw. Children's Hosp., 1976-79; med. dir. Great Lakes Hemophilia Found., 1976-79. Armour and Hyland Labs. grantee, 1969-72, 72-76, Med. Coll. of Wis. grantee, 1976-79, HEW grantee, 1976-79, Cutter Labs. grantee, 1981-82, 82-83; recipient Rsch. Funds award U. Calif.-Davis, 1981-82, Outstanding Alumnus award U. Chgo., 1981. Fellow Am. Acad. Pediatrics; mem. Am. Fedn. for Clin. Rsch., N.Y. Acad. Scis., Nat. Hemophilia Found., Am. Chem. Soc. (biochemistry sect., med. chemistry sect.), Hemostasis Assn. of Calif., Internat. Soc. Thrombosis and Hemostasis, Am. Heart Assn. Coun. on Thrombosis Basic Sci. Coun., Am. Soc. Hematology, Am. Soc. for Exptl. Pathology, World Fedn. Hemophilia, Am. Assn. Blood Banks, Am. Soc. Pediatric (hematology and oncology credentials and by-laws com., membership com.), Alpha Omega Alpha. Office: U Nev Sch Medicine 2040 W Charleston Blvd Ste 200 Las Vegas NV 89102-2206

LAZO, JOHN, JR., physician; b. Passaic, N.J., Nov. 29, 1946; s. John and Mary (Beley) L.; m. Donnalynn Margaret Materna, July 22, 1972; children: Jonathan Christopher, Ashley Jude. BS, Fairleigh Dickinson U., 1974; MD, Univ. Autonoma de Guadalajara, Mexico, 1978. Diplomate Am. Bd. Emergency Medicine. Intern Akron (Ohio) City Hosp., 1980-81, resident in emergency medicine, 1981-83, chief resident in emergency medicine, 1982-83; med. dir. emergency svcs. Parma (Ohio) Comty. Gen. Hosp., 1986-93, vice-chmn. emergency dept., 1995—; dir. Paramedic Edn. Program, Parma, 1986-93; bd. dirs. Advantage Health Ptnrs. Sgt. USAF, 1966-70. Fellow Am. Coll. Emergency Physicians; mem. NEOSEM. Republican. Russian Orthodox. Home: 10010 Gatewood Dr Cleveland OH 44141-3615 Office: Parma Community Gen Hosp 7007 Powers Blvd Cleveland OH 44129-5437

LAZOWICK, ANDREA LEE, pharmacist; b. Phila., Mar. 3, 1970; d. Ellis and Toby (Forman) L. BS in Pharmacy, Phila. Coll. Pharmacy and Sci., 1992; PharmD, Nova-Southeastern U., North Miami Beach, Fla., 1994. Lic. pharmacist, Fla., Pa. Pharmacist CVS Pharmacy, Phila., 1992, Truco Drugs, North Miami Beach, 1992-93, Pulmonary Prescription Providers, Hallandale, Fla., 1993; psychopharmacy splty. resident Albany (N.Y.) Coll. Pharmacy, 1994-95; asst. prof. pharmacy practice Fla. A&M U., Miami, 1995—; clin. pharmacist in psychiatry, Fla. A&M U., 1995—, VA Med. Ctr., Miami; faculty liaison Am. Soc. Health Sys. Pharmacists, Bethesda, Md., 1995—. Contbr. articles to profl. jours.; invited referee Annals of Pharmacotherapy Jour., 1995—. Mem. Broward Advocates for the Mentally Ill, Plantation, Fla., 1995—, OC Found., Miami, 1995—; participant "Healthy People 2000", Atlanta, 1995—. Mem. Am. Assn. Colls. of Pharmacy, Am. Coll. Clin. Pharmacy, Am. Soc. Health-Sys. Pharmacists, Am. Pharm. Assn., Mental Health Assn., Fla. Soc. Health-Sys. Pharmacists, Fla. Pharmacy Assn. Democrat. Jewish. Office: Florida A&M Univ 1500 NW 12th Ave Ste 1126 Miami FL 33136

LAZUTKA, JUOZAS RIMANTAS, geneticist; b. Vilnius, Lithuania, Mar. 12, 1960; s. Stanislovas and Liudvika (Lisenkaite) L.; m. Veronika Dedonyte, Jan. 9, 1986; children: Justas, Greta, Raminta. Degree, Vilnius State U., 1982; PhD, Inst. Gen. Genetics, Moscow, 1987; DSc, Vilnius U., 1994. Jr. research fellow dept. botany and genetics Vilnius U., 1982-87, sci. researcher ecol. genetics lab., 1987-92, sr. sci. rschr. ecol. genetics lab., 1992-94, chief rschr., 1994—; guest researcher Lund U., 1993. Author: Sister Chromatid Exchanges, 1990; contbr. articles to profl. publs. Fellow Lithuanian Soc. Genetics and Breeding. Home: Stanevičiaus 14-81, 2029 Vilnius Lithuania Office: Vilnius U EGL, 21 Čiurlionis St, 2009 Vilnius Lithuania

LAZZARA, DENNIS JOSEPH, orthodontist; b. Chgo., Mar. 14, 1948; s. Joseph James and Jacqueline Joan (Antonini) L.; m. Nancy Ann Pirhofer, Dec. 18, 1971; children: Kristin Lynn, Bryan Matthew, Matthew Dennis, Kathryn Marie, David Brady. BS, U. Dayton, 1970; DDS, Loyola U., 1974. MS in Oral Biology, 1976, cert. orthodontics, 1976. Practice dentistry specializing in orthodontics, Geneva, Ill., 1976—; mem. dental staff Delnor Community Hosp., Geneva and St. Charles, Ill., 1976—; sec. dental staff, Geneva, 1978-80, v.p., 1980-82, pres., 1982-84, exec. com., 1982-84. Leader Boy Scouts Am., 1988-90. Recipient Award of Merit, Am. Coll. of Dentists, 1974, Harry Sicher honorable mention Council on Research, Am. Assn. Orthodontists, 1977. Mem. Am. Assn. Orthodontists, Midwestern Soc. of Orthodontists, Ill. Soc. Orthodontists, ADA, Fox River Valley Dental Soc. (bd. dirs. 1983-86), Blue Key Nat. Honor Soc. Roman Catholic. Avocations: sailing, golf. Office: PO Box 431 Geneva IL 60134-0431

LEACH, KAY T., critical care nurse, administrator; b. Brazil, Ind., Oct. 11, 1953; d. David M. and Tamiko (Ishiguru) Oberholtzer; m. Ronald Leach, June 12, 1982; children: Brian, Kristen, Brittany, Ronald Ian. BSN, Ind. State U., 1975, MSN, 1989. Cert. emergency nurse, ACLS. House supr. Union Hosp., Terre Haute, Ind., ICU staff nurse, dir. emergency dept. Mem. Emergency Nurses Assn., Sigma Theta Tau, Phi Kappa Phi.

LEACH, ROBERT ELLIS, physician, educator; b. Sanford, Maine, Nov. 25, 1931; s. Ellis and Estella (Tucker) L.; m. Laurine Seber, Aug. 20, 1955; children: Cathy, Brian, Michael, Craig, Karen, Diane. AB, Princeton U., 1953; MD, Columbia U., 1957. Diplomate Am. Bd. Orthopedic Surgery (treas. 1986-93). Resident orthopedic surgery U. Minn., 1957-62; orthopedic surgeon Lahey Clinic, Boston, 1964-68; chmn. dept. Lahey Clinic, 1968-70; prof., chmn. dept. Boston U. Med. Sch., 1970—; head physician U.S. Olympic Team, 1984; chmn. sports medicine coun. U.S. Olympic Com., 1984-93; vice chmn. sports medicine coun. U.S. Tennis Assn., 1988—. Editor-in-chief Am. J. Sports Med.; contbr. articles to profl. jours. Served to lt. comdr. USNR, 1962-64. Am., Brit., Canadian Orthopedic Travelling fellow, 1971; Sports Medicine Man of the Yr., 1988. Mem. Am. Acad. Orthopedic Surgeons, Continental Orthopedic Soc. (sec. 1966), Am. Orthopedic Assn. (pres. 1994), Am. Orthopedic Soc. Sports Medicine (pres. 1983), Longwood Cricket Club. Home: 40 Rockport Rd Weston MA 02193-1428 Office: 230 Calvary St Waltham MA 02154-8366

LEADBETTER, MARK RENTON, JR., orthopedic surgeon; b. Phila., Nov. 7, 1944; s. Mark Renton and Ruth (Protzeller) L.; m. Letitia Ashby, July 28, 1973 (div. June 1990); m. Jan Saker, 1991. BA, Gettysburg Coll., 1967; MSc in Hygiene, U. Pitts., 1970; MD, Temple U., 1974. Surg. intern Univ. Hosps., Boston, 1974-75, resident in surgery, 1975-76; emergency room physician Sturdy Meml. Hosp., Attleboro, Mass., 1976-78; resident in orthopaedics U. Pitts., 1978-81; orthopaedic physician Rockingham Meml. Hosp., Harrisonburg, Va., 1981-82, courtesy staff, 1982—; pvt. practice, Staunton, Va., 1982—; mem. active staff King's Daus. Hosp., Staunton, 1982—; active staff Samaritan Hosp., Moses Lake, Wash.; courtesy staff Columbia Basin Hosp., Ephrata, Wash. Contbr. articles to med. jours.; patentee safety syringes, safety cannulas, designer of medecal equipment. Mem. Am. Coll. Sports Medicine, So. Med. Assn., So. Orthopaedic Assn., County Med. Soc., Nat. Futures Assn. (assoc.). Republican. Home: 660 Coolidge St Moses Lake WA 98837-1877

LEAF, ALEXANDER, physician, educator; b. Yokohama, Japan, Apr. 10, 1920; came to U.S., 1922, naturalized, 1936; s. Aaron L. and Dora (Hural) L.; m. Barbara Louise Kincaid, Oct. 1943; children—Caroline Joan, Rebecca Louise, Tamara Jean. B.S., U. Wash., 1940; M.D., U. Mich., 1943; M.A., Harvard, 1961. Intern Mass. Gen. Hosp., Boston, 1943-44; mem. staff Mass. Gen. Hosp., 1949—, physician-in-chief, 1966-81; resident Mayo Found., Rochester, Minn., 1944-45; research fellow U. Mich., 1947-49; practice internal medicine Boston, 1949-90; faculty Med. Sch., Harvard, 1949—, Jackson prof. clin. medicine, 1966-81, Ridley Watts prof. preventive medicine, 1980-90, chmn. dept. preventive medicine and clin. epidemiology, 1980-90, Jackson prof. clin. medicine emeritus, 1990—; Disting. physician VA Medical Ctr. Brockton/W. Roxbury Hosps., Boston, 1992—. Served to capt. M.C. AUS, 1945-46. Recipient Outstanding Achievement award U.

Minn., 1964; vis. fellow Balliol Coll., Oxford, 1971-72; Guggenheim fellow, 1971-72; named Disting. Physician, VA, 1991—. Fellow Am. Acad. Arts and Scis.; mem. NAS, ACP (master), Inst. Medicine, Am. Soc. Clin. Investigation (past pres.), Am. Physiol. Soc., Biophys. Soc., Assn. Am. Physicians (Kober medal 1995). Home: 1 Curtis Cir Winchester MA 01890-1703 Office: Mass Gen Hosp Boston MA 02114

LEAK-COLEMAN, PAMELA SUE, health facility administrator; b. Ionia, Mich., Nov. 4, 1959; d. Edwin Sherrard and Bonnie Alita (Walkington) L. ADN, Kelloggs Community Coll., Battle Creek, Mich., 1981. RN, Calif., Mich. Head nurse Indian Trails Camp, Grand Rapids, Mich., 1983-86; staff nurse Traveling Nurse Corp., Dartmouth, Mass., 1983-87; nurse mgr. pediatrics Bay Shore Med. Group, Torrance, Calif., 1987-88; IV div. coord. Clin. Care Pharmacy, Pasadena, Calif., 1988-90; asst. health care adminstr. Hawthorne (Calif.) Community Group, 1990-91; coord. high risk infants Westside Regional Ctr., 1991—. Mem. Intravenous Nurse Soc.

LEAKE, BRENDA GAIL, enterostomal therapist nurse practitioner; b. Harriman, Tenn., Aug. 5, 1950; d. James Frank and Pauline Ruby (McGuffey) Judd; m. Lee Leake, Aug. 1, 1970 (div. Apr. 1974). AS in Nursing, U. Nev., Las Vegas, 1971, BN, 1986; cert. enterostomal therapist, U. Calif., San Diego, 1975. RN, Nev.; cert. enterostomal therapist, urol. nurse. Staff nurse Humana Hosp. Sunrise, Las Vegas, 1971-73, relief charge nurse, 1973-76, enterostomal therapist, 1976—; speaker Hospice Vol. program, Las Vegas, 1982—, I Can Cope program, Las Vegas, 1984—. Author instructional guide. Vol. Am. Cancer Soc., 1983—, mem. program devel. nurse edn. com. Mem. Intenat. Assn. Enterostomal Therapists (cert.), Nat. Assn. Pediatric Pseudobstructive Soc., Am. Nurses Assn., So. Nev. Nurses Assn., World Council Enterostomal Therapists, Am. Urol. Assn. (cert.), So. Nev. Ostomy Assn. (med. advisor 1976—), Crohns & Colitis Assn., Advanced Practitioners Nursing (cert., program chmn. 1986—), Wound Healing Soc. Republican. Presbyterian. Office: Sunrise Hosp 3186 S Maryland Pky Las Vegas NV 89109-2317

LEAKE, DONALD LEWIS, oral and maxillofacial surgeon, oboist; b. Cleveland, Okla., Nov. 6, 1931; s. Walter Wilson and Martha Lee (Crowe) L.; m. Rosemary Dobson, Aug. 20, 1964; children: John Andrew Dobson, Elizabeth, Catherine. AB, U. So. Calif., 1953, MA, 1957; DMD, Harvard U., 1962; MD, Stanford U., 1969. Diplomate Am. Bd. Oral and Maxillofacial Surgery. Intern Mass. Gen. Hosp., Boston, 1962-63; resident Mass. Gen. Hosp., 1963-64; postdoctoral fellow Harvard U., 1964-66; practice medicine specializing in oral and maxillofacial surgery; asso. prof. oral and maxillofacial surgery Harbor-UCLA Med. Ctr., Torrance, 1970-74, dental dir., chief oral and maxillofacial surgery, 1970—, prof., 1974—; assoc. dir. UCLA Dental Rsch. Inst., 1979-82, dir., 1982-86; prof. extranjero Escuela de Graduados, Asociacion Medica Argentina, 1990—; cons. to hosps.; dental dir. coastal health services region, Los Angeles County, 1974-81; oboist Robert Shaw Chorale, 1954-55; solo oboist San Diego Symphony, 1954-59. Contbr. articles to med. jours.; rec. artist: (albums on Columbia label) The Music of Heinrich Schütz, Stockhausen, Zeitmasse for 5 Winds, Schönberg, Orchestra Variations-Opus 31; freelance musician various film studio orchs., Carmel Bach Festival, 1949, 52-53, 67-81, numerous concerts with Coleman Chamber Music, The Cantata Singers, Boston, Garden St. Chamber Players, Cambridge, Baroque Consortium, L.A., Corona Del Mar Baroque Festival, others; world premieres (oboe works) by Darius Milhaud, William Kraft, Alice Parker, Mark Volkert, Eugene Zádor, Robert Linn. Mem. Commn. on the Future of Rose-Hulman Inst. Tech., Terre Haute, Ind., 1992-93. Recipient 1st prize with greatest distinction for oboe and chamber music Brussels Royal Conservatory Music Belgium, 1956. Fellow ACS; mem. AAAS, Internat. Assn. Dental Rsch., Internat. Assn. Oral Surgeons, Soc. Biomaterials, Biomed. Engring. Soc. (sr. mem.), L.A. County Med. Assn., European Assn. Maxillofacial Surgeons, Brit. Assn. Oral and Maxillofacial Surgeons, Internat. Gesellschaft fur Kiefer-Gesichts-Chirurgie, Internat. Soc. Plastic, Aesthetic and Reconstructive Surgery, Phi Beta Kappa, Phi Kappa Phi. Clubs: Harvard (Boston and N.Y.C.). Home: 2 Crest Rd W Rolling Hills CA 90274-5003 Office: Harbor-UCLA Med Ctr 1000 W Carson St Torrance CA 90502-2004 also: Harbor UCLA Profl Bldg 21840 Normandie Ave Ste 700 Torrance CA 90502-2047

LEAKE, ROSEMARY DOBSON, physician; b. Columbus, Ohio, July 14, 1937; d. Joseph Lawrence and Rosemary Elizabeth (Brockmeyer) Dobson; m. Donald Leake, Aug. 20, 1964; children: John, Elizabeth, Catherine. BA, Ohio State U., 1959, MD, 1962. Diplomate Am. Bd. Neonatal-Perinatal Medicine. Intern, pediatrics Mass. Gen. Hosp., Boston, 1962-63, resident, pediatrics, 1963-64; rsch. fellow Maternal Infant Health Collaborative Study The Boston Lying-In Hosp., Boston, 1965-67; neonatal fellow Stanford U. Hosp., Palo Alto, Calif., 1968-69; co-dir. NIH sponsored perinatal tng. program Harbor-UCLA Med. Ctr., Torrance, 1979, program dir. NIH sponsored perinatal rsch. ctr., 1980—; prof. pediatrics UCLA Sch. of Medicine, L.A., 1982—; dir. regionalized fellowship Harbor-UCLA/King-Drew Med. Ctr., Torrance, 1986-92; chair pediatrics Harbor-UCLA Med. Ctr., Torrance, 1992—; dir. perinatal crisis care program Harbor-UCLA Med. Ctr., Torrance, 1972-76, dir. neonatal ICU, 1974-81, assoc. prof. pediatrics, 1976-82, assoc. chief div. neonatology, 1976-77. Named UCLA Woman of Sci., 1985, Outstanding Woman Acadmician of Yr. Nat. Bd. Award of the Med. Coll. of Pa., 1989; recipient Alumni Achievement award Ohio State U. Sch. Medicine, 1987. Mem. Am. Pediatric Soc., Soc. for Pediatric Rsch. Home: 2 Crest Rd W Rolling Hills CA 90274-5003 Office: Harbor-UCLA Med Ctr 1000 W Carson St Torrance CA 90502-2004

LEÃO, MIGUEL JORGE-FERREIRA, pediatric neurologist; b. Porto, Portugal, Sept. 26, 1960; s. Jorge Oliveira and Maria Lucilia (Vitorino) L.; m. Maria Gabriela Castanheira, Aug. 30, 1985 (div. 1990); 1 child, Mariana. MD, U. Porto, 1984, M Genetics, 1990, M Med. Genetics, 1992. Resident in neurology Hosp. of S. Yoão, Porto, 1987-91, asst. prof. med. genetics faculty medicine, 1987-94, cons. neurogenetics, 1990—, cons. pediatric neurology, 1993—, asst. prof. neurology faculty of medicine, 1995—; specialist med. genetics Ordem Dos Medicos, 1992; gen. sec. standing com. Doctors of the European Cmty., 1991-92; founder Portuguese Assn. Young Med. Doctors, 1989. Contbr. articles to profl. publs. V.p. Juventude Centrista, Porto, 1978-83, pres., 1983-86; founder Found. Portudal XXth Century, 1987; founder Portuguese Soc. Ethics and Politics, 1991. Mem. Portuguese Med. Assn. (gen. sec. no. coun. 1990-92, exec. coun. 1990-92), Portuguese Soc. Genetics, European Soc. Human Genetics, Portuguese Soc. Against Epilepsy, Portuguese Soc. Neurology, N.Y. Acad. Scis. Mem. Social Democrat Party. Roman Catholic. Office: Hosp S João, Dept Neurology/Neurosurgery, 4200 Porto Portugal

LEAPER, DAVID JOHN, surgeon, educator; b. York, Eng., July 23, 1947; s. David Thomas and Gwendoline (Robertson) L.; m. Gillian Margot Fanthorpe, May 31, 1971 (div. July 1992); children: Charles David Edward, Alice Jane Sophia; m. Francesca Ann Hanes, Nov. 4, 1995. MBChB with honors, Leeds Med. Sch., U.K., 1970; MD, Leeds Med. Sch., 1979, ChM, 1982; FRCS, Royal Coll. of Surgeons, Eng., 1975; FRCSEd, Royal Coll. of Surgeons, Edinburgh, 1974. Med. diplomate. Surg. registrar Leeds and Scarborough Hosps., U.K., 1971-75; cancer rsch. campaign fellow Kings Coll. Hosp., U.K., 1976-77; sr. registrar Westminster Hosp., London, 1977-81; prof. surgery U. Hong Kong, 1988-90; sr. lectr. U. Bristol, 1981-95; prof. surgery U. Newcastle-Upon-Tyne, 1995—. Chief editor surg. rsch. comm., 1988—; editl. bd. British Jour. Surgery, 1992—; author/editor: International Surgical Practice, 1992; author: (book series) Your Operation, 1993-94. Chmn. Round Table Britain and Ireland, Thornbury, U.K., 1988-89; mem. dept. health/Hosp. Infection Control, U.K., 1992-94; vice-chmn. hosp. ethic com., Bristol, U.K., 1994-95. Rsch. fellowship grant Southwest Region Eng., 1982, Distinction award Nat. Health Svc., U.K., 1993. Mem. European Wound Mgmt. Assn. (pres. 1994-95), Royal Soc. Medicine U.K. (v.p. sect. surgery 1985-93), Royal Coll. surgeons Eng. (mem. court examiners 1992—, Ethicon Found. award 1976, 82), Surg. Infection Soc. (recorder 1993—), Surg. Rsch. Soc. (com. mem. 1987-89, European fellow 1976), North of Eng. Surg. Soc. Office: U Newcastle Upon Tyne- Surgery, North Tees NHS Trust, TS198PE Cleveland England

LEAPLEY, PATRICIA MURRAY, dietitian; b. Lowell, Mass.; d. Henry J. and Ruth (Slipp) Murray; m. Robert A. Leapley; children: Robert Jr., Deborah, John. BS in Nutrition and Edn., Framingham State Coll., 1959; MS in Allied Health Services, U. North Fla., 1986. Registered dietitian, Washington, cert. diabetes educator; lic. dietitian, Fla. Chief nutrition clinic Walter Reed Army Med. Ctr., Washington, 1976-79; coordinator diabetes program U. South Fla., Tampa, 1979-80; dir. nutrition BLD Nutrition Mgmt. Systems, Clearwater, Fla., 1980-84, Health Care Assocs., Rockville, Md., 1984; clin. nutrition specialist Riverside Hosp., Jacksonville, Fla., 1985-87; dir. nutrition services The Drs. Clinic, Jacksonville, 1987-88; diabetes and lipid nutrition specialist Dept. Vets. Affairs Lake City (Fla.) Med. Ctr. Author (book and slides): Food Facts for Diabetes and Weight Control, 1979; contbr. numerous articles to profl. jours. Served as capt. U.S. Army, 1959-64. Recipient Alumni Achievement award Framingham State Coll., 1979; first dietitian to develop diet for treatment of Phenylketonuria in children, Walter Reed Med. Amry Med. Ctr., 1960. Mem. Am. Assn. Diabetes Educators (bd. dirs. 1980-83, program chair VA/AADE diabetic educators group 1994-95), Am. Dietetic Assn. (exec. bd. 1972-79), Am. Diabetes Assn. (Jacksonville bd. dirs. 1985-93, Washington bd. dirs. 1973-79, coun. on epidemiology sec. 1982-89, chairperson Dept. Vet. Affairs 1993-95), Dept. Vet. Affairs/Am. Assn. Diabetes Educators. Home: PO Box 23398 Jacksonville FL 32241-3398

LEAR, ERWIN, anesthesiologist, educator; b. Bridgeport, Conn., Jan. 1, 1924; s. Samuel Joseph and Ida (Ruth) L.; m. Arlene Joyce Alexander, Feb. 15, 1953; children—Stephanie, Samuel. MD, SUNY, 1952. Diplomate Am. Bd. Anesthesiology, Nat. Bd. Med. Examiners. Intern L.I. Coll. Hosp., Bklyn., 1952-53; asst. resident anesthesiology Jewish Hosp., Bklyn., 1953-54; sr. resident Jewish Hosp., 1955, asst., 1955-56, adj., 1956-58, assoc. anesthesiologist, 1958-64; attending anesthesiologist Bklyn. VA Hosp., 1958-64, cons., 1977—; assoc. vis. anesthesiologist Kings County Hosp. Ctr., Bklyn., 1957-80; staff anesthesiologist Kings County Hosp. Ctr., 1980-81; vis. anesthesiologist Queens Gen. Hosp. Ctr., 1955-67; dir. anesthesiology Queens Hosp. Ctr. Jamaica, 1964-67, cons., 1968—; chmn. dept. anesthesiology Catholic Med. Ctr., Queens and Bklyn., 1958-80; dir. anesthesiology Beth Israel Med. Ctr., N.Y.C., 1981—; clin. instr. SUNY Coll. Medicine, Bklyn., 1955-58; clin. asst. prof. SUNY Coll. Medicine, 1958-64, clin. assoc. prof., 1964-71, clin. prof., 1971-80, prof., vice-chmn. clin. anesthesiology, 1980-81; prof. anesthesiology Mt. Sinai Sch. Medicine. 1981-94, Albert Einstein Coll. of Medicine, 1994—. Author: Chemistry Applied Pharmacology of Tranquilizers; contbr. articles to profl. jours. Served with USNR, 1942-45. Fellow Am. Coll. Anesthesiologists, N.Y. Acad. Medicine (sec. sect. anesthesiology 1985-86, chmn. sect. anesthesiology 1986-87); mem. AMA, Am. Soc. Anesthesiologists (chmn. com. on by-laws 1982-83, dir. 1981—, ho. of dels. 1973—, editor newsletter 1984—, chmn. adminstrv. affairs com., 1987—), N.Y. State Bd. Profl. Med. Conduct, N.Y. State Soc. Anesthesiologists (chmn. pub. relations 1963-73, chmn. com. local arrangements 1968-73, dist. dir. 1972-73, v.p. 1974-75, pres. 1976, bd. dirs. 1972—, chmn. jud. com. 1977-81, assoc. editor Bulletin 1963-77, editor Sphere 1978-84), N.Y. State Med. Soc. (chmn. sect. anesthesiology 1966-67, sec. sect. 1977-81), N.Y. County Med. Soc., SUNY Coll. Medicine Alumni Assn. (pres. 1983, trustee alumni fund 1980), Alpha Omega Alpha. Address: Harriman Dr Sands Point NY 11050

LEARN, RICHARD NORMAN, ophthalmologist; b. San Diego, Feb. 19, 1934; s. Noble Norman and Jean (Duffy) L.; m. Arlene Ann Perozynski, June 21, 1962; children: Victoria, Alison, Kristen, Richard. BA, San Diego State U., 1956; MD, UCLA, 1960. Diplomate Am. Bd. Ophthalmology. Intern USN, San Diego, 1960; resident ophthalmology UCLA, 1964-67; pvt. practice Eye Physicians Med. Group, Inc., El Cajon, Calif., 1967—. Lt. USN, 1960-64. Fellow Am. Acad. Ophthalmology; mem. San Diego County Ophthalmol. Soc. Office: Eye Physician Med Group Inc 225 W Madison El Cajon CA 92020

LEATHER, ROBERT PAUL, vascular surgeon; b. Bklyn., Jan. 31, 1928. BME, Rensselaer Poly. Inst., 1948; MD, Albany Med. Coll., 1954. Diplomate Am. Bd. Surgery, Gen. Surgery, Vascular Surgery. Instr. in surgery Albany (N.Y.) Med. Ctr., 1961-66, co-dir. trauma unit, 1966-75, clin. asst. prof. surgery, 1966-74, assoc. prof. surgery, 1974-83, prof. surgery, 1983—, chief vascular surgery sect., 1986-88, head divsn. gen. surgery, 1988-93, chief vascular surgery sect., 1993—. Contbr. articles to profl. jours. and chpts. to textbooks on vascular surgery. Capt. U.S. Army, 1955-57. Fellow ACS; mem. Am. Surg. Assn., Soc. for Vascular Surgery (bd. dirs., lifeline found.), Eastern Vascular Soc. (pres. 1995-96), Scandinavian Assn. for Thoracic and Cardiovascular Surgery, Am. Assn. for Surgery of Trauma. Office: Albany Med Coll Dept of Surgery 47 New Scotland Ave Albany NY 12208

LEATHERBURY, KEITH CHARLES, surgeon; b. Annapolis, Md., Nov. 15, 1959; s. Charles Oliver and Doris Olea (Toppen) L.; m. Lisa Alane Wilhelmi, May 22, 1982; children: Kasee, Alex. BS in Biology summa cum laude, U. N.D., 1982, MD, 1987. Diplomate Am. Bd. Surgery. Resident in gen. surgery U. Kans., Wichita, 1987-92; staff surgeon Fremont (Nebr.) Med. Assocs. Meml. Hosp. Dodge County, 1992—. Fellow ACS; mem. Fremont C. of C., Phi Beta Kappa. Office: Fremont Med Assocs 2350 N Clarkson Fremont NE 68025

LEATHERS, MARGARET WEIL, foundation administrator; b. Princeton, Ind., Dec. 22, 1949; d. Albert J. and Nora Jewel (Franklin) Weil; m. Charles L. Leathers, June 19, 1971 (div. Dec. 1987); children: Julianna L., Kevin Sean. AB, U. Ill., 1971; MS, Russell Sage Coll., 1979. Cert. tchr., N.Y., health edn. specialist. Employment counselor Snelling & Snelling, Schenectady, N.Y., 1972-76; substitute tchr. Monahasen High/Jr. High Sch., Schenectady, 1978-79; grant abstractor State of N.Y., Albany, 1979; program coordinator Am. Lung Assn. Santa Clara-San Benito Counties, San Jose, Calif., 1982-84, dir. programs, 1984-87, nat. clinic leader trainer, 1986—, acting exec. dir., 1987-88, exec. dir., 1988—. Author: Camp Superstuff Workbook and Teachers Manual, 1983; contbr. articles to profl. publs. and mags. Bd. dirs., officer Santa Clara Valley Coun. Parent-Participating Nursery Schs., 1980-81; resource vol. Lyceum Santa Clara Valley, 1983-87; leader Explorer post Boy Scouts Am., San Jose, 1988; mem. adminstrv. bd. coun. ministries United Meth. Ch.; mem. staff 1st asthma camp Young Tchrs. of Health, Soviet Union, 1989, Seattle, 1990; mem. citizen's oversight com. Local Transp. Commn. for Santa Clara County, 1993—; mem. steering com. for Measure A., 1992. Mem. APHA, Soc. Pub. Health Educators, Am. Sch. Health Assn., Assn. of United Way Agys. (exec. bd. 1993), ALA Calif. Coun. Execs. (v.p. 1994). Democrat. Home: 341 Springpark Cir San Jose CA 95136-2148 Office: Am Lung Assn 1469 Park Ave San Jose CA 95126-2530

LEAV, IRWIN, dean, veterinarian; b. N.Y.C., July 4, 1937; s. Sol and Sadie (Agrenovitz) L.; m. Lois Paula Lefton, Sept. 3, 1961; children: Brett, Ross. BA, Ohio State U., 1959, DVM, 1965. Rsch. fellow Harvard Med. Sch., Boston, 1965-70; asst. prof. Tufts Med. Sch., Boston, 1970-79, assoc. prof., 1980-89; assoc. dean Tufts Vet. Sch., Boston, 1978-93; prof. Tufts Vet. and Med. Schs., Boston, 1986—; cons. U.S. Army, 1972—, TSI Corp., Worcester, Mass., 1986—. Contbr. articles to profl. jours. including Cancer Jour., Jour. Nat. Cancer Inst., Am. Jour. Pathology, Cancer Rsch. With USAF, 1961-62. Mem. Am. Coll. Vet. Pathologists, Am. Vet. Med. Assn., New England Soc. Pathologists. Jewish. Office: Tufts Vet Sch Dept Pathology 136 Harrison Ave Boston MA 02111-1800

LEAVERTON, DAVID RUNYAN, psychiatrist; b. Dallas, Sept. 7, 1936; m. Elaine M. Rubenstein; children: Lisa G., Julie L., Jenny M., Dan, Joshua A. Steinitz, Ben R. BS in Chemistry, Colo. State U., 1958; MD, U. Colo., 1961. Lic. psychiatrist, Colo., Md. Intern pediatrics U. Fla., Gainesville, 1961-62; resident pediatrics U. Fla., 1962-64, resident psychiatry, 1967-69, fellow child psychiatry children's mental health unit, 1969-71, instr. child psychiatry, pediatrics, 1970-71; asst. prof. Coll. Medicine Ohio State U., 1971-74; assoc. prof., coord. child psychiatry tng. U. Calif., Davis, 1974-78; assoc. prof., div. dir. Albany Med. Coll. Union U., 1978-79; from assoc. prof., dir. dir. to assoc. clin. prof. Balt. Sch. Medicine U. Md., 1979-82; pvt. practice, 1971—; med. dir. A. Q. Jones Lab. Alachua County Pub. Schs., 1967-70; cons. child psychiatry Fla. Sch. Deaf and Blind, 1969-71, Alachua County Pub. Schs., 1970-71, Gallagher Svcs., 1985—, Crownsville St. Hosp. Adolescent Unit, 1987-88, Martin Pollak Project, 1989—, Chesapeake Ctr., 1990—, others; dir. crisis intervention svcs. Columbus (Ohio) Childrens Hosp., 1973-75. Contbr. articles to profl. jours. Head coach Girls Softball, 1973-79; asst. coach Youth Ice Hockey, 1973-81; parent coop. com. Holmes Jr. High Sch., Davis, 1975; trustee Sacramento Diabetes Assn., 1975-78; organizer, leader Sierra Backpacking for Children with Diabetes, 1975-78; chmn. No. Calif. Diabetes Bike-a-thon, 1976-77; organizer, co-leader CAREs Program, 1977-79, 81-83; bd. dirs. Glen Oban Community Assn. Fellow Am. Psychiatric Assn., Am. Orthopsychiatric Assn.; mem. Am. Acad. Child and Adolescent Psychiatry, Md. Psychiatric Soc. (dist. br. APA), Md. Regional Coun. Child Psychiatrist. Home: 1331 Kinloch Cir Arnold MD 21012-2133

LEBARON, FRANCIS NEWTON, biochemistry educator; b. Framingham, Mass., July 26, 1922; s. Paul Burrows and Dorothy (Lamson) LeB.; m. Margaret Lenore Shaw, July 8, 1953; 1 child, Geoffrey Shaw. S.B., MIT, 1944; M.A., Boston U., 1948; Ph.D., Harvard U., 1951. Assoc. biochemist McLean Hosp., Belmont, Mass., 1957-64; asso. biol. chemist Harvard U. Med. Sch., 1959-64; asso. prof. biochemistry U. N.Mex. Med. Sch., 1964-69, prof., 1969-83, chmn. dept., 1971-78, chmn. ad hoc nutrition planning commn., 1969; vis. scholar Mass. Inst. Tech., 1974-75. Editorial bd.: Jour. Neurochemistry, 1965-74; Contbr. articles to profl. jours. Served with USNR, 1943-46. Mem. Am. Chem. Soc., Biochem. Soc. (London), Am. Soc. Biol. Chemists, AAAS, Internat. Soc. Neurochemistry, Am. Soc. Neurochemistry (pres. 1969-71), Theta Delta Chi. Home: PO Box 779 Mashpee MA 02649-0779

LEBARON, RUTHANN HAYES, biology educator, management consultant; b. Denver, Nov. 8, 1925; d. John Edward and Anna Elizabeth (Hansen) Hayes; m. Marshall John LeBaron, Sept. 7, 1948 (div. Feb. 1980); children: Anne, Michael Roy. BA cum laude, U. Colo., 1946; MA in Zoology, Mt. Holyoke Coll., 1948; postgrad., U. Idaho, 1948-70. Instr. histology U. Idaho, Moscow, 1948-49; from asst. prof. to assoc. prof. biology Coll. So. Idaho, Twin Falls, 1965-70, prof., 1970-76, chmn. dept. sci., 1965-73; prof. biology Linfield Coll., McMinnville, Oreg., 1983—, Linn Benton Community Coll., Newport, Oreg., 1986-88, Oreg. Coast Community Coll., Newport, 1988—; bd. dirs. Regional Studies Ctr., Caldwell, Idaho, 1972-77; chmn. bd. dirs. Pacific Communities Hosp., Newport, 1990—, vice chmn. 1992-93. Author: Hormones: A Delicate Balance, 1972; contbr. articles to profl. jours. Pres. Idaho Fedn. Music Clubs, Twin Falls, 1963-65. Recipient award of recognition Oreg. and Wash. Community Coll. Couns., 1988; NSF grantee, 1966, 67, 73. Mem. Am. Inst. Biol. Sci., AAAS, Idaho Acad. Sci. (pres. 1972-73), Phi Beta Kappa, Sigma Xi. Republican. Episcopalian. Home: 1713 Sandpiper Dr PO Box 886 Waldport OR 97394-0886

LEBENGER, KERRY, allergist; b. Bklyn., Jan. 18, 1955. BA, Johns Hopkins U., 1976; MD, N.Y. Med. Coll., N.Y.C., 1980. Diplomate Am. Bd. Internal Medicine, Am. Bd. Allergy and Immunology. Allergist Summit (N.J.) Med. Group, 1985—; clin. instr. Columbia U. Coll. Physicians and Surgeons, 1988—. V.p. Livingston (N.J.) Ednl. Found., 1995—. Fellow Am. Acad. Allergy Asthma and Immunology; mem. Med. Soc. N.J., N.J. Allergy and Immunology Soc. (pres. 1996). Office: Summit Med Group 120 Summit Ave Summit NJ 07901

LEBENSOHN, ZIGMOND MEYER, psychiatrist, educator; b. Kenosha, Wis., Sept. 8, 1910; s. Morris P. and Bertha (Schiffman) L.; m. Mary Bates, Feb. 15, 1940 (dec. May 1975); children—Valerie, Jeremy, Marya Lebensohn Huseby, Lucia Lebensohn Eakle.; m. Nancy Leach Shields, Mar. 18, 1979. Student, U. Wis., 1926-29; B.S., Northwestern U., 1930, M.B., 1933, M.D., 1934. Diplomate: Am. Bd. Psychiatry and Neurology. Intern Cook County Hosp., Chgo., 1934-35; psychiat. med. officer St. Elizabeths Hosp., Washington, 1935-39; chief psychiatry Sibley Meml. Hosp., 1956-76, chief emeritus, 1976—; mem. faculty George Washington U. Med. Sch., 1936-41; clin. prof. clin. psychiatry Georgetown U. Sch. Medicine, 1941—; cons. to govt., 1946—. Mem. editorial bd. Comprehensive Psychiatry, 1965—, Am. Jour. Psychiatry, 1964-75; contbr. articles to profl. jours. Mem. med. adv. panel FAA, 1961-66; mem. D.C. Commnr. Youth Council, 1954-55. Served as med. officer USNR, 1941-45. Kober lectr. Georgetown U., 1962; recipient Seymour Pollak Disting. Achievement award, 1986; Zigmond M. Lebensohn Lectureship established, 1977. Life fellow Am. Psychiat. Assn. (chmn. com. pub. information 1964-67, 70-73, trustee 1967-70); fellow A.M.A.; mem. Assn. Research Nervous and Mental Diseases, Am. Psychopathol. Assn., Group Advancement Psychiatry (chmn. com. psychiatry and law 1966-70), D.C. Med. Soc. (1st v.p. 1953-54, certificate meritorious service 1963), Washington Psychiat. Soc. (pres. 1952), Phi Beta Kappa, Alpha Omega Alpha. Home: 4840 Hutchins Pl NW Washington DC 20007-1528 Office: 2015 R St NW Washington DC 20009-1011

LE BERVET, JEAN YVES, anesthesiologist, consultant; b. Toulon, Provence, France, Feb. 22, 1947; s. Yves Le Bervet and Yvette Broudic; m. Nicole Le Hir, June 1, 1991; 1 child, Jade. MD, Rennes (France) U., 1976; profl. diving & hyperbaric specialist, U. Paris, 1985. Resident psychiatry Bourloud Clinic, Rennes, 1976-77; resident chirurgy Auray Hosp., France, 1976; resident & asst. pediatry, physiology Rennes, 1977-82; chief Functional Unit Anaesthesiology, Rennes, 1990-96. Author: Memento of Anaesthesiology in Maternity, 1989; co-author: Position for Blood-Patch Obstetrics, 1993. Office: CHV Rennes Maternite, 2 Rue l'Motel-Dieu, 35000 Rennes France

LEBLANC, CAROLINE ANNE, nurse, psychotherapist, educator; b. Worcester, Mass., Dec. 11, 1947; d. Leonard Eugene and Gertrude Rita (Plamondon) LeB.; m. Jon Ralph Hager, May 24, 1969; children: Keith Erik Hager, Brant William Hager. BS in Nursing cum laude, Boston Coll., 1969; MS, U.Md., 1978; postgrad. Georgetown U., 1980-83. Pub. health and psychiat. staff nurse, 1969-71; occupational health nurse Def. Supply Agy., Boston, 1971-72; sr. asst. nurse officer USPHS, 1972-74; asst. prof. psychiat. nursing Bloomsburg (Pa.) State Coll., 1978-81; pvt. practice contractural svcs. rural nursing and mental health, clin., ednl. and consultative svcs., Williamsport, Pa., 1977-82; commd. capt. Nurse Corps U.S. Army, 1982; nurse/psychotherapist Walson Army Hosp., Ft. Dix, N.J., 1982-86; clin. nurse specialist, asst. clin. prof. psychiatry Med. Coll. of Ga., Augusta, 1986-89; pvt. practice nursing, psychotherapy, Augusta, 1987-89; pvt. practice psychotherapy, Watertown, N.Y., 1989—; faculty adv. Bloomsburg State Coll. Campus Child Care Center, 1980-81; founder Wilderness Heart Workshops. Founding mem. Balt. Nurses NOW Task Force; founding mem. Wellspring Ctr. for Human Potential, Md., 1974-75. With USPHS, 1972-74, maj. discharged, 1989, res. Cert. specialist in psychiat. and mental health nursing. Mem. Am. Nurses Assn., Am. Orthopsychiat. Assn., N.Y. Nurses Assn., Phi Kappa Phi, Sigma Theta Tau, Sigma Xi. Home and Office: 17926 N Adams Heights Adams NY 13605

LEBLANC, GILBERT ARTHUR, urologist; b. Worcester, Mass., Sept. 27, 1927; s. Arthur Eugene and Regina Lea (Pelletier) L.; m. Helene Marie Kenedy, Feb. 27, 1954; children: Stephen, Michele, Christopher, Dominique. AB, Assumption Coll., 1950; MD, Georgetown U., 1954. Diplomate Am. Bd. Urology. Intern USN, St. Albans, N.Y., 1954-55, resident in urology, 1955-59, asst. chief, 1959-61; chief USN, Newport, R.I., 1961-65, Yokosuka, Japan, 1965-68; chmn. dept. urology USN, Oakland, Calif., 1968-77; chief of urology Holderman Hosp., Yountville, Calif., 1977—. Fellow ACS; mem. Am. Urologic Assn., Soc. Pediatric Urology, Assn. Mil. Surgeons. Republican. Roman Catholic. Home: 280 Crystal Springs Rd St Helena CA 94574 Office: Holderman Hosp Po Box 51 Yountville CA 94599-0057

LEBLANC, HECTOR J., physician; b. New Orleans, June 21, 1939; s. Hector J. and Marion A. (Fenasci) LeB.; m. Barbara Jean Russ, Dec. 28, 1963; children: Russ Raynal, Adrienne Eve LeBlanc Bossio, Anne Danielle. BS, La. State U., 1960, MD, 1965. Diplomate Am. Bd. Neurol. Surgery. Asst. prof. neurosurgery La. State U. Med. Ctr., New Orleans, 1972-79, asst. prof. pathology and neuropathology, 1990—; pvt. practice Olympia, Wash., 1979-84; asst. prof. neurosurgery U. Wash., Seattle, 1984-85, resident in neuropathology, 1985-89; neurosurgeon, cons., tchr. La. State U. Med. Ctr., 1972-79, U. Wash., 1979-85. Author rsch. papers in field. Founding co-dir. La. State U. Neurosci. Brain Bank, New Orleans, 1991. Fellow Am. Coll. Surgeons; mem. Am. Assn. Neuropathology, Am. Assn. Neurol. Surgery, Congress of Neurol. Surgery, Alumni Assn. La. State U. Neurosurgeons (pres. 1989—), La. State Neurosurgical Soc. (sec.-treas. 1974—). Office: La State U Med Ctr Pathology Dept 1901 Perdido St New Orleans LA 70112

LEBOVIC, GAIL SHIRLEY, surgeon; b. L.A., May 19, 1957; d. Ernest and Helen Lebovic. BA, U. Calif., Berkeley, 1979, MA, 1983; MD, George

Washington U., 1986. Diplomate Am. Bd. Surgery. Resident Stanford (Calif.) U. Med. Ctr., 1986-93; intern Santa Clara Valley (Calif.) Med. Ctr.; pvt. practice Palo Alto, Calif., 1993—; mem. staff Gender Dysphoria Clinic, Palo Alto, 1990—, Stanford U. Hosp., 1993—; dir. Bay Area Breast Ctr., Palo Alto, 1994—; bd. dirs. Patient Info. Svcs., Inc. Author: (with others) Current Therapy in Oncology, 1993, Diseases of the Breast, 1994; contbr. numerous articles to profl. jours. State of Calif. grantee, 1994. Fellow ACS, Am. Med. Soc.; mem. Am. Soc. Breast Surgeons (dir. Western Tex. region 1995), Am. Women's Med. Soc., Am. Soc. Outpatient Surgeons, Calif. Med. Assn., Nat. Consortium Breast Ctrs., Soc. for Study Breast Disease, Santa Clara Med. Assn., French Soc. Breast Surgery, Alpha Omega Alpha Honor Med. Soc. Office: Bay Area Breast Ctr 1101 Welch Rd # A-6 Palo Alto CA 94304

LEBOWITZ, MICHAEL DAVID, epidemiologist; b. Bklyn., Dec. 21, 1939; s. Harry and Rachel (Dick) L.; m. Joyce Marian Schmidt, Sept. 9, 1960; children: Jon A., Kira L., Debra M. AB, U. Calif., 1961, MA, 1965; PhC, U. Wash., 1969, PhD, 1971. Resch. assoc. preventive medicine U. Wash., Seattle, 1967-70, rsch. assoc. environ. health, 1970-71; asst. prof. internal medicine U. Ariz., Tucson, 1971-75, assoc. prof. internal medicine, 1975-80, prof. medicine, 1980—, prof. preventive cmty. medicine, 1996—, asst. dir. div. respiratory sci., 1974-84, assoc. dir. Respiratory Sci. Ctr., 1985-96; chair epidemiol. grad. program Ariz. Prevention Ctr., Tucson, 1994—, dir., prof. epidemiol. unit, 1996—; vis. fellow Postgrad. Cardiothoracic Inst., U. London, 1978-79; vis. prof. Groningen U., The Netherlands, 1993, U. Pisa, Italy, 1993; cons. NIH, Bethesda, Md., 1985—, EPA, Washington, 1969—, WHO, 1979—, Italian Nat. Rsch. Coun., 1979—, Polish Nat. Inst. Hygiene and Acad. Scis., 1981—, Hungarian Nat. Inst. Hygiene, 1989—, Pan Am. Health Orgn., 1985—, also numerous others; co-chmn. Indoor Air Pollutants Commn., NAS-NRC, Washington, 1979-81, WHO Guidelines for Studies in Environ. Epidemiology, 1983, WHO-EURO Monographs on Air Quality, 1982-94. Mem. editl. bd.: Jour. Behavioral Medicine, 1977-93, Jour. Air Pollution Control Assn., 1984-88, Pediat. Pulmonology, 1990-95, Archives Environ. Health, 1990—, Am. Rev. Respiratory Diseases, 1993—; co-editor: WHO/Euro Biol. Contaminants, 1990, WHO Europ Priorities in Environ. Epidemiology, 1996; assoc. editor: Jour. Toxicology Indsl. Health, 1984—, Jour. Exposure Analysis Environ. Epidemiology, 1992—; contbr. numerous articles to profl. jours., chpts. to books and monographs. Chmn. Pima County Air Quality Adv. Coun., Tucson, 1975-78; cons. Ariz. State Dept. Health Svcs., 1972—, Ariz. Lung Assn., 1971—, State Dept. Environ. Quality, 1987—, Gov. of Ariz., 1987-93; senator U. Ariz. Faculty Senate, Tucson, 1976-78. Recipient Ariz. Clean Air award Ariz. Lung Assn., 1987; numerous epidemiology/disease grants and contracts, NIH, EPA, FDA, EPRI and others, 1964—. Fellow Am. Coll. Epidemiology, Am. Coll. Chest Physicians, Collegium Ramazzini, Internat. Acad. Indoor Air Sci.; mem. Am. Epidemiol. Soc., Am. Thoracic Soc., Internat. Epidemiol. Assn., European Respiratory Soc., Soc. Epidemiol. Rsch., Internat. Soc. Environ. Epidemiology, Internat. Soc. Exposure Analysis, Hungar Soc. Health (hon.). Office: U Ariz Coll Medicine Prevention Ctr 1501 N Campbell Ave Tucson AZ 85724-5163

LECAPITAINE, JOHN EDWARD, counseling psychology educator, researcher; b. Nov. 21, 1950; s. Vincent Bernard and Evelyn Lucille Le-Capitaine; m. Jessica Dale; 1 child, Katherine Briee. BS, U. Wis., 1973, MS, 1975; D, Boston U., 1980. Rsch. assoc. Dupont Psychol. Edn. Inst., Eau Claire, Wis., 1975-76; counseling and sch. psychologist Martin Luther King. Jr. Ctr., Boston, 1976-78; rsch. cons. Dept. Mental Health, 1985-90; prof. counseling psychology U. Wis., River Falls, 1990—; adj. prof. Boston U., 1981-89. Contbr. poetry, fiction, and acad. articles to profl. jours. Mem. Am. Counseling Assn., Nat. Assn. Sch. Psychologists, Internat. Coun. Psychologists, Assn. Play Therapy, Assn. Multicultural Counseling and Devel., Assn. Humanistic Devel. and Edn., Assn. Counselor Edn. and Supervision, Internat. Soc. Poets, Phi Delta Kappa. Home: 731 Lumphrey Ct River Falls WI 54022-3426 Office: U Wis Ames Bldg River Falls WI 54022

LECHAT, MICHEL FRANÇOIS, epidemiologist, consultant; b. Brussels, Apr. 30, 1927; s. Pierre M. Lechat and Jacqueline H. (Greiner) de Haulleville; m. Edith G. Dasnoy, Mar. 25, 1953; children: Marie, Laurent, Sylvie. Agrege, Cath. U. Louvain, Belgium, 1960; MD, Cath. U. Louvain, 1952; diploma in tropical medicine, Tropical Medicine Inst., Antwerp, Belgium, 1953; MPH, Johns Hopkins U., 1963, PhD, 1966. Med. dir. Leprosy Hosp. of Iyonda, Mbandaka, Zaïre, 1953-59; med. officer Pan Am. Health Orgn., Mexico City, 1965-66; prof. head epidemiology dept. Cath. U. Louvain, Brussels, 1967-92; prof. Tropical Medicine Inst., Antwerp, 1967-80; dir. Rsch. Ctr. Disaster Epidemiology, Brussels, 1978-93; pres. Sch. Pub. Health Cath. U., Louvain, Brussels, 1983-92; cons. Nat. Acad. Scis., Washington, 1976-78, WHO, Geneva, 1969—, UN Internat. Decade for Natural Disaster Reduction, 1990-95. Assoc. editor: Internat. Jour. Epidemiology, 1970-90; contbr. articles to profl. jours. Mem. selection com. King Baudouin award, 1978-95, pres., 1990-95. Recipient Broden-Rodhain award Belgian Soc. Tropical Medicine, 1955, Internat. Ghandi Leprosy award, 1990. Fellow Royal Belgian Acad. for Overseas Sci.; mem. Acad. Europea, Royal Belgian Acad. Medicine, Internat. Leprosy Assn. (pres. 1978-88, pres. emeritus), Soc. Scholars Johns Hopkins U. Home: 109 Rue des Trois- Tilleuls, Brussels Belgium 1170 Office: Sch of Pub Health, EPID 30.34-UCL, Brussels Belgium 1200

LECHELT, EUGENE CARL, psychology educator; b. Edmonton, Alta., Can., Dec. 26, 1942; s. Adolph Carl and Natalie (Klapstein) L.; m. Sandra Dona Morris, Dec. 18, 1965; 1 child, David Patrick. B.Sc., U. Alta., 1964, M.Sc., 1966, Ph.D., 1969. Research assoc., lectr. Princeton U., N.J., 1969-72; asst. prof. dept. psychology U. Alta., Edmonton, 1972-76, assoc. prof., 1976-82, prof., 1982—, chmn., 1986—. Recipient Rutherford Teaching award, 1985, Vol. award Fed. Govt. of Can., 1994; U. Alta. dissertation fellow, 1968-69; Social Scis. Research Council Can. fellow, 1978-79. Mem. Psychonomic Soc., Can. Psychol. Assn., AAAS, N.Y. Acad. Scis., Sigma Xi. Home: 11723-91 Ave, Edmonton, AB Canada T6G 1B1 Office: U Alta, Dept Psychology, Edmonton, AB Canada T6G 2E9

LECHEVALIER, MARY PFEIL, retired microbiologist, educator; b. Cleve., Jan. 27, 1928; d. Alfred Leslie Pfeil and Mary Edith Martin; m. Hubert Arthur Lechevalier, Apr. 7, 1950; children: Marc E.M., Paul R. BA in Physiology-Biochemistry, Mt. Holyoke Coll., 1949; MS in Microbiology, Rutgers U., 1951. Rsch. fellow Rutgers U., New Brunswick, N.J., 1949-51, rsch. assoc. inst. microbiology, 1962-74, from asst. to assoc. rsch. prof., 1974-85, rsch. prof. Waksman inst. microbiology, 1985-91, prof. emerita, 1991—; ind. rschr., 1955-59; microbiologist steroid preparative lab. E.R. Squibb and Sons, New Brunswick, 1960-61; vis. investigator Inst. Biology Czechoslovak Acad. Scis., Svc. de Mycologie Pasteur Inst., Prague, Paris, 1961-62; cons. in field. Contbr. over 100 chpts. to books and articles to rsch. jours.; mem. adv. com. actinomycetes Bergey's Manual of Determinative Bacteriology, 8th edit.; chair adv. com. muriform actinomycetes Bergey's Manual, 9th edit. Assoc. mem. Bergey's Trust, 1989-92. Recipient Charles Thom award Soc. Indsl. Microbiology, 1982, Waksman award Theobald Smith Soc., 1991. Mem. AAAS, Am. Soc. Microbiology (former mem. com. actinomycetales), U.S. Fedn. Culture Collections (exec. com. 1982-85, J. Roger Porter award nominating com. 1983-84, 87-88, chair 1989-90, J. Roger Porter award 1992), N.Am. Mycol. Assn., Soc. Gen. Microbiology, Sigma Xi (pres. Rutgers U. chpt. 1977-78). Home: RR 2 Box 2235 Morrisville VT 05661-9429

LECHNYR, RONALD JOSEPH, psychologist; b. Mpls., July 21, 1942; s. Joseph Albert and Leila (Lilijedahl) L.; m. Celia Ann Filter, Aug. 15, 1964; children: David R., Michelle, Terri A., Sandra M. BA in Clin. Social Work, Wartburg Coll., 1964; MSW in Clin. Social Work, Smith Coll., 1967; DSW in Clin. Social Work, U. Utah, 1973; PhD in Psychology, U. Oreg., 1982. Diplomate Internat. Acad. of Behavioral Medicine & Psychotherapy & Counseling, Am. Acad. Pain Mgmt., Am. Bd. Med. Psychotherapists, Am. Bd. Examiners in Clin. Social Work. Intern Family Svc. Assn. Greater Boston, Boston, 1965-66; intern dept. psychiatry Mass. Gen. Hosp., Boston, 1966-67; commd. helath svc. officer USPHS, 1967; intern Marriage & Family Counseling Clinic U. Utah, Salt Lake City, 1972-73; advanced through grades to chief dept. psychiatry USPHS Med. Ctr., Gallup, N.Mex, 1974-76; post-doctoral resident in psychology Pain Therapy Clinic, Eugene, 1980-83; dir. psychotherapy clinic The Eugene (Oreg.) Hosp. & Clinic, 1976-81; clin. psychologist in pvt. practice Eugene, 1981—; clin. dir., co-founder Oreg. Pain Ctr., Springfield, 1985-91; clin. dir., co-owner Oreg. Health Rehab., Springfield, 1991-96; clin. assoc. dept. psychiatry U. N.Mex., 1973-76; faculty advisor univ. without walls program Loretto Heights Coll., Denver, 1973-76; clin. instr. U. Utah, Salt Lake City, 1972-73; field instr. Portland (Oreg.) State U. 1989-90. Columnist (newspaper) Blackberry Ink, Eugene, 1990-94; contbr. articles to profl. jours. Fellow Am. Orthopsychiat. Assn., Am. Assn. for Marriage and Family Therapy, Biofeedback Cert. Inst. Am.; mem. Oreg. Psychol. Assn., Lane County Psychol. Assn., Am. Pain Soc., Western U.S.A. Pain Soc., Internat. Soc. for Study of Pain, Prescribing Psychologists' Register Inc. (charter mem.), Phi Kappa Phi. Democrat. Lutheran. Home: 1955 McLean Blvd Eugene OR 97405 Office: Dr Ron Lechnyr & Assocs 2440 Willamette St Ste 102 Eugene OR 97405

LECKLITNER, MYRON LYNN, nuclear physician; b. Canton, Ohio, June 16, 1942; s. Myron Devoy and Margaret (Koon) L.; m. Carol Vance, Sept. 1979; 1 child, Tonja Ann. BS in Acctg. and Economics, Pa. State U., 1964; BS in Chemistry and Biology, U. Ala., 1970, MD, 1974. Diplomate Am. Bd. Nuclear Medicine. Intern Lloyd Noland Hosp., Birmingham, Ala., 1974-75, resident in internal medicine, 1975-77; fellow in nuclear medicine and ultrasound, U. Ala.-Birmingham, 1977-79; asst. prof. U. Tex.-San Antonio, 1979-83; assoc. prof. U. South Ala., Mobile, 1983-86, prof., 1986—; dir. diagnostic imaging div., sr. scientist U. South Ala. Cancer Ctr., 1984—. Vis. prof. U. Nuevo Leon, Mex., 1983, U. Oxford, Eng., 1985, 88, Royal Postgrad. Sch. Med., U. London, 1985, and numerous Am. U. Contbr. chpts. to books, articles to profl. jours. Served to capt. U.S. Army, 1964-67. Decorated Bronze Star medal, 1966, Army Commendation medal, 1966, Air medal, 1966. Fellow Am. Coll. Nuclear Physicians (treas. 1988-90, vice chmn. membership com. 1985-87, exec. com. 1985-90, bd. Regents 1985-90, chmn. fin. com. 1986-88, chmn. publs. com. 1994-96); mem. Ala. Soc. Nuclear Medicine (pres. 1985-86, trustee S.E. chpt. 1988-90, 1991—, chmn. govt. affairs com.), Am. Coll. Radiology (nuclear med. mktg. com. 1992—), Soc. Nuclear Med. (bus. advisors group 1990—, socioecons. com. 1991—). Home: 5505 Oak Park Ct Mobile AL 36609-2204 Office: U South Ala Dept Radiology 2451 Fillingim St MSN 301 Mobile AL 36617

LECKMAN, LINDA J., physician; b. Watonga, Okla., Oct. 2, 1947; d. Kenneth L. and Clara I. (Driever) Cordell; m. Scott L. Leckman, June 12, 1983; children: Matthew S., Eric A. BA, Tex. Christian U., 1969; MD, U. N.Mex., 1977. Am. Bd. Surgery. Intern, resident U. Utah Affiliated Hosps., Salt Lake City, 1977-82; Bd. trustees Utah Med. Assn., Salt Lake City, 1986—, Intermountain Health Care, Salt Lake City, 1986—; bd. dirs. Health Insight, Salt Lake City. Fellow ACS; mem. Utah Med. Assn. (trustee), Assn. Women Surgeons, Alpha Omega Alpha. Home: 21st Fl 30 South State St Salt Lake City UT 84111 Office: 9720 S 1300 E #110 Sandy UT 84094

LECLAIR, GARY J., gynecologist; b. Columbus, Ohio, July 11, 1945; s. James B. and Margaret R. (Rosebaugh) L.; m. Rebecca G. Ziegman, July 28, 1990; children: Alan J., Nathan R., Kevin R., Michelle Palmer, Michael Palmer. BS in Zoology, Wash. State U., 1967; MD, Baylor U., 1971; student, N.W. Christian Coll., Eugene, Oreg., 1994—. Diplomate Am. Bd. Ob-gyn. Intern Med. Coll. Va., Richmond, 1971-72; resident Baylor Affiliated Hosps., Houston, 1972-74; chief resident Baylor Affiliated Hosps., 1974-75; asst. chief obstetrics U.S. Army, Tacoma, Wash., 1975-77; past chief ob-gyn. Sacred Heart Gen. Hosp., Eugene, Oreg., 1986-88. Author monthly column Perspectives, 1994—. Past pres. Lane County Med. Soc., Eugene, 1994. Major U.S. Army med. corps, 1975-77. Office: Women's Care 598 E 13th Ave Eugene OR 97401

LECLAIR, SUSAN JEAN, hematologist, clinical laboratory scientist, educator; b. New Bedford, Mass., Feb. 17, 1947; d. Joseph A. and Beatrice (Perry) L.; m. James T. Griffith; 1 child, Kimberly A. BS in med. tech., Stonehill Coll., 1968; postgrad., Northeastern U., Boston, 1972-74; MS in Med. Lab. Sci., U. Mass., Dartmouth, 1977. Cert. clin. lab. scientist; cert. med. technologist. Med. technologist Union Hosp., New Bedford, Mass., 1968-70; supr. hematology Morton Hosp., Taunton, Mass., 1970-72; edn. coord., program dir. Sch. Med. Tech. Miriam Hosp., Providence, 1972-79; hematology technologist R.I. Hosp., Providence, 1979-80; asst. prof. med. lab. sci. U. Mass., Dartmouth, 1980-84, assoc. prof. med. lab. sci., 1984-92, prof. med. lab. sci., 1992—; instr. hematology courses Brown U., Providence, 1978-80; cons. Bd. R.I. Schs. Med. Tech., R.I. Hosp. Div. Clin. Hematology, Cardinal Cushing Gen. Hosp., Charlton Meml. Hosp., St. Luke's Hosp., VA Med. Ctr., Providence, 1984—, Nemasket Group, Inc., 1984-87, Gateway Health Alliance, 1985-87; chair hematology/hemostasis com. Nat. Cert. Agy. for Med. Lab. Pers. Exam. Coun., 1994—. Contbr. articles to profl. jours.; contbr. articles to jours and chpts. to books; author computer software in hematology. Reviewer Nat. Commn. Clin. Lab. Scis., 1986-89; chairperson Mass. Assn. Health Planning Agys., 1986-87; bd. dirs. Southeastern Mass. Health Planning Devel. Inc., (1975-88, numerous other offices and coms.); planning subcom. AIDS Edn. (presentor Info Series). Mem. Am. Soc. Clin. Lab. Sci., Nat. Cert. Agy. for Med. Lab. Pers. (chair Hematology Com. of Exam Coun. 1994—), Am. Soc. Med. Tech. Edn. and Rsch. Fund, Inc. (chairperson 1983-85), Mass. Assn. for Med. Tech. (pres. 1977-78), Southeastern Mass. Soc. Med. Tech. (pres. 1975-76), Alpha Mu Tau (pres. 1993-94). Office: U Mass Dept Med Lab Sci Dartmouth MA 02747

LE CLOIREC, JOSEPH, nuclear medicine physician; b. Quimperle, France, Nov. 14, 1951; s. André and Simone (Mentec) L.C.; m. Brigitte Delaunay, Aug. 18, 1984; children: Julien, Antoine, Etienne. MD, Faculté Rennes, France, 1981; specialist in nuclear medicine, INSTN, Paris, 1984. Asst. U. Rennes, 1985-93; specialist Nat. Cancer Ctr., Rennes, 1993—. Mem. EANM, SFBMN, SMNO (v.p. 1996—). Home: 14 Rue AG de Coligny, 35000 Rennes France Office: CE Marquis, Rue de la Bataille Flandres, 35062 Rennes France

LECUYER-COONS, GEORGEIDA CELENE, nurse, small business owner; b. Clifton, Kans., Jan. 4, 1926; d. George and Ida Marie (Savoie) L.; m. Roger James Freeman (div. 1971); children: George W., Kathryn A., Margaret J., John M.; m. Merlyn D. (Tony) Coons (dec. 1985). BA, Park Coll., Parkville, Mo., 1980; RN, Avila Coll., Kansas City, Mo., 1948. RN, Kans. Med.-surg. staff nurse Research Hosp., Kansas City, Mo., 1966-67; anesthetist Oral Surgeons, Inc., Kansas City, 1967-70; instr. practical nursing Kansas City Bd. Edn., Mo., 1972-75; oncology staff nurse U. Kans. Med. Ctr., Kansas City, Kans., 1975-78; mental health staff nurse VA Hosp., Leavenworth, Kans., 1978-82; gerontology staff nurse VA Hosp., Topeka, 1982-85; ret. VA Hosp., 1985; owner Baby Boomer Hdqrs. of Kans., Salina, 1986—; ednl. cons. VA Hosp. In-Service dept., Topeka. 1982-85; conductor workshops on behaviors, team concept, alcoholism and ageism. Local leader Boy Scouts Am., Girl Scouts U.S., Kansas City, Mo., 1962-66. Served with U.S. Cadet Nursing Corps, 1944-47. Recipient Excellent Bedside Caregiver award U. Kans. Med. Ctr., 1977, Spl. Advancement award VA, 1982. Mem. Nat. Assn. Ret. Fed. Employees, Am. Assn. Ret. Persons. Republican. Roman Catholic. Club: Salina (Kans.) Christian Women's.

LEDEEN, ROBERT WAGNER, neurochemist, educator; b. Denver, Aug. 19, 1928; s. Hyman and Olga (Wagner) L.; m. Lydia Rosen Hailparn, July 2, 1982. B.S., U. Calif., Berkeley, 1949; Ph.D., Oreg. State U., 1953. Postdoctoral fellow in chemistry U. Chgo., 1953-54; rsch. assoc. in chemistry Mt. Sinai Hosp., N.Y.C., 1956-59; rsch. fellow Albert Einstein Coll. Medicine, Bronx, N.Y., 1959; asst. prof. Albert Einstein Coll. Medicine, 1963-69, assoc. prof., 1969-75, prof., 1975-91; prof., dir. div. neurochemistry U. Medicine and Dentistry N.J., Newark, 1991—. Contbr. articles to profl. jours.; dep. chief editor Jour. Neurochemistry. Mem. neurol. scis. study sect. NIH; mem. study sect. Nat. Multiple Sclerosis Soc. NIH grantee, 1963—; Nat. Multiple Sclerosis Soc. grantee, 1967-74; recipient Humboldt prize, Javits Neurosci. Investigator award. Mem. Internat. Soc. Neurochemistry, Am. Soc. Neurochemistry, Am. Chem. Soc., Am. Soc. Biol. Chemists, N.Y. Acad. Sci. Jewish. Home: 8 Donald Ct Wayne NJ 07470-4608 Office: U Medicine and Dentistry NJ Dept Neurosci 185 S Orange Ave Newark NJ 07103-2714

LEDERBERG, JOSHUA, geneticist, educator; b. Montclair, N.J., May 23, 1925; s. Zwi Hirsch and Esther (Goldenbaum) L.; m. Marguerite S. Kirsch, Apr. 5, 1968; children: David Kirsch, Anne. BA, Columbia U., 1944; PhD, Yale U., 1947. With U. Wis., 1947-58; prof. genetics Sch. Medicine, Stanford (Calif.) U., 1959-78; pres. Rockefeller U., N.Y.C., 1978-90, univ. prof. Sackler Found. scholar, 1990—; adj. prof. Columbia U., 1990—; mem. adv. com. med. rsch. WHO, 1971; mem. bd. sci. advisors Affymax N.V., Palo Alto, Hewlett Packard Inc., Palo Alto, Aviron, Mountain View, Calif.; cons. U.S. Def. Sci. Bd., NSF, NIH, NASA, ACDA. Trustee Camille and Henry Dreyfus Found.; bd. dirs. Chem. Industry Inst. Toxicology, N.C. With USN, 1943-45. Recipient Nobel prize in physiology and medicine for rsch. in genetics of bacteria, 1958, U.S. Nat. Medal of Sci., 1989, Alan Newell award ACM, 1996. Fellow AAAS, Am. Philos. Soc., Am. Acad. Arts and Scis., N.Y. Acad. Medicine (hon.), Acad. Universelle Cultures (Paris); mem. Inst. Medicine NAS, Coun. Fgn. Rels., Royal Soc. London (fgn.), N.Y. Acad. Scis. (hon. life gov.), Ordre des Lettres et des Arts (comdr.). Office: Rockefeller U 1230 York Ave Ste 400 New York NY 10021-6307

LEDERIS, KAROLIS PAUL (KARL LEDERIS), pharmacologist, educator, researcher; b. Noreikoniai, Lithuania, Aug. 1, 1920; arrived in Can., 1969; s. Paul Augustus and Franciska (Danisevicius) L.; m. Hildegard Gallistl, Feb. 28, 1952; children: Aldona Franciska, Edmund Paul. Diploma, Tchrs. Coll., Siauliai, Lithuania, 1939; BSc, U. Bristol, U.K., 1958, PhD, 1961, DSc, 1968. Jr. lectr., then lectr. and reader U. Bristol, 1961-69; prof. pharmacology and therapeutics U. Calgary, Alta., Can., 1969-89, prof. emeritus, 1989—; vis. prof. univs. in Fed. Republic Germany, Austria, Chile, Argentina, Sri Lanka, Switzerland, Lithuania, France, , USA, USSR, 1963-79, U. Bristol, 1979, U. Kyoto, Japan, 1980; career investigator, mem., chair grants com. Med. Rsch. Coun., Ottawa, Ont., Can., 1970-89, coun. mem., exec., 1983-90; mem. internat. com. Centres Excellence Networks, Ottawa, 1988-89. Author, editor: 5 books on hypothalamic hormones; editor in chief Jour. Exptl. and Clin. Pharmacology, 1977-89; contbr. approximately 350 book chpts. and articles to profl. jours.; patentee hormonal peptides. Recipient Upjohn award in pharmacology, 1990, various fellowships and scholarships in U.K., Fed. Republic of Germany, U.S.A. Fellow NAS, Royal Soc. Can.; mem. Western Pharmacological Soc. (pres. 1982-83), pharm., physiol., endocrinological, biochem. socs. U.K., Can., U.S., Lithuanian Club (London), Men's Can. Club, Cabot Yacht and Cruise Club (Bristol). Home: 147 Carthew St, Comox, BC Canada V9M 1T4 Office: U Calgary, Health Scis Centre, Calgary, AB Canada T2N 4N1

LEDERMAN, RICHARD JOEL, neurologist; b. Buffalo, Apr. 2, 1939; s. Israel R. and Hazel F. (Fisher) L.; m. Barbara E. Wilson, June 18, 1960; children: Douglas J., Joy, Anne D. AB, Princeton U., 1960; MD, SUNY, Buffalo, 1966, PhD, 1966. Diplomate Am. Bd. Psychiatry and Neurology. Intern in medicine Bronx (N.Y.) Mcpl. Hosp., 1966-67, resident in medicine, 1967-68; rsch. assoc. NIH, Bethesda, Md., 1968-70; resident in neurology Mass. Gen. Hosp., Boston, 1970-73; staff neurologist Cleve. Clinic, 1973—; asst. clin. prof. neurology Case Western Res. U., Cleve., 1976—; clin. assoc. prof. medicine Pa. State U., Hershey, 1989—; assoc. prof. neurology Ohio State U., Columbus, 1993—; profl. adv. bd. Alzheimer's Assn., Cleve., 1992—, chmn. 1996—. Co-editor: Textbook of Performing Arts Medicine, 1991. Bd. trustees Cleve. Chamber Music Soc., 1980-86; bd. trustees Ohio Chamber Orch., Cleve., 1988—. Lt. comdr. USPHS, 1968-70. Fellow Am. Acad. Neurology, Am. Assn. Electrodiagnostic Medicine (bd. dirs. 1988-91); mem. Am. Neurol. Assn., Performing Arts Medicine Assn. (pres. 1991-93). Home: 2731 Shelley Rd Shaker Heights OH 44122 Office: Cleve Clinic Found 9500 Euclid Ave Cleveland OH 44195

LEDERMAN, SALLY ANN, nutrition educator and researcher; b. N.Y.C., July 8, 1937; d. Joseph Edward and Leanora (Galeski) Rossi; m. Lawrence Lederman, Jan. 26, 1958 (div. Feb. 1991); children: Leandra, Evin. BS in Chemistry, Bklyn. Coll., 1957; MS in Nutrition, Columbia U., 1976, PhD, 1980. Analytical chemist U.S. FDA, N.Y.C., 1957-62; lectr. dept. chemistry Bklyn. Coll., 1962-66, 74; postdoctoral fellow Inst. Human Nutrition Columbia U., N.Y.C., 1980-83, postdoctoral fellow obstetrics and biochemistry, 1983, asst. prof. Sch. Pub. Health, 1983-90, assoc. prof. Sch. Pub. Health, 1990-94; prof. Tchrs. Coll., 1994—. Editor: Controversial Issues in Public Health Nutrition, 1983; contbr. articles to profl. jours. Mem. APHA, AAAS, Am. Inst. Nutrition, Am. Women in Sci., N.Y. Acad. Scis. Office: Columbia U Tchrs Coll Box 137 525 W 120th St New York NY 10027

LEDFORD, JOAN FERRIS, physician assistant; b. Yonkers, N.Y., Apr. 25, 1955; d. George Schermerhorn and Elizabeth Muir (Hemmingford) Ferris; m. Robert Mitchell Ledford, June 2, 1989. BA in Biology, Ithaca Coll., 1977. Cert. physician asst. Physician asst. emergency room Dist. Meml. Hosp., Andrews, N.C., 1979-87; instr. Tri-County C.C., Murphy, N.C., 1986-93; physician asst. Lee Arrendale Correctional Inst., Alto, Ga., 1988—, Long Street Clinic, Gainesville, Ga., 1994—. Fellow Am. Acad. Physician Assts. Home: 251 Yonah Post Rd Alto GA 30510 Office: Long Street Clinic Enota St Gainesville GA 30501

LEDGER, WILLIAM JOE, physician, educator; b. Turtle Creek, Pa., 1932. B.A., Princeton U., 1954; M.D., U. Pa., 1958; M.S., Temple U., 1964. Diplomate Am. Bd. Ob-Gyn. Intern Hamot Hosp. Assn., Erie, N.Y., 1958-59; resident Temple U. Hosp., Phila., 1961-64; attending physician Women's Hosp.-Mich. Med. Ctr., 1964-72; assoc. prof. U. Mich., Ann Arbor; prof. U. So. Calif., L.A., 1972-79; Given Found. prof., chmn. ob-gyn. Cornell U. Med. Coll., N.Y.C., 1979—. Served to capt. USMC, 1959-61. Fellow ACS, Am. Coll. Ob-Gyn. Office: NY Hosp-Cornell Med Sch 525 E 68th St New York NY 10021

LEDLEY, FRED DAVID, physician, business executive; b. Washington, Nov. 27, 1954; s. Robert Steven and Terry (Wachtell) L.; m. Tamara Ann Shapiro, June 6, 1976; children: Miriam Esther, Johanna Sharon. BS, U. Md., 1974; MD, Georgetown U., 1978. Intern, resident Harvard Med. Sch., Boston Children's Hosp., Boston, 1978-81; fellow Harvard Med. Sch., MIT, Am. Cancer Soc., Boston, 1981-83; asst. investigator Howard Hughes Med. Inst., Houston, 1986-92; asst. prof. Baylor Coll. of Medicine, Houston, 1986-89, assoc. prof. cell biology and pediatrics, 1989—; v.p. medicine and Sci. found. GeneMedicine, Inc., Houston, 1993—; prin. investigator clin. trial gene transfer into human livers; cons. on gene therapy to NIH and industry. Contbr. over 200 articles to profl. sci. jours. Recipient Upjohn Research award Georgetown U., 1978, Charles Janeway award Harvard Med. Sch./ Children's Hosp., 1981. Mem. AAAS, Am. Soc. for Human Genetics, Soc. for Pediatrics Rsch. (coun. 1993-96), Am. Soc. Study Liver Disease, Soc. for Inherited Metabolic Disease. Office: GeneMedicine Inc 8301 New Trails Dr The Woodlands TX 77381

LEDUC, LOUISE ELIZABETH, pharmacologist, educator, research scientist; b. Lincoln, Nebr., May 6, 1952; d. Thomas Harold and Kathryn Barbara (King) LeD.; 1 child, Kathryn Nicole. BA cum laude, Radcliffe Coll., 1974; PhD, Washington U., 1981. Postdoctoral fellow UCLA Sch. of Medicine, 1981-83; asst. rsch. biochemist U. Calif. Davis Sch. of Medicine, 1983-85; adj. asst. prof. dept. medicine UCLA Rsch. and Edn. Inst., Torrance, 1985-91; assoc. dir. Biochemistry Care, Inflammatory Bowel Disease Ctr. Harbor-UCLA Med. Ctr., 1985-89; asst. prof. Pa. State U. Coll. of Medicine, Hershey, 1991—. Reviewer Gastoreneterology jour., Pharmacology jour.; ad hoc reviewer NIH, 1993, VA Med. Rsch. Svc. Merit Review; contbr. articles to profl. jours. Mem. Berry Twp. Curriculum Com., 1995. Recipient Career Devel. award Crohns and Colitis Found. of Am., 1987-90. Mem. AAAS, Am. Gastroenterology Assn., Am. Soc. Pharmacology and Exptl. Therapeutics (Travel award 1978), Nature Conservancy. Office: Pa State Univ Coll Medicine Dept Pharmacology PO Box 850 Hershey PA 17033

LEE, ALAN GREGORY, health facility administrator; b. Glendale, Calif., July 14, 1955; s. Jock Gim and Rose Patricia (Choy) L.; m. Clarice Ayako Oka, Mar. 9, 1982. BA in Biology/Religion, U. Hawaii at Manoa, Honolulu, 1978; MPH, U. Hawaii, Honolulu, 1980. Lic. nursing home adminstr. Mgmt. analyst Hawaii State Dept. Health-Divsn. Cmty. Hosps., Honolulu, 1981-85; asst. adminstr., COO Maui Meml. Hosp., Wailuku, 1985—; acting adminstr. Lanai Hosp., Lanai City, Hawaii, 1992-93, Kula (Hawaii) Hosp., 1994-95. Bd. mem., past pres. Hospice Maui, Hawaii, 1989-94; bd. mem. Maui (Hawaii) Symphony Orch., 1994-95. Office: Maui Meml Hosp 221 Mahalani St Wailuku Maui HI 96793-2581

LEE, ALISON ANN, healthcare manager; b. Holyoke, Mass., June 30, 1950; d. Robert Keating and Audrey Ethel (Emery) L. BA, Mt. Holyoke Coll., 1975; MA, Cen. Mich. U., 1985; MPH U. Okla., 1990. Med.

technologist Wesson unit Baystate Med. Center, Springfield, Mass., 1973-78; cons. Tulsa City-County Health Dept., 1979-81, Moton Health Center, Tulsa, 1980-84; lead med. technologist St. Francis Hosp., Tulsa, 1978-86; dir. edn. Springer Clinic, Tulsa, 1986-91; mgr. practice devel. Credentials and Health Edn. Found. Health, Rancho Cordova, Calif., 1991-94; assoc. prof. Chapman U., 1992—. Past public edn. chmn., mem. profl. edn. com., bd. dirs. Am. Cancer Soc.; mem. adv. bd. Am. Heart Assn.; mem. Jr. League Sacramento; vol. various community orgns.; dir. edn. and prevention Sacramento AIDS Found. Mem. Am. Soc. Clin. Pathologists, Med. Group Mgmt. Assn. Home: 11801 Fair Oaks Blvd # 12 Fair Oaks CA 95628-2846 Office: 1330 21st St Ste 100 Sacramento CA 95814

LEE, ARTHUR VIRGIL, III, biotechnology company executive; b. Detroit, Nov. 24, 1920; s. Arthur Virgil and Emily S. (Burry) L.; m. Elizabeth Hoppin Chafee, Dec. 8, 1945 (div.); children: Arthur C., Sherrill Ann Rosoff, William J., Henry C.; m. Jean Austin LaMothe, Dec. 30, 1967. BA, Williams Coll., 1942; Indsl. Adminstr. (World War II MBA), Harvard Bus. Sch., 1943. With McKesson & Robbins, Inc., Memphis, 1946-47; ops. mgr. Providence div. McKesson & Robbins, Inc., 1947-63, v.p., mgr. Providence div., 1954-59, with Boston div., 1959-63, with Pitts. div., 1963; asst. dean Harvard U. Bus. Sch., Cambridge, Mass., 1964-65, dir. corp. rels., 1965-72, dir. resources, 1972-73; v.p. Lesley Coll., Cambridge, 1973-77; dir. corp. rels. Tufts U., Medford, Mass., 1977-79; pres. Biotec Internat., Ltd., Williamstown, Mass., 1979-95. Bd. dirs. New Eng. Drug Exchange, 1956-63; trustee Am. Coll. Switzerland, 1978-82, Williamstown Theatre Festival, 1984-94, trustee emeritus, 1994—; mem. Weston Town Fin. Com., 1961-66; mem. adv. bd. Coll. Pharmacy, U. R.I., 1957-58. Lt. USNR, 1942-46. Mem. Taconic Golf Club, Alpha Delta Phi. Congregationalist. Home and Office: 1549 Green River Rd Williamstown MA 01267-3128

LEE, BYUNG IN, neurologist; b. Seoul, Korea, Mar. 31, 1950; s. Woo Choo and Young Ok (Choi) L.; m. Kwang Il Bang; children: Eum Ji, Hong Kyun, Yong Kyun. MD, Yonsei U. Coll. Medicine, Seoul, 1974. Resident in internal medicine St. Joseph Hosp., Chgo., 1979-80; resident in neurology U. Minn., Mpls., 1980-83; fellow clin. electrophysiology Cleve. Clinic, 1983-84; asst. prof. neurology Ind. U., Indpls., 1984-88; asst. prof. neurology Yonsei U., Seoul, 1988-89, assoc. prof., 1989-95, prof. neurology, 1995—, dir. EEG lab., 1988—, dir. epilepsy clinic, 1989—; assoc. dir. EEG lab. Ind. U., Indpls., 1984-88. Contbr. articles to profl. jours. Sec. gen. AOCN, Seoul, 1996—; chmn. Korean Organizing Com. for AOEO, Seoul, 1996—. Capt. Korean Air Force, 1974-77. Mem. Korean Med. Assn., Korean Neurol. Assn. (bd. acad. affairs 1989-93), Am. Acad. Neurology. Office: Yonsei Univ Coll Medicine, Seodaemun-ten, 134 Shinchan-dong, Seoul South Korea

LEE, CARLA ANN BOUSKA, nursing educator; b. Ellsworth, Kans., Nov. 26, 1943; d. Frank J. and Christine Rose (Vopat) Bouska; m. Gordon Larry Lee, July 8, 1967. RN, Marymount Coll., Salina, Kans., 1964; BSN, U. Kans., 1967; MA, Wichita State U., 1972, EdS, 1975, M in Nursing, 1984; PhD, Kans. State U., 1988. RN; cert. family and adult nurse practitioner, advanced nurse adminstr., health edn. specialist. Staff, charge nurse Ellsworth (Kans.) County Vet. Meml. Hosp., 1964-65; critical, coronary, and surg. nurse Med. Ctr. U. Kans., Kansas City, 1966-67; Watkins Meml. Hosp. and Student Health Ctr., 1965-55; asst. dir., chief instr. sch. nursing Wesley Sch. Nursing, Wichita, Kans., 1967-74; asst prof., chairperson Nurse Clinician/Practitioner Dept. Wichita State U., 1974-84; assoc. prof., dir. nurse practitioner program Ft. Hays State U., Hays, Kans., 1992-95; assoc. prof., coord. postgrad. nursing studies Clark Coll., Omaha, 1995—; cons. GRCI's CE Providership, 1994-96; lectr. Wichita State U., 1972-74, mem. grad. faculty, 1993-95; cons. Hays Med. Ctr.-Family Healthcare Ctr., 1993-96, Baker U., Northeastern U., Boston; mem. adv. coun. Kans. Newman Coll.; mem. adv. bd. Kans. Originals, Kans. Dept. Econ. Devel. Project, Wilson; mem. grad. faculty U. Kans. 1993-95; rschr. in field. Author: (with Stroot & Barrett) Fluids and Electrolytes: A Basic Approach, 3d edit., 1984, 4th ed., 1996 (poetry) Seasons: Marks of Life, 1991 (Golden Poet award 1991), Winter Tree, 1995 (Internat. Poet of Merit award 1995), (booklet) Czechoslovakian History, 1988 (honor room Czech Mus. and Opera House, Wilson); author, editor: History of Kansas Nursing, 1987; contbr. articles to profl. jours. Co-founder Kans. Nurses Found., pres., trustee, 1978-93, vol. ARC, 1967-92, bd. dirs., 1977-90; mem. rschr. Gov.'s Commn. Health Care, Topeka, 1990; mem. State of Kans. health care agenda Kans. Pub. Health Assn., 1995; city coord. campaign Sec. State, 1986; vol., lectr. Am. Heart Assn., Am. Cancer Soc., 1967—; election judge Sedgwick County, Kans., 1989-94; chair Nat. Task Force on Care Competence of Nurse Practitioners, 1995; mem. Nat. Task Force on Feasibility of Care Exam. for Nurse Practitioners, 1995. Nurse Practitioner Tng. grantee U.S. Health and Human Svcs.; named Outstanding Cmty. Leader, jaycees, Alumnus of Yr., Kansas U, 1979, marymount Coll., 1987, Poet of Yr., 1995; recipient Tchr. award Mortar Bd. Fellow Am. Acad. Nursing, Am. Acad. Nursing; mem. ANA (nat. and site visitor ANCC), Kans. Nurses Assn. (bd. dirs., treas.), Kans. Alliance Advanced Nurse Practitioners (founder, pres., 1986), Gt. Plains Nurse Practitioners Soc., (founder, pres. 1993), Internat. Soc. Poets (disting.), Alpha Eta (pres. Wichita State U. chpt.), Sigma Theta Tau Internat., Internat. Woman of Yr. Republican. Roman Catholic. Home: 1367 N Westlink St Wichita KS 67212-4238 Office: Clarkson Coll Dept Nursing 101 S 42nd St Omaha NE 68131

LEE, CARLTON K. K., clinical pharmacist, consultant, educator; b. Honolulu, June 17, 1962; s. Hsiang Tsing and Ngan Kar (Ching) Lee; m. Joanne Evelyn Tilley, May 27, 1995. PharmD, U. of the Pacific, 1985; MPH, Johns Hopkins U., 1994. Hosp. pharmacy resident Johns Hopkins Hosp., Balt., 1985-86, clin. staff pharmacist pediatrics dept. pharmacy, 1986-88, sr. clin. pharmacist pediatrics dept. pharmacy, 1988-90, clin. coord. pediatrics dept. pharmacy, 1990—; asst. prof. Sch. Pharmacy, Howard U., Washignton, 1987-88; clin. asst. prof. Sch. Pharmacy, U. Md., Balt., 1989—; instr. pediatrics Sch. Medicine, Johns Hopkins U., Balt., 1992-95, asst. prof., 1995—; cons. Nat. Med. Care Inc., Columbia, Md., 1994, Home Intensive Care Inc., Hunt Valley, Md., 1992-93; founder, pres. Mid-Atlantic Pediatric Pharmacotherapy Specialists, 1993—. Contbg. author: Harriet Lane Handbook, 1990, 93, 96, Newborn Nursery Handbook, 1992, 96; investigational drug advisor Med. Sci. Bull., 1992—; contbr. articles to profl. jours.; author, co-author conf. papers. Mem. Am. Soc. Hosp. Pharmacists , Am. Coll. Clin. Pharmacy, Internat. Assn. Therapeutic Drug Monitoring and Clin. Toxicology. Office: Johns Hopkins Hosp Dept Pharmacy Svcs 600 N Wolfe St Baltimore MD 21287-6180

LEE, DAVID ANSON, ophthalmologist; b. Pine Ridge, S.D., Jan. 28, 1956; s. Robert Ying and Betty (Wang) L. BA, Boston U., 1980, MD, 1980; MS, U. Minn., 1984, MBA UCLA, 1993. Diplomate Nat. Bd. Med. Examiners, Am. Bd. Ophthalmology. Intern Mayo Clinic, Rochester, Minn., 1980-81, resident in ophthalmology, 1981-84; fellow in glaucoma Mass. Eye and Ear Infirmary, Harvard Med. Sch., Boston, 1984-86; instr. in ophthalomology Mayo Med. Sch., 1983-86; asst. prof. ophthalmology UCLA Sch. Medicine, 1986-90, assoc. prof. ophthalmology, 1990-96, 1996—; guest lectr. in ophthalmology Henan Med. Coll., Peoples Republic of China, 1983; chief glaucoma divsn. UCLA, dir. mobil eye clinic. Author: (with J.A. Dyer) Atlas of Extraocular Muscle Surgery, 1984, (with E.J. Higginbotham) Management of Difficult Glaucomas, 1994, New Developments in Glaucoma, 1995; contbr. articles to profl. jours. Recipient Roland P. Mackay award Am. Acad. Neurology, 1980, Nat. Research Service award Nat. Eye Inst., 1984-85; Heed Ophthalmic Found. fellow, 1984-85, Judson Daland fellow Am. Philos. Soc., 1985-87, Heed-Knapp fellow, 1985-86; recipient 3 patents. Mem. Am. AAAS, AMA, Acad. Ophthalmology, Assn. Research in Vision and Ophthalmology, Culver Legion, Boston U. Alumni Assn., Phi Beta Kappa, Sigma Xi, Alpha Omega Alpha. Avocations: fencing, long-distance running, golf, tennis, sailing. Home: 205 S Thurston Ave Los Angeles CA 90049-3123 Office: UCLA Sch Medicine Jules Stein Eye Inst 100 Stein Pla Los Angeles CA 90095

LEE, DAVID AUDREY, plastic surgeon; b. Shreveport, La., Feb. 10, 1944; s. Whitny Aubrey Lee and Theresa Louise (Robinson) Giering; m. Mary Carol Coco, June 27, 1967; children: Christopher David, Elizabeth Robinson. BS, Northwestern State U., 1966; MD, La. State U., New Orleans, 1970. Diplomate Am. Bd. Plastic Surgery, Am. Bd. Hand and Neck Surgery. Resident in otolaryngology Baylor Sch. Medicine, Houston, resident in plastic surgery, 1983-85; pres. Plastic Surgery Practice, Houston, 1985—; med. dir. United Med. Care, Houston, 1993—. Dir. La. Outdoor Drama Assn., 1980-83. Maj. USAF, 9175-77. Mem. Houston Soc. Plastic Surgery (pres. 1995-96), Rotary. Roman Catholic. Office: 6560 Fannin #1760 Houston TX 77030

LEE, DONNA JEAN, retired hospice and respite nurse; b. Huntington Park, Nov. 12, 1931; d. Louis Frederick and Lena Adelaide (Hinson) Munyon; m. Frank Bernard Lee, July 16, 1949; children: Frank, Robert, John. AA in Nursing, Fullerton (Calif.) Jr. Coll., 1966; extension student, U. Calif., Irvine, 1966-74; student, U. N.Mex., 1982. RN, Calif.; cert. Intraventous Therapy Assn. U.S.A. Staff nurse Orange (Calif.) County Med. Ctr., 1966-71, staff and charge nurse relief ICU, CCU, Burn Unit, ER, Communicable Disease, Neo-Natal Care Unit, 1969-71, charge nurse communicable disease unit, 1969-70; staff and charge nurse ICU, emergency rm., CCU, med./surg. units Anaheim (Calif.) Meml. Hosp., 1971-74; charge and staff nurse, relief Staff Builders, Orange, 1974-82; agy. nurse Nursing Svcs. Internat., 1978-89; asst. DON Chapman Convalescent SNF, Orange, 1982; geriatric and pediatrics nurse VNASS, 1985-93; hospice/respite nurse VIA Upjohn Home Healthcare Svcs and VNA Support Svcs. of Orange, 1985-93; ret.; staff relief nurse ICU/CCU various hosps. and labs, including plasmapheresis nurse Med. Lab. of Orange, 1978. Life mem. Republican, pres. task force, 1982—; past mem. Republican adv. com., Rep. Presdl. Trust; mem. Rep. Presdl. Legion of Merit. Mem. AACN, RNCC, RNSC, ADA, ASA, Inst. Noetic Scis., The Heritage Found., Aria, Am. Cancer Soc., Am. Lung Assn., Am. Heart Assn., Nat. Multiple Sclerosis Soc., Easter Seal Soc. Baptist. Home: 924 S Hampstead St Anaheim CA 92802-1740

LEE, EDWARD MORRIS, urologist; b. Houston, June 14, 1934; s. Morris Winfield and Lillian Margaret (Todd) L.; m. Ellen Jane Waddle, July 10, 1965; children: Loren Ellen, Amy Catherine, Jefferson Edward. BA, Baylor U., 1956, MD, 1960. Cert. Am. Bd. Urological Surgeons. Intern Med. Coll. of Va., 1960-61; chief resident urology Vancerbilt Hosp., Nashville, 1964-65; chief urology Brooke Army Hosp., Ft. Sam Houston, Tex., 1965-67, 3rd Field Hosp., Saigon, Viet Nam, 1967-68; pvt. practice Waco, Tex., 1968—. Capt. U.S. Army, 1966-68. Mem. AMA, AUA, Tex. Urological Assn., McLennan County Med. Soc. Home: 3303 Wood Lake Waco TX 76710 Office: 3115 Pine Ste 308 Waco TX 76708

LEE, EMMA MCCAIN, social worker; b. McCormick, S.C., July 8, 1948; d. John Walker and Emma Eliza (Nealous) McCain; m. Lannis Bernard Lee, Dec. 27, 1986; children: Nefertiti McCain, Jasmine Lee; stepchildren: LaTonia, LaStacia, Lannis Bernard Jr., Laterra. BS in Sociology, Paine Coll., 1970; MA in Sociology, Am. U., 1975; EdS, U. S.C., 1995. Cert. criminal justice specialist. Caseworker II Phila. County Bd. Assts. 1972-75; social worker II, human svcs. sr. provider Ga. Dept. Human Resources, Augusta, 1976—. Mem. AACD, Nat. Orgn. Forensic Counselors, Alpha Kappa Mu. Democrat. Office: Ga Dept Human Resources Ga Regional Hosp 3405 Old Savannah Rd Augusta GA 30906-3815

LEE, GARRETT, research administrator, physician, surgeon; b. San Francisco, June 23, 1946; s. Frederick B. and Josephine (Woo) L. BA in Genetics, U. Calif., Berkeley, 1968; MD, U. Calif., Davis, 1972. Diplomate Am. Bd. Laser Surgery. Fellow in cardiology U. Calif., Davis, 1976; dir. cardiac catherization lab. U. Calif.-Davis Med. Ctr., Sacramento 1977-83; dir. rsch. Western Heart Inst., San Francisco, 1984—, No. Calif Heart & Lung Inst., Concord, 1986-92; commr. Med. Bd. Calif., 1989—; chmn. Xintec Corp., Oakland, Calif., 1984-92, DioLase Corp., 1992—. Contbr. over 200 articles to profl. jours. Recipient Physician Recognition award Chinese Am. Physician Soc., 1984. Fellow Am. Coll. Cardiology, Am. Soc. Laser Medicine and Surgery, Am. Coll. Clin. Pharmacology, Am. Coll. Angiology; mem. Am. Heart Assn., Alpha Omega Alpha. Office: Western Heart Inst 450 Stanyan St San Francisco CA 94117-1079

LEE, GILBERT BROOKS, retired ophthalmology engineer; b. Cohasset, Mass., Sept. 10, 1913; s. John Alden and Charlotte Louise (Brooks) L.; m. Marion Corinne Rapp, Mar. 7, 1943 (div. Jan. 1969); children: Thomas Stearns, Jane Stanton, Frederick Cabot, Gilbert Eliot Frazar. BA, Reed Coll., 1937; MA, New Sch. for Social Rsch., 1949. Asst. psychologist U.S. Naval Submarine Base Civil Svc., Psychophysics of Vision, New London, Conn., 1950-53; rsch. assoc. Project Mich., Vision Rsch. Labs., Willow Run, 1954-57; rsch. assoc. dept. ophthalmology U. Mich., Ann Arbor, 1958-72, sr. rsch. assoc., 1972-75, sr. engring. rsch. assoc. ophthalmology, 1975-82, part-time sr. engr. ophthalmology, 1982—; sec. internat. dept., 23d St. YMCA, N.Y.C.; cons. W.K. Kellogg Eye Ctr., Ann Arbor, 1968—. Local organizer, moderator (TV program) Union of Concerned Scientists' Internat. Satellite Symposium on Nuclear Arms Issues, 1986; producer (TV show) Steps for Peace, 1987; designer, builder portable tristimulus Colorimeter; (videotape) Pomerance Awards, UN.; broken lake ice rescue procedure rsch., by one person in a dry suit, all weather conditions, 1966, 89-93 (videotape). Precinct del. Dem. County Conv., Washtenaw County, 1970, 74; treas. Dem. Club, Ann Arbor, Mich., 1971-72, 74-79; vice chmn. nuclear arms control com., 1979; chmn. Precinct Election Inspectors, 1968-75; scoutmaster Portland (Oreg.) area coun. Boy Scouts Am., 1932-39. Capt. AUS, 1942-46, 61-62. Mem. AAAS, Nat. Resources Def. Coun., Fedn. Am. Scientists, N.Y. Acad. Sci., Nation Assocs., ACLU, Sierra Club, Amnesty Internat. Home: 4131 E Pinchot Ave Phoenix AZ 85018-7115

LEE, GINGER, discharge planning supervisor, administrator; b. Cheverly, Md., June 24, 1954. BSN, U. Md., Balt., 1976; M in Health Care Adminstrn., Cen. Mich. U., Washington, 1981. RN, D.C.; cert. cmty. health nurse, cert. in nursing adminstrn., cert. in continuity of care. Head nurse, sr. clin. nurse Walter Reed Army Med. Ctr., Washington, 1988-90, supervisory community health nurse, 1990—, surg. intensive care clin. nurse, dental clin. nurse; neonatal ICU clin. nurse Frankfurt Army Med. Ctr., Fed. Republic Germany, 1984-88. Mem. ANA, U. Md. Alumni Assn., Sigma Theta Tau, Sigma Iota Epsilon.

LEE, GLEN K., dentist; b. Honolulu, Nov. 10, 1950; s. Kenneth Kam Chun Lee and Audrey (Mew Wun) Chun; m. Barbara Lynn Dunnett, Feb. 14, 1981; children: Jayna Christine, Jeffrey Ryan, David Michael. BS, Loyola U., L.A., 1972; DDS, Creighton U., 1976. Pvt. practice Santa Barbara, Calif., 1976—; mem. med. staff St. Francis Hosp., Santa Barbara, 1976—, Santa Barbara Cottage Hosp., 1976—, Goleta Valley Hosp., Goleta, Calif., 1976—. Mem. Santa Barbara Trust for Hist. Preservation; bd. dirs. Hope Sch. Dist. Ednl. Found. Mem. ADA, Am. Acad. Implant Dentistry, Am. Acad. Cosmetic Dentistry, Acoustic Neuroma Assn. Am., Calif. Dental Assn., Santa Barbara-Ventura County Dental Soc., Old Towne Mchts. Assn., Santa Barbara Hist. Soc. Democrat. Roman Catholic. Home: 3641 Tierra Bella Santa Barbara CA 93105-2555 Office: 1919 State St Ste 201 Santa Barbara CA 93101-2430

LEE, GREGORY PRICE, neuropsychology educator; b. Orange, N.J., July 3, 1952; s. John Landon and Olga (Squeo) Lee. BA in Psychology, U. No. Colo., 1975; MA in Clin. Psychology, Lone Mountain Coll., 1975; PhD in Clin. Psychology, Fla. Inst. Tech., 1980. Diplomate Am. Bd. Clin. Neuropsychology, Am. Bd. Profl. Psychology; lic. psychologist, Ga. Predoctoral intern Harlem Valley Psychiat. Ctr., White Plains, N.Y., 1977-78; instr. dept. psychology Coll. V.I., St. Thomas, 1981-82; rsch. assoc. Tex. Rsch. Inst. Mental Sci., Tex. Med. Ctr., Houston, 1983-84; postdoctoral fellow dept. psychology, sect. neuropsychology U. Houston, Baylor Coll. Medicine, 1983-84; postdoctoral fellow dept. neurology U. Wis. Med. Sch., Milw., 1984-86; dir. neuropsychology svc. sect. neurosurgery Dept. Psychiatry Med. Coll. Ga., Augusta, 1986—, mem. student ednl. enrichment program faculty, 1987-89, asst. prof. dept. surgery sect. neurosurgery, 1986-90, assoc. prof. dept. surgery sect. neurosurgery, 1990-95; assoc. prof. dept. psychiatry and health behavior Med. Coll. of Ga., Augusta, 1991-95; prof. depts. of surgery and psychiatry Med. Coll. Ga., Augusta, 1995—; reviewer work samples Am. Bd. Clin. Neuropsychology, 1989—; cons. editor Jour. of the Internat. Neuropsychol. Soc., 1994—. Co-author: Amobarbital Effects and Lateralized Brain Function: The Wada Test; contbr. numerous articles to profl. jours. and chpts. to books. Mem. med. adv. com. Alzheimer's Disease and Related Disorders Assn., 1986—; bd. dirs. Red Devil, Inc., 1985-92. Fellow Nat. Acad. Neuropsychology; mem. APA, Internat. Neuropsychol. Soc. (com. for dictionary neuropsychology 1987—, editor neuroanatomy and clin. neurology sect. dictionary neuropsychology), Am. Acad. Neurology, Am. Epilepsy Soc., Am. Coll. Legal Medicine, Soc. Biol. Psychiatry, Sigma Xi. Office: Med Coll Ga Dept Surgery Sect Neurosurgery Augusta GA 30912-4010

LEE, HI YOUNG, physician, acupuncturist; b. Seoul, Korea, Oct. 18, 1941; came to U.S., 1965, naturalized, 1976; s. Jung S. and Hwa J. (Kim) L.; m. Sun M. Lee, June 4, 1965; children: Sandra, Grace, David. M.D., Yon Sei U., Seoul, 1965. Diplomate Am. Bd. Family Practice. Intern Grasslands Hosp., Valhalla, N.Y., 1965-66; resident VA Hosp., Dayton, Ohio, 1966-70; mem. staff Eastern State Hosp., Medical Lake, Wash., 1970-74; practice family medicine, acupuncturist Empire Med. Office, Spokane, Wash., 1974—; active staff St. Lukes Meml. Hosp., Spokane, 1974—, bd. trustees St. Georges Prep Sch., Wash., 1986— ; courtesy staff Deaconess Med. Center, Spokane, 1974—, Sacred Heart Med. Ctr., Spokane, 1974—. Author: Von Recklinghousen's Disease, 1970 (McDermit award). Elder First Presbyterian Church, Spokane, 1975. Fellow Am. Acad. Family Practice; mem. ctr. for Chinese Medicine, Spokane County Med. Soc., Nat. Acupuncture Research Soc., Christian Med. Soc. Home: 2006 W Liberty Ave Spokane WA 99205-2570 Office: Empire Med Office 17 E Empire Ave Spokane WA 99207-1707

LEE, JAMES RICHARD, ophthalmologist, educator; b. San Diego, July 21, 1939; s. Elynor (Maguire) Lee; m. Lynda Karen Johnson; children: James Nicholas, Johanna Maguire. BA, Yale U., 1961; MD, McGill U., Montreal, Que., Can., 1965. Diplomate Am. Bd. Ophthalmology. Surg. intern N.Y. Hosp., N.Y.C., 1965-66, surg. resident, 1966-67; resident in ophthmology Mass. Eye and Ear Infirmary, Boston, 1970-73, corneal fellow, 1973-75; clin. instr. Harvard U. Med. Sch., Cambridge, 1975—; ophthalmologist Harvard U. Health Svcs., Cambridge, 1980-96. Author: Handbook of Contact Lenses, 1986. Med. officer USN, 1967-69; with Mass. N.G., 1980—, col., 1990—. Fellow ACS; mem. AMA, Mass. Med. Soc., New Eng. Ophthalmic Soc., Mass. Soc. Eye Physicians and Surgeons. Office: 27 Lincoln St Winthrop MA 02152

LEE, JAMES TRAVIS, JR., surgeon; b. Wichita Falls, Tex., Apr. 20, 1943; s. James Travis and Mary Ann (Walker) L. BA, U. Tex., 1964; MS, PhD, U. Ill., 1968; MD, U. Minn., 1975. Diplomate, Am. Bd. Surgery. Intern U. Minn., Mpls., 1975-76, resident, 1976-81; sr. rsch. scientist 3M Co., St. Paul, 1968-72; staff surgeon VA Med. Ctr., Mpls., 1981—; asst. prof. surgery U. Minn., Mpls., 1981-91, assoc. prof. surgery, 1991—; assoc. chief of surgery VA Med. Ctr., 1991—. Fellow ACS. Office: VA Med Ctr 1 Veterans Dr Minneapolis MN 55417-2300

LEE, JAN LOUISE, nursing educator; b. Grundy Center, Iowa, Oct. 30, 1953; d. Robert L. and B. Lucille (Frey) Thede; m. Henry M. Lee. BSN, U. Iowa, 1975; MN, UCLA, 1980; PhD, U. So. Calif., 1988. Patient care coord. Queen of the Valley Hosp., West Covina, Calif., 1977-78; rsch. clin. nurse specialist Wadsworth VA Med. Ctr., L.A., 1980-83; asst. prof. nursing U. So. Calif., L.A., 1983-88, UCLA, 1988-95; dir. undergrad. and non-traditional programs U. Mich. Sch. Nursing, Ann Arbor, 1995—; Mem. ANCC Commn. on cert. Contbr. articles to profl. jours. Grantee NIH, U. So. Calif., UCLA, others. Mem. Mich. Nurses Assn., Sigma Theta Tau (past chpt. pres.). Home: 1336 Waterways Dr Ann Arbor MI 48108 Office: U Mich Sch Nursing 400 N Ingalls Ann Arbor MI 48109-0482

LEE, JAN WAI-TSUN, cardiothoracic surgeon; b. Hong Kong, May 17, 1940; d. George Arthur and King Wan (Lo) L.; m. Frank Chi-Hung Lee, Aug. 11, 1979; 1 child, Daniel Dat-Ning. MBBS, U. Hong Kong, 1964. Intern Queen Mary Hosp., Hong Kong, 1964-65, resident, 1965-67; resident Hosp. Sick Children, Toronto, Ont., 1975-76; resident in cardiovascular surgery St. Michael's Hosp., Toronto, 1974-75; resident in cardiology Toronto Gen. Hosp., 1976; S.H.O. Hosp. Sick Children, London, 1967-68, Hammersmith Hosp., London, 1968-69; rsch. fellow Hosp. Sick Children, Toronto, Ont., Can., 1972-74; clin. asst. St. Michael's Hosp., Toronto, 1977-78; sr. med. officer Grantham Hosp., Hong Kong, 1978-83, cons., cardiothoracic surgeon, 1984—; hon. lectr. U. Hong Kong, 1979—, Granthan Hosp., Hong Kong, 1969-72. Fellow Royal Coll. Surgeons; mem. Hong Kong Cardiol. Soc., Hong Kong Med. Assn., Assn. Thoracic and Cardiovascular Surgeons of Asia., Coll. of Surgeons Hong Kong, Hong Kong Coll. Of Cardiology. Methodist. Office: Grantham Hosp, 125 Wong Chuk Hang Rd, Hong Kong Hong Kong

LEE, JEFFREY EDWIN, surgeon; b. Queens, N.Y., July 6, 1957; s. Edwin Joseph and Miriam Magdalene (Niedhammer) L.; m. Laura Norma Dietch, May 19, 1984 (div. Dec. 9, 1988); m. Joy Kay McFate, Apr. 6, 1991; children: Caitlin Elizabeth, Alicia Colleen. AB magna cum laude, Dartmouth Coll., 1979; MD, Stanford U., 1984. Lic. physician Tex., Hawaii, Calif.; diplomate Am. Bd. Surgery, Nat. Bd. Med. Examiners. Rsch. asst. dept. chemistry Dartmouth Coll., Hanover, N.H., 1978-80; rsch. asst. div. epidemiology dept. family, community and preventive medicine Stanford U., 1981-82; intern dept. surgery Stanford U. Med. Ctr., 1984-85, resident div. gen. surgery, 1985-91, postdoctoral rsch. fellow dept. surgery and pediatrics, 1987-89; clin. fellow gen. surg. oncology dept. gen. surgery U. Tex. M.D. Anderson Cancer Ctr., Houston, 1991-93, postdoctoral rsch. fellow depts. gen. surgery/immunology, 1992, asst. prof. dept. surgical oncology, 1993—; lectr. in field. Contbr. articles to profl. jours. Rufus Choate scholar, 1975-76; NIH Nat. Rsch. Svc. award, 1987-89. Mem. AMA, ACS, Am. Soc. Clin. Oncology, Soc. Surgery of Alimentary Tract, Am. Pancreatic Assn., Am. Assn. Endocrine Surgeons, Soc. Surg. Oncology, Assn. Acad. Surgery, Internat. Assn. Pancreatology, S.W. Surg. Congress, Tex. Med. Assn., Harris County Med. Soc., Houston Surg. Soc., Am. Heart Assn. (cert.), Am. Assn. Cancer Rsch., Am. Gastroenterol. Assn. Home: 3646 Glen Haven Blvd Houston TX 77025-1308 Office: U Tex M D Anderson Cancer Dept Surg Oncology 106 1515 Holcombe Blvd Houston TX 77030-4009

LEE, JEN-SHIH, biomedical engineering educator; b. Kwangtong, China, Aug. 22, 1940; parents Y. and Yao-Ze (Lai) L.; m. Lian-Pin Ma Lee, June 11, 1966; children: Lionel, Grace, Albert. BS, Nat. Taiwan U., 1961; MS, Calif. Inst. Tech., 1963, PhD, 1966. Advance rsch. fellow San Diego Heart Assn., U. Calif., San Diego, 1966-69; asst. prof. dept. Biomedical Engring. U. Va., Charlottesville, 1969-74, assoc. prof., 1974-83, prof., 1983—, chmn. dept. Biomedical Engring., 1988—. Editor: Microvascular Mechanics, 1988; assoc. editor Jour. Biomech. Engring., 1987-93; contbr. articles to Jour. Applied Physiology, Jour. Biomech. Engring., others. Recipient Rsch. Career Devel. award NIH, 1974-80. Fellow ASME, Am. Inst. Med. and Biol. Engring.; mem. IEEE, Am. Physiol. Soc., Microcirculatory Soc., Biomed. Engring. Soc. (bd. dirs. 1991-93, pres. 1994-95), Coun. of Socs. Am. Inst. Med. and Biol. Engring. (bd. dirs. 1995-97, chair 1995-97). Office: U Va Health Sci Ctr Dept Biomed Engring Box 337 Charlottesville VA 22908

LEE, JOHN EVERETT, physician; b. Charlotte, N.C., May 5, 1932; s. William States Lee and Sarah Everett; m. Iona Coker, July 29, 1961; children: Sarah Lee Elson, Jonathan Coker. AB, Princeton U., 1954; MD, Duke U., 1958. Diplomate Am. Bd. Psychiatry & Neurology, Am. Bd. Sleep Medicine. Chief resident neurology N.Y. Hosp., N.Y.C., 1963-64; mem. neurology faculty Med. Coll. Cornell U., N.Y.C., 1965-72; neurologist Atlanta Neurol. Clinic, 1972-92; sleep disorders practitioner Northside Hosp., Atlanta, 1992—; chief of staff Northside Hosp., 1984-86, bd. dirs. Office: Northside Hosp Sleep Disorders Ctr 1000 Johnson Ferry Rd Atlanta GA 30342

LEE, JOSEPH KING TAK, radiologist, medical educator; b. Shanghai, China, Mar. 17, 1947; came to U.S., 1968; s. S.Y. (Zee) Lee; m. Christina Y.M. Tsai, June 2, 1973; children: Alexander, Betsy, Catherine. BSc, Chinese U. of Hong Kong, 1968; MD, Washington U., St. Louis, 1973. Diplomate Am. Bd. Radiology. Intern Washington U. Sch. Medicine, St. Louis, 1973-74, resident, 1974-77, instr. radiology, 1977-78, asst. prof. radiology, 1978-82, assoc. prof. radiology, 1982-86, prof. radiology, 1986-91; prof. radiology, chair dept. radiology U. N.C., Chapel Hill, 1991—; editor Topics in MRI, 1988—. Author, editor: Computed Body Tomography, 1983, Computed Body Tomography with MRI Correlation, 1989, Pocket Atlas of Normal CT Anatomy, 1984, Manual of Clinical Magnetic Resonance Imaging, 1985. Fellow Am. Coll. Radiology; mem. Am. Roentgen Ray Soc., Soc. Uroradiology (bd. dirs. 1988-90), Soc. Computed Body Tomography/MR (pres. 1993-94), Soc. of Chairmen of Acad. Radiology, Radiology Soc. N.Am. Protestant. Office: Univ North Carolina CB 7510 Chapel Hill NC 27599

LEE, KEAT-JIN, otolaryngologist, medical educator; b. Malaysia, Sept. 7, 1940; s. Chengtin Lee and Chooisean Saw; m. Linda Lee, Aug. 20, 1966; children: Kenneth, Lloyd, Mark. BA, Harvard U., 1961; MD, Columbia U., 1965. Diplomate Am. Bd. Otolaryngology, Am. Bd. Laser Surgery. Intern in surgery St. Luke's Hosp. Ctr., N.Y.C., 1965-66; resident in surgery St. Luke's Hosp. Ctr., 1966-67; resident in ear, nose and throat Harvard-Mass. Eye and Ear Infirmary, Boston, 1967-70; tchg. fellow Harvard Med. Sch., Boston, 1969-70; clin. instr. U. Wash., 1970-72, Yale U., New Haven, Conn., 1972-76; asst. clin. prof. Yale U., 1976-91, assoc. clin. prof., 1991—; chief otolaryngology Hosp. of St. Raphael, 1986—; mng. ptnr. So. New Eng. Ear, Nose, Throat & Facial Plastic Surgery Grou, 1989—; founding mem. The Primary & Specialist Med. Ctr., LLC, 1993—; chmn. pub. edn. com. Hosp. of St. Raphael, 1976—, pres. med. staff, 1983, chmn. med. bd., 1983; vice chmn. Healthcare HMO, 1983-86; mem. faculty Medcom Ednl. Products; dir. Ear Rsch. and Ednl. Ctr.; presenter seminars in field. Author: The Otolaryngology Boards, 1973, Essentiial Otolaryngology, 6th edit., 1994, Differential Diagnosis in Otolaryngology, 1978, Metabolic Diseases in Otolaryngology, 1981, Textbook of Otolaryngology-Head and Neck Surgery, 1989; co-author: (with I. Goodrich) The Pituitary: Clinical Aspects of Normal and Abnormal Function, 1987, (with J. Willett) Otolaryngology-Head and Neck Surgery: Specialty Board Review, 1994; editor-in-chief: Comprehensive Surgical Atlases in Otolaryngology-Head and Neck Surgery, Vols. 1-5, 1983; co-editor: (with C.H. Stewart) Ambulatory Surgery and Office Procedures in Head and Neck Surgery, 1986; mem. editl. bd. Ear, Nose and Throat Jour.; contbr. over 40 articles to profl. jours.; participant numerous audio-visual productions in field; developer new air-drills for mastoid, acoustic neuroma and hypophysectomy surgery, voice prosthesis for post-laryngectomized patients. Life mem. Centurion Club of Deafness Rsch. Found., state co-chmn.; mem. credentials com. Am. Acad. Facial Plastic and Reconstructive Surgery, Inc., 1979-86; trustee Orange (Conn.) Congl. Ch., 1978-80. Recipient Presdl. citation for otolaryngology/head and neck surgery AAO-HNS, Washington, 1992. Fellow ACS, Am. Acad. Facial Plastic and Reconstructive Surgery (credentials com. 1979-86), Am. Acad. Otolaryngology-Head and Neck Surgery (faculty, sec.-treas. 1993-96, bd. dirs. 1988-91, sec.-treas. 1993—), Am. Soc. Head and Neck Surgery, Triological Soc. (honorable award for thesis); mem. Am. Acad. Otolaryngol. Allergy, New Eng. Otolaryngol. Soc., Conn. State Med. Soc., New Haven County Med. Soc., Harvard Club So. Conn. (life), Assn. Harvard Chemists. Office: So New Eng Ear Nose & Throat 98 York St New Haven CT 06511

LEE, KYO RAK, radiology educator; b. Seoul, Korea, Aug. 3, 1933; s. Ke Chang and Ok Hi (Um) L.; came to U.S., 1964, naturalized, 1976; MD, Seoul Nat. U., 1959; m. Ke Sook Oh, July 22, 1964; children: Andrew, John. Intern, Franklin Sq. Hosp., Balt., 1964-65; resident U. Mo. Med. Center, Columbia, Mo., 1965-68; instr. dept. radiology U. Mo., Columbia, 1968-69, asst. prof., 1969-71; asst. prof. dept. radiology U. Kans., Kansas City, 1971-76, assoc. prof., 1976-81, prof., 1981—. Served with Republic of Korea Army, 1950-52. Diplomate Am. Bd. Radiology (cert. added qualification in pediat. radiology). Recipient Richard H. Marshak award Am. Coll. Gastroenterology, 1975. Fellow Am. Coll. Radiology; mem. Radiol. Soc. N.Am., Am. Roentgen Ray Soc., Assn. Univ. Radiologists, Kans. Radiol. Soc., Greater Kansas City Radiol. Soc., Wyandotte County Med. Soc., Korean Radiol. Soc. N.Am., Soc., Soc. Pediat. Radiology. Contbr. articles to med. jours. Home: 9800 Glenwood St Shawnee Mission KS 66212-1536 Office: U Kans 39th St and Rainbow Blvd Kansas City KS 66103

LEE, LAWRENCE JAMES, social services administrator; b. Bklyn., Sept. 1, 1942; s. Lawrence and Helen Lee; m. Bernice Chu, June 8, 1979 (dec. Feb. 1991); 1 child, Gregory. BA in Psychology, W.Va. Wesleyan Coll., 1966; MA in Psychology, Hunter Coll., 1974, MSW, 1976. Cert. clin. social worker, N.Y. Chief social worker Union Health Ctr., Internat. Ladies' Garment Workers Union, N.Y.C., 1966-74; rehab. coord. N.Y. state div. Youth-Long Term Treatment Unit, Bronx, N.Y., 1977-78; team leader Lower East Side Family Union, N.Y.C., 1978-80; exec. dir. Chinatown Health Clinic, N.Y.C., 1980; adminstr., supr. Lower Eastside Svc. Ctr., N.Y.C., 1981-85; assoc. dir. agy. rels. United Way N.Y.C., 1985-88; dir. ffamily svcs. div. Victim Svcs. Agy., N.Y.C., 1988—; adv. bd. Gov. Hosp., N.Y.C., 1982-87. Bd. dirs. Chinatown Voter Edn. Alliance, N.Y.C., 1983—, City Vol. Corps, 1987—; pres., bd. dirs. Asian Ams. for Better N.Y., N.Y.C., 1989—; founder Chinese Community Social Svc. Health Coun., N.Y.C., 1979-85. Mem. NASW (N.Y.C. chpt., bd. dirs. 1980-87), Acad. Cert. Social Workers, Social Workers' Coop. (bd. dirs. 1987—). Home: 473 Fdr Dr Apt K1506 New York NY 10002-2024 Office: Victim Svcs Agy 2 Lafayette St New York NY 10007-1307

LEE, LILLIAN VANESSA, microbiologist; b. N.Y.C., June 1, 1951; d. Wenceslao and Ada (Otero) Cancel; B.S. in Biology, St. Johns U., 1972; M.S. in Microbiology, Wagner Coll., 1974; m. Thomas Christopher Lee, June 11, 1972; children—Tovan, John-Peter, Phillip-Michael. Grad. lab. asst. in microbiology Wagner Coll., S.I., N.Y., 1972-74; clin. microbiology technologist Queens Hosp. Center, Jamaica, N.Y., 1974-81, clin. microbiology supr., 1981-84; sect. head microbiology Nyack (N.Y.) Hosp., 1984-93, acting lab. mgr., 1992-93; microbiology mgr. Beth Israel Med. Ctr., N.Y., 1994—. Cert. registered microbiologist and specialist in microbiology, clin. lab. specialist. Mem. Am. Soc. Clin. Pathologists, Am. Soc. Microbiology (N.Y.C. br. coun. mem. 1992—, program com. chair 1993—, N.Y.C. br. nat. coun. 1996), Am. Acad. Microbiology, Med. Mycology Soc., N.Y., N.Y. Acad. Scis., N.Y.C. Soc. Infectious Diseases, Clin. Lab. Mgmt. Assn. (program com. 1996—). Home: 14 Continental Dr West Nyack NY 10994-2803 Office: Beth Israel Med Ctr 1st Ave at 16th St New York NY 10003

LEE, MARGARET ANNE, social worker, psychotherapist; b. Scribner, Nebr., Nov. 23, 1930; d. William Christian and Caroline Bertha (Benner) Joens; m. Robert Kelly Lee, May 21, 1950 (div. 1972); children: Lawrence Robert, James Kelly, Daniel Richard. AA, Napa Coll., 1949; student, U. Calif., Berkeley, 1949-50; BA, Calif. State Coll., Sonoma, 1975; MSW, Calif. State U., Sacramento, 1977. Diplomate clin. social worker; lic. clin. social worker, Calif.; lic. marriage and family counselor, Calif.; tchr. Columnist, stringer Napa (Calif.) Register, 1946-50; eligibility worker, supr. Napa County Dept. Social Services, 1968-75; instr. Napa Valley Community Coll., 1978-83; practice psychotherapy Napa, 1977—; oral commr. Calif. Dept. Consumer Affairs, Bd. Behavioral Sci., 1984—; bd. dirs. Project Access, 1978-79. Trustee Napa Valley C.C., 1983—, v.p. bd., 1984-85, pres. bd., 1986, 90, 95, clk., 1988-89; bd. dirs. Napa County Coun. Econ. Opportunity, 1984-85, Napa chpt. March of Dimes, 1957-71, Mental Health Assn. Napa County, 1983-87; vice chmn. edn. com. Calif. C.C. Trustees, 1987-88, chmn. edn. com., 1988-89, legis. com., 1985-87, bd. dirs., 1989—, 2d v.p., 1991, 1st v.p., 1992, pres., 1993; mem. student equity rev. group Calif. C.C. Chancellors, 1992; bd. dirs. C.C. League Calif., 1992-95, 1st v.p., 1992. Recipient Fresh Start award Self mag., award Congl. Caucus on Women's Issues, 1984. Mem. NASW, Mental Health Assn. Napa County, Calif. Assn. Physically and Handicapped, Women's Polit. Caucus, Calif. Elected Women's Assn. Edn. and Rsch., Am. Assn. Women in Community and Jr. Colls. Democrat. Lutheran. Office: 1100 Trancas St Napa CA 94558-2908

LEE, MATHEW HUNG MUN, physiatrist; b. Hawaii, July 28, 1931; married; 3 children. AB, Johns Hopkins U, 1953; MD, U. Md., 1956; MPH, U. Calif., 1962. Diplomate Am. Bd. Physical Medicine & Rehab. Resident Inst. Physical Medicine & Rehab., NYU, 1962-64, assignee rehab. svc.N.Y. State Health Dept., 1964-65, from asst. prof. to assoc. prof. rehab. medicine, 1965-73, dir. edn. & training dept. rehab. medicine, 1966-68, assoc. dir., 1968, prof. rehab medicine, 1973—; dir. dept. rehab. medicine Goldwater Meml. Hosp., 1968—; assoc. vis. physician Goldwater Meml. Hosp., 1965-68, vis. physician, 1968—, chief electrodiagnosis unit, 1966—, v.p. med. bd., 1969-70, pres., 1971' asst. clin. prof. Coll. Dentistry NYU, 1966-69, clin. asst. prof., 1969-70, clin. assoc. prof., 1970—; cons. Daughters of Israel Hosp., N.Y., 1965-72, Bur. Adult Hygiene, 1965—, Human Resources Ctr., 1966—; asst. attending physician Hosp. NYU, 1968—; med. dir. dept. rehab. medicine N.Y.U., 1989; attending physician Bellevue Hosp. Ctr., 1971—; cons. World Rehab. Fund, Gordon Seagrave & Maryknoll Hosps., Korea, 1969, U.S. Dept. Interior. Fellow Am. Acad. Physical Medicine & Rehab., Am. Coll. Physicians, Am. Pub. Health Assn.; mem. AAAS, Pan-Am. Med. Assn. Office: Jerry Lewis Neuromuscular Dis Ctr Dept Rehab Medicine 400 E 34th St New York NY 10016-4901

LEE, MICHAEL RADCLIFFE, emeritus clinical pharmacology educator; b. Manchester, Eng., Nov. 21, 1934; s. Harry and Jean Adelaide (Radcliffe) L.; m. Judith Ann Horrocks, Aug. 27, 1960; children: Stephen Michael, Karen Elizabeth. BA, Oxford (Eng.) U., 1956, MA, 1961, DPhil, 1966, DM, 1970. Lectr. Oxford U., 1961-69, St. Thomas Hosp., U.K., 1969-71; mng. dir. Weddel Pharms., U.K., 1971-73; sr. lectr. Leeds (Eng.) U., 1973-84; prof. U. Edinburgh (Scotland), 1984-95; cons. pharm. industry, U.K., 1984-95. Author: Renin and Hypertension, 1969, Clinical Toxicology, 1982; contbr. articles to profl. jours. Fellow Royal Coll. Physicians (London), Royal Coll. Physicians (Edinburgh), Royal Soc. (Edinburgh); mem. Brit. Pharmacol. Soc., Internat. Soc. for Hypertension, Assn. Physicians Gt. Britain and Ireland.

LEE, MIN SHIU, polymer engineer, material scientist; b. Taipei, Taiwan, June 30, 1940; s. Thoan Chip and Ping Hsuey (Chen) L.; m. Amy Yen-Mei Su, Apr. 16, 1966; children: Terri Sue, David Marshall. BS, Nat. Taiwan U., 1962; MS, N.Mex. Highland U., 1966; PhD, Case Western Res. U., 1969. Sr. rsch. chemist FMC Corp., Princeton, N.J., 1969-72; sr. rsch. scientist Avicon Corp., Princeton, 1972-76; sr. rsch.scientist Jelco Lab., Johnson & Johnson Co., Raritan, N.J., 1976-79, mgr. material rsch. and sci. svcs., 1979-80, mgr. material and process devel., rsch. and devel. Critikon, Inc. div. Johnson & Johnson, Tampa, Fla., 1980-83, staff cons., 1983-86; sr. scientist Becton Dickinson & Co., 1986-91, mgr. biomaterials Application, 1991—. Contbr. to profl. jours. Chmn. Taiwan Christian Fellowship of Central Jersey, 1972-74; treas. Univ. Chinese Sch. of Princeton, 1977-78; pres. Chinese Christian Ch. in Bay Areas, Fla., 1982-86. Served to 2d lt. Chinese Army, 1962-64. Recipient award Nat. Def. Ministry, 1963; Inst. Sci. Research fellow, 1964-66; chemistry fellow Case Western Res. U., 1966-67. Mem. AAAS, Am. Chem. Soc. (chmn. Dayton sect., investment com. 1989—), N.Y. Acad. Scis., Am. Assn. for Med. Instrumentation and Biomaterials (Johnson & Johnson polymer subcom.), Sigma Xi.

LEE, MOO HEE, pediatrician, pediatric cardiologist; b. Pusan, Korea, Mar. 8, 1942; came to U.S., 1966; s. Sang Mook and Sang Kyung (Oh) L.; m. Jung Won Han, Aug. 8, 1970; children—Michael Jaiwhan, Michelle Nayung, Monica Unjin. B.S., Yonsei U., Seoul, Korea, 1962, M.D., 1966. Intern, Salem Hosp. (Mass.), 1966-67; resident in pediatrics, U. Man., Winnipeg, Can., 1967-69; fellow in pediatric cardiology Case Western Res. U., Cleve., 1969-71; research fellow in cardiovascular physiology Mt. Sinai Hosp., 1971-72; asst. prof. pediatrics and pediatric cardiology, Med. Coll. Ga., Augusta, 1973-75; pediatric cardiologist and pediatrician, Atlanta Heart and Lung Clinic, P.C., Crippled Children's Cardiac Clinic, Atlanta, South Atlanta Pediatrics, P.A., Riverdale, Ga., 1975—. Contbr. articles to profl. jours. including Am. Jour. Cardiology, Circulation, Circulation Research, Am. Jour. Physiology, Jour. of Pediatrics, Pediatrics, Jour. of Electrophysiology. Am. Heart Assn. cardiovascular research fellow, 1972. Fellow Am. Coll. Cardiology; mem. AMA, Med. Assn. Ga., Am. Acad. Pediatrics (Ga. chpt.), Am. Heart Assn. Republican. Methodist. Club: Lions. Home: 105 Broadmoor Dr Fayetteville GA 30214-2715 Office: South Atlanta Pediatrics PA 251 Medical Way Riverdale GA 30274-2522

LEE, MYLES EDWIN, cardiothoracic surgeon; b. Boston, May 3, 1939; s. Charles and Erma (Butman) L.; m. Elizabeth Jachu Lu, Jan. 16, 1988; children: Allison Elizabeth, Evan Preston. BS cum laude, Harvard Univ., 1961; MD, Tufts Medical Sch., 1965. Diplomate Am. Bd. Surgery, Am. Bd. Thoracic Surgery. Cardiothoracic surgeon Cedars-Sinai Medical Ctr., L.A., 1976-87; dir. cardiothoracic surgery Centinela Hosp. Medical Ctr., Inglewood, Calif., 1987—; chmn. dept. surgery Centinela Hosp. Medical Ctr., 1996. Author: Near Misses in Cardiac Surgery, 1992; contbr. articles to profl. jours. Benefactor L.A. County Music Ctr., 1992—; bd. dirs. Snakespeare Globe Ctr., L.A., 1992-95, Am. Heart Assn., 1992. Maj. M.C., U.S. Army, 1971-73. Mem. Am. Assn. Thoracic Surgery, Soc. Thoracic Surgeons, Am. Assn. for Artifical Internal Organs, Am. Coll. Surgeons, Am. Coll. Cardiology, Am. Coll. Chest Physicians. Home: 938 Bel Air Rd Los Angeles CA 90077-2611 Office: Centinela Hosp Medical Ctr 555 E Hardy St 4th Fl E Inglewood CA 90301

LEE, PAUL P., physician, lawyer, consultant; b. Taipei, Taiwan, Sept. 8, 1960; s. Pei-Fei and Julia Lee. BA, U. Mich., 1981, MD, 1986; JD, Columbia U., 1986. Bar: Md. 1987, D.C. 1988. Congl. intern U.S. House Select Commn. on Aging, Washington, 1980; biologist NASA, Cape Canaveral, Fla., 1981; med. intern Beth Israel Hosp., Boston, 1986-87; resident in ophthalmology Johns Hopkins Hosp., Balt., 1987-90; fellow glaucoma Mass. Eye & Ear Infirmary, Boston, 1990-91; asst. prof. U. So. Calif., L.A., 1991-95, assoc. prof., 1995—; cons. health scis. program Rand Corp., Santa Monica, Calif. Contbr. articles to profl. jours. Treas. Blind Children's Ctr. Rsch. fellowship Brookdale Inst. on Aging, 1985, Stone scholar Columbia U. Law Sch., 1985. Mem. AMA, ABA, APHA, Assn. Health Svcs. Rsch., Chinese-Am. Ophthalmology Soc. (treas.), Assn. for Rsch. in Vision and Ophthalmology. Office: Doheny Eye Inst 1450 San Pablo St Los Angeles CA 90033-4615

LEE, PEGGY BOATMAN, nursing educator, community health consultant; b. Greenwood, Miss., Oct. 20, 1950; d. Everette Durrell and Mary Elizabeth (Thompson) Boatman; m. Charles Branch Lee; children: Lindsey Allison, Bradley Everette. ADN, Miss. Delta Jr. Coll., Moorhead, 1974; BSN, Miss. Coll., Clinton, 1987; MS, U. So. Miss., Hattiesburg, 1990. RN, Miss., Ark.; cert. cmty. nurse cons. Asst. charge nurse Bolivar County Hosp., Cleveland, Miss., 1974-77; practical nursing instr. Miss. Delta Jr. Coll., 1977-85; clinic nurse Bolivar County Health Dept., Cleveland, 1987-89; staff nurse, relief charge nurse Bolivar County Hosp., 1987-89; cmty. health nurse Miss. Regional Home Health, Cleveland, 1989-92; instr. nursing Delta State U., Cleveland, 1989-92; asst. prof. nursing Ark. Tech. U., Russellville, 1992—; cmty. health specialist St. Mary's Home Health, Russellville, 1993—; cons. indsl. nursing Ore-Ida Foods, Clarksville, Ark., 1993—. Bd. dirs. Am. Heart Assn., Russellville, 1994; vol. Am. Cancer Soc., Cleveland and Russellville; mem. Dames Club, Russellville, 1992—. Mem. ANA, Ark. Nurses Assn., Ark. for Nurses. Methodist. Home: 1416 Lands End North Russellville AR 72801 Office: Ark Tech U Dept Nursing Russellville AR 72801

LEE, PHILIP RANDOLPH, medical educator; b. San Francisco, Apr. 17, 1924; married, 1953; 4 children. AB, Stanford U., 1945, MD, 1948; MS, U. Minn., 1956; DSc (hon.), MacMurray Coll., 1967. Diplomate Am. Bd. Internal Medicine. Asst. prof. clin. phys. medicine & rehab. NYU, 1955-56; clin. instr. medicine Stanford (Calif.) U., 1956-59, asst. clin. prof., 1959-67; asst. sec. health & sci. affairs U. Calif., San Francisco, 1967-69, chancellor, 1969-72, prof. social medicine, 1969—, dir. inst. health policy studies, 1972-93; asst. sec. U.S. Dept. of Health & Human Services, Washington, D.C., 1993—; mem. dept. internal medicine Palo Alto Med. Clinic, Calif., 1956-65; cons. bur. pub. health svc. USPHS, 1958-63, adv. com., 1978, nat. commn. smoking & pub. policy, 1977-78; dir. health svc. office tech. cooperation & rsch. AID, 1963-65; dep. asst. sec. health & sci. affairs HEW, 1965, asst. sec., 65-69, mem. nat. coun. health planning & devel., 1978-80; co-dir. inst. health & aging, sch. nursing U. Calif., San Francisco, 1980—; pres. bd. dirs. World Inst. Disability, 1984—; mem. population com. Nat. Rsch. Coun.- Nat. Acad. Sci., 1983-86; mem. adv. bd. Scripps Clinic & Rsch. Found., 1980—. Author over 10 books; contbr. articles to profl. jours. Recipient Hugo Schaefer medal Am. Pharm. Assn., 1976. Mem. AAAS, AMA, ACP, Am. Pub. Health Assn., Am. Fedn. Clin. Rsch., Am. Geriatric Soc., Assn. Am. Med. Colls., Inst. Medicine-Nat. Acad. Sci. Office: Dept of Health & Human Servs Public Health Service 200 Independence Ave SW Washington DC 20201-0004*

LEE, PHILLIP DUKEAL KWAIYUEN, pediatric endocrinologist, researcher; b. Honolulu, May 29, 1956; s. Dukeal and Evelyn (Pang) L. BS in Medicine, Northwestern U., 1978, MD, 1980. Diplomate Am. Bd. Pediatrics. Intern U. Tex. Med. Br., Galveston, 1980-81; resident in pediatrics Children's Meml. Hosp., Northwestern U., Chgo., 1981-83; postdoctoral fellow Stanford (Calif.) U., 1983-86; pediatric endocrinologist The Children's Hosp., Denver, 1986-89; mem. staff Barbara Davis Ctr. for Childhood Diabetes, Denver, 1986-89; asst. prof. pediatrics Baylor Coll. Medicine, Houston, 1989—; acting chief diabetes care ctr. Tex. Children's Hosp., Houston, 1990-93; dir. rsch. and sci. affairs Diagnostic Systems Labs., Webster, Tex., 1993—; asst. prof. pediatrics U. Colo. Health Scis. Ctr., 1986-89. Juvenile Diabetes Found. fellow, 1985-86. Mem. Endocrine Soc., Am. Diabetes Assn., Am. Fedn. Clin. Rsch., Soc. In Vitro Biology, Lawson-Wilkins Pediat. Endocrine Soc. Home: 224 Emerson St Houston TX 77006-4567 Office: Diagnostic Systems Labs Inc 445 Medical Center Blvd Webster TX 77598-4217 also: Tex Childrens Hosp Diabetes Care Ctr 6621 Fannin St # 32351 Houston TX 77030-2303

LEE, QWIHEE PARK, plant physiologist; b. Republic of Korea, Mar. 1, 1941; came to U.S., 1965; d. Yong-sik and Soon-duk (Paik) Park; m. Ick-whan Lee, May 20, 1965; children: Tina, Amy, Benjamin. MS, Seoul Nat. U., Republic of Korea, 1965; PhD, U. Minn., 1973. Head dept. plant physiology Korea Ginseng and Tobacco Inst., Seoul, 1980-82; instr. Sogang U., Seoul, 1981, Seoul Women's U., 1981; research assoc. U. Wash., Seattle, 1975-79. Exec. dir. Korean Community Counseling Ctr., Seattle, 1983-86. Named one of 20 Prominent Asian Women in Wash. State, Chinese Post Seattle, 1986. Mem. AAAS. Buddhist. Home: 13025 42nd Ave NE Seattle WA 98125-4624 Office: U Wash Dept Pharm SJ-30 1959 NE Pacific St Seattle WA 98195-0004

LEE, R. DARRELL, hospital administrator, management consultant; b. St. Petersburg, Fla., May 14, 1968; s. J. Randolph and Patricia Ann (Klutts) L. BS in Stats., Fla. State U., 1990, MS in Stats., 1992. Statis. cons. Fla. State U., Tallahassee, 1990-93; project analyst/measurement Tallahassee Meml. Regional Med. Ctr., 1992-93; quality program facilitator All Children's Hosp., St. Petersburg, 1993—; mgmt. cons. St. Petersburg, 1993—; cons. doctoral candidates/pvt. cos.; bd. dirs. State Dept. Labor and Employment Security, Human Resources Divsn., Tallahassee, 1992-93. Performer Body Tune-Up, All Children's Hosp., 1995-96; founding mem. Tallahassee Quality Coun., 1991. Mem. Am. Assn. Therapeutic Humor, Am. Soc. Quality Control, Nat. Assn. Healthcare Quality, Fla. Assn. Healthcare Quality (area II), Am. Statis. Assn. Office: All Childrens Hospital Box 949 801 6th St S Saint Petersburg FL 33701

LEE, RICHARD SCOTT, neurologist; b. Bklyn., Sept. 10, 1949. BS in Chemistry, U. Wis., 1970; MD, SUNY, Buffalo, 1974. Diplomate Am. Bd. Neurology, Am. Acad. Pain Mgmt. Clin. neurologist Martin Meml. Hosp., Stuart, Fla., 1981-90; neurologist Physicians Plus HMO, Madison, Wis., 1991; cons. neurologist Reno (Nev.) Neurol. Assocs., 1992-93; dir. neuroscis. Sierra Summit Rehab., Reno, Nev., 1983-94, No. Nev. Med. Ctr., Reno, 1994—; med. dir. No. Nev. Sleep Disorders Ctr., Sparks, 1995—; cons. neurologist Washoe Med. Ctr., Reno, 1992—, St. Mary's Regional Med. Ctr., 1992—. Contbr. articles to profl. jours. Fellow Am. Acad. Neurology, Royal Soc. Medicine; mem. Am. Acad. Pain Mgmt., Am. Assn. for Study of Headache, Internat. Headache Soc., Am. Sleep Disorders Assn. Office: No Nev Med Ctr 2385 E Prater Way #308 Sparks NV 89434

LEE, RICHARD VAILLE, physician, educator; b. Islip, N.Y., May 26, 1937; s. Louis Emerson and Erma Natalie (Little) L.; m. Susan Bradley, June 25, 1961; children: Matthew, Benjamin. BS, Yale U., 1960, MD cum laude, 1964. Diplomate Am. Bd. Internal Medicine, Am. Bd. Family Practice. Intern Grace-New Haven Hosp., 1964-65, asst. resident in internal medicine, 1965-66, 69-70; fellow in inflammatory disease Yale U., New Haven, 1970-71; practice medicine specializing in internal medicine New Haven, 1969-76, Buffalo, 1976—; family practice Poplar, Mont., 1966-68, Chester, Mont., 1968-69; asst. prof. medicine Yale U., 1971-74, assoc. prof. clin. medicine, 1974-76; prof. medicine SUNY, Buffalo, 1976—, prof. pediatrics, 1985—, adj. prof. anthropology, 1989—, prof. obstetrics, 1992—, chief div. gen. internal medicine, 1979-82, chief div. maternal and adolescent medicine, 1982—, chief div. geog. medicine, 1991—; dir. primary care ctr. Yale-New Haven Hosp., 1975-76, dir. med. clinics, 1971-75; chief med. svc. Buffalo VA Hosp., 1976-79; head dept. medicine Children's Hosp. Buffalo, 1979-96; chief med. officer WHO Collaborating Ctr. for Health in Housing, 1995—; fellow WHO Collaborating Ctr. for Health and Housing, 1985—; cons. internal medicine N.Y. Zool. Soc., 1973—; cons. physician Buffalo Zool. Soc., 1980—; aviation med. examiner, 1980—; med. dir. Ecology and Environment, Inc., Lancaster, N.Y. Sr. editor Current Obstetric Medicine, 1989—; corr. editor Jour. Obstetrics and Gynecology, London, 1989—; mem. editl. bd. Internat. Jour. Environ. Health, 1994—; cons. editor Am. Jour. Medicine, 1976-86; contbr. articles on gen. medicine, infectious diseases, and med. anthropology to med. jours., also articles on med. problems during pregnancy; contbr. chpts. to books on obstetrics. Served with USPHS, 1966-68. Fellow ACP, Am. Acad. Family Practice, Explorers Club N.Y.C., Royal Geog. Soc., Royal Soc. Medicine; mem. AMA, Am. Soc. History of Medicine, Yale China Assn. (trustee 1992—, sec. 1995—), N.Y. Acad. Sci., Am. Fedn. Clin. Rsch. Soc., Gen. Internal Medicine, Am. Soc. Tropical Medicine and Hygiene, Infectious Diseases Soc. Am., Soc. Obstetric Medicine (pres. 1991-93), Am. Coll. Occupl. and Environ. Medicine, Great Lakes Interurban Clin. Club, Alpha Omega Alpa. Home: 7664 E Quaker St Orchard Park NY 14127-2015 Office: 219 Bryant St Buffalo NY 14222-2006

LEE, ROBERT EARL, retired physician; b. North Sydney, N.S., Can., Sept. 26, 1928; came to U.S. 1928, naturalized, 1942; s. Matthew and Amy Roberts (Moulton) L.; m. Sally Gosling, June 23, 1953 (annuled 1967); children: Diane, Cynthia, Susan, Robert; m. Elaine Katherine Chapleau, Dec. 15, 1967. AB, Colgate U., 1948; MD, Cornell U., 1952. Diplomate Am. Bd. Internal Medicine. Intern N.Y. Hosp., Cornell Med. Ctr., N.Y.C., 1952-53, resident, 1955-56, asst. clin. prof. internal medicine Med. Coll.; fellow Manhattan VA Hosp., N.Y.C., 1956-57; cons. internal medicine N.Y. Hosp., Cornell Westchester Div., 1958, dir. med. services, 1967-80, attending physician Burke Rehab., White Plains, 1957-71, cons., 1971-93; attending physician White Plains Hosp., N.Y., 1957-93, St. Agnes Hosp., White Plains, 1971-93; ret., 1993; cons. in medicine Dobbs Ferry Hosp., N.Y., 1968-90; pres. White Plains Hosp. Med. Staff, 1975-76; mem. Westchester County Bd. Mgrs., Div. Lab. and Research, 1970, chmn. 1984—. Bd. dirs. Westchester Council Social Agencies, 1972-77; sr. warden Ch. of St. James the Less, Scarsdale, N.Y., 1988; vol. vol. advisor Scarsdale Ambulance Corps., 1977—; v.p. Greenburgh Nature Ctr., Scarsdale, 1982-84. Served to 1st lt. U.S. Army, 1953-55. Named to Am. Soc. Most Venerable Order of St. John of Jerusalem, 1984 (comdr.). Mem. Westchester County Med. Soc., N.Y. State Med. Soc., ACP, Westchester County Med. Soc. (bd. dirs. 1970-72). Republican. Episcopalian. Clubs: Fox Meadow Tennis (Scarsdale) (pres. 1980-81); Union League. Home: 9 Old Windy Bush Rd New Hope PA 18938-1133

LEE, ROLAND ROBERT, radiologist, educator; b. Cleve., July 18, 1954; s. Chia Huan and Ellen Lee. BS in Physics, Calif. Inst. Tech., 1975; MA in Physics, U. Calif., Berkeley, 1977; MD, UCLA, 1985. Diplomate Am. Bd. Radiology (added qualifications in neuroradiology). Physicist Lawrence Livermore Nat. Lab., Livermore, Calif., 1975-77; intern Harbor-UCLA Med. Ctr., Torrance, Calif., 1985-86; resident in radiology Brigham & Women's Hosp.-Harvard U., Boston, 1986-90; fellow MRI Meml. Magnetic Resonance Ctr., Long Beach, Calif., 1990-91; fellow neuroradiology U. Calif., San Francisco, 1991-92; asst. prof. radiology Johns Hopkins Hosp., Balt., 1992—; cons. radiology and neuroradiology, Balt., 1992—. Author, editor: Spinal Imaging, 1995; contbr. book chpts.: Magnetic Resonance Imaging, 1992, The Adult Spine: Principles and Practice, 1996; contbr. articles to sci. jours. Mem. AMA, Am. Soc. Neuroradiology (sr.), Am. Coll. Radiology, Radiolog. Soc. N.Am. Home: 207 Witherspoon Rd Baltimore MD 21212 Office: Johns Hopkins Hosp Dept Radiology 600 N Wolfe St Baltimore MD 21287

LEE, SHUNG-MAN, nephrologist; b. Canton, Peoples Republic of China, Feb. 22, 1949; came to the U.S., 1968; s. Ning-Woo and Shui-Fong Lee; m. Ellen Poon, Aug., 1976; 1 child, Andrew. BS, U. Toronto, 1972, MD, 1976. Diplomate Am. Bd. Nephrology, Am. Bd. Internal Medicine, Nat. Bd. Med. Examiners. Intern Sunnybrook Med. Ctr. U. Toronto, 1976-77, resident, 1977-78; resident Jewish Gen. Hosp. McGill U., Montreal, 1978-79; clin. fellow in nephrology Billings Hosp. U. Chgo., 1979-81, rsch. fellow, 1981-82; pres., med. dir. Biotronics Kidney Ctr., Beaumont, Tex., 1990—; cons. nephrologist, mem. med. staff St. Elizabeth Hosp., Beaumont, Bapt. Hosp. S.E. Tex., Beaumont, Beaumont Med. Surg. Hosp., 1982-90; med. dir. Cmty. Dialysis Svcs., Beaumont, 1986-90; cons. nephrologist, mem. courtesy staff Dr.'s Hosp., Groves, Tex., Bapt. Hosp., Orange, Tex., Park Place Hosp., Port Arthur, Tex.; clin. asst. prof. U. Tex. Med. Br. at Galveston, 1991—; founder, owner Biotronics Kidney Ctr. Beaumont, Inc.; founder, Lake Charles (La.) Dialysis Ctr. Contbr. articles to profl. jours. Organizer, founding mem. Adult Indigent Clinic for S.E. Tex., Beaumont, 1992—. Rsch. fellow Chgo. Heart Assn., 1981; rsch. scholar Ontario Cancer Soc., 1974, Ann Shepard Meml. scholar in biology, 1970. Fellow ACP; mem.

AMA, Internat. Soc. Nephrology, Internat. Soc. Peritoneal Dialysis, Am. Soc. Nephrology, Jefferson County Med. Soc., So. Med. Assn., Am. Soc. Internal Medicine, Tex. Med. Assn., Chinese-Am. Soc. Nephrology (pres.), New Century Health Care Internat. (pres.). Office: Biotronics Kidney Ctr 2688 Calder St Beaumont TX 77702-1917

LEE, SIN HANG, pathologist; b. Hong Kong, Nov. 17, 1932; came to U.S., 1963, naturalized, 1976; s. Yat Sun and Siu Tsing (Wong) L.; M.D., Wuhan Med. Coll., China, 1956; m. Kee Hung Hau, Dec. 31, 1958; children—Emil, Karen. Intern, South Balt. Gen. Hosp., 1963-64; resident N.Y. Hosp., 1964-66; bacteriologist Sichuan Med. Coll., Chengdu, China, 1956-61; demonstrator in pathology U. Hong Kong, 1961-63; instr. pathology Cornell-N.Y. Hosp., 1966-67; fellow in pathology Meml. Hosp. for Cancer, N.Y.C., 1967-68; asst. prof. McGill U., Montreal, 1968-71; asso. prof. Yale U., 1971-73, asso. clin. prof., 1973—; guest prof. Wuhan Med. Coll. (China), 1984—; attending pathologist Hosp. St. Raphael, New Haven, Conn., 1973—. Diplomate Am. Bd. Pathology. Mem. Royal Coll. Physicians and Surgeons Can., AAAS, Internat. Acad. Pathology, Am. Assn. Pathologists, Pathol. Soc. Great Britain and Ireland, N.Y. Acad. Scis. Contbr. articles in field to profl. jours.; patentee in field. Office: 1450 Chapel St New Haven CT 06511

LEE, STEPHEN SHENG-HAO, dentist; b. Tao-Yuan Hsien, Taiwan, Dec. 14, 1945; came to U.S., 1972; s. Mao-chi Lee and San-Mei Fan; m. Fei-Jen Lo, Oct. 17, 1973; children: Christopher Stephen, Jennifer Stephanie. BS, Nat. Taiwan U., 1969, MS, 1972; PhD, U. Ill., 1976; DDS, Loyola U., Chgo., 1980. Dentist Stephen Lee Dental Clinic, Berwyn, Ill., 1981—; with curriculum com. dental asst. program Morton Coll., 1988. Author Research Publs., 1972. Bd. mem. Taiwan Benevolent Assn. Chgo., 1983. Mem. ADA, Ill. State Denal Soc., Chgo. Dental Soc. Republican. Office: 3239 Grove Ave Berwyn IL 60402-3468 also: 6550 S Cass Ave Westmont IL 60559-3211

LEE, SUSAN, dentist, microbiologist; b. Jellico, Tenn., June 2, 1943; d. Roy Pickerell and Florida Maybell (Weaver) Savage; m. Joseph James Lee, Dec. 30, 1969 (dec. Dec. 1980); 1 child, Susan. BS, Cumberland Coll., 1965; DMD, U. Louisville, 1976. Lic. real estate agt., Ky. Asst. head dept. microbiology Norton Children's Hosp. (formerly Norton Meml. Infirmary, Louisville, 1964-69; head dept. microbiology St. Anthony's Hosp., Louisville, 1969-72; mgr. office, cons. Drs. Med. Plaza, Louisville, 1976-82; dentist Office Richard S. Bonn, DMD, Louisville, 1982-86; hygienist, dentist, cons. Office James Lewis, DMD, Louisville, 1986—; cons. in field, 1982—. Named Hon. Order Ky. Cols. Mem. Louisville Soc. Physicians and Surgeons (sec., treas.), So. Med. Soc., Fraternal Order Police. Republican. Baptist. Home and Office: 6303 Crest Creek Ct Louisville KY 40241-5801

LEE, THOMAS K., dentist, medical educator; b. Seoul, Republic of Korea, Sept. 6, 1964; came to U.S., 1977; s. Yong Joo and Keum Yeon (Cho) L.; m. Shanah Hyunsun Park, Feb. 26, 1995. BA, Northwestern U., 1987; B in Dental Sci., U. Ill., Chgo., 1989, DDS, 1991. Resident GPR Valley Med. Ctr., Fresno, Calif., 1991-92; pvt. practice Sacramento, Calif., 1992-93, L.A., 1996—; resident in advanced prosthodontics UCLA Sch. Dentistry, 1993-95; dir. AEGD program UCLA, 1995—. Cmty. advisor Calif. State U., Sacramento, 1992-93. Mem. ADA, Am. Coll. Prosthodontics, Am. Acad. Osseointegration, Calif. Dental Assn.

LEE, THOMAS WAY, obstetrician, gynecologist; b. Bhamo, Burma, Dec. 20, 1943; s. Way Ywan and Kim Ho (Kyang) L.; married; came to U.S., 1968, naturalized, 1973; I.Sc., U. Rangoon (Burma), 1962; M.B., B.S., Inst. of Medicine, Rangoon, 1967; m. Rita Chan, May 10, 1968; children—Patrician, Jefferey. Cert. Am. Bd. Ob-Gyn. Intern, Rangoon Gen. Hosp., 1967-68, St. Mary's Hosp., Phila., 1968-69; resident in ob-gyn Milard Fillmore Hosp., Buffalo, 1969-72; practice medicine specializing in ob-gyn, Easton, Pa., 1972-73, Upland, Calif., 1973-84; pvt. practice Rancho Cucamonga, Calif., 1984-95, Upland, Calif., 1995—; mem. staffs San Antonio, Drs., Vencor, Ontario (Calif.) Cmty. Hosps., Covina Valley Hosp., West Covina, Calif.; asst. clin. instr. SUNY, Buffalo, 1970-72; teaching staff dept. ob-gyn San Bernardino County (Calif.) Med. Center, 1970-80; chmn. Ob/gyn. Dept. San Antonio Hosp., Calif., 1993—, mem. exec. com., 1993-95. Fellow Am. Coll. Obstetricians and Gynecologists, ACS, Internat. Coll. Surgeons; mem. AMA, Am. Fertility Soc., Am. Assn. Gynecologic Laparoscopists, Calif. Med. Assn., San Bernardino County Med. Soc. (pres. 1984-85), Burma Med. Soc. (pres. 1985-86), San Bernardino-Riverside Obstetrics and Gynecology Soc. Contbr. articles to Jour. Reproductive Medicine. Office: 811 E 11th St Ste 201 Upland CA 91786-4872

LEE, TUNG-KWANG, pathologist, cancer researcher; b. Wuchang, China, Oct. 6, 1934; came to U.S., 1980; s. Jie-Tsai Lee and Chong-Wen Ding; m. You-An Sun, Jan. 30, 1974; 1 child, Hao. MD, Shanghai First Med. Coll., 1955. Resident in surgery and pathology Yubei Med. Sch., Henan, China, 1957-60, tchr. pathology, 1960-78, assoc. prof., 1979-80; Bradshaw fellow Bowman Gray Sch. of Medicine, Winston-Salem, N.C., 1980-81, rsch. assoc., 1981-85; rsch. instr. East Carolina U. Sch. Medicine, Greenville, N.C., 1985-87, rsch. asst. prof., 1988-95, rsch. assoc. prof., 1996—; researcher and speaker in field. Author: (with others) Rheumatology, 1985, Ovarian Tumors, 1984, Clinical Cytology, 1981; contbr. over 60 articles to profl. jours. Bd. dirs., chmn. membership com. Eastern Carolina Multicultural Ctr., Greenville, 1992—. Brown F. Finch Found. grantee 1993. Mem. Am. Assn. Cancer Rsch., Radiation Rsch. Soc., Internat. Acad. Cytology, Internat. Soc. Comparative Oncology, Sigma Xi. Home: 1403 Evergreen Dr Greenville NC 27858-4612 Office: Dept Radiation Oncology Sch of Medicine Leo W. Jenkins Cancer Ctr Greenville NC 27834

LEE, VIVIAN FOSTER, nursing administrator; b. Tallapoosa County, Ala., Sept. 30, 1945; d. James D. Sr. and Cora (Railey) Foster; m. Joseph D. Lee, Oct. 4, 1963; children: Shannon, Joseph D. II. ADN, Troy State U., Montgomery, Ala., 1978; BSN, Troy State U., Phenix City, Ala., 1984, MSN, 1986; postgrad., Samford U.; JD, Birmingham Sch. of Law, 1995. Lic. nursing home adminstr. Dir. dept. psychiatry East Ala. Med. Ctr., Opelika, 1986-87; mgr. nursing program Hillcrest Hosp., Birmingham, Ala., 1987-88; adminstr. clin. coord. Carraway Meth. Hosp., Birmingham, 1988-90, dir. behavioral health, 1990, DON, patient care units, 1990—. Mem. Am. Orgn. Nurse Execs., Ala. Nurses Assn., Ala. Assn. Alcohol and Drug Abuse Counselors, Am. Hosp. Assn., Ala. Orgn. Nurses Execs., Birmingham Regional Orgn. Nurse Execs. (sec./treas.), Sigma Theta Tau, Sigma Delta Kappa. Home: 731 Jasmine Way Birmingham AL 35226

LEE, WOONG MAN, pathologist; b. Seoul, Korea, Dec. 3, 1938; came to U.S., 1967; s. Jay Hyuck and Sung Yong Lee; m. Young Sook Kim, 1968; children: Danny Eugene, Francis Eusun, Peggy Eurie. BS, Seoul Nat. U., 1960, MD, 1964. Asst. resident Albany (N.Y.) Med. Ctr. Hosp., 1967-70, resident, 1970-72, asst. attending pathologist, 1974-79; instr. Albany Med. Coll., 1970-74, asst. prof., 1974-79; attending pathologist Albany VA Hosp., 1974-79; pathologist Glens Falls (N.Y.) Hosp., 1979—. Roman Catholic. Office: Glens Falls Hosp 100 Park St Glens Falls NY 12801-4413

LEEB, CHARLES SAMUEL, clinical psychologist; b. San Francisco, July 18, 1945; s. Sidney Herbert and Dorothy Barbara (Fishstrom) L.; m. Storme Lynn Gilkey, Apr. 28, 1984; children: Morgan Evan, Spencer Douglas. BA in Psychology, U. Calif.-Davis, 1967; MS in Counseling and Guidance, San Diego State U., 1970; PhD in Edn. and Psychology, Claremont Grad. Sch., 1973. Assoc. So. Regional Dir. Mental Retardation Ctr., Las Vegas, Nev., 1976-79; pvt. practice, Las Vegas, 1978-79; dir. biofeedback and athletics Menninger Found., Topeka, 1979-82, dir. children's div. biofeedback and psychophysiology ctr. The Menninger Found., 1979-82; pvt. practice, Claremont, Calif., 1982—; dir. of psychol. svcs. Horizon Hosp., 1986-88; dir. adolescent chem. dependency and children's program Charter Oak Hosp., Covina, Calif., 1989-91; founder, chief exec. officer Rsch. and Treatment Inst., Claremont, 1991—; lectr. in field. Contbr. articles to profl. jours. Mem. Am. Psychol. Assn., Calif. State Psychol. Assn. Office: 937 W Foothill Blvd Ste D Claremont CA 91711-3358

LEECH, JAMES JOHNSTON, neurosurgeon; b. Ft. Leavenworth, Kans., Dec. 3, 1956; s. Lloyd Lorenzo and Virginia Ross (Stiles) L.; m. Susan Lynn Weirick, June 5, 1982 (div. Dec. 1992); children: James J. Jr., Kelly Annin, Joseph Carver; m. Christine Mary Baker, Apr. 5, 1993; 1 child, Michael Ross. BS in Biology, Va. Mil. Inst., 1978; MD, U. Tex., San Antonio, 1982. Diplomate Am. Bd. Neurol. Surgery. Commd. 2nd lt. U.S. Army, 1982, advanced through grades to lt. col., 1994; resident neurosurgery Walter Reed Army Med. Ctr., Washington, 1982-88; attending neurosurgeon Brooke Army Med. Ctr., San Antonio, 1988-91, William Beaumont Army Med. Ctr., El Paso, Tex., 1991-95; chair dept. surgery William Beaumont Army Med. Ctr., El Paso, 1995—. Fellow ACS; mem. AMA, Am. Assn. Neurol. Surgeons, Congress of Neurol. Surgeons, Tex. Med. Assn. Home: 4509 Croton Circle El Paso TX 79924 Office: Wm Beaumont Army Med Ctr Dept Surgery 5005 N Piedras El Paso TX 79920

LEECH, STEPHEN HARRY, laboratory administrator; b. Prestwich, Eng., Mar. 27, 1942; came to U.S., 1962; s. Harry Rowland and Kathleen Hellen (Baker) L.; m. Susan Harriet Black; children: Elspeth, Megan, Sarah, Rebecca; m. Janet Susan Smith, Sept. 28, 1992. MB, ChB, U. Edinburgh, Scotland, 1965; PhD, U. London, 1976. Diplomate Am.Bd. Allergy and Clin. Immunology. Lectr. medicine McGill U., Montreal, Que., Can., 1970-72; clin. rsch. fellow Tumor Immunology Unit, U. Coll. London, 1972-76; asst. prof. dept. medicine La. State U. Med. Ctr., New Orleans, 1976-81, assoc. prof., 1981-86, assoc. prof. biometry/genetics, 1985-87, prof. dept. medicine, 1986-87; prof. clin. immunology Ea. Va. Med. Sch., Norfolk, 1988-93; prof. pathology and lab. medicine Temple U. Sch. Medicine, Phila., 1993—; adj. prof. Old Dominion U., Norfolk, 1992-93. With RAF, 1962-65. Recipient Young Investigators award Nat. Cancer Inst., La. State U. Med. Ctr., New Orleans, 1978-81, Fogarty Internat. fellowship Nat. Cancer Inst., U. Coll. London, 1984. Office: Tempe U Hosp Broad & Ontario Sts Philadelphia PA 19140

LEEDS, ROBERT, dentist; b. Newark, Sept. 8, 1930; s. William David and Gertrude (Greene) L.; m. Joyce Sumner, Nov. 28, 1960; children: Deborah Joyce, Robin Elizabeth. AA, U. Fla., 1953; DDS, Emory U., 1954. Gen. practice dentistry, Miami, Fla. Patentee herpes simplex method of therapy. Served to maj. USAF, 1954-56. Mem. ADA, East Coast Dental Assn., Miami Dental Soc., South Dade Dental Soc. Club: Coral Gables Country (Fla.). Lodges: Shriners, Masons. Avocations: sailing; water skiing; snow skiing. Office: 6437 Bird Rd Miami FL 33155-4827

LEEMAN, CAVIN PHILIP, psychiatrist. educator; b. N.Y.C., Jan. 16, 1932; s. Stephen and May (Cavin) L.; m. Susan Epstein, Aug. 11, 1957 (div. 1983); children: Eve, Jennifer, Raphael; m. Diane Leenheer Zimmerman, Feb. 18, 1984. AB, Harvard U., 1952, MD, 1959. Diplomate Am. Bd. Psychiatry and Neurology. Intern in medicine Mass. Gen. Hosp., Boston, 1959-60; resident in psychiatry Mass. Mental Health Ctr., Boston 1960-62; resident in psychiatry Beth Israel Hosp., Boston, 1962-64, asst. in psychiatry, 1964-66; instr. in psychiatry Harvard Med. Sch., Boston, 1966-75; chief of psychiatry Framingham (Mass.) Union Hosp., 1973-83; lectr. Harvard Med. Sch., 1975-83; assoc. clin. prof. Boston U. Sch. Medicine, 1974-83; chief of psychiatry VA Med. Ctr., Bklyn., 1983-85; clin. dir. psychiatry Univ. Hosp., Bklyn., 1985-96; clin. prof. psychiatry SUNY Health Sci. Ctr., Bklyn., 1984-96, clin. prof. psychiatry emeritus, 1996—; faculty assoc., divsn. humanities in medicine, SUNY Health Sci. Ctr., Bklyn., 1994—; mem. active med. staff Univ. Hosp., Bklyn., 1985—. Contbr. articles to profl. publs. Fellow Am. Psychiat. Assn. (life); mem. Assn. for Acad. Psychiatry, Am. Assn. Gen. Hosp. Psychiatrists, Acad. Psychosomatic Medicine, N.Y. Acad. Medicine, Physicians for Social Responsibility, Physicians for Human Rights, Soc. Bioethics Cons. Office: 344 W 23rd St Ste 1B New York NY 10011

LEEMAN, SUSAN EPSTEIN, neuroscientist, educator; b. Chgo., May 9, 1930; d. Samuel and Dora (Gubernikoff) Epstein; m. Cavin Leeman (div.); children: Eve, Raphael, Jennifer. BA, Goucher Coll., 1951; MA Radcliffe Coll., 1954, PhD, 1958; DS (hon.), SUNY, Utica, 1992; hon. degree, Goucher Coll., 1993. Instr. Harvard Med. Sch., Boston, 1958-59; postdoctoral fellow Brandeis U., Waltham, Mass., 1959-62, 62-66; rsch. assoc., adj. ast. prof., asst. rsch. prof. Brandeis U., Waltham, Mass., 1966-68, 71; asst. prof. Harvard Med. Sch., 1972-73, assoc. prof., 1973-80; prof. U. Mass. Med. Ctr., Worcester, 1980-92, dir. interdept. neurosci. program, 1984-92; prof. Boston U. Sch. Medicine, 1992—; Burroughs Wellcome vis. prof. U.Ky., 1992. Fogarty scholar NAS, 1994; recipient Women in Sci. award N.Y. Acad., 1995. Mem. NAS (197th Lilly lectr. 1994, Fred Conrad Koch award 1994, Women in Sci. award 1995). Office: Boston U Sch Medicine Dept Pharmacology 80 E Concord St Boston MA 02118-2307

LEEMPOEL, PETER J. B., dentist; b. Hilversum, The Netherlands, July 11, 1947; s. André M. C. and Maria (Brölmann) L.; m. Maria J. Th. A. Schellekens, July 25, 1970; children: Sebastiaan, Astrid. Dental degree, U. Nijmegen, The Netherlands, 1970, PhD, 1987. Staff prosthodontist dept. prosthodontic dentistry Nijmegen, 1970-76, sr. staff prosthodontist, assoc. prof. dept. Occlusal Reconstruction, 1976—; sr. staff posthodontist dept. prosthodontic dentistry Brussels, 1982-83. mem. bd. dept. Occlusal Reconstruction, Nijmegen, 1978-82, prosthetic dentistry, Nijmegen, 1974-75; v.p. bd. Faculty Dentistry, Nijmegen, 1979-80, substitute pres. bd., 1980. Author: De Prothetische Behandeling van een Patient met een Edentate Bovenkaak en een Gedeeltelijk Betande Onderkaak, 1986, Die prothetische Versorgung eines Patienten mit zahnlosem Oberkiefer und teilbezahntem Unterkiefer, 1986, Levensduur en Nabehandelingen van Kronen en Conventionele Bruggen in de Algemen Praktijk, 1987. Mem. Fedn. Dentaire Internat., Nederlander Vereniging voor Orale Implantiologie, Assn. Nederlandse Tandartsen. Office: St Canisiussingel 21, 6511 TG Nijmegen The Netherlands

LEENDERS, ALEXANDER C., medical microbiologist; b. Eindhoven, The Netherlands, July 3, 1965; s. Anton Adrianus Canisius Maria and Mathea Augusta Maria (Knoers) L.; m. Marjan Meilindes Wassenaar, May 27, 1994. Atheneum B, St. Joris Coll., Eindhoven, 1983; PhD, U. Utrecht, The Netherlands, 1988, Physicians Degree, 1991. Recruitment selection physician Ministry of Def., Hilversum Utrecht, 1991-92; rschr. in antifungals efficacy U. Rotterdam, The Netherlands, 1992-94; med. microbiologist Hosp. of U. Rotterdam, 1994—. Lt. Dutch armed forces, 1990-91. Mem. Dutch Soc. Microbiology, Dutch Soc. Infectious Diseases, Am. Soc. Microbiology. Roman Catholic. Office: Univ Hosp Dykzigt, Dr Molewaterplein 40, 3015 GD Rotterdam The Netherlands

LEESON, LEWIS JOSEPH, research pharmacist, scientist; b. Paterson, N.J., Apr. 26, 1927; s. Alfred Elias and Rose (Sandow) L.; m. Barbara Rothstein, Dec. 20, 1953; children: Suzanne, Erica, Alex. BS in Pharmacy, Rutgers U., Newark, 1950, MS in Pharm. Chemistry, 1954; PhD in Pharm. Chemistry, U. Mich., 1957. Registered pharmacist, N.J., N.Y., Mich. Pharmacist Mack Drug Co., Paterson, N.J., 1950-52, Fried's Drugs, Paterson, 1952-54; lab. asst. Rutgers U. Coll. Pharmacy, Newark, 1952-54, U. Mich., Ann Arbor, 1954-57; rsch. pharmacist, project leader Lederle Labs., Pearl River, N.Y., 1955-67; dir. product R & D, Union Carbide Co., Greenburgh, N.Y., 1967-69; asst. dir. product R & D, Geigy Pharm., Suffern, N.Y., 1969-71; dir., sr. dir., sr. rsch. fellow Ciba-Geigy Pharm., Summit, N.J., 1971-84; disting. rsch. fellow Ciba-Geigy Corp., Summit, 1984-93, ret., 1993; pres. LJL Assocs. Inc, Pharm. R&D Cons, Montville, N.J., 1993—; Dean Lou Busse lectr. U. Wis., 1993; mem. USP exec. com., 1990-95; NJ. DURC, 1984-89. Editor: Dissolution Technology, 1971; contbr. over 40 articles to profl. jours; patentee in field. Recipient Disting. Alumnus award U. Mich., 1990. Fellow Acad. Pharm. Sci., Am. Assn. Pharm. Scientists; mem. Am. Pharm. Assn., Sigma Xi, Rho Chi, Phi Lambda Upsilon. Jewish. Home and Office: LJL Assocs Inc 134 Ridge Dr Montville NJ 07045-9473

LEEVY, CARROLL MOTON, medical educator, hepatology researcher; b. Columbia, S.C., Oct. 13, 1920; s. Isaac S. and Mary (Kirkl) L.; m. Ruth S. Barboza, Feb. 4, 1956; children: Carroll Barboza, Maria Secora. AB, Fisk U., 1941; MD, U. Mich., 1944; ScD (hon.), N.J. Inst. Tech., 1973, U. Nebr., 1989; HHD (hon.), Fisk U., 1981; M, Am. Coll. Physicians, 1991. Intern Jersey City Med. Ctr., 1944-45, resident, 1945-48, dir. clin. investigation, 1947-57; fellow Banting-Best Inst., U. Toronto, Ont., Can., 1953; research assoc. Harvard U. Med. Sch., Cambridge, Mass., 1959; assoc. prof. U. Medicine and Dentistry of N.J., 1960-64, prof., 1964, Disting. prof., 1990—; physician in chief Univ. Hosp., 1975-91; dir. Liver Ctr. U. Medicine and Dentistry N.J., 1983-85; dir. div. hepatology and nutrition N.J. Med. Sch., 1959-75, acting chmn. dept. medicine, 1966-68, chief of medicine, 1968-71, chmn. dept. medicine, 1975-91; disting. prof. medicine Univ. Hosp., physician in chief, 1975-91; acting chmn. Sammy Davis Jr. Nat. Liver Inst., 1984-86, pres., sci. dir., 1989—; dir. N.J. Med. Sch. Liver Ctr., 1991—; chief medicine VA Hosp., East Orange, N.J., 1966-71; cons. NIH, 1965—, FDA, 1970-80, VA, 1971—, Alcohol aand Nutrition Found., 1970-80, Am. Liver Found., 1979-84; cons. Health Care Fin. Adminstrn., 1990—, mem. adv. com. on liver transplantation, 1991—; mem. Nat. Commn. on Digestive Disease, 1975-78; mem. expert com. on chronic liver disease WHO, 1978; mem. nat. adv. com. digestive disease HHS, 1989-93; chmn. monitoring com. VA Coop. Study on Alcoholic Hepatitis, 1989-94—, VA Rsch. Study on Colchicine Alcoholic Cirrhosis, 1994—. Author: Practical Diagnosis and Treatment of Liver Disease, 1957, Evaluation of Liver Function in Clinical Practice, 1965, 2d edit., 1974, Liver Regeneration in Man, 1973, The Liver and Its Diseases, 1973, Diseases of the Liver and Biliary Tract, 1977, Guidelines for Detection of Drug and Chemical-Induced Hepatotoxicity, 1979, Alcohol and the Digestive Tract, 1981, Standardization of Nomenclature, Diagnostic Criteria and Prognosis for Diseases of the Liver and Biliary Tract, 1994; contbr. numerous articles to med., sci. jours.; patentee in field. Bd. dirs. U. Cape Town, South Africa, 1984—; active Cmty. Congl. Ch. Cmdr. USNR, 1954-59. E.V. Gabriel scholar, 1938, Kellog Med. scholar, 1942; recipient Modern Med. award, 1972, Edward III award, 1973, United Negro Coll. Fund award, 1980, Key to City of Newark, 1981, Key to City of Columbia, S.C., 1987, Key to City of Secaucus, N.J., 1981, 50th N.J. Achievement award U. Medicine and Dentistry N.J., 1995; 40th Anniversary Faculty Honoree, U. Medicine and Dentistry N.J., 1995. Mem. NAACP, ACP (publs. com. 1969-74, master), AMA (vice-chmn., chmn. program com. sect. on gastroenterology 1971-74), AAAS, Am. Assn. for Study Liver Diseases (pres. 1967-68, chmn. steering com. 1968-74, Disting. Svc. award 1991), Internat. Assn. for Study Liver (pres. 1970-74, chmn. criteria com. 1972—), Am. Gastroenterol. Assn. (edn. and tng. com. 1967-71), Assn. Profs. Medicine (Robert Williams Disting. Chmn. award 1991), Assn. Am. Physicians, Soc. Exptl. Biology and Medicine, Am. Soc. Clin. Nutrition, Am. Inst. Nutrition, Nat. Med. Assn. (award 1987, Centenial award 1995), Am. Fedn. Clin. Rsch., Assn. Acad. Minority Physicians (pres. 1986-88, chmn. bd. trustees 1988—, Disting. Achievement award 1995), Internat. Com. on Informatics in Hepatology (chmn. 1986—), Internal Hepatology Informatics Group (chmn. 1984-93), N.J. Acad. Medicine, Phi Beta Kappa, Alpha Omega Alpha, Sigma Pi Phi. Home: 35 Robert Dr Short Hills NJ 07078-1525 Office: UMDNJ Med School 100 Bergen St Newark NJ 07103-2407

LEFEBURE, ALAIN PAUL, family physician; b. Paris, Nov. 17, 1946; s. Rene Julien and Ginette (Peradon) L.; m. Lucia Lefebure; children: Vincent, Benjamin. RN, Sch. Nursing, Paris, 1970; Dr. Medicine, U. Paris 7, 1978. Male nurse Tenon Hosp., Paris, 1970-71; intern Bichat Hosp., Paris, 1974-76; resident Bretonneau Hosp., Paris, 1976-78; lectr. in pediatrics Claude Bernard Hosp., Paris, 1976-81; practice medicine specializing in family medicine Paris, 1981—. Author six langs. med. dictionary Lexica Medica Polyglotta. Dep. Internat. Parliament for Safety and Peace; knight Templars of Jerusalem. Recipient Clarinetist Soloist prize Congratulations from the Jury, 1965. Mem. Comdr. des Lofsensischen Ursiniusordens, Internat. Order of Merit. Office: 2 rue Pierre Mouillard, 75020 Paris France

LEFER, JAY, psychiatrist; b. N.Y.C., June 4, 1930; s. Ben-Zion and Gertrude (Silbermann) L.; m. Anne Griffin, July 26, 1968; children: David Gerard, Theodore Benedict. AB, Columbia U., 1950; MD, U. Lausanne, Switzerland, 1955. Diplomate, Am. Bd. Psychiatry and Neurology. Intern French Hosp., N.Y.C., 1955-57; unit chief Hillside Hosp., N.Y.C., 1959-60; chief resident Yale Med. Sch., New Haven, 1960-62; pvt. practice N.Y.C., 1962—; clin. prof. N.Y. Med. Coll., N.Y.C., 1992. Contbr. articles to profl. publs. Capt. M.C., U.S. Army, 1957-59, Korea. Recipient Gralnick Found. award in psychoanalysis, 1971. Mem. Soc. Liaison Psychiatry (pres. 1978-79, founding mem.), N.Y. Acad. Medicine, Am. Coll. Psychoanalysts. Office: 200 E End Ave New York NY 10128-7831

LEFF, ALAN RICHARD, medical educator, researcher; b. Pitts., May 23, 1945; s. Maurice D. and Grace Ruth (Schwartz) L.; m. Donna Rae Rosene, Feb. 14, 1975; children: Marni, Karen, Alison. AB cum laude, Oberlin Coll., 1967; MD, U. Rochester, 1971. Diplomate Am. Bd. Internal Medicine, Am. Bd. Pulmonary Disease. Intern U. Mich. Hosp., Ann Arbor, 1971-72, resident, 1974-76; fellow U. Calif.-San Francisco, 1976-77, postdoctoral fellow, 1977-79; asst. prof. medicine U. Chgo., 1979-85, assoc. prof.medicine and clin. pharm., 1985-89, prof. medicine, anesthesia and critical care and clin. pharm., 1989—, prof. cell physiology, 1992—, prof. pediatrics, 1993—, prof. pharm. and physical scis., 1993—, dir. pulmonary medicine service, 1984-87, dir. Pulmonary Function Lab., 1979-87, chief sect. pulmonary and critical care medicine, 1987—; dir. NIAID Asthma and Allergic Dis. Coop. Rsch. Ctr., Chgo., 1993—; advisor San Francisco Dept. Pub. Health, 1977-79, Chgo. Dept. Health, 1979—; bd. dirs. Chgo. Lung Assn., 1984-93. Cons. editor Jour. Clin. Invest., editorial bd. Am. Jour. Physiology, Jour. Applied Physiology; editor Am. Jour. Respir. Critical Care Medicine, 1994—; assoc. editor Am. Rev. Respiratory Disease, 1989-94, Pulmonary Pharm., 1987; contbr. articles to profl. jours. Served with USPHS, 1972-74. Recipient Citation of merit Chgo. Lung Assn., 1974; Leopold Schepp Found. fellow, 1967-69. Fellow Am. Coll. Chest Physicians; mem. Am. Fedn. Clin. Research (councilor 1983-86), Am. Soc. Clin. Investigation, Am. Physiological Soc., Cent. Soc. for Clin. Investigation, Assn. Am. Physicians, Sigma Xi. Avocation: music. Home: 5730 S Kimbark Ave Chicago IL 60637-1615 Office: U Chgo Pritzker Sch Medicine Div Biological Scis MC 6076 5841 S Maryland Ave Chicago IL 60637-1463

LEFF, JULIAN PAUL, psychiatry educator; b. London, July 4, 1938; s. Samuel and Vera Miriam (Levy) L.; m. Joan Lillian Raphael, Jan. 31, 1975; children: Michael, Alex, Jessa, Jonty, Adriel. BSc, London U., 1958, MB BS, 1961, MD, 1972. Intern U. Coll. Hosp., London, 1955-62; resident Whittington Hosp., London, 1962-63; career scientist Med. Rsch. Coun., London, 1972—; dir. Team for Assessment of Psychiat. Svcs., London, 1985—, MRC Social and Community Psychiatry Unit, London, 1989-95; prof. social and cultural psychiatry Inst. of Psychiatry, London, 1987—. Author: Psychiatric Examination in Clinical Practice, 1978, Expressed Emotion in Families, 1985, Psychiatry Around the Globe, 1988, Family Work For Schizophrenia, 1992, Principles of Social Psychiatry, 1993. Recipient Starkey prize Royal Coll. of Health, Eng., 1976. Fellow Royal Coll. Psychiatry; mem. Royal Coll. Physicians, Nat. Schizophrenia Fellowship (profl. adv. com. 1987-96), SANE (profl. adv. com. 1990—), Richmond Fellowship (coun. 1988—). Office: MRC Social Psychiatry Sect, Decrespigny Park, London SE5 8AF, England

LEFF, PAUL, pharmacologist; b. London, Feb. 12, 1954; s. Daniel and Eileen (Shaw) L.; m. Tarja Teljovaara, June 28, 1975 (div. 1984); m. Barbara Crack, Dec. 8, 1994; children: Amy Riina, Jacob Paul. BSc in Biochemistry, Manchester U., U.K., 1975, MSc in Biochemistry, 1977, PhD in Biochemistry, 1979. Rsch. scientist Wellcome Rsch. Labs., Beckenham, Kent, Eng., 1979-82, sr. rsch. scientist, 1982-87; mgr. pharmacology dept. Fisons Plc, Loughborough, Leicestershire, Eng., 1987-90, head pharmacology, 1991-95; dir. pharmacology Astra Charnwood, Loughborough, Leicestershire, Eng., 1995—. Editor Tips, 1994—; referee Brit. Jour. Pharmacology, 1981-90, editor, 1991—; contbr. over 60 articles to profl. jours., chpts. to books. Mem. Brit. Pharm. Soc. Office: Astra Charnwood, Bakewell Rd, Loughborough Leicestershire, England LE110RH

LEFFALL, LASALLE D(OHENY), JR., surgeon; b. Tallahassee, May 22, 1930; s. LaSalle Doheny Sr. and Martha (Jordan) L.; m. Ruth McWilliams; 1 child, LaSalle Doheny III. BS, Fla. A&M U., 1948; MD, Howard U., 1952. Intern Homer G. Phillips Hosp., St. Louis, 1952-53; resident Freedmen's Hosp., Washington, 1953-57; fellow Meml. Sloan Kettering Cancer Ctr., N.Y.C., 1957-70; chmn. dept. surgery Howard U. Coll. Medicine, Washington, 1970-95, acting dean, 1970, Charles R. Drew prof. surgery, 1992—. Contbr. articles on cancer to profl. publs. Pres. Soc. Surg. Oncology, 1978-79, Am. Cancer Soc., 1978-79, ACS, 1995-96. Capt. U.S. Army, 1960-61. Recipient St. George medal and citation Am. Cancer Soc., 1977, Nat. Achievement award Black Caucus Dem. Nat. Com., 1982, Exceptional Black Scientist award CIBA-Geigy, 1984. Mem. Internat. Fedn. Surg. Colls. (assoc.), Med. Edn. for South African Blacks (bd. dirs. 1988—). Office: Howard Univ Coll Med 2400 6th St NW Washington DC 20059-0001

LEFFELL, DAVID JOEL, surgeon, dermatologist, educator, researcher; b. Montreal, Feb. 28, 1956; came to U.S., 1973; s. Allen Bernard and Freda (Deckelbaum) L. BS, Yale U., 1977; MD, McGill U., Montreal, 1981.

Diplomate Am. Bd. Dermatology, Am. Bd. Internal Medicine. Resident in internal medicine Meml. Sloan-Kettering Cancer Ctr., N.Y.C., 1981-84; instr. medicine Cornell U. Sch. Medicine, N.Y.C., 1983-84; lectr., fellow dermatologic surgery U. Mich., Ann Arbor, 1987-88; resident in dermatology Yale U. Sch. Medicine, New Haven, 1984-86, assoc. prof. dermatology, plastic surgery and otolaryngology, 1988-96, chief Mohs micrographic surgery and laser surgery, 1988—, dir. Yale skin cancer detection program, 1988—, med. dir. faculty practice plan, 1996—; sci. advisor Nat. Hereditary Hemorrhagic Telangiectasia Found., New Haven, 1991—. Contbg. editor: Jour. Dermatologic Surgery and Oncology; assoc. editor Med. and Surg. Dermatology; mem. editl. bd. Archives of Dermatology; assoc. editor: Geriatric Dermatology; inventor laser fluorescence device to measure photoaging. Recipient Frederic Mohs award Skin Cancer Found., 1988, 91. Mem. Conn. Dermatology Soc. (sec.-treas.). Home: 69 Mumford Rd New Haven CT 06515-2431 Office: Yale Sch Medicine PO Box 208059 New Haven CT 06520

LEFFLER, CAROLE ELIZABETH, mental health nurse, women's health nurse; b. Sidney, Ohio, Feb. 18, 1942; d. August B. and Delores K. Aselage; children: Veronica, Christopher. ADN, Sinclair Community Coll., Dayton, Ohio, 1975. Cert. psychiat. nurse coord. Nurse Grandview Hosp, Dayton, 1961-76; substitute sch. nurse Fairborn (Ohio) City Schs., 1981-82; dir. nursing Fairborn Nursing Home, 1983; psychiat. nurse coord. Dayton Mental Health Ctr., 1984—; mem. exec. bd. 1199. Vol., instr., disaster health nurse ARC; officer, leader, camp nurse for Girl Scouts, Boy Scouts; Ch. Parish Coun. Recipient Fleur de Lis award Girl and Boy Scouts, Svc. award ARC, Fairborn Mayor's Cert. of Merit for Civic Pride, State of Ohio Govs. award Innovation Ohio. Mem. ANA, Ohio Nurses Assn. Home: 29 W Bonomo Dr Fairborn OH 45324-3407

LEFKO, JEFFREY JAY, hospital planner; b. St. Paul, July 15, 1945; s Morris and Dorothy (Mindell) L.; m. Philomena M. Corno, Mar. 6, 1970 (div. Dec. 1984); children: Melissa Ann, Benjamin Scott, Ellen Rachael; m. Mary Wilson, Jan. 10, 1986 (div. June 1989); m. Susan H. Shockley, Jan. 5, 1990. BSBA with distinction, U. Nebr., 1967; M in Hosp. Adminstrn., Washington U., St. Louis, 1969. Adminstrv. resident St. John's Mercy Hosp., St. Louis, 1968-69; nat. fellow Health Services Adminstrn. Am. Hosp. Assn.-Blue Cross Assn., Chgo., 1969-70; v.p. planning/ops. Meth. Hosp. of Ind., Indpls., 1970-75; v.p. Jewish Hosp., St. Louis, 1975-78; v.p. planning Greenville (S.C.) Hosp. System, 1979-88; exec. cons. The Lash Group, Greenville, 1988-90; v.p. planning Union Meml. Hosp., Balt., 1990-93; v.p. planning and mktg. St. Joseph Med. Ctr., Balt., 1993—; adj. instr. Washington U., 1976-78; guest lectr. Duke U., Univ. S.C., Clemson U., Ind. U.; instr. Furman U., Greenville, 1982-84, Med. Univ. of S.C. 1989. Contbr. articles to profl. jours.; contbr. to (book) Guide to Strategic Plannin g for Hosps., 1981; mem. edit. bd. Health Care Strategic Mgmt., 1984—. Mem. Am. Hosp. Ass. (pres. Soc. for Hosp. Planning and Mktg. 1984-85), Am. Coll. of Health Care Execs., Carolinas Soc. of Hosp. Planning (founding mem.), Innocents Soc., Beta Gamma Sigma. Lodge: Rotary. Office: St Joseph Med Ctr 7620 York Rd Baltimore MD 21204-7508

LEFKON, BRUCE WARREN, physician, urologist; b. Jackson Heights, N.Y., June 11, 1942; s. Irving M. and Hinda (Feld) L.; m. Frances MacDonald, Dec. 30, 1968; children: Marc, David, Owen. AB, Columbia U., 1964; MD, SUNY, Bklyn., 1969. Diplomate Am. Bd. Urology. Intern L.A. County Hosp., 1969-70; resident in surgery Beth Israel Hosp., N.Y.C., 1970-71; resident in urology SUNY Downstate Med. Ctr., 1971-74; urologist Urology Group, South Orange, N.J., 1975-80; pvt. practice Livingston, N.J., 1980—; chief urology sect. St. Barnabes Med. Ctr., Livingston, 1996; chief urology sect. Hosp. Ctr., Orange, 1995, bd. trustees, 1986—. Featured as one of two urologists in state in "Doctors Favorite Doctors", N.J. Mag., 1992. Mem. Orange Lawn Tennis Club (bd. govs. 1987-89). Office: 22 Old Short Hills Rd Livingston NJ 07039

LEFKOVITZ, NORMAN WAYNE, neurologist; b. May 26, 1957. BS, U. Akron, 1978; MD, Ohio State U., 1981. Diplomate Am. Bd. Psychology and Neurology, Am. Bd. Electrodiagnostic Medicine. Intern in internal medicine Ohio State U., 1981-82; resident in neurology Case Western Reserve U. Hosp., Cleve., 1982-85; fellow in clin. neurophysiology Vanderbilt U. Hosp., Nashville, 1985-86; pvt. practice neurologist, 1986—. Mem. Am. Acad. Neurology. Home: 60 N Miller Rd Fairlawn OH 44333

LEFKOWITZ, LOUIS HIRSCH, obstetrician-gynecologist; b. Bklyn., Oct. 20, 1937; s. Paul Howard and Bertha (Schulman) L.; m. Patricia Smith; 1 child, Andrew, Philip. BA, U. N.C., 1959; postgrad., U. bologna, 1959-62; MD, N.Y. Med. Coll., 1964. Diplomate Am. Bd. Ob-gyn. Intern Beth Israel Med. Ctr., N.Y.C., 1964-65; resident in ob-gyn N.Y. Med. Coll., Flower Fifth Avenue and Met. Hosp. Ctr., N.Y.C., 1965-69; dir. ob-gyn. dept. Good Samaritan Hosp., Suffern, N.Y., 1988-92. Maj. U.S. Army, 1969-71. Fellow Am. Coll. Ob-Gyns., ACS, Am. Fertility Soc.; mem. Am. Assn. Gynecologic Laparoxopy, Rockland County Med. Soc., N.Y. State Med. Soc. Jewish. Office: Tallman Ob-Gyn PC 134 Route 59 Suffern NY 10901-4917

LEFKOWITZ, ROBERT JOSEPH, physician, educator; b. N.Y.C., Apr. 15, 1943; s. Max and Rose (Levine) L.; children: David, Larry, Cheryl, Mara, Joshua; m. Lynn Tilley, May 26, 1991. B.A., Columbia U., 1962, M.D., 1966. Diplomate: Am. Bd. Internal Medicine. Assoc. prof medicine Duke U., Durham, N.C., 1973-77, prof. medicine, 1977—, James B. Duke prof. medicine, 1982—, prof. biochemistry, 1985—; investigator Howard Hughes Med. Inst., Durham, 1976—. Author: Receptor Binding Studies in Adrenergic Pharmacology, 1978, Receptor Regulation, 1981, Principles of Biochemistry, 1983. Am. Heart Assn. established investigator, 1973-76, Basic Rsch. prize, 1990; recipient Young Scientist award Passano Found., 1978, George Thorn award Howard Hughes Med. Inst., 1979, Oppenheimer award, 1982, Gordon Wilson medal Am. Clin. and Climatol. Assn., 1982, Lita Annenberg Hazen award, 1983, outstanding rsch. award Internat. Soc. for Heart Rsch., 1985, H.B. van Dyke award Coll. Physicians and Surgeons Columbia U., 1986, Steven C. Beering award Ind. U. Sch. Medicine, 1986, N.C. award in Sci., 1987, Internat. award Gairdner Found., 1988, Novo Nordsk Biotech. award, 1990, Biomed. Rsch.award Assn. Am. Med. Colls., 1990, City of Medecin award, N.C., 1991, Columbia U. Coll. of Physicians and Surgeons Alumnus award for Disting. achievements in medicine, 1992, Bristol-Meyers Squibb award for Disting. achievement in Cardiovascular rsch., 1992, The Giovani Lorenzini Prize for Basic Biomedical Rsch., 1992, Columbia U. coll. of Physicians and Surgeons Joseph Mather Smith Prize, 1993, The Endocrine Soc. Gerald D. Aurbach Lectr. award Inst. of Medicine NAS, 1995, J. David Gladstone Insts. Disting. Lecture award, 1996, Bio/Tech. Winter Symposia Feodor Lynen award. Mem. Am. Soc. Biol. Chemists, Am. Soc. Clin. Investigation (counselor, 1982-85, pres.-elect 1986-87, pres. 1987-88), Assn. Am. Physicians (treas. 1989-94), Am. Soc. Pharmacology and Exptl. Therapeutics (John J. Abel award 1978, Goodman and Gilman award 1986), Endocrine Soc., Am. Fedn. Clin. Research (sec.-treas. 1980-83, mem. nat. council 1978-83), NAS, Am. Acad. Arts and Scis., Japanese Biochem.soc. (hon.), Am. Heart Assn. Basic Rsch. Soc. Office: Duke Univ Med Ctr PO Box 3821 Durham NC 27710-0001

LEFLY, DIANNE LOUISE, research psychologist; b. Denver, July 17, 1946; d. Gordon Eugene Boen and Elizabeth (Welsh) Tuveson. AB, U. No. Colo., 1968; MA, U. Colo., 1980; PhD, U. Denver, 1994. Classroom tchr. Adam County Sch. Dist. #12, Thornton, Colo., 1968-77; rschr. John F. Kennedy Child Devel. Ctr., Denver, 1979-81, U. Colo. Health Scis. Ctr., 1981-89, U. Denver, 1989—. Contbr. articles to profl. jours. Mem. Colo. Rep. Party, Denver, 1968—. Scholarship U. No. Colo., 1964-68; fellowship U. Denver, 1989. Mem. Mensa. Republican. Home: 8650 W 79th Ave Arvada CO 80005-4321 Office: U Denver 2155 S Race St Denver CO 80210-4633

LEFOR, ALAN TERENCE, surgical oncologist; b. N.Y.C., Sept. 19, 1956; s. Frank Maarten and Rita (Pollard) L. BS, SUNY, Albany, 1976; MD, SUNY, Syracuse, 1982; MA, Wesleyan U., 1978. Diplomate Nat. Bd. Med. Examiners. Resident in surgery SUNY, Syracuse, 1982-85, sr. resident, 1987-88, chief resident, 1988-89; rsch. fellow surgery br. NIH/Nat. Cancer Inst., 1985-87; assoc. prof. surgery and oncology U. Md., Balt., 1989-96; prof. surgery U. Calif., San Diego, 1996—; surg. oncologist Kern Med. Ctr., Bakersfield, Calif., 1996—. Contbr. articles to profl. jours. Fellow ACS; mem. AMA, Soc. Univ. Surgeons, SSO, Sigma Xi.

LEFORCE, BRUCE RYAN, neurologist; b. Middletown, Ohio, Oct. 9, 1958; s. James Gordon and Judith Ellen (Thomas) LeF.; m. Charlotte Ann (Carla) Volovsek, Sept. 13, 1986; 1 child, Kathryn Ellen. BS in Chemistry cum laude, Rhodes Coll., 1981; MD, U. Louisville, 1985. Intern in internal medicine Wilford Hall Med. Ctr., Lackland AFB, Tex., 1985-86; resident in neurology Wilford Hall Med. Ctr., Lackland AFB, 1986-89; staff neurologist Wilford Hall Med. Ctr., Lakeland AFB, 1990-94; fellow in Epilepsy and clin. neurophysiology Cleve. Clinic Found., 1989-90; pvt. practice in neurologist San Antonio, 1994—; profl. adv. bd. mem. Epilepsy Assn. San Antonio/South Tex., 1993—. Maj. USAF, 1985-94. Mem. AMA, Am. Epilepsy Assn., Tex. Med. Assn., Bexar County Med. Assn. Office: 2829 Babcock Rd #407 San Antonio TX 78229

LEFTON, HARVEY BENNETT, gastroenterologist, educator, author; b. Cleve., May 17, 1944; s. Nat L. and Edith (Waintrup) L.; m. Paulette Lipkowitz, Aug. 24, 1968; children: Allison Rachel, Daniel Adam. BS, U. Pitts., 1966; MD, Jefferson Med. Coll., Phila., 1970. Cert. Nat. Bd. Med. Examiners, Am. Bd. Internal Medicine, Am. Bd. Gastroenterology. Intern medicine Cleve. Clinic, 1970-71, resident internal medicine, 1971-72, fellow gastroenterology, 1972-74; chief gastroenterology Scott AFB, Belleville, Ill., 1974-76; asst. clin. prof. medicine Med. Coll. Pa., Phila., 1976-78, assoc. clin. prof. medicine, 1978-81, clin. prof. medicine, 1981—; cons. gastroenterology Friends Hosp., Belmont Psychiat. Hosp., Pa., 1980—. Contbr. articles to profl. jours. Maj. USAF, 1974-76. Named Outstanding Vol. Physician, Med. Coll. Pa., 1994. Fellow ACP, Am. Coll. Gastroenterology, Coll. Physicians Phila.; mem. Am. Soc. Gastroenterology Endoscopy, Pa. Soc. Gastroenterology, Omicron Delta Kappa. Home: 559 Long Ln Huntingdon Valley PA 19006-2935 Office: 2 Bala Plz Ste IL 22 Bala Cynwyd PA 19004

LEGERTON, CLARENCE WILLIAM, JR., gastroenterologist, educator; b. Charleston, S.C., July 8, 1922; s. Clarence William and Winnie Davis (McMaster) L.; m. Mitzi Foster Herrin, May 31, 1958; children: Clarence William, Mary Pringle, Gregg McMaster. Student, Davidson Coll., 1939-43, BS, 1982; MD, Med. Coll. S.C., 1946. Intern Univ. Hosp., Balt., 1946-47, med. resident, 1947-48; med. resident Duke U. Sch. Medicine, 1951-52, fellow in gastroenterology, 1952-53, instr. medicine, 1950-53; practice medicine specializing in gastroenterology Conway, S.C., 1953-56, Charleston, 1956-66; prof. medicine, dir. div. gastroenterology Med. U. S.C., Charleston, 1966-92; asst. to pres. Med. U. S.C., 1975-80, prof. Emeritus, 1992; vis. prof. Royal United Hosp., Bath, Eng., 1987; cons. Cambridge U. Sch. Medicine (Eng.), 1978; trustee Nat. Found. for Ileitis and Colitis, 1976—; bd. dirs. Coalition Digestive Disease Orgns., 1982—; mem. nat. digestive diseases adv. bd. NIH, Washington; chmn. com. on digestive diseases rsch. ctrs. Nat. Inst. Digestive Diseases, Diabetes, and Kidney Diseases, Washington. Med. dir. Nat. Miss U.S.A. Pageant, 1977-79; dir. Citizens and So. Nat. Bank, Charleston; chmn. Charleston bd., 1974—; bd. dirs. Nations Bank, Charleston, 1992—; vice chmn. Charleston Commn. Public Works, 1959-76; chmn. water supply City of Charleston; pres. Charleston Symphony Orch. Assn., 1967-68; chmn. bd. dirs. Legerton & Co., Inc.; Mem. City Council Charleston, 1959-76, mayor pro-tem, 1960; pres. Charleston County Democratic Conv., 1960; trustee Montreat-Anderson Coll., vice chmn., 1962-74, chmn., 1974-78; trustee Queens Coll., 1965—; bd. visitors Davidson (N.C.) Coll., 1979—, trustee, 1982-84; bd. visitors Warren Wilson Coll., Swannanoa, N.C., 1993—; chmn. bd. Charleston Mcpl. Auditorium; chmn. adv. bd. Comprehensive Health Planning Council, Charleston, Berkeley and Dorchester Counties. Served to capt. AUS, 1948-50. Named Disting. Alumnus, Med. U. of S.C., 1986; recipient Alumni Svc. award Davidson Coll., 1988. Master ACP (gov. S.C. 1978-82); fellow Am. Coll. Gastroenterology (gov. for S.C. 1978-82), Am. Gastroenterology Assn. (chmn. com. on pub. policy and govt. rels. 1982—, governing bd. 1985); mem. S.C. Soc., New Eng. Soc. (pres. 1992—), Coun. Med. socs. (rep. 1980-84), Nat. Alumni Assn. Davidson Coll. (pres. 1983-84), Alpha Omega Alpha, Sigma Phi Epsilon, Alpha Kappa Alpha. Presbyterian (ruling elder 1956—, pres. corp. 1965—, moderator 1963). Clubs: Carolina Yacht (Charleston); Biltmore Forest Country (Asheville, N.C.); The Club at Seabrook Island. Home: 2 1/2 Atlantic St Charleston SC 29401-2746

LEGG, LARRY BARNARD, biology educator; b. Laurel, Miss., Aug. 19, 1941; s. Walter H. and Lillian (Stringer) L.; m. Katherine Sue Bynum, May 30, 1965; 1 child, Elizabeth. BS, U. So. Miss., 1965; MS, Northwestern State U. of La., 1970. Tchr. biology Vidalia (La.) High Sch., 1966-69; instr. biology NW State U. of La., Natchitoches, 1969-70, Mountain View Coll., Dallas, 1970—; broker Tex. Real Estate Commn.; presenter League of Innovation in C.C. Conf. on Computing, 1988-94. Author: Microbiology, 1973, Breeds of Animals, 1975, Biological Science I, 1982, 4th ed. 1989, Biological Science II, 1984, 4th ed., 1990. Mem. Mountain View Coll. Faculty Assn. (v.p. 1986-90, 95, chmn. welfare and benefits 1989-90), Tex. Assn. of Advisers to Health Profession, Lions (pres. Red Bird/Dallas chpt. 1976-77, pres. Duncanville Noon chpt. 1982-83, editor newspaper 1984-85, 87-88, Lion of Yr. 1979-80, life advisor 1989, Gov. Spl. Appreciation award 1983, 87-88, 89, 100% Dep. Dist. Gov. 1987-88, 100% Dist. Cabinet sec.-treas. 1988-89. Home: 1512 Wyndmere Dr De Soto TX 75115-7808 Office: Mountain View Coll 4849 W Illinois Ave Dallas TX 75211-6503

LEGGETT, PHILIP LLOYD, general and laparoendoscopic surgery; b. Houston, July 22, 1953; s. Milbourne Kerlic and Phyllis Ruth (Cline) L.; m. Janet Elizabeth Akeroyd, June 21, 1980; children: Philip Lloyd II, Lauren Elizabeth, Lindsey Anne. BA of Arts Biology, U. Tex., 1975; MD, U. Tex. Med. Br., 1980. Diplomate Am. Bd. Surgery; MD, Tex., La. Intern in surgery Alton Ochsner Med. Found., New Orleans, 1980-81, resident in surgery, 1981-85; surgeon pvt. practice Houston, 1985—; chmn. gen./vascular surgery Houston NW Med. Ctr., Houston, 1993, 94, 1995; sec. gen. staff, 1995; lectr. in field. Contbr. articles to profl. jours. Bd. dirs., founder golf tournament Benefitting Boys/Girls Country of Houston, Hockley, Tex., 1985-95; mem. steer auction Houston Livestock Show, 1992-93, 93-94, 95-96. Fellow ACS, ACS (South Tex. chpt.), Internat. Coll. Surgeons; mem. AMA, Alton Ochsner Surg. Soc., So. Med. Assn., Tex. Med. Assn., Harris County Med. Soc., Soc. Am. Gastrointestinal Endoscopic Surgeons, Tex. Soc. Gastrointestinal Endoscopy, Soc. Laparoendoscopic Surgeons, Ninth Dist. Med. Soc., Am. Soc. for Gastrointestinal Endoscopy, Assn. Am. Physicians and Surgeons, Inc., Internat. Fedn. Socs. of Endoscopic Surgeons. Office: Philip L Leggett MD 800 Peakwood Ste 8B Houston TX 77090

LEGIDO, AGUSTIN, pediatric neurologist; b. Carinena, Spain, Sept. 9, 1957; came to U.S., 1985; s. Agustin and Maria Luisa (Cameo) L.; m. Elvira Isabel Zuazo, July 31, 1992; 1 child, Agustin Javier. BD, Goya Inst., Zaragoza, Spain, 1974; MD, Zaragoza U., 1980; PhD, Bologna U., 1981, Zaragoza U., 1985. Diplomate Am. Bd. Pediat., Am. Bd. Psychiatry & Neurology. Pediat. fellow Clinica Pediatrica II, Bologna, Italy, 1980-81; pediat. residency Hosp. Clin. Universitario, Zaragoza, 1981-85; pediat. neurology fellow Children's Hosp. Phila., 1985-87; neurology rsch. fellow U. Pa. Sch. Medicine, Phila., 1987-88; pediat. resident St. Christopher's Hosp. for Children, Phila., 1988-89, mem. attending staff, 1990—; neurologist Med. Coll. Pa., Phila., 1989-90, cons. in child neurology, 1992—; asst. prof. pediat. and neurology Temple U. Sch. Medicine, Phila., 1990-95, assoc. prof., 1995—; cons. in child neurology Albert Einstein Med. Ctr., Phila., 1993—. Roman Catholic. Office: St Christophers Hosp for Children Dept Neurology Philadelphia PA 19134-1095

LEGLER, DONALD WAYNE, dentist, university dean; b. Mpls., Oct. 2, 1931; s. Ernest W. and Almira (Elness) L; m. Janice Carol Cleworth, June 21, 1938; children: Lori, Lee, Catherine, Christian. BS, U. Minn., 1954, DDS, 1956; PhD, U. Ala., 1966. Lic. dentist Ala., Colo., Minn. Chmn. dept. oral biology U. Ala., Birmingham, 1968-71, 76-80, assoc. prof. dentistry, 1968-74, assoc. prof. microbiology Med. Ctr., 1969-80, asst. dean Sch. Dentistry, 1971-74, assoc. dean for adminstrv. affairs Sch. Dentistry, 1974-75, prof. dentistry, 1974-77, asst. dean for adminstrn., 1977-80; prof. dentistry, assoc. dean for rsch. and advanced edn. Sch. Dentistry U. Minn., Mpls., 1980-83, dir. Ctr. for Aging, 1981-83; prof. dentistry, dean Coll. Dentistry U. Fla., Gainesville, 1983—; curriculum cons. So. Assn. Colls. and Schs., Atlanta, 1973-75. Swedish Med. Rsch. Coun. fellow, 1966-67. Mem. ADA (curriculum cons. coun. on dental edn. 1974-88, commn. on nat. dental exams. 1993—), Fla. Dental Assn. (Dentist of Yr. award 1988), Internat. Assn. Dental Rsch., Am. Assn. Dental Schs. (chmn. coun. deans 1989-90). Office: U Fla Coll Dentistry PO Box 100405 Gainesville FL 32610-0405*

LEGLER, THEODORE REX, II, retired army officer, optometrist, clinical professor; b. Harlan, Ky., May 6, 1946; s. Theodore Rex and Mary Jane (Neese) L.; m. April C. Arington, Aug. 26, 1967; children: Melinda Melodie, Sara Cinnamon, Theodore Rex, III. AB in Optometry, Ind. U., 1968, AB in Zoology, 1969, OD, 1971; MA in Health Svcs. Mgmt., Webster U., St. Louis, 1982; grad. U.S. Army Command and Gen. Staff Coll., Fort Leavenworth, Kans., 1984. Diplomate Nat. Bd. Examiners. Commd. 2d lt. U.S. Army, 1968, advanced through grades to col., 1992; chief optometry clinic U.S. Army, Mannheim, Germany and Fort Ord, Calif., 1971-79; chief optical div. U.S. Army Med. Equipment and Optical Sch., Aurora, Colo., 1979-82; chief optometry svc., Fort Campbell, Ky., 1982-85; mem. faculty Acad. Health Svcs., U.S. Army, 1979-85, Regis Coll., Denver, 1979-82; affiliate prof. So. Coll. Optometry, Memphis, 1982-85, Pa. Coll. Optometry, Phila., 1988-91; chief optometry Svc. USA MEDDAC-Berlin, Fed. Republic Germany, 1985-88, Ft. Jackson, S.C., 1988-91; chief Optometry Svc. 130th Sta. Hosp., Heidlberg, Germany, 1991-95; optometry cons. 7th Med. Command USAREUR, 1991-95; Legion of Merits tech. cons. Surgeon Gen. U.S. Army, 1976-79; affiliate prof. Ind. U. Sch. Optometry, Bloomington, 1982-85. Active regional and nat. level Boy Scouts Am. Recipient Silver Beaver award Boy Scouts Am., 1973,Girls Scout of USA, (life). Fellow Am. Acad. Optometry; mem. VFW (life), Am. Optometric Assn. (Optometric Recognition award 1981-85, 87-92, 94—), Ind. Optometric Assn., Armed Forced Optometric Soc. (svc. award 1979), Assn. Mil. Surgeons U.S.(life), Ind. U. Alumni Assn. (life), Ind. U. "I" Men's Assn., South Carolina SAR & Indiana SAR, (life) Nat. Rifle Assn. (life), Compatriot, Nat. Eagle Scout Assn. (life), Beta Sigma Kappa, Omega Epsilon Phi (life). Republican. Mem. Ch. of Christ. Avocations: scouting, fishing. Home: 2468 E Blackford Ave Evansville IN 47714-2417 Office: I U Sch of Optometry 800 E Atwater Ave Bloomington IN 47405-3680

LEGOFFIC, FRANCOIS, biotechnology educator; b. Pluzunet, France, Nov. 10, 1936; s. Jacques and Marie LeGoffic; m. Marie-Thérèse Castel, Nov. 28, 1957; 1 child, Marc. Dr 3e Cycle, U. Paris, 1962, Dr Sci., 1963. Various positions Nat. Ctr. Sci. Rsch., France, 1962-74; prof. Ecole Nationale Supérieure de Chimie de Paris, 1975—; bd. dirs. UA 1389 du Centre Nat. de la Recherche Scientifique; vis. prof. Rolla U., 1975. Contbr. over 350 articles to Organic Chemistry, Biochemistry, Biotechnology and Microbiology; holder 20 patents. Recipient award Chem. Soc. France, 1968, Acad. Pharmacy, 1971, Acad. Scis., 1993; named Officier palmes academiques, 1994. Home: 42 rue Jean Georget, 92140 Clamart France Office: ENSCP, 11 rue Pierre Marie Curie, 75231 Paris France

LEHAR, THOMAS J., oncologist; b. Mpls., Nov. 7, 1933; s. Joseph L. and Marie (Capitola) L.; m. Barbara Osborn, June 23, 1964; 1 child, Shilpa Katherine. BA, BS, U. Minn., 1955, MD, 1958, MS, 1965. Intern Mpls. Gen. Hosp., 1958-59; resident Mayo Clinic, Rochester, Minn., 1959-60, 62-66; pvt. practice Sharp Rees-Stealy Med. Group, San Diego, 1966—; clin. prof. medicine U. Calif., San Diego, 1974—. Lt. USNR, 1960-62. Fellow ACP (gov. So. Calif. region III 1980-84); mem. Am. Soc. Clin. Oncology. Office: Sharp Rees-Stealy Med Group 2001 4th Ave San Diego CA 92101

LEHEW, WILLETTE LEWIS, obstetrician, gynecologist; b. Washington, Feb. 1, 1935; s. Allen Edwin and Roweno (Radcliff) L.; m. Myrene Putnam; children: Allen, Julie Anne, William, Scott. BS, Hampden-Sydney (Va.) Coll., 1957; MD, U. Va., Charlottesville, 1961. Resident East Va. Med. Sch., Norfolk, 1961-65; pvt. practice Norfolk, 1965—; assoc. prof. Ea. Va. Med. Sch., Norfolk; bd. dirs. Doctors Ins. Co. Va. Mem. Va. Coun. for Teenage Pregnancy Prevention; bd. trustees Hampden Sydney Coll., 1992-95, Med. Coll. of Hampton Rds., 1992—, vice rector, 1994-96, rector 1996—. Recipient Algernon-Sydney award Hampden-Sydney Coll., 1985. Fellow Am. Coll. Obstetricians and Gynecologists (Va. sect. chair 1995—); mem. South Atlantic Assn. Obstetricians and Gynecologists (v.p. 1989-90, pres. 1991-92), Seaboard Med. Soc. (pres. 1982), Va. Ob-Gyn. Soc. (sec.-treas. 1986-90, pres. 1992—), Norfolk Acad. Medicine (pres. 1982), Norfolk Yacht and Country Club (pres. 1983-85). Methodist. Home: 1209 S Fairwater Dr Norfolk VA 23508-1116 Office: Ob-Gyn Assn Tidewater 880 Kempvill Rd Norfolk VA 23502

LEHIGH, GEORGE EDWARD, medical group consultant, management consultant; b. Graettinger, Iowa, Feb. 3, 1927; s. Earl F. and Rachel F. (Baker) L.; m. Karla Bair; children: Bruce V., Susan Paige. Student, N.D. State U., 1944-45, W.Va. U., 1945; BA, Buena Vista Coll., 1948; postgrad., Drake U., 1949-50. Tchr. secondary schs., Iowa, 1953-54; prin. secondary schs., Iowa and Minn., 1948-51, 57-58; jr. exec. World Ins. Co., 1951-54; field cons. Profl. Mgmt. Midwest, Waterloo, Iowa, 1954-57; bus. adminstr. Mankato (Minn.) Clinic, 1958-70; adminstr. Austin (Tex.) Diagnostic Clinic, 1970-75, Jackson (Tenn.) Clinic, P.A., 1975-77; exec. adminstr. Thomas-Davis Clinic, P.C., Tucson, 1977-80; dir. adminstrn. law firm Brown, Maroney, Rose, Baker & Barber, Austin, 1980-82; exec. adminstr. Capitol Anesthesiology Assn., Austin, 1982-89; pres. A.P.S. Practice Mgmt., Inc., 1984-85; dir., treas. Profl. Health Services, Inc., Tucson, 1977-80. Bd. dirs. Credit Bur., Mankato, 1960-70, pres., 1967. Fellow Am. Coll. Med. Practice Execs.; mem. Med. Group Mgmt. Assn., Austin-Cen. Tex. Assn. Legal Adminstrs. (pres. 1981-82), Anesthesia Adminstrn. Assembly (chmn. 1983-85). Republican. Methodist.

LEHMAN, JOSEPH MANN, dermatologist; b. El Campo, Tex., Sept. 2, 1924; s. Alphonse Norman and Annie (Levine) L.; m. Sylvia Moss, June 20, 1948; children: Michele, Michael, Rene. MD, Southwestern U., Dallas, 1948; cert. dermatology, U. Pa., 1961. Diplomate Am. Bd. Dermatology. Intern Baylor Hosp., Dallas, 1948-49; pvt. practice gen. medicine O'Donnell, Tex., 1949-56; prin. Lehman Dermatology Clinic, Lubbock, Tex., 1961—; cons. Meth. Hosp., Lubbock, St. Mary's Hosp., Lubbock, 1961—. Capt. USAR, 1956-58. Fellow Am. Acad. Dermatology; mem. Tex. Med. Assn., Lubbock, Garza, Crosby County Med. Soc., Resident's Coun. Tex. Tech. U. Jewish. Office: 3715 21st St Lubbock TX 79410-1219

LEHMAN, RALPH A. W., neurosurgeon; b. July 21, 1937. AB, Harvard U., 1958, MD, 1962. Surgical resident Mass. Gen. Hosp., Boston, 1962-64; neurosurgical resident Washington U., St. Louis, 1966-69, asst. prof. neurosurgery, 1969-72; asst. & assoc. prof. neurosurgery U. Colo. Med. Ctr., Denver, 1972-78; prof. neurosurgery Pa. State U., Hershey, 1978—. Capt. U.S. Army, 1964-66. Mem. Am. Assn. Neurol. Surgeons, Am. Coll. Surgeons, Congress Neurol. Surgeons, Soc. Neurol. Surgeons. Office: Univ Hosp Divsn Neurosurgery 500 University Dr Hershey PA 17033

LEHMAN, RICHARD M., neurosurgeon; b. Phila., May 27, 1938; s. James A. Lehman and Adelaide (Asadorian) Lehman-Rea; m. Judith Burden; children: Michael, Allison, Jennifer; m. Sylvia Lewis, Dec. 3, 1989. BS, Princeton U., 1958; MD, Temple U., 1962. Diplomate Am. Bd. Neurol. Surgery. Assoc. prof. Robert Wood Johnson Med. Sch. U. Medicine & Dentistry N.J., New Brunswick, 1991—; co-chmn. Neuro/Ortho Spine Conf. Robert Wood Johnson Med. Sch., 1991—. Contbr. articles to profl. jours. Mem. AMA, ACS, Am. Assn. Neurol. Surgeons, Am. Epilepsy Soc., Am. & World Soc. Stereotactic & Functional Neurosurgery, Med. Soc. N.J., N.J. Neurosurg. Soc., Acad. Medicine N.J., Phila. Coll. Physicians, Middlesex County Med. Soc., European Soc. Stereotactic & Functional Neurosurgery. Office: U Medicine & Dentistry NJ Robert W Johnson Med Sch CAB Ste 2100 125 Patterson St New Brunswick NJ 08901

LEHMANN, HEINZ EDGAR, psychiatrist, consultant, researcher; b. Berlin, July 17, 1911; came to Can., 1937, naturalized, 1948; s. Richard and Emmy (Grönke) L.; m. Annette Joyal, July 28, 1940; 1 child, François. Abiturium, Mommsen Gymnasium, Berlin, 1929; M.D., U. Berlin, 1935; LL.D. (hon.), U. Calgary, Can., 1980. Clin. dir. Douglas Hosp., Montreal, Que., Can., 1947-66; dir. research Douglas Hosp., 1966-67; prof. psychiatry McGill U., Montreal, 1965—; emeritus prof. McGill U., 1981—, chmn. dept. psychiatry, 1970-74; cons. 4 Montreal hosps., 1976—; dep. commr. research N.Y. State Office Mental Health, Albany, 1980—. Contbr. over 300 articles to profl. jours., chpts. to books. Decorated officer Order of Can., 1975; recipient Albert Lasker award Lasker Found., 1957, Heinz Lehmann Rsch. award N.Y. State Office of Mental Health, 1990. Fellow Internat. Coll. Neuropsychopharmacology (pres. 1970-72), Can. Coll. Neuropsychopharmacology (Heinz Lehmann ann. award 1983), Que. Psychiat. Assn. (Heinz Lehmann ann. award 1986); mem. Am. Coll.

Neuropsychopharmacology (pres. 1965-66, life), Am. Psychiat. Assn. (life), Royal Soc. Can. Office: 1033 Pine Ave W, Montreal, PQ Canada H3A 1A1

LEHMANN, ROLF RICHARD, biologist, anatomist, educator; b. Genthin, Germany, Aug. 29, 1934; s. Karl Richard Johannes and Charlotte Margarete Alma (Helmecke) L.; m. Evelyn Margarete Thomas, May 24, 1963; 1 child, Sven Oliver. D of natural sci., U. Freiburg, Baden-Wurttemberg, 1965; Dr. habilitation, U. Münster, Westphalia, Germany, 1982. Rsch. assoc. dept. zoology U. Freiburg, Baden-Wurttemberg, 1965-66; rsch. assoc. dept. biology U. Rochester, N.Y., 1966-68, U. Freiburg, 1968-72; asst. prof. U. Southern Calif., L.A., 1973-75; researcher inst. arteriosclerosis U. Münster, Germany, 1975-80; lectr. dental sch. U. Münster, 1980-84, lectr. dept. anatomy, 1984-91, prof. dept. anatomy, 1991—; cons. Sickness Ins. Fund, Westphalia, 1983—. Author: Ecology of the Mouth, 1991, (videotape) Prevention and Oral Hygiene in Secondary Dentition, 1988; co-editor, co-author: Liver Transplantation in Children, 1993, State of Prevention and Therapy in Human Arteriosclerosis and Animals, 1978; co-author: Laser in Orthopedics, 1991, (video) Biotope Oral Cavity, 1996; contbr. articles to profl. jours. Recipient Fgn. Fellowship award Study Found. of German People 1966, Annual Sci. award Ministry for Rsch. and Tech. 1976, Internat. Video award French Dental Assn. 1985, 94. Mem. Internat. Assn. for Dental Rsch., European Orgn. for Caries Rsch., Soc. German Scientists and Physicians, German Soc. for Dentistry, German Dental Soc., German Anatomical Soc., German Assn. for Laser Medicine. Home: Bammeltring 29, D-48366 Laer Germany Office: U Münster Inst Anatomy, Vesaliusweg 2-4, D-48129 Münster Germany

LEHR, JEFFREY MARVIN, immunologist, allergist; b. N.Y.C., Apr. 29, 1942; s. Arthur and Stella (Smellow) L.; m. Suzanne Kozak, June 10, 1946; children: Elisa, Alexandra, Vanessa. BS, City Coll., Bklyn., 1963; MD, NYU, 1967. Resident, fellow Beth Israel Hosp., N.Y.C., 1968-72; resident in allergy/immunology, internal medicine Roosevelt Hosp., N.Y.C., 1968-72; allergist, immunologist Monterey, Calif., 1974—. Chmn. Monterey Bay Ari Pollution Hearing Bd., 1982-95; v.p. Lyceum of Monterey, 1977-83. Fellow Am. Acad. Allergy/Immunology, Am. Coll. Allergy/Immunology, Am. Assn. Cert. Allergists; mem. Am. Lung Assn. (v.p. 1989-91), Monterey County Med. Soc. (pres. 1988-89). Office: 798 Cass St Monterey CA 93940-2918 also: 262 San Jose St Salinas CA 93901-3901

LEHRER, JOEL FREDRIC, otolaryngologist; b. Bklyn., May 2, 1941; s. Isidore and Helen (Barach) L.; m. Nancy-Dean Murray, June 15, 1962; children: Brian, Hilary. AB, Cornell U., 1952; MD, SUNY, Bklyn.; 1956. Diplomate Am. Bd. Otolaryngology. Intern Kings Co. Hosp., Bklyn., 1956-57, resident in otolaryngology, 1959-61; resident in otolaryngology Mt. Sinai Hosp., N.Y.C., 1961-63, fellow, 1963-64; pvt. practice N.Y.C., 1964-73, Teaneck, N.J., 1968—; chief dept. otolaryngology Bergen Pines Hosp., Paramus, N.J., 1977-83, Holy Name Hosp., Teaneck, 1979-85, v.p., pres. physicians orgn., trustee. Contbr. articles to med. jours. Trustee First Option Health Plan, Red Bank, N.J., First Option Health Plan, Inc.; patroller Nat. Ski Patrol, Haystacks Mountain, Vt., 1973-88. Capt. M.C. USAF, 1957-59. Fellow ACS, Am. Neurootology Soc.; mem. Med. Soc. N.J., Bergen County Soc. Otlaryngologists (pres. 1987-91, Lotos Club (N.Y.C., pres. 1987-91). Office: 315 Cedar Ln Teaneck NJ 07666-3442

LEHRER, RANDEE H., health facility administrator; b. Queens, N.Y., June 12, 1958. BSN, U. S.C., 1979; MBA, U. Tampa, 1987. RN, Tex. Staff nurse Richland Meml. Hosp., Columbia, S.C., 1979-80, St. Joseph's Hosp., Tampa, Fla., 1980-82; dir. nursing and comm. health svcs. Med. Pers. Pool, Tampa, 1982-83; coord. devel. Tampa Bay Health Plan, St. Petersburg, Fla., 1983-84; dir. health svcs. Physicians Health Plan Fla., Tampa, 1985-88; mgr. mgmt. consulting svcs. Ernest & Young, Tampa, 1988-90; dir. mgmt. consulting svcs. Tampa Bay Assn., Tampa, 1990-91; adminstrv. dir. St. Joseph Children's Hosp., Tampa, 1991-93; dir. managed care Tex. Children's Hosp., Houston, 1993-95; pres. Tex. Children's Health Plan, Houston, 1995—.

LEHRER, RUTH JEANNETTE, social work supervisor; b. N.Y.C., Apr. 17, 1923; d. Samuel and Mollie (Berman) Kinbar; widowed. BS, Hunter Coll., 1944; MSW, Columbia U., 1946. Med. social worker Jewish Hosp. of Bklyn., 1946; social worker N.Y. Assn. for New Ams., N.Y.C., 1946-50; med. social worker Maimonides Hosp., Bklyn., 1950-51; social worker Jewish Family Svc. Assn., Essex County, N.J., 1951-58; med. social worker Mt. Sinai Hosp., N.Y.C., 1958-59; social worker N.Y. Guild for Jewish Blind, N.Y.C., 1959-61, Wiltwyck Sch. for Boys, N.Y.C., 1961-64; sr. social worker Lincoln Hosp. Community Mental Health Ctr., Bronx, N.Y., 1964-67; instr. Albert Einstein Sch. Medicine, 1964-67; sr. social work supr. Maimonides Hosp. Community Mental Health Ctr., Bklyn., 1967—. Mem. NASW. Home: 129 W 89th St New York NY 10024-1908

LEHRMAN, NATHANIEL SAUL, retired psychiatrist; b. May 26, 1923. SB cum laude, Harvard U., 1942; MD, Albany Med. Coll., 1946. Diplomate Am. Bd. Psychiatry and Neurology; cert. psychoanalysis. Rotating intern Jewish Hosp. of Bklyn., 1946-47; resident in psychiatry Bellevue Hosp., N.Y.C., 1947-48; psychiat. tng. Hillside Hosp., Glen Oaks, N.Y., 1950-51, Creedmoor Hosp., 1951-52; pvt. practice Great Neck, N.Y., 1953-64; staff psychiatrist Kings Park (N.Y.) State Hosp., 1964-67; supervising psychiatrist, chief of svc., asst. dir. Bronx (N.Y.) State Hosp., 1967-73; clin. dep. dir. Kingsboro Psychiat. Ctr. Kingsboro Psychiat. Ctr./Bklyn. State Hosp., 1973-78; staff psychiatrist rsch. Creedmoor Psychiat. Ctr., Queens Village, N.Y., 1978-81; pvt. practice rsch. and writing, 1981-91, ret., 1991. Contbr. articles to med. jours. Pres., Nob Hill Pool Club, Roslyn, N.Y., 1982, v.p., 1988-89. Capt. M.C., AUS, 1948-50. Recipient New Frontiers award, Am. Friends Jerusalem Mental Health Ctr., 1989. Fellow Am. Psychiat. Assn. (life, cert. in adminstrv. psychiatry 1975).

LEHRMAN, ROY EDWARD, dentist; b. Decatur, Ind., Sept. 5, 1953; s. Roy Herman and Mary Adeline (Holthouse) L.; m. Brenda Gail Stone, June 12, 1980; children: Alexander Edward, Olivia Anne. BA, Ind. U., 1975; DDS, Emory U., 1980. Dentist Central State Hosp., Milledgeville, Ga., 1980-81; pvt. practice Milledgeville, 1981—. Pres. Am. Cancer Soc., Milledgeville, 1984-86, treas. 1986-88; mem. Parish Coun., 1983—, bldg. and fin. com., 1986—, Eucharistic minister, 1985—, pres. elect 1991; bd. dirs. Baldwin County Coun. on Child Abuse, 1989—. Named to Outstanding Young Men in Am., 1987, 88, 89; recipient Outstanding Svc. award, Am. Cancer Soc., 1985. Master Acad. Gen. Dentistry (dental care chmn. 1990-92, cen. dist. dir. 1991-92, newsletter editor 1992-93); mem. ADA (Recognition award 1987), Ga. Acad. Gen. Dentistry (pres. elect 1993-94, pres. 1994-95), Ga. Dental Assn., Oconee Dental Study Club (founder, charter pres.), Cen. Dist. Dental Assn., Milledgeville C. of C. (Small Bus. Owner of Yr. 1987), Milledgeville Exch. Club (pres. 1986-87, treas. 1987-88, v.p. 1985-86, Exchangite of Yr. 1986), KC (Grand Knight 1988-89, Dep. Grand Knight 1987-88, fin. sec. 1993—), Delta Sigma Delta (treas. 1977-78, pres. 1978-80, Sr. Appreciation award 1980). Republican. Roman Catholic. Home: 3638 Sussex Dr NE Milledgeville GA 31061-9339 Office: 530 W Thomas St Ste F Milledgeville GA 31061-2744

LEHRNER, LAWRENCE MARSHALL, physician; b. Cin., Feb. 9, 1949; s. Harold Nathan and Ruth (Begun) L.; m. Marilyn Jacobs, Aug. 23, 1970 (div.); children: Stephanie, David. BS, Ind. U., 1971, PhD, 1974, MD, 1975. Diplomate Am. Bd. Internal Medicine, Nephrology. Resident in internal medicine William Beaumont Army Hosp., El Paso, Tex., 1976-79, internist, 1979-80; fellowship in nephrology Southwestern Med. Sch., Dallas, 1980-82; nephrologist U.S. Army Inst. of Surg. Rsch., San Antonio, 1982-85; internist Aspen Med., Las Vegas, 1985-87; nephrologist Nephrology and Endocrine Assocs., Las Vegas, 1987—; chief dept. medicine Humana Hosp. Sunrise, Las Vegas, 1991-92, med. exec. com., 1991-92, chief nephrology, 1989-90, dir. utilization rev., 1989-90. Contbr. numerous articles to profl. jours. Trustee B'nai B'rith Nate Mack Lodge, Las Vegas, 1992—, pres., 1988-89, v.p. membership, 1987-88; vice chmn. Nev. Physicians Caucus, Las Vegas, 1991. Maj. U.S. Army, 1976-85. Fellow ACP; mem. AMA, Internat. Soc. Nephrology, Am. Soc. Nephrology, Sigma Xi, Phi Eta Sigma. Jewish. Home: 187 Reed Ln Henderson NV 89014 Office: Nephrology & Endocrine Assocs 500 S Rancho Dr # 12 Las Vegas NV 89106-4844

LEHTONEN, LIISA ANNIKKI, pediatrician; b. Oulu, Finland, Dec. 14, 1962; d. Pekka and Anja (Leskinen) L. MD, Oulu (Finland) Med. Sch., 1986; degree in pediat., Turku (Finland) U., 1993, PhD, 1994, degree in neonatology, 1996. Gen. practitioner Health Ctr., Tornio, Finland, 1986-87; resident Ctrl. Hosp., Kajaani, Finland, 1987-90; resident in pediat. U. Hosp., Turku, Finland, 1990-93, fellow in neonatology, 1993-96; rsch. fellow McGill U.-Montréal Children's Hosp. Rsch. Inst., 1996—; pvt. practice, Turku, 1990—. Mem. Finnish Soc. Pediat., Finnish Soc. Perinatology. Home: Henrikinkatu 1 A 30, 20500 Turku Finland Office: Turku U Hosp, Kiinamyllynkatu 4-8, 20520 Turku Finland

LEIBOWITZ, MORTON MITCHEL, internist, educator; b. Bklyn., Dec. 25, 1939; s. Jacob and Chaye (Rozman) L.; m. Ruth Weinberg, Feb. 21, 1993; children: David, Mindy, Joshua. BA, CUNY, 1961; MD, NYU, 1965. Diplomate Am. Bd. Internal Medicine. Intern Bellevue Hosp., N.Y.C., 1965-66, resident in internal medicine; fellow N.Y. Hosp., N.Y.C.; pvt. practice, N.Y.C., 1971—; spl. cons. Hosp. Plan N.Y., N.Y.C.; instr. clin. medicine NYU Sch. Medicine, N.Y.C., asst. prof., until 1979, assoc. prof., 1979—; vis. prof. Meier Hosp., Kfor Saba, Israel. Sr. asst. surgeon USPHS, 1966-70. Fellow ACP, Am. Coll. Cardiology; mem. Am. Soc. Echocardiography, N.Y. Heart Assn., New York County Med. Soc., Alpha Omega Alpha. Office: NY Med Assocs 907 Fifth Ave New York NY 10021

LEICHTMAN, HARRY MACGREGOR, psychologist; b. Washington, Nov. 3, 1949; s. Edwin Sylvester and Dorothy Esther (Moore) L.; m. Susan Turriff, Aug. 26, 1978; children: Andrew, Jeffrey. B.A., Coll. William and Mary, 1972; M.A., Northwestern U., 1975, Ph.D., 1978. Lic. psychologist, Mass. Predoctoral clin. intern Judge Baker Children's Ctr., Boston, 1975-76; assoc. dir. Wediko Children's Svcs., Boston, 1976-82; cons. delinquency sect. Judge Baker Children's Ctr. and Childrens Hosp., Boston, 1979-80; orgnl. cons., 1981—; dir. HaML Clin. Assocs., Needham, Mass., 1982—; instr., clin. asst. prof. Northeastern U., 1991—. Author: Helping Work Environments Work, 1996. Fellow Mass. Psychol. Assn., Am. Orthopsychiat. AsSn.; mem. Mass. Coun. of Human Svc. Providers, Assn. Family and Conciliation Ctrs., Soc. for Rsch. in Child Devel. Home: 26 Whitney Rd Newton MA 02160-2429 Office: HaML Clin Assocs 388 Hillside Ave Needham MA 02194-1221

LEIER, CARL VICTOR, internist, cardiologist; b. Bismarck, N.D., Oct. 20, 1944; married; 3 children. BA, Creighton U., 1965, MD cum laude, 1969. Diplomate Am. Bd. Internal Medicine, Cardiovascular Medicine, Critical Care Medicine, Geriatric Medicine, Nat. Bd. Med. Examiners; lic. med., surgical Nebr., med. Ohio. Intern Ohio State U. Coll. Medicine, Columbus, 1969-70, med. resident (instr.) dept. medicine, 1971-73, chief resident (instr.), 1973-74, fellowship divsn. cardiology, 1974-76; pathology resident dept. pathology St. Vincent Hosp., Worcester, Mass., 1970-71; trainee NIH Tng. Grant, 1974-75; asst. prof. medicine cardiology dept., Ohio State U. Coll. Medicine, Columbus, 1976-80, asst. prof. pharmacology, 1976-80, assoc. prof., 1980-84, faculty mem. grad. sch., 1980—, dir. rsch. divsn. cardiology, 1980-83, James W. Overstreet prof. of medicine, 1983—, prof. of medicine divsn. cardiology, 1984—, prof. pharmacology, dept. pharmacology, 1984—, dir. divsn. cardiology, 1986—; internship selection com. dept. medicine, Ohio State U., 1973-74, hosp. procedures com. Ohio State U. Hosps., 1973-74; mem. pharmacology and therapeutics com. Ohio State U. Hosps., 1976-80; mem. rsch. com. ctrl. Ohio chpt. Am. Heart Assn., 1977-84, bd. trustees, 1979-88, exec. rsch. com., 1979-84, vice chmn. rsch. com., 1980-82, chmn. rsch. peer rev. com., 1982-84, v.p., 1984-86, pres. elect, 1986-88; numerous other coms.; cons. cardiorenal adv. bd. Smith-Kline Labs., 1982-85, com. on cardio-vascular rsch. and devel., 1982-85., AMA on Drugs and Tech., 1985—, Lilly-Elanco devel. ractopamine, 1989; mem. ad hoc adv. com. on carvedilol in congestive heart failure, Smith, Kline and Beacham Pharms., 1991, ad hoc adv. com. on PDEI devel., McNeil Pharms., 1991, ad hoc adv. com. for clin. trials on Ibopamine, Zambon Pharms., 1993, sci. adv. com. Ohio State Univ. Brain Tumor Rsch. Ctr., 1993—, data safety monitoring bd., Otsuka Vesnarinone Trials, 1993— mem. chmn. Annual Sci. Sessions Planning Com. of the Am. Coll. of Cardiolog, 1996-97; vis. prof., lectr. and presenter at numerous sci. confs., insts. in U.S. and internationally. Editor: (book) Cardiotonic Drugs, 1986, 2d rev. edit., 1991; co-author (with H. Boudoulas) CardioRenal Disorders and Diseases, 1986, 2d edit., 1992 (with J. Vincent) Critical Care Medicine: Recent Advances in Cardiovascular Medicine, 1990; contbr. more than 40 chpts. to other medical books and almost 200 articles to peer reviewed jours. including: Vascular Surgery, Archives of Internal Medicine, Circulation, Brit. Heart Jour., Jour. Electrocardiology, Clinical Pharmacologic Therapy, Chest, Am. Jour. Medicine, Jour. Cardiovascular Pharmacology, Am. Heart Jour., Geriatrics, Annals of Internal Medicine and others; editor in chief Congestive Heart Failure: Index and Revs., 1988—; mem. editorial bds. of ten medical jours. concerned with heart diseases, the review bds. of others including New Eng. Jour. Medicine, Internat. Jour. Cardiology, Jour. of Lab. and Clin. Medicine. Recipient Upjohn award, 1969, Lange Scholar award, 1969, Golden Apple Student Tchg. award, 1973, 75, Young Investigator award Ctrl. Ohio Heart Chpt., Am. Heart Assn., 1976-78, Rsch. Recognition award, 1978; named One of Best Doctors of Columbus, Columbus Monthly, 1992. Fellow Am. Coll. Clin. Pharmacology, Coun. on Clin. Pharmacology, Am. Heart Assn., Am. Coll. Cardiology, Am. Coll. Physicians, Coun. on Geriatric Cardiology; mem. AAAS, Ohio State Med. Assn., Am. Fedn. for Clin. Rsch. Ctrl. Soc. for Clin. Rsch., Am. Soc. Clin. Investigation, Assn. Univ. Cardiologists, Internat. Soc. for Heart Rsch., Internat. Soc. Cardiovascular Pharmacotherapy, Assn. Profs. of Cardiology. Office: Ohio State Univ Med Ctr Divsn Cardiology Columbus OH 43210

LEIFER, MARVIN WILLIAM, physician; b. Albany, N.Y., Feb. 8, 1945; Seymour and Anne (Swidler) L.; m. Lynn Joy Burkes, Nov. 14, 1976. BA, Univ. Chgo., 1966; MD, SUNY, Bklyn., 1970. Diplomate: Am. Bd. Psychiatry and Neurology. Intern L.I. Jewish Med. Ctr., New Hyde Park, N.Y., 1970-71; resident in psychiatry Albert Einstein Coll. Medicine, Bronx, N.Y., 1971-74, rsch. fellow in psychopharmacology, 1974-76; dir. univ. psychiat. svcs. SUNY, Stony Brook, N.Y., 1976-77; dir. outpatient psychopharmacology svcs. Bellevue Hosp. Ctr., N.Y.C., 1977-81; dir. clerkship program in psychiatry NYU Sch. of Medicine, 1981-83; dir. cen. evaluation svc. Bellevue Psychiatric Hosp. Outpatient Clinics, N.Y.C., 1981-83; dir. outpatient dept. St. Vincent's Hosp. Westchester, Harrison, N.Y., 1983-90; dir., chmn. dept. psychiatry Helene Fuld Med. Ctr., Trenton, N.J., 1990-94; med. dir. addiction recovery svcs. U. Medicine and Dentistry N.J., Piscataway, 1994—; asst. prof. SUNY, Stony Brook, 1976-77; asst. prof. NYU Sch. of Medicine, 1977-82; clin. assoc. prof. NYU, 1982-83; clin. assoc. prof. N.Y. Med. Coll., Valhalla, 1983-90; clin. assoc. prof. N.J. Medicine and Dentistry N.J., 1990—. Author and co-author articles in profl. jours. Recipient: individual rsch. fellowship, NIMH, 1974-76. Mem. Am. Psychiat. Assn., Am. Soc. Addiction Medicine (cert.). Office: Helene Fuld Med Ctr 185 W End Ave New York NY 10023-5539 also: 42 N Tulane St Princeton NJ 08540

LEIFERT, MELVYN MARTIN, orthodontist, dental educator; b. Bklyn., Sept. 23, 1942; s. Morris and Ida (Gumer) L.; m. Ellen J. Simels, Oct. 4, 1972; children: John L., Michael F. BS, CCNY, 1963; DDS, SUNY, Buffalo, 1967, cert. proficiency, 1969. Diplomate Am. Bd. Orthodontics. Pres., pvt. practice Melvyn M. Leifert, D.D.S., P.C., N.Y.C., 1969—; asst. attending orthodontist French and Poly Clinic Hosp., N.Y.C., 1970-76; assoc. prof. dentistry Columbia U. Sch. Dentistry and Oral Surgery, N.Y.C., 1974—. Organizer, planner, dir. Teen Health Happening, Poly Clinic Hosp., N.Y.C., 1973. Scholar N.Y. State Regents Coll. Fellow N.Y. Acad. Dentistry, N.Y. Acad. Orthodontics (founder 1994), Sigma Xi, Omicron Kappa Upsilon (Faculty award 1988); mem. Am. Assn. Orthodontists. Home: 14 Rutland Rd Great Neck NY 11020 Office: 30 Fifth Ave New York NY 10011

LEIFMAN, HOWARD DAVID, psychotherapist, consultant; b. Miami, Fla., Aug. 24, 1956; s. Harvey and Renee (Ellis) L. BA, Syracuse U., 1977, MA, 1978; MSW, NYU, 1987, postgrad., 1992—. Cert. social worker. Acct. exec. Bozell & Jacob, N.Y.C., 1978-79; acct. supr. PR AIDS, N.Y.C., 1979-81; dir. mktg. Hearst Corp.-King Features, N.Y.C., 1982-84; acct. dir. West Glen Com., N.Y.C., 1984-86; dir. social svcs. Stuyvesant Poly. Clinic, N.Y.C., 1987-88; dir. spl. svcs. NYU, N.Y.C., 1988-94; cons. Towers Perrin Health, Valhalla, N.Y., 1994—; workshop leader Stern Sch. Bus., N.Y.C., 1989—; bd. dirs. Appleby Found., 1985—; cons. for Fortune 500 cos. Mem. NASW, Coll. Placement Coun. Democrat. Jewish. Office: Towers Perrin Health 100 Summit Lake Dr Valhalla NY 10595

LEIGH, HOYLE, psychiatrist, educator, writer; b. Seoul, Korea, Mar. 25, 1942; came to U.S., 1965; m. Vincenta Masciandaro, Sept. 16, 1967; 1 child, Alexander Hoyle. MA, Yale U., 1982; MD, Yonsei U., Seoul, 1965. Diplomate Am. Bd. Psychiatry and Neurology. Asst. prof. Yale U., New Haven, 1971-75, assoc. prof., 1975-80, prof., 1980-89, lectr. in psychiatry, 1989—; dir. Behavioral Medicine Clinic, Yale U., 1980-89; dir. psychiat. cons. svc. Yale-New Haven Hosp., 1971-89; chief psychiatry VA Med Ctr., Fresno, Calif., 1989—; prof., vice chmn. dept. psychiatry U. Calif., San Francisco, 1989—, head dept. psychiatry, 1989—; cons. Am. Jour. Psychiatry, Archives Internal Medicine, Psychosomatic Medicine. Author: The Patient, 1980, 2d edit., 1985, 3d edit., 1992; editor: Psychiatry in the Practice of Medicine, 1983, Consultation-Liaison Psychiatry: 1990's & Beyond, 1994. Fellow ACP, Internat. Coll. Psychosomatic Medicine (v.p.), Am. Acad. Psychosomatic Medicine; mem. AMA, AAUP, World Psychiat. Assn. Office: U Calif Dept Psychiat 2615 E Clinton Ave Fresno CA 93703-2223

LEIGHNINGER, DAVID SCOTT, cardiovascular surgeon; b. Youngstown, Ohio, Jan. 16, 1920; s. Jesse Harrison and Marjorie (Lightner) L.; m. Margaret Jane Malony, May 24, 1942; children: David Allan, Jenny. BA, Oberlin Coll., 1942; MD, Case Western Res. U., 1945. Intern Univ. Hosps. of Cleve., 1945-46, resident, 1949-51, asst. surgeon, 1951-68; rsch. fellow in cardiovascular surgery rsch. lab. Case Western Res. U. Sch. Medicine, Cleve., 1948-49, 51-55, 57-67, instr. surgery, 1951-55, sr. instr., 1957-64, asst. prof., 1964-68, asst. clin. prof., 1968-70; resident Cin. Gen. Hosp., 1955-57; practice medicine specializing in cardiovascular surgery, Cleve., 1957-70; pvt. practice medicine specializing in cardiovascular and gen. surgery Edgewater Hosp., Chgo., 1970-82, staff surgeon, also dir. emergency surg. services, 1970-82; staff surgeon, also dir. emergency surg. svcs. Mazel Med. Ctr., Chgo., 1970-82; emergency physician Miner's Hosp., Raton, N.Mex., 1982-83, 84-85, No. Colfax County Hosp., Raton, 1983-84, Mt. San Rafael Hosp., Trinidad, Colo., 1984-85; assoc., courtesy, or cons. staff Marymount Hosp., Cleve., Mt. Sinai Hosp., Cleve., Geauga Community Hosp., Chardon, Ohio, Bedford Community Hosp (Ohio), 1957-70. Tchr. tng. courses in CPR for med. personnel, police, fire and vol. rescue workers, numerous cities, 1950-70. Served to capt., M.C., AUS, 1946-48. Recipient Chris award Columbus Internat. Film Festival, 1964, numerous other award for sci. exhibits from various nat. and state med. socs., 1953-70; USPHS grantee, 1949-68. Fellow Am. Coll. Cardiology, Am. Coll. Chest Physicians; mem. AMA, N.Mex. Med. Assn., Colfax County Med. Assn., Ill. Med. Assn., Chgo. Med. Assn., U. Cin. Grad. Sch. Surg. Soc. Contbr. numerous articles to med. jours., chpts. to med. texts; spl. pioneer research (with Claude S. Beck) in physiopathology of coronary artery disease and CPR; developed surg. treatment of coronary artery disease; achieved 1st successful defibrillation of human heart, 1st successful reversal of fatal heart attack; provided 1st intensive care of coronary patients. Home: HC 68 Box 77 Fort Garland CO 81133-9708

LEIGHTON, LESLIE STEVEN, gastroenterologist; b. N.Y.C., Jan. 18, 1952; s. Fred Victor and Sitty (Hess) L.; m. Deborah Gilda Perl, Apr. 25, 1982; children: Andrew David, Lauren Sophia, Jennifer Ellen, Rachel Johanna. BA with high distinction, U. Va., 1974; MD, Johns Hopkins U., 1978. Diplomate Am. Bd. Internal Medicine, Am. Bd. Gastroenterology. Intern, then resident in medicine NYU-Bellevue Hosp., N.Y.C., 1978-81; gastroenterology fellow Brigham and Women's Hosp., Boston, 1981-84; teaching asst. NYU Sch. Medicine, N.Y.C., 1980-81; clin. fellow Harvard Med. Sch., Boston, 1981-83, rsch. fellow, 1983-84; pvt. practice Peachtree Gastroenterology, P.C., Atlanta, 1984—; clin. instr. Emory U. Sch. Medicine, Atlanta, 1986-90, clin. asst. prof. medicine, 1990—; chmn. dept. internal medicine Ga. Bapt. Med. Ctr., 1991-94; asst. clin. prof. medicine Med. Coll. Ga., 1992—; staff physician Piedmont Hosp., Atlanta, 1984—. Vice chmn. Nat. Found. Ileitis and Colitis, Atlanta, 1989-91, chmn., 1991-93. Mem. AMA, Med. Assn. Atlanta, Am. Gastroenterol. Assn., Am. Coll. Physicians, Am. Coll. Gastroenterology, Druid Hills Golf Club, Buckhead Club. Office: Peachtree Gastroenterol PC 95 Collier Rd NW Ste 4075 Atlanta GA 30309-1721

LEIGHTON, RICHARD F., dean. BA, Western Md. Coll., 1951; MD, U. Md., 1955. Diplomate Am. Bd. Internal Medicine (Specialty Cardiovascular Disease). Intern U. Hosp., Balt., 1955-56; flight surgeon USN, 1956-58; resident Ohio State U. Hosp., 1959-61, resident, cardiology fellow, 1961-64; from asst. prof. to assoc. prof. medicine Coll. Medicine Ohio State U., 1965-74, dir. coronary care unit, 1968-69, dir. cardiac catheterization labs., 1970-74; prof. medicine, chief cardiology Med. Coll. Ohio, 1974-90, acting chmn. dept. medicine, 1988, vice chmn., 1988-90, v.p. acad. affairs, dean Sch. Medicine, 1990-95, sr. v.p. acad. affairs, dean Sch. Medicine, 1995—. Editl. bd. La Lettre du Cardiologue, 1985—; contbr. numerous articles to profl. jours. Fellow ACP, Am. Coll. Cardiology (gov. Ohio chpt. 1985-88), Am. Heart Assn (coun. circulation, epidemiology, clinical cardiology, coun. rep. Ohio 1977-80), Royal Soc. Medicine; mem. Ctrl. Soc. Clin. Rsch., Societe Francaise Cardiologies (corr.), Alpha Omega Alpha. Office: Med Coll Ohio Off Dean Toledo OH 43699*

LEIKIN, JERROLD BLAIR, emergency room physician, toxicologist; b. Chgo., Aug. 28, 1954; s. Mitchell and Evelyn (Ucitel) L.; m. Robin Ellen Goldman, June 6, 1982; children: Scott Michael, Eryn Nicole. BS, U. Iowa, 1976; MD, Chgo. Med. Sch., 1980. Diplomate Am. Bd. Internal Medicine, Am. Bd. Emergency Medicine, Am. Bd. Med. Toxicology, Am Bd. Quality Assurance and Utilization Rev. Physicians. Resident Evanston (Ill.) Hosp., 1980-82, Northwestern Meml. Hosp., Chgo., 1982-84; fellow Cook County Hosp., Chgo., 1984-87; chief med. emergency svcs. U. Ill. Hosp., Chgo., 1984-88; assoc. dir. Rush Emergency Svcs. Rush Presbyn. St. Luke Med. Ctr., Chgo., 1988—, med. dir. Rush Poison Control Ctr., 1989—; cons. Underwriter Labs., Northbrook, Ill., 1991—; reviewer Jour. Clin. Toxicology, Omaha, 1990—. Co-author: Poisoning and Toxicology Handbook; contbr. articles to profl. jours. Fellow ACP, Am. Coll. Emergency Physicians; mem. AMA (adv. bd. AMA Jour.), Am. Acad. Clin. Toxicology. Office: Rush Presbyn St Luke Med Ct 1753 W Congress Pky Chicago IL 60612-3809

LEIS, HENRY PATRICK, JR., surgeon, educator; b. Saranac Lake, N.Y., Aug. 12, 1914; s. Henry P. and Mary A. (Disco) L.; m. Winogene Barnette, Jan. 8, 1944; children: Henry Patrick III, Thomas Frederick. BS cum laude, Fordham U., 1936; MD, N.Y. Med. Coll., 1941. Diplomate Am. Bd. Surgery. Intern Flower and Fifth Ave Hosps., N.Y.C., 1941-42, resident, 1943-44, 46-49, attending surgeon, chief breast service, 1960-81; resident in surgery Kanawa Valley Hosp., Charleston, W.Va., 1942-43; attending surgeon, chief breast service Met. Hosp., N.Y.C., 1960-81, emeritus chief breast service, 1982—; attending surgeon Coler Meml. Hosp., N.Y.C., 1960-76; chief breast surgery Cabrini Hosp. Med. Ctr., 1978-85, cons. breast surgery, 1985—; emeritus surgeon Lenox Hill Hosp.,, N.Y.C., 1980-83, hon. surg. staff, 1984—; hon. surg. staff Drs. Hosp., N.Y.C.; hon. surg. staff, cons. breast surgery Breast Diagnostic Ctr. Columbia Grand Strand Regional Med. Ctr., Myrtle Beach, S.C., 1985—; liason officer Am. Coll. Surgeons Commn. on Cancer; attending surgeon Westchester County Med. Ctr., 1977-81, emeritus surgeon, 1982—; clin. prof. surgery U. S.C. Sch. Medicine, Breast Surg. Oncology, Columbia, 1985—; hon. dir. breast cancer ctr., cons. in breast surgery Winthrop Univ. Hosp., Mineola, 1971—; cons. in breast surgery VA Hosp., Columbia, S.C., 1985—; cons. in breast surgery St. Claires Hosp., N.Y.C., 1979; attending surg. staff Richland Meml. Hosp., Columbia, 1986-90; clin. prof. surgery, 1960-81, prof. emeritus, 1982—, co-dir. Inst. Breast Diseases, 1978-82, emeritus, 1982—, chief breast svc. N.Y. Med. Coll., 1960-81, emeritus, 1982—; cons. in breast surgery SUNY Div. Rehab., 1965—, Med. and Surg. Specialists Plan N.Y.; mem. Am. Joint Com. on Breast Cancer Staging and End Results; v.p. N.Y. Met. Breast Cancer Group, 1975-76, pres., 1977-79; cons. Med. Advs. Selective Svc. System, N.Y.C. Alumni trustee N.Y. Med. Coll., 1971-76; adv. coun. Fordham Coll. Pharmacy, 1968; bd. dirs. Hall Fame and Mus. Surg. History and Related Scis. Author: Diagnosis and Treatment of Breast Lesions: The Breast, 1970, Management of Breast Lesions, 1978, Breast Cancer: Conservative and Reconstructive Surgery, 1989, Breast Lesions: Diagnosis and Treatment, 1988; co-editor: Breast; hon. editor Internat. Surgery Jour.; mem. editorial bd. jour. Senolgia, 1982—, Breast: An Internat. Jour.; contbr. articles to profl. jours. Mem. Women's Cancer Task Force of S.C. Capt. M.C., AUS, 1944-46, PTO. Decorated knight Grand Cross Equestrian Order Holy Sepulchre Jerusalem, knight Mil., Order of Malta, Knight Noble Co. of the Rose; recipient award of Merit Am. Cancer Soc., 1969, 87, cert. and award for outstanding and devoted services to indigent sick City N.Y., 1965, Dr. George Hohman Meml. medal, 1936, N.Y. Apothecaries medal,

1936, Internat. cert. merit for disting. service to surgery, 1970, award of merit N.Y. Met. Breast Cancer Group, 1976, medal of Ambrogino (Italy), 1977, Service award of Honor N.Y. Med. Coll., 1969, medaille d'Honneur (France), medal of City of Paris, 1979. Fellow ACS (cancer liaison physician Surgeons commn. on Cancer 1987—, Peruvian Acad. Surgery (hon.), Am. Acad. Compensation Medicine, Am. Soc. Clin. Oncology, Am. Assn. Cancer Rsch., Am. Geriatrics Soc., Indsl. Med. Assn., Internat. Coll. Surgeons (1st v.p. 1973-74, pres. 1977-78, v.p., chmn. coun. examiners U.S. sect. 1962-68, pres. 1971, Svc. award of honor 1971), Internat. Paleopathology Assn. (founder), N.Y. Acad. Medicine, N.Y. Coun. Surgeons, Royal Soc. Health (Eng.); mem. AMA, AAAS, AAUP, Am. Cancer Soc. (com. breast cancer), Am. Med. Writers Assn., Am. Profl. Practice Assn., Assn. Am. Med. Colls., Am. Coll. Radiology (com. mammography and breast cancer), Assn. Mil. Surgeons U.S., Cath. Physicians Guild (pres. N.Y. 1970-78), Gerontol. Soc., Internat. Platform Assn., N.Y. Cancer Soc., N.Y. County Med. Soc., N.Y. Surg. Soc., Pan Am Med. Assn. (v.p. N.Am. sect. on cancer 1967—), Pan Pacific Surg. Assn. (v.p. 1980, Resfficers Assn. U.S., Soc. Acad. Achievement (editorial bd. 1969—), Nat. Consortium Breast Ctrs. (bd. dris. 1991—), Soc. Med. Jurisprudence, Soc. Nuclear Medicine Surg. Soc. N.Y. Med. Coll., WHO, World Med. Assn., Alumni Assn. N.Y. Med. Coll. (gov. 1960—, pres. 1971), Assn. Mil. Surgeons U.S., Catholic War Vets Assn., VFW, Hollywood Acad. Medicine (hon.), Alpha Omega Alpha, Phi Chi; hon. mem. Argentine Soc. Mammary Pathology, Argentina Cardiac and Thoracic Surg. Soc., Ecuador Med. Assn., Mo. Surg. Soc., Venezuela Surg. Soc., Italian Surg. Soc., S.C. Oncology Soc., So. Med. Assn. Club: Surf, Rotary. Lodge: K.C. (4th deg.).

LEITE, CARLOS ALBERTO, physician, medical educator; b. Rio de Janeiro, Feb. 2, 1939; s. Indayassu and Munira (Raed) L. BSc, Coleg. Ext. Sao Jose, Rio de Janeiro, 1956; MD, U. Brazil, Rio de Janeiro, 1962, PhD, 1972. Intern Rochester (N.Y.) Gen. Hosp., 1963-64; resident Henry Ford Hosp., Detroit, 1964-65; resident, fellow, researcher Jackson Meml. Hosp. and U. Miami, Fla., 1965-68; ltd. practice Nanticoke Meml. Hosp., Seaford, Del., 1968; prof. medicine U. Fed. de Rio de Janeiro, 1972—; emeritus prof. medicine Faculty Medicine Soc. Ens. Sup. Nova Iguacu, Rio de Janeiro, 1986—; dir. Hosp. de Nova Iguacu-Posse, Rio de Janeiro, 1991; instr. medicine Fac. Nac. Med., U. Fed. Rio de Janeiro, 1963-72; chief in-patient ward Santa Casa da Misericordia Hosp., Rio de Janeiro, 1968-72, chief outpatient dept., 1968-76, cons. physician surg. unit, 1969—; chercheur visitant temporaire Inst. Pasteur, Paris, 1988; prof. U. Fed. Rio de Janeiro, Brazil, 1993; prof. medicine Univ. Fed. Fluminense, 1994; expert cons. for EMBRATEL. Med. writer Today's Medicine/Jour. Commerce, 1975—; editor: Metabolic Aspects of 95% Pancreatic Resection, 1971, Medicine, Logique and Reasoning, 1992, Limited Abduction of the Thumb-A New Physical Sign, 1992, Signs and Manoevers in Physical Diagnosis, 1992; editor: Crural Hernias, 1993; contbr. articles to profl. jours. 2d lt. Brazilian Army, 1961-62. Recipient Carlos Chagas medal State of Guanabara, 1972, medal Tiradentes, 1992, Pedro Americo medal, 1993; prize Argentine Meeting of Gastroenterology, 1971. Fellow ACP, Colegio Interamericano de Medicos y Cirurjanos; mem. N.Y. Acad. Scis., Am. Venereal Disease. Brazilian Coll. Surgeons, Clube Monte Libano (counsel mem. 1972—). Home: 70 Rua Redentor Apt 101, Ipanema, 22421-030 Rio de Janeiro Brazil Office: Ste 302, 595 Rua Visconde de Piraja, 22410-003 Rio de Janeiro Brazil

LEITENBERGER, WILLIAM EUGENE, psychotherapist; b. Johnstown, Pa., May 7, 1940; s. Edward Karl and Jane L. (Inscho) L.; m. Sharon Ann Swick, Aug. 13, 1963; 1 child, William E. Jr. BS in Psychology, U. Pitts., Johnstown, Pa., 1986; MA in Clin. Psychology, Edinboro U. Pa., 1987. Chief psychologist State Correctional Instn., Dept. Corrections, Somerset, Pa., 1993—. Bd. dirs. Cambria County Adults and Children with Learning Disabilities, Johnstown, 1989—; asst. advisor Explorer Post 91, Johnstown, 1989—. With USN, 1959-61. Mem. Laurel Mountain Psychol. Assn.(pres. elect). Home: 404 Penn Ave PO Box 399 Jerome PA 15937 Office: State Correctional Instn Somerset Dept Corrections 1590 Walters Mill Rd Somerset PA 15510-0001

LEITER, EDWARD HENRY, scientist; b. Columbus, Ga., Apr. 17, 1942; m. Susan Shaw, Sept. 5, 1964. BS, Princeton U., 1964; MS, PhD in Cell Biology, Emory U., 1968. Fellow U. Tex., Austin, 1968-71; asst. prof. CUNY, Bkyn., 1971-74; assoc. staff scientist Jackson Lab., Bar Harbor, Maine, 1974-75, staff scientist, 1975-90, sr. staff scientist, 1990—. Recipient rsch. award Am. Diabetes Assn., 1995. Office: Jackson Lab Bar Harbor ME 04609

LEITHART, PAUL WALTER, physician, consultant; b. Columbus, Ohio, Jan. 29, 1921; s. Otto Theodore and Marie Elizabeth (Koch) L.; m. Mildred Woelke, June 19, 1953; children: Paul W. II, Theodore John, Peter James. BA, Capital U., 1943, BS, 1944; MD, Ohio State U., 1948. Cert. in addiction medicine. Grad. asst. Ohio State U., Columbus, 1944-45; intern Miami Valley Hosp., Dayton, Ohio, 1949; resident Mt. Carmel Hosp., Columbus, 1950; pvt. practice Columbus, 1951-91; univ. physician Capital U., Columbus, 1952-59; addictive medicine physician St. Anthony's Hosp., Columbus, 1973-85; med. dir. Parkside Lodge, Gahanna, Ohio, 1983-92, outpatient dir., 1992-93. Program host WCVO Radio. Elder St. Paul's Luth. Ch., 1960—; mem. exec. com. Ohio Dist. Am. Luth. Ch., Columbus, 1957-64; researcher on convalescent homes Mayor's Task Force, Columbus, 1970s. Named Ohio Patriot of Yr. John Birch Soc., 1968. Mem. Am. Assn. Physicians and Surgeons (pres. 1969-70, bd. dirs. 1964-92), Am. Soc. Addictive Medicine, Bible Sci. Assn. (bd. dirs. 1970-88), Sertoma Internat. (Freedom award 1961). Home: 750 Fairway Blvd Columbus OH 43213-2514

LEITZKE, JACQUE HERBERT, psychologist, corporate executive; b. Watertown, Wis., Dec. 25, 1929; s. Herbert Wilbert and Ruth Valberg (Stavenow) L.; m. Mary Annis Lacey, June 20, 1950 (div. Nov. 1963); children: Keith Alan, Sari Dawn, Thora Jacquelynne. BS, U. Wis., Madison, 1955; MA, Kent State U., 1958. Lic. psychologist, Wis., Ill., N.Y. Sch. psychologist Bur. Child Guidance, N.Y.C., 1959-61; clin. psychologist Bur. of Child Guidance, Neenah, Wis., 1961-64; clin. psychologist, psychotherapist Winnebago County Guidance Ctr., Neenah, Wis., 1961-64; sch. psychologist Waukegan City (Ill.) Sch. Dist. 61, 1965-66; clin. psychologist Wis., Ill., 1967-78; corp. pres., CEO Psychometrics Internat. Corp., Watertown, 1979—. Author: Definitively Incorporeal Human Intelligence Itself; originator intelligence test Abecedarian Measure of Human Intelligence, 1979. Trustee Human Intelligence Rsch. Found. Served with USAF, 1948-51. Mem. APA, Mensa. Home: 1153 Boughton St Apt 807 Watertown WI 53094-3106 Office: Psychometrics Internat Corp PO Box 247 Watertown WI 53094-0247

LEIVA, WILLIAM ARTHUR, biomedical company executive; b. Tehachapi, Calif., Aug. 31, 1948; s. Arthur Murray and Madoline Irene (Cowan) L.; m. Karen Marie Laversin, July 4, 1970; children: Michael W. (dec.), Stephanie M. BA, Whittier Coll., 1970, MS, 1972. Cert. nuclear med. technologist. Rsch. assoc. UCLA Sch. Medicine, 1972-73; mem. staff Beckman Instruments, Fullerton, Calif., 1973-84; v.p. Innotron Diagnostics, Irvine, Calif., 1984-86, Hycor Biomedical, Garden Grove, Calif., 1986-88, Sensor Diagnostics, Irvine, 1988-89; pres., chief exec. officer Medix Biotech, Foster City, Calif., 1989—. Contbr. articles to Bus. Mktg. Mag., numerous others. Office: Medix Biotech Inc 1531 Industrial Rd San Carlos CA 94070

LEJNIEKS, L. ARNO, healthcare management, educator; b. Latvia, Nov. 18, 1928; came to U.S., 1950; s. Reinis Arnold and Alma (Nelke) L.; m. Jean Marie Rittenhouse, June 10, 1958; children: Laura, Dianne, Lisette. BS in Chemistry, Pacific Union Coll., 1954; MD, Loma Linda U., 1958. Diplomate: Am. Bd. Internal Medicine. Sr. med. dir. Americare, Sacramento, 1984-86; clin. prof. endocrinology U. Calif., Davis, 1985—; pres. Intergrated Healthcare Adminstrs., Sacramento, 1991—. Pres. Sacramento Diabetes Assn., 1986-87; chmn. bd. dirs. Found. Health Plan, Sacramento, 1978-86. Capt. U.S. Army, 1960-62. Mem. ACP, Am. Coll. Physician Execs., Endocrine Soc., Navy League, Comstock Club (pres., bd. dirs. 1986, 87). Republican. Seventh Day Adventist. Office: Integrated Healthcare Adminstrs 2335 American River Dr Ste 301 Sacramento CA 95825

LEMA, MARK JOSEPH, anesthesiologist; b. Buffalo, June 18, 1949; s. Joseph Patrick and Grace Lucille (Sante) L.; m. Suzanne Czamara, Jan. 7, 1972; children: Gareth, Jordan, Bethany. BA in Polit. Sci., Canisius Coll., 1972; MS in Natural Scis., SUNY, Buffalo, 1976, PhD in Physiology, 1978; MD, SUNY, Bklyn., 1982. Lic. physician, N.Y., Mass.; diplomate with pain mgmt. qualifications Am. Bd. Anesthesiology, assoc. examiner; diplomate Nat. Bd. Med. Examiners. Intern S.I. Hosp., 1982; clin. fellow in anesthesiology Brigham and Women's Hosp., Boston, 1983-84; instr. anesthesiology Med. Sch. Harvard U., Boston, 1985-87; asst. prof. anesthesiology Sch. Medicine SUNY, Buffalo, 1987-94, assoc. prof., 1994—, dir. rsch. dept. anesthesia, 1987-92, vice-chmn. acad. affairs dept. anesthesiology, 1992—; chmn. anesthesiology Roswell Park Cancer Inst., 1987—, chief chronic pain svc., 1988—; vis. prof. SUNY, Buffalo, Naval Med. Command, Bethesda, Md., Cornell U., Dartmouth-Hitchcock Med. Ctr., Lebanon, N.H., SUNY, Syracuse, Cairo U., U. Rochester, SUNY, Bklyn., SUNY, Stony Brook, La. State U., Harvard U., Rush Med. Sch., Alleghany Gen. Hosp.; lectr. hosps., univs., 1983—; prin. investigator in anesthesiology various orgns. Mem. Am. Pain Soc., Internat. Assn. for Study of Pain, Am. Soc. Anesthesiologists, Am. Soc. Regional Anesthesia (bd. dirs.), Anesthesia History Assn., Internat. Anesthesia Rsch. Soc., Med. Soc. State of N.Y., Anesthesia Patient Safety Found., Med. Soc. County Erie, N.Y. State Soc. Anesthesiologists (bd. dirs.). Roman Catholic. Office: Roswell Park Cancer Inst Buffalo NY 14263

LEMAK, LAWRENCE JOHN, orthopaedic surgeon; b. Pitts., June 10, 1943; s. John and Irene (Hornak) L.; m. Georgine Ann Janosko, June 26, 1965; children: John, David, Matthew. BS, U. Pitts., 1965; MD, U. Ala., Birmingham, 1969. Diplomate Am. Bd. Orthopaedic Surgeons. Resident orthopaedics U. Pitts., 1969-74; fellowship dir. Am. Sports Medicine, Birmingham, 1986—; pres. Health South Med. Ctr., Birmingham, 1986—; founder Ala. Sports Medicine and Orthopaedic Ctr., Birmingham, 1986—; team doctor Samford U., Birmingham, 1987—, Auburn (Ala.) U., 1994—; med. coord. World Football League, divsn. NFL, Birmingham and N.Y.C., 1992—; med. dir. Maj. League Soccer, 1995; co-med. dir. Ladies Profl. Golf Assn., Birmingham and Daytona Beach, Fla., 1992—; chmn. bd. Ala. Sports Found., Birmingham, 1995—. Maj. U.S. Army, 1974-76. Lawrence J. Lemak scholarship in his honor Samford U., Birmingham, 1994—. Mem. Am. Orthopaedic Soc. Sports Medicine, Am. Acad. Orthopaedic Surgeons, Arthioscopy Assn. N.Am., Med. Assn. State Ala., Jefferson County Med. Soc., Birmingham Regional Sports Devel. Coun., Birmingham C. of C. (bd. trustees 1992—, vice chmn. sports devel. com. 1994—). Office: Ala Sports Medicine 1201 11th Ave S Ste 200 Birmingham AL 35209

LEMANSKE, ROBERT F., JR., allergist, immunologist; b. Milw., 1948. MD, U. Wis., 1975. Diplomate Am. Bd. Pediats., Am. Bd. Allergy and Immunology. Intern U. Wis. Hosp., Madison, 1975-76, resident in pediats., 1976-78, asst. prof. medicine. Fellow Am. Acad. Pediats., Am. Acad. Allergy and Immunology. Office: Clin Sci Ctr 600 Highland Ave Madison WI 53792-0002*

LEMANSKI, LARRY FREDRICK, medical educator; b. Madison, Wis., June 5, 1943; s. Fredrick Everett and Marjery Ulila (Hill) L.; m. Sharon Lee Wulf, Aug. 6, 1966; children: Scott Fredrick, Jennifer Lee. BS, U. Wis., Platteville, 1966; MS, Ariz. State U., 1968, PhD, 1971. Asst. prof. U. Calif., San Francisco, 1975-77; assoc. prof. U. Wis., Madison, 1977-79, prof., 1979-83; prof., chmn. dept. anatomy and cell biology SUNY, Syracuse, 1983—, dir. cell and molecular biology doctoral tng. program and consortium, 1987—; rsch. prof. biology Syracuse U., 1988—; mem. ad hoc rev. panel NIH. Adult leader for Boy Scouts Am., mem. nat. staff Boy Scout Jamboree 1989, coun. tng. chmn., 1992—. Officer USAR, 1965-69. Recipient Pres'. award Rsch. SUNY HSC, 1987, Disting. Alumnus award U. Wis., 1990, Profl. Excellence award N.Y. State/United Univ. Professions, 1990; NIH fellow, 1968-71, 71-73, Muscular Dystrophy fellow, 1973-75; grantee NIH, 1975—. Mem. AAAS, Am. Heart Assn. (Wis. affiliate rsch. com. 1982-83, Louis N. Katz Rsch. prize 1978, Outstanding Rsch. award 1982, Established Investigator award 1976-81), Electron Microscopy Soc. Am., Am. Assn. Anatomists, Am. Soc. Cell Biology (congrl. liaison com. 1993—), Soc. Devel. Biology, Am. Assn. Anatomy Chmn., N.Y. Acad. Scis., Masons (3d degree master), Sigma Xi, Beta Beta Beta. Methodist. Home: 4163 Coye Rd Jamesville NY 13078-9780 Office: SUNY Coll Medicine Dept Anatomy Cell Biol Syracuse NY 13210

LEMBERGER, AUGUST PAUL, university dean, pharmacy educator; b. Milw., Jan. 25, 1926; s. Max N. and Celia (Gehl) L.; m. Charlyne A. Young, June 30, 1947; children: Michael, Mary, Thomas, Terrence, Ann, Kathryn, Peter. BS, U. Wis., 1948, PhD, 1952. Sr. chemist Merck & Co., Inc., Rahway, N.J., 1952-53; asst. prof. U. Wis. Sch. Pharmacy, 1953-57, assoc. prof., 1957-63, prof. pharmacy, 1963-69; prof. pharmacy, dean U. Ill. Coll. Pharmacy, Chgo., 1969-80; prof. pharmacy, dean U. Wis.-Madison Sch. Pharmacy, 1980-91, ret., 1991; sec. Wis. Pharmacy Internship Bd., 1965-69; conf. dir. Nat. Indsl. Pharm. Research Conf., 1966-69; mem. Am. Council on Pharm. Edn., 1978-84, v.p., 1980-84. Served to 1st lt. AUS, 1944-46. Recipient Kiekhofer Meml. Teaching award U. Wis., 1957, citation of merit, 1977, Disting. Pharmacist award Wis. Pharm. Assn., 1969, Higuchi Lecture award Acad. Pharm. Sci. and Tech., Japan, 1989, Pres.' award Wis. Soc. Hosp. Pharmacists, 1991, Alumnus of Yr. award Pharmacy Alumni Assn., 1991. Fellow AAAS, Am. Found. for Pharm. Edn. (Disting. Svc. Profile award 1990), Acad. Pharm. Scis., Am. Assn. Pharm. Scientists; mem. Am. Soc. Hosp. Pharmacists, Am. Assn. Colls. Pharmacy (past com. chmn., exec. com. 1971-74, chmn. coun. deans 1975-77, chmn. sect. tchrs. of pharmacy Conf. Tchrs., hon. pres. 1993-94), Acad. Pharm. Scis. (v.p. 1976-77, pres. 1983-84), Am. Pharm. Assn. (mem. jud. bd. 1976-79, trustee 1985-88, treas. 1989-90, hon. pres. 1996-97), Wis. Pharm. Assn., Sigma Xi, Rho Chi (v.p. 1979-81, pres. 1981-83). Home: 7439 Cedar Creek Trl Madison WI 53717-1538 Office: 425 N Charter St Madison WI 53706-1508

LEMEGA, ROMAN WASYL, clinical psychologist; b. Haddington, Scotland, Sept. 17, 1949; s. William and Maria (Budnyk) L.; m. Denise Brenda Sheridan, July 25, 1973; children: Jennifer, Roman Jr., Will. BA, Seton Hall U., 1971; MA, Fairleigh Dickinson U., 1973; PhD, Hofstra U., 1985. Lic. psychologist, N.J., N.Y. Psychiat. asst. Clara Maas Meml. Hosp., Belleville, N.J., 1971-73; psychology intern Bergen Pines County Hosp., Paramus, N.J., 1973-74; clin. psychologist Morris County Guidance Ctr., Morris Plains, N.J., 1974-79, North Jersey Devel. Ctr., Totowa, N.J., 1979-90, Psychol. Cons. Group, Upper Montclair, N.J., 1985-89; dir. dept. psychology Woodbridge (N.J.) Devel. Ctr., 1990—; pvt. practice Florham Park, N.J., 1985—; cons. psychologist Morris County Assn. for Retarded Citizens, Morris Plains, 1988-90; cons. clin. psychologist Cmty. Access Unltd., Elizabeth, N.J., 1994—; chmn. psychology adv. com. to commr. Dept. Human Svcs., State of N.J., 1990-94; chmn. N.J. Psychol. Assn. Com. on Utilization Profl. Svcs., 1990—, com. of legis. affairs, 1991—, task force on pub. policy, 1994—;. Coach travel teams Florham Park Soccer Club, 1985—; coach Florham Park Baseball, 1985-90, Florham Park Basketball, 1988-93. Mem. N.J. Psychol. Assn., Am. Psychol. Assn., Am. Assn. Mental Retardation, Assn. for the Advancement of Behavior Therapy, N.J. Acad. Psychology, Morris County Psychologists. Roman Catholic. Home: 3 Midwood Dr Florham Park NJ 07932-1810

LEMEN, RICHARD ALAN, epidemiologist, medical administrator; b. Paola, Kans., July 23, 1943; s. Warren S. and Blanche (Hirt) L.; m. Kimble M. Varner; children: Monica D. (dec.), Wendy L., Tyler M. B.A., Central Meth. Coll., 1967; M.S., U. Mo., 1969; PhD, U. Cin., 1992. Dist. sanitarian Mo. Div. Health, Macon, 1966-67; epidemiologist Nat. Inst. Occupational Safety and Health, USPHS, Cin., 1970-73; biometry br. chief Nat. Inst. Occupational Safety and Health, USPHS, 1974-76, asst. chief industry wide studies br., 1978-80, dir. div. standards devel. and tech. transfer, 1980-88, dir. Washington office, asst. dir. Nat. Inst. Occupational Safety and Health, 1988-91, dep. dir., 1991—, acting dir., 1993-94; asst. surgeon gen. USPHS, 1995—; assoc. prof. divsn. environ. and occupational health Emory U., Atlanta, 1993—; bd. govs. Tri-State Air Com., 1974-76; mem. working group Internat. Agy. Research on Cancer, WHO; mem. VA adv. com. on herbicides, 1979-80; mem. Asbestos Sch. Hazards Safety Task Force, U.S. Dept. Edn., 1980-82; vice chmn. subcom. Risk Assessment of Com. to Coordiante Environ. and Health Related Programs, USPHS; chmn. asbestos ingestion task force, interag. coordination com. for environ. research USPHS; chair Nat. Symposium on Prevention of Leading Work-Related Diseases and Injuries, Occupational Cancer, 1985, Disorders of Reproduction, 1986, Assn. Schs. Pub. Health and Nat. Inst. Occupational Safety and Health, USPHS; mem. expert panel on Occupational Health, WHO, 1993—; vol. assoc. profl dept. Environ. Helath U. Cin., 1994—. Author: Workplace Exposure to Asbestos, 1980; editor: Dust and Disease, 1979; contbr. chpts. to profl. books. Served with U.S. Army, 1967-69; served to rear adm. USPHS, 1970—. Decorated Army Commendation medal, others; recipient Meritorious Svc. medal USPHS, 1988, Commendation medal, 1981, 85, Disting. Svc. medal, 1991, Surgeon Gen's Exemplary Svc. medal, 1993; recipinet Disting. Alumni award Ctrl. Meth. Coll., 1989, I.W. Abel award for pub. svc. AFL-CIO, 1994, Alice Hamilton sci. award for occupational safety and health, 1993. Fellow Collegium Ramazzini; mem. Soc. Occupational and Environ. Health (dir. 1980-82, bd. dirs. 1992—), Mil. Surgeons U.S., Commd. Officers Assn. of USPHS, Beta Beta Beta. Office: Nat Inst Occupational Safety & Health 1600 Clifton Rd Atlanta GA 30333*

LEMIEN, HENRY LESTER, JR., laboratory administrator; b. Norwalk, Conn., Dec. 26, 1934; s. Henry Lester Sr. and Helen E. (Allison) LeM.; m. Betty Jean Fendley, Nov. 28, 1953; children: Deborah Ann LeMien Legg, Henry L. III. BSc, U. Ala., 1959; postgrad., USAF Air War Coll., 1973. Rep. Ayerst Labs., Birmingham, Ala., 1959-66; clin. rsch. assoc. Ayerst Labs., Chgo., 1966-71; clin. pharmacology coord. Ayerst Labs., Montreal, Que., Can., 1971-76; asst. to med. dir. Ayerst Labs., N.Y.C., 1976-78, mgr. ops.-med., 1978-88; mgr. ops.-med. affairs Wyeth-Ayerst Labs., St. Davids, Pa., 1988—. Sr. instr. State Conn. Fire Commn., Meriden, 1977-88; asst. chief West Redding (Conn.) Fire Dept., 1985-88; safety officer Eat Whiteland (Pa.) Fire Dept., 1992—; safety chmn. Upper Mainline (Pa.) Fire Dept. Chiefs, 1995—. Mem. N.Y. Acad. Sci., Drug Info. Assn. Republican. Methodist. Home: RD #1 Charlestown 8 Ridgewood Rd Malvern PA 19355-9629 Office: Wyeth-Ayerst Labs PO Box 8299 Philadelphia PA 19101-0082

LEMIEUX, DAVID ROBERT, school psychologist; b. Hartford, Conn., Feb. 25, 1957; s. Edward Joseph and Phyllis Marie (Sheehan) L.; m. Alicia Anna Szewczyk, Aug. 4, 1990. BA, Holy Cross Coll., 1979; MS, U. Hartford, 1981, specialist degree in sch. psychology, 1987. Cert. sch. psychologist. School psychologist Manchester (Conn.) Pub. Schs., 1982, Vernon (Conn.) Pub. Schs., 1982-83, East Hartford (Conn.) Pub. Schs., 1983-85, Windsor (Conn.) Pub. Schs., 1985—. Eucharistic min. St. Bridget's Ch., Manchester, 1988-90. Mem. Conn. Assn. Sch. Psychologists. Republican. Roman Catholic. Home: 1166A Middle Tpke W Manchester CT 06040-1807 Office: Windsor Conn Pub Schs 601 Matianuck Ave Windsor CT 06095-3540

LEMIRE, DAVID STEPHEN, school psychologist, educator; b. Roswell, N.Mex., May 23, 1949; s. Joseph Armon and Jeanne (Longwill) L.; BA, Linfield Coll., 1972, MEd, 1974; EdS, Idaho State U., 1978; postgrad. U. Wyo.; EdS in Ednl. Adminstrn. and Instructional Leadership, U. Wyo., 1988; postgrad. U. Wyo. Cert. sch. counselor, student pers. worker, psychology instr., Calif. Sch. counselor, psychol. technician and tchr. Goshen County Sch. Dist. 1, Torrington, Wyo., counselor Aspen High Sch., Aspen, Colo.; sch. counselor Unita County Sch. Dist., Evanston, Wyo., coord. R&D Lifelong Learning Ctr. 1986-87; dir. spl. svcs. and sch. psychologist Bighorn County Sch. Dist. #4, Basin, Wyo., 1989-90; sch. psychologist Sweetwater County Sch. Dist. #2, Green River, Wyo., 1990-91; dir. housing, residence supr. Pratt (Kans.) Community Coll., 1991-92; pres. David Lemire Software Enterprises, Evanston; dir. Inst. for Advanced Study of Thinkology. Mem. ASCD, Nat. Assn. Sch. Psychologists (cert.), Am. Psychol. Assn. Former editor WACD Jour.; former mng. editor Jour. Humanistic Edn.; contbr. articles to profl. jours. Address: PO Box 6266 Kansas City KS 66106-0266 also: Creative Therapeutics Adminstrv Offices 2390 Riviera St Reno NV 89509-1144

LEMLEY, DOUGLAS EDWIN, internist, rheumatologist; b. Wheeling, W.Va., Apr. 29, 1956; s. Fred LeMoyne and Ruth Ann (Gamble) L.; m. Barbara Lynn Freedy, Sept. 1, 1991. BA in Biology, W.Va. U., 1978, MD, 1982. Diplomate Am. Bd. Internal Medicine. Resident in internal medicine U. Fla., Gainesville, 1982-85; fellow in rheumatology Georgetown U., Washington, 1985-87; rheumatologist H&M Med. Clinic, Concord, N.C., 1987-91, Greensboro (N.C.) Med. Assocs., 1991—; cons. asst. prof. Duke U., Durham, N.C., 1987—; speaker at health fairs, support groups. Contbr. articles to profl. jours. Mem. AMA, ACP, Am. Coll. Rheumatology, Arthritis Found. (Carolinas chpt. bd. dirs.). Republican. Office: Greensboro Med Assocs 1511 Westover Ter Greensboro NC 27408-7122

LEMMON, WILLIAM THOMAS, JR., surgeon; b. Phila., June 11, 1934; s. William T. and Madeleine (Pierce) L.; m. Jean Moyer, Sept. 30, 1961; children: Kelly, Tracy. AB, Princeton U., 1956; MD, Jefferson U., 1960. Diplomate Am. Bd. Gen. Surgery. Intern Jefferson Med. Coll. Hosp., Phila., 1960-61, resident in surgery, 1961-63, 65-67, instr. surgery, attending staff physician, 1967-73; pres. Lemmon Surg. Assocs., Ltd., Lansdale, Pa., 1973—. Lt. comdr. USPHS, 1963-65. Mem. Alpha Omega Alpha. Home: 102 Tanglewood Dr Lansdale PA 19446-1615 Office: Lemmon Surg Assocs Ltd 2031 N Broad St Ste 147 Lansdale PA 19446-1063

LEMONCELLI, JOHN JOSEPH, psychology educator; b. Archbald, Pa., May 4, 1948; s. Samuel L. and Mary Jean (McAndrew) L.; m. Margaret A. Kolmansberger, June 12, 1971; children: Mark James, Mauri Theresa. BA, U. Scranton, 1971, MS, 1972; EdD, Temple U., 1983. Lic. psychologist, Pa. Dir. community svcs. Luzerne-Wyoming County Mental Health, Wilkes-Barre, Pa., 1973-83; lectr. U. Scranton, Pa., 1984-87; psychologist intern G.D. Boroios, M.D. & Assocs., Scranton, 1983-87; psychologist Forum Psychol. Assn., Scranton, 1987—; assoc. prof. Marywood Coll., Scranton, 1987—; instr. Pa. State Police Commn., Harrisburg, 1980—; cons. Sister Servants IHM, 1989—, clergy Diocese of Scranton, 1989—. Contbr. articles to profl. jours., 1978—. CCD tchr. St. Thomas Aquinas Ch., Archbald, 1981—; bd. dir. Commn. on Cath. Edn., Scranton, Pa., 1989—. Recipient Prevention Progress award, Pa. Consultation Coun., 1981, Exemplary Svc. award, 1982; named Disting. Svc. Profl., Counseling and Devel. Assn., 1990. Mem. Pa. Consultation and Edn. Assn. (pres. 1981), No. Psychology Assn., Pa. Counseling Assn., Am. Psychology Assn., Pa. Psychol. Assn., Chi Sigma Iota. Democrat. Office: Marywood Coll Chs Dept Counseling Ps Scranton PA 18503

LEMONS, ROSEMARY MARIE HOEFLINGER, molecular biologist; b. Vincennes, Ind., Apr. 3, 1954; d. Lawrence Melvin and Gisela Johanna (Hansch) Lemons; m. Joseph Paul Hoelinger, Oct. 13, 1983; children: Joseph Kyle Lemons, Lawrence Keith Lemons. BS in Microbiology, Ind. U., 1977. From rsch. asst. to rsch. assoc. II U. Mich., Ann Arbor, 1977—. Contbr. articles to New Eng. Jour. Medicine, Jour. Biol. Chemistry, Analytical Biochemistry, Jour. Cell Biology. Participant Women-in-Sci., Ann Arbor, 1987—, Youth Mentoring Program, 1995—. Office: U Mich 300 NIB Rm 1187 Ann Arbor MI 48109-0408

LEMPEL, RITA, neurologist; b. Antwerp, Belgium, Aug. 26, 1950; came to U.S., 1975.; MD, Free U. Brussels, 1975. Diplomate Am. Bd. Psychiatry and Neurology. Intern in medicine L.I. Jewish Med. Ctr., Jamaica, N.Y., 1975-76; resident in neurology NYU Med. Ctr., N.Y.C., 1976-79, fellow in electromyography Rusk Inst., 1979-80; pvt. practice N.Y.C., 1981—; ind. med. examiner various ins. cos., N.Y.C. and boroughs, 1985—; expert witness for compensation and arbitration, 1985—; neurology cons. to legal profession, 1985—. Home and Office: 435 E 65th St Apt 9G New York NY 10021-6971

LENARD, JOSEPH ARVID, orthodontist; b. Phila., June 21, 1946; s. Joseph Bertil and Ruth M. (Browne) L.; m. Judy Jakowatz, June 20, 1971. BCE, Ga. Tech., 1969; MBA, Fla. State U., 1973; DDS, U. N.C., 1982; cert. in orthodontics, U. Conn., 1984. Diplomate Am. Bd. Orthodontics. Mech. design engr. Pratt Whitney Aircraft, West Palm Beach, Fla., 1969-72; comml. loan adminstrn. First Union Nat. Bank, Charlotte, N.C., 1973-77; orthodontist Pinehurst, N.C., 1984—. Recipient Table Clinic award Internat. Coll. Dentists, Chapel Hill, N.C., 1981, Dentsply Internat., 1981, Dental Sch. award Am. Soc. Orthodontics; fellow Nat. Inst. Dental Rsch., 1981. Mem. ADA, Am. Assn. Orthodontics, Sandhills Dental Assn., Christian Med. and Dental Soc., Spurgeon Dental Soc., Beta Gamma Sigma, Sigma Iota Epsilon. Republican. Evangelical. Home: 515 E Massachusetts Ave Southern Pines NC 28387-6139 Office: 105 Turnberry Way Pinehurst NC 28374-8509

LENCIONI, RICCARDO ANTONIO, radiologist, researcher; b. Lucca, Tuscany, Italy, June 13, 1961; s. Odilio and Natalia (Carli) L. MD cum laude, U. Pisa, Italy, 1986, certification in gastroenterology, 1990, postgrad. degree diagnostic ultrasound, 1990, postgrad. degree interventional ultrasound, 1990, certification in radiology cum laude, 1994. Resident dept. surgery U. Pisa, Italy, 1986-90, resident dept. radiology, 1990-94, staff dept. radiology, 1992-95, asst. prof., residency Sch. Radiology, 1995—; coord. postgrad. course in interventional ultrasound, 1991-95; tchr. postgrad. course computed tomography, 1992-95, postgrad. course MRI, 1993-95, Erasmus course on abdominal MRI, 1994—; vis. prof. Emory U. Sch. Medicine, Atlanta, 1994; invited spkr. over 125 nat. and internat. congresses. Author: Ultrasound of the Breast, 1993; contbr. numerous articles to internat. profl. jours. Recipient 1st place sci. paper European Seminar Liver Tumors, Bonn, Germany, 1991, Cert. Merit Sci. Paper European Congress Radiology, Vienna, Austria, 1993. Mem. Radiol. Soc. N.Am., Am. Roentgen Ray Soc., European Soc. Magnetic Resonance, Italian Soc. Med. Radiology, Italian Soc. Interventional Radiology (bd. dirs. 1996-2000). Home: Via Matteo Trenta, I-55100 Lucca Italy Office: U Pisa Dept Radiology, Via Roma 67, I-56100 Pisa Italy

LENERTZ, THOMAS CLARENCE, hospital administrator; b. Mankato, Minn., Sept. 5, 1936; s. Clarence Robert and Nona Cathryn (Dorn) L.; m. Patricia Ann Muellerleile, July 16, 1960; children: Laura Marie, Bradley Thomas. BA in Bus. Adminstrn., Mankato State U., 1960. Auditor Arthur Andersen & Co., Mpls., 1960-65; asst. controller Am. Rehab. Found., Mpls., 1965-68; asst. adminstr. Mt. Sinai Hosp., Mpls., 1968-73; exec. v.p. Riverview Healthcare Assn., Crookston, Minn., 1973-95, pres., CEO, 1995—; chmn., dir. North Star Hosp. Mut., Bermuda, 1977-87; dir. Agassiz Health Systems Agy., Grand Forks, N.D., 1983—, Polk County Group Homes, 1985-87; mem. com. of inspection North Star Hosp. Mut. Ins.; mem. Crookston program improvement audit com. U. Minn., preceptor Crookston health mgmt. program; mem. health mgmt. program Concordia Coll., Minn. Care Regional Coordinating Bd.; chmn. svc. delivery com. Minn. REgional Coordinating Bd.; bd. dirs. United Way of Crookston, Minn., 1981-87; trustee Minn. Hosp. Assn., 1981-85, 89-91; treas. MHHP/MHHA Dist. A.; mem. adv. com. N.W. Tech. Coll., East Grand Forks, Minn. Served with U.S. Army, 1956-58, PTO. Recipient William G. Follmer award Hosp. Fin. Mgmt., 1969, Robert H. Reeves award, 1973, Disting. Svcs. award Minn. Hosp. Assn., 1991, Torch & Shield award U. Minn., 1993. Mem. Am. Colls. Hosp. Execs. Roman Catholic. Lodges: Lions, Eagles, K.C. Avocations: fishing; winemaking; gardening. Home: 511 Euclid Ave Crookston MN 56716-2509 Office: Riverview Healthcare Assn 323 S Minnesota St Crookston MN 56716

LENFANT, CLAUDE JEAN-MARIE, physician; b. Paris, Oct. 12, 1928; came to U.S., 1960, naturalized, 1965; s. Robert and Jeanine (Leclerc) L.; children: Philipe, Bernard, Martine Lenfant Wayman, Brigitte Lenfant Martin, Christine. B.S., U. Rennes, France, 1948; M.D., U. Paris, 1956; D.Sc. (hon.), SUNY, 1988. Asst. prof. physiology U. Lille, France, 1959-60; from clin. instr. to prof. medicine physiology and biophysics U. Wash. Med. Sch., 1961-72; asso. dir. lung programs Nat. Heart, Lung and Blood Inst. NIH, Bethesda, Md., 1970-72; dir. div. lung diseases Nat. Heart, Lung and Blood Inst. NIH, 1972-80; dir. Fogarty Internat. Center NIH, 1980-82, assoc. dir. internat. research, 1980-82; dir. Nat. Heart, Lung and Blood Inst., 1982—. Assoc. editor: Jour. Applied Physiology, 1976-82, Am. Jour. Medicine, 1979-91 ; mem. editorial bd.: Undersea Biomed. Research, 1973-75, Respiration Physiology, 1971-78, Am. Jour. Physiology and Jour. Applied Physiology, 1970-76, Am. Rev. Respiratory Disease, 1973-79; editor-in-chief: Lung Biology in Health and Disease. Fellow Royal Coll. Physicians; mem. Assn. Am. Physicians, Am. Soc. Clin. Investigation, French Physiol. Soc., Am. Physiol. Soc., N.Y. Acad. Scis., Undersea Med. Soc., Inst. of Medicine of Nat. Acad. Sci., USSR Acad. Med. Scis., French Nat. Acad. Medicine. Home: 13201 Glen Rd Gaithersburg MD 20878-8855 Office: Nat Heart Lung & Blood Inst Bldg 31A Rm 5A52 Bethesda MD 20892

LENGELER, JOSEPH W., genetics educator; b. Burg-Reuland, Belgium, Apr. 29, 1937; s. Philipp A. and Anna K. (Jousten) L.; m. Marie-Luise Reusse, Aug. 27, 1966; children: Jorg Ph., Klaus B. Staatsexamen, U. Cologne, Fed. Republic Germany, 1962, D. in Natural Scis., 1966; D. in Natural Scis. Habilitation, U. Regensburg, Fed. Republic Germany, 1976. Asst. U. Cologne, 1966-69; rsch. assoc. Harvard U., Boston, 1969-72; asst. U. Cologne, 1972-73; asst. U. Regensburg, 1973-80, prof., 1980-84; prof. U. Osnabrück, Fed. Republic Germany, 1984—. Editor Molecular & Gen. Genetics, 1985—. Office: U Osnabrück, Barbara Str 11, D 49069 Osnabruck Germany

LENHART, MICHAEL E., pediatrician, neonatologist; b. Lawrence, Kans., Sept. 5, 1951; s. Ervin Eugene and Letha Lucile (Clemings) L.; m. Giselle Susan White, Nov. 23, 1978; children: Luke, Sandra. BS, Southwestern Coll., 1982; DO, Kirksville Coll. Osteo. Med., 1987. Diplomate Am. Osteo. Bd. Pediatrics. Intern Okla. Osteo. Hosp., Eugene, 1988; resident in pediat. Tulsa Regional Med. Ctr., Drs. Hosp. (Columbus, Ohio), 1990; fellow in neonatology Miami Valley Hosp. (Dayton, Ohio), Drs. Hosp., 1992; pvt. practice Tulsa, 1992—; dir. neonatal svcs. Columbia Tulsa Regional Med. Ctr., 1992—, chmn. dept. pediatrics, 1994—. Chmn. Windsor Lake Homeowners Assn., Owasso, Okla., 1994—; chmn. transp. com. St. Matthews United Meth. Ch., Tulsa, 1996—, mem. pastor parish rels. com., 1996—. Mem. Am. Acad. Osteopathy. Am. Osteo. Assn., Am. Coll. Osteo. Physicians, Nat. Perinatal Assn., Okla. Osteo. Assn., Tulsa Dist. Osteo. Assn. Republican.

LENNARD-JONES, JOHN EDWARD, gastroenterologist; b. Bristol, Eng., Jan. 29, 1927; s. John Edward and Kathleen Mary (Lennard) Jones; m. Verna Margaret Down, Feb. 19, 1955; children: David, Peter, Andrew, Timothy. BA, Corpus Christi Coll, Cambridge, Eng., 1947, MA, 1951; MD, U. Cambridge, 1965. Mem. jr. med. staff U. Coll. Hosp., Manchester Royal Inf., Ctrl. Middlesex Hosp., 1953-61; sr. registrar Central Middlesex Hosp., London, 1961-63; mem. med. rsch. coun. gastroenterology rsch. unit Ctrl. Middlesex Hosp., London, 1963-74; cons. physician U. Coll. Hosp., London, 1965-74; prof. gastroenterology London Hosp. Med. Coll., 1974-87; cons. gastroenterologist St. Mark's Hosp., London, 1965-92; chmn. med. adv. com. Nat. Assn. for Colitis and Crohn's Disease, 1979-90. Contbr. articles to profl. jours. Cir. steward Meth. Ch., 1985-91. Fellow Royal Coll. Physicians (London) (mem. coun. 1986-89, chmn. gastroenterology com. 1985-88), Royal Coll. Surgeons (London), U. Coll. (London), Royal Soc. Medicine (hon.); mem. Brit. Soc. Gastroenterology (hon. mem., pres. 1983, hon. sec. 1965-70, chmn. clin. svcs. com. 1986-90), Swedish Soc. Gastroenterology (hon.), Swiss Soc. Gastroenterology (hon.), French Soc. Coloproctology (hon.), Ileostomy Assn. (hon.), Anthenaeum. Home: 72 Cumberland St, Woodbridge 1P12 4AD, England Office: St Marks Hosp, Northwick Park, Watford Rd, Harrow HA1 3UJ, England

LENNON, DAVID M., physician assistant, educator; b. Sturgis, Mich., May 12, 1953; s. Martin Elwood and Donna Faye (Cheney) L.; m. Pamela Sue Hunt, Jan. 23, 1976; children: Michelle Lorraine, Brian Thomas. ASN, Hillsborough C.C., Tampa, Fla., 1981; BS Physician Asst., Trevecca Nazarene Coll., 1983, MEd in Adminstrn./Supervision, 1994. RN, Fla., Tenn. Physician asst. Pvt. Practice of George W. Robertson MD, Lebanon, Tenn., 1983-89; physician asst. dept. surgery Humana Hosp.-McFarland, Lebanon, 1989-90; dir. edn. Birman and Assocs. Inc., Cookeville, Tenn., 1990-92; chair dept. of physician asst. Trevecca Nazarene U., Nashville, 1992—; pres. Dictation Resources Inc., Nashville, 1993—. Innkeeper Room in the Inn homeless shelter, Nashville, 1992. Fellow Am. Acad. Physician Assts. (bd. dirs. Tenn. chpt. 1994—), Am. Assn. Surgeon Assts.; mem. Tenn. Coalition of Health Care Providers. Mem. Ch. of the Nazarene. Home: 5217 Windypine Dr Nashville TN 37211 Office: Trevecca Nazarene U 333 Murfreesboro Rd Nashville TN 37210

LENOIR, ALLEN ADRED, infectious diseases physician; b. Birmingham, Ala., Nov. 15, 1954; s. Adred Clarence and Eunice Audry (Glass) L.; m. Anna Elizabeth Baron, Mar. 24, 1984; children: Andrew Allen, Dana Courtney. BS, Birmingham So. Coll., 1977; MD, U. Ala., 1981. Diplomate Am. Bd. Pediatrics. Resident in pediatrics U. Tenn. Coll. Medicine, Memphis, 1981-84; fellow in pediatric infectious diseases Washington U., St. Louis, 1984-87; cons. in infectious diseases Miami (Fla.) Children's Hosp., 1987—; physician Pediatric Infectious Diseases Assocs., Miami. Contbr. articles to profl. publs. Mem. AMA, Am. Acad. Pediatrics, Am. Soc. Microbiology, Pediatric Infectious Disease Soc., Infectious Disease Soc. Am., Sabin Soc., Phi Beta Kappa. Baptist. Office: Pediatric Infectious Diseases Assocs 3200 SW 60th Ct Ste 206 Miami FL 33155

LENOX, ANGELA COUSINEAU, healthcare consultant; b. Vergennes, Vt., Dec. 12, 1946; d. Romeo Joseph and Colombe Mary (Gevry) C.; m. Donald Allen Lenox, Oct. 5, 1969 (div.); 1 child, Tiffanie Jae. RN diploma, Albany Med. Ctr. Sch. Nursing, 1969; BS, Barry U., 1982; M of Health Mgmt., St. Thomas U., 1990. Cert. in profl. healthcare quality. Intravenous therapist Holy Cross Hosp., Ft. Lauderdale, Fla., 1979-91; utilization review coord. North Borward Hosp., Pompano Beach, Fla., 1984-89; med. staff quality mgr. Humana Bennett, Plantation, Fla., 1990-91; med. resource analyst Hermann Hosp., Houston, 1991-93; assoc. mgr. quality improvement The Prudential, Sugarland, Tex., 1993-95; cons. ACL Cons., Houston, 1995—. Contbr. articles to profl. jours. 1st lt. U.S. Army res., 1991—. Mem. Tex. Gold Coast Assn. Healthcare Quality, Tex. Soc. Quality Assurance, Nat. Assn. Healthcare Quality. Home & Office: 8523 Dawnridge Dr Houston TX 77071-2441

LENT, JOHN E., physician; b. Fall River, Mass., May 4, 1941; s. James W. and Margaret A. (Sedlock) L.; m. Barbara A. Dunphy; children: Christopher, Margaret, Anne, John J., Kathryn. BA, Coll. of Holy Cross, 1962; MD, Georgetown U., 1966. Diplomate in internal medicine and cardiovascular diseases Am. Bd. Internal Medicine. Intern Milwaukee County Gen. Hosp., 1965-66; cardiologist in pvt. practice Fond du Lac, Wis. Bd. dirs. Marian Coll., Fond du Lac, 1986-89; trustee St. Joseph Ch., Fond du Lac, 1987-89. Lt comdr. USN, 1970-72. Fellow Am. Coll. Cardiology; mem. ACP, Wis. State Med. Soc. Physician of Yr., Dist. 5 1995), Fond du Lac County Med. Soc., Alpha Omega Alpha. Roman Catholic. Home: PO Box 222 Fond Du Lac WI 54936 Office: Aurora Med Group 50 N Portland St Fond du Lac WI 54935

LENTZ, EDWARD ALLEN, consultant retired health administrator; b. Superior, Wis., May 30, 1926; s. Otto Albert and Martha Mary Ann (Gruhel) L.; m. Margaret Ann Denier, May 30, 1952; 1 child, Elizabeth Ann Clark. BS, U. Cin., 1951; MHA, Wayne State U., Detroit, 1957. Asst. dir. Pub. Health Fedn., Cin., 1954-57; dir. health planning United Cmty. Coun., Columbus, Ohio, 1957-62; asst. dir. Columbus Hosp. Fedn., 1962-65; assoc. exec. dir. Ohio Hosp. Assn., Columbus, 1965-69; exec. dir. Health Planning Assn. of Ohio River Valley, Cin., 1969-70; asst. prof. grad. program in health svcs. adminstrn. Coll. of Medicine, Ohio State U., Columbus, 1970-72, adj. assoc. prof. preventive medicine, 1957—; dep. dir. med. care adminstrn. Ohio Dept. Health, Columbus, 1972-75; pres., CEO Med. Advances Inst., Columbus, 1975-79; v.p. corp. devel. Mt. Carmel Health System, Columbus, 1979-95; cons. Mt. Carmel Health System, 1995—; cons. cmty. health planning USPHS. Contbr. articles to profl. jours. Mem., chair Ohio Dept. Human Svcs./Ohio Med. Care Adv. Com., Columbus, 1975—; bd. dirs., vice chair Netcare Corp., Columbus, 1989—. Served with USN, 1944-46; 1st lt. U.S. Army, 1951-53, Korea. Recipient Spl. Citation for hosp. planning and mktg. in Ohio and Delbert L. Pugh Conf., Ohio State U. Coll. Medicine and Ohio Hosp. Assn., 1991. Fellow Am. Pub. Health Assn. (bd. dirs., vice chmn. bd. trustees 1979-83); mem. Ohio Pub. Health Assn. (pres. 1969-70), Am. Assn. Areawide Planning Agencies (pres. 1969-70), Ohio Hosp. Assn. Soc. for Hosp. Planning and Mktg. (pres. 1987-88), Columbus Rotary (com. chair). Presbyterian. Home: 585 Keyes Ln Worthington OH 43085

LENTZ, LINDA KAY, school psychologist, learning disability educator; b. Dayton, Ohio, Aug. 13, 1936; d. Harry E. and Mary E. (Swinger) Denlinger; m. Paul Dean Lentz, May 5, 1955; children: Lisa Kay Heaton, David Paul. BS, U. Dayton, 1981, MS, 1985; MEd, Wright State U., 1987. Cert. tchr., Ohio. Tchr., owner Springboro (Ohio) Pre-sch., 1974-83; tchr. learning disabilities Franklin (Ohio) City Schs., 1983-87; sch. psychologist Montgomery County Bd. Edn., 1987-92. Mem. Springboro Bd. Edn., 1981-84; chairperson Help through Edn. Leads to Prevention, Springboro, 1982-85. Recipient Community Involvement award Springboro Jaycees, 1983, Disting. Service award Springboro Jaycees, 1984, William Holden Jennings Scholar award U. Dayton, 1986-87. Mem. Nat. Assn. Sch. Psychologists, Nat. Assn. for Children with Learning Disabilities, Ohio Assn. for Children with Learning Disabilities, Ohio Assn. for Counseling and Devel. Presbyterian. Home: 7241 Mountain Trl Dayton OH 45459-3151

LENTZ, RICHARD DAVID, psychiatrist; b. Passaic, N.J., Jan. 27, 1942; s. Harold Arthur and Ruth (Bitterman) L.; m. Joan Ellen Sacks, June 25, 1983; children: Daniel Keith, Andrew Simon. Student, John Hopkins U., 1959-61; AB cum laude, NYU, 1964; MS in Pathology, U. Rochester, 1969, MD with distinction, 1969. Diplomate Am. Bd. Psychiatry and Neurology, Am. Bd. of Pediatrics, Am. Bd. of Pediatric Nephrology. Intern U. Minn. Hosps., Mpls., 1969-70, resident in pediatrics, 1970-71, fellow in pediatric nephrology, 1972-74; resident in neurology and pediatrics Washington U., St. Louis, 1971-72; resident in psychiatry, fellow consultation-liaison U. Minn. Hosps., Mpls., 1979-81; chief pediatric nephrology Walter Reed Army Med. Ctr., Washington, 1974-76; instr. dept. of pediatrics Georgetown Med. Ctr., Washington, 1975; asst. prof. U. Md., Balt., 1978; cons. psychiatrist Park Nicollet Clinic/HSM, St. Louis Park, Minn., 1981—, vice chmn. dept. psychiatry, 1981-85, chmn. patient rels., 1983-95, risk mgmt. com., ops. com., dir. Medctr. Health Plan, 1985-90; chmn. risk mgmt. Health Sys. Minn., St. Louis Park, Minn., 1995—; from clin. asst. prof. to assoc. prof. U. Minn., Mpls., 1981-90; clin. prof. U. Minn., 1990—; chmn. psychiatry Abbott-Northwestern Hosp., Mpls., 1991-92; assoc. dir. profl. assessment program Abbott-Northwestern Hosp., 1993; cons. Courage Ctr., Mpls., Comprehensive Epilepsy Ctr., Bill Kelly House, numerous others. Contbr. articles to profl. jours. Maj. U.S. Army, 1974-76. Mem. Am. Psychiat. Assn., Minn. Med. Assn., Hennepin County Med. Soc. Office: Park Nicollet Med Ctr 2001 Blaisdell Ave Minneapolis MN 55404-2414

LENTZ, THOMAS LAWRENCE, biomedical educator, dean, researcher; b. Toledo, Mar. 25, 1939; s. Lawrence Raymond and Kathryn (Heath) L.; m. Judith Ellen Pernaa, June 17, 1961; children: Stephen, Christopher, Sarah. Student, Cornell U., 1957-60; MD, Yale U., 1964. Instr. in anatomy Yale U. Sch. Medicine, New Haven, 1964-66, asst. prof. of anatomy, 1966-69, assoc. prof. of cytology, 1969-74, assoc. prof. of cell biology, 1974-85, prof. of cell biology, 1985—, asst. dean for admissions, 1976—, vice chmn. cell biology, 1992—; mem. cellular and molecular neurobiology panel NSF, 1987-88, mem. cellular neurosci. panel, 1988-90; mem. neurology B-1 study sect. Nat. Inst. Neurol. Disorders and Stroke, NIH, 1996. Author: The Cell Biology of Hydra, 1966, Primitive Nervous Systems, 1968, Cell Fine Structure, 1971; contbr. over 90 articles to sci. publs. Vice chmn., chmn. Planning and Zoning Commn., Killingworth, Conn., 1979—; active Killingworth Hist. Soc. Recipient Conn. Fedn. Planning and Zoning Agys. award, 1995, Citizen of Yr. award Killingworth Lions Club, 1993; fellow Trumbull Coll., Yale U.; grantee NSF, 1968-92, Dept. Army, 1986, NIH, 1987—. Mem. AAAS, Am. Soc. Cell Biology, Soc. for Neurosci., N.Y. Acad. Scis., Appalachian Mountain Club (trails com., Warren Hart award 1995), Appalachian Trail Conf., Mt. Washington Obs., Wonalancet Out Door Club, Alpha Omega Alpha. Republican. Mem. United Ch. of Christ. Office: Yale U Sch Medicine Dept Cell Biol 333 Cedar St PO Box 208002 New Haven CT 06520-8002

LENZ, TOMAS, nephrologist, researcher; b. Wilzenberg, Germany, Aug. 16, 1956; s. Albrecht and Irmgard Lenz; m. Martina Helga Schuessler; 1 child, Christian. MD, U. Mainz, 1982 Intern Teaching Hosp.-Wiesbaden, Germany, 1982-83; resident Free U. Berlin, 1983-86, clin. fellow, 1989-92; clin. fellow Cornell U., N.Y.C., 1986-89; med. adviser E. Merck, Darmstadt, 1992-93; attending nephrologist U. Frankfurt/Main, 1993—. Contbr. articles to profl. jours. Rsch. fellow Nat. Kidney Found. N.Y. & N.J., 1988-89. Mem. Am. Soc. Hypertension, Am. Soc. Nephrology. Home: Grunewaldstr 6, 63225 Langen Germany Office: U Hosp, Theodor Stern Kai 7, 60590 Frankfurt Germany

LENZER, IRMINGARD ISOLDE, psychology educator; b. Munich, Fed. Republic Germany; arrived in Can., 1969; d. Johann and Maria (Pfaffinger) L.; children: Alexander Lemond, Anna Lemond. BA in Psychology, UCLA, 1964; PhD in Psychology, Ind. U., 1969. Asst. prof. psychology St. Mary's U., Halifax, N.S., Can., 1969-73, assoc. prof., 1973-81, prof., 1981—. Mem. Internat. Neuropsychol. Soc., Assn. for Treatment of Sexual Abusers. Home: 1232 Edward St, Halifax, NS Canada B3H 3H4 Office: St Mary's U Dept Psychology, Robie St, Halifax, NS Canada B3H 3C3

LEO, MARGARET ELEANOR, social worker; b. San Bernardino, Calif., Aug. 15, 1937; d. James Buell and Frances Clara (Stone) Chessington; m. Arnold Leo, Apr. 14, 1958 (div. 1973); children: Erik, Melissa. BA in Art and Edn., Hunter Coll., 1970; MEd in Elem. Edn. and Counseling, Antioch U., 1973; MSW, Smith Coll., 1985. Lic. social worker, Mass., Vt. Clin. social worker N.Y. State Edn., 1986-94; family therapist Fordham Tremont Cmty. Mental Health Ctr., Bronx, 1990-93; therapist Human Resource Ctr., Athol, Mass., 1993-94; dir. Putney (Vt.) Family Svcs., 1994—; union del. Local 1199, N.Y.C., 1990-93. Home: RR 3 Box 108 Putney VT 05346-9311

LEÓN, FELIX IVAN, pulmonologist; b. Santurce, P.R., Mar. 17, 1948; s. Felix Antonio and Irma (Rivero) L.; m. Nicole Lucienne Soto, Mar. 24, 1972; children: Michelle, Annette. Student, U. Colo., 1965-68; MD, U. P.R., 1972. Diplomate Am. Bd. Internal Medicine, Am. Bd. Pulmonary Disease. Instr. in medicine U. P.R. Med. Sch., San Juan, 1975-76; fellow in pulmonary disease Wash. U. Med. Sch., St. Louis, 1976-78; assoc. prof. medicine U. Ctrl. Del Caribe, Cayey, P.R., 1978-84; prof. medicine U. Ctrl. Del Caribe, Bayamon, P.R., 1986-88, head dept. medicine, 1986-88; pvt. practice pulmonology San Juan Office, 1984-86, 93—; chief pulmonary fellowship San Juan City Hosp., 1988-93; sr. respiratory dist. cons. P.R. Indsl. Commn., San Juan, 1978—; treas. 1st Pan Am. Congress Diseases of Chest, San Juan, 1989-96. Capt. U.S. Army, 1977-78. Fellow ACP, Am. Coll. Chest Physicians, Am. Coll. Cardiology. Roman Catholic. Office: 1329 Jesus J. Pinero Caparra Terrace PR 00923

LEONARD, ANGELINE JANE, psychotherapist; b. McKeesport, Pa., Dec. 9, 1940; d. Paul James Franklin and Jane Angeline (McKee) L.; m. Tom L. Kregel, Aug. 25, 1962 (div. 1970). BFA, U. Okla., 1962; MA in Art History, UCLA, 1965; MA in Clin. Art Therapy, Immaculate Heart Coll., 1980; PhD in Clin. Psychology, Cambridge Grad. Sch., 1991. Lic. marriage, family, child counselor, Calif., marriage and family counselor, N.C.; registered, bd. cert. art therapist; cert. hypnotherapist, guided imagery; lic. sci. of mind practitioner. Tchr. San Gabriel (Calif.) Mission High Sch., 1964-66, L.A. Valley Coll., Van Nuys, 1966-90, L.A. Unified Sch. Dist., 1980-90; pvt. practice psychotherapy, Reseda, Calif., 1982—; spkr. in field. Author: California Art Therapy Trends, 1993; author of poems. Bd. dirs., v.p. Ch. of Religious Sci., North Hollywood, Calif., 1989-93. Mem. Am. Art Therapy Assn., Am. Assn. Marriage and Family Therapists, Artist Equity Assn. (sec.), Calif. Assn. Marriage and Family Therapists, So. Calif. Art Therapy Assn. (bd. dirs.), No. Calif. Art Therapy Assn. Democrat. Home and Office: 19520 Vose St Reseda CA 91335-3637

LEONARD, BRIAN EDMUND, psychopharmacology educator; b. Winchester, Hampshire, Eng., May 30, 1936; s. Harold Edmund and Dorothy (Coley) L.; m. Helga Frieda Emilie Mühlpfordt, Nov. 13, 1959; children: Ingrid Jenifer, Heide Jean. BSc with honors, U. Birmingham (Eng.), 1959, PhD, 1962; DSc, Nat. U. Ireland, 1977. Lectr. U. Nottingham (Eng.), 1962-68; tech. officer I.C.I. Pharms. Div., Macclesfield, Eng., 1968-71; group leader Organon Internat. B.V., Oss, The Netherlands, 1971-74; prof. pharmcology dept. Univ. Coll., Galway, Ireland, 1974—; mem. Royal Irish Acad., Ireland, 1982—; chmn. edn. com. Collegium Internat. Neuropsychopharmacol., 1989—, treas., 1992—. Author: Fundamentals of Psychopharmacology, 1992; editor: Antidepressants, 1990, Benzodiazepines, 1990; editorial bd. 8 internat. jours.; contbr. over 300 articles to profl. jours. Mem. Internat. Soc. Study Stress (coun. 1989), Nat. Drugs Adv. Bd., Brit. Assn. Psychpharmacology (pres. 1988-90), Am. Coll. Neuropsychopharmacology (fng. corr.), Royal Coll. Psychiatry (assoc.). Office: U Coll Pharmacology Dept, Galway Ireland

LEONARD, ELISE ROBERTA, ophthalmologist; b. Bklyn., Nov. 23, 1953; d. Paul I. and Sylvia R. (Tracer) L.; m. Arnold M. Semel, July 4, 1976; children: Arin, Jessica. BA, NYU, 1974, MD, 1978. Diplomate Am. Bd. Ophthlmology, Am. Bd. Eye Surgery. Intern in internal medicine L.I. Jewish Hosp., New Hyde Park, N.Y., 1978-79, resident in ophthalmology, 1979-82; pvt. practice Plantation, Fla., 1982—; bd. dirs. Found. for Advanced Eye Care, Sunrise, Fla.; founder, pres. Women Physicians of South Fla., 1987-92. Bd. dirs. Women in Distress, Ft. Lauderdale, 1995-96, Temple Beth Torah, Tamarac, Fla., 1995-96. Fellow Am. Acad. of Ophthalmology; mem. Am. Soc. Cataract and Refractive Surgery, Am. Coll. of Eye Surgeons, Am. Med. Women's Assn., Women in Ophthalmology, Women Physicians of South Fla. (pres. 1987-92). Jewish. Office: Ste 214 1776 N Pine Island Rd Plantation FL 33322 also: 1732 Univ Dr Pembroke Pines FL 33024

LEONARD, HUBERT ARNOLD, neurologist; b. Astoria, Oreg., Mar. 18, 1945; s. Hubert F. and June (Groth) L. AB, Brown U., 1967; PhD in Biochemistry, U. Oreg., 1971, MD, 1973. Diplomate Am. Bd. Neurology, Am. Bd. Psychiatry. Med. resident UCLA, 1973-74; neurology resident U. Oreg., 1974-77; dir. neurology resident program Good Samaritan Hosp., Portland, 1977-79; neurologist pvt. practice, Portland, 1979—; tchr. nursing biochemistry Oreg. Health Scis. U., 1969, 70, 71, tchr. med. neuroanatomy, 1975, 76; lectr. and presenter in field. Contbr. articles to profl. jours. Bd. dirs. Ballet Oreg., Portland, 1981-88. Grantee Sandoz Pharm., 1979-82, 95, Eli Lilly Labs., 1982-90, Glaxo Pharms., 1989-90, 90-91, 93-94, 94-95, 95; Biochemistry fellow NIH, 1967-70. Mem. Am. Assn. for Study of Headaches, Am. Acad. Neurology, North Pacific Soc. Neurology and Psychiatry, Oreg. Med. Assn., Med. Soc. of Greater Portland. Office: Neurological Clinic 1040 NW 22d Portland OR 97210

LEONARD, JULIET MITCHELL, physician assistant; b. Washington, June 21, 1959; d. George Hunt and Betty Ann (Gantz) Mitchell; m. Charles William Leonard Jr., Sept. 10, 1983; children: Stephanie Ann, Chase Edward. BS in Biology, Salem Coll., 1981; cert. physician asst., U. N.C., 1983. Physician asst. George H. Mitchell, M.D., Washington, 1984—. Mem. Acad. Acad. Physician Assts. Republican. Episcopalian. Home: 712 Cornell St Apt 6 Fredericksburg VA 22401

LEONARD, SUSAN RUTH, psychologist, consultant; b. Mineola, N.Y., June 15, 1955; d. Donald Edward Leonard and Jane (Solomon) Hertzberg. BA, L.I. U., 1977; MA, U. N.C., 1980, PhD, 1985. Lic. psychologist, N.C. From instr. to asst. prof. psychology dept. Wake Forest U., Winston-Salem, N.C., 1984-86, staff psychologist counseling ctr., 1985-89; clin. psychologist Manoogian Psychol. Assocs., Winston-Salem, 1986—; cons. Ctr. for Creative Leadership, Greensboro, N.C., 1985-92. Vol. United Way, Winston-Salem, 1990-91; mem. adv. com. Family Svcs., Family Violence, Winston-Salem, 1987-90; trustee Resource Ctr. for Women and Ministry in South, 1989-91; bd. dirs. AIDS Task Force, Winston-Salem, 1989-92, Youth Opportunities Inc., Winston-Salem, 1990-92, 93—, AIDS Care Svc., Winston-Salem, 1991-95, Cancer Svcs., Winston-Salem, 1996—. Mem. APA, AAUW, Assn. Women in Psychology, N.C. Psychol. Assn. Office: Manoogian Psychol Assocs 1338 Ashley Sq Winston Salem NC 27103

LEONARD, WALTER RAYMOND, retired biology educator; b. Scott County, Va., July 5, 1923; s. Homer Stanley and Minnie Eunice (Neal) L.; m. Alice Ann McCaskill, Sept. 1, 1951; children—Leslie Ann, Walter Raymond. B.A., Tusculum Coll., Greeneville, Tenn., 1946; M.A., Vanderbilt U., 1947, Ph.D., 1949. Mem. faculty Wofford Coll., Spartanburg, S.C., 1949-93; John M. Reeves prof. biology Wofford Coll., 1954-87, William R. Kenan Jr. prof. biology, 1987-93, William R. Kenan Jr. prof. emeritus, 1993—; instl. rev. bd. mem. Spartanburg Regional Med. Ctr., 1994—; faculty athletic rep. NCAA. Served with USAAF, 1942-43. Named to Sports Hall of Fame, Tusculum Coll., 1983; Walter Raymond Leonard scholarship created Wofford Coll., 1973; W. Ray Leonard award established Beta Beta Beta, 1993; W. Ray Leonard Retirement Fund established Former Students Wofford Coll., 1993. Mem. AAAS, S.C. Acad. Sci., Scabbard and Blade (hon.), Lamda Chi Alpha (named to Hall of Fame 1996), Letterman's Club (hon.). Methodist. Home: 110 Pinetree Cir Spartanburg SC 29307-2938 Office: Wofford Coll N Church St Spartanburg SC 29301

LEONARDI, MARCO M., neuroradiologist; b. Rome, May 23, 1944; s. Giuseppe M. and Paola E. (Boriani) L.; m. Adrianna C. Dall'Occa Dell'Orso, Apr. 16, 1969; 1 child, Nicola O. Diploma, Maturita Classica

Liceo, Venezia, Italy, 1961; MD, U. Padua, Italy, 1967, Radiologist, 1969. Asst. radiologist Civil Hosp., Udine, Italy, 1968-71, asst. neuroradiologist, 1971-74, chief neuroradiology sect., 1974-80, head neuroradiology dept., 1980-93; head neuroradiology dept. Univ. Hosp., Milan, Italy, 1993—; asst. prof. neuroradiology U. Milan, 1995—. Founder, editor in chief Rivista di Neuroradiologia Jour., 1988—; founder, pub. editor: Interventional Neuroradiology; contbr. articles to profl. jours./publs., author books in field. Mem. Italian Assn. Neuroradiology (pres. 1986-90), European Soc. Neuroradiology (sec.-gen. 1993—), Am. Soc. Neuroradiology (corr. mem.), Radiol. Soc. N.Am., World Fedn. Neuroradiol. Socs. (chmn. Commn. for Publs. in Neuroradiology), Hungarian Soc. Neuroradiology (hon.). Home: Via del Pratello 8, I-40122 Bologna Italy Office: IRCCS Ospedale Maggiore, Via Francesco Sforza 35, I-20122 Milan Italy

LEONE, CHARLES RUSSELL, JR., ophthalmologist; b. Erie, Pa., Mar. 11, 1935; s. Charles Russell and Jessie Florence (Chimenti) L.; m. Ellen Kay Warren, Nov. 15, 1958; children: Charles III, Jeffrey J., Randolph T., Phillip C. BA, U. Va., 1956; MD, Temple U., 1960; MSc, Ohio State U., 1965. Diplomate Am. Bd. Ophthalmology. Intern St. Vincent Hosp., Erie, 1960-61, surg. resident, 1961-62; ophthalmology resident Ohio State Univ., Columbus, 1963-66; fellow in eye plastic surgery Manhattan Eye and Ear Hosp., N.Y.C., 1966-67; fellow eye mastic surgery Univ. Ala. Eye Found. Hosp., Birmingham, 1966-67; John Mustarde preceptee Canniesburn Hosp., Glasgow, Scotland, 1971; mem. adv. com. Edmund P. Spaeth Found., Phila., 1977—. Author: Atlas of Orbital Surgery, 1991; co-author: Eye Plastic Surgery Manual, 1983, Eye Plastic Surgery, 1990; mem. editl. bd. Ophthalmic Plastic Surgery Jour., 1983—; contbr. articles to profl. jours. Mem. Soc. to Prevent Blindness, San Antonio, 1968, Tex. Med. Assn. Political Action, Austin, 1968. Capt. USAF, 1962-63. Fellow ACS, Am. Soc. Ophthalmic Plastic and Reconstructive Surgery (charter, sec. 1975-77, v.p. 1982-83), Am. Acad. Ophthalmology (Honor award 1979, Sr. Honor award 1990); mem. San Antonio Soc. Ophthalmology (pres. 1977-78, 91-92), Orbital Soc. (charter mem.). Republican. Roman Catholic. Office: 7950 Floyd Curl Dr San Antonio TX 78229-3916

LEONE, DOLORES MADELINE, retired psychiatric health care administrator; b. Jersey City, N.J., Oct. 14, 1931; d. Frank and Mary (Critelli) L. Diploma in Nursing, Jersey City Hosp., 1952; BS in Nursing, Loretto Heights Coll., 1966; MS in Nursing, U. Colo., 1968; Cert. in Alcohol Studies, Rutgers U., 1971. RN, Colo. Staff mem. Jersey City Hosp. Med. Ctr., 1952; camp nurse YMHA and YWHA Camps, Milford, Pa., 1952; head nurse and suprv. BS Pollak Hosp., Jersey City, 1952-57; indsl. nures Corona Corp., Jersey City, 1957-59; sr. staff nurse Vets. Adminstrn. Hosp., Denver, 1959-64; clin. specialist, dir. psychiatric nursing N.W. Community Mental Health Ctr., Denver, 1968-73; mental health coordinator Colo. Div. Mental Health, Denver, 1973-74; pub. health nursing cons. Colo. Dept. of Health, Denver, 1974-78; dir. adminsrtv. services and edn. Bethesda PsycHealth Sytem, Denver, 1978-90; ret., 1990. Co-author Creative Health Services, 1976; contbr. articles to profl. jours. National Inst. Mental Health grantee, 1964-68; named Outstanding Psychiatric Nurse Clinician, 1984. Democrat. Roman Catholic.

LEONE, LUCILE P., retired health administrator; b. Ohio, 1902; m. Nicholas C. Leone, 1952. BA, U. Del., 1924; BS, Johns Hopkins U., 1927; MS, Columbia U., 19929; 9 hon degrees. Staff nurse Johns Hopkins Hosp., Balt., 1927-29; instr., prof. U. Minn., Mpls., 1929-41; comdt. Student Nursing Svc. USPHS, 1941-42, dir. Cadet Corps Program, 1942-48, chief nurse officer, asst. surgeon gen., 1948-66; assoc. dean nursing Tex. Woman's Coll., 1977-82; advisor internat. students Sch. Nursing U. Calif., San Francisco, 1978-83. Mem. Inst. Medicine/Nat. Acad. Sci. Address: 1400 Geary Blvd San Francisco CA 94109*

LEONG, JO-ANN CHING, microbiologist, educator; b. Honolulu, May 15, 1942; d. Raymond and Josephine Ching; m. Oren T.H. Leong; children: Kara Elise, Jonathan Raymond. BA in Zoology, U. Calif., Berkeley, 1964; PhD in Microbiology, San Francisco Sch. Medicine, 1971. Postdoctoral rsch. assoc. dept. biochemistry U. Calif., San Francisco, 1971-75, asst. rsch. virologist Cancer Rsch. Inst., 1975; asst. prof. Oreg. State U., Corvallis, 1975-80, assoc. prof., 1980-86, prof., 1986-92, disting. prof., 1992—, chairperson, 1996—; grant reviewer Sea Grant, NSF, CRIS, USDA, NIH; cons. Am. Microscan, 1986. Co-author: Retroviruses and Differentiation, 1982, Molecular Approaches to Bacteria and Viral Diseases of Fish, 1983, Fish Vaccination, 1988, Viral Vaccines for Aquaculture, 1993, Human Endogenous Retroviruses, 1994, DNA Vaccines for Fish, 1996; virology editor Diseases of Aquatic Organisms. Coord. Women in Sci. Career Workshop, Portland (Oreg.) State U., 1977. Recipient Dernham Rsch. Fellowship, Am. Cancer Soc., 1973-75, fellowship Giannini Found. for Med. Rsch., 1973, Rsch. award Sigma Xi, 1990; named NORCAS prof. Batelle NW Labs, 1976, Disting Prof. Oreg. State U. Alumni Assn., 1991. Fellow Am. Acad. Microbiology; mem. AAAS, AAUP (exec. bd. 1982), European Assn. of Fish Pathologists, Am. Soc. Microbiology, Am. Soc. Virology, Am. Fisheries Soc. (fish health sect.), Assn. Women in Sci., Am. Assn. Cancer Rsch. Office: Oreg State U Dept Microbiology Corvallis OR 97331

LEONG, SUE, retired community health and pediatrics nurse; b. Alameda, Calif., Feb. 15, 1930; d. Leong Dai Sun and Leong San See. BS, U. Calif., San Francisco, 1953; MPH, U. Mich., 1963; MA, San Francisco Theol. Sem., 1958. Cert. sch. nurse, sch. nurse practitioner, nurse specialist. Head nurse Lafayette Clinic, Detroit; pub. health nurse San Francisco Health Dept.; assoc. dir. Ecumenical Campus Ctr., Ann Arbor, Mich.; sch. nurse practitioner Ann Arbor Pub. Schs.; adj. asst. prof. U. Mich. Contbr. articles to profl. jours. Mem. NEA, Mich. Assn. Sch. Nurses (Disting. Svc. award 1990, Dorothy Christy award 1993). Home: 1506 Golden Ave Ann Arbor MI 48104-4327

LEOPOLD, GEORGE ROBERT, radiologist; b. Lewistown, Pa., 1937. MD, U. Pitts., 1962. Intern York Hosp., 1962-63; resident U. Pitts., 1965-68; chmn., prof. dept. radiology U. Calif., San Diego. Mem. Am. Coll. Radiology (Gold medal 1996), AIUM, ARRS, AUR, RSNA. Office: U Calif San Diego Med Ctr 8756 200 W Arbor Dr San Diego CA 92103-8756

LEOPOLD, MARTIN ROBIN, ophthalmologist; b. Bklyn., Apr. 3, 1952; s. Robert Wallace and Phila (Banner) L.; m. Karen Kravarik, Apr. 13, 1975; children: Yona Ruth, David Karol, Daniel Robert. BA in Physics with honors, Hofstra U., 1974; MD, Cornell U., 1978. Diplomate Am. Bd. Ophthalmology; lic. MD, N.Y. Intern Northport (N.Y.) VA Hosp., 1979; resident in ophthalmology Mt. Sinai Hosp., N.Y.C., 1980-82; med. retina fellow NYU/Belleview Hosp., N.Y.C., 1983; pvt. practice Fishkill, N.Y., 1983—; instr./lectr. Mt. Sinai Med. Ctr., N.Y.C., 1992—; investigator Wyeth-Ayerst for Tolrestat, Nat. Eye Inst.-HEDS Study. Author: Ultrasound in Medicine, 1979, AIDS: The Epidemic of Kaposis Sarcoma and Opportunistic Infections, 1984; contbr. articles to profl. jours. Mem. Dutchess County Traffic Safety Bd., Poughkeepsie, N.Y., 1985-88. Citibank Med. scholar, 1975-78. Fellow ACS, Am. Acad. Ophthalmology; mem. AMA, Am. Soc. Cataract and Refractive Surgery, N.Y. State Med. Soc., Dutchess County Med. Soc. (rep. ins. 1989-91), Phi Beta Kappa. Office: Hudson Valley Eye Surgeons 335 Rt 52 Fishkill NY 12524

LEOUNG, GIFFORD S., physician; b. N.Y.C., July 8, 1953; s. Will and Judy (Yuen) L.; m. Mee Mee Kiong, May 21, 1989; children: Jasmine, Mitchell. BS, Columbia U., 1975; MD, Cornell U., 1979. Resident in internal medicine Washington Hosp. Ctr., 1979-82; fellow in infectious diseases U. Calif./San Francisco Gen. Hosp., 1983-85; fellow in pulmonary medicine U. Calif. Davis/VA Hosp., Martinez, 1985-86; asst. clin. prof. medicine U. Calif., San Francisco, 1988—; pvt. practice specializing in infectious diseases San Francisco, 1989—; med. dir. HIV care St. Francis Meml. Hosp., San Francisco, 1994—. Contbr. articles to profl. jours. Recipient CIBA award for cmty. svc., 1977; numerous awards and commendations for work in AIDS. Mem. ACP, Calif. Med. Assn., Am. Soc. Microbiology, Am. Thoracic Soc., Am. Coll. Chest Physicians, Bay Area Infectious Disease Soc., Infectious Disease Soc. Am. Office: 1199 Bush St # 400 San Francisco CA 94109

LEPE, XAVIER, dentist, educator; b. Chgo., June 19, 1956; s. Javier and Dolores G. (Pimienta) L.; m. Rosa Irene Pelayo, Dec. 17, 1983; children: Melinda Yvette, Xavier Adrian. BS, U. Guadalajara, Mex., 1976, DDS, 1980; prosthodontic cert., Loyola U., Chgo., 1985, MS, 1987. Substitute asst. prof. U. Guadalajara, 1981-82; clin. instr. Loyola U., 1983-85, asst. prof., 1986-93; asst. prof. U. Wash., Seattle, 1993—. Contbr. articles, revs. to profl. publs. Bd. dirs. Chgo. Boys and Girls Club, 1982-83; soccer coach Snoking Youth Club, Edmonds, Wash., 1995-96. Mem. ADA, Wash. State Dental Soc., Am. Assn. Dental Schs., Internat. Assn. Dental Rsch., Wash. State Soc. Prosthodontics, Phi Omega Dental Fraternity. Roman Catholic. Office: U Wash Box 357456 Seattle WA 98195-7456

LEPORE, MARIE ANN, home care nurse; b. Bronx, N.Y., Aug. 21, 1946; d. John Paul and Lillian Josephine (Lucenta) LePore; 1 child, Marie Ann Bank. Student, Cambridge Acad., 1982, S.I., N.Y., 1983, Barton Sch., 1986, Laurel Sch.Med. recruit, 1986; A. Specialized Bus., I.C.S., Scranton, Pa., 1995, A in Computer Specialist in Sci., 1996; DegreeMed. Dental Asst., Laurel Sch. for Med. Recruit, N.Y. Home care nurse Dept. Social Svcs., N.Y.C., 1975-78; home health care worker Massive Home Health Svcs., Bronx, N.Y., 1978-82; home careworker Puerto Rican Home Care Svcs., Bronx, N.Y., 1982-84; home care nurse Entea Home Care, Bronx, N.Y., 1986-89, Montefiore Hosp., Bronx, 1989—; dental asst. Recipient numerous professional awards. Home: 3304 White Plains Rd Bronx NY 10467-5703 Office: 925 Oak St Scranton PA 18515

LEPORT, PETER CARY, surgeon; b. N.Y.C., Jan. 15, 1949; s. Hyman Bert Leport; m. Christina Rizza, Dec. 1984; children: Franciso, Aurora, Christopher. BA, SUNY, Binghamton, 1970; MD, SUNY, Bklyn., 1975. Diplomate Am. Bd. Surgery. Intern Kings County Hosp., Bklyn., 1974-75, resident, 1975-78; Bd. dirs. Ayn Rand Inst. Mem. ACS, Am. Free Choice in Medicine. Office: 11180 Warner Ave Ste 461 Fountain Valley CA 92708

LEPPERT, PHYLLIS CAROLYN, obstetrician/gynecologist; b. Phila., July 7, 1938; d. Walter Jennings and Alice (Brubach) L. BS, Columbia U., 1961, MS, 1964; MD, Duke U., 1973; PhD, Columbia U., 1986. Diplomate Nat. Bd. Med. Examiners, Am. Bd. Obstetrics and Gynecology. Clin. scholar Duke U., Durham, N.C., 1973-74; resident in pediatrics Duke U. Med. Ctr., Durham, 1974-76; resident in ob-gyn. Yale U. Med. Sch., New Haven, 1976-79; assoc. in ob-gyn. Columbia U., N.Y.C., 1979-81, asst. prof. ob-gyn., 1981-88; vis. prof. Tokyo (Japan) Coll. of Pharmacy, Hachioji, 1989; chmn. dept. ob-gyn. Rochester (N.Y.) Gen. Hosp., 1989—; from assoc. prof. to prof. U. Rochester Sch. of Medicine and Dentistry, 1989—; mem. adv. com. women's health initiative program NIH, 1993—; mem. N.Y. State Coun. on Grad. Med. Edn., 1994—, mem. subcom. on health care reform and financing, mem. subcom. on med. edn. consortium; mem. Bd. Profl. Med. Conduct, N.Y., 1990—. Co-editor: The Extracellular Matrix of the Reproductive Tract, 1991; contbr. numerous articles to profl. jours. Mem. Monroe County Bd. Health, 1992—; bd. dirs. Maternity Ctr. Assn., N.Y.C., 1988—, Preferred Care, Rochester, 1990-94, Riverdale Mental Health Assn., 1986-89, St. Luke/Roosevelt Hosp., N.Y.C., 1986-88; mem. vestry Christ Ch. Riverdale, Bronx, N.Y., 1984-86; mem. adv. com. Office of Tech., U.S. Congress, 1984. Berlex Found. Internat. rsch. fellow, 1989. Fellow ACOG; mem. AAAS, Am. Coll. of Ob-Gyn (com. on the underserved), Soc. for Exptl. Medicine, N.Y. Obstet. Soc., Soc. for Gynecol. Investigation, Am. Soc. Profs. of Ob-Gyn., Monroe County Med. Soc. Office: Rochester Gen Hosp 1425 Portland Ave Rochester NY 14621-3001

LEPPLA, DAVID CHARLES, pathology educator; b. Denver, July 22, 1953; s. Charles Frederick and Lucille Josephine (Schneider) L. BS, Seattle U., 1975; MD, Colo. U., 1979. Diplomate Am. Bd. Pathology. Intern in internal medicine U. Tex. Health Sci. Ctr., Dallas, 1979-80, fellow in mineral metabolism and endocrinology, 1980-82, rsch. assoc., 1982-83; resident in pathology Marshall U. Sch. Medicine, Huntington, W.Va., 1984-87, chief resident in pathology, 1987-88, asst. prof., 1988—. Fellow Am. Soc. Clin. Pathology (alt. to adv. com. 1990); mem. AAAS, Alpha Omega Alpha. Office: Marshall U Sch Medicine 1542 Spring Valley Dr Huntington WV 25704-9388

LERCH, MARKUS M., gastroenterologist; b. Hilden, Germany, Sept. 30, 1957; s. Hans H. and Ruth (Dietel) L.; m. Gudrun Dahmen. MD, Freiburg (Germany) U. Bd. cert. internal medicine and gastroenterology. Intern dept. medicine Freiburg U. Med. Sch., 1983-84, resident dept. pathology, 1984; resident dept. gastroenterology Aachen Tech. U., Germany, 1984-89; rsch. fellow cell biology U. Milan, 1989-90; postdoctoral fellow Harvard Med. Sch., Boston, 1990-92; attending physician dept. medicine and gastroenterology Ulm U., Germany, 1992-94; sr. scientist dept. molecular biology Max-Planck-Inst Biochemie, Martinsried, Germany, 1994-96; asst. prof. medicine U. Saarland, Homburg, Saar, 1996—. Editor: Textbook on Gastrointestinal Emergencies, 1996; contbr. articles to profl. jours. Recipient rsch. scholarship to Italy and U.S., 1989-92, Adolf-Kussmaul prize in gastroenterology Germany, 1993. Mem. Gastrointestinal Rsch. Group of Am. Gastroenterological Assn., Am. Pancreatic Assn. Office: Medizinische Klinik II, UniKlinik Saar, 66421 Homburg Germany

LERIT, DELIA TUMULAK, school nurse; b. Lapulapu City, The Philippines, July 16, 1954; d. Nephtali and Presentacion (Tubongbanua) Tumulak; m. Felix Lerit, Jr., Apr. 9, 1983; children: Vanessa Joy, Chloe Mae. BSN, Velez Coll. Nursing, Cebu City, The Philippines, 1975; health svc. credential, Calif. State U., L.A., 1990, MSN, 1995. RN, Calif., B.C., Can. Staff nurse White Meml. Med. Ctr., L.A., Vancouver (B.C.) Gen. Hosp., Shaughnessy Hosp., Vancouver; sch. nurse L.A. Unified Sch. Dist. Named Employee of Month, 1986. Mem. Philippine Nurses Assn., L.A. Coun. Sch. Nurses, Sigma Theta Tau.

LERITZ, DANIEL RAYMOND, pharmaceutical company executive, consultant; b. St. Louis, Jan. 24, 1945; s. Joseph D. and Agnes (Lyons) L.; m. Retta J. Schoen, Nov. 9, 1974; children: Daniel, Retta. BS in Chem., St. Louis U., 1966; MBA, Washington U., 1971. Loss control cons. The Hartford Ins. Group, St. Louis, 1970-71; mgr. new products Carboline Co., St. Louis, 1971-78; acct. exec./dir. mktg. BHN Advt., St. Louis, 1978-80; mgr. sales Carnegie div. Rexall Corp., St. Louis, 1980-81; mgr. western sales The Vitarine Co., Inc., Springfield Gardens, N.Y., 1981-82; mgr. sales Pvt. Formulations, Inc., Edison, N.J., 1982-87; pres. The Leritz Co., Inc., St. Louis, 1985—; bd. dirs. Nutri-Pac Corp., Interstate Foods Mktg., Ltd. Coauthored numerous articles. Bd. dirs. Am. Cancer Soc., Mo., 1980; chmn. bd. trustees York Woods, Mo., 1984; mem. alumni bd. St. Louis U. High. Mem. Am. Chem. Soc., Assn. Drug & Chem. Industry of Mo., Norwood Hills Country Club, Delta Sigma Phi. Roman Catholic. Home: 1 Cricket Ln Saint Louis MO 63144-1021 Office: The Leritz Co Inc 2652 Melvin Ave Saint Louis MO 63144-2551

LERMAN, STEVEN ELLIOT, occupational medicine physician; b. N.Y.C., May 10, 1958; s. Harold and Mildred (Fried) L.; m. Wendy Schwimmer, June 21, 1981; children: Kevin Louis, Alysa Beth. BA, Rutgers Coll., 1980; MD, Washington U., 1984; MPH, Robert Wood Johnson Med. Sch., 1988. Resident in internal medicine Sinai Hosp., Balt., 1984-86; resident in occupational medicine Robert Wood Johnson Med. Sch., Piscataway, N.J., 1986-88; med. dir. Exxon, Baytown, Tex., 1988-90, dir. medicine and environ. health, 1990—; mem. site visit team Coun. on Edn. for Pub. Health, Washington, 1994; adj. assoc. prof. occupational medicine U. Tex. Health Sci. Ctr. Contbr. articles to profl. jours. Bd. dirs. Am. Cancer Soc., Baytown, 1990-91. Mem. Am. Coll. Occupational Medicine, AMA, Tex. Med. Assn. (com. on the environment 1991—), Tex. Chem. Coun. (environ. health com. 1991-92). Jewish. Office: Exxon Baytown Chem Plant PO Box 4004 Baytown TX 77522

LERNER, CHARLES J., physician; b. Chgo., Apr. 16, 1941; s. Louis and Julia K. Lerner; m. Shirley Farkas, July 2, 1961; children: Nancy, Wendy. BS, U. Chgo., 1962; MD, St. Louis U., 1966. Diplomate Am. Bd. Internal Medicine. Physician San Antonio, Tex., 1972—; instr. U. Tex. Sch. Medicine, San Antonio, 1973-77, asst. prof., 1977-78, assoc. prof. medicine, 1978-86, clin. prof. medicine, 1986—; med. adv. bd. So. Tex. Blood Tissue, San Antonio, 1987—, trustee, 1989—; hosp. epidemologist, San Antonio Comm. Hosp., 1983—. Author: (book) Health Hints for Traveler, 1990. Mem. Northside Sch. Dist. Vopat Coun., San Antonio, 1990-91. Mem. Tex. Infectious Disease Soc. (sec. 1989-93, pres. 1993-94), Infectious Disease Soc. Am., Soc. Hosp. Epidemiology, Internat. Soc. Travel Medicine. Office: San Antonio Infectious Disease Cons 8042 Wurzbach # 280 San Antonio TX 78229

LERNER, LEONARD JOSEPH, endocrinology and pharmacology educator; b. Roselle, N.J.; s. Hyman and Esther (Honig) L. BS in Pharmacy, Rutgers U., 1943, BA, 1951, MS, 1953, PhD, 1954. Head endocrine rsch. sect. William S. Merrell Co. (now Marion Merrell Dow), Cin., 1954-58; head endocrinology sect. Squibb Inst. for Med. Rsch., New Brunswick, N.J., 1958-65, dir. dept. endocrinology, 1965-70; dir. dept. endocrinology Lepetit Rsch. Labs. div. Dow Lepetit, Milan, Italy, 1971-77; rsch. prof. dept. ob-gyn and pharmacology Jefferson Med. Coll., Thomas Jefferson U., Phila., 1977—, prof. pharmacology, 1988—; adj. prof. Sch. Nursing, U. Pa., Phila., 1990—; cons. NIH, WHO, FDA, various other govt and non-profit orgns., 1958—, pharm. cos., 1977—; mem. numerous sci. adv. bds., coms. and rev. bds. Mem. editorial bd. Steroids, Transactions of N.Y. Acad. Scis., others; contbr. articles to profl. jours.; patentee in field. Bd. dirs. N.J. affiliate Am. Diabetes Assn., 1990-92. With AUS, 1944-46. Grantee in field. Fellow AAAS, N.Y. Acad. Scis. (vice chair, then chair sect. biomedicine 1968-72); mem. Endocrine Soc., Am. Assn. Cancer Rsch. (mem. program com., Cain Meml. award 1989), Soc. Study of Reproduction (animals in rsch. com.), Am. Physiology Soc., Am. Soc. for Reproductive Medicine, Soc. for Exptl. Biology and Medicine, Sigma Xi. Home: C5 Windsor Castle Cranbury NJ 08512-1412 Office: Thomas Jefferson U Dept Pharmacology 1020 Locust St Philadelphia PA 19107-6731

LERNER, MILDRED SHERWOOD, clinical psychologist, psychoanalyst, psychotherapist; b. N.Y.C., Mar. 29, 1929; d. Samuel Jerome and Rose (Malina) Sherwood; children—Andrew Roy, Julie Sue. B.A. with honors, CCNY, 1951, M.A., 1952; Ph.D., NYU, 1957. Pvt. practice psychology N.Y.C., 1962—; supr. N.Y. Clinic Mental Health, N.Y.C.; instr. adult edn. CCNY, N.Y.C., 1952-54; chief psychologist High Point Hosp., Port Chester, N.Y., 1954-61; bd. dirs., tng. analyst, tchr. Nat. Psychol. Assn. for Psychoanalysis, N.Y.C., 1968—; dean student tng. Nat. Psychol. Assn. for Psychoanalysis, 1968-72, pres., 1972-74, v.p., 1986—; prof. Womanschool, N.Y.C., 1974-76; dir. grad. program in psychoanalysis Internat. Grad. U. Leysin, Switzerland, 1975-76; therapy cons. Canyon Ranch, 1989—. Contbr. articles to profl. jours. Trustee Chamber Ballet U.S.A. Alvin Johnson scholar, 1951; Psychology fellow, CCNY, 1952-54. Fellow Am. Psychol. Assn.; mem. AAUW, N.Y. State Psychol. Assn., N.Y. Soc. Clin. Psychologists, Am. Assn. Psychotherapy, Psychotherapists in Pvt. Practice, Am. Humanistic Psychol. Assn., Am. Group Psychol. Assn., Mcpl. Art Soc., NY. Acad. Sci.; Nat. Arts Club (music chmn.), Psi Chi. Address: 2 Fifth Ave Apt 19A New York NY 10011-8842 also: Canyon Ranch 8600 E Rockcliff Rd Tucson AZ 85715-9733

LERNER, ROBERT, surgeon, educator; b. N.Y.C., Mar. 1, 1929; s. Gerson and Gertrude Lerner; m. Pilar Lerner, May 17, 1962; children: David B., Charles A. BA, NYU, 1949; MS, Columbia U., 1950; MD, U. Basel, Switzerland, 1955. Rotating intern, resident in surgery Jewish Hosp. of Bklyn., 1956-60; fellow in head and neck surgery Meml. Sloan-Kettering Cancer Ctr., N.Y.C., 1961; clin. prof. surgery SUNY, Bklyn., 1962—; attending surgeon Jewish Hosp. Bklyn., N.Y., 1962-78, dir. surgery, 1978-88; med. dir. Lymphedema Svcs., PC, N.Y.C., 1989—. Fellow ACS, Internat. Coll. Surgeons. Office: Lymphedema Svcs PC 360 East 57 St New York NY 10022

LERNER, ROBERT GIBBS, medical educator; b. Bklyn., Mar. 30, 1936; s. Morris and Sarah (Kludke) L.; m. Helen Marjorie Halpern, Aug. 31, 1958; children: Rachel Ann, Marcia Lynn, Sharon Ruth. AB, NYU, 1956, MD, 1960. Diplomate Am. Bd. Internal Medicine. Teaching asst. NYU Sch. Medicine, N.Y.C., 1961-62; instr. U. So.Calif. Sch. Medicine, 1965-67; from asst. prof. to prof. medicine N.Y. Med. Coll., N.Y.C., 1967-81; prof. medicine, chief hematology N.Y. Med. Coll., Valhalla, 1981—, acting chmn. dept. medicine, 1996—; cons. FDA, Rockville, Md., 1972-78, NIH, Bethesda, Md., 1976, 95. Contbr. articles to profl. jours. Served to capt. M.C., U.S. Army, 1963-65. Recipient Research Career Devel. award NIH, 1971. Fellow ACP, Soc. for the Study of Blood, (pres. 1995); mem. Island Peer Review Orgn. (bd. dirs. 1995). Home: 11 Dell Dr Tuckahoe NY 10707-1203 Office: NY Med Coll Grasslands Rd Valhalla NY 10595

LERNER, STEPHEN ALEXANDER, microbiologist, physician, educator; b. Chgo., Oct. 4, 1938; s. David G. and Florence (Trace) L.; m. June 6, 1963 (div. 1990); children: Deborah, Daniel, Susan; m. Aug. 18, 1991. AB magna cum laude, Harvard U., 1959, MD magna cum laude, 1963. Intern, then resident Peter Bent Brigham Hosp., 1963-65; rsch. assoc. NIH, 1965-68; postdoctoral fellow Stanford (Calif.) U., 1968-71; asst. prof. then assoc. prof. U. Chgo., 1971-86; prof. of medicine Wayne State U., Detroit, 1986—; convenor Soviet-Am. Symposium Antibiotics and Chemotherapy, Moscow, 1988. Editor: Aminoglycoside Ototoxicity, 1981; mem. editl. bd. Antimicrobial Agts. and Chemotherapy, 1981—, European Jour. Clin. Microbiology and Infectious Diseases, 1992—; contbr. articles to profl. jours. With USPHS, 1965-67. Recipient Borden Rsch. award, 1963. Fellow Infectious Disease Soc. Am., Am. Acad. Microbiology (com. on awards); mem. Am. Soc. Microbiology (chmn. antimicrobial chemotherapy 1987-88, divsn. group rep. 1990-92, councillor 1990-92, chmn. confs. com. 1993-96, internat. coord. com. 1993—, chmn. 1996—), Inter-Am. Soc. for Chemotherapy (pres. 1986-88, bd. dirs., chmn. 1988-93), Internat. Soc. Chemotherapy (exec. com. 1987-93), Phi Beta Kappa, Sigma Xi, Alpha Omega Alpha. Democrat. Jewish. Office: Harper Hosp Div Infectious Diseases 3990 John R Detroit MI 48201-2018

LERNER, THEODORE RAPHAEL, dentist; b. Bklyn., Sept. 28, 1932; s. Meyer and Tillie (Brimberg) L.; student Washington and Jefferson Coll., 1950-53; DDS, U. Pa., 1957; m. Barbara Ellen Bernstein, June 29, 1974; children by previous marriage: Andrea Holly, Evan Andrew. Practice dentistry, specializing in endodontics, Bklyn., 1957-93, Forest Hills, N.Y., 1968-93, Boca Raton, Fla., 1992—. Diplomate Am. Bd. Endodontics. Fellow Internat., Am. colls. dentists, Am. Assn. Endodontists; mem. ADA, 2d Dist. Dental Soc. (pres. 1971), Dental Soc. State of N.Y. (pres. 1983), Fla. Dental Assn. Home: 7040 Lions Head Ln Boca Raton FL 33496-5931 Office: 2499 Glades Rd Ste 204 Boca Raton FL 33431-7201

LERUT, HUGO LOUIS ARMAND JUSTINE, surgeon; b. Tienen, Brabant, Belgium, June 10, 1942; s. Robert and Simone (Knaepen) L.; m. Anne-Marie Jenné, Aug. 22, 1970; children: Sophie, Evelyne. MD, Kath. U. Leuven, Belgium, 1967, Lic. Phys. Edn., 1974. Surgeon H. Heart Hosp., Tienen, 1975, St. Andrews Hosp., Lubbeek, Belgium, 1975-94; coroner forensic medicine Leuven, 1980—; evaluator phys. damage for ins. co.; lectr. pediat. surgery Nursing Sch., Leuven, 1976-76; lectr. med. physiology Inds. U. Leuven, 1982-84, sec., coord. med. edn. for students in medicine. Contbr. articles to profl. jours.; edit. bd. Acta Chirurgica Belgica. Vice pres. Med. Commn. Brabant; trustee Orgn. for Disabled, tienen. Mem. Order of Medicine, Orde van den Prince Antwerp. Roman Catholic. Home: O L Vrouw Broedersstraat 5, 3300 Tienen Belgium

LESCOE, RICHARD JOHN, physician; b. Pa., Nov. 2, 1925; s. Charles and Mary Lescoe; children: Donna Lee, Linda Ann, Debora; m. Jean Sharley Taylor, Apr. 23, 1978; guardian of Stephanie. BS, U. Pitts., 1948, MD, 1949; JD, West Los Angeles Ch. Law, 1970. Diplomate Am. Bd. Gen. Surgery, Thoracic Surgery, Medicine in Law. Pvt. practice S.W. L.A., Calif., 1956-88; med. officer Bur. of Prisons, L.A., 1986-96. Capt. USAF, 1954-56. Fellow ACS, Am. Coll. Legal Medicine, Soc. Thoracic Surgery. Home: 986 Cornell Rd Pasadena CA 91106-4039

LESKO, BETTY HARDT, health care facility executive; b. Tyler, Tex., Aug. 13, 1945; d. John Wesley and Mary Martha (Carson) H.; m. Edmund M. Lesko, Oct. 11, 1969; children: Catherine, John, Richard. BA cum laude, Southwestern U., 1967; MA, So. Meth. U., 1968. Cert. tchr., Tex. Instr. Cen. Tex. Coll., Killeen, 1968-69; v.p. Roanoke Valley Anesthesia, Rocky Mt., Va., 1970—. Treas., pres. Roanoke Acad. Medicine Aux., 1976-79, 84-87; treas. Jr. League Roanoke Valley, 1979-83, pres., 1982-83; vol. ARC, Roanoke, 1989-91; membership chmn. S.W. Va. Opera Soc., Roanoke, 1977-79; treas., v.p. Roanoke Valley Speech and Hearing Ctr., 1988-91; bd. dirs. Planned Parenthood of the Blue Ridge; treas. Art Mus. Western Va., 1995-96, bd. dirs. Am. Cancer Soc., Rocky Mount and Roanoke, 1987-96, pres., 1993-95. Presbyterian. Home and Office: 100 Adam Perry Rd Rocky Mount VA 24151-9761

LESKO, RONALD MICHAEL, osteopathic physician; b. Homestead, Pa., Mar. 25, 1948; s. Andrew Paul and Elizabeth Ann (Tarasovic) L.; m. Helena Alexandra Shalayeva, July 29, 1990. BS, U. Pitts., 1970; DO, Coll. Osteo. Medicine & Surgery, Des Moines, 1973; MPH, Loma Linda U., 1985. Diplomate Am. Osteo. Bd. Family Physicians, Am. Osteo. Bd. Preventive Medicine (bd. dirs., chmn. pub. health rep., chmn. bd. exam. com. 1991-97). Famiy physician pvt. practice Port Richey, Fla., 1974-80; flight surgeon USN, NAS Chase Field Beeville, Tex., 1981-83; resident gen. preventive medicine Loma Linda (Calif.) U. Med. Ctr., 1983-85; pvt. practice family and preventive medicine, pvt. practice, Del Mar, Calif., 1988—; flight surgeon, capt. USNR, NAS Miramar, San Diego, 1988-95; ret. USNR, Loma Linda, Calif., 1996; attending physician ambulatory care svc. J.L. Pettis Meml. VA Hosp., Loma Linda, Calif., 1986-88; staff physician Scripps Meml. Hosp., La Jolla, Calif., 1990—; lectr., 1985—; cons. Jour. Am. Osteo. Assn., Chgo., 1987, phys. rediness div. USN, Washington, 1988; med. advisor blue ribbon adv. com. Nutrition Screening Initiative, Washington, 1991. Contbr. articles to med. jours.; rschr. in nutrition and metabolism in human physiology. Med. adviser March of Dimes Suncoast chpt., New Port Richey, 1977-79; bd. dirs. Fla. Gulf Health Systems Agy., Region IV, 1977-79, Price-Pottenger Nutrition Found., San Diego, 1988—. Fellow Am. Osteo. Coll. Occupational and Preventive Medicine (trustee 1989-91, chmn. pub. health divisional com. 1989-91), Am. Coll. Preventive Medicine; mem. APHA, Am. Osteo. Assn., San Diego Osteo. Med. Assn., Osteo. Physicians and Surgeons Calif., Am. Coll. Family Physicians-Osteo., U.S. Naval Flight Surgeons. Office: 13983 Mango Dr Ste 103 Del Mar CA 92014-3146

LESLIE, BRUCE ROBERT, physician; b. N.Y.C., Apr. 7, 1947; s. Stephen Howard and Lillian (Osinoff) L.; m. Leslie Ellen Gerwin, July 3, 1978; 1 child Jonathan Gerwin Leslie. AB, Harvard Coll., 1967; MD, Harvard Med. Sch., 1972; MSPH, Tulane Sch. Pub. Health, 1991. Bd. cert. in internal medicine, nephrology; recert. in internal medicine. Asst. prof. med. Cornell U. Med. Coll., N.Y.C., 1978-83; physician Ochsner Clin., New Orleans, 1983—. Lt. comdr. USPHS, 1974-76. Fellow Am. Coll. Physicians; mem. Am. Soc. Nephrology. Office: Ochsner Clin 1514 Jefferson Hwy New Orleans LA 70121-2429

LESLIE, CHARLES J., medical facility administrator; b. N.Y.C., Jan. 23, 1939; s. Charles Joseph and Alice (Clark) L.; m. Nancy, June 10, 1960; children: C.J., Jeffrey. BS, Columbia U , 1964. From v.p. to pres. Pyne X-Ray Corp., San Francisco, N.Y.C., 1965-86; pres. Fuji Med. Sys. USA, Stamford, Conn., 1987—. Mem. Marin Yacht Club, Manhasset Bay Yacht Club, Stamford Club, Winged Foot Golf Club, San Francisco Olympic Club. Office: Fuji Med Sys USA 333 Ludlow Stt Stamford CT 06902

LESLIE, M(ERLE) RUSSELL, JR., orthopaedic surgeon; b. Pitts., May 12, 1936; s. Merle Russell and Anne Louise (Blessing) L.; m. Virginia Lee Heinz, Nov. 28, 1964; children: Scott, Lisa, Craig, Kristen. AB, Dartmouth Coll., 1958; MD, U. Pitts., 1962. Diplomate Am. Bd. Orthopaedic Surgery. Pvt. practice, Pitts., 1970—. Capt. M.C., U.S. Army, 1963-65. Fellow ACS, Am. Acad. Orthopaedic Surgeons (cert. added qualifications in surgery of hand). Republican. Presbyterian. Home: 119 Springhouse Ln Pittsburgh PA 15238 Office: Oakland Orthopaedic Assocs 5020 Centre Ave Pittsburgh PA 15206

LESLIE, ROBERT ANDREW, physician; b. Eldorado, Kansas, June 19, 1931; s. Robert Wilson and Eleanor Bertha (Cumming) L.; m. Lynette Leslie. MD, Duke Univ., 1955. Dispensary SAC, USAF, APO 147, N.Y., 1956-58; medical officer U.S. Naval Repair Facility, San Diego, 1958-61; physician Seaview Medical, Long Beach, Calif., 1961-63, Carl G. Johnson, Long Beach, Calif., 1963-75; physician, medical dir. ACACIA Medical, Anaheim, Calif., 1975-80; physician Health Affilites, Long Beach, 1980-86; intra medical group L.A., 1986-92; physician Reservoir Medical Group, Pomona, Calif., 1992—; utilization com., Long Beach Hosp., 1984-85, medical com., 1984-85. With USAF, 1956-58. Mem. Soc. Contemporary Medicine and Surgery, Rotary Club, Am. Legion. Home: 243 Berkeley Ave Irvine CA 92715 Office: Reservoir Med Group 945 Holt St Pomona CA 91767

LESNE, MICHEL, research pharmacologist, educator; b. Tournai, Belgium, Jan. 27, 1943; s. Alphonse and Simone (Gennart) L.; children: Philippe, Vincent. Pharmacist degree, U. Louvain, Belgium, 1965, PhD in Pharm. Scis., 1969, clin. biology specialist, 1977; degree in pharmacokinetics, Pharm. Sch., London, 1972. Rsch. asst. Nat. Rsch. Fund, Belgium, 1965-69, 1969-71; assoc. prof. pharmacology Cath. U. Louvain, 1971-75, prof., 1975-79, full prof., 1979-87, pres. Sch. Pharmacy, 1977-80, acad. sec. Faculty Medicine, 1980-84; assoc. prof. U. Montreal, Que., Can., 1987-96; dir. R & D dept. Searle European Devel. Ctr., Mont St. Guibert, Belgium, 1987-89, sr. dir., 1989-93; scientific adv. Lilly Mont Saint Guibert Devel. Ctr., Mont Saint Guibert, Belgium, 1993—; prof. U. Laval, Quebec, 1990—; prof. pharmacokinetics U. Brussels, 1980-81. Co-author 4 books; also over 300 articles; patentee in field. Recipient Alumni prize Univ. Found. Belgium, 1977; Joseph Lepoix prize Belgium Acad. Medicine clinical toxicology, 1980, Pharm. Scis. prize, 1986. Mem. Belgian Soc. Pharm. Scis. (bd. dirs. 1985-94), Belgian Assn. Clin. Biology Specialists (bd. dirs. 1986-92), Am. Assn. Pharm. Scientists, French Assn. Pharmacologists, Belgian Soc. Physiology and Pharmacology, French Acad. Pharmacy. Home: 33 BB Ave St Pancrace, B-1950 Kraainem Belgium Office: Lilly Mont Saint Guilbert Devel Ctr, 11 rue Granbonpré, B-1348 Mont Saint Guibert Belgium

LESSEM, JAN NORBERT, pharmaceuticals executive; b. Malmo, Sweden, Apr. 7, 1948; s. Slom and Frida (Marcus) L.; m. Eva K. Löfquist, July 11, 1976; children: Martin A., Sarah E. MD, U. Lund, 1974, PhD, 1982. Med. diplomate. Intern, then resident in cardiology; assoc. prof. U. Lund, Sweden, 1981-82; med. dir. Merck, Sharp & Dohme, Rahway, N.J., 1982-83, Bristol-Myers, Evansville, Ind., 1983-85; sect. head cardiology div. Syntex Research, Palo Alto, Calif., 1986-87, sr. dept. head cardiology div., 1987-90; dir. clin. investigation SB Pharma., Phila., 1991-95; med. dir. Takeda Am., Princeton, N.J., 1995—. Contbr. over 150 articles to profl. jours. Bd. dirs. Am. Swedish Hist. Mus., Phila., 1992—. Fellow Am. Coll. Cardiology, Coll. of Physicians Phila., Swedish Soc. Cardiology, Royal Swedish Coll. Med. Jewish Youth. Club: Jewish (Malmo) (pres. 1966-73). Office: Takeda am Ste 207 101 Carnegie Ctr Princeton NJ 08540

LESSER, ERWIN, clinical psychologist, educator; b. Phila., Jan. 14, 1929; s. Jack and Fannie (Belkin) L.; m. Sima Faye Altshuler, June 26, 1955; children: Ann, David, Fran. BS, Pa. State U., 1950, MS, 1954, PhD, 1955. Diplomate in clin. psychology Am. Bd. Prof. Psychology; diplomate in clin. hypnosis Am. Bd. Psychol. Hypnosis. Sr. psychologist Allentown (Pa.) State Hosp., 1955-56; chief psychologist Guidance Ctr. Northampton and Monroe Counties, Easton, Pa., 1956-58, Variety Children's Hosp., Miami, Fla., 1962-68; clin. psychologist, asst. prof. U. Miami, Coral Gables, Fla., 1958-62, adj. prof., 1987—; dir. Reading and Learning Ctr., Miami, 1970-75; assoc. prof. Fla. Sch. Profl. Psychology, Miami, 1978-81; pvt. practice, South Miami, Fla., 1962—; cons. in psychology Cath. Home for Children, Miami, 1968-70; co-owner Forensic Neuropsychology Assocs., 1994—. Contbr. articles to profl. jours. Chmn. edn. com. Mental Health Assn., Miami, 1964-67, Temple Beth Am, South Miami, 1966-75. Erwin Lesser award named in his honor Temple Beth Am, 1973. Mem. APA, Fla. Psychol. Assn. (pres. 1987), Dade County Psychol. Assn. (pres. 1967-69, Disting. Svc. award 1984), Nat. Acad. Neuropsychology, Internat. Neuropsychology Soc. Democrat. Office: 6601 SW 80th St Ste 206 Miami FL 33143-4661

LESSER, GERSHON MELVIN, physician, lawyer, medical and legal media commentator; b. N.Y.C., Apr. 3, 1933; s. Herman and Dora (Kronfeld) L.; m. Michelle Elyse Lesser; children: Hadrian, Aaron, Jason. BA, UCLA, 1954; MD, U. So. Calif., 1958; JD, UWLA, 1977. Atty. in pvt. practice L.A., 1977-82; med. dir. Westside Hosp., Am. Med. Inc., Beverly Hills, 1964-75; pvt. practice cardiology L.A., 1963-92; mem. pres.'s coun. Salk Inst., La Jolla, Calif.; broadcaster KGIL Radio, San Fernando Valley, 1984-92, KCRW-Nat. Pub. Radio, Santa Monica, Calif., 1980-94; med. broadcaster KTTV, Hollywood, Calif., 1984-86; med. dir. CD, L.A., 1978-89; adj. prof. law U. West L.A. Sch. Law, 1980-87; instr. internal medicine and med. malpractice, U. So. Calif. Sch. Medicine, L.A., 1963-80. Author: Growing Younger, 1987, When You Have Chest Pain, 1989; TV commentator Alive and Well, USA Cable, L.A., 1984-95. Fellow Am. Coll. Legal Medicine, Royal Soc. Health, Am. Coll. Angiology, Am. Coll. Geriatrics; mem. ABA, Am. Acad. Preventive Medicine, Am. Coll. Thoracic Medicine, Am. Coll. Cardiology, Am. Soc. Internal Medicine, Calif. Bar Assn., L.A. Bar Assn., Salerni Collegium, Fhi Delta Epsilon. Office: Atkons Agy 8484 Wilshire Blvd Ste 205 Beverly Hills CA 90211

LESSER, LORYN SARI, mental health counselor; b. Bridgeport, Conn., Aug. 11, 1950; d. Bertram Britwar and Roslyn Vivian (Ment) L.; BA with honors, Richmond Coll., CUNY, 1971; MA with honors, Montclair State Coll., 1973; Montessori tng. cert. Fairleigh Dickinson U., 1975; postgrad. George Washington U.; PhD, Walden U., 1984; m. Wallace Kleid, July 1, 1979; children: Micah Saul, Matthew Brett. Founder, dir. Mountaineer Montessori Sch., Charleston, W.Va., 1975-76; founding dir. counseling Women's Health Center, Charleston, 1976-77; family planning clinic asst., counselor dept. ob-gyn George Washington U., 1978-79; cert. clin. mental health counselor Suburban Mental Health Assn., Balt., 1979-81; mem. faculty psychology Catonsville Coll., Balt., 1979-91; founder, cert. clin. mental health counselor Womancare, Balt. 1982—; psychologist Rosewood Ctr., 1989-90; supr. JVS, 1990-93; program dir. dept. edn. Dundalk C.C., 1982-83; mem. exec. planning com. Md. Conf. on Families, 1979-80. Bd. dirs. Coalition for Optional Parenthood Edn., Washington, 1978-79, Womancare, 1981—; exec. dir. Balt. City Commn. Women, 1984-86. Mem. Nat. Acad. Cert. Clin. Mental Health Counselors (dir. 1979-85), Am. Mental Health Counselors Assn. (dir. 1978-79), Am. Assn. State Counseling Bds. (exec. dir. 1995—), Am. Assn. Counseling and Devel., Md. Assn. Counseling and Devel., Md. Mental Health Counselors (exec. bd., pres. 1985-86), Md. Bd. Examiners Profl. Counselors (chairperson 1986-94). Jewish.

LESSICK, MIRA LEE, nursing educator; b. Hazleton, Pa., Jan. 25, 1949; d. Jack H. and Shirley E. (Frumkin) L. Diploma in nursing, Albany (N.Y.) Med. Ctr., 1969; BSN, Boston U., 1972; MS, U. Colo., 1973; PhD, U. Tex., 1986. Staff nurse Boston City Hosp. and Mass. Gen. Hosp., 1969-72; instr. to asst. prof. nursing, genetics clinician U. Rochester, N.Y., 1973-79; asst. prof. nursing, practitioner Rush U., Chgo., 1986-91, assoc. prof. nursing, 1992—. Contbr. articles to profl. jours. Recipient Bd. of Govs. award, Excellence in Pediatric Nursing award Albany Med. Ctr., 1969, Outstanding Nurse Recognition award March of Dimes Birth Defects Found., 1991, Recognition award for Individual Contbn. to Maternal-Child Health Nat. Perinatal Assn., 1993. Mem. AAAS, ANA, APHA, Internat. Soc. Nurses in Genetics (chair rsch. com.), Assn. Women's Health, Obstetric, and Neonatal Nurses, Am. Soc. Human Genetics, Chgo. Nurses Assn. (legis. com. 1990-91), N.Y. Acad. Scis., Midwest Nursing Rsch. Soc., Sigma Theta Tau (Luther Christman award for excellence in published writing 1993), Phi Kappa Phi. Home: 4180 N Marine Dr Apt 612 Chicago IL 60613-2210 Office: Rush U Coll Nursing 301 SSH Chicago IL 60612

LESTAGE, DANIEL BARFIELD, retired naval officer, physician; b. Jennings, La., July 7, 1939; s. Henry Oscar Jr. and Juliet Xavier (Barfield) L.; m. Helen Newcomer, Mar. 9, 1963; children: Juliet Lestage Hirsch, Diane Lestage Davis, Daniel B. Jr. Grad., La. State U., 1959, MD, 1963; grad., Naval Sch. Aviation, 1964; MPH, Tulane U., 1969; diploma, Indsl. Coll. Armed Forces, 1978. Diplomate Am. Bd. Preventive Medicine (trustee 1988-94), Am. Bd. Family Practice. Commd. ensign USN, 1962, advanced through grades to rear adm., 1986; rotating intern Charity Hosp., New Orleans, 1963-64; resident in family practice Lafayette (La.) Charity Hosp., 1964; student flight surgeon Naval Sch. Aviation Medicine, Pensacola, Fla., 1964; staff flight surgeon/med. officer Carrier Air Wing 16 USS Oriskany, NAS Lemoore, Calif., 1965-67; sr. med. officer Naval Med. Clinic, NAS New Orleans, 1967-68, USS John F. Kennedy, Norfolk, Va., 1971-73; resident in aerospace medicine Naval Aerospace Med. Inst., Pensacola, 1969-71; sr. med. officer Br. Clinic, Jacksonville NAS, 1973-77; chief preventive medicine dept. Naval Regional Med. Ctrs., Jacksonville, 1973-77; spl. asst. to surgeon gen. Navy Bur. Medicine and Surgery Dept. Navy, Washington, 1978-81; head operational medicine br., aeromed. advisor Office of Chief Naval Ops., Washington, 1978-81; dir. clin. svcs., dir. med. edn., exec. officer Naval Regional Med. Ctr., Portsmouth, Va., 1981-83; commancing officer Naval Hosp., Millington, Tenn., 1983-84; comdr. U.S. Naval Med. Command, London, 1984-86; fleet med. officer U.S. Naval Forces Europe, 1984-86; fleet surgeon U.S. Atlantic Fleet, Norfolk, 1986-88; command surgeon U.S. Atlantic Command U.S. Atlantic Command/Supreme Allied Comdr., Norfolk, 1986-89; asst. dir. naval medicine Office of Chief Naval Ops., 1989; insp. gen. Navy Bur. of Medicine and Surgery, 1989-90; comdr. Naval Med. Ctr., Portsmouth, Va., 1990-92; corp. med. dir. Blue Cross/Blue Shield of Fla., Jacksonville, 1992-95, v.p. med. ops., 1995—; asst. dean Ea. Va. Med. Sch., Norfolk, 1981-83, assoc. dean, 1990-92; del. AMA ho. of dels from Aerospace Med. Assn., 1993—; del. Fla. Med. Assn. ho. of dels. from Fla Soc. Preventative Medicine, 1995—. Dir. Blood Bank, Jacksonville, 1973-77; bd. dirs. Cath. Family Svcs., Portsmouth, 1981-83, Fraser-Millington Mental Health Ctr., Memphis, 1983-84. Decorated Legion of Merit with four oak leaf clusters, Meritorious Svc. medal, Air medal with oak leaf cluster, Navy Commendation medal; recipient Physician's Recognition award AMA, 1972, 75, 78, 81, 85, 88, 91, 94, 97. Fellow Am. Coll. Physicians, Am. Coll. Preventive Medicine, Am. Acad. Family Physicians, Aerospace Med. Assn. (pres. 1988-89); mem. AMA (del. 1993—), Fla. Acad. Family Physicians (bd. dirs. 1995-98), Fla. Soc. for Preventive Medicine (pres. 1995-96), Fla. Med. Assn. (del. 1995—), VFW, Am. Legion, Internat. Acad. Aviation and Space Medicine, Am./Fla. Coll. of Occupl. and Environ. Medicine, Rotary, Elks. Roman Catholic. Home: 1782 Long Slough Walk Orange Park FL 32073-7033 Office: Blue Cross/Blue Shield Fla 8657 Baypine Rd Jacksonville FL 32256-7513

LESTER, DAVID, psychology educator; b. London, June 1, 1942; came to U.S. 1964; s. Harry and Kathleen (Moore) Lester; m. Bijou Yang, Apr. 2, 1950; 1 child, Simon. BA, Cambridge U., Eng., 1964; MA, Cambridge U., 1968, Brandeis U., Waltham, Mass., 1966; PhD, Brandeis U., 1968, Cambridge U., 1991. Asst. prof. Wellesley (Mass.) Coll., 1967-69; dir. Suicide Prevention & Crisis Svc., Buffalo, 1969-71; prof. psychology Richard Stockton State Coll., Pomona, N.J., 1971—. Author: Why Women Kill Themselves, 1988, Questions and Answers about Suicide, 1989, Questions and Answers About Murder, 1991, Serial Killers, 1995, Theories of Personality, 1995; contbr. articles to profl. jours. Mem. Am. Assn. Suicidology, Internat. Assn. Suicide Prevention (v.p. 1989-91, pres. 1991-95). Home: Stonegate Ct # 5 Blackwood NJ 08012-5356 Office: Richard Stockton Coll Richard Stockton Coll Pomona NJ 08240-0195

LESTRADET, HENRI GEORGES, pediatrics educator; b. Esternay, Marne, France, Feb. 17, 1921; s. Georges and Henriette (Tanneur) L; m. Marie-Anne Woimant, May 14, 1948; children: Francois, Anne, Luc, Marie Odile, Claire, Marie. Lic. Scis., Sorbonne U., Paris, 1942; MD, U. Paris, 1945, Agregation in Medicine, 1960. Chief pedicatrics svc. Assistance Publique, Paris, 1960-88; prof. pediatrics Faculty Medicine, Paris, 1968-90, prof. emeritus, 1990—; pres., found. Aide Aux Jeunes Diabetique, France, 1955-89, Internat. Study Group Diabetes in Children and Adolescents, 1976. Author: Le Diabète de l'Enfant, 1967-80, L'Enfant et son diabète, 1992. Lt. French mil., 1944-45. Decorated Legion of Honor. Mem. Nat. Acad. Medicine. Roman Catholic. Home: 7 Place du Tertre, Paris 75018, France

LETSOU, GEORGE VASILIOS, cardiothoracic surgeon; b. Boston, 1958; s. Vasilios George and Helen (Valacellis) L.; m. Jane Elizabeth Carter, June 1, 1985; children: Christopher George, Philip Taylor, John Carter. AB magna cum laude, Harvard U., 1979; MD, Columbia U., 1983. Diplomate Am. Bd. Surgery, Am. Bd. Thoracic Surgery. Resident in gen. surgery Yale-New Haven Hosp., 1983-88, chief resident and instr. surgery, 1987-88, clin. fellow in cardiothoracic surgery, 1988-89, Cystic Fibrosis Found. fellow in cardiopulmonary transplantation, 1988-89, Winchester scholar in cardiothoracic surg. rsch., 1989-90, resident in cardiothoracic surgery, 1990-91; chief resident in cardiothoracic surgery, 1991-92; Houston; attending surgeon Yale-New Haven Hosp., 1992-95; instr. surgery Yale U., New Haven, 1987-88, 91-92, asst. prof. surgery, 1992-95; attending surgeon Yale-New Haven Med. Ctr., 1992-95; Meth. Hosp., Ben Taub Hosp., Houston, 1995—; assoc. prof. surgery Baylor Coll. Medicine, Houston, 1995—. Mem. AMA, ACS, Am. Coll. Cardiology, Am. Coll. Chest Physicians, Soc. Thoracic Surgeons. Office: Dept Surgery One Baylor Plaza Ste 4040 Houston TX 77030

LETTON, ROBERT WARREN, surgeon; b. Selma, Ala., June 12, 1963; s. Robert Warren and Geraldine (Ashton) L.; m. Donna Kathryn Porter, July 9, 1988; children: Haley Ashton, Lewis Conrad. BS, Davidson Coll., 1985; MD, U. Ky., 1990. M.D., N.C. Intern gen. surgery Bowman Gray Sch. Medicine, Winston-Salem, N.C., 1990-91; resident gen. surgery Bowman Gray Sch. Medicine, 1991-94, Bradshaw rsch. fellow, 1994-95, chief resident in gen. surgery, 1995-96, instr. gen. and pediatric surgery, 1996-97; instr. Advanced Trauma Life Support, Winston Salem, 1992—. Capt. USAR, 1990-95. Mem. AMA, ACS, SAGES, Soc. Critical Care Medicine, Assn. Acad. Surgeons, Shock Soc., Phi Beta Kappa, Alpha Omega Alpha. Democrat. Office: Box 2216 Med Ctr Dr Winston Salem NC 27157

LEUKEFELD, CARL GEORGE, researcher, educator; b. Lake Forest, Ill., May 14, 1943; s. Karl Frederick and Berta (Link) L.; BS, Mo. Valley Coll., 1965; MSW, U. Mich., 1967; DSW, Cath. U. Am., 1975; cert. Harvard Sch. Public Health, 1980; m. Sara Ann Huffstutler, Aug. 13. 1966; children: Sarabeth, Karl Austin, Marianne. Program dir. Boys Club, Pontiac, Mich., 1966; commd. lt. USPHS, 1967, advanced through grades to capt. 1980; mental health officer, L.A., 1967-71; mental health adv., Rockville, Md., 1971-73; staff asst., then spl. asst. Nat. Inst. on Drug Abuse, USPHS, Rockville, Md., 1975-77, dep. dir., acting dir. div. of resource devel., 1978-81, dep. dir., then dir. div. prevention and treatment devel , 1981-82, acting dir., dep. dir. div. clin. rsch., 1982-90; prof. psychiatry, dir. Ctr. Drug and Alcohol Rsch. U. Ky., Lexington, 1990—; principal investigator NIH, Aids Rsch., 1993, Inst. for Women Substance Abuse Treatment, 1993, Ctr. for Substance Abuse Treatment, 1993, Ky. State Substance Abuse Needs Assessment, Drug Addictions Treatment, 1995; detailed to Naval Mil. Personnel Command, 1983, chief health svcs. officer USPHS, 1984-89; fellow mental health career devel. program NIMH, 1973-75. Mem. social work career devel. com. USPHS, chair. social work career devel. com., 1982, chairperson social work profl. adv. subcom. 1983; mem. Intra-Agy. Task Force Emergency Preparedness, 1987-90; adj. faculty Va. Commonwealth U., 1986-90. Editor jour. National Health Line, Health and Social Work, Jour., 1987-90, AIDS Edn. and Prevention, 1989—; cons. editor Jour. Primary Prevention; mem. editorial bd. Jour. Social Work Rsch., 1990-93, Jour. Mental Health Adminstrn., Substance Use and Misuse; co-editor books including Responding to AIDS: Psychosocial Initiatives, 1987, 89, Improving Drug Abuse Treatment, 91, Treatment in Prisons and Jails, 1992, Cocaine Treatment: Research and Clinical Perspective, 1992, Getting Funded, 1994, Prevention Research, 1995; contbr. articles to profl. jours. Decorated Commendation medal, 1978, 83, Outstanding Service medal, Meritorious Service medal, 1987, Pub. Health Svc. citation, 1988, 90; recipient Torch award Am. Humanics Found., 1978, Disting. Alumni award Cath. U. of Am., 1994; named to Honorable Order of Ky. Cols. State of Ky., 1991. Mem. Nat. Assn. Social Workers (chmn. commn. on health and mental health 1985-87, co-chair fund devel., Whitham/Knee awards), Acad. Cert. Social Workers, AAAS, Nat. Acads. Practice, Am. Public Health Assn., Assn. Mil. Surgeons (chmn. med. service corp. sect. 1987), Commd. Officers Assn. USPHS (bd. dirs. 1984-90), Alcohol and Drug Abuse Problems Am., Social Work Coun., Am. Pub. Health Assn., Am. Correctional Assn., Soc. Clin. Social Workers (bd. dirs. Bluegrass chpt. 1990-92), Am. Probation and Parole Assn., Tau Kappa Epsilon, Alpha Phi Omega, Pi Gamma Mu. Presbyterian (elder). Home: 1121 Sheffield Pl Lexington KY 40509-2018 Office: U Ky Coll Medicine Annex 2 Rm 210 Lexington KY 40536-0080

LEUPIN, LUCA, oncologist, hematologist; b. Bern, Switzerland, July 5, 1945; s. Hans Emil and Maria Rosetta (Carlevaro) L.; m. Catherine Elisabeth Beguelin, Apr. 7, 1971; children: Nicolas, Olivier-Xavier, Jerôme-Thierry. Degree, Med. Sch., Bern, 1973; MD, U. Bern, 1982, postgrad., 1982, 87. Resident Pathol. Inst. U. Bern, 1974-75; resident Citizen's Hosp. of Solothern, Switzerland, 1975-78; resident Med. Policlinic Univ. Hosp. of Bern, 1977-79, resident dept. hematology, 1981-83; intern Policlinic of oncohematology U. Hosp. Geneva, 1979-81; pvt. practice Bern, 1983—; resident, cons. Sclem-Clinic, Bern, 1983—. Contbr. articles to profl. jours. Mem. Swiss Soc. for Internal Oncology, Catonal Soc. for Hematology-Oncology (pres. 1990—). Liberal. Roman Catholic. Office: Dufourstrasse 45, CH-3005 Bern Switzerland

LEUSCH, MARK STEVEN, microbiologist; b. Cleve., June 8, 1961; s. Thomas Arthur and Elaine Margaret (Torma) L.; m. Cindy June Campos, Feb. 4, 1989; children: Steven Alexander, Kristen Denise. BA, U. Ariz., 1984, PhD, 1990. Postdoctoral assoc. Monsanto Co., St. Louis, 1990-92; scientist healthcare div. Procter and Gamble Co., Cin., 1992—; devel. team Crest Gum Care, 1995, Clean Mint Scope, 1994; tech. support for advt. claims Scope, 1994. Contbr. articles to profl. jours. including Infection and Immunity, Pros. NAS, Biochem. and Biophys. Rsch. Commn., Gene. Mem. Internat. Assn. Dental Rsch., Am. Soc. Microbiology. Roman Catholic. Office: Health Care Rsch Ctr PO Box 8006 Mason OH 45040

LEUTY, GERALD JOHNSTON, osteopathic physician and surgeon; b. Knoxville, Iowa, July 23, 1919; s. John William and Mable Reichard (Johnston) L.; m. Martha L. Weymouth, Jan. 24, 1940 (div. 1957); children: Maxine Joanne, Robert James, Gerald Johnston Jr., Karl Joseph; m. Norma Jean Hindman, Dec. 30, 1969; children: Barbara Jayne, Patrick Jack. AB, Kemper Mil. Sch., Boonville, Mo., 1939; postgrad., Drake U., Des Moines, 1944-45; DO, Des Moines Coll. Osteopathy, 1949; embalmer, Coll. Mortuary Sci., St. Louis, 1941. Mortician/embalmer Cauldwell-McJihon Funeral Home, Des Moines, 1939-40; aero. engr. Boeing Aircraft Co., Wichita, Kans., 1941-42; osteopathic physician and surgeon Knoxville (Iowa) Osteopathic Clinic, 1949-56; dir. Leuty Osteopathic Clinic, Earlham, Iowa, 1957-77; osteopathic physician and surgeon in pvt. practice Santa Rosa, Calif., 1977—; prof. clin. med. Coll. Osteopathic Medicine of the Pacific, Pomona, Calif., 1985—. With U.S. Army, 1942-46. Named Physician of the Yr., 6th Dist. Iowa Osteopathic Soc., 1975, Disting. Leadership award, Am. Biog. Inst., 1988, others. Fellow Internat. Co.. Angiologists; mem. Am. Osteopathic Assn. (ho. of dels., life mem. 1989), Iowa Osteopathic Soc. (pres. 6th dist. 1974), Soc. Osteopathic Physicians, No. Calif. Osteopathic Med. Soc. (pres. 1981), Osteopathic Physicians and Surgeons of Calif (pres. 1982), Am. Acad. Osteopathy (chmn. component socs. com. 1988, Calif. div. pres. 1987), North Coast Osteopathic Med. Assn. (pres. 1992), Am. Med. Soc. Vienna (life mem.), Am. Legion (6th dist. comdr. 1974-75), Lions (pres. 1946). Republican. Presbyterian. Home: 5835 La Cuesta Dr Santa Rosa CA 95409-3914

LEUZ, CHRISTOPHER AUGUSTUS, III, medical missionary, plastic surgeon; b. Edison, Pa., June 8, 1937; s. Christopher Augustus and Laura Evelyn (Tyson) L.; m. Lois Olive Gross, June 23, 1962; children: Kimberly Lynn, Laura Gross. Diploma, Phila. Bible Inst., 1958; BA, Goshen Coll., 1960; MD, Temple U., 1964; diploma in Tropical Medicine, Leopold II Sch. Tropical Med., Antwerp, Belgium, 1974. Diplomate Am. Bd. Plastic Surgeons, Am. Bd. Hand Surgeons. Missionary doctor Vietnam Mennonite Ctrl. Comty., Akron, Pa., 1965-68; missionary doctor Zaire Mennonite Ctrl. Comty., Akron, 1974-78; missionary doctor Taiwan Gen. Conf. Mennonite Ch., Newton, Kans., 1978-85, 92—; staff doctor Goshen (Ind.) Gen. Hosp., 1985-92, Elkhart (Ind.) Gen. Hosp., 1985-92; acting med. dir. Mennonite Christian Hosp., Taiwan, 1982-83; med. vice supt., 1993-95. Compiler: (reference book) Leuz Index of Plastic Surgery, 1976; contbr. articles to profl. jours. Fellow Am. Coll. of Surgeons; mem. Am. Soc. Plastic and Reconstructive Surgeons, Am. Assn. for Hand Surgery, Mennonite Med. Assn.

LEVA, NEIL IRWIN, psychotherapist, hypnotherapist; b. N.Y.C., Sept. 18, 1929; s. Charles and Alice Lee (Peirce) L.; m. Jean Kathryn Walters, Dec. 4, 1952 (div. May, 1988); children: Steven L., Michael N., Scott A.; m. Susan Mary Callagy, Aug. 12, 1988. BA in Govt., U. Tex., 1963; MA in Systems Mgmt., U. So. Calif., 1973; MA in Psychology, Cath. U. Am., 1976; MSW, U. Md., 1990. Diplomate in clin. social work. Commd. 2d. lt. U.S. Army, 1953, advanced through grades to col., 1976, retired, 1976; with psych. factors div. Quadraennial Bd. for Rev. of Mil. Compensation, Washington, 1974-76; psychotherapist Village Counselling Ctr., Potomac, Md., 1978-86, Met. Psychotherapist Group, Bethesda, 1986-90, Village Counseling Ctr., Potomac, Md., 1990—; human factors cons. The Artery Orgn., Washington, 1978-83, Montgomery County Schs., Rockville, Md., 1979-81. Decorated D.F.C., Bronze Star with V device and 4 oak leaf clusters, Air Medal with V device and 10 oak leaf clusters, Purple Heart, Legion of Merit. Mem. NASW, DAV, Am. Assn. Family Counselors, Internat. Transactional Analysis Assn., Mil. Order of Purple Heart, Am. Legion. Democrat. Home: 10011 Counselman Rd Potomac MD 20854-5019 Office: Village Counseling Ctr 10011 Counselman Rd Potomac MD 20854-5019

LEVEILLE, GILBERT ANTONIO, food products executive; b. Fall River, Mass., June 3, 1934; s. Isidore and Rose (Caron) L.; divorced; children: Michael, Kathleen, Edward; m. Carol A. Phillips, Aug. 7, 1981. B in Vocat. Agriculture, U. Mass, 1956; MS, Rutgers U., 1958, PhD, 1960. Prof. nutritional biochemistry U. Ill., Urbana, 1965-71; chmn. dept. food sci. and human nutrition Mich. State U., East Lansing, 1971-80; dir. nutrition and health sci. Gen. Foods Corp., Tarrytown, N.Y., 1980-86; v.p. for rsch. and tech. svcs. Nabisco Inc., East Hanover, N.J., 1986—. Author: The Set Point Diet, 1985 (N.Y. Times nonfiction bestseller); also over 300 articles. Served to 1st lt. U.S. Army, 1960-62. Recipient rsch. award Poultry Sci. Assn., 1965, Disting. Faculty award Mich. State U., 1980. Mem. AAAS, Am. Chem. Soc., Am. Inst. Nutrition (pres. 1988-89, Mead Johnson rsch. award 1971), Am. Soc. for Clin. Nutrition, Inst. Food Technologists (pres. 1983-84, fellow 1983, Carl Fellers award 1992). Office: Nabisco Inc PO Box 1944 East Hanover NJ 07936-1944

LEVENDUSKY, PHILIP GEORGE, clinical psychologist, administrator; b. Lowell, Mass., Oct. 21, 1946; s. Harry George and Phyllis Mary (Gowgill) L.; m. Cynthia Ann Becton; 1 child, Jason Philip. BA magna cum laude, U. Mass, 1968; MS, Wash. State U., 1971, PhD, 1973. Diplomate Am. Bd. Profl. Psychology. Asst. to dir. Human Rels. Ctr., Wash. State U., Pullman, 1971-73; asst. psychologist McLean Hosp., Belmont, Mass., 1974-82; assoc. psychologist McLean Hosp., Belmont, 1982-92, psychologist, 1992—, dir. cognitive behavior therapy unit, 1974-94, dir. ambulatory care, 1991-93, asst. gen. dir., 1993-95, dir. ambulatory care svcs., 1994-95, v.p. network devel., 1995—, chmn. dept. psychology, dir. clin. tng.; instr. psychiatry Harvard Med. Sch., 1974-88, asst. prof., 1989—; dir. Levendusky and Assocs., Arlington, Mass., 1980—; Bd. dirs. Pullman Mgmt., Manchester, Mass., 1976-80, Feeding Ourselves, 1980, Anorexia Bulemia Care, 1991-93; dir. Bain & Co., Employee Consultation, Boston, 1987—; cons. Va Hosp., Boston, 1977-85, Boston Cardiovascular Health, 1983-85, Mass. Dept. Mental Health, 1987—; mem. Mass. Bd. Psychology, Boston, 1988-93. Contbr. articles to profl. jours., mags., newspapers; author book chpts.; guest numerous TV and Radio programs, Boston. Mem. Am. Psychol. Assn., Assn. Advancement Behavior Therapy, New Eng. Soc. of Behavior Analysis and Therapy (bd. dirs. 1991), Phi Beta Kappa. Republican. Roman Catholic. Home: . Manchester by the Sea MA 01944-1405 Office: McLean Hosp 115 Mill St Belmont MA 02178-1041

LEVENE, SHIRLEY SCHECHTER, psychotherapist; b. N.Y.C., Oct. 10, 1917; d. William and Edith (Herman) Goldsmith; m. Jack Levene, Nov. 1983; children: Judith Schechter Lasko, Ruth Schechter Rubinow. BA, Vassar Coll., 1938; MS, Columbia U., 1942; cert. analytic group psychotherapy, Postgrad. Ctr. Mental Health, 1968, cert. supervision of individual and group therapy, 1971. Psychotherapist Family Consultation Svc., Eastchester, N.Y.; pvt. practice psychotherapist White Plains, N.Y. Contbr. articles to profl. jours. Fellow AGPA; mem. NASW (diplomate), Eastern Group Psychotherapy Soc. (past pres.), N.Y. Soc. Clin. Social Work Psychotherapists (diplomate N.Y. State cert. social worker). Home: 111 Miles Ave White Plains NY 10606-3816

LEVENSALER, WALTER LOUIS, human resources consultant; b. Somerville, Mass., Jan. 18, 1934; s. Leon Walter and Elizabeth Mary (Adreani) L.; m. Mary Frances Cronin, Sept. 26, 1964; children: Karen, Linda, Renee. BBA, Northeastern U., Boston, 1961; MA in Sociology, Northeastern U., 1977. Wage and salary analyst ITEK Corp., Lexington, Mass., 1960-62, personnel adminstr., 1962-65; personnel adminstr. MITRE Corp., Bedford, Mass., 1965-68; wage and salary adminstr. Univ. Hosp., Boston, 1968-70, personnel dir., 1970-73, adminstr. labor relations, 1973-76, adminstr. personnel, 1976-82, adminstr. human resources, 1982-88; ind. cons., 1988—; wage and salary cons. New Eng. Rehab. Hosp., Woburn, Mass., 1982-83; labor rels. cons. Resthaven Nursing Home, Roxbury, Mass., 1980—, Armenian Nursing Home, Jamaica Plain, Mass., 1984-86; pers. cons. Martha's Vineyard (Mass.) Hosp., 1978-82, Nevins Home, Methuen, Mass., 1990—, Orthopedic Assn. of Portland, Maine, 1991—, Litle & Co., Salem, N.H., 1991—, Days Hotel, Manchester, N.H., 1992-93, Walnut St. Ctr., Somerville, Mass., 1994, 95, 96. Com. mem. Town of Acton (Mass.) Personnel Bd., 1977-83. Served with USAF, 1952-56. Mem. Am. Soc. Personnel Adminstrs., Am. Acad. Polit. and Social Scis., Am. Mgmt. Assn., Mass. Health Care Human Resources Assn. (pres. 1976-77), Indsl. Relations Research Assn., N.E. Geneol. & Hist. Soc., Boston Mus. Sci., N.E. O.D. Network. Democrat. Roman Catholic. Office: 300 Somerville Ave Somerville MA 02143

LEVENSON, ROBERT MONTIE, retired physician; b. Yakima, Wash., Jan. 10, 1921; s. Montie T. and Ellen (Sharkey) L.; m. Marie E. Hofmeister, Sept. 21, 1947; children: Robert Jr., Albert D., David A., Nancy, Linda, Mary. MD, U. Louisville, 1946. Diplomate Am. Bd. Internal Medicine, 1955. Intern King County Hosp., Seattle, 1946-47; pvt. practice in internal medicine Seattle, 1954-88; resident Providence Hosp., Seattle, 1949-51, U. Calif. Hosp., San Francisco, 1951-52; clin. prof. U. Wash. Med. Sch., Seattle, 1974—. Trustee Swedish Hosp. Med. Ctr., Seattle, 1985-88, King County Med. Blue Shield, Seattle, 1985—, J.L. Locke Trust, Seattle, 1974—. Fellow Am. Coll. Cardiology, Am. Coll. Physicians, Council Clin. Cardiology; mem. Am. Heart Assn. (award of merit 1982). Home: 3406 72nd Pl SE Mercer Island WA 98040-3342

LEVENTHAL, ALAN, physiotherapist; b. Bklyn., Mar. 3, 1930; s. Harry Gabriel and Lillian (Brodsky) L.; student N.Y. U., 1947-49; B.S. magna cum laude, Ithaca Coll., 1952, M.S. in Physiotherapy, 1954; m. Joan Lois Eckstein, Mar. 31, 1957; 1 son, David Adam. Staff Physiotherapist Jewish Chronic Disease Hosp., Bklyn., 1952-57; chief physiotherapist Maimonides Hosp. Bklyn., 1957-67; co-chmn. physiotherapy dept. Victory Meml. Hosp., Bklyn., 1967—; pvt. practice physiotherapy, Bklyn., 1952—; guest lectr. N.Y. U., 1974, 78, SUNY Downstate Med. Center, 1975-78; clin. asso. Sch. Health Professions, N.Y.U., 1978—; pres. physiotherapy grievance com. N.Y. State Edn. Dept., 1965-67; mem. regional adv. group N.Y. Met. Regional Med. Plan; mem. doctoral program com. L.I. U. Mem. Council Lic. Physiotherapists N.Y. State (chmn.), United Socs. Physiotherapists (nat. legis. dir.), N.Y. Soc. Continuing Edn. in Phys. Therapy (v.p.), Am. Phys. Therapy Assn., N.Y. State Soc. Physiotherapists (editor-in-chief jour. 1960-63, pres. 1968-73, Meritorious Service award 1981). Jewish. Lodge: Masons. Home: 125 Girard St Brooklyn NY 11235-3009 Office: 1318 Newkirk Ave Brooklyn NY 11226-7359

LEVENTHAL, BENNETT LEE, psychiatry and pediatrics educator, administrator; b. Chgo., July 6, 1949; s. Howard Leonard and Florence Ruth (Albert) L.; m. Celia G. Goodman, June 11, 1972; children: Matthew G., Andrew G., Julia G. Student, Emory U., 1967-68, La. State U., 1968-70; BS, La. State U., 1972, postgrad., 1970-74, MD, 1974. Diplomate Am. Bd. Psychiatry and Neurology in Psychiatry, Am. Bd. Psychiatry and Neurology, Child Psychiatry; lic. physician N.C., La., Ill., Va. Undergrad. rsch. assoc. Lab. Prof. William A. Pryor dept. chemistry, La. State U., 1968-70; house officer I Charity Hosp. at New Orleans, 1974; resident in psychiatry Duke U. Med. Ctr., Durham, N.C., 1974-78, chief fellow divsn. dept. psychiatry, 1976-77, chief resident dept. psychiatry, 1977-78, clin. assoc. dept. psychiatry, 1978-80; staff psychiatrist, head psychiatry dept. Joel T. Boone Clinic, Virginia Beach, Va., 1978-80; staff psychiatrist, faculty mem. dept. psychiatry Naval Regional Med. Ctr., Portsmouth, Va., 1978-80; asst. prof. psychiatry and pediats. U. Chgo., 1978-85, dir. Child Psychiatry Clinic, 1978-85, dir. Child and Adolescent Psychiatry Fellowship tng. program, 1979-88; psychiat. cons. Caledonia State Prision/Halifax Mental Health Ctr., Tillery, N.C., 1976-77, Fed. Correctional Inst., Butner, N.C., 1977-78; cons. Norfolk Cmty. Mental health Ctr., 1978-80; adj. prof. psychology, biopsychology, and devel. psychology U. Chgo., 1990, adj. assoc. prof. dept. psychology and com. on biopsychology, 1987-90; meed. dir. Child Life and Family Edn. program Wyler Children's Hosp. of U. Chgo., 1983-95; dir. child and adolescent programs Chgo. Lakeshore Hosp., 1986—; Pfizer vis. prof. dept. psychiatry U. P.R., 1992; examiner Am. Bd. Psychiatry and Neurology in Gen. Psychiatry and Child Psychiatry, 1982—; mem. steering com. Harris Ctr. for Devel. Studies, U. Chgo., 1983—; mem. com. on evaluation of GAPS project AMA, 1993—; treas. Chgo. Consortium for Psychiat. Rsch., 1994; pres. Ill. Coun. Child and Adolescent Psychiatry, 1992-94; vis. scholar Hunter Inst. Mental Health and U. New Castle, NSW, Australia, 1995; mem. Gov.'s Panel on Health Svcs., 1993-94; prof. psychiatry & pediats. U. Chgo., 1990—, chmn. dept. psychiatry, 1991—; presenter in field. Mem. editl. bd. Univ. Chgo. Better Health Letter, 1994—; cons. editor: Jour. Emotional and Behavioral Disorders, 1992-96; reviewer: Archives of Gen. Psychiatry, 1983—, Biol. Psychiatry, 1983—, Am. Jour. Psychiatry, 1983—, Jour. AMA, 1983—, Jour. Am. Acad. Child and Adolescent Psychiatry, 1983—, Sci., 1983—; book rev. editor Jour. Neuropsychiatry and Clin. Neuroscis., 1989-92, mem. editl. bd., 1989-92; contbr. articles to profl. jours. Lt. comdr. M.C., USNR, 1978-80. Recipient Crystal Plate award Little Friends, 1994, Individual Achievement award Autism Soc. Am., 1991, Merit award Duke U. Psychiat. Resident's Assn., 1976, Bick award La. Psychiat. Assn., 1974; Andrew W. Mellon Found. faculty fellow U. Chgo., 1983-84; John Dewey lectr. U. Chgo., 1982. Fellow Am. Acad. Child and Adolescent Psychiatry (Outstanding Mentor 1988, dep. chmn. program com. 1979—, chmn. arrangements com. 1979—, new rsch. subcom. for ann. meeting 1986—, mem. work group on rsch. 1989—), Am. Psychiat. Assn. (Falk fellow, mem. Ittleson Award Bd. 1994-97, mem. Am. Psychiat. Assn./Wisniewski Young Psychiatrists Rsch. Award Panel 1994—), Am. Acad. Pediats., Am. Orthopsychiat. Assn.; mem. AAAS, Am. Coll. Psychiatrists, Brain Rsch. Inst., Ill. Coun. Child and Adolescent Psychiatry, Ill. Psychiat. Soc., Soc. for Rsch. in Child Devel., Soc. of Profs. of Child and Adolescent Psychiatry, Soc. Biol. Psychiatry, Nat. Bd. Med. Examiners, Mental Health Assn. Ill. (profl. adv. bd. 1991—), Sigma Xi. Office: U of Chgo Pritzker Sch of Medicine 5841 S Maryland Ave Chicago IL 60637-1463

LEVENTHAL, LAWRENCE JAY, rheumatologist, educator; b. N.Y.C., June 5, 1958; s. Samuel and Anne Leventhal; m. Linda Currao, May 15, 1988; 2 children. BA in Biology magna cum laude, Brandeis U., 1980; MD, Hahnemann U., 1984. Resident in internal medicine Albert Einstein Med. Ctr., Phila., 1984-87; fellow in rheumatology U. Pa., Phila., 1987-90; clin. assoc. in medicine U. Pa., 1989-91, clin. asst. prof. medicine, 1989-91, 91—; clin. asst. prof. Med. Coll. Pa., Phila., 1990—; dir. arthritis rsch. edn. Presbyn. Hosp., Phila., 1990-93; assoc. chief rheumatology Grad. Hosp., Phila., 1993—. Author: Primer of Rheumatic Disease, 1994; editor: Jour. Clin. Rheumatology; contbr. articles to profl. jours. Fellow ACP, Am. Coll. Rheumatology; me. AMA (physicians recognition award 1987—), Am. Soc. Internal Medicine, Phila. Rheumatism Soc. Office: Grad Hosp 1800 Lombard St Philadelphia PA 19146-1414

LEVER, ANDREW MICHAEL LINDSAY, physician, consultant, educator; b. Trincomalee, Sri Lanka, June 23, 1953; arrived in U.K., 1953; s. Ivor Lindsay Douglas and Sylvia Marion (Tannock) L.; m. Elizabeth Ann O'Donnell, July 24, 1981; children: Robert Andrew, Jonathan Patrick, Gillian Elizabeth. BSc in Biochemistry, U. Wales, Cardiff, Eng., 1975, B in Medicine and Surgery, 1978, MD, 1987. Med. position U. Hosp. of Wales, Eng., 1978-79, U. Newcastle, Eng., 1979-80; med. position Clin. Rsch. Ctr., London, 1980-82, rsch. fellow, 1983-85; Wellcome trust lectr. Royal Free Hosp., London, 1985-88; rsch. fellow Dana-Farber Cancer Inst., Boston, 1988-89; physician, sr. lectr., cons. St. George's Hosp., London, 1989-91; univ. lectr. in medicine Cambridge U., 1991—. Inventor HIV based viral vector system; contbr. articles to profl. jours. Med. Rsch. Coun. grantee, 1989—. Fellow Royal Coll. Physicians, Royal Coll. Physicians Edinburgh; mem. AAAS, Royal Coll. Physicians Scotland, Assn. Physicians Gt. Britain, Med. Rsch. Soc., Brit. Soc. for Study of Infection, Royal Coll. Pathologists. Office: Dept of Medicine, Addenbrooke's Hosp, Cambridge CB2 2QQ, England

LEVERE, RICHARD DAVID, physician, academic administrator, educator; b. Bklyn., Dec. 13, 1931; s. Samuel and Mae (Fain) L.; m. Diane L. Gonchar, Jan. 15, 1978; children: Elyssa C., Corinne G., Scott M. Student, NYU, 1949-52; MD, SUNY, N.Y.C., 1956. Intern Bellevue Hosp., N.Y.C., 1956-57, resident, 1957-58; resident Kings County Hosp., 1960-61; asst. prof. medicine SUNY Downstate Med. Center, 1965-69, assoc. prof., 1969-73, prof., 1973-77, vice-chmn. dept. medicine, 1975-77, chief hematology/oncology div., 1970-77; asst. prof. Rockefeller U., 1964-65; prof., chmn. dept. medicine N.Y. Med. Coll., 1977-93, vice dean, 1991-93; med. dir. Westchester County Med. Ctr., 1991-92; v.p. med. affairs St. Agnes Hosp., 1991-93; sr. v.p. The Bklyn. Hosp. Ctr., 1994—; assoc. dean, prof. medicine NYU Sch. Medicine, 1994—; adj. prof. Rockefeller U., 1973—. Contbr. articles to profl. jours. Bd. dirs. Leukemia Soc. Am., 1970-85, Am. Heart Assn., 1978-94; trustee Our Lady of Mercy Med. Ctr., 1993-96. NIH grantee, 1971-76, 65-86. Fellow ACP (gov. N.Y. State 1990-94, pres. N.Y. State chpt. 1992-93, Physician Recognition award 1986), N.Y. Acad. Medicine; mem. Harvey Soc., Am. Soc. Clin. Investigation, Soc. Study of Blood (pres. 1973-74), Soc. Devel. Biology, Am. Soc. Pharm. Exptl. Therapeutics (William Dock Teaching award, Tinsley Harrison Rsch. award), Den Tiroler Adler-Ordern of Austria, Alpha Omega Alpha. Home: 5 Seymour Pl W Armonk NY 10504-2516 Office: Bklyn Hosp Ctr 121 Dekalb Ave Brooklyn NY 11201-5425

LEVETT, JAMES MICHAEL, cardiothoracic surgeon; b. Waterloo, Iowa, Mar. 24, 1949; s. Charles John and Gertrude Clara (Radischat) L.; m. Paula Kathleen Vernon, Sept. 20, 1986; children: Christine, Catherine, Suzanne, Mary. BA, Carleton Coll., 1970; MD, U. Iowa, 1974. Diplomate Am. Bd. Surgery, Am. Bd. Thoracic Surgery. Internship and residency U. Chgo. Hosp. and Clinics, 1974-81, asst. prof. cardiac surgery, 1982-85; postdoctoral fellow Med. Ctr. Duke U., Durham, N.C., 1981-82; asst. prof. surgery Robert Wood Johnson Med. Sch., New Brunswick, N.J., 1985-87, assoc. prof. surgery, 1988; dir. surg. rsch. Deborah Rsch. Inst., Browns Mills, N.J., 1985-88; staff surgeon Deborah Heart and Lung Ctr., Browns Mills, 1985-88; clin. assoc. prof. surgery U. Iowa, Iowa City, 1988-94; cardiothoracic surgeon Surg. Specialists, P.C., Cedar Rapids, Iowa, 1988-94; chmn. dept. of surgery Luth. Gen. Hosp., Park Ridge, Ill., 1994—; clin. prof. surgery U. Chgo. Hosps. and clins., 1995—; bd. dirs. St. Luke's Health Care Found., Cedar Rapids. Contbr. over 80 articles and abstracts to profl. publs. Rsch. grantee Deborah Rsch. Inst., 1987, Am. Heart Assn. N.J., 1988-89, Iowa, 1990-91, Mercy Med. Ctr., Iowa, 1989-92. Mem. ACS, Am. Coll. Cardiology, Am. Assn. Thoracic Surgery, Am. Heart Assn., Soc. Thoracic Surgeons. Home: 1850 S Windridge Dr Lake Forest IL 60045 Office: Dept of Surgery Luth Gen Hosp 1775 Dempster St Park Ridge IL 60068-1143

LEVEY, GERALD SAUL, physician, educator; b. Jersey City, N.J., Jan. 9, 1937; s. Jacob and Gertrude (Kantoff) L.; m. Barbara Ann Cohen, June 4, 1961; children: John, Robin. AB, Cornell U., 1957; MD, N.J. Coll. Medicine, 1961. Diplomate: Am. Bd. Internal Medicine. Med. intern Jersey City Med. Ctr., 1961-62, asst. med. resident, 1962-63; postdoctoral fellow dept. biol. chemistry Harvard U. Med. Sch., 1963-65; med. resident Mass. Gen. Hosp., Boston, 1965-66; clin. assoc. clin. endocrinology br. Nat. Inst. Arthritis and Metabolic Diseases NIH, Bethesda, Md., 1966-68, clin. assoc. Nat. Heart and lung Inst., 1968-69, sr. investigator Nat. heart and Lung Inst., 1969-70; assoc. prof. medicine U. Miami Sch. Medicine, Fla., 1970-73, prof. medicine, 1973-79; prof., chmn. dept. medicine U. Pitts. Sch. Medicine, 1979-91; physician-in-chief Presbyn.-Univ. Hosp., Pitts., 1979-91; sr. v.p. for med. and sci. affairs Merck and Co., Inc., Whitehouse Sta., N.J., 1991-94; provost med. scis., dean Sch. of Medicine UCLA, 1994—; Harold Jeghers lectr. N.J. Coll. Medicine, 1977; Marian Blankenhorn lectr. Cin. Soc. Internal Medicine, 1982; co-prin. investigator Nat. Study of Internal Medicine Manpower, 1984—. Mem. editorial bd.: Endocrinology, 1972-76, Am. Jour. Physiology, 1972-76, Jour. Applied Physiology, 1972-76, Annals of Internal Medicine, 1981-84; cons. editor: Hosp. Medicine, 1981-91; contbr. articles to profl. jours. Bd. dirs. Am. Jewish Com., Miami, 1975-79; mem. United Jewish Fedn. Pitts. Leadership Devel., 1981-82; bd. dirs. Jewish Family and Children's Services, 1982-83. NIH grantee, 1971-91; Fla. Heart Assn. grantee, 1971-74. Fellow ACP; mem. AMA, Am. Thyroid Assn. (mem. membership com. 1977-80), Am. Fedn. Clin. Rsch. (councillor so. sect. 1973-76, pres. so. sect. 1977-78), Am. Soc. Clin. Investigation, Endocrine Soc., Assn. Profs. Medicine (chmn. ad hoc com. for use of animals in rsch., 1982-85, chmn. task force on internalmedicine manpower 1983-90, nat. pres. 1990-91), So. Soc. Clin. Investigation, Soc. Gen. Internal Medicine, Assn. Am. Physicians, Alpha Omega Alpha. Home: 1132 Laurel Way Beverly Hills CA 90210-2221 Office: UCLA 10883 Le Conte Ave Los Angeles CA 90024-3010*

LEVIN, ARNOLD MURRAY, social worker, psychotherapist; b. Bklyn., Dec. 26, 1924; s. William and Pauline (Kramer) L.; m. Elaine M. Zimmerman, Dec. 19, 1946 (dec. Aug. 1971); children: Michael, Nancy Jo Noteman, Amy Louise. BA, U. Mass., 1948; MA, U. Chgo., 1950, PhD, 1975; Cert., Chgo. Inst. Psychoanalysis, 1955. ACSW, LCSW, BCD. Case worker Jewish Family Svcs., Chgo., 1950-53; group therapist Portal House Clinic Alcoholism, Chgo., 1952-55; exec. dir. Family Svc., Mental Health Ctr. So. Cook County, Park Forest, Ill., 1953-60; pvt. practice in social work Chgo., 1960—; founder, pres. Inst. Clin. Social Work, Chgo., 1979—; bd. dirs. Jewish Childrens Bur., Chgo., 1987—; founder, pres., Ill. Soc. Clin. Social Workers, Chgo., 1971-76; mem. 90 for the 90's, Ill. Author: Private Practice of Psychotherapy, 1983. Sgt. U.S. Army, 1943-46. NIMH grantee, 1971; recipient Gov.'s award, Chgo., 1975, Alumnus of Yr. award U. Chgo., 1976. Mem. Nat. Registry of Health Care Providers in Clin. Social Wk. (bd. dirs. 1985-88), Nat. Fedn. Socs. for Clin. Social Work (founder 1971-75). Home: 3180 N Lake Shore Dr 11G Chicago IL 60657 Office: 151 N Michigan #809 Chicago IL 60601

LEVIN, BERNARD, physician; b. Johannesburg, Republic of South Africa, Apr. 1, 1942; came to U.S. 1966, naturalized 1972; m. Ronelle DuBrow; children: Adam, Katherine. MD, U. Witwatersrand, 1964. Resident Presbyn. St. Lukes Hosp., Chgo., 1966-68; rsch. fellow U. Chgo., 1968-71; NIH fellow U. Chgo., 1971-72; instr. medicine U. Chgo., 1971-73, asst. prof. medicine, 1973-78, assoc. prof., 1979-84; prof. med., chmn. dept gastrointestinal oncology and digestive diseases, U. Tex. Med. Ctr. M.D. Anderson Hosp., Houston, 1984-94, Robert R. Herring prof., 1986-91, Ellen F. Knisely chair, 1991-94, v.p. for Cancer Prevention (ad interim), 1992-94, v.p. for Cancer Prevention, 1994—, Betty Marcus chair 1994—; mem. large bowel cancer working group Nat. Cancer Inst., 1984-85; cons. spl. study sect. Nat. Cancer Inst., 1976-84, chair nat. adv. com. on colorectal cancer, 1990—. Contbr. articles to profl. jours.; mem. editorial bd. Pancreas, Jour. Nat. Cancer Inst. J. Clin. Oncology USPHS grantee, 1976-80; Melamid Found. Gift, U. Chgo., 1978-83; NCI grantee, 1980-84, others. Fellow ACP, Am. Coll. Gastroenterology; mem. AAAS, Am. Assn. Cancer Rsch., Am. Gastroenterol. Assn., Am. Soc. Gastrointestinal Endoscopy, Am. Pancreatic Assn, Am. Soc. Preventive Oncology, Internat. Assn. Pancreatology, Am. Soc. Clin. Oncology, Am. Cancer Soc. (chair nat. adv. com. on colorectal cancer), Sigma Xi. Jewish. Office: UT M D Anderson Cancer Ctr 1515 Holcombe Blvd 203 Houston TX 77030-4095

LEVIN, DOUGLAS M., gastroenterologist; b. N.Y.C., Feb. 9, 1944; s. Virginia Helen Smith Levin; m. susan Slifkin, Aug. 25, 1968; children: Rachel Slifkin, Rebecca. AB cum laude, Harvard U., 1965; MD, NYU, 1969. Diplomate Am. Bd. Internal Medicine with subspecialty in gastroenterology. Intern Yale-New Haven Med. Ctr., 1969-70, resident in internal medicine, 1970-71; clin. assoc. NIH, Bethesda, Md., 1971-74; fellow in gastroenterology U. Chgo., 1974-76; gastroenterologist Columbus (Ohio) Med. Ctr., 1976-95, Columbus Med. Gastroenterology, 1995—; clin. assoc. prof. Ohio State U., Columbus, 1977—; sect. gastroenterology Riverside Meth. Hosp.; assoc. Mt. Carmel Hosp.; courtesy staff Ohio State U. Hosps. Contbr. articles to profl. jours. Mem. Bd. of Health, Upper Arlington, Ohio, 1979-83. Lt. comdr. USPHS, 1971-74. Fellow ACP, Am. Coll. Gastroenterology; mem. AMA, Am. Gastrointestinal Assn., Am. Assn. Study of Liver Disease, Columbus Soc. Internal Medicine (program chmn. 1979-80, sec.-treas. 1981, v.p. 1981-82, pres. 1983-84), Alpha Omega Alpha.

LEVIN, HAL ALAN, psychiatrist; b. Bklyn., Feb. 13, 1935; s. David and Rose M. (Rosen) L.; children of former marriage: Julie Levin Keith, Susan Levin Davis, Mark D. Levin; m. Sharon Greenleaf, Feb. 9, 1973; children: Anne Levin Warrick, Julie Elizabeth, Alisa M., Kimberly L. Grimes, Christopher Lenk. BS, Roosevelt U., 1958; MD, Tulane Med. Sch., New Orleans, 1967. Diplomate Am. Bd. Psychiatry and Neurology, Am. Bd. Forensic Examiners, Am. Bd. Forensic Medicine. Intern Norfolk (Va.) Gen. Hosp., 1967-68; resident in psychiatry Sheppard & Enoch Pratt Hosp., Towson, Md., 1968-70, Crownsville (Md.) Hosp., 1970-71; fellow in forensic psychiatry U. So. Calif., L.A., 1983-84; staff psychiatrist Atascadero (Calif.) State Hosp., 1971-72; pvt. practice psychiatry San Bernardino, Calif., 1972-85; asst. prof. clin. psychiatry Mich. State U., East Lansing, 1985-86; asst. dir. mental health State of Mich., Lansing, 1985-86; dir. mental health State of Ariz., Phoenix, 1986-87; pvt. practice psychiatry Tempe, Ariz., 1987—; cons. psychiatrist San Bernardino County Hosp., 1972-85, San Bernardino Superior Ct., 1972-85; dir. Desert Valley Clinic, Apple Valley, Calif., 1973-80; med. dir. Big Bear (Calif.) Psychiat. Clinic, 1980-84; med. dir. Ctr. for Behavioral Health, Tempe, 1989—. cons. Jewish Family Svcs., Tempe, 1990—, Interfaith Counseling, Mesa, Ariz., 1991—. Mem. AMA, Am. Psychiat. Assn., Ariz. Med. Assn., Am. Acad. Psychiatry & the Law, Am. Bd. Forensic Examiners, Friends of Phoenix Symphony. Democrat. Office: 5410 S Lakeshore Dr # 103 Tempe AZ 85283-2171

LEVIN, HENRY STUART, ophthalmologist; b. Bklyn., Mar. 30, 1954; m. Susan A. Hodgson, June 24, 1990. BS, SUNY, Stony Brook, 1975; MD, Mt. Sinai Sch. Medicine, 1980. Diplomate Am. Bd. Ophthalmology. Med. intern Westchester County Med. Ctr., 1980-82; resident in ophthalmology N.Y. Med. Coll., 1982-85; pvt. practice New Rochelle, NY, 1988—. Office: 421 Huguenot St New Rochelle NY 10801

LEVIN, JONATHAN MINAR, neurologist; b. Cleve., Oct. 15, 1962; s. Jacob and Myrtle (Srochi) L.; m. Marjorie Ross, June 5, 1994. BA, Yale U., 1984; MD, Emory U., 1988; MPH, Harvard U., 1993. Diplomate Am. Bd. Psychiatry and Neurology. Intern in internal medicine U. Tex.- Southwestern/Parkland Meml. Hosp., Dallas, 1988-89; resident in neurology Harvard-Longwood Neurol. Tng. Program, Boston, 1989-92; fellow neurosci. McLean Hosp./Harvard Med. Sch., Belmont, Mass., 1992-95; dir. lab. for cerebral blood flow McLean Hosp., Belmont, 1995—; acad. practice, Belmont, 1995—. Mem. Am. Acad. Neurology, Soc. Magnetic Resonance, Internat. Soc. Cerebral Blood Flow and Metabolism. Office: McLean Hosp Brain Imaging Ctr 115 Mill St Belmont MA 02178

LEVIN, LINDA ROSE, mental health counselor; b. Des Moines, June 29, 1951; d. Morris Sam and Betty Francis (Burns) Nemirovski; m. Michael Arthur Levin, Feb. 25, 1971; children: David Bradley, Shane Michael. Student, Grandview Jr. Coll., 1969-70; BS in Psychology, Ottawa Univ., 1992, MA in Counseling, 1994. Cert. hypnotherapist, advanced hypnotherapist. Asst. dir. trade practice Better Bus. Bur., Phoenix, 1980-83; program coord. Carnation Health and Nutrition Ctr., Phoenix, 1983-85; v.p. AAA Telephone Answering Svc., Phoenix, 1985-90; past state of Ariz. rep. Toughlove, Phoenix, 1988-90; counselor level II, resident advisor Wayland Family Ctrs., Phoenix, 1990-91; case mgr. for the serious mentally ill Community Care Network, Phoenix, 1991-92; pvt. practice in hypnotherapy Counseling Ctr. for Personal Growth, Phoenix, 1992—. Vol. arbitrator Better Bus. Bur., 1983—. Mem. Am. Arbitration Assn. Democrat. Jewish. Office: Counseling Ctr for Personal Growth 13231 N 35th Ave A-10 Phoenix AZ 85029-1233

LEVIN, NORMAN LEWIS, biology educator; b. Hartford, Conn., Mar. 31, 1924; s. Joseph and Fannie (Sosin) L.; m. Shirley Alleen Ginsberg, Sept. 1950; children: Faye Deborah, Alan Jeffrey. BS, U. Conn., 1948, MS, 1949; PhD, U. Ill., 1956. Teaching asst. U. Ill., Champaign, 1953-56, instr. zoology, 1956-57; vis. asst. prof. biology Westminster Coll., Fulton, Mo., 1957-58, asst. prof., 1958-60; fellow in tropical medicine Sch. of Medicine La. State U., 1959; instr. biology Bklyn. Coll., 1960-64, asst. prof., 1964-71, assoc. prof., 1971-76, prof., 1976—, dep. chmn. dept., 1983—; mem. evaluation panel NSF, Washington, 1968, 71, 74; reader advanced placement exams. Ednl. Testing Svc., Princeton, N.J., 1978-84. Contbr. articles to profl. jours. With AUS, 1942-45, PTO. Fellow AAAS; mem. Am. Soc. Parasitologists, Am. Soc. Zoologists, Am. Soc. Tropical Medicine and Hygiene, Am. Microscopical Soc., Helminthological Soc. Wash., Sigma Xi, Phi Sigma. Office: CUNY Bklyn Coll Ave H and Bedford Ave Brooklyn NY 11210

LEVIN, WARREN MAYER, family practice physician; b. Phila., Aug. 20, 1932; s. Israel and Clara Deborah (Cherim) L.; m. Marsha Ann Beinstein, Dec. 24, 1955 (div. 1975); children: Beth Ann, Julie Ruth; m. Frances Susan Teitler, Mar. 20, 1982; 1 child, Erika Alexandra. BS, Ursinus Coll., 1952; MD, Jefferson Med. Coll., 1956. Diplomate Am. Bd. Family Pracitce, Am. Bd. Bariatric Medicine, Am. Bd. Environ. Medicine, Am. Bd. Chelation Therapy. Intern U.S. Naval Hosp., Newport, R.I., 1956-57; pvt. practice S.I., N.Y., 1959-74; founder, med. dir. Heights Holistic Health Ctr., Bklyn., 1974-79, World Health Med. Group, N.Y.C., 1979-94; physician Physicians for Complementary Medicine, N.Y.C., 1994—. Contbr. to books: Nutrition in Pregnancy, 1981, Challenging Orthodoxy, 1991, Alternative Medicine, 1994. Bd. govs. Internat. Coll. Applied Nutrition, 1974-76. Lt. Med. Corps

USNR, 1956-59. Recipient Disting. Pioneer in Alternative Medicine award Found. for Advancement of Innovative Medicine Fund, 1995, Presdl. Commendation, Am. Coll. for Advancement in Medicine, 1995. Fellow Am. Assn. Environ. Medicine, Am. Coll. Nutrition, Am. Acad. Family Practice. Office: Physicians ComplementaryMedicine 24 W 57th St Ste 701 New York NY 10019

LEVIN, WILLIAM COHN, hematologist, former university president; b. Waco, Tex., Mar. 2, 1917; s. Samuel P. and Jeanette (Cohn) L.; m. Edna Seinsheimer, June 23, 1941; children: Gerry Lee Levin Hornstein, Carol Lynn Levin Cantini. B.A., U. Tex., 1938, M.D., 1941; M.D. (hon.), U. Montpellier, 1980. Diplomate: Am. Bd. Internal Medicine. Intern Michael Reese Hosp., Chgo., 1941-42; resident John Sealy Hosp., Galveston, Tex., 1942-44; mem. staff U. Tex. Med. Br. Hosps., Galveston, 1944—, assoc. prof. internal medicine, 1948-65, prof., 1965—; Warmoth prof. hematology U. Tex. Med. Br., 1968-86, Ashbel Smith prof., 1986—, pres., 1974-87; past chmn., past mem. cancer clin. investigation rev. com. Nat. Cancer Inst., past. mem. Bd. Sci. Counselors. Exec. com., mem. nat. bd. Union Am. Hebrew Congregations; trustee Houston-Galveston Psychoanalytic Found., 1975-78, Menil Found., 1976-83. Recipient Nicholas and Katherine Leone award for adminstrv. excellence, 1977; decorated Palmes Académiques France. Fellow ACP, Internat. Soc. Hematology; mem. Am. Fedn. Clin. Research, Central Soc. Clin. Research, Am. Soc. Hematology, Phi Beta Kappa, Sigma Xi, Alpha Omega Alpha. Office: Am Indemnity Co PO Box 1259 Galveston TX 77553-1259

LEVINE, AARON M., physiatrist; b. Bronx, N.Y., Mar. 5, 1947; s. David and Dorothy (Moshman) L.; m. Susan F. Labelle, Sept. 4, 1983; children: Danielle, Robert, Phillip, Ethan. BS, U. Pitts., 1967, MD, 1971. Diplomate Am. Bd. Phy. Medicine and Rehab., Am. Bd. Electodiagnostic Medicine. Intern gen. surgery U. Ill. Chgo., 1971-73; resident orthopaedics Hosp. Joint Diseases, N.Y.C., 1973-76; resident phys. medicine Baylor Coll. Medicine, Houston, 1978-80, asst. prof., 1980-84; staff physician MacGregor Clinic, Houston, 1984-86; med. dir. Harris Meth. Hosp., Ft. Worth, 1986-87; pvt. practice Ft. Worth, 1987-88; asst. med. dir. Mt. Sinai Hosp., Hartford, Conn., 1988-90; med. dir. Meml. Inst. Rehab., Houston, 1990—. Asst. editor Postgraduate Medicine, 1986-90. Maj. U.S. Army, 1976-78. Mem. Tex. Med. Assn. (del. rehab. div.). Home: 4210 Misty Heather Ct Houston TX 77059-5521 Office: Meml Inst of Rehab 11914 Astoria Blvd Houston TX 77089-6064

LEVINE, ALAN S., health science administrator; b. N.Y.C., Aug. 11, 1944; s. Howard E. and Sylvia (Greenberg) L.; m. Renie Levine, June 11, 1967; children: Lisa R., Scott P. BS, Monmouth Coll., 1966; PhD, U. Del., 1971. Rsch. assoc. Kans. U., Lawrence, 1971-72; staff fellow NIH, Bethesda, Md., 1972-74, sr. staff fellow, 1974-76; health scientist adminstr. Nat. Heart, Lung and Blood Inst., Bethesda, 1977-86, blood diseases br. chief, 1986-91, chief cellular hematology br., 1881-94, dir. blood diseases program, 1994—. Editor: Molecular Biology of Hemopoiesis, 1988, Molecular Biology of Erythropoiesis, 1989, Molecular Biology of Haematopoiesis, 1990, 2d edit., 1994. Recipient Hour-Glass award Cooley's Anemia Found., N.Y.C., 1989, Merit award NIH, 1992. Mem. AAAS, Am. Soc. Hematology, Internat. Soc. for Exptl. Hematology.

LEVINE, ALEXANDER, physician, ophthalmologist; b. N.Y.C.; s. Milton and Sylvia (Minsky) L.; m. Rosalind Levine, June 12, 1962; children: Eric, Karen, Kenneth. BA, U. Rochester, 1958, MD, 1962; postgrad. in Ophthalmology, NYU, 1963-64. Diplomate Am. Bd. Ophthalmology. Resident in ophthalmology Boston City Hosp., 1964-67; pvt. practice Brockton, Mass., 1967—; clin. instr. ophthalmology Tufts Med. Sch., Boston, Boston U. Med. Sch. Fellow Am. Acad. Ophthalmology and Otolaryngology; mem. New Eng. Ophthalmology Soc., Mass. Med. Soc. Office: 830 Oak St Brockton MA 02401

LEVINE, ARLENE BRADLEY, cardiologist; b. Williamsburg, Va., Nov. 30, 1954; d. Warren Francis and Brigitte (Looke) Bradley; m. T. Barry Levine, July 4, 1987; children: Lionel Marc, Edlyn Victoria. BA, Barnard Coll., 1975; MD, Harvard Med. Sch., 1979. Internal medicine intern Peter Bent Brigham Hosp., Boston, 1979-80; resident in internal medicine Brigham and Women's Hosp., Boston, 1980-82; fellow in cardiology Beth Israel Hosp., Boston, 1982-85; sr. staff U. Tex. Health Sci. Ctr., San Antonio, 1985-86; assoc. dir. cardiac cath. lab. Harper Hosp., Detroit, 1986-88; assoc. dir. heart failure and transplant program Henry Ford Hosp., Detroit, 1990—. Contbr. articles to profl. jours. Fellow Am. Coll. Cardiology; mem. Soc. for Heart Lung Transplant, Am. Heart Assn. Office: Henry Ford Hosp K-14 2799 W Grand Blvd Detroit MI 48202

LEVINE, BARRY WILLIAM, internist; b. Everett, Mass., Mar. 21, 1940; s. Irvine and Betty (Nemon) L.; m. Ellen S. Haas, June 30, 1963; children: Susan, Rachel. BA, Dartmouth Coll., 1962, BS in Medicine, 1963; MD, Harvard U., Boston, 1965. Diplomate Am. Bd. Internal Medicine, Am. Bd. Pulmonary Disease. Intern Presbyn. St. Lukes Hosp., Chgo., 1965-66; resident Harvard Svc./Boston City Hosp., 1966-68; fellow in pulmonary disease Mass. Gen. Hosp., Boston, 196870; intern Presbyn.-St. Lukes Hosp., Chgo., 1965-66, resident in medicine, 1966-67; resident in medicine Boston City Hosp.-Harvard U., 1967-68; fellow Mass. Gen. Hosp., Boston, 1968-70; asst. in medicine Mass. Gen Hosp., Boston, 1970-80, assoc. physician, 1980—. Bd. dirs. North Haven Devel. Corp., 1984—. Fellow ACP; mem. Masons, Shriners. Home: 14 Manor House Rd Newton MA 02159

LEVINE, DONALD PAUL, infectious disease specialist; b. Detroit, Apr. 25, 1945; s. Louis L. and Lily (Lorber) L.; m. Diane Lynn Mendelson, Aug. 1, 1982; children: Miriam T., Carl D., Max N., Hannah R. BA, U. Mich., 1967; MD, Wayne State U., 1972. Diplomate Am. Bd. Infectious Diseases, Diplomate Am. Bd. Internal Medicine. Intern, resident Wayne State U. Affiliated Program; chief sect. infectious diseases Detroit Receiving Hosp.; asst. prof. Wayne State U., Detroit, 1978-83, assoc. prof., 1983-94, prof., 1994—. Editor: Infections Intravenous Drug Abusers, 1990. Office: Detroit Receiving Hosp 4201 Saint Antoine St Detroit MI 48201-2153

LEVINE, ELLIOT L., ophthalmologist; b. Columbus, Ohio, Mar. 23, 1961; s. Norman and Shirley Irene (Douglas) L.; m. Rosana Silva, May 5, 1991; children: Jordan Nathan, Samuel Alexander. BSChE, Ohio State U., 1983, MD, 1987. Diplomate Am. Bd. Ophthalmology. Intern Riverside Meth. Hosp., Columbus, 1987-88; resident Georgetown U., Washington, 1988-91; ophthalmologist Eye Cons. of Atlanta, 1991—, sec.-treas., 1995—. Home: 1104 Westbrooke Way Atlanta GA 30319 Office: Eye Consultants of Atlanta 95 Collier Rd Atlanta GA 30309

LEVINE, EUGENE, health services researcher; b. N.Y.C., Jan. 11, 1925; s. Maurice and Rebecca (Spector) L.; m. Barbara Jean Stevenson, July 23, 1971; m. Julia Raisner, June 26, 1948 (div. July 1971); children: Gary Mitchell, Jeffrey Howard, Douglas Edward. BBA, CCNY, 1948; MPA, NYU, 1950; PhD, Am. U., 1960. Statistician N.Y.C. Health Dept., 1948-50; chief rsch. and statistics div. nursing USPHS, Washington, 1950-77, dep. dir. div. health professions analysis, 1977-80; cons. Levine Assocs., Kensington, Md., 1982-93; prof. Grad. Sch. Nursing Uniformed Svcs. U. Health Scis., Bethesda, Md., 1993—; cons. Nat. League Nursing, N.Y.C., 1984-88, Indian Health Svc., Washington, 1986—, NAS, Washington, 1981-84; adj. prof. Georgetown U., Washington, 1982-91. Author: Better Patient Care through Nursing Research, 1986 (award ANA 1988), Needs for Environmental Health Personnel, 1988, Nursing Practice in the UK and North America, 1993, Preparing Nursing Research for the 21st Century, 1994; editor Proc. Nursing Productivity Conf., 1987; also articles. With USAAF, 1942-45, ETO. Mem. APHA, Am. Statis. Assn., Nat. League for Nursing (Outstanding Svc. award Washington chpt. 1971), Assn. for Health Svcs. Rsch. Democrat. Jewish. Home: 8135 Inverness Ridge Rd Potomac MD 20854-4014 Office: Rm 400 B 11426 Rockville Pike Ste 400 B Rockville MD 20852-3007

LEVINE, GARY IRA, family practice physician; b. Detroit, Mar. 22, 1951; s. Stanley and Sylvia (Udow) L.; m. Deborah Labas, Oct. 8, 1977; children: Arielle, Katrina. BS, U. Mich., 1972; MD, Wayne State U., 1976. Diplomate Am. Bd. Family Practice. Asst. prof. family medicine East Carolina U. Sch. of Medicine, Greenville, N.C., 1980-87, U. Ky., Lexington, 1981-91; assoc. prof. family medicine Mercer U., Macon, Ga., 1991-96; assoc. prof. family medicine East Carolina State U., Greenville, N.C., 1996—, inpatient coord. dept. family medicine, 1996—; adv. group Am. Bd. Family Practice, Lexington, 1990—. Author: (with others) 5 ML-Clinical Conduct, 1993-95. Mem. Alpha Omega Alpha. Office: East Carolina U Sch Med Dept Family Medicine Moye Blvd Greenville NC 27858

LEVINE, GEOFFREY, pharmacist; b. Sept. 2, 1942. BS in Pharmacy, Temple U., 1965, MS in Radiol. Health, 1967; PhD in Environ. Health Engring., Northwestern U., 1978. Bd. cert. in nuclear pharmacy; lic. pharmacist, Pa. Pharmacist Profl. Practice-Community Peoples Drug Stores, 1965-67; radioisotope chemist Abbott Labs., Chgo., 1966-68; dir. radiopharmaceutical svcs. U. Pitts. Health Ctr., 1972-93; asst. prof. radiology U. Pitts. Sch. Medicine, 1972-83, assoc. prof., 1983-95; nuclear pharmacist Presbyn.-Univ. Hosp., 1972-95; dir. nuclear pharmacy Cen. Imaging Svcs., Inc., 1985-93; assoc. mem. Pitts. Cancer Inst., 1987-89, 89-95, clin. dir. Monoclonal Antibody Ctr., 1993-95; mem. adj. faculty U. Pitts. Sch. Pharmacy, 1981; clin. prof. Allegheny County C.C., 1984—; mem. Radiation Safety Com. U. Pitts. Med. Ctr., Radioactive Drug Rsch. Com. and Human Use Subcom. Radioactive Materials, 1972—; cons. U. Pitts. Med. Ctr., dir., pres. 900 comm., 1995—. Contbr. numerous articles to profl. jours. and publs. Recipient AEC-AUA-ANL fellowship, USPHS traineeship, Teaching assistantship, W.P. Murphy fellowship; recipient Plaque, Am. Pharm. Assn., 1978. Mem. AAAS, Am. Pharm. Assn., Health Physics soc., Soc. Nuclear Medicine, Pa. Coll. Nuclear Medicine and Nuclear Physicians, Sigma Xi, Rho Chi. Home: 6360 Monitor St Pittsburgh PA 15217-2720

LEVINE, GEORGE ARTHUR, plastic surgeon, educator; b. Bklyn., May 20, 1935; s. William and Rose (Finkelstein) L.; m. Jean Ann Schipsi, Apr. 16, 1972; children: Richard, Stephen, Heather. BA, NYU, 1956, DDS, 1961; MD, N.Y. Med. Coll., 1965. Diplomate Nat. Bd. Med. Examiners, Am. Bd. Surgery, Am. Bd. Plastic Surgeons. Intern Jackson Meml. Hosp., Miami, Fla., 1965-66, resident, 1966-68; resident Hahnemann Med. Coll. Hosp., Phila., 1968-70; plastic surgical resident U. of Utah Affiliated Hosps., Salt Lake City, 1970-72; clin. instr. plastic surgery U. Miami Sch. Medicine, Miami, 1973-85, clin. asst. prof. plastic surgery, 1985—; practice medicine specializing in plastic and reconstructive surgery Miami, 1973—; chief div. plastic surgery Bapt. Hosp. of Miami, 1987—, Ambulatory Ctr. of Miami, 1985—. Fellow ACS; mem. Am. Soc. Plastic Reconstructive Surgeons, Southeastern Soc. Plastic and Reconstructive Surgeons, Fla. Soc. Plastic and Reconstructive Surgeons, Greater Miami Soc. Plastic and Reconstructive Surgeons, Am. Soc. for Aesthetic Plastic Surgery. Jewish. Office: 8700 N Kendall Dr Miami FL 33176-2206

LEVINE, GWENN KAREL, hospital administrator; b. Jersey City, Mar. 11, 1945; d. Milton and Mildred (Cohen) Karel; m. Ronald W. Levine, Jan. 28, 1967 (div. Nov. 1979); children: David Trevor, Joshua Loren. BA in Politics with honors, Brandeis U., 1966; postgrad. in pub. adminstrn., NYU, 1966-67; MA in Polit. Sci., Fordham U., 1975, PhD in Polit. Sci., 1992. Intern U.S. Congress, Washington, summer 1965; planning assoc. Bergen-Passaic Health Systems Agy., Hackensack, N.J., 1977-81; dir. program devel. Bergen-Passaic Hosp. and Physician Council, Totowa, N.J., 1981; dir. program planning St. Joseph's Hosp. and Med. Ctr., Paterson, N.J., 1981-89, v.p. planning and mktg., 1989-95, v.p. strategic planning, 1995—; mem. policy and plan devel. com. N.J. Statewide Health Coordinating Coun., Trenton, 1987-91; chmn. N.J. Comprehensive Rehab. Adv. Com.. 1988-89. Mem. Mayor's Health Planning Task Force, Paterson., N.J., 1989-90. Recipient Silver award Health Services Div. Am. Mktg. Assn., 1986. Mem. Hosp. Planning and Mktg. Soc. N.J. (sec.-treas. 1984, v.p. 1985, pres. 1986, Ann. Achievement award 1989). Democrat. Office: St Joseph's Hosp and Med Ctr 703 Main St Paterson NJ 07503-2621

LEVINE, HAROLD GRUMET, health professions educator, consultant; b. Pitts., Nov. 1, 1931; s. David and Mollie (Wedner) L.; m. Paula Lea Goldbaum, July 4, 1955; children: Steven Robert, Ruth Ellen Levine Bernstein. BA in Edn., U. Pitts., 1953; MPA SUNY, Albany, 1963; postgrad., Loyola, Chgo., 1968-69. Pers. examiner N.Y. State Civil Svc. Dept., Albany, 1956-59; supr. test devel. N.Y. State Edn. Dept., Albany, 1959-65; sr. assoc. med. edn. Coll. Medicine U. Ill., Chgo., 1965-69; dir. edn. Am. Soc. Med. Tech., Houston, 1969-71; dir. rsch. in med. edn. Med. Br., U. Tex, Galveston, 1971-81, asst., assoc. to prof. dept. preventive medicine community health, 1971—, spl. asst. med. edn., 1981-85, ednl. specialist, 1985—, prof. dept. pediatrics, 1985—; cons. in field, 1965—; chmn. Health Scis. Consortium, Chapel Hill, N.C., 1974-76, rev. com. Rsch. in Med. Edn. Conf., Washington, 1982-85, So. Group on Med. Edn., 1979-81. Contbr. articles to profl. jours. Adminstr. Jewish Marriage Encounter Tex., Houston, 1976-85; co-leader Gt. Books Discussion Group, Galveston, 1971-81, 88—; prin. Galveston Community Jewish Religious Sch., 1982-87; pres. Galveston County Jewish Welfare Assn., 1984-86, 89-91. With U.S. Army, 1953-55. Mem. Am. Ednl. Rsch. Assn., Nat. Coun. Measurement in Edn. (program com. 1978-79), Ambulatory Pediatric Assn. (edn. com. 1988—), Jewish Marriage Encounter (regional bd. dirs. 1980-84), U. Tex. Talkers Toastmasters Club (treas. 1985-87, pres. 1991), B'nai Brith, B'nai Israel Men's Club. Democrat. Home: 7654 Chantilly Cir Galveston TX 77551-1627 Office: U Tex Med Br Children's Hosp Galveston TX 77550

LEVINE, HARVEY ROBERT, retired biology educator, parasitologist, entomologist; b. N.Y.C., Sept. 15, 1931; s. William and Molly (Heinberg) L.; m. Rosalyn Freides, Oct. 7, 1956; children: Nancy Levine Fichman, David. BS, CCNY, 1953; MS, U. Mass., 1955, PhD, 1958; postgrad. Ind. U., 1955-56. Cert. in med. entomology Am. Registry Profl. Entomologists. Faculty Bemidji State U., Minn., 1958—, prof., 1965-68; prof. biology Quinnipiac Coll., Hamden, Conn., 1968-96, prof. emeritus, chmn. dept. biol. sci., 1968-76, 93-94, dir. Title II Math. Sci. Computer Inst., 1991-93. Contbr. articles to profl. jours. Trustee Quinnipiac Coll., Hamden, 1984-93. Grantee NSF, HEW. Mem. NRTA, Soc. Vector Ecologists, Conn. Sci. Tchrs. Assn., Conn. Sci. Suprs. Assn., Entomol. Soc. Am., Am. Fedn. Tchrs., Am. Assn. for Lab. Animal Sci., Am. Mus. Natural History, Sigma Xi, Phi Kappa Phi, Beta Beta Beta, Alpha Phi Sigma. Jewish. Avocations: philately, gardening, computers. Home: 8799 Holly Ct #103 Tamarac FL 33321

LEVINE, HOWARD SETH, family physician; b. N.Y.C., Jan. 21, 1961. BS in Psychology, SUNY, Stony Brook; DO, Kirksville (Mo.) Coll. Osteo. Medicine and Surgery, 1987. Diplomate Am. Osteo. Bd. Family Practice, Am. Bd. Family Medicine, Am. Bd. Geriatric Medicine. Intern Kennedy Meml. Hosp./Univ. Medicine and Dentistry of N.J., Newark, 1987-88, resident in family practice, 1983-90; pvt. practice Bayonne, Jersey City, N.J., 1990—; asst. clin. prof. Pa. State U., 1993—; attending physician dept. internal medicine Bayonne Hosp., 1990—, Greenville Hosp., 1990—, mem. credential com., 1994—, mem. dietary com., 1994; attending physician dept. family practice Christ Hosp., 1990—, mem. transfusion com., 1993—; attending physician dept. family practice St. Francis Hosp., 1990—, chmn. dept., 1993; attending physician Hamilton Pk. Nursing Home, 1990—, Jewish Geriatric Home, 1990—, St. Anne's Nursing Home, 1990-93, Luth. Nursing Home, 1991-92; geriatric fellow Stratford Nursing Home, 1988-90; team physician Jersey City State Coll., 1990—, Camden County Football League, 1989-90; sports medicine physician, school physician St. Peter's Coll., Jersey City, 1990-93; cons. sports medicine Jersey City Dept. Recreation, St. Anthony's H.S., Dickinson H.S., Ferris H.S., St. Dominic's H.S.; lectr. in field. Vol. swim tchr. autistic and handicapped children, SUNY-Stony Brook, 1978-83; vol. swim coach h.s. swim club, Stony Brook, 1979-83; vol. Spl. Olympics, Stony Brook, 1979-83; vol. tutor Kirkland Coll. Osteo. Medicine and Surgery, 1985-87, vol. alumni telethon N.Y./N.J. area, 1990, chmn., 1994; vol. student physician Planned Parenthood, Kirksville, Mo., 1987-88; vol. AIDS sensitivity tng. Bayonne Cmty. Mental Health Ctr., 1990; contbr. pub. svc. announcements on effects of cigarette smoking for pub. radio, 1992; vol. physician and drug test escort N.Y.C. Marathon, 1989-94; vol. physician N.J. Waterfront Marathon, 1989, Millrose Games, 1989, Mercedes Mile, 1990, Nat. Indoor Championships of Track and Field, 1990, Meadowlands Invitational Track and Field Meet, 1990. Named All-Am. Swimmer, 1983; recipient Eastern Collegiate Athletic Conf. award, 1983. Mem. Am. Osteo. Assn., Am. Coll. Osteo. and Family Practitioners, Internat. Marathon Dirs. Assn., N.J. Assn. Osteo. Physicians and Surgeons, Hudson County Osteo. Assn. (treas. 1990—), Pres.'s Club Kirksville Coll. Osteo. Medicine, Iota Tau Sigma (past pres.). Office: Steinbaum-Levine Assocs 789 Ave C Bayonne NJ 07002

LEVINE, JANE SHEILA, nurse, health insurance consultant; b. Bklyn., Jan. 2, 1946; d. Irving Richard and Ann (Odell) Levine; m. Robert Nevin Stewart, Sept. 1, 1988. Grad., Bellevue Sch. Nursing, 1966; student Am. U., 1966-67, Marymont Manhattan Coll., 1967, Fla. Internat. U., 1976-78. Staff nurse Washington Hosp. Ctr., 1966; nurse N.Y. Office Paramount Pictures, 1967-68; operating room nurse Beth Israel Hosp., N.Y.C., 1968-70; pub. health nurse Bellevue Hosp., N.Y.C., 1970-74; regional rep. N.Y. State Nurses Assn., 1974-75; asst. dir. nursing Parkway Gen. Hosp., Miami, Fla., 1975-77; dir. Staff Builders, Miami, 1977-78; v.p. for nursing Westchester Gen. Hosp., Miami, 1978-80; dir. nursing services Med. Personnel Pool Am., 1981-82; founder Elder Designs Inc., 1982-91; health, life and fin. counsel Equitable Life Assurance, Miami, 1983-86; brokerage cons. Springfield/Monarch Ins. Brokers, 1986; founder, employee benefits counselor Fin. Designs, 1987—; founder, pres. World Impact Now, Inc., 1988-90, Home Health HiTech Nursing and Woundcare Specialist, 1991—. Mem. Am. Nurses Assn., Fla. Nurses Assn., Nat. Assn. Life Underwriters, Nat. Assn. Health Underwriters, Fla. Assn. Health Underwriters. Home: Regency Lakes 5220 Eagle Cay Way Coconut Creek FL 33073

LEVINE, JANICE CAROL, nurse; b. Detroit, Jan. 22, 1942; d. James Edward and Marjorie Ann (Brumitt) Smith; children: Colleen, Lana, James, John; m. Herbert Levine. Degree in Practical Nursing, E.C. Goodwin Tech. Coll.-New Britain Gen. Hosp., 1969; diploma in Nursing, Tunxis Community Coll., 1981; student in familty therapy porgram, U. Conn., 1983-84; student, Mid State Sch. Family Therapy, 1984-85. RN Conn.; cert. psychiat. and mental health nursing A.N.A. Lic. practical nurse Geri-Care, Farmington, Conn., 1969-71; staff nurse for pvt. physician, New Britain, Conn., 1971-75, NCCB, Bristol, Conn., 1975-81; supr. nursing Nursing Care Ctr. Bristol, Bristol, 1981-84, Elmcrest Psychiat. Inst., Portland, Conn., 1984-86; exec. dir. families domestic violence Coping Ctr., Middletown, Conn., 1986—; lectr. on drugs and family violence various pub. schs. Mem. exec. bd. New Haven chpt. Am. Heart Assn., 1986; bd. dirs. sexual assault crisis service Middlesex County, 1987-88, Nat. Orgn. Victim Assistance, 1988, Am. Heart Assn. Middlesex County, 1986-88. Mem. Am. Nurses Assn., Nat. Assn. Female Execs. Office: Coping Ctr 32 Washington St Middletown CT 06457-4739

LEVINE, JAY ALAN, cardiologist; b. Bklyn., Aug. 7, 1941. BA cum laude, NYU, 1962, MD, 1966. Diplomate Nat. Bd. Med. Examiners, Am. Bd. Internal Medicine, Cardiovascular Disease. Intern, resident Kings County Hosp., Bklyn., 1966-68, resident, 1970-71; fellow cardiology NYU, 1971-72; rsch. fellow cardiology Peter Bent Brigham Hosp., Boston, 1972-74; staff physician Miami Heart Inst., Miami Beach, Fla., 1974—; asst. instr. medicine SUNY, Downtown Med. Ctr., 1970-71; tchg. asst. NYU, 1971-72, clin. instr. U. Miami, Coral Gables, Fla., 1974-75, clin. asst. prof., 1975-82, clin. assoc. prof., 1982-89, clin. prof., 1989—; staff physician Mt. Sinai Hosp., Miami Beach, 1974—; attending physician Miami Heart Inst., 1974—. Contbr. articles to profl. jours. Maj. U.S. Army, 1968-70. Mem. ACP, AMA, Am. Soc. Echocardiography, Am. Soc. Internal Medicine, Am. Coll. Chest Physicians (Coun. Critical Care), Am. Coll. Cardiology, Am. Coll. Angiology, Am. Fedn. Clin. Rsch., Fla. Med. Assn., Dade County Med. Assn., Mass. Heart Assn. (Samuel A. Levine fellow 1973-74), Am. Heart Assn. (Coun. Clin. Cardiology), Greater Miami Heart Assn., Phi Beta Kappa, Alpha Omega Alpha. Office: Cardiology Assocs 2925 Aventura Blvd Ste 300 North Miami Beach FL 33180

LEVINE, JEROME, psychiatrist, educator; b. N.Y.C., July 10, 1934; s. Abraham and Sadie (Glowatz) L.; children: Ross W., Lynn R., Andrew R. BA, U. Buffalo, 1954, MD, 1958. Intern, then psychiat. resident E.J. Meyer Meml. Hosp., Buffalo, 1958-61; sr. psychiat. resident St. Elizabeth's Hosp., Washington, 1961-62; staff psychiatrist USPHS Hosp., Lexington, Ky., 1962-64; research psychiatrist, asst. chief psychopharmacology research br. NIMH, 1964-67, chief of br., 1967-81, chief pharmacologic and somatic treatments research br., 1981-84; research prof. psychiatry U. Md. Sch. Medicine, Balt., 1985-94; dep. dir. Nathan Kline Inst. for Psychiat. Rsch., Orangeburg, N.Y., 1994—; rsch. prof. psychiatry NYU, 1994—; instr. psychiatry Johns Hopkins Med. Sch., 1964-72; vis. prof. U. Pisa, Italy, 1977. Author books and papers on psychopharmacology, clin. trial methodology, somatic treatment assessment for psychiat. disorders. Mem. Soc. Clin. Trials, Am. Psychiat. Assn. (Hofheimer Research prize 1970), Am. Coll. Neuropsychopharmacology, Collegium Internationale Neuropsychopharmacologicum, Am. Soc. Clin. Pharmacology and Therapeutics. Home: 15 Stony Hollow Chappaqua NY 10514-2014 Office: Nathan Kline Inst Bldg 37 140 Old Orangeburg Rd Orangeburg NY 10962

LE VINE, JEROME EDWARD, retired ophthalmologist, educator; b. Pitts., Mar. 23, 1923; s. Harry Robert and Marian Dorothy (Finesilver) L.; m. Marilyn Tobey Hiedovitz, Apr. 14, 1957; children: Loren Robert, Beau Jay, Janice Lynn. B.S., U. Pitts., 1944; M.D., Hahnemann Med. Sch., Phila., 1949; postgrad. in ophthalmology U. Pa., 1951-52. Diplomate Am. Bd. Disability Cons., Am. Bd. Quality Assurance & Utilization Rev. Intern, St. Francis Hosp., Pitts., 1949-50; resident in ophthalmology Jefferson U. Med. Sch. Hosp., Phila., 1952-54; ophthalmologist Leech Farm VA Hosp., Pitts., 1955-59; chief eye dept. Stanocola Clinic, Baton Rouge, 1959-64; sole practice medicine specializing in ophthalmology, Baton Rouge, 1959-86; cons. La. State U., East La. State Hosp. Infirmary, Villa Feliciana Geriatric Hosp., disability dept. Social Security Adminstrn., div. blind La. State Pub. Welfare dept.; mem. staff Our Lady of the Lake Hosp., Baton Rouge Gen. Hosp., Women's Hosp.; instr. spl. edn. U. Southeastern La., 1971. Mem. Am. Bd. Quality Assurance and Utilization Rev., 1990. Served with MC, AUS, 1942-44. Fellow Am. Geriatric Soc., Royal Soc. Health; mem. AMA, La. State Med. Soc., East Baton Rouge Parish Med. Soc., 6th Dist. Med. Soc., New Orleans Acad. Ophthalmology, So. Med. Assn., La. Med. Soc., Baton Rouge Parish Med. Soc., Pi Lambda Phi, Phi Delta Epsilon. Democrat. Jewish. Office: PO Box 66787 Baton Rouge LA 70896-6787

LEVINE, MACY IRVING, physician; b. Johnstown, Pa., May 19, 1920; s. Elliott B. and Ida (Leuin) L.; m. Evelyn B. Levine, June 28, 1948; children: Alan, Amy, Paul, Robert. BS, U. Pitts., 1940, MD, 1943. Diplomate Am. Bd. Internal Medicine, Am. Bd. Internal Medicine in Allergy. Intern U. Pitts. Med. Ctr., 1944; resident in allergy VA Hosp., Aspinwall, Pa., 1947-48, resident in medicine, 1948-49; fellow in medicine Lahey Clinic, Boston, 1950-51; USPHS postdoctoral fellow in medicine Peter Bent Brigham Hosp.-Harvard Med. Sch., Boston, 1951-52; pvt. practice Pitts., 1952—; clin. prof. medicine U. Pitts. Sch. Medicine. Editor: Monograph on Insect Allergy, 1995; editor Bull. of the Allegheny County MEd. Soc., 1975-86, Pitt Medicine Med. Alumni Assn., U. Pitts., 1987—; contbr. more than 70 articles to profl. jours. Bd. dirs. Self Help Group Network, 1989-95, B'nai Israel Congregation, Pitts., 1965-71, Hebrew Free Loan Assn. Pitts., 1980—. Capt. U.S. Army, 1944-46, PTO. Recipient Disting. Svc. award Am. Acad. Allergy and Immunology, 19087, Frederick M. Jacob, M.D. Physician Merit award for Outstanding Svc. Allegheny County Med. Soc., 1988. Fellow Am. Acad. Allergy, Asthma and Immunology (v.p. 1982-83, Outstanding Vol. Clin. Faculty award 1996), Pa. Allergy Assn. (pres. 1970-71, Spl. Recognition award 1989), ACP; mem. Pitts. Allergy Soc. (pres. 1959-61), U. Pitts. Med. Alumni Assn. (pres. 1976-77), U. Pitts. Alumni Assn. (pres. 1984-85). Home: 220 N Dithridge St Apt 400 Pittsburgh PA 15213

LEVINE, MARC M., pediatric cardiologist; b. N.Y.C., Aug. 12, 1947; s. Abraham and Cele (Josepher) L.; m. Priscilla Anne Leicht, Aug. 25, 1974; children: Arielle, Elana, Joshua. BA in Biology, SUNY, Buffalo, 1968; MD, Med. Coll. of Wis., Milw., 1972. Diplomate Am. Bd. Pediatric Cardiology, Am. Bd. Pediatrics. Intern in pediatrics Long Island Jewish Hosp.-Hillside Med. Ctr., New Hyde Park, N.Y., 1972-73, resident in pediatrics, 1973-75, fellow in pediatric cardiology, 1978-81; asst. prof. pediatrics Med. Coll. Ohio, Toledo, 1981—. Lt. comdr. USN, 1975-78. Fellow Am. Acad. Pediatrics, Am. Coll. Cardiology.

LEVINE, MARION HOLENA, medical librarian; b. N.Y.C., Feb. 21, 1939; d. John and Elizabeth (Miazga) Holena; m. Donald Martin Levine, Feb. 16, 1964 (div. Nov. 1976); children: Richard Benjamin, Carolyn Holena. BA, Hunter Coll., 1961; MLS, Columbia U., 1964; MS in Health Care Adminstrn, Hartford Grad. Ctr., 1990. Reference libr., head biblio. sect. Columbia Med. Libr., N.Y.C., 1964-67; coord. document delivery svc., head reference dept. Harvard Med. Libr., Boston, 1976-82; asst. dir. libr. U. Conn. Health Ctr., Farmington, 1982-86, assoc. dir. libr., 1986—; co-prin. investigator Nat. Network Librs. of Medicine, Farmington, 1991—. Co-editor: Current Serials in Countway, 1979. Mem. Med. Libr. Assn. (membership com. 1991-94, chair 1993-94, instrnl. devel. subcom. 1992-93, chair internat. coop. com. and sect. 1988, chair taskforce 1990-92, chair Cunningham fellow itinerary subcom. 1986-87), North Atlantic Health Sci. Libr. (exhibits com. 1995—, Cert. of Appreciation 1991, chair task force on ann. meeting 1993, treas. 1981-87), Conn. Assn. Health Sci. Librs. (membership com. 1995—, coord. Conn. Hosp. Libr. Survey 1986), Capital Region Libr. Coun. (planning com. 1988—, co-chair legis. com. 1984, chair interlibr. loan task force 1983), Kehilat Chaverim (archivist, steering com. 1994—). Office: Univ Conn Health Ctr Lyman Maynard Stowe Libr PO Box 4003 Farmington CT 06034-4003

LEVINE, RAPHAEL KREVSKY, orthopedic surgeon; b. Allentown, Pa., May 10, 1940; s. Herman Arthur and Marcia (Krevsky) L.; m. Letha S. Schwartz, Feb. 14, 1965; children: Zalman, Shoshana, Chava, Yehoshua, Batya. BA, Brandeis U., 1961; MD, Jefferson Med. Coll., Phila., 1965. Resident in orthop. surgery Columbia/Presbyn. Hosp., N.Y.C., 1970-72; fellow in orthop. surgery Columbia/Presbyn. Hosp., 1972-73; attending orthop. surgeon Pascack Valley Hosp., Westwood, N.J., 1974—; chief children's surg. svcs. Helen Hayes Hosp., West Haverstraw, N.Y., 1973-85, chief orthopedics, 1980-84. Contbg. author: The Child With Disabling Illness, 1976. Pres. Congregation Shomrei Emunah, Englewood, N.J., 1990-91. Lt. comdr. USN, 1966-69, Vietnam. Mem. Med. Soc. N.J. (Profl. Svc. award 1986), Bergen County Med. Soc. (vice chmn. jud. com. 1991—, sec.-treas. 1994—). Jewish. Home: 171 E Linden Ave Englewood NJ 07631 Office: Westwood Orthop Group PA 354 Old Hook Rd Westwood NJ 07675

LEVINE, RICHARD, plastic surgeon; b. Bklyn., Mar. 27, 1948; m. Jean Allan; children: Allyson, David, Elizabeth, Meredith. BA in Math., SUNY, Buffalo, 1968, DDS with honors, 1972, MD with honors, 1974. Diplomate Am. Bd. Plastic Surgery, Am. Bd. Med. Examiners. Glenn Leak fellow in head and neck cancer Sloan-Kettering Meml. Hosp., N.Y.C., 1971; postdoctoral rsch. fellow-oral pathology SUNY, Buffalo, 1972-73; U.S. Army Burn Unit U.S. Army Inst. Surg. Rsch., Ft. Sam Houston, Tex., 1976-77; surg. oncology Roswell Pk. Meml. Inst., Buffalo, 1977, 78; resident in gen. surgery SUNY, Buffalo Gen. Hosp., Buffalo, 1975-78; resident in plastic surgery SUNY, Buffalo, 1978-80, clin. asst. prof. Dept. Oral Pathology, 1972-75, from clin. asst. instr. to asst. prof. Dept. Surgery, 1974-81; clin. assoc. prof. Dept. Surgery U. Tex. Health Sci. Ctr., San Antonio, 1984—; chief of plastic surgery Charleston (S.C.) VA Hosp., 1980-81; attending surgeon Charleston County Hosp., Med. U. S.C., 1980-81; courtesy staff various, 1981-85; sec. med. staff, med. exec. bd. Village Oaks Regional Hosp., San Antonio, 1985—; chmn. divsn. Plastic Surgery 5 San Antonio Hosps., 1996—; chief of staff-elect Bapt. Meml. Hosp. Sys., San Antonio, 1996—; NE Regional Bds. fellow, Nat. Bd. Dental Examiners. Contbr. articles to profl. jours. Fellow ACS, Internat. Coll. Surgeons, Am. Coll. Oral and Maxillofacial Surgery; mem. Am. Soc. for Aesthetic Plastic Surgery, Am. Burn Assn., Am. Cleft Palate Assn., Am. Soc. Plastic and Reconstructive Surgeons, Internat. Soc. for Aesthetic Plastic Surgery, Internat. Assn. for Maxillofacial Surgery, Lipoplasty Soc. N.Am., San Antonio Surg. Soc., San Antonio Soc. Plastic Surgeons (sec.-treas. 1987-88), Tex. Med. Assn., Bexar County Med. Soc., Tex. Soc. Plastic Surgeons. Office: 8500 Village Dr Ste 102 San Antonio TX 78217-5510

LEVINE, RICHARD A., physician; b. Miami Beach, Fla., July 6, 1953; s. Morris Joseph and Sybil Rosalie (Panossian) L.; m. Lidia Foffu, Nov. 14, 1982; children: Mitchell, Kimberly, David. BS cum laude in zoology, U. Fla., 1975; MD, Universita di Roma, Rome, 1982. Diplomate Am. Bd. Internal Medicine, added qualifications in geriatric medicine; cert. Fed. Aviation Adminstrn. Med. Examiner; lic. Va., Fla. Resident in internal medicine U. Va. Affiliated Hosps., Roanoke-Salem, Va., 1983-86; pvt. practice Boca Raton, Fla., 1987—; bd. dirs. South Fla. Health Care Assocs., Boca Raton, 1994; lectr. in field. Dir. med. edn. com. Am. Cancer Soc., Boca Raton, 1990. Fellow Am. Coll. Physicians; mem. AMA, Fla. Med. Assn., Palm Beach County Med. Soc. (bd. dirs. 1994), Va. Med. Soc. Office: 800 NW 13th St Boca Raton FL 33486

LEVINE, ROBERT JOHN, physician, educator; b. N.Y.C., Dec. 29, 1934; s. Benjamin Bernard and Ruth Florence (Schwartz) L.; m. Jeralea Fooshee Hesse, Nov. 28, 1987; children from previous marriage: John Graham, Elizabeth Hurt Braun. Student, Duke U., 1951-54; MD with distinction, George Washington U., 1958. Diplomate Am. Bd. Internal Medicine. Med. house officer Peter Bent Brigham Hosp., Boston, 1958-59, asst. resident in medicine, 1959-60; clin. assoc. Nat. Heart Inst., Bethesda, Md., 1960-62, investigator, 1963-64; chief med. resident VA Hosp., West Haven, Conn., 1962-63; mem. faculty depts. medicine and pharmacology Yale U., New Haven, 1964-73, chief sect. clin. pharmacology, 1966-74, prof. medicine, lectr. pharmacology, 1973—; mem. med. staff Yale-New Haven Med. Ctr., 1964-68, attending physician, 1968—; mem. Conn. Adv. Com. on Foods and Drugs, 1967-82, sec. 1969-71, chmn., 1971-73; mem. adv. com. AIDS program U.S. HHS, 1989-95; cons. Nat. Commn. Protection of Human Subjects of Biomed. and Behavioral Rsch., 1974-78; bd. dirs. Medicine in the Pub. Interest, Inc., 1976—, sec., 1983—. Author: Ethics and Regulation of Clinical Research, 1981, 2d edit., 1986; co-editor: Ethics and Research on Human Subjects: International Guidelines, 1993; editor Clin. Rsch., 1971-76, IRB: Rev. Human Subjects Rsch., 1978—; contbr. numerous articles to profl. jours. Mem. Conn. Humanities Coun., 1983-89, chmn. 1988-89, Coun. Internat. Orgn. Med. Scis., co-chmn. steering com. revision internat. ethical guidelines for biomed.rsch. involving human subjects, 1991-93. Multiple rsch. grantee. Fellow ACP, Am. Coll. Cardiology, The Hastings Ctr.; mem. AAAS (coun. del. 1987-91), Am. Soc. Clin. Investigation, Am. Soc. Clin. Pharmacology and Therapeutics (bd. dirs. 1981-85), Am. Fedn. Clin. Rsch. (nat. coun. 1967-76, exec. com. 1971-76), Am. Soc. Pharmacology and Exptl. Therapeutics (exec. com. 1974-77), Am. Soc. Law, Medicine and Ethics (bd. dirs., pres. 1989-90, 94-95), Pub. Responsibility in Medicine and Rsch. (bd. dirs.), Soc. for Bioethics Consultation (bd. dirs. 1988-94), Sigma Xi, Alpha Omega Alpha. Office: Yale U Sch Medicine 333 Cedar St New Haven CT 06520-8010

LEVINE, RONALD H., physician, state official; b. N.Y.C., Mar. 30, 1935; m. Elizabeth P. Kanof; children—Mitchell, Rebecca Ann. BS, Union Coll., Schenectady, N.Y., 1955, DSc (hon.), 1990; MD, SUNY-Bklyn., 1959; MPH, U. N.C., 1967. Officer USPHS, Raleigh, N.C., 1963-65; chief communicable disease br. N.C. State Bd. Health, Raleigh, 1965-67, chief community health sect., 1968-73; asst. dir., dep. dir. N.C. Div. Health Services, Raleigh, 1974-81, state health dir., 1981—. Recipient Stevens award N.C. Assn. Local Health Dirs., 1982. Fellow Am. Acad. Pediatrics, Am. Pub. Health Assn., Am. Coll. Preventive Medicine, mem. N.C. Pub. Health Assn. (pres. 1974-75, Reynolds award 1973), Wake County Med. Soc. (pres. 1978), N.C. Med. Soc. Office: Dept Environ Health & Natural Resources PO Box 27687 512 N Salisbury St Raleigh NC 27604-1118

LEVINE, STEPHEN BARRY, pediatric ophthalmologist; b. Bklyn., Oct. 22, 1942; s. David and Rickey (Nedboy) L.; m. Susan Joanne Zane, Aug. 28, 1966; children: Deborah, Laurie, Jennifer. BS in Chemistry, Washington Coll., 1963; MD, SUNY, 1967. Diplomate Am. Acad. Ophthalmology. Intern Kings County Hosp., N.Y.C., 1967-68; resident in ophthalmology Mt. Sinai Hosp., N.Y.C., 1970-73; pres. Pediatric Eye Care of Atlanta, PC, 1974—. Lt. comdr. USPHS, 1968-70. Summer Rsch. fellow SUNY Downstate Med. Ctr., 1964, 65, 66; Fellowship Award grantee Seeing Eye, Inc., 1973-74, Heed Ophthalmic Found., 1973-74. Mem. Atlanta Ophthal. Sco. (pres. 1991-92), Med. Assn. Ga., Med. Assn. Atlanta, Assn. Pediatric Ophthalmology & Strabismus, Soc. Heed Fellows. Home: 230 N Chambord Dr NW Atlanta GA 30327-4587 Office: Pediatric Eye Care 5671 Peachtree Dunwoody Rd NE Atlanta GA 30342-5000

LEVINE, STEVEN RICHARD, neurologist, researcher; b. Bay Shore, N.Y., June 29, 1955; s. Harry Arnold and Elaine Judith (Fink) L.; m. Joanne Miriam Traurig; children: Aaron Marc, David Benjamin, Aliza Rachael. BS, U. Mich., 1977; MD, Med. Coll. Wis., 1981. Resident in neurology U. Mich. Med. Ctr., Ann Arbor, 1982-85; fellow in cerebrovascular disease Henry Ford Hosp., Detroit, 1985-87, staff neurologist, dir. clin. stroke svc., 1987—. Mem. editl. Bd. Stroke, Henry Ford Hosp. jour., 1990—. Rsch. fellow Am. Heart Assn., 1986-87; recipient Harold G. Wolff Lectr. award Am. Assn. Study of Headache; grantee NIH-NINDS, 1990-95. Fellow Stroke Coun. Am. Heart Assn. (chmn. Mich. unit 1991-93); mem. Phi Beta Kappa. Jewish. Office: Henry Ford Hosp Health Scis Ctr Neur K-11 2799 W Grand Blvd Detroit MI 48202-2689

LEVINSKY, NORMAN GEORGE, physician, educator; b. Boston, Apr. 27, 1929; s. Harry and Gertrude (Kipperman) L.; m. Elena Sartori, June 17, 1956; children—Harold, Andrew, Nancy. A.B. summa cum laude, Harvard U., 1950, M.D. cum laude, 1954. Diplomate Am. Bd. Internal Medicine. Intern Beth Israel Hosp., Boston, 1954-55; resident Beth Israel Hosp., 1955-56; commd. med. officer USPHS., 1956; clin. assoc. Nat. Heart Inst., Bethesda, Md., 1956-58; NIH fellow Boston U. Med. Center, 1958-60; practice medicine, specializing in internal medicine and nephrology Boston, 1960—; chief of medicine Boston City Hosp., 1968-72, 93—; physician-in-chief, dir. Boston U. Med. Ctr. Hosp., Boston, 1972—; asst. prof., then assoc. prof. medicine Boston U., 1960-68, Wesselhoeft prof., 1968-72, Wade prof. medicine, 1972—, chmn. dept. medicine, 1972—; mem. drug efficacy panel NRC; mem. nephrology test com.-Am. Bd. Internal Medicine, 1971-76: mem. gen. medicine B rev. group NIH; mem. comprehensive test com. Nat. Bd. Med. Examiners, 1986-89; chmn. com. to study end-stage renal disease program Nat. Acad. Scis./Inst. Medicine, 1988-90, chmn. com. on Xenografts, 1995. Editor (with R.W. Wilkins) Medicine: Essentials of Clinical Practice, 3d edit., 1983, (with R. Rettig) Kidney Disease and the Federal Government, 1991; contbr. chpts. to books, sci. articles to med. jours. Recipient Distinguished Teacher awd., Am. Coll. of Physicians, 1992. Master ACP; mem. AAAS, Am. Fedn. Clin. Rsch., Am. Soc. Clin. Investigation, Am. Heart Assn., Assn. Am. Physicians, Am. Physiol. Soc., Assn. Profs. Medicine (sec., treas. 1984-87, pres.-elect 1987-88, pres. 1988-89), Am. Soc. Nephrology, Inst. Medicine NAS, Interurban Clin. Club (pres. 1985-86), Phi Beta Kappa, Alpha Omega Alpha. Home: 20 Kenwood Ave Newton MA 02159-1439 Office: Boston U Med Ctr 75 E Newton St Boston MA 02118-2340

LEVINSON, ARNOLD IRVING, allergist, immunologist; b. Balt., 1944. MD, U. Md. Sch. Medicine, 1969. Intern Balt. City Hosps., 1969-70, resident internal medicine, 1970-71; fellow U. Pa., Phila., 1973-75, assoc. prof. neurology, 1987—. Mem. AAI, AFCR, AFEB, ASCI, Brit. Soc. Immunology. Office: U Pa Hospital 3400 Spruce St Philadelphia PA 19104-4219*

LEVINSON, BRUCE ARTHUR, optometrist; b. Syracuse, N.Y., Apr. 19, 1965; s. Jordan Malcome and Miriam Margaret (Wolff) L.; m. Darlene Louise Levinson, Aug. 21, 1994. Ed., Buffalo State Coll., 1988; DOptometry, New Eng. Coll. Optometry, Boson, 1992. Optometrist Med. and Surg. Ophthalmology, Binghamton, N.Y., 1992, Health Svcs. Assn., Syracuse, N.Y., 1992-94, J.M. Levinson-Optometrist, Syracuse, 1994—, John MacDaniel, O.D., Syracuse, 1994—; dir. optometric rels. Cataract, Cornea and Refractive Ctr., George O. Temnycky, M.D., Syracuse, 1995—. Contbr. articles to profl. jours. Optometrist, Vision USA, Syracuse, 1994-96. Fellow Am. Acad. Optometry; mem. Ctrl. N.Y. Optometric Soc. (treas. 1993-95, v.p. 1995-96), N.Y. State Soc. Optometric Soc. (chair membership com. 1993), Am. Optometric Soc. Home: 1622 Westmoreland Ave Syracuse NY 13210 Office: 2806 Court St Syracuse NY 13208

LEVINSON, HARRY, psychologist, educator; b. Port Jervis, N.Y., Jan. 16, 1922; s. David and Gussie (Nudell) L.; m. Roberta Freiman, Jan. 11, 1946 (div. June 1972); children—Marc Richard, Kathy, Anne, Brian Thomas; m. Miriam Lewis, Nov. 23, 1990. BS, Emporia (Kans.) State U., 1943, MS, 1946; PhD, U. Kans., 1952. Coordinator profl. edn. Topeka State Hosp., 1950-53, psychologist, 1954-55; dir. div. indsl. mental health Menninger Found., Topeka, 1955-68; visiting prof. MIT, 1961-62, U. Kans. Bus. Sch., 1967, Texas A&M U., 1976; Thomas Henry Carroll-Ford Found. distinguished vis. prof. Harvard Grad. Sch. Bus., Boston, 1968-72; adj. prof. Coll. Bus. Adminstrn., Boston U., 1972-74; lectr. Harvard Med. Sch., 1972-85; adj. prof. Pace U., 1972-83; clin. prof. psychology Harvard Med. Sch., 1985-92, emeritus prof., 1992—; head sect. orgnl. mental health Mass. Mental Health Ctr., 1983-92; pres. The Levinson Inst., 1968-91, chmn. bd., 1991—; mem. Am. Bd. Profl. Psychology, 1972-80, chmn., 1978-80; Ford Found. prof. Mathur Inst., Jaipur India, 1974; conducted internat. course on social psychiatry Finnish Govt. Inst., 1979. Author: Emotional Health In the World of Work, 1964, Executive Stress, 1970, The Exceptional Executive (McKinsey Found. and Acad. Mgmt. awards), 1968 (James A. Hamilton Hosp. Adminstrs. Book award), Organizational Diagnosis, 1971, The Great Jackass Fallacy, 1973, Psychological Man, 1976, Casebook for Psychological Man; (with S. Rosenthal) CEO: Corporate Leadership in Action (Am. Coll. Health Care Adminstrs. Book award 1986), 1984, Ready, Fire, Aim, 1986, Designing and Managing Your Career, 1989, Career Mastery, 1992. Chmn. Kans. adv. com. U.S. Civil Rights Commn., 1962-68; chmn. Topeka Human Relations Commn., 1967-68. Served with F.A. AUS, 1944-46. Recipient Perry Rohrer Cons. Psychology Practice award, 1984, Career award Mass. Psychol. Assn., 1985, First award Soc. Psychologists in Mgmt.; Eminent scholar in bus. Fla. Atlantic U., 1995. Fellow APA (award for disting. profl. contbn. to knowledge 1992); mem. AAAS, Acad. Mgmt., Authors Guild. Home: 225 Brattle St Cambridge MA 02138-4623

LEVINSON, JOHN MILTON, obstetrician, gynecologist; b. Atlantic City, Aug. 17, 1927; m. Elizabeth Carl Bell; children: Patricia Anne, John Carl, Mark Jay. BA, Lafayette Coll., Easton, Pa., 1949; MD, Thomas Jefferson U., 1953. Diplomate Am. Bd. Ob-Gyn. Intern Atlantic City Hosp., 1953-54; Am. Cancer Soc. clin. fellow Jefferson Med. Coll. Hosp., Phila., 1954-55; resident in ob-gyn. Del. Hosp., Wilmington, 1955-57; pvt. practice ob-gyn. Wilmington, 1957-85; prof. dept. ob-gyn. Jefferson Med. Coll., Thomas Jefferson U., Phila., hon. clin. prof., 1990—; sr. attending physician emeritus Med. Ctr. Del., Wilmington, 1986—; attending chief dept. ob-gyn. St. Francis Hosp., Wilmington, chief emeritus, 1986-92; founder, pres. Aid for Internat. Medicine, Inc., 1966—; med. dir., chief surgeon Quark Expeditions, 1991-95; cons. Riverside Hosp., 1972-86, Wilmington Pa. Blue Shield, 1982—: cons. gynecology U.S. VA, 1974-85; founding mem., treas., bd. dirs. Physicians Health Svcs., Del., Ltd., 1985-87; vis. prof., cons., ship's surgeons, practicing physician various orgns. in Africa, Antarctica, Arctic regions, Ctrl. Am., Europe, S.E. Asia,, S.W. Asia, 1963—; lectr. in field; internat. med. cons. to Sen. Edward M. Kennedy, 1967—; chmn. Antarctic expdns. study group to advise NSF, 1992-93; co-chmn. Com. for Safety in Arctic and Antarctic Frontier Expeditions, 1992-93. Author: Shorebirds: The Birds, the Hunters, the Decoys, 1991; contbr. articles to profl. jours., book chpts. Bd. dirs. Del. com. Project H.O.P.E., 1965-75, ARC, 1968-70, Charles A. Lindbergh Fund, Inc., 1985-90; trustee Blue Cross/ Blue Shield Del., Inc., 1968-86, Brandywine Coll., 1972-77; bd. dirs. Nat. Assn. Blue Shield Plans, 1971-77; mem adv. com. Trinity Alcohol and Drug Program, 1978-85; mem. Del. Gov.'s Commn. on Health Care Cost Mgmt., 1985-87; bd. dirs. founding mem. World Affairs Coun. Wilmington Inc, v.p., 1981-86; pres. Rockland Mills Cmty. Assn., 1992-94. With USN, 1945-47; col. M.C., USAFR, 1984-87. Recipient Brandywine award Brandywine Coll., 1968, cert. of appreciation for med. svcs. Ministry of Health, Republic of Vietnam, 1963-66, commendation Pres. of U.S., 1971, The Eisenhower award People to People Internat., 1986, Commemorative medal Charles A. Lindbergh Fund, 1987, Phila. Explorers award 1987, Citation for Outstanding Contbn. to People of Del., Med. Soc. Del., 1992. Fellow Am. Assn. Ob.-Gyns., Royal Geog. Soc. London; mem. AMA, Am. Assn. Gyn. Laporoscopists (founding, bd. dirs.), Del. Obstetric Soc. (pres. 1980-82), Phila. Obstetric Soc., Med. Soc. Del. (Citation of Merit award 1992), New Castle County Med. Soc., Soc. Ob-Gyn. Vietnam (hon.), Ducks Unltd. (sponsor, mem. Del. com. 1980-92), Explorers Club (fellow 1966—, chmn. Phila. chpt. 1983-85, bd. dirs. 1981-88, pres. N.Y.C. 1985-87), Univ. and Whist Club Wilmington (life, bd. govs. 1961-64), Rotary (bd. dirs. local club 1991-93), Theta Chi (pres. 1945) Phi Beta Pi (pres. 1952), Kappa Beta Phi (pres. 1952). Home: 55 Millstone Ln Rockland DE 19732

LEVINSON, RASCHA, psychotherapist; b. N.Y.C., Nov. 27, 1930; d. Frank Alfred and Goldye Dena (Preiser) Cohen; m. Monroe Louis Levinson, Oct. 6, 1955 (div. 1973); 1 child, Nadia Levinson Fogel. BA, NYU, 1960; MSW, Columbia U., 1962; Tng. in Hypnosis, Milton Erickson Soc., N.Y.C., 1992-93. Lic. social worker, N.Y. Pvt. practice N.Y.C., 1970—; psychotherapist Wasington Sq. Inst., N.Y.C., 1973-74; intake therapist Women's Psychotherapy Referral Svcs., N.Y.C., 1973-76; supr. psychotherapy Mid-Hudson Cons. Ctr., Wappinger Falls, N.Y., 1974-83; workshop leader New Sch. Social Rsch., N.Y.C., 1980-87. Fellow Soc. Clin. Social Workers (pres. Westchester chpt. 1986-88); mem. Assn. for Women in Psychology, N.Y.C. Coalition for Women's Mental Health (bd. dirs. 1986-89), Advanced Feminist Therapy Inst. (editor newsletter 1990-92). Office: 55 Central Park W # 1B New York NY 10023-6003

LEVINSON, WARREN EDWARD, physician, microbiologist, educator; b. N.Y.C., Sept. 28, 1933; s. Jay Raymond and Claire (Grossman) L.; m. Barbara Boykin, Aug. 12, 1965. BS, Cornell U., 1953; MD, U. Bufflao, 1957; PhD, U. Calif., Berkeley, 1965. Diplomate Nat. Bd. Med. Examiners. Commd. lt. USN, 1957; flight surgeon USN, Alameda, Calif., 1958; faculty Sch. of Med. U. Calif., San Francisco, 1967—. Author: Medical Microbiology and Immunology, 1989, 4th edit. 1996. Mem. Planning Commn., Mill Valley, Calif., 1978-80, 1988-90; mem. Mill Valley City Coun., 1990—, vice mayor, 1991-92, mayor, 1992-93. Mem. AAAS, Am. Soc. Microbiology, Calif. Acad. Scis., Alpha Omega Alpha (med. hon. soc.). Home: 183 Molino Ave Mill Valley CA 94941-2742 Office: U Calif Dept Microbiology 510 Parnassus Ave Box 0414 San Francisco CA 94143

LEVINSTONE, BERTRAM, surgeon; b. N.Y.C., Nov. 11, 1921; s. Aaron and Etta Miriam (Goldstein) L.; m. Mildred Dolores Rothfeld, Nov. 16, 1946; children: Edward Ira, Daniel Everett. BS, Muhlenberg Coll., 1942; MD, U. Pa., 1945. Diplomate Am. Bd. Surgery. Intern Newark Beth Israel Med. Ctr., 1945-46, surg. resident, 1947-50; pvt. practice Newark, Maplewood, N.J., 1951-77, West Orange, N.J., 1977—; attending surgeon St. Barnabas Med. Ctr., Livingston, N.J., 1951—, clin. chief surgery, 1980-83; sr. attending surgeon Newark Beth Israel Med. Ctr., 1951—; attending surgeon St. James Hosp., Newark, 1953—; surg. cons. U.S. VA Hosp., Lyons, N.J., 1953-88; med. dir. Harrison (N.J.) Alloys, 1953-89, Penick Corp., Newark, 1953-94, Mannkraft Corp., Newark, 1953—; clin. instr. surgery N.Y. Med. Coll., N.Y.C., 1963-66; clin. assoc. prof. surgery U. Medicine and Dentistry N.J., N.J. Med. Sch., Newark, 1970—; lectr. surgery Mt. Sinai Med. Sch., N.Y.C., 1983-86; regional med. dir. Aetna Health Plans N.J., Parsippany, 1987—. Trustee Jewish News of Metrowest, East Orange, N.J., 1955-60, Jewish Family Svc. Metrowest, Florham Park, N.J., 1963-93; mem. Cmty. Rels. Com. Metrowest, East Orange, 1983-96; exec. com. Met. Orch., West Orange, 1972—; med. com. Am. Cancer Soc., 1983-94, vice chmn., 1984. Fellow ACS (chmn. cancer liason program for N.J.), Internat. Coll. Surgeons, Acad. Medicine N.J. (pres. 1981-82); mem. AMA, Med. Soc. N.J. (ho. dels. 1980—), N.J. Gastroent. Soc., N.J. Soc. Surgeons, Oncology Soc. N.J. (pres. 1991-92), Essex County Med. Soc. (editor bull. 1973-78), Orange Lawn Tennis Club. Home: 15 Riggs Ct Basking Ridge NJ 07920-1037 Office: 769 Northfield Ave West Orange NJ 07052-1106

LEVINTHAL, CHARLES FREDERICK, research psychologist; b. Cin., July 6, 1945; s. Sam and Mildred Carolyn (Greenburg) L.; m. Beth Ellen Kuby, Dec. 16, 1973; children: David Justin, Brian Ross. AB, U. Cin., 1967; MA, U. Mich., 1968, PhD, 1971. Lic. psychologist, N.Y. Asst. prof. Hofstra U., Hempstead, N.Y., 1971-78, assoc. prof., 1978-87, prof., 1987—. Author: Messengers of Paradise: Opiates and the Brain, 1988, Introduction to Physiological Psychology, 3d edit., 1990, Drugs, Behavior, and Modern Society, 1996; contbr. articles to profl. jours. With USAR, 1968-74. Fellow Woodrow Wilson Found., 1967, NSF, 1967-71. Mem. Am. Psychol. Assn., Soc. Neurosci. Jewish. Home: 9 Royal Oak Dr Huntington NY 11743-4427 Office: Hofstra U 1000 Hempstead Tpke Hempstead NY 11550-1090

LEVIS, DONALD JAMES, psychologist, educator; b. Cleve., Sept. 19, 1936; s. William and Antoinette (Stejskal) L.; children: Brian, Katie. Ph.D., Emory U., 1964. Postdoctoral fellow clin. psychology Lafayette Clinic, Detroit, 1964-65; asst. prof. psychology U. Iowa, Iowa City, 1966-70, assoc. prof., dir. research and tng. clinic, 1970-72; prof. SUNY-Binghamton, 1972—. Author: Learning Approaches to Therapeutic Behavior Modification, 1970, Implosive Therapy, 1973; cons. editor: Jour. Abnormal Psychology, 1974-80, Jour. Exptl. Psychology, 1976-77, Behavior Moedifications, 1977-81, Behavior Therapy, 1974-76, Clin. Behavior Therapy Rev., 1978—; contbr. articles to profl. jours. Served to capt. AUSR, 1958-66. Fellow Behavior and Therapy Research Soc. (charter, clin.), Am. Psychol. Assn.; mem. Assn. Advancement Behavior Therapy (publ. bd. 1979-82), AAAS, Psychonomic Soc., N.Y. State Psychol. Assn., Sigma Xi. Home: 48 Riverside Dr Binghamton NY 13905-4402 Office: SUNY at Binghamton Dept Psychology Binghamton NY 13901

LEVIT, EDITHE JUDITH, physician, medical association administrator; b. Wilkes-Barre, Pa., Nov. 29, 1926; m. Samuel M. Levit, Mar. 2, 1952; children: Harry M., David B. BS in Biology, Bucknell U., 1946; MD, Woman's Med. Coll. of Pa., 1951; DMS (hon.), Med. Coll. Pa., 1978; DSc (hon.), Wilkes U., 1990. Grad. asst. in psychology Bucknell U., 1946-47; intern Phila. Gen. Hosp., 1951-52, fellow in endocrinology, 1952-53, clin. instr., assoc. in endocrinology, 1953-57, dir. med. edn., 1957-61, cons. med. edn., 1961-65; asst. dir. Nat. Bd. Med. Examiners, Phila., 1961-67; assoc. dir., sec. bd. Nat. Bd. Med. Examiners, 1967-75, v.p., sec. bd., 1975-77, pres., chief exec. officer, 1977-86, pres. emeritus, life mem. bd., 1987—; cons. in field, 1964—; mem. adv. coun. Inst. for Nuclear Power Ops., Atlanta, 1988-93; bd. dir. Phila. Electric Co. Contbr. articles to profl. jours. Bd. dirs. Phila. Gen. Hosp. Found., 1964-70; bd. dirs. Phila. Council for Internat. Visitors, 1966-72; bd. sci. counselors Nat. Library Medicine, 1981-85. Recipient award for outstanding contbns. in field of med. edn. Commonwealth Com. of Woman's Med. Coll., 1970; Alumni award Bucknell U., 1978; Disting. Dau. of Pa. award, 1981; Spl. Recognition award Assn. Am. Med. Colls., 1986; Disting. Service award Fedn. State Med. Bds., 1987; Master A.C.P. Fellow Coll. Physicians of Phila.; mem. Inst. Medicine of Nat. Acad. Scis., AMA, Pa., Phila. County med. socs., Assn. Am. Med. Colls., Phi Beta Kappa, Alpha Omega Alpha, Phi Sigma. Home: The Rittenhouse 210 W Rittenhouse Sq Philadelphia PA 19103-5726

LEVITAS, ANDREW STEPHEN, child psychiatrist, educator; b. Bklyn., Feb. 17, 1948; s. Louis and Laura (Perlman) L.; m. Phyllis Malin, Apr. 19, 1970; children: Joshua, Matthew. BS, Union Coll., 1968; MD, Albert Einstein Coll. Medicine, 1972. Diplomate Am. Bd. Psychiatry and Neurology. Intern Montefiore Hosp. and Med. Ctr., Bronx, N.Y., 1972-73; resident in psychiatry Downstate-Kings County Hosp. Ctr., Bklyn., 1973-75; fellow in child psychiatry U. Colo. Health Scis. Ctr., Denver, 1975-77, asst. clin. prof., 1982-86; staff psychiatrist Denver Children's Hosp., 1977-79; pvt. practice Denver, 1979-86; asst. prof. U. Nebr. Med. Ctr., Omaha, 1986-88; asst. prof. U. Medicine and Dentistry N.J. Sch. Osteo. Medicine, Cherry Hill, 1988-96, assoc. prof. clin. psychiatry, 1996—; med. dir. div. prevention and treatment of devel. disorders Sch. Osteo. Medicine, Cherry Hill, 1992—; cons. psychiatrist T.I.M. House, Devel. Pathways, Aurora, Colo., 1982-86; mem. sci. adv. bd. Fragile-X Soc., Denver. Contbr. numerous articles to profl. jours. Mem. MLA, Am. Psychiat. Assn., Am. Acad. Child and Adolescent Psychiatry. Office: U Medicine and Dentistry NJ Sch Oste Medicine Dept Psy 2250 Chapel Ave Cherry Hill NJ 08002-2051

LEVITON, ADINA PLATT, rehabilitation consultant; b. N.Y.C., July 9, 1962; d. George L. and Naomi D. Platt. BA, SUNY, Albany, 1983; MA, George Washington U., 1985; PhD in Counseling and Consultation, grad. cert. in Gerontology, U. Md., 1994. Cert. rehab. counselor, profl. counselor, Md., rehab. provider, Va. Crisis hotline counselor SUNY, Albany, 1983; rehab. counselor Va. Dept. Rehab. Svcs., Alexandria, 1985; spl. student svcs. counselor U. D.C.; pvt. practice, McLean, Va., 1984—; intern vocat. rehab. Nat. Rehab. Hosp., Washington, 1991-92; rehab. counselor screener Office of Worker's Compensation Programs, Washington, 1994; ptnr. Rehab. Consulting Group, Springfield, Va., 1995—. Mem. ACA, Am. Rehab. Counseling Assn., Assn. Adult Devel. and Aging, Nat. Rehab. Assn., Nat. Rehab. Counseling Assn., Nat. Assn. Pvt. Rehab., Am. Soc. on Aging, Chi Sigma Iowa. Office: PO Box 3542 Mc Lean VA 22103

LEVITSKY, DMITRII IVANIVICH, biochemist; b. Moscow, Dec. 11, 1951; s. Ivan Ivanovich Levitsky and Serafima Ilyinichna Berkhin; m. Nataliya Grigoryievna Voloshina, June 16, 1979; children: Olga, Alexander. BS, Moscow State U., 1976, PhD, 1981; DSc, Russian Acad. Scis., 1992. Scientist Moscow State U., 1976-88; sr. scientist A.N. Bakh Inst. Biochemistry, Russian Acad. Scis., Moscow, 1988-92, head scientist, 1992—; head rsch. group A.N. Bakh Inst. Biochemistry, Russian Acad. Scis., 1993—. Author: Myosin and Biological Motility, 1982, Domain Structure of the Myosin Head, 1994; contbr. sci. papers to profl. jours. Fogarty grantee

NIH, 1993-95, Internat. Sci. Found. grantee, 1994-95. Office: AN Bakh Inst Biochemistry, Leninsky prosp 33, 117071 Moscow Russia

LEVITT, LEROY PAUL, psychiatrist, psychoanalyst; b. Wilkes-Barre, Pa., Jan. 8, 1918; s. Samuel and Paula (Goldstein) L.; divorced; children: Steven C., Susan M., Jeremy W., Sara H.; m. Jane A. Glaim, Apr. 7, 1971. B.S., Pa. State U., 1939; M.D., Chgo. Med. Sch., 1943; postgrad., Inst. Psychoanalysis, Chgo., 1950-59. Diplomate: Am. Bd. Psychiatry and Neurology. Intern Beth David Hosp., N.Y.C., 1943; resident Elgin (Ill.) State Hosp., 1947-49; pvt. practice, specializing in psychiatry and psychoanalysis Chgo., 1949—; prof. psychiatry Chgo. Med. Sch., 1949-76, dean, 1966-73; dir. Ill. Dept. Mental Health, 1973-76; v.p. Mt. Sinai Hosp. Med. Ctr., Chgo., 1976-82, chmn. dept. psychiatry, 1982-87, dir. med. edn., 1987-88; prof. psychiatry Rush Med. Coll., 1977-89, prof. emeritus, 1989—; mem. staff Naples Community Hosp., 1989-95; cons. Blue Cross-Blue Shield, 1977-80, Nat. Council Aging, Ill. Psychiat. Inst.; mem. Mayor's Commn. on Aging, 1955-60. Pres. Chgo. Bd. Health, 1979-83; bd. dirs. Med. Ctr. YMCA, Med. Careers Council; bd. govs. Inst. of Medicine of Chgo. Med. Soc. Served to capt. M.C. AUS, 1944-46. Named Prof. of Year Chgo. Med. Sch., 1964, Tchr. of Year Ill. Psychiat. Inst., 1966, Chicagoan of Yr. in Medicine, 1970; WHO fellow Europe, 1970; recipient Sinai Health Service award, 1986. Fellow Am. Psychiat. Assn. (life), Am. Acad. Psychoanalysis, Am., Internat. psychoanalytic assns., Ill. Psychiat. Soc. (pres.), Chgo. Inst. Medicine, Am. Coll. Psychiatrists, Am. Coll. Psychoanalysts (pres. 1983, Laughlin award 1985), Sigma Xi, Alpha Omega Alpha, Phi Lambda Kappa (Gold medal sci. award). Home: 222 Harbour Dr Naples FL 34103-4022

LEVITT, MIRIAM, pediatrician; b. Lampertheim, Germany, June 10, 1946; came to U.S., 1948; d. Eli and Esther (Kingston) L.; m. Harvey Flisser, June 25, 1967; children: Adam, Elizabeth, Eric. AB, NYU, 1967; MD, Albert Einstein Coll. Medicine, Yeshiva U., 1971. Diplomate Am. Bd. Pediatrics. Intern Montefiore Med. Ctr., Bronx, N.Y., 1970-71, resident in pediatrics, 1971-73, attending pediatrician, 1975—; dir. outpatient svcs. pediatrics Bronx-Lebanon Hosp., N.Y.C., 1973-77; instr. pediatrics Albert Einstein Coll. Medicine, N.Y.C., 1973-76, asst. prof. clin., 1976—; med. staff Lawrence Hosp., Bronxville, N.Y., 1978—, dir. pediatrics, 1988—; sch. physician Bronxville Bd. Edn., 1983—. Fellow Am. Acad. Pediatrics; mem. Westchester County Med. Soc. Office: 1 Pondfield Rd Bronxville NY 10708-3706

LEVITT, SEYMOUR HERBERT, physician, radiology educator; b. Chgo., July 18, 1928; s. Nathan E. Levitt and Margaret (Chizever) D.; m. Phillis Jeanne Martin, Oct. 31, 1952 (div. Oct. 1981); children: Mary Jeanne, Jennifer Gaye, Scott Hayden; m. Solveig I. Ostberg, Feb. 6, 1983. B.A., U. Colo., 1950, M.D., 1954. Diplomate: Am. Bd. Radiology (trustee). Intern Phila. Gen. Hosp., 1954-55; resident in radiology U. Calif. at San Francisco Med. Center, 1957-61; instr. radiation therapy U. Mich., Ann Arbor, 1961-62, U. Rochester, N.Y., 1962-63; asso. prof. radiology U. Okla., Oklahoma City, 1963-66; prof. radiology, chmn. div. radiotherapy Med. Coll. Va., Richmond, 1966-70; prof., head dept. therapeutic radiology U. Minn., Mpls., 1970—; cons. in field. Exec. bd. Am. Joint Com. for End Result Reporting and Cancer Staging; com. radiation oncology studies Nat. Cancer Inst. Bd. dirs., mem. exec. com. Am. Cancer Soc., 1990-95. With M.C., AUS, 1955-57. Recipient Disting. Svc. award U. Colo., 1988. Fellow Am. Coll. Radiology (bd. chancellors, Gold medal 1995), Royal Coll. Radiology (hon.); mem. Am. Radium Soc. (sec. 1981-83, pres. 1983-84, Janeway medal 1989), Radiol. Soc. N.Am. (bd. dirs. 1991—), Am. Assn. Cancer Rsch., Am. Cancer Soc. (pres. Minn. divsn. 1979-80, nat. bd., exec. com.), Am. Roentgen Ray Soc., Soc. Chairmen of Acad. Radiation Oncology Programs (pres. 1974-76), Internat. Soc. Radiation Oncology (pres. 1981-85), Soc. Nuclear Medicine, Am. Soc. Clin. Oncology, Am. Soc. Therapeutic Radiologists (exec. bd. 1974-78, pres. 1978-79, chmn. bd. 1979-80, Gold medal 1991), Deutsche Rontgengesellschaft Gesellschaft fur Medizinische Radiologie E.V. (hon.), Phi Beta Kappa, Sigma Xi., Alpha Omega Alpha. Home: 7233 Lewis Ridge Pkwy Minneapolis MN 55439-1106 Office: U Minn PO Box 436 Minneapolis MN 55455

LEVITZKY, MICHAEL GORDON, physiology educator; b. Elizabeth, N.J., Jan. 3, 1947; s. Edward and Shirley Edith (Worfman) L.; m. Ellen M. de Roxtro (div. Dec. 1984); m. Elizabeth Seeliger Gouaux, Mar. 13, 1985; children: Edward Benjamin, Sarah Elizabeth. BA, U. Pa., 1969; PhD, Albany Med. Coll., Union U., 1975. Instr. physiology Albany (N.Y.) Med. Coll., 1974-75; asst. prof. physiology La. State U. Med. Ctr., New Orleans, 1975-80, assoc. prof., 1980-85, prof., 1985—; adj. prof. Tulane U. Med. Ctr., New Orleans, 1990—. Author: Pulmonary Physiology, 1982, 2d edit., 1986, 3d edit., 1991, 4th edit., 1995; co-author: Introduction to Respiratory Care, 1990. Nat. Heart, Lung and Blood Inst. grantee, 1976-78, 78-86. Mem. Am. Physiol. Soc. (edn. com. 1988-91), Am. Thoracic Soc., N.Y. Acad. Scis., Soc. for Exptl. Biology and Medicine, Sigma Xi. Office: La State U Med Ctr Dept Physiology 1901 Perdido St New Orleans LA 70112-1328

LEVY, ALBERT, family physician; b. Stanleyville, Zaire, Nov. 8, 1948; came to U.S., 1977; s. Moise and Eugenie J. (Menache) L.; children: Antonia G., Eric M. MD, Fed. U. Brazil, Rio de Janeiro, 1973, MS in Field Medicine, 1976. Diplomate Am. Bd. Family Physicians, Am. Bd. Family Practice, Am. Bd. Geriatric Medicine. Chief family medicine sect. Our Lady of Mercy Hosp., Bronx, N.Y., 1989—; pvt. practice family medicine Manhattan Family Practice, N.Y.C., 1990—; physician Montefiore Med. Ctr., Bronx, 1994—; asst. clin. prof. dept. family medicine Albert Einstein Coll. Medicine, Bronx, N.Y., 1994—; asst. prof. N.Y. Med. Coll., Valhalla, N.Y., 1994—; with Beth Israel Med. Ctr., 1986, St. Luke's/Roosevelt Med. Ctr., 1986, Lenox Hill Hosp., 1995. Fellow Am. Acad. Family Physicians, Royal Soc. Medicine, (Eng.), N.Y. Acad. Medicine; mem. AMA, Am. Geriatric Soc., World Orgn. Nat. Colls./Acads. Family Physicians, N.Y. Acad. Scis., Med. Soc. State of N.Y., N.Y. County Acad. Family Physicians (v.p. 1992), Soc. Tchrs. Family Medicine. Jewish. Home: 311 Wilton Rd Westport CT 06880 also: 25 Sutton Pl S New York NY 10022 Office: Manhattan Family Practice 911 Park Ave New York NY 10021

LEVY, BARRY EDWARD, neurologist; b. Balt., Jan. 10, 1951. BA, Johns Hopkins U., 1972; MD, U. Md., 1976. Diplomate Am. Bd. Psychiatry and Neurology. Intern in internal medicine Md. Gen. Hosp., Balt., 1976-77; resident in neurology U. Md., 1977-80; pvt. practice Louisville, 1980-81, Park Ridge, Ill., 1981—; asst. prof. neurology Rush Med. Coll., Chgo., 1995—; dir. sleep disorders ctr. Holy Family Med. Ctr., Des Plaines, Ill., 1994—. Mem. AMA, Am. Acad. Neurology, Am. Sleep Disorders Assn. Office: 444 N Northwest Hwy Park Ridge IL 60068

LEVY, BENJAMIN, medical research executive; b. N.Y.C., June 12, 1937; s. Martin Luther and Alice (Marks) L.; m. Ellen Lois Goldberg, Sept. 1, 1963; children: Michael, Daniel, Mark. BS, Union Coll., Schenectady, N.Y., 1956; MD, N.J. Coll. Medicine, 1960. Diplomate Am. Bd. Internal Medicine. Intern Jersey City Med. Ctr., 1960-61; resident Boston City Hosp., 1961-63; fellow NIH, N.Y.C., 1963-65; practice internal medicine Hartford (Conn.) Hosp., 1965-83; research dir., pres. Nat. Med. Research Corp., Hartford and Brussels, 1983-96; also bd. dirs. Nat. Med. Research Corp., Hartford; exec. v.p., dir. rsch., chmn. bd. Scirex Corp., 1996—; dir. courses, lectr. Ctr. for Profl. Advancement, New Brunswick, N.J., 1985-92; exec. v.p. rsch. dir., chmn. bd. Scirex Corp., 1996—. Contbr. articles to profl. jours. Bd. dirs. Conn. Opera Co., Hartford, 1978-82; trustee Westwood Hill Assn., West Hartford, Conn., 1980-95. Recipient numerous grants for med. research. Mem. AMA, Am. Soc. Clin. Pharmacology and Therapeutics, Conn. Med. Soc., Drug Info. Assn., Soc. for Clin. Trials, Am. Coll. CLin. Pharmacology, Am. Heart Assn., Hartford C. of C. (coms. 1984—), Hartford Club, Tumblebrook Country Club (Bloomfield, Conn.), Admiral's Cove Country Club (Jupiter, Fla.), Hartford Club (life). Home: 47 Westwood Rd West Hartford CT 06117-2253 Office: Scirex Corp 25 Main St Hartford CT 06106-1806

LEVY, DAVID ALFRED, immunology educator, physician, scientist; b. Washington, Aug. 27, 1930; s. Stanley A. and Blanche B. (Berman) L.; m. Annette Levy-Badoux; children: Jill, William, Stanley. BS, U. Md., 1952, MD, 1954. Diplomate Am. Bd. Internal Medicine, Am. Bd. Allergy and Immunology. Intern, resident in medicine U. Hosp., Balt., 1954-59; physician VA Hosp., Balt., 1961-62; fellow dept. microbiology Sch. Medicine Johns Hopkins U., 1962-66, asst. prof. radiol. sci. Sch. Hygiene and Pub. Health, Sch. Medicine, 1966-68, assoc. prof. Sch. Hgiene and Pub. Health, Sch. Medicine, 1968-71, prof. radiol. sci. and epidemiology Sch. Hygiene and Pub. Health, Sch. Medicine, 1972-73, prof. biochemistry Sch. Hygiene and Pub. Health, Sch. Medicine, 1973-82, with joint appointments in epidemiology and medicine Sch. Medicine, 1973-82, in pathobiology Sch. Medicine, 1980-82, prof. immunology and infectious diseases Sch. Medicine, 1982-86; mem. FDA Panel on Rev. of Allergenic Extracts, 1975-83; mem. allergy and immunology rev. com. Nat. Inst. Allergy and Infectious Diseases, 1975-77; adj. dir. Centre d'Immunologie et de Biologie, Pierre Fabre, S.A., 1985-90; cons. to pharm. industry, 1990—. Editorial bd. Clin. Immunology and Immunopathology, 1971-76, Revue d'Allergologie Française; contbr. articles to med. jours. and books. Sci. dir. Centre d'Allergie, Hopital Rothschild, Paris, 1991—. With U.S. Army, 1959-61. Fellow Am. Acad. Allergy and Immunology; mem. Internat. Union Immunol. Socs. (vice chmn. allergen standardization subcom. 1980-83), Am. Assn. Immunologists, French Soc. Allergology, Sigma Xi. Home and Office: 11 Quai St Michel, 75005 Paris France

LEVY, DAVID EDWARD, neurologist, researcher, educator; b. Washington, May 10, 1941; s. Maurice W. and Celia (Blue) L.; m. Ellen Kaplan, June 7, 1943. A.B., Harvard U., 1963, M.D., 1968. Diplomate Am. Bd. Internal Medicine, Am. Bd. Psychiatry and Neurology. Intern, then resident in medicine N.Y. Hosp. Cornell Med. Ctr., N.Y.C., 1968-70, resident in neurology, 1970-72; instr. Cornell U. Med. Coll., N.Y.C., 1972-75, asst. prof. neurology, 1975-80, assoc. prof., 1980—. Contbr. numerous articles, abstracts on stroke and coma to profl. jours. Recipient Tchr.-scientist award Andrew W. Mellon Found., 1975-77; established investigator Am. Heart Assn., 1978-83; Robert Wood Johnson Found. grantee, 1981-87. Fellow ACP; mem. Am. Neurol. Assn. Office: Cornell U Med Coll A-569 1300 York Ave New York NY 10021-4805

LEVY, DAVID LAWRENCE, emergency medicine educator; b. Huntington, N.Y., Jan. 4, 1968; s. Dalton and Pearl (Shulman) L. BS in Biochemistry, SUNY, Stony Brook, 1990; DO, N.Y. Coll. Osteo. Medicine, 1994. Chief intern Good Samaritan Hosp. Med. Ctr., West Islip, N.Y., 1994-95; resident emergency medicine L.I. Jewish Med. Ctr., New Hyde Park, N.Y., 1995—. Recipient Outstanding Promotion of Osteo. Medicine, NYCOM, 1992, Cmty. Svc. award Med. Soc. State N.Y., 1994. Mem. Am. Coll. Emergency Physicians, Am. Coll. Osteo. Emergency Physicians, Emergency Medicine Residents' Assn., Assn. Emergency Physicians, Am. Osteo. Assn. Soc. for Acad. Emergency Medicine. Office: LI Jewish Med Ctr Dept Emergency Medicine Lakeville Rd New Hyde Park NY

LEVY, ELI SAUL, social work educator; b. Bklyn., June 18, 1929; s. Benjamin and Mollie (Weitz) L.; m. Doris Shapiro, May 24, 1953; children: Sherry Eileen, Bonnie Karen, Sondra Gail, Benjamin Samuel. AB, Bklyn. Coll., 1951; MS in Social Svc., Boston U., 1953; PhD, NYU, 1974. Youth bd. worker South Bronx YMHA, YWHA, Bronx, N.Y., 1953; dir. teen. activities Williamsburg YMHA, YWHA, Bklyn., 1956-58; psychiat. social worker Hillside Hosp., Glen Oaks, N.Y., 1958-61, dir. activities therapy, 1961-67; student unit supr. Lincoln Hosp., Bronx, 1967-70; asst. prof. social work Rutgers U., New Brunswick, N.J., 1970-74; assoc. prof. social work Yeshiva U., N.Y.C., 1974—; adj. prof. sociology Nassau Community Coll., Garden City, N.Y., 1968—; cons. N.J. Civil Svc. Bd., Trenton, 1970-73. Contbr. articles to profl. jours. Chmn. youth com. Young Isreal, Oceanside, N.Y., 1962-65, bd. dirs., 1965-93. Cpl. U.S. Army, 1953-55. Mem. NASW, Nat. Conf. Jewish Communal Svc. Office: Yeshiva U Wurzweiler Sch Social Work 2495 Amsterdam Ave New York NY 10033-3312

LEVY, ELLIOT GENE, physician; b. Kansas City, Mo., Oct. 15, 1946; s. Jerry and Sarah A. (Lesser) L.; m. Deborah Lynn Benovitz, Aug. 24, 1971; children: Jonathan, Emily, Daniel. BS, Northwestern U., 1967, MD, 1971. Intern U. Pa., Phila., 1971-72; resident Washington U., St. Louis, 1972-74; pvt. practice North Miami Beach, Fla., 1975—. Fellow ACP; mem. Am. Diabetes Assn., Am. Thyroid Assn., Endocrine Soc., Thyroid Found. Am. Republican. Jewish.

LEVY, GERHARD, pharmacologist; b. Wollin, Germany, Feb. 12, 1928; came to U.S., 1948, naturalized, 1953; s. Gotthold and Eliesabeth (Luebeck) L.; m. Rosalyn Mincer, June 8, 1958; children: David, Marc, Sharon. B.S., U. Calif. at San Francisco, 1955, Pharm.D., 1958; Dr. honoris causa, Uppsala (Sweden) U., 1975, Phila. Coll. Pharmacy and Sci., 1979, L.I. U., 1981, U. Ill., 1986, Hoshi U., Japan, 1996. Asst. prof. pharmacy U. Buffalo, 1958-60; asso. prof. pharmacy State U. N.Y. at Buffalo, 1960-64, prof. biopharmaceutics, 1964-72, distinguished prof. pharmaceutics, 1972-75, chmn. dept. pharmaceutics, 1966-70, univ. disting. prof. emeritus, 1995; vis. prof. Hebrew U., Jerusalem; cons. WHO, 1966, Bur. Drugs Adv. Panel System, FDA, 1971-74; mem. com. on problems of drug safety NRC, 1971-75; mem. pharmacol.-toxicol. com. NIH, 1971-75. Mem. editorial bd. Jour. Pharm. Sci, 1970-75, Clin. Pharmacology and Therapeutics, 1969—, Internat. Jour. Clin. Pharmacology, 1968-78, Drug Metabolism and Disposition, 1973-78, Jour. Pharmacokin Biopharm, 1972—, Internat. Jour. Pharm., 1977-95, Jour. Pharmacobi-Dynamics, 1979-93, Pharm. Res., 1983-95; contbr. articles to profl. jours. Served with AUS, 1950-51. Recipient Ebert prize, 1969, Am. Pharm. Assn. Research Achievement award, 1969, McKeen Cattell award Am. Coll. Clin. Pharmacology, 1978, Host-Madsen medal Internat. Pharm. Fedn., 1978, Oscar B. Hunter award in exptl. therapeutics Am. Soc. Clin. Pharmacology and Therapeutics, 1982, Volwiler Research Achievement award Am. Assn. Colls. Pharmacy, 1982, Scheele award Swedish Acad. Pharmaceutical Scis., 1992, 1st Lifetime Achievement in the Pharm. Scis. award Internat. Pharm. Assn., 1994; named Alumnus of Year U. Calif. Sch. Pharmacy Alumni Assn., 1970. Fellow Am. Pharm. Assn., Acad. Pharm. Scis. (Takeru Higuchi Research prize 1983), AAAS; mem. Inst. Medicine of Nat. Acad. Scis., Am. Assn. Pharm. Scientists (Dale E. Wurster Rsch. award 1992), Am. Soc. Exptl. Pharmacology and Therapeutics. Home: 169 Surrey Run Buffalo NY 14221-3321 Office: SUNY Sch Pharmacy Amherst NY 14260

LEVY, HAROLD BERNARD, pediatrician; b. Shreveport, La., Apr. 27, 1918; s. Phillip and Ida (Sperling) L.; m. Betty Ann Friedenthal, Nov. 29, 1942; children—James, Charles, Roger, Judy Levy Harrison. B.S., La. State U., 1937; M.D., 1940. Diplomate Am. Bd. Pediatrics. Intern, Tri-State Hosp., Shreveport, 1940-41; resident in pediatrics Shreveport Charity Hosp., 1946-48; practice medicine specializing in pediatrics, Shreveport, La., 1948—; co-med. dir. Caddo Found. for Exceptional Children, 1953—; founder, dir. spl. clinic for learning disabilities La. Handicapped Children's Services, 1955—; clin. assoc. prof. pediatrics La. State U. Med. Sch., Shreveport, 1973—; faculty mem. Nat. Coll. Juvenile Justice, Reno, 1975—; mem. staff Schumpert, Willis-Knighton, Doctors, La. State U. hosps.; Pres., Shreveport Summer Theater, 1953; pres. Caddo-Bossier Safety Council, 1959-60. Served to maj. M.C., USAAF, 1942-46. Recipient Brotherhood citation NCCJ, 1976; Spl. recognition award La. Assn. Children with Learning Disabilities, 1976; Axson-Choppin award La. Pub. Health Assn., 1983. Mem. Am. Acad. Cerebral Palsy and Devel. Medicine (pres. 1983), Am. Acad. Pediatrics, La. Med. Soc., So. Med. Assn., AMA, Orton Dyslexia Soc., Sigma Xi Republican. Jewish. Club: East Ridge Country. Author: Square Pegs, Round Holes, The Learning Disabled Child in the Classroom and at Home, 1973; contbr. articles to profl. jours. Home: 6026 Dillingham Ave Shreveport LA 71106-2131 Office: 865 Margaret Pl Ste 316 Shreveport LA 71101-4542

LEVY, HAROLD JAMES, physician, psychiatrist; b. Buffalo, Feb. 15, 1925; s. Sidney Harold and Evelyn (Sperling) L.; m. Arlyne Adelstein, July 3, 1958; children: Sanford Harvey, Richard Alan, Kenneth Lee. MD, U. Buffalo, 1946. Diplomate in psychiatry Am. Bd. Neurology and Psychiatry. Intern Erie County Med. Ctr., Buffalo, 1946-47, asst. resident in psychiatry, 1947-48, asst. chief psychiatry, 1953-58, attending psychiatrist, 1957-90; cons. psychiatrist Erie County Med. Ctr., 1990—; fellow in psychosomatic medicine Med. Sch. U. Buffalo, Erie County Med. Ctr., 1950-53; psychiatrist Buffalo, 1950—; mem. courtesy staff Millard Fillmore Hosp., 1957, clin. asst., 1958, asst. attending physician, 1959-63, assoc. attending physician, 1963-64, attending physician, 1964-90, chmn. dept. psychiatry, 1968-90, cons., 1990—; attending psychiatrist BryLin Psychiat. Hosp. (formerly Linwood Bryant Hosp.), Buffalo, 1955—, clin. dir. psychiatry, 1966-91; staff psychiatrist Psychiat. Clinic, Family Ct. Erie County, N.Y., 1959-63, psychiat. dir. clinic, 1963-80; mem. courtesy staff in psychiatry St. Joseph's Intercommunity Hosp., Buffalo, 1969-71, cons. in psychiatry, 1971—; cons. in psychiatry St. Francis Hosp., 1972-91, Sisters of Charity Hosp., 1985—; asst. in psychiatry Med. Sch. SUNY, Buffalo, 1950-52, instr. 1952-55, assoc. 1955-70, clin. asst. prof. 1970-86, clin. assoc. prof., 1986—; mem. psychiat. staff Rosa Coplon Jewish Home and Infirmary, 1957-72, chmn. dept. psychiatry, 1969-72; staff psychiatrist Chronic Disease Rsch. Inst., sect. on alcoholism Med. Sch. SUNY, Buffalo, 1950-53; psychiat. cons. Dent Clinic Found. Millard Fillmore Hosp., 1967—, Lafayette Gen. Hosp., Buffalo, 1973-85. Pres. Lemezo Enterprises Inc., Buffalo, 1970, Sanricken Enterprises Inc., Buffalo, 1970—; mem. exec. com. Blue Shield Western N.Y. Served to capt. M.C., AUS, 1948-50. Fellow Am. Psychiat. Assn. (life, pres. Western N.Y. dist. br. 1969-70), Am. Soc. Psychoanalytic Physicians, Am. Soc. Advancement Electrotherapy; mem. AMA, Israel Med. Assn., N.Y. State Med. Soc., Erie County Med. Soc. (chmn. com. on mental health, econs. com., publ. com. for bull. 1959-78), Buffalo Acad. Medicine, Maimonides Med. Soc. (pres. 1968-69), N.Y. State Soc. Med. Rsch., Western N.Y. Neuropsychiat. Soc. (pres.-elect 1965-66), Western N.Y. Psychiat. Assn. (pres. 1974-75), Gen. Alumni Assn. SUNY, Buffalo (treas. exec. bd. 1967-69, numerous offices), SUNY-Buffalo Sch. Medicine Alumni Assn. (past pres., numerous offices), Med. Students' Aid Soc. (past nat. pres., chmn. bd. dirs. 1990-92), B'nai B'rith (exec. com. Anti Defamation League), Cherry Hill Colf and Country Club, Alpha Omega Alpha, Phi Lambda Kappa (nat. dir., past nat. v.p., past nat. pres., chmn. bd. dirs. 1990-92), Beta Sigma Rho. Home: 47 Longleat Dr Buffalo NY 14226-4114 Office: Psychiat Assocs of Western NY 2740 Main St Buffalo NY 14214-1702

LEVY, HERMAN ABRAHAM, retired internist; b. Chgo., Aug. 4, 1908; s. Joseph and Elizabeth (Sternberg) L.; m. Sadel Rita Prosterman, Nov. 25, 1932; children: Charles G., Gerald E., Marcia R. Levy Wingard. BS in Medicine, Loyola U., Chgo., 1930, MD, 1932. Diplomate Am. Bd. Internal Medicine. Intern Cook County Hosp., Chgo., 1932-33, resident in pathology, 1933-34; practice medicine specializing in allergic diseases Chgo., 1934—; asst. emeritus prof. medicine, U. Ill., Chgo., 1986—. Contbr. articles on hypoparathyroidism to profl. jours. Served to 1st lt., U.S. Army, 1932-34. Fellow Am. Coll. Allergy and Immunology, Am. Acad. Allergy and Immunology, Ill. Soc. Allergy and Immunology, Am. Coll. Physicians, Am. Geriatric Soc., Internat. Soc. Medicine. Jewish.

LEVY, JENNIFER YATES, psychologist; b. Riverside, Calif., Sept. 13, 1952; d. Jules David and Natalie (Weisberg) Y. BA, U. Mass., Boston, 1974; MEd, Boston U., 1975; PhD, George Washington U., 1986. Lic. clin. psychologist, Va. Lectr. in psychology Newbury Jr. Coll., Boston, 1975-76, No. Va. C.C., Woodbridge, 1978-80, George Mason U., Fairfax, Va., 1982; mental health therapist Prince William County, Dumfries, Va., 1982-86; resident in psychology Family Counseling Ctr., Manassas, Va., 1986-87, clin. dir., 1987—; co-founder, co-dir. Turning Points Domestic Violence Program, Dumfries, 1978-80; group co-leader Individual Devel. Assn., Quantico, Va., 1984-85. Author: Healing the Harm Done, 1995. Bd. dirs. Sexual Assault Victims Advocacy Svcs., Prince William County, Va., 1990-93; troop leader Girl Scouts U.S., Woodbridge, Va., 1991-95; mem., past mem. steering com. Domestic Violence Cmty. Coalition, Prince William County, 1991-95. Mem. APA, Va. Psychol. Assn. Office: Family Counseling Ctr 9300 Grant Ave # 300 Manassas VA 22110

LEVY, JEROME, dermatologist; retired naval officer; b. Bklyn., Aug. 17, 1926; s. Alexander and Pauline (Wollkof) L.; m. Leona Elsie Eligator, June 6, 1948; children—Andrew B., Eric J., Peter C., David J. Student, Wesleyan U., 1944-45; postgrad., 1952-54; A.B., Yale U., 1947; M.D., Albany Med. Coll., 1958. Diplomate Am. Bd. Dermatology. Commd. ensign M.C., U.S. Navy, 1957, advanced through grades to capt., 1972; intern U.S. Naval Hosp., Newport, R.I., 1958-59; resident U.S. Naval Hosp., Phila., 1960-62, U. Pa. Grad. Sch. Medicine, Phila., 1962-63; chief dept. dermatology U.S. Naval Hosp., Memphis, 1963-67, Yokosuka, Japan, 1967-70, Long Beach, Calif., 1974-75; head outpatient dermatology clinic San Diego Naval Hosp., 1970-72; sr. med. officer Keflavik, Iceland, 1972-74; ret., 1975; med. dir. dermatology Westwood Pharm Co., Buffalo, 1975-82; acting chief dermatology dept. Buffalo Gen. Hosp., 1981-82; cons. Erie County Health Dept., 1979-82; clin. assoc. prof. SUNY, Buffalo Med. Sch., 1980-82; practice medicine specializing in dermatology, Coronado, Calif., 1982-90. Contbr. articles to med. jours. Decorated Navy Commendation medal, Joint Service Commendation medal; Knight's Cross of the Order of Falcon (Iceland). Fellow Am. Acad. Dermatology, ACP; mem. AMA, So. Med. Assn., Assn. Mil. Surgeons, U.S., Navy League, Alpha Omega Alpha. Republican. Jewish. Home: 3352 Lucinda St San Diego CA 92106-2932

LEVY, KENNETH JAY, psychology educator, academic administrator; b. Dallas, Sept. 18, 1946; s. Reuben and Ruth (Okon) L.; children: Ryan S., Scott D. BA, U. Tex., 1968, MA, 1969; PhD, Purdue, 1972. Asst. prof. psychology SUNY, Buffalo, 1972-75, assoc. prof., 1976-73, prof., 1979—, chmn. dept. psychology, 1976-78, dean social scis., 1978-82, various adminstrv. positions, 1985—, assoc. provost, 1987—. Contbr. numerous articles to profl. jours.; editorial cons. Psychometrika. Home: 39 Shire Dr S East Amherst NY 14051-1816 Office: SUNY at Buffalo Capen Hall Buffalo NY 14260

LEVY, LAURENT D., physician, radiologist; b. Constantine, Algeria, Sept. 13, 1957; s. Jean Claude L. and Jeannine S. Cohen-Adad; m. Monique L. Baranes, May 16, 1960; children: Meryl, Jean-Charles. Baccalaureat, Lyceé Janson de Sailly, Paris, 1975; MD, C.H.U. Broussais Hotel Dieu, Paris, 1983. Cert. Radiology Bd., Paris. Resident Hopital Tenon, Paris, 1983-84, Hopital Raymond Poincaré, Paris, 1984-85; with Hopital St. Louis, Paris, 1985-86, Inst. Radiologie, Paris, 1986—; cons. Hopital Saint Louis, Paris, 1986-92. Co-author: Mammography Atlas, 1991, Computed Tomography of Kidneys, 1991, Ultrasound Atlas of Prostate, 1992, Imaging of the Prostate, 1994. Mem. French Soc. Radiology, French Soc. Gyn. Home: 7 Rue du General Bertrand, 75007 Paris France Office: Inst Radiologie, 31 Ave Hoche, 75008 Paris France

LEVY, LEWIS LAWRENCE, neurologist; b. N.Y.C., Feb. 18, 1922; s. Jack Ellis and Ida (Schwartz) L.; m. Dorothy E. Bensing, June 16, 1946; children: Robert, Susan, Joan, David. AB, Temple U., 1943, MD, 1946. Diplomate Am. Bd. Psychiatry and Neurology; lic. MD, Pa., N.Y., Ky., Conn. Intern Temple U. Hosp., Phila., 1946-47; capt. U.S. Army Med. Corps, 1947-49; resident in neurology VA Hosp., Louisville, 1949-50; resident in psychiatry VA Hosp., Bronx, N.Y., 1950-51; fellow in neurology U. Louisville Med. Sch., 1951-52, instr. in medicine, asst. prof. medicine, 1952-53, 53-54; asst. clin. prof. neurology Yale U. Sch. Medicine, 1954-64, assoc. clin. prof. neurology, 1964-71, clin. prof. neurology, 1971—; chief neurology svc. VA Hosp. Med. Ctr., 1955-83; sr. staff Yale New Haven Hosp., 1956—; dir. stroke acute care unit VA Med. Ctr., 1971-76, chief cerebrovascular sect., 1979-83. Contbr. numerous articles to profl. jours. Fellow Am. Acad. Neurology; mem. Am. Neurol. Assn., Assn. for Rsch. of Nervous and Mental Disease. Home: 230 Pleasant Point Rd Branford CT 06405-5610

LEVY, LOUIS ALAN, neurosurgeon; b. N.Y.C., Feb. 25, 1939; s. Leon Simeon and Ina E. (Eisenberg) L.; divorced; children: Sierra-Lorri Anne, Jennifer Levy Martin, Robert, Alan, Susan Levy Roberts, Johanna Levy Scholberg. BA, U. Calif., Santa Barbara, 1962; MD, U. So. Calif., L.A., 1964. Diplomate Am. Bd. Neurol. Surgeons. Intern L.A. County/U. So. Calif. Gen. Hosp., 1964-65, resident neurology, 1970-73; gen. surgery resident L.A. County-U. So. Calif./Harbor Gen. Hosp., Torrance, 1965-66; clin. assoc. prof. Sch. Medicine U. Nev. Fellow ACS. Home: 864 Marsh Ave Reno NV 89509

LEVY, MARGUERITE F., psychology educator, researcher; b. Buffalo, Dec. 20, 1925; d. Matthias and Mary Elizabeth (deStasio) Fine; m. Louis Harold Levy, May 23, 1925; B.A., U. Buffalo, 1952; M.A., NYU, 1964, Ph.D., 1968. Licensed psychologist. Research scientist NYU, N.Y.C., 1968-69; research assoc. CUNY, 1969-70; asst. prof. Queens Coll., CUNY, Flushing, 1970-76; dir. research and evaluation Community Mental Health Ctr., Paterson, N.J., 1976-77; dir. research Med. and Health Research Assn., N.Y.C., 1978-82; adj. Baruch Coll.; adj. CUNY, 1982-85, assoc. prof., 1985-90; cons. pvt. practice, 1990— cons. Bd. Edn., Bklyn., 1975-76, Bd. Higher Edn., N.Y.C., 1972-73, Columbia U., N.Y.C., 1978, Fashion Inst. Tech., SUNY, N.Y.C., 1983-85. Editor: Research and Theory in Developmental Psychology, 1983; assoc. editor The Corporation and Its Publics, 1963. Contbr. articles to profl. jours. Fellow NIMH-USPHS, NYU, 1966-67;

recipient Creative Talent award Am. Inst. Research, 1967-68. Fellow APA; mem. N.Y. State Psychol. Assn. (pres. social div. 1977-78, 83-84), Sigma Xi. Club: Women's City (N.Y.C.) (sec. 1983-85). Home: 241 Sackett St Brooklyn NY 11231-3604

LEVY, MARLON FRANTZ, surgeon; b. Paris, Oct. 26, 1959; came to U.S., 1969; children: Piet, Henri. BA cum laude, U. Dallas, 1981; MD, U. Tex., Dallas, 1985. Diplomate Am. Bd. Surgery. Intern Med. Coll. Wis., Milw., 1985-91; staff tranplant surgeon Baylor U. Med. Ctr., Dallas, 1992—. Mem. med. editorial adv. bd. Transplant Internat. jour.; contbr. articles to profl. jours. Fellow ACS; mem. AMA, Am. Assn. Study of Liver Disease, Am. Soc. Transplant Surgeons, Soc. Critical Care Medicine, Transplantation Soc., Southwestern Surg. Congress, Tex. Med. Assn., Tex. Med. Found., Tex. Transplant Soc. Office: Baylor U Med Ctr Transplant Svcs 3500 Gaston Ave Dallas TX 75246

LEVY, MICHA, physician; b. Vienna, Austria, June 3, 1938; arrived in Israel, 1938; s. Mordecai Max and Margot (Altmann) L.; m. Lydia Beraha, Feb. 14, 1962; children: Tamar, Jonathan. MD, Hebrew U., Jerusalem, 1964; MS, Harvard U., 1973. Cert. specialist in internal medicine. Resident Hadassah U. Hosp., Jerusalem, 1966-71, head clin. pharmacology, 1975-88, chmn. dept. medicine, 1989—; sr. investigator Boston Collaborative Drug Surveillance Program, 1972-74; prof. medicine Hebrew U., Jerusalem, 1984—; chmn. Internat. Study of Agranulocytosis, 1979-86; vis. prof. Cornell U. Med. Coll., 1980, Boston U., 1986, U. Erlangen, 1995. Author 2 books; contbr. over 150 scientific papers to profl. jours. Lt. col. Israel Defence Forces, ret. Recipient Humboldt-Meitner award, 1995. Mem. Israel Soc. Internal Medicine (chmn. 1990-93), Israel Soc. Clin. Pharmacology (chmn. 1994—). Office: Hadassah U Hosp, Kiryat Hadassah, Jerusalem 91-120, Israel

LEVY, MICHAEL SCOTT, psychologist; b. Newburgh, N.Y., Oct. 23, 1953; s. Beverly (Kalish) Mark; m. Laurie Paige Bristow, Aug. 19, 1978; 1 child, Brianna Nicole. BA, Boston U., 1975; PhD, Calif. Sch. Profl. Psychology, Berkeley, 1981. Lic. psychologist, Mass. Staff psychologist Chenango County Mental Health Clinic, Norwich, N.Y., 1981-83; consulting psychologist Delphi Ctr., Reading, Mass., 1983-86; clin. dir. dual diagnosis unit Met. State Hosp., Waltham, Mass., 1984-91; dir. of psychology Dr. Solomon Carter Fuller Mental Health Ctr., Boston, 1991-92; clin. dir. Ctr. for Behavioral Medicine Norcap, Southwood Community Hosp., Norfolk, Mass., 1992-96; clin. instr. in psychology, med. sch. Harvard U., Cambridge, Mass., 1987-94; pvt. practice Andover, Mass., 1986—; program dir. Choate Health Mgmt. The Psychiatric Ctr. Health Alliance Hosp., Fitchburg, Mass., 1996—; consulting psychologist Project COPE, Lynn, Mass., 1984-85; mem. faculty Colgate U., Hamilton, N.Y., 1983, Ctr. Addiction Studies, Cambridge, 1987—. Contbr. chpts. to books, articles to profl. jours. Mem. adv. com. ARC Boston, Lexington, Mass., 1988—; bd. dirs. Ea. Middlesex Coun. Children, Wakefield, Mass., 1984-87. Mem. APA, Mass. Psychol. Assn. Jewish. Home: 7 Island Way Andover MA 01810-6044 Office: 2 Elm Sq Andover MA 01810-3668

LEVY, MORTON GERALD, pediatrician; b. N.Y.C., June 24, 1936; s. Samuel and Leah (Yagoda) L.; m. Arlene Carol Sakowitz Levy, June 8, 1958; children: Jay Barry, Mitchell Keith, Anita Caren. AB, Washington U., St. Louis, 1957; MD, SUNY, Bklyn., 1961. Diplomate Am. Bd. Pediatrics. Intern Kings County Hosp. Ctr., Bklyn., 1961-62; resident Mt. Sinai Hosp., N.Y.C., 1962-64; pvt. practice Roslyn Heights, N.Y., 1977—; clin. asst. prof. pediatrics Cornell U. Coll. Medicine, N.Y.C., 1973; attending in pediatrics North Shore U. Hosp., Manhasset, N.Y., 1983; med. dir. Cleft Palate Clinic North Shore Hosp., Manhasset, 1985; mem. staff Schneider Childrens Hosp., New Hyde Park, 1969. Capt. M.C. U.S. Army, 1964-66. Fellow Am. Acad. Pediatrics; mem. N.Y. State Med. Soc., Nassau County Med. Soc. Office: 73 Garden St Roslyn Heights NY 11577

LEVY, NEAL D., psychotherapist; b. Bklyn., Dec. 30, 1951. BA, Yeshiva U., 1973; MSW, Wurzweiler Sch. Social Work, 1976; cert., Hunter Coll., 1980; PhD, Columbia Pacific U., 1981. Diplomate Am. Bd. Examiners in Clin. Social Wk.; cert. social worker, N.Y., ACSW; lic. emergency med. technician, N.Y. Co-founder, clin. dir. Jewish Inst. for Family Therapy, Rego Park, N.Y.; clin. dir. Ohel Children's Home and Family Svc., Bklyn.; asst. prof. Wurzweiler Sch. Social Work, N.Y.C.; pvt. practice psychotherapist Rego Park; pub. speaker, workshop leader, presenter on family and marital rels. Mem. NASW (diplomate). Home: 66-05 Booth St Rego Park NY 11374

LEVY, NORMAN B., psychiatrist, educator; b. N.Y.C., 1931; s. Barnett Theodore and Lena (Gulnick) L.; m. Lya Weiss (dec.); children: Karen, Susan, Joanne; m. Carol Lois Spiegel, 1 son, Robert Barnett. B.A. cum laude, NYU, 1952; M.D., SUNY. Diplomate: Am. Bd. Psychiatry and Neurology (examiner). Intern Maimonides Med. Center, Bklyn.; resident physician in medicine U. Pitts.-Presbyn. Hosp.; resident in psychiatry Kings County Hosp. Center, Bklyn.; instr. psychiatry State U. N.Y. Downstate Med. Center Coll. Medicine, Bklyn.; asst. prof. State U. N.Y. Downstate Med. Center Coll. Medicine, assoc. prof., prof.; presiding officer faculty State U. N.Y. Downstate Med. Center Coll. Medicine (Coll. Medicine), assoc. dir. med-psychiat. liaison service; prof. psychiatry, medicine, surgery and coordinator psychiat. liaison services N.Y. Med. Coll.; clin. prof. psychiatry, adj. prof. of medicine Health Science Ctr. SUNY, Bklyn., 1992—; dir. liaison psychiatry divsn. Westchester County Med. Ctr., 1980-95, mem. exec. com. med. staff, 1981-85, 89-92; dir., consultation-liaison and emergency psychiatry Coney Island Hosp., Bklyn., 1996—; clin. prof. psychiatry and adj. prof. medicine SUNY, Health Sci. Ctr. at Bklyn., 1996—; vis. prof. psychiatry and medicine So. Ill. U. Sch. Medicine; vis. prof. psychiatry John A. Burns Sch. Medicine, U. Hawaii, 1981; coord. 1st Internat. Conf. Psychol. Factors in Hemodialysis and Transplantation, 1978, 2d-10th Internat. Confs. on Psychonephrology; cons. NIMH; chief med. svcs. USAF Hosp., Ashiya, Japan. Author: (with others), editor: Living or Dying: Adaptation to Hemodialysis, 1974, Psychonephrology I: Psychological Factors in Hemodialysis and Transplantation, 1981, Men in Transition: Theory and Therapy, 1982, Psychonephrology II: Psychological Problems in Kidney Failure and their Treatment, 1983; contbr. articles to jours., chpts. to textbooks in field.; assoc. editor: Gen. Hosp. Psychiatry, 1978-82, sect. editor, 1982—; sect. editor: Internat. Jour. Psychiatry in Medicine, 1977-78; mem. editorial bd., book rev. editor Jour. Dialysis and Transplantation, 1979—; mem. editorial bd. Resident and Staff Physician, 1981-91, Internat. Jour. Artificial Internat. Organs, 1983-93, Geriatric Nephrology and Urology, 1990—, Kidney: A Current Survey of World Literature, 1990—. Served to capt. M.C., USAF. Served to capt. M.C., USAF. Recipient Willaim A. Console Master Tchr. award, SUNY, Brooklyn, 1991; Thomas P. Hackett award Acad. Psychosomatic med., 1993. Fellow ACP, Am. Coll. Psychiatrists, Am. Psychiat. Assn. (pres. Kings County dist. br. 1981-82), Internat. Coll. Psychosomatic Medicine, Acad. Psychosomatic Medicine; mem. AAAS, Am. Psychosomatic Soc. (coun. 1994—), N.Y. Acad. Scis., Psychonephrology Found. (pres. 1978—), Assn. Acad. Psychiatry, Internat. Soc. Nephrology, Am. Soc. Nephrology, Am. Assn. Artificial Internal Organs, Soc. Liaison Psychiatry (bd. dirs. 1979-80, sec. 1980-81, pres.-elect 1991-92, pres. 1992-94, bd. dirs. 1995—), Phi Beta Kappa, Sigma Xi. Home: 169 Westminster Rd Brooklyn NY 11218-3445 Office: Coney Island Hosp Dept Psychiatry Brooklyn NY 11235

LEVY, ROBERT ISAAC, physician, educator, research director; b. Bronx, N.Y., May 3, 1937; s. George Gerson and Sarah (Levinson) L.; m. Ellen Marie Feis, 1958; children: Andrew, Joanne, Karen, Patricia. B.A. with high honors and distinction, Cornell U., 1957; M.D. cum laude, Yale U., 1961. Intern, then asst. resident in medicine Yale-New Haven Med. Ctr., 1961-63; clin. assoc. molecular diseases Nat. Heart, Lung and Blood Inst., Bethesda, Md., 1963-66, chief resident, 1965-66, attending physician molecular disease br., 1965-80, head sect. lipoproteins, 1966-80, dep. clin. dir. inst., 1968-69, chief clin. services molecular diseases br., 1969-73, chief lipid metabolism br., 1970-74, dir. div. heart and vascular diseases, 1973-75, dir. inst., 1975-81; v.p. health scis., dean Sch. Medicine Tufts U., Boston, 1981-83, prof. medicine, 1981-83; v.p. health scis. Columbia U., N.Y.C., 1983-84, prof., 1983-88, sr. asst. v.p. health scis., 1985-87; pres. Sandoz Research Inst., East Hanover, N.J., 1988-92; pres. Wyeth-Ayerst Rsch. Wyeth-Ayerst Labs div. Am. Home Products, Phila., 1992—; attending physician Georgetown U. med. div. D.C. Gen. Hosp., 1966-68; spl. cons. anti-lipid drugs FDA. Editor: Jour. Lipid Rsch., 1972-80, Circulation, 1974-76, Am. Heart Jour., 1980-90; contbr. articles to profl. jours. Served as surgeon USPHS, 1963-66. Recipient Kees Thesis prize Yale U., 1961; Arthur S. Flemming award, 1975; Superior Service award HEW, 1975; Rsch. award and Van Slyke award Am. Soc. Clin. Chemists, 1980; Roger J. Williams award, 1985; award Humana Heart Found., 1988. Mem. Am. Heart Assn. (mem. coun. on atherosclerosis), Am. Inst. Nutrition, Am. Fedn. Clin. Rsch., N.Y. Acad. Scis., Am. Soc. Clin. Nutrition, Am. Soc. Clin. Investigation, Am. Coll. Cardiology, Inst. Medicine of Nat. Acad. Scis., Am. Soc. Clin. Pharmacology and Therapeutics, Assn. Am. Physicians, Phi Beta Kappa, Sigma Xi, Alpha Omega Alpha, Alpha Epsilon Delta, Phi Kappa Phi. Office: Wyeth-Ayerst Rsch PO Box 8299 Philadelphia PA 19101-0082

LEVY, RONALD, medical educator, researcher; b. Carmel, Calif.. B.S., Harvard U.; M.D., Stanford U., 1968. Diplomate Am. Bd. Internal Medicine. Intern Mass. Gen. Hosp., Boston, 1968-69; researcher Mass. Gen. Hosp., 1969-70; Helen Hay Whitney Found. fellow in dept. chem. immunology Weizmann Inst. Sci., Rehovot, Israel, 1973-75; mem. faculty Stanford U., Calif., 1975—, now assoc. prof. dept. medicine-oncology. Co-recipient (with G. Telford) 1st award for cancer research Armand Hammer Found. Mem. ACP, Am. Soc. Clin. Oncology. Office: Stanford U Dept Medicine-Oncology 300 Pasteur Dr Palo Alto CA 94304-2203

LEVY, ROSS STUART, medical educator; b. Bklyn., Jan. 26, 1951; s. Zachary Franklin and Rhoda (Fuerth) L.; m. Janet Sisman, Aug. 8, 1982; children: Adam, Andrew, Alana. BS, CUNY, 1973; MD, Albert Einstein Coll. Medicine, 1976. Diplomate Am. Bd. Dermatology. Med. intern Montefiore Hosp., Bronx, N.Y., 1976-77, resident in internal medicine, 1977-78; resident, then chief resident in dermatology Albert Einstein Coll. Medicine, Bronx, 1978-81, instr., 1981-82, asst. prof., 1982-88, assoc. clin. prof., 1988—; dir. divsn. dermatology North Ctrl. Bronx Hosp., 1983-93; dir. dermatologic laser Montefiore Hosp., 1983-93; dir. dermatologic surgery Albert Einstein Coll. Medicine, 1985—. Contbr. articles to profl. jours. Fellow Am. Acad. Dermatology, Am. Soc. Dermatologic Surgery, Am. Soc. Laser Medicine and Surgery; mem. Am. Soc. Acad. Dermatologic Surgeons, N.Y. State Dermatologic Soc., Greater N.Y. Dermatologic Soc., Westchester County Med. Soc. Office: Mt Kisco Med Ctr 90 S Bedford Rd Mount Kisco NY 10549-3408

LEVY, S. WILLIAM, dermatologist; b. San Francisco, Sept. 28, 1920; s. Joseph and Dora (Taylor) L.; m. Elisabeth Rellstab, Mar. 17, 1974; children: David Lewis, Ann Louise. BS, U. Calif., San Francisco, 1943, MD, 1949. Practice medicine specializing in dermatology San Francisco; research dermatologist Biomechanics Lab., U. Calif., San Francisco; mem. staff Children's Hosp., Mt. Zion Hosp. and Med. Center; cons. to Letterman Army Hosp.; central med. adv. Calif. Blue Shield, San Francisco; clin. prof. dermatology U. Calif.; cons. in field. Author: Skin Problems of the Amputee, 1983; co-author: The Skin in Diabetes, 1986, Dermatology, 3rd edit., 1992, Dermatology in General Medicine, 4th edit., 1993, Atlas of Limb Prosthetics, 2d edit., 1992, Cutis, 1995. Served with USN, 1943-46. Recipient Lehn and Fink Gold Medal award. Fellow Am. Acad. Dermatology (Gold medal); mem. San Francisco Dermatol. Soc. (pres.), Pacific Dermatologic Assn. (v.p.), AMA, Calif. Med. Assn. (sci. council 1977-84), San Francisco Med. Soc. Office: Ste 203 599 Sir Francis Drake Blvd Greenbrae CA 94904

LEVY, SANDRA, nurse; b. N.Y.C., Jan. 28, 1942; d. Solomon and Esther (Rosenthal) L. Student, Beth Israel Hosp. Sch. Of Nursing, 1959-61; AAS in Nursing, CUNY, Queens, 1965; BSN, Adelphi U., 1971; Postgrad., Pierce Coll., 1983. RN, N.Y., Calif.; cert. sch. nurse tchr., N.Y., tchr., N.Y. Staff nurse Long Island Jewish Hosp., New Hyde Park, N.Y., 1965-67; asst. instr. Queens Hosp. Ctr. Sch. of Nursing, Jamaica, N.Y., 1967-71; pvt. duty nurse N.Y. State Employment Service, N.Y.C., 1970-71; head nurse Queens Hosp. Ctr., Jamaica, 1971-73; tchr. nursing N.Y.C. Bd. Edn., 1973-83; tchr. homemaker home health aides Evening Trade Sch. Bd. Edn. N.Y.C., 1980-82; staff nurse relief Staff Builders Health Care Svcs., Sherman Oaks, Calif., 1983-92; relief nurse Profl. Staffing, Granada Hills, Calif., 1992-94; mental health nurse L.A. County-OV/UCLA Med. Ctr., Sylmar, Calif., 1994—. Democrat. Jewish.

LEVY, WAYNE DAVID, psychiatrist; b. Balt., Sept. 18, 1958; s. Alfred and Gertrude (Levinson) L.; m. Ann Fay-Ling, Sept. 4, 1992. BS in Chemistry summa cum laude, Loyola Coll., Balt., 1980; MD, Emory U., 1984. Diplomate Am. Bd. Psychiatry and Neurology. Commd. officer U.S. Army, 1984-90, advanced through grades to maj., 90-93; res. maj., 1993—; intern, then resident in psychiatry Walter Reed Army Med. Ctr., Washington, 1984-88; div. psychiatrist 2d Inf. Div., Korea, 1988-89; staff psychiatrist Tripler Army Med. Ctr., Honolulu, 1989-93; resigned, 1993; psychiatrist Kaiser Permanente Med. Group, 1993—. Maj. USAR, 1981-84, 93—. Presdl. scholar Loyola Coll., 1976. Mem. Am. Psychiat. Assn.

LEW, ARTHUR, psychiatrist; b. N.Y.C., Feb. 22, 1944. AB, Columbia U., 1964; MD, SUNY, Bklyn., 1968; grad., Psychoanalytic Inst. of NYU, N.Y.C., 1988. Diplomate Am. Bd. Psychiatry and Neurology, Am. Bd. Child Psychiatry. Intern Queens Hosp., Honolulu, 1968-69; resident in psychiatry SUNY, 1969-72, fellow child psychiatry, 1971-72, 74-75; pvt. practice N.Y.C., 1972—; assoc. clin. prof. psychiatry N.Y. Med. Coll., 1975—; dir. psychiatry Sound Shore Med. Ct., Westchester, N.Y., 1985—; supervising psychiatrist NYU Med. Ctr., N.Y.C., 1986—; mem. faculty Psychoanalytic Inst. of NYU Med. Ctr., 1989—. Maj. USAF, 1972-74. Mem. Am. Psychiat. Assn., Am. Psychoanalytic Assn., Internat. Psychoanalytic Assn., Psychoanalytic Assn. N.Y., Westchester Psychoanalytic Soc. (pres. 1994-96). Office: 55 E 93d St New York NY 10128 also: 225 Lyncroft Rd New Rochelle NY 10804

LEWALLEN, WILLIAM M., JR., ophthalmologist; b. McGregor, Tex., Aug. 31, 1927; s. William M. and Lois Pauline (Sherrill) L.; m. Katherine Louise Mosley, June 12, 1947 (div. Nov. 1985); children: Margaret Anne, William Michael, Susan, Cynthia. BS, Southern Meth. Univ., 1944; MD, Southwestern Med. Coll. Tex., 1947. Diplomate Am. Bd. Otolaryngology, Am. Bd. Ophthalmology. Internship Baylor Univ., Dallas, 1947-48; residency otolarygology Southwestern Medical Coll., Dallas, 1948-50; residency ophthalmology Jefferson Davis Hosp., Houston, 1953-54; pvt. practice Pueblo, Colo., 1955—; asst. clin. prof. Univ. Colo. Medical Sch., Denver, 1956—; cons. Colo. State Hosp., 1956—, U.S. VA Hosp., Ft. Lyon, Colo., 1956—; chief ophthalmology St. Mary-Corwin Hosp., 1970-72, exec. com., 1970-74. Contbr. articles to profl. jours. Bd. dirs. YMCA, Pueblo, 1958-60; pres. bd. dirs. Rocky Mountain Coun. Boy Scout Am., 1960-72; mem. sch. bd. Pueblo Sch. Bd. Dist. 60, 1959-71, pres. sch. bd., 1967-69; pres., chmn. bd. dirs. Pueblo Blvd. Bank, 1979-83, pres. Rotary Club, 1975-76, dir., 1974-77. Lt. comdr. U.S. Navy, 1950-52. Fellow Am. Acad. Ophthalmology. Republican. Protestant. Home and Office: William Lewallen MD 205 Dunsmere Ave Pueblo CO 81004

LEWANDOWSKI, THEODORE CHARLES, psychology educator; b. Phila., Apr. 26, 1945; s. Theodore A. and Teresa M. Lewandowski; m. Regina F. Blake, Sept. 21, 1968; children: Michael T., Joan T. BA, Villanova U., 1967, MS, 1969; CAGS, Temple U., 1979. Lic. psychologist, Pa. Lectr. Villanova (Pa.) U., 1974-79; prof. Delaware County Coll., Media, Pa., 1969—; lectr. Thomas Jefferson U., Phila., 1981—; credential evaluator Pa. State Bd. Psychology, Harrisburg, 1987—, vice-chairperson, 1980-86; mem. Pa. Drug, Device and Cosmetic Bd., Harrisburg, 1987-92. Author: Abnormal Psychology Case Interviews, 1971; co-author: Instructor's Manual to accompany Understanding Abnormal Behavior, 1971. Emergency coord. for Ea. Pa. Am. Radio Relay League, Newington, Conn., 1989-92. Mem. APA (state liaison 1970-72), Am. Ednl. Rsch. Assn., Am. Psychol. Soc., Ea. Psychol. Assn., Pa. Psychol. Assn. (stds. com. 1973-74), Pa. Ednl. Rsch. Assn. Office: Delaware County Coll 901 S Media Line Rd Media PA 19063-1094

LEWENT, JUDY CAROL, pharmaceutical executive; b. Jan. 13, 1949. BA, Goucher Coll., 1970; MS in Mgmt., MIT, 1972. With corp. fin. dept. E.F. Hutton & Co., Inc., 1972-74; asst. v.p. for strategic planning Bankers Trust Co., 1974-75; sr. fin. analyst corp. planning Norton Simon, 1975-76; div. contr. Pfizer, Inc., 1976-80; dir. acquisitions and capital analysis Merck & Co., Inc., Whitehouse Station, N.J., 1980-83, asst. contr., 1983-85, exec. dir. fin. evaluation and analysis, 1985-87, v.p., treas., 1987-90, v.p. fin., CFO, 1990-92, sr. v.p., CFO, 1993—. Office: Merck & Co Inc PO Box 100 One Merck Dr Whitehouse Station NJ 08889-0100

LEWERT, ROBERT MURDOCH, microbiologist, educator; b. Scranton, Pa., Sept. 30, 1919; s. Philip John and Nell (Bertholf) L.; m. Evelyn P. Allen, Feb. 19, 1948; children—Philip Allen, Barbara Joan. B.S., U. Mich., 1941; M.S., Lehigh U., 1943; Sc.D., Johns Hopkins, 1948. Diplomate: in parasitology Am. Bd. Microbiologists. Instr. biology Lehigh U., 1941-43, Hobart and William Smith Colls., Geneva, N.Y., 1943-44; instr. dept. bacteriology and parasitology U. Chgo., 1948-52; asst. prof. U. Chgo., 1952-56, assoc. prof. microbiology, 1957-61, prof., 1961-85, prof. emeritus dept. molecular genetics and cell biology, 1985—; Vis. prof. parasitology U. Philippines Inst. Hygiene, 1961, 63-66; mem. com. on parasitic diseases Armed Forces Epidemiological Bd., 1955-73; cons. to surgeon gen. Dept. Army, 1956-75; cons. on parasitic diseases Hines (Ill.) VA Hosp., 1975-82; mem. tropical medicine and parasitology study sect. USPHS, 1965-69, allergy and infectious diseases tng. grant com., 1969-73. Mem. editorial bd.: Jour. Parasitology, 1958-64, Abstracts of Bioanalytic Tech, 1959-63, Jour. Infectious Disease, Am. Jour. Epidemiology, Am. Jour. Tropical Medicine and Hygiene. Served with USNR, 1944-46. Fulbright fellow, 1961; Guggenheim fellow, 1961. Mem. Am. Acad. Microbiology, Am. Soc. Parasitologists, Am. Soc. Tropical Medicine and Hygiene, AAAS, Royal Soc. Tropical Medicine and Hygiene, N.Y. Acad. Scis., Nippon Bijitsu Token Hozon Kyokai (life), Japanese Sword Soc. of U.S. (chmn. 1977-83), Nihontoken Hozon Kai, Kunzan-Sensei Ni Manabu-Kai, Token Soc. Gt. Britian, Sigma Xi. Home: 37 Henry Mountain Rd Brevard NC 28712-9705 Office: 920 E 58th St Chicago IL 60637-1432

LEWETAG, BONITA LOUISE, nursing educator; b. Pitts., Dec. 22, 1955; d. John and Bernice (Molnar) Reekie; m. Walter W. Lewetag III, Feb. 10, 1973; children: Walter W. IV, Brandy Lee. Diploma in nursing, St. Margaret Meml. Hosp., Pitts., 1984; BSN, Clarion U. Pa., 1996. RN, Pa.; cert. advanced cardiac life support, CPR instr.; cert. rehab. nurse. Staff nurse St. Margaret's Meml. Hosp., 1984-85; team leader SCI unit Harmarville Rehab. Ctr., Pitts., 1985-87, nursing edn. specialist, 1987—. Mem. Assn. Rehab. Nurses. Home: PO Box 31 Bairdford PA 15006-0031

LEWEY, SCOT MICHAEL, gastroenterologist, army officer; b. Kansas City, Mo., Sept. 10, 1958; s. Hugh Gene and Janice Vivian (Arnold) L.; divorced; children: Joshua Michael, Aaron Scot, Rachel Anne. BA in Chemistry, William Jewell Coll., 1980; DO, U. Health Scis., 1984. Diplomate Am. Bd. Internal Medicine, Am. Bd. Gastroenterology, Am. Bd. Hepatology, Am. Bd. Pediat. Commd. 2d lt. U.S. Army, 1980, advanced through grades to lt. col., 1994; resident internal medicine and pediatrics William Beaumont Army Med. Ctr., El Paso, Tex., 1985-89; asst. chief pediatric svc. Irwin Army Hosp., Ft. Riley, Kans., 1989-90; asst. chief dept. medicine Irwin Army Hosp., Ft. Riley, 1990, chief emergency med. svcs., 1990; comdr. F co. 701st support bn. 1st inf. Operation Desert Shield Operation Desert Storm U.S. Army, Saudi Arabia, 1990-91; chief dept. pediatrics Munson Army Hosp., Ft. Leavenworth, Kans., 1991-92, chief dept. medicine, 1992-93; fellow in gastroenterology Fitzsimons Army Med. Ctr., Aurora, Colo., staff gastroenterology svc., 1993-95; chief gastroenterology svc. Evans Army Hosp., Ft. Crason, Colo., 1996—; clin. instr. medicine U. Colo. Health Scis. Ctr. Sch. Medicine. Decorated Bronze STar; named Outstanding Young Man of Am.; recipient Jr. Scientist Rsch. award William Baumont Soc. of Army Gastroenterologists, 1994. Fellow ACP, Am. Acad. Pediatrics; mem. AMA (physician recognition award), Am. Coll. Gastroenterology, Am. Osteo. Assn., Am. Gastroenterol. Assn., Am. Soc. Gastrointestinal Endoscopy, Assn. Mil. Osteo. Physicians and Surgeons. Republican. Mem. Christian Ch. Office: Evans Army Hosp Gastroenterology Svc Fort Carson CO 80913

LEWI, DAVID SALOMAO, medical educator; b. Sao Paulo, Brazil, Oct. 12, 1956; s. Moises and Clelia (Grosman) L.; m. Suely Kleiman Rabinovich, Apr. 1, 1982; children: Mayra, Juliana. MD, Pauliste de Medicina, Sao Paulo, Brazil, 1979, master's degree, 1987, PhD, 1991. Coord. ALAS program Pauliste de Medicina, Sao Paulo, Brazil, 1989—, assoc. prof., 1991—. Home: Rue Bahia 684/51, 01244-000 São Paulo Brazil Office: Pauliste de Medicina, Rua Bofucafu 740/Fo-ander, 04023-062 Sao Paulo Brazil

LEWIN, KLAUS J., pathologist, educator; b. Jerusalem, Israel, Aug. 10, 1936; came to U.S., 1968; s. Bruno and Charlotte (Nawratzki L.; m. Patricia Coutts Milne, Sept. 25, 1964; children: David, Nicola, Bruno. Attended, King's Coll. U. London, 1954-55; MB, BS, Westminster Med. Sch. London, Eng., 1959; MD, U. London, 1966. Diplomate Am. Bd. Pathology, Royal Coll. Pathologists (London), lic. Calif. Casualty officer Westminster Med. Hosp., 1960; resident Westminster Hosp. Med. Sch., London, 1960-68; pediatric house physician Westminster Hosp. Med. Sch., Westminster Children's Hosp., 1961; house physician St. James Hosp., Balham, London, 1961; asst. prof. pathology Stanford (Calif.) U., 1970-76; assoc. prof. pathology UCLA, L.A., 1977-80; attending physician Dept. Medicine Gastroenterology divsn. UCLA, Wadsworth, Va., 1978—; prof. pathology UCLA Med. Sch., L.A., 1980—, prof. dept. medicine divsn. gastroenterology, 1986—; divsn. surg. pathology UCLA Ctr. Health Scis.; resident pathologist clinical chemistry, bacteriology, hematology, blood transfusion, serology, Westminster Hosp. Med. Sch., 1961-62, registrar dept. morbid anatomy, 1962-64, rotating sr. registrar morbid anatomy, Royal Devon, Exeter Hosp., 1964-68; vis. asst. prof. pathology, Stanford U. Med. Sch., 1968-70; vice chmn. pathology UCLA, L.A., 1979-86; pres. L.A. Soc. Pathologists Inc., 1985-86; mem. curriculum com. U. Calif. Riverside, 1977-84; cons. Wadsworth VA Hosp., L.A., carcinoma of esophagus intervention study, Polyp Prevention study, Nat. Cancer Inst., Cancer Preservation Studies br., Bethesda, Md., Sepulveda VA Hosp.; mem. various coms. UCLA in field; rschr. structure, function, pathologic disorders of gastrointestinal tract and liver. Author: (with Riddel R., Weinstein W.) Gastrointestinal Pathology and Its Clinical Implications, 1992; edit. bd. Human Pathology, 1986—, Am. Jour. Surg. Pathology, 1990—; reviewer Gastroenterology and Archives of Pathology; contbr. papers, abstracts, review articles to profl. jours., chpts. in books; lectr., presenter in field. Dir. diagnostic Immonuhistochemistry Lab.; mem. diagnostic surg. Pathology svc. Recipient Chesterfield medal Inst. Dermatology, London, 1966; named Arris and Gale lectr. Royal Coll. Surgeons, London, 1968; Welcome Trust Rsch. grantee, 1968; fellow Found. Promotion Cancer Rsch., Tokyo, 1992. Fellow Royal Coll. Pathologists (Eng.); mem. Pathological Soc. Great Britain, Am. Gastroenterology Soc., Gastrointestinal Pathology Soc. (founder, pres. 1985-86, exec. com., edn. com. 1990—), U.S. Acad. Pathology, Can. Acad. Pathology, Assn. Clin. Pathologists, Pathological and Bacteriological Soc. Great Britain, Internat. Acad. Pathology, L.A. Pathology Soc. (bd. dirs.), Calif. Soc. Pathology (edn. com. 1983—), So. Calif. Soc. Gastrointestinal Endoscopy, Arthur Purdy Stout Soc., Gastrointestinal Pathology Soc. (pres., by-laws com., chmn. edn. com., exec. com.). Home: 333 N Las Casas Ave Pacific Palisades CA 90272-3307 Office: UCLA Sch Medicine Dept Pathology 10833 Le Conte Ave Los Angeles CA 90095-1732

LEWIN, MARC ROBERT, physician; b. Toronto, Jan. 26, 1965; s. Raoul and Rachel (Bonstat) L. Student, McMaster U., 1984-86; MD, U. Western Ont., 1990. Diplomate Can. Bd. Family Practice. Club physician Club Med, Eluthra, Bahamas, 1991; vol. physician Calcutta (India) Rescue, 1992; emergency physician York Hosp., Newmarket, Ont., Can., 1993-94, North York Gen. Hosp., Toronto, 1993-94; family physician Med Care Clinic, Toronto, 1993-94; emergency physician Gaston Meml. Hosp., Gastonia, N.C., 1994—; pres., CEO Vitality Health Corp., Charlotte, N.C., 1996—. Office: Gaston Meml Hosp Emergency Dept 2525 Court Dr Po Box 1747 Gastonia NC 28053-1747

LEWIN, PEARL GOLDMAN, psychologist; b. Bklyn., Apr. 25, 1923; d. Frank and Anna (Simon) Goldman; m. Seymour Z. Lewin, Oct. 17, 1943; children: David, Jonathan. BA, Hunter Coll., 1943; MS, U. Mich., 1947; PhD, NYU, 1980. Lic. psychologist, N.Y. Insp. chemist quarter master corps U.S. Army, 1943-45; chemist chem. warfare U.S. Army, Edgewood Arsenal, Md., 1945; asst. psychologist Bur. Psychol. Svcs., U. Mich., Ann Arbor, 1947-48; freelance rsch. asst. chemistry N.Y.C., 1955-71; adj. lectr. CUNY, Bklyn., 1973-74, instr., 1974-79, asst. prof., 1979-80; psychologist Creedmore Psychiat. Ctr., N.Y.C., 1980-82; sr. psychologist Manhattan

Family Ct., N.Y.C., 1982-87; cons., 1987—; mentor Peer Counseling Orgn., Bklyn. Coll., 1976-80, coord. student svcs. New Sch. Liberal Arts, 1974-76, adminstr. acad. regulations, 1974-76. Author: Sexist Humor, 1979. Mem. APA, Pi Lambda Theta, Phi Kappa Phi. Home and Office: 4231 N Walnut Ave Arlington Heights IL 60004-1302

LEWINGER, JEAN ELIZABETH, pediatrics nurse, neonatal intensive care nurse; b. Bklyn., Oct. 30, 1946; d. Donald and Grace W. (Mowat) Gordon; m. Arnold A. Lewinger, Nov. 4, 1967; children: William Anthony, Andrea Jean. Diploma in nursing, Kings County Hosp. Ctr., Bklyn., 1967; BSN, Cedar Crest Coll., 1986; MSN, U. Pa., 1988. Staff nurse neonatal ICU Southside Hosp., Bayshore, N.Y., 1973-76; staff nurse, charge nurse pediatric spl. care unit Ea. Maine Med. Ctr., Bangor, 1976-81, transport nurse, 1977-81; neonatal transport nurse Allentown (Pa.) Hosp., 1981-88, neonatal ICU, 1981-88; neonatal nurse practitioner Pa. Hosp., Phila., 1988-89, Episc. Hosp., Phila., 1989-95, Thomas Jefferson U. Hosp., Phila., 1995—; CPR instr.; nurse laision for neonatal support group, Phila.; regional instr. neonatal resuscitation program. Contbr. articles to profl. publs. Mem. NAACOG (cert. neonatal intensive care practitioner, cert. neonatal intensive care nurse), AHWONN, Nat. Assn. Neonatal Nurses, Am. Bd. Examiners, Ob-Gyn. Nurses, Nat. Perinatal Assn., Pa. Perinatal Assn., Phila. Perinatal Assn., Delaware Valley Assn. Neonatal Nurses.

LEWINTER, PAUL, internist; b. Bklyn., Feb. 23, 1931; s. Arthur and Regina (Rezak) L.; m. Shirlee Bubis, Jan. 3, 1956; children: Jody G., Donna E., Andrew S. BA, Columbia U., 1951; MD, SUNY, Bklyn., 1955. Diplomate Am. Bd. Internal Medicine, Nat. Bd. Med. Examiners, Geriat. Med. Intern Long Island Jewish Hosp., New Hyde Park, N.Y., 1955-56; resident in medicine V.A. Hosp., Bklyn., 1956-58; fellow in medicine Yale U. Sch. of Medicine, 1958-59; pvt. practice Fanwood, N.J., 1961—; sr. attending physician, Mullenberg Hosp., Plainfield, N.J., 1961-96, clin. assoc. prof., U. Med. and Dentistry, New Brunswick, N.J., 1972-96. Contbr. articles to profl. jours. Physician to the homeless, Union Co., N.J., 1990-96. Capt. U.S. Army, 1959-61. Recipient Advanced Achievement in Internal Med., Am. Bd. Internal Med., 1987. Fellow ACP, Am. Coll. Gastroenterology, Am. Geriat. Soc., Am. Coll. Utilization Rev. Physicians, Am. Coll. Nutrition. Home: 1974 Winding Brook Way Scotch Plains NJ 07090 Office: 346 South Ave Fanwood NJ 07023

LEWIS, ALAN BENEDICT, pediatric cardiologist; b. N.Y.C., Jan. 6, 1945; s. Lee Nathan and Esther (Miller) L.; m. Shirley Sheinbek, July 27, 1969; children: Michael Joshua, Lisa Beth. BS, CCNY, 1966; MD, NYU, 1970. Diplomate in pediatrics and pediatric cardiology Am. Bd. Pediatrics. Pediatric intern Albert Einstein Coll. Medicine, Bronx, N.Y., 1970-71, resident in pediatrics, 1971-72; fellow in pediatric cardiology U. Calif., San Francisco, 1972-74; asst. prof. pediatrics U. So. Calif. Sch. Medicine/Children's Hosp. L.A., 1974-80, assoc. prof., 1980-87, prof., 1987—; pres. Univ. Children's Med. Group, L.A., 1995—. Contbr. numerous articles to profl. jours. Capt. U.S. Army, 1971-77. Am. Heart Assn. rsch. grantee, 1977-80, Norris Found. grantee, 1980-83. Fellow Am. Acad. Pediatrics, Am. Coll. Cardiology; mem. Soc. for Pediatric Rsch., Am. Pediatric Soc. Office: Children's Hosp LA 4650 Sunset Blvd Los Angeles CA 90027

LEWIS, ALAN ERVIN, internist; b. Milw., Feb. 1, 1936; s. Morris and Mildred Lewis; m. Sandra Briskin, Aug. 17, 1961; children: Scott, Brandt. BA, U. Wis., 1957; MD, Marquette U. & Med. Coll. Wis., 1960. Diplomate Am. Bd. Internal Medicine. Asst. prof. medicine Tufts U., Boston, 1967-69; from instr. to assoc. prof. Hahnemann U., Phila., 1969-87; pvt. practice Mesa, Ariz., 1987—; v.p. West Pk. Hosp., Phila.; mem. medicine com., credentials com. Desers Samaritan Hosp., Mesa. Contbr. studies to profl. jours. Lt. USNR, 1961-63. Fellow ACP; mem. Am. Diabetes Assn. (affiliate assn. com., nat. bd. dirs., Ariz. affiliate, pres. chmn. bd. dirs. Phila. affiliate), Am. Assn. Clin. Rsch., Endocrine Soc., Pa. Med. Soc., Phila. County Med. Soc., Ariz. State Med. Soc., Maricopa Med. Soc. Home: 2051 E Calle Maderas Mesa AZ 85213 Office: 1450 S Dobson Mesa AZ 85202

LEWIS, ALAN JAMES, pharmaceutical executive, pharmacologist; b. Newport Gwent, UK. BSc, Southampton U., Hampshire, 1967; PhD in Pharmacology, U. Wales, Cardiff, 1970. Postdoctoral fellow biomedical sci. U. Guelph, Ont., Can., 1970-72; rsch. assoc. lung rsch. ctr. Yale U., 1972-73; sr. pharmacologist Organon Labs., Ltd., Lanarkshire, Scotland, 1973-79; rsch. mgr. immunoinflammation Am. home products Wyeth-Ayerst Rsch., Princeton, N.J., 1979-82, assoc. dir. exptl. therapeutics, 1982-85, dir., 1985-87, asst. v.p., 1987-89, v.p. rsch., 1989-93; pres. Signal Pharms. Inc., San Diego, 1994—, pres., CEO, 1996—. Editor allergy sect. Agents & Actions & Internat. Archives Pharmacodynamics Therapy; reviewer Jour. Pharmacology Exptl. Therapy, Biochemical Pharmacology, Can. Jour. Physiol. Pharmacology, European Jour. Pharmacology, Jour. Pharm. Sci. Mem. Am. Soc. Pharmacological and Exptl. Therapeutics, Am. Pheumatism Assn., Mid-Atlantic Pharmacology Soc. (v.p. 1991-93, pres. 1993-94), Pulmonary Rsch. Assn., Inflammation Rsch. Assn. (pres. 1986-88), Pharm. Mfrs. Assn., Internat. Assn. Inflammation Socs. (pres. 1990-95). Office: Signal Pharms Inc 5555 Oberlin Dr Ste 100 San Diego CA 92121-3746

LEWIS, ALVIN EDWARD, pathology educator; b. N.Y.C., Nov. 21, 1916; s. Herman and Libbie (Levy) L.; m. Oct. 23, 1943, (widowed 1974); children: Joan, Elizabeth; m. July, 1, 1976. BA, U. Calif. L.A., 1938; MA, Stanford U., 1939, MD, 1944. Chief, pathology sect, atomic energy project UCLA, 1949-53; dir. clin. labs. Mount Zion Hosp., San Francisco, 1953-66; pathology prof. Mich. State U., East Lansing, 1966-72; pathology prof., chmn. U. S. Ala., Mobile, 1972-74; pathology prof. U. Calif., Davis, 1974-87, prof. emeritus, 1987—; rev. com. mem. Nat. Libr. Medicine, Bethesda, Md., 1972-75, med. quality rev. com. Dist. 3, Sonoma, Calif., 1989-94. Author: Biostatistics, 1966, 1984 (2d ed.), Principles of Hematology, 1970. Lt. (j.g.) USNR, 1945-46. Fellow Coll. Am. Pathologists; mem. Am. Physiol. Soc. Republican. Jewish. Home: 21 Woodgreen St Santa Rosa CA 95409-5921

LEWIS, ANDREW MORRIS, JR., virologist; b. Cheriton, Va., Nov. 28, 1934; s. Andrew Morris and Wilsye (Hamilton) L.; m. Gladys Ruth Shorrock, June 8, 1960; children: T. Reid Lewis, Andrew M. III. BA, Duke U., 1956, MD, 1961. Intern Pediatrics Duke Host., 1961-62, resident, 1962-63; scientist Nat. Inst. Allergy and Infectious Diseases/Lab. Immunopathology/NIH, Bethesda, Md., 1963-86; head viral pathogenesis sect. NIAID/LIP/NIH, Bethesda, Md., 1986-95; med. officer office vaccines, rsch. & rev. Ctr. Biol. Evaluation and Rev., FDA, Rockville, Md., 1995—; Capt. USPHS, 1963. Decorated Commendation medal. Mem. Am. Soc. Microbiology, Am. Soc. Virology, Am. Assn. Immunologists, AAAS, Am. Assn. Cancer Rsch. Office: DVRR/CBER/FDA HFM 400 1401 Rockville Pike Rockville MD 20852-1448

LEWIS, BARRY KENT, cardiologist; b. Chgo., Aug. 2, 1949; s. Seymour and Esther (Rothfeld) L.; m. Marsha Diane Berman, June 6, 1976; children: Jeremy Aaron, Ryan Allen. AB, Boston U., 1971; DO, Kirksville Coll. Osteo. Med., 1976. Diplomate Am. Bd. Internal Medicine, Sub-bd. Cardiology. Physician, asst. prof. Chgo. Coll. Osteo. Medicine, 1984-88; physician, clinician Internal Medicine Clin. Group, Farmington Hills, Mich., 1988—; asst. prof. Mich. State U. Coll. Osteo. Medicine, East Lansing, 1989—; dir. cardiac catheterization lab. Botsford Gen. Hosp., Farmington Hills, 1989—. Capt. U.S. Army, 1977-80, Germany. Fellow Am. Coll. Cardiology, Am. Coll. Osteo. Internists; mem. Am. Osteo. Assn., Am. Heart Assn., Am. Soc. Cardiovascular Interventionalists. Jewish. Home: 34662 Valley Forge Dr Farmington MI 48331-3206 Office: Cardiovascular Clin Group Ste 300W 28080 Grand River Ave Farmington MI 48336-5966

LEWIS, BENJAMIN PERSHING, JR., pharmacist, public health service officer; b. Danville, Ky., June 2, 1942; s. Benjamin Pershing Lewis and Juanita Elizabeth (Garner) Applewhite; m. Patricia Marlene Glover, Aug. 7, 1968; children: Laura Denise, Jason Matthew. BS in Pharmacy, Auburn U., 1966, MS in Pharmacy, 1972; PhD in Health Svcs. Mgmt., Century U., L.A., 1989. Registered pharmacist, Ky., Ala. Instr. Auburn (Ala.) U. Sch. Pharmacy, 1972-73, now affiliate asst. prof.; commd. lt. comdr. USPHS, 1976, advanced through grades to capt., 1985; pharmacy officer Bur. Drugs FDA, Rockville, Md., 1976-82, health scientist adminstr. orphan products devel., 1982-87, AIDS coord., 1987-89; spl. asst. to assoc. dir. Ctr. Biologics Evaluation-Rsch. FDA, Bethesda, Md., 1989-92; dir. regulatory ops. divsn. transfusion transmitted diseases FDA Ctr. Biologics Evaluation and Rsch., Rockville, Md., 1993—. Co-author: Veterinary Drug Index, 1982; editor: FDA Role in AIDS, 1988, The International Ramifications of Drug Development, 1988, Report of the Criticism Task Force on Career Development, 1989; co-editor: Poliovirus Attenuation: Molecular Mechanisms and Practical Aspects, 1993, Combined Vaccines and Simultaneous Administration, 1995; contbr. articles to profl. jours. Officer U.S. Army, 1972-76. Recipient letter of commendation FDA, 1984. Mem. Am. Pharm. Assn., Am. Acad. Pharm. Rsch. and Sci., Am. Soc. for Pharmacy Law, Commd. Officers Assn., USPHS, AAAS, Sigma Xi. Methodist. Home: 24137 Newbury Rd Gaithersburg MD 20882-4009 Office: FDA Ctr Biols Eval and Rsch Div Transfusion Transmitted HFM 310 1401 Rockville Pike Rockville MD 20852-1428

LEWIS, CEYLON SMITH, JR., internist, educator; b. Muskogee, Okla., July 19, 1920. Dir. internat. studies internal medicine Med. Coll., U. Okla., Tulsa. Mem. Inst. Med.-Nat. Acad. Sci. Office: Dept Internal Med U Okla Medical Coll Tulsa OK 74129

LEWIS, CHARLES EDWIN, physician, educator; b. Kansas City, Dec. 28, 1928; s. Claude Herbert and Maudie Friels (Holaday) L.; m. Mary Ann Gurera, Dec. 27, 1963; children—Kevin Neil, David Bradford, Matthew Clinton, Karen Carleen. Student, U. Kans., 1948-49; M.D., Harvard, 1953; M.S., U. Cin., 1957, Sc.D., 1959. Diplomate Am. Bd. Preventive Medicine (Occupl. Medicine). Intern, resident U. Kans. Hosp., 1953-54; trainee USPHS, 1956-58; fellow occupational health Eastman Kodak Co., 1958-59; asst. clin. prof. epidemiology Baylor U. Sch. Medicine, 1960-61; asso. prof. medicine U. Kans. Med. Sch., 1961-62, prof., chmn. dept. preventive medicine, 1962-69; coordinator Kan. Regional Med. Program, 1967-69; prof. social medicine Harvard Med. Sch., 1969-70; prof. pub. health, head div. health adminstrn. UCLA Med. Sch., 1970-72, prof. medicine, div. head, 1972-90; prof., 1972-89; prof. nursing Sch. Nursing UCLA Med. Sch., 1973—, head div. preventive and occupational medicine, 1991-93; dir. Health Svcs. Rsch. Ctr., 1991-93, UCLA Ctr. Health Promotion and Disease Prevention, 1991—; chair acad. senate UCLA, 1995-96; chmn. acad. senate UCLA, 1995-96; cons. Getty Trust, Walt Disney Prodns.; mem. Nat. Bd. Med. Examiners, 1964-68, 8-83, Ct. Commn. on Accreditaiton Health Care Orgns., 1989-95; mem. health svcs. rsch. study sect. USPHS, 1968-76; vis. scholar Annenberg Sch. Comm., U. So. Calif., 1980-81; mem. adv. bd. Hosp. Rsch. and Edn. Trust, 1972-75. Contbr. articles to profl. Jours. Served to capt. USAF, 1954-56. Recipient Ginsberg prize medicine U. Kans., 1954, Glasier award Soc. Gen. Internal Medicine, 1988. Fellow APHA, Acad. Occupl. Medicine; mem. ACP (regent 1988-94, Rosenthal award 1980, Laureate award So. Calif. III 1994, mastership, 1996), Internat. Epidemiology Soc., Assn. Tchrs. Preventive Medicine (pres. coun. 1977-80), Am. Assn. Physicians. Home: 221 S Burlingame Ave Los Angeles CA 90049-3702

LEWIS, DANIEL ALAN, osteopathic physician; b. Moberly, Mo., Aug. 13, 1946; s. Harvey E. and Catherine M. (Graves) L.; m. Sandra K. Botham, June 7, 1970; children: David, Amy, Matthew, Timothy. BS, N.E. Mo. State U., 1975; DO, Kirksville Coll. Osteo. Med., 1980. Intern Kirksville (Mo.) Osteopathic Health Ctr, 1980-81; physician Nat. Health Corps, Richland, Mo., 1981-82, Princeton, Mo., 1982-84; physician Paris (Mo.) Clinic, 1984-94, St. John's Health Ctr./FMO Stockton Clin., Stockton, Mo., 1994—, Family Med. Clinic, Marsfield, Mo., 1995—. With USAF, 1965-68. Mem. Am. Osteopathic Assn., Mo. Assn. Osteopathic Physicians and Surgeons, Am. Coll. of Gen. Practitioners. Baptist. Home: 504 E Hillcrest Stockton MO 65785 Office: Family Med Clin P O Box 69 101 S Pine Marshfield MO 65706

LEWIS, DAVID CARLETON, medical educator, university center director; b. Hartford, Conn., May 19, 1935; s. Theodore and Lillian (Levin) L.; m. Eleanor Grace Levinson, Aug. 23, 1959; children: Deborah, Steven. AB magna cum laude, Brown U., 1957; MD, Harvard U., 1961. Intern Beth Israel Hosp., Boston, 1961-62, jr. resident, 1962-63, chief med. resident, 1966-67, dir. emergency unit and med. outpatient dept., 1969-71; sr. resident U. Hosps. Cleve., 1963-64, Parkland Meml. Hosp., Dallas, 1964-66; fellow U. Tex. Southwestern Med. Hosp., Dallas, 1964-66; Sloan Found. fellow Harvard Med. Sch., Boston, 1971-72; med. dir. Washingtonian Ctr. for Addictions, Boston, 1972-77; dir. div. alcohol and substance abuse Roger Williams Gen. Hosp., Providence, 1976—; dir. program in alcoholism and drug abuse Brown U., Providence, 1976-82, prof. medicine and community health, 1982—, Donald G. Millar prof. alcohol and addiction studies, 1987—, chmn. dept. community health, 1981-86, dir. Ctr. Alcohol and Addiction Studies, 1982—; mem. nat. adv. coun. Nat. Alcohol Inst., Rockville, Md., 1981-85, cons. to dir., 1985—; mem. sci. adv. bd. Children of Alcoholics, 1985—; cons. WHO, 1986—, mem. WHO cocaine global adv. com., 1992-95; chair Physician Consortium on Substance Abuse Edn., 1989—; mem. Carnegie Substance Abuse Adv. com., 1989-92; scholar-in-residence Nat. Inst. Med., 1991-92; mem. adv. panel to U.S. Pharmacopoeia, 1995—; mem. Drug Strategies Nat. Adv. Panel, 1994—; mem. nat. adv. com. Robert Wood Johnson Found. Fighting Back program, 1996—. Author: The Drug Experience: Data for Decision Making, 1970; editor: Providing Care for Children of Alcoholics, 1986; editor Brown U. Digest of Addiction Theory and Application, 1986—; exec. editor Substance Abuse jour., 1984—; contbr. numerous articles to profl. jours. Med. dir. Beacon Hill Free Clinic, Boston, 1968-71; chmn. Mayor's Coun. on Drug Abuse, Boston, 1972-80; mem. nat. adv. com. for fighting back program Robert Wood Johnson Found., 1996—. Grantee Nat. Alcohol and Drug Insts., 1986—, Edward John Noble fellow Harvard U. Med. Sch., 1957-91. Fellow ACP; mem. NAS, Inst. Medicine Study on Treatment Alcohol Problems, Assn. Med. Edn. and Rsch. in Substance Abuse (pres. 1983-88, Excellence in Medicine award 1986), Am. Soc. Addiction Medicine (chair core curriculum com. 1989-96, chair sect. on internal medicine 1990—, bd. dirs.), U.S. Pharmacopea (mem. adv. panel), Brown Med. Alumni Assn. (pres. 1974-76), Phi Beta Kappa, Sigma Xi. Office: Brown Univ Ctr Alcohol & Addiction Studies Box G Providence RI 02912

LEWIS, DAVID JAMES, psychiatrist; b. Montreal, Que., Can., May 28, 1920; s. David Sclater adn Evelyn Doris (Ross) L.; m. Catherine Jefferson Lewis, Dec. 20, 1949; children: David Wilson Ross, Anne S., Peter James, Naomi Catherine, Jane A. Squier. BA, McGill U., Montreal, 1941; MD, U. Toronto, Ont., Can., 1950. Reporter Ottawa (Ont.) Jour., 1939-41; intern Toronto Gen. Hosp., 1950-51; asst. resident Johns Hopkins Hosp., 1952-54, Maudsley Hosp., London, 1954; asst. psychiatrist St. Michael's Hosp., Toronto, 1956-65; to asst. prof. U. Toronto, 1956-65; asst. psychiatrist Royal Victoria Hosp., Montreal, 1965-66; sr. psychiatrist Royal Victoria Hosp., 1966-72; clin. dir. Allan Meml. Inst., Toronto, 1966-71; assoc. prof. psychiatry, coordinator postgrad. edn. in psychiatry McGill U., 1965-71; prof. U. Calgary, Alta., Can., 1971-85; prof. emeritus U. Calgary, 1985—, acting head, 1976-77, 80-81; physician Foothills Hosp. Psychiatry, Calgary, 1971-92, ret., 1992; cons. Mineral Springs Hosp., Banff, Alta., 1972-78; Gov. Royal Humane Soc. Served to lt. comdr. Royal Can. Naval Res., 1941-60. Mentioned in Despatches, 1942; recipient testimonial Royal Humane Soc., 1944. Fellow Royal Coll. Physicians Can. (life), Am. Psychiat. Assn.; mem. Royal Coll. Psychiatry, Can. Med. Assn., Can. Psychiat. Assn., Alpine Club (Canmore, Alta.), U. Calgary Club, Nu Sigma Nu. Home and Office: Serendip, Box 17 Site 3 RR 1, Calgary, AB Canada T2P 2G4

LEWIS, DELBERT O'NEAL, disability consultant, former state official; b. Searcy, Ark., Oct. 15, 1947; s. Scott and Viola Marie (Hodges) L. BA in Psychology and Sociology, Harding U., 1969; 2M Rehab. Counseling, Ark. State U., 1972. Cert. rehab. counselor. With divsn. rehab. svcs. Ark. Dept. Human Svcs., Little Rock, 1972-90, planning specialist, 1978-90; ret., 1990, cons. on disability issues to govt., legal, ednl., and pvt. orgns., 1990—; former staff and advisor Ark. Com. on Equal Access for Handicapped, Interdeptl. Task Force on Rights of Handicapped; former rehab. specialist Disability Determination Svcs. Social Security Adminstrn., Little Rock; former mem. planning coun. CETA and Job Tng. Partnership Act, Little Rock and Pulaski County; guest lectr. on disability issues U. Ark., Little Rock; founding mem., past pres. Ark. Environ. Barriers Coun.; mem. Ark. Adv. Com. to U.S. Commn. on Civil Rights; cons. Emerging Issues Project Inst. for Info. Studies, Washington. Contbr. articles to profl. publs. First Pub. Mem. Ark. Bd. Archs.; former mem. OurWay, Inc., Little Rock; active Ark. Child Find to Implement Edn. for Handicapped Children Act., others. Recipient plaque of appreciation for svcs. as pres. Ark. br. Nat. Rehab. Counseling Assn., 1976, certs. City of Little Rock, 1975-85, First Mover and Shaker award Ark. Gov.'s Commn. on People with Disabilities, 1978, recognition of svc. plaque Ark. Rehab. Assn., 1990, dedicated svc. plaque Ark. Divsn. Rehab. Svcs. Consumer Adv. Coun., 1990, pub. svc. plaque ARKLA Gas Co., 1991, Cert. of Svc. award U.S. Commn. on Civil Rights, Washington, 1995. Fellow Internat. Biog. Assn.; mem. Found. for Sci. and Disability, Gazette Internat. Networking Inst.-Internat. Polio Network, Drug Policy Found., Rehab. Tech. Assn. Home and Office: 2400 Riverfront Dr Apt 12-f Little Rock AR 72202

LEWIS, DONALD L., ophthalmologist; b. New Lexington, Ohio, Aug. 14, 1931; s. David J. and Ethel Grace (Trout) L.; m. Sally Ruth Reeves, Sept. 10, 1960; children: Stephen, Jeffrey. BS in Optometry, Ohio State U., 1954, MD, 1961. Lic. physician, Ohio. Intern Riverside Meth. Hosp., Columbus, Ohio, 1961-62; fellow Mayo Clinic, Rochester, Minn., 1962-66; pvt. practice Columbus, Ohio, 1966—. 1st lt. USAF, 1954-56. Mem. Am. Acad. Ophthalmology, Assn. Mayo Eye Fellows (pres. 1975), Mayo Clinic Alumni Assn., Masons (officer). Methodist. Home: 2400 Onandaga Dr Columbus OH 43221 Office: 3545 Olentangey River Rd Columbus OH 43214

LEWIS, EDWARD B., biology educator; b. Wilkes-Barre, Pa., May 20, 1918; s. Edward B. and Laura (Histed) L.; m. Pamela Harrah, Sept. 26, 1946; children: Hugh, Glenn (dec.), Keith. B.A., U. Minn., 1939; Ph.D., Calif. Inst. Tech., 1942; Phil.D., U. Umea, Sweden, 1982; DSc, U. Minn., 1993. Instr. biology Calif. Inst. Tech., Pasadena, 1946-48, asst. prof., 1949-56, prof., 1956-66, Thomas Hunt Morgan prof., 1966-88, prof. emeritus, 1988—; Rockefeller Found. fellow Sch. Botany, Cambridge U., Eng., 1948-49; mem. Nat. Adv. Com. Radiation, 1958-61; vis. prof. U. Copenhagen, 1975-76, 82; researcher in developmental genetics, somatic effects of radiation. Editor: Genetics and Evolution, 1961. Served to capt. USAAF, 1942-46. Recipient Gairdner Found. Internat. award, 1987, Wolf Found. prize in medicine, 1989, Rosenstiel award, 1990, Nat. Medal of Sci. NSF, 1990, Albert Lasker Basic Med. Rsch. award, 1991, Louisa Gross Horowitz prize Columbia U., 1992, Nobel Prize in Medicine, 1995. Fellow AAAS; mem. NAS, Genetics Soc. Am. (sec. 1962-64, pres. 1967-69, Thomas Hunt Morgan medal), Am. Acad. Arts and Scis., Royal Soc. (London) (fgn. mem.), Am. Philos. Soc., Genetical Soc. Great Britian (hon.). Home: 805 Winthrop Rd San Marino CA 91108-1709 Office: Calif Inst Tech Div Biology 1201 E California Blvd Pasadena CA 91125-0001

LEWIS, EDWIN REYNOLDS, biomedical engineering educator; b. Los Angeles, July 14, 1934; s. Edwin McMurtry and Sally Newman (Reynolds) L.; m. Elizabeth Louise McLean, June 11, 1960; children: Edwin McLean, Sarah Elizabeth. AB in Biol. Sci., Stanford U., 1956, MSEE, 1957, Engr., 1959, PhD in Elec. Engring., 1962. With research staff Librascope div. Gen. Precision Inc., Glendale, Calif., 1961-67; mem. faculty dept. elec. engring. and computer sci. U. Calif., Berkeley, 1967—, dir. bioengring. tng. program, 1969-77, prof. elec. engring. and computer sci., 1971-94, prof. grad. sch., 1994—, assoc. dean grad. div., 1977-82, assoc. dean interdisciplinary studies coll. engring., 1988-96; chair joint program bioengring. U. Calif., Berkeley and San Francisco, 1988-91. Author: Network Models in Population Biology, 1977, (with others) Neural Modeling, 1977, The Vertebrate Inner Ear, 1985, also numerous articles. Grantee NSF, NASA, 1984, 87, Office Naval Rsch., 1990-93, NIH, 1975—; Neurosci. Rsch. Program fellow, 1966, 69; recipient Disting. Teaching Citation U. Calif., 1972; Jacob Javits neurosci. investigator NIH, 1984-91. Fellow IEEE, Acoustical Soc. Am.; mem. AAAS, Assn. Rsch. in Otolaryngology, Soc. Neurosci., Toastmasters (area lt. gov. 1966-67), Sigma Xi. Office: Dept Elec Engring & Computer Scis U Calif Berkeley CA 94720

LEWIS, ERIC ALLEN, cardiologist; b. Phila., Mar. 10, 1959; s. Bernard Paul and Claire (Small) L.; m. Carolyn Theresa Haffner; children: Julie, Michael, Katie. BS, Rutgers Coll., 1981; MD, St. Louis U., 1985. Intern in internal medicine U. Hosp., Jacksonville, Fla., 1985-86; resident in internal medicine U. Hosp., Jacksonville, 1986-88; cardiologist Marple Med., Broomall, Pa., 1992-93, Punja & Shawl, Greenbelt, Md., 1993-95, Citrus Cardiology Cons., Inverness, Fla., 1995—. Fellow Am. Coll. Cardiology; mem. Am. Coll. Physicians. Office: Citrus Cardiology Cons 318 S Line Ave Inverness FL 34452

LEWIS, GLADYS SHERMAN, nurse, educator; b. Wynnewood, Okla., Mar. 20, 1933; d. Andrew and Minnie Elva (Halsey) Sherman; R.N., St. Anthony's Sch. Nursing, 1953; student Okla. Bapt. U., 1953-55; AB, Tex. Christian U., 1956; postgrad. Southwestern Bapt. Theol. Sem., 1959-60, Escuela de Idiomas, San Jose, Costa Rica, 1960-61; MA in Creative Writing, Central (Okla.) State U., 1985; PhD in English Okla. State U. 1992; m. Wilbur Curtis Lewis, Jan. 28, 1955; children: Karen, David, Leanne, Cristen. Mem. nursing staff various facilities, Okla., 1953-57; instr. nursing, med. missionary Bapt. mission and hosp., Paraguay, 1961-70; vice-chmn. edn. commn. Paraguay Bapt. Conv., 1962-65; sec. bd. trustees Bapt. Hosp., Paraguay, 1962-65; chmn. personnel com., handbook and policy book officer Bapt. Mission in Paraguay, 1967-70; trustee Southwestern Bapt. Theol. Sem., 1974-84, chmn. student affairs com., 1976-78, vice-chmn. bd. 1978-80; ptnr. Las Amigas Tours, 1978-80; writer, conference leader, campus lectr., 1959—; adj. prof. English Cen. State U., Okla. (name changed to U. Cen. Okla.), 1990-91; faculty mem., asst. prof. English U. Cen. Okla., 1991-95, assoc. prof., 1996—. Active Dem. com., Evang. Women's Caucus, 1979-80; leader Girl Scouts U.S.A., 1965-75; Okla. co-chmn. Nat. Religious Com. for Equal Rights Amendment, 1977-79; tour host Meier Internat. Study League, 1978-81. Mem. AAUW, Internat. and Am. colls. surgeons women's auxiliaries, Okla. State, Okla. County med. auxiliaries, Am. Nurse Assn., Nat. Women's Polit. Caucus, 1979-80. Author: On Earth As It Is, 1983; Two Dreams and a Promise, 1984, Message, Messenger and Response, 1994; also religious instructional texts in English and Spanish; editor Sooner Physician's Heartbeat, 1979-82; contbr. articles to So. Bapt. and secular periodicals. Home: 14501 N Western Ave Edmond OK 73013-1828

LEWIS, GREGORY WILLIAMS, scientist; b. Seattle, Mar. 3, 1940; s. Delbert Srofe and Eileen Julianne (Williams) L.; m. Stephanie Marie Schwab, Sept. 18, 1966; children: Jeffrey Williams, Garrick Peterson. BS, Wash. State U., 1962, MA, 1965, PhD, 1970. Tchr., rsch. asst. Wash. State U., Pullman, 1965-69; prin. investigator U.S. Army Med. Rsch. Lab., Ft. Knox, Ky., 1970-74; prin. investigator USN Pers. R & D Ctr., San Diego, 1974—, head neurosci. lab., 1980-95, leader security sys., 1981-83, head neurosci. projects office, 1987-89, divsn. head neurosci., 1989-95, sr. prin. scientist, 1995—; cons. in field. Contbr. articles to profl. jours. Bd. dirs., pres. Mesa View Homeowners Assn., Calif., 1980-82; bd. dirs. Santa Fe Homeowners Assn., Calif., 1994-96. Capt. U.S. Army, 1967-74. Fellow Internat. Orgn. Psychophysiology; mem. AAAS, Soc. Neurosci., Internat. Brain Rsch. Orgn., N.Y. Acad. Scis., Soc. Psychophysiol. Rsch., Sigma Xi, Alpha Kappa Delta, Delta Chi, Psi Chi. Home: 410 Santa Cecelia Solana Beach CA 92075-1505 Office: US Navy Pers R&D Ctr 53335 Ryne Rd San Diego CA 92152-7250

LEWIS, HOWARD FRANKLIN, chiropractor; b. Havre de Grace, Md., July 27, 1944; s. Walter Lee and Ruby Jane (Moretz) L.; m. Margaret Colleen Bush, Apr. 8, 1963 (div. 1969); 1 child, Vaughn; m. Cynthia Marie Hoover, Apr. 4, 1970; children: Amy, David. D of Chiropractic, L.A. Coll. Chiropractic, 1971. Diplomate Am. Bd. Chiropractic Radiology; lic. chiropractor Calif., Md. Pvt. practice Lewis Chiropractic Ctr., Bel Air, Md., 1974-85, Fallston, Md., 1985—. Fellow Internat. Coll. Chiropractors; mem. Am. Chiropractic Assn. (mem. coun. on diagnostic imaging, coun. on nutrition), Am. Chiropractic Coll. Radiology, Md. Chiropractic Assn. (chmn. bd. dirs. 1985-86, v.p. 1986, pres. 1987-89, Leadership award 1989, Chiropractor of Yr. award 1990), Md. State Bd. Chiropractic Examiners (v.p. 1994-96, pres. 1996—), Sacro Occipital Rsch. Soc. (bd. dirs. 1992-95, cert.), Christian Chiropractors Assn., Found. Chiropractic Edn. and Rsch. Republican. Office: Lewis Chiropractic Ctr 1621-A Belair Rd Fallston MD 21047-2745

LEWIS, IRVING JAMES, community health educator, health policy analyst, public administrator; b. Boston, July 9, 1918; s. Harry and Sarah (Bloomberg) L.; m. Rose Helen Greenwald, June 15, 1941; children—Deborah Ann, Amy Rebecca, William David. AB, Harvard U., 1939; AM, U. Chgo., 1940. With U.S. Govt., 1942-70; dep. chief internat. div. Bur. Budget, 1959-65; dept. head Intergovtl. Com. European Migration, Geneva, 1957-59; chief health and welfare div. Bur. Budget, 1965-67; dep.

asst. dir. Bur., 1967-68; dep. adminstr. health services and mental health adminstrn. HEW, 1968-70; prof. community health Albert Einstein Coll. Medicine, Bronx, N.Y., 1970-86, prof. emeritus, 1986; ccns. to fed. and state govts. Co-author: The Sick Citadel, A Study of Academic Medicine, 1983; author articles on health policy and fin. Served with CIC AUS, 1 943-46. Recipient Exceptional Svc. award Bur. Budget, 1964; Ann. Career Svc. award Nat. Civil Svc. League, 1969; Brookings Instn. rsch. fellow, 1941; WHO summer fellow, 1977. Assoc. fellow N.Y. Acad. Medicine (com. on medicine and society, chmn. ann. health conf. 1985); mem. APHA, Med. Health and Rsch. Assn., Assn. Am. Med. Colls., Am. Vets. Com. (pres. Washington 1949), Inst. Medicine/NAS, Harvard Club (Washington). Jewish (pres. temple). Home: Apt 623 3310 N Leisure World Blvd Silver Spring MD 20906-5664 Office: Albert Einstein Coll Medicine Bronx NY 10461

LEWIS, JACQUELYN ROCHELLE, nursing administrator; b. Portsmouth, Va., Feb. 24, 1956; d. Everet Darl and Frances Emaline (Pettit) Johnson; m. Philip Alden Lewis Jr., May 20, 1978. Nursing diploma, Iowa Meth. Hosp. Sch. Nursing, 1985; BS, Purdue U., 1979; postgrad., Thomas Coll., 1996; 1985. RN; cert. prof. in healthcare quality. Staff nurse Iowa Lutheran Hosp., Des Moines, 1985-87, U.S. Naval Hosp., Groton, Conn., 1987, Ctrl. Maine Med. Ctr., Lewiston, 1988; quality coord. Kennebec Valley Med. Ctr., Augusta, Maine, 1988—. V.p. Ctrl. Maine Dressage Assn., Auburn, 1996—, sec. 1993-95; usher Prince of Peace Luth. Ch., 1991—. Mem. Maine Assn. Healthcare Quality (skpr.). Office: Kennebec Valley Med Ctr 6 E Chestnut Augusta ME 04330

LEWIS, JONATHAN JOSEPH, surgical oncologist, molecular biologist; b. Johannesburg, South Africa, May 23, 1958; s. Myer Philip and Maisie (Bagg) L.; m. Nanci Lynn Vicedomini, May 20, 1990. MB BCH, Witwatersrand U., Johannesburg, 1982; PhD, Med. Sch., South Africa, 1990. Registrar in surgery Witwatersrand U. Sch. Medicine, 1982-87; postdoctoral assoc. Yale U. Sch. Medicine, New Haven, Conn., 1987-90; chief resident, surgery Yale U. Sch. Medicine, New Haven, 1990-92; fellow dept. surgery Meml. Sloan-Kettering Cancer Ctr., N.Y.C., 1992-94, attending surgeon, asst. mem., 1994—; asst. prof. surgery Cornell Univ. Med. Coll., 1994—. Contbr. articles to profl. jours. Recipient Abelheim medal Med. Coun., 1982, Trubshaw medal Coll. of Surgeons, Johannesburg, 1984; Winston fellow Sloan-Kettering Inst., 1994-95. Fellow Royal Coll. Surgeons; mem. Am. Soc. Cell Biology, Am. Assn. Cancer Rsch., Am. Soc. Clin. Oncology (Young Investigator award 1994), Assn. Acad. Surgeons, Soc. Surg. Oncology, N.Y. Acad. Scis. Jewish. Home: 504 E 63rd St Apt 37S New York NY 10021-7929 Office: Meml Sloan-Kettering Cancer Dept Surgery 1275 York Ave New York NY 10021-6007

LEWIS, LINDA DONELLE, neurologist, educator; b. Columbus, Ohio, Nov. 27, 1939; d. Donald Peter and Ann Elizabeth (Karn) L.; m. Gary Gambuti, Oct. 6, 1979. BS, Bethany Coll., 1961, DSc (hon.), 1981; MD, W.Va. U., 1965. Intern U. Wis., 1965-66; resident in medicine St. Luke's Hosp., N.Y.C., 1966-68; resident in neurology Case Western Res. U., Cleve., 1968-69; sr. resident in neurology Columbia Presbyn. Med. Ctr., N.Y.C., 1969-70, chief resident in neurology, 1970-71;, pvt. practice medicine specializing in neurology, N.Y.C., 1971—; prof. neurology Coll. Physicians and Surgeons, Columbia U., N.Y.C., from 1971, now clin. prof., assoc. dean student affairs, 1979—; cons. in field; mem. N.Y. State Bd. for Profl. Med. Conduct, 1979—. Contbr. articles to sci. jours. Trustee Bethany Coll., 1987—, A.P. Gold Found. Mem. AMA, N.Y. State Med. Soc. (del.), New York County Med. Soc., Am. Assn. Med. Colls., Am. Acad. Neurology, AAAS. Home: 320 Central Park W New York NY 10025-7659 Office: 710 W 168th St New York NY 10032-2603

LEWIS, MARION ELIZABETH, social worker; b. Los Alamos, Calif., Dec. 7, 1920; d. James Henry and Carolina Sophia (Niemann) Eddy; m. William Ernest Lewis, May 30, 1943 (dec. Oct. 1954); children: Doris Lenita Lewis Terrill, Paul William. Student, Jr. Coll., Santa Maria, Calif., 1939-40, Bus. Coll., Santa Barbara, Calif., 1940-41, Alan Hancock Coll., 1958-61, BA in Sociology cum laude, Westminster Coll., Salt Lake City, 1964. Office clk. Met. Life Ins. Co., Santa Barbara, 1942-43; sales clk. Sprouse Reitz Co., Laguna Beach, Calif., 1943-44; office clk. U.S. Army, Santa Maria AFB, 1944-45; sch. crossing guard Calif. Hwy. Patrol, Los Alamos, 1956-58; office clk. Holaday Children's Ctr., Salt Lake City, 1964; social worker Sonoma County Social Svc., Santa Rosa, Calif., 1964-78, ret., 1978; sales rep. Avon Products, Los Alamos, 1957-61; sales clk. Gen. Store, Los Alamos, 1957-59; office clk. Sonoma County Pub. Health Dept., 1979-80. Deacon Presbyn. Ch., 1956—, moderator Presbyn. Women, 1990-91, vice moderator, 1989-90, sem. rep., 1978-80, 92-94. Mem. AAUW, R.I. Geneal. Soc., Sonoma County Geneal. Soc., Calif. Automobile Assn., Nat. Geographic Soc., Sonoma County Assn. Ret. Employees, Commonwealth Club Calif., Sequoia Club, Westminster Coll. Alumni Assn., Alpha Chi (alumni chpt.). Republican. Home: 61 Sequoia Cir Santa Rosa CA 95401-4992

LEWIS, MARTHA NELL, expressive arts therapist, massage therapist, counselor, director; b. Atlanta, Mar. 4, 1944; d. Clifford Edward and Nell (Shropshire) Wilkie; m. Jeffrey Clark Lewis, Aug. 20, 1966 (div. Aug. 1986); children: John Martin, Janet Michelle Teal. BA, Tex. Tech. U., 1966; massage therapy, The Winters Sch., 1991; MA, Norwich U., 1994. Registered expressive therapist, massage therapist, therapeutic massage and bodywork, massage therapist instr. Geophys. analyst Shell Oil Co., Houston, 1966-68; photogravity specialist Photogravity, Inc., Houston, 1972-80; tchr. music Little Red Sch. House, Houston, 1974-75; sec., treas. Lewis Enterprises, Inc., Houston, 1976-83; regulatory supr. Transco Energy Co., Houston, 1983-92; expressive arts therapist Shalom Renewal Ctr., Splendora, Tex., 1995—, River Oaks Health Alliance, Houston, 1995—; also bd. dirs. Shalom Renewal Ctr. and River Oaks Health Alliance, 1995—; nat. exec. dir., pres. Music for Healing and Transition Program, Houston, 1994—; massage therapist, Houston, 1991—. Advisor youth Corpus Christi Ch., Houston, 1970-80; vocalist, instrumentalist Sounds of Faith Folk Group, Houston, 1978—; harpist Houston Harpers Harp Ensemble, 1990-92; instr. exercise, body awareness Transco Energy Co. Fitness Ctr., Houston, 1990-92; vol. The Inst. for Rehab. and Rsch., Houston, 1989-90, Houston Hospice, 1992—, Houston Healing Healthcare Project, 1993—; vol. Healing Environ. Coun. St. Luke's Episc. Hosp., 1993—, lay chaplain, 1994—; founder The Winters Sch. Massage Therapy Care Team, Houston, 1991—. Mem. Internat. Expressive Arts Therapy Assn., Am. Holistic Nurses Assn., Am. Harp Soc., Internat. Folk Harp Assn., Am. Massage Therapy Assn., Nat. Soc. Fund Raising Execs., Exec. Dir.'s Forum, Space City Ski Club (asst. trip coord. 1991-92), Houston Sigma Kappa Found. (bd. dirs.), Sigma Kappa Alumnae Assn. (pres. Houston chpt. 1974-76, nat. collegiate province officer 1981-85, Houston Alumnae of Yr. 1981, Tex. Alumnae of Yr. 1980, Pearl Ct. award 1991). Roman Catholic. Home: 6400 Christie Ave # 4202 Emeryville CA 94608

LEWIS, MARY ANN, nursing educator; b. Kansas City, Mo., Aug. 1, 1937; m. Charles Edwin Lewis, Dec. 27, 1963; children: Kevin, David, Matthew, Karen. BS in Nursing, U. Kans., 1962; MS in Nursing, Boston U., 1963; DrPH, UCLA, 1984. cert. adult nurse practitioner. Instr. pub. health nursing U. Kans., Kansas City, Mo., 1963-66; coordinator pub. health nursing Children's Mercy Hosp., Kansas City, 1966-68; research health specialist UCLA, 1971-73, project dir. Primex Family Nurse Practice, 1972-76, adj. asst. prof. nursing, 1976-80, adj. prof. nursing and medicine, 1980-86, asst. prof. nursing, 1986—, prof., 1989—; chair faculty UCLA Sch. Nursing, 1992—; cons. internat. health Health Resources Adminstrn., Washington, 1978—; bd. dirs. Maxicare Rsch. and Edn. Found., L.A.; cons. Asthma and Allergy Found. Am., L.A., Washington; ad hoc reviewer NIH. Author: Health Decision-Making, 1980; bd. dirs., editorial bd. The Nurse Practitioner, 1981—; contbr. articles to profl. jours. Com. mem. AIDS Project, Los Angeles, 1986-88. Fellow Am. Acad. Nursing; mem. AAUW, ANA, APHA, Assn. for History of Nursing, Chironians of UCLA Sch. Nursing (co-chmn. 1987—), Sigma Theta Tau. Office: UCLA Sch Nursing 10833 Le Conte Ave Los Angeles CA 90024

LEWIS, MELVIN, psychiatrist, pediatrician, psychoanalyst; b. London, May 18, 1926; came to U.S., 1956; s. Abraham George and Kitty (Merrick) L.; m. Dorothy S. Otnow, May 30, 1963; children: Gillian Io, Eric Anthony. M.B., B.S., Guy's Hosp. Med. Sch., London, 1950; D.C.H., 1954; M.A. (hon.), Yale U., 1972. Diplomate Am. Bd. Psychiatry and Neurology, Am. Bd. Child Psychiatry; cert. in psychoanalysis, child and adolescent psychoanalysis. Intern Lambeth Hosp., 1950, Fulham Hosp., 1951 (both Eng); resident in pediatrics Yale U. Sch. Medicine, 1956-57, resident in psychiatry and child psychiatry, 1957-61; instr. psychiatry Yale U. Child Study Center, New Haven, 1961-63; asst. prof. pediatrics and psychiatry Yale U. Child Study Center, 1963-67, assoc. prof., 1967-70, prof. child psychiatry and pediats., 1971—, dir. med. studies, 1970—. Author: Clinical Aspects of Child and Adolescent Development, 1971, 3d edit. (with Fred Volkmar), 1991; editor: Jour. Am. Acad. Child & Adolescent Psychiatry, 1975-87, Child and Adolescent Psychiatry, A Comprehensive Textbook, 1991, 2d edit., 1996; cons. editor: Child and Adolescent Psychiatric Clinics of North America, 1991—. Served with M.C. Royal Army, 1951-53. Fellow Am. Acad. Child and Adolescent Psychiatry, Am. Psychiat. Assn., Royal Coll. Psychiatrists; mem. Royal Soc. Medicine, Am. Pediatric Soc., Am. Psychoanalytic Assn. Home: 10 St Ronan Ter New Haven CT 06511-2315 Office: Yale U Child Study Ctr 333 Cedar St New Haven CT 06510-3206

LEWIS, MICHAEL SETH, health care executive; b. Bklyn., Dec. 11, 1953; s. Irving Abraham and Beatrice Rachel (Fishman) L.; m. Arlene Feigenbaum, June 27, 1976; children: Adam, Sara. BA, Bklyn. Coll., 1974; MS, Fordham U., 1975; MBA, Temple U., 1977. Grad. asst. Temple U., Phila., 1975-77; adminstrv. asst. Cherry Hill (N.J.) Med. Ctr., 1976-77; adminstr. Brachfeld Med. Assocs., Willingboro, N.J., 1977-94; v.p. Founders Health Care Inc., Phila., 1995—. Mem. Mt. Laurel Twp. Budget Steering Com.; fin. v.p. Congregation Beth Tikvah. Mem. Med. Group Mgmt. Assn., Am. Pub. Health Assn., Beta Gamma Sigma. Home: 24 Abington Rd Mount Laurel NJ 08054-4720 Office: Founders Health Care 2115 South St Philadelphia PA 19146

LEWIS, MYRON, physician; b. Memphis, Oct. 16, 1937; s. Joseph and Louise Elizabeth (Ottenheimer) L.; m. Edith Gail Haupt, Nov. 30, 1963; children: Robin, Tracey, Joelle. BA magna cum laude, Dartmouth Coll., 1959; MD, Columbia U., 1963. Cert. in medicine, gastroenterology. Intern, resident Vanderbilt U., Nashville, 1963-65; resident Cornell and Bellvue, N.Y.C., 1965-67; fellow U. Tenn., Memphis, 1969-70, assoc. prof. dept. medicine, 1980—. Asst. editor The Gastroenterologist, 1993—. Lt. comdr. USPHS, 1967-69. Fellow Am. Coll. Physics, Am. Coll. Gastroenterology (master, pres. 1987-88), Phi Beta Kappa. Office: Memphis Gastro Group PC 80 Humphreys Ctr # 220 Memphis TN 38120

LEWIS, NEIL PHILLIP, management psychologist; b. N.Y.C., Dec. 17, 1942; m. Judith Van Der Ploog, Nov. 30, 1979; 1 child, Russell. BA, Hofstra U., 1964; MA, Fordham U., 1966, PhD, 1971. Lic. psychologist, Ga. Cons. Ernst & Young, N.Y.C., 1969-70; mgr. mgmt. devel. Bendix Corp., Southfield, Mich., 1970-73; mgr. Ernst & Young, Detroit, 1973-75; sr. cons. RHR Internat., Atlanta, 1975-85; prin. Lewis Assocs., Marietta, Ga., 1985—; chmn. Mich. State Psychologist Ethics Bd., 1972-75. Contbr. articles to profl. jours. Mem. APA, Soc. Human Resource Mgmt., Oakland County Psychol. Assn. (pres. 1974-75).

LEWIS, PAUL LE ROY, pathology educator; b. Tamaqua, Pa., Aug. 30, 1925; s. Harry Earl and Rose Estella (Brobst) L.; m. Betty Jane Bixby, June 2, 1953; 1 child, Robert Harry. AB magna cum laude, Syracuse U., 1950; MD, SUNY, Syracuse, 1953. Diplomate Am. Bd. Pathology. Intern Temple U. Hosp., Phila., 1953-54; resident in pathology Hosp. of U. Pa., Phila., 1954-58, asst. instr., 1957-58; instr. pathology Thomas Jefferson U. Coll. Medicine, Phila., 1958-62, asst. prof., 1962-65, assoc. prof., 1965-75, prof., 1975-93, prof. emeritus, 1993—; pathologist Thomas Jefferson U. Hosp., 1958-91; attending pathologist Meth. Hosp., Phila., 1975-93, dir. clin. labs., chmn. dept. pathology, 1975-92, consulting pathologist, 1993—; pathologist pvt. practice Phila., 1993—; pres. Penndel Labs. Inc., Ardmore, Pa., 1974-85; cons. VA Hosp., Coatesville, Pa., 1976-85; mem. med. adv. com. ARC Blood Bank, Phila., 1978—. Contbg. author: Atlas of Gastrointestinal Cytology, 1983; contbr. articles to med. jours. 2d lt. USAAF, 1943-46. Fellow Am. Soc. Clin. Pathologists, Coll. Am. Pathologists; mem. AMA, Pa. Med. Soc., Philadelphia County Med. Soc., Internat. Acad. Pathology, Am. Soc. Cytology, Masons, Phi Beta Kappa, Alpha Omega Alpha, Nu Sigma Nu. Republican. Methodist. Home and Office: 521 Baird Rd Merion Station PA 19066-1301

LEWIS, RANDALL JEFFREY, orthopedic surgeon; b. Boston, Jan. 26, 1946; s. Benjamin David and Shirley (Rudolph) Lewis; m. Patricia (Gimbel) Lewis, Sept. 1, 1968; 1 dau., Allison. B.A. summa cum laude, Yale U., 1965, M.D. cum laude, Harvard U., 1969. Diplomate Am. Bd. Orthopaedic Surgery, Nat. Bd. Med. Examiners. Intern, resident in surgery Beth Israel Hosp., Boston, 1969-71; clin. assoc. Nat. Cancer Inst., Bethesda, Md., 1971-73; resident in orthopedic surgery Hosp. Spl. Surgery, N.Y.C. 1973-76; asst. prof. orthopedic surgery George Washington U., Washington, 1976-79, assoc. prof., 1978-81; assoc. clin. prof. surgery, 1981—clin. prof. 1991—, assoc. clin. prof. ortho. surgery, Georgetown U., 1992— ; cons. clin. ctr. NIH, 1976—; cons. and panel mem. FDA sect. orthopedic, rehab. devices, 1980-94 ; med. adv. com. Met. Washington Arthritis Found., 1981-84 . Contbr. articles, abstracts in field to publs. Served as asst. surgeon USPH, 1971-75. Fellow: Am. Acad. Orthopedic Surgeons (bd. councillors 1989-95); mem. D.C. Med. Soc., Washington Orthopedic Soc. (pres. 1989-90), Rheumatism Soc. D.C., Phi Beta Kappa, Sigma Xi. Democrat. Jewish. Office: 2021 K St NW Washington DC 20006

LEWIS, RICHARD HARLOW, urologist; b. San Diego, May 14, 1951; s. Charles William Jr. and Gene (Harlow) L.; m. Deanna Elma Boggs, March 14, 1950; children: Richard Harlow Jr., Sara-Grace Dean. BS, Guilford Coll., 1973; MD, Duke U., 1977. Intern Bethesda (Md.) Naval Hosp., 1977-78, residence, 1978-82, chief urology, 1982-85; pvt. practice McIver Clinic, Jacksonville, Fla., 1985—; mng. ptnr. McIver Clinic divsn. Urology Clinic of Fla., Jacksonville, 1994—. Mem. Christian Coalition, Duval County, Fla., 1987—; Rep. precinct rep., Duval County, 1987-90. Lt. comdr. USNR, 1973-85. Winner, Karl Storz Endoscope Photography Contest Karl Storz Corp., 1983. Fellow ACS, Am. Soc. Laser Medicine Surgery, Am. Bd. Laser Surgery, S.E. Surg. Soc.; mem. Am. Urol. Assn. Home: 4900 Arapahoe Ave Jacksonville FL 32210-8336 Office: McIver Clinic 710 Lomax St Jacksonville FL 32204-4004

LEWIS, ROBERT EDWIN, JR., pathology immunology educator, researcher; b. Meridian, Miss., Mar. 11, 1947. BA in Biology and Chemistry, U. Miss., 1969, MS in Microbiology, 1973, PhD in Pathology, 1976; specialty tng., Barnes Hosp., U. Miami Med. Ctr., U. Tenn. Ctr. for Health Scis., City of Memphis Hosps., St. Jude Children's Research Hosp. Instr. pathology, anesthesiology U. Miss. Med. Ctr., Jackson, 1976-77, asst. prof. pathology, 1977-84, asst. prof. anesthesiology, 1977-85, asst. dir. clin. immnuopathology lab., 1978-81, assoc. dir. tissue typing lab., 1980-84, dir. paternity testing lab., 1981—, assoc. dir. clin. immunopathology lab., 1981-84, asst. prof. nurse anesthesiology, 1981-85, assoc. prof. pathology, 1984-91, prof., 1991—, co-dir. clin. immunology, tissue typing lab., 1984—, mem. grad. council, 1981—, prof., 1991—. Co-author: Illustrated Dictionary of Immunology, 1995; editor: (with J.M. Cruse) Concepts in Immunopathology, Vols. 1-8, 1985-91, The Year in Immunology-1984-85, 1985, The Year in Immunology-1986-87, 1987, The Year in Immunology-1988, 1989, The Year in Immunology-1989-90, 1990, Progress in Experimental Tumor Research, Vol. 32, 1987, Contributions to Microbiology and Immunology, Vol. 8, 1986, Vol. 9, 1987, Vol. 10, 1989, Vol. 11, 1989, The Year in Immunopathology, 1987, Complement Profiles, Vol. 1, 1992; sr. editor Pathology and Immunopathology Research, 1982-90, Immunologic Research, 1981—, Transgenics, 1993; series editor Concepts in Immunopathology, The Year in Immunology, Contributions to Microbiology and Immunology; vol. editor Progress in Experimental Tumor Research; immunology editor Dorland's Illustrated Medical Dictionary, 26th and 27th edits.; dep. editor-in-chief Pathobiology, 1990—; contbr. chpts. to books. Am. Cancer Soc. grantee, NIH grantee, Wilson Found. grantee, 1990-95. Fellow Royal Soc. Health; mem. AAAS, Am. Assn. Pathologists, Am. Assn. Immunologists, Clin. Immunology Soc., Can. Soc. Immunology, Reticuloendothelial Soc., Am. Soc. Microbiology, Am. Soc. Histocompatibility and Immunogenetics (co-chmn. publs. com., co-chmn. 1987-95), Exptl. Biology and Medicine, N.Y. Acad. Scis., Miss. Acad. Scis., Sigma Xi. Office: U Miss Med Ctr Pathology Dept 2500 N State St Jackson MS 39216-4500

LEWIS, ROBERT LEE, III, health facility executive; b. San Francisco, Sept. 20, 1949; s. Robert Lee Jr. and Dolores Patricia (Brady) L.; m. Kari B. Hanson, May, 1989; children: Paige Caroline, Caitlin Elizabeth. BS, Calif. State U., Fresno, 1971, MBA, 1978; cert. exec. program, Stanford U., 1983. Ops. officer, adminstrv. asst. to v.p. Security Pacific Nat. Bank, Fresno, 1971-74; service chief County Health Dept., Fresno, 1974-79; adminstrv. dir. clin. labs. Stanford (Calif.) U. Hosp., 1979-84; pres. Western Div. Internat. Clin. Labs., Dublin, Calif., 1984-86; v.p. Performance Health Care, Inc., Danville, Calif., 1986-87; adminstr. Good Samaritan Med. Group, San Jose, Calif., 1987-90; chief exec. officer O'Connor Med. Group, San Jose, 1990-93; CEO Med Cor Health Info. Solutions, Cupertino, Calif., 1993—; adj. faculty Coll. Profl. Studies U. San Francisco, 1988—. Author: Optimizing Productivity: Capital Equipment Acquisition, 1985; mem. editorial bd. Syva Monitor, 1984. Served with USNG, 1971-76. Mem. Med. Group Mgmt. Assn., Fresno Assn. for Retarded (bd. dirs. (1975-78), Health Care Fin. Assn. Home: 1553 Arbor Ave Los Altos CA 94024

LEWIS, ROBERT TURNER, retired psychologist; b. Taft, Calif., June 17, 1923; s. D. Arthur and Amy Belle (Turner) L.; m. Jane Badham, Mar. 23, 1946; children: Jane, William, Richard. BA, U. So. Calif., 1947, MA, 1950; PhD, U. Denver, 1952. Diplomate Am. Bd. Profl. Disability Cons.; lic. psychologist, Calif. Chief psychologist Hollywood Presbyn. Hosp., L.A., 1953-58; dir. psychol. svcs. Salvation Army, Pasadena, Calif., 1958-68; dir. Pasadena Psychol. Ctr., 1964-74; successively asst. prof., assoc. prof. and prof., Calif. State U., L.A., 1952-83, prof. emeritus, 1984—; assoc. dir. Cortical Function Lab., L.A., 1972-84; clin. dir. Diagnostic Clinic, West Covina, Calif., 1983-85; dir. Job Stress Clinic, Santa Ana, Calif., 1985-95. Author: Taking Chances, 1979, A New Look at Growing Older, 1995, Money Hangups, 1995; co-author: Money Madness, 1978; Human Behavior, 1974; The Psychology of Abnormal Behavior, 1961. Served to lt. (j.g.) USNR, 1943-46, PTO. Mem. APA, Calif. State Psychol. Assn. Republican.

LEWIS, ROBERT WELBORN, hospital administrator; b. San Antonio, Apr. 20, 1953; s. Joseph Welborn and Betty Jane (Hillman) L.; m. Lynette Pearl McCoy, May 31, 1975 (div. Dec. 1985); m. Rachael Richardson, 1993. Assoc., Hinds Jr. Coll., Raymond, Miss., 1973; BBA, U. So. Miss., Hattiesburg, 1975, MBA, 1985. CPA, Miss. Medicare auditor Blue Cross and Blue Shield of Miss., Jackson, 1975-76; reimbursement specialist Am. Med. Internat., Houston, 1976-77; acctg. dir. Singing River Hosp. System, Pascagoula, Miss., 1977-81; chief fin. officer Singing River Hosp. System, Pascagoula, 1981—; bd. dirs. Premier Health, Inc., Jackson County Med. Found. Mem. AICPA, Health Care Fin. Mgmt. Assn., Miss. Soc. CPAs. Republican. Baptist. Home: 8 Indian Trl Ocean Springs MS 39564-5020

LEWIS, SANDRA JEAN, internist, cardiologist, educator; b. Portland, Oreg., Apr. 11, 1949; m. James Rosenbaum; children: Lisa, Jennifer. BA in Psychology, Stanford U., 1971, MD, 1977; student, Yale U., 1971-72, U. Conn. Sch. Medicine, 1973-75. Diplomate Am. Bd. Internal Medicine, Am. Bd. Cardiology. Resident Stanford (Calif.) U. Hosp., 1977-80; fellow in cardiology Stanford U., 1980-83; staff physician and cardiologist S. San Francisco Kaiser Hosp., 1984-85, acting chief of cardiology, 1984-85; chief of cardiology Good Samaritan Hosp., Portland, Oreg., 1990-93; chmn. rsch. com. Legacy Heart Svcs., Portland, 1993—; pvt. practice cardiology Portland (Oreg.) Cardiovascular Inst., 1993—; clin. asst. prof. medicine Oregon State U., Portland, 1993—. Contbr. articles and abstracts to profl. jours. Grantee Robert Wood Johnson Found., U. Conn. Sch. Medicine, 1973-75, S.A.V.E. and C.A.R.E., Good Samaritan Hosp., Portland; recipient Young Leadership award Oreg., Gen. Mills, 1967. Fellow Am. Coll. Cardiology (Merck fellow). Office: Portland Cardio Inst 2222 NW Lovejoy Ste 606 Portland OR 97210

LEWIS, THOMAS HOWARD, psychiatrist, educator; b. Red Lodge, Mont., July 28, 1919; s. William Michel and Charlotte Amanda (Johnson) L.; m. Ruth Danielson, May 5, 1944; children: William Richard, Daniel John, Thomas Morgan, Linda Ruth, David Gryffdd. BS, U. Wash., 1941; MD, Duke U., 1946. Commd. lt. USN, 1946, advanced through grades to capt., 1962; resident U.S. Naval Hosp. USN, Bethesda, Md., 1951-53; resident NIMH, 1960; dir. resident tng. in psychiatry Nat. Naval Med. Ctr. USN, 1963-68, chief neurology and psychiatry, 1969-73, ret., 1973; prof. psychiatry Georgetown U., Washington, 1975—. Author: Forgotten Battles Along the Yellowstone, 1985, The Medicine Men, 1990; contbr. over 270 articles on medicine, anthropology, biology, ethnology and anatomy to profl. jours.; assoc. editor Am. Indian Quar., 1975—. Fellow ACP, Am. Psychiat. Assn.; mem. AMA, AAAS, Wash. Psychoanalytic Soc., Wash. Psychiat. Soc., N.Y. Acad. Sci., Sigma Xi, Phi Sigma. Democrat. Clubs: Cosmos, St. David's Soc. (Washington). Home and Office: Box 162 Boyd MT 59013

LEWIS, WILBUR CURTIS, surgeon; b. Okmulgee, Okla., Sept. 10, 1930; s. Charles D. and Eula Alice (Cole) L.; m. Gladys Sherman, Jan. 28, 1955; children: Karen Kay, Mark David, Leanne Gwynneth, Cristen Sue. BS, Okla. Bapt. U., 1952; MD, Okla. U., 1955. Diplomate Am. Bd. Family Practice (charter); ordained to ministry Bapt. Ch. as pastor, 1953. Intern Harris Hosp., Ft. Worth, 1955-56; resident in surgery VA Hosp., Dallas, 1956-57, Univ. Hosp., Oklahoma City, 1965-67; med. missionary So. Bapt. Conv., Costa Rica and Paraguay, 1959-70; pvt. practice medicine specializing in surgery, Oklahoma City, 1970—; leader med. disaster relief team, Honduras, 1975, Guatemala, 1976, Dominican Republic, 1977; surgeon, lectr. Maraciabo, Venezuela, 1989, Taxila, Pakistan, 1990, Bangalore, India, 1990, Guito, Ecuador, 1991, Signatepeque and Teguigalpa, Honduras, 1993; mem. staff Bapt. Hosp., Deaconess Hosp., Mercy Hosp., St. Anthony Hosp., Oklahoma City Hosp.; deacon, mem. meml. trust com. 1st Bapt. Ch., Oklahoma City; former chmn. deacons and social ministries com.; former pastor various chs., Okla. and Paraguay; co-founder, former pres. Baptist Med. Dental Fellowship; lectr. on surgery and burn care topics in Venezuela, Pakistan, India and Equador and Honduras. Past pres. Midwest City C. of C. Capt. USAF, 1957-59. Decorated knight Knights of Malta. Fellow ACS, Internat. Coll. Surgeons; mem. AMA, Internat. Fedn. Surgical Colls., Okla. State Med. Assn. (former del. and alt. del.), Christian Med. and Dental Soc. (former del.), Oklahoma City Surg. Soc., Am. Burn Assn., Internat. Soc. Burn Injuries (burn care com.), Oklahoma City Clin. Soc. Democrat. Home: 14501 N Western Ave Edmond OK 73013-1828 Office: 3141 NW Expressway St Oklahoma City OK 73112-4143

LEWIS, WILLIAM IRVIN, surgeon; b. Dallas, May 6, 1941; m. Kathleen L. Trettel; children: Markell J., Frances S., Pauline L. BA in Physics, U. Dallas, 1966; MD, U. Tex. Med. Sch., San Antonio, 1976. Diplomate Am. Bd. Surgery. Surg. intern U. Minn., 1976-84, transplant fellow, 1984-85; surg. resident Vanderbilt U. Sch. Medicine, Nashville, 1987-88; instr. physics Blinn Coll., Brenham, Tex., 1966-67; dynamics engr. Bell Helicopter, Fort Worth, 1967-72; asst. prof. surgery So. Ill. U. Sch. Medicine, Springfield, 1985-87; pvt. practice Nashville, 1988—; clin. asst. prof. surgery Meharry Med. Coll., Nashville, 1993—; clin. instr. dept. surgery Vanderbilt U. Sch. Medicine, Nashville, 1988—; dir. transplant program Centennial Med. Ctr., Nashville, 1994—. Metabolism and Digestive Disease Rsch. Fellow Nat. Inst. Arthritis, 1982. Mem. AMA (Physician Recognition award 1985-91, 91-94, 95—). Office: 2010 Church St Ste 526 Nashville TN 37203

LEWIS-FERNANDEZ, ROBERTO, psychiatrist; b. Santurce, P.R., Dec. 4, 1958; s. Robert and Piri (Fernandez) Lewis. BA, Harvard U., 1979, M.Theol. Studies, 1982; MD, Yale U., 1986. Resident in psychiatry Cambridge (Mass.) Hosp., 1986-90; fellow in med. anthropology dept. social medicine Dept. Social Medicine, Harvard Med. Sch., Boston, 1990-93; lectr. social medicine Harvard Med. Sch., Boston; med. dir. Bio-Psycho-Social Ctr., Santurce Med. Mall; co-investigator Behavioral Scis. Rsch. Inst., U. P.R. Clin. cases editor Culture, Medicine and Psychiatry. Am. Coll. Psychiatrists Laughlin fellow, 1990, Mead Johnson fellow, 1990, NIMH mini-fellow, 1990, DuPont Warren fellow, 1990-91. Mem. Am. Psychiat. Assn., Am. Soc. Hispanic Psychiatry (bd. dirs.).

LEWITT, MICHAEL HERMAN, physician, educator; b. Hartford, Conn., Nov. 27, 1948; s. Bernard and Celeste (Garfunkel) LeW.; m. Lynne Rubin, Apr. 1, 1979; children: Mattea, Jeremy, Rachel. BA, Lafayette Coll., 1970; MD, Jefferson Med. Coll., 1974; student, Med. Coll. Wis. Diplomate Am. Bd. Preventive Medicine, Am. Bd. Emergency Medicine, Am. Bd. Family Practice. Med. dr. FMC Corp., 1975-78; physician U.S. Steel Corp., 1978-81; staff physician Jeanes Hosp., 1981-84; med. dir. occupational medicine

Chester County Hosp., 1984-90; instr. dept. medicine, dept. surgery Jefferson Med. Coll., Phila., 1983—; pvt. practice, 1990—; cons., 1990—. Fellow Phila. Coll. Physicians, Am. Coll. Emergency Physicians, Am. Coll. Occupational and Environ. Medicine, Am. Acad. Family Practice; mem. Am. Coll. Physicians. Office: Paoli Hosp Occupl Med 255 W Lancaster Ave Paoli PA 19301

LEWITTES, DON JORDAN, clinical psychologist; b. Bklyn., Jan. 21, 1950; s. Morton H. and Laura C. L.; BA, N.Y. U., 1971; PhD, SUNY, Albany, 1976; m. Andrea D. Jordon, June 15, 1978; 1 son, Jason D. Instr. dept. psychiatry Albany (N.Y.) Med. Coll., 1976-78. Diplomate Am. Bd. Med. Psychotherapists, Am. Bd. Disability Cons., Am. Bd. Forensic Examiners. Sr. psychologist Schenectady Shared Services, Ellis Hosp., 1976-77; dir. in-patient services South Richmond-South Beach Psychiat. Center, S.I., N.Y., 1977-81; chief psychologist South Nassau Communities Hosp., Oceanside, N.Y., 1982-87; clin. affiliate prof. psychology St. John's U., 1984-87; project dir. and cons. Nassau Coalition on Child Abuse and Neglect, Hempstead, N.Y., 1989—; psychol. cons. Gracie Sq. Hosp., N.Y.C., 1989-91; expert cons. N.Y.C. Office Legal Affairs/Human Resources Adminstrn., 1991—, Kings County and Manhattan County Dist. Atty's. Office, 1994—; mem. faculty Grad. Sch. Social Svc. Fordham U., 1995—; intern dept. psychiatry Rutgers Med. Sch., Piscataway, N.J., 1974-75. Contbr. articles to profl. jours. Mem. Am. Psychol. Soc., Am. Bd. Forensic Examiners. Home: 501 E 87th St New York NY 10128-7665 Office: 30 Hempstead Ave Rockville Centre NY 11570-4034

LEWKOWITZ, KAREN HELENE, orthodontist; b. Bklyn., Dec. 26, 1956; d. William A. and Janet B. (Kagan) L.; m. Robert Louis Shpuntoff, Dec. 18, 1983; children: Hilana Megan, Ariana Elizabeth. BA magna cum laude, CUNY, 1978; DDS, Columbia U., 1982; cert. in orthodontics, NYU, 1984. Researcher W. M. Krogman Ctr., Children's Hosp. Phila., Pa., 1976; ptnr. Bayside (N.Y.) Orthodontic Assocs., 1984—; pres. med. awareness com. Queens Coll.-CUNY, 1977-78; attending orthodontist, lectr. Jamaica (N.Y.) Hosp., 1984—. Mem. Temple Torah, Little Neck, N.Y., 1988-94, Temple Israel, Great Neck, N.Y., 1994—, Hadassah, Great Neck, 1990—; v.p. of programming Orgn. Rehab. Thru Tng., Lake Success, N.Y., 1991. Mem. ADA, Acad. Gen. Dentistry, Am. Assn. Women Dentists, Am. Assn. Orthodontists, Queens County Dental Soc. (trustee 1985—, historian 1990, treas. 1991, sec. 1992, v.p. 1993, pres.-elect 1994, pres. 1995), Alpha Omega (pres. Columbia U. chpt. 1980-82, pres. Queens-Nassau chpt. 1984-87, Presdl. citation 1986, regent N.Y. met. area 1990, 91). Office: Bayside Orthodontic Assocs 59-01 Springfield Blvd Bayside NY 11364

LEWTER, BILLY RAY, psychology educator; b. Louisville, Aug. 17, 1936; s. Robert Lee and Lena Pearl (Hannah) L.; m. Mary Josephine Knecht, Aug. 17, 1963; children: Jonathan, Amy, Elizabeth, Rachel, David. BA, U. Louisville, 1966; MA, Eastern Ky. U., 1973; PhD, U. Ky., 1979; DLitt, Oxford Grad. Sch., 1985. Assoc. dir. acads. Hong-Kong Christian Coll., 1965-68; instr. psychology Cen. Inst., Manila, 1968-70; asst. prof. psychology Southeastern Coll., Winchester, Ky., 1972-79; assoc. prof. psychology Bryan Coll., Dayton, Tenn., 1980-85; prof. psychology Palm Beach Atlantic Coll., West Palm Beach, Fla., 1985—. Fulbright scholar U.S. Dept. Edn., 1983, 87, 89. Mem. Am. Psychol. Assn. Republican. Home: 2370 Bimini Dr West Palm Beach FL 33406-7760 Office: Palm Beach Atlantic Coll PO Box 24708 West Palm Beach FL 33416-4708

LEWY, JOHN EDWIN, pediatric nephrologist; b. Chgo., Apr. 22, 1935; s. Stanley B. and Lucile (Mayer) L.; m. Rosalind Portnoy, June 9, 1963; children—Karen, Steven. B.A., U. Mich., 1956; M.D., Tulane U., 1960. Diplomate Am. Bd. Pediatrics (oral examiner 1985-89, oral examination com. 1987-91, certifing examination com. on clin. problems 1989—), Am. Bd. Pediatric Nephrology (credentials com. 1981-83). Intern Michael Reese Hosp. Med. Center, Northwestern U., 1960-61, resident in pediatrics, 1961-62; resident in pediatrics Michael Reese Hosp. Med. Center, 1963-64, chief resident, 1964, pediatric nephrology fellow, 1965, dir. sect. pediatric nephrology, 1967-70; fellow dept. pediatrics Cornell U. Med. Coll., 1966, research fellow physiology, 1966-67, asst. prof. pediatrics, 1970-71, asso. prof., 1971-75, prof., 1975-78, dir. div. pediatric nephrology, 1970-78; prof., chmn. dept. pediatrics Tulane U. Hosp., New Orleans, 1978—; physician-in-chief Tulane Hosp. for Children, New Orleans, 1993—; mem. staff Children's Hosp., Med. Ctr. La.; pediatrician La. Handicapped Children's Program; bd. dirs., sci. adv. com. La. End Stage Renal Disease Council. Assoc. editor Jour. Dialysis, 1978—, Jour. Pediatric Nephrology, 1979—; contbr. over 200 articles and abstracts to profl. jours. Mem. profl. adv. com. Nat. Found. March of Dimes; sci. adv. com. U.S. Renal Data System, HHS, 1990—. Served with M.C., USAF, 1962-63. Named Intern of Year Michael Reese Hosp. Med. Center, 1961; recipient award La. Pediatric Soc., 1960. Mem. Inst. Medicine (end stage renal disease com. 1989-91), Am. Acad. Pediatrics, Soc. Pediatric Research, Am. Pediatric Soc., Am. Soc. Pediatric Nephrology (sec.-treas. 1974-80, pres. 1980-81, pub. policy com. 1991—), Am. Soc. Nephrology, Internat. Soc. Nephrology, Midwest Soc. Pediatric Research, AAAS, Salt and Water Club, N.Y. Acad. Scis., Internat. Pediatric Nephrology Assn. (asst. sec. gen. 1977-78), La. State Med. Soc., Assn. Med. Sch. Pediatric Dept. Chairmen, Am. Soc. Artificial Internal Organs, Orleans Parish Med. Soc., Greater New Orleans Pediatric Soc., Nat. Kidney Found. (health and sci. affairs com. 1989—), So. Soc. Pediatric Research, Kidney Found. La. (bd. dirs., med. adv. bd. 1981—, sci. adv. bd. 1982—), Tulane Clin. Sci. Council (chmn. 1980-90, Tulane senate com. on honors 1982-83, senator 1987-90), Alpha Omega Alpha. Home: 700 S Peters St New Orleans LA 70130-1663 Office: 1430 Tulane Ave New Orleans LA 70112-2699

LEWY, ROBERT IRA, internist, hematologist; b. N.Y.C., Oct. 16, 1943; s. Martin and Esfira (Levy) L.; m. Nada Chandler, Apr. 8, 1978; children: Amelia, Adam. BA magna cum laude, Franklin and Marshall Coll., Lancaster, Pa., 1964; MD, U. Pa., 1971. Diplomate Am. Bd. Internal Medicine, Am. Bd. Hematology. Intern Phila. Gen. Hosp., 1972-74; resident Thomas Jefferson U., Phila., 1975-81; pvt. practice Houston, 1981—; assoc. prof. medicine Baylor Coll. Medicine U. Tex. Health Sci. Ctr. Trustee Houston Opera, Houston Symphony. Fellow Am. Coll. Physicians; mem. Am. Coll. Rheumatology, Am. Soc. Hematology, Phi Beta Kappa. Home: 2221 River Oaks Blvd Houston TX 77019 Office: 8181 N Stadium Dr Houston TX 77054

LEWY, ROBERT MAX, physician; b. N.Y.C., Oct. 18, 1945; s. Martin and Ellen (Newmark) L.; m. Barbara, Oct. 4, 1987; children: Jennifer, Sarah. AB, U. Rochester, 1967; MD, U. Medicine and Dentistry N.J., Newark, 1971; MPH, Columbia U., 1977. Diplomate Nat. Bd. Med. Examiners, Am. Bd. Family Practice. Intern Dartmouth Affiliated Hosps., Hanover, N.H., 1971-72; resident Maine-Dartmouth Family Practice Program, Augusta, 1974-75; clin. scholar Columbia U., N.Y.C., 1975-77; dir. employee health svcs. Presbyn. Hosp., Columbia-Presbyn. Med. Ctr., N.Y.C., 1977-88, dir. office physician affairs, 1988-91, sr. v.p. med. affairs, 1991—; assoc. prof. medicine Columbia U., N.Y.C., 1991—. Author: Preventive Primary Medicine, 1981, Employees at Risk, 1991; contbr. articles to profl. jours. With USPHS, 1972-74. Fellow Am. Occupational Med. Assn. (sec. chmn. 1984-88), Am. Coll. Preventive Medicine; mem. Am. Pub. Health Assn., N.Y. Occupational Med. Assn. (bd. dirs. 1985—). Home: 864 Bradley Pky Blauvelt NY 10913-1127 Office: Presbyn Hosp 622 W 168th St New York NY 10032-3702

LEWYCKJ, MYRON I., ophthalmologist; b. Chgo., May 9, 1964. BS, Northwestern U., Evanston, Ill., 1986; MD, Northwestern U., 1988. Diplomate Am. Bd. Ophthalmology. Intern Swedish Covenant Hosp., Chgo., 1989; resident in ophthalmology Northwestern U. Hosp., Chgo., 1992; opthalmologist Felton-Evans Eye Clinics, Valparaiso, Ind., 1992—; instr. tng. residents Nortwestern U., 1995—. Mem. AMA, Am. Acad. Ophthalmology, Ind. State Med. Soc., Ind. Acad. Ophthalmology. Office: Felton-Evans Eye Clinics 2005 Valparaiso St Valparaiso IN 46383

LEY, KLAUS FRIEDRICH, biomedical engineering and physiology educator; b. Frankfurt, Hessen, Fed. Republic Germany, May 1, 1957; s. Walter Georg and Gertraud Irmgard (Frister) Ley; m. Gisela Renate Seifert, Nov. 16, 1984; 1 child, Katharina Gertraud Renate. MD, U. Würzburg, Fed. Republic Germany, 1983. Postdoctoral fellow dept. physiology Freie U., Berlin, 1983-89, rsch. assoc. dept. physiology, 1989-94; postdoctoral fellow dept. physiology Ames-Bioengring., U. Calif., San Diego, 1987-89; assoc. prof. bioengineering U. Va., Charlottesville, Va., U.S.A., 1994—. Assoc. editor Jour. Immunology, 1995—, Microvascular Rsch., 1996—; mem. editorial bd. Am. Jour. Physiology, Heart and Circulatory Physiology, 1993—; contbr. articles to profl. publs. Recipient Sci. award Smith-Kline Beecham Found., 1992; travel grantee Gesellschaft Microcirculation, Oxford, 1984, German Rsch. Coun., 1986; rsch. grantee German Rsch. Coun., 1987-89, 90—. Mem. Am. Physiol. Soc., Microcirculatory Soc. (mem. program com. 1994-96), German Physiol. Soc., European Soc. Microcirculation (Abbott Microcirculation award 1986), German Soc. Microcirculation (v.p. 1994-96). Home: 1412 River Oaks Rdg Charlottesville VA 22901-0638 Office: U Va Med Sch Dept Biomedical Engring PO Box 377 Charlottesville VA 22908-1722

LEY, TIMOTHY JAMES, hematologist, molecular biologist; b. Buffalo Center, Iowa, June 17, 1953; s. William Dean and Clara Ruth (Odland) L.; m. Patricia Ann Hohn, Aug. 21, 1986; children: Amelia, James, Anna. BA, Drake U., 1974; MD, Washington U., St. Louis, 1978. Diplomate Am. Bd. Internal Medicine and Hematology. Resident in medicine Mass. Gen. Hosp., Boston, 1978-80; fellow in hematology NIH, Bethesda, Md., 1980-83, sr. investigator, 1984-86; fellow in hematology and oncology Washington U. Med. Sch., St. Louis, 1983-84, asst. prof. medicine and genetics, 1986-90, assoc. prof. medicine, 1990-93, prof. medicine and genetics, 1993—; dir. Hematopoiesis Rsch. Ctr. Hematopoiesis Rsch. Ctr., St. Louis, 1994—. Contbr. more than 70 articles to profl. jours. Secretary, founding mem. Alison Eberlein Found. for Pediatric Cancer Rsch., Buffalo Center and Washington, 1982-91. With USPHS, 1980-86. Mem. Am. Soc. Hematology, Am. Soc. Biochemistry and Molecular Biology, Am. Fedn. for Clin. Rsch., Am. Soc. for Clin. Investigation, Am. Assn. Physicians, Phi Beta Kappa, Alpha Omega Alpha. Democrat. Presbyterian. Office: Washington U Med Sch Box 8007 660 S Euclid Ave Saint Louis MO 63110

LEYDA, JAMES PERKINS, pharmaceutical company executive; b. Youngstown, Ohio, Oct. 2, 1935; s. Walter Csetus and Dorothy Eleanor (Perkins) L.; m. Barbara Marie Dykstra, Sept. 9, 1967; children: Jason Walter, Jeffrey Albert, Justin Michael. B.S. in Pharmacy, Ohio No. U., 1957; M.Sc. in Pharmacy, Ohio State U., 1959, Ph.D., 1962. Registered pharmacist, Ohio. Devel. chemist Lederle Labs., Pearl River, N.Y., 1962-66; mgr. new product devel. Cyanamid Internat., Pearl River, 1966-69; dir. new product devel. Merrell Internat., N.Y.C. also Westport, Conn., 1969-81, dir. pharmacy research Merrell Dow Pharm., Cin., 1981-83, dir. comml. devel., 1983-89; assoc. dir. product approval Marion Merrell Dow Inc. (name chaned to Hoechst Marion Roussel, Inc.), Cin., 1989-92; mgr. strategic rsch. alliances Hoechst Marion Roussel, Inc., 1992-95. Contbg. Mgr. Strategic Alliances, Hoechst Marion Roussel Inc., 1995—, author: Pharmaceutical Chemistry, 1964; contbr. articles to profl. jours. Recipient Ohio No. U./Bristol Labs. Bristol award, 1957; Richardson Merrell Inc. Lunsford Richardson award, 1960; NIH Predoctoral Fellowship award, 1960. Mem. Am. Pharm. Assn., Acad. Pharm. Scis., N.Y. Acad. Scis., AAAS, Sigma Xi. Avocations: Tennis, golf. Home: 10597 Tanagerhills Dr Cincinnati OH 45249-3634 Office: Hoechst Marion Roussel Inc 2110 E Galbraith Rd Cincinnati OH 45215-6300

LEYDORF, FREDERICK LEROY, lawyer; b. Toledo, June 13, 1930; s. Loftin Herman and Dorothy DeRoyal (Cramer) L.; m. Mary MacKenzie Malcolm, Mar. 28, 1953; children: Robert Malcolm, William Frederick, Katherine Ann, Thomas Richard, Deborah Mary. Student, U. Toledo, 1948-49; B.B.A., U. Mich., 1953; J.D., UCLA, 1958. Bar: Calif. 1959. Assoc. Hammack & Pugh, L.A., 1959-61; ptnr. Willis, Butler, Scheifly, Leydorf & Grant, L.A., 1961-81, Pepper, Hamilton & Scheetz, L.A., 1981-83, Hufstedler & Kaus, L.A., 1983-95; lectr., cons. Calif. Continuing Edn. of Bar, 1965-92; mem. planning com. Probate and Trust Conf., U. So. Calif., 1984-92. Contbg. author: California Non-Profit Corporations, 1969; contbr. articles to profl. jours. Chmn. pub. adminstr.-pub. guardian adv. commn. Los Angeles County Bd. Suprs., 1972-73; bd. dirs. J.W. and Ida M. Jameson Found., 1967—, Western Ctr. on Law and Poverty, Inc., 1980-82, L.A. Heart Inst., 1988-90; mem. legal com. Music Ctr. Found., 1980-95; mem. lawyers adv. coun. Constl. Rights Found., 1982-85; mem. devel. adv. bd. U. Mich. Sch. Bus. Adminstrn., 1984-90; mem. adv. bd. UCLA-CEB Estate Planning Inst., 1979-92; Lt. USNR, 1953-55. Mem. ABA, L.A. County Bar Assn. (bd. trustees 1973-75), State Bar Calif. (chmn. conf. dels. 1977, Alumnus of Yr. award, conf. of dels. 1983, mem. exec. com. estate planning, trust and probate law sect. 1979-80), L.A. County Bar Found. (pres. 1977-79, bd. dirs. 1975-87), Am. Coll. Trust and Estate Counsel, Internat. Acad. Estate and Trust Law (v.p. N.Am. 1978-82), Life Ins. and Trust Coun. L.A. (pres. 1983-84), UCLA Law Alumni Assn. (pres. 1982), L.A. World Affairs Coun., Chancery Club (pres. 1991-92), Jonathan Club, Laguna Hills Golf Club, Phi Delta Phi, Phi Delta Theta. Republican. Lutheran. Home: 3078-D Via Serena S Laguna Hills CA 92653-2771

L'HEUREUX, LAURA ANNE, obstetrician, gynecologist; b. Duarte, Calif., Mar. 29, 1961; d. Roland Joseph and Pamela Algwen (Simpson) L'H.; m. Craig Michael Rundbaken, May 30, 1992. BS in Biol. Scis., Calif. Polytech State U., 1983; DO, U. Osteo. Medicine, 1992. Pub. health investigator L.A. County Health Dept., 1985-86, 88; histology teaching asst. U. Osteo. Medicine & Health Scis., Des Moines, 1939-90; intern Garden City (Mich.) Hosp., 1992-93, ob-gyn. resident, 1993-94; ob-gyn. resident Botsford Gen. Hosp., Farmington Hills, Mich., 1994—. Am. Med. Women's Assn. scholar, 1992. Mem. AMA, Am. Osteo. Assn., Am. Coll. Osteo. Ob-gyn., Am. Assn. Gynecologic Laparoscopists (hon. resident), Mich. Assn. Osteop. Physicians & Surgeons, Phi Delta Epsilon. Home: 49513 Pointe Crossing Plymouth MI 48170 Office: Botsford Gen Hosp 28050 Grand River Ave Farmington Hills MI 48336

LHEVINE, DAVE BERNARD, radiologist, educator; b. Tulsa, May 20, 1922; s. Morris Boise and Sarah Fannie (Fiatt) L.; m. Mary Helen Orr, Dec. 19, 1963 (div. July 1986); children: Rhonda Dean, Paul Morris; m. Catherine Marie Garvey, Mar. 28, 1992. BA, Okla. U., 1943, MD, 1945. Diplomate Am. Bd. Radiology. Intern U.S. Naval Hosp., Bklyn., 1945-46; resident in radiology St. Louis City Hosp., Bklyn., 1948-51, 1948-51; dir. dept. radiology Hillcrest Med. Ctr., Tulsa, 1951-83, dir. dept. radiation therapy, 1983-86; clin. prof. dept. radiation oncology Okla. U., Oklahoma City, 1987-95; vice chmn. dept. radiology Okla. U. Sch. Medicine Tulsa Med. Coll., 1978—; corp. sec. Sterling Oil Co. of Okla., Tulsa, 1987-94. Active Tulsa County Dem. politics. Elected chmn. Tulsa County Dem. Com., 1995. Lt. (j.g.) USN, 1942-47. Fellow Am. Coll. Radiology (hon., emeritus); mem. AMA, Radiol. Soc. of N.Am., Okla. State Radiol. Soc. (pres. 1958). Democrat. Home: 2716 E 26th Pl Tulsa OK 74114-4308 Office: Tulsa Co Dem Party 3930 E 31st St Tulsa OK 74135

LI, ALBERT P., cell biologist, toxicologist; b. Hong Kong, Dec. 6, 1951; came to U.S., 1969; children: Nicole M., Brandon L. BSc, U. Wis., Stevens Point, 1972; PhD, U. Tenn., Oak Ridge, 1976. Rsch. asst. prof. U. N.Mex., Albuquerque, 1976-79; cell biologist Lovelace Inhalation Toxicology Rsch. Inst., Albuquerque, 1979-82; sr. rsch. toxicologist Monsanto Co., St. Louis, 1982-84, rsch. specialist, 1984-85, assoc. fellow, 1985-88, fellow, 1988-92, sr. fellow, 1992-93, head liver biology dept., 1992-93; dir. surgical rsch. inst. St. Louis U. Med. Ctr., 1993-95; rsch. prof. St. Louis U. Med. Sch., 1993-95; v.p. Hepatic Techs., In Vitro Techs., Inc., Balt., 1995—; adj. prof. surgery St. Louis U. Med. Sch., 1989-93; affiliated prof. Washington U., St. Louis, 1991-95; vis. prof. Guang Zhou U., 1990—; chmn. gene-tox work group U.S. EPA, Washington, 1984-93; chmn. mutagenicity subcom. Am. Indsl. Health Coun., Washington, 1990-91; councillor Environ. Mutagen Soc., Washington, 1990-93; chmn. 1st Internat. Symposium on Drug Interaction, 1995. Editor: Toxicity Testing: New Approaches and Applications to Human Risk Assessment, 1985, Genetic Toxicology, 1991, Drug-Drug Interactions: Scientific and Regulatory Perspectives; assoc. editl. bd. Mutation Rsch. jour., 1991. Wis. Legis. scholar, 1969-72. Mem. Environ. Mutagen Soc. (councillor 1990-93), Soc. Toxicology, Internat. Soc. for Studies in Xenobiotics. Office: Hepatic Techs 5202 Westland Blvd Baltimore MD 21227

LI, JAMES, emergency medicine physician; b. Seattle, Jan. 11, 1965. MD, U. Wash., 1992. Resident in emergency medicine Charity Hosp., New Orleans, 1992-94; practice emergency medicine New Orleans, 1994—. Contbr. articles to med. jours. Vol. physician Kikuyu Hosp., Kenya, 1993, Masanga Leprosy Hosp., Sierra Leone, 1993. Mem. Soc. for Acad. Emergency Medicine, Am. Coll. Emergency Physicians, Alpha Omega Alpha. Home: 903 2d St New Orleans LA 70130-5529

LI, JIANMING, molecular and cellular biologist; b. Xinxiang, Henan, China, Oct. 23, 1956; came to U.S., 1983; s. Zhonghe and Zhimei (Liang) L.; m. Wei Xiao, Sept. 27, 1982; children: Christina Bo, Tracy. BS, Wuhan U., 1982; PhD, CUNY, 1989. Assoc. rsch. scientist Yale U., New Haven, 1989—. Contbr. articles to Jour. Cell Biology, Gene, Jour. Bacteriology, others. Recipient Swebilius cancer rsch. award Yale U., 1991. Mem. AAAS, Am. Assn. Cancer Rsch., Am. Soc. Microbiology, N.Y. Acad. Scis. Office: Yale U Sch Medicine 333 Cedar St New Haven CT 06510-3206

LI, JOHN K.J., biomedical engineer, educator; b. Taiwan, Aug. 28, 1950; came to U.S., 1972; s. George Tien-Fu and Yin-Chu (Pan) L.; m. Evangeline Sim, July 14, 1973; children: Michael, Christopher. BSc, U. Manchester, 1972; MS, U. Pa., 1974, PhD, 1978. Rsch. fellow U. Pa., Phila., 1973-77; head biomed. engring., cardiology Presbyn.-U. Pa. Med. Ctr., Phila., 1977-79; asst. prof., assoc. prof. Rutgers U., New Brunswick, N.J., 1979-89; prof. Rutgers U., New Brunswick, 1989—; adj. prof. surgery UMDNJ-Robert Wood Johnson Med. Sch., New Brunswick, 1981—. Author: Arterial System Dynamics, 1987, Comparative Cardiovascular Dynamics of Mammals, 1996; editor: (procs.) 19th NE Bioengring. Conf., 1993, 22d Conf., 1996. Grantee NIH, 1994; recipient Rsch. Initiation award NSF, 1980. Fellow Am. Coll. Cardiology, Am. Coll. Angiology; mem. IEEE (sr., Merit certificates, 1985—, assoc. editor 1987-90, chmn. Engring. in Medicine and Biology Soc. 1985—), Am. Physiol. Soc., Cardiovascular Sys. Dynamics Soc., Am. Heart Assn. (grantee 1980—). Home: 3 Kettering Ct Robbinsville NJ 08691 Office: Dept Biomed Engring Rutgers Univ Piscataway NJ 08855-0909

LI, WEIYE, ophthalmologist, biochemist, educator; b. Zhejiang, China, Oct. 10, 1946; came to U.S., 1990; s. Zhao-ji Li and Qin Yue; m. Xinru Liu, Apr. 12, 1986; 1 child, Yafeng. MD, Peking Second Med. Coll., China, 1970; postgrad., Acad. Med. Scis., China, 1978-80; PhD, U. Pa., 1984. Intern Chao Young Hosp., Peking, 1970-71, resident ophthalmology, 1971-78; rsch. fellow dept. ophthalmology and biochem. grad. sch. Sch. Medicine U. Pa., Phila., 1981-84, postdoctor, asst. prof. dept. ophthalmology Scheie Eye Inst. Sch. Medicine, 1984-85; asst. prof., attending physician ophthalmology Peking Union Med. Coll. Hosp., 1985-86, assoc. prof. ophthalmology, 1986-88, prof. ophthalmology, 1988-93, chmn. dept. ophthalmology, 1989-93; prof. ophthalmology, dir. rsch. dept. ophthalmology, prof. pathology, mem. faculty interdepartmental program molecular biology and biotech. Hahnemann U., Phila., 1990—. Recipient Rsch. award Internat. Juvenile Diabetes Found., 1984-86, 1st Class Sci. and Tech. Advances prize Chinese Ministry Pub. Health, 1988; grantee NIH, 1981-82, 86—, Fight for Sight, Inc., 1982-83, Am. Diabetes Assn., 1990—, Frank E. Snider Trust Fund, 1990—; Postdoctoral fellow Internat. Juvenile Diabetes Found., 1982-84. Mem. Assn. Rsch. in Vision and Ophthalmology, Assn. Chinese Ophthal. Soc. Office: Hahnemann U Dept Ophthalmology MS 209 Broad and Vine Sts Philadelphia PA 19102-1192

LI, YI, health facility investigator; b. Beijing, China, May 28, 1947; came to U.S., 1989; d. Zhiyan and Yunpeng (Zhao) L.; m. Songshun Zhu, Aug. 13, 1970; children: Harry, Jing. MD, Tainjin Med. Coll., 1970, MS, 1981. Physician Tianjin (China) Binjiang Hosp., 1970-72; psychiatrist Tianjin Psychiat. Hosp., 1972-78; neurologist Tianjin Med. Coll. Hosp., 1978-89; asst. rsch. scientist Tianjin Neurol. Inst., 1981-89; rsch. scientist U. Hong Kong, 1986-87; asst. staff investigator Henry Ford Hosp., Detroit, 1991-92, assoc. staff investigator, 1992—. Author: Advances in Pineal Research, 1989, Apoptosis in Cerebral Ischemia, 1994; contbr. articles to profl. jours. Geneva Cantonal U. Ctr. Lab. fellow, 1988-89, Henry Ford Hosp. fellow, 1990-91. Office: Henry Ford Hosp 2799 W Grand Blvd Detroit MI 48202

LIANG, JEROME ZHENGRONG, radiology educator; b. Chongging, Sichuan, China, June 23, 1958; came to U.S., 1981; BS, Lanzhou U., China, 1982; PhD, CUNY, 1987. Rsch. instr. Albert Einstein Coll. Medicine, Bronx, N.Y., 1986-87; rsch. assoc. Duke U. Med. Ctr., Durham, N.C., 1987-89; asst. med. rsch. prof. Duke U. Med. Ctr., 1990-92; asst. prof. SUNY, Stony Brook, 1992—. Contbr. articles to profl. jours. Grantee Soc. Thoracic Radiology, 1994-95, ADAC Rsch. Lab., 1995-96; recipient NIH awards, 1990-94, 95—, AHA award, 1996—. Mem. Assn. Chinese-Am. Sr. Profls., Inc. (trustee 1994—). Office: Dept Radiology SUNY Stony Brook 4th Fl Rm 092 Stony Brook NY 11794

LIANG, TEHMING, dermatologist; b. Tainan, Taiwan, Apr. 14, 1945; came to U.S., 1969; BS, Nat. Taiwan U., Taipei, 1968; PhD, U. Chgo., 1973; MD, U. Miami, Fla., 1987. Rsch. assoc. Ben May Inst., U. Chgo., 1973-76, rsch. asst. prof., 1976-77; sr. rsch. biochemist Merck Sharp & Dohme Rsch. Labs., Rahway, N.J., 1977-81, rsch. fellow, 1981-85; resident in internal medicine Robert Wood Johnson U. Hosp., New Burnswick, N.J., 1987-88; resident in dermatology U. Chgo. Hosps., 1989-91; assoc. prof. dermatology Wright State U., Dayton, Ohio, 1992-95, chn. dept., dir. dermatology residency program, 1994-95; chief dermatology VA Med. Ctr., Dayton, 1992-95; dermatologist pvt. practice, Bolingbrook, Ill., 1995—. Mem. AMA, Am. Soc. Biochemistry and Molecular Biology, Soc. Neurosci., The Endocrine Soc., Soc. Investigative Dermatology, N.Y. Acad. Scis. Office: 454 W Boughton Rd Ste B Bolingbrook IL 60440

LIANG, VERA BEH-YUIN TSAI, psychiatrist, educator; b. Shanghai, China, July 29, 1946; came to U.S., 1970, naturalized, 1978; d. Ming Sang and Mea Ling Chu Tsai; m. Hanson Liang, Nov. 6, 1971; children: Eric G., Jason G. MBBS, U. Hong Kong, 1969. Diplomate Am. Bd. Psychiatry and Neurology. Intern Cambridge Hosp. (Mass.), 1970-71; resident Hillside div. L.I. Jewish Med. Ctr., New Hyde Park, N.Y., 1971-73; fellow Albert Einstein Coll. Medicine, Bronx, N.Y., 1973-75, asst. clin. prof., 1989-95; instr. SUNY, Bklyn., 1975-79; asst. prof. SUNY, Stony Brook, 1979-89; med. dir. Hillside Ea. Queens Ctr., Queens Village, N.Y., 1977-90, 91-92; staff child psychiatrist Schneider Children's Hosp., New Hyde Park, N.Y., 1990-92; sr. psychiatrist South Oaks Hosp., Amityville, N.Y., 1992—; cons. in field. Contbr. articles to profl. jours. Mem. Am. Psychiat. Assn., Am. Acad. Child Psychiatry. Office: South Oaks Hosp 400 Sunrise Hwy Amityville NY 11701-2508

LIAO, JAMES KUANG-JAN, cardiologist, educator; b. Taipei, Taiwan, Sept. 14, 1959; came to U.S., 1964; s. George S. and Helen H. (Huang) L.; m. Olivia Tan-Yu Chan, June 2, 1990; children: Annette, Thomas. BS, UCLA, 1981; MD, U. Calif. San Francisco, 1985. Diplomate Am. B. Internal Medicine, Cardiovascular Medicine. Intern Brigham & Young Women's Hosp., Boston, 1985-86, resident, 1986-88, assoc. physician, 1991—; asst. physician Mass. Gen. Hosp., Boston, 1990-91; instr. medicine Harvard Med. Sch., Boston, 1990-95; asst. prof. medicine Brigham & Women's Hosp., Boston, 1995—. Fellow ACP, Am. Coll. Cardiology; mem. Am. Fedn. for Clin. Rsch., Chinese Am. Med. Soc. (v.p. 1995), Mass. Med. Soc., Am. Heart Assn. (basic sci. coun. 1993—). Republican. Home: 12 Audubon Rd Weston MA 02193 Office: Brigham & Women's Hosp 75 Francis St Boston MA 02115

LIAU, GENE, medical educator; b. Hsing-Chu, Taiwan, Nov. 28, 1954; came to U.S., 1965; BS in Biology, U. N.C., 1977; DPhil, Vanderbilt U., 1982. Postdoctoral fellow Lab. Molecular Biology Nat. Cancer Inst. NIH, Bethesda, Md., 1982-85; assoc. mem. Dept. Cell Biology Revlon Biotech. Rsch. Ctr., Rockville, Md., 1985-87; scientist I Dept. Molecular Biology Am. Red Cross Jerome H. Holland Lab., Rockville, 1987-90, scientist II, 1990—; assoc. prof. Dept. Anatomy George Washington U. Med. Ctr., Washington, 1995—; mem. AHA Vascular Wall Biology Rsch. Study Com., 1992-96, Pathology A Study Sect. NIH, 1994—; invited spkr. in field. Contbr. articles to profl. jours. Arthritis Found. fellow, 1982-85; pub. health svc. grantee, 1988—; recipient Nat. Rsch. Svc. award NIH, 1977-81, Rsch. Career Devel. award, 1990-95. Mem. AAAS, Am. Soc. Cell Biology, Am. Heart Assn. Coun. Basic Sci. (Established Investigator 1990, Grant-in-Aid 1992-95, 95—), Soc. Chinese Bioscientists, Sigma Xi. Home: 14900 Kelley Farm Dr Darnestown MD 20874 Office: Dept Molecular Biology Holland Lab 15601 Crabbs Branch Way Rockville MD 20855*

LIBBERT, EIKE, plant physiologist; b. Osterwieck, Germany, Apr. 22, 1928; s. Walter Wilhelm and Hedwig Sophie (Krelle) L.; m. Waldtraut Anni Koehne, Mar. 24, 1951; 1 child, Lutz. Diploma Biology, U. Greifswald (Germany), 1951, D Natural Scis., 1952; D. Natural Scis., habilitatus, U. Berlin, 1954. Asst. U. Berlin, 1952-55, docent, 1955-59, assoc. prof., 1959-63; dir. Inst. Botany U. Rostock (Germany), 1959-68, prof., 1963-96, head dept. plant physiology and biochemistry, 1968-96. Author: Textbook of Plant Physiology, 5 edits., 1973-93; editor: General Biology, 7 edits, 1976-91; co-editor: Encyclopedia Biology, 3 edits., 1976-81, Dictionary Plant Physiology, 1984. Mem. Rotary Internat. Home: Grohner Kamp 10, D 28759 Bremen Germany

LIBERTI, PAUL ALFONSO, biotechnology executive, inventor, entrepreneur, consultant; b. Lyndhurst, N.J., Mar. 18, 1936; s. Paul Frank and Rose (Pollara) L.; m. Rae Francis, July 1, 1961 (div. Jan. 1996); children: Paul P., Theodore L., Roseanne, Joseph F. AB, Columbia U., 1959; postgrad., Loyola U., Chgo., 1959-61; PhD, Stevens Inst. Tech., Hoboken, N.J., 1966. Prof. biotechnology, immunology Jefferson Med. Coll., Phila., 1968-83, adj. prof., 1984—; pres., founder Immunochem. Assocs., 1981—; pres., founder Immunicon Corp., Huntingdon Valley, Pa., 1984-91, dir. R & D, 1991-95; vis. scientist Inst. for Med. Rsch., London, 1976-77; mem. adv. bd. Ben Franklin Partnership; mem. study sect. NIH/NSF U.S. Army Breast Cancer Program. Mem. adv. bd. Jour. Immunology, Molecular Immunology; contbr. more than 60 articles to profl. jours. Founder, speaker Anti-Drug Program, Bucks County, Pa., 1981-83. Recipient Rsch. Career award NIH, 1971-77. Mem. Am. Assn. Immunologists, Am. Soc. Hematologists, Internat. Soc. Hematopoetic Graft Engring. Home: 1503 Grasshopper Rd Huntingdon Valley PA 19006-5807 Office: Immunicon Corp 1310 Masons Mill Business Park Huntingdon Valley PA 19006-3515

LIBERTINO, JOHN A., physician, surgeon, health facility administrator; b. Brooklyn, N.Y., Apr. 9, 1940; s. John A. and Lucy L. (Yaccarino) L.; m. Mary Jo Paolo, July 20, 1963; children: John P., Chris. Student, NYU, 1957-61; BA, Windham Coll., 1961; MD, Georgetown U., 1965. Resident gen. surgery U. Rochester (N.Y.) Strong Meml. Hosp., 1965-67; resident urology Sch. Medicine Yale U., New Haven, Conn., 1967-70; chmn. dept. urology Lahey Clinic Med. Ctr., Burlington, Mass., 1970—, chief surgery, 1984-96; also chmn. bd., 1995—. Author: Reconstructive Urological Surgery, 3rd edit., 1978, 86, 96, Renovascular Surgery, 1984, Adrenal Surgery, 1992. Fellow Am. Coll. Surgeons (gov. 1986-92), Am. Urol. Assn. (scientific program com., pres. N.E. sect., Hugh Hampton Young award 1988). Office: Lahey Clinic Med Ctr 41 Mall Rd PO Box 541 Burlington MA 02805

LICHTBLAU, SHELDON, orthopedic surgeon; b. Union City, N.J., Feb. 27, 1926; s. Max and Ella (Baumgarten) L.; m. Lucile Makowsky, Nov. 11, 1956; children: Daniel, Joseph, Ethan, Joshua. BS, Rutgers U., 1948; MS, U. Wis., 1949; MB, Chgo. Med. Sch., 1953, MD, 1954. Bd. cert. orthopedics Am. Acad. Orthopaedic Surgeons. Intern L.A. County Hosp., 1953-54; resident gen. surgery Bronx & Bronx VA Hosps., 1954-56; resident orthopedic surgery Hosp. for Spl. Surgery, N.Y.C., 1956-59; asst. attending physician Mt. Sinai Hosp., N.Y.C., 1959-70, assoc. attending physician, 1970—; attending physician Doctor's Hosp., N.Y.C., 1954—, chief orthopedics, 1983-90; chief orthopedics Hebrew Home for Aged, Bronx, 1980—; cons. orthopedics Coler Hosp., Roosevelt Island, N.Y., 1994—. Pres. PTA 5th Grade Sch., Englewood, N.J., 1975; mem. grievance com. N.Y. Acad. Medicine, N.Y.C., 1980-93. With USN, 1944-46. Fellow ACS, Am. Acad. Orthopedic Surgeons, Ea. Orthopedic Surgeons, F.Y. County Med. Soc. Democrat. Jewish. Office: 1100 Park Ave New York NY 10128

LICHTENBERG, DEBORAH A., nurse epidemiologist; b. Boston, May 9, 1952; d. Rose Clair (Martucci) L. BSN, Salem State Coll., 1987. Cert. infection control APIC, CBIC. Nurse epidemiologist Boston City Hosp., 1979-87, Deaconess Hosp., Boston, 1987—; cons. Kendall Healthcare Products Divsn., Mansfield, Mass., 1980—, New England Organ Bank, Boston, 1994-95; mem. adv. bd. Jour. HCMM, Chgo., 1990-92, 3M, Minn., 1995-96. Contbr. articles to profl. jours. Mem. Assn. for Practitioner in Infection Control and Hosp. Epidemiology (pres. 1989-90, bd. dirs. 1985-87, membership dir. 1994-95). Democrat. Roman Catholic. Home: 12 Fiske St Revere MA 02151 Office: Deaconess Hosp 1 Deaconess Rd Boston MA 02215

LICHTENBERG, PHILIP, social work educator; b. Schenectady, N.Y., Oct. 1, 1926; s. Chester and Bertha (Stein) L.; m. Elsa Russell, June 15, 1949; children: Erik Russell, Andrew Adam, Thomas Philip, Peter Alexander. BS, Case Western Res. U., 1948, MA, 1950, PhD, 1952. Lic. psychologist, Pa. Rsch. fellow in clin. psychology Harvard U., 1951-52; rsch. asst. prof. of Psychology NYU, N.Y.C., 1952-54; rsch. psychologist Michael Reese Hosp., Chgo., 1954-57; assoc. social psychologist N.Y. State Dept. of Mental Hygiene, Syracuse, N.Y., 1957-61; from assoc. prof. to prof. social work and social rsch. Bryn Mawr (Pa.) Coll., 1961-96, prof. emeritus, 1996—; bd. dirs. The Gestalt Therapy Inst. of Phila., Bryn Mawr, Pa. Author (book) Psychoanalysis: Radical and Conservative, 1969, Getting Even, 1988, Undoing the Clinch of Oppression, 1990; co-author (book) Motivation for Child Psychiatry Treatment, 1960; contbr. articles to profl. jours. Sgt. USAF, 1944-46, ETO. Mem. Am. Psychological Assn., Coun. on Social Work Edn., AAAS, AAUP, Am. Orthopsychiatric Assn., Pa. Psychological Assn., Bertha Capen Reynolds Soc. Home: 25 S Lowrys Ln Bryn Mawr PA 19010-1402 Office: Bryn Mawr Coll 300 Airdale Rd Bryn Mawr PA 19010-1646

LICHTENFELD, AMY DALE, internist, allergist; b. N.Y.C., Feb. 16, 1959; d. Julius and Judith (Balcourt) L.; m. Jeffrey Michael Loria, Nov. 19, 1989; children: Jessica Brooke, Joshua Daniel. BA, U. Pa., 1980, MD, 198. Diplomate Am. Bd. Internal Medicine, Am. Bd. Allergy and Immunology. Intern, then resident in internal medicine Lenox Hill Hosp., N.Y.C., 1984-87, attending staff emergency room, 1987-88; fellow in allergy and immunology N.Y. Hosp.-Cornell U. Med. Ctr., N.Y.C., 1988-90; pvt. practice, N.Y.C., 1990—. Mem. ACP, AMA, Am. Acad. Allergy, Arthritis and Immunology, Med. Soc. State N.Y., New York County Med. Soc., New York County Allergy Soc. Office: 19 E 80th St New York NY 10021

LICHTENSTEIN, ALICE HINDA, nutritional biochemist; b. N.Y.C.; d. Armand and Adelaide (Goldstein) L.; m. Barry R. Goldin: children: David Aaron Lichtenstein Goldin, Rachel Bella Lichtenstein Goldin. BS, Cornell U., 1971; MS, Pa. State U., 1973, Harvard U., 1975; DSc, Harvard U., 1979. Rsch. assoc. Boston U., 1982-83, asst. prof., 1983-88. scientist II Jean Mayer USDA Human Nutrition Rsch. Ctr. on Aging, Boston, 1988-94, scientist I, 1994—; assoc. prof. sch. nutrition Tufts U., Boston, 1994—; bd. dirs. Edinformer, Marblehead, Mass. Mem. editl. bd. Womens' Letter, 1990-91, Jour. Nutrition, 1993—; contbr. articles to profl. jours. Mem. Am. Inst. Nutrition (new mems. com. 1994—), Am. Soc. Clin. Nutrition, Am. Heart Assn. (basic sci. coun. 1984—, arteriosclerosis coun. 1980—, nutrition com. 1993—, bd. dirs. Greater Boston chpt. 1983-86, rsch. grant peer rev. com. Mass. chpt. 1988-90, chair task force on heart health edn. in young 1986-89, chair sub task force on evaluation task force on heart-health sch. lunch 1992-93), Phi Kappa Phi, Kappa Omicron Nu. Office: Tufts Univ HNRCA USDA 711 Washington St Boston MA 02111

LICHTENSTEIN, ERIC S., endocrinologist; b. N.Y.C., May 5, 1941; s. Sam and Rose L.; m. Maria S. Guoth. BA, Colgate U., 1962; MD, Albert Einstein Coll. Medicine, 1968. Intern in medicine Columbia U Coll. P. & S., Harlem Hosp., N.Y.C., 1968-69; resident in medicine NYU, N.Y. VA Hosp., N.Y.C., 1969-71; attending physician, prin. investigator Walter Reed Army Med. Ctr., Washington D.C., 1971-73; endocrinology fellow Columbia P. & S. Presbyn. Hosp., N.Y.C., 1973-76; chief endocrinologist Hosp. For Joint Diseases, N.Y.C., 1976-79; med. dir. N.H. County Med. Soc., 1979-80; pvt. practice in endocrinology, attending physician Yale N.H. Hosp., 1979-81; with endocrine divsn. Q-LI Med. Group, 1981—; dir. div. endocrinology, diabetes & metabolism North Shore Univ. Hosp., Forest Hills, N.Y., 1986—; pres. Linkirk Inc., N.Y.C., 1973-90; mng. dir. Med. Cybernetics, Inc., N.Y.C., 1991—. Patentee in field. Maj. U.S. Army, 1971-73. Fellow Am. Coll. Physicians, Am. Assn. Clin. Endocrinologists, Am. Coll. Endocrinology; mem. Am. Med. Informatics Assn., The Endocrine Soc. Office: North Shore Univ Hosp 102-01 66th Rd Forest Hills NY 11375

LICHTENSTEIN, LAWRENCE MARK, allergy, immunology educator, physician; b. Washington, May 31, 1934; s. Samuel and Lillian (Colodny) L.; m. Carolyn Eggert, June 15, 1956; children: Elizabeth, Joshua, Rebekah. MD, U. Chgo., 1960; PhD, Johns Hopkins U., 1965. Diplomate: Am. Bd. Allergy and Immunology. Intern, Johns Hopkins Hosp., 1960-61, resident in medicine, 1965-66; asst. prof. medicine Johns Hopkins U. Sch. Medicine, 1966-70, assoc. prof., 1970-75, prof., 1975—, dir. Johns Hopkins Asthma and Allergy Ctr.; mem. Nat. Adv. Allergy and Infectious Diseases Coun. Mem. editorial bd.: Clin. Immunology and Pathology, Immunology, Pulmonary, Allergy; editor 11 books; contbr. articles to profl. jours. Fellow ACP; mem. Am. Soc. Pharmacology and Exptl. Therapeutics, Am. Assn. Immunology (sec., treas.), Am. Fedn. Clin. Rsch., Am. Soc. Clin. Investigation, Am. Acad. Allergy and Immunology (past pres.), Am. Soc. Exptl. Pathology, Collegium Internat. Allergologicum (pres.), Assn. Am. Physicians. Democrat. Jewish. Home: 1600 The Terraces Baltimore MD 21209-3637 Office: John Hopkins Asthma & Allergy Ctr 5501 Hopkins Bayview Cir Baltimore MD 21224-6821

LICHTENSTEIN, STEVEN, gastroenterologist, medical educator; b. Phila., Sept. 26, 1961; s. Herbert and Marlene (Brodsky) L. BA in Biology and Chemistry, Beaver Coll., 1986; DO, Phila. Coll. Osteo. Medicine, 1990. Intern Mercy Cath. Med. Ctr., Darby, Pa., 1990-91; resident in internal medicine Mercy Cath. Med. Ctr., 1991-93, fellow in gastroenterology, 1993-95, attending physician, mem. tchg. staff, 1995—; pvt. practice gastroenterologist Darby, 1995—. Mem. AMA, Am. Soc. Gastrointestinal Endoscopy, Am. Gastroent. Assn., Lambda Omicron Gamma. Office: 1501 Lansdowne Ave Ste 205 Darby PA 19023

LICHTER, PAUL RICHARD, ophthalmology educator; b. Detroit, Mar. 7, 1939; s. Max D. and Buena (Epstein) L.; m. Carolyn Goode, 1960; children: Laurie, Susan. BA, U. Mich., 1960, MD, 1964, MS, 1968. Diplomate Am. Bd. Ophthalmology. Asst. to assoc. prof. ophthalmology U. Mich., Ann Arbor, 1971-78, prof., chmn. dept. ophthalmology, 1978—; chmn. Am. Bd. Ophthalmology, 1987. Editor-in-chief Ophthalmology jour., 1986-94. Served to lt. comdr. USN, 1969-71. Fellow Am. Acad. Opthalmology (bd. dirs. 1981—, pres. 1996, sr. honor award 1986); mem. AMA, Pan Am. assn. Opthalmology (bd. dirs. 1988—, sec.-treas. English speaking countries 1991-95), Mich. State Med. Soc., Washtenaw County Med. Soc., Mich. Opthalmol. Soc. (pres. 1993-95), Assn. Univ. Profs. Opthalmology (trustee 1986-93, pres. 1991-92), Alpha Omega Alpha. Office: U Mich Med Sch Kellogg Eye Ctr 1000 Wall St Ann Arbor MI 48105-1912

LICHTI, DOUGLAS JON, physician, surgeon; b. Hebron, Nebr., Oct. 27, 1955; s. Lawrence Vernon and Edna Faye (Kempf) L.; m. Margaret Gayle Brendel, Sept. 15, 1979; children: Kristin, Brandon, Sara. BS in Chemistry, Nebr. Wesleyan U., Lincoln, 1976; MD, U. Nebr., 1979. Diplomate Am. Bd. Gen. Surgery. Gen. surgery resident U. Kans. Med. Ctr., Kansas City, 1979-84; gen. surgeon North Platte, Nebr., 1984-90, Provo, Utah, 1990—. Fellow ACS; mem. Utah Med. Assn. Republican. Home: 675 S Riverbreeze Dr Orem UT 84058

LICHTIG, LEO KENNETH, health economist; b. Bklyn., Oct. 20, 1953; s. Samuel and Alyne Norma (Strauss) L.; m. Susan Mary Walsh, May 15, 1977; children: Brielle Joy, Danica Jill. BS, MS, Rensselaer Poly. Inst., 1974, PhD, 1976. Asst. prof. SUNY, Albany, 1976-77; project specialist, econometrician N.J. State Dept. Health, Trenton, 1977-82; dir. utilization econs. and rsch. Empire Blue Cross/Blue Shield, Albany, 1982-90; v.p. rsch. and demonstration Health Care Rsch. Found., Albany, 1982-90; v.p. Network, Inc., Randolph, N.J., Latham, N.Y., 1990-94; sr. v.p., chief info. officer Network, Inc., Randolph, 1994—; pvt. practice cons., Latham, 1982-90; mem. nat. diagnosis related group, steering com. health care fin. adminstrn. Yale U., Washington, 1979-81; mem. adj. faculty Russell Sage Grad. Sch. Health Adminstrn., Albany, 1986—, Union Coll. Grad. Mgmt. Inst., Schenectady, N.Y., 1991-92; expert reviewer Health Care Financing Adminstrn., Washington, 1987, 89. Author: Hospital Information Systems for Case Mix Management, 1986; contbg. editor (newsletter) Nat. Report on Computers & Health, 1982-85; contbr. articles to profl. jours. Mem. tech. adv. com. Statewide Planning and Rsch. Coop. System, N.Y. State Dept. Health. Mem. Assn. for Health Svcs. Rsch., Am. Statis. Assn. (com. on privacy and confidentiality 1981-84, subcom. on quality and productivity measures 1988-90), Healthcare Fin. Mgmt. Assn. Office: Network Inc 1572 Sussex Tpke Randolph NJ 07869-1822

LICHTIGER, MONTE, physician, anesthesiologist, educator; b. Bronx, N.Y., July 12, 1939; s. Manuel and Sylvia Lichtiger; m. Barbara Zucker, Aug. 25, 1962; children: Shari Beth, Marcie Dawn, Adam Brett. AB, Columbia U., 1961; MD, Albert Einstein Coll. Medicine, 1965. Staff USAF Wilfred Hall Hosp., San Antonio, 1969-71; instr. U. Miami, Fla., 1969, asst. prof., 1971-74, clin. assoc. prof., 1974-83, clin. prof., 1983—; clin. asst. prof. U. Tex.-San Antonio, 1969-71; bd. dirs. Anesthesiologists Profl. Assurance Trust, Anesthesiologists Profl. Assurance Co. NIH fellow in anesthesiology U. Miami (Fla.), 1966-69. Served with USAF, 1969-71. Vice chmn. anesthesiology dept. Mt. Sinai Med. Ctr., Miami, Fla. Mem. Am. Soc. Anesthesiologists (house of dels., sec.-treas. 1995, 2d v.p. 1996), Fla. Soc. Anesthesiologists (bd. dirs. 1993—), Am. Med. Assn. Jewish. Author: Introduction to the Practice of Anesthesia, 1975, 2d edit., 1978; editor Current Revs. in Clin. Anesthesiology, Current Revs. for Nurse Anesthetists. Office: Mt Sinai Med Ctr 4300 Alton Rd Miami FL 33140-2849

LICHTMAN, ANTON RODNEY, physician; b. Outjo, Namibia, Oct. 2, 1953; s. Joseph Alexander and Stella Juliet (Shapiro) L.; m. Valerie Mercia Hurnimann, Nov. 30, 1990. MB ChB, U. Cape Town, South Africa, 1977; FFA, Coll. Medicine, South Africa, 1985. Diplomate South Africa Med. Dental Coun., Namibia Med. Bd., Gen. Med. Coun. Eng. Intern Oshakati Hosp., Namabia, 1978; med. officer Tygerberg Hosp., South Africa, 1979-80, Northwick Park Hosp., London, 1982-83; sr. med. officer Windhoek (Namibia) Ctrl. Hosp., 1980-82, cons. in intensive care, 1986—; registrar in anesthesiology Groote Schuur Hosp., South Africa, 1983-86; prof. in critical care medicine U. Namibia, 1990—. Exec. mem. Med. Bd. Namibia, 1995—. Mem. South African Soc. Anaesthesiologists, Critical Care Soc. South Africa. Jewish. Home: 19 Hoepfner St, Windhoek Namibia Office: Windhoek Ctrl Hosp, Intensive Care Unit, Windhoek Namibia

LICHTMAN, MARSHALL ALBERT, medical educator, physician, scientist; b. N.Y.C., June 23, 1934; s. Samuel and Vera L.; m. Alice Jo Maisel, June 23, 1957; children—Susan, Joanne, Pamela. AB, Cornell U., 1955; MD, U. Buffalo, 1960. Diplomate Am. Bd. Internal Medicine. Resident in medicine Strong Meml. Hosp., 1960-63; surgeon USPHS and postdoctoral research assoc. Sch. Pub. Health, U. N.C., 1963-65; chief resident and instr. medicine Strong Meml. Hosp., 1965-66; sr. instr. medicine, research trainee in hematology U. Rochester Sch. Medicine, N.Y., 1966-67, asst. prof. medicine, spl. postdoctoral research fellow in hematology, 1968-70, assoc. prof. medicine and radiation biology and biophysics, 1971-74, prof. medicine and radiation biology and biophysics, 1974—, chief hematology unit dept. medicine, 1975-77, co. chief, 1977-89; sr. assoc. dean for acad. affairs and research, 1979-89, dean Sch. of Medicine and Dentistry, 1990-95; exec. v.p. rsch. and med. affairs Leukemia Soc. Am., Inc., 1996—; vis. prof. univs.; lectr. in field. Leukemia Soc. Am. scholar, 1969-74; recipient contracts U.S. Army Research, 1972-78, U.S. Dept. Energy, 1972-80; USPHS grantee, 1971-95. Editor: Abnormalities of Granulocytes and Monocytes, 1975, Hematology for Practitioners, 1978, Hematology and Oncology, 1980, (with W.J. William, E. Beutler, A.J. Erslev) Hematology, 3d edit., 1983, 4th edit., 1990, (with E. Beutler, B. Coller, T.J. Kipps) 5th edit., 1995; (with H.J. Meiselman and P.L. LaCelle) White Cell Mechanics: Basic Science and Clinical Aspects, 1984. Contbr. articles to profl. jours. Master ACP; mem. NIH (hematology study sect., 1982-86), Am. Fedn. Clin. Research, AAAS, Am. Soc. Hematology (pres. 1989), Internat. Soc. Hematology, N.Y. Acad. Scis., Am. Soc. Clin. Investigation, Assn. Am. Physicians, Am. Assn. for Cancer Research, Am. Physiol. Soc., Reticuloendothelial Soc., Soc. Exptl. Biology and Medicine, Am. Soc. Cell Biology. Home: 64 Woodbury Pl Rochester NY 14618-3445 Office: U Rochester Sch Medicine & Dentistry Box 610 601 Elmwood Ave Rochester NY 14642-9999

LICKER, KENNETH IRA, physician; b. Newark, Apr. 7, 1944; s. Milton and Rheda (Sokol) L.; m. Linda Arlene Shaw, Nov. 25, 1965; children: David, Carolyn, Robin, Eric. BA, Montclair (N.J.) State Coll., 1965; MD, N.Y. Med. Coll., 1972. Diplomate Am. Bd. Urology. Urologist North Tex. Clinic Assn., Dallas, 1980-85, S.W. Urology Assocs., Dallas, 1987; pvt. practice urologist DeSoto, Tex., 1987—. Maj. U.S. Army, 1978-80. Fellow ACS; mem. Am. Urological Assn., AMA, Am. Fertility Soc., Sinfonia, Phi Mu Alpha. Jewish. Home: 1325 Green Hills Ct Duncanville TX 75137-2841 Office: 951 York Dr # 102 De Soto TX 75115-2052

LICOPANTIS, DEAN PETER, podiatric surgeon; b. Queens, N.Y., July 5, 1961; s. Peter Gus and Yolanda (Diamantis) L.; m. Katherine J. Kozakis, June 18, 1988. BS, U. Albany, 1983; D of Podiatric Medicine, Pa. Coll. Podiatric Medicine, 1988. Diplomate Am. Bd. Podiatric Orthops., Am. Bd. Podiatric Surgery. Podiatric surg. resident Osteo. Med. Ctr., Phila., 1988-89; podiatric surgeon Ankle & Foot Surgery, P.A., Parsippany, N.J., 1994—; mem. staff Morristown (N.J.) Meml. Hosp., 1995—. Mem. Am. Podiatric Med. Assn., N.J. Podiatric Med. Assn. Greek Orthodox. Office: Ankle and Foot Surgery PA 1130 Rte 46 W Parsippany NJ 07054

LIDOFSKY, STEVEN DAVID, medical educator; b. Bklyn., Jan. 19, 1954; s. Leon Julian and Eleanor Helen (Liebman) L.; m. Elisabeth Tang Barfod, May 3, 1982; children: Benjamin Barfod, Anna Barfod. BA, Columbia U., 1975, PhD, 1980, MD, 1982. Bd. cert. in gastroenterology and internal medicine Am. Bd. Internal Medicine. Intern U. Colo., Denver, 1982-83, resident, 1983-85, chief med. resident, 1985-86; fellow in gastroenterology U. Calif., San Francisco, 1986-90, asst. prof. medicine, 1990—. Contbr. articles to profl. jours. Recipient Liver Scholar award Am. Liver Found., 1990-93, Rsch. award Am. Diabetes Assn., 1996. Mem. Am. Assn. for Study of Liver Diseases, Am. Fedn. for Clin. Rsch., Am. Gastroenterol. Assn. (Fiterman Found. Rsch. award 1994), Calif. Acad. Medicine. Office: Univ Calif San Francisco GI Unit S357 San Francisco CA 94143-0538

LIEBER, RICHARD LOUIS, biomedical engineering scientist, educator; b. Walnut Creek, Calif., Dec. 14, 1956; s. Richard and Janet Elizabeth (Stone) L.; m. Deborah Jane Chippendale, Oct. 22, 1980; children: Katelyn Suzanne, Kristin Michelle. BS with honors, U. Calif., Davis, 1978, PhD, 1982. Biomed. engr. VA Med. Ctr., San Diego, 1983—; assoc. prof. surgery U. Calif., San Diego, 1985—; cons. Pref Med. Products Inc., 1987—. Contbr. sci. papers to profl. publs.; inventor surgical myometor, 1985, adaptive muscle stimulator, 1987. Faculty advisor Inter-Varsity Christian Fellowship, San Diego, 1984—. Recipient Presdl. award Am. Acad. Cerebral Palsy, 1984; State of Calif. Gov.'s scholar, 1974. Mem. IEEE, Orthopaedic Rsch. Soc., Biophys. Soc. (Talbot award 1981), Rehab. Engring. Soc. N.Am., Soc. Neursci., Am. Soc. Biomechanics, Am. Physiol. Soc. Republican. Home: 2816 Jacaranda Ave Carlsbad CA 92009-9216 Office: U Calif Dept Of Orthopaedics # V-151 San Diego CA 92161

LIEBERMAN, EDWIN JAMES, psychiatrist; b. Milw., Nov. 21, 1934. AB, U. Calif., 1955, MD, 1958; MPH, Harvard U., 1963. Intern USPHS Hosp., Staten Island, 1958-59; resident in psychiatry Mass. Mental Health Ctr., 1959-61, Putnam Children's Ctr., Boston, 1962-63, Hillcrest Children's Ctr., 1965-66; asst. clin. prof. Howard U. Sch. Medicine, Washington, 1967-76; assoc. clin. prof. George Washington U. Sch. Medicine, Washington, 1976-87; adj. prof. dept. family and community devel. U. Md., 1987-90; clin. prof. George Washington U. Sch. Medicine, 1990—; pvt. practice Family Inst., Chtd.; psychiatrist extramural program NIMH, 1963-67, chief ctr. for child and family mental health, 1969-73; cons. Peace Corps, 1963-64, UNICEF, 1965-66, WHO, 1974; coord. family therapy Hillcrest Children's Ctr., 1971-74; lectr. Internacia Esperanto Kongresa U., Beijing, 1986; bd. chmn. Ctr. for Population Options, 1981-83; population rsch. adv. com. NIH, 1967-70. Author: Acts of Will: The Life and Work of Otto Rank, 1985, rev. edition, 1993. Capt., med. dir. USPHSR. Fellow APHA (project fir. mental health/family planning 1972-77), Am. Psychiat. Assn.; mem. Esperantic Studies Found. (sec.), Universala Esperanto Asocio (del. in medicine). Office: 3900 Northampton St NW Washington DC 20015-2951

LIEBERMAN, ELLIOTT, urologist; b. Paterson, N.J., May 14, 1951; s. Benjamin and Henrietta (Reback) L.; children: Brian Howard, Dana Elyse. BA in Biochemistry cum laude, Cornell U., 1972; MD, SUNY, Bklyn., 1976. Diplomate Am. Bd. Urology. Intern, gen. resident in surgery Mt. Sinai Hosp., N.Y.C., 1976-78; resident in urology SUNY-Downstate Med. Ctr., Bklyn., 1978-81; active attending staff North Shore U. Hosp., various cities, N.Y.; co-chief divsn. urology North Shore U. Hosp., Plainview, N.Y., 1992—; mem. adv. bd. Vis. Nurse Svc. N.Y.; mem. quality assurance com. White Oaks Nursing Home, Woodbury, N.Y. Mem. AMA, Med. Soc. State N.Y., Nassau County Med. Soc., N.Y. State Urol. Soc. Office: 875 Old Country Rd Ste 301 Plainview NY 11803

LIEBERMAN, FLORENCE, clinical social worker, educator; b. N.Y.C., Apr. 16, 1918; d. Simon and Fredericka (Joseph) Rosenblum; m. Lawrence Lieberman, Sept. 1, 1940; children: Joan, Paul. BA, Hunter Coll., 1938; MSS, Smith Coll., 1956; D in Social Work, Columbia U., 1968. Diplomate Am. Bd. Examiners in Clin. Social Work. Social investigator Dept. Social Svcs., N.Y.C., 1939-46; researcher, cons. for various city govt offices N.Y.C., 1946-56; sr. social worker, student supr., group therapist Madleine Borg Child Guidance Clinic Jewish Family Svcs., N.Y.C., 1956-66; prof. Hunter Coll. Sch. Social Work, N.Y.C., 1966-86; vis. John Milner prof. U. So. Calif., 1988; psychotherapist Scarsdale, N.Y., 1968—. Author: Before Addiction, Clinical Social Work with Children; editor: Clinical Social Workers As Psychotherapists, Child & Adolescent Social Work Jour.; adv. editor Clin. Social Work Jour.; co-editor Aging in Good Health : A Quality Life Style for the Later Years, 1993; contbr. numerous articles to profl. jours. Recipient Van Ophuijsen Meml. award, Jewish Bd. of Guardians, 1964, Day-Garret award Smith Coll. Sch. of Social Work, 1986; named Disting. Practitioner in Social Work, 1983; elected Hall of Fame Hunter Coll. CUNY, 1994. Fellow Internat. Conf. for Advancement Pvt. Practice, Am. Orthopsychiat. Assn.(life); mem. NASW (charter), Am. Group Psychotherapy Assn., N.Y. State Soc. Clin. Social Work Psychotherapy (diplomate). Office: 315 Wyndcliffe Rd Scarsdale NY 10583-4832

LIEBERMAN, HARVEY JOEL, mental health administrator, psychologist; b. Bklyn., Dec. 7, 1943; s. Leonard and Sylvia Lieberman; m. Carol M. Schneider, Apr. 12, 1970; 1 child, Jay. BE, Cooper Union, 1966; MS in Psychology, Pa. State U., 1970, PhD in Clin. Psychology, 1974. Lic. psychologist, N.Y. Dir. Bayview Manor/South Beach Psychiat. Ctr., Bklyn., 1974-79; chief community residential treatment svc. South Beach Psychiat. Ctr., S.I., 1979-87; exec. dir. Inst. for Community Living, Bklyn., 1986-87; dir. treatment svcs. South Beach Psychiat. Ctr., Staten Island, 1987-96; exec. dir. Choices Inst. for Cmty. Living, Bklyn., 1996—; internat. cons. in field; adj. prof. L.I. U., Bklyn., 1985—; vis. assoc. prof. Rutgers U., 1986-88; adj. assoc. prof. NYU, 1991—. Contbr. articles to profl. jours. Fellow Am. Coll. Mental Health Adminstrs.; mem. APA, AAAS, Ea. Evaluation and Rsch. Soc. Home: 31 Oxford Pl Rockville Centre NY 11570-1829

LIEBERMAN, HARVEY MICHAEL, hepatologist, gastroenterologist, educator; b. N.Y.C., Feb. 24, 1949; s. Louis and Ellie (Miller) L.; m. Lewette Alexandra Fielding, Nov. 24, 1985. BA magna cum laude, NYU, 1972, MD, 1976. Intern Bronx (N.Y.) Mcpl. Hosp./Albert Einstein Coll. Medicine, N.Y.C., 1976-77, jr. and sr. resident, 1977-79; fellow in gastroenterology and liver disease Albert Einstein Coll. Medicine, 1979-81, rsch. assoc. Liver Rsch. Ctr., 1983; asst. prof. Albert Einstein Coll. Medicine, Bronx, N.Y., 1984-86; dir. gastroenterology Gouverneur Hosp., N.Y.C., 1986-90; asst. chief gastroenterology Lenox Hill Hosp., N.Y.C., 1992—, founding dir. liver clinic, 1992—; dir. hepatology program, 1994—; ednl. coord. Lenox Hill Hosp., N.Y.C., 1995—; clin. asst. prof. NYU Sch. Medicine, 1986-93, clin. assoc. prof., 1993—; prin. investigator Liver Rsch. Ctr. Albert Einstein Coll. Medicine, 1984-87, vis. scientist, 1992—; med. adv. bd. Crohn's and Colitis Found. of Am., Am. Liver Found., N.Y. chpts., 1987—; researcher in molecular biology of hepatitis B virus and relationship to viral infection and liver cancer. Author: Relationship of Hepatitis B Viral Infection in Serum to Viral Replication, 1983. Recipient Clin. Investigator award NIH, 1984-87. Fellow ACP, Am. Coll. Gastroenterology, N.Y. Acad. Gastroenterology (pres. 1990-91). Office: 345 E 37th St New York NY 10016-3217

LIEBERMAN, JOSEPH ALOYSIUS, III, physician; b. Allentown, Pa., Oct. 15, 1938; s. Joseph Aloysius and Marie Catherine (McDermott) L.; m. Judith Ann Dees, July 23, 1966; children—Lila, Lucy, Joseph IV, Karl. BS,

Georgetown U., Washington, 1960; MD, Jefferson Med. Coll., Phila., 1964; MA in Pub. Health Rutgers U., 1989, Health Policy Fellow, Inst. of Med. Nat. Acad Scis., 1988-89 Deplomate Am. Bd. Family Practice. Family physician Sr/Jr Partnership, Allentown, 1967-68; solo practice family medicine, Allentown, 1968-71; sr. ptnr. West End Med. Group, Allentown, 1971-77; full-time faculty Robert Wood Johnson Med. Sch., Piscataway, N.J., 1977-91, prof., chmn. dept. family medicine, 1982-91; clin. prof. family medicine Jefferson Med. Coll. Thomas Jefferson U., 1991—. chmn. dept. family and community medicine Med. Ctr. of Del., 1991—. Contbr. articles to profl. jours. Served to capt. USAF, 1965-67. Recipient Exceptional Merit award U. Medicine and Dentistry of N.J., 1979-80, 81-82. Republican. Roman Catholic. Office: Med Ctr Delaware Dept Family and Cmty Medicine PO Box 1668 501 W 14th St Wilmington DE 19801-1013

LIEBERMAN, MICHAEL JAY, ophthalmologist; b. N.Y.C., July 8, 1948; s. Murray H. and Bella (Adler) L.; m. Andea Dina Kaplan, Aug. 3, 1969; children: Shira, Shelly, Devorah. BA, Yeshiva U., 1970; MD, N.Y. Med. Coll., Valhalla, 1974. Diplomate Am. Bd. Ophthalmology. Pvt. practice Farmingdale, N.Y., 1978—; staff physician Brunswick Hosp., Amityville, N.Y., 1978—, Mid Island Hosp., Bethpage, N.Y., 1979—, Massapequa Gen. Hosp., Seaford, N.Y., 1978—, North Shore Univ. Hosp., Plainview, N.Y., 1978—. Jewish. Office: 850 Fulton St Farmingdale NY 11735

LIEBERMAN, PHILLIP LOUIS, allergist, educator; b. Memphis, Mar. 20, 1940; m. Barbara; children: Ryan, Lee, Jay. Student, London Sch. Econs., 1961; BA in Sociology, Tulane U., 1962; MD, U. Tenn., 1965. Intern City of Memphis Hosp. U. Tenn., 1965-66, asst. resident internal medicine, 1966-67, assoc. resident internal medicine, 1967-68, chief resident, 1968-69; fellow in allergy, immunology Northwestern U., Evanston, Ill., 1969-71; asst. prof., chief div. allergy, immunology U. Tenn., 1971-74, assoc. prof., chief div. allergy, immunology, 1974-79, prof., chief div. allergy, immunology, 1979—; instr. internal medicine U. Tenn., 1968-69; mem. exec. bd. Joint Coun. of Allergy & Immunology, 1985-90, AAAI rep., 1990; AAAI rep. Mothers for Asthmatics, 1990. Co-editor: Asthma Edition: Abstract-a-Card System, 1991—; contbr. numerous articles, abstracts to profl. publs.; author numerous presentations in field, book chpts., revs. Exec. bd. dirs. Asthma and Allergy Found. of Am., 1990—, mem. med. scientific coun., 1987, chmn., 1990—. Served to cpt. USAR, 1965-71. Mem. Am. Acad. Allergy (com. on alternative forms of therapy, 1980—), Am. Acad. Allergy and Immunology (exec. com. 1983-91, constitution and by-laws com. 1984-87, also chmn. 1985, undergraduate com. 1985, pres.-elect. 1987-88, pres. 1988-89, nominating com. 1987, also chmn. 1989, program com. 1987), Am. Coll. Allergists, Am. Assn. Allergists (sec. 1985), Am. Assn. Certified Allergists (2d v.p. 1986-87, pres. 1989-90), Am. Bd. Allergy and Immunology. Office: U Tenn 300 S Walnut Bend Rd Cordova TN 38018-7293 also: Allergy Assocs 920 Madison Ave Ste 909N Memphis TN 38103-3451

LIEBERMAN, RICHARD MICHAEL, urologist, educator; b. Phila., Nov. 22, 1953; s. Martin and Beverly (Tarcove) L.; m. Janet Averbach, June 22, 1986; children: Matthew, Daniel. BS in Biology, Rensselaer Poly. Inst., 1974; MD, Temple U., 1980. Diplomate Am. Bd. Urology, Nat. Bd. Med. Examiners. Resident in surgery North Shore U. Hosp., Manhasset, N.Y., 1980-82; resident in urology Temple U., Phila., 1982-85; pvt. practice, Allentown, Pa., 1985—; chief urology Lehigh Valley Hosp., Allentown, 1991—; co-dir. genitourinary oncology Morgan Cancer Ctr., Allentown, 1994—; clin. assoc. prof. surgery Pa. State U., Hershey, 1995—. Trustee Lehigh chpt. Am. Cancer Soc., Allentown, 1995—. Fellow ACS; mem. Am. Urol. Assn., Urol. Assn. Pa., Phila. Urol. Soc., Lehigh County Med. Soc. (trustee 1995-97). Office: Ste 235 1259 Cedar Crest Blvd Allentown PA 18103

LIEBERMAN, SHARI, clinical nutritionist; b. Bklyn., June 24, 1958; d. Mort and Sheila (Kolchin) L. BS, NYU, 1979, MA, 1981; PhD, Union Inst., 1993. Cert. Bd. for Nutrition Specialists. Pvt. practice N.Y.C., 1982—; lectr. Health and Med. Conf., 1981—; nutritional cons. and product developer Garden State Nutritionals, Windmill Mktg., Celmark Internat., N.J., 1987—, Home Shopping Club, USA, Can., 1988—, Books Mag. Prodn. USA, 1987—. Author: Design Your Own Vitamin and Mineral Program, 1987, The Real Vitamin and Mineral Book, 1990; contbg. editor Better Nutrition for Today's Living, 1989—, New Life mag., 1989—. Mem. N.Y. Acad. Scis., Am. Preventive Med. Assn. (bd. dirs.), Am. Coll. Nutrition. Office: 100 Lehigh Dr Fairfield NJ 07004-3013

LIEBERT, ARTHUR EDGAR, retired hospital administrator; b. Milw., Nov. 18, 1930; married. B, Lake Forest Coll; MHA, Northwestern U. Adminstrv. resident Rochester (N.Y.) Gen. Hosp., 1953-54, adminstrv. asst., 1954, asst. adminstr., 1957-65, assoc. dir., 1965-70, admitting dir., 1970-73, pres., 1973-93; co-pres. Greater Rochester Health Sys., 1994-96, Greater Rochester Health Sys. Inc., Rochester, 1994-96. Mem. Am. Hosp. Assn. (del.), Hosp. Assn. N.Y. (del.). Home: 611 Dewitt Rd Webster NY 14580-1333

LIEBERT, PETER S., pediatric surgeon, consultant; b. N.Y.C., Feb. 27, 1936; s. Louis M. and Sonia F. (Wolfe) L.; m. Phyllis J. Farkas, Sept. 6, 1960 (div. 1982); 1 child, Peter S., Jr.; m. Mary Ann Rosenfeld, Jan. 22, 1984; 1 stepchild, Lewis Charles. AB, Princeton U., 1957; MD, Harvard Med. Sch., Boston, 1961. Diplomate Am. Bd. Surgery; cert. of spl. competence pediat. surgery. Practice medicine specializing in pediatric surgery Eastchester, N.Y., 1961—; clin. assoc. prof. surgery Columbia U. Coll. Physicians and Surgeons. Author: Color Atlas of Pediatric Surgery; editor: Emergency and Office Pediatrics. Dir. Med. Network for Missing Children. Home: 67 Pleasant Ridge Rd Harrison NY 10528-1232 Office: 270 White Plains Rd Eastchester NY 10707-4412

LIEBETREU, MARK ERNEST, optometrist; b. Detroit, Sept. 24, 1962; s. Ernest Alfred Liebetreu and Darlene Jeanette (Eaton) Novak. OD, Ferris State U., 1986. Staff optometrist pvt. practice med. office, Harperwoods, Mich., 1986-87, Bascom Palmer Eye Inst., Miami, Fla., 1987-89; rsch. asst. Gothenburg (Sweden) U., 1989-91; cir. optometrist Commonwealth Eye Svcs., Lexington, Ky., 1991-95; staff optometrist Eye Health of Ft. Myers, Fla., 1995—; adj. faculty Ferris State U. Contbr. articles to profl. publs. Mem. Am. Optometric Assn., Fla. Optometric Assn., So. Coun. Optometrists. Office: Eye Health of Ft Myers 29 Barkley Cir Fort Myers FL 33907

LIEBLICH, STUART EDWARD, oral and maxillofacial surgeon; b. N.Y.C., Oct. 14, 1955; s. Severyn Bernard and Phyllis (Katz) L.; m. Janet June Bente, Aug. 27, 1983; children: Brett, Margot. BA, Rutgers U., 1977; DMD, U. Pa., 1981. Diplomate Am. Bd. Oral and Maxillofacial Surgery. Intern Kings County/Downstate Med. Ctr., Bklyn., 1981-82, resident in oral and maxillofacial surgery, 1982-84; asst. prof. oral and maxillofacial surgery U. Conn., Farmington, 1984-88; pvt. practice Drs. Piecuch & Lieblich, Avon, Conn., 1988—. Contbr. articles to profl. jours., chpts. to books; editl. bd. Anesthesia Progress, 1993—. Bd. dirs. Farmington Valley MCA, Simsbury, Conn., 1990—. Fellow Am. Assn. Oral and Maxillofacial Surgeons, Am. Dental Soc. Anesthesiology (pres. 1990—); mem. ADA, Conn. Dental Assn., Conn. Dental Soc. Anesthesiology (pres. 1993—). Office: Drs Piecuch & Lieblich 34 Dale Rd #105 Avon CT 06001

LIEBMAN, PAUL ROBERT, vascular surgeon; b. Richmond, Va., Dec. 4, 1945; s. Morris and Helen (Neiman) L.; m. Patricia B. Sherin, Dec. 29, 1973; children: Joseph, Benjamin, Andrew. BS in Zoology, George Washington U., 1967; MD, Georgetown U., 1971. Diplomate Am. Bd. Surgery, Am. Bd. Vascular Surgery. Intern Boston U.-Boston City Hosp., 1971-72, resident in surgery, 1972-73, 77-80, rsch. fellow, 1975-77; vascular fellow Med. Coll. Va., Richmond, 1980-81; attending surgeon St. Mary' Hosp. and Good Samaritan Med. Ctr., West Palm Beach, Fla., 1981—; dir. surgery div. Good Samaritan Med. Ctr., West Palm Beach, 1987—; ptnr. Surg. Specialists of the Palm Beaches, West Palm Beach; mem. adv. bd. Palm Beach County Blood Bank, West Palm Beach, 1991—, metabolic unit Good Samaritan Med. Ctr., West Palm Beach, 1991—. Bd. dirs. Good Samaritan Med. Ctr. Found.; mem. bd. govs. Intracoastal Health Sys. Maj. USAF, 1973-75. Fellow ACS; mem. Internat. Soc. for Cardiovascular Surgery, Southeastern Surg. Congress, So. Assn. for Vascular Surgery, Fla. Vascular Soc. (founding, pres.), Alpha Omega Alpha. Office: Surg Specialists of the Palm Beaches 2511 N Flagler Dr West Palm Beach FL 33407-5914

LIEBOWITZ, NEIL ROBERT, psychiatrist; b. Bklyn., Feb. 5, 1956; s. Harold and Gertrude Liebowitz; m. Judith Linda Ross, Oct. 21, 1952; children: Sarah Michelle, Daniel Geoffery. BA, U. Va., 1978; MD, SUNY, Stony Brook, 1982. Cert. Am. Bd. Psychiatry and Neurology. Intern Greenwich Hosp. Assn., Greenwich, Conn., 1982-83; psychiatry fellow Yale Dept. Psychiatry, New Haven, 1982-86; chief resident psychiatry Yale New Haven Hosp., 1985-86; dir. consultation liaison psychiatry Newington VA Med. Ctr., Newington, Conn., 1986-87; chief mental hygiene clinic Newington VA Med. Ctr., 1986-88; asst. prof. psychiatry U. Conn., Farmington, 1986—; dir. inpatient psychiatry Newington VA Med. Ctr., 1988-89; dir. ambulatory psychiatry John Dempsey Hosp., Farmington, 1989-91; cons. psychiatrist Rocky Hill (Conn.) Vets. Home and Hosp., 1987-88; attending New Britain Gen. Hosp., 1992—; dir. Conn. Anxiety & Depression Treatment Ctr., Farmington, 1994—. Contbr. articles to profl. jours.; co-investigator clin. research Clin. Psychopharmocology, 1988—. Mem. Am. Psychiat. Assn., Conn. Psychiat. Soc., Phi Beta Kappa. Office: Conn Anxiety & Depression Treatment Ctr Farmington CT 06032

LIECHTY, RICHARD DALE, surgeon, educator; b. Lake Geneva, Wis., Oct. 20, 1925; s. Ernest A. and Margaret (Demerath) L.; m. Valerie Jane Grunow, Jan. 1952; children: Robert Mark, Valerie Ann, Richard Cameron. BA, Yale Y., 1950; MD, Northwestern U., 1954. Diplomate Am. Bd. Surgery. Intern, resident U. Mich., Ann Arbor, 1954-59; prof. U. Colo. Med. Sch., Denver, 1971—; asst. prof. U. Iowa Med. Sch., Iowa City, 1960-71. Editor, author: Synopsis of Surgery, 6 edits., 1968-90; contbr. articles and book revs. to profl. jours. Served with USN, 1944-46, PTO. Fellow ACS; mem. Am. Assn. Endocrine Surgeons, We. Surg. Assn. (sec 1981-86, pres. 1986), Denver Acad. Surgeons. Presbyterian. Home: 4900 E Mansfield Denver CO 80237

LIEF, HAROLD ISAIAH, psychiatrist; b. N.Y.C., Dec. 29, 1917; s. Jacob F. and Mollie (Filler) L.; m. Myrtis A. Brumfield, Mar. 3, 1961; Caleb B., Frederick V., Oliver F.; children from previous marriage: Folly Lief Goldberg, Jonathan F. BA, U. Mich., 1938; MD, NYU, 1942; cert. in psychoanalysis, Columbia Coll. Physicians and Surgeons, 1950; MA (hon.), U. Pa., 1971. Intern Queens Gen. Hosp., Jamaica, N.Y., 1942-43; resident psychiatry L.I. Coll. Medicine, 1946-48; pvt. practice psychiatry N.Y.C., 1948-51; asst. physician Presbyn. Hosp., N.Y.C., 1949-51; asst. prof. Tulane U., New Orleans, 1951-54, assoc. prof., 1954-60, prof. psychiatry, 1960-67; prof. psychiatry U. Pa., Phila., 1967-82, prof. emeritus, 1982—; dir. div. family study U. Pa., 1967-81; dir. Marriage Council of Phila., 1969-81, Ctr. for Study of Sex. Edn. in Medicine, 1968-82; mem. staff U. Pa. Hosp., 1967-81, Pa. Hosp., 1981—; clin. prof. psychiatry Jefferson Med. U., 1994—. Author: (with Daniel and William Thompson) The Eighth Generation, 1960; Editor: (with Victor and Nina Lief) Psychological Basis of Medical Practice, 1963, Medical Aspects of Human Sexuality, 1976, (with Arno Karlen) Sex Education in Medicine, 1976, Sexual Problems in Medical Practice, 1981, (with Zwi Hoch) Sexology: Sexual Biology, Behavior and Therapy, 1982, (with Zwi Hoch) International Research in Sexology, 1983, Human Sexuality With Respect to AIDS and HIV Infection, 1989; contbr. numerous articles to pubs. Bd. dirs. Ctr. for Sexuality and Religion; mem. La. State Commn. Civil Rights, 1958-67. Maj. M.C. U.S. Army, 1943-46. Commonwealth Fund fellow, 1963-64; recipient Gold Medal award Mt. Airy Hosp., 1977, Lifetime Achievement award Phila. Psychiat. Soc., 1992. Fellow Phila. Coll. Physicians, Am. Psychiat. Assn. (life), N.Y. Acad. Scis., AAAS, Am. Acad. Psychoanalysis (charter, past pres.), Am. Coll. Psychiatrists (founding), Am. Coll. Psychoanalysts (charter); mem. Am. Assn. Marriage and Family Therapists, Sex Info. and Edn. Council U.S. (past pres.), Group Advancement Psychiatry (life), Am. Soc. Adolescent Psychiatry, Am. Psychosomatic Soc., Assn. Psychoanalytic Medicine (life), Internat. Acad. Sex Rsch., Soc. Sci. Study of Sex, Am. Soc. Sex Educators, Counselors and Therapists, Soc. Sex Therapists and Researchers, World Assn. Sexology (past v.p.), Soc. Exploration of Psychotherapy Integration (adv. bd.), Columbia Club, Mich. Club of Greater Phila., Penn Club of N.Y., Sigma Xi, Alpha Omega Alpha, Phi Eta Sigma, Phi Kappa Phi. Home: 101 S Buck Ln Haverford PA 19041-1104 Office: Ste 719 987 Old Eagle School Rd Wayne PA 19087

LIEF, NINA RAYEVSKY, psychiatrist, educator; b. Liberty, N.Y., Feb. 12, 1907; d. Charles and Lucy (Kalina) Rayevsky; m. Victor F. Lief (dec.); 1 child, Carlotta Lief Schuster. BA, Barnard Coll., 1927; MD, NYU, 1931. Asst. prof. psychiatry Tulane U., New Orleans, 1960-63; assoc. prof. psychiatry N.Y. Sch. Psychiatry, N.Y.C., 1963-68, N.Y. Med. Coll., N.Y.C., 1968-87; pvt. practice specializing in child psychiatry N.Y.C.; cons. prof. psychiatry N.Y. Med. Coll., 1987—. Author: First Year of Life, 1979, Second Year of Life, 1983, Third Year of Life, 1991. Fellow Am. Acad. Psychoanalysis, Am. Acad. Child Psychiatry, Am. Psychiat. Assn., AMA, Am. Acad. Pediatrics; mem. N.Y. Med. Soc. Democrat. Jewish. Office: Ctr for Comprehnsive Health 167 E 97th St New York NY 10029-7305

LIEFER, ALLAN LEE, surgeon; b. Chgo., Dec. 13, 1944; s. Elmer F. and Elsie L. (Yud) L.; m. Louise Stermer, June 11, 1967; children: Heidi, Jonathan, Christopher, Gretchen. BS, U. Ill., Urbana, 1966; MD, U. Ill., Chgo., 1971. Diplomate Am. Bd. Surgery. Intern Cook County Hosp. and Luth. Gen. Hosp., Chgo., Des Plaines, 1971-72; resident in gen. surgery Loyola Affiliated Hosps., Maywood, Ill., 1972-76; surgeon Cmty. Hosp., Sparta, Ill., 1978—; staff Meml. Hosp., Chester, Ill., 1990—, St. Clement Hosp., Red Bud, Ill., 1978—, St. Elizabeths Hosp., Belleville, Ill., 1984—. Mem. unit bd. Am. Cancer Soc., 1976. Maj. U.S. Army, 1976-78. Fellow ACS; mem. AMA, Soc. Am. Gastrointestinal Endoscopic Surgeons, Midwest Surg. Assn., Ill. State Surg. Soc., Randolph County Med. Soc., Ill. State Med. Soc. Republican. Lutheran. Home: #4 Knollwood Dr Chester IL 62233-1415 Office: PO Box 150 1650 State Chester IL 62233-0150

LIEM, HAN, psychiatrist; b. Pekalongan, Java, Indonesia, Mar. 28, 1929; came to U.S., 1968; s. Soen-Lian and Pat-Nio (Tio) L.; m. Frieda Gwat-Lan Lie, Oct. 16, 1960; children: Marina Dewi, Kristina Dini, Elizabeth Julianti. MD, U. Indonesia, Jakarta, 1956. Diplomate Am. Bd. Psychiatry and Neurology. Pvt. practice gen. psychiatry, Mt. Holly, N.J., 1971-75; staff psychiatrist VA, Phila., 1975-87, 95—; assoc. chief VA Mental Health Clinic, Phila., 1987-95; clin. assoc. dept. psychiatry U. Pa., Phila., 1983—. Mem. Nat. Assn. VA Physicians, Assn. Mil. Surgeons U.S. Home: 712 Fitzwatertown Rd Glenside PA 19038-1305 Office: VA Mental Health Clinic University & Woodland Aves Philadelphia PA 19104

LIEN, ERIC L., pharmaceutical executive; b. Hammond, Ind., Apr. 9, 1946; s. Arthur P. and Rowena (Woltz) L.; m. Winifred A. Latham, July 23, 1987; children: Caroline, Steven, Janet, Elizabeth, Jeffrey, Alison. BA, Coll. of Wooster, 1968; MSc, U. Ill., 1971, PhD 1972. Postdoctoral fellow Sch. Medicine U. Pa., Phila., 1972-75; rsch. biochemist Wyeth Labs., Phila., 1975-82, mgr. metabolic disorders, 1982-87, assoc. dir. nutritional rsch., 1987-90; dir. nutritional rsch. Wyeth-Ayerst Labs., Phila., 1990-93, sr. dir. nutritional rsch., 1993—; mem. U.S. delegation CODEX Alimentarius, Washington and Rome, 1988—; mem. tech. adv. group com. on nutrition Am. Acad. Pediatrics, Oak Park, Ill., 1988—; mem. Com. on Nutritional Scis. Infant Formula Coun., Atlanta, 1988—. Contbr. articles to profl. publs., chpts. to books. Recipient award Am. Heart Assn., 1974. Mem. AAAS, Am. Soc. Parenternal and Enteral Nutrition, Am. Inst. Nutrition, Phi Beta Kappa. Episcopalian. Home: 1 Anthony Dr Malvern PA 19355-1973 Office: Wyeth-Ayerst Labs PO Box 8299 Philadelphia PA 19101-8299

LIER, NANCY JEAN, medical educator, administrator; b. Breckenridge, Mich., Sept. 21, 1942; d. Joseph and Lucinda Martha (Feltman) Smolek; m. James William Lier, June 20, 1964; 1 child, Thomas James. BS, Madonna U., 1964; postgrad., U. Kans., 1976-77; MS in Sci. Adminstrn., Cen. Mich. U., 1985. Supr. immunohematology St. Mary's Med. Ctr., Saginaw, Mich., 1964-66, 67-68, supr. bacteriology, 1968-69, dir. sch. med. tech., 1967—; staff technologist Flint (Mich.) Med. Lab., 1966-67; acad. appointments include Grad Valley State U., Allendale, Mich., 1967—, Ctrl. Mich. U., Mt. Pleasant, 1967-92, Saginaw Valley State U., University Center, Mich., 1967—, Madonna U., Livonia, Mich., 1967—, Mich. Tech. U., Houghton, 1967—. Vol. Boy Scouts Am., Frankenmuth, Mich., 1972-83. Mem. Am. Soc. Clin. Pathologists (cert. med. technologist), Am. Soc. Med. Technologists. Republican. Roman Catholic. Office: St Mary's Med Ctr 830 S Jefferson Ave Saginaw MI 48601-2522

LIESEGANG, THOMAS JOHN, ophthalmologist; b. Cleve., Nov. 14, 1945; s. Robert and Bernice (Kachmar) L.; m. Eileen Rita Manion, June 17, 1967; children: Brian, Jason, Alex, Shane. BA, Providence Coll., 1966; MD, NYU, 1970. Diplomate Am. Bd. Ophthalmology. Intern Duke U., Durham, N.C., 1970-71; ophthalmology resident U. Miami, 1973-76, chief resident, 1977-78; fellow in corneal disease Baylor U., Houston, 1976-77; cons. Mayo Clinic Rochester, 1978-86; chmn. dept. ophthalmology Mayo Clinic Jacksonville, Fla., 1986—; mem. Fla. Organ and Tissue Transplantation Adv. Bd., 1993-94; cons. Govt. Panel Evaluating Cataract Surgery, 1992—; reviewer, advisor Fla. Peer Rev. Orgn., 1989—; vis prof. U. Minn., 1979, Mont. Ophthalmol. Soc., 1983, Wis. Ophthalmology Soc., 1983, U. Pitts., 1983, Northwestern U., 1985, Ky. Acad. Eye Surgeons, 1989, Baylor Coll. of Medicine, 1990, John's Hopkins U., 1991, Pitts. Ophthalmol. Soc., 1991, Mayo Clinic Rochester, 1991, New Orleans Acad. Ophthalmology, 1991, Washington Hosp. Ctr., 1991, Fla. Soc. of Ophthalmology, 1992, U. Tenn., Memphis, 1993, Med. U. of S.C., 1993, U. Ottawa, 1993, Med. Coll. of Ga., 1994, Can. Ophthalmol. Assn., 1995. Editl. bd. Mayo Clinic Procs., 1988-91, Am. Jour. Ophthalmology, 1993-96, Ophthalmology World News, 1994—, Cornea, 1995—; sect. editor Duane's Found. of Clin. Ophthalmology, 1993—; contbr. articles to profl. jours. Lt. USN, 1971-73. Fellow Am. Acad. of Ophthalmology (chairperson 1989-96, sec. 1990-96, assoc. examiner 1980—, mem. various coms.); mem. Am. Ophthalmol. Soc., Assn. for Rsch. in Vision and Ophthalmology, Castroviejo Soc., Duval County Med. Soc., S.E. Corneal Group, Dan B. Jones Soc. (pres.), Fla. Med. Assn., Fla. Soc. of Ophthalmology. Roman Catholic. Office: Mayo Clinic Jacksonville 4500 San Pablo Rd Jacksonville FL 32224

LIFSEY, EVELYN P., psychotherapist; b. Belmar, N.J., Apr. 5, 1958; d. Jeremy Allen and Carol Joyce (Goldman) Lifsey; m. Richard Ira Male, Nov. 23, 1985; children: Abraham Y., Daniel O., Sarah Golde, Juliadele M. AB in Psychology cum laude, Harvard U., 1979; MA in Religion with distinction, Iliff Sch. Theology, 1988; postgrad., U. Denver, 1990—. Lic. profl. counselor, Colo. Cmty. organizer Black Hills Alliance, Rapid City, S.D., 1979-83; dir. Western Solidarity, Denver, 1983-86; clinician, dir. nursing home project Jewish Family Svc., Denver, 1989-93; lic. psychotherapist in pvt. practice Denver, 1993—; emergency rm. clinician Health ONE, Denver, 1993-95; assoc. psychotherapist Pike & Assocs., Denver, 1994—; instr. Talmudic Rsch. Inst., Denver, 1995-96. Editor: Keystone to Survival, 1981. Mem. ACA, Nat. Assn. Forensic Counselors. Office: Pike & Assocs Ste 390 190 E 9th Ave Denver CO 80203

LIFSHITZ, BENJI C., physician; b. Bklyn., Aug. 3, 1960. MD, Cornell Univ., 1985. Diplomate Am. Bd. Internal Medicine. Office: Benjamin C Lifshitz 3043 Ocean Ave Ste 205 Brooklyn NY 11235

LIGENZA, ANDREA ANGELA, nurse; b. Lansford, Pa., Apr. 7, 1952; d. Stanley Walter and Mary (Porambo) L. Diploma in Nursing, Hosp. of U. Pa., 1973; BS in Nursing, U. Pa., 1976. RN; cert. nurse practitioner, Pa. Staff nurse Hosp. of U. Pa., Phila., 1973-79, nurse practitioner cardiothoracic surgery sect., 1979-88; preceptor nursing students U. Pa., 1985-91; founder, group leader Self Esteem Workshops, 1986-87; nurse practitioner Cardiothoracic Surg. Assocs. Pa. Hosp., 1988-91, Bryn Mawr Hosp., 1991-93, Primary Care, Drexel Hill, Pa., 1992—. Eucharistic min. Roman Cath. Ch. Mem. Puccini Inst., Sigma Theta Tau. Republican. Avocations: classical music, tennis, travel. Office: 2235 Garrett Rd Drexel Hill PA 19026-1130

LIGGINS, GEORGE LAWSON, microbiologist, diagnostic company executive; b. Roanoke, Va., June 19, 1937; m. Joyce Preston Liggins, Sept. 3, 1966; 1 child, George Lawson Jr. BA, Hampton U., 1962; cert. med. technician, Meharry Med. Sch., 1963; MPH, U. N.C., 1969; PhD, U. Va., Charlottesville, 1975. Med. technician Vets. Hosp., Hampton, Va., 1963-66; rsch. technician U. N.C. Med. Sch., Chapel Hill, 1966-69; postdoctoral fellow Scripps Clinic, La Jolla, Calif., 1975-76, Salk Inst., La Jolla, 1976-77; rsch. mgr. Hyland div. Baxter, Costa Mesa, Calif., 1977-78; R & D dir. diagnostics div. Baxter, Roundlake, Ill., 1978-83; pres., COO Internat. Immunology, Murrieta, Calif., 1983-86; chmn., CEO Bacton Assay Systems, Inc., San Marcos, Calif., 1986—; cons. Beckman Instruments, Inc., Brea, Calif., 1987-90, Paramax divsn. Baxter, Irvine, Calif., 1988-90, Scantibodies Lab., Santee, Calif., 1990-92; presenter in field; mem. virology study Cold Spring Harbor Lab., L.I., N.Y., 1974. Contbr. articles to profl. jours. Fellow NIH, 1975, Am. Cancer Soc., 1976. Mem. Am. Soc. Microbiology, Am. Assn. Clin. Chemistry, Van Slyke Soc. of Am. Assn. Clin. Chemistry, Am. Heart Assn., Nat. Hampton Alumni, Inc. (pres. 1991—), Omega Psi Phi. Republican. Methodist. Office: Bacton Assay Systems Inc 772-A N Twin Oaks Valley Rd San Marcos CA 92069

LIGHAM, DWIGHT PAUL, physician; b. East Orange, N.J., Mar. 14, 1955; s. Chester Kenneth and Pauline Dorthea (Couchinello) L.; m. Patricia A. Ligham; children: Ariell, Zachary. BS, SUNY, Oneonta, 1980, MS, 1984; MD, SUNY, Syracuse, 1992. Tchr. ARC Ctr. for Living Skills, Arkville, N.Y., 1980-81; counselor personal adjustment, placement, vocat. evaluator Otsego County ARC, Oneonta, N.Y., 1981-85; residence counselor-shift coord. Upstate Home for Children's Community Residence Program, Oneonta, 1985-88; resident in anesthesiology Sch. Medicine Yale U., 1996; pain mgmt. physician Cayuga Med. Ctr., Ithaca, N.Y., 1996—. With USN, 1973-79. Mem. AMA, ASA. Home: Cayuga Med Ctr 812 Triphammer Rd Ithaca NY 19850

LIGHT, DOUGLAS BRUCE, biologist, educator; b. N.Y.C., Apr. 9, 1956; s. Jerome E. and Margery R. (Jacobs) L.; children: Erin, Jessica, Rachel. BA in Biology, Colby Coll., 1978; MS in Zoology, U. Minn., 1986, PhD in Physiology, 1986. Cert. 7-12 tchr., Maine. Tchr. biology Winslow (Maine) High Sch., 1978-81; teaching asst., rsch. asst. U. Minn., Mpls., 1981-86; postdoctoral fellow Dartmouth Med. Sch., Hanover, N.H., 1986-88, rsch. assoc., 1988-89; instr. biology Sch. for Life Long Learning, Lebanon, N.H., 1988; prof. Ripon Coll., Wis., 1989—. Contbr. articles to Nature, Sci., Am. Jour. Physiology, Jour. Clin. Investigation, others. Hitchcock Found. grantee, 1988-89; recipient Instrumentation and Lab. Improvement award NSF, 1991, RUI award, 1993. Mem. Am. Physiol. Soc. (Excellence in Rsch. award 1987, Caroline Tum Suden award 1988, May Bumby Severy award 1991, Sr. Class award 1993), Soc. Integrative and Comparative Biology, Biopyhs. Soc., Soc. Gen. Physiologists, Sigma Xi. Office: Ripon Coll Dept Biology 300 Seward St Ripon WI 54971-0248

LIGHT, RICHARD TODD, health consulting company exeucitve, internist; b. Rochester, N.Y., May 1, 1948; s. Glenn Wallace and Gloria C. (Capparelli) L.; m. Susan Kathryn Nelson, Nov. 2, 1974. BS, Yale U., 1970; MD, U. Rochester, 1975. Diplomate Am. Bd. Internal Medicine, Am. Bd. Pathology. Intern Johns Hopkins Hosp., 1975-76, resident, 1976-78; resident clin. pathology U. Minn., Mpls., 1978-79, fellow chem. pathology, med. hematology, 1979-82; asst. prof. Vanderbilt U. Med. Sch., Nashville, 1983-88; dir., asst. chief Nashville VA Med. Ctr. Lab. Svc., 1987-88; assoc. dir. Bristol-Myers Squibb Human Pharmacology, Princeton, N.J., 1988-90; world-wide corp. med. dir. Becton Dickinson Co., Franklin Lakes, N.J., 1990-92; med. dir. CIBA-GEIGY Corp., Summit, N.J., 1992-93; pres. Princeton Clin. Cons., Inc., Lawrenceville, N.J., 1993—. Contbr. articles to profl. jours. Mem. Am. Soc. for Clin. Pharmacology and Therapeutics, Am. Heart Assn., Am. Assn. Clin. Chemistry, Am. Fedn. for Clin. Rsch., Assn. Clin. Lab. Physicians and Scientists, Sigma Xi. Home: C-17 Carver Pl Lawrenceville NJ 08648 Office: Princeton Clin Cons Inc PO Box 6919 Lawrenceville NJ 08648-0919

LIGHT, TERRY RICHARD, orthopedic hand surgeon; b. Chgo., June 22, 1947. BA, Yale U.; MD, Chgo. Med. Sch. Asst. prof. Yale U., New Haven, 1977-80; asst. prof. Loyola U., Maywood, Ill., 1980-82, assoc. prof., 1982-88, prof., 1988-90, Dr. William M. Scholl prof., chmn. dept. orthopaedic surgery, 1991—; attending surgeon Hines (Ill.) VA Hosp., 1980—, Shriner's Hosp., Chgo. and Tampa, Fla., 1981—, Foster McGaw Hosp., Maywood, Ill., 1981—; hand cons., mem. med. adv. bd. DuPage Easter Seal, Villa Park, Ill., 1980—; hand cons. Chgo. White Sox, 1986—. V.p. Frank Lloyd Wright Home and Studio Found., Oak Park, Ill., 1985-88, pres., 1988-90. Fellow ACS, Am. Acad. Orthopaedic Surgeons; mem. Am. Soc. for Surgery of the Hand, Am. Assn. Hand Surgery (bd. dirs. 1990-91), Chgo. Soc. for Surgery of the Hand (sec. 1985-87, pres.-elect 1987-88, pres. 1988-89), Twenty-First

Century Orthopaedic Assn. (pres. 1979—). Office: Loyola U Med Ctr 2160 S 1st Ave Maywood IL 60153-3304

LIGHTDALE, CHARLES J., physician, educator; b. Jersey City, Apr. 25, 1940; s. Harold B. and Dorothy R. (Raynes) L.; m. Reina S. Silverman, Sept. 8, 1968; children: Jenifer, Hallie, Nina, Sarah. AB, Princeton U., 1962; MD, Columbia U., 1966. Intern Yale-New Haven Hosp., 1966-67, med. resident, 1967-68; resident Cornell Med. Coll., N.Y.C., 1968-69; fellow gastroenterology Meml. Hosp., N.Y.C., 1971-73; asst., assoc. attending physician Meml. Sloan-Kettering Cancer Ctr., N.Y.C., 1973-91, attending physician, 1991-93, dir. endoscopic rsch. gastroenterology svc., 1991-93; asst., assoc. prof. clin. medicine Cornell U. Med. Coll., N.Y.C., 1973-92, prof. medicine, 1992-93; prof. clin. medicine Columbia U., N.Y.C., 1993—; attending physician Columbia-Presbyn. Med. Ctr., N.Y.C., 1993—; dir. clin. gastroenterology Columbia-Presbyn. Med. Ctr., 1993—. Editor Gastrointestinal Endoscopy, 1989-96. Fellow ACP, Am. Coll. Gastroenterology (trustee 1982-84); mem. Am. Gastroent. Assn., Am. Soc. Gastointestinal Endoscopy (disting. svc. award 1995, councillor 1995—), N.Y. Gastroent. Assn. (pres. 1988-89), N.Y. Soc. Gastointestinal Endoscopy (master endoscopist 1987, pres. 1981-82), N.Y. Acad. Gastroenterology (pres. 1980-81). Office: Columbia-Presbyn Med Ctr 630 W 168th St PH876 New York NY 10032-3702

LIGMAN, JEFFREY DEAN, psychologist; b. Nashville, Jan. 12, 1958; s. Dean Vincent and Judith Ann (Erickson) L.; m. Pamela Ann Fleider, July 23, 1984; children: Kyle, Kase. BS in Psychology, Colo. State U., 1980; D in Psychology, Forest Inst. Profl. Psychology, 1986. Lic. psychologist, Wis. Staff psychologist Inst. for Motivational Devel., Wauwatosa, Wis., 1986-91; ptnr., owner Midwest Mental Health Cons. Inc., Wales, Wis., 1991-95; owner Alternatives in Psycholog. Consultation S.C., Milw., 1995—; active med. staff Rogers Mental Hosp., Oconomowoc, Wis., 1987—, Charter Hosp., Brown Deer, Wis., 1995; cons. Ancillary Home Health, Wauwatosa, 1993—. Mem. APA, Nat. Register of Health Svc. Providers in Psychology, Phi Beta Kappa. Office: Alternatives in Psych Cons 3333 N Mayfair Rd Ste 101 Milwaukee WI 53222

LIGOTTI, EUGENE FERDINAND, retired dentist; b. N.Y.C., June 10, 1936; s. Eugene A. and Lee (D'Agata) L.; m. Corbina Theresa Loscalzo, Nov. 21, 1959; children: Gina Maria Ligotti Aliperti, Lisa Anne Ligotti Liberatoscioli. BA, Adelphi U., 1958; DDS, NYU, 1962. Pvt. practice Huntington, N.Y., 1962-90; instr. operative dentistry NYU, N.Y.C., 1962-65. Author historic fiction, mystery novels, and screenplays; contbr. articles to profl. jours. and mags.; inventor ValueVac. Founder, pres. Upper Bay Civic Assn., Inc., Huntington, 1979—. Mem. ADA, N.Y. State Dental Soc., Suffolk County Dental Soc., German Shepherd Dog Club (pres. 1971-75), Xi Psi Phi (founder, pres. alumni chpt. 1981-82), Chi Sigma. Republican. Roman Catholic.

LIJTMAER, HUGO NORBERTO, physician; b. Buenos Aires, Argentina, Mar. 26, 1945; came to U.S., 1971; s. Salomon and Berta (Herbstein) L.; m. Ruth M. Michkin, Sept. 11, 1969; children: Fabian S., Martin N. MD, U. Buenos Aires, 1968. Resident Albert Einstein Coll. Medicine, Bronx, 1971-74, attending physician, instr., 1974-75; attending physician The Valley Hosp., Ridgewood, N.J., 1975—, dir. dept. neurosci., 1984-92. Mem. AMA, Am. Acad. Neurology, Med. Soc. N.J., Neurol. Assn. N.J. (pres. 1987-96), Bergen County Med. Soc. Jewish. Office: Neurology Group Bergen County 206 Prospect St Ridgewood NJ 07450

LIKENS, SUZANNE ALICIA, physiologist, researcher; b. Chgo., Nov. 12, 1945; d. Harry Ross and Sibyle Lovelett (Butler) L. BS in Biology, U. N.Mex., 1969, MS in Physiology, 1982. Research asst. biology dept. U. N.Mex, Albuquerque, 1969; sr. research technologist Inhalation Toxicology Research Inst., Albuquerque, 1974-93; lab. scientist II state lab. divsn. N.Mex. Dept. Pub. Health, Albuquerque, 1994—; mgr. dressage horse shows Am. Horse Show Assn./U.S. Dressage Fedn. Contbr. sci. papers and articles to profl. jours. Mem. N.Mex. Mus. Natural History & Sci. Found. Mem. AAAS, N.Mex. Natural History and Sci. Mus. Found. (docent, operator planetarium, lectr. on astronomy), N.Mex. Zool. Soc., N.Mex. Herpetol. Soc. (charter), Cousteau Soc., Women in Sci. and Enging., Am. Horse Show Assn., U.S. Dressage Fedn., N.Mex. Dressage and Combined Tng. Assn., S.W. Dressage Assn. (bd. dirs. 1989-94), N.Y. Acad. Scis., Sigma Xi. Republican. Presbyterian. Home: 1311 Dartmouth Dr NE Albuquerque NM 87106-1803

LILENFIELD, IRWIN, osteopath, surgeon; b. Boston, Oct. 24, 1931; s. Harry and Fannie (Moskowitz) L.; m. Ruth Darlene Peterson, May 27, 1963; children: Dena, Amy. BS, Bklyn. Coll. Pharmacy, 1953; DO, Kirksville Coll., 1963. Diplomate Am. Osteopathic Medicine. V.p. Canton South (Ohio) Med. Ctr. Inc., 1964—; dir. Ambulatory Care Ctr. Doctors Hosp., Massillion, Ohio, 1983-88; med. dir. quality rev. Doctors Hosp., 1984—; asst. prof. family medicine Ohio U., Athens, 1976—; v.p., med. dir. and prin. Health Design Plus, 1988-92; cons. Integrated Med. Resources, 1994—; med. dir. Canton Cmty. Clinic, 1994—. Adv. bd. Am. Cancer Soc. Stark County; Vis. Nurse Soc. Stark County; examining physician Planned Parenthood Stark County, Canton, 1969-72; Canton Boxing Commn., 1974-80. Served with U.S. Army, 1954-56. Fellow Am. Coll. Med. Quality, Am. Coll. Family Practice, Ohio State Soc. Osteo. Family Practice (pres. 1977-78); mem. Am. Acad. Med. Dirs., Am. Hosp. Assn., Am. Coll. Physician Execs., Am. Coll. Healthcare Execs., Am. Bd. Q.A.U.R.P., Nat. Assn. Managed Care Physicians. Home: 921 22nd St NE Canton OH 44714-2038

LILIENFELD, SCOTT OWEN, psychology educator; b. N.Y.C., Dec. 23, 1960. AB, Cornell U., 1982; PhD, U. Minn., 1990. Rsch. asst. U. Minn., Mpls., 1982-86, instr., teaching asst., 1986, 88-89; psychology intern Western Psychiat. Inst. and Clinic, Pitts., 1986-87; rsch. asst. U. Minn., Mpls., 1987-90; asst. prof. psychology SUNY, Albany, 1990-94, Emory U., Atlanta, 1994—. Contbr. articles to profl. jours. Mem. Am. Psychol. Soc. Office: Emory Univ Dept Psychology 206 Atlanta GA 30322

LILIENFIELD, LAWRENCE SPENCER, physiology and biophysics educator; b. Bklyn., May 5, 1927; s. Henry Jacob and Lee (Markman) L.; m. Eleanor Marion Russ, Oct. 22, 1950; children: Jan, Adele, Lisa. BS, Villanova (Pa.) U., 1945; MD, Georgetown U., 1949, MS, 1954, PhD, 1956. Diplomate Nat. Bd. Med. Examiners, Am. Bd. Internal Medicine. Intern Georgetown U. Hosp., Washington, 1949-59, 1949-50, resident in internal medicine, 1950, 52-54, rsch. fellow, 1954-55; instr. medicine Sch. Medicine Georgetown U., Washington, 1955-56, asst. chief cardiovascular rsch. lab., dept. medicine, 1956-63, asst. chief cardiovascular rsch. lab. dept. medicine, 1956-63, assoc. prof. physiology, biophysics and medicine Sch. Medicine, 1961-64, prof. physiology and biophysics Sch. Medicine, 1964-95, prof., chmn. dept. physiology and biophysics Sch. Medicine, 1963-93; attending physician VA Hosp., Washington, 1956-70; cons. USPHS, 1964-69, NASA, 1964-70, U.S. Dept. State, 1967-74; established investigator Am. Heart Assn., 1958; vis. prof. faculty of medicine U. Saigon, Republic of Korea, 1965-74. Contbr. numerous articles to profl. jours. Bd. dirs. Washington Heart Assn., 1962-67, chmn., 1966. With USN, 1945; capt. USAF, 1950-52. Recipient Established Investigator award Am. Heart Assn., 1958; Rsch. Career Devel. award USPHS, 1963, Rsch. Career award, 1963, Kaiser-Permanente Teaching award, 1987; USPHS rsch. and rsch. tng. grantee, 1987. Fellow ACP; mem. Am. Soc. for Clin. Investigation, Am. Physiol. Soc., Soc. for Exptl. Biology and Medicine, Am. Fedn. for Clin. Rsch. (chair ea. sect. 1965-66). Office: Georgetown U Sch Medicine 3900 Reservoir Rd NW Washington DC 20007-2187

LILJESTRAND, JAMES STRATTON, physician administrator, internist; b. Wareham, Mass., May 8, 1941; s. Robert Stratton and Lyla Mae (Kellum) L.; div. 1978; children: Karin E., Norman N.; m. Alice Jane Romanker, Aug. 20, 1983; children: Amy A., Jennelle S. BS, Ohio State U., 1962; MD, Northwestern U., 1966; MPH, Harvard U., 1973. Diplomate Am. Bd. Preventive Medicine. Instr. Harvard Med. Sch., Boston, 1973-75; asst. dean Harvard Sch. Pub. Health, Boston, 1973-76; med. dir., sr. v.p. med. svcs. Braintree (Mass.) Hosp., 1975—; pres. Nat. Assn. Rehab. Facilities, Washington, 1991—; chmn. bd. Rehab. Facilities Svcs., Inc., Washington, 1991—; copr. med. liason Continental Med. Systems, Inc., Mechanicsburg, Pa., 1992—. Contbr. articles to profl. jours. Pres. Alumni Assn. Harvard Sch. Pub. Health, 1980-83. With USPHS, 1967-69. Recipient Membership award Am. Acad. of Physical Medicine and Rehab., Chgo., 1991. Fellow Am. Heart Assn. (mem. stroke coun.), Am. Coll. Preventive Medicine, Am. Coll. Physician Execs. (cert.). Office: Braintree Hosp 250 Pond St Braintree MA 02184-5391

LILLE, SEAN TOMAS, surgeon, researcher; b. N.Y.C., Aug. 22, 1965; s. Philip M. and Patricia G. Lille; m. Diane Faith Lille, Mar. 5, 1996. BA summa cum laude, U. Calif., Berkeley, 1988; MD, U. Ariz., 1992. Lic. physician, Wash. Resident dept. surgery U. Wash., Seattle, 1992-95, sr. rsch. fellow dept. vascular surgery, 1995—. Contbr. articles to profl. jours. Lt. USNR.

LILLEY, DAVID MALCOLM JAMES, molecular biology; b. Colchester, Essex, Eng., May 28, 1948; s. Gerald Albert Thomas and Betty Pamela (Dickerson) L.; m. Patricia Mary Biddle, Mar. 7, 1981; children: Katherine Suzannah, Sarah Anne. BSc, U. Durham, Eng., 1969, PhD, 1973. Lectr. U. Dundee, Scotland, 1981-84, reader, 1984-90, prof., 1990—. Editor: (book series) Nucleic Acids & Molecular Biology, 1987—; contbr. more than 170 articles to sci. jours. Recipient Colworth medal Biochem. Soc., London, 1982, Mendel medal Czech Acad. Scis., Prague, 1994, Prelog medal ETH, Zürich, Switzerland, 1996. Fellow Royal Soc. Edinburgh; mem. European Molecular Biology Orgn. Office: The University, Dundee DD1 4HN, Scotland

LILLIEHÖÖK, J(OHAN) BJÖRN O(LOF), health science association administrator; b. Stockholm, Feb. 12, 1945; s. Nils Olof and Barbro (Brandel) L.; m. E. Margareta Setterberg, Sept. 7, 1968; children: Veronica, Lovisa, Alexandra. LLB, U. Stockholm, 1969. Dist. judge's assessor Dist. Ct. Sollentuna and Farentuna, Solna, Stockholm, Sweden, 1969-72; prin. clk. Swedish Nat. Bd. Immigration, Stockholm, 1972-73; dir., v.p., head regional office Swedish Employers' Confederation, Stockholm, 1973-90; sec.-gen., chief exec. officer Swedish Heart Lung Found., Stockholm, 1990—; chmn. Stockholm New Enterprise Ctr., 1987-90; chair Nordic Assn. in Stockholm, 1993—; trustee. bd. dirs. King Oscar II's Jubilee Found., Stockholm, 1994—; bd. dirs. F.O.F. Rsch. and Progress Found., Stockholm. Chmn. fund raising com., mem. exec. com. Internat. Union Against Tb and Lung Disease, Paris, 1994—; mem. exec. bd. Internat. Soc. and Fedn. of Cardiology, Geneva, 1995—; mem. European Heart Network Coun., 1995—. Mem. Internat. Soc. for Labour Law and Social Security, Sallskapet, SvD Exec. Club, Internat. Soc. and Fedn. Cardiology (exec. bd. 1995—), Rotary (bd. dirs. Stockholm club, pres. 1989-90), European Heart Network. Lutheran. Office: Swedish Heart Lung Found, Kungsgatan 30, S-11135 Stockholm Sweden

LILLO, JOSEPH LEONARD, osteopath, family practice physician; b. Mt. Gilead, Ohio, Aug. 12, 1954; s. Joseph and Betty Jean (Rogers) L.; m. Barbara Anne Burn, June 25, 1976; children: Marie, Michael, Laura. BS in Zoology, Ariz. State U., 1976; DO, Kirksville Coll. Osteo. Med., 1979. Diplomate Am. Bd. Family Practice, Natq. Bd. Examiners in Osteo. Medicine and surgery. Intern Phoenix Gen. Hosp., 1979-80; physician/surgeon Med. Arts P.A., Scottsdale, Ariz., 1980—; mng. ptnr. Granite Reef Devel. Corp., Scottsdale, 1986-88; adminstr. Scottsdale Cmty. Hosp., 1988-89; chmn. dept. family practice Tempe St. Luke's Hosp., 1992-93, chmn. credentials com., 1994-95; med. dir. Scottsdale Convalescent Plaza, 1988-89. Chmn. bd. Am. Cancer Soc., Scottsdale, 1990, bd. dirs., 1987-93; guest faculty Christ the King Cath. Sch., 1987—. Named Physician of the Yr. Scottsdale Cmty. Hosp., 1986. Mem. Am. Coll. Osteo. Family Physicians, Am. Osteo. Assn., Ariz. Osteo. Med. Assn. Republican. Roman Catholic. Home: 3433 E Contessa Cir Mesa AZ 85213 Office: Medical Arts PA 1525 N Granite Reef #16 Scottsdale AZ 85257

LILLY-HERSLEY, JANE ANNE FEELEY, nursing researcher; b. Palo Alto, Calif., May 31, 1947; d. Daniel Morris Sr. and Suzanne (Agnew) Feeley; children: Cary Jane, Laura Blachree, Claire Foale; m. Dennis C. Hersley, Jan. 16, 1993. BS, U. Oreg., 1968; student, U. Hawaii, 1970; BSN, Sacramento City Coll., 1975. Cert. ACLS, BCLS. Staff and charge nurse, acute rehab. Santa Clara Valley Med. Ctr., San Jose, Calif., staff nurse, surg. ICU and trauma unit; clin. project leader mycophenolate mofetil program team Syntex Rsch., Palo Alto. Co-founder, CFO and dir. scientific rsch. Citizens United Responsible Environmentalism, Inc., CURE (internat. non-profit edn./rsch. orgn.). Mem. AACN.

LIM, ALEXANDER RUFASTA, neurologist, clinical investigator, educator, writer; b. Manila, Philippines, Feb. 20, 1942; s. Benito P. and Maria Lourdes (Cuyegkeng) L.; m. Norma Sue Hanks, June 1, 1968; children: Jeffrey Allen, Gregory Brian, Kevin Alexander, Melissa Gail. AA, U. Santo Tomas, Manila, Philippines, 1959, MD, 1964. Intern Bon Secours Hosp., Balt., 1964-65; resident internal medicine Scott and White Clinic, Temple, Tex., 1965-67; resident in neurology Cleve. Clinic, 1967-69, chief resident in neurology, 1969-70, fellow clin. neurophysiology, 1970-71, clin. assoc. neurologist, 1971-72; neurologist, co-founder, co-mng. ptnr. Neurol. Clinic, Corpus Christi, Tex., 1972—; pres., CEO Neurology, P.A., Corpus Christi, 1972-92; chief neurology Meml. Med. Ctr., Corpus Christi, 1975-90, Spohn Hosp., Corpus Christi, 1974-90, Reynolds Army Hosp., Ft. Sill, Okla., 1990-91; clin. assoc. prof. Sch. Medicine U. Tex. Health Sci. Ctr., San Antonio. Mem. editl. bd. Coastal Bend Medicine, 1988-95. Lt. col. Med. Corps, 1990-91. Recipient Army Commendation medal, 1991, Nat. Def. medal U.S. Army, 1991. Mem. AMA, Tex. Med. Assn. (chmn. neurology 1985-86), Tex. Neurol. Soc. (sec. 1986-88, pres. 1989-90), Am. Acad. Neurology, Am. Epilepsy Soc., Am. Acad. Clin. Neurophysiology, Am. Electroencephalographic Soc., So. Electroencephalographic Soc., Am. Acad. Pain Mgmt., Physician Com. Responsible Medicine, Am. Legion, Internat. Platform Assn., KC. Republican. Roman Catholic. Home: 4821 Augusta Cir Corpus Christi TX 78413-2711 Office: The Neurological Clinic 3006 S Alameda St Corpus Christi TX 78404-2601

LIM, DANIEL VAN, microbiology educator; b. Houston, Apr. 15, 1948; s. Don H. and Lucy (Toy) L.; m. Carol Lee, Sept. 2, 1973. BA in Biology, Rice U., 1970; PhD in Microbiology, Tex. A&M U., 1973. Postdoctoral fellow Baylor Coll. Medicine, 1973-76; asst. prof. U South Fla., Tampa, 1976-81, assoc. prof. microbiology, 1981-87, chmn. dept. biology, 1983-85, prof. 1987—; pres. Micro Concepts Rsch. Corp; dir. Inst. Biomolecular Sci., 1988-93; cons. in field. Author: Microbiology, 1989, Introduction to Microbiology, 1995; inventor bacteriological broth. Recipient Outstanding Ph.D. Dissertation in U.S. award Phi Sigma, 1974, Outstanding Contbn. in Sci. and Tech. award Fla. Gov. Fellow Am. Acad. Microbiology; mem. Inter-Am. Soc. Chemotherapy (v.p. 1983-88), Am. Soc. Microbiology (pres. southeastern br. 1990-91, Carski award com. 1983-86, Margaret Green Outstanding Tchr. award). Office: U South Fla 4202 E Fowler Ave LIF 136 Tampa FL 33620-5150

LIM, HWA AUN, research geneticist, bioinformaticist, consultant; b. Alor Setar, Kedah, Malaysia, July 29, 1957; came to U.S., 1981; s. Keng Hoon and Beng See (Tan) L. BSc (hons.), Imperial Coll. of Sci. & Tech., London, 1981; MA, U. Rochester, 1982, PhD, 1986. Rsch. asst. Imperial Coll. of Sci. & Tech., London, 1978-81, U. Rochester, Rochester, N.Y., 1981-85; medical asst. Strong Meml. Hosp., Rochester, N.Y., 1985-86; rsch. assoc. Lab. for Laser Energetics, Rochester, N.Y., 1986-87; rsch. assoc. Fla. State U., Tallahassee, 1987-89, univ. faculty, 1989-95; dir. bioinformatics HYSEQ, Sunnyvale, Calif., 1995—; adj. prof. St. Johns Fisher Coll., Rochester, 1986-87; vis. academician USSR Acad. Scis., Moscow, Kiev, Tbilisi, 1989; prin. investigator Fla. State U., 1989-95. Co-author: Computer Analysis of Genetic Macromolecules: Structure, Function and Evolution, 1994; editor: Electrophoresis, Supercomputing and Genome, 1991, Bioinformatics, Supercomputing and Genome, 1993, Isozymes: Roles in Evolution, Genetics and Physiology, 1994, Bioinformatics and Genome Research, 1994, Gene Families: Structure, Function, Genetics and Evolution, 1996; mng. editor Internat. Jour. Genomic Rsch., 1989—; assoc. editor Internat. Jour. Modern Physics C: Physics and Computers, 1989—; editor Jour. Modelling and Scientific Computing, 1991—; contbr. articles to profl. jours. Mem. rev. panel NSF, Arlington, Va., 1992, Nat. Cancer Inst., Bethesda, Md., 1994; bioinformatics expert UN, Daejon, Korea, Rome, Washington, 1993. Recipient numerous grants. Mem. AAAS, N.Y. Acad. Scis., Internat. Assn. Math. & Computer Modelling, Internat. Human Genome Orgn., Soc. Chinese Bioscientists in Am. (life). Office: HYSEQ 670 Almanor Ave Sunnyvale CA 94086

LIM, JOSEPH DY, oral surgeon; b. Manila, Nov. 2, 1948; s. Celestino Yu and Soledad (Dy) L.; m. Giok Leng Cua, Nov. 10, 1974; children: Joseph Oliver, Alistair Bryan, Kenneth Lester, Mark Andrew. DMD cum laude, U. of the East, The Philippines, 1974. Pres. Filipino-Chinese Dental Found., Inc., 1982-83; mng. dir. Internat. Dental Supply, Inc., Manila, 1982—; pvt. practice Manila, 1975—; pres. Oral Implantology Ctr. of The Philippines, 1992—; co-chmn. trade exhibits Asian-Pacific Dental Congress, 1994; organizing chmn. 12th Internat. Oral Implant Symposium, Manila, 1995; chief Philippine del. 14th Asian-Pacific Dental Congress, Seoul, Republic of Korea, 1989; Philippine del. 16th Asian-Pacific Dental Congress, Kuala Lumpur, Malaysia, 1993; mem. internat. adv. bd. Implant Dentistry Rsch. and Edn. Found. of Internat. Congress Oral Implantologist. Editl. cons. MDS Digest, 1989; contbr. sci. articles to profl. jours. Chmn., team leader Civic Action, Filipino-Chinese Dental Found., Inc., 1981—; pres. Metro Manila Health Group-Dr. Puring Rocamora Meml. Found. Recipient Disting. Svc. award Filipino-Chinese Dental Found., Inc., 1982, Outstanding Achievement award Grace Alumni Assn., Inc., 1995. Fellow Philippine Coll. Oral Maxillo-Facial Surgeons, Internat. Coll. Dentists, Internat. Assn. Oral and Maxillofacial Surgeons, Asian Oral Implant Acad. (hon.), Internat. Congress Oral Implantologist (diplomate, v.p. Asian-Pacific sect., Edn. award 1995); mem. ADA (assoc.), Philippine Dental Assn. (auditor 1982-83, 92-93, 94-95, trustee 1988-89, chmn. trade exhibits 1982-89, Presdl. award of merit 1983, Spkr.'s Bur. 1992—), Manila Dental Soc. (pres. 1989-90, organizer CIVAC team 1982—), U. of the East Dental Alumni Inc. (bd. dirs. 1993—), Fedn. Dentaire Internat. (co-chmn. trade exhibits 1986), Asian-Pacific Dental Fedn., Asian Oral Implant Acad., Assn. Asian Oral Mixillo-Facial Surgeons, Internat. Assn. Dental Rsch., Asian Acad. Craniomandibular Disorders, Assn. Dental Practitioners of Philippines (pres. 1993—), Oral Implantology Ctr. Study Club (founding), Am. Acad. Implant Dentistry, Acad. Osseointegration. Office: Tytana Pla Ste 821, Pla Lorenzo Ruiz Binondo, Manila The Philippines also: Ortigas Ctr Complex, Jollibee Ctr Bldg Ste 202, Pasig, Metro Manila The Philippines

LIM, KASIAN, surgeon, educator; b. Foochien, China, Dec. 6, 1929; arrived in Philippines, 1936; s. Hulay Lim and Oan Yu Ang; m. Flora Ludo, Apr. 8, 1961; 1 child, Arthur Joseph. MD, U. Santo Tomas, Philippines, 1955. Diplomate Am. Bd. Surgery, Philippine Bd. Surgery, Philippine Bd. Thoracic and Cardiovascular Surgery. Assoc. prof. surgery U. Santo Tomas, Philippines; chief dept. surgery, med. dir. Chinese Gen. Hosp. & Med. Ctr., Manila. Mem. Philippine Coll. Surgeons, Philippine Assn. Thoracic and Cardiovascular Surgeons (pres. 1970), Surg. Oncology Soc. of the Philippines.

LIM, M. BLANCHE, nephrologist; b. Cebu, Philippines, Nov. 20, 1947; came to U.S., 1974; d. Antonio and Conchita (Tio) L.; m. J. March Maquilan, June 11, 1974; children: Michael, Melissa, Genevieve. BS, U. San Carlos, 1968; MD, Cebu Inst. Medicine, 1972. Diplomate Am. Bd. Internal Medicine, Am. Bd. Nephrology. Asst. prof. Hahnemann Univ. Hosp., Phila., 1986—; med. dir. BMA Phila. Dialysis, 1986—. Mem. Am. Soc. Nephrology, Internat. Soc. Nephrology. Office: 205 N Broad St Philadelphia PA 29103

LIM, RAMON (KHE-SIONG), neuroscience educator, researcher; b. Cebu City, Philippines, Feb. 5, 1933; came to U.S., 1959; naturalized 1973; s. Eng-Lian and Su (Yu) L.; m. Victoria K. Sy, June 21, 1961; children—Jennifer, Wendell, Caroline. A.B., U. Santo Tomas, Manila, 1953, M.D. cum laude, 1958; Ph.D. in Biochemistry, U. Pa., 1966. Diplomate Am. Bd. Psychiatry And Neurology. Research neurochemist U. Mich., Ann Arbor, 1966-69; asst. prof. biochemistry U. Chgo., 1969-76, assoc. prof. Brain Research Inst., 1976-81; prof. dept. neurology U. Iowa, Iowa City, 1981—, dir. div. neurochemistry and neurobiology, 1981—. career investigator, VA, 1983. Mem. editorial bd. Internat. Jour. Devel. Neurosci., 1984—. Contbr. numerous articles to sci. jours. Research includes isolation and characterization of regulatory brain proteins; growth and differentiation of brain cells; brain chemistry and molecular biology. Grantee NIH, 1971—, NSF, 1979—, VA, 1981—; Art Assn. Philippines 3rd prize, 1957; named Outstanding Overseas Young Chinese, Fedn. Overseas Chinese Orgns., 1961. Mem. Am. Soc. Biochem. Molecular Biology, Internat. Soc. Neurochemistry (vis. lectorship 1986), Am. Soc. Neurochemistry, Soc. Neurosci., Am. Soc. Cell Biology. Avocations: calligraphy, painting, writing, music. Home: 118 Richards St Iowa City IA 52246-3516 Office: U Iowa Iowa City IA 52242

LIM, SHUN PING, cardiologist; b. Singapore, Jan. 12, 1947; came to U.S., 1980; s. Tay Boh and Si Moi (Foo) L.; m. Christine Sock Kian Ng; children: Corinne Xian-li, Damien John Xian-ming, Justin David Xian-an. MBBS with honors, Monash U., Clayton, Australia, 1970, PhD, 1981; M in Medicine, Nat. U. Singapore, 1975; M, Royal Australasian Coll. Physicians, 1975. Rsch. scholar Australian Nat. Health and Med. Rsch. Coun., Canberra, 1978-79; fellow in cardiology Michael Reese Hosp., Chgo., 1980-82; chief noninvasive cardiovascular imaging Cin. V.A.M.C., 1982-86; asst. prof. U. Cin., 1982-86; cardiologist Quain and Ramstad Clinic, Bismarck, N.D., 1986-88; clin. asst. prof. U. N.D., Bismarck, 1986-90; pvt. practice cardiovascular diseases, 1988-91; assoc. prof. medicine U. N.D., 1991-93; clin. assoc. prof. Ohio State U., Columbus, 1993—; dir. catheterization lab. Marion (Ohio) Gen. Hosp., 1991-93; med. dir. Cardiovasc. Cons., Columbus, 1993—; pres. Inst. for Advanced Med. Tech., 1990—, Am. Med. Investments, Inc., 1994—; chmn. ICU com. VA Med. and Regional Office Ctr., Fargo, N.D., 1991-93, chief cardiology sect., 1991-93; founder, med. dir. Cardiovascular Cons., Singapore, 1993—. Contbr. articles to profl. jours.; catheter tip polarographic lactic acid and lactate sensor. Fellow ACP, Am. Coll. Cardiology, Internat. Coll. Angiology, Am. Coll. Angiology, Royal Australian Coll. Physicians, Am. Coll. Chest Physicians, Coun. on Clin. Cardiology of Am. Heart Assn., Soc. Critical Care Medicine, Acad. Medicine Singapore; mem. Am. Fedn. Clin. Rsch., Am. Soc. Echocardiography, Am. Heart Assn. (grantee 1984-85), Ohio State Med. Assn., N.Y. Acad. Scis. (life). Methodist. Office: Cardiovascular Cons Ohio Ste 200 & 220 3545 Olentangy River Rd Columbus OH 43214

LIN, CHIN-CHU, physician, educator, researcher; b. Taichung, Taiwan, Oct. 24, 1935; came to U.S., 1969; naturalized, 1977; s. Kung Yen and Nung (Chiang) L.; m. Sue S. Hsu; children: Jim, John, Juliet. BS, Nat. Taiwan U., 1956, MD, 1961. Diplomate Am. Bd. Ob-Gyn., Am. Bd. Maternal-Fetal Medicine (bd. examiners 1986-89). Rsch. fellow SUNY Downstate Med. Ctr., N.Y.C., 1969-71; resident in ob-gyn Columbia U., N.Y.C., 1972-74; fellow in maternal-fetal medicine Albert Einstein Med. Coll., 1974-76; lectr., staff Nat. Taiwan U. Hosp., Taipei, 1966-69, 1971-72; staff, asst. prof. U. Chgo., 1976-80, assoc. prof., 1980-87, prof., 1987—; maternal-child health adv. com. Dept. of Health, Chgo., 1985-88; frequent keynote spkr. numerous internat. confs. including 12th Asian and Oceanic Congress on Ob-Gyn., 1989, 8th Congress of Fedn. Asian Oceanic Perinatal Soc., Taiwan, 1994, 5th World Congress Ultrasound in Ob-Gyn., Japan, 1995; vis. prof. univs. in U.S., Japan, People's Republic of China, Republic of China, 1981—; keynote spkr., prof. S.J. Chiu Meml. lectures, Taiwan, 1989. Author: Intrauterine Growth Retardation, 1984, The High Risk Fetus, 1993; editor in chief Taiwan Tribune Med. Issues, 1986-89; contbr. over 80 articles to profl. jours., 17 chpts. to books; reviewer for Am. Jour. Ob-Gyn., Jour. Perinatal Medicine, Obstetrics and Gynecology, Jour. Maternal-Fetal Medicine, Jour. Formosan Med. Assn.; pres. 10th ann. meeting N.Am. Taiwanese Profs. Assn., Taiwan, 1990. People to People Ob-Gyn del. to USSR, 1987; bd. dirs. Taiwanese United Fund, 1980—, pres. 1984-85. Selected candidate semifinalist dean of med. sch. Nat. Taiwan U., 1993; disting. scholar lectr. award Formosa Med. Assn., 1981, Kenote Speaker award Asia-Oceanic Congress Perinatology, 1986, 94, 2d Internat. Symposium on Obstetrics and Perinatal Medicine, Beijing, 1988, 28th Sci. Meeting Assn. Ob-gyn., Taiwan, 1988, 12th Asian Oceanic Congress on Obstetrics and Gynecology, 1989, 33d Ann. Meeting Assn. Ob-gyn., Taiwan, 1993, 5th World Congress Ultrasound in Ob-gyn., Japan, 1995. Mem. Am. Coll. Ob.-Gyn. (jour. reviewer 1982—, Purdue Frederick award 1978), N.Am. Taiwanese Profs. Assn. (bd. dirs. 1988-91, bull. editor 1980—, v.p. 1988-89, pres. 1989-90, pres. 10th ann. meeting Taiwan 1990), N.Am. Taiwanese Med. Assn. (chmn. ednl. com. 1984-88, bd. dirs. 1991-93, chmn. scientific program 1994), Taiwanese United Fund (bd. dirs. 1980—, pres. 1984-85), Cen. Assn. Ob.-Gyn., Soc. Perinatal Obstetricians, Internat. Soc. Study Hypertension in Pregnancy, Am. Inst. Ultrasound in Medicine, Chgo. Gynecol. Soc. Office: U Chgo Dept Ob-Gyn 5841 S Maryland Ave Chicago IL 60637-1463

LIN, DORIS BISHYNG, optometrist; b. Tainan, Taiwan, Apr. 23, 1947; came to U.S., 1971; d. Chung-Lee and Shou-Ching Shieh; m. Wunan Lin,

July 10, 1971. BS in Physics, U. Calif., Berkely, 1965; MS, U. Calif. Berkeley, 1974, OD, 1976, PhD, 1993. Cert. tchr., Calif. Optometrist specializing in contact lens, low ision and visual tng., Castro Valley, Calif., 1976—; pub. health adv. bd. mem. Alameda County, Calif., 1993—. Co-chair Pacific Rim Internat. com. U. Calif., Berkeley, 1994—; bd. dirs. Asian Am. Together, Castro Valley, Calif. Mem. Am. Optometrists Assn., Calif. Optometrists Assn., Alameda/Contra Costa Counties Optometry Soc., Rotary Internat. Office: 3550 Castro Valley Blvd Castro Valley CA 94546

LIN, JUNG-CHUNG, microbiologist, researcher; b. Ping Tung, Taiwan, Nov. 15, 1939; came to U.S., 1970; s. Wan-Ho and Kwei-Tzu (Chen) L.; m. Shou-Huei, July 19, 1967; children: Melissa, Richard. PhD, Temple U., 1974. Rsch. asst. unit 2 U.S. Naval Med. Rsch., Taipei, Taiwan, 1965-66; asst. prof. Nat. Def. Med. Coll., Taipei, 1967-70; assoc. mem. Inst. of Zoology Academia Sinica, Taipei, 1967-74; rsch. assoc. U. N.C., Chapel Hill, 1977-80, rsch. asst. prof., 1980-84, rsch. assoc. prof., 1984-90; chief molecular biology sect. Ctrs. for Disease Control, Atlanta, 1990—; adj. prof. Emory U., Atlanta, 1992—. Author chpts. in books; contbr. over 80 articles to profl. jours. Grantee NCI, NIH, NIAID. Mem. AAAS, Am. Soc. for Microbiology, Am. Soc. for Virology, Am. Assn. for Cancer Rsch., Internat. Soc. for Antiviral Rsch., Internat. Assn. for Rsch. on Epstein-Barr Virus and Associated Diseases. Home: 3723 Toxaway Ct Atlanta GA 30341-4622 Office: Ctrs for Disease Control 1600 Clifton Rd NE Atlanta GA 30333-4018

LIN, MING SHEK, allergist, immunologist; b. Taipei, Taiwan, Oct. 11, 1937; came to U.S., 1965; s. Joseph and Tong-Kai (Chan) Lynn; m. Mary Liao, Nov. 22, 1969; children: Jerry, Michael. MD, Nat. Taiwan U., 1964; PhD, U. Pitts., 1974. Diplomate Am. Acad. Allergy and Immunology, Am. Bd. Pediatrics. Asst. prof. U. Pitts. Grad. Sch. Pub. Health, 1976-80; asst. and assoc. prof. dept. pediatrics U. Pitts. Sch. Medicine, 1981—; chief sect. of allergy and immunology Forbes Health System, Pitts., 1987—; pres. Pitts. Allergy Soc., 1994—. Contbr. articles to Jour. Allery and Immunology, Internat. Congress of Immunology, Jour. Allergy, Jour. Pediatrics, Jour. Cellular Immunology. Named Winklestan lectr., 1976. Fellow Am. Soc. for Microbiology; mem. AMA. Home: 81 Locksley Dr Pittsburgh PA 15235-5117 Office: 4099 William Penn Hwy Ste 805 Monroeville PA 15146-2518

LIN, TU, endocrinologist, educator, researcher, academic administrator; b. Fukien, China, Jan. 18, 1941; came to U.S., 1967; s. Tao Shing and Jan En (Chang) L.; m. Pai-Li, July 1, 1967; children: Vivian H., Alexander T., Margaret C. MD, Nat. Taiwan U., Taipei, 1966. Diplomate Am. Bd. Internal Medicine, Am. Bd. Endocrinology and Metabolism. Intern Episcopal Hosp.-Temple U., Phila., 1967-68; resident in medicine Berkshire Med. Ctr., Pittsfield, Mass., 1968-70; fellow in endocrinology Lahey Clinic, Boston, 1970-71, Roger Williams Gen. Hosp.-Brown U., Providence, 1971-73; rsch. fellow in med. sci. Brown U., 1971-73; chief, endocrine sect. WJB Dorn Vet. Hosp., Columbia, S.C., 1975—; asst. prof. U. S.C. Sch. Medicine, Columbia, 1976-80, assoc. prof., 1980-84, prof. medicine, 1984—, prof., dir. divsn. endocrinology, diabetes and metabolism, 1992—; mem. Merit Review Bd. of Endocrinology, Dept. Vet. Affairs, 1990-94. Author: (book chpt.) Disorders of Male Reproductive Function, 1996; mem. editl. bd. Biology of Reproduction, 1990-95, Jour. of Andrology, 1993-96; contbr. articles to med. and profl. jours. Recipient Disting. Investigator award U. S.C. Sch. Medicine, 1981, 88, 95. Fellow ACP; mem. Endocrine Soc., Am. Soc. Andrology (chmn. ann. meeting, coun. 1993-96), Soc. for the Study of Reproduction. Office: U SC Sch Medicine Med Library Bldg Ste 316 Columbia SC 29208

LIN, YUNG-ZEN, pediatrician; b. Kaoshong, Taiwan, June 30, 1956; s. Jin-Yuan and Su-chi (Wang) L.; m. Meng-chuan Hong, May 26, 1984; children: Hsin-Chia, Hsin-Chin. MD, Med. Coll. Nat. Taiwan U., 1981. Resident in pediatrics Nat. Taiwan U. Hosp., Taipei, 1983-87, fellow in allergy and immunology, 1987-88; lectr. Med. Coll. Nat. Taiwan U. Hosp., Taipei, 1995—; attending pediatrician Taipei Mcpl. Chung Hsiao Hosp., 1988—; vis. staff dept. pediatrics Nat. Taiwan U. Hosp., 1988—. Contbr. articles to profl. jours. Lt. Taiwanese Army, 1981-83. Recipient Pediatric Overseas Publ. award Mead Johnson, 1988, 90, Rsch. award Govt. of Taipei, 1989, 91, 92, 95, 96.

LINAM, HAROLD WAYNE, medical technologist; b. Victoria, Tex., June 9, 1935; s. Aaron Burleson and Gladys May (Pridgen) L.; m. Charlene Ophelia Brown, Sept. 2, 1960; children: Gordon Wayne, Rhonda Grace, Lynda Gayle. Student, Victoria Coll., 1955-56; med. lab. technologist, Commonwealth Coll. Scsi., 1962. Health Edn. Welfare cert. Med. technologist DeTar Hosp., Victoria, 1963-68, Citizens Hosp., Victoria, 1968-73; supr. Diagnostic Lab., Victoria, 1973-85; med. technologist Cuero (Tex.) Cmty. Hosp., 1985—. Mem. Am. Med. Technologist (cert.). Baptist.

LINAWEAVER, WALTER ELLSWORTH, JR., physician; b. San Pedro, Calif., Oct. 16, 1928; s. Walter Ellsworth and Catherine Breathed (Bridges) L.; m. Lydia Anne Whitlock, Oct. 6, 1957; children: Catherine Ann, Nancy Alyn, Walter E. III. BA cum laude, Pomona Coll., 1952; MD, U. Rochester, 1956. Diplomate Am. Bd. Allergy and Immunology, Am. Bd. Pediatrics, Am. Bd. Pediatric Allergy. Intern pediatrics Med. Ctr. U. Rochester, N.Y., 1956-57, resident pediatrics Med. Ctr., 1958-59; asst. resident pediatrics Med. Ctr. UCLA, 1957-58; fellow allergy and immunology Med. Ctr. U. Colo., Denver, 1959-61, instr. pediatrics Sch. Medicine, 1961; pvt. practice Riverside (Calif.) Med. Clinic, 1962—; bd. dirs. Riverside Med. Clinic. Elder Presbyn. Ch. Staff sgt. U.S. Army, 1946-48. Inducted into Athletic Hall of Fame Pomona Coll., Claremont, Calif., 1979. Fellow Am. Acad. Allergy and Immunology, Am. Acad. Pediat., Southwestern Pediat. Soc. (emeritus, v.p. 1978), L.A. Acad. Medicine; mem. Riverside County Med. Soc. (councillor), Riverside County Heart Assn. Republican. Home: 1296 Tiger Tail Dr Riverside CA 92506-5475 Office: Riverside Med Clinic 3660 Arlington Ave Riverside CA 92506-3912

LINCHITZ, RICHARD MICHAEL, psychiatrist, pain medicine specialist, physician; b. Bklyn., Mar. 29, 1947; m. Rita A. Colao, Sept. 22, 1973; children: Elise Ann, Michael Benjamin, Jonathan Adam. BA cum laude in Psychology, Cornell U., 1967, MD, 1973; student L.I. Univ., 1967-68, U. Lausanne Med. Sch., 1968-71. Diplomate Am. Bd. Psychiatry and Neurology, Am. Acad. Pain Mgmt., AM. Bd. Pain Medicine. Intern, Moffit Hosp., San Francisco, 1973-74; resident in psychiatry Langley Porter Neuropsychiat. Inst., San Francisco, 1974-77; practice medicine specializing in treatment of chronic pain conditions and psychiatry, Carle Place, N.Y., 1978—; med. dir. Roslyn Mental Health Ctr. (N.Y.), 1978—, Pain Alleviation Center, Carle Place, 1978—. Recipient letter of commendation White House, 1977; Nathan Seligman award Cornell U. Med. Coll., 1973; Nat. Psychiat. Endowment Fund award Langley Porter Neuropsychiat. Inst., 1977; Langley Porter Youth Service award, 1977. Fellow Am. Coll. Pain Medicine; mem. Am. Psychiat. Assn., Acad. Pain Research, Am. Pain Soc., Nassau Psychiat. Soc., Am. Acad. of Pain Medicine (bd. dirs.), Am. Acad. Pain Mgmt. (cert.), Alpha Omega Alpha. Author: Life Without Pain, 1987. Office: 179 Westbury Ave Carle Place NY 11514-1227

LINCICOME, DAVID RICHARD, biomedical and animal scientist; b. Champaign, Ill., Jan. 17, 1914; s. David Rosebery and Olive Iola (Casper) L.; m. Dorothy Lucile Van Cleave, Sept. 1, 1941 (dec. Nov. 1952); children: David Van Cleave, Judith Ann; m. Margaret Stirewalt, Dec. 29, 1953. BS, MS with high honors, U. Ill., 1937; PhD in Tropical Medicine, Tulane U., 1941. Diplomate (emeritus) Am. Bd. Microbiology; diplomate Am. Coll. Animal Physiology; cert. animal scientist Am. Registry Profl. Animal Scientists. Asst. instr. U. Ill., 1937; asst. instr. tropical medicine Tulane U. Med. Sch., 1937-41; asst. prof. parasitology U. Ky., 1941-47, U. Wis. Med. Sch., 1947-49; sr. rsch. parasitologist Du Pont Co., 1949-53; from asst. prof. to full prof. biol. Scis. Howard U., 1953-70; vis. sci. NIH, 1965-66; registrar, Jacob Sheep Conservancy, 1989-96, bd. dirs., 1990—, pres., 1996; vis. scholar Nat. Agrl. Libr. USDA, 1990-92; guest scientist USDA Exp. Sta., Beltsville, Md., 1978—, Naval Med. Rsch. Inst., 1954-62. Founder, editor Exptl. Parasitology, 1949-76; editor Transactions of the Ky. Acad. Sci., 1946-49, Transactions of the Am. Microscopical Soc., 1970-71, Internat. Rev. Tropical Medicine, 1953-63; founder Virology, 1950, Advances in Vet. Sci., 1952. Lt. col. Med. Svc. Corps, U.S. Army, World War II, PTO. Recipient Anniversary award Helminthological Soc., 1975; rsch. grantee NIH, 1958-68. Fellow AAAS, Explorers Club (nat., N.Y.); mem. Helminthological Soc. (pres. 1958, emeritus), Am. Physiol. Soc. (emeritus), Soc. Invertebrate Zoology (emeritus), Am. Soc. Zoologists (emeritus), Am. Soc. Parasitologists, Am. Soc. Cell Biology, Am. Microscopical Soc. (emeritus), Royal Soc. Tropical Medicine (emeritus), Am. Soc. Tropical Medicine (emeritus), Am. Goat Soc. (bd. dirs. 1992—), Am. Dairy Goat Assn. (founder., 1st sec. rsch. found. 1979, bd. dirs. 1972-87), Nat. Pygmy Goat Assn. (bd. dirs. 1976-92, pres. 1979), Natural Colored Wool Growers Assn. (bd. dirs. 1988-94), Jacob Sheep Breeders Assn., Jacob Sheep Soc. (Eng.), Nat. Tunis Sheep Registry (bd. dirs. 1991-93, sec. 1991-92), Soft-coated Wheaten Terrier Club of Am. (mem rescue com. 1993—), Greater Washington D.C. Area Soft-Coated Wheaten Terrier Club (founder, pres. 1991-92), Am. Livestock Breeds Conservancy (bd. dirs. 1994—), Va. State Dairy Goat Assn. (founder, pres. 1976), Midwestern Conf. Parasitologists (founder, 1st sec. 1949), Soc. Exptl. Biology & Medicine (sec. D.C. chpt. 1996, emeritus), Phi Beta Kappa, Sigma Xi (assoc. mem. 1936, mem. 1941, pres. Howard U. chpt. 1962). Home: Frogmoor Farm 3032 Courtney Sch Rd Midland VA 22728-9748 also: PO Box 13 4419 Cambria Ave Garrett Park MD 20896 Office: USDA BARC East Rm 207 Bldg 467 Beltsville MD 20705

LINCLAU, DENISE MARIE, nursing administrator; b. Detroit, Oct. 1, 1951; d. Adolph Francis and Marie Yvonne (DeWolf) L.; m. Donald M. Miller, Apr. 11, 1975 (div.); children: Martin Linclau-Miller, Russell Linclau-Miller. BSN, Wayne State U., 1974; MSA, Cen. Mich. U., 1985; student, Wharton Sch. Exec. Mgmt./, Leonard Davis Inst. Health Care Mgmt., U. Pa., 1988, 94. RN, Mich.; cert. nurse adminstr., critical care, trauma nurse. Instr. nursing edn. St. John Hosp., 1973-85; dir. ednl. svcs. Holistic Health Care, Inc., Warren, Mich., 1985-86; clin. mgr. critical care div. Hutzel Hosp. Detroit Med. Ctr., 1986-88; adminstrv. mgr. critical care div. Harper Hosp. Detroit Med. Ctr., 1988-95; dir. critical care nursing svcs. Detroit Receiving Hosp., Detroit Med. Ctr., 1989-95; asst. v.p. critical care and emergency svcs. Sinai Hosp., Detroit, 1995—; instr. advanced courses (ACLS) Am. Heart Assn., 1982—, instr. basic courses BCLS, 1985—. Instr. and mem. U.S. Power Squadron Grosse Pointe, Mich., 1984—; del. People to People Ambassadors Program to People's Republic of China, 1991. Recipient Nat. Disting. Svc. award Registry Nursing Am. Nurses Assn., 1988. Mem. AAUW, ANA, AACN (Pres. award 1975), Am. Assn. Nursing Execs., Am. Orgn. Nurse Execs., Am. Burn Assn., Am. Assn. Female Execs., Sigma Theta Tau, Sigma Iota Epsilon. Roman Catholic. Home: 1375 Grayton St Grosse Pointe MI 48230-1127

LINCOLN, THOMAS L., pathologist, educator; b. Pitts., Jan. 4, 1929; s. John J. and Jean Gregg Lincoln; m. Nancy, Apr. 15, 1956 (dec. Feb. 1971); children: Elizabeth, John; m. Catherine de La Prée., May 30, 1972; 1 child, Iris. BS, Yale U., 1955, MD, 1960. Diplomat Nat. Bd. Med. Examiners, Anatomical Pathology. Intern in pathology Yale U., New Haven, Conn., 1960-61, resident, 1961-63; rsch. asst. prof. Inst. for Fluid Dynamics and Applied Math./U. Md., 1963-66; assoc. clin. prof., dept. pathology U. So. Calif. Cancer Ctr., L.A., 1975-77, assoc. prof., 1977-87, prof. rsch. pathology, 1987-96; prof. emeritus U. So. Calif. Cancer Ctr.; sr. scientist Sunquest Info. Sys., Tucson, 1995-96; vis. prof. dept. clin. epidemiology and social medicine, St. Thomas's Hosp. Med. Sch., London, 1972; cons./researcher in field. Contbr. articles to profl. jours. Patient advisor Leukemia Soc. of Am., L.A., 1970-82. Mem. Johns Hopkins Med. Soc., Leukemia Soc. of Am., Cosmos Club (Washington), Am. Soc. Clin. Pathology, Coll. of Am. Pathologists, IEEE, AMA, Am. Assn. Med. Systems and Informatics, others. Democrat. Episcopalian. Home: 802 Franklin St Santa Monica CA 90403-2318 Office: Rand Corp 1700 Main St Santa Monica CA 90407

LIND, DAVID SCOTT, surgical oncologist, educator; b. Rochester, Minn., Nov. 26, 1958; s. James F. and Dorothy A. Lind; m. Barbara Kaplan, June 9, 1984; children: Joanna, Jason, Jenny. BS, McMaster U., Hamilton, Ont., Can., 1981; MD, Ea. Va. Med. Sch., Noroflk, 1984. Resident surgery U. Tex., San Antonio, 1984-89; resident surg. oncology Med. Coll. Va., Richmond, 1989-92; asst. prof. dept. surgery U. Fla. Coll. Medicine, Gainesville, 1992—. Home: 8007 SW 43rd Pl Gainesville FL 32608 Office: U Fla Dept Surgery PO Box 100286 Gainesville FL 32610

LIND, SVEN-GUNNAR, dentist; b. Dorotea, Sweden, Oct. 9, 1954; s. Gunnar and Eva (Jakobsson) L.; m. Marilou Jabellana. DDS, U. Umeå, Sweden, 1979. Gen. dentist Kronobergs County Coun., Växjö, Sweden, 1980, Södermanlands County Coun., Eskilstuna, Sweden, 1980-86, 90-91, N/W Armed Forces Hosp., Tabuk, Saudi Arabia, 1986-88, Airbase Dental Clinic, Tabuk, 1988-90, Nordland County Coun., Hattfjelldal, Norway, 1991-92; dentist Västernorrlands County Coun., Örnsköldsvik, Sweden, 1992—. 2nd lt. Swedish Army, 1981. Mem. Swedish Dental Assn. Home: Fäbodvägen 1 B, S-892 50 Domsjö Sweden Office: Doktorsgatan 6, S-892 30 Domsjö Sweden

LINDAHL, JOSEPH EDWIN, physician assistant; b. Logansport, Ind., Nov. 5, 1948; married; 2 children. AS, Baylor/U.S. Army, San Antonio, 1977; BS, U. So. Ill., 1987; MS, Chapman Coll., 1990. NCCPA. With U.S. Army, 1970-90, physician asst., 1977-90; physician asst. Miller Ortho. Clin., Charlotte, N.C., 1990-95, Lipscomb Ortho. Clin., Nashville, 1995—. Fellow Am. Acad. Physician Assts., Soc. Army Physician Assts.; mem. Tenn. Acad. Physician Assts. (v.p.), Physician Assts. Ortho. Surgery (1st pres., past pres.). Office: Lipscomb Clinic 4230 Harding Rd Nashville TN 37205

LINDAUER, THEODORE, psychiatrist; b. N.Y.C., July 17, 1935; s. Harry and Anne (Kurtz) L. AB, Columbia Coll., 1956; MD, U. Pitts., 1960; cert. in adult psychiatry, U. Ill., 1963; cert. in child psychiatry, Harvard U., 1965. Intern Michael Reese Hosp., Chgo.; resident adult psychiatry U. Ill., Chgo.; resident child psychiatry Harvard U., Boston; dir. mental health svcs. L.A. Unified Sch. Dist., 1971-73; asst. clin. prof. UCLA, 1973-75, 79-81; dir. adolescent svcs. Kellogg Psychiat. Hosp., Corona, Calif., 1977-79 med. dir. Hathaway Home for Children, L.A., 1980-82; cons. psychiatrist Chaparral Treatment Ctr., San Bernadino, Calif., 1987-89; cons. Mental health AIDS L.A. Project, Long Beach, Calif., 1987-89; cons. psychiatrist Med. Sq. Counseling Ctr., Garden Grove, Calif., 1987-94. Mem., speaker Common Cause, L.A., 1971—; mem., writer Amnesty Internat., L.A., 1971—. Recipient N.Y. State Regents scholar, 1952-56. Mem. Am. Psychiat. Assn., Am. Assn. Child and Adolescent Psychiatry. Home: 1 Jady Hill Ave J-8 Exeter NH 03833

LINDBERG, C. RONALD, ophthalmologist; b. Chgo., Dec. 20, 1947; s. Carl Victor and Etty Marie Louise Lindberg; m. Marilyn Ann Rue, Sept. 2, 1972; children: Erik, Mark. AB, Augustana Coll., 1970; MS, U. Ill., 1972; MD, U. Ill., Chgo., 1976. Diplomate Am. Bd. Ophthalmology. Intern Pacific Med. Ctr., San Francisco, 1976-77; resident in ophthalmology U. Ill. Eye and Ear Infirmary, Chgo., 1977-80; pvt. practice ophthalmology La Grange, Ill., 1980-91, Western Springs, Ill., 1991—. With USAR, 1970-76. Fellow Am. Acad. Ophthalmology. Lutheran. Office: 915 W 55th St Western Springs IL 60558

LINDBERG, DONALD ALLAN BROR, library administrator, pathologist, educator; b. N.Y.C., Sept. 21, 1933; s. Harry B. and Frances Seeley (Little) L.; m. Mary Musick, June 8, 1957; children: Donald Allan Bror, Christopher Charles Seeley, Jonathan Edward Moyer. AB, Amherst Coll., 1954, ScD (hon.), 1979; MD, Columbia U., 1958; ScD (hon.), SUNY, 1987; LLD (hon.), U. Mo., Columbia, 1990. Diplomate Am. Bd. Pathology, Am. Bd. Med. Examiners (exec. bd. 1987-91). Rsch. asst. Amherst Coll., 1954-55; intern in pathology Columbia-Presbyn. Med. Ctr., 1958-59, asst. resident in pathology, 1959-60; asst. in pathology Coll. Physician and Surgeons Columbia U., N.Y.C., 1958-60; instr. pathology Sch. of Medicine U. Mo., 1962-63, asst. prof. Sch. of Medicine, 1963-66, assoc. prof. Sch. of Medicine, 1966-69, prof. Sch. of Medicine, 1969-84, dir. Diagnostic Microbiology Lab. Sch. of Medicine, 1960-63, dir. Med. Ctr. Computer Program Sch. of Medicine, 1962-70, staff, exec. dir. for health affairs Sch. of Medicine, 1968-70, prof., chmn. dept. info. sci. Sch. of Medicine, 1969-71; dir. Nat. Libr. of Medicine, Bethesda, Md., 1984—; adj prof. pathology U. Md. Sch. Medicine, 1988—, clin. prof. pathology U. Va., 1992—; dir. Nat. Coord. Office for High Performance Computing and Comms., exec. office of Pres., Office Sci. & Tech. Policy, 1992-95; mem. computer sci./engring. bd. Nat. Acad. Sci., 1971-74, chmn. Nat. Adv. Com. Artificial Intelligence in Medicine, Stanford U., 1975-84; U.S. rep. to Internat. Med. Info. Assn./Internat. Fedn. Info. Processing, 1975-84; bd. dirs. Am. Med. Info. Assn., 1992—; adv. coun. Inst. Medicine, 1992—. Author: The Computer and Medical Care, 1968; The Growth of Medical Information Systems in the United States, 1979; editor: (with W. Siler) Computers in Life Science Research, 1975; (with others) Computer Applications in Medical Care, 1982; editor Methods of Info. in Medicine, 1970-83, assoc. editor, 1983—; editor Jour. Med. Systems, 1976—, Med. Informatics Jour., 1976—; chief editor procs. 3d World Conf. on Med. Informatics, 1980; editorial bd. Jour. of AMA, 1991—; contbr. articles to jours. Recipient Silver Cord award Internat. Fedn. for Info. Processing, 1980, Walter C. Alvarez award Am. Med. Writers Assn. 1989, PHS Surgeon Gen.'s medallion, 1989, Nathan Davis award AMA, 1989, Presdl. Disting. Exec. Rank award, Sr. Exec. Svc., Outstanding Svc. medal Uniformed Svcs. U. of the Health Scis., 1992, Computers in Healthcare Pioneer award, 1993; Simpson fellow Amherst Coll., 1954-55; Markle scholar in acad. medicine, 1964-69. Mem. Inst. Medicine of NAS, Coll. Am. Pathologists (commn. on computer policy and coordination 1981-84), Mo. State Med. Assn., Assn. for Computing Machines, Salutis Unitas (Am. v.p. 1981-91), Am. Assn. for Med. Systems and Informatics (internat. com. 1982-89, bd. dirs. 1982, editor conf. procs. 1983, 84), Gorgas Meml. Inst. Tropical and Preventive Medicine (bd. dirs. 1987—), Am. Med. Informatics Assn. (pres. 1988-91), Sigma Xi. Democrat. Club: Cosmos (Washington). Home: 13601 Esworthy Rd Germantown MD 20874-3319 Office: Nat Libr of Medicine 8600 Rockville Pike Bethesda MD 20894-0001

LINDBLAD, WILLIAM JOHN, pharmacologist; b. Glen Head, N.Y., Oct. 14, 1954; s. Herbert Paul and Elizabeth (Kisely) L.; m. Linda Susan Riewald, Aug. 23, 1985; children: Kelsi Anne, Jonathan William. BS, U. Maine, 1976; MS, Cleve. State U., 1977; PhD, U. R.I., 1980. Postdoctoral fellow Med. Coll. Va., Richmond, 1980-81, rsch. asst., 1981-83, asst. prof., 1983-89, assoc. prof., 1989-90; assoc. prof. pharm. scis. Wayne State U., Detroit, 1990—; pres. Yorkshire Pharm. Rsch. Inst., 1996—; pres. Yorkshire Pharms. Rsch. Inst., 1996—. Mng./co-editor: Wound Repair and Regeneration; co-editor: Wound Healing: Biochemical and Clinical Aspects, 1991; contbr. articles to profl. jours., chpts. to books. Community adv. bd. March of Dimes, Richmond, 1988-90. Recipient Probus Club Acad. Achievement award, 1994. Mem. Am. Assn. for Study of Liver Diseases, N.Y. Acad. Scis., Am. Soc. for Pharmacology and Exptl. Therapeutics, The Wound Healing Soc. Office: Wayne State U Dept Pharm Sci 721 Shapero Hall Detroit MI 48202

LINDBURG, DAYTHA EILEEN, physician assistant; b. Emporia, Kans., June 24, 1952; d. Kenneth Eugene and Elsie Eileen (Smith) L. BS cum laude, Kans. State U., 1974; BS magna cum laude, Wichita State U., 1976. Registered cert. physician asst. Physician asst. in family practice Fredrickson Clinic, Lindsborg, Kans., 1976-93; physician asst. in ob/gyn. Mowery Clinic, Salina, Kans., 1993—; cons. McPherson County (Kans.) Health Dept., 1983—. Mem. adv. bd. Riverview Estates Nursing Home, 1980-86; bd. dirs. McPherson County Humane Soc., 1989-93; choir mem. Messiah Luth. Ch., Lindsborg, 1981—, liturgist, 1991—, mem. Altar Guild, 1976—, mem. music and worship com., 1981-88. Kans. Bd. Regents scholar, 1970-71, Kans. State U. scholar, 1972, 73, Smurthwaite scholar, 1970-74. Mem. Assn. of Physician Assts. in Obstetrics and Gynecology, Kans. Acad. Physician Assts., Am. Acad. Physician Asst.

LINDE, LEONARD M., pediatric cardiologist; b. N.Y.C., June 1, 1928; s. Ben and Marsha (Weinberg) L.; m. Shirley Dann, Apr. 22, 1951; children: Bruce D., Lauren G., Brian K., Peter B. BS, U. Calif., Davis, 1947; MD, U. Calif., San Francisco, 1951. Intern Morrisania City (N.Y.) Hosp., 1952; from resident to sr. resident in pediat. L.A. Childrens Hosp., 1952-56; prof. pediat. cardiology UCLA Sch. Medicine, 1956-72; chief pediat. cardiology St. Vincent Hosp., L.A., 1973-87; prof. pediat. cardiology U. So. Calif. Sch. Medicine, L.A., 1988—; med. dir. Marion Davies Clinic, 1957-61; pediat. cons. Crippled Children Svcs. State of Calif., 1957—; chief pediat. cardiology L.A. Heart Inst., St. Vincents Med. Ctr., L.A., 1973-87; internat. adv. bd. Acta Pediat. Japonica, 1992—; book reviewer in field. Mem. editl. bd. USC Jour. Medicine, 1990—; contbr. articles to profl. jours. With med. corps., U.S. Army, 1953-55. UCLA Med. Ctr. fellow, 1956-57. Fellow Am. Acad. Pediat. (coun. on cardiology 1962-68, exec. coun. 1968-75); mem. Am. Pediat. Soc., Soc. Pediat. Rsch. (Ross Pediat. Rsch. award 1962), Western Soc. for Pediat. Rsch. (exec. coun. 1966-69), Calif. Soc. for Pediat. Cardiology, Alpha Omega Alpha, Alpha Zeta. Home: 2733 Manning Ave Los Angeles CA 90064 Office: Childrens Hosp LA 4650 Sunset Blvd Los Angeles CA 90027

LINDE, LUCILLE MAE (JACOBSON), motor-perceptual specialist; b. Greeley, Colo., May 5, 1919; d. John Alfred and Anna Julia (Anderson) Jacobson; m. Ernest Emil Linde, July 5, 1946 (dec. Jan. 27, 1959). BA, U. No. Colo., 1941, MA, 1947, EdD, 1974. Cert. tchr. Calif., Colo., Iowa, N.Y.; cert. ednl. psychologist; guidance counselor. Dean of women, dir. residence C.W. Post Coll. of L.I. Univ., 1965-66; asst. dean of students SUNY, Farmingdale, 1966-67; counselor, tchr. West High Sch., Davenport, Iowa, 1967-68; instr. grad. tchrs. and counselors, univ. counselor, researcher No. Ariz. U., Flagstaff, 1968-69; vocat. edn. and counseling coord. Fed. Exemplary Project, Council Bluffs, Iowa, 1970-71; sch. psychologist, counselor Oakdale Sch. Dist., Calif., 1971-73; sch. psychologist, intern Learning and Counseling Ctr., Stockton, Calif., 1972-74; pvt. practice rsch. in motor-perceptual tng. Greeley, 1975—; rschr. ocumeter survey Lincoln Unified Sch. Dist., Stockton, 1980, 81, 82, Manteca (Calif.) H.S., 1981; spkr. Social Sci. Edn. Consortium, U. Colo., Boulder, 1993; presenter seminars in field. Author: Psychological Services and Motor Perceptual Training, 1974, Guidebook for Psychological Services and Motor Perceptual Training (How One May Improve in Ten Easy Lessons!), 1992, Manual for the Lucille Linde Ocumeter: Ocular Pursuit Measuring Instrument, 1992, Motor-Perceptual Training and Visual Perceptual Research (How Students Improved in Seven Lessons!), 1992, Effects of Motor Perceptual Training on Academic Achievement and Ocular Pursuit Ability, 1992; inventor ocumeter, instrument for measuring ocular tracking ability, 1989, target for use, 1991; patentee in field. Mem. Rep. Presdl. Task Force, 1989-96, trustee, 1991-92, charter mem., 1994—, life mem., 1994-95; mem. Rep. Nat. Com., 1990, 93-96, Rep. Nat. Com. on Am. Agenda, 1993, Nat. Rep. Congl. Com., 1990, 92, 93, 95, 96, Nat. Fedn. Rep. Women, Greeley Rep. Women, 1996; advisor Senator Bob Dole for Pres.; charter mem. Rep. Newt Gingrich's Speaker's Task Force, Senator Phil Gramm's Presdl. Steering Com.; at-large- del. Rep. Platform Planning Com.; team leader Nat. Rep. Rapid Response Network, Campaign America, 1996; active Heritage Found., Attention Deficit Disorder Adv. Group, Christian Bus. Men's Assn., Friends U. N.C. Librs., Citizens Against Govt. Waste, 1996, Concerns of Police Survivors, 1996, Nat. Assn. of Police Org. Recipient Presdl. medal of merit and lapel insignia, 1990, Nat. Rep. Senatorial Com., 1991-96, cert. of appreciation Nat. Rep. Congl. Com., 1992, 95, lapel pin Rep. Senatorial Inner Circle, 1990-96, Rep. Presdl. commemorative honor roll, 1993, Rep. Senatorial Freedom medal, 1994, Rep. Legion of Merit award, 1994, 96, Rep. Congl. Order of Freedom award, 1995, Convention medallion Rep. Senatiroial Inner Cir., 1996, Lapel Pin award RNC, 1996, Leadership citation Rep. Senatorial Inner Cir./ Rep. Nat. Conv., 1996, Legion of Merit Rep. Presdl. exec. com., 1996, Honor cert. House Spkr. Newt Gingrich, 1996; named to Rep. Nat. Hall of Honor, 1992. Mem. AAUP, NAFE, Nat. Assn. Sch. Psychologists and Psychometrists (spkr. at conf. 1976), Nat. Fedn. Rep. Women (name engraved on Ronald Wilson Reagan Eternal Flame of Freedom, 1995, on the Nat. Rep. Victory Monument, Washington, 1996, Rep. Sen. Inner Cir. Conv. Medallion 1996, RNG Mems. Only pin 1996), The Smithsonian Assocs., Nat. Trust for Hist. Preservation, Am. Pers. and Guidance Assn., Nat. Assn. Student Pers. Adminstrs., Nat. Assn. Women Deans and Counselors, Calif. Tchrs. Assn., Internat. Platform Assn., Independence Inst., Assn. Children Learning Disabilities (conf. spkr. 1976), Learning Disabilities Assn. (spkr. internat. conv. 1976), Greeley Rep. Women's Club, Pi Omega Pi, Pi Lambda Theta. Home: 1954 18th Ave Greeley CO 80631-5208

LINDEBERG, HENNING, physician, educator; b. Copenhagen, Dec. 19, 1943; m. Kis Sørensen, Sept. 16, 1978. DDS, Royal Dental Coll., Copenhagen, 1972; MD, Aarhus U., Denmark, 1979; PhD, Royal Dental Coll., Aarhus, Denmark, 1986; DMSci, Aarhus U., 1991. Cert. specialist in oral and maxillofacial surgery, oto-rhino-laryngology. Various positions as registrar in oral surgery and otolaryngology, 1972—; cons. in ENT Namdal Hosp., Norway, 1994; assoc. prof., head lab. for oral pathology, Dept. for Oral and Maxillofacial Surgery and Oral Pathology Royal Dental Coll., Aarhus, 1995—; founder DNA Labs. Aarhus U. Hosp., 1987. Contbr. articles to profl. jours. Fellow Danish Soc. Oto-Laryngology and Head and

Neck Surgery. Office: Dept Maxillofacial Surgery & Oral Pathology, Royal Dental Coll, 8000 Aarhus Denmark

LINDELL, ANDREA REGINA, college dean, nurse; b. Warren, Pa., Aug., 21, 1943; d. Andrew D. and Irene M. (Fabry) Lefik; m. Warner E. Lindell, May 7, 1966; children—Jennifer I., Jason M. B.S., Villa Maria Coll., 1970; M.S.N. Catholic U., 1975, D.N.Sc., 1976; diploma R.N., St. Vincent's Hosp., Erie, Pa. Instr. St. Vincent Hosp. Sch. Nursing, 1964-66; dir. Rouse Hosp., Youngsville, Pa., 1966-69; supr. Vis. Nurses Assn., Warren, Pa., 1969-70; dir. grad. program Cath. U., Washington, 1975-77; chmn., assoc. dean U. N.H., Durham, 1977-81; dean, prof. Oakland U., Rochester, Mich., 1981-90, dean, Schmidlapp prof. nursing U. Cin., 1990—; bd. dirs. CHEMED Corp.; cons. Moorehead U., Ky., 1983. Editor; Jour. Profl. Nursing, 1985; contbr. articles to profl. jours. Mem. sch. bd. Strafford Sch. Dist., N.H., 1977-80; Gov.'s Blue Ribbon Commn. Direct Health Policies, Concord, N.H., 1979-81; vice chmn. New England Commn. Higher Edn. in Nursing, 1977-81; mem. Mich. Assn. Colls. Nursing, 1981—. Named Outstanding Young Woman Am., 1980. Mem. Nat. League Nursing, Am. Assn. Colls. Nursing, Sigma Theta Tau. Democrat. Roman Catholic. Avocations: water skiing; roller skating; reading; fishing; camping;*

LINDEN, JEANNE VICTORIA, pathologist; b. Syracuse, N.Y., Jan. 24, 1958; d. Raymond Edward and Ruth Louise (Hansen) Vanderlinde. BS, Union Coll., Schenectady, 1980; MD, U. Conn., Farmington, 1984, MPH, 1986. Diplomate Am. Bd. Pathology, Clin. Pathology and Transfusion Medicine. Resident dept. lab. medicine U. Conn., 1984-87; dir. blood and tissue resources N.Y. State Dept. Health, Albany, 1987—. Contbr. numerous articles to med. jours. Named outstanding former resident dept. lab. medicine U. Conn., 1993. Fellow Coll. Am. Pathologist; mem. Am. Assn. Blood Banks (chmn. blood data rev. and rsch. com. 1994—), Am. Assn. Tissue Banks (chmn. stds. and procedures com. 1993-95), Am. Med. Women's Assn., Blood Banks Assn. N.Y. State (pres. 1995—). Office: NY State Dept Health Wadsworth Ctr PO Box 509 Albany NY 12201-0509

LINDENMAYER, JEAN-PIERRE, psychiatrist; b. Basel, Switzerland, July 25, 1942; came to U.S. 1969; s. Franz and Celina Aries L. Diploma of Med. & Surgery, U. Basel, Switzerland, 1968. Diplomate Am. Bd. Psychiatry and Neurology. Residency in psychiatry Downstate Med. Ctr., Bklyn., 1973; fellow Doctor of Med. Sci. Program, Downstate Med. Ctr., SUNY, 1974; dir. Psychiatric Inpatient Svc., U. Hosp., Downstate Med. Ctr., Bklyn., 1973-76, Psychiatric Inpatient Svc., Bronx (N.Y.) Mcpl. Hosp., 1977-80; chief of svc. tng. unit Bronx Psychiat. Ctr., 1981-83, dir. Dept. Psychiatry, 1984-86; dir. Schizophrenia Research Program, Albert Einstein Coll. Med., Bronx, 1987-94; dir. psychopharmacology rsch. Manhattan Psychiatric Ctr., N.Y.C., 1994—; asst. prof., SUNY, Bklyn., 1975-77, Albert Einstein Coll. of Med., Dept. Psychiatry, Bronx, 1977-87, assoc. prof., 1987-94., clin. prof., Dept. Psychiatry, N.Y. Univ., 1994—. Co-author: Psychotropic Drugs: Manual for Emergency Management of Overdosage, 1981, Psychiatric Emergencies: Principles and Management of Emergency Medicine, 1985, New Biological Vista of Schizophrenia, 1992; contbr. articles on schizophrenia to profl. jours. Fellow, Am. Psychiatric Assn.; mem. Swiss Med. Assn., Am. Orthopsychiatry Assn. Office: 18 E 77th St New York NY 10021-1722

LINDESAY, JAMES EDWARD BURNET, psychiatry educator; b. Dumfries, Scotland, Nov. 11, 1954; s. Edward Dickson and Mary Elizabeth (Burnet) L. BA, Oxford (Eng.) U., 1976, BM, BCh, 1979, MD, 1990. Lectr. in psychogeriatrics United Med. and Dental Schs., London, 1986-87; sr. lectr. in psychogeriatrics U.M.D.S., London, 1987-91; prof. psychiatry for the elderly U. Leicester (England), 1991-96, head dept. psychiatry, 1996—; hon. cons. in psychogeriatrics Guy's Hosp., London, 1987-91, Leicestershire Mental Health Svc., N.H.S. Trust, Leicester, 1991—; project mgr. R&D for Psychiatry, 1987-91. Co-author: Delirium in the Elderly, 1990; editor: Neurotic Disorders in the Elderly, 1995; contbr. articles to profl. jours. Chmn. Alzheimer's Disease Soc., Leicestershire, U.K., 1994—. Recipient Eric Gregory award Soc. Authors, U.K., 1979. Mem. Royal Coll. Psychiatrists. Office: Leicester Gen Hosp, Gwendolen Rd, Leicester LE5 4PW, United Kingdom

LINDESMITH, LARRY ALAN, physician, administrator; b. Amarillo, Tex., July 27, 1938; s. Lyle J. and Imogene Agnes (Young) L.; m. Patricia Ann Brady, June 6, 1959 (div. Mar. 1973); children: Robert James, Lisa Ann; m. Diane Joyce Bakken, Nov. 22, 1973; children: Abigail Arleen, Nathan Lyle, David Alan. BA, U. Colo., 1959; MD, Bowman-Gray Sch. Medicine, Winston-Salem, N.C., 1963. Diplomate Am. Bd. Internal Medicine, Am. Bd. I.M.-Pulmonary Disease; Nat. Inst. Occupational Safety and Health B Reader; provider ACLS, advanced trauma life support. Medical intern U. Chgo. Hosps., Clinics, 1963-64; I.M. resident U. Colo. Med. Ctr., Denver, 1964-66; pulmonary disease fellowship U. Colo. Med. Ctr., Webb-Waring Lung Inst., Denver, 1966-67; asst. dir. infectious and pulmonary disease svc. Madigan Gen. Hosp., Tacoma, Wash., 1967-69; chief pulmonary disease Gundersen Clinic, Ltd., La Crosse, Wis., 1969-87, chief pulmonary and occupational medicine, 1979-89, chmn. dept. medicine, 1987-93; chief occupational health, preventive medicine, 1988—; bd. govs. Gundersen Clinic, Ltd., 1987-93; adj. prof. phys. therapy U. Wis., La Crosse, 1977-92; cons. VA Hosp., Tomah, Wis., 1977-93, Comty. Meml. Hosp., Winona, Minn., 1996—, Tomah Meml. Hosp., 1995—; clin. asst. prof. internal medicine U. Wis., Madison, 1982-92, clin. assoc. prof., 1992—; med. dir. RESTOR U. Wis., La Crosse, 1986-95, Svcs. to Bus. and Industry Gundersen/Luth. Med. Ctr., La Crosse, 1987-94; mem. occupational medicine boardwriting com. Am. Bd. Preventive Medicine, 1992-96. Contbr. book chpts. and articles to profl. publs. Mem. Air Pollution Control Coun. State of Wis. Dept. Natural Resources, 1978-81; vice-chmn. Bd. Control Luther High Sch., Onalaska, Wis., 1990-93. Maj. USAR, 1968-69; chmn. bd. dirs. Greater La Crosse Area C. of C., 1991. Boettcher Found. scholar, 1955-59; named Pagliara Tchr. of Yr. Gundersen Med. Found., 1984; recipient Dist. Svc. award Am. Lung Assn. Wis., 1988. Fellow Am. Coll. Chest Physicians, Am. Coll. Occupational and Environ. Medicine (assoc., chmn. pvt. practice coun., chmn. occupational lung disorders com.); mem. AMA, Am. Bd. Preventive Medicine (occupational medicine com. 1991-95), Am. Assn. Respiratory Therapy, Clin. Sleep Soc., Am. Thoracic Soc. (Wis. counselor 1978-81), Ctrl. States Occupational Medicine Assn. (bd. govs. 1984-95, pres. 1991), Am. Lung Assn. Wis. (pres. 1975-77), Wis. Thoracic Soc. (gen. conf. chmn. 1987), State Med. Soc. Wis. (chmn. environ. and occupational health com. 1989-91). Republican. Lutheran. Home: W 4965 Woodhaven Dr La Crosse WI 54601 Office: Gundersen Clinic Ltd 1836 South Ave La Crosse WI 54601-5429

LINDEWALD, GUSTAF BERTEL, pharmaceutical company executive; b. Norrköping, Sweden, Dec. 16, 1942; s. Torsten Wilhelm and Gunvor (Jung) L.; m. Birgitta Ingegerd Håkansson, July 19, 1970; children: Nicklas, Staffan, Ola. Pharmacist, Inst. Pharmacy, Stockholm, 1969. Mktg. mgr. ACO, Solna, Sweden, 1973-81; exec. v.p. mktg. ACO/Kabi-Pharmacia, Solna, 1981-87; exec. v.p. ACO Nova, Solna, 1987-88; dir. R&D Procordia Health Food, Bromma, Sweden, 1988-93; exec. v.p. mktg. Friggs AB, Bromma, 1993-95; exec. dir. Anjo/Semper, Stockholm, 1995—; bd. dirs. Anjo A/S, Copenhagen. Author: (periodicals) Reptilen, 1967-68, Informaco, 1981-88. Lt. Swedish Army Svc. Corps. Home: Runristarvägen 17, S 18650 Vallentuna Sweden Office: Anjo Semper, Torsgatan 14, S 10546 Stockholm Sweden

LINDHEIMER, MARSHALL DAVID, nephrologist, researcher; b. N.Y.C., June 28, 1932; s. Gaston L.; m. Jacqueline Paullette Zimmerlin-Lindheimer, Nov. 20, 1958; children: Daniele, Joel, Philippe, Robin, Claire. AB, Cornell U., 1952; MD, U. Geneva, 1960. Am. Bd. Internal Medicine, Am. Bd. Nephrology. Intern Rochester (N.Y.) Gen. Hosp., 1961-62; resident internal medicine Bklyn. VA Hosp., 1962-63; chief resident internal medicine Brookdale Hosp., Bklyn., 1963-64; fellow in nephrology Boston U. Sch. Medicine, 1964-66; sr. instr. Case Western Reserve U., Cleve., 1966-68; asst. prof. medicine Northwestern U., Chgo., 1969-70; from asst. to full prof. medicine, ob./gyn., pharmacology U. Chgo., 1970—. Author: Medical Disorders During Pregnancy, 2d edit., 1996 and 3 other med. books. contbr. over 270 articles to profl. jours. Named fellow ad eundum Royal Coll. Ob.-Gyn., London, 1994. Fellow Am. Coll. Physicians, Am. Heart Assn. (high blood pressure rsch. coun.); mem. Int. Soc. Study High Blood Pressure in Pregnancy (pres. 1990-92, Chesley award 1988). Office: U Chgo Dept Medicine 5841 S Maryland Ave Chicago IL 60637-1463

LINDLEY, BARRY DREW, medical educator; b. Orleans, Ind., Jan. 25, 1939; s. Paul Lemuel and Martha (Drew) L.; m. Sondra Patterson, June 20, 1964 (div. 1980); children: Theodore Drew, Matthew Bishop, Sarah Jeannette; m. Elizabeth Price, Apr. 24, 1982. BA, DePauw U., 1960; PhD, Western Res. U., 1964. Postdoctoral fellow Karolinska Inst., Stockholm, 1964-65; asst. prof. Western Res. U., Cleve., 1965-68; assoc. prof. Case-Western Res. U., Cleve., 1968-84, prof. physiology, 1984-93, assoc. dean, 1985-93, acting chmn. of anatomy, 1988-93; vice chancellor for acad. affairs U. Ark. for Med. Scis., Little Rock, 1993—, dean Grad. Sch., prof. physiology and biophysics, 1993—; vis. scientist ARC unit of Invertebrate Physiology, Cambridge, Eng., 1972, Duke U. Marine Lab., Beaufort, N.C., 1973; mem. physiology study sect. NIH, Bethesda, Md., 1975-79; com. mem. Nat. Bd. Med. Examiners, Phila., 1986-91; bd. visitors DePauw U., Greencastle, Ind., 1989-92; faculty fellow Liaison Com. on Med. Edn., 1988; vis. lectr. in med. illustration Cleve. Inst. Art, 1993-94; adj. prof. applied health scis. Tulane U. Sch. Pub. Health and Tropical Medicine, 1994—; mem. sci. adv. bd. Nat. Ctr. for Toxicol. Rsch., 1995—; cons.-evaluator North Ctrl. Assn. Colls. and Schs., 1996—. Contbr. numerous articles to sci. jours. Deacon Calvary Presbyn. Ch., Cleve., 1971; asst. scoutmaster Cleve. area Boy Scouts Am., 1987, supernumerary Cleve. Opera, 1988-93; bd. dirs. Kenneth J. Pennebaker Ctr., 1994—. Recipient Med. Faculty award Lederle Found., 1967-70, Career Devel. award NIH, 1971-76; disting. scholar Camille and Henry Dreyfus Found., DePauw U., 1983. Mem. Am. Physiol. Soc. (membership com. 1973-76), Biophys. Soc., Soc. Gen. Physiologists, Assn. Anatomy Chmn., MidSouthern Watercolorists, 1994—. Office: U Ark for Med Scis 4301 W Markham St # 541 Little Rock AR 72205-7199

LINDLEY, NORMAN DALE, physician; b. Henrietta, Tex., July 18, 1937; s. Hardie Lindley and Hope (Clement) Mourant; m. Luise Ann Moser, May 29, 1964; children: Norman Dale Jr., Roger Paul. BS, N.Mex. Highlands U., 1960; MD, U. Colo., 1964. Diplomate Am. Bd. Ob-Gyn. Rotating intern Kans. City (Mo.) Gen. Hosp., 1964-65; resident in ob-gyn. St. Joseph Hosp., Denver, 1965-68; med. officer USAF, Cheyenne, Wyo., 1968-70; pvt. practice physician Alamogordo, N.M., 1970—; dir. N.Mex. Found. for Med. Care, Albuquerque, 1985-88, N.Mex. Med. Rev. Assn., Albuquerque, 1985-88; physician liaison Am. Assn. Med. Assts., Chgo., 1987-93; physician advisor N.Mex. Soc. Med. Assts., 1984—. Bd. dirs. Otero County Boys and Girls Club, Alamogordo, 1977—, pres., 1979-81; bd. dirs. Otero County Assn. for Retarded Citizens, 1985-91, pres., 1989-90; bd. dirs. Otero County chpt. Am. Cancer Soc., 1970-72. Capt. USAF, 1968-70. Rsch. grantee NSF, 1959, 60. Fellow Am. Coll. Ob-Gyn.; mem. AMA, Am. Fertility Soc., Am. Inst. Ultrasound in Medicine, Am. Soc. Colposcopists and Cervical Pathologists, M.Mex. Med. Soc. (councilor 1985-88), Otero County Med. Soc. (pres. 1972-73, 83-84), Rotary (pres. White Sands chpt. 1981-82, bd. dirs. 1988-89, Svc. Above Self award 1979, Paul Harris fellow 1987). Home: 2323 Union Ave Alamogordo NM 88310-3849 Office: Thunderbird Ob-Gyn 1212 9th St Alamogordo NM 88310-5842

LINDO, CLINTON LEOPOLD, JR., internist, medical educator; b. Chgo., June 28, 1960; s. Clinton Leopold Sr. and Frances Olivia (Wallace) L.; m. Sandra Elaine Smith, Oct. 12, 1991; children: Nya Elaine, Jackson Farri. BS, Washington U., 1982; MD, Yale U., 1986. Diplomate Am. Bd. Internal Medicine, 1987. Intern U. Calif., San Francisco, 1986-87, resident, 1987-89, chief resident, 1989-90; asst. prof. clin. medicine U. Chgo., 1990-94; asst. dir. internal medicine residency Oakwood Hosp. and Med. Ctr., Dearborn, Mich., 1994—; dir. med. student edn. Oakwood Hosp. and Med. Ctr., Dearborn, 1994—; clin. asst. prof. medicine U. Mich. Med. Sch., Ann Arbor, 1995—. Mem. ACP, Soc. Gen. Internal Medicine. Office: Oakwood Hosp & Med Ctr 18108 Oakwood Blvd Dearborn MI 48123

LINDO, J. TREVOR, psychiatrist, consultant; b. Boston, Feb. 12, 1925; s. Edwin and Ruby Ianty (Peterson) L.; m. Thelma Elaine Thompson, Sept. 22, 1962. BA, NYU, 1946; cert. in pre-clin. studies, U. Freibourg, Switzerland, 1953; MD, U. Lausanne, Switzerland, 1957. Lic. psychiatrist, N.Y., Conn. Clin. instr. Columbia U., N.Y.C., 1965-75, asst. clin. prof., 1975-82, assoc. clin. prof., 1982-85; attending psychiatrist Bedford-Stuyvesant Cmty. Mental Health Clinic, Bklyn., 1976-86, med. dir., 1986—; attending psychiatrist Harlem Hosp. Ctr., N.Y.C., 1964-75; vis. psychiatrist Interfaith Hosp., Bklyn., 1976-85; psychiat. cons. Bklyn. Bur. Cmty. Svc., 1980, Marcus Garvey Manor, Bklyn., 1982-86; candidate Nat. Bd. Forensic Examiners, 1995. Co-chairperson com. Dr. Thomas Matthew, N.Y.C., 1974. With U.S. Mcht. Marine, 1947-51. Fellow Am. Coll. Internal Physicians; mem. Nat. Med. Assn., Am. Psychiat. Assn., Provident Clin. Soc. (v.p. 1980-82, parliamentarian 1982—), Bklyn. Psychiat. Soc., Black Psychiatrists of Am. Office: 1265 President St Brooklyn NY 11213-4237 also: Bedford Stuyvesant Cmty Mental Health Ctr 1406 Fulton St Brooklyn NY 11216-2606

LINDSAY, JON ROBERT, oral surgeon; b. Indpls., Aug. 13, 1938; s. Hamlin Berry and Beulah Beatrice (Bunch) L.; m. Judilynn Marie Theisen, Apr. 19, 1975 (dec. Jan. 1989); 1 child, Devon Marie Foster Poore; m. Orian Elizabeth Tolton, Oct. 24, 1995. BS, Ind. U., 1961, DDS, 1964. Diplomate Am. Bd. Oral and Maxillofacial Surgery. Oral surgery intern Lincoln Hosp., N.Y.C., 1964-65; didactic Boston U., 1965-66; oral surgery resident Valley Med. Ctr., Fresno, Calif., 1966-68; ober asst. Dental Sch., U. Bern, Switzerland, 1968-71; pvt. practice oral surgery Fresno, 1972-80, Monterey, Calif., 1980-82, San Jose, Calif., 1982—. Author: Introduction to CP/M Assembly Language, 1982, CP/M-86 Assembly Language Programming, 1986. Fellow Am. Assn. Oral & Maxillofacial Surgery; mem. ADA, Calif. Dental Assn. Office: 2121 Alexian Dr San Jose CA 95116

LINDSAY, JUNE CAMPBELL MCKEE, communications executive; b. Detroit, Nov. 14, 1920; d. Maitland Everett and Josephine Belle (Campbell) McKee; BA with honors in Speech (McGregor Fund Mich. grantee), U. Mich., 1943; Electronics Engring. certificate Signal Corps Ground Signal Svc., 1943; postgrad. (Inst. Gen. Semantics grantee), U. Chgo., 1944-45, N.Y. U. (Armour grantee), 1945-46, Columbia U., 1946-47, Wayne State U., 1960-64, U. Mich., 1964-70, 78—; MA, Specialist-in-Aging Cert., Inst. of Gerontology, 1982; m. Powell Lindsay, Nov. 25, 1967; 1 child, Kristi Costa-McKee. Coord., activator McKee Prodns., Detroit, 1943-56, Being Unltd., 1957—, InterBeing, Inc., 1979—, M.U.T.U.A.L. A.I.D., 1981—; info. dir. Suitcase Theatre, Inc., Lansing and Ann Arbor, Mich. Cons. Cornelian Corner Detroit, Inc., 1957-63, Islamic Ctr. Found. Soc., Detroit, 1959-62, City Ann Arbor Human Rels. Commn., 1966-68, Urban Adult Edn. Inst., Detroit, 1968-69, Mich. Bell Tel. Co., Detroit, 1969, African Art Gallery Founders, Detroit Inst. Arts, 1964, WKAR-TV, Mich. State U., 1971—. Mem. Nat. Caucus, Ctr. for Black Aged; bd. dirs. Mus. Youth Internat., Saline, Mich., Ann Arbor Community Devel. Corp. Chaplain's asst. Univ. Hosp., Ann Arbor, 1971-72; program dir. People-to-People, Ann Arbor, 1971-72; Suitcase Theatre tour coord. Brit. Empire's Leprosy Relief Assn., 1972—; assembly cons. Baha'i Faith, 1960—; mem. Comprehensive Health Planning Coun. S.E. Mich., Baha'i Internat. Health Agy., Inst. for Advancement of Health, Mission Health, Catherine McAuley Health Ctr. Share and Care Support Group. Recipient Award for Excellence Mich. Ednl. Assn., 1971, Mich. Assn. Classroom Tchrs., 1972; exec. dir. Powell Lindsay Meml. Program in Theatre and Communications, Louhelen Baha'i Sch. and Residential Coll., U. Mich., Flint, Mott Community Coll., 1988—. Mem. ACLU, Soc. for Individual Responsibility, Am. Women in Radio and TV, Broadcast Pioneers, Am. Fedn. Advt., Internat. Platform Assn., Gray Panthers, Planetary Citizens, Am. Assn. Adult and Continuing Edn., Am. Pub. Health Assn., Wellness Assocs., Mich. Assn. Holistic Health, Internat. Health Found., Inst. Study Conscious Evolution, Am. Soc. on Aging, Mich. Health Coun., Nat. Coun. on Aging, U.S., Assn. Humanistic Psychology, Assn. Holistic Health, Internat. Soc. for the Study of Subtle Energies and Energy Medicine, Nat. Inst. for the Clin. Application of Behavioral Medicine, Assn. Baha'i Studies, Mental Health Assn. in Mich., Mich. Soc. Gerontology, Washtenaw County Council on Aging, Nat. Coun. Sr. Citizens, Am. Assn. Ret. Persons, People's Med. Soc., Giraffe Soc., Living Tao Found., World Future Soc., Nat. Trust for Hist. Preservation, Orgn. Devel. Inst. (registered orgn. devel. profl. 1988), UN Assn. of the U.S.A. Home: 2339 S Circle Dr Ann Arbor MI 48103-3442

LINDSAY, KATHRYN MARITA, mental health nurse; b. Phila., Mar. 15, 1949; d. William Bernard and Jane Mary (Brady) l. Diploma, Pa. Hosp., Phila., 1970; BS in Sociology, St. Joseph's U., Phila., 1979; BSN, U. State of N.Y., Albany, 1991; MSN in Pub. Health Nursing, LaSalle U., Phila., 1993. RN, Pa., N.J., Del.; cert. psychiat./mental health nurse, nursing adminstr. Staff nurse, hemodialysis St. Agnes Hosp., Phila., 1974-75; staff nurse, psychiatry Pa. Hosp., Phila., 1970-72, evening supr., 1972-74, asst. nursing dir., 1976-80, nursing dir., 1980-93, program coord., 1994—; adj. faculty in nursing Neumann Coll., Aston, Pa, 1994—; bd. dirs. Supportive Older Woman's Network, Phila., 1995—; adj. clin. prof. Widener U., Chester, Pa., spring 1994; cons. behavioral health LaSalle Neighborhood Nursing Ctr., Phila., 1995—, Maternity Care Coalition, Phila., 1995. Advocacy activist Babies First, Phila., 1995—. Breast Health Inst. grantee, 1995. Mem. APHA, Am. Psychiat. Nurses Assn., Nat. League for Nursing, Pub. Health Nurses Promoting Health Neighborhoods, Coll. Physicians of Phila., Sigma Theta Tau. Democrat. Roman Catholic. Home: 1336 E Susquehanna Ave Philadelphia PA 19125 Office: Pa Hosp Women's Mental Health Prog 111 N 49th St Philadelphia PA 19139

LINDSAY, PEGGY ANNE, nurse, educator, consultant, school nurse; b. Torrance, Calif., June 19, 1947; d. Francis M. and Frances M. (Bacon) Knight; m. John Lindsay, Dec. 2, 1967; children: Chris, Rob. AA, El Camino Coll., 1967; BS, Chapman Coll., 1979; MA, U. of Redlands, 1980. RN, Calif. Dir. edn. County of San Bernardino, San Bernardino, Calif., 1981-91; instl. nurse San Bernardino (Calif.) County Sheriff's Dept., 1991-92; sch. nurse Hesperia (Calif.) Unified Sch. Dist., 1992—. Contbr. articles to Modern Nurse mag., other publs. Vol. Internat. Relief Teams, Inc., Liga, Inc.; bd. dirs. ARC, Victorville, Calif. Mem. ANA, North Am. Nursing Diagnosis Assn., Calif. Sch. Nurse Assn., So. Calif. Nursing Diagnosis Assn., Inland Area Health Edn. Coun. Home: 15032 Ash St Hesperia CA 92345-4205

LINDSEY, WILLIAM FRANK, surgeon; b. Elmhurst, Ill., July 31, 1950; s. John Schaffer and Rhea Isabel (Russell) L.; m. Sheila Colleen Stack, May 1976; children: Melissa, Daniel, Meghan, Kathryn. BS with honors, U. Ill., 1972; MD, U. Ill., Chgo., 1976. Resident in gen. surgery Cook County Hosp., Chgo., 1976-83; rsch. in surg. oncology U. Ill. Hosp., Chgo., 1978-80; clin. assoc. NIH, Chgo., 1979-80; clin. fellow Am. Cancer Soc., Chgo., 1979-80, 82-83; fellow in surg. oncology U. Ill. Hosp., Chgo., 1983-84; attending Cook County Hosp., 1983-85; attending Oneida (N.Y.) City Hosp., 1985—, chief surgery, 1990-91, chief med. staff, 1992-93; asst. prof. surgery U. Ill., Chgo., 1983-85; mem. governing bd. Blue Cross / Blue Shield, Utica, N.Y., 1996—. Contbr. articles to profl. jours. Chmn. bldg. com. Tri-Valley YMCA, Oneida, 1990-92. Fellow ACS; mem. AMA, Soc. Laparoendoscopic Surgeons, Am. Soc. Gen. Surgeons, Connective Tissue Oncology Soc., Med. Soc. Madison County (pres. 1993-95). Office: Oneida Surg Group 357 Genesee St Oneida NY 13421

LINDSLEY, DAVID FORD, neurophysiology educator; b. Cleve., May 18, 1936; s. Donald and Ellen (Ford) L.; m. Elizabeth McBride, Aug. 20, 1960; children—Eric, Karen, Victoria. A.B., Stanford U., 1957; Ph.D. in Anatomy and Neurophysiology, UCLA, 1961. Postdoctoral fellow, Moscow, 1961-62, U. Cambridge, Eng., 1962-63; asst. prof. Stanford U. Med. Sch., 1963-67; assoc. prof. U. So. Calif. Med. Sch., 1967—. Co-author: Basic Human Neurophysiology, 1984. Contbr. articles to profl. jours. Guggenheim fellow, 1974-75. Mem. Soc. Neurosci., Internat. Brain Research Orgn., Am. Assn. Anatomists, Am. Physiol. Soc. Republican. Home: 517 11th St Santa Monica CA 90402-2901 Office: U So Calif Dept Physiology 1333 San Pablo St Los Angeles CA 90033-4526

LINDSLEY, DONALD BENJAMIN, physiological psychologist, educator; b. Brownhelm, Ohio, Dec. 23, 1907; s. Benjamin Kent and Mattie Elizabeth (Jenne) L.; m. Ellen Ford, Aug. 16, 1933; children: David Ford, Margaret, Robert Kent, Sara Ellen. A.B., Wittenberg Coll. (now Univ.), 1929, D.Sc. (hon.), 1959; A.M., U. Iowa, 1930, Ph.D., 1932; Sc.D. (hon.), Brown U., 1958, Trinity Coll., Hartford, Conn., 1965; D.Sc. (hon.), Loyola U. Chgo., 1969; Ph.D. (hon.), Johannes Gutenberg U., Mainz, W.Ger., 1977. Instr. psychology U. Ill., 1932-33; NRC fellow Harvard U. Med. Sch., 1933-35; research assoc. Western Res. U. Med. Sch., 1935-38; asst. prof. psychology Brown U.; also dir. psychol. and neurophysiol. lab. Bradley Hosp., 1938-46; dir. war research project on radar operation Yale, OSRD, Nat. Def. Research Com., Camp Murphy and Boca Raton AFB, Fla., 1943-45; prof. psychology Northwestern U., 1946-51; prof. psychology, physiology, psychiatry and pediatrics UCLA, 1951-77, prof. emeritus, 1977—, mem. Brain Research Inst., 1961—, chmn. dept. psychology, 1959-62; William James lectr. Harvard, 1958; Univ. Research lectr. U. Calif. at Los Angeles, 1960; Phillips lectr. Haverford Coll., 1961; Walter B. Pillsbury lectr. psychology Cornell U., 1963; vis. lectr. Kansas State U., 1966, Tex. A & M U., 1980; Mem. sci. adv. bd. USAF, 1947-49; undersea warfare com. NRC, 1951-64; cons. NSF, 1952-54; mem. mental health study sect. NIMH, 1953-57; neurol. study sect. Nat. Inst. Neurol. Diseases and Blindness, 1958-62; cons. Guggenheim Found., 1963-70, mem. edl. adv. bd., 1970-78; chmn. behavioral scis. tng. com. Nat. Inst. Gen. Med. Scis., 1966-69; mem. behavioral biology adv. panel AIBS-NASA, 1966-71; mem. space sci. bd. NAS, 1967-70; mem. com. space medicine, 1969-71; mem. Calif. Legis. Assembly Sci. and Tech. Coun., 1970-71. Cons. editor Jour. Exptl. Psychology, 1947-68, Jour. Comparative and Physiol. Psychology, 1952-62, Jour. Personality, 1958-62; mem. editorial bd. Internat. Jour. Physiology and Behavior, 1965-77, Exptl. Brain Rsch., 1965-76, Developmental Psychobiology, 1968-82, Neurosci. and Behavioral Physiology, 1976—; contbr. numerous articles on physiol. psychology, neurosci., brain and behavior to sci. jours., also numerous chpts. in books. Trustee Grass Found., 1958-95, emeritus trustee, 1996—. Awarded Presdl. Cert. of Merit (for war work), 1948; recipient Disting. Sci. Achievement award Calif. Psychol. Assn., 1977, Disting. Sci. Contbn. award Soc. Psychophysiol. Rsch., 1984, Disting. Grad. award Dept Psychology U. Iowa, 1987, Disting. Alumnus award for Achievement U. Iowa, 1988, Gerard prize (with H.W. Magoun) Soc. Neurosci., 1988, Gold Medal award Am. Psychol. Found., 1989, Hon. Life Mem. award Dept. Psychobiology, U. Calif., Irvine, 1989; Guggenheim fellow Europe, 1959, hon. fellow UCLA Sch. Medicine, 1986. Mem. Nat. Acad. Scis. (chmn. com. long duration missions in space 1967-72, mem. space sci. bd.), Am. Psychol. Assn. (Disting. Sic. Contbn. award 1959), Am. Physiol. Soc., Soc. Exptl. Psychologists, Am. Electroencephalographic Soc. (pres. 1964-65, hon. mem. 1980—, Herbert Jasper award 1994), AAAS (v.p. 1954, chmn. sect. J. 1977), Midwest Psychol. Assn. (pres. 1952), Am. Acad. Cerebral Palsy, We. Soc. Electroencephalography (hon. mem. with great distinction, pres. 1057, Wilder Penfield award and lectr. 1996), We. Psychol. Assn. (pres. 1959-60), Am. Acad. Arts and Scis., Internat. Brain Rsch. Orgn. (reas. 1967-71), Soc. Neurosci. (Donald B. Lindsley prize in behavioral neurosci. established in his name), Finnish Acad. of Sci. and Letters (fgn. mem.), Sigma Xi, Alpha Omega Alpha, Gamma Alpha, Phi Gamma Delta. Conglist. Home: 471 23rd St Santa Monica CA 90402-3125

LINDSTROM, DONALD FREDRICK, JR., priest; b. Atlanta, July 18, 1943; s. Donald Fredrick Sr. and Elizabeth (Haynes) L.; m. Marcia Pace, Dec. 30, 1983; children: Christopher, Eric, Ashley, Ellison. ABJ, U. Ga., 1966; MDiv, Va. Theol. Sem., 1969; JD, Woodrow Wilson Coll. Law, 1977; postgrad., U. West Fla., 1984. Lic. marriage and family therapist. Broadcast journalist radio and TV Atlanta and N.Y.C., 1961-68; priest Episcopal ch., 1969—; rector Episcopal Ch. Mediator, Meridian, Miss., 1991—; pvt. practice as marriage and family therapist, Pensacola, Fla., 1983-91; ecumenical officer Diocese of Ctrl. Gulf Coast, 1989-91, Miss., 1992—; bd. visitors Kanuga Conf. Ctr., 1993—; guest chaplain U.S. Ho. of Reps., nat. prayer breakfast, 1994; mem. ecumenical staff gen. conv. Episcopal Ch., 1994. Writer, producer The Cry for Help, The Autumn Years. Chaplain Atlanta Police Dept., 1975-78, Meridian Police Dept., 1995—; pres. N.W. Fla. chpt. Nat. Kidney Found., 1987-88; mem. Leadership Atlanta, 1975; bd. dirs. Leadership Pensacola; trustee Fla. Trust for Hist. Preservation. Mem. Am. Assn. for Marriage and Family Therapy (clin.), Mental Health Assn. (life, bd. dirs. Pensacola 1986-88), Navy League, Order of Holy Cross (assoc.), Bailli (pres.), Confrerie de la Chaine des Rotisseurs, Bailliage de Meridian, Alpha Tau Omega, Sigma Delta Chi, Delta Gamma Kappa. Office: Episcopal Ch Mediator 3825 35th Ave Meridian MS 39305-3617

LINDSTROM, ERIC EVERETT, ophthalmologist; b. Helena, Mont., Nov. 28, 1936; s. Everett Harry and Nan Augusta (Johnson) L.; BS, Wheaton Coll., 1958; MD, U. Md., 1963; MPH, Harvard U., 1966; m. Nancy Jo Alexander, July 24, 1960; children: Laura Ann, Eric Everett. Intern,

Madigan Army Med. Center, Tacoma, Wash., 1963-64; resident in aerospace medicine Sch. Aerospace Medicine, Brooks AFB, Tex., 1966-68, resident in ophthalmology Brooke Army Med. Ctr., Ft. Sam Houston, Tex., 1972-75; surgeon 12th combat aviation group U.S. Army, Vietnam, 1968-69, chief profl. svcs. and aviation medicine Beach Army Hosp., Ft. Wolters, Tex., 1969-72; asst. chief ophthalmology clinic Madigan Army Med. Center, Tacoma, 1975-76; now with Lindstrom Eye Clinic; med. dir. Palo Pinto County (Tex.) Mental Health Clinic., 1970-72; cons. Tex. State Rehab. Com., 1971-72; chmn. bd. trustees South Cen. Regional Med. Ctr.; sr. aviation med. examiner, FAA; flight surgeon Miss. ANG, ret. Deacon First Bapt. Ch., Laurel, 1978—; bd. dirs. Laurel Salvation Army. Decorated Bronze Star, Air medal with 2 oak leaf clusters, Meritorious Svc. medal. Diplomate Am. Bd. Preventive Medicine, Am. Bd. Ophthalmology. Fellow ACS, Am. Coll. Physician Execs., Am. Coll. Preventive Medicine, Aerospace Med. Assn. (assoc.), Am. Acad. Ophthalmology; mem. AMA, FAA (sr. aviation med. examiner), Am. Acad. Cataract and Refractive Surgery, Miss. Med. Assn. (trustee), Miss. EENT Assn., South Miss. Med. Soc., Southern Med. Assn., La.-Miss. EENT Assn., Flying Physicians Assn., Soc. Mil. Ophthalmologists, Soc. of USAF Flight Surgeons, Alliance of Air N.G. Flight Surgeons, Aircraft Owners and Pilots Assn., Nu Sigma Nu. Club: Kiwanis. Home: 809 Cherry Ln Laurel MS 39440-1651 Office: Lindstrom Eye Clinic PO Box 407 Laurel MS 39441-0407

LINDSTROM, JON MARTIN, medical research scientist; b. Moline, Ill., Oct. 9, 1945; s. Herbert Martin and Melnotte Elanore (Anderson) L.; m. Dona Meiko Chikaraishi, June 29, 1969 (div. 1972); m. Suzanne Stevenson, Nov. 23, 1977; children—Laurel Anne, Kara Martine, Jon Kenneth. BA, U. Ill., 1967; PhD, U. Calif.-San Diego, 1971. Asst. prof. Salk Inst., La Jolla, Calif., 1973-78, assoc. prof., 1978-83, assoc. prof. and mem., 1983-90, trustee prof. U. Pa. Med. Sch. Dept. Neurosci., 1990—. Author over 250 articles; discovered cause of myasthenia gravis; patentee radioimmunoassay for myasthenia gravis; mem. editorial bd. Jour. Neuroimmunology. Mem. Sci. adv. com. Muscular Dystrophy Assn. Grants and awards include NIH, Jacob Javits award, Muscular Dystrophy Assn., Sloan Found., McKnight Found., Onassis Found., Office Naval Research, U.S. Army. Home: 110 Rock Rose Ln Radnor PA 19087-3736 Office: U Pa Med Sch 217 Stemmler Hall Philadelphia PA 19104-6074

LINEHAN, ALLAN DOUGLAS, prosthodontist; b. L.A., Dec. 30, 1954; s. Charles K. and P. Alene (Rohrbaugh) L.; m. Anita J. Peterson, Aug. 1, 1981; children: Chelsea L., Keegan H. BA, Lewis & Clark Coll., 1978; D in dental medicine, Oreg. Health Scs. Ctr., 1983; MS in prosthodontics, Univ. Tex., 1993. Diplomate Am. Bd. Prosthodontics. Gen. dental officer USAF Clinic Kadena, Okinawa, Japan, 1983-86, USAF Clinic Bitburg, Bitburg, Germany, 1986-90; prosthodontic resident Wilford Hall USAF Medical Ctr. Lackland Air Force Base, San Antonio, 1990-93; chief of prosthodontics 10th Dental Squadron USAF Acad., Colorado Springs, Colo., 1993—. Contbr. articles to profl. jours. Dir. for fundraising Explorer Elem. Sch., Colo. Springs, 1995—. Recipient John J. Sharry Prosthodontic Rsch. competition award Am. Coll. Prosthodontics, 1993, Tylman Rsch. grant Am. Acad. Fixed Prosthodontics, 1992. Fellow Am. Coll. Prosthodontics; mem. Acad. Gen. Dentistry, Psi Omega (v.p. 1979-83). Home: 3337 Birnamwood Dr Colorado Springs CO 80920 Office: 10th Medical Group SGD 2348 Sijan Dr Ste 2A41 U S A F Academy CO 80840

LING, GEOFFREY SHIU FEI, neurologist, pharmacologist, educator; b. Balt., Oct. 14, 1956; s. Alfred Soy Chiu and Helen (Moshang) L.; m. Shari Miura. BA, Washington U., St. Louis, 1977; PhD, Cornell U., 1982; MD, Georgetown U., 1989. Enlisted U.S. Army, 1989; postdoctoral fellow Meml. Sloan-Kettering Cancer Ctr., N.Y.C., 1982-84, rsch. assoc., 1984—; instr. Cornell U. Med. Coll., N.Y.C., 1985—; intern in neurology Walter Reed Army Med. Ctr., 1986, resident in neurology, 1990—; fellow in neurosci. critical care Johns Hopkins Hosp., Balt., 1993—; attending physician critical care medicine and neurology Walter Reed Army Med. Ctr., 1995—; dir., asst. prof. divsn. critical care medicine depts. anesthesiology, neurology, surgery Uniformed Svcs. Univ. Health Scis., Bethesda, Md., 1995—; lectr. N.Y. Hosp. (surgeon asst. program), N.Y.C., 1980—. Contbr. articles to profl. jours. Damon Runyon-Walter Winchell Cancer Fund fellow, 1982. Capt. MC, U.S. Army, 1989—. Mem. AAAS, Soc. for Neurosci., N.Y. Acad. Scis., Am. Fedn. for Clin. Rsch., Sigma Xi. Presbyterian. Avocations: karate; running. Office: Walter Reed Army Med Ctr Dept Neurology Washington DC 20307

LING, KATHRYN WROLSTAD, health association administrator; b. Watertown, Wis., Aug. 3, 1943; d. Jeffrey Harold and Constance Devina (Egre) Wrolstad; stepchildren: Renee Rainey, Roz Harper. BS in History and Polit. Sci., U. Wis., 1965. Supr. recreation ARC, DaNang, Cam Ran Bay, VietNam, 1968; assoc. exec. dir. Am. Cancer Soc., Evanston, Ill., 1968-71, exec. dir., 1971-73; exec. dir. Montgomery County Unit Am. Cancer Soc., Md., 1973-76, cons. income devel., 1976, dir., profl. edn. cancer incidence and end results, 1976-78, dir. income devel., 1978-82; exec. dir. Am. Cancer Soc., Chgo., 1982-84; assoc. exec. dir. Alzheimer's Disease and Related Disorders Assn., Chgo., 1985-87, v.p. community svcs., 1988-91, sr. v.p. chpt. Family Svcs. and Edn. divsn., 1991-93; cons. Nat. Aphasia Assn.; pres. The Leadership Edge, Chgo.; chmn. bd. dirs. Kaleidoscope. Mem. Soc. Non-Profit Orgn. (chmn. bd. dirs.). Home: 1255 N Sandburg Ter Chicago IL 60610

LINGMAN, GÖRAN KRISPIN, obstetrician, gynecologist, consultant, educator; b. Amal, Sweden, Dec. 27, 1949; s. Gunnar Krispin and Maj-Stina (Göransson) L.; m. Runa Bodil Rubin, Sept. 21, 1974; children: Markus, Oskar. MD, U. Gothenburg, Sweden, 1976; PhD, U. Lund, Sweden, 1985. Intern Cen. Hosp., Helsingborg, Sweden, 1976-78; resident in ob-gyn Cen. Hosp., 1978-82; cons. Cen. Hosp., Helsingborg, Sweden, 1986-89, KFSH & RC, Riyadh, Saudi Arabia, 1989-90; cons. dept. ob-gyn. Cen. Hosp., Helsingborg, Sweden, 1990; assoc prof. U. Lund, 1987—; bd. dirs. Flowteckab. Contbr. numerous articles in field to med. jours. Mem. Swedish Soc. Ob-Gyn. (bd. dirs. 1988-89), Svenska Läkarsällskapet, Svenska L kareförbundet, Svdnska Överläkarforbundet, Helsingborgs Läkarsällskap (bd. dirs. 1991-92), N.Y. Acad. Scis. Office: Cen Hosp, Dept Ob-Gyn, 25187 Helsingborg Sweden

LINHARDT, ROBERT JOHN, medicinal chemistry educator; b. Passaic, N.J., Oct. 18, 1953; s. Robert J. and Barbara A. (Kelley) L.; m. Kathryn F. Burns, May 31, 1975; children: Kelley, Barbara. BS in Chemistry, Marquette U., 1975; MA in Chemistry, Johns Hopkins U., 1977, PhD in Organic Chemistry, 1979; postgrad., Mass. Inst. Tech., 1979-82. Rsch. assoc. Mass. Inst. Tech., Cambridge, 1979-82; asst. prof. U. Iowa, Iowa City, 1982-86, assoc. prof., 1986-90, prof. medicinal and natural products chemistry, 1990—, prof. chem. and biochem. engring., 1996—, F. Wendell Miller Disting. prof., 1996; cons. in field.; interacad. exchange scientist to USSR NAS, 1988. Mem. editl. bd. Applied Biochemistry and Biotech., 1985—, Carbohydrate Rsch., 1990—, Analytical Biochemistry, 1991—, Jour. Biol. Chem., 1995—; contbr. numerous articles to profl. jours. Johnson and Johnson fellow MIT, 1981; NIH grantee, 1982-95. Mem. AAAS, Am. Chem. Soc. (Horace S. Isbell award Carbohydrate Chemistry 1994), Soc. Glycobiology. Office: U Iowa Coll Pharmacy Phar # 303A Iowa City IA 52240

LINHART, JOSEPH WAYLAND, cardiologist, educational administrator; b. N.Y.C., Feb. 7, 1933; s. Joseph and Myrla Watson (Wayland) L.; m. Marilyn Adele Voight, Sept. 1, 1956; children: Joseph, Mary-Ellen, Richard, Jennifer, Donna-Lisa, Daria. BS, George Washington U., 1954, MD, 1958. Diplomate Am. Bd. Internal Medicine with subspecialty in cardiovascular diseases. Intern Washington Hosp. Ctr., 1958-59; resident George Washington U. Hosp., Washington, 1959-60, Duke U. Hosp., Durham, N.C., 1961; fellow Duke U. Hosp., Durham, 1960, 62-63, Nat. Heart Inst./Johns Hopkins Hosp., Bethesda/Balt., Md., 1963-64; asst. prof. medicine U. Fla., Gainesville, 1964-67; clin. assoc. prof. U. Miami, Fla., 1967-68; assoc. prof. medicine U. Tex., San Antonio, 1968-71; prof., dir. cardiology Hahnemann Med. Coll., Phila., 1971-75; prof., chmn. dept. medicine Chgo. Med. Sch., 1975-79, Oral Roberts U., Tulsa, 1979-83; prof. medicine U. South Fla., Tampa, 1983-92; prof., regional chmn. medicine Tex. Tech. U., Odessa, 1992-93; prof. medicine La. State U., Shreveport, 1993—; chief med. svc. VA Med. Ctr., Shreveport, 1993—, acting chief of staff, 1996—; cons. in cardiology and med./legal questions. Contbr. over 131 articles to profl. jours.; author 4 books. Mem. med. adv. com. YMCA, Niles, Ill., 1976-79; bd. govs. Phila. Heart Assn., 1972-75; mem. rsch. coun. Okla. Heart Assn., Tulsa, 1980-83. Fellow ACP, Am. Coll. Cardiology; mem. AAAS, Planetary Soc., Nat. Space Soc., Astron. Soc. of Pacific, Alpha Omega Alpha. Republican. Home: 324 Colony Bend Shreveport LA 71115 Office: Overton Brooks VA Med Ctr 510 E Stoner Ave Shreveport LA 71101

LINK, DEBORAH ANN, nurse; b. Flint, Mich., July 2, 1954; d. Donald Paul and Ruth Ellen (Rubel) L. Cert. practical nursing, Mott C.C., 1974; diploma, Hurley Sch. Nursing, 1980; BS in Health Care, U. Mich., Flint, 1993. Cert. ACLS, BLS provider. Staff nurse Flint Osteo. Hosp., 1980-90, 95—, asst. nurse mgr., 1990-91, staff nurse, 1991-93, clin. coord. family practice, 1993-95. Mem. AAcn (Greater Flint chpt.), Job's Daus. Presbyterian.

LINK, DEBORAH SHAW, psychiatrist, psychoanalyst; b. Boston, Apr. 19, 1933; d. Lawrence and Helen Louise (Fernald) Shaw. BA, Smith Coll., 1955; MA, Yale U., 1956; MD, Albert Einstein Coll. Medicine, 1971; grad., N.Y. Psychoanalytic Inst., 1984. Diplomate Am. Bd. Psychiatry and Neurology, Am. Psychoanalytic Assn. Resident Bronx Mcpl. Hosp., 1971-74; pvt. practice New Canaan, Conn., 1974—. Fellow Am. Coll. Psychoanalysts; mem. Am. Psychiat. Assn., Am. Psychoanalytic Assn., N.Y. Psychoanalytic Soc., Internat. Psychoanalytical Assn. Home and Office: 97 Marvin Ridge Rd New Canaan CT 06840-6904

LINK, HARTMUT, internist; b. Kirchheim, Germany, Nov. 1, 1951; s. Gerhard and Charlotte (Renk) L.; married; children: Cornelia, Alexander, Andreas. Degree in medicine, Univ. Tubingen, Germany, 1976, MD, 1977; postgrad., Hochschule Hannover, Germany, 1989. Intern Dept Internal Medicine, Univ. Med. Ctr., Tubingen, 1977-78, resident in internal medicine, Hematology & Oncology, 1978-80, chief resident in internal medicine, 1980-85; staff bone marrow transplant unit Dept. Hematology/Oncology Med. Sch. Hannover, 1985—, assoc. dir., 1985—. Mem. German Soc. Internal Medicine, German Soc. Hematology and Oncology, Paul Ehrlich Soc. Chemotherapy, European Group for Blood and Bone Marrow Transplantation, Am. Soc. Hematology, European Hematology Assn. Office: Med Sch Hannover Dept Hemat/Onc, Koustanty Gutschowstr 8, Hannover D-30625, Germany

LINKE, HARALD A.B., microbiology educator, consultant; b. Bautzen, Fed. Republic Germany, Aug. 18, 1936; came to U.S., 1967; s. Helmuth and Kathe Linke; m. Christa Bolte, Dec. 21, 1971; 1 child, Arthur. BSc, Humboldt U., Berlin, 1961; MSc, U. Gottingen, Fed. Rep. Germany, 1963, PhD, 1967; prof. oral microbiology. Postdoctoral fellow Rutgers U., New Brunswick, N.J., 1967-69; rsch. microbiologist Allied Chem. Corp., Morristown, N.J., 1969-72; rsch. assoc. Waksman Inst. Rutgers U., 1972-73; prof. NYU, 1973—. Co-author: Developments in Sweeteners-3, 1987; co-patentee method of reducing dental caries. Mem. Am. Soc. Microbiology, German Chem. Soc., European Orgn. Caries Rsch., Internat. Assn. Dental Rsch., U.S. Fedn. Culture Collections, N.Y. Acad. Scis., Sigma Xi. Home: 138 Barnard St Highland Park NJ 08904-3510

LINKER, ROBERT WILLIAM, III, cardiothoracic and vascular surgeon; b. Louisville, June 21, 1952; s. Robert William Jr. and Mary Lucille (Lipps) L.; m. Margaret Alyce Waits, May 9, 1981; children: Robert W. IV, Meaghan Kathleen, Caroline Rose. BA in Chemistry, U. Louisville, 1974, MD, 1978. Asst. prof. surgery Med. U. S.C., Charleston, 1985-86; staff thoracic surgeon Nurton Hosp., Louisville, 1986—; chief surgery Meth. Hosp., Louisville, 1990-92; chmn. surg. care appraisal Norton Hosp., 1991—. Chmn. annual golf tounrament Cystic Fibrosis Found., Louisville, 1989—. Fellow Am. Coll. Surgeons; mem. AMA, So. Thoracic Surg. Assn., Soc. Thoracic Surgeons. Republican. Roman Catholic. Office: Kentuckian Surg Assocs 234 E Gray St #458 Louisville KY 40202

LINKNER, EDWARD JAMES, physician; b. Detroit, May 15, 1949; s. Leonard S. and Ronnie Miller (Feigenbaum) L.; m. Debra Lynn Edelson, June 22, 1969; children: Justin, Lauren, Evan, Adam, Alex. BS, Mich. State U., 1970; MD, U. Mich., 1974. Diplomate Am. Bd. Internal Medicine, Am. Bd. Med. Examiners; cert. physician, Mich. Resident St. Joseph Mercy Hosp./U. Mich. Med. Sch., Ann Arbor, 1974-77; pvt. practice, founding mem. Ann Arbor Family Practice Assocs., P.C., 1977-90; solo pvt. practice Ann Arbor, 1990—; clin. faculty, lectr. dept. family practice U. Mich. Med. Sch., Ann Arbor, 1977—; co-founder Inst. Psychology and Medicine, 1979; founder Castle Remedies, 1982—; founding mem. Rehab. Health Ctr., 1984—; co-founder, co-dir. The Pkwy Ctr., 1987—. Chair physicians com. Wastenaw County United Way, 1984; bd. dir. Ann Arbor Sr. Citizens Guild, 1978-83; mem. Comprehensive Health Planning Coun. Southeastern Mich., 1983-86. Mem. ACP, Am. Acad. Family Practice, Am. Coll. Preventive Medicine, Am. Holistic Med. Assn. (trustee, sec. 1996—), Am. Bd. Holistic Medicine (trustee), Am. Assn. Naturopathic Physicians, Mich. Acupuncture Coalition (trustee), Am. Inst. Homeopathy, Internat. Acad. Preventive Medicine, Inst. for Advancement of Health, Mich. Acad. Family Physicians, Mich. State Med. Soc., Physicians for Social Responsibility, Royal Soc. Medicine, Wastenaw County Med. Soc., Assn. for Children with Social and Learning Disorders, Am. Numismatic Assn., Am. Numismatic Soc., Humane Soc. U.S., Internat. Health Found., others. Jewish. Address: 2345 S Huron Pkwy Ann Arbor MI 48104-5124

LINKO, LAURI TAPANI, lung disease specialist; b. Viipuri, Finland, Dec. 12, 1931; s. Iivo and Elli Elisabeth (Olkkonen) L. MD, U. Helsinki, 1957; lung disease specialist, U. Turku, Finland, 1966; grad. in x-ray protection, Instn. of X-ray Shelter, Finland, 1978. Asst. Dr. Pori Mcpl. Hosp., Finland, 1958-59, Kantonspital, Frauenfeld, Switzerland, 1959-60; dept. Dr. Reuma Found. Hosp., Heinola, Finland, 1965-66; dept. Dr. Satalinna Lung Hosp., Harjavalta, 1960-65, 67-68, asst. chief Dr., 1968-71; Dr. for welfare outpatiens lung disease dept. Kanta-Häme Ctr. Hosp., Hämeenlinna, 1971-89, asst. chief Dr. of Lung Disease Dept, 1989-91; retired, 1991; Drs. occupational trust man Kanta-Häme Ctr. Hosp., Hämeenlinna, 1977-91. Lt. Med. Svc., 1958, Res. Mem. Finnish Lung Drs. Assn. Conservative. Lutheran. Home: Rauhank 2 H 97, 13100 Hämeenlinna 10, Finland

LINKUS, KIMBERLY A., occupational therapist; b. Elizabeth, N.J., Feb. 19, 1957; d. Bonnaventure and Emily (Malinowsky) L. BS in Occupational Therapy, U. Pa., 1979; MA in Devel. Disabilities, NYU, 1982. Registered occupational therapist. Dir. occupational therapy Rahway (N.J.) Hosp.; OT-cognitive therapist Lifestyle Inst., JFK Med. Ctr., Edison, N.J.; dir. occupational therapy The Head Injury Ctr. at Plaza Med., Camden, N.J.; clin. care coord. occupational therapy Neurologic Ctr. at Cortland (N.Y.); clin. practice dir. occupational therapy Nova Care; dir. in-patient rehab. Med. Ctr. of Ocean County, N.J., Ea. N.Y., N.J.; clin. coord. of occupl. therapy N.E. Pa. Region Nova Care Inc.; presenter 5th annual symposium Nat. head Injury Found., instr. neuro-rehab. lab, Kenka Coll., N.Y. Mem. Am. Occupational Therapy Assn., N.J. Occupational Therapy Assn., N.Y. State Occupational Therapy Assn. (co-chmn. Cen. dist.). Home: 13 Cherry St Lakewood NJ 08761

LINNAN, JUDITH ANN, psychologist; b. Pasadena, Calif., July 11, 1940; d. Robert Emmet Linnan and Jane Thomas (Shutz) H.; m. Ralph Theodore Comito, Feb. 1, 1964 (div. Mar. 1975); children: Matthew, Andrew, Kristine. BA, U. Portland, 1962; MS, Calif. State U., Long Beach, 1974; PhD, CCI Internat. U., 1982; postgrad., Newport Psychoanalytical Inst., 1984-87, 95—. Lic. MFCC pupil pers., lic. rsch. psychoanalyst. Probation officer L.A. County Probation Dept., 1962-63; social worker L.A. County Dept. Probation and Social Svcs., 1963-69; counselor Huntington Beach (Calif.) Free Clinic, 1970-73, counseling ctr., Calif. State U., Long Beach, 1973-74; psychologist Fullerton (Calif.) Union High Sch. Dist., 1975-80, Psychiat. Med. Group, Orange County, Calif., 1981-82; psychologist, dir. Berkeley Psychol. Svcs., Placentia, Calif., 1982—; pvt. practice psychotherapist Huntington Beach, 1975—; founder, dir. Pacific Acad., Fullerton, 1981-82; dir. human resources So. Calif. Coll. Optometry, Fullerton, 1986—; cons., expert witness Orange County Social Svcs., 1992—; dir. student parent program Placentia Sch. Dist., 1993—. Democrat. Roman Catholic. Office: Berkeley Psychol Svcs 101 N Kraemer Blvd Ste 125 Placentia CA 92670-5000

LINS, ROBERT LOUIS, nephrologist, clinical investigator; b. Antwerp, Belgium, Feb. 6, 1949; s. Jean Louis and Maria-Louisa (Sels) L.; m. Clara J. Dubois, Sept. 21, 1974; children: Muriel, Sofie, Veronique. MD, U. Gent (Belgium), 1974; internist, U. Antwerp (Belgium), 1979, nephrologist, 1981. Nephrologist Stuivenberg Hosp., Antwerp, Belgium, 1979-84, head of dept. nephrology and hypertension, 1984—; head clin. rsch. unit Bio-pharma n.v., Antwerp, Belgium, 1987—; cons. various hosps., Antwerp, 1983; lectr. U. Antwerp, 1986—. Author books with internat. publ.; contbr. numerous articles to profl. jours. with internat. publ. Mem. Flemish Belgian Soc. Nephrology (pres. 1991-94), Belgian Hypertension Com. (sec. 1994—), European Renal Assn., Internat. Soc. Nephrology, European Soc. Hypertension, Nat. Kidney Found. Home: Hazelarenstr 7, 2020 Antwerp Belgium Office: A Z Stuivenberg Dept Nephrology, Lange Beeldekenstr 267, 2060 Antwerp Belgium

LINSENMEYER, TODD ALAN, medical educator, physician. Student, Whittier (Calif) Coll., 1971-72; BS with honors, Stanford U, 1975; MD, U. Hawaii, 1979. Diplomate Am. Bd. Urology, Am. Bd. Phys. Medicine and Rehab. Surg. intern Queen's Hosp., Honolulu, 1979-80; resident urology Tripler Amy Med. Ctr., Honolulu, 1980-84; resident physical medicine and rehab. Stanford (Calif.) Med. Ctr., 1986-89; clin. asst. prof. surgery U. Medicine and Dentistry/N.J. Sch. Medicine, Newark, 1989-95, asst. prof. rehab. medicine, 1989—, asst. prof. surgery, 1995—, assoc. prof. rehab. medicine, 1996—; asst. chief urology 98th Gen. U.S. Army Hosp., Nuremberg, Germany, 1984-86; dir. urology Kessler Inst. Rehab. Medicine, West Orange, N.J., 1989—; cons. urodynamics Dept. Vets. Affairs Med. Ctr., East Orange, 1991—; vis. prof. phys. medicine and rehab. Stanford U., 1992; reviewer Male Spinal Cord Injury Fertility Program: Miami Project for Cure of Paralysis, 1994; mem. sci. adv. bd. Paralyzed Vets. Am., 1995—; mem. grant rev. com. NIH, 1991, 92; mem. adv. com. Spinal Cord Injury Practice Consortium, 1995—, mem. steering com., 1995—; chmn. autonomic dysreflexia practice parameter guideline com. SCI Practice Parameter Consortium, 1995—; presenter various meetings, orgns., confs. Contbr. articles to profl. jours., chpts. to books. Maj. M.C. U.S. Army, 1980-87. Recipient 2nd pl. award paper competition ACS, Honolulu, 1984; grantee Sprague Dawley Rat Eastern Paralyzed VA, 1992-93, NIH, 1992-95, VA, 1995-98, Am. Paraplegia Soc., 1995-96. Mem. AMA, Am. Paraplegia Soc. (bd. dirs. 1993—, membership com. 1990, chmn. membership com. 1992-94, chmn. clin. practice parameter com. 1995—), Am. Spinal Cord Injury Assn. (mem. urology com. sexuality and disability 1991—, mem. program com., publs. com. 1994—), Am. Acad. Phys. Medicine and Rehab., Am. Congress Rehab. Medicine (mem. nat. task force on sexuality and disability 1988—), Am. Urodynamics Soc. (assoc.), Assn. Acad. Physiatrists, Am. Urol. Assn. Office: Kessler Inst Rehab 1199 Pleasant Valley Way West Orange NJ 07052

LINSEY, MICHAEL S., nephrologist; b. L.A., July 28, 1954; m. Ellen Reiko. BS in Biochemistry, UCLA, 1973; MD, U. Calif., Davis, 1977. Diplomate Am. Bd. Internal Medicine with subspecialty in nephrology. Intern Cedars Sinai Med. Ctr., L.A., 1977-78; resident in medicine U. Calif.-Davis, Sacramento, 1978-80, fellow in nephrology, 1980-82; pvt. practice Pasadena, Calif., 1982—; med. dir. Clinishare-Dialysis, Pasadena, 1985-90, 55 Congress Dialysis Ctr., Pasadena, 1985-90, Huntington Dialysis Ctr., Pasadena, 1990—; prin. investigator Normal Hemotocrit Cardiac Study Amgen, Inc., Pasadena, 1993—. Recipient Clin. Tchr. award Huntington Meml. Hosp., 1987. Fellow ACP; mem. Am. Soc. Nephrology, Am. Soc. for Apheresis, Internat. Soc. Nephrology, Internat. Soc. Peritoneal Dialysis, Calif. Med. Assn., Phi Beta Kappa, Alpha Omega Alpha. Office: 808 S Fair Oaks St Pasadena CA 91105

LINZ, ANTHONY JAMES, osteopathic physician, consultant, educator; b. Sandusky, Ohio, June 16, 1948; s. Anthony Joseph and Margaret Jane (Ballah) Linz; m. Kathleen Ann Kovach, Aug. 18, 1973; children: Anthony Scott, Sara Elizabeth. BS, Bowling Green State U., 1971; D.O., U. Osteo. Med. and Health Scis., 1974. Diplomate Nat. Bd. Osteo. Examiners; bd. cert., diplomate Am. Osteo. Bd. Internal Medicine, Internal Medicine, Med. Diseases of Chest and Critical Care Medicine. Intern Brentwood Hosp., Cleve., 1974-75, resident in internal medicine, 1975-78; subsplty. fellow in pulmonary diseases Riverside Meth. Hosp., Columbus, Ohio, 1978-80; med. dir. pulmonary svcs. Sandusky (Ohio) Meml. Hosp., 1980-85; med. dir. cardio-pulmonary svcs. Firelands Community Hosp., Sandusky, 1985—; cons. pulmonary, critical care and internal medicine, active staff sect. internal medicine, chmn. dept. medicine, head div. pulmonary medicine Firelands Community Hosp., 1985—; cons. staff dept. medicine Good Samaritan Hosp., 1982-85, sect. internal medicine specializing pulmonary diseases; cons. pulmonary, critical care, and internal medicine Providence Hosp., Sandusky, Mercy Hosp., Willard, Ohio; clin. prof. internal medicine Ohio U. Coll. Osteo. Medicine; clin. prof. medicine Univ. Health Scis. Coll. Osteo. Medicine, Kansas City, Mo.; clin. asst. prof. med. Med. Coll. of Ohio at Toledo; adj. prof. applied scis. Bowling Green State U.; mem. respiratory tech. adv. bd. Firelands Campus, Bowling Green State U., 1983—; med. dir. Respiratory Therapy program., Bowling Green State U., 1984—. Author, contbr. articles and abstracts to profl. jours. Water safety instr. ARC, 1965—; med. dir., clin. rsch. investigator Camp Superkid Asthma Camp, 1984—; bd. trustees Stein Hospice, 1986-90. Recipient Edward Ruff Comty. Svc. award Am. Lung. Assn., 1985, Master Clinician award Ohio U. Coll. Osteopathic Medicine, 1987, Golden Rule award J.C. Penney, 1990, Disting. Alumna/Alumnus award Firelands Coll., Bowling Green State U., 1995. Fellow Am. Coll. Chest Physicians, Am. Coll. Critical Care Medicine, Am. Coll. Osteo. Internists; mem. AAAS, European Thoracic Soc., Am. Osteo. Assn., Ohio Osteo. Assn. (past pres., past v.p., past sec.-treas., acad. trustees 5th dist. acad.), Am. Heart Assn., Am. Thoracic Soc., Ohio Thoracic Soc., Am. Lung Assn. (pres., 1st v.p., med. adv. bd. chmn., exec. bd. dirs., bd. dirs. Ohio's So. Shore sect. 1984—), Nat. Assn. Med. Dirs. Respiratory Care, Ohio Soc. Respiratory Care (med. adviser/dir. 1982—), So. Critical Care Medicine, Am. Coll. Physicians (Ohio chpt.), Found. Critical Care (mem. Founder's Cir.), Sandusky Yacht Club, Sandusky chpt.), Alpha Epsilon Delta, Beta Beta Beta, Pi Kappa Alpha, Atlas Med. Fraternity. Roman Catholic.

LION, ROBERT T., emergency room nurse; b. St. Marys, Pa., May 11, 1973; s. Stephen Andrew and Alice Rose (Collins) L. ASN, U. Pitts., 1993, BSN, 1995. RN, BSN, HP, Pa.; cert. ACLS, PALS, BTLS, EMT paramedic. Paramedic St. Marys (Pa.) Area Ambulance Svc., 1991—; mem. nursing staff St. Marys (Pa.) Regional Med. Ctr., 1993—; instr. EMMCO East Inc., St. Marys, 1994—, Am. Heart Assn., St. Marys, 1994—; data collector rsch. study effects of heparin transport patients, 1994. Vol. sch. nurse Sacred Heart Cath. Sch., St. Marys, 1994—; asst. scoutmaster Boy Scouts Am. Sacred Heart Troop 95, St. Marys, 1989—. Republican. Roman Catholic. Home: 705 Ford Rd Saint Marys PA 15857 Office: St Marys Regional Med Ctr 763 Johnsonburg Rd Saint Marys PA 15857

LIPFIELD, RICHARD, marriage, family and child counselor; b. N.Y.C., Aug. 26, 1941; s. Henry and Shirley (Stahl) L. BA in Bus. Adminstrn., Adelphi U., 1963; MA in Clin. Psychology, Antioch U., San Francisco, 1987. Pvt. practice marriage, family and child counseling Mill Valley, Calif. Author: Adult Children of Alcoholics Recovery Picture Book, 1985. Home: 752 Marin Dr Mill Valley CA 94941 Office: 160 Throckmorton Mill Valley CA 94941

LIPINSKI, BARBARA JANINA, psychotherapist, psychology educator; b. Chgo., Feb. 29, 1956; d. Janek and Alicja (Brzozkiewicz) L.; m. Bernard Joseph Burns, Feb. 14, 1976 (div. 1985). B of Social Work, U. Ill., Chgo., 1978; MFCC, MA, U. Calif., Santa Barbara, 1982; PhD, U. So. Calif., 1992. Diplomate Am. Bd. Forensic Medicine; cert. tchr., Calif., psychology tchr., Calif.; cert. adminstr., non-pub. agent; lic. marriage, family and child therapist; bd. cert. forensic examiner. Police svc. officer Santa Barbara (Calif.) Police Dept., 1978-79; peace officer Airport Police, Santa Barbara, 1979-80; emergency comms. Univ. Police, Santa Barbara, 1980-82; facilitator, instr. Nat. Traffic Safety Inst., San Jose, Calif., 1981-87; assoc. dir. Community Health Task Force on Alcohol and Drug Abuse, Santa Barbara, 1982-86; instr. Santa Barbara C.C., 1987-88; patients' rights adv. Santa Barbara County Calif. Mental Health Adminstrn., 1986-89; pvt. practice psychotherapist Santa Barbara, 1985—; faculty mem., clin. coord. Pacifica Grad. Inst., Carpinteria, Calif., 1989—; intern clin. psychology L.A. County Sheriff's Dept., 1991-92, cons. Devereaux Found., Santa Barbara, 1993-95, Ctr. for Law Related Edn., Santa Barbara, 1986; cons., trainer Univ. Police Dept.,

Santa Barbara, 1982, 89. Vol. crisis work Nat. Assn. Children of Alcoholics, L.A., 1987; crisis intervention worker Women in Crisis Can Act, Chgo., 1975-76; vol. counselor Santa Barbara Child Sexual Assault Treatment Ctr.-PACT, Santa Barbara, 1981-82. Recipient Grad. Teaching assistanship U. So. Calif., 1990-92. Mem. APA, Am. Profl. Soc. on Abuse of Children, Am. Coll. Forensic Examiners, Internat. Critical Incident Stress Found., Calif. Assn. Marriage and Family Therapists, Internat. Soc. for Traumatic Stress Studies. Home: 301 Los Cabos Ln Ventura CA 93001 Office: Pacifica Grad Inst 249 Lambert Rd Carpinteria CA 93013-3019

LIPKIN, BERNICE SACKS, computer science educator; b. Boston, Dec. 21, 1927; d. Milton and Esther Miriam (Berchuck) Sacks; m. Lewis Edward Lipkin; children: Joel Arthur, Libbe Lipkin Englander. BS in Biology, Chemistry, Northeastern U., 1949; MA in Psychology, Boston U., 1950; PhD in Experimental Psychology, Columbia U., 1961. Rsch. and devel. scientist Directorate Sci. and Tech., CIA, Washington, 1964-70; scientist dept. computer sci. U. Md., Greenbelt, 1971-72; health sci. adminstr. NIH, Bethesda, Md., 1972-88; cons. computerized text analysis, data exploration L+B and Co., Bethesda, 1989—. Author: String Processing and Text Manipulation in C, 1994; editor: Picture Processing and Psychopictorics, 1970; contbr. articles on computer-based text searches and data analysis to profl. publs. Cerebral Palsy Soc. fellow in neurophysiology, 1961-62; NIH trainee, 1955-58. Mem. AAAS, IEEE, APA, Soc. Neurosci., Optical Soc. Am., Assn. Computing Machinery, Sigma Xi. Jewish. Office: 9913 Belhaven Rd Bethesda MD 20817-1733

LIPKIN, DAVID ERNEST, physician; b. N.Y.C., Sept. 1, 1942; s. Herman and Marion (Bender) L.; m. Shelly Marsha Silver, June 29, 1968; children: Gary, Cindy, Elizabeth, Cathy. BA cum laude, Adelphi U., 1965; MD, Howard U., 1969. Diplomate Am. Bd. Internal Medicine. Pvt. practice Phila., 1972—. Mem. AMA, Montgomery County Med. Soc., Am. Soc. Internal Medicine, Pa. Med. Soc., Alpha Omega Alpha. Office: 1335 Tabor Rd Philadelphia PA 19141

LIPKIN, MARY CASTLEMAN DAVIS (MRS. ARTHUR BENNETT LIPKIN), retired psychiatric social worker; b. Germantown, Pa., Mar. 4, 1907; d. Henry L. and Willie (Webb) Davis; m. William F. Cavenaugh, Nov. 8, 1930 (div.); children: Molly C. (Mrs. Gary Oberbillig), William A.; m. Arthur Bennett Lipkin, Sept. 15, 1961 (dec. June 1974). Student, Pa. Acad. Fine Arts, 1924-28; postgrad., U. Wash., 1946-48, seattle Psychonalytic Assn., 1959-61. Nursery sch. tchr. Miquon (Pa.) Sch., 1940-45; caseworker Family Soc. Seattle, 1948-49, Jewish Family and Child Service, Seattle, 1951-56; psychiat. social worker Stockton (Calif.) State Hosp., 1957-58; supr. social service Mental Health Research Inst., Fort Steilacoom, Wash., 1958-59; engaged in pvt. practice, Bellevue, Wash., 1959-61. Former mem. Phila. Com. on City Policy. Former diplomate and bd. mem. Conf. Advancement of Pvt. Practice in Social Work; former mem. Chestnut Hill women's com. Phila. Orch; mem. Bellevue Art Mus., Assoc. Am. Assn. of U. Women, Wing Luke Mus. Mem. ACLU, LWV, Linus Pauling Inst. Sci. and Medicine, Inst. Noetic Scis., Menninger Found., Smithsonian Instn., Union Concerned Scientists, Physicians for Social Responsibility, Center for Sci. in Pub. Interest, Asian Art Council, Seattle Art Mus., Nature Conservancy, Wilderness Soc., Sierra Club. Home: 10022 Meydenbauer Way SE Bellevue WA 98004-6041

LIPMAN, BERNARD, internist, cardiologist; b. St. Joseph, Mo., June 14, 1920; s. Harry and Sarah K. (Kross) L.; m. Leslie Joy Garber, Apr. 23, 1949; children: Lawrence Alan, Robert Bruce, Bradford Craig, William Lloyd. A.B., Washington U., 1941, M.D., 1944. Diplomate: Am. Bd. Internal Medicine, Am. Bd. Cardiology. Intern Barnes Hosp., St. Louis, Newington Hosp.-Yale Med. Sch.; resident in medicine Barnes Hosp., 1947-49; teaching fellow U. Wash. Med. Sch., 1949-50; mem. faculty Emory U. Sch. Medicine, Atlanta, 1950—; clin. prof. medicine Emory U. Sch. Medicine, 1978-83, clin. prof. emeritus, 1983—; mem. staff St. Joseph Hosp., Grady Hosp., Piedmont Hosp., Emory U. Hosp., West Paces Ferry Hosp.; dir. heart sta. St. Joseph Hosp.; co-dir. Giddings Heart Clinic. Co-author Lipman-Massie Clinical Electrocardiography, 8th edit., 1989, ECG Pocket Guide, 1987; contbr. articles to med. jours. Co-trustee Albert Steiner Found. Served to capt. M.C. AUS, 1945-47. Fellow A.C.P., Am. Coll. Cardiology (emeritus); mem. Am. Heart Assn. (mem. council clin. cardiology), Am. Fedn. Clin. Research, Am. Soc. Internal Medicine, Phi Beta Kappa, Sigma Xi, Alpha Omega Alpha. Home: 2652 Brookdale Dr NW Atlanta GA 30305-3504

LIPNIK, MORRIS JACOB, physician; b. Detroit, Aug. 27, 1922; s. Louis and Lillian (Portney) L.; m. Lois Russine Wertheimer, Dec. 8, 1946; children: Susan, Carol. BA, Wayne State U., 1943, MD, 1946. Diplomate Am. Bd. Dermatology. Intern, Detroit Receiving Hosp., 1946-47; resident Johns Hopkins Hosp., Balt., 1947-48, Hosp. of U. Pa., 1949-51; practice medicine specializing in dermatology, Southfield, Mich., 1953—; mem. staff Sinai Hosp., Detroit, 1954-60, Cottage Hosp., Grosse Pointe, Mich., 1957-60, St. John Hosp. Detroit, 1954-60, Mt. Carmel Hosp., Detroit, 1966—, Beaumont Hosp., 1986—, St. Joseph Hosp., Pontiac, Mich., 1990—, Grace Hosp., Detroit, 1990—; spl. lectr. U. Detroit Dental Sch., 1958-63; adj. clin. prof. dermatology Marygrove Coll., Detroit, 1979—. Contbr. articles to med. jours. Mem. Founders' Soc. Detroit Inst. Arts, 1962; pres. Center Theatre, Detroit, 1963; patron Detroit Symphony Orch., 1978, Mich. Opera Theatre, Detroit, 1980, Detroit Community Music Sch., 1981, 82, 83. Served to capt. AUS, 1947-49. Mem. Mich. Dermatol. Soc., AMA, Am. Acad. Dermatology, Renaissance (Detroit), Fairlane Club (Dearborn), Knollwood Country Club, Bonita Bay Country Club, Phi Delta Epsilon. Office: 29829 Telegraph Rd #103-107 Southfield MI 48034-1330

LIPOMI, MICHAEL JOSEPH, health facility administrator; b. Buffalo, Mar. 9, 1953; s. Dominic Joseph and Betty (Angelo) L.; children: Jennifer, Barrett, M. Conner. BA, U. Ottawa, 1976; MS in Health Adminstrn., U. Colo., 1994. Mktg. dir. Am. Med. Internat. El Cajon Valley Hosp., Calif., 1980-83; dir. corp. devel. Med. Surg. Ctrs. Am., Calif., 1983-85; exec. dir. Stanislaus Surgery Ctr., Modesto, Calif., 1985—. Author: Complete Anatomy of Health Care Marketing, 1988; co-host med. TV talk show Health Talk Modesto. Bd. dirs. Am. Heart Assn., Modesto, 1988-89; pres. Modesto Community Hospice, 1987-88; active local govt.; sec.-treas. Modesto Industry and Edn. Council, 1989. Mem. Calif. Ambulatory Surgery Assn. (pres. 1988-89, mem. legis. com. 1994, mem. rsch. and edn. found. bd. 1994—), No. Calif. Assn. Surgery Ctrs. (pres. 1986-88), Federated Ambulatory Surgery Assn. (mem. govt. rels. com. 1988, bd. dirs. 1989—, chmn. govt. rels. com. 1990), Modesto C. of C. (bd. dirs. 1989-92), Rotary. Office: Stanislaus Surgery Ctr 1421 Oakdale Rd Modesto CA 95355-3359

LIPPA, ERIK ALEXANDER, ophthalmologist; b. Mpls., Nov. 7, 1945; s. Walter and Cecilie (Buchman) L.; m. Linda Susan Mottow, Mar. 6, 1980; children: David Abram, Andrew Moss. BS, Calif. Inst. Tech., 1967; MS, U. Mich., 1968, PhD in Math., 1971; MD, Albert Einstein Coll. Medicine, 1980. NATO postdoctoral fellow Oxford (Eng.) U., 1971-72; asst. prof. Purdue U., West Lafayette, Ind., 1972-78; med. intern NYU Med. Ctr./Manhattan (N.Y.) VA Hosp., 1980-81; resident ophthalmology Ill. Eye and Ear Infirmary, Chgo., 1981-84; ophthalmologist St. Paul, 1984-85; asst. dir. clin. rsch. Merck & Co. Inc., West Point, Pa., 1985-89, dir. clin. rsch., 1989-93; dir. med. affairs Allergan, Inc., Irvine, Calif., 1993—; adj. clin. asst. prof. Jefferson Med. Coll., Phila., 1986-91, adj. clin. assoc. prof., 1991—; clin. assoc. U. Pa., Phila., 1987-93; asst. surgeon Wills Eye Hosp., Phila., 1991-93, instr., 1986-91. Author: Mathematics for Freshmen in the Life Sciences, 1976; contbr. articles to profl. jours. Treas. Cub Scout Pack #665, Ft. Washington, Pa., 1988-93. Fellow Am. Acad. Ophthalmology; mem. AMA, Assn. Rsch. in Vision and Ophthalmology, Internat. Soc. Eye Rsch., Am. Glaucoma Soc., European Glaucoma Soc., Sigma Xi, Tau Beta Pi. Home: PO Box 16517 Irvine CA 92623-6517 Office: Allergan Inc 2525 Dupont Dr Irvine CA 92612-1531

LIPPE, PHILIPP MARIA, neurosurgeon, educator; b. Vienna, Austria, May 17, 1929; s. Philipp and Maria (Goth) L.; came to U.S., 1938, naturalized, 1945; m. Virginia M. Wiltgen, 1953 (div. 1977); children: Patricia Ann Marie, Philip Eric Andrew, Laura Lynne Elizabeth, Kenneth Anthony Ernst; m. Gail B. Busch, Nov. 26, 1977. Student Loyola U., Chgo., 1947-50; BS in Medicine, U. Ill. Coll. Medicine, 1952, MD with high honors, 1954. Rotating intern St. Francis Hosp., Evanston, Ill., 1954-55; asst. resident gen. surgery VA Hosp., Hines, Ill., 1955, 58-59; asst. resident neurology and neurol. surgery Neuropsychiat. Inst., U. Ill. Rsch. and Ednl. Hosps., Chgo., 1959-60, chief resident, 1962-63, resident neuropathology, 1962, postgrad. trainee in electroencephalography, 1963; resident neurology and neurol. surgery Presbyn.-St. Luke's Hosp., Chgo., 1960-61; practice medicine, specializing in neurol. surgery, San Jose, Calif., 1963—; instr. neurology and neurol. surgery U. Ill., 1962-63; clin. instr. surgery and neurosurgery Stanford U., 1965-69, clin. asst. prof., 1969-74, clin. assoc. prof., 1974-96, clin. prof. 1996—; staff cons. in neurosurgery O'Connor Hosp., Santa Clara Valley Med. Ctr., San Jose Hosp., Los Gatos Cmty. Hosp., El Camino Hosp. (all San Jose area); chmn. divsn. neurosugery Good Samaritan Hosp, 1989—; founder, exec. dir. Bay Area Pain Rehab. Center, San Jose, 1979—; clin. adviser to Joint Commn. on Accreditation of Hosps.; mem. dist. med. quality rev. com. Calif. Bd. Med. Quality Assurance, 1976-87, chmn., 1976-77. Served to capt. USAF, 1956-58. Diplomate Am. Bd. Neurol. Surgery, Nat. Bd. Med. Examiners, Am. Bd. Pain Medicine. Fellow ACS, Am. Coll. Pain Medicine (bd. dirs. 1991-94, v.p. 1991-92, pres. 1992-93); mem. AMA (Ho. of Dels. 1981—), Am. Coll. Physician Execs., Calif. Med. Assn. (Ho. of Dels. 1976-80, sci. bd., council 1979-87, sec. 1981-87, Outstanding Svc. award 1987), Santa Clara County Med. Soc. (coun. 1974-81, pres. 1978-79, Outstanding Contbn. award 1984, Benjamin J. Cory award 1987), Chgo. Med. Soc., Congress Neurol. Surgeons, Calif. Assn. Neurol. Surgeons (dir. 1974-82, v.p. 1975-76, pres. 1977-79), San Jose Surg. Soc., Am. Assn. Neurol. Surgeons (chm. sect. on pain 1987-90, dir. 1983-86, 87-90, Disting. Svc. award 1986, 90), Western Neurol. Soc., San Francisco Neurol. Soc., Santa Clara Valley Profl. Standards Rev. Orgn. (dir., v.p., dir. quality assurance 1975-83), Fedn. Western Socs. Neurol. Sci., Internat. Assn. for Study Pain, Am. Pain Soc. (founding mem.), Am. Acad. Pain Medicine (sec. 1983-86, pres. 1987-88, Philipp M. Lippe Disting. Svc. award 1995, exec. med. dir. 1996—), Am. Bd. Pain Medicine (exec. v.p., 1994—), Alpha Omega Alpha, Phi Kappa Phi. Assoc. editor Clin. Jour. of Pain; contbr. articles to profl. jours. Pioneered med. application centrifugal force using flight simulator. Office: 2100 Forest Ave Ste 106 San Jose CA 95128-1422

LIPPER, STEVEN, psychiatrist, educator; b. Boston, July 17, 1943; s. Philip and Tillie (Levine) L.; m. Susan Fay Shapiro, July 27, 1969; children—Rachel Margaret, Charles Nathan. A.B. magna cum laude, Harvard Coll., 1964; postgrad. Yale U. Sch. Medicine, 1964-65, 67-68; Ph.D., Boston U., 1970, M.D., 1972. Diplomate Nat. Bd. Med. Examiners. Resident in psychiatry N.C. Meml. Hosp., Chapel Hill, 1972-75; clin. assoc. NIMH, Bethesda, Md., 1975-77; staff psychiatrist VA Med. Ctr., Ann Arbor, Mich., 1977-82; asst. prof. psychiatry U. Mich. Med. Sch., Ann Arbor, 1977-80, assoc. prof., 1980-82; staff psychiatrist VA Med. Ctr., Durham, N.C., 1982—; assoc. prof. psychiatry Duke U., Durham, 1982-92, assoc. clin. prof., 1993-95, clin. prof. psychiatry and behavioral scis., 1995—. Served with USPHS, 1975-77. Recipient John M. Murray prize in psychiatry, 1972; Anclote Manor award in psychiatry N.C. Meml. Hosp. Dept. Psychiatry, 1975; Honored Tchr. Psychiatry Duke U., 1984. Fellow. Am. Psychiat. Assn.; mem. N.C. Psychiat. Assn., AAAS, So. Psychiatric Assn., Fedn. Am. Scientists, N.Y. Acad. Scis., Phi Beta Kappa, Sigma Xi, Alpha Omega Alpha. Contbr. chpts. to books, articles to profl. jours. Office: Psychiatry Service VA Med Ctr 508 Fulton St Durham NC 27705

LIPPERT, CHRISTOPHER NELSON, dentist, consultant; b. N.Y.C., Apr. 17, 1952; s. Raymond Joseph and Shirley Ann (Nelson) L.; m. Valerie Jo Schlager, Nov. 4 1989. BS, U. Cin., 1975; DDS, Emory U., 1979. Dentist John W. Regenos DDS, Inc., Cin., 1979-87; pres., dentist Lippert & Wilkes DDS, Inc., Cin., 1987—; cons. Teret's Syndrome Found., Cin., 1983—, Health Am., Cleve., 1985-90; lectr. Ohio State U., 1981-89. Bd. dirs. Creekwood Condominiums, Cin., 1985-86. Mem. ADA, Am. Acad. Fixed Prosthodontists, Ohio Dental Assn., Ohio Acad. Practice Adminstrn., Cin. Dental Soc. (peer rev. com. 1985—), Midwest Med. Found. (bd. dirs. 1984-88), Phi Eta Sigma, Sigma Alpha Epsilon, Psi Omega.

LIPPERT INDIG, JOAN, medical writer; b. Glen Cove, N.Y., Dec. 3, 1951; d. Joseph Jr. and Mary Jane Lippert; m. Benjamin C. Indig, May 22, 1982. BA, Mount Holyoke Coll., 1974. Personal sec. Harcourt Brace Jovanovich, N.Y.C., 1974-75; editl. asst. Good Housekeeping Mag., N.Y.C., 1975-76, writer, 1976-78; mng. editor Sci. Digest Mag., N.Y.C., 1978-80, Health Mag., N.Y.C., 1980-85; freelance med. writer. Contbr. articles to mags. Parent chair Hastings Nursery Sch., Hastings-on-Hudson, N.Y., 1990-91; deacon 1st Reformed Ch., Hastings-on-Hudson, 1989-92, elder, 1996—; bd. mem. Hudson River Nursery Sch., Dobbs Ferry, N.Y., 1995—, pres. 1996—. Recipient Journalism award Am. Soc. Plastic and Reconstructive Surgeons, 1989. Mem. Am. Soc. Journalists and Authors.

LIPPINCOTT, JONATHAN RAMSAY, healthcare executive; b. Cin., Dec. 26, 1946; s. Morss d'Isay and Virginia Yvonne (Peugnet) L.; m. Nancy Todd Smith, Feb. 22, 1975; children: Jonathan J.E., Michael R.T. BA, Yale U., 1968; MLitt, Oxford U., 1972. Program research analyst human resources adminstrn. City of New York, 1973-76; exec. asst. to dir. med. ctr. U. Cin. Med. Ctr., 1977, asst. sr. v.p., 1977-84; fellow in HMO planning policy & mgmt. Harvard Community Health Plan, Brookline, Mass., 1985-86; assoc. sr. v.p. U. Cin. Med. Ctr., 1984-94; assoc. dir. U. Cin. Hosp., 1993-94; sr. v.p., chief strategic officer Health Alliance Greater Cin., 1994—; exec. dir. bus. devel. Alliance Ptnrs., 1996—; trustee, chmn., bd. Southwestern Ohio Sr. Svcs. Inc., Maple Knoll Village, 1993-96; bd. dirs., sec., treas. Univ. Health Maintenance Orgn., Inc., 1989-93; exec. bd. dirs. The Health Initiative, Cin.; co-dir. U. Cin. Inst. Health Policy and Health Svcs. Rsch., 1993-96. Contbr. articles to cons. and acad. mags. Pres., bd. trustees Little Miami, Inc., Cin., 1984-85; steering com., chmn. health & human svcs. session Leadership Cin., 1983-84; vice chmn. Cin. Transp. Study Com., 1984-85. Mem. Am. Assn. Med. Colls. (midwest regional chmn. group on inst. planning 1991-93), Am. Coll. Health Care Execs., Cin. C. of C. (health care com.). Office: Health Alliance Greater Cin 2060 Reading Rd Ste 400 Cincinnati OH 45202

LIPPINCOTT, JOSEPH ARTHUR, psychologist; b. Somerville, N.J., Mar. 11, 1956; s. Donald John and Mary Rose (Vince) L.; m. Ruth Bale, Aug. 11, 1984. BSN, Seton Hall U., 1978; MS in Psychiat. Nursing, Rutgers U., 1981; PhD, Lehigh U., 1991. Psychiat. nurse Lyons (N.J.) VA Med. Ctr., 1978-79; psychotherapist Prince Georges County Community Mental Health Ctr., Clinton, Md., 1981-86, Lenape Valley Found., Richboro, Pa., 1986-87; coll. counselor Lehigh U., Bethlehem, Pa., 1987-90; assoc. prof. Kutztown (Pa.) U., 1990—; adj. faculty Northampton Community Coll., Bethlehem, 1986-87; cons. Prince Georges County Parole/Probation, Marlboro, Md., 1981-86, Ortho Pharms., Raritan, N.J., 1980. Mem. ACA, ANA (coun. advanced practitioners in psychiat. nursing), Sigma Theta Tau, Chi Sigma Iota (Outstanding Rsch. award 1990). Home: 810 Tower Rd Alburtis PA 18011-2351

LIPPMAN, MARC ESTES, pharmacology educator; b. Bklyn., Jan. 15, 1945. BA, Cornell U., 1964; MD, Yale U., 1968. Intern Osler med. svc. Johns Hopkins Hosp., Balt., 1968-69, asst. resident, 1969-70; clin. assoc. leukemia svc. Nat. Cancer Inst., NIH, Washington, 1970-71, clin. assoc. lab. biochemistry, 1971-73, sr. investigator med. br., 1974-88, head med. breast cancer sect., 1976-88; clin. prof. medicine & pharmacology, uniformed svc. U. Health Sci., 1978—; dir. Vincent T. Lombardi Cancer Ctr. Georgetown U., Washington, 1988—, prof. medicine & pharmacology, 1988—; mem. merit rev. bd. oncology Vet. Adminstrn. Med. Rsch. Svc., 1977-81, endocrine treatment com. Nat. Surg. Adjuvant Breast Project, 1977-86; cons. dept. pharmacology George Washington Sch. Medicine, 1978-89; co-chmn. Gordon Rsch. Conf. on Hormone Action, 1984, chmn., 1985; treas. Internat. Congress Hormones & Cancer, 1984—; mem. adv. bd. Nat. Alliance Breast Cancer Orgn., 1986—; mem. stage III monitoring com. Nat. Surg. Adjuvant Project Breast & Bowel Cancers, 1987-89; bd. trustees Am. Cancer Soc., Washington, 1989-92; mem. sci. adv. bd. Coordinated Coun. Cancer Rsch., 1989—; hon. dir. Y-ME, Nat. Orgn. Breast Cancer Info. & Support, 1990—; Woodward vis. prof., mem. Sloan-Kettering, 1990; Sidney Sachs Meml. lectr. Case Western Reserve, 1985, D.R. Edwards lectr. Tenovus Inst., Wales, 1985, Gosse lectr. Dalhousie U., Halifax, N.S., 1987, Transatlantic lectr. Brit. Endocrine Socs., 1989, Barofsky lectr. Howard U., 1990, Rose Kushner Meml. lectr. Long Beach Meml. Med. Ctr., 1990, Constance Wood Meml. lectr. Hammersmith Hosp., Eng., 1991. Endocrinology fellow Yale Med. Sch., 1973-74; recipient Mallinckrodt award Clin. Radioassay Soc., 1978, D.R. Edwards medal Tenovus Inst., 1985, Transatlantic medal Brit. Endocrine Socs., 1989, Tiffany award of Distinction, Komen Found., 1989. Richard and Hinda Rosenthal Found. award Am. Assn. Cancer Rsch. 1994. Fellow ACP, Am. Fedn. Clin. Rsch., Am. Soc. Cell Biology, Am. Assn. Cancer Rsch. (program com. 1986), Am. Soc. Clin. Oncology (program com. 1987-89, chmn. local organizing com. 1989-90), Endocrine Soc. (pub. affairs com. 1980-81, Edward B. Astwood Lecture award 1991), Metastasis Rsch. Soc.; mem. Assn. Am. Physicians, Am. Soc. Clin. Investigators (program com. 1988), Am. Soc. Biol. Chemists. Office: Lombardi Career Center Research Bldg 3970 Reservoir Rd NW, Rm E501 Washington DC 20007*

LIPPMANN, BRUCE ALLAN, rehabilitative services professional; b. Balt., Aug. 29, 1950; s. Allan L. and Phyllis Marie (Bunyea) L.; m. Barbara Jean Wood, May 26, 1973 (div. Aug. 1979); m. Susan K. Shampanier, Feb. 1, 1981 (div. Nov. 1990); m. Frances G. Scruggs, Dec. 31, 1991; children: Joshua Rae Holt, Stuart Holt, Joshua Lippmann, Grant Lippmann. BA, U. Md., Catonsville, 1972; MS, Loyola U., 1979; cert., San Diego Inst., 1989; postgrad., Calif. Sch. Profl. Psychology, 1992-93. Cert. rehab. counselor, ins. rehab. specialist. Social worker Md. Children's Ctr., Catonsville, 1970-72; vocat. cons. St. Md. Workers Compensation Commn., Balt., 1975-79; sr. counselor McGuinness Assocs., Fresno, Calif., 1980-84; pres., chief exec. officer Sierra Rehab. Svcs. Inc., Fresno, 1984-91; vocat. counselor Fresno, 1991-94; health care mgr. GAB Robins N.Am. Inc., Fresno, 1994—; cons. Doctors Med. Ctr., Modesto, Calif., 1989-92, Calif. Ctr. Rehab. Svcs., Fresno, 1986-89, U.S Dept. Labor, San Francisco, 1984—; curriculum cons. Microcomputer Tng. Inst., Fresno, 1986-91. Mem. Metro Circle-Fresno Metro Mus., 1986—, Fresno Zool. Soc., 1985—, Fresno Arts Mus., 1984—, Bulldog Found., Fresno State U., 1985-91. With U.S. Army, 1972-75. Mem. APA, Central Calif. Rehab. Assn. (pres. 1984-85), Nat. Assn. Rehab. Profls. (Counselor of Yr. 1987, Pvt. Sector Rehab. Counselor or Yr. 1988), Calif. Nat. Assn.Rehab. Profls. Pvt. Sector (membership com. 1984-85, Meritorious Svc. 1985, Cert. of Recognition 1986), Calif. Assn. Rehab. Profls., Nat. Rehab. Assn., Nat. Rehab Counseling Assn. Democrat. Jewish. Office: 1477 E Shaw Ave Ste 100 Fresno CA 93710-8021

LIPPMANN, HEINZ ISRAEL, physician, educator, researcher; b. Breslau, Fed. Republic of Germany, May 21, 1908; came to U.S., 1940; s. Felix and Sophie (Moskiewicz) L.; m. Alisa Moscato, Mar. 15, 1936; children: Ruth Lippmann Gordon, Robert, Lawrence. MD, U. Berlin, 1931, U. Genoa, Italy, 1933. Diplomate Italian Med. Bd., diplomate Am. Bd. Phys. Medicine and Rehab. Asst. prof. Albert Einstein Coll. Medicine, N.Y.C., 1955-59, assoc. prof., 1959-69, prof. rehab. medicine, 1969-, prof. emeritus, 1976—, chief peripheral vascular diseases clinic, 1957—; cons. rehab. medicine St. Joseph Hosp., Paterson, N.J., Englewood (N.J.) Hosp., E-O VA Med. Ctr., East Orange, N.J., 1960-93. Fellow Am. Coll. Physicians (life); mem. AMA (sr.), N.Y. Acad. Medicine (life), N.Y. Acad. Scis. (life), Am. Acad. PMR (sr., Disting. Clinician 1986), Am. Congress Rehab. Medicine (sr., Gold Medal 1959), N.J. State Med. Soc. (sr.). Home: 2 Berol Close Chappaqua NY 10514-2305 Office: Albert Einstein Coll of Medicine 1600 Tenbroeck Ave Bronx NY 10461-2008

LIPPMANN, MICHAEL, physician, educator; b. N.Y.C., June 30, 1944; s. Ernest and Margot (Rosenow) L.; m. Julie Ann Cohn, June 8, 1969; children: Elisa, Sara. BS, CCNY, 1966; MD, SUNY, Buffalo, 1970. Intern medicine Bronx Mcpl. Hosp. Ctr., N.Y.C., 1970-71; sr. asst. surgeon USPHS-NIOSH, Morgantown, W.Va., 1971-73; resident medicine Yale New Haven Hosp., New Haven, 1973-75; fellow Bronx Mcpl. Hosp., N.Y.C., 1975-76; attending pulmonary Albert Einstein Med. Ctr., Phila., 1977—; chief pulmonary disease Albert Einstein Med. Ctr., 1980—; prof. medicine Temple U. Sch. Medicine, Phila. Contbr. articles on pulmonary diseases to profl. jours. Pres. Camp Ramah Poconos, Lake Como, Pa., 1988-91. Fellow ACP, Am. Coll. Chest Physicians; mem. Am. Thoracic Soc., Soc. Critical Care Medicine. Democrat. Jewish. Office: Albert Einstein Med Ctr York & Tabor Philadelphia PA 19141

LIPPNER, LEWIS ALAN, health facility administrator; b. Bklyn., Mar. 10, 1948; s. Sid and Ruth L. Fellow Internat. Health & Econs., U. Oslo, Norway, 1968; BA in Econs., U. Pitts., 1969; MA in Health Care Adminstrn., George Washington U., 1972. Resident King's County Hosp. Ctr., Bklyn., 1971-72; facilities planning and fin. cons. Block, McGiboney & Assocs./Health and Hosp. Cons., Silver Springs, Md., 1972-73; asst. dir., planner The Bklyn. Hosp./Bklyn.-Cumberland Med. Ctr., 1973-75; asst. hosp. adminstr., COO John E. Runnells Hosp. of Union County, Berkley Heights, N.J., 1975-78; adminstr. Johnston R. Bowman/Rush Presbyn. St. Luke's Med. Ctr., Chgo., 1978-82; asst. v.p. adminstrv. affairs Rush Presbyn. St. Luke's Med. Ctr., Chgo., 1983-88; COO Lincoln Hosp. Med. Ctr., N.Y.C., 1988-90; chief exec. officer Fairfield Hills Hosp., Newtown, Conn., 1990-91; dep. commr. Westchester (N.Y.) County Med. Ctr.; CEO, exec. dir. Orthopaedic Assocs. N.Y., P.C., 1993-95; adminstr. Psychiatry Inst. Bergen Pines County Hosp., 1996—; adminstr. fin. cons. Pritzker Med. Sch., U. Chgo. Hosp. & Clins., 1988; planning cons. Internat. Sci. and Tech. Inst., Washington, 19881 network devel. cons. Managed Care Orgns. and Physicians Groups, 1988-89. Univ. scholar U. Pitts., 1967-69; recipient Frederick Schaeffer Meml. fellowship U. Oslo, Norway, 1968, U.S. Pub. Health traineeship George Washington U., 1970-71. Mem. Am. Coll. Healthcare Execs., Am. Hosp. Assn., Chgo. Health Execs. Forum, George Washington U. Alumni Assn. for Health Svcs. Adminstrn., Omicron Delta Epsilon.

LIPPOLD, ROLAND WILL, surgeon; b. Staunton, Ill., May 1, 1916; s. Frank Carl and Ella (Immenroth) L.; m. Margaret Cookson, June 1, 1947; children: Mary Ellen Lippold Elvick, Catherine Anne Lippold Rolf, Carol Sue Lippold Webber. BS, U. Ill., 1940, MD, 1941. Diplomate Am. Bd. Surgery. Intern Grant Hosp., Chgo., 1941-42, resident in surgery, 1942-43, 47-48; resident in surgery St. Francis Hosp., Evanston, Ill., 1946-47; fellow in pathology Cook County Hosp., Chgo., 1947-48, resident in surgery, 1949-50; practice medicine specializing in surgery Chgo., 1950-53; also asst. in anatomy U. Ill., Chgo., 1950-53; practice medicine specializing in surgery Sacramento, 1953-68; chief med. officer No. Reception Ctr.-Clinic, Calif. Youth Authority, Sacramento, 1954-68, chief med. services, 1968-79; cons. in med. care in correctional instns.; cons. Calif. State Personnel Bd. Contbr. articles to med. publs. Chmn. Calif. Expn. Hall of Health, 1971-72. Comdr. M.C., USNR, 1943-73, PTO. Mem. Sacramento Surg. Soc., Sacramento County Med. Soc., Calif. Med. Assn., AMA, Assn. Mil. Surgeons U.S., Sacramento Hist. Soc. (life). Republican. Lutheran. Home: 1811 Eastern Ave Sacramento CA 95864-1724

LIPPY, KAREN DOROTHY FETHE, nursing administrator; b. Balt., July 2, 1946; d. Vernon Harold and Dorothy Margaret (Wirth) Fethe; m. Robert Eugene Lippy, July 29, 1972; 1 child, Jarrod Blaire. BS in Nursing, U. Md., Balt, 1972, MS in Nursing, 1975. Cert. clin. specialist in adult psychiat./mental health nursing; cert. in nursing adminstrn.-advanced. Clin. nurse specialist Springfield Hosp. Ctr., Sykesville, Md., 1975-79, asst. dir. nursing, 1979-86, dir. nursing, 1986—; clin. nurse specialist Reentry Mental Health Svcs., Westminster, Md., 1983—; mem. task force on RN standards of practice Md. State Bd. Nursing; mem. patient rights, classification, RN job specification, and credentialing/privileging task forces Md. Mental Hygiene Adminstrn. Recipient Gov.'s Citation for Excellence, State of Md., Achievement in Nursing Adminstrn., Md. Dept. Mental Hygiene. Mem. ANA, Md. Nurses Assn. (dist. bd. dirs.), Sigma Theta Tau, Phi Kappa Phi. Home: 2519 Bird View Rd Westminster MD 21157-8309

LIPS, DANIEL LEE, cardiologist; b. Trenton, Mo., July 20, 1955; s. Argaylis Morgan and Lorraine Martha (Grote) L.; m. Martha Jeanne Beardslee, Dec. 19, 1987; children: Margaret Eileen, Erin Michelle, Anne Marie. BA summa cum laude, Macalester Coll., 1977; MA, Oxford U., 1980; MD, Washington U., 1983. Diplomate Am. Bd. Internal Medicine. Intern in medicine Barnes Hosp./Wash. U. Sch. of Medicine, St. Louis, 1983-84, resident in medicine, 1984-86, rsch. assoc. in medicine, 1986-90, fellow in cardiology, 1990-92, fellow in interventional cardiology St. Vincent Hosp., Indpls., 1992-93; staff cardiologist Northside Cardiology, St. Vincent Hosp., Indpls., 1993—; chmn. cardiac database St. Vincent Hosp. and Ind. Heart Inst., Indpls., 1995—. Contbr. articles to profl. jours. Rhodes scholar Rhodes Trust, 1977. Mem. AMA, Ind. State Med. Soc., Indpls. Med. Soc., Am. Coll. Cardiology, Ind. Heart Inst., Phi Beta Kappa, Alpha Omega

Alpha. Office: Northside Cardiology Ste 200 8333 Naab Rd Indianapolis IN 46260

LIPSCOMB, PAUL ROGERS, orthopedic surgeon, educator; b. Clio, S.C., Mar. 23, 1914; s. Paul Holmes and Mary Emma (Rogers) L.; m. Phyllis M. Oesterreich, July 20, 1940; children—Susan L. Nachbaur, Paul Rogers. B.S., U. S.C., 1935; M.D., Med. U. S.C., 1938; M.S. in Orthopaedic Surgery, Mayo Found., U. Minn., 1942. Diplomate Am. Bd. Orthopaedic Surgery (sec. 1968-71, pres. 1971-73). Intern Cooper Hosp., Camden, N.J., 1938-39; resident in orthopaedic surgery Mayo Clinic, Rochester, Minn., 1939-43, asst. to staff orthopaedic surgery, 1941-43, staff assoc., 1943-69, v.p. staff, 1963; cons. Methodist, St. Mary's hosps., 1943-69; mem. faculty Mayo Grad. Sch. U. Minn., 1944-69, prof. orthopaedic surgery, 1961-69; mem. univ. senate from U. Minn. (Mayo Grad. Sch.), 1963-67; past mem. grad. and admissions com. and joint com. Grad. Sch. U. Minn. and Mayo Grad. Sch.; prof., chmn. dept. orthopedic surgery (Sch. of Medicine, U. Calif.), Davis, 1969-81, prof. emeritus, 1981—; pres. staff Sacramento Med. Center, 1980-81; mem. staff Woodland Clinic, 1981-86; ret., 1992; v.p. Woodland Clinic Research and Edn. Found., 1982-84, pres., 1984-85; hon. vis. prof. orthopaedics U. Auckland, New Zealand, 1978; cons. Disability Evaluation Group, Sacramento, 1988-92. Contbr. numerous articles to profl. jours. Mem. Am. Acad. Orthopedic Surgery (chmn. com. sci. investigation 1955-56, chmn. instrl. course com., editor instrl. course lectures 1961-63, chmn. com. on arthritis 1970), Orthopaedic Rsch. Soc. (chmn. membership com., mem. exec. com. 1956), AMA (chmn. orthopaedic sect. 1965), ACS, Am. Orthopaedic Assn. (pres. 1974-75), Western Orthopaedic Soc., Internat. Soc. Orthopaedic Surgery and Traumatology, Ctrl., Internat. orthopaedic clubs, New Zealand Orthopaedic Assn. (corr.), Sacramento County, Yolo County med. socs., Sterling Bunnell Found. (trustee 1984-86), Calif. Med. Assn., Sigma Xi, Alpha Omega Alpha. Presbyterian. Home: 749 Sycamore Ln Davis CA 95616-3432

LIPSITT, LEWIS PAEFF, psychology educator; b. New Bedford, Mass., June 28, 1929; s. Joseph and Anna Naomi (Paeff) L.; m. Edna Brill Duchin, June 8, 1952; children: Mark, Ann. BA, U. Chgo., 1950; MS, U. Mass., 1952; PhD, U. Iowa, 1957. Instr. dept. psychology Brown U., Providence, 1957, asst. prof., 1958-61, assoc. prof., 1961-66, prof., 1966-96, dir. Child Study Ctr., 1967-92, Wriston lectr., 1993—, prof. emeritus psychology, med. sci. and human devel., 1996—, rsch. prof. psychology, 1996—; mem. Gov.'s Adv. Commn. on Mental Retardation, 1963-66; cons. NIH; mem. edn. task force Model Cities Program, Providence, 1969-71; fellow Stanford Ctr. for Advanced Study in Behavioral Scis., 1979-80; vis. scientist NIMH, 1986-87; chair steering com. nat. child care project NICHHD, 1994—. Co-author: Child Development, 1979; founder, editor: Infant Behavior and Devel., 1978-82; founding co-editor: Advances in Child Development and Behavior, 1963-70, 78-82; co-editor: Research Readings in Child Psychology, 1963, Experimental Child Psychology, 1971, Advances in Infancy Research, Self-regulatory Behavior and Risk Taking, 1991; contbr. articles to profl. jours. Bd. dirs. Providence Child Guidance Clinic, 1960-63; trustee Butler Hosp., Providence, 1965-84; mem. bd. sci. counselor Nat. Ins. Child Health and Human Devel., 1984-88; nat. co-dir. Lee Salk Family Ctr., Kidspeace, Allentown, Pa., 1993—. Recipient Mentor award for lifetime achievement AAAS, 1995, Profl. Achievement citation U. Chgo., 1995; USPHS Spl. Rsch. fellow, 1966, Guggenheim fellow, 1972-73, USPHS fellow, 1973. Fellow AAAS (Lifetime Mentor award 1994), APA (exec. com. divsn. devel. psychology 1967-70, pres.-elect divsn. devel. psychology 1979-80, pres. divsn. devel. psychology 1980-81, bd. sci. affirs 1985-88, exec. dir. for sci. 1990-91, sci. officer 1991-92, Nicholas Hobbs award 1990); mem. AAUP, Soc. Rsch. in Child Devel., Internat. Soc. Study of Behavioral Devel. (membership sec. 1981-83, exec. com. 1984-89), Am. Psychol. Soc. (founding mem., charter fellow, bd. dirs. 1989-90), Can. Inst. for Advanced Rsch. (chair adv. com. human devel. group 1995—).

LIPSKY, LINDA ETHEL, business executive; b. Bklyn., June 2, 1939; d. Irving Julius and Florence (Stern) Ellman; m. Warren Lipsky, June 12, 1960 (div. Sept. 1968); 1 child, Phillip Bruce; m. Jerome Friedman, Jan. 17, 1988. BA in Psychology, Hofstra U., 1960; MPS in Health Care Adminstrn., Long Island U., 1979. Child welfare social worker Nassau County Dept. Social Service, N.Y., 1960-64; adminstr. La Guardia Med. Group of Health Ins. Plan of Greater N.Y., Queens, 1969-72; cons. Neighborhood Service Ctr., Bronx, N.Y., 1973-78; dir. ODA Health Ctr., Bklyn., 1978-82; pres. Millin Assocs., Inc., Nassau, N.Y., 1982—. Mem. Health Care Fin. Mgmt. Assn., Nat. Assn. Community Health Ctrs., Nat. Assn. Female Execs., Cmty. Health Ctr. Assoc. of N.Y., Hofstra U. Alumni Assn. (mem. senate 1984—, chairperson membership com. 1985—), Pi Alpha Alpha. Republican. Jewish. Avocations: cooking, writing, reading. Office: Millin Assocs Inc 521 Chestnut St Cedarhurst NY 11516-2223

LIPSMAN, JOSHUA BAR, health officer; b. Newport Beach, Calif., Aug. 14, 1956; s. Alexander and Claire Louise (Kaplan) L. BA, U. Chgo., 1978, MS, 1979; MD, Albert Einstein Coll. Med., 1983; MPH, U. N.C., 1990. Diplomate Am. Bd. Family Practice, Am. Bd. Preventive Medicine. Intern, resident in family practice St. Paul-Ramsey Med. Ctr. (U. Minn. affiliate), 1983-86; staff physician Indian Health Svc., Pine Ridge, S.D., 1986-89; bur. chief clin. health svcs. City Houston Dept. Health and Human Svcs., 1989-91; dist. health officer Va. Dept. Health, Alexandria, 1991—; pres. Va. Acad. Preventive Medicine and Pub. Health, 1995-96; adj. inst. Georgetown U. Sch. Med., 1993; adj. assoc. prof. health care scis. George Washington Sch. Medicine, 1993; chmn. health officers com. Coun. Govts., 1995-96, mem. adv. bd. Whitman Walker Clin. No. Va., 1996; pres. Va. Acad. Preventive Medicine and Pub. Health, 1995—. Fellow Ctrs. for Disease Control Pub. Health Leadership Inst., 1992. Fellow Am. Coll. Preventive Medicine, Am. Acad. Family Physicians; mem. Am. PUb. Health Assn., Alexandria Med. Soc. (sec. 1996), Capital Area Physicians Human Rights (pres. 1993-95). Office: Alexandria Health Dept 517 N Saint Asaph St Alexandria VA 22314

LIPSON, ACE, physician; b. Providence, Mar. 11, 1947; s. Julius and Betty (Salk) L.; m. Linda Novack, Dec. 30, 1972; children: Elena, Zachary.. BA, NYU, 1969; MD, Washington U., St. Louis, 1973. Intern George Washington U., Washington, 1973-74, resident, 1974-76, asst. prof., 1978-82, assoc. clin. prof., 1982—; physician pvt. practice, Washington, 1981—. Contbr. articles to profl. jours. Endocrinology fellow Johns Hopkins Hosp., Balt., 1976-78. Fellow Am. Coll. Physicians, Am. Assn. Clin. Endocrinologists; mem. Am. Diabetes Assn., Nat. Adrenal Found., D.C. Med. Soc., Endocrine Soc., Jacobi Med. Soc. (pres. 1996). Office: 2141 K St NW #600 Washington DC 20037

LIPSON, STEPHEN DUNCAN, urologist; b. Boston, Feb. 2, 1948; s. Herbert William and Lillian Elizabeth (Zach) L.; m. Karent Ann Luoma (div.); 1 child, Mathew Adam; m. Jean Marie Esserwein; children: Andrew, Rebecca, Daniel, David, Timothy. BA magna cum laude, Princeton U., 1970; MD, U. Cin., 1974. Diplomate Nat. Bd. of Med. Examiners, Am. Bd. Urology. Intern in gen. surgery The Johns Hopkins Hosp., Balt., 1974-75, resident in gen. surgery, 1975-76; fellow cancer rsch. and surgery The Surgery Br. of Nat. Cancer Inst., NIH, Bethesda, 1976-78; resident in gen. surgery The Fifth Harvard Surg. Svc., Boston, 1978; resident and chief resident, instr. in urology Mass. Gen. Hosp., Harvard Med. Sch., Boston, 1979-82; pvt. practice urology The Vickers Urologic Inst., Augusta, Maine, 1982-83, Susquehanna Urologic Assocs. Ltd., Williamsport, Pa., 1993—; staff urologist The Williamsport Hosp., 1983—, Divine Providence Hosp., 1983—, Muncy Valley Hosp., 1983—. Contbr. articles to profl. jours. Lt. comdr. USPHS, 1976-78. Fellowship NSF, Princeton U., 1969, Am. Cancer Soc., Mass. Gen. Hosp., 1980. Fellow ACS; mem. Am. Urol. Assn. (mid atlantic sect.), Am. Assn. of Clin. Urologists, Pa. Med. Soc., Lycoming County Med. Assn., Pa. Urologic Assn., Mensa, Sigma Xi. Home: 1242 Deerfield Dr Williamsport PA 17701 Office: Urologic Assocs Ltd Ste 206 1705 Warren Ave Williamsport PA 17701

LIPSON, STEVEN MARK, cliniical virologist, educator; b. Bklyn., May 25, 1945; s. Jonas and Ana (Soltz) L.; m. Heleen P. Bleiweiss, Apr. 21, 1971; children: Tracy J., Jennifer B. BS in Biology, Long Island U., 1967; MS in Microbiology, Marine Sci., C.W. Post Coll., 1972; PhD in Cell Biology, Microbiology, N.Y.U., 1981. Radioactive materials cert., N.Y. State Dept. Health. Rsch. assoc. immunology lab. Dept. Neoplastic Diseases Mt. Sinai Sch. Medicine, N.Y.C., 1980-84; chief virology lab., assoc. dir. divsn. microbiology Nassau County Med. Ctr. Dept. of Pathology, East Meadow, N.Y., 1984-90; dir. virology lab., asst. prof. microbiology in medicine North Shore U. Hosp. N.Y.U. Sch. of Medicine, Manhasset, N.Y., 1990—; acting dir. Flow Cytometry/Cellular Immunology Lab. North Shore U. Hosp. N.Y.U. Sch. of Medicine, Manhasset, 1995—; cons. Enzo Biochem, N.Y.C., Becton, Dickenson and Co., Research Triangle Park, N.C., Roche Diagnostic Systems, Nutley, N.J., BioMerieux Vitek, Inc., Rockland, Mass; mem. profl. adv. panel Med. Lab. Advisor, 1994—, adjunct edtl. bd. Clin. Reviews in Microbiology, 1995, Manual of Clin. Microbiology, 1995. Author: Clinical Microbiology Procedures Manual (Virology), 1993; contbr. articles to 42 profl. peer reviewed publs.; presenter over 60 abstracts at sci. meetings. Vol. lectr. Kiwanis Club, Long Island, 1985-90; vol. N.Y. Hall of Sci., Queens, 1996. Mem. Am. Soc. for Microbiology (N.Y. City Br.), Nat. Soc. for Microbiology, Long Island Infectious Dis. Soc. Office: North Shore U Hosp NYU Sch Medicine Labs Dept 300 Community Dr Manhasset NY 11030

LIPSTEIN, STEVEN H., medical administrator; b. Wilmington, Del., Mar. 15, 1956; s. Leonard and Nannette (Allen) L.; m. Susan Ullman, Sept. 15, 1984; children: Greg, Ross, Kate. BA, Emory U., 1978; MHA, Duke U., 1980. Spl. asst. to pres. John Hopkins, Balt.; asst. program dir. Commonwealth Fund Task Force, Balt., 1983-87; dir. program devel. and mktg. John Hopkins Hosp. Health Sys., Balt., 1984-88; dir. clin. ops., med. John Hopkins Hosp. Sch. of Medicine, Balt., 1988-89; mgmt. cons. John Hopkins Hosp. Med. Svc. Corp., Balt., 1992-93; program dir. John Hopkins Hosp. Adminstrv. Fellowship, Balt., 1989-93; exec. dir. John Hopkins Hosp. Outpatient Ctr., Balt., 1989-93; v.p. ambulatory care programs and svc. John Hopkins Hosp., Balt., 1992-93, v.p. adminstrn., 1993-94; exec. v.p. U. Chgo. Hosps., 1994—; bd. dirs. Johns Hopkins Med. Svcs. Corp., Balt., 1993-94. Co-author: Decnetralized Management in Teaching Hospitals, 1984. Referendum com. mem. Dist. 181 Schs., Hinsdale, Ill., 1995. Office: U Chicago Hosps 5841 S Maryland Chicago IL 60637

LIPTON, LESTER, ophthalmologist, entrepreneur; b. N.Y.C., Mar. 14, 1936; s. George and Rita (Steinbaum) L.; m. Harriet Arfa, June 25, 1960; children: Sherri, Brandi, Shawn. BA, NYU, 1959; MD, Chgo. Med. Sch, 1964. Rsch. fellow Chgo. Med. Sch., 1959-60; intern Brookdale Hosp. Ctr., Bklyn., 1964-65; resident Harlem Eye and Ear Hosp., N.Y.C., 1965-68; assoc. attending Polyclinic French hosps., N.Y.C., 1968-75; asst. attending physician, ophthalmologist, surg. instr. St. Clare's Hosp., N.Y.C., 1975—; attending ophthalmologist Cabrini Med. Ctr., N.Y.C., 1982—, St. Vincent's Hosp., N.Y.C., 1995—; founder Lipton Eye Clinic, N.Y.C., 1981—; v.p. Van Arfa Realty, N.Y.C., 1984-88; pres. H&L Realty, Suffern, N.Y., 1981—; mem. bd. dirs. Salisbury (Conn.) Pub. Health Nursing Assn. Mem. U.S. Congl. Adv. Bd.; mem. bd. deacons Congregationalist Ch. With AUS, 1956-58. Named Internat. Amigo, OAS; recipient Presdl. Citation for outstanding community svc., 1991. Mem. N.Y. Med. Soc., Am. Assn. Individual Investors, Bronx High Sch. Sci. Alumni Assn., Sharon Country Club, United Shareholders Assn., Internat. Platform Assn., Wider Quaker Fellowship, Vanderbilt U. Cabinet Club. Republican. Home: Interlaken Estates Lakeville CT 06039 also: 1199 Park Ave New York NY 10128-1711 Office: Lipton Eye Clinic 51 E 90th St New York NY 10128-1205

LIPTZIN, BENJAMIN, psychiatrist; b. N.Y.C., Sept. 17, 1945; s. David Murray and Mollie (Brody) L.; m. Sharon Leslie Rothstein, June 10, 1968; children: Shoshanna, Daniel, Deborah. BA, Yale U., 1966; MD, U. Rochester, N.Y., 1971. Diplomate Am. Bd. Psychiatry and Neurology. Resident in psychiatry U. Va. Hosp., Charlottesville, 1971-74; med. officer NIMH, Rockville, Md., 1974-78; dir. geriatric psychiatry McLean Hosp., Belmont, Mass., 1978-89, asst. gen. dir., 1989-90; chief dept. psychiatry Baystate Med. Ctr., Springfield, Mass., 1990—; prof., dep. chmn. dept. psychiatry Tufts U. Sch. Medicine, 1990—. Contbr. articles to profl. jours. With USPHS, 1972-78. Recipient Acad. award NIMH, 1983. Fellow Am. Psychiat. Assn. (trustee-at-large 1992-95), Gerontol. Soc. Am.; mem. AMA, Am. Coll. Psychiatrists. Democrat. Jewish. Office: Baystate Med Ctr Dept Psychiatry 140 High St Springfield MA 01199-1000

LIQUORI, JOSEPH JOHN, social worker; b. N.Y.C., Aug. 6, 1939; s. John and Pompeia (Dimino) L.; m. Margaret Mohl, Aug. 22, 1964; children: Patrice, Denise, Jason. BA, St. John's U., 1961; MSW, Fordham U., 1965. Cert. social worker, N.Y.; bd. cert. diplomate social work. Psychotherapist Catholic Charities, N.Y.C., 1962-73, Ind. Cons. Ctr., N.Y.C., 1972-85; clin. dir. Pelham Bay Counsellling Ctr., N.Y.C., 1984—; sr. med. social worker Albert Einstein Hosp., N.Y.C., 1987—; cons. in field. Chairperson patient and community svc. com. Nat. Kidney Found., exec. com., trustee. Home: 1937 Hobart Ave Bronx NY 10461-4015

LISAK, ROBERT PHILIP, physician, researcher, educator; b. Bklyn., Mar. 17, 1941; s. Irving Arthur and Sylvia Lillian (Kadish) L.; m. Deena Freda Penchansky, Aug. 2, 1964; children: Ilene Ann, Michael Loren. BA, NYU, 1961; MD, Columbia U., 1965; MA (hon.), U. Pa., 1976. Diplomate Am. Bd. Neurology. Intern in medicine Montefiore Hosp. and Med. Ctr., Bronx, 1965-66; rsch. assoc. NIMH, Bethesda, Md., 1966-68; resident in medicine Bronx Mcpl. Med. Ctr., 1968-69; resident in neurology Hosp. of the U. of Pa., Phila., 1969-72; with Sch. of Medicine U. Pa., Phila., 1972-87, prof. neurology Sch. of Medicine, 1980-87, vice chmn. dept. neurology Sch. of Medicine, 1985-87; prof., chmn. dept. neurology Sch. of Medicine Wayne State U., Detroit, 1987—; mem. adv. bd. Guillain-Barre Syndrome Internat., Wynnewood, Pa., 1985—; mem. med. adv. bd. Myasthenia Gravis Found., Chgo., 1988—, Nat. Multiple Sclerosis Soc., N.Y.C., 1988—. Co-author: Myasthenia Gravis, 1982; editl. bd. Jour. Neuroimmunology, 1984—, Muscle and Nerve Jour., 1981-86, 92-95, Neurology, 1981-86, Annals of Neurology, 1990-95; contbr. articles to profl. jours. With USPHS, 1966-68. Fulbright rsch. scholar, London, 1978-79; recipient Disting. Teaching award U. Pa., 1985, Drs. award Myasthenia Gravis Found., 1991. Fellow Am. Acad. Neurology (sci. issues com. 1987-93); mem. Am. Neurol. Assn. (membership com. 1989-91, chmn. 1990-91, sci. program com. 1994—), Internat. Soc. Neuroimmunology (exec. com. 1987-91, sec.-treas. 1991-95), Am. Assn. Immunologists, Soc. for Neurosci., Norwegian Neurol. Assn., Royal Soc. Medicine. Office: Wayne State U Sch Medicine 6E-UHC 4201 St Antoine Detroit MI 48201

LISBON HEYLIGER, GENEVA, psychiatric nurse; b. Charleston, S.C., Nov. 9, 1938; d. Cullem and Dora (Moore) Lisbon; m. Lambert Heyliger, Aug. 23, 1980; children: Glenn, Alston, Erma. Cert., Helene Fuld Sch. Practical Nursing, 1959; AS, Hostas Community Coll., 1975. Charge and med. nurse Hosp. for Joint Disease, N.Y.C., 1959-62; relief nurse obstets. unit Med. U. of S.C., 1962-63, staff nurse, 1963-68, asst. charge nurse med./surg. unit, relief nurse ICU and Drug and Alcohol Unit, 1968-75; relief nurse psychiat., charge nurse med./surg. unit County Hosp., Charleston, 1976-77; oncology charge nurse med./surg. unit Roper Hosp., Charleston, 1977-80; staff nurse III Dept. Health div. Mental Health, Alcohol and Drug Dependency, 1981—. Mem. VINA (bd. dirs.), Health Ctr.

LISKOW, BARRY IRWIN, psychiatrist, educator; b. Cin., Jan. 6, 1943; s. Sidney Bernard and Rose (Ganson) L.; m. Linda Jane Blackwell, June 24, 1972; children: Samantha, Michael. BA, Columbia Coll., 1964, MD, 1968. Diplomate Am. Bd. Psychiatry and Neurology. Intern U. N.Mex., Albuquerque, 1968-69; resident dept. psychiatry Washington U., St. Louis, 1969-72; chief psychiatry VA, Iowa City, 1974-79; assoc. prof. psychiatry U. Kans., Kansas City, 1979-86; chief alcohol treatment unit VA, Kansas City, 1979-86, chief psychiatry, 1989—; chief of staff VA, Columbus, 1986-89; asst. prof. psychiatry U. Iowa, Iowa City, 1974-79; prof. clin. psychiatry Ohio State U., columbus, 1986-89; prof. psychiatry U. Kans., 1989—. Co-author: Psychotropic Drug Handbook, 1976, 7th edit. 1996; contbr. over 50 articles to profl. jours. Lt. comdr. USPHS, 1972-74. Mem. APA, Rsch. Soc. Alcoholism. Office: Kansas City VA Med Ctr 4801 Linwood Blvd Kansas City MO 64128

LISOWITZ, GERALD MYRON, neuropsychiatrist; b. Johnstown, Pa., May 28, 1930; s. Charles Gerson and Tillie (Cohen) L.; m. Amelia Josephine Rozzando, Mar. 1, 1976 (div. June 1967); children: Mara, Scott, Laurie, Carlyn, Linda. BS magna cum laude, U. Pitts., 1953, MD, 1955. Diplomate Am. Bd. Neurology in Psychiatry. Intern Montefiore Hosp., Pitts., 1955-56; psychiat. resident, teaching fellow Western Psychiatric Inst. & Clinic, 1956-59; psychiatric trainee Phila. Psychoanalytic Inst., 1958, Pitts. Psychoanalytic Inst., 1962-72; clin. instr. dept. psychiatry Sch. Medicine U. Pitts., 1961-80; pvt. practice gen. psychiatry, 1969—; ptnr. Psychiat. Assocs., Pitts., 1969-83; cons. in field. Contbr. articles to profl. jours. Bd. dirs., advisor Westmoreland County Mental Health Dept., Greensburg, 1970-85. Capt. U.S. Army, 1959-61. Mem. AMA, Am. Psychiat. Assn., Am. Assn. Clin. Psychiatrists, Pa. Med. Soc., Pa. Psychiat. Assn., Westmoreland County Med. Soc., Western Pa. Psychiat. Soc., Phila. Psychiat. Assn., Pitts. Psychiat. Soc., Pitts. Med. Forum, Phi Delta Epsilon. Home: 3 Foxwood Ln Greensburg PA 15601 Office: 419 W Pittsburgh St Greensburg PA 15601

LIST, ALAN, medical educator; b. York, Pa., Oct. 13, 1954; s. Francis and Ruth L.; m. Kimberly Nodorp, Sept. 9, 1995. BS, MS, Bucknell U., Lewisburg, Pa., 1976; MD, Coll. Medicine, Lewisburg, Pa., 1980; attended, Good Samaritan Med. Ctr., Phoenix, 1980-83. Diplomate Nat. Bd. Med. Examiners, Am. Bd. Internat Medicine. Oncology fellow Vanderbilt U. Med., Nashville, 1983-85, hematology fellow, 1985-86; clin. rsch. assoc. Dept. Med. Ethics, Nashville, 1985-86; chief sect. of oncology/hematology VA Med. Ctr., Phoenix, 1986-88; staff physician oncology/hematology VA Med. Ctr., Tucson, 1988-91; acting dir. clin. hematology Ariz. Cancer Ctr., Tucson, 1989-91; asst. prof. sect. hematology/oncology Dept. Medicine, Coll. Medicine U. Ariz., Tucson, 1988—; asst. rsch. scientist cancer biology program Ariz. Cancer Ctr., Tucson, 1992—; clin. dir. BMT program U. Ariz. Cancer Ctr., Tucson, 1992—; assoc. prof. medicine sect. hematology/oncology, Dept. Medicine, Coll. Medicine U. Ariz., Tucson, 1994—. Patentee in field. Recipient award for meritorious rsch. in biological scis. Phi Sigma, 1976, Nat. Rsch. Svc. award NIH, 1985-86, Clin. Fellowship award Am. Cancer Soc., 1983-84, Merit award Gen. Motors Cancer Rsch. Found., 1991; named Tchr. of the Yr. Good Samaritan Med. Ctr. VAMC, 1986-87. Home: 4725 N Camino Escuela Tucson AZ 85718

LIST, NOEL DAVID, medical educator; b. Apr. 25, 1940; m. Lesley Ellen List; children: David, Jessica, Nancy, Melanie. BS, NYU, 1960; MD, SUNY, N.Y.C., 1965; MPH, Harvard U., 1967. Asst. prof. medicine and preventive medicine U. Md. Sch. Medicine, Balt., 1972-84; assoc. prof. medicine Duke U. Med. Sch., Durham, N.C., 1984-89; assoc. prof. medicine, chief geriatric medicine Chgo. Med. Sch., 1989-94, head geriatric ctr., 1989-94; prof. medicine, prof. family and preventive medicine U. S.C. Sch. Medicine, Columbia, 1994—; chair ethics and guardmanship consul State of Md., Balt., 1980-83. Fellow Am. Geriatric Soc.; mem. AMA, ATPM, Am. Gerontol. Soc., Gerontol. Soc. S.C., Columbia Med. Soc. Home: 3740 North Shore Rd Columbia SC 21206 Office: JF Byrnes Ctr Geri Med Ed Box 119 2100 Bull St Columbia SC 29202

LISTER, JOHN W., physician; b. Germany, Jan. 10, 1932; came to U.S., 1936.; s. Jacob and Elli A. (Modlinger) L.; m. Caroline Cooper, Dec. 24, 1960; children: Jacqueline, Michelle. BA, NYU, 1954; MD, U. of Basel (Switzerland), 1959. Dir EKG sta. Mt. Sinai Hosp., Miami Beach, Fla., 1967-68; dir. electrophys. lab. Miami Heart Inst., Miami Beach, 1969-88; chmn. of cardiology Cleveland Clinic, Ft. Lauderdale, Fla., 1988-91; dir. electrophys. lab. Broward County Med. Ctr., Ft. Lauderdale, 1991—. Fellow ACP, Am. Coll. Cardiology, Clin. Coun. Am. Heart Assn. (pres. Miami chpt. 1979). Office: The Greater Ft. Lauderdale Heart Group 3536 N Federal Hwy Fort Lauderdale FL 33308

LISTERUD, MARK BOYD, retired surgeon; b. Wolf Point, Mont., Nov. 19, 1924; s. Morris B. and Grace (Montgomery) L.; m. Sarah C. Mooney, May 26, 1954; children: John, Mathew, Ann, Mark, Sarah, Richard. BA magna cum laude, U. Minn., 1949, BS, 1950, MB, 1952, MD, 1953. Diplomate Am. Bd. Surgery. Intern King County Hosp., Seattle, 1952-53; resident in surgery U. Wash., Seattle, 1953-57; practice medicine specializing in surgery Wolf Point, 1958-93; mem. admission com. U. Wash. Med. Sch., Seattle, 1983-88; instr. Dept. Rural and Community Health, U. N.D. Med. Sch., 1991. Contbr. articles to med. jours. Mem. Mont. State Health Coordinating Council, 1983, chmn. 1986—; bd. dirs. Blue Shield, Mont., 1985-87. Served with USN, 1943-46. Fellow Am. Coll. Surgeons, Royal Soc. Medicine; mem. N.E. Mont. Med. Soc. (pres.), Mont. Med. Assn. (pres. 1968-69), AMA (alt. del., del. 1970-84). Clubs: Montana, Elks. Home: Rodeo Rd Wolf Point MT 59201 Office: 100 Main St Wolf Point MT 59201-1530

LISTGARTEN, MAX ALBERT, periodontics educator; b. Paris, May 14, 1935; came to U.S., 1968; s. Samuel and Etla (Weber) L.; m. Eileen Anne Gregory, July 3, 1963; children: Karen, Sheralyn, Michael. DDS, U. Toronto, 1959; cert. in periodontics, Harvard U., 1963; MA (hon.), U. Pa., 1971; PhD (hon.), U. Athens, 1993. Research assoc. Harvard U., Boston, 1963-64; asst. prof. periodontics U. Toronto, Can., 1964-67, assoc. prof., 1967-68; assoc. prof. U. Pa., Phila., 1968-71, prof., 1971—; vis. prof. U. Gothenburg, Sweden, 1976-77, U. Berne, 1988-89; cons. Nat. Inst. Dental Research, Bethesda, Md., 1979-88, FDA, Rockville, Md., 1992—; cons. in field. Author textbooks and numerous articles on various aspects of periodontal anatomy, microbiology, histopathology, and diagnosis. Recipient Periodontology award William J. Gies Found., 1981; named Disting. Alumnus, Harvard U., 1986, U. Pa., 1994. Fellow AAAS, Am. Acad. Periodontology (Clin. Rsch. award 1987); mem. ADA, Am Assn. for Dental Rsch. (pres. 1991-92), Internat. Assn. Dental Rsch. (award for basic rsch. in periodontology 1973). Jewish. Office: U Penn-School of Dental Medicine Dept of Periodontics 4001 Spruce St Philadelphia PA 19104-4118

LISTINSKY, JAY JOHN, radiologist, researcher; b. Milw., Nov. 9, 1951; s. August John and LaVerne Ruth (Schooley) L.; m. Catherine Morstatter, June 18, 1977. BS, U. Wis., 1974; PhD, U. Chgo., 1979, MD, 1982. Diplomate Am. Bd. Radiology. Resident in radiology U. Louisville Hosps., 1982-83; resident in radiology Strong Meml. Hosp., Rochester, 1983-86, fellow in nuclear magnetic resonance rsch., 1986-87; asst. prof. radiology U. Rochester, N.Y., 1987-88, U. Ala., Birmingham, 1988—. Contbr. articles and book revs. to med. jours. Recipient nat. rsch. svc. award NIH, 1976-78. Mem. AMA, Radiol. Soc. N.Am., Am. Inst. Ultrasound in Medicine, Internat. Soc. Magnetic Resonance in Medicine. Office: U Ala Hosp Dept Radiology 619 S 19th St Birmingham AL 35233

LISTON, MARY FRANCES, retired nursing educator; b. N.Y.C., Dec. 17, 1920; d. Michael Joseph and Ellen Theresa (Shaughnessy) L. BS, Coll. Mt. St. Vincent, 1944; MS, Catholic U. Am., 1945; EdD, Columbia, 1962; HHD (hon.), Allentown Coll., 1987. Dir. psychiat. nursing and edn. Nat. League for Nursing, N.Y.C., 1958-66; prof. Sch. Nursing, Cath. U. Am., Washington, 1966-78; dean Sch. Nursing, Cath. U. Am., 1966-73; prof. Marywood Coll., 1984-87; spl. assignment Imperial Med. Center, Tehran, Iran, 1975-78; dep. dir. for program affairs Nat. League for Nursing, N.Y.C., 1978-84. Mem. Sigma Theta Tau. Home: 182 Garth Rd Scarsdale NY 10583-3863

LIT, ALFRED, experimental psychologist, vision science educator, engineering psychology consultant; b. N.Y.C., Nov. 24, 1914; s. Oscar Zachery and Elsie (Jaro) L.; m. Imogene Speegle, Jan. 27, 1947. B.S., Columbia U., 1938, A.M., 1943, Ph.D., 1948. Lic. psychologist, N.Y., optometrist, N.Y. Prof. optometry Columbia U., N.Y.C., 1946-56; rsch. psychologist U. Mich., Ann Arbor, 1956-59; head human factors Bendix Systems Div., Ann Arbor, 1959-61; prof. psychology Southern Ill. U., Carbondale, 1961-83; prof. emeritus, 1983—; research prof. optometry Schnurmacher Inst. for Vision Research, State Coll. Optometry, SUNY, 1984-86; mem. adv. bd. Emeritus Coll., So. Ill. U., Carbondale, 1986—. Contbr. chpts in books and articles on vision sci. and psychology to sci. jours. Adv. NRC Com. on vision Nat. Acad. Scis., Washington, 1960—. Served to 1st lt. U.S. Army, 1943-46, PTO. Recipient Research award Sigma Xi, So. Ill. U., 1972; Outstanding Educator of Am. award So. Ill. U., 1975. USPHS, NSF grantee, 1962-85. Fellow Am. Optometric Assn., Am. Psychol. Assn., AAAS, Optical Soc. Am., N.Y. Acad. Scis., N.Y. Acad. Optometry (hon.), Soc. Engring. Psychology. Achievements include developming a portable-computer-operated visual display system useful in the early detection of pathology in the visual centers or pathways. Avocation: music. Home: 451 Lake Dr Murphysboro IL 62966-5956 Office: So Ill Univ Dept Psychology Carbondale IL 62901

LITCHFIELD, JEAN ANNE, nurse; b. Gary, Ind., Oct. 6, 1942; d. Donald Kleine and Helen Louise (Sweet) Eller; m. Norman E. Stone, Dec. 27, 1965 (div. Aug. 1973); children: Diana, David, Julie; m. Frank Litchfield, Jan. 26, 1974. Lic. practical nurse, Ind. U. Vocat. Tech. Coll., 1973; AS in Biology, Richland C.C., 1991; BSN, Millikin U., 1993; MSN, Ind. State U., 1995. RN, Ind., Ill. Nurse asst. St. Anthony Hosp., Terre Haute, Ind., 1960-73, nurse, 1973-74; charge nurse psychiatric ward St. Mary's Hosp., Decatur,

Ill., 1974—; instr. allied nursing and health divsn. Richland C.C., Decatur, 1995—; mem. student welfare com. Millikin U., Decatur, 1991-92. Recipient 1st place art award 1984, 85, 86, 2d place art award 1984, 85, 2d place County Fair, 1985, Gold Poet award World of Poetry, 1989, Silver Poet award, 1990; named Most Caring Nurse St. Mary's Hosp. 1990, Clara Compton scholar, St. Mary's Hosp., 1993, 94, scholar Am. Legion, 1992. Mem. Internat. Platform Assn., Barn Colony Artists (treas. 1986-88), Phi Theta Kappa, Beta Sigma Phi (treas. 1976-78), Alpha Tau Delta (treas. 1991-92, pres. 1992-93), Sigma Theta Tau Internat. Home: 1680 N 30th St Decatur IL 62526-5416

LITLE, PATRICK ALAN, psychologist, educator; b. Pomona, Calif., Nov. 14, 1946; s. Ralph and Doris Elizabeth (Little) L. m. Patricia J. Litle, Oct. 18, 1986; children: Lauren, Philip. MusB, U. Redlands, 1968; MA, Calif. State U., Long Beach, 1982; PhD, U. Del., 1986. Cert. tchr., Va., Calif. Band dir. Chesapeake Public Schs., Va., 1973-75; music therapy intern Lanterman State Hosp., Pomona, Calif., 1977; music therapist Coll. Hosp., Cerritos, Calif., 1977-78; instr. psychology U. Del., 1980—; clin. psychology intern Perry Point VA Med. Center, Md., 1981-82, health scis. specialist, 1984-86; clin. psychology intern Los Angeles VA Outpatient Clinic, 1982-83; psychology technician Coatesville VA Med. Ctr., 1983-84, clin. psychologist, 1986—. Contbr. 20 articles to profl. jours. Served with USN, 1969-72. Mem. Am. Psychol. Assn., Nat. Assn. Music Therapy (registered music therapist), Psychomusicology Soc., Phi Kappa Phi. Home: 4 Forest Creek Dr Hockessin DE 19707-2018 Office: Coatesville VA Med Ctr Psychology Service Coatesville PA 19320

LITMAN, KERRY C., physician; b. L.A., May 5, 1959; s. Marshall Girson and Norma Riva (Rothblatt) L.; m. Edith Tabangcura, July 4, 1982; 1 child, Cody Tabangcura. BS, U. Calif. San Diego, 1981; MD, UCLA, 1985. Resident Santa Monica (Calif.) Hosp., 1985-88; physician Kaiser Colton (Calif.) Clinic, 1988—; physician Kaiser Permanente, Fontant, Calif., 1990—. Office: Kaiser Colton Clinic 789 S Cooley Dr Colton CA 92324

LITMAN, ROBERT BARRY, physician, author, television and radio commentator; b. Phila., Nov. 17, 1947; s. Benjamin Norman and Bette Etta (Saunders) L.; m. Niki Thomas, Apr. 21, 1985; children: Riva Belle, Nadya Beth, Caila Tess, Benjamin David. BS, Yale U., 1967, MD, 1970, MS in Chemistry, 1972, MPhil in Anatomy, 1972, postgrad. (Life Ins. Med. Rsch. Fund fellow) Yale U., Univ. Coll. Hosp., U. London, 1969-70; Am. Cancer Soc. postdoctoral rsch. fellow Yale U., 1970-73. Diplomate Am. Bd. Family Practice. Resident in gen. surgery Bryn Mawr (Pa.) Hosp., 1973-74; USPHS fellow Yale U. Sch. Medicine, 1974-75; pvt. practice medicine and surgery, Ogdensburg, N.Y., 1977-93, San Ramon, Calif., 1993—; mem. med. staff A. Barton Hepburn Hosp., 1977-93, John Muir Med. Ctr., 1993—, San Ramon (Calif.) Regional Med. Ctr., 1993—, also chmn. med. edn.; commentator Family Medicine Stas. WWNY-TV and WTNY-Radio, TCI Cablevision, Contra Costa T.V.; clin. preceptor dept. family medicine State Univ. Health Sci. Ctr., Syracuse, 1978—. Author: Wynnefield and Limer, 1983, The Treblinka Virus, 1991, Allergy Shots, 1993; contbr. articles to numerous sci. publs. Pres. Am. Heart Assn. No. N.Y. chpt., 1980-84. Fellow Am. Coll. Allergy, Asthma, and Immunology, Am. Acad. Family Physicians; mem. AMA (Physicians Recognition award 1970—), Calif. State Med. Assn., Alameda-Contra Costa County Med. Assn., Joint Coun. Allergy and Immunology, Nat. Assn. Physician Broadcasters (charter), Acad. Radio and TV Health Communicators, Book and Snake Soc., Gibbs Soc. of Yale U. (founder), Sigma Xi, Nu Sigma Nu, Alpha Chi Sigma. Home and Office: PO Box 1857 San Ramon CA 94583-6857

LITRENTA, FRANCES MARIE, psychiatrist; b. Balt., June 25, 1928; d. Frank P. and Josephine (DeLuca) L. AB, Coll. Notre Dame Md., 1950; MD, Georgetown U., 1954. Diplomate Am. Bd. Psychiatry and Neurology. Rotating intern St. Agnes Hosp., Balt., 1954-55, asst. resident in psychiatry, 1955-56; fellow in psychiatry Univ. Hosp., Balt., 1956-57; fellow in child psychiatry Georgetown U. Hosp., Washington, 1957-59; clin. instr. psychiatry Med. Ctr. Georgetown U., Washington, 1959-63; clin. asst. prof. Med. Ctr. Georgetown U., 1963-72, clin. assoc. prof. psychiatry Med. Ctr., 1972-87; pvt. practice Balt., 1959—; cons. St. Vincent's Infant Home, Balt., 1965-75; mem. coun. to dean Georgetown U. Sch. Medicine, 1977-93. Fellow Am. Acad. Child and Adolescent Psychiatry, Am. Orthopsychiat. Assn. (life); mem. Am. Psychiat. Assn. (life), Md. Psychiat. Soc. (life), Georgetown Med. Alumni Assn. (nat. comm. chmn. 1987-90, class co-chmn. 1974-87, class comm. chmn. 1987—, bd. dirs. 1989—, gov. 1989-95, senator 1995—, Founder's award 1994). Office: 6110 York Rd Baltimore MD 21212-2697

LITSCHER, GERHARD, biomedical engineer, researcher; b. Graz, Styria, Austria, July 24, 1958; s. Wolfgang and Erika Litscher; m. Ursula Litscher, July 13, 1985; 1 child, Daniela. PhD, U. Tech., Graz, Austria, 1987. Rsch. asst. dept. med. informatics Inst. Biomed. Engring., Graz, 1984-90; biomed. engr. dept. anesthesiology U. Graz, 1990—. Author: Multivariable Non-Invasive Intensive Care Monitoring, 1994 (Hoechst award 1995). Recipient Theodor Körner Sci. prize for brain function monitoring, 1987, award for sci. and rsch. Govt. of Styria, 1991. Office: U Graz Dept Anesthesiology, Auenbruggerplatz 29, A-8036 Graz Austria

LITSKY, BERTHA YANIS, microbiologist, artist; b. Chester, Pa., Jan. 2, 1920; d. Edward Bernard and Hattie (Howell) Meade; m. Martin Yanis, June 27, 1942 (dec.); children: Libby Nesvold, Rosalind Yanishevsky; m. Warren Litsky, July 27, 1965 (dec. July 1994). BSc, Phila. Coll. Pharmacy, 1942; MPA, NYU, 1964; PhD, Walden U., 1974. Lic. med. technologist. Head dept. bacteriology Assoc. Labs., Phila., 1942-44; asst. supr. prodn. Nat. Drug Co., Swiftwater, Pa., 1944-45; rsch. bacteriologist U. Pa., Phila., 1945-50; cons. microbiologist Phila., 1950-56; head dept. bacteriology S.I. Hosp., N.Y.C., 1956-65; rsch. assoc. U. Mass., Amherst, 1965—; nurse cons. Bingham Assocs. Fund New Eng. Med. Ctr. Hosp., Boston, 1965-85. Author: An Administrative Program for Hospital Sanitation, 1966, Food Service Sanitation, 1973; contbr. chpts. to books; contbr. more than 115 articles to profl. jours. Troop mother Girl Scouts USA, S.I., 1953-60; judge Acad. Sci., N.Y.C., 1953-60; aided students in project for Sci. Fair, N.Y.c., 1953-62; mem. animal control com. Town of Amherst, 1978-80; sanitation cons. Town Hall, Amherst, 1994—; v.p. Friends of Amherst Stray Animals, 1980—; mem. fundraising com. MSPCA, Boston, 1995. Recipient scholarship NYU, 1964, Editl. award, Hosp. Mgmt., 1964, 65, 68, Annual Alumni award Phila. Coll. Pharmacy and Sci., 1979, Leonard A. Leipus award Am. Soc. for Hosp. Ctrl. Svc. Pers., 1982, 9th Annual Dr. John J. Perkins Meml. award Surgicot, Inc., 1983, Pub. Svc. award Assn. Surg. Technologists, 1983, 85, Appreciation award N.C. Assn. for Hosp. Ctrl. Svc. Pers., 1987, Pioneer in Infection Control award Smith Bros. Whitehaven, Ltd., 1992, among others. Mem. APHA, Am. Hosp. Assn., Am. Soc. Microbiology, Internat. Assn. for Hosp. Ctrl. Svc. Material Mgmt. (Pres.'s award 1992), Amherst Club. Home: 9 Kettle Pond Rd Amherst MA 01003 Office: U Mass Amherst MA 01003

LITT, IRIS FIGARSKY, pediatrics educator; b. N.Y.C., Dec. 25, 1940; d. Jacob and Bertha (Berson) Figarsky; m. Victor C. Vaughan, June 14, 1987; children from previous marriage: William M., Robert B. AB, Cornell U., 1961; MD, SUNY, Bklyn., 1965. Diplomate Am. Bd. Pediatrics (bd. dirs. 1989-94), sub-specialty bd. cert. in adolescent medicine. Intern, then resident in pediat. N.Y. Hosp., N.Y.C., 1965-68; assoc. prof. pediat. Stanford U. Sch. Medicine, Palo Alto, Calif., 1982-87, prof., 1987—, dir. divsn. adolescent medicine, 1976—, dir. Inst. for Rsch. on Women and Gender, 1990—; bd. dirs. Youth Law Ctr., San Francisco. Editor Jour. Adolescent Health. Mem. Soc. for Adolescent Medicine (charter), Am. Acad. Pediatrics (award sect. on adolescent health), Western Soc. Pediatric Rsch., Soc. Pediatric Rsch., Am. Pediatric Soc., Inst. of Medicine/NAS. Office: 750 Welch Rd Ste 325 Palo Alto CA 94304

LITTLE, ANGELA CAPOBIANCO, nutritional science educator; b. San Francisco, Jan. 12, 1920; d. Alfredo Agosto and Elizabeth (Kruse) Capobianco; m. George Gordon Little, Nov. 8, 1947; 1 child, Judith Kristine. BA, U. Calif., Berkeley, 1940, MS, 1954, PhD, 1969. Specialist jr. to asst. to assoc. U. Calif., Berkeley, 1958-69, food scientist, 1969-85, assoc. prof. to prof, 1977-85, prof. emeritus, 1985—, acad. ombudsman, 1985-87, 89-91; cons. in field; v.p., bd. dirs. Math/Sci. Network, Berkeley; vis. scholar U. Wash., Seattle, 1976-77, Kans. State U., Manhattan, 1972; mem. faculty Fromm Inst., U. San Francisco, 1992—. Author: Color of Foods, 1962. Nutritional adv. bd. Project Open Hand, San Francisco, 1989-91, vol., 1988-91, UNICEF, San Francisco, 1986-89, St. Francis Hosp., 1992—. Rsch. grantee Robert Woods Johnson Found., 1989-90, others 1960-85. Mem. Am. Soc. Wine and Food (bd. editors), N.Y. Acad. Scis., Am. Women in Sci., San Francisco Acad. Sci., San Francisco Mus. Soc., U. Calif. Berkeley Emeritii Assn. (pres. 1991-93), Women are Good News (co-founder, co-chair 1991—), Am. Assn. for History of Medicine, Bay Area History of Medicine Club (pres.-elect 1995—), Sigma Xi. Home: 85 Cleary Ct Apt 3 San Francisco CA 94109-6518 Office: U Calif Dept Nutritional Scis Berkeley CA 94720

LITTLE, BRIAN W., pathology educator, administrator; b. Boston, Dec. 15, 1945; m. Pamela Little; children: Kristin B., Eric W. BA in Physics, Cornell U., 1967; MD, U. Vt., 1973, PhD in Biochemistry, 1977. Diplomate in neuropathology and anatomic and clin. pathology Am. Bd. Pathology; lic., Pa. Attending pathologist neuropathology SUNY, Stony Brook, 1984-87, Lehigh Valley Hosp., Allentown, Pa., 1987—; assoc. prof. pathology Hahnemann U. Sch. Medicine, Phila., 1989-94; dir. of edn. Lehigh Valley Hosp., Allentown, 1991-94; assoc. prof. pathology-neuropathology Med. Coll. of Pa./Hahnemann U., Phila., 1994—, assoc. dean for affiliate affairs, 1994-95, sr. assoc. dean for affiliate affairs and grad. med. edn., 1995—. Office: Med Coll Pa/Hahnemann U Broad and Vine Philadelphia PA 19102-1192

LITTLE, DOUGLAS JONATHAN, internist; b. Oak Ridge, Tenn., Apr. 22, 1945; s. James Conrad and Sarah Frances (Burnam) L. BA with honors, U. Tenn., 1967; MD, U. N.C., 1971. Diplomate Am. Bd. Internal Medicine. Internship Emory U. Affiliated Hosps., Atlanta, 1971-72, residency, 1972-74, fellowship in cardiology, 1975-76; pvt. practice internal medicine and cardiology, Sanford, N.C., 1978—; chief staff Ctrl. Carolina Hosp., Sanford, 1985, chmn. ICU com., 1980=93. Mem. ACP, N.C. Med. Soc., Lee County Med. Soc. Office: 136 Carbonton Rd Sanford NC 27330-4000

LITTLE, JOHN BERTRAM, physician, radiobiology educator, researcher; b. Boston, Oct. 5, 1929; s. Bertram Kimball and Nina (Fletcher) L.; m. Francoise Cottereau, Aug. 4, 1960; children—John Bertram, Frederic Fletcher. A.B. in Physics, Harvard U., 1951; M.D., Boston U., 1955. Diplomate Am. Bd. Radiology. Intern in medicine Johns Hopkins Hosp., Balt., 1955-56; resident in radiology Mass. Gen. Hosp., Boston, 1958-61; fellow Harvard U., Cambridge, Mass., 1961-63; from instr. to assoc. prof. radiobiology Harvard Sch. Pub. Health, Boston, 1963-75; prof. Harvard Sch. Pub. Health, 1975—, chmn. dept. physiology, 1980-83, James Stevens Simmons prof. radiobiology, 1987—; dir. Kresge Ctr. Environ. Health, Boston, 1982—; cons. radiology Mass. Gen. Hosp., Boston, 1965—, Brigham and Women's Hosp., Boston, 1968—; chmn. bd. sci. counsellors Nat. Inst. Environ. Health Sci., 1982-84; bd. sci. counsellors Nat. Toxicology Program, 1988-92; mem. sci. coun. Radiation Effects Rsch. Found., Hiroshima, Japan, 1993—; bd. dirs. on radiation effects rsch. Nat. Acad. of Scis. Mem. editorial bd. numerous nat. and internat. jours.; contbr. chpts. to books and articles to profl. jours. Mem. coun. Nat. Coun. on Radiation Protection and Measurements, 1993—; trustee various hist. and cultural orgns. Capt. U.S. Army, 1956-58. Am. Cancer Soc. grantee, 1965-68; recipient numerous rsch. and grants NIH, 1968—; named one of Outstanding Investigator grantee Nat. Cancer Inst., 1988—. Mem. AAAS (coun. in med. scis. 1988-91), Radiation Rsch. Soc. N.Am. (pres.-elect 1985, pres. 1986-87), Am. Assn. Cancer Rsch., Am. Physiol. Soc., Health Physics Soc., Am. Soc. Photobiology. Office: Harvard U Dept Radiobiology 665 Huntington Ave Boston MA 02115-6021

LITTLE, JOHN REVELEY, neurosurgeon; b. Regina, Sask., Can., Apr. 9, 1946; came to U.S., 1971; s. George Albert Little and Sylvia Irene (Reveley) Richter; m. Barbara JoAnne Cory, Mar. 21, 1976 (div. Oct. 1982); children: Jennifer, Collin, Amanda; m. Veora Marie Davis, July 20, 1984; 1 child, Katherine. MD, U. Sask., 1970; MS, U. Minn., 1974. Diplomate Am. Bd. Neurol. Surgery. Resident in neurosurgery Mayo Clinic, Rochester, Minn., 1971-75; lectr. McGill U., Montreal, Que., Can., 1975-77, asst. prof., 1977-79; staff neurosurgeon Cleve. Clinic, 1979-90, chmn. dept. neurosurgery, 1987-90, program dir. neurosurgery residency tng. program, 1985-90; med. dir. Internat. SPine Inst., Naples, Fla., 1994—. Editor: Clinical Neurosurgery, 1984-87; co-editor: Stroke and the Extracranial Vessels, 1984; mem. editorial bd. Stroke, 1981-86, Neurosurgery, 1984-89; contbr. numerous articles to profl. jours. Recipient Gov. Gen.'s medal, Gov. Gen. of Can., 1964; rsch. grantee Med. Rsch. Coun. Can., 1978, Nat. Inst. Neurol. and Communicative Disorders and Stroke, Washington, 1986, 87. Fellow Royal Coll. Surgery of Can. (medal 1979), Am. Coll. Surgeons; mem. Am Heart Assn. (stroke coun., exec. com. 1987-90), Congress Neurol. Surgeons (exec. com. 1987-91, v.p. 1990-91), Ohio State Neurosurg. Soc. (sec. 1986-88, v.p. 1988-89, sec.-treas. joint sect. on cerebrovascular surgery 1987-89m chmn. 1989-90). Office: 680 Goodlette Rd N Naples FL 33924

LITTLE, JULIA ELIZABETH, surgeon; b. Holly Hill, Fla., June 7, 1961; d. Richard Pangborn and Martha Lee (Pierson) L.; m. William Francis Vorder Bruegge, June 22, 1991; children: Martha Anne, Ruth Helen. B-SChemE, Va. Tech., 1983; MD, Harvard U., 1987. Diplomate Am. Bd. Surgery. Commd. officer U.S. Army, 1983, advanced through grades to maj.; intern, resident Walter Reed AMC, Washington, 1987-92; staff gen. surgeon Womack AMC, Ft. Bragg, N.C., 1992-96; discharged U.S. Army, 1996; pvt. practice gen. surgery Clinton, N.C., 1996—. Nursery dir. 1st Presbyn. Ch., Fayetteville, N.C., 1996—. Fellow ACS. Presbyterian. Home: 7682 Heriot Dr Fayetteville NC 28311-9408

LITTLE, LAWRENCE ALAN, health facility administrator; b. Downey, Calif., Jan. 23, 1947; s. Eugene R. and Naomia Little. Student, Long Beach City Coll., 1964-66; PharmD, U. Calif., San Francisco, 1970. Registered pharmacist, Calif., Nev. Pharmacist French Hosp., San Francisco, 1970-76, asst. dir. pharmacy, 1976-80, dir. pharmacy, 1980-81; assoc. dir. pharmacy Herrick Hosp., Berkeley, Calif., 1981-82; dir. pharmacy Herrick Hosp., Berkeley, 1982-86; dir. pharmacy Alta Bates Med. Ctr., Berkeley, 1986-96, dir. pharmacy respiratory svcs., 1996—; mem. nat. adv. com. Purchase Connection Pharmacy, L.A., 1980-88; mem. nat. pharmacy coun. Vol. Hosps. Am., Dallas, 1994—; asst. clin. prof. U. Calif. Sch. Pharmacy, San Francisco, 1981—. Pres. bd. dirs. Herrick Credit Union, Berkeley, 1985-87. Mem. Am. Soc. Health Sys. Pharmacists. Office: Alta Bates Med Ctr 2450 Ashby Ave Berkeley CA 94705

LITTLE, ROBERT COLBY, physiologist, educator; b. Norwalk, Ohio, June 2, 1920; s. Edwin Robert and Eleanor Thresher (Colby) L.; m. Claire Campbell Means, Jan. 20, 1945; children—William C., Edwin C. A.B., Denison U., 1942; M.D., Western Res. U., 1944, M.S., 1948. Intern Grace Hosp., Detroit, 1944-45; USPHS postdoctoral research fellow Western Res. U., 1948-49; resident internal medicine Crile VA Hosp., Cleve., 1949-50; asst. prof. physiology, then assoc. prof. physiology and medicine U. Tenn. Sch. Medicine, 1950-54; rsch. participant Oak Ridge Inst. Nuclear Studies, 1952; dir. clin. research Mead Johnson & Co., 1954-57; lectr. medicine U. Louisville, 1955-57; dir. cardio pulmonary labs. Scott and White Clinic, Scott Sherwood and Brindley Found., Temple, Tex., 1957-59; prof. physiology, asst. prof. medicine Seton Hall Coll. Medicine and Dentistry, 1957-64, acting chmn. dept. physiology, 1961-63; prof. physiology, chmn. dept., also asst. prof. medicine Ohio State U. Sch. Medicine, 1964-73; prof. physiology, prof. medicine Med. Coll. Ga. Sch. Medicine, Augusta, 1973-89, chmn. dept. physiology, 1973-86, prof., chmn. emeritus, 1989—; cons. in field. Author: Physiology of the Heart and Circulation, 1977, 2d edit., 1981, 3d edit., 1985, 4th edit., 1989; editor: Physiology of Atrial Pacemakers and Conductive Tissues, 1980; contbr. articles to profl. jours. Served to capt. M.C. AUS, 1945-47. Mem. Am. Physiol. Soc., So. Soc. Clin. Investigation, Am. Heart Assn., Soc. Exptl. Biology and Medicine, Am. Fedn. Clin. Research, Sigma Xi, Sigma Chi, Alpha Kappa Kappa, Alpha Omega Alpha. Home: 523 Brandon Village 4275 Owens Rd Evans GA 30809

LITTLE, WILLIAM CAMPBELL, cardiologist, physiologist; b. Cleve., May 1, 1950; s. Robert Colby and Claire (Means) L.; m. Constance Lydia Loydall, June 9, 1975; children: John Campbell, Elizabeth Loydall. BA in Physics, Oberlin Coll., 1972; MD, Ohio State U., 1975. Diplomate Am. Bd. of Internal Medicine, Am. Bd. Cardiovascular Disease. Intern, then resident in internal medicine U. Va. Hosp., 1975-78; fellow in cardiology Sch. of Medicine U. Ala.; instr. U. Ala. Sch. Medicine, Birmingham, 1980-81; asst. prof. medicine U. Tex. Health Sci. Ctr., San Antonio, 1981-84, assoc. prof. medicine, 1984-86; assoc. prof. medicine Bowman Gray Sch. Medicine, Winston-Salem, N.C., 1986-89, prof. medicine, 1989—, chief cardiology, 1990—; cons. study sect. NIH, Bethesda, Md., 1987—. Co-author: (book) Physiology of the Heart and Circulation, 1989; contbr. over 100 articles on cardiac physiology and clin. cardiology to profl. publs. Recipient Established Investigator award Am. Heart Assn., 1986-91, Young Investigator award So. Sec. Am. Fedn. Clin. Rsch., 1991; grantee NIH, 1985—. Mem. Am. Coll. Cardiology, Am. Physiological Soc. (Lamport award 1987), Am. Soc. Clin. Investigation (Harrison award 1993), Assn. Univ. Cardiologists. Presbyterian. Office: Bowman Gray Sch Medicine Medical Ctr Blvd Winston Salem NC 27157

LITTLEFIELD, JOHN WALLEY, physiology educator, geneticist, cell biologist, pediatrician; b. Providence, Dec. 3, 1925; s. Ivory and Mary Russell (Walley) L.; m. Elizabeth Legge, Nov. 11, 1950; children: Peter P., John W., Elizabeth L. M.D., Harvard U., 1947; MHS, Johns Hopkins U, 1992. Diplomate: Am. Bd. Internal Medicine. Intern Mass. Gen. Hosp., Boston, 1947-48; resident in medicine Mass. Gen. Hosp., 1948-50, staff, 1956-74, chief genetics unit children's service, 1966-73; asso. in medicine Harvard U. Med. Sch., 1956-62, asst. prof. medicine, 1962-66, assoc. prof. pediatrics, 1966-69, prof. pediatrics, 1970-73; prof., chmn. dept. pediatrics Johns Hopkins U. Sch. Medicine, Balt., 1974-85; pediatrician-in-chief Johns Hopkins U. Hosp., 1974-85; prof., chmn. dept. physiology Johns Hopkins U. Sch. Medicine, Balt., 1985-92. Author: Variation, Senescence and Neoplasia in Cultured Somatic Cells, 1976. Served with USNR, 1952-54. Guggenheim fellow, 1965-66; Josiah Macy Jr. Found. fellow Oxford U. Mem. NAS, Am. Acad. Arts and Scis., Am. Soc. Biol. Chemists, Am. Soc. Clin. Investigation, Tissue Culture Assn., Soc. Pediatric Rsch., Am. Soc. Human Genetics, Am. Pediatric Soc., Assn. Am. Physicians, Phi Beta Kappa, Alpha Omega Alpha, Delta Omega. Home: 304 Golf Course Rd Owings Mills MD 21117-4114 Office: Johns Hopkins U Sch Medicine Dept Physiology Baltimore MD 21205

LITTLEFIELD, VIVIAN MOORE, nursing educator, administrator; b. Princeton, Ky., Jan. 24, 1938; children: Darrell, Virginia. B.S. magna cum laude, Tex. Christian U., 1960; M.S., U. Colo., 1964; Ph.D., U. Denver, 1979. Staff nurse USPHS Hosp., Ft. Worth, Tex., 1960-61; instr. nursing Tex. Christian U., Ft. Worth, 1961-62; nursing supr. Colo. Gen. Hosp., Denver, 1964-65, pvt. patient practitioner, 1974-78; asst. prof. nursing U. Colo., Denver, 1965-69, asst. prof., clin. instr., 1971-74, asst. prof., 1974-76, acting asst. dean, assoc. prof. continuing edn., regional perinatal project, 1976-78; assoc. prof., chair dept. women's health care nursing U. Rochester Sch. Nursing, N.Y., 1979-84; clin. chief ob-gyn., nursing U. Rochester Strong Meml. Hosp., N.Y., 1979-84; prof., dean U. Wis. Sch. Nursing, Madison, 1984—; cons. and lectr. in field. Author: Maternity Nursing Today, 1973, 76, Health Education for Women: A guide for Nurses and Other Health Professionals, 1986; mem. editorial bd. Jour. Profl. Nursing; contbr. articles to profl. jours. Bur. Health Professions Fed. trainee, 1963-64; Nat. Sci. Service award, 1976-79. Mem. MAIN, AACN (bd. dirs.), NLN (bd. dirs.), Am. Acad. Nursing, Am. Nurses Assn., Consortium Prime Care Wis. (chair), Health Care for Women Internat., Midwest Nursing Research Soc., Sigma Theta Tau (pres. Beta Eta chpt., co-chair coun nursing practice and edn. 1995). Avocations: golf, biking. Office: U Wis Sch Nursing 600 Highland Ave # H6 150 Madison WI 53792-0001

LITTLEJOHN, MARK HAYS, radiologist, b. Detroit, Apr. 11, 1936; s. Maurice Mark and Elizabeth Dowell (Metcalf) L.; children from previous marriage: M. Hays, Sara J.; m. Karla Ann McGinnis, Apr. 16, 1983; 1 stepchild, Bradford D. Schwartz. BS, Northwestern U., 1958, MD, 1961. Diplomate Am. Bd. Radiology, Am. Bd. Nuclear Medicine. Intern, Luth. Hosp., Ft. Wayne, Ind., 1961-62; resident VA Rsch. Hosp., Chgo., Northwestern U. Med. Sch., Chgo., 1962-65; staff radiologist Ireland Army Hosp., Ft. Knox, Ky., 1965-66, chief radiology, 1966-67; staff radiologist St. Mary Nazareth Hosp., Chgo., 1968-80, chief nuclear medicine, 1975-80; instr. in radiology Northwestern U. Med. Sch., 1968-71; dir. dept. radiology Cannon Meml. Hosp., Banner Elk, N.C., 1980—, chief of staff, 1987-89; cons. 1st U.S. Army, 1966-67. Served to capt. U.S. Army, 1965-67. Mem. AMA (Physician's recognition award 1971, 74, 77, 80, 84, 90, 93, 96), Am. Coll. Radiology, Am. Coll. Nuclear Physicians, (charter), Am. Inst. Ultrasound in Medicine, Radiology, Soc. N.Am., Soc. Nuclear Medicine, Pi Kappa Epsilon. Avocations: sculpture, painting. Home: PO Box 188 Blowing Rock NC 28605-0188 Office: PO Box 1167 Banner Elk NC 28604-1167

LITTLEJOHN, OLIVER MARSILIUS, university administrator; b. Cowpens, S.C., Sept. 29, 1924; s. Thomas C. and Lillie Kate (Coveney) L.; m. Beverly Sue Seastrunk, Dec. 18, 1948; children: Daniel Oliver, Susan Katherine. B.S. in Chemistry, U. S.C., 1948, B.S. in Pharmacy cum laude, 1949; M.S. in Pharmacy, U. Fla., 1951, Ph.D., 1953. Instr. pharmacy U. S.C., 1948-49; pharmacist Smith Drug Store, Spartanburg, S.C., 1949-50; grad. asst. U. Fla., 1952-53; asst. prof. pharmacy, head dept. So. Coll. Pharmacy, 1953-56; prof. pharmacy, head dept. U. Ky., 1956-57; dean, prof. pharmacy So. Sch. Pharmacy, Mercer U., 1957-84, v.p., 1983-88; retired, 1988; Del. U.S. Pharmacopeial Conv., 1960, 70, 75, 80. Contbr. articles to profl. jours. Served with inf. AUS, 1943-46, ETO. Decorated Bronze Star, Purple Heart, Combat Inf. badge. Fellow Am. Found. Pharm. Edn.; mem. Am., Ga. pharm. assns., Am. Assn. Colls. Pharmacy, Sigma Xi, Omicron Delta Kappa, Rho Chi, Gamma Sigma Epsilon, Phi Sigma., Phi Kappa Phi. Baptist (deacon). Home: 6485 Bridgewood Valley Rd NW Atlanta GA 30328-2903

LITTLETON, JESSE TALBOT, III, radiology educator; b. Corning, N.Y., Apr. 27, 1917; s. Jesse Talbot and Bessie (Cook) L.; m. Martha Louise Morrow, Apr. 17, 1943 (dec. 1994); children: Christine, Joanne, James, Robert, Denise; m. Mary Lou Durizch, Mar. 25, 1995. Student, Emory (Va.) and Henry Coll., 1934-35. Johns Hopkins U., 1935-39; MD, Syracuse U., 1939-43. Diplomate Am. Bd. Radiology, Intern Buffalo Gen. Hosp., 1943; resident in medicine, surgery and radiology Robert Packer Hosp., Sayre, Pa., 1946-51, assoc. radiologist, 1951-53, chmn. dept. radiology, 1953-76; prof. radiology U. South Ala., Mobile, 1976-87, prof. emeritus, 1987—; cons. in field. Author textbooks (3); contbr. chpts. to books and 100 articles to profl. jours., sci. exhibits to profl. confs. Served to capt. U.S. Army MC, 1944-46; Pacific. Fellow Am. Coll. Radiology; mem. AMA, Radiol. Soc. N.Am., Am. Roentgen Ray Soc., Ala. Acad. Radiology, Med. Assn. Ala., French Soc. Neuroradiology, Sigma Xi, Alpha Omega Alpha. Republican. Methodist. Club: Country of Mobile (Ala.). Research on conventional tomography, phys. principles, equipment devel. and testing and clin. applications; transp. and radiology of acutely ill and traumatized patient; angiography, devel. first sheet film serialograph; devel. of equipment for sectional radiographic anatomy. Home: 5504 Churchill Downs St Theodore AL 36582-9622 Office: U South Ala Med Ctr 2451 Fillingim St Mobile AL 36617-2238

LITTMAN, EDWARD, physician; b. N.Y.C., Mar. 4, 1935; s. Morris and Gertrude (Goldberg) L.; m. Elaine Becker, Aug. 10, 1961; children: Jay, Karen. BA, Cornell U., 1957; MD, Chgo. Med. Sch., 1961. Intern Michael Reese Hosp., Chgo., 1961-62; resident Jersey City (N.J.) Med. Ctr., 1962-63, Montefiore Hosp., Bronx, 1965-66; fellow in renal disease Mt. Sinai Hosp., N.Y.C., 1963-65; physician Norwalk (Conn.) Med. Group, 1968-86, pvt. practice, Norwalk, 1986—; chief sect. nephrology Norwalk Hosp., 1970—, dir. dialysis unit, 1972—, sr. attending, 1975—; bd. trustees Norwalk Hosp., 1986-91; clin. instr. Yale U., New Haven, Conn., 1976-77, asst. clin. prof., 1977-81, assoc. clin. prof., 1981—; lectr. Chgo. Med. Sch., 1987—. Contbr. articles to profl. jours. Vice chmn. adv. bd. Kidney Found., Conn., 1978-81, chmn. med. adv. bd., 1981-84; chmn. ESRD Network Coord. Coun., Conn., 1979-81. Capt. U.S. Army, 1966-68. Fellow ACP. Office: Norwalk Hosp Maple St Norwalk CT 06856

LITTON, KIMBERLEY ANN, critical care nurse; b. Somerset, Ky., Oct. 5, 1956; d. Charles D. and Ruby J. (West) L. BSN, U. Tex., Galveston, 1981; BA in Biology, Tex. Tech U., 1979; MS in Nursing, U. Nev., Reno, 1988. CCRN, cert. clin. nurse specialist, cert. BCLS-CPR instr., advanced life support certification. Staff nurse post anesthesia recovery U. Tex. Med. Branch, Galveston; staff nurse per diem Sparks (Nev.) Family Hosp.; staff nurse, charge nurse post anesthesia care unit Washoe Med. Ctr., Reno; critical care clin. specialist, critical care educator Osteopathic Med. Ctr. Tex., Ft. Worth; cardiovasc. clin. nurse specialist Hillcrest Bapt. Med. Ctr., Waco, Tex., All Saints Episc. Hosp., Ft. Worth. Mem. cardiovascular nurses edn.

task force Am. Heart Assn. Recipient Clin. Practice award Sigma Theta Tau, 1990. Mem. AACN, Am. Soc. Post Anesthesia Nurses, Alpha Lambda Delta, Sigma Theta Tau. Office: All Saints Episc Ch 1400 8th St Arlington TX 76014

LITTON, STEPHEN FREDERICK, orthodontist; b. Bklyn., Jan. 8, 1943; s. Murray A. and Eda (Schwartz) L.; m. Bonnie Lee Tarnoff, July 4, 1965; children: Jeremy Lawrence, Jonathan Randall. BA, BS with distinction, U. Minn., 1965, DDS, 1967, cert. in orthodontics, 1970; PhD, 1972. Tchg. asst. dept. anatomy, rsch. fellow Sch. Dentistry, U. Minn., Mpls., 1967-72, asst. prof. dept. anatomy, 1972-85; pvt. practice gen. dentistry, Mpls., 1967-70, pvt. practice orthodontics, 1970—; co-dir. orthodontics Children's Hosp., Mpls., 1972-83, mem. active staff, 1972—; orthodontic cons. Pilot City Regional Health Ctr., Mpls., 1972-73, chief dentistry Mt. Sinai Hosp., Mpls., 1979-83; cons. orthodontic treatment panel State of Minn., St. Paul, 1979-84; mem. med. adv. bd. Nat. Sjogren's Syndrome Assn., 1990—, co-chmn., 1994-96, mem. med. adv. bd. Twin City-Minn. chpt., 1988—. Bd. dirs. Herzl Camp, 1982-87. Fellow USPHS, 1967-72. Mem. ADA, Am. Assn. Orthodontists, Minn. Dental Assn., Mpls. Dist. Dental Soc. (del. or alt. del. to Minn. Dental Assn. 1981-83, 85-87, 91, exec. coun. 1984-85, 92-94, sec.-treas. 1996—), Midwestern Soc. Orthodontists (bd. dirs. 1994—, newsletter editor 1996—, alt. del. to Am. Assn. Orthodontists 1996), Minn. Assn. of Orthodontists (exec. bd. 1983—, pres. 1989-90), Northside Dental Study Club (exec. bd. 1986-90, pres. 1988-89), Alpha Omega (pres. 1966-67), Omicron Kappa Upsilon, Sigma Alpha Mu (pres. 1963). Office: Ste 220 7575 Golden Valley Rd Golden Valley MN 55427 also: 3604 Cedar Ave S Minneapolis MN 55407

LITTOOY, FRED NELSON, peripheral vascular surgeon; b. Kansas City, Mo., May 6, 1943; s. Fred Clyde and Helen Virginia (Johnson) L.; m. Martha Sue Gilbert, Aug. 1, 1965 (div.); children: Fred Cameron, Heather Lynn, Chandra Renee, Stephanie Amber. AB, U. Kans., 1965, MD, 1969. Intern, resident U. Calif., San Francisco, 1969-72, 74-76, wound healing rsch., 1972-74, fellow in peripheral vascular surgery, 1976-77; from asst. prof. to prof. surgery Loyola U. Med. Ctr., Maywood, 1977—; staff physician, chief divsn. peripheral vascular surgery Hines VA Med Ctr, Hines, Ill., 1996—. Mem. editl. bd. Vascular Surgery, 1995—. Fellow Am. Coll. Surgeons; mem. Internat. Soc. for Cardiovasc. Surgery, Soc. for Vasc. Surgery, Ctrl. Surgical Assn., Western Surgical Assn., Midwestern Vascular Surg. Soc. (treas. 1985-88, pres. 1991). Office: Loyola U Med Ctr 2160 S 1st Ave Maywood IL 60153 also: Hines VA Med Ctr Vascular Surgery Divsn Hines IL 60141

LITVAK, RONALD, psychiatrist; b. Cleve., Aug. 11, 1938; s. Albert and Ruth (Jaffe) L.; m. Betty Ann Resnick, Aug. 14, 1960; children: Alan, Diane, Amy. BA, Case Western Res. U., 1960; MD, Ohio State U., 1964, MS, 1968. Diplomate Am. Bd. Psychiatry and Neurology, Am. Bd. Forensic Psychiatry; lic. Ohio. Intern in internal medicine Ohio State U. Hosp., Columbus, 1964-65, resident in psychiatry, 1965-68; chief resident in psychiatry Profl. Staff Ohio State U. Hosp., Columbus, 1967-68; practice medicine specializing in psychiatry Columbus, Ohio, 1964—; dir. outpatient svcs. Harding Hosp., Worthington, Ohio, 1979-83, pres. med. staff, 1980; cons. Ohio Dept. Mental Health and Mental Retardation, 1970-78, Chillicothe VA Hosp., 1970-71, Columbus Police Dept., Worthington Police Dept., Ohio State Hwy Patrol, Indsl. Commn. of Ohio, Ohio Atty. Gen., State Med. Bd. of Ohio, Supreme Ct. of Ohio, Bd. of Commrs. and Grievances and Discipline of the Bar, Columbus City Atty., U.S. Dept. Labor, U.S. Dept. State. Contbr. articles to profl. jours. Served to maj. Med. Service Corps, U.S. Army, 1968-70. Recipient Cert. of Achievement Comdr. U.S. Walson Army Hosp., Ft. Dix, N.J., 1970, Letters of Commendation, Officers in Tng. Brigade, Ft. Dix, N.J. Fellow Am. Psychiat. Assn.; mem. AMA, Ohio State Med. Assn., Ohio Psychiat. Assn., Psychiat. Soc. Cen. Ohio, Acad. Medicine of Columbus and Franklin County, Am. Acad. Psychiatry and the Law. Home: 1195 Circle On The Grn Columbus OH 43235-1208 Office: 1170 Old Henderson Rd # 201 Columbus OH 43220-3661

LITWACK, ARLENE DEBRA, psychotherapist, psychoanalyst, consultant, educator; b. Brookline, Mass., July 18, 1945; d. Hyman and Bessie Litwack. BA cum laude, Boston U., 1967; MS, Columbia U., 1969; postgrad. Ctr. for Mental Health, N.Y.C., 1981; psychoanalyst cert. Inst. for Psychoanalytic Tng. and Rsch., 1993. Caseworker Pride Treatment Ctr., Douglaston, N.Y., 1969-73, supr., 1973-78, sr. worker, 1978-80; pvt. practice psychotherapy and psychoanalyst, N.Y.C., 1980— mem. faculty Inst. for Mental Health Edn., Englewood, N.J., 1983-89; clin. cons. N.Y. Spaulding for Children, 1989; bd. dir. child therapy dept. L.I. Consultation Ctr., Rego Park, N.Y., 1980-85; faculty workshop leader Human Svcs. Workshops, N.Y.C.; adj. faculty Fordham U., 1991—; mem. faculty, supr., chair object rels. Psychoanalytic Study Ctr., 1991—. Contbr. articles to profl. jours. Mem. N.Y. State Soc. of Clin. Social Worker, Nat. Assn. of Social Workers. Home: 115 4th Ave Apt 3E New York NY 10003-4907

LITWIN, MARTIN STANLEY, surgeon; b. Florence, Ala., Jan. 8, 1930; s. Ben and Rose L.; m. Cheryl Denise Mason; children: Anna Marie, Rebecca, Benjamin, Martin. BS, U. Ala., 1951, MD, 1955. Diplomate Am. Bd. Surgery. Intern Michael Reese Hosp., Chgo., 1955-56; asst. in surgery to chief surg. resident Peter Bent Brigham Hosp., Boston, 1956-65; pvt. practice specializing in surgery New Orleans; asst. prof. to assoc. prof. surgery Tulane Med. Sch., New Orleans, 1966-75; prof. surgery Tulane Med. Sch., 1975—, assoc. dean, med. dir. faculty practice, 1976—, Robert and Viola Lobrano prof. surgery, 1977—; chmn. continuing edn., 1979-93; clin. investigator VA Hosp., West Roxbury, Mass., 1964-66; vis. surgeon Charity Hosp. of La., 1966; active staff Tulane Med. Ctr. Hosp., 1977—; univ. staff Touro Infirmary, 1967—. Contbr. articles to profl. jours.; assoc. editor Emergency Medicine, 1969-84. 1st lt. to col. USAR-MC, 1956-80. Fellow ACS; mem. Assn. Am. Med. Colls. (chmn. steering com. 1994—, Group on Faculty Practice), Am. Coll. Phys. Execs., Am. Burn Assn., Am. Surg. Assn., Am. Assn. Surgery of Trauma, Am. Surg. Assn., Am. Assn. Surgery of Trauma, Soc. Surg. Assn., Soc. Med. Assn., Southeastern Surg. Congress, La. Med. Soc., New Orleans Surg. Soc. (pres. 1989), Orleans Parish Med. Soc. (mem. hosp. com. 1983), European Soc. Exptl. Surgery, Internat. Surg. Soc., Assn. Acad. Surgery, Soc. Surgeons of Alimentary Tract, Soc. Univ. Surgeons, Brigham Sur. Alumni Assn., Tulane Surg. Soc., others. Address: 5591 Bellaire Dr New Orleans LA 70124-1001 Office: Tulane U Med Ctr 1415 Tulane Ave New Orleans LA 70112-2605

LIU, ANDREW TZE CHIU, chemical researcher and developer; b. Hong Kong, July 20, 1929; came to U.S., 1947; s. Yan Tak and Dorothy M. K. (Kwok) L.; m. Helena L. Y. (Chang), Feb. 7, 1956; children: Genevia K. M., Andrea K. Y. BS, Ind. U., 1951; MS, U. Mass., Lowell, 1953; PhD, London U., 1961; DIC, Imperial Coll., London, 1962. Engr. Textile Rsch. Inst., Beijing, 1955-59; tech. officer I.C.I. Ltd., Manchester, Eng., 1961-67; rsch. chemist E.I. du Pont and Nemours & Co., Beaumont, Tex., 1967-71; chief exec. officer LIU Industries, Hong Kong, 1971-77; coord. new ventures Conoco, Inc., Ponca City, Okla., 1977-80; v.p. Continental Overseas Oil, Inc., Houston, 1980-85; chief exec. officer China Ctr. for Tech. Devel., Houston, 1985-88; dir., sr. rsch. scientist Dentsply Internat., York, Pa., 1988-93; spl. projects mgr. Bisco, Inc., Itasca, Ill., 1994—; advisor Ctr. Internat. Bus. Studies Tex. A&M U., College Station, 1986-89. Author: Science and Technology Policy, 1983. Recipient Disting. Svc. award, E. I. du Pont, Wilmington, Del. Mem. ADA (subcom. direct filling working group), Internat. Assn. Dental Rsch., Am. Chem. Soc., Soc. Plastic Engrs., Am. Soc. Materials. Home: 150 W Saint Charles Rd 711 Lombard IL 60148 Office: Bisco Inc 1500 W Thorndale Ave Itasca IL 60143-1133

LIU, CHING-TONG, research physiologist; b. Kiangsu, China, Oct. 19, 1931; s. Lien Yi and Su Ju (Ku) L.; m. In-May Hsin, Feb. 28, 1970; children: Rex, Grace, Jeannette, Christine. BS, Nat. Taiwan U., 1956; MS, U. Tenn., Memphis, 1959, PhD, 1963. Assoc. research biologist Sterling-Winthrop Research Inst., Renssalaer, N.Y., 1965-66; asst. prof. physiology Baylor Coll. Medicine, Houston, 1966-73, adj. prof., 1979—; rsch. physiologist dept. aerobiol. and product evaluation U.S. Army Med. Rsch. Inst. Infectious Diseases, Ft. Detrick, Md., 1973—; adviser postdoctoral rsch. assocs. NRC, Washington. Contbr. numerous articles to profl. jours; rsch. activities emphasize organ dynamic functional changes and systemically integrated relationships of pathogenesis during toxemias; the possible linkages between celluar released chem. mediators and organ dysfunction have been postulated and presently under study. Recipient Outstanding Performance award U.S. Army, 1976-77, Superior Performance award, 1980-81, Exceptional Performance rating, 1982-84, Merit Performance award, 1984-87. Mem. Soc. Exptl. Biology and Medicine, Am. Physiol. Soc., Am. Soc. Pharmacology and Exptl. Therapeutics. Home: 7915 W 7th St Frederick MD 21702-2801 Office: Fort Detrick USAMRIID Toxinology Divsn Frederick MD 21702-5011

LIU, DAVID TEK YUNG, obstetrician, gynecologist, medical educator; b. Sandakan, Sabah, Malaysia, Apr. 26, 1941; arrived in Australia.; s. Tsu Shya and King Yeu (Leung) L.; m. Pamela Margaret Thwaites, July 26, 1973; 1 child, Natasha Harriet. M.B.B.S., U. Sydney, Australia, 1966; MPhil in Biomed. Engring., U. Sussex, U.K., 1975; MD, U. Nottingham, U.K., 1991. Intern Women's Hosp., Sydney, Australia, 1968-69; rsch. fellow Sussex U., 1971-74; rsch. registrar, lectr. U. London, 1974-76, lectr., 1976-81; lectr., sr. registrar U. Nottingham, 1981—; clin. dir. ob-gyn. Nottingham City Hosp.; cons. in field; co-founder, co-chmn. Nottingham Charity Appeal for Prenatal Diagnosis, 1981—. Author/editor: Chorion Villus Sampling, Labour Ward Manual, 1981, 2d edit., 1987, Practical Gynaecology, 1989; inventor Liu sampler, 1983. Fellow Royal Coll. Obstetricians and Gynecologists, Royal Australian Coll. Obstetricians and Gynecologists; mem. Nottingham County Sailing Club. Office: Nottingham City Hosp, Dept OB-Gyn, Hucknall Rd, Nottingham NG5 1PB, England

LIU, DON, ophthalmologist, medical researcher; b. Nanjing, China, July 17, 1947; came to the U.S., 1964; s. Robert Ching Ming and I. Tu Liu; m. Helen Cheng, June 21, 1975; children: David, Grace, Glory, Daniel. BS in Physics, Purdue U., 1969; MS in Physics, U. Mass., 1971; MD, SUNY, Buffalo, 1977. Dir. oculoplastics/orbit. Ford Hosp., Detroit, 1982-90; dir. oculoplastics/orbit. svc. U. So. Calif.-L.A. County Hosp., L.A., 1990—; assoc. dir. tech. transfer U. So. Calif., 1995—; organizer Internat. Conf. U.S.A., China and Hong Kong, Taiwan, 1985, 87, 89, 92, 93, 95; cons. to med. industries, state govt. and the Chinese govt. on health care; sci. referee Ophthalmology, 1990, Am. Jour. Ophthalmology, 1991—, Ophthalmic, Plastic and Recontructive Surgery, 1991—, Ophthalmic Surgery and Lasers, 1994—; mem. adv. bd. Med. Books for China, Internat., 1985—. Contbr. numerous book chpts. and articles to textbooks and profl. jours.; mem. editl. bd. numerous jours. Campaign fundraiser Mike Woo for Mayor, L.A., 1993; So. Calif. coord. Bush/Quayle, 1992, L.A.; sponsor San Marino (Calif.) Sch. Dist., 1990—; active Boy Scouts Am., Amnesty Internat., ch. activities. Recipient numerous tchg. awards, hon. degrees and titles from Chinese med. instns. Fellow ACS, Am. Acad. Facial Plastic and Reconstructive Surgery (com. mem. 1992-96), Am. Soc. Ophthalmic, Plastic and Reconstructive Surgery (fellowship dir. 1994—, Outstanding fellow 1981), Am. Acad. Ophthalmology (hon. award 1994), Am. BdOphthalmology (assoc. examiner 1991—); mem. AMA, Chinese Am. Ophthalmologic Soc.(sec.-treas. 1988-92), Internat. Soc. Ocuplastic Surgeons (bd. dirs.), Com. of 100. Home: 1066 Kewen Dr San Marino CA 91108-1013

LIU, GRANT T., neurologist, neuro-ophthalmologist; b. Minn., Apr. 9, 1962; s. Shean-Lin and Ai-Yu (Lin) L.; m. Geraldine Watts; children: Alessandra, Jonathan. AB, Harvard U., 1984; MD, Columbia U., 1988. Diplomate Am. Bd. Psychiatry and Neurology. Intern Columbia-Presbyn. Hosp., N.Y.C., 1988-89; resident in neurology Beth Israel, Children's, Brockton-West Roxbury VA Hosps., Boston, 1989-92; fellow in neuro-ophthalmology Children's Hosp., Phila., 1992-93; intern Columbia-Presbyn. Hosp., N.Y.C., 1988-89; resident in neurology Beth Israel, Children's, Brockton-West Roxbury VA Hosps., Boston, 1989-92, Brigham and Women's Hosp., 1989-92; fellow in neuro-ophthalmology Bascom Palmer Eye Inst., Phila., 1992-93; asst. prof. neurology and ophthalmology U. Pa. Sch. Med., Phila., 1993—. Contbr. articles to profl. jours. Mem. Am. Acad. Neurology. Office: Hosp U Pa 3400 Spruce St Philadelphia PA 19104

LIU, KHANG-LEE, dentist, educator; b. China, Aug. 5, 1939; came to U.S., 1972, naturalized, 1982; s. T.P. and K.H. (Lu) L.; m. Nancy S.Y. Lee (div.); children: Christine, Helen. B.D.S., Nat. Def. Med. Ctr., Faculty of Dentistry, Taipei, 1964; MA, U. Chgo., 1974. Asst., Nat. Def. Med. Ctr., Taipei, Taiwan, 1964-67; instr. Med. Ctr., Republic of China, 1968-72; asst. prof. U. Chgo., 1972-76; assoc. prof. Nat. Def. Med. Ctr., 1976-77; from asst. prof. to assoc. prof. dentistry Northwestern U., Chgo., 1977—; dir. McCormick Boys and Girls Dental Clin. Pres. midwest chpt. Coun. on Chinese Cultural Renaissance, 1984—. Mem. ADA, Chgo. Dental Soc., Am. Soc. Dentistry for Children, Internat. Assn. Dental Rsch., Am. Acad. Pediatric Dentistry, Chinese Am. Dentist Assn. (charter mem., 1st pres. 1990). Office 2158-B S Archer Ave Chicago IL 60616

LIU, MAN-NAN HAMILTON, dermatologist; b. TTainan, Taiwan, China, Dec. 20, 1953; m. I-Yuahn Wu; children: Daniel, Janny, Ruby. MB, Nat. Def. Med. Ctr., Taipei, 1969; M.Med.Sci., U. Minn., 1986. Diplomate Am. Bd. Dermatology. Cons. dermatologist Tri-Svc. Gen. Hosp., Taipei, 1986-88; sect. chief dept. dermatology Vets. Gen. Hosp., Taipei, 1988—. Bd. editors Am. Jour. Dermatology, 1994-96, Chinese Med. Jour., 1988-96, Clin. Medicine, 1988-96. Named Best Tchr. of the Yr. Vets. Gen. Hosp., 1989. Mem. Chinese Dermatologic Soc. (exec. com. 1996), SLE Club (hon. mem. exec. com. 1994-96). Office: Veterans General Hosp., 201 Sect 2 Shih-Pai Rd, Taipei 112, Taiwan

LIU, MAW-SHUNG, physiologist, dentist; b. Taiwan, Republic of China, Feb. 2, 1940; came to U.S., 1968; s. Chao-Tung and Chian (Hwang) L.; m. Min-Chau Chang, Sept. 15, 1966; 1 child, Chien-Ye. DDS, Kaohsiung Med. Coll., Taiwan, 1964; PhD, U. Ottawa, Can., 1976. Cert. by Coun. Nat. Bd. Dental Examiners. Intern in pathology U. Ky., Lexington, 1963-69; instr. physiology La. State U. Med. Ctr., New Orleans, 1974-76, asst. prof., 1976-78; assoc. prof. Bowman Gray Sch. Med. Wake Forest U., Winston-Salem, N.C., 1978-82; prof. St. Louis U. Sch. Medicine, 1982—; vis. prof. Beijing Med. U., 1984—, Zhejiang Med. U., 1986, Kaohsiung Med. Coll., 1989—, Chang Gung Med. Coll., 1989—; mem. surgery, anesthesiology and trauma study sect. NIH, 1988-92. Mem. editl. bd. Circulatory Shock, 1982-93, Shock, 1993—; contbr. over 60 articles and 60 papers to profl. jours. Named hon. prof. Nanjing Med. Univ., 1984, Hunan Med. Univ., 1988; grantee Nat. Heart Lung and Blood Inst., Inst. Gen. Med. Sci., 1977—. Mem. Internat. Soc. Heart Rsch., Am. Physiol. Soc., The Shock Soc. Office: St Louis U Sch Medicine Dept Pharm & Physiol Sci 1402 S Grand Blvd Saint Louis MO 63104-1004

LIU, STEPHEN H., orthopedic surgeon; b. Taipei, Taiwan, Apr. 24, 1960; s. Tang-Kue and Li-Su L.; m. Machi Matsumura, July 7, 1991; 1 child, Seiji. BS cum laude, UCLA, 1982; MD, U. So. Calif., 1986. Diplomate Am. Bd. Orthopedic Surgery. Fellow in orthopaedic sports medicine Hughston Clinic, Columbus, Ga., 1991; asst. prof. dept. orthopedic surgery UCLA Sch. Medicine, 1992—; chief sports medicine VA Wadsworth Med. Ctr., L.A., 1995—. Author 5 books, contbr. numerous articles to profl. jours. Am. Orthopedic Sports Medicine Soc. travelling fellow, 1996. Fellow Am. Acad. Orthopedic Surgeons; mem. Orthopedic Rsch. Soc., Arthfoscopy Assn. N.Am., Internat. Soc. Knee Surgery, Phi Beta Kappa. Home: 728 N Roxbury Dr Beverly Hills CA 90210

LIU, ZHONG-PING, natural medicine specialist; b. Beijing, People's Republic of China, June 5, 1958; came to U.S., 1986; s. De-Rang Liu and Yin-Mei Zhang. BS in Plant Protection, Hunan Agrl. Coll., Changsha, Hunan, China, 1981; AAS in Data Processing Tech., Del. Tech., Wilmington, 1990; BS in Computer Info. Systems, Goldey-Beacom Coll., Wilmington, 1991; postgrad., Samra U. Cert. in advanced English as a second lang., Del. Tech.; cert. in ornamental hort. Longwood Gardens, Inc. Gardener Gaotian Econ. Plant Garden, Shaodong, Hunan, China, 1975-78; asst. rschr. Hunan Inst. Plant Protection, Changsha, Hunan, China, 1982-84; curator Jiangsu Inst. Botany/Nanjing Bot. Garden Mem. Sun Yat-Sen, Nanjing, Jiangsu, China, 1984-86; horticulturist Longwood Gardens, Inc., Kennett Square, Pa., 1986-87; computer lab. asst. Goldey-Beacom Coll., Wilmington, Del., 1990-91, sr. asst./computer cons., 1991-94; observer, intern Samra U., L.A., 1995—. Contbr. rsch. articles to profl. jours. Mem. Calif. Chinese Medicine Assn. Home: PO Box 3273 Alhambra CA 91803-0273

LIVENGOOD, RICHARD VAUGHN, healthcare executive; b. Offerle, Kans., Mar. 24, 1934; s. C. Earl and Wynona Mae (Block) L.; m. D. Joanne Desler, Aug. 11, 1962; children: Linda Renee, John David. BS in Edn., Eastern Ill. U., 1956; student, Kings Fund Coll., London, 1972; MHA, Duke U., 1973. Instr., coach Rockford (Ill.) Sch. Bus. and Engring., 1959-64; asst. adminstr. Freeport (Ill.) Meml. Hosp., 1964-68; asst. adminstr. finance Manatee Meml. Hosp., Bradenton, Fla., 1968-71; v.p. Charleston (W.Va.) Area Med. Ctr., 1973-75; pres. Lakeview Med. Ctr., Danville, Ill., 1975-88; pres., CEO Providence Meml. Hosp., El Paso, 1988-92; COO Santa Rosa Health Care Corp., San Antonio, 1992-93; pres., CEO Marion (Ill.) Meml. Hosp., 1993—. Fellow Am. Coll. Healthcare Execs., Hosp. Fin. Mgmt. Assn., Ill. Hosp. Assn. (trustee 1981-88, chmn. 1987); mem. Tex. Hosp. Assn. (trustee 1989-91), Am. Hosp. Assn., S.W. Healthcare Execs. (pres. 1990-91), VHA S.W. (bd. dirs. 1988-91), Lakeview Meml. Found. (bd. dirs. 1979-87), El Paso Hosp. Coun. (bd. dirs. 1988-91). Methodist. Home: 1810 Paula Ln Marion IL 62959-1425 Office: Marion Meml Hosp Marion IL 62959

LIVINGOOD, CLARENCE S., dermatologist; b. Elverson, Pa., Aug. 7, 1911; s. Clarence A. and Eliza (Zerr) L.; m. Louise Sinclair Woelpper, Oct. 24, 1947; children: Wilson, Louise S., Clarence, Susan, Elizabeth. B.S., Ursinus Coll., 1932, D.Sc. (hon.), 1982; M.D., U. Pa., 1936. Diplomate Am. Bd. Dermatology (exec. dir. 1968-92, exec. cons. 1993—). Intern, then resident dermatology Hosp. U. Pa., 1936-41; asst. prof. dermatology U. Pa. Med. Sch., 1946-48, U. Pa. Med. Sch. (Grad. Sch.), 1946-49; chief dermatology Children's Hosp. Pa., 1946-48; prof., chmn. dept. dermatology Jefferson Med. Sch., Phila., 1948-49, U. Tex. Sch. Medicine, 1949-53; chmn. dermatology dept. Henry Ford Hosp., Detroit, 1953-76; chmn. emeritus Henry Ford Hosp., 1976—; team physician Detroit Tigers Baseball Club, 1967—; clin. prof. dermatology U. Mich. Sch. Medicine; mem. com. on cutaneous diseases AFEB, 1956-72; chief cons. dermatology VA, 1953-59; sec.-gen. XII Internat. Congress Dermatology, 1962; mem. Am. Bd. Med. Spltys., 1963-92, mem. exec. com., 1974-76, spl. award, 1993; mem. residency rev. com. for dermatology AMA, 1957-67; mem. adv. com. Nat. Disease and Therapeutic Index, 1974—; bd. dirs., treas. Coun. Med. Splty. Socs., 1976-80, mem. liaison com. on grad. med. edn., 1978-83; mem. Accreditation Coun. for Grad. Med. Edn., 1977-83. Author: (with D.M. Pillsbury, M.B. Sulzberger) Manual of Dermatology; contbr. articles to med. jours. Trustee Dermatology Found., 1965-71, ECFMG, 1975-79. Served to lt. col. M.C. AUS, 1942-46. decorated Bronze Star, Legion of Merit; recipient Profl. Achievement award Wayne County Med. Soc., 1993, Dermatology Fedn. Practitioner of Yr. award, 1993. Fellow Am. Acad. Dermatology (dir., past pres., Gold medal 1975, Masters in Dermatology 1985, Presdl. Citation 1987, C.S. Livingood Ann. Lectureship established 1993), ACP; mem. AMA (ho. of dels., chmn. sect. dermatology 1958, Disting. Svc. award 1990), Soc. Investigative Dermatology (past pres., Stephen Rothman award 1980), Am. Dermatol. Assn. (past pres., dir. 1964-68, named hon. mem. 1981), Am. Bd. Dermatology (diplomate, exec. dir. 1968-92, exec. cons. 1993—), Coll. Physicians Phila., Pacific Dermatol. Soc. (hon. mem.), Phila. Dermatol Soc., Detroit Dermatol. Soc. (past pres.), Mich. Med. Soc. (jud. council, ho. dels. 1974-80), Med. Cons. Soc. World War II, Assn. Mil. Dermatologists, Detroit Acad. Medicine, Assn. Maj. League Team Physicians, Assn. Dermatology Argentina (corr.), N.Y. Acad. Scis. (internat. congress dermatology), Danish Soc. (hon.), Indian Assn. Dermatologists (hon.), Brit. Dermatol. Soc. (hon.), Yugoslavian Dermatol. Soc. (hon.), Israel Dermatol. Soc. (hon.), N.Y. Dermatol. Soc. (hon. 1992), 18th World Congress Dermatology (hon. pres. 1992). Clubs: Grosse Pointe, Witenagemote. Home: 345 University Pl Grosse Pointe MI 48230-1635 Office: Henry Ford Hosp 2799 W Grand Blvd Detroit MI 48202-2608

LIVINGSTON, DAVID MORSE, biomedical scientist, physician, internist; b. Cambridge, Mass., Mar. 29, 1941; s. Arthur Joshua and Phyllis Freda (Kanters) L.; m. Jacqueline Gutman, June 23, 1963 (div. 1983); m. Emily Rabb, Jan. 25, 1986; children: Catherine Ellen, Julie. AB cum laude, Harvard U., 1961; MD magna cum laude, Tufts U., 1965. Diplomate Nat. Bd. Med. Examiners, Am. Bd. Internal Medicine. Intern, resident Peter Bent Brigham Hosp., Boston, 1965-67; rsch. assoc., sr. staff fellow, sr. investigator NCI-NIH, Bethesda, Md., 1967-69, 71-73; rsch. fellow in biol. chemistry Harvard Med. Sch., Boston, 1969-71, asst. prof. medicine, 1973-76, assoc. prof. medicine, 1976-82, prof. medicine, 1982-92; Emil Frei III prof. medicine Harvard Med. Sch., 1992—; v.p. Dana-Farber Cancer Inst., Boston, 1989-91; dir., physician-in-chief Harvard Med. Sch., Boston, 1991-95, Emil Frei III prof. medicine, 1992—, chmn. res. exec. com., 1995—. Mem. editorial bd. Virology jour., 1989—; editor BBA Revs. on Cancer, 1988—; contbr. articles to profl. jours. Mem. sci. adv. com. Damon Runyan-Walter Winchell Cancer Fund, N.Y.C., 1988-92, chmn. sci. adv. com., 1989-92; bd. dirs. Cancer Rsch. Fund, 1992—, mem. exec. com., 1994—; vice chmn. sci. adv. com. Pexcoller Found., Trento, Italy, 1994—; mem. sci. adv. bd. Inst. Cancer Rsch., Fox Chase, Pa., 1991—, Lineburger Comprehensive Cancer Ctr., U. N.C., Chapel Hill, 1993-95, MIT Cancer Ctr., 1994—, Fred Hutchinson Cancer Ctr., 1992—. Comdr. USPHS, 1967-73. Recipient Claire & Richard Morse award for Rsch., Dana-Farber Cancer Inst., 1991. Mem. NAS, Am. Soc. for Clin. Investigation, Assn. Am. Physicians, Am. Soc. Biol. Chemistry and Molecular Biology, Am. Soc. Microbiology, Am. Soc. Virology, Inst. Medicine of NAS, Met. Club Washington, St. Botolph Club, Univ. Club (N.Y.C., Boston), Alpha Omega Alpha. Office: Dana-Farber Cancer Inst 44 Binney St Boston MA 02115-6013

LIVINGSTON, GORDON STUART, psychiatrist; b. Memphis, June 30, 1938; s. Stanton Knowlton and Barbara (Keegan) L.; m. Katharine Stuart Lowry, Feb. 4, 1961 (div. June 1975); children: Kirsten, Nina, Michael; m. Clare Vickers King, Mar. 19, 1977; 1 child, Emily. BS, U.S. Mil. Acad., 1960; MD, Johns Hopkins U., 1967. Commd. 2nd lt. U.S. Army, 1960; intern Walter Reed Gen. Hosp. U.S. Army, Washington, 1967-68; regimental surgeon 11th Armored Cavalry Regiment U.S. Army, Vietnam, 1968-69; resigned U.S. Army, 1969; resident psychiatry Johns Hopkins Sch. Medicine, Balt., 1969-72; fellow in child psychiatry Johns Hopkins Sch. Medicine, 1972-74; psychiatrist Columbia Med. Plan, Columbia, Md., 1974-77; chief psychiatry Columbia Med. Plan, 1977—; asst. prof. psychiatry Johns Hopkins U. Sch. Medicine, Balt., 1972—. Author: Only Spring, 1995; contbr. articles to profl. jours. and newspapers. Mem. Am. Psychiat. Assn., Md. Regional Coun. on Child Psychiatry, AMA. Democrat. Home: 5993 The Bowl Columbia MD 21045-3830 Office: Columbia Med Plan Knoll North Dr # 2 Columbia MD 21045-2298

LIVINGSTON, LAWRENCE C., retired nursing administrator; b. Greenville, Fla., Feb. 12, 1944; s. Abraham Livingston Sr. and Estella (Evans) Woody; m. Clifford B. Livingston, Aug. 7, 1965; children: Vernona, Otis, Lesa, Melissa. ADN, Manatee Jr. Coll., Bradenton, Fla., 1971. RN; cert. in nursing adminstrn. Staff nurse Manatee Meml. Hosp., Bradenton, 1971-72, nurse, surg. and urology units, 1972-78, supr., asst. dir. nurses, 1978-86; nursing mgr., 1986-94, ret., 1994. Home: 1016 25th St E Palmetto FL 34221-2616

LIVINGSTON, LOUISA ROSE, psychologist; b. Highland Park, Mich., Oct. 10, 1942; d. Albert and Mildred Loraine (Bos) Feldman; m. Philip Melancthon Powell, Dec. 29, 1962 (div. Mar., 1989); children: David, Aaron, Robert; m. Martin S. Livingston, May 30, 1992. BS, Roosevelt U., 1966; MS, U. Chgo., 1969, PhD, 1973. Intern in psychology VA Hosp., Newington, Conn., 1973-75; instr. So. Conn. State Coll., New Haven, 1975-76; psychologist Austin (Tex.) Evaluation Ctr., 1979-80, 81-82; dep. dir. gen. clin. svcs. Austin Child Guidance & Evaluation Ctr., 1982-86; sch. psychologist San Rafael (Calif.) Schs., 1980-81; instr. S.W. Tex. State U., San Marcos, 1978-79; adj. prof. dept. psychology U. Tex., Austin, 1984-88, clin. coord. learning abilities Child-Family Practicum Ctr., 1986-87; pvt. practice psychology; active Interagy. tng., 1989-90; mem. state task force for childrens svcs., 1990. Chmn. Cub Scouts Pack No. 54, 1977-78; v.p. pub. affairs Austin Alliance for Mentally Ill, 1987-89; mem. Nat. Alliance for Mentally Ill, Tex. Alliance for Mentally Ill., adv. com. Children & Adolescent Svc. System Program, Tex., 1989; bd. dirs. Capital Area Mental Health Ctr., 1985-86, task force on transitional living Tex. Protection & Adv., Inc., 1989; cellist Austin Community Orch., 1983-85. Lic. psychologist, health services provider, Tex. 1978-92, N.Y., 1992—. Fellow Am. Orthopsychiat. Assn.; mem. APA, Am. Assn. Marital and Family Therapy, Am. Group Psychotherapy Assn. (clin. mem.), Assn. Psychoanalytic Self Psychology (program com. 1993—), Tng. and Rsch. Inst. Self Psychology (candidate). Democrat. Home: 159 E 30th St Apt 18B New York NY 10016-7388 Office: 127 E 30th St Apt 3D New York NY 10016-7373

LIVOLSI, VIRGINIA ANNE, pathologist; b. N.Y.C., July 29, 1943; d. Epifanio and Mary Ann (LaPorta) LiV. BS cum laude, Coll. Mt. St. Vincent, N.Y.C., 1965; MD, Columbia U., 1969; MA honoris cause, U. Pa., 1983. Instr. pathology Columbia U., N.Y.C., 1973-74; attending pathologist Yale-New Haven Hosp., 1974-83; asst. prof. Yale U. Sch. Medicine, 1974-79, assoc. prof., 1979-83; dir. cytology Yale U., 1975-77; dir. surg. pathology Hosp. U. Pa., Phila., 1983-94, vice chair anat. pathology, 1994—, prof. pathology, 1983—. Mem. U.S. and Can. Acad. Pathology, Am. Soc. Clin. Pathologists (abstract rev. com. 1991—, practice parameters com. 1993-95), Arthur Purdy Stout Soc. Surg. Pathologists (sec. 1987-93, pres.-elect 1995—), Am. Thyroid Assn., Coll. Am. Pathologists, Assn. Dirs. Anatomic and Surg. Pathology (v.p. 1995—). Office: Hosp U Pa 3400 Spruce St # F6042 Philadelphia PA 19104

LIVONIA, ROBERT ANGELO, family practice physician, former military officer; b. Toulouse, France, Oct. 1, 1927; came to U.S., 1953; s. Charles Livonia and Alice T. Kyia; m. Barbara Livonia; 1 child, Chuck. DVM, Ecole Nat. Veterinaire, Toulouse, France, 1950; PhD in Pharmacology, Faculty de Med. Pharmacy, Toulouse, France, 1953; MA, Wayne State U., 1956; DO, U. Osteo. Med. Health Scis., 1960. Diplomate Am. Osteo. Bd. Family Practice; cert. BLS, ACLS. Clin. lab. asst. Kirksville Hosp., Mo., 1960-61; intern James Taylor Hosp., Bangor, Maine, 1961-62; pvt. practice Keser Falls, Maine, 1962-74; commd. USAF, 1974, advanced through grades to col.; chief hosp. svcs., also pres. med. bds. and CME USAF Hosp., 1974-75; hosp. comdr. USAF Hosp., Karamursel, Turkey, 1975-77; col., chmn. primary care clinic and emergency David Grant USAF Med. Ctr., Travis AFB, Calif., 1977-81; vice chmn. med. gen. clinic and emergency Irwin Army Hosp., Ft. Riley, Kans., 1981-83, chief PEC, practitioner in primary care and emergency, 1983-87; ret., 1987; physician, chief emergency room, nursing home dir. Reynolds County Meml. Hosp., Ellington, Mo., 1989-90; physician Ft. Leonard Wood (Mo.) Army Hosp., 1990-92, Van Buren Clinic, AMI Lucy Lee Hosp., Poplar Bluff, Mo., 1993, Med. Clinic, St. Joseph, Mo., 1993, Healthline-Meramec Med. Clinic, Sullivan, Mo., 1994, Meml. Health Br. East Clinic, Jefferson City, Mo., 1994, Healthway Family Practice, Potosi, Mo., 1994—. Author: Application of Zen Philosophy for Remaking American Industry, 1985; contbr. articles to profl. jours. Decorated chevalier Legion d'Honneur (France), D.S.M., Army Legion of Merit medal, Humanitarian Svc. medal, Air Force Commendation medal, Air Force Meritorious Svc. medal, Army Meritorious Svc. medal, Air Force Longevity Svc. award; recipient Recognition cert. USAFE Retrospective Patient Care Workshop, 1976, Appreciation cert. Cuban Resettlement Program, 1980. Mem. Am. Coll. Gen. Practice, Am. Coll. Emergency Physicians, Maine Osteo. Assn., Am. Osteo. Assn., Coll. Pediatrics Osteo. (assoc. mem.), Adv. Soc. Parasitilogy, Am. Clin. Chemist Assn., Nutrition of Today Soc., United Naval Inst., Am. Med. Soc. Vienna, Austria (life mem.), Am. Diabetic Assn., Am. Coll. Osteo. Family Physicians, Assn. Mil. Surgeons U.S., Mil. Assn. Osteop. Physicians Surgeons. Republican. Baptist. Office: Healthway Family Practice Potosi MO 63664

LIVORNESE, DOUGLAS SCOTT, internist; b. Somerville, N.J., Feb. 18, 1964; s. Lawrence Louis and Joan Ann (Hembrook) L.; m. Mary Eileen Walter, Oct. 28, 1989. BA in Chemistry, Lafayette Coll., 1986; MD, U. Med. & Dentistry N.J., 1990. Diplomate Am. Bd. Internal Medicine. Resident Med. Coll. Pa., Phila., 1990-94, postdoctoral fellow pulmonary and critical care, 1994—. Mem. ACP, Am. Coll. Chest Physicians, Am. Thoracic Soc., Soc. Critical Care Medicine. Office: Med College Pa 3300 Henry Ave Philadelphia PA 19129

LJUTIĆ, DRAGAN, internist; b. Šibenik, Croatia, Oct. 20, 1956; s. Marko and Dara (Radić) L.; m. Vjekoslava Raos, Sept. 20, 1980; children: Marko, Andela. MD, Sch. Medicine, Zagreb, Croatia, 1980; MS, Sch. Medicine, Rideka, Croatia, 1988; specialist in internal medicine, Sch. Medicine, Zagreb, 1989, PhD, 1991. House officer House of Pub. Health, Split, Croatia, 1980-82; physician House of Pub. Health, Makarska, Croatia, 1980-82; family physician House of Pub. Health, Makarska, 1982-85; registrar in internal medicine Clin. Hosp. Split, 1985-88, Clin. Hosp. Rebro, Zagreb, 1988-89; specialist in internal medicine Clin. Hosp. Split, 1989—; hon. registrar in nephrology renal unit Guy's Hosp., London, 1992; head divsn. nephrology Clin. Hosp. Split, 1990; asst. prof. medicine Sch. Medicine, Zagreb, 1994. Contbr. articles to med. jours. Mem. Internat. Soc. Nephrology (award 1992), European Renal Assn., European Dialysis and Transplantation Soc., Brit. Coun. (award 1993). Roman Catholic. Home: A G Matoša 14, 21000 Split Croatia Office: Clin Hosp Split, Spinčićeva 1, 2100 Split Croatia

LLAMAS, LUIS, pathologist; b. Mexico City, Apr. 28, 1948; came to U.S., 1975; s. Leopoldo and Rosalia (Cervantes) L.; m. Helia Nunez, Apr. 26, 1974; children: Elisa, Luis Leopoldo. BS, U. Mex., Mexico City, 1966; intern, IMSS, 1972; MD, U. Mex., Mexico City, 1973. Diplomate Am. Bd. Pathology. Resident in pathology Creighton U. Affiliated Hosps., Omaha, Nebr., 1975-76, U. Tex. M.D. Anderson Cancer Ctr., Houston, 1976-79; resident in pathology U. Tex. Med. Sch., Houston, 1982-84, asst. prof. clin. pathology, 1984-86; pathologist Doctors' Hosp., Laredo, Tex., 1986-88; dir. labs. Mercy Regional Med. Ctr., Lardeo, Tex., 1988—. Home: 1014 Castle Heights Dr Laredo TX 78041-2865 Office: Mercy Regional Med Ctr 1515 Logan Ave Laredo TX 78040-4617

LLEWELLYN, CHARLES ELROY, JR., psychiatrist; b. Richmond, Va., Jan. 16, 1922; s. Charles Elroy and Pearl Ann (Shield) L.; m. Grace Eldridge, Sept. 25, 1948; children: Charles Elroy III, George E. (dec.), Richard S. BS, Hampden-Sydney Coll., 1943; MD, Med. Coll. Va., 1946; MS in Psychiatry, U. Colo., 1953. Diplomate Am. Bd. Psychiatry and Neurology; lic. marriage and family therapist, N.C. Intern psychiatry Tucker Hosp., Inc., Richmond, 1946-47, asst. to staff, 1948-50; intern gen. medicine Bellevue Hosp., N.Y.C., 1947-48; fellow psychiatry Colo. Psychopathic Hosp. and U. Colo. Med. Ctr., Denver, 1950-53; assoc. dept. psychiatry Duke U., Durham, N.C., 1955-56, asst. prof., 1956-63, assoc. prof., 1963-87; asst. dir. adult psychiat. outpatient clinic Duke U. Med. Ctr., Durham, 1955-56, head adult psychiat. outpatient div., 1956-76, acting head divsn. cmty. and social psychiatry, 1976-81, chief tng. divsn. cmty. and social psychiatry, 1976-85, head divsn. cmty. and social psychiatry, 1985-87; pvt. practice Durham, 1987—; psychiat. cons., supr., seminar dir. pastoral counseling tng. programs Duke U. Med. Ctr., 1965-87, dir. student mental health svc. Duke U., 1959-68; psychiat. cons. N.C. Divsn. Social Svcs., 1955-79, N.C. Medicaid Program, 1971-75, N.C. Med. Peer Rev. Found., Inc., 1975-79; sr. psychiat. cons. Family Cons. Svc., Durham, 1966-87; mem.-at-large N.C. Substance Abuse Profl. Ctr. Bd., 1984-89; part-time cons., med. dir. Durham Substance Abuse Treatment Ctr., 1968-88. Contbr. articles to profl. jours, chpts. to books. Mem. adv. bd. Durham County Drug Counseling and Evaluation Svc., 1972-79; bd. dirs. Family Counseling Svc. Durham, 1973-78, pres., 1975; bd. dirs. United Health Svcs., 1975-84; trustee Epworth United Meth. Ch., 1959-62, dir. cmty. ministries com., 1961-62; cubmaster Boy Scouts Am., 1960-66; mem. ch. campus rels. com. The Meth. Ctr., Duke U., 1964-66. Capt. U.S. Army, 1953-55. Recipient Outstanding Profl. Human Svcs. Am. Acad. Human Svcs., 1974-75; grantee U.S. Inst. Mental Health, 1967-71. Fellow Am. Psychiat. Assn. (life); mem. AMA (life), Am. Group Psychotherapy Assn., Pan Am. Med. Soc. (life), Am. Assn. Marriage and Family Therapy, Carolinas Group Psychotherapy Soc. (treas. 1983-94), N.C. Med. Soc. (life), N.C. Assn. Marriage and Family Therapists, Mental Health Assn. N.C., Durham-Orange County Med. Soc. (life). Office: 3308 Chapel Hill Blvd Ste 110 Durham NC 27707-2643

LLEWELLYN, THOMAS SYLVESTER, III, radiologist, educator; b. Tulsa, June 13, 1936; s. Thomas Sylvester and Agnes Marie (Quinn) L.; m. Lana Jean Holder, Aug. 7, 1976; children: Bronwen Kay, Deirdre Ann, Cristin Marie. BS, U. Tulsa, 1958; MD, U. Okla., 1961. Diplomate Am. Bd. Radiology. Intern St. John Hosp., Tulsa, 1961-62; resident U. Mo. Med. Ctr., Columbia, 1964-67; instr. U. Mo. Med. Ctr., 1967-68; radiologist St. Francis Hosp., Tulsa, 1968—, clin. prof., 1995—; clin. asst. prof., assoc. prof. U. Okla. Health Sci. Ctr., Tulsa, 1978-95, clin. prof., 1995—; pres. Radiol. Cons. Tulsa. Bd. dirs. 12 & 12 Transition House, Tulsa. Capt. U.S. Army, 1962-64. Mem. AMA, Okla. Radiol. Soc., Okla. Med. Soc., Am. Soc. Emergency Radiology, Tulsa County Med. Soc., Am. Coll. Radiology, Radiol. Soc. N.Am., Soc. Cardiovasc. and Interventional Radiology, Flying Physicians Assn., Alpha Omega Alpha. Republican. Roman Catholic. Office: St Francis Hosp 6161 S Yale Ave Tulsa OK 74136-1902

LLINÁS, RODOLFO RIASCOS, medical educator, researcher; b. Bogota, Colombia, Dec. 16, 1934; came to U.S., 1959, naturalized, 1973; s. Jorge Enrique (Llinas) and Bertha (Riascos) L.; m. Gillian Kimber, Dec. 24, 1965; children: Rafael Hugo, Alexander Jorge. B.S., Gimnasio Moderno, Bogota, 1952; M.D., U. Javeriana, Bogota, 1959; Ph.D., Australian Nat. U., 1965; M.D. (hon.), U. Salamanca, Spain, 1985; PhD (hon.), U. Barcelona, Spain, 193, U. Nacional Bogota, Colombia, 194. Research fellow Mass. Gen. Hosp.-Harvard U., 1960-61; NIH research fellow in physiology U. Minn., Mpls., 1961-63, assoc. prof., 1965-66; assoc. mem. AMA Inst. Biomed. Research, Chgo., 1966-68, mem., 1970, head neurobiology unit, 1967-70; assoc. prof. neurology and psychiatry Northwestern U., 1967-71; guest prof. physiology Wayne State U., 1967-74; professorial lectr. pharmacology U. Ill.-Chgo., 1967-68, clin. prof., 1968-72; prof. physiology, head neurobiology div. U. Iowa, 1970-76; prof., chmn. physiology and biophysics NYU, N.Y.C., 1976—; Thomas and Suzanne Murphy prof. neurosci. NYU, 1985—; mem. neurol. sci. research tng. com. Nat. Inst. Neurol. Diseases and Stroke, NIH, 1971-73; mem. neurology A study sect. div. research grants NIH, 1974-78; assoc. neurosci. research program MIT, 1974-83; mem. U.S. Nat. Com. for IBRO, 1978-81; acting chmn. U.S. Nat. Com. For IBRO, 1982, chmn., 1983-89, exec. com., 1985—; mem. sci. adv. bd. Max-Planck Inst. for Psychiatry, Munich, 1979-83; professorial lectr. Coll. de France, Paris, 1979, Nat. Poly. Inst., Mexico City, 1981; IBRO internat. lectr., S.Am., 1982; McDowall lectr. King's Coll., London, 1984. Author: (with Hubbard and Quastel) Electrophysiological Analysis of Synaptic Transmission, 1969; editor: Neurobiology of Cerebellar Evolution and Development, 1969, (with W. Precht) Frog Neurobiology: A Handbook, 1976; chief editor: Neurosci., 1974—; mem. editorial bd.: Jour. Neurobiology, 1980—; mem.: Pfluegers Archives, 1981—, Jour. Theoretical Neurobiology, 1981—. Recipient John C. Krantz award U. Md., 1976, Einstein Gold medal UNESCO, 1991, Signoret award in cognition, Fondation Ipsen La Salpâtrière, Paris, 1994. Mem. NAS, Soc. For Neurosci. (council 1974-78), Am. Physiol. Soc. (Bowditch Lectr. 1973), Am. Soc. Cell Biology, Biophys. Soc., Harvey Soc., Internat. Brain Research Orgn., N.Y. Acad. Scis., Alpha Omega Alpha (hon.). Office: NYU Med Ctr 550 1st Ave New York NY 10016-6481

LLOYD, CECIL RHODES, pediatric dentist; b. Corpus Christi, Tex., Aug. 18, 1930; s. Cecil Rhodes Hilbun and Cidney W. (Linxwiler) Lloyd; m. Donna Mae Thomas, Dec. 31, 1955 (div. 1973); children: James Michael, Leigh Ann, Lisa Kendall; m. Glenda Sue Williams, Dec. 31, 1979; children: Lauren Cecily, Sutton Rhodes. Student, La. State U., 1949, La. Tech. Inst., 1950, Centenary Coll., 1952-54; DDS, Loyola U., New Orleans, 1958. Pediatric dentist Shreveport, La., 1958—; cons. pediatric dentistry Barksdale AFB, La., 1970—. Chmn. Cen. YMCA, Shreveport, 1974, met. bd., 1969, Ind. Bowl Football Classic, Shreveport, 1984, 85, Fellowship Christian Athletes, 1986; bd. dirs. Riverside Hosp., Bossier, La., 1982-84; pres.-elect Sports Found., 1989, pres., 1990; founder Sports Mus. of Champions, Shreveport-Bossier; interim mem. Shreveport City Coun., 1990. Named Southwestern Handball Hall of Fame, 1996. NW La. Dental Assn., La. Dental Assn., ADA, Am. Acad. Pediatric Dentistry, La. Bd. Dentistry (pres., 1969-70, 77-78, 83-84), Ark.-La.-Tex. Dental Congress (chmn. 1979-80). Republican. Baptist. Office: 927 Shreveport Barksdale Hwy Shreveport LA 71105-2205

LLOYD, CHARLES HEYWOOD, dental materials scientist; b. Sinoia, Rhodesia, Sept. 15, 1947; arrived in Scotland, 1976; s. Frank Eric and Jane Wray (McCrudden) L.; m. Elizabeth Ann Mead, Feb. 1, 1971; children: Katharine Jane, David Charles, Rebecca Ann. BSc, U. Birmingham, Eng., 1969, PhD, 1973. Rsch. assoc. U. Birmingham, 1972-76; lectr. U. Dundee, Scotland, 1976-85; sr. lectr. U. Dundee, 1985-89, reader, 1989—; cons. ICI Dental, Macclesfield, U.K., 1984-89; mem. European Concerted Action Program BE7317 Biomaterials, 1996—. Mem. Internat. Assn. Dental Rsch. (mem. Brit. divsn. councilor Brit. divsn. 1992-95), Inst. Materials (London), Brit. Stds. Com. for Dental Materials, Internat. Stds. Com. for Dental Materials. Office: U Dundee Dental Sch, Park Pl, DD1 4HN Dundee Scotland

LLOYD, DOUGLAS SEWARD, physician, public health administrator; b. Bklyn., Oct. 16, 1939; s. Heber Hughes and Virginia Seward (Chamberlin) L. A.B. in Chemistry, Duke U., 1961, M.D., 1971; postgrad., Old Dominion U., 1965-67; M.P.H. in Health Planning, U. N.C., 1971. Diplomate Am. Bd. Preventive Medicine. Intern in pediatrics Duke U., Durham, N.C. 1971-72; clin. scholar Duke U., 1972, resident in family practice, 1972-73; commr. health Conn. Dept. Health Services, 1973-87; assoc. med. dir. Nat. Med. Rsch. Corp., Hartford, Conn., 1987-89; pres. Doug Lloyd Assocs., Farmington, Conn., 1989-92; assoc. adminstr. Health Resources and Svcs. Adminstrn., Rockville, Md., 1992—; lectr. Yale U., Conn., 1973-87; chmn. bd. Pub. Health Found., 1984-87. Contbr. articles to profl. jours. Served to capt. USNR. Recipient Lange Publ. award, 1971, McCormick award for excellence in pub. health, 1987. Fellow Am. Coll. Preventive Medicine; mem. AMA, Am. Pub. Health Assn., Assn. State and Territorial Health Ofcls. (past pres.). Home: 11410 Stonewood Ln Rockville MD 20852-4543 Office: Health Resources & Svcs Adminstrn 5600 Fishers Ln Rockville MD 20857-0001

LLOYD, EVAN DEAN, optometrist; b. Salt Lake City, Aug. 20, 1961; s. Bruce Anders and Gayle Claire (Ashworth) L.; m. Monique Moes, July 16, 1988; children: Natasha Kelsey, Ashley Nicole. BA, U. Utah, 1987; OD, So. Calif. Coll. Optometry, 1991. Optometrist Sugarhouse Vision Clinic, Salt Lake City, 1991—, Nebo Vision Clinic, Nephi, Utah, 1991—, Fox Park Vision Clinic, West Jordan, Utah, 1993—, Great Basin Vision Clinic, Delta, Utah, 1994—; mem. pub. rels. com. Intermountain Managed Eye Care, Salt Lake City, 1994—. Advancement chmn. Boy Scouts Am., Sandy, Utah, 1995—. Mem. Am. Optometric Assn., Utah Optometric Assn. Office: Sugerhouse Vision Clinic 2178 S 900 E Salt Lake City UT 84106

LLOYD, GEOFFREY JOHN, consultant physician; b. Dartford, Kent, Eng.; s. John Llewellyn and Queenie Ellen Lloyd; m. Coral Ann; 1 child, Tamsin Coral. BSc with honors, London U., 1967, MB BChir, 1970; LLB, London & Wolverhampton Univs., 1994. Gen. med. coun. cert. for gen. medicine. House officer Profl. unit Med. Sch., 1970-71; sr. house officer Luter Hosp., 1971-73; registrar Royal Free Hosp. Med. Sch., 1973-74, sr. registrar, 1974-77; cons. physician Ahmadi, Kuwait, 1974, 77-86, Royal Free Hosp. Med. Sch., 1986-89, Awali, Bahrain, 1989-90; pvt. practice London. Contbr. articles and papers to profl. publs. Fellow Royal Coll. Physicians (London), Royal Soc. Medicine; mem. Brit. Med. Students Assn. (pres. 1968-69), Internat. Fedn. Med. Students Assn. (pres. 1969-70. Office: 21 Devonshire Pl, London W1N 1PD, England

LLOYD, LEWIS KEITH, JR., surgery and urology educator; b. Shreveport, La., Sept. 18, 1941; s. Lewis Keith Sr. and Cidney (Linxwiler) L.; m. Karen Hansen, June 9, 1970; children—Kristine Elizabeth, Lewis Keith III, Kevin Hansen. Student, Centenary Coll., 1959-62; M.D., Tulane Med. Sch., 1966. Diplomate Am. Bd. Urology. Intern USPHS Hosp., Norfolk, Va., 1966-67; resident in urology Tulane U. Med. Sch., New Orleans, 1970-74; from asst. to assoc. prof. surgery U. Ala., Birmingham, 1974-77, prof., 1981—; dir. Urol. Rehab. Rsch. Ctr., Birmingham, 1978, dir. urol. divsn., 1995; chmn. exec. com. Univ. Hosp., 1988-90. Adminstrv. bd. Highlands Meth. Ch., Birmingham, 1983-90; trustee Ala. chpt. Multiple Sclerosis Soc., Birmingham, 1984-85, 92—; bd. dirs. Am. Spinal Injury Assn., 1986-92. Lt. comdr. USPHS, 1966-70, Vietnam. Mem. AMA (Billings Gold medal 1978), Am. Urol. Assn. (bd. dirs. Southeastern sect. 1991-94), Am. Spinal Injury Assn., Birmingham Urology Club (pres. 1981-82), Greystone Golf Club. Republican. Clubs: Birmingham Urology (pres. 1981-82); Mountain Brook Swim and Tennis, Summit Club. Office: U Ala Med Sch 606 MEB Birmingham AL 35294

LLOYD, MICHAEL L., nursing administrator, educator; b. Miami, Ariz., Jan. 17, 1954; s. James Warren and Willa Mae (Jackson) Lloyd; m. Glynnis Morrill; 1 child, Amanda. Diploma, Mesa (Ariz.) Community Coll., 1974; BSN, Ariz. State U., 1976. RN, Colo., Ariz. Instr. nursing Gateway Community Coll., Phoenix, 1984-90; dir. nurses PRN, Phoenix, 1990-93; staff nurse PACU Montrose (Colo.) Meml. Hosp., 1993-96, mgr. surg. svcs., 1996—. Contbr. articles to profl. jours. Mem. ASPAN, AORN, Ariz. Assn. Health Care Agys., Ariz. Nurse Network, Ariz. Nurses Assn., Colo. Nurses Assn.

LLOYD, RAY DIX, health physicist, consultant; b. Mar. 10, 1930; s. Ray Ernest and Dixie (Penrose) L.; m. Louise Mortensen, July 10, 1954; children: Thomas R., Janna L. Brady, Alan T., Christopher R., Heather L. Smith. BS, U. Utah, 1954, MS, 1956, PhD, 1974; postgrad., U. Southwestern La., 1959, La. State U., 1960. Diplomate Am. Bd. Health Physics; recert. Rsch. asst. radiobiology divsn. U. Utah, 1961, rsch. assoc. radiobiology divsn., 1961-64, rsch. instr. dept. anatomy, radiobiology divsn., 1964-74, rsch. assoc. prof. dept. pharmacology, radiobiology divsn., 1979-84, rsch. prof. dept. pharmacology, radiobiology divsn., 1984-86, rsch. prof. Sch. Medicine, 1986-92, part-time rsch. prof. Sch. Medicine, 1992—; adj. asst. prof. dept. mechanical engring. U. Utah, 1975-90; cons. numerous orgns, health sys., and projects including Hale and Dorr, attys., Boston, Life Sys., Inc., Cleve., BioTrace, Salt Lake City, Plateau Resources, Ltd., Grand Junction, Colo., Hercules Aerospace, Magna, Utah, Mini-Dose Labs., Golden, Colo., Western Analytical Labs., Salt Lake City, 1979-94, Holy Cross Hosp., Salt Lake City, U.S. Dept. Justice, Nat. Cancer Inst; mem. Nat. Coun. Radiation Protection and Measurements, 1980-86, 86-92, consociate mem., 1992—; mem. radiol. health adv. com. Utah State Divsn. Health. Assoc. editor: (jour.) Health Physics, 1990-92, (book) Delayed Effects of Bone Seeking Radionuclides; reviewer: Radiation Rsch., Health Physics, Radiat. Protection, Internat. Jour. Radiation Biology, others; contbr. numerous articles to jours., chpts. to books, abstracts and tech. papers; patentee radiation detector. M sgt. U.S. Army, 1948-52, Korea, 1951-52. Fellow Health Physics Soc.; mem. Am. Acad. Health Physics, Radiation Rsch. Soc., Health Physics Soc. (Great Salt Lake chpt.), Utah br. Am. Assn. for Lab. Animal Sci., Internat. Radiation Protection Assn., Sigma Xi, Phi Kappa Phi, Gamma Theta Upsilon. Office: U Utah Radiobiology Lab Bldg 586 Salt Lake City UT 84112

LO, EDDY KONG CHUAN, medical epidemiologist, public health physician; b. Sitiawan, Perak, Malaysia, Oct. 20, 1937; s. Ho Chin Lo and Kim Hong Ong; m. Chee Kah Yeo, Dec. 12, 1964; children: Anthony, Joanne, Daniel. MB BS, Melbourne U., 1964; DPH, Sydney U., 1968; MSc in Epidemiology and Tropical Pub. Health, Harvard U., 1974. Jr. resident med. officer Royal Hobart (Tasmania) Hosp., 1965; sr. resident med. officer Austin Hosp., Heidelberg, Australia, 1966, pediatric registrar, 1967; chief div. epidemiology Pub. Health Inst., Kuala Lumpur, Malaysia, 1969-76; asst. dir. health svcs. Ministry of Health, Kuala Lumpur, Malaysia, 1976-87, dep. dir. vectorborne diseases control program, 1987-88; med. svcs. advisor in epidemiology Dept. Health Housing and Community Svcs., Canberra, Australia, 1987-93; gen. practice in family and preventive medicine Immediate Health Care Med. Ctr., Wanniassa/Canberra, 1993—; mem. expert panel on global surveillance of diseases WHO, Geneva, 1979-89, Scientific Working Group of Epidemiology WHO, 1978-83; bd. dirs. Kah Chuan Holdings S/B, Kuala Lumpur. Decorated A.M.N., King of Malaysia, 1982. Fellow Australian Faculty Pub. Health Medicine (founder), Gideons Internat.; mem. Malaysian Med. Assn. (chmn. anti-smoking com. 1972-82), Malaysian Soc. Health (gen. sec. 1969-75, pres. 1980), Malaysian Coll. Gen. Practitioners (founder), Internat. Epidemiol. Assn., Australian Soc. HIV Medicine, Australasian Epidemiol. Assn., Australian Pub. Health Assn., Harvard Club Australia, Lake Club (Kuala Lumpur). Methodist. Home: 2 Tasman Pl, 45 Gilmore Crescent, Carram ACT ACT, Australia 2605

LO, STEVE, hematologist, oncologist; b. Hong Kong, Aug. 28, 1958; came to U.S., 1965; s. Chun Ying and Pui Mei (Wong) L.; m. Jami Keogan, Jan. 21, 1989; children: Michael, Caylin, Ana. BA summa cum laude, Harvard U., 1981, MD, 1985. Intern, resident Brigham and Women's Hosp., Boston, 1985-88; hematology/oncology fellow Dana Farber Cancer Inst., Boston, 1988-92; hematologist, oncologist Hematology Oncology, P.C., Stanford, Conn., 1992—. Recipient Physician Scientist award NIH, 1989-92. Office: Bennett Cancer Ctr 34 Shelburne Rd Stamford CT 06902

LO, YING-SUI ARCHIE, cardiologist; b. Hong Kong, May 25, 1952; s. Ying-Shek and Lee-Kwan (To) L. BS, U. Wis., 1975; MD, U. Chgo., 1978. Resident L.A. County USC Med. Ctr., 1978-81; fellow in cardiology Northwestern U. Med. Ctr., Chgo., 1985-86, Stanford (Calif.) U. Med. Ctr., 1986-87; cons. cardiologist Hong Kong Adventist Hosp., 1987—; cons. cardiologist Hong Kong Sanatorium Hosp., 1994—; hon. clin. tutor Chinese U. Hong Kong, 1993—. Contbr. articles to profl. jours. Fellow Am. Coll. Cardiology, Am. Heart Assn., Royal Coll. Physicians Canada, ACP, Royal Coll. Physicians Glasgow, Hong Kong Acad. Medicine; mem. Rotary. Office: Ste 306 Ctrl Bldg, Pedder St, Hong Kong Hong Kong

LOARIE, THOMAS MERRITT, healthcare executive; b. Deerfield, Ill., June 12, 1946; s. Willard John and Lucile Veronica (Finnegan) L.; m. Stephanie Lane Fitts, Aug. 11, 1968 (div. Nov. 1987); children: Thomas M., Kristin Leigh Soule. BSME, U. Notre Dame, 1968; Student, U. Minn., 1969-70, U. Chgo., 1970-71, Columbia U., 1978. Registered profl. engr., Calif. Prodn. engr. Honeywell, Inc., Evanston, Ill., 1968-70; various positions Am. Hosp. Supply Co., Evanston, Ill., 1970-83, pres. Heyer-Schulte divsn., 1979-83; pres. COO Novacor Med. Corp., Oakland, Calif., 1984-85, also bd. dirs.; pres. ABA Bio Mgmt., Danville, Calif., 1985-87; chmn., CEO Keravision, Inc., Fremont, Calif., 1987—; founder, chmn., med. device CEO Roundtable, 1993—; asst. prof. surgery Creighton U. Med. Sch., Omaha, 1986-94; speaker in field. Contbr. articles on med. tech. and pub. policy to Wall St. Jour., others. Bd. dirs. Marymount Sch. Bd., 1981-84; bd. dirs. United Way Santa Barbara, 1981-84, assoc. chairperson, 1982-83, treas., 1983. Named One of 50 Rising Stars: Exec. Leaders for the 80's Industry Week mag., 1983. Mem. Assn. for Rsch. in Vision and Ophthalmology, Contact Lens Assn. Ophthalmology, Med. Mktg. Assn., Health Industry Mfrs. Assn. (spl. rep. bd. dirs. 1993—), Am. Entrepreneurs for Econ. Growth. Roman Catholic. Office: KeraVision Inc 48630 Milmont Dr Fremont CA 94538-7353

LOBAR, BRUCE IAN, neurologist; b. Washington, June 7, 1953; s. Caspar Bernard and Edith (Goldstein) L.; m. Patricia Elizabeth Mulligan, Nov. 7, 1981; children: Bryan Thomas, Sean Miles. BA in Psychology, U. Md., 1975, MA in Human Devel., 1976; MD, Am. U. Caribbean, Plymouth, Monserrat, 1982. Diplomate Am. Bd. Psychiatry and Neurology. Pvt. practice, Staunton, Va., 1986-90, Salisbury, Md., 1990-95, Harrisonburg, Va., 1996—. Mem. Am. Acad. Neurology, Am. Soc. Internal Medicine, Va. Neurol. Soc., Rockingham County Med. Soc. Address: 624 Eastern Shore Dr #A Salisbury MD 21804-5962

LOBEL, CHARLES IRVING, physician; b. Phila., Nov. 9, 1921; s. Maurice and Dora (Barnett) L.; m. Julia Valentine Skellchock, June 12, 1955; children: Meredith Anne Lobel-Angel. AA, San Jose State U., 1948; student, Stanford U., 1948-49; MD, U. So. Calif., 1953. Physician Permanente Med. Group, Inc., South San Francisco, 1954-65; physician, courtesy staff Chope Community Hosp., San Mateo, Calif., 1965-89, Sequoia Hosp., Redwood City, Calif., 1965—; physician Permanente Med. Group, Inc., Redwood City, Calif., 1965-95; clin. prof. medicine div. rheumatology Stanford U. Sch. Medicine, 1965—; chief profl. edn. Kaiser Found. Hosp., Redwood City, 1968-80, rehab. coord, 1968-80, pres med. staff, 1968-70; mem. Calif. Med. Assn. Staff Survey Com., San Francisco, 1970-90; mem. 4th dist. Bd. Med. Quality Assurance State Calif., 1979-84. 1st Lt. U.S. Army, 1942-46. Decorated Combat Infantry Badge, Bronze Star, Presdl. Unit citation, 3 Battle Stars. Fellow Am. Acad. Family Physicians, Am. Coll. Rheumatology; mem. AMA, AAAS, San Mateo County Med. Soc. (bd. dirs. 1975-78), Calif. Med. Soc. (alt. del. 1979-83), N.Y. Acad. of Sci., Am. Heart Assn., Royal Soc. of Med., Med. Friends of Wine, Arthritis Found. No. Calif., Phi Delta Epsilon. Office: Stanford U Clinic Dept Rheumatology 900 Blake Wilbur Dr Palo Alto CA 94304-2205

LOBIS, ROBERT ALAN, psychiatrist; b. Phila., Dec. 2, 1942; s. Milton and Theresa (Laster) L.; children: Samantha, Seth. BA, U. Pa., 1964; MD, Harvard U., 1968. Diplomate Am. Bd. Psychiatry and Neurology. Assoc. dir. mental health div. Leonard Morse Hosp., Natick, Mass., 1976-87; dir. child and adolescent svcs. Inst. of Living, Hartford, Conn., 1987-93; med. dir. Riverview Hosp., Middletown, Conn., 1993-95; sr. psychiatrist Choate Health Mgmt., Stoneham, Mass., 1995—; instr. Harvard U. Med. Sch., 1976-80; asst. prof. Tufts U. Med. Sch., Boston, 1980-87, U. Conn. Med. Sch., Farmington, 1988-93; asst. prof. Yale Med. Sch., 1993-95. Fellow Am. Acad. Child and Adolescent Psychiatry; mem. Am. Psychiat. Assn., Am. Psychoanalytic Assn., Aesulaplan.

LOBITZ, WALTER CHARLES, JR., physician, educator; b. Cin., Dec. 13, 1911; s. Walter Charles and Elsa (Spangenberg) L.; m. Caroline Elizabeth Rockwell, July 11, 1942; children: Walter Charles III, John Rockwell, Susan Hastings. Student, Brown U., 1930-31; B.Sc., U. Cin., 1939, M.B., 1940, M.D., 1941; M.Sc., U. Minn., 1945; M.A. (hon.), Dartmouth, 1958; LL.D., Hokkaido U., 1976. Diplomate Am. Bd. Dermatology (bd. dirs. 1955-64, pres. 1962). Intern Cin. Gen. Hosp., 1940, resident medicine, 1941; fellow Mayo Found., 1942-45; 1st asst. Mayo Clinic, 1945-47; chmn. sect. dermatology Hitchcock Clinic, Hanover, N.H., 1947-59; bd. dirs. Hitchcock Clinic, 1955; faculty Dartmouth Med. Sch., 1947-59, prof. dermatology, 1957-59; prof. dermatology, head div. U. Oreg. Med. Sch., 1959-69, chmn. dept., 1969-77; prof. Oreg. Health Scis. Univ., until 1980; emeritus prof. U. Oreg. Health Scis. Ctr., 1980—; area cons. VA, 1949-59; mem. commn. cutaneous diseases Armed Forces Epidemiologic Bd., 1965-75; cons., mem. gen. med. study sect. USPHS, 1961-65; mem. grant rev. com. United Health Found., 1964-65; cons. dermatology tng. grants com. NIAMD, 1966-70; cons. VA Hosp., U. Oreg. Med. Sch., 1959—; civilian cons. to surgeon gen. USAF, 1969-79; U.S. Air Force-Nat. cons. to Surgeon Gen., 1970-80; Dohi Meml. lectr. Japanese Dermatol. Assn., 1964; lectr. U. Copenhagen, Denmark, 1969, 74. Author numerous articles in field.; Co-editor: The Epidermis; editorial bd.: Jour. Investigative Dermatology, 1958-61, Excerpta of Medicine, 1961-78, Clinics in Dermatology, 1982; mem. editorial bd.: Archives Dermatology, 1960-77, chief editor, 1963-68. Trustee Dermatology Found., Med. Research Found. Oreg., 1972, exec. com., 1977-80, v.p., 1975-76, pres., 1977-78; music adv. com. Oreg. Symphony Orch., 1970-73; mem. Oreg. Ballet Council, 1974; bd. govs. Hitchcock Hosp., 1955; trustee Hitchcock Found., 1958-59, exec. com., 1958-59. Recipient Outstanding Achievement award U. Minn., 1964, Disting. Alumni award U. Cin. Coll. Medicine, 1995; dedication of Lobitz-Jillson Libr., Dartmouth-Hitchcock Med. Ctr., 1992; decorated Japanese Order of the Sacred Treasure, Gold Rays with neck ribbon, Emperor of Japan, 1993. Fellow ACP, Am. Acad. Dermatology (hon., bd. dirs. 1958-61, 66-69, pres. 1969, gold medal 1985, Master in Dermatology 1987), Phila. Coll. Physicians (hon.); mem. AMA, AAAS, Am. Dermatol. Assn. (bd. dirs. 1962-67, pres. 1972, hon. 1982), Soc. Investigative Dermatology (hon., v.p. 1952, bd. dirs. 1953-58, pres. 1957, Stephan Rothman medal for disting. achievement 1989), N.H., Multnomah County, Oreg., med. socs., N.Y. Acad. Scis., Pacific N.W. Dermatol. Assn. (pres. 1971), Pacific Dermatol. Assn., Israel Dermatol. Assn. (hon.), N.W. Soc. Clin. Rsch., Oreg. Dermatol. Soc. (pres. 1969), Portland Acad. Medicine, Am. Fedn. Clin. Rsch., Pacific Interurban Clin. Club (councilor 1971), Internat. Soc. Tropical Dermatology, Assn. Univ. Profs. Dermatology (founder, bd. dirs. 1961-66, pres. 1965-66), Soc. Venezolana de Dermatologia & Leprologia (hon.), French Soc. Dermatology, Brit. Assn. Dermatology, Assn. parala Investigacion Dermatologica (Venezuela), Soc. Dermatol. Danicae, Italian, Japan, Hokkaido, Sapporo derm. socs., Sigma Xi, Pi Kappa Epsilon, alpha Omega Alpha. Presbyn. Home: 2211 SW 1st Ave Portland OR 97201-5060

LOCEY, MARTIN LAWRENCE, diagnostic radiologist; b. Kalamazoo, Nov. 7, 1953; s. William Laverne and Teresa Ellen (Knapp) L.; children: Christopher, Rachel, Phillip, Matthew. BS, King Coll., 1975; MD, U. Fla., 1979. Diplomate Am. Bd. Radiology. Resident Brooke Army Med. Ctr., San Antonio, Tex., 1983; chief computerized tomography Womack Army Hosp., Fayetteville, N.C., 1983-85; dir. radiology Crisp Imaging Assocs., Cordele, 1985-94; dir. Crisp Imaging Assocs., Cordele, Ga., 1995—; radiology cons., mammography cons., various orgns., Fayetteville. Maj. U.S. Army, 1979-85. Fellow Am. Coll. Radiology; mem. Radiol. Soc. N.Am. Roman Catholic. Home: 1412-A Pecan St Cordele GA 31015

LOCHAMY, RICHARD EDWARD, physician; b. Gadsden, Ala., Jan. 28, 1955; s. Edward Harold and Edna Louise (Farrar) L.; m. Marlene Ruth Hebert, June 3, 1978; 1 child, Chelsea Pri. BS, U. Tex., Galveston, 1980; MD, Autonomous Universidad de Guadalajara, Mexico, 1988. Pvt. practice physician Junction City, Kans., 1993—; med. dir. Geary County Diabetes Assn., Junction City, 1995—. Recipient John J. Calabro award for House Officer of the Year St. Vincent's Hosp., 1993. Mem. AMA, Kans. Med. Assn. Office: 1106 St Marys Rd # 306 Junction City KS 66441

LOCHEN, GREGORY ROBERT, ophthalmology; b. Milw., Sept. 11, 1946; s. Robert Earl and Marjorie Ruth (Huxtable) L.; m. Suzanne Ella Mueller, Sept. 6, 1969; children: Eric Matthew, Kristen Anne. BS, U. Wis., 1968, MD, 1972. Pvt. practice Waukesha, Wis., 1977—. Vol. soccer coach Brookfield Soccer Club, 1982-92. Fellow Am. Acad. Ophthalmology, Am. Coll. Surgeons. Protestant. Office: Medical Eye Assocs 1111 Delafield St Waukesha WI 53188

LOCKE, EDWIN ALLEN, III, psychologist, educator; b. N.Y.C., May 15, 1938; s. Edwin Allen and Dorothy (Clark) L.; m. Anne Hassard, June 13, 1968. B.A., Harvard U., 1960; M.A., Cornell U., 1962, Ph.D., 1964. Assoc. research scientist Am. Inst. Research, 1964-66, research scientist, 1966-70; asst. prof. psychology U. Md., College Park, 1967-69; assoc. prof. U. Md., 1969-70, assoc. prof. bus., mgmt. and psychology, 1970-73, prof., 1973-96; chmn. faculty mgt. and orgn. Coll. Bus. and Mgmt. U. Md., College Park, 1984-96. Author: A Guide to Effective Study, 1975; co-author: Goal Setting: A Motivational Technique That Works, 1984, A Theory of Goal Setting and Task Performance, 1990, The Essence of Leadership, 1991; editor: Generalizing from Laboratory to Field Settings, 1986; cons. editorial bd. Organizational Behavior and Human Decision Processes, J. Applied Psychology; contbr. articles to profl. jours. Office Naval Research grantee, 1964, 79; NIMH grantee, 1967; Army Rsch. Inst. grantee, 1993. Fellow APA, Acad. Mgmt., Am. Psychol. Soc., Soc. Indsl. and Orgnl. Psychology (Disting Scientific Contbn. award 1993). Home: 30 Old Mill Bottom Rd N Annapolis MD 21401 Office: U Md Coll Bus and Mgmt College Park MD 20742

LOCKE, STEVEN ELLIOT, psychiatrist; b. Englewood, N.J., Dec. 2, 1945; m. Joanne Callahan, 1984; children: Alexandra Callahan Locke, Graham Sahl Bengen. AB, Cornell U., 1968; MD, Columbia U., 1972. Diplomate Am. Bd. Psychiatry and Neurology. Rotating intern Mt. Zion Hosp. and Med. Ctr., San Francisco, 1972-73; resident in psychiatry McLean Hosp., Belmont, Mass., 1974-77; clin. fellow in psychiatry Med. Dept. MIT, Cambridge, 1976-77; fellow in psychosomatic medicine Boston U. Sch. Medicine, 1977-78; asst. attending physician U. Calif., Berkeley, 1973-74; clin. assoc. in psychosomatic med. U. Hosp., Boston, 1977-79; assoc. in psychiatry Beth Israel Hosp., Boston, 1980-84, asst. psychiatrist, 1985-87, assoc. psychiatrist, 1987—, dir. med. student edn., psychiatry dept., 1989-95; rsch. psychiatrist to U. Health Svc., Harvard U., Cambridge, 1976-81, psychology dept. MIT, 1983-85; dir. Computers in Psychiatry, Ctr. for Clin. Computing, Harvard Med. Sch., 1987—; dir. psychiatry Beth Israel/Children's Hosp. Med. Care Ctr., Lexington, Mass., 1993-94; asst. prof. Harvard Med. Sch., 1987—, MIT, 1993—; chief behavioral medicine Harvard Pilgrim Health Care, 1995—; instr. various acads., instns.; numerous coms. and task force including AIDS Task Force, Beth Israel Hosp., 1987—, psychiatry dept. Harvard Med. Sch., 1987—; mem. Sci. Adv. Coun., Inst. for Advancement of Health, 1983-91, Commonwealth, Bolinas, Calif., 1987—. Assoc. editor: Biofeedback and Self-Regulation jour., 1984-87; series editor: Psychological and Behavioral Treatments of Medical Disorders, 1984-88; editorial bd. Medical Psychotherapy, Psychotherapy and Psychosomatics, 1987-91, M.D. Computing, Am. Health, Am. Jour. Health Promotion, Psychoanalytic Quarterly, others; contbr. articles to profl. jours. Active Mass. Div. Am. Cancer Soc., 1977-80, chmn. task force on support groups, 1979-80. Recipient Young Investigator award, Nat. Cancer Inst., 1980-83, Columbia Presbyn. Med. Soc. Rsch. award, 1972, Hon. Mention Scientific Exhibit, AMA, 1977, First Prize Scientific Exhibit, Am. Coll. Emergency Physicians, 1977; named Daniel Alpern Rsch. Fellow, Columbia U. Coll. Physicians and Surgeons, N.Y.C., 1971-72, Rsch. Fellow in Biobehavioral Sci., Boston U. Sch. of Medicine, 1978-80. Fellow Am. Psychiat. Assn.; mem. Mass. Psychiat. Soc. (pub. affairs com. 1989—), Am. Psychosomatic Soc. (chair pub. affairs com. 1993—), Soc. Behavioral Medicine, Boston Computer Soc., Am. Group Psychotherapy Assn., Am. Med. Informatics Assn., Am. Soc. Clin. Exptl. Hypnosis, Internat. Soc. Clin. Hypnosis, Am. Psychosomatic Soc. (chair pub. affairs com., coun. 1996—, program com.). Home: 27 Camden Rd Newton MA 02166-1503 Office: Beth Israel Hosp 330 Brookline Ave Boston MA 02215-5400

LOCKE, TIMOTHY JOHN, cardiothoracic surgeon; b. Leicester, Eng., Nov. 14, 1954; s. Peter Robert and Ann (Eyre) L.; m. Anne Brennan, July 30, 1977; children: Victoria, Alexandra, Jonathan. M.B.Ch.B., Sheffield (Eng.) U., 1978, MD, 1989. Registrar Freeman Hosp., Newcastle-upon-Tyne, Eng., 1984-87; sr. registrar No. Gen. Hosp., Sheffield, Eng., 1987-90; clin. fellow Mayo Clinic, Rochester, Minn., 1989; cons. No. Gen. Hosp., Sheffield, 1990—; dir. Heart and Lung Transplant Unit No. Gen. Hosp., 1992—; examiner Royal Coll. Surgeons, Edinburgh, 1995—. Contbr. chpts. to books. Fellow Royal Coll. Surgeons (Edinburgh); mem. Soc. Cardiothoracic Surgeons, Brit. Med. Assn., Internat. Soc. Heart and Lung Transplantation. Office: No Gen Hosp Cardio Surgery dept, Herries Rd, Sheffield S5 7AU, England

LOCKEBY, KYLE E., JR., health care administrator, consultant; b. Avon Park, Fla., Aug. 4, 1927; s. Kyle E. and Lorine (Haire) L.; m. Mary Helen Paul, July 27, 1950; children: Mary Lorine Horn, Paul Edward Lockeby. Degree in Bus. Adminstrn., Bryant Coll., Smithfield, R.I., 1949, degree in Bus. Adminstrn. (hon.), 1987. Diplomate Fla. State Bd. Nursing Home Examiners. Owner Huntington Square, Inc., Daytona Beach, Fla., 1969—; adminstr. Huntinton Square Convalarium, Daytona Beach, Fla., 1969-77; pres. Jenkins-Lockeby Assocs, Inc., Daytona Beach, Fla., 1971—; adminstr. Daytona Beach Geriatric Ctr., Daytona Beach, Fla., 1975-79; regional dir. Mediplex, Inc., Jackson, Mich., 1975-80; adminstr. St. Catherine's La Bouré Manor, Jacksonville, Fla., 1979-80; chmn. bd. Sr. Am. Mgmt., Inc., Daytona Beach, 1994—; chmn. Fla. State Bd. Nursing Home Adminstrs., Tallahassee, 1973-80; mem. Health Planning Coun. Northeast Fla., 1979-82. Dir. emeritus Living Gifts Found. for Coun. on Aging, Daytona Beach, 1986; lif emem. U.S. Jaycees Melbourne chpt., 1957—. Fellow Am. Coll. Health Care Adminstrn.; mem. Am. Health Care Assn., Fla. Health Care Assn. (Walter M. Johnson award 1975), Rotary. Democrat. Episcopal. Home: 2201 S Peninsula Dr Daytona Beach FL 32118 Office: Jenkins-Lockeby Assocs. 410 N Halifax Ave Daytona Beach FL 32118

LOCKEY, RICHARD FUNK, allergist, educator; b. Lancaster, Pa., Jan. 15, 1940; s. Stephen Daniel and Anna (Funk) L.; m. Carol Lee Madill, July 3, 1982; children: Brian Christopher, Keith Edward. B.S., Haverford Coll., 1961; M.D., Temple U., 1965; M.S., U. Mich., 1972. Diplomate Am. Bd. Internal Medicine, Am. Bd. Allergy and Immunology. Intern Temple U. Med. Sch., Phila., 1965-66; asst. resident internal medicine Univ. Hosp. U. Mich., Ann Arbor, 1966-67, resident, 1966-68, fellow in allergy and immunology, 1969-70; asst. prof. medicine U. South Fl. Coll. Medicine, Tampa, 1973-77, assoc. prof. medicine, 1977-83, asst. dir. div. allergy and immunology, 1979-82, dir. allergy and immunology, 1982—, prof. medicine, 1983—, prof. pediats., 1983—, prof. pub. health, 1987—; asst. chief sect. allergy and immunology VA Hosp., Tampa, 1973-82, chief sect. allergy and immunology, 1983—; mem. allergenic adv. com. FDA, 1985-89. Editor: Allergy and Clinical Immunology, 1980 co-editor: (with S.C. Bukantz) Fundamentals of Immunology and Allergy, 1987, (with S.C. Bukantz) Principles of Immunology and Allergy, 1987, JAMA Primer on Allergic and Immunologic Diseases, 1987, (with S. C. Bukantz) Allergen Immunotherapy, 1991, (with M. Levine) Monograph on Insect Allergy, 1995; contbr. articles to profl. jours. and chpts. to books; author monographs. Served to maj. USAF, 1971-73. Named Outstanding Med. Specialist, Town and Country Mag., 1989, Claude P. Brown Meml. lectr. Assn. Clin. Scientists, ADA, 1981, Disting. Visitor Ann. Meeting of Coll. of Medicine, Republic of Costa Rica, 1979, spl. mem. Internat. Sci. Bd. Pharmacia Allergy Rsch. Found., 1992—; recpient Alumni Achievement award Temple U. Sch. of Medicine Alumni Assn., 1990, Outstanding Leadership in Chpt. Devel. and Patient Support, Nat. Asthma and Allergy Found. of Am. award, 1992, Cert. of Appreciation, Fla. Med. Assn., 1992. Fellow ACP, AAAS, AMA, Am. Coll. Chest Physicians, Am. Acad. Allergy and Immunology (chmn. com. on insects 1978-81, chmn. undergrad. and grad. edn. com. 1982-88, com. on occupational lung disease 1982—, chmn. com. on standardization of allergenic extracts 1983-86, exec. com. mem. at large 1986-88, historian 1988-89, sec. 1989-90, treas. 1990-91, pres.-elect 1991-92, pres. 1992-93, Am. Bd. Allergy and Immunology (bd. dirs. 1993—), Soc. Allergy and Immunology of Cordoba, Argentina (hon.), John M. Sheldon U. of Mich. Allergy Soc. (councilor 1977-80, pres. 1980-82), Fla. Allergy and Immunology Soc. (sec.-treas. 1979-80, pres. 1981-82), Southeastern Allergy Assn., Hillsborough County Med. Assn., Joint Coun. Allergy and Immunology, Clin. Immunology Soc., Fla. Thoracic Soc., Univ. Club, Carrollwood Village Club. Clubs: Carrollwood Village (Tampa), University. Home: 3909 Northampton Way Tampa FL 33624-4443 Office: U So Fla VA Hosp 13000 Bruce B Downs Blvd Tampa FL 33612-4745

LOCKMAN, LAWRENCE ALLEN, pediatric neurologist; b. Cleve., Nov. 4, 1937; s. Maurice and Rose Alice (Printz) L.; m. Nancy Jo Mattie, June 24, 1962 (div. 1981); children: Paula Jo, Miriam Ellen; m. Dianne Lynn McClay, Jan. 2, 1982; children: Kristian Alfred Brogger, Rachel Charlotte Lockman. AB, Brown U., 1959; MD, Western Res. U., 1963. Diplomate Am. Bd. Pediatrics, Am. Bd. Psychiatry and Neurology. Asst. prof. U. Minn., Mpls., 1971-78, assoc. prof., 1978—. Assoc. editor Pediatric Neurology jour., 1984—. Capt. USAF, 1966-68. Fellow Am. Acad. Pediatrics, Am. Acad. Neurology; mem. Child Neurology Soc. (sec., treas.), AAAS, Sigma Xi. Home: 5247 Clinton Ave Minneapolis MN 55419-1464 Office: Div Pediatric Neurology 445 Umhc 12 169 Pwb Minneapolis MN 55455

LOCKWOOD, BARBARA LYNN, podiatrist; b. Erie, Pa., July 8, 1952; d. Theodore Raymond and Barbara Ann (Loesch) L. BS, John Carroll U., 1974; DPM, Ohio Coll Podiatric Medicine, 1979. Pvt. practice Erie, Pa., 1980—. Mem. Mensa. Home: 8622 Gudgeonville Rd Girard PA 16417 Office: 938 Powell Ave Erie PA 16505

LOCKWOOD, FRANCES MANN, clinical psychologist; b. Washington, June 20, 1946; d. Ernest Daniel Mann and Thelma Gertrude (Gheen) Hubert; m. Bruce Robert Lockwood, May 10, 1975; children: Kathleen Gail, Karen Ann. BA, U. Richmond, 1968; MA, U. Tenn., 1971, PhD, 1973. Lic. psychologist, Tenn., Va. Intern. VA Hosp., Memphis, 1971-72; staff psychologist children's youth program Helen Ross McNabb Ctr., Knoxville, Tenn., 1973-75; staff psychologist, asst. dir. psychology Commonwealth Psychiat. Ctr., Richmond, Va., 1975-77; pvt. practice as clin. psychologist, Arlington and Alexandria, Va., 1978-81, Jackson, Tenn., 1982-93; staff psychologist Pathways, Inc., 1993—; coord. children's and youth svcs. West Tenn. Behavioral Ctr., 1993-95; bd. dirs. In-Home Care Planning, Inc., 1987-89, Montessori Ctr. of Jackson, 1991—. Mem. Child Abuse Rev. Team, Madison County, Tenn., 1985-90, Child Protection Investigative Team, 1994—; mem. steering com. Jackson chpt. Assn. Children With Learning Disabilities, 1985; mem. Leadership Jackson, 1985; sec. Andrew Jackson PTA, 1987-88. Mem. APA, Tenn. Psychol. Assn. (ins. com. 1984-85, Leadership Conf. 1990-91), Southeastern Psychol. Assn., Jackson Bus. & Profl. Women's Club (2d v.p. 1985, pres. 1986-87), Psi Chi (Book award 1968). Home: 148 Laurie Cir Jackson TN 38305-3045 Office: Ste 216 1804 Hwy 45 Bypass Jackson TN 38305-3906

LODER, JUDITH A., sexual abuse program administrator; b. N.J., Dec. 10, 1947; d. Vincent and Agnes (Milko) Aquavia; m. Daniel J. Loder, Feb. 6, 1969; children: Lisa, Stacy, Daniel. AS, Ocean County Coll., 1982; BSW, Stockton State Coll., 1985; MSW, Rutgers U., 1986. Cert sch. social workers, rape counselor, cert. crisis intervention instr.; diplomate in clin. social work. Crisis intervention counselor St. Francis Counseling Ctr., Long Beach Island, N.J.; supr. emergency svcs. Shore Mental Health Ctr., Lakewood, N.J.; family therapist CPC Mental Health Svcs., Freehold, N.J.; program dir. Family Growth Program of Cath. Charities. Mem. NASW, Parents United (coord. Monmouth County chpt.), Am. Profl. Soc. on the Abuse of Children, N.J. Network for the Treatment of Sex Offenders, Acad. of Cert. Social Workers, Phi Theta Kappa. Home: 44 Hillcrest Rd Holmdel NJ 07733-1600

LODWICK, GWILYM SAVAGE, radiologist, educator; b. Mystic, Iowa, Aug. 30, 1917; s. Gwylim S. and Lucy A. (Fuller) L.; m. Maria Antonia De Brito Barata; children by previous marriage: Gwilym Savage III, Philip Galligan, Malcolm Kerr, Terry Ann. Student, Drake U., 1934-35; B.S., State U. Iowa, 1942, M.D., 1943. Resident pathology State U. Iowa, 1947-48, resident radiology, 1948-50; fellow, sr. fellow radiologic and orthopedic pathology Armed Forces Inst. Pathology, 1951; asst., then asso. prof. State U. Iowa Med. Sch., 1951-56; prof. radiology, chmn. dept. U. Mo. at Columbia Med. Sch., 1956-78, research prof. radiology, 1978-83, interim chmn. dept. radiology, 1980-81, chmn. dept. radiology, 1981-83, prof. bioengring., 1969-83, acting dean, 1959, assoc. dean, 1959-64; assoc. radiologist Mass. Gen. Hosp., 1983-88, radiologist, 1988-91; hon. radiologist Mass. Gen. Hosp., Boston, 1991—; vis. prof. dept. radiology Harvard Med. Sch., 1983-93; cons. in field; vis. prof. Keio U. Sch. Medicine, Tokyo, 1974; chmn. sci. program com. Internat. Conf. on Med. Info., Amsterdam, 1983; trustee Am. Registry Radiologic Technologists, 1961-69, pres., 1964-65, 68-69; mem. radiology tng. com. Nat. Inst. Gen. Med. Scis., NIH, 1966-70; com. radiology Nat. Acad. Scis.-NRC, 1970-75; chmn. com. computers Am. Coll. Radiology, 1965, Internat. Commn. Radiol. Edn. and Info., 1969-73; cons. to health care tech. div. Nat. Ctr. for Health Services, Research and Devel., 1971-76; dir. Mid-Am. Bone Tumor Diagnostic Ctr. and Registry, 1971-83; adv. com. mem. NIH Biomed. Image Processing Grant Jet Propulsion Lab., 1969-73; nat. chmn. MUMPS Users Group, 1973-75; mem. radiation study sect. div. research grants NIH, 1976-79, mem. study sect. on diagnostic radiology and nuclear medicine div. research grants, 1979-82, chmn. study sect. on diagnostic radiology div. research grants, 1980-82; mem. bd. sci. counselors Nat. Library of Medicine, 1985, chmn. 1987-89; dir. radiology Spaulding Rehab. Hosp., 1986-92. Adv. editorial bd. Radiology, 1965-86, cons. to editor, 1986-91; adv. editorial bd. Current/Clin. Practice, 1972-88; mem. editorial bd. Jour. Med. Systems, 1976—, Radiol. Sci. Update div. Biomedia, Inc., 1975-83, Critical Revs. in Linguistic Imaging, 1990; mem. cons. editorial bd. Skeletal Radiology, 1977-92, Contemporary Diagnostic Radiology, 1978-80; assoc. editor Jour. Med. Imaging, 1988—. Served to maj. AUS, 1943-46, ETO. Decorated Sakari Mustakallio medal Finland; named Most Disting. Alumnus in Radiology, State U. Ia. Centennial, 1970; recipient Sigma Xi Research award U. Mo., Columbia, 1972, Gold medal XIII Internat. Conf. Radiology, Madrid, 1973, Founder's Gold medal Internat. Skeletal Soc., 1990. Fellow AMA (radiology rev. bd. coun. med. edn., coun. rep. on residency rev. com. for radiology 1969-74), Am. Coll. Radiology (co-chmn. ACR-NEMA standardization com. 1983-90, NEMA Med. Tech. Leadership award 1995); mem. NAS Inst. Medicine, Am. Coll. Med. Informatics (founding), Nat. Acad. Practice in Medicine, Radiol. Soc. N.Am. (3d v.p. 1974-75, chmn. ad hoc com. representing assoc. scis. 1979-87, chmn. assoc. scis. com. 1981-87), Assn. Univ. Radiologists, Mo. Radiol. Soc. (1st pres. 1961-62), Salutis Unitas; hon. mem. Portuguese Soc. Radiology and Nuclear Medicine, Tex. Radiol. Soc., Ind. Roentgen Soc., Phila. Roentgen Ray Soc., Finnish Radio. Soc. (ho.), Rotary, Harvard of Boston Club, Cosmos, Alpha Omega Alpha. Home: 3900 Galt Ocean Dr Apt 307 Fort Lauderdale FL 33308-6622

LOE, EMMETT BAXTER, social worker; b. Haskell County, Tex., Dec. 28, 1924; s. Stephen Rals and Ellie Lorene (Baker) L.; m. Ruby Nell Ketchersid, Sept. 12, 1946; children: Ronald Wayne, Karen June, Kimberley Grant, Melinda Michelle. Student, Howard Payne U., 1964-66, Amarillo, Coll., 1970-71, West Tex. State U., 1971-72. Ordained to ministry Ch. of Christ, 1961. With Amerada Petroleum Corp., Gaines County, Tex., 1950-61; pastor chs. Brownwood, Tex., 1961-66, Odessa, Tex., 1966-69; chmn. bd. Christian Relief Fund, Amarillo, Tex., 1975—; lectr. in field. Editor Gospel Tidings mag., 1965-75. Bd. dirs. Southwestern Bible Inst., San Angelo, Tex., 1980-83. With USN, 1944-46. Mem. Evang. Council for Fin. Accountability, Amarillo Ministerial Alliance (pres.), Christian Ministries Mgmt. Assn., Rotary (Paul Harris Fellow, pres. Amarillo chpt. 1978-79, chaplain City of Amarillo 1987-89). Republican. Home: 2521 Walnut St Amarillo TX 79107-2047 Office: 4606 River Rd Amarillo TX 79108-5202

LÖE, HARALD, dentist, educator, researcher; b. Steinkjer, Norway, July 19, 1926; s. Haakon and Anna (Bruem) L.; m. Inga Johansen, July 3, 1948; children: Haakon, Marianne. DDS, U. Oslo, 1952; D in Odontology, 1961; hon. degree, U. Gothenburg, 1973, Royal Dental Coll., Aarhus, 1980, U. Athens, 1980, Cath. U., Leuven, 1980, U. Lund, 1983, Georgetown U., 1983, U. Bergen, 1985, U. Md., 1986, U. N.J., 1987, Royal Dental Coll., Copenhagen, 1988, U. Toronto, 1989, U. Detroit, 1990, S.C. Med. U., 1990, U. Helsinki, Finland, 1992, Pacific U., 1993, U. Milan, Italy, 1994. Instr. Sch. Dentistry, Oslo U., 1952-55; rsch. assoc. Norwegian Inst. Dental Rsch., 1956-62; Fulbright rsch. fellow, rsch. assoc. dept. oral pathology U. Ill., Chgo., 1957-58; Univ. rsch. fellow Oslo U., 1959-62, assoc. prof. dept. periodontology, 1960-61; prof. dentistry, chmn. dept. periodontology Royal Dental Coll., Aarhus, Denmark, 1962-72; asso. dean, dean-elect Royal Dental Coll., 1971-72; prof., dir. Dental Rsch. Inst. U. Mich., Ann Arbor, 1972-74; dean, prof. periodontology Sch. Dental Medicine U. Conn., Farmington, 1974-82; dir. Nat. Inst. Dental Rsch. Nat. Inst. Dental Rsch., Bethesda, Md., 1983-94; univ. prof. Sch. Dental Medicine U. Conn. Health Ctr., Farmington, 1994—; vis. prof. periodontics Hebrew U., Jerusalem, 1966-67; hon. prof. Med. Scis. U. Beijing, 1987; cons. WHO, NIH. Contbr. over 300 articles to sci. publs. With Norwegian Army, 1944-48. Recipient 75th Anniversary award Norwegian Dental Assn., 1958, Aalborg Dental Soc. prize, Denmark, 1965, William J. Gies Periodontology award, 1978, Alfred C. Fores medal, U.S. Surgeon Gen.'s medal and Exemplary award, 1988, Internat. award Swedish Dental Assn., 1989, Harvard medal, 1992, Scandinavian Pub. Health award, 1994; decorated Knight of Danebrog by Queen of Denmark, 1972, Comdr. of Royal Norwegian Order of Merit by King of Norway, 1989. Mem. AAAS, ADA (gold medal 1994, Callahan medal 1995, Spenadel medal 1995), Am. Coll. Dentists, Nat. Acad. Inst. Medicine, Danish Dental Assn., Am. Acad. Periodontology, Am. Assn. Dental Rsch. (hon. mem.), Am. Soc. Preventive Dentistry (internat. award), Mass. Dental Soc. (internat. award), Internat. Assn. Dental Rsch. (award for basic rsch. in periodongology 1969, pres. 1980), Internat. Coll. Dentists, Scandinavian Assn. Dental Rsch. Office: U Conn Health Ctr Sch Dental Medicine Farmington CT 06030-1710

LOEB, DEANN JEAN, nurse; b. West Union, Iowa, Aug. 1, 1960; d. Dale Alfred and Annagene Helen (Suhr) Ungerer; m. Thomas Allan Loeb, Sept. 1, 1985; children: Ryan, Jennifer, Andrea, Cody. Diploma in nursing, NE Iowa Tech. Inst., 1982. Lic. practical nurse, Iowa. Laundry aide Good Samaritan Ctr., West Union, 1977, kitchen aide, cook, 1977-79, nurses asst., 1979-81, practical nurse, 1982-84; practical nurse Ind. (Ind.) Care Ctr., 1985-89, Dr. Jose C. Aguiar, Waterloo, Iowa, 1989-93, Dr. John Musgrave-Dr. Mary O'Connell, Waterloo, Iowa, 1993-94; nurse Waterloo Asthma and Allergy Clinic, 1994—. Leader Brownies, asst. leader Girl Scouts U.S.; tchr. Bible, Sunday sch., mem. parish bd. edn., mem. parish life com. Zion Jubilee Luth. Ch., Jesup, Iowa. Republican. Home: 7144 Spring Creek Rd Jesup IA 50648-9568

LOEB, GERARD SERGE, medical director; b. Paris, June 3, 1949; s. Georges and Catherine (Sender) L.; m. Eve Amar, July 1, 1976; children: Michaël, Yaël. MD, Paris U., 1976. Pvt. practice medicine, 1976-89; med. dir. Yamanouchi Pharma, Charenton-le-Pont, France, 1989—. Author: Semaine des hopitaux de Paris, 1978, Le Concours Medical, 1985-87, 90, 94, Revue du Rhumatisme, 1994, Osteoporosis Int, 1995, annales de Dermatologie et de Venereologie, 1995. Mem. French Nat. Com. for Drug Safety, Paris, 1986-90. Office: Yamanouchi Pharma, 10 Place de la Coupole BP 105, 94223 Charenton-le-Pont Cedex France

LOEB, LAURENCE, psychiatrist; b. N.Y.C., Nov. 23, 1929; s. Herman Kaufman and Ruth Theresa (Mayer) L.; m. Saralta Padawer, Dec. 8, 1957; children: Jennifer, Alison, Diana. BS, U. Cin., 1949; MD, SUNY, Bklyn., 1953. Diplomate Am. Bd. Psychiatry and Neurology, Am. Bd. Forensic Psychiatry. Intern L. I. Coll. Hosp., Bklyn., 1953-54; fellow in child adolescent psychiatry Albert Einstein Coll. Medicine, Bronx, N.Y., 1959-60; pvt. practice Hartsdale, N.Y., 1959—; resident in psychiatry N.Y. Hosp.-Westchester Div., 1954-55, 57-59; supervising psychiatrist Grasslands Hosp., Valhalla, N.Y., 1960-61; chief psychiatrist edn. Grasslands Hosp., 1961-62, clin. dir. edn., 1962-64; clin. instr. psychiatry Albert Einstein Coll., Bronx, N.Y., 1959-62; clin. asst. prof. psychiatry Albert Einstein Coll., 1962-65, Cornell U. Med. Coll., N.Y.C., 1965-69; clin. assoc. prof. psychiatry Cornell U. Med. Coll., 1970—; adj. prof. law Pace U., White Plains, N.Y., 1978—; cons. USMA, West Point N.Y., 1968-82, U.S. Dept. Defense, Washington, 1966—, Adoption Soc. Westchester, White Plains, 1970-78, Bedford Hills (N.Y.) Correctional Facility, 1980—. Co-author, co-editor: The Schizophrenic Syndrome, 1968; contbr. articles to profl. jours. Adv. bd. Scarsdale (N.Y.) Adult Sch., 1970-71, bd. trustees, 1971-77. Capt. USMC, AUS, 1955-57. Recipient Pediatrics award Kings County Med. Soc., Bklyn., 1953. Fellow Am. Psychiat. Assn. (life), Am. Soc. Adolescent Psychiatry (life); mem. Westchester County Med. Soc., Psychiat. Soc. Westchester (pres.

1971-72), Am. Acad. Psychiatry and the Law, Argentine Soc. Psychiatry and Psychology Childhood Assn. (hon.). Jewish. Office: 180 E Hartsdale Ave Hartsdale NY 10530-3544

LOEB, VIRGIL, JR., oncologist, hematologist; b. St. Louis, Sept. 21, 1921; s. Virgil and Therese (Meltzer) L.; m. Lenore Harlow, Sept. 8, 1950 (dec. Nov. 1987); children: Katherine Loeb Doumas, Elizabeth Loeb McCane, David, Mark; m. Elizabeth Moore, Dec., 1990. Student, Swarthmore Coll., 1938-41; MD, Washington U., St. Louis, 1944. Diplomate Am. Bd. Internal Medicine. Intern Barnes and Jewish Hosps., St. Louis, 1944-45; resident in internal medicine, research fellow in hematology Barnes Hosp., St. Louis, 1947-52; med. faculty Washington U., St. Louis, 1951—, prof. clin. medicine, 1978-96, prof. emeritus clin. medicine, 1996—; practice medicine specializing in oncology and hematology St. Louis, 1956-96; cons., clin. researcher; dir. Cen. Diagnostic Labs., Barnes Hosp., 1952-68; staff numerous hosps., 1951-96; cons. Nat. Cancer Inst., 1966-96, chmn. cancer clin. investigation rev. com., 1966-69, mem. diagnostic research adv. com., 1972-75, bd. sci. counselors, DCPC, 1983-87; mem. oncology merit rev. bd. VA, 1971-75. Contbr. author books, articles to profl. jours. Bd. dirs. Am. Cancer Soc., mem. nat. adv. com., 1969—, pres. Mo. div., 1983-85, nat. pres., 1986-87; bd. dirs. St. Louis Blue Cross and Blue Shield, Bi-State Red Cross; trustee John Burroughs Sch., 1966-69. Served with M.C. AUS, 1945-47. Fellow ACP; mem. Cen. Soc. Clin. Research, Inst. Medicine of Nat. Acad. Sci., Am. Assn. Cancer Research, Internat. Soc. Hematology, Am. Soc. Hematology, St. Louis Soc. Internal Medicine (pres. 1974), Am. Soc. Clin. Oncology, Am. Assn. for Cancer Edn., St. Louis Met. Med. Soc. (hon.), Sigma Xi, Alpha Omega Alpha. Home: 24 Deerfield Rd Saint Louis MO 63124-1412 Office: Barnes Hosp 1 Barnes Hospital Plz Saint Louis MO 63110

LOEFF, DEBORAH SUSAN, pediatric surgeon; b. Chgo., Apr. 14, 1950; d. Harold M. and Phyllis Ann (Saxon) L. BA, Sarah Lawrence Coll., N.Y.C., 1972; MD, Rush Med. Coll., Chgo., 1977. Intern, resident in gen. surgery U. Utah Med. Ctr., Salt Lake City, 1978-84; fellow in clin. nutrition Babies Hosp./Columbia-Presbyn-St. Luke's Med. Ctr., N.Y.C., 1981-82; fellow in pediatric surery Hosp. for Sick Children, Toronto, 1984-87; asst. prof. surgery U. Ill., Chgo., 1987-91; attending surgeon Cook County Hosp., Chgo., 1987—; asst. prof., head sect. pediatric surgery Rush-Presbyn. St. Luke's Med. Ctr., Chgo., 1990—; attending surgeon Christ Hosp., Oak Lawn, Ill., 1995—. Co-author: Shackleford's Surgery of the Alimentary Tract, 1995. Fellow ACS, Am. Acad. Pediatrics (surg. sect.); mem. Ill. Pediatric Surg. Assn., Can. Assn. Pediatric Surgeons, Brit. Assn. Pediatric Surgeons. Office: Midwest Pediat Surg Assocs PC 4400 W 95th St Oak Lawn IL 60453

LOEFFLER, ROBERTA LYNN, physician general practice; b. Hill City, Kans., Feb. 10, 1956; d. Ervin Lloyd and Marilyn (Hodel) L.; m. J. Timothy Fey, Oct. 24, 1992. BS in Chemistry, Emporia State U., 1978; MS in Chemistry, Purdue U., 1980; MD, Washington U., St. Louis, 1984. Lic. physician, Mo. Resident in medicine Jewish Hosp., St. Louis, Mo., 1984-87; chief resident in medicine Jewish Hosp., St. Louis, 1987-88, physician emergency dept., 1988-90; dir. student health Washington U., St. Louis, 1990-92; physician pvt. practice Ctrl. Med. Group, St. Louis, 1989—. Recipient 3M fellowship Purdue U. Mem. ACP, St. Louis Met. Med. Soc. Roman Catholic. Office: Ctrl Med Group 4932 Forest Park St Ste 7B Saint Louis MO 63108

LOELLGEN, HERBERT HANS, cardiologist; b. Bonn, Fed. Republic Germany, Jan. 5, 1943; s. Artur and Maria (Decker) L.; m. Inge Horres, Apr. 28, 1944; children: Ruth, Deborah, Noëmi, Eva. MD, Rheinische Friedrich Wilhelms U. Bonn, 1968; PhD, U. Mainz, 1979. Asst. prof. U. Mainz, Fed. Republic Germany, 1970-72, 77-78, Hosp. Bethanien, Moers, Fed. Republic Germany, 1973-76; vice-head dept. cardiology U. Freiburg, Fed. Republic Germany, 1978-82; head dept. med., cardiology Hosp. Limburg, Fed. Republic Germany, 1983-85, Mcpl. Hosp. Remscheid, Fed. Republic Germany, 1986—. Author: Ergometrie, 1983, Kardiopulmonale Funktionsdiagnostik, 1983, 3d edit., 1995, EKG-Beurteilung, 1986; (with G. Meuret) Reanimation, 1988, 2d edit. 1995; editor: Herz-Rhythmusstörungen, 1983, Progress in Ergometry, 1984, Advances in Ergometry, 1990. Chmn. working group ergometry UNESCO; mem. Med. Bd. German Astronauts. Fellow Am. Coll. Cardiology, Am. Heart Assn. (internat.); mem. Assn. Sports Medicine (pres. 1986—), Aerospace Med. Assn. (space medicine br.), several internat. and nat. med. socs. Roman Catholic. Home: Bermesgasse 32B, D-5630 Remscheid Germany Office: Mcpl Hosp, Burger Str 211, D-2897 Remscheid Germany

LOERAKKER, JO ANN KATHERINE, chiropractic physician; b. Springfield, Ill., Dec. 9, 1941; d. Joseph Francis and Virginia Ann (Seifert) L.; m. Frederick Frank, Jr., Jan. 12, 1980. BA, U. Ill., 1964, MS, 1965; BS, Nat. Chiropractic Coll., Lombard, Ill., 1979, D of Chiropractic, 1979. Cert. disability rating, Nat. Bd. Chiropractic Examiners. Research asst. Loyola U., Hines, Ill., 1965-66; acting head Electron Microscopy, Michael Reese Hosp., Chgo., 1966-67; info. specialist Quaker Oats Co., Barrington, Ill., 1967-68; assoc. prof. Wilbur Wright Coll., Chgo., 1968-79; assoc. chiropractor Frank Chiropractic Clinic, Miami, Fla., 1980-81; owner Gallatin Chiropractic Clinic, Gallatin, Tenn., 1981—; lectr. Vol. State Community Coll., Gallatin, Tenn., 1981—; panelist, speaker, Ill. Chemical Council, Chgo., 1967-68. Bd. dirs. Ill. Walking Horse Assn., Springfield, Ill., 1970, 72-73, sec. 1971; Colo. equine dir. Morris Animal Found., 1974-75, 76; sec. ann. horse show Lions Club, Gallatin. Mem. Fla. Chiropractic Assn., Sumner Saddle Club (v.p. 1989). Republican. Roman Catholic. Home: 1061 Hwy 25 Gallatin TN 37066-6102 Office: Gallatin Chiropractic Clin 590 Hartsville Pike Gallatin TN 37066-2450

LOEW, FRANKLIN MARTIN, medical and biological scientist; b. Syracuse, N.Y., Sept. 8, 1939; s. David Franklin and Sarah (Adelaide) L.; children: Timothy, Andrew. B.S., Cornell U., 1961, D.V.M., 1965; Ph.D., U. Sask., 1971. Lic. veterinarian; diplomate Am. Coll. Lab. Animal Medicine. Research asst. R.J. Reynolds Co., Winston-Salem, N.C., 1965-66; research asst. Tulane U., New Orleans, 1966-67; prof. U. Sask., Saskatoon, Can., 1967-77; dir. comparative medicine Johns Hopkins U., Balt., 1977-82; dean Sch. Vet. Medicine, Tufts U., Boston, 1982-95, Henry and Lois Foster prof. comparative medicine, 1985-95; v.p. Tufts U. Devel. Corp. Inc., Boston, 1991-95; pres. Tufts Biotech. Corp., Boston, 1993-95; dean Coll. Vet. Medicine, Cornell U., Ithaca, N.Y., 1995—; cons. Can. Coun. Animal Care, Ottawa, Ont., 1969-84; mem. life scis. com. Nat. Acad. Sci., Washington, 1981-88, chmn. Inst. Lab. Animal Resources, 1981-87; mem. FDA Commn. on Sr. Biomed. Rsch. Svc. Credentials, 1995—; N.B. lectr. Am. Soc. Microbiology; mem. nat. adv. bd. Ctr. on Bioethics Lit., Kennedy Inst. Georgetown U., 1986—; Schofield lectr. U. Guelph, Can.; Smith lectr. U. Sask.; Schalm lectr. U. Calif.; univ. lectr. Tex. A&M U.; bd. dirs. Mass. Biotech. Rsch. Inst., Commonwealth BioVentures, Inc.; mem. sci. adv. com. Harvard Primate Rsch. Ctr., 1988—, Mass. Health Resources Inst.; sci. and tech. adv. com. State of Mass., 1988-92; mem. USDA Sec.'s Adv. Com. Nat. Rsch. Initiative, 1992—; pres. Tufts Biotech. Corp., 1993-95; bd. trustees Marine Biol. Lab., 1990-94, New Eng. Aquarium, 1991-95, Guys Drug Rsch. Unit, U.K., 1993-94; mem. panel animal health Nat. Rsch. Coun., 1992—. Author: Vet in the Saddle, 1978; editor: Laboratory Animal Medicine, 1984; contbr. numerous articles to profl. jours. Chmn. bd. trustees Boston Zool. Soc., 1984-88; trustee Worcester Acad. 1984-90; mem. Nat. Ctr. Rsch. Resources adv. coun. NIH, 1988-92, Blue Ribbon adv. coun. USDA, 1987-91; bd. dirs. Ea. States Exhbn.m 1988-85; bd. dirs. Mass. SPCA, 1996—;mem. bus. bd. Pharmacia & Upjohn, 1996—. Decorated Queen Elizabeth II Jubilee medal Gov.-Gen. Can., 1977; Med. Rsch. Coun. Can. fellow, 1969-71; recipient Charles River prize Am. Vet. Med. Assn., 1988, named Vet. of Yr., 1989; recipient Disting. Svc. award Mass. Vet. Med. Assn., 1992. Mem. NAS/Inst. Medicine, AAAS, Am. Inst. Nutrition, Soc. Toxicology, Assn. Am. Vet. Med. Colls. (pres. 1985-86), Am. Coll. Lab. Medicine (bd. dirs. 1979-82), Nat. Acads. Practice, Fedn. Am. Socs. for Exptl. Biology, Am. Antiquarian Soc., Mass. Agrl. Club. Office: Cornell U Coll Vet Medicine Ithaca NY 14853-6401

LOEWENSTEIN, JOSEPH EDWARD, endocrinologist, medical educator; b. Crockett, Tex., Nov. 25, 1937; s. Joseph Meyer and Ethel Lois (Fallis) L.; m. Marjorie Marie Thomson, Aug. 16, 1958; children: Sarah F., Edward B. BA with highest honors, U. Tex., 1959; MD cum laude, Washington U., 1963. Diplomate in internal medicine, endocrinology and metabolism Am. Bd. Internal Medicine. Intern internal medicine Barnes Hosp., St. Louis, 1963-64, resident internal medicine, 1967-69; rsch. assoc. Nat. Cancer Inst., NIH, Bethesda, Md., 1964-66; staff mem. Nat. Cancer Inst., NIH, Bethesda, 1966-67; fellow in metabolism Washington U., St. Louis, 1969-70, instr. internal medicine, 1970; asst. prof. medicine La. State U., Sch. Medicine, Shreveport, 1970-73, assoc. prof. medicine, 1973-78, prof. medicine, 1978-84, clin. prof. medicine, 1984-91, chief sect. of endocrinology and metabolism, 1970-84; pvt. cons. practice of endocrinology and metabolism Shreveport, 1984-91; chief divsn. endocrinology and metabolism, dept. medicine Meridia Huron Hosp., Cleve., 1991—; assoc. clin. prof. medicine Case Western Res. U., Cleve., 1992—; cons. endocrinologic and metabolic drugs adv. com. U.S. FDA, Rockville, Md., 1976, 84-85, mem. endocrinologic and metabolic drugs adv. com., 1980-84, chmn., 192-84, cons. fertility and maternal health drugs adv. com., 1982-83. Mem. editl. bd. Jour. Intensive Care Medicine, 1993—; contbr. articles to profl. jours. Bd. govs. Gilbert and Sullivan Soc. of Shreveport, 1970-91, pres., 1973-76; bd. dirs. Shreveport Opera, 1972-91, pres., 1975-78; bd. dirs. Am. Diabetes Assn. La. Affiliate, Baton Rouge, 1985-90; trustee Diabetes Assn. Greater Cleve., 1992—; v.p. edn. Cleve. Opera League, 1994-96. Lt. USPHS, 1964-67. Fellow ACP; mem. The Endocrine Soc., Phi Beta Kappa, Alpha Omega Alpha. Office: Meridia Huron Hosp Dept Medicine 13951 Terrace Rd Cleveland OH 44112

LOEWY, DAVID MICHAEL, ophthalmologist; b. Detroit, Nov. 6, 1955; s. Sheldon and Anne (Cooperstein) L.; m. Mary Jill Bailey, May 10, 1981; children: Shannon Mary, Evan Michael. BA magna cum laude, Wayne State U., 1977; MD, U. Mich., 1981. Diplomate Am. Bd. Ophthalmology. Intern Henry Ford Hosp., Detroit, 1981-82; resident in ophthalmology Ea. Va. Med. Sch., Norfolk, 1982-85, chief resident, 1984; pvt. practice, Bartow, Fla., 1985-87, Winter Haven, Fla., 1987—. Contbr. articles to med. jours. Fellow ACS, Am. Acad. Ophthalmology; mem. AMA, Fla. Med. Assn., Am. Soc. Cataract and Refractive Surgery, Polk County Med. Assn. (program chmn. 1989-90, pres. 1996—), Fla. Soc. Ophthalmology, Eye Bank Assn. Am., Winter Haven C. of C., Phi Beta Kappa. Home: 49 Skidmore Rd Winter Haven FL 33884-3039 Office: Eye Clinic Mid-Fla 407 Avenue K SE Winter Haven FL 33880-4126

LOFLAND, GARY KENNETH, cardiac surgeon; b. Milford, Del., Mar. 5, 1951; s. Joseph Sudler and Doris Louise (Peters) L.; m. Janice Marie Show, Feb. 3, 1979; children: Kiernan Sudler, Glennis Kathleen. BA cum laude, Boston U., 1969, MD cum laude, 1975. Diplomate Am. Bd. Surgery, Am. Bd. Thoracic Surgery; lic. physician, Va., N.Y., Mont., N.C. Intern, jr. asst. resident in surgery Duke U. Med. Ctr., Durham, N.C., 1975-81; rsch. fellow dept. surgery Duke U. Med. Ctr., Durham, 1979-81, sr. asst. resident in surgery, 1981-84, chief resident in surgery, 1984-85, teaching scholar in cardiac surgery, 1985-86; sr. registrar in cardiothoracic surgery Hosp. for Sick Children, London, 1986-87; dir. cardiovascular surgery Children's Hosp. of Buffalo, 1987-88; asst. prof. surgery SUNY, Buffalo, 1987-88; assoc. prof. surgery/pediatrics, Med. Coll. Va., Richmond, 1988-94, dir. pediatric cardiac surgery/med. dir. cardiac surgery ICU, 1988-94; clin. prof. surgery Georgetown U., Washington, 1994—; dir. Columbia/HCA Ctr. Congenital Heart Disease, Richmond, 1994—. Editorial rev. bd. Progress in Pediatric Cardiology, Year Book of Thoracic Surgery; contbr. articles to profl. jours. Pres. Am. Heart Assn., Richmond; mem. bd. trustees Transplant Found. Lt. comdr. USPHS, 1977-79. Recipient Univ. Hosp. Trustees award, Boston, 1975; HEW/USPHS commendation medal, 1979. Mem. AMA, Am. Heart Assn., Assn. for Acad. Surgery, Internat. Soc. for Heart Transplantation, Med. Soc. Va., Richmond Acad. Medicine, Richmond Surg. Soc., So. Thoracic Surg. Assn., Soc. for Thoracic Surgeons, Congenital Heart Surgeons Soc., , Alpha Omega Alpha. Home: 740 Lee Rd PO Box 126 Crozier VA 23039 Office: Columbia/HCA Ctr Congenital Heart Disease 7602 Forest Ave Ste 208 Richmond VA 23229

LOFTON, KEVIN EUGENE, medical facility administrator; b. Beaumont, Tex., Sept. 29, 1954. BS, Boston U., 1976; M Health Care Adminstrn., Ga. State U., 1979. Adminstrv. resident Meml. Med. Ctr., Corpus Christi, Tex., 1978-79; adminstr. emergency svcs. Univ. Hosp., Jacksonville, Fla., 1979-80, adminstr. material mgmt., 1980-81, asst. exec. dir. ambulatory care, 1981-82, asst. v.p. ambulatory svcs., 1982-83, v.p. profl. svcs., 1983-86; exec. v.p. Univ. Med. Ctr., Jacksonville, 1986-90; exec. dir. Howard Univ. Hosp., Washington, 1990-93; assoc. v.p., exec. dir. U. Ala. Hosp., Birmingham, 1993—. Contbr. articles to profl. publs. Fellow Am. Coll. Health Care Execs. (R.S. Hudgenw award 1993); mem. Am. Hosp. Assn., Nat. Assn. Health Svcs. Execs. (pres.-elect). Home: U Ala Hosp Room 246/OHB 2112 Lake Heather Way Hoover LA 35242 Office: U Ala Hosp 619 19th St Rm 246/OHB Birmingham AL 35233*

LOGAN, BRUCE DAVID, physician; b. Salem, Mass., Nov. 17, 1945; s. Jack Merill and Miram Jane (Buckley) L.; m. Ann Marie Viola, Mar. 24, 1983; children: Annaleah, Jennifer Mary. BA, Colby Coll., 1967; MD, Columbia U., 1972. Dir. ambulatory care Beekman Hosp., N.Y.C., 1981-87; pvt. practice N.Y.C., 1987—; chief of medicine N.Y. Downtown Hosp., N.Y.C., 1991—; clin. assoc. prof. medicine Cornell U. Med. Coll. Mem. AAAS, AMA, Assn. Program Dirs. in Internal Medicine, Phi Beta Kappa.

LOGAN, CHARLES WILBUR, urologist; b. Nashville, Sept. 12, 1934; s. J. Wilbur and Lillie Mae (Polk) L.; m. Joyce Whitley Martin, Apr. 18, 1964; children: Russell, Christopher, Karen. BA in English Lit., So. Meth. U., 1956; MD, Vanderbilt U., 1960. Diplomate Am. Bd. Urology. Intern surgery Cornell Med. Ctr., N.Y.C., 1961-62; resident gen. surgery Baylor Med. Ctr., Houston, 1963, resident urology surgery, 1963-65; assoc. prof. urology U. Ark., Little Rock, 1967—; staff Bapt. Med. Ctr., Little Rock, 1967—; staff St. Vincent Infirmary, Little Rock, 1967—, chief surgery, 1980-84; vice chief urology Doctors Hosp., Little Rock, 1993-94, chief urology, 1995—. Bd. dirs. Vis. Nurses Assn., 1989—; past bd. dirs. Our House, Little Rock, St. James United Meth. Ch. Capt. U.S. Army, 1965-67. Recipient Founders medal Vanderbilt Med. Sch. Mem. AMA (alt. del. 1994), ACS (Ark. chpt., past pres., past sec., gov. 1990—), Am. Assn. Clin. Urologists (bd. dirs. 1993—), Am. Urol. Assn. (South Ctrl. sect. health policy coun. rep.), Ark. Med. Soc. (chmn. coun., pres.-elect), Ark. Urol. Assn. (past pres., past sec., South Ctrl. sect. rep.), Ark. Lithotripsy Inst. (pres.), Pulaski County Med. Soc. (past pres., councilor), Endourol. Soc., Pediat. Urol. Soc., Ark. Travelers Baseball Club (bd. dirs., v.p.), Ark. Gov.'s Task Force on Healthcare, BCBS MRC Com., Am. Coll. Surgeons (sec. bd. govs.), Rotary, Phi Beta Kappa, Alpha Omega Alpha. Office: Urology Assocs PA 500 S University Ave Little Rock AR 72205-5302

LOGAN, DAVID BRUCE, health care administrator; b. Grand Rapids, Mich., Jan. 30, 1942; s. Wesley Goldsmith and Ernestine (Sovereen) L.; m. Joann Fern Jordan, Nov. 5, 1961; children: Jennifer, Julie, Jeanine, David II, Douglas, Dean. MusB, U. Mich., 1964; B Zoology with honors, Mich. State U., 1970; MBA, U. Ill., 1978. Tchr. sci. Flint (Mich.) Pub. Schs., 1970-71; health care adminstr. USAF, Mpls., 1971-75; asst. chief, med. adminstrn. svc. trainee VA, Mpls., 1975-76; asst. chief med. adminstrn. svc. VA, Danville, Ill., 1976-78; asst. med. dist. coord. VA Med. Dist. 15, Indpls., 1978-80; med. dist. coord. VA Med. Dist. 8, Durham, N.C., 1980-87; nat. disaster med. system mgr. VA, Salisbury, N.C., 1987—. Dir. choir Kirk of Kildaire Presbyn. Ch., 1981-85; asst. scoutmaster, scoutmaster Boy Scouts Am., 1978-94. Capt. USAF, 1964-68, lt. col. Res. ret. Fellow Am. Coll. Healthcare Execs., Soc. Air Force Res. Med. Officers, Air Force Assn., Res. Officers Assn. (bd. dirs. Minn. 1973-74, jr. v.p. for air 1974-75). Office: Dept VA Med Ctr 1601 Brenner Ave Salisbury NC 28144-2515

LOGAN, JOHN LANDISS, physician; b. Shelbyville, Ill., Apr. 19, 1945; s. Manford Alexander and Drusilla Ruth (Rumrill) L.; m. Rita Janet Starriett, Aug. 27, 1984 (div. Feb. 1993); 1 child, Ryan Alexander. BS, U. Ill., 1967, MD, 1971. Diplomate Am. Bd. Urology. Surgery resident Torrance, Calif., 1971-73; urology resident Kaiser Permanente, L.A., 1973-76; attending urologist Kaiser Permanente, Harbor City, Calif., 1976-79; urologist, pvt. practice Camarillo, Calif., 1979-92, Durango, Colo., 1992—. Bd. dirs. United Way, La Plata, Colo., 1995, Am. Cancer Soc., Ventura, Calif., 1984-86. Mem. Am. Urology Assn., Rotary. Office: San Juan Urology Assocs 2901 N Main Ave Durango CO 81301

LOGAN, LEE ROBERT, orthodontist; b. L.A., June 24, 1923; s. Melvin Duncan and Margaret (Seltzer) L.; m. Maxine Nadler, June 20, 1975; children: Fritz, Dean, Scott, Gigi, Chad, Casey. BS, UCLA, 1952; DDS, Northwestern U., 1956, MS, 1961. Diplomate Am. Bd. Orthodontics. Gen. practice dentistry, Reseda, Calif., 1958-59; practice dentistry specializing in orthodontics, Northridge, Calif., 1961—; pres. Lee R. Logan DDS Profl. Corp.; mem. med. staff Northridge Hosp., Tarzana Hosp.; owner Maxine's Prodn. Co.; owner Maxine's Talent Agy.; guest lectr. UCLA, U. So. Calif., dir dental edn. Northridge Med. Ctr. Contbr. articles to profl. jours. Served to lt. USNR, 1956-58. Named (with wife) Couple of Yr. Autistic Children Assn., 1986; recipient Nat. Philanthropy award, 1987, 1st Pl. winner Austistic Jogathon, 1981-95, 1st Pl. Mem. Am., San Fernando Valley Dental Assn. (v.p.), Am. Assn. Orthodontists, Pacific Coast Soc. Orthodontists (dir., pres. so. sect. 1974-75, chmn. membership 1981-83), Found. Orthodontic Research (charter mem.), Calif. Soc. Orthodontists (chmn. peer rev. 1982-93), G.V. Black Soc. (charter mem.), Angle Soc. Orthodontists (pres. 1981-82, bd. dirs. 1982-95, nat. pres. 1985-87, dir. 1985—), U.S.C. Century Club Fraternity, Xi Psi Phi, Chi Phi. Home: 4830 Encino Ave Encino CA 91316-3813 Office: 18250 Roscoe Blvd Northridge CA 91325-4226

LOGE, FRANK JEAN, II, hospital administrator; b. Redlands, Calif., May 28, 1945; s. J. Phillip Loge and Helen M. (Booker) Loge Power; m. Sharon Lee Entrekin, Feb. 11, 1967; children—Frank III, Christopher, Gregory. BA, Claremont Men's Coll., Long Beach, Calif., 1967; MBA, Calif. State U.-Long Beach, 1969; postgrad., UCLA Sch. Pub. Health, 1972-73. Mgr. mgmt. analysis UCLA, 1972-73, asst. dir. fin., 1973-74; dir. fin. U. Calif. Davis Med. Ctr., Sacramento, 1975-79, dep. dir. hosp. and clinics, 1979-84, dir. hosp. and clinics, 1984—. Office: U Calif Davis Med Ctr 2315 Stockton Blvd Sacramento CA 95817-2201*

LOGEMANN, JERILYN ANN, speech pathologist, educator; b. Berwyn, Ill., May 21, 1942; d. Warren F. and Natalie M. (Killmer) L.; BS, Northwestern U., 1963; MA, 1964, PhD, 1968. Grad. asst. dept. communicative disorders Northwestern U., 1963-68; instr. speech and audiology DePaul U., 1964-65; instr. dept. communicative disorders Mundelein Coll., 1967-71; research assoc. depts. neurology and otolaryngology and maxillofacial surgery Northwestern U. Med. Sch., Chgo., 1970-74, asst. prof., 1974-78, dir. clin. and research activities of speech and lang., 1975—, assoc. prof. depts. neurology, otolaryngology and comm. scis. and disorders, 1978-83, prof., 1983, chmn. dept. communication scis. and disorders, 1982—, Ralph and Jean Sundin Prof. of Comm. Scis. and Disorders, 1995—; mem. assoc. staff Northwestern Meml. Hosp., 1976—, N. Chgo. VA Hosp., 1983—, Evanston (Ill.) Hosp., 1988—, Children's Meml. Hosp., Chgo., 1988—; cons. in field; assoc. dir. cancer control. Ill. Comprehensive Cancer Council, Chgo., 1980-82. Mem. rehab. com. Ill. div. Am. Cancer Soc., 1975-79, chmn., 1979—; mem. upper aerodigestive tract organ site com. Nat. Cancer Inst., 1986-89. Postdoctoral fellow Nat. Inst. Neurologic Disease, Communicative Disorders and Stroke, Northwestern U., 1968-70; fellow Inst. Medicine Chgo., 1981—; grantee Nat. Cancer Inst., 1975—, Am. Cancer Soc. , 1981-82; Honors award Conn. Speech Lang. Hearing Assn., 1995, Appreciation award Coun. Grad. Programs in Comms. Scis. and Disorders, 1995, Cellular One award Vanderbilt U. Fellow Am. Speech, Lang. and Hearing Assn. (pres.-elect 1993, pres. 1994, past pres. 1995), Inst. Medicine; mem. Internat. Assn. Logopedics and Phoniatrics, AAUP, Acoustic Soc. Am. (program com. Chgo. regional chpt.), Linguistic Soc. Am., Speech Comm. Assn., Am. Cleft Palate Assn., Ill. Speech and Hearing Assn. (DiCarlo award 1988), Chgo. Heart Assn., Chgo. Speech Therapy and Auditory Soc. Author: The Fisher-Logemann Test of Articulation Competence, 1971, Evaluation and Treatment of Swallowing Disorders, 1983; Manual for the Videofluorographic Evaluation of Swallowing, 1985, 93; assoc. editor Jour. Speech and Hearing Disorders, Jour. Head Trauma Rehab., Dysphagia jour., 1978-82. Office: Northwestern U Med Sch 303 E Chicago Ave Chicago IL 60611-3008 also: Dept Comm Sci & Disorder 2299 Sheridan Rd Evanston IL 60208-0837

LOGIO, THOMAS, colon and rectal surgeon; b. Jersey City, Sept. 17, 1941; m. Eloise DeDonato; children: Jill, Lia, Kim, Thomas, Michael. BS, St. Peters Coll., 1963; MD, St. Louis U., 1967. Diplomate Am. Bd. Surgery, Am. Bd. Colon and Rectal Surgery. Intern U. Chgo. Hosp. and Clinics; asst. resident U. Chgo.-Pa. Hosp.; chief resident Pa. Hosp.; resident in colon and rectal surgery Muhlenberg Hosp.; surgeon Summit (N.J.) Colon & Rectal Surg. Assn.; assoc. in clin. surgery Columbia U., N.Y.C. Mem. AMA, ACS (pres. Union County bd.), N.J. Med. Soc., N.J. Soc. Colon & Rectal Surgeons, N.Y. Soc. of Colon and Rectal Surgeons, Union County Med. Soc. (1st v.p.). Office: Summit Colon & Rectal Surg Assn 137 Summit Ave Summit NJ 07901-2800 also: 315 Elmora Ave Elizabeth NJ 07208

LOGIUDICE, ELAINE A., nursing administrator; b. Sellersville, Pa.; d. William and Miriam (Yoder) Anders; m. Guy LoGiudice. BS, Columbia U., 1961; MSN, Cath. U. Am., 1982. Cert. nurse administr., advanced; cert. quality mgr. Dept. chairperson, instr. Washington Hosp. Ctr. Sch. Nursing, Washington, 1974-82; asst. dir. nursing Prince George's Gen. Hosp., Cheverly, Md., 1982-85; dir. maternal-child health psychology D.C. Gen. Hosp., Washington, 1986—; coord. NSG standards & practice Bon Secaro St. Joseph Hosp., Port Charlotte, Fla., 1996—; project dir. RWJ grant D.C. Gen. Hosp., 1994-96. Mem. ANA.

LOGOSSO, RONALD DANIEL, plastic surgeon; b. Bklyn., July 24, 1938; s. Louis Paul and Angela (Scotto) L.; m. Lillian Anne Lacapria; children: Anne Michele, Ronald Daniel, Marisa Claudia. AA, George Washington U., 1957, BS, 1959; MD, Georgetown U., 1963. Diplomate Am. Bd. Plastic Surgery, Nat. Bd. Med. Examiners. Intern, resident in surgery, resident in plastic surgery Nassau County Med. Ctr., to 1971; attending surgeon Nassau County Med. Ctr., East Meadow, N.Y., 1971-95, Cmty. Hosp. of Smithtown, N.Y., 1971-95, St. John's Episcopal Hosp., Smithtown, 1971—, U. Hosp. Stonybrook, N.Y., 1993—; dir., CEO Horizons in Plastic Surgery, Stonybrook, 1986—; cons., advisor Protocare, Smithtown, 1990-93. Capt. U.S. Army, 1965-67. Fellow Am. Soc. Plastic Surgeons, Am. Assn. Cosmetic Surgeons, Internat. Acad. Cosmetic Surgeons. Republican. Roman Catholic. Home: 19 Tanager Ln Northport NY 11768 Office: Horizons in Plastic Surgery 2500 Rte 347 Bldg 14-D Stony Brook NY 11790

LOGUE, A(NDREW) DOUGLAS, psychiatrist; b. Erie, Pa., Dec. 1, 1938; children: Douglas H., William A., Richard T.; m. Judith R. Logue. BS in Biochemistry, Yale U., 1960; MD, Johns Hopkins U., 1964. Diplomate Am. Bd. Psychiatry and Neurology, Am. Bd. Profl. Disability Cons., Am. Bd. Forensic Examiners, Am. Bd. Forensic Medicine, Am. Acad. Experts in Traumatic Stress. Intern in surgery Johns Hopkins U., 1964-65, resident in psychiatry, 1965-68; dep. chief resident psychiatry Johns Hopkins U., Balt., 1967-68; pvt. practice Balt., 1970—, Princeton, N.J., 1989—; psychiatrist Sinai Hosp., 1972-84. Maj. U.S. Army, 1968-70. Howard County Community Psychiatry fellow, 1967-68. Mem. Am. Psychoanalytic Assn., Internat. Psychoanalytic Assn., Atlantic Soc. for Psychoanalytic Tng., Inst. for Psychotherapy and Psychoanalysis of N.J. Home: 159 Valley Rd Princeton NJ 08540-3442 Office: 20 Nassau St Ste 513 Princeton NJ 08542-4509 also: 829 Park Ave Baltimore MD 21201-4869

LOGUE, JAMES NICHOLAS, epidemiologist; b. Duryea, Pa., June 18, 1946; s. James and Lucille (Polen) L.; m. Mary Frances Carey, Nov. 25, 1972; children: Melissa, Jimmy, Jeffrey. BS, Kings Coll., 1968; MPH, U. Mich., 1971; DrPH, Columbia U., 1978. Statistician Warner Lambert Co, Morris Plains, N.J., 1969-70, 71-73; sr. med. biostatistician Ciba-Geigy Co., Summit, N.J., 1973-78; epidemiologist GEOMET Technologies, Inc., Rockville, Md., 1978-80; supervisory epidemiologist US FDA, Rockville, 1980-82; dir. divsn. environ. health assessment Pa. Dept. Health, Harrisburg, 1982—. Office: Pa Dept of Health PO Box 90 Harrisburg PA 17120

LOGUE, JUDITH R., psychoanalyst, educator; b. Phila., Aug. 21, 1942; d. Martin and Laura (Goldman) Kirshenbaum; AB in Govt., Wheaton (Mass.) Coll., 1963; MSW, Rutgers U., 1966, PhD, Rutgers U. Grad. Sch. Arts and Scis., 1983; grad. N.Y. Center for Psychoanalytic Tng., 1978; m. Stephen Felton, Feb. 8, 1966 (div. Aug. 1989); 1 dau., Jane Jennifer; m. A. Douglas Logue, Feb. 14, 1990. Clin. social worker VA, Newark, 1967; psychotherapist Santa Barbara (Calif.) Mental Health Services, 1967-69; supr. Santa Barbara Counselling Center, 1967-69; pvt. practice psychoanalysis, 1969—; psychoanalyst, therapist Fifth Ave. Center for Psychotherapy, N.Y.C., 1969-72; instr. Marymount Manhattan Coll., 1971; psychotherapy supr. clin. faculty, dept. psychiatry Rutgers U. Med. Sch., New Brunswick, N.J., 1972-75, teaching asst. Grad. Sch. Social Work, 1974-76; vis. lectr. Bryn Mawr

Coll. Sch. Social Work and Social Research, 1980; mem. faculty N.Y. Center for Psychoanalytic Tng., 1980—, N.J. Inst. Psychoanalysis and Psychotherapy, 1982—. Bd. dirs. N.Y. Ctr. for Psychoanalytic Tng., Inst. for Psychoanalysis and Psychotherapy N.J. Faculty, 1982—. NIMH fellow, 1965; diplomate Am. Bd. Psychotherapy. Recipient Disting. Faculty award Atlantic County Psychoanalytic Soc., 1987. Fellow N.J. Soc. for Clin. Social Work; mem. AAUP, APA (div. 39, sect. 1), NASW, Conf. Psychoanalytic Psychotherapists, Nat. Assn. for Advancement Psychoanalysis, Groves Conf. on Family, Acad. Cert. Social Workers, Soc. for Psychoanalytic Tng. (bd. dirs. 1983—, dir. social sci. program 1983-86). Mem. editorial bd. jour. Current Issues in Psychoanalytic Practice, 1983—; contbr. articles to profl. jours. Home and Office: 159 Valley Rd Princeton NJ 08540-3442

LOH, HORACE H., pharmacology educator; b. Canton, Republic China, May 28, 1936. BS, Nat. Taiwan U., Taipei, Republic China, 1958; PhD, U. Iowa, 1965. Lectr. dept. pharmacology U. Calif. Sch. Medicine, San Francisco, 1967; assoc. prof. biochem. Wayne State U., Detroit, 1968-70; lectr., rsch. assoc. depts. psychiatry, pharmacology Langley Porter Neuropsychiatric Inst. U. Calif. Sch. Medicine, San Francisco, 1970-72, assoc. prof. depts. psychiatry, pharmacology Langley Porter Neuropsychiatric Inst., 1972-75, prof. depts. psychiatry, pharmacology Langley Porter Neuropsychiatric Inst., 1975-88; prof., head dept. pharmacology U. Minn. Med. Sch., Mpls., 1989—, Frederick and Alice Stark prof., head dept. pharmacology, 1990—; chmn. annual meeting theme com. on receptors Fedn. Am. Socs. for Exptl. Biology, 1984; mem. exec. com. Internat. Narcotic Rsch. Conf., 1984-87, chair sci. program annual meeting, 1986; mem. adv. com. Nat. Tsing Hua U. Inst. Life Scis., Taiwan, Republic China, 1985-89; mem. exec. com. Com. on Problems of Drug Dependence, Inc., 1985-88; mem. sci. adv. coun. Nat. Found. for Addicitive Diseases, 1987—; cons. U.S. Army R & D Dept. Defense, 1980-84. Mem. editorial adv. bd. Life Scis., 1978—, Substance and Alcohol Abuse, 1980—, Neurochemistry Internat., 1980-88, Neuropharmacology, 1982—, Neurosci. Series, 1982-83, Annual Rev. Pharmacology and Toxicology, 1984-89, Jour. Pharmacology and Exptl. Therapeutics, 1987—; assoc. editor Annual Rev. Pharmacology and Toxicology, 1990-95, CRC Critical Rev. in Pharmacological Scis., 1987-88; author 56 book chpts; editor 1 book; contbr. 300 articles to profl. jours. Recipient Career Devel. award USPHS, 1973-78, 78-83, Rsch. Scientist award, 1983-88, 1989-94, Humboldt award for sr. U.S. scientists (Fed. Republic Germany), 1977. Mem. Am. Coll. Neuropsychopharmacology (honorific awards com. 1988—), Am. Soc. Pharmacology and Exptl. Therapeutics (program com. 1976-86, trustee bd. publs. 1987-93, com. on confs. 1990-93), Soc. Chinese Bioscientists in Am. (pres. 1985-86), Western Pharmacology Soc. (councilor 1980-83, pres. 1984-85). Office: U Minn Med Sch Dept Pharmacology 3 249 Millard Hall Minneapolis MN 55455

LOHMAN, HELENE, therapist; b. Denver; m. Michael Lohman; children: Benjamin, Justin. BS in Occupl. Therapy, Colo. State U.; MA in Health Edn., U. Nebr. Occupl. therapist St. Joseph Hosp., Omaha; occupl. therapist, dept. coord. Bergan Mercy Hosp., Omaha; asst. prof. Creighton U., Omaha; bd. intern Rose Blunkin Home; cons. Clarkson Coll. Author/editor: Introduction to Splinting: A Problem Solving Approach; contbr. articles to profl. jours. Mem. Am. Occupl. Therapy Assn., Nebr. Occupl. Therapy Assn. (reimbursement chair 1987-90). Office: Creighton Univ 2500 California Plz Omaha NE 68178

LOHMANN, GEORGE YOUNG, JR., neurosurgeon, hospital executive; b. Scranton, Pa., Aug. 9, 1947; s. George Young Lohmann and Elizabeth (Nichols) Frantzen; m. Joette Calabrese, May 15, 1973 (div. 1981); m. Rosemary Ei-Ling Ma, Sept. 24, 1988; 1 child, Norelle Christa Victoria. AB in Chemistry with honors, Hobart Coll., 1968; MD, SUNY, Buffalo, 1972. Diplomate Am. Bd. Neurol. Surgeons, Am. Acad. Pain Specialists. Resident gen. surgery Wesley Meml. Hosp., Chgo., 1972-73; from jr. resident to chief resident Georgetown U. Hosp., Washington, 1975-79; asst. med. dir. West Side Orgn., Chgo., 1973-74; emergency physician St. James Hosp., Chicago Heights, Ill., 1973-74; pvt. practice Baton Rouge, 1979-81, 81-84; dir. dept. neurosurgery Brookdale Hosp. Med. Ctr., Bklyn., 1984-93; pres. Bklyn. Neurosurg. Svcs., Inc., 1985—; mem. Med. Dir. Com., Risk Mgmt. Com., Exec. Quality Assurance Com., 1987-93; mem. Med. Bd. Com., 1985-93, Exec. Bd. Com., 1984-93, Pain Mgmt. Com., 1988-91. Named to Compton-Connolly Guide to Best Physicians in the New York Met. Area; patentee in field; contbr. articles to profl. jours. Mem. adv. bd. Ctr. Latin Affairs, Baton Rouge, 1982-84; mem. Senatorial Inner Cir., 1988; bd. trustees Christian Victory Ctr., Hempstead, N.Y., 1986-88; fellow Am. Coll. Pain Mgmt. Fellow ACS; mem. AMA, Am. Assn. Neurologic Surgeons (mem. trauma sect.), N.Y. State Neurosurg. Soc., N.Y. Soc. Neurosurgery, Congress Neurologic Surgeons (spine sect., sect. on trauma), Tex. State Med. Soc., Midland County Med. Soc., So. Med. Soc. Presdl. Roundtable, Shanhai Tiffin Club, Donyin Sister City Assn., Senatorial Inner Circle, Midland C. of C., Midland-Odessa Symphony and Choral Soc.

LOIUDICE, THOMAS ANTHONY, gastroenterologist, researcher; b. Wilmington, Del., Dec. 3, 1942; s. Dominick and Carmela (Vignola) LoI.; m. Jean Anne Lang, June 20, 1970; children: Christopher, Mark. BS, St. Joseph's U., 1966; DO, Chgo. Coll., 1972. Diplomate Am. Bd. Family Practice, Am. Bd. Internal Medicine, Am. Bd. Nutrition; lic. physician Tenn., Pa., Ind., Ohio, N.Y., Fla. Intern U. Health Ctr. Pitts. Hosp., 1972-73, jr. asst. resident in inernal medicine, 1973-74, sr. asst. resident in internal medicine, 1974, fellow cardiology, 1975; fellow gastroenterology and clin. nutrition Union U., Albany, N.Y., 1975-77; pres. Akron (Ohio) Gastroenterology Assocs., Inc., 1978—; instr. Northeastern Ohio U., Akron, 1977-83, asst. prof., assoc. prof. gastroenterology, 1983-91, prof., 1991—, head subsect. nutrition, 1986—; sec.-treas. Tri-County Emergency Med. Svc., Inc., 1983—; clin. rsch. assoc. Smith, Kline & French Labs., 1983—; mem. sr. teaching staff St. Thomas Med. Ctr., Akron, chief nutrition, head nutritional support team, 1989—; mem. courtesy staff Barberton Citizens Hosp., Barberton, Ohio, Cuyahoga Falls (Ohio) Gen. Hosp.; mem. jr. staff Akron Gen. Med. Ctr.; mem. staff Akron City Hosp.; speaker in field. Contbr. numerous articles to So. Med. Jour., Gastroeterology, Ob/Gyn., Am. Jour. Gastroenterology, Am. Jour. Digestive Diseases, Am. Jour. Clin. Nutrition, N.Y. Jour. Medicine, and other. Grantee William H. Rorer, Smith Kline and French, Ortho Pharm. Corp., Glaxo Pharm. Fellow ACP, Am. Coll. Angiology, Am. Coll. Gastroenterology, Am. Coll. Nutrition, Royal Soc. Medicine (Eng., affiliate); mem. AMA, AAAS, Am. Coll. Emergency Physicians, Am.Soc. Contemporary Medicine and Surgery, Am. Soc. Internal Medicine, Am. Gastroenterology Assn., Am. Assn. for Study Liver Disease, Am. Soc. Gastrointestinal Endoscopy, Am. Fedn. Clin. Rsch., Ohio Med. Assn., Ohio Soc. Internal Medicine, Northeastern Ohio Soc. Gastrointestinal Endoscopy, Summit County Med. Soc. Roman Catholic. Office: Akron Gastroenterology Assoc 444 N Main St Ste 324 Akron OH 44310-3110

LOKIETEK, WLADYSLAW ZYGMUNT, orthopedist; b. Tertre, Hainaut, Belgium, Aug. 8, 1941; s. Wladyslaw and Teresa (Palaszewska) L.; m. Suzanne Christiaens, July 6, 1967; children: Sophie-Claude Marie, Wladyslaw-François Sabine, Ludmila-Cecile-Lucie, Catherine-Pierre Marie. MD, U. Louvain, Belgium, 1968, PhD, 1982. Intern St. Boniface Hosp., Winnipeg, Man., Can., 1967-68; rsch. fellow Columbia U., N.Y.C., 1971-72; pediatric orthop. resident A.I. DuPont Inst., Wilmington, Del., 1972-73; chief orthop. unit scoliosis Cath. U. Louvain, 1973, chief orthop. ward, 1983, assoc. prof., 1982-90, prof., 1990—; chief orthopediat. rsch., 1982—; coord. Belgian-Polish Orthop. Coop., 1992; mem. Bur. Groupe Etude Scoliosis, France, 1980; cons. med. rel. U. Cracow, Poland, 1992; organizer orthop. coop. UCL, Cracow, 1992. Assoc. editor Jour. Pediatric Orthop., 1987; contbr. numerous articles to pediatric jours. Mem. Scoliosis Rsch. Soc. (U.S.), European Pediatric Orthopediat. Soc., Belgian Assn. Pediatric Orthopediat. (pres. 1987). Office: St Luc Univ Hosp, Ave Hippocratic 1200, Brussels Belgium also: Cath U Louvain, Dept Orthopediat, Mont-Godinne Belgium

LOKYS, LINDA J., dermatologist; b. Poughkeepsie, N.Y., July 30, 1954. BA, Vassar Coll., 1972; MS, Columbia U., 1982; MD, Albany Med. Coll., 1987. Diplomate Am. Bd. Dermatology. Dermatologist Diagnostic Clinic, Clearwater, Fla., 1991—. Office: Diagnostic Clinic 3131 McMullen Booth Rd Clearwater FL 34685

LÖLLGEN, HERBERT, cardiologist; b. Bonn, Germany, Jan. 5, 1943; s. Artur and Maria (Decker) L.; m. Inge Horres, Nov. 18, 1969; children: Ruth, Deborah, Noëmi, Eva. MD, U. Bonn, 1967; PhD, U. Mainz (Germany), 1979. Asst., intern Med. Sch., U. Mainz, 1970-72, asst., 1976-78; asst. med. dept. Hosp., Moers, Germany, 1973-75; rsch. fellow Aug Krogh Inst., Copenhagen, 1975; vice head dept. cardiology U. Freiburg (Germany), 1978-82; head dept. cardiology Acad. Hosp., Limburg, Germany, 1983-85, Mcpl. Hosp., Acad. Hosp., U. Bochum, Remscheid, Germany, 1986—; chmn. Working Group on Ergometry, 1985-93; mem. med. bd. German Astronauts, Cologne, 1980—. Author 11 books on ergometry and emergency medicine; mem. editl. bd. nat. and internat. sci. jours. With German Army, 1970. Fellow Am. Coll. Cardiology, Am. Heart Assn.; mem. Sports Medicine Assn. (pres.), Nordrhein (pres 1986—), German Coun. on Resuscitation. Roman Catholic. Home: Bermesgasse 32 b, D-42897 Remscheid Germany Office: Mcpl Hosp, Burger Str 211, D-42859 Remscheid Germany

LOLLI, FRANCESCO, neurologist, researcher; b. Florence, Italy, Oct. 30, 1958; s. Gualtiero and Anita (Bascialla) L. MD, U. Florence, 1983; postgrad., U. Florence, 1991; PhD, Karolinska Inst., Stockholm, 1992. Diplomate Italian Bd. Neurology. Registrar in neurology Univ. Hosp., Florence, 1991-93, sr. registrar in neurology, 1994—; docent specialization in neurophysiology U. Florence, 1994—. Author: Infezione da HIV de sistema nervoso e alterazioni B e T cellulari, 1982. Mem. Italian Assn. Forensic Pathology. Office: Dept Neurology & Psychiatry, Viale Morgagni 85, 50134 Florence Italy

LOMAX, DONALD HENRY, physician; b. Lexington, N.C., Dec. 30, 1921; s. William Henry and Bessie Ida (Young) L.; m. Marie Smith, Dec. 14, 1947; children: Susan, Don, Melissa, Sally, Ann, Laurie, John. BS, Wake Forest U., 1948; MD, U. N.C., 1951. Diplomate Am. Bd. Family Practice. Intern Letterman Gen. Hosp., San Francisco, 1951-52, Mather AFB Hosp., 1952-53; attending physician Rowan Regional Med. Ctr., 1953—, chief of staff, trustee; pvt. practice Salisbury, N.C., 1953—. Past med. dir. N.C. Cerebral Palsy Assn. Capt. USAF, 1942-46, 51-53. Fellow Am. Acad. Family Physicians; mem. N.C. Acad. Family Physicians (past dir., past chmn. sci. com.), N.C. Med. Soc., So. Med. Assn. Office: 1710 W Innes St Salisbury NC 28144

LOMAX, JAMES WELTON, psychotherapist; b. San Antonio, Dec. 7, 1944; s. James Welton and Dolores (Farley) L.; m. Nancy Robinson, Sept. 3, 1966; children: Laura, Heather, Lisa. BA magna cum laude, Rice U., 1967; MD, Baylor U., 1971. Cert. in psychoanalysis. Asst. coord. Baylor Psychiatry Residency, Houston, 1977-79; asst. prof. psychiatry Baylor Coll. Medicine, Houston, 1977-83; assoc. coord. Baylor Psychiatry Residency, 1979-81, coord., 1981-82, dir., 1982—; assoc. prof. clin. psychiatry Baylor Coll. Medicine, 1983-89, prof. psychiatry, 1989—, acting chmn. dept. psychiatry, 1990-91, assoc. chmn. dept. psychiatry, 1991—. Bd. trustees Inst. Religion, Tex. Med. Ctr., 1995—. With USPHS, 1972-74. Names Outstanding Student in Psychiatry, Baylor Coll. Medicine, 1971. Fellow Am. Psychiat. Assn., Am. Coll. Psychiatrists (Falk fellow 1975-77), Am. Coll. Psychiatrists; mem. Am. Assn. Dirs. Psychiatry Residency Tng. (pres. 1994-95), Phi Beta Kappa, Delta Phi Alpha. Home: 4801 Maple Bellaire TX 77401 Office: Baylor Coll Medicine One Baylor Plz Ste 619D Houston TX 77030

LOMBARDI, ADOLPH VINCENT, orthopaedic surgeon; b. Phila., Jan. 12, 1956; s. Adolph Vincent and Emilia Lombardi; m. Anne Theresa Palmer, Jan. 12, 1985; children: Adolph V. III, Joanna, Karlenna. BS, St. Joseph's Univ., 1977; MD, Temple Univ., 1981; orthopaedic surgery, Albert Einstein Med. Ctr., 1986. Diplomate Am. Bd. Orthopaedic Surgery, Nat. Bd. Medical Examiners. Internship Temple Univ. Hosp., Phila., 1981-82; residency Albert Einstein Medical Ctr., Phila., 1982-86; residency pediatric orthopaedic surgery Shriners Hosp. Crippled Children, Phila., 1984; residency hand surgery Thomas Jefferson Univ. Hosp. Hand Rehab. Ctr., Phila., 1985; fellowship Ohio State Univ. St. Anthony Medical Ctr., Columbus, 1986, Nat. Hosp. Orthopaedics and Rehab., Arlington, Va., 1987; clinical asst. prof. orthopaedic surgery Ohio State Univ., Columbus, 1996—, clinical asst. prof. biomedical engring., 1996—; dir. medical rsch. Ohio Orthopaedic Inst., 1996—; active Grant Medical Ctr., Columbus, assoc. Park Medical Ctr., dir. medical rsch., Grant Orthpaedic Inst., 1990-95; chmn. orthopaedic sect. Grant Medical Ctr., 1996—. Contbr. numerous articles to profl. jours. Vol. physician Faith Missions Homeless, Columbus, 1996—. Fellow Am. Acad. Orthopaedic Surgeons, Am. Coll. Surgeons, Internat. Coll. Surgeons; mem.AMA, Internat. Soc. of the Knee, The Knee Soc., The Hip Soc., Assn. Arthritic Hip and Knee Surgery, Mid-Am. Orthopaedic Assn., Ohio Orthopaedic Soc., Ohio State Medical Assn., Am. Assn. Tissue Banks, Ohio Assn. Physician Assts., Columbus Orthopaedic Soc., Albert Einstein Medical Ctr. Orthopaedic Alumni, St. Joseph's Univ. Medical Alumni, Alpha Epsilon Delta (v.p. 1975-77), Bhaffrey Biological Soc. (treas. 1975-77). Home: Emilia's Estate 17 New Albany Farms Rd New Albany OH 43054 Office: Joint Implant Surgeons Inc 720 East Broad St Columbus OH 43215

LOMBARDO, RICHARD JAMES, emergency physician; b. Manchester, Conn., July 22, 1944; s. Corado James and Constance Marie (Sapienza) L.; m. Sandra Lee Haag, May 24, 1969 (dec. Jan. 1975); children: Terri Lyn, Karin Michelle; m. Sandra Lynn Rockneberg, May 21, 1976; 1 child, Amanda Lee; stepchildren: Michael DeHaan, Darrin DeHaan. BS, Trinity Coll., Hartford, Conn., 1966; MD, U. Medicine and Dentistry N.J., Newark, 1970. Family practice staff physician Tipton County Hosp., Covington, Tenn., 1973-78, Randolph County Med. Ctr., Pocahontas, Ark., 1979-86; emergency physician, med. dir. emergency dept. Springfield (Mo.) Cmty. Hosp., 1987-92; emergency physician Rsch. Belton (Mo.) Hosp., 1992—, Rsch. Med. Ctr., Kansas City, Mo., 1992—; chief of staff Tipton County Hosp., 1978, Randolph County Med. Ctr., 1984. Lt. USN, 1971-73. Mem. Met. Med. Soc., Mo. State Med. Assn. Home: 705 Sandpiper Raymore MO 64083 Office: Rsch Belton Hosp 17065 S 71 Hwy Belton MO 64012

LONDON, BERTON LEE, cardiology; b. Detroit, Jan. 4, 1930; s. Julius David and Rose Sarah (Goldberg) L.; m. Beverly Jane Falk, Aug. 12, 1946 (div. Oct. 1994); children: Julia Holloway, Laura Rousseau, James London. BS, U. Mich., 1950, MD, 1954. Diplomate Am. Bd. Internal Medicine. Pres. Cardiovasc. Assocs., Southfield, Mich., 1964—; chmn. cardiology Grace Hosp., Detroit, 1973-85; clin. asst. prof. internal medicine Wayne State U., Detroit, 1973-96. Capt. U.S. Army, 1956-58, Germany. Fellow Am. Coll. Physicians, Am. Coll. Cardiology. Office: Cardiovasc Assocs 27177 Lanser Southfield MI 48034

LONDON, DAVID BRUCE, psychiatrist; b. Chgo., Sept. 25, 1948. AB, George Wash. U., 1970, MD, 1974. Diplomate Am. Bd. Psychiatry and Neurology, Am. Bd. Adolescent Psychiatry. Intern in internal medicine George Wash. U., Washington, 1974-75; fellow in psychiatry Yale U., New Haven, 1975-78, forensic fellow in psychiatry, 1984-86; clin. and research fellow Yale Psychiat. Inst., New Haven, 1978-80; sr. staff psychiatrist Inst. of Living, Hartford, Conn., 1980-82; pvt. practice Madison, Conn., 1982—, Waterford, Conn., 1984—; cons. in psychiatry Waterford Country Sch., 1983—, Madison (Conn.) Youth Svcs., 1987-90, Norwich (Conn.) Ct. Diagnostic Clinic, 1988—; med. dir. Chem. Addiction Recovery Enterprise, New London, Conn., 1987-91, asst. clin. prof. psychiatry Yale U., New Haven, 1987; cons. psychiatrist Act Team Gilead House, Middletown, Conn., 1994-95. Contbr. articles to profl. jours. Mem. Am. Psychiat. Assn., Am. Acad. Psychiatry and the Law, Am. Soc. Adolescent Psychiatry, Am. Acad. Med. Acupuncture. Office: Ste 320 567 Vauxhall St Ext Waterford CT 06385-4341 also: 147 Durham Rd PO Box 1158 Madison CT 06443

LONDON, GARY WAYNE, neurologist; b. Alexandria, La., Sept. 21, 1943; s. Arthur Jack and Aileen Ida (Friedman) L.; m. Susan Tolkan, June 19, 1965; children: David, Jeremy, Benjamin. BSM, Northwestern U., 1965, MD, 1968. Diplomate Nat. Bd. Med. Examiners, Am. Bd. Psychiatry and Neurology, Am. Bd. Electrodiagnostic Medicine; lic. Md., D.C., Va., Calif., Bur. Narcotic and Dangerous Drugs. Intern U. Calif. Affiliated Hosps., L.A., 1968-69; resident in neurology U. Mich., Ann Arbor, 1969-70; resident in neurology dept. neurosci. U. Calif. San Diego, 1972-74; neurologist in pvt. graoup practice Drs. Mayle, London & Einbinder, LLC, Bethesda, Md., 1974—; affiliated with hosps. including Montgomery (Md.) Gen. Hosp., Holy Cross Hosp., Suburban Hosp., Shady Grove Adventist Hosp., Potomac Ridge Med. Ctr., Montgomery County, Md., Sibley Meml. Hosp., George Washington U. Hosp., Washington; clin. instr. neuroscis. U. Calif., San Diego, 1973-74; adj. asst. clin. prof. neurology George Washington U. Sch. Medicine and Health Scis., 1985—. Contbr. articles to profl. jours., chpt. to book. Mem. steering com. Washington chpt. of Weissmann Inst., 1993—; v.p. Hebrew Home of Greater Washington, Rockville, Md., 1993—. Fellow Am. Acad. Neurology, Royal Soc. Medicine; mem. AMA, ACP, Am. Assn. Electrodiagnostic Medicine (liason to Nat. Coalition for Rsch. in Neurolog. and Comm. Disorders 1984-94), Am. Med. Electroencephalographic Assn., Am. Acad. Clin. Neuropsychology, Am. Soc. Clin. Evoked Potentials, Am. Epilepsy Soc., Am. Soc. Neurol. Rehab., Am. Soc. Neuroimaging, N.Y. Acad. Scis., Russell W. DeJong Soc., Md. Neurol. Soc., Md. State Med. Soc., Jacobi Soc. Washington, Phi Delta Epsilon (pres. Washington grad. club 1982-83), Phi Eta Sigma. Republican. Jewish. Office: Camalier Bldg 10215 Fernwood Rd Ste 301 Bethesda MD 20817

LONDON, IRVING MYER, physician, educator; b. Malden, Mass., July 24, 1918; s. Jacob A. and Rose (Goldstein) L.; m. Huguette Piedzicki, Feb. 27, 1955; children: Robert L.J., David T. AB summa cum laude, Harvard U., 1939, MD, 1943; DSc (hon.), U. Chgo., 1966. Sheldon Traveling fellow Harvard U., 1939-41, Delamar research fellow med. sch., 1940-41; intern Presbyn. Hosp., N.Y.C., 1943; asst. resident Presbyn. Hosp., 1946-47, asst. physician, 1946-52, assoc. attending physician, 1954-55; Rockefeller fellow in medicine Coll. Physicians and Surgeons, Columbia U., 1946-47; instr. Columbia U., 1947-49; asso. in medicine Coll. Phys. and Surg., Columbia U., 1949-51; asst. prof. Coll. Phys. and Surg., Columbia, 1951-54, assoc. prof., 1954-55; prof., chmn. dept. medicine Albert Einstein Coll. Medicine, N.Y.C., 1955-70; vis. prof. medicine Albert Einstein Coll. Medicine, 1970—; prof. biology MIT, 1969-89, prof. emeritus, 1989—; vis. prof. medicine Harvard Med. Sch., 1969-72, prof. medicine, 1972-89, prof. emeritus, 1989—; dir. div. health scis. and tech. Harvard and MIT, 1969-85, prof. medicine, 1972—, Grover M. Hermann prof. health scis. and tech., 1977-89, prof. emeritus, 1989—; dir. Whitaker Coll. Health Scis., Tech. and Mgmt., MIT, 1978-83; dir. med. service Bronx Mcpl. Hosp. Center, 1955-70; Phi Delta Epsilon lectr. U. Colo., 1962, Harvey lectr., 1961; Jacobaeus lectr., Stockholm, Sweden, 1964; vis. scientist Pasteur Inst., Paris, 1962-63; Commonwealth Fund fellow, 1962-63; Alpha Omega Alpha lectr. Yale, Boston U., Columbia, SUNY Downstate Med. Center, U. Chgo.; Harry L. Alexander vis. prof. Washington U., St. Louis, 1968; Alpha Omega Alpha vis. prof. Johns Hopkins U., 1970; Eugene A. Stead Jr. vis. lectr. Duke Med. Center, 1970; Cons. to Surgeon Gen., AUS, 1957-60; chmn. metabolism study sect. USPHS, 1961-63; Med. fellowship bd. Nat. Acad. Scis., NRC, 1955-64; mem. bd. sci. cons. Sloan Kettering Inst., 1960-72; bd. sci. counselors Nat. Heart Inst., 1964-68; exec. com. Health Research Council, City N.Y., 1958-63; mem. sci. adv. council Pub. Health Research Inst., N.Y.C., 1958-63; mem. adv. com. to dir. NIH, 1966-70, nat. cancer adv. bd., 1972-76; physician Brigham and Women's Hosp., 1972-83, sr. physician 1983—; chmn. research group Nat. Commn. on Arthritis, 1975-76; chmn. adv. com. Div. Health Scis., Inst. Medicine, 1979-82; mem. Bd. Sci. Counselors, NIADDK, 1979-83; bd. dirs., cons. Johnson and Johnson, 1982-89. Asso. editor: Jour. Clin. Investigation, 1952-57; mem. editorial bd.: Am. Jour. Medicine, 1965-79. Bd. dirs. Philippe Found. Capt. AUS, 1944-46. Recipient Theobald Smith award in med. scis. AAAS, 1953; Bloomfield medal and lectr., Lady Davis Inst., 1986. Fellow Am. Acad. Arts and Scis.; mem. Am. Soc. Biol. Chemists, Am. Soc. Clin. Investigation (pres. 1963-64), Nat. Acad. Scis. (mem. bd. medicine 1967-70, mem. exec. com. Inst. Medicine 1970-72), Internat. Soc. Hematology, Soc. Exptl. Biology and Medicine, Assn. Am. Physicians, Nat. Acad. Scis., Phi Beta Kappa, Alpha Omega Alpha. Office: Harvard U-MIT Div Health Scis and Tech 77 Massachusetts Ave Cambridge MA 02139-4301

LONDON, ROGER DAVID, internist; b. N.Y.C.. BA, Cornell U., 1973; MD, Mount Sinai U., 1977; MBA, Columbia U., 1996. Resident in medicine Columbia Presbyn. Med. Ctr., N.Y.C., 1977-80; postdoctoral fellow Yale Sch. Medicine, New Haven, Conn., 1980-83; asst. chief dialysis Bronx VA Med. Ctr., 1983-84; asst. attending Mount Sinai Hosp., N.Y.C., 1986—; asst. prof. medicine Mount Sinai Med. Sch., N.Y.C., 1985—, dir. home dialysis, 1985—. Reviewer Am. Jour. Physiology, Jour. Lab. Clin. Medicine; contbr. articles to profl. jours. Mem. N.Y. Acad. Sci., Am. Soc. Nephrology, Am. Fed. for Clin. Rsch., Internat. Soc. Nephrology. Home: 137 E 66th St 5B New York NY 10021 Office: Mount Sinai Med Ctr Box 1147 1 Gustave Levy Pl New York NY 10021-6130

LONDON, WILLIAM LORD, pediatrician; b. Durham, N.C., Nov. 1, 1930. MD, U. N.C., 1955. Intern Children's Med. Ctr., Boston, 1955-56, resident, 1956-57, 59-60, fellow in pediatric hematology, 1960-61; mem. staff Durham (N.C.) Gen. Hosp.; clin. assoc. prof. Duke U., Durham. Fellow Am. Acad. Pediatrics; mem. AMA. Office: 2609 N Duke St # 801 Durham NC 27704-3019*

LONECK, BARRY MARTIN, social work educator, researcher; b. Erie, Pa., Dec. 5, 1954; s. Francis and Mary Gertrude (Gent) L.; m. Andrea Bernice Fabrizi, Aug. 6, 1977; children: Heather, Gabrielle, Kimberly, Stephanie. BA, Case Western Res. U., 1976, MS in Social Adminstrn., 1978, PhD, 1985. Alcoholism counselor, researcher The Lakeland Inst., Lorain, Ohio, 1981-89; asst. prof. Sch. of Social Welfare SUNY, Albany, 1989—. Co-author: (monograph) Research and Development of An Alcohol Abuse Prevention Program at Case Western Res. U., 1980; contbr. numerous articles to profl. jours. Faculty mem. Ctr. for Study of Issues in Publ. Mental Health, Albany; bd. dirs. Pahl, Inc., Troy, N.Y. Rsch. fellow Nat. Assn. State Mental Health Program Dirs. Rsch. Inst., 1991-93. Mem. NASW, Acad. Cert. Social Workers (cert.), United Univ. Professions. Roman Catholic. Home: 15 Cedar Ln Gansevoort NY 12831-1055 Office: SUNY Sch Social Welfare 135 Western Ave Albany NY 12203-1011

LONG, AMELIA ROSE, psychologist; b. Altus, Okla., Feb. 15, 1944; d. Everett Bailey Holland and Edna Odessa Amelia (Donnohue) Holland Sweetland; adopted by George R. Sweetland; m. Deryl Wayne Long, Aug. 8, 1963 (div. 1976); children: Katherine Kimberley, Kenneth Wayne, Amy Nicole. BA, Ball State U., 1979, MA, 1982, PhD in Counseling Psychology, 1986. Lic. psychologist, N.D. Psychologist N.W. Human Svc. Ctr., Williston, N.D., 1985—; pvt. practice Williston, 1989—. Mem. APA. Unitarian Universalist. Home: 1216 6th Ave E Apt 4 Williston ND 58801-4439 Office: NW Human Svc Ctr 316 2d Ave W Williston ND 58801-5218 also: 417 1st Ave E Williston ND 58802-0962

LONG, CHARLES WILLIAM, child and adolescent psychiatrist; b. Helena, Ark., Sept. 22, 1947; s. Benjamin Asa and Laura Jo (Underwood) L.; m. Heather Barbara Murray, Sept. 19, 1987; children: Charles William 2d, Lindsay Catherine. BS in Biology and Chemistry, Ark. State U., 1969; MD, U. Ark., Little Rock, 1976. Diplomate in gen. psychiatry and child and adolescent psychiatry Am. Bd. Psychiatry and Neurology. Chief resident in psychiatry William S. Hall Psychiat. Inst., Columbia, S.C., 1978-79; from instr. to asst. prof. dept. neuropsychiatry U. S.C. Sch. Medicine, Columbia, 1978-80, asst. clin. prof., 1980-82; chief child and adolescent psychiatry WSHPI, Columbia, 1978-80; pvt. practice Columbia, 1982-88; from vice chief to chief psychiatry Bapt. Med. Ctr., Columbia, 1983-87; med. dir. Psychiat. Health Svcs., Columbia, 1987-88; pvt. practice Charter Hosp. Charleston, S.C., 1988-95, assoc. med. dir., 1994-95; assoc. med. dir. Charter Hosp., Charleston, S.C., 1993-95; pres. med. staff Charter Hosp. Charleston, 1993-95; med. dir. Charter Behavior Health Sys., Charleston, 1995, Behavior Resources, Greenville, S.C., 1995; psychiat. cons. Univ. Devel. Disability, Columbia, 1982-83. Mem. Am. Psychiat. Assn., Am. Acad. Child Psychiatry, Am. Soc. Adolescent Psychiatry, S.C. Med. Assn., Greenville Med. Soc.

LONG, DAVID MICHAEL, JR., pharmaceutical executive, cardiothoracic surgeon; b. Shamokin, Pa., Feb. 26, 1929; s. David Michael and Elva (Christ) L.; m. Donna Rae Long, Feb. 26, 1954; children: Kurt, Raymond, Carl, Grace, Carolyn, Ruth. BS magna cum laude, Muhlenberg Coll., Allentown, Pa., 1951; MS, Hahnemann U., Phila., 1954, MD, 1956; PhD, U. Minn., 1965. Lic. physician, Ariz., Calif., Colo., Ill., Md., Minn., Pa., Tex.; diplomate Nat. Bd. Med. Examiners, Am. Bd. Surgery, Am. Bd. Thoracic Surgery; cert. trauma provider, advanced life support; advanced cardiac life support. Intern Hahnemann U. Hosp., Phila., 1956-57; resident in surgery U. Minn., Mpls., 1957-65, fellow in surgery, 1957-61, 63-65, fellow in physiology, 1959-61; pres., chmn. bd. Long Labs., San Diego, 1984-85; chmn., dir. rsch. Fluoromed Pharm., Inc., San Diego, 1985-89; chmn., dir. sci. Alliance

Pharm. Corp., La Jolla, Calif., 1989-91; pres., chmn. Abel Labs., Inc., Spring Valley, Calif., 1991—; mem. faculty Hahnemann U., 1953-54, U. Calif., San Diego, 1973-92, U. Minn., 1959-61, 63-64, Naval Med. Sch., 1962, Chgo. Med. Sch., 1965-67, Cook County Grad. Sch. Medicine, 1965-73, U. Ill., 1967-73; cons. Chgo. State Tuberculosis Sanitarium, 1967-72; asst. dir. dept. surg. rsch. Hektoen Inst. for Med. Rsch. of Cook County Hosp., 1965-68, dir., 1968-73, assoc. attending staff, 1965-73; attending staff West Side VA Hosp., 1966-73, U. Ill. Hosp., 1967-73, Villa View Hosp., 1973-85, AMI Valley Med. Ctr., 1973-85, Grossman Dist. Hosp., 1973-85, Alvarado Cmty. Hosp., 1973-85, Sharp Meml. Hosp., 1973-84; head divsn. cardiovasc. and thoracic surgery U. Ill., 1967-73; cons. continuing med. edn. com. Grossmont Dist. Hosp., 1985—; mem. continuing med. edn. com. Sharp Healthcare Sys., 1994—; cons. Docent Corp., 1975-76; com. mem. consensus devel. com. Thrombolytic Therapy in Thrombosis, NIH/FDA, 1980. Contbr. numerous articles and abstracts to profl. jours., chpts. to books; editl. bd. Current Surgery, 1967-89; co-editor Hematrix, 1982-85. Bd. dirs. Rsch. Assocs. of Point Loma Nazarene coll., San Diego, chmn., 1984-85; bd. trustees Muhlenberg Coll., Allentown, Pa., 1992—, chmn., 1994—; bd. dirs. Grossmont Hosp. Found., Grossmont Hosp., La Mesa, Calif., 1992—; co-chmn. Calif. divsn. of campaign of Muhlenberg Coll., 1992-93; chmn. Campaign of Grossmont Hosp. Found. for David and Donna Long Cancer Treatment Ctr. and Cardiac Diagnosis Ctr., 1992-94; co-chmn. Campaign for Health Ctr., Point Loma Nazarene Coll., San Diego, 1992-94. Rsch. fellow Heart Assn. Southeastern Pa., 1953-54, Student Senate of Hahnemann U., 1955; trainee Nat. Cancer Inst., 1957-58, Nat. Heart Inst., 1958-60, 63-64; spl. rsch. fellow Nat. Heart Inst., 1960-61; established investigator Minn. Heart Assn, 1964-65; Muhlenberg Coll. scholar, 1947-51, Hahnemann U. scholar, 1952-55, Luth. Brotherhood Leadership scholar, 1951. Fellow ACS, Am. Coll. Chest Physicians (sec. cardiovascular surgery com. 1976-78), Am. Coll. Cardiology; mem. AAAS, AMA, Am. Assn. Thoracic Surgery, Am. Assn. Anatomists, Internat. Cardiovascular Surgery Soc., Internat. Soc. for Artificial Cells and Immobilization Biotechnology, Am. Heart Assn., Am. Physiol. Soc., Am. Thoracic Soc., Assn. for Advancement of Med. Instrumentation, Cajal Soc. Neuroanatomy, Calif. Med. Assn., Internat. Soc. Surgery, Internat. Soc. Hemorheology (founding mem.), N.Y. Acad. Sci., San Diego County Med. Soc., Soc. Thoracic Surgeons, Soc. Univ. Surgeons, Warren H. Cole Soc., Western Thoracic Surg. Soc. Lutheran. Office: Abel Laboratories Inc Ste 108 2737 Via Orange Way Spring Valley CA 91978

LONG, DONLIN MARTIN, surgeon, educator; b. Rolla, Mo., Apr. 14, 1934; s. Donlin M. and Davene E. (Johnson) L.; m. Harriett Page, June 13, 1959; children: Kimberley Page, Elisabeth Merchant, David Bradford. Student, Jefferson City Jr. Coll., 1951-52; M.D., U. Mo., 1959; Ph.D., U. Minn., 1964. Diplomate: Am. Bd. Surgery. Intern U. Minn. Hosps., Mpls., 1959-60; resident U. Minn. Hosps., 1960-64; resident in neurosurgery Peter Bent Brigham and Children's Hosp. Med. Center, Boston, 1965; practice medicine specializing in neurosurgery Balt., 1973—; asst. prof. dept. neurosurgery U. Minn. Hosps., 1967-70, neurosurgeon, 1967-73, asso. prof., 1970-73; neurosurgeon-in-chief dept. neurosurgery Johns Hopkins Hosp., 1973—; prof. and chmn. dept. neurosurgery Johns Hopkins U., 1973—; mem. prin. staff Applied Physics Lab., 1976—; cons. neurosurgery Mpls. VA Hosp., 1967-73, John F. Kennedy Inst., 1977, Balt. City Hosp., 1973—. Contbr. numerous articles on neuropathology and surgery to profl. jours.; contbr. to book chpts. in field. Served with USPHS, 1965-67. Mem. Soc. Neurosci., Am. Assn. Neuropathologists, Soc. Neurol. Surgeons, AAAS, AMA, Balt. Neurol. Soc., Internat. Assn. Study of Pain, Internat. Soc. Pediatric Neurosurgery, William T. Peyton Soc., Congress Neurol. Surgeons, Johns Hopkins Med. and Surg. Assn., Electron Microscopy Soc. Am., Md. Neurosurg. Soc., Am. Acad. Neurosurgery, Am. Assn. Neurol. Surgery, Neurol. Soc. Am., Cajal Club, Sigma Xi, Omicron Delta Kappa, Alpha Omega Alpha, Phi Eta Sigma, Pi Mu Epsilon, Mystical 7. Home: 9 Blythewood Rd Baltimore MD 21210-2401 Office: Johns Hopkins Hosp Dept Neurosurgery Meyer 7-109 600 N Wolfe St Baltimore MD 21205-2110

LONG, DORANNE LOUISE, physical therapist; b. Honolulu, May 10, 1959; d. James S. And Barbara D. (Sax) L. BS in Physical Therapy, U. Puget Sound, 1981; MS in Physical Therapy, Mass. Gen. Hosp. Inst. Health, 1988. Physical therapist North Lincoln Hosp., Lincoln City, Oreg., 1981-84, Physical Therapy and Hand Rehab. Clinic, Yakima, Wash., 1984-87, Rougue Valley Physical Therapy Clinic, Grants Pass, Oreg., 1988-90; pvt. practice Grants Pass, 1990-95, Abel Ctr. for Rehab. Therapies, Inc., Grants Pass, 1995—. Mem. Am. Physical Therapy Assn., Oreg. Physical Therapy Assn.

LONG, EDWIN TUTT, surgeon, data base company executive; b. St. Louis, July 23, 1925; s. Forrest Edwin and Hazel (Tutt) L.; m. Mary M. Hull, Apr. 16, 1955; children: Jennifer Ann, Laura Ann, Peter Edwin. AB, Columbia U., 1944, M.D., 1947. Diplomate Am. Bd. Surgery, Am. Bd. Thoracic Surgery. Rotating intern Meth. Hosp., Bklyn., 1947-78; surg. intern U. Chgo. Clinics, 1948-49, resident in gen. surgery, 1952-55, resident in thoracic surgery, 1955-57; asst. prof. surgery U. Chgo., 1957-59; thoracic and cardiovascular surgeon, chief surgery dept. Watson Clinic, Lakeland, Fla., 1960-69; asso. prof. surgery U. Pa., Phila., 1970-73; thoracic and cardiovascular surgeon Allegheny Cardiovascular Surg. Assocs., Pitts, 1973-88; exec. v.p. Mailings Clearing Ho. and Roxbury Press, Inc., 1988-90, pres., 1990—, chmn., bd. dir., 1991—; dir. Watson Clinic Rsch. Found., 1965-69; bd. dirs. Roxbury Press, Inc., Cardiac Telecom, Inc., Pitts. Pressure Vectorography Rsch. grantee Alfred P. Sloan Found., 1963; patentee gas sterilizer, 1969. Capt. USAF, 1950-52. Mem. ACS, Am. Coll. Cardiology, Internat. Soc. for Cardiovascular Surg., Allegheny Vascular Soc. (pres. 1987), Ea. Vascular Soc. (founding mem.), Soc. Thoracic Surgery (founding mem.), Direct Mktg. Assn., Midwest Bioethics Ctr., Kansas City Club, Rotary, Sigma Xi, Beta Theta Pi. Home: 1415 Torrey Pines Dr Columbia MO 65203-4830 Office: Roxbury Press Inc 601 E Marshall St Sweet Springs MO 65351-0295

LONG, ELIZABETH ANN, physical therapist; b. Indpls., Nov. 28, 1961; d. Alfred and Irene (Prost) Schoepf; m. Bradford Keith Long, June 22, 1985. BS, U. Md., 1984. Registered phys. therapist, Md. Staff phys. therapist Greater Washington Ortho. Group, Silver Spring, Md., 1984-85, Kensington Phys. Therapy, Wheaton, Md., 1985-87; chief phys. therapist Office of Drs. Ghovanlou & Townsend, Greenbelt, Md., 1987-89; staff phys. therapist Potomac Home Health Care, Rockville, Md., 1986-90, clin. rehab. supr., 1991—. Mem. Honors Admission Com., U Md., 1980-82. Recipient Malinoski award Md. Assn. Home Care, 1994. Mem. Am. Phys. Therapy Assn. (Md. chpt. 1984—, sect. on orthopedics 1985-90, sect. on geriatrics 1988—, sect. on cmty. health 1992—, reimbursement com. mem. 1994—), Md. Assn. Home Care (chairperson phys. therapy spl. interest group 1994-96), U. Md. Alumni Bd. Republican. Presbyterian. Home: 15037 Joshua Tree Rd North Potomac MD 20878-2548

LONG, HUEY BILLY, education educator; b. Grand Ridge, Fla., Apr. 9, 1935; s. Melvin Durward Sr. and Ramona Bernice (Robinson) L.; m. Marie Ward, June 10, 1954; children: Huey B., Pamela Anne Long Cleghorne, Mark Stafford. BS, Fla. State U., 1957, MS, 1958, PhD, 1966. Info. and edn. forester Fla. Forest Svc., Lakeland, 1958-62; asst. br. chief I&E br. Fla. Forest Svc., Tallahassee, 1962-63; dir. pub. rels. City of Tallahassee, 1963-66; assoc. dir. Urban Rsch. Ctr. Fla. State U., Titusville, 1966-67, dir. Urban Rsch. Ctr., asst. prof., 1967-69; assoc. prof. edn. U. Ga., Athens, 1969-72, dir. grad. studies Coll. Edn., 1972-82, assoc. dean rsch. and grad studies, 1974-82; Kellogg prof., dir. Pub. Mgrs. Ctr. U. Okla., Norman, 1987—. Author: Adult Learning: Research and Practice, 1983; author, editor 20 books. Mem. citizens adv. com. City of Titusville, 1967-69; exec. dir. Pub. Adminstrn. Continuing Edn. Svc., Titusville, 1966-69; pres. Long Enterprises, Norman, 1970—; pres. Apalachee Audubon Soc., Tallahassee, 1964-66; v.p. Fla. Audubon Soc., Maitland, 1962-68; bd. dirs. Fla. Nature Conservancy, Tallahassee, 1964-66. Armand Hammer fellow U. So. Calif., 1984; UCLA-USC fellow, 1984. Mem. Am. Assn. Adult and Continuing Edn. (bd. dirs. 1971-78, pres. 1976-77). Republican. Baptist. Home: 4409 Balmoral Ct Norman OK 73072-3163 Office: U Okla Coll Edn Van Vleet Oval Norman OK 73019

LONG, JOHN PAUL, pharmacologist, educator; b. Albia, Iowa, Oct. 4, 1926; s. John Edward and Bessie May L.; m. Marilyn Joy Stookesberry, June 11, 1950; children: Jeff, John, Jane. B.S., U. Iowa, 1950, M.S., 1952, Ph.D., 1954. Research scientist Sterling Winthrop Co., Albany, N.Y., 1954-56; asst. prof. U. Iowa, Iowa City, 1956-58, asso. prof., 1958-63, prof. pharmacology, 1963—, head dept., 1970-83. Author 315 research publs. in field. Served with U.S. Army, 1945-46. Recipient Abel award Am. Pharm. Assn., 1958; Ebert award Pharmacology Soc., 1962. Mem. Am. Soc. Pharm. Exptl. Therapy, Soc. Exptl. Biol. Medicine. Republican. Home: 1817 Kathlin Dr Iowa City IA 52246-4617 Office: U Iowa Coll Medicine Dept Pharmacology Iowa City IA 52242

LONG, KERRY JEAN, pharmaceutical company executive; b. Joliet, Ill., Oct. 28, 1948; d. Robert Armand and Marilyn Jean (Burt) L. BS in Chemistry, St. Mary's Coll., Notre Dame, Ind., 1970; MBA, U. Chgo., 1978. Analytical chemist Gillette Co., Chgo., 1970-74, Ctrl. Soya Co., Chgo., 1974-75; analytical chemist G. D. Searle, Skokie, Ill., 1975-78, supr. quality control, 1978-81; mgr. quality control G. D. Searle, Skokie and San Juan, P.R., 1981-82, University Park, Ill., 1982-84; dir. quality assurance G. D. Searle, Skokie, 1984-87, sr. dir. quality assurance, 1987-93, v.p. corp. quality assurance, 1993—. Mem. St. Mary's Coll. Alumnae (v.p. 1984-87), U. Chgo. Women's Bus. Group. Democrat. Roman Catholic. Office: G D Searle & Co 5200 Old Orchard Rd Skokie IL 60077-1034

LONG, KEVIN JAY, medicolegal consultant; b. Chgo., May 19, 1961. Student, Chgo. Med. Sch., 1983-86; BS in Math./Stats., Loyola U., Chgo., 1985; postgrad., John Marshall Law Sch., 1988-90. Researcher Cons. in Neurology, Ltd., Skokie, Ill., 1981-84, Assn. for Women's Health Care, Ltd., Chgo., 1982-83; researcher dept. neurology U. Ill., Chgo., 1985-86; law clk. Steven K. Jambois, Chgo., 1989; med. paralegal Hilfman & Fogel, P.C., Chgo., 1989-92; internal medicolegal cons. Robert A. Clifford & Assocs., Chgo., 1992; medicolegal cons. Chgo., 1992—. Contbr. articles to Current Problems in Obstetrics and Gynecology, Archives of Neurology, Archives of Internal Medicine, Pediatrics, Clin. Electroencephalography, Am. Jour. Medicine, Hosp. Pharmacy, Pediatric Emergency Care, Quality Management in Health Care, Houston Medicine, Nursing Quality Connection. Mem. Nat. Hon. Soc. Secondary Schs., Assn. Trial Lawyers Am., Am. Med. Student Assn., N.Y. Acad. Scis., Blue Key Nat. Hon. Frat., Beta Beta Beta Biol. Honor Soc., Alpha Epsilon Delta Premed. Honor Soc. Jewish. Home and Office: Ste 3-South 1325 W North Shore Ave Chicago IL 60626-4763

LONG, MARK ALEXANDER DIETTERICH, psychologist; b. Boston, July 29, 1954; s. Lewis M.K. and Barbara Sue (Dietterich) L.; m. Pamela Gayle Gibbles, Aug. 1, 1987. BA, Earlham Coll., 1976; MEd, James Madison U., 1977; EdD, W.Va. U., 1986. Diplomate Am. Bd. Prof. Disability Cons.; lic. psychologist, Va., N.C. Commd. USN, 1983, advanced through grades to Comdr.; instr. W.Va. U., Morgantown, 1981-84; clin. psychology intern USN, Bethesda, Md., 1983-84; clin. psychologist USN, Camp Le Jeune, N.C., 1984-86, 91-95, Thrasher-Faber Assocs., Norfolk, Va., 1987-89, Comprehensive Mental Health Svcs., Virginia Beach, Va., 1986-89; psychologist Carolina Psychol. Health Svcs., Jacksonville, N.C., 1989-91, Thrasher-Faber Assocs., Virginia Beach, Va., 1991-95; psychologist Family Advocacy program Naval Med. Ctr., Portsmouth, 1996—. Mem. Am. Psychol. Assn., Am. Bd. Profl. Disability Cons. Office: Family Advocacy Dept Naval Med Ctr 6500 Hampton Blvd Norfolk VA 23508

LONG, MICHAEL LINDSAY, ophthalmologist; b. Ottumwa, Iowa, Dec. 17, 1944; s. Wallace Hansen and Mary Agnes (Lindsay) L.; m. Dianne Ruth Koenen, Aug. 11, 1967; children: Craig, Sarah, Suzanne. BS, U. Iowa, 1967, MD, 1970. Intern Butterworth Hosp., Grand Rapids, Mich., 1970-71; resident in ophthalmology Mayo Clinic, Rochester, Minn., 1973-77; pvt. practice North Iowa Eye Clinic, Mason City, 1977—; sr. ophthalmic registrar Ahmadu Bello U., Zaria, Nigeria, 1976-96. Capt. USAF, 1971-73. Fellow Am. Acad. Ophthalmology; mem. AMA, Iowa Med. Soc., Iowa Acad. Ophthalmology, Alpha Omega Alpha. Methodist. Home: 14 Old Farm Rd Mason City IA 50401 Office: North Iowa Eye Clinic 3121 4th St SW Mason City IA 50401

LONG, RALPH STEWART, clinical psychologist; b. Pitts., Feb. 23, 1926; s. Ralph S. and Virginia (Hawk) L.; m. Vera Lazorchak, June 16, 1951; children: Karen Virginia, Brian Reed, Lauri Michelle. BS, Lock Haven U., 1950; MEd, Pa. State U., 1951; PhD, Washington U., St. Louis, 1965. Lic. psychologist, Tex. Commd. 2d lt. USAF, 1951, advanced through grades to lt. col., 1968; psychologist various hosps. USAF, U.S. and Europe, 1951-71; ret., 1971; dir. psychol. svcs. Community Ctr. Mental Health, Mental Retardation, Wichita Falls, Tex., 1971-72; psychol. cons. Family Counseling Ctr., Wichita Falls, 1972-74; dir. psychol. svcs. Nueces County Mental Health-Mental Retardation Community Ctr, 1974-77; dir. Corpus Christi Counseling Ctr./Physicians-Surgeons Hosp., Tex., 1977-79, Psychol. Cons., Corpus Christi, 1979-82; exec. dir. Personal Dynamics Inst., Corpus Christi, 1982—, dir., 1988—; instr. dept. psychology McKendree Coll., Lebanon, Ill., 1962-63; instr. So. Ill. U., 1962-64; adj. prof. human rels. Webster U., Webster Groves, Mo., 1976-79, 88-93; adj. prof. psychology Del Mar Coll., Corpus Christi, 1977-83, adj. prof. bus. adminstrn., 1991-93; cons. Tex. Dept. Corrections, 1988-90; bd. dirs. Ctr. Creative Living, 1986—; cons., trainer Crisis Svcs., 1980—; profl. adv. bd. North Tex. Regional Coun. Alcoholism, 1971-74, Mental Health Assn. Coastal Bend, 1974-83, Wichita Mental Health Assn., 1965-67, 70-74; adj. prof. Embry-Riddle U., Corpus Christi, 1991-93; consulting psychologist Nueces County Juvenile Justice Ctr., Corpus Christi, 1992—, Warm Springs Rehab. Ctr., Corpus Christi, 1992—, MCC Managed Behavioral Care, Inc., Eden Prairie, Minn., 1992—, Champus Provider, 1972—; bd. dirs. Consumer Credit Counseling Svc. South Tex., 1983-92, emeritus, 1993—. Contbr. to profl. jours.; presenter in field. Charter mem. U.S. Holocaust Meml. Mus. With USN, 1944-51. Named Am. Man Sci., 1962. Fellow Soc. Air Force Clin. Psychologists; mem. APA, DAV, VFW, Am. Inst. Hypnosis, U.S. Holocaust Meml. Mus. (charter), Libr. of Congress Assocs. (charter), Tex. Assn. Mental Health (exec. com. 1980-83), Air Force Assn., Nat. Register Health Svc. Providers in Psychology, Smithsonian, Sierra Club, Am. Assn. Ret. Persons, Masons, Shriners, Sigma Xi. Office: Personal Dynamics Inst 1819 S Brownlee Blvd Corpus Christi TX 78404-2901

LONG, SARAH S., pediatrician; b. Portland, Oreg., Oct. 31, 1944. MD, Jefferson Med. Coll., 1970. Intern St. Christopher Hosp. for Children, Phila., 1970-71, resident, 1971-73; fellow pediatric and infant depts. Temple U. Sch. Medicine, Phila., 1973-75; staff St. Christopher Hosp. for Children, Phila., 1975—; prof. Temple U. Sch. Medicine, 1975—; Diplomate Am. Bd. Pediatrics. Office: St Christopher Child Hosp Erie Ave at Front St Philadelphia PA 19134*

LONG, WALKER ANDERSON, pediatric cardiologist, pharmaceutical executive; b. Cleve., Mar. 9, 1949; s. William Lunstord and Rebecca (Williams) L.; m. Wendy Jane Dascomb, June 1, 1970 (div. Nov. 1995); children: Joshua, Millie, Hadley. BA, U. N.C., Chapel Hill, 1971, MD, 1976. Resident in med.. and pediatrics U. N.C., Chapel Hill, 1976-79, fellow neonatology, 1979-81, fellow pediatric cardiology, 1981-83, rsch. asst. prof., 1983-90, rsch. assoc. prof., 1990-96, assoc. prof., 1996—; sr. clin. rsch. scientist Wellcome Rsch. Labs., Research Triangle Park, N.C., 1983-90; head pulmonary sect. Wellcome Rsch. Labs., Research Triangle Park, 1990-92, dir. cardiopulmonary medicine, 1992-93; editor Jour. Pharm. Medicine, 1994—. Contbr. articles to profl. jours., chpts. to books; editor book: Fetal and Neonatal Cardiology, 1990. Fellow Am. Coll. Cardiology; mem. Alpha Omega Alpha. Episcopalian. Office: UNC-CH Div Pediat Cardiology 311 Burnett-Womack Bldg 229 Chapel Hill NC 27599-7220

LONG, WILLIAM MCMURRAY, physiology educator; b. Greenville, S.C., Nov. 9, 1948; s. William McMurray and Cecile Mae (Ariail) L.; m. Kathleen Webb, Mar. 18, 1971 (dec. Oct. 1990); m. Marianne Castrén, July 22, 1992. BA, Tulane U., 1970, BS, 1974; PhD, La. State U., 1980. Rsch. assoc. Med. Ctr. La. State U., New Orleans, 1974-75; pathology extern Charity Hosp. of La., New Orleans, 1975-80; Nat. Rsch. Svc. Award fellow Pa. State Med. Ctr., Hershey, 1980-82; rsch. assoc. Mt. Sinai Med. Ctr., Miami Beach, Fla., 1983-89; rsch. physiologist VA Med. Ctr., Miami, Fla., 1982-89; asst. prof. medicine U. Miami, 1982-89; asst. prof. physiology U. N.D., Grand Forks, 1989-94; CFO OBI Lab. Co., 1994—; cons. VA Med. Ctr., Miami, 1991; ad hoc reviewer Am. Jour. Physiology, Bethesda, Md., 1990-91, Va. Ctrl. Office, 1987-90; dir. Minority Access to Rsch. Careers, U. N.D., Ah'jo'gun to the Baccalaureate. Author: Non-Steriodal Agents in Sepsis Syndrome, 1989, (with others) Airways: Asthma, Bronchietasis and Emphysema, 1992; contbr. articles to profl. jours. Chmn. Nat. Letter-In Com., New Orleans, 1968, Cliff Solar Fund, New Orleans, 1973; cood. Spring Jazz Festival, New Orleans, 1970. Recipient Rsch. award Bush Found., 1990, Nat. Rsch. Svc. award NIH, 1980-82; grantee NIH, 1986-89, Fla. Lung Assn., 1984-85, VA, 1986-90, Am. Heart Assn. Dakota affiliate, 1991-93, Nat. Inst. Gen. Med. Scis., 1992—. Mem. Am. Physiol. Soc., Am. Thoracic Soc., N.Y. Acad. Scis., Da Vinci Soc. (sec. 1987-88). Home: 1023 Reeves Dr Grand Forks ND 58201-5646 Office: OBI Labs 1023 Reeves Dr Grand Forks ND 58201

LONGENECKER, STEPHEN CARROLL, physician; b. Reading, Pa., Nov. 13, 1960; s. Roger Neil and Louise Carole (Pray) L.; m. Lisa Scornavacchi, Nov. 3, 1984; children: Stephen, Andrew, Mary. BS, Albright Coll., 1982; MD, Temple Univ., 1986. Gen. surgery internship Temple Univ. Hosp., Phila., 1986-87, orthopaedic surgery residency, 1989-91; staff orthopaedic surgeon Reading Hosp. & Medical Ctr., 1991—; group practice Orthopaedic Assocs. Reading, 1991—. Fellow Am. Acad. Orthopaedic Surgeons, AMA, Berks County Medical Eastern Orthopaedic Assoc. Lutheran. Office: Orthopaedic Assn Reading 401 W Buttonwood Dr Reading PA 19611

LONGFELLOW, LAYNE ALLEN, psychologist, educator, author, lecturer; b. Jackson, Ohio, Oct. 23, 1937; s. Hershel Herman and Opal Edna (Pursley) L. BA in Psychology magna cum laude with honors, Ohio U., 1959; MA, U. Mich., 1961, PhD, 1967. Asst. prof. psychology Reed Coll., Portland, Oreg., 1967-68; postdoctoral fellow Dr. Carl Rogers, La Jolla, Calif., 1968-70; asst. prof. psychology Prescott (Ariz.) Coll., 1970-71, chmn. dept., 1971-72, acad. v.p., 1972-74; dir. exec. seminars Menninger Found., Topeka, 1975-78; dir. wilderness exec. seminars Banff Ctr., Alta., Can., 1978-86; pres. Lecture Theatre, Inc., Prescott, Ariz., 1981—; dir. Inst. for Human Skills, 1985—; internat. lectr., cons. in field; adj. faculty Union Grad. Sch. and Humanistic Psychology Inst., 1974-84. Composer: Ten Songs, 1969, Uncommon Festival of Christmas, 1974; creator Body Talk, 1970, The Feel Wheel, 1972, The Mountain Waits, 1983 (Gold medal N.Y. Festival of TV); video producer, author: Generations of Excellence, 1992, Beyond Success, 1993, Sustainable Growth, 1994, Healty, Wealthy and Wise, 1994; author: (with W.M. Hubbard) Visual Feast, 1995. Active Found. for Ethics and Meaning. Woodrow Wilson fellow, NSF fellow, NIMH fellow. Mem. APA, Nat. Speakers Assn., Nature Conservancy, Phi Beta Kappa. Office: Lecture Theatre Inc PO Box 4317 Prescott AZ 86302-4317

LONGINO, GRADY ESTES, physician; b. Atlanta, Sept. 17, 1923; s. Dick Randolph and Mary Evelyn (Estes) L.; m. Patricia Eleanor Bohinick, Aug. 28, 1952; children: Katherine Parker, Lynn Watkins, Frances Seel. MD, Emory U., 1947. Cert. geriatrics Am. Bd. Internal Medicine. Intern Coney Island Hosp., 1947-48; asst. resident Grady Meml. Hosp., Atlanta, 1948-49; med. intern Lawson VA Hosp., Atlanta, 1949-50; asst. resident Atlanta VA Hosp., 1952-54; pvt. practice associated with Dr. H.G. Estes Atlanta, 1954-55; staff physician Dublin (Ga.) VA Hosp., 1955-56, chief of medicine, 1956-58; pvt. practice, ptnr. Clark & Daughtrey Med. Group, Lakeland, Fla., 1958-67; staff physician CArl Vinson VA Hosp., Dublin, 1967-90; dist. health dir. Dist. 5 Unit 1 of Ga. Dept. Human Resources, 1992—. Lt. USNR, 1950-52, ret. comdr., Korea. Fellow Am. Coll. Physicians. Home: 115 Ramsey St Dublin GA 31021-4035

LONGNECKER, DAVID E., anesthesiologist, educator; b. Kendallville, Ind., 1939. MD, Ind. U., 1964, MA in Anesthesiology, 1968. Diplomate Am. Bd. Anesthesiology. Intern Blodgett Meml. Hosp., Grand Rapids, Mich., 1964-65; resident in anesthesiology U. Ind., 1965-69; asst. prof. dept. anesthesiology U. Mo., 1970-73; assoc. prof. dept. anesthesiology U. Va., Charlottesville, 1974-78, prof., 1978-88; Robert D. Dripps prof., chmn. dept. anesthesia U. Pa., Phila., 1988—. With USPHS, 1968-70. Mem. Am. Soc. Anesthesiology, Inst. Medicine. Office: U Pa Health Sys Dept Anesthesia 3400 Spruce St Philadelphia PA 19104

LONGO, MARGARET FAY, surgeon; b. Alexandria, La., July 4, 1936; d. Joseph Phillip and Mary Margaret (Cangelosi) L. BA, Our Lady of Lake Coll., 1958; MD, La. State U., 1962. Diplomate Am. Bd. Surgery. Intern, house staff Confederate Meml. Med. Ctr., Shreveport, La., 1962-63; surg. resident St. Mary's Hosp., Rochester, Minn., 1963-66, Rochester (Minn.) Meth. Hosp., 1963-66, 67; asst. surg. cons. Mayo Clinic, Rochester, 1967; mem. surg. staff Lafayette (La.) Gen. Hosp., 1968-89, chmn. dept. surgery, 1971; mem. surg. staff Our Lady of Lourdes Hosp., Lafayette, 1968-89; coord. quality/utilization mgmt. Lafayette Gen. Med. Ctr., 1990-92; mem. vis. surg. staff Lafayette Charity Hosp., 1968-72; critical care cons. on trauma Acadiana Emergency Med. Svcs. Coun., 1977-79. Chmn. med. div. United Givers Fund, 1971, 83; co-chmn. Acadian Right to Life Com., 1974; mem. Acadiana Arts Coun., 1977-79; bd. dirs. Lafayette Natural History Mus. Assn., 1978-81, 81-84, Emergency Med. Svcs. Coun., 1978-83, United Givers Fund Lafayette, Inc., 1979—; advisor Acadiana chpt. Am. Assn. Med. Assts., 1978-83; mem. Bayou coun. Girl Scouts U.S., 1982-85, adv. com. Hospice Acadiana, 1983-90, Trustees' Acad., Our Lady of the Lake Coll., 1981—. Recipient Best Original Research award Tex. Acad. Sci., 1956, cert. of merit award, 1956; Minn. Surg. Essay award Minn. Surg. Soc., 1966; Surg. Travel award Mayo Found.-Mayo Clinic, 1967; Physician's Recognition award AMA, 1974-77, 78-80, 80-83, 83-86, 86-89, 89-92, 92-96, 95—; Outstanding Alumni award Our Lady of Lake, U. San Antonio, 1976; scholastic scholar, Our Lady of Lake Coll., 1954-58. Fellow ACS (pres. La. chpt. 1983-84, gov.-at-large, regent), Am. Coll. Gastroenterology; mem. AAAS (hon.), Priestley Soc. (dir. 1977-80, pres. 1982-83), Undersea Med. Soc., Doctors Mayo Soc., So. Med. Assn., Southeastern Surg. Congress, La. Med. Soc., Minn. Med. Soc., Surg. Assn. La. (dir. 1976-79, pres. 1990), Am. Coll. Physician Execs., Lafayette Parish Med. Soc., Mayo Clinic Alumni Assn. (v.p. 1983-85, pres. 1987-89). Roman Catholic. Contbr. articles to profl. jours.

LONGUEVILLE, JACQUES JOSEPH, medical educator; b. Quaregnon, Hainaut, Belgium, Aug. 23, 1935; s. Arthur Hubert and Clementine Zoe (Wautelet) L.; m. Monique Albert Verdonck, Aug. 9, 1960; children: Michel, Philippe, Serge, Vincent, Nathalie. MD, U. Louvain (Belgium), 1960. Lic. specialist in internal medicine, 1965. Resident City Hosp., Chatelet, Belgium, 1960-62; resident U. Med. Ctr., Louvain, 1962-65, chef de clinique adjoint, 1966-77; chef de clinique associe U. Med. Ctr., Brussels, 1977-87, chef de clinique, 1987—, clin. prof., 1991—; fellow P.H.S. Jersey City Med. Ctr., 1965-66; mem. Drug Registration Com., Bruxelles, 1982—. Mem. Internat. Soc. Internal Medicine, European Assn. Cancer Rsch., Royal Soc. Medicine (London), Am. Soc. Clin. Oncology, European Soc. Med. Oncology, N.Y. Acad. Scis., Rotary (pres. 1991-92). Roman Catholic. Home: Rte de Rixensart 71, B-1300 Limal Brabant, Belgium Office: Cliniques U St-Luc, Ave Hippocrate 10, B-1200 Bruxelles Brabant, Belgium

LONIEWSKI, EDWARD GERARD, orthopedic surgeon; b. Detroit, Apr. 19, 1961; s. Edward Anthony and Joanne (Rohrig) L.; m. Melissa Dawn McMurray, Oct. 5, 1991; children: Tess Maria, Carly Louise. BA, Mich. State U., 1986, DO, 1990. Intern Botsford Hosp., Farmington Hills, Mich., 1990-91; resident orthopedics Botsford Hosp., Farmington Hills, 1991-95; fellow revision joint arterioplasty U. Chgo., 1995-96; orthopedic surgeon McPherson Hosp., Howell, Mich., 1996—; sec. Intern Resident Com., Chgo., 1991-96. Recipient Andrew Taylor Still award, 1995, Resident Achievement award, 1995, Burroughs-Wellcome Cmty. Achievement award, 1995; rsch. fellow Am. Osteo. Assn., Chgo., 1994-95. Mem. Am. Osteo. Assn. (sec. intern/resident com. 1991-96). Roman Catholic. Office: McPherson Hosp 620 Byron Howell MI 48843

LOO, MARITTA LOUISE, military officer, nurse; b. Denver, Feb. 6, 1945; d. William Del Rio and Audrey Elaine (Fromholz) Dugan; m. Albert W.S. Loo, June 26, 1971 (div. Apr. 1976). Diploma, St. Mary's, Kansas City, Mo., 1966; BS in Health Svcs. Adminstrn., Calif. U., Navato, 1986; student, Army War Coll., 1986-87. RN, Tex. From staff to head nurse Kansas City Gen. Hosp., Mo., 1966-69; shift charge, emergency nurse St. Mary's Hosp., Kansas City, 1969-71; research nurse office of Dr. J. Willoughby, Kansas City, 1970-71; dir. critical care Dallas-Ft. Worth Med. Ctr., Grand Prairie, Tex., 1974-86; rev. supr. Tex. Med. Found., 1988-92; asst. dir. home health Dallas-Ft. Worth Med. Ctr., Grand Prairie, 1993—; freelance leadership trainer, mgmt. cons., 1985-93; owner, mgr. Masavic Properties, Inc., Ft. Worth, 1979—; co-chmn. Tex. Adj. Gen.'s adv. coun., Austin, 1985-86; spl. advisor Am. Security Coun., Washington, 1985, nat. advisor, 1985-87; rep. Partnership For Peace program, Prague, 1995; mem. Congl. Bd. for candidate selection Annapolis Acad., 1995—; comdr. med. unit Tex. Air N.G., 1996—; motivational spkr., 1994—. Contbr. articles to mags., 1984—. Resource coord. ARC, Carlisle, Pa., 1986-87; mem. Cath. Adults, Arlington, Tex. Served to capt. USAF, 1971-74; col. Air N.G., 1975—, Desert Shield, 1990, Desert Storm, 1990-91. Recipient honored vol. award ARC, 1982, Profl. Devel. award Tex. Adj. Gen.'s Adv. Coun., 1986, Rare Joint Forces award, 1995; named one of Notable Women of Tex., 1985. Mem. ANA, DAV (bronze leader comdrs. club), AACN (bd. advisors 1983, office Ft. Worth chpt. 1984-86), N.G. Assn. (del. 1984—), Air Force Assn., Am. Legion. Republican. Roman Catholic. Home: 2433 Parkwood Grand Prairie TX 75050-1727

LOOK, JANET K., psychologist; b. Bklyn., Mar. 11, 1944; d. Harry and Isabelle (Chernoff) Kaplan; divorced; children: Howard, Erika (dec.). AB, NYU, 1964; EdM, Rutgers U., 1967, EdD, 1976. Lic. psychologist; cert. sch. psychologist. Asst. examiner Ednl. Testing Svc., Princeton, N.J., 1964-66; instr. Rutgers U., New Brunswick, N.J., 1968-69; psychologist Seattle Pub. Schs., 1991—; pvt. practice Kirkland, Wash., 1993—; adj. instr. U. Conn., Waterbury, 1973-91; appearances on various TV and radio shows including the Today Show; interviews include Litchfield County Times, 1987, Waterbury Rep.-Am., 1983-87, Manchester Jour. Inquirer, 1986, Danbury News-Times, 1985; presenter APA, San Francisco, 1991, Nation's Concern and Its Response, U. Wis., Milw., 1991, Nat. Assn. Sch. Psychologists, Dallas, 1991, Divorce Issues Inst., So. Conn. State U., New Haven, 1989. Author: (with others) The Troubled Adolescent, 1991; contbr. articles to newspapers, including N.Y. Times. Mem. APA, Wash. State Psychol. Assn., Nat. Assn. Sch. Psychologists, Wash. State Assn. Sch. Psychologists (area rep., bd. dirs. 1991-93). Office: 1104 Market St Kirkland WA 98033-5441

LOOMIE, LEO STEPHEN, psychiatrist; b. N.Y.C., Dec. 31, 1916; s. Leo Stephen and Loretta Felicia (Murphy) L.; m. Araceli Maria Riera, Dec. 27, 1941 (div. 1963); children: Adrienne, Leo S., Loretta; m. Helen Green, May 25, 1971 (dec.). BA, Fordham Coll., 1938; MD, Columbia U., 1942. Intern Bklyn. Naval Hosp., 1942-43; resident in psychiatry Menninger Clinic, Topeka, Kans., 1947-49; pvt. practice N.Y.C., 1950—; med. dir. N.Y. Psychoanalytic Inst., 1956-73. Lt. USN, 1946-47. Fellow Am. Psychiat. Assn., Am. Psychoanalytic Assn. (chmn. membership com. 1961-66); mem. N.Y. Psychoanalytic Soc., N.Y. State Med. Soc., Regency Whist Club, South Fork Country Club. Home and Office: 150 E 77th St New York NY 10021-1922

LOOMIS, EARL ALFRED, JR., psychiatrist; b. Mpls., May 21, 1921; s. Earl Alfred and Amy Louise (Shore) L.; m. Victoria Malkerson, June 2, 1944 (div.); children: Rebecca Marie Keith, Kathleen Victoria, Jennifer Lee; m. Lucile Meyer, July 1, 1962 (dec. 1967); 1 child, Amy Windeler; m. Anita Muriel Peabody, Mar. 22, 1969. MD, U. Minn., 1945. Diplomate Am. Bd. Psychiatry and Neurology, Am. Bd. Adult and Child Psychiatry. Intern in internal medicine, pediatrics Univ. Hosp., Boston, 1945-46; resident Western Psychiat. Hosp., Pitts., 1946-48, Hosp. U. Pa., Phila., 1948-50; assoc. prof. child psychiatry U. Pitts. Sch. Medicine, 1952-56; prof. psychiatry and religion Union Theol. Sem., N.Y.C., 1956-63; chief div. child psychiatry St. Luke's Hosp., N.Y.C., 1956-62; rsch. fellow U. Geneva (Switzerland) Inst. Jean-jacques Rousseau, 1962-63; med. dir. Blueberry Treatment Ctr./Severly Emotionally Ill Children, Bklyn., 1963-81; prof. psychiatry Med. Coll. Ga., Augusta, 1980-90; pvt. practice, cons. Vet. Hosp., Charter Hosp. of Augusta, 1985-95; cons. U.S. VA Hosp., Augusta, 1985-95; cons. Gracewood Sch. and Hosp., Augusta, 1983-89, Eisenhower Army Med. Ctr., Augusta, 1983—. Author: The Self in Pilgrimage, 1960; contbr. articles to profl. jours. Lt. (j.g.) USNR, 1950-52. Rsch. grant NIMH, 1956-63, travel grant, 1962-63, U.S. Info. Svcs., 1963. Fellow Am. Psychiat. Assn. (chair psychiatry and religion 1955-60); Group for the Advancement of Psychiatry (chair psychiatry and religion 1959-62), Am. Psychoanalytic Assn., Psychoanalytic Study Group of S.C. (founder, pres. 1981-88). Home and Office: 1002 Katherine St Apt 6 Augusta GA 30904-6141 also: PO Box 697 125 Cove Cir Greenport NY 11944

LOOMIS, WILLIAM FARNSWORTH, biology educator; b. Boston, Sept. 17, 1940; s. William F. and Violet (Amory) L.; m. Patricia Hasegawa, Aug. 21, 1981; children: Catherine Amory, Emily Farnsworth. BS, Harvard U., 1962; PhD, MIT, 1965. Prof. biology U. Calif., San Diego. Author: Developmental Biology, 1986. Mem. Soc. Devel. Biology (pres.). Office: U Calif-San Diego Dept Biology # B-022 La Jolla CA 92093

LOONEN, ANTON JOSEPH MARIA, clinical pharmacologist; b. Vlijmen, The Netherlands, July 4, 1953; s. Hendrikus Johannes and Maria Cornelia Lamberta (Jansen) L.; m. Carmen Jeannet Soe-Agnie, Jan. 11, 1980 (div. 1984). MSc, U. Amsterdam, The Netherlands, 1976, PharmD, 1978, PhD, 1980; MD, U. Nymegen, The Netherlands, 1996. Jr. asst. U. Amsterdam, 1975-76, jr. staff mem., 1977-80; clin. pharmacologist Reinier van Arkel/Coudewater/Medictr., 's-Hertogenbosch/Rosmalen/Vught, The Netherlands; external clin. advisor Dutch Drug Registration Bd., Rijswijk, 1984-89; sec., mem. Found. Adv. Clin. Rsch. Psychiatry, Hilversum, 1985—. Author: Farmaca, Psychofarmaca Klinisch Onderzoek, 1987; contbr. articles to profl. jours. Mem. Collegium Internat. Neuropsychopharmacologicum, European Coll. Neuropsychopharmacology. Roman Catholic. Office: Psychiat Hosp, Reinier van Arkel, PO Box 10.150, 5260 GB Vught The Netherlands

LOOP, FLOYD D., health, medical executive; b. Lafayette, Ind., Dec. 17, 1936; s. Floyd Addison and Marie D. L.; m. Bernadine P. Healy, Aug. 17, 1985; children: Alison, Frederick, Kendall, Bartlett, Marie. BS, Purdue U., 1958; MD, George Washington U., 1962. Diplomate: Am. Bd. Surgery, Am. Bd. Thoracic Surgery. Intern, resident in gen. surgery George Washington U., 1962-64, chief resident, 1967-68; fellow in cardiac surgery Cleve. Clinic Found., 1968-70, staff surgeon thoracic and cardiovascular surgery, 1971-75, chmn. dept. thoracic and cardiovascular surgery, 1975-89, chmn. bd. govs., chief exec. officer, 1989—. Mem. Editorial bd. Jour. Thoracic and Cardiovascular Surgery, 1979-85, Am. Jour. Cardiology, 1978-83, Am. Heart Jour, 1980—, Clin. Cardiology, 1979—, Jour. Cardiac Surgery, 1986—, Jour. Cardiothoracic Anesthesia, 1986—, Cleve. Clinic Jour. Medicine, Perfusion. With M.C. USAF, 1964-66. Decorated Brazilian Order of Merit. Fellow ACS (adv. council for cardiothoracic surgery 1986—), Am. Coll. Cardiology (Theodore and Susan B. Cummings Humanitarian award 1975); mem. Am. Assn. Thoracic Surgery (treas. 1984—, mem. council 1984—), Am. Surg. Assn., Soc. Thoracic Surgeons, Am. Coll. Chest Physicians (bd. regents 1986—), Thoracic Surgery Dirs. Assn., Am. Heart Assn. (exec. com. of council on cardiovascular surgery 1985—, Paul Dudley White citation for internat. service 1980), Am. Soc. Artificial Internal Organs Soc. Vascular Surgery. Office: Cleve Clinic Found 1 Clinic Ctr 9500 Euclid Ave Cleveland OH 44195-0001

LOPATIN, DENNIS EDWARD, immunologist, educator; b. Chgo., Oct. 26, 1948; s. Leonard Harold and Cynthia (Shifrin) L.; m. Marie S. Ludmer, June 6, 1971 (div. 1983); 1 child, Jeremy; m. Constance Maxine McLeod, July 24, 1983. BS, U. Ill., 1970, MS, 1972, PhD, 1974. Postdoctoral fellow Northwestern U. Med. Sch., Chgo., 1974-75; rsch. scientist U. Mich., Ann Arbor, 1976-90, prof., 1982—. Contbr. articles to sci. jours. Mem. Am. Assn. Immunologists, Am. Soc. Microbiology, Internat. Assn. Dental Rsch., Sigma Xi. Office: U Mich Sch Dentistry Ann Arbor MI 48109-1078

LOPER, JOHN CAREY, molecular genetics and environmental toxicology, research scientist, educator; b. Hadley, Pa., June 21, 1931; s. Clark M. and Anna B. (Carey) L; m. Dorothy L. Moredock, Dec. 23, 1956; children: John T., Robert D., Christopher L. BA, Western Md. Coll., 1952; MS, Emory U., 1953; PhD, The Johns Hopkins U., 1960. Instr. to asst. prof. St. Louis U. Sch. Medicine, 1960-63; asst. prof. U. Cin. Coll. Medicine, 1963-66, assoc. prof., 1966-74, prof. microbiology, 1974-88, prof. environ. health, 1979—, prof., assoc. dir. dept. molecular genetics, biochemistry and microbiology, 1988—; environ. cons., 1984—; prin. investigator U. Cin./Nat. Inst. Environ. Health Scis. Superfund Basic Rsch. Program, 1991—. Contbr. articles to profl. jours. 1st lt. Med. Svc. Corp, 1954-56. Vis. fellow genetics Australian Nat. U., Camberra, 1971; Grad. Sch. fellow U. Cin; Rsch. grantee. Mem. Am. Genetics Soc., Am. Soc. Microbiology, Am. Chem. Soc., Am. Soc. Biochem. Molecular Biology. Democrat. Office: U Cin Coll Medicine Dept Molecular Genetics Biochem Microbio Cincinnati OH 45267-0524

LOPES, JOHN ALEX, microbiologist; b. Nandakhal, India, Mar. 6, 1937; came to U.S., 1969; s. Alex J. and Joanna A. Lopes; m. Rose J., May 2, 1955; children: William, Lily, Leena, Irene. MSc, U. Bombay, 1963; PhD, U. Waterloo, Ont., Can., 1969. Tchg. fellow U. Waterloo (Can.), 1966-69; postdoctoral fellow U. Conn. Sch. Medicine, Farmington, 1969-71; assoc. rsch. scientist NYU Sch. Medicine, N.Y.C., 1971-73; asst. dir., sr. scientist Haffkine Inst., Bombay, 1973-76; mgr. R&D Hindustan Lever Rsch. Ctr., Bombay, 1976-78; sr. microbiologist Diversey Corp., Wyandotte, Mich., 1981-89; pres., dir. tech. Microcide, Inc., Troy, Mich., 1990—. Contbr. articles to profl. jours.; 2 patents on disinfecting composition; patent for sanitizing activity of n-octenylsuccinic acid, 2 patents on sanitization compositions, non-alcoholic mouthwash and cysticidal activities. Mem. Am. Soc. for Microbiology, Am. Bd. Bioanalysis, Can. Soc. Microbiology. Home: 2209 Niagara Dr Troy MI 48083-5933

LOPEZ, ALFONSO ASTRERO, JR., physician; b. Naga City, Philippines, Aug. 5, 1939; s. Alfonso Lopinto and Josefina (Astrero) L.; m. Pazcelita Valeriano, Oct. 15, 1965; children: John Vincent, Julie Lisa, Alfonso III, Chrissy Ann. AA, U. of the East, Quezon City, Philippines, 1958, MD, 1963. Diplomate Am. Bd. of Surgery. Chief dept. surgery Mercy-Meml. Med. Ctr., St. Joseph, Mich., 1988; sec. Soc. of Philippine Surgeons in Am., Chgo., 1990-94, pres., 1995, 1995—. Fellow ACS. Home: 690 Greenbrook Cir Saint Joseph MI 49085 Office: 1818 Langley Saint Joseph MI 49085

LOPEZ, ANTONIO VINCENT, education educator; b. Montgomery, Ala., Apr. 24, 1938; s. Joseph Charles and Eva Mae (Hall) Maschi. BS in Pharmacy, Auburn U., 1959, MS, 1961; PhD, U. Miss., 1966. Asst. prof. Mercer U. Sch. Pharmacy, Atlanta, 1966-68, assoc. prof., 1968-74, prof., 1974-96, assoc. dean for student affairs, 1994-96, prof. emeritus, 1996—, dept. chmn. Sch. Pharmacy, 1967-78, asst. dean, 1978-80, assoc. dean, 1980-85, dir. student affairs, 1985-94. Author: Exploring Mental Health, 1974. Pres. Met. Coun. on Alcohol and Drugs, Atlanta, 1985-86; bd. dirs. Families in Action, Atlanta, 1981-86; active Ga. Alcohol and Drug Abuse Adv. Coun., 1978-83; treas. Ga. Opera Co., Atlanta, 1976. Recipient Cert. of Recognition Ga. Citizens Coun. on Alcoholism, 1986, Cert. of Appreciation State of Ga., 1984, Lederle Labs. Faculty Rsch. award, 1967, 72. Mem. Am. Coll. Apothecarie, Ga. Pharm. Assn., Phi Lambda Sigma, Rho Chi, Kappa Psi (Tchr. of Yr. 1976-89), Kappa Epsilon. Republican. Roman Catholic. Office: Mercer U 3001 Mercer University Dr Atlanta GA 30341-4115

LOPEZ, CAROLYN CATHERINE, physician; b. Chgo., Oct. 13, 1951; d. Joseph Compean and Angela (Silva) L. BS, Loyola U., Chgo., 1973; MD, U. Ill., 1978. Diplomate Am. Bd. Family Practice. Intern, resident Rush/Christ Hosp., Chgo., 1978-81; med. dir. Wholistic Health Ctr., Oak Lawn, Ill., 1981-82; clin. dir. Anchor HMO, Oak Brook, Ill., 1982-84, assoc. med. dir., 1984-87; med. dir. Chgo. Pk. Dist., 1987-91; v.p. Rush Access HMO, Chgo., 1992-93; asst. dean Rush Med. Coll., 1990-93; med. dir. Rush Access HMO, Chgo., 1991-93, v.p., 1992-93; v.p. for profl. affairs Rush Anchor HMO, 1993; sr. v.p. and chief med. officer Rush-Prudential Health Plans, 1993-95; chair dept. family practice Cook County Hosp., 1996—. Primary Care Policy fellow USPHS, 1993. Mem. AMA, APHA, Am. Acad. Family Physicians, Chgo. Med. Soc., Ill. State Med. Soc., Am. Coll. Physicians Execs., Ill. Acad. Family Physicians (bd. dirs. 1987-89, speaker 1990-91, bd. chair 1990-91, pres.-elect 1991-92, pres. 1992-93, alt. del. to Am. Acad. Family Physicians 1992—), Am. Med. Women's Assn. Roman Catholic. Office: Cook County Hosp Dept Family Practice 1900 W Polk Chicago IL 60612

LOPEZ, GUILLERMO, obstetrician-gynecologist, educator; b. Bogota, Colombia, Oct. 3, 1919; came to U.S., 1944; s. Pedro P. and Sofia (Escobar) L.; m. Jeannie Pareja, July 16, 1955; children: Monica, Diana, Roberto, John G. MD, U. Nacional, Bogota, 1943; MS in Ob-Gyn, St. Louis U., 1947; asst. etranger, U. Paris, 1954. BE Am. Bd. Ob-Gyn. Intern Hosp. San Juan de Dios, U. Nacional, Bogota, 1942-43; resident in ob-gyn St. Louis U. Group Hosps., 1944-47; head gynecol. svc. San Juan de Dios Hosp., U. Nacional, Bogota, 1949-53, prof. of ob-gyn, 1951, assoc. dean clin. scis., 1965-66; head dept. gynecol. Inst. Nacional Cancer, Bogota, 1950-68; rsch. assoc. UCLA Harbor Gen. Hosp., 1967-68; head population div. Colombian Assn. Med. Schs., Bogota, 1969-73; head dept. gynecology, obstetrics and reproduction Centro Medico de los Andes, Fundacion Santa Fe, Bogota, 1981-88; rsch. prof. dept. community and family health Coll. Pub. Health, U. South Fla., Tampa, 1989—; seminar cons., tchr. mother and child care Peruvian Assn. Acad. Med. programs, Paracas, Peru, 1970; pres. Corp. Cen. Regional Population, Bogota, 1973-89; cons. Pan-Am. Health Orgn. (WHO), UN Fund for Population Activities (UNFPA), 1989—; bd. dirs. Bogota Health Div., 1981-82; presenter in field. Editor: Reproduction, 1979, editor Reproductive Health in Americas, 1992; contbr. articles to profl. jours., including Am. Jour. Ob-Gyn., Med. Cir., Panamerican Health Orgn., Editorial Fotolito Garcia e Hijos, others. Bd. dirs. Floridians for a Sustainable Population. Fellow ACS, Am. Coll. Ob-Gyn.; mem. N.Y. Acad. Scis., Am. Fertility Soc., Nat. Acad. Medicine Colombia, Fla. Ob-Gyn. Soc., Am. Pub. Health Assn. Home: 6118 Kipps Colony Dr W Saint Petersburg FL 33707-3970 Office: U South Fla Coll Pub Health 13201 Bruce B Downs Blvd Tampa FL 33612-3805

LOPEZ, LEONARDO V., internist; b. Havana, Cuba, Nov. 6, 1946; came to U.S., 1962; s. Marcelino Vicente and Martha (Barredo) L.; m. Kim D. Donley, Jan. 2, 1982; children: Janette, Leo, Andrea, Vanessa Justine. BS, U. Miami, 1968, MD, 1972. Diplomate Am. Bd. Internal Medicine, Am. Bd. Cardiovascular Medicine. Cert. Am. Bd. Quality Assurance and Utilization Rev. Chief med. resident, dir. med. ICU Miami (Fla.) VA Hosp., 1975; pvt. practice Miami, 1977—; asst. clin. prof. medicine U. Miami Sch. Medicine, 1977-87; chief dept. medicine Coral Gables (Fla.) Hosp., 1988-90; sr. attending staff Mercy Hosp., Miami; active staff Coral Gables Hosp.; courtesy staff Kendall Med. Ctr., South Miami Hosp.; bd. dirs. Coral Gables PHO, 1994—, chmn. 1996; trustee Coral Gables Hosp., 1994—; pilot reviewer IMCARE, Washington, 1993—. Fellow Am. Coll. Cardiology, Am. Coll. Chest Physicians, Am. Bd. Quality Assurance Utilization Review; mem. ACP, Am. Soc. Internal Medicine, Am. Heart Assn., Cuban Soc. Internal Medicine. Office: 2602 SW 37th Ave #701 Miami FL 33133

LOPEZ, MANUEL, immunology and allergy educator; b. Bucaramanga, Colombia, Sept. 30, 1939; came to U.S., 1971; married; 4 children. BS, Colegio San Pedro Claver, Bucaramanga, 1956; MD, Univ. Javeriana, Bogota, Colombia, 1963. Diplomate Am. Bd. Allergy and Immunology, Am. Bd. Diagnostic Lab. Immunology. Intern Hosp. San Juan De Dios, Bucaramanga, 1962-63, resident, 1963-64, med. dir., 1969-71; clin. and rsch. fellow dept. medicine allergy unit Harvard U. and Harvard Med. Sch. at Mass. Gen. Hosp., Boston, 1964-68; dir. med. rsch. Univ. Indsl. De Santander, Bucaramanga, 1968-69; dir. immunology svc. lab. La. State Med. Ctr., New Orleans, 1971-74; asst. prof. medicine med. ctr. La. State U., New Orleans, 1971-74; from clin. asst. prof. to assoc. prof. med. sch. Tulane U., New Orleans, 1974-89, prof., 1989—, dir. immunology diagnostic lab. med. sch., 1974-83, dir. clin. immunology labs., 1983—, program dir. allergy and immunology tng. program, 1990—, acting chief sect. allergy and clin. immunology, 1990-91, chief, 1991—; mem. med.-sci. adv. com. Asthma and Allergy Found. Am., 1986-89; ad hoc mem. immunological sci. study sect. NIH, 1987, allergy and clin. immunology spl. reviewer immunology and transplantation rsch. com., 1988, mem. gen. clin. rsch. ctrs. com. 1993—; reviewer merit rev. grants VA, 1988, 89, 90; grant program reviewer Ctrs. of Excellence, Dept. Health and Human Svcs., 1991; mem. allergic products adv. com. FDA, 1993—; mem. spl. rev. com. Nat. Inst. Allergy and Infectious Diseases, 1993; presenter in field. Mem. editl. bd. Jour. Allergy and Clin. Immunology, 1986-94, reviewer, 1987-88; contbr. articles to profl. jours. and chpts. to books. Fellow John Simmon Guggenheim Meml. Found., 1964-66. Fellow Am. Acad. Allergy and Clin. Immunology (mem. internat. com. 1986-89, mem. immunotherapy of asthma com. 1987—, mem. Latin Ctrl. and South Am. com. 1987—, chmn. internat. grant aids 1988-89, mem. continuing med. edn. com. 1992-94), Am. Coll. Chest Physicians; mem. Am. Assn. Immunologists, Am. Fedn. Clin. Rsch., Am. Thoracic Soc., U.S.-Colombian Med. Assn. (pres. IX Congress 1989), La. Allergy Soc., N.Y. Acad. Scis., Southeastern Allergy Assn., Assn. Med. Lab. Immunologists, Internat. Assn. Aerobiology, Cordoba Allergy Soc. (hon.), Sigma Xi. Office: Tulane U Med Sch Clin Immunology Sect 1700 Perdido St Fl 3 New Orleans LA 70112-1210

LOPEZ, MARVIN JOSE, surgeon, educator; b. Leon, Nicaragua, Oct. 23, 1947; s. Roberto and Azucena (Ramirez) L.; m. Linda G. Lopez, Feb. 16, 1969; children: Marvin, Anna, Christopher, Robert. MD, U. Autonoma Guadalajara, Mex., 1970. Internship Regina Grey Nuns' Hosp., Regina, Sask., Can., 1970-71, 73-74; residency in surgery The Montreal Gen. Hosp./McGill U., Can., 1974-79; fellowship in surg. oncology Ellis Fischel Cancer Ctr., Columbia, Mo., 1979-80; asst. prof. surgery U. Mo., Columbia, 1979-88; assoc. chief surgery Ellis Fischel Cancer Ctr., Columbia, 1979-88; assoc. prof. surgery Washington U., St. Louis, 1988-92; dir. ctr. for breast care St. Elizabeth's Med. Ctr., Boston, 1992—, chief gen. and oncol. surgery, vice chmn. dept. surgery, 1992—; prof. surgery Sch. Medicine Tufts U., Boston, 1995—; mem. cancer clin. investigation com. NIH, 1990-91. Contbr. over 80 articles to profl. jours. Fellow ACS (v.p. Mo. chpt. 1992—), Am. Coll. Nutrition, Royal Coll. PHysicians and Surgeons Can., Am. Cancer Soc.; mem. AMA, AAAS, Am. Assn. for Cancer Edn., Am. Radium Soc., Am. Soc. Clin. Oncology, Am. Soc. Liver and Pancreas Surgery, Am. Soc. Parenteral and Enteral Nutrition, Assn. for Acad. Surgery, New Eng. Surg. Soc., Soc. Internat. de Chirurgiae, Soc. Pelvic Surgeons, Boston Surg. Soc., Can. Assn. Gen. Surgeons, Ctrl. Surg. Assn., Collegium Internat. Chirurgiae Digestivae, Mass. Med. Soc., Soc. Am. Gastrointestinal Endoscopic Surgeons, Soc. Head and Neck Surgeons, Soc. for Surgery of the Alimentary Tract, Soc. Surg. Oncology, Southwestern Surg. Congress. Office: St Elizabeth's Med Ctr Seton Gen Surgery 736 Cambridge St MOB 406 Boston MA 02135

LÓPEZ-GONZÁLEZ, MIGUEL ÁNGEL, biochemical otorhinolaryngologist, researcher; b. Seville, Andalucia, Spain, Apr. 27, 1953; s. Miguel López-Velázquez and Paulina González-Ramírez; m. Petra Lorente-García; children: Carmen, Ana. MD, U. Seville, PhD. Cert. specialist in labor medicine; cert. specialist in biochemistry and otorhinolaryngology. Biochemist Pub. Health, Madrid, 1980-84; labor physician Pub. Inst., Madrid, 1985; clin. pathologist Pub. Health, Seville, 1986; fellow in med. oncology Charing Cross Hosp., London, 1987-88; clin. pathologist Pub. Health, Seville, 1989-93, otorhinolaryngologist, 1994—. Contbr. articles to profl. jours. Grantee Edn. Ministry, 1974-80. Mem. Otorhinolaryngology Soc. (grantee 1995). Office: Hosp Virgen Del Rocío, Manuel Siurot S/N, 41013 Seville Spain

LOPEZ-NAVARRO, EDUARDO LUIS, family therapist; b. Santiago de Cuba, Oriente, Cuba, June 29, 1959; came to U.S, 1970; s. Eduardo Regino and Alicia Del Pilar (Navarro) Lopez. BA, UCLA, 1982; MS in Psychology with honors, Calif. State U., L.A., 1991. Counselor L.A. Unified Sch. Dist., 1982-90; family therapist Family Counseling Svcs., San Gabriel, Calif., 1990-93; program coord. El Centro del Pueblo, L.A., 1993—; family therapist Hillsides Home for Children, Pasadena, Calif., 1992—, El Centro Del Pueblo, L.A., 1993—; dir. North Ctrl. L.A. Family Preservation Project; cons. (counselor) UCLA/Valley Alternative Magnet Sch., Van Nuys, 1990; rsch. asst. UCLA/Fernald Sch., 1981; lectr. in field; expert presenter and cons. various TV programs including Univision and Telemundo Networks, L.A., 1993—. Contbr. articles to profl. jours.; author video: The World of Perpetual Night: Insights into the Psychology of Street Prostitution, 1990. Counselor Hollywood Sunset Cmty. Clinic, L.A., 1986-89; family counselor St. Matthias Ch.; mem. san Gabriel Valley Child Abuse Coun.; educator/trainer Latino Family Preservation, L.A., 1994. Am. Assn. for Marriage and Family Therapy Minority fellow, 1981; recipient Counseling Dept. Spl. Recognition award Hollywood Sunset Cmty. Clinic, 1988, Exito Internat. award. Mem. Calif. Assn. Marriage and Family Therapists, Am. Assn. Marriage and Family Therapists. Roman Catholic. Office: El Centro Del Pueblo 1157 Lemoyne St Los Angeles CA 90026-3206

LOPKER, ANITA MAE, psychiatrist; b. San Diego, May 25, 1955; d. Louis Donald and Betty Jean (Sayman-Campbell) L. BA magna cum laude, U. Calif., San Diego, 1978; MD, U. Rochester, 1982. Diplomate Nat. Bd. Med. Examiners, Am. Bd. Forensic Examiners. Intern in internal medicine Yale U. Sch. Medicine-Greenwich Hosp., 1982-83; resident in psychiatry Yale U. Sch. of Medicine, 1983-86; postdoctoral fellow Yale U. Sch. Medicine, New Haven, Conn., 1982-86; clin. instr. Yale U. Sch. Medicine, New Haven, 1986-88; pvt. practice specializing eating disorders and Lyme disease Westport, Conn., 1987—; cons. psychiatrist Yale-New Haven Hosp Lyme Disease Study Clinic, 1987—, Yale U. Lyme Disease Rsch. Project, 1986—, Alcoholism and Drug Dependency Coun., Inc., 1989-90; internat. lectr. on Lyme psychiat. syndrome; nat. lectr. on eating disorders, substance abuse. Contbr. articles to profl. jours. Founding mem. Nat. Mus. for Women in the Arts, Washington, 1987; patron Menninger Found.; bd. dirs. The Fairfield Orch., 1993-96. Recipient Benjamin Rush prize in psychiatry U. Rochester Sch. Medicine, 1982. Mem. AAAS, Am. Psychiat. Assn., Conn. Psychiat. Soc., World Fedn. Mental Health (life), Menninger Found., Alpha Omega Alpha, Phi Beta Kappa. Home: 27 Strathmore Ln Westport CT 06880-4700 Office: 7 Whitney Street Ext Westport CT 06880-3761

LOPUKHIN, MICHAEL, psychotherapy consultant; b. Tver, USSR, Russia, June 7, 1931; came to U.S., 1949; s. Alexis and Thekla (Meyendorff) L.; m. Elizabeth Koulomzin, Aug. 29, 1954; children: Olga, Tatiana, Alexandra, Andrei. MSW, Columbia U., 1963; BA in Psychology, Adelphi U., 1958. CSW. Pub. asst. City of N.Y. Dept. of Welfare, N.Y., 1958-59, Rockland County Det. of Welfare, Pomona, N.Y., 1959-65; mental health clinic Westchester Jewish Community Scvs., White Plains, N.Y., 1965-80; prv. practice psychotherapy, Hawthorne, N.Y., 1980—; cons. Pre-school Children Mental Health Scarsdale YWHA, N.Y., 1968-70, Orthodox Edn. Dept. Am. Orthodox Ch., Crestwood, N.Y., 1969-75. Contbr. articles to profl. jours. Steering com. Stewardship in Orthodox Ch. Am., Scarsdale, N.Y., 1988-90; chmn. Russian Gift of Life, Westchester, 1995. Home: 142 Amsterdam Ave Hawthorne NY 10532-1637 Office: 142 Amsterdam Ave Hawthorne NY 10532-1637

LORBACHER, PETER, internist, hematologist; b. Essen, Germany, July 1, 1936; s. Wilhelm and Hilde (Schrod) L.; m. Brigitte Gymnich, July 3, 1963; children: Marcus, Louisa, Frank, Dominik. Dr med, U. Düsseldorf, 1960; Habilitation, U. Bonn, 1969, apl. Prof., 1973. Rsch. fellow, resident Freiburg, Bonn and Boston; staff physician German Clinic for Diagnostics, Wiesbaden, Fed. Republic Germany. Contbr. articles on cytochemistry of blood and bone marrow cells to med. jours. Mem. Deutsche Gesellschaft fuer Haematologie und Onkologie, Internat. Soc. Hematology, Rotary (pres. Wiesbaden-Kochbrunnen 1986-87). Roman Catholic. Home: Nerotal 77, D-65193 Wiesbaden Germany Office: Deutsche Klinik Diagnostik, Aukammallee 33, D-65191 Wiesbaden Germany

LORBER, DANIEL LOUIS, endocrinologist, educator; b. N.Y.C., Sept. 21, 1946; s. Jerome Zachary Lorber and Ruth (Frank) Cook. AB, Columbia U., 1968; MD, Albert Einstein, 1972. Diplomate Am. Bd. Internal Medicine, Endocrinology and Metabolism. Intern medicine Bronx (N.Y.) Municipal Ctr., 1972-73; resident medicine Albert Enstein, Bronx, 1973-75; fellow in endocrinology Vanderbilt U., Nashville, 1975-77; from asst. prof. to asst. dean NYU Sch. Medicine, N.Y.C., 1977-84; from asst. clin. prof. to assoc. clin. prof. Albert Einstein Coll. Medicine, Bronx, 1984-94; clin. assoc. prof. Cornell U. Med. Coll., 1994—; dir. endocrinology N.Y. Hosp. Med. Ctr. of Queens, N.Y., 1994—; med. dir. Diabetes Control Found., Flushing, N.Y., 1985—. Editor in chief Practical Diabetology Magazine, 1987—. Fellow ACP; mem. Am. Diabetes Assn. (bd. dirs. N.Y. State affiliate 1996—), Endocrine Soc. Democrat. Jewish. Office: Diabetes Control Found 138-26 58th Ave Flushing NY 11355-5232

LORBER, MORTIMER, physiology educator; b. N.Y.C., Aug. 30, 1926; s. Albert and Frieda (Levin) L.; m. Eileen Segal, May 20, 1956; children: Kenneth, Stephanie. BS, NYU, 1945; DMD cum laude, Harvard U., 1950, MD cum laude, 1952. Diplomate Nat. Bd. Med. Examiners. Rotating intern A.M. Billings Hosp., 1952-53; resident in hematology Mt. Sinai Hosp., N.Y.C., 1953-54, asst. resident in medicine, 1957; asst. resident medicine Georgetown U. Hosp., Washington, 1958; instr., asst. prof. dept. physiology and biophysics Georgetown U., Washington, 1959-68, assoc. prof., 1968; lectr. physiology U.S. Naval Dental Sch., Bethesda, Md., 1962-70, Walter Reed Army Inst. Dental Rsch., Washington, 1963-70; guest scientist Naval Med. Rsch. Inst., Bethesda, 1978-83. Contbr.: The Merck Manual, 14th, 15th and 16th edit., 1982, 87, 92; contbr. articles to profl. jours. Lt. USNR, 1954-56. Recipient Lederle Med. Faculty award Lederle Co., Pearl River, N.Y., 1960-63, USPHS Rsch. Career Devel. award Nat. Inst. Dental Rsch., Bethesda, 1963-70; grantee Am. Cancer Soc., USPHS. Mem. Am. Physiol.

Soc., Am. Soc. Hematology, Assn. Rsch. in Vision and Ophthalmology, Internat. Assn. Dental Rsch. Jewish. Home: 5823 Osceola Rd Bethesda MD 20816-2032 Office: Georgetown U Sch Medicine 3900 Reservoir Rd NW Washington DC 20007-2187

LORCH, MARJORIE PERLMAN, linguist; b. Balt., Nov. 20, 1956; arrived in Eng., 1985; d. Bennard Bloch and Miriam Lois (Walfish) Perlman; m. Richard Samuel Lorch, Jan. 14, 1985; children: Emily Madeleine Saskia, Nicholas Peter Frederick. BA in Linguistics and Anthropology, Washington U., St. Louis, 1978; PhD in Lang. Behavior, Boston U., 1986. Clin. fellow Washington U. Med. Sch., St. Louis, 1976-78; rsch. asst. Aphasia Rsch. Ctr. VA Med. Ctr., Boston, 1979-85; rsch. Nat. Hosp. for Neurology and Neurosurgery, London, 1989-91; lectr. applied linguistics Birkbeck Coll., U. London, 1985—. Author: (book chpts.) Handbook of Neurological Speech and Language Disorders, 1995, Morphology, Phonology and Aphasia, 1990, The Characteristics of Aphasia, 1989, The Biological Foundations of Gesture, 1986. Mem. Internat. Clin. Linguistics and Phonetics Assn., Am. Speech-Lang. Hearing Assn., Acad. Aphasia, Phi Beta Kappa. Office: Birkbeck Coll, 43 Gordon Sq, London WC1H OPD, England

LORD, JAMES LORIN, dentist; b. Ellensburg, Wash., Nov. 20, 1937; s. James Roy and LaVerda (Murtol) L.; m. Linda Lord, Dec. 29, 1964 (div. May 1979); children: Steve, Jeff, Eric. BS in Zoology, Wash. State U., 1960; DDS, U. Wash., 1964, MSD in Prosthodontics, 1970, Cert. in Restorative Dentistry, 1970; Cert. in Osseointegrated Implants, U. Goteborg/Inst. Applied Bio., Sweden, 1983. Lic. dentist, Wash. Pvt. practice gen. dentistry Garfield, Wash., 1964-65; pvt. practice gen. dentistry Seattle, 1966-70, pvt. practice part-time limited to prosthodontics, 1970-74, pvt. practice half-time limited to prosthodontics, 1974-76, pvt. practice prosthodontics, 1976—; instr. prosthodontics U. Wash., Seattle, 1965-71, asst. prof., 1971-73, part-time 1973-74, asst. prof. grad. faculty, 1971-74, assoc. prof. prosthodontics, 1974-76, clin. asst., 1976-86, clin. prof., 1986—; attending staff U. Wash. Hosp., 1966-76, Providence Med. Ctr., 1991-92. Contbr. numerous articles to profl. jours. Recipient Outstanding Instr. award Class of 1971 U. Wash., 1967-68, Most Outstanding Dental Instr. Class of 1972, 1968-69, Outstanding Instr. award Class of 1976, 1973-74, Instr. of Yr. award Class of 1978, 1975-76; USPHS grantee, 1963. Fellow Am. Coll. Dentists, Internat. Coll. Dentists, Acad. Prosthodontics (exec. coun. 1989—); mem. ADA, Am. Coll. Prosthodontics (bd. dirs. 1992-94), Am. Prosthodontic Soc., Am. Soc. for Geriatric Dentistry, Pacific Coast Soc. Prosthodontics (exec. coun. 1977, 86-90, pres. 1990-91, membership chair 1993-94), Fedn. Prosthodontic Orgns. (chmn. dental practice 1981-83, pres. 1990-91), Wash. State Soc. Prosthodontists (pres. 1985), Wash. Dental Assn. (exec. coun. 1988-92, legis. dir. 1992-93, alt. del. to ADA house 1989-92, del. 1995, rep. to WSDLA critical issues com. 1994-95), U. Wash. Dental Alumni Assn. (pres. 1977), Seattle King County Dental Assn. (pres. 1987-88, del. WSDA house 1990-94, exec. coun. 1982-86, other coms.), Psi Omega, Omicron Kappa Upsilon. Home: 3237 12th Ave W Seattle WA 98119 Office: 10212 5th Ave NE #240 Seattle WA 98125

LORD, JERE WILLIAMS, JR., retired surgeon; b. Balt., Oct. 12, 1910; s. Jere Williams and Evelyn (Pope) L.; m. June Harrah, Dec. 6, 1941; children: Harrah, Jere W. III, Lonna; m. Margaret Humphreys Graham, Feb. 13, 1971. A.B., Princeton U., 1933; M.D., Johns Hopkins U., 1937. Diplomate Am. Bd. of Surgery. Intern Surgery N.Y. Hosp., Cornell U. Med. Coll., 1937-38, intern pathology, 1938-39, asst. resident surgeon, 1939-44, resident surgeon, 1944; vis. surgeon. 4th Div., Bellevue Hosp.; cons. surgeon U. Hosp.; prof. clin. surgery N.Y.U.; instr. surgery and surgeon to out-patients N.Y. Hosp., Cornell U. Med. Coll., 1944-45; mem. med. bd. Doctors Hosp.; attending surgeon Manhattan State Hosp., 1945-48; cons. surgeon Greenwich (Conn.) Hosp., Hackensack Hosp., Paterson Gen. Hospital, Elizabeth Horton Meml. Hosp., Middletown., N.Y., Norwalk Hosp., Conn., Central Suffolk Hosp., Riverhead, N.Y., Arden Hill Hosp., Goshen, N.Y., St. Agnes Hosp., White Plains, N.Y., St. Luke's Hosp., Newburgh, N.Y., Putnam Community Hosp., Carmel, N.Y.; chief vascular surgery Columbus Hosp., N.Y.C. Awarded 3d essay prize; Am. Urol. Assn., 1942. Fellow ACS; mem. N.Y. Gastroent. Assn. (pres. 1956), Am. Assn. Surgery of Trauma, Soc. for Vascular Surgery, N.Y. Soc. for Cardiovascular Surgery (pres. 1957-59), N.Y. Soc. for Thoracic Surgery (pres. 1961-62), N.Y. Heart Assn. (pres. 1957-59), N.Y. Surg. Soc., Eastern Surg. Soc. (pres. 1982), Am., Pan-Pacific, So. surg. assns., Internat. Cardiovascular Soc., James IV Assn. Surgeons (sec. 1967-75). Democrat. Episcopalian. Clubs: Ivy (Princeton); Pithotomy (Johns Hopkins); Bedford Golf and Tennis. Home: Greenwich Rd Bedford NY 10506

LORD, OTTIS KERMIT, JR., social psychologist; b. Hazlehurst, Ga., Jan. 26, 1943; s. Ottis Kermit Sr. and Alma (Warnock) L. AS, S. Ga. Coll., 1963; BA, Ga. So. Coll., 1968; postgrad., U. Ga. Caseworker I Bacon County Dept. Family Children Svcs., Alma, Ga., 1970-72; clk. labor cost Cook and Co., Hazlehurst, 1972; jr. buyer Miles Mill Supply, Hazlehurst, 1973; grad. asst. Sociology Dept. U. Ga., Athens, 1980-84; ind. rschr. Hazlehurst, 1984—. Home: RR 3 Box 1335 Hazlehurst GA 31539-9565

LOREFICE, LAURENCE SANTO, psychiatrist; b. N.Y.C., May 11, 1950; s. Lawrence Salvatore and Gemma (Patrone) L.; m. Mary Ellen Foulds; children: Jeanne, Kristine, Luke. BA, Johns Hopkins U., 1971; MD, U. Pa., 1975; MPH, Harvard U., 1979. Diplomate Am. Bd. Psychiatry and Neurology. Internship and resident in psychiatry Mass. Gen. Hosp., Boston, 1975-78, fellow in social and community psychiatry, 1978-79; chief resident Outpatient Clinic Erich Lindemann Mental Health Ctr., Boston, 1977-78; clin. fellow psychiatry Med. Sch. Harvard U., 1975-79; chief psychiatrist Day Treatment Program, mem. staff Mt. Sinai Med. Ctr., N.Y.C., 1979-80; dir. Intermediate Care Treatment Unit Westchester County (N.Y.) Med. Ctr., 1980-82; dir. Washington Heights Outpatient Clinic N.Y. State Psychiat. Inst., 1982-84; assoc. chief dept. psychiatry Stamford (Conn.) Hosp., 1986—; instr. N.Y. Med. Coll., Valhalla, 1980-82, clin. asst. prof. psychiatry, 1985—; asst. clin. prof. psychiatry Coll. Physicians and Surgeons Columbia U., N.Y.C., 1982-95; pvt. practice Old Greenwich, Conn., 1978—. Contbr. articles to profl. jours. Fellow Am. Psychiat. Assn. Home and Office: 404 Sound Beach Ave Old Greenwich CT 06870-2222

LOREI, JOHN MICHAEL, emergency medicine physician, educator; b. Erie, Pa., Jan. 8, 1960; s. John Albert and Evelyn Esther (Lokasiewicz) L.; m. Carol Joan Wagner, Oct. 19, 1987; children: Alison Wagner, Emily Marie. BS, U. Iowa, 1983, MD, 1987. Diplomate Am. Bd. Emergency Medicine. Resident in emergency medicine U. Pitts., 1987-90, chief resident, 1989-90; staff physician in emergency medicine St. Luke's Hosp. Kansas City, Mo., 1990—; chmn. emergency svcs. St. Luke's Northland Hosp., Kansas City, 1993—; assoc. clin. prof. medicine U. Mo., Kansas City, 1991—. Fellow Am. Coll. Emergency Physicians; mem. Alpha Omega Alpha. Office: St Luke's Northland Hosp 5830 NW Barry Rd Kansas City MO 64154

LORELLI, JOHN PETER, physician assistant, clinical microbiologist; b. N.Y.C., Apr. 17, 1943; 1 child, John Peter Jr. BA, CUNY, 1973, MA, 1981; BS, Touro Coll., 1983. Registered physician asst., N.Y.; cert. clin. lab. supr. in microbiology, N.Y.C. Clin. microbiologist Albert Einstein Coll. Medicine, Bronx, N.Y., 1965-81, physician asst., trainer, evaluator physician asst. students, 1985-88; physician asst. med. dept. N.Y.C. Dept. Sanitation, 1984-85; pvt. practice, N.Y.C., 1988-94; physician asst. Bronx Mcpl. Hosp. Ctr., 1994—; presenter Am. Soc. for Microbiology 79th Meeting, 1979. Mem. Am. Acad. Physician Assts., N.Y. State Soc. Physician Assts. Office: 2532 Bathgate Ave Bronx NY 10458

LOREMAN, LORIE, internist; b. Abington, Pa., Aug. 6, 1961; d. James Mallard and Mary Eleanor (Ulrich) L. BS, Chestnut Hill Coll., 1983; DO, Phila. Coll. Osteo. Medicine, 1987. Intern Allentown Osteo. Med. Ctr., 1987-88; med. intern Albert Einstein Med. Ctr., Phila., 1988-89; med. resident Abington (Pa.) Meml. Hosp., 1989-91, chief med. resident, 1991-92; pulmonary fellowship St. Elizabeth's Hosp., Boston, 1992-94; pulmonary attending Doylestown (Pa.) Hosp., 1994—. Mem. Am. Assn. of Physicians Human Rights, San Francisco, 1989. Recipient Med. Excellence award Syntex Pharms., 1992. Mem. ACP, AMA; mem. Am. Coll. Chest Physicians, Am. Osteo. Assn., Am. Thoracic Soc., Kappa Gamma Pi. Home: 5502 Jillian Way Pipersville PA 18947 Office: Coyne Med Assocs 5039 Swamp Rd Ste 402 Fountainville PA 18923

LORENCEAU, BERNARD JEAN, plastic surgeon; b. Boulogne, France, July 7, 1947; s. Bernard Sven and Monique (Rust) L.; m. Dominique Sebilleau, June 25, 1970; children: Pauline, Elise, Camille. MD, Janson de Sailly, Paris, 1968. Intern in medicine Hosp. Orleans, France, 1970-71; intern Hosp. Paris, 1973-78, resident, 1978-81; chief plastic surgery unit Hosp. Pontoise, France, 1981—; asst. chief Microsurgery Research Lab., St. Louis, France, 1976-85; expert in plastic surgery Wur D'appel, 1982—. Contbr. articles to profl. publs. Mem. French Plastic and Reconstructive Surgery Soc., French Coll. Plastic Surgeons. Roman Catholic. Office: 24 Rue Lalo, 75116 Paris France also: 2 pladu general de Gaulle, 95300 Pontoise France

LORENTE, RODERICK DANA, optometrist; b. Lynn, Mass., Mar. 9, 1949; s. Roderick Mariano and Cassie V. (Petrykowski) L.; m. Carol Ann London, Jan. 1, 1972 (div. 1987); m. Mary Carlstrom, June 13, 1993. BA, Northeastern U., 1971; OD, New Eng. Coll., 1975. Optometrist G. Burtt Holmes & Assoc., Worcester, Mass., 1975-83, Peabody Med. Assocs. (was Med. East Community Health Plan), Peabody, Mass., 1986—; pvt. practice Belmont, Mass., 1979-84; mgr. clin. programs Soft Contact Lens div. Am. Optical (named changed to Ciba Vision Care), Framingham, Mass., 1984-86, Atlanta, 1984-86; asst. prof. New Eng. Coll. Optometry, Boston, 1983—. Contbr. articles to profl. jours. Mem. Am. Optometric Assn., New Eng. Coun. Optometrists, Mass. Soc. Optometrists (contact lens com. 1980-84), Belmont Lions, Beta Nu. Home: 62 Crescent Hill Ave Arlington MA 02174-2530 Office: Peabody Med Assocs Northshore Mall Peabody MA 01960-1600

LORENTZ, WILLIAM BEALL, pediatrician; b. Glenville, W.Va., July 8, 1937; s. William Beall and Mary Gay (Garrett) L.; m. Anne Lynne Hickman, June 20, 1960 (div. Aug. 30, 1977); children: Pamela Lynne, Lisa Anne, William Chad; m. Suzy Vernice Gibson, Sept. 5, 1977. BA, W.Va. U., 1959; MD, Jefferson Med. Coll., 1963. Diplomate Am. Bd. Pediatrics, Sub-board of Pediatric Nephrology. Internship Harrisburg (Pa.) Polyclinic Hosp., 1963-64, resident in pediatrics, 1964-65; resident in pediatrics U. Tex. Med. Br., Galveston, Tex., 1965-67; med. corp USN, Quantico (Va.) Naval Hosp., 1967-69; fellow in renal physiology U. N.C. Sch. of Medicine, Chapel Hill, 1969-71; asst. prof. pediatrics U. Tex. Med. Br., Galveston, 1971-74, Bowman Gray Sch. Medicine, Winston-Salem, N.C., 1974-75; assoc. prof. pediatrics Bowman Gray Sch. Medicine, Winston-Salem, 1975-81; prof. pediatrics Bowman Grey Sch. Medicine, Winston-Salem, 1981—; assoc. chief staff N.C. Bapt. Hosp., 1991—; med. dir. Medcost, Winston-Salem, 1989—; cons. physician Allegheny Regional Hosp., Low Moor, Va., 1988; pres. Piedmont Med. Found., Winston-Salem, 1983-88. Contbr. articles to profl. jours. Lt. comdr. USN, 1966-69. Mem. Soc. for Pediatric Rsch., Am. Pediatric Soc., Am. Acad. Pediatrics. Am. Soc. Nephrology, Am. Soc. for Pediatric Nephrology. Democrat. Presbyterian. Office: Bowman Gray Sch Medicine 300 S Hawthorne Rd Winston Salem NC 27157-0002

LORENZ, LINDA LEE, human services administrator, consultant; b. Meadeville, Pa., May 25, 1957; d. Richard Leo and Nancy Lee (Sherman) Shaw; children: Lee Mugweru Karanja, Daniel Gakuo Karanja. Student Summer Inst. Linguistics, U. Wash., 1976; BA in Linguistics and Spanish, Gordon Coll., 1978; literacy cert., Mary Mount Coll., 1981. Cert. sexual assault counselor/child advocate. Resource developer VISTA, Salem, Mass., 1978-79; group home tutor Orange County Dept. Edn., Santa Ana, Calif., 1981; staff editor Quest Publ. Co., Brea, Calif., 1981-84; documentation specialist CXC, Irvine, Calif., 1984-86; tech. writer Emulex Corp., Costa Mesa, Calif., 1986-88; sr. tech. writer ICL/North Am., Irvine, Calif., 1988-90; coord. victim svcs. Wild Iris Women's Svcs., Bishop, Calif., 1990-92; dir. T L Cons., Big Pine, Calif., 1990—; exec. dir. Inyo-Mono Advs. for Community Action, Inc., Bishop, 1992-93; dir. Starpointe Communications Group, 1994—; cons. Shanel Corp., San Jose, Calif., 1991, Am. Indian Opportunity Corp., Big Pine Reservation, Calif., 1990-91; cons. instr. ICL/North Am., 1991-92, cons. tech. writer, 1990—. Contbr. Intercontinental Dictionary Series; editor Biomed. Tech., 1984; staff editor Jour. Clin. Engring., 1984. Legis. chmn. Inyo County (Calif.) Rep. Women, 1991-93; coord. crisis line Wild Iris Women's Svcs., Inyo-Mono Counties, 1990-91; child adv. Ct.-Appointed Spl. Advs., Orange County, Calif., 1990. Mem. NAFE, Soc. Tech. Communication (award of achievement 1990), Rotary (group study exch. alt. team 1992). Office: T L Cons PO Box 653 Big Pine CA 93513-0653

LORENZ, RUEDIGER, neurosurgeon; b. Niederfischbach, Fed. Republic Germany, Sept. 9, 1932; s. Johannes and Ena (Mueller) L. m. Gunde Hussmann, Feb. 13, 1959; children: Matthias, Mechthild. Study of medicine U. Bonn and Goettingen, 1951-1956; Dr. Med. U. Goettingen, 1956; Dr.h.c. U. Zaragoza, 1991. Med. tng. in internal medicine, gen. pathology, gen. surgery, ob-gyn, 1957-1959. Spl. tng. in gen. surgery 1959-1962, neurophysiology 1963, neurosurgery 1962. Specialist in neurosurgery 1967. Habilitation for Neurosurgery U. Giessen 1971; prof. neurosurgery U. Giessen Faculty Medicine, 1973-80; prof. and chmn. neurosurgery, head dept. Univ. Hosp., Frankfurt, 1980—. Recipient Disting. medal Govt. Germany ,1993. Mem. Am. Soc. Neurological Surgeons (hon.), Med. Acad. Zaragoza (Spain) (hon.), Med. Acad. Burma (hon.), Med. Acad. Argentina (hon.), Polish Soc. Neurosurgeons (hon.), Andalusian Soc. Neurosurgeons (hon.). Contbr. articles in field to profl. jours., chpts. in books, monographs. Home: Lerchesbergring 86a, D-60598 Frankfurt Germany Office: Leiter der Klinik fuer Neurochirurgie, 2-16 Schleusenweg, D-60528 Frankfurt Germany

LORENZEN, ROBERT FREDERICK, ophthalmologist; b. Toledo, Ohio, Mar. 20, 1924; s. Martin Robert and Pearl Adeline (Bush) L.; m. Lucy Logsdon, Feb. 14, 1970; children: Roberta Jo, Richard Martin, Elizabeth Anne. BS, Duke, 1948, MD, 1948; MS, Tulane U., 1953. Intern, Presbyn. Hosp., Chgo., 1948-49; resident Duke Med. Center, 1949-51, Tulane U. Grad. Sch., 1951-53; practice medicine specializing in ophthalmology, Phoenix, 1953—; mem. staff St. Joseph's Hosp., St. Luke's Hosp., Good Samaritan Hosp., Surg. Eye Ctr. of Ariz. Pres. Ophthalmic Scis. Found., 1970-73; chmn. bd. trustees Rockefeller and Abbe Prentice Eye Inst. of St. Luke's Hosp., 1975—. Recipient Gold Headed Cane award, 1974; named to Honorable Order of Ky. Cols. Fellow ACS, Internat. Coll. Surgeons, Am. Acad. Ophthalmology and Otolaryngology, Pan Am. Assn. Ophthalmology, Soc. Eye Surgeons; mem. Am. Assn. Ophthalmology (sec. of ho. of dels. 1972-73, trustee 1973-76), Ariz. Ophthal. Soc. (pres. 1966-67), Ariz. Med. Assn. (bd. dirs. 1963-66, 69-70), Royal Soc. Medicine, Rotary (pres. Phoenix 1984-85). Republican. Editor in chief Ariz. Medicine, 1963-66, 69-70. Office: 367 E Virginia Ave Phoenix AZ 85004-1202

LORENZO, JOSEPH ANTHONY, endocrinologist, educator; b. N.Y.C., Nov. 11, 1948; s. Anthony J. and Mary (Emma) L.; m. Pam Seton, July 8, 1973; children: Alexander, Gregory. BS, Rensselear Poly. Inst., 1970; MD, SUNY, Bklyn., 1974. Diplomate Am. Bd. Internal Medicine, Am. Bd. Endorcrinology and Metabolism. Intern in internal medicine U. Ill., Chgo., 1974-75, resident, 1975-77; fellow in endocrinology and metabolism U. Conn., Farmington, 1977-79, instr. medicine, 1979-80, asst. prof., 1980-87, assoc. prof., 1987-96, prof., 1996—; staff physician div. endocrinology dept. medicine VA Med. Ctr., Newington, Conn., 1982—, acting assoc. chief staff for rsch., 1993-95, mem. clin. exec. bd., 1993-95, dep. assoc. chief staff for rsch., 1995—; referee Jour. Clin. Investigation, Endocrinology, Jour. Clin. Endocrinology and Metabolism, Am. Jour. Physiology, Calcified Tissue Internat., Bone; ad hoc reviewer merit rev. bd. VA, 1985-93, NSF, 1987, 88; site visitor Nat. Cancer Inst., 1987, 93; mem. med.-clin. rev. panel U. Conn. Rsch. Found., 1988-89. Dep. editor Jour. Bone and Mineral Rsch., 1990; contbr. articles to med. jours., chpt. to book. Recipient new investigator rsch. award NIH, 1982-85, rsch. assoc. career devel. award VA, 1983-88; grantee USPHS, 1988-97, G.D. Searle, 1991-93. Mem. AAAS, Endocrine Soc., Am. Soc. for Bone and Mineral Rsch., Conn. Endocrine Soc. Office: VA Med Ctr Bldg 5 Rsch 555 Willard Ave Newington CT 06111

LORINCZ, ALBERT BELA, physician, educator; b. Budapest, Hungary, Sept. 6, 1922; came to U.S., 1922, naturalized, 1944; s. Frank Coleman and Theresa (Csore) L.; m. Ann Marie Callaghan, Mar. 23, 1946; children: Margaret Alice, Albert Gregory, Paul Francis, Ann Elizabeth, Thomas Andrew, Catherine Bernadette, Peter Henry. B.S. in Biochemistry, U. Chgo., 1944, M.D., 1946. Diplomate: Am. Bd. Obstetrics and Gynecology. Intern Ill. Central Hosp., Chgo., 1946-47; resident obstetrics and gynecology Chgo. Lying-In Hosp., 1949-53; asst. prof. obstetrics and gynecology U. Chgo. Med. Sch., 1958-61, prof., 1966-71; clin. prof. Stanford U. Sch. Medicine, 1971—; prof. obstetrics and gynecology, chmn. dept. Creighton U. Sch. Medicine, 1961-66; dir. dept. obstetrics and gynecology Creighton Meml.-St. Joseph's Hosp., Omaha, 1961-66; chmn. dept. obstetrics and gynecology Archbishop Bergan Mercy Hosp., Omaha, 1964-66; chief obstetrics Booth Meml. Hosp., Omaha, 1961-66; cons. VA Hosp., Omaha, also; Douglas County Hosp., Omaha, 1962-66; attending physician Chgo. Lying-In Hosp., Billings Hosp., Chgo., 1966-71; med. dir., chief obstetrics and gynecology Valley West Gen. Hosp., Los Gatos, Calif., 1971-75; chief staff Valley West Gen. Hosp., 1976, 84; mem. staff O'Connor Hosp., San Jose Hosp.; mem. staff, sec. dept. ob-gyn Santa Clara Valley Med. Ctr., bd. dirs., 1982-88; mem. staff Alexian Bros. Hosp., Good Samaritan Hosp., others. Contbr. articles to profl. jours. Mem. med. adv. bd. Nat. Found.-March of Dimes; bd. dirs. Santa Clara Valley PSRO, 1978-84. Served to 1st lt., M.C. AUS, 1944-46; to lt. col. 1948-58; col. Res., 1966-82 (ret.). Fellow ACS, Am. Coll. Obstetricians and Gynecologists; mem. AAAS, Am. Assn. Gynecologic Laparoscopists, Am. Chem. Soc., N.Y. Acad. Scis., Am. Fertility Soc., Am. Inst. Chemists, Assn. Profs. Gynecology and Obstetrics, Gynecol. Soc. for Study Breast Disease, Am. Soc. Reproductive Medicine, Am. Geriatric Soc., Royal Soc. Medicine (affiliate), Omaha-Midwest Clin. Soc., Chgo., San Francisco gynecol. socs., AMA, World Med. Assn., Am. Assn. for Lab. Animal Sci., Central Assn. Ostetricians and Gynecologists, Am. Assn. for Maternal and Infant Health, Assn. Mil. Surgeons U.S., Reticuloendothelial Soc., Shufelt Soc. Santa Clara County, Pan Pacific Surg. Assn., Peninsula Gynecologic Soc., AAUP, Internat. Fertility Assn., Pan Am. Med. Assn., Am. Soc. Abdominal Surgeons, Pro-Life Med. Assn. Calif. (pres.), Am. Assn. Pro-Life Obstetricians and Gynecologists, Assn. for Advancement Med. Instrumentation, Santa Clara Valley PSRO (pres., dir.), Calif. Assn. Obstetricians and Gynecologists, Sigma Xi. Democrat. Roman Catholic. Club: Central Travel. Home: 18816 Devon Ave Saratoga CA 95070-4606 Office: 15899 Los Gatos Almaden Rd Los Gatos CA 95032-3739

LORING, DAVID WILLIAM, neuropsychologist, researcher; b. Richmond, Ind., July 13, 1956; s. Richard William and Janet (Teetor) L.; m. Debra Rogers, Jan. 5, 1980 (div. 1983); m. Sherrill Rabon, July 30, 1988; children: Jason Michael, Sarah Elizabeth, Rachel Erin. BA, Wittenberg U., 1978; PhD, U. Houston, 1982. Diplomate Am. Bd. Profl. Psychology. Postdoctoral fellow dept. neurology Coll. of Medicine Baylor U., Houston, 1982-83; instr. div. neurosurgery U. Tex. Med. Br., Galveston, 1983-85; asst. prof. dept. neurology Med. Coll. Ga., Augusta, 1985-89, assoc. prof. dept. neurology, 1989-94, prof., 1994—; lectr. Parke-Davis Nat. Speakers Bur., 1991—. Author: Amobarbital Effects and Lateralized Brain Function, 1992; cons. editor Clin. Neuropsychologist Jour., 1991—, Jour. Epilepsy, 1991—, Jour. Clin. and Exptl. Neuropsychology, 1993—, Aging and Cognition, 1993—, Jour. Internat. Neuropsychol. Soc., 1994—; contbr. articles to Jour. Clin. and Exptl. Neuropsychology, Neuropsychologia, Archives of Neurology, Neurology. Mem. Internat. Neuropsychol. Soc. (bd. govs. 1991-94), Am. Epilepsy Soc., Am. Psychol. Assn., Am. Acad. Neurology (assoc.). Home: 147 Savannah Pt North Augusta SC 29841-3568 Office: Med Coll Ga Dept Neurology Augusta GA 30912

LORING, RICHARD WILLIAM, psychotherapist; b. Bronx, N.Y., May 26, 1928; s. William Maurice and Jeannette Edith (Bass) L.; B.A., DePauw U., 1952; M.A., Ind. U., 1954; Ph.D., Columbia Pacific U., 1982; m. Janet Teetor, Aug. 22, 1953; children—Steven, David, Lynne. Psychiat. social worker Richmond (Ind.) State Hosp., 1954-56; asst. dir. Tippecanoe County Mental Health Center, Lafayette, Ind., 1956-62; exec. dir. Venango County Mental Health Center, Oil City, Pa., 1962-71; adminstr. Mental Health/Mental Retardation Authorities, Oil City, 1970-71; dir. Venango Human Services Center, Franklin, Pa., 1971-75; clin. program dir., dir. consultation and edn. Erie County Mental Health Dept.; pvt. practice psychotherapy, Oil City, 1976—; mem. staff dept. psychiatry Oil City Hosp., sr. psychotherapist Vets. Adminstrn. Vietnam Vets. Outreach Program, 1986—; part-time prof. sociology DePauw U., 1956-62; part-time prof. psychology Pa. State U., 1968-69; field prof. U. Pitts., 1969-74; prof. sociology Clarion State Coll., part-time, 1972-73; part-time prof. mental health counseling Gannon Coll., 1975, clin. advisor Physician Asst. Preceptorship, 1986-95; spl. cons. Corps Chaplains, U.S. Army, 1971-75; mem. profl. adv. com. Crippled Children and Adults Com., 1971-75; mem. profl. adv. com. Clarion State Coll. Sch. Nursing, 1981-94 . Bd. dirs. Pa. Mental Health Assn., 1969-77, mem. exec. com., 1973-77; del., mem. task force White House Conf. on Aging, 1971; del. Nat. Conf. on Mental Health, 1975; bd. dirs. Franklin Light Opera Co., 1970-74; chmn. project rev. com. Venango Regional Comprehensive Health Planning, 1973-75; chmn. Gt. Lakes Forum on Primary Prevention in Mental Health, 1976; chmn. N.W. Pa. Family Planning Council, 1974; mem. N.W. region steering com. Pub. Com. for Humanities in Pa., 1971-74. Served with AUS, World War II. Named Boss of Yr., Ft. Venango chpt. Nat. Secs. Assn., 1972. Fellow Am. Assn. Social Psychiatry; mem. ACA, Psychiat. Outpatient Centers Am. (exec. sec. 1966-74), Am. Pub. Health Assn., Am. Assn. Mental Health Counseling, Am. Coll. Clinic Adminstrs. Editor: Selected Papers of Psychiatric Outpatient Centers, 1967; Psychiatric Outpatient Centers and Low Income Populations, 1968. Home: 406 W 7th St Oil City PA 16301-3040 Office: Venango Int Med Assocs 1 Memorial Dr Oil City PA 16301-2137

LORNTZ, JOYCE HANSCOM, family and marriage counselor; b. Astoria, Oreg., Aug. 9, 1945; d. Russell Loring and Ouida Eloise (Sprague) Hanscom; m. E. John Lonrtz, Sept. 14, 1969; children: Breyette, Tarina. BS in Edn., Atlantic Union Coll., South Lancaster, Mass., 1968, AS in Nursing, 1969, MPH, 1987, MA, 1990; PhD, Walden U., 1992. Nat. cert. counselor. Chaplain Loma Linda (Calif.) U. Med. Ctr., 1990-91; assoc. pastor Fletcher (N.C.) SOA Ch., 1991—; speaker family life workshops in east and west coastal regions; pres. Women in Ministry, SE Calif. Conf. Seventh-day Adventists; co-chmn. Chaplains for Women in Ministry, Adventist Chaplains Ministry. Mem. AACD, Am. Mental Health Counselors Assn. Home and Office: PO Box 429 Fletcher NC 28732-0429

LORTON, SHARON KAY, optometrist, educator; b. Newton, Iowa, Feb. 23, 1947; d. James Edgar and Helene Marie (Christiansen) L. BS in Phys. Edn., St. Cloud (Minn.) State U., 1969, MS in Health Edn., 1977; BS in Visual Sci., Pacific U., Forest Grove, Oreg., 1981, OD, 1985. Cert. Nat. Bd. Optometry, Minn. Bd. Optrometry, Wis. Bd. Optometry. Tchr., health educator, coach Rocori H.S., Cold Spring, Minn., 1969-81; instr. St. Cloud Vocat. Tech. Coll., 1987-89; optometrist St. Cloud Optometry Clinic, 1985-86; optometrist Midwest Vision Ctrs. Inc., St. Cloud, 1986—, dir. optometric svcs., 1989-95; mem. optometric adv. bd. St. Cloud Vocat. Tech. Coll., 1987-90; vol. Mid Minn. Health Clinic, St. Cloud Hosp., 1991—; lectr. for profl. orgns. Active Minn. Girl Scouts. PEO grantee, 1984; named to Outstanding Young Women of Am., 1984. Mem. Am. Optometric Assn., Minn. Optometric Assn. Office: Family Eyewear 2824 Divison St Saint Cloud MN 56301

LOSADA-PAISEY, GLORIA, psychologist; b. Havana, Cuba, Apr. 20, 1957; came to U.S., 1962; d. Manuel Benito and Maria del Pilar (Fernandez) Losada; m. Timothy John Henry Paisey, June 4, 1983 (div. June 1989); 1 child, Monica Paisey. BA, Fla. Internat. U., 1980; D Psychology, Nova U., 1984. Lic. psychologist, Conn. Pre-doctoral psychology fellow Yale U., New Haven, 1983-84; clin. psychologist State of Conn. Dept. Mental Retardation Southbury Tng. Sch., Southbury, Conn., 1984-86, State of Conn. Dept. Mental Retardation New Haven Ctr., New Haven, 1986-88; dir. psychol. svcs. State of Conn. Dept. Mental Retardation Region 6, Waterford, Conn., 1988-92; clin. psychologist Conn. Dept. Children and Youth Svcs., Middletown, Conn., 1992—; pvt. practice psychology, Waterbury, 1986—; dir. treatment program for mentally retarded offenders Southbury Tng. Sch., State of Conn., 1984-86. Mem. APA, New Eng. Psychol. Assn. Democrat. Roman Catholic. Office: 265 Meriden Rd Waterbury CT 06705-2001

LOSSE, CATHERINE ANN, pediatric nurse, critical care nurse, educator, clinical nurse specialist; b. Mount Holly, N.J., Mar. 12, 1959; d. David C. and Bernice (Lewis) L. Diploma, Helene Fuld Sch. Nursing, 1980; BSN magna cum laude, Thomas Jefferson U., 1986; MSN, U. Pa., 1989; postgrad., Widener U., 1995—. RN, N.J., Pa., Del.; cert. pediatric nurse, cert. pediatric critical care nurse; cert. PALS provider, BLS instr. Staff nurse adult med.-surg. Meml. Hosp. Burlington County, Mount Holly, N.J., 1980-81; staff nurse pediatric home care Newborn Nurses, Moorestown, N.J., 1986-87; clin. nurse II surg. intensive care Deborah Heart & Lung Ctr., Browns Mills, N.J., 1986-87, clin. nurse III pediatric cardiology, 1981-86, 87—; ednl. nurse specialist critical care The Children's Hosp., Phila., 1992-94; instr. nursing of families, maternal-child health, pediat., geriatrics Burlington County Coll., 1994-96; staff nurse pediatric home care Bayada Nurses, Burlington, N.J., 1995—; clin. instr. pediatrics Thomas Jefferson U., 1990; clin. instr. adult med. surg. Burlington County Coll., 1991. Mem. ANA, AACN (CCRN, pediat. spl. interest cons. 1995-96), Nat. Assn. Pediatric Nurse Assocs. and Practitioners, Soc. Pediat. Nurses, N.J. State Nurses Assn. (mem. cabinet on continuing edn. rev. team III 1992-96, mem. forum for nursing in advanced practice 1994—), Am. Heart Assn. (cert. instr. PALS and BLS, bd. dirs. Burlington County br. 1995—, vice chairperson cmty. site com. 1995—), Sigma Theta Tau. Home: 253 Spout Spring Ave Mount Holly NJ 08060-2041

LOTHANE, HENRY ZVI, psychiatrist, psychoanalyst; b. Lublin, Poland, May 21, 1934; married March 29, 1959; 1 child, Shara. MD, H.U. Hadassah, 1962. Cert. Am. Bd. Psychiatry and Neurology. Intern Beilinson (Israel) Hosp., 1961-62; psychiat. resident Talbieh (Israel) Psychiat. Hosp., 1962-63, Strong Meml. Hosp., Rochester, N.Y., 1963-66; unit chief Hillside Hosp., 1966-69; pvt. practice, 1966—; asst. prof., assoc. prof. psychiatry Mt. Sinai Sch. Medicine, N.Y.C., 1969—; assoc. attending Mt. Sinai Hosp., N.Y.C., 1969—. Co-author books on psychiatry and psychoanalysis; contbr. articles on psychiatry and psychoanalysis to profl. jours. Fellow Am. Psychiat. Assn., Am. Acad. Psychoanalysis; mem. N.Y. County Med. Soc., Internat. Psychoanalytic Assn., Union of Concerned Psychoanalysts and Psychotherapists (past pres.). Office: 1435 Lexington Ave New York NY 10128-1625

LOTKE, PAUL A., orthopedic surgery; b. Sept. 9, 1937; m. Dorothy Sue Lotke; 3 children. MD, U. Pa., 1963. Intern Univ. Hosp., Madison, Wis., 1963-64; resident Hosp. for Spl. Surgery, N.Y.c., 1964-71; prof. orthopedic surgery U. Pa. Hosp., Phila., 1971—. Editor: (book) Master Techniques of Knee Surgery, 1995; contbr. numerous articles to med. jours., chpts. to med. texts. Lt. USN, 1964-66. Mem. Knee Soc. (pres. 1985), Phila. Orthopedic Soc. (pres. 1985), Phila. Rheumatism Soc. (pres. 1986), Hosp. Spl. Surgery Soc. (pres. 1994). Office: Hosp Univ Pa 3400 Spruce St Philadelphia PA 19104

LOTSCH, RICHARD CHARLES, osteopath; b. Waverly, Pa., Oct. 3, 1961; s. Charles Francis and Doris Emily (Shuster) L.; m. June Pamela Dennis, Sept. 21, 1985. BS, Hahnemann U., 1985; DO, Phila. Coll. Osteo. Medicine, 1996. Cert. physician asst. Emergency paramedic Lower Providence Ambulance, Eagleville, Pa., 1985-87; staff physician asst. Mont. County Emergency Svc., Norristown, Pa., 1985-87, 92-95; med. physician asst. USAF, 1987-92; emergency medicine resident Albert Einstein Med. Ctr., Phila., 1996—. Troop com. chmn. Boy Scouts Am., Cannon AFB, N.Mex., 1991-92, asst. scoutmaster, 1988-91; vol. paramedic Lower Providence Ambulance, Eagleville, 1982-85, asst. ambulance chief, 1982. Capt. USAF, 1987-92. Decorated Air Force Commendation medal, USAF, Air Force Health Professions scholar, 1992. Mem. Am. Coll. Emergency Physicians (student mem.), Assn. Mil. Osteo. Physicians and Surgeons (student mem.), Am. Osteo. Assn., Am. Acad. Family Physicians (student mem.), Am. Coll. Osteo. Family Physicians (student mem.). Office: Albert Einstein Med Ctr 5501 Old York Rd Philadelphia PA 19141

LOTSPEICH, KURT, optometrist; b. Westwood, Calif., Dec. 28, 1955; s. Dennis Ray and Akiko (Kinosita) L. BS, Calif. State U., 1978; OD, Ill. Coll. Optometry, 1982. Pvt. practice Clearwater, Fla., 1982—. Republican. Home: 4300 Ridgemoor Dr N Palm Harbor FL 34685 Office: Ste 1069 27001 US Hwy 19 North Clearwater FL 34621

LOTT, IRA TOTZ, pediatric neurologist; b. Cin., Apr. 15, 1941; s. Maxwell and Jeneda (Totz) L.; m. Ruth J. Weiss, June 21, 1964; children: Lisa, David I. BA cum laude, Brandeis U., 1963; MD cum laude, Ohio State U., 1967. Intern Mass. Gen. Hosp., Boston, 1967, resident in pediatrics, 1967-69, resident in child neurology, 1971-74; clin. assoc. NIH, Bethesda, Md., 1969-71; from clin. rsch. fellow to asst. prof. Harvard Med. Sch., Boston, 1971-82; clin. dir. Eunice Kennedy Shriver Ctr. for Mental Retardation, Waltham, Mass., 1974-82; assoc. prof. U. Calif., Irvine, 1983-91, prof., 1992—; chmn. dept. pediatrics U. Calif., Irvine, 1992—, dir. pediatric neurology, 1983—; pres. Prof. Child Neurology, Mpls., 1992—. Editor: Down Syndrome-Medical Advances, 1991; contbr. articles to profl. jours. Sec., treas. Child Neurology Soc., Mpls., 1987-90. Lt. comdr. USPHS, 1969-71. NIH grantee, 1974—; recipient Career Devel. award Kennedy Found., 1976. Fellow Am. Acad. Neurology; mem. Am. Pediatric Soc., Am. Neurol. Assn., Nat. Down Syndrome Soc. (sci. acad. bd. 1985—), Western Soc. for Pediatric Rsch. (councillor 1989-91). Office: U Calif Irvine Med Ctr Dept Pediatrics 101 The City Dr S # 27 Orange CA 92668-3201

LOTTY, KATHLEEN MARY, nurse, physician assistant; b. Hartford, Conn., Sept. 29, 1949; d. John Lewis and Helen Loretta (Bergan) Muska; m. Robert Wayne Lotty, May 7, 1983; children: Sara, Alexandra. RN, Children's Hosp. Sch. Nursing, 1970; PA, Yale U., 1984; BS in health scis., Charter Oak State Coll., 1995. RN, Mass., Conn., N.Y. Operating rm. nurse Children's Hosp., Boston, 1970-72, 74-81, Med. Coll. Va., Richmond, 1972-74, Cardiac Surg. Team Children's Hosp., Boston, 1979-81. Speaker Trumbull (Conn.) PTA, 1990, 91. Mem. Mill Plain Improvement Soc. (v.p. 1994—).

LOTUACO, LUISA GO, pathologist; b. Gapan, Nueva Ecija, Philippines, Jan. 29, 1938; d. Galicano Yuzon and Alicia (Go) L.; m. George Garrett Shepherd; 1 child, Lara. Student, U. Santo Tomas, Manila, Philippines, MD cum laude, 1960. Diplomate Am. Bd. Coll. Am. Pathology. Pathologist, Manila Sanitarium and Hosp., Manila, Philippines, 1969-72; mem. pathology faculty Kansas U., Kansas City, 1972, 1974-94; pathologist St. Catherine Hosp., East Chgo., Ind., 1973-74, VA Med. Ctr., Kansas City, Mo., 1974-94; chief pathology and lab. medicine John Pershing VA Med. Ctr., Poplar Bluff, Mo., 1994-96, chief of staff, 1995—. Paul Harris fellow, 1996. Fellow Coll. Am. Pathology, Am. Assn. of Clin. Pathologists; mem. U.S. and Canadian Acad. Pathologists, Am. Assn. Blood Banks, Philippine Med. Soc. of Kansas City (pres. 1981-83), Am. Med. Women's Assn., Philippine Med. Soc. Avocations: stamps; ceramics; antiques, opera, classical music. Home: 14111 Christy Ln Poplar Bluff MO 63901 Office: John Pershing VA Med Ctr 1500 N Westwood Blvd Poplar Bluff MO 63901-3318

LOTZE, EVIE DANIEL, psychodramatist; b. Roswell, N.Mex., Mar. 6, 1943; d. Wadsworth Richard and Lee Ora (Norrell) Daniel; m. Christian Dieter Lotze, June 9, 1963; children: Conrad, Monica. BA cum laude, La. State U., 1964; MA, Goddard Coll., 1975; PhD, Union Inst., Cin., 1990. Dir. Casa Alegre, Hogares, Albuquerque, 1979-80; pvt. practice Riyadh, Saudi Arabia, 1980-83, Silver Spring, Md., 1983-85; dir. Gulf States Psychodrama Tng., Houston, 1986-88; founder, dir. Innerstages Psychodrama Tng., Houston, 1988-94; program devel. cons. in tng. Children's Nat. Med. Ctr., Washington, 1994-96; pvt. practice Paris, 1996—; supr. Houston Area psychodramatists, 1988—; tng. cons. Assn. Applied Psychologists, Moscow, 1992—; cons. in field. Author: (tng. manual) Clinical Psychodrama Training Manual, 3 vols., 1990. Bd. dirs. Interact Theater, Houston, 1992. Mem. Am. Group Psychotherapy Assn., Internat. Coun. Psychologists. Democrat. Lutheran.

LOTZE, MICHAEL T., surgeon; b. Altadena, Calif., July 11, 1952; s. Thomas Hilary and Joanone Bernice (Bellas) L.; m. Joan Harvey, June 25, 1977; children: Thomas, Anna, Michael, Jenette. BA, Northwestern U., 1973, MD with hons., 1974. Diplomate Am. Bd. Surgery, Nat. Bd. Med. Examiners; lic. N.Y., Minn., Md., Pa. Jr. fellow in Surgery M.D. Anderson Tumor Inst., Houston, Tex., 1975; intern, resident Stong Meml. Hosp., Rochester, N.Y., 1975-76; asst. resident in surgery Stong Meml. Hosp., Rochester, 1976-77; fellow surgery br. Nat. Cancer Inst., Bethesda, Md., 1978-80; sr. and chief resident surgery, instr. U. Rochester, N.Y., 1980-82; asst. prof. surgery Uniformed Svcs. U. of Health Scis., Bethesda, Md., 1983-88; assoc. prof. surgery Uniformed Svcs. U. of Health Scis., Bethesda, 1988-90; prof. surgery, molecular genetics and biochemistry chief sect. surgical oncology U. Pitts., 1990—; co-dir. human gene therapy program Pitts. Genetics Inst., 1991—; co-dir. divsn. biol. therapeutics Pitts. Cancer Inst., 1992—; mem. numerous groups involved in rsch. on melanoma and other cancers including: coord. NIH Melanoma Working Group, 1985-87, Rev. Bd. United Cancer Coun., Inc., Rochester, 1985-87, chmn. spl. study sect. Exptl. Immunology NIH, 1990, mem. planning com. NIH Consensus Devel. Conf. on Diagnosis and Treatment of Early Melanoma, 1991, mem. search com. Chair U. Pitts. Med. Ctr. dir. radiation oncology, 1992, Mellon Dickson Prize com. U. Pitt. Sch. Medicine, 1993-95; vis. prof. Duke Univ, Durham, N.C., 1987, Acad. Sinica/Veteran's Gen. Hosp, Tapei, Taiwan, 1993; co-organizer Keystone Symposium on Cellular Innunity and the Immunotherapy of Cancer, Park City, Utah, 1990, Keystone Symposium on Melanoma and Biology of the Neural Crest, Taos, N. Mex., 1992. on Cellular Immunity and the Immunotherapy of CancerII, Taos, 1993; organizer 2d Internat. Congress on Biol. Response Modifiers, San Diego, 1993. Contbr. over 280 articles to profl. jours. including Jour. Am. Med. Assn., New Eng. Jour Medicine, Immunology, Exptl. Immunology and others; presenter at about 200 sci. workshops, confs., symposiums.; editor: (with others) (books) Cellular Immunity and the Immunotherapy of Cancer, 1990, Current Cancer Therapy, 1994, Regional Therapy of Advanced Cancer, 1996; producer films on Ultrasound Imaging, Laser surgery and other Spectacular Problems in Surgery, 1986, Immunotherapy Vidoe Handbook, 1992, Resection of a Giant Lipoma, 1995; assoc. editor The Cancer Jour., 1995; mem. edtl. bd. European Cytokine Jour., 1988, Jour. Immunotherapy, 1990, Jour. Immunology, 1990-95, Contemporary Oncology, 1990-94, Gen. Surgery and Laparoscopy News, 1991, Melanoma Rsch., 1991, Therapeutic Immunology, 1993, Gene Therapy (Nature), 1995 and others. Med. Officer, Nat. Health Svc. Corps, 1977-78. Named Ann. Edith Hamilton Cancer Lectr., Genesee Hosp., Wasyl Pluta Cancer Ctr., Rochester, N.Y., 1986; Virginia Mason Rsch. Ctr. Disting. Lectr., Seattle, 1990, Ann. John Palmer Lectr., U. Toronto, Can., 1991, 10th Hinshaw Lectr. U. Rochester, 1991, Sommer Meml. Lectr. Portland, Oreg., 1994, El Tabah Lectr., McGill U., Montreal, Can., 1995, 1st Peter Fink Lectr., Meml. Sloan Kettering, 1995; grantee: NIH, 1992-96, 92-94, 94-99, 95, 95-99 and others, VA RAG, 1991-93. Fellow Am. Coll. Surgeons; mem. AMA, Am. Assn. Cancer Rsch. (program com. 1991), Am. Assn. Immunology (program com. 1990, 92), Am. Soc. Clin. Oncology, Assn. Acad. Surgery, Cell Transplant Soc., Clin. Immunological Soc. (program com. 1993), Soc. for Analytical Cytology, Soc. for Surgical Oncology (program com. 1992, 93, clin. affairs com. 1991-93), Soc. Univ. Surgeons, Soc. for Biologic Therapy (program com. 1991-93), World Assn. Hepato-Pancreatico-Biliary Surgery. Office: Univ Pitts 200 Lathrop St Pittsburgh PA 15201

LOUARD, AGNES A., social work educator; b. Savannah, Ga., Mar. 10, 1922; d. Jospeh B. and Agnes (Hollinger) Anthony; m. V. Benjamin Louard (dec. Aug. 1986); children: Rita Jean, Diane C. Louard-Michel, Kenneth A. BA, U. Pa., 1944; MA, Fisk U., 1945; MSW, Columbia U., 1948; post-grad., NYU Sch. Edn., 1970-72. Asst. to dir. South Broad St. U.S.O., Phila., 1945-46; supr. children and teen activity Manhattanville Neighborhood Ctr., N.Y.C., 1948-50, supr. children's div., 1950-52; dir. recreation and edn. Union Settlement Assn., N.Y.C., 1952-57; dir. East Harlem Project, N.Y.C., 1958-59; sr. caseworker Speedwell Svcs. for Children, Inc., N.Y.C., 1959-61, Leake and Watts Children's Home, Yonkers, N.Y., 1962-63; dir. recreation A. Holly Patterson Home for Aged and Infirmed, Uniondale, N.Y., 1963-65; field instr. Sch. Social Work Columbia U., N.Y.C., 1965-67, asst. prof. Sch. Social Work, 1967-71, assoc. prof. sch. social work, 1971-92; adj. prof. Sch. Social Work Columbia U., N.Y.C., 1992—; couns. Harlem Youth Bd., N.Y.C., Headstart Program, N.Y.C., 1966-68, James Weldon Johnson Ctr., N.Y.C., 1967-69, CCNY Psychol. Ctr., 1969-70, Volt-Headstart Op., Schenectady, N.Y., 1970, Atlantic City, 1972, Harlem Hosp., 1971-73, Spence Chapin Foster Care and Adoption Svcs. Agy., N.Y.C., 1973—; trainer summer Headstart Progs., NYU, 1967-68; mem. staff E.P.D.A. Guidance Inst., Queens Coll., 1969. Trustee Union Chapel, Oak Bluffs, Martha's Vineyard, Mass., 1975—, Union Chapel, Oak Bluffs, 1975—, sec., 1995—; mem. adv. bd. YWCA, New Harlem, N.Y., 1985-88; bd. dirs., past pres. Harriet Tubman Cmty. Ctr., Hempstead, N.Y., 1964-86; bd. dirs. Pleasant Ave. Day Care Ctr., 1987—, Peninsula Counselling Ctr., Woodmere, N.Y., 1972—, pres., 1985-88, Schumburg Corp., 1989—, trustee, 1994-96; v.p. Allen Neighborhood Care Team, 1995—. Mem. NAACP, NASW, ACLU, Common Cause, Women's City Club (trustee 1991—). Democrat. Home: 560 Riverside Dr Apt 6L New York NY 10027-3240 Office: Columbia U Sch Social Work 622 W 113th St New York NY 10025-7982

LOUBE, SAMUEL DENNIS, physician; b. Rumania, Aug. 26, 1921; came to U.S., 1922, naturalized, 1927; s. Harry and Rebecca (Pollack) L.; m. Emily Wallace, Apr. 14, 1976; children—Julian M., Jonathan B., Susan C., Karen E., Patricia A., Pamela B., Brian R. A.B., George Washington U., 1941, M.D. cum laude, 1943. Diplomate: Am. Bd. Internal Medicine. Intern, then resident in medicine Gallinger Municipal Hosp., Washington, 1943-46; physician USPHS, 1946-48; postdoctoral fellow NIH, 1948-50; research fellow in endocrinology Michael Reese Hosp., Chgo., 1948-49; research fellow in metabolism and endocrinology May Inst. Jewish Hosp., Cin., 1949-50; mem. faculty George Washington U. Med. Sch., 1950-89, clin. prof. medicine, 1975-89, prof. emeritus, 1989; practice medicine specializing in endocrinology and metabolic diseases, Washington, 1950-88, mem. Washington Internal Medicine Group, 1965-88; former chmn. dept. medicine, chief sect. endocrinology Sibley Meml. Hosp. Contbr. articles to med jours. Fellow ACP; mem. AMA, Am. Diabetes Assn., Endocrine Soc., Am. Soc. Internal Medicine, Diabetes Assn. D.C. (past pres.), Jacobi Med. Soc. (past pres.). Jewish.

LOUCKS, VERNON R., JR., healthcare products and services company executive; b. Evanston, Ill., Oct. 24, 1934; s. Vernon Reece and Sue (Burton) L.; m. Linda Kay Olson, May 12, 1972; 6 children. B.A. in History, Yale U., 1957; M.B.A., Harvard U., 1963. Sr. mgmt. cons. George Fry & Assos., Chgo., 1963-65; with Baxter Travenol Labs., Inc. (now Baxter Internat. Inc.), Deerfield, Ill., 1966—, exec. v.p., 1976, also bd. dirs., pres., chief oper. officer, 1980, chief exec. officer, chmn., 1987—; bd. dirs. Dun & Bradstreet Corp., Emerson Electric Co., Quaker Oats Co., Anheuser-Busch Cos.; bd. advisors Nestlé U.S.A. Trustee Rush-Presbyn.-St. Luke's Med. Ctr.; assoc. Northwestern U. 1st lt. USMC, 1957-60. Recipient Citizen Fellowship award Chgo. Inst. Medicine, 1982, Nat. Health Care award B'nai B'rith Youth Svcs., 1986, William McCormick Blair award Yale U., 1989, Semper Fidelis award USMC, 1989, Disting. Humanitarian award St. Barnabas Found., 1992, Alexis de Tocqueville award for community svc. United Way Lake County, 1993; named 1983's Outstanding Exec. Officer in the health-care industry Fin. World; elected to Chgo.'s Bus. Hall of Fame, Jr. Achievement, 1987. Mem. Health Industry Mfrs. Assn. (chmn. 1983), Bus. Roundtable (conf. bd., mem. policy com.), Bus. Coun. Clubs: Chgo. Commonwealth, Commercial, Mid-America; Links (N.Y.C.). Office Baxter Healthcare Corp One Baxter Pkwy Deerfield IL 60015

LOUGHARY, THOMAS MICHAEL, dentist; b. Beardstown, Ill., June 13, 1959; s. Thomas Giels and Beverly Ann (Marshall) L.; m. Vicki Lynne Shaneman, May 25, 1986 (div.); children: Thomas Michael II, Victoria Paige. Student, Knox Coll., 1977-80; DMD, So. Ill. U., Alton, 1984. Dentist Pla. Dental Ctr., Jacksonville, Ill., 1984-90, Dental Assocs. of Jacksonville, 1991—; gen. practice dentistry Beardstown Dental Assocs., 1985—; staff dentist Passavant Hosp., Jacksonville, Ill.; cons. Cass County Cancer Assn., Virginia, Ill., 1986—, Beardstown Board Edn., 1980—. Soloist Jacksonville Symphony Soc., 1984, 87; dir. Beardstown Community Theater, 1990-91, Jacksonville Theater Guild, 1990; chmn. Cass County Cancer Soc., 1989—. Recipient monetary cert. Phi Gamma Delta Ednl. Found., 1980. Mem. ADA, Chgo. Dental Soc., G.V. Black Dental Soc., Jacksonville C. of C., Kiwanis, Elks, Internat. Assn. of Orthodontics and Edn. (chmn. St. Louis advanced orthodontic study club). Republican. Lutheran. Home: 5 Guy Dr Jacksonville IL 62650-9400 Office: Dental Assocs Jacksonville 1515 W Walnut Blvd # 10 Jacksonville IL 62650-1910

LOUGHEAD, JEFFREY LEE, physician; b. Mystic, Conn., May 11, 1957; s. Lawrence L. and Alice M. L.; m. Melinda K., Apr. 29, 1995; children: Brittany, Molly. BA, Miami U., 1979; MD, U. Cin., 1983. Diplomat Am. Acad. Pediatrics. Intern Children's Hosp. Med. Ctr., Cin., 1983-84, resident, 1984-86, chief resident, 1986-87; fellow in neonatal-perinatal medicine U. Cin., 1987-90; med. dir. spl. care unit Good Samaritan Hosp., Dayton, 1991-95; dir. quality assurance Children's MEd. Ctr., Dayton, 1991—, physician advisor nursing rsch. com., 1993—, clin. dir., 1995—. Author: (chpts.) Principles of Perinatal and Neonatal Metabolism, 1991, Current Pediatric Therapy, 1996. Fellow Am. Coll. Nutrition (Young Investigator award 1988), Am. Acad. Pediatrics. Office: Childrens Med Ctr 1 Children's Plz Dayton OH 45404

LOUGHLIN, KEVIN RAYMOND, urological surgeon, researcher; b. N.Y.C., Aug. 10, 1949; s. Raymond Gerard and Josephine (McGrath) L. AB, Princeton U., 1971; MD, N.Y. Med. Coll., 1975. Diplomate Nat. Bd. Med. Examiners, Am. Bd. Urology. Surgery instr. Harvard Med. Sch. Brigham & Women's Hosp., Boston, 1983-86, asst. prof. surgery Harvard Med. Sch., 1986-90, dir. urologic rsch., 1987—, assoc. prof. surgery Harvard Med. Sch., 1991—; staff urologist Dana Farber Cancer Inst., Boston, 1991—; dir. urologic rsch. Brigham and Women's Hosp., Boston, 1987—. Contbr. over 90 articles to profl. jours. Fellow Am. Cancer Soc., 1982-83, Nat. Kidney Found., 1980-81. Fellow ACS; mem. AAAS, Am. Soc. Andrology, Am. Soc. Clin. Oncology, Am. Urologic Assn., Boston Surg. Soc., Soc. for Basic Urologic Rsch. Home: 30 Lime St Boston MA 02108-1103 Office: Brigham & Womens Hosp 75 Francis St Boston MA 02115-6110

LOUGHMAN, BARBARA ELLEN, immunologist researcher; b. Frankfurt, Ind., Oct. 26, 1940; d. Jimmie Jewel and Ruth Eileen (Hoyer) Evers; m. Terry B. Loughman, June 28, 1962 (dec.); children: Lance Evers Loughman, Chad Elliott Loughman. BS, U. Ill., 1962; PhD, Notre Dame U., 1972. Rsch. scientist Ames Research Labs., Elkhart, Ind., 1962-72; staff fellow NIH, Balt., 1972-74; from research assoc. to research mgr. The Upjohn Co., Kalamazoo, Mich., 1974-84; dir. immunology research Monsanto Co., St. Louis, 1984-85; sr. dir. immunology diseases research G.D. Searle/Monsanto Co., St. Louis, 1986-88; dir. project mgmt. Rorer Cen. Research, Horsham, Pa., 1988-91; dir. internat. drug regulating affairs Marion Merrell Dow, Kansas City, Mo., 1991-95; v.p. devel.svcs. Internat. Med. Tech. Cons., Inc., Lenexa, Kans., 1995—. Contbr. over 20 articles to profl. jours. 1. Mem. AAAS, Am. Acad. Asthma Allergy and Immunology, Am. Assn. Immunology. Office: Internat Med Tech Cons Inc 16300 College Blvd Lenexa KS 66219

LOUIE, ERIC K., cardiologist; b. Chgo.; s. David S. and Eleanor (Towne) L.; m. Karen Giguere, May 6, 1979; children: Andrew, Steven. AB, Harvard U., 1972, MD, 1977. Diplomate Am. Bd. Internal Medicine, Am. Bd. Cardiovasc. Diseases. Intern Brigham and Women's Hosp., Boston, 1977-78, resident, 1978-79; fellow U. Chgo., 1979-81; asst. prof. medicine Uniformed Svcs. Univ., Bethesda, Md., 1981-85; asst. physician to the President The White House, Washington, 1981-84; asst. prof. medicine U. Ill., Chgo., 1985-88; assoc. prof. medicine to prof. medicine Loyola U. Med. Ctr., Maywood, Ill., 1988—, assoc. dir. divsn. cardiology, 1996—. Contbr. over 100 articles and revs. to profl. jours., and chpts. to books, in field of cardiovasc. diseases. Pres. Met. Chgo. chpt. Am. Heart Assn., 1996—. Comdr. USNR, 1981-91. Fellow Am. Coll. Cardiology, Am. Heart Assn. Coun. on Clin. Cardiology; mem. Chgo. Soc. Echocardiography (pres. 1992-94). Office: Loyola Univ Med Ctr 2160 S First Ave Maywood IL 60153

LOUIE, KAREN GIGUERE, internist, medical oncologist, educator; b. Lowell, Mass., July 10, 1950; d. Joseph H. and Mildred E. (Murphy) Giguere; m. Eric K. Louie, May 6, 1979; children: Andrew D., Steven M. BS cum laude, Brandeis U., 1972; MD, Harvard U., Boston, 1979. Diplomate Am. Bd. Internal Medicine, Am. Bd. Med. Oncology, Nat. Bd. Med. Examiners. Lab. technician Mass. Eye and Ear Infirmary, Boston, 1974-75; blood bank technician Boston Hosp. for Women, 1975-76; intern, then jr. resident in medicine U. Chgo. Hosp., 1979-81; sr. asst. resident Washington VA Hosp., 1981-82; med. staff fellow Nat. Cancer Inst., Bethesda, Md., 1982-85; pvt. practice, Hinsdale, Ill., 1985—; staff mem. Hinsdale Hosp., 1985—, Good Samaritan Hosp., Downers Grove, Ill., 1994—, Elmhurst (Ill.) Hosp., 1995—; asst. prof. clin. medicine Northwestern U., Chgo., 1985—; mem. Ill. Cancer Coun., Chgo., 1989-92; affiliate mem. Nat. Surg. Adjuvant Breast and Bowel Project. Contbr. articles and abstracts to med. jours. Alt. mem. Oak Brook (Ill) Cmty. Caucus, 1994—; pres. Oak Brook Little League, 1995—. Sachar fellow Brandeis U., 1970-71, Collins fellow Harvard U. Med. Sch., 1975-76. Fellow ACP; mem. Am. Soc. Clin. Oncology, Am. Assn. for Cancer Rsch.k, Gynecologic Oncology Group (affiliate), Ea. Coopr. Oncology Group (affiliate). Office: Hinsdale Hematology Oncology 908 N Elm St Hinsdale IL 60521

LOUIE, MAY, neurologist, educator; b. Hong Kong, May 31, 1963; (parents Am. citizens); BA in Chemistry, Cornell U., 1984; MD, Meharry Med. Coll., Nashville, 1988. Diplomate Am. Bd. Neurology, Nat. Bd. Med. Examiners. Intern St. Barnabas Med. Ctr., Livingston, N.J., 1988-89; resident, tchg. fellow Boston City Hosp. and Affiliates Program, 1989-92; EMG/Neuromuscular Diseases fellow, clin. fellow in Neurology Brown U./R.I. Hosp., Providence, 1992-93; staff neurologist Goddard Med. Assocs., Brockton, Mass., 1993—; clin. instr. in Neurology Tufts U., Medford, Mass., 1993—. Contbr. articles to profl. jours. Mem. Combined Jewish Philanthropies. Mem. AMA, Mass. Med. Soc., Am. Acad. Neurology, Chinese Am. Med. Soc. Office: 1 Pearl St Brockton MA 02401-2800

LOUIE, RONALD RICHARD, pediatric hematologist, oncologist; b. Columbus, Ohio, Nov. 11, 1954. BA, Case Western Reserve U., 1976; MD, Med. Coll. Ohio, 1980. Diplomate in pediatrics and pediatric hematology-oncology Am. Bd. Pediatrics. Pediatric hematologist and oncologist Group Health Coop., Seattle, 1988—; clin. asst. prof. pediatrics U. Wash., Seattle, 1988—. Vol. pediatrician and hematologist Internat. Dist. Cmty. Health Ctr., Seattle. Fellow Am Acad. Pediatrics: mem. Am. Soc. Clin. Oncology, Children's Cancer Group (affiliate investigator). Office: Group Health Cooperative 200 15th Ave E Seattle WA 98112

LOUIS, RENÉ PAUL, orthopedist, department chairman, spine surgeon, educator; b. Manosque, Provence, France, June 8, 1933; s. Francois Louis and Emilienne Breuza; m. Janine Louise Molinier, Dec. 22, 1956; children: Ghislaine, Claude, Christian. MD, Med. Sch. Marseilles, France, 1958. Anatomy chief aid Med. Sch. of Marseilles, 1956-66; res. in surgery Pub. Hosps., Marseilles, 1956-66; prof. of Anatomy and Orthopedics Med. Sch. and Hosp. U., Dakar, Senegal, 1966-71; prof. and surg. dept. chief Med. Sch. Marseilles, 1971—, orthopedics chief of dept. and chief prof., 1971—. Author: Surgery of the Spine, 1982. Lt. Health Svc., 1959-61, France. Mem. French Orthopedic Soc., Cervical Spine Research Soc., Internat. Soc. for Study of Lumbar Spine, Golf Salette, SOFCOT (pres.). Roman Catholic. Home: 4 Impasse Roc Fleuri, 13008 Marseilles France Office: Hosp De La Conception, 147 Bd Baille, 13005 Marseilles France

LOUREIRO-DIAS, MARIA DA CONCEIÇÃO, microbiologist, educator; b. Mesão Frio, Portugal, Feb. 22, 1947; d. Fernando and Maria Alice (Silva-Dias) L.-D.; m. Mil-Homens, Feb. 1, 1972; children: João, Rita. Degree in chem. engring., Inst. Superior Tecnico, Lisbon, 1972; PhD in Biology, New U., Lisbon, 1986. Rsch. asst. Gulbenkian Inst. Sci., Oeiras, Portugal, 1981-89, investigator, 1989—; prof. Tech. U., Lisbon, 1986—; active Internat. Commn. on Yeasts; cons. Quasis Quality & Environment, Lisbon, 1979-83. Contbr. articles to profl. jours. Mem. Soc. Portuguesa de Bioquimica, Soc. Portuguesa de Microbiologia, Biochem. Soc., Planetary Soc. Office: Gulbenkian Inst Sci, 2781 Oeiras Portugal

LOURENCO, RUY VALENTIM, physician, educator; b. Lisbon, Portugal, Mar. 25, 1929; came to U.S., 1959, naturalized, 1966; s. Raul Valentim and Maria Amalia (Gomes-Rosa) L.; children: Peter Edward, Margaret Philippa. M.D., U. Lisbon, 1951. Intern Lisbon City Hosps., 1951-53, resident internal medicine, 1953-55; instr. U. Lisbon, 1955-59; fellow dept. medicine Columbia U.-Presbyn. Med. Ctr., N.Y.C., 1959-63; asst. prof. medicine N.J. Coll. Medicine, 1963-66, assoc. prof., 1966-67; practice medicine specializing in pulmonary medicine, 1967—; assoc. prof. medicine and physiology U. Ill. Coll. Medicine, Chgo., 1967-69, prof., 1969-89, Foley prof. medicine, 1978-89, chmn. dept. medicine, 1977-89, exec. head dept. medicine, 1983-89; dir. respiratory rsch. lab. Hektoen Inst., Chgo., 1967-71; dir. pulmonary medicine Cook County Hosp., Chgo., 1969-70; attending physician U. Ill. Med. Ctr., Chgo., 1967-89; dir. pulmonary sect. and labs U. Ill. Med. Ctr., 1970-77, physician-in-chief, 1977-89, pres. med. staff, 1980-81; prof. medicine and physiology, dean N.J. Med. Sch. U. Medicine and Dentistry N.J., Newark, 1989—; cons. task force on rsch. in respiratory diseases NIH, 1972, mem. pathology study sect., 1972-76; mem. rev. bd. Spl. Ctrs. of Rsch. program, 1974; cons. career devel. program VA, 1972-76; mem. nat. com. Rev. Sci. Basis of Respiratory Therapy, 1973-74; pres. exec. com. U. Hosp., Newark, 1989—; mem. bd. govs. Hackensack U. Hosp., 1993—; mem. step II USMLE and fin. com. Nat. Bd. Med. Examiners, 1994—; mem. bd. trustees Bergen Pines County Hosp., 1994—. Editorial bd. Jour. Lab. and Clin. Medicine, 1973-77, 84-91, Am. Rev. Respiratory Diseases, 1985-91; contbr.

numerous articles on pulmonary diseases, respiratory physiology and biochemistry to med. jours. Fellow AAAS, Am. Coll. Chest Physicians, ACP (pres. Ill. chpt. 1974-75, vice chmn. com. on environ. health 1981-82, gov. 1988-90, 93-95); mem. Assn. Am. Med. Colls. (coun. of deans 1989—, exec. com. project 3000 by 2000), Am. Fedn. Clin. Rsch., Am. Heart Assn., Am. Physiol. Soc., Am. Soc. Clin. Investigation, Am. Thoracic Soc. (chmn. sci. assembly 1974-75, bd. dirs. 1987-90, chmn. com. on internat. rels. 1989-91), Am. Soc. Internal Medicine, Chgo. Soc. Internal Medicine (pres. 1988-89), Am. Lung Assn. (com. smoking and health 1981-84), Internat. Acad. Chest Physicians and Surgeons (chmn. nominating com. 1984-90), Chgo. Lung Assn. (bd. dirs. and mem. exec. com. 1974-82), Soc. Exptl. Biology and Medicine, Sigma Xi, Alpha Omega Alpha, Phi Kappa Phi. *

LOURIE, IRA SANDERS, psychiatrist; b. N.Y.C., Jan. 2, 1941; s. Reginald Spenser and Lucille B. (Radin) L.; m. Bonita F. Liss, Aug. 15, 1965; children: Eli M., Jennifer D. BA, George Washington U., 1964, MD, 1968. Diplomate Am. Bd. Psychiatry and Neurology. Intern San Francisco Gen. Hosp., 1968-69; resident Mass. Mental Health Ctr., Boston, 1969-71, Judge Baker Child Guidance Ctr., Children's Hosp., Boston, 1971-73; coord. child abuse program NIMH, Rockville, Md., 1973-76; dep. chief Ctr. for Studies of Child & Family Mental Health, NIMH, Rockville, 1976-79, asst. dir. div. mental health svcs., 1979-81; med. dir. Regional Inst. for Children and Adolescents, Rockville, 1981-83; dir. Child & Adolescent Svc. System Program, Rockville, 1983—; chief child and family support br. Child & Family Support Branch, NIMH, Rockville, 1988-91; mental health policy cons. Human Svc. Collaborative, Washington, 1991—; asst. clin. prof. child psychiatry Georgetown U. Sch. Medicine, Washington, 1979—; cons. in field; med. dir. Pressley Ridge Schs. of Md., 1996—. Bd. dirs. Karma Acad., Rockville, 1975-78; commr. Farmland Athletic Assn., Rockville, 1979-83. Recipient Freda London award Am. Assn. Psychiat. Svcs. for Children, 1973, Outstanding Svc. award USPHS, 1983. Fellow Am. Orthopsychiat. Assn. (treas. 1989-91); mem. Am. Acad. Child & Adolescent Psychiatry, Am. Psychiat. Assn., Am. Soc. for Adolescent Psychiatry. Democrat. Jewish. Home: 6706 Old Stage Rd Rockville MD 20852-4330 Office: Human Svc Collaborative 2262 Hall Pl NW Washington DC 20007-1838

LOURY, SHARON DIANE, community health nurse, educator; b. Stamford, Conn., Apr. 30, 1946; d. Thomas Mellor and Ethel Caroline (Sundberg) Kuttroff; m. Neal Houghton Loury, Jan. 23, 1967; 1 child, Jennifer Paige. BSN with honors, Calif. State U., L.A., 1994, MSN, 1994. RN, Calif., N.C. Staff nurse San Dimas (Calif.) Cmty. Hosp., 1984-85; home health nurse Glendora (Calif.) Cmty. Hosp.-Home Care Plus, 1985-87; staff nurse Arcadia (Calif.) Outpatient Surgery Ctr., 1987-88; instr. ARC, L.A., 1993-94, Citrus Coll., Glendora, 1993-94; clin. instr. Calif. State U., L.A., 1993-94, East Carolina U., Greenville, N.C., 1995—; dir. pilot project Neighborhood Wellness Ctr., 1994. Mem. ANA, Nat. League for Nursing, Sigma Theta Tau. Home: 108 Arbor Dr Greenvillee NC 27858 Office: East Carolina U Sch Nursing Greenville NC 27858-4353

LOUW, DAP, psychologist, educator; b. Windhoer, Namibia, Feb. 17, 1946; s. Daniel and Annalu (Burger) L.; m. Anet Elizabeth Davel, June 24, 1972; children: Antoinette, Dappie. MA in Criminology, U. Pretoria, South Africa, 1970, PhD in Criminology, 1973; MA in Psychology, Potch U., South Africa, 1975, PhD in Psychology, 1978. Cert. clin. psychologist. Lectr. U. Pretoria, South Africa, 1968-73; lectr. Potch U., 1974-77, sr. lectr., 1978-82, prof., 1983-90, vice dean, 1983-90; prof. psychology U. Orange Free State, Bloemfontein, South Africa, 1991—, head Centre Behavioral Scis., 1993—. Author, editor: Dictionary of Psychology, 1979, Introduction to Psychology, 1982, Human Development, 1986, Abnormal Psychology, 1989. Recipient Stals award for psychology South African Acad. Sci. and Arts, 1991. Mem. Psyssa, South African Soc. Forensic Psychology (pres. 1990-94), Internat. Coun. Psychology (bd. dirs. 1989-93). Home: Hennie Potgieter St 33, Bloemfontein 9300, South Africa Office: U Orange Free State, PO Box 339, Bloemfontein 9300, South Africa

LOUX, NORMAN LANDIS, psychiatrist; b. Souderton, Pa., June 27, 1919; s. Abram Clemmer and Martha Wasser (Landis) L.; m. Esther Elizabeth Brunk, June 4, 1941; children—Philip Michael, Elizabeth Ann, Peter David. Student, Eastern Mennonite Coll., 1940-42; B.A., Goshen Coll., 1943; M.D., Hahnemann Med. Coll., 1946; postgrad., Yale, 1950-51. Intern Hahnemann Hosp., Phila., 1947; gen. practice medicine Souderton, 1947-48; psychiat. resident Butler Hosp., Providence, 1949-50; chief service, clin. dir., asst. supt. Butler Hosp., 1951-55; founder Penn Found. Mental Health, Inc., Sellersville, Pa., 1955; med. dir. Penn Found. Mental Health, Inc., 1955-80; chief Psychiat. Svc. Grand View Hosp., Sellersville, 1955-80; pres. med. staff Grand View Hosp., 1963-64; exec. com., joint conf. com. Mem. Gov.'s Adv. Com. for Mental Health and Mental Retardation, 1955-80; mem. Pa. State Bd. Pub. Welfare, 1971-85. Bd. dirs. Dock Woods Retirement Community, 1989—, Adult Communities Total Svcs. Inc., 1990—. Co-recipient Earl D. Bond award, 1964; recipient Achievement award Souderton Lions Cub, 1963, Community Svc. award B'nai B'rith, 1976, citation for achievements Mennonite Med. Assn., 1978; dept. of psychiatry Grand View Hosp. rededicated in his name, 1992. Fellow Am. Psychiat. Assn., A.C.P., Pa. Psychiat. Soc., Am. Coll. Psychiatrists; mem. AMA, Pa., Bucks County med. socs., Group for Advancement Psychiatry, Southeastern Mental Health Assn., Acad. Religion and Mental Health. Mem. Mennonite Ch. Home: 138 Cowpath Rd Souderton PA 18964-2007 Office: Penn Found Mental Health Inc PO Box 32 Sellersville PA 18960-0032

LOUX, PETER CHARLES, anesthesiologist; b. Phila., Feb. 1, 1949; s. Theodore Clewell and Agnes Elva (Eichelman) L.; m. Jean Alyce McCluskey, Sept. 27, 1975; children: Tara Jean, Kimberly Marie. Student, Ea. Bapt. Coll., St. David's, Pa., 1967-68; BS in Biology, Widener Coll., Chester, P., 1971; DO, Phila. Coll. Osteo. Medicine, 1975. Diplomate Am. Bd. Anesthesiology. Resident USPHS, Staten Island (N.Y.C.), 1975-78; fellowship Milton S. Hershey Med. Ctr. Pa. State U., Hershey, 1978-79, asst. prof. Anesthesiology Milton S. Hershey Med. Ctr., 1979-83; pvt. practice Huntsville, Ala., 1983-95; ptnr. Comprehensive Anesthesia Svcs., Huntsville, 1995—; clin. assoc. prof. Anesthesiology and Surgery U. Ala. Sch. Medicine, Huntsville, 1993—; co-med. dir. Surgery Ctr. of Huntsville, 1985-86; chief divsn. of Anesthesiology Huntsville Hosp., 1986-87. Contbr. articles to profl. jours. Mem. St. Mark's Luth. Ch. (constitution com., 1987, long-range planning com., 1989, fellowship com., 1986). Lt. cmdr. USPHS, 1975-78. Mem. AMA, Am. Soc. Anesthesiologists, Ala. State Soc. Anesthesiologists (pres. 1993-95, alt. del. to Am. Soc. Anesthesiologists 1989, 91, del. 1990, 92), Madison County Med. Soc. (anesthesiology rep. to exec. bd. 1987-92, dist. 5 rep. to Ala. State Soc. Anesthesiologists 1987-92). Soc. Critical Care Medicine, Am. Soc. Regional Anesthesia. Home: 1606 Drake Ave Huntsville AL 35802-1057 Office: Comprehensive Anesthesia Svcs 201 Sivley Rd Ste 500 Huntsville AL 35801-5151

LOVAAS, JUDITH B., public health nurse; b. Rochester, N.Y., Jan. 1, 1939; d. Alfred Ralph and Alberta Jean (Miller) Barker; m. Arvin Lovaas, Aug. 17, 1963; children: Steven, Perri. BSN, U. Rochester, 1960, MS, 1963. Coord. practical nursing program Larmer County Voc-Tech. Ctr., Ft. Collins, Colo.; nursing adminstr. Health Care Ctr. Colo. State U., Ft. Collins, health educator Student Health Ctr.; DON Hospice of Larimer County; pub. health nurse Larimer County Health Dept. Mem. ANA, Colo. Nurses Assn., Colo. Pub. Health Assn.

LOVE, SHIRLEY BELLE, psychotherapist; b. N.Y.C.; d. Morris and Rachel Greenstein; m. Sidney I. Love; children: Carolyn Beth Love Bersak, Jeanine Deborah Love Dropkin. BA, Bklyn. Coll., 1944; MSW, Columbia U., N.Y., 1948; PhD, Heed U., 1980. Cert. psychoanalyst, Nat. Assn. Advancement Psychoanalysis, 1974; diplomate Clin. Social Worker, Nat. Assn. Social Workers. Founder, faculty supr. Manhattan Ctr. Psychoanalytic Studies, N.Y.C., 1970—; faculty Phila. Sch. Psychoanalysis, 1976—; faculty supr. Internat. Sch. Social Services, N.Y.C., 1977—; co-founder, co-dir., faculty, supr. Riverdale Seminars, 1981—. Co-founder, v.p. Riverdale YM-YWHA, 1967-73. Fellow Clin. Social Work Psychotherapist, Inc., Am. Orthopsychiat. Assn. (life); mem. NASW, Assn. Modern Psychoanalysis. Office: 30 E 60th St New York NY 10022-1008

LOVE, SIDNEY IRWIN, psychologist, psychotherapist; b. N.Y.C., Feb. 12, 1922; s. Irving Daniel and Dora (Sokol) L.; m. May 9, 1948; children: Carolyn Beth, Jeanine Deboral. BS, CCNY, 1946; MSW, Columbia U., 1948; PhD, Heed U., 1978. Lic. psychologist, N.Y.; lic. social worker, N.Y. Assoc. therapist Child Guidance Inst. Jewish Bd. of Guardians, N.Y.C., 1948-61; asst. prof. dept. edn. Stony Brook br. SUNY, L.I., 1961-64; founder, mem. faculty Ctr. for Modern Psychoanalysis in N.Y., N.Y.C., 1971-81; founder, gen. dir. seminars Riverdale (N.Y.) Seminars in Modern Analytic Psychotherapy, 1981—; pvt. practice, N.Y.C. and Riverdale, 1952—. Contbr. articles to profl. jours. Sgt. U.S. Army, 1942-45, World War II, ETO. Decorated Bronze Star, Purple Heart. Fellow Am. Orthopsychiat. Assn. (life); mem. Nat. Psychol. Assn. for Psychoanalysis, NASW, Coun. for Health Svc. Providers in Psychology. Home: 2727 Palisade Ave Bronx NY 10463-1018 Office: 30 E 60th St New York NY 10022-1008

LOVEDAY, WILLIAM JOHN, hospital administrator; b. Lynn, Mass., Nov. 4, 1943; Married. B, Colby Coll., 1967; MHA, U. Chgo., 1970. Adminstrv. asst. Meml. Med. Ctr., Long Beach, Calif., 1970-71, asst. adminstr., 1971-74, v.p., 1974-82, exec. v.p., 1982-88; pres., chief exec. officer Meth. Hosp. Ind., Inc., Indpls., 1988—. Home: 7828 Traders Cove Ln Indianapolis IN 46254-9614 Office: Meth Hosp Ind PO Box 1367 Indianapolis IN 46206-1367*

LOVEJOY, JENNIFER G., medical educator; b. Seattle, Mar. 30, 1961; d. Roland William and Deborah (Daniels) L.; m. Tom Stone McNees, Mar. 19, 1988. BS in Zoology magna cum laude, Duke U., 1982; MA in Psychobiology, Emory U., 1986, PhD in Psychobiology, 1988. Rsch. tech. pediatric virology Duke U. Med. Ctr., Durham, N.C., 1982-83; grad. fellow psychobiology dept. psychology Yerkes Primate Rsch. Ctr., Atlanta, 1983-88; rsch. fellow endocrinology and metabolism, dept. medicine Emory U. Sch. Medicine, Atlanta, 1988-89, instr. in medicine dept. medicine, 1989-91; asst. prof. obesity, diabetes and metabolism sect. Pennington Biomed. Rsch. Ctr., La. State U., Baton Rouge, 1991—; clin. asst. prof. rsch. dept. ob-gyn. La. State U., Sch. Medicine, New Orleans, 1993—; lab. specialist glycolipid biochemistry dept. pathology U. Va. Med. Ctr., Charlottesville, 1985; introductory psychology lectr. Oglethorp U., Atlanta, 1990; lectr. and seminar leader in field. Contbr. chpts. to books and articles to profl. jours. Recipient Nat. Rsch. Svc. award NIH-NIDDK, 1989-91, New Populations award The Obesity Found., 1990. Mem. Am. Diabetes Assn. (coun. mem. nutritional sci. and metabolism, Frances O. Hazzard award 1992, Career Devel. award 1993—, clin. rsch. grantee 1996), Am. Inst. Nutrition, Am. Soc. for Clin. Nutrition, Assn. for Women in Sci., N.Am. Assn. for the Study of Obesity, Internat. Assn. for the Study of Obesity, Soc. for the Study Ingestive Behavior, Sigma Xi. Office: Pennington Biomed Rsch Ctr 6400 Perkins Rd Baton Rouge LA 70808

LOVEJOY, JOHN FLETCHER, JR., orthopedist; b. Jacksonville, Fla., Sept. 15, 1938; s. John F. Sr. and Margaret (McCabe) L.; m. Harriet Ellen Jackson, Oct. 8, 1966; children: Ellen Lovejoy Holman, John F. III. BA in History, Duke U., 1960; BS in Chemistry, U. Fla., 1962, MD, 1966. Intern Med. Coll. Ga., Augusta, 1966-67; resident in orthop. surgery Ga. Bapt.-Scottish Rite Hosps., Atlanta, 1967-71; pvt. practice Jacksonville, Fla.; clin. instr. orthop. U. Fla. Health Sci. Ctr., Jacksonville, 1974—; mem. tissue com. St. Luke's Hosp., 1977-86, chmn. program com., 1978, 86-87, mem. antibiotic utilization/infection control com., 1978-84, mem. surg. rev. com., 1983-86, mem. utilization rev. com., 1990—, mem. anticoagulation task force, 1994; mem. libr. com. Bapt. Meml. Hosp., 1977-79; pres. staff Nemours Children's Hosp., 1978-80, mem. clin. coordinating com., 1980-85; pres. med.-dental staff Hope Haven Med., 1977-79; spkr. in field. Contbr. articles to profl. jours. Bd. dirs. Spina Bifida Found., 1974-75, Riverside Presbyn. Day Sch., 1977-79, Jacksonville Marine Inst., 1982—; co-chmn. crippled children's com. Morocco Temple, 1974—; chmn. Doctors for Ford Com., 1976; mem. nat. com. Physicians for Reagan-Bush, 1984, Physicians for Bush-Quayle, 1992; mem. vestry All Sts. Episc. Ch., 1979-82; pres. Hope Haven, Jacksonville, 1977-79; mem. exec. bd. dirs. Boy Scouts Am., 1978, asst. scoutmaster Troop 94, 1979-86, adv. bd., 1995—; sec.-treas. Navy League, 1984-86, program chmn., 1986-87, pres., 1990; bd. dirs. Commodores League, 1986—, flag commodore, 1990; mem. citizens' adv. com. automated skyway express project, 1977-82; mem. study group indigent health care aides task force Jacksonville Cmty. Coun., 1989-90; bd. dirs. Hope House Children's Clinic & Family Ctr., 1978—. Lt. comdr. USN, 1971-73. Recipient Orthop. Resident's award Ga. Orthop. Soc., 1967, 70. Fellow Am. Acad. Orthop. Surgeons (diplomate, chmn. regional membership com. 1986, bd. councilors 1993—, local chmn. joint parade 1994, chmn. state orthop. socs. com. 1995, task force on certs. of added qualification 1994, task force on guidelines 1994—); mem. AMA, So. Med. Assn., Fla. Orthop. Soc. (exec. bd. 1979-84, program chmn. 1981-82, coun. on specialty medicine 1987, pres.-elect 1989, pres. 1990), Fla. Med. Assn., N.E. Fla. Orthop. Soc. (sec.-treas. 1981-82, pres. 1983), Duval County Med. Soc. (chmn. membership com. 1977-79, treas. 1979-81, sec. 1980-81, pub. agys. com. 1981-82, bd. dirs. 1982—, pres. profl. liaison com. 1983, pres. found. for med. care 1982-86, chmn. orthop. sect. med. specialties com. 1983, v.p. 1983-86, pres.-elect 1987, pres. 1988, pres. Jacksonville Area Physicians for Better Govt. 1993-95), Meniak Club (bd. dirs. 1979-81, sec. 1982, pres.-elect 1988, pres. 1989), Fla. Yacht Club, The River Club, Epping Forest Yacht Club, Masons, Shriners. Home: 6408 San Jose Blvd W Jacksonville FL 32217 Office: Orthop Clin Jacksonville 4203 Belfort Rd Ste 215 Jacksonville FL 32216

LOVELACE, ELAINE COLWELL, psychologist; b. Nordeg, Alta., Can., May 12, 1947; d. Stephen Paul and Hilda Gwendolyn (Miller) Hencley; m. David Wayne Lovelace; children: Caroline, Meredith, Adrian. BSEd with honors, U. Ill., 1968; MS in Edn. Psychology with honors, U. Utah, 1977; PhD in Clin. Psychology, Ga. State U., 1988. Lic. psychologist, Ga., sch. psychologist, Ga. Tchr. Anaheim (Calif.) City Schs., 1968-72, Salt Lake City Schs., 1975-76; therapist The Children's Ctr., Salt Lake City, 1976-77; sch. psychologist Ft. Worth Ind. Sch. Dist., 1977-78; psychologist, tchr. Coweta County Schs., Newnan, Ga., 1978-79, psychologist, therapist, 1979-86, dir. psychology, 1987-90, coord. psychology and counseling, 1990-94; psychology intern VA Med. Ctr., Tuskegee, Ala., 1986-87; pvt. practice Newnan, 1988—; Presentor workshops. Contbr. articles to profl. jours. Edmund J. James scholar U. Ill., 1964-68. Mem. Am. Psychol. Assn., Nat. Assn. Sch. Psychologists, Alpha Lambda Delta (scholastic honorary). Episcopalian.

LOVELACE, ROBERT FRANK, health science facility administrator, researcher; b. Elizabethton, Tenn., Oct. 7, 1950; s. Douglas Clayton and Doris Ivalee (Guy) L.; m. Diane Marie Wamsley, June 3, 1972; children: Jason Robert, Geoffrey Mark. BS, Phila. Coll. Bible, 1972; MA, Ea. Sem., Phila., 1974; PhD, Temple U., 1988. Lic. nursing home adminstr. Adminstr. research The Franklin Inst., Phila., 1974-79, adminstr. contracts, 1979-81; dir. research adminstrn. The Grad. Hosp., Phila., 1981-88; adminstr. Elm Terr. Gardens, Lansdale, Pa., 1988-95, pres., 1995—; adj. lectr. Temple U., Phila., 1983-86, Wilkes Coll., 1986-90, Rutgers U., 1989-93, St. Joseph's U., 1993—; exec. dir., sec.-treas. Gradtech, Phila., 1985-88. Contbr. articles to profl. jours. V.p., bd. dirs. Elm Terr. Gardens, Lansdale, 1986-88; dir. bd. Christian edn. 1st Bapt. Ch., Lansdale, 1985-88, 90-96, chmn. program com., 1987-90, chmn. worship svcs. com., 1992, chmn. search com., 1995. Mem. Am. Coll. Health Care Adminstrs., Nat. Coun. Univ. Rsch. Adminstrs., Soc. Rsch. Adminstrs. (mem. editorial bd. jour. 1986-90), Rsch. and Devel. Mgmt. Assn. Republican. Home: 553 Millers Way Lansdale PA 19446-4059 Office: Elm Terr Gardens 660 N Broad St Lansdale PA 19446-2361

LOVELL, ANTHONY PHILIP, cardiologist; b. Hyannis, Mass., June 18, 1940; s. Herbert and Valjean (VanDerVeer) L.; m. Kathleen Pelkey, Mar. 23, 1968; children: Alyssa, Andrew. BA, Yale U., 1963, MD, 1967. Intern, resident U. Calif., San Francisco, 1967-70; resident USPHS Hosp., San Francisco, 1970-72; fellow W.H. VA Hosp., West Haven, Conn., 1972-73; ptnr. Cardiology Group of Springfield, Mass., 1973—; assoc. clin. prof. medicine Tufts Med. Sch., Boston, 1994-96. Bd. dirs. Springfield Symphony Orch., 1993-96. Lt. comdr. USPHS, 1970-72. Fellow Am. Coll. Cardiology. Office: Ste 410 2 Med Center Dr Springfield MA 01107

LOVERME, PAUL JOSEPH, plastic and reconstructive surgeon; b. Washington, Sept. 23, 1951; s. Stephen Russell and eleanor Gertrude (Alcott) LoV.; m. Kathleen Marie Cowen, May 25, 1973; children: Melissa Lee, Corey Paul, Christopher Todd. BA in Biology cum laude, Boston U., 1973; MD, U. Med./Dentistry of N.J., Newark, 1978. Diplomate Am. Bd. Surgery, Am. Bd. Plastic Surgery (added qualification in surgery of the hand), Nat. Bd. Med. Examiners; lic. physician, N.J. Intern in surgery U. Medicine and Dentistry of N.J., 1978-79, resident in surgery, 1979-82, rsch. fellow, 1980-81, adminstrv. chief resident in surgery, 1982-83; clin. fellow head, neck and oncologic surgery Am. Cancer Soc., 1981-82; resident in plastic surgery Med. Coll. Ohio, 1983-84, chief resident in plastic surgery, 1984-85; pvt. practice Advanced Aesthetics Plastic Surgery Ctr., Bloomfield, N.J., 1985—; clin. asst. prof. U. Medicine and Dentistry of N.J., Newark, 1985—, dir. edn. in plastic surgery, 1987—, dir. cleft palate and craniofacial team, 1987—; sec. dept. surgery Montclair Cmty. Hosp., 1988-90, chmn. house physician and outpatient svcs., 1990-93; del. med. adv. com. Blue Cross/Blue Shield of N.J., 1990—. Contbr. numerous articles to profl. jours. Vol. Healing the Children; mem. Glen Ridge (N.J.) Bd. Health, 1991—; mem. Father's Club, Delbarton Sch., 1991—; mem. Friends of Glen Ridge Libr.; soccer coach Glen Ridge Athletic Assn., 1985-86, 90, baseball coach, 1989; soccer boosters mem. Delbarton Sch., 1991-93, football boosters, 1994-96. Mem. AMA (Physician Recognition award 1981, 84, 87, 90, 93, 95), Am. Soc. Aesthetic Plastic Surgeons, Am. Soc. Plastic and Reconstructive Surgeons (mem. young plastic surgeons com. 1990-93, socio-econ. com. 1990-94, pub. rels. com. 1994—), N.E. Soc. Plastic Surgery, N.Y. Regional Soc. Plastic and Reconstructive Surgeons, Acad. Medicine of N.J., N.J. Soc. Plastic Surgeons (pres. 1996—, profl. fee rev. com. 1989—, chmn. ins. liaison com. 1991—), Essex County Med. Soc. (3d party rev. com. 1990-92, cancer com. 1990—, legis. com. 1990—, speakers bur. 1993—, sr. citizens rels. com. 1989-94), N.J. Medicine and Dentistry N.J. Alumni Assn. (bd. trustees 1989-93), N.J. Med. Soc., Soc. Surgeons of N.J., Am. Cleft Palate and Craniofacial Soc., Lipoplasty Soc., Plastic Surgery Ednl. Found., N.Y. Area Boston U. Alumni Assn. Roman Catholic. Office: Adv Aesthetics Plastic Surg 557 Broad St Bloomfield NJ 07003

LOVIN, KATHLEEN ANN, physician assistant; b. Dallas, May 10, 1954; d. Daniel LeGrande and Marjorie Ellen (Coleman) Rader; m. Mark Alan Lovin, Dec. 21, 1991. BA, U. Tex. Galveston, 1983; MS, U. Hartford, 1984. Resident physician asst. Mt. Sinai Hosp., U. Conn., Hartford, 1983-84; physician asst. rschr. U. Tex. Health Scis. Ctr., Dallas, 1984-85; clin. physician asst. Valley Health Sys., Huntington, W.Va., 1985-88, 90-92, Cross Lanes (W.Va.) Family Practice, 1992—; instr. physician asst. Coll. W.Va., Beckley, 1995—; bd. dirs. Kanawha Home Health, Dunbar, W.Va., 1995-96, March of Dimes, Huntington, 1986-87. With USN, 1973-90. Fellow Am. Acad. Physician Assts. (cert., state rep. 1992), Navy Assn. Physician Assts. (Physician Asst. of Yr. 1988), W.Va. Assn. Physician Assts. (com. chair 1987, 88, 90). Office: Cross Lanes Family Practice 5480 Big Tyler Rd Cross Lanes WV 25313

LOVITT, MATTHEW ALAN, general surgeon; b. Denver, Oct. 3, 1960; m. Kelly T. Lovitt; children: Joseph, Nick, Catherine. AB, Stanford U., 1982; MD, Vanderbilt U., 1986. Diplomate Am. Bd. Surgery. Resident in gen. surgery Baylor U. Med. Ctr., Dallas, 1986-91, chief resident in gen. surgery, 1990-91; attending surgeon, maj. USAF, Sheppard AFB, Tex., 1991-94; chief surg. svcs. USAF, Shepherd AFB, Tex., 1991-94; active attending John Peter Smith Hosp., Ft. Worth, Tex., 1994—; provisional staff Baylor U. Med. Ctr., Dallas, 1996—. Fellow ACS (assoc.); mem. Am. Soc. Gen. Surgeons, Southwestern Surg. Congress, Tex. Med. Assn., Tarrant County Med. Assn. Office: John Peter Smith Hosp Dept of Surgery 1500 S Main St #303 OPC Fort Worth TX 76104

LOVROVICH, ANTHONY THOMAS, orthodontist; b. Tacoma, Wash., Sept. 17, 1949; s. Anton Thomas and Marie Yovanna (Bogetich) L.; m. Sharon Akemi Fujita, Aug. 11, 1973; children: Adam Thomas, Michael Anthony George, Andrew Paul. BA, U. Wash., 1973, BS, 1976, DDS, 1981. Staff dentist Pacific Med. Ctr., Seattle, 1983-87; resident in orthodontics Eastman Dental Ctr., Rochester, Minn., 1987-89; pvt. practice orthodontics Seattle, 1989—. Mem. Am. Dental Assn., Am. Assn. Orthodontists, Pacific Coast Soc. Orthodontists, Seattle-King County Dental Soc. (treas. 1993-94, sec. 1994-95, exec. coun. 1995-96). Republican. Roman Catholic. Office: 4540 Sand Point Way NE #140 Seattle WA 98105

LOW, FRANK NORMAN, anatomist, educator; b. Bklyn., Feb. 9, 1911; s. William Wans and Hilda (Nelson) L. BA, Cornell U., 1932, PhD, 1936; DSc (hon.), U. N.D., 1983. Postdoctoral Charlton fellow Sch. Medicine Tufts Coll., Boston, 1936-37; instr. to asst. prof. U. N.C., Chapel Hill, 1937-45; assoc. Sch. Medicine U. Md., Balt., 1945-46; assoc. prof. U. W.Va., Morgantown, 1946; asst. prof. Johns Hopkins Med. Sch., Balt., 1946-49; assoc. prof. to prof. anatomy Sch. Medicine La. State U., New Orleans, 1949-64, vis. prof., 1981—; rsch. prof. anatomy U. N.D., Grand Forks, 1964-81, emeritus, 1981—, Chester Fritz Disting. prof., 1975-77; mem. regional rev. bd. Am. Heart Assn., Grand Forks, 1971-74. Author: (with J.A. Freeman) Electron Microscopic Atlas of Normal and Leukemic Human Blood, 1958; assoc. editor Am. Jour. Anatomy, 1971-91; contbr. over 100 rsch. articles to profl. jours. Participant People's Republic China-U.S. exchange program, People to People; citizen amb. Soviet Union, 1991; del. Anniversary Caravan '91, People to People Internat., Russia, Uzbekistan. Mem. Am. Assn. Anatomists (exec. com. 1976-80, Henry Gray award 1989), Am. Soc. Cell Biology, La. Soc. Electron Microscopy (chmn. 1962), Am. Assn. History of Medicine, World Trade Ctr. (New Orleans), Sigma Xi (pres. U. N.D. chpt. 1977). Office: La State Med Ctr Dental Sch 1100 Florida Ave New Orleans LA 70119-2714

LOW, MARISSA E., health care administrator; b. San Francisco; d. Fred and Winifred L. AA, Fashion Inst. of Design and Mdse., 1979; Cert. Corp. Communications, Calif. State U.-Long Beach, 1987; BSBA, U. Redlands, 1992. Assoc. area mgr. Buffums, Glendale, Calif., 1979-80; asst. buyer Buffums, Long Beach, Calif., 1981-83; mdse. control mgr. Buffums, Long Beach, 1983-86, advt. mgr., 1987-89; account rep. CompuMed, Culver City, Calif., 1989-91; physician recruiter Pioneer Ind. Physician Network, Artesia, Calif., 1991-92; provider rels. mgr. Mullikin Ind. Physician Assn., Long Beach, Calif., 1992-93; dir. provider rels. Mullikin Ind. Physician Assn., Daly City, 1993-94; regional network mgr. AHI Healthcare Systems, Inc., San Mateo, Calif., 1994-95; regional contracts mgr. Nat. Health Plans, Modesto, Calif., 1996—. Judge Miss Lakewood Pageant of Beauty, 1987; vol. Long Beach Conv. and Visitors Coun., 1987, Am. Cancer Soc. 1996; pub. rels. chmn. March of Dimes, Calif., 1986; v.p. programs, spl. projects, chmn. bd. dirs., nomination com. chmn. Women's Coun., 1985-91; sec. Women's Bus. Conf., 1985; com. mem. Interval House Le Bal des Papillons. Recipient Cert. Appreciation Orange County Commn. on Status of Women, 1991, Interval House, 1991. Mem. NAFE, Am. Mktg. Assn., Group Health Assn. of Am., Acad. Health Svcs. Mktg. (chmn. managed care com. Health Futures Forum 1992), Healthcare Fin. Mgmt. Assn. Office: 1005 W Orangeburg Ave Ste B Modesto CA 95350-4163

LOW, WALTER CHENEY, neuroscience and physiology educator; Madera, Calif., May 11, 1950; s. George Chen and Linda Quan (Gong) L.; m. Margaret Mary Schwarz, June 4, 1983; children: Matthew Mangan, Elizabeth Catharine. BS with honors, U. Calif.-Santa Barbara, 1972; MS, U. Mich., 1974, PhD, 1979. Postdoctoral fellow U. Cambridge, Eng., 1979-80, U. Vt., Burlington, 1980-83; asst. prof. physiology Ind. U. Sch. Med., Indpls., 1983-84, asst. prof. physiology, biophysics and med. neurobiology, 1984-89, assoc. prof. physiology, biophysics and medical neurobiology, 1989-90; assoc. prof. physiology, neurosurgery, physiology & neurosci. U. Minn. Med. Sch., Mpls., 1990-93; dir. lab. for Neurol Transplantation, 1990—; prof. Neurosurgery, Physiology and Neurosci., 1993—; dir. Lab for Cell and Gene Therapies, 1995—; assoc. dir. Algheimer's Disease Ctr., 1995—; dir. grad. program in physiology and biophysics, Sch. Medicine Ind. U., 1985-88. Contbr. numerous publs. to profl. jours. on brain rsch. Established Investigator Award Am. Heart Assn., 1990—. Recipient Individual Nat. Rsch. Svc. award Nat. Heart, Lung and Blood Inst., 1981-83, Nat. Inst. Neurol., Communicative Disorders and Stroke, 1979, Bank of Am. Lab. Scis. award, 1968; grantee NIH, 1984, 85, 87-92, Alzheimers Disease Assoc. award, 1988-89, Am. Parkinsons Disease Assoc. award, 1993-94, Am. Cancer Soc. award, 1994-95, Am. Heart Assn., 1987-90; Rackham U. Mich., 1976-78; internat. programs travel Ind. U., 1984; AGAN rsch. fellow Am. Heart Assn., 1980-81; Rotary scholar, 1968-69. Mem. AAAS, Soc. for Neurosci. (pres. Indpls. chpt. 1985-87), Am. Soc. for Neural Transplantation (sec. elect. 1994-95), Internat. Brain Rsch. Orgn., Calif. Scholastic Fedn. (life), N.Y. Acad Sci., Sigma Xi. Avocations: tennis, cross-country skiing, sailing. Office: U Minn Med Sch Dept Neurosurgery Box 96 UMHC 420 Delaware St SE Minneapolis MN 55455-0374

LOWE, CAMERON ANDERSON, dentist, endodontist, educator; b. Alcester, S.D., Dec. 19, 1932; s. Richard Barrett and Emma Louise (Anderson) L.; m. Doris Teresita Franquez, Dec. 23, 1957; children: Barrett, Steven, Leslie. Student, George Washington U., 1951-53, U. Va., 1955-56; DDS, Georgetown U., 1956-60; cert. residency in endodontics, U.S. Naval Dental Sch., 1967-69. Commd. lt. (j.g.) U.S. Navy Dental Corps, 1953, advanced through grades to capt., 1976, ret., 1978; pvt. practice endodontist Newport News, Va., 1978-81; assoc. prof. dentistry emeritus Old Dominion U., Norfolk, Va., 1991, asst. chair Sch. Dental Hygiene, 1985-89; adj. asst. prof. Med. Coll. Va.-Va. Commonwealth U. Sch. Dentistry, Richmond, 1979-81. Contbr. articles to profl. jours. Tutor adult literacy, 1994-96; coord. Neighborhood Watch, 1994-96; pack and troop chmn. Boy Scouts Am., Guam, 1969-72, Virginia Beach, Va., 1972-78. With USN, 1953-55. Mem. Assn. Mil. Surgeons of U.S., Am. Assn. Endodontists, Am. Acad. Oral Medicine, Am. Dental Assn., Va. Acad. Endodontics, USN Assn. Endodontists, Peninsula Dental Soc., Sigma Alpha Epsilon, Delta Sigma Delta, Sigma Phi Alpha (Dental Hygiene Honor Soc.). Republican. Methodist. Home: 1497 Wakefield Dr Virginia Beach VA 23455-4541

LOWE, DAVID HENRY, plastic surgeon; b. Washington, Mar. 18, 1950; s. Ernest and Ruth (Glaser) L.; m. Susan Jane Blehm; children: Scott, Arron, Danielle. BA, U. Va., 1972; MD, Ea. Va. Med. Sch., 1977. Diplomate Am. Bd. Plastic Surgery. Resident East Va. Med. Sch., Norfolk, 1977-80; resident in plastic surgery Johns Hopkins Hosp., Balt., 1980-82, fellow in plastic surgery, 1982-83; fellow in hand surgery Union Meml. Hosp., Balt., 1983; pvt. practice Annapolis, Md., 1984—. Fellow ACS; mem. AMA, Am. Soc. Anesthetic Plastic Surgery, Am. Soc. Plastic and Reocnstructive Surgery, John Staigo Davis Soc. Office: 2448 Holly Ave Annapolis MD 21401

LOWE, JOHN BURTON, molecular biology educator, pathologist; b. Sheridan, Wyo., June 13, 1953; s. Burton G. and Eunice D. Lowe. BA, U. Wyo., 1976; MD, U. Utah, 1980. Diplomate Am. Bd. Pathology. Asst. med. dir. Barnes Hosp. Blood Bank, St. Louis, 1985-86; instr. Sch. of Medicine Washington U., St. Louis, 1985, asst. prof. Sch. of Medicine, 1985-86; asst. investigator Howard Hughes Med. Inst., Ann Arbor, Mich., 1986-92, assoc. investigator, 1992—; asst. prof. Med. Sch. U. Mich., Ann Arbor, 1986-91, assoc. prof. Med. Sch., 1991-95, prof. Med. Sch., 1995—. Contbr. articles to Jour. Biol. Chemistry, Genes and Devel., Nature, Cell. Office: U Mich Howard Hughes Med 1150 W Medical Center Dr Ann Arbor MI 48109-0650

LOWE, MARGARET, podiatrist; b. Portland, Oreg., Sept. 23, 1942; d. Jack and Gene Edith (McMunn) L.; 1 child, Jack Alexander Lowe LeMieux. BS, Portland State U., 1966; MS, No. Ill. U., 1973; D in Podiatric Medicine, Calif. Coll. Podiatric Med., San Francisco, 1978. Lic. podiatrist, Calif. Planner health and human svcs. City-County Planning Com., Rockford, Ill., 1968-72; adminstr. Crusader's Clinic Assoc., Rockford, Ill., 1972-73; pvt. practice Oakland, Calif., 1978—; podiatry clinic dir. Agnews Devel. Ctr., San Jose, Calif., 1993—. VISTA vol. U. Oreg. Health Scis. Ctr., Portland, 1974-75; vol. San Francisco AIDS Found., 1995—. Recipient Cmty. Svc. award Unitarian Ch., 1973. Mem. Am. Soc. Aging, Lesbian-Gay Aging Issues Network. Democrat. Jewish. Office: 4179 Piedmont Ave # 201 Oakland CA 94611

LOWE, MICHAEL CRAIG, pharmacologist; b. Colfax, Wash., July 24, 1942; s. Judson Nathaniel and Joyce Leland (Johnson) L.; B.S. in Zoology, Wash. State U., 1964; M.S. in Pharmacology (USPHS fellow), U. Wash., 1968, Ph.D. in Pharmacology (USPHS fellow), 1970; m. Constance Rita Birr, Sept. 1, 1961; children: Laurie Lynne, Jamison Anne, Todd Michael Johnson, Robert Michael Judson. Asst. prof. U. Wash., Seattle, 1973-78; Cancer expert Lab. of Toxicology, Nat. Cancer Inst., NIH, Bethesda, Md., 1978-83, acting chief toxicology Nat. Cancer Inst., 1980-82; health scientist adminstr. Nat. Heart, Lung and Blood Inst., NIH, Bethesda, 1983-85; v.p. toxicology ICF-Clement, Washington, 1985-88; prin. Weinberg Cons. Group, Washington, 1988—; cons. toxicology FDA, EPA, Dept. of Justice. V.p., citizens adv. coun. Lake Washington Sch. Dist., Kirkland, Wash., 1975-76; coach Montgomery Soccer, Inc., Bethesda, 1979-81; team rep. Montgomery County Swim League, Bethesda, 1981-84, rules chmn., bd. dirs., 1985-88. NIH grantee, 1975-78; Nat. Merit Scholar, 1960; Pharm. Mfrs. Assn. Found. Pharmacology and Morphology fellow, 1971-73. Mem. AAAS, Electron Microscopy Soc. Am., Western Pharmacology Soc., Am. Soc. Pharm. and Exptl. Therapeutics, Catecholamine Club. Democrat. Congregationalist. Researcher cardiovascular pharmacology, toxicology of antineoplastic agts, environmental risk assessment. Home: 8904 Liberty Ln Potomac MD 20854-3638 Office: Weinberg Group 1220 19th St NW Ste 300 Washington DC 20036-2405

LOWE, OARIONA, dentist; b. San Francisco, June 17, 1948; d. Van Lowe and Jenny Lowe-Silva; m. Evangelos Rossopoulos, Dec. 18, 1985; 1 child, Thanos G. BS, U. Nev., Las Vegas, 1971; MA, George Washington U., 1977; DDS, Howard U., 1981; pediatric dental cert., UCLA, 1984. Instr. Coll. Allied Health Scis. Howard U., Washington, 1974-76, asst. prof., 1976-77; research asst. Howard U. Dental Sch., Washington, 1977-81; resident gen. practice Eastman Dental Ctr., Rochester, N.Y., 1981-82; dir. dental services City of Hope Med. Ctr., Duarte, Calif., 1984-86; chief dental staff Whittier (Calif.) Presbyn. Hosp., 1992-94; asst. prof. Loma Linda (Calif.) U., 1991—; vis. lectr. pediatric dentistry UCLA; mem. oral cancer task force Am. Cancer Soc., Pasadena, Calif., 1985—. Contbr. articles to profl. jours. Del. People to People Internat. Mem. ADA, Am. Soc. Dentistry for Children (v.p.), Nat. Soc. Autistic Children, Calif. Dental Assn., Am. Acad. Pediatric Dentistry, San Gabriel Valley Dental Soc. (chmn. 1991—), Sigma Xi, Alpha Omega. Republican. Presbyterian. Office: 8135 Painter Ave Ste 202 Whittier CA 90602-3154

LOWELL, EDWARD HERBERT, psychiatrist; b. Newark, N.J., Feb. 23, 1929; s. Harry A. and Rosalind L. (Lowenstein) L.; div.; children: Troy D., Brett A., Allegra S. AB, Drew U., 1950; MD, Hahnemann Med. Coll., 1954. Diplomate Am. Bd. Psychiatry and Neurology. Intern Newark Beth Israel Hosp., 1954-55; resident Manhattan VA Hosp., N.Y.C., 1957-59, Kings County Hosp. Ctr., Bklyn., 1959-60; cons. N.J. Commn. for Blind and Visually Handicapped, 1961—, Newark Bd. Edn., 1961-69, Pequannoch (N.J.) Valley Mental Health Ctr., 1962-64. Contbg. author chpt. in Psychiatry Almanac, 1981. Capt. U.S. Army, 1955-57, Japan. Mem. Essex County Med. Soc., N.J. Med. Soc., Am. Psychiatry Assn., N.J. Psychiatric Assn., Tri-County Psychiatric Assn. Home and Office: 372 Harding Dr South Orange NJ 07079-1339

LOWELL, JANET ANN, nurse; b. Greenfield, Mass., Dec. 12, 1946; d. Edward Franklin and Helen Elizabeth (Walker) A; m. Brian Theodore Lowell, Oct. 22, 1965 (div. 1982); children: David Earle, Jennifer Lee. AS, Greenfield Community Coll., 1984; BSN summa cum laude, Norwich U., 1991. RN, Mass.; cert. breast self-exam instr. Sec. U. Md., Far East Div., Tokyo, 1966-68; receptionist, sec., prodn. supr. Greenfield (Mass.) Paper Box Co., Inc., 1975-81; staff nurse Franklin Med. Ctr., Greenfield, 1984-85, Farren Meml. Hosp., Turners Falls, Mass., 1985-88; nursing supr. Hospice in Franklin County, Greenfield, 1988-90; staff ednl. coord. Farren Care Ctr., Turners Falls, Mass., 1990-91; staff nurse oncology, hematology Dartmouth Hitchcock Med. Ctr., Lebanon, N.H., 1991-94, clin. rev. case facilitator, 1994-95, 95—; continuing care nurse patient and family svcs. Dartmouth Hitchcock Med. Ctr., 1995—; mem. Am. Cancer Soc. Profl. Edn. Com., Greenfield, 1986-89; mem. mission com., rep. mission coun. Farren Care Ctr., Turners Falls, 1990-91; rep. to nursing profl. practice coun. Dartmouth Hitchcock Med. Ctr., Lebanon, 1991-94, mem. bereavement support group, 1995—. Recipient Hap Adams scholarship, 1983, Ethel Dow Wells scholarship, 1982-84, Fred B. Wells scholarship, 1982-84, Greenfield Community Coll., Franklin Med. Ctr. scholarship, Franklin Med. Ctr., 1983. Mem. Oncology Nursing Soc. (cert., Vt./N.H. chpt.), Mohawk Woman's Club (chpt. treas. 1979-80, pres. 1980-81), Nat. Oncology Nursing Soc. Office: Dartmouth Hitchcock Med Ctr One Medical Center Dr Lebanon NH 03756

LOWENFELS, ALBERT BROWNOLD, surgeon, educator; b. New Rochelle, N.Y., May 10, 1927; s. Albert Lowenfels and Corrine (Brownold) L.; m. Doris Rosett Becker, June 20, 1948; children: Kate, Charles, Robert, Ann. BS, U. Vt., 1948; MD, NYU, 1952. Diplomate Am. Bd. Surgery. Intern Bellevue Hosp., N.Y.C., 1952-53; resident in surgery NYU, 1953-58; assoc. dir. dept. surgery Westchester County Med. Ctr., Valhalla, N.Y., 1966—; pvt. practice, 1958-66; prof. surgery N.Y. Med. Coll., Valhalla, 1979—, prof. community and preventive medicine, 1981—; vis. scientist Internat. Agy. for Rsch. on Cancer, WHO, Lyon, France, 1977—. Author: Alcoholic Patient in Surgery, Companion Guide to Surgery; contbr. articles on surgery, epidemiology, alcoholism and pub. health to profl. jours. Recipient award Smithers Found., Mill Neck, N.Y., 1969—. Mem. ACS, Am. Gastroent. Assn., Phi Beta Kappa. Office: NY Med Coll Munger Bldg Valhalla NY 10595

LOWENGART, RUTH ANN, physician; b. Cedar Rapids, Iowa, Nov. 13, 1954; d. Otto B. and Margaret O. L. BS, U. Wis., 1975; MS in Occupl. Medicine, U. So. Calif., 1986, MD, 1981. Diplomate Am. Bd. Preventive Medicine, Am. Bd. Internal Medicine. Physician Contra Costa County, Martinez, Calif., 1989-90, Alta Bates Occupl. Health, Berkeley, Calif., 1991-95; pvt. practice Medford, Oreg. Mem. ACP, Am. Coll. Occupl. Environ. Medicine, Am. Assn. Orthop. Medicine, Jackson County Med. Soc., Oreg. Med. Assn. Office: 786 State St Medford OR 97504-8441

LOWENSOHN, RICHARD IRWIN, medical educator, physician; b. Los Angeles, Jan. 1, 1944; s. Robert Henry and Judy Pearl (Kaplan) L.; m. Diane Loretta Martin, June 24, 1975; children: Erin, David, Joshua. BSEE, Stanford U., 1965; MD, U. So. Calif., 1970. Diplomate Am. Bd. Ob-Gyn; cert. maternal fetal medicine. Intern U. So. Calif.-Los Angeles County Med. Ctr., Los Angeles, 1970-71; resident in ob-gyn Women's Hosp. div. U. So. Calif.-Los Angeles County Med. Ctr., Los Angeles, 1971-75; asst. prof. ob-gyn U. So. Calif., Los Angeles, 1977-78, Pritzker Sch. Medicine, Chgo., 1978-83; perinatologist Alta Bates Hosp., Berkeley, Calif., 1983-86; assoc. prof. ob-gyn Oreg. Health Scis. U., Portland, 1986—, chief obstetrics, dir. maternal-fetal medicine, 1987-96; pres. RI Lowensohn MD Inc., Oakland, Calif., 1984-86; mem. Oreg. Maternity Care Access Commn., 1992-95; v.p. Health Outcome Technologies, Inc., 1994—; v.p. Healthy Start Washington County. Chair health adv. coun. March of Dimes, Lewis & Clark chpt.; bd. trustees Cong. Beth Israel. Fellow Am. Coll. Ob-Gyn.; mem. Soc. Perinatal Obstetricians, Oreg. Med. Assn., Tau Beta Pi. Democrat. Jewish. Office: Oreg Health Scis U Dept Ob-Gyn 3181 SW Sam Jackson Park Rd Portland OR 97201-3011

LOWENSTEIN, ALFRED SAMUEL, cardiologist; b. Frankfurt, Germany, Oct. 19, 1931; came to U.S., 1938; s. Ernst and Babette (Stern) L.; m. Mirjam Stern, June, 1957 (div. Feb. 1981); children: Esther, David, Eve; m. Lucy Zilbersweig, Nov. 1, 1981; children: Elie, Daniel, Ariel. BA cum laude with honors in German, NYU, 1953; MD, SUNY, Bklyn., 1957. Intern Montefiore Hosp., Bronx, N.Y., 1957-58, resident, 1959-60, fellow in cardiology, 1960-61; resident Bklyn. VA Hosp., 1958-59; fellow in cardiology St. Vincent's Hosp., N.Y.C., 1970-72; internist Far Rockaway, N.Y., 1963-70; attending cardiologist Beilenson Hosp., Petah Tikva, Israel, 1972-75; pvt. practice Cedarhurst, N.Y., 1975-93. Capt. U.S. Army, 1961-63. Fellow Am. Coll. Cardiology, N.Y. Cardiol. Soc.; mem. AMA, N.Y. State Nassau County Med. Soc., Phi Beta Kappa. Jewish. Office: 1490 Broadway Hewlett NY 11557-1432

LOWENTHAL, RICHARD MARK, neurologist; b. Cin., July 14, 1942; s. Gerson and Irma May (Pushin) L.; m. Toni Louise Ach, June 16, 1967 (dec. 1982); children: Sarah, Anna; m. Barbara K. Goodspeed Chen, Nov. 23, 1986; stepchildren: Christian Chen, Marisa Chen. AB cum laude, Harvard U., 1964; MD, U. Chgo., 1968. Diplomate Am. Bd. Psychiatry and Neurology (examiner 1984-88). Med. intern U. Chgo. Hosps., 1968-69; resident neurology U. Calif., San Francisco, 1971-74, rsch. fellow, 1974-75, instr., 1975-76; asst. clin. prof. U. So. Calif., L.A., 1980-83, assoc. clin. prof., 1983—; neurologist Sansum Med. Clinic, Santa Barbara, 1976—; chmn. dept. neurology Cottage Hosp., Santa Barbara, 1979-82, vice chmn., 1990-92, chmn. dept. neurology and neurosurgery, 1992—; bd. dirs. Nat. Multiple Sclerosis Soc. Channel Islands, 1980—, chmn. profl. adv. com., 1980-90; dir. Muscular Dystrophy Assn. Clinic, Santa Barbara. Lt. commdr. USPHS, 1969-71. Recipient L.J. Henderson prize Harvard Coll., 1964. Fellow Am. Acad. Neurology (mem. edn. com. 1984—). Office: Sansum Med Clinic PO Box 1239 Santa Barbara CA 93102-1239

LOWERY, BARBARA J., psychiatric nurse, educator. RN, Reading Hosp. Sch., 1958; MSN, Villanova U., 1966; NSN, U. Pa., 1968; EdD, Temple U., 1973. Staff nurse, head nurse Danville State Hosp., Pa., 1958-62; unit and hosp. supr. Norristown (Pa.) State Hosp., 1960-63, instr. nursing edn., 1963-65; dir. nursing edn. Ea. Pa. Psychiat. Inst., 1968-69; instr. Sch. Nursing, U. Pa., Phila., 1970-72, assoc., 1972-73, from asst. prof. to assoc. prof., 1973-87, prof., 1987—, chmn. psychiat. mental health nursing, 1978-84, ombudsman, 1984-86, dir. Robert Wood Johnson clin. nurse scholars program, 1986-91; cons. in field. Author, co-author chpts. to books; assoc. editor Nursing Rsch., 1978-83. Fellow Am. Acad. Nursing; mem. NAS. Office: U Pa Sch Nursing 34th and Spruce Sts Philadelphia PA 19104*

LOWERY, PATRICIA ANN, surgeon; b. Chgo., July 21, 1941; arrived in Ghana, 1978; d. Martin Joseph and Catherine (O'Brien) L. BA, Notre Dame Coll., 1967; MD, Georgetown U., 1971. Diplomate Am. Bd. Surgery. Intern St. Vincent's Hosp. and Med. Ctr., N.Y.C., 1971-72, resident in surgery, 1972-76, acting dir. surg. ICU, 1976-77; clin. instr. surgery NYU, N.Y.C., 1975-77; sr. med. officer, surgeon Holy Family Hosp., Berekum, Ghana, 1978-79, Sunyani (Ghana) Regional Hosp., 1979—; surgeon Ministry Health, Ghana, Brong-Ahafo, Ghana, 1979—. Fellow Am. Coll. Surgeons, West African Coll. Surgeons; mem. AMA, Ghana Med. Assn., Assn. Women Surgeons, Soc. Critical Care Medicine. Democrat. Roman Catholic. Home: PO Box 1095, Sunyani Ghana Office: Sunyani Regional Hosp, PO Box 27, Sunyani Ghana

LOWITZ, GLENN HOWARD, clinical psychologist; b. Clarksdale, Miss., July 12, 1952; s. Ralph and Berthe (Mosrow) L.; m. Ellen Finkelstein, May 30, 1976; children: David, Brett. PhD, U. Miss., 1979. Staff psychologist Ark. Children's Hosp., Little Rock, 1979-83; pvt. practice clin psychology Little Rock, 1983—. Chmn., mem. case com. Jewish Fedn. Ark., 1980—, pres., 1992-94. Mem. APA, Ark. Psychcl. Assn. Office: 11219 Financial Ctr Pky 310 Little Rock AR 72211-3858

LOWN, BERNARD, cardiologist, educator; b. Utena, Lithuania, June 7, 1921; came to U.S., 1935; s. Nisson and Bella (Grossbard) L.; m. Louise Charlotte Lown, Dec. 29, 1946; children—Anne Lown Green, Frederick, Naomi Lown Lewiton. BS summa cum laude, U. Maine, 1942, DS (hon.), 1982; MD, Johns Hopkins U., 1945; DSc (hon.), Worcester State Coll., 1983, Charles U., Prague, 1987, Bowdoin Coll., 1988, SUNY, Syracuse, 1988, Columbia Coll., Chgo., 1989; LLD (hon.), Bates Coll., Lewiston, Maine, 1983, Queen's U., Kingston, Ont., Can., 1985; LHD (hon.), Colby Coll., 1986, Thomas Jefferson U., 1988; PhD (hon.), U. Buenos Aires, 1986; D honoris causa, Autonomous U. Barcelona, Spain, 1989; D Univ. (hon.), Hiroshima (Japan) Shudo U., 1989. Asst. in pathology Yale U.-New Haven Hosp., 1945-46; intern in medicine Jewish Hosp., N.Y.C., 1947-48; asst. resident in medicine Montefiore Hosp., N.Y.C., 1948-50; research fellow in cardiology Peter Bent Brigham Hosp., Boston, 1950-53, asst. in medicine, 1955-56, dir. Samuel A. Levine Cardiovascular Research Lab., 1956-58, jr. assoc. in medicine, 1956-62, research assoc. in medicine, 1958-59, assoc. in medicine, 1962-63, sr. assoc. in medicine, 1963-70, dir. Samuel A. Levine Coronary Care Unit, 1965-74, physician, 1973-81, sr. physician, 1982—; asst. in medicine Harvard U., Boston, 1955-58, asst. prof. medicine dept. nutrition Sch. Pub. Health, 1961-67, assoc. prof. cardiology, 1967-73, prof. cardiology, 1974—, dir. cardiovascular research lab. Sch. Pub. Health, 1961—; cons. in cardiology Newton-Wellesley Hosp., Mass., 1963-77, Beth Israel Hosp., Boston, 1963-94, Children's Hosp. Med. Ctr., Boston, 1964-82; spl. cons. WHO, Copenhagen, 1971; coordinator U.S.-USSR Coop. Study, 1973-81; mem. lipid metabolism adv. com. NIH, Bethesda, Md., 1975-79; vis. prof., lectr., guest speaker numerous univs., hosps., orgns. Author: (with Samuel A. Levine) Current Advances in Digitalis Therapy, 1954; (with Harold D. Levine) Atrial Arrhythmias, Digitalis and Potassium, 1958, (with A. Malliani) Neural Mechanisms and Cardiovascular Disease, 1986; mem. editorial bd. Circulation, Coeur et Medecine Interne, Jour. Electrocardiology; mem. editorial adv. bd. Jour. Soviet Research in Cardiovascular Diseases; contbr. numerous articles to profl. jours.; mem. internat. adv. bd. Internat. Med. Tribune, 1987—; inventor cardioverter; introduced Lidocaine as antiarrythmic drug. Recipient Modern Medicine award, 1972, Ray C. Fish award and Silver medal Tex. Heart Inst., Houston, 1978, A. Ross McIntyre award and Gold medal U. Nebr. Med. Ctr., Omaha, 1979, Richard and Hinda Rosenthal award Am. Heart Assn., 1980, George W. Thorn award Brigham and Women's Hosp., 1982, 1st Cardinal Medeiros Peace medallion, 1982, Nikolay Burdenko medal Acad. Med. Scis. USSR, 1983; co-recipient Peace Edn. award UN Edn., Sci. and Cultural Orgn., 1984, Beyond War award, 1984, Nobel Peace prize, 1985, Ghandi Peace award, 1985, New Priorities award, 1986, Andres Bello medal 1st class Ministry Edn. and Ministry Sci., Venezuela, 1986, Gold Shield, U. Havana, Cuba, 1986, Dr. Tomas Romay y Cahcon Medallion Acad. Sci., Havana, 1986, George F. Kennan award, 1986, Fritz Gietzelt Medaille Council of Medico-Sci. Socs. of German Democratic Republic, 1987; named hon. citizen City of New Orleans, 1978, Pasteur award Pasteur Inst., Leningrad, USSR, 1987, Alumni Humanitarian award U. Maine, Orono, 1988, Internat. Peace and Culture award Soka Gokkai, Tokyo, 1989, Golden Door award Internat. Inst. Boston, 1989; named Disting. Citizen and recipient Key to City Buenos Aires, 1986. Fellow Am. Coll. Cardiology; mem. Am. Soc. for Clin. Investigation, Am. Heart Assn., Assn. Am. Physicians, AAAS, Physicians for Social Responsibility (founder, 1st pres. 1960-70), U.S.-China Physicians Friendship Assn. (pres. 1974-78), Internat. Physicians for Prevention Nuclear War (pres. 1980-93); mem. Brit. Cardiac Soc. (corr.), Cardiac Soc. Australia and New Zealand, Swiss Soc. Cardiology, Belgian Royal Acad. Medicine, Acad. Medicine of Columbia (hon.), Harvard Club (Boston), Nat. Acad. Scis. (sr. mem. inst. medicine), Phi Beta Kappa, Alpha Omega Alpha. Club: Harvard (Boston). Office: Lown Cardiovascular Group PC 21 Longwood Ave Brookline MA 02146

LOWRIE, DOUGLAS BRUCE, microbiologist, researcher; b. New Castle Tyne, Northumberland, U.K., Aug. 8, 1944; s. Arthur Bruce and Victoria Norton (Smith) L.; m. Margaret Brenda Giles, Sept. 20, 1969; children: Helen Grace, Eve Alison. BS in Bacteriology, U. Birmingham, Eng., 1966, PhD in Microbiology, 1970. Rsch. fellow U. Birmingham, 1969-72; sci. staff Med. Rsch. Coun., London, 1972—; hon. lectr. Royal Postgrad. Med. Sch., 1977, hon. sr. lectr., 1982; C.L. Oakley lectr. Path. Soc. Gt. Britain and Ireland, 1981. Mem. editl. bd. Microbial Pathogenicity. Fellow Royal Coll. Pathologists; mem. Soc. Gen. Microbiology, Biochem. Soc., Brit. Soc. Immunology, Brit. Soc. Cell Biology, Am. Soc. Microbiology, Med. Rsch. Club. Office: Nat Inst for Med Rsch, The Ridgeway, Mill Hill, London England NW7 1AA

LOWRY, JOHN CHRISTOPHER, maxillofacial surgeon; b. Timperley, Eng., June 6, 1942; s. Arnold Leslie and Betty (Hornby) L.; m. Valerie Joyce Smethurst, July 6, 1968; children: Michelle Victoria, Jonathan Karl. BDS, U. Manchester Dental Sch., 1963; M.B.Ch.B, U. Manchester Med. Sch., 1970; F.R.C.S., Royal Coll. Surg. of Edinburgh, 1985; M.R.C.S. L.R.C.P., Royal Coll. Surg.& Physicians, 1969, 70. Cert. MHS/MHSM, 1993; registered Gen. Med. Coun., Gen. Dental Coun. House surgeon U. Dental Hosp., Manchester, 1963; sr. house officer Manchester Royal Infirmary, Manchester, 1964; registrar plastic & maxillofacial Bradford/Wakefield, Yorkshire, 1965; house surgeon, house physician to professorial units U. Hosp., South Manchester, 1971; sr. house officer Surg. Units Plastic/Orthopaedic Withington Hosp., Manchester; sr. registrar Manchester Royal Infirmary, North/South Manchester, 1972-76; cons. surgeon North Western Health Authority, Manchester, 1976—; examiner Gen. Dental Coun., Eng., 1988—, U. Manchester Cell & Structural Biology, 1976—, Royal Coll. Surgeons of Eng., 1991—, Royal Coll. Surgeons of Egin, 1993—; referee Brit. Jour. Oral and Maxillo Facial Surgery, 1976—; Jour. Cranio-Maxillo Facial Surgery, 1992—. Fellow Leverhulme Travelling Brit. Assn. Oral and Maxillofacial Surgeons, Royal Coll. Surgeons, Eng., 1974-75. Fellow Brit. Assn. Oral & Maxillofacial Surgeons, Royal Coll. Surgeons of Eng., Manchester Med. Soc., Internat. Assn. Oral and Maxillofacial Surgeons; mem. European Assn. Cranio-Maxillofacial Surgery; mem. bd. Faculty Royal Coll. Surgeons, Eng., 1993—, specialist adv. com. 1994—. Home: The Valley House, 50 Ravenswood, Bolton BL1 5TL, England Office: Dept Maxillofacial Surgery, Bolton General Hospital, Minerva Rd, Farnworth Bolton BL4 OJR, England

LOWRY, OLIVER HOWE, pharmacologist, biochemist; b. Chgo., July 18, 1910; married Adrienne Clark, 1935; children: Susan, Emily, Charles, Stephen, John. BS, Northwestern U., 1932; MD and PhD in Biochemistry, U. Chgo., 1937; DSc (hon.), Wash. U., 1981. Oliver H. Lowry lectr. prof. exptl. instr. biochemistry Harvard Med. Sch., 1937-42; mem. staff Pub. Health Rsch. Inst., N.Y., 1942-44, assoc. chief divsn. physiology and nutrition, 1944-47; prof. pharmacology Wash. U., 1947-79, head dept., 1947-76, dean, 1955-58, emeritus disting. prof. pharmacology Sch. Medicine, 1979—; Commonwealth Found. fellow Carlsberg Lab., Copenhagen U., 1939. Recipient Borden award Assn. Am. Med. Colls., 1955. Mem. NAS, Am. Soc. Pharmacology and Exptl. Therapeutics, Am. Soc. Biol. Chemistry, Am. Chem. Soc. (Midwest award 1962, Scott award 1963), Histochem. Soc., AAAS, Harvey Soc., Am. Acad. Arts and Scis., Royal Danish Acad. Sci. Office: Washington Unif Dept of Pharmacology Sci 660 S Euclid Ave Saint Louis MO 63110-1010*

LOYA, PRAXEDES, social services administrator; b. Riverside, Calif., Nov. 14, 1938; s. Jose Luz and Guadalupe (Arevalo) Loya. AA, Riverside City Coll., 1958; BA, San Jose State U., 1961; MSW, U. Washington, 1971. Social supr. II Riverside County DPSS, Riverside; social svc. supr. II Riverside County, Riverside. Sgt. U.S. Army, USAF, 1963-68. Recipient Community Svc. award City of Riverside, 1980, 85. Mem. NASW, CSWO (past pres. and treas.), ERC, OIC (past treas.), CAAA (past nominations com.), LGFR (chmn.), CSSRC (bd. dirs.), CSA. Home: 5510 Magnolia Ave Riverside CA 92506-1819

LOZANO, JOSE, nephrologist; b. San Vicente, El Salvador, Feb. 11, 1941; came to U.S., 1968; s. Jose E. and Transito Maria (Mendez) L.; m. Hilda Berganza, Jan. 27, 1965; children: Jose E., Claudia Maria. MD, U. El Salvador, 1965. Diplomate Am. Bd. Internal Medicine, Am. Bd. Nephrology. Rotating intern Nat. Med. Ctr., San Salvador, El Salvador, 1963-64; asst. resident in internal medicine Rosales Hosp., San Salvador, 1965-66, resident in internal medicine, 1966-67, chief resident in internal medicine, 1967-68; resident in internal medicine Baylor U. Affiliated Hosps., Houston, 1968-70, fellow in nephrology, 1970-71, 73-74; asst. prof. medicine U. El Salvador, 1971-72; internist and nephrologist Social Security Hosp., San Salvador, 1971-72; instr. in medicine Baylor Coll. Medicine, Houston, 1974-75, asst. prof. medicine in nephrology, 1975-76, clin. asst. prof. medicine, 1976-80; mem. staff internal medicine St. Elizabeth Hosp., Beaumont Med./Surg. Hosp., Bapt. Hosp., Beaumont, Tex., 1976; med. dir. Golden Triangle Dialysis Ctr., Beaumont, 1977—, BMA Jasper, Jasper, Tex., 1986, BMA Orange, Orange, Tex., 1987-90; med. dir. Golden Triangle Dialysis Ctr., Beaumont, 1977; med. dir. BMA Jasper, Tex., 1986, Orange, Tex., 1987-90; mem. Kidney Health Care Adv. Com., 1981-82; pesenter in field. Contbr. articles to profl. publs. Mem. AMA, ACP, Am. Soc. Nephrology, Internat. Soc. Nephrology, Tex. Med. Assn., Harris County Med. Soc., Jefferson County Med. Soc., Am. Coll. Physicians Execs., Physicians for A Nat. Health Plan. Home: 4655 Ashdown St Beaumont TX 77706-7723 Office: Beaumont Nephrology Assocs 3282 College St Beaumont TX 77701-4610

LOZITO, DEBORAH ANN, osteopathic internist; b. Paterson, N.J., Jan. 20, 1960; d. Joseph Anthony and Geraldine Anita (Note) L. BS, Montclair State U., 1982; DO, Phila. Coll. Osteo. Medicine, 1987. Diplomate Am. Bd. Osteo. Internists. Physician-in-tng. Union (N.J.) Hosp., 1987-91; physician Hawthorne (N.J.) Med. Assocs., 1991—. Mem. AMA, Am. Osteo. Assn., N.J. Assn. Osteo. Physicians and Surgeons, Am. Coll. Osteo. Internists. Office: Hawthorne Med Assocs 484 Lafayette Ave Hawthorne NJ 07506

LOZITO, JOHN C., neurologist. BS, Stetson U., 1965; MD, U. Miami, 1969. Diplomate Am. bd. psychiatry and Neurology, Am. acad. Pain Mgmt.; cert. Am. Bd. Electroencephalography. Intern Wilford Hall, San Antonio, 1969-70; resident U. Miami, Fla., 1973-76; neurologist Melbourne (Fla.) Neurologic, 1976-91; pvt. practice Melbourne, 1991—; mem. staff Holmes Regional Med. Ctr., Melbourne, Palm Bay (Fla.) Cmty. Hosp.; mem. staff, past chief of staff Sea Pines Rehab. Hosp., Melbourne; cons. in field. Contbr. articles to profl. jours. With USAF, 1971-73. Mem. AMA, Am. Acad. Neurology, Am. Assn. Study Headache, Am. Epilepsy Soc., Am. Med. EEG Assn., Am. Soc. Neuro Imaging (cert.), Am. Acad. Pain Mgmt.,

Fla. Med. Soc., Fla. Soc. Neurology, Brevard County Med. Soc., So. Clin. Neurologic Soc. Office: 1333 Pine St Melbourne FL 32901

LUBAN, NORMAN ALAN, neurologist; b. N.Y.C., Dec. 27, 1945; s. Morris and Lillian L.; m. Naomi Corman, May 23, 1971; children: Matthew, Benjamin. BA, SUNY, Buffalo, 1967; MD, Albert Einstein Coll. Medicine, 1971. Intern Bellevue Hosp., N.Y.C., 1971-72; rsch. assoc. NIH, Bethesda, Md., 1972-74; resident Presbyn. Hosp., N.Y.C., 1974-77; pvt. practice neurology Bethesda, 1977—. Physician Community for Creative Non-Violence, Washington, 1990—. Lt. comdr. USPHS, 1972-74. Recipient Bernton award Providence Hosp., D.C., 1979. Fellow Am. Acad. Neurology. Jewish. Home: 4101 Leland St Bethesda MD 20815-5033 Office: 1160 Varnum St NE # 314 Washington DC 20017

LUBAR, JOEL F., psychology educator; b. Washington, Nov. 16, 1938; s. Raymond and Barbara Frances (Pollak) L.; m. Judith Ostrovsky; children: Sandra Gita, Edward Justin. BS, U. Chgo., 1960, PhD, 1963. Lic. psychologist, Tenn. Asst. prof. psychology U. Rochester, N.Y., 1963-67; assoc. prof. U. Tenn., Knoxville, 1967-71, prof., 1971—; co-dir. Southeastern Biofeedback Inst., Knoxville, 1971—; dir. biofeedback svcs. Pain and Neuroscis. Ctr. St. Mary's Hosp., Knoxville, 1984-88. Contbr. papers in field. Mem. profl. adv. bd. Epilepsey Found. Am., 1979-83. Demonstration grantee Dept. Edn., 1981-82. Fellow N.Y. Acad. Scis.; mem. Am. Psychol. Assn., Soc. for Neurosci., Biofeedback Soc. Am., Biofeedback Cert. Inst. Am. (bd. dirs. 1983-86, cert.), Assn. Applied Psychophysiology and Biofeedback (pres. 1996—), Sigma Xi. Home: 405 Anteelah Trl Knoxville TN 37919-6675 Office: U Tenn Dept Psychology 310A Austin Peay Knoxville TN 37996-0900

LUBECK, MARVIN JAY, ophthalmologist; b. Cleve., Mar. 20, 1929; s. Charles D. and Lillian (Jay) L. A.B., U. Mich., 1951, M.D., 1955, M.S., 1959. Diplomate Am. Bd. Opthamology; m. Arlene Sue Bitman, Dec. 28, 1955; children: David Mark, Daniel Jay, Robert Charles. Intern, U. Mich. Med. Ctr., 1955-56, resident ophthalmology, 1956-58, jr. clin. instr. ophthalmology, 1958-59; pvt. practice medicine, specializing in ophthalmology, Denver, 1961—; mem. staff Rose Hosp., Porter Hosp., Presbyn. Hosp., St. Luke's Hosp.; assoc. clin. prof. U. Colo. Med. Ctr. With U.S. Army, 1959-61. Fellow ACS; mem. Am. Acad. Ophthalmology, Denver Med. Soc., Colo. Ophthalmol. Soc. Home: 590 S Harrison Ln Denver CO 80209-3517 Office: 3600 E Alameda Ave Denver CO 80209-3803

LUBER, HOWARD J., dermatologist; b. Milw., May 21, 1956. BS, Yale U., 1978; MD, U. Wis., 1982. Bd. cert. internal medicine and dermatology. Dermatologist Southwest Skin Specialists, Scottsdale, Ariz., 1989—. Mem. Am. Cancer Soc. (bd. dirs.), Ariz. Dermatology Soc. (sec.-treas. 1994-96), Phoenix Dermatology Soc. (pres. 1994-96). Office: Southwest Skin Specialists 4845 E Thunderbird Rd Scottsdale AZ 85254

LUBIC, LOWELL GERALD, neurologist, medical educator; b. Pitts., Oct. 2, 1926; m. Janet K. Kimball; children: Leslie Finkel, Jennifer Pakula. BS, U. Pitts., 1946, MD, 1950. Intern Montefiore Hosp., Pitts., 1950-51, resident in internal medicine, 1951-52; resident in neurology Neurol. Inst., N.Y.C., 1952-54, Western Psychiat. Inst. and clinic, Pitts., 1954-55; asst. prof. clin. neurology U. Pitts., 1957-85, prof. clin. neurology, 1985—; neurologist in pvt. practice Neurol. Neurosurg. Assocs., Pitts., 1956—. Active Pres. Reagan/Bush campaigns. Capt. USAFR. Republican. Jewish. Home: 1878 Shaw Ave Pittsburgh PA 15217 Office: Neurol Neurosurg Associates 3470 Fifth Ave Pittsburgh PA 15213

LUBIC, RUTH WATSON, association executive, nurse midwife; b. Bucks County, Pa., Jan. 18, 1927; d. John Russell and Lillian (Kraft) Watson; m. William James Lubic, May 28, 1955; 1 son, Douglas Watson. Diploma, Sch. Nursing Hosp. U. Pa., 1955; BS, Columbia U., 1959, MA, 1961, EdD in Applied Anthropology, 1979; Cert. in Nurse Midwifery, SUNY, Bklyn., 1962; LLD (hon.), U. Pa., 1985; DSc (hon.), U. Medicine and Dentistry, N.J., 1986; LHD (hon.), Coll. New Rochelle, 1992; DSc (hon.), SUNY, Bklyn., 1993; LHD (hon.), Pace U., 1994. RN, Pa. Mem. faculty Sch. Nursing, N.Y. Med. Coll.; mem. faculty Maternity Ctr. Assn., SUNY Sch. Nurse-Midwifery, Downstate Med. Ctr.; staff nurse through head nurse Meml. Hosp. for Cancer and Allied Disease, N.Y.C., 1955-58; clin. assoc. Grad. Sch. Nursing N.Y. Med. Coll., N.Y.C., 1962-63; parent educator, cons. Maternity Ctr. Assn., N.Y.C., 1963-67, gen. dir., 1970-95; dir. clin. projects., 1995—; cons. in midwifery, nursing and maternal and child health Office of Pub. Health and Sci. HHS, 1995—; adj. prof. divsn. nursing, NYU, 1995—; bd. dirs., v.p. Am. Assn. for World Health U.S. Com. for WHO, 1975-94, pres. 1980-81; mem. bd. maternal child and family health NRC, 1974-80; mem. Commn. on Grads. Fgn. Nursing Schs., 1979-83, v.p. 1980-91, treas., 1982-83; bd. govs. Frontier Nursing Svc., 1982-92; bd. dirs. Pan Am. Health Edn. Found., pres. 1987-88; vis. prof. King Edward Meml. Hosp., Perth, Australia, 1991; Kate Hanna Harvey vis. prof. cmty. health nursing Frances Payne Bolton Sch. Nursing Case Western Res., 1991; Lansdowne lectr. U. Victoria, B.C., Can., 1992. Author: (with Gene Hawes) Childbearing: A Book of Choices, 1987; contbr. articles to profl. jours. Recipient Letitia White award, Florence Nightingale medal, 1955, Rockefeller Pub. Svc. award, 1981, Hattie Hemschemeyer award, 1983, Alumnae award Sch. Nursing U. Pa., 1986, Tchrs. Coll. Columbia U., 1992, Disting. Svc. award Francis Payne Bolton Sch. Nursing, 1993, MacArthur Fellowship award, 1993, Hon. Recognition N.Y. State Nurses Assn., 1993, Nurse-Midwifery Faculty award Columbia U., 1993, Spirit of Nursing award Vis. Nurses Svc. N.Y., 1994, Maes-MacInnes award Divsn. Nursing NYU, 1994, Hon. recognition ANA, 1994; named Maternal-Child Health Nurse of Yr., ANA, 1985. Fellow AAAS, Am. Acad. Nursing, N.Y. Acad. Medicine, Soc. for Applied Anthropology, Am. Coll. of Nurse Midwives; mem. APHA (mem. com. on internat. health, sec. maternal and child health coun. 1982, mem. governing coun. 1986-89, mem. nominating com. 1987, mem. action bd. 1988-90), Am. Coll. Nurse-Midwives (v.p. 1964-66, pres.-elect 1969-70), Soc. Applied Anthropology, Inst. Medicine of NAS, Nat. Assn. Childbearing Ctrs. (pres. 1983-91), Herman Biggs Soc. (sec., treas. 1989-90), Cosmopolitan Club, Sigma Theta Tau.

LUBIN, MICHAEL FREDERICK, physician, educator; b. Phila., Mar. 20, 1947; s. Leonard and Ethel Sybil (Stern) L. BA, Johns Hopkins U., 1969, MD, 1973. Resident Emory U. Affiliated Hosp., Atlanta, 1973-76; asst. prof. medicine Emory U. Sch. Medicine, Atlanta, 1976-82, assoc. prof. medicine, 1982—, dir. div. gen. medicine, 1989-95; dir. preoperative clinic Grady Hosp., Atlanta, 1995—; chmn. housestaff evaluation com. Dept. medicine Emory U. Sch. Medicine; chmn. pharmacy and therapeutics com. Grady Hosp. Editor: Medical Management of the Surgical Patient, 1982, 3d rev. edit., 1995, Med. Rounds, 1988-90; mem. editl. bd. I-M: Internal Medicine, 1992-95; contbr. to Med. Knowledge Self Assessment Program X, 1994. Mem. alumni coun. Johns Hopkins U., 1995—. Hartford scholar in Geriatrics UCLA, 1984-85. Fellow ACP; mem. Am. Geriatrics Soc., Soc. Gen. Internal Medicine. Office: Emory U Sch Medicine 69 Butler St SE Atlanta GA 30303-3033

LUBKIN, VIRGINIA LEILA, ophthalmologist; b. N.Y.C., Oct. 26, 1914; d. Joseph and Anna Fredericka (Stern) L.; m. Arnold Malkan, June 6, 1944 (div. 1949); m. Martin Bernstein, Aug. 28, 1949; children: Ellen Henrietta, James Ernst, Roger Joel, John Conrad. BS summa cum laude, NYU, 1933; MD, Columbia U., 1937. Diplomate Am. Bd. Ophthalmology. Intern Harlem Hosp., N.Y.C., 1938-40; asst. resident neurology Montefiore Hosp., N.Y.C., 1940, asst. resident pathology, 1940-41, fellow in ophthalmology, 1941-42; resident ophthalmology Kings County Hosp., Bklyn., 1942-43, Mt. Sinai Hosp., N.Y.C., 1943-44; attending ophthalmologist, assoc. clin. prof. emeritus Mt. Sinai Sch. Medicine, 1944—; also sr. attending surgeon N.Y. Eye and Ear Infirmary, Mt. Sinai Sch. Medicine; pvt. practice N.Y.C., 1945-90; surgeon, now sr. surgeon N.Y. Eye and Ear Infirmary, 1945—; rsch. prof. N.Y. Med. Coll., 1986—; co-creator, now chief of rsch. bioengineering lab. N.Y. Eye and Ear Infirmary (name now The Aborn), N.Y.C., 1978—; creator first grad. course in oculoplastics and bi-yearly symposia in devel. dyslexia Mt. Sinai Sch. Medicine; educator courses in psychosomatic ophthalmology Am. Acad. Ophthalmology, 1950-60, educator course in complications of blepharoplasty, 1980-90; bd. dirs. Jewish Guild for the Blind; tchr. surg. opthalmology in French Cameroon, Presbyn. Mission, 1951; lectr. in numerous countries including India, 1976, 92, Pakistan, 1976, 84, China, 1978, Sri Lanka, 1979, South Africa, 1982, Singapore, 1984, Thailand, 1984, Argentina, 1986, Peru, 1987. Author: (with others) Ophthalmic Plastic and Reconstructive Surgery, 1989; contbr. articles to profl. jours. Bd. dirs. Ctr. fo Environ. Therapeutics, 1995. Grantee Intraocular Lens Implant Mfrs., 1989. Fellow AMA, AAAS, Am. Soc. Ophthalmic Plastic and Reconstructive Surgery (founding), Am. Coll. Surgeons, N.Y. Acad. Medicine, N.Y. Acad. Scis., Am. Acad. Ophthalmology, Am. Soc. Cataract and Refractive Surgery, PanAm. Soc. Ophthalmology, N.Y. Soc. Clin. Ophthalmology, Soc. Light Treatment and Biol. Rhythms, Phi Beta Kappa, Alpha Omega Alpha. Home: 1 Blackstone Pl Bronx NY 10471-3607 Office: NY Eye and Ear Infirmary Apt 2C Residence Bldg 310 E 14th St New York NY 10003-4200

LUBMAN, RICHARD L., physician, research scientist; b. Bklyn., Dec. 10, 1956; m. Sue Ann Feinberg; children: Rachel Susannah, Louisa Natalie. BA, Cornell U., 1977; MD, SUNY, Bklyn., 1981. Diplomate Nat. Bd. Med. Examiners, Am. Bd. Internal Medicine. From intern to chief resident in internal medicine SUNY-Kings County Hosp.-Bklyn. VA Med. Ctr., Bklyn., 1981-85; fellow pulmonary and critical care medicine N.Y. Hosp.-Cornell Med. Ctr., N.Y.C., 1985-88; instr. medicine Cornell U. Med. Coll., N.Y.C., 1988-91; asst. prof. medicine U. So. Calif., L.A., 1991—. Recipient Initial Investigator award Am. Heart Assn., 1993-95; J. Burns Amberson fellow N.Y. Lung Assn., 1986-88, fellow Parker B. Francis Found., 1988-91. Fellow Am. Coll. Physicians, Am. Coll. Chest Physicians; mem. Am. Thoracic Soc., Am. Heart Assn., Am. Physiol. Soc. Office: Univ So Calif 2011 Zonal Ave HMR 900 Los Angeles CA 90033

LUCÀ-MORETTI, MAURIZIO, scientist, nutrition researcher; b. Rome, June 2, 1945; s. Giuseppe and Elena (Moretti) L.; m. Anna Grandi, Jan. 2, 1974; 1 child, Elena. BS, Ministry of Edn., Caracas, Venezuela, 1969; PhD in Allied Health Scis., Pacific Western U., 1990, DSc in Human Nutrition, 1990; MD (hon.), Universidad Santo Tomas, La Paz, Bolivia, 1994; MPH (hon.), Inst. Superiore di Studi Sanitari, Rome, 1995. Rschr. Inst. Italiano di Terapia Fisica e Medicina Interna, Rome, 1974-76, sr. rschr., 1976-78, dir. rsch., 1978-80; dir. rsch. Inst. Italiano di Terapia Fisica e Medicina Interna, Caracas, Venezuela, 1980-88; dir. human nutrition rsch. program and AIDS rsch. program InterAm. Med. and Health Assn., Boca Raton, Fla., 1989—, pres., 1989—; gen. sec. World Acad. Medicine, 1992—; prof. emeritus Pacific We. Univ., New Orleans, 1992; invited prof. Univ. di Chiete, Italy, 1991, Univ. de Asuncion, Paraguay, 1992, Univ. di Roma, Rome, 1995; hon. prof. Univ. de Granada, Spain, 1994, Univ.Nacional Pedro Enrique Ureña, Santo Domingo, Dominican Rep., 1994, Inst. Superiore di Studi Sanitari, 1996. Recipient medal Univ. Asuncion, Paraguay, 1992, medal Univ. Granada, Spain, 1993. Fellow NAS (Dominican Rep.), Royal Nat. Acad. Medicine Spain, Royal Acad. Scis. Spain, Royal Acad. Medicine Salamanca, Royal Acad. Medicine Granada, Royal Acad. Medicine Valencia, Royal Acad. Medicine of Zaragoza, Nat. Acad. Medicine Bolivia, Nat. Acad. Medicine Ecuador, Nat. Acad. Medicine Paraguay, Nat. Acad. Medicine Dominican Rep., Acad. Medicine Maracaibo. Office: InterAm Med and Health Assn 3025 Saint James Dr Boca Raton FL 33434-3370

LUCARINI, JAMES WALTER, otolaryngologist; b. Mt. Holly, N.J., Nov. 12, 1956; s. James Vincent and Eva Maria (Saraca) L.; m. Donna Lorraine Casey, Sept. 29, 1991; 1 child, Kara Elizabeth. AB magna cum laude, Harvard U., 1979; MD, Yale U., 1983. Surg. intern U. Pa., Phila., 1983-84; resident in otolaryngology Mass. Eye and Ear Infirmary, Boston, 1984-88; staff otolaryngologist New Eng. Deaconess Hosp., Boston, 1988-93; pvt. practice otolaryngology Dedham Med. Assocs., Newton, Mass., 1993—; clin. instr. Harvard Med. Sch., Boston, 1989—, Tufts Sch. Medicine, Boston, 1995—. Contbr. articles to profl. jours. Fellow ACS, Am. Soc. for Head and Neck Surgery; mem. New Eng. Otolaryngol. Soc. Roman Catholic. Office: Dedham Med Assocs 2000 Washington St # 460 Newton MA 02162

LUCAS, HOWARD CHARLES, SR., ophthalmologist; b. Lakeland, Fla., May 7, 1924; s. Charles Robert and Zelma Louise (Hilty) L.; m. Leone Marjorie DeLelys, July 1, 1950 (dec. Dec. 1989); children: Leora, Louise, Gordon, Howard Charles Jr. BS in Chemistry, U. Fla., 1947; MD, Cornell U., 1951. Diplomate Am. Bd. Ophthalmology. Resident in surgery Geneseee Hosp., Rochester, N.Y., 1951-53; pvt. practice Winter Haven, Fla., 1953-57, 60—; resident in ophthalmology Presbyn. Med. Ctr., N.Y.C., 1957-60; mem. staff Winter Haven Hosp., 1953—, pres. med. staff, 1970. With U.S. Army, 1943-46. Mem. AMA, Am. Acad. Ophthalmology, Phi Beta Kappa. Home: 7317 Crystal Beach Rd Winter Haven FL 33880-5152 Office: 560 Avenue K SE Winter Haven FL 33880-4203

LUCAS, MELINDA ANN, pediatrician, educator; b. Maryville, Tenn., June 27, 1953; d. Arthur Baldwin and Dorthy (Shields) L. BA, Maryville Coll., 1975; MS, U. Tenn., 1976, MD, 1981; postgrad., U. Tenn. Law Sch., 1992-93. Diplomate Am. Bd. Pediatrics; lic. dr. N.Y., Tenn. Intern in pediatrics U. Rochester, N.Y., 1981-82, resident in pediatrics, 1982-84; pvt. practice, Maryville, 1984-85; emergency room pediatrician U. Tenn. Med. Ctr., Knoxville, 1985-90, dir. child abuse clinic, 1987-90, pediatric intensivist, 1987—, acting dir. pediatric ICU, 1990-92, mem. faculty, 1988—; mem. Pediatric Cons., Inc. Knoxville; physician rep. Project Search Working Symposium, 1990—. Contbr. articles to profl. jours. Mem. Blount County Foster Care Rev. Bd., Maryville, Tenn., 1985-93, Blount County Exec. Bd. Maryville Coll. Alumni Assn., 1988-92. Fellow U. Tenn. Genetics Ctr., 1988-89, pediatric critical care fellow U. Mich., 1995-96; scholar United Presbyn. Ch., 1971, Mary Lou Braly scholar, 1971-74; grantee AAP-NHTSA for Safe Ride Program. Fellow Am. Acad. Pediatrics; mem. AMA (Physician Recognition award 1984-87, 88-91, 91-94, 94-97), Am. Profl. Soc. on Abuse of Children, Tenn. Pediatric Soc. (co-chmn. accident and injury prevention com. 1993-95), Knoxville Area Pediatric Soc., Soc. Critical Care Medicine (abstract reviewer 1991, 92, 93, 94). Methodist. Home: 1608 Mcilvaine Dr Maryville TN 37803-6230

LUCCA, JOHN JAMES, retired dental educator; b. Bklyn., July 12, 1921; s. Thomas and Marie (Ciancia) L.; m. Mary A. Pascarell, June 22, 1946; children—Diane, Eileen, Denise, Nancy, John, William. A.B., NYU, 1941; D.D.S., Columbia, 1947. Diplomate: Am. Bd. Prosthodontics. Research fellow prosthetics Columbia Dental Sch., 1949-52, asst. prof., 1952-57, assoc. prof., 1957-64, head clin. prosthodontics; and postgrad. instr. 1st, 10th Dist. dental socs., 1954-87, prof. dentistry, 1964-87, dir. div. prosthodontics; prof. emeritus Columbia U., 1987—; cons. Westchester County Med. Ctr.; attending emeritus Presbyn. Hosp.; cons., lectr. U.S. Naval Dental Sch.; mem. examination com. N.E. Regional Bd. Dental Examiners; mem. med. staff Valley Hosp. Contbr. to dental jours., chpts. to various textbooks. Extraordinary minister of the Eucharist, 1974—; mem. parish council Mt. Carmel Ch., 1985—; hon. police surgeon N.Y.C. Police Dept., 1964—. Served with AUS, 1943-44. Recipient Ella M. Ewell medal Columbia, 1947. Fellow N.Y. Acad. Dentistry, Internat. Coll. Dentists Am. Coll. Dentists, Greater N.Y. Acad. Prosthodontics (pres. 1968), Internat. Coll. Prosthodontists, Am. Acad. Osseo Integration, Am. Coll. Prosthodontics (charter, pres. N.J. state sect. 1979-81); mem. Am. Equilibration Soc., First Dist. Dental Soc. (chmn. prosthodontia sect. 1971), Am. Prosthodontics Soc., William Jarvie Rsch. Soc., Chgo. Acad. Dental Rsch., Knight of Malta, Omicron Kappa Upsilon (pres. Epsilon Epsilon chpt. 1967). Home: 524 Eastgate Rd Ridgewood NJ 07450-2204

LUCE, EDWARD ANDREW, plastic surgeon; b. Syracuse, N.Y., Mar. 5, 1940; s. Edward Andrew and Constance Faith (Jones) L.; m. Rebecca Sue Wall; children: Darcie, Michael. BS, U. Dayton, 1961; MD, U. Ky., 1965. Diplomate Am. Bd. Surgery, Am. Bd. Plastic Surgery (chmn. 1990-91). Resident in surgery Barnes Hosp., St. Louis, 1965-71; resident in plastic surgery Johns Hopkins Hosp., Balt., 1971-73, asst. prof. plastic surgery, 1973-75; assoc. prof. plastic surgery U. Ky., Lexington, 1975-87, prof. plastic surgery, 1987-95, chief plastic surgery, 1975-95; chief plastic surgery VA Hosp., —, 1975-95; Kiehn-DesPrez prof. surgery Case Western Reserve U., Cleve., 1995—; chief plastic surgery U. Hosps. of Cleve., 1995—, VA Hosp., Cleve., 1995—; attending plastic surgeon St. Joseph Hosp., Lexington, 1975-95, Good Samaritan Hosp., Lexington, 1978-95, Humana Hosp., Lexington, 1982-95; Kiehn-DesPrez Prof. and Chief of Plastic Surgery, Case Western Reserve U. and Univ. Hosps. of Cleveland; pres. Assn. Acad. Chmn. of Plastic Surgery, 1989-90, Am. Soc. Maxillofacial Surgeons, 1990-91, Southeastern Soc. Plastic and Reconstructive Surgeons, 1992-93. Pres. U. Ky. Med. Alumni Assn., 1977-78; pres. John Hoopes Plastic Surgery Found., 1993. Recipient Clinician of Yr., Am. Assn. Plastic Surgeons, 1990. Mem. Plastic Surgery Ednl. Found. (pres. 1993-94), Am Coll. Surgeons, Am. Surg. Assn., So. Surg. Assn., Am. Soc. Plastic and Reconstructive Surgeons, Soc. Head and Neck Surgeons. Office: Univ Hosp Lakeside Plastic Surgery 11100 Euclid Ave Cleveland OH 44106

LUCEK, DONALD WALTER, surgeon; b. Rockford, Ill., Jan. 26, 1945; s. Walter Joseph and Magdalen Mary (Kazunas) L.; m. Mary Philomena Keany, July 6, 1968; children: Patricia, Donald Jr., Michael, Stephen. BA, U. Ill., 1970, MD, 1974. Diplomate Am. Bd. Surgery. Intern Boston U., resident in surgery, clin. instr. surgery, 1980-87, asst. clin. prof. surgery, 1987—; surgeon Milton (Mass.) Hosp., 1979—, pres. med. staff, 1993, chief of surgery, 1993-95, chmn. tissue and transfusion, 1987-93, chmn. operating rm. com., 1993-94. Pres. Milton Office Condo Assn., 1990-94; med. examiner Commonwealth of Mass., Norfolk County, 1989—. Fellow ACS, Mass. Med. Soc.; mem. AMA, Boston Surg. Soc., Mass. Medicolegal Soc. Office: 100 Highland St Milton MA 02186

LUCHETTE, FREDERICK A., surgeon; b. Sharon, Pa., Aug. 9, 1954; s. Albert and Rosemary (Songer) L.; m. Barbara Ann O'Brien, Aug. 31, 1985; children: Richard, Matthew, Claire, Katherine. BA, Thiel Coll., 1976; MS, U. Louisville, 1978, MD, 1981. Diplomate Am. Bd. Surgery. From clin. instr. to asst. prof. surgery SUNY, Buffalo, 1981-93; assoc. prof. surgery U. Cin., 1994—. Fellow Am. Coll. Surgeons; mem. Am. Assn. Surgery of Trauma, Am. Trauma Soc., Eastern Assn. Surgery of Trauma, Soc. Critical Care Medicine, Surgical Infection Soc. Roman Catholic.9. Office: U Cin Med Ctr 231 Bethesda Ave MS 0558 Cincinnati OH 45267

LUCHINS, ABRAHAM SAMUEL, psychologist, emeritus educator; b. Bklyn., Mar. 9, 1914; s. Morris Aaron and Anne Rissa (Yompolsky) L.; m. Edith H. Luchins, Oct. 10, 1942; children—David, Daniel, Jeremy, Anne, Joseph. B.A. cum laude, Bklyn. Coll., 1935; M.A., Columbia U., 1936; Ph.D., NYU, 1939. Research asst. New Sch. Social Research, N.Y.C., 1936-42; instr. to assoc. prof., chmn. dept. psychology Yeshiva U., N.Y.C., 1940-49; dir. tng. Mental Hygiene Clinic, VA, 1947-49; assoc. prof. psychology McGill U., Montreal, Que., Can., 1949-54; prof. psychology U. Oreg., Eugene, 1954-58, U. Miami, Coral Gables, Fla., 1958-62; prof. psychology SUNY-Albany, 1962-84, prof. emeritus, 1984—; adj. prof. psychology Rensselaer Poly. Inst., Troy, N.Y., 1986—; personnel cons. to clin. psychologist U.S. Army, 1943-46; cons. in clin. psychology Queen Mary's Hosp., Montreal, 1949-54, Oreg. State Hosp., Salem, 1954-58; cons. Communication and Attitude Change Project, Yale U., New Haven, 1949-54; scientist-writer sci. courses, Rensselaer Poly. Inst., 1964-65. Contbr. articles to profl. jours.; author: Revisiting Wertheimer's Seminars, vols. I and II, 1978; lectr. in field. NIH grantee, 1968-73; Air Force grantee, 1965. Fellow Am. Psychol. Assn.; mem. Am. Ednl. Research Assn., Sigma Xi. Jewish. Avocations: gardening; walking; reading. Address: 53 Fordham Ct Albany NY 12209-1192

LUCHINS, DANIEL JONATHAN, psychiatrist; b. N.Y.C., July 1, 1948; s. Abraham Samuel and Edith (Hirsch) L.; children: Kerith, Matthew. BSc, McGill U., Montreal, Que., Can., 1971, MD, 1973. Diplomate Am. Bd. Psychiatry and Neurology; cert. geriatric psychiatry. Vis. scientist NIMH, Washington, 1977-81; assoc. prof. U. Chgo., 1981—; med. coord. mental health Ill. Dept. Mental Health, Chgo., 1989-91; chief of adult psychiatry U. Chgo., 1991-93; assoc. dir. for clin. svcs. Ill. Dept. Mental Health, Chgo., 1995—; mem. Ill. Gov.'s Adv. Com. on Alzheimer Disease, 1986-90; mem. Gov.'s Task Force on Mental Health, 1986; mem. consensus panel on surgery for treatment of epilepsy NIH, Bethesda, Md., 1990. Contbr. articles to profl. publs. Recipient A.E. Bennett award Soc. Biol. Psychiatry, Geriatric Mental Health acad. award NIMH, 1984-87. Fellow Am. Psychiat. Assn.; mem. Ill. Psychiat. Assn. (councillor 1989-91, pres. 1995). Jewish. Office: Dept Psychiatry Univ Chgo 5841 S Maryland Ave Chicago IL 60637-1463

LUCIANI, SISTO, pharmacology, researcher; b. Perugia, Umbria, Italy, Dec. 24, 1936; s. Fausto and Antonietta (Moschetti) L.; m. Paola Fioretti, July 27, 1963; children: Claudia, Giovanni Battista, Marta, Matteo. D of Pharmacy, U. Padova, Perugia, 1959; MD, U. Padova, 1969; PhD in Pharmacology, U. Padova, Perugia, 1971. Asst. prof., biochemistry U., Perugia, 1960-62; asst. prof., pharmacology U., Padova, Italy, 1962-70, assoc. prof., pharmacology, 1970-75; prof.. pharmacology U., Padova, 1975—; chmn. dept. pharmacology, U. Padova, 1986-90; vis. scholar Fulbright Biochemistry, Harvard U., 1980-82, Fulbright Physiology, Tufts U., 1990-91. Editor: Atracyloside, 1978, Calcium Ion-Sabbatani Symposium, 1986. E.M.B.O. Physiology fellow U. Munich, 1972, NATO Biochemistry fellow Harvard U., 1982. Mem. Italian Soc. Pharmacology (bd. dirs. 1984-88), Italian Soc. Toxicology, Biochem. Soc., N.Y. Acad. Sci. Office: Dept Pharmacology U, Largo Meneghetti 2, 35131 Padova Italy

LUCIO, DANIEL CHRISTOPHER, internist; b. New Orleans, Apr. 18, 1961; s. Benjamin Andrew and Joan Fay (Rodriquez) L.; m. Michelle Marie Fonseca, May 7, 1992; 1 child, Henri Daniel. BS in Biol. Scis., U. New Orleans, 1984, MS in Biol. Scis., 1989; MD, La. State U. New Orleans, 1992. Lic. MD, La. Resident Ochsner Med. Found., New Orleans, 1992-95; staff physician West Jefferson Med. Ctr., Marrero, La., 1995—. Mem. AMA, ACP, So. Med. Assn., Phi Kappa Sigma (Mem. of Yr. 1984). Office: The Family Doctors' 1111 Med Ctr Blvd Ste N401 Marrero LA 70072

LUCK, DENNIS NOEL, biologist, educator, researcher; b. Durban, Natal, South Africa, Dec. 8, 1939; s. Peter Burvill and Eva Annie (Taylor) L.; m. Joan Burchall, Jan. 18, 1969; 1 child, Roy Burvil. BSc, U. Natal, South Africa, 1961, MSc, 1963; DPhil, Oxford U., Oxford, Eng., 1966. Lectr. in biochemistry U. Natal, South Africa, 1966-69; vis. asst. prof. Baylor Coll. Medicine, Houston, 1969-70; asst. prof. zoology U. Tex., Austin, 1970-72; asst. prof., assoc. prof. biology Oberlin (Ohio) Coll., 1972-82, prof., 1982—, chmn., 1995—; cons. Gilford Instrument Labs., Oberlin, 1980-82, The Oberlin Sci. Co., 1989-90. Contbr. more than 20 articles to profl. jours. including Nature, Molecular Endocriniolgy, DNA, Procs. NAS, Biochimica et Biophysica Acta, Protein Engring.; speaker at maj. sci. meetings, 1988, 90, 94. Recipient Eleanor Roosevelt Internat. Cancer fellowship Internat. Union Against Cancer, Geneva, Switzerland, 1978-79; grantee NSF, 1975-80, 1984—. Mem. Endocrine Soc., Biochem. Soc. London, Am. Soc. for Microbiology, Am. Soc. for Cell Biology, Am. Soc. for Biochemistry and Molecular Biology. Home: 240 Oak St Oberlin OH 44074-1518 Office: Dept Biology Kettering Hall Oberlin OH 44074

LUCKENBACH, ALEXANDER HEINRICH, dentist; b. Heidenheim, Fed. Republic Germany, Aug. 1, 1956; s. Siegfried and Gertraud (Hirsch) L.; m. Christine O. Heckmann, June 13, 1987. DDS, U. Tuebingen, Fed. Republic Germany, 1981; DMD, U. Tuebingen, 1983. Clin. dentist U. Tuebingen, 1983-85, asst. prof. dept. prosthodontics, 1986—, v.p. R&D, cons., 1988—, staff ZMK-Klinik, 1989%; tech. design cons. Girrbach Dental Co., Pforzheim, Fed. Republic Germany, 1985—; pres. Advanced Dental Computer Techs. Co., Tuebingen, 1991—. Author software; patentee techniqes for dental appliances, computer aided 3D joint movement recording system. Fellow German Gesellschaft F. Zahn, Mund and Kieferheilkunde, German Rsch. Soc. (spl. rsch. unit implantology), Apple Programmers and Developers Assn. Office: Praxis Bus Park, Zettachring 4, D-70567 Stuttgart Germany

LUCKMANN, KENNETH FREDERICK, gastroenterologist; b. Plainfield, N.J., Dec. 25, 1945; s. Frederck H. and Adele S. Luckman; m. Jerralyn Wall, Aug. 1, 1970; children: Keith, Craig, Clark. BS, Johns Hopkins U., 1968; MD, Vanderbilt U., 1972. Diplomate internal medicine and gastroenterology Am. Bd. Internal Medicine. Intern and resident Vanderbilt Univ. Hosps., Nashville, 1972-75; fellow gastroenterology U. Tex. Health Sci. Ctr., San Antonio, 1975-77; pres. Oak Ridge (Tenn.) Gastroenterology Assoc. PC, 1978—; bd. dirs. Preferred Health Partnership, Knoxville, Tenn., 1988—. Contbr. articles to profl. jours. Fellow ACP; mem. AMA, Am. Gastroenterologic Assn., Am. Soc. Gastrointestinal Endoscopy, Tenn. Med. Assn., Roane-Anderson County Med. Soc. (pres. 1980-81), So. Med. Assn., Am. Soc. Internal Medicine, Briarcliff Cmty. Club (pres. 1996). Office: Oak Ridge Gastroenterology Assoc PC 988 Oak Ridge Tpke Ste 40L Oak Ridge TN 37830-6930

LUCKSINGER, THOMAS SHELLEY, lawyer; b. Austin, Tex., July 12, 1941; s. Thomas W. and Beatrice A. (Shelley) L.; m. Sarah Nesmith, May 21, 1972; children: Shel, Melissa, Todd, Brett. BBA, U. Tex., 1964, JD, 1967. Bar: Tex. 1967, U.S. Dist. Ct. (so. dist.) Tex. 1967, U.S. Tax Ct. 1967, U.S. Supreme Ct. 1967. Tax specialist Haskins & Sells, Houston, 1967-71; ptnr. Lucksinger, Holland & Wylie, Houston, 1971-73, Wood, Lucksinger & Epstein, Houston, 1973-91, Vinson & Elkins, Houston, 1991-92; pres., CEO NYL Care Health Plan, Houston, 1992—; lectr. in field. Contbr. articles to legal publs. Bd. dirs. Harris County Mcpl. Utility Dist. 82, 1971-76, pres. 1973-76; bd. dirs. Allegro Ballet, 1975-77, Houston Symphony, Houston Forum, Houston March of Dimes, Houston Better Bus. Bur., Tex. Taxpayers and Rsch. Assn.; vice-chmn. Houston Rodeo Lamb Com.; mem. healthcare com. Greater Houston Partnership; mem. Am. Red Cross-Houston Area. Mem. Tex. Bar Assn. (past chmn. health law sect.), Nat. Healthcare Lawyers Assn., Tex. Soc. CPA, Order of Barristers. Office: NYL Care Health Plan 2425 W Loop S Ste 1000 Houston TX 77027-9999

LUCKY, ANNE WEISSMAN, dermatologist; b. N.Y.C., May 11, 1944; d. Jacob and Gertrude (Tetelman) Weissman; m. Paul A. Lucky, May 19, 1972; children: Jennifer, Andrea. BA, Brown U., 1966; MD, Yale U., 1970. Diplomate Nat. Bd. Med. Examiners, Am. Bd. Pediatrics/subspecialty of pediatric endocrinology, Am. Bd. Dermatology. Intern and resident in pediatrics The Children's Hosp. Med. Ctr., Boston, 1970-73; fellow in human genetics and pediatrics Yale U. Sch. Medicine, New Haven, Conn., 1973-74; resident in dermatology Yale U. Sch. Medicine, 1979-81, instr. pediatrics, 1980-81, assoc. prof. dermatology and pediatrics, 1981-83; clin. assoc. Reprodn. Rsch. Br./Nat. Inst. Child Health/NIH, Bethesda, Md., 1974-76; asst. prof. pediatrics Wyler Children's Hosp./Pritzker Sch. Med./U. Chgo. Hosps., 1976-79; assoc. prof. dermatology, pediatrics U. Cin. Coll. Medicine, 1983-88; pvt. practice Dermatology Assocs. of Cin, Inc., 1988—; pres. Dermatology Rsch. Assocs., Inc., Cin., 1988—; dir. Dermatology Clinic Children's Hosp. Med. Ctr., Cin., 1989—; vol. prof. dermatology and pediatrics U. Cin. Coll. Medicine, 1988-94. Editorial bd. Pediatric Dermatology, 1982—, Archives of Dermatology, 1983-94; contbr. numerous articles to profl. jours., publs. Recipient the Janet M. Glasgow Meml. Scholarship, Am. Women's Med. Assn., 1970, the Ramsey Meml. Scholarship award Yale U. Sch. Medicine, 1968, others; grantee USPHS, 1964-66, 67, 68-70, NIH, 1977-79, 79-82, 82-87, 84-87, 87-93, others. Mem. Lawson Wilkins Pediatric Endocrine Soc., Soc. for Pediatric Endocrinology (bd. dirs. 1984-87, pres. 1990-91), Am. Acad. Dermatology, Soc. Investigative Dermatology, Soc. for Dermatologic Genetics of the Am. Acad. Dermatology, Endocrine Soc., Acad. Medicine/Cin. Women's Faculty Assn./The Children's Hosp. Med. Ctr., Women's Derm. Soc. (bd. dirs. 1993—), Ohio State Med. Assn., Soc. Pediatric Rsch., Cin. Derm. Soc. (pres. elect 1995-96), Phi Beta Kappa, Sigma Xi, Alpha Omega Alpha. Office: Derm Assocs of Cin 7691 Five Mile Rd Cincinnati OH 45230

LUCORE, CHARLES LEE, cardiologist; b. Southington, Conn., Apr. 30, 1957; s. Charles Earl and Eleanor Christina Lucore; m. Paula F. Sorensen, Sept. 25, 1982; children: Alexander Charles, Jordon Mari. AB, Colgate U., 1979; MD, Duke U., 1983. Diplomate Am. Bd. Internal Medicine, Am. Bd. Cardiovasc. Diseases. Intern N.Y. Hosp.-Cornell Med. Ctr., N.Y.C., 1983-84, resident, 1984-86; cardiovasc. postdoctoral rsch. fellow Sch. Medicine Wash. U., St. Louis, 1986-88, clin. cardiology fellow, 1988-89, invasive cardiology fellow, 1989-90, asst. prof. medicine and interventional cardiology, 1990-92; interventional cardiologist Prairie Cardiovasc. Consultants, Ltd., Springfield, Ill., 1992—; co-dir. cardiac catherization lab. St. John's Hosp., Springfield, Ill., 1992—, chmn. dept. cardiology, 1994—, mem. Prairie Edn. and Rsch. Coop. Coord., 1995—, mem. exec. com., 1996—, mem. exec. com. Prairie Cardiovasc. Consultants, Ltd., 1995—; asst. clin. prof. medicine So. Ill. U., Springfield, Ill., 1992—. Recipient Rsch. award Corvas Internat., 1991. Fellow Am. Coll. Cardiology; mem. ACP, Am. Heart Assn. (thrombosis coun. 1989—, coun. on cardiology 1994—, grantee 1992, 93), Phi Beta Kappa, Beta Beta Beta. Office: Prairie Cardiovasc Cons Ltd 301 N 8th St Ste 3B-301 Springfield IL 62701

LUDDEN, DEBORAH ANN, community health nurse; b. Freeport, N.Y., Mar. 4, 1958; d. John F. and Josephine Turant; children: Paul Thomas, Jeremy, Joshua, Corey. AAS, Nassau Community Coll., Garden City, N.Y., 1984; cert. in health adminstrn., U. Scranton, Pa., 1988. RN, Pa., N.Y. Staff nurse Drs. Officenter, Hicksville, N.Y.; asst. adminstr. Golden Care Northeast Pa., Pittston; dir. profl. svcs. House Calls Inc., Kingston, Pa., Above All Home Health and Hospice, Clarks Summit, Pa., A Home Health, Kingston, Pa., Assoc. Family Home Care, Kingston, Pa. Mem. Plains Rotary.

LUDDEN, THOMAS MARCELLUS, pharmaceutical research scientist; b. Kansas City, Mo., Jan. 16, 1946; s. Thomas Marcellus and Dorothea Naomi (Thompson) L.; m. Mary C. Hendra, Oct. 23, 1967 (div. Feb. 1979); children: Johnny Thomas, Susan Nicole; m. Linda Kay Schroeder, Nov. 29, 1979; children: Jon Paul Goggin, Marc A. Goggin. BS in Pharmacy, U. Mo., Kansas City, 1969, PhD in Pharmacology, 1973. Lic. pharmacist, Mo. Asst. prof. U. Tex., Austin, 1975-80, assoc. prof., 1980-85, prof. pharmacology, 1985-91; expert/cons. Ctr. for Drug Evaluation and Rsch. FDA, Rockville, Md., 1991-92; dir. divsn. biopharmaceutics FDA, 1992-95; Parke-Davis prof. and chair, Dept. Pharm. Scis. Coll. Pharmacy U. Nebr. Med. Ctr., Omaha, 1995—; vis. rsch. assoc. Ohio State U., Columbus, 1974-75; part-time expert cons. FDA, Rockville, Md., 1987-91. Office: U Nebr Med Ctr Dept Pharm Scis Coll Pharmacy 600 S 42d St Omaha NE 68198

LÜDERITZ, BERNDT, cardiologist; b. Braunschweig, Fed. Republic Germany, Mar. 26, 1940; s. Bernhard and Theda (Winter) L.; m. Hedwig Muschol, Nov. 29, 1969; children: Florian, Martin, Stephan. MD, U. Heidelberg, Fed. Republic Germany, 1965. Cert. Med. State Bd., Munich, 1965. Intern U. Munich, 1965-67; resident U. Munich and Göttingen, 1967-74; asst. prof. cardiology U. Göttingen, Fed. Republic Germany, 1972-79; assoc. prof. cardiology U. Munich, 1979-83; prof. chmn. dept. medicine, cardiology U. Bonn, Fed. Republic Germany, 1983—; chmn. German Working Group on Cardiac Pacing, 1983-88. Editor: (book) Cardiac Pacing, 1976, Interventional Electrophysiology, 1991; co-editor: (book) Myocardial Failure, 1977; mem. editorial bd. PACE, 1981, Intervention Cardiol., 1988. Fellow Am. Coll. Cardiology, Am. Heart Assn.; mem. German CArdiac Soc. (exec. bd. 1984-88, Arthur Weber prize 1980), N.Am. Soc. Pacing and Electrophysiology, Internat. Cardiac Pacing and Electrophysiology Soc. (bd. dirs.). Lutheran. Home: 10 Erich-Böger, D-5300 Bonn Germany Office: U Bonn Dept Medicine and Cardiology, 25 Sigmund Freud Str, D-5300 Bonn Germany

LUDLOW, MARVIN O., endodontist, educator; b. Salt Lake City, Nov. 20, 1941; s. Marvin and Ruthe (Oldham) L.; m. Karen Wallace, June 28, 1965; children: John, Mark, Kristina, LeAnna. DDS, U. Mo., 1969; MS, U. Nebr., 1974. Pvt. dental practice American Fork, Utah, 1969-70; instr. operative dentistry Univ. Nebr., Lincoln, 1970-72, asst. prof. endodontics, 1972-76; assoc. prof. endodontics Creighton Univ., Omaha, 1976-79, chmn. endodontics, 1979—; pvt. endodontic practice, Omaha, 1976—, cons. VA Hosp., Omaha, 1985—. Contbr. articles to profl. Bishopric LDS Ch., Omaha, 1985-88, youth tchr., 1988-92, adult tchr., 1993-96; explorer scout adv. Creighton Univ. Post, Omaha, 1980-96. Mem. Nebr. Assn. Endodontics, OKU (pres. Alpha Alpha chpt. 1975, Upsilon chpt. 1989). Mem. LDS Ch. Office: Creighton Univ Dept Endodontics 2500 California St Omaha NE 68178

LUDLUM, DAVID BLODGETT, pharmacologist, educator; b. N.Y.C., Sept. 30, 1929; s. C. Daniel and Elsie B. (Blodgett) L.; B.A., Cornell U., 1951; Ph.D., U. Wis., 1954; M.D., N.Y.U., 1962; m. Carlene L. Dyke, Dec. 23, 1952; children: Valerie Jean Ludlum Wright, Kenneth David. Research scientist Dupont Co., Wilmington, Del., 1954-58; intern Bellevue Hosp., N.Y.C., 1962-63; asst. prof. pharmacology Yale U., 1963-68; assoc. prof. U. Md., 1968-70, prof., 1970-76; prof. pharmacology Albany (N.Y.) Med. Coll., 1976-86 , chmn. dept. pharmacology, 1976-80, prof. medicine, 1980-86, dir. oncology research, 1980-86; prof. pharmacology and medicine U. Mass. Med. Sch., 1986—; adj. prof. chemistry Rensselaer Poly. Inst., Troy, N.Y., 1977-80; vis. prof. oncology Johns Hopkins U., 1973-76; vis. prof. Courtauld Inst., London, 1970. WARF fellow, 1951-52; NSF fellow, 1952-54; Am. Heart Assn. fellow, 1960-62; recipient NIH Research Career Devel. award 1968; Markle scholar in acad. medicine, 1967-72; lic. physician, N.Y., Conn., Md. Mem. Am. Soc. Pharmacology and Exptl. Therapeutics, Am. Soc. Clin. Pharmacology and Therapeutics, Am. Assn. Cancer Research, Am. Soc. Biochem. and Molecular Biology, Am. Chem. Soc., Phi Beta Kappa, Sigma Xi, Phi Kappa Phi, Alpha Omega Alpha. Assoc. editor Cancer Rsch., 1980-87, 89—; contbr. articles to profl. jours.; patentee in field; grantee in field. Home: 24 Linda Ct Delmar NY 12054-3512 Office: U Mass Med Sch Worcester MA 01655-0126

LUDVIGSEN, CARL WILLIAM, JR., lawyer, physician, consultant; b. Palo Alto, Calif., Mar. 21, 1953; s. Carl William Sr. and Florence (Burkhalter) L.; m. Ilana Nora Airth-Kindree, Dec. 25, 1987. BA, U. Colo., 1974; PhD, MD cum laude, Washington U., St. Louis, 1980; JD, Creighton U., 1988. Bar: Nebr. Resident in clin. pathology U. Minn., Mpls., 1980-82, clin. chemistry fellow, 1982-83; dir. chemistry U. Nebr. Med. Ctr., Omaha, 1983-86; emergency room physician Lutheran Hosp., Bryan Meml. Hosp., Omaha, 1986-87; cons. Med.-Legal Cons., Omaha, 1986—; dir. emergency room, clin. physician, nursing home physician Sandstone (Minn.) Area Med. Group, 1988; exec. v.p., COO Lab. One, Shawnee Mission, Kans., 1989—. Recipient Young Investigators award Acad. Clin. Lab. Physician Scientists, Seattle, 1982. Mem. ABA, Nebr. Bar Assn., Omaha Bar Assn., AMA, Clin. Assn. Pathology, AAAS. Office: Reference Lab PO Box 2035 Shawnee Mission KS 66201-1035

LUDWIG, HEINZ, oncologist; b. Vienna, Mar. 21, 1947; s. Johann and Margarethe (Trandl) L.; m. Birgit Schreiner, July 8, 1989; children: Michael, Claudia. MA, U. Vienna, 1971, asst. prof., 1983, prof., 1985. Rsch. asst. Inst. Immunologie, Vienna, 1971-74; clin. asst. dept. medicine Vienna, 1974-81, sr. registrar, 1981-83, asst. prof., 1983-85; prof., 1985-90; head dept. medicine and med. oncology Wilhelminenspital, Vienna, 1990—. Contbr. articles to profl. jours. Sec. Austrian Cancer Soc., Vienna, 1986-89, pres., 1989-92, Austrian Forum Against Cancer, 1993—. Recipient Sci. award Municipality of Vienna, 1985. Mem. Am. Assn. Cancer Rsch. (corr.). Home: Kaulbachstr 19, A-1120 Vienna Austria Office: Wilhelminenspital Dept Med Oncology, Montleartstr 37, 1-1160 Vienna Austria

LUDWIG, IRENE HELEN, ophthalmologist, researcher; b. N.Y.C., Dec. 30, 1954; d. Peter F. and Eva H. (Assenheim) L.; children: Keith Donald, Peter Gregory. BA summa cum laude, CUNY, 1975; MD, Cornell U., 1979. Diplomate Am. Bd. Ophthalmology, Nat. Bd. Med. Examiners. Resident in gen. surgery U. Va. Hosp., Charlottesville, 1979-80; resident in ophthalmology Cleve. Clinic Found., 1980-83; sr. staff fellow NIH, Bethesda, Md., 1983-85; fellw pediatric ophthalmology Children's Hosp. Nat. Med. Ctr., Washington, 1985-86; staff attending ophthalmologist Mary Imogene Bassett Hosp., Cooperstown, N.Y., 1986-91; clin. asst. prof. ophthalmology Albany (N.Y.) Med. Coll., 1986-91; instr. in clin. ophthalmology Columbia U., N.Y.C., 1986-91; attending ophthalmologist Eye Ctr. South, Dothan, Ala., 1991-92; asst. prof. ophthalmology La. State U. Eye Ctr., New Orleans, 1992—; Contbr. to scientific jours. Recipient Joseph P. Collins Found. scholarship, 1976-79. Fellow Am. Acad. Ophthalmology; mem. Am. Assn. Pediatric Ophthalmology and Strabismus, Assn. for Rsch. in Vison and Ophthalmology, Costenbader Soc., N.Y. State Med. Soc. Office: La State Univ Eye Center 2020 Granier St Ste B New Orleans LA 70112

LUDWIG, KARL DAVID, psychiatrist; b. Johnstown, Pa., June 9, 1930; s. Karl Döring and Kathryn Bride (Palmer) L.; m. Darlene Ann Fisher, July 9, 1959; children: John D., Karl David Jr., Elizabeth Ann Craig, Mark D., Michael D. BA in Biology, St. Vincent Coll., 1952; postgrad., Pa. State U., 1952-53, St. Mary's Sem. & Univ., Balt., 1953-54; MD, U. Pitts., 1960. Intern U.S. Naval Hosp., Phila., 1960-61; resident psychiatry Ea. Pa. Psychiat. Inst., Phila., 1961-64; fellow psychiat. rsch. and teaching Jefferson Med. Coll., Phila., 1964-66; rsch. psychiatrist, dir alcoholism program Friends Hosp., Phila., 1966-73; staff psychiatrist Haverford State Hosp., Haverford, Pa., 1964-71; cons. in psychiatry VA Hosp., Coatesville, Pa., 1968-70; chief outpatient svcs. Northeast Community Mental Health Ctr., Phila., 1973; clin. dir. Northeast Community Mental Health Ctr., 1973-80; supt. Dixmont State Hosp., Sewickley, Pa., 1980-81; dir. inpatient psychiatry Sewickley Valley Hosp., Sewickley, 1981-95; asst. med. dir. Staunton Clin., 1990-95; pres. med. staff Friends Hosp., Phila., 1969-71, Northeast Community Mental Health Ctr., Phila., 1974-75. Pres. Phila. Navy chpt. Res. Officers Assn. of U.S., 1976-77, dept. Pa., 1978-79; bd. trustees Valley Care Assn., Sewickley, 1983-93; bd. dirs. Valley Care Nursing Home, Sewickley, 1983-93. Capt. med. corps USNR, ret. Fellow Am. Psychiat. Assn., Psychiat. Physicians Pa. (pres. 1990-91); mem. AMA, Pitts. Psychiat. soc. (pres. 1985-86), Pa. Med. Soc., Allegheny County Med. Soc., Am. Legion, Assn. Mil. Surgeons U.S., Navy League U.S., Mil. Order World Wars. Republican. Roman Catholic. Home and Office: 2168A Reis Run Rd Pittsburgh PA 15237-1425

LUDWIGS, ULF GERHARD, cardiologist; b. Lidingö, Sweden, Mar. 21, 1958; s. Yngve and Inga-lill Ludwigs; m. Ingrid Almlid, Sept. 4, 1987; children: Mathilda Viktoria, Siri Elisabeth. MD, Carolinian Inst. Stockholm, 1982, PhD, 1996. Asst. physician dept. medicine Sodersjukhuset, Sweden, 1982-84; rsch. fellow U. Ala. at Birmingham, 1984-85; asst. physician Med. Intensive Care Unit, Södersjukhuset, Sweden, 1985-92; sr. physician Med. Intensive Care Unit, Södersjukhuset, 1992—. Contbr. articles to profl. jours. Mem. Swedish Med. Assn, European Soc. Intensive Care Medicine. Mem. Swedish Ch. Office: MIVA, Sodersjukhuset, 118 83 Stockholm Sweden

LUEBBERT, CHRISTIAN, nursing manager, researcher; b. Luebbecke, NRW, Germany, Mar. 26, 1957; s. Heinrich and Elsbeth (Nierste) L.; m. Ulrike Fernkorn, June 30, 1983; children: Marius, Juliane. H.S. diploma, Hardtberg-Gymn., Bonn, Germany, 1977. RN, 1981; cert. anaesthesiology and intensive care, 1983. Nurse Städt Kliniken Bielefeld-Mitte, Germany, 1981; head nurse of anaesthesia Städt Kliniken Bielefeld-Mitte, 1985-92, nursing mgr., 1992—; co-dir. AG autologuous transfusion, Ulm, Germany, 1992-95. Contbr. articles to jours. in field, chpt. to book. Fellow Deutsche Gesellschaft für Fachkrankenpflege, AG autologuous transfusion. Home: AM Alten Dreisch 59, 33605 Bielefeld Germany Office: Staedt Kliniken Bielefeld-Mitte, Teutoburger Str 50, 33604 Bielefeld Germany

LUECKE, ELEANOR VIRGINIA ROHRBACHER, civic volunteer; b. St. Paul, Mar. 10, 1918; d. Adolph and Bertha (Lehman) Rohrbacher; m. Richard William Luecke, Nov. 1, 1941; children: Glenn Richard. Joan Eleanor Ratliff, Ruth Ann. Student, Macalester Coll., St. Paul, 1936-38, St. Paul Bus. U., 1938-40. Author lit. candidate and ballot issues, 1970—; producer TV local issues, 1981—; contbr. articles to profl. jours. Founder, officer, dir., pres. Liaison for Inter-Neighborhood Coop., Okemos, Mich., 1972—; chair countrywide special edn. millage proposals, 1958, 1969; trustee, v.p., pres. Ingham Intermediate Bd. Edn., 1959-83; sec., dir. Tri-County Cmty. Mental Health Bd., Lansing, 1964-72; founder, treas., pres. Concerned Citizens for Meridian Twp., Okemos, 1970-86; mental health rep. Partners of the Americas, Belize, Brit. Honduras, 1971; trustee Capital Area Comprehensive Health Planning, 1973-76; v.p., dir. Assn. Retarded Citizens Greater Lansing, 1973-83; chair, mem. Cmty. Svcs. for Developmentally Disabled Adv. Coun., 1973—; dir., founder, treas. Tacoma Hills Homeowners Assn., Okemos, 1985—; facilitator of mergers Lansing Child Guidance Clinic, Clinton and Easton counties Tri-County Cmty. Mental Health Bd., Lansing Adult Mental Health Clinic, founder. Recipient Greater Lansing Cmty. Svcs. Coun. "Oscar," United Way, 1955, state grant Mich. Devel. Disabilities Coun., Lansing, 1983, Disting. award Mich. Assn. Sch. Bds., Lansing, 1983, Pub. Svc. award C.A.R.E.ing, Okemos, 1988, Earth Angel award WKAR-TV 23, Mich. State U., East Lansing, 1990, Cert. for Cmty. Betterment People for Meridian, Okemos, 1990, 2nd pl. video competition East Lansing/Meridian Twp. Cable Comm. Commn., 1990, 1st pl. award video competition, 1992; Ingham Med. Hosp. Commons Area named in her honor, Lansing, 1971. Mem. Advocacy Orgn. for Patients and Providers (dir. 1994—). Home: 1893 Birchwood Dr Okemos MI 48864-2766

LUEDKE, PATRICIA GEORGIANNE, microbiologist; b. Milw., May 4, 1956; m. Michael Andrew Luedke, July 15, 1978; children: Christopher M., Sean P. BS, Marquette U., 1978, postgrad., 1981-82. Registered med. technologist; registered microbiologist; specialist microbiology. Med. technologist Med.-Surgical Clinic, Milw., 1978-79, Milw. County Hosp., 1979, Fort Atkinson (Wis.) Meml. Hosp., 1979-88, Franciscan Shared Lab., Wauwatosa, Wis., 1988—; cons. Forensic Rsch. Assocs., Oconomowoc, Wis., 1978—. Mem. Am. Soc. Microbiology, Am. Soc. Clin. Pathologists, N.Y. Acad. Scis. Home: 739 Elizabeth St Oconomowoc WI 53066-3703

LUEPKER, RUSSELL VINCENT, epidemiology educator; b. Chgo., Oct. 1, 1942; s. Fred Joeseph and Anita Louise (Thornton) L.; m. Ellen Louise Thompson, Dec. 22, 1966; children: Ian, Carl. BA, Grinnell Coll., 1964; MD with distinction, U. Rochester, 1969; MS, Harvard U., 1976; PhD (hon.), U. Lund, Sweden, 1996. Intern U. Calif., San Diego, 1969-70; resident Peter Bent Brigham Hosp., Boston, 1973-74; cardiology fellow Peter Bent Brigham Hosp./Med., Boston, 1974-76; asst. prof. divsn. epidemiology med. lab. physiol. hygiene U. Minn., Mpls., 1976-80, assoc. prof., 1980-87, prof. divsn. epidemiology and medicine, 1987—, dir. divsn. epidemiology, 1991—; cons. NIH, Bethesda, Md., 1980—, U. So. Calif., L.A., 1985—, Armed Forces Epidemiology Bd., 1993—; vis. prof. U. Goteborg, Sweden, 1986, Ninewells Med. Sch., Dundee, Scotland, 1995. Lt. comdr. USPHS, 1970-73. Harvard U. fellow, 1974-76, Bush Leadership fellow, 1990; recipient Prize for Med. Rsch. Am. Coll. Chest Physicians, 1970, Nat. Rsch. Svc. award Nat. Heart, Lung and Blood Inst., Bethesda, 1975-77, Disting. Alumni award Grinnell Coll., 1989. Fellow ACP, Am. Coll. Cardiology, Am. Heart Assn. Coun. on Epidemiology (chmn. 1992-94), Am. Heart Assn. Sci. Sessions (program com. chair 1995—), Am. Coll. Epidemiology; mem. Delta Omega Soc. (Nat. Merit award 1988). Office: Univ Minn Sch Pub Health Div Epidemiology 1300 S 2nd St Ste 300 Minneapolis MN 55454-1015

LUEPNITZ, ROY ROBERT, psychologist, consultant, small business owner, entrepreneur; b. Ft. McClellan, Ala., June 3, 1955; s. Carl A. and Helen Elizabeth (Brown) L.; m. Mary Kinloch Bush, Dec. 18, 1981; 1 child, Noel. BA cum laude, Southwestern U., 1979; MS in Counseling Psychology, U. So. Miss., 1981; PhD in Counseling Psychology, Tex. A & M U., 1985. Diplomate Am. Bd. Froensic Examiners; cert. health svc. provider in psychology, Tex.; cert. travel agt.; registered treator of sex offenders; bd. cert. forensic examiner. Intern, vol. Austin (Tex.) State Hosp., 1978-79; counselor Univ. Counseling Psychology Clinic, Hattiesburg, Miss., 1980; master level psychologist Pine Belt Mental Health Ctr., Hattiesburg, 1981, Tex. Rehab. Commn., Bryan, 1981-82; grad. tchr. Tex. A & M Univ.. College Station, 1982-83; psychologist Brazos Valley MHMR Authority, Bryan, 1983-84; mental health dir. Brazos Valley MHMR Authority, Bryan, 1984-86; psychologist Tom Edwards, PhD, Bryan, 1987; pvt. practice psychologist College Station, 1987—; cons. Dept. Human Svcs., Bryan, 1987—, Brazos Valley MHRA, Bryan, 1987—, Sandstone Psychiatry, College Station, 1990—, HCA Greenleaf Hosp., College Station, 1991—, various chs., schs., govt. agys., 1983—; Noel's Wonderful World of Travel, Village Square Office Park. Sec. Miss. APGA, 1979-81; active sex offender's assessment/treatment program. Mem. Assn. Treatment of Sexual Abuses, Am. Assn. Christian Counselors, Nat. Register Health Svc. Providers in Psychology, Tex. Psychol. Assn., Brazos Valley Psychol. Assn. Republican. Methodist. Home: 1200 Noel Ct College Station TX 77845-3803 Office: Brazos Valley Christian Counseling 2748 Longmire Dr College Station TX 77845-5424

LUFT, HAROLD S., health economist; b. Newark, N.J., Jan. 6, 1947; s. George and Kay (Grossman) L.; m. Lorraine Ellin Levinson, May 24, 1970; children: Shira Levinson, Jana Levinson. A.B., Harvard U., 1968, AM, 1970, Ph.D., 1973. Systems analyst, rsch. asst. Harvard Transport Rsch., Cambridge, Mass., 1965-68; systems analyst Harvard Econ. Rsch. Project, Cambridge, Mass., 1968-72; instr. econs. Tufts U., Medford, Mass., 1972-73; postdoctoral fellow Harvard Ctr. Community Health, Boston, 1972-73; asst. prof. health econs. Stanford U., Calif., 1973-78; prof. health econs., acting dir. Inst. Health Policy Studies, U. Calif., San Francisco, 1978—; cons. Applied Mgmt. Scis., Silver Spring, Md., 1979—, Robert Wood Johnson Found., Princeton, N.J., 1982—; study sect. Nat. Ctr. Health Svcs., Rockville, Md., 1981-83; mem. coun. Agy. for Health Care Policy and Rsch. Author: Poverty and Health, 1978, Health Maintenance Organizations, 1981, 2d edit., 1988, (with Deborah Garnick, David mark, Stephen McPhee) Hospital Volume, Physician Volume, and Patient Outcomes, 1990, HMOs and the Elderly, 1994; contbr. chpts. to books, articles to profl. jours. Advisor, fin. planning com. Mid-Peninsula Health Service, Palo Alto, Calif., 1984—. NSF fellow, Carnegie Found. fellow, Grad. Prize fellow Harvard U., 1968-72, fellow Ctr. for Advanced Study in Behavioral Scis., 1988-89. Mem. Am. Pub. Health Assn., Am. Econ. Assn., Inst. Medicine, Western Econ. Assn., Assn. for Health Svcs. Rsch. (bd. dirs.). Home: 1020 Ramona St Palo Alto CA 94301-2443 Office: U Calif Inst for Health Policy Studies 1388 Sutter St Fl 11 San Francisco CA 94109-5427

LUFTMAN, MARTIN JASON, plastic and reconstructive surgeon; b. Boston, June 13, 1950. BA, Brown U., Providence, 1972; MD, U. Cin., 1976. Diplomate Am. Bd. Plastic Surgery. Resident N.C. Bapt. Hosp., Bowman Gray Sch. Medicine, 1976-79, Med. Coll. Ohio, Toledo, 1979-81; pvt. practice Lexington, Ky., 1981—; chief surgery Ctrl. Bapt. Hosp., Lexington, 1993-94, chief dept. plastic surgery, 1990—; asst. prof. U. Ky. Med. Ctr., Lexington, 1982—. Recipient award for excellence Cin. Surg. Soc., 1976. Fellow ACS; mem. Am. Soc. Plastic and Reconstructive Surgeons, Southeastern Soc. Plastic and Reconstructive Surgeons, Am. Soc. Aesthetic Plastic Surgery, Ky. Soc. Plastic and Reconstructive Surgeons (pres. 1986). Home: 3336 Lyon Dr Lexington KY 40513 Offce: 1401 Harrodsburg Rd B360 Lexington KY 40504

LUI, FRED Y.H., nephrologist; b. China, May 4, 1954; came to U.S., 1962; BS, Stanford U., 1976, MD, 1980. Pvt. practice Burlingame, Calif., 1985—; asst. clin. prof. U. Calif.-San Francisco Med. Sch., 1987—; med. dir. renal svcs. Miles-Peninsula Hosps., San Mateo, Calif., 1988—; chief dept. medicine Chinese Hosp., San Francisco, 1993—; v.p. bd. dirs. Transpacific Renal Network, Larkspur, Calif., 1994—. Fellow ACP; mem. Nat. Kidney Found. (rsch. fellowship grant 1984), Internat. Soc. Nephrology, Calif. Med. Assn., Renal Physicians Assn., Phi Beta Kappa. Office: 1828 El Camino Real # 805 Burlingame CA 94010

LUJAN, HENRY JOHN, surgeon; b. Cochabamba, Bolovia, Jan. 16, 1965; came to U.S., 1965; s. Enrique Rudolfo Lujan and Virginia Montaño; m. Renee Cespedes, June 29, 1996. BA in Biology, U. Chgo., 1986; MD, U. Ill., Chgo., 1990. Diplomate Am. Bd. Surgery. Resident dept. surgery Finch U. Health Sci./Chgo. Med. Sch. at Mt. Sinai Hosp., 1990-96; fellow colon and rectal surgery Orlando (Fla.) Regional Med. Ctr., 1996—. Mem. Bolivian Am. Med. Assn. Roman Catholic. Home: 1445 N State Pkwy # 2604 Chicago IL 60610

LUKAS, ELSA VICTORIA, radiobiologist, radiobiochemist; b. Baden nr. Vienna, Austria, Feb. 28, 1927; d. Johann and Victoria (Hauer) L.; Degree for High Sch. Tchrs., U. Vienna, 1952, Ph.D., 1955; DSc in Physics, Biology and Physiology (hon.) Marquis Giuseppe Scicluna Internat. U., 1987; PhD in Physics (hon.), Albert Einstein Internat. Acad. Found., 1990. Researcher, Max Planck Inst. Biophysics, Frankfurt/Main, Federal Republic Germany, 1959-64, Path. Inst. Justus Liebig U., Giessen, Fed. Republic Germany, 1961-64, Oak Ridge Nat. Lab., U. Radiation Biology, U. Tenn., Knoxville, 1964-67; high sch. tchr., country insp. schs., Vienna, 1967—; research. Author numerous publs. on biochem. effects of ionizing radiation in living cells, especially in their nucleic acids. Recipient Dr. J. Kowarschick award, 1957, Dr. Karl Luick award 1957, Theodor Kö rner prize 1960, Alexander von Humboldt award, 1961, Vibert Douglas award Internat. Fedn. Univ. Women, 1962, medal of honor Am. Biog. Inst., 1987, Golden Acad. award, 1991, Profl. of Yr. nomination, 1991, Cert. of Merit as Foremost Woman of the 20th Century Internat. Biog. Centre, Cambridge, Eng., 1987; named hon. citizen of State of Tenn., 1965, Woman of Yr. Am. Biog. Inst., 1990; Fulbright Hays scholar, 1964; inducted to Am. Biog. Inst's. 5,000 Personalities of the World Hall of Fame, N.C., 1989. Mem. Biophys. Soc., Radiation Research Soc., Soc. German Scientists and Physicians, Austrian Biochem. Soc., Am. Inst. Biol. Scis., Soc. Parapsychology, German Bot. Soc., Soc. German Biologists, Gregor Mendel Soc., Soc. Austrian Chemists, Univ. Assn. Alma Mater Rudolphina. Roman Catholic. Home: 60 Elisabethstrasse, Baden 2500, Austria

LUKASIK, JOHN PETER, JR., therapist, counselor, school psychologist; b. Scranton, Pa., June 19, 1947; s. John Peter and Mary Ann (Minich) L.; 1 child, Thomas Volk. BA in Mgmt., Park Coll., 1980; MA in Counseling, Webster U., 1982; MS in Counselor Edn., U. Scranton, 1990; cert. Sch.

Psychologist, Marywood Coll., 1993, postgrad., 1996. Enlisted U.S. Army, 1968, advanced through grades to chief warrant officer, ret., 1988; athletic dir. Cath. Youth Ctr., Scranton, 1989-91; psychotherapist Children's Svc. Ctr., Wilkes Barre, Pa., 1990-91; therapist, counselor Specialized Counseling Svcs., Scranton, 1989-90; sch. psychologist, guidance counselor Bishop Hannan High Sch., Scranton, 1991—. Mem. sch. psychology adv. bd. Marywood Coll., Scranton. Mem. APA, ASCD, NASP, ACA. Republican. Roman Catholic. Home: 101 Bengar Dr Scranton PA 18505-3421 Office: Bishop Hannan H S 330 Wyoming Ave Scranton PA 18503-1224

LUKASZCZYK, JOHN JAMES, surgeon; b. Bethlehem, Pa., July 15, 1958; s. Thomas Andrew and Dorothy Helena (Matyas) L.; m. Margaret Mary Barnacle, Nov. 26, 1988; children: John, Rebecca. BS, Villanova (Pa.) U., 1980; MD, Hahnemann U., Phila., 1984. Diplomate Am. Bd. Surgery. Resident in surgery Hahnemann U., Phila., 1984-90, clin. instr. surgery, 1989-95; staff surgeon St. Luke's Hosp., Bethelehem, 1990—, Muhlenberg Hosp. Ctr., Bethelehem, 1990—. Mem. Northampton County Med. Soc. (bd. dirs. 1996—). Office: Surgical Assocs Bethlehem 701 Ostrum St # 602 Bethlehem PA 18015-1153

LUKE, WILLIAM J., osteopath; b. Alameda, Calif., July 1, 1934; s. William J. and Rowena (Will) L.; widowed; 1 child, William J. BS, Loma Linda U., 1957; DO, Kansas City Coll. Osteopathy, 1971. Osteopath West Thomas Family Med. Ctr., Phoenix, 1972—. Office: West Thomas Family Med Ctr 4660 W Thomas Rd Phoenix AZ 85031

LUKEN, MARTIN GERARD, neurosurgeon; b. Chgo., Nov. 2, 1947; married; 3 children. BS cum laude, Georgetown U., 1969; MD, Columbia U., 1973. Diplomate Am. Bd. Neurol. Surgery. Intern. asst. resident Osler Med. Svc., John Hopkins Hosp., Balt., 1973-75; asst. resident dept. surgery U. Ill. Hosp., 1975-76; asst., chief resident dept. neurosurgery Neurol. Inst. N.Y., 1976-80; attending neurosurgeon dept. neurosurgery Michael Reese Hosp. and Med. Ctr., Chgo., 1980—, Ingalls Meml. Hosp., 1984—, Little Company of Mary Hosp., Chgo., 1990—, St. James Hosp. and Med. Ctr., 1993—, Children's Meml. Hosp., 1994—; cons. neurosurgeon South Chicago Cmty. Hosp., 1980—, South Shore Cmty. Hosp., 1980—; mem. courtesy staff dept. neurosurgery Mercy Hosp. and Med. Ctr., 1987—; mem.-at-large med. bd. Humana/Michael Reese Hosp., 1991-94; presenter in field. Contbr. articles to profl. publs. Rsch. grantee NSR, 1968. Mem. ACS, Am. Assn. Neurol. Surgeons, Congress Neurol. Surgeons (ann. resident award 1978), Chgo. Med. Soc. (bd. govs. S.E. br. 1990—), Phi Beta Kappa. Office: 55 E Washington St Ste 2700 Chicago IL 60602

LULL, ROBERT JOHN, nuclear medicine physician, educator; b. Buffalo, Aug. 23, 1940; s. Joseph J. and Margaret L.; m. Dorothy Lee Murtha, Feb. 2, 1965 (div. 1987); children: Jonathan C., Benjamin D. AB in Biochemistry, Canisius Coll., 1962; MD, Union U., 1966. Diplomate Nat. Bd. Med. Examiners, Am. Bd. Internal Medicine, Am. Bd. Nuclear Medicine; lic. Calif., Tex., N.Y. Commd. U.S. Army, 1966, advanced through ranks to col., 1980, ret., 1990; rotating intern Brooke Army Med. Ctr., San Antonio, Tex., 1966-67; resident internal medicine Brooke Army Med. Ctr., San Antonio, 1967-70; fellow nuclear medicine Wm. Beaumont Army Med. Ctr., El Paso, Tex., 1970-72; chief nuclear med. svc. Brooke Army Med. Ctr., San Antonio, 1972-76, Letterman Army Med. Ctr., San Francisco, 1976-90; assoc. dir. nuclear medicine dept. San Francisco Gen. Hosp., 1990-91; clin. prof. radiology and lab. medicine U. Calif. San Francisco, 1990—, dir. nuclear medicine residency, 1991—; dir. nuclear medicine dept. San Francisco Gen. Hosp., 1991—; bd. dirs. Calif. Radioactive Materials Mgmt. Forum, Sacramento, Calif., 1986—; cons., mem. adv. com. FDA, Washington, 1991—. Contbr. 30 peer rev. articles med. jours., chpts. to 7 med. books; reviewer for 8 med. jours.; editor (audio visual med. series) AIMS program, 1987-89. Nuclear medicine cons. Surgeon Gen., U.S. Army, Washington, 1977-90; senate appointee Citizen's Adv. Com. on Nuclear Emergencies, Calif., 1989-92; nuclear cons. to bd. San Francisco Med. Soc., 1994—; commr. Calif. Southwestern Low Level Radioactive Waste Compact, 1995—; bd. dirs. Nat. Assn. Cancer Patients, 1995—. Recipient Boss of Yr. award No. Calif. chpt. Am. Bus. Women's Assn., 1979, Legion of Merit award U.S. Army, Presidio of San Francisco, 1990. Fellow Am. Coll. Nuclear Physicians (bd. dirs. 1988—, pres. Calif. chpt. 1990-93, nat. pres. 1992-93, Pres. award 1995), Am. Coll. Physicians; mem. Am. Coll. Radiology (com. mem. 1990-95), Radiol. Soc. N. Am., Soc. Nuclear Medicine (pres. Calif. chpt. 1986-87, Silver medal 1972-83. Office: San Francisco Gen Hosp Nuclear Medicine Dept NH 1001 Portrero Ave Rm G100 San Francisco CA 94110

LULLI, BONNIE JEAN, medical group administrator; b. Cin., Jan. 1, 1943; d. Richard Roland and Mary Elizabeth (Kinzer) Lang; m. Arden Darryl Allen, Jan. 30, 1972 (div. Jan. 1988); 1 child, John C.; m. Gordon Agusto Lulli, Sept. 2, 1989. BA in Bus., Calif. State U., Northridge, 1965. Office mgr. Dr. Richard Clancy, Glendale, Calif., 1963-68; bus. mgr. Dr. Vivagene Loop, Glendale, 1969-75; bus. and office mgr. Dr. Robert B. Gold, Santa Ana, Calif., 1975-87; gen. mgr. So. Calif. Assoc. Plastic Surgeons-Expert Med. Mgmt. Corp., Anaheim, 1987-89; bus. adminstr. Meml. Cardiology Med. Group, Inc., Long Beach, Calif., 1990—; owner Physicians' Med. Ins. Billing Svc., Huntington Beach, Calif., 1975-90; mem. physicians' office mgrs.' task force Long Beach Meml. Med. Ctr., 1994—. Sec. Fountain Valley (Calif.) Youth Baseball, 1980-86; Stephen min., class instr. Roman Cath. Ch., Huntington Beach. Mem. Med. Group Mgmt. Assn., Profl. Assn. Health Care Office Mgrs. Home: 8771 Burlcrest Dr Huntington Beach CA 92646 Office: Meml Cardiol Med Group Inc 2898 Linden Ste 120 Long Beach CA 90806-1554

LUM, ADRIENNE ANN, optometrist; b. Leland, Miss., Dec. 25, 1959; d. Eugene and Sue Jean (Wong) L.; m. David A. McDonald, Dec. 29, 1990. BA, U. Miss., 1981; OD, U. Houston, 1985. Optometrist Azar Eye Clinic, New Orleans, 1986, Vision Plaza, New Orleans, 1987-96. Mem. Am. Optometric Assn., La. State Optometric Assn. Office: Vision Plaza 9391 Cortana Pl Baton Rouge LA 70815

LUMB, WILLIAM VALJEAN, veterinarian; b. Sioux City, Iowa, Nov. 26, 1921; m. Lilly Carlson, 1949; 1 child, John W. DVM, Kans. State U., 1943; MS, Tex. A&M U., 1953; PhD in Vet. Medicine, U. Minn., 1957. Intern, resident Angell Meml. Animal Hosp., Boston, 1946-48; from instr. to assoc. prof. medicine and surgery Tex. A&M U., 1949-52; asst. prof. clin. surgery Colo. State U., 1954-58; assoc. prof. surgery and medicine Mich. State U., 1958-60; assoc. prof. medicine Coll. Vet. Medicine, Colo. State U., Ft. Collins, 1960-63, dir. surg. lab., 1963-79, prof. surgery, 1963-81, emeritus prof., 1981—. Mem. AVMA, AAAS, Am. Coll. Vet. Anesthesiologists, Am. Coll. Vet. Surgeons, Nat. Acad. Sci., N.Y. Acad. Sci., Am. Assn. Vet. Clinicians, Am. Coll. Vet. Surgery. Office: Vet Teaching Hosp Colo State U Fort Collins CO 80521*

LUMBIGANON, PISAKE, obstetrician/gynecologist; b. Khon Kaen, Thailand, Aug. 28, 1953; s. Narong and Tasanee (Thirasas) L.; m. Pagakrong Teptanavatana, Jan. 4, 1979; children: Disajee, Supanat. MD, Ramathibodi, Bangkok, Thailand, 1976; MS, U. Pa., Phila., 1991. Diplomate Bd. Ob-Gyn. Thailand. Intern Ramathibodi Hosp., Bangkok, 1976-77, resident, 1977-80; lectr. Khon Kaen U., 1980-82, asst. prof., 1982-87, assoc. prof., 1987—, dept. chmn., 1987-91, asst. dean rsch., 1989-92; cons. WHO, Rangoon, 1984, Geneva, 1987, 91, 92, 93, 94, 95, 96, Johns Hopkins Programme of Internat. Edn. for Gynecology and Obstetrics, Cairo, 1991, Jarkatar, 1992, Nairobi, Kenya, 1993. Mem. editl. bd. British Med. Jour. Postdoctoral fellowship Rockefeller Found., 1982-83, rsch. grant, 1984, WHO, 1984, 90, IDRC, 1986, Mother Care, 1995. Mem. Internat. Epidemiol. Assn., Thai Med. Assn., Thai Coll. Ob-Gyn. Buddhist. Home: 6/3 Klangmuang Rd, Khon Kaen 40000, Thailand Office: Khon Kaen U, 123 Mitraparb Rd, Khon Kaen 40002, Thailand

LUMENG, LAWRENCE, physician, educator; b. Manila, Aug. 10, 1939; came to U.S., 1958; s. Ming and Lucia (Lim) Lu; m. Pauline Lumeng, Nov. 26, 1966; children: Carey, Emily. AB, Ind. U., 1960, MD, 1964, MS, 1969. Intern U. Chgo., 1964-65; resident Ind. U. Hosps., Indpls., 1965-67, fellow, 1967-69, asst. prof. Sch. of Medicine, 1971-73, assoc. prof. Sch. of Medicine, 1974-79, prof. Sch. of Medicine, 1979—, dir. div. gastroenterology and hepatology Sch. of Medeine, 1984—; chief gastroenterology sect. VA Med. Ctr., Indpls., 1979—; mem. merit rev. bd. VA. Cen. Office, Washington, 1981-84; mem. alcohol biomed. res. rev. com. NIAAA, Washington, 1982-86; mem. grant rev. panel USDA, Washington, 1985—. Contbr. articles to profl. jours. Maj. U.S. Army, 1969-71. Fellow ACP; mem. Am. Soc. Clin. Investigation, Am. Soc. Biol. Chemists, Rsch. Soc. on Alcoholism (treas. 1985-87, sec. 1987-89), Am. Gastroenterological Assn., Am. Assn. for the Study of Liver Diseases. Office: Ind U Med Ctr 975 W Walnut St Indianapolis IN 46202-5181*

LUMIA, FRANCIS JAMES, internist; b. Trenton, N.J., Apr. 24, 1941; s. Joseph and Rose (Amodio) L.; m. Carolyn King, May 2, 1970; children: Margaret E., Joseph J. BA, U. Chgo., 1963, MD, 1967. Diplomate Am. Bd. Internal Medicine, Am. Bd. Quality Assurance and Utilization Rev. Intern and resident in medicine George Washington U. Hosp., Washington, 1967-70, fellow in cardiology, 1970-72; attending physician Northport VAH, L.I., N.Y., 1972-77; asst. prof. medicine SUNY, Stony Brook, 1972-77; attending physician Deborah Heart and Lung Ctr., Browns Mills, N.J., 1977—, co-dir. sect. of Nac medicine, 1990—, asst. chair cardiology, 1991—; physician advisor Peer Rev. Orgn. of N.J., East Brunswick, N.J., 1985—, sanctions com., 1994—; governing coun. Med. Soc. of N.J., Lawrenceville, 1987—. Contbr. articles to profl. jours. Recipient Washington Spl. Clin. fellow Heart Assn., 1971-72. Fellow ACP, Am. Coll. Cardiology, Acad. of Medicine of N.J., Am. Coll. Med. Quality, Am. Coll. of Angiology; mem. Am. Coll. Physician Execs. Roman Catholic. Office: Deborah Heart & Lung Ctr 200 Trenton Browns Mills NJ 08015

LUMPKIN, JOHN ROBERT, public health physician, state official; b. Chgo., July 28, 1951; s. Frank and Beatrice (Shapiro) L.; m. Mary S. Blanks, Jan. 28, 1984; children: Alia, John R. Jr. BS, Northwestern U., Evanston, Ill., 1973; MD, Northwestern U., Chgo., 1974; MPH, U. Ill., Chgo., 1985. Diplomate Am. Bd. Emergency Medicine. Intern U. Chgo. Hosps., 1975, resident anesthesiology, 1976-78, vice chmn. emergency medicine, 1981-84; asst. prof. U. Chgo., 1978-84; asst. dir. emergency medicine South Chgo. Hosp., 1984-85; staff physician St. Mary of Nazareth Hosp., Chgo., 1985; assoc. dir. Ill. Dept. Pub. Health, Springfield and Chgo., 1985-90, dir., 1990—; cons. Egyptian Ministry Health, Cairo, 1986-90; mem. sec.'s adv. com. on injury control Ctrs. for Dis. Control, Atlanta, 1989-93. Fellow Am. Coll. Emergency Physicians (bd. dirs. 1987-93); mem. Soc. Tchrs. Emergency Medicine (pres. 1981-82), Ill. Coll. Emergency Physicians (pres. 1982-83, Bill B. Smiley award 1986), Assn. State and Territorial Health Ofcls. (pres. 1995-96). Office: Ill Dept Pub Health 100 W Randolph St Ste 6-600 Chicago IL 60601-3219

LUMSDEN, ROBERT DOUGLAS, plant pathologist; b. Washington, June 21, 1938; s. George Napier and Mary Louise (Shropshire) L.; m. Valerie Theresa Brook, June 11, 1960; children: Douglas Robert, Thomas Brook. BS, N.C. State U., 1961, MS, 1963; PhD, Cornell U., 1966. Rsch. leader Biocontrol Plant Diseases Lab. USDA/ARS, Beltsville, Md., 1966—. Co-editor: Biotechnology of Fungi, 1989, Pest Management: Biologically Based Technologies, 1993; patentee in field. NDEA fellow Cornell U., 1963, NIH fellow U.S. HHS, 1965. Fellow Am. Phytopathol. Soc.; mem. Phi Kappa Phi, Sigma Xi. Office: USDA Beltsville Agrl Rsch Ctr Beltsville MD 20705

LUNA, GREGORY KEVIN, surgeon; b. Oakridge, Oreg., Sept. 26, 1953. AS cum laude, North Idaho Coll., Coeur d'Alene,, 1972; BS summa cum laude, U. Idaho, 1974; MD, U. Colo., 1978; MPH, U. Wash., 1987. Diplomate Am. Bd. Surgery, qualifications insurg. critical care and vascular surgery; lic. physician, Wash., Ont.; cert. ATLS, ATLS instr. Surg. resident U. Wash. Allifiated Hosps., Seattle, 1978-80, 81-84; preventive medicine resident U. Wash., Seattle, 1987, acting instr. dept. surgery, 1984-87, asst. prof., 1987-89, clin. asst. prof., 1991—; vascular fellow U. Ottawa, Ont., Can., 1988-89, asst. prof. dept. surgery, 1989-90; emergency rm. physician Valley Gen. Hosp., Renton, Wash., 1980-81; dir. emergency rm. surg. svcs. Harborview Med. Ctr., Seattle, 1984-89; dir. ICU Valley Med. Ctr., Renton, Wash., 1991—, blood svcs. com., emergency svcs. com., ICU com., 1990—; mem. organ procurement adv. com. N.W. Kidney Ctr., 1988-89; epidemiological cons. Mont. Critical Illness and Trauma Found., 1988—; presenter various orgns., meetings, confs. Contbr. articles to profl. jours., chpts. to books. Fellow ACS (state com. on trauma, vice chmn. edn. 1988—); mem. AAAS, Am. Trauma Soc., King County Med. Soc., Assn. Acad. Surgery, Henry M. Harkins Surg. Soc., Seattle Surg. Soc., North Pacific Surg. Assn., North Pacific Vascular Soc., Phi Kappa Phi. Home: 104 W 5th Ave Spokane WA 99204-2480 Office: U Wash Dept Surgery Seattle WA 99204

LUNAN, CHARLES BURNETT, obstetrician, gynecologist; b. London, Great Britain, Sept. 28, 1941; s. Andrew Burnett and Jean Clarke (Orr) L.; m. Helen Russell Ferrie, Mar. 6, 1973; children: Kirsteen, Robert, Donald. MBChB, U. Glasgow, Scotland, 1965, MD, 1977; MRCOG, Royal Coll. of Ob/Gyn., U.K., 1970. FRCS, FRCOG. Lectr. ob/gyn U. Aberdeen, Scotland, 1973-75; sr. lectr. U Nairobi, Kenya, 1975-77; cons. in maternal and child health WHO, Bangladesh, 1984-85; cons. obstetrician Greater Glasgow Health Bd., Scotland, 1977—; cons. Overseas Devel. Adminstrn., Bangladesh, 1990. Contbg. author: History of Rottenrow, 1984, Sterilization Counselling, 1985, Infection in Labour, 1990. Mem. Royal Medico-Chirurgical Soc. Glasgow (treas. 1982-90, pres. 1991-92). Home: 1 Moncrieff Ave Lenzie, G66 4NL Glasgow Scotland Office: Royal Maternity Hosp, Rottenrow, G4 ONA Glasgow Scotland

LUND, DORIS HIBBS, retired dietitian; b. Des Moines, Nov. 10, 1923; d. Loyal Burchard and Catharine Mae (McClymond) Hibbs; m. Richard Bodholdt Lund, Nov. 9, 1946; children: Laurel Anne, Richard Douglas, Kristi Jane Lund Lozier. Student, Duchesne Coll., Omaha, 1941-42; BS, Iowa State U., 1946; postgrad., Grand View Coll., Des Moines, 1965; MS, Iowa State U., 1968. Registered dietitian, lic. dietitian. Clk. Russell Stover Candies, Omaha, 1940-42; chemist Martin Bomber Plant, Omaha, 1942-43; dietitian Grand Lake (Colo.) Lodge, 1946; tailoring instr. Ottumwa Pub. Schs., 1952-53; cookery instr. Des Moines Pub. Schs., 1958-62; dietitian Calvin Manor, Des Moines, 1963; home economist Am. Wool Coun./Am. Lamb Coun., Denver, 1963-65, The Merchandising Group of N.Y., 1965-68, Thomas Wolff, Pub. Rels., 1968-70; home economist weekly TV program Iowa Power Co., 1968-70; cons. in child nutrition programs Iowa Dept. Edn., Des Moines, 1970-95; ret. Nutritioneering, Ltd., 1995; Mem. Iowa Home Economists in Bus. (pres. 1962-63), PEO, Pi Beta Phi (Iowa Gamma chpt. pres. 1945-46). Pres. Callanan Jr. H.S. PTA, 1964, Roosevelt H.S. PTA, 1966; pres., mem. Ctrl. Presbyn. Mariners, Des Moines; ruling elder, clk. of session Ctrl. Presbyn. Session, Des Moines, 1972-78; bd. dirs. Ctrl. Found., 1996; amb. Friendship Force Internat., 1982—. Duchesne Coll. 4 yr. scholar. Mem. Iowa Home Economists in Bus. (pres. 1962-63), PEO, Pi Beta Phi (pres. 1945-46). Republican. Home: 105 34th St Des Moines IA 50312-4526

LUND, SUSAN ELLEN, nursing consultant; b. Dayton, Ohio, Dec. 3, 1947; d. Joseph Edwin and Eva Lucille (Hollingsworth) Weiss. Diploma St. Patrick Sch. Nursing, Missoula, Mont., 1968; BA in Liberal Studies, Linfield Coll., 1976, MS in Edn. Portland State U., 1992. RN, Mont., Oreg. Staff nurse St. Patrick Hosp., Missoula, Mont., 1965, Providence Hosp., Portland, Oreg., 1968-78, asst. head nurse, 1970-71, head nurse dialysis, 1971-75; nurse assoc. Dr. Fredrick Orether, Portland, 1971-75; owner, Sam Lund Med./Legal Rsch. and Investigation, Portland, 1978—; nurse cons. to ins. co. and lawyers, Portland; presenter in field. CPR instr. Am. Heart Assn., Portland, 1979-88, affiliate faculty, 1986-88. Mem. City Council of Maywood Park, Oreg., pres., 1980-86; bd. dirs. Guardianship Advocacy Protective Services, 1986—. Democrat. Office: 8040 NE Sandy Blvd Ste 300 Portland OR 97213-7100

LUNDBERG, GEORGE DAVID, II, medical editor, pathologist; b. Pensacola, Fla., Mar. 21, 1933; s. George David and Esther Louise (Johnson) L.; m. Nancy Ware Sharp, Aug. 18, 1956 (div.); children: George David III, Charles William, Carol Jean; m. Patricia Blacklidge Lorimer, Mar. 6, 1983; children: Christopher Leif, Melinda Suzanne. AA, North Park Coll., Chgo., 1950; BS, U. Ala., Tuscaloosa, 1952; MS, Baylor U., Waco, Tex., 1963; MD, Med. Coll. Ala., Birmingham, 1957; ScD (hon.), SUNY, Syracuse, 1988, Thomas Jefferson U., 1993, U. Ala., Birmingham, 1994, Med. Coll. Ohio, 1995. Intern Tripler Hosp., Hawaii; resident Brooke Hosp., San Antonio; assoc. prof. pathology U. So. Calif., Los Angeles, 1967-72, prof., 1972-77; assoc. dir. labs. Los Angeles County-U. So. Calif. Med. Ctr., 1968-77; prof., chmn. dept. pathology U. Calif.-Davis, Sacramento, 1977-82; v.p. scientific info., editor Jour. AMA, Chgo., 1982—, editor in chief scientific publ., 1991-95; editor in chief AMA Sci. Info. and Multimedia, Chgo., 1995—; vis. prof. U. London, 1976, Lund U., Sweden, 1976; prof. clin. pathology Northwestern U., Chgo., 1982—; adj. prof. health policy Harvard U., Boston, 1993—; vis. prof. pathology, 1994-96. Author, editor: Managing the Patient Focused Laboratory, 1975, Using the Clinical Laboratory in Medical Decision Making, 1983, 51 Landmark Articles in Medicine, 1984, AIDS From the Beginning, 1986, Caring the the Uninsured and Underinsured, 1991, Violence, 1992; contbr. articles to profl. jours. Served to lt. col. M.C., U.S. Army, 1956-67. Fellow Am. Soc. Clin. Pathologists (past pres.), Am. Acad. Forensic Sci.; mem. N.Y. Acad. Scis., Inst. Medicine, Alpha Omega Alpha. Democrat. Episcopalian. Office: JAMA 515 N State St Chicago IL 60610-4320

LUNDBLAD, ROGER LAUREN, research director; b. San Francisco, Oct. 31, 1939; s. Lauren Alfred and Doris Ruth (Peterson) L.; m. Susan Hawly Taylor, Oct. 15, 1966 (div. 1985); children: Christina Susan, Cynthia Karin. BSc, Pacific Luth. U., 1961; PhD, U. Wash., 1965. Rsch. assoc. U. Wash., Seattle, 1965-66, Rockefeller U., N.Y.C., 1966-68; asst. prof. U. N.C., Chapel Hill, 1968-71, assoc. prof., 1971-77, prof. pathology and biochemistry, 1977-91; adj. prof., 1991—; dir. sci. tech. devel. Baxter-Biotech, Duarte, Calif., 1991—; vis. scientist Hyland div. Baxter Healthcare, Glendale, Calif., 1988-89. Author: Chemical Reagents for Protein Modification, 1984, 2d edit., 1990; editor: Chemistry and Biology of Thrombin, 1977, Chemistry and Biology of Heparin, 1980, Techniques in Protein Modification, 1994; editor-in-chief: Biotechnology and Applied Biochemistry, 1996—; contbr. articles to profl. jours. Recipient Career Achievement award U. N.C., 1986. Mem. Am. Soc. Biochem. Molecular Biology, Am. Soc. Microbiology, Am. Heart Assn., Sigma Xi. Office: Baxter Biotech Hyland Divsn 1720 Flower Ave Duarte CA 91010-2923

LUNDE, DONALD THEODORE, physician; b. Milw., Mar. 2, 1937; m. Marilynn Krick; children: Montgomery, Christopher, Glenn, Evan, Bret. BA with distinction, Stanford U., 1958, MA in Psychology, 1964, MD, 1966. Diplomate Nat. Bd. Med. Examiners. Ward psychologist Palo Alto (Calif.) VA Hosp., 1965-66, chief resident in psychiatry, 1969-70, assoc. chief tng. and research sect., 1970-72, acting chief tng. and research sect., 1971-72; intern in internal medicine Palo Alto/Stanford Hosp., 1966-67; resident in psychiatry Stanford (Calif.) U. Sch. Medicine, 1967-69, instr. psychiatry, 1969-70, asst. prof. psychiatry, 1970-75, dir. med. sch. edn. in psychiatry, 1971-74, clin. assoc. prof. psychiatry, 1978-89, clin. prof. psychiatry, 1989—; lectr. Law Sch. Stanford U., 1971-81; staff physician Atascadero (Calif.) State Hosp., 1968. Author books and articles in field. Served with USN, 1958-61. Fellow Am. Psychiat. Assn., Am. Coll. Forensic Psychiatry; mem. No. Calif. Psychiat. Soc., Phi Beta Kappa, Alpha Omega Alpha. Office: Stanford U 900 Welch Rd Ste 400 Palo Alto CA 94304-1804

LUNDQUIST, DANA R., health insurance executive; b. Mpls., Sept. 12, 1941; s. R. Dana and Mary Jane (Norton) L.; children: Brenda A., Sheila R. BA, Valparaiso U., 1963; postgrad., U. Hawaii, 1963-64, U. Colo., 1963; MBA, U. Chgo., 1966. Adminstrv. asst. U. Chgo. Hosps. and Clinics, 1966-67, asst. supt., 1967-68, asst. dir., 1968-70; officer, bd. dirs. affiliates Hamot Health Systems, Inc., Erie, Pa., 1970-92, pres. parent co., 1981-92, cons. to bd., 1992—; cons. Blue Cross Western Pa., 1992-93, sr. v.p.,1993—; lectr. grad. program in hosp. adminstrn. U. Chgo., 1967-70; mem. Erie County Hosp. Coun., 1978-92, pres., 1982; bd. dirs. Hosp. Coun. Western Pa., 1978-92, vice chmn.; exec. com. Pa. Coun. Teaching Hosps., 1986-90; adv. coun. risk mgmt. Pa. Hosp. Ins. Co., 1982-90, bd. dirs. Vol. Hosps. Am. of Pa., 1985-92, chmn. bd.; bd. visitors The Behrend Coll., Pa. State U., 1990-92; bd. dirs. Pa. Med. Coll., 1991-92, Hardware Hawaii, 1989—. Mem. Erie Conf. on Community Devel., 1981-92, bd. dirs., 1988-92; bd. dirs. N.W. Pa. Buy Right Coun., 1986-92, United Way Erie County, 1983-92; mem. pres.'s coun. Villa Maria Coll., Erie, 1981-90, bd. incorporators Gannon U., Erie, 1981-92; mem. governing bd. St. Paul's Luth. Ch., Erie, 1973-78, v.p., 1974-78; mem. Erie Down Town Coalition Steering Com., 1990-92, chmn., 1991-92, numerous other activities. Mem. Am. Coll. Healthcare Execs. (former regents adv. coun. Pa.); mem. Am. Hosp. Assn. (governing coun. sect. met. hosps. 1987, alt. ho. of dels. 1988), Hosp. Assn. Pa. (polit. action com. 1981-92), Pa. C. of C., U. Chgo. Hosp. Alumni Assn. (exec. com. 1967-70, 87-92, sec.-treas. 1988, pres. 1990-91), Downtown Athletic Club, Rotary. Home: PO Box 22130 Pittsburgh PA 15222-0130 Office: Blue Cross Western PA 5th Ave Pl Ste 3012 Pittsburgh PA 15222-3099

LUNDQUIST, PER BIRGER, physician, medical illustrator, artist, surgeon; b. Stockholm, Jan. 20, 1945; s. Birger Richard Emanuel and Karin Margareta Beata (Bernstone) L.; m. Margareta Ulvas, June 7, 1967 (div. 1975); children: Karolina, Jonas Petter; m. Maria Cecilia Mahlberg, Oct. 21, 1989; children: Sara, Richard. BSc AAM, U. Toronto, 1971; MD, Karolinska Inst., Stockholm, 1978; student, Art Students League, 1967-68; postgrad., Ariz. Heart Inst., 1993-94. Gen. vascular surgery residency Karolinska Hosp., Stockholm, 1978-83; handsurgery Sabbatsbergs Hosp., 1982-83; fellow in cardiovascular surgery Baylor Med. Ctr., Dallas, 1983-84; family practice tng. and rsch. Akademiska Hosp., Uppsala, Sweden, 1988-90; family, surg. practice Stureplan & Östermalm, Stockholm, 1991-95; author, illustrator, lectr. Med. Communications PBL, Stockholm, 1991—; med. illustrator dept. Art as Applied to Medicine, Toronto, 1970, Audio Visual Svcs. Regional Hosp., Linkoping, Sweden, 1971—; rschr. endoluminal grafts and endovascular surgery. Author, artist: Svenska Dagbladet, 1989, Allmanmedicin, 1990, Cardiovascular Training Program, 1990-91, Human Interferon Production Purpose, 1984; illustrator: The Five Senses, 1972-73, Human Blood Lipids, 1990; exhibits Vastervik, 1987, Stockholm, 1988, Helsingborg, 1989, Uppsala, 1994. Mem. N.Y. Acad. Scis., Am. Heart Assn. (coun. arteriosclerosis, epidemiology, vascular surgery), Swedish Med. Assn., Swedish Assn. Family Physicians, Stockholm Med. Assn., Internat. Soc. Endovascular Surgery. Home: 31 Roslagsgatan, 113 55 Stockholm Sweden Office: Karolinska Hosp Dept Surg, Divsn Vascular Surgery, 171 76 Stockholm Sweden also: Östermalms Med Office, Humlegårdsgatan 4, 114 46 Stockholm Sweden

LUNDY, JANET CECILE, histotechnologist; b. Laverty, Okla., May 20, 1942; d. Cecil LeRoy and Grace (Arnold) Parish; student pub. schs., Chickasha, Okla.; m. J. W. Lundy, Oct. 20, 1963. Histology technician Presbyn. Hosp., Oklahoma City, 1960-68; supr. histotech. Okla. Health Scis. Ctr., Oklahoma City, 1968-71; supr. histotech. Hillcrest Osteo. Hosp., Oklahoma City, 1972-75; supr., histotechnologist Bapt. Med. Center Okla., Oklahoma City, 1975-83; founder, operator Precision Histology Lab Inc., 1983—; mem. adj. faculty Oscar Rose Jr. Coll. (now Rose State Coll.), 1978-83; founding officer Post Burn Support Group Okla., Inc., 1989. Mem. steering com. Linwood Pl. Neighborhood Assn., 1980-82. Mem. Okla. Soc. Histotechnologists, Nat. Soc. Histotech., Am. Soc. Clin. Pathologists (assoc.). Mem. Ch. Nazarene. Home: 3132 NW 22nd St Oklahoma City OK 73107-3018

LUNGSTROM, LEON GEORGE, retired biology educator, entomologist; b. Kans., July 22, 1915; s. George and Jennie (Ekstrom) L.; m. Linda Kay Greenwalt, Nov. 20, 1965; children: Michael Harlan, Laura Christine. BS, Bethany Coll., Lindsborg, Kans., 1940; MS, Kans. State U., 1946, PhD, 1950. Entomologist USPHS, Kans., Mo., 1945, Kansas City, Kans., Mo., 1949-52; instr. biology Bethany Coll., 1946-47, prof., 1952-81, Milfred Riddle McKeown disting. prof. sci., 1979, prof. emeritus, 1981—; team leader on mosquito rsch. HEW, Tex., Ark., La., Ga., Tenn., 1964; cons. Lindsborg Mosquito Control Com., 1989-90. Author: History of Natural Science and Mathematics at Bethany College, 1990; contbr. articles to Trans. Kans. Acad. Sci. Mem. McPherson County Hist. Soc., McPherson, Kans., 1961, also past pres.; bd. dirs. McPherson County Old Mill Mus., Lindsborg, 1976—, co-dir., 1980-84. With Med. Svc. Corps, AUS, 1942-43. Faculty fellow NSF, Stanford U., 1959-60, grantee Ariz. State U., 1962, U. Okla., 1965,Tulane U., 1970. Democrat. Lutheran. Home: 518 E Lincoln St Lindsborg KS 67456-2427

LUNN, JOSEPH SCOTT, physician, educator; b. Oneonta, N.Y., July 11, 1931; s. William H. and Dorothy Elizabeth (Hanks) L.; m. Janet Lenore Novko, Aug. 16, 1952 (div. 1978); children: Gregory Scott, Daniel Joseph, Susan Elizabeth; m. Marilyn Stevens Chew, Jan. 21, 1983 (dec. 1992); m. Ramona Carter, Jan. 30, 1993. BA, Conn. Wesleyan U., 1953; MD, SUNY

Health Scis. Ctr., 1958. Diplomate Am. Bd. Internal Medicine. Intern, then resident in medicine SUNY Health Scis. Ctr., Syracuse, 1958-62; surgeon USPHS, Atlanta, 1963-64, fellow in infectious diseases, 1964-65; attending physician Mary Imogene Bassett Hosp., Cooperstown, N.Y., 1969-80, physician-in-chief, 1974-80; clin. prof. Coll. Physicians & Surgeons Columbia U., N.Y.C., 1979-80; prof. Med. Coll. of Ga., Augusta, 1980—. Contbr. articles to profl. jours. Fellow ACP; mem. APHA, Assn. for Health Scis. Rsch., Physicians for a Nat. Health Plan, Alpha Omega Alpha. Home: 5167 Huntfield Rd Evans GA 30809-9713 Office: Med Coll of Ga Dept Of Medicine Augusta GA 30912

LUNSFORD, THOMAS RAY, orthotist, mechanical engineer; b. Clayton, N.Mex., Oct. 31, 1940; s. Roy McCall and Ola Oran (Jackson) L.; m. Brenda Rae Quortrup, Feb. 12, 1966. BSEE, U. Tex., El Paso, 1962; MS in Nuclear Engring., UCLA, 1969. Bd. cert. orthotics Am. Bd. for Cert. in Orthotics and Prosthetics. Sr. engr. N.Am. Aviation, Inc., L.A., 1963-69; engring. mgr. Nat. Cash Register, Hawthorne, Calif., 1969-76; chief orthotist Rancho Los Amigos Med. Ctr., L.A., 1976-93, The Inst. for Rehab. and Rsch., Houston, 1993-96; pres. Lone Star Orthotics, Inc., Houston, 1996—; clin. dir. orthotics and prosthetics Calif. State U. Dominguez Hill, Carson, Calif., 1978-93; dir. orthotic rsch. Rehab. Engring. Ctr., Downey, Calif., 1990-93; asst. prof. Baylor Coll. Medicine, Houston, 1993—; pres. Kit Sys., Houston, 1980—, Am. Acad. Orthotists and Prosthetists, Alexandria, Va., 1993; commr., exec. bd. Commn. on Accreditation of Allied Health Profs., Chgo., 1994—; chmn. long range orthotics cert. exam. Am. Bd. for Cert. Orthotics and Prosthetics, Alexandria, 1995—. Author: Strength & Materials in Orthotics and Prosthetics, 1996; rsch. editor Jour. Prosthetics and Orthotics, 1987—. Active Toastmasters Internat., Hawthorne, Calif., 1974-85. Recipient Article of the Yr. awards Am. Acad. Orthotics and Prosthetics, 1987, 93, 94, 95; grantee Nat. Inst. for Disability and Rehab. Rsch., Bethesda, Md., 1990-93, NASA, Houston, 1995-98. Home: 39 Halfmoon Ct The Woodlands TX 77380 Office: Lone Star Orthotics Inc 8399-L Ameda Rd Houston TX 77054

LUNTZ, MAURICE HAROLD, ophthalmologist; b. Capetown, South Africa, July 27, 1930; came to U.S. 1978; s. Montague Bernard and Sarah Marian (Friedman) L.; m. Angela June Myerson, June 21, 1956; children—Melvyn Howard, Caryn Susan, David Sean. M.B., Ch.B., Capetown U., 1952; M.D., U. Witwatersrand, Johannesburg, S. Africa, 1964. Diplomate Am. Bd. Ophthalmology. Lectr. ophthalmology Oxford U. (Eng.), 1960-62; prof., chmn. ophthalmology Witwatersrand U., 1964-78; dir. ophthalmology Beth Israel Med. Ctr., N.Y.C., 1978-89; chief glaucoma svc. Manhattan Eye, Ear & Throat Hosp., 1989—, pres., bd. surgeon dirs., 1992-95; prof. Mt. Sinai Sch. Medicine, N.Y.C., 1978—; cons. Merck, Sharp & Dohme, N.J., 1980-82. Author: Uveitis, 1983; Glaucoma Surgery, 1984 second edition, 1995; editorial bd. Highlight Ophthalmology, Panama, 1970—; contbr. articles to profl. jours.; producer movie Glaucoma Surveys, 1970. Fellow Royal Coll. Surgeons (Edinburgh). Mem. Academia Ophthalmologica Internationalis. Office: 121 E 60th St New York NY 10022-1109

LUPIANI, DONALD ANTHONY, psychologist; b. N.Y.C., June 7, 1946; s. Louis and Josephine (Boccia) L.; m. Linda Moyik, June 20, 1970; 1 child, Jennifer. BA, Iona Coll., 1968; MA, Columbia U., 1971, PhD, 1973; postdoctoral, Behavior Therapy Inst., White Plains, N.Y., 1976. Lic. psychologist, N.Y. Clin. assoc. Columbia U., N.Y.C., 1974-85, Fordham U., Bronx, N.Y., 1979-81; dir. psychology and spl. edn. svcs. Riverdale Country Sch., Bronx, 1973-87; chief psychologist Franciscan Order of Priests, N.Y.C., 1983—; pvt. practice Yonkers, N.Y., 1975—; dir. spl. svcs. Riverdale Country Sch., Bronx., 1973-87; bd. dirs. St. Ursula Learning Ctr., Mt. Vernon, N.Y. Contbr. articles to profl. jours. Bd. dirs., mem. The St. Ursula Learning Ctr. Fellow Am. Orthopsychiat. Assn., Am. Coll. Psychology, Am. Acad. Sch. Psychology; mem. APA, N.Y. State Psychol. Assn., Westchester County Psychol. Assn. (chmn. ethics com. 1980-87). Roman Catholic. Home and Office: 227 Mile Square Rd Yonkers NY 10701-5369

LUPULESCU, AUREL PETER, medical educator, researcher, physician; b. Manastiur, Banat, Romania, Jan. 1, 1923; came to U.S., 1967, naturalized, 1973; s. Peter Vichentie and Maria Ann (Dragan) L. MD magna cum laude, Sch. Medicine, Bucharest, Romania, 1950; MS in Endocrinology, U. Bucharest, 1965; PhD in Biology, Faculty of Scis., U. Windsor, Ont., Can. Diplomate Am. Bd. Internal Medicine. Chief Lab. Investigations, Inst. Endocrinology, Bucharest, 1950-67; research assoc. SUNY Downstate Med. Ctr., 1968-69; asst. prof. medicine Wayne State U., 1969-72; assoc. prof., 1973—; vis. prof. Inst. Med. Pathology, Rome, 1967; cons. VA Hosp., Allen Park, Mich., 1971-73. Author: Steroid Hormones, 1958, Advances in Endocrinology and Metabolism, 1962, Experimental Pathophysiology of Thyroid Gland, 1963, Ultrastructure of Thyroid Gland, 1968, Hormones and Carcinogenesis, 1983, Hormones and Vitamins in Cancer Treatment, 1990; reviewer for various sci. jours.; contbr. chpts., numerous articles to profl. publs.; research on hormones and tumor biology; studies regarding role of hormones and vitamins in carcinogenesis. Fellow Fedn. Am. Socs. for Exptl. Biology; mem. Electron Microscopy Soc. Am., Soc. for Investigative Dermatology, N.Y. Acad. Sci., AMA (physician's recognition award 1983, 86), Am. Soc. Cell Biology, Soc. Exptl. Biology and Medicine, AAAS. Republican. Home: 21480 Mahon Dr Southfield MI 48075-7525 Office: Wayne State U Sch Medicine 540 E Canfield St Detroit MI 48201-1928

LURIA, ZELLA HURWITZ, psychology educator; b. N.Y.C., Feb. 18, 1924; d. Hyman Hurwitz and Dora (Garbarsky) H.; m. Salvador Edward Luria, Apr. 18, 1945; 1 child, Daniel David. BA, Bklyn., 1944; MA, Ind. U., 1947, PhD, 1951. lic. clin. psychologist, Mass. Ford Found. postdoctoral fellow U. Ill., Urbana, 1951-53, Russell Sage found. fellow, 1953-56, clin. researcher, 1954-58; asst. prof. psychology Tufts U., Medford, Mass., 1958-62, assoc. prof., 1962-70, prof., 1970—; psychiatry lectr. Mass. Gen. Hosp., Boston, 1970-79; vis. scholar Stanford U., 1977, 83; vis. prof. UCLA, 1992, 94, U. Mich., 1993. Sr. author: Psychology of Human Sexuality, 1979, Human Sexuality, 1987. Postdoctoral fellow USPHS, Paris, 1963-64, Bunting fellow Radcliffe Coll., 1989-90; Mellon Found. Faculty grantee Wellesley Coll., 1979-80. Mem. Tufts U. Am. Assn. Univ. Profs. (pres. 1986-87). Office: Tufts Univ Dept Of Psychology Medford MA 02155

LURIE, ABRAHAM, social worker, educator; b. N.Y.C., Oct. 18, 1917; s. Isidore and Celia (Kulak) L.; m. Nettie Manheim, June 14, 1948; children: Susan, Debra. BS, CCNY, 1941; ML, Ohio State U., 1943; MS, Columbia U., 1948; PhD, NYU, 1964. Psychiat. social worker Mannhattan State Hosp., N.Y.C., 1947-48, Project Follow-Up, Bellevue Hosp., N.Y.C., 1948-50; dir. social work Hillside Hosp., Queens, N.Y., 1950-73, L.I. Jewish Hillside Hosp., Queens, 1973-84; prof. Adelphi U., Garden City, N.Y., 1984-89; prof. social work SUNY, Stony Brook, 1989—; cons. VA Northport (N.Y.) Hosp., 1970—, Nassau County Mental Health Assn., Mineola, N.Y., 1984—. Editor: Social Work in Mental Health, 1976; co-editor: Social Work with Group Health, 1982, Social Work Administration, 1985. Bd. dirs. Nassau County Mental Health Assn., 1984-87; now bd. dirs. Variety Pre-Schoolers, Syosset, N.Y. Named Social Worker of Yr. Israel Cummings Found., 1966; recipient Ida M. Cannon award Am. Hosp. Assn., 1978, Hy Wiener Lecture award Soc. Hosp. Social Workers, 1985, Sy Silverberg award L.I. Jewish/Hillside Hosp., 1986; Brookdale Found. exch. fellow, 1978. Fellow Am. Orthopsychiat. Assn.; mem. Nat. Assn. Social Worker, Acad. Cert. Social Workers, Am. Assn. Marriage and Family Therapy, Am. Assn. Psychiat. Social Work (nat. v.p. 1955-56), Soc. Hosp. Social Work (nat. pres. 1978-79), Nat. Acad. Practice (Disting. Practitioner). Office: Health Scis Ctr Suny Sch Social Welfar Stony Brook NY 11794

LURIE, SOL DAVID, physician; b. Johannesburg, Transvaal, Republic of South Africa, May 23, 1928; came to U.S., 1977; s. Mendel Isaac and Anne Ray (Gishen) L.; m. Ruth Levy, Oct. 22, 1961; children: Karen, Rhona, Wendy, Lesley, Melanie. Diploma in Pharmacy, Witwatersrand Coll., Johannesburg, 1948; MD, U. Witwatersrand, Johannesburg, 1956; postgrad studies in Mediation, Dispute Mediation Svcs., Dallas, 1994. Diplomate Am. Bd. Family Practice; mem. Faculty of Gen. Practice (Republic of South Africa). Residency U. of Witwatersrand Johannesburg Gen. Hosp., Johannesburg, 1957-58; pvt. practice Richardson, Tex., 1977—; mem. staff Humana Hosp. Med. City, Dallas, chmn. dept. medicine, 1981; pres. Jewish Family Svc., Dallas, 1989-91; active Humana Med. Ctr., Dallas, Richardson Med. Ctr. Named Vol. of Yr., Gov. Tex., 1989. Fellow Am. Acad. Family Practice. Office: 2085 Promenade Ctr Richardson TX 75080-5479

LUSCH, CHARLES JACK, physician; b. Lehighton, Pa., Feb. 15, 1936; s. Charles Norman and Loretta (Gaumer) L.; m. Carole Faye Eckart, Aug. 17, 1957; children: Marjorie, Susan, Stephen, Robert. AB in Biology magna cum laude, Lafayette Coll., Easton, Pa., 1957; MD, Temple U., 1961. Diplomate in med. oncology, hematology, internal medicine, forensic medicine; diplomate Am. Bd. Forensic Medicine. Pres. Berks Hematology-Oncology Assocs., Reading, Pa., 1968—; chief sect. of med. oncology & hematology Reading Hosp. & Med. Ctr., Reading, 1970—; dir. Pa. State Hemophilia Ctr., Reading Hosp. & Med. Ctr., 1973—; v.p. Lusch Motor Parts, Lehighton, Pa., 1975—; chief sect. med. oncology & hematology Community Gen. Hosp., Reading, 1980—; asst. chief medicine Reading Hosp. and Med. Ctr., 1986—; med. dir. Pocono Internat. Raceway, 1980-85; chmn. institutional rev. bd. Reading Hosp. and Med. Ctr., 1986—, dir. continuing med. edn., 1987—; med. dir. Berks County Hospice, Berks County Vis. Nurse Assn., Reading, 1987—; dir. oncology svcs. Reading Hosp. and Med. Ctr., 1990—; med. adv. com. Pa. Blue Shield, Camp Hill, Pa., 1987—; bd. dirs. Berks Home Health Car, Reading Cancer Ctr., Reading Hosp.; malpractice cons. Med. Protective Ins. Co., Ft. Wayne, Ind., 1985—; cons. in hematology and oncology Pottsville (Pa.) Hosp. and Good Samaritan Hosp., 1975—; clin. asst. prof. medicine Pa. Med. Sch., 1984—, Pa. State Med. Sch., 1981—, Temple U. Med. Sch., clin. assoc. prof. 1990; sr. clin. instr. Mahnemann U. Med. Sch., 1968—; prin. investigator Ea. Coop Oncology Group, 1975-90, Nat. Surg. Adj. & Breast Project, 1986—. Contbr. articles to profl. jours.; editor The Med. Record (regional med. jour.), 1970-71. Advisor Future Physicians Am., Reading, 1965; bd. dirs. Berks County unit Am. Cancer Soc., Reading, 1968-78, Keystone Cmty. Blood Bank, Reading, 1970-80; adv. com. The Women's Ctr., Reading Hosp., 1987-88; mem. bd. divsn. ch. soc. Evang. Luth. Ch. Am., Chgo.; pres. ch. coun. Atonement Luth. Ch., Wyomissing, Pa. Lt. comdr. USPHS, 1965-67. Fellow ACP; mem. Pa. Soc. Hematology-Oncology (sec.-treas. 1986-87), Am. Soc. Clin. Oncology, Am. Soc. Hematology, Am. Fedn. Clin. Rsch., Acad. Hospice Physicians (publs. com. 1989—), U.S. Amateur Ballroom Dance Assn. (past pres. Reading chpt.), Sports Car Club Am.. Phi Beta Kappa, Alpha Omega Alpha. Republican. Lutheran. Home: 1617 Meadowlark Rd Wyomissing PA 19611 Office: Berks County Oncology Assoc 301 S 7th Ave Reading PA 19611-1410

LUSK, JUANITA ROSANNE, telemetry, cardiac nurse; b. Ft. Worth, Apr. 21, 1960; d. Charles Edward Karges and Nada Faye (Ray) Serna; m. Bruce Wayne Smith, Sept. 1, 1978 (div. July 1987); children: Alan Smith, Aaron Smith; m. Robert Donald Lusk, March 3, 1988; children: Ty Lusk, Linsday Lusk, Jonathan Lusk, Camern Lusk. AAS, Tex. A&M U., Denison, Tex., 1993; student, Tex. A & M Univ. RN, Tex.; cert. nurse clinician. Staff, aide Home Hospice, Sherman, Tex., 1987-88; staff RN, relief charge nurse Wilson N. Jones Hosp., Sherman, 1993-94, St. Joseph's Hosp., Bryan, Tex., 1994-95; med. ICU/stepdown charge nurse Wilson N. Jones Hosp., 1995-96; nurse clinician Cardiac Solutions, Dallas, 1996—; vol./disaster nurse ARC, Denison, 1991—. Leader Boy Scouts Am., 1989-92, Girl Scouts U.S., 1988-90. Republican. Baptist. Home: Rte 2 Box 506 Whitesboro TX 76273

LUSMAN, PAUL ALAN, allergist; b. Bklyn., Aug. 19, 1940; s. Sol and Lena (Ades) L.; m. Barbara Phyllis Helfenbein, Mar. 23, 1969; children: Joel, Debra, Rebecca. AB, Columbia Coll., 1961; MD, Albert Einstein Coll. Medicine, 1965. Lic. M.D., N.Y. Pvt. practice specializing in allergy-immunology Port Jefferson, N.Y., 1972-96; clin. asst. prof. medicine SUNY, Stony Brook, 1980—; allergy cons. St. John's Hosp., Smithtown, N.Y., 1976—, Brookhaven Meml. Hosp., Patchogue, N.Y., 1975—; attending physician John T. Mather Meml. Hosp., Port Jefferson, 1973—, St. Charles Hosp., Port Jefferson, 1973—, Good Samaritan Hosp, Bay Shore, N.Y., 1985—. Lt. comdr. USNR, 1968-70. Fellow Am. Acad. Asthma, Allergy and Immunology, Am. Coll., Asthma, Allergy and Immunology, Am. Acad. Pediatrics. Office: Paul A Lusman MD PC 120 N Country Rd Port Jefferson NY 11777

LUSTERMAN, DON-DAVID, psychologist; b. Bklyn., Sept. 7, 1932; s. Edward Aaron and Helen Fleurette (Greenwald) L.; m. Judith Grace Singer, July 26, 1953; children: Eliezer, Noam, Gavi. MusB, U. Mich., 1954, MusM, 1955; MS in Edn., Hofstra U., 1966; PhD, Yeshiva U., 1973. Lic. psychologist, N.Y.; diplomate Am. Bd. Profl. Psychology Family. Instr. music Hebrew Union Coll., N.Y.C., 1959-62; tng. supr. fed. project, vocat. cons. Hofstra U., Hempstead, N.Y., 1965; intern VA, Bklyn. & Bronx, 1968-70; intern Roosevelt Hosp., N.Y.C., 1969-70, vis. family therapist, 1970-71; asst. prof. edn. psychology Hofstra U., Hempstead, 1971-77, ad. prof., coord. family counseling program, 1977-82; pvt. practice Baldwin, N.Y., 1974—; exec. dir. Am. Bd. Family Psychology, Baldwin, N.Y., 1982-85; cons. in field. Co-author: The Teacher as Learning Facilitator, 1979; co-editor: Integrating Family Therapy: Handbook of Family Psychology & Systems Theory, 1995; cons. in field. Voter registration worker Congress of Racial Equality, Riverhead, N.Y., 1962-63; mem. Baldwin Human Rights Commn., 1962-65, Physicians for Social Responsibility, Washington, 1985—. Fellow Am. Psychol. Assn., 1987, Am. Assn. Marriage and Family Therapy, 1988. Fellow Am. Psychol. Assn., Am. Orthopsychiatric Assn., Am. Assn. Marital and Family Therapy, Acad. Family Psychology ; mem. Internat. Family Therapy Assn., Am. Family Therapy Assn. (charter), N.Y. Psychol. Assn., N.Y. Assn. Marital and Family Therapy, Nassau County Psychol. Assn., Israel Assn. Marital and Family Therapy. Jewish. Home and Office: 856 Mckinley St Baldwin NY 11510-4648

LUSTGARTEN, JACQUELINE SIEGEL, ophthalmologist; b. N.Y.C., Oct. 21, 1946; m. Eli S. Lustgarten, Apr. 10, 1970; children: Ephram, Jonathan. BA in Math., Queens Coll., 1967; MA in Math, Boston U., 1969; MD, Rutgers Med. Sch., 1977. Diplomate Am. Bd. Ophthalmology. Instr. math. Boston U., 1969-71; rsch. asst. in anesthesia Mass. Gen. Hosp., Boston, 1974; intern N.W. Meml. Hosp., Chgo., 1977-78, resident in ophthalmology, 1978-81; resident pediat. ophthalmology Children's Meml. Hosp., Chgo., 1980-81; fellow in glaucoma Mt. Sinai Sch. Medicine, N.Y.C., 1981-82, from clin. instr. to assoc. clin. prof., 1982-84, assoc. clin. prof., 1984—; clin. asst. Mt. Sinai Hosp., N.Y.C., 1981-82, asst. attending, 1982-87, assoc. attending, 1987—, ophthalmology resident selection com., 1984-88, quality assurance com., 1988-92; attending Elmhurst Gen. Hosp., N.Y.C., 1982-85, Hackensack (N.J.) Med. Ctr., 1983—, Pascack Valley (N.J.) Hosp., 1984—; cons. Bronx VA Hosp., New York, 1981—; clin. rsch. coord Schering Plough Corp, Bloomfield, N.J., 1972-73; biostatistician, computer programmer Harvard U./Mass. Gen. Hosp., Boston, 1968-72; presenter in field. Contbr. articles to profl. pubs. Fellow Am. Acad. Ophthalmology (new tech. task force 1991-92); mem. AMA, Assn. Rsch. Vision Ophthalmology, Am. med. Women's Assn., Acad. Medicine N.J., Bergen County Med. Soc. (cons. judicial com. 1991-93), N.J. Acad. Ophthalmology and Otolaryngology, Women in Ophthalmology (bd. dirs. 1991—, sec., treas. 1992—), Am. Glaucoma Soc. Home: 130 Kinderkamack Rd Ste 302 River Edge NJ 07661

LUSTIBER, LAURIE ANN, speech pathologist; b. Boston, Jan. 23, 1956; d. Charles Joseph and Marguerite Elizabeth (Murphy) Ferguson; m. Peter Michael Lustiber, Nov. 8, 1980; 1 child, Gregory Charles. AB cum laude, Harvard Coll., 1978; MS, Boston U., 1980. Cert. speech pathologist. Speech pathologist New England Rehab. Hosp., Woburn, Mass., 1980-83, asst. dir. speech pathology, 1983-85, dir. speech pathology, 1985; supr. speech pathology Burke Rehab. Hosp., White Plains, N.Y., 1985-86; mgr. speech pathology Providence Hosp., Cin., 1986-88; v.p. phys. medicine and rehab. Franciscan Health Sys. Cin., 1988-89; pvt. practice Monroe, Conn., 1990—. Mem. Am. Speech and Hearing Assn., Conn. Assn. Rehab. Facilities, Ohio Assn. Rehab. Facilities (bd. mem. 1989). Democrat. Roman Catholic. Home and Office: 182 Meadows End Rd Monroe CT 06468

LUSTMAN, PATRICK J., psychiatrist. Recipient Am. Diabetes Clin. Rsch. grantee, 1996. Office: Washington U Sch Med 660 S Euclid Ave Saint Louis MO 63110-1010

LUSZKI, WALTER ALOISE, clinical psychologist; b. Detroit; s. Peter A. and Elizabeth (Kisiel) L.; m. Margaret B. Barron, Mar. 15, 1950. BA, U. Mich., 1937, MA, 1949; EdD, U. Ga., 1964. Commd. 2d lt. U.S. Army, 1939, advanced through grades to lt. col., 1960; sr. psychologist U. Mich. Med. Ctr., Ann Arbor, 1964-66; chief psychologist Coastal Carolina Rehab. Ctr., Charleston, S.C., 1966-69; clin. psychologist Charleston, 1969—. Author: Psych Yourself to Better Tennis, 1971, How to Test Your Dog's IQ, 1980, How to Test Your Cat's IQ, 1981, Winning Tennis Through Mental Toughness, 1982, A Rape of Justice, 1991, Join the Army: 20 Adventurous Army Years, 1991; contbr. articles to profl. jours. Mem. Am. Psychol. Assn., S.C. Psychol. Assn., S.E. Psychology Assn., Charleston Area Psychology Assn. Unitarian. Home: 502 E Indian Ave Folly Beach SC 29439 Office: Dr. Walter A Luszki 165 Maple St Charleston SC 29403-3348

LUTHER, GEORGE AUBREY, orthopedic surgeon; b. Keokuk, Iowa, Dec. 11, 1933; s. George August and Leda (Galbraith) L.; m. Dorothy Gould Luther, Aug. 18, 1956; children: Melinda, George Bradley. AB, Cen Meth. U., 1955; MD, Vanderbilt U., 1959. Diplomate Am. Bd. Orthopaedic Surgery. Intern Vanderbilt U. Hosp., Nashville, 1959-60, resident, 1961-64, instr., 1964; resident St. Louis City Hosp., 1960-61; pres. St. Louis Orthopedic Inst., 1965—; pres. med. staff St. Joseph Hosp., St. Louis, 1982-83; trustee St. Joseph Hosp., 1981-84. Contbr. article profl. jours. Served to maj. U.S. Army, 1967-69. Fellow Am. Acad. Orthopedic Surgery, ACS (admissions com. 1982—); mem. AMA, Mo. Orthopedic Soc. (v.p. 1985-86, pres. 1986-87), St. Louis Metro. Med. Soc. (counselor 1983-85), Vanderbilt Orthopedic Soc. (pres. 1981-82), Tenn. Soc. of St. Louis. Republican. Methodist. Club: Bellerive Country. Home: 177 Ladue Oaks Ct Saint Louis MO 63141-8128

LUTHER, JOHN STAFFORD, biology educator, consultant; b. L.A., April 5, 1943; s. John Andrew and Marcia (Stafford) L.; divorced; 1 son, David. BA, Beloit (Wis.) Coll., 1965; MA, Calif. State Coll., Hayward, 1968. Mem. faculty dept. biology Merritt Coll., Oakland, Calif., 1968-70; mem. faculty Coll. of Alameda (Calif.), 1970—, chmn. sci. and math. div., 1973-75; cons. Environ. Impacts Reports, 1972—; leader natural history trips, 1978—. Mem. Oakland (Calif.) Mus. Assn., 1972—; tchr. natural sci. docent program Oakland Mus., 1987—; mem. Ednl. Use Adv. Com., East Bay Regional Park Dist., 1981—. Mem. Western Field Ornithologists (pres. 1978-81, dir. 1975-91), Calif. Bird Records Com. (sec. 1976-81), Sierra Club, Am. Birding Assn., Golden Gate Audubon Soc., Nature Conservancy, Point Reyes Bird Obs., Alameda County Breeding Bird Atlas (bd. dirs.), Oakland Zoo-East Bay Zool. Soc., Calif. Acad. Scis. Contbr. articles to Western Birds; mem. editorial bd. Western Birds. Home: 6511 Exeter Dr Oakland CA 94611-1641 Office: Coll of Alameda 555 Atlantic Ave Alameda CA 94501

LUTHER, RONALD B., medical products executive; b. Brookfield, Mo., Apr. 25, 1932; s. Alberta (Straub) Luther. BS, U. Mo., 1954. V.p. Lucky Tiger, Kansas City, Mo., 1963-67; gen. mgr. McGaws Labs, Ga. and, Mex., 1967-74; pres. Wm. Harvey Rsch. CRB and Cardiovascular, Tustin, Calif., 1974-78, Luther Med. Products, Inc., Tustin, Calif., 1978—. patentee in field. Capt. USMC, 1954-63; col. Confederate Air Force, 1980—. Mem. Masons, Shriners. Republican. Home: 530 King Rd Newport Beach CA 92663 Office: Luther Med Products Inc 14332 Chambers Rd Tustin CA 92680

LUTHER, THOMAS WILLIAM, physician; b. Milw., Feb. 27, 1925; s. Elmer Charles and Ida Martha (Sohrweide) L.; children: Brian Thomas, Siri Karen Luther Witt. BS, U. Wis., 1947, MD, 1950. Diplomat Am. Bd. Dermatology. Bd. dirs. Tri-Cmtys. Crime Reduction Coalition, Meenah-Menasha, Wis., 1994-96. Lt. USN, 1943-54. Fellow Am. Acad. Dermatology; mem. AMA, Wis. Med. Soc., Wis. Dermatologic Soc., Appleton Rotary. Home: 1936 Palisades Dr Appleton WI 54915

LUTTON, LEWIS MONTFORT, biology educator, researcher; b. Cin., July 14, 1945; s. Edwin Scott and Virginia (Melchior) L.; m. Marianne C. Hendow, Nov. 26, 1982; children: Wolf M., Bram V. BA, Swarthmore Coll., 1968; PhD, Cornell U., 1976. Instr. Allegheny Coll., Meadville, Pa., 1974-75, asst. prof., 1975-80; with Mercyhurst Coll., Erie, Pa., 1980-83, assoc. prof., 1983-92, prof., 1992—; rsch. assoc. Brooks Air Force Base Armstrong Labs., San Antonio, Tex., 1990-91; chmn. sci. divsn. Mercyhurst Coll., 1986-90, chmn. honors program, 1982-90, chmn. biology dept., 1992—, premed. advisor, 1981-96. Contbr. articles to profl. jours. Mem. AAAS, Nat. Assn. Biology Tchrs., Soc. for Neursci., Soc. for Biological Rhythms, Phi Kappa Phi, Sigma Xi. Unitarian. Home: 4706 Upland Dr Erie PA 16509-2248 Office: Mercyhurst Coll Glenwood Hls Erie PA 16504

LUTWAK, NANCY RUTH, physician; b. N.Y.C., Jan. 16, 1950; d. Edgar and Rose (Tucker) Selwyn; m. Erwin Lutwak, Mar. 7, 1968. BA, Bklyn. Coll., 1971; MD, Albert Einstein Coll. Medicine, 1984. Intern Montefiore Med. Ctr., Bronx, N.Y., 1984-85; resident Montefiore Med. Ctr., Staten Island U. Hosp., 1985-89; fellow Westchester County Med. Ctr., 1989-91; attending physician Cath. Med. Ctr., Elmhurst, N.Y., 1991—; physician St. Johns Queens Hosp., Elmhurst, N.Y., 1991—. Mem. Am. Coll. Emergency Physicians, Physicians for a Violence Free Soc., Coalition Physicians Against Family Violence.

LUTZ, LAWRENCE JOSEPH, family practice physician; b. Detroit, Dec. 16, 1949; s. Stephen A. and Eva B. (Groh) L.; m. Joan Regedanz, Dec. 27 (div. 1986); m. Ruthanne Rocki Ramsey, Apr. 29, 1989; 1 child, Alex Joseph. BS in Computer Sci., U. Mich., 1972; MD, Wayne State U., 1976; MSPH, U. Utah, 1982. Resident Saginaw Coop. Hosp., 1976-79; Robert Wood Johnson fellowship U. Utah, 1979-81; mem. faculty, divsn. dir. U. Utah, Salt Lake City, 1981-89; mem. faculty U. Colo., Denver, 1989-93; mem. faculty, chair family medicine and preventive medicine Emory U., Atlanta, 1993—.

LUTZ, MYRON HOWARD, obstetrician, gynecologist, surgeon, educator; b. N.Y.C., June 26, 1938; s. Morris David and Rose (Greenblatt) L.; m. Judy Cohen, Aug. 6, 1963; children: Mark Steven, Sheri Lutz Barnett, Kenneth Ian. BA, Columbia U., 1960; MD, NYU, 1964. Diplomate Am. Bd. Ob-Gyn., Am. Bd. Gynecologic Oncology. Intern Phila., Gen. Hosp., 1964-65; resident in ob-gyn. Albert Einstein Coll. Medicine, Bronx, N.Y., 1965-69; fellow M.D. Anderson Hosp., Houston, 1971-72, U. Miami (Fla.) Sch. Medicine, 1972-73; asst. prof. ob-gyn. Med. U. S.C., Charleston, 1973-76, co-dir. gynecology oncology, 1973-77, clin. assoc. prof. ob-gyn., 1977—, clin. assoc. prof. surgery, 1986—; pvt. practice, Charleston, 1973—; mem. cancer adv. bd. Roper Hosp., Charleston, 1993—; star TV mid-day talk show, 1990—. Author pub. svc. ednl. tapes on gynec. problems; mem. editl. bd. House Calls mag., 1992—. Bd. dirs. Am. Cancer Soc., Charleston, 1974-75, v.p., 1975-76, pres., 1976-78; bd. dirs. Trident Acad., Charleston, 1982-86, Hospice, Charleston, 1984-86. Maj. M.C., U.S. Army, 1969-71. Fellow ACOG, ACS; mem. AMA, Am. Radium Soc., Am. Soc. Clin. Oncology, Soc. Gynecologic Oncologists, Felix Rutledge Soc., S.C. Med. Soc., S.C. Oncology Soc., Charleston Med. Soc. Home: 55 Chadwick Dr Charleston SC 29407 Office: 1606 Ashley River Rd Charleston SC 29407

LUUS, GEORGE AARNE, physician; b. Estonia, Apr. 23, 1937; s. Edgar and Aili (Poldmaa) L.; M.D., U. Toronto (Ont., Can.), 1962; m. Margit Jaanusson, Sept. 14, 1962 (div. 1983); children—Caroline Anna Elizabeth, Clyde Gregory Edgar, Lia Esther Isabelle; m. 2d, Donna Gervais Martell, Oct. 1, 1983. Intern Toronto East Gen. and Orthopaedic Hosp.; practice medicine specializing in family medicine, Sault Sainte Marie, Ont., 1963—; mem. Algoma Dist. Med. Group, 1966—; sec. med. staff Gen. Hosp., 1972—, v.p., bd. dirs., 1973. Adv. bd. Can. Scholarship Trust Found., 1976-77. Mem. Algoma West Med. Acad. Lodge: Rotary. Home: 42 Linstedt St, Sault Sainte Marie, ON Canada P6B 3H9 Office: 240 McNabb St, Sault Sainte Marie, ON Canada P6B 1Y5

LUX, KATHLEEN MARY, community health educator, nurse; b. Columbus, Ohio, Nov. 17, 1953; d. Donald Gregory and Harriet Hope (Harmer) L. BS, Ohio State U., 1975; MS, U. Hawaii, 1988; PhD, Ohio State U., 1992. Cert. health edn. specialist. Asst. charge nurse Doctor's North Hosp., Columbus, 1975-76; team leader Ohio State U. Hosp., Columbus, 1976-77; flight nurse USAF, 1977-84; EMT instr. City Colls. Chgo., 1981-82; nursing and health svcs. chair ARC, Rhein Main, Fed. Republic Germany, 1984-85; parent educator, clinic coord. Kapiolani Hosp., Honolulu, 1985-86; family planning nurse student and health svcs. U. Hawaii, Honolulu, 1986-87, rsch. asst., 1988; grad. teaching assoc. Ohio State U., Columbus, 1988-92, lectr., 1992-93, asst. prof., 1993—. Mem.

APHA, AAHPERD, Res. Officer's Assn., Ohio Assn. Health, Phys. Edn., Recreation and Dance (exec. dir. 1993—), Sigma Theta Tau, Eta Sigma Gamma, Phi Kappa Phi. Republican. Roman Catholic. Office: Ohio State U 212 Pomerene Hall 1760 Neil Ave Columbus OH 43210-1221

LUX, MARY FRANCES, clinical microbiology educator; b. Erie, Pa., Sept. 7, 1947; d. George Henry and Eleanor Marie (Gossman) L.; m. William Patrick Bryson, Sept. 24, 1967 (div. Oct. 1988); children: Elizabeth Bryson Taylor, Patricia Bryson, Kathryn Bryson, William Bryson. BS in Med. Tech., U. Miss., 1970, BA in Secondary Edn., 1984, MS in Biol. Scis., 1987, PhD in Biol. Scis., 1990. Cert. med. technologist, Am. Soc. for Clin. Pathologists. Staff technologist North Miss. Med. Ctr., Tupelo, 1970-75; chief staff technologist Hillcrest Hosp., Calhoun City, Miss., 1975-86; rsch. asst. U. Miss., University, 1985-90; asst. prof. U. So. Miss., Hattiesburg, 1990—. Contbr. articles to profl. jours. Mem. Am. Soc. Microbiology, Am. Soc. Clin. Sci., Miss. Acad. Sci. (sect. chair 1993, 95), Miss. Soc. Med. Tech., Sigma Xi. Roman Catholic. Office: Univ So Miss Box 5134 Hattiesburg MS 39406

LUXENBERG, JAY S., medical facility administrator; b. Newark, N.J.; s. Allen and Marilyn (Juman) L.; m. Jan Uhley, July 11, 1982; children: Adam, Evan. BS, Rensselaer Polytechnic Inst., 1979; MD, Albany Med. Coll., 1979. Diplomate Am. Bd. Internal Medicine, Am. Bd. Geriatric Medicine. Intern Mt. Zion Hosp. and Med. Ctr., San Francisco, 1979-80, resident in internal medicine, 1980-82; fellow in geriatric medicine Mt. Zion/U. Calif., San Francisco, 1982-84; med. staff fellow Nat. Inst. on Aging/NIH, Bethesda, Md., 1984-87; pvt. practice geriatrics and internal medicine San Francisco, until 1996; MD Jewish Home for Aged, San Francisco, 1996—; assoc. clin. prof. U. Calif., San Francisco, 1992—, asst. clin. prof., 1987-92, clin. assoc., 1982-84, dir. fellowship program in geriatric medicine, 1991-95. Contbr. articles to profl. jours. Bd. dirs. Family Caregiver Alliance, San Francisco, 1992—; mem. physician's adv. com. UCSF/Mt. Zion Ctr. on Aging, San Francisco, 1987—, others. Office: Jewish Home for Aged 302 Silver Ave San Francisco CA 94102

LUXENBERG, MALCOLM NEUWAHL, ophthalmologist, educator; b. Philipsburg, Pa., July 29, 1935; s. Maurice and Henrietta (Neuwahl) L.; m. Sandra Diane Rosen, June 16, 1957; children: Steven Neuwahl, Cathy Ann. Student, Tulane U., 1953-56; M.D., U. Miami, Fla., 1960. Diplomate: Am. Bd. Ophthalmology. Intern Cin. Gen. Hosp., 1960-61; resident in neurology U. Vt. Affiliated Hosps., Burlington, 1961-63; resident in ophthalmology Bascom Palmer Eye Inst., U. Miami-Jackson Meml. Hosp., Miami, Fla., 1963-66; asst. prof. ophthalmology Coll. Medicine, U. Iowa, Iowa City, 1968-70; chief ophthalmology service VA Hosp., Iowa City, 1968-70; practice medicine specializing in ophthalmology West Palm Beach, Fla., 1970-72; clin. asst. prof. ophthalmology Bascom Palmer Eye Inst., Sch. Medicine, U. Miami, 1971-72; prof., chmn. dept. ophthalmology Med. Coll. Ga., Augusta, 1972—; cons. ophthalmology VA Hosp., Augusta, 1972—; Sr. surgeon USPHS, 1966-68; bd. dirs. Am. Bd. Ophthalmology. Recipient Outstanding Civilian Service Medal Dept. of Army, 1986. Mem. AMA, Am. Acad. Ophthalmology (hon. award 1986), Am. Ophthalmol. Soc., Assn. Univ. Profs. in Ophthalmology (pres. 1982-83), Ga. Soc. Ophthalmology, Med. Assn. Ga., Richmond County Med. Soc. Home: 512 Scotts Way Augusta GA 30909-3238 Office: Med Coll Ga Dept Ophthalmology Augusta GA 30912

LYBARGER, JEFFREY ALLEN, epidemiology research administrator; b. Granite, Ill., 1951. MD, So. Ill. U., 1976. Diplomate Am. Bd. Gen. Preventive Medicine, Am. Bd. Preventive Medicine in Pub. Health, Preventive Medicine and Occupl. Medicine. Intern in pediat. St. Louis U. Glennon Hosp., 1976-77; resident in occupl. medicine U. Cin., 1979-81; resident in pub. health, pub. medicine Ctrs. for Disease Control, Atlanta, 1982-84; dir. Agy. for Toxic Substances and Disease Registry Divsn. Health Studies, Atlanta. Mem. Soc. for Epidemiol. Rsch., Soc. for Occupl. and Environ. Health, Internat. Soc. for Environ. Epidemiology. Office: Agy Toxic Subs/Disease Reg Divsn Health Studies 1600 Clifton Rd NE Mail Stop E31 Atlanta GA 30333*

LYBARGER, MARJORIE KATHRYN, nurse; b. Holland, Mich., Apr. 23, 1956; d. Richard Simon and Mary Kathryn (Homan) Denuyl; m. John Steven Lybarger, Aug. 22, 1981; children: Ashley Ann, Ryan Christopher. BA in Psychology, Biola U., Calif., 1979, BS in Nursing, 1984. RN, Calif. Staff nurse Presbyn. Intercommunity Hosp., Whittier, Calif, 1985-86, Healthcare Med. Ctr., Tustin, Calif., 1986-88; staff nurse med.-telemetry unit Friendly Hills Regional Med. Ctr., La Habra, Calif., 1988-90; staff nurse telemetry unit Riverside (Calif.) Community Hosp., 1990-93; staff nurse med. telemetry unit St. Anthony's Ctrl. Hosp., Denver, 1993-94; staff nurse cardiovascular intermediate care unit St. Anthony's Ctr., Denver, 1994—. Mem. Acad. Med.-Surg. Nurses (Rocky Mountain chpt.), Gamma Phi Beta. Republican. Home: 8489 W 95th Dr Broomfield CO 80021-5330

LYDA, TIMOTHY STUART, cardiothoracic surgeon; b. Woodland, Calif., Oct. 16, 1959; s. Stuart Davison and Jo Anne (Koenecke) L.; m. Virginia Inez Montgomery; children: Stuart C., Lindsay K., T. Logan. BS, Tex. A&M U., 1981, MS, 1982; MD, U. Tex. Health Sci. Ctr., San Antonio, 1986. Diplomate Am. Bd. Surgery, Am. Bd. Thoracic Surgery. Intern in gen. surgery U. Tex. Health Sci. Ctr., 1986-87, resident in gen. surgery, 1987-91, fellow in cardiovascular surgery, 1991-93, chief resident cardiothoracic surgery, 1992-93; pvt. practice cardiothoracic surgery San Antonio, 1993—; chief of cardiovascular and thoracic surgery svc. North Ctrl. Bapt. Hosp., San Antonio, 1996—, N.E. Bapt. Hosp., San Antonio, 1996—. Fellow Am. Coll. Chest Physicians, So. Surg. Congress; mem. J. Bradly Aust Surg. Soc., Bexar County Cardiology Soc., Alpha Omega Alpha. Office: Thoracic and Cardiac Surg Group 7950 Floyd Carl Ste 1005 San Antonio TX 78229

LYDON, MAUREEN ELLEN, nurse, administrator; b. Evergreen Park, Ill., Apr. 4, 1956; d. Thomas Joseph and Mary Bernadine (Buckley) Gallagher; m. Terence Michael Lydon, Sept. 29, 1989. BSN, St. Xavier Coll., 1979; MS, U. Ill., Chgo., 1994. Cert. quality assurance and utilization rev. profl. Am. Assn. Quality Assurance and Rev. Profls. Staff RN ob-gyn. Mercy Hosp. & Med. Ctr., Chgo., 1979-80; staff RN oper. rm. Palos Cmty. Hosp., Palos Hills, Ill., 1980-81; staff RN neonatal ICU Little Company of Mary Hosp., Evergreen Park, Ill., 1981-82; RN, fin. cons. Med. Charge Analysis, Chgo., 1982-85; RN, office mgr. Thomas D. Davin, M.D.. Evergreen Park, 1985-86; RN, mktg. cons. Profl. Detailing Inc., Chgo., 1986; RN coord. utilization rev. Health Care Comfare, Lombard, Ill., 1986-87; RN coord., quality assurance St. Mary of Nazareth Hosp., Chgo., 1987-88; RN coord. quality assurance, utilization rev., discharge planning, Chgo., 1988-90; RN coord., bill audit St. Mary of Nazareth Hosp., Chgo., 1990-92; RN mgr. utilization rev. West Side VA Med. Ctr., Chgo., 1992—. Block capt. S.W. Beverly Improvement Assn., Chgo., 1995; active Ill. Young Dems., Chgo., 1993—, Irish Am. Alliance, 1994—. Mem. ANA, Ill. Nurses Assn., Assn. for Health Care Quality, Am. Assn. Utilization Mgmt. Nurses (cert. profl.). Roman Catholic. Office: West Side VA Med Ctr 820 S Damen Ave Chicago IL 60612

LYMAN, GARY HERBERT, epidemiologist, cancer researcher, educator; b. Buffalo, Feb. 24, 1946; s. Leonard Samuel and Beatrice Louise L.; children: Stephen Leonard, Christopher Henry. BA, SUNY-Buffalo, 1968, MD, 1972; MPH, Harvard U., 1982. Diplomate: Am. Bd. Internal Medicine (med. oncology, hematology). Resident in medicine U. N.C.-Chapel Hill, 1972-74; fellow in oncology Roswell Park Meml. Inst., Buffalo, 1974-77; rsch. instr. medicine SUNY Med. Sch.-Buffalo, 1974-77; mem. faculty U. South Fla. Coll. Medicine, Tampa, 1977—, assoc. prof. medicine, 1980-86, prof. medicine, 1986—, dir. div. med. oncology, 1979-93, chief medicine H. Lee Moffitt Cancer Ctr. and Rsch. Inst., prof. epidemiology and biostats., 1988—. Co-author: Geriatric Oncology, 1992; contbr. articles to profl. jours., chpts. to books. Spl. fellow Leukemia Soc. Am., 1976-77; postdoctoral fellow biostats. Harvard U., 1981-82; spl. clin. fellow Roswell Park Meml. Inst., Buffalo, 1975-76. Fellow ACP, Am. Coll. Preventive Medicine, Am. Coll. Clin. Pharm.; mem. Am. Soc. Clin. Oncology. Current work: Cancer clinical trials, biostatistics, epidemiology, clinical decision analysis. Office: 12902 Magnolia Dr Tampa FL 33612-9416

LYMAN, HOWARD B(URBECK), psychologist; b. Athol, Mass., Feb. 12, 1920; s. Stanley B(urbeck) and Ruth Mary (Gray) L.; A.B., Brown U., 1942; M.A., U. Minn., 1948; Ph.D., U. Ky., 1951; m. Patricia Malone Taylor, May 4, 1966; children—David S., Nancy M., D. Jane Lyman Paraskevopoulos; stepchildren—Richard P. Taylor, Martha C. Kitsinis, Robert M. Taylor, David P. Taylor. Acting dir. student personnel E. Tex. State Tchrs. Coll., Commerce, 1948-49; counselor, research asst. univ. personnel office U. Ky., Lexington, 1949-51; research psychologist tests and measurements U.S. Naval Exam. Center, Norfolk, Va. and Gt. Lakes, Ill., 1951-52; asst. prof. psychology U. Cin., 1952-62, asso. prof., 1962-85 , prof. emeritus, 1986—; dir. Acad. Edn. and Research in Profl. Psychology Ohio 1975-84. Served with AUS, 1942-46. Licensed psychologist, Ohio. Fellow APA, Am. Psychol. Soc.; mem. Ohio Psychol. Assn. (dir. 1960-84, Disting. Svc. award 1974), Midwestern, Cin. psychol. assns., Assn. Measurement and Evaluation in Guidance, Nat. Council Measurement in Edn., Internat. Council of Psychologists, Cheiron Soc., Authors Guild, Psi Chi. Author: Single Again, 1971; Test Scores and What They Mean, 5th edit., 1990; editor Ohio Psychologist, 1967-79. Home: 3422 Whitfield Ave Cincinnati OH 45220-1525

LYMAN, JOHN B., ophthalmologist; b. Portland, Oreg., Sept. 26, 1945; s. Howard Watson and Janet Virginia (Bingner) L.; m. Margie Huhta, Mar. 16, 1973 (div. June 1979); children: Matthew, Jefferson; m. Marva Joyce Nebeker, Feb. 13, 1981; children: Meredith, Tara, Mason, Blake, Austin. BA, U. Oreg., 1969, MD, 1974. Diplomate Am. Bd. Ophthalmology, Am. Bd. Eye Surgery. Med. dir. Oreg. Eye Surgery Ctr., Eugene, 1988-92; pvt. practice Eugene, 1979-95, Bountiful, Utah, 1995—. Office: 520 Medical Dr Bountiful UT 84010-4930

LYMAN, RUTH ANN, psychologist; b. Nashville, Ark., Feb. 2, 1948; d. Oren Ernest and Frances Emeline (Urban) Frerking. BS, U. Ala., 1969, MA, 1972, PhD, 1974, MPA, 1986. Lic. psychologist, Ala. Cons. Ohio Coun. Community Mental Health Ctrs., Columbus, 1983, Ellard-Harper Found., Birmingham, Ala., 1983; resource cons. Ala. State Legis. Task Force on Child Abuse & Neglect, Montgomery, 1984-86; chief mental health sect., clin. psychologist U. Ala., Tuscaloosa, 1973-75; exec. dir. Western Mental Health Ctr., Birmingham, 1975-87; pvt. practice clin. psychologist Birmingham, 1988—; bd. dirs. Med. Bus. Mgmt., Inc.; mem. dept. psychiatry steering com. Brookwood HOsp., Birmingham, 1990—; adj. clin. prof. dept. psychology U. Ala., 1973-75, 77—. Author: (with others) Behavior Modification in Children: Case Studies and Illustrations from a Summer Camp, 1974, Outpatient Psychiatry: Progress, Treatment, Prevention, 1985, Administrative Discretion and the Implementation of Public Policy, 1986; contbr. articles to profl. jours. Treas., exec. com. Alcoholism Recovery Svcs., Inc., 1978-87; mem. adv. com. Nat. Alliance for the Mentally Ill., Birmingham, 1986-87, Pers. Bd. Jefferson County, 1978-82, chair, 1982, legis. com. chair, 1980-81; mem. Group Home Adv. Com., 1976-83; bd. dirs. Ala. NCCJ, 1979-82; mem. task force Birmingham Regional Health Systems Agy., Inc., 1977-79, mental health subcom., com. chair, 1979; chair by-laws com. Head Start Policy Coun., Birmingham, 1976-78; v.p. Ala. Coun. Community Health, 1987, stds. com., 1982, planning com., 1980-81, 83-85, sec., treas. and exec. com., 1978-79; bd. dirs., program co-chair Women's Network Birmingham, 1986; adv. com. Mental Health Assn. of Jefferson County, 1976-87. Named Birmingham Career Woman of the Yr., 1981. Mem. APA, NAFE, Southeastern Psychol. Assn., Ala. Psychol. Assn. (chair ad hoc com. for psychologists in pub. agys. 1985-86, chair ethics com. 1990, sec. 1990-92, pres. 1996), Birmingham Regional Assn. Lic. Psychologists (co-chair steering com. and cmty. edn. com. 1989-90, pres. 1991), Assn. for Advancement of Psychology, Assn. Lic. Psychologists in Ala., Women's Network of Birmingham (bd. dirs., co-chair program 1986), Zonta Internat.

LYNCH, BENJAMIN LEO, oral surgeon educator; b. Omaha, Dec. 29, 1923; s. William Patrick and Mary (Rauber) L.; m. Colleen D. Cook, Nov. 10, 1956; children: Kathleen Ann, Mary Elizabeth, Patrick, George, Martha, Estelle. BSD, Creighton U., 1945, DDS, 1947, MA, 1953; fellow, U. Tex., 1947-48; MSD, Northwestern U., 1954. Diplomate Am. Bd. Oral and Maxillofacial Surgery. Asst. instr. oral surgery Creighton U., 1948-50, instr., 1950-52, asst. prof., 1952-53; dean Creighton U. (Sch. Dentistry), 1954-61, assoc. prof. oral surgery, 1954-55, prof. oral surgery, 1957-86, prof. emeritus, 1986—, dir. oral surgery dept., 1954-67; also coordinator grad. and postgrad. programs; chief oral surgeon Douglas County Hosp., Omaha, 1951-63; pres. dental staff Children's Meml. Hosp., Omaha, 1952, 59; co-founder cleft palate team Children's Meml. Hosp., 1959; chmn. dept. dentistry Bergan-Mercy Hosp., Omaha, 1963-68; mem. exec. com., head dental staff Luth. Hosp., 1963-66; bd. dirs. Nebr. Dental Service Corp., 1972-78, pres., 1974-78; treas. Children's Meml. Hosp. Med.-dental staff, 1979-81; guest lectr. Walter Reed Grad. Sch. Medicine, 1957-58. Mem. Omaha-Douglas County Health Bd., 1966-68, v.p., 1967, pres., 1968; exec. com. Nebr. divsn. Am. Cancer Soc., 1963-67; bd. dirs. Nebr. Blue Cross, 1968-89, Creighton U. Alumni Coun., Omaha chpt., 1989-91; trustee United Cath. Social Svcs., 1989-95; adv. bd. to dean Creighton U. Dental Sch., 1984—, vice chmn., 1992-93, chmn., 1993-94; pres. Creighton U. Graybackers, 1991-94. Served at Walter Reed U.S. Army Med. Ctr., 1955-57. Recipient Alumni merit award Creighton U., 1978; named one of Ten Outstanding Young Omahans, 1952, 53, 58; inducted into Nebr. Dental Hall of Fame, 1981. Fellow Am. Coll. Dentists (pres. Nebr. chpt. 1973-74); mem. Am. Soc. Oral Surgeons, Midwest Soc. Oral Surgeons, Nebr. Soc. Oral Surgeons (founder 1957, pres. 1961), Nebr. Dental Soc. (trustee 1964-66), Omaha Dist. Dent Soc. (pres. 1963-64), Am. Coll. Oral-Maxillofacial Surgeons (founding mem.), Nebr. Soc. Dental Anesthesiology (founder, 1st pres.), Alpha Sigma Nu, Omicron Kappa Epsilon, Delta Sigma Delta. Home: 509 S Happy Hollow Blvd Omaha NE 68106-1224

LYNCH, DIANE R., health care executive, lawyer; b. Phila., Jan. 2, 1949; d. Willie and Bruce (Purnell) Brown; divorced. BS, Kean Coll., Union, N.J.; MS, Columbia U.; JD, Antioch Sch. Law, Washington. Health care exec. Hosp. Ctr. of Orange, N.J.; lobbyist Lynch Assocs., New Brunswick, N.J. Trustee St. Peter's Med. Ctr., New Brunswick, 1993—, Renaissance 2000, New Brunswick, 1992—; mem. New Brunswick Bd. Edn.; mem. alumni bd. D.C. Law Sch., Washington, 1994—. Home: 79 Lawrence St New Brunswick NJ 08901

LYNCH, DONALD FRANCIS, JR., urological oncologist; b. Buffalo, Oct. 16, 1946; s. Donald Francis and Catherine Theresa (Gibbons) L.; m. Mary Carole Flannery, Oct. 5, 1968; children: Donald Francis III, Sean E., Kathleen M. Student, Va. Mil. Inst., 1964-67; MD, U. Va., 1971. Diplomate Am. Bd. Urology, Am. Bd. Med. Hypnosis. Commd. ensign USN, 1968, advanced through grades to capt., 1985; intern U.S. Naval Hosp., San Diego, 1971-72, urology resident, 1975-79; chmn. urology dept. U.S. Naval Hosp., Portsmouth, Va., 1980-83; resigned, 1983; ret. USNR, 1991; urology fellow Meml. Sloan-Kettering Cancer Ctr., N.Y.C., 1979-80; urologic oncologist Danville (Va.) Urologic Clinic, 1983-93, Sentara Cancer Inst., Norfolk, Va., 1993—; assoc. prof. urology Ea. Va. Med. Sch., 1993—; pres. med. staff Meml. Hosp., Danville, 1991—; sr. aviation med. examiner FAA, Washington, 1983—. Contbr. articles to profl. jours. Fellow ACS; mem. Am. Urolog. Assn., Soc. Surg. Oncology, Am. Soc. Clin. Oncology, Am. Soc. Clin. Hypnosis, Am. Radio Relay League, Nat. Eagle Scout Assn. Roman Catholic. Office: Sentara Cancer Inst River Pavilion # 203 600 Gresham Dr Norfolk VA 23507-1904

LYNCH, DONALD FREDERICK, psychology educator; b. Augusta, Maine, Dec. 31, 1950; s. Donald and Phyllis (Willett) L. BA, U. Maine, 1973, MEd, 1974. Cert. social worker; lic. profl. clin. counselor. Complex coord. U. Maine, Orono, 1974-77; outpatient therapist Community Health and Counseling Svcs., Bangor, Maine, 1977-84, dir. outpatient svcs., 1984-86; asst. prof. psychology Unity (Maine) Coll., 1986-92, assoc. prof. psychology, 1992—; cons. Maine State Dept. Corrections, Augusta, 1985—, St. Michael's Ctr., Bangor, Maine, 1987—; dir. peer counseling program Unity Coll., 1987—; state, nat. and internat. mental health trainer. Mem. New Eng. Assn. Ednl. Opportunity Program Pers. Home: 2188 Kennebel Rd Newburgh ME 04444 Office: Unity Coll Quaker Hill Rd Unity ME 04988

LYNCH, GEORGE MICHAEL, family practice physician; b. Seneca Falls, N.Y., June 20, 1952; s. Victor Kamerer and Jane (Sutherland) L.; m. Kathryn Louise Lavrich, Feb. 24, 1979; children: Matthew Michael, Michelle Louise, Meredith Morgan. BS in Psychology, Pa. State U., 1974; MD, Jefferson Med. Coll., 1978. Diplomate Am. Bd. Family Practice. Pvt. practice family physician Herndon, Va., 1981—; 1st vice chmn. Physicians' Care Health Plan, Arlington, Va., 1984-89; chmn. med. audit com. Fair Oaks Hosp., Fairfax, Va. , 1984-86, chmn. bylaws com, 1996—; med. dir., chmn. of the bd. Reston Nursing Assn., 1985; chmn. Reston Hosp. Dept. Family Practice, 1994-96. Fellow Am. Acad. Family Physicians; mem. Fairfax County Med. Assn. Office: Ste 340 13350 Franklin Farm Rd Herndon VA 22071

LYNCH, HARRY JAMES, biologist; b. Glenfield, Pa., Jan. 18, 1929; s. Harry James and Rachel (McComb) L.; m. Pokum Lee Lynch. BS, Geneva Coll., Beaver Falls, Pa., 1957; PhD, U. Pitts., 1971; postgrad. Bio-Space Tech. Tng. Program, NASA and U. Va., 1970. Clin. chemist West Penn Hosp., Pitts., 1955-56; grad. teaching asst. U. Pitts., 1966-71, sr. teaching fellow, 1971; postdoctoral fellow MIT, Cambridge, 1973-75, rsch. assoc. dept. nutrition, lab. neuroendocrine regulation, 1973-75, lectr., 1976-81, rsch. scientist dept. brain and cognitive sci., 1982-92; cons. Ctr. for Brain Scis. and Metabolism Charitable Trust, 1992—. Contbr. more than 60 articles on the pineal gland to profl. jours. and books; patentee on implantable programmed microinfusion apparatus, 1981. With USN, 1950-54. NIH postdoctoral fellow 1971-73. Mem. Soc. Light Treatment and Biol. Rhythms. Democrat. Office: MIT E25-615 77 Massachusetts Ave Cambridge MA 02139-4301

LYNCH, HENRY THOMSON, medical educator; b. Lawrence, Mass., Jan. 4, 1928; s. Henry F. and Eleanor (Thomson) L.; m. Jane Smith, Nov. 9, 1951; children—Patrick, Kathleen, Ann. B.S., Okla., 1951; M.A., Denver U., 1952; M.D., U. Tex., Galveston, 1960. Intern St. Mary's Hosp., Evansville, Ind., 1960; resident U. Nebr. Sch. Medicine, 1961-64, sr. clin. cancer trainee, 1964-66; practice medicine specializing in internal medicine and medical oncology Omaha, 1967—; asst. prof. medicine U. Tex. M.D. Anderson Hosp., Houston, 1966-67; assoc. prof. Creighton U. Sch. Medicine, Omaha, 1967-70; prof., chmn. dept. preventive medicine and pub. health Creighton U. Sch. Medicine, 1970—, prof. medicine, 1982—. Editor: Hereditary Factors in Carcinoma, 1967, Dynamic Genetic Counseling for Clinicians, 1969, Cancer and You, 1971, Skin, Heredity and Malignant Neoplasms, 1972, Cancer Genetics, 1975, Genetics and Breast Cancer, 1981, Cancer Associated Genodermatoses, 1982, Colon Cancer Genetics, 1985, Biomarkers, Genetics and Cancer, 1985, also numerous sci. articles. Served with USNR, 1944-46. Recipient Bristol-Myers Squibb Co. unrestricted cancer rsch. grantee, 1996. Mem. Am. Soc. Human Genetic, Am. Soc. Clin. Oncology, Am. Assn. Cancer Research, Alpha Omega Alpha. Home: 9406 Douglas St Omaha NE 68114-3838

LYNCH, JOSEPH PATRICK, III, physician; b. Boston, July 1, 1947; m. Evelyn Shuer; children: Michael David, Daniel Patrick, Lindsay Kelly. BA cum laude, Harvard U., 1969; MS, Dartmouth Med. Sch., 1971; MD, Harvard U., 1973. Diplomate Am. Bd. Internal Medicine, Am. Bd. Pulmonary Disease. Intern, then resident in internal medicine U. Mich. Med. Ctr., Ann Arbor, 1973-76, fellow in pulmonary disease, 1976-78; instr. to assoc. prof. U. Mich., Ann Arbor, 1978-94, prof. divsn. pulmonary and critical care medicine, 1994—, acting divsn. chief pulmonary and critical care medicine, 1985-87; mem. editl. bd. Seminars of Respiratory Infection, Clin. Pulmonary Medicine; reviewer Chest, Am. Review Respiratory Disease, Am. Jour. Med Sci., Archives of Internal Medicine, JAMA; editor Seminars of Respiratory and Critical Care Medicine, 1997; lectr. in field. Contbr. over 160 articles to profl. jours. Fellow Am. Coll. Chest Physicians (gov. Mich. chpt., 1994-96, mem. original investigations com., 1993-94, mem. steering com. sect. cardiopulmonary infections, 1993-95, chmn. sect. cardiopulmonary infections, 1994-95, designated regent and vice-chair coun. govs., 1994-95, chair, 1995-96, mem. exec. com. bd. regents, 1995-96, chair gov.'s nominating com., 1995-96); mem. Am. Thoracic Soc. (mem. com. on health care policy and clin. practice, 1994-95, Mich. Thoracic Soc. Internat. Soc. Heart and Lung Transplantation. Office: U Mich 3916 Taubman Box 0360 Ann Arbor MI 48109

LYNCH, PETER JOHN, dermatologist; b. Mpls., Oct. 22, 1936; s. Francis Watson and Viola Adeline (White) L.; m. Barbara Ann Lanzi, Jan. 18, 1964; children: Deborah, Timothy. Student, St. Thomas Coll., 1954-57; B.S., U. Minn., 1958, M.D., 1961. Intern U. Mich. Med. Center, 1961-62, resident in dermatology, 1962-65; clin. instr. U. Minn., 1965; chief dermatology and venereal disease Martin Army Hosp., Columbus, Ga., 1966-68; asst. prof. to asso. prof. dermatology U. Mich. Med. Center, 1968-73; asso. prof. to prof. dermatology U. Ariz., Tucson, 1973-86; chief sect. dermatology U. Ariz., 1973-86, asso. head dept. internal medicine, 1977-86; prof., head dermatology U. Minn. Med. Sch., Mpls., 1986-95; med. dir. ambulatory care U. Minn. Health System, 1993-95; prof., chmn. dept. dermatology U. Calif., Davis, 1995—. Author: (with S. Epstein) Burckhardt's Atlas and Manual of Dermatology and Venereology, 1977, Dermatology for the House Officer, 1982, 3d edit., 1994, (with W.M. Sams) Principels and Practice of Dermatology, 1992, 2 edit., 1996, (with I.E. Edwards) Genital Dermatology, 1994. Served with AUS, 1966-68. Served with AUS, 1966-68. Decorated Army Commendation Medal; recipient Disting. Service award for faculty U. Mich., 1970, Disting. Faculty award U. Ariz., 1981. Mem. Am. Acad. Dematology (bd. dirs. 1974-78, v.p. 1991-92), Assn. Profs. Dematology (bd. dirs. 1976-80, pres. 1994—), Internat. Soc. Study of Vulvar Disease (bd. dirs. 1976-79, pres. 1983), Soc. Investigative Dermatology, Am. Bd. Dermatology (bd. dirs. 1984-89), Gougerot Soc. (Bronze Medal award), Alpha Omega Alpha. Democrat. Roman Catholic. Home: 332 Sandpiper Dr Davis CA 95616 Office: U Calif Dept Dermatology 1605 Alhambra Blvd # 2300 Sacramento CA 95816

LYNCH, PRISCILLA A., nursing educator, therapist; b. Joliet, Ill., Jan. 8, 1949; d. LaVerne L. and Ann M. (Zamkovitz) L. BS, U. Wyo., 1973; MS, St. Xavier Coll., Coll., 1981. RN, Ill. Staff nurse Rush-Presbyn.-St. Luke's Med. Ctr., Chgo., 1977-81, psychiat.-liaison cons., 1981-83, asst. prof. nursing, unit leader, 1985—; mgr. and therapist Oakside Clinic, Kankakee, Ill., 1987—; mem. adv. bd. Depressive and Manic Depression Assn., Chgo., 1986—; mem. consultation and mental health unit Riverside Med. Ctr., Kankakee, 1987—; speaker numerous nat. orgns. Contbr. numerous abstracts to profl. jours., chpts. to books. Bd. dirs. Cornerstone Svcs. Recipient total quality mgmt. award Rush-Presbyn.-St. Luke's Med. Ctr., 1991. Mem. ANA, Ill. Nurses Assn. (coms.), Coun. Clin. Nurse Specialists, Profl. Nursing Staff (sec. 1985-87, mem. coms.). Presbyterian. Home: 606 Darcy Ave Joliet IL 60436-1673

LYNCH, SEAN DENNIS, health care executive; b. Bethlehem, Pa., Apr. 1, 1957; s. Bernard Joseph Jr. and Elizabeth (Murphy) L.; m. Kimberly Ann Lynch, 1995. BA, East Stroudsburg U., 1981; postgrad., Lehigh U., 1981-83, Dale Carnegie Leadership Inst., 1981, 86. Supr. Community Found. for Human Devel., Sellersville, Pa., 1983-85, asst. dir., 1985-87; program supr. partial hospitalization Kids Peace, Allentown, Pa., 1987-95, mkt. analyst, 1995; v.p. Stoff's Personal Home Health Care, Bethlehem, Pa., 1995—. Mem. Fountain Hill (Pa.) Borough Coun., 1986—, v.p. 1989; mem. Fountain Hill Hist. Soc., 1991—; mem. drug task force Northampton County, Pa., 1990—, Lehigh Valley Child Care Coalition, 1990—, Northampton County Anti-Drug Initiative, 1990—. Mem. Am. Mgmt. Assn., Fountain Hill Jaycees (state rep. 1988-91), Holy Name Soc., Bethlehem Rugby Club, Mack Ski Club, Alpha Chi Rho. Democrat. Roman Catholic. Home: 615 Lechauweki Ave Bethlehem PA 18015 Office: Wiley House L610 Emmaus Ave Allentown PA 18103

LYNCH, STEPHANIE NADINE, clinical psychologist; b. Cambridge, Mass., Apr. 11, 1951; d. Jeremiah and Irma C. (Gauntt) L.; m. Rickey Bernard Silverman, Apr. 17, 1983; children: Jason Frederick, Leonard Jeremiah, Rachel Elizabeth. PhD in Clin. Psychology, Case Western Res. U., 1977. Lic. psychologist, Mass., cert. psychologist, N.H. Staff psychologist Reading (Pa.) Hosp. & Med. Ctr., 1977-79, St. Elizabeth's Hosp., Brighton, Mass., 1979-81; atty. Silverman & Assocs., Plaistow, N.H., 1981-95; pvt. practice Derry, N.H., 1995—; clin. instr. Tuft U. Sch. Medicine, Boston, 1980-89; cons. Parkland Hosp., Derry, N.H., 1990—, Cath. Med. Ctr., Manchester, N.H., 1990—, St. Elizabeth's Hosp., Brighton, Mass., 1980—, Holy Family Hosp., Methuen, Mass., 1981—. Co-author: (chpt.) Handbook of Innovative Psychotherapies, 1981. Pres. No. New England Down Syndrome Congress, Maine, N.H., Vt., 1988-90. Mem. APA, Mass. Psychol. Assn. Office: 44 Birch St Ste 202 Derry NH 03038

LYNCH, THOMAS, retired psychiatry educator; b. Dublin, Ireland, Nov. 17, 1922; s. Fionan and Bridget (Slattery) L.; m. Sheila O'Donovan, Sept. 17, 1956; children: Mairead, Niall, Timothy, Sally-Ann, Fionnuala. MD, U.

Ireland, 1946. Intern Richmond Hosp., Dublin, 1946-47; house officer St. Patrick's Hosp., Dublin, 1948-51, staff psychiatrist, 1954-61; sr. med. officer Maudsley Hosp., London, 1952-53; resident med. supt. St. Otteran's Hosp., Waterford, Ireland, 1961-68; clin. dir. St. Brendens Hosp., Dublin, 1968-88; prof. psychiatry, chmn. dept. Royal Coll. Surgeons, Dublin, 1968-90, prof. emeritus, 1990—; clin. dir. Ea. Health Bd., Dublin, 1968-88. Author: Psychiatric Notes for Medical Students, 1984. Capt. Waterford Golf Club, 1965-66, pres., 1967-68. Fellow Am. Psychiat. Assn. (hon. corr. 1981); mem. Royal Coll. Physicians Ireland (Harry Masesy Miles gold medal 1946, McNaughton Jones gold medal 1946, coun. scholar), Royal Coll. Psychiatrists (v.p. 1981-83), Mental Health Assn. Ireland (hon. sec. 1965), Milltown Golf Club (capt. 1981-82). Roman Catholic. Home: 44 South Hill, Dartry, Dublin 6, Ireland Office: Royal Coll Surgeons, St Stephen's Green, Dublin 2, Ireland

LYND, PRISCILLA ANN, pediatrician; b. Ironton, Ohio, Feb. 4, 1942; d. Jacob Edward and Margaret (Richards) L. BA, U. Ky., 1964, MD, 1968. Diplomate Am. Bd. Pediatrics. Internship U. Ky., Lexington, 1968-69; residency U. Va., Charlottesville, 1969-70; residency, fellowship U. Ky., Lexington, 1970-73, asst. prof. pediatrics, 1973-78, pediatrician pvt. practice, 1978—; bd. dirs. Cen. Ky. Blood Ctr., Lexington, 1980—. Contbr. articles to profl. jours. Pres. Fayette County Young Reps., Lexington, 1974; exec. v.p. Ky. YRs, 1975, chmn. 6th dist., 1974-76. Mem. Ky. Med. Assn., Fatette County Med. Soc., Bluegrass Pediatrics Soc., Fayette County Master Gardeners. Republican. Methodist. Office: 3320 Tates Creek Rd Lexington KY 40502-3400

LYNDAKER, STEVEN LEHMAN, internist; b. Watertown, N.Y., Nov. 15, 1963; s. Norman Jacob and Phyllis Joy (Lehman) L.; m. Shereen Evelyn Palmer, Aug. 19, 1989. BA, Hamilton Coll., 1986; MD, U. Rochester, 1990. Diplomate Am. Bd. Internal Medicine. Resident U. Rochester, 1990-93, chief resident in medicine, 1993-94; mem. med. attending staff Baystate Med. Ctr., Springfield, Mass., 1994—; sr. clin. instr. Tufts Sch. Medicine, Boston, 1994—; preceptor of med. residents Baystate Internal Medicine Program, Springfield, 1994—. Mem. Am. Coll. Physicians, Physicians for Social Responsibility. Democrat. Mem. United Ch. of Christ. Office: Boston Rd Med Assocs 2377 Boston Rd Wilbraham MA 01095

LYNN, DEBORAH JOANNE, neurologist, researcher; b. Columbus, Ohio, Apr. 30, 1958; d. Arthur Dellert Jr. and Pauline Judith (Wardlow) L.; m. Jeffrey Lee Huntley, Apr. 12, 1986; children: Katherine Lynn Huntley, Patricia Claire Huntley. BA, Amherst Coll., 1980; MD, Ohio State U., 1984. Diplomate Am. Bd. Internal Medicine, Am. Bd. Psychiatry and Neurology. Intern in internal medicine Strong Meml. Hosp. U. Rochester, N.Y., 1984-85, resident in internal medicine, 1985-87, resident neurology, 1987-90; fellow in neuromuscular disease dept. neurology Ohio State U., Columbus, 1990-92; asst. prof. neurology Ohio State U., 1992—. Contbr. articles to profl. jours., chpts. to books. Mem. professorial adv. com. Nat. Multiple Sclerosis Soc. mid-Ohio chpt., Columbus, 1994—. Mem. ACP, Am. Acad. Neurology. Episcopalian. Office: Ohio State U Med Ctr 453 Means Hall 1654 Upham Dr Columbus OH 43210

LYNN, PAMELA ANN, nursing administrator; b. Washington, Sept. 7, 1961; d. Martin Joseph and Margaret Arliene (Clark) L. BSN, Cath. U. Am., 1983; min.'s cert., Wash. Psychic Inst., 1991; MS in Orgn. Devel., Ctrl. Wash. U., 1996. RN, D.C., Wash. Nurse Children's Hosp. and Med. Ctr., Washington, 1983-85; nurse U. Wash. Med. Ctr., Seattle, 1985-86, asst. head nurse, 1986-89, nurse mgr., 1989-92, coordinated care project mgr., 1992-96; internal cons., 1996—. Mem. cmty. activity com. Ch. of Divine Man, Seattle, 1990-92, mem. fin. com., 1991-92, trustee, 1992—, pres., 1995-96. Recipient Nurse Excellence award U. Wash. Med. Ctr., 1989. Mem. ASTD, Puget Sound Orgn. Devel. Network, Assn. for Quality and Participation, Nat. Orgn. Devel. Network, Am. Orgn. Nurse Execs., Mountaineers, Sigma Theta Tau. Office: U Wash Med Ctr Orgn Devel Tng/Quality Impr Box 25 6054 Seattle WA 98195-6054

LYNN, VALERIE ROEMER, psychotherapist; b. Pitts., Jan. 31, 1927; d. Carl and Sylvia (Huot) Roemer; m. Kenneth Schuyler Lynn, Sept. 23, 1948; children: Andrew S., Elisabeth, Sophia. BA, Wellesley Coll., 1948; MS, Simmons Sch. Social Work, 1968. Diplomate Acad. Cert. Social Workers. Caseworker Robert Breck Brigham Hosp., Boston, 1959; social worker Chestnut Lodge, Rockville, Md., 1969-80; pvt. practice psychotherapy, 1980—. Pres. Friends of Historic Preservation, Inc., Washington, 1988—. Mem. NASW, Greater Washington Soc. Clin. Social Workers. Home and Office: 1709 Hoban Rd NW Washington DC 20007-2036

LYON, ISOLDA YVETTE, dietitian; b. Managua, Nicaragua, Nov. 10, 1954; came to U.S., 1982; naturalized citizen 1989; d. Lauriston Edmund and Teresa del Carmen (Rodriguez) Burey; m. Ward Burton Lyon, Mar. 25, 1983; children: Jessica Yvette, Angelica Isolda. BS in Nutrition and Dietetics, U. San Carlos, Guatemala, 1978. Registered dietitian; lic. dietitian; cert. food and beverage mgr., correctional officer. Nutritionist Health Ministry, Managua, Nicaragua, 1975-77; cons. Welfare Ministry and Health Ministry, Managua, Nicaragua, 1978-79; prof. faculty Ctrl. Am. U., Managua, Nicaragua, 1981; dietitian Nestle Co., Managua, Nicaragua, 1979-82; nutritionist Harris County Hosp. Dist., Houston, 1983-85; food svc. dir. Carnegie Gardens Nursing, Melbourne, Fla., 1985-86; food svc. supr. Wuesthoff Hosp., Rockledge, Fla., 1986-87; sgt., food svc. mgr. Tex. Dept. of Corrections, Rosharon, Tex., 1987-88; dir. dietary svcs. Washington Sq. Devel. Svcs. Inc., Titusville, Fla., 1988—. Mem. Dem. Party, Managua, 1981-82. Named Employee of Yr., Carnegie Gardens, 1985, Intelligent Employee of the Yr., Devel. Svcs., 1992. Mem. Am. Dietetic Assn., Dietetics in Devel. and Psychiat. Disorders, Clin. Nutrition Mgmt., Dietetics in Phys. Medicine and Rehab., Space Coast Dietetic Assn. (pres. 1995-96), Nicaraguan Nutritionist and Dietetic Assn. (treas. 1979-82), Ctrl. Am. and Panama Nutritionist Dieticians Assn. Republican. Roman Catholic. Home: 847 Tiffany Pl Rockledge FL 32955 Office: Washington Sq Devel Svcs 1401 N US Highway 1 Titusville FL 32796-1310

LYON, JOANNE B., psychologist; b. Little Rock, June 2, 1943; d. F. Ike and Marie (Graham) Beyer; m. Jas. Sherod Lyon, Dec. 1971 (div. Sept. 1975), m. John M. Lofton, May 22, 1983 (dec. Feb. 1990). BA, Webster U., 1966; MEd, U. Mo., St. Louis, 1976, PhD, 1986. Lic. psychologist, Kans. Reading specialist Rockwood Sch. Dist., St. Louis, 1976-79; psychology cons. handicapped component St. Louis Head Start, 1982-83; intern Topeka State Hosp., 1983-84; dir. partial hosp. programs Family Svc. & Guidance Ctr., Topeka, 1985-89; pvt. practitioner and joint owner Shadow Wood Clin. Assocs., Topeka, 1989—; clin. supr. Family Svc. & Guidance Ctr., Topeka, 1989-93; behavioral scis. regulatory bd. Psychology Adv. Com., 1996—. Mem. exec. bd. Interfaith of Topeka, 1995—, I Have a Dream Coalition, 1994—, Psychology Advisory Bd. Behavioral Sci. Regulatory Bd.; bd. dirs. Temple Beth Sholom Sisterhood, 1996—. Sherman scholar U. Mo., St. Louis, 1982. Mem. APA, Kans. Psychol. Assn., Am. Orthopsychiatric Assn., Soc. for Personality Assessment, Internat. Platform Assn. Jewish. Home: 3030 SW Arrowhead Rd Topeka KS 66614-4134 Office: Shadow Wood Clin Assocs 2933 SW Woodside Dr Topeka KS 66614-4181

LYON, JOSEPH LYNN, physician, medical educator; b. Salt Lake City, May 13, 1939; s. Thomas Edgar and Hermana (Forsberg) L.; m. June Fetzer, July 3, 1964; children: Natalee, Joseph, Stephen, Maryanne, Rachael, Janet. BS, U. Utah, 1964, MD, 1967; MPH, Harvard U., 1969. Diplomate Am. Bd. Preventive Medicine. Intern U. Calif., San Diego, 1967-68; resident Harvard U., 1968-70, Utah State Health Dept., 1971-72; asst. prof. U. Utah, Salt Lake City, 1974-80, assoc. prof., 1980-90, prof., 1990—. Contbr. articles to profl. jours. Mem. Soc. for Epidemiologic Rsch. (sec.-treas. Balt. chpt. 1993). Mem. LDS Ch. Office: U Utah Coll Dept of Medicine Salt Lake City UT 84132

LYON, MARK CHRISTOPHER, pharmaceutical industry executive; b. Johnson City, Tenn., Nov. 5, 1961; s. William James III and Yvonne (Fisher) L.; m. Lisa D. Taylor, June 1, 1985; children: Morgan Taylor, Mark Christian, Matthew James. BBA, East Tenn. State U., 1984; postgrad., Am. Grad. Sch. Internat. Mgmt. Mgr. Gen. Shale, Atlanta, 1985; field salesman The Upjohn Co., Kingsport, Tenn., 1985-87; hosp. salesman The Upjohn Co., Winston Salem, N.C., 1987; health sci. assoc. The Upjohn Co., Balt., 1988-90; regional trainer The Upjohn Co., Richmond, Va., 1990; dist. mgr. The Upjohn Co., Roanoke, Va., 1990-94; leadership devel. Upjohn Co., Kalamazoo, Mich., 1994-95; bus. devel. mgr. Pharmacia and Upjohn, Inc., 1995—, U.S. managed care mktg. execc., 1996—. Mem. 1st Reformed Ch. Republican. Home: 5026 Queen Victoria Ln Kalamazoo MI 49009 Office: 7000 Portage Rd Kalamazoo MI 49001-0102

LYON-LOFTUS, GREGORY THOMAS, family physician, psychologist; b. Washington, July 16, 1944; s. Joseph Phillip and Margaret Mary (Boland) Loftus; m. Diana Joan Lyon, July 12, 1975; children: Michael Thomas, Anthony Eric. BA, Wheeling (W.Va.) Jesuit Coll., 1966; MA, Mich. State U., 1970, PhD, 1975, MD, 1977. Diplomate Am. Bd. Family Practice, Am. Bd. Geriatrics. Intern dePaul Hosp., Norfolk, Va., 1978-79; resident in family practice Ea. Va. Med. Sch., Norfolk, 1978-81; dir. emergency med. svcs., acting dir. mental health svcs. Indian Health Svc., USPHS, Keams Canyon, Ariz., 1982-84; pvt. practice, Mont Alto, Pa., 1984—. Officer USPHS, 1982-84. Mem. Am. Acad. Family Practice, Pa. Acad. Family Practice (del. 1990—), Am. Diabetes Assn. (bd. dirs. Waynesboro, Pa. chpt. 1987—), Rotary (bd. dirs. Waynesboro 1990—). Roman Catholic. Home: 916 E Main St Waynesboro PA 17268-2337 Office: Mont Alto Family Practice 6155 Anthony Hwy Mont Alto PA 17237

LYONS, BARBARA ANN, physician assistant; b. Monticello, N.Y., Jan. 15, 1954; d. Arthur Bolen and Ellen Agnes (Carswell) L.; m. Edward James Beazley, May 2, 1986; children: Elizabeth Lyons, Emily Lyons. BA, Eisenhower Coll., 1976; BS, physician asst. cert., Baylor Coll. Medicine, 1979; MA, U. Houston-Clear Lake, 1986. Clin. physician asst. Baylor-Meth.-Lipid Rsch. Clinics, Houston, 1979-81; instr. U. Tex. Med. Br., Galveston, 1981-84, asst. prof., 1984-89, assoc. prof. dept. physician asst. studies, 1989—. Author, co-editor: Educating Patients: A Practical Approach, 1996, HIV Manual for Health Care Professionals, 1993; contbr. articles to profl. jours.; mem. editl. bd. Physician Asst., 1992—. Vol. Westwood Elem. Sch., Friendswood, Tex., 1995-96, Friendswood Area Swim Team, 1996. Recipient Robert J. Luchi Disting. Alumni award Baylor Coll. Medicine, 1992. Fellow Am. Acad. Physician Assts.; mem. Assn. Physician Asst. Programs, Phi Kappa Phi. Home: 300 Woodstream Circle Friendswood TX 77546 Office: Dept Physician Asst Studies 301 University Blvd Box 1028 Galveston TX 77555-1028

LYONS, NATALIE BELLER, family counselor; b. Habana, Cuba, Apr. 3, 1926; d. Herman Lawrence and Jennie (Engler) B.; widowed, Apr. 18, 1986; children: Anne, Sara. BS in Surveying and Land Appraising, Inst. Vedado, Habana, Cuba, 1943; BA, U. Mich., 1946; MEd, U. Miami, Fla., 1967. Family counselor, mem. staff furniture design and mfg. co. George B. Bent, Gardner, Mass., 1953-58; tchr. H.S., Winchendon, Mass., Hollywood, Fla., 1962; tchr. parochial sch., Ft. Lauderdale, Fla., 1963-64; family counselor Miami, 1967—; project dir. Cen. Am. fisheries program Peace Corps, 1972-74; counselor Svc. Corp. of Ret. Execs., Miami, 1993, bd. dirs., 1994—; bd. dirs., mem. Com. for Accuracy in Mid East Reporting, 1990—. Pres. Miami region Hadassah, 1989-91; bd. dirs. Greater Miami Jewish Fedn., 1985—; bd. dirs. Miami Civic Music Assn., 1985—; bd. dirs. women's divsn. Greater Miami Jewish Fedns. Cmty. Rels. Coun.; mem. nat. bd. dirs. nat. women's divsn. Am. Soc. for Technion, 1991—, pres. 1984-86; co-chair Pro-Israel Rally, Tri County, 1991, Joint Action Com., Miami, 1989-91; trg. dir. Los Amigos de las Ams., 1975—; founder, dir. Cmty. Inst. Jewish Studies, Hollywood, Fla., 1962-64. Recipient Leadership award Hadassah, 1987, honoree Am. Soc. for Technion Scholarship Fund, 1991; named Woman of Yr., Hadassah, 1991. Democrat.

LYONS, PAULA MARIE, physician; b. Phila., Apr. 9, 1957; d. John Joseph Jr. and Beatrice Johanna (Koenderman) L.; m. Jeffrey John Meffert, May 18, 1980; children: Austin Lyons Meffert, Ian Lyons Meffert. BA, U. Tex. Austin, 1977; MD, U. Tex. San Antonio, 1981. Diplomate Am. Bd. Family Practice; lic. Tex. Staff physician, capt. USAF Regional Hosp., Langley AFB, Va., 1984-86; physician Coll. Village Clinic, Anchorage, 1986-89; physician Tex. Med. Clinic, San Antonio, 1989—, clin. med. dir., 1995—; clin. instr. U. Tex. Med. Sch., San Antonio, 1990—. Fellow Am. Acad. Family Physicians; mem. Tex. Med. Assn., Tex. Acad. Family Physicans (Alamo chpt.), Bexar County Med. Soc.

LYONS, RICHARD CHAPMAN, former urologist; b. Corry, Pa., Nov. 23, 1919; s. Arch C. and Araline (Drought) L.; m. Norma Lydia Wright, Dec. 25, 1945; children: Dorothy A., John C., Sanford D., Timothy R., Valerie A. Grad. U. Pa., 1941; MD, U. Pitts., 1944. Diplomate Am. Bd. Urology. Intern, St. Elizabeth Hosp., Washington, 1945; resident, Mayo Clinic, Rochester, Minn., 1945-46, 48-50; civilian physician U.S. Army, 1946-47; chmn. dept. urology, Hamot Med. Ctr., Erie, Pa., 1955-68, practitioner, surgeon, 1950-86, founder, head urology residency program, 1958-68; hon. mem. med. staffs St. Vincent Health Ctr., Erie, 1951-86; mem. Pa. State Bd. Med. Edn. and Licensure, 1971-85, chmn., 1976-78, 81-85; dir. NW Pa. Corp., Oil City, Mellon-North, Erie; mng. ptnr. Lyons Properties Ltd. Partnership. Trustee Gannon U. Named Disting. Pennsylvanian, Gannon U., 1981. Recipient Integrity award Soc. for Advancement Intergrity in Pub. Life. Fellow ACS (gov. 1975-81); mem. AMA, Pa. Med. Soc., Erie County Med. Soc., Pa. Urologic Assn. (pres. 1974), Mayo Clinic Alumni Assn., Mayo Urol. Alumni Assn. (pres. 1976), Erie Club, Kahkwa Club, Erie Yacht Club, Univ. Club (Pitts.), Elks. Republican. Roman Catholic. Home: 52 Royal Palm Dr Fort Lauderdale FL 33301-1409

LYONS, STEPHEN H., medical educator; b. Rochester, Minn., June 15, 1951; s. Henry R. and Margaret (Mumway) L. AS in EMT, Santa Fe C.C., 1985. Cert. EMT-Paramedic, Colo.; cert instr. ACLS, BTLS, EMT. EMS coord Crested Butte First Protection Dist.; flight paramedic, program cons. Shands Teaching Hosp., U. Fla., Gainesville; trauma technologist dept. emergency medicine George Washington U., Washington; surg. asst. pvt. practice gen. surgery Gainesville; dir., CEO EMSED; pres., owner Wilderness Profl. Tng., Crested Butte, Colo.; instr. Wilderness Med. Assocs., Bryant Pond, Maine, Wilderness Medicine Inst., SOLO West, Pitkin, Colo.; cons. Wilderness Med. Assocs., NASAR Wilderness Med. Programs; faculty instr. NASAR Ednl. Programs, Fairfax, Va.; instr. emergency care courses Georgetown U. Sch. of Medicine, Washington. Past instr. trainer Aquatics, First Aid & CPR, Small Craft Safety, ARC; past program coord. EMS Assoc./Tech. Degree Programs, Santa Fe C.C., Gainesville, Fla.; mem. State of Colo. EMS Task Force; guide Wildwater, Ltd., Section IV, Chattooga River. Mem. Nat. Assn. EMTs, Nat. Assn. Search and Rescue, EMT Assn. of Colo., Nat. Assn. EMS Physicians, Wilderness Med. Soc. Office: Wilderness Profl Tng PO Box 759 602 Butte Ave #1 Crested Butte CO 81224

LYRER-GAUGLER, PHILIPPE ALEXANDER, neurologist; b. Basel, Switzerland, Sept. 19, 1957; s. Siegfried Adolf and Laure (Bembassat) Lyrer; m. Astrid Gertrud Gaugler, June 22, 1984. Diploma in medicine, U. Basel, 1983, MD, 1984. Commd. lt. Swiss Army, 1981, advanced through grades to capt., 1987; resident in neurology Univ. Hosp., Basel, 1987-92, clin. fellow, 1993—. Contbr. articles on multiple sclerosis, cerebrovascular diseases and magnetic resonance to med. jours. Fellow Swiss Neurol. Soc., Swiss Soc. Neuroradiology (sci. prize 1990); mem. Am. Acad. Neurology (clin. assoc.).

LYTLE, GLENN HERBERT, surgeon, educator; b. Rochester, N.Y., Feb. 19, 1948; s. Theodore Lemerz and Cynthia (Wooden) L.; children: Sheridan, Melissa, Gregg, Jonathan, Kaylan. BA, Princeton U., 1970; MD, U. Rochester, 1974. Diplomate Am. Bd. Surgery. Resident in surgery Yale U., New Haven, Conn., 1974-79; pvt. practice surgery Chambersburg (Pa.) Surg. Assn., 1979-87; assoc. prof. surgery Oral Roberts U., Tulsa, Okla., 1987-89; assoc. prof., vice chair surgery U. Okla. Coll. Medicine, Tulsa, 1989—; chief of surgery VA Med. Ctr.-Muskogee, Okla., 1993—; mem. exec. bd. Assn. for Sug. Edn., 1995—. Contbr. articles to profl. jours. Bd. dirs., vice chair Sch. Bd., Tulsa, 1990—. Office: Univ Okla Coll Medicine 2808 S Sheridan Tulsa OK 74129

LYTTON, BERNARD, urology educator; b. London, June 28, 1926; came to U.S., 1962; s. Morris and Pearl (Zuckerberg) L.; m. Norma M. Mendle, Oct. 28, 1963; children: Sharon, Simon, Timothy, Jennifer. MB, BS, U. London, 1948. Prof., chief urology Yale Univ. Sch. U., New Haven, 1967-87; Donald Gultrie prof. surgery Yale Univ. Sch. U., 1987—; Master Jonathan Edwards Coll. Yale U., 1987—. Fellow ACS, Royal Coll. Surgeons (England); mem. Am. Urol. Assn. (Hugh Hampton Young award 1985, pres. New Eng. sect. 1974), Am. Assn. Genio-Urinary Surgeons, Clin. Soc. Genio-Urinary Surgeons, Soc. Pelvic Surgeons. Home: 70 High St New Haven CT 06511 Office: Yale U Sch Medicine Sect Urology PO Box 208041 YPB 322 New Haven CT 06520-8041

LYTTON, LINDA ROUNTREE, marriage and family therapist, test consultant; b. Suffolk, Va., Mar. 30, 1951; d. John Thomas and Anne Carolyn (Edwards) Rountree; m. Daniel Michael Lytton, June 23, 1973; 1 child, Seth Daniel. BS, Radford U., 1973; MS, Va. Poly. Inst. and State U., 1992. Collegiate profl. cert. Tchr., cons. Fauquier County Pub. Schs., Warrenton, Va., 1973-74, Chesterfield County Pub. Schs., Richmond, Va., 1974-78, Williamsburg (Va.)-James City Pub. Schs., 1979-83, Prince William County Pub. Schs., Manassas, Va., 1983-89; hist. area interpreter Colonial Williamsburg Found., 1978-79; outpatient therapist Prince William County Community Svcs. Bd., 1989-91, emergency svcs. therapist, therapist cons., 1991-93; marriage and family therapist Employee Assistance Svc., Inc., Manassas, 1993—; pvt. practice Ashton Profl. Ctr., 1996—; cons. Horizons for LEarning, Inc., Richmond, 1989—. Great Books LEader, 1993—. Mem. Am. Assn. Marriage and Family Therapy, Va. Assn. Marriage and Family Therapy, Internat. Assn., Marriage and Family Counselors, Sigma Kappa (life). Home: 12046 Market Square Ct Manassas VA 20112-3214

MA, HONG, plant molecular biologist, educator; b. Shanghai, People's Republic of China, Oct. 19, 1960; came to U.S., 1980; s. Zhe and Linsun (Hu) M.; m. Yi Hu, Aug. 10, 1987; 1 child, Jason J. BA summa cum laude, Temple U., 1983; PhD, MIT, 1988. Teaching asst. MIT, Cambridge, 1983-84, rsch. asst., 1984-88; postdoctoral fellow Calif. Inst. Tech., Pasadena, 1988-90; staff investigator Cold Spring Harbor (N.Y.) Lab., 1990-91, sr. staff investigator, 1992—; adj. faculty SUNY, Stony Brook, 1991—; mem. faculty SUNY-Cold Spring Harbor Lab.-Brookhaven Joint, 1991—; adviser undergrad. rsch. program Cold Spring Harbor Lab., 1991—; mem. panel NIH Biol. Study Sect., 1995; spkr. in field. Reviewer articles for Genetic, Molecular Cell Biology, Molecular Gen. Genetics, Plant Cell, Plant Jour., Plant Molecular Biology; contbr. articles to profl. jours. Mem. selection com. Ptnrs. for Future High Sch. Students, Cold Spring Harbor, N.Y., 1991—; mentor high sch. student rsch. project Westinghouse Talent Competition, 1993. MIT fellow, 1983, Helen H. Whitney Found. fellow, 1988; NSF rsch. grantee, 1990, 91, 94, USDA rsch. grantee, 1991, 92, 94, 95, Am. Cancer Soc. rsch. grantee, 1995; Am. Cancer Soc. jr. faculty rsch. awardee, 1994. Mem. AAAS, Genetic Soc. Am., Am. Soc. Microbiology, Internat. Soc. Plant Molecular Biologists, Assn. Chinese Students and Scholars in Life Scis., Soc. Chinese Bioscientists Am., N.Y. Acad. Scis. Office: Cold Spring Harbor Lab 1 Bungtown Rd Cold Spring Harbor NY 11724-2209

MAANY, IRADJ, psychiatrist; b. Tehran, Iran, May 21, 1941; came to U.S., 1969; s. Mohammad Maany and Anisea Eshraghi; m. June 22, 1971; children: Veda, Pouyan. MD, Tehran U., 1967, grad., 1967; postgrad., U. Pa., 1973-74, Temple U., 1973-74. Intern Henry Ford Hosp., Detroit, 1969-70; resident Ypsilanti (Mich.) State Hosp., 1970-71; psychiat. resident East Pa. Psychiat. Inst., Phila., 1971-73; asst. prof. U. Pa., Phila., 1974-76, clin. assoc. prof., 1977—. Mem. APA.

MAAS, ANTHONY ERNST, pathologist; b. Utrecht, The Netherlands, May 6, 1926; came to U.S., 1959; s. Willem A. and Tono Clara (Bonebakker) M.; m. Julia Margaret Lampley, July 7, 1962; children: Willem Fulton, Julie Estelle, Anthony Ernst Jr. BS, U. Utrecht, 1948, MD, 1953. MD, Pa.; cert. anatomical and clin. pathologist. Asst. pathologist United Hosp., Port Chester, N.Y., 1965-66; assoc. pathologist Polyclinic Hosp., Harrisburg, Pa., 1966-74; assoc. pathologist Holy Spirit Hosp., Camp Hill, Pa., 1974-90, dir. labs., 1990—; dir. labs. Harrisburg State Hosp., Harrisburg, 1990—. Contbr. articles to profl. jours. Fellow Am. Coll. Pathologists, Am. Soc. Clin. Pathologists; mem. AMA, Dauphin County Med. Soc., Torch Club of Harrisburg (pres.) 1983. Republican. Presbyn.

MAASS, ALFRED ROLAND, health science consultant; b. Plymouth, Wis., Apr. 14, 1918; s. George Edward and Mabel (Eichenberger) M.; m. Eleanor Anderson, Jan. 26, 1947; children: Andrew, David, Philip. BS, Antioch Coll., 1942; MS, U. Wis., 1948, PhD, 1950. Abbott lab. fellow Argonne Nat. Labs., North Chicago, Ill., 1950; sr. biochemist Smith Kline & French Labs., Phila., 1951-56, group leader biochemistry dept., 1956-57, asst. sect. head biochemistry dept., 1957-62, sect. head biochemistry dept., 1962-67, assoc. dir. biochemistry dept., 1967-75, assoc. dir. biol. rsch., 1975-78, dir. analytical biochemistry dept., 1978-79, dir. analytical biochemistry dept. preclin. devel., 1980-81, dir. sci. adminstrn., 1981-82; radiol. safety chair Smith Kline & French Labs., 1952-75, worldwide dir., 1974-78. Contbr. numerous articles to profl. jours. Lt. (j.g.) USNR, 1944-46, PTO. Recipient Maurice K. Goddard State award, 1986, Outstanding Pa. Tree Farmer Am. Forest Coun., 1989,. Outstanding Norhteastern Tree Farmer, 1990. Home: RR 2 Box 50 New Milford PA 18834-9616

MAAT, BENJAMIN, radiation oncologist; b. Vlaardingen, The Netherlands, Apr. 17, 1947; s. Teunis and Evelien (van de Ridder) M.; m. Suzanne Faase, Dec. 19, 1969; children: Arthur, Menno, Michiel. MD, State U. Leiden, 1973, PhD, 1986. Intern State U. Hosp. Leiden, The Hague, The Netherlands, 1971-72; resident in radiother St. Johannes de Deo Hosp., The Hague, 1976-77; intern Dr. Daniel den Hoed Kliniek Rotterdam Radiotherapeutisch Inst., 1977-80; scientist Radiobiologic Inst. TNO, Dutch Health Orgn., Delft, The Netherlands, 1971-80; cons. radiotherapist Dr. B. Verbeeten Inst., Tilburg, The Netherlands, 1980—; cons. neuro-oncologist St. Elisabeth Hosp., Tilburg, 1980—; cons. radiotherapist St. Nicolaas Hosp. and St. Elizabeth Hosp., Tilburg, 1980—. Author: The Use of Anticoagulants in Antimetastatic Therapy, 1986; contbr. articles to profl. jours. Police doctor Mcpl. Police, Delft, 1976-80. Mem. European Orgn. Rsch. Treatment of Cancer (Brain Tumor Group and Radiotherapy Group), Dutch Soc. Radiotherapy, Dutch Soc. Radiobiology, European Soc. Therapeutic Radiation Oncology, Dutch Soc. Neurology. Home: Regge 93, N Brabant, 5032 RB Tilburg The Netherlands Office: Dr B Verbeeten Inst, Brugstraat 10, 5042 SB Tilburg The Netherlands

MABEE, JOHN RICHARD, physician assistant, educator; b. San Francisco, Sept. 18, 1956; s. Robert John and Mary Sachiko (Nose) M.; m. Cheryl Ann Saxton, June 24, 1978 (div. Aug. 1995); children: Jonathan, Alan. BS, Regents Coll., 1981; MS, Calif. State U., L.A., 1991; postgrad., Union Inst., Cin., 1994—. Cert. physician asst., Nat. Commn. Cert. Physician Assts. Physician asst. resident dept. emergency medicine Los Angeles County/U. So. Calif. Med. Ctr., 1984-85, emergency medicine physician asst. Calif. med. ctr., 1985—; rsch. asst. dept. biology Calif. State U., L.A., 1987-88, lectr., 1988-91, physician asst., 1992; rsch. physician asst. U. So. Calif. Emergency Medicine Assocs., L.A., 1993-95, clin. instr. dept. emergency medicine, 1994—, conscious sedation adv. com., 1995—, lectr. sch. medicine, 1995—. Contbr. articles to profl. jours. Named Alumnus of Yr., Emergency Medicine Physician Asst. Residency, 1994. Fellow Am. Acad. Physician Assts.; mem. Soc. Emergency Medicine Physician Assts. (founding, election com., 1988—). Democrat. Home: 717 S Almansor St A Alhambra CA 91801 Office: LAC-USC Med Ctr Unit I Rm 1060 1200 N State St Los Angeles CA 90033

MABREY, WILLIAM THOMAS, ophthalmologist; b. Little Rock, Aug. 30, 1956; s. Thomas Anthony and Betty (Chronister) M.; m. Christy Hendricks, July 3, 1982; children: William Thomas Sr., John Allen, Matthew Chronister. BA in Chemistry, U. Ark., Fayetteville, 1979; MD, U. Ark., Little Rock, 1983. Bd. cert. ophthalmology. Resident ophthalmology U. Ark. Med. Sch., Little Rock, 1984-88; fellow retina and vitreous Dever Eye Ctr., Portland, Oreg., 1988-89; mem. profl. staff Bapt. Med. Ctr., St. Vincent Med. Ctr., Little Rock, 1989—; vice chief sect. ophthalmology Bapt. Med. Ctr., Little Rock, 1996-97. Contbr. chpts. to books. Recipient Burton scholarship U. Ark. Med. Sch., Little Rock, 1982. Fellow Am. Acad. Ophthalmology (chmn. Diabetes 2000 Ark. chpt. 1993—); mem. Am. Ophthalmology Soc. (dir. Diabetes 2000 1985-96), Am. Med. Soc., Ark. Med. Soc., Pulaski County Med. Soc., Phi Beta Kappa, Alpha Omega Alpha. Roman Catholic. Home: 4309 Deer Park Dr Little Rock AR 72212 Office: Marie Eye Clinic Med Towers I Ste 990 9601 Lile Dr Little Rock AR 72205

MACAGBA, RUFINO L., JR., physician, international agency executive; b. San Fernando, Philippines, Feb. 3, 1933; came to U.S., 1974; s. Rufino N. Sr. and Crispina (Lorenzana) M.; m. Victoria D. Reyes, Apr. 10, 1957; children:

Carol Lynn, Rufino III, Jonathan, Michelle. MD, U. Philippines, Manila, 1957; MPH, UCLA, 1975. Hosp. adminstr., chief surgeon Lorma Hosp., San Fernando, 1960-74; internat. health advisor World Vision Internat., Calif., 1975-88, exec. mgmt. trainer, 1982-84; pres. Lorma Hosp. and Coll., 1980—, Health Devel. Internat., Calif., 190—; internat. health coord. Food for the Hungry, Scottsdale, Ariz., 1990-95, head internat. tech. and managerial svcs., 1994-95; dir. MBA program Pacific Christian Coll., Fullerton, Calif., 1995—; freelance cons. to World Vision Relief and Devel., Inc., Monrovia, Calif., World Bank, Washington, U. of the Nations, Kona, Hawaii, Mercy Corps Internat., Portland, Oreg., Food for the Hungry Internat. Author books and booklets, including: Health Care Guidelines for Use in Developing Countries, 1977, Hospitals and Primary Health Care, 1984, What World Vision Staff Should Know About AIDS, 1987, (with Mike O. Minodin) Selected Publications for Community Health Care, 1987, also articles. Mem. Nat. Coun. for Internat. Health (bd. dirs. 1978-80), Internat. Hosp. Fedn. (travelling fellow 1982-84), Health Devel. Internat. (pres. 1991-95). Republican. Christian. Home: 1352 Briarcroft Rd Claremont CA 91711-3001 Office: Pacific Christian Coll MBA Program 2500 E Nutwood Ave Fullerton CA 92631

MACARIO, ALBERTO JUAN LORENZO, physician; b. Naschel, Argentina, Dec. 1, 1935; came to U.S., 1974, naturalized, 1980; s. Alberto Carlos and Maria Elena (Giraudi) M.; MD, Nat. U. Buenos Aires, 1961; m. Everly Conway, Mar. 16, 1963; children: Alex, Everly. Intern, Ramos Mejia Hosp., Buenos Aires, 1958-60, resident 1960; resident Rivadavia Hosp., Buenos Aires, 1961-62, physician-hematologist, 1962-64; fellow NRC Argentina, Buenos Aires, 1964-69; head dept. radioactive isotopes Inst. Hematological Investigations, Nat. Acad. Medicine Argentina, Buenos Aires, 1967-69; Eleanor Roosevelt fellow Internat. Union Against Cancer, Dept. Tumorbiology, Karolinska Inst., Stockholm, 1969-71; mem. sci. staff Lab. Cell Biology, NRC Italy, Rome, 1971-73; head Lab. Immunology, Internat. Agy. Rsch. on Cancer, WHO, Lyons, France, 1973-74; research scientist Brown U., Providence, 1974-76, Div. Labs. and Rsch., N.Y. State Dept. Health, Albany, 1976-79; chief hematology Clin. Lab. Center, N.Y. State Dept. Health, Albany, 1979-81, dir. clin. and exptl. immunology sect. Lab. Medicine Inst., 1981-83; rsch. physician, 1981—, Wadsworth Ctr. for Labs. and Rsch. N.Y. State Dept. of Health; prof. Dept. Biomed. Scis. Sch. Pub. Health U. at Albany, 1985—, mem. senate at SUNY Albany, N.Y., 1989-94; adj. prof. pathology and lab. medicine Albany Med. Coll., 1991—; grant reviewer for nat. and internat. agys.; manuscript reviewer for sci. jours. Recipient Diploma de Honor prize Nat. U. Buenos Aires, 1961, Bernardino Rivadavia prize Nat. Acad. Medicine Argentina, 1967, Ciencia e Investigation prize Argentinian Soc. Advancement Sci., 1967; Ford Found.-NAS travel fellow, 1968, Eleanor Roosevelt fellow, 1969. Mem. Scandinavian Soc. Immunology, Italian Assn. Immunologists, French Soc. Immunology, Am. Assn. Immunologists, Am. Soc. Microbiology (sect. editor Manual of Clin. Lab. Immunology 5th edit. 1994—), Am. Soc. Investigative Pathology. Achievements include patents in field; discovered primary myeloperoxydase deficiency in leucocytes; developed method for immunologic identification of bacteria that produce methane gas; discovered antigenic diversity of these bacteria in natural and manufactured ecosystems; described structural topography of methanogenic bacteria and population dynamics in granular microbial consortia; found novel multicellular forms of archaebacteria; isolated for the first time the genes in the dnaK locus from an archaebacterium. Editor multivol. treatise Monoclonal Antibodies Against Bacteria and treatise Gene Probes for Bacteria; contbr. articles to profl. jours., chpts. to books. Office: Empire State Pla/Dept Health Wadsworth Ctr Labs Rsch PO Box 509 Albany NY 12201

MACARTHUR, JOHN DUNCAN, surgeon; b. Duluth, Miss., Jan. 17, 1934; m. Gretchen MacArthur; children: John, Andrew, Heather. BS, U. Minn., 1956, MD, 1960. Diplomate Am. Bd. Surgery. Intern Peter Bent Brigham Hosp., Boston, 1960-61, resident, chief resident, 1961-67; Peters Traveling fellow St. Mary's Hosp., London, 1963-64; instr. surgery, tutor med. sci. Harvard Med. Sch., Boston, 1968-72, asst. prof. surgery, 1972-73, asst. clin. prof. surgery, 1973-79, lectr. surgery, 1985—; sr. lectr. surgery Tufts Med. Sch., Boston, 1973-75, assoc. clin. prof., 1975-79; assoc. clin. prof. surgery Yale U., New Haven, 1979—, preclin. tutor, 1985—; chmn. Com. on Trauma, Conn., 1994—; chmn. surgery Bridgeport (Conn.) Hosp., 1979—. Co-author: Post-Traumatic Pulmonary Insufficiency, 1969, Operative Anatomy of the Abdomen, 1975, E.D. Assessment of Injured Patients, 1992; contbr. articles to profl. jours. Pres. Regional Coun. EMS, Fairfield, Conn., 1988-95; deacon Greenfield Hill Ch., Fairfield, Conn., 1984-88. Fellow ACS (pres. Conn. chpt. 1995—); mem. Conn. Soc. Bd. Surgeons (pres. 1987), Alpha Omega Alpha. Home: 138 Evergreen Hill Rd Fairfield CT 06430 Office: Bridgeport Hosp 267 Grant St Bridgeport CT 06610

MACARTY, JOHN DAVID, optometrist; b. Okla. City, Okla., Nov. 14, 1963; s. John Walker Macarty and Lois Joan (Towe) Whisler; m. Lori Ann Braley, Aug. 1, 1995; children: Alyssa Renee, Kristen Nicole. BS in Biology, Southwestern Okla. State U., 1986; D in Optometry, Northeastern Okla. State U., 1991. Diplomate Bd. of Optometry. Optometrist pvt. practice Altus, Okla., 1991-95; med. optometrist, dir. Western Okla. Eye Ctr., Altus, 1995—. Bd. dirs. United Way of Altus, Jackson County, Okla., 1995—; grad. Leadership Altus, 1994. Mem. Am. Optometric Assn., Okla. Optometric Assn., Altus C. of C., Rotary Club of Altus (bd. dirs. 1994-95, pres.-elect 1997), Red River Investment Club, Altus (sec. 1994—). Republican. Methodist. Home: 716 Lark St Altus OK 73521 Office: Western Okla Eye Ctr 1415 N Main St Altus OK 73521

MACAVINTA-TENAZAS, GEMORSITA, family physician; b. Numancia, Aklan, Phillippines, Dec. 18, 1938; came to U.S., 1967; d. Dominador Zalazar and Georgina Estrada (Tabanera) Macavinta; m. Salvador Torrefiel Tenazas Jr., Apr. 18, 1963; children: Alan, Alex, Albert, Alfred. BA, Far Ea. U., Manila, 1959, D of Medicine, 1964. Diplomate Am. Bd. Family Practice. Intern North Gen. Hosp., Manila, 1963-64; pvt. practice Manila, 1965-67; extern Chinese Gen. Hosp., Manila, 1965-67; with St. Joseph Med. Ctr., Burbank, Calif., 1967-69; chief cytotechnologist Cancer Screening Svcs., North Hollywood, Calif., 1969-73; resident in family practice medicine Health Scis. Ctr., Tex. Tech. U., Lubbock, 1974-75; staff physician VA Outpatient Clinic, L.A., 1975—. Recipient physician recognition awards AMA, 1973-85, 92-94; named Disting. Alumna, Aklan Acad., Philippines, 1991. Fellow Am. Acad. Family Physicians; mem. Calif. Acad. Family Physicians, Filipino Asian-Pacific VA Employees Soc. (pres. L.A. chpt. 1988—), Aklanons of Am. (pres. 1988—, 1st Mrs. Aklan 1986-89), Far Ea. U. Med. Alumni Assn. (asst. sec. 1988—). Roman Catholic. Office: VA Outpatient Clinic 425 S Hill St Los Angeles CA 90013-1110

MACCALLUM, (EDYTHE) LORENE, pharmacist; b. Monte Vista, Colo., Nov. 29, 1928; d. Francis Whittier and Berniece Viola (Martin) Scott; m. David Robertson MacCallum, June 12, 1952; children: Suzanne Rae MacCallum Barslund and Roxanne Kay MacCallum Batezel (twins), Tracy Scott, Tamara Lee MacCallum Johnson, Shauna Marie MacCallum Bost. BS in Pharmacy U. Colo., 1950. Registered pharmacist, Colo. Pharmacist Presbyn. Hosp., Denver, 1950, Corner Pharmacy, Lamar, Colo.. 1950-53; rsch. pharmacist Nat. Chlorophyll Co., Lamar, 1953; relief pharmacist, various stores, Delta, Colo., 1957-59, Farmington, N.Mex., 1960-62, 71-79, Aztec, N.Mex., 1971-79; mgr. Med. Arts Pharmacy, Farmington, 1966-67; cons. pharmacist Navajo Hosp., Brethren in Christ Mission, Farmington, 1967-77; sales agt. Norris Realty, Farmington, 1977-78; pharmacist, owner, mgr. Lorene's Pharmacy, Farmington, 1979-88; tax cons. H&R Block, Farmington, 1968; cons. Pub. Svc. Co., N.Mex. Intermediate Clinic, Planned Parenthood, Farmington; first woman registered pharmacist apptd. N.Mex. Bd. Pharm., 1982-92. Author numerous poems for mag. Advisor Order Rainbow for Girls, Farmington, 1975-78. Mem. Nat. Assn. Bds. Pharmacy (com. on internship tng., com. edn., sec., treas. dist. 8, mem. impaired pharmacists adv. com., chmn. impaired pharmacists program N.Mex., 1987—, mem. law enforcement legis. com., chmn. nominating com. 1992), Nat. Assn. Retail Druggists, N.Mex. Pharm. Assn. (mem. exec. coun. 1977-81), Order Eastern Star (Farmington). Methodist. Home and Office: 1301 Camino Sol Farmington NM 87401-8075

MACCARIO, MAURICE MALCOLM, oral and maxillofacial surgeon, consultant; b. Newark, Jan. 17, 1942; s. Melchiorre Malcolm and Susan (Bocchino) M.; m. Rosemarie Agnes Nocera; children: Lenora, Marcus. BA, Villanova U., 1964; DDMedicine, Fairleigh Dickinson U., 1968. Diplomate Am. Bd. Oral and Maxillo Facial Surgery. Intern Bklyn. Jewish Hosp., 1969; resident Bklyn. Vets. Hosp., 1970; chief resident Bklyn. Cumberland Med. Ctr., 1971; sr. registrar North Staffordshire Royal Infirmary, Eng., 1971-72; tchr. oral surgery Bklyn. Hosp., 1972-82; pvt. practice Oakland, N.J., 1972—; assoc. dir. dentistry Valley Hosp., Ridgewood, 1996—; assoc. dir. oral surgery Valley Hosp., 1996—; staff Valley Hosp., Ridgewood, N.J., 1971—, dir. dentistry, 1980-88, assoc. dir. dentistry and oral surgery, 1996—; cons. St. Joseph Hosp., Paterson, N.J., 1971—. Contbr. articles to profl. jours. V.p. Oakland (N.J.) Rep. Club, 1986-88. Fellow Am. Assn. Oral and Maxillofacial Surgeons, Oral Surgery Soc. N.J., Am. Mensa Soc. Roman Catholic. Home: 160 Long Hill Rd Oakland NJ 07436-3113 Office: 180 Ramapo Valley Rd Oakland NJ 07436-2524

MACCARTHY, JOHN PHILLIP, internist; b. Spokane, Wash., June 12, 1944; s. Raymond Joseph and Lorraine Mary (Rafferty) MacC. BA in Philosophy, St. Norbert Coll., DePere, Wis., 1967; MA in Religious Edn., Fordham U., 1972; MD, Loyola U., Chgo., 1977. Diplomate Am. Bd. Internal Medicine. Intern, resident internal medicine Hennepin County Med. Ctr., Mpls., 1977-80; primary care physician Centro San Jose, Aucayacu, Peru, 1980-82; med. dir. St. Jude Hosp., St. Lucia, W.I., 1982-85, Centro de Salud Sta. Clotilde, Iquitos, Peru, 1985—. Recipient Stritch award Loyola U., Chgo., 1988. Office: Apt 216, Centro Salud Clotilde, Iquitos Peru

MACCARTY, COLLIN STEWART, neurosurgeon; b. Rochester, Minn., Sept. 20, 1915; s. W.C. MacCarty; married; 3 children. AB, Dartmouth Coll., 1937; MD, Johns Hopkins U., Balt., 1940; MS in Neurosurgery, U. Minn., 1944. Diplomate Am. Bd. Neurol. Surgery. Surg. house officer Johns Hopkins Hosp., Balt., 1940-41; fellow in neurosurgery Mayo Found., Rochester, 1944; instr. neurol. surgery on grad. faculty U. Minn., Rochester, 1947-53, asst. prof., 1953-57, assoc. prof., 1957-61, prof., 1961-73; prof. Mayo Med. Sch./U. Minn., Rochester, 1973-80, assoc. dir. grad. edn., 1975-77, dir., 1977-80, prof. emeritus, 1980—; mem. neurosurg. staff Mayo Clinic, Rochester, 1946-75, sr. cons., 1975, chmn. med. staff, 1965-66; sec. for congress affairs World Fedn. Neurosurg. Socs., 1965-69, chmn. program com., mem. liaison com., mem. adminstrv. coun.; adv. com. to dean Dartmouth Med. Sch., 1968-72, bd. overseers, 1973—, chmn. bd., 1977-79; adv. bd. Bur. of Medicine and Surgery, Dept. of Navy, 1970; nat. cons. in neurosurgery Air Force, Wilford Hall Hosp., Lackland AFB, Tex., 1971; cons. in neurosurgery to Surgeon Gen., USN, 1977-80; vis. prof. neurosurgery Western Res. U., Cleve., 1966, Johns Hopkins U., 1969, U. Okla., 1971, Ohio State U., 1977, U. Tex., 1979; Caldwell lectr. Am. Roentgen Ray Soc., 1974; Elsberg lectr. N.Y. Soc. Neurol. Surgery, 1981. Author: (monograph) The Surgical Treatment of Intracranial Meningiomas, 1961; co-author: Primary Intramedullary Tumors of the Spinal Cord and Filum Terminale, 1964; contbr. over 158 articles to various med. jours. With USN, 1944-46. Mem. AMA (residency rev. com., sect. on med. edn. 1967-72), ACS, Am. Assn. Neurol. Surgeons (v.p. 1965, pres. 1970, bd. dirs. 1965-73, del. to World Fedn. 1973-77), Neurosurg. Soc. of Am. (v.p. 1954, pres. 1959, rep. to AANS bd. dirs. 1965-69), Minn. Med. Assn., Zumbro Valley Med. Soc., Minn. Soc. Neurol. Scis., Soc. Neurol. Surgeons, So. Minn. Med. Assn., Minn. Neurosurg. Soc., Found. for Internat. Edn. in Neurol. Surgery, Inc., Societa Italiana de Neurochirurgia (corr. mem.), Egyptian Soc. Neurol. Surgeons (hon.), Japan Soc. Neurol. Surgeons (hon.), Internat. Travellers Club, Neurosurg. Travel Club, Sigma Xi (chpt. pres. 1979-80). Home: HC 60 Box 71A Cable WI 54821-9510

MACCIONE, JOANNE COLACI, nursing home administrator; b. Waterbury, Conn., Aug. 7, 1947; d. Louis Colaci and Edith (Serafine) Santopietro; m. Richard D. Maccione, May 18, 1968; children: Ryan Louis, Courtney Paige. Diploma in Nursing, Waterbury Hosp., 1973; BS in Human Svcs., N.H. Coll., 1987. RN, Conn.; LPN, Conn.; lic. nursing home adminstr., Conn. LPN Waterbury Hosp., 1966-69, staff nurse, 1969-86; infection control nurse Abbott Terrace Health Ctr., Waterbury, 1986-87, asst. adminstr., 1987-88, adminstr., 1988-95; adminstr. Laurelwood Rehab. and Skilled Nursing Ctr., Ridgefield, Conn., 1994—. Chairperson for sr. subcom. Visions for Waterbury Task Force, 1993-94; 1st v.p., 2d v.p., pres. Woodbury Jr. Women's Club. Recipient Women in Leadership award YWCA, Waterbury. Mem. Am. Coll. Health Care Adminstrs., Waterbury Hosp. Sch. Nursing Alumni Assn., Ridgefield C. of C. Republican. Roman Catholic. Office: Laurelwood Rehab & Skld Nsg 642 Danbury Rd Ridgefield CT 06877

MACCLEAN, WALTER LEE, dentist; b. Sheridan, Wyo., July 10, 1935; s. Edward Satterlee and Eleanor Elizabeth (Weir) Mac.; m. Nancy Lee Strale, Sept. 4, 1965 (div. 1975); children: David Satterlee, Carrie Lynn. BS with honors, U. Wyo., 1957, postgrad., 1958; DMD, U. Oreg., Portland, 1962. Mil. dental adv. Korean Mil. Adv. Group, Wonju, 1962-63; chief dental svc. Dugway Chem. Testing Ctr., Utah, 1965-68; pvt. dental practice Cheyenne, Wyo., 1968-70; assoc. prof. Sheridan Coll., Wyo., 1970-76; staff dentist VA Hosp. Med. Ctr., Ft. Meade, S.D., 1976—; 1976-93, ret., 1993; cons., lectr. Health Edn. Program Svc., Ft. Meade, 1984-93. With U.S. Army 1962-68. Mem. ADA. Episcopalian. Home: PO Box 450 Hardin MT 59034-0450 also: Highbourne House, 13-15 Marylebone High St, London W1M 3PE, England

MACCOBY, MICHAEL, psychologist, consultant; b. Mount Vernon, N.Y., Mar. 5, 1933; s. Max and Dora (Steinberg) M.; m. Sandylee Weille, Dec. 19, 1959; children: Anne Maccoby Berglöf, Izette Maccoby Folger, Nora, Max. AB, Harvard U., 1954, PhD, 1960; psychoanalyst, Mexican Inst. Psychoanalysis, Mexico City, 1964. Pvt. practice psychotherapy & psychoanalysis Mexico, Washington, 1961-89; dir. Project on Tech., Pub. Policy and Human Devel., Cambridge, Mass., 1978-90, Project on Tech., Wk. and Character, Washington, 1970—; pres. The Maccoby Group, Washington, 1989—; dir. SMG N.Am., San Francisco, 1989—; cons. in field. Co-author: Social Character in a Mexican Village, 1970, A Prophetic Analyst, 1996; author: The Gamesman, 1976, The Leader, 1981, Why Work, 1988, 2d edit., 1995, Sweden at the Edge, 1991. Fellow APA, Am. Anthropol. Assn., Soc. for Applied Anthropology; mem. Nat. Acad. Pub. Adminstrs., Cosmos Club. Home: 4825 Linnean Ave NW Washington DC 20008-2124 Office: The Maccoby Group PC 1700 K St NW Ste 306 Washington DC 20006-3817

MACCORMACK, J(OHN) NEWTON, epidemiologist; b. Chester, S.C., Aug. 3, 1936; s. Eugene Little and Mary Alice (Mayfield) MacC.; m. Amy Jean Guill, June 1, 1963; children: Mary Kathryn, Forrest Stuart. BA, Duke U., 1958; MD, U. N.C., 1962, MPH, 1968. Diplomate Am. Bd. Preventive Medicine. Intern Med. Coll. Va., Richmond, 1962-63; resident Dist. Health Dept., Chapel Hill, N.C., 1965-67; chief communicable disease control N.C. Divsn. Health Svcs., Raleigh, 1968-83; dir. epidemiology divsn. N.C. Dept. Environ. Health and Natural Resources, Raleigh, 1984-94, chief gen. communicable disease control sect., 1994—. Mem. Raleigh Community Band, Cary (N.C.) Town Band. Mem. N.C. Pub. Health Assn. Office: NC Dept Environ Health and Natural Resources PO Box 27687 Raleigh NC 27611-7687

MACDONALD, ANITA, pediatric dietitian; b. Preston, England, Apr. 20, 1956; d. Thomas and Connie (Lawrenson) Jenkinson; m. John MacDonald. BSc, Leeds Poly., 1979. Registered dietitian. Dietitian Derby Royal Infirmary, U.K., 1979-80; pediat. dietitian St. James U. Hosp., Leeds, U.K., 1980-92; chief pediat. dietitian Birmingham Children's Hosp., U.K., 1992—; tutor Leeds U., 1985-92; dietetic adv., med. com. Galactosaemia Support Group, 1994—; chmn. Internat. Cystic Fibrosis Nutrition Group, 1994—. Mem. Br. Dietetic Assn. (organizer pediat. working group 1990—), Nat. Soc. Phenylketonuria (med. com. 1990-94), Br. Pediat. Assn. (child care excellence award 1993, pediat. award 1987, Mead Johnson award 1983/85), West Midlands Pediat. Group (coord. 1992—), Br. Inherited Metabolic Disease Group. Office: Birmingham Children's Hosp, Ladywood Middleway, Birmingham B16 8ET, England

MACDONALD, DAVID RICHARD, industrial psychologist; b. Dowagiac, Mich., May 20, 1953; s. Jerrold Brewster and Shirley Ann (Shaffer) MacD.; m. Mary Elizabeth Olson, Dec. 20, 1975 (div. Sept. 5, 1995); 1 child, Sarah Ann; m. Cathleen Jean Carlson, July 25, 1996. AS, Southwestern Mich. Coll., 1973; BBA, Western Mich. U., 1975, MA, 1976, EdS, 1979; PhD, Mich. State U., 1986. Announcer, boardman WDOW AM/FM, Dowagiac, Mich., 1969-72; mgmt. devel. specialist Interstate Motor Freight System, Grand Rapids, Mich., 1977-79; sr. mgmt. tng. instr. GTE Gen. Telephone Co. Mich., Muskegon, 1979-82; cons. human resources devel. Steelcase, Inc., Grand Rapids, 1982-86, mgr. performance devel., 1986—; asst. prof. grad. mgmt. Aquinas Coll., Grand Rapids, 1983—; cons., speaker in field; facilitator, program dir. Devel. Dimensions Internat., Pitts., 1981; facilitator Alamo Learning Systems, Southfield, Mich., 1983, 86, Wilson Learning Corp., Eden Prairie, Minn., 1983; job analysis program mgr. Barry M. Cohen & Assocs., Largo, Fla., 1985. Co-chair United Way Steelcase campaign, Grand Rapids, 1986. Mem. ASTD (sec. W. Mich. chpt. 1977-79), Soc. Indsl.-Orgnl. Psychology, Am. Psychol. Assn., Nat. Soc. for Performance and Instrn., Mensa, Phi Kappa Phi. Republican. Home: 2306 Prospect Ave SE Grand Rapids MI 49507-3159 Office: PO Box 1967 Grand Rapids MI 49501-1967

MACDONALD, JEROME EDWARD, school psychologist, consultant; b. Newark, Aug. 16, 1925; s. Jerome A. and Olvinia Regina (McKenna) MacD.; m. Nan Elizabeth Kennington, June 2, 1951; children: Jerome C., Mary Jane, Charles, Blanche Kohler, Ruth, Gregory, Paul, Robert, Carol Arbing. BS, Niagara U., 1947, MA (grad. fellow), 1950; MA in Ednl. Psychology (experienced tchr. fellow), profl. diploma in sch. psychology, Jersey City State Coll., 1970; postgrad., Fordham U., 1950-55. Asst. prof. philosophy Seton Hall U., South Orange, N.J., 1948-55; lectr. in philosophy, edn. Seton Hall U., South Orange, 1955-61; tchr. English Newark Pub. Schs., 1955-60, guidance counselor, 1960-62, chmn. dept., 1963-69, psychologist, 1969-71; psychologist Metuchen (N.J.) Pub. Schs., 1971-86; vis. tchr. NDEA Reading Inst. Bowling Green (Ohio) U., 1966-67; extern psychologist N.J. Diagnostic Ctr., Menlo Park, 1969; consulting psychologist Dept. Health and Social Svcs., P.E.I., Can., 1987—. Editor: (with Eli Levinson) The English Curriculum in Secondary Schools: Ninth Grade, 1964. Troop treas. Boy Scouts Am., 1967-69. With inf., AUS, 1943-46. Decorated Bronze Star medal. Mem. Nat. Assn. Sch. Psychologists, Internat. Reading Assn., NEA, Am. Psychol. Assn., N.J. Psychol. Assn., N.J. Assn. Sch. Psychologists, Middlesex County Sch. Psychologists Assn. (pres. 1976-77, 81-82), Psychol. Assn. Prince Edward Island, N.J. Catholic Tchrs. Guild (pres. 1966), VFW, Am. Legion, DAV, Holy Name Soc., Can. Legion, Mensa, Phi Delta Kappa, Lions. Roman Catholic. Home: PO Box 71, 1 MacDonald Rd Cavendish, North Rustico, PE Canada C0A 1X0

MACDONALD, JOHN STEPHEN, oncologist, educator; b. Bklyn., June 2, 1943; s. John Stephen and Margaret (Martin) M.; m. Mary Suzanne Stock, July 11, 1964; children: Margaret Wilson, John Stephen, Kathleen Lenore, Frederick Stock. A.B., Dartmouth Coll., 1965, B.M.S., 1967; M.D., Harvard U., 1969. Diplomate Am. Bd. Internal Medicine (mem. med. oncology com. 1989-93, chmn. med. oncology self edn. process com. 1993—). Intern and resident in medicine Beth Israel Hosp., Boston, 1969-71; clin. assoc. immunology and med. oncology Nat. Cancer Inst., Bethesda, Md., 1971-74; assoc. dir. cancer therapy evaluation program, div. cancer treatment Nat. Cancer Inst., 1979-82, med. oncologist Washington Clin., 1982-84; instr., asst. prof., then assoc. prof. medicine Georgetown U., Washington, 1974-79; clin. assoc. prof. Georgetown U., 1979-84, George Washington U., 1980-84; prof. medicine, chief div. hematology-oncology U. Ky., Lexington, 1984-89, assoc. dir. Markey Cancer Center, 1984-89; prof. medicine, chief sect. med. oncology, dir. cancer ctr. Temple U., Phila., 1989—; chmn. gastrointestinal cancer com. S.W. Oncology Group, 1985—. Editor-in-chief: Cancer Treatment Reports, 1979-82; co-editor: Gastrointestinal Oncology, 1992; mem. editorial bd. Jour. Clin. Oncology, 1988-91; contbr. over 180 articles to med. jours. Bd. mgmt. YMCA, 1979-84; bd. dirs. CYO, 1979-84. Served with USPHS, 1971-74. Jr. faculty clin. fellow Am. Cancer Soc., 1974-76. Fellow ACP; mem. Am. Fedn. Clin. Research, Am. Soc. Clin. Oncology, Am. Assn. for Cancer Research, Am. Cancer Soc. (bd. dirs. Phila. chpt. 1994—). Roman Catholic. Home: 522 Ridgeview Ln Villanova PA 19085-1715 Office: Temple U PO Box 38346 3322 N Broad St Philadelphia PA 19140-5102

MACDONALD, KENNETH GORDON, JR., surgeon; b. Charleston, W.Va., Sept. 6, 1954; s. Kenneth Gordon and Ellen Nora (Cook) M.; m. Jane Ethel Miller, May 19, 1979; children: Gloria Jane, Clara Ellen, Elizabeth Jeanne. BS in Biology cum laude, Washington and Lee U., Lexington, Va., 1976; MD, W.Va. U., 1981. Diplomate Am. Bd. Surgery, Nat. Bd. Med. Examiners; lic. physician N.C.; cert. ATLS, ATLS instr. Intern in internal medicine N.C. Bapt. Hosp., Bowman-Gray Sch. Medicine, Winston-Salem, 1981-82, resident in gen. surgery, 1982-84; resident in gen. surgery Pitt County Meml. Hosp./East Carolina U. Sch. Medicine, Greenville, 1984-86, chief resident in gen. surgery, 1986-87; clin. instr. surgery East Caroline U. Sch. Medicine, Greenville, 1987-88, asst. prof. surgery, 1988-93, assoc. prof. surgery, 1993—, chief gastrointestinal surgery and surg. endoscopy, 1989—; lectr. in field. Assoc. editor Current Surgery, 1990—; contbr. articles to profl. jours., chpts. to books. Mem. exec. bd. East Carolina coun. Boy Scouts Am., 1988-93, chmn. health and safety com., 1988—; participant 3d ann. corp. spelling bee Literacy Vols. of America/Pitt County, 1993. Ciba-Geigy Corp. grantee, 1993, Roerig/Pfizer Pharms. grantee. Fellow ACS (1st prize for presentation 1986), Southeastern Surg. Congress; mem. AMA, Am. Soc. Bariatric Surgery (chmn. program com., ex-officio mem. exec. coun. 1991, 92, exec. coun. 1992-95, pres.-elect 1995-96), Assn. Acad. Surgery, Assn. for Surg. Edn., N.C. Med. Soc., Pitt County Med. Soc., So. Am. Gastrointestinal Endoscopic Surgeons, Soc. for Surgery of Alimentary Tract, Walter J. Pories Soc. (founding mem.), Sigma Xi. Office: East Carolina Univ Sch of Medicine Dept of Surgery Greenville NC 27858

MACDONALD, MICHAEL JOSEPH, physician, administrator; b. Lafayette, Ind., Aug. 22, 1962; s. Hugh Joseph and Joan Evelyn (Ruel) MacD. AA, Brevard C.C., 1982; BS, Fla. State U., 1984, BA, 1986; DO, Southeastern U., 1990; MPH, Harvard U., 1995. Intern family practice USN, Jacksonville, Fla., 1990-91; flight surgeon candidate USN, Pensacola, Fla., 1991-92; flight surgeon USN, South Weymouth, Mass., 1992-94; occupl. medicine resident Harvard U., Boston, 1994-96; occupational med. specialist Health First Physicians, Melbourne, Fla., 1996—, co-dir., 1996—. Contbr. articles to profl. jours. Active Make-a-Wish Found., Boston, 1994-96. Lt. USN, 1990-94; lt. comdr. USNR, 1995—. Mem. AMA, Am. Osteo. Assn., Harvard Club, Fla. State Alumni Assn. Republican. Roman Catholic. Home: 8651 Sylan Dr Melbourne FL 32901 Office: Health First Physicians Inc 1051 S Hickory St Melbourne FL 32901

MACDONALD, PAUL CLOREN, biologist, physician. MD, U. Tex., 1955. Prof. ob-gyn. and biochemistry Cecil H. & Ida Cecil Green Ctr. Reproductive Biol. Scis., 1974—, dir. endocrinology, 1974—. Mem. Inst. Medicine, Nat. Acad. Scis. Office: Green Ctr Reproductive Biol 5323 Harry Hines Blvd Dallas TX 75235*

MACDONALD, RICHARD GALLOWAY, podiatrist; b. Evanston, Ill., Dec. 31, 1936; s. Hugh and Edith (Jersild) M.; m. (Sally) Jean Anderson, July 1, 1961; children: Richard B., Philip A., Anne Macdonald Wheeden. D of Podiatric Medicine, Ill. Coll. Podiatric Medicine, 1960. Diplomate Am. Bd. Podiatric Surgery, Am. Coun. Cert. Podiatric Physicians and Surgeons. Preceptor, resident U.S. Army, 1961-64; podiatrist Richard G. Macdonald DPM, PC, Peoria, Ill., 1965—; podiatrist St. Francis Med. Ctr., Peoria, Meth. Med. Ctr., Peoria, Proctor Hops., Peoria, Peoria Day Surgery Ctr., Peoria, Peoria Ambulatory Surgery Ctr.; cons. VA Out Patient Clinic, Peoria, 1988-94, Fed. Correctional Instn., Pekin, Ill., 1995—; lectr. in field. Mem. sch. bd. Dist. # 52 Sch. Bd., Washington, 1977-80. Capt. U.S. Army, 1960-65. Fellow Am. Coll. Podiatric Physicians; mem. Am. Podiatric Med. Assn., Ill. Podiatric Med. Assn. (pres. Zone II), Peoria Rotary Club (bd. dirs., sec. 1966—), Alpha Gamma Kappa. Home: 609 Yorkshire Dr Washington IL 61571 Office: Richard G Macdonald 515 NE Glen Oak Ave Ste 312 Peoria IL 61603

MACDONALD, ROSS ALEXANDER, pharmaceutical company executive; b. Castlemaine, Victoria, Australia, Apr. 19, 1958; s. Donald Marshall and Helen (Lindsay) M.; m. Sharon Anne O'Brien, Nov. 10, 1990. BSc with honors, Monash U., Melbourne, Australia, 1981, PhD, 1986; Grad. Diploma Bus. Adminstrn., Swinburne U., 1993. Rsch. fellow Royal Children's Hosp., Melbourne, 1986-88; cons. analyst Roach Tilley Grice, Melbourne, 1987-88; sci. affairs mgr. AMRAD Corp., Melbourne, 1988-91, rsch. projects mgr., 1991-93, bus. devel. mgr., 1993-95, group bus. devel. mgr., 1995—. Contbr. articles to profl. jours. Recipient scholarship Australian Govt., 1973, Monash U., 1981, Rsch. award Royal Children's Hosp., 1987. Mem. Australian Alpine Club (chmn. 1989—), N.Y. Acad. Scis. Office: AMRAD Corp, 17-27 Cotham Rd, Kew VIC 3101, Australia

MACDONALD, STEPHEN HUGH, physician, reserve naval officer; b. Lafayette, Ind., Aug. 22, 1962; s. Hugh Joseph and Joan Ruth (Ruel) MacD. AA, Brevard Community Coll., 1982; BS, Fla. State U., 1984, BA, 1986; DO, Southeastern U. Health Scis., 1990; MPH, Harvard U., 1995. Commd. lt. USN, 1990; intern in family practice Naval Hosp., Pensacola, Fla., 1990-91; flight surgeon USNR, Beaufort, S.C., 1992-94; resident occupl. medicine Harvard U., Cambridge, Mass., 1994-96. Lt. comdr. USNR, 1996. Republican. Roman Catholic. Home: 8651 Sylvan Dr Melbourne FL 32904-2427

MACDOUGALL, COLIN NEIL, gastroenterologist, consultant; b. Colchester, Essex, Eng., Aug. 16, 1949; arrived in Rhodesia (now Zimbabwe), 1955; s. William Aitken and Pauline Audrey (Maxted) MacD.; m. Mary Elizabeth Parker, Nov. 2, 1972; children: Caroline, Robert, Helen. MB BChir, Birmingham U., Salisbury, Eng., 1973. Registered physician, U.K.; cert. good standing; cert. specialist register, Zimbabwe. Med. registrar Repatriation Gen. Hosp., Perth, Australia, 1979-81; lectr. U. Zimbabwe, Harare, 1982-85; cons. physician, gastroenterology Mil. Hosp., Khamis Mushayt, Saudi Arabia, 1985-87, Harare, 1987-92; cons. gastroenterologist Mil. Hosp., Jeddah, Saudi Arabia, 1992-94; cons. physician, gastroenterologist Harare, 1994—; dir. postgrad. edn. King Fahd Mil. Hosp., Jeddah, 1993-94. Fellow Royal Coll. Physicians; mem. South African Gastroenterol. Soc., Gastroenterol. Soc. Australia. Office: 53 Baines Ave, Harare Zimbabwe

MACDOUGALL, JOHN DUNCAN, surgeon; b. Indpls., Mar. 4, 1925; s. Duncan Campbell and Beulah Stewart (Ward) MacD.; m. Inga Margaretha Tranberg, Oct. 6, 1951 (div. Oct. 1990); children: Stewart Andrew, Eric Matthew, Victoria Suzanne MacDougall Korb; m. Barbara Lee Mayse, Nov. 1, 1990; children: Katherine Jane, James William. BS, Ind. U., 1948; MD, Ind. U., Indpl., 1951. Diplomate Am. Bd. Surgery, Am. Bd. Thoracic Surgery. Pvt. practice Indpls., 1957-93; pres. med. staff St. Francis Hosp., Beech Grove, Ind., 1975, pres. adv. bd., 1993-95, chmn. governing bd. trustees, 1995—; chmn. bd. dirs. Physician's Ins. Co. of Ind., Indpls., 1987—. Adv. com. Ind. U. Sch. Medicine, Indpls., 1989—, pres. dean's coun., 1992-95; mem. Ind. Govs. Task Force on Organ Transplantation, Indpls., 1986-89; pres. Ind. Med. Polit. Action Com., Indpls., 1992—. With U.S. Army, 1943-46; ETO. Decorated Bronze Star medal. Fellow ACS; mem. AMA (del., chmn. Ind. delegation), Ind. State Med. Assn. (pres. 1987-88), Indpls. Med. Soc. (pres. 1978-79), Orgn. State Med. Assn. Pres. (pres. 1994-95), Nat. Med. Vets. Assn. (bd. dirs. 1992—), Masons, Indpls. Lit. Club. Republican. Episcopalian. Home: 7202 Dean Rd Indianapolis IN 46240-3628 Office: Physicians Ins Co of Ind Ste 300 8425 Woodfield Crossing Indianapolis IN 46240

MACDUFFEE, ROBERT COLTON, family physician, pathologist; b. Princeton, N.J., Apr. 23, 1923; s. Cyrus Colton and Mary Augusta (Bean) MacD.; m. Elizabeth Ann Jessup, Aug. 30, 1984; children: Martha, Jennifer, Susan. BS, U. Chgo., 1944, MD, 1946. Diplomate, Am. Bd. Pathology, Am. Bd. Family Practice. Asst. prof. pathology Hahnemann Med. Sch., Phila., 1959-60; chief clin. pathologist Grad. Hosp. U. Pa., Phila., 1960-63; pathologist Lock Haven (Pa.) Hosp., 1963-64; pathologist, chief Altoona (Pa.) Hosp., 1964-71; pathologist, assoc. SmithKline Labs., Tampa, Fla., 1971-84; dir. walk-in clinic Naples (Fla.) Med. Ctr., 1984-93; ret., 1994. Maj. MC, U.S. Army, 1946-54, Korea. Fellow Coll. Am. Pathologists. Presbyterian.

MACE, JOHN WELDON, pediatrician; b. Buena Vista, Va., July 9, 1938; s. John Henry and Gladys Elizabeth (Edwards) M.; m. Janice Mace, Jan. 28, 1962; children: Karin E., John E., James E. B.A., Columbia Union Coll., 1960; M.D., Loma Linda U., 1964. Diplomate: Am. Bd. Pediatrics, Sub-bd. Pediatric Endocrinology. Intern U.S. Naval Hosp., San Diego, 1964-65, resident in pediatrics, 1966-68; fellow in endocrinology and metabolism U. Colo., 1970-72; asst. prof. pediatrics Loma Linda (Calif.) U. Med. Center, 1972-75, prof., chmn. dept., 1975—; med. dir. Loma Linda U. Children's Hosp., 1990-92, physician-in-chief, 1992—. Contbr. articles to profl. jours. Treas. Found. for Med. Care San Bernardino County, 1979-80, pres., 1980-82; mem. Congl. Adv. Bd., 1984-87; pres. So. Calif. affiliate Am. Diabetes Assn., 1985-86, dir., 1987-89; chmn. adv. bd. State Calif. Children's Svcs., 1986—; bd. dirs. So. Calif. Children's Cancer Svcs., 1993-94, Loma Linda Ronald McDonald House, 1991—, Aetna Health Plans of Calif., 1993-95; bd. dirs. Loma Linda U. Health Care, 1995—. Named Alumnist of Yr., Loma Linda U. Sch. Medicine, 1994. Mem. AAAS, N.Y. Acad. Sci., Calif. Med. Soc. (adv. panel genetic diseases State Calif., 1975—), Western Soc. Pediatric Rsch., Lawson Wilkens Pediatric Endocrine Soc., Assn. Med. Pediatric Dept. Chmn., Am. Acad. Pediatrics, Sigma Xi, Alpha Omega Alpha. Office: Loma Linda U Children's Hosp 11234 Anderson St Loma Linda CA 92354

MACE, MARTIN CHARLES, oral and maxillo-facial surgeon, consultant; b. Winchester, Hampshire, England, Aug. 5, 1945; m. Frances Mace, Dec. 19, 1969; children: Alasdair, Richard. BDS, Guys Hosp., London, 1967; LDS, Royal Coll. of Surgeons, England, 1967; MBBS, Guys Hosp., London, 1973; FDS, Royal Coll. Surgeons, England, 1974. House surgeon Guys Hosp., London, 1968, 73; registrar Eastman Dental Hosp., London, 1974-75; sr. registrar Queen Victoria Hosp., East Grinstead, 1975-76, Guys Hosp., London, 1976-78; cons. Stoke Mandeville Hosp., Buckinghamshire, 1978—; hon. clin. tutor Guys Hosp., London, 1980—. Co-author: (books) General Dental Treatment, 1986, Currrent Surgical Practice, 1990. vice chmn. Dentist's Provident Soc., London, 1984—; chmn. Dentist's Ins. Com., London, 1996. Fellow British Assn. Oral and Maxillo-facial Surgeons. Office: Stoke Mandeville Hosp, Mandeville Rd, HP218AL Aylesbury Buckinghamshire England

MACE, SHARON ELIZABETH, physician; b. Syracuse, N.Y., Oct. 30, 1949; d. James Henry and Leona Helen (Bednarski) M. BS, Syracuse U., 1971; MD, SUNY, 1975. Intern and resident in pediatrics Case-Western Res. U. Hosps., Cleve., 1975-77, fellow in cardiology, 1977-79, instr. dept. emergency medicine, 1980—; rsch. assoc. div. investigative medicine Mt. Sinai Med. Ctr., Cleve., 1979-80, staff physician depts. emergency medicine and investigative medicine, 1979-86, coord. emergency medicine residency program; asst. dir. dept. emergency medicine Mt. Sinai Med. Ctr.; dir. emergency dept. Saratoga Hosp., Saratoga Springs, N.Y., 1986-88; dir. emergency dept. St. Mary's Hosp., Rochester, N.Y., 1988-91; dir. emergency dept. St. Elizabeth Hosp., Utica, N.Y., 1991-94; assoc. dir. observation unit Cleve. Clin. Gound., 1995—; former instr. Case Western Res. U. Sch. Medicine; helicopter flight physician; instr. Advanced Cardiac Life Support. Contbr. articles to med. jours. Mem. Am. Coll. Emergency Physicians (edn. com., bd. dir. N.Y. chpt., bd. dirs. N.Y. and Ohio chpts., chmn. N.Y. sect.), Soc. Academic Emergency Medicine. Congregationalist. Home: 11961 Laurel Rd Chesterland OH 44026-1757 Office: Cleve Clinic Found Desk E-19 9500 Euclid Ave Cleveland OH 44195

MACE, TERESA ANN, geriatrics nurse; b. San Diego, Mar. 10, 1967; d. E Clayton Knight and Patricia Lee (Doggette) Humphries; married; children: Steven J., Clayton Alexander. Diploma in nursing, Moultrie Area Tech. Sch., 1992. LPN, Ga., Va.; cert. BLS Am. Heart Assn. Patient care coord. Horizon Health Ctr., Athens, Ga., 199294; LPN charge nurse Beverly Manor of Portsmouth, Va., 1994, Mannings Convalescent Home, Portsmouth, Va., 1994—. Leader Girl Scouts U.S., Moultrie, 1988-89; vol. ARC, Ga., 1991-93, 94-95. Mem. Nat. Fedn. LPN. Democrat. Baptist.

MACER, GEORGE ARMEN, JR., orthopedic hand surgeon; b. Pasadena, Calif., Oct. 17, 1948; s. George A. and Nevart Akullian M.; m. Celeste Angelle Lyons, Mar. 26, 1983; children: Christiana Marilu, Marina Lynn, Emily Sue. BA, U. So. Calif., 1971, MD, 1976. Diplomate Am. Bd. Med. Examiners, Am. Bd. Orthopaedic Surgery; cert. surgery of hand. Intern Meml. Hosp. Med. Ctr., Long Beach, Calif., 1976; resident Orthopaedic Hosp./U. So. Calif., 1977-81; pvt. practice hand surgery Long Beach, 1983—; asst. clin. prof. orthopaedics U. So. Calif., Long Beach, 1983-89, 1990—; cons. hand surgery svc. Rancho Los Amigos Hosp. Downey, 1990—; cons. Harbor UCLA Med. Ctr., Torrance, 1983—. Joseph Boyes Hand fellow, 1982; mem. AMA, Calif. Med. Assn., L.A. County Med. Assn., Western Orthopaedic Assn., Am. Soc. for Surgery of Hand, Am. Acad. Orthopaedic Surgery. Republican. Office: 3550 Linden Ave Ste 2 Long Beach CA 90807 also: 8635 W 3d St Ste 965W Los Angeles CA 90048

MAC FADYEN, BRUCE VISCHER, JR., physician, surgeon; b. Phila., Nov. 4, 1942; s. Bruce V. and Renee S. (Smith) MacF.; BS, Wheaton Coll., 1964; MD, Hahnemann Med. Coll., 1968; m. Rosemary Mortensen, June 18, 1965; children: Sharon Ruth, Deborah Renee, Bruce Vischer, Christina Elizabeth. Intern, Hosp. of U. Pa., 1968-69, asst. resident gen. surgery, 1969-72, Hermann Hosp., Houston, 1972-73, chief resident surgery, 1973-74; research fellow Harrison dept. surg. rsch. U. Pa. Sch. Medicine, Phila., 1971-72; practice medicine specializing in surgery, Phila., 1968-72, Houston, 1972—; asst. instr. surgery U. Pa., Phila., 1969-72; instr. surgery U. Tex. Med. Sch., Houston, 1973-74, asst. prof. surgery, 1974-77, assoc. prof. surgery, 1977-90, prof. surgery, 1990—; mem. staff Hermann, Meml. S.W., Diagnostic, Park Plaza, St. Joseph's hosps., Houston. Diplomate Am. Bd. Surgery. Fellow ACS; mem. Assn. Acad. Surgery, Am. Soc. Parenteral and Enteral Nutrition, Soc. Surgery of Alimentary Tract, Internat. Soc. Parenteral Nutrition, Soc. Surg. Oncology, Am. Cancer Soc. (dir. 1976-80), Harris County Med. Soc., AMA, Tex. Med. Assn., Christian Med. Soc., Tex. Surg. Soc., Ravdin-Rhoads Surg. Soc., Am. Soc. Laser Medicine and Surgery, Collegium Internat., Soc. Am. Gastrointestinal Endoscopic Surgeons, Am. Soc. Gastrointestinal Endoscopy. Contbr. numerous articles on nutrition, surgery, oncology and endoscopy to med. jours. Home: 303 Glenchester St Houston TX 77079-7154 Office: 6431 Fannin St Houston TX 77030-1501

MACGREGOR, ALEX M. C., surgeon; b. Invergowrie, Scotland, Dec. 15, 1932; m. Christine Ann McNaughton, June 16, 1964; children: Gregor, Callum, Gylla. MD, U. St. Andrews, Scotland, 1958. Cardiovascular rschr. U. So. Calif., 1964-65, Dundee (Scotland) Royal Infirmary, 1969-70. Fellow ACS, Royal Coll. Surgeons (Edinburg, Scotland); mem. AMA, Alachua County Med. Soc., Am. Coll. Legal Medicine, Am. Soc. Abdominal Surgeons, Am. Soc. Bariatric Surgery (pres.), Am. Soc. Parenteral and Enteral Nutrition, Assn. Acad. Surgery, AvMed-SantaFe Healthcare, Fla. Acad. Family Physicians, Fla. Assn. Nutritional Support, Fla. Ind. Physicians Assn., Fla. Med. Assn., Fla. Physicians Assn., Fla. Surg. Soc., Gainesville Area C. of C., Nat. Bariatric Surgery Register, N.Am. Assn. for Study of Obesity, North Fla. Assocs., Royal Soc. Medicine, Soc. Laparoendoscopic Surgeons, Southeastern Surg. Congress, So. Med. Assn. Office: Gainesville Surg Group PA 6717 NW 11th Pl Ste C Gainesville FL 32605

MACGREGOR, GRAHAM ALEXANDER, medical educator; b. St. Albans, Eng., Apr. 1, 1941; s. Alexander Brittan and Sybil Philip (Hawkey) MacG.; m. Christiane Bourquin, Feb. 11, 1968; children: Annabelle, Vanessa, Christopher. Student, Marlborough Coll., Wiltshire, Eng., 1955-59; BA, MA, Cambridge U., 1964; MB, BChir, Middlesex Hosp., London, 1967. House physician Middlesex Hosp. and Hammersmith Hosp., London, 1967-69; lectr. St. Thomas' Hosp., London, 1970-73; sr. registrar Charing Cross Hosp., London, 1973-79, sr. lectr., 1979-89; prof. cardiocascular medicine St. George's Hosp., London, 1989—. Author: Hypertension in Practice, 1987, 2d edit., 1995, Low Salt Diet Book, 1989, 2d edit., 1992; contbr. sci. papers to profl. publs. Fellow Royal Coll. Physicians; mem. Brit. Hypertension Soc. (treas.), Internat. Soc. Hypertension, Assn. Physicians, Am. Soc. Hypertension. Office: St George's Hosp Dept Medicine, Cranmer Ter, London SW17 ORE, England

MACGREGOR, JAMES THOMAS, toxicologist; b. N.Y.C., Jan. 14, 1944; s. James and Phyllis (Bowman) MacG.; m. Judith Anne Anello, July 12, 1969; 1 child, Jennifer Lee. BS in Chemistry, Union Coll., Schenectady, N.Y., 1965; PhD in Toxicology, U. Rochester, 1970. Diplomate Am. Bd. Toxicology. Postdoctoral fellow U. Calif., San Francisco, 1970-72; dir. food safety rsch. USDA, Berkeley, Calif., 1972-88; assoc. prof. U. Calif., Berkeley, 1978-88; pres. Toxicology Consulting Svcs., Danville, Calif., 1988-90; dir. toxicology lab. SRI Internat., Menlo Park, Calif., 1990—; mem. numerous nat. and internat. profl. coms. and working groups. Mem. editorial bd.: Environ. Molecular Mutagenesis, N.Y.C., 1986-88, Mutation Res., Amsterdam, 1989-91, Mutagenesis, Oxford, 1989-93. Recipient Alexander Hollender award, 1995. Mem. Am. Assn. Cancer Rsch., Soc. Toxicology, Environ. Mutagen Soc. (treas. 1986-89, pres. 1992-93), Genetic Environ. Toxicology Assn. No. Calif. (pres. 1982). Office: SRI Internat 333 Ravenswood Ave Menlo Park CA 94025-3453

MACGREGOR, REBECCA, medical and surgical nurse; b. Canon City, Colo., Nov. 13, 1958; d. Archie Robert, Jr. and Jeanette Ruth (Wilson) MacG. BS, U. No. Colo., 1981. RN, Colo., N.Mex. Relief supr. Salida (Colo.) Hosp.; staff nurse St. Mary-Corwin Hosp., Pueblo, Colo.; nurse mgr. Dept. Vet. Affairs Med. Ctr., Albuquerque.

MACHADO, CHRISTIAN E., cardiologist; b. Havana, Cuba, May 12, 1961; came to U.S., 1978; s. Christian and Seida J. (Tormes) M.; m Kelly E. Machado, July 8, 1988; children: Alexandra I., Gabriell E. BA in Sci., Palm Beach (Fla.) Coll., 1980; MD, St. Domingo Inst. Tech., Dominican Republic, 1985. Diplomate Am. Bd. Internal Medicine with subspecialty in cardiology, electrophysiology and pacing. Chief resident Wayne State U., Detroit, 1989-90, chief cardiology fellow, 1993-94; dir. arrythmia svcs. Heart Care Inst. of Tampa, Fla., 1994—, dir. pacemaker clinic, 1994; dir. electrophysiology Univ. Cmty. Hosp., 1994—; Sci. editor Med. Letter of Nicaraguan Am. Med. Assn., 1994; contbr. articles to profl. jours. Fellow Am. Coll. Cardiology, Am. Coll. Chest Physicians; mem. ACP, N.Am. Soc. Pacing and Electrophysiology, Am. Heart Assn. (mem. coun.). Office: Heart Care Institute 14320 Bruce B Downs Tampa FL 33647

MACHELL, DAVID FRANCIS, academic and counseling psychologist; b. Manchester, Conn., Apr. 11, 1950; s. Ernest Robert and Teresa (Madden) M.; BS, Ctrl. Conn. State U., 1976; MS in Psychology, MS Counseling, 1978; EdD, Fordham U., 1984; m. Phyllis A. Smith, Nov. 5, 1971. Approved clin. supr., Conn.; cert. alcoholism counselor, cert. substance abuse counselor, cert. clin. supr. Exec. dir. Alcoholism Rehab. Center, New Britain, Conn., 1978-82; approved chief adminstr. Conn. Dept. Mental Health, New Britain, 1978-82; adj. prof. Western Conn. State U., Danbury, 1980-81, asst. prof. justice, law adminstrn., 1981-86, assoc. prof., 1986-91, prof., 1991—, chair divsn. justice and law adminstrn., 1993—; treatment cons. Hartford Correctional Center, 1978-82, Guenster Rehab. Center, Bridgeport, 1982-85; clin. dir. Meridian Found. Inc., Stamford, Conn., 1985-87; pvt. practice in cmty. psychology COES, Watertown, Conn., 1987—; com. mem. adv. bd. on clin. supervision Conn. Alcohol and Drug Abuse Commn., Hartford, 1979-81; mem. adv. council on criminal justice Cath. Family Services, New Britain, 1978-82; clin. mental health counselor, dept. psychiatry New Britain Gen. Hosp., 1976-78; exec. dir. Resurrection House, Inc., New Britain; bd. dirs. Conn. Addiction Cert. Bd. Mem. exec. bd. Tri-County Alcoholism Council, Middletown, Conn., 1979-82. Mem. APA, Nat. Acad. Cert. Clin. Mental Health Counselors, Conn. Assn. Alcohol Agys. (exec. bd. 1979-81), Assn. Labor-Mgmt. Adminstrs. and Consultants on Alcoholism, New England Psychol. Assn. (bd. dirs.), Conn. Criminal Justice Assn. Roman Catholic. Home: 1650 Litchfield Rd Watertown CT 06795-1012 Office: Western Conn State U Divsn Justice and Law Administrn Westside Campus Danbury CT 06810

MACHEMER, ROBERT, ophthalmologist; b. Muenster, Germany, Mar. 16, 1933; came to U.S., 1966, naturalized, 1972; s. Helmut and Erna M.; m. Christine Haller, July 28, 1961; 1 dau., Ruth. Student, univs. Muenster, Freiburg, Germany, Vienna, Austria, 1953-59, med. diploma, 1959; MD, U. Freiburg, 1959; MD (hon.), U. Goettingen, Germany, 1988. Diplomate Am. Bd. Ophthalmology. Rotating intern Germany, 1960-61; fellow in gen. pathology Univ. Inst. of Pathology, Freiburg, Germany, 1961-62; resident in ophthalmology Augenklinik der Universitaet Goettingen, Germany, 1962-65; sci. asst. U. Goettingen, 1962-68; Akademischer Austauschdienst research fellow Bascom Palmer Eye Inst., U. Miami, Fla., 1966-67, Nat. Council to Combat Blindness research fellow, 1967-68, instr. ophthalmology, 1968-70, asst. prof. ophthalmology, 1970-74, assoc. prof., 1974-78, prof., 1978; prof., chmn. dept. ophthalmology Duke U. Eye Center, 1978-91, Helena Rubinstein Found. prof., 1983—; mem. staff VA Hosp., Miami, 1969-78; chief sect. ophthalmology VA Hosp., 1969-71; mem. staff VA Hosp., Durham, N.C., 1978-80; mem. policy adv. group, diabetic retinopathy vitrectomy study NIH, 1978-80, mem. study exec. com., 1977-80, mem. data monitoring com. early treatment diabetic retinopathy study, 1980-88, mem. study sect., 1982-84. Author: (with T. Aaberg) Vitrectomy, 1979; mem. editorial bd. Am. Jour. Ophthalmology, 1979—, Graefe's Archive, 1982—; contbr. numerous articles related to retinal detachment and vitreous surgery to med. pubs. Recipient Hermann Wacker award Club Jules Gonin, 1972, Trustees award Rsch. to Prevent Blindness, 1978, von Graefe prize German Ophthal. Soc., 1981, Pisart Vision award N.Y. Lighthouse for the Blind, 1987, Ernst Jung prize for Medicine Jung Stiftung for Sci. and Rsch., Hamburg, Germany, 1993; Rsch. to Prevent Blindness Louis B. Mayer scholar, 1971. Fellow Royal Australian Coll. Ophthalmologists (hon.); mem. AMA, Am. Acad. Ophthalmology, Pan. Am. Assn. Ophthalmology, Am. Ophthalmol. Soc., Retina Soc. (award of merit in retina research 1980), N.C. Med. Soc., Club Jules Gonin (pres. 1986-88), Assn. Research in Vision and Ophthalmology (Proctor medal and lectr. 1988). Office: Duke U Med Ctr Box 3802 Durham NC 27710

MACHERAS, PANAYOTIS, pharmacist educator; b. Piraeus, Greece, Sept. 27, 1947; s. Evangelos and Helen (Sideromenos) M.; m. Chryssanthi, Sept. 29, 1973; children: Evangelos, Spiros. B of Pharmacy, U. Athens, Greece, 1970, PhD, 1977; PhD, U. London, Eng., 1981. Lic. pharmacist. Asst. lectr. dept. pharmacy U. Athens, Greece, 1975-77, lectr., 1978-83, asst. prof., 1984-87; vis. assoc. prof. coll. of pharmacy U. Mich., Ann Arbor, 1988; assoc. prof. dept. pharmacy U. Athens, 1987-93, dir. Biopharmaceutics-Pharmacokinetics lab., 1991-93, prof. pharmacy, 1993—; mem. sci. coun. Nat. Orgn. of Drugs, Greece, 1983-89; mem. com. 5th European Congress of Pharm. Sci., Pharm. Rsch., European Jour., Pharm. Sci., Jour. Biochem. and Biophys. Methods. Author: Biopharmaceutics, 1984, 91, Greek National Formulary, 1986, Quantitative Calculations in Pharmaceutical Practice and Research, 1993, Biopharmaceutics of Orally Administered Drugs, 1995; editor Pharmakeftiki, 1987—; contbr. more than 60 articles to profl. jours.; reviewer Biopharmaceutics and Pharmacokinetics. Home: 19 Drakou, 11742 Athens Greece Office: U of Athens, Panepistimiopolis, 15771 Athens Greece

MACHIDA, CURTIS A., research molecular neurobiologist; b. San Francisco, Apr. 1, 1954. AB, U. Calif., Berkeley, 1976; PhD, Oreg. Health Scis. U., 1982. Postdoctoral scientist Oreg. Health Scis. U., Portland, 1982-88; asst. scientist div. neurosci. Oreg. Regional Primate Research Ctr., Beaverton, 1988-95, assoc. scientist divsn. neuroscience, 1995—; rsch. asst. prof. biochemistry and molecular biology Oreg. Health Scis. U., 1989-95, mem. faculty neurosci. and molecular and cell biology grad. programs, 1989—, adj. assoc. prof. biochemistry and molecular biology. Editorial cons. Oreg. Health Scis. U. News, 1984-87; ad-hoc reviewer Endocrinology Molecular Pharmacology, NSF; contbr. articles to profl. jours. Established investigator Am. Heart Assn., 1994—. Recipient Leukemia Assn. award, 1981, Tartar award Med. Rsch. Found. Oreg., 1980; NIH fellow, 1980-82, 85-87, grantee, 1989, 95. Mem. AAAS, ASBMB, Am. Soc. Microbiology, Soc. Neurosci., AHA Basic Scis. Coun. Office: Div Neurosci Oreg Regl Primate Rsch Ctr Beaverton OR 97006

MACHLIN, LAWRENCE J., nutritionist, biochemist, educator; b. N.Y.C., June 24, 1927; s. Morris Louis and Lilly (Manevitz) M.; m. Ruth Beerman, May 30, 1953; children: Marc, Steven, Paul. BS, Cornell U., 1948, M in Nutritional Sci., 1949; PhD, Georgetown U., 1953. Nutritional biochemist USDA, AEC, Beltsville, Md., 1949-56; group chief Monsanto Co., St. Louis, 1956-73; sr. group chief Hoffman-La Roche Inc., Nutley, N.J., 1973-85, dir., 1985-92; pres. Nutrition Rsch. and Info. Inc., Livingston, N.J., 1993—; lectr. in nutrition Washington U., St. Louis, 1969-72; adj. prof. nutrition NYU, 1977-82; adj. assoc. prof. nutrition in medicine Cornell U., 1979—; Samuel Brody lectr. U. Mo., Columbia, 1988; Gladys Emerson Vis. prof. UCLA, 1990. Editor: Vitamin E, 1980, Handbook of Vitamins, 1984, rev. edit. 1991; co-editor: Vitamin Intake & Health, 1991; contbr. over 120 articles to profl. jours. Mem. Am. Inst. Nutrition, Am. Soc. Clin. Nutrition, N.Y. Acad. Scis., N.Y. Lipid Club, Soc. for Exptl. Biology and Medicine. Home: 18 Locust Pl Livingston NJ 07039-1213 Office: Hoffmann-LaRoche Inc 45 Eisenhower Dr Paramus NJ 07652-1429

MACHTIGER, HARRIET GORDON, psychoanalyst; b. N.Y.C., July 27, 1927; d. Michael J. and Miriam D. (Rand) Gordon; BA, Bklyn. Coll., 1947; dipl. with distinction, U. London, 1966, PhD, 1974; m. Sidney Machtiger, Feb. 7, 1948; children: Avram Coleman, Marcia Gordon, Bennett Rand. Tchr., Phila. Pub. Schs., 1962-64; ednl. therapist Child Guidance Tng. Center, London, 1966-68; ednl. therapist Sch. Psychol. Svc., Inner London Edn. Authority, 1968-70; therapist Paddington Day Hosp., London, 1970-71, London Centre for Psychotherapy, 1971-74, Staunton Clinic, U. Pitts., 1974-78; pvt. practice psychoanalysis, Pitts., 1976—; pres. C.G. Jung Ctr., Pitts., 1976-81; cons. in field. Mem. S.W. Pitts. Community Mental Health, 1976-78; past dir. Pitts. program Inter-Regional Soc. Jungian Analysts, 1975-85. Recipient award for Disting. Contributions to Advancement in Edn., Pa. Dept. Edn., 1962; Social Sci. Rsch. Coun. award, 1973; cert. psychologist, Pa. Fellow Am. Orthopsychiat. Assn.; mem. APA, N.Y. Assn. Analytical Psychologists, Pa. Psychol. Assn., Brit. Psychol. Soc., Brit. Assn. Psychotherapists, Assn. Child Psychology and Child Psychiatry. Home: 207 Tennyson Ave Pittsburgh PA 15213-1415 Office: 123 Cathedral Mansions 4716 Ellsworth Ave Pittsburgh PA 15213-2851

MACINTOSH, HOUSTON HOOD, psychiatrist; b. Springfield, Mass., Feb. 29, 1936. MD, U. Rochester, N.Y., 1961. Pvt. practice Washington, 1970—. Capt. USAF, 196-567. Fellow Am. Psychiat. Assn.; mem. Washington Psychoanalytic Soc. (treas. 1985-91), Am. Psychoanalytic Assn. Office: 330 Maryland Ave NE Washington DC 20002-4980

MACK, HENRY RUSSELL, JR., oral and maxillofacial surgeon; b. New Haven, Conn., Oct. 16, 1956; s. Harry Russell and Virginia (Hayden) M.; m. Stephanie Brunson, Sept. 22, 1957; children: Russell, Caroline. DDS, U. Mich., 1982; MD cum laude, U. Ala., 1988. Pvt. practice Nashville, 1988—. Mem. ADA, Am. Assn. of Oral Surgeons, Nashville Acad. of Medicine, Tenn. Soc. of Oral Surgeons, Pi Tau Sigma. Republican. Presbyterian. Home: 9580 Clove-croft Rd Franklin TN 37067 Office: 5802 Nolensville Rd #103 Nashville TN 37211

MACK, WILLIAM JOSEPH, psychotherapist, rehabilitation specialist; b. Evergreen Park, Ill., Mar. 5, 1943; s. Arol Ruth (Tallut) M.; m. Margaret Crace McCullom, Jan. 8, 1966 (div. Aug. 1979); children: William, Amy; m. Joan Kinnon, May 22, 1987; stepchildren: Margaret, Wendy, Douglas, Suzanne. BA, U. Dayton, 1965; cert., Ind. State U., Terre Haute, 1980; MA, Ball State U., 1983; M Health Scis., Governors State U., 1994; Doctorate, Am. Inst. Hypnotherapy, 1995. Lic. social worker, Ill.; cert. addictions counselor, clin. hypnotherapist, Ill.; nat. cert. master addictions counselor; lic. clin. profl. counselor, Ill. Mktg. rep. Texaco Inc., Lockport, Ill., 1969-73; med. rep. Merrell-Dow, Kokomo, Ind., 1973-82; program coordinator Pilsen Vocat., Chgo., 1983-85; dir. sheltered workshop Edgewater Community Mental Health Ctr., Chgo., 1985-88; mem. staff Edgewater Uptown Community Mental Health Ctr., Chgo., 1988-92; program dir. Community Counseling Ctrs. Chgo., 1992-96; mgr. adult health ctr. Chgo. Commons, 1996—; adj. faculty mem. Kendall Coll.; therapist Vet. Ctr., Chicago Heights, Ill., 1984-85. Instr. first aid ARC, Chgo., 1986. Served with U.S. Army, 1965-68; Res. ret. Mem NASW. Internat. Assn. PsychoSocial Profls., Am. Assn. Profl. Hypnotherapists, Mktg. Execs. for Sheltered Workshops, Chgo. Soc. Clin. Hypnosis, Am. Legion, Ret. Officers Assn. Democrat. Roman Catholic. Home: 2755 W Farragut Ave Chicago IL 60625-3508 Office: Chgo Commons Adult Health Ctr 1258 W 51st St Chicago IL 60609

MACKAY, CYNTHIA JOHNSON, ophthalmologist; b. N.Y.C., Sept. 20, 1942; d. Francis Edgar and Helena Noel (Edey) Johnson; m. Malcolm Mackay, August 29, 1964; children: Robert Livingston, Hope Winthrop. BA cum laude, Harvard U., 1964; MD, SUNY, Bklyn., 1977. Diplomate Nat. Bd. Med. Examiners, Am. Bd. Ophthalmology. Tchr. sci. The Dana Hall Sch., Wellesley, Mass., 1964-66; researcher Time-Life Books, N.Y.C., 1966-67; tchr. geography The Nightingale-Bamford Sch., N.Y.C., 1967; tchr., chmn. sci. dept. St. Ann's Episcopal Sch., Bklyn., 1968-73; intern The Lenox Hill Hosp., N.Y.C., 1977-78; resident in ophthalmology Edward S. Harkness Eye Inst. of Presbyn. Hosp., N.Y.C., 1978-81, Heed fellow in ocular genetics and retina, 1981-82; ophthalmologic practice with others N.Y.C., 1982-85, pvt. practice in ophthalmology,

1985—; assoc. clin. prof. Columbia U. Coll. Physicians and Surgeons, N.Y.C., 1985—; assoc. att. ophthalmologist Edward S. Harkness Eye Inst., 1985—; bd. dirs. Helen Keller Services for the Blind, Bklyn., Inst. for Visual Scis., N.Y.C. Contbr. articles to med. jours. Fellow Heed Found., 1981-82. Fellow Am. Acad. Ophthalmology; mem. N.Y. State Ophthal. Soc., The Assn. for Research in Vision and Ophthalmology. Home: 2 Montague Terrace Brooklyn NY 11201-2105 Office: 69 E 71st St New York NY 10021

MACKELLAR, KEITH ROBERT, hospital administrator; b. Chgo., Dec. 26, 1943; s. Duncan Harvey and Julie Marie MacK.; m. Deborah Marie Boone, Aug. 26, 1967; children: Andrea Kathleen, Bethany Kristine. AA, Morton Coll., 1969; B in Orgnl. Behavior, Northwestern U., 1978; M in Human Resources, Loyola U. Chgo., 1987. Dir. Ill. Masonic Med. Ctr., Chgo., 1967-74, Northwestern Meml. Hosp., Chgo., 1974-80; div. dir. AMA, Chgo., 1980-89; dir. human resources Physicians & Surgeons Hosp., Shreveport, La., 1989-91; v.p. human resources Eastern N.Mex. Med. Ctr., Roswell, 1991—; chmn. N.Mex. Hosp. Workers Compensation Bd. Sec. Sch. Bd. Dist. #88, Bellwood, Ill., 1980-83. Sgt. USMC, 1962-66, Vietnam. Mem. Am. Coll. Healthcare Execs., Am. Soc. Healthcare Human Resources Assn., Am. Mgmt. Assn., Soc. Human Resources Mgmt., N.Mex. Healthcare Human Resources Assn. (pres.-elect 1995—), Rotary Internat., Leadership Roswell Alumni Assn. (pres. 1995). Baptist. Home: 808 La Paloma Roswell NM 88201 Office: Eastern NMex Med Ctr 405 W Country Club Rd Roswell NM 88201

MACKEN, DANIEL LOOS, physician, educator; b. Rochester, N.Y., May 7, 1933; s. Daniel Edward and Mary Frances (Loos) M.; children: Elizabeth Redford, Diana Loos; m. Maria Luisa Medina de Palma, Nov. 16, 1979. AB, Holy Cross Coll., Worcester, Mass., 1955; postgrad., Yale U., 1956-57; MD, Boston U., 1960. Resident Roosevelt & Columbia-Presbyn. Hosps., N.Y.C., 1960-63; fellow Am. Heart Assn., 1964-65; dir. coronary care unit Walter Reed Gen. Hosp., Washington, 1968; staff rsch. physician Walter Reed Army Inst. of Rsch., Washington, 1970; instr. Columbia U., N.Y.C., 1966-78, asst. clin. prof., 1979—; pres. Medica Found., Inc., N.Y.C., 1971—; bd. dirs. Medica Endowment Fund, N.Y.C.; vis. lectr. U. saigon, Vietnam, 1969. Contbr. chpts. in book and articles to profl. jours. Lt. Col. U.S. Army, Med. Corp, 1967-70, Vietnam. Recipient Bronze Star medal U.S.A. 1970; Vietnam Cross 1969. Fellow Am. Coll. Cardiology, Royal Soc. Medicine, N.Y. Acad. Medicine, Harvey Soc.; mem. AMA, Assn. Mil. Surgeons of U.S., Am. Heart Assn., Met. Govs. Island Officers Club. Republican. Roman Catholic. Home: 570 Park Ave New York NY 10021-7370 Office: Columbia-Presbyn Med Ctr 161 Ft Washington Ave New York NY 10032-3713

MACKENZIE, RONALD ALEXANDER, anesthesiologist; b. Detroit, Mar. 31, 1938; s. James and Elizabeth (McIvor) M.; m. Nancy Lee Vogan, Aug. 25, 1962; children: Margaret, James. BS, Alma Coll., 1961; DO, Kansas City Coll., 1967. Diplomate Am. Bd. Anesthesiology. Resident in anesthesiology Detroit Osteo. Hosp., 1970-72, Cleve. Clinic, 1972-73; resident in anesthesiology Mayo Clinic, Rochester, Minn., 1973-74, cons. in anesthesia, 1974—; vice-chmn. dept. anesthesiology Mayo Clinic, 1988—. Pres. Minn. Orch., Rochester, 1987-89. Fellow Am. Coll. Anesthesiologists; mem. Am. Soc. Anesthesiologists (bd. dirs. 1983-87, sec. 1991—), Sigma Xi. Office: Mayo Clinic 200 SW 1st St Rochester MN 55905

MACKEY, RICHARD ANDREW, social worker, educator; b. Danvers, Mass., Oct. 31, 1935; s. Elias Joseph and Alice (Powers) M.; m. Eileen Frances Rawa, June 11, 1960; children: Gregory, Lynn, John. AB, Merrimack Coll., 1957; MSW, Cath. U., 1959, DSW, 1966. Lic. social worker. Social caseworker Cath. Charities, Buffalo, 1959-60; psychiat. social worker NIMH, Bethesda, 1960-66; clin. social worker pvt. practice, Westwood, Mass., 1970—; prof. Boston Coll., Chestnut Hill, Mass., 1966—; editorial bd. Jour. of Ind. Social Work, 1986—. Author: Ego Psychology and Clinical Practice, 1985, Lasting Marriages: Men and Women Growing Together, 1995; contbr. over 40 articles and profl. papers. With USPHS, 1960-66. Named Outstanding Profl. in Human Svcs., 1988, Outstanding Educator of Am., 1973. Mem. NASW. Office: Boston Coll Chestnut Hill MA 02167-3807

MACKINNEY, A. CLINTON, physician; b. Flint, Mich., June 20, 1956; s. Arthur C. and Lois E. (Lineberry) MacK; m. Ellen A. Forsythe, June 4, 1988. AB, Miami U., Oxford, Ohio, 1978; MD, Med. Coll. Ohio, 1982. Diplomate Am. Bd. Family Practice, added qualifications in geriatrics. Resident Mayo-St. Francis Hosp., La Crosse, Wis., 1982-85; family physician Mercy Family Care, Cresco, Iowa, 1985—; nat. leader Cmty. Health Svc. Devel.; lectr. profl. confs. Contbr. articles to profl. jours. Founder Cresco Health Adv. Partnership, 1995. Recipient Spl. Recognition award USPHS, 1986. Fellow Am. Acad. Family Physicians (mem. com. 1992-95); mem. AMA, Nat. Rural Health Assn., Am. Coll. Physician Execs., Healthcare Forum, Iowa Acad. Family Physicians (pres. 1995). Office: Mercy Family Care 321 8th Ave Cresco IA 52136

MACKINNON, ROGER ALAN, psychiatrist, educator; b. Attleboro, Mass., Feb. 13, 1927; s. Irville Herbert and Helen (Junk) MacK.; m. Florence Lundgren, Apr. 8, 1949 (div. 1970); children: Carol Louise, Stuart Alan; m. Nadine Trasenster, May 28, 1971. Student, Princeton U., 1944-46; MD, Columbia U., 1950, Cert. Psychoanalytic Med., 1957. Diplomate Am. Bd. Psychiatry and Neurology. Intern E.W. Sparrow Hosp., Lansing, Mich., 1950-51; resident in psychiatry N.Y. State Psychiatric Inst., N.Y.C., 1951-52, 52-54; chief psychiatry Vanderbilt Clinic, Presbyn. Hosp., N.Y.C., 1959-77; prof. clin. psychiatry Coll. Physicians & Surgeons, Columbia U., N.Y.C., 1986—; tng., supervising analyst Columbia U. Psychoanalytic Ctr., 1970—, asst. dir. for selection, 1981-91, dir., 1991—; attending psychiatrist Presbyn. Hosp., N.Y.C., 1972—, N.Y. State Psychiatric Inst., N.Y.C., 1972—; asst. examiner Am. Bd. Psychiatry and Neurology, 1960-70; lectr. in field. Coauthor textbook: The Psychiatric Interview, 1971, The Psychiatric Evaluation, 1986; contbr. articles to profl. jours., chpts. to books. Lt. USNR, 1952-54. Recipient George Goldman award, Columbia U. Psychoanalytic Ctr., 1989, George E. Daniels Merit award Assn. for Psychoanalytic Medicine, 1995. Fellow Am. Psychiat. Assn. (life), N.Y. Acad. Medicine; mem. Am. Psychoanalytic Assn., N.Y. Psychiat. Soc. (pres. 1987-88). Home: 11 Edgewood Ter Tenafly NJ 07670-2909 Office: 11 E 87th St New York NY 10128-0527 also: Columbia U Ctr Psychoanalytic Tng Rsch 722 W 168th St New York NY 10032-2603

MACKINTOSH, FREDERICK ROY, oncologist; b. Miami, Fla., Oct. 4, 1943; s. John Harris and Mary Carlotta (King) MacK.; m. Judith Jane Parnell, Oct. 2, 1961 (div. Aug. 1977); children: Lisa Lynn, Wendy Sue; m. Claudia Lizanne Flournoy, Jan. 7, 1984; 1 child, Gregory Warren. BS, MIT, 1964, PhD, 1968; MD, U. Miami, 1976. Intern then resident in gen. medicine Stanford (Calif.) U., 1976-78, fellow in oncology, 1978-81; asst. prof. med. U. Nev., Reno, 1981-85, assoc. prof., 1985-92, prof. medicine, 1992—. Contbr. articles to profl. jours. Fellow ACP; mem. Am. Soc. Clin. Oncology, Am. Cancer Soc. (pres. Nev. chpt. 1987-89, Washoe chpt. 1988-90), No. Nev. Cancer Coun. (bd. dirs. 1981-92), No. Calif. Cancer Program (bd. dirs. alt. 1983-87, bd. dirs. 1987-91). Office: Nev Med Group 781 Mill St Reno NV 89502-1320

MACKLIN, MARTIN RODBELL, psychiatrist; b. Raleigh, N.C., Aug. 27, 1934; s. Albert A. and Mitzi (Robdell) M.; m. Ruth Chimacoff (div.); children: Meryl, Shelley; m. Anne Elizabet Warren, May 25; children: Alicia, Aaron. BME, Cornell U., 1957, M in Indsl. Engring., 1958; PhD in Biomed. Engring., Case Western Res. U., 1967, MD, 1977. Diplomate Am. Bd. Psychiatry and Neurology; cert. in alcoholism and other drug dependencies Am. Soc. Addiction Medicine. Investigator Am. Heart Assn., Cleve., 1969-74; vis. fellow U. Sussex, Brighton, England, 1970; assoc. prof. biomed. engring. Case Western Res. U., 1972-81, asst. prof. psychiatry, 1981—; clin. dir. Horizon Ctr. Hosp., Warrensville Township, Ohio, 1981-83; adminstrv. dir. Riverview Psychiat. Assocs., 1983-94; med. dir. Woodside Hosp., 1989-94; v.p. med. affairs Geauga Hosp., Chardon, Ohio, 1994—; psychiat. cons. Glenbeigh Hosp., Ohio and Fla.; cons. various indsl. cos. Contbr. articles to profl. jours; patentee in field. NIH rsch. grantee Kellogg Found., Cleve., 1967-81; Laughlin fellow Am. Coll. Psychiatry, 1980. Mem. Am. Psychiat. Assn., Am. Coll. Physician Execs., Cleve. Acad. Medicine, Cleve. Psychiat. Soc. Home: 348 N Chestnut St Jefferson OH 44047-1130

MACKLIN, RUTH, bioethics educator; b. Newark, Mar. 27, 1938; d. Hyman and Frieda (Yaruss) Chimacoff; m. Martin Macklin, Sept. 1, 1957 (div. June 1969): children: Meryl, Shelley Macklin Taylor. BA with distinction, Cornell U., 1958; MA in Philosophy, Case Western Res. U., 1966, PhD in Philosophy, 1968. Instr. in philosophy Case Western Res. U., Cleve., 1967-68, asst. prof., 1968-71, assoc. prof., 1971-76; assoc. for behavioral studies The Hastings Ctr., Hastings-on-Hudson, N.Y., 1976-80; vis. assoc. prof. Albert Einstein Coll. Medicine, Bronx, N.Y., 1977-78, assoc. prof., 1978-84, prof. dept. epidemiology and social medicine, 1984—; cons. NIH, 1986—; advisor WHO, Geneva, 1989: apptd. mem. White House Adv. Com. on Human Radiation Experiments, Washington, 1994—. Author: Man, Mind and Morality, 1982, Mortal Choices, 1987, Enemies of Patients, 1993, Surrogates and Other Mothers, 1994; contbr. articles to ethics, law and med. jours. Fellow The Hastings Ctr., Inst. Medicine of NAS, Am. Philos. Assn. (life), Am. Pub. Health Assn., Am. Soc. Law, Medicine and Ethics; mem. Internat. Assn. Bioethics (bd. dirs.), Am. Assn. Bioethics (bd. dirs.), Phi Beta Kappa. Democrat. Office: A Einstein Coll Medicine Dept Epidemiology & Social Medicine 1300 Morris Park Ave Bronx NY 10461-1926

MACKLIN, THOMAS JACK, hospital human resources executive, consultant; b. Milw., Sept. 9, 1947; s. Lawrence Fritz and Blanche Caroline (Riekkoff) M.; m. Colleen Louise Hensiak, Oct. 30, 1971; children: Caitlin Laura, Ian Thomas. BS, U. Wis., Milw., 1970, MA, 1973; PhD, Ind. U., 1979. Mgmt. cons. Standard Bus. Rsch., Chgo., 1973-74; internal cons. Imperial-Eastman Corp., Niles, Ill., 1974-76; vis. prof. U. N.Mex., Albuquerque, 1978-79; lectr. U. Wis., Milw., 1979-80; dir. human resource svcs. Nat. Cons. and Tng. Inst., Milw., 1980-84; mgr. tng. and devel. St. Joseph's Hosp., Milw., 1984-88, mgr. employee rels. and orgn. devel., 1988-90; dir. human resources St. Joseph's Hosp., Asheville, N.C., 1990—; adj. prof. Cardinal Stritch Coll., Marquette, Keller Grad. Sch. Mgmt., 1980-88; presenter in field. Contbr. articles to profl. jours. Chmn. St. Joseph Hosp. orgn. com. United Way, 1984-89; orgn. liaison Black Achievers, Milw., 1989-90, INROAD'S Wis., Milw., 1989-90; bd. dirs. A Child's Place Child Devel. Ctr., Asheville, 1992—, pres. 1995—; mem. diversity com. Mission and St. Joseph's Health Sys., 1994—; orgn. liaison U. N.C. Asheville Mgmt. Interns, 1991—. Grantee State of Wis., 1983-84. Mem. Soc. Human Resource Mgmt., N.C. Healthcare Human Resource Assn. (bd. dirs., exec. com. 1992-94), Western N.C. Human Resource Assn. Home: 27 Cherokee Trl Fletcher NC 28732-9436 Office: St Joseph's Hosp 428 Biltmore Ave Asheville NC 28801-4502

MACKMAN, GARY STEVEN, ophthalmologist; b. Milw., June 11, 1950; s. Arthur and Rose (Rittberg) M.; m. Barbara Ann Martini, July 26, 1972; children: Darren, Whitney. BS, U. Wis., 1972, MD, 1976. Diplomate Am. Bd. Ophthalmology. Intern, resident U. Wis., Madison, 1977-80; cornea and external disease fellow U. Fla., Gainsville, 1980-81; pvt. practice Phoenix, 1981—; clin. lectr. U. Ariz., Tucson, 1994—; chmn. dept. ophthalmology Bapt. Hosp., Phoenix, 1988-93; vice-chmn. dept. ophthalmology St. Joseph's Hosp., 1988-89. Contbr. articles to profl. jours.; presenter in field. Fellow Am. Bd. Ophthalmology; mem. AMA, Internat. Soc. Cataract and Refractive Surgery, Contact Lens Assn., Phoenix Opthal. Soc. (pres. 1995-96). Office: Phoenix Ophthalmologists 777 E Brill St Phoenix AZ 85006

MACKNIN, CAROL JEAN HYMAN, psychiatrist; b. Cleve., Mar. 2, 1950; d. Lawrence and Florence (Goldberg) Hyman; m. Michael Larry Macknin; 2 children. BS in Edn. summa cum laude, Ohio State U., 1972; MEd, Boston Coll., 1973; student, Wellesley Coll., 1978-79; MD, Case Western Res. U., 1985. Diplomate Am. Bd. Psychiatry, Am. Bd. Neurology. Intern then resident U. Hosp. Cleve. and VA Hosp., 1986-90; staff psychiatrist Lake County Mental Health Ctr., Mentor, Ohio, 1990-92; pvt. practice Cleve., 1990—; tchr. blind and visually impared Perkins Sch. for The Blind, Boston, 1973-75, Medford (Mass.) Sch. Dist., 1975-78; sr. clin. instr. Case Western Res. U., Cleve., 1990—. Troop leader Girl Scouts Am., Cleve., 1993—. Mem. Am. Psychiatric Assn., Women Faculty Orgn. Case Western Res. U. Office: 24100 Chagrin Blvd # 470 Beachwood OH 44122

MACKS, GERALD CHARLES, management professional; b. Balt., July 8, 1942; s. Solomon S. and Miriam K. M.; m. Judith Goldstein, Aug. 6, 1968; children: Daniel E., Aaron D. BS in Indsl. Engring., Johns Hopkins U., 1964; MS, George Washington U., 1969. Indsl. engr. Western Electric Co., Balt., 1964-66; project dir. Cmty. Sys. Found., Balt., 1966-71; mgmt. analyst NIH Clin. Ctr., Bethesda, Md., 1971—; bd. dirs. Md. Hosp. Assn., Lutherville, 1981—, Soc. for Health Sys., Atlanta, 1994-96, HIMSS, Chgo., 1986-87. Co-author: Productivity Measurement System, 1993. Citizens Adv. Com. for Gifted Edn., Towson, Md., 1985—. Diplomate Am. Coll. Healthcare Execs. Office: NIH Clin Ctr 10/2C146 MSC 1504 Bethesda MD 20892

MACLAREN, NOEL KEITH, medical educator; b. Christ Church, New Zealand, July 28, 1939; came to U.S., 1973; s. James Keith and Pearl Agnes (Rainey) M.; children: Sophie, Kristy; m. Sunita Schil, July 28, 1996. BB ChB, U. Otago, 1963. Asst. prof. pediatrics U. Md. Sch. Medicine, Balt., 1973-74, assoc. prof. pediatrics, 1975-78; prof. pathology & pediatrics U. Fla. Coll. Medicine, Gainesville, 1978—; dir. clin. chemistry Shands Teaching Hosp., Gainesville, 1978-86; prof., chmn. dept. pathology and lab. medicine U. Fla., Gainesville, 1987—; prof. comparative and exptl. pathology U. Fla. Coll. Vet. Medicine, Gainesville, 1990—; treas. Internat. Immunology Diabetes Workshop, 1990—, pres., 1990—; editl. bd. Autoimmunity Jour., Paris, 1987—; med. adv. com. Nat. Disease Rsch. Interchange Group, Phila., 1982—. Recipient Connaught Nova Nordisk award, Toronto, Can., 1994, David Rumbough Sci. award, N.Y.C., Juvenile Diabetes Found., 1995. Office: U Fla Coll Medicine Dept Pathology PO Box 100275 Gainesville FL 32610

MACMAHON, BRIAN, epidemiologist, educator; b. Sheffield, Eng., Aug. 12, 1923; came to U.S. 1952; s. Desmond and Gladys (Nelson) MacM.; m. Heidi Marie Graber, Aug. 28, 1948; children—Michael, Kevin, Kathleen Louise, Mary Anne. M.B., Ch.B., U. Birmingham, Eng., 1946, Ph.D., 1952, M.D., 1955; M.S., Harvard U., Boston, 1953; DMS (hon.), U. Athens, Greece, 1976; DSc (hon.), SUNY, Buffalo, 1986. Ship surgeon Alfred Holt & Co., Liverpool, Eng., 1946-48; assoc. prof. SUNY Downstate Med. Ctr., Bklyn., 1955-57, prof., 1957-58; prof., chmn. dept. epidemiology Harvard Sch. Pub. Health, Boston, 1958-89, emeritus prof. epidemiology, 1989—. Author: Epidemiologic Methods, 1960, Epidemiology: Principles and Methods, 1970, 2d edit., 1996; editor: Cancer Causes and Control, 1990; contbr. articles to profl. jours. Recipient Edwards Meml. medal U. Wales, 1974; Lucy Wortham James award Soc. Surg. Oncology, 1978; John Snow award Am. Pub. Health Assn., 1980; Lemuel Shattuck award Mass. Pub. Health Assn., 1982, Prix Antoinne Lacassague Ligue National Francaise Contre le Cancer; Am. Cancer Soc. Medal of Honor, 1995. Fellow Am. Pub. Health Assn.; mem. Am. Epidemiol. Soc. Home: 89 Warren St Needham MA 02192-3115 Office: Harvard Sch Pub Health 677 Huntington Ave Boston MA 02115-6028

MACMILLAN, FRANCIS PHILIP, physician; b. Everett, Mass., June 19, 1937; s. Edward Joseph and Katherine H. (Hogan) M.; m. Nancy Marie Mirabello, May 18, 1963; children: Frank, Edward, Paul, John, Kerry. BS, Boston Coll., 1959; MD, N.Y. Med. Coll., 1964. Diplomate Am. Bd. Internal Medicine, Am. Bd. Gastroenterology. Intern Boston City Hosp., 1964-65, resident in internal med., 1965-66; resident Boston VA Hosp., Jamaica Plains, Mass., 1966-68; practice medicine specializing in gastroenterology Pentucket Med. Assn., Inc., Haverhill, Mass., 1968—; pres. med. staff Hale Hosp., Haverhill, 1975-78, chief of medicine, 1980-82; cons. in gastroenterology Lawrence (Mass.) Gen. Hosp., Holy Family Hosp., Methuen, Mass., Anna Jaques Hosp., Newburyport, Mass. Contbr. articles to profl. jours. Served to maj. USAR, 1968-71. Fellow Am. Coll. Physicians. Mem. Am. Med. Assn., Mass. Med. Assn., Am. Soc. Internal Med., Am. Gastroent. Assn., New England Endoscopy Soc. (pres. 1996—). Roman Catholic. Club: Haverhill Golf and Country (bd. dirs. 1983-86). Office: One Parkway Haverhill MA 01830 also: 203 Turnpike St North Andover MA 01845

MACMILLAN, ROBERT FRANCIS, director university service; b. Easton, Pa., Oct. 3, 1925; s. William F. and Margaret (Woodruff) M.; m. Dolores G., June 7, 1952; 1 child, R. David. BS in Elec. Engring., Lafayette Coll., 1949; BD, Southern Bapt. Theol. Sem., 1952, ThM and MRE, 1954, 56; PhD, Am. U., 1969. Lic. psychologist, Pa. Assoc. pastor 1st Bapt. Ch., Washington, 1955-69; dir. psychol. svcs. U. Pa., East Stroudsburg, 1969—; pres., Assn. Pa. State Coll. U Faculty, 1980—. Chmn. Monroe County Planning Commn., Stroudsburg, 1974-85. Sgt. U.S. Army, 1943-46. Mem. Am. Psychol. Assn. Home: 32 Club Ct Stroudsburg PA 18360-1548 Office: East Stroudsburg U Dept of Psychol Stroudsburg PA 18301

MACMULLEN, JEAN ALEXANDRIA STEWART, nurse, administrator; b. N.Y.C., Feb. 21, 1945; d. John Douglas and Isabella Stewart (Park) MacM. Diploma in nursing, Lenox Hill Hosp., N.Y.C., 1965; BS in Nursing, Adelphi U., 1969, MS in Nursing, 1971; MA in Anthropology, U. South Fla., 1978. Nurse renal disease unit N.Y. Hosp., N.Y.C., 1971-72; clin. nurse specialist VA Hosp., Tampa, Fla., 1972-76, med./surg. coord., 1976-82; assoc. chief nurse VA Med. Ctr., Gainesville, Fla., 1982-93; assoc. med. ctr. dir. nursing VA Med. Ctr., Montgomery, Ala., 1993—. Jour. editor Am. Assn. Nephrology Nurses, Pitman, N.J., 1980-82, referee, adviser, 1983—; contbr. numerous articles to profl. publs. Mem. Fla. Nurses Assn. Republican. Episcopalian. Office: VA Med Ctr 215 Perry Hill Rd Montgomery AL 36109-3725

MACMURREN, HAROLD HENRY, JR., psychologist, lawyer; b. Jersey City, Sept. 18, 1942; s. Harold Sr. and Evelyn (Almone) MacM.; m. Margaret Bartro, Nov. 21, 1970. BA, William Paterson Coll., Wayne, N.J., 1965; MA, Jersey City Coll., 1973; EdD, St. Johns U., N.Y.C., 1985; JD, Rutgers U., 1989. Cert. secondary tchr., N.J.; Bar: N.J. 1989. Instr. Wanaque (N.J.) Bd. Edn., 1965-66, cons. psychologist, 1983-84; instr. Elmwood Park (N.J.) Bd. Edn., 1967-70; coll. faculty mem., psychologist Assoc. Clinic, Jersey City, 1971-72; cons. psychologist Rockaway (N.J.) Bd. Edn., 1972-83; intern lawyer Environ. Law Clinic, Newark, N.J., 1988-89; cons. psychologist Pequannock (N.J.) Bd. Edn., 1984—; coord. of child study team Sandyston Walpack Sch. System; adj. prof. William Paterson Coll.; spkr. and writer in field. Mem. ABA, NEA, N.J. Edn. Assn., N.J. Psychologist Assn., N.J. Bar Assn., Sierra Club, Phi Delta Kappa. Home: 4 Systema Pl Sussex NJ 07461-2833 Office: Pequannock Board of Ed Pequannock NJ 07440

MACOSKO, PAUL JOHN, II, psychotherapist; b. Erie, Pa., May 15, 1952; s. Paul Sr. and Susan Ann (Miraldi) M.; m. Marsha Gail Blystone, July 1, 1978; children: Paul John III, Benjamin Jamison. BA in Psychology, Mercyhurst Coll., 1976; postgrad., Grand Rapids Bapt. Bible Sem., and Edinboro U., 1976-78; MA in Bibl. Counseling, Grace Theol. Sem., Winona Lake, Ind., 1983; DPhil, Oxford U., 1992. Protective svc. caseworker I Trumbull County Children's Svcs. Bd., Warren, Ohio, 1976-77; counselor Regular Bapt. Children's Agy., St. Louis, 1978-81; coord. devel. dual diagnosis program Dr. Gertrude A. Barber Ctr., Erie, 1987-92; pvt. practice marriage, family and crisis counseling Erie, 1984-94; dir. Christian Care Ministry Grace Bapt. Ch., Erie, 1992-94; outpatient therapist The achievement Ctr., Erie, 1994—. Mem. ACA, Am. Assn. Christian Counselors, Assn. Religious and Value Issues in Counseling, Pa. Counseling Assn., Nat. Disting. Svc. Registry. Baptist. Office: 3933 Oxer Rd Erie PA 16505-3345

MACOUL, KENNETH L., eye surgeon; b. Methuen, Mass., May 25, 1940; m. Carole Ann Nihan; children: Katherine, Michael, Ann. BS in Engring., MIT, 1961; MD, Tufts U., 1965. Diplomate Am. Bd. Surgery. Resident in eye surgery Stanford U., Palo Alto, Calif., 1966-69; pvt. practice specializing in eye surgery Lawrence, Mass., 1969—. Contbr. numerous articles to profl. jours. Office: 280 Haverhill St Lawrence MA 01840-1208

MACOVSKI, ALBERT, electrical engineering educator; b. N.Y.C., May 2, 1929; s. Philip and Rose (Winogr) M.; m. Adelaide Paris, Aug. 5, 1950; children—Michael, Nancy. B.E.E., City Coll. N.Y., 1950; M.E.E., Poly. Inst. Bklyn., 1953; Ph.D., Stanford U., 1968. Mem. tech. staff RCA Labs., Princeton, N.J., 1950-57; asst. prof., then assoc. prof. Poly. Inst. Bklyn., 1957-60; staff scientist Stanford Research Inst., Menlo Park, Calif., 1960-71; fellow U. Calif. Med. Center San Francisco, 1971-72; prof. elec. engring. and radiology Stanford U., 1972—, endowed chair, Canon USA prof. engring., 1991—; dir. Magnetic Resonance Systems Research Lab.; cons. to industry. Author. Recipient Achievement award RCA Labs., 1952, 54; award for color TV circuits Inst. Radio Engrs., 1958; NIH spl. fellow, 1971. Fellow IEEE (Zworykin award 1973), Am. Inst. Med. Biol. Engring., Optical Soc. Am., Internat. Soc. Magnetic Resonance in Medicine (former trustee); mem. NAE, Inst. of Medicine, Am. Assn. Physicists in Medicine, Sigma Xi, Eta Kappa Nu. Jewish. Home: 2505 Alpine Rd Menlo Park CA 94025-6314 Office: Stanford U Dept Elec Engring Stanford CA 94305

MACQUIDDY, JEAN ELIZABETH, health organization administrator; b. Watsonville, Calif., May 22, 1943; d. Thomas Malcolm and Elizabeth Geary (Wilson) MacQ.; m. Peter Mills Baptiste, Dec. 11, 1939 (div. Sept. 1977); children: Geary, Ruth. BA, Mills Coll., 1965; MBA, Northeastern U., 1982. Staff asst. Harvard Sch. of Edn., Cambridge, Mass., 1965-67; staff asst. Market Structure Studies, Cambridge, 1967-68; conv. coord. Interactive Learning Systems, Brighton, Mass., 1968-69; adminstrv. asst. Harvard Law Sch., Cambridge, 1969-70; exec. officer Harvard Med. Sch., Boston, 1971-84; bus. planning mgr. Allied Health & Scientific Products, Andover, Mass., 1984-85; adminstrv. officer Mass. Eye and Ear Infirmary, Boston, 1985—. Mem. Med. Group Mgmt. Assn., Harvard Cooperative Soc. (bd. dirs. 1980-84). Episcopalian. Home: 107 North Ave Weston MA 02193-2033

MACRAE, DAVID HASKINS, physician; b. Waukegan, Ill., Oct. 15, 1954; s. Kenneth Liebold and Donna Marie (Haskins) MacR.; m. Nella Cozette van der Giessen, Oct. 27, 1973; children: Ian, Anna, Andrew, Alec. BS summa cum laude, U. S. Ala., 1979, MD, 1983. Diplomate Am. Bd. Internal Medicine; added qualifications in geriatrics. Asst. prof. U. S. Ala., Mobile, 1986-88; pvt. practice West Mobile Internal Medicine, 1988—; chmn. med. exec. bd. Knollwood Park Hosp., Mobile, 1990; bd. advisors Allen Meml. Home, Mobile, 1991—; med. dir. Bay Manor Nursing Home, Mobile, 1990—; pres. med. staff, Mercy Med. Hosp., Mobile, 1989. Author: (book) Problems in Critical Care, 1989. Cubmaster Boy Scouts Am., Mobile, 1992-95. With USN, 1972-76, Japan. Mem. Buccaneer Yacht Club, Alpha Chi, Phi Kappa Phi, others. Office: West Mobile Internal Med 3401 Medical Park Dr Mobile AL 36693

MAC TAVISH, LAWRENCE SCOTT, podiatrist; b. San Antonio, Tex., Nov. 26, 1947; s. William Alexander and Evelyn Marie (Moyer) Mac T.; m. Lesley Jean Bowser, June 14, 1969 (div. Dec. 1992); children: Lawrence Scott II, Kevin Ryan, Amanda Kathleen, Michelle Yvette Lozano, Apr. 17, 1993. BS in Biology, Baylor U., 1970; BS and DPM, Calif. Coll. Podiatric Medicine, San Francisco, 1974. Diplomat Am. Bd. Podiatric Medicine. Podiatrist Foot Ctr.-Northwest Houston, 1983—; past chief of staff Tex. Outpatient Surg. Hosp., Houston; chmn. peer rev. com., 1978-92. Mem. No. Harris County C. of C., Houston, 1976-96; exec. sec. Chrysler Adv. Bd., 1984-95; past bd. dirs. March of Dimes. Fellow Am. Coll. of Foot and Ankle Surgeons; mem. Am. Podiatric Med. Assn. (del. Tex. 1985-96), Tex. Podiatric Med. Assn. (govtl. affairs chmn.), Northgate Country Club (bd. dirs. 1985-96). Republican. Baptist. Office: Foot Ctr of Northwest Houston 17215 Red Oak # 102 Houston TX 77090

MADDEN, ARTHUR ALLEN, nuclear pharmacist, educator; b. Atlanta, Sept. 19, 1960; s. Arthur Allen and Lillian Brandon (Vaughan) M.; m. Rebecca Kaye Teague, June 25, 1988; 1 child, Kelley Vaughan. BA in English, U. of the South, Sewanee, Tenn., 1982; BS in Pharmacy, U. S.C., 1988, PharmD, 1990. Registered pharmacist, N.C., S.C.; bd. cert. nuclear pharmacist, 1994. Poison control specialist Palmetto Poison Ctr., Columbia, 1988-90; relief pharmacist Wal-Mart, Columbia, 1989-91; dir. S.C. Nuclear Pharmacy, Columbia, 1990-91; nuclear pharmacist Syncor Internat. Corp., Columbia, S.C., 1991-95; radiation safety cons. Syncor Internat. Corp., Columbia, 1990-95; dir. Cosource Nuclear Pharmacy Geodax Tech., Inc., Columbia, 1995—; mem. faculty U. S.C. Sch. Medicine, Columbia, 1990—, asst. prof. Coll. Pharmacy, 1990—; third party ins. expert, Columbia, 1983-93; mem. ad hoc com. for infectious disease policy. Mem. Am. Pharm. Assn., Am. Soc. Hosp. Pharmacists, S.C. Nuclear Medicine Soc., S.C. Sch. Medicine Hemotology/Oncology Jour. Club, Bd. Pharm. Specialties-Nuclear Pharmacy, Phi Lambda Sigma (sec. 1987-89), Order of the Thistle, Order of the Highlander. Home: 4626 Reamer Ave Columbia SC 29206-1541 Office: Cosource Nuclear Pharmacy 2501 Main St Columbia SC 29201

MADDEN, ROBERT EDWARD, surgeon, educator; b. Oak Park, Ill., Sept. 16, 1925; s. Joseph Edward and Gertrude Celelia (McGowan) M.; m. Susan Ann Hale, May 24, 1958; children: Robert Joseph, Lisa Marie, Karen Louise, Kevin Francis. BS in Medicine, U. Ill., Chgo., 1950, MS in Biochemistry, 1952, MD, 1952. Diplomate Am. Bd. Surgery, Bd. Thoracic Surgery. Assoc. in surgery U. Ill. Coll. Medicine, Chgo., 1957-58; sr. surgeon Nat. Cancer Inst., Bethesda, Md., 1959-60; asst. prof. surgery N.Y. Med. Coll., N.Y.C., 1961-66, assoc. prof., 1966-71; prof. N.Y. Med. Coll., Valahlla, 1971—; mem. N.Y. State Health Rsch. Coun., Albany, 1976—. Author: (with Lippincott) Problems In General Surgery, 1988; editor: Gastrointestinal Bieeding, 1987; editor-in-chief N.Y. Med. Quarterly, 1979-90; contbr. articles to profl. jours. With U.S. Army, 1943-46. Recipient Borden Undergrad. Rsch. award Borden Corp., 1952; postdoctoral fellow Am. Cancer Soc., 1958-59. Fellow ACS; mem. Internat. Soc. Cardiovascular Surgery, Soc. Internat. Chirurgie, Am. Assn. Cancer Edn. (pres. 1979), N.Y. Cancer Soc. (pres. 1975-76), N.Y. State Cancer Progress Assn. (pres. 1975-76), Knights of Holy Sepulchre, Knights of the Order of Malta, Pi Gamma Mu. Republican. Roman Catholic. Home: 6 Crows Nest Rd Bronxville NY 10708-4802 Office: NY Med Coll Munger Pavilion Valhalla NY 10595

MADDOX, TOM SMITH, JR., ophthalmologist; b. Greenville, Ky., Sept. 28, 1943; s. Tom Smith and Maryanna (Jenkins) M.; m. Jackie C. Calhoun, July 15, 1967; children: Tom, Jeffrey, Austin. BA, Murray State U. 1965; MD, U. Ky., 1969. Intern Charity Hosp., New Orleans, 1969-70; resident U. Ky., Lexington, 1970-73; chief ophthalmology U.S. Navy, Charleston, S.C., 1973-75; pvt. practice medicine specializing in ophthalmology, Owensboro, Ky., 1975—; staff ophthalmologist Owensboro-Daviess County Hosp., Mercy Hosp., Owensboro Ambulatory Surgery Ctr. Contbr. articles to profl. jours. Mem. Owensboro Ind. Bd. Edn., 1980— (chmn. bd. dirs. 1991—), Ky. Sch. Bd. Assn., 1980—, bd. dirs. 1989-95; bd. dirs. Ky. Soc. to Prevent Blindness; mem. dean's adv. com. U. Ky. Coll. Medicine; pres. ch. bd. Disciples of Christ Ch., 1990 Served to lt. comdr. USN, 1973-75. Fellow Am. Acad. Ophthalmology; mem. Am. Soc. Cataract and Refractive Surgery. Assn., AMA, Daviess County Med. Soc., Ky. Acad. Eye Physicians and Surgeons (pres. 1985—), Ky. Academic Assn. (bd. dirs.), Kiwanis (pres. 1980-81). Democrat. Avocations: jogging, golf, photography. Home: 1210 Griffith Ave Owensboro KY 42301-2815 Office: Physicians Eye Ctr 2845 Farrell Cres Owensboro KY 42303-1393

MADEDDU, PAOLO, cardiologist; b. Sassari, Sardinia, Italy, July 2, 1952; s. Andrea and Lidia (Spano) M.; m. Maria Laura De Cherchi, Sept. 20, 1980; children: Andrea, Francesca. MD, U. Sassari, Italy, 1976, postgrad., 1980. Sr. rschr. Clinica Medica, U. Sassari, 1978—, sr. physician, 1980—, prof. pharmacology, prof. therapy, 1993—; fellow, vis. rschr. Henry Ford Hosp., Detroit, 1986-88; referee sci. jours. Hypertension, Jour. Hypertension, 1994; cons. dept. biochemistry, molecular biology U. Charleston, S.C., 1990; spkr. at many sci. meetings. Contbr. over 140 articles to profl. jours. Grantee Sci. Ministry, Univ. Ministry, 1988—. Mem. Coun. for High Blood Pressure Rsch., Internat. Soc. Nephrology, Internat. Soc. Hypertension. Democratic-Socialist. Roman Catholic. Home: Viale Adua 13, 07100 Sassari Sardinia Italy Office: Clinica Medica, Vaile S Pietro, 07100 Sassari Sardinia Italy

MADEWELL, JOHN E., radiologist. MD, U. Okla., 1969. Intern Madigen Gen. Hosp., Tacoma, 1969-70; resident in diagnostic radiology Walter Reed Med. Ctr., Washington, 1970-73; fellow in radiol. pathology Armed Forces Inst. Pathology, Washington, 1973-74; radiologist Milton S. Hershey Med. Ctr.; prof., chmn. dept. Milton S. Hershey Med. Ctr./Pa. State U. Mem. ACR, ARRS, AUR, ISS, RSNA. Office: Pa State U Coll Medicine Hershey Med Ctr Dept Radiol PO Box 850 Hershey PA 17033-0850*

MADHUSOODANAN, SUBRAMONIAM, psychiatrist, educator; b. Trivandrum, India, Sept. 7, 1947; came to U.S., 1976; s. Subramoniam Pillai and Leelavathi K. Amma; m. Rama Sivathanu, Feb. 5, 1976 (div. Feb. 1991); children: Leena, Deepa; m. Gunjan Jain, Sept. 12, 1991; 1 child, Neha. MBBS, Trivandrum Med. Coll., 1971; Diploma in Otorhinolaryngology, Kurnool (India) Med. Coll., 1975; MD, SUNY, 1992. Diplomate in psychiatry and geriatric psychiatry Am. Bd. Psychiatry and Neurology, Am. Bd. Quality Assurance and Utilization Physicians. Instr. Mt. Sinai Sch. Medicine, CUNY, 1978-82; asst. attending psychiatrist Mt. Sinai Svcs., City Hosp. Ctr. at Elmhurst, N.Y., 1979-81; med. dir. outpatient alcohol program St. John's Episcopal Hosp., Far Rockaway, N.Y., 1983—, acting dir. psychiatry, 1984-86, assoc. chair psychiatry, 1986—, program dir. geriatric psychiatry fellowship program, 1993—; dir. psychiatry Peninsula Hosp., Far Rockaway, 1985-94; clin. asst. prof. dept. psychiatry SUNY Downstate Med. Ctr., Bklyn., 1989-95, 1995—; cons. psychiatrist St. John's Nursing Home, Peninsula Nurses Home, Far Rockaway Nursing Home, Lawrence Nursing Home, Rockaway Care Ctr., Brookhaven Nursing Home Haven Manor, 1981—. Mem. Am. Psychiat. Assn., Am. Geriatric Psychiatry Assn., World Fedn. Mental Health, Am. Geriatric Soc., Queens County Psychiat. Soc., Lawrence Assn. Democrat. Hindu. Home: 249 Broadway Lawrence NY 11559-1511 Office: St John's Episcopal Hosp 327 B 19th St Far Rockaway NY 11691

MADLANG, RODOLFO MOJICA, urologic surgeon; b. Indang, Cavite, The Philippines, Apr. 9, 1918; came to U.S., 1953; s. Simeon Fajardo and Eugenia R. (Mojica) Madlangsacay; m. Lourdes Recto Gregorio, Dec. 8, 1946; children: Cesar, Rodolfo G., Mercy Lynn. AA, U. Philippines, Manila, 1939, MD, 1945. Diplomate Am. Bd. Urology. Resident in gen. surgery Philippine Gen. Hosp., Manila, 1946-49; resident in urology St. Francis Hosp., Peoria, Ill., 1953-55; asst. prof. physiology Far Ea. U. Inst. Medicine, Manila, 1956-58, cons. in urology, 1956-58; attending urologist St. Catherine Hosp., East Chicago, Ind., 1958-81, chief surgery, 1977-79; attending urologist St. Margaret Hosp., Hammond, Ind., 1960-81; chief urology U.S. VA Outpatient Clinic, L.A., 1982—. Fellow ACS; mem. AMA, Am. Urol. Assn., Pan Pacific Surg. Assn., Assn. Mil. Surgeons of the U.S., Ind. State Med. Assn., N.Y. Acad. Scis. Republican. Roman Catholic. Office: VA Outpatient Clinic 351 E Temple St Los Angeles CA 90012-3328

MADORE, JOYCE LOUISE, gerontology nurse; b. Madison, Kans., Dec. 15, 1936; d. Lionel Wiedmer and Mary Elizabeth (Piley) Murphy; m. Robert Madore, Aug. 15, 1969; children: Carl, Clay. BS, Emporia State U., 1980; diploma, Newman Hosp., 1981. RN, Kans., Mo.; cert. gerontol. nurse, non profit adminstr., nursing home adminstr. Med. charge nurse St. Mary's Hosp., Emporia, Kans., 1971-72; dir. nursing Madison (Kans.) Manor, 1974-81, 82-83; staff nurse Newman Meml. Hosp., Emporia, 1981-82; dir. Daybreak Adult Day Svcs., dir. HELP program Springfield (Mo.) Area Coun. of Chs., 1983—; mem. Gov.'s Com. to Establish Rules and Regulations on Adult Day Care Patients State of Mo.; cons. U. Mo. Coop. Extension Svc. Program Guides on Adult Day Care. Contbr. video Understanding Aging Program; developer Home Guide for the Homebound, 1996. Named one of Outstanding Nurses in Mo. St. Louis U., 1989. Mem. NANA, AFE, Adult Day Care Assn. (past sec., exec. past v.p. 1989-91), Mo. Nurses Assn., Mo. Adult Day Care assn. (pres. 1991-95, Exec. award 1995), Mo. League of Nursing. Home: 171 Hilltop Oaks Ln Sparta MO 65753-8911

MADORY, JAMES RICHARD, hospital administrator, former air force officer; b. Staten Island, N.Y., June 11, 1940; s. Eugene and Agnes (Gerner) M.; m. Karen James Clifford, Sept. 26, 1964; children: James E., Lynn Anne, Scott J., Elizabeth Anne, Joseph M. BS, Syracuse U., 1964; MHA, Med. Coll. Va., 1971. Enlisted USAF, 1958; x-ray technician Keesler Area Med. Ctr., Biloxi, Miss., 1959-62; commd. 2d lt. USAF, 1964, advanced through grades to maj., 1978; x-ray technician Keesler Area Med. Ctr., Biloxi, Miss., 1959-62; adminstr. Charleston (S.C.) Clinic, 1971-74, Beale Hosp., Calif., 1974-77; assoc. adminstr. Shaw Regional Hosp., S.C., 1977-79; ret. USAF, 1979; asst. adminstr. Raleigh Gen. Hosp., Beckley, W.Va., 1979-81; adminstr., dir., sec. bd. Chesterfield Gen. Hosp., Cheraw, S.C., 1981-87; pres., CEO Grand Strand Hosp., Myrtle Beach, S.C., 1987-95, trustee, 1987-95; cons. in health care adminstrn. Horry County Planning Commn., 1995—; cons. Healthcare Adminstrs., 1995—; mem. adv. bd. Cheraw Nursing Home, 1984-85. Contbr. articles to profl. publs. Chmn. bd. W.Va. Kidney Found., Charleston, 1980-81; chmn. youth bd. S.C. TB and Respiratory Disease Assn., Charleston, 1972-73; county chmn. Easter Seal Soc., Chesterfield County, S.C., 1984-85; campaign crusade chmn. Am. Cancer Soc., Chesterfield County, 1985-86; chmn. dist. advancement com. Boy Scouts Am., 1987-90; bd. dirs. Horry County United Way, 1989-91, Horry County Access Care, 1989-91; trustee Cheraw Acad., 1982-85, Grand Strand Gen. Hosp., 1987-94, Coastal Acad., 1988-90; commr. Horry County Planning Commn., 1995—. Decorated Bronze Star, Vietnamese Cross of Gallantry, Vietnamese Medal of Honor; named to S.C. Order of Palmetto Gov. David Beasley, 1995. Fellow Am. Coll. Hosp. Adminstrs., Am. Coll. Health Care Execs; mem. S.C. Hosp. Assn. (com on legislation 1984-86, trustee 1989-94), Am. Acad. Healthcare Adminstrs., Cheraw C. of C. (bd. dirs. 1982-83), Rotary (pres. 1984-85). Republican. Roman Catholic. Home and Office: 3710 Kinloch Dr Myrtle Beach SC 29577

MADOW, LEO, psychiatrist, educator; b. Cleve., Oct. 18, 1915; s. Solomon Martin and Anna (Meyers) M.; m. Jean Antoinette Weisman, Apr 16, 1942; children: Michael, Robert. AB, Western Res. U., 1937, MD, 1942; MA, Ohio State U., 1938. Diplomate Am. Bd. Psychiatry and Neurology. Intern Phila. Gen. Hosp., 1942-43; resident Phila. Gen. Hosp., Jefferson Hosp., Inst. Pa. Hosp., 1943-46; practice medicine specializing in psychiatry Phila., 1948—; prof., chmn. dept. neurology Med. Coll. Pa., Phila., 1958-65; prof., chmn. dept. psychiatry and neurology Med. Coll. Pa., 1965-70, prof., chmn. dept. psychiatry, 1970-81, clin. prof. psychiatry Hershey Med. Ctr., 1982—; sr. cons. psychiatry Inst. Pa. Hosp., Phila., 1975—; tng. analyst, past pres. Phila. Psychoanalytic Inst.; past pres., mem. med. staff Inst. Pa. Hosp. Author: Anger, 1972, Love, 1983, Guilt, 1989; editor: Dreams, 1970, Sensory Deprivation, 1970, Psychomimetic Drugs, 1971, Integration of Child Psychiatry with Basic Resident Program, 1975. Served to capt. AUS, 1944-46. Named Outstanding Educator of Am. Med. Coll. Pa., 1972. Fellow ACP, Am. Psychiatric Assn. (life), Phila. Psychiatric Soc. (Lifetime Achievement award 1991) (past pres.), Am. Coll. Psychiatrists, Am. Coll. Psychoanalysts (pres. 1989-90, Laughlin award 1990); mem. Am. Psychoanalytic Assn., Am. Neurol. Assn., Phila. Psychoanalytic Soc. (past pres.), Alpha Omega Alpha, Phi Soc. Home: 135 Sibley Ave Narberth PA 19072-1318 Office: Inst of Pa Hosp 111 N 49th St Philadelphia PA 19139-2718

MADSEN, LYNN ELISE, psychologist, author; b. Great Falls, Mont., June 21, 1953; d. Paul Walter and Barbara Lee (Evensen) Madsen; m. John Michael Murphy, June 26, 1983; children: Evan Patrick, Kyle Peter, Katherine Louise. BS, U. Calif., Davis, 1979; MA, U. Minn., 1983, PhD, 1986. Lic. psychologist, Minn. Therapist Fredrickson & Assocs., St. Paul, 1983-85; counselor CHART-Career Counseling, Mpls., 1981-84; clinic dir. Lakeland Counseling Ctr., Edina, Minn., 1986-90; pvt. practice psychology Edina, 1990—; cons. Tex. Midwives Assn., Houston, 1995. Author: Rebounding From Childbirth, 1994. Mem. core com. theol. insights program, Coll. of St. Catherine, St. Paul, 1995. U. Calif.-Davis Student Rsch. awardee, 1979. Mem. Minn. Women Psychologists. Office: 7101 York Ave S #345 Edina MN 55435

MADURA, JAMES ANTHONY, surgical educator; b. Campbell, Ohio, June 10, 1938; s. Anthony Peter and Margaret Ethel (Sebest) M.; m. Loretta Jayne Sovak, Aug. 8, 1959; children: Debra Jean, James Anthony II, Vikki Sue. BA, Cogate U., 1959; MD, Western Res. U., 1963. Diplomate Am. Bd. Surgery. Intern in surgery Ohio State U., Columbus, 1963-64, resident in surgery, 1966-71; asst. prof. Surgery Ind. U., Indpls., 1971-76, assoc. prof. Surgery, 1976-80, prof. Surgery, 1980—; dir. gen. surgery Ind. U. Sch. Medicine, Indpls., 1985—. Contbr. articles to profl. jours. Capt. U.S. Army, 1964-66, Vietnam. Fellow Am. Coll. Surgeons; mem. Cen. Surg. Assn., Western Surg. Assn., Soc. Surgery Alimentary Tract, Midwest Surg. Assn., Internal Biliary Assn., Assn. Acad. Surgeons, The Columbia Club. Republican. Roman Catholic. Home: 9525 Copley Dr Indianapolis IN 46260-1422 Office: Indianapolis U Dept of Surgery 545 Barnhill Dr #205 Indianapolis IN 46202-5112*

MAECHTLE, MARY ANN, obstetrical nurse; b. Port Washington, Wis., Dec. 24, 1970; d. Bernard George and Chelene Catherine (Ebert) Golownia; m. Robert Dean Maechtle, Aug. 10, 1991; 1 child, Jacob Steven. BSN, Concordia U., Mequon, Wis., 1993. RN, Wis. Obstet. nurse St. Michael Hosp., Milw., 1993—; counselor Resolved Through Sharing, 1993—. Home: 220 Martin Dr # 2 Fredonia WI 53021 Office: St Michael Hosp 2400 W Willard Ave Milwaukee WI 53209

MAERSCH, NANCY KAY, laboratory manager; b. Norfolk, Nebr., May 11, 1942; d. Ambrose Pryor and Angela Gertrude (Goergen) Jordan; m. Frank C. Maersch, May 11, 1968; 1 child, Todd F. BS in Med. Tech., Mt. Marty Coll., 1963; MA in Health Care Adminstrn., Cen. Mich. U., 1981. Diplomate Lab. Medicine; clin. lab. scientist; specialist in hematology. Med. technologist Madison (Wis.) Gen. Hosp. Lab., 1963-64, hematology sect. head, 1964-72, hematology specialist, 1973-79, hematology sect. head, 1979-80, lab. customer svc. rep., 1980-82, mgr. adminstrv. svc. and mktg., 1982-85; mgr. mobile diagnostics Meriter Gen. Med. Labs., Madison, 1985-87, mgr. client svcs., 1987-89, mgr. lab. ops., 1990—; bd. dirs. Dane County Cytology Ctr., Madison. Chair Edgefest event Edgewood H.S. Aux., 1987-92; mem. Bus. Forum, Madison, 1989—; vol. Ronald McDonald House; bd. dirs. parents assn. Marquette U., 1993—. Mem. Am. Soc. Clin. Lab. Sci., Wis. Soc. Clin. Lab. Sci. (sec. 1967-70, 76-80), Clin. Lab. Mgmt. Assn., Wis. chpt. Clin. Lab. Mgmt. Assn. (bd. dirs., pres.-elect 1995-96), Madison Area Lab. Suprs., Madison Civics Club. Roman Catholic. Home: 3105 Nottingham Way Madison WI 53713-3457 Office: Gen Med Labs 36 S Brooks St Madison WI 53715-1304

MAFFEI, STEPHEN ROGER, medical products executive, treasurer; b. N.Y.C, July 24, 1939; s. Roger S. and Catherine E. (Premo) M.; m. Barbara A. Tomek, Apr. 15, 1961; children: Stephen, Matthew, Joseph. BS, U. Bridgeport, 1960; MBA, Pace U., 1976. Analyst Dun & Bradstreet, N.Y.C., 1961-63; sr. analyst Burlington Industries, N.Y.C., 1963-66; asst. treas. U.S. Mineral, Stanhope, N.J., 1966-71; sec.-treas. Mueller Group, Alpha, N.J., 1971-73; chief fin. officer, v.p., sec.-treas. Landis & Gyr Inc., Elmsford, N.Y., 1973-84; chief fin. officer, v.p. fin., treas. Meadox Meds. Inc., Oakland, N.J., 1984-92; bd. dirs. Ramco Inc., Dumont, N.J., Watershed Inc., Englishtown, N.J. Home: 2 Trenton Ave Lavallette NJ 08735-2717 Office: Maffei Inc PO Box 487 Marlboro NJ 07746

MAGALSKI, ANTHONY, internist; b. Cleve., Apr. 3, 1963. MD, Washington U., St. Louis, 1989. Intern U. Tex. Southwestern Affiliated Hosp., Dallas, 1989-90, resident, 1990-92, fellow in cardiology, 1992—. Recipient Clinician-Scientist award Am. Heart Assn., 1995-96. Mem. ACP, Am. Coll. Cardiology, AMA. Office: U Tex Southwestern Med Ctr 5232 High Meadow Dr Dallas TX 76051-4284*

MAGARGAL, WELLS WRISLEY, biochemist; b. Worthington, Mass., Nov. 25, 1950; s. Charles Raymond and Helen Marion (Bartlett) M.; divorced; children: Wrisley Ann, Spencer Lee. BA, Pa. State U., 1972; PhD, U. Mass., 1978. Resident Johns Hopkins U., Balt., 1978-82; asst. prof. U. Ala., Birmingham, 1982-88; sr. rsch. cell biochemist Lederle Labs., Pearl River, N.Y., 1988—; asst. prof. Rockland C.C., Suffern, N.Y., 1992—. Mem. Am. Chem. Soc., Am. Soc. Cell Biology, Soc. In Vitro Biology. Office: Lederle Labs 401 N Middletown Rd Pearl River NY 10965

MAGEE, GEORGE PATRICK, therapist; b. Bryn Mawr, Pa., Dec. 22, 1940; s. James Cyril and Catherine Louise (Starkey) M. BA, Villanova U., 1964; MA, Augustinian Coll., Washington, 1968; MS, Biscayne Coll., Miami, Fla., 1977; DSc, Northwestern U., 1979. Cert. addictions counselor, Pa.; ordained priest Roman Cath. Ch., 1968; joined Order St. Augustine. Assoc. dir. human svcs. Villanova (Pa.) U., 1981-85; assoc. pastor for social svcs. St. Rita Ch., Phila., 1986; family therapist West Covina (Calif.) Hosp., 1986-89; primary therapist Harrison Recovery Program of Med. Coll. Pa., Phila., 1989-90; edn. specialist Mirmont Treatment Ctr., Lima, Pa., 1990—; founder, CEO The Fifth Station, Inc., Drexel Hill, Pa., 1994—; priest Augustinian Fathers, Villanova, 1968—; lectr. on spirituality; recreational therapist. Mem. Nat. Orgn. Alcohol and Drug Counselors, Pa. Coun. Alcohol and Drug Counselors, K.C. (4th degree). Democrat. Home: Bonner Faculty House Lansdowne Avenue Rd Drexel Hill PA 19026-1196

MAGEE, MICHAEL JOSEPH, physician; b. Kinston, N.C., June 13, 1953; s. Albert Joseph and Okalena (Gwyn) M.; m. Deborah Ruth Deason, June 18, 1977; children: Shane Michael, Paul Joseph. BS, Auburn U., 1974; MD, U. Tenn., 1977. Diplomate Am. Bd. Internal Medicine, cert. in internal medicine, med. oncology, hematology. Resident in internal medicine Bapt. Meml. Hosp., Memphis, 1977-80; fellow med. oncology Meml. Sloan-Kettering, N.Y.C., 1980-82; fellow hematology Vanderbilt U., Nashville, 1982-83; asst. dir. internal medicine residency Bapt. Hosp/Univ. Tenn., Nashville, 1983-86; pvt. practice Bapt. Hosp., Nashville, 1986—; asst. prof. medicine U. Tenn., 1984. Bd. mem. Tenn. chpt. Leukemia Soc. Am., Nashville, 1983-89, Cumberland chpt. Nat. Hemophilia Found., Nashville, 1983-86, Alive Hospice, Nashville, 1984-89; mem. founding session East Brentwood (Tenn.) Presbyn. Ch., 1988-91, Sunday sch. tchr., 1994—; coach Civitan Youth Baseball, 1988—, YMCA Soccer, 1993-94, YMCA Youth Basketball, 1994-95. Fellow ACP; mem. Am. Soc. Clin. Oncology, Am. Soc. Hematology. Office: Ste 503 222 22nd Ave N Nashville TN 37203

MAGEE, WALTER BULKELEY, toxicologist; b. Newark, July 13, 1954; s. Walter Bulkeley and Dorothy (Adams) M.; m. Mona Teresa Rawlins, June 26, 1982 (div. Nov. 1985); m. Marcia Carabell, Feb. 1, 1995. BS in Toxicology, Northeastern U., Boston, 1994, BA in German Lang. and Lit., 1994. Exec. gen. mgr. Sony Acres Farm, Colt's Neck, N.J., 1979-82; CEO N.J. Thoroughbred Sales Agy., Colt's Neck, 1981-82; regulatory assoc. Hampshire Chem. Corp., Lexington, Mass., 1993-95; cons. toxicologist in regulatory affairs Rochelle, Va., 1995—. Author/editor: Catalog for Sales Agency, 1981-82. Mem. Nat. Steeplechase Assn. Episcopalian. Home and Office: Ellinwood Farm HCR03 Box 383 Rochelle VA 22738

MAGEN, JED GARY, child psychiatrist; b. Des Moines, Iowa, May 10, 1953; s. Myron Shimon and Ruth May Magen; m. Carol Ann Barrett, June 18, 1978; children: Benjamin Barrett, Zachary Barrett. BA, Oakland U., 1975; DO, Coll. Osteopathic Medicine and Surgery, Des Moines, 1978. Cert. in gen. psychiatry. Intern Botsford Gen. Hosp., Farmington Hills, Mich., 1978-79; with Ind. Health Service, Bowler, Wis., 1979-82; resident in psychiatry, fellow in child psychiatry U. Mich., 1982-86; clin. instr. psychiatry, research fellow Inst. Social Research U. Mich., 1986-88; chief resident child psychiatry U. Mich., 1984-1985, dept. chief, 1985-86; asst. prof., residency tng. dir. dept psychiatry Mich. State U., East Lansing, 1988—, dir. of residency tng., 1991—; reviewer Jour. Am. Acad. Child & Adolescent Psychiatry. Served with USPHS, 1979-82. mem. Am. Psychiat. Assn., Am. Osteopathic Assn. Am. Coll. Neuropsychiatry. Home: 2045 Belding Ct Okemos MI 48864-3657 Office: Mich State U 105B E Fee Hall East Lansing MI 48824-1316

MAGEN, MYRON SHIMIN, osteopathic physician, educator, university dean; b. Bklyn., Mar. 1, 1926; s. Barney and Gertrude Beatrice (Cohen) M.; m. Ruth Sherman, July 6, 1952; children—Jed, Ned, Randy. D.O., Coll. Osteo. Medicine and Surgery, 1951; Sc.D. (hon.), U. Osteo. Medicine and Health Scis., Des Moines, 1981. Rotating intern Coll. Hosp., Des Moines, 1951-52, resident in pediatrics, 1953-54; chmn. dept. pediatrics Coll. Osteo. Medicine and Surgery, Des Moines, 1958-62, Riverside Osteo. Hosp., Trenton, Mich., 1962-68, Detroit Osteo. Hosp., 1965-67; med. dir., dir. med. edn. Zieger-Botsford Hosps., Farmington, Mich., 1968-70; prof. pediatrics Mich. State Coll. Osteo. Medicine, East Lansing, 1970—, dean, 1970—; mem. spl. med. adv. group to chief med. dir. VA, 1973-77; mem. grad med. edn. nat. dv. com. HHS, Washington, 1978-80; James Watson disting. lectr. Ohio Ostio Assn., 1974, Grad. Med. Edn. Nat. Adv. Com.; Watson Meml. lectr. Am. Coll. Osteo. Pediatricians, 1987; chair Mich. Med. Schs. Coun. Deans, 1979-84, 90-91; mem. PEW Health Professions Com., 1991—. Contbr. articles to profl. jours. Served with USN, 1943-45. Recipient Disting. Service award Okla. Coll. Osteo. Medicine and Surgery, 1975; Founder's medal Tex. Coll. Osteo. Medicine, 1978; Mem. Am. Assn. Colls. Osteo. Medicine (pres. 1977), Am. Osteo. Assn. (com. edn., chair com. on colls. 1987-90, La. Burns lectr. 1977, chair bur. profl. edn. 1990-92), Am. Coll. Osteo. Pediats. (pres. 1965-66), Mich. Assn. Osteo. Physicians and Surgeons. Home: 1251 Farwood Dr East Lansing MI 48823-1831 Office: Mich State Univ Coll Osteopathic Medicine 308 E Fee Hall East Lansing MI 48824-1316

MAGEN, NED ALAN, emergency physician; b. Dallas, July 23, 1956; s. Myron S. and Ruth May (Sherman) M.; m. Charlissa Renee Roundtree, June 19, 1994; children: Maurissa, Darryl. BS, Western Mich. U., 1978; DO, U. Health Scis., Des Moines, 1981. Diplomate Am. Bd. Emergency Physicians. Resident emergency medicine Mich. State U., East Lansing, 1986-88; emergency dept. physician Ctrl. Peninsula Gen. Hosp., Soldotna, Alaska, 1989—, dir. emergency dept., 1991—; med. advisor Kenai City (Alaska) Fire Dept., 1990—. Bd. dirs. Peninsula Home Health, Kenai, 1990—. With USPHS, 1982-85. Fellow Am. Coll. Emergency Physicians; mem. Am. Osteo. Assn., Alaska Osteo. Assn., Am. Coll. Emergency Physicians, Am. Coll. Osteo. Physicians, Am. Coll. Physicians Execs. Home: PO Box 926 Soldotna AK 99669 Office: Central Peninsula Gen Hosp 250 Hospital Pl Soldotna AK 99669

MAGENHEIM, DOUGLAS A., internist; b. Cin., Nov. 13, 1961; s. Herbert G. and Eileen (Steinberg) M.; m. Amy S. Dresnin, Jan. 1, 1996. BA in Chemistry and Polit. Sci., Miami U., 1984; MD, U. Cin., 1988; postgrad., Xavier U., 1995—. Diplomat Am. Bd. Internal Medicine. Intern Univ. Hosp./U.Cin., 1988-89, resident, 1989-91; practice internal medicine Cin., 1991—; mem. staff Jewish Hosps., Christ Hosp., Univ. Hosp., Bethesda Hosp., Cin. Recipient Top Young Physician award Ohio State Med. Assn., 1995. Fellow ACP; mem. AMA, Tristate Med. Assn. (v.p., bd. dirs. 1994-95), Cin. Soc. of Internal Medicine, Ohio State Med. Assn. (del. 1992—). Office: Premier Med Assocs 2925 Vernon Pl #200 Cincinnati OH 45219-2430

MAGENHEIM, MARK JOSEPH, physician, epidemiologist, educator; b. Deland, Fla., Nov. 1, 1947; s. Milton David and Dolores Ella (Raithel) M. BA cum laude, Wash. U., 1969; MPH, Yale U., 1971; MD with honors, McMaster U., 1974. Diplomate Am. Bd. Preventive Medicine, Am. Bd. Pub. Health, Am. Bd. Family Medicine. Health officer, prof. Oreg. State U., Corvallis, 1976-78; prof. cmty. health U. Sierra Leone, Freetown, West Africa, 1978-81; asst. prof. McMaster U., Hamilton, Ont., Can., 1978-83; asst. state health officer State of Fla., Tallahassee, 1989-91; health officer Sarasota (Fla.) County Pub. Health Dept., 1984-95; med. dir. Hospice of S.W. Fla., Sarasota, 1994—; adj. prof. U. South Fla., Tampa, 1985—; mem. staff Doctor's Hosp. Sarasota. Author, editor Clinics in Geriatric Medicine, 1986, (with others) Practice of Geriatrics, 1986; contbr. articles to profl. jours. Bd. dirs. Children & Youth Consortium, Sarasota, 1989—, Health Care Planning Coun., Sarasota, 1992—. Recipient Surgeon Gen.'s medallion of excellence USPHS, 1989, award of commendation, 1989, Leadership award Ctrs. for Disease Control, 1991-92; recipient numerous grants. Fellow Royal Soc. Tropical Medicine and Hygiene; mem. Pub. Health Leadership Soc. (chair 1993-95), Fla. Pub. Health Leadership Inst., Fla. Pub. Health Assn., Fla. Med. Assn., Fla. Soc. for Preventive Medicine, Sarasota County Med. Soc. (chair pub. health com. 1987—). Home: 3412 Clark Rd - 234 Sarasota FL 34231-8406 Office: Hospice of SW Fla 6055 Rand Blvd Sarasota FL 34238-5189

MAGGIO, CINDY MICHELE, pharmacist; b. Hempstead, N.Y., Apr. 8, 1959; d. Henry Howard and Helen (Epstein) Simon; m. May 10, 1986. AA in Scis., Miami-Dade C.C., Miami, Fla., 1981; BS in Microbiology, U. Fla., 1983, BS in Pharmacy, 1986; PharmD, Nova-Southeastern U., 1990. Pharmacy intern Super-X Drugs, West Miami, Fla., 1985, Bapt. Hosp., Miami, 1986; clin. pharmacist I Jackson Meml. Hosp., Miami, 1987-90, staff pharmacist (part-time), 1995-96; cons. pharmacist Hospice-Care, Inc., Miami, 1990-92; program mgr., clin. specialist HIV/AIDS Dept. Vets. Affairs, Miami, 1990—; mem. com. on admissions Nova-Southwestern U., 1996; instr. pharmacology I Fla. Coll. Physician Assts., Miami, 1996. Co-author: Primary Care Handbook/Amb HIV/AIDS, 1995. Recipient Patient Care award South Fla. Soc. Hosp. Pharmacists, 1989, 95. Mem. Am. Coll. Clin. Pharmacists, Am. Soc. Health Sys. Pharmacists, South Fla. Soc. Health Sys. Pharmacists, Kappa Epsilon. Home: 14918 SW 132 St Miami FL 33186 Office: Dept Veteran Affairs Pharmacy Svcs 1201 NW 16th St Miami FL 33125

MAGID, GAIL AVRUM, neurosurgeon, neurosurgery educator; b. Chgo., Oct. 15, 1934; s. Harry M. and Henrietta (Busch) M.; m. Janet Louise Reinhardt, June 15, 1962 (div.); children: Allison Magid London, Jonathan Alward; m. Roseanne Cipra Muirhead, Sept. 4, 1982. BSc, U. Ill., 1954;

MD, Chgo. Med. Sch., 1958. Diplomate Am. Bd. Neurol. Surgery. Intern Cook County Hosp., Chgo., 1958-59; resident, then fellow neurol. surgery Mayo Clinic, Rochester, Minn., 1959-61, 63-65; clin. instr. neurosurgery U. Calif., San Francisco, 1965-70, asst. clin. prof., 1970-79, assoc. prof., 1979—; chmn. Dominican Neurol. Inst., Santa Cruz, Calif., 1975—; bd. dirs. Dominican Found.; cons. neurosurgery U.S. Army, San Francisco Gen. Hosp. Assoc. editor: Clinical Neurosurgery, 1974. Bd. dirs. Santa Cruz Symphony Assn., 1983-85, U. Calif. Friends of Arts, Santa Cruz, 1985-86. Served to lt. comdr. USN, 1961-63. Fellow ACS, Internat. Coll. Surgeons; mem. AMA, Calif. Med. Assn., Internat. Soc. Pediatric Neurosurgeons, Am. Assn. Neurol. Surgeons, Western Neurosurg. Soc., Cong. Neurol. Surgeons, San Francisco Neurol. Soc. (pres.-elect 1991, pres. 1992), St. Francis Yacht Club (San Francisco). Republican. Home: 241 4th Ave Santa Cruz CA 95062-3815 Office: 1661 Soquel Dr Santa Cruz CA 95065-1709

MAGILL, ROSALIND MAY, psychotherapist; b. Albany, N.Y., Apr. 27, 1944; d. Fenton Elliot Sr. and Rosalind Pearl (Gross) M.; m. Theodore T. Solomon, May 18, 1970 (div. 1980). Student, N.Y. Inst. Tech., 1963-64, Pace Coll., 1970-71; cert. in process piping design, Voorheese Tech. Inst., 1968; MEd in Counseling and Psychology, Cambridge Coll., 1994. Lic. master pipefitter, Mass.; EIT. Piping designer Badger Am., Inc., Cambridge, Mass., 1976-77; tchr. advanced math. Vision-in-Action, Natick, Mass., 1977-80; plumbing designer R. G. Vanderweil Assocs., Boston, 1980-81; vol. counselor alcohol/substance abuse social detox program Bergen County Hosp., Paramus, N.J., 1981-83; field engr. United Engrs. and Constructors, Phila., 1983-84; tchr. spl. edn. math. and sci. Amesbury (Mass.) High Sch., 1984-85; resident engr. Hoyle, Tanner Assocs., Londonderry, N.H., 1985-86; resident engr., constrn. mgr. dept. environ. mgmt. Commonwealth of Mass., Boston, 1986-89; clin. supr., counselor substance abuse Positive Lifestyles, Mattapan, Mass., 1990-93; dir. Respond Program, substance abuse therapist Ctr. for Family Devel., Lowell, Mass., 1993-94, dir. Respond Program, 1994—; counselor alcoholism and substance abuse Serenity House/Gift of Serenity, 1977-80; counselor substance abuse Baldpate Hosp., Georgetown, Mass., 1984.85. With USMC, 1962. N.Y. State Regent's scholar, 1962. Mem. ACA, Internat. Assn. Addictions and Offender Counselors, Women's Ordination Conf., Daus. Bilitis (pres. N.Y. chpt. 1968-70), Matachine Soc. (bd. dirs. 1968-70).

MAGIONCALDA, DONALD GERARD, oncologist; b. N.Y.C., Oct. 25, 1946; s. Albert J. and Marie T. (Rigney) M.; m. Marie T. Cinquemani, Dec. 27, 1969. BS, St. Bonaventure U., 1968; MD, SUNY, Bklyn., 1972. Bd. cert. in hematology, med. oncology, internal medicine. Med. intern SUNY Downstate/Kings County Hosp., 1972-73, resident in medicine, 1973-75; dir. med. oncology Kennebec Valley Med. Ctr., Augusta, Maine, 1978—; adj. clin. professor Dartmouth Family Practice Residency, Augusta, Maine, 1983—. Chmn. Maine Cancer Prevention & Control Adv. Com., Augusta, 1986—; dir., past pres. Maine div. Am. Cancer Soc., Brunswick, 1985—; chmn. Maine Coalition for Smoking or Health, 1995-96, dir. med. care devel., 1987—. Mem. Am. Soc. Clin. Oncology, Am. Soc. Hematology, Maine Med. Assn. Office: Kennebec Valley Med Ctr 6 E Chestnut St Augusta ME 04330-5717

MAGLACAS, A. MANGAY, nursing researcher. BSN, Vanderbilt U.; MPH, U. Minn.; DPH, Johns Hopkins U.; DS (hon.), U. Ill., 1987. Chief sci. for nursing divsn. health manpower devel. WHO, Cologny, Switzerland; adj. prof. Coll. Nursing, U. Ill., Chgo.; various vis. prof. positions in U.S., The Philippines, Thailand, Papua New Guinea, Japan, USSR, Australia; cons. in field. Rockefeller fellow, 1964-67; Fulbright-Smith-Mundt scholar, 1952-54. Mem. Internat. Coun. Nurses (bd. dirs.), NAS (fgn. assoc.). Office: 59 Chemin de Planta, CH-1223 Cologny Switzerland

MAGLIATO, HENRY J., orthopedic surgeon; b. N.Y.C., June 8, 1933; s. E. Henry and Anna (Carillo) M.; m. Teresa Joan Dabulis, Aug. 29, 1959; children: Todd Andrew, Lisbeth Ann. BS cum laude, Fordham U., 1954; MD, SUNY, 1958. Diplomate Am. Bd. Orthopedic Surgery. Attending orthopedic surgeon St. Luke's-Roosevelt-Columbia Hosp., N.Y.C., 1963—; police surgeon N.Y.C. Police Dept., 1981—. Fellow Am. Acad. Orthopedic Surgeons, Am. Coll. Surgeons, Am. Soc. Indsl. Medicine, Internat. Assn. Chiefs of Police, N.Y. State Soc. Orthopedic Surgeons, N.Y. County Med. Soc. Republican. Roman Catholic. Office: 860 5th Ave New York NY 10021-5856

MAGLIO, GESOMINA V., clinical social worker; b. Mar. 23, 1956. MSW, Fordham U., 1982, D Social Work, 1995. Diplomate Am. Bd. Examiners in Clin. Social Work. Clin. social worker, psychotherapist N.J., 1984—; pvt. practice, 1984—; adj. prof. Coll. of St. Elizabeth, Convent Station, N.J., 1996. Fellow Am. Orthopsychiat. Assn.; mem. NASW, Acad. Cert. Social Works,, N.Y. State Soc. Clin. Social Workers, Nat. Registry Health Care Providers in Clin. Social Work.

MAGNANI, MAURO, biochemist, dean; b. S. Giovanni Marignano, Italy, Apr. 9, 1953; s. Vittorio and Lidia (Casadei) M.; m. Maddalena Ligi, Oct. 10, 1976; children: Paolo, Marco. Doctorate, U. Urbino, Italy, 1976. Asst. prof. U. Urbino, 1977-82; assoc. prof. U. Urbino, Eng., 1982-86; prof. U. Urbino, 1986—; dean U. Urbino, Haifa, Israel, 1996—; vis. rschr. U. Birmingham, Eng., 1980; vis. prof. Technion, Haifa, Israel, 1983. Co-editor: Red Blood Cell Aging, 1991, The Use of Resealed Erythrocytes, 1992; contbr. numerous articles to sci. jours.; patentee in field. Grantee EEC, govt. and pvt. orgns., 1980—. Mem. Biochemical Soc., Internat. Soc. Use of Resealed Erythrocytes (past pres. 1991-93). Roman Catholic. Office: U Urbino, Via Saffi 2, 61029 Urbino PS, Italy

MAGNES, HARRY ALAN, physician; b. Orange, N.J., Dec. 3, 1948; s. Sam and Shirley (Daniels) M.; m. Patricia Bruce, Mar. 25, 1989; 1 child, Carlos Fontiveros. AB in Biology magna cum laude, Brown U., 1970; MD, Yale U., 1974. Cert. Am. Bd. Internal Medicine. Intern, resident internal medicine U. Iowa Hosps. and Clinics, 1974-77; ptnr., med. dir., pres., CEO Gallatin Med. Clinic, Downey, Calif., 1977—; pres., CEO Gallatin Med. Corp., Downey, Calif., 1992-94; med. dir., bd. dirs. Gallatin Med. Found., Downey, Calif., 1993—; staff physician Downey Cmty. Hosp., 1977-96, Presbyn. Intercmty. Hosp., 1992—; bd. dirs. Primehealth of So. Calif.; clin. instr. Rancho Los Amigos Hosp., Downey, 1981-83. Author: Rheumatic Fever in Connecticut, 1974. James Manning scholar Brown U., 1968. Mem. ACPE, Healthcare Assn. So. Calif., Primehealth So. Calif. (bd. dirs. 1995—, exec. com. 1996—), Am. Coll. Med. Practice Execs., Am. Med. Group Assn. (med. policy com. 1994—), Med. Group Mgmt. Assn., Sigma Xi, Phi Beta Kappa. Office: Gallatin Med Found 10720 Paramount Blvd Downey CA 90241-3306

MAGNESS, RHONDA ANN, microbiologist; b. Stockton, Calif., Jan. 30, 1946; d. John Pershing and Dorothy Waneta (Kelley) Wetter; m. Barney LeRoy Bender, Aug. 26, 1965 (div. 1977); m. Gary D. Magness, Mar. 5, 1977; children: Jay D. (dec.), Troy D. BS, Calif. State U., 1977. Lic. clin. lab. technologist, Calif., med. technologist; cert. clin. lab. scientist. Med. asst. C. Fred Wilcox, MD, Stockton, 1965-66; clk. typist Dept. of U.S. Army, Ft. Eustis, Va., 1967, Def. Supply Agy., New Orleans, 1967-68; med. asst. James G. Cross, MD, Lodi, Calif., 1969, Arthur A. Kemalyan, MD, Lodi, 1969-71, 72-77; med. sec. Lodi Meml. Hosp., 1972; lab. aide Calif. State U., Sacramento, 1977; phlebotomist St. Joseph's Hosp., Stockton, 1978-79; supr. microbiology Dameron Hosp. Assn., Stockton, 1980—. Active Concerned Women Am., Washington, 1987—. Mem. AAUW, Calif. Assn. Clin. Lab. Technologists, San Joaquin County Med. Assts. Assn., Nat. Geog. Soc., Nat. Audubon Soc. Baptist. Lodge: Jobs Daus. (chaplain 1962-63). Home: 9627 Knight Ln Stockton CA 95209-1961 Office: Dameron Hosp Lab 525 W Acacia St Stockton CA 95203-2405

MAGNESS, WALTER BONHAM, orthodontist, educator; b. Houston, Dec. 13, 1932; s. Walter Bonham and Lillian Ida (Wagner) M.; m. Marcille Elaine Nerger, Aug. 6, 1960; children: Marc Bonham, Marlene Elaine, Mary Lynn. AA, Angelo State U., San Angelo, Tex., 1952; DDS, U. Tex., Houston, 1956, cert. in orthodontics, 1960. Assoc. prof. clin. orthodontics U. Tex. Dental Br., 1960-88, clin. prof., 1988—; pvt. practice, Houston, 1960—; bd. dirs. Am. Bd. Orthodontics, St. Louis, 1974-80, pres., 1980-81. Contbr. articles to dental jours. Capt. USAF, 1956-58. Fellow Am. Coll. Dentists; mem. ADA, Am. Assn. Orthodontists (Todd Dewell award 1988), Southwestern Soc. Orthodontists (Martin Dewey award 1990), Charles Tweed Orthodontic Study Group (pres. 1976), U. Tex. Orthodontic Alumni (pres. Houston 1974, Yellen-Schoverling award 1988). Home: 12211 Perthshire Houston TX 77024-2442 Office: 902 Frostwood Ste 300 Houston TX 77024-2442

MAGNO, JOANA H., cardiologist, medical educator; b. Yokohama, Japan, Nov. 19, 1954; d. Dominador Lara and Hisako (Harada) M.; m. Henry Ankeny Tucker, Nov. 17, 1990; children: John Henry, Margaret. BA, Yale U., 1976; MD, U. Wash., 1981. Diplomate Am. Bd. Internal Medicine, Am. Bd. Cardiology. Intern and resident in internal medicine Sch. of Medicine, U. Hawaii, Honolulu, 1981-84, chief resident, 1984-85, asst. clin. prof., 1987—; cardiology fellow U. Calif., San Francisco, 1985-87. Fellow Am. Coll. of Cardiology; mem. ACP, Am. Heart Assn. (bd. dirs. 1987-94). Office: 1329 Lusitana #707 Honolulu HI 96813

MAGNUSON, HAROLD JOSEPH, physician; b. Halstead, Kans., Mar. 31, 1913; s. Joseph Simeon and Margaret Ethel (Matson) M.; m. Ruth Prusia, Feb. 16, 1935 (dec. 1941); children: Karen Margaret Magnuson Mauro), Ruth Ellen; m. Kathryne I. Bause, Dec. 20, 1941 (dec. 1993). AB, U. So. Calif., 1934, MD, 1938; MPH, Johns Hopkins U., 1942. Diplomate: Am. Bd. Preventive Medicine (mem. bd. 1964-75, vice chmn. occupational medicine 1968-75). Intern Los Angeles County Gen. Hosp., 1937-39; research fellow A.C.P., 1939-40; instr. medicine U. So. Calif., 1939-41; commd. asst. surgeon USPHS, 1941, med. dir., 1952; instr. medicine Johns Hopkins, 1943-46; research prof. exptl. medicine U. N.C., 1946-55; chief div. occupational health USPHS, 1956-62; ret., 1962; prof. internal medicine U. Mich. Sch. Medicine, prof. indsl. health, 1962-76, prof. emeritus, 1976—; chmn. dept. U. Mich. Sch. Pub. Health; also dir. U. Mich. Sch. Pub. Health (Inst. Indsl. Health), 1962-69; asso. dean U. Mich. Sch. Pub. Health (Sch. Pub. Health), 1969-76; Mem. U.S. delegation ILO Conf., 1958, 59; Chmn. U.S. indsl. toxicology delegation to, USSR, 1963. Fellow A.C.P., A.A.A.S., A.M.A. (chmn. sect. preventive medicine 1966, Hektoen bronze medal 1956), Am. Acad. Occupational Medicine, Am. Pub. Health Assn. (chmn. sect. occupational health 1966, Indsl. Med. Assn., Knudsen award 1970); mem. Soc. Clin. Investigation, Soc. Exptl. Biology and Medicine, Soc. Exptl. Pathology, Mich. Indsl. Med. Assn. (pres. 1965-66), Internat. Congress Indsl. Medicine (v.p. 1969), Rammazzini Soc., Phi Beta Kappa, Sigma Xi, Alpha Omega Alpha, Delta Omega. Home: 18755 W Bernardo Dr Apt 1125 San Diego CA 92127-3023

MAGNUSSON, TOMAS HERBERT, dentist, researcher; b. Linköping, Sweden, Apr. 1, 1949; s. Herbert Gustav and Iris Viola (Wetterström) M.; m. Annica Birgitta Hedmo, Oct. 11, 1969; children: Malin, Jenny, Cecilia. LDS, Faculty Odontology, Göteborg, Sweden, 1974, D of Odontology, 1981, docent/reader, 1986. Dentist Pub. Dental Svc., Jokkmokk, Sweden, 1974-80; head of dept. of stomatognathic physiology Pub. Dental Svc., Luleå, Sweden, 1980-88; sr. cons. dept. stomatognathic physiology Pub. Dental Svc., Jönköping, Sweden, 1988—. Author or co-author 5 textbooks in field of stomatognathic physiology/occlusion; contbr. numerous papers to internat. sci. jours. Mem. Soc. Oral Physiology, Swedish Soc. Stomatognathic Physiology. Home: Swedenborgsgatan 66 B, S-55448 Jönköping Sweden Office: Inst Postgrad Dental Edn, S-55111 Jönköping Sweden

MAGOUN, THATCHER, VI, surgeon; b. Worcester, Mass., Sept. 19; s. Thatcher and Mary (Stewart) M.; m. Nina Fell Morris, Sept. 1, 1938; 1 child, Sean Stewart. BS, Franklin & Marshall U., 1959; MD, Temple U., 1963. Intern Abington (Pa.) Hosp., 1963-64; resident The Queen's Hosp., Honolulu, 1964-67; intern Abington (Pa.) Meml. Hosp.; resident Queens Hosp., Honolulu, 1967-68, Temple U., Phila.; surgeon Waimea (Hawaii) Clinic, 1972-76; chief of staff Kauai Vets. Meml. Hosp., Waimea, 1975-76; surgeon Kauai Med. Group, Lihue, Hawaii, 1976—; chief of staff Wilcox Meml. Hosp., Lihue, 1979-80, chmn. dept. surgery, 1981—. Major U.S. Army, 1969-72. Mem. ACS; mem. Coll. Physicians Phila., Pan Pacific Surg. Soc., Hawaii Surg. Assn., Masons, Alpha Omega Alpha. Republican. Baptist. Home: 3781 Papalina Rd Kalaheo HI 96741 Office: Kauai Med Group 3-3420 B Kuhio Hwy Lihue HI 96766

MAGRUDER, G. BROCK, ophthalmic surgeon; b. Orlando, Oct. 6, 1931; s. Clarence Cephas and Mary Kathryn (Rogers) M.; m. Susan Anne McKenzie, Feb. 23, 1957 (div. May. 1975); m. Polly Fulkerson, Aug. 29, 1980; children: G. Brock Jr., Douglas M., James Bailey, John Tanner. MD, Emory U., 1956. Diplomate Am. Bd. Ophthalmology, Am. Bd. Eye Surgeons. Intern internal medicine Duke Univ. Hosp., Durham, N.C., 1957; resident in internal medicine Strong Meml. Hosp., Rochester, N.Y., 1958; resident in ophthalmology N.Y. Hosp.-Cornel Med. Ctr., 1958-61; vice chief ophthalmology Bethesda (Md.) Naval Hosp., 1961-63; pvt. practice Orlando, Fla., 1963—; past chief medicine Orlando Regional Med. Ctr.; past pres. Ctrl. Fla. Soc. Ophthalmology. Trustee Crummer Bus. Sch., Orlando, 1991—. Lt. cmdr. U.S. Navy, 1961-63. Mem. AMA, AM. Acad. Ophthalmology, Am. Soc. Cataract and Refractive Surgeons, Fla. Med. Assn., Fla. Soc. Ophthalmology (past pres.), Fla. Soc. Prevention of Blindness, Orange County Med. Soc. Republican. Episcopal. Office: Magruder Eye Inst 116 W Sturtevant St Orlando FL 32806

MAGUIRE, CHARLOTTE EDWARDS, retired physician; b. Richmond, Ind., Sept. 1, 1918; d. Joel Blaine and Lydia (Betscher) Edwards; m. Raymer Francis Maguire, Sept. 1, 1948 (dec.); children: Barbara, Thomas Clair II. Student, Stetson U., 1936-38, U. Wichita, 1938-39; BS, Memphis Tchrs. Coll., 1940; MD, U. Ark., 1944. Intern, resident Orange Meml. Hosp., Orlando, Fla., 1944-46; resident Bellevue Hosp. and Med. Ctr., NYU, N.Y.C., 1954, 55; instr. nurses Orange Meml. Hosp., 1947-57, staff mem., 1946-68; staff mem. Fla. Santarium and Hosp., Orlando, 1946-56, Holiday House and Hosp., Orlando, 1950-62; mem. courtesy and cons. staff West Orange Meml. Hosp., Winter Garden, Fla., 1952-67; active staff, chief dept. pediatrics Mercy Hosp., Orlando, 1965-68; med. dir. med. svcs. and basic care Fla. Dept. Health and Rehab. Svcs., 1975-84; med. exec. dir., med. svcs. divsn. worker's compensation Fla. Dept. Labor, Tallahassee, 1984-87; chief of staff physicians and dentists Ctrl. Fla. divsn. Children's Home Soc. Fla., 1947-56; dir. Orlando Child Health Clinic 1949-58; pvt. practice medicine Orlando, 1946-68; asst. regional dir. HEW, 1970-72; pediat. cons. Fla. Crippled Children's Commn., 1952-70, dir., 1968-70; med. dir. Office Med. Svcs. and Basic Care, sr. physician Office of Asst. Sec. Ops., Fla. Dept. Health and Rehab. Svcs.; clin. prof. dept. pediat. U. Fla. Coll. Medicine, Gainesville, 1980-87; mem. Fla. Drug Utilization Rev., 1983-87; real estate salesperson Investors Realty, 1982—; bd. dirs. Stavros Econ. Ctr. Fla. State U., Tallahassee; mem. pres.'s coun. Fla. State U., U. Fla., Gainesville. Mem. profl. adv. com. Fla. Center for Clin. Services at U. Fla., 1952-60; del. to Midcentury White House Conf. on Children and Youth, 1950; U.S. del from Nat. Soc. for Crippled Children to World Congress for Welfare of Cripples, Inc., London, 1957; pres of corp. Eccleston-Callahan Hosp. for Colored Crippled Children, 1956-58; sec. Fla. chpt. Nat. Doctor's Com. for Improved Med. Services, 1951-52; med. adv. com. Gateway Sch. for Mentally Retarded, 1959-62; bd. dirs. Forest Park Sch. for Spl. Edn. Crippled Children, 1949-54, mem. med. adv. com., 1955-68, chmn., 1957-68; mem. Fla. Adv. Council for Mentally Retarded, 1965-70; dir. central Fla. poison control Orange Meml. Hosp.; mem. orgn. com., chmn. com. for admissions and selection policies Camp Challenge; participant 12th session Fed. Exec. Inst., 1971; del. White House Conf. on Aging, 1980. Mem. AMA (life), Nat. Rehab. Assn., Am. Congress Phys. Medicine and Rehab., Fla. Soc. Crippled Children and Adults, Ctrl. Fla. Soc. Crippled Children and Adults (dir. 1949-58, pres. 1956-57), Am. Assn. Cleft Palate, Fla. Soc. Crippled Children (trustee 1951-57, v.p. 1956-57, profl. adv. com. 1957-68), Mental Health Assn. Orange County (charter mem.; pres. 1949-50, dir. 1947-52, chmn. exec. com. 1950-52, dir. 1963-65), Fla. Orange County Heart Assn., Am. Med. Women's Assn., Am. Acad. Med. Dirs., Fla. Med. Assn. (chmn. com. on mental retardation), Orange County Med. Assn., Orange Med. Soc. (life), Fla. Pediatric Soc. (pres. 1952-53), Fla. Cleft Palate Assn. (counselor-at-large, sec.), Nat. Inst. Geneal. Rsch., Nat. Geneal. Soc., Assn. Profl. Genealogists, Tallahassee Geneal. Soc., Fla. State U. Found. Inc. (bd. dirs. Stavoris Ctr. for Econ. Edn.). Club: Governors. Home: 4158 Covenant Ln Tallahassee FL 32308-5765

MAHAGNA, HAMZI, anesthesia technician; b. Um-El Fahem, Israel, July 3, 1955; arrived in New Zealand, 1986; s. Mahmoud and Wagiha Mahagna; m. Alison Prime; children: Yasmin, Maya. Student, Jerusalem U., 1971, Nursing Sch., Jerusalem, 1973. Office: Waikato Hosp, Anesthesia Dept, Hamilton New Zealand

MAHAN, KIERAN THOMAS, podiatric surgeon, educator; b. Stamford, Conn., Feb. 13, 1953; s. John Anthony and Evelyn (Riley) M.; m. Blair Marie Wallace, Aug. 21, 1976; children: Sean, Caitlin, Patrick, Brendan. BS, U. Toronto, Ont., Can., 1974; MS, U. Bridgeport, 1976; D of Podiatric Medicine, Pa. Coll. Podiatric Medicine, Phila., 1980. Diplomate Am. Bd. Podiatric Surgery. Chief resident Dr.'s Hosp., Tucker, Ga., 1982-83; asst. prof. podiatric surgery Pa. Coll. Podiatric Medicine, Phila., 1983-86, prof., v.p. acad. affairs, 1986—; permanent faculty, founding bd. trustees The Podiatry Inst., Tucker, 1990—; bd. dirs. Nat. Bd. Podiatric Med. Examiners; disting. practitioner Nat. Acad. of Practice. Contbr. over 80 articles, chpts. to profl. publs. Fellow Am. Coll. Foot and Ankle Surgeons; mem. Am. Poliatric Med. Assn., AO Alumni Assn., Am. Coll. Podopediatrics, Am. Assn. Colls. of Podiatric Medicine (chmn. coun. of deans 1987). Roman Catholic. Office: Pa Coll Podiatric Medicine 810 Race St Philadelphia PA 19107-2406

MAHENDROO, PREM PRASAD, biophysical sciences facility administrator, medical sciences educator; b. India, July 4, 1931; came to U.S., 1956; s. Raghunath Prasad and Satgurpyari (Segal) M.; m. Indu Surat Malhotra, Sept. 8, 1962; children: Mala, Sanjay. MA in Applied Math., Punjab U., India, 1955; PhD in Physics, U. Tex., Austin, 1960. From asst. prof. to prof. physics, dir. lab biophysics Tex. Christian U., Ft. Worth, 1960-81; rsch. fellow, dir. spectroscopy R&D Alcon Labs., Inc., Ft. Worth, 1981-82, rsch. fellow, dir. physics R&D, 1982-88, dir. new tech./instrumentation, 1988-89, dir. phys. scis. rsch., 1989—; vis. prof. U. Nottingham, Eng., 1973-74; adj. prof. of pharmacology U. North Tex., Health Science Ctr. at Ft. Worth U.; mem. congl. liaison com. for the consortium of biomed. rsch. socs. (ACCB, ASBM, Biophy Soc., GSA); cons. various indsl. rsch. labd., 1960-81. Reviewer, contbr. over 60 articles on physical scis., biophysics and ophthalmology to profl. jours. Recipient Fulbright award Internat. Edn. Agy., N.Y., 1956; cancer sci. fellow Nat. Cancer Inst. of NIH, Bethesda, Md., 1976-78; rsch. grantee Office Sci. Rsch., USAF, R&D Ctr., U.S. Army, NSF, NIH, Robert A. Welch Found., Indsl. R&D Labs. Fellow AAAS, APS, Tex. Acad. Sci.; mem. Assn. for Rsch. in Vision and Ophthalmology, Internat. Soc. Magnetic Resonance in Medicine, Biophys. Soc. Home: 6413 Poco Ct Fort Worth TX 76133-5217 Office: Alcon Labs Inc R2-19 6219 South Fwy Fort Worth TX 76134-2001

MAHER, BRENDAN ARNOLD, psychology educator, editor; b. Widnes, Eng., Oct. 31, 1924; came to U.S., 1955; s. Thomas F. and Agnes (Power) M.; m. Winifred Barbara Brown, Aug. 27, 1952; children: Rebecca, Thomas, Nicholas, Liam, Niall. B.A. with honours, U. Manchester, Eng., 1950; M.A., Ohio State U., 1951, Ph.D., 1954; student, U. Ill. Med. Sch., 1952-53; A.M. (hon.), Harvard, 1972. Diplomate: Am. Bd. Examiners in Profl. Psychology. Psychologist Her Majesty's Prison, Wakefield, Eng., 1954-55; instr. Ohio State U., 1955-56; asst. prof. Northwestern U., 1956-58; asso. prof. La. State U., 1958-60; lectr. Harvard, 1960-64; chmn. Center Research Personality, 1962-64; prof. U. Wis., 1964-67, 71-72; vis. fellow U. Copenhagen, 1966-67, vis. fellow and research scientist, 1979; prof. psychology Brandeis U., 1967-72; dean Brandeis U. (Grad. Sch.), 1969-71, dean faculty, 1971-83; E. C. Henderson prof. psychology, 1983—; prof. Harvard U., 1972—, chmn. dept. psychology and social relations, 1973-78, chmn. dept. psychology, 1987-89, dean Grad. Sch. Arts and Scis., 1989-92; assoc. psychologist McLean Hosp., Belmont, Mass., 1968-77; psychologist McLean Hosp., 1977-84; cons. in medicine Peter Bent Brigham Hosp., Boston, 1977-85; cons. in psychology Mass. Gen. Hosp., 1977—. Author: Principles of Psychopathology, 1966, Introduction to Research in Psychopathology, 1970, A Passage to Sword Beach, 1966; co-editor: National Research Council: Research Doctorate Programs in the United States, 1995; editor Progress in Exptl. Personality Rsch., 1964-87, Jour. Cons. and Clin. Psychology, 1972-78; cons. editor Rev. Personality and Social Psychology, Clin. Psychology Rev. Served with Brit. Royal Navy, 1943-47. Fellow AAAS, Am. Psychol. Soc.; mem. Brit. Psychol. Assn. (chartered psychologist U.K.), Soc. Rsch. in Psychopathology (pres. 1985-87). Office: Harvard U William James Hall Cambridge MA 02138 also: Giffords Island, Mahone Bay, NS Canada

MAHER, CHARLES ANDREW, psychology educator; b. Bayonne, N.J., June 23, 1944. BA, Montclair State Coll., 1966, MA, 1969; profl. diploma in psychology, Kean Coll., 1973; PhD in Psychology, Rutgers U., 1976. Lic. psychologist, N.J.; cert. supt., N.J.; cert. Internat. Bd. Trainers; diplomate Bd. Adminstrv. Psychology. Tchr. of handicapped Southington (Conn.) Pub. Schs., 1966-68; sch. psychologist Kearny (N.J.) Pub. Schs., 1968-73; dir. spl. svcs. Somerville (N.J.) Pub. Schs., 1973-75, asst. supt. schs., 1975-79; assoc. prof. Rutgers U., New Brunswick, N.J., 1979-83, prof., chair dept. applied psychology, 1983—; cons. Wis. Dept. Pub. Instrn., Madison, 1985—, N.J. Dept. Labor, Trenton, 1988—, Chgo. White Sox, N.Y. Yankees, 1989—, Gen. Motors Corp., Rowe Internat.; dir. Inst. Program Planning/Evaluation, Piscataway, N.J., 1991—. Author: Planning and Evaluating Services, 1985, Self Management, 1986; editor Spl. Svcs. jour., 1980—; contbr. articles to profl. jours. Fellow APA (div. v.p. 1986-88, Am. Psychol. Soc., Am. Assn. for Applied and Provacative Psychology. Office: Rutgers U Grad Sch Psychology PO Box 819 Piscataway NJ 08855-0819

MAHER, CORNELIUS CREEDON, III, neurologist, toxicologist; b. N.Y.C., Jan. 30, 1949; s. Cornelius Creedon Jr. and Hester (Sullivan) M.; m. Lynn Marie Elliott, July 15, 1972; children: Christa, Cornelius IV, Kimberley. BS in Chemistry, Boston Coll., 1969; MS in Chemistry, U. Mich., 1973, PhD in Chemistry and Environ. Health, 1976; MD, St. Louis U., 1986. Rsch. fellow Brookhaven Nat. Lab., Upton, N.Y., 1969; rsch. fellow then lectr. U. Mich., Ann Arbor, 1969-76; rsch. assoc. Children's Hosp. Med. Ctr., Boston, 1976-77; indsl. toxicologist West Allis (Wis.) Meml. Hosp., 1977-82; commd. 2d lt. U.S. Army, 1982, advanced through grades to lt. col.; intern in neurology Letterman Army Med. Ctr., San Francisco, 1986-87, resident in neurology, 1987-90; staff neurologist William Beaumont Army Med. Ctr., El Paso, 1990-94; chief outpatient neurology clinic Walter Reed Army Med. Ctr., Washington, 1994—. Contbr. articles to profl. jours. Mem. AMA, Am. Acad. Neurology, Am. Chem. Soc., Assn. Mil. Surgeons, N.Y. Acad. Scis., Sigma Xi, Phi Lambda Upsilon, Alpha Chi Sigma. Office: Neurology Dept Walter Reed Army Med Ctr Washington DC 20307

MAHER, JOHN FRANCIS WALLACE, physician; b. Milw., Sept. 3, 1953; s. John Francis Wallace and Georgene (Stoppel) M.; m. Mertz Ethel Wilson, Oct. 20, 1990; children: John Wallace, Elizabeth Rose. BS in Zoology with honors, U. Wis., 1976; MD, Loyola U., 1981. Physician pvt. practice, Torrance, Calif., 1986—; clin. asst. prof. U. Calif., San Diego, 1986—. Contbr. articles to profl. jours. Med. mission work Focus, Haiti, 1980. Fellow Am. Acad. Ophthalmology; mem. Am. Soc. Cataract and Retinal Surgery, ORange County Soc. Ophthalmology, L.A. County Med. Assn., Lions (eyecare screening 1986—), Phi Eta Sigma. Roman Catholic. Home: 3820 Newton St Torrance CA 90505 Office: 21320 Hawthorne Blvd #216 Torrance CA 90503

MAHER, JOHN PATRICK, public health physician administrator, educator; b. Bklyn., Sept. 30, 1933; s. John P. and Kathleen G. (Power) M.; m. Maryellyn Cooney, Aug. 5, 1967; children: Ann Marie, James A., Rachel Anne, Christopher F. BS, St. Peter's Coll., 1956; MD, SUNY, Bklyn., 1960; MPH, Harvard U., Boston, 1968. Lic. physician, Pa. Intern Highland Hosp., Rochester, N.Y., 1960-61; med. resident Misericordia Hosp., Phila., 1963-66; resident in pub. health N.Y.C. Health Dept., 1967-70, pub. health physician, 1968-70, dist. health officer Bedford Stuyvesant, 1970-71, borough health officer S.I., 1971; asst. prof. pub. health Cornell U., N.Y.C., 1970-71; dir. ambulatory and community svcs. Mercy Cath. Med. Ctr., Phila., 1971-76; 1st clin. dir. Brookdale Social Health Ctr. for the Aging; dir. ambulatory medicine Mt. Sinai Hosp., N.Y.C., 1976-78; dir. Chester County Health Dept., West Chester, Pa., 1978—; instr. pub. health West Chester U., 1980—. Co-editor: Outpatient Medicine, 1980; contbr. articles to profl. jours. Profl. adv. com. Am. Lung Assn. Southeastern Pa.; mem. Inter-Agy. Execs. Coun., Cmty. Svc. Coun. of Chester County; coach Cath. Youth Orgn. Baseball; coach, umpire Little League Baseball. Capt. U.S. Army, 1961-63, Vietnam. Mem. AMA, Pa. Med. Soc. (vice chmn. commn. on pub. health and toxic substances), Pa. Pub. Health Assn., Chester County Med.

Soc. (contbg. editor Healthwise). Republican. Roman Catholic. Office: Chester County Health Dept 601 Westtown Rd Ste 290 West Chester PA 19382-4542

MAHER, L. JAMES, III, molecular biologist; b. Mpls., Nov. 28, 1960; s. Louis James and Elizabeth Jane (Crawford) M.; m. Laura Lee Moseng, July 2, 1983; children: Elizabeth Lillian, Christina Ailene. BS in Molecular Biology, U. Wis., 1983, PhD in Molecular Biology, 1988. Fellow U. Wis., Madison, 1983-84, rsch. asst., 1984-88; postdoctoral fellow Calif. Inst. Tech., Pasadena, 1988-91; asst. prof. molecular biology Eppley Inst., U. Nebr. Med. Ctr., Omaha, 1991-95; assoc. prof. biochem. molecular biology Mayo Found., Rochester, Minn., 1995—. Editorial bd. Antisense Rsch. & Devel. Jour., 1991—; contbr. articles to profl. jours. Musician, Madison Symphony Orch., 1983-88, Calif. Inst. Tech. Symphony Orch., L.A., 1988-91. Gosney fellow, 1988; Am. Cancer Soc. postdoctoral fellow, 1988. Mem. AAAS, Phi Beta Kappa. Evangelical Christian Ch. Office: Mayo Found Dept Biochem and Molec Biol 200 1st St SW Rochester MN 55905

MAHER, TIMOTHY JOHN, pharmacologist, educator; b. Boston, Nov. 24, 1953; s. Robert Daniel and Veronica Irene (Cody) M.; m. Barbara Jean Walz, Aug. 20, 1977; children: Andrew Michael, Matthew Edward, Elizabeth Irene, Johnathan Daniel. BS, Boston State Coll., 1976; PhD, Mass. Coll. Pharmacy, 1980. Asst. prof. Mass. Coll. Pharmacy, Boston, 1980-83, assoc. prof., 1983-87, prof., 1987—, chmn., 1987-93, dir. pharm. scis., 1994—, Sawyer prof. pharm. scis., 1994—; postdoctoral fellow MIT, Cambridge, 1983-88, lectr., 1988—; bd. dirs. Mass. Soc. Med. Rsch., Chelmsford, 1985—; adv. bd. Mass. Poison Control System, Boston, 1990—. Contbr. 75 articles to profl. jours. Roman Catholic. Office: Mass Coll Pharmacy 179 Longwood Ave Boston MA 02115-5804

MAHER, VINCENT F., academic administrator, educator, lawyer; b. Dublin, Ireland, Mar. 5, 1955; s. Denis V. and Bridget (Breen) M.; m. Ann M. Avitabile, May 26, 1979; 1 child, Elisabeth. BS, Coll. Mt. St. Vincent, 1979; MS, Columbia U., 1982; JD, Queens Coll., CUNY, 1986; MA, Fordham U., 1992; Profl. Diploma, U. Cambridge, Eng., 1993. Bar: N.J. 1987, N.Y. 1988, U.S. Dist. Ct. N.J. 1987, U.S. Dist. Ct. (ea. and so. dists.) N.Y. 1989; CRNA; RN, N.Y. Staff nurse anesthetist NYU/Bellevue, N.Y.C., 1983-84, St.Luke's/Roosevelt Hosp. Ctr., N.Y.C., 1980-86; cons. atty. Gair, Gair, Conason, Steigman and Mackauf, N.Y.C., 1995—; chmn. health svcs. adminstrn. Iona Coll., New Rochelle, N.Y., 1989—; nat., internat. lectr. Contbr. articles to profl. jours.; mem. editl. bd. Health Care Analysis, Jour. N.Y. State Nurses Assn., Jour. Nursing Law, Internat. Jour. Value Based Mgmt., others. Bd. dirs. Inst. Health Care Mgmt. Mem. ABA, ANA, AMWA, NHLA, N.Y. Bar Assn., Am. Pub. Health Assn., World Acad. on Med. Law, Am. Soc. Healthcare Execs., others. Office: Iona Coll 715 North Ave New Rochelle NY 10801-1890

MAHESH, VIRENDRA BHUSHAN, endocrinologist; b. India, Apr. 25, 1932; came to U.S., 1958, naturalized, 1968; s. Narinjan Prasad and Sobhagyawati; m. Sushila Kumari Aggarwal, June 29, 1955; children: Anita Rani, Vinit Kumar. BSc with honors, Patna U., India, 1951; MSc in Chemistry, Delhi U., India, 1953, PhD, 1955; DPhil in Biol. Sci, Oxford U., 1958. James Hudson Brown Meml. fellow Yale U., 1958-59; asst. research prof. endocrinology Med. Coll. Ga., Augusta, 1959-63; assoc. research prof. endocrinology Med. Coll. Ga., 1963-66, prof., 1966-70, Regents prof. endocrinology, 1970-86, Robert B. Greenblatt prof., 1979—, chmn. endocrinology, 1972-86, chmn., Regents prof. physiology and endocrinology, 1986—, chmn. physiology and endocrinology, 1986—; dir. Ctr. for Population Studies, 1971—; mem. reproductive biology study sect. NIH, 1977-81, mem. human embryology and devel. study sect. NIH, 1982-86, 90-93, chmn., 1991-93. Contbr. articles to profl. jours., chpts. to books; editor: The Pituitary, a Current Review, Functional Correlates of Hormone Receptors in Reproduction, Recent Advances in Fertility Research, Hirsuitism and Virilism, Regulation of Ovarian and Testicular Function, Excitatory Amino Acids: Their Role in Neuroendocrine Function; mem. editl. bd. Steroids, 1963—, Jour. of Clin. Endocrinology and Metabolism, 1976-81, Jour. Steroid Biochemistry and Molecular Biology, 1991—, Assisted Reproductive Tech./Andrology, 1993—; mem. adv. bd. Maturitas, 1977-81. Recipietn Rubin award Am. Soc. Study Sterility, 1962, Billings Silver medal, 1965; Best Tchr. award freshman class Sch. Medicine, Med. Coll. Ga., 1969, Outstanding Faculty award Sch. Medicine, 1992, Outstanding Faculty award Sch. Grad. Studies, 1981, 94, Disting. Teaching award, 1988, Excellence in Rsch. award Grad. Faculty Assembly, 1987-91, 93-95; Disting. Scientist award Assn. Scientist Indian Origin in Am., 1989, rsch. grantee NIH, 1960—. Mem. Chem. Soc. (Eng.), Soc. Biochem. and Molecular Biol., Soc. Neurosci., Endocrine Soc., Soc. for Gynecologic Investigation, Internat. Soc. Neuroendocrinology, Soc. for Study Reproduction (Carl G. Hartman award 1996), Am. Physiol. Soc., Internat. Soc. Reproductive Medicine (pres. 1980-82), Soc. Exptl. Biology and Medicine, Am. Fertility Soc., Am. Assn. Lab. Animal Sci., N.Y. Acad. Scis., AAUP, Sigma Xi. Office: Med Coll of Ga Dept Physiology & Endocrinology Augusta GA 30912-3000

MAHIG, MICHAEL EDWARD, internist; b. Columbus, Ohio, July 17, 1962; s. Joseph and Dolores Jean (Mann) M. AA, Oxford of Emory U., 1982; BA, Emory U., 1984, BS in Math. and Computer Sci., 1984; MD, Yale U., 1988. Diplomate Am. Bd. Internal Medicine. Intern in internal medicine New Eng. Deaconess Hosp., Boston, 1988-89, resident in internal medicine, 1989-91; internist South Brevard Med. Clinic HMA, Barefoot Bay, Fla., 1994—. Maj. USAF, 1991-94. Mem. Phi Beta Kappa. Office: South Brevard Med Clinic 7901 Ron Beatty Blvd Barefoot Bay FL 32978

MAHL, GEORGE FRANKLIN, psychoanalyst, psychologist, educator; b. Akron, Ohio, Nov. 27, 1917; s. Floyd Alexander and Margaret (Strecker) M.; m. Martha Jane Fenn, Jan. 10, 1944; 1 dau., Barbara Jessica. A. B., Oberlin Coll., 1939, M.A., 1941; PhD, Yale U., 1948; certificate, Western New Eng. Inst. Psychoanalysis, 1962. Asst. psychology Oberlin Coll., 1939-41; rsch. asst. in psychology Yale U., New Haven, 1941-42, mem. faculty, 1947—, prof. psychiatry and psychology, 1964-88, prof. emeritus, 1988—; tchr. Western New Eng. Inst. Psychoanalysis, 1961-85, pres., 1972-74. Served to 1st lt. AUS, 1942-46. Fellow AAAS, APA; mem. Ea. Psychol. Assn., Western New Eng. Inst. Psychoanalysis, Western New Eng. Psychoanalytic Soc., Internat. Psychoanalytical Assn., Inst. Psychoanalytic Tng. and Rsch. (N.Y.). Home: 106 Bayard Ave North Haven CT 06473-4303

MAHLER, HALFDAN THEODOR, physician, health organization executive; b. Vivild, Denmark, Apr. 21, 1923; s. Magnus and Benedicte (Suadicani) M.; m. Ebba Fischer-Simonsen, Aug. 31, 1957; children: Per Bo, Finn. MD, U. Copenhagen, 1948, postgrad. degree in pub. health; LLD (hon.), U. Nottingham, Eng., 1975; MD (hon.), Karolinska Inst., Stockholm, 1977; Docteur, de l'Universite des Scis. Sociales de Toulouse, France, 1977; DPH (hon.), Seoul Nat. U., 1979; ScD (hon.), U. Lagos, Nigeria, 1979, Emory U., 1989; MD (hon.), Warsaw Med. Acad., 1980; LHD, U. Nacional Federico Villareal, Lima, Peru, 1980; LHD (hon.), U. Gand, Belgium, 1983, CUNY, 1989; MD (hon.), Charles U., Prague, 1982, Mahidol U., Bangkok, Thailand, 1982, Aarhus U., Denmark, 1988, U. Copenhagen, 1988, Aga Khan U., Pakistan, 1989; LHD (hon.), U. Nacional Autonoma de Nicaragua, 1983; Dr. honoris causa, The Semmelweis U. of Medicine, Budapest, Hungary, 1987; LLD (hon.), McMaster U., Can., 1989; DSc (hon.), SUNY, 1990; MD (hon.), U. Newcastle Upon Tyne, 1990; LLD (hon.), U. Exeter, 1990; LLD (honoris causa), U. Toronto, 1990. Specialized tng. in TB, active field of internat. pub. health work; planning officer mass Tb campaign Ecuador, 1950-51; sr. officer nat. Tb program WHO, India, 1951-61; chief Tb unit, Hdqrs., WHO, Geneva, 1962-69, sec. to expert adv. panel on Tb, 1962-69, dir. project systems analysis, 1969-70, asst. dir.-gen. div. health services and div. family health, 1970-73, dir.-gen., 1973-88, dir.-gen. emeritus, 1988; sec. gen. Internat. Planned Parenthood Fedn., 1989-95. Contbr. articles on epidemiology and control of Tb, polit., social, econ, and technol. priorities in health sector, application of systems analysis to health care problems to profl. jours. Decorated Grand Officier de l'Ordre Nat. du Benin, 1975, Grand Officier de l'Ordre Nat. du Voltaique, Upper Volta, 1978, comdr. de l'Ordre Nat. du Mali, 1982, Grand Officer de l'Ordre du Merite de la Rep. du Senegal, 1982, comdr. 1st class Order White Rose (Finland), Grand Officier de l'Ordre nat. malgache, Madagascar, 1987, Grand Cross Icelandic Order of the Falcon, 1988, Grand Cordon of Order Sacred Treasure, Japan, 1988, Bourgeoisie d'Honneur, Geneva, Switzererland, Grand Croix De L'Ordre De Merite, Luxenbourg, 1990; recipient Jana Evangelisty Purkyne medal (Presdl. award) Prague, 1974, Comenius U. gold medal Bratislava, 1974, Carlo Forlanini gold medal Federazione Italiana contro la Tubercolosi et le Malattie Polmonari Sociali Rome, 1975, Ernest Carlsens Found. Prize Copenhagen, 1980, Georg Barfred-Pedersen prize Copenhagen, 1982, Hagedorn medal and prize Denmark, 1986, Freedom From Want medal Roosevelt Inst., 1988, Storkors Af Dannebrogsordenen, Denmark, 1988; hon. prof. U. Nacional Mayor de San Marcos, Lima, Peru, U. Chile Faculty of Medicine, Beijing Med. Coll., Rep. of China, Shanghai Med. U.; Bartel World Affairs fellow Cornell U., 1988; U.N. Population award, 1995, Andrija Stampar award, 1995. Fellow Royal Coll. Physicians (London), Faculty Community Medicine of Royal Colls. Physicians U.K. (hon.), Indian Soc. for Malaria and other Communicable Diseases (hon.), Royal Soc. Medicine (London) (hon., U.K.-U.S. Hewitt award 1992), London Sch. Hygiene and Tropical Medicine (hon.); mem. Med. Assn. Argentina (hon.), Latin Am. Med. Assn. (hon.), Italian Soc. Tropical Medicine (hon.), Belgium Soc. Tropical Medicine (assoc.), Societe medicale de Geneve (hon.), Union internationale contre la Tuberculose (hon.), Societe francaise d'Hygiene, de Medecine sociale et de Genie sanitaire (hon.), Uganda Med. Assn. (hon. life), Coll. Physicians and Surgeons, Bangladesh Royal Coll. Gen. Practitioners (ad eundem), List of Honour of the Internat. Dental Fedn., Am. Pub. Health Assn. (hon.), Nat. Acad. Medicine Mex. (hon.), Nat. Acad. Buenos Aires (hon.), Swedish Soc. Medicine (hon.), Brit. Medal Assn. (hon. fgn. corr. 1990). Home and Office: 12 Chemin du Pont-Ceard, CH 1290 Versoix Switzerland

MAHLER, HOWARD SAMUEL, psychiatrist; b. Bklyn., July 21, 1952; s. Eugene and Mildred (Winnick) M. BS, SUNY, Albany, 1974; MD, Med. Coll. Wis., 1979. Diplomate Am. Bd. Psychiatry and Neurology. Intern and resident sch. medicine Wash. U., St. Louis, 1979-83; Staff psychiatrist Malcolm Bliss Mental Health Ctr., St. Louis, 1983-84; psychiatrist II Kingsboro Psychiat. Ctr., Bklyn., 1986—. Mem. Am. Psychiat. Assn., AMA, Phi Beta Kappa. Office: Kingsboro Psychiat Ctr 681 Clarkson Ave Brooklyn NY 11203-2125

MAHMOUD, ADEL, infectious diseases, tropical medicine physician; b. Cairo, Egypt, Aug. 24, 1941; came to U.S., 1972; s. Abdel Fattah and Fathia (Osman) M.; m. Sally L. Hodder, Jan. 31, 1993. MD, Cairo U., 1963; MPH, Ain Shams U. Cairo, 1967; PhD, U. London, 1971. Lic. Ohio. Asst. lectr. Ain Shams Med. Sch., Cairo, 1965-68; fellow WHO U. London, 1969-72; postdoctoral fellow, instr., prof. Case We. Res. U., Cleve., 1973-80, chief divsn. geog. medicine, 1977-87, John H. Hord prof., chmn., 1987—; physician-in-chief Univ. Hosps., Cleve., 1987—; mem. adv. bd. Nat. Allergy and Infectious Diseases, Bethesda, Md., Fogarty; program project NIH, Bethesda, 1994; program dir. Howard Hughes Med. Inst., 1996. Editor: The Eosinophil in Health and Disease, 1979, Tropical and Geographical Medicine, 1990. Mem. Natural History Mus., Cleve. Fellow Infectious Diseases Soc. Am.; mem. Am. Soc. Clin. Investigations, Assn. Am. Physicians, Inst. Medicine. Home: 18900 S Park Blvd Shaker Heights OH 44122 Office: Case Western Reserve Univ Univ Hosps of Cleveland 11100 Euclid Ave Cleveland OH 44106

MAHMOUD, IBRAHIM YOUNIS, biology educator, physiology researcher; b. Baghdad, Iraq, Sept. 9, 1933; came to U.S., 1949; s. Younis Mahmoud and Najjia Mehdi Al-Rajjab; m. Laurice Wynette Shelton, June 6, 1965; children: Sherri, Najjia, Yasamin, Julie, Lara. BS, U. Ark., Monticello, 1953; MS, U. Ark., 1955; PhD, U. Okla., 1960. Cert. biologist, herpetologist. Prof. biology Northland Coll., Ashland, Wis., 1960-63; assoc. prof. biology U. Wis., Oshkosh, 1963-68, prof. biology, 1968—; adj. prof. zoology U. Fla., Gainesville, 1989; radiation safety officer U. Wis., Oshkosh, 1984-88. Author: (with others) Turtles: Perspectives and Research, 1979; contbr. articles to profl. jours. Bd. mem. Fox Valley Islamic Soc., Neenah, Wis., 1991. Recipient Duncan Rsch. award, 1982, Men of Achievement award (Eng.), 1984, John McNaughton Rosebush Univ. Professorship award, 1991. Mem. AAAS, Am. Soc. for Ichthyologists and Herpetologists, Am. Soc. Zoologists, N.Y. Acad. Scis., Sigma Xi (pres. 1986). Moslem. Home: 5708 Wild Rose Ln Oshkosh WI 54904-9554 Office: U Wis 142 Halsey Sci Bldg Oshkosh WI 54901

MAHNKE, KURT LUTHER, psychotherapist, clergyman; b. Milw., Feb. 18, 1945; s. Jonathan Henry and Lydia Ann (Pickron) M.; m. Dana Moore, Mar. 19, 1971; children: Rachel Lee, Timothy Kurt, Jonathan Roy. BA, Northwestern Coll., Watertown, Wis., 1967; MDiv, Wis. Luth. Sem., 1971; MA, No. Ariz. U., 1984. Cert. profl. counselor, marriage and family therapist, ind. clin. social worker. Pastor Redeemer/Grace Luth. Chs., Phoenix & Casa Grande, Ariz., 1971-75, St. Philips Luth. Ch., Milw., 1975-78, 1st Luth. Ch., Prescott, Ariz., 1978-82; counselor NAU Counseling/Testing Ctr., Flagstaff, Ariz., 1983-84, Wis. Luth. Child & Family Svc., Wausau, Wis., 1984-86; area adminstr. Wis. Luth. Child & Family Svc., Appleton, Wis., 1986-89; founder, psychotherapist Family Therapy & Anxiety Ctr., Menasha, Wis., 1989—; part-time min. St. Paul Luth. Ch., Appleton, 1993-94; presenter Nat. Police Week, Washington, 1995-96, 13th Nat. Conf. on Anxiety Disorders, Charleston, S.C., 1993; cons. editor Northwestern Pub. House, Milw., 1990—; adj. faculty Fox Valley Tech. Coll., Appleton, 1993—. Cons. editor Counseling at the Cross, 1990; contbr. articles to profl. publs. Cons. Wis. Evang. Luth. Synod, Milw., 1986—; cons. crisis counselor Fox Valley Luth. H.S., Appleton; crisis counselor Critical Incident Stress Debriefing Team, Fox Cities, 1991—; active Fox Cities Cmty. Counsel; victim crisis response coord. Appleton Police Dept., 1996—. Mem. ACA, Am. Mental Health Counselors Assn., Anxiety Disorders Assn. Am. (charter), Internat. Assn. Marriage and Family Counselors, Assn. Specialists in Group Work, Nat. Anxiety Found., Obsessive Compulsive Found., Wis. Outpatient Mental Health Facilities. Republican. Lutheran. Office: Family Therapy/Anxiety Ctr 1477 Kenwood Ctr Menasha WI 54952-1160

MAHON, KATHLEEN MELANIE, ophthalmologist; b. Santa Fe, N.Mex., Jan. 2, 1948; d. Walter S. and Lorraine Kahn; m. William Mahon; 1 child, William. BS in Pharmacy cum laude, U. N.Mex., 1970, MD, 1975. Diplomate Nat. Bd. Med. Examiners, Am. Bd. Ophthalmology, Am. Bd. Quality Assurance and Utilization Rev. Physicians; lic. physician N.Mex., Tex., Nev., Calif., Ariz. Intern U. So. Calif./L.A. County Gen. Hosp., 1975-75; resident in ophthalmology U. Fla./Shands Teaching Hosp., Gainesville, 1976-79; fellow in pediatric ophthalmology U. Tex. Med. Br., Houston, 1979-80; pvt. practice Las Vegas, 1980—; clin. prof. dept. surgery/pediatrics and divsn. chief divsn. ophthalmology U. Nev., Reno; active staff Sunrise Hosp., Univ. Med. Ctr., Desert Springs Hosp., Valley Hosp.; chief pediatric ophthalmology, vice chief of staff Sunrise Children's Hosp., 1995—; contbg. physician The Doctors Book of Home Remedies for Children; lectr. in field. Contbr. articles to profl. jours.; editl. adv. bd. Ophstart - Cooper Vision, Total Eye Care, 1989; sr. editor: Infant Vision;. Chmn. concept com. Ronald McDonald House, 1984—, v.p. fundraising, bd. dirs., 1989-93, 94—, del. to internat. meeting, Chgo., 1990; bd. dirs. Ronald McDonald Children's Charities, 1989-93; mem. health edn. adv. bd. Clark County C.C., 1986; bd. dirs. Frontier coun. Girl Scouts U.S., 1983-85, Big Bros./Big Sisters, 1983-84; UNICEF liaison for So. Nev., 1983-84; vol. vision screening pub./pvt. schs. annually; bd. dirs. Nev. Children's Hosp. Assn. Named Woman of Achievement in health profession Las Vegas C. of C., 1988, woman of Achievement in Health, Soroptimist, 1990, Woman of Distinction Frontier coun. Girl Scouts U.S., 1992; recipient Centennial Disting. Alumni award U. N.Mex., 1989; Del Webb Found. grantee. Fellow ACS (coun. mem. Nev. chpt. 1995), Am. Coll. Med. Quality, Am. Acad. Pediatrics (sr. cons., tech. reviewer), Am. Acad. Ophthalmology; mem. AMA, AAUW, Am. Assn. Pediatric Ophthalmology and Strbismus (pub. info. com., profl. rels. com.), Clark County Med. Assn., Internat. Assn. Ocular surgeons, Internat. Soc. Refractive Keratoplasty, Internat. Strabismological Assn., Las Vegas Ophthal. Soc., Nev. Med. Assn., Nev. Ophthal. Soc., Pacific Coast Oto Ophthal. Soc., Pan Am. Assn. Ophthalmology, Assn. Women Surgeons (Nev. state rep.), Las Vegas Pediatric Soc. (pres. 1993-95), Am. Coll. Physician Execs., Rotary of Las Vegas, Am. Med. Women's Assn., Women in Ophthalmology, Soroptimists of Greater Las Vegas, Mortarboard, Rho Chi. Office: 3201 S Maryland Pkwy #400 Las Vegas NV 89109

MAHONEY, GERALD T., medical facility administrator; b. Rochester, Minn., Nov. 10, 1933. AA, Rochester C.C., 1953; BS, Mankato State U., 1958. Constrn. supr. Murry Drake & Towey, 1958-59; credit counselor Mayo Clinic, Rochester, Minn., 1959-67, sys. and procedures specialist, 1967-69, adminstrv. asst., 1969-86; asst. to assoc. adminstr. St. Mary's Hosp. of Rochester, 1986-93, adminstr., 1993—. Mem. Am. Coll. Health Care Execs. (assoc.). Home: 1019 NW 1st St Rochester MN 55902 Office: St Mary's Hosp 1216 SW 2d St Rochester MN 55902*

MAHONEY, LESLIE A., home health administrator; b. New Haven, Conn., Sept. 24, 1943; d. Carl Oscar and Marie Ethne (Loughery) West; children from previous marriage: Sean, Daniel. Grad., New Rochelle Hosp Sch. Nursing, 1964; BSN cum laude, Calif. State U., Dominques Hills, 1991. RN, N.Y.; CCRN. Evening nurse supr. Valley Med. Ctr., Fresno, Calif., 1978-80, head nurse med. ICU, 1980-87, crisis resource nurse, 1990-91; coord. recovery care ctr. Fresno (Calif.) Surgery Ctr., 1988-89; dir. critical care Island Hosp., Anacortes, Wash., 1992-94, coord. quality assurance, 1994-95, dir. home health svc., 1994—. Vol. Skagit Valley Hospice, Mt. Vernon, Wash., 1994—. Mem. AAUW (mem. membership com. 1993-94, chair polit. action 1993-94), AACN, Soc. Ambulatory Care Profls., Home Care Assn. Wash. Office: Island Hosp 1211 24th St Anacortes WA 98221

MAHONEY, LISA REEVES, dermatologist; b. N.Y.C., June 6, 1947; d. Jesse Waring and Mary Watkins (Reeves) M.; m. David Woods, Dec. 24, 1986 (div. Jan., 1990). BS, NYU at Washington Square, 1969; MD, NYU, 1974. Diplomate Am. Bd. Dermatology. Intern in medicine NYU Med. Ctr., N.Y.C., 1974-75; resident in dermatology U. Calif. Med. Ctr., San Francisco, 1975-78; attending dermatologist JT Mather Meml. Hosp., Port Jefferson, N.Y., 1979—, St. Charles Hosp., Port Jefferson, 1979—; pvt. practice Port Jefferson, 1979-90, Miller Place, N.Y., 1990—. Mem. Rotary Club of Port Jefferson. Mem. Am. Acad. Dermatology, N.Y. Dermatol. Soc., Suffolk Dermatol. Soc., Suffolk County Med. Soc., Long Island Dermatology Assn., Alpha Omega Alpha. Office: L Reeves Mahoney MD 565 Route 25 A Miller Place NY 11764

MAHONEY, MARGARET ELLERBE, foundation executive; b. Nashville, Oct. 24, 1924; d. Charles Hallam and Leslie Nelson (Savage) M.; BA magna cum laude, Vanderbilt U., 1946; LHD (hon.), Meharry Med. Coll., 1977, U. Fla., 1980, Med. Coll. Pa., 1982, Williams Coll., 1983, Smith Coll., 1985, Beaver Coll., 1985, Brandeis U., 1989, Marymount Coll., 1990, Rush U., 1993, SUNY, Bklyn., 1994, N.Y. Med. Coll., 1995. Fgn. affairs officer State Dept., Washington, 1946-53; exec. assoc., assoc. sec. Carnegie Corp., N.Y.C., 1953-72; v.p. Robert Wood Johnson Found., Princeton, N.J., 1972-80; pres. Commonwealth Fund, N.Y.C., 1980-94; pres. MEM Assocs., Inc., N.Y.C., 1995—. Contbr. articles to profl. jours. Trustee John D. and Catherine T. Mac Arthur Found., 1985—, Dole Found., 1984—, Smith Coll., 1988-93, Columbia U., 1991—, Goucher Coll., 1995—; vis. fellow Sch. Architecture and Urban Planning, Princeton U., 1973-80; bd. dirs. Council on Found., 1982-88; mem. N.Y.C. Commn. on the Yr. 2000, 1985-87, MIT Corp., 1984-89; bd. govs. Am. Stock Exchange, 1987-92; adv. bd. Office of the Chief Med. Examiner, N.Y.C., 1987—, Barnard Coll, Inst. Med. Research, 1986-92; vice chmn. N.Y.C. Mayor's Com. for Pub./Pvt. Partnerships, 1990-93; bd. dirs. Alliance for Aging Rsch., 1987—, Overseas Devel. Coun., 1988—, Nat. Found. Center for Disease Control and Prevention, Inc., 1994—; mem. vestry Parish of Trinity Ch., 1982-89, 91-95; active Atlantic Fellowships Selection Com., 1994—. Recipient Frank H. Lahey Meml. award, 1984, Women's Forum award, 1989, Walsh McDermott award, 1992, Disting. Grantmaker award Coun. Founds., 1993, Edward R. Loveland award Am. Coll. Physicians, 1994, Special Recognition award AAMC, 1994, Merit medal Lotos Club, 1994, Terrance Keenan Leadership award in Health Philanthrophy, Grantmakers in Health, 1995. Mem. AAAS, Inst. Medicine of NAS, Am. Acad. Arts and Scis., Am. Philos. Soc., Coun. Fgn. Rels., Fin. Women's Assn. N.Y., N.Y. Acad. Medicine (vice chmn. bd. govs.), N.Y. Acad. Scis., Alpha Omega Alpha. Office: MEM Assocs Inc 521 Fifth Ave Ste 2010 New York NY 10175

MAHONY, JOHN FRANCIS, renal physician; b. Sydney, Australia, June 6, 1940; s. Francis Joseph and Mary Kathleen (Sexton) M.; m. Marie Therese Brereton, Aug. 18, 1967; children: Ann Marie, Catherine, Paul, Stephanie, Andrew, Claire, Emily, John, Luke. MBBS with honors, U. Sydney, Australia, 1963. Resident, registrar St. Vincents Hosp., Sydney, Australia, 1963-68; renal fellow UNI Colorado Med. Ctr., Denver, Colo., U.S.A., 1968-70; renal physician Sydney Hosp., Australia, 1970-79, dir. renal unit, 1979-83; dir. Sydney Dialysis Ctr., Australia, 1979—; renal physician Royal North Shore Hosp., Sydney, Australia, 1983—; clin. assoc. prof. U. Sydney, Australia, 1993—; renal physician cons. Royal Newcastle Hosp., Gosford Dist. Hosp., Australia; chmn. Transplant Adv. Com., Sydney, 1995—. Editor: Hormones and the Kidney, 1980; contbd. articles to profl. jours. Fellow Royal Australasian Coll. Physicians; mem. Australian New Zealand Soc. Nephrology (exec. officer 1988-90), Transplantation Soc. of Australia and New Zealand (councellor 1992—), N.Y. Acad. Scis. Office: Royal North Shore Hosp, Pacific Highway, Saint Leonards NSW 2065, Australia

MAICKEL, ROGER PHILIP, pharmacologist, educator; b. Floral Park, N.Y., Sept. 8, 1933; s. Philip Vincent and Margaret Mary (Rose) M.; m. Lois Louise Pivonka, Sept. 8, 1956; children: Nancy Ellen Maickel Ward, Carolyn Sue Maickel Anderson. B.S., Manhattan (N.Y.) Coll., 1954; postgrad., Poly. Inst. Bklyn., 1954-55; M.S., Georgetown U., 1957, Ph.D., 1960. Biochemist Nat. Heart Inst., Bethesda, Md., 1955-65; assoc. prof. pharmacology Ind. U., 1965-69, prof., 1969—, head sect. pharmacology med. scis. program, 1971-77; prof. pharmacology and toxicology, head dept. Sch. Pharmacy and Pharmacal Scis. Purdue U., West Lafayette, Ind., 1977-83, dir. lab. animal program Purdue U., West Lafayette, 1988—; acting v.p. product acquisition and devel. BetaMED Pharms., Inc., Indpls., 1983-84. Adv. editor: Pergamon Press, 1970-88; adv. editorial bd.: Neuropharmacology, 1974-88. Bd. dirs. TEAMS, Inc., 1981-87, Am. Coun. on Sci. and Health, 1993—; trustee AAALAC, 1992-96. Recipient Alumni award in medicine Manhattan Coll., 1972. Fellow AAAS, Am. Coll. Neuropsychopharmacology, Am. Inst. Chemists (bd. dirs. 1989-92, pres.-elect 1992-94, pres. 1994-96, chmn. 1996—), Royal Soc. Chemistry, Collegium Internat. de Neuro-Psychopharmacologicum; mem. ASTM, Am. Chem. Soc., Am. Soc. Pharmacology and Exptl. Therapeutics, Am. Soc. Clin. Pharmacology and Therapeutics, Soc. Forensic Toxicologists, Internat. Assn. Chiefs Police, Internat. Soc. Psychoneuroendocrinology, N.Y. Acad. Scis., Soc. Neurosci., Soc. Toxicology, Sigma Xi, Rho Chi. Home: 3567 Canterbury Dr Lafayette IN 47905-3714 Office: R E Heine Pharmacy Bldg Purdue Univ Lafayette IN 47907-1334

MAIER, ALFRED, neuroscientist; b. Bamberg, Bavaria, Fed. Republic of Germany, Sept. 16, 1929; came to U.S., 1958; s. Johan and Barbara (Rauh) M. BS in Zoology, Calif State U., Long Beach, 1967; PhD in Anatomy, UCLA, 1972. Postdoctoral fellow Dept. Kinesiology, UCLA, 1972-74; instr. Dept. Cell Biology U. Ala., Birmingham, 1974-76, asst. prof, 1976-80, assoc. prof., 1980-89, prof., 1989—; sr. scientist cell adhesion and matrix rsch. ctr. U. Ala., Birmingham; rsch. sabbatical Faculty Biology U. Konstanz, Fed. Republic of Germany, 1984, Dept. Physiology U. Otago, Dunedin, New Zealand, 1990; vis. prof. Faculty of Biology, U. Konstanz, 1985, '86. Contbr. articles and sci. papers to profl. jours and seminars. Recipient Pres.'s award for Excellence in Tchg., U. Ala., 1994, Didactic Instr. of Yr. Sch. Dentistry, 1993, 94, Best Basic Sci. Instr. Sch. Dentistry, 1978, 79, 83, 84. Mem. Soc. for Neurosci., Am. Assn. Anatomists.

MAIER, ROBERT HAWTHORNE, biology educator; b. N.Y.C., Oct. 26, 1927; s. Ernest Henry and Clara Louise M.; m. Jane Hiob, Aug. 31, 1952; children: Pamela, David, Daniel. BS, U. Miami, 1951; MS, U. Ill., 1952, PhD, 1954. Asst. dean Grad. Coll., U. Ariz., 1966-67; asst. chancellor for instrn. and research U. Wis., Green Bay, 1967-69, vice chancellor and dep. chancellor, prof., 1969-75, prof. sci. and environ. change, public and environ. adminstrn., 1975-79; vice chancellor acad. affairs East Carolina U., Greenville, N.C., 1979-83; prof. exptl. surgery, biology, polit. sci. East Carolina U., 1983—, dir. Trace Element Ctr., Sch. Medicine, 1984—, adj. prof. physics, 1996—; pres., chmn. Nat. Investment Advisors, Inc., 1984—, M 4, Inc., 1988—; bd. dirs. Agronomic Sci. Found.; mem. coun. biotech. U. N.C.; reviewer NC Tech. Devel. Authority, 1989—, NRC, 1990—. Contbr. articles to profl. jours. Bd. dirs. Lakeland chpt. ARC, 1978-79, Children's Svcs. Ea. N.C., 1987-94; mem. Edn. Task Force, City of Green Bay, 1977-78, N.C. State Panel Advancement of Women in Adminstrn., 1981-84, Gov.'s Commn. on Future of N.C., 1981-84; treas. Ronald McDonald House, 1987-94; mem. Vision Task Force, Global Transpark Devel. Commn., Kinston, N.C., 1996—. With U.S. Army, 1954-56. Fellow AAAS, Am. Inst.

Chemists, Am. Soc. Agronomy, Soil Sci. Soc. Am.; mem. Am. Chem. Soc., Am. Inst. Biol. Scis. Presbyterian. Office: East Carolina U Sch Med Surgery Dept Greenville NC 27858-4354

MAIESE, KENNETH, neurologist; b. Audubon, N.J., Dec. 5, 1958; s. Charles and Margaret (Fioretti) M. BA summa cum laude, U. Pa., 1981; MD, Cornell U., 1985. Intern N.Y. Hosp., 1985-86, resident in neurology, 1986-89, asst. attending physician, 1989-94; asst. prof. Cornell U. Med. Coll., N.Y.C., 1989-94; assoc. prof. dept. neurology, Ctr. Molecular Medicine and Genetics, Sch. Medicine Wayne State U., Detroit, 1994—, dir. Lab. Molecular and Cellular Cerebral Ischemia, 1994—; with, 1995—; dir. neurol. diagnosis N.Y. Hosp., 1991-94. Author: Neurology and General Medicine, 1989, Neurological and Neurosurgical ICU Medicine, 1988; contbr. articles to Neurology, Jour. Cerebral Blood Flow and Metabolism, Jour. Intensive Care Medicine, Jour. Neurosci., Jour. Neurosci. Rsch., Neurosci. Lett., Jour. Brain Rsch. doseph Collins scholar, 1981-85, Grupe Found. scholar, 1985; grantee NIH, 1990—, Nat. Stroke Assn., 1992-94, Alzheimer's Assn., 1994—, Am. Heart Assn., 1995—, United Cerebral Palsy Found., 1995—, Janssen Found., 1995—; recipient Young Scientist award Jours. Cerebral Blood Flow, 1991, Hoechst Investigaror award, 1993, Robert G. Siekert award in stroke, 1994, Johnson and Johnson Disting. Investigator award, 1996. Mem. Am. Acad. Neurology, N.Y. Acad. Scis., Assn. for Rsch. in Nervous and Mental Diseases, Am. Neurol. Assn., Soc. Neurosci. Roman Catholic. Office: Wayne State U Sch Medicine 6E-19 Univ Health Ctr Dept Neurology 4201 Saint Antoine St Detroit MI 48201-2153

MAILLOUX, RAYMOND VICTOR, health services administrator; b. Haverhill, Mass., Feb. 8, 1959; s. Raymond Alfred and Elaine Irene (Tourville) M.; m. Donna Ann Murphy, Aug. 1, 1981; children: Matthew, Michael. BS, U. Lowell, 1980; MBA, N.H. Coll., 1984. Lic. nursing home adminstr., N.H., Mass. Comptroller Home Health Svcs., Haverhill, 1980-84; instr. Northern Essex C.C., Haverhill, 1984-86; adminstr. St. John's Nursing Home, Lowell, Mass., 1984-87; dir. health care svcs. N.H. Catholic Charities, Manchester, 1987—. Mem. Am. Coll. Health Care Adminstrs., Am. Health Care Assn. (region I non-proprietary com. rep. 1993—), N.H. Health Care Assn. (pres. 1993, 94), New Eng. Gerontol. Assn. (v.p. 1987—). Home: 238 Jennifer Dr Chester NH 03036 Office: NH Catholic Charities 215 Myrtle St Manchester NH 03104

MAIMONE, ROBERT, oral and maxillofacial surgeon; b. Bklyn., July 31, 1955; s. Salvatore and Jeanette (Barbieri) M.; m. Alexandra Elizabeth Winslow, Aug. 29, 1992; 1 child, Matthew. BA in Natural Scis., Johns Hopkins U., 1977; DDS, NYU, 1982. Diplomate Am. Bd. Oral and Maxillofacial Surgery. Resident in maxillofacial surgery Montefiore Hosp. Med. Ctr., Bronx, N.Y., 1982-86; pvt. practice, N.Y.C., 1991—; lectr. advanced dental lasers, N.Y.C., 1995. Mem. steering com. Mens Christian Fellowship, Manhasset (N.Y.) Bapt. Ch., 1995-96, promise keepers point man, 1995=96, tchr. adult Christian edn., 1996. Mem. ADA, Am. Dental Soc. Anesthesiology. Home: 163 Onderdonk Ave Manhasset NY 11030 Office: 71 Broadway Ste 1415 New York NY 10006

MAINOR, ROBERT, family physician; b. Macon, Ga., Apr. 3, 1923; s. James Thaddeus and Iva (Davis) M.; m. Alma Louise Allen, June 12, 1946; children: Janet, Robert Jr. BS, U. Ga., 1947; MD, Med. Coll. Ga., 1951. Diplomate Am. Bd. Family Practice. Intern Madigan Army Hosp., 1951-52; pvt. practice Smyrna, Ga. 1st lt. U.S. Army, 1942-46, ETO, 51-53. Decorated Bronze Star medal with cluster, Purple Heart medal with cluster. Mem. AMA, AAFP, Med. Assn. Ga., Ga. Acad. Family Physicians (pres. 1967). Office: 2874 King St Smyrna GA 30080-3506

MAIOLO, JOSEPH ANTHONY, internist, educator; b. Morgantown, W.Va., Dec. 31, 1935; s. Joseph and Florence (Valentine) M.; m. Florence Sandra Angle, June 10, 1961; children: Michael Anthony, Jean Marie, Andrew Joseph. AB, W.Va. U., 1957, BS, 1959; MD, Med. Coll. Va., 1961. Diplomate Am. Bd. Internal Medicine. Intern Lewis Gale Hosp., Roanoke, Va., 1961-62; resident Beckley (W.Va.) Meml. Hosp., 1962-64, W.Va. U. Med. Ctr., Morgantown, 1964-65; pres. So. W.Va. Health Svcs., Beckley, 1985-95, So. W.Va. Clinic Inc., Beckley, 1985-95; chmn. dept. medicine Raleigh Gen. Hosp., Beckley, 1991-93; clin. prof. medicine Marshall U. Sch. Medicine, Huntington, W.Va., 1983—. Capt. M.C., U.S. Army, 1967-69. Mem. ACP, AMA, W.Va. State Med. Assn., Raleigh County Med. Soc. Office: So WVa Clinic 250 Stanaford Rd Beckley WV 25801-3142

MAIORIELLO, RICHARD PATRICK, otolaryngologist; b. Phila., Mar. 17, 1936; s. Gesumino Theodore and Angelina (Del Rossi) M.; A.B., U. Pa., 1960; M.D., Jefferson Med. Coll., 1964; M.S., Thomas Jefferson U., 1972; m. Susan Hemenway, Mar. 6, 1979; children—Gabriel, Angela, Richard. Commd. 2d lt., U.S. Air Force, 1963, advanced through grades to col., 1977; ret., 1979; intern Keesler Hosp., 1965-67; chief flight medicine USAF Base, Bitburg, W. Ger., 1965-68; resident in otolaryngology Thomas Jefferson Hosp., Phila., 1968-71, 72-73; fellow in physiology Thomas Jefferson U., 1971-72; dir. med. edn. Andrews AFB, 1974-78; assoc. prof. uniformed services Univ. Health Scis., 1978-79; assoc. prof. Northeastern Ohio U. of Medicine, 1983—; mem. staff Aultman Hosp., 1979—; assoc. staff Timken Mercy Med. Ctr., 1981—, Union Hosp., 1988—; cons. otolaryngology to Surgeon Gen., 1977—; pres. Mid-Ohio Dressage Assn. Served with USNR, 1954-58. Decorated Air Force Commendation medal; diplomate Nat. Bd. Med. Examiners, Am. Bd. Otolaryngology. Fellow ACS, Am. Soc. Head and Neck Surgery; mem. Am. Acad. Otolaryngology, Am. Acad. Facial Plastic and Reconstructive Surgery, Am. Assn. Cosmetic Surgery, Vail Cosmetic Surg. Soc., Hanoverian Soc. (exec. v.p.), U.S. Dressage Fedn. (chmn. all-breeds coun.), Centurion Club. Republican. Roman Catholic. Office: 1445 Harrison Ave NW Canton OH 44708-2620

MAIR, DOUGLAS DEAN, medical educator, consultant; b. Mpls., May 29, 1937; s. Lester Alexander and Irene Clare (Fisher) M.; m. Joanne Mary Elliott, Aug. 18, 1963; children: Scott, Michele, Todd. BA, U. Minn., 1959, MD, 1962. Bd. cert. pediats. and pediat. cardiology. Cons. Mayo Clinic, Rochester, Minn., 1971—; from asst. prof. pediats. to assoc. prof. pediats. Mayo Med. Sch., Rochester, 1972-80, prof. pediats., 1980—, assoc. prof. internal medicine, 1978—. Contbr. numerous articles and book chpts. to profl. publs. Capt. USAF, 1966-67.

MAIS, DALE EUGENE, chemist, pharmacologist; b. South Bend, Ind., Mar. 24, 1952; s. Rollin Charles and Violet Maybel (Paine) M.; m. Ellen Maria Barrell, May 9, 1976; children; James Charles, Maryellen Clare. BS in Chemistry, Ind. U., 1974, MS in Organic Chemistry, 1977, PhD in Pharmacology, 1983. Undergrad. rsch. asst. Ind. U., Bloomington, Ind., 1972-74, teaching asst. in chemistry, grad. rsch. asst., 1973-77, 74-77; mgr. organic synthesis Lafayette (Ind.) Pharmacal Inc., 1977-79; teaching asst. anatomy, grad. rsch. asst. Ind. U., Bloomington, 1979-80, 79-83; postdoctoral fellow, asst. prof. Med. U. of S.C., Charleston, 1983-86, 86-89; sr. pharmacologist dept. cardiovascular pharmacology Eli Lilly and Co., Indpls., 1989-92; adj. assoc. prof. Ind. U. Sch. of Medicine, Indpls., 1990-92; sr. rsch. scientist Ligand Pharm., Inc., San Diego, 1992—; expert analyst Organic Chemistry Edition of Chemtracts, 1990—. Editor: Eicosanoids in the Cardiovascular and Renal Systems, 1988; patentee in field; contbr. numerous articles to profl. jours. and chpts. to books. Named Ira E. scholar Ind. U., 1974, Drug Sci. Found. scholar, 1983-86; recipient Grad. Grant-in-Aid, Ind. U., 1982, 83, Nat. Rsch. Svc. award, 1983-86, First Pl. in Postdoctoral Divsn. of Student Rsch. Day Competition, 1984, 85, Louis N. Katz Basic Rsch. award-Finalist, 1985. Mem. Am. Socs. of Pharmacology and Exptl. Therapeutics, Am. Chem. Soc., S.C. Acad. Sic., Sigma Xi. Office: Ligand Pharms 9393 Towne Centre Dr Ste 100 San Diego CA 92121-3016

MAISEL, LOUIS M., ophthalmologist; b. N.Y.C., July 3, 1961; s. Theodore M. and Stella (Gray) M.; m. Grace Rague s, Nov. 11, 1990; children: Remy, Zoe. AB, Vassar Coll., 1983; MD cum laude, SUNY, Bklyn., 1988. Diplomate Am. Bd. Ophthalmology. Intern Long Island Jewish Med. Ctr., New Hyde Park, N.Y.; resident Nassau County Med. Ctr., East Meadow, N.Y.; vitreoretinal fellow Vitreoretinal Found., Memphis, 1992-93; vitreoretina specialist N.Y. Med. Group PC, N.Y.C., 1993—; pvt. practice vitreoretina specialist, Hicksville, N.Y., 1993-95. Fellow Am. Acad. Ophthalmology; mem. AMA, Med. Soc. State N.Y., N.Y. State Ophthalmology Soc. Office: NY Med Group PC 215 E 95th St New York NY 10128

MAISLIN, ISIDORE, hospital administrator; b. N.Y.C., Aug. 4, 1919; s. Solomon and Rose (Baruch) M.; m. Frances Mussman, Jan. 18, 1948; children—Wendy Sue (Mrs. Neil Robbins), Steven William. B.S., Columbia, 1950, M.S., 1951. Asso. dir. Albert Einstein Med. Center, Phila., 1950-59; asso. dir. Mt. Sinai Hosp. Greater Miami, Mimai Beach, Fla., 1959-63; adminstr. Scranton (Pa.) Gen. Hosp., 1963-64; exec. dir. Jewish Home of Eastern Pa., Scranton, 1964-67; adminstr. South Mountain (Pa.) Restoration Center, 1967—. Served with AUS, 1943-46. Fellow Am. Coll. Hosp. Adminstrs., Am. Pub. Health Assn., Royal Soc. Health. Home and Office: 535 Colfax Ave Scranton PA 18510-2364

MAIZE, JOHN CHRISTOPHER, dermatology educator; b. Elizabeth, N.J., July 23, 1943; s. Donald Adam and Caroline Marie (Costanzo) M.; m. Janice Lee Bentley, May. 21, 1966; children: Sandra Kristine Tolly, John C. Jr., Jennifer Lee. MD, U. Mich., 1968. Diplomate Am. Bd. Dematology. Intern U. Mich., Ann Arbor, 1968-69, residency in dermatology, 1969-72; asst. prof. dermatology SUNY, Buffalo, 1972-77, assoc. prof., 1977-80; assoc. prof. Med. U. of S.C., Charleston, 1980-83, prof., 1983-89, prof., chmn. dept. dermatology, 1989—; editor-in-chief Am. Jour. Dermatology, 1986-90; dir. Am. Bd. Dermatology, 1990—. Author: Pigmented Lesions of the Skin, 1987. Fellow Am. Acad. Dermatology, Am. Soc. Dermapathology (pres. 1995); mem. Am. Dermatol. Assn., Internat. Soc. Dermatopathology (sec. 1987-89, pres. 1989-91), S.C. Med. Assn., S.C. Dermatol. Assn. Roman Catholic. Office: Med U SC 171 Ashley Ave Charleston SC 29425-0001

MAJD, MASSOUD, radiology and nuclear medicine educator; b. Yazd, Iran, July 23, 1935; came to U.S., 1961; s. Jalil and Khadijeh Majd; m. Fereshteh H.S. Javadi, June 23, 1968; children: Kurosh, Katayoon. MD, Tehran U., 1960. Diplomate Am. Bd. Radiology, Am. Bd. Nuclear Medicine. Intern Deaconess Hosp., Buffalo, 1961-62; resident Georgetown U., Washington, 1962-66, instr. radiology, 1965-66, 68-70; asst. prof. Pahlavi U., Shiraz, Iran, 1966-68; asst. prof. George Washington U., 1970-72, assoc. prof., 1972-79, prof. radiology and pediatrics, 1979—; radiologist, dir. pediatric nuclear medicine Children's Nat. Med. Ctr., Washington, 1968—; adj. prof. radiology Georgetown U., 1981—; staff radiologist Georgetown U. Hosp., 1965-66; radiologist Pahlavi U. Hosps, Shiraz, 1966-68; assoc. staff radiology Children's Med. Ctr., 1968-72, sr. attending staff radiology, 1972—, founder dir. sect. nuclear medicine, 1969—; presenter in field. Contbr. chpts. to books and articles to profl. jours. Fellow Soc. Uroradiology, Am. Coll. Radiology, Am. Coll. Nuclear Physicians, Am. Acad. Pediatrics; mem. Am. Roetgen Ray Soc., Radiologic Soc. N.Am., European Soc. Pediatric Radiology (affiliate), Soc. Pediatric Radiology, Soc. Nuclear Medicine, Pediatric Imaging Coun., John Caffey Soc. Home: 8605 Stirrup Ct Potomac MD 20854-4843 Office: Childrens Nat Med Ctr 111 Michigan Ave NW Washington DC 20010-2970

MAJERUS, PHILIP WARREN, physician; b. Chgo., July 10, 1936; s. Clarence Nicholas and Helen Louise (Mathis) M.; m. Janet Sue Brakensiek, Dec. 28, 1957; children: Suzanne, David, Juliet, Karen. BS, Notre Dame U., 1958; MD, Washington U., 1961. Resident in Medicine Mass. Gen. Hosp., Boston, 1961-63; research assoc. NIH, Bethesda, Md., 1963-66; asst. prof. biochemistry Washington U., St. Louis, 1966-75, asst. prof. medicine, 1966-69, assoc. prof. medicine, 1969-71, prof. medicine, 1971—, dir. div. hematology, 1973—, prof. biochemistry, 1976—. Mem. editorial bd. numerous jours. and profl. mags.; contbr. numerous articles to profl. jours. Recipient numerous awards including Am. Cancer Soc. Faculty Rsch. Assoc. award, 1966-75, Disting. Career award for Contbns. to Hemostasis Internat. Soc. for Thrombosis and Hemostasis, 1985, Alumni/Faculty award Washington U. Sch. Medicine, 1986, The Robert J. and Claire Pasarow Found. award, 1994. Fellow ACP; mem. NAS, Inst. Medicine of NAS, Am. Acad. Arts and Scis., Assn. Am. Physicians, Am. Soc. Hematology (pres. 1991), Am. Fedn. Clin. Rsch., Am. Soc. Biol. Chemists, Am. Soc. Clin. Investigation (pres. 1981-82), Sigma Xi, Alpha Omega Alpha. Home: 7220 Pershing Ave Saint Louis MO 63130 Office: Wash Univ Sch of Med Internal Med Saint Louis MO 63110

MAJORS, NELDA FAYE, physical therapist; b. Houston, Aug. 3, 1938; d. Columbus Edward and Mary (Mills) M. Cert. in Phys. Therapy, Hermann Sch. Phys. Therapy, Houston, 1960; BS, U. Houston, 1963. Lic. phys. therapist, Tex. Staff therapist Tex. Med. Ctr. Hermann Hosp., Houston, 1960-61; phys. therapist Chelsea Orthopedic Clinic, Houston, 1961-63; dir. phys. therapy Meml. Hosp. Southwest, Houston, 1963-75; owner, pres. Nelda Majors, Inc., Houston, 1975—; mem. profl. adv. bd. Logos Home Health Agy., Houston, 1985-86; adv. dir. 1st Northwestern Bank, Houston. Active Meml. Dr. Meth. Ch., Houston, 1983—; ptnr. Houston Proud Ptnr., 1986—; founder, pres. Instnl. Safety Advs. Inc., 1994—; bd. dirs. Texans for the Improvement of Long Term Care Facilities, 1995—. Named All Am. Softball Pitcher, Amateur Softball Assn., 1964, All-Regional and All-State Pitcher, Tex. Amateur Softball Assn., 1954-70; named to Houston Amateur Softball Assn. Softball Hall of Fame, 1994. Mem. Am. Phys. Therapy Assn. (pvt. practice sect.), Tex. Phys. Therapy Assn., U. Houston Alumni Assn., E. Cullen Soc. (U. Houston), N.W. Crossing Optimist Club (Houston, charter mem., bd. dirs.), River Oaks Rotary (Houston), Phi Kappa Phi. Republican. Club: U. Houston Cougar.

MAJORS, RICHARD GEORGE, psychology educator; b. Ithaca, N.Y.; s. Richard G. II and Fannie Sue Majors; legal guardian: Lillian A. McGill. AA, Auburn (N.Y.) Community Coll., 1974; BA in History, Plattsburgh State Coll., 1977; PhD in Ednl. Psychology, U. Ill., 1987. Various social svc. positions, 1976-79; probation officer, ct. investigator Plattsburgh, 1979; clin. intern McKinley Health Ctr., Urbana, Ill., 1981; rsch. asst. U. Minn., Mpls., 1981, U. Ill., Urbana, 1981-84; instr. Parkland Community Coll., Champaign, Ill., 1985; rsch. asst. U. Ill., Champaign, 1985-86; postdoctoral fellow U. Kans., Lawrence, 1987-89; postdoctoral fellow, clin. fellow Harvard Med. Sch., Boston, 1989-90; asst. prof. psychology U. Wis. System, 1990-93; sr. rsch. assoc. The Urban Inst., Washington, 1993-95; vis. fellow, scholar The David Walker Rsch. Inst., Mich. State U., 1995—; vis. fellow, scholar David Walker Rsch. Inst. Mich. State U.; presenter in field. Co-author: Coolpose: The Dilemmas of Black Manhood in America, 1992, The American Black Male: His Present Status and Future, 1994; founder Jour. of African Am. Men. Named one of Outstanding Young Men of Am., 1987. Fellow APA (predoctoral minority fellow 1984); mem. Nat. Coun. African Am. Men (chmn., co-founder), Soc. for Psychol. Study of Ethnic Minority Issues, Am. Orthopsychiat. Assn., Greenpeace, Kappa Delta Pi, Phi Delta Kappa. Office: David Walker Rsch Inst Mich State U B421 West Fee Hall East Lansing MI 48824

MAJZUN, RICK S., health services administrator; b. San Diego, Oct. 3, 1969; m. Shannon Michele, June 26, 1993. B Journalism, U. Mo., 1991; MHA, Washington U., St. Louis, 1994. Sales rep. Cola Cola Enterprises, St. Louis, 1992; evening/night adminstr. Barnes Hosp., St. Louis, 1992-94; adminstrv. fellow Henry Ford Health Sys., Detroit, 1994-95, planning analyst, 1995—; cons. EME, Inc., St. Louis, 1993-94, ICM, Inc., St. Louis, 1993-94. 1st lt. U.S. Army, 1991—. Mem. Am. Coll. Healthcare Execs. Office: Henry Ford Health Sys 1 Ford Pl Detroit MI 48202

MAK, GILBERT KWOK KWONG, pediatric dentist, researcher; b. Hong Kong, 1963; came to U.S., 1987.; s. Lun and Sze Mak. B in Dental Surgery, U. London, 1986; Licentiate in Dental Surgery, Royal Coll. Surgeons, London, 1987; postgrad. cert. in pediat. dentistry, U. So. Calif., L.A., 1990. Asst. house surgeon Guy's Hosp. Dental Sch. U. London, 1986, researcher dept. oral medicine and oral pathology, 1987; resident in pediatric dentistry U. So. Calif., 1987, clin. teaching faculty dept. pediatric dentistry, 1987—; resident in dentistry Children's Hosp. L.A., 1987-90, Long Beach Med. Ctr., 1990; asst. prof. U. So. Calif., L.A., 1990—; pvt. practice L.A., 1990—; attending physician Millier's Children Dental Residency Program Long Beach Meml. Med. Ctr., 1991—; with Dulwich Coll., London, 1980-82; univ. senator U. So. Calif., L.A., 1992-93. Contbr. articles to profl. jours. Recipient Fencing Bronze Proficiency award Amateur Fencing Assn., 1982, Med. Sickness Soc. Elective award Guy's Hosp. Dental Soc., 1986, Malleson Prize for Dental Rsch. Guy's Hosp., London, 1985, NIH Physician Scientist award, 1991—; USPHS grantee, 1987-88, 88-89; Dean's fellow U. So. Calif. Sch. Dentistry, 1989-90;. Mem. Internat. Assn. for Dental Rsch., Am. Acad. Pediatric Dentistry, ADA, Brit. Soc. for Dental Rsch., Brit. Dental Assn., Am. Soc. Dentistry for Children, Alumni Assn. Student Clinicians of ADA, Calif. Dental Assn., Harbor Dental Soc. Office: PO Box 661059 Arcadia CA 91066-1059

MAK, KOON HOU, cardiologist, researcher; b. Singapore, June 23, 1961; s. Kok Thye and Ayen (Fong) M.; m. Li-Hwei Sng, May 1, 1993. B of Medicine, B of Surgery, Nat. U. of Singapore, 1985, M of Medicine (internal medicine), 1989; diploma, Singapore Bible Coll., 1990. House officer Ministry of Health, Singapore, 1985, med. officer trainee, 1988-89, registrar, 1991-92; intern Nat. Univ. Hosp., Singapore, 1986; med. officer Ministry of Defense, Singapore, 1986-87; head clin. br., med. officer (cardiology) Med. Classification Ctr. Cen. Manpower Base, Singapore, 1987-88; ag registrar Singapore Gen. Hosp., 1990-91, registrar dept. cardiology, 1991—; examining med. officer Civil Aviation Bd., Singapore, 1988-89, 92; clin. tchr. Nat. U. Singapore, 1989—; clin. supr. Singapore Armed Forces, 1990; vis. cardiology specialist Ministry Def., 1990—. Contbr. sci. papers to profl. jours. Speaker Singapore Lion and Lioness Club, 1988; dr. Orissa (India) Follow-Up, 1990; participant Japan Internat. Coop. Agy., 1990; mem. com. Singapore Nat. Heart Week, 1990, 92, 93, Singapore Cancer Soc.(chmn. Stay Fresh club 1992—, Smoke Free Day 1992-93). Capt. Med. Svcs., Singapore Armed Forces, 1986-88, res., 1988—. Recipient Sch. Merit award Raffles Instn., Singapore, 1979, Lim Boon Keng medal, Singapore Med. Assn. medal and First Meckie Book prize Nat. U. Singapore, 1985; named Dr. of the Yr., 1964; local merit scholar Pub. Svc. Commn., Singapore, 1980. Fellow Acad. Medicine, ACP; mem. Royal Coll. Physicians Edinburgh, Royal Coll. Physicians and Surgeons Glasgow, Singapore Cardiac Soc., N.Y. Acad. Scis., Singapore Cancer Soc. Stay Fresh Club (mem. com.), Singapore Nat. Heart Assn. (bd. dirs. 1993). Methodist. Office: Tan Tock Seng Hosp, Dept Cardiology Moulmein Rd, Singapore 1130, Singapore

MAK, LAI WO, physician; b. Hong Kong, Jan. 31, 1946; s. Cham Kwong and Sing Kwan (Tong) M.; m. Ying Chun Yuen, Aug. 3, 1972; children: Wing Lun, Dun Ping. MBBS, U. Hong Kong, 1968, MD, 1974; PhD, U. London, 1975. Lectr. in med. U. Hong Kong, 1969-78; research asst. U. London Royal Postgrad. Med. Sch., 1972-75; hon. lectr. medicine U. Hong Kong, 1978-92; gen. practice medicine Hong Kong, 1978—. Fellow Royal Coll. Physicians, Hong Kong coll. Physicians, Hong Kong Acad. Medicine; mem. Soc. Physicians of Hong Kong (pres. 1981-82). Office: 49 Queen's Road Central 1F, Hong Kong Hong Kong

MAK, TAK WAH, biochemist, educator; b. Canton, Republic of China, Oct. 4, 1946; s. Kent and Linda (Chan) M.; m. Shirley Lau, June 7, 1969; children: Julie Shi-Lan, Jennifer Shi-yan. BSc, U. Wis., 1967, MSc, 1969; PhD, U. Alta., Edmonton, Can., 1972; ScD (hon.), Carlton U., Ottawa, 1989, Laurentian U., 1992. Research asst. U. Wis., Madison, 1967-69, U. Alta., Edmonton, 1969-72; postdoctoral fellow U. Toronto, Ont., Can., 1972-74, asst. prof., 1974-78, assoc. prof., 1978-84, prof., 1984—; sr. staff scientist Ontario Cancer Inst., Toronto; dir. and research v.p. Amgen Inst.; vis. prof. U. Wis., Madison, 1980; hon. prof. Beijing Union Med. U., 1986—. Editor: Molecular and Cellular Biology of Hemopolitic Stem Cell Differentiation, 1981, Molecular and Cellular Biology of Neiplasia, 1983, Cancer: Perspective for Control, 1986, The T Receptor, 1987, AIDS: Ten Years Later, 1991; contbr. over 250 sci. articles. Recipient E.W.R. Steacie prize, 1986, Ayerst award Can. Biochem. Soc., 1985, Emil Von Behring prize Marburg (Germany) U., 1986, Gairdner Internat. award Gairdner Found., 1989, McLaughlin medal Royal Soc. Can., 1990, King Faisal Internat. prize for medicine King Faisal Found., 1995; hon. mem. Beijing Union Med. U., 1986, rsch. award Can. Found. for AIDS Rsch., 1992, Alfred P. Sloan, Jr. medal GM, 1996; E.W.R. Steacie fellow Nat. Sci. and Engring. Rsch. Coun. Can., 1984. Fellow Royal Soc. London (King Faisal Internat. prize of medicine 1995); mem. Royal Soc. Can. (McLaughlin medal 1990), Chinese Acad. Med. Sci. (hon.). Home: 130 Glen Rd, Toronto, ON Canada M4W 2W3 Office: Ont Cancer Inst, 610 University Ave Rm 8-712, Toronto, ON Canada M5G 2M9

MAKANT, J(OSEPH) EARLE, JR., osteopathic physician, medical consultant; b. Pawtucket, R.I., Mar. 16, 1929; s. Joseph Earle and Ruth Elizabeth (Perkins) M.; m. Audrey Roberts, Sept. 7, 1950 (div. Sept. 1962); children: Jeffrey Earle, Diane Elizabeth; m. Barbara Ruth Whalin, Jan. 1, 1983. AB, U. R.I., 1951; DO, Phila. Coll. Osteo. Medicine, 1956; MD, Midwestern U., Arcadia, Mo., 1963. Family practitioner Newtown Square, Pa., 1957-75; commd. major U.S. Air Force, 1975, advanced through grades to col., 1985, ret., 1987; chief primary care Dover (Del.) AFB, 1975-77; dir. aeromed. svcs. Andrews AFB, Washington, 1977-81; command surgeon Air Force Res., Warner Robins, Ga., 1981-82; hosp. comdr. USAF Hosp., Seymour Johnson AFB, Goldsboro, N.C., 1982-85; dep. asst. sec. for health Dept. Corrections, Tallahassee, 1985-89; med. cons. Office of Disability Determinations, Tallahassee, 1989-92. Decorated Legion of Honor; recipient Gov.'s citation State of Md., 1980. Fellow Am. Coll. Physician Execs.; mem. AMA, Mil. Order of World Wars (comdr. 1990-91), SAR, Nat. Sojourners, Masons. Republican. Episcopalian. Home: 1286 Millstream Rd Tallahassee FL 32312-2548

MAKARI, GEORGE JACK, psychiatrist; b. Plainfield, N.J., July 9, 1960; s. Jack George and Odette (Tamer) M.; m. Arabella Ogilvie, Oct. 7, 1989. BA, Brown U., 1982; MD, Cornell U., 1987. Lic. physician, N.Y. Columnist Washington Tribune, Washington, 1982-83; resident psychiatrist N.Y. Hosp., N.Y.C., 1987-91; Reader's Digest rsch. fellow N.Y. Hosp., 1991-94, asst. prof. psychiatry, 1994—. Contbr. articles to profl. jours. Mem. Am. Psychiatric Assn., History of Psychiatry Sect. of N.Y. Hosp. Office: N Y Hosp 525 E 68th St New York NY 10021-4873

MAKAROWSKI, WILLIAM STEPHEN, rheumatologist; b. Elmira, N.Y., Dec. 31, 1948; s. William John and Irene (Obuhanich) M.; m. Barbara Ann Payne; children: Elizabeth, Kathleen, Mary Lou. BS cum laude, Saint Bonaventure U., 1970; MD, Loyola-Stritch Coll., 1974; Rheumatology fellow, Cleve. Clinic, 1977-79. Diplomate Nat. Bd. of Med. Examiners, Am. Bd. of Pain Practice Mgmt. Resident in internal medicine Robert Packer Hosp., Sayre, Pa., 1974-77; pvt. practice Erie, Pa., 1984; chief rheumatology div. St. Vincent Hosp., Erie, Pa., 1979-86; med. dirs. Musculo Occupational Rehab. Pain Mgmt. Program Great Lakes Rehab. Hosp., Erie, Pa., 1986-92, pres., 1991-93; cons. Shriner's Hosp., Erie, 1980—, Metro Health Ctr., 1980-93, VA Hosp., 1981—; mem. Hamot Med. Ctr. med. dept., 1979—; clin. asst. prof. Gannor U. Author: Living with Pain; columnist: The Joint Achievement newsletter, 1981-88. Chmn. med. adv. bd. The Lupus Found., 1987-89; advisor Arthritis Discussion Group, 1981-91; mem. bd. govs. Arthritis Found., 1981-91. Fellow Am. Coll. Rheumatology (founding); mem. AMA, Pa. Med. Soc., Erie County Med. Soc., So. Med. Assn., Am. Pain Soc., Internat. Soc. for Rheumatic Therapy, Can. Pain Soc., Erie Yacht Club, Kahkwa Country Club, Erie Club, Aviation Club. Home: 5075 Tramarlac Ln Erie PA 16505-1350 Office: Rheumatology Assocs NW Pa 1781 W 26th St Erie PA 16508-1256

MÄKELÄ, KARI KALEVI, medical physicist, consultant; b. Stockholm, Apr. 12, 1960; arrived in Finland, 1984; m. Paula Marjatta Kesti, May 24, 1988; children: Henri, Toni. BS, Australian Nat. U., 1984; MS, U. Helsinki, Finland, 1986; Licentiate Tech., Tampere U. Tech., Finland, 1993, PhD, 1996. Cert. hosp. physicist. Hosp. physicist Tampere U. Hosp., 1984-89; dir. Clinica Salud, Spain, 1989-91; sr. hosp. physicist Tampere U. Hosp., 1991-92; asst. prof. Tampere U. Tech., 1992, rsch. fellow Acad. Finland, 1993; sr. hosp. physicist Seinäjoki Ctr. Hosp., Finland, 1994—; dir. Finn-Casa Ltd., Finland, 1989—; rsch. fellow Ragnar Granit Inst., Finland, 1992—; cons. Tampere U. Hosp., 1994; lectr. Ostrobotnia Sch. Health Svcs., 1994. Author: Sähköiset Aivomme, 1994; editor: Handbook of Clinical Neurophysiology, 1996; inventor in field. Grantee Instrumentation Sci. Found., 1986, Wihuri Found., 1992, Wilpori laisen Osakonnan Rsch. Found., 1987. Mem. Internat. Fedn. for Med. and Biol. Engring., Internat. Orgn. Med. Physics, Rotary. Office: Seinäjoki Cen Hosp, Hanneksenrinne 7, 60220 Seinäjoki Finland

MAKER, HOWARD SMITH, neurology educator; b. N.Y.C., Oct. 29, 1930; s. Charles Gilbert and Sylvia (Smith) M.; m. Myra Lois Chitroo, Feb. 21, 1965; children: Elizabeth sylvia, Ellen Judith. BA, NYU, 1956; MD, SUNY, Bklyn., 1956. Intern Montefiore Hosp., Bronx, 1956-57; resident Mt. Sinai Med. Ctr., N.Y.C., 1957-60; asst. prof. Mt. Sinai Sch. Medicine, N.Y.C., 1968-86, prof. neurology, 1986—; prof. neurology Albert Einstein Coll. Medicine, Bronx, 1994—; assoc. dir. neurology Beth Israel Med. Ctr.,

N.Y.C., 1996—. Contbr. articles to profl. jours. Neurochemistry fellow Harvard Med. Sch., Boston, 1962-65, rsch. fellow Mt. Sinai Sch. Medicine, 1965-68; State of N.Y. scholar, 1952-56. Fellow Am. Acad. Neurology; mem. Am. Assn. Rsch. Rsch. Neurology, Am. Soc. Neurochemistry, Am. Naval Assn. (elected mem.), Mass. Med. Soc., Internat. Soc. Neurochemistry, Phi Beta Kappa. Home: 299 Piermont Rd Closter NY 07624 Office: Beth Israel Med Ctr 16th St & 1st Ave New York NY 10003

MAKHIJA, MOHAN, nuclear medicine physician; b. Bombay, Oct. 1, 1941; came to U.S., 1969; m. Arlene Zambito, Nov. 11, 1978. MD, Bombay U., 1965. Diplomate Am. Bd. Nuclear Medicine, Am. Bd. Radiology; cert. spl. competence in nuclear radiology. Resident in radiology Morristown (N.J.) Meml. Hosp., 1972-75; resident in nuclear medicine Yale-New Haven Hosp., 1975-76; post-doctoral fellow Yale U. Sch. Medicine, New Haven, 1976-77; jr. attending physician Helene Fuld Med. Ctr., Trenton, N.J., 1977-78; acting dir. dept. nuclear medicine Monmouth Med. Ctr., Long Branch, N.J., 1978, dir. nuclear medicine sect., 1979—, asst. attending radiology, 1978-80, assoc. attending radiology, 1980-83, attending radiologist, 1983—; sr. instr. Hahneman U., Phila., 1978-80, clin. asst. prof., 1980-83, clin. assoc. prof., 1983-91, clin. prof., 1991-94, clin. prof. of Radiologic Scis., Med. Coll. of Pa. and Hahnemann U., 1994—; radiol. cons. to N.J. State Bd. Med. Examiners., 1994. Contbr. articles to profl. jours. Fellow ACP, Am. coll. Nuclear Physicians (spkr. ho. of dels. 1992-93), Am. Coll. Radiology; mem. Monmouth County Med. Soc. (pres. 1991-92), Radio Soc. N.J. (chmn. nuclear medicine 1988-94, treas. 1994-95, sec. 1995-96, v.p. 1996-97), Indo-Am. Soc. Nuclear Medicine (pres. 1992-93), Soc. Nuclear Medicine (bd. govs. greater N.Y. chpt. 1992—). Home: 5 High Ridge Rd Ocean NJ 07712-3460 Office: Monmouth Med Ctr 300 2nd Ave Long Branch NJ 07740-6300

MAKI, DENNIS G., medical educator, researcher, clinician; b. River Falls, Wis., May 8, 1940; m. Gail Dawson, 1962; children: Kimberly, Sarah, Daniel. BS in Physics with honors, U. Wis., 1962, MS in Physics, 1964, MD, 1967. Diplomate Am. Bd. Internal Medicine, Am. Bd. Infectious Diseases, Am. Bd. Critical Care Medicine. Physicist, computer programmer Lawrence Radiation Lab., AEC, Livermore, Calif., 1962; intern, asst. resident Harvard Med. unit Boston City Hosp., 1967-69, chief resident, 1972-73; with Hosp. Infections sect. Ctrs. for Disease Control, USPHS, Atlanta, 1969-71; acting chief nat. nosocomial infections study Ctr. for Disease Control, USPHS, Atlanta, 1970-71; sr. resident dept. medicine Mass. Gen. Hosp., 1971-72, clin. and research fellow infectious disease unit, 1973-74; asst. prof. medicine U. Wis., Madison, 1974-78, assoc. prof., 1978-82, prof., 1982—; hosp. epidemiologist, U. Wis. Hosp. and Clinic, Madison, 1974—; Ovid O. Meyer chair in medicine U. Wis., Madison, 1975—, head sec. infectious diseases, 1979—; attending physician Ctr. for Trauma and Life Support U. Wis., 1976—; clinician, rschr., educator in field; mem. program com. Intersci. Conf. on Antimicrobial Agts. and Chemotherapy, 1987-94; mem. Am. Bd. Critical Care Medicine, 1989-95. Sr. assoc. editor Infection Control and Hosp. Epidemiology, 1979-93; mem. editl. bd. Jour. Lab. and Clin. Investigation, 1980-86, Jour. Critical Care, 1985—, Jour. Infectious Diseases, 1988-90, Critical Care Medicine, 1989-94; contbr. articles to med. jours. Recipient 1st award for disting. rsch. in Antibiotic Rev., 1980, Internat. CIPI award, 1994, numerous teaching awards and hon. lectrs. Fellow ACP, Am. Coll. Chest Physicians, Infectious Diseases Soc. Am. (coun. 1993-96), Soc. for Critical Care Medicine, Surg. Infection Soc.; mem. Soc. Hosp. Epidemiologists Am. (pres. 1990, program com. ann. meeting 1992-96), Ctrl. Soc. for Clin. Rsch., Am. Soc. Microbiology, Am. Fedn. Clin. Rsch., Alpha Omega Alpha (nat. bd. dirs. 1983-89). Office: U Wis Hosp and Clinics H4/574 Madison WI 53792

MAKI, JERROLD ALAN, health system executive; b. Duluth, Minn., Sept. 4, 1947; s. Willio John and Eleanor Edla (Savela) M.; m. Carolyn Helen Dack, Aug. 2, 1969; children: Eric Edward, Emily Miriam, David Dack. BA cum laude, U. Min., Duluth, 1969; MHA, U. Min., Mpls., 1973. Lic. nursing home adminstr., Ohio. Asst. to supr. Investors Diversified Svcs., Inc., Mpls., 1969-71; assoc. adminstr. North Ottawa Community Hosp., Grand Haven, Mich., 1973-77; v.p. St. Mary's Hosp., Grand Rapids, Mich., 1977-80, Bapt. Med. Ctr., Oklahoma City, 1980-85; exec. v.p., COO Svc. Frontiers, Inc., Lafayette, Ind., 1985-86; exec. v.p., COO Mercy Med. Ctr., Springfield, Ohio, 1986-90, pres., CEO, 1990-95, bd. dirs., 1987-95; sr. v.p. Mercy Health System-We. Ohio, Springfield, 1995-96; pres., CEO Mercy Health Sys.-Western Ohio, Springfield, 1996—, also bd. dirs.; sr. v.p. Mercy Health System, Cin., 1996—; chairperson accreditation and quality com. Ohio Hosp. Assn., 1993—; pres. Mercy Health Ventures, 1996—; chmn. bd. dirs. Mercy Primary Care, 1996—; bd. dirs. Mercy Managed Care, Ltd. Bd. dirs. Mental Health Svcs. Clark County, Springfield, 1987—, Friends of Mercy, Springfield, 1988-95, Springfield Physician-Hosp. Orgn., 1991—; v.p. Springfield Acad. for Cmty. Leadership, 1988-89; bd. deacons for ch., 1990-92, bd. trustees, 1993—, Mercy Found., 1996—. Fellow Am. Coll. Healthcare Execs.; mem. Springfield C. of C., Springfield CountryClub, Rotary. Presbyterian. Home: 2006 W Mile Rd Springfield OH 45503-2732 Office: Mercy Health Sys-Western Ohio 1 S Limestone St Ste # 600 Springfield OH 45501-0688

MAKINS, JAMES EDWARD, retired dentist, dental educator, educational administrator; b. Galveston, Tex., Feb. 22, 1923; s. James and Hazel Alberta (Morton) M.; m. Jane Hopkins, Mar. 4, 1943; children: James E. Jr., Michael William, Patrick Clarence, Scott Roger. DDS, U. Tex.-Houston, 1945; postdoctoral, SUNY-Buffalo, 1948-49. Lic. dentist, Tex. Practice dentistry specializing in orthodontics, Lubbock, Tex., 1949-77; dir. clinics Dallas City Dental Health Program, 1977-78; dir. continuing edn. Baylor Coll. Dentistry, Dallas, 1978-92, ret., 1992, prof. emeritus Baylor Coll. Dentistry. Author: (book chpt.) Handbook of Texas, 1986. Chmn. profl. div. United Fund, Lubbock, 1958; pres. Tex. State Bd. Dental Examiners, Austin, Tex., 1968; instl. chmn. United Way, Dallas, 1983. Served to lt. comdr., USNR, 1945-47. Recipient Community Service award W. Tex. C. of C., Abilene, 1968, Clinic award Dallas County Dental Soc., 1981. Fellow Am. Coll. Dentists, Internat. Coll. Dentists; mem. Tex. Dental Assn. (life, v.p. 1954, Goodfellow 1973), West Tex. Dental Assn. (pres. 1955), Am. Assn. Dental Examiners, Park City Club, Rotary, Omicron Kappa Upsilon. Methodist. Avocation: dental history.

MAKMAN, MARIANNE WERTHEIM, psychiatrist, educator; b. Vienna, Austria, June 17, 1936; came to U.S., 1938; d. John Hans and Herta (Fuchs) Wertheim; m. Maynard H. Makman, Sept. 27, 1959; children: Judith, Lisa. BA, Swarthmore Coll., 1958; MD, Case-Western Res. U., 1962. Diplomate Am. Bd. Psychiatry and Neurology. Intern in medicine Georgetown U. Hosp., Washington, 1962-63; resident in psychiatry Jacobi Hosp.-Albert Einstein Med. Coll., Bronx, N.Y., 1965-69, instr., then asst. clin. prof., 1970—; pvt. practice, Larchmont, N.Y., 1969—. Fellow Am. Psychiat. Assn. (program chmn. local dist. br., mem. ethics com., com. on women, chmn. cross-cultural psychiatry). Office: 1815 Palmer Ave Ste 1 Larchmont NY 10538

MAKOTO, ASASHIMA, biology educator, researcher; b. Niigata, Japan, Sept. 6, 1944; m. Yoshiko Hasei, Nov. 24, 1975; children: Nobuko, Hiromitsu. B., Tokyo Kyoiku U., Tokyo, 1967; MS, Tokyo U., 1969, DSc, PhD, 1972. Rsch. asst. Berlin Free U., 1972-74; assoc. prof. Yokohama (Japan) City U., 1974-84, prof., 1985-93; prof. Tokyo U., 1994—. Author: Mechanism of Development, 1983, Modern Biology, 1985; editor: Fundamentals of Space Biology, 1990, Development Growth Difference, 1994, Zoology Science, 1994. Recipient Eto Acad. Found. prize, 1990, Zool. Soc. Japan prize, 1990, Inoue Acad. Found. prize, 1991, Kihara Meml. Life Sci. Found. prize, 1994, Siebold prize Humboldt Found. (Germany), 1994. Mem. Zool. Soc. Japan (councilor 1986—), Japanese Soc. Devel. Biologists (councilor 1986—), Internat. Soc. Devel. Biologists (editor Devel. Growth Differences 1993—, Zool. Sci. 1993—). Office: Tokyo U, Dept Biology, 3-8-7 Komaba Meguro-ku, Meguro-ku Tokyo 153, Japan

MAKOWKA, LEONARD, medical educator, surgeon; b. Toronto, Ont., Can., Nov. 25, 1953. MD, U. Toronto, Can., 1977, MS in Pathology, 1979, PhD in Pathology, 1982. Intern in surgery The Mount Sinai Hosp., Toronto, Ont., Can., 1977-78; with gen. surgery course U. Toronto, Can., 1978; Can. fellow med. rsch. coun., dept. surgery and pathology Toronto Gen. Hosp., U. Toronto, Can., 1978-82; rsch. assoc., dept. surgery and pathology U. Toronto, Can., 1982; asst. resident gen. surgery Toronto Gen. Hosp., Can., 1982; sr. resident gen. surgery Women's Coll. Hosp., 1983; chief resident surgery Toronto Western Hosp., Can., 1983-84; fellow in hepatobiliary surgery Toronto Gen. Hosp., Can., 1984-85; rsch. assoc. dept. surgery and pathology U. Toronto, Can., 1984-85, asst. prof. dept. surgery and pathology, 1985; asst. prof. surgery, dept. surgery U. Pitts., Pa., 1986-87, assoc. prof. surgery, dept. surgery, 1987-89; dir. surgery and transplantation svcs., dept. surgery Cedars Sinai Med. Ctr., 1989-92; prof. surgery UCLA Med. Sch., 1989—; chmn. dept. surgery, dir. transplantation svcs. Cedars Sinai Med Ctr., 1992—; exec. dir. comprehensive liver disease & treatment ctr. St. Vincent Med. Ctr., L.A., 1995—; vis. asst. prof. U. Pitts., Pa., 1985; lectr. in the field. Contbr. to over 345 jours. Recipient Charles E. Frost Bronze medal, 1979, Royal Coll. Physicians and Surgeons of Can. Surgery medal, 1980, 85, First Place award Second Annual Assembly of Gen. Surgeons, 1979, Gallie Bateman Essay award, 1980, Davis and Geck Surgical Essay award, 1981-82, Can. Found. of Ileitis and Colitis Rsch. award, 1981, U. Toronto Rsch. Papers award, 1981; Charles E. Frost scholar, 1979, Schering scholar Am. Coll. Surgeons, 1981; Graham Campbell fellow Faculty of Medicine U. Toronto, 1982, Centennial fellow Med. Rsch. Coun. of Can., 1985-87; named Humanitarian of the Yr. World Children's Transplant Fund, 1992. Mem. Alpha Omega Alpha. Office: St Vincent Med Ctr Institute Plz 2200 W Third St Los Angeles CA 90057

MALA, THEODORE ANTHONY, physician, consultant; b. Santa Monica, Calif., Feb. 3, 1946; s. Ray and Galina (Liss) M.; children: Theodore S., Galina T.; m. Cynthia A. Lindquist, July 2, 1996; 1 stepchild, Rebecca Smith. BA in Philosophy, DePaul U., 1972; MD, Autonomous U., Guadalajara, Mex., 1976; MPH, Harvard U., 1980. Spl. asst. for health affairs Alaska Fedn. Natives, Anchorage, 1977-78; chief health svcs. Alaska State Div. of Corrections, Anchorage, 1978-79; assoc. prof., founder, dir. Inst. for Circumpolar Health Studies, U. Alaska, Anchorage, 1982-90; founder Siberian med. rsch. program U. Alaska, Anchorage, 1982, founder Magadan (USSR) med. rsch. program, 1988; commr. Health and Social Svcs. State of Alaska, Juneau, 1990-93; pres. chief exec. officer Ted Mala, Inc., Anchorage, 1993—; pres., ptnr. Mexican-Siberian Trading Co., Monterrey, Mex., 1994—; mem. Alaska rsch. and publs. com. Indian Health Svc., USPHS, 1987-90; advisor Nordic Coun. Meeting, WHO, Greenland, 1985; mem. Internat. Organizing Com., Circumpolar Health Congress, Iceland, 1992-93; chmn. bd. govs. Alaska Psychiat. Inst., Anchorage, 1990-93; cabinet mem. Gov. Walter J. Hickel, Juneau, 1990-93; advisor humanitarian aid to Russian Far East U.S. Dept. State, 1992—; cons. USAID on U.S.-Russian Health Programs, 1994. Former columnist Tundra Times; contbr. articles to profl. jours. Trustee United Way Anchorage, 1978-79; chmn. bd. trustees Alaska Native Coll., 1993—. Recipient Gov.'s award, 1988, Outstanding Svc. award Alaska Commr. Health, 1979, Ministry of Health citation USSR Govt., 1989, Citation award Alaska State Legislature, 1989, 90, 94, Commendation award State of Alaska, 1990, Alaska State Legislature, 1994, Honor Kempton Svc. to Humanity award, 1989, citation Med. Comty. of Magadan region, USSR, 1989; Nat. Indian fellow U.S. Dept. Edn., 1979. Mem. Assn. Am. Indian Physicians, N.Y. Acad. Scis., Internat. Union for Circumpolar Health (permanent sec.-gen. 1987-90, organizing com. 8th Internat. Congress on Circumpolar Health 1987-90). Office: 205 E Dimond Blvd Ste 544 Anchorage AK 99515-1909

MALACH, MONTE, physician; b. Jersey City, Aug. 15, 1926; s. Charles and Yetta (Pascher) M.; m. Ann Elaine Glazer, June 15, 1952 (dec. June 1989); children: Barbara Sandra, Cathie Tara, Matthew David; m. Barbara Meryl Lipstein, Dec. 24, 1994; stepchildren: Heather Ilene, Jennifer Beth, Matthew Howard. BA, U. Mich., 1949, MD, 1949. Diplomate Am. Bd. Internal Medicine, Nat. Bd. Med. Examiners. Intern Beth Israel Hosp., Boston, 1949-50; resident Beth Israel Hosp., 1950-51, chief resident, 1951-52; chief resident Kings County Hosp., Bklyn., 1954-55; practice medicine specializing in internal medicine and cardiology Bklyn., 1955—; dir. CCU Bklyn. Hosp., 1955-91, dir. emeritus CCU, 1991—; med. dir. Medicare IPRO Downstate N.Y., 1990—; pres. profl. staff Bklyn. Hosp., 1966-69, chmn. med. bd., 1971-72; attending staff Caledonian Hosp., pres. profl. staff, 1984-85; pres. profl. staff Bklyn. Hosp.-Caledonian Hosp., 1987-89, chmn. med. bd., 1988-89; cons. Kings County Hosp.; tchg. fellow Tufts U. Med. Sch., 1951-52; instr. medicine Downstate Med. Ctr., Bklyn., 1955-59, clin. asst. prof. medicine, 1959-68, clin. assoc. prof., 1969-76, clin. prof., 1976—; clin. prof. medicine NYU Med. Ctr., 1994—; bd. dirs. Bay St. Landing One Owners Corp., 1985-87; v.p. Ocean View Condos, 1989-90, pres., 1990-95. Kings County committeeman Democratic Party, 1964, 65. Served with USNR, 1944-46, to 1st lt. M.C. U.S. Army, 1952-54. Recipient 1st Prize for Crisis Mgmt. Habitat Mag., 1987. Fellow Am. Coll. Chest Physicians, ACP, Am. Coll. Cardiology (task force Health Care Quality Improvement Initiative 1996—); mem. AMA (chmn. sect. coun. on internal medicine 1980), N.Y. Heart Assn., Am. Soc. Internal Medicine (trustee 1975-79, sec.-treas. 1979—, pres. elect 1981, pres. 1982-83, chmn. investment com. 1985-93), N.Y. State Soc. Internal Medicine (pres. 1973-74, dir. 1966-84, chmn. Bklyn. chpt., v.p. 1971, award of merit 1978), Bklyn. Soc. Internal Medicine (mem. council 1965, pres. 1969-72), Med. Soc. State of N.Y. (chmn. sect. internal medicine 1976, chmn. med. care ins. com. 1988-93), Federated Council for Internal Medicine (chmn. 1979-80), Med. Soc. County Kings (censor 1985-91). Office: 55 Rugby Rd Brooklyn NY 11226-2607

MALACHOWSKY, MARTIN NORMAN, physician; b. Glen Ridge, N.J., June 19, 1929; s. Louis and Lena (Sirotkin) M.; m. Zelda L. Rutenberg, Dec. 25, 1951; children: Jeffrey Wayne, Chris Alan. BA, Columbia Coll., 1950; MD, SUNY, 1953. Diplomate Am. Bd. Obstetrics and Gynecology. Intern Mountainside Hosp., Montclair, N.J., 1953-54, resident, 1954-55; physician obstetrics Geisinger Meml. Hosp, Danville, Pa., 1958-60; resident physician, 1957-58; physician obstetrics Monmouth Med. Ctr., Long Branch, N.J., 1957-58, sr. attending physician ob-gyn.; pvt. practice Monmouth Med. Ctr., Long Branch, 1960—; clin. asst. prof. ob-gyn. Hahnemann Med. Coll. Capt. U.S. Air Force, 1954-57. Fellow Am. Coll. Obstetricians and Gynecologists, Am. Coll. Surgeons; mem. AMA, N.J. Obstetrical and Gynecologic Soc., Soc. Surgeons of N.J., N.J. Med. Soc., Monmouth County Med. Soc., N.J. Acad. Medicine, Am. Fertility Soc., Am. Assn. Gynecologic Laparoscopist. Jewish. Office: Pavilion Ob/Gyn Assocs 127 Pavilion Ave Long Branch NJ 07740 also: 502 Candlewood Commons Howell NJ 07731-2170

MALAMENT, IRWIN BERNARD, podiatrist; b. Bklyn., Dec. 3, 1950; s. Harry Joseph and Evelyn (Kasten) M.; m Jane Ann Wolff, Aug. 25, 1974; children: Michelle, Laura. BS in Sys. Engring., Poly. Inst. Bklyn., 1972; D of Podiat. Medicine, Pa. Coll. Podiat. Medicine, 1979; MS in Biomed. Engring., U. Miami, 1973. Diplomate Am. Bd. Podiat. Surgery. Resident in podiat. surgery Westview Hosp., Indpls., 1980, podiatrist, 1981—; podiatrist Putnam County Hosp., 1985—, Winona Hosp. Ctr., 1985—, Culver Union Hosp., 1991—, Hendricks Cmty. Hosp., 1992—, Meth. Hosp., 1993—, Physician's Care Outpatient Surgery Ctr., 1993—, St. Vincent's Hosp., 1994—; dir. residency tng. Westview Hosp., 1987-90, pres. podiatry staff, 1984-86; mem. radiologic tech. cert. com. Ind. State Bd. of Health, 1993-94; pres. Artemis, Inc., Indpls., 1995-96; cons., scoring judge Nat. Bd. Podiatry Examiners, Princeton, N.J., 1988-90, Podiat. Med. Licensing Exam. for States, Washington, 1989—; cons. Hene Specialty Meat Co., Indpls., 1995-96. Contbr. articles to profl. jours. Bd. dirs. Hoosier Safety Coun., Indpls., 1994-95; contbr. Greater Indpls. Coun. on Alcoholism, 1995. Fellow Coll. Foot and Ankle Surgeons; mem. Am. Podiat. Med. Assn. (del. Ho. of Dels. 1994-95), Ind. Podiat. Med. Assn. (dir. continuing med. edn. 1982-84, chmn. ethics and patient inquiry com. 1992-94, 2d v.p. 1992-93, chmn. continuing edn. com. 1994, 1st v.p. 1994, pres.-elect 1995, pres. 1996). Office: Irwin B Malament DPM 3410 N High School Rd # C Indianapolis IN 46224

MALANGA, CARL JOSEPH, pharmacologist; b. N.Y.C., Aug. 26, 1939; s. Joseph John and Carolina Jennie (Graziano) M.; m. Mary Lou Villano, July 31, 1966; 1 child, C.J. III. BS, Fordham U., 1961, MS, 1967, PhD, 1970. Instr. Fordham U. Coll. Pharmacy, Bronx, 1964-70; from asst. prof. to assoc. dean W.Va. Univ. Sch. Pharmacy, Morgantown, 1970—. Democrat. Roman Catholic. Home: 2202 Surrey Dr Morgantown WV 26505 Office: W Va Univ Sch Pharmacy 1137 HSN PO Box 9500 Morgantown WV 26506

MALASANOS, LOIS JULANNE FOSSE, nursing educator; b. LaPorte City, Iowa, Sept. 1, 1928; d. Lewis Reginald and Hennetta Marie Fosse; widowed; children: John, Toree. BSN, U. Tex., 1948; BA in Gen. Sci., U. Iowa, 1952; MA in Nursing Edn., U. Chgo., 1959; PhD in Physiology, U. Ill., 1973. Assoc. dir. nursing U. Iowa Hosps., Iowa City, 1950-51, staff charge nurse, 1951; instr. operating room Sch. Nursing, Michael Reese Hosp., Chgo., 1951-58; charge nurse, med.-surg. U. Chgo. Billings Hosp., 1952-59; pvt. duty nurse Ill., 1959-60; charge nurse, maternal-infant nursing Weiss Meml. Hosp., Chgo., 1963-66; asst. prof. Loyola U., Chgo., 1966-69; teaching asst. in physiology U. Ill., Chgo., 1969-73, assoc. prof., assoc. head gen. nursing dept. Coll. Nursing, 1973-76, prof., assoc. head gen. nursing dept., 1976-80; prof., dean Coll. Nursing U. Fla., Gainesville, 1980-95, Disting. Svc. prof., 1995—; instr. anatomy and physiology Cook County Hosp., Chgo., 1973; lectr. endocrinology Chgo. Coll. Osteopathic Medicine, 1973-80; active Pres. Clinton's Task Force on Health Care, 1993; cons. Am. Assn. Med. Colls., 1977-78, Am. Heart Assn., 1977-94, Am. Jour. Nursing, 1978-79, Gainesville (Fla.) Vets. Ctr., 1980-95, Lake Butler Receiving Ctr., 1980—; presenter papers in field; cons. to numerous colls. and univs. regarding curriculum, nursing care and endocrinology; chair Deans and Dirs. of Fla. Colls. Nursing, 1981-89; chair edn. com. State Bd. Nursing, 1983, 87, chair probable course com.; vis. prof. Dokuz English U.. Izmir, Turkey, 1995-96. Co-author, editor: Manual of Medical Surgical Nursing, 1983, Translating Comitment to Reality, 1986, Health Assessment, 1977 (Am. Jour. Nursing Book of Yr. award 1977), 4th edit., 1989; editor: Vital Signs, 1981-90, Fla. Cancer Nursing News, 1983-84; co-editor: Fla. Nursing Rev., 1986-90; mem. editl. rev. bd. Image, 1980—; editl. cons. Nursing, 1982—; manuscript referee Rsch. in Nursing and Health, 1980—, Jour. Profl. Nursing, 1985—; chairperson adv. com. Nursing Outlook, 1986-91, Peer Rev., 1986—; contbr. more than 100 articles, revs. to profl. jours. Mem. nursing com., scholarship com. and rsch. rev. com. Am. Cancer Soc., Tampa, Fla., 1980—. Recipient Bronze medal Fla. Heart Assn., 1986, Silver medal Fla. Heart Assn., 1989, 93; named Disting. Alumnus U. Tex. Med. Br., 1985; named to Disting. Faculty, Albany State U., 1988, Hall of Fame, U. Tex. Med. Br., 1992; NEH fellow, 1981; Fulbright awardee to Turkey, 1995-96. Mem. ANA (mem. coun. nurse rschrs.), AACN, AAAS, AAUP, Am. Acad. Nursing (mem. pub. com. 1986-89) Am. Assn. Higher Edn., Am. Assn. Colls. Nursing, Fla. Nurses Assn. (mem. dist. 10), Fla. League Nursing, Nat. League Nursing (mem. coun. baccalaureate and higher degree programs. Dirs. award 1995), So. Regional Edn. Bd., Sigma Xi, Sigma Theta Tau, Phi Kappa Phi (pres. 1987-88). Office: U Fla Coll Nursing PO Box 100197 Gainesville FL 32610-0197

MALATESTA, VICTOR JULIO, JR., clinical psychologist, researcher; b. Wilmington, Del., Apr. 3, 1951; s. Victor J. and Gloria Marie (Faenza) M.; B.A., U. Del., 1973; M.S., U. Ga., 1975, Ph.D., 1978, cert. in gerontology, 1980, cert. in clin. psychology, 1981. Lic. psychologist, Pa., S.C. Psychology intern Med. U. S.C. and Charleston VA Hosp., 1980-81; asst. prof. psychiatry, dir. Psychol. Assessment Ctr., 1981-83; asst. prof. psychiatry Med. U. S.C., 1983—; clin. assoc. prof. psychiatry Inst. Pa., U. Pa. Hosp., Phila., 1989—, dir. behavioral therapy, 1983—; cons. in gerontology, human sexuality, behavioral treatment. Contbr. numerous articles to profl. jours., book chpts. Mem. APA, Southeastern Psychol. Assn., Assn. for Advancement Behavior Therapy, So. Soc. Psychology and Philosophy, Assn. Med. Sch. Profs. Psychology. Home: 515 W Pleasant Grove Rd West Chester PA 19382-7119 Office: Inst of Pa Hosp 111 N Street Philadelphia PA 19139

MALAY, MARCELLA MARY, nursing educator, administrator; b. Nashua, N.H., Mar. 18, 1948; d. John H. and Helyn (Sullivan) M. BSN, U. Del., 1970; MS, Boston U., 1977; postgrad., Mass. Coll. Pharmacy, Boston. RN, Mass. Instr. Faulkner Hosp., Boston, 1973-76, New England Deaconess Hosp., Boston, 1975-87; asst. prof. Mass. Coll. Pharmacy, Boston, 1987—; edn. specialist New Eng. Bapt. Hosp., Boston, 1987-93, DON, 1993-95, dir. edn., quality improvement and rsch., 1996—. Mem. teleconf. adv. com. Tufts Med. Sch. Mem. ANA, Mass. Nurses Assn., Sigma Theta Tau. Home: 97 Hampden Dr Apt 2D Norwood MA 02062-5466

MALBERT, CHARLES HENRI, gastroenterologist; b. Auch, France, Jan. 12, 1961; s. Jean and Anne (Pheline) M. DVM, Ecole Vet. Toulouse, France, 1984; PhD, Inst. Nat. Polytechnique, France, 1987, habilite a diriger des Recherches, 1990. Attache scientifique INRA, St. Gilles, France, 1984-89, in charge rsch. 2, 1989-90, in charge rsch. 1, 1990—. Co-author: Antro-Pyloro-Duodenal Coordination, 1990, Advances in the Innervation, 1992, Nutrition des Ruminants, 1995; author software. Lt. French Mil., 1988-89. Recipient Prix de Assn. Francaise de Nutition, 1994. Mem. Am. Physiol. Soc., Assn. Physiologistes, European Gastro Intestinal Soc., Club Francais de Motricite Digestive. Office: INRA, Porcines Station de Recherches, 35590 Saint Gilles France

MALBRAIN, MANU LUDOVIC NELLY GUIDO, internist; b. Dendermonde, Belgium, Dec. 25, 1965; s. Hubert Desire and Marie-Louise (De Geyter) M.; m. Bieke Elvire Depré, Mar. 27, 1993; children: Jacco, Milan. Degree in Latin and math., H. Maagd Coll., 1983; MD maxima cum laude, Cath. U., 1991; degree in painting & drawing, Acad. Fine Arts, Overyse, Belgium, 1995. Health care worker Psychiat. Instn., Mortsel, Belgium, 1987; co-asst. pediatrics Royal Hosp. for Sick Children, Bristol, United Kingdom, 1989; intern U. Hosp. Gasthuisberg, Leuven, Belgium, 1989-90, resident in internal medicine, 1993-95; resident in internal medicine Stuivenberg Gen. Hosp., Antwerp, Belgium, 1991-93, resident in intensive care medicine, 1995—. Contbr. articles to profl. jours. Organizer cultural events Rotaract Dendermonde, 1984-91; organizer, tchr. rock and roll dance courses, Leuven, 1986-93. Mem. Belgian Haematological Soc., Belgian Soc. Internal Medicine, Belgian Soc. Gastroenterology. Roman Catholic. Home: Dreef 1, B-3360 Lovenjoel Belgium Office: U Hosp Gasthuisberg, Herestraat 49, B-3000 Leuven Belgium

MALCOLM, DAWN GRACE, family physician; b. L.A., Nov. 3, 1936; d. Thomas N. and Grace S. (Salisian) M. BA, UCLA, 1959; MD, Med. Coll. Pa., 1973. Diplomate Am. Bd. Family Practice. Tchr. elem. music Fullerton (Calif.) Sch. Dist., 1960-61; tchr. Ahlman Acad., Kabul, Afghanistan, 1961-65; intern and resident in family practice Kaiser Found. Hosp., L.A., 1973-76; family physician So. Calif. Permanente Med. Group, L.A., 1976—; mem. faculty family practice residency program Kaiser Found. Hosp., L.A., 1976—. Fellow Am. Acad. Family Physicians. Office: So Calif Permanente Med Grp 4747 Sunset Blvd Los Angeles CA 90027-6021

MALDEN, JOAN WILLIAMS, physical therapist; b. Bayshore, N.Y., Apr. 14; d. Sidney S. and Myrtle L. (Williams) Siegel; B.S., N.Y. U., 1957; m. Alan A. Chasnov, Jan. 20, 1951; children—Marc, Robin, Debra and David (twins); m. 2d, Miroslav Mladenovic, Sept. 14, 1967; 1 child, Kristine. Phys. therapist hosps. and orgns. in N.Y.C. area, 1956-57; phys. therapist Brunswick Hosp. Center, Amityville, N.Y., 1968-69; pvt. practice phys. therapy, Wantagh, N.Y., 1968—; licensure examiner, N.Y. State; cons., tchr. in field; lectr. NYU, Citizen Amb. Program to China; clin. coord. Hunter Coll., Daemen Coll., NYU, Columbia U., SUNY at Stony Brook, Touro Coll., Springfield Coll., Mercy Coll., Russell Sage Coll.; researcher in field; contbr. articles to profl. jours. Pres. internat. scholarships com. Massapequa chpt. Am. Field Service, 1962-64. Mem. Am. Acad. Cerebral Palsy, Am. Phys. Therapy Assn. (past chmn. polit. action com. N.Y. chpt., past chmn. L.I. dist.), AAUW (pres. Massapequa chpt. 1962-64), N.Y. State Soc. Continuing Edn. in Phys. Therapy, L.I. Assn. Ind. Phys. Therapists, Airplane Owners and Pilots Assn., Ninety-Nines, Exptl. Aviation Assn., Farmingdale Flyers (officer). Democrat. Unitarian. Home: 35 S Bay Ave Massapequa NY 11758-7847 Office: Wantagh Med Plz 3305 Jerusalem Ave Wantagh NY 11793-2028

MALECKI, JEAN MARIE, public health director; b. Miami, Mar. 27, 1953; d. Raymond Edward and Patricia Ann (Diehl) Mortimer; m. Peter John Malecki, Apr. 11, 1981; 1 child, Heather Marie. BS, Fairfield U., 1971; MD, N.Y. Med. Coll., 1975; MPH, U. Miami Sch. Medicine, 1985. Diplomate Nat. Bd. Medical Examiners, Am. Bd. Preventive Medicine and Pub. Health. Acting med. dir. HRS Palm Beach County Pub. Health Unit, Lake Worth Br., Lake Worth, Fla., 1983—; dir. Grad. Programs in Pub. Health, 1989—; med. dir. HRS/Palm Beach County Pub. Health Unit, West Palm Beach, Fla., 1989—; adj. asst. prof. dept. epidemiology and pub. health U. Miami Sch. Medicine, 1988—; chairperson Residency Adv. Com. Gen. Preventive Medicine and Pub. Health, 1986-89; pres. Healthy Start Coalition of Palm Beach County, 1992—; lectr. in field. Contbr. articles to profl. jours. Recipient Up and Comer award, 1990, Citation for Scholastic Achievement Am. Med. Women's Assn., 1979, Cor Et Manus award N.Y. Med. Coll., 1979, award Alpha Omega Alpha. Mem. AMA, APHA, Am. Cancer Soc. (Vol. of Yr. award 1991), Fla. Med. Assn., Fla. Pub. Health

Assn., Palm Beach County Med. Soc. Office: HRS Palm Beach County PO Box 29 West Palm Beach FL 33402-0029

MALEK, REZA SAID, urological surgeon; b. Aug. 22, 1940; s. Said and Banoo (Rais) M.; m. Haleh F. Rassa, Feb. 9, 1980. MB, BS, U. London, 1964; MS in Urology, U. Minn., 1971. Diplomate Am. Bd. Urology. Intern St. Mary's Hosp., Eastbourne, Eng., 1964-65, Lister Hosp., Hitchin, Eng., 1964-65; resident, sr. house officer St. Thomas's Hosp., U. London, 1965-66, Mayo Grad. Sch. Medicine, Rochester, Minn., 1967-71; rsch. fellow in calculous disease of urinary tract, vis. clin. surgeon Bowman-Gray Sch. Medicine, Winston-Salem, N.C., 1971-72; instr. urology Mayo Clinic, Rochester, 1972-74, asst. prof., 1974-76, assoc. prof., 1976-91, prof., 1991—; adviser to regional dir. WHO, 1972; cons. urology Mayo Clinic, 1972—. Fellow ACS, Royal Coll. Physicians and Surgeons of Can., Am. Soc. for Laser Medicine and Surgery; mem. AMA, Minn. Med. Assn., Zumbro Valley Med. Soc., Sigma Xi. Home: 1523 Camelback Ct NE Rochester MN 55906-8960 Office: Mayo Clinic 200 1st St SW Rochester MN 55905-0001

MALERMAN, ARNOLD JOEL, orthodontist, educator; b. Phila., Aug. 20, 1943; s. Vernon and Eve (Resow) Malerman; m. Joyce Fraida Manulkin, June 19, 1966; 1 child, Paige. Student, Pa. State U., 1961-62; degree, Temple U., 1964, DDS, 1968; cert. orthodontics, U. Pa., 1972. Clinician Sausser Dental Health Ctr Thomas Jefferson U. Hosp., 1972-76; clin. instr. U. Pa. Sch. Dental Medicine, 1973-82, clin. asst. prof., 1982-85, clin. assoc. prof. orthodontics, 1985—; asst. dentist Children's Hosp. Phila., 1973-75, assoc. dentist, 1975-79; vis. instr. Albert Einstein Med. Ctr. No. divsn., 1989-90. Sec., bd. dirs., Sterling Model's, Inc., 1977-86, Aerial Toys, Inc., 1977-86, Pa. Reimbursenent, Inc., 1991—; mem. adv. bd. Ovations-The Club at the Spectrum, 1981-83, Parent's Network, 1987-90. Capt. USAF. Recipient award Omicron Kappa Upsilon, 1968, award John Coleman Soc. Oral Medicine, 1968, award James R. Cameron Oral Surgery Soc., 1968. Mem. ADA, Am. Assn. Orthodontics, Am. Soc. Dentistry for Children, Internat. Assn. Dentistry for Children, Internat. Assn. Dentistry for the Handicapped, Pa. Dental Assn. (alt. del. from 2d Dist. Dental Soc.), Phila. County Dental Soc., Mid-Atlantic Soc. Orthodontists, Pa. Soc. Orthodontists, Phila. Soc. Orthodontists (pres.-elect 1988, pres. 1989), Bucks-Mont Orthodontic Study Assn. (sec., treas. 1972-80), Scotia Connections Study Group, Alpha Omega. Republican. Jewish. Home: 840 Timber Ln Dresher PA 19025 Office: Dresher Profl Ctr Ste 1 830 Twining Rd Dresher PA 19025

MALES, JAMES LOWELL, endocrinologist; b. Sayre, Okla., Mar. 21, 1940; s. Lowell Lawrence and Lorena Gladys (Savage) M.; m. Helle Lykke-Hansen, June 30, 1962; 1 child, Mikael Lowell. BS, S.W. Okla. U., 1962; MD, U. Okla. Health Sci. Ctr., 1966. Diplomate Am. Bd. Internal Medicine. Staff endocrinologist Oklahoma City Clinic, 1974—, dir., 1978-80, 89-92. Contbr. articles to profl. jours. Maj. U.S. Army, 1972-74. Fellow ACP; mem. Am. Diabetes Assn., Am. Thyroid Soc., Endocrine Soc. Office: Oklahoma City Clinic 701 NE 10th St Oklahoma City OK 73104

MALHOTRA, HARISH KUMAR, psychiatrist; b. Lahore, India, Dec. 4, 1945; came to U.S., 1973; s. Sohan Lal and Krishna (Kamla) M.; m. Mahamaya Malhotra, Oct. 26, 1972; children: Gautam, Rahul. MB, BS, Govt. Med. Coll., Amritsar, India, 1967; MD in Psychiatry, Postgrad. Inst. Med. Edn., Chandigarh, India, 1972. Diplomate Am. Bd. Psychiatry and Neurology. Resident in psychiatry Postgrad. Inst. Med. Edn. and Rsch., 1969-72; resident in psychiatry Coll. Medicine and Dentistry N.J., Newark, 1973-75, med. dir. div. drug abuse, 1976-77; pvt. practice Elizabeth, N.J., 1977-82, New Providence, N.J., 1982-84, Springfield, N.J., 1985-93, Summit, N.J., 1993—; staff psychiatrist Overlook Hosp., Summit, 1982—, St. Barnabas Med. Ctr., Livingston, N.J.; pres. A Gift of Info. Inc., New Providence, N.J., 1988—; pub. med. edn. cassettes. Contbr. articles to psychiat. jours. Mem. Am. Psychiat. Assn., Oriental Numismatic Soc. Avocation: Indian coins. Office: 33 Overlook Rd Ste 212 Summit NJ 07901-3561

MALHOTRA, VIVEK, medical educator. BS with honors, Stirling U., 1982; DPhil in Biochemistry, Oxford U., 1985. Asst. prof. biology U. Calif., San Diego, 1990-95, assoc. prof. biology, 1995—. Contbr. articles to profl. jours. Recipient Established Investigator award Am. Heart Assn., 1995; postdoctoral fellow Stanford U., 1985-90, Am. Cancer Soc., Calif., 1988-90; Pirie-Reid scholar, Oxford U., 1982-85, Basil O'Connor Starter scholar, March of Dimes, 1992-95. Office: U Calif Dept Biology La Jolla CA 92093-0347*

MALIA, JOANNE SWINDLEHURST, microbiologist; b. Manchester, N.H., Jan. 14, 1958; d. John Robert and Eleanor Ruth (Rogler) Swindlehurst; m. Mark Anthony Malia III, Apr. 20, 1991; children: Mark Anthony IV, Jonathan Patrick. BA in Biology, Notre Dame Coll., 1979; MS in Microbiology, U. Conn., 1982; MS in Applied Mgmt., Lesley Coll., 1986. Nurse's aide maternity and nursery Concord (N.H.) Hosp., 1974-79; teaching asst. U. Conn., Storrs, 1980-82; rsch. asst. Tufts Med. Sch., Boston, 1982-83; scientist biochemistry Cambridge (Mass.) Rsch. Lab., 1983-85, scientist molecular biology, 1985-86, sr. scientist tech. assessment, 1986-88; scientist annotator Max Planck Inst. for Biochemistry, Martinsried, Germany, 1988-90; cons. tech. transfer Johnson & Johnson, New Brunswick, N.J., 1989-90; mgr. clin. ops. adminstrn. IBRD-Rostrum Global, Irvine, Calif., 1990—. Mem. Am. Soc. for Microbiology, Drug Info. Assn., Spl. Librs. Assn., Gesellschaft für Biologische Chemie, Canadian Assn. for Clin. Microbiology and Infectious Diseases, European Soc. Clin. Microbiology and Infectious Diseases. Congregationalist. Home: 24612 Bunbury Lake Forest CA 92630 Office: IBRD-Rostrum Global 2525 Campus Dr Irvine CA 92715

MALIHA-NEBUS, JEANETTE E., school nurse; b. Warwick, N.Y., Aug. 15, 1935; d. Charles George Yopp and Charlotte Kathleen (Donley) Keyser; children: Roxane E. Turner, Nadine C. Collard. RN, Middletown (N.Y.) Psychiat. Ctr. Sch. Nursing, 1956; AA, Orange County Community Coll., Middletown, 1970; BS in Psychology, SUNY, New Paltz, 1972; BSN, Mount St. Mary Coll., Newburgh, N.Y., 1977; MS in Counselor Edn., L.I. U., 1979. RN, N.Y., N.J.; cert. sch. nurse, tchr., N.Y. Staff nurse Middletown (N.Y.) Psychiat. Ctr., 1958-59, from staff nurse to head nurse to nurse instr. dept. staff devel. and Sch. Nursing to nurse supr., 1967-80; pvt. duty nurse Horton Hosp., Middletown, 1957-58, 59-60; staff nurse Valley Hosp., Ridgewood, N.J., 1964-67; coord. clin. care Community Gen. Hosp., Harris, N.Y., 1982-84; sch. nurse Middletown Enlarged City Sch. Dist., 1988—. Mem. ANA (coun. psychiat.-mental health nursing 1991—), AAUW, Am. Sch. Health Assn., Nat. Assn. Sch. Nurses, Nat. Women's Hall of Fame, N.Y. State Nurses Assn., N.Y. State Assn. Sch. Nurses, RN Club Middletown, Women's Univ. Club Middletown, Warwick Hist. Soc., Sigma Theta Tau (Mu Epsilon chpt.). Home: 19 Overhill Rd Middletown NY 10940-3003

MALIN, HOWARD GERALD, podiatrist; b. Providence, Dec. 2, 1941; s. Leon Nathan and Rena Rose (Shapiro) M. AB, U. R.I., 1964; MA, Brigham Young U., 1969; BSc, Calif. Coll. Podiatric Medicine, 1969, DPM, 1972; MSC, Pepperdine U., 1978; postgrad. in classic, U. So. Calif., 1983—. Diplomate Am. Bd. Podiatric Pub. Health, Am. Bd. Podiatric Orthopedics. Extern in podiatry VA Med. Ctr., Wadsworth, Kans., 1971-72, Marine Corps Res. Dept., San Diego, 1972; resident in podiatric medicine and surgery N.Y. Coll. Podiatric-Medicine, N.Y.C., 1972-73; resident in podiatric surgery, instr. in podiatric surgery N.Y. Coll. Podiatric Medicine, N.Y.C., 1973-74; pvt. practitioner in podiatric medicine and surgery Bklyn., 1974-77; mem. staff Prospect Hosp., Bronx, N.Y., 1974-77; chief podiatry service, mem. staff, cons. sports medicine David Grant U.S. Air Force Med. Ctr., Travis AFB, Calif., 1977-80; chief podiatric sect., mem. staff VA Med. Ctr., Martinsburg, W.Va., 1980—; instr. edml. devel. program VA Med. Ctr., Martinsburg, W.Va., 1980—; clin. prof. med. sci. Alderson-Broaddus Coll., U. Osteopathic Medicine and Health Scis.; adj. prof. Barry U. Sch. Podiatric Medicine; dir. extern program Pa. Coll. Podiatric Medicine. Editorial rev. bd. Jour. Contemporary Podiatric Physician, 1991—. Lt. col. USAF, 1977-80, with Res. Fellow Am. Coll. Foot Orthopedics, Am. Coll. Podiatric Physicians, Am. SOc. Podiatric Medicine (past pres., archivist), Am. Soc. Podiatric Radiologists (v.p., archivist), Royal Soc. Health; mem. Am. Acad. Podiatric Sports Medicine (assoc.), Assn. Mil. Surgeons U.S. (life), Am. Coll. Podiatric Surgery (assoc.), Am. Assn. Podiatric Med. Writers (archivist), Phi Kappa Theta, Phi Kappa Psi. Home: 210 Shenandoah Rd Apt 2D Martinsburg WV 25401-3723 Office: VA Med Ctr Dept Podiatry Martinsburg WV 25401

MALIN, THOMAS H., orthopaedic surgeon, educator; b. Frackville, Pa., Oct. 26, 1939; m. Elisabeth Malin; children: Greg, Carol, Janet. BS, Pa. State U., 1961; MD, Jefferson Med. Coll. Phila., 1965. Diplomate Am. Bd. Orthopaedic Surgery. Intern Harrisburg (Pa.) Poly. Hosp., 1965-66, resident in gen. surgery, 1966, 69; resident in orthopaedic surgery U. Pitts. Health Ctr., 1969-72; rheumatoid fellow St. Margaret's Hosp., Pitts., 1972; pvt. practice, Camp Hill, Pa., 1972—; clin. assoc. prof. surgery Pa. State U. Coll. Medicine-Hershey Med. Ctr., 1972—; chief dept. orthopaeics Holy Spirit Hosp., Camp Hill, 1994-97, mem. exec. com., 1994—. Lt. M.C., USN, 1966-69. Fellow ACS, Am. Acad. Orthopaedic Surgery (bd. councilors 1993—); mem. AMA, Ea. Orthopaedic Soc., Pa. Orthopaedic Soc. (pres. 1991-92), Pa. Med. Soc., Dauphin County Med. Soc. (chmn. legis. action team 1986-89). Office: Cumberland Orthopaedic Assocs Ltd 99 November Drive Camp Hill PA 17011

MALINDZAK, GEORGE STEVE, JR., cardiovascular physiology, biomedical engineer; b. Cleve., Jan. 3, 1933; s. George Steve Sr. and Mary (Zemancik) M.; m. Marianne Beamer, June 27, 1959; children: Katherine, Scott, Edward, Eric. AB cum laude in Chemistry and Biology, Western Res. U., 1956; MSc in Physiology and Biophysics, Ohio State U., 1959, PhD in Physiology and Biophysics, 1961; postgrad., MIT, 1963-65. Metallurgist Thompson & Co., Cleve., 1956-57; from instr. to asst. prof. dept. physiology Bowman Gray Sch. Medicine, Winston-Salem, N.C., 1962-68, assoc. prof., 1968-73; rsch. physiologist U. N.C.-EPA, Chapel Hill, 1973-76; prof., chmn. dept. physiology N.E. Ohio U. Coll. Medicine, Rootstown, 1976-85; prof., chmn. dept. biomed. engring. La. Tech. U., Ruston, 1985-88; health sci. adminstr. NIH, Nat. Inst. Environ. Health Scis., Rsch. Triangle Park, N.C., 1988—; cons. Internat. Chelation Rsch. Found., 1982—, Tech. Adv. Svc. for Attys., 1979—. Contbr. more than 133 articles and abstracts to profl. publs. Mem. U.S. Power Squadron (boating), 1967—. With U.S. Army, 1950-53. Grantee NIH, 1961-73, N.C. Heart Assn., 1962-73, EPA, 1973-76, Am. Heart Assn., 1977-85. Mem. AAAS, Am. Soc. Engring. Edn., Am. Physiol. Soc., Am. Soc. Pharmacology and Exptl. Therapeutics, Assn. Chmn. Depts. Physiology, IEEE Engring. in Medicine and Biology Group, Biomed. Engring. Soc., Am. Heart Assn. (basic sci. coun.), Assn. Computing Machinery, AAUP, Biophys. Soc., La. Engring. Soc., Sigma Xi, Beta, Beta, Beta, Alpha Eta Mu. Home: 5201 Smallwood Ct Raleigh NC 27613-6113 Office: Nat Inst Environ Health Sci PO Box 12233 Durham NC 27709-2233

MALINOSKI, FRANK JOSEPH, general practice physician; b. Troy, N.Y., Sept. 4, 1954; s. Frank and Ruth Elizabeth (Martin) M.; m. Judith Ann Sanders, May 23, 1981; children: Wayne D. Peschel, Matthew C. BA, Colby Coll., Waterville, Maine, 1976; PhD, Rutgers U., 1981; MD, Albany (N.Y.) Med. Sch., 1985. Commd. U.S. Army, 1981, advanced through grades to maj.; intern Brooke Army Med. Ctr., San Antonio, 1985-86; physician U.S. Army Med. Research Inst. Infectious Diseases, Frederick, Md., 1986-92; resigned U.S. Army, 1992; dir. clin. rsch. Lederle-Praxis Biols., Rochester, N.Y., 1992-96; v.p. med. affairs NABI, Rockville, Md., 1996—; cons. Frederick Med. Ctr. Clinic, Walkersville, Md., 1987-92; affiliate staff Frederick Meml. Hosp., 1987-92. Contbr. articles to profl. jours. Mem. Frederick County Substance Abuse Coun., 1988-92, Drug Utilization Rev. Bd. of Md., Balt., 1989-92, Instn. Biosafety Com., 1988-92. Nat. Cancer Inst. fellow, 1978-81; Cystic Fibrosis Found. fellow, 1979-80; N.Y. State Health Research Council fellow, 1981-82. Mem. AMA, Am. Soc. Microbiology, Am. Soc. Virology, Am. Soc. Torpical Medicine and Hygiene, Am. Assn. Family Physicians. Republican. Home: 2 Wild Hunt Ct Laytonsville MD 20882 Office: NABI 12276 Wilkins Ave Rockville MD 20852

MALINVERNI, ALBERTO FERRUCCIO, physician; b. Granozzo, Novara, Italy, Dec. 23, 1947; s. Livio Pietro and Maria Antonietta (Aina) M.; m. Carla Volta, June 1, 1985; 1 child, Laura. MD cum laude, U. Milan, Italy, 1972; radiology specialization, U. Tourin, Italy, 1976. Jr. radiology Hosp. Novara, Italy, 1973-80, sr. radiology, 1980-91; chief of staff Hosp. Borgosesia, Italy, 1991—. Contbr. articles to prof. jours. Lt. medicine Aeronautica Italiana, 1974. Mem. Associazione Italiana Radiologia Medica. Roman Catholic. Home: Via Vicenza 34, 28100 Novara Italy Office: Ospedale Degli Infermi, Piazzale Lora 1, 13011 Borgosesia Italy

MALIS, BERNARD JAY, pharmacologist; b. Phila., Feb. 25, 1923; s. Louis J. and Jennie L. (Josselowitz) M.; children: David Joel, Alexa Faith, Olga Lee, Kenneth Andrew, Jonathan Martin. BSc in Pharmacy and Chemistry, Phila. Coll. Pharmacy and Sci., 1944, MSc in Pharmacology/Indsl. Chemistry, 1947. Registered pharmacist, Pa., N.J. Pres. Ogontz Manor Pharmacies, Inc., Phila., 1950-56; dir. pharmacy and cosmetics Sav-Fair, Food Fair Stores, Phila. and Miami, 1956-58; rsch. dir. Haelan Labs., Phila., 1958-60; prin BJM Assocs., Phila., 1960-85, ret., 1985; U.S. del. Fedn. Internat. Pharm., The Hague, 1960-80; bd. incorporators The Phila. Coll. of Pharmacy and Sci., 1950-80. Contbr. articles to profl. jours. including The Explorers Jour. Chmn. The Forum, Phila., 1988-90; assoc. fgn. policy rsch. inst. and Middle East coun. divsn. U. Pa., univ. mus. archaeology and anthropology. Recipient Legion of Honor award Chapel of Four Chaplains, 1989; named Col. Gov. Wallace G. Wilkinson, 1988. Fellow Royal Soc. (London), AAAS; mem. Am. Pharm. Assn. (life), Acad. of Pharm. Rsch. and Sci., C. of C. (ambassador 1985-91), The Pickwick Club, Am. Legion (Benjamin Franklin Post), Navy League, Masons (hon. life mem.), The Explorers Club (chmn. 1990-91, Rotary (dir. club and found. 1988-90). Home and Office: The Warwick Hotel 1701 Locust St Ste 1502 Philadelphia PA 19103-6114

MALISH, DAVID MARC, physician; b. Phila., Dec. 29, 1947; s. Irvin and Esther (Divor) M.; m. Robin Malish, June 16, 1976 (div. 1990); children: Jennifer, Scott; m. Shari Boxer, Sept. 26, 1992; 1 child, Jack. BS, Knox Coll., 1969; MD, Hahnemann U., 1973. Diplomate Am. Bd. Internal Medicine, Am. Bd. Allergy and Immunology. Intern Hahnemann Hosp., Phila., 1973-74; internal medicine resident Monmouth Med. Ctr., Long Branch, N.J., 1974-76; fellow in allergy and immunology Kaiser Found. Hosp.-Sunset facility, UCLA Immunodeficiency Clinic, Children's Hosp., L.A., 1976-78; locum tenems Drs. Cenci and Krall, West Hartford and Hartford, Conn., 1978-79; pvt. practice San Jose, Calif., 1979—; staff internist Monte Villa Hosp., Morgan Hill, Calif., 1979-81; med. dir., staff internist Good Samaritan Recovery Ctr., Good Samaritan Hosp., San Jose, 1991-94, med. cons. Samaritan Pain Ctr., San Jose. Bd. dirs. Am. Lung Soc., Santa Clara, 1980—; med. dir. Camp Superstuff-Asthmatic Camp for Children, 1985—; head pediat. asthma sect. Am. Lung Assn., Santa Clara County, 1994—; mem. fin. bd. for physicians Com. to Reelect Congressman Norm Mineta. Fellow Am. Acad. Allergy and Immunology, Am. Coll. Allergy; mem. Am. Acad. Physicians, Calif. Soc. Addiction Medicine (cert.), Santa Clara Med. Assn. Office: 2505 Samaritan Dr Ste 606 San Jose CA 95124

MALKASIAN, GEORGE DURAND, JR., physician, educator; b. Springfield, Mass., Oct. 26, 1927; s. George Dur and Gladys Mildred (Trombley) M.; m. Mary Ellen Koch, Oct. 16, 1954; children: Linda Jeanne, Karen Diane, Martha Ellen. AB, Yale U., 1950; MD, Boston U., 1954; MS, U. Minn., 1963. Diplomate Am. Bd. Ob-Gyn. Intern Worcester (Mass.) City Hosp., 1954-55; resident in ob-gyn Mayo Grad. Sch. Hosp., Rochester, Minn., 1955-58, 60-61; mem. faculty Mayo Med. Sch., 1962—, prof. ob-gyn, 1976—, chmn. dept. ob-gyn, 1976-86. Author articles in field. Served to lt. comdr. M.C., USNR, 1958-60. Named Tchr. of Yr., Mayo Grad. Sch. Medicine, 1973, 77, Alumnus of Yr., Boston U. Sch. Med., 1990. Mem. ACS, Am. Coll. Obstetricians and Gynecologists, Am. Gynecol. and Obstet. Soc., Am. Radium Soc., Soc. Gynecologic Oncologists, Assn. Profs. Ob-gyn., N.Am. Ob-gyn. Soc., Ctrl. Assn. Obstetricians and Gynecologists, Minn. Soc. Obstetricians and Gynecologists, Am. Coll. Obstetricians and Gynecologists (pres. 1989-90), Zumbro Valley Med. Soc. (exec. dir. 1996—). Home: 1750 11th Ave NE Rochester MN 55906-4215 Office: Mayo Clinic 200 1st St SW Rochester MN 55905-0001

MALKIN, STANLEY LEE, neurologist; b. Pitts., Nov. 11, 1942; s. Maurice and Bessie Beatrice (Serbin) M.; children: Justin Ross, Keith Richard. BA with honors, U. Pa., 1964; MD, U. Pitts., 1968; Intern, Montefiore Hosp., Pitts., 1968-69; resident in neurology Columbia-Presbyn. Med. Center, N.Y.C., 1969-72; chief neurology service Wright-Patterson AFB, Dayton, Ohio, 1972-74; practice medicine specializing in neurology, N.Y.C.; attending staff Mt. Sinai Hosp.; former dir. Neuro-Diagnostic Lab, Englewood; asst. clin. prof. neurology Mt. Sinai Sch. of Medicine; founder Bergen-Passaic Tomography Center, Fairlawn, N.J.; neurology cons. Regent Hosp.; med. dir. Pain Suppression Labs., Inc.; med. dir. Efficient Health Systems, Inc.-N.Y.C. Healthline; founder, med. dir., exec. v.p. Hosp. Diagnostic Equipment Corp., 1987—; pres. Cancer Treatment Holdings, Inc, 1993-95, dir. 1993-94, sr. med. dir. 1995—; founder Montvale Med. Imaging Assocs. (N.J.), N.Y. Med. Imaging, N.Y.C., Hosp. Diagnostic Equipment Corp. Co-mcpl. coord. Ft. Lee Citizens for McGovern, 1972; ptnr. Sall/Myers Med. Assocs., prin. 1995—; mem. Edgewater Rent Control Bd., 1978, Nat. Headache Found. Maj. M.C., USAF, 1972-74. Diplomate Am. Bd. Psychiatry and Neurology, Nat. Bd. Med. Examiners. Mem. Am. Acad. Neurology, Am. Assn. Electrodiagnostic Medicine, Am. Soc. Neuro-Imaging (charter), Am. Med. EEG Soc., Am. Assn. for Study of Headache, Nat. Headache Found., Internat. Headache Soc., N.Y. Acad. Scis., N.Y.U. Bellevue Psychiat. Soc. Office: 120 W 44th St Ste 701 New York NY 10036 also: 136 E 57th St Ste 600 New York NY 10022

MALKINSON, FREDERICK DAVID, dermatologist; b. Hartford, Conn., Feb. 26, 1924; s. John Walter and Rose (Volkenheim) M.; m. Una Zwick, June 15, 1979; children by previous marriage: Philip, Carol, John. Student, Loomis Inst., 1937-41; 3 yr. cert. cum laude, Harvard U., 1943, D.M.D., 1947, M.D., 1949. Intern Harvard-Beth Israel Hosp., Boston, 1949-50; resident in dermatology U. Chgo., 1950-54, from instr. to assoc. prof. dept. dermatology, 1954-68; prof. medicine and dermatology U. Ill., Chgo., 1968-71; chmn. dept. dermatology Rush Med. Coll. and Rush-Presbyn.-St. Luke's Med. Ctr., Chgo., 1971-92, Clark W. Finnerud, M.D. prof. dept. dermatology, 1981-95; trustee Sulzberger Inst. Dermatol. Comm. and Edn., 1976-96; pres. Sulzberger Inst. Dermatol. Communication and Edn., 1983-88, 93-96. Editor: Year Book of Dermatology, 1971-78; chief editor: AMA Archives of Dermatology, 1979-83; bd. editors, 1976-84, Jour. AMA, 1979-83; editorial cons. World Book Medical Encyclopedia, 1991—; contbr. articles and abstracts to profl. jours., chpts. to books. Active Evanston (Ill.) Libr. Bd., 1988-94, pres., 1993-94. With M.C. USN, 1950-52. Grantee U.S. Army, 1955-61, USPHS, 1962-73. Mem. AAAS, Am. Acad. Dermatology (v.p. 1987-89, dir. 1964-67), Am. Dermatol. Assn., Soc. Investigative Dermatology (v.p. 1978-79, dir. 1963-68), Am. Fedn. Clin. Rsch., Cen. Soc. Clin. Rsch., Radiation Rsch. Soc., Assn. Profs. of Dermatology (dir. 1982-85), Dermatology Found. (trustee 1980-93, pres. 1983-85), Nat. Coun. on Radiation Protection and Measurements (mem. com. on cutaneous radiobiology 1986-92), Chgo. Dermatol. Soc. (pres. 1964-65, Gold Medal award 1992), Chgo. Lit. Club.

MALLENBAUM, SIDNEY, neurologist; b. Milford, Conn., July 14, 1960; s. Victor Mallenbaum; m. Rita Hixson, June 15, 1986; children: Joshua John, Isaac Chaim. BSc, McGill U., Montreal, Que., Can., 1982; MD, U. N.C., 1986. Diplomate Am. Bd. Psychiatry and Neurology, Am. Bd. Electrodiagnostic Medicine. Intern in internal medicine Royal Victoria Hosp., Montreal, 1986-87; resident in neurology Montreal Neurol. Inst. and Montreal Neurol. Hosp., 1987-90, chief resident, 1989; active staff and cons. neurologist Virginia Beach (Va.) Gen. Hosp., 1990—; pvt. practice, Virginia Beach, 1990—; cons. neurologist Sentara Bayside Hosp., Virginia Beach, 1990—; prin. investigator Stroke Treatment with Ancrod Trial, Lubeluzole in Acute Ischemic Stroke Study, Thrombolytic Therapy in Acute Ischemic Stroke Trial; electrodiagnostic cons. Dynamic Engring. Corp., Madison, Wis., 1992—; lectr. Va. Pediat. Soc., Virginia Beach, 1993. Univ. scholar McGill U., 1978-79, faculty scholar, 1979-80. Fellow Am. Assn. Electrodiagnostic Medicine; mem. Am. Acad. Neurology, Virginia Beach Med. Soc. Office: Neurol Cons Va Beach Inc 1008 First Colonial Rd Ste 101 Virginia Beach VA 23454-3002

MALLERY, BERRELL, psychologist. BA in Psychology, CUNY-Hunter Coll., 1975; MS in Psychology, Yeshiva U., 1977, Specialist Cert., 1979, PhD in Psychology, 1980. Lic. psychologist, N.Y.; cert. sch. psychologist, N.Y., N.J. Intern N.Y.C. Evaluation and Placement Unit/Bd. Edn., 1975-76, St. Matthew Luth. Sch., N.Y.C., 1976-77; rsch. asst. Montefiore Hosp., 1977-78; intern Bronx (N.Y.) Devel. Svcs./Albert Einstein Coll. of Medicine, 1977-78; NIH internship fellow St. Luke's Hosp. Ctr., N.Y.C., 1978-79; staff psychologist Youth Devel. Clinic of Coll. Medicine and Dentistry of N.J., Newark, 1980-81; sch. psychologist Buckingham Sch., Bklyn., 1981; psychotherapist New Hope Guild Ctr., Bklyn., 1981-84; sr. staff psychologist S.I. (N.Y.) Mental Health Soc., 1982—; pvt. practice N.Y.C., 1983—; presenter workshops in field. Contbr. articles to profl. jours. Recipient NIMH fellowship and scholarship, 1976-77. Mem. APA, Ea. Psychol. Assn., Assn. Play Therapy, Coun. For Nat. Register Health Svcs. Providers in Psychology, N.Y. State Psychol. Assn. (mem. student affiliate steering com. 1976-77), N.Y. Acad. Scis. Address: 89 Bleecker St Apt 3F New York NY 10012-1526

MALLETTE, PHYLLIS SPENCER COOPER, medical/surgical nurse; b. Chestertown, Md., Nov. 18, 1944; d. Charles P. and Elma (Brown) Spencer; children: Winsor A. Cooper, III and Elma Cooper Henderson; m. Arthur E. Mallette, June 5, 1982. ASN, Rutgers U., 1965; BSN cum laude, Trenton State Coll., 1978. Cert. critical care, IV therapy, acute respiratory care, OSHA regulations, advanced coronary care, med. office mgmt., case mgmt., utilization rev.; RN, Md., N.J., Pa. Nurse delivery room St. Francis Med. Ctr., Trenton, N.J., 1971-73; nurse ICU Delaware Valley Med. Ctr., Langhorne, Pa., 1973-74; coord. nights Robert Wood Johnson U. Hosp., New Brunswick, N.J., 1974-75; occupational health RN Warner-Lambert/Parke-Davis Co., Morris Plains, N.J., 1977-79; sr. profl. rep. hosp., coord. sales tng. Merck Human Health Svcs. Divsn., Phila., 1979-89; co-coord. 400 trainee field force expansion Merck Sharp & Dohme, Denver, 1989; clin. nurse Johns Hopkins Hosp., Balt., 1989-90; office mgr. Arthur E. Mallette, M.D., Pikesville, Md., 1990-94; quality mgmt. specialist United Health Care, Inc., Balt., 1994—; med. cons. N.J. Pub. TV, Trenton, 1974. Mem. Sigma Theta Tau. Democrat. Methodist. Home: 10 Dodworth Ct Apt 303 Timonium MD 21093-2033 Office: United Health Care Inc 814 Light St Baltimore MD 21230-3945

MALLEY, WILLIAM JOSEPH, health care facility administrator; b. Youngstown, Ohio, Nov. 7, 1949; s. William Joseph and Ruth Ann (Kasony) M.; m. Marjorie Ann Chapon, Aug. 19, 1972; children: Maureen, William, Sean, Keith, Katelyn. AS, Community Coll. Allegheny County, Pitts., 1972; BS, Indiana U. Pa., 1975; MS, U. Pitts., 1981. Registered respiratory therapist; cert. pulmonary function technologist. Respiratory technician/therapist St. Elizabeth Hosp., Youngstown, Ohio, 1969-70; respiratory therapist Allegheny Gen. Hosp., Pitts., 1972-73; instr. sch. respiratory care Ind. U. Pa./West Penn Hosp., Pitts., 1973-78, dir. clin. edn. sch. respiratory care, 1978-81, program dir., 1981—; item writer, therapist, technician Nat. Bd. for Respiratory Care, 1978-83. Author: Clinical Blood Gases: Application and Noninvasive Alternatives, 1990. Mem. baptism com. St. Elizabeth Ch., Baldwin, Pa., 1977-87. Mem. Am. Assn. Repiratory Care, Pa. Soc. Repiratory Care (bd. dirs. 1982), Pa. Assn. for Respiratory Therapy Educators (pres. 1983-85), West Pa. Respiratory Mgrs. Assn. (v.p. 1983, chmn. edn. com. 1982-84, pres. 1995), Indiana U. Pa. Alumni Assn. (exec. bd. 1992-96, v.p. 1995-96), Phi Kappa Phi, Lambda Beta. Roman Catholic. Home: 254 Toura Dr Pittsburgh PA 15236-4509 Office: West Penn Hosp Sch Respiratory Care 4800 Friendship Ave Pittsburgh PA 15224-1722

MALLIN, SANFORD RICHARD, medical science educator; b. Milw., Jan. 12, 1933. BS, U. Wis., 1954, MD, 1957. Diplomate Am. Bd. Internal Medicine. Intern Mt. Sinai Hosp., Milw., 1957-58; resident in internal medicine Hahnemann Hosp. and Med. Coll., 1958-60; fellow in metabolic and endocrine rsch. Michael Reese Hosp., Chgo., 1960-62; instr. medicine Chgo. Med. Sch., 1961-62; clin. instr. medicine Marquette (Wis.) Sch. Medicine, 1962-68; asst. clin. prof. mediicne, then assoc. clin. prof. Med. Coll. Wis., Milw., 1968-81, clin. prof. medicine, 1981—; assoc. clin. prof. medicine U. Wis. Sch. Medicine, Madison, 1975-80, clin. prof. medicine, 1980—, preceptor, 1968-75. Contbr. numerous articles to profl. jours. Fellow ACP, Am. Coll. Endocrinology; mem. AMA, Am. Fedn. Clin. Rsch., Endocrine Soc. (clin. endocrinology initiatives com., postgrad. edn. com.), Am. Assn. Clin. Endocrinologists, Am. Diabetes Assn. (ctrl. coun. 1973-75, pres. 1974, bd. dirs. 1964-82, 85-90), Milw. Acad. Medicine (pres. 1976), Am. Soc. Internal Medicine (house of dels. 1995—), Wis. State Med. Soc., Med. Soc. Milw. County (pres. 1991), N.Y. Acad. Scis., Milw. Internists Club.

MALLOT, MICHAEL E., gastroenterologist; b. N.Y.C., Mar. 11, 1943; s. Sam and Ruth (Bernstein) M.; m. Anita Claire Sopian, Dec. 15, 1963 (div. Dec. 1990); children: Scot, Darren; m. Kathleen A. Rizzo, Apr. 22, 1995. BA, UCLA, 1964; MD, U. Calif., Irvine, 1968. Diplomate Am. Bd. Internal Medicine. Resident in internal medicine U. Calif., Orange, 1968-71, 73-75; pvt. practice L.A., 1975-92, Nacogdoches, Tex., 1993—. Maj. U.S. Army, 1971-73. Fellow Am. Coll. Gastroenterology; mem. AMA, ACP, Am. Soc. Gastrointestinal Endoscopy, Tex. Med. Assn., Alpha Omega Alpha. Office: Nacogdoches Gastroent PA 1225 N Mound St Nacogdoches TX 75961

MALLOW, ALISSA JANE, social worker; b. Bklyn., Oct. 8, 1959; d. Gerald Mallow and Marcia (Bunkin) Goldberg; m. Kenneth P. Humbert, Nov. 4, 1990. BA, SUNY, Stony Brook, 1981; MSW, Adelphi U., 1983, postgrad., 1994—. Social worker Assn. for the Advancement of The Blind and Retarded, Jamaica, N.Y., 1983-84, Syosset (N.Y.) Community Hosp., 1984-87; social work therapist North Shore U. Hosp., Manhasset, N.Y., 1987-90; program coord. North Shore U. Hosp., Glen Cove, N.Y., 1990-94; coord. outreach, edn. and tng. North Shore U. Hosp., Glen Cove, 1994—. Contbr. articles to profl. jours. Mem. NASW, Acad. Cert. Social Workers. Office: North Shore U Hosp Saint Andrews Lane Glen Cove NY 11542

MALLOY, BERNARD MATHIS, psychiatrist; b. Chgo., Sept. 2, 1928; s. John Cyril Malloy and Jennie (May) Mathis; m. Dorothy I. Davis, July 1, 1958 (div. 1976); children: John Davis, Bernard Jr., Elizabeth Grace; m. Patricia A. Davidge, Mar. 6, 1982. AB, Lambuth Coll., 1951; MD, Vanderbilt U., 1954. Diplomate Am. Bd. Psychiatry and Neurology. Intern Vanderbilt U. Hosp., Nashville, 1954-55, resident, 1955-56; resident Payne Whitney Clinic, N.Y.C., 1956-58; clerkship Nat. Hosp. for Neural Disabilities (Queens Sq.), London, 1958; chief psychiat. div. CIA, Washington, 1963-84; asst. clin. prof. Georgetown U. Med. Ctr., Washington, 1972—; staff Sibley Meml. Hosp., Washington. Sgt. U.S. Army, 1946-48. Fellow Am. Psychiat. Assn., So. Psychiat. Assn.; mem. AMA, Chevy Chase Club, Met. Club. Office: 3 Washington Cir NW Ste 403 Washington DC 20037-2356

MALM, RONALD L., physician; b. Cheyenne, Wyo., June 29, 1966; s. Kendrick E. and Linda K. (Conger) M. BS, U. Wyo., 1988; DO, U. Health Scis., 1992. Diplomate Am. Bd. Family Medicine. Intern Granview Hosp. and Med. Ctr., Dayton, Ohio, 1992-93; resident Smoky Hill Family Practice, Salina, Kans., 1993-95; physician A.L. Gruber & P.J. Schiel, M.D., P.C., Cheyenne, Wyo., 1995—. MEm. Wyo. Med. Soc., Laramie County Med. Soc., Am. Acad. Family Physicians, Wyo. Acad. Family Physicians, Soc. Tchrs. Family Medicine (Resident Tchrs. award 1995). Office: 5416 Education Dr Cheyenne WY 82009

MALMO, DAVID PAUL, substance abuse counselor; b. Saginaw, Mich., Sept. 23, 1948; s. Curtis G. and Gloria J. (Crandall) M.; m. Diane M. Ruszczyk, Apr. 15, 1972 (div. Mar. 1989); children: Adam J., Melissa A.; m. Janis K. Lemke, June 17, 1995. Student, Delta Coll., 1969; BS in Edn., Ctrl. Mich. U., 1971, postgrad., 1974. Cert. apprentice counselor, Mich. Tchr. Newaygo (Mich.) County Schs., 1973-77; coord. substance abuse prevention Life Counseling Svcs., Fremont, Mich., 1977-80; employment counselor Five CAP, Inc., Big Rapids, Mich., 1981-83, Mecosta Osceola Career Ctr., Big Rapids, Mich., 1984; ctr. dir. Human Aid, Inc., Reed City, Mich., 1985—. Bd. dirs. Osceola Cmty. Corrections, Reed City, 1986—, Mecosta Osceola Child Abuse and Neglect, Big Rapids, 1988-95; vice chairperson Osceola Children's Coun., Reed City, 1995—, Human Svc. Coord. Body, Reed City, 1990—; mem. team Crisis Response Team, Reed City, 1988—, Multidiscipline Team, Reed City, 1985—; mem. Future Planning Com., Reed City, 1995—, Substance Abuse Task Force, 1995—. Methodist. Home: 2149 Dagget Pierson MI 49339 Office: Human Aid Inc PO Box 143 834 S Chestnut Reed City MI 49677

MALMQUIST, CARL PHILLIP, psychiatrist; b. St. Paul, Mar. 10, 1934; s. Phillip C. and Lillian Viola (Kahler) M.; m. Arlyn Virginia Bodal (dec. 1984); children: Derek, Jay. BA summa cum laude, U. Minn., 1954, MD, 1958, MS in Philosophy of Sci., 1961. Diplomate Am. Bd. Psychiatry and Neurology, Am. Bd. Child Psychiatry, Am. Bd. Adult Psychiatry; cert. forensic psychiatry, added qualification in forensic psychiatry. Intern U. Minn., 1962-63, Columbia Med. Ctr., N.Y.C., 1963-64; assoc. prof. dept. psychiatry U. Mich., 1965-67; assoc. prof. Inst. Child Devel. U. Minn., Mpls., 1967-70, prof., dir. child and adolescent psychiatry, 1971-72, prof. criminal justice, 1972-80, prof. social psychiatry, dept. sociology, 1980—; cons. Hennepin County, Mpls., 1967—, Dist. Ct., 1969—; mem. commn. of mentally disabled ABA, 1985. Author: Adolescent Development, 1980, Homicide: Psychiatric Perspectives, 1996; mem. editl. bd. Psychiat. Anns., 1981; contbr. articles to profl. jours. Fellow Am. Psychiat. Assn. (mem. commn. on jud. action 1994—), Am. Coll. Psychiatrists, Am. Orthopsychiat. Assn., Am. Acad. Child Psychiatry, Am. Acad. Psychiatry and Law, Am. Coll. Forensic Psychiatry; mem. Group for Advancement Psychiatry. Episcopalian. Home: 5010 Bruce Ave Minneapolis MN 55424-1318 Office: U Minn 6600 France Ave S Ste 545 Minneapolis MN 55435-1804

MALNIG, LAWRENCE R., psychologist; b. N.Y.C., Oct. 17, 1916; s. Joseph E. and Rose (Rosa) M.; m. Laura Itteilag, Feb. 24, 1945; children: Anita, Julie. BA, CUNY, 1938; MA, Columbia U., 1940; PhD, NYU, 1959. Lic. psychologist, N.J. Interpreter Wall St. Bank, N.Y.C., 1940-45; instr. fgn. language Wagner Coll., N.Y.C., 1946-48; instr. French, Spanish and Italian St. Peter's Coll., Jersey City, N.J., 1948-52, dir. counseling ctr., 1952-92; ret., 1992; Pres., publisher Abbott Press, 1988—. Author: Peacocks on Parade, 1955, What Can I Do With A Major In...?, 1975, 2d edit., 1984; contbr. articles to profl. jours. Trustee Englewood (N.J.) Coll., 1950-52, Bd. of Edn., Ridgefield, N.J., 1965-70, Elizabeth Seton Coll., Yonkers, N.Y., 1971-88; environ. commn. Ridgefield Municipality, 1980-82, 92—. Mem. AACD, Am. Psychol. Assn., N.J. Psychol. Assn. Home and Office: 626 Abbott Ave Ridgefield NJ 07657-1706

MALO, TEMISTOCLES, obstetrician and gynecologist; b. Panama, Republic of Panama, Oct. 8, 1926; s. Aristoteles and Candelaria Norberta (Iglesias) M. Student, U. Panama, 1949; BS, Tulane U., 1950; MD, 1954. Diplomate in ob-gyn. Intern Santo Tomas Hosp., Panama, 1954-55; resident in ob-gyn. Gorgas Hosp., Ancon, Panama, 1955-56; med. officer Coco Solo Hosp., Cristoval, Panama, 1956-58, chief ob-gyn., 1961-79, med. dir., 1978-79; resident in ob-gyn. Jackson Meml. Hosp., Miami, Fla., 1958-61; med. officer ob-gyn. Gorgas Army Hosp., Ancon, 1980-93; pvt. practice Ancon, 1993—. Fellow ACOG (chmn. Panama sect. 1995), Alpha Omega Alpha. Home: 509 Parita Pl, Ancon Republic of Panama Office: Apartado 1432, Balboa Ancon Republic of Panama

MALOFF, BRUCE L., pharmacologist; b. Syracuse, N.Y., Aug. 26, 1953; s. Paul and Leah (Gilot) M.; m. Amy B. Miller, Aug. 14, 1976. BS, Syracuse U., 1973; PhD, SUNY, Albany, 1978. Instr. Sch. Medicine U. Rochester (N.Y.), 1978-81, sr. instr., 1981; rsch. pharmacologist DuPont Co., Wilmington, Del., 1981-86, sr. rsch. pharmacologist, 1987-88; dir. biochem. pharmacology Panlabs, Inc., Bothell, Wash., 1988-90, dir. pharmacology mktg. and sales, 1991-92; dir. regional divsn. East Coast Panlabs, Inc., Wilmington, Del., 1992-94; dir. corp. devel. USA Bio-Rsch. Labs., Ltd., Montreal, Que., Can., 1994-95, head mktg. and sales, 1995-96, v.p. bus. devel., 1996—. Fellow U. Rochester, 1978-81. Mem. Am. Soc. Pharmacology and Exptl. Therapeutics, Endocrine Soc. Office: Bio-Rsch Labs Ltd, 87 Senneville Rd, Montreal, PQ Canada H9X 3R3

MALONE, MICHAEL JOSEPH, neurology educator, retired; b. Portland, Maine, Apr. 28, 1930; s. Patrick J. and Margaret M. (Ridge) M.; m. Dorothy Helen Corcoran, July 4, 1956; 1 child, Michael P. AB, Boston Coll., 1951; MD, U. Georgetown, 1956. Cert. Am. Bd. Psychiatry and Neurology. Rsch. assoc. Harvard Med. Sch., Boston, 1963-65, clin. investigator, 1965-68; asst. prof. neurology Boston U. Med. Sch., Boston, 1968-70; prof. neurology George Washington U., Washington, 1970-75; chief child neurology Children's Hosp. Nat. Med. Ctr., Washington, 1970-75; prof. neurology and pediatrics Boston U. Med. Sch., 1975-85; prof. neurology Med. U. S.C., Charleston, 1985-96, prof. emeritus in neurology, 1996—; chief neurology svc. VA Med. Ctr., Charleston, 1985—; cons. pediatric neurology USAH Walter Reed, Washington, 1970-80, USNH Bethesda (Md.), 1970-80; cons. NIH Clin. Ctr., Bethesda, 1970-80. Contbr. articles to profl. jours., 1963—. Mem. adv. coms. S.C. Assn. on Aging, Columbia, 1986—; bd. dirs. Area Adminstrn. Agy. Trident, Charleston, 1987—; chmn. med. adv. com., bd. dirs. Charles Webb Easter Seal Ctr., Charleston, 1987—. Capt. U.S. Army, 1957-59. Recipient clin. investigatorship Rsch. Svc. Va., 1965-68; rsch. grantee NIH, 1968—, Am. Heart Assn., 1968—, Rsch. Svc. Va., 1968—. Democrat. Roman Catholic. Home: 27 Johnson Rd Charleston SC 29407-7514 Office: Med Univ SC Dept Neurology 171 Ashley Ave Charleston SC 29425-0001

MALONE, SUE ANDERSON, information systems specialist, educator; b. Chattanooga, Apr. 18, 1930; d. Thomas E. and Camie M. (Dean) Anderson; m. (dec.); children: Mick Z., Tacea C., Kerry P. BS in Health Care Mgmt., Fla. Internat. U., 1977, BS in Med. Record Admin., 1979; MPA, U. Mo., Kansas City, 1981. Registered record adminstr. Dir. med. record dept. King's Daughters Hosp., Madison, Ind., 1967-70; dir. med. record svcs. Gwinnett County Hosp. Authority, Lawrenceville, Ga., 1970-72, Imperial Point Med. Ctr., Ft. Lauderdale, Fla., 1972-79; assoc. prof. health info. mgmt. edn. U. Kans. Med. Ctr., Kansas City, 1979—, chmn. dept., 1981—; cons. Bottomley & Assocs., Duluth, Ga., 1987—; critical reviewer W.B. Saunders Co., 1988; cons. numerous health care facilities; speaker in field. Contbr. articles to profl. jours. Vol. Children's Miracle Network Telephon, 1987-88. Recipient Disting. Teaching award U. Kans. Amoco Found., 1984. Mem. NAFE, Am. Health Info. Mgmt. Assn., Kans. Health Info. Mgmt. Assn. (chmn. continuing edn.-program chmn.), Kansas City Area Health Info. Mgmt. Assn., Am. Bus. Women's Assn. (v.p. Mo.-Kans. Star chpt. 1988-89, Woman of Yr. 1989). Baptist. Office: U Kans Med Ctr 39th And Rainbow Kansas City KS 66160

MALONE, WINFRED FRANCIS, health scientist; b. Revere, Mass., Feb. 10, 1935; s. Winfred and Margurite (Meehan) M.; m. Eleanor Malone, Aug. 1974. BS, U. Mass., 1957, MS, 1961; MS, Rutgers U., 1963; PhD, U. Mich., 1970. Health scientist Nat. Cancer Inst., Bethesda, Md., 1970-81, chief chemoprevention br., 1981-95, acting assoc. dir., 1991-93; chief ACRES Nat. Cancer Inst., 1995—. Contbr. articles on drug devel. scis. to profl. jours. Mem. AAAS, Am. Coll. Toxicology, N.Y. Acad. Scis., Drug Info. Assn. Home: 3209 Wake Dr Kensington MD 20895-3216 Office: Nat Cancer Inst EPN # 201 Bethesda MD 20892

MALONEY, ANITA L., speech and language pathologist; b. Boston, Jan. 20, 1961; d. John and Anita J. (Martignetti) M. BS in Communication Disorders and Psychology, Worcester (Mass.) State Coll., 1983; MS in Communication Disorders, Emerson Coll., 1985. Speech-lang. pathologist Franklin Med. Ctr., Greenfield, Mass., 1985-87, Morton Hosp., Taunton, Mass., 1987-89, Bradley Hosp., East Providence, R.I., 1989-91, Lang. Cognitive Devel. Ctr., Jamaica Plain, Mass., 1991-94, Cambridge/Somerville Early Intervention, 1994—; pvt. practice speech lang. pathologist specializing in children with Autism, 1990—. Fellow Mass. Speech, Hearing and Lang. Assn. Home: 27 Wedgewood St Quincy MA 02171-1028

MALONEY, DIANE MARIE, legal nurse consultant; b. Aug. 15, 1951; d. John J. and Ruthe E. (Fournier) Perron; m. Patrick J. Maloney, Apr. 26, 1975; children: Melissa, Sheamus. Grad., Miller Hosp. Sch. Nursing, St. Paul, 1970; degree, Inver Hills Community Coll., Inver Grove Heights, Minn., 1988, cert. in paralegal/medical studies, 1989. Orthopedic specialist St. Luke's Hosp., St. Paul; head nurse Otolaryngology Profl. Assocs., St. Paul; charge nurse Southview Health Ctr., West St. Paul, Minn.; legal nurse cons. Milavetz and Assocs., Bloomington, Minn.; with Milavetz, Gallop & Milavetz, Edina, Minn. Mem. NAACOG, Am. Assn. Legal Nurse Cons., Minn. Assn. Legal Nurse Cons. (steering com.), Interstitial Cystits Assn.

MALONEY, FRANCIS PATRICK, physiatrist, educator; b. Pitts., Mar. 4, 1936; s. Francis Barrington and Esther Elizabeth (Kuhn) M.; m. Kathryn Brassell Anderson, June 25, 1960 (dec. June 6, 1987); children: Timothy J., Kevin P., J. Christopher; m. Billie Barbara Galloway, Feb. 14, 1990. BA, St. Vincent Coll., 1958; MD, U. Pitts., 1962; MPH, Johns Hopkins U., 1966. Diplomate Am. Bd. Phys. Medicine and Rehab., Am. Bd. Preventive Medicine, Am. Bd. Med. Mgmt. Intern St. Francis Hosp., Pitts., 1962-63; resident gen. preventive medicine Johns Hopkins U. Sch. of Hygiene & Pub. Health, Balt., 1965-67; fellow medicine, med. genetics Johns Hopkins U. Sch. of Medicine, Balt., 1966-68; resident phys. medicine and rehab. U. Minn., Mpls., 1968-70; staff physician Sister Kenny Inst., Mpls., 1970-72; asst. clin. prof. U. Minn., Mpls., 1970-72; asst. prof. phys. medicine and rehab., assoc. prof. U. Colo., Denver, 1972-78, 78-84; prof. head div. of rehab. medicine U. Ark., Little Rock, 1984-91, prof., chmn. dept. phys. medicine and rehab., 1991—; med. dir. Bapt. Rehab. Inst., Little Rock, 1985—; chief rehab. medicine svc. VA Med. Ctr., Little Rock, 1984—. Editor: Interdisciplinary Rehabilitation of Multiple Sclerosis and Neuromuscular Disease, 1984; editor, author: Physical Medicine & Rehabilitation State of the Art Reviews, 1987, Primer on Management, 1987, Rehabilitation of Aging, 1989, Management for Rehabilitation Medicine II, 1993; alt. editor: Archives of Physical Medicine and Rehabilitation, 1989-93. Mem. exec. bd. Greater No. Colo. Chpt. of Muscular Dystrophy Assn. of Am., 1972-82; spl. edn. adv. com. Cherry Creek Sch. Dist., Denver, 1975, vice chmn., 1976, chmn., 1977; med. advisor Denver Commn. on Disabled and Coun. on Aging, Denver, 1980-82, Denver Commn. on Human Svcs., 1982-84; external examiner King Saud U. Med. Sch., Saudi Arabia, 1983; med. adv. bd. Ark. Multiple Sclerosis Soc., Little Rock, 1985-88; chmn. chmn's. coun. Assn. Acad. Physiatrists, Indpls., 1992-94. Fellow Am. Acad. Phys. and Rehab.; mem. AMA, Am. Congress of Rehab. Medicine, Am. Acad. Cerebral Palsy, Am. Pub. Health Assn., Am. Bd. Physical Medicine and Rehbilitation (dir. 1988—), Soc. for Exptl. Biology and Medicine, Assn. Acad. Physiatrists, Ark. Med. Soc., Pulaski County Med. Soc., Soc. for Neuroscis. Office: U Ark Med Scis 4301 W Markham Slot #602 Little Rock AR 72205

MALONEY, MILFORD CHARLES, retired internal medicine educator; b. Buffalo, Mar. 15, 1927; s. John Angelus Maloney and Winifred Hill; m. Dione Ethyl Sheppard. BS, Canisius Coll., 1947, postgrad., 1947-49; MD, U. Buffalo, 1953. Diplomate Am. Bd. Internal Medicine. Rsch. chemist Buffalo Electrochem. Co., 1947-49; intership Mercy Hosp./Georgetown U., 1953-54; med. residency Buffalo VA Hosp., 1954-56; cardiology fellow Buffalo Gen. Hosp., 1956-57; chmn. dept. medicine Mercy Hosp., 1969-94; program dir., internal medicine residency Mercy Hosp., Buffalo, 1972-89; with steering com. Assn. Program Dirs. in Internal Medicine, 1976, coun. mem., 1977-80; clin. prof. medicine SUNY, Buffalo, 1981-94; trustee Am. Soc. Internal Medicine, 1984-90; edn. leader med. seminar Am. Soc. Internal Medicine, Austria, Switzerland, France, 1987, Argentina, Brazil, Paraguay, 1988; bd. dirs. Internal Medicine Ctr. for Advancement and Rsch. Edn.; pres. Heart Assn. Western N.Y., Buffalo, 1969; sr. cancer rsch. physician Roswell Park Meml. Cancer Inst., 1959-62; mem. internal medicine liaison com. N.Y. State, 1980-90. Editor (newsletter) N.Y. State Soc. Internal Medicine, 1972-78. bd. dirs. Health Systems Agy. Western N.Y., Buffalo, 1981; exec. com., bd. dirs. Blue Cross Western N.Y., Buffalo, 1987; bd. regents Canisius Coll., Buffalo, 1987—; mem. pres. assocs. SUNY, Buffalo. Capt. M.C., U.S. Army, 1957-59. Recipient Merit award N.Y. State Soc. Internal Medicine, 1980, Man of Yr. award Heart Assn. Western N.Y., 1982, Ann. Honoree award Trocai Coll., 1986, Disting. Alumni award Canisius Coll., 1991, Berkson Excellence award in Tchg. and Art of Medicine, SUNY at Buffalo, 1992, Outstanding Med. Tchg. Attending award Mercy Hosp./SUNY Med. Residents, 1994; named to Sports Hall of Fame, Canisius Coll., 1978. Fellow ACP (Upstate Physician Recognition award 1989), Am. Coll. Cardiology; mem. AMA (SUNY rep. 1986-94, rep. to sect. med. schs. at ann. meetings 1984-94, chmn. sect. on internal medicine 1990-91), Am. Soc. Internal Medicine (bd. dirs. internal medicine purchasing group, trustee 1984-90, pres. 1990-91, chmn. long range planning com., rep. to Federated Coun. on Internal Medicine 1990-91, rep. to AMA nat. practice parameters and guidelines com. 1989-91), N.Y. State Soc. Internal Medicine (pres.), Alumni Assn. SUNY (pres. 1975), Med. Soc. County Erie (pres. 1969), Va. Soc. Internal Medicine (hon.). Home: 116 Cove Point Ln Williamsburg VA 23185-8613

MALONEY, ROBERT KELLER, ophthalmologist, medical educator. AB in Mathematics summa cum laude, Harvard U., 1979; MA in Philosophy, Politics and Econs., Oxford (Eng.) U., 1981; MD, U. Calif., San Francisco, 1985. Diplomate Am. Bd. Ophthalmology. Rsch fellow dept. physiology Cambridge (Eng.) U., 1985; intern U. Calif., L.A., 1985-86; resident Wilmer Ophthalmol. Inst. Johns Hopkins Hosp., Balt., 1986-89; head fellow cornea and refractive surgery Emory U., Dept. Ophthalmology, Atlanta, 1989-91; asst. prof. ophthalmology UCLA Sch. Medicine, Jules Stein Eye Inst., 1991—; cons. Premier Laser Systems, for devel. of Erbium-YAG sys. for corneal refractive surgery. Contbr. numerous articles to profl. jours.; presenter and spkr. in field; assoc. editor (N.Am.) Jour. Refractive and Corneal Surgery, 1991-95; internat. editl. bd. European Jour. Implant and Refractive Surgery, 1995; reviewer Am. Jour. Ophthalmology, Ophthalmology, Archives of Ophthalmology, Jour. Cataract and Refractive Surgery, Ophthalmic Surgery and Lasers. Rhodes scholar, 1979, Heed Found. fellow, 1989-90, Heed/Knapp fellow, 1990-91, John Harvard scholar, 1978; recipient Detur and Edward Whitaker prizes, Harvard U., Rsch. to Prevent Blindness Career Devel. award, 1992. Mem. Am. Acad. Ophthalmology (long-range planning com. 1989-92, quality of care com. 1987-91, retina preferred practice pattern subcom., refractive errors preferred practice pattern subcom.; chmn. ann. meeting program com. for young ophthalmologists, 1990-92; adv. group to ad hoc com. on orgnl. design 1991, young ophthalmologists' com. 1992-94; Honor award 1993), Assn. Rsch. in Vision and Ophthalmology, Internat. Soc. Refractive Surgery, Calif. Assn. Ophthalmology, Max Fine Corneal Soc., Phi Beta Kappa. Office: UCLA Sch Medicine Jules Stein Eye Inst 100 Stein Plaza Los Angeles CA 90024-7003

MALOOF, JANE, radiologist; b. Sydney, NSW, Australia, Jan. 30, 1968; came to U.S., 1993; d. Clement Joseph and Rabina Maloof; m. Richard M. Rashid, Apr. 25, 1993. MBBS, Sydney U., 1990. Intern, resident Royal Prince Alfred Hosp., Sydney, 1990-91; radiology registrar Repatration Hosp. Concord, Sydney, 1992-93; assoc. radiology rsch. W.Va. U., Morgantown, 1993-94, resident radiology, 1994—. Contbr. articles to profl. jours. Mem. AMA, Am. Assn. Women Radiologists, Radiol. Soc. N.Am. (resident rsch. program 1995), Roentgen Ray Soc. Office: West Virginia Univ Radiology Dept HSS PO Box 9235 Morgantown WV 26506

MALOUF, JOSEPH F., cardiologist; b. Beirut, Sept. 13, 1949; s. Fredrick and Nida (Makdisi) M.; m. Nesrene Tibi, Dec. 20, 1976; children: Samer Fredrick, Nadine. BS, Am. Univ. Beirut, 1971, MD, 1975. Diplomate Am. Bd. Internal Medicine, Am. Bd. Cardiovasc. Diseases. Fellow in cardiology Columbia/St. Luke's Hosp., N.Y.C., 1977-79, Mt. Sinai Hosp., N.Y.C., 1979-80; from asst. prof. to assoc. prof. internal medicine Am. Univ. Beirut Sch. Medicine, 1980-87; head div. cardiology King Fahad Nat. Guard Hosp., Riyadh, Saudi Arabia, 1987-92; cons. cardiovasc. diseases Mayo Clinic-Jacksonville, Fla., 1992—; dir. echocardiography lab. Am. U. Beirut, 1980-87; from asst. prof. to assoc. prof. Mayo Med. Sch., Rochester, Minn., 1992—. Mem. Internat. Soc. Cardiovasc. Ultrasound (bd. dirs. 1992—, counsel 1992—). Home: 13152 Biggin Church Rd S Jacksonville FL 32224 Office: Mayo Clinic 4500 San Pablo Rd Jacksonville FL 32224

MALOUF, PETER JOHN, dermatology resident; b. Hereford, Tex., Mar. 3, 1969; s. Hanna and Linda (Masso) M. BS in Biology, S.W. Tex. State U.; DO, U. Noth Tex. Diplomate Nat. Bd. Med. Examiners. Owner, operator Fabric Store, Friona, Tex. Contbr. articles to profl. jours. Mem. Habitat for Humanity, Mentor Program. Roman Catholic. Home: 4558 Dove Tree Ct Fort Worth TX 76137

MALT, RONALD A., surgeon, educator; b. Pitts., 1931; married, 3 children. A.B., Washington U., 1951; M.D., Harvard U., 1955. Diplomate Am. Bd. Surgery, Am. Bd. Thoracic Surgery, Am. Bd. Vascular Surgery. Resident Mass. Gen. Hosp., Boston, 1955-56, 58-62, chief gastrointestinal surg. sect., 1972—; from asst. in surgery to assoc. prof. surgery Harvard U. Med. Sch., Boston, 1962-74, prof., 1975—. Co-author: Regeneration of Liver and Kidney, 1972. Editor: Colonic Carcinogenesis, 1983, Complex Operations, 1984, Surgical Techniques Illustrated, 1985, The Practice of Surgery, 1993, Oxford Textbook of Surgery, 1994 co-editor: Micromolecular Synthesis and Growth, 1967; assoc. editor New Eng. Jour. Medicine, Boston, 1966-93. Contbr. articles to profl. jours. Served to lt. comdr. USNR, 1956-62. Mem. Am. Surg. Assn., Am. Soc. Clin. Investigation, Am. Physiol. Soc., Internat. Cardiovascular Surgery Soc., Soc. Surg. Oncology, Societe Internat. Chirurgie, Somerset Club, St. Botolph Club, Thursday Evening Club, Clug of Odd Vols. Republican. Episcopalian. Achievements include first replantation of a severed limb, 1962; development of replantation surgery. Office: Mass Gen Hosp Boston MA 02114-2620

MALTSBERGER, JOHN TERRY, psychiatrist; b. Cotulla, Tex., Dec. 18, 1933; s. John Terry and Ruth (Rogers) M.; children: Joshua, Eliza, Noah. AB, Princeton U., 1955; MD, Harvard U., 1959. Diplomate Am. Bd. Psychiatry and Neurology. Intern Pa. Hosp., Phila., 1960; resident in child and adult psychiatry Mass. Mental Health Ctr., Boston, 1960-65, assoc. dir., 1967-69; staff psychiatrist Harvard U. Health Svcs., Cambridge, Mass., 1969-75; clin. dir. psychiatry Jamaica Plain VA Med. Ctr., Boston, 1977-80; staff psychiatrist Mass. Gen. Hosp., Boston, 1979—; sr. psychiatrist Cambridge (Mass.) Hosp., 1989-91; assoc. psychiatrist McLean Hosp., Belmont, Mass., 1991—; psychoanalytic tng. Psychoanalytic Inst., Boston, 1970, instr. in psychiatry Harvard Med. Sch., Boston, 1967-76, lectr. on psychiatry, 1980—; assoc. clin. prof. Tufts U. Med. Sch., Boston, 1976-81; bd. dirs. Am. Suicide Found., N.Y.C., 1989; editorial bd. Suicide and Life Threatening Behavior Jour., 1989; lectr. in field. Author: Suicide Risk, 1986, The Church of the Advent, First Years, 1985; contbr. articles to profl. jours. Fellow Am. Psychiat. Assn.; mem. Mass. Med. Soc., Boston Psychoanalytic Soc. and Inst. (chmn. faculty 1984-87), Am. Assn. Suicidology, Somerset Club. Office: McLean Hosp 39 Fuller St Brookline MA 02146

MALTZ, ROBERT, surgeon; b. Cin., July 21, 1935; s. William and Sarah (Goldberg) M.; m. Sylvia Moskowitz, Aug. 24, 1958; children: Mark Edward, Deborah Lynn, Steven Alan, David Stuart. BS in Zoology, U. Cin., 1958, MD, 1962. Diplomate Am. Bd. Otolaryngology, 1970. Intern Cin. Gen. Hosp., 1962-63; resident Barnes Hosp., St. Louis, 1965-69; asst. prof. surgery Stanford U. Med. Ctr., Palo Alto, Calif., 1969-71; asst. prof. otolaryngology U. Cin. Med. Ctr., 1971-75, assoc. prof. otolaryngology, 1975—; dir. dept. otolaryngology Jewish Hosp., Cin., 1992—; chief, div. head and neck surgery, dept. otolaryngology and maxillofacial surgery U. Cin. Med. Ctr., 1972-76; bd. dirs. Cancer Control Council, U. Cin. Med. Cntr.; cons. Bur. Crippled Children's Svcs., State of Ohio; mem. med. records com. Cin. Gen. Hosp., utilization rev. com., tissue com., Holmes Hosp., Med. Audit Com., Tissue Com., Cin. Gen. Hosp., med. records com. Jewish Hosp.; on staff VA Hosp., Cin., Children's Hosp. Med. Ctr., Holmes Hosp., Bethesda Hosp., Cin., Christ Hosp., Shriners Burn Inst., Cin., Our Lady of Mercy Hosp.; del. to numerous profl. confs.; mem. health affairs adv. com. Cmty. Mut. Ins. Co.; mem. mng. bd. PIE Mut. Ins. Co.; bd. dirs. UCATS, 1995—; instr. short term courses in field. Contbr. articles to profl. jours. Bd. dirs. Jewish Community Rels. Coun.; mem. faculty adv. com. U. Cinn., mem. med. alumni exec. coun. Capt. USAF, 1963-65, PTO. USPHS fellow, 1968-69; grantee Eli Lilly Co. grantee, 1971-76, Burroughs Wellcome Co., 1972. Fellow ACS, Am. Acad. Facial and Reconstructive Surgery (edn. com. 1972, future plans com. 1973-75, sci. program com., budget and fin. com. 1975, chmn. credentials com., no. sect. 1980-85), Royal Soc. Health, Internat. Cosmetic Surgeons, Am. Acad. Cosmetic Surgeons, Am. Assn. Cosmetic Surgeons (sec.-treas. 1976-81); mem. Am. Acad. Otolaryngology and Head and Neck Surgery, Am. Coun. Otolaryngology, Soc. Univ. Otolaryngologists, Pan-Am. Assn. Oto-Rhino-Laryngology and Broncho-Esophagology, Ohio State Med. Assn., Cin. Acad. Medicine (chmn. pub. rels. com. 1980, trustee 1992-95, legis. com. 1985—, treas. 1993-95, chmn. commn. com. 1994—, pres. 1996, editl. bd. 1994—, chmn. specialty soc. com. 1995), U. Cin. Alumni Assn. (bd. govs., sec. 1994, fin. v.p. 1995, 1st v.p. 1996), Cin. Ear, Nose and Throat Soc., Ulex Club, Metro Club, Losantiville Country Club, Queen City Racquet Club, Omicron Delta Kappa, Sigma Sigma, Sigma Alpha Mu. Home: 2601 Willowbrook Dr Cincinnati OH 45237-3725 Office: 10496 Montgomery Rd Cincinnati OH 45242-5220

MALTZMAN, IRVING MYRON, psychology educator; b. Bklyn., May 9, 1924; s. Israel and Lillian (Mass) M.; m. Diane Seiden, Aug. 21, 1949; children—Sara, Kenneth, Ilaine. B.A., N.Y. U., 1946; Ph.D., State U. Iowa, 1949. Mem. faculty UCLA, 1949—, assoc. prof., 1957-60, prof. psychology, 1961—, chmn. dept., 1970-77. Co-author: Handbook of Contemporary Soviet Psychology, 1969. Fellow APA, AAAS; mem. Phi Beta Kappa, Sigma Xi. Home: 11260-22B Overland Ave Culver City CA 90230-5559

MALUF, NOBLE SUYDAM RUSTUM, retired surgeon; b. Cairo, Nov. 30, 1913; came to U.S., 1933; s. Maluf Bey and Eugé Waked. BSc, Am. U.,

Cairo, 1933; MSc, PhD, Cornell U., 1936; MD, Harvard U., 1946; ChM, U. Liverpool, Eng., 1967. Diplomate Am. Bd. Surgery, Am. Bd. Urology. Clin. asst. urology Baylor U. Coll. Med., 1953-55; chief urology VA Hosp., Houston, 1953-55; staff urologist various Kaiser Found. Hosps., Calif., 1956-59; prosecutor in gross anatomy U. Minn. Sch. Medicine, 1960-61; registrar gen. surgery Eng., 1961-62; staff gen. surgeon AUS, 1964-65; chief urology World Med. Found., Laguna Hills, Calif., 1969-70; pvt. surg. practice L.A., 1971-72; dir. surg. residency tng. Appalachian Regional Gen. Hosp., Beckley, W.Va., 1973-74; assoc. dir. surg. residency tng. Kern County Gen. Hosp., Bakersfield, Calif., 1974-75; asst. dir. surg. residency tng. Huron Road Hosp., Cleve., 1976; pvt. practice, rsch. Cleve., 1977-80; pvt. practice, gen. surgery and urology Blythe, Calif., 1980-82; ret., 1985; del. Internat. Vascular Conf., London, 1981. Contbr. numerous articles to profl. jours. Capt. AUS, 1948-50, U.S. and Austria. Sterling fellow Yale U., New Haven, 1936-37, Hon. fellow 1937-39, Johnston Scholar Johns Hopkins U., Balt., 1939-40. Fellow Royal Coll. Surgeons (Can.), Royal Coll. Surgeons (Glasgow); mem. Am. Physiol. Assn., Am. Assn. Anatomists. Home: 12500 Edgewater Dr Lakewood OH 44107

MALVEAUX, FLOYD J., academic dean. Dean Howard U. Med. Sch., Washington. Office: Howard U Med Sch 520 W St NW Washington DC 20059*

MANALO, PACITA BARBAZA, physician, pathology educator; b. Manila, Philippines, May 17, 1932; d. Carlos and Magalena (Barbaza) M.; m. Hector C. De Los Santos, Aug. 5, 1982. A.A., U. Santo Tomas, Manila, 1950; M.D., U. Santo Tomas, Manila, 1955; M.S. in Pathology, Northwestern U., Chgo., 1963. Diplomate Am. Bd. Pathology. Rotating intern General Rose Meml. Hosp., Univ. Colo., Denver, 1955-56; resident in pathology St. Joseph's Hosp., Denver, 1956-59; resident clin. pathology Evanston (Ill.) Hosp. and Northwestern Univ., 1959-60, Postdoctoral fellow in pathology, 1960-61; pathologist anatomic surg. pathology, cytopathology VA Med Ctr., Reno, Nev., 1975-83, chief anatomic pathology service, 1983—; attending pathology Evanston Hosp., Ill., 1961-75, dir. cytology, cytogenetics, 1961-75, dir. Blood Bank, 1967-75, dir. Sch. Med. Tech., 1970-75, instr. pathology residency tng. program in anatomical and clin. pathology, 1961-75; mem. staff Washoe Med. Ctr., St. Mary's Hosp., Reno. Instr. pathology Northwestern Univ. Med. Sch., Chgo., 1960-67, asst. prof. pathology, 1967-74, assoc. prof. pathlogy, 1974-75; vis. prof. pathology Karolinska Inst. and Huddinge Hosp., Sweden, 1974; assoc. prof. pathology U. Nev. Sch. Medicine, Reno, 1975—, acting chmn. dept. lab. medicine and pathology, 1982-84, med. dir. med. tech. program, 1980-84. Contbr. numerous articles to various publs. Mem. blood donor recruitment program Northsuburban Blood Center, Northbrook, Ill., 1971-75, mem. med. adv. bd., 1971-75; mem. commn. allied health fields Washoe County Med. Soc., 1979-80; mem. clin. com. No. Nev. Cancer Council, 1977-81; mem. med. adv. com. Reno Planned Parenthood No. Nev., Reno, 1981-87; chmn. advance gifts com., med. dir. Easter Seal Treatment Ctr., Sparks, Nev., 1976-79, 1979-80; bd. dirs. Easter Seal Soc. Crippled Children Nev., Sparks, 1976-79; chmn., coordinator tumor bd., cancer bd. VA Med. Ctr., 1978—; mem. med. students admissions com. U. Nevada, Sch. Medicine, Reno, 1975—; bd. dirs. Nev. Easter Seal Soc., Reno, 1976-79. Research grantee Chgo. and Ill. Heart Assn., 1964-72, G. D. Searle & Co., Chgo., 1968-69, Eli Lilly Co., Indpls., 1969-71, Reno Cancer Center, 1980-81. Republican. Roman Catholic. Home: 3455 San Mateo Ave Reno NV 89509-5048 Office: VA Med Ctr 1000 Locust St Reno NV 89520-0102 also: U Nev Sch Medicine Manville Bldg Reno NV 89557

MANART, FRANK DAVID, cardiovascular surgeon; b. L.A., Sept. 19, 1947; s. Frank and Olga (Gavic) M.; m. Katherine Ann Nuttall, June 2, 1979; children: Andrew Scott, Katherine Jane. BA magna cum laude, U. So. Calif., 1969; MD, George Washington U., 1974. Diplomate Am. Bd. Surgery, Am. Bd. Thoracic Surgery. Resident in gen. surgery U. Colo. Health Scis. Ctr., Denver, 1974-79, resident in cardiovascular surgery, 1979-81; ptnr., cardiovascular surgeon Cardiovascular Inst., Mountain View, Calif., 1982-84, Rainer-Sadler Assocs., Denver, 1984-87, Denver Cardiac Surgery, 1987—; assoc. clin. prof. surgery U. Colo. Health Scis. Ctr. Contbr. chpts. to books, articles to profl. jours. Fellow ACS, Am. Coll. Cardiology, Am. Coll. Chest Physicians; mem. Denver Acad. Surgery. Democrat. Lutheran. Office: Denver Cardiac Surgery 2005 Franklin St I #700 Denver CO 80205

MANASSE, GABRIEL OTTO, psychiatrist; b. Durham, N.C., Feb. 10, 1942; s. Ernst Moritz and Marianna (Bernhard) M.; m. Judy Wikler, June 4, 1964 (div. 1971); 1 child, Katherine Elinor Goldstein; m. Patricia Catherine Arthur, Dec. 11, 1971; children: Jeffrey Lawrence, Emily Marie. Student, U. N.C., 1960-62; BA, U. Mich., 1964; MD, Temple U., Phila., 1969. Diplomate Am. Bd. Psychiatry and Neurology. Intern USPHS Hosp., San Francisco, 1969-70; gen. med. officer in psychiatry USPHS Hosp., 1970-72; resident in psychiatry UCLA, 1972-75, Tavistock Clinic, London, 1974-75; staff psychiatrist Brentwood VA Med. Ctr., L.A., 1975-79; adminstrv. scholar VA, Washington, 1979-81; chief psychiatry svc. Tucson VA Med. Ctr., 1981-88; assoc. dep. dir. strategic planning Vets Health Svc. & Rsch. Adminstrn., Dept. Vets Affairs, Washington, 1988-92; spl. asst. for clin. strategic planning Vets. Health Adminstn., Dept. Vets. Affairs, Washington, 1992-93; acting dep. assoc. dep. chief med. dir. hosp. based svcs. Vets. Health Adminstrn., Dept. Vets. Affairs, Washington, 1993-96, chief cons. acute care hosp. based svcs., 1996—; asst. clin. prof. dept. psychiatry UCLA, 1976-79; clin. asst. prof. georgetown U., 1980-81; assoc. clin. prof. psychiatry U. Ariz., 1981-88; clin. asst. prof. Howard U., 1989—; mem. profl. staff Commn. on Future Structure of Vets. Health Care, 1990-92. Contbr. articles to profl. jours. With USPHS, 1969-72. Fellow Am. Psychiat. Assn.; mem. A.K. Rice Inst. (pres. Washington-Balt. Ctr. 1991-94). Home: 11018 Stillwater Ave Kensington MD 20895-1101 Office: Dept VA 810 Vermont Ave NW Washington DC 20420-0001

MANCALL, ELLIOTT LEE, neurologist, educator; b. Hartford, Conn., July 31, 1927; s. Nicholas and Bess Tuch M.; m. Jacqueline Sue Cooper, Dec. 27, 1953; children: Andrew Cooper, Peter Cooper. BS, Trinity Coll., Hartford, 1948; MD, U. Pa., 1952. Diplomate Am. Bd. Psychiatry and Neurology (dir. 1983-91, dir. emeritus, 1991—). Intern Hartford Hosp., 1952-54; clk. in neurology Nat. Hosp. Nervous Disease, London, 1954-55; asst. resident neurology Neurol. Inst. N.Y., 1955-56; resident neuropathology Mass. Gen. Hosp., 1956-57, also clin. and research fellow, 1957-58; teaching fellow neuropathology Harvard Med. Sch., 1956-57; asst. prof. neurology Jefferson Med. Coll., 1958-64, asso. prof., 1964-65; prof. medicine Hahnemann Med. Coll. and Hosp., 1965-76, prof. neurology, chmn. dept., 1976-93; prof. neurology Jefferson Med. Coll., Phila., 1995—, Med. Coll. Pa.-Hahnemann U., 1993-95; dir. Hahnemann U. ALS Clinic; chmn. bd. dirs. Phila. Profl. Standards Rev. Orgn., 1981-84; del. Am. Bd. Med. Specialties, 1984—. Author: (with others) The Human Cerebellum: A Topographical Atlas, 1961, (with B.J. Alpers) Clinical Neurology, 1971, Essentials of the Neurological Examination, 1971, 81; contbr. numerous articles to profl. jours. Served with USN, 1945-47. Recipient Christian R. and Mary F. Lindback award, 1969; Oliver Meml. prize ophthalmology U. Pa., 1952. Fellow Am. Acad. Neurology (alt. del. to AMA 1982-86, gen. editor CONTINUUM 1991—); mem. Am. Neurol. Assn., Am. Assn. Neuropathology, Assn. Rsch. in Nervous and Mental Diseases, Soc. Neurosci., AAUP, Pa. Med. Peer Rev. Orgn. (dir. 1979-84), Phila. Neurol. Soc., Alpers Soc. Clin. Neurology, Coll. Physicians Phila., Sydenham Coterie, Phila. County Med. Soc., Pa. State Med. Soc., AMA (sec.-treas. sect. coun. neurology 1983-86), Am. Med. Soc. on Alcoholism, Neurology Intersoc. Liaison Group, Intersoc. Com. Neurol. Resources, Assn. Univ. Prof. Neurology (pres. 1988-90), Soc. for Exptl. Neuropathology, Am. Bd. Med. Specialties (exec. bd., chair COSEP, 1992—), Am. Bd. Psychiatry and Neurology (v.p. 1990, del. to Am. Bd. Med. Specialties, emeritus dir. 1991—), Pa. Blue Shield (profl. adv. coun. 1991—). Home: PO Box 498 Lafayette Hill PA 19444 Office: 1025 Walnut St Philadelphia PA 19107

MANCHESTER, CAROL ANN FRESHWATER, psychologist; b. Coshocton, Ohio, Sept. 30, 1942; d. James M. and Kathleen C. (Call) Freshwater; m. Crosby Manchester, Mar. 16, 1963 (dec. 1973). BS, Ohio State U., 1963, MS, 1973, PhD, 1977. Diplomate Internat. Soc. Psychotherapy and Behavioral Medicine, Am. Bd. Forensic Examiners. Elem. counselor Columbus (Ohio) Pub. Schs., 1973-79; counselor Regional Alcoholism & Tng. Ctr., Columbus, 1977-79; therapist Beechwold Clinic, Columbus, 1977-80; counselor Gifted and Talented Program, Columbus, 1979-81; dir. Freshwater Mental Health Clinic, Columbus, 1982—; asst. clin. prof. Coll. Medicine Ohio State U., 1990-95; instr. psychology Urbana Coll., Columbus, 1977-79; dir. Freshwater Clinic, Columbus, 1983—; bd. dirs. Ecole Francaise, Columbus, 1985—; cons. Columbus Cmty. Hosp., 1988—, Mt. Carmel Med. Ctr., Park Med. Ctr., Columbus, 1990—; presenter in field. Author: Affective Model The Gifted and Talented Handbook for Columbus Public Schools, 1981. Active Gov.'s Task Force on Child Abuse, Columbus. Recipient Disting. Svc. award Ohio Counselor's Assn., Valley Forge Freedom award. Mem. ACLU, AOA, Am. Acad. Cert. Neurotherapists (v.p. 1993, 94, diplomate, exec. bd. dirs.), Am. Acad. Neurobrainwave Therapists (v.p.), Soc. of Neuronal Regulation (v.p.), Nat. Soc. Clin. Hypnosis, Meninger Soc., Internat. Soc. Post Traumatic Stress, Internat. Soc. Multiple Personality Disorder, Assn. Applied Psychophysiology and Biofeedback, Ohio Psychol. Assn., Delta Omicron, Tau Beta Sigma. Office: Freshwater Clinic 6065 Glick Rd Ste C Powell OH 43065-9604

MANCINI, MARY CATHERINE, cardiothoracic surgeon, researcher; b. Scranton, Pa., Dec. 15, 1953; d. Peter Louis and Ferminia Teresa (Massi) M. BS in Chemistry, U. Pitts., 1974, MD, 1978; postgrad. in Anatomy and Cellular Biolog, La. State U. Med. Ctr., 1994—. Diplomate Am. Bd. Surgery (speciality cert. critical care medicine), Am. Bd. Thoracic Surgery. Intern in surgery U. Pitts., 1978-79, resident in surgery, 1979-87; fellow pediatric cardiac surgery Mayo Clinic, 1987-88; asst. prof. surgery, dir. cardiothoracic transplantation Med. Coll. Ohio, Toledo, 1988-91; assoc. prof. surgery, dir. cardiothoracic transplantation La. State U. Med. Ctr., Shreveport, 1991—. Author: Operative Techniques for Medical Students, 1983; contbr. articles to profl. jours. Rsch. grantee Am. Heart Assn., 1988; recipient Pres. award Internat. Soc. Heart Transplantation, 1983, Charles C. Moore Tchg. award U. Pitts., 1985, Internat. Woman of Yr. award Internat. Biog. Inst., Eng., 1992-93, Internat. Order of Merit award, 1995, Nina S. Braunwald Career Devel. award Thoracic Surgery Found. Fellow ACS, Am. Coll. Chest Physicians, Internat. Coll. Surgeons (councillor 1991—); mem. Assn. Women Surgeons, Rotary (gift of life program 1991). Roman Catholic. Office: La State U Med Ctr 1501 Kings Hwy Shreveport LA 71103-4228

MANCLARK, CHARLES ROBERT, microbiologist, researcher; b. Rochester, N.Y., June 22, 1928; s. Charles and Mary (Powell) M.; m. Doloras Jolly, Dec. 19, 1953; children: Charles Scott, Timothy Brooks. BS in Biology, Calif. Poly. State U., 1953; PhD in Bacteriology, UCLA, 1963. Rsch. and teaching asst. UCLA, 1956-61; asst. prof. Calif. State U., Long Beach, 1961-64; rsch. bacteriologist UCLA, 1963-65; asst. prof. U. Calif., Irvine, 1965-67; chief lab. of pertussis Ctr. for Biologics Evaluation and Rsch., Bethesda, Md., 1967-93; dir. WHO Collaborating Ctr., Bethesda, 1978-93; cons. WHO, UN, Pan. Am. Health Orgn., UNICEF and many fgn. countries worldwide, 1971—. Author of 2 lab. manuals for bacteriology; editor of 9 books on pertussis and pertussis vaccine; contbr. over 100 articles to profl. jours. Patentee in field. Cpl. U.S. Army, 1953-55. Recipient Merit award FDA, 1985, Group Recognition award 1989, medal Institutos de Salud, Lima, Peru, 1980, Disting. Svc. award for biomed. rsch. Dept. HHS, 1992; named Honored Alumnus in Sci. and Math., Calif. Poly. State U., 1992; Univ. fellow in microbiology UCLA, 1960. Fellow Am. Acad. Microbiology; mem. Am. Soc. for Microbiology, Internat. Assn. Biol. Standardization, Sigma Xi, Beta Beta Beta (pres. Epsilon Pi chpt. 1952-53). Home & Office: 3236 Braemar Dr Santa Barbara CA 93109-1067

MANCUSI-UNGARO, HAROLD RAYMOND, JR., plastic surgeon; b. Newark, May 6, 1947; s. Harold Raymond Sr. and Freda (Liebman) M.-U.; m. Carol Marian Caruso, June 18, 1979 (div. May 1988); children: Harold Themistocles, Marianna Caruso; m. Susan Ruth Brittain Jackson, Dec. 30, 1988. BA cum laude, Yale U., 1969, MD, 1973. Diplomate Am. Bd. Plastic Surgery, Am. Bd. Surgery. Asst. prof. surgery U. Tex. Health Sci. Ctr., Houston, 1982-86; asst. prof. surgery, dir. burn unit U. Colo. Health Scis. Ctr., Denver, 1986-88; assoc. prof., chief div. plastic surgery, dir. burn unit U. N.Mex. Med. Ctr., Albuquerque, 1988-90; pvt. practice Beaumont, Tex., 1990—; pres. med. staff S.E. Tex. Rehab. Hosp., Beaumont, 1992-93, 94-95; chmn. surgery Bapt. Hosp. S.E. Tex., 1993, Beaumont Regional Med. Ctr., 1994. Author: Michelangelo: The Bruges Madonna and the Piccolomini Altar, 1971; contbr. articles to profl. jours., chpts. to books. Mem. Masons, Shriners, Bailli, Beaumont Chaine des Rotisseurs. Office: SE Tex Plastic Surgery Inc 2965 Harrison St Ste 315 Beaumont TX 77702-1150

MANDAC, BENJAMIN REYES, pediatric rehabilitation physician; b. Philippines, Jan. 8, 1956. BS, UCLA, 1979; MD, U. Calif. Davis, 1984. Diplomate Am. Bd. Pediatrics. Staff pediatrician Catherine McAuley Health Ctr., Ann Arbor, Mich., 1987-90; asst. prof. Loma Linda (Calif.) U. Med. Ctr., 1990-92; dir. pediat. rehab. Santa Clara Valley Med. Ctr., San Jose, Calif., 1992—; med. dir. spina bifida clinic Lucile Salter Packard Children's Hosp., Palo Alto, Calif., 1993—; med. cons. Calif. Children's Svcs., Monterey, Calif., 1994—.

MANDAVA, NAGESWARA RAO, surgeon, oncologist; b. India, Nov. 22, 1955; came to U.S., 1968; s. Babu Rao and Vidyadhari (Kakarla) M.; m. Lakshmi Yalamanchili, Aug. 18, 1981; children: Ashok, Sri Vidya, Anupa. MBBS, Andhra (India) U., 1981. Gen. surgical resident Cath. Med. Ctr., Jamaica, N.Y., 1981-86; dir. surgery St. John's Queens Hosp.; surgical oncology fellow Roswell Park Meml. Inst., Buffalo, N.Y., 1986-89; asst. prof. surgery Cornell U. Med. Coll., 1993—.

MANDECKI, WLODEK, molecular biologist; b. Warsaw, Poland, Aug. 29, 1951; s. Stefan Mandecki and Cecylia (Sobolewska) Mandecka; m. Wanda Michalska, Apr. 24, 1977; children: Michael, Thomas, Joanna. MS, U. Warsaw, 1975; PhD, Polish Acad. Scis., 1979. Postdoctoral researcher UCLA, L.A., 1980, U. Wis., Madison, 1980-81, U. Colo., Boulder, 1981-83; group leader, lab. head Abbott Labs., Abbott Park, Ill., 1983—. Contbr. over 50 articles to profl. jours. Mem. Protein Soc., AAAS. Office: Abbott Labs Viral Discovery D90D 1401 Sheridan Rd North Chicago IL 60064

MANDEL, H(AROLD) GEORGE, pharmacologist; b. Berlin, June 6, 1924; came to U.S., 1937, naturalized, 1944; s. Ernest A. and Else (Crail) M.; m. Marianne Klein, July 25, 1953; children: Marcia Mandel Halgren, Audrey Lynn Mandel Todd. BS, Yale U., 1944, PhD, 1949. Lab. instr. in chemistry Yale U., 1942-44, 47-49; research asso. dept. pharmacology George Washington U., 1949-50, asst. research prof., 1950-52, assoc. prof. pharmacology, 1952-58, prof., 1958—, chmn. dept. pharmacology, 1960—; Advanced Commonwealth Fund fellow Molteno Inst. Cambridge (Eng.) U., 1956; Commonwealth Fund fellow U. Auckland (N.Z.) and U. Med. Scis., Bangkok, Thailand, 1964; Am. Cancer Soc. Eleanor Roosevelt Internat. fellow Chester Beatty Research Inst. London, 1970-71; Am. Cancer Soc. scholar U. Calif., San Francisco, 1978-79; fellow Med. Research Council toxicology unit, Carshalton, Eng., 1986; Burroughs Wellcome Rsch. travel grant, Carshalton, 1988; hon. rsch. fellow dept. biochemistry and molecular biology U. Coll., London, 1993, 96; mem. cancer chemotherapy com. Internat. Union Against Cancer, 1966-73, fellow, Lyon, France, 1989; mem. external rev. com. Howard U. Cancer Research Center, 1972-74 ; cons. Bur. Drugs, 1975-79, EPA, 1978-82; mem. toxicology adv. com. FDA, 1975-78; mem. med. research service merit rev. bd. in alcoholism and drug dependence VA, 1975-78; mem. cancer spl. program adv. com. Nat. Cancer Inst., 1974-78, chmn., 1976-78; mem. Nat. Large Bowel Cancer Project Working Cadre, 1980-84; mem. com. on toxicology NRC-Nat. Acad. Sci., 1978-82; mem. Kettering award selection com. Gen. Motors Cancer Research Found., 1979-81. Editorial bd.: Jour. Pharmacology and Exptl. Therapeutics, 1960-65, field editor, 1978-94; editorial bd.: Molecular Pharmacology, 1965-69, Rsch. Comm. in Chem. Pathology, Pharmacology, 1972—, Cancer Drug Delivery, Selective Cancer Therapeutics, 1983-92, Cancer Research, 1974-76, assoc. editor, 1977-81. Served with AUS, 1944-46. Recipient John J. Abel award in pharmacology Eli Lilly and Co., 1958, Disting. Achievement award Washington Acad. Scis., 1958, Golden Apple Teaching award AMA, 1969, 85. Mem. AAAS, Am. Chem. Soc., Am. Soc. Biochemistry and Molecular Biology, Am. Soc. Pharmacology and Exptl. Therapeutics (pres. 1973-74), Am. Assn. Cancer rsch., Assn. Med. Sch. Pharmacology (pres. 1976-78), Nat. Caucus of Basic Biomed. Sci. Chairs (chmn. 1991—), Cosmos Club (Washington), Sigma Xi, Alpha Omega Alpha. Democrat. Home: 4956 Sentinel Dr Bethesda MD 20816-3594 Office: George Washington U Dept Pharmacology 2300 I St NW Washington DC 20037-2337

MANDEL, LEWIS RICHARD, pharmaceutical company executive; b. Bklyn., Nov. 13, 1936; s. Murray and Belle (Teller) M.; m. Rochelle Holtzman, Mar. 27, 1960; children: Beth, Susan, Stefanie. BS, Columbia U., 1958, PhD, 1962. Registered pharmacist, N.Y., N.J., Pa. Lectr. in biochemistry, then asst. prof. pharmacology Columbia U., N.Y.C., 1961-64; rsch. biochemist Merck & Co., Inc., Rahway, N.J., 1964-76, dir. biochemistry, 1976-79, sr. dir. univ. and indsl. rels., 1979-89, exec. dir. indsl. and acad. rels., 1989—, exec. dir. external sci. affairs worldwide, 1993. Patentee in field; contbr. articles to profl. publs. Grantee NIH, 1963-64; recipient Wellcome travel award Burroughs Wellcome, 1963. Mem. Am. Soc. Pharmacology and Exptl. Therapeutics, Am. Soc. Biochemistry and Molecular Biology. Office: Merck and Co Inc PO Box 2000 Rahway NJ 07065-0900

MANDEL, SHELDON LLOYD, physician, dermatologist; b. Mpls., Dec. 6, 1922; s. Maurice and Stelle R. M.; m. Patricia E., Oct. 15, 1978; 1 child, Melissa A. BA, U. Minn., Mpls., 1943, BS, 1944, BM, 1946, MD, 1946. Diplomate Am. Bd. Dermatology, 1953. Pvt. practice dermatology Mpls., 1951—; prof. clin. dermatology U. Minn., Mpls., 1970—. Contbr. articles to profl. jours. Capt. MC, AUS, 1947-49. Fellow Royal Soc. Medicine (Britain), Am. Acad. Dermatology (life); mem. AMA, Minn. Med. Soc., Noah Worcester Dermatological Soc. (bd. dirs. 1988-91), Internat. Dermatological Soc. Home: 2828 Burnham Blvd Minneapolis MN 55416 Office: Downtown Dermatology 552 Med Arts Bldg Minneapolis MN 55402

MANDELBAUM, DOROTHY ROSENTHAL, psychologist, educator; b. N.Y.C., May 18, 1935; d. Benjamin Daniel and Rachael (Osofsky) Rosenthal; m. Seymour Jacob Mandelbaum, Aug. 19, 1956; children: David Gideon, Judah Michael, Betsy Daniella. AB cum laude, Hunter Coll., 1956; PhD, Bryn Mawr Coll., 1975. Lic. clin. psychologist, Pa. Tchr., Valley Road Sch., Princeton, N.J., 1956-59; instr. ednl. psychology dept. Temple U., Phila., 1970; asst. prof. dept. edn. Rutgers U., Camden, N.J., 1974-80, assoc. prof., 1980—, dir. women's studies, 1981-86, chair edn. dept., 1986-91, pres. faculty senate, 1990-91. Author: Work, Marriage and Motherhood: The Career Persistence of Female Physicians, 1981; contbr. articles on psychology of women and med. edn. to profl. publs. Dir. Am. Liver Found., 1991-93. AAUW predoctoral fellow, 1973-74. Mem. AAUP, APA. Home: 2290 N 53rd St Philadelphia PA 19131 Office: Rutgers U Camden NJ 08102

MANDELBAUM, ISABEL LEE, toxicologist, biology educator; b. Sept. 29, 1946; s. Herbert Isaac and Mary (Levine) m. B.A., Bklyn. Coll., 1967; Ph.D., U. Pa., 1975; postdoctoral Thomas Jefferson U., 1981-83. Asst. prof. biology LaSalle Coll., Phila., 1974-81; toxicologist NUS Corp., Wayne, Pa., 1984-86, Roy F. Weston, Inc., 1986—; sci. editor Info. Ventures, Phila., 1984—. Author: Physiology, A Self-Study Guide, 1978. Inst. of Neurol. Scis. fellow, 1967-68; Nat. Inst. Environ. Health Scis. fellow, 1981-83. Mem. Soc. Toxicology, Soc. Devel. Biology, Soc. Environ. Toxicology and Chemistry, Sigma Xi, Phi Beta Kappa. Avocations: flower photography; modern dance; old house restoration. Office: Roy F Weston Inc 1 Weston Way West Chester PA 19104

MANDELKERN, MARK ALAN, physics and radiology educator; b. N.Y.C., Jan. 28, 1943; s. Sydney and Minerva (Bernstein) M.; m. Margot A. Metzner, Jan. 1, 1980; children: India, Benjamin, Seth. BA, Columbia U., 1963; PhD, U. Calif., Berkeley, 1967; MD, U. Miami, 1975. Diplomate Am. Bd. Nuclear Medicine. Intern U. Calif., Irvine, 1976; nuclear medicine resident UCLA, 1982-84; prof. physics and radiology U. Calif., Irvine, 1968—; chief Positron Emission Tomography Ctr., West L.A. Va. Med. Ctr., 1984—; clin. prof. UCLA, 1988—. Office: U Calif Physics Dept Irvine CA 92717

MANDELL, MARSHALL, physician, allergist, consultant; b. N.Y.C., Feb. 4, 1922; s. Albert and Beatrice (Roth) M.; m. Thelma Sylvia Cantor, Aug. 1, 1944 (div. 1974); children: Joan Arlene, Steven Marshall, Nori Lyn; m. Sandra Jane Bodnar, Dec. 6, 1988. BA in Zoology, U. Conn., 1943; MD, L.I. Coll. Medicine, 1946. Diplomate Am. Bd. Pediats., Am. Bd. Allergy, Am. Bd. Allergy and Immunology. Intern in pediats. Yale U. Med. Sch./New Haven Hosp., 1946; jr. resident in pediats. St. Louis Children's Hosp./Washington U., 1946-49; resident in pediats. Gen. Hosps. #1 and #2, Kansas City, Mo., 1950; instr., clin. asst. N.Y. Med. Coll., 1955-58, asst. prof. allergy, 1958-80; adj. prof. nutrition and allergy U. Bridgeport, Conn., 1976-90; cons. in allergy and clin. ecology in mental illness Fuller Meml. Sanitarium, South Attleboro, Mass., 1972-76. Author: 5-Day Allergy Relief, 1979, Lifetime Arthritis Relief, It's Not Your Fault You're Fat Diet; editor: Let's Have Healthy Children; contbr. more than 30 articles to profl. jours. Capt. U.S. Army, 1942-49. Recipient Huxley Soc. Founders medal. Fellow Am. Coll. Allergy, Asthma, and Immunology, Am. Acad. Environ. Medicine (Jonathan Formam gold medal), Acad. Orthomolecular Medicine (Spl. Commendation for Contbns. to Mental Illness), Internat. Acad. Nutrition and Preventive Medicine; mem. Lions (pres. Norwalk club 1956-58), Phi Sigma Delta (pres. 1941-43). Home and Office: 6721 Oakmont Way Bradenton FL 34202

MANDELL, WALLACE, psychology educator, consultant; b. N.Y.C., Jan. 25, 1928; s. Harry Zalman and Lillian (Weisman) M.; m. Sara Rebeca Kabakow, Dec. 24, 1966; children: David Samuel, Rachel, Batya, Avram Moses. B Social Studies, CCNY, 1948; MS, Yale U., 1951; PhD, NYU, 1954; MPH, Johns Hopkins U., 1959. Lic. psychologist, N.Y., Md. Mental health rsch. cons. Tex. Health Dept., Austin, 1956-60; dir. rsch. S.I. (N.Y.) Mental Health Soc., 1960-68; prof. mental hygiene Johns Hopkins U. Sch. Pub. Health, Balt., 1968—; chmn. Dept. of Mental Hygiene, 1993—; cons. Nat. Inst. on Alcoholism, Nat. Inst. on Drug Abuse, NIMH. Author: Workers Who Drink, 1978; contbr. articles to various publs. With U.S. Army, 1954-56. Fellow APHA (governing coun.); mem. APA. Democrat. Jewish. Home: 3932 Cloverhill Rd Baltimore MD 21218-1707 Office: Johns Hopkins U Sch Pub Health 624 N Wolfe St Baltimore MD 21205-2110

MANDERS, KARL LEE, neurosurgeon; b. Rochester, N.Y., Jan. 21, 1927; s. David Bert and Frances Edna (Cohan) Mendelson; m. Ann Laprell, July 28, 1969; children: Karlanna, Maidena; children by previous marriage: Karl, Kerry, Kristine. Student, Cornell U., 1946; MD, U. Buffalo, 1950. Diplomate Am. Bd. Neurol. Surgery, Am. Bd. Clin. Biofeedback, Am. Bd. Hyperbaric Medicine, Am. Bd. Pain Medicine, Nat. Bd. Med. Examiners. Intern U. Va. Hosp., Charlottesville, 1950-51, resident in neurol. surgery, 1951-52; resident in neurol. surgery Henry Ford Hosp., Detroit, 1954-56; pvt. practice Indpls., 1956—; med. dir. Cmty. Hosp. Rehab. Ctr. for Pain, 1973—; chief hosp. med. and surg. neurology Cmty. Hosp., 1983, 93; coroner Marion County, Ind., 1977-85, 92-96. Served with USN, 1952-54, Korea. Recipient cert. achievement Dept. Army, 1969. Fellow ACS, Internat. Coll Surgeons, Am. Acad. Neurology; mem. Am. Assn. Neurol. Surgery, Congress Neurol. Surgery, Internat. Assn. Study of Pain, Am. Assn. Study of Headache, N.Y. Acad. Sci., Am. Coll. Angiology, Am. Soc. Contemporary Medicine and Surgery, Am. Holistic Med. Assn. (co-founder), Undersea Med. Soc., Am. Acad. Forensic Sci., Am. Assn. Biofeedback Clinicians, Soc. Cryosurgery, Pan Pacific Surg. Assn., Biofeedback Soc. Am., Acad. Psychosomatic Medicine, Pan Am. Med. Assn., Internat. Back Pain Soc., North Am. Spine Soc., Am. Soc. Stereotaxic and Functional Neurosurgery, Soc. for Computerized Tomography and Neuroimaging, Ind. Coroners Assn. (pres. 1979), Royal Soc. Medicine, Nat. Assn. Med. Examiners, Am. Pain Soc., Midwest Pain Soc. (pres. 1988), Am. Acad. Pain Medicine, Cen. Neurol. Soc., Interurban Neurosurg. Soc., Internat. Soc. Aquatic Medicine, James A. Gibson Anat. Soc., Am. Bd. Med. Psychotherapists (mem. profl. adv. council), James McClure Surg. Soc., Brendonwood Country Club, Highland Country Club. Home: 5845 High Fall Rd Indianapolis IN 46226-1017 Office: 7209 N Shadeland Ave Indianapolis IN 46250-2021

MANDIA, STEPHEN ERNEST, urologist; b. Engelwood, N.J., Dec. 30, 1958; s. Ernest James and Anita Joan (Turrisi) M. BS, Georgetown U., Washington, 1980; MSA in Health Svcs. Adminstrn., Cen. Mich. U., Mt. Pleasant, 1996; MD, Georgetown U., 1984. Diplomate Am. Bd. Urology. Surgery resident St. Vincent's Med. Ctr., Bridgeport, Conn., 1984-85; commd. ensign USN, 1980, advanced through grades to comdr., 1995; flight surgeon USN, San Diego, 1985-88, urology resident, 1988-92; head urology dept. USN, Rota, Spain, 1992-94, chief surg. svcs., 1994; urologist USN, Jacksonville, Fla., 1994—; assoc. clin. prof. Uniformed Svcs. U. of Health

Scis., Bethesda, Md., 1994—. Fellow ACS; mem. AMA, Am. Urol. Assn., Fla. Med. Assn. (bd. govs. 1995—). Republican. Roman Catholic. Office: US Naval Hosp 2080 Child St Jacksonville FL 32214

MANDLER, GEORGE, psychologist; b. Vienna, Austria, June 11, 1924; came to U.S., 1940, naturalized, 1943; s. Richard and Hede (Goldschmied) M.; m. Jean Matter, Jan. 19, 1957; children: Peter Clark, Michael Allen. B.A., NYU, 1949; M.S., Yale U., 1950, Ph.D., 1953; postgrad., U. Basel, Switzerland, 1947-48. Asst. prof. Harvard U., 1953-57, lectr., 1957-60; prof. U. Toronto, Ont., Can., 1960-65; prof. psychology U. Calif., San Diego, 1965-94, chmn. dept. psychology, 1965-70, prof. emeritus, 1994—; dir. Ctr. Human Info. Processing, U. Calif., San Diego, 1965-90; hon. rsch. fellow Univ. Coll. London., 1977-78, 82-90, vis. prof., 1990—. Author: Mind and Emotion, 1975, (German edit.), 1980, Mind and Body, 1984, (Japanese edit.), 1987, Cognitive Psychology, 1985, Japanese edit., 1991; contbr. articles and revs. to profl. jours.; editor: Psychol. Rev., 1970-76. Served with U.S. Army, 1943-46. Fellow Ctr. for Advanced Study in Behavioral Scis., 1959-60; vis. fellow Oxford U., Eng., 1971-72, 78; Guggenheim fellow, 1971-72. Fellow AAAS, Am. Acad. Arts and Scis.; mem. AAUP, Am. Assn. Advancement Psychology (1974-82); Psychonomic Soc. (governing bd., chmn. 1983), Am. Psychol. Soc., Am. Psychol. Assn. (pres. div. exptl. psychology 1978-79, pres. div. gen psychology 1982-83, mem. coun. reps. 1978-82, William James prize 1986), Internat. Union Psychol. Scis. (U.S. com. 1985-90), Soc. Exptl. Psychologists, Fedn. Behavioral Psychol. and Cognitive Scis. (pres. 1981). Home: 1406 La Jolla Knoll La Jolla CA 92037-5236 Office: U Calif San Diego Dept Psychology La Jolla CA 92093-0109 also: 3 Perrins Lane, London NW3 1QY, England

MANDRAVELIS, PATRICIA JEAN, healthcare administrator; b. Hanover, N.H., May 7, 1938; d. William J. and Ruth E. (Darling) Bartis; m. Anthony M. Mandravelis, Nov. 8, 1959; children: Michael A., Tracy J. Diploma in nursing, Nashua (N.H.) Meml. Hosp. Sch. Nursing; BS in Psychology, Sociology, New Eng. Coll.; MBA, N.H. Coll., 1989. Cert. nursing adminstr., advanced nursing adminstr. Staff nurse Nashua Meml. Hosp. (name now So. N.H. Regional Med. Ctr.), 1959-60, obstet. nurse, 1962-65, charge nurse, 1969-71, supr., 1971-76, assoc. dir. nursing, 1976-81, dir. nursing, 1981-83, asst. exec. dir. nursing, 1983-87, v.p. nursing, 1987-91; v.p. ops., chief operating officer Nashua Meml. Hosp., 1991-95; v.p. cmty. health and wellness S. N.H. Regional Med. Ctr., Nashua, 1995—. Contbr. articles to profl. jours. Bd. dirs. deNicola Women's Ctr., Nashua, 1987-95, Nashua Vis. Nurse Program, 1986-88; v.p. Nashua chpt. ARC, 1985-87; bd. dirs. Home Health Hosp., 1988-94, chmn. bd., 1991-93, vice chmn. bd., 1993-94; mem. citizens adv. bd. W.R. Grace, 1989—. Mem. Am. Coll. Healthcare Execs., Nat. League of Nursing, Am. Nurses Assn., Am. Orgn. Nurse Execs., N.H. Nurses Assn., N.H. Orgn. Nurse Execs., Sigma Theta Tau. Office: So NH Regional Med Ctr 8 Prospect St Nashua NH 03060-3925

MANDRI, DANIEL FRANCISCO, psychiatrist; b. Camaguey, Cuba, Apr. 22, 1950; came to U.S., 1962; s. Adalberto Froilan and Estrella (Pereiro) M.; m. Monica A. Ruffing, May 21, 1983; children: Nicholas, Natalie. MD, U. Cen. Del Este, Dominican Republic, 1977. Diplomate Am. Bd. Psychiatry and Neurology. With internal medicine PGY-1 Christ Hosp., Oak Lawn, Ill., 1979-80; with psychiatry PGY 2 plus 3 U. Miami/Jackson Meml. Hosp., Miami, Fla., 1980-82, chief resident psychiatry, 1982-83; pvt. practice psychiatry Coral Gables, Fla., 1983-86; dir. acute care unit Broward County Mental Health Div., Hollywood, Fla., 1986-87; dir. psychiat. svcs. Douglas Gardens Community Mental Health Ctr., Miami, 1987—, Douglas Gardens Home and Hosp. for the Aged, Miami, 1989-92; asst. instr. psychiatry dept. of psychiatry U. Miami, 1982-83. Mem. N.Y. Acad. Scis., Am. Psychiatry Assn., World Psychiat. Assn., World Fedn. for Mental Health, Am. Assn. Community Psychiatrists. Office: Douglas Gardens Cmty Mental Health Ctr 701 Lincoln Rd Miami FL 33139-2879

MANDUANO, JOEY MORGAN, osteopathic physician and surgeon, educator; b. Ada, Okla., Apr. 16, 1947; s. Joseph Patrick Manduano and Ester Fay (Heath) Bailey; m. Nancy Olen Medley, Apr. 15, 1978; 1 child, Lindsey Morgan; 1 child from previous marriage: Anna Lynn. BS, Panhandle State U., Goodwell, Okla., 1969; DO, Kansas City Coll. Osteo Med., 1973. Diplomate Am. Osteopathic Bd. Surgery; cert. in plastic and reconstructive surgery, gen. surgery. Jr. resident in gen. surgery Am. Osteo. Assn., Tulsa, 1973-76, sr. resident in gen. surgery, 1976-78; pvt. practice gen. surgery Tulsa, 1978-89; resident in plastic and reconstructive surgery Am. Osteo. Assn., N.Y.C., 1989-91; chief of surgery Tulsa Regional Med. Ctr., 1984-86; fellow in plastic (cosmetic) surgery Am. Osteo. Assn., Santa Monica, Calif., 1991; fellow in burn surgery Am. Osteo. Assn., Valhalla, N.Y., 1990; attending dept. of surgery div. plastic & reconstructive Tulsa (Okla.) Regional Med. Ctr; adj. faculty Okla. State U. Coll. Osteo. Medicine. Contbr. articles to profl. jours. Vol. screening physician Am. Cancer Soc., Tulsa, 1981; vol. sch. physician Tulsa Pub. Schs., 1983; lectr. Tulsa Emergency Med. Svcs., 1985. Fellow Am. Coll. Osteo. Surgeons; mem. Am. Osteo. Assn., Okla. Osteo. Assn., Tulsa Dist. Osteo. Assn. Democrat.

MAÑÉ GARZÓN, FERNANDO, pediatrics educator; b. Montevideo, Uruguay, Jan. 24, 1925; s. Alberto and Maria Herminia Garzón; m. Maria Elena Lezica Alvear, Aug. 24, 1954; children: Florencia, Ana Elena, Teodelina, Silvina, Maria Rosa, Fernando. BA, Lycée Francais, Montevideo. Extern Ministerio Salud Publica, Montevideo, 1949-50, intern, 1950-54; beca artigas U. Uruguay, Montevideo, 1951; asst. faculty of medicine Clinic of Pediatrics U. Paris, 1954-56, Jefe clinica faculty of medicine Clinic of Pediatrics, 1957-60; asst. clinica faculty of medicine Clinic of Pediatrics U. Montevideo, 1960-64, prof. agregado Clinic of Pediatrics, 1964-84, prof. zoology faculty sci., 1966-81, prof. titular Clinic of Pediatrics, 1984—, prof. history medicine, 1985-93, prof. emeritus Clinic of Faculty Medicine, 1993—, prof. clin. genetics, 1993—; jefe pediatria Direc. Gen. Seguridad Social, Montevideo, 1960, Centro Asist. Sindicato Medico, Montevideo, 1961. Author: Pedro Visca, 1984, Claude Bernard, Vilardebo, 1990, Cien Años Darwinismo, 1990, Susviela Guarch, 1991, Estrazulas, 1991, El Gringo de Confianza, 1993, No es para tanto mi tí Vida de H. Muñoz, 1995, Admirabilis Celsus, 1995, Historia de la Ciencia en el Uruguay, 1996; editor: journal Soc. Uruguaya Historia Med., 1980-95. Mem. Am. Soc. Parasitology, Sociedad Pediatria Uruguay, Sociedad Uruguaya Historia Medicine. Home: Casilla de Correo 157, Montevideo Uruguay

MANENTI, JOHN MARK, family practice physician; b. Youngstown, Ohio, Sept. 8, 1961; s. John Richard and Gay Ellen (Smith) M.; m. Karen Lynne Molson, May 19, 1990; 1 child, Victoria Gabrielle. BA in Biology, Hiram Coll., 1983; DO, Ohio U., 1988. Intern Youngstown Osteo. Hosp., 1988-89; resident in family practice Youngstown Osteo. Hosp., 1992-94; pvt. practice Youngstown, 1989-92, East Liverpool (Ohio) Family Practice, 1994—; clin. instr. family medicine Ohio U. Coll. Osteo. Medicine, Athens, 1989—. Mem. Am. Osteo. Assn., AMA, Ohio Osteo. Assn., Ohio State Med. Soc. Roman Catholic. Office: East Liverpool Family Pract 16761 Saint Clair Ste B East Liverpool OH 43920

MANFREDI, MARIO ERMINIO, neurologist educator; b. Genoa, Liguria, Italy, Aug. 5, 1934; s. Leonardo Carlo and Alessandra (Bianchetti) M.; m. Maddalena Irene Canepa, June 6, 1966; children: Carlo Luigi, Giovanni Walter. MD, U. Genoa, Italy, 1958, Bd. in Neuropsychiatry, 1961; Libera Docenza, Nat. Examination, Rome, Italy, 1966, Idoneita Primariale, 1970. Rsch. fellow Nat. Rsch. Coun., Genoa, Italy, 1962-63; asst. prof. U. Genoa, Italy, 1964-70; fellow NIH Washington U., St. Louis, 1966-67; asst. prof. U. Rome Sapienza, 1970-84; prof. U. Aquila, 1972-75; prof. neurology Nat. U. Somalia, Mogadishu, 1976; prof. U. Rome Sapienza, 1984—; cons. neurologist Santa Corona Hosp., Pietra Ligure, Italy, 1965, Nuovo Regina Margherita Hosp., Rome, 1970-81. Contbr. numerous articles to profl. jours. Grantee Nat. Rsch. Coun., 1969—, Ministry of Health, 1980—. Mem. Italian League Against Epilepsy (councillor 1973-79), Italian Soc. EEG (councillor 1978-80), Italian Soc. Neurology (treas. 1978-81, sec. 1981-83), Internat. Med. Soc. Motor Disturbances (pres. 1986-88), FOREP Epilepsy and Related Syndromes Rsch. Found. (pres. 1989—). Home: Via Montevideo 21, 00198 Rome Italy Office: Dept Neurosciences, Viale dell'Universita 30, 00185 Rome Italy

MANGANIELLO, LOUIS OTTO JOSEPH, neurosurgeon; b. Waterbury, Conn., June 6, 1915; s. Angelo M. and Raimonda (Membrino) M.; m. Carol Graham Pryor, June 11, 1950; children—Carol Helen, Victoria R. A.B., Harvard U., 1937; M.D., U. Md., 1942; J.D., Augusta Law Sch., 1967. Diplomate Am. Bd. Neurol. Surgery. Intern, Univ. Hosp., Balt., 1942-43, resident in neurol. surgery, 1946-50; pvt. practice medicine specializing in neurosurgery, Augusta, Ga., 1951—; mem. staff Univ. Hosp., Doctors Hosp., St. Joseph Hosp., Augusta; mem., past pres. composite state bd. Med. Examiners Ga.; cons. VA Hosp., Augusta; dir. Blue Cross/Blue Shield; assoc. prof. neurosurgery Med. Coll. Ga., 1951—. Served with USN, 1942-46. Bd. dirs. ARC. Fellow ACS; mem. AMA, Richmond County Med. Soc., Med. Assn. Ga., Am. Assn. Neurol. Surgery, Congres Neurosurgeons, So. Neurosurg. Soc., Southeastern Surg. Congress, Am. Assn. Cancer Research, Am. Assn. Med. Colls., Internat. Assn. Lex and Sci., Ga. Neurosurg. Soc. (past pres.). Club: Country of Augusta, Pinnacal. Lodge: Rotary. Contbr. articles to profl. jours. Home: 656 Milledge Rd Augusta GA 30904-4388

MANGANO, JOSEPH JAMES, health services administrator; b. Bad Canstatt, West Germany, Feb. 18, 1956; s. Joseph Anthony and Eleanor Aida (Landino) M. BA, N.C. State U., 1976; MPH, U. N.C., 1973; MBA, Fordham U., 1985. Data mgr. Profl. Standards Review Orgn., N.Y.C., 1978-81; planner Columbia-Presbyn. Med. Ctr., N.Y.C., 1981-83; asst. dir. Health & Hosps. Corp., N.Y.C., 1983-86; cons., adj. prof. various univs., N.Y.C., 1987-91; newsletter editor Faulkner & Gray Pub., N.Y.C., 1991—. Author: Health Information Management, 1993, Living Legacy: How 1964 Changed America, 1993; contbr. articles to profl. jours. Home and Office: 786 Carroll St Brooklyn NY 11215

MANGANO, MICHAEL F., federal official. AB, Villanova U., 1968; postgrad., U. Md., 1968-69. Dep. inspector gen. Office Evaluation & Inspections, 1988-94; prin. dept. Office Inspector Gen. HHS, 1994—. Mem. adv. bd. Evaluation Practice; assoc. editor Evaluation Review; contbr. articles to profl. jours. Recipiente Presdl. Meritorious Exec. Rank award, 1987, Profl. Devel. award Inspector Gen., 1991, Myrdal Govt. Svc. award Am. Evaluation Assn., 1991, Exemplary Svc. award Surgeon Gen., 1992. Office: Office of Inspector Gen 330 Independence Ave SW Washington DC 20201*

MANGER, WILLIAM MUIR, internist; b. Greenwich, Conn., Aug. 13, 1920; s. Julius and Lilian (Weissinger) M.; m. Lynn Seymour Sheppard, May 30, 1964; children: William Muir, Jr., Lilian Wade (Mrs. Porter Fleming), Stewart Sheppard, Charles Seymour. BS, Yale U., 1944; MD, Columbia U., 1946; PhD, Mayo Found., U. Minn., 1958. Intern, Presbyn. Hosp., N.Y.C., 1946-47, resident, 1949-50; fellow internal medicine Mayo Found., 1950-55; asst. physician Presbyn. Hosp., 1957—; dir. Manger Rsch. Found., 1961-77; clin. asst. vis. physician Columbia div. Bellevue Hosp., 1964-68; asst. attending physician NYU Bellevue Hosp. 1969-77; assoc. attending physician, 1977-83, attending physician, 1983—; instr. medicine Columbia U. Coll. Phys. and Surg., 1957-66, assoc. medicine, 1966-70, lectr., 1981—; asst. attending physician Presbyn. Hosp., 1966-68; asst. clin. prof. medicine N.Y.U. Med. Ctr., 1968-75, assoc. clin. prof. medicine, 1975-83, prof. clin. medicine, 1983—; mem. devel. com. Mayo Clinic, 1981-87; vice chmn. bd. Manger Hotels, Inc., 1957-73. Mem. bd. govs. St. Albans Sch., Washington, 1958-64, 67-73, 83-89, chmn., 1967-69; trustee Found. Rsch. in Medicine and Biology, 1971-77, Buckley Sch., 1975-85, Found. for Advancement Internat. Rsch. in Microbiology, 1977-82, Thyroid Found., 1980-85; mem. bd. visitors Boston U. Med. Sch., 1992—; trustee Found. for Depression and Manic Depression, 1978-89, pres., 1980-89; elder Presbyn. Ch., 1968-70, 92-93, trustee, 1962-67, 80-84, deacon, 1959-61. Lt. (j.g.) M.C., USNR, 1947-49. Recipient Mayo Found. Alumni award for Meritorious Rsch., 1955, Disting. Alumnus award, 1992. Diplomate Nat. Bd. Med. Examiners, Am. Bd. Internal Medicine. Fellow ACP, Acad. Psychosomatic Medicine, Am. Geriatric Soc., Coun. on Geriatric Cardiology, N.Y. Acad. Medicine (admission com. 1976-78, edn. com. 1979-92), Am. Coll. Cardiology, Am. Coll. Clin. Pharmacology, Royal Soc. Health, Am. Inst. Chemists; trustee Nat. Hypertension Assn. (chmn. 1977—), AMA, Am. Soc. Internal Medicine, N.Y. State Med. Soc., N.Y. County Med. Soc., Am. Heart Assn. (fellow council on circulation and council for high blood pressure rsch.), Nat. High Blood Pressure Edn. Program (mem. Coord. Com.), Inter-Am. Soc. Hypertension, Internat. Soc. Hypertension, Am. Soc. Hypertension, Am. Thoracic Soc., N.Y. Acad. Sci., AAAS, Am. Physiol. Soc., Am. Chem. Soc., Am. Soc. Pharmacology and Exptl. Therapeutics, Am. Soc. for Clin. Pharmacology and Therapeutics, Clin. Autonomic Rsch. Soc., Am. Autonomic Soc., Med. Strollers, N.Y.C., Endocrine Soc., Pan Am. Med. Assn., Harvey Soc., Soc. Exptl. Biology and Medicine, Rsch. Discussion Group (founding mem., sec.-treas. 1958-80), Am. Fedn. Clin. Rsch., Am. Soc. Nephrology, Royal Soc. Medicine (affiliate), Fellows Assn. Mayo Found. (v.p., pres. 1953), Mayo Alumni Assn. (v.p. 1981-82, exec. com. 1981-89, pres. elect 1982-85, pres. 1985-87), Catecholamine Club (founder, sec.-treas. 1967-80, pres. 1981-82), Doctors Mayo Soc., Albert Gallatin Assos., New Eng. Soc., S.R. (chmn. admissions com. 1959-67, bd. mgrs. 1959-67, 69-70), Soc. Colonial Wars, Sigma Xi, Nu Sigma Nu, Phi Delta Theta, Explorers, Meadow (L.I., N.Y.); Univ.; Yale; N.Y. Athletic (N.Y.C.); Southampton Bathing Corp.; Jupiter Island. Co-author: Chemical Quantitation of Epinephrine and Norepinephrine in Plasma, 1959, Pheochromocytoma, 1977, Clinical and Experimental Pheochromocytoma, 1996; author: Catecholamines in Normal and Abnormal Cardiac Function, 1982; editor, contbr. Hormones and Hypertension, 1966; editor: Am. Lecture Series in Endocrinology, 1962-75; guest editor First Irvine H. Page Internat. Hypertension Rsch. Symposium, 1990; contbr. articles to profl. and lay jours. Achievements include research on the mechanism of salt-induced hypertension, and on pheochromocytoma. Home: 8 E 81st St New York NY 10028-0201

MANGION, RICHARD MICHAEL, health care executive; b. Haverhill, Mass., Apr. 26, 1941; s. Michael Anthony and Evelyn (Cote) M.; m. Gail Elizabeth Donne, Apr. 27, 1968; children: Catherine Jean, James Richard, Ian Kyle. BBA, Suffolk U., 1963; MBA, Syracuse U., 1965; MPH, U. Calif., Berkeley, 1972. Asst. adminstr. Nashua (N.H.) Meml. Hosp., 1972-75, assoc. adminstr., 1975-77; pres. and chief exec. officer Harrington Meml. Hosp., Southbridge, Mass., 1977—; lectr. U. N.H., Durham, 1972-74. Pres. Tri-Community Devel. Corp., Southbridge, 1983-88. Capt. USAF, 1966-70. Fellow Am. Coll. Health Care Execs. (regent Mass. area B 1995—); mem. Am. Hosp. Assn., Mass. Hosp. Assn., Ctrl. Mass. Hosp. Coun. (pres. 1982-84), Ctrl. Mass. Health Care Found., Tri-Cmty. C. of C. (pres. 1983-84). Democrat. Roman Catholic. Club: Hosp. Supts. Lodge: Rotary. Home: 50 Old Village Rd Sturbridge MA 01566-1069 Office: Harrington Meml Hosp 100 South St Southbridge MA 01550-4051

MANGO-HURDMAN, CHRISTINA ROSE, psychiatric art therapist; b. Garden City, N.Y., May 13, 1962; d. Camillo Andrew and Dorothy Mae (Harrison) Mango; Keith Hurdman, Sept. 11, 1993; 1 child, Clarissa Rose Hurdman. BFA summa cum laude, Coll. of New Rochelle, 1984; MA, NYU, 1987. Registered art therapist; cert. structural family therapy tng.; cert. psycho-edn. multi family therapy tng. Art therapist Bronx Mcpl. Hosp. Ctr., 1984-88; art therapist, clin. supr. Fordham-Tremont Cmty. Mental Health Ctr., Bronx, 1988—; art therapy fieldworker Bronx State Hosp., 1984, art therapy intern Bronx Children's Hosp., 1985, Saint Lukes Hosp., N.Y.C., 1986. Contbr. articles to profl. jours. Mem. N.Y. Art Therapy Assn., No. N.J. Art Therapists Assn., Am. Art Therapy Assn. Home: 11 Turnure St Bergenfield NJ 07621-2035

MANGUN, CLARKE WILSON, JR., public health physician, consultant; b. Iowa Falls, Iowa, Feb. 12, 1919; s. Clarke Wilson and Vallie Hazel (Hoffman) M.; m. Edith Lauretta DuBois, May 13, 1945; children: Edith Ann, Nancy June, Laura Jane. BS, U. Iowa, 1940, MD, 1943; MPH, Columbia U., 1947. Diplomate Am. Bd. Preventive Medicine. Commd. officer USPHS, 1945-66; med. adminstr. Am. Heart Assn., Chgo. 1966-67, Chgo. Heart Assn., 1967-68, AMA, Chgo., 1969-80; long-term cons. Abbott Labs., North Chicago, Ill., 1980—. Recipient award Nat. Bd. Med. Examiners, 1944. Fellow APHA, Am. Coll. Preventive Medicine; mem. AMA (Physician's Recognition award, 1970-96), Ill. State Med. Soc., Chgo. Med. Soc. Home: 733 S Greenwood Ave Park Ridge IL 60068-4539

MANHOLD, JOHN HENRY, medical dentistry educator, author, consultant; b. Rochester, N.Y., Aug. 20, 1919; s. John Henry and Helen Martha (Shulz) M.; m. Beverly Schecter, 1953 (div. 1969) 1 child (dec.); m. Enriqueta Andino, Mar. 20, 1971. BA, U. Rochester, 1940; D.M.D., Harvard U., 1944; MA, Washington U., 1956. Instr. Tufts U. Coll. Medicine, Boston, 1948-50; asst. prof., chmn. gen. and oral pathology Washington U. Coll. Dentistry, St. Louis, 1954-56; from asst. prof. to prof., chmn. dept. gen. and oral pathology Seton Hall Coll. Medicine and Dentistry (now called U. Medicine and Dentistry N.J.), Newark, 1956-87; med. dir., Woog Internat., 1987-89; cons. Johnson & Johnson, New Brunswick, N.J., 1960-70, Richardson-Vicks, Shelton, Conn., 1981-87, Los Produits Associes, Geneva, Switzerland, 1965-87, Health Care Devel. Group, N.J., Pa., Consumer Communications Network, N.Y., Conn., others, 1990—. Author: Introductory Psychosomatic Dentistry, 1956; Outline of Pathology, 1960; Clinical Oral Diagnosis, 1965; Tissue Respiration and Oxigenating Agents, 1977; Practical Dental Management: Patients and Practice, 1984; (with others) Handbook of Pathology, 1987. Editor: Illustrated Dental Terminology: A Lexicon for the Dental Profession, 1985. Editor Clinical Preventive Dentistry jour., 1979-92. World wide lectr. Contbr. numerous articles to profl. jours. Named to Sr. Soc. Harvard Sch. Dental Medicine, 1984, Disting. Alumni Harvard U., 1989; recipient Pres. award Alumni Assn. U. Medicine and Dentistry N.J., 1980, Letter of Appreciation Asara Mihara former minister Japan, 1980, Cert. Achievement U. Md., 1965. Fellow Am. Coll. Dentists, Internat. Coll. Dentists, Acad. Psychosomatic Medicine; mem. APA, Acad. Psychosomatic Medicine (pres. 1977-78, sec. 1975-76, treas. 1970-75), Am. Soc. Clin. Pathologists, Internat. Assn. Dental Rsch., St. Petersburg Yacht Club, Pasadena Yacht and Country Club, Palm Aire Country Club, Sigma Xi. Home and Office: 6848 Country Lakes Cir Sarasota FL 34243-3801

MANIS, FRANKLIN RALPH, psychology educator; b. Whittier, Calif., Feb. 17, 1953; s. Armen Haig and Betty Ruth (McKee) M.; m. Janice Ann Stockl, Jan. 12, 1976; children: Lauren Christine, Caroline Marie, Julia Michelle. BA magna cum laude, Pomona Coll., 1975; PhD, U. Minn., 1981. Instr. U. Minn., Mpls., 1979-81; asst. prof. psychology U. So. Calif., Los Angeles, 1981-86, assoc. prof., 1987—. Contbr. articles on cognitive devel., reading disabilities to profl. jours. Research grantee U. So. Calif., Los Angeles, 1983, NIH, 1985—. Mem. Am. Psychol. Soc., Soc. Research in Child Devel., Orton Dyslexia Soc., Phi Beta Kappa. Office: U So Calif Dept Psychology University Park Los Angeles CA 90089

MANISCALCO, ANTHONY GERARD, neurologist; b. N.Y.C., Feb. 19, 1951; s. Dominick Walter and Anna (Friscia) M.; m. Margaret Rose Hasenauer, June 11, 1972; children: Dominic, Andrea, Peter. BS in Biology, Seton Hall U., South Orange, N.J., 1972; MD, U. Bologna, Italy, 1978. Diplomate Am. Bd. Neurology, Am. Bd. Internal Medicine. Intern Maimonides Med. Ctr., Bklyn., 1978-81; resident in neurology St. Vincent's Hosp. & Med. Ctr. N.Y., 1981-84; ptnr. Neurology Assocs., Bklyn., 1985—; chief neurology divsn. Victory Meml. Hosp., Bklyn., 1992—; asst. clin. prof. neurology SUNY, Bklyn., 1992—. Mem. Am. Acad. Neurology, Med. Soc. State N.Y., King County Med. Soc. Roman Catholic. Office: Neurology Assocs 117 70th St Brooklyn NY 11209

MANKIN, HENRY JAY, physician, educator; b. Pitts., Oct. 9, 1928; s. Hyman Isaac and Mary (Simons) M.; m. Carole Jane Pinkney, Aug. 20, 1952; children: Allison Joan, David Philip, Keith Pinkney. B.S. magna cum laude, U. Pitts., 1952, M.D., 1953; M.A. (hon.), Harvard U., 1973. Diplomate Am. Bd. Orthopaedic Surgery (mem. bd. 1976-82, pres. bd. 1980-81). Intern U. Chgo. Clinics, 1953-54; resident orthopaedics Hosp. for Joint Diseases, N.Y.C., 1957-60; instr. orthopaedics U. Pitts. Sch. Medicine, 1960-62, asst. prof., 1962-64, assoc. prof., 1964-66; dir., prof. orthopaedics Hosp. for Joint Diseases and Mt. Sinai Sch. Medicine, 1966-72; chief orthopaedics Mass. Gen. Hosp., Boston, 1972-96; Edith M. Ashley prof. orthopaedics Harvard Med. Sch., 1972—; mem. surgery B study sect. NIH, 1969-73; mem. adv. com. on surg. treatment FDA, 1973-75; corporator Boston Five Cent Savs. Bank, 1982-83; mem. exec. com. Am. Bd. Med. Spltys., 1982-85; adv. council on grad. med. edn., 1986-96; mem. Nat. Arthritis Avd. Bd., 1986-89; mem. human resources and research rev. group A Nat. Inst. Arthritis, Metabolism and Digestive Diseases, 1981-85, chmn., 1983-85. Assoc. editor Arthritis and Rheumatism, 1967-77, Jour. Bone and Joint Surgery, 1967-82; mem. editorial bd. Jour. Orthopedic Research, 1982-85; trustee Jour. Bone and Joint Surgery, 1985-91, chmn. bd., 1988-91; contbr. numerous articles to profl., med. jours. Served to lt. comdr. USNR, 1955-57. Fellow ACS, Royal Coll. Surgeons (hon.); mem. Am. Acad. Orthopaedic Surgeons, Acad. Orthopaedic Soc. (pres. 1991-92), Am. Orthopaedic Assn. (pres. 1982-83), Orthopaedic Research Soc. (pres. 1969-70), Musculoskeletal Tumor Soc. (pres. 1991-92), Brit. Orthopaedic Research Soc., Argentine Orthopedic Assn. (hon.), N.Y. Acad. Medicine (chmn. orthopaedic sect. 1971-72), Am. Rheumatism Assn., Soc. Internat. Chirurgerie Orthopaedice et Traumatologia, Hip Soc., Interurban, Forum Orthopaedic clubs, Brit. Orthopaedic Assn. (hon.), Can. Orthopaedic Assn. (hon.), Australian Orthopaedic Assn. (hon.), N.Z. Orthopaedic Assn. (hon.), Japanese Orthopaedic Assn. (hon.), Israel Orthopaedic Assn. (hon.), Thai Orthopaedic Assn (hon.). Home: 185 Dean Rd Brookline MA 02146-4201 Office: Mass Gen Hosp 32 Fruit St Boston MA 02114-2620

MANLEY, AUDREY FORBES, medical administrator, physician; b. Jackson, Miss., Mar. 25, 1934; d. Jesse Lee and Ora Lee (Buckhalter) Forbes; m. Albert Edward Manley, Apr. 3, 1970. A.B. with honors (tuition scholar), Spelman Coll., Atlanta, 1955; M.D. (Jesse Smith Noyes Found. scholar), Meharry Med. Coll., 1959; MPH, Johns Hopkins U.-USPHS traineeship, 1987; LHD (hon.), Tougaloo (Miss.) Coll., 1990, Meharry Med. Coll., Nashville, 1991; LLD (hon.), Spelman Coll., 1991. Diplomate: Am. Bd. Pediatrics. Intern St. Mary Mercy Hosp., Gary, Ind., 1960; from jr. to chief resident in pediatrics Cook County Children's Hosp., Chgo., 1960-62; NIH fellow neonatology U. Ill. Rsch. and Ednl. Hosp., Chgo., 1963-65; staff pediatrician Chgo. Bd. Health, 1963-66; practice medicine specializing in pediatrics Chgo., 1963-66; assoc. Lawndale Neighborhood Health Ctr. North, 1966-67; asst. med. dir., 1967-69; asst. prof. Chgo. Med. Coll., 1966-67; instr. Pritzker Sch. Medicine, U. Chgo., 1967-69; asst. dir. ambulatory pediatrics, asst. dir. pediatrics Mt. Zion Hosp. and Med. Center, San Francisco, 1969-70; med. cons. Spelman Coll., 1970-71, med. dir. family planning program, chmn. health careers adv. com., 1972-76; med. dir. Grady Meml. Hosp. Family Planning Clinic, 1972-76; with Health Services Adminstrs., Dept. Health and Human Services, 1976—; commd. officer USPHS, 1976—; chief genetic diseases services br. Office Maternal and Child Health, Bur. Community Health Services, Rockville, Md., 1976-81; acting assoc. adminstr. clin. affairs Office of Adminstr. Health Resources and Services Adminstrn., 1981-83, chief med. officer, dep. assoc. adminstr. planning, evaluation and legis., 1983-85; sabbatical leave USPHS Johns Hopkins Sch. Hygiene and Pub. Health, 1986-87; dir. Nat. Health Service Corps.; asst. surgeon gen., 1988; dep. asst. Sec. for Health USPHS/HHS, 1989-93, acting asst. Sec. Health, 1993, dep. asst. Sec. Health/intergovtl. affairs, 1993-94; dep. surgeon gen., acting dep. asst. sec. for minority health USPHS, 1994-95; acting surgeon gen., 1995—; mem. U.S. del. UNICEF, 1990-94. Author numerous articles, reports in field. Trustee Spelman Coll., 1966-70. Recipient Meritorious Svc. award USPHS, 1981, Mary McLeod Bethune award Nat Coun. Negro Women, 1979, Dr. John P. McGovern Ann. Lectureship award Am. Sch. Health Assn., Disting. Alumni award Meharry Med. Coll., 1989, Spelman Coll. 108 Founder's Day Convocation, 1989, Disting. Svc. medal USPHS, 1992, Hildrus A. Poindexter award OSG/PHS, 1993, numerous other svc. and achievement awards. Fellow Am. Acad. Pediatrics; mem. Nat. Inst. Medicine of Nat. Acad. Sci., Nat. Med. Assn., APHA, AAUW, AAAS, Spelman Coll. Alumnae Assn., Meharry Alumni Assn., Operation Crossroads Africa Alumni Assn., Delta Sigma Theta (hon.). Home: 2807 18th St NW Washington DC 20009-2205 Office: 200 Independence Ave SW Washington DC 20201-0004*

MANLEY, BARBARA LEE DEAN, occupational health nurse, hospital administrator, safety and health consultant; b. Washington, Nov. 5, 1946; d. Robert L. Dean and Mary L. (Jenkins) Dean Smallwood. BS, St. Mary-of-the-Woods, Terre Haute, Ind., 1973; MA, Central Mich. U., 1981. Cert. occupl. health nurse specialist. Indsl. nurse Ford Motor Co., Indpls., 1973-80; employee health nurse Starplex, Inc., Washington, 1981-84, Doctor's Hosp., Lanham, Md., 1984-85; regional occupational health nurse coordinator Naval Hosp., Long Beach, Calif., 1985-88; project mgr. East Coast Health Care Network, Inc., San Francisco, 1980-84; occupl. health nurse cons. HHS, Washington, 1980-84; occupational health and safety cons., mgr. FPE Group, Torrence, Calif., 1988-91; safety and loss control mgr. Assn. Calif. Hosp. Dists., Sacramento, 1991-93, v.p. loss control svcs., 1993-96; exec. dir. Quantum Inst., Sacramento, 1996—; part-time lectr. Compton (Calif.) Coll., 1986. Vol. ARC, Ft. Lewis, Wash., 1974-76, Ft. Harrison, Ind., 1978-80; counselor Crisis Hot-Line, Laurel, Md., 1981-83, Laurel Boy's and Girls Club, 1981-84. Recipient Navy's Meritorious Civilian Svc. Medal, 1989, Women of Excellence award Long Beach Press-Telegram Newspaper Guild, 1990, LCM Profl. of Yr. Acad. Loss Control Mgmt., 1995. Fellow Acad. Ambulatory Nursing Adminstrs. (Honor plaque 1981); mem. SCVAOHN (chair govt. affairs 1994—), Assn. Exec. Females, Am. Nurses Assn., Nat. Safety Mgmt. Soc. (2d v.p. 1992-96, 1st v.p. 1996—), Am. Assn. Occupational Health Nurses, Assn. Occupl. Healthcare Profls. (sec. 1986-88, conf. chairperson 1988, Outstanding Nurse of Yr. 1987), Fed. Safety and Health Council, Cen. Mich. U. Alumni Assn. (sec. 1985-88), Chi Eta Phi (regional bd. dirs. 1978-81). Presbyterian. Avocations: reading; crocheting; traveling; music. Office: Assn Calif Hosp Dists 2260 Park Towne Cir # Cl Sacramento CA 95825-0402

MANLOVE, STEPHEN PAUL, psychiatrist; b. St. Paul, Minn., June 11, 1955; s. Gerald Herald and Joanne Ella (Turner) M.; m. Margaret Ann Saunders, June 9, 1982; children: Kezia, Erin, Luke. BA, St Olaf Coll., 1977; MD, Univ. Minn., 1982. Diplomate Am. Bd. Psychiatry and Neurology, Am. Bd. Internal Medicine. Staff psychiatrist West River Mental Health Ctr., Rapid City, S.D., 1987-89; owner and psychiatrist Manlove Pscyhiatric Group, Rapid City, S.D., 1989-96. Co-founder and pres. bd. Wellspring Inc., Rapid City, 1989—; bd. dirs. Western Providers Physician Orgn., Rapid City, 1996. Mem. Am. Psychiatric Assn. (dep. rep. 1993-96), Am. Coll. Physicians, AMA. Home: 5408 Quail Dr Rapid City SD 57702 Office: Manlove Psychiatric Group 809 South St # 303 Rapid City SD 57701

MANLY, CAROL ANN, speech pathologist; b. Canton, Ohio, Nov. 21; d. William George and Florence L. (Parrish) M.; m. William Merget, Sept. 19, 1992; children: William, John. MA, U. Cin., 1970; PhD, NYU, 1988. Instr. U. Cin. Med. Ctr., 1970-72; asst. dir. Goldwater Hosp. NYU, 1972-83; pvt. practice N.Y.C., 1983—; cons. Mary Manning Walsh Home, N.Y.C., 1974-85, Beth Israel Med. Ctr.-North Divsn., N.Y.C., 1983—; adj. asst. prof. NYU, 1989-90, C.W. Post campus L.I. U., Brookville, 1990—. Author: (with others) Current Therapy in Physiatry, 1984, Communication Disorders of the Older Adult: A Practical Handbook for Health Care Professionals, 1993; contbr. articles to profl. jours. Mem. N.Y. Acad. Scis., Am. Speech-Lang.-Hearing Assn., N.Y. State Speech-Lang.-Hearing Assn., N.Y. Neuropsychology Group, NOW. Office: 360 E 65th St Ste 21D New York NY 10021-6726

MANN, JONATHAN MAX, international agency administrator, public health director; b. Boston, July 30, 1947; s. James and Ida (Laskow) M.; m. Marie-Paule Bondat, Jan. 30, 1970; children: Naomi, Lydia, Aaron. BA, Harvard U., 1969, MPH, 1980; MD, Washington U., St. Louis, 1974. Epidemic intelligence service officer USPHS, Ctrs. Disease Control, Atlanta and Santa Fe, 1975-77; med. epidemiologist, dir. AIDS research program, Kinshasa, Zaire, 1984-86; dir. global program AIDS, WHO, Geneva, 1986-90; state epidemiologist, chief med. officer N.Mex. Health Dept., Santa Fe, 1977-84. Mem. editorial bd. Control of Communicable Diseases in Man, Western Jour. Medicine, 1984—. Contbr. articles to profl. jours. Recipient Spl. Commendation N.Mex. Med. Soc., 1980, Friend of N.Mex. Journalism award Sigma Delta Chi, 1979, Disting. Service award School Nursing Com., 1979. Fellow Am. Coll. Preventive Medicine (Recognition award 1982), Am. Coll. Epidemiology; mem. Santa Fe County Med. Soc. (treas. 1981-82, pres. 1983-84), U.S.-Mex. Border Health Assn., Am. Pub. Health Assn.*

MANN, MARION, physician, educator; b. Atlanta, Mar. 29, 1920; s. Levi James and Cora (Casey) M.; m. Ruth Maurine Reagin, Jan. 16, 1943; children: Marion Jr., Judith (Mrs. Kenneth Walk). B.S. in Edn, Tuskegee Inst., Ala., 1940; M.D., Howard U., 1954; Ph.D., Georgetown U., 1961, D.Sc. (hon.), 1979; D.Sc. (hon.), U. Mass., 1984; grad., U.S. Army Command and Gen. Staff Coll., 1965, U.S. Army War Coll., 1970. Diplomate: Nat. Bd. Med. Examiners, Am. Bd. Pathology. Intern USPHS Hosp., Staten Island, N.Y., 1954-55; resident Georgetown U. Hosp., 1956-60; practice medicine, specializing in pathology Washington, 1961—; instr. pathology Georgetown U., 1960-61; professorial lectr. Georgetown U. (Sch. Medicine), 1970-73; asst. prof. pathology Howard U. Coll. Medicine, 1961-67, assoc. prof., 1967-70, prof., 1970, dean, 1970-79; v.p. rsch. Howard U., 1988-91. Capt. AUS, 1942-50; brig. gen. Res. Mem. Inst. Medicine, Nat. Acad. Scis., Alpha Omega Alpha. Mem. United Ch. of Christ. Home: 1453 Whittier Pl NW Washington DC 20012-2845 Office: 520 W St NW Washington DC 20001-2337

MANN, OSCAR, physician, internist, educator; b. Paris, Oct. 13, 1934; came to U.S., 1953; s. Aron and Helen (Biegun) M.; m. Amy S. Mann, July 19, 1964; children: Adriana, Karen. AA with distinction, George Washington U., 1958; MD cum laude, Georgetown U., 1962. Diplomate Am. Bd. Med. Examiners, Am. Bd. Internal Medicine, Am. Bd. Internal Medicine subspecialty Cardiovascular Disease; cert. advanced achievement in internal medicine; re-cert. in internal medicine. Intern Georgetown U. Med. Ctr., Washington, 1962-63, jr. asst. med. resident, 1963-64, clin. fellow in cardiology with Proctor Harvey program, 1965-66; sr. asst. resident in medicine Georgetown U. Hosp., Washington, 1964-65; clin. prof. medicine Georgetown U. Sch. Medicine, 1985—; nat. chmn. med. alumni fund Georgetown U. Med. Sch., Washington, 1993-95; pvt. practice internal medicine and cardiology, Washington, 1966—; mem. Med.-Nursing Audit Com., CME adv. com., teaching. adv. com., Opthamology dept. rev. com., surgery dept. rev. com., faculty com., search com. for a new dean for acad. affairs Georgetown U. Med. Ctr.; appointed coun. to the dean Georgetown U. Sch. Medicine, 1977—; mem. Instnl. Self Study Task Force. Contbr. articles to profl. jours. Served with the U.S. Army, 1953-55. Recipient Mead Johnson Postgrad. Scholar ACP, 1964-65, Physicians Recognition award AMA, 1987-96, Advanced Achievement in Internal Medicine, 1987. Fellow ACP, Am. Coll. Cardiology, Am. Coll. Chest Physicians; mem. AMA, Am. Soc. Internal Medicine, Am. Heart Assn. (coun. clin. cardiology), Med. Soc. D.C., Cosmos Club, Georgetown U. Alumni Assn. (chmn. med. alumni bd. 1995—, bd. govs. 1993—, chair med. alumni bd. 1995—), Alpha Omega Alpha, Phi Delta Epsilon. Home: 4925 Weaver Ter NW Washington DC 20016-2660 Office: Foxhall Internists PC 3301 New Mexico Ave NW Washington DC 20016-3622

MANN, STEVEN GERALD, radiologist; b. Phila., June 20, 1944; s. Hillard and Jeanette (Abrams) M.; m. Andrea I. Honey Krase, July 6, 1969; children: Heather Avery, Stephanie Anne. BA, Central High Sch., Phila., 1961; postgrad., Temple U., 1961-64; MD, Hahnemann U., 1968. Intern Montefiore Hosp, N.Y.C., 1968-69; fellow Royal Marsden (Cancer) Hosp., London, 1973-74; resident Saroni Tumor Inst., San Francisco, 1971-73; fellow, instr. U. Rochester (N.Y.), 1974-77; attending physician Albert Einstein Med. Ctr., Phila., 1977-80; v.p. Santa Cruz (Calif.) Radiation, 1980—; ptnr. S&M Leasing, Santa Cruz, 1989—; v.p., treas. Santa Cruz Radiation, 1980—. Author: (with others) Lung Cancer, 1982; contbr. articles to profl. jours. Pres. Am. Cancer Soc., Santa Cruz, 1984-86, Temple Beth El, Calif., 1988-89. Lt. comdr. USN, 1969-71. Acad. scholar Temple U., 1961-64; Radiation Therapy Oncology Group grantee Einstein Med. Ctr., Phila., 1977-80; Am. Cancer Soc. fellow Royal Marsden Hosp., London, 1973-74. Mem. AMA, Am. Coll. Radiology (chmn. practice accreditation com in radiation oncology), Am. Soc. Therapeutic Radiologists, Am. Radium Soc. (Resident Essay award 1973), Am. Soc. Clin. Oncology, European Soc. Therapeutic Radiology and Oncology, Endocurietherapy Soc., Santa Cruz County Med. Soc. (pres.-elect 1994-95, pres. 1995-96). Republican. Jewish. Home: 469 Camino Al Barranco Watsonville CA 95076-1508 Office: Santa Cruz Radiation 1575 Soquel Dr Santa Cruz CA 95065-1700

MANN, STEWART, cardiologist; b. Sheffield, Eng., Sept. 23, 1948; s. A. Leslie and Meta (Stewart) M.; m. Sheila G. Jones, Aug. 2, 1975; children: Graham, Eleanor, Catherine. BA, U. Oxford, 1970, BM, BCh, 1973, DM, 1985. Intern Kings Coll. Hosp., London, 1974-75; resident Northwick Park Hosp., Harrow, Eng., 1975-77, rsch. fellow cardiology, 1977-80; registrar Gen. Infirmary, Salisbury, Eng., 1980-81, Royal Infirmary, Bristol, Avon, Eng., 1981-82; sr. registrar, rsch. fellow Royal North Shore Hosp., Sydney, NSW, Australia, 1982-84; sr. registrar St. Mary' Hosp., London, 1984-85; cardiologist Hutt & Wellington Hosps., New Zealand, 1986—; mem. Wellington Area Ethics Com., 1992—. Author: (with others) Autonomic Failure, 1984. Trustee Hutt (New Zealand) Hosp. Heart Trust, 1987—. Fellow Royal Australian Coll. Physicians, Royal Coll. Physicians; mem. Action on Smoking Health, Cardiac Soc. Australia and New Zealand (hon. sec.-treas. 1987-91). Home: 134 Knights Rd, Lower Hutt 6009, New Zealand Office: Hutt Hosp Cardiology Dept, High St Pvt Bag 31907, Lower Hutt New Zealand

MANN, TRUE SANDLIN, psychologist, consultant; b. Longview, Tex., Aug. 4, 1934; d. Bob Murphy and Stella True (Williams) Sandlin; m. Jack Matthewson Mann, Sept. 4, 1954 (div. Dec. 1989); children: Jack Matthewson Jr., Bob Sandlin, Daniel Williams, Nathaniel Currier. BS, Stephen F. Austin State U., Nacogdoches, Tex., 1973, MA, 1977; PhD, East Tex. State U., 1982. Lic. psychologist, Tex., Ark. Instr. Stephen F. Austin State U., 1975-76, vis. asst. prof. psychology, 1986-87; instr. East Tex. State U., Commerce, 1980-81; postdoctoral fellow Southwestern Med. Sch., Dallas, 1982-83; pvt. practice, Longview, Tex., 1983-92; psychologist dept. family practice U. Tex. Health Sci. Ctr., Tyler, 1990-92; dir. psychol. svcs. St. Michael's Hosp., Texarkana, Tex., 1992-93; cons. psychologist, Longview, 1993—; weekly newspaper columnist HARBUS, Cambridge Mass., 1959-60; cons. Made-Rite Co., Longview, 1989—. Mem. candidate com. Assoc. Reps. Tex., Austin, 1990—; bd. dirs. Mental Health Assn. Tex., 1977-82, 84-92, Longview Symphony, 1995, Longview Mus. of Art, 1995; mem. Leadership Tex., 1988—. Mem. APA, Tex. Psychol. Assn. Episcopalian. Home: 1309 Inverness St Longview TX 75601-3548 Office: 1203 Montclair St Longview TX 75601-3565

MANNE, DEBORAH SUE, oncology nurse, consultant, dental hygienist; b. Vincennes, Ind., Nov. 20, 1954; d. Charles Kenneth and Susan Jane (Fox) Thornberry; m. Marshall Stanley Manne, Dec. 21, 1985; children: Matthew, Melissa Manne Zucker. AA, Maplewoods C.C., Kansas City, Mo., 1973; BS in Dental Hygiene, U. Mo., 1975; BSN, St. Louis U., 1991. RN, reg. dental hygienist, Mo. Dental hygienist Dr. Marshall S. Manne, St. Louis, 1978—, office nurse, 1991—; RN CIRCLE Jewish Hosp., St. Louis, 1993—; coord., cons. Oncology Dental Support Svcs., St. Louis, 1992; mem. curriculum rev. com. dental hygiene program St. Louis C.C., 1993; mem. adv. bd. ACCESS Dental Hygiene Jour., 1994—. Contbr. articles to profl. jours. Bd. dirs., v.p. Am. Cancer Soc., St. Louis, 1992-93, chair Gt. Am. Smokeout, 1992, mem. Breast Cancer task force, 1994—; mem. profl. adv. com. Wellness Cmty., St. Louis, 1994—. Recipient Vol. Recognition award Am. Cancer Soc., 1992, Mo. Dental Hygienist of Yr. award, 1995. Mem. Am. Dental Hygienists Assn. (council on pub. rels.), Oncology Nursing Soc. (chair oral care focus group), Mo. Dental Hygienists' Assn. (pres.), Greater St. Louis Hygienists' Assn. (pres.). Home: 11617 Larkmont Dr Creve Coeur MO 63141 Office: Oncology Dental Support Svc 3009 N Ballas Rd #211 Saint Louis MO 63131

MANNICK, JOHN ANTHONY, surgeon; b. Deadwood, S.D., Mar. 24, 1928; s. Alfred and Catherine Elizabeth (Schuster) M.; m. Alice Virginia Gossard, June 9, 1952; children—Catherine Virginia, Elizabeth Eleanor, Joan Barbara. BA, Harvard U., 1949, MD, 1953. Diplomate: Am. Bd. Surgery (dir. 1971-77). Intern Mass. Gen. Hosp., 1953-54, resident in surgery, 1956-60; instr. in surgery to asst. prof. Med. Coll. Va., 1960-64; asso. prof. to prof. surgery Boston U., 1964-76, chmn. div. surgery, 1973-76; Moseley prof. surgery Harvard U., 1976-94, Moseley Disting. prof. surgery, 1994—; dir. ednl. programs Harvard Med. Internat., 1994—; chmn. dept. surgery Peter Bent Brigham Hosp. and Brigham and Women's Hosp., Boston, 1976-94; dir. ednl. programs Harvard Med. Internat., 1994—; mem. surgery, anesthesiology and trauma study sect. NIH, 1978-82, mem. medicine study sect., 1967-70; rsch. com. Med. Found., Inc., 1970-76. Author: (with others) Modern Surgery, 1970, Core Textbook of Surgery, 1972, Surgery of Ischemic Limbs, 1972, The Cause and Management of Aneurysms, 1990; mem. editorial bd. AMA Archives of Surgery, 1973-84, Clin. Immunology and Immunopathology, 1972-84, Surgery, 1982—, Brit. Jour. Surgery, 1982-92, European Jour. Vascular Surgery, 1988—; mem. editorial bd. Advances in Surgery, 1979—, editor, 1984-86; mem. editorial bd. Jour. Vascular Surgery, 1984—, assoc. editor, 1990—; also articles. Served to capt. M.C. USAF, 1954-56. Markle scholar in acad. medicine, 1961-66. Fellow ACS (gov.), Royal Coll. Surgeons (hon., Eng.), Royal Coll. Surgeons (hon., Edinburgh); mem. Am. Fedn. Clin. Rsch., Am. Assn. Immunologists, Am. Soc. Exptl. Pathology, Soc. Clin. Investigation, Soc. Clin. Surgery, Soc. Univ. Surgeons, Soc. Surg. Chmn. (sec. 1985-87, pres. 1987-88), Am. Surg. Assn. (pres. 1989-90), Internat. Cardiovascular Soc. (recorder N.Am. chpt., 1973-76, pres. 1991-92, internat. v.p. 1993), Soc. Vascular Surgery (pres. 1981), N.E. Surg. Soc., New Eng. Soc. Vascular Surgery (pres. 1994-95), So. Surg. Assn., So. Soc. Vascular Surgery, Surg. Infection Soc., Halstead Soc., Phi Beta Kappa. Home: 81 Bogle St Weston MA 02193-1056 Office: 75 Francis St Boston MA 02115-6110

MANNING, BROWN ROTHWELL, physician assistant; b. Knoxville, Tenn., Jan. 2, 1951; s. Robert Cooper and Mary Elizabeth (Robertson) M.; m. Deborah Hansen, Sept. 24, 1977 (div. Oct. 1994); children: Christopher Brown, Andrea Deborah; m. Dianne K. Binzel, Oct. 20, 1995. BS, U. Ga., 1974; B of Med. Sci., Emory U., 1975; MPH, U. Ala., Birmingham, 1985. Cert. physician asst. Clin. physician asst. Jefferson Clinic, P.C., Birmingham, Ala., 1976-86; dir. Emory U. physician asst. program Emory U., Atlanta, 1986-90; instr. U. Fla. physician asst. program U. Fla., Gainesville, 1990-92; clin. physician asst. Jefferson Clinic, P.C., Birmingham, Ala., 1992—; chmn. Accreditation Rev. Com. on Edn. for Physician Assts., Marshfield, Wis., 1990-95; mem. adv. com. Ga. State Bd. Med. Examiners, Atlanta, 1987-90, Ala. Bd. Med. Examiners, Montgomery, 1995—; cons. Fla. Correctional Med. Authority, Tallahassee, 1991-95. Commr. Commn. on Accreditation of Allied Helath Edn. Programs, Chgo., 1994—. Fellow Am. Acad. Physician Assts., Ala. Soc. Physician Assts. (pres. 1984-85, Outstanding Mem. award 1986), Epsilon Delta. Episcopalian. Home: 3233 Ridgely Dr Birmingham AL 35243 Office: Jefferson Clinic PC 1526 Fifth Ave S Birmingham AL 35233

MANNING, DONALD E, psychiatrist, educator; b. Bluefield, W.Va., Dec. 24, 1945; s. Earl and Regina Manning; m. Agnes Thompson; children: Jennifer, Mark. BA in Chemistry, Duke U., 1968; MD, Med. U. S.C., 1972. Diplomate in psychiatry Am. Bd. Psychiatry and Neurology (sr. examiner 1989—), added qualifications in geriatric psychiatry. Resident in psychiatry Med. U. S.C., 1972-75, dir. rsch. tng., asst. dean, 1976-82; assoc. prof. psychiatry Emory Sch. Medicine, Atlanta, 1982-86, vice chmn. psychiatry, 1986-90, prof. psychiatry, 1986—, acting chmn. psychiatry, 1990-91, dir. Ctr. for Geriatrics, 1991—; chief psychiatry Wesley Woods Geriatric Ctr., Atlanta, 1988-89, v.p. med. affairs, 1991—. Contbr. articles to profl. publs. Fellow Am. Coll. Psychiatrists, Am. Psychiat. Assn.; mem. Am. Acad. Psychiatry and the Law, Am. Coll. Physician Execs., Ga. Psychiat. Physicians Assn. (pres. 1991-92), Am. Assn. Geriatric Psychiatrists. Home: 3185 Arden Rd NW Atlanta GA 30305 Office: Emory U Ctr Geriatrics 1817 Clifton Rd NE Atlanta GA 30329

MANNING-WEBER, CLAUDIA JOY, medical radiography administrator, consultant; b. Oak Park, Ill., Mar. 17, 1950; d. Charles Lawrence and Carrie Joy (Lund) Manning. AAS, Coll. of DuPage, 1980; BA with honors, Nat. Coll. of Edn., 1986, MS, 1989. Registered med. radiography technologist, Am. Registry of Radiologic Technologists; cert. med. radiography technologist, Ariz.; cert. adult and continuing edn. tchr., Ariz. State Cmty. Coll. Bd. Faculty Coll. of DuPage, Glen Ellyn, Ill., 1987-90, South Suburban Coll., South Holland, Ill., 1989-91; mentor tchr. Prescott (Ariz.) Coll., 1992—; dir. Ariz. Continuing Edn. Svcs., Avondale, 1992—; clin. instr. Phoenix Bapt. Hosp., 1992-93; program dir. PTR Bryman Sch., 1993-95; program dir. med. radiography Apollo Coll., 1995—; contbr., cons. EDUMED Co., Lakeville, Minn., 1995—; treas. ASSRT, Mesa, Ariz., 1993-94; cons. Coll. of DuPage, 1988-91. Author: Distance Delivered Education in Nuclear Medicine Technology, 1989. Mem. ASCD, AAUW, Internat. Soc. Radiographers and Radiologic Technicians, Assn. for Educators in Radiologic Sci., Am. Soc. Radiologic Technologists, Ariz. State Soc. Radiologic Technologists (ednl. dir. 1992-93, treas. 1993-94, seminar presenter 1991, 92), Delta Kappa Gamma. Home: 10938 W Bermuda Dr Avondale AZ 85323 Office: Apollo Coll 2701 W Bethany Home Rd Phoenix AZ 85017

MANNINO, JOSEPH ROBERT, JR., family practice physician; b. Altoona, Pa., May 6, 1941; m. Rosemary Kathleen McGrath, Apr. 8, 1978; 1 child, Angela Christine. BS in Physiology, Juniata Coll., Huntingdon, Pa., 1963; MA, East Carolina U., 1965; student, Phila. Coll. Osteo. Medicine, 1965-67; PhD, Colo. State U., 1974; DO, Kansas City Coll. Osteo. Medic, 1971. Diplomate Am. Osteo. Bd. Family Practice. Tchg. asst. in physiology East Carolina U., Greenville, N.C., 1965; coord. rsch. Phila. Coll. Osteo. Medicine, 1966-67; rsch. fellow Colo. State U., Ft. Collins, 1968-69; intern Rocky Mountain Hosp., Denver, 1971-72; pvt. practice Denver, 1972-77; asst. prof. gen. practice Kansas City (Mo.) Coll. Osteo. Medicine/U. Health Ctr., 1977-80; prof. family medicine Ohio U. Coll. Osteo. Medicine, Athens, 1981-94, Nova Southeastern U. Coll. Osteo. Medicine, North Miami Beach, Fla., 1994-96; asst. dir. med. edn. Rocky Mountain Hosp., Denver, 1972-73, mem. active med. staff dept. gen. practice, 1972-79, tchr. postdoctoral course in endocrinology, 1974-77, dir. med. edn., 1975-77; prin. investigator endocrine basis of essential hypertension, 1972-77; tchr. predoctoral course in gen. endocrinology Kansas City Coll. Osteo. Medicine, 1975-76, 77-80, dir. med. edn., 1977-80, mem. active med. staff dept. family medicine, 1977-80; dir. gen./family practice residency program Doctors Hosp., Columbus, Ohio, 1980-94, mem. active med. staff dept. gen. practice, 1980-86, tchr. postdoctoral course in clin. endocrinology, 1980-94, family practice residency rep. ednl. coun., 1980-94, mem. sr. attending med. staff dept. gen. practice, 1986-94, mem. pharmacy and therapeutics com., 1986-94, chmn. human-use subcom., 1986-88, chmn. institutional rev. com., 1988-94, chmn. drug use evaluation com., 1990-94; dir. med. edn., program dir. family practice residency program North Broward Hosp. Dist., Ft. Lauderdale, Fla., 1994-96; clin. assoc. Cleve. Clinic, Fla., 1996—; cons. State Bd. Registration for Healing Arts of Mo., 1979—; med. cons. Comprehensive Rev. Tech., Inc., Columbus, 1989-91, Nationwide Ins. Co., Columbus, 1990-94, Ohio State Med. Bd., 1992—; lectr. in field. Editl. cons. Hosp. Formulary, 1986—, Jour. Family Practice, 1991—; contbr. articles to profl. jours. Trustee Rocky Mountain Hosp., Denver, 1975-77. Recognized for Innovation in Improving Health Care Quality Mgmt. Am. Coll. Physician Execs.; named Gen. Practicioner of Yr. Ohio State Soc. Am. Coll. Gen. Practitioners in Osteo. Medicine and Surgery, 1992. Fellow Am. Coll. Osteo. Family Practice, Am. Soc. Colposcopy and Cervical Pathology, Am. Soc. Laser Medicine and Surgery; mem. Am. Osteo. Assn. (internship/residency inspector 1977—), Am. Coll. Osteo. Family Physicians (com. on evaluation and edn. 1990—, com. on rsch. 1990—, chmn. 1990-93, grants implementation com. 1991—, program chmn. ann. meeting 1991—, residency program dirs. workshop 1991-95, task force on practice guidelines 1993—, Fla. state soc.), Am. Coll. Gen. Practicioners in Osteo. Medicine and Surgery (sr. residency cons., inspector 1980—), N.Y. Acad. Sci., Endocrine Soc., Am. Coll. Cryosurgery, Fla. Soc. Osteo. Medicine (Broward County Acad.), Chi Beta Phi, Sigma Xi.

MANOHARAN, THOMAS, pharmacist; b. Vellore, Madras, India, June 5, 1935; came to U.S., 1976; s. Joshua Elias and Annal (David) T. Diploma in compounding, Christian Med. Coll. Hosp., Vellore, 1955, diploma in pharmacy, 1962; B in Pharmacy, Madras Med. Coll., 1966; M in Pharmacy, Nagpur (India) U., 1974; postgrad., Idaho State U., 1993—. Pharmacist Christian Med. Coll. Hosp., Vellore, 1955-65; asst. chief pharmacist Christian Med. Coll. Hosp., Madras, 1965-76; pharmacist Met. Hosp. Ctr., N.Y.C., 1978-84, asst. dir. pharmacy, 1984-95, assoc. dir., 1995—. Author: Manufacturing of Parenteral Fluids in Small Hospital Pharmacy, 1970. Mem. Am. Soc. Hosp. Pharmacists. Home: 92-31 57th Ave Apt 6M Elmhurst NY 11373-5067 Office: Met Hosp Ctr Pharmacy 1901 1st Ave New York NY 10029-7418

MANON-ESPAILLAT, RAMON, neurologist; b. Dominican Republic, Feb. 2, 1956; came to U.S., 1984; s. Ramon and Thelma (Espaillat) M.; m. Dinorah Matos, Apr. 29, 1978; 1 child, Yorell. BS in Chemistry magna cum laude, U. P.R., 1976, MD, 1980. Diplomate Am. Bd. Psychiatry and Neurology, Am. Bd. Clin. Neurophysiology, Am. Bd. Sleep Medicine, Am. Bd. Electrodiagnostic Medicine; lic. physician, N.J., Pa., Ohio, P.R. Med. intern U. P.R., 1980-81, resident in neurology, 1981-84; clin. neurophysiology fellow U. Tex., Houston, 1984-85; asst. prof. neurology Case Western Res. U., Cleve., 1984-90; sleep disorder fellow Ohio State U., Columbus, 1988; assoc. prof. neurology Temple U., Phila., 1990-93, dir. clin. neurophysiology, dir. epilepsy program, 1990-93, dir. sleep lab., 1990-93; dir. epilepsy program, clin. assoc. prof. neurology Thomas Jefferson Med. Sch., Phila., 1993—; pvt. practice Neurology and Neurophysiology Assocs., Phila.; active staff Thomas Jefferson U. Hosp., Meth. Hosp., St. Agnes Hosp., Cooper Hosp., Grad. Hosp., Magee Rehab. Hosp., Wills Eye Hosp. all 1993—. Ad hoc reviewer Neurology Jour., 1987—; contbr. numerous articles and abstracts to profl. jours., chpts. to books.; book reviewer: Advances in Neurology, Vol. 66: Epilepsy and the Functional Anatomy of the Frontal Lobe, 1995. Bd. dirs. Epilepsy Found. Phila., 1992-93. Fellow Am. Sleep Disorder Assn., Am. Assn. Electrodiagnostic Medicine; mem. Am. Acad. Neurology, Am. Epilepsy Soc., Am. EEG Soc. Office: Neurology/Neurophys Assocs 125 S 9th St Philadelphia PA 19107

MANOS, NICHOLAS GEORGE, dental technician; b. N.Y.C., Oct. 14, 1954; s. George Nicholas and Elizabeth Ann (Flanagan) M.; m. Patricia Ann Kaisen, Aug. 4, 1979; children: Cassandra, Cynthia. BS in Biology, Manhattan Coll., Bronx, N.Y., 1976; AAS in Dental Tech., N.Y.C. Cmty. Coll., Bklyn., 1979; MS in Higher Edn. Adminstrn., Baruch Coll., Manhattan, 1985. Cert. dental technician, Nat. Bd. Certification. Chair D.L.T. dept. N.Y.C. Tech. Coll., 1993—; curriculum cons. Commn. on Dental Accrediatation, Chgo., 1990—; spkr. Nat. Bd. Certification, Alexandria, Va., 1990—; pres. Greater N.Y. Cert. Dental Technologists Group, Bklyn., 1990—. Contbr. articles to profl. pubs., 1984-92. Republican. Roman Catholic. Office: N.Y.C. Tech Coll 300 Jay St Brooklyn NY 11201

MANOV, LESLIE JOAN BOYLE BRONN (LESLIE JOAN BOYLE MANOV BRONN), radiologist, medical administrator; b. White Plains, N.Y., Aug. 23, 1948; d. Myles Joseph and Harriet Geib (Warburton) Boyle; m. Gregory A. Manov; children from previous marriage: Jay Alexander Bronn, Natasha Nisa Bronn; children from current marriage: John Joseph Manov, Ann Esther Manov. BS, Ohio State U., 1970, MD, 1976. Diplomate Am. Bd. Radiology. Intern internal medicine Ohio State U. Hosp., Columbus, 1976-77, resident internal medicine, 1977-78, resident diagnostic radiology, 1978-81; chief radiology service VA Outpatient Clinic, Columbus, 1981-86; chief diagnostic radiology service Allen Park (Mich.) VA Hosp. Med. Ctr., 1986-87, chief nuclear medicine and diagnostic radiology services, 1987-94; chief radiology svc. Miami (Fla.) VA Med. Ctr., 1994—; clin. asst. prof. radiology Ohio State U. Coll. Medicine, 1981-86, Wayne State U. Sch. Medicine, 1986-94, U. Miami Sch. Medicine, 1995—. Mem. AMA, Am. Coll. Radiology, Radiol. Soc. N.Am., Assn. VA Chiefs of Radiology, Am. Assn. Women Radiologists, Am. Women's Med. Assn., Am. Inst. Ultrasound in Medicine, South Dade Women's Physicians, South Fla. Radiology Soc., Fla. Radiological Soc., Phi Beta Kappa, Alpha Lambda Delta. Office: Miami VA Med Ctr Radiology Svc Miami FL 33146

MANOWITZ, PAUL, biochemist, researcher, educator; b. Monticello, N.Y., Dec. 13, 1940; s. Jacob M. and Rose (Levine) M.; m. Joyce L. Swartz, June 16, 1968; children: Neal J., Lauren H. BA in Chemistry with honors, Cornell U., 1962; PhD in Biochemistry, Brandeis U., 1967. Postdoctoral fellow NYU Sch. Medicine, 1967-70, instr., 1970-72; asst. prof. psychiatry U. Medicine and Dentistry N.J. Robert Wood Johnson Med. Sch., Piscataway, 1972-78, assoc. prof. psychiatry, 1978-96, assoc. prof. psychiatry and neurology, 1991-96, prof. psychiaty and neurology, 1996—; rsch. cons. VA Med. Ctr., Lyons, N.J., 1987—. Editorial bd. Jour. of Studies on Alcohol, 1993—; contbr. articles to profl. jours. Grantee Nat. Inst. on Alcohol Abuse and Alcoholism, UNICO Found. Mem. AAAS, Am. Soc. for Neurochemistry, Internat. Soc. for Biomed. Rsch. on Alcoholism, Soc. Biol. Psychiatry, Rsch. Soc. on Alcoholism, Soc. for Neurosci., World Fedn. of Socs. Biol. Psychiatry. Home: 7 Guernsey Ln East Brunswick NJ 08816-3506 Office: U Medicine and Dentistry NJ Robert Wood Johnson Med Sch 675 Hoes Ln Piscataway NJ 08854-5635

MANSBERGER, ARLIE ROLAND, JR., surgeon; b. Pitts., Oct. 13, 1922; s. Arlie Rol and Mayme (Smith) M.; m. Anna Ellen Piel, July 27, 1946; children—Ellen Lynn, John Arlie, Leigh Ann. B.A., Western Md. Coll., 1943, D.Sc. (hon.), 1974; M.D., U. Md., 1947, D.Sc. (hon.), 1978. Diplomate: Am. Bd. Surgery (dir., vice chmn.). Intern U. Md. Hosp., 1947-49, resident in surgery, 1947-54; chief wound shock br. biophysics div. Army Chem. Center, 1954-56; instr. surgery U. Md., 1956-59, asst. prof., 1959-61, asso. prof., 1961-69, prof. surgery, 1969-73; clin. dir. shock-trauma unit, 1962-73; prof. surgery, chmn. dept. Med. Coll. Ga., Augusta, 1973-91; prof. surgery emeritus, chmn., 1991—; cons. surgeon Dwight David Eisenhower Army Med. Center, VA Hosp. Editor: Essence of General Surgery, 1975; chmn. editorial bd.: Bull. U. Md, 1971-73; editor-in-chief: The Am. Surgeon,

1973-89; surg. editor: Resident and Staff Physician, 1979-91; contbr. articles to profl. jours., chpts. to books. Trustee Western Md. Coll., 1971—, Med. Research Found. Ga., 1973-91; bd. dirs. Nicholas J. Pisican Found., 1993—. Served to col. U.S. Army, 1943-46, 54-56. Recipient Man of Yr. award U. Md., 1970, 72, Golden Apple teaching award U. Md., 1968, 72, Disting. Faculty award Med. Coll. Ga., 1979, Gold Medal Alumni award U. Md., 1989, Disting. Svc. award (medal) Southeastern Surg. Congress, 1990. Fellow A.C.S. (gov.); mem. Am. Surg. Assn., Soc. Univ. Surgeons, So. Surg. Assn., Soc. Internationale de Chirurgie, Am. Assn. Surgery of Trauma, Southeastern Surg. Congress, Soc. Surgery of Alimentary Tract, AMA, Soc. Consultants to Armed Forces, Med. Assn. Ga. (editorial bd. 1987-92), Am. Bd. Family Practice (bd. dirs. 1987-92), 29th Div. Assn., Alpha Omega Alpha. Episcopalian. Home: One 7th St Unit 1502 Augusta GA 30901-1343 Office: Dept Surgery Med Coll Ga Augusta GA 30912

MANSCHRECK, THEO CLYDE, research psychiatrist; b. New Haven, June 21, 1945; s. Clyde Leonard and Ardis (Taylor) M.; m. Judy Laughery; children: Christopher, Laura Heidi. BA, Carleton Coll., 1967; MD, Cornell U., 1971; MPH, Harvard U., 1971; AM (hon.), Dartmouth, 1993; MA (hon.), Brown U., 1996. Diplomate Am. Bd. Psychiatry and Neurology. Intern San Francisco Gen. Hosp., 1971-72; resident Mass. Gen. Hosp., Boston, 1972-75, chief acute psychiatry svc., 1975-76, fellow in consultation psychiat., 1976-77, chief lab. for clin. and exptl. psychopathology, 1977—; chief adult inpatient svc., Lindemann Mental Health Ctr. Mass. Gen. Hosp., 1980-83; clin. dir. Harbor Area and Lindemann Mental Health Ctr., 1983-90; dir. schizophrenic disorders clinic Mass. Gen. Hosp., 1983-90, sr. psychiatrist, 1990—; prof. psychiatry Dartmouth Med. Sch., N.H. Hosp., Concord, 1989-94; prof. psychiatry and human behavior Brown U. Sch. Medicine, 1994—, also dir. pub. psychiatry, schizophrenia rsch. program, 1994—; assoc. prof. Harvard U. Med. Sch., Boston, 1984-89, lectr. psychiatry, faculty rsch. assoc. dept. psychology, 1990; cons. drug evaluation program, AMA, 1985. Editor: Psychiatric Medicine Update, 1979, 81, 84; contbr. over 100 articles to sci. jours. Pre-med advisor Harvard U., 1983-89; resident tutor, then faculty assoc., 1983-89. Fulbright rsch. award, 1985-86; recipient Rand Award. Fellow Am. Psychiat. Assn., Mass. Psychiat. Soc., Soc. Biol. Psychiatry, Assn. Rsch. in Nervous and Mental Disease, N.Y. Acad. Sci., Soc. for Rsch. in Psychopathology. Office: Harvard Med Sch Corrigan Mental Health Ctr 49 Hillside St Fall River MA 02720

MANSELL, PETER WILLIAM ANSON, oncologist, retired; b. London, Sept. 19, 1936; came to U.S., 1972; divorced; children: Claire, Sophie, Tom. BA, Cambridge U., Eng., 1958, MA, 1962; LMSSA, London U., 1961; MB, MCH, St. Bartholomews Hosp., Eng., 1962. Rsch. assoc. Bristol U., Eng., 1965-72; instr. surgery Tulane U., New Orleans, 1972-74; dir. medicine, oncology McGill U., Montreal, Que., Can., 1974-77; dir., div. edn. and tng. Cancer Ctr. State Fla., Miami, 1977-81; prof. medicine M.D. Anderson Cancer Ctr., Houston, 1981—; med. dir. Inst. Immunological Disorders, Houston, 1986-87; cons. ICN Viratek Inc., Costa Mesa, Calif., 1989-90; pvt. practice Houston, 1989-91; pres. Q3V Inc., 1989—; v.p. R & D, med. dir. Immudyne, Houston, 1994-95; retired, 1995; assoc. corp. med. dir. Pasteur Merieux Connaught, Paris, 1992-94; med. dir. MIDH Labs., France, 1995—; med. cons. Pasteur Merieux Connaught. Author, co-author 20 books; contbr. articles to profl. jours. Fellow Am. Coll. Preventive Medicine, Royal Coll. Surgeons; mem. AMA, Am. Soc. for Clin. Oncology, Physicians Assn. for AIDS Care (pres. 1989-91). Home: 512 W 34th St Houston TX 77018-7650

MANSEN, THOMAS J., nursing educator; b. Holland, Mich., Aug. 8, 1950; s. Albert F. and Donna N. (Hendrickson) M.; m. Cheryl Mock, June 24, 1978; 1 child, Cameron David. BSN, U. Mich., 1973; MS, U. Utah, 1977; PhD, U. Tex., Austin, 1988. Asst. prof. Westminster Coll., Salt Lake City, Hope Coll., Mich.; assoc. prof. U. Utah Coll. Nursing, Salt Lake City. Mem. ANA, Nat. League Nursing, Sigma Theta Tau (pres. Gamma Rho chpt. 1990-92). Home: 6753 S 1530 E Salt Lake City UT 84121-2731

MANSFIELD, CARL MAJOR, radiation oncology educator; b. Phila., Dec. 24, 1928; m. Sarah Lynn Flower; children: Joel, Kara. AB in Chemistry, Lincoln U., 1951; postgrad., Temple U., 1952; MD, Howard U., 1956; ScD (hon.), Lincoln U., 1991. Diplomate Am. Bd. Radiology, Am. Bd. Nuclear Medicine. Rotating intern Episcopal Hosp., Phila., 1956-57, resident in radiology, 1957-58, 60, 61-62; resident in radiation therapy and nuclear medicine Thomas Jefferson Med. Coll. Hosp., Phila., 1960-61, NIH fellow in radiation therapy and nuclear medicine, 1962-63, instr. radiology, chief div. nuclear medicine, 1964-65, Chernicoff fellow in pediatric radiation therapy, 1964-66, assoc. in radiology, chief div. nuclear medicine, 1966-67, asst. prof. radiology, chief div. nuclear medicine, 1967-69, assoc. prof. dept. radiation therapy and nuclear medicine, chief sect. of ultrasound, 1970-74, prof., chief div. nuclear medicine and sect. of ultrasound, 1974-76, prof., chmn. dept. radiation therapy and nuclear medicine, 1983-95; assoc. dir. divsn. cancer treatment Nat. Cancer Inst. NIH, Bethesda, Md., 1995—; NIH postdoctoral fellow in radiation therapy Middlesex Hosp. and Med. Sch., London, 1963-64; lectr. in radiology U. Pa. Sch. Medicine, Phila., 1967-73; vis. prof. radiation therapy and nuclear medicine Hahnemann Med. Coll. Hosp., 1971; sabbatical leave Myerestein Inst. Radiotherapy, Middlesex Hosp. and Med. Sch., London, 1972-73; mem. grad. faculty in radiation biophysics U. Kans. Med. Ctr., Kansas City, 1977-83, prof. , chmn. dept. radiation therapy, 1976-83; chmn. dept. radiation therapy Menorah Med. Ctr., Kansas City, Mo., 1977-83. Author 2 books, also author or co-author over 129 articles in med. jours. Served with USAF, 1958-60. Fellow Am. Coll. Radiology, Coll. Physicians of Phila., Am. Coll. Nuclear Medicine; mem. AMA, Am. Coll. Radiology, Am. Cancer Soc. (dir.-at-large, nat. bd. dirs. 1981-85, med. and sci. com. 1981-88, profl. edn. com. 1981-88, pres. Phila. divsn. 1989), Am. Radium Soc. (pres. 1988), Radiation Rsch. Program Nat. Cancer Inst. (dir.), Sigma Xi. Office: NIH Bldg EPN Rm 800 Bethesda MD 20892

MANSFIELD, PATRICK DAVID, anesthesiologist; b. Louisa, Va., June 15, 1942; s. Patrick Roosevelt and Susie Ann (Scott) M.; div. Oct. 1987; children: Aida Patricia, Daniel Patrick. BS, Va. State U., 1964; diploma, Am. U., 1969; MD, Georgetown U., 1973. Diplomate Am. Acad. Pain Mgmt. Intern Georgetown U., Washington, 1973-74, resident, 1974-77, radiologist, 1977-78, anesthesiologist, 1978-82; anesthesiologist Alexandria (Va.) Hosp., 1982—. Sgt. U.S. Army, 1965-69. Mem. Am. Soc. Anesthesia, Am. Soc. Regional Anesthesia, Va. Soc. Anesthesia, U.S. Com. UNICEF, World Wildlife Fedn. Home: 5405 Gunston Ln Camp Shrimp MD 20746 Office: Anesthesia Assoc Ltd PO Box 9203 Alexandria VA 22304

MANSFIELD, TOBI ELLEN, psychologist; b. Miami Beach, Fla., Oct. 4, 1949; d. Murray Irwin and Rose Turner (Plansky) Mantell; 1 child, Mia Michelle. BA, U. Miami, Fla., 1974; MA, Norwich U., Montpelier, Vt., 1982; PhD, Union Inst., Cin., 1987. Mental health counselor South Dade Crisis Intervention, Miami, Fla., 1978-80; adj. faculty Miami Dade Community Coll., 1977-80; clin. assoc. Miami Psychotherapy Inst., 1980-88; adj. faculty Nova U., 1984-87, U. Miami Med. Sch., 1988-90; psychologist, dir. Miami Wellness Ctr., 1987—; mem. med. staff South Fla. Inst. for Reproductive Medicine. Contbr. articles to profl. jours. Mem. APA, Am. Bd. Med. Psychotherapists (assoc.), Royal Soc. Medicine, Am. Soc. for Reproductive Medicine. Office: Miami Wellness Center Ste # 106 9150 SW 87th Ave Miami FL 33176-2311

MANSKE, PAUL ROBERT, orthopedic hand surgeon, educator; b. Ft. Wayne, Ind., Apr. 29, 1938; s. Alfred R. and Elsa E. (Streufert) M.; m. Sandra H. Henricks, Nov. 29, 1975; children: Ethan Paul, Claire Bruch, Louisa Hendricks. BA, Valparaiso U., 1960, DSc (hon.), 1985; MD, Washington U., St. Louis, 1964. Diplomate Am. Bd. Surgery. Surg. intern U. Wash., Seattle, 1964-65, surg. resident, 1965-66; orthopedic surg. resident Washington U., St. Louis, 1969-72; hand surgery fellow U. Louisville, 1971; instr. orthopedic surgery Washington U. Med. Sch., St. Louis, 1972-76, asst. prof. orthopedic surgery, 1976-83, prof., 1983—, chmn. dept., 1983-95. Editor-in-chief Jour. Hand Surgery, 1996—; contbr. more than 215 articles and abstracts to profl. jours. Lt. comdr. USN, 1966-69, Vietnam. Lt. comdr. USN, 1966-69, Vietnam. Fellow AMA, Am. Acad. Orthopaedic Surgery, Am. Orthopaedic Assn.; mem. Am. Soc. Surgery of the Hand, Alpha Omega Alpha. Lutheran. Office: Washington Univ Dept Orthop Surgery 1 Barnes Hosp Plz Saint Louis MO 63110

MANSO, GILBERT, physician; b. Havana, Cuba, Dec. 16, 1942; s. Gilberto F. and Gricelda (Jimenez) M.; came to U.S., 1959, naturalized, 1968; B.A., U. Tex., Austin, 1965; M.D., U. Tex. Med. Br., Galveston, 1969; student U.S. Air Force Sch. Aerospace Medicine, 1970; children from previous marriage: Wayne, Tammy, Seth. Cert. comml., multiengine, instrument rated pilot. Rotating intern Meml. Bapt. Hosp., Houston, 1969-70; chief of staff Cochran Meml. Hosp., Morton, Tex., 1974-76; health officer Cochran County, Tex., 1974-76; chmn. med. care evaluation com. Tidelands Hosp., Channelview, Tex., 1976-77, vice-chief of staff, 1977-78, chief of staff, 1978—; mem. faculty U. Tex. Health Science, Houston, asst. prof. dept. family medicine; pres. The Whole Health Ctr., Houston, 1976—. Pres., Manso Airmotive; bd. dirs. The Living Ctr. one of the pioneers in wholistic medicine in Tex., Houston; mem. med. adv. bd. Am. Reflexology Assn. Author: The Diabetes & Hypoglycemia Cope Book. Served to maj. MC USAF, 1970-75, Vietnam 1970-71. Decorated Air medal and 2 oak leaf clusters. Diplomate Am. Bd. Family Practice. Fellow Am. Acad. Family Practice; mem. AMA, Tex. Med. Assn., Harris County Med. Soc., Am. Holistic Med. Assn., Internat. Wine and Food Soc. (bd. dirs. 1981-84), Houston Acad. Family Practice, Am. Coll. Emergency Physicians, Chaine de Rotisseurs, New Warriors. Republican. Office: 5177 Richmond Ave Ste 125 Houston TX 77056-6736

MANSON, ROBERTO R., surgeon, educator; b. Santa Fe, Argentina, Feb. 21, 1941; s. Roberto E. and Valentina C. (Troiani) M.; m. Amalia Buffo, June 11, 1966; children: Roberto Jose, Pablo Andres, Carolina Amalia, Sebastian, Ana Amelia. MD, Facultad Medicina, Tucuman, Argentina, 1965. Diplomate Am. Bd. Surgery, Am. Bd. Colon and Rectal Surgery. Intern St. John Hosp., Detroit, 1966-67; resident Mayo Grad. Sch., Rochester, Minn., 1967-72; staff mem. Carle Clinic, Urbana, Ill., 1972-81, Saustrio Mirodelo, Tucuman, 1981—; dir. Sonotuo Niodelo, Tucuman, 1990—; asst. prof. U. Ill., 1973-81, U. Tucuman, 1983—. Mem. Argentina Soc. Surgery, Argentina Acad. Surgery. Republican. Roman Catholic. Office: Saustrio Mirodelo, 25 de Royo 559, 4000 San Miguel Tucuman Argentina

MANSOUR, KAMAL A., cardiothoracic surgeon; b. Nov. 25, 1929; m. Sylvia Cleopatra Sideros, June 19, 1956; 1 child, Sylvia Frederica. M.B., B.Ch., Ein Shams U., Cairo, Egypt, 1954. Diplomate Am. Bd. Surgery, Am. Bd. Thoracic Surgery; lic. physician, Ga. Intern Tanta (Egypt) Gen. Hosp., 1954-55; surgeon Bapt. Hosp., Ajlun, Jordan, 1956-60, Gaza, Egypt, 1961-62; asst. resident in surgery Ch. Home & Hosp., Balt., 1962-63; asst. and chief resident in surgery Ga. Bapt. Hosp., Atlanta, 1963-66; asst. and chief resident cardio thoracic surgery Emory U. Hosp., Atlanta, 1966-68; pvt. practice specializing in cardiothoracic surgery Atlanta, 1968—; active staff Emory U. Hosp., Grady Meml. Hosp., Crawford W. Long Hosp., Henrietta Egleston Children's Hosp., VA Hosp., Piedmont Hosp.; instr. surgery Emory U. Sch. Medicine, 1968-71, asst. prof. surgery, 1971-76, assoc. prof. surgery, 1976-87, prof. cardiothoracic surgery, 1987—. Contbr. numerous articles to profl. jours. Fellow ACS, Am. Coll. Cardiology, Am. Coll. Chest Physicians, Am. Coll. Angiology, Southeastern Surg. Congress; mem. Council on Critical Care, Am. Assn. Thoracic Surgery, Am. Heart Assn., Soc. Thoracic Surgeons, So. Thoracic Surg. Assn. Internat. Coll. Surgeons (vice regent Ga.), Am. Thoracic Soc., Ga. Surg. Soc., AMA, Med. Assn. Ga., Med. Assn. Atlanta, N. Am. Soc. Pacing and Electrophysiology, Internat. Soc. for Diseases of the Esophagus, Gen. Thoracic Surg. Club. Home: 823 Lullwater Rd NE Atlanta GA 30307-1239 Office: The Emory Clinic 1365 Clifton Rd NE Atlanta GA 30307-1013

MANSOUR, M. ASHRAF, vascular surgeon, medical educator; b. Cairo, Egypt, Oct. 2, 1956; came to U.S., 1982; m. Julie Nigg, May 25, 1984. MD, Cairo U., 1980. Diplomate Am. Bd. Surgery, added qualifications in critical care surgery and gen. vascular surgery. Surgery resident U. Colo., Denver, 1984-89, chief resident, 1989-90; staff surgeon Denver Gen. Hosp., 1990-91, Denver VA Med. Ctr., 1990-91; instr. surgery U. Colo., Denver, 1990-91; asst. chief gen. surgery Martin Army Hosp., Ft. Benning, Ga., 1991-93; vascular surgery fellow So. Ill. U., Springfield, 1993-95; clin. asst. prof. surgery Uniformed Svcs. Univ. H.S., Bethesda, Md., 1993—; asst. prof. surgery Loyola U. Sch. of Medicine, Maywood, Ill., 1995.; affiliate faculty Am. Heart Assn., Denver, 1990-92. Major U.S. Army Med. Corps, 1991-93. Mem. AMA, S.W. Surg. Congress, Soc. Critical Care Medicine, Soc. Am. Gastrointestinal Endoscopic Surgeons, Ill. State Med. Soc., Peripheral Vanular Surgery Soc. Office: Loyola Univ Med Ctr Dept Surgery K-352900-3 2160 S First Ave Maywood IL 60153-3304

MANSTEIN, CARL HOWARD, plastic surgeon; b. Phila., Jan. 13, 1951; s. George and Marial Louise (Boyor) M.; m. Marla Sue Cohen, Sept. 7, 1986; children: Arielle Nicole, Samuel Max, Ely Lev. AB cum laude, Amherst Coll., 1972; MD, Temple U., 1976. Chief plastic surgery Jeanes Hosp., Phila., 1985—; assoc. prof. surgery Temple U. Sch. Medicine, Phila., 1984—. Internat. bd. reviewers Jour. Plastic & Reconstructive Surgery, 1986—. Fellow Am. Coll. Surgeons; mem. Am. Soc. Plastic & Reconstructive Surgeons, Sigma Xi. Office: 7500 Central Ave Ste 210 Philadelphia PA 19111

MANSUKHANI, SUNDER HASHMATRAI, pathology educator; b. Hyderabad, Sindh, Pakistan, Jan. 14, 1931; came to U.S., 1969; s. Hahmatrai C. and Putli H. (Shahani) M.; m. Devika B. Kripalani, Sept. 2, 1961; children: Kiron, Ashwin, Sharad. B in Medicine and Surgery, B.J. Med. Coll., Ahmedabad, India, 1954; DPH, Bombay U., 1958; MD, Grant Med. Coll., Bombay, 1959. Diplomate Am. Bd. Pathology. Resident Sir J.J. Hosps./U. Bombay, 1956-59; intern Presbyn. Hosp.-U. Pitts., 1961-62; sr. lectr. Grant Med. Coll., Bombay U., 1959-67; prof. pathology Mahatma Gandhi Med. Coll., Jamshedpur, India, 1967-69; rsch. assoc. U. Pitt. Med. Sch., 1969-71; assoc. prof. pathology Med. Coll. Pa., Phila., 1971-76, prof. pathology, 1976—; chmn. pathology and lab. medicine Bucks County Campus, Med. Coll. Hosp., Warminster, Pa., 1991-94; pres. S.J. Pathology Assocs., 1989—; prof. pathology Hahnemann U., Phila., 1994—; dir. med. edn. in pathology Med. Coll. Pa., Phila., 1971-79; dir. continuing med. edn. Zurbrugg Meml. Hosps., Riverside, N.J., 1979-91. Contbr. abstracts, articles to profl. jours. Fellow Royal Coll. Pathologists (Eng.), Am. Soc. Clin. Pathologists; mem. Internat. Acad. Pathology, Am. Assn. Physicians from India (bd. trustees 1990, chmn. health sys. reform 1995, Spl. Achievement award 1987, 88). Home: 103 N Riding Dr Moorestown NJ 08057-1311

MANTAS, JOHN, health informatics educator; b. Athens, Greece, Oct. 1, 1954; s. Gerassimos and Despina (Deliolanis) M. BSc with honors, U. Manchester, Eng., 1979, MSc, 1980, PhD, 1983. Teaching asst. U. Manchester, 1979-81, rsch. fellow, 1981-83; researcher Greek Armed Forces, Athens, 1983-85; lectr. U. Athens, 1985-87, asst. prof., 1987-92, assoc. prof., 1992—, coord. prof. Erasmus course, 1989—; mem. tech. panel Aim Office, European Econ. Communities, Brussels, 1990, evaluator telematics, 1991, project ptnr., 1989-91, coord. Erasmus Bur., 1991; head delegation European Standardization Com., Brussels, 1990-91. Author: Introduction to Informatics, 1989, MSc Course in Health Informatics, 1990, Health Informatics, 1990. European Econ. Communities fellow 1989-90, grantee, 1989-91. Mem. IEEE, Inst. Elec. Engrs., Assn. Computer Machinery, Internat. Fuzzy Sets Assn., Pattern Recognition Soc. Christian Orthodox. Home: PO Box 77313 P Faliro, GR-17510 Athens Greece Office: U Athens, 75 Mikras Asias St, GR-11527 Athens Greece

MANTERO-ATIENZA, EMILIO, psychiatrist, epidemiologist; b. Seville, Spain, Jan. 23, 1958; came to U.S., 1984; s. Jose Mantero and Marina Atienza. MD, U. Seville, Spain, 1981; MPH in Epidemiology, U. Miami Sch. Medicine, Fla., 1988; PhD, U. Seville Grad. Sch., Spain, 1990. Diplomate Am. Bd. Psychiatry and Neurology; lic. Fla. Staff physician Spanish Health Ctrs., Madrid, Seville, 1981-84; rsch. coord. Clin. Pharmacology Assocs., Miami, Fla., 1984-85; rsch. assoc. dept. pharmacology U. Miami, Fla., 1985-87; Am. Heart Assn. fellow dept. pharmacology U. Miami, 1987-88, rsch. asst. prof. dept. epidemiology, 1989-91, clin. asst. prof. dept. epidemiology and pub. health, 1991—; resident in psychiatry Jackson Meml. Hosp. U. Miami Sch. of Medicine, Fla., 1991-94; attending physician alcohol disorders rsch. unit dept. psychiatry U. Miami Sch. of Medicine, Fla., 1995—; med. dir. St. Thomas Comty. Mental Health Ctr., Coral Gables, Fla., 1995—; hosp. privileges at Mt. Sinai Med. Ctr., Cedars Med. Ctr., South Miami Hosp., Mercy Hosp., Deering Hosp., Miami Heart Inst., Coral Gables Hosp.; seminar conductor Dept. Pharmacology U. Miami Sch. of Medicine, 1986-88; lectr. in basic nutrition Trinity Sr. H.S., Dade County, Fla., lectr. in nutrition, Fla. Internat. U., 1987-89, Metro-Dade Police Dept., Miami, 1988-89; instr. Pub. Health Nutrition, U. Miami Sch. of Medicine, 1989-93, Geriatic Edn. Ctr. Dept. Psychiatry, U. Miami Sch. Medicine. Contbr. articles to profl. jours., chpts. to books; over 60 abstracts from scientific proceedings and confs. Vol. AIDS Watch South Fla., 1989; AIDS Epidemiology Rsch. Cable-TAD Program; seminar conductor on Chronic Fatigue Syndrome to comty. based orgns., 1989, 90; mem. Cure AIDS Now, 1989, 91; vol. Body Positive Resource Ctr., 1989, 92, Biopsychosocial Ctr. for Studies on AIDS, 1991, 92, 93, 94. Recipient NIH postdoctoral fellowship, 1987, Clinician Sci. award, Am. Heart Assn., 1987-88, 88-89; grantee: NIH, 1986-91, 1988-91, 1988-93, 1989-92, Am. Heart Assn. Fla. Affiliate 1987-88, 87-89, 88-89, NIH and Fogarty Internat. Ctr., 1988-93, Human Health Svcs., 1988-91, Fla. Cystic Fibrosis Found., 1988-89, 1988-89, NIAAA, 1993-95. Fellow So. Assn. Geriatric Medicine, Am. Coll. Clin. Pharmacology; mem. AMA, Am. Soc. Clin. Nutrition, So. Med. Assn., Am. Inst. Nutrition, N.Y. Acad. Sci., Am. Psychiat. Assn., Fla. Psychiat. Assn., Am. Soc. Addiction Medicine, Fla. Pub. Health Assn., Am. Coun. on Sci. and Health, Physicians for a Nat. Health Program, Nat. Coun. for Internat. Health, Soc. Latinoam. de Nutricion, Fla. Med. Assn., Southeastern Med. Soc. Home: 278 Palm Ave Miami Beach FL 33139-5142 Office: 444 Brickell Ave Ste 701 Miami FL 33131

MANTHEI, ROBIN DICKEY, research technician; b. Tucson, May 16, 1956; d. Wilbur Dunbar French and Barbara Dickey; m. Joel Robert Manthei, Sept. 4, 1976; children: Nicholas Robert, Charles Dickey. AS, Augsburg Coll., 1976; cert. med. lab. technician, Med. Inst. Minn., 1978; BS, U. Minn., 1994. Med. lab. technician Lufkin Med. Lab., Mpls., 1978-82; jr. scientist U. Minn., Mpls., 1982-86; rsch. tech. Mayo Found., Rochester, Minn., 1986-89; chpt. leader Young Astronaut Program, 1987-94; jr. scientist Inst. Human Genetics U. Minn., 1989-90; rsch. asst. Mpls. Med. Rsch. Found., 1990-93; lab. instr. North Hennepin C.C., Brooklyn Park, Minn., 1994—. Contbr. articles in field. Mem. DAR. Episcopalian. Home: 7630 Lanewood Ln N Maple Grove MN 55311-2670

MANTHEY, FRANK ANTHONY, physician, director; b. N.Y.C., Dec. 2, 1933; s. Frank A.J. and Josephine (Roth) M.; m. Douglas Susan Falvey, Sept. 14 1958 (div. 1979, dec. 1989); children: Michael P., Susan M., Peter J.; m. Doris Jean Pulley, Oct. 11, 1979. BS, Fordham U., 1954; MD, SUNY, Syracuse, 1958. Diplomate Am. Bd. Anesthesiology, Am. Bd. Med. Examiners. Intern Upstate Med. Ctr., Syracuse, 1958-59; resident in anesthesiology Yale-New Haven Med. Ctr., 1962-64; physician Yale-New Haven Hosp., 1964-75; pvt. practice medicine Illmo, Mo., 1975-79; dir. Manthey Med. Clinic, Elkton, Ky., 1979—; clin. instr. anesthesiology Yale U. Med. Sch., New Haven, 1964-69, asst. clin. prof. anesthesiology, 1969-75; cons. Conn. Dept. Aeros., Hartford, 1969-70; sr. med. examiner Fed. Aviation Adminstrn., Illmo, 1975-79. Contbr. articles to profl. jours. Chmn. gen. works Little Folks Fair, Guilford, Conn., 1967-71; mem. Rep. Town Com., Guilford, 1969-75; chmn. Guilford Sch. Bldg. Com., 1973-75. Capt. USAF (M.C.), 1956-62. Mem. Ky. Med. Assn., Aerospace Med. Assn. (assoc. fellow 1973-75), Flying Physicians Assn. (v.p. NE chpt. 1973-75, v.p. nat. 1974-75, 79-80, bd. dirs. 1970-73, 75-78, bd. dirs. nat. 1975-78), Aircraft Owners and Pilots Assn., Mercedes Benz Club Am., Alpha Kappa Kappa. Home: 105 Sunset Dr Elkton KY 42220-9257 Office: Manthey Family Practice Clinic 203 Allensville St PO Box 368 Elkton KY 42220

MANTHORPE, ROLF, medical educator; b. Copenhagen, July 19, 1942; s. Christian and Ruth (Kjaer) M.; m. Tove Bunken, Dec. 4, 1965; 1 child, Martin. Student, U. Frederiksberg, Denmark, 1961; MD, U. Copenhagen, 1969, D in Medicine, 1983. Resident, registrar U. Hosps. in Copenhagen, 1969-78; sr. registrar State U. Hosp., Denmark, 1978-84; assoc. prof. dept. rheumatology Malmo U. Hosp., Malmö, Sweden. Editor: 1st International Seminar on Sjögren's Syndrome, 1986. Home: Vejlesoeparken 11, DK-2840 Holte Denmark Office: Malmo U HOsp, Sjogrens Syndrome Rsch Ctr, S-205 02 Malmö Sweden

MANTILLA, GONZALO C., JR., pediatrician; b. Quito, Ecuador, Nov. 2, 1943; came to U.S., 1965; s. Gonzalo M. Mantilla and Victoria Cabeza de Vaca; m. Marthalicia Calisto; children: Martita, Sebastian, Gigi, Victoria. MD, U. Ctrl., Quito, 1971; postgrad., U. Fla., 1971-76. Diplomate Am. Bd. Pediatrics. Asst. prof. U. Fla., Gainesville, 1976-93; v.p. Met. Hosp., Quito, 1985-90; dean USFQ Med. Sch., Quito, 1993—; pvt. practice. Editor: Salud Infantil, 1987. Advisor Health Ministry, Ecuador, 1985-93. Fellow Am. Acad. Pediatrics. Home: 4900 N Ocean Bl #1203 Fort Lauderdale FL 33308

MANTOVANI, JOHN FRANCIS, neurologist, educator; b. St. Louis, Jan. 17, 1949. BA cum laude, U. Evansville, 1971; MD, U. Mo., 1974. Diplomate Am. Bd. Pediatrics, Am. Bd. Psychiatry and Neurology. Resident pediatrics, neurology, fellow child neurology Washington U. & St. Louis Childrens Hosp., 1974-79; practitioner adult & child neurology Dean Clinic, Madison, Wis., 1979-84; dir. child neurology, vice chmn. dept. pediatrics St. John's Mercy Med. Ctr., St. Louis, 1984—; clin. asst. prof. neurology U. Wis., Madison, 1980-84; instr. clin. pediatrics and neurology Washington U., St. Louis, 1985-95, asst. prof. clin. pediatrics. and neurology, 1995—. Contbr. articles to profl. jours. Mem. AMA, Am. Acad. Pediatrics, Am. Acad. Cerebral Palsy and Developmental Medicine (com. mem. 1985-87, 1989-91, bd. dirs. 1994—), Am. Acad. Neurology, Am. Bd. Electroencephalography, Child Neurology Soc., Alpha Omega Alpha. Office: Ste 5009 621 S New Ballas Rd Saint Louis MO 63141-8200

MANTZELL, BETTY LOU, school health administrator; b. Brookville, Pa., Oct. 16, 1938; d. Elmer William and Wilda Mae (Enterline) M. Diploma, Ind. (Pa.) Hosp. Sch. Nursing, 1959; BSN, Case Western Res. U., 1969, MA, 1978; cert. supr. ednl. adminstrn., Cleve. State U., 1983; cert. supr., John Carroll U., 1989. RN, Ohio, Pa. Oper. rm. nurse Univ. Hosps. of Cleve., 1963-69; sch. nurse various locations Cleve. Pub. Schs., 1969-85, coord. sch. nurses, 1976-85, acting asst. supr. health svcs., 1985-86, supr. health svcs., 1986—; mem. adv. com. to baccalaureate nursing program Cleve. Stae U.; prevention of blindness adv. com. Cleve. Sight Ctr.; active All Kids County Consortium Cleve. Dept. Pub. Health; mem. sch. health com. Acad. Medicine Cleve.; Frances Payne Bolton Sch. Nursing, mem. alumni assn.; clin. instr. cmty. health nursing Case We. Res. U., Cleve., 1988-90, women's connection; mem. coun. econ. opportunities Greater Cleve.; mem. adv. com. Headstart Health Svcs. Mem. Am. Sch. Health Assn., Nat. Assn. Sch. Nurses, Ohio Assn. Sch. Nurses, Northeastern Ohio Assn. Sch. Nurses, Ohio Assn. Secondary Sch. Adminstrs., Cleve. Coun. Adminstrs. and Suprs., Cleve. Med. Libr. Assn. Office: Jane Addams Bus Careers Ctr Office Health Svcs Rm 206 2373 E 30th St Cleveland OH 44115

MANY, RICHARD J., physician assistant; b. Albany, N.Y., July 11, 1949; s. James Leslie and Marilyn (Day) M.; m. Ellen C. Steele, Mar. 7, 1931; children: Kelly Day, Erin Elizabeth. AAS, Hudson Valley C.C., Troy, N.Y., 1974; AAS/PA, Albany (N.Y.) Med. Coll., 1976. Registered physician asst. Physician asst. Mark R. Levy, MD, Troy, 1976-77; asst. med. dir. Rensselaer Poly. Inst., Troy, 1977—; staff physician asst. Bellevue Maternity Hosp., Schenectady, N.Y., 1990-95. With USNR, 1968-74. Mem. Am. Coll. Health Assn., Am. Assn. Physician Asst., N.Y. Soc. Physician Asst.

MANYAK, MICHAEL JOHN, urologist, educator, researcher; b. Flint, Mich., Mar. 25, 1951; m. Rebecca Bringham; children: Rachel, Susannah, Timothy. BA, U. Notre Dame, 1973; MD, U. of East, Manila, 1979. Intern, then resident in gen. surgery Booth Meml. Med. Ctr., Flushing, N.Y., 1980-82; resident in urology George Washington Univ. Med. Ctr., Washington, 1982-84, chief resident, 1984-85, instr. urology, 1988-89, asst. prof., 1989-91, assoc. prof., 1991—; mem. adv. bd. Nat. Kidney and Urological Disease, 1992—; dir. urological rsch. George Washington U. Med. Ctr., 1992—, acting chmn. 1995. Contbr. articles to profl. jours. Fellow Nat. Cancer Inst., 1985-88; scholar Am. Urol. Assn., 1986-88. Fellow Explorers Club (vice chmn. Washington group, nat. co-chmn. for chpts., nat. bd. dirs. 1996); mem. Internat. Soc. Cryptozoology (field med. advisor), Am. Urol. Assn. (chmn. tech. coun. 1995). Office: George Washington Univ Med Ctr 2150 Pennsylvania Ave NW Washington DC 20037-2396

MAPLE, OPAL LUCILLE, school psychologist; b. Canton, Ill., Nov. 15, 1935; d. Dwight Willard and Eileen Beatrice (Cadwalader) Beaty; m. Gilbert

Roy Maple, June 30, 1967 (dec. 1985). BA, Wheaton (Ill.) Coll., 1958; MS, We. Ill. U., 1962. Cert. sch. psychologist, Ill. Tchr. Community Dist. #5, Cuba, Ill., 1958-60, Community Dist. #66, Canton, Ill., 1960-61; asst. dean women Moody Bible Inst., Chgo., 1961-64; sch. psychologist intern Chgo. Pub. Schs., 1964-65; sch. psychologist Peoria (Ill.) pub. schs., 1965-69, Waukegan (Ill.) pub. schs., 1969-81, Knox-Warren Spl. Edn., Galesburg, Ill., 1986—. Co-author pre-sch. test, 1975. Deaconess, treas. Antioch Evang. Free Ch., 1971-81; deaconess, fin. sec. Bethel Bapt. Ch., Galesburg, 1982—. Mem. Cen. Ill. Sch. Psychologists Assn. (pres. 1967-68), Ill. Psychol. Assn. (sec. 1977-79), DAR, Knox County Genealogical Soc., Nat. Assn. Sch. Psychologists, Ill. Sch. Psychologists Assn. Republican. Baptist.

MAPOU, ROBERT LEWIS, neuropsychologist; b. Washington, May 28, 1955; s. Albert and Phyllis Helen (Smul) M.; life ptnr. Michael Jerome Zufall, Jan. 14, 1978. BS, U. Md., 1977; MA, Emory U., 1981, PhD, 1985. Diplomate in Clin. Neuropsychology Am. Bd. Profl. Psychology; lic. psychologist, Md., W. Va. Staff neuropsychologist Greenery Rehab. Ctr., Boston, 1986-88; assoc. dir. neuropsychology Am. Neurosci. Ctrs., Gaithersburg, Md., 1988-90; neuropsychology dir. behavioral medicine rsch. program Henry M. Jackson Found. Advancement Mil. Medicine, Washington, 1990-92; sr. scientist behavioral prevention program Henry M. Jackson Found. for Advancement of Mil. Medicine, Washington, 1992-96; neuropsychology dir. Ctr. Neuro-Rehab., Bethesda, Md., 1996—; asst. clin prof. Tufts U., Boston, 1986-88; ad hoc grant reviewer NIMH, Bethesda, 1989—, clin. neuropsychologist William Stixrud PhD and Assocs., 1990—; adj. asst. prof. Dept. Psychiatry Uniformed Svcs. U. Health Scis., Bethesda, 1991-94; rsch. assoc. prof. Dept. Psychiatry Uniformed Svcs. U. Health Scis., Bethesda, 1995, rsch. asst. prof. Dept. Neurology, 1995—; clin. assoc. prof. Dept. Neurology, Gerogetown U. Sch. Medicine, Washington, 1991—; reviewer Psychol. Bull., 1989, Jour. Comty. Psychology, 1988; presenter at profl. confs. Sr. editor Clinical Neuropsychological Assessment: A Cognitive Approach, 1995; mem. editorial bd. Jour. of Head Trauma Rehab., 1991; contbr. articles to profl. jours. Mem. APA, Internat. Neuropsychol. Soc., Nat. Acad. Neuropsychology, Sigma Xi, Phi Beta Kappa, Phi Kappa Phi, Eta Kappa Nu, Phi Eta Sigma. Home: 2522 Sutcliffe Terr Brookeville MD 20803

MAPP, FREDERICK EVERETT, biology educator; b. Atlanta, Oct. 12, 1910; s. Thaddeus Henry and Willie Anne (Johnson) M.; m. Betty Elizabeth Lewis, Mar. 31, 1963; children: William M. Boyd Jr., Robert A. Boyd. BS, Morehouse Coll., 1932; MS, Atlanta U., 1934; MA, Harvard U., 1942; PhD, U. Chgo., 1950. Tchr. Washington High Sch., Atlanta, 1933-40; assoc. prof. Knoxville (Tenn.) Coll., 1944-46; lectr. Roosevelt Coll., Chgo., 1948-50; prof., chmn. Tenn. State U., Nashville, 1951-52; prof., chmn. Morehouse Coll., Atlanta, 1952-73, prof., 1973—. Trustee Friendship Bapt. Ch., Atlanta, 1980—. Mem. Omega Psi Phi, Sigma Xi, Phi Beta Kappa. Democrat. Home: 703 Waterford Rd NW Atlanta GA 30318-7148

MARAGGUN, ZENAIDA EDUARTE, microbiologist, serologist, educator; b. Canan, Lapaz, The Philippines, Feb. 14, 1950; came to U.S., 1973; d. Antonio and Leonora (Adriatico) Eduarte; m. Ver V. Maraggun, Sept. 23, 1972; children: Jonathan, Clint. BS, St. Louis U., 1970; postgrad. in Biology, Northwestern State U., 1990-91. Cert. tchr., La.; cert. med. technologist, Assn. Med. Technologists; cert. CLS, La. Tchr. sci. Holy Spirit Acad., The Philippines, 1970-73; registered med. asst. Tripler Army Hosp., Honolulu, 1977-78; supr. med. reception Alpha Therapeutic Co., Honolulu, 1978-81; med. lab. technician Byrd Meml. Hosp., Leesville, La., 1981-84, microbiology technologist, 1995; partime med. lab. technician Bayne-Jones Army Hosp., Ft. Polk, La., 1984-89, microbiology/serology supr., 1989—; counsellor Equal Employment Opportunity, Dept. of Army, Ft. Polk, 1985-90. Coord. Asian Pacific Festivities, 1991, 96. Mem. Filipino-Am. Assn. (pres. 1995-96, v.p. 1996—). Home: 1602 Amour Dr Leesville LA 71446 Office: Bayne Jones Army Cmty Hosp Fort Polk LA 71459

MARANGI, DONALD, cardiologist, educator; b. Elizabeth, N.J., Feb. 18, 1955; s. Dominick and Joan M.; m. Margaret, Sept. 15, 1984; 1 child, Anthony Nicholas. BS, Seton Hall U., 1977, MS, 1980; MD, Far Eastern U., 1984. Diplomate Am. Bd. Pediatrics, Am. Bd. Cardiology. Resident in pediatrics Med. Ctr. Del., Wilmington, 1984-87; fellow in pediat. cardiology St. Christopher Hosp. for Children, Phila., 1987-90; fellow in electrophysiology Med. U. S.C., Charleston, 1990-91; asst. prof. U. Fla., Jacksonville, 1991—. Fellow Am. Coll. Cardiology; mem. Fla. Med. Assn., Duval County Med. Soc. Roman Catholic. Office: Wolfson Childrens Hosp Jacksonville FL 32209

MARANO, ANTHONY JOSEPH, cardiologist; b. White Plains, N.Y., Apr. 14, 1934; s. Anthony Joseph and Mary Antoinette (Perrotta) M.; m. Mary Regina Marbach, Aug. 23, 1958; children—Thomas, Kathryn, Michele. B.A., Williams Coll., 1956; M.D., Cornell Med. Coll., 1960. Diplomate Am. Bd. Internal Medicine, Am. Bd. Cardiovascular Disease. Intern Bellevue Hosp., N.Y.C., 1960-61; resident St. Luke's Hosp., N.Y.C., 1961-63; NIH fellow in cardiology Mt. Sinai Hosp., N.Y.C., 1963-64, research assoc., 1964-75; clin. assoc. in medicine Coll. Physicians and Surgeons, N.Y.C., 1970-86; pres. med. staff White Plains Hosp., 1984-86, chief cardiology, 1985-91, chief cardiology emeritus, 1991—, bd. dirs., 1983-88; cons. in cardiology Burke Rehab. Ctr.; med. dir., founder Paramedic Ambulance, White Plains, 1976-82. Contbr. articles to med. jours. Trustee Pace U., N.Y.C., 1975—, Home Savs. Bank, White Plains, 1973-90; bd. dirs. YMCA, White Plains, 1978-82 ; team physician White Plains High Sch., 1967—; cons. physician Dept. Pub. Safety, White Plains, 1968—; cons. physician City of White Plains Sch. System, 1994—; bd. dirs. Westchester County Sports Hall of Fame, 1993—; alumni trustee Tyng Found., Williams Coll., 1994—. Tyng scholar Williams Coll., 1952-59; recipient Outstanding Achievement award Emergency Med. Services Council, 1982. Fellow ACP, Am. Coll. Cardiology; mem. AMA, Am. Coll. Sports Medicine, Am. Heart Assn., N.Y. State Heart Assn. (bd. dirs. 1982-85), Westchester Heart Assn. (v.p. 1983-86, pres. 1987-90), Phi Beta Kappa. Clubs: University (White Plains) (pres. 1970-71); Westchester Country (Harrison, N.Y.). Avocations: tennis, skiing, gardening. Home: 9 Fairway Dr White Plains NY 10605-4107 Office: 20 Old Mamaroneck Rd White Plains NY 10605-2060

MARASCIULLO, DAVID LOUIS, clinical psychologist; b. Bklyn., Apr. 24, 1929; s. Joseph and Josephine Elizabeth (Maresca) M.; m. Rosella Margaret Devine, Sept. 1, 1962; children: Paul, Janene, Mark. BA cum laude, Niagara (N.Y.) U., 1957; MA, Fordham U., Bronx, 1959; PhD, St. John's U., Jamaica, N.Y., 1969; forensic tng., N.Y.C. Family Ct., 1991; substance abuse tng., Nassau County Psychol. Inst., 1995-96; cert. in substance abuse treatment, Am. Coll. Profl. Psychology, 1996. Lic. psychologist, N.Y.; sch. psychologist, Pa., N.Y. Asst. prof. psychology Villanova (Pa.) U., 1959-61; rsch. fellow psychology U. Ark., Fayetteville, 1961-62; clin. psychologist Vocat. Adv. Svc., N.Y.C., 1962-63, Bur. Child Guidance, N.Y.C., 1963-68; sr. sch. psychologist USFD #3, Huntington, N.Y., 1968-69; sch. psychologist CHSD #3 Bellmore/Merrick (N.Y.), 1969-86; dir. pupil svcs. Wyandanch (N.Y.) Pub. Schs., 1987-89; supervising psychologist Pederson-Krag Clinic, Huntington, 1990—; cons. psychologist South Oaks Hosp., Amityville, 1970—, Employees Med. Rev., Suffolk County, N.Y., 1986-94, Syosset Hosp., 1972-80, Huntington Hosp., 1992—; adj. clin. instr. Hofstra U., Hempstead, N.Y., 1972-84; adj. prof. psychology dept. St. John's U., Jamaica, N.Y., 1994—. Contbr. articles to profl. jours. With U.S. Army, 1953-55. Mem. APA, NASP, N.Y. State Psychol. Assn. (pres. 1988), Suffolk County Psychol. Assn., Nassau County Psychol. Assn. (pres. 1985). Roman Catholic. Home and Office: 18 S Hollow Rd Huntington Station NY 11746-6140

MARASCO, JOSEPH A., JR., radiologist. Physician dept. radiology Forbes Regional Hosp., Monroeville, Pa. Recipient Gold award Am. Coll. Radiology, 1995. Office: Forbes Regional Hosp Dept Radiology 2570 Haymaker Rd Monroeville PA 15146

MARATEA, JAMES MICHAEL, healthcare administrator, editor, consultant; b. Riverside, N.J., Nov. 26, 1946; s. Domenic J. and Martha C. (Moloney) M.; m. Linda Jean Morgan, Sept. 6, 1970; children: Jennifer A., Jill M., Patrick J. BS in Bus. Adminstrn., Trenton (N.J.) State Coll., 1973; MA in Mgmt., Cen. Mich. U., 1977. Staff technologist Del. Valley Hosp., Bristol, Pa., 1966-68; supr. Zurbrugg Meml. Hosp., Riverside, 1968-74; v.p. Maratea Med. Lab., Riverside, 1966-84; rep. Thomas Jefferson U., Phila., 1974-75, lab. mgr., 1975-85, adminstr. dept. clin. and anatomic pathology, 1985-93, adminstr. clin. lab. and emergency svcs., 1992—; adminstr. Dept. of Pathology and Emergency Svcs., Thomas Jefferson U., Phila., 1993—; cons. to maj. league baseball, N.Y.C., 1990—; instr. Thomas Jefferson U., 1985—; mem. Univ. Hosp. Cons. Tech. Adv. Com., Chgo., 1989—. Contbg. author: Sharpening Management Skills, A Laboratorian's Guide, 1978; contbr. articles to profl. jours. Mem. Camden County (N.J.) Com., 1991—; v.p. Merchantville (N.J.) Rep. Club, 1991, pres., 1992; mem. Bd. Health, Merchantville, 1986—. Recipient MLO Writing award Med. Econs., 1977, 80, 81, 82. Mem. Am. Med. Technologists, Clin. Lab. Mgmt. Assn. (v.p. Delaware Valley 1981-82, pres. 1982-84), Am. Soc. Med. Technologists, Am. Bd. Bionalysts. Roman Catholic. Home: 118 Westminster Ave Merchantville NJ 08109-2640 Office: Thomas Jefferson U 11th and Walnut Sts Philadelphia PA 19107

MARATOS-FLIER, ELEFTHERIA, medical educator, physician; b. N.Y.C., Dec. 15, 1951; d. Costas and Anna (Domenikos) Maratos; m. Jeffrey Scott Flier, Dec. 7, 1975; children: Sarah, Lydia. BS, NYU, 1972; MD, Mt. Sinai Sch. Medicine, N.Y.C., 1976. Intern and resident George Washington U. Hosp., Washington, 1976-78; resident Beth Israel Hosp., Boston, 1978-79; rsch. fellow Harvard Sch. Pub. Health, Boston, 1980-81; fellow Joslin Diabetes Ctr., Boston, 1981-82; instr. Brigham & Women's Hosp., Harvard Med. Sch., Boston, 1982-87, asst. prof., 1987—. Contbr. articles to Sci., Jour. Cell Biology, Jour. Virology, Jour. Clin. Investigation. Mary K. Iacocca Rsch. fellow, 1981. Mem. Am. Soc. Virology, Am. Microbiol. Assn., Am. Diabetes Assn., Phi Beta Kappa. Office: Joslin Diabetes Ctr One Joslin Pl Boston MA 02215*

MARAZZITI, DONATELLA, psychiatrist, researcher; b. Baschi, Italy, Dec. 12, 1956; s. Francesco and Maria (Carletti) M.; m. Giancarlo Gambinotti, June 22, 1986. Degree in Medicine and Surgery, Sch. Medicine, Pisa, Italy, 1981. Resident Dept. Psychiatry U. Pisa, Italy, 1981-85; fellow Norwegian Govt., Oslo, Norway, 1983; gen. practitioner Italian Health Svc., Pescia, Italy, 1983-92; asst. prof. Dept. Psychiatry Splty. Sch. Psychiatry U. Pisa, Italy, 1987—. Contbr. over 300 publications in internat. jours. and 3 monographs; author: current Insights in OCD, 1994. Recipient Nat. award Formenti, 1989, Ole Rafaelsen award CINP, Kyoto, Japan, 1990, Internat. award ECNP, Montecarlo, 1991. Mem. Italian Soc. Psychiatry, Itlaian Soc. Neuroscience, European Neuroscience Assn., European Coll. Neuropharmacology, Internat. Soc. for Neurochemistry, Internat. Soc. Psychoneuroendocrinology, European Assn. for Psychiatry, Am. Soc. for Biol. Psychiatry, N.Y. Acad. Sci. Roman Catholic. Home: via 27 Aprile 91, 51017 Pescia Italy Office: Univ of Pisa Dept Psychiatry, via Roma 67, 56100 Pisa Italy

MARBLE, HOWARD BENNETT, JR., dentist, oral surgeon; b. Shelburne Falls, Mass., June 14, 1923; s. Howard Bennett Sr. and Lucille Ina (Smith) M.; m. Barbara L Sisson (div.); children: Robert T., Cynthia L. Judith A., Thomas H, Stephen P.; m. Carol Frances Lemon. Student, Brown U., 1941-44; DMD, Tufts U., 1947. Diplomate Am. Bd. Oral and Maxillofacial Surgery. Commd. lt. USN, 1949, advanced through grades to capt.; head oral surgery dept. Naval Dental Sch. Nat. Naval Med. Ctr., Bethesda, Md., 1964-69; retired USN, 1969; prof. oral surgery Med. Coll. Ga. Sch. Dentistry, Augusta; chief dental services VA Med. Ctr., Augusta. Mem. ADA, Ga. Soc. Oral and Maxillofacial Surgery, Am. Soc. Maxillofacial Surgery, Am. Coll. Maxillofacial Surgery.

MARCH, WAYNE FRONT, ophthalmologist, educator; b. Dayton, Ohio, June 8, 1947; s. Abraham W. and Jacqueline F. March. BS, Northwestern U. Chgo., 1966, MD, 1971. Diplomate Am. Bd. Ophthalmology, Laser Surgery. Intern USPHS Hosp., San Francisco, 1971-72; resident ophthalmology Northwestern U. Chgo., 1972-75; NIH postdoctoral fellow U. Wis., Madison, 1975-76; NIH rsch. assoc. U. Iowa, Iowa City, 1976-78; asst. prof., assoc. prof. U. Okla., Oklahoma City, 1978-83, prof., 1983-91, George Lynn Cross rsch. prof., 1991—; prof. U. Tex. Med. Br., Galveston, 1991—, chmn. dept. ophthalmology and visual scis., 1991—, Robertson-Poth chair, 1991—; vice chmn. Pvt. Practice Plan, Galveston, 1994—. Editor: Advances in Ophthalmic Laser Therapy, 1983, Practical Ophthalmic Problems, 1984, Ophthalmic Lasers: A Second Generation, 1989, Practical Laser Surgery, 1989, Laser in Opftalmologia, 1994. Grantee Rsch. to Prevent Blindness, 1996—. Mem. AAUP, Am. Acad. Ophthalmology, Assn. for Rsch. in Vision and Ophthalmology, Am. Glaucoma Soc., Internat. Soc. for Laser Surgery, French Acad. Ophthalmology (hon.). Office: Univ Tex Med Branch 700 University Blvd 3d Fl Galveston TX 77550

MARCHALONIS, JOHN JACOB, immunologist, educator; b. Scranton, Pa., July 22, 1940; s. John Louis and Anna Irene (Stadner) M.; m. Sally Ann Sevy, May 5, 1978; children: Lee, Elizabeth, Emily. A.B. summa cum Laude, Lafayette Coll., 1962; Ph.D., Rockefeller U., 1967. Grad. fellow Rockefeller U., 1962-67; fellow Am. Cancer Soc. Walter and Eliza Hall Inst. Med. Research, 1967-68; asst. prof. biomed. scis. Brown U., 1969-70; head molecular immunology lab. Walter and Eliza Hall Inst. Med. Research, Melbourne, Australia, 1970-76; head cell biology and biochemistry sect. Frederick Cancer Research Ctr., 1977-80; prof. adj. faculty dept. pathology U. Pa., 1977-83; prof., chmn. dept. biochemistry and molecular biology Med. U. S.C., Charleston, 1980-88; prof., chmn. dept. microbiology and immunology U. Ariz., Tucson, 1988—, prof. pathology, 1991—, prof. medicine, 1992—; bd. dirs. Am. Type Tissue Culture Collection. Author: Immunity in Evolution, 1977; editor: Comparative Immunology, 1976, the Lymphocyte: Structure and Function, 1977, (with N. Cohen) Self/Non-Self Discrimination, 1980, (with G.W. Warr) Antibody as a Tool, 1982, The Immunobiology and Molecular Biology of Parasitic Infections, 1983, Antigen-Specific T Cell Receptors and Factors, 1987, The Lymphocyte: Structure and Function, 2d edit., 1987, (with Carol Reinisch) Defense Molecules, 1989, (with Gregory Beck, Edwin L. Cooper and Gail S. Habicht) Primordial Immunity, 1994; edtl. bd. jours. in field. Active Nat. Commn. Damon Runyon-Walter Winchel Cancer Fund. Named among 1,000 most highly cited sci. authors Inst. for Sci. Info.; Frank R. Lillie fellow, 1974; grantee in field. Fellow Am. Inst. Chemists, Am. Acad. Microbiology; mem. AAAS, Am. Assn. Immunology, Am. Soc. Biol. Chemists, Sigma Xi, Phi Beta Kappa. Episcopalian. Home: 5661 N Camino Arturo Tucson AZ 85718-3933 Office: U Ariz Health Scis Ctr Tucson AZ 85724

MARCHAM, TIMOTHY VICTOR, pharmacist; b. New Britain, Conn., June 15, 1943; s. John Nelson and Eileen Agnes (Mannings) M. BS in Pharmacy, U. Conn., 1966. Staff pharmacist Kensington (Conn.) Pharmacy, Inc., 1968-72, New Britain Meml. Hosp., 1972-75; cons. pharmacist Health Care Cons. Corp., West Hartford, Conn., 1976-85; staff pharmacist Conn. Dept. Mental Health/Cedarcrest Regional Hosp., Newington, 1978-85; dir. pharmacy Conn. Dept. Mental Health/Cedarcrest Regional Hosp., 1985-91, N.C. Dept. Corrections, 1992—; corporator New Britain (Conn.) Gen. Hosp., 1974—. Radiol. officer Civil Preparedness/Emergency Mgmt. Div., Town of Plainville, Conn., 1965-91; life mem. New Britain Gen. Hosp. Aux.; pres. New Britain Meml. Hosp. Credit Union, 1974-75; provider, SAC officer Health Systems Agy. of North Cen. Conn., 1976-82. Capt. CAP, 1974—. Fellow Am. Soc. Cons. Pharmacists; mem. Am. Pharm. Assn., Am. Soc. Hosp. Pharmacists, Conn. Pharm. Assn. (awards and scholarship), Conn. Soc. Hosp. Pharmacists, Pharmacy Alumni Assn. U. Conn. (life), N.C. Pharm. Assn., N.C. Soc. Hosp. Pharmacists, Moore County Pharm. Assn. Republican. Episcopalian. Home: 106 Atwater Ct 1196 Seven Lakes N West End NC 27376

MARCHASE, RICHARD BANFIELD, cell biologist, educator; b. Sayre, Pa., Mar. 12, 1948; s. Nicholas and Vivian H. (Banfield) M.; m. Susan Elizabeth Darrow, Apr. 14, 1979; children: Nicholas Darrow, Allison Elizabeth. BS in Engring., Cornell U., 1970; PhD in Biophysics, Johns Hopkins U., 1976; postgrad. Duke U., 1978. Muscular Dystrophy Assn. postdoctoral fellow div. neurology, Duke U. Med. Ctr., 1976-77, USPHS postdoctoral fellow dept. anatomy, 1977-78, asst. prof. anatomy, 1978-86; assoc. prof. cell biology and anatomy U. Ala.-Birmingham, 1986—. Recipient Hamilton Watch award Cornell U., 1970, award Juvenile Diabetes Found., 1995; NSF grad. fellow, 1970-73, Presdl. Young Investigator grantee, 1982-87; Danforth Found. grad. fellow, 1973-76; Nanaline H. Duke scholar, 1982-85; USPHS grantee. Mem. AAAS, Am. Soc. Cell Biology, Am. Soc. Zoology, Assn. of Anatomy, Cell Biology, and Neurobiology Chairpersons (pres. 1995—), Internat. Soc. Devel. Neurosci., Sigma Xi. Contbr. chpts. to books, articles to profl. jours. Home: 2717 Country Wood Way Birmingham AL 35243-2447 Office: U Ala Dept Cell Biology Birmingham AL 35294*

MARCHENESE, KARL JAMES, ophthalmologist; b. Geneva, N.Y., Aug. 26, 1948; s. James Vincent and Ramona Kathleen (Wayman) M.; m. Raquel C. Lansigan, Mar. 30, 1970; children: Kira Lainie, Karl Ryan. BS, Bucknell U., 1970; MD, U. Rochester, 1974. Diplomate Am. Bd. Ophthalmology. Intern, then resident Strong Meml. Hosp. U. Rochester, 1974-79; clin. asst., prof. ophthalmology U. Rochester (N.Y.) Sch. Medicine and Dentistry, 1980—. Bd. dirs. F.F. Thompson Found., Canandaigua, N.Y., 1992—. Fellow Am. Acad. Ophthalmology (bd. counselors 1991-93); mem. AMA, N.Y. State Ophthalmol. Soc. (pres. 1992-93), N.Y. Soc. for Clin. Ophthalmology, Ontario County Med. Soc. (pres. 1985). Office: Eye Care Ctr 325 West St Canandaigua NY 14424

MARCHESE, CRISTIANA ALESSANDRA, geneticist, chemist; b. Torino, Italy, Nov. 7, 1953; d. Gian Stefano Alessandro and Giacomina (Bosco) M.; children: Olmo Giovanni, Tommaso Beniamino and Nicola Benedetto (twins). Maturita' scientifica, Liceo S.S.G. Ferraris, Torino, 1972; MD, U. Torino, 1979, degree in clin. chemistry, 1984; degree in med. genetics, U. La Sapienza, Rome, 1989. Asst. clin. chemist Children Hosp., Torino, 1980-81; asst. med. geneticist dept. med. genetics Molinette Hosp., Torino, 1984-89, aiuto dept. med. genetics, 1990; aiuto clin. chemistry dept. Mauriziano Hosp., Torino, 1991—; cons. geneticist dept. Mauriziano Hosp., Torino, 1990—; elected to physicians com. Molinette Hosp., Torino, 1988-90. U. So. Calif. fellow, 1981, 83. Mem. Am. Soc. Human Genetics, Clin. Genetics Soc., Twins and Multiple Births Assn., N.Y. Acad. Sci. (asst. gen. medicine, citogen medicine). Office: Ospedale Mauriziano Umberto I, Largo Turati 62, Torino I 10128, Italy

MARCHESI, VINCENT T., biochemist, educator; b. N.Y.C., Sept. 4, 1935; married, 1959; three children. BA, Yale U., 1957, MD, 1963; PhD in Pathology, Oxford (Eng.) U., Eng., 1961. Intern, resident in pathology Wash. U., Bethesda, Md., 1963-65; rsch. assoc. cell biology Rockefeller U., New Haven, 1965-66; staff assoc. Nat. Cancer Inst., 1966-68; chief sect. chem. pathology Nat. Inst. Arthritis, Metabolism & Digestive Disorders, 1968-77; Anthony N. Brady prof. pathology Sch. Medicine Yale U., 1977—; dir. Boyer Ctr. Molecular Medicine Yale U., New Haven, 1987—; cons. Miles Pharm., West Haven, Conn., 1982—. Bd. dirs. Am. Cyanamid, N.J., 1992-94. Lt. comdr. USPHS, 1966-72. Mem. Inst. Medicine-NAS, Histochem. Soc., N.Y. Acad. Sci., Am. Soc. Cell Biology. Office: Yale U Sch Medicine Dept Pathology Brady Meml Lab New Haven CT 06520 also: Boyer Ctr Molecular Medicine 205 Congress Ave New Haven CT 06519*

MARCHI, LORRAINE JUNE, association executive; b. San Francisco, June 5, 1923; d. Leopold Pulverman and Josephine Lillian (Trieber) Heiman; m. Gene Marchi, Apr. 10, 1943 (div. 1973); children: Gene, Jeffrey, Debra, Beth; m. Robert L. Fastie, Oct. 21, 1973. Student Stanford U., 1941-42, U. Calif.-Berkeley, 1942-43. Founder Com. To Aid Visually Handicapped Children, San Francisco, 1954-57; pres. Aid to Visually Handicapped, San Francisco, 1957-59; founder, exec. dir. Nat. Assn. for Visually Handicapped, San Francisco, 1972—; sec. Calif. Conf. for Exceptional and Rehab. Needs, San Francisco, 1955-66; chmn. bd. Langley Porter Neuropsychiat. Inst., San Francisco, 1966-73. Recipient spl. svc. award Los Angeles County Soc. Ophthalmology, 1971; honor award Am. Acad. Ophthalmology and Otolaryngology, 1971, Lifetime Achievement award Nat. Assn. for Visually Handicapped, 1989; cert. of appreciation Am. Acad. Ophthalmology, 1978; named Woman of Yr. San Francisco sect. Nat. Council Jewish Women, 1957, one of Ten Disting. Women San Francisco Examiner Bay Area, 1959. Home: 305 E 24th St New York NY 10010-4011

MARCHUK, DOUGLAS ALAN, medical educator; b. Cleve., July 17, 1956. BS in Biology cum laude, U. Dayton, 1978; MS in Microbiology, U. Conn., 1980; PhD in Molecualr Genetics and Cell Biol., U. Chgo., 1985. Postdoctoral U. Mich. Med. Sch., Ann Arbor, 1987-91, asst. rsch. scientist, 1991-93; asst. prof. genetics Duke U. Med. Ctr., Durham, N.C., 1993—; vis. asst. prof. biology Hope Coll., Holland, Mich., 1985-87; lectr. in field. Mem. editorial bd. jour. Genome Rsch., 1993—; ad hoc reviewer jours.; contbr. chpts. to books and numerous articles to profl. jours. Mem. med. adv. bd. Hereditary Hemorrhagic Telengietasis Found., 1992—. Baxter Found. scholar, 1983—; grantee NIH, 1992—, Share Found., 1992-93, Am. Heart Assn., 1995—, Sandoz Pharms. Corp., 1995, Baxter Found., 1993—. Mem. Alpha Sigma Tau. Office: Duke U Med Ctr Rm 265 CARL Bldg Box 3175 Research Dr Durham NC 27710*

MARCO, DAVID DUANE, biomedical engineer; b. Apollo, Pa., Feb. 3, 1951; s. Peter M. and Jean M. (Merlo) M.; m. Nancy Elizabeth Bierman, Nov. 16, 1985; 1 child, Phoebe Elizabeth. BS in Biomed. Engring., Rensselaer Polytechnic Inst., 1973. Operating engr. Shock & Trauma Unit Albany (N.Y.) Med. Ctr., 1973-75; research technician Abcor Inc., Boston, 1975-76; clin. engr. Boston U. Med. Ctr. Hosp., 1975-77; field clin. engr. Arco/Med. Products, San Francisco, 1977-81; sales rep. Siemens-Elema, Oakland, Calif., 1981-85; field clin. engr. Pacesetter, Oakland, 1985—, western field clin. engr. mgr., 1993—. Contbr. articles to profl. jours. Mem. Shiloh Christian Fellowship, Oakland, 1983, dist. dir., 1991-95. Mem. N.Am. Soc. Pacing and Electrophysiology. Republican. Office: Pacesetter Inc Ste A150 3470 Mount Diablo Blvd Lafayette CA 94549-3917

MARCONI, FRANCO, plastic surgeon; b. Rome, Nov. 5, 1947; s. Federico and Vittoria (Martelli Castaldi) M.; m. Annalena Minghetti, Feb. 6, 1992; children: Alfredo, Benedetta. MD, U Bologna, Italy, 1972; Specialist Plastic Surgery, U. Padova, Italy, 1978. Diplomate European Bd. Plastic Surgery. Emergency rm. asst. Hosp., Ascoli Piceno, Italy, 1973-79; plastic surgery asst. Hosp., Bologna, 1979-89, dep. chief plastic surgery, 1989—; temporary prof. plastic surgery U. Bologna, 1992—; cons. plastic surgery Hosp., Bentivoglio, Italy, 1988—. Author: Vascular Microsurgery, 1985; contbr. articles to profl. jours. Lt. Italian Army, 1974-75. Recipient honors Serra Meml. Hosp., Sun Valley, 1978. Fellow ACS, Italian Soc. Plastic Surgery, Italian Soc. Surgery, Internat. Soc. Esthetic Plastic Surgery, European Soc. Surg. Oncology. Roman Catholic. Home: Via Pratello 35, 40122 Bologna Italy Office: Galleria Ugo Bassi 1, 40121 Bologna Italy

MARCOTTE, BRIAN MICHAEL, business executive, consultant; b. Lewiston, Maine, May 29, 1949; s. Roland Louis and Eileen Frances (Hopkins) M. BS, Stonehill Coll., 1971; MA, Clark U., 1973; PhD, Dalhousie, Halifax, N.S., Can., 1977; postgrad., McGill U., 1987, U. Maine, 1988. Asst. prof. biology dept. U. Victoria, Can., 1977-80; asst. prof. McGill U., Montreal, Que., Can., 1980-87; dir. State of Maine Marine Scis. Lab., West Boothbay Harbor, 1987-92; pres., dir. Strategic Analysis, Inc., Portland, Providence, Maine, RI, 1991—; dir. SAI Found., Portland, Providence, Maine, RI, 1991—; founder, dir. HIV/AIDS Rsch. and Clin. Care Libr., 1991—. Author 3 books and 17 technical and advisory reports; contbr. numerous articles to profl. jours. Linnean Soc. London fellow, 1985. Recipient Pub. Svc. Commendation U.S. Dept. Commerce, 1991. Mem. AAAS, N.Y. Acad. Scis. Democrat. Roman Catholic.

MARCOUX, JULIA A., midwife; b. St. Helens, England, Aug. 7, 1928; d. Robert Patrick and Margaret Mary Theresa (White) Ashall; m. Albert Marcoux, Apr. 23, 1955; children: Stephen, Ann Marie, Richard, Michael, Maureen, Patrick, Margaret, Julie. Diploma, Withington Hosp., Manchester, England, 1950; grad., Cowley Hill Hosp., St. Helens, England, 1952; BS in Pub. Adminstrn., St. Joseph's Coll. RN, Conn.; lic. midwife, Conn. Nurse, labor, delivery rm. and nursery Day Kimbal Hosp., Putnam, Conn.; sch. nurse Marianapolis Prep. Sch., Thompson, Conn.; occupational nurse U.S. Post Office, Hartford, Conn.; pvt. duty and gerontology nurse Conn. Contbr. articles to profl. jours. Named Internat. Cath. Family of Yr., 1982.

MARCUCELLA, HENRY, psychologist, educator; b. Brookline, Mass., July 12, 1942; s. Henry and Elinor (DiZacomo) M.; m. Jayne Bradley, Apr. 25, 1965; children: Wendy, Henry. AB, Northeastern U., 1965; AM, Boston U., 1967, PhD, 1972. Asst. prof., assoc. prof. Boston U., 1972-90, prof., 1990-93, chmn. dept. psychology, 1993—; bd. advisors Cambridge (Mass.) Ctr. Behavioral Studies, 1986—; bd. dirs. Greater Boston Phobia Soc., 1987-88.

Contbr. chpts. in books and articles to profl. jours. Grantee NSF, Nat. Inst. Alcohol and Alcoholism. Mem. APA, Internat. Soc. Biomed. Rsch. on Alcoholism, Rsch. Soc. on Alcoholism, Psychonomic Soc., Behavioral Pharmacology Soc. Office: Boston U Dept Psychology 64 Cummington St Boston MA 02215-2407

MARCUS, ANDREW JAMES, osteopath, orthopaedic surgery; b. Flushing, N.Y., June 29, 1964; s. Michael Norman and Joan Ann (Silverman) M.; m. Kathleen Joy Kasper, Oct. 2, 1994. BS cum laude, Rider U., 1986; DO, N.Y. Coll. Osteo Medicine, 1990. Diplomate Nat. Bd. Osteo. Med. Examiners. Rotating intern Cmty. Gen. Osteo. Hosp., Harrisburg, Pa., 1990-91, resident in orthopaedic surgery, 1991-95; pvt. practice, Lehighton, Pa., 1995—, Palmerton, Coaldale, Pa., 1995—. Mem. Am. Coll. Orthopaedic Surgeons, Am. Osteo. Assn., Am. Osteo. Acad. Orthopaeics, Pa. Osteo. Med. Assn.

MARCUS, DAVID DONALD, medical associaton executive; b. Detroit, Jan. 22, 1943; s. Nathan Israel and Jeanette (Sokol) M.; m. Leah Ruth Powell, Nov. 27, 1974; children: Emily Mirah, Lauren Aliza. BA, U. Mich, 1964; MA, U. Calif., Berkeley, 1966, PhD, 1972; MMgmt., Northwestern U., Evanston, Ill., 1980. Vis. lectr. dept. English and comparative lit. U. Calif., Irvine, 1971-72; asst. prof. U. Ill., Chgo., 1972-76; program dir. Northwestern Meml. Hosp., Chgo., 1976-80; dir. socioecon. research info. AMA, Chgo., 1980-88; dir. health care fin. Tex. Med. Assn., Austin, 1988—; asst. to dir. Ctr. for Mental Health and Psychiat. Services, Am. Hosp. Assn., Chgo., 1979-80. Contbr. articles to profl. jours. Mem. Am. Assn. Med. Soc. Execs., Tex. Soc. Assn. Execs. Democrat. Jewish. Home: 7300 W Rim Dr Austin TX 78731-2043 Office: Tex Med Assn 401 W 15th St Austin TX 78701-1665

MARCUS, DEVRA JOY COHEN, internist; b. Bronx, N.Y., Sept. 5, 1940; d. Benjamin and Gertrude (Siegel) Cohen; m. Robert A. Marcus, Apr. 1963 (div. 1974); children: Rachel, Adam; m. Michael J. Horowitz, Mar. 2, 1975; 1 child, Naomi. BA, Brandeis U., 1961; MD, Stanford U., 1966. Diplomate Am. Bd. Internal Medicine. Intern in internal medicine Stanford U., 1966-67, resident, 1967-68; gen. internist D.C. Dept. Pub. Health, 1968-69, Cardozo Neighborhood Health Ctr., Washington, 1969-73; med. dir. East of the River Health Assn., Washington, 1973-75; fellow in infectious disease Washington Hosp. Ctr., 1975-77; gen. internist Police and Fire Clinic, Washington, 1977-78; gen. internist, pvt. practice Washington, 1977—; assoc. clin. prof. medicine George Washington U. Med Ctr., Washington, 1978—; gen. internist World Bank, Washington, 1978-81; ptnr. Traveller's Med. Svc. D.C., 1980-82; gen. internist Community of Good Hope Med. Clinic, Washington, 1984-85; assoc. clin. prof. medicine Georgetown U. Med. Ctr., Washington, 1987—; preceptor Georgetown U. Hosp., 1986—. Contbr. articles to profl. jours. Exec. com. Woodley Park Citizen's Assn., 1979-80; chair mayor's adv. com. on prevention, 1982-83; bd. dirs. Exodus Youth Svcs., 1987-89. Fellow ACP; mem. AMA (Physicians Recognition award, 1981, 84, 87, 90, 93), Med. Soc. D.C. (credentials com., communicable disease com., founder com. on women 1983, pres. 1985-87, med. ethics and judiciary com. 1987-91, judiciary coun. 1992-96). Home: 1205 Crest Ln Mc Lean VA 22101-1837 Office: 2021 K St NW Washington DC 20006

MARCUS, EDWIN LEE, pediatrician; b. Bklyn., Jan. 19, 1928; s. Benjamin and Fanny (Schulman) M.; m. Catherine M. Reid, May 19, 1956; children: Sheila, Jacqueline, Anne. AB, Columbia Coll., 1947; MD, NYU, 1950; MPH, U. Mich., 1958. Intern Lenox Hill Hosp., N.Y.C., 1950-51; resident dept. pediatrics U. Mich., Ann Arbor, 1953-56; pvt. practice Taylor, Mich., 1959-76; clin. rschr. Warner Lambert, Ann Arbor, 1976-86; pvt. practice HF Med. Group, Woodhaven, Mich., 1986-92; divsn. dir. pediatrics Henry Ford Med. Group, Fairlane, Dearborn, Mich., 1992—. 1st lt. M.C., U.S. Army, 1951-53, Korea. Office: Henry Ford Med Group 19401 Hubbard Dearborn MI 48126

MARCUS, ERIC ROBERT, psychiatrist; b. N.Y.C., Feb. 16, 1944; s. Victor and Pearl (Maddow) M.; m. Eslee Samberg, Nov. 24, 1985; children: Max, Pia. AB, Columbia U., 1965; MD, U. Wis., 1969. Diplomate Am. Bd. Psychiatry and Neurology. Intern NYU Med. Ctr. Bellevue Hosp., 1969-70; resident Columbia Presbyn. Med. Ctr.-N.Y. State Psychiatric Inst., 1972-75; dir. St. Marks Free Clinic, N.Y.C., 1971-75; from co-dir. to dir. neuropsychiatric/diagnostic treatment unit Columbia-Presbyn. Med. Ctr., N.Y.C., 1975-84; dir. med. student edn. in psychiatry Columbia U. Coll. Physicians and Surgeons, N.Y.C., 1981—; supervising-tng. analyst Ctr. for Psychoanalytic Tng.-Rsch. Columbia U. Ctr. for Psychoanalytic Tng.-Rsch., N.Y.C., 1995—; bd. govs. student health Columbia U., 1986—. Author: Psychosis and Near Psychosis, 1992; mem. editorial bd. The Psychoanalytic Study of Society, 1989-94; contbr. articles to profl. jours. Recipient Weber rsch. award Columbia U. Psychoanalytic Ctr., 1991, O'Connor Teaching award, 1995. Fellow Am. Psychiat. Assn. (Roeske award 1991), Am. Psychoanalytic Assn., Am. Coll. Psychoanalysts, N.Y. Acad. Medicine. Office: Columbia U Dept Psychiatry 722 W 168th St New York NY 10032-2603

MARCUS, HAROLD, physician, health facility administrator; b. N.Y.C., May 28, 1915; s. Abraham and Yetta (Salb) M.; m. Beatrice Falk, Apr. 27, 1943; children: Robert Michael, Alan David. BS, Columbia U., 1935; BS in Medicine, W.Va. U., 1936; MD cum laude, Boston U., 1939. Diplomate Nat. Bd. Med. Examiners, Am. Bd. Internal Medicine. Intern Maimonides Med. Ctr., Bklyn., N.Y., 1939-41; resident in pathology Nassau County Med. Ctr., Hempstead, N.Y., 1941, 46, resident in internal medicine, 1947-48; resident in neurology Kingsbrook Med. Ctr., Bklyn., 1948-49; pvt. practice Bklyn., 1949-88; chief medicine Internat. Ladies Garment Workers Union Health Ctr., N.Y.C., 1953—. Contbr. articles to profl. jours. Lt. col. U.S. Army, 1941-46. Decorated Bronze Star; recipient Merit Citation Gen. Chiang Kai Shek, China, 1945. Mem. ACP, Phi Delta Epsilon. Home: 180 Marlborough Rd Brooklyn NY 11226-4510

MARCUS, JOEL DAVID, pediatrician; b. Bklyn., June 16, 1932. BA, Columbia Coll., 1954; MD, George Washington U., 1958. Diplomate Am. Bd. Pediats. Rotating intern/pediat. resident The Jewish Hosp. of Bklyn., 1958-61; pvt. practice Rye, N.Y., 1963—; attending pediatrician United Hosp., Port Chester, N.Y., 1963—. Sch. pediatrician Rye Sch. Sys., 1963—. Capt. USAF, 1961-63. Fellow Am. Acad. Pediats. Office: 33 Cedar St Rye NY 10580

MARCUS, LINDA SUSAN, dermatologist; b. Brooklyn; d. Nathaniel and Eugenia (Portnay) Marcus; m. Ronald Carlin, July 5, 1976; children: Robert Adam, Neal Marc. BS, Adelphi U., Garden City, N.J., 1970; MD, Downstate Med. Sch., Brooklyn, 1975. Diplomate Am. Bd. Dermatology. Intern Long Island (N.Y.) Jewish Med. Ctr., 1975-76; resident in dermatology Columbia-St. Luke's, N.Y.C., 1976-77, Boston U.-Tuft's, 1977-79; pvt. practice Wyckoff, N.J., 1980—. Contbr. articles to profl. jours. Mem. Am. Acad. Dermatology, Am. Soc. Dermatology Surgeons, Internat. Soc. Dermatology Surgeons. Office: 271 Godwin Ave Wyckoff NJ 07481-2057

MARCUS, NORMAN H., cardiologist; b. N.Y.C., Oct. 20, 1952; Married; 2 children. BS, Cornell U., 1973; MD, NYU, 1977. Diplomate Am. Bd. Internal Medicine, Cardiovascular Diseases, Clin. Cardiac Electrophysiology; lic. Pa. Intern, resident Yale-New Haven (Conn.) Hosp., 1977-80; fellow cardiology U. Pa. Hosp., Phila., 1980-82, rsch. fellow cardiac electrophysiology, 1982-83; staff physician Lehigh Valley Hosp., Allentown, Pa., 1983—; clin. asst. prof. U. Pa., Phila., 1983-89, Pa. State U., 1995—; med. staff Allentown Osteo. Med. Ctr., 1995—, Presbyn. Med. Ctr. Phila., 1993—, Miners Meml. Med. Ctr., Coaldale, Pa., 1993—. Presenter in field; contbr. articles to profl. jours. Grantee Am. Heart Assn., 1981-83. Fellow Am. Coll. Cardiology; mem. N.Am. Soc. for Pacing and Electrophysiology, Tau Beta Pi, Eta Kappa Nu, Alpha Omega Alpha. Office: Cardiovascular Assocs Ste 2300 1210 S Cedar Crest Blvd Allentown PA 18103

MARCUS, RANDALL EVAN, orthopaedic surgery educato; b. N.Y.C., Feb. 10, 1950; s. Irwin M. and Dorthy (Mann) M.; m. Anne Mulligan, June 2, 1984; 1 child, Blair Mulligan. BS in Biochemistry magna cum laude, Tulane U., 1972; MD, La. State U., 1975. Diplomate Am. Bd. Orthopaedic Surgery (written exam. com. question-writing task force 1983—, written recert. exam. question-writing task force 1991-92). Fellow Nufield dept. orthopaedic surgery Oxford (Eng.) U., 1980-81; internat. fellow dept. surgery U. Basle, Switzerland, 1981; sr. fellow dept. orthopaedics U. Wash.-Harborview Med. Ctr., Seattle, 1981; asst. clin. prof. Tulane U. Sch. Medicine and La. State U. Sch. Medicine, New Orleans, 1984-85; rotating surg. intern Case Western Res. U. Sch. Medicine, Cleve., 1975-76, asst. resident in gen. surgery, 1976-77, resident in orthopaedics, 1977-79, chief resident, 1979-80, postdoctoral fellow, 1977-80, instr., 1981-82, asst. prof., 1982-83, 86-91, assoc. prof., 1992—, dir. divsn. foot and ankle surgery, 1987—; attending orthopaedic surgery Univ. Hosps. Cleve., 1981—, dir. divsn. foot and ankle surgery, 1987—; cons. orthopaedic surgeon VA Hosp., Cleve., 1981—, clin. chief regional prosthetic amputee clinic, 1989—; vis. prof. NYU Sch. Medicine, 1989, Cath. U. Med. Ctr., 1992, U. Cin. Med. Ctr., 1993, Albert Einstein Med. Ctr., Phila., 1993, La. State U. Sch. Medicine, 1994, Nippon U. Sch. Medicine, Tokyo, 1995, Hirosaki (Japan) U. Sch. Medicine, 1995, Greenville (S.C.) Med. Ctr., 1995; presenter to local, nat. and internat. med. and sci. socs., 1981—. Author: Orthopaedics: Problems in Primary Care, 1991; editor: Trauma in Children, 1986; bd. editors Today in Medicine, 1989-95; contbr. articles to med. jours.; patentee for multi-use femoral intramedullary nail. Bd. dirs. Cleve. Health Mus., 1992—; mem. med. adv. bd. ARC No. Ohio, 1992—; mem. orch. tomorrow steering com. Cleve. Mus. Arts Assn., 1992-93. Grantee Robert J. Frackelton Fund, 1982-84, Orthopaedic Rsch. and Ednl. Found., 1983-85, Univ. Hosps. Cleve., 1986, NIH, 1987-93, Smith and Nephew Richards grantee, 1990-93, OrthoBiotech grantee, 1992. Fellow ACS, Am. Acad. Orthopaedic Surgeons; mem. AMA, Clin. Orthopaedic Soc., Orthopaedic Trauma Assn., Am. Orthopaedic Foot and Ankle Soc., Internat. Soc. Orthopedics and Traumatology, Cleve. Orthopaedic Soc. (bd. dirs. 1986-89), Innominatum Med. Soc. Cleve. (bd. dirs. 1988-93, sec.-treas. 1988-90, pres. 1990-91), Cleve. Aesculapian Med. Soc. (bd. dirs. 1991-95, pres. 1993-94), Charles H. Herndon Case Western Res. U. Orthopaedic Alumni Soc. (pres. 1984-91), Pasteur Club Cleve., Phi Beta Kappa, Sigma Xi. Office: Case Western Res U Sch Medicine Univs Hosps Cleve 11100 Euclid Ave Cleveland OH 44106

MARCUS, RICHARD WARREN, pediatrician, educator; b. Englewood, N.J., Apr. 23, 1955; s. Melvin and Lillian Marcus; m. Deborah J. Fox, Aug. 26, 1979; children: Melanie, Alison. BA, Rutgers Coll., 1977; MD, N.J. Med. Sch., 1982. Diplomate Nat. Bd. Med. Examiners, Am. Bd. Pediatrics. Intern-resident in pediatrics Univ. Medicine and Dentistry of N.J. Children's Hosp. N.J., Newark, 1982-85; assoc. attending physician Clara Maass Med. Ctr., Belleville, N.J., 1985-90; attending physician Clara Maass Med. Ctr., Belleville, 1990—; assoc. attending physician Mountainside Hosp., Montclair, N.J., 1987-92, attending physician, 1994—; dir. dept. pediatrics Mountainside Hosp., Montclair, 1995—; clin. asst. prof ped. UMDNJ, Newark, 1996—, clin. asst. prof. family med., 1996—; clin. instr. dept. pediatrics U. Medicine and Dentistry of N.J., 1987-93. preceptor 1st and 4th yr. students, 1992-95, clin. asst. prof., 1993—; clin.asst. prof. pediatrics, Seton Hall Grad. Sch. Med. Edn., Orange, N.J., 1990—; lectr. Mountainside Hosp. Montclair, La Maze Lectr. Series, 1991—. Bd. dirs. Clifton (N.J.) Jewish Ctr. 1990-92, v.p. 1992—, chmn. bd. edn. religious sch., 1992—; mem. physicians adv. com. on lead poisoning N.J. Dept. Health, 1992—. Named Henry Rutgers scholar Rutgers Coll., New Brunswick, 1977. Fellow Am. Acad. Pediatrics (mem. sect. on adolescent health 1994—); mem. AMA, N.J. Pediatric Soc. Office: 242 Washington Ave Nutley NJ 07110-1956

MARCUS, ROBERT MARTIN, physician; b. N.Y.C., Mar. 2, 1964; s. Richard Victor and Myrna Betty (Manoff) M.; m. Evelyn Rosa Morales, Nov. 7, 1992. BA, Brandeis U., 1986; MD, SUNY, Stony Brook, 1990. Intern, resident Emory U. Affiliated Hosps., Atlanta, 1990-93; physician pvt. practice, Atlanta, 1993-94, Piedmont Clinic, Atlanta, 1994—. Mem. Am. Coll. Physicians. Office: Piedmont Physicians 4890 Roswell Rd Atlanta GA 30342

MARCUS, STEVEN MATTHEW, toxicologist; b. Bklyn., July 14, 1942; s. Jack M. and Fanny Theda (Cohen) M.; m. Amy Jane Rubin, Aug. 11, 1968; children: Jayme, Joshua, Leigh. BS in Biology, Bklyn. Coll., 1963; MD, Med. Coll. Va., 1967. Diplomat Am. Bd. Med. Toxicology, Am. Bd. Pediatrics; lic. physician, N.J., N.Y., Va. Intern NYU Bellevue Hosp., N.Y.C., 1967-68, resident in pediatrics, 1968-69; resident in pediatrics Bronx Mcpl. Hosp. Ctr., N.Y.C., 1969-70; asst. dir. dept. pediatrics Newark Beth Israel Med. Ctr., Newark, 1972—; asst. prof. pediatrics preventive and community medicine Coll. Medicine & Dentistry N.J., 1972-82; med. dir. Inst. for Child Study, Kean Coll., Union, N.J., 1976-82; project dir. N.J. Poison Info. and Edn. System, 1980—; assoc. prof. clin. pediatrics U. Medicine & Dentistry N.J., 1982—; dir. N.J. Poison Info. and Edn. System, Newark, 1983—, N.J. AIDS Hotline, Newark, 1988—. Co-author: Ambulatory Pediatric Care, 1988, Current Emergency Therapy, 1984, 85, Experimental and Clinical Toxicokinetics, 1984, Preventing Mental Retardation and Other Disorders, 1980, The Clinical Practice of Emergency Medicine, 1991; editor: Pediatric Emergency News; contbg. editor: Poisindex, 1983—. Pres. Bd. Health, Twp. Vill. South Orange, N.J., 1991-93; active Gov. Coun. on Prevention Mental Retardation, Gov. Coun. on Emergency Med. Svcs., Commrs. Occupational Health Svc. Adv. Panel, Commrs. Coun. on Dioxin Contamination and Risk Assessment, 1983-84, Commrs. Coun. on Ethylene Dibromide and Risk Assessment, 1983-84. Harvard Med. Sch. fellow, 1979-80. Fellow Am. Acad. Pediatrics (councilman, chmn. accident prevention and safety com. N.J. chpt.), Am. Acad. Clin. Toxicology; mem. AMA, AAAS, Med. Soc. the State N.J., Essex County Med. Soc., N.Y. Acad. Sci., Am. Coll. Emergency Physicians, Am. Coll. Preventive Medicine, Ambulatory Pediatric Assn. Office: 201 Lyons Ave Newark NJ 07112-2027

MARDER, HAROLD K., pharmaceutical executive; b. Pitts., May 15, 1949; s. Joseph and Fannie (Talenfeld) M.; m. Jewel D. Slesnick, Mar. 31, 1985. BA, Washington & Jefferson, 1971; MD, U. Pitts., 1975. Asst. prof. U. Cin., 1981-82; pediatric nephrologist Cin. Children's Hosp., 1981-82; pvt. practice Phila., 1982-83; assoc. dir. clin. rsch. Wyeth Labs., Phila., 1983-85, dir. clin. rsch., 1985-87; sr. dir. clin. rsch. Wyeth-Ayerst Rsch., Phila., 1987-92, asst. v.p. clin. rsch., 1992-93, v.p. nutritional R&D, 1994-96, v.p. strategic devel., 1995—. Contbr. articles to profl. jours. Mem. Am. Soc. Nephrology, Am. Soc. Hypertension, Am. Acad. Pediats., Internat. Soc. Nephrology. Office: Wyeth-Ayerst Labs PO Box 8299 Philadelphia PA 19101

MARDER, MICHAEL ZACHARY, dentist, researcher, educator; b. N.Y.C., Aug. 30, 1938; s. Jospeh Theodore and Rhea (Greenspun) M.; (widowed); children: Sherri Ellen, Robert Whitney. Student, Tufts U., 1959; D.D.S., Columbia U., 1963. Diplomate: Am. Bd. Oral Medicine. Practice dentistry N.Y.C., 1963-66, 68—; asst. Sch. Dental and Oral Surgery, Columbia U., N.Y.C., 1963-66, instr., 1968, asst. clin. prof., 1968-72, assoc. clin. prof., 1972-76, clin. prof. dentistry, 1976—, researcher, 1963—; dir. oral medicine, 1972-84, dir. clin. cancer tng., 1993—; asst. attending dental surgeon Presbyn. Hosp., 1972-76; assoc. attending dentist, 1976-82, attending dentist, 1982—; cons. Good Samaritan Hosp., Suffern, N.Y.; lectr. in field. Author 2 textbooks in dental medicine; contbr. chpts. to med. and dental textbooks, articles to profl. jours. Served to capt. U.S. Army, 1966-68. Recipient Cert. of Achievement U.S. Army, 1968. Fellow N.Y. Acad. Dentistry; mem. ADA, Internat. Assn. Dental Rsch., Am. Acad. Oral Medicine, Frist Dist. Dental Soc. N.Y., Omicron Kappa Upsilon, Sigma Xi. Office: 119 W 57th St New York NY 10019-2303

MÅRDH, PER-ANDERS, bacteriology educator; b. Stockholm, Apr. 9, 1941; s. Gustav-Adolf and Inga-Greta MÅrdh. MD, U. Lund, Sweden, 1968, PhD cum laude, 1972. Intern, resident Lund U. Hosp., 1968-84; lectr., reader U. Lund, 1969-81; prof. bacteriology U. Uppsala, Sweden, 1984—; dir. WHO Coll. Centre, Lund, 1984—, Inst. Clin. Bacteriology, Uppsala, 1984—; dir. Uppsala U. Ctr. for Std. Rsch., Uppsala, 1990—; sci. advisor Swedish Bd. Health and Welfare, 1984—. Author/editor 17 books; author med. videos, 1988-93; contbr. articles to profl. jours. Mem. Scandinavian Soc. Travel, Medicine and Health (chmn. hdqrs. 1991—), Internat. Orgn. Tourist Health (bd. mem. 1988—), European Assn. Chlamydia Rsch. (chmn. 1988-92). Office: Uppsala Inst Clin Bacteriology, Box 552, S-75122 Uppsala Sweden

MARDIS, HAL KENNEDY, urological surgeon, educator, researcher; b. Lincoln, Nebr., Apr. 4, 1934; s. Harold Corson and Marie (Swaim) M.; m. Janet Reimers Schenken, June 22, 1956; children: Michael Corson, Anne Lucille, Jeanne Marie. BS, U. Nebr., Lincoln, 1955; MD, U. Nebr., Omaha, 1958. Diplomate Am. Bd. Urology. Intern Nebr. Meth. Hosp., Omaha, 1958-59, med. dir. The Stone Ctr., 1966—; resident in urology Charity Hosp. La., New Orleans, 1959-62, chief resident in urology, 1962-63; pvt. practice Omaha, 1965—; instr., asst. prof. La. State U. Sch. Medicine, New Orleans, 1963-65; asst. prof., assoc. prof. surgery U. Nebr. Med. Ctr., 1965-85, prof., 1985—; investigator North Cen. Cancer Treatment Group, Rochester, Minn., 1988—, Technomed Internat., Inc., Danvers, Mass., 1988—; cons. Boston Sci. Corp., Watertown, Mass., 1988—. Assoc. editor Jour. Stone Disease; contbr. articles to Jour. AMA, So. Med. Jour., Jour. Urology, Urology, Urol. Clinics N.Am., Seminars in Interventional Radiology. Sec., pres. Omaha Symphony Assn., 1973-76; advisor United Arts Omaha, 1983-88. Recipient Outstanding Contbn. award dept. surgery U. Nebr. Med. Ctr., 1990. Fellow ACS; mem. AMa (del. med. staff sect. 1983-86), Am. Urol. Assn. (pres. South Cen. chpt. 1990-91, 1st prize 1976, best clin. exhibit award 1977), Am. Lithotripsy Soc. (pres. 1989-90), Alpha Omega Alpha (pres. 1991-92). Republican. Office: The Urology Ctr 111 S 90th St Omaha NE 68114-3907

MARDJETKO, STEVEN MICHAEL, surgeon; b. Hammond, Ind., Jan. 21, 1956; m. Karen Kozlowski, Jan. 26, 1988; children: Stephanie, Mac. BS, Ill. Benedictine Coll., Lisle, 1978; MD with honors, U. Ill., Chgo., 1982. Diplomate Am. Bd. Orthop. Surgery. Intern U. Ill., Chgo., 1982-83, resident in orthopedic surgery, 1983-87; spinal deformity fellow Rush Presbyn. St. Lukes Hosp., Chgo., 1987-88, pediatric orthopedic fellow, 1989-90; chief spine surgery Cook County Hosp., Chgo., 1988-90, chief pediatric othopedics, 1992—; chief spine surgery Cardinal Glendon Hosp., Chgo., 1990-92; asst. prof. Rush Presbyn. St. Luke Spine Deformity Svc., 1992—; lectr. U. Ill.; cons. Shriners Hosp. Crippled Children, Chgo., 1992—. Co-author: Disorder of the Lumbo Pelvic Junction, 1996, Infantile and Juvenile Scoliosis, 1996; assoc. editor: Text Boook of Spinal Surgery, 1996. Fellow Am. Acad. Orthop. Surgeons, Am. Acad. Pediatrics, Pediatric Orthop. Soc.; mem. Scoliosis Rsch. Soc. (sic. com., program com., edn. com.), N.Am. Spine Soc. Office: # 440 1725 W Harrison St Chicago IL 60612

MARECEK, JEANNE ANN, psychologist, educator; b. Berwyn, Ill., May 28, 1946; d. Frank J. and Josephine (Serio) M. BS, Loyola U., Chgo., 1968; MS, Yale U., 1971, PhD, 1973. From asst. prof. to prof. psychology Swarthmore (Pa.) Coll., 1972—, chmn. dept., 1986-91, 94-95; Fulbright sr. lectr., Sri Lanka, 1988. Co-author: Making a Difference: Psychology and the Construction of Gender; contbr. numerous articles to profl. jours. and chpts. to books. Bd. dirs. Women in Transition, Phila., 1980-86; vice patron Nest, Hendala, Sri Lanka, 1995—; bd. dirs. Women's Therapy Ctr., Phila. Various fed. research grants. Mem. APA, Ea. Psychol. Assn., Assn. for Asian Studies, Am. Inst. Sri Lanka Studies (sec. 1994-95). Office: Swarthmore Coll Dept Psychology 500 College Ave Swarthmore PA 19081

MARES, ABRAHAM JACOB, pediatric surgeon; b. Bucharest, Romania, May 15, 1935; arrived in Israel, 1941; s. Samuel and Pauline (Bercovici) M.; m. Ofra Disatnik, May 3, 1962; children: Eyal, Sharon Mares-Klauzner, Michal. MD, Hadassah-Hebrew U., 1962. Intern Beilinson Med. Ctr., Petach Tiqva, Israel, 1961, resident, 1963-65; resident Beth Israel Hosp., Boston, 1965-68; chief resident Children's Hosp., L.A., 1968-69; chief physician, surgeon Pondville State Cancer Hosp., Walpole, Mass., 1969-70; sr. staff surgeon Soroka Med. Ctr., Be'er Sheba, Israel, 1970-71, chief dept. pediatric surgery, 1971—; sr. lectr. Ben Gurion U., Faculty Health Scis., Be'er Sheba, 1974-81, assoc. prof., 1981-88, prof. surgery, 1988—, vice dean, 1984-86. Contbr. articles to profl. jours. Maj. Israeli Defence Forces Res., 1963-89. Fellow Am. Coll. Surgeons; mem. British Assn. Pediatric Surgeons, Israeli Soc. pediatric Surgeons. Home: 3 Arava St, 84965 Omer Israel

MARES, FRANK JAMES, ophthalmologist; b. El Paso, Tex., Oct. 1, 1951; s. Presciliano Percy and Ascencion Maria (Sisneros) M.; m. Barbara Jean Sais, Feb. 27, 1977. B.S., Colo. State U., 1973; M.D., U. N.Mex., 1977. Diplomate Am. Bd. Ophthalmology. Intern Good Samaritan Hosp., Portland, Oreg., 1977-78; resident in ophthalmology Oreg. Health Scis. U., Portland, 1978-81, fell in pediatric ophthalmology, 1981-82, fell in glaucoma, 1983; chief ophthalmology VA Hosp., Albuquerque, 1982-83; practice medicine specializing in ophthalmology and glaucoma, Albuquerque, 1983—; council mem. Nat. Inst. Gen. Med. Scis., NIH, Bethesda, Md., 1974-78; asst. clin. prof. Oreg. Health Scis. Ctr., Portland, 1981-82, 83, U. N.Mex. Med. Ctr., Albuquerque, 1983—. Fellow Am. Acad. Ophthalmology; mem. Greater Albuquerque Med. Assn., N.Mex. Ophthalmol. Soc., Alpha Omega Alpha, Alpha Kappa Phi. Roman Catholic. Office: Eye Assocs of NMex 806 Grand NE Albuquerque NM 87102

MARESCA, LUIGI, cardiovascular surgeon; b. Naples, Italy, Mar. 19, 1949; came to U.S., 1974; s. Benedetto and Francesca (Zezza) M.; m. Carlotta Bonato, May 30, 1977; children: Betino, Barbara. MD, Cath. U. of Rome, 1973. Diplomate Am. Bd. Thoracic Surgery. Jr. surg. resident McKeesport (Pa.) Hosp., 1974-76, gen. surg. resident, 1976-79; clin. instr. gen. surgery Mich. State U., Saginaw, 1980-81; chief gen. surg. resident Saginaw (Mich.) Coop. Hosp., 1980-81; cardiothoracic fellow Cleve. Clinic, 1981-82, chief gen. thoracic surg. resident, 1982; thoracic and cardiovasc. surg. resident Ohio State U. Hosp., Columbus, 1983-84; clin. instr. thoracic/cardiovasc. surgery Ohio State U. Hosp., 1983-84; pvt. practice Great Lakes Cardiovasc. Surgery P.C., Saginaw, 1985—; clin. asst. prof. surgery Mich. State U., Lansing. Contbr. articles to profl. jours. Lt. med. corps, Italian Army, 1975-76, Brescia, Italy. Fellow ACS, Am. Coll. Cardiology, Am. Coll. Chest Physicians; mem. Mich. Soc. Thoracic Surgeons, Saginaw Surg. Soc. Office: Great Lakes Cardiovascular Surgery PC 4701 Towne Ctr Rd #301 Saginaw MI 48604

MARESCHI, JEAN PIERRE, biochemical engineer; b. Pinzano, Italy, Apr. 11, 1937; s. Thomas and Marie Mareschi; m. Françoise Comte, Feb. 11, 1966. B in Math., Paris, 1957; degree in biochem. engring., Inst. Nat. Sci. Appl. Lyon, Lyon, France, 1962; PhD, U. Paris Faculty Pharmacy, 1993. Cert. adminstrn. indus.; cert. biochem. engr., Nutrition Toxicology Regulatory. Researcher French Army Lab., Lyon, 1962-64; head lab. Rsch. Ctr., Sterling Winthrop, Dijon, 1964-70; head lab. fermentation rsch. and mktg. Air Liquide, Grenoble and Paris, France, 1970-75; dir. sci. asst. Hoffman La Roche, Paris, 1975-82; dir. relation sci. regulatory Danone Group, Paris, 1982-89, dir. internat. affairs, 1989—; mem. mng. com. sci. schs., Lyon, 1991. Contbr. articles to sci. nutrition publs.; patentee in field of fermentation. Chevalier Tastevin. Clos Vougeot, Cote d'Or, France, 1991, Agrl. Merit award Ministry of Agr., France, 1992. Mem. Internat. Life Sci. Inst. Europe (bd. dirs., mem. exec. com., vice chmn. 1991). Home: 16 BD du Parc, 92200 Neuilly-Seine France Office: DANONE, 7 Rue de Teheran, F75008 Paris France

MARFUGGI, RICHARD ANTHONY, plastic surgeon; b. Rutland, Vt., Aug. 3, 1950. BA in Biology, Coll. of the Holy Cross, 1972; MD, U. Vt., 1976. Diplomate Am. Bd. Plastic Surgery. Intern in surgery U. Health Ctr. Hosps., Pitts., 1976-77, resident gen. surgery, 1977-78; resident gen. surgery Ea. Va. Grad. Sch. Medicine, Norfolk, 1978-81; resident plastic surgery Inst. Reconstructive Plastic Surgery, NYU Med. Ctr., N.Y.C., 1981-83; presenter in field. Contbr. articles to profl. jours. Fellow ACS; mem. AMA (Physician Recognition award), Am. Soc. Plastic and Reconstructive Surgeons, Med. Soc. State N.Y., N.J. State Med. Soc., Union County Med. Soc., John Marquis Converse Plastic Surgery Soc., C.F. Reynolds Med. Hist. Soc., Harbison Surg. Soc., Alpha Sigma Nu, Alpha Epsilon Delta. Office: 10 Broadway Denville NJ 07834

MARG, ELWIN, physiological optics, optometry educator; b. San Francisco, Mar. 23, 1918; s. Sigmund and Fannie (Sockolov) M.; m. Helen Eugenia Kelly, Apr. 1, 1942; 1 child, Tamia. AB, U. Calif., Berkeley, 1940, PhD, 1950. Asst. prof. vision sci. U. Calif., Berkeley, 1950-56, assoc. prof., 1956-62, prof., 1962—; bd. dirs., v.p., Minerva Found., Berkeley. Author: Computer Assisted Eye Examination, 1980; also articles. Served to lt. col. USAF, 1941-46, 50-52, ETO. NSF fellow, Nobel Inst. Stockholm, 1957, Guggenheim, Madrid, 1964; recipient Miller Research Professorship U. Calif.-Berkeley, 1967. Fellow AAAS, Optical Soc. Am., Am. Acad. Optometry; mem. Soc. Neurosci., Assn. Rsch. Vision and Ophthalmology, Internat. Soc. Magnetic Resonance in Medicine. Office: U Calif Sch Optometry Berkeley CA 94720-2020

MARGEN, SHELDON, public health educator, nutritionist emeritus; b. Chgo., May 19, 1919; s. Paul and Sarah M.; m. Jeanne Carmel Sholtz, Mar. 16, 1943; children: Claude, Paul, Peter, David. BA, UCLA, 1938, MA, 1939; Md, U. Calif., San Francisco, 1943. Diplomate Am. Bd. Internal Medicine. Assoc prof. U. Calif. ., Berkeley, 1963-68, prof. pub. health and nutrition, 1968-89, prof. emeritus, 1989—; cons., mem. adv. coms. NIH, WHO,; bd. dirs. Omnicare. Cin., 1980—. Editor-in-chief U. Calif. Wellness Letter; author and editor 10 books on Nutrition and/or Pub. Health. Bd. dirs. Calif. Wellness Found., Woodland Hills, 1991—. Capt. Army Med. Corps,1943-48, ETO. Grantee, NIH, State of Calif., Ford Found. and many others. Fellow Am. Inst. Nutrition and many other profl. orgns. in fields of ntutrition and pub. health. Office: Univ Calif Sch of Pub Health Berkeley CA 94720

MARGO, KENNETH CRAIG, counselor; b. Oklahoma City, Apr. 22, 1953; s. Marvin Kenneth and Bobbie June (Cravens) M.; m. Laura Leslie Brooks, June 19, 1980. BA in Psychology, Centenary Coll., Shreveport, La., 1975; MEd in Counseling Psychology, Ctrl. State U., Edmond, Okla., 1978. Lic. profl. counselor, Okla., Wyo. Staff psychologist Okla. Children's Meml. Hosp., Oklahoma City, 1978-82; psychologist, clinic dir. Lincoln County Guidance Ctr., Chandler, Okla., 1982-84; pvt. practice Oklahoma City, 1984-86, 89-90; staff psychologist Mental Health Svcs. So. Okla., Ardmore, 1986-88; therapist, staff devel. coord. St. Joseph's Childrens Home, Oklahoma City, 1988-89; supr. outpatient substance abuse program Ctrl. Wyo. Counseling Ctr., Casper, 1990—. Mem. Okla. Youth and Suicide Task Force, Oklahoma City, Health Planning Commn., Chandler. Mem. ACA, Am. Mental Health Counselors Assn., Wyo. Mental Health Counselors Assn., Wyo. Counseling Assn., Okla. Assn. Counseling & Devel. (pres. 1989). Office: Ctrl Wyo Counseling Ctr 1200 E 3rd St Ste 330 Casper WY 82601-2933

MARGOLIN, CARL M., psychotherapist; b. N.Y.C., Jan. 23, 1939; s. Samuel and Henrietta (Kressel) M.; B.A., CUNY, 1961; M.S.W., Columbia U., 1965; postgrad. Nat. Psychol. Assn. for Psychoanalysis, 1968-70; m. Susie Echols Watts, Feb. 10, 1964; children—Christopher, Andrew; m. Paula Jean Beatty, March 26, 1993. Sr. psychiat. social worker W.J.C.S., White Plains, N.Y., 1964-76; psychotherapist Whitehill Counseling Service, Yorktown Hights, N.Y., 1973-76; pvt. practice psychotherapy, 1976—; tng. supr. Yeshiva U., 1972-76. Mem. exec. com. No. Westchester Mental Health Council, 1973-79, chmn. planning com., 1975-79. Cert. social worker, N.Y. State. Mem. Nat. Assn. Social Workers (diplomate), Acad. Cert. Social Workers, Soc. Clin. Social Work Psychotherapists (bd. cert. diplomate in clin. social work). Office: 19 Long Ridge Rd Bedford NY 10506

MARGOLIN, SOLOMON BEGELFOR, pharmacologist; b. Phila., May 16, 1920; s. Nathan and Fannie (Begelfor) M.; m. Gerda Levy, Jan. 17, 1947 (div. Feb. 1985); children: David, Bernard, Daniel; m. Nancy A. Cox, Apr. 30, 1987. BSc, Rutgers U., 1941, MSc, 1943, PhD, 1945. Asst. Rutgers U., New Brunswick, N.J., 1943-45; rsch. biologist Silmo Chem. Co., Vineland, N.J., 1947-48; rsch. pharmacologist Schering Corp., Bloomfield, N.J., 1948-52, dir. pharmacology dept., 1952-54; chief pharmacologist Maltbie Labs., Belleville, N.J., 1954-56; chief pharmacologist Wallace Labs, Carter-Wallace, Inc., Cranbury, N.J., 1956-60, dir. pharmacology dept., 1960-64, v.p. biol. rsch., 1964-68; pres. AMR Biol. Rsch., Inc., Princeton, N.J., 1968-78; from prof., chmn. pharmacology dept. to emeritus prof. St. George's (Grenada) U. Sch. Medicine, 1978—; pres. MARNAC, Inc., Dallas, 1990—. Author: Harper's Handbook Therapeutic Pharmacology, 1981; author: (with others) Physiological Pharmacology, 1963, World Review, Nutrition & Dietetics, 1980; contbr. over 50 articles to profl. jours. including Annals of Allergy, Proc. Soc. Exptl. Biol. & Med., Nature. Mem. AAAS, Endocrino Soc., Am. Chem. Soc., Soc. Exptl. Biology and Medicine, Am. Soc. Pharmacology and Exptl. Therapeutics, N.Y. Acad. Scis., Drug Information Assn. Home: 6723 Desco Dr Dallas TX 75225-2704 Office: Marnac Inc 6723 Desco Dr Dallas TX 75225-2704

MARGOLIS, GERALD JOSEPH, psychiatrist, psychoanalyst; b. Bronx, N.Y., May 7, 1935; s. Max and Sophie (Siegel) M.; A.B., U. Rochester, 1957; M.D., U. Chgo., 1960; postgrad. Inst. Phila. Assn. Psychoanalysis, 1972; m. June Edelman Greenspan, July 13, 1976; children: David J., Peter S., Steven J. Intern, psychiat. resident, Upstate Med. Center, SUNY, Syracuse, 1960-64, instr. psychiatry, 1966-67; from instr. to clin. prof. psychiatry Med. Sch., U. Pa., Phila., 1967—; practice medicine specializing in psychiatry and psychoanalysis, Cherry Hill, N.J.; tng. and supervising analyst Inst. of Phila. Assn. for Psychoanalysis. Served with M.C., USAF, 1964-66. Diplomate Am. Bd. Psychiatry and Neurology. Mem. Am. Psychoanalytic Assn. (cert.), Am. Psychiat. Assn., AMA, Phila. Assn. for Psychoanalysis (tng. and supervising analyst), Phi Beta Kappa. Club: B'nai B'rith. Contbr. articles to profl. publs. Home: 408 Park Ln Moorestown NJ 08057-2000

MARGOLIS, ROBERT ALLEN, psychologist; b. Bklyn., June 3, 1947; s. Frank and Elsie (Tabachnick) M.; m. Francine Cherry; children: Rachel Beth, Adam Jared. BA, Bklyn. Coll., 1971; MA, New Sch. for Social Rsch., 1980; PhD, Hofstra U., 1992. Lic. psychologist, N.Y. Tchr. emotionally handicapped N.Y.C. Bd. Edn., 1970-90, sch. psychologist, 1990—; pvt. practice psychologist Bellmore, N.Y., 1992—; cons. psychologist Young Adult Inst., N.Y.C., 1990-94; guest lectr. Suicide Prevention Resources, N.Y.C., 1993-95. Author, editor (manual) Benavior Modification Systems, 1987, (resource guidee) The Test Resource Guide, 1988. Mem. U.S. Holocaust Mus. (charter). Office: 2442 Bellmore Ave Bellmore NY 11710

MARGOLIS, SIMEON, physician, educator; b. Johnstown, Pa., Mar. 29, 1931; s. Edward Charles and Bella (Kantor) M.; m. Mary Alice Kahl, May 29, 1954; children: Karen Ann Margolis Griswold, Susan, Amy Elizabeth. BA, Johns Hopkins U., 1953, MD, 1957, PhD, 1964. Intern Johns Hopkins Hosp., Balt., 1957-58, asst. resident, 1958-59; sr. asst. surgeon USPHS, Bethesda, Md., 1959-61; rsch. fellow Johns Hopkins Sch. Medicine, Balt., 1961-64; chief resident Johns Hopkins Hosp., 1964-65; asst. prof. medicine and biol. chemistry Johns Hopkins Sch. Medicine, Balt., 1965-68, assoc. prof., 1968-77, prof., 1977—, assoc. dean acad. affairs, 1984-90, assoc. dean faculty affairs, 1990-92; mem. metabolism study sect. NIH, Bethesda, 1971-75, mem. gen. clin. rsch. ctrs. com., 1976-80, mem. nat. diabetes bd., 1984-88; mem. endocrine and metabolic drugs adv. com. FDA, Rockville, Md., 1979-82. Editor Johns Hopkins Med. Letter Health After 50, 1991—; contbr. articles to profl. jours., chpts. to books. Pres. 3d Dist. Citizens, Balt., 1970. Sr. asst. surgeon USPHS, 1959-61. Nat. Heart Inst. grantee, 1965-85. Mem. Am Diabetes Assn., Endocrine Soc., Am. Soc. Clin. Investigation, Am. Soc. Biol. Chemists, Am. Inst. Nutrition, Am. Soc. Clin. Nutrition, Coun. Atherosclerosis Rsch. Office: Johns Hopkins Hosp Blalock Bldg Rm 904 Baltimore MD 21287-4904

MARGULIES, ANDREW MICHAEL, chiropractor; b. Bklyn.; s. Irving R. and Marion (Steiner) M.; m. Lorraine Raffa, Dec. 23, 1990; children: Samantha Cara, Maxwell Scott. D. Chiropractic, Palmer Coll. Chiropractic, Davenport, Iowa, 1981; MSc in Spinal Biomechanics, Intercontinental U., 1995. Diplomate Nat. Bd. Chiropractic, Am. Acad. Pain Mgmt., Am. Bd. Disability Analyst (sr. disability analyst), Am. Bd. Disability Analysts; cert. chiropractic sports physician. Dir., chiropractic physician Margulies Chiropractic and Sports Injuries Ctr., Massapequa, N.Y., 1981—; chiropractor, mem. med. team N.Y. Long Island Marathon, 1986—, USA/Mobil Track and Field Nat. Championships, 1991—; cons. Massapequa Rd. Runners, Long Island, 1985—. Recipient Silver Star award Markson/Svc. to Community, Flushing, N.Y., 1984, Markson Mgmt. Annual award, 1984, Community Svc. and Profl. award Success Systems, 1993. Fellow Am. Acad. Applied Spinal Biochem. Engring.; mem. APHA, AAAS, N.Y. Acad. Scis., Am. Chiropractic Assn. (coun. on sports injuries and phys. fitness, coun. on diagnostic imaging), Found. for Chiropractic Edn. and Rsch., N.Y. Chiropractic Coun. Office: Margulies Chiropractic and Sports Injury Ctr 1148 Hicksville Rd Massapequa NY 11758-1222

MARGULIES, PAUL, internist, endocrinologist; b. N.Y.C., Nov. 28, 1944; s. Ralph and Tillie (Sher) M.; m. Leslie Hoffer, June 18, 1967; children: Elizabeth, Suzanne. BS in Biochemistry, U. Chgo., 1966, MD, 1970. Diplomate Am. Bd. Internal Medicine with subspecialty in endocrinology and metabolism. Med. intern N.Y. Hosp., N.Y.C., 1970-71, resident in medicine, 1973-75; fellow in endocrinology Cornell U. Med. Coll., N.Y.C., 1975-76; physician-in-chg. endocrinology dept. North Shore Univ. Hosp., Manhasset, N.Y., 1979-85, in chg. Endocrinology Clinic, 1979—, attending physician, 1989—; clin. assoc. prof. medicine Cornell U. Med. Coll., N.Y.C., 1991—; med. dir. Nat. Adrenal Diseases Found., Great Neck, N.Y., 1985. Contbr. articles to profl. jours. Capt. U.S. Army, 1971-73. Fellow ACP, Am. Coll. Endocrinology; mem. Am. Thyroid Assn. Office: 444 Community Dr Manhasset NY 11030

MARGULIES, STANLEY IRA, radiologist; b. Balt., Jan. 6, 1935; s. Oscar and Anne (Hendin) M.; m. Karen Mintz, Feb. 13, 1962 (div. 1991); 1 child, Robin; m. Jenny Cohen Pardo, Nov. 27, 1994. AB, MA, Johns Hopkins U., 1956, MD, 1960. Diplomate Am. Bd. Nuclear Medicine, Am. Bd. Radiology. Intern gen. surgery U. Hosp. of Cleve., 1960-61, asst. resident, 1961-62; asst. resident and fellow radiology Johns Hopkins Hosp. and Univ., Balt., 1964-67, fellow in acad. radiology, 1966-67; fellow in acad. radiology Nat. Inst. of Gen. Med. Sci.-U.S. Dept. of Health, 1966-67; instr. radiology Johns Hopkins U. Sch. of Medicine, Balt., 1967-68; radiologist Johns Hopkins Hosp., Balt., 1967-72, asst. prof. radiology, 1969-70, assoc. prof. radiology, 1970-72; clin. assoc. prof. radiology U. Miami Sch. of Medicine, 1972-74; radiologist Meml. Hosp. Pembroke, Pembroke Pines, Fla., 1995—, Hollywood (Fla.) Med. Ctr., 1974—; radiologist, chief of radiology Meml. Hosp. and Meml. Healthcare System, Hollywood, 1972—; v.p. radiology InPhyNet Med. Mgmt. Inc., Ft. Lauderdale, Fla., 1995—; radiologist Meml. Hosp. West, 1992—; bd. govs. Fla. Patient's Compensation Fund., 1983—, vice chair, 1990—; mem. med. malpractice ins. adv. coun. State of Fla., 1982-83; mem. med. radiation adv. com. Dept. Health and Human Svcs., Washington, 1982-86; bd. dirs. InPhynet Med. Mgmt. Mem. DPR's Vol. Expert Witness program, 1993—; bd. dirs. Statewide Health Coun. of Fla., 1982-90, Broward Regional Health Planning Coun., Inc., Fla., 1982-93, South Fla. Blood Svc., 1982-85, Holocaust Meml. Ctr., 1982-87; exec. com., nat. com. Am. Israel Pub. Affairs com., Washington, 1981-86; dist. rep. for nat. elections, polit. edn. com. Fla. Med. Polit. Action Com., 1981-92, bd. dirs.; mem. nat. exec. com., bd. dirs. Am. Assocs. of Ben Gurion U. of Negev, Israel N.Y.C., 1979—; campaign cabinet Nat. Jewish Appeal, 1976-78; bd. dirs. Jewish Fedn. of South Broward, 1975-88, others. Fellow Am. Coll. Radiology (Fla. chpt.); mem. AMA, Radiol. Soc. of N.Am., Radil. Alumn i Assn. of Johns, Hopkins Med. and Surg. Alumni Assn., Fla. Med. Assn. Home: 920 Washington St Hollywood FL 33019-1922 Office: 3501 Johnson St Hollywood FL 33021

MARGULIS, ALEXANDER RAFAILO, physician, educator; b. Belgrade, Yugoslavia, Mar. 21, 1921; came to U.S., 1946; s. Rafailo and Olga (Weiss-Belic) M.; m. Hedvig Hricak, Feb. 26, 1983; 1 son, Peter Hricak-Margulis. Student, U. Belgrade, 1939-41, 45-46; MD, Harvard U., 1950; hon. doctorates, Aix-Marseille U. Sch. Medicine, 1980, Med. Coll. Wis., 1986, Cath. U. Louvain, 1986, Karolinska Inst., Stockholm, 1986, U. Munich, 1987, U. Toulouse, 1987, U. Montpellier, 1993. Diplomate Am. Bd. Radiology. Intern Henry Ford Hosp., Detroit, 1950-51; resident in radiology U. Mich. Hosps., 1951-53; jr. clin. instr. U. Mich., 1953-54; instr., then asst. prof. U. Minn., 1954-59; asst. prof. sch. medicine Washington U., St. Louis, 1959-60, assoc. prof. to prof., 1960-63; prof. radiology, chmn. dept. U. Calif., San Francisco, 1963-89, dir. magnetic resonance Sci. Ctr., assoc. chancellor spl. projects, 1989-93; spl. cons. to vice chancellor U. Calif.; radiologist in chief U. Calif. Hosps., 1963-89; cons. VA Hosp., Letterman Gen. Hosp., San Francisco, U.S. Naval Hosp., Oakland, Calif.; cons. in radiology Office Surgeon Gen., 1967-71. Author (with others) Roentgen Diagnosis of Abdominal Tumors in Childhood, 1957; co-editor Alimentary Tract Roentgenology; editorial bd. Calif. Medicine, 1964-74, Radiology, 1975-93; assoc. editor Investigative Radiology, 1980-89; editor Opinion in Radiiology, 1988-91. Served to capt. AUS, 1957-59. Recipient J.P. Allyn medal P. Roberts Rsch. Inst., 1989. Fellow Faculty Radiologists (hon.); sr. mem. Nat. Acad. Scis.-Inst. Medicine; mem. AMA (cons. drugs 1961—), Royal Coll. Radiologists, Roentgen Ray Soc., Assn. Univ. Radiologists (pres. 1966-67, chmn. adv. com. acad. radiology 1971), Am. Gastroenterology Assn., Soc. Chmn. Acad. Radiology Depts. (pres. 1968-69), Radiol. Soc. N.Am., San Francisco Radiol. Soc. (pres. 1973-74), Rocky Mountain Radiol. Soc. (hon.), Calif. Acad. Medicine (pres. 1978), Soc. Magnetic Resonance in Medicine (pres. 1983), Serbian Acad. Scis. (fgn.), Russian Acad. Med. Scis. (fgn.). Home: 8 Tara Hill Rd Belvedere Tiburon CA 94920-1554 Office: Univ Calif 3333 California St Ste 16 San Francisco CA 94118-1944

MARHUE, BRIAN KENNETH ANTHONY, optometric physician; b. Port-of-Spain, Trinidad, Oct. 28, 1961; s. Kenneth Augustin and Diana (Timp) M.; m. Danielle Leila Maree Webster, June 20, 1987; children: Aaron Dayne, Brittnie Tayler. BSc in Physiol. Optics, U. Ala., 1989, OD, 1991. Cert. optometric physician, Fla. Optometric dir. Eye Ctrs. Fla., Ft. Myers, 1991—; proctor Sch. Optometry U. Ala., Birmingham, 1995—, U. Montreal, 1995—. Vol. eye care mission worker Surg. Eye Expeditions, El Salvador, 1994, Students of Optometry Serving Humanity, Guatemala, 1990; estab. free clinic for indigent population Nations Assn., Ft. Myers, 1995—, dir., 1995—; soccer coach YMCA, Ft. Myers, 1995—. Fellow Am. Acad. Optometry, 1995. Mem. Am. Optometric Assn. (contact lens sect., sports vision sect.), Fla. Optometric Assn., S.W. Fla. Optometric Assn. (sec. 1995-96), Nat. Acad. Sports Vision. Home: 8220 Arborfield Ct Fort Myers FL 33912

MARIANS, KENNETH JAY, biochemist, educator; b. Bklyn., Nov. 23, 1951; s. Edward L. and Rose (Joffe) M.; m. Susan Rabbiner, June 8, 1975. BS in Chemistry, Poly. Inst. of Bklyn., 1972; PhD in Biochemistry, Cornell U., 1976. Asst. prof. Albert Einstein Coll. of Medicine, Yeshiva U., Bronx, 1978-83, assoc. prof., 1983-84; assoc. mem. Meml. Sloan-Kettering Cancer Ctr., N.Y.C., 1984-88, mem., 1988—, chmn. molecular biology dept., 1991—; cons. NIH, Bethesda, Md., 1989—. Contbr. articles to profl. jours. NIH grantee, 1978—. Office: Meml Sloan Kettering Cancer Ctr 1275 York Ave New York NY 10021-6007

MARIMÓN, SANTIAGO SUÑOL, economist; b. Barcelona, Spain, Apr. 17, 1945; s. Santiago Aguilera and Roser Figueras (Suñol) M.; m. Pilar Bastida SanJuan, July 21, 1972; children: Victor, David. MBA, Escuela Superior de Administración y Dirección de Empresas, Barcelona, Spain, 1971. Credit mgr. Bankunion, Barcelona, Spain, 1973-74; gen. mgr. Interconsultor, Barcelona, Spain, 1975-78, Hosp. Sant Pau, Barcelona, Spain, 1979-80, Hosp. and C.B., Sabadell, Spain, 1981-86; dir. Hosp. Sabadell, Spain, 1987-89; gen. mgr. Unitat de diagnòstic per la Imatge d'Alta Tecnologia, Sabadell, Spain, 1990-95; dir. info. syss. Consorci Hospitalari Catalunya, Barcelona, 1995—; cons. Catalan Hosps. Consortium, Barcelona, 1981—; v.p. Catalunya Savs. Bank, Barcelona, 1982-84, bd. dirs. Co-author: (book) Evaluación Económica de Technologías Sanitarias, 1990, Mercados y Competencia en el Sistema Sanitario, 1994; co-author: El estado del bienestar, 1995. City bd. dirs. Iniciativa per Catalunya, Barcelona, 1986-87. Mem. Catalan Health Econs. Coll. (v.p. 1993-94), Spanish Health Econs. Assn. (v.p. 1990-93), Spanish Hosp. Mgrs. Assn. Office: Consorci Hospitalari De Catalunya, Passeig de Gràcia 28 6è 1a, 08007 Barcelona Spain

MARINCHAK, ROGER ALAN, medical educator; b. Milw., Nov. 27, 1952; s. Steve M. and Jeanne (Nichols) Leabhart; m. Lyn Mary Bauman, Jan. 27, 1988; children: Jamie, Jordan. BA, Franklin & Marshall Coll., 1973; MD, Med. Coll. Pa., 1977. Diplomate Am. Bd. Internal Medicine, Am. Bd. Clin. Cardiac Electrophysiology, Am. Bd. Cardiovascular Disease. Intern Med. Coll. Pa., Phila., 1977-78, resident, chief resident, 1978-80, instr. medicine, 1983-85, asst. prof., 1985-89, clin. instr. emergency medicine, 1985-86, clin. assoc. prof. medicine, 1990—; assoc. prof. medicine Thomas Jefferson U. Coll. Medicine, Phila., 1990—; asst. sect. internal medicine St. Francis Hosp., Wilmington, Del., 1980-84, Med. Ctr. Del. (formerly Wilmington Med. Ctr., 1980-85; staff physician Southbridge Med. Adv. Coun., Inc., Wilmington, 1980-83, med., dental staff Hosp. of Med. Coll. Pa., 1985—, many others; presenter in field. Contbr. articles to profl. jours., chpts. to books. Rsch. grantee numerous orgns.; Fellow Hosp. Med. Coll. Pa., 1983-86. Fellow Am. Coll. Physicians, Am. Coll. Cardiology, Am. Coll. Chest Physicians, Am. Heart Assn. (coun. clin. cardiology); mem. Am. Coll. Clin. Pharmacology. Am. Fedn. Clin. Rsch., N.Am. Soc. Pacing and Electrophysiology, Physiological Soc. Phila.Cardiac Electrophysiology Soc., Alpha Omega Alpha. Office: Mainline Cardiology Cons The Lankeman Hosp Med Office Bldg E Ste 556 Wynnewood PA 19096

MARINER, WILLIAM MARTIN, chiropractor; b. Balt., Jan. 2, 1949; s. William Joseph and Ellen (Dexter) M. AA, Phoenix Coll., 1976; BS in Biology, L.A. Coll. of Chiropractic, 1980, D Chiropractic summa cum laude, 1980; DD (hon.), Universal Life Ch., Modesto, Calif., 1986. Health food restaurant mgr. Golden Temple of Conscious Cookery, Tempe, Ariz., 1974-75; health food store mgr. Guru's Grainery, Phoenix, 1975; physical therapist A.R.E. Clinic, Phoenix, 1975-76; research dir., founder G.R.D. Healing Arts Ctr., Phoenix, 1974-77; aminstrv. asst., acad. dean L.A. Coll. Chiropractic, Whittier, Calif., 1977-80; faculty Calif. Acupuncture Coll., L.A., 1978-80; ednl. cons. Avanti Inst., San Francisco, 1985-91; found, dir., head clinician Pacific Healing Arts Ctr., Del Mar, Calif., 1980-93, Mt. Shasta, Calif., 1993—; ednl. cons. John Panama Cons., San Francisco, 1991—. Patentee in field. Co-dir. "We Care We Share" Charitable Orgn., San Diego, 1985-86. Named Outstanding Sr., L.A. Coll. Chiropractic, 1980. Mem. San Diego Chiropractic Soc., Calif. Chiropractic Assn., Am. Chiropractic Assn., Internat. Coll. Applied Kinesiology, Holistic Dental Assn., Brit. Homopathic Assn., Rotary. Office: Pacific Healing Arts Ctr PO Box 192 Mount Shasta CA 96067-0192

MARINO, CAROL ESTHER MASON, family practice physician; b. Cin., Sept. 29, 1961; d. Harvey Waldo and Felicia Josephine (Catino) Mason; m. Vincent J. Marino, June, 3, 1994. BFA, Ohio U., 1984, MS, 1986, DO, 1992. Diplomate Am. Bd. Osteo. Medicine. Intern Grandview Hosp., Dayton, Ohio, 1993-94, resident in family practice, 1994-96; resident in pathology Kettering (Ohio) Med. Ctr., 1993-94; chief resident family practice Grandview Hosp., Dayton, Ohio, 1995; pvt. practice Dayton, 1996—; sports medicine physician Womens Volleyball, Cin., 1996; physician cons. Peach Orchard, Dayton, 1996; resident instr. Grandview Hosp., Dayton, 1996. Mem. Am. Bd. Osteo. Family Practice (bd. cert.), Am. Osteo. Assn., Ohio Osteo. Assn., Dayton Dist. Acad. Osteo. Medicine. Roman Catholic. Home: 114 E Peach Orchard Ave Dayton OH 45419 Office: Bd Cert Family Practice 3012 Sudbury Ln Kettering OH 45420

MARINO, IGNAZIO ROBERTO, transplant surgeon, researcher; b. Genova, Italy, Mar. 10, 1955; s. Pietro Rosario and Valeria (Mazzanti) M.; m. Rossana Parisen-Toldin, Sept. 15, 1990; 1 child, Stefania Valeria. Maturità-Classica, Coll. of Merode, Rome, 1973; MD, Cath. U., Rome, 1979. Diplomate Nat. Bd. Gen. Surgery, Nat. Bd. Vascular Surgery. Intern, then resident Gemelli U. Hosp., Rome, 1979-84; temp. asst. dept. surgery Cath. U., Rome, 1981, asst. prof. surgery, 1983-92; asst. prof. surgery Transplantation Inst., U. Pitts., 1991-95; assoc. prof. surgery Transplantation Inst./U. Pitts., 1995—; prof. surgery postgrad. Sch. Microsurgery, Exptl. Surgery U. Milan, 1994—; prof.surgery Sch. Medicine U. Perugia, 1994—; attending surgeon U. Pitts. Med. Ctr., Pitts., 1991—; assoc. dir. transplant divsn. VA Med. Ctr., Pitts., 1992—; attending surgeon Children's Hosp. Pitts., 1993—; mem. surg. team 1st and 2d baboon to human liver transplants U. Pitts. Med. Ctr., 1992, 93, dir. European med. divsn., 1995—; sci. journalist Agenzia Nazionale Stampa Associata, 1992—; mem. nat. ad hoc donations com. United Network for Organ Sharing, 1995—. Author: New Technique in Extracorporeal Circulation, 1985 (Ann. prize Italian Soc. Surgery 1986), New Technique in Liver Transplantation, 1986 (De Angelis award 1986); contbr. more than 300 articles to profl. jours. Mem. Italian Ordine Giornalisti, 1994—. Grantee Italian Nat. Coun. Rsch., 1979, 86, 87, 88, 89-93, Gastroenterology Soc., 1988; recipient award Instituto Nazionale Previdenze Dirigenti Aziende Industriali, 1982. Mem. ACS, Am. Soc. Transplantation Surgeons, Am. Soc. Transplant Physicians, Italian Soc. Surgery, Transplantation Soc. (grant 1988), European Soc. for Organ Transplantation, Soc. Surgeons Under 40 (Ann. prize 1986), Cell Transplant Soc. (founding mem.), Acad. Surg. Rsch., Soc. Critical Care Medicine, Internat. Liver Transplantation Soc., Assn. Italian Correspondents in N.Am. (assoc.), Xenotransplantation Club (founding mem.). Home: Corso Italia 29, Rome 00198, Italy Office: Univ Pitts Transplant Inst 4 Falk Clinic 3601 5th Ave Pittsburgh PA 15213-3403

MARINO, JOSEPH ANTHONY, oral and maxillofacial surgeon, consultant; b. Scranton, Pa., Mar. 26, 1962; s. Paul Anthony and Dolores Ann (Andriole) M.; m. Amy Elizabeth Schlier, May 20, 1989; children: Jason Anthony and Justin Anthony (twins). BA in Natural Scis., Johns Hopkins U., 1984; DMD, Tufts U., 1988, oral and maxillofacial surg. cert., 1992. Diplomate Am. Bd. Oral and Maxillofacial Surgery. Pvt. practice, Brockton, Mass., 1992—; oral surgery cons. Pilgrim Health Care, Quincy, Mass., 1994—. Patentee for articulator mount. Mem. ADA, Am. Assn. Oral and Maxillofacial Surgery (diplomate), Mass. Soc. Oral and Maxillofacial Surgery, Mass. Dental Soc. (peer rev. com. 1994—), Omicron Kappa Upsilon. Republican. Roman Catholic. Office: 1351 Main St Brockton MA 02401

MARINO, ROBERT PETER, physician; b. Providence, R.I., Jan. 17, 1967; s. Peter Joseph and Lillian Judith (Zinno) M.; m. Maribeth Jennifer Porreca, May 17, 1992; 1 child, Michaela Krystal. BS, Providence Coll., 1989; DO, Chgo. Coll. Osteopathic Med, 1993. Diplomate Am. Bd. Osteopathy. ALS instr. Cranston (R.I.) YMCA, 1985-89; aquatic coord. Chgo. Coll. Medicine, Downers Grove, Ill., 1990-91, Downers Grove YMCA, Downers Grove, Ill., 1990-91; intern Chgo. Coll. Medicine, Chgo., 1993-94, family practice physician, 1994—, urgent care physician, 1996—; asst. prof. osteopathic medicine Midwestern Univ., Downers Grove, 1990—. Mem. AMA, Am. Osteo. Assn., Am. Coll. Asteo. Family Physicians, Am. Coll. Osteo. Physicians/Surgeons, Am. Coll. Emergency Physicians, Am. Coll. Osteo. Emergency Physicians. Roman Catholic.

MARIO, ERNEST, pharmaceutical company executive; b. Clifton, N.J., June 12, 1938; s. Jerry and Edith (Meijer) M.; m. Mildred Martha Daume, Dec. 10, 1961; children: Christopher Bradley, Gregory Gerald, Jeremy Konrad. B.S. in Pharmacy, Rutgers U., 1961; M.S. in Phys. Scis., U. R.I., 1963, Ph.D. in Phys. Scis., 1965. Registered pharmacist, R.I., N.Y. Vice pres. mfg. Smith Kline Corp., Phila., 1975-77; v.p. mfg. ops. U.S. Pharm. Co. (divsn. E. R. Squibb), New Brunswick, N.J., 1977-79; v.p., gen. mgr. chem. div. E. R. Squibb, Princeton, N.J., 1979-81; pres. chem. and engring. div., sr. v.p. Squibb Corp., Princeton, 1981-84; v.p. Squibb Corp., 1984-86; pres., COO Glaxo Inc., 1986-88, chmn., CEO, 1988, chmn., 1989-91; CEO Glaxo Holdings plc, 1989-93, dep. chmn., 1991-93; co-chmn., CEO, Alza Corp., Palo Alto, Calif., 1993—; grad. asst., instr. U. R.I., Kingston, 1961-66; research fellow Inst. Neurol. Diseases, Bethesda, Md., 1963-65. Contbr. articles to profl. jours. Trustee Duke U., Rockefeller U., U. R.I. Found.; mem. pres.'s coun. U. R.I.; chmn. Am. Found. for Pharm. Edn.; bd. dirs. Nat. Found. Infectious Diseases, Antigenics, Pharm. Product Devel., Stanford Health Svcs., Tech. Mus. Innovation; mem. Calif. gov.'s coun. on biotech. Office: Alza Corp 950 Page Mill Rd Palo Alto CA 94304-1012

MARIS, CHARLES ROBERT, surgeon, otolaryngologist; b. Champaign, Ill., Nov. 24, 1948; s. Harold Franklin and Marjorie Ellen (Beermann) M.; m. Karen Lynne Richardson, Dec. 27, 1970; children: Katherine, Emily, Charles Jr. BS, Eastern Ill. U., 1971; MD, U. Ill., 1975. Diplomate Am. Bd. Surgery, Am. Bd. Otolaryngology. Resident in otolaryngology U. Nebr. Med. Ctr., Omaha, 1982; chief of surgery Sarah Bush Lincoln Health Ctr., Mattoon, Ill., 1984-85, chmn. exec. com., 1985, 89, 94, chief of staff, 1986, 90, 95; bd. dirs. 1st Mid-Ill. Bank & Trust. Mem. Charleston Community Unit Dist. #1 Sch. Bd., 1984-88. Lt. Col. U.S. Army Reserve, 159th Mash (Operation Desert Storm) 1990-91. Named one of Outstanding Young Men in Am., 1985. Fellow Am. Coll. Surgeons, Am. Acad. Otolaryngology-Head and Neck Surgery, Am. Acad. Facial Plastic and Reconstructive Surgery. Republican. Methodist. Office: 200 Lerna Rd South Mattoon IL 61938-9252

MARK, HARRY HORST, ophthalmologist, researcher; b. Breslau, Germany, Jan. 21, 1931; came to U.S., 1957; s. Lothar and Ruth Mark. MD, U. Vienna, Austria, 1957. Diplomate Am. Bd. Ophthalmology. Intern George Washington U., Washington, 1957; resident Boston U., 1958-60, SUNY, Bklyn., 1960-62; pvt. practice New Haven, 1963—; attending ophthalmologist Yale-New Haven Hosp., 1963—, St. Raphael Hosp., New Haven, 1963—. Author: Optokinetics, 1982; contbr. articles to profl. jours. Home: 16 Broadway North Haven CT 06473 Office: 2 Church St S New Haven CT 06519

MARK, HOWARD IRWIN, oral and maxillofacial surgeon; b. Derby, Conn., Mar. 30, 1929; s. Harry and Jean Ethel (Akabas) M.; m. Sheila Berger, June 24, 1951; children—Robin Ann, Brian David, Steven Robert, Elliot Jay. Student Georgetown U., 1946-48; D.M.D., Tufts U., 1952. Diplomate Am. Bd. Oral and Maxillofacial Surgery. Resident in oral and maxillofacial surgery N.Y. Hosp., N.Y.C., 1952-54; fellow in oral surgery U.

Ala. Med. Ctr., Birmingham, 1954-55; dir. div. dentistry Mt. Sinai Hosp., Hartford, Conn., 1970-94 ; pres. med. staff, 1984-86, corporator, 1985—; assoc. prof. oral maxillofacial surgery U. Conn. Sch. Dental Medicine, Farmington, 1972—; pvt. practice oral and maxillofacial surgery, Hartford and Middletown, Conn., 1957-96; attending in oral surgery Hartford Hosp., 1965—, Middlesex Meml. Hosp., 1972—; cons. in oral surgery VA Home and Hosp., Rocky Hill, Conn., 1975—. Contbr. articles to profl. jours. Chmn. troop com. troop 164, Boy Scouts Am., West Hartford, Conn., 1980-94; corporator Middlesex Meml. Hosp., 1977—; mem. dental gifts bd. Hartford Jewish Fedn., 1972—. Served to capt. U.S. Army, 1955-57. Fellow Am. Assn. Oral and Maxillofacial Surgeons (trustee 1973-77, Committeeman of yr. award 1973), Am. Dental Soc. Anesthesiology, Am. Coll. Dentists, Internat. Coll. Dentists, Internat. Assn. Oral Surgeons; mem. Hartford Dental Soc. (pres. 1972-73), Conn. Dental Assn. (editor. Jour. 1985—), Omicron Kappa Upsilon. Democrat. Jewish. Club: Probus of Greater Hartford (pres. 1965-66). Lodge: Odd Fellows. Avocations: photography; gardening; hiking; camping; tennis. Home: 101 W Ridge Dr West Hartford CT 06117-2039 Office: 100 Constitution Plaza Hartford CT 06103

MARK, JAMES B. D., surgeon; b. Nashville, June 26, 1929; s. Julius and Margaret (Baer) M.; m. Jean Rambar, Feb. 5, 1957; children: Jonathan, Michael, Margaret, Elizabeth, Katherine. B.A., Vanderbilt U., 1950, M.D., 1953. Intern, resident in gen. and thoracic surgery Yale-New Haven Hosp., 1953-60; instr. to asst. prof. surgery Yale U., 1960-65; asso. prof. surgery Stanford U., 1965-69, prof., 1969—, Johnson and Johnson prof. surgery, 1978—, head div. thoracic surgery, 1972—, assoc. dean clin. affairs, 1988-92; chief staff Stanford U. Hosp., 1988-92; governing bd. Health Systems Agy., Santa Clara County, 1978-80; sr. Fulbright-Hays fellow, vis. prof. surgery U. Dar es Salaam, Tanzania, 1972-73. Mem. editl. bd.: Jour. Thoracic and Cardiovasc. Surgery, 1986-94, World Jour. Surgery, 1995—; contbr. numerous articles to sci. jours. Bd. dirs. Stanford U. Hosp., 1992-94. With USPHS, 1955-57. Fellow ACS (pres. No. Calif. chpt. 1980-81), Am. Coll. Chest Physicians (pres. 1994-95); mem. Am. Assn. Thoracic Surgery, Am. Surg. Assn., Western Surg. Assn., Pacific Coast Surg. Assn., Halsted Soc. (pres. 1984), Western Thoracic Surg. Assn. (pres. 1992-93), Calif. Acad. Medicine (pres. 1978), Santa Clara County Med. Soc. (pres. 1976-77). Home: 921 Casanueva Pl Stanford CA 94305-1001 Office: Stanford U CVRB Surgery Med Ctr Stanford CA 94305

MARK, JONATHAN B., physician, educator; b. Schenectady, N.Y., Oct. 17, 1952; s. Irving and Adele (Gold) M.; m. Christine Ball, June 24, 1978; children: Benjamin Adam, Zachary Eric. AB, Harvard Coll., 1974; MD, Stanford U., 1978. Diplomate Nat. Bd. Med. Examiners, Am. Bd. Anesthesiology. Instr. anesthesia Brigham and Women's Hosp., Boston, 1982-88, asst. prof. anesthesiology, 1988-92; assoc. prof. anesthesiology Duke U. Med. Ctr., Durham, N.C., 1992—. Office: VA Med Ctr 508 Fulton St 112C Durham NC 27705

MARK, LAURENCE PETER, anesthesiology educator; b. N.Y.C., Jan. 30, 1953; s. Lester Charles and Muriel Harriet (Widman) M.; m. Elizabeth Sue Collier, Aug. 29, 1982; children: Torin and Ryan (twins). BS in Physics, Harvey Mudd Coll., 1975; MD, Columbia U., 1979. Diplomate Am. Bd. Anesthesiology, Nat. Bd. Med. Examiners. Intern surgery St. Vincent's Hosp., N.Y.C., 1979-80; resident anesthesia Mass. Gen. Hosp., Boston, 1980-82; anesthesia fellow Mass. Gen. Hosp., 1982-83; asst. prof. anesthesiology Presbyn. Hosp., Columbia U., N.Y.C., 1983—; med. dir. pre-admission unit, coord. cost-consignment anesthesiology dept. Columbia-Presbyn. Med. Ctr., N.Y.C., 1991—; expert witness Kopff, Nardelli & Dopf, N.Y.C., 1988—; article reviewer Anesthesia and Analgesia; bd. dirs. Columbia-Presbyn. Phsycians Network. Mem. Am. Soc. Anesthesiologists, N.Y. State Soc. Anesthesiologists (speaker closed cir. anesthesiology postgrad. assembly 1988). Democrat. Jewish. Home: 210 W 90th St Apt 9B New York NY 10024-1243 Office: Columbia U 622 W 168th St New York NY 10032-3702

MARK, RICHARD KUSHAKOW, internist; b. N.Y.C., Feb. 11, 1951; s. Eugene and Gertrude (Kushakow) M.; m. Harriet Bass, Sept. 17, 1989; children: Sabrina, Ari Etan. BS, Hofstra U., 1972; MD, U. Autonomous Guadalajara, 1976, SUNY, Bklyn., 1977. Diplomate Am. Bd. Internal Medicine. Resident in medicine Maimonides Med. Ctr., Bklyn., 1977-82; clin. instr. medicine Downstate Med. Ctr., Bklyn., 1982-90, asst. prof. medicine, 1990-93; prof. clin. medicine CUNY, 1993—; pvt. practice internal medicine Bklyn., 1982—; dept. attending emergency Cabrini Med. Ctr., N.Y.C., 1982-84. Author: Consumer's Guide to Preventive Medicine, 1996. Mem. N.Y.C. Coalition for the Homeless, 1986—, The Children's Fund., N.Y.C., 1990—. Recipient community svc. award Borough of Bklyn., 1986. Mem. AMA (physician's recognition award 1984-93), Acad. Medicine, Inter-Am. Coll. Medicine, King's County Med. Soc. Democrat. Jewish. Office: 8200 21st Ave Brooklyn NY 11214-2506

MARK, STEPHEN LEONARD, forensic psychiatrist; b. Williamsport, Pa., Oct. 2, 1947; m. Jean Lois Dickson Mark; children: Daniel, Elizabeth, Alexander. BA, Temple U., 1969; MD, U. Tex., Galveston, 1974. Cert. Am. Bd. Psychiatry and Neurology. Resident U. Tex. Med. Br., 1974-77; pvt. practice psychiatry Waco, Tex., 1977—. Pres. Cen. Tex. Zoo Soc., Waco, 1988-89; mem. chancellor's coun. U. Tex., Austin, 1980—. Recipient Physicians Recognition award AMA. Mem. Titus Harris Psychiat. Soc. (counselor 1984-86), Tex. Med. Assn., Am. Acad. Psychiatry and the Law, McLennan County Med. Soc., U. Tex. Med. Br. Alumni Assn. (pres. 1989-90). Office: 405 Londonderry Dr Ste 202 Waco TX 76712

MARKER, CAROLYN G. SMITH, nursing consultant; b. Wichita, July 6, 1945; d. Jack M. and Nadine R. (Hayes) Smith; m. Charles E. Marker III, Feb. 5, 1978. BSN, Tex. Women's U., 1967; MS in Nursing, Cath. U. Am., 1971. RN. Staff nurse St. Joseph's Hosp., Houston, 1967-69, Providence Hosp., Washington, 1969-71; clin. specialist Sibley Meml. Hosp., Washington, 1971-76; dir. nursing Anne Arundel Gen. Hosp., Annapolis, Md., 1976-81; educator Resource Application, Inc., Balt., 1981-88; cons. Marker System, Inc., Severna Park, Md., 1988—; adj. faculty Anne Arundel C.C., Annapolis, 1978-79; speaker and presenter in field. Author: Setting Standards for Professional Nursing, 1988; contbr. articles to profl. jours. Mem. ANA, Am. Hosp. Assn., Nursing Mgmt. Congress Am. (presenter), Orgn. Nurse Execs., Sigma Theta Tau. Republican. Home: 262 Whistling Pine Rd Severwa Park MD 21146 Office: Marker Systems Inc PO Box 309 Severna Park MD 21146

MARKEWICH, MAURICE ELISH (REESE MARKEWICH), psychiatrist, musician; b. Bklyn., Aug. 6, 1936; s. Arthur and May (Elish) M.; A.B., Cornell U., 1958; M.S. in Social Work, Columbia U., 1960; M.D., N.Y. Med. Coll., 1970; certificate Center for Modern Psychoanalytic Studies, 1976; m. Linda Lawner, June 19, 1960; children—Jennifer Beth, Melissa Ann. Social worker Jewish Family Service, N.Y.C., 1961-64; resident Beth Israel Med. Center, N.Y.C., 1970-73; practice medicine specializing in psychiatry, N.Y.C., 1973—; mem. staff Beth Israel Med. Center; jazz musician, 1954—; pianist, flutist Reese Markewich Quintet, 1955-60; various appearances N.Y. State. Served with U.S. Army, 1960-61. Cert. social worker, N.Y.; lic. physician, N.Y. Mem. Am. Psychiat. Assn., Med. Soc. County N.Y., Club: Masons. Author music books: Inside Outside, 1967; The Definitive Bibliography of Harmonically Sophisticated Tonal Music, 1970; The New Expanded Bibliography of Jazz Compositions Based on the Chord Progressions of Standard Tunes, 1974; Jazz Publicity II, 1974. Home: Bacon Hill Town of Mount Pleasant Pleasantville NY 10570 Office: 207 E 16th St New York NY 10003

MARKHAM, JEROME DAVID, internist, educator, consultant; b. Rockville Centre, N.Y., Jan. 27, 1917; s. Benjamin and Sophia (Newmark) Markowitz; m. Sara Elizabeth Farber, 1941; children: Shelley, Richard Bryan, Barbara Frances. BA, Columbia Coll., 1937; MD, Med. Coll. Va., 1941. Diplomate Am. Bd. Internal Medicine. Intern Queens Gen. Hosp., Jamaica, N.Y., 1941-42; asst. resident in medicine Mt. Sinai Hosp., N.Y.C., 1946-47; sr. resident VA Hosp., Richmond, Va., 1947-48; pvt. practice Richmond, 1948-68; assoc. in physiology Med. Coll. of Va., Richmond, 1950-53, asst. prof. of applied physiology, 1953-57, clin. assoc. in medicine, 1955-84, clin. assoc. prof., 1984-88, clin. assoc. prof. emeritus, 1988—; ptnr. Group Associated Internists, Inc., Richmond, 1968-84; cons. Va. State Bd. Medicine, 1988; peer rev. cons. for Medicare/Champus Office of the Med. Dir., Med. Soc. of Va. Rev. Orgn., 1989-94; malpractice rev. panelist Supreme Ct. Va. Contbr. articles to profl. jours. Ofcl. rep. Columbia U.; mem. med. com. Beth Sholom Home for Aged, 1964-66, bd. dirs., 1964-67; co-chmn. adult edn. com. Temple Beth Ahabah, 1951-54. Capt. M.C., U.S. Army, 1942-46, ETO, NATOUSA. Decorated Bronze Star; The J. David Markham Annual Lectureship established by Div. Gen. Internal Medicine and Primary Care Med. Coll. Va., 1988—. Fellow ACP; mem. Am. Heart Assn. (mem. coun. clin. cardiology), Am. Soc. Internal Medicine, Va. Soc. Internal Medicine, Med. Soc. Va., Richmond Acad. Medicine, Columbia U. Alumni Club (past pres.). Home: 7101 Glen Pky Richmond VA 23229-7506

MARKHAM, RAYMOND E., JR., physician; b. Roanoke, Va., Oct. 25, 1951; m. Virginia Mary Markham, June 19, 1976; 3 children. BS in Chemistry, Roanoke Coll., 1974; MD, U. Va., 1977. Diplomate in internal medicine and hematology Am. Bd. Internal Medicine; lic. physician, N.Y., Ind. Intern, resident in internal medicine Strong Meml. Hosp./U. Rochester, N.Y., 1977-80, instr., fellow in medicine, hematology unit, 1980-82; attending physician Monroe Cmty. Hosp., Rochester, 1980-81; assoc. physician divsn. hematology/oncology Meth. Hosp. and Winona Meml. Hosp., Indpls., 1982—; cons. in hematology/oncology Hendricks Cmty. Hosp., Danville, Ind., 1983—; clin. asst. prof. medicine Ind. U. Sch. Medicine, Indpls., 1984—; chief oper. officer, chmn. physicians exec. com. Meml. Clinic, Indpls., 1990—; interim med. dir. cancer ctr. Meth. Hosp. of Ind., Indpls., 1994—. Contbr. articles to profl. jours. Mem. ACP, Am. Soc. Clin. Oncologists, Am. Soc. Hematologists, Ind. State Med. Soc., Marion County Med. Soc., Am. Cancer Soc. (chmn. colorectal cancer task com. 1984-85), Leukemia Soc. Am. (profl. edn. com. 1984-88). Home: 3399 Eden Hollow Pl Carmel IN 46033 Office: Meml Clinic of Indpls 3266 N Meridian St Indianapolis IN 46208

MARKLEY, KENNETH ALAN, psychologist; b. Harrisburg, Pa., Sept. 30, 1933; s. Charles Donald and Gladys Elizabeth (Wallis) M.; m. Susan Watson, Sept. 14, 1957; children: Jennifer Elaine, Christopher David. BA, Dickinson Coll., 1955; postgrad. Syracuse U., 1955-57; MA, NYU, 1959; postgrad. Ref. Episcopal Sem., 1966-68; HHD, Clarkesville Sch. Theology, 1976 Sch. psychologist Central Dauphin Schs., Harrisburg, 1959; exec. dir. United Cerebral Palsy Treatment Center, Camp Hill, Pa., 1960-64; eastern dir. Narramore Christian Found. and Rosemead (Calif.) Grad. Sch. Psychology, 1964—; mem. faculty Dickinson Coll., Carlisle, Pa., 1963-64; propr. Oldtimers Antique Clocks; ordained to gospel ministry Evangelical Ch. Alliance, 1978. Bd. dirs. many community, civic, religious orgns. Served to 1st lt. Adj. Gens. Corps, AUS, 1955-57. Certified psychologist, Pa.; diplomate Am. Psychotherapy Assn. Mem. Am. Acad. Human Services, Am. Psychol. Assn., Pa. Psychol. Assn., Am. Assn. for Counseling and Dvel., Pa. Counseling Assn., Christian Assn. Psychol. Studies, Phi Kappa Psi. Mem. Brethren in Christ. Author: Our Speaker This Evening, 1974; contbr. to Psychology for Living mag. Address: Narramore Christian Found 104 N 26th St Camp Hill PA 17011-3616

MARKMAN, HOWARD J., psychology educator; b. Oct. 27, 1950; s. Arnold J. and Claire (Fox) M.; m. Fran Dickson, June 29, 1980; children: Mathew Lee, Leah Deborah. BA, Rutgers U., 1972; MA in Clin. Psychology, Ind. U., 1976, PhD in Clin. Psychology, 1977. Lic. clin. psychologist, Colo. Assoc. instr. psychology Ind. U., 1973-75; psychology trainee, consultation team Monroe County Community Mental Health Ctr., Bloomington, Ind., 1975-76; clin./community psychology intern U. Colo. Sch. Medicine, Denver, 1976-77; asst. prof. psychology Bowling Green (Ohio) U., 1977-80, U. Denver, 1980-83; dir. Denver Ctr. for Marital and Family Studies, U. Denver, 1980—; dir. clin. tng. U. Denver, 1983-86, assoc. prof. psychology, 1983-89, prof. psychology, 1989—; presenter in field. Author: Couples' Guide to Communication, 1976, Prevention and Relationship Enhancement Program, 1980, We Can Work it Out, Fighting for your Marriage; mem. editorial bd. Jour. Consulting and Clin. Psychology, 1988-90, Behavioral Assessment, Jour. Family Psychology, Contemporary Psychology, Am. Assn. for Marriage and Family Therapy, Am. Jour. Family Therapy; guest assoc. editor Behavioral Assessment, 1989, Human Communication Rsch.; contbr. articles and reviews to profl. jours. Bd. dirs. Assn. Children and Youth, Boulder, Colo., 1985-86. NIMH grantee, 1980-82. Fellow APA; mem. NIMH (adhoc reviewer 1980—), NSF (adhoc reviewer 1980—), APA, Internat. Soc. Social and Personal Relationships (world conf. planning com. 1990—), Colo. Psychol. Assn. (co-chmn. 1990—), Nat. Coun. on Family Rels., Am. Assn. Marriage and Family Therapy (clin. mem.), Rocky Mountain Conf. Family Rels. (bd. dirs.). Democrat. Jewish. Office: Univ of Denver Ctr Marital & Family Studies Dept of Psychology Denver CO 80208

MARKOE, ARNOLD MICHAEL, radiation oncologist; b. N.Y.C., Apr. 15, 1942; s. Joseph Markoe and Claire (Hershkowitz) Markoe Berger; m. Tana Kates, Sept. 3, 1967; 1 child, Zaharah. BA, Adelphi U., 1963; MS, U. Rochester, 1966; ScD, U. Pitts., 1972; MD, Hahnemann U., 1977. Diplomate, Am. Bd. Radiology (Therapeutic Radiology). Rsch. assoc. Albert Einstein Coll. Medicine, Bronx, N.Y., 1966-69; USPHS postdoctoral fellow Allegheny Gen. Hosp., Pitts., 1972-73; Am. Cancer Soc. spl. postdoctoral fellow Hahnemann Med. Coll., Phila., 1975-77; from sr. instr. to assoc. prof. radiation oncology Hahnemann U., Phila., 1977-89; staff physician Jackson Meml. Hosp., Miami, Fla., 1990—; mem Sylvester Comprehensive Cancer Ctr., Miami, 1990—; assoc. prof. radiation oncology U. Miami, 1989-92, prof., 1992—, interim chmn. radiation oncology Sch. Medicine, 1994-96; chmn., 1996—; staff physician U. Miami Hosp. & Clinics, 1990—, VA Hosp., Miami, 1996—; cons. Anna Bates Leach Hosp. of Bascom-Palmer Eye Inst., 1990—, Cancergrams Info. Ventures, Inc., Phila., 1989-92; spl. site vis. radiation oncology Accreditation Coun. for Grad. Med. Edn., 1986—; adv. bd. radiation therapy tech. tng. program Gwynedd-Mercy Coll., Gwynedd Valley, Pa., 1988-89, Miami Dade C.C./Jackson Meml. Hosp. Consortium, 1989—, med. advisor, 1995—; adv. panel Radiation Oncology Self-Assessment Program, 1992—. Mem. editl. bd. Am. Jour. Clin. Oncology, 1991—, Radiation Oncology Investigations, 1992—; rev. Cancer, 1994—, Jour. Neuro-Oncology, 1994—; contbr. articles to profl. jours., chpts. to med. textbooks. Grantee, Soc. Nuclear Medicine, 1976; named One of Best Drs. in Am., 1996. Mem., Am. Radium Soc., Am. Soc. Clin. Oncology, Am. Coll. Radiology, Am. Coll. Radiation Oncology. Am. Soc. Therapeutic Radiation Oncology, So. Med. Soc., Fla. Med. Soc., Dade County Med. Soc., Fla. Soc. Clin. Oncology, Alpha Omega Alpha, Beta Beta Beta.

MARKOV, MARKO SPIRIDONOV, biophysicist; b. Tcherven Brjag, Bulgaria, Dec. 5, 1941; came to the U.S., 1990; s. Spiridon M. and Radka K. (Kostova) M.; m. Mariana Dimitrova, Aug. 29, 1946; 1 child, Julia. BS, Sofia U., 1963, MS, 1967, PhD, 1980. Asst. prof. Sofia (Bulgaria) U., 1969-85, prof. biophysics, 1985-92; v.p. rsch. Electropharmacology Inc., Pompano Beach, Fla., 1995—; rsch. prof. Mt. Sinai Med. Ctr., N.Y.C., 1991—; vis. rsch. prof. Oakland U., Rochester, Mich., 1990. Mem. editl. bd. Electro and Magnetbiology, 1986—; author: Electromagnetic Field and Biomembranes, 1988. Home: 22198 Appleton Dr Boca Raton FL 33428 Office: Electropharmacology Inc 2301 NW 33 Ct Ste 102 Pompano Beach FL 33069

MARKOVCHICK, VINCENT J., surgeon; b. Hazleton, Pa., 1944. MD, Temple U., 1970. Intern Presbyn. Med. Ctr., Denver, 1970-71; resident emergency medicine U. Chgo. Hosps.-Clinics, 1974-76; mem. staff Denver Gen. Hosp.; assoc. prof. U.Colo. Health Sci. Ctr. Mem. Am. Coll. Emergency Physicians, Colo. Med. Soc., STEM. Office: Denver Gen Hosp Emergency Medicine Dept 777 Bannock St Denver CO 80204-4507*

MARKOVITZ, LAWRENCE JAY, cardiothoracic surgeon; b. N.Y.C., Feb. 5, 1955; s. Jacob and Nellie (Salomon) M.; m. Andrea Linda D'Auria, Nov. 7, 1993. BA, Columbia U., N.Y.C., 1976; MD, Mt. Sinai Med. Sch., 1980. Diplomate Am. Bd. Surgery, Am. Bd. Thoracic Surgery. Resident Mt. Sinai Hosp., N.Y.C., 1980-86, fellow, 1989-90; resident U. Pa., Phila., 1986-89; attending surgeon St. Francis Hosp., Roslyn, N.Y., 1990-91, The Valley Hosp., Ridgewood, N.J., 1991-95, Luther-Midelfort-Mayo, Eau Claire, Wis., 1995—. Contbr. articles to profl. jours. Fellow ACS, Am. Coll. Cardiology, Am. Coll. Chest Physicians; mem. AMA, Am. Soc. Thoracic Surgeons. Home: 138 Emerson Ct Mahwah NJ 07430-3173*

MARKOWITZ, ALAN HARVEY, cardiothoracic surgeon; b. Ft. Riley, Kans., Mar. 25, 1944; s. Benjamin Frank and Miriam Edith (Sirota) M.; m. Cathy Ann Pollard, Oct. 27, 1990; children: Jonathan, Jenifer. AB, U. Rochester, 1965; MD, Albany Med. Coll., 1970. Diplomate Am. Bd. Surgery, Am. Bd. Thoracic Surgery. Gen. surg. resident Case Western Res. U., Cleve., 1970-72; thoracic surgery resident U. Hosp. Cleve., 1974-78; asst. prof. surgery Upstate Med. Sch.-SUNY, Syracuse, 1978-81; clin. asst. prof. surgery Case Western Res. U., Sch. Medicine, Cleve., 1981—; profl. fellow Weatherhead Sch. of Mgmt., Case Western Res. U., Cleve., 1993-94. Contbr. articles to profl. jours. Lt. comdr. USN, 1972-74. Fellow ACS; mem. Soc. Thoracic Surgeons, Am. Assn. Acad. Surgery, Am. Coll. Chest Physicians, Alpha Omega Alpha. Office: Mt Sinai Cardiothoracic Assn Inc-Mt Sinai Med Ctr 1 Mt Sinai Drive Cleveland OH 44106

MARKOWITZ, JOEL, psychiatrist; b. N.Y.C., Mar. 23, 1927; s. Idel and Mina (Fleischer) M.; m. Elizabeth Jane Rich, June 30, 1952; children: John, Adam, Anne. BA, Cornell U., 1949; MD, Columbia U., 1953. Attending assoc. clin. instr. Mount Sinai Hosp., N.Y.C., 1970—; pvt. practice adult and adolescent psychiatry, 1957—; cons. Jewish Child Care Assn., N.Y.C., 1957-59. Contbr. articles to profl. jours. With USN, 1945. Home: 285 Central Park W New York NY 10024-3006

MARKOWITZ, JOHN C., psychiatrist; b. N.Y.C., Oct. 11, 1954; s. Joel and Elizabeth Jane (Rich) M.; m. Kathleen F. Clougherty, Mar. 28, 1980; 1 child, Caitlin Clougherty Markowitz. BA, Columbia Coll., N.Y.C., 1976; MA, Columbia U. GSAS, N.Y.C., 1978; MD, Columbia Coll. of Physicians and Surgeons, N.Y.C., 1982. Intern. Payne Whitney Clin., N.Y. Hosp., N.Y.C., 1982-83, Psychiatric res., 1983-86, chief res., 1986-87; instr. in psychiatry Cornell U. Med. Coll., N.Y.C., 1986-89, asst. prof. of psychiatry, 1989-94, assoc. prof. clin. psychiatry, 1994—; lectr. psychiatry Columbia U. Coll. Physicians and Surgeons, N.Y.C., 1993—; edit. cons. Psychiat. Svcs., Jour. of Psychotherapy Practice and Rsch., Washington. Author of numerous psychiatric chpts. and articles, 1984—. Recipient Individual Faculty Scholar Award, Nat. Inst. of Men. Health, Rockville, Md., 1988-91, APA/Burroughs Wellcome Fellowship, Washington, 1984-86. Mem. Am. Psychiat. Assn. (sci. program com. 1984-95, legis. rep. N.Y. County Dist. br. 1987-93, memm. com. on AIDS 1986—). Office: Payne Whitney Clinic NY Hosp 445 E 68th St New York NY 10021-4873

MARKOWITZ, PHYLLIS FRANCES, mental health services administrator, psychologist; b. Malden, Mass., Sept. 2, 1931; d. Abraham and Rose (Kaplan) Kalishman: children: Gary Keith, Carol Diane Donnelly. AB, Harvard U., 1972, EdM, 1974; EdD, Boston U., 1987. Lic. psychologist; lic., cert. social worker, Mass.; cert sch. psychologist, secondary English and social studies tchr., Mass. Rsch. asst. Boston Coll., Newton, Mass., 1971-73; social worker Combined Jewish Philanthropies, Boston, 1973-74; instr. Harvard U., Cambridge, Mass., 1974-75, counselor, 1974-79; supr. Dept. Social Svcs., Newton and Marlborough, Mass., 1979-88; area dir. case mgmt. and tng., 1988-94, area coord. medically-mentally ill, 1988—, chair consumer/family empowerment project, 1992—; area dir. Svcs. Integration, 1994-95; project dir. Sup. Employment Svcs., 1994-95; area dir. Clin. Svcs., 1995—; area Ams. with Disabilities coord. Dept. Mental Health, Boston, 1995—; instr. human devel. U. Mass., Boston, 1990—. Grantee Radcliffe Inst., 1972; recipient Rsch. scholar award Boston U., 1981-82. Mem. APA, Mass. Psychol. Assn. Office: Dept Mental Health 20 Vining St Boston MA 02115-6115

MARKOWITZ, RICHARD IRA, radiologist. BA, Queens Coll., 1965; MD, SUNY, Syracuse, 1969. Diplomate Am. Bd. Radiology. Intern Thomas Jefferson Univ. Hosp., Phila., 1969-70; resident in diagnostic radiology Univ. Pa. and Presbyn.Univ. Pa. Medical Ctr., Phila., 1970-73; fellow in pediatric radiology St. Christopher's Hosp. for Children, Phila., 1973-74, assoc. attending radiologist, 1974-79; attending radiologist Yale-New Haven Hosp., New Haven, Conn., 1979-88; deputy radiologist in chief, sr. attending radiologist The Children's Hosp. Phila., 1988—; attending radiologist Hosp. Univ. Pa., Phila., 1989-95; assoc. prof. diagnosite radiology and pediatrics Yale Univ. Sch. Medicine, 1981-88; assoc. prof. radiology dept. radiology Univ. Pa. Sch. Medicine, 1988-94, prof. radiology dept. radiology, 1994—; asst. prof. radiology Temple Univ. Sch. Medicine, 1974-77, asst. prof. pediatrics, 1975-77, assoc. prof. radiology and pediatrics, 1977-79; vis. scientist Armed Forces Inst. Pathology, 1995; editorial reviewer numerous jours. Author: Consulting Radiologist Pediatric Infectious Diseases: Principles and Practice, 1995; contbr. numerous articles to profl. jours. With U.S. Army Res., 1973-79. Recipient AMA Physician Recognition award, 1981, 86, Editor's Recognition award for Outstanding Reviewing, 1986-89, Editor's Recognition award Radiology, 1993. Mem. Am. Coll. Radiology, Soc. Pediatric Radiology, Assn. Univ. Radiologists, Radiological Soc. N.Am., Soc. Thoracic Radiology, Pa. Radiology Soc., Phila. Roentgen Ray Soc., Phila. Coll. Physicians. Office: The Children's Hosp Phila Dept Radiology 34th St and Civic Ctr Blvd Philadelphia PA 19104

MARKOWSKA, ALICJA LIDIA, neuroscientist, researcher; b. Warsaw, Poland, Aug. 22, 1948; came to U.S., 1986; d. Marian Boleslaw and Eugenia Krystyna (Wodzynska) Pawlak; m. Janusz Jozef Markowski, Oct. 23, 1971; children: Marta Agnieszka, Michal Jacek. BA, MSc, Warsaw U., 1971; PhD, Nencki Inst., Warsaw, 1979. Postdoctoral fellow Nencki Inst., 1979-81, asst. prof., 1981-86; assoc. rschr. Johns Hopkins U., Balt., 1987-91, rsch. scientist, 1991-92, prin. rsch. sci., prof., 1992-94, head of neuromnemonic lab., 1994—; vis. fellow Czechoslovak Acad. Sci., Prague, 1981; rschr., lectr. U. Bergen, Norway, 1983; vis. faculty Johns Hopkins U., 1986-87; cons. Sigma Tau & Otsuka Co., Italy, Japan, 1990-92. Reviewer Neurobiology of Aging, 1992—, Behavioral Brain Rsch., 1992—' contbr. chpts. to Preoperative Events, 1989, Prospective on Cognitive Neuroscience, 1990, Encyclopedia of Memory, 1992, Neuropsychology of Memory, 1992, Methods in Behavioral Pharmacology, 1993. Grantee Nat. Inst. Age, 1993—, NSF, 1990-93, NIH, 1992—. Mem. AAAS, Soc. for Neuroscience, Internat. Brain Rsch., N.Y. Acad. Sci. Home: 1301 Kingsbury Rd Owings Mills MD 21117-1343 Office: Johns Hopkins U 34th Charles St Baltimore MD 21218

MARKS, ANDREW ROBERT, molecular biologist; b. N.Y.C., Feb. 22, 1955; s. Paul Alan and Joan Harriet (Rosen) M.; m. Margaret Foster, Jan. 14, 1984; children: Joshua, Daniel, Sarah. BA (magna cum laude), Amherst Coll., 1976; MD, Harvard Med. Sch., 1980. Diplomate Am. Bd. Internal Medicine; cert. in cardiovascular diseases. Intern, resident Mass. Gen. Hosp., Boston, 1980-83, cardiology fellow, 1985-87; fellow genetics Harvard Med. Sch., Boston, 1983-85, instr. medicine, 1987-90; asst. prof. molecular biology Mt. Sinai Sch. Medicine, N.Y.C., 1990-93; assoc. prof. molecular biology and medicine, 1993—; Fishberg prof. medicine in cardiology Mt. Sinai Sch. Medicine, N.Y.C., 1995—; Contbr. articles to profl. jours. Mem. Sierra Club, 1986—. Established investigatorship, Am. Heart Assn., 1993. Recipient Clinician-Scientist award Am. Heart Assn., 1986, Excellence in Rsch. award Am. Fedn. for Clin. Rsch., 1990, Syntex Scholars award, 1991. Mem. Am. Assn. Biol. Chemistry and Molecular Biology, Am. Assn. Cell Biology, Biophys. Soc., Harvey Soc., Sierra Club. Office: Mt Sinai Sch Med CUNY 1 Gustave L Levy Pl New York NY 10029-6504

MARKS, EDWARD STANFORD, psychologist; b. Allentown, Pa., Feb. 9, 1936; s. Samuel A. and Grace C. (Cannon) M.; m. Barbara R. Barsky; children: Steven, Howard, Mindy. BA, Temple U., 1957; MA, U. Md., 1960, PhD, 1962. Lic. psychologist, Pa., N.J.; cert. Nat. Bd. Cert. Counselors, Nat. Register Health Svc. Providers in Psychology. Dir. extension svcs. B'nai B'rith Vocat. Svc., Phila., 1961-63; chief psychologist N.E. Community Mental Health Ctr., Phila., 1963-67; career counseling dir. Wordsworth Acad., Ft. Washington, 1967-79; dir. ctr. career svcs. JEVS, Phila., 1979-80; sch. psychologist Trenton (N.J.) Bd. Edn., 1980—; pvt. practice, Wyncote, Pa., 1967—. Author: A Handbook of Entry Strategies for School Consultation, 1995, (with others) Mysteries of the Mind, 1972, Psychology in Action, 1976. Fellow APA, ACA, Pa. Psychol. Assn. (past sec.), Soc. Clin. Psychologists (past v.p. human svcs. ctr. Phila. chpt., chair continuing edn. com.), Nat. Assn. Sch. Psychologists (past pres.). Office: Wyncote House # 10A Wyncote PA 19095

MARKS, EUGENE MELVIN, physician; b. Buffalo, July 5, 1921; s. Sidney M. and Marcia Maud (Tritchler) M.; m. Edna Mildred Aranibar, Nov. 25, 1943; children: James, Catherine, Joanne, Judith, Elizabeth, Edward. BA in Biology, U. Buffalo, 1943, MD, 1946. Diplomate Am. Bd. Preventive Medicine in Occupational Medicine. Intern E.J. Meyer Meml. Hosp., Buffalo, 1946-47, resident in internal medicine, 1947-48; plant physician E.I. duPont de Nemours & Co., Niagara Falls, N.Y., 1952-58; med. supr. E.I.

duPont de Nemours & Co., Buffalo, 1958-68; pvt. practice Alden, N.Y., 1953-64; corp. med. dir. Remington Arms Co., Bridgeport, Conn., 1968-85, contract physician, 1985-89; dist. med. cons. State Div. Rehab. Svcs., Conn., 1968-74, 85—. Mem. Commn. on Aging, Newtown, Conn., 1990—. Fellow Am. Coll. Occupational and Environ. Medicine (dir. 1982-85), Am. Coll. Preventive Medicine; mem. Am. Diabetes Assn., Am. Occupational Medicine Assn. (del. 1972-82, 85-89, dir. 1982-85), Conn. Occupational Medicine Assn. (pres. 1973), Am. Lung Assn. Conn., Newtown Rotary (chmn. com. 1969-75). Home: 22 Grand Pl Newtown CT 06470-2114

MARKS, FLORENCE CARLIN ELLIOTT, nursing informaticist; b. Louisville, Ky., Oct. 15, 1928; d. David Carlin and Anna Marie (Lance) Elliott; m. George Edward Marks, Mar. 18, 1961; children: Mary Ellen Marks Fox, Ruth Ann, Charles Douglas. BS in Chemistry, Zoology, U. Cin., 1949; BSN, U. Minn., 1953, M of Nursing Adminstrn., 1956. RN, Minn. From staff nurse to asst. head nurse U. Minn. Hosps., Mpls., 1953-54; staff nurse Marseilisbog Hosp., Aarhaus, Denmark, 1954-55; nursing supr. U. Minn. Hosps., Mpls., 1956-61, spl. asst. to dir. of nursing svc., 1962; rsch. asst. Hill Family Found. Nursing Rsch. Project, Mpls., 1966-69; writer U. Minn. Sch. of Nursing, Mpls., 1976; cons. U. Minn. Sch. of Nursing, 1976, 1978; nursing program specialist Hennepin County Med. Ctr., Mpls., 1978-84, nursing info. systems dir., cons., 1987—; nursing utilization system coord. U. Minn. Hosps., Mpls., 1984-87; cons. Creative Nursing Mgmt., 1992—; speaker, lectr. various nursing confs. in U.S. Contbr. articles to profl. publs., chpts. to profl. books, posters, abstracts; co-author: (with Joan Williams) (TV series) TLC, 1953 (McCall's award 1954); editor: Tomorrow's Nurse, 1960-62; Minn. Nursing Accent (commemorative issue 60th anniversary) May, 1965. Prin. flutist St. Anthony Civic Orch., 1975—, bd. dirs., 1988-92, adminstrv. bd. Hennepin Ave. United Meth. Ch., 1974-77, tchr., 1966-83 intermittently, cmty. outreach ministry, chair adv. com., 1992-95; mem. U. Minn. Sch. Nursing Densford Recognition Com., 1992-96; troop leader Mpls. coun. Girl Scouts USA, 1971-85, bd. dirs., 1977-79, svc. unit mgr., 1973-77; den leader Cub Scouts Webelo den, Viking coun. Boy Scouts Am., 1977-79; v.p. Wilshire Park PTSA, 1975-76, pres., 1976-77. Recipient Thanks Badge Greater Mpls. Girl Scout Coun. Mem. Minn. Nurses Assn. (various coms., bd. dirs. 1959-61), Minn. League for Nursing, Minn. Heart Assn. (profl. edn. com. 1959-61), Nursing Info. Discussion Group (chmn. Twin City program com. 1985-91, 95—), U. Minn. Sch. Nursing Alumni Assn. (bd. dirs. 1963-67, pres. 1965-66), Mortar Bd., Zeta Tau Alpha, Tau Beta Sigma, Sigma Theta Tau (bd. dirs. Zeta chpt. 1969-73, 89-91, pres. 1972-73, heritage com. 1990). Home: 3424 Silver Lake Rd NE Minneapolis MN 55418-1605

MARKS, FREDRIC, physician; b. Feb. 20, 1933. BS, Pa. State U., 1954; MD, Chgo. Med. Sch., 1958. Diplomate Am. Bd. Plastic Surgery. Attending physician St. Vincents Med. Ctr., Staten Island, N.Y., 1971—; clin. instr. Downstate U., Brooklyn, N.Y., 1973—; chief plastic surgery Dr.'s Hosp., Staten Island, N.Y., 1975—, Staten Island U. Hosp., 1978—; full attending physician Beth Israel Med. Ctr., N.Y.C., 1995—; vis. physician Kings County, Brooklyn, N.Y., 1973—. Home: 1460 Victory Blvd Staten Island NY 10301

MARKS, GERALD, surgeon; b. Bklyn., Apr. 14, 1925; s. Maurice and Lee (Leib) M.; m. Barbara Ann Hendershot, Nov. 25, 1950; children: Richard M., James M., John H. Grad., Villanova U., 1945; M.D., Jefferson Med. Coll., 1949. Diplomate: Am. Bd. Surgery, Am. Bd. Colon and Rectal Surgery (examiner). Intern Jefferson Med. Coll. Hosp., Phila., 1949-51, resident in surgery, 1952-57, resident in proctology, 1953-54; asst. dir. Tumor Clinic Jefferson Med. Coll. Hosp., 1959-68; practice medicine specializing in gen. and colorectal surgery Phila., 1957—; asst. chief surgery Phila. Gen. Hosp., 1957-70, chief Proctology Clinic, 1968-70, coordinator student surg. edn. Jefferson Surg. Service, 1960-70; asst. attending physician in surgery Thomas Jefferson U. Hosp., 1957-95, sec. med. staff, 1974-77, dir. Comprehensive Rectal Cancer Ctr., Colorectal Surgery Residency Program, exec. dir. Colorectal Surgical Found., 1984-95, co-dir. Colorectal Cancer Genetics Ctr.; dir. div. internat. surg. edn. and practice Ctr. for Research in Med. Edn. and Health Care; instr. surgery Jefferson Med. Coll., 1958-67, assoc. in clin. surgery, 1967-68, clin. assoc. prof. surgery, 1974-78, prof., 1978-95; chief sect. colorectal surgery, cons. in colon-rectal surgery Pa. Hosp.; cons. in colon-rectal surgery VA Hosp., Coatesville, Pa., 1959—, San Juan, P.R., 1968—, Wilmington, Del., 1977—; cons in colon-rectal surgery USN Regional Med. Ctr., Phila., 1977—; Edgar Deissler prof. surgery Allegheny U. Health Scis., 1995—, dir. comprehensive rectal cancer ctr., 1995—, dir. GI surg. endoscopy, 1995; adj. prof. surgery U. Pa. Sch. Medicine. Sr. editor Surg. Endoscopy, Ultrasound and Interventional Techniques Jour.; assoc. editor Diseases of the Colon and Rectum Jour., 1977—; cons. editor Pa. Medicine; editl. cons. bd. mem. Gen. Surgery News, 1991, Jour. Surg. Techn.; contbr. articles to profl. jours.; developed colonscopic colon teaching model. Chmn. com. SAGES Internat. Rels. Served with USN, 1943-46; served to capt. M.C. USAF, 1951-52. Recipient 7th Ann. Jonathan M. Wainwright award, Moses Taylor Hosp., Scranton, Pa., 1989. Mem. ACS (rep. to bd. govs. 1983, council Met. Phila. chpt.), AMA, Pa. Soc. Colon and Rectal Surgery (pres. 1981-82), Am. Soc. Colon and Rectal Surgeons (v.p. 1989), Am. Soc. Clin. Oncology, Internat. Soc. Univ. Colon and Rectal Surgeons, Coll. Physicians Phila., Internat. Fedn. Socs. Endoscopic Surgeons (pres. 1991—), Royal Soc. Medicine (affiliate), Ea. Surg. Soc., Phila. Acad. Surgery (mem. council), Pa. Med. Soc., Phila. County Med. Soc. (bd. dirs., v.p., chmn. publs. com., pub. affairs com., v.p. 1986—), Soc. Surgery Alimentary Tract, Am. Soc. Gastrointestinal Endoscopy (honoree ann. Gerald Marks lectureship), Italian Soc. Gastrointestinal Endoscopy (hon.), Soc. Am. Gastrointestinal Endoscopic Surgeons (founder, pres. 1980, bd. govs., honoree Annual Gerald Marks Lectureship, chmn. internat. rels. com.), Italian Soc. Surgery (hon.), Northeastern Soc. Colon and Rectal Surgeons (past pres.), Jefferson Vol. Faculty Assn. (pres. 1973-74), Am. Soc. Colon and Rectal Surgeons (v.p. 1989—), Alpha Omega Alpha. Home: 45 Fairview Rd Narberth PA 19072-1328 Office: 227 N Broad St Ste 100 Philadelphia PA 19107 also: Allegheny U Health Scis Dept Surgery Broad and Vine Sts MS 413 Philadelphia PA 19102-1192

MARKS, HELENA LIN, medical technologist; b. Peking, China, Oct. 6, 1935; came to U.S., 1955, naturalized, 1961; d. Kung and Shu-Fan (Lee) Lin; BA in Math. and Physics, Hunter Coll., N.Y.C., 1972; m. John S. Marks, Nov. 28, 1958 (dec. 1973); children: John Lin, Paul Lee. Supr. chemistry lab. Tompkins County Hosp., Ithaca, N.Y., 1962-64; supr. labs. Calvary Hosp., Bronx, N.Y., 1964-67; med. technologist N. Cen. Hosp., Bronx, N.Y., 1977-86, Nyack (N.Y.) Hosp., 1986—; real estate saleswoman. Mem. Am. Soc. Clin. Pathologists, N.Y.C. Med. Lab. Suprs. Home: 10 Twin Elms Ln New City NY 10956-5811

MARKS, JAMES GARFIELD, JR., dermatologist; b. Trenton, N.J., May 19, 1945; s. James Garfield and Lavinia May (Ellis) M.; m. Joyce Lynne Turner, Aug. 9, 1969; 1 child, Shannon. BA, Wilkes Coll., 1967; MD, Temple U., 1971. Intern Geisinger Med. Ctr., Danville, Pa., 1971-72; resident Wilford Hall USAF Med. Ctr., San Antonio, 1975-78; staff dermatologist Pa. State U. Coll. Medicine, Hershey, 1980—, asst. prof., 1980-85, assoc. prof., 1985-91, prof. medicine, 1991—; clin. instr. dermatology U. Tex. Health Sci. Ctr., San Antonio, 1978-80. Author: Contact and Occupational Dermatology, 1992, Principles of Dermatology, 1993, (with others) Principles of CLinical Diagnosis, 1992, Principles and Practice of Dermatology, 1990, Occupational Skin Diseases, 1990, Conn's Current Therapy, 1988, 89; contbr. articles to profl. jours. Bd. dirs. Braun Sta. East Cmty., 1976. Lt. col. USAF, 1972-80. Decorated Meritorious Svc. Commendation meadl; Am. Acad. Dermatology Exch. fellow, 1984; recipient Roerig Pharms. Challenges in Dermatology Ednl. award, 1982. Mem. Am. Acad. Dermatology, Am. Contact Dermatitis Soc., N.Am. Contact Dermatitis Group, Pa. Acad. Dermatology, Phila. Dermatology Soc., European Soc. Contact Dermatitis, World Fragrance Rsch. Team, Soc. Investigative Dermatology, Assn. Mil. Dermatologists, Dermatology Found., Agromedicine Consortium, Lions (v.p. 1982, pres. 1983). Office: Hershey Med Ctr 500 University Dr Box 850 Hershey PA 17033

MARKS, JAMES S., public health service administrator; b. May 13, 1948. AB cum laude, Williams Coll., 1969; MD, SUNY, Buffalo, 1973; MPH, Yale U., 1980. Diplomate Am. Bd. Pediatrics. Intern in pediat. U. Calif., San Francisco, 1973-74, resident in pediat., 1974-75, chief resident pediatric outpatient dept., 1975-76; resident in preventive medicine Ctrs. for Disease Control, Atlanta, 1977-78; fellow Robert Wood Johnson Clin. Scholars Program Yale U., New Haven, Conn., 1978-80; resident in preventive medicine Ctrs. for Disease Control, Atlanta, 1981-82, chief epidemiology and rsch. br., nutrition divsn., 1982-84, asst. dir. preventive medicine residency program, 1985-87, dir. divsn. reproductive health, 1987, coord. for chronic disease control activities, 1987-88, acting dir. divsn. diabetes transl., 1988-89, acting dir. divsn. chronic disease control, 1990-91, dir. divsn. reproductive health, 1992-95, dir. Nat. Ctr. Chronic Disease Prevention/Health Promotion, 1995—; adj. assoc. prof. Emory U. Sch. Pub. Health, Atlanta, 1990—; editor Chronic Disease Notes and Reports, 1989-92; clinic physician Planned Parenthood of San Francisco Teen Clinic, San Francisco, 1975-76; cons. physician Ohio Dept. Health Bur. Preventive Medicine, 1978-79; cons. PAHO Consultative Group on Perinatal Care, Washington, 1982, WHO Malaysia Ministry of Health, 1982, 83, WHO Maternal and Child Health Unit Geneva, 1983, World Bank China Program Third Health Project, 1988, 1991, World Bank Poland, Health Promotion/Chronic Disease Prevention, 1992, World Bank China, Seventh Health Project, 1993. Contbr. articles to profl. jours, chpts. to books. Exec. sec. Diabetes Tech. Adv. com., 1989-92; liaison mem. Nat. Diabetes Adv. Bd., 1988-89; mem. Diabetes Mellitus Interagy. Coording. com., 1988-89; mem. subcom. adult edn., Am. Cancer Soc., 1987-92; staff White House Task Force on Infant Mortality, 1989; presenter in field. Epidemic Intelligence Svc. Officer USPHS Field Svcs. Divsn., 1976-78. Recipient Alexander D. Langmuir award, 1978, CDC Group award, 1984, Commendation Medal USPHS, 1984, and many other awards and citations. Fellow Am. Coll. Epidemiology; mem. APHA (active in com. work), Am. Epidemiol. Soc., Soc. Epidemiol. Rsch., Am. Acad. Pediat. (com. pediatric rsch. 1994-95), Internat. Epidemiol. Assn., Physicians for Social Responsibility, Soc. on Med. Decision Making, Epidemic Intelligence Svc. Alumni Assn., Sigma Xi. Home: 3158 Kings Arms Court Atlanta GA 30345 Office: Ctrs for Disease Control Health Promotion Chronic Disease Prevention Atlanta GA 30333*

MARKS, JEFFREY ALAN, podiatrist; b. Johnstown, Pa., June 21, 1960; s. A.L. and Joanne Lee (Dietz) M.; m. Kathryn Nancy Smith, June 16, 1984; children: Cayleigh Megan, Jason Alan, Joshua Dietz. BS in Biology, Millersville U., 1982; DPM, Pa. Coll. Podiatric Medicine, 1987. Diplomate Am. Coll. Podiatric Surgery. Surg. resident St. Joseph Hosp., Phila., 1987-91; fellow in surgery Malmo (Sweden) Gen. Hosp., 1991; pvt. practice Mechanicsburg, Pa., 1991—; assoc. pvt. practice Martin Foot & Ankle Ctr., York, Pa., 1993—; active staff Harrisburg (Pa.) Hosp., 1992—, Holy Spirit Hosp., Camp Hill, Pa., 1991—, Seidle Meml. Hosp., Mechanicsburg, Pa., 1991—, York (Pa.) Hosp., 1992—. Contbr.: (book) Textbook of Foot and Ankle Surgery. Mem. Nat. Ski Patrol (OEC instr. 1992—). Lutheran. Office: 940 Century Dr Mechanicsburg PA 17055

MARKS, JON OWEN, physician; b. Bklyn., Dec. 28, 1946; s. Peter J. and Lily I. (Fagelson) M.; m. Ellen A. Zimmerman, June 10, 1967 (div.); m. Eileen M. Rich; children: Ian, Lana, Laura. BS in Aerospace Engring., NYU, 1967, MS in Aerospace Engring., 1969; MD, N.Y. Med. Coll., 1976. Diplomate Am. Bd. Urology. Rsch. engr. Grumman Aerospace, Bethpage, N.Y., 1969-72; resident Lenox Hill Hosp., N.Y.C., 1976-78, 78-81; staff urologist Beth Israel Med. Ctr., N.Y.C., 1981-84; physician pvt. practice, N.Y.C., 1984—; med. dir. Met. Lithotriptor Assocs., N.Y.C., 1987—, Repro Lab, N.Y.C., 1994—. Mem. AMA, Am. Urologic Assn., Am. Soc. Reproductive Medicine, Am. Lithotripsy Soc., Endourology Soc., Soc. Urology and Engring., Tau Beta Pi, Sigma Gamma Tau. Home: 170 Crest Dr Tarrytown NY 10591 Office: Urologic Assocs 55 E 9th St New York NY 10016

MARKS, PAUL ALAN, oncologist, cell biologist, educator; b. N.Y.C., Aug. 16, 1926; s. Robert R. and Sarah (Bohorad) M.; m. Joan Harriet Rosen, Nov. 28, 1953; children: Andrew Robert, Elizabeth Susan Marks Ostrer, Matthew Stuart. AB with gen. honors, Columbia U., 1945, MD, 1949; D in Biol. Sci. (hon.), U. Urbino, Italy, 1982; PhD (hon.), Hebrew U., Jerusalem, Israel, 1987, U. Tel Aviv, 1992. Fellow Columbia U. Coll. Physicians and Surgeons, 1952-53, assoc., 1955-56, mem. faculty, 1956-82, dir. hematology tng., 1961-74, prof. medicine, 1967-82, prof. human genetics and devel., 1969-82, dean faculty of medicine, v.p. med. affairs, 1970-73, dir. Comprehensive Cancer Ctr., 1972-80, v.p. health scis., 1973-80, Frode Jensen prof. medicine, 1974-80; prof. medicine and genetics Cornell U. Coll. Medicine, N.Y.C., 1982—, prof. medicine Grad. Sch. Med. Scis., 1983—; instr. Sch. Medicine, George Washington U., 1954-55; cons. VA Hosp., N.Y.C., 1962-66; attending physician Presbyn. Hosp., N.Y.C., 1967-82; pres., CEO Meml. Sloan-Kettering Cancer Ctr., 1980—; attending physician Meml. Hosp. for Cancer and Allied Diseases, 1980—; mem. Sloan-Kettering Inst. for Cancer Rsch., 1980—; adj. prof. Rockefeller U., 1980—; vis. physician Rockefeller U. Hosp., 1980—; hon. staff N.Y. Hosp., 1981—; bd. sci. counselors divsn. cancer treatment Nat. Cancer Inst., 1980-83; mem. steering com. Frederick Cancer Rsch. Facility Nat. Cancer Inst., 1982-86; chmn. program adv. com. Robert Wood Johnson Found., 1983-89; mem. Gov.'s Commn. on Shoreham Nuclear Plant, 1983; mem. Mayor's Commn. Sci. and Tech. City of N.Y., 1984-87; mem. adv. com. on NIH to Sec. HHS, 1989-90, 93—, external adv. com. Intramural Rsch. Program Rev. NIH; mem. gov. com. NYPRHA, 1996; mem. coun. biol. scis. Pritzker Sch. Medicine U. Chgo., 1977-88; first lectr. Nakasone Program for Cancer Control U. Tokyo, 1984; Ayrey fellow, vis. prof. Royal Postgrad. Med. Sch. U. London, 1985; William Dameshek vis. prof. hematology Mt. Sinai Med. Ctr., 1985; nat. vis. com. CUNY Med. Sch., 1986-89; trustee Feinberg Grad. Sch. Weizmann Inst. Sci., Rehovot, Israel, 1986—; William H. Resnick lectr. in medicine Stamford Hosp., 1986; disting. faculty lectr. M.D. Anderson Hosp. U. Tex., 1986; Maurice C. Pincoffs lectr. U. Md., Balt., 1987; Japan Soc. Hematology Disting. lectr., 1989; vis. prof. Coll. de France, 1988; Alpha Omega Alpha vis. prof. N.Y. Med. Coll., 1990; Mario A. Baldini vis. prof. Harvard Med. Sch., 1991; mem. sci. adv. bd. City of Hope Nat. Med. Ctr., Duarte, Calif., 1987-92, Raymond and Beverly Sackler Found., Inc., 1989, Jefferson Cancer Inst., Phila., 1989, Hong Kong Cancer Inst., U. Hong Kong, 1994; mem. Found. Biomed. Rsch., 1989—; advisor Third World Acad. Sci.; mem. sci. adv. com. Imperial Cancer Rsch. Fund, 1994; mem. bd. govs. Friends of Sheba Med. Ctr., Tel Hashomer. Editor: Monographs in Human Biology, 1963; author 9 books; contbr. over 350 articles to profl. jours.; mem. editl. bd. Blood, 1964-71, assoc. editor, 1976-77, editor-in-chief, 1978-82; assoc. editor Jour. Clin. Investigation, 1967-71; mem. editl. bd. Cancer Treatment Revs., 1981—, Cancer Preventions, 1989, Sci., 1990; guest editl. bd. Japanese Jour. Cancer Rsch., 1985—; assoc. editor Molecular Reprodn. and Devel., 1988—; expert analyst Chemistry and Molecular Biology edit. of Chemtracts, 1990-92; mem. adv. bd. Internat. Jour. Hematology, 1992, Stem Cells; bd. contbg. editors Blood Cells, Molecules and Diseases, 1994, Comité des Sages, 1994. Trustee St. Luke's Hosp., 1970-80, Roosevelt Hosp., 1970-80, Presbyn. Hosp., 1972-80, Metpath Inst. Med. Edn., 1977-79; mem. jury Albert Lasker awards, 1974-82; bd. govs. Weizmann Inst., 1976—; bd. dirs. Revson Found., 1976-91, Am. Found. for Basic Res. Israel, Israel Acd. Scis., 1991; mem. tech. bd. Milbank Meml. Fund, 1978-85; bd. govs. Friends of Sheba Med. Ctr., Tel Hashomer. Recipient Charles Janeway prize Columbia U., 1949, Joseph Mather Smith prize, 1959, Stevens Triennial prize, 1960, und. award in med. rsch., 1965, Columbia U. Coll. Physicians and Surgeons Disting. Achievement medal, 1980, Centenary medal Inst. Pasteur, 1987, Disting. Oncologist award Hipple Cancer Ctr. and Kettering Ctr., 1987, Found. for Promotion of Cancer Rsch. medal, 1984 (Japan), Disting. Svc. medal Robert Wood Johnson Found., 1989, Outstanding Achievement award in hematopoiesis U. Innsbruck, 1991, Pres.'s Nat. Medal Sci., 1991, Gold medal for Disting. Acad. Accomplishments, Coll. Physicians and Surgeons, 1994, Joseph Mather Smith prize Columbia U., 1995, Japan Found. for Cancer Rsch. award, 1995; John Jay award for disting. profl. achievement, Columbia Coll., N.Y., 1996; Commonwealth Fund fellow Pasteur Inst., 1961-62. Master ACP, Coll. Phys. Surgeons; fellow AAAS, Royal Soc. Medicine, Am. Acad. Arts and Scis., Pasteur Inst. Paris; mem. NAS (chmn. sect. med. genetics, hematology and oncology 1980-83, chmn. Acad. Forum Adv. Com. 1980-81, mem. coun. 1984-87, del. biol. warfare com. Internat. Security and Arms Control 1986-89), Royal Soc. Medicine (London), Inst. Medicine (mem. coun. 1973-76, chmn. com. study resources clin. investigation with NAS 1988), Red Cell Club (past chmn.), Am. Fedn. Clin. Rsch. (past councillor Ea. dist.), Am. Soc. Clin. Investigation (pres. 1972-73), Am. Soc. Biol. Chemists, Am. Soc. Human Genetics (past mem. program com.), Am. Assn. Cancer Rsch., Assn. Am. Cancer Insts. (bd. dirs. 1983-88), Soc. Cell Biology, Am. Soc. Hematology (pres.-elect 1983, pres. 1984, chmn. adv. bd. 1985), Assn. Am. Physicians, Econ. Club (n.y.C.), Harvey Soc. (pres. 1973-74), Internat. Soc. Devel. Biologists, Italian Assn. Cell Biology and Differentiation (hon.), Chinese Anti-Cancer Assn. (hon.), Soc. for Devel. Biology, Japanese Cancer Assn. (hon.), Japan Soc. Hematology (Disting. lectr. 1989), Internat. Leadership Ctr. on Longevity and Soc. Interurban Clin. Club, Soc. for Study Devel. and Growth, Third World Acad. Scis., Sci. Adv. Hong Kong Cancer Inst., U. Hong Kong, Weizmann Inst. Sci. (gov. emeritus, Israel), Health Scis. Adv. Coun. Columbia U., Century Assn., Econ. Club, N.Y.C., Univ. Club N.Y.C., Alpha Omega Alpha. Office: Meml Sloan-Kettering Cancer Ctr 1275 York Ave New York NY 10021

MARKS, RONALD BARRY, oral and maxillofacial surgeon; b. Shreveport, La., Oct. 23, 1942; s. Ralph Lewis and Selma (White) M.; m. Nat Allison Marks, Nov. 28, 1970; children: Alan Edward, Spencer Rowan. BA in Chemistry, La. State U., 1964; DDS, Loyola U., 1970. Diplomate Oral and Maxillofacial Surgery. Residency oral and maxillofacial surgery Charity Hosp., New Orleans, 1970-73; oral and maxillofacial surgeon Alexandria (La.) Oral Surgery Assoc., R.L.L.P. Mem. State Bd. Dentistry, Southeastern Soc. Oral and Maxillofacial Surgeons (pres. 1992-93), Am. Assn. Oral and Maxillofacial Surgeons (pres. 1992-93), La. Dental Assn. (pres. 1985-86), La. Dental Soc. (pres. 1982-83), 8th Dist. Dental Soc. (pres. 1978-79), Alexandria C. of C. (polit. affairs com.). Jewish. Office: Alexandria Oral Surgery 1403 Peterman Dr Alexandria LA 71301

MARKS, SHARON LEA, primary school educator, nurse; b. Arroyo Grande, Calif., June 12, 1942; d. Donald Elmore and Gertrude (Grieb) Shaffer; m. George Conrad Schmidt, June 23, 1963 (div. 1975); children: Kerrilynn, Robert, Marianne; m. Keith Dalton Marks, June 4, 1978; children: Joseph, Erik, Alice. Diploma, Sch. Nursing Samuel Merritt Hosp., 1963; BS in Nursing, Lewis and Clark State Coll., 1984, BS in Mgmt., 1986. RN, Calif., Wash. Staff nurse Vesper Meml. Hosp., San Leandro, Calif., 1968-74; night nurse supr. Tuolumne Gen. Hosp., Sonora, Calif., 1975; nurse Orleans (Calif.) Search and Rescue Team, 1975-78; instr. nursing Pasadena (Calif.) City Coll., 1978-79; resource coord. learning ctr. div. health sci. Spokane (Wash.) Community Coll., 1979-84; staff nurse Kootenai Med. Ctr., 1979-85; instr. North Idaho Coll., Coeur d'Alene, 1984-85; staff nurse North Idaho Home Health, Coeur d'Alene, 1985-86; coord. br. office Family Home Care, Spokane, 1986-87; devel., dir. Good Samaritan Home Health Plummer, Idaho and Fairfield, Washington, 1987-88; mgr. patient svcs. VNS Seattle-King County, Tukwila, Wash., 1988-89; co-owner, v.p. The Wooden Boat Shop, Seattle, 1989—; primary sch. tchr. Marisposa Sch., 1994-95, Corona Sch., 1996—; owner Marks and Assocs., 1994—; instr. in emergency med. tech. Orleans campus Coll. Redwoods, Eureka, Calif., 1977-78; book reviewer Brady Co., Besterfield and Assocs., 1994; film reviewer Olympia Media Info. Mem. Nat. Head Injury Found., Wash. State Head Injury Found. Office: 11884 4th St Yucaipa CA 92399

MARKS, SPENCER JONATHAN, director communicable disease control; b. N.Y.C., Mar. 12, 1950; s. George and Elaine (Weiner) M.; m. Susan Louise Houston, Mar. 28, 1992; children: Austin Lee Hamm, David Houston, Jason Houston. BA in Sociology, SUNY, New Paltz, 1974; MPA, Russell Sage Coll., 1983. Pub. health advisor N.Y. State Dept. Health, Albany, 1974-75; social worker Ulster County Health Dept., Kingston, N.Y., 1975; dir. communicable disease control div. Dutchess County Dept. Health, Poughkeepsie, N.Y., 1975—; mem. med. adv. bd. Planned Parenthood, Poughkeepsie, 1984—; mem. infection control com. Vassar Bros. Hosp., Poughkeepsie, 1984—, St. Francis Hosp., Poughkeepsie, 1984—; mem. Mid-Hudson Valley Lyme disease adv. coun., 1991—; adj. faculty psychology dept. grad. divsn. Marist Coll.; project dir. Ryan White Title I EMA; ex-officio Title I Planning Coun. Mem. ACTU community adv. bd. Albany Med. Coll. Mem. N.Y. State Pub. Health Assn. (bd. dirs. Mid-Hudson chpt.). Office: Dutchess County Health Dept 387-391 Main St Poughkeepsie NY 12601

MARKS, STUART DAVID, ophthalmologist; b. Columbus, Ohio, Apr. 25, 1957; s. Jack and Joan (Krause) M.; m. Susan Leigh Ziegler, July 27, 1985; children: Rachel, Geoffrey. BA, Emory U., 1979; MD, Ohio State U., 1983. Diplomate Am. Bd. Ophthalmology. Intern Riverside Meth. Hosp., Columbus, 1983-84; resident in ophthalmology Ohio State U., Colubmus, 1984-87; ophthalmologist Augusta (Ga.) Assoc. in Ophthalmology, 1990—; chief divsn. ophthalmology U. Hosp., Augusta, 1992-96; clin. instr. dept. ophthalmology Emory U., 1988-96, Atlanta VA Hosp., 1988-96, Med. Coll. Ga. VA Hosp., 1996. Landacre Rsch. Soc. award, 1983. Fellow Am. Acad. Ophthalmology; mem. Ga. Soc. Ophthalmology (chmn. program and edn. com. 1993-95, coun. mem. 1994—); Southern Med. Assn., Med. Assn. Ga., Richmond County Med. Soc. Office: Augusta Assoc in Oph 811 13th St Ste 14 Augusta GA 30921

MARKS, VINCENT, pathologist; b. London, June 10, 1930; s. Lewis Meyer and Rose (Goldbaum) M.; m. Averil Rosalie Sherrard, Feb. 10, 1957; children: Alexandra Louise, Lewis Adam. BA, Brasenose Coll., Oxford, 1951; BM, BCh., St. Thomas' Hosp., London, 1954; DM, Brasenose Coll., 1969. Resident pathologist St. George's Hosp., London, 1957-58; rsch. fellow Med. Rsch. Coun., Eng., 1958-60; sr. lectr. Inst. of Neurology, London, 1957-61; dir. labs. Epsom, Eng., 1962-70; prof. U. Surrey, Guildford, Eng., 1970-95, dean medicine European Inst. Health and Med. Sci., 1996—; bd. dirs. Quatro Biosys., Manchester, Eng., Clifmar Assocs., Guildford, Biostat Ltd., Stockport, U.K.; cons. Chem. Path. Royal Surrey County Hosp., St. Luke's Hosp., Guildford, 1970-95. Author: Hypoglycaemia, 1964, 81; editor: Scientific Foundations of Clinical Biochemistry, 1986, 94. Fellow Royal Coll. Physicians (Edinburgh), Royal Coll. Physicians (London), Royal Coll. Pathologists (v.p.); mem. Brit. Acad. Experts. Home: 1 Boxgrove House, Guildford GU1 2PP, England Office: U Surrey, Stirling House Stirling Rd, Guildford GU2 5RF, England

MARLENS, HANNA STEINER, psychologist; b. Vienna, Austria, Apr. 6, 1928; came to U.S., 1939; d. Bruno and Meta (Hoffman) Steiner; m. Alvin M. Marlens, Apr. 8, 1950; children: Steve, Neal. BA, Queens Coll., 1950; MA, CUNY, 1951; PhD, N.Y. U., 1959. Diplomate Am. Bd. Profl. Psychology; cert. sch. psychology, N.Y. Psychology intern Kings County Hosp., Bklyn., 1951-52; staff psychologist Dept. Pediatrics SUNY, Bklyn., 1952-54; rsch. psychologist Downstate Med. Schl., Bklyn., 1954-70; adj. prof. C.W. Post Coll., Brookville, N.Y., 1978-79; cons. psychologist Advanced Ctr. Psychotherapy, Hempstead, N.Y., 1972-75; rsch. cons. Ednl. Testing Svc. Inc., Princeton, N.J., 1970-77; sch. psychologist West Islip (N.Y.) PUbl. Schs., 1963—; cons. Pub. Group, Allyn Bacon, 1979-89; lctr. 1963—. Author: (with others) Psychological Differentiation, 1962. Mem. APA, N.Y. Psychol. Assn., Sch. Psychologists N.Y., N.Y. Soc. Clin. Psychologists, Suffolk County Psychol. Assn. (bd. dirs., 1972-75), Nassau County Psychol. Assn. (bd. dirs. 1977-85). Home: 15 Robin Ln Huntington NY 11743-6513 Office: West Islip Sch Dist Beach St West Islip NY 11795

MARLER, LINDA SUSAN, microbiologist; b. Bloomington, Ind., May 28, 1951; d. Lynne Lionel and Lucille Elizabeth (Widman) Merritt; B.S. in Med. Tech., Ind. U., 1973, M.S. in Allied Health Edn., 1978; m. David William Marler, May 21, 1977 (div.); children—Brian David, Brittney Lynne. Med. technologist, then sr. med. technologist Ind. U. Med. Center, Indpls., 1973—, edn. coordinator dept. microbiology, 1974—, asst. prof. div. allied health Sch. Medicine, 1978-84, assoc. prof., 1984—; speaker in field; contbr. articles to profl. jours. Mem. Am. Soc. Microbiology, South Central Assn. Clin. Microbiologists (teleconf. chairperson, 1988-91, pres.-elect 1992, pres. 1993). Methodist. Office: Fesler 409 1120 South Dr Indianapolis IN 46202-5135

MARLETT, JUDITH ANN, nutritional sciences educatr, researcher; b. Toledo. BS, Miami U., Oxford, Ohio, 1965; PhD, U. Minn., 1972; postgrad., Harvard U., 1973-74. Registered dietitian. Therapeutic and metabolic unit dietitian VA Hosp., Mpls., 1966-67; spl. instr. in nutrition Simmons Coll., Boston, 1973-74; asst. prof. U. Wis., Madison, 1975-80, assoc. prof. dept. nutritional scis., 1981-84, prof. dept. nutritional scis., 1984—; cons. U.S. AID, Leyte, Philippines, 1983; acting dir. dietetic program dept. Nutritional Scis. U. Wis., 1977-78, dir., 1985-89; cons. grain, drug and food cos., 1985—, adv. bd. U. Ariz. Clin. Cancer Ctr., 1987-95; sci. bd. advisors Am. Health Found., 1988—; reviewer NIH, 1982—. Mem. editl. bd. Jour. Sci. of Food and Agrl., 1989—, Jour. Food Composition and Analysis, 1994—; contbr. articles to profl. jours. Mem. AAAS, NIH (Diabetes amd Digestive and Kidney Disease spl. grant rev. com. 1992-96), Am. Inst. Nutrition, Am.

Dietetic Assn., Am. Soc. Clin. Nutrition, Inst. Food Technologists, Am. Assn. Cereal Chemists. Office: U Wis Dept Nutritional Sci 1415 Linden Dr Madison WI 53706-1527

MARLETTA, MICHAEL, biochemistry educator, researcher, pharmacologist; b. Rochester, N.Y., Feb. 12, 1951; m. Margaret Gutowski, 1991. BA, SUNY, 1973; PhD in Pharmacol. Chemistry, U. Calif., 1978. Fellow MIT, Cambridge, 1978-80, from asst. prof. to assoc. prof. toxicology, 1980-87; assoc. prof. med. chemistry U. Mich., Ann Arbor, 1987-91, assoc. prof. biol. chemistry, 1989-91, John G. Searle prof. med. chemistry, prof. biol. chemistry, 1991—. John D. and Katherine T. MacArthur fellow, 1995; recipient award for excellence in environ. health rsch. Lovelance Inst., Albuquerque, 1995. Mem. AAAS, Am. Soc. Biochem. and Molecular Biology, Am. Chem. Soc., Am. Assn. Cancer Rsch. Office: U Michigan Dept Med Biol Chemistry Ann Arbor MI 48109

MARLING, PATRICIA LYNN, nursing educator; b. Lansing, Mich., May 30, 1951; d. Russell David and Elizabeth Helen (Miltz) Cotè; m. Bruce M. VanderLind, Aug. 8, 1970 (div.); children: Burke T., Brady R.; m. L. Bradley Marling, June 13, 1981; 1 child, Dustin Reed. BS in Nursing, U. Tex., Arlington, 1981. RN, Tex. Labor/delivery nurse John Peter Smith County Hosp., Forth Worth, Tex., 1981-86; sch. nurse/health tchr. St. John the Apostle Sch., Fort Worth, Tex., 1985—; labor/deliver/nursery nurse Baylor Hosp., Gravepine, Tex., 1990-92; pres. Parents Orgn. Leonard Music Inst., Fort Worth, 1994-95, bd. dirs. Sec./treas. Boy Scouts Am., Bedford, Tex., 1991-93. Mem. Am. Sch. Health Assn., Am. Sch. Nurses Assn., Tex. Sch. Nurses Assn., Alpha Chi, Sigma Theta Tau. Roman Catholic. Home: 3908 Hillwood Way Bedford TX 76021 Office: St John the Apostle Sch 7421 Glenview Dr Fort Worth TX 76180

MARMER, ELLEN LUCILLE, pediatrician; b. Bronx, N.Y., June 29, 1939; d. Benjamin and Diane (Goldstein) M.; m. Harold O. Shapiro, June 5, 1960; children: Cheri, Brenda. BS in Chemistry, U. Ala., 1960; MD, U. Ala., Birmingham, 1964. Cert. Nat. Bd. Med. Examiners; diplomate Am. Bd. Sports Medicine, Bd. Pediatrics, Bd. Qualified and Eligible Pediatric Cardiology, Bd. cert. sports medicine. Intern Upstate Med. Ctr., Syracuse, N.Y., 1964-65, resident, 1965-66; fellow in pediatric cardiology Columbia Presbyn. Med. Ctr.-Babies Hosp., N.Y.C., 1967-69; pvt. practice Hartford, Vernon, Conn., 1969—; examining pediatrician child devel. program Columbia Presbyn. Med. Ctr.-Babies Hosp., N.Y.C., 1967, instr. pediatrics, 1967-69; dir. pediatric cardiology clinic St. Francis Hosp., Hartford, 1970-80; asst. state med. examiner, Tolland County, Conn., 1974-79; sports physician Rockville (Conn.) High Sch., 1976—; advisor Cardiac Rehab. com., Rockville, 1984-90; mem. bd. examiners Am. Bd. Sports Medicine, 1991—, chmn. credentials com., 1991—. Mem. Vernon Town Coun., 1985-89; bd. dirs. Child Guidance Clinic, Manchester, Conn., 1970—; life mem. Tolland County chpt. Hadassah, v.p., 1969-70, pres., 1970-72, bd. dirs., 1973-74; mem. B'nai Israel Congregation and Sisterhood, Vernon, 1969—, chmn. youth commn., 1970-72. Recipient Outstanding Svc. award Indian Valley YMCA, 1985. Fellow Am. Acad. Pediatrics, Am. Coll. Cardiology, Am. Coll. Sports Medicine (bd. examiners 1991—, chmn. credentials com. 1991—); mem. Conn. Med. Soc., Am. Heart Assn. (mem. coun. cardiovascular disease in young 1969—, chmn. elect New Eng. regional heart com. 1990-91), Conn. Heart Assn. (bd. dirs. 1974-75, 83-84, pres. 1986-88), Heart Assn. Greater Hartford (bd. dirs. 1970-89, mem. exec. com. 1972-73, 79-84, pres. 1982-84), Tolland County Med. Assn. (sec. 1971-72), Vis. Nurse and Community Care Tolland County, LWV (state program chairperson Vernon chpt. 1971-73). Democrat. Jewish. Office: 520 Hartford Tpke Vernon Rockville CT 06066-5037

MARMION, BARRIE PATRICK, microbiologist; b. Alverstoke, Hants, Eng., May 19, 1920; arrived in Australia, 1962; s. Joseph Patrick and Melita (Brian) M.; m. Diana Ray Newling, Sept. 26, 1953; 1 child, Jane. MBBS, London U., 1942, DSc, 1963, MD, 1947; Hon. doctorate, Adelaide U., 1990. Bacteriologist to sr. bacteriologist Pub. Health Lab. Svc., Eng., 1943-62; found. prof. microbiology Monash U. Med. Sch., Melbourne, 1962-68; Robert Irvine prof. of bacteriology Edinburgh (Scotland) U. Med. Sch., 1968-78; dir. div. med. virology and clin. prof. Inst. of Med. and Vet. Sci., 1978-85; vis. prof. Adelaide U., 1985—; cons. Commonwealth Serum Labs., Melbourne. Author/editor: Mackie and Mac Cartney Medical Microbiology; contbr. articles to profl. jours. Recipient Dist. Fellow award Coll. Pathologists, 1987. Mem. Australian Soc. Microbiology (pres. 1984-86, hon. life), Australian Soc. for Infectious Disease (pres. 1982-83, hon. life), Order Australia AO. Home: 14 Birksgate Dr, Urrbrae South Australia 5064, Australia

MARMOR, JUDD, psychiatrist, educator; b. London, May 1, 1910; came to U.S., 1911, naturalized, 1916; s. Clement K. and Sarah (Levene) M.; m. Katherine Stern, May 1, 1938; 1 son, Michael Franklin. AB, Columbia U., 1930, MD, 1933; DHL, Hebrew Union Coll., 1972. Diplomate: Am. Bd. Psychiatry and Neurology, Nat. Bd. Med. Examiners. Intern St. Elizabeth Hosp., Washington, 1933-35; resident neurologist Montefiore Hosp., N.Y.C., 1935-37; psychiatrist Bklyn. State Hosp., 1937; psychoanalytic tng. N.Y. Psychoanalytic Inst., N.Y.C., 1937-41; pvt. practice psychiatry, psychoanalysis and neurology N.Y.C., 1937-46, L.A., 1946—; instr. assoc. in neurology Columbia Coll. Physicians and Surgeons, 1938-40; adj. neurologist, neurologist-in-charge clinic Mt. Sinai Hosp., N.Y.C., 1939-46; lectr. New Sch. Social Rsch., N.Y.C., 1942-43; instr. Am. Inst. Psychoanalysis, N.Y.C., 1943; lectr. psychiatry N.Y. Med. Coll., 1944-46; lectr. social welfare UCLA, 1948-49, vis. prof. social welfare, 1949-64, clin. prof. psychiatry sch. medicine, 1953-80, adj. prof. psychiatry, 1980—; vis. prof. psychology U. So. Calif., 1946-49; tng. analyst, also pres. So. Calif. Psychoanalytic Inst., 1955-57; sr. attending psychiatrist L.A. County Gen. Hosp., 1954—; dir. divs. psychiatry Cedars-Sinai Med. Ctr., L.A., 1965-72; Franz Alexander prof. psychiatry U. So. Calif. Sch. Medicine, 1972-80, emeritus, 1980—; sr. cons. regional office social svc. VA, L.A., 1946-50; cons. psychiatry Brentwood VA Hosp., Calif., 1955-65; mem. Coun. Mental Health of Western Interstate Commn. Higher Edn., 1966-72. Editor: Sexual Inversion-The Multiple Roots of Homosexuality, Modern Psychoanalysis: New Directions and Perspectives, Psychiatry in Transition: Selected Papers of Judd Marmor, Homosexual Behavior: A Modern Reappraisal; (with S. Woods) The Interface Between the Psychodynamic and Behavioral Therapies, Psychiatrists & Their Patients: A National Study of Private Office Practice; (with S. Elsenstein and N.A. Levy) The Diadic Transaction: An Investigation into the Nature of the Psychotherapeutic Process; (with P. Nardi and D. Sanders) Growing Up Before Stonewall; mem. editl. bd. Am. Jour. Psychoanalysis, Contemporary Psychoanalysis, Archives Sexual Behavior; contbr. articles in field to profl. jours. Served as sr. attending surgeon USPHS USNR, 1944-45. Fellow Am. Psychiat. Assn. (life mem., pres. 1975-76), N.Y. Acad. Medicine (life mem.), Am. Acad. Psychoanalysis (pres. 1965-66), Am. Orthopsychiat. Assn. (dir. 1968-71), AAAS, Am. Coll. Psychiatrists; mem. AMA, Calif. Med. Assn., Group for Advancement Psychiatry (dir. 1968-70, pres. 1973-75), Am. Fund for Psychiatry (dir. 1955-57), So. Calif. Psychiat. Soc., So. Calif. Psychoanalytic Soc. (pres. 1960-61), Am. Psychoanalytic Assn., Los Angeles County Med. Soc., Phi Beta Kappa, Alpha Omega Alpha. Home: 655 Sarbonne Rd Los Angeles CA 90077-3214 Office: 1100 Glendon Ave Ste 921 Los Angeles CA 90024-3513

MARMOR, MICHAEL FRANKLIN, ophthalmologist, educator; b. N.Y.C., Aug. 10, 1941; s. Judd and Katherine (Stern) M.; m. C. Jane Breeden, Dec. 20, 1968; children: Andrea K., David J. AB, Harvard U., 1962, MD, 1966. Diplomate Am. Bd. Ophthalmology. Med. intern UCLA Med. Ctr., 1967; resident in ophthalmology Mass. Eye and Ear Infirmary, Boston, 1970-73; asst. prof. ophthalmology U. Calif. Sch. Medicine, San Francisco, 1973-74; asst. prof. surgery (ophthalmology) Stanford (Calif.) U. Sch. Medicine, 1974-80, assoc. prof., 1980-86, prof., 1986—, head. div. ophthalmology, 1984-88, chmn. dept., 1988-92, dir. Basic Sci. Course Ophthalmology, 1993—; mem. assoc. faculty program in human biology Stanford U., 1982—; chief ophthalmology sect. VA Med. Ctr., Palo Alto, Calif., 1974-84; mem. sci. adv. bd. No. Calif. Soc. to Prevent Blindness, 1984-92, Calif. Med. Assn., 1984-92, Nat. Retinitis Pigmentosa Found., 1985-95. Author: The Eye of the Artist, 1996; editor: The Retinal Pigment Epithelium, 1975, The Effects of Aging and Environment on Vision, 1991; editor-in-chief Doc. Ophthalmologica, 1995—; editl. bd. Healthline, Lasers and Light in Ophthalmology; contbr. more than 175 articles to sci. jours., 25 chpts. to books. Mem. affirmative action com. Stanford U. Sch. Medicine, 1984—. Sr. asst. surgeon USPHS, 1967-70. Recipient Svc. award Nat. Retinitis Pigmentosa Found., Balt., 1981, Rsch. award Alcon Rsch Found., Houston, 1989; rsch. grantee Nat. Eye. Inst., Bethesda, Md., 1974-94. Fellow Am. Acad. Ophthalmology (bd. councillors 1982-85, pub. health com. 1990-93, rep. to NAS com. on vision 1991-93, Honor award 1984, Sr. Honor award 1996); mem. Internat. Soc. Clin. Electrophysiology of Vision (v.p. 1990—), Assn. Rsch. in Vision and Ophthalmology, Internat. Soc. for Eye Rsch., Macula Soc. (rsch. com.), Retina Soc. Democrat. Office: Stanford U Sch Medcine Dept Ophthalmology Stanford CA 94305

MARNEY, SAMUEL ROWE, physician, educator; b. Bristol, Va., Feb. 15, 1934; m. Elizabeth Ann Bingham, Oct. 1, 1966; children: Samuel Rowe III, Annis Morison. BA in Chemistry, U. Va., 1955, MD, 1960. Staff physician VA Hosp., Nashville, 1968-69, clin. assoc., 1969-71, clin. investigator, 1971-74, staff physician, infectious disease and allergy cons., 1974—; asst. prof. medicine Med. Ctr. Vanderbilt U., Nashville, 1971-76, assoc. prof. 1976—, dir. allergy and immunology, 1974—; vis. investigator Scripps Clinic and Rsch. Found., La Jolla, Calif., 1973-74. Capt. USAF, 1962-64, Korea. Fellow ACP, Am. Acad. Allergy and Immunology, Am. Coll. Allergy and Immunology; mem. Southeastern Allergy Assn. (pres. 1986-87, Hal M. Davison Meml. award, 1981), Tenn. Soc. Allergy and Immunology. Home: 4340 Sneed Rd Nashville TN 37215-3242 Office: Vanderbilt U Med Ctr Allergy & Immunology 1500 21st Ave S Ste 3500 Nashville TN 37212

MAROHN, ANN ELIZABETH, health information professional; b. Grand Rapids, Mich., Feb. 26, 1946; d. Luther Alfonse and Mary Inez (Pinkstaff) M. BS, Ind. U., 1968; MS, SUNY, Buffalo, 1978. Asst. med. record dir. Highland Park (Mich.) Gen. Hosp., 1968-70; asst. dir. med. record svcs. Meml. Hosp., Elmhurst, Ill., 1970-73; dir. med. record tech. program Alfred (N.Y.) State Coll., 1974-76; mem. faculty med. record adminstrn. dept. Lincoln Coll., Melbourne, Australia, 1977-78, Kean Coll., Union, N.J., 1984-85, Med. U. S.C., Charleston, 1985-87; mem. faculty health record dept. Ferris State Coll., Big Rapids, Mich., 1979-80; dir. health info. mgmt. Armstrong State Coll., Savannah, Ga., 1980-84, dir. med. record dept. Tucson Gen. Hosp., 1988-89, N.D. State Hosp., Jamestown, 1990-92; cons. Prospective Payment Specialists, Tucson, 1992-93; health info. mgr. Sierra Med. Ctr., El Paso, Tex., 1993-94; dir. health info. mgmt. program Southern U., Shreveport, La., 1994—; cons. Oglethorpe Ctr., Savannah, 1983-84. Columnist Australian Med. Record Jour., 1981-87, Communique 1981-84, Palmetto Breeze, 1985-87, Progress Notes, 1984-85. Recipient disting. mem. award Ga. Med. Record Assn., 1984. Mem. NAFE, Am. Health Info. Mgmt. Assn., Ariz. Health Info. Mgmt. Assn. (program chmn. 1988-89, sec. 1989—), Tex. Health Info. Mgmt. Assn. (dist. III v.p.), La. Health Info. Mgmt. Assn., N.W. La. Health Info. Mgmt. Assn., Assembly on Edn. Episcopalian. Home: 215 Sand Beach Blvd 1205 Shreveport LA 71105

MARON, ARTHUR, pediatrician, medical administrator; b. Asbury Park, N.J., Apr. 15, 1933; s. Isidore Chaim and Sadie (Raskin) M.; m. Lynn Sunshine Maron, Aug. 5, 1956 (dec. Aug. 1994); children: Stuart Glenn, Andrea Kim, Scott Michael; m. Ruth Fuerth, Dec. 17, 1995. BS in Biology, Rutgers U., 1954; MD, Union U., 1958; MPA in Health Care, Seton Hall U., 1994. Diplomate Am. Bd. Pediats. Rotating intern USPHS Hosp., Norfolk, Va., 1958-59; pediat. resident Babies Hosp., Newark, 1961-63; pvt. practice specializing in pediats. West Orange, N.J., 1963-94; dir. med. edn. St. Barnabas Med. Ctr., Livingston, N.J., 1988—; pres. Med. Practice Assocs., Roseland, N.J., 1990-93; pres. med. staff St. Barnabas Med. Ctr., Livingston, 1991-93; med. dir. Found. Health Plan, Short Hills, N.J., 1989-91; bd. dirs. Alliance Ind. Acad. Med. Ctrs. Mem. bd. health West Orange Twp., 1970-90, Roseland Bd., 1996—; chmn. physicians divsn. United Jewish Appeal, 1994—. Recipient Maimonides award State of Israel Bonds, 1992. Fellow Am. Acad. Pediats. (bd. dirs., chmn. 1982-88, Presdl. award 1989); mem. AMA, (residency rev. com. for pediats. 1989-96, chmn. 1994-96, nat. residency matching program, bd. dirs. 1996—), Am. Hosp. Assn. (com. on med. edn. 1996—). Jewish. Office: St Barnabas Med Ctr 94 Old Short Hills Rd Livingston NJ 07039

MARONEY, JANE P., state legislator; b. Boston, July 29, 1923; d. John Henry and Mary (Boland) Perkins; m. John Walker Maroney, July 7, 1956; children: Jane Maroney El Dahr, John Walker Jr. Student, Radcliffe Coll., 1940-41; studnet, Katharine Gibbs Sch., 1941-42; LHD (hon.) Golden Beacon Coll., 1995. Elected official Del. Gen. Assembly, Dover, 1978—. Chmn. Del. Family Law Commn., 1990—, Health and Human Devel. Com., 1984—; moderator, panelist Pub. Policy Conf., annually; bd. dirs. YWCA, New Castle County, (J.Thompson Brown award 1992), Child Care Connection, Coord. Coun. Children with Disabilities, chmn. 1990-91; mem. adv. bd. Rockwood Mus., Del. Hospice, Girl Scouts Del., Del. Internat. Yr. of Family, March of Dimes, Coalition for Literacy, Inst. Human Behavior; past mem. Jr. League Wilmington. Named 1 of 10 Best Rep. Legislators of Yr. Pres. Reagan, 1985; recipient Outstanding Svc. to Children award Acad. Pediatrics, Disting. Svc. award Del. Bar Assn., Alfred R. Shands Disting. Svc. award, 1992, Order of Merit award U. Del., 1993, J. Donaldson Brown Disting. Svcs. award Children and Family Svcs. Del. to Dr. & Rep. Maroney, 1992; named to Women's Hall of Fame, Del., 1996. Roman Catholic. Home: 4605 Concord Pike Wilmington DE 19803-1406 Office: Del House of Reps PO Box 1901 Dover DE 19903-1901

MAROTTA, CHARLES ANTHONY, neuroscientist, psychiatric researcher; b. N.Y.C., Apr. 12, 1945; s. Joseph and Angelina (Brancato) M.; m. Rosalind Victoria Kearney, Apr. 4, 1981; children: Gianna Christina, Liliana Catherine. BS, CCNY, 1965; MD, Duke U., 1969; MPhilosophy, Yale U., 1972, PhD, 1975. Resident in psychiatry Mass. Gen. Hosp., Boston, 1973-76; dir. alzheimer rsch. program Mass. Gen. Hosp., Boston and Belmont, 1980-92; dir. neurobiology lab. Mass. Gen. Hosp., Boston, 1985-92, psychobiologist, 1986-92; clin. fellow Harvard Med. Sch., Boston, 1974-76, instr. psychiatry, 1976-77, assoc. prof. psychiatry, 1983-92; chief molecular neurobiology lab. McLean Hosp., Belmont, Mass., 1983-92; dir. div. psychiatric neurosci. Brown U., Providence, 1992—, prof. psychiatry and human behavior, 1992, prof. neurosci., 1993—; affiliate neurosci. program Harvard U., 1982-92; mem. study sect. extramural rsch. program Nat. Inst. on Aging, 1983; advisor WHO, Geneva, Switzerland, 1985; mem. med. and sci. adv. bd. Alzheimer's Assn., 1986-89; mem. com. on hon. degrees Brown U. 1995-96; cons. in field. Editor: Neurofilments, 1983; mem. editl. bd., assoc. editor Alzheimer's Disease and Associated Disorders, 1986—, Jour. Geriatric Psychiatry and Neurology, 1986—, Jour. Psychiat. Rsch., 1989—; contbr. articles to profl. jours.; patentee in field. Advisor Office Career Svcs. Harvard U., Cambridge, 1975—. Recipient MacArthur award MacArthur Found., Chgo., 1981, Neurosci. Devel. award McKnight Found., Mpls., 1985, Alzheimer Rsch. award Wood-Kalb Found., 1985, Disting. grant Sandoz Found. for Gerontol. Rsch., Princeton, N.J., 1988, Met. Life Found. award, 1990; McKnight Found. scholar, Mpls., 1977. Mem. AAAS, Am. Soc. for Neurochemistry, Am. Soc. for Biochemistry and Molecular Biology, Am. Assn. Neuropathologists, Am. Psychiatric Assn., Am. Geriatrics Soc., Internat. Soc. Neurochemistry, Internat. Brain Rsch. Orgn., Mass. Psychiatric Soc., World Psychiatric Assn., Soc. for Exptl. Neuropathology, Soc. for Neurosci., Assn. Rsch. Nervous Mental Diseases.

MAROTTA, MICHAEL P., physician assistant; b. N.Y.C., June 8, 1955; s. Pasquale and Virginia (Bonomo) M.; m. Rona Beth Rosmarin, Mar. 9, 1980; children: P. Joseph, Marisa Elizabeth. AS in Enging. Sci., Coll. S.I., 1975, BS in Econs. and Psychiatry, 1977. Cert. physician asst. Mem. house staff St. Barnabas, N.Y.C., 1979; surgery St. Vincent's, S.I., 1980; mem. emergency dept. Ira Davenport, Bath, N.Y., 1980; mem. house staff Yonkers (N.Y.) Gen., 1981-85; internal medicine Norwalk (Conn.) Hosp., 1985—. Fellow Am. Acad. Physician Assts.; mem. Conn. Assn. Physician Assts., N.Y. Assn. Physician Assts. Roman Catholic.

MARPLES, RICHARD RANSFORD, microbiologist; b. London, June 22, 1934; s. Brian John and Mary Joyce (Ransford) M.; m. Juliet Evelyn Falconer, Apr. 3, 1961; children: David, Nicola. MSc in Zoology, U. Otago, Dunedin, New Zealand, 1957; BM, Oxford U., Eng., 1961; MRC of Pathology, Royal Coll. Pathology, London, 1971, FRC of Pathology, 1981. Registered med. practitioner. Sr. house officer Bristol (Eng.) Royal Infirmary, 1962-63; demonstrator U. Bristol, 1963-64; rsch. fellow U. Pa., Phila., 1964-69, asst. prof. microbiology, 1969-73; cons. Cen. Pub. Health Labs., London, 1973—; dep. dir. Lab. Hosp. Infection, London, 1979—; sec. Internat. Union of Microbiol. Soc. sub-com., London, 1984—. Contbr. articles to profl. publs. Fellow Royal Coll. Pathologists; mem. Brit. Med. Assn., Brit. Soc. Chemotherapy, Hosp. Infection Soc., Assn. Med. Microbiologists, Nat. Trust. Office: Cen Pub Health Lab, 61 Colindale Ave, London NW9 5AT, England

MARQUART, CHRISTOPHER LOUIS, neurosurgeon; b. Wheeling, W.Va., Aug. 2, 1955; s. Louis August and Beatrice Anne (Pagenparm) M.; m. Marisa Dee Boggs, Apr. 16, 983; children: Matthew Christopher, Andrew Stuart. AB in Biology magna cum laude, W.Va. U., 1977, MD, 1981. Diplomate Am. Bd. Neurol. Surgery. Gen. surgery intern Ind. U., Indpls., 1981-82, neurosurgery resident, 1982-87; attending neurosurgeon Wheeling (W.Va.) and OVMC Hosp., 1987—; clin. asst., prof. W.Va. U. Hosp., 1989; chmn. intensive care unit OVMC, Wheeling, 1989—; chmn. dept. neuroscis. OVMC/Wheeling Hosp., 1994. Mem. AMA, Ohio County Med. Soc., Congress of Neurol. Surgeons, Neurosurg. Soc. of the Virginias, W.Va. Med. Soc., W.Va. Neurosurg. Soc. (v.p.), Am. Trauma Soc., Am. Assn. of Neurol. Surgeons, Jacob Schwinn Study Club, Alpha Omega Alpha, Alpha Epsilon Delta, Phi Kappa Phi. Republican. Roman Catholic. Office: 40 Medical Park Ste 406 Wheeling WV 26003-6392

MARR, KENDALL CHEN, physician, cardiologist; b. N.Y.C., Mar. 10, 1948; s. Gilbert and Margaret Marr; m. Lianne C. Marr, Aug. 7, 1970; children: Jonathan, Cara Ann. BS, MIT, 1969; MD, Johns Hopkins U., 1973. Diplomate in internal medicine and cardiovascular disease Am. Bd. Internal Medicine. Resident in medicine Cleve. Met. Hosp., 1973-75; clin. assoc. Nat. Cancer Inst., Nat. Heart, Lung & Blood Inst., NIH, Bethesda, Md., 1975-77; clin. fellow dept. cardiology Cedars-Sinai Med. Ctr., L.A., 1977-79; clin. cardiologist West Hills (Calif.) Med. Group, 1979—; co-dir. dept. cardiology West Hills Regional Med. Ctr., 1992—, chair dept. medicine, 1984-85. Lt. comdr. USPHS, 1975-77. Fellow ACP, Am. Coll. Cardiology. Office: West Hills Med Group 7230 Med Ctr Dr 5th Fl West Hills CA 91307

MARRA, SAMUEL PATRICK, retired pharmacist, small business owner; b. Sault Ste Marie, Mich., Apr. 15, 1927; s. Leonard and Nancy (Clement); m. Jeanette L. Rohr, Sept. 2, 1949; children: Rebecca, Nancy, David, Dana, Janet. BS in Pharmacy, Ferris State Coll., 1949. bd. dirs. Chem. Bank, No. States Bancshares, Chem. Bank North. Bd. dirs. Houghton Lake Edn. Found.; pres. Houghton Lake Grenadier Band; co-chmn. Scheutte for Congress, Roscommon County, 1984, 86. Mem. Nat. Assn. Retail Druggists. Republican. Home: 10672 W Houghton Lake Dr Houghton Lake MI 48629-9725

MARRIOTT, MARCIA ANN, human resources administrator, educator, consultant; b. Rochester, N.Y., Mar. 21, 1947; d. Coyne and Alice (Schepler) M.; children: Brian, Jonathan. AA, Monroe C.C., Rochester, 1967; BS, SUNY, Brockport, 1970, MA, 1975; PhD, S.W. U. La., 1985. Program adminstr. N.Y. Dept. of Labor, N.Y.C., 1970-75; employment mgr. Rochester Gen. Hosp., 1975-77, salary adminstr., 1982—; dir. wage and salary dept. Gannett Newspapers, Rochester, 1977-80; compensation and benefits adminstr. Sybron Corp., Rochester, 1980-82; instr. N.Y. State Sch. Indsl. Rels., Cornell U., N.Y.C., 1976-79; assoc. prof. Rochester Inst. Tech., 1978—, Monroe C.C., 1981—, dir. career adv. coun., 1989—; cons. in field; dir. Rochester Presbyn. Home, 1987-91, 96—; dir. area hosp. coun. Kidney Svc. Ctrs., Rochester, 1988-91. Author: (pamphlets) Guideline for Writing Job Descriptions, 1983, Redesigning the Performance Appraisal, 1996, Skill Based Job Descriptions for Sterile Processing Technicians: A Total Quality Approach, 1994, (manual) Career Planning Manual, 1985, (booklet) Guideline for Writing Criteria-Based Job Descriptions, 1988, Skill-based Job Descriptions: A Quality Approach, 1994, Redesigning the Performance Appraisal Process, 1996. Campaign mgr. Carter Campaign Commn., Rochester, 1975; mem. coun. Messiah Luth. Ch., Rochester, 1991-94. Davenport-Hatch Found. grantee, 1973, Wegman Found. grantee, 1975. Mem. Am. Compensation Assn., Single Adopted Parents Group (pres. 1988-93). Office: Rochester Gen Hosp 1425 Portland Ave Rochester NY 14621-3001

MARROCCO, GUY RUSSELL, pathologist; b. N.Y.C., Apr. 2, 1938; s. Guy D. Marrocco and Antoinette R. (Gulli) Mackray; m. Sigrun Eyle; 1 child, Christopher. BS, Columbia U., 1960; MD, U. Bologna, 1965; MPH, U. Mass., 1989. Diplomate Am. Bd. Pathology. Intern Bklyn. Cumberland Med. Ctr., N.Y.C., 1965-66; resident in pathology U. Vt. Med. Ctr., Burlington, 1970-75; cons. pathologist Project Hope, Montego Bay, W.I., 1975-76; pathologist Cooley Dicksinson Hosp., Northampton, Mass., 1976—; cons. pathologist Kabul Afghanistan Care Medico, 1973, Care Medico, ICA Pedu, Quitos, Peru, 1981-83, AMI, Saudi Arabia, 1982; physician Himalayan Health Care, Tibling Nepal, 1993-95. Bd. dirs. Riverside Industries, Easthampton, Mass., 1991—. Maj. U.S. Army, 1966-70. Fellow Am. Soc. Clin. Pathologists, Coll. of Am. Pathologists, Internat. Acad. of Pathology; mem. Mass. Med. Soc., Paleo Pathology Assn. Democrat. Roman Catholic. Home: 41 Columbus Ave Northampton MA 01060

MARRS, CARL FREDERICK, microbiology educator; b. Seattle, Oct. 7, 1953; s. Carl L. and Patricia (Cardwell) M.; m. Julia E. Richards, Mar. 28, 1981; children: Adrian, Colin. BS in Chemistry, U. Wash., 1975; PhD in Molecular Biology, U. Wis., 1982. Scientist Cetus-Palo Alto (Calif.) Corp., 1983-84; postdoctoral fellow Stanford (Calif.) U., 1984-85; asst. prof. U. Mich., Ann Arbor, 1985-92, assoc. prof., 1992—. Contbr. articles to profl. jours. Achievements include research studies on bacterial pili, especially type 4 and pili on Haemophilus influenzae and on urinary tract infections. Office: U Mich Dept Epidemiology 109 Observatory St Ann Arbor MI 48109-2029

MARRS, TIMOTHY CLIVE, toxicologist; b. Edenbridge, Kent, England, Aug. 27, 1945; s. Wallace McCabe and Barbara Nancy (Hobson) M. BM, BCh, London U., 1968, MSc, 1975, MD, 1978, DSc, 1995. Intern Westminster Med. Sch., London, 1969, resident pathologist, 1970-75; intern West Middlesex Hosp., London, 1969; cons. pathologist St. Steven's Hosp., London, 1975-80; med. officer Ministry of Def., Salisbury, England, 1980-84, sr. med. officer, 1984-90, 90—. Editor: Clinical and Experimental Toxicology of Cyanides, 1987, Clinical and Experimental Toxicology of Organophosphates, 1991, A Textbook of Basic and Applied Toxicology, 1994, Chemical Warfare Agents Toxicology and Treatment, 1996. Fellow Royal Soc. Medicine, Royal Coll. Pathologists; mem. Soc. Toxicology, British Toxicology Soc. Home: Pinehurst Four-Elms Rd, Edenbridge TN8 6AQ, England Office: Skipton House Dept Health, London Rd, London SE1 6LW, England

MARSALISI, FRANK BERNARD, obstetrician-gynecologist; b. N.Y.C., Feb. 11, 1955; s. Bernard J. and Margaret (Sievers) M.; m. Elinor Miranda, June 21, 1978; children: Elinor Clarissa, Frank Phillip, Christina Danielle, Priscilla Alexis. BS in Biology, Fordham U., 1977; MD, Mich. State U., 1983; postgrad., U. South Fla., 1987. Diplomate Am. Bd. Ob-Gyn., Nat. Bd. Med. Examiners. Rsch. asst. USV Pharm., Tuckahoe, N.Y., 1977-78; rsch. assoc. Upjohn Co., Kalamazoo, Mich., 1978-79; resident dept. ob-gyn. U. South Fla/Tampa Gen. Hosp., 1983-87; adminstrv. chief resident dept. ob-gyn U. South Fla., Tampa, 1986-87, clin. asst. prof., 1988—; dir. ob-gyn. Ruskin Migrant and Cmty. Health Ctr., Ruskin, Fla., 1987-91; dir. gynecology, ob-gyn. residency program Bayfront Med. Ctr., St. Petersburg, Fla., 1991—; sec.-treas. ob-gyn. sect. Tampa Gen. Hosp., 1990-91. Contbr. articles to profl. jours. Recipient Regional Health Adminstr.'s award USPHS, 1991, Nat. Faculty award Coun. on Resident Edn. in Ob-Gyn., 1994; named Tchr. of Yr. Bayfront Med. Ctr., 1992, 93. Fellow ACOG; mem. AMA, Am. Uro-Gynecologic Soc., Fla. Ob-Gyn. Soc., Phi Beta Kappa. Office: 500 7th St S Saint Petersburg FL 33701

MARSCHALL, MATTHIAS LAJOS, anesthesiologist; b. Masonmagyaróvár, Hungary, Oct. 25, 1946; arrived in Germany, 1972; s. Lajos and Marta (Marossy) M.; m. Dagmar D. Berg, Mar. 29, 1974; children: Kendra, Melanie. MD, Semmelweis Med. Sch., Budapest, Hungary, 1971. Diplomate German Bd. Anesthesiology. Intern in pediats., ob/gyn., surgery, neurology, psychiatry, and internal medicine Tchg. Hosp. Semmelweis Med. Sch., Budapest, Hungary, 1970-71; resident dept. surgery Postgrad. Med. Sch., Budapest, 1971-72; resident dept. anesthesiology U. Dusseldorf, Fed. Republic Germany, 1972-77, Harvard Med. Sch., Boston, 1978-79; assoc. dir. anesthesiology Southampton Hosp., L.I., N.Y., 1979-80; sr. assoc. anesthesia Sarepta Hosp., Bielefeld, Fed. Republic Germany, 1980-83; chief anesthesia Evang. Hosp., Wulfrath, Fed. Republic Germany, 1983-92; pvt. practice anesthesiology Cologne and Dusseldorf, Germany, 1993—. Mem. Internat. Assn. for Study of Pain. Roman Catholic. Office: Königsallee 60F, 40212 Düsseldorf Germany

MARSH, CLARE TEITGEN, retired school psychologist; b. Manitowoc, Wis., July 7, 1934; d. Clarence Emil and Dorothy (Napiezinski) Teitgen; m. Robert Irving Marsh, Jan. 30, 1955; children: David, Wendy Marsh Tootle, Julie Marsh Domino, Laura Marsh Beltrame. MS in Ednl. Psychology, U. Wis., Milw., 1968. Sch. psychologist Milw. Pub. Schs., 1975-76; lead psychologist West Allis (Wis.)-West Milw. Pub. Schs., 1968-95; sch. psychologist Wauwatosa (Wis.) Pub. Schs., 1987; instr. Milw. Sch. Engring., 1989-90, Alverno Coll., 1990-91. NDEA fellow, 1966-68. Mem. Internat. Sch. Psychologists Assn., Nat. Assn. Sch. Psychologists (del.), Suburban Assn. Sch. Psychologists (pres. 1976-77, 86-87), Wis. Assn. Sch. Psychologists (pres. 1990-91, chmn. membership com. 1980-84, sec. 1985-89, chmn. conv. 1987), Wis. Fedn. Pupil Svcs., Phi Kappa Phi, Pi Lambda Theta (pres.), Kappa Delta Pi, Phi Delta Kappa, Sigma Tau Delta, Alpha Chi Omega. Home: 14140 W Honey Ln New Berlin WI 53151-2442

MARSH, DAVID, medical products company executive; b. Bayonne, N.J., Jan. 23, 1945; s. Harry Joseph and Stephanie (Bachinsky) M.; m. Carol Jakuboski, Dec. 15, 1968. BA, Seton Hall U., 1966. Regional sales mgr. Terumo Corp., Piscataway, N.J., 1979-80; mktg. mgr. Terumo Corp., Piscataway, 1980-83, nat. sales mgr., 1983-84; nat. sales mgr. Renal Systems, Inc., Mpls., 1984-85; pres. David Marsh Assocs., Long Valley, N.J., 1985-86; sales and mktg. mgr. Kestrel div. of Ryder Internat. Corp., Arab, Ala., 1986-89; dir. of sales Toray Mktg. & Sales (Am.), Inc., N.Y.C., 1989-90; dir. sales and mktg. Toray Mktg. and Sales (Am.), Inc., Houston, Tex., 1990-94, dir. med. device dept., 1995—. With USAR, 1966-72. Mem. Acad. for Health Svcs. Mktg., Am. Mktg. Assn., Assn. for Advancement of Med. Instrumentation, Nat. Renal Adminstrs. Assn., Nat. Assn. Nephrology Technologists. Republican. Roman Catholic. Home: 95 W Wedgemere Cir The Woodlands TX 77381-4194

MARSH, DONALD JAY, college dean, medical educator; b. N.Y.C., Aug. 5, 1934; m. Wendy G. Clough; 2 children. AB, U. Calif., Berkeley, 1955; MD, U. Calif., San Francisco, 1958. Intern in medicine UCLA Hosp., 1958-59; postdoctoral fellow dept. physiology NYU, 1959-60, instr. dept. physiology, 1960-61, asst. prof. physiology and biophysics, 1963-67, assoc. prof. physiology and biophysics, 1967-71; prof. biomed. engring. U. So. Calif., 1971-92, prof., chmn. dept. physiology and biophysics, 1978-92, prof. medicine, 1982-92, rsch. prof. physiology and biophysics, 1992—; prof. physiology Brown U., Providence, 1992—, dean medicine and biol. scis., 1992—, Frank L. Day prof. biology, 1995—; mem. engring. in medicine and biology tng. com. NIH, 1973, cardiovascular renal study sect., 1983-86, ad hoc mem. med. lab. scis. rev. com., 1976, inst. gen. med. scis. adv. com., 1982; ad hoc reviewer NSF; mem. rsch. com. Am. Heart Assn., 1979-82, rev. coms. for grants-in-aid, pub. affairs com., 1986-88; cons. com. interdisciplinary rsch. Nat. Rsch. Coun.- Inst. of Medicine, 1989; mem. med. schs. sect. task force AMA, 1994—; lectr. in field. Mem. editorial bd. Annals of Biomed. Engring., 1972-74, mng. editor, 1974-78; mem. editorial bd. Am. Jour. Physiology and Jour. of Applied Physiology, 1972-76, Am. Jour. Physiology: Regulatory, Integrative and Comparative Physiology, 1977-79, Am. Jour. Physiology: Renal, Fluid and Electrolyte Physiology, 1977-82, 88-94, Am. Jour. Physiology: Modelling Methodology Forum, 1984-91; guest reviewer Biophys. Jour., Circulation Rsch., Jour. Clin. Investigation, Jour Theoretical Biology, Kidney Internat., Sci., Pfluegers Archiv European Jour. Physiology; contbr. articles to profl. jours., chpts. to books. Named Career Scientist, Health Rsch. Coun. N.Y., 1964-71; Spl. fellow NIH, 1970-71; NIH grantee, 1963—. Fellow AAAS; mem. Assn. Am. Med. Colls. (coun. of deans), Am. Soc. Nephrology, Am. Physiol. Soc. (com. on coms. 1980-83, chmn. renal sect. 1982-83, long range planning com. 1990-93), Biophys. Soc., Microvascular Soc., Soc. Gen. Physiologists, Soc. Math. Biology (nominating com. 1983, publs. com. 1984-85, bd. dirs. 1986-88), Alpha Omega Alpha. Home: 148 Pratt St Providence RI 02906-1411 Office: Brown U Sch of Medicine Box G-A1 Providence RI 02912

MARSH, JOHN CHARLES, physician, educator; b. Richmond, Va., Sept. 17, 1933; s. Charles Franklin and Chloro Nancy (Thurman) M.; m. Carol Jean Butters, June 16, 1956; children: David, Virginia, John. BS, Coll. of William and Mary, 1955; MD cum laude, Yale U., 1959. Diplomate Am. Bd. Internal Medicine; subspecialty in medical oncology. Intern, asst. resident Boston City Hosp., 1959-61; clin. assoc. Nat. Cancer Inst., Bethesda, Md., 1961-63; clin. fellow, hematology U. Utah, Salt Lake City, 1963-64, chief clin. fellow, 1964-65, rsch. fellow, hematology, 1965-67; asst. prof. medicine and pharmacology Yale U., New Haven, Conn., 1967-70, assoc. prof. medicine and pharmacology, 1970-77, prof. of medicine and lectr. in pharmacology, 1977—; dir. Yale GI Cancer Unit, Yale Cancer Ctr., New Haven, 1986—; acting chief, med. oncology and hematology, dir. Cancer Ctr., West Haven VA Med. Ctr., Conn., 1991-93; prin. investigator Ea. Coop. Oncology Group, New Haven, 1973—. Author/co-editor: (book) Cancer Therapy, 1982; contbg. author books in field; contbr. articles to profl. jours. Pres. Am. Cancer Soc., Conn. Divsn., 1987; chmn. adminstrv. bd. First and Summerfield United Meth. Ch., New Haven, 1988-95. Capt. USPHS, 1961-63, Bethesda. Recipient Bronze medal Am. Cancer Soc., Conn., 1987. Mem. Am. Soc. Clin. Oncology (mem. com. 1975-76), Am. Assn. for Cancer Rsch., Am. Soc. Hematology (mem. chmn. 1971-73), Am. Fedn. Clin. Rsch., Internat. Soc. Hematology, Phi Beta Kappa, Alpha Omega Alpha. Democrat. Methodist. Home: 43 Marion Dr North Haven CT 06473 Office: Yale Sch of Medicine Sect of Medical Oncology 333 Cedar Street Box 208032 New Haven CT 06520-8032

MARSH, TODD ALLEN, medical administrator; b. Jacksonville, Fla., Dec. 30, 1969. B of Health Scis., U. Ky., 1994. Lic. nursing home adminstr., Ky. Asst. adminstr. Regency Health Care Ctr., Louisville, 1993-94; adminstr. Klondike Manor Health Care Ctr., Louisville, 1994—. Mem. Am. Coll. Health Care Adminstrs., Ky. Assn. Health Care Facilities (legis. com. 1995). Home: 1091 Mallard Creek Louisville KY 40207 Office: Klondike Manor 3802 Klondike Ln Louisville KY 40218

MARSH, WILLIAM LAURENCE, retired research pathology executive; b. Cardiff, Wales, Great Britain, Apr. 21, 1926; came to U.S., 1969; s. William and Violet (Hill) M.; m. Jean Beryl Margaret Hill, June 6, 1952; children: Christine Margaret, Nicholas John. Fellow, Inst. Med. Lab. Sci., London, 1954, Inst. Biology, London, 1969; PhD, Columbia Pacific U., 1968; fellow, Royal Coll. Pathologists, London, 1985. Lab. chief Regional Blood Transfusion Ctr., Brentwood, Eng., 1955-69; assoc. investigator N.Y. Blood Ctr., N.Y.C., 1969-79, investigator, 1980-83, sr. investigator, 1984-87; sr. v.p. rsch. Lindsley Kimball Rsch. Inst. of N.Y. Blood Ctr., N.Y.C., 1987-94; ret.; editorial bd. Transfusion jour., 1979-91, Blood Transfusion and Immunohematology jour., 1980-86; sci. reviewer various jours. Author chpts. on human blood groups in textbooks, 1965-91; contbr. over 250 articles to profl. jours. Recipient Blood Donors award of merit Blood Donor Assn., Eng., 1961. Fellow Inst. Med. Lab. Sci. (Race prize 1976), Inst. Biology, Royal Coll. Pathologists; mem. Internat. Soc. Blood Tranfusion, Am. Assn. Blood Banks (Dunsford Meml. award 1975, Emily Cooley award 1988, Grove-Rasmussen award 1990, Karl Landsteiner award 1995), Am. Soc. Clin. Pathologists (Philip Levine Outstanding Rsch. award 1993), Brit. Soc. Hematology, Brit. Soc. Blood Transfusion. Home: 101 Hillcrest Dr Moneta VA 24121-3003 Office: NY Blood Ctr S310 E 67th St New York NY 10021-6204

MARSHAK, HILARY WALLACH, psychotherapist, owner; b. N.Y.C., May 27, 1950; d. Irving Isaac and Suni (Fox) Wallach; m. Harvey Marshak, Jan. 1, 1981; children: Emily Fox, Jacob Randall. BA, U. Conn., Storrs, 1973; MSW, N.Y.U., 1992; cert., Inst. for Study of Culture, and Ethnicity, N.Y.C., 1994. Cert. social worker, N.Y. Tchr. English Glastonbury (Conn.) High Sch., 1973, U. Autonoma de Guerrero, Acapulco, Mexico, 1974; adminstrv. asst. 4M Pub. Svcs. Corp., N.Y.C., 1975, bus. mgr.; exec. v.p. Vitalmedia Enterprises Inc., N.Y.C., 1977-87, pres., chief exec. officer, 1987—; psychotherapist Fifth Ave. Ctr. Counseling and Psychotherapy, N.Y.C., 1992-95; pvt. practice N.Y.C., 1992—; mktg. cons. Frana Ltd., London, 1988-89. Editor: Before the Bar, 1978-80, Guide to Higher Edn., 1980; reviewer vol 32, The Jour. of Sex Rsch. Founder Women's Radical Caucus, U. Conn., 1970; broadcaster Sta. WHUS; bd. dirs. N.Y. Theater Ballet, 1990—, Am. AIDS Assn., 1992—; mem. writers coun. Writers in Performance series Manhattan Theater Club. Recipient 2nd Place Flowers Ulster County Agrl. Fair, New Paltz, N.Y., 1987, 1st Place Herbs, 1988. Mem. NASW, Am. AIDS Assn. (bd. dirs. 1992—), Soc. for Sci. Study of Sex, Sex Edn. and Info. Coun. of U.S., Nat. Coun. Family Rels. Jewish. Home and Office: 95 Horatio St Apt 629 New York NY 10014-1533

MARSHAK, ROBERT REUBEN, former university dean, medical educator, veterinarian; b. N.Y.C., Feb. 23, 1923; s. David and Edith (Youselovsky) M.; m. Ruth Emilie Lyons, Dec. 4, 1948; children: William Lyons, John Ball, Richard Best.; m. Margo Post Marshall, June 25, 1983. Student, U. Wis., 1940-41; D.V.M., Cornell U., 1945; D.V.M. (hon.), U. Bern, 1968; M.A. (hon.), U. Pa., 1971. Diplomate: Am. Coll. Vet. Internal Medicine (charter). Practice vet. medicine Springfield, Vt., 1945-56; prof., chmn. dept. medicine Sch. Vet. Medicine, U. Pa., Phila., 1956-58; prof. medicine Grad. Sch. Medicine, 1957-64; chmn. dept. clin. studies Sch. Vet. Medicine, 1958-73; dir. Bovine Leukemia Research Center, 1965-73; dean Sch. Vet. Medicine, 1973-87; co-dir. Center on Interactions Animals and Soc., 1975-79, also mem. grad. group com. in comparative med. scis.; prof. medicine, chief sect. epidemiology and pub. health Sch. Vet. Medicine U. Pa., 1990-93, prof. medicine emeritus, 1993—; mem. adv. bd. Pa. Dept. Agr., 1973-87; chmn. Gov.'s Study Group on Horse Racing Industry in Pa., 1979; mem. del. to evaluate vet. med. and rsch. Chinese Ministry Agr.; mem. adv. com. Stroud Water Rsch. Ctr., 1992—; mem. adv. coun. Coll. Vet. Medicine, Cornell U., 1993—. Sr. co-editor Advances in Veterinary Science and Comparative Medicine; contbr. numerous articles to sci. jours. Bd. dirs. Humane Soc. U.S., 1978-82, Bide-a-wee Home Assn., 1980-85; sci. adv. bd. mem. Sch. Vet. Medicine The Hebrew U., Jerusalem, 1984—; chmn. external com. Sch. Vet. Medicine Tuskegee U.; trustee Upland Country Day Sch., 1988-91; mem. animal adv. com. City of Phila., 1989-93. Served with AUS, 1943-44. Recipient Disting. Veterinarian award Pa. Vet. Med. Assn., 1984, Barnraiser award Pa. Farmers Assn., 1987. Fellow Phila. Coll. Physicians; mem. AAAS, John Morgan Soc. (pres. 1967-68), Am. Assn. Cancer Rsch., Am. Vet. Med. Assn., Pa. Vet. Med. Assn, NAS Inst. Medicine (sr.), Pa. Livestock Assn. (dir.), Westminster Kennel Club, James A. Baker Inst. for Animal Health (mem. adv. coun. 1977—), Phila. Soc. for Promoting Agr., Pa. Friends of Agr. Found., Phila. Zool. Soc. (bd. dirs. 1986-87), Sigma Xi, Phi Zeta.

MARSHALL, BARRY JAMES, gastroenterologist; b. Kalgoorlie, Western Australia, Australia, Sept. 30, 1951; came to U.S., 1986; s. Robert William and Marjory Jean (Donald) M.; m. Adrienne Joyce Feldman, Dec. 27, 1972; children: Luke, Bronwyn, Caroline, Jessica. MBBS, U. Western Australia, Perth, 1974, postgrad., 1986. Intern Sir Charles Gairdner Hosp., Western Australia, 1975-76, resident, 1976-77, med. registrar, 1977-78; med. registrar Royal Perth Hosp., Western Australia, 1979-82; med. registrar Fremantle Hosp., Western Australia, 1983-84, microbiology register, 1984; research scientist Royal Perth Hosp., Western Australia, 1985-86; research fellow U. Va. Sch. Med., Charlottesville, 1986-87, asst. prof. medicine, 1988—; cons. Procter and Gamble Co., Cin., 1984—, Delta West Perth, 1985—; bd. dirs. JARM Pty. Ltd., Perth, 1987—. Inventor Clotest (rapid urease test), 1985, Carbon-14 Urea Breath Test, 1985; co-discoverer Helicobacter Pylori bacilli in stomach of patients with gastritis and peptic ulcers, 1984; first person to culture Helicobacter Pylori bacilli. Named one of Outstanding West Australians, Perth Jaycees, 1985; research grantee Australian Nat. Health and Med. Research Council, 1985-86; recipient Albert Lasker Clinical Medical Rsch. award Albert and Mary Lasker Foundation, 1995. Fellow Royal Australian Coll. Physicians, Am. Coll. Gastroenterology; mem. Australian Med. Assn., Australian Gastroent. Soc. Office: U Va Med Ctr Dept Internal Medicine PO Box 145 Charlottesville VA 22908

MARSHALL, COURTNEY ALLEN, health services administrator; b. Machias, Maine, Sept. 18, 1950; m. Sandra K. Marshall, Sept. 10, 1987; children: Ilana, Danielle. BA, Stanford U., 1972; MBA, Ind. U., 1982. Lic. health adminstr. Occupl. therapist The Counseling Ctr., Bangor, Maine, 1972-74; psychiat. technician Bloomington (Ind.) Hosp., 1972-76; asst. adminstr. Marshall Health Care, Machias, Maine, 1977; med. records supr. Ind. U., 1978-83; adminstr. Forum Group Inc., Wilmington, Del., 1983-86, Beverly Enterprises, Wilmington, Del., 1986-88; life ins. agt. Prudential/ United, Wilmington, Del., 1988-90; social worker/quality control specialist State of Del., Wilmington, 1990-94; adminstr. Emily Bissell Hosp. and Gov. Bacon Health Ctr., Wilmington, 1994—; adminstr. cons., Del., 1986-90. Candidate Prattville (Ala.) City Coun., 1983. Mem. Am. Coll. of Health Care Adminstrs., Stanford Alumni Assn. (life). Home: 404 Baynard Blvd Wilmington DE 19803 Office: 3000 Newport Gap Pike Wilmington DE 19808

MARSHALL, DAVID, orthodontist; b. Syracuse, N.Y., Feb. 4, 1914; s. Moses and Fanny (Bagelman) Salutsky; B.S., Syracuse U., 1932-35; D.D.S., U. Md., 1938-42; postgrad. Columbia, 1943-45, Tufts Coll., Northwestern U.; children from previous marriage: Robert Andrew, Howard Randy, Douglas S. (dec.), Susan Beth, Robin (dec.); m. Marjorie Kaufman, Sept. 7, 1973. Practice dentistry specializing in orthodontics, Syracuse, mem. staff St. Joseph's Hosp., Crouse-Irving Hosp., University Hosp., Meml. Hosp.; mem. cons. School Speech, Syracuse U.; orthodontic cons. N.Y. State Health Dept.; lectr. in field, producer sci. exbns., Anat. Mus. Recipient Hektoen medal AMA, 1970. Diplomate Am. Bd. Orthodontists. Fellow Royal Soc. Medicine; mem. ADA, N.Y. Dental Soc., Syracuse Dental Soc., 5th Dist. Dental Soc., Syracuse C. of C., Northeastern (qualifying com.), Am. orthodontists socs., Pierre Fauchard Acad. Contbg. author textbooks dentistry and orthodontics; contbr. articles to dental publs; contbr. work to Anatomical Mus. Home: 5231 Brockway Ln Fayetteville NY 13066-1705 Office: 1124 E Genesee St Syracuse NY 13210-1912

MARSHALL, DON ALFREDO, psychiatrist; b. Frankfurt, Ky., Dec. 26, 1954; s. Don Alfredo Sr. and Roumania (Mason) M. BA, Yale U., 1973, MD, 1977. Asst. med. dir. Meriden (Conn.) Wallingford Hosp., 1981-83; med. dir. Hartford (Conn.) Cmty. Meml. Health Ctr., 1983-86; forensic psychiatrist Greater Cmty. MHC-Springfield (Conn.), 1983-86; psychiatrist pvt. practice, Dayton, Ohio, 1987-90; med. dir. stress ctr. Adams County Meml. Hosp., Decatur, Ind., 1990-95; psychiatrist pvt. practice, Ft. Wayne, Ind., 1990—; assoc. med. dir., med. dir. addictions svcs. Park Ctr., Inc., Ft. Wayne, Ind., 1995—; clin. supr. Addicted Women & Children Program, Ft. Wayne, 1991-94; chmn. med. rev. com. Alcohol Abuse Deterant Program, Ft. Wayne, 1991—, bd. dirs. Mem. Am. Assn. Gen. Hosp. Psychiatrists, Am. Soc. Addiction Medicine, Am. Assn. Med. Rev. Officers (diplomate), NAACP, Urban League. Home: 5010 Southwood Ave Fort Wayne IN 46807 Office: Ft Wayne Psychol Svcs 6131 Stoney Creek Dr Fort Wayne IN 46825

MARSHALL, DONALD THOMAS, medical technologist; b. Omaha, June 9, 1955; s. William A. and Alma J. (Jorgensen) M.; m. Beverly Ann Everett, Sept. 22, 1990. Med. tech., Pikes Peak Inst. Med. Tech., 1977; EMT, Pikes Peak C.C., Colorado Springs, 1979; PhD of Religion, Universal Life Ch., 1995, D of Metaphysics (hon.), 1995. Registered med. technologist; cert. clin. lab. technologist. Technician x-ray/med. St. Joseph Hosp. of Plains, Cheyenne Wells, Colo., 1977-79; technician med. lab. Conejos County Hosp., La Jara, Colo., 1979-84; med. technologist Nat. Health Lab., Englewood, Colo., 1984-91; lab. tech. cons. neighborhood health program Denver Dept. Health and Hosps., 1996—. EMT, fireman La Jara Vol. Fire Dept., 1979-84, Meritorious Svc. Citation, 1983. Mem. Internat. Soc. Clin. Lab. Tech., Am. Med. Technologists, East Denver Masonic Lodge Ancient, Free and Accepted Masons (Master 1994). Republican.

MARSHALL, EDWIN COCHRAN, optometrist, educator; b. Albany, Ga., Mar. 31, 1946; children: Erin, Erika. BA, Ind. U., 1968, OD, 1971, MS, 1979; MPH, U. N.C., 1982. Cert. Ind. Bd. Optometry, Ga. Bd. Optometry. Asst. prof. optometry Ind. U., Bloomington, 1973-77, assoc. prof. optometry, 1977-92, prof. optometry, 1992—, chair clin. scis. Sch. Optometry, 1983-92, assoc. dean Sch. Optometry, 1992—. Prentice Soc. fellow, 1990. Fellow Am. Acad. Optometry (diplomate chair 1990-93); mem. APHA (vision care chair 1988-90), Nat. Optometric Assn. (exec. dir. 1981—), Ind. Optometric Assn. (pub. health dir. 1992—), Nat. Optometric Assn. (pres. 1979-81, (Founders' award 1987), Am. Optometric Assn. (nof. and data chair 1986-89), Black Congress on Health, Law and Econs. (steering com. 1994—), Delta Omega. Office: Ind U Sch Optometry 800 E Atwater Bloomington IN 47405

MARSHALL, FRAY FRANCIS, urology educator; b. N.Y.C., Aug. 27, 1944; s. Victor Fray and Barbara (Walsh) M.; m. Lindsay Wheatley, Oct. 6, 1975; children: Wheatley, Brooks. BA, U. Va., 1965, MD, 1969. Diplomate Am. Bd. Urology. Asst. prof. Urology Johns Hopkins Hosp., Balt., 1975-79, assoc. prof. Urology, 1979-86, prof. Urology, 1986—, dir. adult Urology, 1990—. Editor (books) Urologic Complication, 1990, Textbook of Operative Urology, 1996. Office: Johns Hopkins Hosp Dept Urology Marburg 150 601 N Wolfe St Baltimore MD 21287-2101

MARSHALL, JOHN CROOK, internal medicine educator, researcher; b. Blackburn, Lancashire, Eng., Feb. 28, 1941; came to U.S., 1976; s. Albert Acey and Marion Miller (Crook) M.; m. Marilyn Dallas Parry, Sept. 20, 1969; children—Samantha Jane, Susannah Crook. B.S., Victoria U., Manchester, Eng., 1962, M.B., Ch.B., 1965, M.D., 1973. Diplomate Am. Bd. Internal Medicine, Am. Bd. Endocrinology and Metabolism. Intern Manchester Royal Infirmary, 1965-66; resident Brompton Hosp., Nat. Heart Hosp., London, 1966-69; resident Hammersmith Hosp., 1966-69, research fellow, London, 1969-72; lectr. U. Birmingham, Eng. 1972-76; assoc. prof. internal medicine U. Mich., Ann Arbor, 1976-79, prof., 1979-90; chief endocrinology and metabolism, 1991—; prof. U. Va., Charlottesville, 1987—; sci. counselor NIH, Bethesda, Md., 1983—. Editor Endocrinology Jour., 1979-96; editor: Endocrinology Text, 1990; contbr. articles to profl. jours. NIH grantee 1977-87. Fellow Royal Coll. Physicians, Royal Soc. Medicine, ACP; mem. Central Soc. for Clin. Research (council 1983—), Assn.. Am. Physicians, Am. Soc. for Clin. Investigation, Am. Clin. and Climatological Soc. Anglican. Avocations: vintage racing cars; golf; tennis.

MARSHALL, KEITH, pharmaceutical consultant; b. Leeds, Yorkshire, Eng., June 17, 1929; came to U.S., 1976; s. Thomas George and Dorothy (Bickerdike) M.; widowed; children: Neil Anthony, Carol Louise, Christopher Ian. BSC, London U., 1963; PhD, U. Bradford, 1970. Cert. pharm. chemist. Dir. Risdales Chemists, Leeds, Eng., 1954-56; lectr. Bradford Inst. Tech., Eng., 1956-60; head indsl. pharmacy unit U. Bradford, Eng., 1960-76; research dir. Colorcon Inc., Westpoint, Pa., 1976-78; dir. Inst. Applied Pharm.Scis., East Brunswick, N.J., 1978-83; assoc. dir. Smith Kline & French Labs., Phila., 1983-92; pres. Keith Marshall Assocs. Cons. Firm, 1992—; adj. prof. U. R.I., Kingston, 1985—, Phila. Coll. Pharmacy and Sci., 1986—, U. Md., 1994—. Author: Modern Pharmaceutics, 1987, Industrial Pharmacy: Theory and Practice, 1987. Served with M.C., Brit. Army, 1948-50. Fellow Assn. Am. Pharm. Scientists; mem. Royal Pharm. Soc. Gt. Britain, Fedn. Internat. Pharmacy. Home: 10 Royal Dr Brick NJ 08723-6731 Office: 144 Tices Lane East Brunswick NJ 08816

MARSHALL, KENNETH ALLAN, plastic and reconstructive surgeon; b. Boston, Dec. 28, 1938; s. Nathan Harold and Mary (Elizabeth) Creagh; m. JoAnne T. Burrows, Feb. 10, 1968; children: Torrey A., C. Adrian. AB, Harvard U., 1960; MD, Columbia U., 1964. Diplomate Am. Bd. Surgery, Am. Bd. Plastic Surgery. Resident in gen. surgery Harvard Surg. Svc., 1964-66, Boston City Hosp., 1969-72; fellow Shriners Burns Inst., Mass. Gen. Hosp., Boston, 1970; resident in plastic surgery U. Va., Charlottesville, 1973-75; pvt. practice Cambridge and Boston, Mass., 1975—; instr. in surgery Harvard Med. Sch., Cambridge, 1975-83, asst. prof. surgery, 1983—; chief div. of plastic surgery Mt. Auburn Hosp., Cambridge, 1990—. Contbr. articles to profl. jours. Lt. comdr. USNR, 1966-69. Mem. ACS, Am. Soc. Plastic and Reconstructive Surgery, Am. Burn Assn., Plastic Surg. Rsch. Coun., Am. Assn. Plastic Surgeons, Mass. Med. Soc., New Eng. Soc. Plastic Surgery (pres. 1993-94), Northeastern Soc. Plastic Surgery, Mass. Soc. Plastic Surgery (sec. 1985-89, pres. 1989-91), Am. Assn. Hand Surgery, New Eng. Soc. Plastic Reconstructive Surgery (sec.-treas. 1991—, pres. 1993-94). Office: Drs Office Bldg 300 Mount Auburn St Ste 306 Cambridge MA 02138-5600

MARSHALL, L. B., clinical lab scientist; b. Chgo., Feb. 10; s. Gillman and Ethel (Robinson) M.; m. Esther Wood, Sept. 28, 1961; children: Lester B. III, Kiti B., Lelani. Grad. U. Calif., Berkeley; AA, City Coll. San Francisco, 1957; BS in Podiatric Medicine, U. Puget Sound, 1961; ScD, London Inst., Eng., 1972. Pres., Med. Offices Health Svcs. Group Inc., San Francisco, 1964—. Mem. NAACP. With U.S. Army, 1947-53. Decorated Bronze Star, Med. Combat Badge; recipient Cert. Appreciation Pres. Nixon, 1973, Urban League, 1973, Calif. Dept. Human Resources, 1973. Mem. Am. Calif. Assns. Med. Technologists, Calif. State Sheriff's Assn. (assoc.), Oyster Point Yacht Club, Press Club, Commonwealth Club (San Francisco).

MARSHALL, LAURENCE PAUL, social services administrator; b. Portland, Maine, Aug. 12, 1951; s. James Edward and Jane Wynne (Horslin) M.; 1 child, Luke Paul. BA in Social Work, U. So. Maine, 1973; MSW, U. Louisville, 1976. Cert. social worker. Rsch. technician Human Svcs. Dept. Inst., Portland, 1973-75; dir. discharge planning and aftercare Elan One, Poland Spring, Maine, 1976-80; regional planner Maine Dept. Mental Health, Augusta, 1980-82; program dir. Four County Mental Health Svcs., St. Charles, Mo., 1982-85; dir. Friendship House, Dover, N.H., 1985-89, Pioneer House, Salem, Mass., 1989—; mem. faculty Nat. Clubhouse Expansion Project, N.Y.C., 1988—. Mem. Nat. Assn. Social Workers. Home: 151 Indigo Hill Rd Somersworth NH 03878-3018 Office: Pioneer House 34 St Peter St Salem MA 01970-3820

MARSHALL, PHYLLIS ELLINWOOD, mental health system executive, consultant; b. Kansas City, Mo., Dec. 20, 1929; d. Herbert Dwight and Mildred (Gillham) Ellinwood; m. John D. Reich, July 1, 1950 (div. 1964); children: Martha Reich Millican, Michael David, Donald Martin; m. C. Randolph Marshall, Nov. 27, 1969. BA, Washington U., St. Louis, 1951, MSW., 1969. Adult program dir. St. Louis YWCA, 1962-64, dir. decentralized programs, 1964-67; alcoholism caseworker Malcolm Bliss Mental Health Ctr., St. Louis, 1968; exec. dir. Cobb County YWCA, Ga., 1969-72; dir. Coastal Area Cmty. Mental Health Ctr., Brunswick, Ga., 1973-77; dir. Mental Health Svcs., Ga. Dept. Human Resources, Atlanta, 1977-84; exec. dir. Integrated Mental Health, Inc., Rochester, N.Y., 1984-92; exec. dir. No. Va. Mental Health Inst., 1992-95; mgr. MHMRSA Reorgn. Alexandria, Va., 1995—; cons. NIMH, Washington, 1979-84, So. Regional Edn. Bd., Atlanta, 1979-84, N.Y. State Office Mental Health, Albany, 1980-84, State of Ill. Dept. Mental Health, 1988, WHO, 1989, Ont., Can., 1990-91, The Netherlands, 1991-92, independent behavioral health cons., 1996—; with mental health programs in Ohio, Mich., Ariz., Md., S.C.; rep. to health care reform com. Mental Health Liaison Group; co-chair Metro Atlanta Deinstitutionalization Task Force, 1983-85; bd. dirs. Children Have All Rights, Legal, Ednl. and Emotional, Menninger Found. project, Atlanta, 1983-84; bd. dirs. Fingerlakes Health Systems Agy., Rochester, 1985-92, bd. dirs., 1991-92; adviser WHO, 1989; chair Monroe County Adv. Com. on Women's Issues, 1992, chmn., 1991-92; mem. mental health liaison group Com. on Health Care Reform, Washington, 1994—. Contbg. author: Perspectives in Mental Health, 1980, New Directions for Mental Health Svcs., 1988, New Frontiers in Mental Health, 1989; contbr. articles to profl. publs. Bd. dirs. Human Resources Credit Union, Atlanta, 1982-84. Recipient Boss of Yr. award Brunswick Jaycees, 1977, Good Friend award Brunswick Mental Health Assn., 1977, Cmty. Mental Health award Atlanta U., 1980, Outstanding Achievement award Am. Soc. for Pub. Adminstrn., 1990. Mem. AAUW (chpt. pres. 1978), Assn. Mental Health Adminstrs. (chair health policy com. 1995—), Ga. Assn. Community Mental Health Ctrs. (pres. 1975-77), Rochester Women's Network (bd. dirs., treas. 1990-92). Avocations: ocean sailing, music, tennis.

MARSHALL, RICHARD EDWARD, medical educator; b. Long Beach, N.Y., July 30, 1933; s. Robert E. M. and Florence (Klein) House; m. Judy M. Moftey, June 22, 1958; children: Linda Kathy. BA, Wesleyan U., 1954; MD, Yale U., 1962. Intern Barnes Hosp., St. Louis, 1962-63; resident Nadwar Heart Inst., Bethesda, Md., 1963-67, U. Wash., Seattle, 1967-71; asst. prof. Washington U., St. Louis, 1981-86; prof. Case Western Res. U., Cleve., 1986-89; prof. Mich. State Med. Sch., East Lansing, 1989-91, dir. pediatrics, 1991-93; dir. neonatal, maternity & ob-gyn. depts. Newark Med. Sch., 1993—. Mem. Soc. Emergency Physicians, Phi Beta Kappa, Sigma Xi. Home: 21 Alpine Dr Morristown NH 01960 Office: Newark Med Sch 189 S Orange Ave Newark NJ 07103

MARSHALL, ROBERT JOSEPH, psychologist, psychoanalyst; b. Passaic, N.J., Nov. 15, 1928; s. Joseph S. and Mary (Latosinski) Majuschak; m. Simone Paulette Verniere, Sept. 13, 1953; children: Gabrielle, Annette. BS, Rutgers U., 1950; MS in Edn., CCNY, 1951; PhD, SUNY, Buffalo, 1958; cert. in pschotherapy and psychoanalysis, Postgrad. Ctr. Mental Health, N.Y.C., 1964-68. Diplomate Am. Bd. Profl. Psychologists; lic. psychologist, N.Y. Pvt. practice N.Y.C., 1959—; psychologist Lincoln Hall, Lincolndale, N.Y., 1965-75; mem. faculty Ctr. for Modern Psychoanalytic Studies, N.Y.C., 1985—, Derner Inst., Adelphi U., Garden City, N.Y., 1985—. Author: Resistant Interactions, 1983, (with S. Marshall) Transference-Counter Transference Matrix, 1988. 1st lt. USMSC, 1954-59. Home: 300 E 74th St New York NY 10021-3712 Office: 1150 Fifth Ave Ste 1C New York NY 10128-0724

MARSHALL, STEVEN EDWARD, critical care nurse; b. Rantoul, Ill., Sept. 21, 1972; s. James Raleigh and Linda Sue (Wise) M.; m. Margaret Alice Bailey, Dec. 2, 1993. Student, Danville (Va.) C.C., 1990-91; diploma in Nursing, Danville Regional Med. Ctr. Sch. Nursing, 1993. RN, Va.; ACLS, BLS, Am. Heart Assn. Profl. nursing asst. Piedmont Prime Care, Inc., Danville, 1992-93, RN, 1993; RN ICU/CCU Danville Regional Med. Ctr., Danville, 1993—; RN ICCU Moorehead Meml. Hosp., Eden, 1996—; RN, Va.; CCRN; cert. ACLS BLS. Vol. firefighter Tunstall Vol. Fire Dept., Dry Fork, Va., 1989—. Mem. AACN. Baptist. Home: 4492 Strawberry Rd Chatham VA 24531 Office: Moorehead Meml Hosp ICCU ICU/CCU 117 East Kings Hwy Eden NC 27288

MARSHALL, V. BLAKE, physician; b. Coatesville, Pa., June 17, 1958; s. Virgil Blake and Carol Camella (Swisher) M. Student, Va. Polytechnic Inst., 1976-77; BA, U. of Pa., Phila., 1980; DO, Phila. Coll. Osteopathic Med., 1985. Diplomate Am. Bd. Internal Med. Physician pvt. practice, Palm Beach Gardens, Fla., 1988-94, Paragon Med. Assocs., Ft. Lauderdale, Fla., 1995—. Mem. Med. Adv. Com., Cmty. Rsch. Initiative, Miami. Office: Paragon Med Assocs 3061 E Commercial Blvd Fort Lauderdale FL 33308

MARSHALL, WAYNE KEITH, anesthesiology educator; b. Richmond, Va., Feb. 9, 1948; s. Chester Truman and Lois Ann (Tiller) M.; m. Dale Claire Reynolds, June 18, 1977; children: Meredith Reynolds, Catherine Truman, Whitney Wood. BS in Biology, Va. Poly. Inst. and State U., 1970; MD, Va. Commonwealth U., 1974. Diplomate Am. Bd. Anesthesiology, Nat. Bd. Med. Examiners; bd. cert. in pain mgmt. Surg. intern U. Cin., 1974-75, resident in surgery, 1975-77; resident in anesthesiology U. Va. Coll. Medicine, Charlottesville, 1977-79, rsch. fellow, 1979-80; asst. prof. anesthesia Pa. State U. Coll. Medicine, Hershey, 1980-86, assoc. prof., 1986-95, assoc. clin. dir. oper. rm., 1982-95, dir. pain mgmt. svc., 1984-95, chief divsn. pain mgmt., 1992-95; prof., chmn. dept. anesthesiology Med. Coll. Va., Richmond, 1995—; med. dir. operating rms. MCV Hosp., 1995—; moderator nat. meetings. Mem. editorial bd. Am. Jour. Anesthesiology, 1987—, Jour. Neurosurg. Anesthesiology, 1988—; contbr. articles and abstracts to med. jours. Recipient Antarctic Svc. medal NSF, 1980. Mem. AMA, Soc. Neurosurg. Anesthesia and Critical Care (sec.-treas. 1985-87, v.p. 1987-88, pres. 1989-90, bd. dirs. 1985-91), Assn. Univ. Anesthetists, Am. Soc. Anesthesiologists (del. ASA ho. of dels. 1990-92), Internat. Anesthesia Rsch. Soc., Pa. Soc. Anesthesiology. Republican. Baptist. Office: VCU Med Coll Va Dept Anesthesiology PO Box 980695 Richmond VA 23298-0695

MARSHALL, WILLIAM EMMETT, biotechnology company executive, biochemistry researcher; b. Chgo., July 21, 1935; s. William E. and Margaret (Fitzgerald) M.; m. Bonnie M. Dallman, June 10, 1961; children: Elizabeth, Stephanie, William. BS, U. Ill., 1957, MS, 1959, PhD, 1961. Asst. prof. U. Minn. Med. Sch., Mpls., 1961-67; dir. tech. devel. Gen. Foods Corp., White Plains, N.Y., 1967-83; pres. Microbial Genetics div. Pioneer Hi-Bred Internat. Inc., Johnston, Iowa, 1983-91, pres. Microbial Environ. Svcs. div., 1989-91; pres. Immunom Techs. Inc., Bedford Hills, N.Y., 1991—; mem. Grace Commn. U.S. Govt., 1982-83; chmn. adv. bd. Nat. Agrl. Research and Extension Users, Washington, 1983-88; mem. panel on new devel. in biotech. Office of Tech. Assessment, Washington, 1986-90; vice-chmn bd. dirs. Rodale Inst., Emmaus, Pa., Keystone (Colo.) Adv. Panel on Biotech.; mem. adv. com. on intellectual property matters to Gen. Agreement on Trade and Tariffs; mem. adv. bd. NSF Ctr. for Microbial Ecology, Mich. State U., 1990—; adj. assoc. prof. dept. microbiology N.Y. Med. Coll., Valhalla, 1992—. Contbr. articles to profl. jours.; patentee in field. Recipient award of Merit U. Ill., 1994. Mem. AAAS, Iowa Acad. Sci. (awards and recognition com.). Club: Univ. (Washington). Office: NY Med Coll Dept Microbiology & Immunology Valhalla NY 10507

MARSHALL, WILLIAM GENE, JR., physician, surgeon; b. Henderson, Ky., Jan. 19, 1953; s. William Gene Sr. and Jo Ann (Wolford) M.; m. Marsha Ann Radosevich, Feb. 16, 1985. Student, Johns Hopkins U., 1971-73; MD, U. Ky., 1977. Intern, then resident in gen. surgery U. Ala., Birmingham, 1977-82; fellow thoracic and cardiovascular surgery U. Iowa, Iowa City, 1982-84; asst. prof. surgery Washington U., St. Louis, 1985-88; staff surgeon Watson Clinic, Lakeland, Fla., 1988-90, Hamot Med. Ctr., Erie, Pa., 1990-91; pvt. practice S.E. Cardiovascular Assocs., Dothan, Ala., 1992—. Fellow ACS, Am. Coll. Cardiology, Am. Coll. Chest Physicians; mem. So. Thoracic Surgery Assn., Soc. Thoracic Surgeons, Internat. Soc. Cardiovascular Surgeons, Alpha Omega Alpha. Roman Catholic. Office: Southeastern Cardiovascular 2431 W Main St Ste 1001 Dothan AL 36301-1217

MARSHALL, WILLIS HENRY, psychiatrist; s. Willis Henry Sr. and Pauline Elizabeth (Murphy) M.; m. Carolyn Mae Kowalski; children: Louann Lorinda Marshall Johnson, John Willis. AB cum laude, U. Evansville, 1957; MD, Ind. U., 1961. Intern Detroit Meml. Hosp., 1961-62; resident psychiatry Mental Health Inst., Cherokee, Iowa, 1965-67, 69-70, staff psychiatrist, 1967-69; staff psychiatrist Mental Health Ctr., Muskegon, Mich., 1970-71; pvt. practice psychiatry Madison, Tenn., 1974-85, Bowling Green, Ky., 1987—; staff psychiatrist chief admission svc., staff psychiatrist treatment unit Mid. Tenn. Mental Health Inst., Nashville, 1984-85, staff psychiatrist evaluation unit forensic svcs. div., 1985-87, chief of staff, 1986-87; forensic psychiatrist State of Tenn., 1985-87; part-time staff psychiatrist Ottawa County Mental Health Ctr., Grand Haven, Mich., 1971-73, Tenn. Dept. Mental Health and Mental Retardation Mid. Tenn. Mental Health Inst., Nashville, 1981-83, Lifeskills, Inc., Glasgow, Ky., Franklin, Ky., 1987-89; psychiat. cons. Allegan County Mental Health Ctr., Allegen, Mich., 1973; med. svcs.. cons. dept. of forensic svcs. Mid. Tenn. Mental Health Inst., Nashville, 1983-84; clin. asst. prof. psychiatry dept. allied health Trevecca Nazaraene Coll., Nashville, 1985-87; part-time pvt. practice psychiatry, Muskegon, Mich., 1970-74, Madison, Tenn., 1986-87; assoc. clin. dir. mental health unit Med. Ctr., Bowling Green, Ky., 1987-91; preceptor, asst. clin. prof. physician asst. program U. Ky., 1988-91; acting med. dir. Rivendell Children's Psychiat. Hosp., Bowling Green, 1989; med. dir. adult mental health unit Rivendell of Ky., 1992-94. Commd. officer, surgeon USPHS, 1962-65. Recipient AMA Physicians Recognition award, 1969, 79, 83, 86, 89, 92, Exemplary Psychiatrist award Nat. Alliance for Mentally Ill, 1993. Mem. Am. Psychiat. Assn. (art assn. 1976—), Ky. Med. Assn., Warren County Med. Soc., Am. Profl. Practice Assn., Am. Acad. Clin. Psychiatrists, Am. Physicians Art Assn., NRA, Nat. Geog. Soc., AAA Automobile Club, Gallatin Gun Club, Alpha Omega Alpha. Home: 315 Matlock Pike Bowling Green KY 42104-7431 Office: Commonwealth Med Plz 720 E 2nd St Ste 207 Bowling Green KY 42101-1706

MARSIK, FREDERIC JOHN, microbiologist; b. Camden, N.J., June 22, 1943; s. Ferdinand Vincent and Helen (Reidl) M.; children: Terri Jean, Kristi Ann Marsik McCann. BA, Lebanon Valley Coll., 1965; MS, U. Mo., 1970, PhD, 1973. Diplomate Am. Bd. Med. Microbiology. Postdoctoral clin. microbiology staff Hartford (Conn.) Hosp., 1973-76; asst. prof. Sch. Medicine, U. Va., Charlottesville, 1976-80; tech. dir. microbiology and serology Children's Hosp. Wis., Milw., 1980-84; assoc. prof. microbiology and internal medicine Sch. Medicine, Oral Roberts U., Tulsa, 1984-87; dir. microbiology Crozer-Chester Med. Ctr., Upland, Pa., 1987-88; dir. R&D Becton Dickinson Microbiology Systems, Cockeysville, Md., 1988—; mem. adv. com. Milw. Area Tech. Coll., Milw., 1983-84, Tulsa Jr. Coll., 1985-87; mem. rev. bd. Clin. Lab. Sci. Publ., Washington, 1990—. Contbr. chpts. to textbooks. Treas. Rose Fire Co. and Ambulance Svc., New Freedom, Pa., 1989—; bd. govs. New Freedom Community Ctr., 1989—; mem. adult edn. com. So. York County Sch. Dist., Glen Rock, Pa., 1989—. Lt. col. USAR. Recipient Best Rsch. Project award S.W. Assn. for Clin. Microbiology, 1984. Mem. Am. Soc. Microbiology (mem. lab. practices com. 1990—), Am. Soc. Med. Tech., N.Y. Acad. Scis. Congregationalist. Home: 6 Keesey Rd New Freedom PA 17349-9638 Office: Becton Dickinson 250 Schilling Cir Cockeysville MD 21031-1103

MARSTON, ROBERT QUARLES, university president; b. Toano, Va., Feb. 12, 1923; s. Warren and Helen (Smith) M.; m. Ann Carter Garnett, Dec. 21, 1946; children: Ann, Robert, Wesley. B.S., Va. Mil. Inst., 1943; M.D., Med. Coll. Va., 1947; B.Sc. (Rhodes scholar 1947-49), Oxford (Eng.) U., 1949; B.Sc. 6 hon. degrees. Intern Johns Hopkins Hosp., 1949-50; resident Vanderbilt U. Hosp., 1950-51; resident Med. Coll. Va., 1953-54, asst. prof. medicine, 1954; asst. prof. bacteriology and immunology U. Minn., 1958-59; asso. prof. medicine, asst. dean charge student affairs Med. Coll. Va., 1959-61; dean U. Miss. Sch. Medicine, 1961-66; dir. U. Miss. Sch. Medicine (Med. Center), 1961-65, vice chancellor, 1965-66; asso. dir. div. regional med. programs NIH, 1966-68; adminstr. Fed. Health Services and Mental Health Adminstrn., 1968; dir. NIH, Bethesda, Md., 1968-73; scholar in residence U. Va., Charlottesville, 1973-74; Disting. fellow Inst. of Medicine, Nat. Acad. Scis., 1973-74; pres. U. Fla., 1974-84, pres. emeritus, emeritus prof. medicine, emeritus prof. fish and aquaculture; bd. dirs. Johnson and Johnson, Nat. Bank Alachua, Wackenhut Corp.; chmn. bd. dirs. Cordis Corp.; chmn., mem. Fla. Marine Fisheries Commn. Author articles in field. Chmn. Commn. on Med. Edn. for Robert Wood Found.; chmn. Safety Adv. Bd. Three Mile Island. chmn. adv. com. med. implications of nuclear war NAS; exec. coun. Assn. Am. Med. Coll., 1964-67; past chmn. exec. com. Nat. Assn. State Univs. and Land Grant Colls., chmn., 1982. 1st lt. AUS, 1951-53. Decorated Knight of North Star (Sweden); Markle scholar, 1954-59; hon. fellow Lincoln Coll. Oxford U. Fellow Am. Pub. Health Assn.; mem. Inst. Medicine of NAS, AAAS, Am. Hosp. Assn. (hon.), Nat. Med. Assn. (hon.), Assn. Am. Rhodes Scholars, Assn. Am. Physicians, Assn. Am. Med. Colls. (disting. mem.), Am. Clin. and Climatol. Assn., Soc. Scholars Johns Hopkins, Alpha Omega Alpha. Episcopalian. Home: 19810 Old Bellamy Rd Alachua FL 32615

MARTELL, JOHN RAYMOND, JR., orthopaedic surgeon; b. McKeesport, Pa., Feb. 3, 1955; s. John Raymond Sr. and Mary (Rowe) M.; m. Roberta Ann Agosti, May 3, 1975; children: Candice, Nicole, John III. BS, U. Pitts., 1977; MD, Jefferson Med. Coll., 1981. Diplomate Am. Bd. Med. Examiners, Am. Bd. Orthop. Surgery. Surg. intern William Beaumont Army Med. Ctr., El Paso, Tex., 1981-82; resident in orthops. Dwight G. Eisenhower Army Med. Ctr., Ft. Gordon, Ga., 1982-86; chief orthop. svc. Kenner Army Cmty. Hosp., Ft. Lee, Va., 1986-88; mem. attending staff Walter Reed Army Med. Ctr., Washington, 1988-90; orthop. surgeon Steele Orthopaedic Ctr., Greenville, Pa., 1990-91, Triangle Orthopedic Assocs., Pitts., 1991-95, Orthop. Inst. North Ala., P.C., Decatur, 1995—; mem. attending staff Pky. Med. Ctr. Hosp., Decatur, 1995—, Hartselle (Ala.) Med. Ctr., 1995—; chief sports medicine svc., quality assurance officer Walter Reed Army Med. Ctr., 1988-90; team physician Duquesne U., Pitts., 1992-94. Maj. U.S. Army, 1981-90. Fellow Am. Acad. Orthop. Surgeons; mem. AMA (del. young physicians sect. 1992), Am. Coll. Sports Medicine, Pa. Med. Soc. (del. Pitts. chpt. 1991, mem. governing coun. young physicians sect. 1991—), Allegheny County Med. Soc. (del. Pitts. chpt. 1991), Pa. Orthop. Soc., Ea. Orthop. Soc. Office: Orthop Inst North Ala PC 2422 Danville Rd Ste B Decatur AL 35603-9999

MARTENS, DONALD MATHIAS, orthodontist; b. Coleman, Wis., June 25, 1925; s. Harry Alfred and Emma Genevive (Laurent) M.; m. Fern Ann Krejcarek, June 24, 1950; children: Daniel, Nance, Dean, Cathy, Cynthia, Linda, James, Jeffrey, Michele. DDS, Marquette U., 1952. Diplomate Internat. Bd. Orthodontics. Practice dentistry specializing in orthodontics Green Bay, Wis., 1952—; pres. San Luis Manor, Inc., Green Bay, 1973-86. Pres. Martens Found., Green Bay, 1982—. Served with USAAF, 1943-46. Fellow Am. Acad. Orthodontics (pres. 1971-72); mem. Brown Door Kewaunee Dental Soc. (pres. 1964), Fedn. Orthodontics Assn. (pres. 1979-81). Republican. Roman Catholic. Lodge: Optimist (pres. Green Bay club 1964). Home: 3853 Tamarack Dr Green Bay WI 54313-4816

MARTIG, JOHN FREDERICK, anesthesiologist; b. Salem, Oreg., Mar. 19, 1947; s. Kenneth W. and Virginia P. (Young) M.; m. Susan J. Chinworth; children: Daniel R., Thomas. A of Tech. Arts, Olympic Coll., 1968, AS, 1972; BSEE, U. Wash., 1974; DO, COMP, 1987. Cons. Rockwell Internat., Anaheim, Calif., 1984, Honeywell, Silverdale, Wash., 1985; resident Ball Meml. Hosp., Muncie, Ind., 1987-89; physician Drs. Imediate Med. Ctr., Muncie, Ind., 1988—; resident Met. Hosp., Grand Rapids, Mich., 1990-93; chief anesthesia Jay County Hosp., Portland, Ind., 1993—. With USN, 1969-83. Mem. AMA, Am. Osteo. Assn., Am. Soc. Anesthesiologists, Am. Osteo. Coll. Anesthesiologists, Am. Coll. Osteo. Family Physicians, Am. Soc. Regional Anesthesia, Ind. State Med. Assn. Home: 703 W 7th St Portland IN 47371 Office: Jay County Hosp 500 W Votaw Portland IN

MARTIKAINEN, A(UNE) HELEN, retired health education specialist; b. Harrison, Maine, May 11, 1916; d. Sylvester and Emma (Heikkinen) M.; AB, Bates Coll., 1939, DSc (hon.), 1957, Smith Coll., 1969; MPH, Yale, 1941; DSc, Harvard U., 1964. Health edn. sec. Hartford Tb and Public Health Assn., 1941-42; cons. USPHS, 1942-49; chief health edn. WHO, Geneva, 1949-74; chair internat. affairs N.C. div. AAUW, 1986-94. Trustee Bridgton Acad., North Bridgton, Maine; mem. N.C. Women's Forum, 1984—; bd. dirs. N.C. Ctr. of Laws Affecting Women, Inc.; bd. dirs. West Triangle chpt. UNA-USA; mem. program com. and health and social svcs. coms. Carol Woods Retirement Cmty. Recipient Delta Omega award Yale U.; Nat. Adminstrv. award Am. Acad. Phys. Edn.; Bates Key award; Internat. Service award, France, 1953; Prentiss medal, 1956; spl. medal, certificate for internat. health edn. service Nat. Acad. Medicine for France, 1959; Profl. award Soc. Pub. Health Educators, 1963, Benjamin Elijah Mays award Bates Coll. Alumni Assn., 1989. Fellow APHA (chmn. health edn. sect., Excellence award 1969); mem. AAUW, LWV (Chapel Hill, N.C. br. 1987—), Women's Internat. League for Peace and Freedom, U.S. Soc. Pub. Health Educators, Internat. Union Health Edn. (Parisot medal, tech. adviser), Acad. Phys. Edn. (assoc.), N.C. Coun. Women's Orgns. (mem. coun. assembly 1988-92, Women of Distinction award 1989), Phi Beta Kappa. Home: 3113 Carol Woods 750 Weaver Dairy Rd Chapel Hill NC 27514

MARTIN, ALESSANDRO, gastroenterologist, educator; b. Padova, Italy, Aug. 9, 1949; s. Antonio Martin and Elda Zambon; m. Rafaella Pagano, July 30, 1988; 1 child, Antonio. Degree in medicine, U. Padova, 1976. Resident U. Padova, 1975-76, sr. rsch. fellow, 1981—; rsch. fellow U. Manchester, Eng., 1978-79; cons. gastroenterologist several hosps., Veneto, 1980—; del. European Bd. Gastroenterology, 1993—; cons. educator Smith-Kline Found. of Italy, 1985-96. Editor: Medical Ethics, 1988, The Right to Health, 1989; mem. editl. com. Jour. Pedagogia Medica, 1977—; mem. editl. staff Italian Jour. Gastroenterology, 1990—. 2d lt. Italian Army Health Svc., 1976-78, capt. res., 1978—. Mem. Italian Soc. for med. Edn. (founding mem.). Office: U Padova Divsn Gastroentero, Via Giustiniani 2, 35100 Padova Italy

MARTIN, ALFRED, pharmacy educator; b. Pitts., May 1, 1919; s. Alfred Nicholas and Rachel (Church) M.; m. Mary Ziegler, July 27, 1945; children: Neil, Douglas. BS, Phila. Coll. Pharmacy and Sci., 1942; MS, Purdue U., 1948, PhD, 1950. Asst. prof. Temple U., 1950-53, assoc. prof., 1953-55, dean, prof. phys. medicinal chemistry Sch. Pharmacy, 1968-72; assoc. prof., then prof. Purdue U., 1955-66; prof. Med. Coll. Va., 1966-68; prof., dir. Drug Dynamics Inst., Coll. Pharmacy U. Tex., 1973-78, Coulter R. Sublett prof. indsl. pharmacy Drug Dynamics Inst., Coll. Pharmacy, 1977-88, emeritus Coulter R. Sublett prof. Drug Dynamics Inst., Coll. Pharmacy, 1988—; vis. lectr. Am. Assn. Colls. Pharmacy, 1963, 64; lectr. Indsl. Pharmacy Conf., Arden House, N.Y.C., 1966, 67; Pfeiffer Research fellow Center Applied Wave Mechanics, Paris, 1962; indsl. cons., 1961—; vis. pharm. scientist U. Manchester (Eng.), 1976. Author: Physical Pharmacy, 4th edit., 1993; editor pharmaceutics sect. Remington's Pharmaceutical Sciences, 1970, 75, 80, 85. Served with USMCR, 1942-46, PTO. Decorated Navy Air medal, Navy Gold star; recipient Sturmer lecture award Phila. Coll. Pharmacy and Sci., 1967, ann. alumni award, 1980, Kauffman lecture award Ohio State U., 1970, Disting. Alumnus award Purdue U., 1985, Roland T. Lakey Hon. Lecture award Coll. of Pharmacy Wayne State U., 1990. Fellow Acad. Pharm. Rsch. and Sci.; mem. Am. Chem. Soc., Am. Pharm. Assn. (Ebert medal 1967, Rsch. Achievement award 1967), Sigma Xi, Rho Chi (Nat. award 1968). Home: 5404 Ridge Oak Dr Austin TX 78731-4816

MARTIN, ANTHONY KEITH, surgeon; b. Macon, Ga., Apr. 6, 1962; s. James Kenneth and Jo Ann (Washburn) M.; m. Patricia Louise Childs, May 21, 1988; children: Taylor Childs, Clatus William, Alexander Craig. BS, Davidson Coll., 1984; MD, Mercer U., 1988. Resident Bapt. Med. Ctrs., Birmingham, Ala., 1988-93; surgeon pvt. practice, Macon, Ga., 1993—. Fellow ACS; mem. AMA, Ga. Surg. Soc., MAcon Surg. Soc., Bibb County Med. Soc. Republican. Methodist. Office: 380 Hosp Dr Ste 360 Macon GA 31201

MARTIN, BRYAN LESLIE, allergist, immunologist; b. Macomb, Ill., June 25, 1954; s. George Albert and Vernal Louise (Stutsman) M.; m. Deborah Ann Schettig, June 22, 1979; children: Emily, Stephanie Scott. BA, St. Vincent Coll., 1976; postgrad., Ohio U., 1976-79; DO, U. Osteo. Medicine/Hlth. Scis., 1984; M of Mil. Art and Sci., Command & Staff Officer Coll., 1994. Diplomate Am. Bd. Internal Medicine, Am. Bd. Allergy and Immunology, Nat. Bd. Osteo. Med. Examiners. Commd. 2d lt. U.S. Army, 1980, advanced through grades to maj., 1990—, comdr. med. troop 3d armored cavalry regiment, 1990-91; resident in internal medicine William Beaumont Army Med. Ctr., 1987-90, chief med. resident, 1990-91; with U.S. Army Command and Gen. Staff Coll., 1993-94. Student body pres. U. Osteopathic Medicine and Health Scis., Des Moines, 1981-82. Allergy/immunology fellow Fitzsimons Army Med. Ctr., Aurora, Colo., 1991-93; Health Professions scholar U.S. Army, 1980-84; decorated Bronze star. Fellow Am. Coll. Allergy, Asthma and Immunology (fellow-in-tng. rep. to bd. regents 1991-93, chmn. fellow-in-tng. sect. 1992-93); mem. ACP, AMA (del. resident physicians sect. 1991-93, young physicians sect. 1993—), Am. Acad. Allergy and Immunology, Am. Osteo. Assn. (del. 1981-83), Dustoff Assn., Nat. Med. Vets. Soc., Sigma Sigma Phi. Office: Chief Allergy/Immunology Ireland Army Cmty Hosp Fort Knox KY 40121-5520

MARTIN, CHARLES NEIL, JR., health care management company executive; b. Florence, Ala., Dec. 11, 1942; s. Charles Neil Sr. and Hazel Lucy (Hawkins) M. BS, So. Coll., Chattanooga, 1964. Adminstr. El Reposo Nursing Home, Florence, 1964-66, Parkwood Convalescent Ctr., Chattanooga, 1966-67; project dir. Tenn. Hosp. Assn., Nashville, 1967-68, asst. dir., 1968-69; v.p. Gen. Care Corp., Nashville, 1969-76, exec. v.p., 1976-79, pres., chief operating officer, 1979-80; sr. v.p. HCA, Nashville, 1980-85, exec. v.p., 1985-87, also bd. dirs.; pres., chief operating officer HealthTrust, Inc. - The Hosp. Co., Nashville, 1987—; bd. dirs. Equicor, Nashville, 1986—. Bd. dirs. Cystic Fibrosis Found., Nashville, 1987. Office: Ornda Healthcorp 3401 W End Ave Ste 700 Nashville TN 37203-1070*

MARTIN, CHERI CHRISTIAN, health services administrator; b. Nashville, Mar. 9, 1956; d. Jesse Thomas and Eloise (McClain) Christian; m. George A. Martin, June 25, 1977 (div. May 1995); children: Matthew Alexander, Kristin Leigh. BS in Family Resources and Consumer Scis., U. Wis., 1977; cert. healthcare mgmt., U. St. Thomas, 1991. Asst. buyer Dayton Hudson, Mpls., 1978-79, assoc. buyer, 1979-81; instr. Nat. Coll., Mpls., 1981-82; mgr. store Conmo Shoes, Inc., Mpls, 1982-83; patient svcs. rep. Group Health, Inc., Mpls., 1984-89, dental mgr., 1989-94, regional mgr., 1994—; cert. facilitator the Seven Habits of Highly Effective People, 1996. Cert. facilitator (seminar) The Seven Habits of Highly Effective People, 1996. Mem. Minn./Dakota Assn. Patient Reps. (v.p. 1989-90), U. Wis. Alumni Assn., Group Health Social Club Mpls. (pres. 1987-89).

MARTIN, CLYDE VERNE, psychiatrist; b. Coffeyville, Kans., Apr. 7, 1933; s. Howard Verne and Elfrieda Louise (Moehn) M.; m. Barbara Jean McNeilly, June 24, 1956; children: Kent Clyde, Kristin Claire, Kerry Constance, Kyle Curtis. Student Coffeyville Coll., 1951-52; AB, U. Kans., 1955; MD, 1958; MA, Webster Coll., St. Louis, 1977; JD, Thomas Jefferson Coll. Law, Los Angeles, 1985. Diplomate Am. Bd. Psychiatry and Neurology. Intern, Lewis Gale Hosp., Roanoke, Va., 1958-59; resident in psychiatry U. Kans. Med. Ctr., Kansas City, 1959-62, Fresno br. U. Calif.-San Francisco, 1978; staff psychiatrist Neurol. Hosp., Kansas City, 1962; practice medicine specializing in psychiatry, Kansas City, Mo., 1964-84; founder, med. dir., pres. bd. dirs. Mid-Continent Psychiat. Hosp., Olathe, Kans., 1972-84; adj. prof. psychology Baker U., Baldwin City, Kans., 1969-84; staff psychiatrist Atascadero State Hosp., Calif., 1984-85; clin. prof. psychiatry U. Calif., San Francisco, 1985—; chief psychiatrist Calif. Med. Facility, Vacaville, 1985-87; pres., editor Corrective and Social Psychiatry, Olathe, 1970-84, Atascadero, 1984-85, Fairfield, 1985—. Contbr. articles to profl. jours. Bd. dirs. Meth. Youthville, Newton, Kans. 1965-75, Spofford Home, Kansas City, 1974-78. Served to capt. USAF, 1962-64, ret. col. USAFR. Oxford Law & Soc. scholar, 1993. Fellow Am. Psychiat. Assn., Royal Soc. Health, Am. Assn. Mental Health Profls. in Corrections, World Assn. Social Psychiatry, Am. Orthopsychiat. Assn.; mem. AMA, Assn. for Advancement Psychotherapy, Am. Assn. Sex Educators, Counselors and Therapists (cert.), Assn. Mental Health Adminstrs. (cert.), Kansas City Club, Masons, Phi Beta Pi, Pi Kappa Alpha. Methodist (del. Kans. East Conf. 1972-80, bd. global ministries 1974-80). Office: PO Box 3365 Fairfield CA 94533-0587

MARTIN, DALE, vocational rehabilitation executive; b. N.Y.C., May 10, 1935; d. Byron Pink Molter and Ruth (Nobel) Gestram; m. Robert A. Wishart, Dec. 13, 1985; children by previous marriage: Elizabeth, Devon. BS, U. Conn., 1957. RN, cert. case mgr., ins. rehab. specialist, lic. rehab. counsellor, Mass. Dental asst. Hempstead, N.Y., 1951; with Wesson Maternity Hosp., Springfield, Mass., 1957-58, Huntington Hartford Meml. Hosp., Pasadena, Calif., 1958-59; office mgr. Indsl. By Products Inc., Kalamazoo, Mich., 1969-72; controller Indsl. By Products Inc., Chgo., 1970-74; cons. Mgmt. Resources Inc., Broomall, Pa., 1978-81; cons., owner Martin-Collard Assocs., Inc., Monmouth Beach, N.J., 1980-84; cons., owner, chmn. bd. dirs. MCA, Inc., Boston, 1984—; bd. dirs. Consortium Advantage, Inc., Boston; ind. rep. JewelWay Internat., Inc., Platinum Exec.; cons. Viewfinder, Old Chatham, N.Y., 1987—, Phoenix Inc., Global Explorations, Inc. Contbr. articles to profl. jours.; painter, sculptor. Bd. govs. Rumson-Fair Haven H.S., N.J., 1976-78; benefit tennis co-chair Jordan Hosp.-White Cliffs County Club. Mem. Nat. Assn. Rehab. Profls. in Pvt. Sector (forensic sect., past rep. region I to bd. dirs.), Nat. Rehab. Assn. (pvt. sector group), Internat. Assn. Psychosocial Rehab. Specialists, New Eng. Claims Assn., Individual Case Mgmt. Assn., Mass. Nurses Assn. (chmn. image com. 1984-85), Town Club (v.p.), Mountain Lakes Ski Club (founder), Jr. Women's Club, Jr. League, Sigma Theta Tau, Alpha Delta Pi. Office: MCA Inc PO Box 1617 Sagamore Beach MA 02562 also: MCA Inc PO Box 789 Port Salerno FL 34992-0789

MARTIN, DALE ALISON, counseling, psychology; b. Selma, Ala., May 4, 1941; s. Ted C. and Omie Lee (Frith) M.; m. Blanche Waters, June 23, 1962; 1 child, Alyssa. BS cum laude, Samford U., 1964; MS, Fla. State U., 1966, PhD, 1970. Lic. profl. counselor; cert. counselor; cert. career counselor. High sch. tchr. Bay County Bd. Pub. Instrn., Panama City, Fla., 1964-65; grad. asst. dept. guidance and counseling Fla. State U., Tallahassee, 1966-67; psychometrist VA Guidance Ctr., Fla. State U., Tallahassee, 1967, dir., counselor, 1967-69; dir. Univ. Counseling Svcs. and Test Ctr. Troy (Ala.) State U., Montgomery, Ala., 1969-71; asst. prof. dept. counselor edn. Troy State U., Montgomery, Ala., 1971-76; assoc. prof. dept. counseling and human devel. Troy (Ala.) State U., Montgomery, Ala., 1976-81, prof., chmn. dept. counseling, human devel. and psychology, 1981-88, prof., dean div. counseling, edn. and psychology, 1988-95; panel vocat. experts Office Hearing and Appeals, Social Security Adminstrn., U.S. Govt., Montgomery, 1974—; vocat. cons., career counselor Disability Hearings and Ct. Cases for Workmen's compensation, R.R. Retirement Bd., Montgomery and Ala. area, 1978—. Deacon First Bapt. Ch., Montgomery, 1979—. Mem. APA, ACA, Assn. Counselor Edn. and Supervision, Nat. Career Devel. Assn., Phi Delta Kappa, Omicron Delta Kappa.

MARTIN, DANIEL C., surgeon, educator; b. St. Louis, Apr. 7, 1946; s. Dan Allen and Ruth Keel (Fields) M.; m. Glenn Ann Blakemore, July 7, 1970; children: Josh, Adam. BS in Physics, Emory U., 1968, MD, 1972. Diplomate Am. Bd. Ob-Gyn. Rsch. asst. physics and radiology Emory U., Atlanta, 1968-69; intern, resident, fellow, instr. The Johns Hopkins Med. Instns., Balt., 1972-77; from asst. prof. to clin. asst. prof. U. Tenn., Memphis, 1977-90, clin. assoc. prof., 1990—; surgeon Reproductive Surgery, P.C., Memphis, 1977—; reproductive surgeon Bapt. Meml. Hosp., 1977—;

dir. gynecologic laser and endoscopy workshops, 1982-93. Editor: (textbooks) Lasers in Endoscopy, 1990, Laparoscopic Appearance of Endometriosis, 1990, Manual of Endoscopy, 1990, Atlas of Endometriosis, 1993, Endoscopic Management of Gynecologic Disease, 1996. Basketball coach Grace St. Luke's Ch., Memphis, 1992-95. Picker Found. fellow Emory U., 1969; Tex. Assn. Ob-Gyn. hon. fellow, 1989; recipient Bridges trophy for athletics Emory U., 1968, Codman surg. award, 1982, 83, Video award Am. Fertility Soc., 1992; named one of Best Drs. Am. Woodward and White Inc., 1992. Mem. ACOG (sect. chair jr. fellows Md.), Tenn. Med. Assn., Memphis and Shelby County Med. Soc. (comm. com.), Am. Nat. Std. Inst. (subcom. on laser safety in med. facility), Am. Assn. Gynecol. Laparoscopists (pres. 1990-91, Videoendoscopy award 1993), Gynecologic Surgery Soc. (pres. 1994-96), Sigma Pi Sigma. Office: Reproductive Surgery PC # 100 1717 Kirby Pkwy Memphis TN 38120-4331

MARTIN, DANIEL RICHARD, pharmaceutical company executive; b. Lima, Peru, June 9, 1937; s. James Marion and Clemmy Caroline (Valencia) M.; m. Barbara Artemis Cyrus, June 23, 1962; children: Daniel Richard Jr., John Alexander, Christopher Andrew. BA, Cornell U., 1958; MS, Columbia U., N.Y.C., 1959. Area sales supr. Schering Corp., Bloomfield, N.J., 1960-64; assoc. McKinsey & Co., N.Y.C., 1964-69; treas. Harper & Row, Pubs., N.Y.C., 1969-72; mng. dir. Merck & Co., Rahway, N.J., 1972-77; group v.p. Bell & Howell Co., Chgo., 1977-80; pres. Howland Martin Corp., N.Y.C., 1980-85; pres. Sterling Europe, Middle East, Africa Sterling Drug, Inc., N.Y.C., 1986-89; pres., CEO E-Z-EM, Inc., Westbury, N.Y., 1990—; adj. prof. mgmt. Pace U., N.Y.C., 1996—. Co-chmn. Accion Internat., Cambridge, Mass., 1988—; trustee Bangor (Maine) Theol. Sem., 1991—; dir. Americas Found.; bd. dirs., fin. com. White Plains (N.Y.) Hosp. Decorated Order of Merit (Ecuador). Mem. Coun. on Fgn. Rels., Americas Soc., Univ. Club (N.Y.C., Chgo.), Cornell Club (N.Y.C.). Republican. Congregationalist. Home: 2 Dolma Rd Scarsdale NY 10583-4506 Office: E-Z-EM Inc 717 Main St Westbury NY 11590-5021

MARTIN, DAVID ALLEN, medical educator; b. Harrisonburg, Va., Jan. 5, 1957. BA, Goshen (Ind.) Coll., 1980; MD, Ind. U., 1984. Diplomate Am. Bd. Ob-gyn. Resident in ob-gyn. Ind. U. Med. Ctr., Indpls., 1984-88; fellow in ob-gyn. U. N.C., Chapel Hill, 1988-90; clin. instr. U. N.C. Sch. Medicine, Chapel Hill, 1988-90; asst. prof. dept. ob-gyn. U. Fla., Gainesville, 1990-95. Grantee Am. Cancer Soc., 1988, 89; recipient Nat. Faculty Tchg. award Coun. on Resident Edn. for Ob-gyn., 1995. Fellow ACS, Am. Coll. Ob-gyn.; mem. AMA, Soc. Gynecologic Oncologists, Fla. Med. Assn., Tenn. Med. Assn., Fla. Soc. Gynecologic Oncologists. Office: 101 Blount Ave Ste 400 Knoxville TN 37920

MARTIN, DAVID EDWARD, health sciences educator; b. Green Bay, Wis., Oct. 1, 1939; s. Edward Henry and Lillie (Luckman) M. B.S., U. Wis., 1961, M.S., 1963, Ph.D., 1970. Ford Found. research trainee Wis. Regional Primate Ctr., Madison, 1967-70; asst. prof. health scis. Ga. State U., Atlanta, 1970-74, assoc. prof., 1974-80, prof., 1980-91, regents prof., 1992—; affiliate scientist Yerkes Primate Rsch. Ctr., Emory U., Atlanta, 1970—; U.S. rep. to Internat. Olympic Acad., 1978; sports medicine rsch. assoc. U.S. Olympic Com., 1981-84; chmn. sports scis. U.S.A. Track and Field; mem. coaching staff U.S. teams to world championships in distance running, Rome, 1982, Gateshead, Eng., 1983, Budapest, Hungary, 1994, head coach, Paris, 1980, Madrid, 1984, Hiroshima, Japan, 1985, Warsaw, Poland, 1987, Antwerp, Belgium, 1991; mem. Olympic med. support group Atlanta Olympic Games. Author: Laboratory Experiments in Human Physiology, 4th edit., 1980, The Marathon Footrace, 1979, La Corsa Di Maratona, 1982, The High Jump Book, 1982, 2d edit., 1987, Respiratory Anatomy and Physiology, 1987, Training Distance Runners, 1991, German edit., 1992, Spanish edit., 1995; contbr. articles to profl. jours. Trustee Ga. Found. for Athletic Excellence. Recipient fed. and univ. grants for physiol. research; named Disting. prof. Ga. State U., 1975, 81, 85. Fellow Am. Coll. Sports Medicine; mem. Internat. Soc. Olympic Historians, Am. Physiol. Soc., Atlanta Track Club. Home: 510 Coventry Rd Apt 13A Decatur GA 30030-5038 Office: Ga State U Dept Cardiopulmonary S Atlanta GA 30303

MARTIN, DONALD CREAGH, surgeon; b. Port Chester, N.Y., Mar. 7, 1937; s. Donald Creagh and Margaret Eleanor (Dobson) M.; m. Jacqueline Anne Poole, Sept. 25, 1965; children: Samuel, Joseph. BA in Econs., Yale U., 1958; MD, U. Pa., 1962. Diplomate Am. Bd. Surgery. Intern, Pa. Hosp., Phila., 1962-63, resident in gen. surgery and pathology, 1965-67, 69-71, 72-74, instr. anatomy, 1968-69, 71-72; practice gen. surgery, White Plains, N.Y., 1974-78, Toledo, 1978—; rsch. asst. dept. surgery Guy's Hosp., London, 1967-68; mem. staff Toledo, Mercy, Riverside, St. Charles Hosps. and St. Vincent Med. Ctr.; clin. asst. prof. surgery Med. Coll. Ohio, Toledo, 1980—. Trustee Toledo Cmty. Hosp. oncology program, 1987-93; bd. dirs. Lucas County chpt. Am. Cancer Soc., 1983-90; med. adv. bd. Aetna of NW Ohio, 1993—. Served with M.C., USNR, 1963-65. Fellow ACS, Am. Coll. Nutrition; mem. AAAS, Toledo Surg. Soc. (councillor 1992-95, pres. 1995-96), Soc. Internat. Chirurgie, World Assn. for Hepato-Pancreato-Biliary Surgery (founder), Am. Hepato-Pancreato-Biliary Assn., 1994—; Republican. Contbr. articles to med. jours.; mem. editl. bd. Toledo Medicine, 1995—. Office: 2109 Hughes Dr Ste 600 Toledo OH 43606-5104

MARTIN, FRANCIS PAUL, pediatrician; b. N.Y.C., June 3, 1924; s. John Francis and Anna Catherine (Mollers) M.; m. Barbara Elizabeth Kelsey, Sept. 11, 1948; children: Katherine, Therese, Francis, Jeanne, Deborah, James, Thomas, Lawrence, Kenneth, Margaret, Daniel. BS, U. Notre Dame, 1945; MD, NYU, 1948. Diplomate Am. Bd. Pediatrics. Resident pediatrics King County Hosp., Bklyn., 1948-50, Brooke Army Hosp., San Antonio, 1951-52; pvt. practice Lynbrook, Rockville Ctr., N.Y., 1955—; assoc. prof. pediatrics NYU Med. Ctr., N.Y.C., 1966-86; dir. pediatrics Mercy Med. Ctr., Rockville Centre, 1989-93; cons. in pediatrics Winthrop U. Med. Ctr., Mineola, N.Y., 1981—; dir. Smith Barney Funds, Inc., N.Y.C. Contbr. articles to profl. jours., chpts. to books. Mem. bishop's com. Rockville Ctr. Diocese Quality of Life, 1987; bd. dirs. Marty Lions Found., 1981—; lector St. Agnes Cathedral, 1956—. Named Man of the Yr. Notre Dame Club of N.Y., 1962; mem. NYU Athletic Hall of Fame, 1990. Fellow Am. Acad. Pediatrics; mem. AMA, N.Y. State Med. Soc., Nassau County Med. Soc. Roman Catholic. Home: 321 N Village Ave Rockville Centre NY 11570-2327 Office: 2000 N Village Ave Rockville Centre NY 11570-1001

MARTIN, FRANKLIN MCLAIN, physician; b. Washington, Apr. 14, 1955; s. Franklin Townsend and Barbara (Fraser) M.; m. Cynthia Reynolds Minsch, Sept. 1, 1979; children: David T., Daniel G., Douglas F. BA in biophysics, U. Pa., 1977; MD, Georgetown U., 1982. Diplomate Am. Bd. Surgery, Am. Bd. Gen. Surgery, Am. Bd. Surg. Critical Care. Commd. ensign USN, 1978, advanced through grades to comdr., 1993, res., 1993; resident Nat. Naval Med. Ctr., Bethesda, Md., 1982-87; ship's surgeon USS Am. CV-66, Norfolk, Va., 1987-88; staff surgeon Naval Med. Ctr., San Diego, 1988—; pvt. practice Escondido, Calif., 1992-93; physician Southwest Surg. Assocs., Escondido, 1994—; chmn. dept. trauma Palomar Med. Ctr., Escondido, 1994-95, chmn. dept. surgery, 1996—; clin. asst. prof. surgery Uniformed Svcs. U. Health Scis., Bethesda, 1985—. Contbr. articles to prof. jours. Asst. scoutmaster Boy Scouts Am., San Diego, 1991. Office: 488 E Valley Pkwy Ste 311 Escondido CA 92025

MARTIN, GARY JOSEPH, medical educator; b. Chgo., Mar. 12, 1952; m. Helen Gartner; children: Daniel T., David G. BA in Psychology, U. Ill., 1974, MD, 1978. Diplomate Am. Bd. Internal Medicine, Am. Bd. Cardiovascular Disease, Nat. Bd. Med. Examiners; lic. physician, Ill. Intern, resident internal medicine Northwestern U. Med. Sch., Chgo., 1978-81, instr. medicine, 1981-82, asst. prof. medicine, 1984-90, assoc. prof., 1990—, divsn. chief, divsn. gen. internal medicine, 1988—; cardiology fellow Loyola U. Med. Ctr., 1982-84; attending physician Northwestern Meml. Hosp./Northwestern Med. Faculty Found., Chgo., 1984—; chief med. resident, attending physician Northwestern Meml. Hosp., Chgo., 1981-82; faculty and course dir. Nat. Ctr. for Advanced Med. Edn., 1984—; chmn. outpatient utilization rev. and quality assurance com., 1985—; chmn. Northwestern Meml. Hosp./Lakeside VA Rsch. Com., 1988-91; dir. tng. gen. internal medicine residency program, 1985—; bd. dirs. com. Northwestern Med. Faculty Found., 1993—; cons. health care divsn. Ernst & Young, 1991—; peer reviewer Faculty Devel. Rev. Com. Panel 1, 1994. Contbr. articles to profl. jours. Fellow Buehler Ctr. on Aging. Fellow Am. Coll. Cardiology; mem. ACP, Am. Fedn. Clin. Rsch., Soc. Gen. Internal Medicine, Am. Heart Assn., Soc. Med. Decision Making. Home: 215 N Home Park Ridge IL 60068-3029 Office: Northwestern U Med Sch Divsn Gen Internal Medicine 303 E Ohio Ste 300 Chicago IL 60611*

MARTIN, GEORGE, psychologist, educator; b. L.A., May 8, 1940; s. George Leonard and Margaret (Padigamus) M.; m. Penny Harrell, June 22, 1963 (div. 1986); children: Jeni, Kimberle. BA, UCLA, 1965; MA, Calif. State U., L.A., 1967; MS, Calif. State U., Fullerton, 1994. Systems analyst L.A. Dept. Water & Power, 1965-67; project coord. L.A. Police Dept., 1967-70, edn. cons., 1980-83; alcohol researcher Pomona (Calif.) Coll., 1970-73; tng. systems researcher Lanterman State Hosp., Pomona, 1973-77; prof. psychology Mt. San Antonio Coll., Walnut, Calif., 1970—, dir. rsch., 1986-94. Contbr. articles to profl. jours. Rsch. dir. Orange County Dem. Party, 1985-86. With U.S. Army, 1959-61. Grantee Nat. Inst. Law Enforcement, 1967-70, Nat. Inst. Alcohol, 1970-74. Mem. APA, NSA. Home: 1313 N Grand Ave Ste 326 Walnut CA 91789-1317 Office: Mt San Antonio Coll 1100 N Grand Ave Walnut CA 91789-1341

MARTIN, GEORGE M., pathologist, gerontologist, educator; b. N.Y.C., June 30, 1927; s. Barnett J. and Estelle (Weiss) M.; m. Julaine Ruth Miller, Dec. 2, 1952; children: Peter C., Kelsey C., Thomas M., Andrew C. BS, U. Wash., 1949, MD, 1953. Diplomate Am. Bd. Pathology, Am. Bd. Med. Genetics. Intern Montreal Gen. Hosp., Quebec, Can., 1953-54; resident-instr. U. Chgo., 1954-57; instr.-prof. U. Wash., Seattle, 1957—; vis. scientist Dept. Genetics Albert Einstein Coll., N.Y.C., 1964; chmn. Gordon Confs. Molecular Pathology, Biology of Aging, 1974-79; chmn., nat. res. Plan on Aging Nat. Inst. on Aging, Bethesda, Md., 1985-89; dir. Alzheimer's Disease Rsch. Ctr. U. Wash., 1985—. Editor Werner's Syndrome and Human Aging, 1985, Molecular Aspects of Aging, 1995; contbr. articles in field to profl jours. Active Fedn. Am. Scientists. With USN, 1945-46. Recipient Allied Signal award in Aging, 1991, Rsch. medal Am. Agy. Assn., 1992, Kleemeier award, 1994; named Disting. Alumnus, U. Wash. Sch. Medicine, 1987; USPHS rsch. fellow dept. genetics, Glasgow U., 1961-62; Eleanor Roosvelt Inst. Cancer Rsch. fellow Inst. de Biologie, PHysiologie, Chimie, Paris, 1968-69; Josiah Macy faculty scholar Sir William Din Sch. Pathology, Oxford (Eng.) U., 1978-79, Humboldt Disting. scientist dept. genetics U. Wurzburg, Germany, 1991. Fellow AAAS, Gerontol. Soc. Am. (chmn. Biol. Sci. 1979, Brookdale award 1981), Tissue Culture Assn. (pres. 1986-88); mem. Inst. Medicine, Am. Assn. Univ. Pathologists (emeritus), Am. Soc. Human Genetics, Am. Soc. Investigative Pathology. Democrat. Home: 2223 E Howe St Seattle WA 98112-2931 Office: U Wash Sch Medicine Dept Pathology Sm # 30 Seattle WA 98195

MARTIN, JACK, physician; b. Northport, Ala., Aug. 11, 1927; s. Marvin Oscar and Glenavis (Rice) M.; m. Ann Inman, Apr. 7, 1957; children: Sarah, Richard, Charles Randall, Robert. BS, U. Ala., 1949; MD, Valderbilt U., 1953. Intern Charity Hosp., New Orleans, 1953-54; resident in adult and child psychiatry Cin. Gen. Hosp., Richardson, Tex., 1954-58; dir. child psychiatry U. Tex. Health Scis. Ctr., Dallas, 1958-67; med. dir. Shady Brook Res. Ctr., Richardson, 1963-81; physician pvt. practice, Dallas, 1981—. With USNR, 1945-47. Independent. Episcopalian. Office: 3636 Dickinson St Dallas TX 75219

MARTIN, JAMES DOUGLAS, neurologist; b. Cullman, Ala., Dec. 10, 1926; s. Charles L. and Sylvia J. (Johnson) M.; m. Elizabeth Mason, June 22, 1956; children: James, Julia, Ann. BA, Vanderbilt U., 1949, MD, 1959. Diplomate Am. Bd. Psychiatry and Neurology. Med. intern U. Va., Charlottesville, Va., 1959-60; neurology resident U. Va., Charlottesville, 1960-63; fellow in neuropathology Harvard Med. Sch., Boston, 1963-65; asst. prof. neurology W. Va. U., Morgantown, 1965-70, assoc. prof., 1970-72, prof., 1972—. Fellow Am. Acad. Neurology. Office: W Va Univ Dept Neurology PO Box 9180 Morgantown WV 26506-9180

MARTIN, JAMES LLOYD, pharmacist; b. Augusta, Ga., June 30, 1949; s. Lloyd Franklin and Phyllis Pearl (Studin) M.; m. Karen Nancy Phillips, Sept. 2, 1972; children: Kara, Jamie, Krista, Jimmy. BS in Biology, Ga. So. U., 1971; BS in Pharmacy, U. Ga., 1974. Registered pharmacist, Ga. Pharmacist Burke Drug Co., Waynesboro, Ga, 1974-75, Super X Drug Co., Statesboro, Ga., 1975-78; pharmacist, owner Coll. Pharmacy, Inc., Statesboro, 1978—. Chmn. Bulloch County Alcohol and Drug Task Force, 1991—; chmn. Statesboro Downtown Devel. Authority; trustee First Methodist Ch., Statesboro, 1993—. Recipient Pharmacy Leadership award Menck, Sharpe & Dohme, Hilton Head, S.C., 1990, Bowl of Hygiia (community pharmacist leader), Ga., 1994; named Pharmacist of Yr., Phi Delta Chi, 1990. Mem. Ga. Pharm. Assn. (pres. 1989, bd. dirs. 1981—, chmn. bd. 1990, chmn. polit. action com. 1991—, chmn. audit com. 1991—), Nat. Assn. Retail Druggists (nat. officer 1989—; exec. com., chmn. nat. coms. 1989—), Acad. Ind. Pharmacy (bd. dirs.), Sigma Phi Epsilon (sec., treas. alumni bd.). Methodist. Home: 6 Golf Club Cir Statesboro GA 30458-9163 Office: Coll Pharmacy Inc 19 S Main St Statesboro GA 30458-6005

MARTIN, JAY HERBERT, psychoanalysis and English educator; b. Newark, Oct. 30, 1935; s. Sylvester K. and Ada M. (Smith) M.; m. Helen Bernadette Saldini, June 9, 1956; children: Helen E., Laura A., Jay Herbert. AB with honors, Columbia U., 1956; MA, Ohio State U., 1957, PhD, 1960; PhD in Psychoanalysis, So. Calif. Psychoanalytic Inst., 1983. Instr. English Pa. State U., 1957-58; instr., then asst. to assoc. prof. English and Am. Studies Yale U., New Haven, Conn., 1960-68; prof. English and comparative culture U. Calif., Irvine, 1968-79; asst. prof. psychiatry and human behavior, clin. supr. residency program Calif. Coll. Medicine Calif. Coll. Medicine U. Calif., Irvine, 1978-96; Leo S. Bing prof. English and Am. lit. U. So. Calif., Irvine, 1979-96, dir. undergrad. program in Am. studies, 1968-69, dir. program in comparative culture, 1969-71, dir. edn. abroad program, 1971-75, dir. grad. studies dept. English, 1980-83; Shirley H. Gould prof. humanities Claremont McKenna Coll., Claremont, Calif., 1996—; instr. psychoanalysis So. Calif. Psychoanalytic Inst., 1984-96; Bicentennial prof. Am. lit. and culture Moscow State U., USSR, 1976; vis. Parmenter lectr. Children's Hosp., San Francisco, 1989, Ann. William Faulkner Lecture, 1991, Herman Serota Found. lecture, 1992; cons. to pub. houses; lectr. USSR, Poland, Norway, France, Costa Rica, Fed. Republic Germany, Brazil, Can., U. London, Hebrew U., Jerusalem, Seoul, Rep. Korea, Bergen, Norway; dir. NEH summer sems., 1976, 77; mem. evaluation com. dept. pvt. post-secondary edn. State of Calif., 1986; cons. numerous univs., pubs., NEA, NEA, J.S. Guggenheim Found., Calif. Coun. for Humanities and Pub. Policy, U.S. Congress Com. on Edn. and Labor; faculty assoc. Coun. Internat. Exch. of Scholars; frequent speaker profl. orgns. and sems., univs., confs., hosps. Author: (criticism and biography) Conrad Aiken: A Life of His Art, 1962, Harvests of Change: American Literature 1865-1914, 1967, Nathanael West: The Art of His Life, 1970 (U. Calif. Friends Libr. award), Robert Lowell, 1970, Always Merry and Bright. The Life of Henry Miller, 1978, (U. Calif. Friends of Libr. award, Phi Kappa Phi Best Faculty Publ. prize U. So. Calif., transl. in French, Japanese and German), (fiction) Winter Dreams: An American in Moscow, 1979, Who Am I This Time, Uncovering the Fictive Personality, 1988 (Burlington No. Found. award 1989); Swallowing Tigers Whole, 1996, A Corresponding Leap of Love: Henry Miller, 1996, Henry Miller's Dream Song, 1996;author one hour radio drama, William Faulkner. Sound Portraits of Twentieth-Century Humanists, starring Tennessee Williams, Glenn Close, Colleen Dewhurst, Nat. Pub. Radio, 1980; author sects. 24 books including most recently American Writing Today, vol. I, 1982, The Haunted Dusk: American Supernatural Fiction, 1820-1902, 1983, Frontiers of Infant Psychiatry, vol.II, 1986, Centenary Essays on Huckleberry Finn, 1985, Robert Lowell: Essays on the Poetry, 1987, William Faulkner: The Best from American Literature, 1989, The Homosexualities: Reality, Fantasy and the Arts, 1991, Life Guidance Through Literature, 1992, Biography and Source Studies, 1995, William Faulkner and Psychology, 1995, Psychotherapy East and West, 1996; contbr. numerous articles and revs. to profl. jours., bulls., L.A. Times Book Rev., Partisan Rev., N.Y. Times Book Rev., Internat. Rev. Psycho-Analysis, Am. Lit., London Times Lit. Supplement, Psychoanalytic Quarterly; editor: Winfield Townley Scott (Yale series recorded poets), 1962, Twentieth Century Interpretations of the Waste Land: A Collection of Critical Essays, 1968, Twentieth Century Views of Nathanael West, 1972, A Singer in the Dawn: Reinterpretations of Paul Laurence Dunbar (with intro.), 1975, Economic Depression and American Humor (with intro.), 1986, The Theory and Practice of the Contemporary American Short Story, 1996; mem. editl. bd. Am. Lit., 1978-81, Humanities in Society, 1979-1983; editor-in-chief Psychoanalytic Edn., 1984-89; appearances on TV and adio including Connie Martinson Talks Books, Barbara Brunner Nightline, Sonya Live in L.A., Oprah Winfrey Show, 1988-89. Pres. Friends of Irvine Pub. Libr., 1974-75; mem. Com. for Freud Mus. Recipient Fritz Schmidl Meml. prize for rsch. applied psychoanalysis Seattle Assn. Psychoanalysis, 1982, Marie H. Briehl prize for child psychoanalysis, 1982, Franz Alexander prize in psychoanalysis, 1984; Morse rsch. fellow, 1963-64, Am. Philos. Soc. fellow, 1966, J.S. Guggenheim fellow, 1966-67, Rockefeller Found.humanities sr. fellow, 1975-76, Rsch. Clin. fellow So. Calif. Psychoanalytic Soc. 1977-81, Rockefeller fellow, Bellagio, Italy, 1983, NEH sr. fellow, 1983-84. Mem. So. Calif. Am. Studies Assn. (pres. 1969-71), Am. Studies Assn. (exec. bd. 1969-71, del. to MLA Assembly 1974, chmn. Ralph Gabriel prize com. 1975-77), MLA (chmn. prize com. Jay B. Hubbell Silver medal in Am. lit. 1978-84), Nat. Assn. Arts and Letters (prize com. 1987-88), Nat. Humanities Faculty (advisor to Valhalla High Sch., El Cajon, Calif. 1979-81), Nat. Am. Studies Faculty, Internat. Psychoanalytic Assn., Internat. Assn. Empirical Aesthetics, Internat. Assn. U. Profs. English, Internat. Karen Horney Soc., Phi Beta Kappa. Home: 18651 Via Palatino Irvine CA 92715-3445

MARTIN, JEAN ANN, school administrator, educational diagnostician; b. Omaha, June 27, 1942; d. Clarid Fee and Frances Catherine (Dugan) McNeil; m. Robert William Martin, Dec. 28, 1968. BS, Pa. State U., 1963; MEd, U. Del., 1968. Cert. English tchr., Pa., N.Y., Del., reading specialist, Va., N.Y., Del., secondary prin., reading supr., dir. of instrn., Del. Tchr. English Neshaminy Sch. Dist., Langhorn, Pa., 1963-65; tchr. English and reading Unionville (Pa.) Sch. Dist., 1965-68; tchr. reading Jamesville-DeWitt (N.Y.) Sch. Dist., 1968-69, South Colonie Sch. Dist., Albany, N.Y., 1969-70; tchr. English Bethlehem Cen. Sch. Dist., Delmar, N.Y., 1970-71, Smyrna (Del.) Sch. Dist., 1971-73; reading specialist, tchr. English Delmar Sch. Dist., 1973-88; reading specialist Accomack (Va.) County Schs., 1988-93; sch. adminstr., diagnostician Silver Lake Ctr., Middletown, Del., 1994—. Past pres. Lioness, Delmar. Mem. ASCD, Del. ASCD, Va. Reading Assn. (bd. dirs. 1989-93, editorial adv. bd. Reading in Va. 1990-92), Ea. Shore Reading Coun. Va. (pres. 1989-91), Sussex County Orgn. for Reading Excellence (pres. 1980-81), Diamond State Reading Assn. (pres. 1985-86), Del. Assn. Sch. Adminstrs., Internat. Reading Assn., Coun. for Exceptional Children, Cedar Shores Condominium Assn. (sec.), Lions Club (Onancock, Va.), Alpha Delta Kappa (past pres. Theta chpt. and Del.). Home: 33 E 6th St New Castle DE 19720-5087 Office: Silver Lake Ctr PO Box 423 493 E Main St Middletown DE 19709

MARTIN, JEANNE ROCKWELL, physician assistant; b. Johnson City, N.Y., Sept. 24, 1950; d. Dewey Carlton and Jeanne Marie (Case) Rockwell; m. Christopher William Martin, June 17, 1972; children: Kristen Lee, Katie Lynn. BSN, Hartwick Coll., 1972; BS Physician Asst., Med. U. S.C., 1996. RN; cert. physician asst., Ga., 1980. Staff nurse, supr. AO Fox Hosp., Oneonta, N.Y., 1972-76; nurse practitioner, physician asst. Mark J. Meiler, MD, Oneonta, 1976-93, Aiken, S.C., 1994—; physician asst. Hartwick Coll., Oneonta, 1988-93. Bd. dirs. Indian Hills Girl Scout Coun., Binghamton, N.Y., v.p., 1989-93. Mem. Am. Assn. Physician Assts., Aiken C. of C., Aiken Steeplechase Assn. Republican. Episcopalian. Home: 124 Live Oak Rd Aiken SC 29803 Office: Mark J Meiler MD 148 University Pkwy Aiken SC 29801

MARTIN, JERRY DARREL, orthopedic surgeon; b. Gladewater, Tex., Jan. 13, 1952; s. David Preston and Malda (Hammond) M.; m. Cynthia Knowles, June 10, 1974; children: Elizabeth Ann, Daniel Austin. BS, U. Tex., 1974; MD, U. Tex., Galveston, 1978. Intern in gen. surgery U. Tex., Galveston, 1978-79, resident in orthop. surgery, 1979-83; pvt. practice Huntsville, Tex., 1983—. Fellow Am. Acad. Orthop. Surgeons; mem. AMA, Tex. Med. Assn., Tri County Med. Soc., Eggers Soc. (pres. 1992-93), Alpha Omega Alpha. Office: 2950 I45 Ste 5 Huntsville TX 77340

MARTIN, JOHN THOMAS, physician, author, educator; b. Cleve., June 8, 1924; s. Clarence Henry and Clara May (Feeney) M.; m. Marion Elizabeth George, Feb. 18, 1946; children: Thomas R., David B., Richard G., Janet E., Patricia L., Robert W. MD, U. Cin., 1948. Commd. 1st lt. USAF, 1949, advance through grades to maj., 1953; resident in anesthesiology Lackland AFB Hosp., San Antonio, 1953-55; asst. chief USAF Sch. Anesthesiology, Lackland AFB, 1955-57; attending anesthesiologist Baylor U. Hosp., Dallas, 1957-58; cons. dept. anesthesiology Mayo Clinic, Rochester, Minn., 1958-72; head Meth sect. anesthesiology Mayo Clinic, 1966-72; chmn. dept. anesthesiology Ochsner Med. Ctr., New Orleans, 1972-74; clin. assoc. prof. anesthesiology Tulane U. Sch. Medicine, New Orleans, 1972-74; prof. anesthesiology Med. Coll. Ohio, Toledo, 1974-90; chmn. dept. anesthesiology Med. Coll. Ohio, 1980-89, emeritus prof. anesthesiology, 1990—. Editor, author: Positioning Patients Anesthesia/Surgery, 1978, 2d edit., 1987, 3d edit., 1996; editor ASA Handbook of Hosp. Facilities for Anesthesia, 1972, 2d edit., 1974; contbr. articles to profl. jours. Chmn. conductor selection com. Rochester Symphony Orch., 1963-66; pres. Rochester Civic Music, 1965. Mem. Internat. Anesthesia Rsch. Soc. (chmn. 1979-81, trustee 1965-90), Minn. Soc. Anesthesiologists (pres. 1966-67), Ohio Soc. Anesthesiologists (pres. 1988-89), Am. Med. Writers Assn. (pres. Minn. chpt. 1970-71), Assoc. Physicians Med. Coll. Ohio (bd. dirs. 1974-89), Am. Soc. Anesthesiology, Sigma Xi, Alpha Omega Alpha, Sigma Chi, Phi Chi. Republican. Home: 4605 Woodland Ln Sylvania OH 43560-3221 Office: Med Coll of Ohio Toledo PO Box 10008 Toledo OH 43699

MARTIN, JOSEPH BOYD, neurologist, educator; b. Bassano, Alta., Can., Oct. 20, 1938; s. Joseph Bruce and Ruth Elizabeth (Ramer) M.; m. Rachel Ann Wenger, June 18, 1960; children: Bradley, Melanie, Douglas, Neil. BSc, Eastern Mennonite Coll., Harrisonburg, Va., 1959; MD, U. Alta., 1962; PhD, U. Rochester, N.Y., 1971; MA (hon.), Harvard U., 1978; ScD (hon.), McGill U., 1994, U. Rochester, 1996. Resident in internal medicine Univ. Hosp., Edmonton, Alta., 1962-64; resident in neurology Case-Western Res. U. Hosps., 1964-67; rsch. fellow U. Rochester, N.Y., 1967-70; mem. faculty McGill U. Faculty Medicine, Montreal, Que., Can., 1970-78; prof. medicine and neurology, neurologist-in-chief Montreal Neurol. Inst., 1976-78; chmn. dept. neurology Mass. Gen. Hosp., Boston, also Dorn prof. neurology Harvard U. Med. Sch., 1978-89; dean Sch. Medicine U. Calif., San Francisco, 1989-93; chancellor U. Calif., San Francisco, 1993—; mem. med. adv. bd. Gairdner Found., Toronto, 1978-83; adv. council neurol. disorders program Nat. Inst. Neurol., Communicative Disorders and Stroke, 1979-82. Co-author: Clinical Neuroendocrinology, 1977, The Hypothalamus, 1978, Clinical Neuroendocrinology: A Pathophysiological Approach, 1979, Neurosecretion and Brain Peptides: Implications for Brain Functions and Neurological Disease, 1981, Brain Peptides, 1983; editor Harrison's Principles of Internal Medicine, Clin. Neuroendocrinology 2d edit., 1987. Recipient Moshier Meml. gold medal U. Alta. Faculty Medicine, 1962, John W. Scott gold med. award, 1962; Med. Research Council Can. scholar, 1970-75. Mem. NAS, Internat. Soc. Neuroendocrinology (coun. 1980—), Am. Neurol. Assn. (pres. 1990), Am. Physiol. Soc. (Bowditch lectr. 1978), Royal Coll. Phys. and Surg. Can., Endocrine Soc., Soc. Neurosci., Am. Soc. Clin. Investigation, Assn. Am. Physicians, Am. Acad. Arts and Scis., Inst. of Medicine, Nat. Adv. Coun., Nat. Inst. Aging. Office: U Calif 513 Parnassus Ave Ste 126 San Francisco CA 94122-2722

MARTIN, KEVIN JOHN, nephrologist, educator; b. Dublin, Ireland, Jan. 18, 1948; came to U.S., 1973; s. John Martin and Maura (Tighe) M.; m. Grania E. O'Connor, Nov. 16, 1972; children: Alan, John, Ciara, Audrey. MB BCh, Univ. Coll. Dublin, 1971. Diplomate Am. Bd. Internal Medicine, Am. Bd. Nephrology. Intern St. Vincent's Hosp., Dublin, 1971-72, resident, 1972-73; resident Barnes Hosp., St. Louis, 1973-74, fellow, 1974-77; asst. prof. Washington U., St. Louis, 1977-84, assoc. prof., 1984-89; prof., dir. div. nephrology St. Louis U., 1989—. Contbr. numerous articles to med. jours. Office: Saint Louis Univ Med Ctr 3635 Vista Ave Saint Louis MO 63110-2539

MARTIN, LAURENT MICHEL, oncologist; b. Suresnes ile de France, France, Mar. 26; s. Michel Joseph and Josette Roberte (Frankart) M.; m. Patricia Quetier, Sept. 17, 1986; children: Charlene, Alexandre. MD, Fac. Medecine Paris XII; Diplome d'etude Appsolaudie, 1992. Intern Hosp. Necher, Paris, 1985, Hosp. St. Louis, Paris, 1989; Hosp. St. Louis, Inst. Gustave Roussy, 1990, CHU Henri Hondou Creteil, 1991; tnr. rschr. INSERM, Villejuif, France, 1991-92; oncologist SNU Mondor, Créteil, France, 1992-94; dir. Centre D'Oncologie, Le Havre, France, 1995—; dir. health edn.

program Koudougou, Burkima Faso, 1986-88. Mem. Eau, Agr., Santé en Milieu Tropical, Paris, 1986. With WHO, 1986-88. Recipient award ICCR, Kyoto, 1992. Mem. European Soc. Therapeutic Radiology and Oncology, Internat. Conf. of Radiology and Radiotherapy. Home: La Fougeraie, 76430 Oudalle France Office: Centre D'Oncologie, 29 Rue, Guillaume de Conquerant, 76600 Le Havre France

MARTIN, LESTER W., pediatrician, surgeon; b. Edwards, Mo., Aug. 15, 1923; s. Wade Hampton and Elizabeth (Moore) M.; m. Joan Belanger; children: Sarah, Betsy, Susan, Janet, David. BS, U. Mo., 1945, BSc in Medicine, 1947; MD, Harvard U., Boston, 1949. Instr. Cornell Med. Sch., N.Y.C., 1950-51, Harvard Med. Sch., Boston, 1952-57; asst./assoc. prof. U. Cin., 1957-65, prof. surgery, 1965-91, prof. emeritus, 1991—; dir. pediatric surgery Cin. Children's Hosp., 1957-91; Felton Bequest prof. pediatric surgery U. Melbourne, Australia, 1972; study group mem. NIH, 1963-65, site visitor, 1977-78; assoc. examiner Am. Bd. Surgery, 1958, 64, 70, 74, 78, 80, 82, 84, 86; surg. cons. Cin. chpt. Cystic Fibrosis Rsch. Found., Hamilton County Diagnostic Clinic for Mentally Retarded, Soldiers and Sailors Home for Children, Xenia, Ohio; vis. prof. Meth. Hosp., Indpls., 1969, Med. Coll. Va., Richmond, 1967, SUNY-Upstate Med. Ctr., Syracuse, 1980, U. South Fla., Tampa, 1974, Mich. State U., Edward W. Sparrow Hosp., Lansing, Mich., 1977, Mayo Clinic, Rochester, Minn., 1976, U. Ariz., 1978, Johns Hopkins U., Balt., 1982, Northeastern Ohio Coll. Medicine and St. Elizabeth Hosp., Youngstown, Ohio, 1983, U. Colo. and Denver Children's Hosp., 1983, Yale U., New Haven, 1986, Tohoku U., Sendai, Japan, 1987, Escola Paulista de Medicina, Sao Paulo, 1988, U. Louisville, 1988, Cornell U./ Northshore Hosp., 1990; lectr. in field. Contbr. over 157 articles to profl. jours.; editl. bd. Jour. Pediatric Surgery; assoc. editor: Pediatric Therapy, 6th edit., 1980. 1st lt. U.S. Army, 1951-52. Named Hon. citizen, State of Tex., 1973; recipient Renal Transplant Recognition award Children's Hosp. Cin., 1985, Founders award Cin. Pediatric Soc., 1988, Citation of Merit U. Mo.-Columbia Alumni Assn. and Sch. Medicine, 1989, Daniel Drake award U. Cin., 1990, Award of Excellence, 1990. Mem. Kansas City Surg. Soc. (hon.), St. Paul Surg. Soc. (hon.), Philippine Coll. surgeons (hon.), Royal Australasian Coll. Surgeons (hon.), Mont Reid Surg. Soc. (hon.), Brazilian Surg. Soc. (hon.), Columbian Pediatric Surg. Soc. (hon.), Houston Surg. Soc. (hon.), Japanese Pediatric Surg. Soc. (hon.), Alpha Omega Alpha. Office: Childrens Hospital Dept Pediatric Surgery 3333 Burnet Ave Cincinnati OH 45229

MARTIN, LISA WARSINGER, cardiologist; b. Washington, July 28, 1952; m. Neil F. Martin, June 23, 1974; children: David, Joshua, Rebecca. AB, Harvard U., 1974; MD, U. Fla., 1980. Diplomate in internal medicine and cardiovascular Am. Bd. Internal Medicine. Intern Johns Hopkins Hosp., Balt., 1980-81, resident, 1981-83; fellow in cardiology George Washington U., Washington, 1983-86; pvt. practice, Falls Church, Va. Fellow Am. Coll. Cardiology. Office: 201 N Washington St Falls Church VA 22046

MARTIN, LOUIS FRANK, surgery and physiology educator; b. Troy, N.Y., Nov. 7, 1951; s. Eugene Lavern and Lois Jane (Perkins) Martin; m. Deborah Lynn Tjarnberg, Mar. 12, 1977; children: Jesse Tjarnberg, James Casey, Tyler Gene. BA, Brown U., 1973, MD, 1976; MS in Health Administrn., U. Louisville, 1993. Diplomate Am. Bd. Surgery. Resident in gen. surgery U. Wash. Affiliated Hosps., Seattle, 1977-78; resident in gen. surgery U. Louisville, 1978-83, rsch. fellow trauma rsch. and health care ednl. adminstrn., 1980-82; asst. prof. surgery Pa. State U., Hershey, 1983-88, asst. prof. physiology, 1986-88, assoc. prof. surgery and cellular and molecular physiology, 1988-92; prof. surgery, assoc. chmn. dept. La. State U., New Orleans, 1992—, prof. health svcs. rsch./pub. health, 1994—; prof. neurosci., 1995—; med. dir. St. Charles Weight Mgmt. Ctr. La. State U., New Orleans, 1995—; vis. scientist INSERM, Poste ORange, France, 1990-91; cons. TENET Health Care Corp. MEd. Affairs Dept., 1995—. Mem. editorial bd. Shock, 1994; contbr. articles to newspapers and profl. jours. Recipient Loyal Davis Traveling Surg. scholar ACS, 1990, Clin. Investigator award NIH, 1985-90. Mem. ACS, Am. Coll. Critical Care Medicine, Am. Coll. Physician Execs., Am. Physiol. Soc., Assn. for Acad. Surgery (councilman 1988-90), Collegium Internat. Chirurgiae Digestivae, Soc. Internat. Chirurgie, Soc. Univ. Surgeons. Home: 3005 Palm Vista Dr Kenner LA 70065-1560 Office: La State U Dept Surgery 1542 Tulane Ave New Orleans LA 70112-2825

MARTIN, LYNN THOMAS, plastic surgeon; b. Stevens Point, Wis., Sept. 21, 1951; s. Harlan E. and Mary A. Martin; m. Sharon Robinson, Dec. 30, 1984; children: Jacob, Jessica. BA with honors in Molecular Biology, U. Wis., 1973, MD, 1977. Diplomate Am. Bd. Otolaryngology, Head and Neck Surgery, Am. Bd. Plastice and Reconstructive Surgery. Resident otolaryngology U. Oreg., Portland, 1978-82; resident plastic surgery U. Wis., Madison, 1982-84; plastic surgeon Gundersen Clinic, Ltd., LaCrosse, Wis., 1984—. Contbr. articles to profl. jours. Mem. Am. Soc. Plastic and Reconstructive Surgeons, Midwestern Soc. Plastice and Reconstructive Surgeons, Wis. Soc. Plastic Surgeons, Wis. State Med. Soc., County Med. Soc. Office: Gundersen Clinic Ltd 1836 South Ave La Crosse WI 54601

MARTIN, MICHAEL, internist; b. Hamburg, Germany, Oct. 27, 1932; s. Carlotto and Anneliese (Rahtjen) M.; m. May 18, 1966. MD, U. Hamburg, 1961. Intern Anatomy Inst., Freiburg, Fed. Republic of Germany, 1963-66; resident Aggertalklinik Clinic for Vascular Disease, Cologne, Fed. Republic of Germany, 1967-69, 72-77, U. Hosp., Bonn, Fed. Republic of Germany, 1969-72; Lectr. for internal medicine and angiology U. Bonn, 1971; head geriatric dept. Mcpl. Hosp., Duisburg, 1977—; lectr. U. Bonn, 1972, prof. medicine, 1977. Author: Geriatric Medicine for Students, 1980, The 36-Hour Day (transl.), 1986, Streptokinase in Chronic Arterial Disease, 1988, Die Kurzzeitlyse mit Ultrahoher Streptokinase, 1988, Phlebologische Krankheitsbilder, 1990, Therapieschemata Geriatrie, 1991, Fibrinolytische Behandlung peripherer Arterien und Venenverschlüsse, 1994; editor: New Concepts in Streptokinase Dosimetry, 1978. Mem. Internat. Coll. Angiology, German Geriatrics Soc. (v.p.), British Geriatrics Soc., Deutsche Gesellschaft fur Angiologie, Gesellschaft fur Thrombose-und Hämostaseforschung, Deutsche Gesellschaft für Innere Medizin. Office: Städtische Kliniken, Zu den Rehwiesen 9, Duisburg D-47055, Germany

MARTIN, PAUL DOUGLAS, organ transplant recovery coordinator, educator; b. St. Louis, Sept. 26, 1961; s. Floyd Clarence and Beverly Joann (Harpending) M.; m. Sueann Clark, Sept. 12, 1987; children: Kristina Ann, James Floyd, Matthew Douglas. ADN, Austin Peay State U., 1982, BS in Biology, 1987. EMT, Tenn., N.C. Staff nurse ICU Nashville (Tenn.) Gen. Hosp., 1982-84, charge nurse ICU, 1984-85, staff nurse emergency rm., 1985-86, charge nurse emergency rm., 1986-88; staff nurse cardiac cath lab. Parkview Med. Ctr., Nashville, 1988-89; organ recovery coord. Tenn. Donor Svcs., Nashville, 1989-91, sr. coord., 1991-92; supr. recovery svcs. Carolina Organ Procurement Agy., Raleigh-Durham, N.C., 1992—; paramedic clin. instr. Vol. State Coll., Gallatin, Tenn., 1986-91. Mem. AACN, N.Am. Transplant Coords. Assn (cert. procurement transplant coord., edn. com. 1991—, pub. rels. com. 1994-95), Am. Assn. Tissue Banks (cert. tissue bank specialist). Baptist. Office: Carolina Organ Procurement Agy W Gate Plz 3622 Lyckan Pky Ste 6002 Durham NC 27707-2545

MARTIN, PETER ROBERT, psychiatrist, pharmacologist; b. Budapest, Hungary, Sept. 6, 1949; came to U.S.,1980; s. Nicholas M. and Eva (Horvat) M.; m. Barbara Bradford, Dec. 23, 1985; 1 child, Alexander Bradford. BSc with honors, McGill U., Montreal, Que., Can., 1971, MD, CM, 1975; MSc, U. Toronto (Ont., Can.), 1978. Diplomate Am. Bd. Psychiatry and Neurology, Psychiatry, Addiction Psychiatry. Resident Dept. Medicine U. Toronto, Can., 1975-76, Psychiatry, U. Toronto, 1978-80; fellow Clin. Pharmacology Addiction Rsch. Found., Toronto, 1976-78; chief Sect. Clin. Sci., Nat. Inst. on Alcohol Abuse & Alcoholism, Bethesda, 1983-86; assoc. prof. Vanderbilt U. Sch. Medicine, Nashville, 1986-92, prof., 1992—; dir. Addiction Rsch. Ctr. Vanderbilt U., Nashville, 1994—, chief psychiatrist Vanderbilt Addiction Care Ctr., 1995—; vis. scientist Lab. of Clin. Sci., NIMH, Bethesda, Md., 1980-83; investigator John F. Kennedy Ctr. for Rsch. on Human Devel., Nashville, 1993—. Fellow Royal Coll. Physicians (Can.), Am. Psychiatric Assn.; mem. AAAS, Am. Soc. Clin. Pharmacology and Therapeutics, Am. Acad. Addiction Psychiatry, Am. Coll. Psychiatrists, Rsch. Soc. on Alcoholism, Internat. Soc. Biomed. Rsch. in Alcoholism. Office: Vanderbilt U Sch Medicine Dept Psychiatry MCN A2205 Nashville TN 37232

MARTIN, ROBERT JAMES, physician, surgeon; b. Omaha, Oct. 16, 1936; s. James Wicher and Frances Olivia (Dickerson) M.; m. Nancy Lynn Janssen, July 10, 1960; children: Susan Haselhoff, James Martin. BS, U. Nebr., 1957; MD, U. Nebr., Omaha, 1961. Diplomate Am. Bd. Surgery. Intern Nebr. Meth. Hosp., Omaha, 1961-62; resident in surgery U. Kans. Med. Ctr., Kansas City, 1962-66; surgeon Sioux Valley Meml. Hosp., Cherokee, Iowa, 1968-95; gen. surgeon Sioux Valley Med. Assocs., 1994—; cons. surgeon State Mental Health Inst., Cherokee, 1968-95; high sch. atheltic team physician. Bd. mem. Cherokee Cmty. Sch. Dist., Cherokee, 1969-78; bd. dirs. Cherokee Econ. Devel. Corp., 1978-80. Caprt USAF, 1966-68. Fellow Am. Coll. Surgeons; mem. Sigma Nu (pres. 1956-57), Phi Chi (pres. 1959-60). Republican. Methodist. Home: 700 Walnut Cherokee IA 51012 Office: Sioux Valley Med Assocs 300 Sioux Valley Dr Cherokee IA 51012

MARTIN, ROBERT JOHN, psychologist, educator; b. Chgo., May 13, 1943; s. Robert J. and Mildred R. (Blumhagen) M.; m. Suzanne Louise Wildhalen, July 6, 1946; children: Joan, Andrew. PhD, U. Ill., 1972. Prof. N.E. Mo. State, Kirksville, 1972—; psychologist RJM Assocs., Moberly, Mo., 1980-94, Macon, Mo., 1994—; consulting psychologist Moberly Regional Med. Ctr., 1988-94. Author: Teaching Through Encouragement, 1980, A Skills and Strategies Handbook for Working with People, 1983. Mem. APA, Lead Mgmt., Am. Soc. for Cybernetics, William Glaser Inst. Home and Office: 805 Sunset Dr Macon MO 63552

MARTIN, STEVEN S., insurance company executive; b. Horton, Kans., Aug. 14, 1956; s. Bob D. and Pattie L. Martin; m. Amy M. Haddad, Mar. 17, 1984. Cert. in gerontol. nursing, U. Nebr., Omaha, 1989; MA in Gerontology, U. Nebr., 1992; BSN, Washburn U., 1979. With St. Francis Med. Ctr., Topeka, 1976-78; staff Menninger Found., Topeka, 1978-80, assoc. nursing coord., 1980; co-founder, v.p. HealthCheck, Inc., Topeka, 1980-82; regional mgr., cons. Health Programs divsn. Upjohn HealthCare Svcs., 1982-84; founding dir. Am. HomeCare, Omaha, 1984-86; reimbursement adminstr. Blue Cross & Blue Shield Nebr., Omaha, 1986-89; dir. health svcs. rsch. Menninger Found., Topeka, 1989-93, v.p. health svcs. rsch. and reimbursement, 1993—; sr. v.p., founder Pro Pax Svcs., Inc., 1994—; co-leader nursing study tour, USSR, 1987, People's Republic China, 1989; mem. inpatient cost mgmt. project adv. com. Blue Cross Blue Shield, 1990. Contbr. chpt. to: High Tech Home Care, 1987. State worksite edn. chairperson Nebr. div. Am. Cancer Soc., 1986; mem. exec. com. Wellness Coun. of the Midlands, Omaha, 1984; mem. adv. bd. Sch. Nursing, Coll. of St. Mary, Omaha, 1985; hon. mem. adv. bd. Omaha Hospice Assn., 1990; bd. dirs. The Friendship Program, Omaha, 1985, pres. bd. dirs., 1988. Mem. ANA (cert. cmty. health nurse), APHA, Assn. Health Svcs. Rsch., Nebr. Nurses Assn., Health Care Fin. Mgmt. Assn. (nat. and AK-SAR-BEN chpts.), Sigma Theta Tau (Eta Kappa chpt.).

MARTIN, TOMAS DITTO, physician; b. Lufkin, Tex., Jan. 16, 1956; s. Juan Enrique and Cordelia (Ditto) M.; m. Sally Jones, Aug. 22, 1981; children: Monica Anne, John Everitt. BS in Microbiology, Tex. A&M U., 1977; MD, U. Tex., Houston, 1981. Diplomate in Am. Bd. Surgery, Am. Bd. Thoracic Surgery. Asst. prof. surgery Emory U., Atlanta, 1990-92; chief cardiothoracic surgery Atlanta VA Hosp., 1990-92; asst. prof. surgery U. Fla., Gainesville, 1989-90, assoc. prof. surgery, chief adult cardiovascular surgery, 1993—. Author: Diagnostic and Therapeutic Cardiac Catheterization, 1993, Cardiopulmonary Bypass, 1995; contbr. articles to profl. jours. Fellow ACS, Am. Coll. Chest Physicians, Am. Coll. Cardiology; mem. AMA, Soc. Thoracic Surgeons, Assn. Acad. Surgery, Southeastern Surg. Congress, Fla. Med. Assn., Alachua County Med. Soc. Office: U Fla Dept Surgery Box 100286 Gainesville FL 32610-0286

MARTIN, VIRVE PAUL, licensed professional counselor; b. Tallinn, Estonia, Nov. 19, 1928; came to U.S., 1949; d. Walter Gerhard and Alice (Haas) Paul; m. Albert Lynn Martin Jr., May 31, 1952; children: Lynda Lee, Elaine Lynne, Monique Louise. Student, U. Heidelberg, Germany, 1948-49; BA, Wesleyan Coll., Macon, Ga., 1952; MA, U. Minn., 1970. Cert. profl. counselor, Ga. Interpreter Internat. Refugee Orgn., Nuremberg, Frankfurt, Heidelberg, Fed. Republic of Germany, 1947-49; bookkeeper, receptionist DeKalb Nat. Bank, Atlanta, 1955-56; rsch. asst. Kenny Inst., Mpls., 1966-67; vocat. evaluator Dept. Human Resources, Atlanta, 1970-73, rehab. counselor, 1973—; interpreter Mpls. C. of C., 1963-65, Dem. Nat. Conv., Atlanta, 1988; attaché Estonian Olympic Com. 1996 Olympics, Atlanta. Writer, editor World Pen Pals, 1964-66. V.p., bd. dirs. Ms. JCs, Minn., 1959-62; pres. Valley View Mothers' Club, Bloomington, Minn., 1961-62. Mem. AAUW, Nat. Rehab. Assn., Ga. Rehab. Assn. (membership chair 1988), Ga. Mental Health Counselors Assn. Home: 1106 Norwich Cir NE Atlanta GA 30324-2908 Office: Dept Rehab Svc 1800 Peachtree St NW Ste 444 Atlanta GA 30309-2505

MARTIN, WAYNE A., clinical social worker; b. N.Y.C., Jan. 26, 1945; s. Bernard and Juliet (Aurbach) M.; m. Barbara Jo Goodman, Aug. 16, 1970; 1 child, Jason David. BA in Social Sci., Fla. State U., 1966; MS, Columbia U., 1968; postgrad. Old Dominion U., 1978—. Lic. clin. social worker, Va., cert. diplomate. Day camp dir. Jewish Cmty. Ctr., Norfolk, Va., 1968-71, children's dept. dir., 1968-69, youth dept. dir., 1969-71; psychiat. social worker Psychiat. Assocs., Ltd., Portsmouth, Va., 1971-77; clin. social worker Human Resource Inst., Norfolk, 1977-79; part-time caseworker Cath. Home Bur., Hampton, Va., 1977-78; primary therapist Charter Colonial Inst., Newport News, Va., 1980-91; pvt. practice clin. social work, Virginia Beach, Norfolk and Newport News, 1980—; program coord. for adolescent psychiat. unit Peninsula Psychiat. Hosp., Hampton, Va., 1979-80; field supr. Va. Commonwealth U. Sch. Social Work, 1978-84, Norfolk State U. Sch. Social Work, 1982—; chmn. adv. com. Upjohn Health-care Svcs., 1979-80; dir. social svcs. Colonial Hosp., Newport News, 1995—; oral examiner/ adviser Va. Bd. Social Work. Chmn., Crisis Ctr., 1977-78; pres. Arnold Gamsey Lodge of B'Nai B'rith, 1975-77; 1st v.p. B'nai Brith, Va. State Assn., 1977-78, pres., 1979-80, mem. B'Nai B'rith dist. 5 bd. govs., 1978—, 3d v.p./treas. dist. 5, 1983-84, 1st v.p., 1985-86, pres.-elect 1986-87, pres. 1987-88, chmn. dist. 5 personnel com., bd. govs. B'nai B'rith Internat., 1986-88, 94—; chmn. Hillel Found. for State of Va., 1978-79, 90—; bd. dirs. Jewish Community Ctr., Norfolk, 1973-79, Anti-Defamation League; exec. bd. Temple Israel Synagogue, 1981-84, pres. Men's Club, 1981-82, temple sec., 1982-84. Recipient Charles Olshansky Lodge Svc. award B'nai Brith, 1991, Outstanding Svc. Presdl. citation, 1991; named Outstanding Lodge Pres., B'nai Brith, 1977, Outstanding State Pres., 1980, Man of Yr., Va. State Assn. B'nai B'rith, 1980. Mem. NASW (v.p. Hampton Roads unit 1974-76, dist. chmn. 1982-83 state dir. 1977-83), Va. Soc. Clin. Social Work (bd. dirs. Ea. Va. chpt. 1989-96, pres. 1991-95), Nat. Fed. Socs. Clin. Social Work (bd. dirs. 1991-95), Acad. Cert. Social Workers (bd. cert. diplomate), ACLU, Kappa Delta Pi, Phi Alpha Theta, Pi Sigma Alpha. Democrat. Jewish. Club: Mogul Ski (v.p. 1970-71) (Norfolk). Home: 1827 Longdale Dr Norfolk VA 23518-4943 also: Colonial Practice Assocs 708 Mobjack Pl Newport News VA 23606

MARTIN, WILLIAM COLLIER, hospital administrator; b. Atlanta, Aug. 16, 1926; s. William Henry and Lillian (Collier) M.; BS, U. Ga., 1950; diploma Charlotte Meml. Hosp., 1952; postgrad. U. Okla., 1969; m. Alice Elizabeth Nickle, Jan. 12, 1952; children: Mary Anne, Patricia Jean, William Collier, Nancy Lee. Operating room technician Athens (Ga.) Gen. Hosp., 1949-50; hosp. adminstrn. intern/resident Charlotte (N.C.) Meml. Hosp., 1950-52; hosp. adminstr. Rockmart-Aragon Hosp., Rockmart, Ga., 1952-54; asst. hosp. adminstr. St. Agnes Hosp., Raleigh, N.C., 1954-56; hosp. adminstr. Florence-Darlington Tb. Sanitorium, Florence, S.C., 1956-58; commd. 1st lt. MSC, U.S. Army, 1959, advanced through grades to lt. col.; adj. U.S. Army Hosp., Ft. Campbell Ky., 1959; comdg. officer med. co. U.S. Army Hosp., 1959-61; comdg. officer U.S. Army Med. Svc. Detachment, Ft. Gulick, C.Z., 1961-64; exec. officer 5th Evacuation Hosp., Ft. Bragg, N.C., 1964, comdg. officer, 1964-65; adj. personnel officer 55th Med. Group, Ft. Bragg, 1965-66, Qui Nhon, Republic Vietnam, 1966-67; comdg. officer 47th Gen. Hosp., Fitzsimons Gen. Hosp., Denver, 1967-68; exec. officer Evans Health Care Facility, Ft. Buckner, Okinawa, 1968-69; dir. security plans and ops. U.S. Army Med. Ctr., Camp Kue, Okinawa, 1969-71; med. ops. officer VII Corps, Moehringen, W.Ger., 1971-73; chief tng., exercises and readiness U.S. Army Med. Command, Europe, Heidelberg, W.Ger., 1973-74; dir. security plans and tng. Fitzsimons Army Med. Ctr., 1974-77, ret., 1977; guest lectr. health care adminstrn. U.S. Army Med. Command in Europe, 1973-74; exec. dir. Thomas Rehab. Hosp., Asheville, N.C., 1977-78; chmn. Pub. Health Trust of Escambia County, Pensacola, Fla., 1979-86; guest lectr. to profl. assns., civic orgns. and mil. units, 1965—; mem. N.C. Gov.'s Adv. Com. on Rehab. Ctrs., 1977-78; mem. regional Hospice Program for NW Fla., Inc., 1979-80, chmn., bd. dirs., 1980-83, exec. dir., 1983-85; mgmt. cons. Pensacola (Fla.) Habatat for Humanity, Inc., 1986-88, Niceville (Fla.) Mktg. Resources, 1986-87, Dan Laumpking Mgmt. Cons., Fairhope, Ala., 1986-87. Mem. Pres.'s Com. on Employment of the Handicapped, 1978; sec. United Meth. Bd. Pastoral Care and Counseling, 1988-90; mem., v.p., bd. ministries Pensecola Dist. United Meth. Ch., Inc., 1988—; dir. lay speaking, bd. laity, council on ministries Ala.- West Fla. Conf. United Meth. Ch., 1988—; mem. Health and Human Services task force of citizens goals for Pensacola, 1981-86; vice chmn. adminstrv. bd. Pine Forest United Meth. Ch., Pensacola, 1979-86; mem. fin. com., 1979-86; dir. for lay speaking Pensacola Dist. United Meth. Ch., 1985-88; bd. dirs. Hispanic Minorities, Inc., 1986-93, Meth. Homes for the Aging, Inc., 1988—, Pastoral Counseling, Care and Tng., Inc., 1990-95. Served with USN, 1944-46. Decorated Legion of Merit, Bronze Star; Vietnam Royal Cross of Gallantry with bronze palm; cert. lay speaker of United Meth. Ch. Fellow Am. Acad. Med. Adminstrs.; mem. Am. Soc. Tng. and Devel. (dir. 1977-78), Ret. Officers Assn., Assn. of U.S. Army (dir. Denver-Centennial chpt. 1974-77, Greater Gulf Coast chpt. 1979-86), U.S. Power Squadrons, V.F.W., Phi Delta Theta. Democrat. Club: Masons.

MARTIN, WILLIAM OWEN, III, ophthalmologist; b. Atlanta, Oct. 10, 1937; s. William Owen and Gertrude Ellen (Harris) M.; m. Ann Rogers Poten, Oct. 6, 1962; children: Christopher, Virginia, Gayle (dec.). BA, Yale U., 1958; MD, Emory U., 1962. Ophthalmologist pvt. practice, Atlanta, 1968-91. Capt. USAF, 1963-65. Fellow Am. Acad. Ophthalmology, Ga. Soc. Ophthalmology. Office: Ste 3000 95 Collier Rd NW Atlanta GA 30309

MARTIN, YVONNE CONNOLLY, pharmaceutical company executive; b. St. Paul, Minn., Sept. 13, 1936; d. Elvert Farrell and Irene Mildred (Aitken) C.; m. William Brady Martin, Dec. 14, 1963; children: Margaret Anne, Catherine Irene. BA, Carleton Coll., 1958; PhD, Northwestern U., Evanston, Ill., 1964. Pharmacology asst. Abbott Labs, North Chgo., Ill., 1958-60, sr. pharmacologist, 1964-67; sr. pharmacologist Abbott Labs, Abbott Park, Ill., 1968-70, assoc. rsch. fellow, 1970-74, rsch. fellow, 1974-85, sr. project leader, 1983—, sr. rsch. fellow, 1985—; instr. in chemistry Northwestern U., 1963-64; vis. instr. Pomona Coll., Claremont, Calif., 1967-68. Author: Quantitative Drug Design, 1978; Editor: Paths to Better and Safer Drugs, 1989; contbr. articles to profl. jours. Recipient predoctoral fellowship NSF, Northwestern U., 1960-63. Fellow, AAAS; mem. Am. Chem. Soc., Am. Crystall. Assn., Molecular Graphics Soc., Protein Soc., Phi Beta Kappa, Sigma Xi. Office: Abbott Labs D47E AP10 100 Abbott Park Rd Abbott Park IL 60064-3500

MARTINA, BENEDICT FRANZ, cardiologist; b. Wattwil, St. Gallen, Switzerland, Mar. 20, 1957; s. Franz and Beatrix (Christ) M.; m. Petra Fehrenbach, Oct. 27, 1990; children: Sophie, Franz. MD, U. Basel, Switzerland, 1982. Intern, asst. dept. surgery St. Clara Hosp., Basel, 1983-84; resident internal medicine Univ. Clinics, Bern and Basel, 1985-87; resident cardiology Herz-Zentrum, Bad Krozingen, Germany, 1987-89; resident cardiology Univ. Clinic, Basel, 1987-89, attending physician internal medicine, 1989-90, attending physician med. outpatient dept., 1991-94; dep. chmn. med. outpatient dept. and emergency dept. Univ. Hosp., Basel, 1994—. Co-author: Differix Internal Medicine, 1994, Memorix (Cardiology), 1996. Mem. Swiss Soc. Internal Medicine, Swiss and European Soc. Cardiology. Home: Saint Alban Anlage 50, 4052 Basel Switzerland Office: Univ Hosp, Petersgraben 4, 4031 Basel Switzerland

MARTIN-CANNICI, CYNTHIA ELAINE, clinical psychologist; b. Matador, Tex., Aug. 25, 1953; d. Barney Joe and Cloria Martella (Neatherlin) Martin; m. Rick A. McCorkle, Sept. 25, 1982; children: Brandt Martin Cannici, Huxley Anne Martin McCorkle, Darcy Jane Martin McCorkle. BA summa cum laude, North Tex. State U., 1977, MS, 1980, PhD, 1984. Cert. psychologist, Ark.; licensed clin. psychologist, Tex.; registered sex offender treatment provider; diplomate Profl. Assn. of Custody Evaluators, Am. Bd. Forensic Examiners. Tex. Asst. dir. Denton Area Crisis Ctr., Tex., 1975-77; dir. psychol. services children's inpatient unit, U. Ark. for Med. Scis., Little Rock, 1982-84; psychologist Mental Health Mental Retardation Svcs. of Texoma, Sherman, Tex., 1984-85; ind. practice, Sherman, 1985—; cons. Grayson County Juvenile Alternatives, Sherman, 1985—, Grayson County Juvenile Probation, 1985—, Fannin County Juvenile Probation, 1985—, Grayson County Sheriff's Dept., 1985—, Denison Police Dept., 1986—, Grayson County Dist. Cts., 1985—, Grayson County Child Protective Svc., 1986—, Grayson County Teen Ct., 1987, Fannin County Child Protective Svcs., 1987—, The Family Connection, 1987—, Fannin County Adult Probation, 1989—, Cooke County Child Protective Svcs., 1989—, Grayson County Adult Probation, 1991—, Grayson County CASA, 1994—; counselor CETA Youth Program, Denton, 1981; foster parent Survival House, Denton, 1979-81; chmn. prevention Greater Little Rock Cmty. Mental Health Ctr. Adv. Bd., 1982-84; cons. Women's Crisis Ctr., Sherman, 1985—, Sherman Boy's Club, 1985, Sherman Kerr East Ctr., 1985—. Contbr. papers to profl. publs. and confs. Vol. Grayson County Foster Parent Assn., 1987—; program chmn. Montessori PTA, Little Rock, 1983; vol. Denton County Big Bros. Big Sisters, 1980; guardian ad litem Charleston Family Ct. System, S.C., 1978; mem. adv. bd. Grayson County Juvenile Alternatives, 1985—, Tex. Dept. Human Svcs., 1992—; bd. dirs. Sexual Abuse Intervention Network Tex., 1992—, Sherman Little League, 1991, Theatricks Children's Theater. Recipient Letter of Commendation U. Ark. Med. Scis., 1984; named one of Outstanding Young Women in Am., 1986. Mem. APA, ASCAP, Am. Bd. Forensic Examiners, Tex. Psychol. Assn., Tex. Coalition for Juvenile Justice, Am. Assn. Counsel for Children. Avocations: reading, crafts, games.

MARTIN-COMIN, JOSE, nuclear medicine physician; b. Obon, Spain, Oct. 19, 1948; s. Manuel and Manuela (Comin) M.; m. Anna Miralles Casellas; 1 child, Isis. BS, U. San Miguel, 1965; MD, U. Ctrl., Barcelona, 1972, specialist in nuclear medicine, 1980. Asst. prof. pharmacology U. Ctrl., Barcelona, 1972-75; resident Hosp. Clinic, Barcelona, 1976-78; staff physician Hosp. de Bellvitge, Barcelona, 1978-87, clin. chief, 1987—. Editor: Radiolabelled Blood Cells, 1994; contbr. articles to profl. jours. Mem. Soc. Catalana Medicina Nuclear (pres. 1994-95), European Assn. Nuclear Medicine (task group coord. 1994-97), Soc. Espanola Medicina Nuclear (pres.-elect 1995—), Internat. Soc. Radiolabelled Blood Elements (pres. 1995-97). Home: c/ Rocafort 151, 08015 Barcelona Spain Office: CSUB Hosp de Bellvitge, Feixa 1 Larga s/n, 08907 Barcelona Spain

MARTINEZ, AUGUSTO JULIO, neuropathologist; b. Saint Cruz Sur, Camagüey, Cuba, Apr. 12, 1930; came to U.S., 1962; s. Augusto M. and Aurora (Avila) M.; m. Josephine Bridget O'Donnell, Oct. 15, 1966; children: Killeen Josephine, Bridget Elizabeth, Mary Ondina. BS, Inst. Camagüey, 1950; MD, U. Havana, Cuba, 1959. Asst. prof. Med. Coll. of Va., Richmond, 1969-71, assoc. prof., 1974-76; assoc. prof. U. Tenn., Memphis, 1972-74; prof. pathology U. Pitts., 1976—; neuropathologist Presbyn. U. Hosp., Pitts., 1976—, Montefiore U. Hosp., Pitts., 1989—. Author: Freeliving Amebas, 1985. Named Mem. of Honor Med. Soc. of Cataluna, Barcelona, Spain, 1986, Extraordinary Mem. Soc. of Neuropathologists, Buenos Aires, 1991. Republican. Roman Catholic. Home: 111 Emily Dr Pittsburgh PA 15215-1009 Office: Presbyn Hosp DeSoto & O'Hara Streets Pittsburgh PA 15213

MARTINEZ, CINDY LEE, nursing administrator; b. Alliance, Ohio, July 13, 1952; d. Harold L. and Edna Jane (Stultz) Becker; 1 child, Deborah. BA, Chapman Coll., 1988, MA in Counseling Psychology, 1994; AS, Victor Valley Coll., 1981. RN, Calif. Sch. nurse St. Joseph's Sch., Barstow, Calif., 1982-89; labor and delivery nurse Barstow (Calif.) Community Hosp., 1983—; marriage-family-child counselor Women's Group Therapy, Marine Corps Logistics Base, Barstow, 1986-90, adolescent group facilitator, stress mgmt. instr., 1994—. Home: 34927 Norwich Ct Barstow CA 92311-3622

MARTINEZ, JOHN G., surgeon. BA in Biology, U. Colo., 1977; MD, U. Wash., 1982. Diplomate Am. Bd. Surgery; cert. laser surgery, laproscopic surgery, advanced trauma life support instr. Intern St. Joseph Presbyn. Hosps., Denver, 1982-83; intern gen. surgery Highland Gen. Hosp., Oakland, Calif., 1985-86; gen. surgery resident U. Nev., Las Vegas, 1986-90, chief resident gen. surgery, 1989-90; gen., vascular and thoracic surgeon Medford, Oreg., 1990-91, Fort Collins, Colo., 1991—; operating rm. tech. U. Colo. Med. Ctr., Denver, 1973-77; vet. asst., Denver, 1974-76; gen. med. officer Indian Health Svcs., Tuba City, Ariz., 1983-85; dir. trauma Providence Hosp., Medford; med. dir. trauma Poudre Valley Hosp., Fort Collins; med. dir. Wound Care Ctr. Sgt. USN, 1970-73. Office: Fort Collins Surg Assoc 1217 Riverside Ave Fort Collins CO 80524-3218

MARTÍNEZ, LUÍS OSVALDO, radiologist, educator; b. Havana, Cuba, Nov. 27, 1927; came to U.S., 1962, naturalized, 1967; s. Osvaldo and Felicita (Farinas) M.; children: María Elena, Luís Osvaldo, Alberto Luis; m. Nydia M. Ceballos. MD, U. Havana, 1954. Intern Calixto García Hosp., Havana, 1954-55; resident in radiology Jackson Meml. Hosp., Miami, Fla., 1963-65, fellow in cardiovascular radiology, 1965-67; instr. radiology U. Miami, 1965-68, asst. prof., 1968, clin. asst. prof., 1968-70, assoc. prof., 1970-76, prof., 1976-91, clin. prof., 1991-94; chief radiol. svcs. VA Med. Ctr., 1991—; assoc. dir. dept. radiology Mt. Sinai Med. Ctr., Miami Beach, Fla., 1969-91, chief div. diagnostic radiology, 1970-91, dir. residency program in diagnostic radiology; dir. Spanish Radiology Seminar. Reviewer Am. Jour. Radiology, Radium Therapy and Nuclear Medicine, 1978; contbr. articles to profl. jours. Former pres. League Against Cancer. Recipient Medaille Antoine Beclere ICR-89, 1989, Carlos J. Finlay Gold medal Cuban Med. Congress in Exile, 1990. Mem. AMA, AAUP, Radiol. Soc. France (hon. 1991), Internat. Soc. Lymphology, Interam. Coll. Radiology (pres.), Internat. Coll. Surgeons, Internat. Coll. Angiology, Internat. Soc. Radiology, Interam. Coll. Radiology (Gold medal 1975), Cuban Med. Assn. in Exile, Am. Coll. Chest Physicians (assoc.), Radiol. Soc. N.Am., Am. Coll. Radiology, Am. Roentgen Ray Soc., Am. Assn. Fgn. Med. Grads., Am. Profl. Practice Assn., Am. Thoracic Soc., Pan Am. Med. Assn., Am. Assn. Univ. Radiologists, Brit. Inst. Radiology, Am. Heart Assn. (mem. council cardiovascular radiology), Faculty Radiologists, Soc. Gastrointestinal Radiologists, Am. Geriatrics Soc., Am. Coll. Angiology, Royal Coll. Radiologists, Am. Soc. Therapeutic Radiologists, Assn. Hosp. Med. Edn., Am. Coll. Med. Imaging, Interasma, So. Med. Assn., N.Y. Acad. Scis., Fla. Thoracic Soc., Fla. Radiol. Soc., Dade County Med. Assn., Greater Miami Radiol. Soc., Cuban Radiol. Soc. (sec.), Can. Assn. Radiologists, Soc. Thoracic Radiologists (founding mem.), Emeritus mem., Am. Coll. of Angiology, 1989, Emeritus mem., Am. Heart Assn., 1992; hon. mem. numerous med. socs. of Mex., Cen. and S.Am. Roman Catholic. Office: 1201 NW 16th St Miami FL 33125-1624

MARTINEZ, MARIA DOLORES, pediatrician; b. Cifuentes, Cuba, Mar. 16, 1959; d. Demetrio and Alba Silvia (Perez) M.; m. James David Marple, Apr. 25, 1992. MD, U. Navarra, Pamplona, Spain, 1984. Med. diplomate. Resident in pediatrics Moses Cone Hosp., Greensboro, N.C., 1986-89; pvt. practice Charlotte, N.C., 1989-93, Mooresville, N.C., 1993—; with Univ. Med. Hosp., Tucson. Mem. AMA, Am. Acad. Pediatrics, N.C. Med. Soc., Mecklenburg County Med. Soc. Republican. Roman Catholic. Office: Univ Med Hosp 1501 Campbell Ave Tucson AZ 85741

MARTINEZ, RICHARD MANUEL, pediatrician; b. Tampa, Fla., Nov. 28, 1954; s. Herman and Mercedes (Salinero) M.; m. Peggy D. Duffy, Apr. 7, 1984; children: Michael, Julia, Joseph, Katie. BS, U. Fla., 1976; MD, U. So. Fla., 1979. Diplomate Nat. Bd. Med. Examiners, Am. Bd. Pediatrics, Am. Bd. Pediatric Cardiology; lic. MD, Ohio, Fla. First year resident in pediatrics Children's Hosp. Med. Ctr., Cin., 1979-80, resident in pediatrics, 1980-82, ambulatory fellow, 1982-83, cardiology fellow, 1983-86; staff pediatric cardiologist All Children's Hosp., St. Petersburg, Fla., 1986—; med. dir. non-invasive sect. cardiology All Children's Hosp., St. Petersburg, 1991—; clin. assoc. prof. pediatrics U. South Fla. Coll. of Medicine; co-dir. Adult Congenital Heart Disease Ctr., U. South Fla. Contbr. articles to profl. jours. Grantee Southwestern Ohio chpt. Am. Heart Assn., 1985-86. Fellow Am. Coll. Cardiology, Am. Acad. Pediatrics; mem. AMA, Fla. Med. Assn., Am. Heart Assn., Am. Soc. Endocardiography, Am. Inst. Ultrasound in Medicine, Soc. Pediatric Echocardiography, Hillsborough County Med. Soc., Hillsborough County Pediatric Soc., Fla. Pediatric Soc., Fla. Assn. Pediatric Cardiologists, Pinellas County Pediatric Soc., Fla. Physicians Assn., North Am. Soc. Pediatric Exercise Medicine. Office: Pediatric Cardiology Assocs 880 Sixth St S Ste 280 Saint Petersburg FL 33701

MARTINEZ, VICTOR J., surgeon, lawyer; b. Tampa, July 27, 1934; s. David and Mary (Fernandez) M.; m. Aline Guerra, June 10, 1956; children: Victor Daniel, Katherine Ann. BS, U. Fla., 1955; MD, U. Miami, Fla., 1959, JD, 1990. Diplomate Am. Bd. Surgery, Am. Bd. Thoracic and Cardiovascular Surgery; cert. health care risk mgr., Fla. Med. dir. HRS/Pub. Health unit, Tampa, 1991-93, Hills County HHS, Tampa, 1993-96; asst. prof. surgery U. South Fla. Sch. Medicine, Tampa, 1973—; pvt. practice medicine Tampa, 1968—, pvt. practice law, 1992—. Comdr. USPHS, 1964-66. Named Hispanic Man of Yr., Tampa, 1996. Mem. Kiwanis, Masons (32 degree), Shriners. Democrat. Roman Catholic. Home: 77 Martinique Ave Tampa FL 33606 Office: 405 W Azeele Tampa FL 33606

MARTINEZ-ARRARAS, JOAQUIN, cardiologist; b. Madrid, Oct. 26, 1959; came to the U.S., 1982; s. Carlos and Maria Teresa (Arraras) Martinez-Caro; m. Mercedes Unzurrunzaga Iturbe, June 5, 1985; children: Carlos, Reyes. MD, U. Navarra, 1982. Diplomate Am. Bd. Cardiovascular Disease, Am. Bd. Internal Medicine. Intern, resident in internal medicine Interfaith Med. Ctr., Bklyn., 1985-88; resident in clin. cardiology Hosp. St. Raphael, New Haven, Conn., 1988-90, fellow in interventional cardiology, 1990-91; physician Heart Inst. for Care, Amarillo, Tex., 1991-92; v.p. Panhandle Cardiovascular Clinics, Amarillo, 1992—; CCU dir., mem. utilization rev. com. High Plains Bapt. Hosp., Amarillo, 1994—, quality assurance com., 1994—; mem. quality improvement com. N.W. Tex. Hosp., Amarillo, 1995—, credentials com., 1995—; mem. physician adv. com. Prudential Health Plan Amarillo, 1996. With Spanish Army. Rsch. fellow in children's exercise physiology U. Navarra, 1983-84. Fellow Am. Coll. Cardiology; mem. AMA, Tex. Med. Assn., Potter-Randall County Med. Soc. Roman Catholic. Office: Panhandle Cardiovascular Clinics PA 1901 Medi-Park Ste # 1015 Amarillo TX 79106

MARTINEZ-CALATAYUD, JOSÉ, analytical chemistry educator; b. Onteniente, Valencia, Spain, Mar. 23, 1945; s. José Maria and Encarnacion (Calatayud) Martinez; m. Remedios Ferrero-Mico, July 31, 1972; children: Eugenia Martinez, Alberto Martinez. BSc in Chemistry, U. Valencia, 1968, PhD, 1972. Asst. tchr. U. Valencia, 1968-70, adj. tchr., 1970-80, prof. analytical chemistry, 1990—; prof. titular Centro Estudios Universitarios, Valencia, 1974—; dir. C.E.U., Valencia, 1992—. Author: Alchemists: mystics, savants, rascals. . ., 1992, Glow Injection Analysis of Pharmaceuticals. Automation in the Laboratory, 1996; contbr. to ency. Comprehensive Analytical Chemistry, 1995. Mem. Royal Soc. Chemistry, Soc. Espanola Quimica Analitica, F.C. Quimicas (sec.). Roman Catholic.

MARTINEZ-LOPEZ, JORGE IGNACIO, internist, cardiologist, educator, consultant; b. Santurce, P.R., Oct. 5, 1926; s. Jorge Martinez-Rivera and Dolores (Lopez) Martinez; m. Mona Hagan, June 12, 1950 (div. 1982); children: Jorge Alan, Anthony James, Ricardo, Matthew Joseph; m. Glenda Gayle Tomlinson, Mar. 4, 1983. MD, La. State U., 1950. Diplomate Am. Bd. Internal Medicine, Am. Bd. Cardiovascular Diseases. Intern Arecibo Dist. Hosp., P.R., 1950-51; resident in internal medicine La. State U. Medicine Svcs., Charity Hosp. La., New Orleans, 1954-57; trainee in cardiology, instr. dept. medicine La. State U. Med. Ctr., 1957-59, asst. prof., 1960-63, assoc. prof., 1963-70, prof., 1970-86, prof. emeritus, 1986—; clin. prof. dept. internal medicine Tex. Tech. U. Health Scis. Ctr., Lubbock, 1988; prof. dept. internal medicine Tex. Tech. U. Health Science Ctr., El Paso, 1988—; mem. staff R. E. Thomason Gen. Hosp., El Paso; cardiologist Heart Sta., Charity Hosp. La., 1960-75, dir. dept. cardiology, 1975-86, vis. physician, 1957-64, sr. vis. physician, 1964-86; cardiologist Hotel Dieu, New Orleans, 1961-86, dir. cardiology dept., 1970-75; dir. cardiac work evaluation unit Delgado Rehab. Ctr., New Orleans, 1967-86; cons. cardiology Edward F. Hebert Meml. Hosp., USN, Gretna, La., 1977-78; bd. govs. Orleans Parish Med. Soc., 1974-76; v.p. New Orleans Acad. Internal Medicine, 1969-70, pres., 1970-71. Contbr. more than 200 articles to profl. jours. Col. U.S. Army, 1951-53, 86-88, res. 1953-88, ret. Scholar Govt. P.R., 1947-50. Fellow Am. Coll. Cardiology, Am. Coll. Chest Physicians, Am. Coll. Physicians; mem. Am. Heart Assn. (fellow Coun. Clin. Cardiology, La. bd. dirs. 1965-86, v.p. 1972-73, pres.-elect 1973-74, pres. 1974-75, El Paso div. pres.-elect 1989-90, pres. 1990-91, bd. dirs. 1989—), Assn. Army Cardiology, La. State Med. Soc., Res. Officers Assn. (La. dept. surgeon 1963-69, 74-75, pres. Chpt. 19, 1963-69). Office: Tex Tech U Health Science Ctr 4800 Alberta Ave El Paso TX 79905-2709

MARTINEZ-MALDONADO, MANUEL, medical service administrator, physician; b. Yauco, P.R., Aug. 25, 1937; s. Manuel Martinez and Josefa Maldonado; m. Nivia Elena Rivera, Dec. 18, 1959; children: Manuel, David, Ricardo, Pablo. BS, U. P.R., 1957; MD, Temple U., 1961. Diplomate Am. Bd. Internal Medicine (assoc. mem. nephrology com. 1982-86), Am. Bd. Nephrology. Intern St. Charles Hosp., Toledo, 1961-62; resident VA Hosp., San Juan, 1962-65, chief resident, 1964-65; instr. U. Tex. Southwestern Med. Sch., Dallas, 1967-68; asst. prof. medicine Baylor Coll. Medicine, Houston, 1968-71, assoc. prof. medicine, 1971-73, prof. medicine, dir. renal sect., 1973; prof. medicine U. P.R. Sch. Medicine, 1973-90, prof. physiology, 1974-90; prof. medicine U. Caribbean, Bayamon, P.R., 1980-90; chief med. services VA Hosp., San Juan, 1973-90, dir. renal metabolic lab, 1973-90; prof., vice chmn. dept. medicine Emory U. Sch. Medicine, 1990—; chief med. svcs., assoc. chief of staff for ambulance care Atlanta VA Med. Ctr.; chief, med. svcs., assoc. chief of staff Ambulance Care VA Med. Ctr., Atlanta; mem. nat. adv. bd. gen. medicine, B study sect. Nat. Inst. Arthritis, Metabolism and Digestive Diseases NIH; mem. bd. sci. counselors, sci. advisors com. Nat. Heart, Lung and Blood Inst., Nat. Insts. Health. Author: La Voz Sostenida, 1984, Palm Beach Blues, 1986, Por Amor al Arte, 189; film critic for El Reportero, 1983-86, El Mundo, 1987-90; contbr. over 200 med. rsch. articles to sci. jours.; editor or co-editor of 11 books on renal pharmacology, nephrology, physiology; mem. editl. bd. U. P.R. Press, numerous profl. jours.; editor-in-chief Am. Jour. of Med. Scis., 1994-97. Mem. health com. Poplar Dem. Com., P.R., 1982-84; mem. Com. 500th Anniversary of Discovery Am., P.R., 1987-92; mem. com. on human rights Inst. of Medicine, Washington, 1987-92. Recipient Lederle Internat. award, 1966-67, Scholar award Macy Faculty, 1979-80, Grand Mobil prize medicine Mobil Oil Corp., 1981, Disting. Alumnus award Temple Med. Sch., 1988, Presdl. award Nat. Kidney Found, 1988, Donald W. Seldin medal 1994, Disting. Physician award P.R. Hosps. Assn., 1988, Orden del Cafetal award Municipality of Yauco, 1989; named one of Outstanding Med (medicine) P.R. C. of C., 1976, Fed. Supr. Employee of Yr., Fed. Execs. Assn., P.R., 1977. Fellow ACP, AAAS, Coun. for High Blood Pressure Rsch., Am. Heart Assn. (hypertension rsch. coun.; mem. Inst. Medicine NAS, Am. Soc. Nephrology (legis. liaison com., chmn. audit com. 1988), So. Soc. Clin. Investigation (sec.-treas. 1983-85, pres. 1985-86, Founders medal 1990), Am. Soc. for Clin. Investigation, Nat. Kidney Found. (chmn. sci. adv. bd. 1987-89, Donald W. Seldin medal, chmn. pub. policy com. 1992-94, pub. svc. medal), Latin Am. Soc. Nephrology (v.p. 1987-91, pres. elect 1991-94, pres. 1994-96), Inter-Am. Soc. Hypertension Assn. (bd. govs., chmn. 8th Sci. Congress 1989), U.S. Pharmacopeial Convention Cardio Renal Drugs Com., Assn. Am. Physicians, Inst. Medicine, Alpha Omega Alpha. Office: VAMC Med Svc 1670 Clairmont Rd Decatur GA 30033-4004

MARTINEZ-O'FERRALL, JOSÉ A., public health physician, retired air force officer; b. San Juan, P.R., Oct. 30, 1936. BS in Math., U. P.R., 1955, MD, 1959; MPH, U. Calif., Berkeley, 1967; grad., Flight Surgeon Sch., Brooks AFB, Tex., 1960, Sch. Aerospace Medicine, Brooks AFB, Tex., 1969, Air War Coll., Maxwell AFB, Ala., 1973. lectr., presenter in field. Intern Mercy Hosp., Buffalo, 1960; commd. capt. USAF, 1960, advanced through grades to col., 1975; chief of aviation medicine Ben Guerir Air Base, Morocco, 1960-61; chief of profl. svcs. and aviation medicine Zaragoza Air Base, Spain, 1961-64; chief of aerospace medicine Davis-Monthan AFB, Tucson, 1964-66; amb. health clinic med. dir. Bien Hoa, Vietnam, 1969-70; resident in preventive and aerospace medicine Brooks AFB, San Antonio, 1967-69, Scott AFB, Belleville, Ill., 1968-69; hosp. comdr., med. dir. Altus AFB, Altus, Okla., 1970-72; command surgeon, dir. base med. svcs. USAF So. Command, Albrook AFB, Canal Zone, 1973-76; team chief USAF Med. Inspection, Norton AFB, Calif., 1976-78; comdr., med. dir. USAF Med. Ctr., Clark Air Base, The Philippines, 1978-80; dep. surgeon USAR Air Tng. Command, Randolph AFB, Tex., 1980-81; vice comdr. Wilford Hall USAF Med. Ctr., Lackland AFB, Tex., 1982-85; hosp. comdr., med. dir. Laughlin AFB, Del Rio, Tex., 1985-88; med. cons. USAF Mil. Pers. Ctr., Randolph AFB, 1988-90; ret., 1990; preventive medicine cons. Al-Hada Armed Forces Hosp., Taif, Saudi Arabia, 1990-95; prev. medicine cons. Al-Hada Armed Forces Hosp., Taif, Saudi Arabia, 1991-95; apptd. by USAF Surgeon Gen. to represent U.S. Medicine in the Air Forces of Ams., Ecuador, Dominican Republic, Bolivia, Chile, Argentina and Colombia. Contbr. articles to med. jours. Decorated Legion of Merit with oak leaf cluster, Bronze Star with V, Bronze Star, Air Medal with oak leaf cluster; Gallantry Cross with palm (Vietnam); Republic of Vietnam Campaign medal; Vietnamese Honor medal; Vietnam Svc. medal; recipient George Washington medal Freedom Found., 1971, 73; scholar U. P.R., 1952-59; fellow NIH, summer 1956. Fellow Am. Coll. Preventive Medicine (assoc.), Aerospace Med. Assn. (assoc.); mem. AMA, Assn. Mil. Surgeons U.S., Soc. Hosp. Epidemiology Am., U.S.-Mex. Border Health Assn., Soc. USAF Flight Surgeons, Air Force Assn., Fed. Med. Exec. Inst. (life), Soc. Med. Grads. U. P.R. Sch. Medicine, Phi Chi. Home: 10602 Benchmark Way San Antonio TX 78213-1945

MARTINEZ-PIÑEIRO, LUIS, urologist, educator; b. Madrid, Feb. 3, 1961; s. Jose Antonio Martinez-Piñeiro and Alicia Lorenzo; m. Teresa Piñeiro, Mar. 9, 1991. MD, U. Autonoma, Madrid, 1985, PhD, 1991. Cert. European Bd. Urology, European Assn. Urology; cert. Spanish and European Bd. Urology. Resident in urology La Paz Hosp., Madrid, 1986-91; hon. prof. urology U. Autonoma, Madrid, 1990-91; postdoctoral rsch. fellow U. Calif., San Francisco, 1991-92; assoc. prof. urology U. Autonoma, Madrid, 1992—; cons. urologist La Paz Hosp., Madrid, 1991—. Co-author: (surg. video) European Association Urology, 1988 (Best Video award 1988); assoc. editor: Archivos Españoles Urologia, 1991-96; contbr. rsch. articles to profl. jours. Grantee Fondo Investigacion Sanitaria, 1991; recipient ednl. commn. for fgn. med. grads., U.S., 1985. Mem. Internat. Soc. Urology, European Urol. Assn., Spanish Urol. Assn. (grantee for fgn. studies 1991), Am. Urol. Assn. Office: Pz Conde Valle Suchil 17 1B, 28015 Madrid Spain

MARTINEZ-PONS, MANUEL, psychology educator; b. Dominican Republic, Apr. 19, 1940; s. Manuel and Alsacia (Gorsd) Martinez. BGS, U. Nebr., 1973, PhD, 1977, MS, 1975; PhD, CUNY, 1988. Contbr. articles to profl. jours. Home: PO Box 310379 Brooklyn NY 11231-0379 Office: Brooklyn Coll Sch Of Edn Brooklyn NY 11210

MARTIN-LANGTRY, DONNA CATHERINE, speech pathology and audiology services professional; b. Kingston, Pa., June 27, 1958; d. Stephen Joseph and Rita (Dress) Martin; m. Douglas P. Langtry, Nov. 25, 1983. BS in Communications Disorders, Kutztown State Coll., 1980; MA in Communication Disorders, U. Maine, Orono, 1982. Speech/lang. pathologist Ea. Maine Med. Ctr., Bangor, 1982-85, Head Injury Ctr. at Lewis Bay, Hyannis, Mass., 1985-88; sr. speech/lang. pathologist Head Injury Ctr. at Lewis Bay, Hyannis, 1986-88, program case mgr., 1988-90; speech/lang. pathologist Harwich Sch. Dist., Harwich, Mass., 1990-94, Nauset Sch. Dist., Orleans, Mass., 1994—; cons. Cape Cod Collaborative, Hyannis, Mass., 1990—; pvt. practice cons. dysphagia and swallowing disorders, 1991—. Mem. Am. Speech Lang. Hearing Assn., Nat. Head Injury Foun., Mass. Speech Lang. Hearing Assn. Home: 25 Mansion St West Harwich MA 02671-1106

MARTINS, ANTONIO GENTIL, pediatric and plastic surgeon; b. Lisbon, Portugal, July 10, 1930; s. António Augusto da Silva and Maria Madalena Gentil; m. Maria Guilhermina Ivens Ferraz Jardim; children: António Vasco, Inêz Maria, Luis Carlos, Teresa Maria, Ana Maria, Rita Maria, Sofia Maria, Joao Manuel. MD, Faculdade de Medicina, Lisbon, 1953; degree in Pedagogical Scis., Faculdade de Letras, Lisbon, 1954. Diplomate in Pediatric and Plastic Surgery. Intern Hospitals Civis de Lisbon, 1954-56; scholar Brit. Council, London, 1956-57; registrar Alder Hey Hosp., Liverpool, 1958-59; pediatric surgeon Hosp. D.Estefânia, Lisbon, 1965; founder, former head and cons. pediatric dept. Inst. Português Oncologia de Francisco Gentil, Lisbon, 1960-88, cons. pediatric surgery, 1986-92; prof. pediatric surgery Faculdade de Ciências Médicas, Lisbon, 1986-92; dir. pediatric surgery Hosp. D.Estefânia, Lisbon, 1987-92; cons. EEC Pediatric Oncology, 1991. Editor: Proc.Luso-Brasilian Met. Plastic Surg, 1970, (jour.) Revista da Ordem dos Médicos, 1980-86. Cons. WHO, Prague, Czechoslovakia, 1977; mem. working group Council of Europe Human Rights, Italy, 1981-82. Recipient Diploma of Honor Cuban Med. Assn. in Exile, Miami, 1983, Keys to City of Miami and Dade County, Fla., 1983; named Grande Official da Ordem do Infante D. Henrique, 1984. Mem. CPCEE, CIO, UEMS, Med. Students Assn. (pres. 1952), Ordem dos Medicos (pres. 1978-86), World Med. Assn. (pres. 1981-83), Portuguese Soc. Plastic Surgery (pres. 1968-74), Portuguese Soc. Pediatric Surgeons (pres. 1975-84, 91-92), World Fedn. Assn. Pediatric Surgeons (coun. mem. 1983-89), Internat. Soc. Pediatric Oncology (sci. com. mem. 1982-84); hon. mem. Brasilian Soc. Pediatric Surgeons, Spanish Soc. Pediatric Surgeons, Greek Soc. Pediatric Surgeons, Internat. Assn. Aesthetic Plastic Surgery, Portuguese League Against Cancer (pres. So. br. 1988—, pres. gen. assembly 1988-90, gen. sec. 1992—). Roman Catholic. Club: Internat. Futebol, Lisbon. Home: Rua D Francisco Manuel, de Melo 1-3D, 1000 Lisbon Portugal Office: Ave Antonio Augusto, Aguiar 22-1-D, 1000 Lisbon Portugal

MARTINS-GREEN, MANUELA, cell biologist; b. Luso, Moxico, Angola, Dec. 30, 1947; came to U.S., 1973; d. Joaquim P. and Maria Alice (Marques) Martins; m. Harry W. Green, II, May 15, 1975; children: Alice, Harry, Maria Green. BS, U. Lisbon, 1970; MS, U. Calif., Riverside, 1975; PhD, U. Calif., Davis, 1987. Chief scientist EM lab Agronomical Sta., Oeiras, Portugal, 1970-73; electron microscopist, dept. ophthalmology U. Calif., Davis, 1975-82; postdoctoral researcher Lawrence Berkeley Lab., U. Calif., 1987-88, rsch. scientist, 1992-93; adj. asst. prof. Rockefeller U., 1991-92; asst. prof. biology U. Calif., Riverside, 1993—; vis. lectr. U. Wuhan, China, 1988. Contbr. articles to profl. jours., books. Recipient Nat. Rsch. Svc. award, 1988-91, NIH traineeship, 1986-87; Fulbright Travel grantee Internat. Exch. Scholars, Riverside, 1973, NIH grantee, 1992—; dept. fellow U. Calif., Riverside, 1973-75, Regents fellow, 1985, Regents Faculty fellow U. Calif.-Riverside, 1995-96. Mem. Am. Cancer Soc., Am. Soc. for Cell Biology, Am. Soc. Devel. Biology, Elec. Microscopy Soc. of Am., Women for Cell Biology, Wound Healing Soc., Phi Kappa Phi. Office: U Calif Dept Biology Riverside CA 92521

MARTINSON, IDA MARIE, nursing educator, nurse, physiologist; b. Mentor, Minn., Nov. 8, 1936; d. Oscar and Marvel (Nelson) Sather; m. Paul Varo Martinson, Mar. 31, 1962; children—Anna Marie, Peter. Diploma, St. Luke's Hosp. Sch. Nursing, 1957; B.S., U. Minn., 1960, M.N.A., 1962; Ph.D., U. Ill., Chgo., 1972. Instr. Coll. St. Scholastica and St. Luke's Sch. Nursing, 1957-58, Thornton Jr. Coll., 1967-69; lab. asst. U. Ill. at Med. Ctr., 1970-72; lectr. dept. physiology U. Minn., St. Paul, 1972-82; asst. prof. Sch. Nursing U. Minn., 1972-74, assoc. prof. rsch., 1974-77, prof., dir. rsch., 1977-82; prof. dept. family health care U. Calif., San Francisco, 1982—, chmn. dept., 1982-90; vis. rsch. prof. Nat. Taiwan U., Def. Med. Ctr., 1981; vis. prof. nursing Sun Yat-Sen U. Med. Scis., Guang Zhou, Republic of China, Ewha Women's U., Seoul, Korea; vis. prof. nursing Frances Payne Bolton Sch. Nursing, Case Western Res. U., Cleve., 1994—; chair, prof. dept. health scis. Hong Kong Poly. U., 1996—. Author: Mathematics for the Health Science Student, 1977; editor: Home Care for the Dying Child, 1976, Women in Stress, 1979, Women in Health and Illness, 1986, The Child and Family Facing Life Threatening Illness, 1987, Family Nursing, 1989, Home Health Care Nursing, 1989; contbr. chpts. to books, articles to profl. jours. Active Am. Cancer Soc. Recipient Book of Yr. award Am. Jour. Nursing, 1977, 80, 87, 90, Children's Hospice Internat. award, 1988, Humanitarian award for pediatric nursing, 1993; Fulbright fellow, 1991. Mem. ANA, Coun. Nurse Rschrs., Am. Acad. Nursing, Inst. Medicine, Sigma Xi, Sigma Theta Tau. Lutheran. Office: U Calif Family Health Care Nursing San Francisco CA 94143-0606

MARTON, LAURENCE JAY, clinical pathologist, educator, researcher; b. Bklyn., Jan. 14, 1944; s. Bernard Dov and Sylvia (Silberstein) M.; m. Marlene Lesser, June 27, 1967; 1 child, Eric Nolan. BA, Yeshiva U., 1965, DSc (hon.), 1993; MD, Albert Einstein Coll. Medicine, 1969. Intern Los Angeles County-Harbor Gen. Hosp., 1969-70; resident in neurosurgery U. Calif.-San Francisco, 1970-71, resident in lab. medicine, 1973-75, asst. research biochemist, 1973-74, asst. clin. prof. depts. lab. medicine and neurosurgery, 1974-75, asst. prof., 1975-78, assoc. prof., 1978-79, prof., 1979-92, asst. dir. div. clin. chemistry, dept. lab. medicine, 1974-75, dir. div., 1975-79, acting chmn. dept., 1978-79, chmn. dept., 1979-92; dean med. sch. U. Wis., 1992-95, prof. pathology and lab. medicine and oncology, 1992—; prof. dept. human oncology U. Wis., Madison, 1993-95. Co-editor: Polyamines in Biology and Medicine, 1981; Liquid Chromatography in Clinical Analysis, 1981; Clinical Liquid Chromatography, vol. 1, 1984, vol. 2, 1984. Served with USPHS, NIH, 1971-73. Recipient Rsch. Career Devel. award Nat. Cancer Inst., Disting. Alumnus award Albert Einstein Coll. Medicine, 1992. Mem. Am. Assn. Cancer Rsch., AAAS, Acad. Clin. Lab. Physicians and Scientists, Am. Investigative Pathology, Am. Soc. Clin. Pathologists, Soc. Analytical Cytology, Alpha Omega Alpha. Jewish. Home: 5810 Tree Line Dr Fitchburg WI 53711-5826 Office: U Wis Med Sch McArdle Lab Cancer Rsch 1400 University Ave Madison WI 53706*

MARTONI, CHARLES J., dean; b. Pitts., Aug. 24, 1936; s. John and Virginia (Caputo) M. A.A., Community Coll. Allen County, 1969; B.S., California State Coll. (Pa.), 1971, M.A., 1977; M.S., Duquesne U., 1976, M.Ed., 1972; Ph.D., U. Pitts., 1988. Cert. counselor, nat. and Pa. Asst. dir. fin. aid Boyce Campus Community Coll. Allen County, Monroeville, Pa., 1971-73, dir. fin. aid, 1973-76, dir. fin. aid and counseling, 1976-80, dean of students, 1980—; mem. exec. bd. Tri-State Conf. on Steel. Mayor Swissvale, Pa., 1982-90; pres. Coun. Swissvale, 1990, Mon Valley Initiative. With U.S. Army, 1958-60. John Hart scholar, 1970; named Outstanding Alumnus, Boyce Campus, Community Coll. Allen County, 1978. Mem. Pa. Personnel and Guidance Assn., Pa. Mayors Assn., Nat. Assn. Student Personnel Administrs., Am. Assn. Counseling and Devel., Nat. Cert. Counselors. Democrat. Roman Catholic. Home: 7114 Church St Pittsburgh PA 15218-2434 Office: City Hall Swissvale PA 15218

MARTORELL, MARIO FRANCISCO, psychologist, educator; b. Guanabacoa, Havana, Cuba, Dec. 3, 1942; came to U.S., 1974; s. Mario Lazaro Inocente and Flor Maria (Borrell) M. MA in Chemistry, Montclair State Coll., 1978; Advanced Cert. in Adminstrn., CCNY, 1980; MS in Edn., L.I. U., 1983; PhD in Sch. Psychology, Fordham U., 1991. Cert. sch. psychologist, tchr., N.Y., N.J.; diplomate Am. Coll. Forensic Examiner. Tchr. Havana Bd. of Edn., 1961-69; dir. comml. dept. Barcelona Import, Inc., Spain, 1972-74; bilingual tchr. of chemistry N.Y.C. Bd. Edn., 1974-79, coord. high sch. prog. Nat. Alliance for Bus., 1979-80, coord., supr. CCOED prog., 1980-84, asst. chmn. com. on handicapped, 1984-85, bilingual sch. psychologist, 1989—; bilingual sch. psychologist Manhattan Regional Bd. Edn., N.Y.C., 1984-86, interim acting clin. supr. of sch. psychologists, 1987-89; prof. psychology Mercy Coll., Dobbs Ferry, N.Y., 1985—; bilingual psychol cons. N.J. Edn. Dept., 1993—; prof. CCNY Coll. Edn., 1993—; asst. prof Long Island U. Sch. Psychology Program, Grad. Ctr., 1993—. Author sci. curriculum, 1976. Active the Cuban Am. Nat. Found., Washington, 1990, Nat. Assn. Bilingual Edn., 1992. Recipient scholarship L.I. U., Bklyn. Campus, 1983, Outstanding Achievement award CCNY, 1980, fellowship NSF, Washington, 1979, Fordham U. Doctoral Dissertation award Phi Delta Kappa, 1992. Fellow Am. Bd. Forensic Medicine; mem. Am. Psychol. Assn. (doctoral dissertation award 1991), Nat. Assn. Sch. Psychologists, Am. Ednl. Rsch. Assn., N.Y. State Sch. Psychologist Assn., Ea. Psychol. Assn., Kappa Delta Pi, Psi Chi. Democrat. Roman Catholic. Home: 20 49th St Weehawken NJ 07087-7204 Office: Bd of Edn 516 W 181 St New York NY 10033

MARTTILA, JAMES KONSTANTIN, pharmacy administrator; b. Soudan, Minn., Oct. 25, 1948; s. Walter Konstantin and Verena (Oliver) M.; m. Kathleen A. Meyerle, Dec. 27, 1980; 1 child, Andrew. BS in Pharmacy, U. Minn., 1971, PharmD, 1972; MBA, Coll. St. Thomas, St. Paul, 1984. Lic. pharmacist, Minn. Prof. Coll. Pharmacy U. Minn., Mpls., 1973-86; dir. pharmacy, adminstr. Mayo Med. Ventures Mayo Found. Med. Edn., Research, Rochester, Minn., 1987—; cons. pharmacy Pharm. Cons. Svc., Mpls., 1975-86; chief operating officer Pharm. Svc. Corp., Mpls., 1975-87. Fellow Am. Soc. Cons. Pharmacists; mem. Am. Soc. Hosp. Pharmacists, Am. Pharm. Assn. (Schwartz award 1979). Office: Mayo Med Ventures Clinic 200 1st St SW Rochester MN 55905-0001

MARTUZA, ROBERT L., neurosurgeon; b. Wilkes-Barre, Pa., July 1, 1948. BA, Bucknell U., Lewisburg, Pa., 1969; MD, Harvard U., 1973. Diplomate Am. Bd. Neurol. Surgery. Intern. surgery Harvard Med. Sch., Boston, 1980-81, asst. prof., 1981-86, assoc. prof., 1986-91; prof., chmn. dept neurosurgery Georgetown U., Washington, 1991—; Dir. Georgetown Brain

Tumor Ctr., Washington, 1993—, Mass. Gen. Hosp. Neurofibromatosis Clinic, Boston, 1990-91; chair Decade of the Brain Task Force, Chgo., 1994—. Contbr. articles to profl. jours. Recipient Von Recklinghanson award Nat. NF Found., N.Y.C., 1989. Mem. Am. Acad. Neurol. Surgeons, Soc. Neurol. Surgery (Grass award), Am. Assn. Neurol. Surgeons, Congress Neurol. Surgeons. Office: Georgetown U Dept Neurosurgery 3800 Reservoir Rd NW Washington DC 20007*

MARTY, RAYMOND, nuclear physician; b. Bklyn., Oct. 26, 1929; s. Harry Kenneth and Pearl (Bailin) M.; B.A., UCLA, 1952; M.D., U. Lausanne (Switzerland), 1959; m. Carole M. Perry, Jan. 25, 1960. Intern, Hosp. Good Samaritan, Los Angeles, 1960-61; resident in diagnostic radiology Albert Einstein Sch. Medicine, Bronx, N.Y., 1962; fellow radiation therapy Stanford Med. Sch., 1962-63; dir. out patient clinic St. Joseph's Hosp., San Francisco, 1963-65; fellow Tumor Inst., Seattle, 1965-66, mem. staff, 1966—, dir nuclear medicine/ultrasound, 1967—; assoc. clin. prof. nuclear medicine tech. Seattle U. Med. Sch., 1972—; asst. clin. prof. nuclear medicine U. Wash. Med. Sch., Seattle, 1974—. Mem. AMA, Am. Coll. Radiology, Radiol. Soc. N.Am., Am. Coll. Nuclear Physicians, Soc. Nuclear Medicine, N.Y. Acad. Scis., Fedn. Am. Scientists, AAAS. Clubs: Seattle Yacht, Columbia Tower (Seattle); La Chaine des Rotisseurs; Lahaina Yacht (Maui, Hawaii). Contbr. articles to profl. jours. Home: 4607 103rd Ln NE Kirkland WA 98033-7638 Office: 1229 Madison St Ste 1150 Seattle WA 98104-1357

MARTZ, WILLARD HARRY, physician; b. Camden, N.J., Dec. 2, 1934; s. Willard Weldon and Lena (Waldner) M. BA, Rutgers U., 1956; MD, Temple U., 1960. Intern Mt. Sinai Greater Miami, Miami Beach, Fla., 1960-61; resident VA, Long Beach, Calif., 1963-66; dermatologist So. Calif. Permanente Med. Group, L.A., 1966-69; pvt. practice Miami Beach, 1969-71; assoc. prof. clin. dermatology U. Miami, 1980-94, prof. clin. dermatology, 1994—; cons. VA Hosp. of Miami. Fellow Am. Acad. Dermatology, Pacific Dermatology Assn.; mem. Nature Conservancy, Union of Concerned Scientists, Ctr. for Marine Conservation, Sierra, Alpha Omega Alpha. Office: Med Offices 1688 Meridian Ave Ste 421 Miami FL 33139-2700

MARUYAMA, KOSHI, pathologist, educator; b. Sapporo, Hokkaido, Japan, Feb. 19, 1932; s. Kotaro and Eiko (Nakamura) M.; m. Rumy Misawa, May 6, 1961; children: Nariyuki, Narihiro, Yumie. MD, U. Hokkaido Sch. Medicine, 1957, PhD, 1962. Diplomate Japanese Bd. Pathology. Staff pathologist Nat. Inst. Leprosy Research, Tokyo, 1962-65, Nat. Cancer Ctr. Research Inst., Tokyo, 1965-67; assoc. prof., assoc. virologist U. Tex. M.D. Anderson Hosp. and Tumor Inst., Houston, 1967-75; dir. dept. pathology Chiba Cancer Ctr. Rsch. Inst., Japan, 1975—; vis. prof. Dalian Med. U., 1995—. Contbr. articles to profl. jours. Assoc. editor: Japanese Jour. Cancer Clinic, 1978—, The Cancer Bull., 1978-89, The Year Book of Cancer, 1978. Trustee Tex. Gulf Coast chpt. Leukemia Soc. Am., Houston, 1973-75. Bd. dirs. Japan Br. Internat. Acad. Pathology, 1995—; trustee U. Tex. Japan Execs., 1996—. Leukemia Soc. Am. scholar, 1968; hon. prof. Liaoning Cancer Hosp. and Inst., Shenyang, 1992; mem. world com. The Internat. Assn. Comparative Rsch. on Leukemia and Related Diseases, 1993—; recipient Culture Promotion award The Tsuchiya Found., 1995. Fellow N.Y. Acad. Sci., Japanese Pathol. Soc., Japanese Cancer Assn., Japan Soc. Reticuloendothelial System; mem. Am. Assn. Cancer Research, AAAS, Am. Soc. Microbiology, Am. Assn. Investigative Pathology, Japan Assn. Hosp. Pathologists, Internat. Assn. Comparative Research on Leukemia and Related Diseases, Internat. Soc. for Preventive Oncology, Internat. Acad. Pathology (bd. dirs. Japan br. 1995—). Office: Chiba Cancer Ctr Rsch Inst, Dept Pathology 666-2 Nitona-cho, Chuo-ku Chiba 260, Japan

MARUYAMA, TORU, medical educator; b. Hachioji, Tokyo, June 15, 1956; s. Kinji and Kazuko (Wakamatsu) M.; m. Atsuko Uchida, July 23, 1959; children: Jun-ya, Haruka, Wataru. MD, Kyushu U., Japan, 1995. Lectr. Kyushu U., Beppu, Japan, 1991-92, Fukuoka, Japan, 1992—. Co-author: The Cardiomyopathic Heart, 1994, The Adapted Heart, 1994; contbr. articles to profl. jours. Home: Morooka 1-25-46-201, Fukuoka 816, Japan Office: Kyushu U, Maidashi 3-1-1 Higashi-ku, Fukuoka 812, Japan

MARVEL, WANDA FAYE, home health clinical consultant; b. Price, Utah, Nov. 10, 1951; d. Albert Jr. and Hazel A. Marvel; m. John M. Robinsin Jr. ADN, Westark Community Coll., 1978; BSN, U. Mo., 1986, MSN, 1993. Cardiac nurse Bapt. Med. Ctr., Little Rock, 1978-79; ICU staff nurse Ellis Fischel Cancer Ctr., Columbia, Mo., 1982-84; staff nurse emergency svc., med. ICU U. Mo., Columbia, 1984-87; head nurse surgery dept. Ellis Fischel Cancer Ctr., Columbia, 1987-89; rsch. asst. U. Mo., Columbia, 1988-89; asst. dir. Columbia Regional Hosp. Home Health, 1990-92; area v.p. HealthCor, Inc., Dallas, 1993-94, clin. cons., 1995—; guest lectr. Columbia Coll. RN Completion, 1989; clin. instr. Cen. Meth. Coll., Fayette, Mo., 1987; bd. dirs. Carpe Diem Hospice, Inc. Vol. Hospice Cen. Mo., Columbia, 1990; bd. dirs. Hospice Found., Columbia, 1990-91. Recipient Grad. Nurse Assn. scholarship U. Mo., 1989, Nursing Fund scholarship, 1989, Superior Grad. Achievement award, 1990. Mem. AAUW, ANA, Grad. Nurses Assn. (pres. 1988-89), Oncology Nurses Soc., Emergency Nurses Assn. (chmn. govtl. 1988), Sigma Theta Tau.

MARVIN, JOHN BINGHAM "JACK", psychologist; b. Burlington, Vt., Dec. 15, 1935; s. Benjamin Jesse Warrell and Pearl Emmaline Gibson; adopted s. Merrill Morton and Adelia (Johnson) M.; m. Deanna Hart, Sept. 17, 1955; children: Paul, Dawn, Valerie, Timothy, Peter. BA, U. Vt., 1957, MA, 1959; postgrad., Boston U., 1964-68. Lic. psychologist; cert. Nat. Register of Health Providers in Pschology. Asst. dir. mental health Vt. Dept. Health, Burlington, 1960-62, acting dir. mental health, 1962-63; asst. dir. cmty. svcs. Vt. Dept. Mental Health, Montpelier, 1963-64; psychologist intern Brookline (Mass.) Mental Health Ctr., 1964-65; doctoral fellow Boston U. Human Rels. Ctr., 1965-67; dir. counseling tng. U. Maine in New England Ctr., Durham, N.H., 1967-68; pres. Assocs. Human Resources, Concord, Mass., 1967-74, exec. dir., 1979-85, pres., 1985—; exec. officer Young Elders of Am., Littleton, Mass., 1994—; pres., mem. faculty Gestalt Inst. New England, Concord, Mass., 1975-79; co-chmn. dept. human behavior Oblate Coll., Natick, Mass., 1972-74; cons. USN Human Resources, Newport, R.I., Digital Equipment Corp., Shrewsbury, Mass., 1987-90; mem. task force on prevention of compulsive gambling Mass. Coun. on Compulsive Gambling, Boston, 1992-93. Cons. San Diego County Dept. Health Svcs., Alcohol and Drug Abuse Svcs., 1994. Mem. Am. Adoption Congress (life, v.p. 1995—), Nat. Assn. Children Alcoholics (state del. 1988-91, bd. dirs. Mass. chpt. 1988-92), Mass. Coalition for Children, Coalition for Responsible Medicare and Medicaid Reform, Assn. for Treatment and Tng. in the Attachment of Children, Nat. Assn. for Family Based Svcs., Mass. Sr. Health Care Coalition, Open Door Soc. (bd. dirs. Mass. chpt.), Adoption Professionals Network. Home and Office: Assocs for Human Resources 20 Nagog Hill Rd Littleton MA 01460-2212

MARVIT, ROBERT CHARLES, psychiatrist; b. Lynn, Mass., Jan. 23, 1938. BS summa cum laude, Mass. Coll. Pharmacy, 1960; MD, Tufts U., 1964; M.Sc., Harvard U., 1970. Intern New Eng. Med. Ctr., Pratt Diag. Hosp., 1964-65; resident in psychiatry, neuropsychol. medicine Mass. Gen. Hosp., Boston, 1967-70; pvt. practice medicine, specializing psychiatry Honolulu, 1970—; prof. pub. health U. Hawaii, Honolulu, 1974-78, adj. prof. Sch. Pub. Health, 1978—; forensic advisor Hawaii Mental Health Div., 1977—; dir. Health Info. Sys. Office, Dept. Health, 1976-80; cons. in field; lectr. in field. Contbr. articles to profl. jours. Served with USPHS, 1965-67 to lt. comdr. Recipient Alpha Omega Alpha Research award Tufts U., 1963. Fellow Am. Coll. Preventive Medicine, Internat. Soc. Social Psychiatry of Am. Pub. Health Assn., Am. Psychiat. Soc.; mem. Am. Acad. Psychiatry and the Law, Hawaii Psychiat. Soc., AAAS, Harvard Med. Soc., Boston Soc. Neurology and Psychiatry, Hawaii Neurol. Soc., Internat. Soc. Neurosci., Am. Acad. Forensic Psychiatry, Alpha Omega Alpha. Home: 929 Pueo St Honolulu HI 96816-5234 Office: 1314 S King St Ste 759 Honolulu HI 96814-1942

MARX, KENNETH ALLEN, health services administrator; b. Balt., July 23, 1960; s. Robert Simon and Harriet Ann (Stern) M.; m. Linda Frances Hayward, May 28, 1989; 1 child, Dagan Curtis Hayward Marx. BS, Va. Poly. Inst. and State U., 1982; MA, U. Iowa, 1990, MBA, 1990. Pharmacy technician Northwestern Meml. Hosp., Chgo., 1987-88; adminstrv. resident U. Iowa Hosps. and Clinics, Iowa City, 1991-92, adminstrv. fellow, 1992-93, adminstrv. assoc., 1993—. Sec., bd. dirs. Iowa City Ronald McDonald House, 1994-95, bd. dirs., 1993—; big bro. Big Bros./Big Sisters, Johnson County, Iowa, 1991-93. Mem. Am. Coll. Healthcare Execs., Beta Gamma Sigma. Office: Univ of Iowa Hosps/Clinics 200 Hawkins Dr Iowa City IA 52242

MARX, ROBERT JOSEPH, surgeon; b. St. Louis, Jan. 22, 1953; s. Arthur William Marx and Dorothy Shirley (Leibov) Henschke; m. Rebecca Steel, May 28, 1978; 1 child, Anna. BA, Westminster Coll., 1975; BS, U. Mo., 1978; MS, N.E. Mo. State U., 1983; DO, Kirksville Coll. Osteo., 1987. Diplomate Nat. Bd. Osteo. Med. Examiners; cert. gen. surgery Am. Osteopathic Bd. Surgery. Intern Normandy Osteopathic Hosp, St Louis, 1987-88; resident Deaconess med. Ctr. North and West, St Louis, 1989-93; gen. surgeon Youngstown (Ohio) Osteo. Hosp., 1993—, Northside Med. Ctr., Youngstown, Ohio, 1995—. Maj. U.S. Army, 1989—. Mem. Am. Osteo. Assn., Am. Coll. Osteo. Surgeons, Ohio Osteo. Assn., Mo. Osteo. Assn., AMA, Soc. Laprascopic Surgeons. Home: 5198 Sampson Dr Youngstown OH 44505 Office: 1323 Florencedale Ave Youngstown OH 44505

MARZANO, PATRICK WAYNE, osteopath; b. Far Rockaway, N.Y., Apr. 19, 1966; s. Patrick Eugene and Mary Natlie (Caparelli) M. BS in Life Sci. cum laude, N.Y. Inst. Tech., 1988; DO, N.Y. Coll. Osteo. Medicine, 1991. Diplomate Nat. Bd. Osteo. Med. Examiners. Rotating intern St. Barnabas Hosp., Bronx, N.Y., 1991-92; resident, then chief resident dept. ob-gyn. Brookdale Hosp., Bklyn., 1992—. Fellow ACOG (jr.); mem. AMA, Am. Osteo. Assn. Office: Brookdale Hosp 1 Brookdale Plz Brooklyn NY 11212

MARZLUFF, WILLIAM F., medical educator; b. Washington, May 7, 1945. BA in Chemistry magna cum laude, Harvard Coll., 1967; PhD in Biochemistry, Duke U., 1971; postdoc. student in Biology, Johns Hopkins U., 1971-74. From asst. prof. to prof. chemistry Fla. State U., Tallahassee, 1974-84, prof. chemistry, 1984-91; prof., dir. program molecular biology, biotech. U. N.C., Chapel Hill, 1991—; cons. physiology course MBL, Woods Hole, 1976; istr. sci. summer and math. camp Fla. State U., 1985, dir. program molecular biophysics, 1986-91; acting chmn. dept. biochem. and biophysics, U. N.C., 1994—; mem. rsch. com. Fla. Divsn. Am. Cancer Soc., 1977-91, chmn. summer rsch. fellowship subcom., 1979-83, 90-91; mem. site visit team NIH, 1980-88, ad hoc mem. molecular cytology study sect., 1982-85, ad hoc mem. molecular biology study sect., 1982-83, 86, 88, 89, mem. molecular biology study sect., 1989-91, chmn. molecular biology study sect., 1991-93; mem. cell biology panel NSF, 1987-89, mem. rev. panel biological ctrs., 1987-90; lectr. in field. Co-editor: Histone Genes: Organization and Expression, 1984; mem. editl. bd. Gene Expression; contbr. over 80 articles to profl. pubs. MBL fellow, 1975, NIH fellow; recipient Career Devel. award USPHS, 1975-80, tchg. award Program Med. Scis., 1978. Address: 5116 Green Meadows Rd Hillsborough NC 27278*

MASAHITO, NAGASAKA, physician; b. Fukuoka, Japan, Jan. 22, 1924; s. Kiyohito and Yaeko (Iwamitsu) N.; m. Setsuko Yokoyama, Apr. 19, 1955; 1 child, Shoichiro. MD, U. Tokyo, 1947, D Med. sci., 1959. Cert. med. diplomate. Rsch. fellow U. Tokyo, 1949-52, asst., 1951-53, 1962-70, lectr., 1970-83; asst. dir. Tachikawa Sogo Hosp., Tokyo, 1984-89, advisor, 1989—. Mem. Japanese Coll. Angiology (spl. mem.), Japan Soc. Internal Medicine (local councillor 1986—), Japanese Circulation Soc. (local hon. mem.), Japan Soc. Applied Physiology (spl. mem.), Japan Soc. Nephrology (merit mem.). Home: 5-15-13 Higashinakano, Nakanoku, Tokyo 164, Japan Office: Tachikawa Sogo Hosp, 1-16-15 Nishikicho Tachikawashi, Tokyo 190, Japan

MASCALCHI, MARIO, neuroradiologist; b. Florence, Italy, Sept. 28, 1959; s. Tullio and Ann Maria (Mainardi) M. MD, U. Florence, 1984, PhD, 1993. Diplomate in neurology, diagnostic radiology. Staff neuroradiologist Azienda Ospedaliera Pisana, Pisa, Italy, 1992—; cons. Sect. of Magnetic Resonance, Italian Soc. of Med. Radiology, 1995-96. Contbr. articles to profl. jours. With Italian Army, 1984-85. Mem. Soc. of Magnetic Resonance, Am. Acad. of Neurology, Associazione Italiana Neuroradiologia. Office: Cattedra di Radiologia U, Di Pisa Via Roma 67, 56100 Pisa Italy

MASCARENHAS, DANIEL NEVILLE, cardiologist, educator; b. Bombay, India, July 21, 1955; came to U.S., 1985; s. Peter Francis and Juliet (Baretto) M.; m. Suzette Barreto, Sept. 6, 1991; children: Francis Raphael, Erica Juliet. MBBS, Gordhandas Sunderdas Med. Coll, Bombay, 1980; MD, GS Med. Coll., Bombay, 1985. Diplomate Am. Bd. Internal Medicine, Am. Bd. Cardiology. Asst. clin. prof. anatomy N.Y. Coll. Osteo. Med., Long Island, 1985-86; resident in internal medicine Woodhull Med. Ctr., Bklyn., 1986-89; fellow in cardiology St. Vincent Hosp., Worcester, Mass., 1989-92; fellow in intervention cardiology U. Mass. Med. Ctr., Worcester, 1992-93; staff cardiologist Warren Hosp., Phillipsburg, N.J., 1994—; staff cardiologist St. Lukes Hosp., Bethlehem, Pa., 1994—; nuclear cardiologist, intervention cardiologist Easton (Pa.) Hosp., 1994—. Postgrad. Merit scholar Bombay U., 1982-84. Fellow ACP, Am. Coll. Cardiologists, Am. Coll. Chest Physicians; mem. Am. Soc. Nuclear Cardiologists. Office: Two Rivers Cardiology 1235 22nd St Easton PA 18042

MASCHAK-CAREY, BARBARA JEAN, clinical nurse specialist; b. Johnstown, Pa., July 20, 1947; d. Stephen Daniel and Ernestine Agnes (LaBuda) Maschak; m. Francis X. Carey, Dec. 3, 1977; children: Justin Francis, Lisa Jean. RN, Mercy Hosp. Sch. Nursing, Johnstown, Pa., 1968; BSN, U. Pa., 1972, MSN, 1980, postgrad. cert. diabetes educator Am. Assn. Diabetes Educators, clin. nurses specialist, ANA. Staff nurse med. nursing dept. Hosp. U. Pa., Phila., 1968-72, staff nurse med. intensive care unit, 1972-73, primary nurse provider med. diabetes, cardiac, ambulatory, 1973-80, staff devel. instr. for diabetes and hypertension edn., 1975-80, coord. of diabetes edn. program, 1975-85, chairperson patient edn. com., 1985-88, diabetes clin. nurse specialist, 1980—; adj. clin. preceptor grad. program. Sch. Nursing U. Pa., 1980—; rsch. nurse coord. diabetes control and complications trial U. Pa. Med. Ctr., 1985-93, trial coord. Epidemiology of Diabetes Intervention and Complications Study, 1994—; mem. endocrine adv. panel U.S. Pharmacopoeia Conv., Inc., 1991—, ind. cons., 1992; ind. cons. Windemere Comms., Inc., 1992, Becton Dickenson Corp., 1992; reviewer Diabetes Educator, 1989—; mem. faculty pump therapy symposiumMinimed Technologies, Princeton, N.J., 1991, 93; mem. faculty clin. edn. program Four Seasons Hotel, 1990; developer, coord., lectr. dept. med. nursing Hosp. U. Pa., 1983-84; cons. Met. Home Health Svc. Corp., 1985-86; mem. facilty 1st ann. conf. men.-surg. and geriatric nursing Am. Jour. Nursing Chgo., 1989, Phila. Dietetic Assn., Del. chpt. Soc. Nutrition Edn., 1989, Clin. edn. program Md. cad. Family Physicians, Annapolis, 1990, clin. edn.program N.J. affiliate, 1990, clin. edn. program Phila. dept. health physicians Phila. County Med. Soc., 1990; lectr., presenter in field. Co-author: Goals for Diabetes Education; contbr. articles to profl. jours. Recipient Alleyen Von Son award for Outstanding Teaching Tool Am. Assn. Diabetes Edn., 1984. Mem. Am. Assn. Diabetes Educators, Am. Diabetes Assn. (Outstanding Health Care Profl. Educator award 1993, mem. com. on sci. and med. programs 1984-86, task force for profl. membership 1986-87, ad hoc reviewer of health edn. abstracts 1987, bd. dirs. 1986-89, facilty on conf. recognition 1988-89, reviewer tng. 1988-90, sec. coun. edn. 1989-91, edn. program rev. panel 1991-93, ADA applications reviewer 1987—, program chair coun. edn. 1992-93, profl. sect. adv. panel 1992-94, chairperson edn. coun. 1992, program co-chair, presenter Post-Grad. Course, Boston 1994, assoc. editor 1995—), Am. Diabetes Assn. Pa. Affiliate, Inc. (transition com. 1989-90, profl. edn. com.1990-91, exec. com. 1991, chmn. profl. activities com. 1991, bd, dirs. 1990-92, assoc. editor 1995—), Am. Diabetes Assn. Phila. Affiliate, Inc. (mem. various coms. including exec. com. 1979-89, chmn. diabetes educators coun. 1983-89, active speakers bur. 1979—, profl. edn. com. 1991, pres. Phila chpt. 1990-92, pres. 1993), Sigma Theta Tau. Home: 461 W Abbottsford Ave Philadelphia PA 19144-4766 Office: Hosp of the U Pa 3400 Spruce St Philadelphia PA 19104

MASCHIO, GIUSEPPE, nephrology educator; b. Treviso, Veneto, Italy, July 20, 1935; s. Bonaventura and Maria (Lovisotto) M.; m. Emilia Zanette, May 27, 1962; children: Claudia, Silvia. MD, U. Padua, Italy, 1959. Fellow dept. internal medicine U. Padua, 1959-61, assoc. prof. nephrology, 1971-74, prof. nephrology, 1975—; dir. postgrad. sch. nephrology, U. Verona, Italy, 1981—. Capt. Italian San. Svc., 1961-62. Office: Civil Hosp, Div Nephrology, 37126 Verona Italy

MASEK, MARK JOSEPH, laboratory administrator; b. Joliet, Ill., June 13, 1957; s. Glenn James and Helen Margaret (Gleason) M.; m. Theresa Marie Norton, Oct. 24, 1987. BJ, U. Ill., 1979. Reporter The Daily Illini, Champaign, 1976-79, Joliet Herald-News, 1978-79; columnist, editor Elgin (Ill.) Daily Courier-News, 1979-88; editor The Daily Herald, Arlington Heights, Ill., 1988-90; publs. mgr. Argonne (Ill.) Nat. Lab., 1990—. V.p. Recycle Now-Joliet, 1991—; active City of Joliet Environ. Commn., 1993-96; bd. dirs. Will County Habitat for Humanity, 1994—. Recipient 1st pl. pub. svc. award Ill. AP Editor's Assn., 3d pl. pub. svc. award, 1980, 2d pl. columns award No. Ill. Newspaper Assn., 1982, 1st pl. columns award Nat. Newspaper Assn., 1982. Mem. Soc. Profl. Journalists, Mensa. Democrat. Roman Catholic. Office: Argonne Nat Lab 9700 Cass Ave Argonne IL 60439-4803

MASHBURN, KIMBERLY JOY NEEDHAM, healthcare administrator; b. St. Charles, Mo., Mar. 10, 1957; d. Earl David and Marie Cecelia (Stahlschmidt) Needham; m. Douglas Newton Mashburn, Dec. 8, 1979; children: David Nicholas, Jennifer Marie. BS in Nursing, U. Tenn., 1979. RN, Tenn. Staff nurse U. Tenn. Hosp., Knoxville, 1979-80; pediatric nurse Dr. Donald Larmee, Knoxville, 1980-81; staff devel. coord. Ft. Sanders Regional Med. Ctr., Knoxville, 1981-85; dir. adminstrv. and support svcs. Thompson Cancer Survival Ctr., Knoxville, 1986-91; dir. spl. projects Ft. Sanders Alliance, Knoxville, 1991-94, dir. bus. and network devel., 1994-95; pres., CEO Beacon Health Svcs., Inc., Chattanogga, 1995—. Mem. Childcare adv. bd., Knoxville, 1987, Knoxville Jr. League, 1988. Mem. Am. Coll. Healthcare Execs. (assoc.), Am. Mgmt. Assn., Tenn. League for Nursing (chmn. 1984-86), AIDS Response Knoxville (bd. dirs. 1987-88), Am. Cancer Soc. (nursing edn. com. 1985—, pub. edn. chmn. 1988-89, bd. dirs. 1990—), Med. Group Mgmt. Assn., Delta Delta Delta. Office: 979 E 3d St Ste 1001 Chattanooga TN 37403

MASHIACH, SHLOMO, gynecologist; b. Tel Aviv, Mar. 14, 1937; s. Nissim and Adina Mashiach; m. Ilit Atias Papo; children: Guy, Roy. MD, Hebrew Univ., 1962; cert. of specialist, Israel Ministry of Health, 1972. Physician-in-charge/ultrasonic lab and clinic Dept. Ob/Gyn. Sheba Med. Ctr., Tel Hashomer, Israel, 1975, dep. dir., 1975-79, dir., 1979—, physician in-charge program, 1981; head of acad. divsn. Tel Aviv Univ. Med. Sch., 1982-86, prof. ob-gyn., 1985—; adv. com. ob-gyn. Dir. Gen. of Israel Ministry of Health, 1984-88; mem. senate Tel Aviv Univ., 1988—, incumbant chair for prevention and treatment of congenital defects, 1994—. Editl. bd. In-Vitro Fertilization and Transfer Plenum Pub. Co., 1984, Jour. Perinatal Medicine; contbr. articles to profl. jours. Capt. Med. Corps. Rsch. grant Israel Family Planning Assn., 1975, Mifal Hapayis, 1976, Ministry of Health, 1980, Paz Co., 1980. Mem. Internat. Fedn. of Ob-Gyn. (exec. bd.), European Soc. for Human Reproduction, Israel Med. Assn. (exam. bd. of the scientific coun.), Israel Assn. of Perinatal Medicine, Israel Endocrine Soc., European Soc. for Human Reproduction (internal adv. com. 1992), Israel Soc. of Ob-Gyn. (pres. 1992—), Israel Soc. for Reproductive Rsch. (pres. 1967-91). Home: 50 Dizengoff St, Tel Aviv Israel Office: Dept Ob-Gyn, Chaimshebia Med Ctr, Tel Hashomer 52621, Israel

MASHIN, JACQUELINE ANN COOK, medical sciences consultant; b. Chgo., May 11, 1941; d. William Hermann and Ann (Smidt) Cook; m. Fredric John Mashin, June 7, 1970; children: Joseph Glenn, Alison Robin. BS, U. Md., 1984. Cert. realtor. Adminstrv. asst. CIA, Washington, 1963-66; asst. to mng. dir. Aerospace Edn. Found., Washington, 1966-74; exec. asst. to asst exec. dir. Air Force Assn., Washington, 1974-79; v.p., ptnrship. owner Discount Linen Store, Silver Spring, Md., 1979-81; asst. regional polit. dir. Office of Pres.-elect, Washington, 1980-81; confidential asst. to dir. Office of Personnel Mgmt. (US), Washington, 1981-83; spl. asst. to dep. dir. Office of Mgmt. and Budget, Washington, 1983-86; dir. internat. communications and spl. asst. to commr. Dept. of the Interior, Washington, 1986-89, cons., 1989-93; with Washington Hosp. Ctr., 1993—. Pres. Layhill Civic Assn., Silver Spring, Md., 1980; state chmn. Md.'s Reagan Youth Delegation, Annapolis, Md., 1980; state treas., office mgr. Reagan-Bush State Hdqrs. of Md., Silver Spring, 1980; mem. Women's Com. Nat. Symphony Orch. Mem. Air Force Assn. (life), Aux. Salvation Army (life), Am. League Lobbyists, Internat. Platform Assn., U.S. Capital Hist. Soc., Women's Nat. Rep. Club (N.Y.C.), Indian Springs Country Club. Republican. Home and Office: 2429 White Horse Ln Silver Spring MD 20906-2243

MASHMAN, JAN HOWARD, neurologist, educator, rehabilitation administrator; b. N.Y.C., Oct. 3, 1939; s. Jack and Dorothy (Dimondstein) M.; m. Susan Lee Zuckerman, Aug. 13, 1959; children: Walter, Pamela. BA with honors, U. Vt., 1961, MD cum laude, 1965. Intern in medicine Montefiore Hosp. Med. Ctr., Bronx, 1965-66; resident in neurology Albert Einstein Coll. Medicine, Bronx, 1966-69, chief resident in neurology, 1968-69; pvt. practice Associated Neurologists, P.C., Danbury, Conn., 1971—; asst. clin. prof. neurology Yale Med. Sch., New Haven, Conn., 1980—; med. dir. Datahr Rehab. Inst., Brookfield, Conn., 1984—; bd. dirs. MedCtr. Home Health Care, Brookfield; chmn., v.p. profession adv. com. Western Conn. M.S. Soc., Norwalk, 1980-92. Contbr. articles to profl. jours. Maj. USAF, 1969-71. Recipient Mosby scholarship award, Med. Sch. faculty, 1965. Fellow Am. Acad. Neurology (cert. neurology, polit. action com. 1990-95); mem. Conn. Neurol. Soc. (pres. 1988—), Fairfield County Neurology Soc. (pres. 1975-85, polit. action com. 1995), Briard Club Am., Alpha Omega Alpha, Sigma Xi. Jewish. Office: Associated Neurologists PC Ste 300 69 Sand Pit Rd Danbury CT 06810

MASI, DALE A., research company executive, social work educator; b. N.Y.C.; d. Alphonse E. and Vera Avella; children: Eric, Renee, Robin. BS, Coll. Mt. St. Vincent; MSW, U. Ill.; D Social Work, Cath. U. Lectr. Sch. Social Svcs., Ipswitch, Eng., 1970-72; project dir. occupational substance abuse program, asso. prof. Boston Coll. Grad. Sch. Social Work, 1972-79; dir. Office Employee Counseling Svc., Dept. Health/Human Svcs., Washington, 1979-84; pres. Masi Research Cons., Inc., 1984—; prof. U. Md. Grad. Sch. Social Work, 1980—; adj. prof. U. Md. Coll. Bus. and Mgmt., 1980—; mem. IBM Mental Health Adv. Bd., 1990-95; cons. IBM, Toyota, Mobil Chm., The Washington Post, U.S. Ho. Reps., U.S. Postal Svc., White Hous, WHO, Bechtel Corp., other orgns. in pub. and pvt. sector; bd. advisors Employee Assistance mag. and Nat. Security Inst.; USIA Ampart lectr. on alcohol, drugs and AIDS in the workplace. Author: Human Services in Industry, Organizing for Women, Designing Employee Assistance Programs, Drug Free Workplace, AIDS Issues in the Workplace: A Response Model for Human Resource Management, The AMA Handbook for Developing Employee Assistance and Counseling Programs, Evaluating Your Employee Assistance and Managed Behavioral Care Program; also over 40 articles. Fulbright fellow, 1969-70; AAUW postdoctoral fellow; NIMH fellow, 1962-64; recipient award Employee Assistance Program Digest; named to Employee Assistance Program Hall of Fame. Mem. AAUW, NASW (Internat. Rhoda G. Sarnat award 1993), Acad. Cert. Social Workers, Employee Assistance Profls. Assn. (nat. individual achievement award 1983), Fulbright Assn. (nat. bd.). Democrat. Roman Catholic. Office: 500 23d St NW Ste 202 Washington DC 20037-2801

MASKIN, STEVEN LLOYD, physician; b. N.Y.C., Sept. 8, 1958; s. Sol and Dorothy Faith (Gottlieb) M.; m. Angela Eve Zolper, Sept. 24, 1994. BA magna cum laude, Washington U., 1980; MD, St. Louis U., 1984. Diplomate Am. Bd. Ophthalmology. Intern St. John's Mercy Med. Ctr., St. Louis, 1984-85; resident in ophthalmology U. Tex. Health Sci. Ctr., San Antonio, 1985-88; rsch. fellowship in ophthalmology U. Miami (Fla.) Sch. Medicine, 1988-90, clin. fellowship dept. ophthalmology, 1990-91; appointed med. adv. bd. Ctrl. Fla. Lion's Eye and Tissue Bank, 1992, appointed med. dir., 1995; presenter in field. Author: (chpt.) Ophthalmology Clinics of North America; contbr. articles to profl. jours. Recipient scholarship Grass Found., 1978, Tng. grant NIH, 1988-89, grant Bascom Palmer Eye Inst., 1989-90. Fellow ACS; mem. AMA, Assn. for Rsch. in Vision and Ophthalmology, Am. Acad. Ophthalmology, Am. Bd. Ophthalmology, Fla. Soc. Ophthalmology, Fla. Med. Assn., Hillsborough County Med. Assn., Tampa Bay Opthalmol. Soc. Office: Steven L Maskin MD PA 508 S Habana Ave # 350 Tampa FL 33609

MASLACH, CHRISTINA, psychology educator; b. San Francisco, Jan. 21, 1946; d. George James and Doris Ann (Cuneo) M.; m. Philip George Zimbardo, Aug. 10, 1972; children: Zara, Tanya. B.A., Harvard-Radcliffe Coll., 1967; Ph.D., Stanford U., 1971. Prof. psychology U. Calif.-Berkeley, 1971—. Author: Burnout: The Cost of Caring, 1982; co-author: Influencing Attitudes and Changing Behavior, 1977, Maslach Burnout Inventory (rsch.

scale), 1981, 2d edit., 1986, 3d edit., 1996, Experiencing Social Psychology, 1979, 2d edit., 1984, 3d edit., 1993, Professional Burnout, 1993. Recipient Disting. Teaching award, 1987, Best Paper award Jour. Orgnl. Behavior, 1994. Fellow AAAS, APA, Am. Psychol. Soc., Soc. Clin. and Exptl. Hypnosis (Henry Guze rsch. award 1980), We. Psychol. Assn. (pres. 1989); mem. Soc. Exptl. Social Psychology. Democrat. Office: U Calif Tolman Hall #1650 Dept Psychology Berkeley CA 94720-1650

MASLANSKY, CAROL JEANNE, toxicologist; b. N.Y.C., Mar. 3, 1949; d. Paul Jeremiah and Jeanne Marie (Filiatrault) Lane; m. Steven Paul Maslansky, May 28, 1973. BA, SUNY, 1971; PhD, N.Y. Med. Coll., 1983. Diplomate Am. Bd. Toxicology; cert. gen. toxicology. Asst. entomologist N.Y. State Dept. Health, White Plains, 1973-74; sr. biologist Am. Health Found., Valhalla, N.Y., 1974-76; rsch. fellow N.Y. Med. Coll., Valhalla, 1977-83, Albert Einstein Coll. Medicine, Bronx, N.Y., 1983; copr. toxicologist Texaco, Inc., Beacon, N.Y., 1984-85; prin. GeoEnviron. Cons., Inc., White Plains, N.Y., 1982—; lectr. in entomology Westchester County Parks and Preserves, 1973—, lectr. toxicology and hazardous materials, 1985—. Author: Air Monitoring Instrumentation, 1993, (with others) Training for Hazardous Materials Team Members, 1991 (manual, video) The Poison Control Response to Chemical Emergencies, 1993. Mem. Harrison (N.Y.) Vol. Ambulance Corps., 1986-91, Westchester County (N.Y.) Hazardous Materials Response Team, 1987—. Monsanto Fund Fellowship in Toxicology, 1988-90; grad. fellowship N.Y. Med. Coll., 1977-83. Mem. AAAS, Nat. Environ. Health Assn., N.Y. Acad. Sci., Am. Coll. Toxicology, Am. Indsl. Hygiene Assn., Environ. Mutagen Soc.

MASON, BERT E., podiatrist; b. Ryderwood, Wash., Mar. 17, 1944; s. Jean Grenette and Bette Evelyn (Phillips) M.; m. Rachel Nell Hall, May 17, 1991. BA with honors, U. Calif., San Diego, 197l; B in Basic Med. Sci., Calif. Coll. Podiatric Medicine, 1975; D Podiatric Medicine, Calif. Coll. Podiatric Med., 1977. Diplomate Am. Bd. Podiatric Surgery, Am. Bd. Podiatric Orthopedics, Am. Acad. Pain Mgmt. Pvt. practice Fairfield, Calif., 1977-79; chief podiatry sect., dir. podiatric residency VA Med. Ctr., Huntington, W.Va., 1983-87; pvt. practice San Diego, 1987-89; chief podiatry svc., dir. podiatric residency program VA Med. Ctr., Huntington, W.Va., 1993—; asst. prof. podiatric surgery Ohio Coll. Podiatric Medicine, Cleve., 1984-87, 1993—; asst. prof. dept. surgery and community medicine Marshall U. Sch. Medicine, Huntington, 1985-87; v.p. Smith Hanna Med. Group; assoc. prof. of podiatric medicine, Coll. of Podiatric Medicine, Osteo. U. and Health Scis., De Moines, 1993—. Alumni mem. scholarship com., U. Calif., San Diego, 1988—. Maj. U.S. Army, 1979—, chief Podiatry Sect. Ft. Knox, Ky., Ireland Army Hosp. 1980-83, Individual Augmentee Health Svcs. Command, 1983—. Luth. Hosp. Soc. scholar, 1968. Fellow Am. Coll. Foot Surgeons, Am. Coll. Foot Orthopedics, Am. Assn. Hosp. Podiatrists; mem. AAAS, Am. Podiatric Med. Assn., Am. Acad. Pain Mgmt. (diplomate), West. Va. Podiatry Group (pres.), U. Calif. San Diego Alumni Assn. (bd. dirs.). Republican. Home: 350 Grand Blvd Huntington WV 25705-3612 Office: VA Med Ctr Dept Podiatry Huntington WV 25704

MASON, CHARLES PERRY, biology educator; b. Newport, R.I., Aug. 12, 1932; s. Charles Perry and Bernice (Passmore) M.; m. Harriet Gale, Sept. 7, 1958; children: Grant Vause, Gale Perrie. BS, U. R.I., 1954; MS, U. Wis., 1958; PhD, Cornell U., 1961. From asst. prof. to assoc. prof. Hamline U., St. Paul, 1961-67; from assoc. prof. to full prof. Gustavus Adolphus Coll., St. Peter, Minn., 1967—; vis. scientist Gray Freswater Biol. Inst., Navarre, Minn., summers 1978, 79, 81, 85; ecol. cons. Northern States Power Co., Minn., summer 1973; dir. wild rice rsch. Green Giant Co., Le Sueur, Minn., summer 1969. Contbr. articles to Ecology, Science, Jour. Wash. Acad. Science, Japan. Lindberg grantee Charles A. Lindberg Fund Inc., 1984, IMPULL grantee, 1984, NSF grantee, 1985. Mem. Phycological Soc. Am., Internat. Phycological Soc., Sigma Xi. Office: Gustavus Adolphus Coll Biology Dept Saint Peter MN 56082

MASON, DEAN TOWLE, cardiologist; b. Berkeley, Calif., Sept. 20, 1932; s. Ira Jenckes and Florence Mabel (Towle) M.; m. Maureen O'Brien, June 22, 1957; children: Kathleen, Alison. BA in Chemistry, Duke U., 1954, MD, 1958. Diplomate Am. Bd. Internal Medicine, Am. Bd. Cardiovasc. Diseases, Nat. Bd. Med. Examiners. Intern, then resident in medicine Johns Hopkins Hosp., 1958-61; clin. assoc. cardiology br., sr. asst. surgeon USPHS, Nat. Heart Inst., NIH, 1961-63, asst. sect. dir. cardiovascular diagnosis, attending physician, sr. investigator cardiology br., 1963-68; prof. medicine, prof. physiology, chief cardiovascular medicine U. Calif. Med. Sch., Davis-Sacramento Med. Center, 1968-82; dir. cardiac ctr. Cedars Med. Ctr., Miami, Fla., 1982-83; physician-in chief Western Heart Inst., San Francisco, 1983—; chmn. dept. cardiovascular medicine St. Mary's Med. Ctr., San Francisco, 1986—; co-chmn. cardiovascular-renal drugs U.S. Pharmacopeia Com. Revision, 1970-75; mem. life scis. com. NASA; med. rsch. rev. bd. VA, NIH; vis. prof. numerous univs., cons. in field; mem. Am. Cardiovascular Splty. Cert. Bd., 1970-78. Editor-in-chief Am. Heart Jour., 1980—; contbr. numerous articles to med. jours. Recipient Research award Am. Therapeutic Soc., 1965; Theodore and Susan B. Cummings Humanitarian award State Dept.-Am. Coll. Cardiology, 1972, 73, 75, 78; Skylab Achievement award NASA, 1974; U. Calif. Faculty Research award, 1978; named Outstanding Prof. U. Calif. Med. Sch., Davis, 1972. Fellow Am. Coll. Cardiology (pres. 1977-78), A.C.P., Am. Heart Assn., Am. Coll. Chest Physicians, Royal Soc. Medicine; mem. Am. Soc. Clin. Investigation, Am. Physiol. Soc., Am. Soc. Pharmacology and Exptl. Therapeutics (Exptl. Therapeutics award 1973), Am. Fedn. Clin. Research, N.Y. Acad. Scis., Am. Assn. U. Cardiologists, Am. Soc. Clin. Pharmacology and Therapeutics, Western Assn. Physicians, AAUP, Western Soc. Clin. Research (past pres.), Phi Beta Kappa, Alpha Omega Alpha. Republican. Methodist. Club: El Marcero Country. Home: 44725 Country Club Dr El Macero CA 95618-1047 Office: Western Heart Inst St Mary's Med Ctr 450 Stanyan St San Francisco CA 94117-1079

MASON, EARL JAMES, JR., pathologist, educator b. Marion, Ind., Aug. 26, 1923; s. Earl James and Grace A. (Leer) M.; student Marion Coll., 1940-41; B.S. in Medicine, Ind. U., 1944, A.B. in Chemistry, 1947, M.A. in Bacteriology, 1947; Ph.D. in Microbiology, Ohio State U., 1950; M.D., Western Res. U., 1954; m. Eileen Gursansky, Dec. 2, 1967. Diplomate Am. Bd. Nuclear Medicine. Teaching asst. dept. bacteriology Ind. U., 1945-47; research fellow depts. ophthalmology and bacteriology Ohio State U., Columbus, 1947-48, teaching asst. dept. bacteriology, 1948-50; Crile research scholar Western Res. U., Cleve., 1951-53; Damon Runyon cancer research fellow dept. pathology Western Res. U.-Cleve. City Hosp., 1951-56; dept. chief dept. pathology USPHS Hosp., San Francisco, 1956-58; fellow pathology U. Tex. Postgrad. Sch. Medicine, M.D. Anderson Hosp. and Tumor Inst., Houston, 1958-59; asst. prof. dept. pathology Baylor U. Coll. Medicine, 1959-60; asst. pathologist Jefferson Davis Hosp., 1959-60; asst. pathologist Michael Reese Hosp. and Med. Center, Chgo., 1960-61; assoc. dir. dept. pathology, dir. dept. biol. scis. Mercy Hosp., 1960-65; dir. labs. St. Mary Med. Ctr., Gary and Hobart, Ind., 1965-94, cons. pathology and nuclear medicine, 1994—; assoc. prof. pathology Chgo. Med. Sch., 1966—; clin. prof. pathology Ind. U. Med. Sch., 1976—; clin. prof. Inst. Critical Care Medicine, Palm Springs, Calif., 1996—. Diplomate Am. Bd. Pathology in anat. and clin. pathology, radioisotopic pathology and dermatopathology, Am. Bd. Nuclear Medicine. Mem. Coll. Am. Pathologists, Am. Assn. Pathologists and Bacteriologists, Am. Soc. Clin. Pathologists, Internat. Acad. Pathologists, Am. Soc. Exptl. Pathology, Am. Assn. Cancer Research, Am. Assn. Blood Banks, Am. Soc. Hematology, Am. Acad. Dermatology, Soc. Nuclear Medicine, Lake County Med. Soc., Am. Soc. Cytology, Sigma Xi. Research on cellular origin of antibodies and virus-cell interactions. Home: 64465 Via Risso Palm Springs CA 92264-0236 Office: 1500 S Lake Park Ave Hobart IN 46342-6638

MASON, EDWARD EATON, surgeon; b. Boise, Idaho, Oct. 16, 1920; s. Edward Files and Dora Bell (Eaton) M.; m. Dordana Fairman, June 18, 1944; children—Daniel Edward, Rose Mary, Richard Eaton, Charles Henry. B.A., U. Iowa, 1943, M.D., 1945; Ph.D. in Surgery, U. Minn., 1953. Intern, resident in surgery Univ. Hosps., Mpls., 1945-52; asst. prof. surgery U. Iowa, 1953-55, assoc. prof., 1956-60, prof., 1961-91, prof. emeritus, 1991—, chmn. gen. surgery, 1978-91; cons. VA Hosp.; trainee Nat. Cancer Inst., 1949-52. Author: Computer Applications in Medicine, 1964, Fluid, Electrolyte and Nutrient Therapy in Surgery, 1974, Surgical Treatment of Obesity, 1981; developer gastric bypass and gastroplasty for treatment of obesity; contbr. articles profl. jours. Served to lt. (j.g.) USNR, 1945-47. Fellow ACS; mem. AMA, Am. Surg. Assn., Western Surg. Assn., Soc. Univ. Surgeons, Internat. Soc. Surgery, Ctrl. Surg. Assn., Soc. Surgery Alimentary Tract, Am. Thyroid Assn., Am. Soc. Bariatric Surgery, Sigma Xi, Alpha Omega Alpha. Republican. Presbyterian. Home: 5 Melrose Cir Iowa City IA 52246-2013 Office: University Hosp Dept of Surgery Iowa City IA 52242

MASON, ELIZABETH JANE, nursing consultant; b. Uniontown, Pa., Aug. 22, 1935; d. William Sherman and Margaret Catherine (Luman) M. Diploma in nursing, Presbyn. U. Hosp., Pitts., 1956; BSN, U. Pitts., 1959; MSN, Wayne State U., 1962; PhD in Edn., U. Wis., 1972. Instr. anatomy and physiology, clin. instr. med.-surg. nursing Presbyn. U. Hosp. Sch. Nursing, 1959-61; instr. nursing U. Pitts., 1962-66; asst. prof. med. and surg. nursing U. Wis., Madison, 1966-70; assoc. prof. med.-surg. nursing Va. Commonwealth U., Richmond, 1972-76, assoc. prof. for ednl. planning and devel., 1975-76; asst. dir. undergrad. edn., asst. prof. Ohio State U., Columbus, 1976-80; dir. grad. program nursing adminstrn. and edn., assoc. prof. U. Pitts. Sch. Nursing, 1980-85; internat. cons. interdisciplinary standards quality management and the clinical costs of healthcare, 1985—. Author: How to Write Meaningful Nursing Standards, 1978, 3d edit. 1994, How To Write Meaningful Standards of Care; patentee software, Excelcare, multidisciplinary decision support system. USPHS pre-doctoral fellow, 1970-72. Mem. ANA, Am. Ednl. Rschrs. Assn., Pi Lambda Theta, Sigma Theta Tau.

MASON, EMANUEL JOEL, psychology educator; b. N.Y.C., Aug. 7, 1943; s. Murray Aaron and Natalie (Josephson) M.; m. Susan B. Spreiregen, Apr. 9, 1944; children: Sara Beth, Sandra Lisa. BS in Psychology, CCNY, 1965; MEd in Ednl. Psychology, Temple U., 1969, EdD in Sch. Psychology, 1972. Lic. psychologist, Ky.; nat. cert. sch. psychologist. Sch. psychologist Edgewater Twp. Schs., Edgewater Park, N.J., 1969-72; faculty in sch. and ednl. psychology U. Ky., Lexington, 1972-96, chmn. dept. ednl. and counseling psychology, 1988-93; prof. counseling and sch. psychology Northeastern U., Boston, 1996—. Co-author: Computers in Schools, 1985, Understanding and Conducting Research, 1989; contbr. articles to profl. jours. 2nd lt. to capt. U.S. Army, 1965-67. Fellow Am. Psychol. Assn. (editor div. 16 newsletter 1978-81, Lightner Witmer award, div. sch. psychologists 1978), Am. Psychol. Soc.; mem. AAUP, Am. Ednl. Rsch. Assn., Nat. Assn. Sch. Psychologists (state del. 1977). Office: Northeastern Univ (LA203) Dept Counseling Psychology Boston MA 02115

MASON, GEORGE ROBERT, surgeon, educator; b. Rochester, N.Y., June 10, 1932; s. George Mitchell and Marjorie Louise (Hooper) M.; m. Grace Louise Bransfield, Feb. 4, 1956; children: Douglas Richard, Marcia Jean, David William. BA, Oberlin Coll., 1955; MD with honors, U. Chgo., 1957; PhD in Physiology, Stanford U., 1968. Diplomate: Am. Bd. Surgery (examiner 1977-80, dir. 1980-86), Bd. Thoracic Surgery. Teaching asst. pathology U. Chgo., 1954-56; rotating intern U. Chgo. Clinics, 1957-58; tchg. asst. surgery, NIH postdoctoral fellow, USPHS fellow surgery Stanford U., 1960-62; from asst. resident in surgery to sr. and chief resident in surgery Stanford U. Hosps., 1962-66; mem. faculty Stanford Med. Sch., 1965-71, assoc. prof., 1970-71; prof., chmn. dept surgery U. Md. Med. Sch., Balt., 1971-80; also prof. physiology; prof., chmn. dept. surgery U. Calif., Irvine, 1980-89; chief surgical svc. Hines (Ill.) VA Hosp., 1990-95; prof. surgery and thoracic cardiovascular surgery Loyola U. Med. Ctr., 1990—; chmn. dept. thoracic and cardiovasc. surgery Loyola U. Med. Ctr., Maywood, Ill., 1995—; mem. residency review com. for surgery, 1981-87. Contbr. to profl. jours., med. textbooks. Served to capt. M.C., USAF, 1958-60. Giannini fellow Stanford U., 1966-67; recipient Markle scholarship in acad. medicine, 1968-74. Mem. ACS, Am. Assn. Thoracic Surgeons, Am. Coll. Chest Physicians, Am. Physiol. Soc., Am. Gastroent. Assn., Pacific Coast Surg. Assn., Assn. Acad. Surgery, Ctrl. Surg. Soc., So. Surg. Soc., Chgo. Surg. Soc., Am. Surg. Assn., Western Surg. Assn., Soc. Thoracic Surgeons, Ill. Thoracic Surg. Soc. (pres. 1994-95), Halsted Soc., Chesapeake Vascular Soc., Soc. Internat. Chirurgie, Soc. Clin. Surgery, Soc. for Surgery Alimentary Tract, Soc. Univ. Surgeons. Home: PO Box 3877 Oak Brook IL 60522-3877 Office: EMS LUMC Rm 6240 Bldg 110 2160 S First Ave Maywood IL 60153

MASON, GREGG C., orthopedic surgeon; b. 07281958Schenectady, N.Y., July 28, 1958. BS in Chemistry magna cum laude, Allegheny Coll., 1980; MD, U. Pitts., 1984. Diplomate Am. Bd. Orthop. Surgery, Nat. Bd. Med. Examiners. Gen. surgery intern U. Colo./U. Colo. Med. Ctrs., Denver, 1984-85; orthop. rsch. fellow U. Pitts., 1985-86, resident in orthop. surgery, 1986-89; pvt. practice Orthop. Surgeons, Inc., Erie, 1992—; active staff St. Vincent Med. Ctr., St. Vincent Surgery Ctr., Hamot Med. Ctr., Union City Meml. Hosp.; lectr. in field. Contbr. articles to profl. jours. Comdr. M.C. USNR, 1980—. Recipient Outstanding Student Rsch. award U. Pitt. Sch. Medicine, 1984, Harold Henderson Sankey Orthop. award, 1984; rsch. grantee Competitive Med. Rsch. Fund., Presbyn.-Univ. Hosp. of Pitts., 1986-87, U. Pitts. Rsch. Devel. Fund, 1986-87. Disting. Alden scholar 1977, 78, 79, 80, Sandra Doane Turk scholar, 1979, Armed Svcs. Health Professoins scholar, 1981-84. Mem. AMA, Am. Acad. Orthop. Surgeons (teaching seal 1993), Pa. Orthop. Soc. (Best Rsch. Paper 1987, 88), Erie Orthop. Soc., U. Pitts. Med. Ctr. Orthop. Alumni., Am. Orthop. Soc. of Sports Medicine (Cabaud award 1988), Ea. Orthop. Assn. (Founders award 1988), Phi Beta Kappa. Office: Orthopaedic Surgeons Inc 204 W 26th St Erie PA 16508

MASON, JAMES OSTERMANN, public health administrator; b. Salt Lake City, June 19, 1930; s. Ambrose Stanton and Neoma (Thorup) M.; m. Lydia Maria Smith, Dec. 29, 1952; children: James, Susan, Bruce, Ralph, Samuel, Sara, Benjamin. BA, U. Utah, 1954, MD, 1958; MPH, Harvard U., 1963, DPH, 1967. Diplomate Am. Bd. Preventive Medicine. Intern Johns Hopkins Hosp., Balt., 1958-59; resident in internal medicine Peter Bent Brigham Hosp.-Harvard Med. Service, Boston, 1961-62; chief infectious diseases Latter-day Saints Hosp., Salt Lake City, 1968-69; commr. Health Services Corp., Ch. of Jesus Christ of Latter-day Saints, 1970-76; dep. dir. health Utah Div. Health, 1976-78, exec. dir., 1979-83; chief epidemic intelligence service Ctr. Disease Control, Atlanta, 1959, chief hepatitis surveillance unit epidemiology br., 1960, chief surveillance sect. epidemiology br., 1961, dep. dir. bur. labs., 1964-68, dep. dir. of Ctr., 1969-70; dir. Ctrs. for Disease Control, Atlanta; adminstr. Agy. for Toxic Substances and Disease Registry, 1983-89; acting asst. sec. health HHS, Washington, 1985, asst. sec. for health, acting surgeon gen., 1989-90, asst. sec. for health, 1990-93; asst. prof. dept. medicine and preventive medicine U. Utah, Salt Lake City, 1968-69; assoc. prof., chmn. div. community medicine, dept. family and community medicine U. Utah, 1978-79; v.p. planning, devel., prof. preventive medicine and biometrics Uniformed Svcs. U. Health Scis., 1993-94; 2nd quorum of Seventy LDS Ch., 1994—; physician, cons. to med. services Salt Lake VA Hosp., 1977-83; clin. prof. dept. family and community medicine, U. Utah. Coll. Medicine, 1979-83, clin. prof. dept. pathology, 1980-83; clin. prof. community health Emory U. Sch. Medicine, 1984-86; chmn. joint residency com. in preventive medicine and pub. health Utah Coll. Medicine, 1975-80; mem. Utah Cancer Registry Research Adv. Com., 1976-83; mem. adv. com. Utah Ctr. Health Stats., 1977-79; chmn. bd. Hosp. Coop. Utah, 1977-79; chmn. exec. com. Utah Health Planning and Resource Devel. Adv. Group, 1977-79; chmn. Utah Gov.'s Adv. Com. for Comprehensive Health Planning, 1975-77; mem. recombinant DNA adv. com. NIH, 1979-83; mem. Gov.'s Nuclear Waste Repository Task Force, 1980-83, chmn., 1980-82; bd. dirs. Utah Health Cost Mgmt. Found., 1980-83; mem. adv. com. for programs and policies Ctrs. for Disease Control, 1980; mem. com. on future of local health depts., Inst. Medicine, 1980-82; mem. exec. com., chmn. tech. adv. com. Thrasher Research Found., 1980-89; mem. Robert Wood Johnson Found. Program for Hosp. Initiatives in Long-Term Care, 1982-84; mem. sci. and tech. adv. com. UNDP-World Bank-WHO Spl. Programme for Research and Tng. in Tropical Diseases, 1984-89; mem. Utah Resource for Genetic and Epidemiologic Research, 1982-85, chmn. bd., 1982-83; U.S. rep. WHO Exec. Bd., 1990-93. Author: (with H.L. Bodily and E.J. Updyke) Diagnostic Procedures for Bacterial, Mycotic and Parasitic Infections, 5th edit., 1970; (with M.H. Maxell, K.H. Bousfield and D.A. Ostler) Funding Water Quality Control in Utah, Procs. for Lincoln Inst., 1982; contbr. articles to profl. jours. Mem. nat. scouting com. Boy Scouts Am., 1974-78. Recipient Roche award U. Utah, 1957, Wintrobe award U. Utah, 1958, Disting. Alumni award U. Utah, 1973, Adminstr. of Yr. award Brigham U., 1980, spl. award for outstanding pub. svc. Am. Soc. Pub. Adminstrn. 1984, Disting. Svc. medal USPHS, 1988, LDS Hosp. Deseret Found. Legacy of Life award, 1992, Gorgas Medal and Scroll, 1993. Mem. Inst. Medicine of NAS, AMA, Am. Pub. Health Assn. (task force for credentialing of lab. personnel 1976-78, program devel. bd. 1979-81), Utah State Med. Assn. (trustee 1979-83), Utah Acad. Preventive Medicine (pres. 1982-83), Utah Pub. Health Assn. (pres. 1980-82, Beatty award 1979), Sigma Xi, Alpha Epsilon Delta, Phi Kappa Phi, Alpha Omega Alpha, Delta Omega. Mem. LDS Ch. Lodge: Rotary. Office: LDS ChThe 70 47 E South Temple St Salt Lake City UT 84150 also: Africa Area Adminstrv Office, POBox 1218, Lonehill 2062, South Africa

MASON, JAMES STEPHEN, orthopedic surgeon, educator; b. Sewickley, Pa., Feb. 9, 1958; s. William Eugene and Elizabeth (Jula) M.; m. MaryLynn DeLembo, Aug. 29, 1981; children: Tyler Joseph, Jennifer Elizabeth. BS, Allegheny Coll., Meadville, Pa., 1980; DO, New Eng. Coll. Osteo. Medicine, Biddeford, Maine, 1984. Bd. cert. Am. Osteo. Bd. Orthopedic Surgery. Commd. 2d lt. USAF, 1985, advanced through grades to lt. col.; staff physician USAF Hosp., Robins AFB, Ga., 1985-87; asst. chief emergency dept. USAF Hosp., 1986-87; staff orthopedic surgeon 72d Med. Group, Tinker AFB, Okla., 1991—; chief orthopedic surgery 72d Med. Group, Tinker AFB, 1992-94, chief surgery, 1992-96, dir. surg. svcs., 1996—; clin. instr. orthopedics U. Okla. Health Svcs. Ctr./VA Med. Ctr., Oklahoma City, 1991—; examiner clin., oral bds. Am. Osteo. Bd. Orthopedic Surgery, 1995—. Mem. Am. Osteo. Assn., Soc. Mil. Orthopedic Surgeons, Am. Osteo. Acad. Orthopedics (chmn. liaison to Armed Svcs. Com., 1995-96). Home: 2309 Powderhorn Edmond OK 73034-6829

MASON, JENNIFER ANN GRAVES, medical/surgical nurse; b. Tacoma, Feb. 10, 1965; d. Glen Edward and Marlene June (Freel) Graves; m. Robert Joseph Mason, June 19, 1993. BSN, U. Portland, 1987, MS, 1992. Cert. adult nurse practitioner. Nurse Ballard Community Hosp., Seattle, 1990-95; asst. prof. Seattle (Wash.) Pacific Univ., 1992—. Home: 6200 Sand Point Way NE Apt 402 Seattle WA 98115-7968

MASON, JOAN ELLEN, nurse; b. Reading, Pa., June 29, 1947; d. Richard Lenhart and Mary Jane (Miller) Fritz; m. W. Davis Mason, Feb. 12, 1977. RN, Temple U. Hosp. Sch. Nursing, 1968; BS in Nursing Edn., Temple U., 1971, EdM in Health Edn., 1981; postgrad. U. Pa. Staff nurse Temple U. Hosp., 1968-71; nursing instr. Phila. Gen. Hosp. Sch. Nursing, 1971-76; coordinator staff devel. Meml. Hosp., Roxborough, Phila., 1976-84; clin. editor Springhouse Corp., Pa., 1984-94; clin. data coord. for Smithkline Beecham, 1995—; instr. continuing edn. programs. Contbr. articles to profl. jours. Mem. NAFE, Am. Nurses Assn., Pa. Nurses Assn. (dist. 1), Ea. Pa. Nursing Dx. Assn., Temple U. Nurses Alumni Assn., Victorian Hist. Preservation Soc., Hist. Accommodations of Cape May, Cape May Bed and Breakfast Assn., N.J. Bed and Breakfast Assn., Am. Bed and Breakfast Assn., Mid-Atlantic Ctr. for the Arts, Mus. Nursing History, Inc., Phila. Libr. Republican. Home: 430 S 42nd St Philadelphia PA 19104-4045

MASON, LINDA ANN, health company executive; b. Columbus, Ohio, Mar. 31, 1947; d. Lloyd Walter and Ann Elizabeth (Seely) M.; m. Clifford A. Bridges, Sept. 14, 1968 (div. Dec. 1982); 1 child, David Lloyd Bridges. BA summa cum laude, Ohio U., 1969; MA, Kutztown (Pa.) U., 1985. Ptnr. Brownback, Masons & Assocs., Allentown, Pa., 1982—; bd. dirs. Allentown Rescue Mission. Bd. dirs. Lehigh Valley Nursing Mothers. Mem. Internat. Soc. for the Study of Dissociation (co-presenter 1985, 86, 89), Lehigh Valley Psychol. Assn., Acad. Cert. Neurotherapists, Am. Bd. Forensic Examiners, Mortar Bd., Phi Beta Kappa. Home: 1702 W Walnut St Allentown PA 18104-6741 Office: Brownback Mason & Assocs 1702 W Walnut St Allentown PA 18104-6741

MASON, MICHAEL DOYLE, orthopaedic surgeon; b. Media, Pa., Sept. 11, 1956; s. Mary Joan (Fellger) Wendl; m. Ilene Ann Schiff, Oct. 6, 1979; children: Tyler Matthew, Adam Kyle. BS, Westchester State U., 1983; DO, Phila. Coll. Osteopathic Medicine, 1987; internship, Community Gen. Hosp., Harrisburg, Pa. Diplomate Am. Osteopathic Bd. of Orthopaedic Surgery. Resident in orthpaedic surgery Cmty. Gen. Hosp., Harrisburg, Pa., 1987-92; clin. fellow in adult reconstruction Brigham and Womens Hosp., Boston, 1992-93; clin. instr. orthopaedic surgery Harvard Med. Sch., Boston, 1992-94; asst. prof. orthopaedic surgery Boston U. Sch. Medicine, 1994—; recipient of grant to be technical instr. Johnson & Johnson Orthopaedics Divsn., Mass., 1992-95; recipient of grant to be technical cons. Osteonics, Inc., N.J., 1995, 96. Contbr. articles to profl. jours. With U.S. Army, 1975-76. Mem. Am. Osteopathic Assn., Am. Osteopathic Assn. of Orthopaedic Surgeons, Mass. Osteopathic Assn. (treas. 1993-96). Office: Arthritis Spine and Reconstructive Surgery 930 Commonwealth Ave Boston MA 02215

MASON, MILES HERBERT, III, surgeon; b. San Diego, Oct. 2, 1947; s. Miles Herbert Jr. and Elizabeth (Deal) M.; m. Sandra Ulmer, June 17, 1972; children: Stephanie, Lisa, Miles IV. Diploma, Oxford Coll. of Emory U., 1967; BA, Emory U., 1968; MD, Med. Coll. of Ga., 1972. Intern Baylor U. Med. Ctr., Dallas, 1972-73; surgery resident Med. Coll. of Ga., Augusta, 1973-74, Baylor U. Med. Ctr., Dallas, 1974-77; pvt. practice in gen. surgery Duluth, Ga., 1979—; hosp. staff Gwinnett Hosp. System, Lawrenceville, Ga., 1979—; bd. dirs. Wachovia Bank, Lawrenceville; bd. mem. Southcare Med. Alliance; mem. adv. bd. First Nat. Bank. of Atlanta; chief of staff Gwinnett Hosp. system, Lawreceville, 1981-88. Bd. mem. Gwinnett County Div. Am. Cancer Soc.; affiliate faculty Ga. Chpt. Am. Heart Assn. Lt. Comdr. USNR, 1977-79. Decorated Naval Achievement award, 1978. Fellow ACS, Ga. Surgical Soc., Southeastern Surgical Congress; mem. AMA, Me. Assn. Ga., So. Med. Assn., Gwinnett-Forsyth Med. Soc. Home: 3398 E Whippoorwill Dr Duluth GA 30136-5330 Office: 3255 Mcclure Bridge Rd Duluth GA 30136-3223

MASON, MITCHELL GARY, emergency nurse; b. Nelsonville, Ohio, Aug. 11, 1957; s. Homer Frank and Margaret Louise (Lehman) M. Student, Capital U., Columbus, Ohio, 1975-76; BSEd, Ohio U., Athens, Ohio, 1981; ADN, Hocking Tech. Coll., Nelsonville, Ohio, 1985; postgrad., Barry U., Miami Shores, Fla., 1991. Instr. med. terminology Hocking Tech. Coll., Nelsonville, 1984-85; staff nurse Hocking Valley Community Hosp., Logan, Ohio, 1974-86; trauma nurse specialist, assoc. head nurse Jackson Meml. Hosp., Miami, Fla., 1986—. Home: 316 W 194th Ave Pembroke Pines FL 33029-5456

MASON, SARA SMITH, managed healthcare consultant; b. Rochester, N.Y.; d. Harry F. and Louise S. (Sullivan) Smith; m. Larry S. Mason, Oct. 14, 1972. BA, Lewis and Clark Coll., Portland, Oreg., MA in Tchg.; MBA, U. Oreg., 1987. Dir. N.W. area Intracorp., Portland, 1979-90; dir. ops. Western region Ptnrs. In Exec. Solutions, Irvine, Calif., 1990-91; asst. v.p. group and casualty svcs. ETHIX Nat., Portland, Oreg., 1992-94; managed care product mgr. Fireman's Fund Ins. Cos., Portland, 1994-95; exec. v.p. Cyber Metrix, Beaverton, Oreg., 1995—. Mem. med. subcom. Worker's Compensation, Salem, Oreg., 1987. Mem. Oreg. Exec. MBA Alumni Bd. (bd. dirs.), Nat. Assn. Rehab. Profl. in Pvt. Sector, Portland City Club (bus. labor com. 1990-91). Office: Firemans Fund Ins Cos 101 SW Main St Ste 710 Portland OR 97204-3215

MASON, TERRY WAYNE, university counseling service director; b. Balt., May 13, 1955; s. Milton P. and Bertha Mason; m. Teresa Faye Smith, Apr. 20, 1985; children: Trey, Travis. BA, Cornell Coll., 1977; PhD, Tex. Tech U., 1982. Lic. psychologist, Tex. Staff counselor Lubbock (Tex.) Mental Health/Mental Retardation, 1978-81; counseling psychology intern Iowa State U., Ames, 1981-82; cons., co-prin. investigator U.S. Dept. Labor, Beckley, W.Va., 1982-85; counseling psychologist Brazos Psychol. Assocs., College Station, 1986—; assoc. dir. Tex. A&M U. Student Counseling Svc., College Station, 1985-93; pres., ptnr. Omega Organizational Consultants, College Station, 1989-93. Mem. Assn. Univ. and Coll. Counseling Ctr. Dirs. (bd. dirs. 1995—), Phi Beta Kappa. Home: 3705 Fletcher Blvd Ames IA 50010-4167 Office: Iowa State Univ Student Counseling Svc Student Svcs Bldg 3rd Fl Ames IA 50011

MASON, WILLIAM A(LVIN), psychologist, educator, researcher; b. Mountain View, Calif., Mar. 28, 1926; s. Alvin Frank and Ruth Sabina (Erwin) M.; m. Virginia Joan Carmichael, June 27, 1948; children: Todd, Paula, Nicole, Hunter. B.A., Stanford U., 1950, M.S., 1952, Ph.D., 1954. Asst. prof. U. Wis.-Madison, 1954-59; research assoc. Yerkes Labs. Primate Biology, Orange Park, Fla., 1959-63; head dept. behavioral sci. Delta Primate Research Ctr., Tulane U., Covington, La., 1963-71; prof. psychology, research psychologist U. Calif., Davis, 1971—, leader behavioral biology unit Calif. Primate Rsch. Ctr., 1972-96; bd. dirs. Jane Goodall Inst., 1978-92, Karisoke Rsch. Ctr., 1980-86. Mem. Editorial bd. Animal Learning and Behavior, 1973-76, Internat. Jour. Devel. Psychobiology, 1980-92, Internat. Jour. Primatology, 1980-90; contbr. numerous articles to profl. jours., chpts. to books. With USMC, 1944-46. USPHS spl. fellow, 1963-64. Fellow AAAS, APA (pres. divsn. 6 1982, disting. sci. contbn. award 1995), Am. Psychol. Soc., Animal Behavior Soc.; mem. Internat. Primatological Soc. (pres. 1976-80, 81-84), Am. Soc. Primatologists (pres. 1988-90, disting. primatologist award), Internat. Soc. Devel. Psychobiology (pres. 1971-72, Best Paper of Yr. award 1976), Sigma Xi. Home: 2809 Anza Ave Davis CA 95616-0257 Office: U Calif Regional Primate Rsch Ctr Davis CA 95616

MASON, WILLIAM VANHORN, dermatologist; b. Pitts., Jan. 8, 1930. AB, Harvard U., Cambridge, Mass., 1951; MD, Baylor Coll. Medicine, Houston, 1961. Diplomate Am. Bd. Dermatology. Pvt. practice Albuquerque, 1979—; clin. assoc. prof. dermatology U. N.Mex. Sch. Medicine, Albuquerque, 1986—. LTJG USN, 1951-54. Mem. Phi Beta Kappa, Alpha Omega Alpha. Office: 201 Cedar SE # 404 Albuquerque NM 87106

MASOVER, GERALD KENNETH, microbiologist; b. Chgo., May 12, 1935; s. Morris H. and Lillian (Perelgut) M.; m. Bonnie Blumenthal, Mar. 30, 1958 (dec. 1992); children: Steven, Laurie, David; m. Lee H. Tower, Mar. 25, 1995. BS, U. Ill., Chgo., 1957, MS, 1970; PhD, Stanford U., 1973. Registered pharmacist, Calif., Ill. Owner, operator Ropert Pharmacy, Chgo., 1960-68; rsch. assoc. Stanford U. Med. Sch., Palo Alto, Calif., 1974-80; assoc. rsch. cell biologist Children's Hosp., Oakland, Calif., 1980-83; rsch. microbiologist Hana Biologics, Berkeley, Calif., 1983-86; pharmacist various locations, 1970—; quality control sect. head Genentech, Inc., South San Francisco, 1986-90, quality control sr. microbiologist, 1990—. Contbr. articles to profl. jours., chpts. to books. 1st Lt. USAR, 1957-66. NSF predoctoral fellow, 1970-73; NIH rsch. grantee, 1974-78. Mem. Soc. In Vitro Biology, Internat. Orgn. for Mycoplasmology, Parenteral Drug Assn., Am. Soc. Microbiology, Sigma Xi. Jewish. Home: 4472 24th St San Franicisco CA 94114 Office: Genentech Inc 460 Point San Bruno Blvd South San Francisco CA 94080-4918

MASSA, MARY CATHERINE, dermatologist, medicine educator; b. Jersey City, Dec. 22, 1951; d. Vito and Florence (Carbutti) M.; m. Walter G. Barr, June 16, 1979; children: Walter G. Jr., Maria, Luke. BS in Biology, St. Peters Coll., Jersey City, 1973; MD, Loyola U., Maywood, Ill., 1976. Diplomate Am. Bd. Internal Medicine, Am. Bd. Dermatology, Am. Bd. Dermatopathology, Nat. Bd. Med. Examiners. Intern in medicine Loyola U. Hosp., 1976-77, resident, 1977-79; resident in dermatology Mayo Clinic, Rochester, Minn., 1979-82; fellow in dermatopathology U. Chgo., 1982-83; asst. prof. medicine Loyola U. Med. Ctr., 1983-87, asst. prof. pathology, 1986-87, assoc. prof. medicine and pathology, 1987—, chief sect. dermatology, 1986-92, dir. divsn. dermatology, 1992—; lectr. U. Ill., Chgo., 1985—; attending physician Hines (Ill.) VA Hosp., 1984—; mem. cons. med. staff HCA Riveredge Hosp., 1988-91; guest Dermatologic Drugs Adv. Com., Washington, 1992; mem. dermatologic drugs adv. com. FDA, 1995; vis. prof. Mayo Clinic, 1985; numerous lectures in field; reviewer Archives Dermatology, 1985—, Jour. Am. Acad. Dermatology. Contbr. numerous articles and abstracts to med. jours. Scholar Loyola U., 1975; travel grantee Clin. Cases in Dermatology, 1990. Fellow ACP; mem. Am. Acad. Dermatology, Soc. for Investigative Dermatology, Am. Soc. Dermatopathology, Assn. Profs. Dermatology, Am. Fedn. Clin. Rsch., Scleroderma Clin. Trials Consortium (charter), Ill. Dermatologic Soc., Chgo. Dermatol. Soc., Chgo. Med. Soc., Alpha Omega Alpha. Roman Catholic. Office: Loyola U Med Ctr 2160 S 1st Ave Maywood IL 60153

MASSA, SALVATORE PETER, psychologist; b. Queens, N.Y., Aug. 5, 1955; s. Joseph and Marie Massa; AAS, Orange County Community Coll., 1975; BA in Psychology, Queens Coll., 1977; MA, St. John's U., 1978, profl. diploma, 1979, PhD, 1985; m. Patricia Louise Kathryn Kelley, Mar. 12, 1979; children: Kathryn Kelley, Kristopher Kelley, KayLynn Kelley, Patrick Kelley, Grace Kelley. Lic. psychologist, N.Y.; nat. cert. sch. psychologist. Intern psychologist Sagamore Children's Psychiat. Hosp., Melville, N.Y., 1978-79; habilitation supr. Suffolk Child Devel. Center, Smithtown, N.Y., 1979; staff psychologist Cumberland Mental Health Center, Bklyn., 1979-81; asst. program dir., dir. clin. services Rhinebeck (N.Y.) Country Sch., 1981-87; cons. psychologist Brookwood Ctr., 1985-86, Anderson Sch., 1987-89, Renssalaer Columbia Greene BOCES, 1987—; chmn. Com. on Spl. Edn., 1991—, Com. on Presch. Edn., 1991—; sch. psychologist Red Hook Cen. Sch. Dist., cons. psychologist Rhinebeck Cen. Sch. Dist., 1986-90, chmn. profl. conf. com., 1986-87, Anderson Sch., 1987-88; cons. Columbia County Assn. for Retarded Citizens, Rehab. Programs, Inc., 1989; adj. prof. Marist Coll., Poughkeepsie, N.Y., 1989—. Head football coach YMCA winter league, 1979-81; asst. football coach Rhinebeck Country Sch., 1982; coach Germantown Little League, Germantown Winter Basketball League. Recipient public service award for vol. work Middletown State Hosp., 1975; spl. recognition award Internat. Council Psychology, 1981; cert. sch. psychology, N.Y. Mem. Am. Psychol. Assn. (divs. pediatric psychology, psychotherapy, sch. psychology, neuropsychology), Eastern Psychol. Assn., Internat. Council Psychologists, Hudson Valley Psychol. Assn., Nat. Assn. Sch. Psychologists, Nat. Soc. Autistic Children. Democrat. Roman Catholic. Contbr. papers to profl. confs.; co-author study on relaxation tng. in residential treatment.

MASSEY, CLINTON EDWARD, neurosurgeon; b. Charlotte, N.C., Oct. 31, 1947; s. Robert Lee and Mary Alice (Grier) M.; m. Carolyn Jean Spaduzzi, May 23, 1970; children: Heather Christine, Lauren Ashley. BS, Presbyn. Coll., 1970; MD, Med. Coll. Ga., 1978. Diplomate Am. Bd. Neurol. Surgery. Intern Med. Coll. Ga., 1978-79, resident, 1979-84; pvt. practice, Augusta, Ga., 1984—; bd. dirs. Walton Rehab. Hosp., Augusta, St. Joseph Hosp., Augusta. Bd. dirs. March of Dimes, Augusta, 1989—. 2d lt. U.S. Army, 1970. Mem. AMA, Am. Assn. Neurol. Surgery, Congress Neurol. Surgeons, Ga. Neurosurg. Soc. Republican. Home: 67 Conifer Cir Augusta GA 30909-4508 Office: Summerville Neurosurgery PC 2100 Central Ave Ste 1 Augusta GA 30904-6709

MASSEY, LODIE BUNCE, administrator; b. Port Arthur, Tex., Sept. 23, 1948; s. Thomas Jefferson and Peggy Joyce (Rising) Henderson; m. Harvey Bunce III, Jan. 25, 1969 (div. Dec. 1984); children: Jessica Leigh, T.H. Beau; m. Jack Alan Massey, Apr. 30, 1988. BS, U. Tex., Galveston, 1975; MA, U. Houston, 1985. Cert. physician asst.; lic. chem. dependency counselor, Tex. Physician asst. U. Tex. Med. Br., Galveston, 1975-79; asst. med. dir. Gulf Coast Mental Health Mental Retardation Ctr., Galveston & Brazoria Co., Tex., 1979-81, dir. spl. svcs., 1984-90, dir. substance abuse svc., 1990-95; asst. prof. Sch. Allied Health, U. Tex. Med. Br., Galveston, 1981-84, clin. asst. prof., 1984—; dir. correctional psychiatric svcs. U. Tex. Med. Br. Dept. Criminal Justice Managed Care, 1995—; cons., physician asst. psychiatry Metrana Mgmt., Galveston, 1987-95; mem. adv. bd. Mayor's Coalition for a Drug-Free Galveston, 1992—, chmn., 1995; bd. mem. Assn. Substance Abuse Svc. Providers Tex., 1993-95; mem. adv. bd. Mayor's Com. on Handicapped and Sr. Citizens, Galveston, 1987-90. Author ann. reports The Gulf Coast Mental Health Mental Retardation Ctr., 1984-90; editor All Ctr. News, 1984-90, Update Sch. Allied Health Scis. Newsletter U. Ex. Med. Br., 1987-90; dir. videotape Reflections - A 20 Year History of the Gulf Coast Center, 1990. Active edn., tng., CPR, cmty. rsch. Jr. League, Galveston County, Tex., 1983-86. Named Outstanding Alumni, Dept. Physician Asst. Studies, U. Tex. Med. Br., Galveston, 1986; recipient Comm. awards Nat. Assn. Mental Health Info. Officers, 1987, 88, 89. Fellow Am. Acad. Physician Assts.; mem. Tex. Acad. Physician Assts., Leadership galveston Alumni Assn. (bd. dirs. 1988-89, chair publs. com. 1988-89), Sch. Allied Health Scis. Alumni Assn. U. Tex. Med. Br. (bd. dirs. 1986-92), Galveston C. of C. (chair edn. com. 1986-88). Office: UTMB TDJC Managed Care 301 University Blvd Galveston TX 77555-1008

MASSEYEFF, RENÉ FRANCIS, medical reference laboratory executive; b. Paris, Sept. 1, 1927; s. Sacha Masseyeff and Yvonne Marie-Louise (Dehoulle) Rosenwald; m. Christine Truong Ngoc, Apr. 5, 1965 (div. Apr. 1973); children: Veronique, Claire, Yann; m. Marie France Elbaz, Jan. 26, 1974; 1 child, Nicolas. MD, U. Paris, 1952. Scientist ORSTOM, Yaounde, Cameroon, 1952-57; prof. biochemistry Univ. Med. Sch., Dakar, Senegal, 1958-68; prof. immunology U. Nice (France) Faculty Medicine, 1969-87; dir. Lab. Analyses Biologiques, Nice, 1987—; mem. Nat. Univs. Coun., France, 1980-85. Author: La Faim, 1956; editor: L'Alpha Foetoproteine, 1973, Immunoenzymatic Techniques, 1983; editor-in-chief Methods of Immunological Analysis, 1993—. Mem. Permanent Nat. Com. Med. Biology, Paris, 1983—. Decorated chevalier Nat. Order of Merit (Senegal and France). Mem. Am. Assn. Immunologists, French Soc. Immunology (bd. dirs. 1979-81), French Soc. Clin. Biology (bd. dirs. 1985-89), Am. Assn. for Clin. Chemistry. Office: Labs Analyses Biol Spec, 57 Rte de Canta Gallet, 06200 Nice France

MASSIE, BILLIE ANNE, neuroscience nurse; b. New London, Ohio, Mar. 14, 1939; d. Clinton Frederick and Mildred Eleanor (Triplett) Frank; m. Boyd O. Massie, Aug. 24, 1958; children: Charles Daniel, Shirley Anne Massie Bixby, Patricia Elaine Massie Rzesnowiecky. Grad., M.B Johnson Sch. Nursing, North Windham, Maine, 1972; BS in Pub. Adminstrn., St. Joseph's Coll., 1984. RN, Fla., Ohio; cert. med.-surg. nurse, ANA, CPR instr. Staff nurse Elyria (Ohio) Meml. Hosp., 1972-86; asst. head nurse neurosci. unit Tampa (Fla.) Gen. Hosp., 1986-91, head nurse neurosci. unit, 1991-95, instr. medications, 1993-94, case mgr. med.-surg. divsn, 1995—; home health nurse Assoc. Health Care Svcs. Inc., 1991-95; procedure com. Tampa Gen. Hosp., 1988-91, contbr. radio advertisement, 1990, instr. medications, 1993-94; presenter King's Theory 1994. Mem. fin. com. Asbury United Meth. Ch., New Port Richey, Fla., chairperson children's home. Mem. ANA, Am. Assn. Spinal Cord Injury Nurses (com. on bylaws, policy and procedures 1990-92, 10th anniversary task force), Nat. Spinal Injury Assn. (bd. dirs., treas. Tampa Bay chpt. 1990—), World Fedn. Neurosci. Nurses, Am. Assn. Neurosci. Nurses (treas. Tampa Bay chpt. 1990-94, pres. 1994—), Fla. Orgn. Nurse Execs. (coun. nurse mgr. affiliates 1991—), Fla. Nurses Assn., Tampa Gen. Nat. Mgmt. Assn., Nat. Mgmt. Assn. (instr. 1994, chmn. programs 1995—), Order Ea Star, Sigma Theta Tau. Office: Tampa Gen. Hosp PO Box 1289 Tampa FL 33601-1289

MASSIMINI, ELIZABETH L., podiatrist; b. Phila., Apr. 10, 1963; d. Mario Vincent and Elizabeth Concetta (Pascuccio) M. DPM, Pa. Coll. Podiatric Medicine, 1989. Diplomate Am. Bd. Podiatric Surgery. Assoc. Dr. Lee S. Cohen Assocs., Ridley Park, Pa., 1990-94; pvt. practice Springfield, Pa., 1994—. Fellow Am. Coll foot Surgeons; mem. Am. Podiatric Med. Assn., Pa. Podiatric Med. Assn., Rheumatoid Soc. Office: 1001 Baltimore Pike Ste 111 Springfield PA 19064

MASSION, WALTER HERBERT, anesthesiologist, educator; b. Eitorf, Ger., June 4, 1923; came to U.S., 1954; s. Rudolf and Margarethe (Polch) M.; m. Rose Marie Kumin, July 15, 1956; children: Birgit, Stuart, Iris. BS, U. Cologne, Ger., 1948; MD, U. Heidelberg, 1951, U. Bonn, 1951. Diplomate German Bd. Anesthesiology. Intern U. Zurich Hosps., 1951-52; trainee WHO Anesthesiology Centre, Copenhagen, 1952-53; asst. prof. physiology U. Basel, Switzerland, 1953-54; postdoctoral fellow U.S. Nat. Acad. Sci., Rochester, N.Y., 1954-56; asst. prof. anesthesiology U. Okla. Med. Ctr., Oklahoma City, 1957-61, assoc. prof., 1961-67; prof. anesthesiology, physiology and biophysics U. Okla. Health Sci. Ctr., Oklahoma City, 1967-88, prof. emeritus, 1988; prin. investigator NATO Collaborative Rsch. Project, Oklahoma City and Homburg, 1988-95. Editor: Hemorrhage/Anesth. Requirements, 1974, Multiple Trauma, 1984, Critical Care Cardiology, 1988; contbr. over 125 articles to profl. jours. Hon. consul Fed Republic Germany, Oklahoma City, 1980-95. Grantee WHO, 1953, U.S. Nat. Acad. Scis., 1954, NIH, 1959-88; Fulbright scholar, 1985; named Newsmaker of the Yr., Okla. Press Assn., 1964, Alexander von Humboldt prize, 1974; decorated Order of Merit 1st class Fed. Republic Germany, 1990. Office: Univ Okla Health Sci Ctr PO Box 26901 Oklahoma City OK 73126

MASSON, JOHN ROLAND, social worker; b. Manchester, N.H., Sept. 26, 1953; s. Roland D. and IreneM. (St. Laurent) M. BA, U. N.H., 1975; MSW, Simmons Coll., Boston, 1980. Lic. independent clin. social worker, Mass. Clin. social worker New England Home for Little Wanderers, Boston, 1980-84; dir. child and family svcs. Cmty. Counseling of Bristol County, Taunton, Mass., 1984-94, program coord., 1994-96. Active Social Workers for Peace and Nuclear Disarmament, Boston, 1985-95. Fellow Am. Orthopsychiat. Assn.; mem. NASW. Home: 657 Cottage St New Bedford MA 02740-5545 Office: Community Counseling 170 High St Taunton MA 02780-3536

MASSOT, CHRISTIAN THIERRY, physician; b. Huy, Liege, Belgium, June 21, 1960; s. Christian Adolphe and Leopoldine (Cloetens) M.; m. Marie-Anne Josee Neve, Sept. 10, 1988; children: Julien Christian, Virginie Marianne. MD, U. Liege, 1985; degree in tropical medicine, Inst. Tropical Medicine, Antwerp, 1986; cert. in statistics, epidemiology, Free U. Brussels, 1991. Student asst. U. Liege, 1982-84; med. supr. Medecins sans Frontieres, Abeche, Chad, Belgium, 1986-87; mem. staff Hosp. St. Joseph, Liege, 1991-92; med. supr. Medecins sans Frontieres, Kasaji, Zaire, 1988-90; med. field coord. Medecins sans Frontieres, Ruwaished, Jordan, 1990; med. Medecins san Frontieres, Vinh, Vietnam, 1992; expert on drugs tender for 4 C.I.S. republics EEC, 1992; head of mission Medecins sans Frontieres, Cluj, Romania, 1993-94; physician Carolo Cardio Sante, Charleroi, 1995—, Ville-Sante, La Louviere, 1996, Observatoire de Sante du Hainaut, Mons, Belgium, 1995—. Mem. Equipe Technique, CercleSci. Interfacultaire U. Liege (treas. 1980-82, chmn. 82-85). Home: 2 Pl d'Ormeignies, 7802 Ath Belgium Office: Observatoire de Sante, 1 rue St Antoine, 7021 Havre, Mons Belgium

MASSURA, EILEEN KATHLEEN, family therapist; b. Chgo., July 25, 1925; d. John William and Loretta (Feil) Stratemeier; m. Edmund Karamanski, July 24, 1948 (dec.); children: John, Kathleen; m. Alfred Massura, Aug. 30, 1963; children: Michael, Kathryn, Mark. BS in Nursing, DePaul U., 1963; MS in Nursing, St. Xavier Coll., 1971. RN; cert. family therapist. Dir. nurses Franklin Blvd. Hosp., Chgo., 1958-62; adminstr. Mich. Ave Hosp., Chgo., 1962-64; instr. St. Xavier Coll., Chgo., 1972-74, Joliet (Ill.) Jr. Coll., 1972-81; family therapist Oak Lawn (Ill.) Family Svc., 1978-88; prof. nursing Govs. State U., University Park, Ill., 1981-89; family therapist McCarthy & Assocs., Oak Lawn, 1982-93, Massura & Assocs., Oak Lawn, 1994—; preceptor to grads. St. Xavier Coll., 1980-90, Govs. State U., 1980-89; co-leader Clin. Study Med./Surg. Nursing, Moscow, 1984; presenter Am. Nursing Rev., Ala., Fla., Va., Pa., Tex., Md., 1985-86. Leader Campfire Girls, Oak Lawn, 1964-74; co-leader Orient/Am. Med./ Surg. Nursing, 1987; mem. Marist Women's Bd., Chgo., 1978-82. Bro. Rice Women's Bd., Chgo., 1969-72; Luth. Family Svc. Bd. Day Care for Srs., 1988-89. Grantee HEW, 1969-71; named Disting. Nurse Alumnae, St. Xavier Coll., 1985; named Nursing Prof. of Yr., Govs. State U., 1983. Mem. Am. Nurses Assn. (nominating com. 1982-87), Ill. Nurses Assn. (program com. 1980-84), Am. Assn. Marital and Family Therapists, Cath. Order Foresters, Sigma Theta Tau (v.p. 1971-75). Roman Catholic. Office: 5660 W 95th St Oak Lawn IL 60453-2380

MAST, ERIC EDWARD, physician; b. Marion, Ind., Apr. 28, 1968; s. Larry Edward and Nancy Marlene (Bates) M.; m. Jodyn Elizabeth Halter, June 19, 1993. BA, Anderson U., 1989; DO, Ohio Univ. Coll., 1993. Intern Firelands Cmty. Hosp., Sundusky, Ohio, 1993-94; resident family practice Munson Med. Ctr., Traverse City, Mich., 1994-96. Vol. Belize med. misison Faith Reformed Ch., 1996. Mem. Am. Osteo. Assn., Am. Coll. Osteo. Family Practioners, Christian Med. Soc. (vol. Ecuador med. mission, chpt. pres. 1989-90). Office: 1019 Pierce St Sandusky OH 44870

MASTER, STEVEN BRUCE, clinical psychologist; b. Phila., May 27, 1953; s. Hyman and Gertrude (Steiner) M. BA, Muhlenberg Coll., 1975; MS, Villanova U., 1980; PhD, Temple U., 1987. Lic. psychologist, Pa., N.J. Counselor Pottstown (Pa.) Area Drug Rehab. Program, 1979-80, dir. residential treatment, 1980-82; cons. Effective Tng. Cons., Kimberton, Pa., 1980-82; pvt. practice Turnersville, N.J., 1987—, Devon, Pa., 1990—. Contbr. articles to profl. publs. Bd. dirs., pres. Help Counseling, Inc., 1987—; mem. Coventry Canine Search and Rescue, 1989-92. Office: 410 Lancaster Ave Ste 208 Devon PA 19333-1588

MASTERS, GARY EVERETT, librarian, educator; b. Fresno, Calif., July 3, 1941; s. Jess Franklin and Lois May (Cain) M.; m. Ella Suzanne Tilson, Dec. 27, 1972. BA, Tex. Tech. U., 1969; MLS, North Tex. State U., 1976, PhD, 1987. Info. specialist CIA, Washington, Vietnam, 1969-75; sci. librarian North Tex. State U., Denton, 1976-87; asst. prof. Uniformed Svcs. U. Health Scis., Bethesda, Md., 1987-93; libr. automated svcs. Tex. A&M Internat. U., Laredo, 1994—; database coord. for Vietnam med. records and counter narcotics tactical ops. med. support reports. Sgt. U.S. Army, 1965-67. Mem. Tex. Libr. Assn. Democrat. Methodist. Office: Tex A&M Internat U 5201 University Blvd Laredo TX 78041-1999

MASTERS, ROBERT EDWARD LEE, psychotherapist, neural researcher, human potential educator; b. St. Joseph, Mo., Jan. 4, 1927; s. Robert and Katherine (Leeper) M.; m. Jean Houston, May 8, 1965. BA in Philosophy, U. Mo., 1951; PhD in Clin. Psychology, Humanistic Psychology Inst., 1974. Dir. Library of Sex Research, N.Y.C., 1962-66, Sensory Imagery Program, 1965-68; dir. research Found. for Mind Research. N.Y.C. and Pomona, N.Y., 1965—; dir. Zarathustra Project, Pomona, 1980—; co-dir. Human Capacities Tng. Program, Ramapo, N.J., 1982—; pres. Kontrakundabuffer Corp.; Pomona, 1983—; pvt. practice psychotherapy, neural re-edn., aging and geropsychology programs; prin. tchr. Psychophys. Method Tchr. Tng. Programs, 1980—; pres. Human Capacities Corp.; Pomona, 1982—; prin. tchr. Hypnotherapist Tng., Pomona, 1982—. Author: books (27) including Eros and Evil, 1962, Mind Games, 1972, Listening to the Body, 1978, Psychophysical Method Exercises Vols. I-VI, 1983, The Goddess Sekhmet, 1987, The Masters Technique, 1987, Neurospeak, 1994, The Way to Walk, 1996; (with J. Houston) Varieties of Psychedelic Experience, 1966; also sci. publs., poetry, fiction, essays, lit. and art criticism, book revs. Served with USN, 1945-46, PTO. Grantee Erickson Found, 1966, Kleiner Found., 1968, Babcock Found, 1970, Doris Duke Found., 1972. Fellow Am. Acad. Clin. Sexologists (founder), Mem. Am. Psychol. Assn., Can. Psychol. Assn., N.Y. Acad. Scis., Am. Anthrop. Assn., Am. Bd. Sexology (clin. supr.), Am. Assn. Sex Educators, Counselors and Therapists, AAAS, Assn. Humanistic Psychology. Office: Found Mind Rsch PO Box 3300 Pomona NY 10970-0523

MASTERSON, JAMES FRANCIS, psychiatrist; b. Phila., Mar. 25, 1926; s. James Francis and Evangeline (O'Boyle) M.; m. Patricia Cooke, Jan. 28, 1950; children: James F., Richard K., Nancy. BS, U. Notre Dame, 1947; MD, Jefferson Med. Sch., Phila., 1951. Diplomate Am. Bd. Psychiatry, Am. Bd. Neurology. Intern Phila. Gen. Hosp., 1951-52; resident in psychiatry Payne Whitney Clinic, N.Y. Hosp., N.Y.C., 1952-55, chief resident, 1955-56, dir. adolescent OPD, 1956-66, head adolescent program, 1968-75, asst. attending psychiatrist, 1956-60, assoc. attending psychiatrist, 1960-70, attending psychiatrist, 1970—, dir. The Symptomatic Adolescent Research Project, 1957-67; dir. Masterson Group, P.C. for Study and Treatment Personality Disorders, N.Y.C., 1977—. Author: Psychotherapy of the Borderline Adolescent, Psychotherapy of the Borderline Adult, Countertransference, Narcissistic Personality Disorder, The Real Self, The Psychiatric Dilemma of Adolescence, The Test of Time: From Borderline Adolescent to Functioning Adult; contbr. articles to profl. jours. Fellow Am. Psychiat. Assn., Am. Coll. Psychoanalysts; mem. AMA, Am. Coll. Psychoanalysis, N.Y. Soc. Adolescent Psychiatry (founder, past pres.), N.Y. County Med. Soc. Office: 60 Sutton Pl S New York NY 10022-4168

MASTERSON, LINDA HISTEN, medical company executive; b. N.Y.C., May 21, 1951; d. George and Dorothy (Postler) Riddell; m. Robert P. Masterson, March 6, 1982; m. William J. Histen, May 24, 1971 (div. 1979). BS in med. tech., U. R.I., 1973; MS in microbiology, U. Md., 1977; student, Wharton U. Pa., Phila., 1988. Med. technologist various hosps., 1972-78; microbiology specialist Gen. Diagnostics, Warner-Lambert, Morris Plains, N.J., 1978-80; from tech. sales rep. to dir. internat. mktg. Micro-Scan, Baxter Internat., Sacramento, 1980-87; dir. mktg. Ortho Diagnostics, Johnson & Johnson, Raritan, N.J., 1987-89; sr. v.p. mktg/sales GenProbe, San Diego, 1989-92; v.p. mktg./sales Bio Star, Boulder, Colo., 1992-93; exec. v.p. Cholestech Inc., Hayward, Calif., 1994—; bd. dirs. U.S. Alcohol Testing of Am., Inc., Rancho Cucamonga, Calif. Tribute to women in industry Young Women's Christian Assn., N.J., 1989. Mem. Biomedical Mktg. Assn., Med. Mktg. Assn., Phi Kappa Phi. Office: Cholestech Inc 5347 Investment Blvd Hayward CA 94541-9999

MASTIN, ROBERT ELDON, obstetrician, gynecologist; b. Harlinger, Tex., May 17, 1940; s. Harold Miner and Tressie Syril (Thrasher) M.; m. Linda Sue Forbes, July 17, 1940; children: Laura Lynn, Lisa Kay, Paul Alan, Mark Robert. BS, Baylor U., 1962, MD, 1966. Dimplomate Am. Bd. Ob/Gyn. Commd. ensign USN, 1965, advanced through grades to lt. comdr., 1973; resident hosp. USN, Oakland, Calif., 1968-71; staff physician USN, Corpus Christi, Tex., 1971-73; pvt. practice Corpus Christi, 1973—. Fellow ACS, Am. Coll. Ob/Gyn.; mem. AMA, Am. Fertility Soc., Tex. Med. Assn., Rotary. Office: 3240 Fort Worth St # 100 Corpus Christi TX 78411-2459

MASTRANGELO, JOHN J., podiatrist; b. Rome, N.Y., Nov. 2, 1952; s. John Patrick and Clara Florence (Casillo) M.; m. Rosanne Seccurra, July 31, 1976; children: John, Robert, Matthew. BS, Utica Coll., 1974; DPM, Ohio Coll. Podiatric Medicine, 1978. Diplomate Am. Acad. Ambulatory Foot Surgeons. Pvt. practice Rome and Oneida, N.Y., 1979—; staff Rose Hosp,, Rome, 1979-83, Rome Meml. Hosp., 1979—, Oneida Health Ctr., 1979—, Cmty. Meml. Hosp., Hamilton, N.Y., 1980—; cons. in field. Chmn. Rome Heart Com., 1980-81; mem. parish coun. St. John the Bapt. Roman Cath. Ch., 1986-89; mem. Bd. Edn., 1989— (clerk 1991-93, pres. 1994-96); adv. bd. Salvation Army, Rome, 1993—. Office: 214 W Bloomfield St Rome NY 13440 also: 100 Washington Ave Oneida NY 13421

MASTRINI, JANE REED, social worker, consultant; b. Lincoln, Nebr., July 23, 1948; d. William Scott and Ellen (Daly) Cromwell; m. Charles James Mastrini, July 19, 1969. BA, Western State Coll., Gunnison, Colo., 1970; MSW, U. Denver, 1980. Lic. social worker Colo.; cert. alcohol counselor Colo. and nat. Tchr. Flandreau (S.D.) Indian Sch., 1970; social worker S.D. Dept. Welfare, Pierre, 1970-75; child care worker Sacred Heart Home, Pueblo, Colo., 1975-76; counselor Fisher Peak Alcohol Treatment Ctr., Trinidad, Colo., 1976-77; family therapist West Nebr. Gen. Hosp., Scottsbluff, 1980-81; adolescent coord. St. Luke's Hosp., Denver, 1981-86; exec. dir. New Beginnings At Denver, Lakewood, Colo., 1986-90; pres. Counseling Dimensions of Colo., Denver, 1990-92; trainer Mile High Inst., 1987-93; outpatient mgr. Arapahoe House, 1992-94; therapist Kaiser Permanente, Denver, 1994—; cons. Colo. Counseling Consortium, Denver, 1984-90; field work supr. U. Denver, 1983—. Lectr., group leader Colo. Teen Inst., Denver, 1984-85. Mem. NASW (cert.), P.E.O. (pres. 1984-87, 94-95), Colo. Counseling Consortium, Colo. Assn. Addiction Treatment Programs (v.p. 1991-92). Democrat. Episcopalian. Home: 11785 W 66th Pl # D Arvada CO 80004-2473 Office: Kaiser Permanente CDTP 10230 E Dakota Ave Denver CO 80219

MASTROIANNI, LUIGI, JR., physician, educator; b. New Haven, Nov. 8, 1925; s. Marion (Dallas) M.; m. Elaine Catherine Pierson, Nov. 4, 1957; children: John James, Anna Catherine, Robert Luigi. AB, Yale U., 1946; MD, Boston U., 1950, DSc (hon.), 1973; MA (hon.), U. Pa., 1970. Diplomate Am. Bd. Ob-gyn. and Reproductive Endocrinology and Infertility. Intern, then resident ob.-gyn. Met. Hosp. N.Y., 1950-54; fellow rsch. Harvard Med. Sch. and Free Hosp. for Women, Boston, 1954-55; instr. dept. ob-gyn. Sch. of Medicine Yale U., New Haven, 1955-56, asst. prof. ob.-gyn. dept., 1956-61; prof. U. Calif., L.A., 1961-65; chief ob-gyn Harbor Gen. Hosp., L.A., 1961-65; William Goodell prof. ob.-gyn., chmn. dept. U. Pa. Sch. of Medicine, Phila., 1965-87, William Goodell prof. ob.-gyn. dept., dir. human reproduction div., 1987—. Contbr. numerous articles to profl. jours. Recipient Squibb prize Pacific Coast Fertility Soc., 1965, Christian R. and Mary Lindback award, 1969, Gold medal Barren Found., 1977, King Faisal prize in medicine, 1989, Pub. Recognition award Assn. Profls. of Gynecology and Obstets., 1990, Disting. Svc. award Soc. Study Reproduction, 1992, Axel Munthe award, 1996. Mem. ACS, Am. Gyneol. and Obstet. Soc., Am. Gynecol. Club, Am. Soc. for Reproductive Medicine, Am. Physiol. Soc., Am. Coll. Obs.-Gyns., Inst. Medicine of NAS, Soc. Gynecology Investigation, Soc. for Exptl. Biology and Medicine, Endocrine Soc., Soc. for Study Reproduction (Disting. Svc. award 1992), Pacific Coast Fertility Soc. (hon.), Cen. Assn. Ob-Gyns. (hon.), Tex. Assn. Ob.-Gyns. (hon.), N.C. Gynecol. Soc. (hon.), Assn. Profs. Ob-Gyns., Brazilian Fertility Soc. (hon.), Italian Soc. Ob-Gyns. (hon.). Argentina Fertility Soc. (hon.), Peruvian Fertility Soc. (hon.), Sociedad Espanola de Fertilidad (hon.), Israel Soc. Ob-Gyn. (hon.), Uruguan Soc. Sterility and Fertility (hon.), Inst. Medicine, Sigma Xi, Alpha Omega Alpha. Home: 561 Ferndale Ln Haverford PA 19041-1614 Office: Hosp U Pa 3400 Spruce St Philadelphia PA 19104

MASUDA, GOHTA, physician, educator; b. Tokyo, Nov. 21, 1940; s. Ryota and Chiyo (Ikeuchi) M.; m. Mitsuko Taguchi, May 14, 1983. MD, Keio U., 1966, PhD, 1977. Intern, Keio Univ. Hosp., Tokyo, 1965-67; instr. Keio U., Tokyo, 1967-74, 76-78; asst. prof. Kitasato U., Kanagawa-Ken, Japan, 1974-76; chief dept. infectious diseases Tokyo Met. Komagome Hosp., 1978-95; dir. dept. infectious diseases Tokyo Met. Komagome Hosp., 1995—; asst. prof. Toho U., Tokyo, 1985—, Keio U., 1986—, Gunma U., 1989—, Juntendo U., 1995—. Contbr. articles to profl. jours. Mem. Japanese Assn. for Infectious Diseases, Japan Soc. Chemotherapy, Am. Soc. Microbiology, Brit. Soc. for Antimicrobial Chemotherapy. Buddhist. Home: 1-14-12-305 Komagome, Toshima-ku 170 Tokyo Japan Office: Tokyo Met Komagome Hosp Dept Infectious Diseases, 3-18-22 Honkomagome, Bunkyo-ku 113 Tokyo Japan

MASULLO, ALFREDO SALVATORE, dermatologist; b. Weehawken, N.J., June 27, 1949; s. Gustavo and Natalina (Caridi) M.; m. Linda Masullo, 1983. BA, Rutgers U., 1971; MD, U. Medicine and Dentistry N.J., Newark, 1975. Diplomate Am. Bd. Dermatology. Intern in internal medicine U. Medicine and Dentistry N.J., 1975-76, resident, 1976-77; resident in dermatology St. Lukes, Roosevelt and Columbia-Presbyn. Med. Ctr., N.Y.C., 1977-80; pvt. practice, Hackensack, N.J., 1980—; attending physician Hackensack Univ. Med. Ctr., 1980—, Holy Name Hosp., Teaneck, N.J., 1980—. Fellow Am. Acad. Dermatology; mem. AMA. Office: 120 Prospect Ave Hackensack NJ 07601-2256

MASYS, DANIEL RICHARD, medical school director; b. Columbus, Ohio, Mar. 6, 1949; s. Paul John and Jane Marie (Mollenauer) M.; m. Linda Suzanne Bross, June 2, 1974; 1 child, Christopher. AB in Biochemistry, Princeton U., 1971; MD, Ohio State U., 1974. Diplomate Am. Bd. Internal Medicine. Staff hematologist, oncologist U.S. Naval Hosp., San Diego, 1980-84; chief ICRDB br. NIH, Bethesda, Md., 1984-86; dir. Lister Hill Nat. Ctr. Nat. Libr. Medicine, Bethesda, Md., 1986-94; dir. informatics and assoc. clin. prof. Sch. Medicine U. Calif., San Diego, 1994—. Assoc. editor Acad. Medicine jour., 1988-91. Mem. high performance computing White House Office of Sci., Washington, 1991-94; rep. Fed. Networking Coun., Washington, 1991-94. Capt. USPHS, 1984-94. Fellow ACP, Am. Coll. Med. Informatics (exec. com. 1989-92); mem. Am. Med. Informatics Assn. (bd. dirs. 1992-95, assoc. editor jour. 1993—, Pres.'s award 1992), Alpha Omega Alpha. Office: Univ of Calif San Diego Sch of Medicine 9500 Gilman Dr Rm 1317 La Jolla CA 92093-0602

MATARASSO, ALAN, plastic and reconstructive surgeon; b. N.Y.C., Oct. 19, 1953; s. Daniel and Ethel (Hakim) M. BA magna cum laude, Boston U., 1975; MD, U. Miami, Miami, Fla., 1979. Diplomate Nat. Bd. Med. Examiners, Am. Bd. Plastic Surgery. Intern in dept. of gen. surgery Albert Einstein Coll. Med., Montefiore Med. Ctr., Bronx, N.Y., 1979-80, resident in dept. surgery, 1980-82, chief resident dept. of gen. surgery, 1982-83, resident dept. of plastic surgery, 1983-84, chief resident dept. of plastic surgery, 1983-84; fellow aesthetic surgery Manhattan Eye, Ear and Throat Hosp., NYU Med. Ctr., N.Y.C., 1985, asst. attending surgeon, 1985—; clin. asst. prof. plastic surgery Albert Einstein Coll. Medicine, 1985—; attending surgeon St. Luke's/Roosevelt Hosp. Ctr., 1986—, N.Y. Eye and Ear Infirmary, 1986—, Doctors Hosp., 1988—. Contbr. chpt. Encyclopedia of Flpas, Clinics in Plastic Surgery, Mastery in Plastic Surgery; instrnl. course vol. Plastic Surgery Ednl. Found.; numerous profl. presentations; contbr. articles to profl. jours. Bd. dirs. Sephardic Home For The Aged, Bklyn. Recipient Physicians Recognition award AMA, 1994; named one of Best Drs. in Am. Am. Health Mag., 1996, N.Y. Mag., 1996, Castle-Connolly Guide to the Best Drs., N.Y. Metro Area. Fellow ACS; mem. Am. Soc. Plastic and Reconstructive Surgery (various coms.), Northeastern Soc. Plastic Surgeons, Soc. for Acad. Surgeons, Royal Soc. Medicine, Am. Cleft Palate Assn., Pan Am. Med. Soc. Office: 1009 Park Ave New York NY 10028-0936

MATCHAEL, MICHAEL FREDRICK, laboratory manager; b. Carthage, Mo., Sept. 2, 1943; s. Joseph Leonard Sr. and Gladys Marie (Baker) M.; m. Mary Louise Haynes, July 28, 1961; children: Michael Jr., Mary Kim. Grad. high sch., Carthage, Mo. Trainee lab. Upsher Lab., Joplin, Mo., 1959-63; technician Upsher Lab., Sedalia, Mo., 1964-68; med. technologist Bothwell Regional Health Ctr., Sedalia, 1968-95, lab. mgr., 1995—. Recipient Disting. Achievement award Nat. AMT, 1973. Mem. Mo. State Soc. AMT (state treas. 1970-71, pres. 1972-74, Technologist of Yr. 1972). Republican. Home: 1405 E 15th Apt #21 Sedalia MO 65301 Office: Bothwell Regional Health Ctr 601 E 14th Sedalia MO 65301

MATELES, RICHARD ISAAC, biotechnologist; b. N.Y.C., Sept. 11, 1935; s. Simon and Jean (Phillips) M.; m. Roslyn C. Fish, Sept. 2, 1956; children: Naomi, Susan, Sarah. BS, MIT, 1956, MS, 1957, DSc, 1959. USPHS fellow Laboratorium voor Microbiologie, Technische Hogeschool, Delft, The Netherlands, 1959-60; mem. faculty MIT, 1960-70, assoc. prof. biochem. engring., 1965-68; dir. fermentation unit Jerusalem, 1968-77; prof. applied microbiology Hebrew U., Hadassah Med. Sch., Jerusalem, 1968-80; vis. prof. dept. chem. engring. U. Pa., Phila., 1978-79; asst. dir. rsch. Stauffer Chem. Co., Westport, Conn., 1980, dir. rsch., 1980-81, v.p. rsch., 1981-88; sr. v.p. applied scis. IIT Rsch. Inst., Chgo., 1988-90; proprietor Candida Corp., Chgo., 1990—. Editor: Biochemistry of Some Foodborne Microbial Toxins, 1967, Single Cell Protein, 1968, Jour. Chem. Tech. and Biotech., 1972—; contbr. articles to profl. jours. Mem. Conn. Acad. Sci. Engring., 1981—; mem. vis. com., dept. applied biol. sci. MIT, 1980-88; mem. exec. com. Coun. on Chem. Rsch., 1981-85. Fellow Am. Inst. Med. and Biol. Engring.; mem. AICE, AAAS, SAR, Am. Chem. Soc., Am. Soc. Microbiology, Soc. for Gen. Microbiology U.K., Inst. Food Technologists, Soc. Chem. Ind. (U.K.) Union League, Sigma Xi. Home: 150 W Eugenie St # 46 Chicago IL 60614-5839 Office: 175 W Jackson Blvd Chicago IL 60604-2601

MATERIA, KATHLEEN PATRICIA AYLING, nurse; b. Jersey City, Nov. 7, 1954; d. Donald Anthony and Muriel Cecilia (Joyce) Ayling; m. Francis Peter Materia, June 5, 1983; children: Christopher Michael, Donna Nicole. BS in Nursing, Fairleigh Dickinson U., 1976. RN. Critical care nurse Palisades Gen. Hosp., North Bergen, N.J., 1976-87, grad. nurse, 1976-77; nurse CCU, North Hudson Hosp., Weehawken, N.J., 1977-78. Mem. Alpha Sigma Tau. Democrat. Roman Catholic. Avocations: bowling, dancing.

MATERNA, THOMAS WALTER, ophthalmologist; b. Passaic, N.J., Oct. 24, 1944; s. Anthony and Ann (Popowich) M.; m. Jorunn Pauline Aronsen, Aug. 18, 1973; children: Richard C., Barbara L. BA, Coll. Holy Cross, Worcester, Mass., 1966; MD, SUNY, N.Y.C., 1971; MBA, Rutgers U., Newark, 1990. Diplomate Am. Bd. Ophthalmology. Intern N.Y. Hosp.-Cornell U. Med. Ctr., N.Y.C., 1971-72; resident N.Y. Eye and Ear Infirmary, N.Y.C., 1975-78; pvt. practice ophthalmology San Francisco, 1986; ophthalmologist N.J. Eye Physicians & Surgeons, Newark; pres., CEO, US Try Zub Ent., Inc., Newark, Bizmore Internat., Inc., Luiv, Ukraine. Com. mem. N.J. Sch. for the Arts, Montclair, 1991—. Lt. USN, 1972-74, comdr. USNR, 1974—. Fellow ACS, Am. Acad. Ophthalmology; mem. Rotary, Army-Navy Club. Democrat. Roman Catholic. Home: 87 Lorraine Ave Montclair NJ 07043-2304 Office: NJ Eye Physicians and Surgeons 20 Ferry St Newark NJ 07105-1420

MATES, SHARON, medical association administrator; b. N.Y.C., Feb. 20, 1953. BS in Scis., Ohio State U., 1973; PhD in Neuroscis., Washington U., 1981. V.p. corp. fin. and analyst Bridgmere Capital, San Francisco, 1986-88; pres. North American Vaccine Inc., Beltsville, Md., 1989—; bd. dirs. AMVAX. Mem. AAAS, Am. Soc. for Microbiology, Biotech. Industry Orgn., Internat. Assn. Biol. Stds., N.Y. Acad. Sci. Office: North American Vaccine Inc 12103 Indian Creek Ct Beltsville MD 20705

MATHENY, ADAM PENCE, JR., child psychologist, educator, consultant, researcher; b. Stanford, Ky., Sept. 6, 1932; s. Adam Pence and Dorotha (Steele) M.; m. Ute I. Debus, July 10, 1962 (div.); m. Mary P. Tolbert, June 24, 1967 (div.); children—Laura Steele, Jason Gaverick. B.S., Columbia U., 1958; Ph.D., Vanderbilt U., 1962. Sr. human factors engr. Martin Aerospace div., Balt., 1962-63; instr. Johns Hopkins U. Med. Sch., 1963-65; staff fellow Nat. Inst. Child Health and Human Devel., 1965-67; from asst. prof. to prof. pediatrics U. Louisville Med. Sch., 1967-86, assoc. dir. to dir. Louisville Twin Study, 1986—. mem. review panel NIH, 1991-95. Served with USN, 1951-55. Fellow Internat. Soc. Twin Research, Am. Psychol. Assn., Am. Psychol. Soc.; mem. Soc. Research Child Devel., AAAS, Behavior Genetics Assn., Internat. Soc. Behavior Devel., Internat. Soc. Infant Study, Phi Beta Kappa, Sigma Xi. Co-author: Genetics and Counseling in Medical Practice, 1969; contbr. articles to profl. jours.

MATHENY, SAMUEL COLEMAN, academic administrator; b. Stanford, Ky., Dec. 2, 1941; s. Samuel Ferdinand and Elise Elizabeth (Coleman) M. BA, Emory U., 1963; MD, U. Ky., 1967; MPH, UCLA, 1974. Dist. health officer Alhambra Health Dist., L.A. County Health Svcs., 1975-77; chmn. U. Soc. Calif., Divsn. Family Medicine, L.A., 1977-81; assoc. dir. Santa Monica (Calif.) Residency, 1981-83; prof. dept. family medicine U. So. Calif., L.A., 1992-93; chmn. dept. family practice U. Ky. Coll. Medicine, Lexington, 1993—. Capt. USPHS, 1968-71, 86-92. Mem. Assn. Depts. Family Planning. Office: U Ky Coll Medicine Dept Family Practice Clinic Lexington KY 40536

MATHER, ELIZABETH VIVIAN, health care executive; b. Richmond, Ind., Sept. 19, 1941; d. Willie Samuel and Lillie Mae (Harper) Fuqua; m. Roland Donald Mather, Dec. 26, 1966. BS, Maryville (Tenn.) Coll., 1963; postgrad., Columbia U., 1965-66. Tchr. Richmond Community Schs., 1963-67, Indpls. Pub. Schs., 1967-68; systems analyst Ind. Blue Cross Blue Shield, Indpls., 1968-71, Ind. Nat. Bank, Indpls., 1971; med. cons. Ind. State Dept. Pub. Welfare, Indpls., 1971-78, cons. supr., 1978-86; systems analyst Ky. Blue Cross Blue Shield, Louisville, 1988-89; contracts specialist Humana Corp., Louisville, 1989—. Active Rep. Cen. Com. Montgomery County, Crawfordsville, 1976-86, Centenary Meth. Ch., adminstrv. bd., 1990. Mem. DAR (treas. 1963-66, sec. 1978-86). Home: 6106 Partridge Pl Floyds Knob IN 47119 Office: Humana Corp 500 W Main St Louisville KY 40201-1438

MATHES, DOROTHY JEAN HOLDEN, occupational therapist; b. Paterson, N.J., Mar. 13, 1953; d. Cornelius Fred and Dorothy Johanna (Ferguson) Holden; m. Clayton Derald Mathes, May 26, 1973 (div. Dec. 1984); children: Christy, Carl, Chuck, Chad; m. Elie Youssef Hajjar, Oct. 4, 1989. BS in Occupational Therapy, Tex. Woman's U., Denton, Tex., 1988; MA in Occupational Therapy, Tex. Woman's U., 1995. Lic. occupational therapist, Tex.; cert. pediatric occupational therapist. Occupational therapy cons. Lakes Regional -SOCS, ECI, 1988—. Mem. Am. Occupational Therapy Assn., Tex. Occupational Therapy Assn. Home: 2608 Woodhaven St Denton TX 76201-1340 Office: Lakes Regional SOCS-ECI 3969 Teasley Lane Denton TX 76205

MATHES, STEPHEN JOHN, plastic and reconstructive surgeon, educator; b. New Orleans, Aug. 17, 1943; s. John Ernest and Norma (Deutsch) M.; m. Jennifer Tandy Woodbridge, Nov. 26, 1966; children: David, Brian, Edward. BS, La. State U., 1964; MD, La. State U., New Orleans, 1968. Diplomate Am. Bd. Surgery, Am. Bd. Plastic Surgery (dir. 1993—). Asst. prof. surgery Wash. U., St. Louis, 1977-78; assoc. prof. U. Calif., San Francisco, 1978-84, prof. surgery, 1984, prof. surgery, anatomy and cell biology, 1984-85, also bd. dirs. craniofacial anomalies; head plastic surgery sect. U. Mich., Ann Arbor, 1984-85, prof. surgery, 1984-85; prof. surgery, head plastic and reconstructive surgery div. U. Calif., San Francisco, 1985—. Author: (textbook) Clinical Applications for Muscle and Musculocutaneous Flaps, 1983 (Best Med. Book award Physician's category, Am. Med. Writer's Assn., 1983); contbr. articles to profl. jours. Recipient 1st prize plastic surgery scholarship contest, Plastic Surgery Edn. Found., 1981, 83, 84, 86; grantee NIH, 1982-85, 86—. Fellow ACS; mem. Am. Assn. Plastic Surgery, Plastic Surgery Research Council (pres.-elect 1986), Am. Soc. Surgery of Hand, Soc. Univ. Surgeons. Republican. Episcopalian. Home: 30 Trophy Ct Burlingame CA 94010-7434 Office: U Calif San Francisco Dept Surgery San Francisco CA 94143-0932

MATHESON, DONALD SAMUEL, obstetrician and gynecologist; b. Aruba, Jan. 23, 1957; came to U.S., 1968; s. Alix Barry; m. Yasmine Gaynel Genevive McCormack, June 10, 1985; children: Monisha, Kinnari. BS, CCNY, 1979; MD, Thomas Jefferson Med. Sch., Phila., 1983. Diplomate Am. Bd. Ob-Gyn. Intern St. Vincent's Hosp. and Med. Ctr., N.Y.C., 1983-84, resident in ob-gyn., 1984-87; clin. instr. St. Vincent's Hosp. and Med. Ctr., 1987—; practice medicine, specializing in ob-gyn. N.Y.C.; bd. dirs. Brownsville Devel. Corp., Bklyn.; cons. Everest Internat., Atlanta, 1991—; lectr. Kaplan, Milan, 1995. Mem. AMA, Am. Coll. Ob-Gyn., Am. Assn. Gynec. Laparascopists. Christian. Office: 103 Fifth Ave New York NY 10003

MATHESON, LINDA, retired clinical social worker; b. Martna, Estonia, Dec. 29, 1918; came to U.S., 1962, naturalized, 1969; d. Endrek and Leena Endrekson; m. Charles McLaren Matheson, Feb. 5, 1955. Diploma, Inst. for Social Scis., Tallinn, Estonia, 1944; MS, Columbia U., 1966; D in Social Work, Columbia U., 1974. Diplomate clin. social work. Social work officer UN Rehab. and Resettlement Assn., Germany, 1946-48; social worker Victorian Mental Hygiene, Australia, 1955-62; rsch. assoc., social work project dir. Arthritis Midway Ho., N.Y.C., 1966-68; rschr. Columbia Presbyn. Med. Center, N.Y.C., 1971-75; field instr. Columbia U. Sch. Social Work, 1977-79, Columbia Presbyn. Med. Ctr., NYU Sch. Social Work, 1989-90; ret., 1992. Family Found. fellow, 1966, 89-90; NIMH grantee, 1969-72. Mem. Nat. Assn. Social Workers, Nat. Wildlife Fedn., Center for Study of Presidency, Smithsonian Assn., English Speaking Union, Alliance Francaise, Columbia U. Alumni Assn., Internat. Platform Assn., Met. Mus. of N.Y. Lutheran. Home: 30-95 29th St Astoria NY 11102-2735

MATHESON, NINA W., medical researcher. Prof., dir. William H. Welch Med. Libr., Balt., 1985-94; prof. emeritus Jouns Hopkins U., Balt., 1994—. Named Disting. prof. nursing Vanderbilt Sch. Nursing, 1976-82. Office: John Hopkins Univ William H. Welch Medical Libr 720 Rutland Ave Baltimore MD 21205-2109*

MATHEWS, BARBARA EDITH, gynecologist; b. Santa Barbara, Calif., Oct. 5, 1946; d. Joseph Chesley and Pearl (Cieri) Mathews; AB, U. Calif., 1969; MD, Tufts U., 1972. Diplomate Am. Bd. Ob-Gyn. Intern, Cottage Hosp., Santa Barbara, 1972-73, Santa Barbara Gen. Hosp., 1972-73; resident in ob-gyn Beth Israel Hosp., Boston, 1973-77; clin. fellow in ob-gyn Harvard U., 1973-76, instr., 1976-77; gynecologist Sansum Med. Clinic, Santa Barbara, 1977—; faculty mem. ann. postgrad. course Harvard Med. Sch.; bd. dirs. Sansum Med. Clinic, vice chmn. bd. dirs., 1994-96; dir. ann. postgrad course UCLA Med. Sch. Bd. dirs. Meml. Rehab. Found., Santa Barbara, Channel City Club, Santa Barbara, Music Acad. of the West, Santa Barbara, St. Francis Med. Ctr., Santa Barbara; mem. citizen's continuing edn. adv. council Santa Barbara C.C.; moderator Santa Barbara Cottage Hosp. Cmty. Health Forum. Fellow ACS, Am. Coll. Ob-gyn.; mem. AMA, Am. Soc. Colposcopy and Cervical Pathology (dir. 1982-84), Harvard U. Alumni Assn., Tri-counties Obstet. and Gynecol. Soc. (pres. 1981-82), Phi Beta Kappa. Clubs: Birnam Wood Golf (Santa Barbara). Author: (with L. Burke) Colposcopy in Clinical Practice, 1977; contbg. author Manual of Ambulatory Surgery, 1982. Home: 2105 Anacapa St Santa Barbara CA 93105-3503 Office: 317 W Pueblo St Santa Barbara CA 93105-4355

MATHEWS, JAMES EVERT, surgeon; b. Pampa, Tex., Nov. 22, 1936; s. John Evert Mathews and Eunice (Jones) Estridge; m. Rosemary O. Lindsey, Aug. 25, 1938. BS, Tex. Christian U., 1957, Tex. Wesleyan Coll., 1959; MD, Tulane U., 1964. Diplomate Am. Bd. Surgery. Intern John Peter Smith Hosp., Ft. Worth, 1964-65; resident in surgery Scott & White Hosp. and Clinic, Temple, Tex., 1967-71; surgeon VA Hosp., Temple, Tex., 1971-72, Malone-Hogan Clinic, Big Spring, Tex., 1972—. Capt. U.S. Army, 1965-67. Office: Malone Hogan Clinic 1501 W 11th Pl Big Spring TX 79720

MATHEWS, JOHN N., pediatrician; b. Quilon, Kerala, India, Feb. 4, 1937; s. Geevarghese and Saramma (Chacko) M.; m. Marie M. Mathews, Sept. 1, 1969; children: Santhosh, Kusum, Vijay, Geetha. MD, Trivandrum Med. Coll., Kerala, 1958; MS, Queen's U., Kingston, Ont., Can., 1964. Pvt. practice Enfield & Windsor Locks, Conn., 1971-88; med. dir. pediatric outpatient dept. St. Mary's Hosp., Troy, N.Y., 1988-90; pediatrician Conn. Valley Pediatric Ctr., Windsor, 1990—. Fellow Royal Coll. Physicians Can., Am. Acad. Pediatrics; mem. Conn. State Med. Sco., Hartford County Med. Assn. Office: Conn Valley Pediatric Ctr 1080 Day Hill Rd Windsor CT 06095

MATHEWS, PAUL JOSEPH, allied health educator; b. Washington, Aug. 17, 1944; s. Paul Joseph and Ruth Irene (O'Malley) M.; m. Loretta Jeanne Calvo; children: Heather Marie, Amy Elizabeth, Timothy Hunter. AS, Quinnipiac Coll., 1971, BS, 1975; MPA, U. Hartford, 1978; EdS, U. Mo., Kansas City, 1989. Registered respiratory therapist; lic. respiratory therapist, Kans. Instr., clin. coord. New Britain (Conn.) Gen. Hosp., 1971-74; instr. Quinnipiac Coll., Hamden, Conn., 1974-76; chief respiratory therapy dept. Providence Hosp., Holyoke, Mass., 1974-80, dir. cardiology/neurology, 1977-80, asst. dir. planning, 1980-81; asst. prof. U. Kans. Sch. Allied Health, Kansas City, 1981-88, assoc. prof. respiratory care edn., 1988—, chmn. dept. respiratory care edn., 1981-93, assoc. prof. phys. therapy Grad. Sch., 1992—; U. Kans.; adj. assoc. prof. Ctr. on Aging U. Kans. Med. Ctr., 1987—; hon. prof. U. Costa Rica, San Jose, 1987—; cons. FDA, 1988, NIH, 1988, 89, SUNY, Stony Brook, 1990, USPHS, 1994, 95. Mem. editl. bd. Nursing, 1989—, Neonatal Intensive Care, 1990, Jour. Respiratory Care Edn., 1993—, Respiratory Therapy, 1988, Respiratory Therapy Intern, 1991; author audio tapes in field; contbr. articles to profl. jours., chpts. to books. Recipient Creative Achievement award Puritan-Bennett Corp., 1984, 85, A. Gerald Shapiro award N.J. Soc. for Respiratory Care, 1990; internat. fellow Project HOPE, 1987, 92. Mem. Am. Assn. Respiratory Care (bd. dirs. 1984-87, v.p. 1987, pres.-elect 1988, pres. 1989), Am. Coll. Chest Physicians, Sigma Xi, Lambda Beta, Phi Lambda Theta. Home: 8844 Hemlock Dr Overland Park KS 66212-2946 Office: U Kans 39th and Rainbow Blvd Kansas City KS 66103

MATHEWS, SUSAN MCKIERNAN, health care executive; b. N.Y.C., May 28, 1946; d. Thomas Joseph and Eileen Ann (Looschen) McK.; m. Robert Emmett Mathews, June 17, 1967 (div.); children: Colin Robert, Brendan Robert, Devin Robert, Kiernan Robert. Diploma in nursing, St. Francis Sch. Nursing, 1966; BS in Health Adminstrn., St. Joseph's Coll., 1979; MS in Pub. Svc. Adminstrn., Russell Sage Coll., 1983; PhD in Health Adminstrn., Columbia Pacific U., 1985. RN, N.Y. Utilization rev. analyst N.Y. State Office Mental Retardation & Devel. Disabilities, Albany, 1980-83; with Empire Blue Cross & Blue Shield, Albany, 1983-86, dir. instl. utilization rev., cons. in field, 1986-88; pres., COO Corp. Health Dimensions, Troy, N.Y., 1988-92, pres., 1992—; spkr. in field. Mem. bus. adv. bd. SUNY Coll., New Paltz; grad. Capital Leadership, 1990; mem. pres. coun. Sage Colls., 1994. Recipient Excellence in Mgmt. Pvt. Sector award, 1992. Mem. Med. Group Mgmt. Assn., Albany Colonie Regional C. of C. (chmn. 1996), Rensselaer County C. of C. (Woman of Achievement award 1994), The 50 Group. Roman Catholic. Office: Corp Health Dimensions 500 Federal St Ste 601 Troy NY 12180-2832

MATHEWS, WAYNE A., medical association administrator; b. Omaha, Sept. 20, 1953; s. Gerald W. and Carol J. (Francis) M.; m. Patricia Maria Miller, Dec. 12, 1979; children: Nathaniel, Ben, Joel, Luke. BS, U. Nebr., 1981; MS in Epidemiology, U. Ill., 1995. NCCPA, ACLS, ATLS. Dir. student health U. Nebr., Omaha, 1981; physician asst. UNMC Orthop., Omaha, 1982; hosp. adminstr. Norfolk (Nebr.) Regional Ctr., 1983-84; physician asst., cons. epidemiology Carle Clinic, Urbana, Ill., 1989-94; dir. emergency medicine Kirby Hosp., Monticello, Ill., 1994—; cons. Health Com. Consulting., Champaign, Ill., 1995—; COO Atwood (Ill.) Rural Health Clinic, 1995—; chmn. Ill. Telemedicine Adv. Bd., Springfield, 1995; devel. ptnr. Netscape Software, 1995. Contbr. articles to profl. jours. Med. missionary, East Africa, 1992. With USN, 1972-76. Fellow Am. Acad. Physician Assts. (editl. adv. 1990—), Soc. Emergency Medicine Physician Assts., Nebr. Acad. Physician Assts. (scholar 1981); mem. Ill. Rural Health Assn. (advisor, exemplary project 1995), Ill. Acad. Physician Assts. Home: 1204 S Prospect Ave Champaign IL 61820 Office: Kirby Hosp 1111 N State St Monticello IL 61856

MATHEWS, WILLIAM EDWARD, neurological surgeon, educator; b. Indpls., July 12, 1934; s. Ples Leo and Roxie Elizabeth (Allen) M.; m. Eleanor Jayne Comer, Aug. 24, 1956 (div. 1976); children: Valerie, Clarissa, Marie, Blair; m. Carol Ann Koza, Sept. 12, 1987; 1 child, William Kyle. BS, Ball State U., 1958; DO, Kriksville Coll. Osteopathic Medicine, 1961; MD, U. Calif., L.A., 1962; student, Armed Forces Trauma Sch., Ft. Sam Houston, Tex., 1967-68. Diplomate Am. Bd. Neurol. and Orthopedic Surgery, Am. Bd. Pain Mgmt., Am. Bd. Indsl. Medicine, Am. Bd. Spinal Surgeons (v.p. 1990-92). Intern Kirksville (Mo.) Osteopathic Hosp., 1961-62; resident neurosurgery Los Angeles County Gen. Hosp., 1962-67; with Brookes Army Hosp., Ft. Sam Houston, 1967-68; with 8th field hosp. U.S. Army Neurosurgeon C.O. & 933 Med. Corp, Vietnam, 1968-69; chief neurosurgery Kaiser Med. Group, Walnut Creek, Calif., 1969-77; staff neurosurgeon Mt. Diablo Med. Ctr., Concord, Calif., 1977—; chief resident neurosugery Los Angeles County Gen. Hosp., 1962-67; chief neurosurgery Kaiser Permanente Med. Group, Walnut Creek, 1969-77; comdg. officer 933d Med. Detachment Vietnam R.V.N., 1968-69; asst. prof. Kriksvelle Coll. Osteopathic Medicine, 1958-62; asst. lecturing prof. Neuroanatomy U. Calif. Coll. of Medicine, 1962-65. Author: (jour./book) Intracerebral Missile Injuries, 1972, Early Return to Work Following Cervical Disc Surgery, 1991; contbr. articles to profl. jours. Mem. adv. com. Rep. Presdl. Selection Com.Maj. U.S. Army, 1967-69, Vietnam. Recipient Disting. Svc. award Internat. Biography, 1987; scholar Psi Sigma Alpha, 1989. Fellow Congress Neurol. Surgeons (joint sect. on neurotrauma), Royal Coll. Medicine, Am. Acad. Neurologic and Orthopedic Surgeons (pres. 1981-82); mem. AMA, Calif. Med. Assn., San Francisco Neurologic, Contra Costa County Med. Soc. Roman Catholic.

MATHEWS, WILLIAM FRANKLIN, physician assistant, software developer; b. Gainesville, Fla., Feb. 28, 1947; s. Harold Franklin and Verna Florence (Pooler) M.; m. Johnna Jean Hamlin, June 30, 1967; children: Tonya, Jennifer, Christina. AAS, Lake Sumter Jr. Coll., Leesburg, Fla., 1970; B Health Sci., cert. physician assoc., Duke U., 1974. Cert. Nat. Assn. on Cert. Physician Assts.; cert. physician asst., Fla. Physician asst. pvt. surgery practice, Pensacola, Fla., 1974-75, Indian Health Svc., Princeton, Maine, 1980-81; pvt. practice, Bonifay, Fla., 1975-80; physician asst. Fla. State Prison, Starke, 1981—; software developer Fla. N.G., Starke, 1990—. Author: Guidelines for Patient Evaluation, 1985, 18D Credentialing Book, 1991; also articles. Instnl. rep. Boy Scouts Am., Bonifay, 1979; bishop LDS Ch., Bonifay, 1979, exec. sec., Lake City, Fla., 1994—; computer Bull. Bd. Sys. operator Fidonet, Raiford, Fla., 1987. With USN, 1967; with N.G., 1983, 91, capt. 1994—. Recipient Disting. Svc. award Fla. State Prison, 1982, 90. Fellow Am. Acad. Physician Assts.; mem. Fla. Acad. Physician Assts. (charter), Assn. Mil. Surgeons U.S., Undersea and Hyperbaric Med. Soc. (assoc.), Soc. Army Physician Assts., N.G. Officers Assn. U.S., Bradford-Union County Computers Group (founder). Republican. Office: Fla State Prison PO Box 747 Starke FL 32091

MATHEWSON, HUGH SPALDING, anesthesiologist, educator; b. Washington, Sept. 20, 1921; s. Walter Eldridge and Jennie Lind (Jones) M.; m. Dorothy Ann Gordon, 1943 (div. 1952); 1 child, Jane Mathewson Holcombe; m. Hazel M. Jones, 1953 (div. 1978); children: Geoffrey K., Brian E., Catherine E. Brock, Jennifer A. Jehle; m. Judith Ann Mahoney, 1979 (div. 1990). Student, Washburn U., 1938-39; A.B., U. Kans., 1942, M.D., 1944. Intern Wesley Hosp., Wichita, Kans., 1944-45; resident anesthesiology U. Kans. Med. Ctr., Kansas City, 1946-48; pvt. practice specializing in anesthesiology Kansas City, Mo., 1948-69; chief anesthesiologist St. Luke's Hosp., Kansas City, 1953-69; med. dir., sect. respiratory therapy U. Kans. Med. Ctr., 1969-92, assoc. prof., 1969-92, prof., 1975-92, prof. anesthesiology emeritus, respiratory care edn., 1992—; examiner schs. respiratory therapy, 1975—; oral examiner Nat. Bd. Respiratory Therapy; mem. Coun. Nurse Anesthesia Practice, 1974-78; prof. phys. therapy edn., 1993—. Author: Structural Forms of Anesthetic Compounds, 1961, Respiratory Therapy in Critical Care, 1976, Pharmacology for Respiratory Therapists, 1977; contbr. articles to profl. publs.; mem. editorial bd. Anesthesia Staff News, 1975-84; assoc. editor: Respiratory Care, 1980—, cons. editor, 1980—, editor-in-chief Respiratory Mgmt., 1989-92. Trustee Kansas City Mus., Kansas City Conservatory of Music, 1993—. Served to lt. comdr. USNR, 1956. Recipient Bird Lit. prize Am. Assn. Respiratory Therapists, 1976. Mem. Mo. Soc. Anesthesiologists (pres. 1963), Kans. Soc. Anesthesiologists (pres. 1974-77), Kans. Med. Soc. (council), Phi Beta Kappa, Sigma Xi, Lambda Beta (hon.). Office: Kans Med Ctr 39th and Rainbow Blvd Kansas City KS 66103

MATHEWSON, JOHN JACOB, emergency and family practice physician; b. Greenville, Ill., Sept. 20, 1924; s. Henry Adolph and Grace Elizabeth

(Kimbro) M.; m. Patricia Lou Hendrix, Aug. 31, 1946; children: John Jeffry, Craig T., Susan Patricia. AB, Greenville Coll., 1948; BS, U. Ill., Chgo., 1950, MD, 1952. Bd. cert. Am. Bd. Emergency Medicine, AAFB. Physician Pana (Ill.) Med. Group, 1954-71; emergency physician St. Johns Hosp., Springfield, Ill., 1971-74; assoc. prof. emergency medicine Tex. Tech. U. Sch. Medicine, Lubbock, 1974-78; dir., chair emergency dept. Lakeland (Fla.) Regional Med. Ctr., 1978-82; physician Flatonia (Tex.) Med. Clinic, 1982-84; emergency physician Watson Clinic, Lakeland, 1984-95; emergency and family physician Mult Hosp. and Fayette-Lavaca Family Med. Ctr., Lakeland and Shiner, Tex., 1995—; bd. med. advisors Spectrum Emergency Med. Care, St. Louis, 1979-82; med. advisor Polk County Emergency Med. Svc., Lakeland, 1979—; tchr., organizer 1st course in emergency medicine Tex. Tech. U. Sch. Medicine, 1976; clin. asst. prof. U. So. Fla., Tampa, 1985—. Contbr. articles to med. jours. Mem. sch. bd., Pana, 1965. Col. U.S. Army, 1943-84. Mem. Polk County Med. Soc. (pres. 1993, del. 1992-95, trustee 1993-95), Fla. Coll. Emergency Physicians (bd. dirs. 1985-91), Christian County Med. Soc. (past pres. 1961-62). Home: 70 Country Club Ln Mulberry FL 33860

MATHIAS, ROBERTO S., physician, educator; b. São Paulo, Apr. 10, 1945; s. Assib S. and Judith S. (Pitombo) M.; m. Ligia A. Silva Telles, Mar. 30, 1985; children: Julia, Gustavo. MD, U. São Paulo, 1970, Anesthesiology Specialist, 1973. TSA Brazilian Soc. Anesthesiology. Supr. obstetric anesthesia Hosp. Clinicas, São Paulo, 1975-85; asst. prof. U. São Paulo, 1986-90, dr., prof., 1990-96; chief of clinics Sch. Medicine U. São Paulo, 1994-96. Lt. Brazilian Army, 1971-72. Home: Al Campinas 139/41, 01404-000 São Paulo SP, Brazil

MATHIES, ALLEN WRAY, JR., physician, hospital administrator; b. Colorado Springs, Colo., Sept. 23, 1930; s. Allen W. and Esther S. (Norton) M.; m. Lewise Austin, Aug. 23, 1956; children: William A., John N. BA, Colo. Coll., 1952; MS, Columbia U., 1956, PhD., 1958; MD, U. Vt., 1961. Rsch. assoc. U. Vt., Burlington, 1957-61; intern L.A. County Hosp., 1961-62; resident in pediatrics L.A. Gen. Hosp., 1962-64; asst. prof. pediatrics U. So. Calif., L.A., 1964-68, assoc. prof., 1968-71, prof., 1971—, assoc. dean, 1969-74, interim dean, 1974-75, dean, 1975-85, head physician Communicable Disease Svc., 1964-75; pres., CEO Huntingtom Meml. Hosp., Pasadena, Calif., 1985-94; pres., CEO So. Calif. Healthcare Sys., Pasadena, 1992-95, pres. emeritus, 1995—; bd. dirs. Pacific Mut. Contbr. articles to med. jours. Bd. dirs. Occidental Coll. With U.S. Army, 1953-55. Mem. Am. Acad. Pediatrics, Infectious Disease Soc. Am., Am. Pediatric Soc., Soc. Pediatric Rsch. Republican. Episcopalian. Home: 314 Arroyo Dr South Pasadena CA 91030-1623 Office: Huntington Meml Hosp PO Box 7013 Pasadena CA 91109-7013

MATHIEU, PETER LOUIS, physician, banker; b. Woodstock, Vt., June 23, 1924; s. Pierre L. and Ida Veronica (Racine) M.; m. Betty Burkhardt, May 30, 1950; children: Elizabeth, Gretchen, Joan, Amy. BS in Biology-Chemistry, Coll. of Holy Cross, 1946; MD, St. Louis U., 1948. Diplomate Am. Bd. Pediatrics, Am. Bd. Allergy and Immunology. Resident R.I. Hosp., 1948-50; resident in pediatrics Boston Children's Hosp., 1950-52; pvt. practice Providence, 1955—; mem. staff R.I. Hosp., Women and Infants Hosp.; dir. pediatrics St. Joseph's Hosp., Providence, 1971-82; mem. staff Roger Williams, Pawtucket Meml. hosps.; clin. asst. prof. pediatrics Med. Sch., Brown U., Providence, 1974—; dir. metabolic svcs. R.I. Health Dept., Providence, 1955-74; med. dir. St. Vincent's Ctr., 1955—, St. Aloysius Home for Adolescents, Greenville, R.I., 1960-84, R.I. Sch. for Deaf, Providence, 1960—; dir. Cath. Social Svcs., Providence, 1955—; bd. dirs. lst Fin. Corp., Providence. Author: Allergy Equilibrium, 1960; former newspaper columnist, host weekly radio program. Mem. AMA, Am. Acad. Pediatrics, Am. Acad. Allergy, New Eng. Med. Soc. (pres. 1982-83), R.I. Med. Soc. (pres. 1981), Providence Med. Assn. (pres. 1974), Nat. Assn. State Med. Socs. (pres. 1983), Staff Phys. Soc. R.I. (pres. 1975), Rotary. Roman Catholic. Office: Comprehensive Health Svcs 255 Waterman St Providence RI 02906-5210

MATHIS, BEVERLY J., osteopath; b. Tulsa, Nov. 8, 1950; d. Augustus and Betty Jane (Heasley) Baker; m. Frank D. Mathis, Dec. 23, 1972; children: Molly Marie, Andrew Allen. B Health, U. Okla., Oklahoma City; DO, Okla. StateU., 1981. Diplomate Am. Bd. Nephrology, Am. Bd. Internal Medicine, Am. Osteo. Bd. Internal Medicine. Asst. prof. medicine Oral Roberts U., Tulsa, 1988-90; staff physician Tulsa Regional Med. Ctr., 1986—; dir. dialysis CDC Pryor, Okla., 1995—; asst. dir. dialysis Tulsa Regional Med. Ctr., 1986—, chief staff, 1994-96. Trustee, vice chmn. bd. Tulsa Regional Med. Ctr., 1996—; trustee Okla. Organ Sharing Network, Oklahoma City, 1992—, Tulsa City County Health Dept., 1995—,TRMC Physican Hosp. Orgn., Tulsa, 1995—; mem. Zoofriends, Tulsa, 1993—; supporting mem. PHilbrook Mus., Tulsa, 1987—. Mem. Am. Osteo. Assn., Am. Diabetes Assn. (trustee 1992-95), Am. Soc. Nephrology, Am. Coll. Osteo. Internists, Okla. Osteo. Assn. (Rookie Physician of Yr. 1987), Tulsa Osteo. Med. Soc. Office: Osteo Physicians Tulsa 802 S Jackson #225 Tulsa OK 74127

MATHIS, DAVID EDWIN, physician, educator; b. Quitman, Ga., Sept. 7, 1964; s. S. Edwin Mathis and Lyrice Emma (Shiver) McCranie; m. Allison Paige Scheetz, Feb. 13, 1993. BS, BA, Emory U., 1986; MD, Mercer U., 1990. Diplomate Am. Bd. Internal Medicine, Nat. Bd. Med. Examiners. Intern, then resident in internal medicine Mercer U. & Med. Ctr. Ctrl. Ga., Macon, 1990-93; dir. ambulatory resident medicine Med. Ctr. Ctrl. Ga., Macon, 1994—; instr. medicine Mercer U. Sch. Medicine, Macon, 1993-94, asst. prof. medicine, 1994—, dir. ambulatory medicine, 1994—; mem. consulting staff Ctrl. Ga. Rehab. Hosp., Weeler County Hosp., Taylor Regional Hosp., 1993-95; prin. investigator ClinTrails/Merck, 1993-94; co-investigator ALLHAT, Nat. Heart Lung Inst. of NIH. Contbr. articles to profl. jours. and chpt. to book. Mem. AMA (physician's recognition award 1993, 96), ACP, Am. Geriatrics Soc., Am. Soc. Internal Medicine, So. Med. Assn., N.Y. Acad. Scis. Baptist. Office: Mercer U Sch Medicine Dept Internal Medicine 857 Orange Terr Macon GA 31201

MATHISEN, HOWARD, psychologist, minister; b. Bklyn., June 3, 1938; s. Olaf and Hjordis K. (Skjaerum) M.; B.A., Taylor U., 1960; M.Div., Phila. Theol. Sem., 1963; postgrad. Luth. Theol. Sem., 1964-65; M.A. in Religion, Concordia Sem., 1967; postgrad. Rutgers U., 1975, Assumption Coll., 1971-76; D.Min., Andover Newton Theol. Sch., 1976. m. Kathleen Ann Poce, Sept. 20, 1980 (dec. Oct. 1987); children—Randi Sue, Lisa Jane; m. Carolynn Ann Burroughs, Aug. 22, 1992. Ordained to ministry Lutheran Ch., 1962; pastor Christ Meml. Ch., Phila., 1962-66, Zion Luth. Ch., Webster, Mass., 1967-73; dir. Human Svcs. Ctr., Hubbard Regional Hosp., Webster, 1973-81; pvt. practice psychology, Boylston, Mass., 1976-81; co-dir. Counseling Affiliates, Worcester, Mass., 1981—; asst. pastor Concordia Luth. Ch., Worcester, 1976—; dir. min. asst. program New England Synod, Luth. Ch., 1991—; adj. instr. psychology Nichols Coll., Dudley, Mass., 1981, Assumption Coll., Worcester, Mass., 1983-86. Dean cen. Mass. Conf. New Eng. Synod, Luth. Ch., 1988-90; bd. dirs. Luth. Svc. Assn. New Eng., 1973-87, vice chmn., 1983-85, chmn., 1985-87; bd. dirs. Luth. Home of Worcester, 1987-92, chmn. 1987-89; chmn. bldg. com. Luth. Nursing Home, Worcester, 1977-79; chmn. Family Svcs. Com., 1981-83; mem. Mass. Adv. Com. Continuing Edn. for Nursing, 1979-81; bd. dirs. Family Planning Svcs. Ctrl. Mass., 1975-81; mem. tech. adv. subcom. substance abuse Ctrl. Mass. Health Sys. Agy., 1979-80. Lic. psychologist, Mass., Marriage and Family therapist, Mass.; cert. sex therapist; diplomate in marital and sex therapy Am. Bd. Family Psychology; diplomate Am. Bd. Sexology. Fellow Acad. of Family Psychology, Am. Acad. of Clin. Sexologists, mem. Am. Psychol. Assn., Am. Assn. Marriage and Family Therapy, Mass. Psychol. Assn., Mass. Assn. Marriage and Family Therapy, New England Soc. Clin. Hypnosis. Home: 6 Camelot Cir Dudley MA 01571-6110 Office: 52 Ward St Worcester MA 01610-1902

MATHOG, ROBERT H., otolaryngologist, educator; b. New Haven, Apr. 13, 1937; s. William and Tiby (Gans) M.; m. Donna Jane Rabinowitz, June 14, 1964; children: Tiby, Lauren, Heather, Jason. BA, Dartmouth Coll., 1960, MD, NYU, 1964. Diplomate Am. Bd. Otolaryngology, Am. Bd. Facial Plastic and Reconstructive Surgery. Asst. prof. U. Minn., Mpls., 1971-76, assoc. prof., 1976-77; prof., chmn. Wayne State U., Detroit, 1977—; chief Harper Hosp., Detroit, 1977—; mem. adv. coun. MDCD, Washington; bd. dirs. Dol Harder Rehab. Inst. Author 2 books; contbr. over 250 articles to profl. pubs. Maj. USAF, 1969-71. Fellow AMA, Am. Laryngol. Assn. (council 1994-96), Soc. Univ. Otolaryngologists (pres. 1995), Am. Triological Soc. (v.p. 1995), Am. Soc. Facial Plastic Surgery (v.p. 1981). Office: Dept Otolaryngology Head & Neck Surgery 4201 Saint Antoine Detroit MI 48201

MATICH-MARONEY, JEANNE M., social worker; b. Flushing, N.Y., Mar. 8, 1964; d. Anthony and Regina (Byrnes) M. BS, NYU, 1985, MSW, 1986, PhD, 1996. Cert. social worker, N.Y. Assoc. program dir. Shield Inst. Recipient 1985 NYU Dean's Merit award, NYU Founder's Day award, NYU Alumnae Assn. Key Pin award. Mem. NASW, Nat. Assn. for Dually Diagnosed. Home: 4926 Douglaston Pky # 1L Flushing NY 11362-1052 Office: 39-09 214th Pl Bayside NY 11361-2123

MATIKAINEN, MARTTI JUHANI, gastroenterologist; b. Helsinki, Finland, Aug. 24, 1948; s. Kullervo and Aino Johanna (Kuokka) M.; m. Marja Tuulikki Nikunen, July 24, 1971; children: Terhi, Taru, Tiina, Markku. MD, U. Helsinki, 1982. Sr. house officer Ahmadu Bello U. Nigeria, 1975-76; house officer Etela-Saimaa Ctrl. Hosp., Finland, 1976-77, Helsinki U. Ctrl. Hosp., 1977-81; hosp. surgeon Tampere U., Finland, 1981-87, chief surgeon gastroenterology, 1987—. Co-author: Decision Making in Colorectal Surgery, 1995. Lt. medicine Finnish Army. Mem. Nordic Soc. Surgery (coun. colorectal sect. 1992), Internat. Soc. Univ. Colon and Rectal Surgeons, Finnish Soc. Gastroenterology. Home: Jousikatu 17, F-33530 Tampere Finland Office: Tampere Univ Hosp, Box 2000, F-33521 Tampere Finland

MATILAINEN, RIITTA MARJA, pediatrician, pediatric neurologist; b. Hankasalmi, Finland, Dec. 10, 1948; s. Paavo Eskil and Lyyli Dagmar M. Licentiate Medicine, U. Turku, Finland, 1974; student pediatrics, U. Kuopio, Finland, 1982, student ped. neurology, 1988, MD, 1988. Gen. practice medicine Communal Health Svc., Heinola, Finland, 1974-77; asst. surgeon Childrens Hosp. U. Kuopio, Finland, 1977-82, asst. surgeon pediatric neurology, 1983-84; asst. surgeon neurology Vaajasalo Hosp., Kuopio, Finland, 1982-83; sub-chief med. officer Vaajasalo Hosp., Kuopio, 1984-86, chief physician pediatric neurology, 1987-93. Author: (with others) A Multidisciplinary Case Control Study of Mental Retardation in Children of Four Birth Cohorts, 1985; The Significance of Intrauterine Growth Retardation for the Prognosis of Preterm Children, 1988, MBD and Rehabilitation Report on a Group Therapy; Effect of Vigabatrium on Epilepsy in Mentally Retarded Children, 1988; contbr. articles to profl. jours. Mem. Jr. C. of C. (exec. v.p. youth sect.). Home: Kasarmik 10 C 39, SF-70110 Kuopio Finland Office: Childrens Hosp U Kuopio, Kaartokatu 9, SF-70218 Kuopio 21, Finland

MATIN, ABDUL, microbiology educator, consultant; b. Delhi, India, May 8, 1941; came to U.S., 1964, naturalized, 1983; s. Mohammed and Zohra (Begum) Said; m. Mimi Keyhan, June 21, 1968. BS, U. Karachi, Pakistan, 1960, MS, 1962; PhD, UCLA, 1969. Lectr. St. Joseph's Coll., Karachi, 1962-64; research assoc. UCLA, 1964-71; sci. officer U. Groningen, Kerklaan, The Netherlands, 1971-75; from asst. prof. to full prof. microbiology and immunology Stanford U., Calif., 1975—; prof. Western Hazardous Substances Rsch. Ctr. Stanford U., 1981—; cons. Engenics, 1982-84, Monsanto, 1984-86, Chlorox, 1992-93; chmn. Stanford Recombinant DNA panel; mem. Accreditation Bd. for Engring. and Tech.; mem. panel Yucca Mountain Microbial Activity, Dept. of Energy, mem. study sect.; participant DOE, NABIR program draft panel; convenor of microbiol. workshop and confs.; rev. panel DOE environ. mgmt. program. Mem. editl. bd. Jour Bacteriology, Ann. Rev. Microbiol.; reviewer NSF and other grants; contbr. numerous publs. to sci. jours. Fellow Fulbright Found., 1964, NSF, 1981-92, Ctr. for Biotech. Rsch., 1981-85, EPA, 1981—, NIH, 1989-92, Coll. BioTech., U.N. Tokten, 1987, DOE, 1993—, Dept. Agrl., 1995—. Mem. AAAS, AAUP, Am Soc. for Microbiology (Found. lectr. 1991-93), Soc. Gen. Microbiology, Soc. Indsl. Microbiology, No. Soc. Indsl. Microbiology (bd. dirs.), Biophys. Soc., Am. Chem. Soc. Home: 690 Coronado Ave Stanford CA 94305-1039 Office: Stanford U Fairchild Sci Bldg Dept Microbiology & Immunology Stanford CA 94305-5402

MATJASKO, M. JANE, anesthesiologist, educator; b. Harrison Twp., Pa., 1942. MD, Med. Coll. Pa., 1968. Diplomate Am. Bd. Anesthesiology (bd. dirs.). Resident in anesthesiology Md. Hosp., Balt., 1968-72; prof., chmn. anesthesiology U. Md., Balt.; appt. U. Md. Hosp., Balt. Mem. Am. Soc. Anesthesiologists, Assn. Univ. Anesthesiologists. Office: U Md Hosp Dept Anesthesiology 22 S Greene St Baltimore MD 21201-1544*

MATLOFF, MARK ALEXANDER, psychologist; b. Bklyn., Feb. 15, 1950; s. Simon and Eudice Rose (Strom) M.; m. Elaine S. Meyers, Oct. 23, 1977; one child, Daniel Aaron. BA, CUNY, 1971; MS, Auburn U., 1974, PhD, 1977. Diplomate Internat. Acad. Behavioral Medicine, Counseling and Psychotherapy; cert. in thought field therapy at diagnostic level, cert. thought field therapy algorithms tchr., Inst. Rational-Emotive Therapy. Clin. psychology intern Bradley Ctr. Psychiat. Hosp., Columbus, Ga., 1976-77; clin. psychologist Burwell Psychoednl. Ctr., Carrollton, Ga., 1977-78; staff psychologist Warren (Pa.) State Hosp., 1978-81; pvt. practice psychology Olean, N.Y., 1981-83; program dir. community svcs. team Madison County Dept. Mental Health, Wampsville, N.Y., 1983-85; pvt. practice psychology Syracuse, N.Y., 1985—; cons. POMCO, Syracuse, 1986—, VA, Syracuse, 1988—, Madison County Day Treatment Ctr., Oneida, N.Y., 1983-84; cert. supr. Inst. Rational-Emotive Therapy, N.Y.C., 1989—. Assoc. fellow Inst. Rational-Emotive Therapy, N.Y.C., 1983. Mem. APA, Cen. N.Y. Psychol. Assn. Home and Office: 209 Oaknont Dr Syracuse NY 13214-1533

MATSON, PAMELA ANNE, environmental science educator; b. Eau Claire, Wis., Aug. 3, 1953. BS, U. Wis., 1975; MS, Ind. U., 1980; PhD, Oreg. State U., 1983. Prof. U. Calif., Berkeley, 1993—. MacArthur fellow, 1995; recipient award for excellence in environ. health rsch. Lovelance Inst., Albuquerque, 1995. Mem. Am. Acad. Arts & Scis., Nat. Acad. Sci. Office: U Calif Dept Sci Policy and Mgmt Dept Environ Science Berkeley CA 94720-3110

MATSUO, FUMISUKE, physician, educator; b. Iida, Japan, Dec. 24, 1942; came to U.S., 1969; s. Riichi and Utako (Sasaki) M.; m. Ruth Ann Smith, May 24, 1975; children: Jocelyn, Bryan. MD, Kyoto (Japan) Prefectural U. Medicine, 1968. Asst. prof. U. Iowa, Iowa City, 1975; asst. prof. U. Utah, Salt Lake City, 1975-79, assoc. prof., 1979-87, prof., 1987—; dir. EEG Lab. Univ. Hosp., Salt Lake City, 1975—. Contbr. articles to profl. jours. Fellow Am. Acad. Neurology, Am. Clin. Neurophysiology Soc.; mem. AMA, Soc. Neuroscis., Am. Epilepsy Soc., Epilepsy Assn. Utah (bd. dirs. 1978-81, 87-89), Western EEG Soc. (bd. dirs. 1983-86, sec.-treas. 1989-90, pres. 1991-92). Home: 1353 S 1900 E Salt Lake City UT 84108-2219 Office: U Utah Med Ctr 50 N Medical Dr Salt Lake City UT 84132-0001

MATSUYAMA, JOY REIKO, pharmacist, educator; b. Mpls., July 15, 1964; d. Eugene Seiichi and Jayne Yurie (Kuwata) M.; m. Eric Timothy Krening, July 28, 1991; 1 child, Jared Timothy. BS in Pharmacy, U. Wash., 1987, Pharm. D, 1989. Bd. cert. pharmacotherapy specialist. Hosp. clin. pharmacist, resident Harborview Med. Ctr., Seattle, 1987-89; geriatric clin. pharmacy resident Vets. Affairs Med. Ctr, Boise, Idaho, 1989-90; ambulatory care clin. pharmacist Vets. Affairs Med. Ctr., Boise, 1990-91; adj. faculty Idaho State U., Pocatello, 1990-91, asst. prof. pharmacy practice, 1991-96; coord. pharmacy edn. and profl. practice Queen's Med. Ctr., Honolulu, 1996—; pharmacist in med. awareness program Sr. Health Svcs., Boise, 1991—. Editl. bd., reviewer Annals of Pharmacotherapy, Cin., 1992—; contbr. articles to profl. jours. Mem. Am. Assn. Colls. Pharmacy, Am. Coll. Clin. Pharmacy, Am. Soc. Health Sys. Pharmacists, Idaho Soc. Health Sys. Pharmacists (chair coun. on edn. 1992-94, excellence in rsch. award 1st pl. 1994), Rho Chi. Office: Queen's Med Ctr 1301 Punchbowl St Honolulu HI 96813

MATTEI, FRANK ANTHONY, orthopaedic surgeon; b. Phila., Nov. 13; s. Joseph Anthony and Maria Michelle (Melfi) M.; m. Beadina Doris Pologruto, Mar. 31, 1962; 1 child, Frank Joseph. BS in Biology, Villanova U., 1942; MD, Jefferson Med. Coll., 1945. Diplomate Am. Bd. Orthopaedic Surgery. Intern St. Mary Hosp., Phila., 1945-46; resident in orthops. Phila. Gen. Hosp., 1948-50, Children's Hosp., 1951; instr. orthops. Jefferson Med. Coll., 1951-59; clin. asst. prof. Hahneman Med. Coll., 1959—; pvt. practice Phila., 1951—; chmn. orthops. St. Agnes Med. Ctr., 1952-89, emeritus in orthops., 1989—; chmn. orthops. St. Luke Med. Ctr., 1955-89; chief orthopedist Penal Sys., Phila., 1971-89; prof. surgery Podiatric Coll. Medicine, Phila., 1971-73. Dir. Paris Corp., Burlington, N.J.; pres. Unico National, Phila., 1964, Franklin House Inc., Glassboro, N.J., 1976—. Capt. U.S. Army, 1946-48. Fellow ACS, Regional Trauma Com., Phila. Orthop. Soc., Pa. Orthop. Soc., Jefferson Orthop. Soc.; mem. AMA, Phila. County Med. Soc. Office: 1421 S Broad St Philadelphia PA 19147-4919

MATTELAER, PIERRE MARCEL MARIA, medical director; b. Kortrijk, Belgium, July 13, 1949; s. Bernard and Renee (Blancke) M.; m. Marie-Christine Van Nuffel, May 22, 1974; children: Benjamin, Pieter, Alexander. MD, Cath. U., Louvain, Belgium, 1974; postgrad., Seminaire Belge, Brussels, 1984. Dep. mktg. dir. Roche, Belgium, 1977-80; med. dir. Labaz-Sanofi, Belgium, 1980-85, Beecham, Belgium, 1986-90, Smithkline Beecham, Genval, Belgium, 1990—. Office: Smithkline Beecham, Rue du Tilleul, B 1332 Genval Belgium

MATTERSON, JOAN MCDEVITT, physical therapist; b. Bryn Mawr, Pa., Feb. 24, 1949; d. William J. and Wanda Jean (Edwards) McD.; children: Brian, Jennie, Kira. BS in Biology, St. Joseph's U., Phila., 1973; cert. in phys. therapy, U. Pa., 1974. Assoc. pharmacologist, researcher immunology and arthritis Progressive Phys. Therapy, P.A., Wilmington, Del., 1976-93, pediatric phys. therapist, 1974-81, pres., 1976-95; rehab. cir. Achievement Rehab.; phys. therapist Liberty Home Health, 1995—; rehab. dir. Office of Joan Matterson, 1995—, Integrated Health Svcs.- Kent. Smyrna, Del., 1996—; lectr. in field of low level laser therapy. Dep. gov. Am. Biog. Rsch. Inst.; mem. adv. bd. Internat. Biographical Rsch. Inst., Cambridge, England. Mem. Am. Soc. Laser Medicine and Surgery, Internat. Platform Assn., Am. Phys. Therapy Assn., Am. Acad. Pain (assoc.), Inst. Noetic Sci., Am. Bd. Forensic Examiners.

MATTHEWS, DARYL BRUCE, psychiatrist; b. Cleve., Sept. 26, 1947; s. David Earle and Esther Ann (Seifter) M.; m. Esther Solomon, Dec. 24, 1979; children: Max, Jacob. BA in Human Biology, Johns Hopkins U., 1969, MD, 1973, PhD in Sociology, 1977. Diplomate Am. Bd. Psychiatry and Neurology, Am. Bd. Forensic Psychiatry. Asst. prof. psychiatry Boston U., 1976-81; assoc. prof. U. Va., Charlottesville, 1981-82; assoc. clin. prof. U. Hawaii, Honolulu, 1982-90; prof., dir. edn. U. Ark., 1990-95; clin. prof. U. Hawaii, Honolulu, 1995—. Author: Disposable Patients, 1981; contbr. articles to profl. jours. Jewish. Office: 1435 Kuhio Hwy # 206 Kapaa HI 96746

MATTHEWS, FRANK, pathologist; b. Chgo., Feb. 13, 1931; s. Warren B. and Martha Nancy (Eakes) M.; m. Elizabeth Jean Wilson, June 13, 1953; children: Susanna Dell, Margaret Ann, Beverly Jean. BS, Emory U., 1951; MD, U. Mich., 1954. Diplomate Am. Bd. Pathology. Intern Boston City Hosp., 1954-55; resident pathology U. Mich., 1955-59; chief pathologist DeKalb Med. Ctr., Decatur, Ga., 1961—; active staff Decatur Hosp., Eastside Med. Ctr., Rockdale Hosp.; pres. PSPA Reg. Lab., Decatur, 1970-78; cons. Ga. Bd. Health, 1967-70, Blood Bank, ARC, 1965—. Contbr. articles to profl. jours. Mem. Coll. Am. Pathologists (bd. govs. 1977-84, pathologist of the yr. 1984), Atlanta Soc. Pathologists (pres. 1963), Ga. Assn. Pathologists (pres., bd. dirs.), DeKalb Med. Soc. (pres. 1987), Rotary (pres. 1987-88). Methodist. Home: 2544 River Oak Dr Decatur GA 30033-2803 Office: DeKalb Med Ctr 2701 N Decatur Rd Decatur GA 30033-5918

MATTHEWS, MICHAEL KUKUVKA, JR., neurology educator; b. Somerset, Pa., June 20, 1950; s. Michael Kukuvka and Helen Gertrude (Boyers) M.; m. Irene Beth Frederick, July 7, 1973; children: Bethany, Timothy, Katrina. BS, U. Pitts., 1972; PhD, U. Pa., 1976; MD, U. Nebr., 1985. Diplomate Nat. Bd. Med. Examiners, Am. Bd. Psychiatry & Neurology (examiner 1993—). Asst. prof. psychology Yankton (S.D.) Coll., 1977-80; med. intern Albany (N.Y.) Med. Ctr., 1985-86, resident in neurology, 1986-89; fellow in behavioral neurology Boston U., 1989-90; asst. prof. neurology Med. Coll. of Pa., Phila., 1990-95; assoc. prof. neurology Med. Coll. of Pa., Hahnemann U., Phila., 1995—; meam. adv. bd. Gwynedd Square Ctr., Phila., 1992—, Alzheimer's Found., Phila., 1992—; med. cons. Inst. Cognitive Prosthetics, Bala Cynwyd, Pa., 1993—. Author: (with others) Neuroimaging: A Companion to Adams & Victors Principles of Neurology, 1995; contbr. articles to profl. jours. Asst. coach, vol. Yankton High Sch. Gymnastics Team, 1977-80; asst. coach Penn Valley (Pa.) Baseball League, 1994. Rsch. grantee NIH, 1978. Mem. AAAS, Am. Acad. Neurology, Phila. Neurol. Soc., Behavioral Neurology Soc., Phi Beta Kappa. Office: Med Coll of Pa 3300 Henry Ave Philadelphia PA 19129

MATTHEWS, SHERMAN ERVIN, JR., social services administrator; b. Chattanooga, May 4, 1948; s. Sherman J. and Mary K. (Powell) M.; m. Brenda Jones, May 2, 1970; children: Kimberly Diane, Erika Lannette. BA in Sociology, Ky. State U., 1971; postgrad., U. Tenn., Chattanooga, 1974-76. Emergency substitute tchr., Chattanooga, 1971; family counselor Assn. Day Care Agy., Chattanooga, 1971-72; drug counselor day program Community Action Agy., Chattanooga, 1972-73; juvenile probation officer Tenn. Dept. Correction, Chattanooga, 1973-86, supervisory probation officer III, 1986-88, mgr. juvenile probation I, 1988-89; regional dir. SE region Tenn. Dept. Youth Devel., Chattanooga, 1989—; adj. prof. U. Tenn., 1978. Bd. dirs. Operation PUSH; mem. adv. bd. and steering com. PUSH-Excel Program, Chattanooga, 1979, now bd. dirs.; mem. Unity Group, Chattanooga; mem. Chattanooga Pub. Sch. Bd. Edn. Dist. 5, 1990—. Recipient award Excel Adv. Bd., 1983, Key to City, City of Chattanooga, 1988. Mem. NAACP (bd. dirs. Chattanooga 1989), Masons (32 degree, master mason), Shriners, Kappa Alpha Psi, Alpha Phi Omega. Democrat. Baptist. Home: 2808 Terry Ct Chattanooga TN 37411-1065 Office: Tenn Dept Youth Devel 540 Mccallie Ave Chattanooga TN 37402-2089

MATTHEWS, WENDY SCHEMPP, psychologist, researcher; b. Bridgeport, Conn., Feb. 4, 1945; d. Harry Edward and Julie Schempp; m. Robert J. Matthews, Aug. 16, 1969 (div. June 1984); 1 child, Avery. BA, Beaver Coll., 1966; MA, Cornell U., 1971, PhD, 1975; cert., Université de Paris, 1972. Rsch. assoc. Harvard U., Cambridge, Mass., 1977-78; jr. fellow N.J. Div. Human Svcs., Trenton, 1978; clin. assoc. prof. U. of Medicine & Dentistry of N.J., New Brunswick, 1979—; dir. children's ctr. Contemporary Psychology Inst., Skillman, N.J., 1983-87; pediatric psychologist N.J. Div. Youth & Family Svcs., Trenton, 1987—; pvt. practice Princeton, N.J., 1987—. Author: He & She: How Children Develop Their Sex Role Identity, 1977; contbr. articles to profl. jours.

MATTIE, HERMAN, internist; b. Amsterdam, May 4, 1933; s. Antonius Hermanus and Maria A.E. (De Bruin) M.; m. Lucie M. J. De Boer, Jan. 21, 1961; children: Christiaan H.F., Erik H., Roelof Th, Herbert J. MB, U. Amsterdam, 1956, MD, 1959; PhD, State U. Leiden, Netherlands, 1972. Asst. Pharmacol. Lab., Amsterdam, 1961-62; trainee internal medicine OLVG, Amsterdam, 1962-65; rsch. asst. Pharmacol. U., Leiden, 1965-73; head Div. Clin. Pharmacol., U. Leiden, 1973-85; internist Dept. Infectious Disease, U. Hosp., Leiden, 1967—; assoc. prof. State U., Leiden, 1974—; mem. exec. com. Internat. Ther. Union, Paris, 1981; mem. adv. com. Nat. Ctr. for Monitoring of Adverse Drug Reactions, Rijswijk. Editor Pijninformatorium, 1979—. 1st lt. Meds., 1959-60. Mem. Am. Soc. Microbiology, Infectious Disease Soc. Am., Brit. Pharmacol. Soc., Internat. Assn. Study of Pain, N.Y. Acad. Scis., Netherlands Soc. Clin. Pharmacology (life, founder), European Soc. Biomodulation and Chemotherapy (founder, com.). Roman Catholic. Home: Zoeterwoudsesingel 17, 2313 AZ Leiden The Netherlands Office: U Hosp, Post Box 9600, 2300 RC Leiden The Netherlands

MATTISON, ELISA SHERI, organizational psychologist; b. Grand Rapids, Mich., Apr. 24, 1952; d. Andrew and Loraine R. Wierenga. BS cum laude, Western Mich. U., 1974, MA, 1979; postgrad., Fielding Inst., 1990. Trainer No. Inst., Anchorage, 1980; mgmt. cons., trainer Alaska Assocs. Human Devel. Inc., Anchorage, 1980-82; job devel. specialist Collins, Weed and Assocs., Anchorage, 1982-83; owner, pres., cons. Mattison Assocs. Inc., Anchorage, 1992—; mem. adj. faculty Anchorage Community Coll., 1981-82; work environment and design conslt. ARCO Alaska Inc., 1983-86; cons. Employee Assts. Cons. Alaska, Anchorage, 1982; v.p. Human Resource Mgmt. and Mktg. Alaskan Fed. Credit Union, 1986-90; asst. dir. degree completeion program, adult and continuing edn., Alaska Pacific U., 1990-92, adj. faculty, 1990—. Mem. Am. Soc. Tng. and Devel., Soc. Human Resource Mgmt. Contbr. articles to profl. pubs. Office: 3910 Iona Circle Anchorage AK 99507-3344

MATTISON, JOEL, plastic surgeon; b. Arcadia, Fla., Dec. 29, 1931; s. William L. and Millie B. Mattison; m. Jean Morris, June 5, 1955; children: Lewis, Karl. AB, Davidson Coll., 1951; MDiv, Princeton Sem., 1954; MD, Duke U., 1961. Diplomate Am. Bd. Plastic Surgery, Am. Bd. Quality Assurance and Utilization Rev. Physicians. Intern surgery Duke U. Med. Ctr., Durham, N.CD., 1961; resident plastic surgery U. Fla., Gainesville, 1964-69; practice medicine specializing in plastic surgery Tampa, Fla., 1969-95; clin. prof. surgery U. South Fla., Tampa; frequent lectr. on med. ethics. Contbr. articles on med. ethics, Am. antiques and decorative arts to profl. jours. Recipient Disting. Alumnus award Princeton Sem., 1991. Fellow ACS; mem. Am. Soc. Plastic Surgeons, Southeastern Soc. Plastic Surgeons (Outstanding Achievement award 1985), Fla. Soc. Plastic Surgeons, Rotary. Presbyterian. Home: 847 S Newport Ave Tampa FL 33606-2934 Office: St Joseph's Hosp Dept Util Mgmt Tampa FL 33677-4227

MATTMAN, LIDA HOLMES, microbiologist, educator; b. Denver, July 31, 1912; d. Eureka Spurgeon and Lillie Edith (Henry) Holmes; children: Sandra, Paul. BA, U. Kans., 1933, MA, 1934; PhD, Yale U., 1940. Head clin. labs. UN Relief and Rehab., 1944; sr. bacteriologist dept. pub. health Commonwealth of Mass., Boston, 1947-48; instr. Wayne State U., Detroit, 1949-85; instr. immunology Oakland U., Rochester, Mich., 1986; rsch. investigator, emeritus prof. Wayne State U., Detroit, 1986—; prof. Howard Hughes Inst. Immunology, 1992, 94; cons. immunology U.S. Dept. Justice, Detroit, NSF. Author: Cell Wall Deficient Forms, 1975, Cell Wall Deficient Forms, Stealth Pathogens, 1992; contbr. chpts. to books and numerous articles to profl. jours. AMA grantee, Am. Thoracic Soc. grantee, Damon Runyon Soc. grantee, Mich. Cancer Soc. grantee, Mich. Heart Assn. grantee, Detroit Tuberculosis Soc. grantee, Wayne County Tuberculosis Soc. grantee, USPHS grantee, Wayne State U. grantee, Yale U. scholar, U. Pa. rsch. fellow. Mem. Am. Soc. Microbiology (pres. Mich. br.), Mich. Acad. Scis. (chmn. med. div.). Home: 319 Rivard Blvd Grosse Pointe MI 48230-1625 Office: Wayne State U Biology Dept Detroit MI 48202

MATTOCKS-WHISMAN, FRANCES, nursing administrator, educator; b. Cedar Vale, Kans., Dec. 20, 1945; d. Thomas Emerson and Lavonna Laura (Myers) McKinney; m. Jim L. Whisman, Nov. 6, 1981; stepchildren: Toni Zweigart, Gay Asbell, Jenny Watts, Beth Whisman. Diploma, William Newton Sch. Nursing, Winfield, Kans., 1966; student, Tulsa Jr. Coll., Cen. State U., Edmond, Okla., Graceland Coll., Lamoni, Iowa, 1989—. RN; cert. operating room nurse. Operating room nurse Hillcrest Med. Ctar., Tulsa, 1968-72, 74-76; office mgr. Myra A. Peters, M.D., 1972-76; pvt. duty nurse Homemakers Upjohn, Inc., Tulsa, 1976-77; staff nurse, head nurse, insvc. instr. Doctors Med. Ctr., Inc., Tulsa; co-dir. Sch. Surg. Tech. Tulsa County Area Vo-Tech. Sch., 1981-89; asst. dir. transplantation/retrievals Tulsa chpt. ARC, 1989; staff nurse, infection control coord. Wetumka (Okla.) Gen. Hosp., 1989-91; dir. nurses Bristow (Okla.) Meml. Hosp., 1991-93; br. mgr. Doctors Homecare, Sapulpa, Okla., 1993—; br. supr. Sapulpa and Mannford offices Doctors Homecare, 1994-95; instr. Wes Watkins Area Vo-Tech. Sch., Wetumka, 1989-90; cons. ARC, Tulsa chpt. Transplantation, 1990. Contbr. articles to profl. jours. Active ARC. Mem. NEA, Nat. Assn. Orthopedic Nurses, Nat. League for Nursing, Am. Vocat. Assn., Okla. Vocat. Assn., Okla. Edn. Assn., Concerned Oklahomans for Nurse Edn., Assn. Operating Rm. Nurses, Infections Control. Nurses. Home: RR 1 Box 154 Okemah OK 74859-9733 Office: Columbia Homecare-Okla 405 S Main Sapulpa OK 74066

MATTSON, JOY LOUISE, oncological nurse; b. Moline, Ill., Feb. 1, 1956; d. Norman O. and Jeannette (Squier) M.; m. Duncan F. Crannell, Sept. 9, 1988. BA magna cum laude, Bates Coll., 1977; MTS, Harvard U., 1982; BSN magna cum laude, Rutgers U., Newark, 1988; MLS, Rutgers U., 1993. RN, N.J. Staff nurse oncology Muhlenberg Reg. Med. Ctr., Plainfield, N.J., 1987-88; staff nurse St. Lawrence Rehab. Ctr., Lawrenceville, N.J., 1988-89; clin. rsch. asst. G.H. Besselaar Assocs., Princeton, N.J., 1990-91; med. writer Convatec, Skillman, N.J., 1991-92, G.H. Besselaar Assocs., Princeton, N.J., 1992-94; clin. safety assoc. Pfizer Inc., N.Y.C., 1994—. Mem. Phi Beta Kappa. Home: 5 Tudor City Pl Apt 508 New York NY 10017

MATTSON, MARLIN ROY ALBIN, health facility administrator, psychiatry educator; b. Bellingham, Wash., Apr. 25, 1939; s. Conrad Roy and Ruth Viola (Thompson) M. BA, U. Wash., 1961, MD, 1965. Diplomate Am. Bd. Psychiatry and Neurology. Intern and resident in medicine Cornell U. program at Bellevue and Meml. Hosps., N.Y.C., 1965-67; resident in psychiatry Payne Whitney Clin. The N.Y. Hosp., N.Y.C., 1969-72, chief resident in psychiatry, 1972-73, asst. med. dir., 1973-89, assoc. med. dir., 1989—; asst. med. dir. quality assurance Westchester Div. The N.Y. Hosp., White Plains, 1979-89, assoc. med. dir. quality assurance, 1989-93; head of quality assurance program Dept. Psychiatry The N.Y. Hosp., N.Y.C., 1979-94; asst. prof. psychiatry Cornell U. Med. Coll., N.Y.C., 1973-79, assoc. prof. clin. psychiatry, 1979—; bd. visitors Manhattan Psychiat. Ctr., 1991—; bd. dirs. N.Y. County Health Svcs. Rev. Orgn., N.Y.C., 1983-95; mem. stds. com. Utilization Rev. Accreditation Commn., 1996—. Editor Manual of Psychiat. Quality Assurance, 1992; contbr. numerous articles to profl. jours. Capt. U.S. Army Med. Corp., 1967-69, Korea. Fellow Am. Psychiat. Assn. (mem. nat. com. on quality assurance 1988-95, chmn. 1992-95, mem. com. campus peer rev. program 1984-86, sec. N.Y. County dist. br. 1987-91, pres.-elect 1991-92, pres. 1992-93, co-pres. 1995-96, assembly rep. 1996—), N.Y. Acad. Medicine (com. pub. health 1984-92, sec. sect. on psychiatry 1993-94, chmn. 1994-95); mem. N.Y. State Psychiat. Assn. (chmn. peer rev. com. 1982-95, mem. com. econ. affairs 1995—). Republican. Episcopalian. Home: 501 E 87th St Apt 4J New York NY 10128-7609 Office: NY Hosp Payne Whitney Psychiat Clinic 525 E 68th St New York NY 10021-4873

MATTSON, RICHARD HENRY, neurologist, educator; b. Waterbury, Conn., May 9, 1931; s. George F. and Edith O. (Curtis) M.; m. Elena Mary Hill, June 13, 1954; children: Richard Jr., Gail Mattson-Gates, Catherine. BS, Yale U., 1953, MA (hon.), 1967; MD, Boston U., 1957; MS, U. Minn., 1962. Intern Wilford Hall USAF Hosp., San Antonio, 1957-58, chief neurology, cons. to surgeon gen., 1962-67; resident in neurology Mayo Clinic, Rochester, Minn., 1958-62; asst. clin. prof. neurology U. Tex. Med. Br., Galveston, 1964-67; asst. chief and chief of neurology VA Med. Ctr., West Haven, Conn., 1967-92; from asst. prof. to prof. neurology Yale U. Sch. Medicine, New Haven, 1967—, dir. med. studies dept. neurology, 1985—, dir. residency tng. program dept. neurology, 1985—, dir. clin. neurosci. curriculum, 1990—, vice chmn. for acad. affairs, 1995—; dir. NIH Yale Epilepsy Program Project, 1985—; cons. VA Ctrl. Office, 1967—, NIH, 1974—, various pharm. cos. Author: Antiepileptic Drugs, and other related books; contbr. over 200 articles to profl. jours. Recipient H.V. Jone award Mayo Found., 1962, Best Clin. Trial award Internat. League Against Epilepsy, 1988, Amb. award, Internat. League Against Epilepsy, 1990. Fellow Am. Acad. Neurology, Am. EEG Soc.; mem. Am. Neurol. Assn., Am. Epilepsy Soc. (pres. 1986-87, Wiliam G. Lennox award 1994), Begg Honor Soc.

MATTURRO, PETER JOHN, social worker; b. Corona, N.Y., Aug. 4, 1953; s. Anthony Francis and Bridget Anne (Campbell) M.; m. Mary Martha Mahoney, June 10, 1978; children: Elizabeth Mary, David Peter, Laura Elaine. AS, CUNY, 1973, BA, 1976; MPA cert., Marist Coll., Poughkeepsie, N. Y.; M in Social Work, Fordham U. 1980. cert. Social Worker, N.Y. Adoption, social worker St. Cabrini, Inc., West Park, N.Y., 1978-80; program dir. Kingston (N.Y.) Children's Home, 1980-82; psychiatric social worker Rockland Children's Psychiatric Ctr., Newburgh, N.Y., 1982-88; supr. Fordham U., 1987-88; coord. intensive case mgmt. Rockland Children's Psychiat. Ctr., Newburgh, N.Y., 1988—; ct. apptd. spl. asst., Kingston, N.Y., 1987-88. Home: 230 Marcott Rd Kingston NY 12401-8318

MATUSIEWICZ, DAVID THOMAS, optometrist; b. S.I., N.Y., Apr. 5, 1967; s. Thomas Stanley and Lenore Frances (Kula) M.; m. Kathryn Debra Matusiewicz, Feb. 24, 1993. BS in Biology cum laude, Glassboro (N.J.) State Coll., 1988; BS in Visual Scis., Pa. Coll. Optometry, 1988, OD, 1991. Cert. in treatment and mgmt. ocular diseases Internat. Assn. Bds. Examiners in Optometry; cert. Therapeutic Pharm. Agts. Bd. Pvt. practice, Chadds Ford, Pa., 1991-93, Point Pleasant, W.Va., 1992-93, Newark, Del., 1993-94; owner, CEO Vision Ctr. of Del., Newark, 1994—. coord. for State of Del., VISION U.S.A., 1995. Mem. Am. Optometric Assn., Del Optometric Assn. (exec. com.), W.Va. Optometric Assn., New Castle C. of C. Home: 847 Broadfield Dr Newark DE 19713 Office: Vision Ctr Del 317 E Main St Newark DE 19711

MATUSZAK, ALICE JEAN BOYER, pharmacy educator; b. Newark, Ohio, June 22, 1935; d. James Emery and Elizabeth Hawthorne (Irvine) Boyer; m. Charles Alan Matuszak, Aug. 27, 1955; children: Matthew, James. BS summa cum laude, Ohio State U., 1958, MS, 1959; postgrad., U. Wis., 1959-60; PhD, U. Kans., 1963. Registered pharmacist, Ohio, Calif. Apprentice pharmacist Arensberg Pharmacy, Newark, 1953-58; rsch. asst. Ohio State U., Columbus, 1958, lab. asst., 1958-59; rsch. asst. U. Wis., Madison, 1959-60, U. Kans., Lawrence, 1960-63; asst. prof. U. of the Pacific, Stockton, Calif., 1963-67, assoc. prof., 1971-78, prof., 1978—; vis. fgn. prof. Kobe-Gakuin U., Japan, 1992. Contbr. articles to profl. jours. Recipient Disting. Alumna award Ohio State U. Coll. Pharmacy, 1994; NIH grantee, 1965-66. Fellow Am. Pharm. Assn. (chmn. basic scis. 1990); mem. Am. Assn. Colls. of Pharmacy (chmn. chemistry sect. 1979-80, bd. dirs. 1993-95), Am. Inst. History of Pharmacy (exec. coun. 1984-88, 90-92, 92-95, chmn. contributed papers 1990-92, pres.-elect 1995—), Cert. of Commendation 1990), Am. Chem. Soc., Internat. Fedn. Pharmacy, Acad. Pharm. Rsch. Sci. (pres. 1993-94), Coun. Sci. Soc. Pres., U.S. Adopted Names Coun. U.S. Pharmacopeial Conv., Sigma Xi, Rho Chi, Phi Kappa Phi, Kappa Epsilon (Unicorn award, award of merit 1995), Lambda Kappa Sigma, Delta Zeta. Democrat. Episcopalian. Home: 1130 W Mariposa Ave Stockton CA 95204-3021 Office: U of the Pacific Sch of Pharmacy Stockton CA 95211

MATUSZEK, JOHN MICHAEL, JR., environmental scientist, educator, consultant; b. Worcester, Mass., Nov. 30, 1957; s. John Michael and Felicia Martha (Shandruk) M.; m. Roberta Eva Coonan, Nov. 30, 1957; children: Debra-Jane Y., John Michael III, Kevin P., Jennifer R. BS with distinction, Worcester Poly. Inst., 1957; PhD, Clark U., 1962. Dept. mgr. Teledyne Isotopes, Westwood, N.J., 1964-71; rsch. scientist N.Y. State Health Dept., Albany, 1971—; adj. prof. Rensselaer Poly. Inst., Troy, N.Y., 1977—; prof. SUNY, Albany, 1996—. Lt. comdr. USPHS, 1962-64. Home: 82 McGuffey Ln Delmar NY 12054 Office: NY State Dept Health Empire State Plz PO Box 509 Albany NY 12201-0509

MATZICK, KENNETH JOHN, hospital administrator; b. Chgo., May 31, 1943; married. B, U. Iowa, 1965, MHA, 1967. Adminstrv. resident VA Med. Ctr., Iowa City, 1966; adminstrv. resident Morristown (N.J.) Meml. Hosp., 1967-68, asst. to exec. v.p., 1968-69; asst. dir. William Beaumont Hosp., Royal Oak, Mich., 1969-76; dir. William Beaumont Hosp., Troy, Mich., 1976-83; v.p., hosp. dir. William Beaumont Hosp., Royal Oak, 1983—. Home: 1204 Shore Club Dr Saint Clair Shores MI 48080-1565 Office: William Beaumont Hosp 3601 W 13 Mile Rd Royal Oak MI 48073-6712*

MATZKIN, WILLIAM LIONEL, psychiatrist; b. N.Y.C., Apr. 24, 1922; s. David George and Anna (Speizer) M. BS, CCNY, 1950; DO, Chgo. Coll. Osteopathy, 1954; D of Medicine, Calif. Coll. Med., 1962. Bd. eligible Am. Bd. Psyciatry and Neurology. Intern St. Elizabeth Hosp., Washington, 1964-65; resident in psychiat. medicine L.A. County Hosp., 1962-63, Met. Hosp., N.Y.C., 1963-64; resident in psychiat. medicine, child psychiatry fellow Hillcrest Children's Ctr., Washington, 1965-67; resident in psychiat. medicine, psychiat. teaching fellow Freedman's Hosp., Washington, 1967-68; med. dir. Pastoral Inst., Washington, 1968-69; sr. attending physician Washington Hosp. Ctr., 1969-72. Mem. Am. Psychiat. Assn. Home and Office: 209 Hardy Pl Rockville MD 20852-1223

MAUCK, HENRY PAGE, JR., medical and pediatrics educator; b. Richmond, Va., Feb. 3, 1926; s. Henry Page and Harriet Hutcheson (Morrison) M.; m. Janet Garrett Horsley, May 14, 1955; children—Henry Page III, John Waller. B.A., U. Va., 1950, M.D., 1952. Diplomate: Am. Bd. Internal Medicine. Intern Henry Ford Hosp., Detroit, 1952-53; resident Med. Coll. Va., Richmond, 1953-56; asst. prof. medicine and pediatrics Med. Coll. Va., 1961-66, assoc. prof., 1966-72, prof., 1972—; fellow in cardiology Am. Heart Assn., 1956-57; cons. cardiology Langley Field Air Force Hosp., Hampton, Va., McGuire's VA Hosp., Richmond. Contbr.: chpt. to Autonomic Control of Cardiovascular System, 1972; contbr. articles to sci. jours. Served with U.S. Army, 1944-46. Fellow ACP, Am. Coll. Cardiology (former gov. Va.); mem. Am. Physiol. Soc., So. Soc. Clin. Investigation, Am. Fedn. Clin. Research, So. Soc. Clin. Research. Presbyterian. Home: 113 Oxford Cir W Richmond VA 23221-3224 Office: Med Coll Va PO Box 281 Richmond VA 23202-0281

MAUDERLY, JOE LLOYD, pulmonary toxicologist; b. Strong City, Kans., Aug. 31, 1943; s. Joseph Park and Violet May (Cox) M.; m. Cheryl Gaines, Jan. 31, 1965; children: Laurie Jean, Jameson Lynn. BS, Kans. State U., 1965, DVM, 1967. Respiratory physiologist Inhalation Toxicology Research Inst., Albuquerque, 1967-89, supr. pathophysiology group, 1976-89, dir., 1989—; rsch. prof. medicine U. N.Mex., Albuquerque, 1988—, clin. prof. pharmacy, 1990—; cons. in field. Assoc. editor Fundamental Applied Toxicology, 1989-94; contbr. articles to profl. jours., chpts. to books. Served to capt. USAF, 1967-69. Mem. Am. Thoracic Soc. (chmn. assembly of environ. and occupational health 1991-93, long-range planning com. 1991-94, sci. adv. com. 1993-96, editl. bds., inhalation toxicology and exptl. lung rsch.), Am. Physiol. Soc., Am. Vet. Med. Assn., N.Mex. Vet. Med. Assn., Soc. of Toxicology, Exptl. Aircraft Assn. Republican. Home: 4517 Banff Dr NE Albuquerque NM 87111-2829 Office: Inhalation Toxicology Rsch Inst PO Box 5890 Albuquerque NM 87185-5890

MAUDGAL, DHARAM PAL, gastroenterologist; b. Tewar, Punjab, India, Sept. 19, 1943; arrived in Eng., 1971; d. Ratti Ram and Poorna Devi (Vashisht) Sharma; m. Malkito Sanghera Maudgal, Oct. 28, 1973 (div. 1994); 1 child, Davinder Dharam. FSc, D.A.V. Coll., Ambala City, India, 1961; MBBS, Govt. Med. Coll., Patiala, India, 1967; PhD in Medicine, St. George's Med. Sch., London, 1981. House officer Rajenara Hosp., Patiala, 1967-68; med. registrar Med. Coll. Hosp., Rohtak, India, 1968; med. officer State Electricity Bd., Haryana, India, 1968-70; sr. house officer Coventry (Eng.) & Warks Hosp., 1971-72, Gen. Hosp., South Shields, Eng., 1972-73, Tynemouth Infirmary, North Shields, Eng., 1973-74; med. registrar Salford (Eng.) Royal Hosp., 1974-75; from rsch. fellow to sr. med. registrar St. George's Hosp., London, 1975-83; cons. physician Manor House Hosp., London, 1983—; cons. gastroenterologist Edgware Gen. Hosp., 1995—, Barnet Gen. Hosp., 1995—; hon. assoc. con. gastroenterologist St. George's Hosp. Med. Sch., London, 1986—; hon. cons. gastroenterologist Northwick Park Hosp., Harrow, Eng., 1987-95; med. dir. London Med. Bur., Edgware, Eng., 1984—. Author: Hypothermia, Medical and Social Aspects, 1987; contbr. articles to profl. jours. Instr. meditation in cmty. Recipient Gold medals, Punjabi U., India, 1967, Silver medal, Govt. Med. coll., 1967, Merit scholarship, Punjab U., 1959. Fellow Royal Coll. Physicians London, Royal Soc. Medicine; mem. Brit. Soc. Gastroenterology, Brit. Med. Assn., Assurance Med. Soc., Indian Med. Assn. U.K., South Harrow Tennis Club. Hindu. Home: 107 Harrowes Meade, Middlesex HA8 8RS, England Office: Manor House Hosp, North End Rd, London NW11, England

MAUER, ALVIN MARX, physician, medical educator; b. LeMars, Iowa, Jan. 10, 1928; s. Alvin Milton and Bertha Elizabeth (Marx) M.; m. Theresa Ann McGivern, Dec. 2, 1950; children: Stephen James, Timothy John, Daria Maureen, Elizabeth Claire. B.A., State U. Iowa, 1950, M.D., 1953. Intern Cin. Gen. Hosp., 1953-54; resident in pediatrics Children's Hosp. Cin., 1954-56; fellow in hematology dept. medicine U. Utah, Salt Lake City, 1956-59; dir. div. hematology Children's Hosp. Cin., prof. dept. hematology, 1959-73; prof. dept. pediatrics U. Cin. Coll. Medicine, 1959-73; prof. pediatrics U. Tenn. Coll. Medicine, Memphis, 1973—, prof. medicine, 1983—, chief med. oncology/hematology; dir. cancer program U. Tenn. Coll. Health Scis.; dir. St. Jude Children's Research Hosp., Memphis, 1973-83; mem. hematology study sect. NIH; mem. clin. cancer investigation rev. com. Nat. Cancer Inst.; mem. com. on maternal and infant nutrition NRC. Author: Pediatric Hematology, 1969; editor: The Biology of Human Leukemia, 1990. Served with U.S. Army, 1946. Mem. Am. Soc. Hematology (pres. 1980-81), Assn. Am. Cancer Insts. (pres. 1980), am. Acad. Pediatrics (com. on nutrition), Am. Assn. Cancer Edn., Am. Soc. Clin. Investigation, Am. Fedn. Clin. Rsch., Assn. Am. Physicians, Am. Pediatric Soc., Cen. Soc. Clin. Investigation, Cen. Soc. Clin. Rsch., Internat. Soc. Hematology (pres. 1988-90, chmn. 1992-96, bd. councilors 1992-96), Am. Cancer Soc. (pres. Tenn. divsn. 1992-93), Midwest Soc. Pediat. Rsch., N.Y. Acad. Scis., Soc. Pediat. Rsch., Am. Assn. Cancer Rsch., Phi Beta Kappa, Sigma Xi, Alpha Omega Alpha. Democrat. Roman Catholic. Office: U Tenn Memphis Cancer Ctr N327 Van Vleet Bldg 3 S Dunlap St Memphis TN 38103-4907

MAUGHAN, WILLARD ZINN, dermatologist; b. Riverside, Calif., Apr. 21, 1944; s. Franklin David and Martha Charlotte (Zinn) M.; m. Rona Lee Wilcox, Aug. 20, 1968; children: Julie Anne, Kathryn Anita, Willard Wilcox, Christopher Keith. Student, Johns Hopkins U., Balt., 1962-64; BS, U. Utah, 1968, MD, 1972. Diplomate Am. Bd. Dermatology. Intern Walter Reed Army Med. Ctr., Washington, 1972-73; fellow Mayo Clinic, Rochester, Minn., 1976-79; pvt. practice Ogden, Utah, 1979—. Contbr. articles to profl. jours. Commr. Boy Scouts Am., Weber County, Utah, 1980-84, dist. chmn., 1993-94, assoc. mem. bd. dirs. Trapper Trails coun., 1995—; pres. Am. Cancer Soc., Weber County, 1985-86. Maj. U.S. Army, 1971-76. Recipient Dist. award of merit Boy Scouts Am., 1985, Silver Beaver award 1994. Fellow ACP, Am. Acad. Dermatology, Royal Soc. Medicine (London); mem. N.Y. Acad. Scis., Kiwanis Club, Alpha Omega Alpha, Phi Sigma Iota. Republican. Mormon. Home: 2486 W 4550 S Roy UT 84067-1944 Office: 3860 Jackson Ave Ogden UT 84403-1956

MAUKSCH, INGEBORG GROSSER, nursing educator; d. Frederick and Claire (Tauber) G.; children from previous marriage: Lawrence Bernard, Valerie. Ph.D., U. Chgo., 1969; D.Sc. (hon.), Syracuse U., 1979. Valere Potter disting. svc. prof. nursing Vanderbilt U. Sch. Nursing, Nashville; sr. program cons. Robert Wood Johnson nurse faculty fellowships in primary care program Vanderbilt U. Sch. Nursing, 1976—; mem. Presdl. Com. on Nat. Health Inst. Author: (with M. Miller) Implementing Change in Nursing, 1981, Systematic Patient Medication Record Review, 1980; mem. editorial bd.: Nursing Outlook, Nurse Educator. Mem. U.S. Holocaust Meml. Council. Recipient Alumni Achievement award Columbia U., 1979. Mem. Am. Nurses Assn. (hon.), Am. Acad. Nursing, Nat. Acad. Scis., Tenn. Nurses Assn. Office: Vanderbilt U Sch Nursing Nashville TN 37240*

MAUL, STEPHEN BAILEY, biotechnology executive; b. Parkersburg, W.Va., Jan. 11, 1942; s. Charles Bailey and Virginia (Stephens) M.; m. Patricia Harbison, June 17, 1967; children: Lydia B., Deborah K., Rachel M. BS in Chemistry, Alilene Christian U., 1963; PhD in Chemistry, U. Tex., 1969. Rsch. assoc. MIT, Cambridge, 1969-70; sr. scientist antibiotic fermentation devel. Eli Lilly & Co., Indpls., 1970-74; mgr. bioengring. Shering Corp., Union, N.J., 1974-76; v.p. Sylvan Spawn Lab., Inc., Kittanning, Pa., 1976-86; pres. Mycorr Tech., Inc., Pitts., 1987—; v.p. Plant Health Care Inc., Pitts., 1995—. Patentee in field; contbr. chpts. to books. Rsch. grantee USDA, 1989, 90—. Home: RR 1 Box 282 Worthington PA 16262-9731 Office: Mycorr Tech Inc 440 William Pitt Way Pittsburgh PA 15238-1330

MAUL, TERRY LEE, psychologist, educator; b. San Francisco, May 6, 1946; s. Chester Lloyd and Clella Lucille (Hobbs) M.; AB, U. Calif., Berkeley, 1967, MA, 1968, PhD, 1970; student Coll. San Mateo, 1964-65; m. Gail Ann Retallick, June 27, 1970 (div. Dec. 1986); 1 son, Andrew Eliot. Prof. psychology San Bernardino Valley Coll., San Bernardino, Calif., 1970—, chmn. dept., 1979-82; researcher self-actualization. Mem. AAUP (chpt. pres. 1971-73), Am. Psychol. Assn., Audubon Soc., Mensa, Nature Conservancy, Rachel Carson Council, Wilderness Soc., Sierra Club. Democrat. Author: (with Eva Conrad) Introduction to Experimental Psychology, 1981; (with Gail Maul) Beyond Limit: Ways to Growth and Freedom, 1983; contbg. author other psychol. texts. Home: 6155 Bluffwood Dr Riverside CA 92506-4605 Office: San Bernardino Valley Coll 701 S Mount Vernon Ave San Bernardino CA 92410-2705

MAULE, TAMARA LEE, optometrist; b. Spokane, Wash., Mar. 22, 1963; d. Donald and Tara (Pennington) M.; m. David Lee Fish, Aug. 24, 1991. BS, Stetson U., 1985; OD cum laude, So. Coll. Optometry, Memphis, 1989. Cert. optometric physician, Fla. Pvt. practice, Boca Raton, Fla., 1990—; mem. optometric adv. coun. Cole Vision Corp., Cleve., 1992-94. Operating editor O.D. Exch., 1994. Mem. Am. Optometric Assn., Fla. Optometric Assn., Paul Beach County Optometric Soc., Lions (past treas., sec., pres. Lake Worth, Lion of Yr. award 1992), Beta Sigma Kappa. Lutheran. Office: 8903 W Glades Rd Bay A1-4 Boca Raton FL 33433

MAULIK, NILANJANA, medical educator; b. Dec. 22, 1960. BS in Chemistry, St. Xavier's Coll., 1981; MS in Biochemistry, U. Coll. Sci., 1983, PhD in Biochemistry, 1990. Asst. prof. dept. surgery U. Conn. Sch. Medicine, Farmington, 1994—; lectr. in field. Jr. Rsch. fellow U. coll. Sci., Calcutta, India, 1983-85, Sr. Rsch. fellow, 1985-90, Postdoctoral fellow U. Conn. Sch. Medicine, 1992-92, Am. Heart fellow, 199294; Nat. Merit scholar, 1978; recipient Young Investigator award Am. Coll. Angiology, 1992, Internat. Soc. Angiology, 1994. Mem. Am. Soc. Biochemistry and Molecular Biology, Am. Heart Assn. (cardiovascular coun.), N.Y. Acad. Sci. Internat. Soc. Heart Rsch., Soc. Biol. Chemists, Indian Sci. Congress Assn. (life). Office: U Conn Sch Medicine Dept Surgery Farmington CT 06030-1110

MAULION, RICHARD PETER, psychiatrist; b. Rosario, Argentina, Sept. 2, 1949; s. Peter Henry and Vivien Ormsby (Gough) M.; m. Renee Vander Hayden de Maulion, July 24, 1982; 1 child, Maximillian. BS, Colegio Salesiano San Jose, Rosario, ARgentina, 1967; MD, U. Nacional de Rosario, 1980. Diplomate Am. Bd. Psychiatry and Neurology, Am. Acad. Psychoanalysis, Am. Acad. Addiction Medicine, Am. Acad. Pain Mgmt., Am. Bd. Forensic Examiners. Intern Kans. U., Kansas City, 1981-82; resident in psychiatry Tulane U., New Orleans, 1983-86, fellow in psychoanalytic medicine, 1984-87; pvt. practice gen. psychiatry Covington, La., 1986-87; pvt. practice psychiatry Ft. Lauderdale, 1987—; founder, med. dir. The Rose Inst., Ft. Lauderdale, Fla., 1988—; sec. med. exec. com., chmn. quality assurance com., The Retreat Hosp., Sunrise, Fla., 1994—; med. dir. Anxiety and Depression prog., CPC Ft. Lauderdale Hosp., 1989-90; med. dir. Acad. Medicine and Psychology, Ft. Lauderdale, 1988-89, CEPHAS Prog., HSA Greenbrier Neuropsychiat. Hosp., Covington, La., 1986-87, chief med. staff, 1987; clin. instr. psychiatry Tulane U. Med. Ctr., 1986-87; pres. med. exec. com., chief med. staff, chmn. quality assurance com. Retreat Hosp., 1992—; workshop speaker; radio program host The Rose Institute Hour; lectr. in field; cons. in field. Host ednl.-cmty. svc. radio program The Rose Inst. Hour, 1995—. Mem. pub. health com. for the Health and Human Svcs. Bd., Dist. 10; mem. alcohol, drugs and mental health com.. Fellow Am. Acad. Psychoanalysis, Am. Bd. Forensic Examiners, Interam. Coll. Physicians and Surgeons; mem. AMA, Am. Psychiat. Assn., Am. Acad. Psychoanalysis, Am. Soc. Clin. Hypnosis, Fla. Med. Assn. (Med. Speaker of Yr. award, 1st pl. radio, 2nd pl. t.v., 1990, del. 1993—), Fla. Psychiat. Soc. (coun. mem. 1993-94), Broward County Psychiat. Soc. (med. exec. com., pres. 1994-95), Broward County Med. Assn. (chmn. physicians recovery network com., bd. dirs.), Broward County Psychiat. Soc. (pres. 1993—), M.I.N.D. Home: PO Box 350033 Fort Lauderdale FL 33335-0033

MAUN, RICHARD ANGUS, surgeon; b. Detroit, Nov. 21, 1943; s. Mark Emmet and Eleanor Theresa (Wagner) M.; m. Barbara Ann Penland, Mar. 8, 1969; children: Mark Emmet II, Brendan Liam. BA, Yale U., 1965; MD, Columbia U., 1969. Diplomate Am. Bd. Surgery. Intern San Francisco Gen. Hosp., 1969-70; surgery resident U. Calif. Hosp., 1970-71, 73-74; ortho resident San Francisco Ortho Rsch., 1974-77; med. staff Presbyn. Hosp., Whittier, Calif., 1977—; chmn. dept. surgery Presbyn. Hosp., Whittier, 1986, chief of staff, 1990; chmn. regional admissions Am. Acad. Orthopedic Surgery, Whittier, 1988; med. staff Whittier Hosp., 1993—; assoc. clin. prof. surgery U. So. Calif., L.A., 1983—. Lt. comdr. USNR, 1971-73. Fellow ACS, Am. Acad. Ortho. Surgery; mem. Western Orthopaedic Assn. Home: Whittier Ortho Surgery 15141 E Whittier Rd Whittier CA 90603

MAUPAY, WALTER R., JR., healthcare company executive; b. Phila., Feb. 28, 1939; s. Walter R. Sr. and Margaret M. (Mueller) M.; children: Margaret E., Walter R. III. BS in pharmacy, Temple U., 1961; MBA, Lehigh U., 1970. Sales rep. Merck, Sharpe & Dohme, West Point, Pa., 1961-64, hosp. rep., 1964-68, sales mgr., 1968-71, mktg. mgr., 1971-80, nat. coord., 1980-84; v.p. healthcare Calgon Vestal, St. Louis, 1985-88, pres., 1988-95; bd. dirs. Kensey Nash, Exton, Mo., 1995—; chmn. C.V. Labs., London, 1989-94; bd.

dirs. Polymedica, Boston, 1990-94, Calgon Corp., Pitts., 1988-93. Mem. Lehigh Alumni Assn. Home: 328 Doulton Pl Saint Louis MO 63141

MAURER, BRIAN THOMAS, physician assistant; b. Pottsville, Pa., Aug. 27, 1953; s. Ronald Louis and Lorraine Mae Maurer; m. Maria Encarnacion Camiña, Apr. 8, 1976; children: Ian, Joshua, Sara, Emily. BS, Hahnemann U., Phila., 1979; MS, U. Hartford, 1983. Cert. physician asst. With Lancaster (Pa.) Neighborhood Health Ctr., 1979-81; pediatric physician asst. Mt. Sinai Hosp., Hartford, 1981-87, Gerald Calnen, M.D., Enfield, Conn., 1987-93, Enfield Pediatric Assocs., 1993—; clin. asst. prof. Hahnemann U., Phila., 1980-87. Fellow Am. Acad. Physician Assts., Conn. Acad. Physician Assts., Soc. Physician Assts. in Pediatrics. Episcopalian. Office: Enfield Pediatric Assoc 141-B Hazard Ave Enfield CT 06082

MAURER, HANS HILARIUS, pharmacology educator; b. Homburg, Germany, Nov. 25, 1950; s. Hilarius Andreas and Elisabeth (Greff) M.; m. Claudia Regina Kessler, Oct. 9, 1981; children: Christine, Johannes. Lic. in pharmacy, U. Saarland, Saarbrücken, Germany, 1977, PhD, 1983, Habilitation, 1988. Asst. prof. pharmacology U. Saarland, 1983-88, univ. lectr., 1988-92; prof. pharmacology/toxicology, head dept. toxicology U. Saarland, Hamburg, Germany, 1992—. Author: (with Pfleger and Weber) Mass Spectral and GC Data, 1985, 92, Mass Spectral Library, 1987, 2d edit., 1993, (with De Zeeuw, Franke, and Pfleger) Gas Chromatographic Retention Indices, 1992, (with Schaefer) Diagnosis and Therapy of Intoxications, 1993. Capt. M.C., German Army, 1977-78. Mem. German Pharm. Soc. (chpt. pres. 1990-92), Soc. Toxicology and Forensic Chemistry (treas. 1987—), Internat. Assn. Forensic Toxicologists, Internat. Assn. Therapeutic Drug Monitoring Clin. Toxicology, German Soc. Pharmacology and Toxicology, Toxicol. Soc. Belgium and Luxembourg, Lions Club Internat. Roman Catholic. Office: U Saarland, Univ Clinics, D-66421 Homburg Germany

MAURER, HAROLD MAURICE, pediatrician; b. N.Y.C., Sept. 10, 1936; s. Isador and Sarah (Rothkowitz) M.; m. Beverly Bennett, June 12, 1960; children: Ann Louise, Wendy Sue. A.B., N.Y. U., 1957; M.D., SUNY, Bklyn., 1961. Diplomate Am. Bd. Pediatrics, Am. Bd. Pediatric Hematology-Oncology. Intern pediatrics Kings County Hosp., N.Y.C., 1961-62; resident in pediatrics Babies Hosp., Columbia-Presbyn. Med. Center, N.Y.C., 1962-64; fellow in pediatric hematology/oncology Columbia-Presbyn. Med. Center, 1966-68; asst. prof. pediatrics Med. Coll. Va., Richmond, 1968-71; asso. prof. Med. Coll. Va., 1971-75, prof., 1975—, chmn. dept. pediatrics, 1976-93; dean U. Neb. Coll. Medicine, Omaha, 1993—; chmn. Intergroup Rhabdomyosarcoma Study; exec. com. Pediatric Oncology Group; mem. cancer clin. investigation rev. com. NIH. Editor: pediatrics, 1983, Rhabdomyosarcoma and Related Tumors in Children and Adolescence, 1991; mem. editorial bd. Am. Jour. Hematology, Journal Pediatric Hematology and Oncology, Medical and Pediatric Oncology, 1984—; contbr. articles to profl. jours. Mem. Youth Health Task Force, City of Richmond., Gov.'s Adv. Com. on Handicapped.; mem. nat. com. on childhood cancer Am. Cancer Soc., bd. dirs. Va. div. Served to lt. comdr. USPHS, 1964-66. NIH grantee, 1974—. Mem. Am. Acad. Pediatrics (com. oncology-hematology), Am. Soc. Hematology, Soc. Pediatric Rsch., Am. Pediatric Soc., Va. Pediatric Sic. (exec. com.), Assn. Med. Sch. Pediatric Dept. Chmn., Internat. Soc. Pediatric Oncology, Am. Soc. Clin. Oncology, Va. Hematology Soc., Am. Assn. Cancer Rsch., Am. Cancer Soc., Am. Soc. Pediatric Hematology (v.p. 1990-91, pres. 1991-93), Sigma Xi, Coun. Deans AAMC, Gov.'s Blue Ribbon Commn., Alpha Omega Alpha. Republican. Jewish. Home: 9822 Ascot Dr Omaha NE 68114-3848 Office: U Neb Coll Medicine 600 S 42nd St Omaha NE 68105-1002

MAURER, ROBERT (STANLEY), osteopathic physician; b. Bklyn., Feb. 10, 1933; s. Gustav and Hilda Maurer; A.B. in Chemistry, U. Pa., 1953; D.O., Phila. Coll. Osteo. Medicine, 1962; m. Beverly Greenberg, Sept. 4, 1960; children: Ellen Jo, David, Andrew. Cert. Am. Bd. Quality Assurance and Utilization Rev. Physicians, 1989, Am. Coll. Family Practice, 1977. Intern, Phila. Coll. Osteo. Medicine, 1962-63; gen. practice osteo. medicine, Woodbridge Twp., N.J., 1963-93; mem. med. staff JFK Med. Ctr., Edison, N.J., chmn. utilization rev., 1985-95; mem. med. staff Kennedy Med. Hosp., Stratford, N.J., 1992—; dir. Med. Inter-Ins. Exch. N.J., 1977-96; police and fire surgeon City Iselin; assoc. prof. clin. family medicine N.J. Sch. Osteo. Medicine; clin. asst. prof. Robert Wood Johnson Med. Sch.; dir. alumni affairs UMDNJ Sch. Osteo. Medicine, 1986-96. Mem. N.J. State Gov.'s Task Force on Med. Malpractice, 1985-89; chmn. legis. com. N.J. State Med. Underwriters, 1981-95; mem. Congl. Dist. Health Care Coun., 1994—; candidate for N.J. State Senate, 1983, for N.J. State Assembly, 1987. Lt. USNR, 1953-58; Korea. Named Physician of Yr., 1990; recipient Spl. Recognition award N.J. State Assembly, 1990. Fellow Am. Osteo. Coll. Rheumatology; (exec. sec. 1993-96), mem. VFW, N.J. Council Ambulatory Physicians (v.p. 1977-80), N.J. Assn. Osteo. Physicians and Surgeons (pres. 1976-77), Middlesex County Osteo. Soc. (pres. 1973-74), Am. Osteo. Assn., N.J. Osteo. Edn. Found. (pres. 1985-89), Physicians Rev. Orgn. (bd. dirs. N.J. 1987-96), Am. Coll. Utilization Rev. Physicians, Phila. Coll. Osteo. Medicine Alumni Assn. (pres. 1981, sec. 1991-96).

MAURISSEN, JACQUES PAUL JEAN, toxicologist; b. Liège, Belgium, Feb. 11, 1947; came to U.S., 1972; s. Paul and Hubertine (Albert) M.; m. Ghislaine Marcelle Dallemagne, July 22, 1972; 1 child, Stéphanie. MA in Psychology, U. Liège, 1970; PhD. in Toxicology, U. Rochester, 1979. Instr. U. Rochester, N.Y., 1980-82; sr. rsch. toxicologist The Dow Chem. Co., Midland, Mich., 1982-85, project leader, 1985-89, rsch. leader, 1989-93, rsch. assoc., 1993-95, assoc. scientist, 1995—; editorial bd. Neurotoxicology, 1986—. Contbr. articles to Toxicology, Neurosci., Computer Sci. Fellow APA; mem. Soc. Toxicology, Soc. for Neurosci., Int. Neurotoxicology Assn. Office: The Dow Chemical Co 1803 Bldg Toxicology Midland MI 48674

MAURO, KATHLEEN, pediatric nurse practitioner, clinical researcher; b. Fairview, N.J., Mar. 14, 1947; d. Gennaro J. and Catherine M. (Covone) Mauro; m. Martin L. Dresner, June 10, 1982; children: Kira, Kurt, Noah. BSN, Long Island U., 1970; MN, U. Wash., 1981; PhD, U. Mich., 1995. RN, Ariz.; cert. pediatric nurse practitioner. Commd. 2d lt. U.S. Army Nurse Corps, 1970, advanced through grades to lt. col., 1990, nurse practitioner, 1970-93, ret., 1993; clin. rschr., fellow U. Ariz., Tucson, 1995—. Civilian Tng. scholarships U.S. Army, 1979-81, 86-89; Rackham Dissertation grantee U. Mich., 1989. Fellow Nat. Assn. Pediatric Nurse Practitioners and Assocs. (pres. mil. chpt. 1990). Office: U Ariz Coll Nursing Nursing Dept Tucson AZ 85721

MAVES, MICHAEL DONALD, medical association executive; b. East St. Louis, Ill., Oct. 14, 1948. BS, U. Toledo, 1970; MD, Ohio State U., 1973; MBA, U. Iowa, 1988. Lic. physician, Iowa, Mo., Ill., D.C.; diplomate Am. Bd. Otolaryngology. Rsch. fellow Ohio State U. Coll. Medicine, Columbus, 1977; fellow head and neck surgery Columbia-Presbyn. Med. Ctr., N.Y.C., 1978, U. Iowa Hosps. and Clinics, Iowa City, 1980-81; asst. prof. otolaryngology, head and neck surgery Ind. U. Sch. Medicine, Indpls., 1981-84; asst. prof. otolaryngology, head and neck surgery U. Iowa Hosps. and Clinics, Iowa City, 1984-87, assoc. prof., 1987-88; chmn. dept. otolaryngology St. Louis U. Sch. Medicine, St. Louis, 1988-94; exec. v.p. Am. Acad. Otolaryngology, Head and Neck Surgery, Alexandria, Va., 1994—; lectr. in field. Contbr. articles to profl. jours. Capt. U.S. Army, 1974-76. Recipient numerous awards including Honor award and Pres.'s award Am. Acad. Otolaryngology-Head and Neck Surgery; named one of Best 1000 Physicians in U.S., 1992, 94, One of Best 400 Cancer Doctors in Am., Good Housekeeping, 1992. Fellow ACS; mem. AMA (RBRVS update com.), Am. Cancer Soc., others. Office: Am Acad Otolaryngology One Prince St Alexandria VA 22314

MAVROS, GEORGE S., clinical laboratory director; b. Adelaide, Australia, Oct. 14, 1957; came to U.S., 1970; s. Sotirios George and Angeliki (Korogiannis) M.; m. Renee Ann Cuddeback, June 24, 1979. BA in Microbiology, U. South Fla., 1979, MS in Microbiology, 1987; MBA, Nova U., 1991; PhD in Health Sci. Mgmt., LaSalle U., 1995. Cert. lab. dir. Nat. Certifying Agy. for Clin. Lab. Pers.; diplomate Am. Coll. Health Care Execs. Med. technologist Jackson Meml. Hosp., Dade City, Fla., 1979-81; microbiology supr. HCA Bayonet Point-Hudson Med. Ctr., Hudson, Fla., 1981-82, dir. labs., 1982-88; lab. mgr., adminstrv. and tch. dir. Citrus Meml. Hosp., Inverness, Fla., 1988—; lab. cons. HCA Oak Hill Hosp., Spring Hill, Fla., 1983-84; cons. lab. info. systems Citation Computer Systems, St. Louis, 1983—, Hosp. Corp. of Am., Nashville, 1986; instr. Microbiology Pasco Hernando Com. Coll., New Port Richey, Fla., 1986-88, Inst. Biolog. Scis. Cen. Fla. Community Coll., Lecanto, 1989—; bd. dirs. Gulf Coast chpt. Clin. Lab. Mgrs. Assn., Tampa, Fla., 1987, pres., 1987-89. Parish pres. Greek Orthodox Ch. of West Cen., Inverness, Fla.; chmn. Bayonet Point Hosp. Good Govt. Group, Hudson, 1986-88. Mem. APHA, Am. Mgmt. Assn., Am. Soc. Microbiology, Am. Soc. Clin. Pathologists (cert. in lab. mgmt.), Am. Soc. Med. Technologists (cert.), Fla. Soc. Med. Technologists, Clin. Lab. Mgmt. Assn. (pres. Gulf Coast chpt. 1988-90), Am. Assn. Clin. Chemists, Am. Acad. Microbiology (cert.), Fla. State Bd. Clin. Lab. Pers. (chmn. 1994). Democrat. Clubs: Greek Orthodox Youth Am. (Clearwater, Fla.). Lodges: Order of DeMolay, Sons of Pericles (sec.). Home: 6 Byrsonima Ct W Homosassa FL 34446-4610 Office: Citrus Meml Hosp 502 W Highland Blvd Inverness FL 34452-4720

MAXA, ROBERT L., physician; b. Pitts., July 19, 1951; s. Robert L. and Elfrida Erna (Zech) M.; m. Rhonda Reese Hood, Dec. 4, 1976; children: Aaron Robert, Allison Rebecca, Bradley William. BS, Gannon U., 1975; postgrad., Edinboro State U., 1980-83; DO, Kirksville Coll. of Osteo. Medicine, 1987. Diplomate Am. Bd. Osteo. Family Physicians. Pvt. practice Erie, Pa., 1989-95; ptnr., owner Presque Isle Family Practice, Erie, 1995—; mem. staff Metro Health Ctr., Erie, 1989-95, chief of staff, 1993, 94, bd. dirs., 1993, 94; mem. tchg. faculty Phila. Coll. Osteopathy, Kirksville Coll. Osteopathy, Lake Erie Coll. Osteopathy. Bd. dirs. ARC, Erie, 1991. Mem. AMA, Am. Coll. Osteo. Family Physicians, Am. Osteo. Assn., Pa. Osteo. Med. Assn., Pa. Med. Assn., Erie County Med. Assn. Republican. Lutheran. Office: Presque Isle Family Medicine 2564 W 12th St Erie PA 16505

MAXIMOVICH, STANLEY PAUL, plastic and reconstructive surgeon; b. Chgo., June 17, 1957. BS in Biology with honors, Brown U., 1979; MD, Rush U., 1983. Bd. cert. Am. Bd. Plastic Surgery. Gen. surgery tng. Loyola U. Med. Ctr., Maywood, Ill., 1983-86, plastic surgery tng., 1986-89; pvt. practice Hinsdale, Ill., 1989—. Contbr. articles to profl. jours. Mem. AMA, Am. Coll. Surgeons, Am. Soc. Plastic and Reconstructive Surgeons, Ill. State Med. Soc., Chgo. Med. Soc. Office: 40 S Clay St Ste 237 W Hinsdale IL 60521

MAXSON, MARK JAY, engineer; s. Dale E. and Nancy H. BS in Indsl. Engring., Iowa State U., 1975; MA in Orgn. and Mgmt., U. Phoenix, 1994; postgrad., Stanford U., 1994. Mfg. engr. Harnischfeger, Cedar Rapids, Iowa, 1975-77; plant engr. Square D, Cedar Rapids, 1977-87; facility mgr. Lifescan, a Johnson & Johnson Co., Milipitas, Calif., 1987-91, staff engr., 1991—. Mem. Internat. Pers. Mgmt. Assn. Office: Lifescan Johnson & Johnson Co 1000 Gibraltar Dr Milpitas CA 95035

MAXWELL, LEO CHAMBERS, physiologist; b. Ithaca, N.Y., Nov. 28, 1941; s. Rodney Leroy and Caroline (Chambers) M.; m. Ann Christine DeDell, Aug. 22, 1965; children: Daniel, Laura. BS, SUNY, Cortland, 1965, MS, 1966; PhD, U. Mich., 1971. Rsch. investigator U. Mich., Ann Arbor, 1974-77, asst. rsch. scientist, 1977-79; asst. prof. U. Tex. Health Sci. Ctr., San Antonio, 1979-83, assoc. prof., 1983—. Recipient Outstanding Internat. Student Advisor award, 1989. Mem. Am. Heart Assn., Am. Physiol. Soc., Am. Coll. Sports Medicine. Office: U Tex Health Sci Ctr 7703 Floyd Curl Dr San Antonio TX 78284-6200

MAXWELL, ROBERT ALLAN, JR., internist, oncologist, hematologist; b. Leavenworth, Kans., Apr. 2, 1933; s. Robert Allan and Aileen Wyman (Bowers) M.; m. Elsa June Lahr, Aug. 4, 1962; children: Carolyn Lahr, Jennifer Anne, Robert Allan III. BA, Yale U., 1954; MD, U. Louisville, 1958. Diplomate Am. Bd. Internal Medicine, subspecialty med. oncology and hematology. Assoc. physician Abington (Pa.) Meml. Hosp., 1968-82; internship Thomas Jefferson Univ. Hosp., Phila, 1958-59, residency, 1959-62; fellowship in hematology Charlotte Drake Cardeza Found. Thomas Jefferson Univ. Hosp., 1962-63; sr. physician Abington (Pa.) Meml. Hosp., 1982—. Pres. Am. Cancer Soc., Abington br., 1979-81. Capt. USAR, 1963-65. Mem. Montgomery County Med. Soc., St. Andrews Soc. Phila., Huntingdon Valley Country Club. Republican. Episcopalian. Home: 1450 Stockton Rd Meadowbrook PA 19046-1131 Office: Abington Hematology Oncology 1245 Highland Ave Abington PA 19001-3714

MAY, BRETT ALAN, psychologist; b. Grand Rapids, Mich., Aug. 29, 1962; s. Melvyn Virgil and Patricia Mae (Bloomfield) M.; m. Lisa Beth Owen, Nov. 3, 1984; children: Brittany Lee, Rebecca Anne. BS in Psychology with honors, Mich. State U., 1985, MA in Clin. Psychology, 1988, PhD in Clin. Psychology, 1992. Lic. psychologist, Mich. Primary prevention coord., sexual assault prevention program Mich. State U., East Lansing, 1988-90, instr., 1990-91; intern in psychology Pine Rest Christian Hosp., Grand Rapids, 1991-92, clin. psychologist, 1992—; mental health therapist Cmty. Support Svcs., Lansing, Mich., 1991-95; mem. faculty Pine Rest ADD Inst., Grand Rapids, 1995—; dir. Pine Rest Psychol. Consultation Ctr., 1996—. Contbr. articles to profl. jours. Named Outstanding Young Men of Am., 1989; recipient Robert P. O'Neil award Mich. Psychol. Assn., 1990; grantee Pine Rest Found., 1992-94, Frye Found., 1995. Office: Pine Rest Christian Hosp 300 68th St SE Grand Rapids MI 49501

MAY, EVERETTE LEE, pharmacologist, educator; b. Timberville, Va., Aug. 1, 1914; married, 1940; 4 children. AB, Bridgewater Coll., 1935; PhD in Organic Chemistry, U. Va., 1939. Rsch. chemist Nat. Oil Products Co., 1939-41; from assoc. chemist to sr. chemist NIH, 1941-53; from scientist to sr. scientist Commd. Corps., 1953-58, scientist dir., 1959; chief sect. med. chemistry Nat. Inst. Arthritis and Metabolic Disorders, USPHS, 1960-78; adj. prof. pharmacology Med. Coll. Va., 1974-77, prof. pharmacology, 1977—; mem. expert adv. panel, 1958-78; chem. adv. panel mem. Walter Reed Army Inst., 1965—; ad hoc review com. Nat. Cancer Inst., 1978. Mem. Am. Chem. Soc. (E.E. Smissman award 1979, Nathan B. Eddy Meml. award 1981, Alfred Burger Medicinal Chemistry award 1992). Home: 1626 Logwood Cir Richmond VA 23233

MAY, JAMES M., medical educator, medical researcher; b. Oklahoma City, Aug. 20, 1947; married; 2 children. BS, Yale Coll., 1969; MD, Vanderbilt U., 1973. Diplomate Am. Bd. Internal Medicine, Am. Bd. Endocrinology and Metabolism. Intern Vanderbilt U., Nashville, 1973-74, assoc. prof. medicine, 1986—, assoc. prof. molecular physiology and biophysics, 1993—; resident in medicine Johns Hopkins Hosp., Balt., 1974-75; fellow in endocrinology U. Wash., Seattle, 1975-78; asst. prof. medicine Med. Coll. Va., Richmond, 1978-83, assoc. prof. medicine, 1983-86; mem. award com. dept. medicine Vanderbilt U., 1992—; mem. awards com. Summer Diabetes Program, Diabetes Rsch. and Tng. Ctr., 1994—. Mem. editl. bd. Metabolism, 1996—; contbr. articles to profl. jours. Recipient Nat. Rsch. Svc. award NIH, 1975-78, grantee, 1993, 95; recipient Poncin Fund award, 1975-78. Mem. Am. Diabetes Assn. (pres. Va. affiliate 1985-86, chmn. rsch. com. Tenn. affiliate 1990-92, Rsch. award 1996), Am. Fedn. Clin. Rsch. (sec.-treas. So. sect. 1983-86, nat. councilor 1983-88, pres.- elect and pres. 1986-88), Am. Soc. Clin. Investigation, So. Soc. Clin. Investigation, Alpha Omega Alpha. Office: Vanderbilt U Med Ctr Divsn Endocrinology & Diabetes 715 Med Rsch Bldg II Nashville TN 37232-6303

MAY, MARGRETHE, allied health educator; b. Tucson, Ariz., Oct. 6, 1943; d. Robert A. and Margrethe (Holm) M. BS in Human Biology, U. Mich., 1970, MS in Anatomy, 1986. Cert. surg. technologist. Surg. technologist Hartford (Conn.) Hosp., 1965-68, U. Mich. Hosps., Ann Arbor, 1968-70; asst. operating room supr. U. Ariz. Med. Ctr., Tucson 1971-72; coord. operating room tech. program Pima Coll., Tucson, 1971-76; prof., coord. surg. tech. and surg. first asst. programs Delta Coll., University Center, Mich., 1978—; commr. Commn. on Accreditation of Allied Health Ednl. Programs, Chgo., 1994—, Coun. Accreditation and Unit Recognition, 1994-96. Editor: Core Curriculum for Surgical Technology, 3d edit., 1990, Core Curriculum for Surgical First Assisting, 1993; contbr. articles to profl. jours. Mem. Assn. Surg. Technologists (bd. dirs. 1987-89, pres.-elect 1989-90, pres. 1990-91, on-site visitor program accreditation 1974—, chmn. exam writing com. 1981, liaison coun. on cert. co-chmn. 1977, chmn. 1978, sec.-treas. 1979, chmn. accreditation review com for edn. in surg. tech. 1994—), Am. Soc. Law, Medicine and Ethics, Mich. Assn. Allied Health Professions (sec. 1994—), Nat. Network Health Career Programs in Two-Year Colls. Home: 2506 Abbott Rd Apt P-2 Midland MI 48642-4876 Office: Delta Coll Allied Health Divsn University Center MI 48710

MAY, STEPHEN JAMES, pharmacist; b. London, May 2, 1963; s. James Robert and Margaret Dorothy Holmes M. BPharm, Bath U., 1984. Prereg. pharmacist East Berkshire Health Authority, 1984-85; resident pharmacist Leicester Gen. Hosp., 1985-87; pharmacist Regional Drug Information Ctr., Leicester, 1987-88; sr. info. pharmacist Univ. Hosp. Queens Med. Ctr., Nottingham, 1988—. producer: (computerized drug info. database software) Di-Scan, 1993, (pharmacy intervention program) PILS, 1995. Mem. UKCPA, Guild of Hosp. Pharmacists (local rep. 1988—). Mem. Ch. of England. Office: Drug Info Ctr-Pharmacy Dept Univ Hosp, Queens Med Ctr, NG7 2UM Nottingham England

MAY, TODD JAY, osteopath; b. Cedar City, Utah, Oct. 29, 1965; s. Jay Allen and Elma Jean (Alldredge) M.; m. Juanita Johns, Mar. 23, 1991; children: Alexia JoAnne, Sydney Morgan. BS, So. Utah U., 1990; DO, Coll. Osteo. Medicine, 1994. Tchg. asst. Coll. Osteo. Medicine, Pomona, Calif., 1991-92; resident U. Nev. Sch. Medicine, Las Vegas, 1994—, chief resident, 1996—; asst. team physician U. Nev. Las Vegas, 1995—. Cub master Boy Scouts Am., Las Vegas, 1996—. Lt. USNR Med. Corps, 1994—. Mem. Am. Acad. Family Practice, Am. Osteopath Assn., Am. Osteopath Acad. of Sports Medicine, Assn. Mil. Osteo. Physicians and Surgeons, N.Am. Hunting Club. Republican. Mem. LDS Ch. Office: Dept Family & Cmty Medicine 6375 W Charleston Blvd Las Vegas NV 89102

MAY, VIRGINIA ANNE, physical therapist; b. Washington, Mar. 25, 1951. AAS in Phys. Therapy Asst., No. Va. C.C., Annandale, 1979; BS in Phys. Therapy, Old Dominion U., 1988, MS in Pediat. Phys. Therapy, 1994. Lic. phys. therapist, Va.; cert. pediat. clin. specialist. Phys. therapy asst., phys. therapist Therapy Assocs., Norfolk, Va., 1984-89; phys. therapy asst. Practical Care, Virginia Beach, Va., 1984-88, Virginia Beach (Va.) Health Dept., 1984-88, Commonwealth Health Care, Virginia Beach, 1984-88; phys. therapist Children's Home Health, Norfolk, 1988—; staff phys. therapist Children's Hosp. Kings Daus., Norfolk, 1989-92; staff phys. therapist neonatal ICU Virginia Beach (Va.) Gen. Hosp., 1992; owner Beach Phys. Therapy 4 Kids, Virginia Beach, 1993—; lectr. and mem. various coms. Old Dominion U., Norfolk, Va., 1994—. Mem. Am. Phys. Therapy Assn. (regional coord. affiliate affairs 1982, mem. on-site accreditation team phys. therapy asst. programs 1983-88, chmn. affiliate spl. interest group 1983, mem. nat. conf. planning com. 1986-88), Va. Phys. Therapy Assn. (del. 1992, 94, 95, 96, chmn. membership com. Tidewater dist. 1989-92, chmn. quality assurance/reimbursement com. Tidewater dist. 1988-89, chmn. task force on utilization of the phys. therapy asst. 1990-92, v.p. pediat. spl. interest group 1994-96, mem. ethics com. Tidewater dist. 1995—, task force on vols. in action 1995-96, bd. dirs. Tidewater dist. 1992-96, others), Neuro-Devel. Treatment Assn., Virginia Beach Interagency Coordinating Coun. Home: 2276 Trant Lake Dr Virginia Beach VA 23454 Office: Sch Cmty Health Professions& Phys Therapy Old Dominion Univ Norfolk VA 23529-0288

MAYBERG, MARC R., neurosurgeon; b. Mpls., Feb. 25, 1951; s. Donald MacMillan and LaVerle (Wright) M.; m. Teresa Slee, Sept. 7, 1991; 1 child, Matthew MacMillan. BA, Harvard U., 1974; MD, Mayo Med. Sch., Rochester, Minn., 1984. Diplomate Am. Bd. Neurol. Surgery, Nat. Bd. Med. Examiners. Intern in surgery Tufts-New England Med. Ctr., Boston, 1978-79; resident in neurosurgery Mass. Gen. Hosp., Boston, 1979-84; fellow Nat. Hosp. for Nervous Diseases, London, 1985; from asst. prof. to prof. neurol. surgery U. Wash., Seattle, 1989-90; adj. prof. U. Washington, 1992—; asst. chief neurosurgery Seattle Vet. Adminstrn. Med. Ctr., 1989—;. Editl. bd. Stroke, 1991—, Neurosurgery, 1991—, Perspectives in Neurosurgery, 1988—, Stroke Clin. Updates, 1994—, Jour. Stroke & Cerebrovasc. Disease, 1990—, Videotape Jour. CNS, 1990—, JAMA, 1988—. Grantee NIH, 1987—, Vet. Adminstrn., 1986—. Fellow Am. Coll. Surgeons, Am. Heart Assn.; mem. AMA, Am. Assn. Neurol. Surgeons, Congress Neurol. Surgeons, Am. Acad. Neurol. Surgeons, Wash. State Neurol. Soc., Internat. Skull Base Soc. Office: U Wash Dept Neurosurgery 1959 NE Pacific St Seattle WA 98295

MAYBERRY, WILLIAM EUGENE, retired physician; b. Cookeville, Tenn., Aug. 22, 1929; s. Henry Eugene and Beatrice Lucille (Maynard) M.; m. Jane G. Foster, Dec. 29, 1953; children: Ann Graves, Paul Foster. Student, Tenn. Tech. U., 1947-49; M.D., U. Tenn., 1953; M.S. in Medicine, U. Minn., 1959; D.H.L. (hon.), Jacksonville U., 1983. Diplomate Am. Bd. Internal Medicine. Intern U.S. Naval Hosp., Phila., 1953-54; resident Mayo Grad. Sch. Medicine, Rochester, Minn., 1956-59; mem. staff New Eng. Med. Ctr., Boston, 1959-60, Nat. Inst. Arthritis and Metabolic Diseases, 1962-64; cons. internal medicine, endocrine research and lab. medicine, chmn. dept. lab. medicine Mayo Clinic, Rochester, 1971-75, bd. govs., 1971-87, vice chmn., 1974-75, chmn., chief exec. officer, 1976-87, prof. lab. medicine, 1971—, prof. medicine, 1983-92; asst. in medicine Tufts U. Med. Sch., 1959-60; mem. faculty Mayo Grad. Sch. Medicine and Mayo Med. Sch., 1960-92; trustee Mayo Found., 1971-87, vice chmn., 1974-85, pres. 1986-87, chmn. bd. devel. 1988—; trustee Minn. Mut. Life Ins., 1983-92; bd. dirs. George A. Hormel & Co., 1986-92. Mem. editorial bd. (Jour. of Clin. Endocrinology and Metabolism), 1971-73; contbr. articles to profl. jours. Trustee Mpls. Soc. Fine Arts, 1983-91, Cumberland U., 1984-86, Twin Cities Pub. TV, Inc., 1991-92, trustee, 1991-92; bd. overseers Mpls. Coll. Art and Design, 1983-86, U. Minn. Sch. Mgmt., 1985-88; bd. dirs. Greater Rochester Area Univ. Ctr., 1986-87, Minn. Acad. Excellence Found., 1986-87, U.S. West-Minn. Exec. Bd., 1988-92; rep. Congl. Dist. I State of Minn. Compensation Council, 1986; chmn. Presdl. Commn. on Human Immunodeficiency Virus Epidemic, 1987. Recipient Disting. Alumni award Tenn. Technol. U., 1976, chair of excellence in bus. adminstrn. named in his honor, 1989; recipient Outstanding Alumni award U. Tenn., 1982, Med. Exec. Award Am. Coll. Med. Group Adminstrs., 1986; rsch. fellow NIH, 1959-60, Am. Cancer Soc., 1962-64; NIH research grantee, 1965-71. Fellow ACP; mem. Inst. Medicine of NAS, Am. Thyroid Assn., Am. Clin. and Climatological Soc., Endocrine Soc., Soc. Med. Adminstrs., Am. Acad. Med. Dirs., Am. Coll. Physician Execs. (bd. regents 1983, vice chmn. 1985-86), Sigma Xi. Clubs: Mpls. Club, Rochester Golf & Country, The Club at Pelican Bay (Naples, Fla.). Home: 826 Rue De Vl Naples FL 33963-8531 Office: Emeritus Siebens 9 200 1st St SW Rochester MN 55905-0001*

MAYEDA, KAZUTOSHI, biologist, educator; b. Santa Monica, Calif., June 17, 1928; s Haruju and Kohana (Matsuuchi) M.; m. Miwako Shimizu Waki, June 1949; children: Karen, Kathy, Michael. BS, U. Utah, 1957, MS, 1958, PhD, 1961. Diplomate Am. Bd. Med. Genetics. Asst. prof. biology Wayne State U., Detroit, 1961-66, assoc. prof., 1966-72, prof., 1972—; dir. cytogenetics Oakwood Hosp, Dearborn, Mich., 1987—; rsch. assoc. Nat. Inst. Genetics of Japan, Mishima, 1970-71; genetic counselor Mott Ctr., Wayne State U. Med. Sch., 1976-87; genetics cons. Children's Hosp. of Mich., Detroit, 1975—. Bd. dirs. Am. Citizens for Justice, Detroit, 1988—; pres. Detroit JACL, 1970, 75, 80, 85, 90, v.p. Nat. JACL, San Francisco, 1980-82; mem. Japanese Am. Citizens League. Sgt. U.S. Army, 1958-60. Recipient Grad. award Sigma Xi, 1961; named to Ethnic Hall of Fame, Internat. Inst. of Detroit, 1987.

MAYER, BERNADETTE BERVIN, physician; b. Aug. 30, 1954; d. Gabriel and Carmela (Meo) Bervin; m. Wolfgang Mayer, June 19, 1975; children: Nicole, Anthony, Elizabeth. BS in Biology with honors, U. Ill., 1977, MD, 1981. Diplomate Am. Bd. Internal Medicine. Internship Ill. Masonic Med. Ctr., Chgo., 1982-83, residency, 1982-85; physician Resurrection Immediate Care Ctr., Chgo., 1985-90, Michael Reese (Humana) HMO, Chgo., 1990-94; pvt. practice Resurrection Med. Ctr., Chgo., 1994—; module leader Michael Reese HMO, 1991-94. Mem. AMA, Chgo. Med. Soc., Ill. State Med. Soc. Office: Bernadette Mayer M D 5365 W Devon Ave Chicago IL 60646

MAYER, DAVID ALAN, general and vascular surgeon; b. Jan. 24, 1950. BA suma cum laude, Lafayette Coll., Pa., 1970; MD, Cornell U. Med. Coll., N.Y.C., 1974. Lic. N.Y. 1975, Fla. 1978. Fellow in surgery Meml. Hosp. Sloan Kettering Cancer Ctr., 1977-78; resident in surgery The N.Y. Hosp. Cornell Med. Ctr., 1973-78; gen. and vascular surgeon Huntington Med. Group, 1978—; dir. surg. ICU; instr. in surgery SUNY, U. Hosp. at Stony Brook; clin. affiliate in surgery The N.Y. Hosp., Cornell Med. Ctr.; clin. assoc. prof. surgery N.Y. Med. Coll. Contbr. articles and presentations to profl. jours. Fellow ACS, Internat. Coll. Surgeons, Am. Soc. Abdominal

Surgeons, Am. Coll. Angiology, Soc. for Minimally Invasive Therapy, N.Y. Metro. Breast Cancer Group, Soc. Am. Gastrointestinal Endoscopic Surgeons, Am. Soc. Gen. Surgeons, Surg. Soc. of The N.Y. Med. Coll. Home: 18 Wayside Ln Lloyd Harbor NY 11743 Office: Huntington Med Group 180 E Pulaski Rd Huntington Station NY 11746

MAYER, IRA EDWARD, gastroenterologist; b. Bklyn., July 31, 1951; s. Elias M. and Mollie (Taxerman) M.; m. Celeste Ann Sivak, Mar. 13, 1976; children: Madelaine Rose, Amanda Beth. BS, Bklyn. Coll., 1972; MD, N.Y. Med. Coll., 1975. Diplomate Am. Bd. Internal Medicine, Am. Bd. Gastroenterology, Nat. Bd. Med. Examiners. Asst. resident in internal medicine N.Y. Med. Coll., 1975-76; resident in internal medicine Met. Hosp. Ctr., N.Y.C., 1976-78; fellow Digestive Diseases div. Emory U., Atlanta, 1978-80; assoc. attending gastroenterologist Maimonides Med. Ctr., Bklyn., 1980—, chmn. patient care com., 1984—; clin. instr. medicine SUNY Health Sci. Ctr., Bklyn., 1980-81, instr. medicine, 1981-83, clin. asst. prof. medicine, 1983—. Author: (with others) Digestive Diseases, 1983, Medicine, 1983; contbr. articles to profl. jours. Fellow ACP, Am. Coll. Gastroenterology; mem. Am. Gastroent. Assn., Am. Soc. for Gastrointestinal Endoscopy, N.Y. Acad. Scis., N.Y. Acad. Gastroenterolgy, N.Y. Soc. for Gastrointestinal Endoscopy, Med. Soc. for the State of N.Y. Jewish. Office: 2560 Ocean Ave Brooklyn NY 11229-4507

MAYER, JACQUELINE P., managed care administrator; b. Bklyn., Oct. 15, 1957; d. Frank and Vincenza (Cusamano) Pepine; m. Walter Mayer, Apr. 21, 1979; 1 child, Walter Jr. BA, Am. Internat. Coll., 1978; MA, Hofstra U., 1987. Asst. adminstr. Cmty. Health Plan, New Hyde Park, N.Y., 1988-92; mgr. instnl. contracting Empire Blue Cross Blue Shield, N.Y.C., 1988-93; managed care coord. L.I. Jewish Hosp., New Hyde Park, 1992-93; dir. provider rels. Health Ins. Plan of Greater N.Y., N.Y.C., 1993-95; exec. dir. Beth Israel Physician Hosp. Orgn., N.Y.C., 1995—. Mem. Healthcare Fin. Mgmt. Assn. Office: Beth Israel PHO 1st Ave at 16th St New York NY 10003

MAYER, LAWRENCE S., biostatistician, epidemiologist; b. Milw., Nov. 14, 1946; s. Andrew Gabriel and Goldie (Goldman) M.; m. Sally Roberts, Dec. 1, 1985. BS, BA, Ohio State U., 1967, 68, MS, 1969, MD, 1970, PhD, 1971; MA, U. Pa., 1980. Asst. prof. Va. Poly. Inst., Blacksburg, 1971-73; assoc. prof. Princeton U., 1973-79; assoc. prof. and dir. Wharton Sch., U. Pa., Phila., 1979-83; vis. scholar Stanford U., Palo Alto, Calif., 1982-83; Erskine fellow U. Canterbury, N.Z., 1989; med. dir. Office of Rsch. Good Samaritan Med. Ctr., Phoenix, 1983—; prof. biostats. Ariz. State U., Phoenix, 1983—; adj. prof. Sch. Pub. Helath and Medicine, Johns Hopkins U., Balt., 1990—; cons. in field. Contbr. articles to profl. jours. Mem. com. on malpractice reform Ariz. Supreme Ct., 1989-93. Fellow Royal Statis. Soc. London; mem. Soc. for Epidemiologic Rsch., Am. Statis. Soc., Biometric Soc., AAAS, Am. Pub. Health Assn., Phi Beta Kappa. Home: 3607 N 55th Pl Phoenix AZ 85018-4545 Office: 1300 N 12th St Ste 509 Phoenix AZ 85006

MAYER, PATRICIA LYNN SORCI, mental health nurse, educator; b. Chgo., July 22, 1942; d. Ben and Adonia (Grenier) Sorci; 1 child, Christopher David Mayer. AGS with high honors, Pima Community Coll., Tucson, 1983; BSN with honors, U. Ariz., 1986, MS in Nursing, 1987. RN, Ariz.; cert. addictions counselor, chem. dependency therapist; lic. pvt. pilot. Nurse educator Tucson. Contbr. articles to profl. jours. Mem. Nat. Nurses Soc. on Addictions, Phi Kappa Phi, Sigma Theta Tau, Pi Lambda Theta, Golden Key.

MAYER, PETER PAUL, physician, geriatric medicine consultant; b. Nottingham, Eng., May 25, 1943; s. Martin Wilhelm and Clara (Feibelman) M.; m. Janet Mary Emery, Aug. 12, 1969 (div. Jan. 1993); children: David, Andrew, Timothy, Christopher. BA in Animal Physiology, Oxford U., 1965, MA in Animal Physiology, 1968. Jr. med. tng. Nat. Health Svc., Birmingham, 1968-74; sen. reg. geriatric medicine East Birmingham Hosp., 1974-75; clin. lectr. geriatric medicine U. Birmingham, 1975-77; cons. in geriatric medicine South/Cen. Birmingham Health Authority, 1977—; dir. clin. svc. geriatric medicine South Birmingham Health Authority, Birmingham, 1986-92; dir. clin. strategy elderly svcs. Southern Birmingham Community Health Trust, 1992—; chmn., mem. svcs. com. West Midlands Regional Health Authority, Birmingham, 1990—; chmn. Crossroads Care, South Birmingham, 1991—; asst. dir. West Midlands Inst. Geriatric Medicine, Birmingham, 1989-93, dir., 1993—; mem. editorial bd. TRIPOD. Contbr. articles to profl. jours. Com. mem. local Liberal Party, Birmingham, 1969-70. State scholar Ministry of Edn., 1961, Goldsmid Entrance scholar Univ. Coll. Hosp., London, 1965; Churchill Found. fellow, 1988; rsch. grantee West Midlands R.H.A., Chest Heart Stroke Found., 1990. Fellow Royal Coll. Physicians; mem. Brit. Med. Assn., Midland Med. Soc. (sec. 1989-92, pres. 1992-93), Brit. Geriatrics Soc. (policy com., audit facilitator 1988-95, chmn. spl. interest group on health promotion 1994—), Prospect Hall (bd. dirs. 1980—), Birmingham Care Units (bd. dirs. 1991-92), Birmingham Age Concern (exec. com. 1989-92), Brit. Geriatrics Soc., Rotary (Edgbaston Conv. 1990—). Jewish. Home: 16 Bryony Rd, Selly Oak, Birmingham B29 4BU, England Office: Dept Geriatric Medicine, Selly Oak Hosp Raddlebarn 121, Birmingham B29 6JT, England

MAYER, RICHARD EDWIN, psychology educator; b. Chgo., Feb. 8, 1947; s. James S. and Bernis (Lowy) M.; m. Beverly Linn Pastor, Dec. 19, 1971; children: Kenneth Michael, David Mark, Sarah Ann. BA with honors, Miami U., Oxford, Ohio, 1969; MS in Psychology, U. Mich., 1971, PhD in Psychology, 1973. Vis. asst. prof. Ind. U., Bloomington, 1973-75; asst. prof. psychology U. Calif., Santa Barbara, 1975-80, assoc. prof., 1980-85, prof., 1985—, pres., chmn. dept., 1987-90; vis. scholar Learning Rsch. and Devel. Ctr., U. Pitts., 1979, Ctr. for Study of Reading, U. Ill., 1984. Author: Foundations of Learning and Memory, 1979, The Promise of Cognitive Psychology, 1981, Thinking, Problem Solving, Cognition, 1983, 2d edit., 1992, BASIC: A Short Course, 1985, Educational Psychology, 1987; editor: Human Reasoning, 1980, Teaching and Learning Computer Programming, 1988; editor jours. Instructional Sci., 1983-87, Educational Psychologist, 1983-89. Sch. bd. officer Goleta (Calif.) Union Sch. Dist., 1981—. NSF grantee, 1975-88. Fellow APA (divsn. 15 officer 1987—, G. Stanley Hall lectr. 1988), Am. Psychol. Soc.; mem. Am. Ednl. Rsch. Assn. (divsn. C officer 1986-88), Psychonomic Soc. Democrat. Jewish. Office: U Calif Dept Of Psychology Santa Barbara CA 93016

MAYER, RICHARD FREDERICK, neurologist, educator; b. Olean, N.Y., June 2, 1929; s. Frank W. and Rosemond F. (Bush) M.; m. Janet R. Bury, Oct. 10, 1959; children: Kathryn, Andrea, Julianna, Christopher, Randall. BS, St. Bonaventure U., 1950; MD, SUNY, Buffalo, 1954. Diplomate Am. Bd. Psychiatry and Neurology. Fellow in neurology Mayo Clinic, Rochester, Minn., 1955-56; clin. fellow Harvard Med. Sch., Boston, 1956-60, rsch. assoc. in neurology, 1960-66; prof. neurology U. Md. Medical Sch., Balt., 1966—; rsch. fellow U. London Nat. Hosp., 1958-59; guest worker NIH, Bethesda, Md., 1975-76; mem. Myasthenia Gravis Found., N.Y.C., 198—, Charcot-Marie-Tooth Med. Found., N.Y.C., 1989—. Contbr. rsch. articles to Clin. Neurophysiology, Pathophysiology of the Motor Unit, Studies in Myasthenia Gravis, Pathophysiology of Peripheral Nerve, Treatment in Guillain Barre Syndrome. Lt. USN, 1958-60. Grantee NIH, 1968-75, 85-93; recipient cert. VA Med. Bd., Washington, 1982. Fellow Am. Acad. Neurology; mem. Am. Neurol. Assn., Am. Assn. Neuropathologists, Soc. Neurosci. Democrat. Roman Catholic. Office: U Md Med Ctr 22 S Greene St Baltimore MD 21201-1544

MAYER, ROBERT SAMUEL, physician; b. Detroit, Jan. 13, 1962; s. Jack J. and Beatrice (Susskind) M.; m. Sherry J. Weinstein-Mayer, June 15, 1986; children: Aimee, Rachel, Elana. BS, Northwestern Univ., 1984, MD, 1986. Diplomate Am. Bd. Indep. Medical Examiners, Diplomate Am. Bd. Electrodiagnostic Medicine, Am. Bd. Physical Medicine & Rehabilitation. Residency Rush-Marianjoy-Oak Forest, Chgo., 1987-90; internship medicine Rush-Presbyn. St. Luke's Medical Ctr., Chgo., 1986-87; residency program dir. Rush-Marianjoy Residency in Physical Medicine & Rehab., 1996—, assoc. residency program dir., 1994-96; medical dir. Employee Health Svcs., 1994—, Ill. Mcpl. Retirement Fund, Oak Brook, Ill., 1992—; medical dir. rehabilitation svcs. Vencor Hosp. Chgo., Northlake, Ill., 1991-93; physiatrist Rehabilitation Medicine Clinic, Wheaton, Ill., 1990—; asst. prof. dept. physical medicine & rehabilitation Rush Medical Coll., Chgo., 1991—; instr. Loyola Univ. Stritch Sch. Medicine, Maywood, Ill., 1990-91; medical records com. Rush-Presbyn. St. Luke's Medical Ctr., 1993; com. edn. appraisal Rush Medical Coll., Chgo.,1992-95; chair edn. com. Am. Medical Student Assn., 1985-86; medical cons. Met. Life Ins., 1992-94; cons. medical dir. Physical Medicine & Rehab. Health Care Compare Corp., Downers Grove, Ill., 1990-94; attending physician RPSLMC, Chgo., 1991—, Grant Hosp., Chgo., 1991—, Westlake Hosp., Melrose Park, Ill., 1991—, Oak Park Hosp., 1990%; cons. physician Marianjoy Rehab. Ctr., Wheaton, 1990—; lectr. in field. Contbr. numerous articles to profl. jours. Rsch. adv. com. United Cerebral Palsy Assn., 1991. Recipient Elkins award Am. Bd. PM&R, 1990, Best Doctor in Am. award Woodward/White, 1996, Innovation grant Nat. Inst. Disability & Rehabilitation Rsch., 1992. Fellow Am. Acad. Physical Medicine & Rehab., Am. Assn. Electrodiagnostic Medicine, Assn. Spine, Sports, Occupational Rehab.; mem. AMA, Assn. Acad. Physiatrists, Chgo. Medical Soc., Ill. State Medical Soc. Office: Rehab Medicine Clinic 1725 W Harrison St Chicago IL 60612

MAYER, STEPHEN EDWARD, respiratory therapist; b. St. Louis, Aug. 5, 1954; s. Marvin Edward and Viola Geraldine (Jack) M.; m. Susan Helen De Neui, Aug. 26, 1978; children: Holly, Bethany, Valerie. B.S., Iowa State U., 1977. Respiratory therapist Iowa Methodist Med. Ctr., Des Moines, 1978-80, supr. pediatric respiratory care, 1980-82, dir. respiratory care, 1982-89; salesman pharm. Schering Labs., 1989—; chmn. blood donor drive, 1984-85. Mem. adv. com. Des Moines Area Community Coll., 1982-89, chmn., 1986-87; mem. health policy adv. com. Rep. Party, 1989-90; bd. dirs. Am. Lung Assn. Iowa, 1993—. Mem. Iowa Soc. Respiratory Care (bd. dirs. 1984-85, pres.-elect, 1987, pres. 1988, immediate past pres. 1989). Republican. Mem. Open Bible Ch. Avocations: hunting, fishing, outdoors. Office: Shering Labs 3515 48th St Des Moines IA 50310-3221

MAYER, SUSAN LEE, nurse; b. N.Y.C., Feb. 10, 1946; d. Hans and Frieda (Schein) Abramson; BSN, Hunter Coll., 1968; MA, NYU, 1974, EDd., Tchrs. Coll., Columbia U., 1974, Tchrs Coll. Columbia U., 1996; cert. in gerontology Yeshiva U.; cert. tchr. Adelphi U., 1987; m. Steven Mayer, June 24, 1973; children: Jason, Stuart, Richard, Deborah. Staff nurse ICU-CCU, Montefiore Hosp., Bronx, N.Y., 1968; organizer CCU, Jewish Meml. Hosp., N.Y.C., 1968; supr., adminstr. Morrisania City Hosp., N.Y.C., 1969-76; instr. Adelphi Univ., Garden City, N.Y., 1977-78; substitute nurse Gt. Neck (N.Y.) Pub. Schs., 1980-90; adj. instr. Queensborough Community Coll.; 1987—; tchr. CPR, 1972—, 85—; lectr. PTA groups, 1981-82; rsch. asst. to dean Sch. Nursing Adelphi U., 1987—; part-time staff nurse Winthrop U. Hosp., Mineola, N.Y., 1987-90, per diem nurse, 1987-90; instr. Dept. Nursing Edn. Bronx Mcpl. Hosp. Ctr. (now Jacobi Med. Ctr.), 1990-96, asst. prof. Helene Fuld Sch. Nursing, 1996—; adj. instr. Bronx C.C., 1992; adj. asst. prof. Iona Coll. Sch. Nursing; presenter 17th Ann. Internat. Assn. for Human Caring Conf., 2nd Internat. & Interdisciplinary Health/Rsch. Symposium; lectr. in field. Contbr. articles to profl. jours including Nursing & Health Care. Bd. dirs. Gt. Neck Synagogue, 1981-91, v.p. Sisterhood, 1978-79, pres., 1979-81; former bd. dirs. Russell Gardens Assn.; founder Work for Share, Zedek Hosp., 1977—; pres. fin. sec. L'Chaim chpt. Hadassah Nurse Coun. N.Y. State Regents scholar, 1963. Mem. ANA, Assn. Orthodox Jewish Scientists, Nat. League Nursing, N.Y. Counties Registered Nurses Assn., Am. Assn. for History of Nursing, Hadassah Nurses Coun. (fin. sec. L'Chaim chpt.), N.Y. Assn. Nurse Execs., Sigma Theta Tau, Kappa Delta Pi. Democrat. Home: 28 Laurel Dr Great Neck NY 11021-2827

MAYER, TIMOTHY AGNEW, dentist; b. Abilene, Tex., June 17, 1945; s. Tully August M. BA, Trinity U., San Antonio, 1967; DDS, Baylor U., 1971. Pvt. practice dentistry, Pharr, Tex., 1973—; bd. dirs. Tex. Dental Polit. Action Com., Austin, Alamo Bank Tex. Mem. editorial adv. com. Tex. Dental Jour., 1987-88; mem. steering com. Am. Heart Assn.; state chmn. Pierre Fauchard Acad., 1986-88. Served to capt. USAF, 1971-73. Champion in golf Plantation C.C., 1989, 90. Fellow Am. Coll. Dentists, Internat. Coll. Dentists, Pierre Fauchard Acad.; mem. Acad. Gen. Dentistry, ADA (del. 1980-84, 86-87), Tex. Dental Assn. (v.p. 1983-85, council chmn. 1981—, cert. appreciation 1984, 85, disting. service award 1985, mem. editorial adv. bd. Tex. Dental Jour. 1987—), Rio Grande Valley Dental Soc. (pres. 1977-78), SW Prosthetic Soc. (pres. 1986-87), Southwest Soc. Oral Medicine, Tex. Scuba Divers Rio Grande Valley Club (pres. 1984-85), Golf Club at Cimarron (Golf Club Champion 1995), Rotary (area rep. 1985-86, pres. 1984-85, Outstanding Rotarian of Year 1984-85, Paul Harris fellow 1986). Avocations: golf, scuba, underwater photography, softball, swimming. Home: 1700 Larkspur Ave Mcallen TX 78501-3855 Office: 310 S Cage Blvd Pharr TX 78577-4845

MAYER, WALTER BREM, physician, neurologist; b. Charlotte, N.C., Mar. 10, 1935; s. Walter Brem and Helen (Dainis) M.; m. Anne Powning, Aug. 3, 1936; children: Penelope, Kimball, Allison, Courtney. AB, Princeton U., 1956; MD, Duke U., 1960. Diplomate Am. Bd. Neurology. Physician Emory Clinic, Atlanta, 1967-70, Atlanta Neurol. Clinic, 1970-95, Peachtree Neurol. Clinic, Atlanta, 1995—; clin. prof. neurology Emory U. Med. Sch., Atlanta, 1980—. Author: Fundamentals of EEG Technology, Vol. II, 1989; co-author: Fundamentals of EEG Technology, Vol. I, 1983; contbg. author: Medicine for the Practicing Physician, 1993. Mem. adv. bd. Trust for Pub. Land, Atlanta, 1994, 95. Episcopalian. Office: Peachtree Neurol Clinic PC 25 Prescott St NE Atlanta GA 30308

MAYERHOFF, DAVID ISAK, psychiatrist; b. N.Y.C., Sept. 3, 1958; s. Jonah and Bernice (Eisleman) M. BA magna cum laude, Yeshiva U., 1979; MD with selected honors, SUNY Downstate, Bklyn., 1983. Cert. Am. Bd. Psychiatry and Neurology, Nat. Bd. Med. Examiners. Intern L.I. Jewish Med. Ctr., New Hyde Park, N.Y., 1983-84; resident Hillside Hosp. div. LIJMC, Glen Oaks, N.Y., 1984-87; clin. rsch. fellow, staff attending Hillside Hosp. div. LIJMC, 1987-89, rsch. attending, psychiatrist, 1989-91; attending psychiatrist Aftercare Clinic, 1991-93; dir. ambulatory mental health svcs., dept. quality assurance Nassau County Medical Ctr., East Meadow, N.Y., 1994—; asst. prof. psychiatry SUNY, Stony Brook, 1994—; staff psychiatrist New Hope Guild, Bklyn., 1986; asst. prof. psychiatry Albert Einstein Coll. of Medicine, Bronx, N.Y. Contbr. to sci. jours. Summer rsch. fellow Downstate Clin. Rsch. Ctr., Bklyn., 1981. Mem. Am. Psychiat. Assn., AMA, N.Y. Acad. Scis. Republican. Jewish. Office: Nassau County Medical Ctr Bldg J 2201 Hampstead Tpke E Meadow NY 11554

MAYERS, ALAN ELSAS, scientist administrator; b. N.Y.C., Oct. 1, 1932; s. Morris Augustus and Roslyn Louise (Elsas) M.; m. Emily Patricia Jackson, Dec. 18, 1959; children: Douglas James, Patricia Jackson. AB, Princeton U., 1954; MS, Boston U., 1959; PhD, Stanford U., 1965. Asst. prof. communication rsch. Tulane U., New Orleans, 1965-67; rsch. psychologist USPHS, Arlington, Va., 1967-69; sci. rev. adminstr. health care tech. sect. Agy. for Health Care Policy and Rsch., Rockville, Md., 1969-93; cons., 1994—. With U.S. Army, 1954-57. Mem. Am. Pub. Health Assn., Soc. Med. Decision Making, Soc. Gen. Internal Medcine. Democrat. Methodist. Home: 1718 Wilmart St Rockville MD 20852-4143

MAYERS, STANLEY PENROSE, JR., public health educator; b. Phila., Nov. 9, 1926; s. Stanley Penrose and Margaret Amelia (Thorpe) M.; m. Virginia Lee Lytle, Aug. 25, 1951 (dec. Oct. 1990); children: Douglas Lytle, Kenneth Stanley, Daniel John, Andrew William; m. Patricia Ann Harne Hulsey, Mar. 6, 1993. BA, U. Pa., 1949, MD, 1953; MPH, Johns Hopkins U., 1958. Diplomate Am. Bd. Preventive Medicine. Intern Phila. Gen. Hosp., 1953-54; resident Arlington County Health Dept., Va., 1954-55; health dir. Henry-Martinsville-Patrick Health Dist., Martinsville, Va., 1955-57; regional dir. Va. State Health dept., Richmond, 1958-59; dist. state health officer N.J. State Dept. of Health, Trenton, 1959-62; asst. prof. and asst. dean Johns Hopkins Sch. Hygiene and Pub. Health, Balt., 1962-65; dir. Arlington County Dept. of Human Resources, Arlington, Va., 1965-71; prof. Health Planning and Adminstrn. Program Pa. State U., Univ. Pk., Pa., 1971-74, 88—; prof. in charge Pa. State U., Univ. Park, Pa., 1974-78; chmn. Pa. State U., Univ. Pk., Pa., 1979-88; assoc. dean undergrad. studies Coll. Health and Human Devel. Pa. State U., Univ. Pk., 1989-92, assoc. dean acad. studies Coll. Health and Human Devel., 1992-95; faculty assoc. Johns Hopkins U. Sch. Medicine, Balt., 1965-75; clin. assoc. prof. Georgetown U. Sch. Medicine, Washington, 1965-71; cons. VA, 1985—. Author numerous reports, articles and surveys on pub. health. Mem. Arlington Optimist Club, 1979-72, pres. 1970-71; bd. dirs. Centre County Family Planning Svcs., Bellefonte, Pa., 1972-79. With USN, 1945-46. Recipient Outstanding Achievement award Dept. Community Medicine, Georgetown U. Sch. Medicine, 1968, Saubel award Coll. of Human Devel., Pa. State U., 1985. Fellow Am. Coll. Preventive Med., Am. Pub. Health Assn. (chmn. membership com. health officer's sect. 1968-70, mem. nominating com. health adminstrn. sect. 1970-72, chmn. com. to draft a statement on local health agy. responsibilities 1973-74); mem. AMA, Arlington County Med. Soc. (Wellborn award 1971), Centre County Med. Soc. (pres. 1978), Med. Soc. Va., Met. Washington Health Officers Assn. (sec. 1967-71), Am. Assn. Pub. Health Physicians (pres. Va. chpt. 1970-71), Pa. Med. Soc. (mem. Ho. of Dels. for Centre County 1974-76, 81—, treas. 1973-74, 85—, sec. 1974-76, v.p. 1976, pres. elect 1977, pres. 1978), University Club (State College, Pa.), Phi Beta Kappa. Episcopalian. Home: 648 Wiltshire Dr State College PA 16803-1450 Office: Pa State U Rm 201 Human Devel Bldg University Park PA 16802

MAYERSAK, JEROME STEPHEN, urologist; b. Superior, Wis., July 4, 1938; s. Joseph Walter and Libby Jean (Conroy) M.; BA, Johns Hopkins, 1960; MD, George Washington U., 1964; m. Priscilla M. Kurtzweil, Mar. 27, 1976; children: Kathlyne Mary, Priscilla Kathlyne, Tzena Lynne. Intern dept. surgery George Washington U. Hosp., Washington, 1964-65, resident in urology, 1966, chief resident, 1968; resident in surgery D.C. Gen. Hosp., 1965-66, resident in urology, 1966-67, sr. resident, 1967; resident in urology George Washington U. Sch. Medicine, 1966-69; sr. resident VA Hosp., 1968, chief resident, Washington, 1969; practice medicine specializing in urology, Wisconsin Rapids, Wis., 1969-71, Merrill, Wis., 1971—; urologist Med. Arts Group, Wisconsin Rapids, 1969-71; mem. staff Taylor County Meml. Hosp., Medford, Wis., 1970—, Good Samaritan Health Ctr. (formerly Holy Cross Hosp.), Merrill, Wis., 1971—, Tri-County Meml. Hosp., Whitehall, Wis., 1971—, Wausau Hosp. Ctr., Wis., 1985—; mem. cons. staff Riverview Hosp., Wisconsin Rapids, 1969-73, Sacred Heart Hosp., Tomahawk, Wis., 1971—, Wild Rose (Wis.) Community Meml. Hosp., 1970—, Neillsville (Wis.) Meml. Hosp., 1969-73; jr. cons. to St. Elizabeth's Hosp., Washington, 1968-69; clin. staff privileges U. Minn. Hosps. and Clinic, dept. urology, Minneapolis; urologist J.S. Mayersak Svc. Corp., Merrill, 1971—; cons. urologist Langlade County Meml. Hosp., Antigo, Wis., Eagle River (Wis.) Hosp., Park Falls (Wis.) Hosp. Chmn. adv. airport com. to Airport Commn., Merrill, Wis., 1970-75; bd. dirs. Tri-County Meml. Hosp.; mem. peer review com. N. Cen. Health Protection Plan. Fellow William Beaumont Hon. Research Soc., St. George Cancer Soc., Internat. Coll. Surgeons; mem. AMA, State Med. Soc. Wis., Am. Assn. Physicians and Surgeons, Am., Internat. socs. nephrology, Minn. Urology Soc. (charter), Twin Cities Urol. Socs., Endourol. Soc., Flying Physicians Assn., Wis., Lincoln County (pres. 1974-78, 87), Aerospace med. socs., Am. Soc. Microbiology, A.C.S., Am. Coll. Utilization Rev. Physicians, Va. Acad. Scis., Pan Am. Med. Assn., Renal Physicians Assn., Royal Soc. London, Asociación Médica Panamericana, Sociedad Ecquatoriana de Urología (hon.), Am. Fertility Soc., Am. Soc. for Laser Medicine and Surgery, Inc., Am. Lithotripsy Soc., Internat. Platform Assn., AAAS, Mensa, Soc. Profl. Pilots (charter), Sigma Xi, Nu Sigma Nu. Lodges: Elks, Moose. Home and Office: 717 Tee Lane Dr Merrill WI 54452-3430

MAYES, GLENN, social worker; b. Aug. 23, 1955; s. Johnny and Lillie (Hopper) M. BS, Cameron U., 1977; MSW, U. Okla., 1984. Cert. profl. healthcare quality; lic. social worker, Okla.; bd. cert. diplomate clin. social worker. Dir. spl. svcs. Jim Taliaferro C.M.H.C., Lawton. Mem. NASW (S.W. chpt. br. chmn. nominations and leadership com.), Nat. Assn. Healthcare Quality, Acad. Cert. Social Workers. Home: 6112 NW Birch Ave Lawton OK 73505-4442

MAYES, MAUREEN DAVIDICA, physician, educator; b. Phila., Oct. 16, 1945; d. David M. and Marguerite Cecilia (Fineran) M.; m. Charles William Houser, Dec. 18, 1976; children: David Steven, Edward Charles. BA, Coll. Notre Dame, 1967; MD, Ea. Va. Med. Sch., 1976; MA in Pub. Health, U. Mich., Ann Arbor, 1994. Resident in internal medicine Cleve. Clinic Found., 1977-79, fellow in rheumatology, 1979-81; asst. prof. medicine W.Va. U., Morgantown, 1981-85; asst. prof. medicine Wayne State U., Detroit, 1985-90, assoc. prof. medicine, 1990—; dir. scleroderma unit Wayne State U., Detroit, 1991—. Contbr. articles to profl. jours. Pres. bd. United Scleroderma Found., 1988-89, mem. med. adv. bd., 1995—; bd. trustees Mich. chpt. Arthritis Found. Robert Wood Johnson scholarship EVMS, 1972, NIH fellow, 1993-94, NIAMS Sr. Rsch. fellowship, 1994; recipient Lower award Cleve. Clinic Found., 1981. Fellow Am. Coll. Rheumatology (mem. ctrl. region coun. 1995—), Am. Coll. Physicians; mem. Am. Fedn. Clin. Rsch., Mich. Rheumatism Soc. Office: Wayne State U Hutzel Hosp 4707 Saint Antoine St Detroit MI 48201-1427

MAYFIELD, PEGGY JORDAN, psychologist; b. Atlanta, Aug. 4, 1934; d. Claude Emmett and Ruby Earnestine (Hutchison) Jordan; children: Steven Jay, David Lee. BA with high honors, Agnes Scott Coll., 1956; MEd, Ga. State U., 1971, SEd, 1976, PhD, 1978. Diplomate Am. Bd. Adminstrv. Psychology; lic. psychologist, Ga., cons. indsl. & orgnl. psychology. Tchr. music, Atlanta, 1956-70; exec. dir. Hi Hope Ctr., Lawrenceville Ga., 1971-74; devel. service chief program dir. Gwinnett Rockdale Newton Mental Health and Mental Retardation Service, Lawrenceville, 1974-78; owner, dir. Gwinnett Mental Health Assocs., Lilburn, Ga., 1978-85; pres. So. Clinic, Inc.; pvt. practice clin. psychologist in assessment counseling consultation, Lawrenceville, 1982-94; pres. Child Train, Inc. 1993—; owner Jay Lee Enterprises; pres. Mayfeild Cons. Svcs., Child Train, Inc.; cons. Creative Enterprises, Lawrenceville, 1978-82; adjudicator Nat. Guild Piano Tchrs., Austin, Tex., 1979—. Author community project reports, ednl. materials; workshop presenter depression in children & adolescents. Named to Hall of Fame, Nat. Guild Piano Tchrs., 1962-63; HEW fellow, 1969-71; recipient Community Program award Ga. Assn. Retarded Citizens, 1973, Nat. Tng. award, Nat. Assn. Retarded Citizens. Mem. APA, Am. Assn. Marriage and Family Therapists, Ga. Psychol. Assn., Phi Beta Kappa. Avocations: music, writing, reading, fishing, travel. Office: So Clinic Inc 3444 Club Dr Lawrenceville GA 30244

MAYFIELD, RONALD KEITH, endocrinologist; b. Morgantown, W.Va., July 15, 1950; s. Albert Keith and Mary Kathleen (Lemley) M.; m. Karen Elizabeth Gaspar, Dec. 27, 1970; children—Douglas Keith, Cortnie Anne. M.D., W.Va. U., 1975. Diplomate Am. Bd. Internal Medicine (cert.), Am. Bd. Endocrinology and Metabolism. Intern in internal medicine W.Va. U. Sch. Medicine, Charleston Area Med. Ctr., 1975-76, resident, 1976-78; fellow in endocrinology-metabolism and nutrition Med. U. S.C., Charleston, 1978-80, instr. medicine, 1980-81, asst. prof., 1981-86, asst. prof. lab. medicine, 1983-86, assoc. prof. medicine, pathology and lab. medicine, 1986-92, prof. medicine, pathology and lab. medicine, 1992—; staff physician, 1980—; cons. in endocrinology Med. U. Hosp., Charleston VA Med. Ctr., Charleston Meml. Hosp.; dir. specialized diagnostic and therapeutic unit VA Med. Ctr., 1984—; assoc. dir. Gen. Clin. Rsch. Med. Ctr. U. So. Calif., 1988-95, dir. fellowship tng. endocrinology, 1995—. Bd. govs. scholar W.Va. U. Sch. Medicine, 1971-75; Mosby scholar W.Va. U. Sch. Medicine, 1972; Health Scis. Developing scholar Med. U. S.C., 1988; recipient Spl. Emphasis Rsch. Career award NIH, 1980-85; named to Best Doctors Am.-Southeast, endocrinology. Fellow ACP; mem. Assn. Subspecialty Profs., Am. Diabetes Assn. (research-rev. com. 1986-89, outstanding profl. service award S.C. affiliate 1983, bd. dirs. S.C. affiliate 1981-88), Am. Fedn. Clin. Rsch., So. Soc. for Clin. Investigation, Endocrine Soc., Alpha Epsilon Delta. Republican. Contbr. articles to profl. jours. Home: 537 Rice Planters Ln Mount Pleasant SC 29464 Office: 171 Ashley Ave Charleston SC 29425-0001

MAYFIELD, SANDRA JEANNE, recreational therapist, consultant; b. Mpls., Aug. 28, 1942; d. Glen Douglas and Ellynore (Kukko) M. BS in Recreation, San Jose State U., 1967, MS in Therapeutic Recreation, 1979. Cert. recreation therapist, Calif., therapeutic recreation specialist. Recreation asst. supr. Sunnyvale (Calif.) Park and Recreation Dept., 1960-67; dir. recreation Santa Clara Valley Med. Ctr., San Jose, Calif., 1967—; lectr. San Francisco State U., 1976-78; instr. San Jose State U., 1986-88, Tex. Women's U., Denton, 1989; cons. Western Med., Hayward, Calif., 1978-79; bd. dirs. Horizons West; chmn., presenter numerous local, state and nat. workshops and conf. sessions; mem. steering com. Coma to Community Bain Trauma Conf., 1988-95; Calif. Bd. Rec. personnel certification, 1993—. Author: Protocols in Therapeutic Recreation, 1989, Quality Assurance and Continuous Quality Improvement, 1992; co-author: Facilitating a Desired Leisure

Lifestyle, 1987. Recipient Disting. Recreation Alumnus award San Jose State U., 1983, Alumnus of Yr. award dept. recreation and leisure studies, 1988. Mem. Nat. Therapeutic Recreation Soc. (bd. dirs. 1983-89, pres. 1988-89, Disting. Svc. award 1995), Calif. Park and Recreation Soc. (pres. therapeutic recreation sect. 1981-83, state bd. dirs. 1981-83, chmn. recreation therapy licensure task force 1983-95, Outstanding Therapeutic Recreator award 1985, Citation 1988, Fellowship award 1993). Democrat. Office: Santa Clara Valley Med Ctr 751 S Bascom Ave San Jose CA 95128-2604

MAYHALL, C. GLEN, internal medicine educator; b. St. Louis, Feb. 17, 1939; s. Orville Green and Mary Beatrice (Trulove) M.; m. Kathryn Ann Rompel, June 12, 1965; children: Lisa, Michelle, Mark. BA, Washington U., St. Louis, 1961; MD, Baylor U., 1966. Diplomate Am. Bd. Internal Medicine, Am. Bd. Infectious Diseases. Intern in internal medicine Barnes Hosp., St. Louis, 1966-67, resident in internal medicine, 1967-68, fellow in infectious diseases, 1973-75; resident in internal medicine St. Luke's Hosp., St. Louis, 1971-73; asst. prof. Med. Coll. Va., Richmond, 1975-80, assoc. prof., 1980-87, prof., 1987-89; prof. U. Tenn., Memphis, 1990-93; prof. internal medicine U. Tex. Med. Br., Galveston, 1994—; hosp. epidemiologist Med. Coll. Va. Hosps., Richmond, 1975-89, Regional Med. Ctr., Memphis, 1990-93, U. Tex. Med. Br. Hosps., Galveston, 1994—. Editor: Hospital Epidemiology and Infection Control, 1995. Maj. U.S. Army, 1968-71. Fellow Infectious Disease Soc. Am.; mem. Soc. for Healthcare Epidemiology of Am. (pres. 1991). Episcopalian. Office: U Tex Med Br Sealy Smith Profl Bldg Galveston TX 77555-0835

MAYHER, WILLIAM EDGAR, III, neurosurgeon; b. Columbus, Ga., Nov. 5, 1938; s. William Edgar Jr. and Frances Hicks (Lummus) M.; m. Jo Anne Mullis, June 9, 1963; children: William Roy, Brant Edgar, Anne Mullis. Student, Tulane U., 1956-58; BS, U. Ga., 1960; MD, Med. Coll. Ga., 1964. Diplomate Am. Bd. Neurol. Surgery. Intern in surgery Grady Meml. Hosp. Emory U., Atlanta, 1964-65; resident in neurosurgery Coll. of Ga., Augusta, 1965-70; practice medicine specializing in neurosurgery Neurosurg. Assocs., Albany, Ga., 1970—; chmn. bd. dirs. Blue Cross and Blue Shield of Ga., 1980-90; chmn. bd. dirs. Gray Communications Sys. Mem. ACS, AMA, Am. Assn. Neurol. Surgeons, Congress Neurol. Surgeons, Ga. Neurosurg. Soc. (pres. 1989-90), So. Neurosurg. Soc., Ga. Surg. Soc., Rotary Club Albany, Med. Coll. Ga. Found. (bd. dirs. 1994—). Republican. Episcopalian. Home: 2520 E Doublegate Dr Albany GA 31707-9241 Office: Neurosurg Assocs P C 804 13th Ave Albany GA 31701-1328

MAYHEW, ERIC GEORGE, cancer researcher, educator; b. London, Eng., June 22, 1938; came to U.S., 1964; s. George James and Doris Ivy (Tipping) M.; m. Barbara Doe, Sept. 28, 1966 (div. 1976); 1 child, Miles; m. Karen Caruana, Apr. 1, 1978 (div. 1994); children: Ian, Andrea: m. Ludmila Khatchatrian, June 29, 1995. BS, U. London, 1960, MS, 1963; PhD, 1967; DSc, U. London, 1993. Rsch. asst. Chester Beatty Rsch. Inst., London, 1960-64; cancer rsch. scientist Roswell Pk. Meml. Inst., Buffalo, 1964-68, sr. cancer rsch. scientist, 1968-72, assoc. cancer rsch. scientist, 1979-93, dep. dir. exptl. pathology, 1988-93; assoc. rsch. prof. SUNY, Buffalo, 1979-93; prin. scientist The Liposome Co., Princeton, N.J., 1993—; ad-hoc mem. NIH study sects., 1982-94. Editor jour. Selective Cancer Therapeutics, 1989-91; contbr. articles to Jour. Nat. Cancer Inst., Cancer Rsch. and many other profl. jours. Grantee NIH, Am. Heart Assn., and pvt. industry, 1972-93. Mem. Am. Assn. Cancer Rsch., N.Y. Acad. Sci. Office: The Liposome Co Princeton Forestal Ctr One Research Way Princeton NJ 08540

MAYHUGH, LISA JAYNE, medical oncology nurse; b. Wheeling, W.Va., May 26, 1958; d. John H. and Mary Virginia (Bryan) Barton; m. James A. Mayhugh, Nov. 26, 1977; children: Whitney, Tyler. ADN, Clark State C.C., Springfield, Ohio, 1985; BSN summa cum laude, Franklin U., Columbus, Ohio, 1994. RN, Ohio; cert. med.-surg. nurse. Nurse Cmty. Hosp., Springfield, 1983—, nurse mgr., 1993—. Christian. Home: 1700 Merrydale Rd Springfield OH 45503 Office: Cmty Hosp 2615 E High St Springfield OH 45502

MAYNARD, CHARLES DOUGLAS, radiologist; b. Atlantic City, Sept. 11, 1934; m. Mary Anne Satterwhite; children—Charles D., Deanne, David. B.S., Wake Forest U., 1955, M.D., 1959. Diplomate Am. Bd. Radiology (trustee, sec.-treas., v.p. 1992-94, pres. 1994—). Intern U.S. Army Hosp., Honolulu, 1959-60; resident N.C. Baptist Hosp., 1963-66; dir. Nuclear Medicine Lab., 1966-77; asst. dean admissions Bowman Gray Sch. Medicine, 1966-71, asso. dean student affairs, 1971-75, prof. radiology, chmn. dept., 1977—; guest examiner Am. Bd. Radiology. Author: Clinical Nuclear Medicine, 1969; mem. editorial bd. Academic Radiology, Yearbook of Diagnostic Radiology, Contemporary Diagnostic Radiology. Mem. Leadership Winston-Salem, Triad Leadership Network; bd. dirs. Downtown Devel. Corp., 1995—, Winston-Salem Bus., Inc., 1995—. Mem. AMA, Soc. Nuclear Medicine (past pres.), Am. Coll. Radiology (past bd. chancellors, past chmn. commn. on nuclear medicine), Radiol. Soc. N.Am. (sec.-treas.), Assn. Univ. Radiologists, Soc. Chairmen Radiology Depts. (past pres.), Acad. Radiology Rsch. (bd. dirs. 1995—), Am. Bd. Radiology (bd. trustees 1987—, pres. 1994—), Am. Bd. Med. Specialists, Greater Winston-Salem C. of C. (bd. dirs.). Office: Medical Center Blvd Dept Radiology Winston Salem NC 27157

MAYNARD, GEORGE FLEMING, III, hospital administrator; b. Tupelo, Miss., Mar. 29, 1947; s. George Fleming Jr. and Shirley Lindsey (Russell) M.; m. Janie White, Aug. 16, 1969; children: George Fleming IV, Benjamin Hoyle. BA in Sociology, U. Miss., 1969; MS in Social Work, U. Tenn., 1972. Child welfare supr. Miss. Dept. Pub. Welfare, Pontotoc, 1972-74; exec. dir. Lift, Inc., Tupelo, 1974-77; dir. devel. and pub. relations North Miss. Med. Ctr., Tupelo, 1977-82; v.p. pub. affairs United Health Svcs., Binghamton, N.Y., 1982-87; exec. v.p. Orlando (Fla.) Regional Healthcare Found., 1987—. Contbr. articles to profl. jours. Mem. Miss. Econ. Coun., Jackson, 1981-82; mem. exec. com. Bayhill Invitational, Orlando, 1987—; bd. dirs. Broome County Cmty. Charities, Endicott, N.Y., 1984-87; mem. Leadership Miss., 1980, Leadership Orlando, 1988, Econ. Devel. Commn.; Eagle scout Boy Scouts Am.; elder Metro Ch. of Christ; lay missionary Varna Bulgaria. Recipient MacEachern award Am. Soc. Hosp. Pub. Relations, 1979. Fellow Assn. Healthcare Philanthropy; mem. Health Systems Devel. Network (rpes. 1994-97), Planned Giving Coun. Ctrl. Fla. (pres. 1994-95), Rotary (pres. Tupelo chpt. 1980-82). Home: 451 Longmeadow Ln Longwood FL 32779-6011 Office: Orlando Regional Healthcare 1414 Kuhl Ave Orlando FL 32806-2008

MAYNARD, KENNETH IRWIN, medical educator, researcher; b. San Fernando, Trinidad, Jan. 17, 1963. Student, Howard U., 1982; BSc with honors, Univ. Coll., London, 1986, MSc, 1987, PhD, 1991. Postdoctoral rsch. assistantship Univ. Coll., London, 1991; postdoctoral rsch. fellow Stroke Rsch. Lab. Neurosurg. Svc. Mass. Gen. Hosp., Harvard Med. Sch., Boston, 1991-93, postdoctoral rsch. fellow neurophysiology lab. Neurosurg. Svc., 1993—; tchg. fellow dept. neurobiology Harvard Med. Sch., Boston, 1992, instr. in surgery, 1995—. Ad hoc reviewer Jour. Vascular Rsch., 1991, Neurosci. Letters, 1995, Vision Rsch., 1996; contbr. articles to profl. jours.; presenter in field. Mem. parish pastoral coun. St. Joseph's Cath. Ch., Boston, 1992-95, chmn. stewarship commn., 1996—; advisor regional com. ctrl. region on stewardship for Archdiocese of Boston, 1995—. Fellow Am. Heart Assn. (mem. stroke coun., minority scientist devel. award 1996); mem. AAAS, Soc. for Neurosci. (NINDS travel fellow for minority neuroscientists 1995), Am. Assn. Neurosurg. Surgeons (adj. assoc. mem. joint sect. on cerebrovascular surgery 1995), Congress of Neurosurg. Surgeons, Internat. Soc. of Cerebral Blood Flow and Metabolism (jr. mem., Young Scientist Bursary award 1993). Office: Mass Gen Hosp Dept Neurosurgery Edwards 414 32 Fruit St Boston MA 02114

MAYNOR, MELANIE MARY, nurse anesthetist; b. Greensboro, N.C., Feb. 16, 1965; d. Luther Vernice and Hazel Betty (Bullock) Maynor. BS in Respiratory Therapy, Med. Coll. Ga., Augusta, 1988; BSN, U. Tenn., Memphis, 1992; postgrad., Raleigh Sch. Nurse Anesthesia, 1993—. RN, N.C.; registered respiratory therapist, Ga. Staff/supr. respiratory therapist Med. Ctr. Ctrl. Ga., Macon, 1988-91; cardiothoracic ICU nurse N.C. Bapt. Hosp., Winston-Salem, 1992—. Mem. Am. Assn. Nurse Anesthetists, Sigma Theta Tau. Home: 632 Georgetown Rd Raleigh NC 27608

MAYO, CLYDE CALVIN, organizational psychologist, educator; b. Robstown, Tex., Feb. 2, 1940; s. Clyde Culberson and Velma (Oxford) M.; m. Jeanne Lynn McCain, Aug. 24, 1963; children: Brady Scott, Amber Camille. BA, Rice U., 1961; BS, U. Houston, 1964, PhD, 1972; MS, Trinity U., 1966. Lic. psychologist, Tex. Mgmt. engr. LWFW, Inc., Houston, 1966-72, sr. cons., 1972-78, prin., 1978-81; ptnr. Mayo, Thompson, Bigby, Houston, 1981-83, founder Mgmt. and Personnel Systems, Houston, 1983—; counselor Interface Counseling Ctr., Houston, 1976-79; dir. Mental Health HMO Group, 1985-87; instr. St. Thomas U., Houston, 1979—, U. Houston Downtown Sch., 1972, U. Houston-Clear Lake, 1983-88, U. Houston-Central Campus, 1984—; dir. mgmt. devel. insts. U. Houston Woodlands and West Houston, 1986-1991, adj. prof. U. Houston, 1991—. Author: Bi/Polar Inventory of Strengths, 1978, LWFW Annual Survey of Manufacturers, 1966-1981. Coach, mgr. Meyerland Little League, 1974-78, So. Belles Softball, 1979-80, S.W. Colt Baseball, 1982-83, Friends of Fondren Library of Rice U., 1988—; charter mem. Holocaust Mus. Mem. Soc. Indsl. Organizational Psychologists, Tex. Indsl. Orgnl. Psychologists (founder, bd. dirs. 1995—), Houston Psychol. Assn. (membership dir. 1978, sec. 1984), Tex. Psychol. Assn., Am. Psychol. Assn., Bus. Execs. for Nat Security, Houston Area Indsl. Orgnl. Psychologists (bd. dirs. 1989-92), Forum Club. Methodist. Club: Meyerland (bd. dirs. 1988-92, pres. 1991). Home: 8723 Ferris Dr Houston TX 77096-1409 Office: Mgmt and Personnel Systems 4545 Bissonnet St Bellaire TX 77401

MAYO, GEORGE DOUGLAS, psychologist; b. Somerville, Tenn., Feb. 3, 1917; s. James Laurence and Margaret Gibbs (Green) M.; m. Mildred Dulcie Harris, Aug. 5, 1942; 1 child, George Douglas Jr. Student, U. Tenn., Martin, 1935-37; BS, Memphis State U., 1939; MA, George Peabody Coll., 1941; PhD, Ohio State U., 1949. Asst. prof. naval sci. and tactics Rice U., Houston, 1945-46; assoc. prof. psychology Birmingham (Ala.)-So. Coll., 1948-50; dir. pers. and tng. rsch. Naval Air Tech. Tng. Command, 1950-73; dir. Ctr. for Instructional Rsch. and Svc. Memphis State U., 1974-79; owner Mayo Psychol. Svcs., 1979—, Memphis, 1979—; adj. prof. dept. founds. edn. Memphis State U., 1974-79, cons. Ctr. for Nuclear Studies, 1979-84; cons. Am. Tech. Inst., Brunswick, Tenn., 1985-88. Author: (with Philip DuBois) The Complete Book of Training, 1987; editor: (with Burl Gilliland) Learning and Instructional Improvement Digests, 1979; (with Philip DuBois) Research Strategies for Evaluating Training, 1970; editor Pers. and Tng Bulletin, Memphis, 1979-84; contbr. articles to profl. jours. Sustaining mem. Rep. Nat. Com., Washington, 1981—. Capt. USN, 1941-46, res., ret. Decorated Purple Heart; recipient Meritorious Civilian Svc. award Dept. Navy, 1967, Superior Civilian Svc. award Dept. Navy, 1973; named to Athletic Hall of Fame, Memphis State u., 1982. Fellow APA; mem. Southeastern Psychol. Assn., So. Soc. for Philosophy and Psychology, M Letterman Club (Memphis State U. pres. 1983), Emeritus Club (Memphis State U. pres. 1988, 93). Methodist. Home: 3148 Homewood Dr Memphis TN 38128-4413 Office: Mayo Psychol Svcs 3148 Homewood Dr Memphis TN 38128-4413

MAYO, OLIVER, biology researcher; b. Adelaide, Australia, May 29, 1942; s. Eric Elton and Edith Janet Allen (Simpson) M.; m. Margaret Gwendoline Burton, Aug. 11, 1967; children: Charles, Rebecca, Rupert. BSc, U. Adelaide, 1964, BSc with honors, 1965, PhD, 1968, diploma in bus. mgmt., 1976, DSc, 1989. Chartered Statistician, RSS. Head. biometry sect. Waite Agrl. Rsch. Inst. U. Adelaide, 1971-89, dean Faculty Agrl. Sci., 1986-88; chief div. animal prodn. Commonwealth Sci. and Indsl. Rsch. Orgn., Sydney, NSW, Australia, 1989—. Author: The Theory of Plant Breeding, 1980, R. Austin Freeman, 1980, Natural Selection and its Constraints, 1983, The Wines of Australia, 1986. Fellow Australian Acad. Sci., Australian Acad. Tech. Scis. and Engring.; mem. Russian Acad. Agrl. Sci. (fgn.). Home: 146 Hereford St, Forest Lodge NSW 2037, Australia Office: CSIRO Div Animal Prodn, Locked Bag 1 Delivery Ctr, Blacktown NSW 2148, Australia

MAYO, STEVEN WADDELL, pharmacist; b. Dallas, Dec. 19, 1960; s. Travis V. and Lola (Waddell) M.; m. Kristin M. Allred. BS in Pharmacy, NE La. U., 1984; postgrad., Centenary Coll. La., 1993—. Registered pharmacist, La. Regional sales exec., cons. La. Moulding & Supply Co., Shreveport, 1982-90; pharmacist Albertson's Pharmacy, Shreveport, 1985-87; mgr. med. rsch. support Boots Pharms. USA, Inc., Shreveport, 1987-92; sr. dir. Biomedical Rsch. Group, Inc., Austin, Tex., 1992-95; pres , founder ClinNet Clin. Rsch. Network, Austin, 1995—. Safety officer Shreveport Power Squadron, 1986-90. Mem. Am. Pharm. Assn., La. Pharm. Assn., Drug Info. Assn., Assocs. of Clin. Pharmacology, Rho Chi, Kappa Psi. Home: 8007 Caribou Parke Cv Austin TX 78726-4020

MAYO, WALKER PORTER, thoracic surgeon, medical historian, educator; b. Prestonsburg, Ky., Sept. 20, 1922; s. Walker Porter and Reba (Harkey) M.; m. Helen Norma Prevost, June 20, 1952; children: Camille Lynn, Walker Porter III, Patrice Lee, Lionel Prevost. MD, U. Louisville, 1946; MS in Physiology, U. Mich., 1950; MA in History, U. Ky., 1985, PhD in History, 1988. Diplomate, Am. Bd. Surgery, Am. Bd. Thoracic Surgery. Intern Parkland City-County Hosp., Dallas, 1946-47; rsch. fellow U. Mich., 1949-50; resident in surgery U. Louisville/VA Hosp., 1950-52; resident in thoracic surgery U. Mich., 1952-54; pvt. practice Lexington, Ky., 1954-84; med. historian, prof. surgery William Osler program U. Ky. Med. Ctr., Lexington, 1988—; asst. clin. prof., assoc. clin. prof. surgery, U. Ky., Lexington, 1962-78, assoc. clin. prof. physician asst. program, 1978-80, dir. respiratory therapy program, 1979-80, clin. prof. surgery, 1989—; reviewer, cons., Choice mag. Contbr. numerous articles to med. publs. Lt. (j.g.) USNR, 1947-49. Fellow ACS; mem. Fayette County Med. Soc., Ky. Med. Assn., AMA, Ky. Surg. Soc.,Lexington Surg. Soc., John Alexander Soc., So. Thoracic Surg. Soc. (founding mem.), Soc. Thoracic Surgery (founding mem.), Am. Coll. Chest Physicians (pres. Ky. div. 1959), Am. Cancer Soc. (pres. Ky. div. 1961-62). Democrat. Methodist. Home: 4009 Streamwater Pl Lexington KY 40515-6050

MAYOCK, ROBERT LEE, internist; b. Wilkes-Barre, Pa., Jan. 19, 1917; s. John F. and Mathilde M.; m. Constance M. Peruzzi, July 2, 1949; children: Robert Lee, Stephen Philip, Holly Peruzzi. B.S., Bucknell U., 1938; M.D., U. Pa., 1942. Diplomate Am. Bd. Internal Medicine. Intern Hosp. U. Pa., Phila., 1943-44; resident Hosp. U. Pa., 1944-45, chief med. resident. 1945-46, attending physician, 1946—; chief pulmonary disease Phila. Gen. Hosp., 1955-72, chief pulmonary disease sect., 1959-72, sr. cons. pulmonary disease sect., 1972—; asst. prof. clin. medicine U. Pa., 1949-59, assoc. prof. 1959-70, prof. medicine, 1970-87, prof. emeritus, 1987—; mem. med. adv. com. for Tb Commonwealth of Pa., 1965-74, mem. med. adv. com. on chronic respiratory disease, 1974-92, chmn. adv. com., 1981-90; mem. subsplty bd. pulmonary disease Am. Bd. Internal Medicine, 1965-76; nat. bd. dirs. Am. Lung Assn., 1983-92, local bd. dirs., 1961, local pres., 1966-69, dir. at large, 1983—. Contbr. articles in field to med. jours. Served to capt. U.S. Army, 1952-54. Fellow ACP, Am. Coll. Chest Physicians (regent 1972-79), Phila. Coll. Physicians; mem. AMA, Am. Thoracic Soc., Am. Fedn. Clin. Rsch., Am. Heart Assn., Pa. Lung Assn. (dir. 1976—), N.Y. Acad. Scis., Pa. Med. Soc., Phila. County Med. Soc., Physiology Soc. Phila., Laennec Soc. Phila., Merion Cricket Club, Westmoreland Club, Swiftwater Res., Sigma Xi. Home: 244 Gypsy Ln Wynnewood PA 19096-1113 Office: U Penn Ravdin Blgd 3rd Fl Ste F Philadelphia PA 19104

MAYOL, ROBERT FRANCIS, pharmaceutical researcher; b. Springfield, Ill., Nov. 11, 1941; s. Alexander Louis and Gertrude Elizabeth (Link) M.; m. Bonnie Jean Meirink, July 26, 1962 (div. July 1981); children: Michele, Matthew, Bryan, Nicole; m. Karen Lee Kastning, Aug. 15, 1985. BA in Chemistry, So. Ill. U., 1964; PhD in Biochemistry, St. Louis U., 1968. Predoctoral fellow St. Louis U., 1964-68; postdoctoral fellow Calif. Inst. Tech., Pasadena, 1968-70; pharm. researcher Bristol-Myers Squibb Co., Evansville, Ind., 1970-87, Wallingford, Conn., 1987—. Contbr. numerous articles to profl. jours.; patentee in field. USPHS fellow, 1964-68, 68-70. Mem. AAAS, Am. Soc. Pharmacology and Exptl. Therapeutics, N.Y. Acad. Sci., Clin. Pharm. Therapeutics, Endocrine Soc., Sigma Xi (pres. Evansville chpt. 1980-85). Home: 56 Green Ln Durham CT 06422-1903 Office: Bristol Myers Squibb Pharm Rsch Inst 5 Research Pky Wallingford CT 06492-1927

MAYOR, GILBERT HAROLD, pharmaceutical executive, consultant, researcher; b. Detroit, Sept. 12, 1939; s. Bela B. and Selma (Keisler) M.; m. Marcia Joan Wommack, Nov. 2, 1968 (div.); children: Aaron Michael, Jonathan Thomas, Leah Elizabeth. BS, Wayne State U., 1961, MD, 1965. Diplomate Am. Bd. Internal Medicine, Am. Bd. Nephrology, Am. Bd. Clin. Pharmacology, Nat. Bd. Med. Examination. Intern, asst. in medicine Washington U. Sch. Medicine/Barnes Hosp., St. Louis, 1965-66, asst. resident, asst. in medicine, 1968-69; resident U. Mich. Med. Ctr., Ann Arbor, 1969-70, fellow divsn. endocrinology and metabolism, 1970-71, fellow nephrology divsn., 1971-72, instr. dept. internal medicine, 1972-73; asst. prof. dept. internal medicine U. Mich., Ann Arbor, 1973-75; asst. prof. medicine and surgery Mich. State U., Lansing, 1976-78, assoc. prof. medicine, 1978-82, prof. medicine, chief divsn. nephrology, 1982-86; med. affairs The Upjohn Co., Kalamazoo, Mich., 1986-88; sr. dir. med. affairs Boots Pharms., Inc., Chgo., 1988-95, Knoll Pharms. Co. (formerly Boots Pharms., Inc.), Mt. Olive, N.J., 1995—; vis. rsch. scientist Ctr. for Human Growth and Devel. U. Mich., Ann Arbor, 1977-82; mem. faculty Ctr. for Environ. Toxicology Mich. State U., East Lansing, 1981-85, adj. prof. dept. physiology, 1986-89; clin. assoc. medicine U. Chgo., 1992-95; adj. assoc. clin. prof. Mount Sinai Sch. Medicine, N.Y.C., 1995. Contbr. articles to profl. jours.; assoc. editor: Am. Jour. Therapeutics, 1994; mem. editl. bd., manuscript cons. Am. Jour. Kidney Disease, 1981, Annals Internal Medicine, 1985-88; manuscript cons. Kidney Internat., Nephron. Capt. U.S. Army, 1966-68. Fellow AACE, SEGA, ACP (mem. program com. Mich. chpt. 1982-86), Am. Coll. Endocrinology, Am. Coll. Clin. Pharm.; mem. AMA (physicians recognition award 1971, 78, 87), Am. Soc. Nephrology, Am. Thyroid Assn. (mem. archives and history com. 1994—), Am. Acad. Pharm. Physicians (hon. life), Assn. Clin. Endocrinologists (mem. Am. com.), Internat. Soc. Nephrology, The Endocrine Soc., Pharm. Mfrs. Assn. (chmn. med. rels. com. 1988-92). Office: Knoll Pharm Co Med Affairs 3000 Continental Dr N Mount Olive NJ 07828-1234

MAYOR, HEATHER DONALD, medical educator; b. Melbourne, Victoria, Australia, July 6, 1930; d. Joseph A. L. and Elizabeth Emily (Boyd) Donald; m. Richard Blair Mayor, May 28, 1956; children: Diana Boyd (Mrs. Russell Hawkins), Philip Hastings. BS, U. Melbourne, Australia, 1949; MS, U. Melbourne, 1951, DSc, 1970; PhD, U. London, 1954. Electron microscopist Nat. Inst. for Med. Research, London, 1952-55; postdoctoral fellow Walter and Eliza Hall Inst., Melbourne, 1955-56; post doctoral fellow Harvard U. Med. Sch., Boston, 1956-60; from asst. prof. to prof. Baylor Coll. Medicine, Houston, 1960—; prof., 1970—; cons. AEC, Washington, 1971—, Nat. Cancer Inst., Bethesda, Md., 1975—, U. Tex. Med. Sch., Houston, 1975—. Contbr. articles and papers to profl. jours.; artist, coordinator Life Shapes, Contemporary Arts Mus. Houston, Tex. art exhbn., 1974. Recipient Disting. award Ctr. for Interaction Man-Sci.-Soc., Houston, 1973, Sir Hiram Maxim award, 1990; named Scientist of Yr., Ency. Britannica, 1992; scholar in residence Rockefeller Inst. and Found., Bellagio, Italy, 1983. Mem. Am. Assn. Immunologists, Biophysical Soc. (program chmn.), Am. Soc. for Cell Biology (program chmn.), Doctors Club, Houstonian Club, Houston Harpsichord Soc. (bd. dirs.). Home: 6 N West Oak Dr Houston TX 77056-2120 Office: Baylor Coll of Medicine 1 Baylor Plz Houston TX 77030-3411

MAYO-SMITH, MICHAEL FOX, physician; b. Exeter, N.H., Nov. 20, 1953; s. Richmond and Nancy (Fox) M.; m. Janet Marie Cronin; children: Michael Fox Jr., Leslie Marie. BA in Chemistry, Amherst Coll., 1976; MA, Hahnemann U., 1980; MPH in Epidemiology, Harvard U., 1986. Diplomate Am. Bd. Internal Medicine, Am. Bd. Emergency Medicine. Am. Bd. Geriatrics, cert. added qualification. Resident in internal medicine Miriam Hosp. Brown U., Providence, 1980-83; chief resident in internal medicine Miriam Hosp. Brown U., Providence, 1983-84; physician in emergency medicine Carney Hosp., Boston, 1984-85, Cambridge (Mass.) City Hosp., 1985-86, Valley Regional Hosp., Claremont, N.H., 1986-87; physician in internal medicine VA Med. Ctr., Manchester, N.H., 1987—, assoc. chief of staff/ambulatory care, 1994—; clin. instr. in medicine Harvard Med. Sch., Boston, 1987—. Contbr. articles to profl. jours. Mem. ACP, Am. Soc. Addiction Medicine (cert.), Soc. Gen. Internal Medicine, Phi Beta Kappa. Home: 15 Meadowood Dr Franklin NH 03235-2118 Office: VA Med Ctr 718 Smyth Rd Manchester NH 03104-7004

MAYRON, LEWIS WALTER, clinical ecology consultant; b. Chgo., Sept. 20, 1932; s. Max and Florence Minette (Brody) M.; married; children: Leslie Hope Mayron Coff, Eric Brian. BS in Chemistry, Roosevelt U., 1954; MS in Biochemistry, U. Ill., 1955, PhD in Biochemistry, 1959. Rsch. assoc. Dept. Biochemistry and Nutrition U. So. Calif., L.A., 1959-61; asst. biochemist Dept. Biochemistry Presby.-St. Luke's Hosp., Chgo., 1961-62; instr. Dept. Biological Chemistry U. Ill., Chgo., 1961-62; biochemistry group leader Tardanbek Labs., Chgo., 1962-63; sr. devel. chemist Abbott Labs., Chgo., 1963-64; asst. attending physician, mem. spl. staff Michael Reese Hosp. and Med. Ctr., Chgo., 1964-66, rsch. assoc. Dept. Allergy Rsch., 1964-66; asst. prof. in biochemistry and physiology Sch. Dentistry Loyola U., Chgo., 1968-71; guest investigator Argonne (Ill.) Nat. Lab., 1973-79; rsch. chemist V.A. Hosp., Hines, Ill., 1968-79; chief clin. radiobiochemist nuclear medicine svc. V.A. Wadsworth Hosp. Ctr., L.A., 1979-83; cons. in clin. ecology, 1980—. Contbr. articles to profl. jours. Mem. Am. Assn. Clin. Chemists, Am. Assn. for the Advancement of Sci., Soc. for Experimental Biology and Medicine, Sigma Xi. Home: 1779 Summer Cloud Dr Thousand Oaks CA 91362-1217

MAYROSE, MONA PEARL, critical care nurse, flight nurse, educator; b. Levittown, N.J., Nov. 3, 1961; d. William Joseph and Sarah (Tanne) Tillis; m. Alan Gary Mayrose, Nov. 1, 1987; 1 child, Kattey; stepchildren: Dale, Brian. BA, NYU, 1982; MSN, Pace U., 1986. Cert. critical care nurse, trauma nurse, staff devel. nurse; instr. ACLS and critical care. Nursery nurse No. Westchester Hosp. Ctr., Mt. Kisco, N.Y., 1987-88; ICU nurse Meth. Hosp., Houston, 1988-89; dir. nursing Golden Age and Winslow Nursing Homes, Houston, 1989; hospice case mgr. Vis. Nurse Assn., Houston, 1989-91; critical care charge nurse Woodlands (Tex.) Meml. Hosp., 1990-92; commd. 1st lt. USAF, 1992, advanced through grades to capt., 1992; charge nurse surg. ICU 59th Med. Wing USAF, Lackland AFB, Tex., 1992-94, critical care educator, 1994-95; flight nurse 23d Aeromed. Evacuation Squadron, Pope AFB, N.C., 1996—. Mem. AACN (bd. dirs. San Antonio chpt.), Nat. Nurses Staff Devel. Orgn., Air Force Assn., Aerospace Med. Assn., Sigma Theta Tau. Jewish. Home: 853 Foxcroft Dr Fayetteville NC 28311

MAYS, CHARLES EDWARD II, physician assistant; b. Montgomery, Ala., Oct. 8, 1961; s. Charles Edward and Roberta (Evans) M.; m. Joyce Yolanda Leftwich, Aug. 20, 1983; children: Shalanda Monique, Charles III, Sheawna Joi. Assoc. Health Sci., CCAF, Montgomery, Ala.; BS in Medicine, U. Nebr. Nat. cert. physician asst., ACLS instr., ATLS. Real estate assoc. ERA Realty, Montgomery, 1983-84; commd. 1st lt. USAF, 1984; med. technician USAF, Warner Robins, Ga., 1984-90; physician asst. USAF, Dover, Del., 1992—, instr. EMT, 1992—; instr. ACLS USAF, Warner Robins and Dover, 1988—. Mem. outreach ministry Calvary Assembly Ch., Dover, 1993—. Mem. Am. Acad. Physician Assts., Soc. Air Forde Physician Assts. Republican. Mem. Full Gospel Ch. Home: 3320 Hemlock Dover DE 19901 Office: 436 Med Group SGOMF 307 Tuskegee Blvd Dover AFB DE 19901

MAYS, PETER KEVIN, biochemist; b. Merton, Surrey, U.K., May 23, 1963; came to U.S., 1990; s. Derek William and Brenda Pauline (Emberson) M. BSc in Chemistry and Pharmacology, U. Nottingham, 1984; PhD Biochemistry, U. London, 1990. Rsch. asst. Sch. Pharmacy Liverpool (U.K.) Polytech., 1984-85; rsch. asst Nat. Heart and Lung Inst., U.K., 1985-90; postdoctoral fellow Dept. Biochemistry & Molecular Biology Jefferson Med. Coll., Phila., 1990-92; staff scientist Organogenesis Inc., Canton, Mass., 1992-96; asst. prof. Coriell Inst. for Med. Rsch., Camden, N.J., 1996; dir. R & D Collagenesis, Inc., Acton, Mass., 1996—. Editl. bd mem. Internat. Jour. Biochemistry and Cell Biology, London, 1995—; patentee in field; contbr. chpt. in book and articles to profl. jours. Grantee Wellcome Trust, 1990; recipient Honor Fell Travel scholarship Brit. Soc. Cell Biology, 1990. Mem. Am. Chem. Soc., Am. Soc. Cell Biology, Biochem. Soc. U.K., N.Y. Acad. Scis. Episcopalian. Home: 2025 Spring Garden St Philadelphia PA 19130 Office: Collagenesis Inc 125 Nagog Park Acton MA 01720

MAZER, MILTON, psychiatrist; b. N.Y.C., Mar. 5, 1911; s. Michael and Rose (Orman) M.; m. Virginia O'Leary, 1949; children: Ruth, Mark F. BA, U. Pa., 1932, MD, 1935. Diplomate Am. Bd. Psychiatry and Neurology. Intern Mt. Sinai Hosp., Phila., 1935-36, mem. staff, 1937-39; resident in internal medicine Montefiore Hosp., Bronx, N.Y., 1936-37; physician VA, Washington and Biloxi, Miss., 1939-42; psychiatry VA, N.Y.C., 1946-48; pvt.

practice N.Y.C., 1948-61, Marthas Vineyard, Mass., 1961—; dir. Marthas Vineyard Mental Health Ctr., 1961-83; instr. Harvard Med. Sch., 1962-72, asst. prof. psychiatry, 1972-76, assoc. clin. prof., 1976-81. Author: People and Predicaments, 1976; co-editor: Outline of Psychoanalysis, 1951; contbr. articles to med. jours. Mem. West Tisbury (Mass.) Dem. Town Com., 1962—; moderator West Tisbury Town Meeting, 1967-77. Capt. M.C., USAAF, 1942-45. Fellow Am. Psychiat. Assn. (life). Office: Music St West Tisbury MA 02575

MAZLEN, ROGER GEOFFREY, physician, clinical pharmacologist and nutritionist; b. Bklyn., Nov. 23, 1937; s. Henry Gershwin and Ann Kurland (Shapero) M.; m. Sandra Phyllis Kuritzky, Aug. 7, 1960; children: James Edward, Vivien Gayle. BS in Biology, Rensselaer Poly. Inst., 1959; MD, SUNY, Bklyn., 1963. Intern, Maimonides Med. Center, Bklyn., 1963-64; resident in medicine, 1964-65; research assoc. NIH, Bethesda, Md., 1965-67; resident in med. ophthalmology Mt. Sinai Med. Center, N.Y.C., 1967-69; asso. med. dir. Pfizer Inc., N.Y.C., 1970-71; asst. dir. clin. research Ayerst Labs., N.Y.C., 1971-75; assoc. dir. clin. research Schering Corp., Bloomfield, N.J., 1975-78; adj. assoc. prof. biology Rensselaer Poly. Inst.; adj. asst. prof. medicine N.Y. Med. Coll.; sr. clin. asst. prof. Mt. Sinai Sch. Medicine; sr. faculty div. endocrinology and metabolism Mt. Sinai Med. Ctr.; sr. attending div. endocrinology and metabolism Mt. Sinai Med. Ctr.; med. cons. Profl. Children's Sch.; cons. in clin. nutrition and metabolism South Oaks Hosp.; med. cons. Terrap Psychol. Assocs. N.Y. Bd. dirs. Bayside Hills Civic Assn., 1970-80; adv. mem. bd. dirs. U.S.A., Inc., 1970-72; founder, chmn. Queens County (N.Y.) Common Cause, 1972-75, vice chmn. N.Y. State, 1974-75; chmn. hyperalimentation com. Astoria Gen. Hosp., N.Y.; cons. in clin. nutrition and metabolism South Oaks Hosp.; dir. Cemitin Am. Nutritiional, 1983-88, also mem. eating disorder adv. bd.; mem. adv. bd. nutrition Roche Nat. Clinic; pres. The Inst. for the Study of CFS and Related Disorders. Served with USPHS, 1965-67. Fellow Am. Coll. Nutrition (sec.-treas.; chmn. council on nutrition and cardiovascular disease 1976-85); mem. Am. Soc. Clin. Pharmacology and Therapeutics, Am. Soc. Internal Medicine, Soc. for Natural Immunity, N.Y. State Soc. Internal Medicine, N.Y. Acad. Scis., Internat. Assn. Eating Disorder Profls., N.Y. Cardiol. Soc., Soc. Biol. Therapy, Muhammad Ali Internat. Sport Youth Athletic Found., Inc. (bd. drs.). Republican. Author: A New Manifesto for Middle America, 1972; (with others) Nutrition and Health Care; contbr. chpt. to Quick Reference to Clinical Nutrition; mem. editorial staff Jour. of the Chiropractic Coun. on Nutrition. Office: 775 Park Ave Ste 155 Huntington NY 11743-3976 also: 148 Tulip Ave Fl 2 Floral Park NY 11001-2705

MAZUMDER, AMITABHA, physician, researcher; b. Calcutta, India, Oct. 28, 1952; s. Bibhuti and Nilima (Deb Chcudhury) M.; m. Shibani Ray, June 29, 1979; children: Nikhilesh, Viveka, Kalyan. BA, Johns Hopkins U., 1973, MD, 1977. Intern and resident Baylor Coll. of Med., Houston, 1977-79; asst. prof. Baylor Coll. Med., Houston, 1983-85; clin. assoc. Nat. Cancer Inst., Bethesda, Md., 1979-82, investigator, 1982-83; asst. prof. M.D. Anderson Hosp., Houston, 1983-85; asst. prof. U. So. Calif. Med. Sch., L.A., 1985-91, dir. bone marrow transplantation unit, dept. hematology, mem. med. student rsch. com., 1985-91, assoc. prof., 1988-91; prof. medicine, dir. bone marrow transplantation Georgetown U. Sch. Medicine Lombardi Cancer Ctr., Washington, 1993—. Contbr. articles to profl. jours., chpts. to books. V.p. Med. Student Govt., Balt., 1977; pres. Youth Forum, Balt., 1976. Served to capt. USPHS, 1979-83. Mem. AAAS, ACP, Am. Assn. Immunologists, Am. Assn. Cancer Research, Am. Soc. Clin. Oncology, Am. Soc. Hematology, Indian Orgns. (Houston chpt. sec. 1979, Balt. sec. 1980-81), Phi Beta Kappa, Alpha Omega Alpha. Democrat. Hindu. Office: Lombardi Cancer Ctr 3800 Reservoir Rd NW Washington DC 20007-2196

MAZUR, LEONARD L., pharmaceutical company executive; b. Ansbach, Germany, Jan. 23, 1945; came to U.S., 1949; s. Walter and Maria (Zatwarnitsky) M.; m. Helena Maria Olijnyk, Nov. 1966; children: Maria, Michael, Irene. BA, Temple U., 1968, MBA, 1975. Mktg. mgr. Cooper Labs., Inc., Fairfield, N.J. and Palo Alto, Calif., 1971-81; dir. product mgmt. Knoll Pharm. Corp. divsn. BASF, Whippany, N.J., 1981-84; v.p. ICN Pharm. Corp., Costa Mesa, Calif., 1984-88; pres., COO Chantal Pharm. Corp., L.A., 1988-89; exec. v.p. Medicis Pharm. Corp., N.Y.C., 1989-93; vice chmn. Cabot Labs., Inc., N.Y.C., 1994—; Patentee in field. Mem. adv. bd. Manor Jr. Coll., Jenkintown, Pa., 1972-78; ind. observer Referendum for Independence, Ukraine, 1991. Roman Catholic. Home: 32 Arden Rd Mountain Lakes NJ 07046-1503

MAZUR, PETER, cell physiologist, cryobiologist; b. N.Y.C., March 3, 1928; s. Paul M. and Adolphia (Kaske) M.; m. Drusilla Stevens, May 28, 1953 (dec. May 1982); 1 child, Timothy Stevens; m. Sara Jo Bolling, June 16, 1984. A.B. magna cum laude, Harvard U., 1949, Ph.D., 1953. NSF postdoctoral fellow, Princeton U., N.J., 1957-59; research staff biology div. Oak Ridge Nat. Lab., 1959—, group leader fundamental and applied cryobiology, 1966—, sci. dir. biophysics and cell physiology, biology div., 1974-75, corporate fellow, 1985; mem. vis. com. biology Harvard U. Bd. Overseers 1972-77; prof. U. Tenn.; mem. Space Sci. Bd. of Nat. Acad., 1975-77. Contbr. articles to prof. jours. Served to capt. USAF, 1953-57. Recipient Author of Yr. award Martin-Marietta Energy Systems, 1985, Disting. Svc. award Am. Assn. Tissue Banks, 1993, R & D 100 award R & D Mag., 1993; Lalor fellow Harvard U., 1952, John Harvard fellow, 1951. Sigma Xi Nat. lectr., 1980. Fellow AAAS; mem. Soc. for Cyrobiology (pres. 1973-74, bd. govs., 1979—), Phi Beta Kappa. Club: Cosmos (Washington). Current work: Cryobiology mechanisms of freezing injury in living cells and tissues. Subspecialties: Cell biology; Biophysics (biology). Home: 125 Westlook Cir Oak Ridge TN 37830-3856 Office: Oak Ridge Nat Lab Biology Divsn PO Box 2009 Oak Ridge TN 37831-8080

MAZZAFERRI, ERNEST LOUIS, physician, educator; b. Cleve., Sept. 27, 1936; s. Joseph and Nanetta (Marinelli) M.; m. Florence Mildred Marolt, Nov. 23, 1957; children: Patricia Marie Atchison, Michael Louis, Sharon Lynne Brown, Ernest Louis. BS cum laude, John Carroll U., 1958; MD, Ohio State U., 1962. Diplomate Am. Bd. Internal Medicine, Am. Bd. Endocrinology and Metabolism. Intern Ohio State U. Hosps., Columbus, 1962-63; resident Ohio State U. Hosps., 1963-64, 66-68; asst. prof. medicine Ohio State U., 1968-70, assoc. prof., 1973-76, prof., 1976-79, dir. div. endocrinology and metabolism, 1975-78; acting dean U. Nev., Reno, 1979-81; prof., chmn. dept. medicine U. Nev., 1978-84, prof. physiology, 1982-84; prof., chmn. dept. medicine, prof. physiology Ohio State U., Columbus, 1984—; pres. Dept. of Medicine Found., 1986—. Author: Endocrinology Case Studies, 3d edit., 1985, Internal Medicine Pearls, 1993; editor: Textbook of Endocrinology, 3d edit., 1986, Contemporary Internal Medicine, 1988, 3d edit., 1990, Advances in Endocrinology and Metabolism, Vol. 6, 1995, Endocrine Tumors, 1993; mem. sci. adv. bd. Western Jour. Medicine, 1993; mem. editl. bd. Jour. Lab. Clin. Medicine, 1987—, Hosp. Practice; contbr. articles to profl. jours. Chmn. Gov.'s Com. on Radiation Fallout in Nev., 1980-84, hosp. ethics com. Ohio State U.; mem. Sec. of Energy Dose Assessment Adv. Com., 1980-84, Agy. for Health Care Policy, Rsch. Cataract Guideline Com., 1991-92. Lt. col. USAF, 1964-72; col. USAR. Decorated Air Force Commendation medal, Meritorious Svc. medal. Fellow ACP (gov. for Nev. 1984-85, chmn. clin. efficacy assessment program com. 1992-95, mem. health and pub. policy com., edn. policy com.); mem. Am. Bd. Internal Medicine (Endocrinology and Metabolism, 1996—), AMA, Am. Thyroid Assn., Am. Diabetes Assn. (pres. Ohio affiliate 1988-89), Endocrine Soc., Am. Clin. and Climatol. Assn., Ctrl. Soc. Clin. Rsch., Am. Coll. Clin. Endocrinology (bd. dirs. 1995-96), Alpha Omega Alpha. Republican. Roman Catholic. Home: 2481 Slate Run Columbus OH 43220-2850 Office: Ohio State U Means Hall 1655 Upham Dr Columbus OH 43210-1251

MAZZAGLIA, ALFIO JOSEPH, podiatric surgeon; b. Lawrence, Mass., Aug. 16, 1932; s. Domenic T. and Rose E. (Ferrante) M. Student, Tufts U., 1949-51; D Podiatric Medicine, Ill. Coll. Podiatric Medicine, 1955. Diplomate Am. Bd. Podiatric Surgery, Am. Bd. Podiatric Orthopedics, Am. Bd. Quality Assurance & Utilization Rev. Chief surgery, dir. interns, clin. prof. surgery Ill. Coll. Podiatric Medicine and Surgery, Chgo., 1955-59; assoc., 1st surg. asst. Henri L. DuVries, DPM, MD, FACS, Chgo., 1954-59; surg. assoc. Charles Guiliano, MD, FACS, 1960-70; guest lectr. Ill. Coll. Podiatric Medicine and Surgery, Chgo., 1971; pvt. practice, Lawrence, Mass., 1961—; assoc. in practice Howar Taylor, MD, FACOS, 1980-87; surg. assoc. Charles Guiliano, MD, 1960-70; Henri L. DuVries, Chgo., 1955-59; dir. surg. seminar courses New Eng. Coll. Foot Surgeons, 1960-61; adj. faculty clinician Ohio Coll. Podiatric Medicine, 1983; physician reviewer Mass. PRO, 1989-94; chmn. coord. foot screening program 131st ann. conv. Am. Dental Assn., 1990; chief podiat. svcs. St. John's Lowell Gen. Hosps., Eliot Hosp., Lowell, Lawrence Gen. Hosp., Cath. Med. Ctr., Manchester, Mass.; lectr. on foot surgery, local anesthesia and surg. wound irrigation to local and nat. orgns.; lectr. U. Mass. Med. Sch., Orthopedic Dept., 1989-90; oral examiner Am. Bd. Podiatric Orthopedics, Chgo., 1993; physician reviewer Mass. Peer Rev. Orgn., 1990-94. Contbg. author: Principles and Practice of Podiatry; also numerous articles; innovator operative procedures for intractable plantar keratosis, hammer toe, ingrown nail, hallux abductovalgus. Named hon. citizen City of Lowell, 1975; recipient citation Mass. Senate, 1988; Italian Coll. club scholar Sons of Italy, 1949. Fellow Am. Assn. Hosp. Podiatrists, Am. Acad. Podiatric Microsurgery, Am. Acad. Ambulatory Foot Surgery, Am. Soc. Podiatric Med., Am. Coll. Foot Surgery, Am. Acad. Podiatric Laser Surgery, Am. Coll. Foot and Ankle Surgeons; mem. Am. Podiatric Med. Assn. (pres. Northeastern divsn. 1981-83, chmn. 1992-95, state pres. 1987-88, com. on hosps. 1988-89, com. on health systems 1990-92, mem. ho. of dels. 1988-91, alt. coun. 1994-95), Mass. Podiatric Med. Soc. (del. ho. of dels. 1994, pres. divsn. III 1995—, trustee 1995—). Office: 338 Ames St Lawrence MA 01841-4113

MAZZEO, JOHN THOMAS, surgeon, educator; b. Newburgh, N.Y., Jan. 11, 1945; s. John Thomas and Nina Rose (Rao) M.; m. Linda Mazzeo; children: Christina, Jack. B.A., Fordham U., 1966; M.D., N.Y. Med. Coll., 1970. Diplomate Am. Bd. Surgery. Resident in gen. surgery N.Y. Med. Coll., N.Y.C., 1970-72, Nat. Naval Med. Ctr., Bethesda, Md., 1974-78; surgeon Surg. Assocs. No. Va., McLean, 1984—; mem. staff Potomac Hosp., Woodbridge, Va., pres. med. staff, 1986—; mem. staff Fairfax Hosp.; assoc. clin. prof. surgery Uniformed Services U. Health Scis., Bethesda, 1978—; clin. assoc. prof. surgery Georgetown U., Washington, 1983—. Trustee No. Va. Peer Rev. Orgn., Falls Church, 1983-84; med. dir, trustee No. Va. chpt. Am. Cancer Soc., 1986—. Served to comdr. USN, 1972-80. Fellow ACS; mem. Va. Surg. Soc., Med. Soc. Va., Fairfax County Med. Soc. Avocation: stone and wood sculpting. Home: 4100 N River St McLean VA 22101 Office: Surg Assocs No Va 2296 Opitz Blvd Ste 260 Woodbridge VA 22191-3300

MAZZONI, BARBARA JEAN, advice nurse; b. Cumberland, Md., July 23, 1949; d. Robert Taylor and Loretta (Miller) McLaughlin; m. Robert A. Mazzoni, Feb. 17, 1979; 1 child, Michael. Diploma, Ch. Home/Hosp. Sch. Nursing, 1971; BS in Nursing, U. Md., 1976. Advice nurse Kaiser Permanente, Lutherville, Md., 1989—; clin. mgr. Greater Balt. Med. Ctr., Towson, Md., 1987-89; nurse clinician U. Md. Hosp., 1978-87. Mem. Md. State Emergency Nurses Assn. (founder; past pres. Met. Balt. chpt.). Home: 670 Post Ln Rock Hill SC 29730-6028

MAZZOTTI, RICHARD RENE, pharmacist; b. Taylorville, Ill., Dec. 8, 1937; s. Rene and Elizabeth Lenore (Gordon) M.; m. Jerri Lynn VanVleet, July 28, 1962; children: Ann Elizabeth, Lisa Lyn. BS, St. Louis Coll., 1961. Lic. registered pharmacist, Mo., Ill.; lic. registered real estate broker, Ill.; registered securities salesperson, Ill.; designated cert. comml. investment mem. Pharmacist, ptnr. Rene's Drug Store, Taylorville, 1957-73; pharmacist, owner Bach's Gen. Discount, Taylorville, 1970-75; owner Ricks Stereo Ctr., Taylorville, 1975-79; pharmacist, owner Union Prescription Ctr., Springfield, Ill., 1973-89; broker Craggs Adams Realtors, Springfield, 1981—; owner Capitol Pharmacy, Springfield, 1989-94. Pres. Taylorville Assn. Commerce and Industry, 1978-79; asst. instr. Real Estate Securities and Syndication Inst., Nashville, 1979; pres. Retail Mchts. Assn., Taylorville, 1967. Mem. Ill. Pharm. Assn. (v.p. 1995—), Springfield Pharmacists Assn. (pres. 1990—), Mo. Pharm. Assn., Am. Pharm. Assn., Nat. Assn. Retail Druggists, Ctrl. Ill. Bd. Realtors (C.C.I.M.) Retailers Nat. Mktg. Inst., Ill. Chpt. Cert. Comml. Investment Mems., Real Estate Securities and Syndication Inst., Ill. Chpt. Real Estate Securities and Hyndication Inst., Capitol Club Ill., Realtors Polit. Action Com. Democrat. Roman Catholic. Home: 1203 Roosevelt Rd Taylorville IL 62568-8909 Office: Ill Dept of Pub Aid 201 S Grand Ave E 3d Fl Springfield IL 62763-0001

MCABEE, THOMAS ALLEN, psychologist; b. Spartanburg, S.C., Mar. 31, 1949; s. Thomas Walker and Doris Lee (Gillespie) McA. Student Ga. Inst. Tech., 1967-69; BA, Furman U., 1971; MA, U. S.C., 1975, PhD, 1979. Clin. counselor Adolescent Inpatient Service, William S. Hall Psychiat. Inst., Columbia, S.C., 1971-73; counselor children's therapeutic camp Columbia Area Mental Health Center, 1974; co-dir. community problems survey Eau Claire Community Project, Columbia, 1975; asst. aging services planner Central Midlands Regional Planning Council, Columbia, 1976; instr. U. S.C., 1976; NSF intern S.C. State Legislature, 1978; research dir. S.C. Legis. Gov.'s Com. on Mental Health and Mental Retardation, Columbia, 1979-80; co-dir. TV project "Feelings Just Are," Columbia Area Mental Health Center, 1980-89, cons., 1977-79; cons. S.C. Protection and Advocacy System for Handicapped Citizens, 1980, 81, S.C. Dept. Mental Health, 1981; psychologist, S.C. Dept. Mental Retardation, 1982-93, S.C. Dept. Disabilities and Spl. Needs, 1993—; mem. deinstitutionalization task force S.C. Developmental Disabilities Council, 1979-80; mem. subcom. State Commr.'s Ad Hoc Com. to Study and Develop Work/Lodge System for S.C., S.C. Dept. Mental Health, 1979-80; mem. Media Task Force of Gov.'s Adv. Com. on Early Childhood Devel. and Edn., 1980-81; chmn. primary prevention public media com. S.C. Dept. Mental Health, 1979-81. Recipient Palmetto Pictures Photography award, 1977; NIMH fellow, 1976-77. Mem. Am. Psychol. Assn., S.C. Psychol. Assn. Home: Rivergate # 821 3900 Bentley Dr Columbia SC 29210-7980 Office: 8301 Farrow Rd Columbia SC 29203-3245

MCADOO, TIM STACEY, health service administrator; b. Union City, Tenn., Apr. 28, 1972. BS, U. Ky., 1994; DD, Charter Ecumenical Ministry, Sacramento, Calif., 1992. LNHA. AIT Louden & Co., Lexington, Ky., 1992, adminstr., 1994—; mem. adv. counsel KIPDA Ombudsman, Louisville, 1995—. Mem. Am. Coll. Health Care Adminstrs., Am. Coll. Health Care Execs.

MCALINDON, MARY NAOMI, nursing administrator; b. Ebensburg, Pa., Oct. 16, 1935; d. S. David and Genevieve (Little) Solomon; m. James Daniel McAlindon, Nov. 25, 1961; children: Robert, Donald, James, Peter, M. Catherine. BSN, Georgetown U., 1957; MA, U. Mich., 1979; EdD, Wayne State U., 1992. RN, Mich. Staff nurse Georgetown U. Hosp., Washington, 1957-59; instr. St. Joseph Hosp., Flint, 1959-62; clin. instr. Mott. C.C., Flint, 1980-81; asst. DON McLaren Hosp., Flint, 1980-89, adminstrv. asst., 1989-92, asst. v.p., 1992-95; clin. informatics mgr. McLaren Health Care Corp., Flint, 1995—. Mem. bd. trustees United Way Genesee County, Flint, 1988-95. Mem. ANA (exec. com. 1991-93), Am. Med. Informatics Assn. (chair nursing group 1993-94), Mich. Nursing Informatics Network (charter), Vis. Nurses Assn. (pres., bd. dirs. 1988-90), Dist. Nurses Assn. (prfes. 1993-96), Nursing Honor Soc. U. Mich. (pres. 1996—). Office: McLaren Health Care Corp 401 S Ballenger Hwy Flint MI 48532-3638

MCALLISTER, RUSSELL GREENWAY, JR., cardiologist, clinical scientist, educator; b. Richmond, Va., Nov. 23, 1941; s. Russell Greenway and Kathryn Lee (Young) McA.; m. Ann Elizabeth Parks, Nov. 9, 1968; children: Kathryn Ann, Edward Russell. BS, Hampden-Sydney Coll., 1963; MD, Med. Coll. Va., 1967. Instr. medicine Vanderbilt U. Coll. Medicine, Nashville, 1969-72; asst. prof. U. Ky. Coll. Medicine, Lexington, 1972-78, assoc. prof., 1978-82, prof., 1982-86; clin. investigator Lexington VA Med. Ctr., 1974-78, assoc. chief of staff for rsch., 1978-86; dir., clinical rsch. Glaxo Inc., Research Triangle Park, N.C., 1986-89; prof. medicine U. N.C. Coll. Medicine, Chapel Hill, 1989-90, Duke U. Med. Ctr., Durham, N.C., 1987—; cons. pharm. cos., 1978-86; v.p., med. dir. Cato Rsch. Ltd., Durham, 1989—. Contbr. numerous articles in profl. jours. Recipient Fogarty Sr. Internat. fellowship, Nat. Inst. of Health, Basel, Switzerland, 1978-79. Fellow Am. Coll. Cardiology, Am. Coll. Physicians, Am. Coll. Clin. Pharm.; mem. Am. Soc. Pharmacology and Therapeutics, Am. Heart Assn., Hope Valley Club (Durham), Keeneland Club (Lexington). Republican. Presbyterian. Home: 3712 Dover Rd Durham NC 27707-5106 Office: Cato Rsch Ltd 4364 S Alston Ave Durham NC 27713-2200

MCANDREW, JANET MARIE, physician assistant; b. Pitts., Apr. 26, 1960; d. Melvin Joseph and Janice Elaine (Vano) McAndrew; m. Ronald Michael Schwoegl, Aug. 3, 1985; 1 child, Daniel Paul Schwoegl. AD, Physician Asst., C.C. of Allegheny County, Pitts., 1984. Cert. physician asst. Physician asst. Alma Illery Med. Ctr., Homewood, Pa., 1987-88, 90-93, Ctr. for Behavioral Medicine, Kittanning, Pa., 1988—; physician asst.-ctrl. testing Shadyside Hosp., Pitts., 1993—; physician asst.-women vet. ctr. Highland Dr. VA Med. Ctr., Pitts., 1995—. Mem. Am. Acad. Physician Assts., Pa. Soc. Physician Assts. Roman Catholic. Home: 538 North Ave Verona PA 15147 Office: VA Med Ctr Highland Dr Pittsburgh PA 15206

MCANDREW, MICHAEL KENNETH, hospital executive; b. Holyoke, Mass., Mar. 21, 1948; s. Michael Kenneth Sr. and Florence (Salha) McA.; m. Sandra Johnson, Oct. 18, 1984; children: Joshua Wayne, Michael Johnson. BS in English, Boston State Coll., 1978; M in Health Adminstrn., Va. Commonwealth U., 1981. V.p. profl. svcs. Galesburg (Ill.) Cottage Hosp., 1981-83; v.p. outreach svcs. Jackson (Tenn.) Madison County Gen. Hosp., 1983-86; pres., chief exec. officer Flaget Meml. Hosp., Bardstown, Ky., 1986-88; chief oper. officer Brazosport Meml. Hosp., Lake Jackson, Tex., 1988-92; sr. v.p. Shannon Med. Ctr., San Angelo, Tex., 1992-96; sr. cons. Quantum Consulting Internat., Austin, 1996—; speaker at seminars. Mem. mayor's adv. com. City of Bardstown, 1988; mem. Leadership Brazosport. Named Ky. Col. Mem. Am. Coll. Healthcare Execs., Lake Jackson C. of C. Democrat. Roman Catholic. Home: PO Box 61412 San Angelo TX 76906-1412 Office: Shannon Med Ctr 120 E Harris Ave San Angelo TX 76903-5904

MCANDREW, ROBERT, dental surgeon, lecturer; b. St. Andrews, Fife, Scotland, Nov. 5, 1963; s. David Coutts and Helen Margaret McKenna (McHale) McA.; m. Moira Barnes, Jan. 6, 1989; children: Amy, Hazel, Fraser. BDS, Dundee (Scotland) U., 1986; Diploma in Restorative Dentistry, Dundee (Scotland) U., Edinburgh. Gen. dental practitioner Northampton, Eng., 1987; house officer Tayside Health Bd., Dundee, 1987; sr. house officer Cen. Manchester Health Authority, Manchester, Eng., 1988-90; registrar Tayside Health Bd., Dundee, 1990-93; sr. registrar in restorative dentistry U. Wales Coll. Medicine, Cardiff, 1993—. Contbr. articles to profl. jours. Rsch. grantee Welsh Scheme, 1993, Oral B, 1993. Fellow RCS (Eng.), RCS (Edinburgh, assoc.). Office: U Wales Coll Medicine, Heath Park, Dept Restorative Dentistry, Cardiff CF4 4XY, Wales

MCANINCH, JACK WELDON, urological surgeon, educator; b. Merkel, Tex., Mar. 17, 1936; s. Weldon Thomas and Margaret (Canon) McA.; m. Barbara B. Buchanan, Dec. 29, 1960 (div. Aug. 1972); m. Burnet B. Sumner, Dec. 29, 1987; children: David A., Todd G., Brendan J. BS, Tex. Tech U., 1958; MS, U. Idaho, 1960; MD, U. Tex., 1964. Diplomate Am. Bd. Urology (trustee 1991—, pres. 1996—). Commd. capt. U.S. Army, 1964-66, advanced through grades to col., 1977, ret., 1977; col. USAR; intern then resident Letterman Army Med. Ctr., San Francisco, 1964-69; chief urol. surgery San Francisco Gen. Hosp., 1977—; prof. urol. surgery U. Calif., San Francisco, 1977—. Editor: Urogenital Trauma, 1985, Urologic Clinics of North America, 1989, Smith's General Urology, 1995; section editor: Early Care of the Injured Patient, 1990, Traumatic and Reconstructive Urology, 1996. Col. US Army, 1964-72. Recipient Disting. Alumnus award Tex. Tech U., 1994. Fellow ACS (gov. 1992—); mem. Am. Urol. Assn. (pres. we. sect. 1992-93, bd. dirs. 1990—, pres. 1996—), Genitourinary Reconstructive Surgeons (pres.), Am. Assn. Surgery Trauma (v.p.), Soc. Univ. Urologists, Am. Bd. Urology (pres. 1996—). Office: San Francisco Gen Hosp Dept Urology 1001 Potrero Ave San Francisco CA 94110-3518

MC ARTHUR, JANET WARD, endocrinologist, educator; b. Bellingham, Wash., June 25, 1914; d. Hyland Donald and Alice Maria (Frost) McA. A.B., U. Wash., 1935, M.S., 1937; M.B., Northwestern U., 1941, M.D., 1942; ScD (hon.), Mt. Holyoke Coll., 1962. Diplomate: Am. Bd. Internal Medicine. Intern Cin. Gen. Hosp., 1941-42, asst. resident in medicine, 1942-43; asst. resident, rsch. fellow in medicine H.P. Walcott fellow clin. medicine Mass. Gen. Hosp., Boston, 1943-47, assoc. physician, 1959-84, assoc. children's svc., 1968-84; instr. Harvard U., 1955-57, asst. prof., 1960-64, assoc. prof., 1964-73, prof., 1973-84, prof. emeritus, 1984—; clin. prof. medicine Boston U. Sch. Medicine, 1984—; adj. prof. Sargent Coll. Allied Health Scis. Boston U., 1982—; mem. reproductive biology study sect. NIH, 1974-78, Com. on Population Studies, 1980-84; co-dir. Vincent Meml. Rsch. Lab., 1977-79; sr. scientist U. London, 1985-86. Author: (with others) Functional Endocrinology from Birth Through Adolescence, 1952; editor: (with Theodore Colton) Statistics in Endocrinology, 1970; contbr. articles to profl. jours. Fellow ACP; mem. AMA, AAAS, Endocrine Soc., Am. Soc. Reproductive Medicine, Am. Assn. Clinical Endocrinologists, Boston Obstetrical Soc., Phi Beta Kappa, Sigma Xi, Alpha Omega Alpha. Home: 19 Brimmer St Boston MA 02108-1025 Office: Boston U 635 Commonwealth Ave Fl 4 Boston MA 02215-1605

MCARTHUR, JUSTIN C., neurologist; b. Reigate, Eng., Feb. 20, 1956; m. Julie Helen Luebbe, Sept. 11, 1982; 1 child, Heather. MB, BS, U. London, 1979; MPH, Johns Hopkins U., 1988. Diplomate Am. Bd. Internal Medicine, Am. Bd. Neurology and Psychiatry. Asst. prof. neurology Johns Hopkins U., Balt., 1985-90, assoc. prof., 1990—, assoc. prof. epidemiology, 1992—, dir. med. clerkship, 1988-95, dir. neurology residency program, 1995—; advisor World Health Orgn., 1988-89, Pres.'s Commn. on AIDS, 1988; chmn. neurology com. AIDS Clin. Trials Group, 1994-96. Author: AIDS and Neurology, 1995; contbr. articles to profl. jours., chpts to books. Sci. adv. com. Am. Found. AIDs Rsch., 1988—. Mem. Am. Acad. Neurology, Am. Neurol. Assn., Alpha Omega Alpha. Office: Johns Hopkins U Meyer 6109 Neurology Baltimore MD 21287

MC ATHIE, MARYLOU, nursing educator; b. Huron, S.D., July 9, 1927; d. John and Agnes Virginia (Mangan) McA.; diploma Oak Park Hosp. unit Loyola U., Chgo., 1948; B.S. in Nursing, DePaul U., 1954, M.S. in Nursing, 1956; Ed.D., U. San Francisco, 1980. Cons. Calif. State Dept. Health, 1961-68; dir. nursing San Joaquin Gen. Hosp., Stockton, Calif., 1960-68; regional nursing cons., spl. asst. Pacific Basin affairs USPHS, HEW, San Francisco, 1968-84; prof. Sonoma State U., 1984-90, prof. emeritus, 1990—; ex officio mem. exec. com. Western Council on Higher Edn. for Nursing. Mem. scholarship com. San Joaquin March of Dimes, 1964-68; bd. dirs. Calif. Nurses Found., 1984—. Recipient award HEW Region IX, 1974, commendation March of Dimes, 1968, citizen's commendation San Joaquin County, 1967, cert. of merit UCLA, 1972, cert. in leadership tng. Western Council on Higher Edn. in Nursing, U. Calif., San Francisco, 1962, cert. in pub. health nursing Calif. Dept. Pub. Health, U. San Francisco, 1964; Spl. Recognition award USPHS, 1984, Recognition award Western Inst. Nursing, 1991, Recognition award Calif. Nurses Assn., 1992. Mem. Am., Calif. (conv. del. 1972, 85, 87, commr. Nursing Edn. 1985-89) nurses assns., Nat., Western (chmn. com. nursing service adminstrs.) leagues for nursing, AAUW, Am. Pub. Health Assn., Western Inst. Nursing, Sigma Theta Tau. Speaker, convs., confs.; Co-author: Professional Trends in Nursing; contbr. to audio and TV tapes, articles to profl. publs. Home: 8109 Arroyo Way Stockton CA 95209-2903 Office: Sonoma State U Dept of Nursing Rohnert Park CA 94928

MCBATH, DONALD LINUS, osteopathic physician; b. Chgo., May 19, 1935; s. Earl and Phyllis (Michalski) McB.; m. Ruth Southerland, Jan. 18, 1956; children: Donald L. Jr., Donna Ruth McBath Bassett, Daniel P. BA in Polit. Sci., U. Fla., 1957, BS in Pre Med., 1962; DO, Kansas City (Mo.) Coll. Osteopathy and Surgery, 1969; MA, St. Leo Coll., 1981. Diplomate Nat. Bd. Examiners; cert. family practice Am. Osteo. Bd. Family Physicians, Correctional Health Profl. Med. Med. dir. various orgns., Dade City, Fla., 1971; chief of staff Jackson Meml. Hosp., Dade City, Fla., 1969—; past chief of staff, med. dir. East Pasco Med. Ctr., Zephyrills, Fla.; med. dir. Pasco County, Hernando County Prison Sys/.Fla.; bd. dirs. East Pasco med. Ctr., Zephrillis; mem. adv. bd. Prudential Health Plan; trustee, pres., exe.c com. Fla. Osteo. Med. Assn.; sports physician Pasco Comprehensive H.S.; med. examiner FAA; Dade City grand marshall, past chmn. adv. coun.; pres., trustee East Pasco Med. Ctr. Found.; assoc. prof. clin. sci. Southeastern U. halth Scis., Miami, Fla.; mem. coun. predoctoral assn. AOA. Trustee St. Leo (Fla.) Coll.; adv. dir. First Union Nat. Bank Fla., Dade City; com. chmn. Hall of Fame Bowl, Pasco County, Fla., 1987. Recipient Pump Handle award Pasco County Health Authority, 1988, Outstanding Contbn. award H.R.S. Pasco County Pub. Health Unit, 1988, Outstanding Svc. award Fla. Interscholastic Athletic Adminstrs. Assn., 1994; named Gen. Practitioner of Yr., Fla. Acad. Gen. Practice, 1990-91. Fellow Am. Coll. Osteo. Family Physicians; mem. Am. Osteo. Assn. (nat. program conv. chmn., conv. com., exhibit adv. com., mem. ho. of dels., coun. on predoctoral edn.), Fla. Soc. Am. Coll. of Gen. Practitioners (nat. conv. com., bd. dirs.

1989-90, pres. 1991-92), Rotary (Dade City chpt. past pres., Paul Harris fellow). Roman Catholic. Home and Office: McBath Med Ctr 13925 17th St Dade City FL 33525-4603

MCBEATH, ANDREW ALAN, orthopedic surgery educator; b. Milw., Mar. 4, 1936; s. Ivor Charles and Lida McBeath; m. Margaret McBeath; children: Craig Matthew, Drew Alan. BS, U. Wis., 1958, MD, 1961. Diplomate Am. Bd. Orthopaedic Surgery (oral examiner). Intern, resident Hartford (Conn.) Hosp., 1961-63; resident in orthopedic surgery U. Iowa, Iowa City, 1963-66; asst. prof. div. orthopedic surgery div. surgery U. Wis., Madison, 1968-72, assoc. prof., 1972-79, prof., 1979—, Frederick J. Gaenslen prof., 1980, acting chmn. div., 1972-75, chmn. div., 1975—. Contbr. over 70 articles, chpt. to books. Capt. M.C., USAF, 1966-68. Mem. AMA, Am. Acad. Orthopaedic Surgeons, Orthopaedic Rsch. Soc., Am. Orthopaedic Assn., Hip Soc., Wis. Orthopaedic Soc., Rotary, Alpha Omega Alpha. Office: U Wis Div Orthopedic Surg G5 361 600 Highland Ave # G5/361 Madison WI 53792-0001

MCBRAYER, REUBEN HILL, physician; b. Dec. 22, 1942; m. Sarah Coles, 1965. BA in Chemistry, U. Richmond, 1963; MD, Med. Coll. Va., 1967. Diplomate Am. Bd. Internal Medicine, Am. Bd. Sleep Medicine. Intern Barnes Hosp., St. Louis, 1967-68, resident, 1968-69; resident Med. Coll. Va., Richmond, 1971-72, fellowship in pulmonary disease, 1972-74; med. dir. respiratory therapy dept. DePaul Hosp., Norfolk, Va., 1974—; med. dir. pulmonary function lab. Sentara Norfolk Gen. Hosp., 1975—, med. dir. respiratory therapy dept., 1982—, med. dir. Sleep Disorders Ctr., 1984—; bd. dirs. DePaul Hosp., 1988-90, chmn. quality assurance com., 1990-91, chmn. med. info. com., 1990-92, immediate past pres. med. staff office, 1989-90, pres. med. staff office, 1988-89, pres.-elect med. staff office, 1987-88, sec./treas. med. staff office, 1986-87, chmn. dept. medicine, 1975-76. Contbr. articles to profl. jours. Mem. bd. Friends of DePaul; usher Ch. of Good Shepherd. With U.S. Army, 1968-71. Recipient numerous grants. Fellow Am. Coll. Physicians, Am. Coll. Chest Physicians (gov. 1996); mem. Am. Med. Soc., Am. Thoracic Soc., Am. Assn. Respiratory Care, Soc. Critical Care Medicine, So. Sleep Soc., , Va. Thoracic Soc. (pres. 1985-87), Norfolk County Med. Soc., Kappa Alpha (pres. 1962), Alpha Omega Alpha, Sigma Zeta, Sigma Xi. Home: 7447 St Francis Ln Norfolk VA 23505 Office: 825 Fairfax Ave Norfolk VA 23507

MCBRIAN, ANDREW KIMBEL, psychologist, educational administrator; b. Peoria, Ill., Sept. 15, 1954; s. Anne Jane (McCaffrey) McB.; m. Elizabeth Pierce Hetzler, June 18, 1988; 1 child, Sarah Frances Hetzler, William Littell. BA, Yale Coll., 1977; MEd, Harvard U., 1984, EdD, 1989. Lic. psychologist. Account exec. McCaffrey & McCall, Inc., N.Y.C., 1977-78; researcher Ctr. for Food and Farm Rsch., Salisbury, Conn., 1980-81; spl. needs tchr. Pine Cobble Sch., Williamstown, Mass., 1981-83; psychology intern mental health clinic Boston U., 1987-88; psychology intern Eliot Community Mental Health, Concord, Mass., 1988-89; psychologist Milton (Mass.) Acad., 1989—; pvt. practice psychologist, Milton and Dedham, Mass., 1991—; pvt. practice ednl. therapist, 1984-94; asst. dir. Salisbury Summer Sch. Reading and English, 1984—, tchr., dept. head, 1976-84, interim dir. 1992, dir., 1996—; ednl. cons. St. Mark's Sch. Southboro, Mass., 1985-88, Roxbury (Mass.) Latin Sch., 1985, Tufts Summer Reading Program, Medford Mass., 1984;. Recipient numerous acad. prizes Suffield Acad., 1970-73, Harvard U. Book prizes, 1972. Mem. Learning Disabilities Network, Am. Assn. for Counseling and Devel., Yale Club N.Y.C., Small Point Club. Home: 44 Chestnut St Dedham MA 02026-4106 Office: Milton Acad Counseling Ctr 170 Centre St Milton MA 02186-3338

MCBRIDE, ANGELA BARRON, nursing educator; b. Balt., Jan. 16, 1941; d. John Stanley and Mary C. (Szczepanska) Barron; m. William Leon McBride, June 12, 1965; children: Catherine, Kara. BS in Nursing, Georgetown U., 1962; LHD (hon.), 1993; MS in Nursing, Yale U., 1964; PhD, Purdue U., 1978; D of Pub. Svc. (hon.), U. Cin., 1983; LLD (hon.), Ea. Ky. U., 1991; DSc(hon.), Med. Coll. of Ohio, 1995. Asst. prof., rsch. asst. inst. Yale U., New Haven, 1964-73; assoc. prof., chairperson Ind. U. Sch. Nursing, Indpls., 1978-81, 80-84, prof., 1981-92, disting. prof., 1992—; assoc. dean rsch. Ind. U. Sch. Nursing, 1985-91, interim dean, 1991-92, univ. dean, 1992—. Author: The Growth and Development of Mothers, 1973, Living with Contradictions, A Married Feminist, 1976, How to Enjoy A Good Life With Your Teenager, 1987; editor: Psychiatric-Mental Health Nursing: Integrating the Behavioral and Biological Sciences, 1996 (Best Book award 1996). Recipient Disting. Alumna award Yale U., Disting. Alumna award Purdue U., Univ. Medallion, U. San Francisco, 1993; Kellog nat. fellow; Am. Nurses Found. scholar. Fellow APA (nursing and health psychology award divsn. 38 1995), Am. Acad. Nursing (past pres.), Nat. Acads. Practice; mem. Midwest Nursing Rsch. Soc. (Disting. Rsch. award 1985), Soc. for Rsch. in Child Devel., Inst. of Medicine, Nat. Acad. Scis., Sigma Theta Tau Internat. (past pres., mentor award 1993). Office: Ind U Sch Nursing 1111 Middle Dr Indianapolis IN 46202-5107

MCBRIDE, MICHAEL ALAN, dentist, educator; b. Memphis, Aug. 20, 1953; s. Robert Patrick and Edna E. (Dinstahl) McB.; m. Jean Ann Lauderdale, Dec. 28, 1974 (div. Oct. 1992); children: Kathryn, Andrew; m. Melody Barrow, Nov. 28, 1992. BS, Union U., 1976; DDS, U. Tenn., 1982; Prosthodontic Cert., VA Med. Ctr., 1994. Bd. eligible prosthodontist. Pvt. practice dentist Memphis, 1982-92; asst. prof. U. Tenn. Dental Sch., Memphis, 1982-92, 94—; resident in prosthodontic VA Med. Ctr., Memphis, 1992-94; pvt. practice prosthodontist Memphis, 1994—. Contbr. articles to profl. jours. Mem. Kingsway Christian Ch., Memphis, 1992—, Union Ave. Bapt. Ch., Memphis, 1981-92. Mem. ADA, Am. Coll. Prosthodontist, Tenn. Dental Assn., Memphis Dental Soc. Office: Ste # 1 5336 Estate Office Dr Memphis TN 38119

MCBRIDE, MICHAEL JOSEPH, psychology educator, administrator; b. Eureka, Calif., Feb. 5, 1945; s. Mark and Anne Josephine (Relgi) McB.; m. Pamela Carol Behring, June 2, 1973; children: Mary Stasha Behring, William Mark Behring. AB in Classical Studies, St. Louis U., 1969, MS, 1975, PhD, 1980. Instr., Jesuit High Sch., Sacramento, 1969-71, S.E. Mo. State U., Cape Girardeau, 1977, Gonzaga U., Spokane, Wash., 1978-96, chairperson dept. psychology, 1984-86, 87-88, 96—; exchange prof. Chongqing (China) U., 1988—. Mem. Am. Psychol. Assn., Soc. for Personality and Social Psychology, Psi Chi. Democrat. Roman Catholic. Home: 1112 E 20th Ave Spokane WA 99203-3434 Office: Psychology Dept Gonzaga U 502 E Boone Ave Spokane WA 99258-1774

MC BRIDE, RAYMOND ANDREW, pathologist, physician, administrator, educator; b. Houston, Dec. 27, 1927; s. Raymond Andrew and Rita (Mullane) McB.; m. Isabelle Shepherd Davis, May 10, 1958 (div. 1978); children: James Bradley, Elizabeth Conway, Christopher Ramsey, Andrew Gore. B.S., Tulane U., 1952, M.D., 1956. Diplomate: Am. Bd. Pathology. Surg. intern Jefferson Davis Hosp., Baylor U. Coll. Medicine, Houston, 1956-57; asst. in pathology Peter Bent Brigham Hosp., Boston, 1957-60; sr. resident pathologist Peter Bent Brigham Hosp., 1960-61; resident pathologist Free Hosp. for Women, Brookline, Mass., 1959; asst. resident pathologist Children's Hosp. Med. Center, Boston, 1960; teaching fellow pathology Harvard Med. Sch., Boston, 1958-61; research trainee Nat. Heart Inst., NIH, HEW, 1958-61; spl. postdoctoral fellow Nat. Cancer Inst., HEW, McIndoe Meml. Research unit Blond Labs., East Grimstead, Sussex, Eng., 1961-63; asst. attending pathologist Presbyn. Hosp., N.Y.C., 1963-65; asst. prof. pathology Coll. Physicians and Surgeons, Columbia U., 1963-65; research asso. Mt. Sinai Hosp., N.Y.C., 1965-68; assoc. prof. surgery and immunogenetics Mt. Sinai Sch. Medicine, N.Y.C., 1965-68; career scientist Health Research Council City N.Y., 1967-73; attending pathologist Flower and Fifth Ave. Hosps., N.Y.C., 1968-78, Met. Hosp. Center, N.Y.C., 1968-78; prof. pathology N.Y. Med. Coll., 1968-78; prof. pathology Baylor Coll. Medicine, Houston, 1978-96, emeritus prof. pathology, 1996—; attending pathologist Harris County Hosp. Dist., Ben Taub Gen. Hosp., Houston, 1978-96; chief pathology svcs. Harris County Hosp. Dist., 1988-96; assoc. staff Meth. Hosp., Houston, 1978-81, active staff to hon. emeritus, 1981-96, 96—; vis. grad. faculty Tex. A & M U., College Station, 1979—; clin. prof. pathology U. Tex. Grad. Sch. Biomed. Scis., Galveston, 1982—, U. Tex. Med. Br., Galveston, 1982—; prof. pathology Libero Istituto Universitario Campus Bio-Medico, Rome, 1993—; adj. prof. dept. stats. Rice U., Houston; mem. sci. com. Libero Istituto Universitario Campus Bio-Medico, Rome, 1991—; exec. dean N.Y. Med. Coll., Valhalla, 1973-75; exec. dir., COO, bd. dirs. Westchester Med. Ctr. Devel. Bd., Valhalla, 1974-76. Mem. editorial bd. Jour. Immunogenetics, Exptl. and Clin. Immunogenetics, European Jour. Immunogenetics; contbr. articles to profl. jours. Bd. dirs. Westchester Artificial Kidney Found., Inc., 1974-78, Westchester Med. Ctr. Libr., 1974-78, Westchester div. Am. Cancer Soc., 1973-78, Magnificat House, 1989-92, Found. for Life, Nat. Bd. Cath. Campaign for Am., 1989—, Tuxedo Libr., 1976-78; co-chmn. Westchester Burn Ctr. Task Force, 1975-76. Grantee Health Research Council, N.Y.C., 1963-73; Grantee Am. Cancer Soc., 1971-72; Grantee NIH, USPHS, 1964—; Grantee NSF, 1965-68. Fellow Royal Soc. Medicine; mem. Transplantation Soc., Soc. for Organ Sharing, Am. Soc. Extpl. Pathology, Reticuloendothelial Soc., AAAS, Am. Assn. Pathologists and Bacteriologists, Soc. for Investigative Pathology, Am. Assn. Immunologists, AAUP, AMA, Tex. Med. Assn., Harris County Med. Soc., Tex. Soc. Pathologists, Coll. Am. Pathologists, Am. Assn. Clin. Pathologists, Houston Acad. Medicine, Houston Soc. Clin. Pathologists, Assn. Am. Med. Colls., Fedn. Am. Scientists, Am., N.Y. cancer socs., Soc. Health and Human Values, Am. Acad. Med. Ethics, Alpha Omega Alpha (hon. med. soc.). Republican. Roman Catholic. Club: Tuxedo (Tuxedo Park, N.Y.). Home: 5001 Woodway Dr Apt 1404 Houston TX 77056-1719 Office: Baylor Coll Medicine Tex Med Ctr Dept Pathology One Baylor Plz Houston TX 77030 Address: via Lancellotti 18, Palazzo Lancellotti, 00186 Rome Italy also: Villa Marignoli, Via PO 2, 00186 Rome 00198, Italy also: Libero Instituto Universitario CBM, Via Longoni 83, 00155 Rome Italy

MCBRIDE, SANDRA TEAGUE, critical care nurse; b. Corinth, Miss., Sept. 13, 1958; d. Clarence R. and Alice (Ingram) T. AAS, Shelby State Community Coll., 1983; BSN, U. North Ala., 1987. RN, Miss., Tenn. Nurse supr. Alcorn County Care, Inc., Corinth, Miss., 1985-87; staff nurse Bolivar (Tenn.) Community Hosp., 1988-90; staff nurse West Tenn. High Security Facility Tenn. Dept. of Corrections, Ripley, 1990-91; staff nurse U.S. Med. Ctr. for Fed. Prisoners, Springfield, Mo., 1991-92, Western Mental Health Inst., Bolivar, 1992—.

MCBRIDE, WANDA LEE, psychiatric nurse; b. Dayton, Ohio, Dec. 13, 1931; d. Owen Francis Staup and Ruby Madonna (Campbell) Inscore; m. Richard H. McBride, July 28, 1951 (div. Mar. 1966); children: Kathleen Kerns, Kimberlee Haley. Diploma, Christ Hosp. Sch., Cin., 1953; student, U. Cin., 1954-55. Cert. psychiat. mental health nurse ANA. Various health-care positions, 1953-66; from supr. 4 acute male units to supr. outpatient dept. Cen. Ohio Psychiat. Hosp., Columbus, 1966-77; supr. hosp., head nurse urology and respiratory diseases flr. St. Anthony Hosp., Okla., 1977-83; shift supr. and coord. child program Willowview Hosp., Spencer, Okla., 1983-88; adminstrv. nursing supr. Grant Ctr. of Deering Hosp., Miami, 1988—, assessment specialist, 1995—; disabilities case mgr. Kemper Nat. Svcs., Plantation, Fla., 1996—. Mem. Gov.'s Com. for Mental Health and Retardation, 1963-66, Logan County Mental Health League, Ohio, 1963-66. Named Nurse of Yr., 1983-90. Mem. Nat. League for Nursing, Mental Health League (past pres.), Lioness Club (past pres.). Republican. Episcopalian. Home: 304 Lakeside Ct Fort Lauderdale FL 33326-2117

MCBURNEY, ELIZABETH INNES, physician, educator; b. Lake Charles, La., Dec. 24, 1944; d. Theodore John and Martha (Caldwell) Innes; divorced, 1980; children: Leanne Marie, Susan Eleanor. BS, U. Southwestern La., 1965; MD, La. State U., 1969. Diplomate Am. Bd. Internal Medicine, Am. Bd. Dermatology. Intern Pensacola (Fla.) Edn. Program, 1969-70; resident in internal medicine Boston U. and Carney Hosps., 1970-72; resident in dermatology Charity Hosp., New Orleans, 1972-74; staff physician Ochsner Hosp., New Orleans, 1974-80; assoc. head of dermatology Ochsner Clinic, New Orleans, 1974-80; clin. asst. prof. Sch. Medicine La. State U., New Orleans, 1976-79, clin. assoc. prof., 1979-90, clin. prof., 1990—; clin. asst. prof. Sch. Medicine Tulane U., New Orleans, 1976-88, clin. assoc. prof., 1988-91, clin. prof., 1991—; mem. staff Northshore Regional Med. Ctr., Slidell, La., 1985—, Slidell Meml. Hosp., 1988—, chmn. CME courses, 1988—; regional dir. Mycosis Fungoides Study Group, Balt., 1974-94. Author: (with others) Dermatologic Laser Surgery, 1990; contbr. articles to profl. jours. Bd. dirs. Slidell Art Coun., 1988—, Camp Fire, New Orleans, 1979-83, Cancer Assn. New Orleans, 1978-83; juror Art in Pub. Places, Slidell, 1989. Fellow ACP; mem. Am. Soc. Dermatologic Surgery (treas. 1991-94, bd. dirs. 1988-91, pres. elect 1995-96, pres. 1996—), Am. Acad. Dermatology (bd. dirs. 1994—), Am. Bd. Laser Medicine & Surgery (bd. dirs. 1991-96), La. Dermatologic Soc. (pres. 1989-90), St. Tammary Med. Soc. (pres. 1988), Phi Kappa Phi, Alpha Omega Alpha. Office: 1051 Gause Blvd Ste 460 Slidell LA 70458-2950

MCBURNEY, LINDA LEE, health facility administrator; b. Denver, June 10, 1942; d. Maurice J. and Dorothy Mae (Whitman) Mooney; m. Kenneth Robert McBurney, June 16, 1962 (div. 1980); children: Scott Robert (dec.), Laura Lynn, Brenda Sue, Valerie Kaye. BSBA, Regis Coll., 1985. Office mgr. elec. co., Lakewood, Colo., 1980; sec. Safeco Ins. Co., Lakewood, 1980-82; office mgr. oil co., Golden, Colo., 1982; from clerical specialist to exec. sec. Cobe Labs., Lakewood, 1982-86; beauty cons. Mary Kay Cosmetics, Lakewood, 1986-87; adminstrv. mgr. Cobe Labs., Lakewood, 1986-89, med. systems mfr., adminstrn. & fin. mgr. worldwide svc. orgn., 1989-90, mgr. customer engring. response ctr., 1990-91; admissions coord. Hospice of Met. Denver, 1992—. Mem. Golden Area Sch. Adv. Com., 1974-80, Jefferson County Sr. High Curriculum Coun., 1980; room mother Kyffin Elem. Sch., Golden, numerous years; vol. Luth. Hosp. Med. Ctr., Wheatridge, Colo., 1973-92; pres. Women's Assn. Arvada (Colo.) Presbyn. Ch., 1979. Mem. AAUW (v.p., mem. com. fundraising program), Assn. Field Svc. Mgrs., Hospice of Metro Denver/Colo. Assn. of Home Health Agys., Gamma Phi Beta. Republican. Home: 11280 W 20th Ave # 36 Lakewood CO 80215-9999 Office: Hospice Metro Denver 425 S Cherry Ste 700 Denver CO 80222-9999

MCBURNEY, ROBERT F., insurance company executive, consultant; b. Pitts., Nov. 17, 1949; s. Robert L. and Mary (Costantino) McB.; m. Pamela A. Stobaugh; children: Robert S., Jeffrey A. Degree in Computer Sci. Elec. Computer Inst. Tech., Pitts., 1969. Mgr. Sun Life of Can., Pitts., 1969-71; dept. head Am. Life Ins. Co., Wilmington, Del., 1971-75; dir. Maccabees Mut., Southfield, Mich., 1975-83; pres., chief exec. officer Govtl. Health Mgrs., Inc., Redford, Mich., 1983-84; exec. v.p. 1st SE Risk Mgmt. of Fla., Inc., Tampa, 1984-86; pres. URS Internat., Tampa, 1984-86; pres. Bankers Risk Mgmt., 1988-93; sr. v.p. Siver Consulting Group, 1993—; cons. group ins. employee benefits, systems, Redford Mcpl. Govt. 1983—. Chmn. bd. Christian Edn., Farmington Hill, 1981-83; bd. dirs. Boys Brigrade Program, Christian Service Brigade, Farmington Hill, 1981-83; state pres. Fla. Assn. Health Underwriters, 1992. Fellow Life Mgmt. Inst. (bd. dirs. Mich. sect. 1983-84), Life Office Mgmt. Assn. (soc. rep. 1983). Republican. Office: Siver Consulting Group 9400 Fourth St N Ste 119 Saint Petersburg FL 33702

MCCABE, JOHN CHARLES, oral surgeon; b. Bklyn., July 27, 1950; s. Vincent James and Helen Cecelia (Byrne) McC.; m. Janet Ellen Tarnowsky, Dec. 18, 1982 (div. June 1993); 1 child, Sean Michael; m. Barbara Ann Carr-Dolan, Jan. 27, 1996. BA, Manhattan Coll., 1972; DDS, Columbia U., 1985, MD, 1990. Diplomate Am. Bd. Oral and Maxillofacial Surgery. Attending physician Presbyn. Hosp., N.Y.C., 1990—; asst. prof. Columbia U., N.Y.C., 1990—, dir. anesthesia and pain control Sch. Dental and Oral Surgery, 1990—; attending surgeon VA Med. Ctr., Bronx, N.Y., 1992—. Asst. scoutmaster Boy Scouts Am., Yorktown Heights, N.Y., 1995—. Fellow Am. Assn. Oral and Maxillofacial Surgeons; mem. AMA, Am. Cleft Palate Assn., N.Y. State Soc. Oral and Maxillofacial Surgeons (Oral Surgery award 1985), N.Y. State Assn. Cleft Palate Ctrs. (bd. dirs.). Roman Catholic. Office: Columbia-Presbyn Med Ctr 620 W 168th St HP-8 New York NY 10032

MCCAFFERY, MARGO, pain consultant, lecturer, author; b. Corsicana, Tex., Sept. 29, 1938; d. Marley William and Mary Katharine (Adams) Smith; m. John Richard Brewer, July 19, 1986; 1 child, Melissa Ruth. BSN, Baylor U., 1959; MS in Nursing, Vanderbilt U., 1961. RN, Calif., Tex. Asst. prof. pediatric nursing UCLA, 1962-70; pain mgmt. cons., lectr., L.A., 1970—; clinician, mgr. pain mgmt. unit Centinela Hosp. Med. Ctr., Inglewood, Calif., 1983-84; mem. adv. bd. Pharmacologic Aspects Nursing, Nursing Jour., Clin. Jour. Pain, Jour. Pain and Sympton Mgmt.; mem. expert adv. com. on cancer pain relief WHO, 1989—. Author numerous books, including Nursing Management of the Patient with Pain, 1972, (with N. Meinhart) Pain: A Nursing Approach to Assessment and Analysis, 1983, (with A. Beebe) Pain: Clinical Manual for Nursing Practice, 1989; producer-writer audio and video tapes. Recipient Linda Richards award Nat. League for Nursing, Disting. Svc. award UCLA, Book of Yr. award Am. Jour. Nursing, Nursing 86 award; scholar Am. Nurses Found.; rsch. grantee NIH, Am. Nurses Found. Mem. ANA, Am. Acad. Nursing, Am. Pain Soc., Internat. Assn. for Study Pain (founding), Nat. Hospice Orgn., Onoclogy Nursing Soc., Sigma Theta Tau (rsch. grantee). Home and Office: 8347 Kenyon Ave Los Angeles CA 90045-2740

MCCAIRNS, REGINA CARFAGNO, pharmaceutical executive; b. Phila., Dec. 23, 1951; d. Carmen Augustus and Regina Mary (Yost) Carfagno; m. Robert Gray McCairns Jr., Nov. 6, 1982. BS, Marymount Manhattan Coll., 1973; MS, Villanova U., 1976; cert. bus., U. Pa., 1982. Rsch. asst. Temple U. Med. Coll., Phila., 1975-77; mfg. supr. William H. Rorer, Ft. Washington, Pa., 1977-79; mgmt. trainee, tech. asst. SmithKline & French Labs., Phila., 1979-80, shift leader antibiotics, 1980-81, validation team mem., 1984-87, validation coord., 1987; mgr. validation svcs. SmithKline Beecham, Phila., 1987-96; quality assurance investigator SmithKline Beecham, King of Prussia, Pa., 1996—. Trustee Country Day Sch. of the Sacred Heart, 1993—. Mem. Parenteral Drug Assn. (bd. dirs. 1985-92, chmn. spring program 1988, 90, chmn. tng. com. 1986-88, chmn. nat. program com. 1990-93), Jefferson Med. Coll. Faculty Wives Club (v.p. 1988-90, program chmn., 1988-90, pres.-elect 1990-92, pres. 1992-94). Democrat. Roman Catholic. Office: SmithKline Beecham UW 2218 Box 1539 709 Swedeland Rd King Of Prussia PA 19406-0939

MCCALL, DOROTHY KAY, social worker, psychotherapist; b. Houston, July 18, 1948; d. Sherwood Pelton Jr. and Kathryn Rose (Gassen) McC. BA, Calif. State U., Fullerton, 1973; MS in Edn., U. Kans., 1978; PhD, U. Pitts., 1989. Lic. social worker. Counselor/intern Ctr. for Behavioral Devel., Overland Park, Kans., 1976-77; rehab. counselor Niagra Frontier Voc. Rehab. Ctr., Buffalo, 1978-79; counselor/instr. dept. motor vehicles Driving While Impaired Program N.Y. State, 1979-80; alcoholism counselor Bry Lin Hosp., Buffalo, 1979-81; instr. sch. social work U. Pitts., 1984, 91; alcohol drug counselor The Whale's Tale, Pitts., 1984-86; sole practice drug and alcohol therapy Pitts., 1986—; faculty Chem. People Inst., Pitts., 1987-89; guest lectr. sch. social work U. Pitts., 1982-87, 89; educator, trainer Community Mental Health Ctr., W.Va., 1986-87, Tenn., 1986; tchr. Tri-Community Sch. System, Western Pa., 1984-87; cons. Battered Women's Shelter, Buffalo, 1980, Buffalo Youth and Alcoholism Abuse program, 1980; lectr. in field. Mem. Spl. Adv. Com. on Addiction, 1981-83; bd. dirs. Chem. People, Task Force Adv. Com., 1984-86; bd. dirs. Drug Connection Hot Line, 1984-86; mem. Coalition of Addictive Diseases, 1984—; co-founder Greater Pitts. Adult Children of Alcoholics Network, 1984; mem. adv. bd. Chem. Awareness Referral and Evaluation System Duquesne U., 1988-93. Recipient Outstanding Achievement award Greater Pitts. Adult Children of Alcoholics Network, 1987, Disting. Svc. award Pa. Assn. for Children of Alcoholics, 1993; Nat. Inst. Alcohol Abuse tng. grantee, 1981; U. Pitts. fellow, 1983. Mem. NASW, Pa. Assn. for Children of Alcoholics (bd. dirs. 1987—, v.p. 1990-94, Disting. Svc. award 1993), Employee Assistance Profls.. Assn. Inc., Am. Soc. for Clin. Hypnosis, Nat. Assn. for Children of Alcoholics, Inst. for Noetic Scis., Internat. Soc. for Study of Subtle Energies and Energy Medicine. Democrat. Office: 673 Washington Rd Pittsburgh PA 15228-1917

MCCALL, RONALD ALVIN, physician assistant, retired air force officer; b. Pomona, Calif., July 30, 1952; s. Raye Aaron and Ruth Hazel (Norton) McC.; m. Carla Diane Beverly Dirks, June 29, 1974; children: Randal A., Robin L., Amy C. AS in Cardiopulmonary Tech., C.C. of Air Force, 1983; BSBA, Wayland Bapt. U., 1983; BS Phys. Asst. Dept., U. Okla., Oklahoma City, 1986. Nat. cert. physician asst.; registered physician asst., Mo. Commd. officer USAF, 1986, advanced through grades to capt.; cardiopulmonary technologist USAF, Sheppard AFB, Tex., 1973-84; physician asst. in family practice USAF, Chanute AFB, Ill., 1986-91; physician asst. in orthopaedics USAF, Langley AFB, Va., 1992-95; ret., 1995; physician asst. Clarke Orthopedic Clinic, Springfield, Mo., 1995—; cons. to command surgeon gen. USAF Air Combat Command, Langley AFB, 1992-95. Mem. Am. Acad. Physician Assts., Physician Assts. in Orthopaedic Surgery (sec., membership chmn.), Soc. Air Force Physician Assts., Mo. Acad. Physician Assts. (bd. dirs.-at-large 1994—), Gideons Internat. Baptist. Home: 5946 S Kimbrough Ave Springfield MO 65810 Office: Clarke Orthopedic Clinic 1000 E Primrose Ste 555 Springfield MO 65807

MC CALLUM, CHARLES ALEXANDER, university official; b. North Adams, Mass., Nov. 1, 1925; s. Charles Alexander and Mabel Helen (Cassidy) McC.; m. Alice Rebecca Lasseter, Dec. 17, 1955; children: Scott Alan, Charles Alexander III, Philip Warren, Christopher Jay. Student, Dartmouth Coll., 1943-44, Wesleyan U., Middletown, Conn., 1946-47; D.M.D., Tufts U., 1951; M.D., Med. Coll. Ala., 1957; D.Sc. (hon.), U. Ala., 1975, Georgetown U., 1982, Tufts U., 1988, Chulalongkorn U., Thailand, 1993, U. Medicine & Dentistry, N.J., 1993. Diplomate Am. Bd. Oral Surgery (pres. 1970). Intern oral surgery Univ. Hosp., Birmingham, Ala., 1951-52, resident oral surgery, 1952-54, intern medicine, 1957-58; mem. faculty U. Ala. Sch. Dentistry, 1956-96, prof., chmn. dept. oral surgery, 1959-65, dean sch., 1962-77; prof., dept. surgery U. Ala. Sch. of Medicine, 1965-96; v.p. for health affairs, dir. U. Ala. Med. Center, Birmingham, 1977-87; pres. U. Ala., Birmingham, 1987-93, chief sect. oral surgery Sch. Dentistry, 1958-65, 68-69, prof., 1959-93, disting. prof., 1993—; mem. nat. adv. dental rsch. coun. NIH, 1968-72; mem. Joint Commn. on Accreditation of Hosps., 1980-91, vice chmn., 1985, chmn., 1987-88. Fellow Am. Coll. Dentists, Internat. Coll. Dentists; mem. ADA (council on dental edn. 1970-76), Am. Assn. Dental Schs. (pres. 1969), Ala. Acad. of Honor, AMA, Am. Soc. Oral Surgeons (trustee 1972-73, pres. 1975-76), Southeastern Soc. Oral Surgeons (pres. 1970), Inst. of Medicine of Nat. Acad. of Scis., Assn. Acad. Health Ctrs. (chmn. bd. dirs. 1984-85), Omicron Kappa Upsilon, Phi Beta Pi. Home: 2328 Garland Dr Birmingham AL 35216-3002 Office: Univ Ala at Birmingham 107 MJH Birmingham AL 35294-2010

MCCAMMON, ANNE WOLTMANN, neurologist; b. L.A., May 15, 1947. AB, Pomona Coll., 1969; MD, Tufts Med. Sch., 1976. Diplomate Am. Bd. Psychology and Neurology. Resident in internal medicine Newton (Mass.)-Wellesley Hosp., 1976-78; resident in neurology U. Tex. Health Scis. Ctr., Houston, 1978-81; staff neurologist MacGregor Med. Assn., Houston, 1981-89; pvt. practice neurology Houston, 1990-94; clin. instr. U. Calif. San Diego Med. Sch., 1995—; clin. instr., clin. asst. prof. U. Tex. Health Scis. Ctr., 1981-94; neurologist Sharp Rees-Stealy Med. Group, San Diego, 1996—. Pres. Physicians for Social Responsibility, Houston, 1985-89. Fellow Am. Acad. Neurology; mem. Calif. Med. Assn., San Diego Neurol. Soc. Office: 5525 Grossmont Ctr Dr La Mesa CA 91944-9012 also: 16870 Bernardo Dr San Diego CA 92127

MCCAMMON, JAMES ANDREW, chemistry educator; b. Lafayette, Ind., Feb. 8, 1947; s. Lewis Brown and Jean Ann (McClintock) McC.; m. Anne Elizabeth Woltmann, June 6, 1969. BA magna cum laude, Pomona Coll., 1969; MA, Harvard U., 1970, PhD, 1976. Research fellow Harvard U., Cambridge, Mass., 1976-78; asst. prof. U. Houston, 1978-81, M.D. Anderson prof. chemistry, 1981-94, dir. Inst. for Molecular Design, 1987-94, prof. biochemistry, 1989-94, adj. prof. chemistry, 1995—; adj. prof. molecular physiology and biophysics Baylor Coll. Medicine, Houston, 1986-94, adj. prof. biochemistry, 1992-94; Joseph E. Mayer chair theoretical chemistry U. Calif., San Diego, 1995—, prof. pharmacology, 1995—. Author: Dynamics of Proteins and Nucleic Acids, 1987. Recipient Tchr.-scholar award Camille and Henry Dreyfus Found., George H. Hitchings award Burroughs-Wellcome Fund, 1987, Computerworld Smithsonian Info. Tech. Leadership award for Breakthrough Computational Sci., 1995; named Alfred P. Sloan Rsch. fellow, 1980. Fellow Am. Phys. Soc.; mem. AAAS, Am. Chem. Soc., Biophys. Soc., Protein Soc., Phi Beta Kappa. Office: U Calif San Diego Dept Chemistry La Jolla CA 92093-0365

MCCANN, MARY CHERI, medical technologist, horse breeder and trainer; b. Pensacola, Fla., July 29, 1956; d. Joseph Maxwell and Cora Marie (Underwood) McC.; m. Robert Lee Spencer, July 20, 1977 (div. Nov. 1983). AA, Pensacola Jr. Coll., 1975; student, U. Md., 1977-78; BS in Biology, Troy State U., 1979; postgrad., U. Fla., 1979. Med. technologist Cape Fear Valley Med. Ctr., Fayetteville, N.C., 1981-85, Doctors Diagnostic Ctr., Fayetteville, 1985-86; sales rep. Waddell & Reed, Fayetteville, 1985-86;

med. technologist Roche Biomed. Lab., Burlington, N.C., 1986-87; lab. mgr. Cumberland Hosp., Fayetteville, 1987-89, Naval Hosp., Pensacola, 1989-90, chemistry supr., 1990-96, night shift supr., 1996—. With U.S. Army, 1976-77. Mem. NAFE, Am. Soc. Clin. Pathologists (registrant), Am. Quarter Horse Assn., Japan Karate Assn., Pinto Horse Assn. Am. Republican. Avocations: horses, karate, guns, oil painting. Home: 300 Dogwood Dr Pensacola FL 32505-5323 Office: Naval Hosp Pensacola Lab Us Hwy 98 Pensacola FL 32512

MCCANN, MICHAEL F., industrial hygienist; b. Toronto, Jan. 19, 1943; s. Jack Francis McCann and Bertha Alice (Singleton) Maher; m. Lois Kaggen, Sept. 26, 1984. BSc with honors, U. Calgary, 1964; PhD in Chemistry, Columbia U., 1972. Sci. tchr. St. Anne's Episc. Sch., Bklyn., 1971-72; sr. technical writer, product safety coord. GAF Corp., N.Y.C., 1973-75; dir. Art Hazards Resource Ctr. Found. for Community of Artists. N.Y.C., 1975-77; founder, pres., exec. dir. Ctr. for Safety in Arts (formerly Ctr. Occupational Hazards), N.Y.C., 1977-96; indsl. hygiene cons., 1975—; adj. faculty N.Y. State Sch. Indsl. and Labor Rels., Cornell U., N.Y.C., 1978, 79; lectr. environ. scis., Sch. Pub. Health, Columbia U., N.Y.C., 1981-92; instr., U. Man., Winnipeg, Can., 1982, 83, adviser, task force on toxicity of art materials, Am. Soc. Testing and Materials, 1980-82; mem. ad hoc com. on heal hazards of arts and crafts materials, Can. Dept. Nat. Health and Welfare, 1981—; mem. adv. bd., Mt. Sinai Occupational Health Clinic, N.Y.C., 1987-95. Author: Health Hazards Manual for Artists, 1975, 4th edit., 1994, Artist Beware, 2d edit., 1994, Lights! Camera! Safety, 1991, Art Safety Procedures for Art Schools and Art Departments, 1992, School Safety Procedures for Art and Industrial Art Programs, 1994; sr. editor Internat. Labor Orgn. Ency. of Occupational Health and Safety, 1995-96; writer, narrator videotape Art Safety: Hazards and Precautions, 1988; contbr. articles on art materials hazards to various publs.; editor profl. publs. Presenter testimony on labeling of art materials, U.S. Ho. of Reps., 1980, N.Y. State Assembly, 1981. Mem. Am. Acad. Indsl. Hygiene, Am. Indsl. Hygiene Assn., Am. Chem. Soc. (chem. health and safety divsn.), N.Y. Com. Occupational Safety and Health (exec. bd. 1977-87, 94—, treas. 1980-85), Am. Pub. Health Assn.

MCCANN-TURNER, ROBIN LEE, child, adolescent analyst; b. Spokane, Wash., Sept. 27, 1945; d. Robert Allen McCann and Mary Lavelle Wilson; m. C. F. Turner, Sept. 10, 1975. BA, U. Mont., 1967; MSW, Wash. U., 1969; cert. child-adolescent psychoanalysis, Hampstead Ctr., London, Eng., 1979. Asst. clin. prof., child and adolescent medicine St. Louis U. Med. Sch., 1984—, Cardinal Glennon Children's Hosp., 1984—; pvt. practice; mem. faculty St. Louis Psychoanalytic Inst., 1982—, chmn. child study group, 1994—, dir. child devel. project, 1994—; mem. ho. of dels. U. Mont., Missoula, 1990—. Mem. APA, NASW, Assn. Child Psychoanalysis, Am. Psychoanalytic Assn. Office: 141 N Meramec Ave Ste 208-209 Clayton MO 63105-3750

MCCARLEY, ROBERT WILLIAM, psychiatrist, educator, researcher; b. Mayfield, Ky., Aug. 17, 1937; s. Robert Smith and Mary Agnes (McGill) McC.; m. Alice Margaret Bowen, Aug. 10, 1968; children: Robert Vinton, Scott William. AB summa cum laude, Harvard U., 1959, MD, 1964. Intern Peter Bent Brigham Hosp., Boston, 1964-65; resident in psychiatry Mass. Mental Health Ctr., Boston, 1965-68; instr. psychiatry Harvard Med. Sch., Boston, 1970-75, asst. prof. psychiatry, 1975-78; co-dir. lab. neurophysiology Mass. Mental Health Ctr., Harvard Med. Sch., Boston, 1975-85, assoc. prof. psychiatry, 1978-84, dir. lab. neurosci., 1985—, prof. psychiatry, 1984—; chair rsch. com. dept. psychiatry Harvard Med. Sch., Boston, 1991—; co-dir. clin. rsch. tng. program Harvard Med. Sch., 1980—; assoc. chief dept. psychiatry Brockton VA Med. Ctr., 1985-93, chief psychiatry, 1994; dep. chief staff mental health svc., 1995—; dir., PI Va. Schizophrenia Ctr., 1995—; cons. Mass. Rehab. Commn., Boston, 1976—, Commonwealth Rsch. Ctr., Boston, 1986; chmn. clin. neurosci. rev. com. NIMH, 1992—. Author: Neuronal Activity in Sleep, 1974, Brainstem Control of Wakefulness & Sleep, 1990; contbr. over 100 articles on neurophysiology of sleep and schizophrenia. Recipient Sr. Investigator award Nat. Alliance for Rsch. on Schizophrenia and Depression, 1993-94; neurophysiology rsch. grantee NSF, 1979-84; career devel. grantee NIMH, 1980-85, neurophysiology rsch. grantee, 1986—, Va. med. rsch. grantee, 1986—. Mem. AAAS, Am. Psychiat. Assn., Soc. for Neurosci., Sleep Rsch. Soc. (exec. sec. 1987-90, pres. 1991), Assn. Profl. Sleep Socs. (vice chair 1987-91), Harvard Club, Neighborhood Club. Democrat. Methodist. Office: Harvard Med Sch/ Brockton VAMC 940 Belmont St # 116A Brockton MA 02401-5596

MCCARROLL, KATHLEEN ANN, radiologist, educator; b. Lincoln, Nebr., July 7, 1948; d. James Richard and Ruth B. (Wagenknecht) McC.; m. Steven Mark Beerbohm, July 10, 1977 (div. 1991); 1 child, Palmer Brooke. BS, Wayne State U., 1974; MD, Mich. State U., 1978. Diplomate Am. Bd. Radiology. Intern/resident in diagnostic radiology William Beaumont Hosp., Royal Oak, Mich., 1978-82, fellow in computed tomography and ultrasound, 1983; radiologist, dir. radiologic edn. Detroit Receiving Hosp., 1984—, vice-chief dept. radiology, 1988-96, chief dept. radiology, 1996—; pres.-elect med. staff Detroit Receiving Hosp., 1992-94, pres., 1994-96; mem. admissions com. Wayne State U. Coll. Medicine, Detroit, 1991—; trustee Detroit Med. Ctr., 1996—; officer bd. dirs. Dr. L. Reynolds Assoc., P.C., Detroit, 1991-94, 96—; presenter profl. confs.; assoc. prof. radiology Wayne State U. Sch. Medicine, Detroit, 1995—. Editor: Critical Care Clinics, 1992; mem. editorial bd. Emergency Radiology; contbr. articles to profl. publs. Mem. AMA, Am. Coll. Radiology (Mich. chpt. sec. 1995—), Radiol. Soc. N.Am., Assn. Univ. Radiologists, Am. Roentgen Ray Soc., Am. Soc. Emergency Radiologists (bd. dirs. 1996—), Mich. State Med. Soc., Wayne/Oakland County Med. Soc., Phi Beta Kappa. Office: Detroit Receiving Hosp 3L-8 4201 Saint Antoine St Detroit MI 48201-2153

MCCARRON, ROBERT FREDERICK, II, orthopedic surgeon; b. Hot Springs, Ark., Oct. 31, 1952; s. Robert Frederick and Irene (Shanks) McC.; m. Vicki Lynn Nichols, June 10, 1977; children: Elizabeth, Jennifer. BS, La. Tech. U., 1974; MD, U. Ark., 1977. Diplomate Am. Bd. Orthopedic Surgery. Intern U. Ark., Little Rock, 1977-78; resident Tex. Tech U., Lubbock, 1978-82, instr. dept. orthopedics, 1983-84, asst. prof., 1984-88; trauma fellow Kantonspittal, Basel, Switzerland, 1982; spine fellow St. Vincent's Hosp., Melbourne, Australia, 1983; pvt. practice orthopedic surgery Conway (Ark.) Orthopaedic and Sports Medicine Clinic, P.A., 1988—; cons. physician U. Cen. Ark., Conway, 1989; chief of surgery Conway Regional Med. Ctr., 1991-94; presenter, exhibitor in field. Contbr. articles to profl. publs. Bd. dirs. Clifton Day Care Ctr., chmn. 1994-95; pres. Conway Regional Physician Hosp. Orgn., 1996, sec., 1995. Fellow Am. Acad. Orthopedic Surgeons, Am. Orthopedic Foot and Ankle Soc.; mem. Ark. Med. Soc., Faulkner County Med. Soc., Ark. Orthopedic Soc., Conway Area C. of C., Sigma Nu. Republican. Mem. Christian Ch. (Disciples of Christ). Office: Conway Orthopaedic Clinic 525 Western Ave Ste 202 Conway AR 72032-4967

MCCARTER, ROBERT HARRIS, psychiatrist, educator; b. N.Y.C., Jan. 31, 1916; s. George William Childs and Dorothy Neilson (Parker) McC.; m. Margaret Douglas, Feb. 19, 1949; children: Madeleine Marie Mullane, Robert Harris Jr., Frank, Charles John, Brian, Bruce. BA, Princeton U., 1938; MD, Thomas Jefferson U., 1942. Diplomate Am. Bd. Psychiatry and Neurology. Intern Pa. Hosp., Phila., 1942-43; resident in neurology Jefferson Hosp., Phila., 1943; resident in psychiatry Mass. Mental Health Ctr., Boston, 1944-47, dir. Southard Clinic, 1947-64; pvt. practice Boston, 1948-81, New Bedford, Mass., 1970-91, Weston, Mass., 1981-90; ret., 1991; sr. assoc. Judge Baker Guidance Ctr., Children's Hosp. Med. Ctr., 1978-90, dir. therapeutic nursery sch., 1970-72; asst. clin. prof. Harvard U. Med. Sch., Boston, 1975-90. Mem. editorial bd. Jour. Preventive Psychiatry, 1981-84. Fellow Am. Psychiat. Assn. (life); mem. AMA, Mass. Med. Soc., Am. Psychoanalytic Assn., New Eng. Coun. Child Psychiatry, Mass. Psychiatric Soc., Boston Psychoanlytic Soc. Home: 1306 Drift Rd Westport MA 02790-1628

MCCARTHY, ANN MARIE, dietician, health facility administrator; b. Corr, Ireland, June 10, 1966; d. Florence Augustine and Noreen Therese (O'Leary) McC. BSc in Human Nutrition with honors, Trinity Coll., Dublin, Ireland, 1988; diploma in Nutrition & Dietetics, Coll. of Tech., Dublin; MBA, U. Coll., Cork, Ireland, 1996. Dietician St. James Hosp., Dublin, Ireland, 1988-90; divsn. mgr. Cow & Gate Nutricia Ireland Ltd., Dublin, 1990—. Mem. Cork MBA Soc. (founder), Irish Nutrition and Dietetic Inst. (award 1988). Office: Cow & Gate Nutricia Ireland Ltd, Burton Hall Rd, Dublin 18, Ireland

MCCARTHY, BARRY WAYNE, clinical psychologist; b. Chgo., Sept. 7, 1943; s. Edward Joseph and Dorothy (Small) McC.; B.A., Loyola U., Chgo., 1965; Ph.D., So. Ill. U., 1969; m. Emily Jeannette McCabe, Nov. 19, 1966; children: Mark, Kara, Paul. Intern, Wood VA Hosp., Milw., 1968-69; psychology cons. Mt. Vernon Ctr. for Community Mental Health, Alexandria, Va., 1970-73; mem. faculty Am. U., Washington, 1969—, prof. psychology, 1978—; ptnr. Washington Psychol. Ctr., 1977—. Diplomate Am. Bd. Profl. Psychology; cert. sex therapist. Mem. Am. Psychol. Assn., Assn. for Advancement of Behavior Therapy, Am. Assn. Sex Educators, Counselors and Therapists, Am. Assn. Marital and Family Therapists. Author: (with M. Ryan and F. Johnson) Sexual Awareness: A Practical Approach, 1975; What You Still Don't Know About Male Sexuality, 1977; (with wife) Sexual Satisfaction After Thirty, 1981, (with wife) Sexual Awareness: Sharing Sexual Pleasure, 1984, Male Sexual Awareness: Increasing Sexual Pleasure, 1988, (with Emily McCarthy) Female Sexual Awareness: Achieving Sexual Fulfillment, 1989, Couple Sexual Awareness: Building Sexual Happiness, 1990, Intimate Marriage: Developing a Life Partnership, 1992, Confronting The Victim Role: Healing From an Abusive Childhood, 1993, Sexual Awareness: Enhancing Sexual Pleasure, 1993. Home: 126 Gills Neck Rd Lewes DE 19958-1407 Office: 4201 Connecticut Ave NW Washington DC 20008-1158

MC CARTHY, FRANK MARTIN, oral surgeon, surgical sciences educator; b. Olean, N.Y., Aug. 27, 1924; s. Frank Michael and Joan (Quinn) McC.; m. Julia Richmond, Nov. 24, 1949; children: Robert Lee, Joan Lee. B.S., U. Pitts., 1943, D.D.S., 1945, M.D., 1949; M.S. in Oral Surgery, Georgetown U., 1954; Sc.D. (hon.), St. Bonaventure U., 1956. Med. intern Mercy Hosp., Pitts., 1949-50; practice oral surgery L.A., 1954-75; teaching fellow Georgetown U., 1952-53; rsch. fellow NIH, 1953-54; prof. oral surgery U. So. Calif. Sch. Dentistry, 1966-75, prof., chmn. sect. anesthesia and medicine, 1975-90, prof. emeritus, 1990—, chmn. dept. surg. scis., 1979-84, assoc. dean adminstrv. affairs, 1977-79, asst. dean hosp. affairs, 1979-84; dir. anesthesiology U.So. Calif. oral surgery sect. L.A. County Hosp., 1958-89; clin. supr., lectr. dental hygiene program Pasadena City Coll., 1992—; v.p. Am. Dental Bd. Anesthesiology, 1984-89; lectr. in field; mem. adv. panel on dentistry sect. anesthesizing agts. Nat. Fire Protection Assn., 1971-79; mem. Am. Nat. Standards Com., 1974-86, 95—; cons. in field. Author: Emergencies in Dental Practice, 1967, rev., 1972, 79, Medical Emergencies in Dentistry, 1982, Safe Treatment of the Medically Compromised Patient, 1987, Essentials of Safe Dentistry for the Medically Compromised Patient, 1989; mem. editorial bd.: Calif. Dental Assn. Jour; contbr. articles to profl. publs. Bd. councilors Sch. Dentistry, U. So. Calif., 1972-75. Served as lt., M.C. USNR, 1950-52. Fellow Internat. Assn. Oral Surgeons (founder), Am. Coll. Dentists, Internat. Coll. Dentists; mem. ADA (editorial bd. jour.), Am. Dental Soc. Anesthesiology (Heidbrink award 1977), Am. Assn. Oral-Max Surgeons (chmn. anesthesia com. 1971), So. Calif. Soc. Oral Surgeons (pres. 1974), Calif., Los Angeles County dental assns., Delta Tau Delta, Psi Omega, Phi Rho Sigma, Omicron Kappa Upsilon. Home and Office: 480 S Orange Grove Blvd Apt 11 Pasadena CA 91105-1720

MCCARTHY, JACK DANIEL, surgeon, educator; b. Chgo., Mar. 13, 1927; s. Elmer Vincent and Helen Vanda (Rogal) McC.; m. Victoria Maria de la Riva, May 9, 1953; children: Leslie Anna, Silvia Rose. PhB, U. Chgo., 1946, MD, 1951. Diplomate Am. Bd. Surgery. Intern then resident in surgery U. Chgo. Clinics, 1951-53, 55-57; resident in surgery U. Mich., Ann Arbor, 1957-59; surgeon Lovelace Med. Ctr., Albuquerque, 1961—; chmn. dept. surgery Lovelace Med. Ctr., 1968-89; clin. prof. surgery U. N.Mex., 1976—; sr. cons. Lovelace Med. Ctr. Contbr. articles to profl. jours. Guggenheim fellow, 1959. Fellow ACS (state cancer liason fellow 1964-82), Southwestern Surg. Cong. (state councillor 1978-86); mem. Western Surg. Assn., F.A. Coller Surg. Soc. (council mem. 1974-76). Libertarian. Office: Lovelace Med Ctr 5400 Gibson Blvd SE Albuquerque NM 87108-4729

MCCARTHY, JAMES TIMOTHY, nephrologist, educator; b. Louisville, Oct. 2, 1952; s. Robert Patrick and Joan Carroll (Riggs) McC.; m. Mary Kathleen Cameron, July 12, 1975; children: J. Timothy, John Patrick, Kathleen Ann-Marie. BA, U. Kans., 1974, MD, 1977. Diplomate Am. Bd. Internal Medicine, Am. Bd. Nephrology. Intern, resident in nephrology Mayo Grad. Sch. Medicine, 1977-83; staff cons. Mayo Clinic, Rochester, Minn., 1983—. Contbr. multiple sci. articles to profl. jours., chpts. to books. Fellow ACP; mem. Am. Soc. Nephrology, Nat. Kidney Found., Internat. Soc. Nephrology, Ctrl. Soc. for Clin. Rsch., Sigma Xi. Office: Mayo Clinic 200 1st St SW Rochester MN 55905

MCCARTHY, KARIN D., optometrist, researcher; b. Copenhagen, May 7, 1959; came to U.S., 1992; d. Finn Louis and Kirsten (Anderson) D.; m. Dennis M. McCarthy, Apr. 3, 1993; children: Kevin, Louise. OD, Coll. of Optometry, Denmard, 1985. Cert. optometrist, contact lens specialist. Optometrist Synoptic, Denmark, 1985-92; rsch. optometrist Vistakon Johnson & Johnson, Jacksonville, Fla., 1992—. Vol. local schs., Ponte Vedra Beach, Fla., 1992—. Fellow Am. Acad. Optometry; mem. Am. Assn. Optometry, Am. Optometric Assn., Assn. for Rsch. in Vision and Ophthalmology, Fla. Optometric Assn. Office: Vistakon 4500 Salisbury Rd Jacksonville FL 32216

MCCARTHY, LAURENCE JAMES, physician, pathologist; b. Boston, Aug. 11, 1934; s. Theodore Clifford and Mary Barrett (Moran) McC.; m. Cynthia Marion DeRoch, Aug. 28, 1978; children: Laurence J. Jr., Jeffrey A., Karen E., Patrick K., Ryan N. BA, Yale U., 1956; student, Georgetown U. Sch. Med., 1956-58; MD, Harvard U., 1960; MS, U. Minn., 1965. Cert. Am. Bd. Pathology, 1965. Intern Boston City Hosp., 1960-61; resident in pathology Mayo Clinic, Rochester, Minn., 1961-65; pathologist Honolulu Heart Program, 1965-67; chief pathology Kelsey-Seybold Clinic, Houston, 1967-68; clin. asst. pathologist M.D. Anderson Hosp., Houston, 1967-68; chief pathology Straub Clinic, Honolulu, 1968-72; assoc. pathologist Wilcox Hosp., Lihue, Hawaii, 1972-74; chief pathology A.R. Gould Hosp., Presque Isle, Maine, 1975-78; assoc. pathologist Kuakini Med. Ctr., Honolulu, 1978—. Med. dir. USPHS, 1965-67. Fellow Coll. Am. Pathologists, Am. Soc. Clin. Pathologists; mem. AMA, Hawaii Soc. Pathologists (pres. 1970), Am. Acad. Forensic Sci., Hawaii Med. Assn., Honolulu County Med. Soc. (del. 1982-83). Roman Catholic. Home: 249 Kaelepulu Dr Kailua HI 96734-3311 Office: Kuakini Med Ctr 347 N Kuakini St Honolulu HI 96817-2372

MCCARTHY, MARY RITA, nursing educator; b. Boston; d. Timothy W. and Catherine M. (Kearns) McC. BS in Nursing, U. Western Ont., London, Ont., Can., 1947; MS in Nursing, St. Louis U., 1964; MEd, Columbia U., 1970, EdD, 1974. Asst. supt., instr. Halifax Infirmary, N.S., Canada, 1945-51; asst. DON, sci. instr. St. Elizabeth Hosp., North Sydney, N.S., 1951-61; asst. supr. nursing Halifax Infirmary, Nova Scotia, Can., 1964; cons. baccaulaureate and higher degree programs Nat. League for Nursing, N.Y.C., 1974-84; dir. nursing edn. Mount St. Vincent U., Halifax, Can., 1965-69; asst. prof. Grad. Program in Nursing U.Md., Balt., 1984-92, acting chair dept. nursing edn., adminstrn., health policy, 1991—; bd. dirs. Tchrs. Coll. Nursing Edn. Alumni Assn. Contbr. articles to profl. jours. Recipient Isabel Hampton Robb award Title II Traineeship for Grad. Study, Nursing Edn. Alumni award for excellence in nursing edn. Tchrs. Coll., Columbia U., N.Y. Mem. ANA, Nat. League for Nursing, N.Y. State Nurses' Assn., Nurses House, Inc., Sigma Theta Tau, Tchrs. Coll. Columbia U. Nursing Edn. Alumni Assn.

MCCARTHY, MICHAEL SHAWN, health care company executive, lawyer; b. Evergreen Park, Ill., May 16, 1953; s. Martin J. and Margaret Anne (McNeill) McC.; m. Jane F. Alberding, Oct. 28, 1988; children: Caroline Margaret, Nicholas Michael. BA, Georgetown U., 1975; MS, U. Ill., 1976; JD, Loyola U., 1980. Bar: Ill. 1980, U.S. Dist. Ct. (no. dist.) Ill. 1980. V.p., sec., gen. counsel Luth. Gen. Health Care System, Park Ridge, Ill., 1980-85, sr. v.p., sec., gen. counsel, 1985-91, sr. v.p. corp. svcs., sec., gen. counsel, 1990-93; chmn., CEO Parkside Sr. Svcs., LLC, Park Ridge, Ill., 1993—; bd. dirs. Cath. Lawyers Guild, Hosps. Organized for Polit. Edn., Juv. Protection Assn. Mem. ABA, Am. Assn. for Preferred Providers Orgn., Ill. Hosp. Assn., Ill. Pub. Health Assn., Ill. State Bar Assn., Chgo. Bar Assn. Roman Catholic. Home: 269 Locust Rd Winnetka IL 60093-3608 Office: Parkside Sr Svcs LLC 205 W Touhy Ave Park Ridge IL 60068

MCCARTHY, PATRICIA BENNETT, social worker; b. N.Y.C., Feb. 28, 1936; d. Walter William Konvalinka and Alice Marsh (Waterman) Bennett; m. Franklin L. McCarthy, Aug. 8, 1964; children: Heather, John. BA, Hood Coll., 1958; MA, U. Chgo., 1962. Diplomate ACSW; lic. social worker, Pa. Psychiat. social worker Univ. Settlement Child Guidance Clinic, N.Y.C., 1962-64, Wilder Child Guidance Clinic, St. Paul, 1964-66, Lane County Mental Health Clinic, Eugene, Oreg., 1966-69; coord. Halfway House for State Mental Patients, Eugene, 1970-72; vol. counselor alcohol program Puget Sound Hosp., Tacoma, 1976-77; vol. counselor, psychiat. cons. Parents Anonymous, Pitts., 1977-79; vol. outpatient counselor Alcohol Treatment Ctr. St. Francis Hosp., Pitts., 1981-83; drug and alcohol counselor Whale's Tale, Pitts., 1988-92; inpatient psychiat. social worker St. Francis Hosp., Pitts., 1992—. Lutheran. Office: St Francis Hospital 400 45th St Pittsburgh PA 15201

MCCARTHY, PAUL LOUIS, pediatrics educator; b. Springfield, Mass., Aug. 9, 1941; s. Alfred Lawrence and Minnie Josephine (Vivian) McC.; m. Barbara Jean Burns, Nov. 30, 1963; children: Paul, Scott, Brian. BA, Dartmouth Coll., 1963; MD, Georgetown U., 1969; MA (in privatum), Yale U., 1982. Diplomate Am. Bd. Pediatrics, Am. Bd. Pediatric Rheumatology. Pediat. intern Children's Hosp., Buffalo, 1969-70, pediat. resident, 1970-72; fellow in ambulatory pediatrics Children's Hosp. Med. Ctr., Boston, 1972-74; asst. prof. pediat. Yale U. Sch. Medicine, New Haven, 1974-78, assoc. prof., 1978-82, prof., 1982—, head gen. pediat., 1985—; Morrison lectr. Geisinger Clinic, Danville, Pa., 1990. Author: Evaluation and Management of Febrile Children, 1985; author 4 monographs; contbr. numerous articles to med. jours., chpts. to books. Fellow Am. Acad. Pediatrics; mem. Ambulatory Pediatric Assn. (pres. 1989-90, Armstrong award 1991), Soc. for Pediatric Rsch., Am. Pediatric Soc. Office: Yale U Sch of Medicine 333 Cedar St New Haven CT 06510-3206

MCCARTNEY, JAMES ROBERT, psychiatrist; b. Elmira, N.Y., Jan. 6, 1932; s. James L. and Edith T. (Tufs) McC; m. Lois McCartney; 4 children. BA, Ohio Wesleyan U., 1952; MD, Columbia U., 1955; MA (Ad Eundem)(hon.), Brown U., 1989. Diplomate Nat. Bd. Med. Examiners, Am. Bd. Pscyhiatry and Neurology, Am. Bd. Geriatric Psychiatry. Intern Boston City Hosp. for Medicine, 1955-56; resdient in psychiatry Elizabeth's Hosp., Washington, 1958-59; assoc. attending psychiatrist then attending psychiatrist North Shore U. Hosp., 1964-80, dir. tng. and edn. dept. psychiatry, 1972-79, chief of liaison svcs., 1973-80, assoc. dir., 1978-80; attending psychiatrist Meadowbrook Hosp., 1961-64; assoc. attending psychiatrist Nassau Hosp., 1964-71; on staff Butler Hosp., 1980—; psychiatrist-in-chief The Miriam Hosp., Providence, 1980—; adv. bd. Mental Health Assn. of Nassau County, 1972-80; cons. impaired physician com. R.I. Med. Soc., 1981—; asst. prof. psychiatry Brown U., Providence, 1980-88, assoc. prof., 1988—. Contbr. articles to profl. jours. Capt. U.S. Army, 1956-58. Fellow ACP, Am. Psychiat. Assn., Acad. of Psychosomatic Medicine; mem. AMA, R.I. Med. Soc., Am. Psychosomatic Soc., Assn. for Acad. Psychiatry, Providence Med. Assn., Am. Assn. Gen. Hosp. Psychiatrists, Gerontol. Soc. of Am., Am. Geriatrics Soc. Office: Miriam Hosp 164 Summit Ave Providence RI 02906-2800

MCCARTY, KENNETH SCOTT, physician, pathologist, educator; b. N.Y.C., Feb. 11, 1948; s. Kenneth Scott and Marketa Maria (Regan) McC.; m. Berrylin June Ferguson, Sept. 1, 1982; children: Kenneth Scott III, Justin, Elizabeth, Winston, Merriweather. BS in Chemistry, Duke U., 1968, MD, 1972, PhD in Pathology, 1973. Diplomate Am. Bd. Internal Medicine, Am. Bd. Pathology, N.C. Bd. Med. Examiners; cert. Pa. Bur. Profl. Affairs. Intern Duke U. Med. Ctr., Durham, N.C., 1971-72, 73-74, resident, 1972-73, 74-75, fellow in clin. endocrinology, 1975-76; fellow in endocrine pathology Duke U. Sch. Medicine, Durham, 1976-77, asst. prof. medicine, 1976-91, from asst. prof. to assoc. prof. pathology, 1977-92; prof. pathology and medicine U. Pitts., 1992—; mem., dir. endocrine oncology labs. Pitts. Cancer Inst., 1993—; cons. Abbott Labs., Chgo., 1987—, Durham Clinic, 1990-93, NIH, Bethesda, Md., 1983—. Contbr. articles to profl. jours. Fellow Coll. Am. Pathologists (insp.); mem. AMA, AAAS, Am. Soc. Internal Medicine, Arthur Purdy Stout Soc. Surg. Pathologists, Internat. Acad. Pathology, Am. Assn. Clin. Endocrinologists, Tissue Culture Assn., Endocrine Soc., U.S. and Can. Acad. Pathology, Sigma Xi. Home: 20 Fairview Manor Pittsburgh PA 15238 Office: U Pitts Med Ctr 200 Lothrop St Pittsburgh PA 15213

MCCARTY, LESLIE PAUL, pharmacologist, chemist; b. Detroit, May 30, 1925; s. Leslie Evart and Ruth Winifred (Clouse) McC.; m. Marie-Jeanne Beullay, May 8, 1976; children: Michael, Patricia, Maureen, Brian. BS, Salem Coll., 1947; MSc, Ohio State U., 1949; PhD, U. Wis., 1960. Diplomate Am. Bd. Toxicology. Rsch. chemist Upjohn Co., Kalamazoo, 1949-55; rsch. leader Dow Chem. Co., Midland, Mich., 1960-92. Contbr. articles to profl. jours.; patentee in field. Served with USNR, 1943-45. Mem. Am. Soc. Pharmacology and Exptl. Therapeutics, Sigma Xi. Avocations: amateur radio, gardening, woodworking. Home: 4588 Flajole Rd Midland MI 48642-9261

MCCARTY, MACLYN, medical scientist; b. South Bend, Ind., June 9, 1911; s. Earl Hauser and Hazel Dell (Beagle) McC.; m. Anita Alleyne Davies, June 20, 1934 (div. 1966); children: Maclyn, Richard E., Dale, Colin; m. Marjorie Steiner, Sept. 3, 1966. AB, Stanford U., 1933; MD, Johns Hopkins U., 1937; ScD (hon.), Columbia U., 1976, U. Fla., 1977, Rockefeller U., 1982, Med. Coll. Ohio, 1985, Emory U., 1987, Wittenberg U., 1989; MD (hon.), U. Cologne, Fed. Republic Germany, 1988; LHD (hon.), Mount Sinai Sch. of Medicine, 1995. House officer, asst. resident physician Johns Hopkins Hosp., 1937-40; assoc. Rockefeller Inst., 1946-48, assoc. mem., 1948-50, mem., 1950—, prof., 1957—, v.p., 1965-78, physician in chief to hosp., 1961-74; research in streptococcal disease and rheumatic fever; Cons. USPHS, NIH. Author: The Transforming Principle: Discovering That Genes are Made of DNA, 1985. Mem. distbn. com. N.Y. Community Trust, 1966-74; chmn. Health Research Council City N.Y., 1972-75; Mem. bd. trustees Helen Hay Whitney Found; chmn. bd. dirs. Pub. Health Research Inst. of N.Y., 1985-92. Served with Naval Med. Research Unit, Rockefeller Hosp. USNR, 1942-46. Fellow medicine N.Y. U. Coll. Medicine, 1940-41; NRC fellow med. scis. Rockefeller Inst., 1941-42; Recipient Eli Lilly award in bacteriology and immunology, 1946, 1st Waterford Biomed. Rsch. award, 1977, Wolf Found. prize in medicine, Israel, 1990, Lasker Spl. Pub. Health award, 1994. Mem. Am. Soc. for Clin. Investigation, Am. Assn. Immunologists, Soc. Am. Bacteriologists, Soc. for Exptl. Biology and Medicine (pres. 1973-75), Harvey Soc. (sec. 1947-50, pres. 1971-72), N.Y. Acad. Medicine (Acad. medal 1979, John Stearns award for lifetime achievement in medicine 1993), Assn. Am. Physicians (Kober medal 1989), Nat. Acad. Scis. (Kovalenko medal 1988), Am. Acad. Arts and Scis., N.Y. Heart Assn. (1st v.p. 1967, pres. 1969-71), Am. Philos. Soc. Home: 400 E 56th St New York NY 10022-4147 Office: Rockefeller U 66th St and York Ave New York NY 10021

MCCAULEY, FLOYCE REID, psychiatrist; b. Braddock, Pa., Dec. 30, 1933; d. John Mitchel and Irene (Garner) Reid; m. James Calvin McCauley, July 15, 1955; children: James Stanley, Lori Ellen. BS in Nursing, U. Pitts., 1956; D.O., Coll. Osteopathic Medicine, Phila., 1972. Bd. eligible in child and adult psychiatry. Intern Suburban Gen. Hosp., Norristown, Pa., 1972-73; resident in adult psychiatry Phila. State Hosp. and Phila. Mental Health Clinic, 1973-75; fellow Med. Coll. of Pa. and Ea. Pa. Psychiat. Inst., Phila., 1975-78; Chief child psychiatry inpatient unit Med. Coll. Pa., Phila., 1978-80; med. dir. Carson ValleySch., Flourtown, Pa., 1980-82; dir. outpatient psychiat. clinic Osteopathic Med. Ctr. Phila., 1980-86; staff psychiatrist Kent Gen. Hosp., Dover, Del., 1986-89; psychiat. cons. Del. Guidance Svcs. for Children, Dover, 1986-91; clin. dir. children's unit HCA Rockford Ctr., Newark, 1991-93; with Kid's Peace Nat. Hosp. for Kids in Crisis, 1993-95, Pa. Found., Sellersville, 1995—; mem. Mental Health Code Rev. Com. for Del., 1991; inducted into the Chapel of Four Chaplains, Phila., 1983; psychiat. cons. Seaford (Del.) Br. of New Eng. Fellowship for Rehab., 1991-93, Cath. Charities Day Treatment Program for 3-6 Yr. Olds, Dover, Del., 1990—; cons. Del. Guidance Day Treatment Program, 1990—; staff psychiatrist Kids Peace Nat. Hosp. for Kids in Crisis, 1993-95, Penn Found., 1995—. Mem. Mayor's Com. for Mental Health, Phila., 1983. Mem. Am.

Osteopathic Assn., Am. Coll. Neuropsychiatrists, Am. Psychiat. Assn., Am. Acad. Child Psychiatrists (Del. br.). Democrat. Methodist.

MCCAULEY, H(ENRY) BERTON, retired public health dentist; b. Duluth, Minn., Dec. 20, 1913; s. Henry Berton and Flora Agnes (Bourassa) McC.; m. Claire Ann Wolff, Dec. 20, 1937. DDS, U. Md., 1936. Lic. dentist, Md. Instr. oral roentgenology U. Md., Balt., 1936-40; Carnegie fellow in dentistry U. Rochester, N.Y., 1940-43, asst. prof. dentistry, cons. Manhattan Project, 1943-45; dir. dental care Balt. City Health Dept., 1949-75; health advisor Office of Mayor, Balt., 1975-77, gen. health adminstr., 1977-80; pres. North Balt. (Mental Health) Ctr., Balt., 1980. Contbr. more than 50 articles to profl. jours. Dir. Cooley's Anemia Found. Md., 1977-93. With USPHS, Nat. Inst. Dental Rsch., 1945-49. Fellow APHA, AAAS, Am. Coll. Dentists (J. Ben. Robinson award 1991), Internat. Coll. Dentists; mem. ADA (life, coun. on dental therapeutics 1943-48, chmn. sect. on pub. health 1968), Internat. Assn. Dental Rsch., Am. Soc. Dentistry for Children (Disting. Svc. award 1978), Am. Assn. Pub. Health Dentistry, Am. Acad. History of Dentistry (Hayden-Harris award 1988, pres. 1990-91), Md. Soc. Dentistry for Children (pres. 1954-55), Md. State Dental Assn. (historian 1959-87, Disting. Svc. award 1986), Md. Pub. health Assn. (pres. 1967-68), Balt. City Dental Soc. (pres. 1973), Nat. Mus. Dentistry (v.p. 1991—), Md. Hist. Soc., Balt. City Life Mus., Walters Art Gallery, Balt. Mus. Art, Mil. Order World Wars (comdr. chpt. 1986-87, dept. 1994-95), Sigma Xi, Omicron Kappa Upsilon. Roman Catholic. Home: 3804 Hadley Sq E Baltimore MD 21218-1807

MCCAULEY, ROGER LEE, psychiatrist; b. Belington, W.Va., Mar. 7, 1943; s. Jewell Welington and Nora Ruth (Ware) McC.; m. Betty Lou Tritsch, June 3, 1967; 1 child, Sara. BS summa cum laude, Alderson-Broaddus Coll., 1965; MD, W.Va. U., 1970. Diplomate Am. Bd. Psychiatry and Neurology. Resident W.Va. U. Hosp., Morgantown, 1970-73; asst. dir. health svcs. W.Va. U. Med. Ctr., Morgantown, 1973-74, dir. adult outpatient svcs. dept. behavioral medicine, 1974-76; psychiatrist Salem Psychiat. Assocs., Winston-Salem, N.C., 1976—; mem. bd. advisors Coun. on Anxiety Disorders, Winston-Salem, 1986—. Mem. AMA, Am. Psychiat. Assn., N.C. Psychiat. Assn., Forsyth County Psychiat. Assn., Forsyth County Med. Soc. Moravian. Home: 7600 Lasater Rd Clemmons NC 27012 Office: Salem Psychiat Assocs 150 Charlois Blvd Winston Salem NC 27103

MCCAUSLAND, CATHERINE LAIRD, critical care nursing educator; b. Honolulu, Mar. 7, 1948; d. Francis H. Jr. and Laird M. (Sullivan) Forbes; m. Warren H. McCausland, June 20, 1987. AA, DeAnza Coll., 1968; BSN, Regents Coll., 1984; MSN, San Francisco State U., 1987. RN, Calif.; cert. critical care nurse. Staff nurse ICU Middlesex Hosp., London; critical care instr. St. Mary's Hosp. & Med. Ctr., San Francisco, dir. nursing edn.; assoc. faculty Profl. Growth Facilitators, San Clemente, Calif., 1990-92. Mem. AACN.

MCCAWLEY, AUSTIN, psychiatrist, educator; b. Greenock, Scotland, Jan. 17, 1925; came to U.S., 1954; s. Austin and Anna Theresa (McBride) McC.; m. Gloria Klein, Feb. 15, 1958; children: Joseph, Tessa. MBCHB, U. Glasgow, 1948. Diplomate Am. Bd. Psychiatry and Neurology; DPM Royal Coll. London. Intern Glasgow Royal Infirmary, Scotland, 1948; resident Inst. Living, Harford, Conn., 1954-57, clin. dir., 1960-66; med. dir. Westchester br. St. Vincent's Hosp., N.Y.C., 1966-72; dir. psychiatry St. Francis Hosp., Hartford, 1972-88; prof. psychiatry U. Conn. Med. Sch., Farmington, 1983-93; pvt. practice, West Hartford, Conn., 1988—. Co-author: The Physician, 1983; contbr. articles to profl. jours. Chmn. Bd. Mental Health, State of Conn., 1981-84, Search Com. for Commr. Mental Health, Conn., 1981; mem. Gov.'s Spl. Task Force on Mental health Policy, Conn., 1982. With RAF, 1948-50. Fellow Am. Psychiat. Assn., Am. Coll. Psychiatry (charter fellow, founder); mem. Conn. Psychiat. Soc. (pres. 1978-79), Hartford Golf Club. Democrat. Roman Catholic. Home: 128 Westmont St West Hartford CT 06117-2926 Office: 18 N Main St West Hartford CT 06107-1919

MCCHESNEY, W. DAVID, orthopedic surgeon; b. Washington, Mar. 30, 1954; s. Robert W. Jr. and Louise (Sanderson) McChesney; m. Anne Elizabeth Day, Aug. 4, 1978; children: Matthew Michael, Claire Lucille. BS in Biology, Boston Coll., Chestnut Hill, Mass., 1976; MS in Physiology, Georgetown U., 1978, MD, 1982. Lic. physician, Tex., D.C.; diplomate Am. Bd. Orthopedic Surgery. Maj. USAF. Fellow Am. Acad. Orthopedic Surgery, Arthroscopy Assn. N.Am.; mem. Soc. Mil. Orthopedic Surgeons, Mid-Am. Orthopedic Assn. Tex. Orthopedic Soc. Office: Cy-Fair Ortho & Sports Medicine 11800 FM 1960 W Houston TX 77065

MCCLANAHAN, DONNA DOWNING, physician assistant; b. Ft. Knox, Ky., Oct. 27, 1950; d. James Arthur and Elizabeth Clay (Downing) McC. BS, Ea. Ky. U., 1972; diploma, U. Ky., 1984. Cert. in primary care Nat. Commn. on Cert. of Physician Assts. House med. officer Fayette County Detention Ctr., Lexington, Ky., 1984-91; physician asst. Office of Dr. Jim Owen, Stamping Ground, Ky., 1991-92; physician asst. emergency rm. St. Joseph Hosp., Lexington, 1994—; mem. selection com. physician asst. studies U. Ky., Lexington, 1994; examiner Nat. Commn. on Cert. of Physician Assts., Lexington, 1994. Bd. dirs. Met. Cmty. Ch., Lexington, 1994—. With U.S. Army, 1974-77. Fellow Am. Acad. Physician Assts., Ky. Acad. Physician Assts. Home: 750 Shaker Dr # 319 Lexington KY 40504-3730 Office: St Joseph Emergency Assn 1 St Joseph Dr Lexington KY 40504

MCCLATCHEY, RONALD THOMAS, optometrist; b. Detroit, Aug. 14, 1946; s. Kenneth Franklin and Helen Est (Thill) McC.; m. Karen Valerie Yon, Oct. 8, 1977; children: Katherine, Kevin, Shannon. BS, Mich. State U., 1969; OD, Ill. Coll. Optometry, 1973. Cert. optometrist, Mich. Pvt. practice Traverse City, Mich., 1974—. Mem. Am. Optometric Assn., Mich. Optometric Assn. (co-chmn. contact lens com., Keyperson award 1988-89), Northwest Mich. Optometric Soc. (past pres.), Traverse City Optimist Club (past pres., photograph Mag. 1982), Traverse City Elks Club. Office: 515 S Union Traverse City MI 49684

MCCLAY, MERI JANE, medical technologist; b. Colorado Springs, Colo., May 9, 1944; d. Charles David and Alice (Livengood) McC.; B.A., U. Oreg., 1966. Med. technologist Sacred Heart Hosp., Eugene, Oreg., 1966-67, Highland Alameda County Hosp., Oakland, Calif., 1967-68; chief technologist Arlington (Tex.) Community Hosp., 1968-72, chief technologist N.E. Med. Ctr., Bonham, Tex., 1972—. Mem. Am. Soc. Clin. Pathologists (registered, affiliate). Presbyterian. Home: PO Box 273 Bonham TX 75418-0273 Office: 504 Lipscomb St Bonham TX 75418-4028

MCCLELLAN, JASON EUGENE, retired internist; b. Bristol, Va., Oct. 6, 1926; s. Eugene Dedrick McClellan and Helen (Rutherford) Davis; m. Jean Kinsey, June 16, 1950; children: Walter, Judy. BS in Chemistry, Coll. William & Mary, 1948; MD, U. Va., 1952. Diplomate Am. Bd. Internal Medicine, Am. Bd. Hematology. Pharmacist mate USNR, Bainbridge, Bethesda, Md., 1944-46; residency U. Va. Hosp., Charlottesville, 1952-55, U. N.C. Meml. Hosp., Chapel Hill, 1955-56; instr. internal medicine U. Va. Hosp., Charlottesville, 1956-57; internist pvt. practice Riverside Hosp., Newport News, Va., 1957-93, cons. hematology, 1957-93; ret., 1993; pres. internal medicine staff Riverside Hosp., Newport News, 1960-61, pres. gen. staff, 1962-63. Contbr. articles to profl. jours. Vol. med. dir. Olde Towne Med. Clinic, Williamsburg, Va., 1933—. With USNR, 1944-46. Fellow Am. Coll. Physicians; mem. Newport News Med. Soc. (pres. 1980-81), Med. Soc. Va., Am. Soc. Hematology, Internat. Soc. Hematology. Republican. Presbyterian. Home: 504 Francis Thacker Williamsburg VA 23185-8235

MCCLELLAN, KEVIN R., ophthalmologist; b. South Bend, Ind., Sept. 21, 1952; s. Edmond L. and Esther E. (Wiesjahn) McC.; m. Mary A. Dougal, Oct. 11, 1986; children: David, Robert. BA, DePauw U., 1994; MD, U. Ill., Chgo., 1979. Intern Ill. Masonic Med. Ctr., Chgo., 1979-80; resident Loyola U. Chgo., Maywood, Ill., 1980-83; mem. staff Resurrection Med. Ctr., Chgo., 1983—. Fellow Am. Acad. Ophthalmology; mem. Alpha Omega Alpha. Office: 7447 W Talcott # 300 Chicago IL 60631

MCCLELLAN, MARY ANN, pediatrics nurse, educator; b. Mar. 29, 1942. BS, Tex. Woman's U., 1964; MN, U. Wash., 1968-69; cert., U. Tex., 1976. Cert. family life educator. Charge nurse Baylor U. Med. Ctr., Dallas, 1964-65; pub. health staff nurse Dallas County Health Dept., Dallas, 1965-68; supervising nurse Okla. State Dept. Health, Oklahoma City, 1969-70, maternal-child health nurse cons., 1971; asst. prof. U. Okla. Coll. Nursing, Oklahoma City, 1971-72; from instr. to asst. prof. Harris Coll. Nursing Tex. Christian U., Ft. Worth, 1972-75; asst. prof. continuing edn. U. Okla. Coll. Nursing, Oklahoma City, 1976-79, assc. prof. baccalaureate program, 1979—, mem. grad. faculty, 1991—; cons. and lectr. in field. Contbr. chpts. to books, articles to profl. jours. Mem. Okla. Nurses Assn. So. Early Childhood Assn., Okla. Early Childhood Assn., Sigma Theta Tau., Phi Kappa Phi. Office: U Okla Coll Nursing PO Box 26901 Oklahoma City OK 73126

MCCLELLAN, ROGER ORVILLE, toxicologist; b. Tracy, Minn., Jan. 5, 1937; s. Orville and Gladys (Paulson) McC.; m. Kathleen Mary Dunagan, June 23, 1962; children: Eric John, Elizabeth Christine, Katherine Ruth. DVM with highest honors, Wash. State U., 1960; M of Mgmt, U. N.Mex., 1980. diplomate Am. Bd. Vet. Toxicology, cert. Am. Bd. Toxicology. From biol. scientist to sr. scientist Gen. Electric Co., Richland, Wash., 1957-64; sr. scientist biology dept. Pacific N.W. Labs., Richland, Wash., 1965; scientist med. research br. div. biology and medicine AEC, Washington, 1965-66; asst. dir. research, dir. fission product inhalation program Lovelace Found. Med. Edn. and Research, Albuquerque, 1966-73; v.p., dir. research adminstrn., dir. Lovelace Inhalation Toxicology Research Inst., Albuquerque, 1973-76, pres., dir., 1976-88; chmn. bd. dirs. Lovelace Biomedical and Environ. Research Inst., Albuquerque, 1988—; pres. Chem. Industry Inst. Toxicology Research, Triangle Park, N.C., 1988—; mem. research com. Health Effects Inst., 1981-92; bd. dirs. Toxicology Lab. Accreditation Bd., 1982-90, treas., 1984-90; adj. prof. Wash. State U., 1980—, U. Ark., 1970-88; clin. assoc. U. N.Mex., 1971-85, adj. prof. toxicology, 1985—; adj. prof. toxicology and occupational and environ. medicine Duke U., 1988—; adj. prof. toxicology U. N.C. Chapel Hill, 1989—; adj. prof. toxicology N.C. State Univ., 1991—; mem dose assessment adv. group U.S. Dept. Energy, 1980-87, mem. health and environ. research adv. com., 1984-85; mem. exec. com. sci. adv. bd. EPA, 1974-95, mem. environ. health com., 1980-83, chmn., 1982-83, chmn. radionuclide emissions rev. com., 1984-85, chmn. Clean Air Sci. Adv. Com., 1987-92, chmn. rsch. strategies adv. com., 1992-94; mem. com. on toxicology NAS-NRC, 1979-87, chmn., 1980-87; bd. dirs. Lovelace Anderson Endowment Found.; mem. com. risk assessment methodology for hazardous air pollution NAS-NRC, 1991-94, com. biol. effects of Radon NAS NRC, 1994—; mem. com. on environ. justice Inst. of Medicine, 1996—; pres. Am. Bd. Vet. Toxicology, 1970-73; mem. adv. council Ctr. for Risk Mgmt., Resources for the Future, 1987—; council mem. Nat. Council for Radiation Protection, 1970—; bd. dirs. N.C. Assn. Biomedical Rsch., 1989-91, N.C. Vet. Medical Found., 1990-95, pres., 1993-94; bd. govs. Rsch. Triangle Inst., 1994—. Contbr. articles to profl. jours. Editorial bd. Jour. Toxicology and Environ. Health, 1980—, assoc. editor, 1982—; editorial bd. Fundamental and Applied Toxicology, 1984-89, assoc. editor, 1987-89; editorial bd. Toxicology and Indsl. Health, 1986—; editor CRC Critical Revs. in Toxicology, 1987—; assoc. editor Inhalation Toxicology Jour., 1987—; mem. edit. bd. Regulatory Toxicology and Pharmacology, 1993—. Recipient Herbert E. Stokinger award Am. Conf. Govtl. Indsl. Hygienists, 1985, Alumni Achievement award Wash. State U., 1987, Disting. Assoc. award Dept. Energy, 1987, 88, Arnold Lehman award Soc. Toxicology, 1992; co-recipient Frank R. Blood award Soc. Toxicology, 1989. Fellow AAAS, Am. Acad. Vet. and Comparative Toxicology, Soc. Risk Analysis; mem. Am. Chem. Soc., Inst. Medicine (elected), NAS, Radiation Research Soc. (sec.-treas. 1982-84, chmn. fin. com. 1979-82), Health Physics Soc. (chmn. program com. 1972, Elda E. Anderson award 1974), Soc. Toxicology (v.p.-elect to pres. 1987-90; inhalation specialty sect. v.p. to pres. 1983-86; bd. publs. 1983-86, chmn. 1983-85), Am. Assn. Aerosol Research (bd. dirs. 1982-94, treas. 1986-90, v.p. to pres. 1990-93), Am. Vet. Med. Assn., Gesellschaft fur Aerosolforschung, Sigma Xi, Phi Kappa Phi, Phi Zeta. Republican. Lutheran. Home: 1111 Cuatro Cerros Trl SE Albuquerque NM 87123-4149 also: 2903 Bainbridge Dr Apt Q Durham NC 27713-1448 Office: Chem Industry Inst Toxicology PO Box 12137 Research Triangle Park NC 27709

MCCLELLAND, JAMES LLOYD, psychology educator, cognitive scientist; b. Cambridge, Mass., Dec. 1, 1948; s. Walter Moore and Frances (Shaffer) McC.; m. Heidi Marsha Feldman, May 6, 1978; children: Mollie S., Heather Ann. BA in Psychology, Columbia U., 1970; PhD in Cognitive Psychology, U. Pa., 1975. Asst. prof. dept. psychology U. California, San Diego, 1974-80, assoc. prof., 1980-84; assoc. prof. Carnegie-Mellon U., Pitts., 1984-85, prof. psychology, 1985—, prof. computer sci., 1987—, acting head psychology, 1989-90, co-dir. Ctr. for Neural Basis of Cognition, 1994—; adj. prof. neurosci. U. Pitts., 1995—; vis. scientist dept. psychology and Ctr. Cognitive Sci., MIT, 1982-84; vis. scholar dept. psychology Harvard U., 1982-84; mem. com. on basic rsch. in behavioral and social scis. NRC, 1985, rev. panel for cognition, emotion and personality NIMH, 1983-87, behavioral scis. rsch. br. assessment panel, 1987-88, Cognitive Functional Neurosci., 1995—; co-organizer NSF workshop on connectionism and cognitive sci., 1986. Author: (with others) Parallel Distributed Processing: Explorations in the Microstructure of Cognition, Vols. I, II, 1986; co-author: A Handbook of Models, Programs, and Exercises, 1988; contbr. numerous articles, reports, book chpts. to profl. publs.; sr. editor Cognitive Sci., 1988-91; mem. editorial bd. Perception and Psychophysics, 1977-82, Jour. of Verbal Learning and Verbal Behavior, 1980-84, Cognitive Sci., 1983-88, Cognitive Neuropsychology, 1983—, (book series) Computational Approaches in Cognitive Sci., 1983—, Cognitive Psychology, 1984—, Jour. Exptl. Psychology: General, 1984-87, Lang. and Cognitive Processes, 1988—, Neural Computation, 1989—. Recipient William W. Cumming prize Columbia U., 1970, Rsch. Scientist Career Devel. award NIMH, 1981-86, 87—; NSF fellow, 1970-73, grantee, 1976-79, 80-84, 86-87, 88—; grantee Office Naval Rsch., 1982-87. Fellow AAAS; mem. Cognitive Sci. Soc. (governing bd. 1988—, chmn. 1991), Psychonomics Soc., Internat. Assn. for Study Attention and Performance (governing bd. 1986—, lectr. 1986), Soc. Exptl. Psychologists (Warren medal 1993), Phi Beta Kappa. Office: Carnegie Mellon U Dept Psychology Pittsburgh PA 15213-3890

MCCLELLAND, MARIANNE JACOB, maternal child health care nurse; b. Baytown, Tex., Nov. 20, 1948; d. Thomas Lionel and Gladys Lena (Henderson) Jacob; m. Jesse Lionel McClelland, Nov. 9, 1985; children: Anne Bennett Dickens, Edward Thomas Bennett. ADN, Lee Coll., Baytown, Tex., 1992. RN, Tex. Staff nurse, labor and delivery U. Tex. Med. Br., Galveston, 1992; staff nurse, maternal child health San Jacinto Meth. Hosp., Baytown, 1992—. Music dir., organist St. Josephs Ch., Baytown; accompanist Pasadena (Tex.) Symphony, Goose Creek Ind. Sch. Dist., Baytown. Mem. AWHONN, ACCN, Phi Theta Kappa (treas. 1991-92). Republican. Roman Catholic. Home: 4707 Spring Ln Baytown TX 77521

MCCLELLAND, RICHARD LEE, dentist; b. Pitts., May 18, 1927; s. William Noble and Pauline Elizabeth (Lee) McC.; m. Elizabeth Anne Michon, Dec. 6, 1958; children: Richard Scott, William Alfred, Robert Craig. BA, Princeton U., 1950; DDS, U. Pa., 1954. Pvt. practice Princeton, N.J., 1958-92; clin. instr. U. Pa. Dental Sch., Phila., 1958-62; mem. exec. com. Med. Ctr. Princeton, 1971-72, past chmn. dental dept.; elected Nat. Dental Surgeon Res. Officers Assn. of U.S., 1972-73. Lt. Dental Corps, USNR, 1954-57, capt., ret. Fellow Am. Coll. Dentists, Internat. Coll. Dentists, Acad. Gen. Dentistry, Acad. Dentistry Internat.; mem. ADA, Am. Prosthodontic Soc., Fedn. Dentaire Internat., Res. Officers Assn., Nassau Club, Princeton Club (N.Y.C.), Rotary (pres. Princeton 1978-79). Republican. Episcopalian.

MC CLELLAND, ROBERT NELSON, surgeon, educator; b. Gilmer, Tex., Nov. 20, 1929; s. Robert Hilton and Verna Louise (Nelson) McC.; m. Connie Logan, May 5, 1958; children: Robert Christopher, Alison, Julie. B.A., U. Tex., Austin, 1952; M.D., U. Tex., Galveston, 1954. Diplomate Am. Bd. Surgery. Rotating intern U. Kans. Med. center, 1954-55; resident in gen. surgery Parkland Hosp., Dallas, 1957-59, 60-62; instr. surgery Southwestern Med. Sch., U. Tex., Dallas, 1962-63; asst. prof. Southwestern Med. Sch., U. Tex., 1963-67, asso. prof., 1967-71, prof., 1971—, Alvin Baldwin prof. surgery, 1977—; examiner Nat. Bd. Med. Examiners. Editor Audio Jour. Rev. Gen. Surgery, 1971-82, Selected Readings in Gen. Surgery, 1974—; contbr. numerous articles to profl. jours., chpts. to books. Served to capt. M.C. USAF, 1955-57. Fellow ACS (mem. grad. edn. com.); mem. AMA, Am. Surg. Assn., Western Surg. Assn., Soc. Surgery of Alimentary Tract, Am. Gastroent. Assn., Southwestern Surg. Soc., So. Surg. Assn., Dallas Soc. Gen. Surgeons (pres. 1987-88), Tex. Surg. Soc., Tex. Med. Assn., Dallas Country Med. Soc., Soc. Internatale de Chiurgie (bd. dirs. Am. chpt.), Phi Beta Kappa, Alpha Omega Alpha. Republican. Lutheran. Home: 3601 Potomac Ave Dallas TX 75205-2110 Office: 5323 Harry Hines Blvd Dallas TX 75235-7200

MCCLELLAND, SHEARWOOD JUNIOR, orthopaedic surgeon; b. Gary, Ind., Aug. 1, 1947; s. Shearwood and Zenobia Pearl (Pruitt) McC.; m. Yvonne Shirley Thornton, June 8, 1974; children: Shearwood III, Kimberly Itaska. AB, Princeton U., 1969; MD, Columbia U., 1974, MPH, 1996. Diplomate Am. Bd. Orthopaedic Surgery. Intern, St. Luke's Hosp., N.Y.C., 1974-75, resident, 1975-76; asst. resident in orthopaedic surgery N.Y. Orthopaedic Hosp., 1976-79; commd. lt. USNR, 1979-82, advanced through grades to lt. comdr., 1980; staff orthopaedic surgeon Nat. Naval Med. Ctr., Bethesda, Md., 1979-82; asst. prof. surgery Uniformed Svcs. U. of Health Scis., 1980-82; acting chief orthopaedic surgery Harlem Hosp. Center, 1983-84, assoc. dir. orthopaedic surgery, 1985-92; acting dir., 1992-94, dir., 1994—; asst. prof. clin. orthopaedic surgery Columbia U., 1983-94, assoc. clin. prof., 1994—; oral examiner Am. Bd. Othopaedic Surgery; mem. N.Y. State Bd. of Profl. Med. Conduct. Annie C. Kane fellow in orthopaedic surgery, 1978-79; fellow in total joint implant surgery Ohio State U., 1982 . Fellow Internat. Coll. Surgeons, ACS, Am. Acad. Orthopaedic Surgeons, N.Y. Acad. Medicine; mem. Assn. Mil. Surgeons of U.S., Eastern Orthopaedic Assn., N.Y. Orthopaedic Hosp. Alumni Assn., Mensa, No. N.J. Princeton Alumni Assn. Office: Harlem Hosp Ctr KP-9101 506 Lenox Ave New York NY 10037-1802

MCCLINTOCK, HOMER GLENN, neurosurgeon; b. Pitts., Oct. 23, 1917; s. Glenn Roy and Alma McClintock; m. Priscille Young, Jan. 15, 1944 (div. 1990); children: Richard, Jeffrey, Priscilla Sue, Mark. BS, U. Pitts., 1941, MD, 1944. Diplomate Am. Bd. Neurosurgery. Mem. staff Mercy Hosp., Pitts., 1952-53; pvt. practice physician Denver, 1953—; assoc. clin. prof. neurosurgery U. Colo., Denver, 1954—; mem. staff U. Zürich, Switzerland, 1967-68. Contbr. articles to profl. jours. Lt. sr. grade USN, 1944-46, PTO. Fellow ACS (chair com. applicants 1981—); mem. Am. Acad. Neurosurgery, Congress Neurol. Surgeons, Western Neurosurg. Soc., Colo. Neurol. Surgeons (pres., founder), Denver Med. Soc., Rotary. Presbyterian. Office: U Colo Divsn Neurosurgery Campus Box C307 4200 E 9th Denver CO 80220

MCCLINTOCK, RICHARD POLSON, dermatologist; b. Lancaster, N.H., Dec. 16, 1933; s. Richard P. and Dorothy Grace (Ramsey) McC.; m. Barbara Wyatt, June 1959 (div. Mar. 1970); children: Peter, Pamela; m. Mary Joy Fitzgerald, Mar. 21, 1970; children: Wayne, Patrick. BA, Dartmouth U., 1956; MD, Harvard U., 1960. Diplomate Am. Bd. Dermatology, Am. Bd. Dermatopathology. Intern in medicine U. N.C., Chapel Hill, 1960-61; resident in dermatology Stanford U., Palo Alto, Calif., 1964-67; pvt. practice Ukiah, Calif., 1967—; clin. instr. dermatology Stanford U., Palo Alto, 1967-78, clin. asst. prof., 1978-86, assoc. clin. prof., 1986-92, lectr., 1992—; mem. hosp. staff Ukiah Valley Med. Ctr., chief of staff, 1974. Contbr. articles to profl. jours. Trustee Found. for Med. Care for Mendocino and Lake Counties, 1990-94, pres., 1992-94. Lt. Med. Corps, USN, 1961-64. Mem. San Francisco Dermatol. Soc., Pacific Dermatol. Assn., Am. Acad. Dermatology, Calif. Med. Soc., Mendocino Lake County Med. Soc., Internat. Soc. Dermatopathology. Office: 723 S Dora St Ukiah CA 95482-5335

MCCLINTOCK, WILLIAM THOMAS, health care administrator; b. Pittsfield, Mass., Oct. 23, 1934; s. Ernest William and Helen Elizabeth (Clum) M.; m. Wendolyn Hope Eckerman, June 22, 1963; children: Anne Elizabeth, Carol Jean, Thomas Daniel. BA, St. Lawrence U., Canton, N.Y., 1956; MBA, U. Chgo., 1959, MHA, 1962. Prodn. planner Corning Glass Works, Corning, N.Y., 1959-60; adminstrv. resident Highland Hosp., Oakland, Calif., 1961-62; adminstrv. asst. Univ. Hosps. of Cleve., 1962-65; asst. adminstr. Presbyn. Hosp., Whittier, Calif., 1965-68; regional asst. Kaiser Found. Hosps., Oakland, Calif., 1968-70; assoc. dir., exec. dir. Conn. Hosp. Planning Commn., New Haven, 1970-75; project dir., lectr. sch. health studies U. N.H., Durham, 1975-77; regional mgr. Tex. Med. Found., Austin, 1977-81; adminstr. Schick Shadel Hosp., Fort Worth, 1981-87; mgmt. cons. George S. May Internat. Co., Park Ridge, Ill., 1987-88; mgr. Nat. Ctr. Rsch. Programs Am. Heart Assn., Dallas, 1988-89; adminstr. Ambulatory Svcs. Health Care of Tex., Ft. Worth, 1990-92; CEO Boundary Community Hosp. & Nursing Home, Bonners Ferry, Idaho, 1992—. 1st lt. U.S. Army, 1957. Fellow Am. Coll. Health Care Execs., Am. Coll. Addiction Treatment Adminstrs.; mem. Am. Hosp. Assn. (life), Am. Heart Assn. (mem. bd. dirs. Idaho/Mont. affiliate 1993—), Idaho Hosp. Assn. (bd. dirs. 1995—), Unity Lodge No. 9, F&AM, N.Y. Republican. Presbyterian. Avocations: book collections, gardening, photography. Home: County Rd 62C PO Box 1226 Bonners Ferry ID 83805-1226 Office: 6640 Kaniksu St Bonners Ferry ID 83805

MCCLURE, JOHN EDWARD, research biomedical scientist, virologist; b. El Campo, Tex., Nov. 20, 1944; s. John and Tillie Margaret (Cervenka) McC.; m. Mary Sue Raymond, Mar. 11, 1973; children: Jonathan Allan, Jennifer Karin. BSc in Chemistry, U. Tex., 1967; PhD in Molecular Virology, Baylor Coll. Medicine, 1994. Rsch. assoc. biochemistry U. Ariz., Tucson, 1968-71, Baylor Coll. Medicine, Houston, 1971-72, U. Tex. Med. Sch., Galveston, 1973-78, George Washington U. Med. Sch., Washington, 1978-82; rsch. assoc. pediatrics Baylor Coll. Medicine, Houston, 1982-85, rsch. instr. pediatrics, 1985—; rsch. scientist immunology Tex. Children's Hosp., Houston, 1985-94; R & D scientist Ramco Labs., Inc., Houston, 1994—; rsch. cons. Hoffmann-LaRoche Inc., Nutley, N.J., 1975-79. Contbr. articles to profl. Jour. Immunology, Cancer Rsch., Cellular Immunology, Molecular Cellular Probes, Prog. in Med. Virology. Mem. Jr. C. of C. (Jaycees), LaMarque, Tex., 1981-82. Co-grantee Nat. Cancer Inst., NIH-USPHS, 1981-82. Mem. AAAS, Am. Soc. for Microbiology, Am. Chem. Soc., N.Y. Acad. Sci. Democrat. Lutheran. Office: Ramco Labs Inc 4507 Mount Vernon St Houston TX 77006-5815

MCCLURE, WILLIAM OWEN, biologist; b. Yakima, Wash., Sept. 29, 1937; s. Rexford Delmont and Ruth Josephine (Owen) McC.; m. Pamela Preston Harris, Mar. 9, 1968 (div. 1979); children: Heather Harris, Rexford Owen; m. Sara Joan Rorke, July 27, 1980. BSc, Calif. Inst. Tech., 1959; PhD, U. Wash., 1964. Postdoctoral fellow Rockefeller U., N.Y.C., 1964-65; rsch. assoc. Rockefeller U., 1965-68; asst. prof. U. Ill., Urbana, 1968-75; assoc. prof. U. So. Calif., L.A., 1975-79; prof. biology, prof. neurology U. So. Calif., 1979—; v.p. sci. affairs Nelson Rsch. & Devel. Co., Irvine, Calif., 1981-82; acting v.p. rsch. & devel. Nelson Rsch. & Devel. Co., 1985-86; dir. program. neurol. info. sci. U. So. Calif., 1982-92, dir. program in psychobiology, 1991—; dir. cellular biology U. So. Calif., 1979-81, dir. neurobiology, 1982-88, dir. prog. psychobiology, 1991—; cons. in field; dir. Marine & Freshwater Biomed. Ctr., U. So. Calif., 1982-83; co-dir. Baja Calif. Expedition of the R/V Alpha Helix, 1974, others; chmn. Winter Conf. on Brain Rsch., 1979, 80, others; lectr. in field; sci. adv. bd. Nelson R & D, 1972-91; mem. bd. commentators Brain and Behavioral Scis., 1978—. Editor or author 3 books; co-editor: Wednesday Night at the Lab; patentee in field; mem. editorial bd. Neurochem. Rsch., 1975-81, Jour. Neurochemistry, 1977-84, Jour. Neurosci. Rsch., 1980-86; contbr. over 100 articles to profl. jours. Bd. dirs. San Pedro and Peninsula Hosp. Found., 1989—, Faculty Ctr., U. So. Calif., 1991-95, San Pedro Health Svcs., 1992—. Scripps Inst. fellow, 1958, NIH fellow, 1959-64, 64-65, Alfred P. Sloan fellow, 1972-76, others; recipient rsch. grants, various sources, 1968—; Intersci. Rsch. Inst. fellow, 1989. Mem. AAAS, Am. Soc. Neurochemistry, Soc. for Neurosci., Am. Soc. Biol. Chemistry and Molecular Biology, Interant. Soc. Neurochemistry, Assn. Neurosci. Depts. and Programs, Univ. Park Investment Group, Bay Surgical Soc., N.Y. Acad. Scis. Republican. Presbyterian. Home: 30533 Rhone Dr Palos Verdes Peninsula CA 90275-5742 Office: U So Calif Dept Biol Scis Los Angeles CA 90089

MCCLURG, JAMES EDWARD, research laboratory executive; b. Bassett, Nebr., Mar. 23, 1945; s. Warren James and Delia Emma (Allyn) McC. B.S., N.E. Wesleyan U., 1967; Ph.D., U. Nebr., 1973. Instr. U. Nebr. Coll. Medicine, Omaha, 1973-76, research instr., 1973-76, clin. asst. prof. Med. Ctr., 1984—; v.p., tech, dir. Harris Labs., Inc., Lincoln, Nebr., 1976-82, exec. v.p., 1982-84, pres., chief exec. officer, 1984—; bd. dirs. Lincoln Mut. Life

Ins. Co., Lincoln Gen. Hosp. (chmn.), Unemed Corp., Lincoln, Harris Labs. Ltd, Belfast No. Ireland. Mem. editorial bd. Clin. Rsch. Practices and Drug Regulatory Affairs, 1984. Contbr. articles to profl. jours. Trustee Univ. Nebr. Found.; mem. Commn. on Human Rights, Lincoln, 1982-85; com. mem. Nebr. Citizens for Study Higher Edn., Lincoln, 1984; chmn. U. Nebr. Found. Recipient ann. research award Central Assn. Obstetricians and Gynecologists, 1982. Mem. Am. Assn. Lab. Accreditation (bd. dirs.). Republican. Clubs: Century (pres. Nebr. Wesleyan U. 1983-84), Nebraska (Lincoln). Lodge: Rotary. Avocation: boating. Office: Harris Labs Inc PO Box 80837 Lincoln NE 68501-0837

MCCLUSKEY, CHARLES JAMES, JR., physician assistant; b. Rockville Center, N.Y., Oct. 16, 1947; s. Charles James McCluskey Sr. and Genevieve Ann (Reaves) Murphy; m. Betsy Ann Dresback, May 9, 1970; children: Charles James III, Christopher James. Student, Broward Jr. Coll., 1967, Weber State Coll., 1971; cert. physician asst., Med. U. S.C., 1975. Cert. physician's asst., Fla., cert. procurement transplant coord. Am. Bd. Transplant Coords. Staff physician asst. George L. Timmons, MD, P.A., Hartsville, S.C., 1975-76; physician asst. U.S. Dept. Justice, Washington, 1977-80, supervisory physician asst., health svc. adminstr., 1980-82; organ procurement coord. U. Fla., Jacksonville, 1982-86; exec. dir. organ procurement ops. U. Fla., Gainesville, 1986—; cons. Japanese Transplant Orgn., Kobe, Osaka, 1989—. Contbr. articles to profl. jours. State dir. S.C. Jaycees, Hartsville, 1975-77; bd. dirs., v.p. Nat. Kidney Found., Jacksonville, 1983-87; bd. dirs. Nielsen Organ Transplant Found., Jacksonville, 1983—. Sgt. USAF, 1970-72. Fellow Am. Acad. Physician's Assts. (liaison transplantation 1975—), N.Am. Transplant Coord. Orgn. (chair edn. 1982—, liaison to Japan 1986-88, Appreciation award 1986); mem. S.E. Organ Procurement Found. (chair procurement presentation 1982—, Appreciation award 1991), United Network for Organ Sharing. Home: 4730 NW 13th Ave Gainesville FL 32605 Office: Organ Procurement Orgn U Fla Box 100286 Gainesville FL 32610

MCCLUSKEY, JEAN ASHFORD, nursing educator, retired; b. Phila., Apr. 27, 1926; d. Charles Robert and Susanna Myers (Smith) Ashford; m. Robert C. McCluskey, June 28, 1947; children: David C., Robert C., Jean Alyce Loux. RN, Jewish Hosp., Phila., 1947; BS in Edn., West Chester (Pa.) State Coll., 1965; EdM, Temple U., PHila., 1970. Coord. practical nursing prog. North Montco AVTS, Lansdale, Pa., 1967-70; dir. dipl. LPN-RN Sch. Nursing Bucks County Grand View Hosp., Sellersville, Pa., 1970-77; dir. Sch. Practical Nursing Sacred Heart Hosp., Norristown, Pa., 1977-93; nursing edn. cons., 1993—. Contbr. articles to profl. jours. Recipient Disting. Svc. award, S.E. Pa. League for Nursing, 1984; named Ky. Col., 1980, others. Mem. Nat. League Nursing (bd. dirs. 1983-87, bd. rvs. CPNP 1987-93).

MCCLUSKEY, NEIL GERARD, gerontologist, educator, literary agent; b. Seattle, Dec. 15, 1920; s. Patrick John and Mary Genevieve (Casey) McC.; m. Elaine Lituchy, June 5, 1977. AB, Gonzaga U., 1944, MA, 1945; Lic. in Sacred Theology, Gen. Theol. Union, Berkeley, 1952; PhD, Columbia U., 1957. Assoc. editor Am. (Nat. Cath. Weekly), N.Y.C., 1955-60; dean sch. edn. Gonzaga U., Spokane, 1960-62, dir. hons. program, 1963-65, v.p. acad., 1963-66; prof. U. Notre Dame, South Bend, Ind., 1966-71, dean, dir. Inst. Studies in Edn., 1968-71; prof., dean profl. studies Lehman Coll. CUNY, 1971-75; dir. Ctr. Gerontol. Studies CUNY Grad. Sch., 1975-81; exec. dir. BHRAGS Social Svcs. Ctr., Bklyn., 1981-84; sr. cons. Retirement Advisors, Inc., N.Y.C., 1985—; pres. Westchester Lit. Agy., 1991—. Author: Public Schools and Moral Education, 1958, Catholic Viewpoint on Education, 1959, Catholic Education Faces Its Future, 1969; author, editor: Aging and Society, 1980, Aging and Retirement, 1981. Bd. dirs. Cath. Big Bros. N.Y., 1985—. Home: 2533 Egret Lake Dr West Palm Beach FL 33413

MCCLUSKEY, TAMARA B., pediatrician; b. Dover, N.J., Aug. 31, 1961; d. Nicholas J. Bertha and Susan M. Bertha Gibbs; m. Michael P. McCluskey, June 11, 1988; 1 child, Michael T. BS, Muhlenberg Coll., Allentown, Pa., 1983; DO, Kirksville Coll. Osteo. Med., 1988. Rotating intern Union (N.J.) Hosp., 1988-89; pediatric resident Monmouth Med. Ctr., Long Branch, N.J., 1989-92; pediatrician Denville (N.J.) Pediatrics, 1992—. Fellow Am. Acad. Pediatrics. Home: 230 North Rd Kinnelon NJ 07405 Office: Denville Pediatrics 140 E Main St Denville NJ 07834

MC COIN, JOHN MACK, social worker; b. Sparta, N.C., Jan. 21, 1931; s. Robert Avery and Ollie (Osborne) McC.; BS, Appalachian State Tchrs. Coll., Boone, N.C., 1957; MS in Social Work, Richmond (Va.) Profl. Inst., 1962; postgrad. U. N.C., 1959-60; PhD, U. Minn., 1977. Lic. master social worker. Social svc. worker Broughton State Hosp., Morganton, N.C., 1958-59, John Unstead State Hosp., Butner, N.C., 1960-61; clin. social worker Dorothea Dix State Hosp., Raleigh, N.C., 1962-63; child welfare case worker Wake County Welfare Dept., Raleigh, 1963-64; psychiat. social worker Toledo Mental Hygiene Clinic, 1964-66; sr. psychiat. social worker N.Y. Hosp.-Cornell U. Med. Ctr. Westchester Divsn., White Plains, 1966-68; social worker VA Hosp., Montrose, N.Y., 1968-73, also vol. mental health worker Westchester County Mental Health Assn. and Mental Health Bd., White Plains, N.Y.; seminar instr. Grad. Sch. Social Work, U. Minn., Mpls., 1973-74; social worker F.D.R. VA Health Care Facility, Montrose, 1975-77; asst. prof. social work U. Wis., Oshkosh, 1977-79, chmn. dept. cmty. liaison com., 1978-79; assoc. prof. social work Grand Valley State Colls., Allendale, Mich., 1979-81; social worker VA Med. Ctr. Battle Creek, Mich., 1981-83; supr. social worker Dept. VA Med. Ctr., Leavenworth, Kans., 1983-94; cons. 44th Gen. Hosp., USAR, Menasha, Wis., 1978-79, 5540th Support Command, USAR, Grand Rapids, Mich., 1979-83; cons. in field; adj. faculty mem. social scis. dept., Kansas City C.C., 1985-89, St. Mary Coll., 1984, Kellogg C.C., Battle Creek, 1981-83; adj. faculty mem. sch. social welfare, U. Kans., Lawrence, 1992. With USMC, 1948-52, USMCR, 1957-72; lt. col. USAR, 1972-91. Recipient Outstanding Performance award VA, 1971, Superior Performance award, 1982, Outstanding Performance award, 1983; grantee NIMH, 1974; cert. social worker, N.Y. Mem. Nat. Assn. Social Workers (social action com. W. Mich. br. 1980-81), Alpha Delta Mu. Democrat. Baptist. Author: Adult Foster Homes: Their Managers and Residents, 1983; founder (with Human Scis. Press), editor Adult Foster Care Jour., 1987-88, Adult Residential Care Jour., 1989-91, independent jour., 1992—; contbr. articles to profl. jours.; presenter in field. Home: 4913 Colonial Way Lawrence KS 66049-3723

MCCOLGIN, STERLING WAYNE, obstetrician, gynecologist; b. Stillwater, Okla., Feb. 12, 1943; s. Quentin PHillips and Katherine Pauline (Bonomo) McC.; m. Sue Blevins, June 17, 1967; children:Lellani, Coby, Ila, Cody. BS, U.S. Mil. Acad., West Point, N.Y., 1967; MD, U. Okla., 1977. Commd. USAF, 1973, advanced through grades to col., 1984; line officer, co. comdr. U.S. Army, Gelnhausen, Germany, 1967-69; inf. co. comdr. 1-12 Inf., 4th Mechanized Inf. Divsn. USAF, Republic of Vietnam, 1969-70; staff officer-co. comdr. U.S. Army, Ft. Carson, Colo., 1970-72; resident David Grant USAF Med. Ctr., Jackson, Miss., 1977-81; chief obstetrics, asst. dept. chmn., asst. clin. prof. Wright State U., 1981-84; chief obstetrics/gynecology, chief hosp. svcs. USAF Hosp., Tyndall AFB, Fla., 1984-86; chief gynecology Keesler Med. Ctr., Keesler AFB, Biloxi, Miss., 1986-88; fellow, instr. maternal fetal medicine dept. ob-gyn. U. Miss. Med. Ctr., Jackson, 1988-90; asst. prof. dept. ob-gyn. U. Colo., Denver, 1990; dir. maternal fetal medicine St. Joseph Hosp., Denver, 1991—; worldwide cons. Air Force Surgeon Gen. in Ob-Gyn., Tyndall AFB, Fla., 1985-88. Contbr. articles to profl. jours., chpts. to books. Fellow Am. Coll. Ob/Gyn.; mem. AMA, Winfred L. Wiser Soc., U.S. Mil. Acad., Soc. Perinatal Obstetricians (Acad. Enrichment award 1989). Office: Midtown 1 Ste 750 2005 Franklin St Denver CO 80205

MCCOLL, IAN, surgeon; b. U.K., June 1, 1933; s. Frederick George and Winifred Edity (Murphy) McC.; m. Jean Lennox McNair, Aug. 27, 1960; children: Alistair James, Caroline Lennox, Mary Knight. MB, BS Surgery, U. London, 1957, MS, 1965. Surgical trainee Guy's Hosp., Hosp. for Sick Children, St. Mark's Hosp., London, 1957-67; sub-dean, surgeon St. Bartholomews Hosp. Med. Coll., London, 1967-71; rsch. fellow Med. Sch. Harvard U., Boston, 1967; prof. surgery Guy's Hosp., London, 1971—. Chmn. govt. inquiry on supplying aids for disabled people, Eng. and Wales, 1985-86; dep. speaker Ho. Lords, 1994—; parliamentary pvt. sec. to Prime Minister, 1994—. Hon. cons. surgeon Brit. Army, 1981—. Named to Brit. Peerage, 1989. Office: 10 Downing, London SW1 AZAA, England

MCCOLLOM, HERBERT FORREST, JR., audiologist; b. Ridley Park, Pa., Sept. 7, 1931; s. Herbert Forrest and Dorothy Mae (Allison) McC.; m. Joan Elizabeth Fleming, June 16, 1956; children: Geoffrey, Mark. BA, Pa. State U., 1953; MEd, Franklin & Marshall, 1959. Cert. clin. competence in audiology, clin. competence in speech-lang. pathology. Tchr. Elizabethtown (Pa.) Schs., 1955-58; itinerant hearing clinician Lancaster (Pa.) County Supt. of Schs., 1958-64; audiologist, exec. dir. Hearing Conservation Ctr., Lancaster, 1966-77; pvt. practice in audiology Hearing Svcs. of Lancaster, 1977—. Co-author: Hearing Aid Dispensing Practice, 1984; contbr. articles to profl. jous. Sgt. Spec./4 U.S. Army, 1953-55. John F. Steinman scholarship Steinman Found., 1964. Fellow Acad. of Dispensing Audiologists (pres. 1986-87, jour. editor 1993-95), Am. Acad. Audiology, Pa. Acad. of Audiology, Am. Speech-Lang.-Hearing Assn. Republican. Office: Hearing Svcs of Lancaster 202 Butler Ave Lancaster PA 17601-6306

MC COLLOUGH, NEWTON CLARK, III, orthopaedic surgeon; b. Butler, Pa., July 17, 1934; s. Newton C. and Margaret Elizabeth (Mattocks) McC.; m. Mary Eva Semanski, Feb. 22, 1968; children—Peter Scott, Amy Marie. B.A., Duke U., 1956; M.D., U. Pa., 1959. Diplomate: Am. Bd. Orthopaedic Surgery. Intern Jackson Meml. Hosp., Miami, Fla., 1959-60; resident in orthopaedic surgery Jackson Meml. Hosp., 1960-64; dir. orthopaedic resident edn. Orange Meml. Hosp., Orlando, Fla., 1965-66; asst. prof. orthopaedics and rehab. U. Miami Sch. Medicine, 1968-72, assoc. prof., 1972-76, prof., vice chmn. dept., 1976-78, prof., chmn. dept., 1978-86; dir. rehab. Jackson Meml. Hosp., Miami, 1972-82, chief orthopedics and rehab., 1978-86; dir. med. affairs Internat. Shriners Hosps. for Crippled Children, Tampa, Fla., 1986—; dir. Am. Bd. for Certification in Prosthetics/Orthotics, 1974-77; mem. Health Planning Council So. Fla. Task Force on Long Term Patient Care, 1974-77; asst. med. dir. Div. of Children's Med. Services, State of Fla., 1975-86; chmn. Statewide Com. for Spinal Cord Injury, 1976-78. Trustee Jour. Bone and Joint Surgery, 1992—, vice chmn., 1996—; contbr. articles to med. jours. Served to lt. comdr. M.C. USNR, 1966-68. Decorated Legion of Merit. Mem. ACS, AMA, Am. Acad. ORthopaedic Surgeons (bd. dirs. 1978-79, 87-92, 2d v.p. 1987-88, 1st v.p. 1988-89, pres. 1989-90), Fla. Orthopaedic Soc. (mem. exec. com. 1978—), Miami Orthopaedic Soc. (v.p. 1978-79), Am. Acad. Orthotists and Prosthetists (hon.), Fla. Med. Soc. Hillsborough County Med. Assn., Am. Congress Rehab. Medicine, Nat. Rehab. Assn., Scoliosos Rsch. Soc., Internat. Soc. Prosthetics and Orthotics, Am. Orthopaedic Assn., Orthopaedic Rsch. and Edn. Found. (trustee 1991—, sec. 1995—), Internat. Soc. Prosthetics and Orthotics (dir. 1980—), Assn. Children's Prosthetic and Orthotic Clinics (pres. 1983-84), Rehab. Engring. Soc. N.Am. (dir. 1980—), Am. Spinal Injury Assn., Internat. Med. Soc. Paraplegia, Pediatric Orthopaedic Soc. (dir. 1983-84, pres. 1984-85), 20th Century Orthopaedic Assn. (treas. 1984-89), Am. Acad. Pediatrics, Phi Beta Kappa, Alpha Omega. Republican. Lutheran. Home: 3206 Mermaid Ct New Port Richey FL 34652-3045 Office: Internat Shriners Hosps for Crippled Children 2900 N Rocky Point Dr Tampa FL 33607-1435

MCCOLLUM, JEAN HUBBLE, medical assistant; b. Peoria, Ill., Oct. 21, 1934; d. Claude Ambrose and Josephine Mildred (Beiter) Hubble; m. Everett Monroe Patton, Sept. 4, 1960 (div. Jan. 1969); 1 child, Linda Joanne; m. James Ward McCollum, Jan. 2, 1971; 1 child, Steven Ward. Student, Bradley U., Ill. Cen. Coll. Stenographer Caterpillar Tractor Co., Peoria, 1952-53, supr. stenographer pool, 1953-55, adminstrv. sec., treas., 1955-60, sec., asst. dept. mgr., 1969-71; med. staff sec. Proctor Cmty. Hosp., Peoria, 1978-82; med. asst. Drs. Taylor, Fox and Morgan, Peoria, 1982-84; freelance med. asst. Meth. Hosp. and numerous physicians, Peoria, 1984-89; office mgr. Dr. Danehower, McLelland and Stone, Peoria, 1989—. Vol. tutor Northmoor Sch., Peoria, 1974-78; bd. dirs., mem. exec. com., com. chmn. Planned Parenthood, Peoria, 1990-92. Recipient Outstanding Performance award Proctor Hosp., 1981, also various awards for svc. to schs., ch. and hosps. for mentally ill. Mem. Nat. Wildlife Fedn., Mensa Internat. (publs. officer, editor 1987-89), Mothers League (treas. 1977), Willow Knolls Country Club (social com. 1989-90), Nature Conservancy, World Wildlife Fund, Forest Park Found., Jacques Cousteau Soc., Wilderness Soc. Methodist. Home: 2822 W Pine Hill Ln Peoria IL 61614-3256

MCCOMBS, MICHAEL MITCHELL, physician; b. New Kensington, Pa., Mar. 11, 1966; s. Allen Dare Jr. and Barbara J. (Johnson) McC.; m. Teresa Ann Spring, Dec. 5, 1995; children: Lauren, Mitchell. BS, U. Pitts., 1992; DO, Phila. Coll. Osteo. Medicine, 1996. Operating room technician Allegheny Gen. Hosp., Pitts., 1989-92; internal medicine resident Doctor's Hosp., Massilon, Ohio, 1996—; co-founder Candace Bypass Program, Phila., 1992-94. Sgt. USAF, 1985-89. Decorated John Lewiston award USAF, Below the Zone award, 1988. Mem. Student Osteo. Surg. Assn. (pres. 1993), Am. Osteo. Assn., Am. Coll. Osteo. Family Practitioners, Ruffed Grouse Soc., NRA, N.Am. Hunting Club, Delta Phi (pres. 1989). Home: 1239 Taylor Ave New Kensington PA 15068

MCCONNAUGHEY, BAYARD H., biology educator; b. Pitts., Apr. 21, 1916; s. Harlow Alexander and Hattie (Cherryman) McC.; m. Evelyn Irene Shirek, June 12, 1950; children: William B., Edward A., John, Rebecca, Diane. BA with highest honors, Pomona Coll., 1938; MA, U. Hawaii, 1941; PhD, U. Calif., Berkeley, 1946. From asst. prof. to prof. U. Oreg., Eugene, 1949-86, prof. emeritus, 1986—; assoc. prof. U. Indonesia, 1963-66; prof. biology World Campus Afloat Semester at Sea, World Cruise, 1974, 88. Author: Introduction to Marine Biology, 1990; contbr. articles to profl. jours. Tech. sgt. U.S. Army, 1942-44. Rsch. fellow Scripps Inst. Oceanography, LaJolla, Calif., 1948. Mem. Phi Beta Kappa, Sigma Xi. Democrat. Unitarian. Home: 1653 Fairmont Blvd Eugene OR 97403

MCCONNELL, BRUCE BOWER, psychiatrist; b. Phila., Mar. 17, 1945; s. Bruce Bower McConnell and Doris Estelle (Barbano) Blanche; m. Gail Kristine Lennstrom, July 4, 1968; children: Derek, Katherine. AB cum laude, Princeton U., 1967; MD, U. Calif., San Francisco, 1971. Diplomate Am. Bd. Psychiatry and Neurology. Intern U. Pa./Phila. Gen. Hosp., 1971-72; resident dept. psychiatry Yale U. Med. Sch., New Haven, 1972-75; chief mental hygiene Hawley Army Hosp., Ft. Harrison, Ind., 1975-77; staff psychiatrist Montrose (N.Y.) VA Med. Ctr., 1977-80; psychiatrist West Haven (Conn.) VA Med. Ctr., 1981-95, Greater Bridgeport Community Mental Health Ctr., Bridgeport, Conn., 1988—; fellow in substance abuse West Haven VA Med. Ctr., 1981-83; asst. clin. prof. Yale U., 1982—. Maj. U.S. Army, 1975-77. Mem. Am. Psychiat. Soc., Conn. Psychiat. Soc., Nat. Assn. vA Physicians, Am. Soc. Addiction Medicine. Congregationalist. Office: Greater Bridgeport Community Mental Health Ctr 1635 Central Ave Bridgeport CT 06610-2717

MCCONNELL, MICHAEL V., medical educator, researcher; b. N.Y.C.. SB, MIT, 1983, SM in Elec. Engring., 1985; MD, Stanford U., 1990. Intern medicine Brigham and Women's Hosp., Boston, 1990-91, jr. asst. resident in internal medicine, 1991-92, cardiology fellow, 1992-96, assoc. physician medicine, 1996—; cardiovasc. imaging fellow Brigham and Women's Hosp., Beth Israel Hosp., Boston, 1995-96; clin. fellow in medicine Harvard Med. Sch., Boston, 1990-93, rsch. fellow in medicine, 1993-96, instr. medicine, 1996—; tech. intern pacing rsch. divsn. Medtronic, Inc., 1982, 83; bioengring. apprentice Micro-Med, Paris, 1985. Contbr. articles to profl. jours. Recipient Undergrad. Rsch. award Uniroyal, 1981, Individual Nat. Rsch. Svc. award NHLBI, 1994, fellowship award for rsch. in cardiac imaging Bracco Diagnostics, Inc.-Soc. for Cardiac Angiography and Interventions, 1995. Mem. Am. Coll. Cardiology, Am. Heart Assn. Coun. Clin. Cardiology (student rsch. fellow 1987, clinician scientist award 1996), Internat. Soc. Magnetic Resonance Medicine, Mass. Med. Soc., Eta Kappa Nu, Sigma Xi, Tau Beta Pi. *

MCCOOEY, TIMOTHY ALEXANDER, health facility administrator; b. Buffalo, N.Y., June 15, 1959; s. Charles Leo and Erma Frances (Gross) McC. BA, Canisius Coll., 1982; M in Hosp. and Healthcare Adminstrn., St. Louis U., 1984. Adminstrv. asst. St. Louis (Mo.) U. Med. Ctr., 1982-84; adminstrv. resident Kenmore (N.Y.) Mercy Hosp., 1983; adminstrv. asst. U. Hosp.-Upstate Med. Ctr., Syracuse, N.Y., 1984-85; asst. administr. Roswell Park Cancer Inst., Buffalo, 1985, Millard Fillmore Health Sys., Buffalo, 1986-91; assoc. hosp. administr. Genesee Meml. Hosp., Batavia, N.Y., 1991-95; v.p. PositiveCare Network (Hospice AIDS), 1995—; adj. faculty D'Youville Coll., 1987-95; pres. Genesee Enterprises, Inc., Batavia, 1993—, WNY Healthcare Exec. Forum, Buffalo, 1994—. Mem. So. Buffalo (N.Y.) Cmty. Devel. Assn., 1984—; mem. Mens Sustaining Soc.-Mercy Hosp., Buffalo, 1986—; core mem. Life Teen-St. Catherine's Ch., 1992-95; mem.-at-large United Way-Genesee/LeRoy, Batavia, 1992-95; adv. bd. mem. Fellowship of Christian Athletes, Buffalo, 1994—; cons. AIDS Cmty. Svcs., 1995. Fellow Am. Coll. Healthcare Execs.; mem. Am. Soc. for Hosp. Risk Mgmt. Democrat. Roman Catholic. Home & Office: 206 S Elmwood Ave Buffalo NY 14201

MCCORD, DON LEWIS, surgeon; b. Vernon, Tex., Aug. 25, 1929; s. Thomas Garfield and Dola (Cavender) McC.; m. Gayle McCord, Mar. 4, 1972; children: Daniel Lindsey, Elizabeth Ann, Melissa Ann Mares, Nicole Pryor. BS in Chemistry, Abilene Christian U., 1949; MD, U. Tex., 1953. Diplomate Am. Bd. Surgery. Intern U. Hosp., Ann Arbor, Mich., 1953-54; resident in surgery U.S. Naval Hosp., Oakland, Calif., 1955-59; asst. chief of surgery U.S. Naval Hosp., Corpus Christi, Tex., 1959-62; pvt. practice Hamilton, Tex., 1962-74; group practice Clifton, Tex., 1974-86; pvt. practice Med. City, Dallas, 1986—, sect. chief gen. surgery, 1990-92; cons. in surgery Hamilton (Tex.) Gen. Hosp., 1988-96, De Leon (Tex.) Hosp. Lt. comdr. USN, 1954-62. Fellow ACS; mem. AMA, Tex. Med. Assn., Dallas County med. Soc., Dallas Soc. Gen. Surgeons, Flying Physicians Assn., Alpha Omega Alpha. Republican. Office: Ste C-608 7777 Forest Ln Dallas TX 75230

MCCORKLE, RUTH, oncological nurse, educator. BS, U. Md., 1968; MA, U. Iowa, 1972, PhD, 1975. Staff nurse CCU Vanvouver (Wash.) Med. Hosp., 1968-69; oncological clin. nurse specialist U. Iowa Hosps. and Clinics, Iowa City, 1971-73; instr. psychiat. nursing and oncological nursing Sch. Nursing, U. Iowa, Iowa City, 1974-75; from asst. prof. to prof. dept. cmty. health care sys. U. Wash., Seattle, 1975-85; prof. adult health and illness divsn. Sch. Nursing, U. Pa., Phila., 1986—, chairperson, 1988-89, dir. Ctr. Advancing Care in Serious Illness, 1989—, dir. cancer control Cancer Comprehensive Ctr., 1990—; mem. nursing sci. rev. com. Nat. Ctr. Nursing Rsch., 1988-92. Contbr. articles to profl. jours. Fellow Am. Acad. Nursing; mem. ANA, NAS, Internat. Soc. Nurses Cancer Care (dir.-at-large 1983-89), Am. Assn. Cancer Edn., Oncology Nursing Soc. (charter mem., mem. rsch. com. 1981-82, dir.-at-large 1983-85). Office: U Pa Sch Nursing 420 Guardian Dr Philadelphia PA 19104-6096

MCCORMACK, DENNIS K., clinical psychologist; m. Nancy K. McCormack; children: Kelly, Karen. BA in Math., Calif. Western U., 1969; MA, U.S. Internat. U., 1971, PhD in Leadership and Human Behavior, PhD in Psychology, 1974, 78. Diplomate Internat. Council Profl. Counseling and Psychotherapy, Am. Inst. Counseling and Psychotherapy, Internat. Acad. Health Care Profls. Pvt. practice family therapist Coronado, Calif.; chief psychologist, Trauma Svc. Group Winn Army Cmty. Hosp., supervisory clin. psychologist, 1994—; chief Family Therapy Winn Army Hosp., 1994—, acting chief Psychology and Psychiatry svcs., 1994—; guest spkr. at numerous clubs, lodges and local orgns. Contbr. articles to profl. jours. Mem. Sr. Citizen Adv. Com., 1982—, Land Use Adv. Com., Coronado, 1979-80; chmn. Coronado Planning Commn., 1978-83, St. Paul's United Meth. Ch., 1978-81, personnel com., 1978-81, mem. adminstrv. bd., 1983—; pres. Coronado Coordinating Council, 1983—; mem. adv. bd. Mil. Affairs Com., 1984—; bd. dirs. Vietnam Vets. Leadership Program, 1984—, Coronado Hosp. Found., 1988—; mem. Southbay Chember Exec. Com., 1986—, Coronado Visitor Promotion Bd., 1986—. Fellow Internat. Council of Sex Edn. and Parenthood of Am. U., Am. Bd. Med. Psychotherapists (clin. assoc.), S.D. Acad. Psychologists (chmn. membership com. 1988—), Coronado C. of C. (pres. 1986—). Office: PO Box 577 Richmond Hill GA 31324-0577

MCCORMICK, DONALD BRUCE, biochemist, educator; b. Front Royal, Va., July 15, 1932; s. Jesse Allen and Elizabeth (Hord) McC.; m. Norma Jean Dunn, June 6, 1955; children: Susan Lynn, Donald Bruce, Michael Allen. B.A., Vanderbilt U., 1953, Ph.D., 1958; postdoctoral fellow, U. Calif., Berkeley, 1958-60. Asst. prof. Cornell U., 1960-63, assoc. prof., 1963-69, prof. nutrition, biochemistry and molecular biology, biol. scis., 1969-79, Liberty Hyde Bailey prof. nutritional biochemistry, 1978-79; chmn. dept. biochemistry Emory U., Atlanta, 1979-94, Fuller E. Callaway prof. biochemistry, 1979—; exec. assoc. dean sci. Emory U. Sch. Medicine, 1985-89; vis. lectr. U. Ill, 1963; Wellcome vis. prof. U. Fla., 1986, Med. Coll. Pa., 1989; Hurley lectr. U. Calif., Davis, 1992; O'Dell lectr. U. Mo., Columbia, 1993; biochem. cons. Interdeptl. Com. on Nutrition for Nat. Def., Spain, 1958; mem. and chmn. nutrition study sect. NIH, 1977-81; mem. diet and health com., dietary guidelines implementation com., vice chmn. food and nutrition bd. NRC, Inst. Medicine, NAS; exec. com., chmn. dept. med. biochemistry, Council Acad. Soc., Am. Assn. Med. Colls., 1984-87. Author: (with others) Spain: Nutrition Survey of the Armed Forces, 1958, Molecular Associations in Biology, 1968, Flavins and Flavin Enzymes, 1968, Flavins and Flavoproteins, 1980, 82, 84, 88, 89, 91, Comprehensive Biochemistry, Vol. 21, 1971, Riboflavin, 1974, Metal Ions in Biological Systems, Vol. 1, 1974, Present Knowledge in Nutrition, 6th edit., 1990, Natural Sulphur Compounds, 1979, Vitamin B6, Metabolism and Role in Growth, 1980, Ann. Rev. of Nutrition, Vol. 1, 1981, Vol. 9, 1989, Mechanisms of Enzymatic Reactions: Stereochemistry, 1986, Chemical and Biological Aspects of Vitamin B6 Catalysis, Part A, 1984, Biochemistry of Vitamin B6, 1987, Textbook of Clinical Chemistry, 1987, 94, Modern Nutrition in Health and Disease, 1988, 94, New Trends in Biological Chemistry, 1990, Chemistry and Biochemistry of Flavins, 1991, Encyclopedia of Human Biology, 1991, Liver, 1994, Molecular Biology and Biotechnology, 1995; editor: Vitamins and Hormones, Vitamins and Coenzymes, Ann. Rev. of Nutrition. Recipient award Bausch and Lomb, 1950, award Mead Johnson, 1970, award Osborne and Mendel, 1978, award Ga. Nutrition Coun., 1989; Westinghouse Sci. scholar, 1950; fellow NIH, 1957-58, 58-60; Guggenheim fellow, 1966-67. Fellow AAAS; mem. Am. Soc. Biochemistry and Molecular Biology, Am. Inst. Nutrition (pres. 1991), Soc. Exptl. Biology and Medicine, Am. Chem. Soc., Am. Inst. Biol. Sci., Biophysics Soc., Fedn. Am. Socs. Exptl. Biology (bd. dirs., LSRO scientific steering group), Microbiol. Soc., Photobiol. Soc., N.Y. Acad. Sci., Protein Soc., Sigma Xi. Home: 2245 Deer Ridge Dr Stone Mountain GA 30087-1129 Office: Emory U Dept Biochemistry Atlanta GA 30322

MCCORMICK, JOSEPH A., orthodontist; b. Darby, Pa., Nov. 27, 1947; s. Joseph A. and Gertrude R. (McGarvey) McC.; m. Maria Theresa McCormick, Oct. 17, 1970; children: Joseph, Michela, John, James. BS in Biology, Villanova U., 1969; DDS, Temple U., 1973, Orthodontics degree, 1975. Diplomate Am. Bd. Orthodontics. Pvt. practice orthodontist Oxford and Lansdowne, Pa., 1993—. Mem. Omicron Kappa Upsilon. Home: 466 Windermere Rd Drexel Hill PA 19026 Office: 2104 Garrett Rd Lansdowne PA 19050 Other: 217 N 5th St Oxford PA 19363

MCCORMICK, KATHLEEN ANN KRYM, geriatrics nurse, computer information specialist, federal agency administrator; b. Manchester, N.H., June 27, 1947. BSN, Barry Coll., 1969; MSN, Boston U., 1971; MS, U. Wis., 1975, PhD, 1978. Capt. nurse officer USPHS; COSTEP nurse USPHS, Staten Island, N.Y., 1968; staff nurse, instr. USPHS, Brighton, Mass., 1970; staff nurse Mercy Hosp., Miami, 1969, St. Elizabeth's Hosp., Brighton, 1970-71; clin. nurse specialist Boston U. Hosp., 1970-71; clin. nurse specialist, instr. U. Wis., Madison, 1971-72; asst. rsch. to chief nursing clin. ctr., dept. Nursing NIH, Bethesda, 1978-83; rsch. nurse, co-dir. inpatient geriatric continence project, Lab. Behavioral Scis., Gerontology Rsch. Ctr. Nat. Inst. Aging, Balt., 1983-88, dir. nursing rsch., 1988-91; dir. office forum quality and effectiveness health care Agy. Health Care Policy and Rsch., Rockville, Md., 1991-93; sr. sci. adviser Agy. Health Care Policy and Rsch., 1993—; adj. asst. prof. Cath. U., Washington, 1979, 82; faculty assoc. U. Md., Balt., 1979-81; ad hoc reviewer biomed. rsch. grants NIH, 1979-80, divsn. nursing rsch. and tng. HRA, 1979-82; instr. Found. Advanced Edn. in Scis., 1981-82; exec. com. Bat. Inst. Aging Liaison Ctr. Nursing Rsch., 1986-91; Surgeon Gen.'s rep. Sec. Alzheimer's Task Force, 1989—; Surgeon Gen. alternate to Bd. Regents Nat. Libr. Medicine, 1989—; co-chair panel guidelines for urinary incontinence in adult, 1990-91; speaker. Editor: Nursing Outlook, 1988-90; mem. editorial staff Mil. Medicine, 1985-93; assoc. editor: Internat. Jour. Tech. and Aging, 1985-87. Recipient award Jour. Acad. Sci., 1965, travel award NSF, 1973, J.D. Lane Jr. Investigator award USPHS Profl. Assn., 1979, Excellence in Writing award Nat. League Nursing/Humana, 1983, award Spl. Recognition Rsch., U. Pa. Sch. Nursing, 1986, Federal Svc. Nursing award, 1987, Surgeon Gen.'s medallion, 1989,; grantee U. Wis.

Grad. Sch., 1977, Upjohn Co., 1977; Queen's Vis. scholar Royal Adelaide (Austrailia) Hosp., 1990. Fellow Am. Acad. Nursing, Royal Coll. Nursing (Australia), Coll. Am. Med. Informatics, Gerontologic Soc. Am. (clin. med. sect., computer program coord. 1985-87, clin. medicine rep. publs. com., Nurse of Yr. 1992), Nat. Acad. Scis. Inst. Medicine; mem. ANA (sec., editor newsletter coun. nurse rschrs. 1980-85, vice chairperson exec. com. coun. computer applications in nursing 1984-86), AACN (strategic planning com. 1987-89, Disting. Rsch. award 1986), Am. Lung Assn./Am. Thoracic Soc. (cert. appreciation mid.-Md. chpt. 1982, 83, 84, chairperson 1983-84, nominating com. 1989, nat. rsch. rev. com.), Am. Med. Informatics Assn., Inst. Medicine, Acad. Medicine, Am. News Women's Club, Internat. Med. Informatics Assn. (working group 8, program com. 1984—), Assn. Mil. Surgeons (sustaining mem. award 1982), Commd. Officers Assn., Met. Area Nursing Rsch. Consortium, Md. Lung Assn. (awards and grants subcom. 1978, 92, v.p. exec. bd. dirs. 1980-87), Capital Spkrs. Club (10 M), Lambda Sigma, Sigma Delta Epsilon (Eloise Gerry grant-in-aid fellow 1979-80), Sigma Theta Tau (grantee 1976). Office: US Agy Health Care Policy Rsch 2101 E Jefferson St Rockville MD 20852-4908

MCCORMICK, KENNETH JOHN, health facility administrator; b. West Monroe, La., Sept. 17, 1966; s. John F. and Dorothy C. (Campbell) Mc. BS in Med. Tech., Northeast La. Univ., 1994. Medical lab. specialist USAF Res., Bossier City, La., 1985-93; medical lab. tech. Green Clinic, Ruston, La., 1993-94; lab. dir. Monroe Medical & Pineville Medical, Monroe, Pineville, La., 1994, Sterlington (La.) Hosp., 1994-96; medical tech. Parkview Medical Ctr., Vicksburg, Miss., 1995—; clin. chemistry, stat lab, immunology dept. supr. Touro Infirmary, New Orleans, La., 1996—; pres. NLU Clinical Lab. Sci. Soc., Monroe, 1995; nominations chmn. La. State Soc. Medical Tech. Contbr. articles to profl. jours. Active Twin Cities Jaycees, 1995. Recipient U.S. Collegiat Achievement award, 1994. Mem. Am. Soc. Clin. Lab. Sci., Am. Soc. Microbiology, La. State Soc. Med. Tech. (Key to the Future award 1995), Am. Assn. Clin. Chem., Am. Soc. Med. Lab. Pers. Republican. Home: Apt N201 3800 Grand Lake Blvd Kenner LA 70065 Office: Touro Infirmary-Pathology 1401 Foucher New Orleans LA 70115-3515

MCCORMICK, KENNETH L., pediatrics educator, researcher. BS in Chem. Engring., U. Pa., 1970; MD, U. Rochester, 1974. Diplomate Am. Bd. Pediatrics, Am. Bd. Pediatric Endocrinology. Intern in pediatrics U. Hosp. Cleve., Case Western Reserve U., 1974-75, resident in pediatrics, 1975-76; instr., rsch. and clin. fellow in pediat. metabolism/diabetes Brown U., Rhode Island Hosp., Providence, 1976-79; asst. prof. pediatrics U. Rochester (N.Y.), 1979-85, assoc. prof. pediatrics, 1985-88; assoc. prof. pediatrics SUNY Health Sci. Ctr., Syracuse, 1988-92; assoc. prof. pediatrics, dir. metabolism and diabetes Med. Coll. of Wis., Milw., 1993—. Mem. editl. bd. Endocrinology, 1993—; reviewer Metabolism, Am. Jour. Diseases in Children, Endocrinology, Am. Jour. of Physiology; contbr. articles and revs. to profl. jours., chpts. to books. NIH fellow, 1978-79; Grantee Kroc Found., 1981-83, NIH, 1982-87, 93—, Wilson Found., 1984-85, Upjohn Co., 1985, Hendricks Found., 1989-90, Squibb Novo, 1994-95, Am. Heart Assn., 1995—. Mem. Am. Diabetes Assn. (bd. dirs. Rochester affiliate 1980-88, grantee 1994-96, Rsch. award 1995), Endocrinology Soc. Office: Med Coll of Wis Dept Endocrinology 8701 Watertown Plank Rd Milwaukee WI 53226

MCCORMICK, MARIE CLARE, pediatrician, educator; b. Haverhill, Mass., Jan. 7, 1946; d. Richard John and Clare Bernadine (Keleher) McC.; m. Robert Jay Blendon, Dec. 30, 1977. BA magna cum laude, Emmanuel Coll., 1967; MD, Johns Hopkins Medical Sch., 1971; ScD, Johns Hopkins, 1978; MA, Harvard, 1991. Diplomate Am. Bd. Pediatrics. Pediatric resident, fellow Johns Hopkins Hosp., Balt., 1971-75; rsch. fellow Johns Hopkins Hosp., 1972-75; asst. prof. U. Ill. Schs. Medicine & Pub. Health, Chgo., 1975-76; pediatrics instr. Johns Hopkins Medical Sch., Balt., 1976-78; asst. prof. healthcare orgn. Johns Hopkins Sch. Hygiene & Pub. Health, 1978-81; asst. prof. pediatrics U. Pa., Phila., 1981-86, assoc. prof. pediatrics, 1986-87; assoc. prof. pediatrics Harvard Medical Sch., Boston, 1987-91; prof., chair. maternal & child health Harvard Sch. Pub. Health, 1992—; prof. pediatrics . Harvard Medical Sch., 1992—; adj. assoc. prof. pediatrics U. Pa., 1987-92; active attending physician, Johns Hopkins Hosp., 1976-81, asst. physician Children's Hosp. Phila., 1981-84, assoc. physician, 1984-86, sr. physician, 1986-87, assoc. pediatrician Brigham & Women's Hosp., 1987, 88—; vis. prof. Wash. U., St. Louis, 1993; editorial bds. Health Svcs. Rsch., 1985-94, Pediatrics in Review, 1986-91, Pediatrics, 1993—; adv. coun. Ctr. Perinatal & Family Health Brigham & Women;s Hosp., 1991—; cons. to numerous coms., orgns. and bds. Contbr. articles to profl. jours. Adv. The David and Lucile Packard Found., 1993-95; bd. dirs. Family Planning Coun. S.E. Pa., 1984-87; chair com. child health Mayor's Commn. Phila., 1982-83. Named Henry Strong Denison scholar Johns Hopkins Sch. Medicine, 1971, Leonard Davis Inst. Health Econs. fellow U. Pa. 1984, First Sumner and Esther Feldberg prof. maternal and child health, 1996; recipient Johns Hopkins U. Soc. Scholars award, 1995, Ambulatory Pediat. Assn. Rsch. award, 1996. Fellow Am. Acad. Pediatrics; mem. AAAS, Ambulatory Pediatrics Assn. (Rsch. award 1996), Soc. Pediatric Rsch. (sr.), Am. Pediatric soc., Am. Pub. Health Assn., Internat. Epidemiological Assn., Assn. Health Svcs. Rsch., Eastern Soc. Pediatric Rsch., Soc. Pediatric Epidemiologic Rsch., Assn. Tchrs. Maternal and Child Health, Mass. Med. Soc., Norfolk Dist. Med. Soc., Mass. Pub. Health Assn., Johns Hopkins U. Soc. Scholars. Office: Harvard Sch Pub Health 677 Huntington Ave Boston MA 02115-6028

MCCORMICK, MARYANN CUPPLES, nursing educator, nursing administrator. Diploma in Nursing, Western Pa. Hosp. Sch. Nursing, Pitts., 1967; BSEd, Calif. U., 1973; BSN, LaRoche Coll., 1989. RN, Pa.; cert. diabetes educator. Diabetes nurse educator Joslin Ctr. for Diabetes, West Penn Hosp., Pitts.; adminstr. coord. West Penn Hosp. Mem. Sigma Theta Tau Internat., Theta Mu. Home: 59 Jaycee Dr Pittsburgh PA 15243-1305

MC CORMICK, WILLIAM FREDERICK, forensic pathologist, neuropathologist; b. Riverton, Va., Sept. 9, 1933; s. Jesse Allen and Elizabeth (Hord) McC.; m. Deanne Bourne Petersen, July 2, 1954; children—William Frederick, Cynthia Anne. BS, U. Chattanooga, 1953; MD, U. Tenn., 1955, MS, 1957. Diplomate Am. Bd. Pathology. Intern Baptist Meml. Hosp., Memphis, 1956; resident in pathology U. Tenn., 1957-60, asst. in pathology, 1957-60, instr., 1960, asst. prof., 1960-64, mem. exec. com., basic med. scis., 1963-64; dep. chief med. examiner Tenn., 1961-63; spl. fellow, instr. neuropathology Columbia U., 1961-62; asso. prof. U. Iowa, 1964-68, prof., 1968-73, chmn. surgery dept. rev. com., 1968-69; prof. pathology, neurosurgery and neurology U. Tex. Med. Br., Galveston, 1973-84, clinical prof. pathology, 1985-89; prof. pathology, neuropathology James H. Quillen Coll. Medicine, East Tenn. State U., 1985—, prof., head forensic pathology, 1989—; asst. chief med. examiner State of Tenn., 1985-87, dep. chief med. examiner, 1987—; cons. in field; vis. scientist Armed Forces Inst. Pathology, Washington, 1965-66; dep. chief med. examiner Galveston County, 1976-84; mem. head injury study group Dept. Transp.; mem. com. NRC, 1978; vis. prof. U. Tenn., U. Pitts., U. Va. Author: (with W. E. Bell) Increased Intracranial Pressure in Children, 1972, 2d edit., 1978, Neurologic Infections in Children, 2d edit, 1981, (with S. S. Schochet, Jr.) Syllabus of Neuropathology, 1973, Atlas of Cerebrovascular Disease, 1976, Neuropathology Case Studies, 1976, 3d edit., 1984, Essentials of Neuropathology, 1979; contbr. (with S. S. Schochet, Jr.) articles to profl. jours. Scoutmaster Bay Area council Boy Scouts Am., 1975-79. Named Milton Helpern Meml. lectr., 1985; recipient Outstanding Contribution award for neuropathology rev. course, AFIP, 1990. Mem. AAAS, AMA, Am. Soc. Human Genetics, Am. Soc. Exptl. Pathology, Assn. Am. Med. Colls., Am. Assn. Pathologists, Am. Assn. Neuropathologists, Nat. Assn. Med. Examiners, N.Y. Acad. Scis., Tex. Med. Assn., Am. Assn. Physical Anthropologists, Am. Acad. Neurologists, Acad. Forensic Sci., Sigma Xi. Home: 120 Niles Wheelock Rd Jonesborough TN 37659-3306 Office: East Tenn State University Dept Forensic Patholog Johnson City TN 37614

MCCOWN, LINDA JEAN, medical technology educator; b. Pitts., Mar. 18, 1953; d. William Earnest and Mary Elizabeth McC. BS, Pa. State U., 1975; MS, U. Pitts., 1979. Cert. med. technologist, clin. lab. scientist. Microbiology aide Pa. State U., University Park, 1973-74; med. technologist, asst. supr., rsch. technologist Children's Hosp. of Pitts., 1975-80; asst. prof. med. tech., assoc. program dir. Ctrl. Wash. U., Ellensburg, 1980—; critiquer, insp. Nat. Accreditation Agy. for Clin. Lab. Scis., Chgo., 1984—; test item writer Nat. Cert. Agy., Washington, 1989—; recruiter Am. Soc. Clin. Pathologists, Chgo., 1988—; lectr., physician asst. program U. Wash., Seattle, 1996. Contbr. articles to profl. jours. Stephen ministry, deacon First Presbyn. Ch., Yakima, Wash., 1992—; bd. dirs. The Campbell Farm, Wapato, Wash., 1990-95; rally chmn. Heifer Project Internat., Wapato, 1991-94. Mem. Am. Soc. for Med. Tech. (mem. commn. on accreditation 1988-91), Wash. State Soc. for Med. Tech. (conv. chair 1992, edn. chair 1986-94, Pres.'s award 1992), Columbia Basin Soc. Clin. Lab. Sci. (pres.-elect 1993, pres. 1994-95), Omicron Sigma. Home: 1305 Jefferson Ave Yakima WA 98902-2528 Office: Ctrl Wash U Ctr Med Tech 1120 W Spruce Yakima WA 98902

MCCOY, CAROL P., psychologist, training executive; b. Bronxville, N.Y., June 14, 1948; d. Rawley Deering and Jane (Wiske) McC.; m. Lanny Gordon Foster, Nov. 29, 1975 (div. 1985). BA, Conn. Coll., 1970; MS in Psychology, Rutgers U., 1974, PhD in Psychology, 1980. Adj. instr. psychology Rutgers U., New Brunswick, N.J., 1974-75; faculty chair dept. social sci. Misericordia Hosp. Sch. Nursing, Bronx, N.Y., 1976-79; tng. and devel. cons. Chase Manhattan Bank N.A., N.Y.C., 1980-85, tng. mgr. internat. consumer banking div., 1985-88, tng. mgr. individual banking, 1988-91; dir. corp. tng. UNUM Life Ins. Co. Am., Portland, Maine, 1991—. Author: Managing a Small HRD Department, 1993. Mem. Am. Soc. Tng. and Devel., Am. Psychol. Assn. Home: 11 Johnson Rd Falmouth ME 04105-1408 Office: UNUM Life Ins Co Am 2211 Congress St Portland ME 04122-0002

MCCOY, DAVID MICHAEL, physician, general surgeon, surgical oncologist; b. Chgo., June 9, 1955; s. Gordon Hugh and Helen Catherine (McNally) McC.; m. Bettina Charlotte Reeb, Apr. 12, 1986; children: Daniel, Jill, Timothy. BS, Loyola Marymount Univ., 1978; MD, Univ. Munich, 1985. Diplomate Am. Bd. Surgery. Intern Univ. Ill., Chgo., 1985-86, resident, 1986-91, surgical oncologist fellow, 1991-92; asst. prof. Tulane, New Orleans, La., 1992—; hosp. staff Rapides Gen. Hosp., Alexandria, La., 1992—, St. Francis Cabrini Hosp., Alexandria, La., 1992—, Huey P. Long Hosp., Pineville, La., 1992—. Contbr. articles to profl. jours. Recipient Fellowship award Am. Cancer Soc. Clinical Oncology, 1991. Fellow Am. Coll. Surgeons; mem. AMA, La. Medical Soc. Republican. Roman Catholic. Home: 6400 Landmark Dr Alexandria LA 71303 Office: Macarthur Surgical Clinic 3311 Prescott Rd Ste 200 Alexandria LA 71301-3983

MCCOY, JOENNE RAE, psychiatric clinic administrator; b. Detroit, Jan. 26, 1941; d. Harlan and Dorothy (Simpson) Heinmiller; children: Harlan Craig, Cathi-Jo. BA, Mich. State U., 1966; MSW, U. Mich., 1983. Tchr. pub. schs., Owosso and Garden City, Mich., 1962-73; psychotherapist, group leader Wayne County Hosp., Mich., 1981-82; psychotherapist East Point, Westland, Mich., 1982-83, Midwest, Dearborn, Mich., 1982-83; owner, dir. Personal Devel. Ctrs., Inc., Plymouth, Mich., 1981—, Co-Dependency Specialists S.E. Mich. Ltd., Livonia, Mich., 1988—, Intergrated Health, 1994—; bd. dirs. Hospice Suport Svcs., Inc., Livonia; cons. Westland (Mich.) Convalescent Ctr., 1983-89; supr. grad. students U. Mich., 1986—; cons., facilitator Women-the Emerging Entrepreneurs, Wayne State U. and Small Bus. Assn., 1985—; chmn. Substance Abuse Com., Plymouth Schs., 1982; cons. Salvation Army, Plymouth. Mem. bd. advisors (newsletter) Personal Performance, Balt., 1986—. Mem. steering com. for neighborhood programs YWCA. Soroptimist scholar, 1982. Mem. NAFE, Internat. Assn. Pediatric Social Workers, Internat. Platform Assn., Mich. Assn. Bereavement Counselors, Families in Crisis: Domestic Violence Inc., Nat. Assn. Social Workers (cert.), Am. Entrepreneurs Assn., Women's Network (pres.), Acad. Cert. Soc. Workers, Agora Club, Passport Club, Agora Club. Avocation: international business and finance. Home: 37644 N Laurel Park Dr Livonia MI 48152-2662 Office: Co-Dependency Specialist SE Mich Ltd Pc 37677 Professional Dr Livonia MI 48154

MCCOY, SANDRA JO, pharmacist; b. Burkesville, Ky., July 30, 1953; d. Jesse Martin and Wanda Lee (Biggerstaff) McC. BS in Pharmacy, Samford U., 1977; D Pharmacy, 1983. Lic. pharmacist Ala., Ky., Tenn. Staff pharmacist St. Vincent's Hosp., Birmingham, Ala., 1977-83; staff pharmacist St. Thomas Hosp., Nashville, 1983—, ptnrs. in excellence quality leadership process trainer, pharmacy dept. coord., 1992—, drug interaction specialist pharmacy, 1992—, profl. achievement system participant, 1994-95; pres. S.J. McCoy Timber, S.J. McCoy Properties; mem. Consumer Mail Panel, Chgo., 1989—; cons. Clin. Mgmt. Cons., Nashville, 1991—; adv. bd. Town and Country Mag. Mem. Opera Guild, Nashville, 1989, mem. com., standing bd. mem., com. event chair, 1994-95, 95-96; mem. Symphony Guild, Nashville, 1992—, Ballet Guild, 1992—, founding mem. Ballet Friends '92, com. chair, 1993-94, 94-95; mem. Friends of Checkwood, Nashville, 1994—, Tenn. Performing Arts Ctr. Friends, 1994—; founding mem. The Abbey Leix Soc. of the O'more Coll. of Design, 1995; stewarship Ky. Dept. Forestry, Ky. Dept. Fish & Wildlife, 1994. Mem. Am. Soc. Hosp. Pharmacists (midyear presentation 1993, 94, alt. del. state of Tenn. 1994), Mid. Tenn. Soc. Hosp. Pharmacists (bd. dirs. 1987-91, sec. 1987-88, pres. elect 1988-89, pres. 1989-90, scholarship com. 1992, poster presentation 1995), Tenn. Soc. Hosp. Pharmacists (membership com. 1989-90), Nashville Area Pharmacists Assn., Lambda Kappa Sigma (Women in Pharm. Leadership in Am. award 1993). Republican. Home: 3415 W End Ave Apt 608 Nashville TN 37203-1025 Office: St Thomas Hosp Dept Pharmacy 4220 Harding Rd Nashville TN 37205-2005

MCCOY, STEVEN R., orthopedist. BA in Zoology, Duke U., 1975, MD, 1979. Diplomate Am. Bd. Orthopedic Surgeons. Intern, resident Duke Med. Ctr., Durham, N.C., 1979-81; resident orthopedic Hosp. for Spl. Surgery, N.Y.C., 1981-84; orthopedist Charlotte Hungerford Hosp., Torrington, Conn., 1984—, pres. med. staff, 1994-96; orthopedist Winsted (Conn.) Meml. Hosp., 1984—, chmn. dept. surgery, 1990-93; dir. Conn. Peer Rev. Orgn., Meriden, 1987-95. Fellow Am. Acad. Orthopedic Surgeons; mem. AMA, Conn. Med. Soc. (Orthopedic br.), Litchfield County Med. Soc. Office: Charlotte Hungerford Hosp 200 Kennedy Dr Torrington CT 06790

MCCOY, SUE, surgeon; b. Charlottesville, Va., Nov. 14, 1935; d. Hulburt Christopher and Evelyn (Savage) McC. AB, Radcliffe Coll., 1957; PhD, Johns Hopkins U., 1964; MD, U. Va., 1980. Diplomate Am. Bd. Surgery. Fellow in physiol. chemistry Johns Hopkins U., Balt., 1964-67; asst. prof. chemistry U. South Fla., Tampa, 1967-69; asst. prof. orthopedics U. Va., Charlottesville, 1969-73, asst. prof. surgery, 1973-78; resident in surgery Hosp. U. Pa., Phila., 1980-83; resident in surgery Cooper Hosp. Rutgers U. Med. Sch., Camden, N.J., 1983-85, asst. prof. surgery, 1985-86; asst. prof. surgery East Tenn. State U., Johnson City, 1986-91, assoc. prof., 1991—. Mem. ACS, Am. Chem. Soc., N.Y. Acad. Sci., Royal Soc. Chemistry, Assn. for Acad. Surgery, Shock Soc., Internat. Soc. Oxygen Transport to Tissue, Am. Fedn. Clin. Rsch., Tenn. Med. Assn., Southeastern Surg. Congress, Assn. for Surg. Edn., Assn. for Women Surgeons, Tenn. Geriatric Assn., Am. Soc. for Parenteral and Enteral Nutrition, Sigma Xi. Home: PO Box 265 Mountain Home TN 37684-0265

MCCRACKEN, ALEXANDER WALKER, pathologist; b. Motherwell, Lanarkshire, Scotland, Nov. 24, 1931; came to U.S., 1968; s. William and Mary Snedden (Walker) McC.; m. Theresa Credgington, June 4, 1960; children: Fiona Jane, Claire Louise. MD, U. Glasgow, Scotland, 1956. Resident in surgery Glasgow Royal Inf., 1956-57; resident in pathology Royal Air Force, U.K., 1957-61, pathologist, 1962-68; fellow in pathology Royal Postgrad. Med. Sch., London, 1961-62; assoc. prof. Med. Sch., U. Tex., San Antonio, 1968-72; prof. Med. Sch., U. Tex., Houston, 1972-73; dir. of microbiology Baylor U. Med. Ctr., Dallas. 1973-81; pres. med. staff, dir. of labs. Meth. Hosps. of Dallas, 1982—; pres. med. staff Meth. Med. Ctr., 1994-95; adj. prof. pathology Baylor U. Coll. Dentistry, Dallas, 1982—; clin. prof. U. Tex. Southwestern Med. Sch., Dallas, 1986—. Author: Pathologic Mechanisms of Human Disease, 1985, Oral and Clinical Microbiology, 1986, Pathology, 1990, (play) Mister Gilbert, 1985, 89. With Royal Air Force, 1957-68. Decorated Gen. Svc. medal. Fellow Royal Coll. Pathologists, Coll. Am. Pathologists; mem. AAAS, AMA, Am. Soc. Microbiology, Tex. Med. Assn., Dallas County Med. Soc., Tex. Soc. Infectious Diseases, Tex. Med. Found., Assn. of Clin. Chemists, Masons. Republican. Anglican. Home: 607 Kessler Lake Dr Dallas TX 75208-3943 Office: Lab Physicians Assn 221 W Colorado Blvd Dallas TX 75208-2363

MCCRACKEN, LINDA, librarian, commercial artist; b. Rochester, N.Y., Apr. 13, 1948; d. Frederick Hugh Craig and Shirley Betty (Shacter) Bickford; m. Alan Cheah, June 13, 1972 (div. 1978); m. Bruce E. McCracken, Sept. 23, 1978 (div. 1985); 1 child, Karen Elizabeth. BA in History, SUNY-Geneseo, 1970, MLS, 1970. Reference libr. Northeastern U., Boston, 1971-72; asst. libr. Burlington Pub. Libr., Mass., 1972-74; rsch. asst. Data Resources, Inc., Lexington, Mass., 1974-76; comml. artist McCracken's, Wolfeboro, N.H., 1973-91; asst. libr. N.H. Vocat.-Tech. Coll., Manchester, 1985-87; libr. N.H. Hosp., Concord, 1987-91. Participant paintings Horseheads Mall Art Show (3rd place award 1968); graphic artist Rare Coin Rev. mag., 1983; layout artist: Market Media Guide, 1979; market rschr. Delahaye Group, Newington, N.H., 1993-94; author Burlington Times-Union, 1973, Pleasant News, 1987-88. Treas. Village Players, Wolfeboro, 1982-83; pub. rels. com. Gov.'s Arts Coun., Wolfeboro, 1982. Mem. State Employees Assn. N.H., Mensa. Avocations: skiing, gardening, singing, acting, hiking. Home: 44 Pine Hill Rd Wolfeboro NH 03894-4330 Office: NH Hosp Dorothy M Breene Meml Libr 105 Pleasant St Concord NH 03301-3852

MCCRAE, KEITH R., medical educator, researcher; b. Springfield, Mass., Dec. 4, 1956; m. Jo Ann; children: Brett, Kristen Ann. BA in Biochemistry summa cum laude, Dartmouth Coll., 1978; MD, Duke U., 1982. Diplomate Am. Bd. Internal Medicine, Am. Bd. Med. Oncology, Am. Bd. Hematology. Resident in internal medicine Duke U. Med. Ctr., Durham, N.C., 1982-85; fellow in hematology and oncology U. Pa., Phila., 1985-89, postdoctoral fellow, 1986-88; co-dir. clin. coagulation lab. U. Pa., 1991-93, dir. clin. coagulation course, 1992-93; rsch. assoc. U. Pa. Sch. Medicine, 1989, lectr. bridge curriculum, 1989-93, asst. prof. medicine, 1990-93, asst. prof. pathology and lab. medicine, 1991-93; lectr. basic curriculum U. Pa. Dental Sch., 1989-92; attending physician Hosp. of U. Pa., 1989-93, Phila. VA Hosp., 1990-93, Temple U. Hosp., 1993—; asst. prof. medicine Temple U. Sch. Medicine, 1993-96, lectr. bridge curriculum, 1993—, assoc. prof. medicine, 1996—; tchg. attending hematology consult svc. U. Pa., 1989-93, tchg. attending hematology oncology inpatient unit, 1992-93; with hematology/oncology outpatient clinic, 1989-93; attending staff mem. hematology consult svc. Temple U. Sch. Medicine, 1993—, attendin staff mem. hematology sickel cell outpatient clinic, 1993—, attending staff mem. gen. internal medicine svc., 1993. Co-author (with M.D. Feldman) Blood: Hemostasis, Transfusion and Alternatives in the Perioperative Period, 1995; jour. reviewer Blood, 1990—, Thrombosis and Haemostasis. 1991—, Annals of Internal Medicine, 1991—, Jour. Biol. Chem., 1992—, Placenta, 1992—, Jour. Exptl. Medicine, 1992—, Platelets, 1992—, Jour. Allergy and Clin. Immunology, 1992—, Cancer Rsch., 1993—, Am. Jour. Hematology, 1993—, Jour. Clin. Oncology, 1994—, Jour. Histochemistry and Cytochemistry, 1994—, Am. Jour. Physiol., 1995—, Thrombosis Rsch., 1995—; contbr. articles to profl. jours., chpts. to books; lectr. in field. Recipient Rsch. award Am. Diabetes Assn., 1995. Mem. AAAS, Am. Heart Assn. (mem. thrombosis coun. 1994—, mem. arteriosclerosclerosis coun. 1994—, mem. southeastern Pa. peer rev. com. B 1995—), Am. Soc. Hematology, Am. Fedn. Clin. Rsch., Phi Beta Kappa. Office: Temple U Sch Medicine Sol Sherry Thrombosis Rsch Ctr 3400 N Broad St Philadelphia PA 19140

MCCRARY, JAMES EDWARD, physician, air force officer; b. Vernon, Tex., Sept. 22, 1958; s. Theodore Lorenzo and Maxine (Willard) McC.; m. Shirl Renee Green, Oct. 31, 1980; children: Angè, Katrina, Shionna, Crystal, James Edward II, Kristopher. BS in Chemistry, U. Tex., Arlington, 1985; DO, Tex. Coll. Osteo. Medicine, 1989. Diplomate Nat. Bd. Osteo. Med. Examiners. Intern Dallas Family Hosp., 1989-90; commd. maj. USAF, 1990; emergency rm. physician USAF, Carswell AFB, Tex., 1990-93; physician USAF, Laughlin, Tex., 1993—; cons. West Dallas Clinic, Isoke Clinic, Dallas, 1990—. Mem. Am. Coll. Gen. Practitioners, Tex. Coll. Gen. Practitioners. Office: USAF 47th Med Group Laughlin A F B TX 78840

MCCRAW, DAVID BRUCE, cardiologist; b. Toronto, Ont., Can., May 12, 1942; s. Donald Fraser and Claire Margaret McCraw; m. Vivian Lorraine Flatt. MD, U. Western Ont., 1966. Intern Montreal (Que., Can.) Gen. Hosp., 1966-67; rsch. fellow Banting Inst. U. Toronto, 1967-68; resident in medicine Montreal Gen. Hosp., 1968-70; fellow in cardiology Sch. Medicine Emory U., Atlanta, 1970-72; chief resident in medicine Montreal Gen. Hosp., 1972-73; asst. prof. Sch. Medicine Emory U., Atlanta, 1973-75, U. Ottawa, Ont., Can., 1975-76; staff cardiologist The Med. Ctr., Pensacola, Fla., 1976—; clin. asst. prof. medicine Emory U. Sch. Medicine, Atlanta, 1978—. Fellow Royal Coll. Physicians and Surgeons of Can., Am. Coll. Cardiology, Am. Heart Assn. (coun. on clin. cardiology 1974). Republican. Roman Catholic. Office: The Med Ctr Clinic PA 8333 N Davis Hwy Pensacola FL 32514-6048

MCCRAW, RONALD KENT, psychologist, osteopath, obstetrician-gynecologist; b. Houston, Dec. 6, 1947; s. Leon Frank and Lorna Mae (Bailey) McC. BA, U. Tex., 1970; MA, U. Tex. Med. Br., Galveston, 1972; PhD, U. South Fla., 1981; diploma Squadron Officers Sch., Air U., 1982-83, Air Command and Staff Coll., 1985-86; DO Tex. Coll. Osteo. Medicine, 1990. Diplomate Nat. Bd. Osteo. Med. Examiners, Internat. Acad. Behavioral Medicine, Counseling and Psychotherapy; lic. psychologist, Tex.; lec. physician, Tex., Mich. Rsch. asst. div. child and adolescent psychiatry U. Tex. Med. Br., 1972-74; grad. asst. div. neuropsychology Fla. Mental Health Inst., Tampa, 1975-76; resident in clin. psychology U. Tex. Health Scis. Ctr., San Antonio, 1977-78; psychometrician Hillsborough Cmty. Mental Health Ctr., Tampa, Fla., 1978-79; clin. psychologist U.S. Air Force Hosp., Chanute AFB, Ill., 1982-86; pvt. practice clin. psychology, 1987-89; intern Detroit Osteo. and Bi-County Hosps., Warren, Mich., 1990-91; resident ob-gyn Detroit Osteo. and Bi-County Cmty. Hosps., 1991-96. Film and book reviewer for AAAS Sci. Books and Films, 1977—, Birth, 1983-88, Jour. Nurse-Midwifery, 1985—; manuscript reviewer Hosp. and Cmty. Psychiatry, 1988, 91—, Military Medicine, 1991—, Patient Care, 1991; editorial bd. Birth Psychology Bull., 1984-87, Health Care of Women Internat., 1984—, American Jour. of Orthopsychiatry, 1992—; abstractor Psychosomatics, 1985-87; contbr. articles to sci. jours. Coach Baytown Girls Softball Assn. (Tex.), 1980-82, Rantoul (Ill.) Ponytail Softball League, 1983-85, Men's Varsity Softball Team, Chanute AFB, Ill., 1983-84, U.S. Slo-Pitch Softball Assn. State and Div. Qualifying Team, 1984. Maj. USAF, 1982-86, USAFR, 1987—. Decorated Commedation medal, 1986, Achievement medal, 1990, Nat. Def. Svc. medal, 1991. Fellow Am. Orthopsychiat. Assn. (program subcom. 1974-76); mem. AMA, Am. Psychol. Assn., Am. Acad. Behavioral Medicine, Soc. Behavioral Medicine, Soc. for Personality Assessment, U. Tex. Ex-Students Assn. (life), Am. Soc. Clin. Hypnosis, Tex. Osteo. Med. Assn., Am. Osteo. Assn., Am. Bd. Med. Psychotherapists (clin. assoc.), Am. Coll. Gen. Practitioners Osteo. Medicine and Surgery, Am. Soc. Psychosomatic ob-Gyn, N.Am. Soc. Pediatric and Adolescent Gynecology Sigma Xi, Psi Chi, Omicron Delta Kappa, Nu Sigma Nu, Phi Beta Pi-Theta Kappa Psi, Sigma Sigma Phi. Baptist. Lodges: Order DeMolay (chevalier), Masons. Home: 26217 Regency Club Dr # 3 Warren MI 48089-6244 Office: Bi-County Community Hosp 13355 E 10 Mile Rd Warren MI 48089-2048

MCCULLAR, BRUCE HAYDEN, oral and maxillofacial surgeon; b. Memphis, June 19, 1953; s. Robert Hayden and Virginia Maria (Daniel) McC; m. Jennifer Hunt, Feb. 15, 1974; 1 child, Michael. BS in Vertebrate Zoology with honors, Memphis State U., 1976; DDS with honors, U. Tenn., 1979. Diplomate Am. Bd. Oral and Maxillofacial Surgery. Intern then resident U. Tenn. Hosp., Memphis, 1980-82; pvt. practice oral and maxillofacial surgery Memphis, 1983—; assoc. prof. dept. oral and maxillofacial surgery U. Tenn., Memphis, 1987—; div. cons. for oral and maxillofacial surgery LeBonheur Children's Med. Ctr. Mem. editorial adv. panel Jour. Dental Econs., 1988. Instr. ACLS, Am. Heart Assn., 1982—. Comdr. USNR, 1985—. Fellow Am. Assn. Oral and Maxillofacial Surgeons, Am. Soc. Dental Anesthesiology, Am. Coll. Oral and Maxillofacial Surgeons, Southeastern Soc. Oral and Maxillofacial Surgeons; mem. ADA, Tenn. Dental Assn., Memphis Dental Soc. (Outstanding New Mem. 1987), Tenn. Soc. Oral and Maxillofacial Surgeons (sec.-treas. 1990-92, v.p. 1993-95, pres. 1996), Memphis Soc. Oral and Maxillofacial Surgeons (pres. 1991-92, sec.-treas. 1990-91), Naval Res. Assn., Assn. Mil. Surgeons of U.S., Memphis C. of C., Rotary Club (East Memphis br.), Chicksaw Country Club, Mensa, Intertel, Psi Omega, Omicron Kappa Upsilon. Republican. Episcopalian. Home: 6597 Oak Estate Dr Memphis TN 38119-6623 Office: 805 Estate Pl Ste 2 Memphis TN 38120-0647

MCCULLOCH, ANNA MARY KNOTT, pharmacy technician; b. Riverdale, Md., Aug. 29, 1964; d. Samuel Eugene and Jean M. (Schildt)

Knott; m. Richard Sears, Nov. 6, 1988; children: John Austen II, Anna Rebecca. Student, W.Va. U., 1982-84; cert., Children's Inst. Lit., 1987. Pharmacy technician Montgomery Gen. Hosp., Olney, Md., 1981-92; med. asst., sec. Dr. Arthur Lomant, Eldersburg, Md., 1986-87; pharmacy technician Frederick (Md.) Meml. Hosp., 1991-95. Mem. Assn. Pharmacy Technicians, Stringband Am., Inc. (v.p. Eldersburg chpt. 1989-90). Roman Catholic. Home: 109 Woodside Ave Thurmont MD 21788-1932

MCCULLOCH, PETER GEORGE, surgeon, educator; b. Chitambo, Serenje, Zambia, Nov. 28, 1956; s. George Morrison and Joan Elizabeth Gertrude (Caves) McC.; m. Carolyn Mitchell, June 7, 1986; children: Shona Lee, Kenneth Peter. MB ChB, U. Aberdeen, Scotland, 1980. House surgeon Glasgow (Scotland) Royal Infirmary, 1980-81; house physician Aberdeen Royal Infirmary, 1981; sr. house officer pediatrics Stobhill Hosp., Glasgow, 1981-82; sr. house officer No. Gen. Hosp., Sheffield, Eng., 1982; surg. registrar Greater Glasgow Health Bd., 1982-85; rsch. fellow dept. surgery U. Glasgow, 1985-87, lectr. dept. surgery, 1989-92; sr. lectr. dept. surgery U. Liverpool, Eng., 1992—; vis. scientist U. Strathclyde, Glasgow, 1989; vis. fellow Nat. Cancer Ctr. Hosp., Tokyo, 1991. Contbr. articles to profl. jours. Br. chmn. Med. Campaign Against Nuclear Weapons, Glasgow, 1986. Recipient Moynihan prize Assn. Surgeons, 1987, TP Gunton award Brit. Med. Assn.; rsch. grantee Cancer Rsch. Campaign, 1987-89. Fellow Royal Coll. Physicians and Surgeons Glasgow (traveling fellow 1988), Royal Coll. Surgeons Edinburgh, Surg. Rsch. Soc. Home: 6 Wrigley's Ln Freshfield, Formby L37 7DR, England Office: Royal Liverpool U Hosp, Dept Surgery, Liverpool L7 8XP, England

MCCULLOUGH, BILLIE GIBSON, pharmacist; b. Muskogee, Okla., Oct. 25, 1924; s. Elmo Weeks and Esther (Gibson) McC.; m. Shirley Ann Hevel, Nov. 22, 1948 (dec. 1976); children—David G., Steven F. B.S. in Pharmacy, Kans. U., 1950. Registered pharmacist, Tex. Pharmacist retail drug stores, Coffeyville, Kans., 1950-52; salesman Eli Lilly & Co., Coffeyville, Waco, Tex., 1954-67; asst. dir. pharmacy Providence Hosp., Waco, 1967—. Served to LCDR, USN, 1942-45, PTO, 1952-53, Korea. Mem. Am. Soc. Hosp. Pharmacists, Tex. Soc. Hosp. Pharmacists, Heart of Tex. Soc. Hosp. Pharmacists. Republican. Episcopalian. Lodge: Masons. Avocations: classical music; study of economics. Home: 5200 Lake Charles St Waco TX 76710-2720 Office: Providence Health Ctr Pharmacy PO Box 2589 Waco TX 76702-2589

MCCULLOUGH, DAVID L., urologist; b. Chattanooga, 1938. MD, Bowman Gray, 1964. Intern U. Hosps. Case Western Reserve U., Cleve., 1964-65, resident in surgery, 1965-66; fellow urology Baylor U. Coll. Medicine, Houston, 1968-69; resident in urology Mass. Gen. Hosp., Boston, 1969-72; chief urologist N.C. Bapt. Hosp., Winston-Salem, 1983—; prof., chmn. urology Bowman Gray, Winston-Salem; pres. Am. Bd. Urology. Mem. ACS, AMA, Am. Urological Assn. (sec. southeastern sect.), Clin. Soc. Urol. Surgeons.

MC CULLOUGH, J. LEE, industrial psychologist; b. Bryn Mawr, Pa., Oct. 3, 1945; s. Leo Francis and Margaret Mary (Hart) McC.; AB, Villanova U., 1967; MA, Ohio State U., 1968, PhD, 1971; m. Bonnie R. Goldberg, Jan. 14, 1979. Teaching asst. Ohio State U., 1967-68, rsch. assoc., 1968-69; assoc. O.P.S. Assos., Columbus, 1970-71; assoc., sr. assoc., sr. prin., v.p. Hay Group, N.Y.C., 1971-90, v.p., dir. fin. svcs. cons., 1990-94; prin. William M. Mercer, Inc., N.Y.C., 1994—; adj. prof. Fordham U. Grad. Sch. Bus., 1984—. Served with AUS, 1972. NSF fellow, 1969; NDEA Title IV fellow, 1970; Univ. Dissertation Year fellow, 1971. Mem. Am., Eastern, Pa., Am. Psychol. Soc., Human Resource Planning Soc., Met. Psychol. Assns. Home: 6 Hereford Dr Princeton Junction NJ 08550-1514

MCCULLOUGH, KATHRYN T. BAKER, social worker, utility commissioner; b. Trenton, Tenn., Jan. 5, 1925; d. John Andrew and Alma Lou (Wharey) Taylor; m. John R. Baker, Sept. 30, 1972 (dec. Oct. 1981); m. T.C. McCullough, May 14, 1988. BS, U. Tenn., 1945, MSW, 1954; postgrad., U. Chgo., 1950, Vanderbilt U., 1950-51. Lic. social worker, Tenn.; emeritus diplomate in clin. social work Am. Bd. Examiners. Home demonstration agt., agrl. extension svc. U. Tenn., Hardeman County, 1946-49; Dyer County, 1949-50; dir. med. social work dept. Le Bonheur Children's Hosp., Memphis, 1954-57; chief clin. social worker clinic mentally retarded children U. Tenn. Dept. Pediatrics, Memphis, 1957-59; clin. social worker Children's Med. Ctr., Tulsa, 1959-60; dir. med. social work dept. Coll. of Medicine U. Tenn., Memphis, 1960-69; dir. community svcs. regional med. program Coll. of Medicine, 1969-76; dir. regional clinic program Child Devel. Ctr. Coll. of Medicine, 1976-85; mem. faculty Coll. of Medicine, Coll. of Social Work U. Tenn., Memphis, 1960-85; social worker admissions rev. bd. Arlington Devel. Ctr., Memphis, 1976—. Author 14 books. Active Gibson County Fedn. Dem. Women, 1987—; commr. Dist. I, Gibson Utility Dist., 1990—. Fellow Am. Assn. Mental Retardation (life); mem. NASW, AAUP, Acad. Cert. Social Workers, Tenn. Conf. on Social Welfare, Sigma Kappa Alumni. Mem. Ch. of Christ. Home: 627 Riverside Yorkville Rd Trenton TN 38382-9513

MCCULLOUGH, ROBERT DALE, II, osteopath; b. Tulsa, June 2, 1937; s. Robert Dale and Roberta Maud (Purdy) McC.; m. Lindell Arlene Wilcox, Sept. 28, 1963; children: Robert Mark, Lori Lindell. Student, Wheaton (Ill.) Coll., 1955-57; BS, N.E. Mo. State U., 1958; DO, Kansas City (Mo.) Coll. Osteopathy, 1958-62. Cert. Am. Osteo. Bd. Internal Medicine, Internal Medicine and Med. Oncology. Gen. practice McCullough Clinic, Tulsa, 1963-68; internal medicine resident Detroit Osteo. Hosp., 1968-71; internal medicine Baker-Todd-McCullough-Sutton, Tulsa, 1971-74; fellow med. oncology M.D. Anderson Hosp., Houston, 1974-75; internal medicine-med. oncology Baker-Todd-McCullough-Sutton, Tulsa, 1975-90; pvt. practice Tulsa, 1990-93; attending staff mem. VA Outpatient Clinic, Tulsa, 1993-94; assoc. med. dir. Blue Cross/Blue Shield of Okla., Tulsa, 1994—; trustee Tulsa Regional Med. Cttr., 1983-88, 90-93; bd. dirs. Okla. Blue Cross Blue Shield, Tulsa, 1983-92, vice chmn., 1991-92; mem. adv. coun. Okla. State U. Coll. Osteo. Medicine, 1988-94, chmn., 1988-90. Mem. bd. of editors Patient Care Magazine, Montvale, N.J., 1988-93. Mem. Okla. State Bd. Health, Oklahoma City, 1983-87, Tulsa City/County Bd. Health, 1988-95, chmn., 1993. Mem. Am. Osteo. Assn. (vice speaker Ho. of Dels. 1986-92, trustee 1993—), Am. Coll. Osteo. Internists, Am. Soc. Clin. Oncology, Okla. Osteo. Assn. (pres. 1982-83), Tulsa Downtown Lions Club, Soc. for Preservation and Encouragement of Barbershop Quartet Singing in Am. Republican. Southern Baptist. Home: 2300 Riverside Dr 10F Tulsa OK 74114-2402 Office: 1215 S Boulder Tulsa OK 74119

MCCULLOUGH, ROBERT WALTER, optometrist; b. Atlanta, Oct. 19, 1951; s. Benjamin Hudson and Isabell Octavia (Booth) McC.; m. Norma Carol Craig, Aug. 7, 1976; 1 child, Benjamin Craig. AS with honors, Middle Ga. Coll., 1971; BS, U. Ga., 1973; OD with honors, So. Coll. Optometry, 1977. Pvt. practice optometry, Jonesboro, Ga., 1979—; cons. Atlanta Fed. Penitentiary, 1979-93; lectr. in field. Bd. dirs. Festival Ballet. Served to lt. USN, 1977-79. U.S. Navy Health Professions scholar, 1975. Mem. Am. Optometric Assn. (Southeastern optometric fed. liaison, mem. eye care benefits exec. com., ethics and values com., pres.-elect 1996—), Ga. Optometric Assn. (chmn. bd. trustees, v.p.), 4th Dist. Optometric Assn. (pres. 1981-82, 95-96), Beta Sigma Kappa, Sigma Alpha Sigma, Phi Theta Kappa. Methodist. Club: Jonesboro Kiwanis (pres. 1981-82). Contbr. articles to profl. jours. Home: 2762 Austin Ln Jonesboro GA 30236-6203 Office: 137 W Mill St Jonesboro GA 30236

MCCULLOUGH-WIGGINS, LYDIA STATORIA, pharmacist, consultant; b. Chgo., May 14, 1948; d. George Robert and Isabell (King) Boulware; m. Robert Dale McCullough, Aug. 1, 1970 (div. Oct. 1977); m. 2d, James Calvin Wiggins, Nov. 3, 1979. Student Wis. State U.-Whitewater, 1966-69; B.S. in Pharmacy, U. Ill.-Chgo., 1972; cert. UCLA, 1976-78. Registered pharmacist, Ill. Registered pharmacy apprentice Lefel Drugs, Chgo., 1971-72; pharmacy mgr. Fernwood Pharmacy, Chgo., 1972-73, Sapstein Bros. Pharmacy, Chgo., 1973-74; dir. pharmacy Martin Luther King Neighborhood Health Ctr., Chgo., 1974-80; pharmacist in charge Walgreens, Chgo., 1980-89; mgr. East End Pharmacy, Oak Park, Ill., 1989-90; rep. The Prudential, La Grange, Ill., 1991-95; registered pharmacist Osco Drugs, Oak Park, 1995—. Bd. dirs. Nia Comprehensive Ctr. Developmental Disabilities, Inc.; mem. coalit. Labor Union Women Exec. Bd. Author: M.L.K. Drug Formulary, 1978. Recipient Cert. of Leadership, YMCA Met. Chgo., 1979; Kizzy award 1980 Black Women Hall of Fame Found., Chgo., 1981; Ann. Med. Achievement award Greater Chgo. Met. Community, 1981. Mem. NAFE, Chgo. Pharmacists Assn., Am. Pharm. Assn., Ill. Pharm. Assn., Nat. Pharm. Assn. (exec. bd.), U. Ill. Alumni Assn. Democrat. Baptist. Club: Christian Novice (pres. 1977-78) (Chgo.). Home: 618 Marshall Ave Bellwood IL 60104-1839

MCCUNE, EDWARD ALLISON, general surgeon; b. Tahlequah, Okla., Nov. 3, 1930; s. Edward Henry and Vera (Allison) McC.; m. Margaret Douglas Rucks, Jan. 29, 1960; children: Allison, Joe, Evelyn, Louisa. Student, Westminster Coll., Fulton, Mo., 1948-50, Northeastern State U., Tahlequah, 1950-51; MD, U. Okla., Oklahoma City, 1955. Diplomate Am. Bd. Surgery. Resident in surgery Univ. Hosp., Oklahoma City, 1955-60; pvt. practice, Enid, Okla., 1962-64, 67—, Oklahoma City, 1965-67; mem. staff St. Mary's Hosp., Enid, 1962-64, 67—, chief surgery, chief staff, trustee, past pres.; mem. staff Bass Hosp., Enid, 1962-64, 67—, chief staff; mem. staff Presbyn. Hosp., Oklahoma City, 1965-67. Mem. Enid City Coun., 1983-87. Capt. USAF, 1960-62. Mem. ACS (pres. Okla. chpt.), Okla. Surg. Assn. (past pres.), Southwestern Surg. Congress, Soc. Am. Gastrointestinal Endoscopic Surgeons, Rotary. Republican. Presbyterian. Office: 330 S 5th St Enid OK 73701

MCCUNE, MARY JOAN HUXLEY, microbiology educator; b. Lewistown, Mont., Jan. 14, 1932; d. Thomas Leonard and Anna Dorothy (Hardie) Huxley; m. Ronald William McCune, June 7, 1965; children: Anna Orpha, Heather Jean. BS, Mont. State Coll., 1953; MS, Wash. State U., 1955; PhD, Purdue U., 1965. Rsch. technician VA Hosp., Oakland, Calif., 1956-59; bacteriologist U.S. Naval Radiol. Def. Lab., San Francisco, 1959-61; teaching assoc. Purdue U., West Lafayette, Ind., 1961-65, vis. asst. prof., 1965-66; asst. prof. Occidental Coll., L.A., 1966-69; asst. rsch. bacteriologist II U. Calif., L.A., 1969-70; affiliate asst. prof. Idaho State U., Pocatello, Idaho, 1970-80, from asst. prof. to prof. microbiology, 1980—; instr. U. Calif., Davis, 1964. Contbr. articles to profl. jours. Pres. AK chpt. PEO, Pocatello, 1988-89; chair faculty senate Idaho State U., 1994-95. David Ross fellow Purdue U., 1964. Mem. AAAS, N.Y. Acad. Sci., Idaho Acad. Sci. (trustee 1989-95, v.p. 1992-93, pres. 1993-94), Am. Soc. for Microbiology (v.p. Intermountain br. 1988-89, pres. 1989-90), Idaho Edn. Alliance for Sci. (bd. dirs.), Sigma Xi, Sigma Delta Epsilon. Presbyterian. Home: 30 Colgate St Pocatello ID 83201-3459 Office: Idaho State U Dept Biol Scis Pocatello ID 83209

MCCURDY, JOHN DENNIS, biochemist, toxicologist; b. Irvington, N.J., Aug. 17, 1942; s. Harris John and Emma Grace (Lang) McC.; m. Patricia Jeanne Mitchell, Aug. 22, 1967; m. Diane Jean Espinoza, Oct. 3, 1981; children: Kristina Marie, Michael John Daniel. BS Fairleigh Dickinson U., 1966; MS, Am. U., 1972, PhD, 1974. Researcher Am. U., Washington, 1969-74; Diplomate Am. Bd. Toxicology. FDA scientist Ctr. for Vet. Medicine, Rockville, Md., 1974—; assoc. rsch. scientist Am. U., 1969-74, rsch. scientist, 1976-90; vis. scientist Howard U., Washington, 1982-83. Contbr. articles and chpts. to profl. jours. Instr., Greater Balt. YMCA, Howard County, 1978, Towson, 1985. Served to capt. U.S. Army, 1966-69. Fellow, Am. Inst. Chemists; mem. Am. Chem. Soc. (bd. mgrs. Washington chpt. 1974), Assn. Official Analytical Chemists, AAAS, N.Y. Acad. Scis., Sigma Xi, Alpha Chi Sigma. Roman Catholic. Clubs: Washington Kendo (Columbia, Md.), Am. Ju-Jitsu Assn. (mem. bd. dirs 1978—, no. regional dir. 1984—). Avocations: martial arts, Ju-Jitsu, Kendo, Iaido. Home: 3949 Sugarloaf Dr Monrovia MD 21770-9113

MCCURDY, LAYTON, psychiatry educator; b. Florence, S.C., Aug. 20, 1935; m. Gwendolyn A. McCurdy, 1958; children: Robert Jr., David Barclay. BS, U. N.C., 1956; MD, Med. U. S.C., 1960. Dimplomate Am. Bd. Psychiatry and Neurology (bd. dirs. 1983-91, pres. 1990); lic. psychiatrist, S.C., N.C., Md., Ga., Pa. Resident in psychiatry N.C. Meml. Hosp., Chapel Hill, 1961-64; with psychiatry tng. br. NIMH, Bethesda, Md., 1964-66; asst. prof. dept. psychiatry Sch. Medicine Emory U., Atlanta, 1966-68; prof., chmn. dept. psychiatry and behavioral scis. Med. U. S.C., 1968-82, prof. psychiatry, v.p. med. affairs, dean, 1990—; prof. psychiatry Sch. Medicine U. Pa., Phila., 1982-90; psychiatrist-in-chief Inst. of Pa. Hosp., Phila., 1982-90; vis. colleague Inst. Psychiatry, U. London, 1974-75; nat. adv. mental health coun. NIMH, 1980-83; apptd. Pa. Adv. Com. for Mental Health and Mental Retardation, 1984-87; chmn. consensus panel on panic disorder NIH, 1991. Recipient Disting. Alumnus award Med. U. S.C., 1988, George C. Ham. Soc., 1990; rsch. fellow NIMH, 1974-75. Fellow Am. Coll. Psychiatrists (bd. regents 1987-90, v.p. 1990-93, pres. 1993-94), Am. Psychiat. Assn. (joint commn. pub. affairs 1981-84, chmn. com. on diagnosis and assessment 1988-94), So. Psychiat. Assn. (bd. regents 1977-80, chmn. bd. regents 1979-80), Royal Coll. Psychiatrists (U.K.); mem. AMA, Assn. for Acad. Psychiatry (pres. 1970-72), S.C. Med. Assn., Charleston County Med. Soc. (exec. com.), Waring Libr. Soc. (pres. 1979-80), Cosmos Club (Washington)., Alpha Omega Alpha. Office: Med U SC Coll Medicine 171 Ashley Ave Ste 601 Csb Charleston SC 29425-0001

MCCUTCHAN, BETTY ANN, counselor; b. Atlanta, May 12, 1931; d. John Elmer and Vivian (Sellers) Segars; m. Richard Shannon McCutchan, Dec. 30, 1955; children: Richard Jr., Jan Elizabeth McCutchan Baugus, Anne McCutchan allen. Diploma, Ga. Bapt. Hosp. Sch. Nursing, 1953; BS in Psychology, East Tex. State U., 1989, MS in Counselor Psychology, 1990. RN, lic. profl. counselor, lic. marriage and family therapist. Campus nurse East Tex. Bapt. U., Marshall, 1953-55; oper. rm. nurse St. Luke's Hosp., Houston, 1956-57, M. D. Anderson Tumor Inst., Houston, 1957-59; sec., treas. McCutchan Pharmacy, Inc., Atlanta, Tex., 1964—; pvt. practice Texarkana, Tex., 1990-95. Author short stories and books for children; contbr. articles to mags. Mem. Amity Study Club, Atlanta, 1964-66; pres. Atlanta Woman's Club, 1980-84. Baptist. Office: 704 W Main St Atlanta TX 75551

MCCUTCHEN, JOHN WARREN, orthopedic surgeon; b. Jefferson City, Mo., Apr. 9, 1950; s. Albert Carroll and Katherine Elizabeth (Chastain) McC.; m. Suzanne Yvonne Sheridan, Aug. 20, 1977; 1 child, Mary Katherine. BS, Harding Coll., 1972; MD, U. Mo., 1976. Intern orthop. U. Tex. San Antonio, 1976-77; resident orthop. U. Tenn., Memphis, 1977-81; surgeon, CEO Jewett Orthop. Clinic, P.A., Winter Park, Fla., 1981—; mem. adv. bd. Ctrl. Fla. Tissue Bank, Orlando, Rhone-Poulenc Rorer, Inc.; bd. regents Liberty U., Lynchburg, Va. Inventor in field. Fellow ACS, Am. Acad. Orthop. Surgeons, Internat. Coll. Surgeons; mem. Soc. Arthritic Joint Surgery, Am. Assn. Hip and Knee Surgeons, Clin. Orthop. Soc., Inc. Republican. Baptist. Home: 779 Suwanee Ct Maitland FL 32751 Office: Jewett Orthop Clinic PA 1285 Orange Ave Winter Park FL 32789

MCDANIEL, CANDACE ANN, osteopathic physician, researcher, educator; b. Dallas, Dec. 16, 1951; d. Wayne Freeman Jr. and Betty Jean (Nichols) Slaughter; m. Stephen Frederick Roberts, May 9, 1977 (div. Aug. 1989); children: Jay Wayne, Morgan Lee, Rosa Lynne, Stephanie Jean; m. Harley Reginald McDaniel, Mar. 11, 1995. BA, So. Meth. U., 1972; MA, Tex. Christian U., 1974; Edn.D, U. Tulsa, 1987; AS, Tulsa Jr. Coll., 1992; BS, Northeastern State U., 1996; DO, Okla. State U., 1996. Staff psychometrist Bartlesville (Okla.) Regl. Edn. Svc. Ctr., 1977-78; search-serve coord. and psychometrist Tulsa-Okmulgee Regl. Edn. Svc. Ctr., 1978-79; dir. spl. svcs. and psychometrist Cath. Diocese of Tulsa, 1980-81; prof. psychology U. Ctr. at Tulsa-Langston U., 1987-93; med. rschr. Fischer Inst. for Med. Rsch., Grand Prairie, Tex., 1993—. Grantee St. John Cardiovasc. Inst., 1986. Mem. Am. Osteo. Assn., Am. Coll. Osteo. Family Physicians. Republican. Methodist. Home: 4602 Chalk Ct Grand Prairie TX 75052 Office: Fischer Inst for Med Rsch 2701 Osler Dr Ste 6 Grand Prairie TX 75051

MCDANIEL, DAVID HENRY, physician; b. Clarksburg, W.Va., May 12, 1952; s. Hubert Harold and Ada Virginia (Henry) McD.; m. Sheila Marie Travis, Sept. 17, 1994. BS in Chemistry cum laude, W.Va. U., Morgantown, 1974, MD, 1978. Diplomate Am. Bd. Dermatology, 1983. Emergency physician Monongalia Gen. Hosp., Morgantown, 1979-82; dir. Laser Ctr. of Va., Virginia Beach, Va., 1982—; asst. prof. clin. dermatology Ea. Va. Med. Sch., Norfolk, 1991—, asst. prof. clin. plastic surgery, 1992—; command cons., Dept. Plastic Surgery Naval Med. Ctr., Portsmouth, Va., 1994—; pres. The Ctr. for Disfigurement, Virginia Beach, 1993—; adv. coun. mem. Disfigurement Guidance Ctr., Scotland, 1994—; pres. David H. McDaniel Cons., Internat., Virginia Beach, 1995—. Contbr. numerous articles to sci. jours. Fellow Am. Acad. Dermatology, Am. Soc. Laser Medicine and Surgery, Am. Soc. Dermatologic Surgery (com. practice mktg. and pub. rels. 1993-96, chair 1996), Internat. Soc. Dermatologic Surgery; mem. Tidewater Dermatology Soc. (pres. 1987-88), Space Dermatology Found. (founding), Va. Space Bus. Roundtable (charter), Phi Lambda Upsilon. Office: Laser Ctr of Va 848 First Colonial Rd Virginia Beach VA 23451

MCDANIEL, ELIZABETH LOGAN, psychologist, educator; b. Youngstown, Ohio; d. Laurence Adair and Henrietta (Villeneuve) Logan; m. David Cotter McDaniel (dec. Feb. 1969); children: David, Steven, Donna, William, Susan. BA, UCLA; MS, U. Ill.; PhD, U. Tex., 1967. Lic. psychologist, marriage and family therapist, profl. counselor, Tex.; registered health svc. provider; nat. cert. sch. psychologist. Prof. psychology S.W. Tex. State U., San Marcos, 1969—; pvt. practice psychology, Austin, 1970-76, San Antonio, 1976—. NIMH fellow, 1964-67. Mem. APA, Nat. Assn. Sch. Psychologists (state del. 1975-79, 81-85, 87-89, WC regional dir. 1989-93), Tex. Psychol. Assn. (pres. 1984-85). Home: 8933 Willmon Way San Antonio TX 78239-1948 Office: 4538 Centerview Ste 160 San Antonio TX 78228

MCDANIEL, MARTHA DAWES, vascular surgeon; b. Boston, Jan. 23, 1953; d. L. Tillman and Mary Eliza (Turner) McDaniel; m. Stephen K. Plume III, July 9, 1983. AB magna cum laude, Harvard U., 1974; MD, Dartmouth Coll., 1977. Vascular surgery fellow Northwestern U. Med. Sch., Chgo., 1982-83; instr. in surgery Dartmouth Med. Sch., Hanover, N.H., 1983-84, asst. prof. surgery, 1984-90, assoc. prof. of surgery, 1990—; chief vascular surgery VA Hosp., White River Junction, Vt. contbr. articles to profl. jours. Recipient VA Career Devel. award, 1988-92. Fellow ACS; mem. Phi Beta Kappa, Alpha Omega Alpha. Office: VA Med Ctr 215 N Main St White River Junction VT 05009

MCDANIEL, RICKEY DAVID, senior living executive; b. Rochester, Minn., Apr. 10, 1946; s. Malcolm David and Elaine (Lee) McD.; m. Shelley Ann Sorensen, May 10, 1980; children: Michael, Mathew, Joseph. AA, Rochester Jr. Coll., 1966; BA, Winona State U., 1969. Clin. mgr. St. Mary's Hosp., Rochester, Minn., 1971-74; long term care adminstr. Roderick Enterprises, Inc., Portland, Oreg., 1974-78; regional dir. Roderick Enterprises, Inc., Portland, 1978-80, v.p. ops., 1980-84; pres. Health Sys. Mgmt. and Devel., L.A., 1984-86; ops. dir. Brim Enterprises, Inc., Portland, 1987-88, v.p., 1988-92, sr. v.p., 1992-93; pres. Brim Sr. Living, Inc., Portland, 1993—; bd. dirs. Brim Homestead, Inc., Portland, Dominican Life Care Svcs., Portland, Belmar, Inc., Portland, also v.p. 1989—; pres. Care Mgmt., Inc., A Fla. Employee Leasing Corp., 1991—; developer alzheimer patients care and housing program, 1993. Cpl. USMC, 1969-71. Republican. Lutheran. Home: 16492 S Arrowhead Dr Oregon City OR 97045-9287 Office: Brim Inc 305 NE 102nd Ave Portland OR 97220-4170

MCDANIEL, SUSAN HOLMES, psychologist; b. Jersey City, Oct. 31, 1951; d. Grover Cleveland and Anna Lou (Toms) McD.; m. David Morton Siegel, July 22, 1984; children: Hanna, Marisa. BA, Duke U., 1973; PhD, U. N.C., 1979. Fellow in family therapy Tex. Rsch. Inst. Mental Scis., Houston, 1980; Supr., staff psychologist W. Monroe Mental Health Ctr., Rochester, N.Y., 1980-82; pvt. practice psychologist Rochester, 1980-88; prof. psychiatry and family medicine U. Rochester Sch. Medicine, 1987—, co-dir. psychosocial edn. dept. family medicine, dir. family therapy tng. program dept. psychiatry, 1988-94, assoc. dir. div. family programs, 1994-96, dir. divsn. family programs, 1996—. Co-author: Systems Consultation, 1986, Family-oriented Primary Care, 1990, Medical Family Therapy, 1992, Counseling Families with Chronic Illness, 1995, Integrating Family Therapy, 1995; co-editor Families, Systems & Health, 1995—; contbr. articles to profl. jours. Recipient Nat. Patient Care award for innovation in family med. edn. Patient Care, Soc. for Tchrs. Family Medicine, 1988. Mem. APA (bd. family divsn., Family Psychologist of Yr. 1995), Am. Family Therapy Acad. (bd. dirs., mem. commn. accreditation marital & family therapy tng. & edn. 1993—), Soc. for Tchrs. Family Medicine. Democrat. Office: Dept Family Medicine 885 South Ave Rochester NY 14620-2318

MCDANIEL, WILLIAM F., III, psychologist, educator; b. Washington, Nov. 26, 1951; s. William F. and Barbara (Burroughs) McD.; m. Sheryl Edmunds, Mar. 8, 1975; 1 child, Justin Dylan. BS, Duke U., 1973; MA, Appalachian State U., 1974; PhD, U. Ga., 1977. Prof. psychology Ga. Coll., Milledgeville, 1977—, chmn. dept. psychology, 1991—; neuropsychologist Ctrl. State Hosp., 1993—. Contbr. over 40 articles to profl. jours. Grantee NSF, 1980—. Mem. Internat. Brain Rsch. Orgn., Soc. for Neurosci., So. Soc. for Philosophy and Psychology, S.E. Psychol. Assn. Office: Ga Coll Dept Psychology PO Box 90 Milledgeville GA 31061-0090

MCDANIEL, WILLIAM JASON, JR., orthopedic surgeon; b. Rutherfordton, N.C., Sept. 22, 1941; s. William Jason Sr. and Edna Grace (Capel) McD.; m. Craig Harris, Aug. 14, 1965; children: Mary Hollingsworth, William Jason III. BS, Davidson Coll., 1963; MD, U. N.C., 1967. Cert. Am. Bd. Orthopaedic Surgery. Internship N.C. Meml. Hosp., Chapel Hill, 1967-68, residency, 1968-72; Instr. N.C. Meml. Hosp., 1972-73; orthopaedic surgeon Raleigh Orthopaedic Clinic, Raleigh, N.C., 1975—; pres. Wake County Med. Soc., Raleigh, 1980-81, Raleigh Orthopaedic Clinic, 1989-91; chief orthopaedic surgery Wake MEd. Ctr., Raleigh, 1985; clin. asst. prof. dept. surgery U. N.C. Med. Sch., Chapel Hill, 1978—. Co-author: The Musculoskeletal System, 1975; Contbr. articles to profl. jours. Pres. Coley Lakes No. 1 Assn., Raleigh, 1988-92; bd. dirs. Citizens for a Safe Glen Eden, Raleigh, 1987. Maj. USAF, 1973-75. Fellow Am. Acad. Orthopaedic Surgeons; mem. Am. Orthopaedic Assn. for Sports Medicine, Arthroscopy Assn. N.Am., N.C. Med. Soc., N.C. Orthopaedic Assn. (pres. 1991-92), So. Orthopaedic Assn. Republican. Presbyterian. Office: Raleigh Orthopaedic Clinic 3515 Glenwood Ave Raleigh NC 27612-4900

MCDERMOTT, PATRICIA ANN, nursing administrator; b. Bklyn., July 10, 1943; d. John J. and Lillian E. (Sweeney) Skelly; m. Joseph Kevin McDermott, Oct. 5, 1963; children: Colleen Mary, John Joseph. Diploma, Kings County Hosp. Ctr. Sch. Nursing, Bklyn., 1963; BS in Health Care Adminstrn., St. Francis Coll., Bklyn., 1979. Staff nurse Kings County Hosp., Bklyn., 1963-66, head nurse outpatient dept., 1966-74; evening supr. Park Nursing Home, Rockaway Park, N.Y., 1974-83; day supr. Hyde Park Nursing Home, Staatsburg, N.Y., 1984-85, DON, 1985—; nurse aide evaluator PRI assessor, MDS, coord. N.Y. State. Active local Girl Scouts U.S.A., 1971-78, Boy Scouts Am., 1978-82, Stella Maris Parents Club, 1978-82, St. Francis de Sales Altar and Rosary Soc., 1970-83, St. Francis de Sales Little League, 1978-80, also softball coach, 1974-77. Republican. Roman Catholic. Avocations: knitting; crocheting; roller skating; bowling; oil painting. Home: 286A Shadblow Ln Clinton Corners NY 12514 Office: Hyde Park Nursing Home RR 9 Staatsburg NY 12580

MC DERMOTT, WILLIAM VINCENT, JR., physician, educator; b. Salem, Mass., Mar. 7, 1917; s. William Vincent and Mary A. (Feenan) McD.; m. Blanche O'Riorden, May 15, 1943 (dec. July 1969); children: Blanche Anne, William Shaw, Jane Travers Hoch; m. Mary Boit Bingham, June 1, 1976 (dec. 1984); m. Frances Weld Gardiner, June 16, 1989 (dec. 1993). A.B., Harvard U., 1938, M.D., 1942. Diplomate: Nat. Bd. Med. Examiners (chmn. surgery test com.), Am. Bd. Surgery. Intern Mass. Gen. Hosp., Boston, 1942; asst. resident surgeon Mass. Gen. Hosp., 1946-49, chief resident surgeon, 1950; practice medicine specializing in surgery Boston, 1951—; mem. staff Mass. Gen. Hosp., 1951—, New Eng. Deaconess Hosp., 1963—; dir. Fifth (Harvard) Surg. Svc. and Sears Surg. Lab. Boston City Hosp., 1963-73; mem. corp. vis. com., 1968—; USPHS fellow dept. biochemistry Sch. Medicine, Yale U., 1949-50; from instr. to prof. surgery Med. Sch. Harvard U., 1951-69, Cheever prof. surgery, 1969-87, prof. surgery emeritus, 1987—, sec. Faculty of Medicine, 1985-87; tutor premed. adv. Cabot House, Harvard Coll., 1989—; vis. prof. pro tem Kings Coll. Hosp. Med. Sch., London, 1960; dir. Harvard Surg. Svc. and Cancer Rsch. Inst., 1973-80; chmn. dept. surgery New Eng. Deaconess Hosp., 1980-85, mem. vis. com., 1987—, bd. dirs. Author four books, over 200 sci. papers; contbr. 12 chapters to books; mem. editorial bd. Jour. Surg. Rsch., 1960-73, Jour. Surg. Oncology, 1970—. Pres. Med. Found., Boston, 1968-70, trustee, 1970-87, hon. trustee, 1987—; bd. trustees Nat. Youth Leadership Forum, 1995—. Maj. M.C. AUS, 1943-46, ETO. Decorated Bronze Star, oak leaf cluster, 5 battle stars; recipient Disting. Alumnus award Harvard U., 1992. Mem. ACS (bd. govs. 1984-90, pres. Mass. chpt. 1980), Soc. Univ. Surgeons, Am. Surg. Assn., Am. Acad. Arts and Scis., New Eng. Surg. Soc. (pres. 1985-86), Boston Surg. Soc. (pres. 1971), Harvard Med. Alumni Assn. (treas.

1965-68, pres. 1975-76, dir. alumni rels. 1987-93, bd. dirs. 1993-95), Harvard Coll. Alumni Assn., Soc. de Chirurgie Internat., Assn. Acad. Surgery, Soc. Surgery Alimentary Tract, Aesculapian Club (pres. 1971), Harvard Club of Boston (bd. govs. 1971-77), Nat. Youth Leadership Forum, Tavern Club, Country Club. Home: 570 Bridge St Dedham MA 02026-4131 Office: New Eng Deaconess Hosp Dept Surgery Boston MA 02215

MCDIARMID, JAMES GEORGE MILTON, plastic surgeon, researcher; b. Beverley, E Yorkshire, England, Sept. 23, 1966; s. Hugh Duncan McDiarmid and Marie Barbara Lautatzis. MB ChB, U. Aberdeen Med. Sch., 1990; MSc, U. London, 1996. Demonstrator in anatomy U. Manchester, 1991-92; sr. house officer in accidents and emergency medicine Withington & Wythenshawe Hosps., Manchester, 1992; sr. house officer in orthopedic/trauma surgery Horton Gen. Hosp., Banbury, 1993; sr. house officer in gen. surgery Royal United Hosp., Bath, 1993-94; sr. house officer in plastic and reconstructive surgery Addenbrooke's Hosp., Cambridge, England, 1994-95; hon. clin. asst. in plastic surgery, rsch. fellow U. Coll. London Hosps., 1995-96; trust med. officer Hazardous Areas Life Support Orgn., Kabul, Afghanistan, 1995. Author: (books) MCQ's in Anatomy for the FRCS, 1993, MCQ's in Physiology for the FRCS, 1993, MCQ's in Pathology for the FRCS, 1993. Fellow Royal Coll. Surgeons of England. Home: 15 Braids Walk Kirk Ella, HU107PB East Yorkshire England

MC DONALD, BARBARA ANN, psychotherapist; b. Mpls., July 15, 1932; d. John and Georgia Elizabeth (Baker) Rubenzer; B.A., U. Minn., 1954; M.S.W., U. Denver, 1977; m. Lawrence R. McDonald, July 27, 1957 (dec. Sept. 1993); children—John, Mary Elizabeth. Diplomate Am. Bd. Social Work; lic. psychotherapist. Day care cons. Minn. Dept. Public Welfare, St. Paul, 1954-59; social worker Community Info. Center, Mpls., 1959-60; exec. dir. Social Synergistics Co., Littleton, Colo., 1970—; cons. to community orgns., Indian tribes. Family therapist , 1979—. Bd. dirs. Vol. Bur. Sun Cities, Ariz., 1988, 89, 90. Named 1 of 8 Women of Yr. and featured on TV spl. Ladies Home Jour., 1974; Clairol scholar, 1974; Am. Bus. Women's Assn. scholar, 1974; Alpha Gamma Delta scholar, 1974. Mem. Minn. Pre-Sch. Edn. Assn. (hon. life), AAUW, Nat. Assn. Social Workers, Ariz. Assn. Social Workers, Assn. Clin. Social Workers, Am. Bus. Women's Assn., U. Minn. Alumni Club (sun cities chpt.), Alpha Gamma Delta (Disting. Citizen award 1975). Club: Altrusa (hon.). Author: Selected References on the Group Day Care of Pre-School Children, 1956; Helping Families Grow: Specialized Psychotherapy with Hearing Impaired Children and Their Families, 1984. Office: 13720 W Franciscan Dr Sun City West AZ 85375-5219

MC DONALD, CHARLES J., physician, educator; b. Tampa, Fla., Dec. 6, 1931; s. George B. and Bertha C. (Harbin) Mc D.; m. Maureen McDonald; children—Marc S., Norman D., Eric S. B.S. magna cum laude, A&T Coll. N.C., 1951; M.S., U. Mich., 1952; M.D. with highest honors, Howard U., 1960. Diplomate: Am. Bd. Dermatology. Rotating intern Hosp. St. Raphael, New Haven, 1960-61; asst. resident in medicine Hosp. St. Raphael, 1961-63; asst. resident in dermatology Yale U., 1963-65, spl. USPHS research fellow, chief resident in dermatology, 1965-66, instr. in medicine and pharmacology, 1966-67, asst. prof. medicine and pharmacology, 1967-68; asst. prof. med. sci. Brown U., 1968-69, assoc. prof., 1969-74, prof., 1974—, dir. dermatology program, 1970-74, head subsect. dermatology, 1974-82, dir. dermatology, 1982—, chair dept. dermatology, 1996—; dir. dermatology Roger Williams Gen. Hosp., 1968—; physician-in-charge dermatology R.I. Hosp., 1989—; mem. com. and task force, chmn. task force on minority affairs Am. Acad. Dermatology, 1975-80; mem. dermatology adv. panel FDA, until 1978, cons., 1978—; mem. pharm. scis. rev. commn. NIH, 1979-83, mem. adv. com. Arthritis, Muscular/Skeletal and Skin Disease Inst., 1993-95; chmn. com. pub. edn., dir., v.p. R.I. divsn. Am. Cancer Soc., 1978-80, pres., 1980-83, bd. dir. nat. soc., 1983—, nat. dir. at large, 1990—, mem. nat. exec. com., 19916; mem. residency rev. com. dermatology ACGME, 1992—. Dermatology editor Postgrad. Medicine; contbr. numerous articles to med. publs. Trustee Howard U., 1993—, chair health affairs com., 1994—, mem. exec. com., 1994—; bd. dirs. Providence Health Care Found., chmn. mem. adv. com., 1976-87; bd. dirs. Providence Fund for Edn.; bd. dirs. Providence Pub. Libr., 1987—, sec., 1991; mem. R.I. State Bd. Edn., 1970-72. Served to maj. USAF, 1952-56. Recipient Disting. Svc. award Hosp. Assn. R.I., 1971, Disting. Alumni award Howard U. Coll. Medicine, 1983, St. George medal nat. divsn. Am. Cancer Soc., 1992. Mem. AAAS, Am. Dermatol. Assn. (bd. dirs. 1995—), New Eng. Dermatol. Assn. (v.p. 1983-84, pres. 1984-85), R.I. Dermatol. Assn., Noah Worcester Dermatol. Assn. (bd. dirs. 1983-86), Soc. Investigative Dermatology, Am. Fedn. Clin. Rsch., Am. Acad. Dermatology (bd. dirs. 1987-91, Nat. Med. Assn. (chmn. sect. dermatology 1973-75), Am. Soc. Clin. Oncology, Dermatology Found. (chmn. sci. com. 1972-76), Assn. Profs. Dermatology (bd. dirs. 1991-94), Sigma Xi, Alpha Omega Alpha, Alpha Kappa Mu, Beta Kappa Chi. Democrat. Office: 825 Chalkstone Ave Providence RI 02908-4728

MCDONALD, JOHN CLIFTON, surgeon; b. Baldwyn, Miss., July 25, 1930; s. Edgar Hone and Ethel (Knight) McD.; m. Martha Dennis, Sept. 9, 1956; children: Melissa Lee, Karen Ann, Martha Knight. B.S., Miss. Coll., 1951; M.D., Tulane U., 1955. Diplomate Am. Bd. Surgery. Intern Confederate Meml. Med. Ctr., Shreveport, La., 1955-56; asst. resident Meyer Meml. Hosp., Buffalo, 1958-62, resident, 1962-63, from asst. attending surgeon to attending surgeon, 1963-68, assoc. dir. surg. research lab., 1965-68; from asst. attending surgeon to attending surgeon Deaconess Hosp., Buffalo, 1965-69, head sect. transplantation, 1966-68; dir. transplantation Charity Hosp. of La., New Orleans, 1969-77, vis. surgeon, 1969-77; clin. asst. surgeon Touro Infirmary, New Orleans, 1969-77; mem. med. staff So. Bapt. Hosp., New Orleans, 1969-77; assoc. mem. dept. surgery Hotel Dieu Hosp., 1969-77; surgeon in chief La. State U. Med. Ctr., Shreveport, 1977—, prof., chmn. dept. surgery, 1977—; asst. prof. surgery SUNY-Buffalo, 1965-68; cons. surgeon various La. Hosps., 1969-77; dir. La. Organ Procurement Program, 1971-77; cons. N.W. La. Emergency Med. Services, 1977—; Buswell research fellow in immunology SUNY-Buffalo, 1963-65, instr. surgery, 1963-65, assoc. prof., 1965-68; assoc. prof. surgery Tulane U. Sch. Medicine, 1969-72, prof., 1972-77, assoc. prof. microbiology and immunology, 1969-77, dir. surg. research labs., 1969-77, dir. transplantation labs., 1969-77, dir. Med. Ctr. Histocampatability Testing Lab., 1969-77. Contbr. articles to med. jours. Served to capt. USAF, 1956-58. Recipient Owl Club award for outstanding teaching Tulane U., 1977; grantee Kidney Found., 1966-67, NIH, 1969—, Schlieder Found., 1970-73, Cancer Assn. Greater New Orleans, 1971-72, La. Regional Med. Program, 1971-73. Mem. AMA, ACS, Am. Assn. Clin. Histocompatibility Testing (founding), Am. Assn. Immunologists, Am. Soc. for Artificial Internal Organs, Am. Soc. Transplant Surgeons (founding, pres. 1987), Buffalo Surg. Soc. (sec. 1968), So. Surg. Assn. (Arthur H. Shipley award 1972, treas. 1988-91, sec. 1991-3, pres. 1993-94), Surg. Assn. La. (dir. 1977—, pres. 1983), Am. Assn. for Surgery of Trauma, Transplantation Soc., Southeastern Surg. Congress, Am. Surg. Assn., Halsted Soc. (pres. 1991), Soc. U. Surgeons, La. Med. Soc., Shreveport Med. Soc., United Network for Organ Sharing (pres. 1986-88). Office: La State U Sch of Medicine Dept Surgery Shreveport LA 71130

MC DONALD, JOSEPH VALENTINE, neurosurgeon; b. N.Y.C., June 7, 1925; m. Carolyn Alice Patricia Petersen, Apr. 30, 1955; children: Judith Katherine McDonald Aquadro, Elizabeth Ann McDonald Iwanicki, Catherine Eleanor McDonald Schneider, Joseph Bede, David Randolph. A.B., Coll. Holy Cross, 1945; M.D., U. Pitts., 1949. Intern St. Vincent's Hosp., N.Y.C., 1949-50; rsch. fellow neuroanatomy Vanderbilt U., 1950-51; gen. surgery asst. resident Cushing VA Hosp., Boston, 1951-52; neurology extern Lenox Hill Hosp., 1952; asst. resident neurosurgery Johns Hopkins Hosp., 1953-55, resident neurosurgeon, 1955-56; practice medicine specializing in neurol. surgery Rochester, N.Y., 1956—; emeritus prof. neurosurgery and neurology U. Rochester Med. Sch. Mem. Soc. Neurol. Surgeons, A.C.S., Am. Assn. Neurol. Surgeons, Congress Neurosurgeons. Home: 800 Allens Creek Rd Rochester NY 14618-3412 Office: Strong Meml Hosp Div Neurosurgery Rochester NY 14642

MCDONALD, LARRY WILLIAM, neuropathologist educator; b. Louisville, Nebr., May 25, 1928; s. Clifford Marion and Tessie Margaret (Higgens) McD.; m. Dorothy Ann Baumgartner, Dec. 26, 1955; children: Laura Ann (dec.), Susan Helen, Lawrence Clifford. BA, U. Calif., Berkeley, 1950; MD, Northwestern U., 1955. Resident in pathology Pondville State Hosp., Walpole, Mass., 1959-60; instr. Harvard U. Med. Sch., Boston, 1961-62; rsch. assoc. U. Calif., Berkeley, 1963-67; assoc. prof. of pathology U. Calif., Davis, 1968-74; prof. Wright State U., Dayton, Ohio, 1975-77; prof. neuropathology U. Ill., Chgo., 1978-94, ret., 1994, prof. emeritus, 1994—. Contbr. articles to Jour. of Neurosurgery, Lab. Investigation, Exptl. and Molecular Pathology, Am. Jour. Pathology. Capt. USAF, 1957-58. Recipient 1st place award Electron Micro Exhibit, Electron Microscopy Soc. of N.Am., 1967. Mem. Internat. Acad. Pathology, AMA (Gold Medal Hektoen award 1968), Am. Assn. Neuropathologists, Coll. Am. Pathologists. Office: Univ Ill Dept Pathology M/C 847 1819 W Polk St Rm 446 Chicago IL 60612-7335

MCDONALD, MAUREEN HELEN, physician, rheumatologist; b. Trenton, N.J., May 6, 1952; d. John James and Mary Theresa (Mikulas) McD. BS in Biology summa cum laude, Tufts U., 1974; MD, U. Pa., 1978. Diplomate Am. Bd. Internal Medicine, sub-bd. Rheumatology. Resident in internal medicine Temple U. Hosp., Phila., 1978-81, fellow in rheumatology, 1981-83; internist, rheumatologist Hill Health Ctr., New Haven, 1983-86; attending physician Yale New Haven Hosp., 1983-86; internist, rheumatologist Maxicare HMO, Langhorne, Pa., 1987-88; attending physician St. Mary Hosp., Langhorne, 1987-88, Mercer Med. Ctr., Trenton, 1988—; rheumatologist Blue Cross/Blue Shield Health Ctr. at Trenton, 1988—, assoc. med. dir. quality and utilization, 1994—. Contbr. articles to profl. jours. Fellow Am. Coll. Rheumatology; mem. AMA (Physicians Recognition award 1989, 92, 95), Phila. Mus. Art, Phi Beta Kappa. Democrat. Roman Catholic. Office: Blue Cross Blue Shield Health Ctr at Trenton 433 Bellevue Ave Trenton NJ 08618

MCDONALD, NANCY ANN, physician assistant; b. Schenectady, N.Y., Feb. 9, 1959; d. Arthur Roderick and Lydia Ann (Giordano) McD. BS in Biology, Ashland (Ohio) U., 1981; student, Bowman Gray Sch. Medicine, 1984-86. Cert. physician asst.; lic., N.Y. Physician asst. Bowman Gray Sch. Medicine, Winston-Salem, N.C., 1986-87, Davidson Cunty Health Dept., Lexington, N.C., 1987-88, Planned Parenthood Health Svcs. Northeastern N.Y., Schenectady, 1988-91, family practice pvt. office, Middleburgh, N.Y., 1995, Ellis Hosp., Schenectady, 1991-95, 95—. Fellow Am. Acad Physician Assts., N.Y. State Soc. Physician Assts.; mem. Capital Area Physician Assts.

MCDONALD, THERESA LAWLOR, nurse practitioner and physician assistant; b. Clinton, Iowa, Oct. 3, 1937; d. Thomas Joseph and Elizabeth (Lawlor) McD.; m. John Harvey Mayo; children: Kelly Mayo, Lorna Mayo, Janis Dochterman. AA, Mt. St. Clara Coll., Clinton, Iowa, 1957; diploma in med. tech., Sch. Med. Tech., Davenport, Iowa, 1959; BSM Physician Asst. Program, U. Iowa, 1974, MA in Edn., 1982, BSN, 1986; Ob-gyn. nurse practitioner, U. Mo., St. Louis, 1992. Advanced RN practitioner Iowa; med. tech. ASCP. Med. technologist James Cahill MD, Preston, Iowa, 1961-68, Anthony Colby MD, Iowa City, Iowa, 1969-72; physician asst. Neighborhood Health Ctr., Rock Island, Ill., 1974-75; medication, treatment nurse Cmty. Care of Clinton County, Charlotte, Iowa, 1989-90; staff nurse Jackson County Pub. Hosp., Maqnokata, Iowa, 1990; nursing instr. Clinton (Iowa) Cmty. Coll. Nursing Program, 1990; tech. writer free lance, Preston, Iowa, 1975-95; physician asst., RN Emma Goldman Clinic for Women, Iowa City, 1975-89, 96; ob.-gyn. nurse practitioner Hillcrest Family Planning Clinic, Dubuque, Iowa, 1992-95; health care cons. freelance, Preston, 1990-95. Author: (books) Gatekeeper Training Manual,1986, The Cervical Cap Handbook, 1988; Contbr. chpts to books also. (1 the Ob-Gyn Book of Yr. 1993). Phone counselor Crisis Ctr., Iowa City, 1971-72, physician asst. and med. technologist Free Med. Clinic, Iowa City, 1971-72, 75; com. mem. JohnsonCounty AIDS Coalition, Iowa City, 1987-89; mem. adminstrv. com. ICARE (Iowa AIDS orgn.), 1988-89.

MCDONALD, WYLENE BOOTH, former nurse, pharmaceutical sales professional; b. Kinston, N.C., Sept. 29, 1956; d. Wiley Truett and Hilda Grey (Brinson) Booth; m. Robert H. McDonald; stepchildren: Stephanie Lynn, Robin Leigh. BSN, Barton Coll., 1979; MSN, East Carolina U., 1984. Pub. health nurse Sampson Co. Health Dept., Clinton, N.C., 1979-81; pub. health coord. New Hanover Co. Health Dept., Wilmington, N.C., 1981-83; med. ctr. liaison Cape Fear Valley Med. Ctr., Fayetteville, N.C., 1984-85; profl. sales rep. Merck, Human Health Div., West Point, Pa., 1985-88; hosp. specialist sales rep. Human Health divsn. Merck, West Point, Pa., 1988-90, sr. prostate health specialist rep., 1990-94; exec. cardiovascular specialist Human Health divsn. Merck, West Point, Pa., ž, 1995—; speaker Coastal Area Perinatal Assn., 1983, Career Week. U. N.C. Sch. Bus., Wilmington, 1987, 88, 89, 93. Fundraiser March of DImes, Fayetteville, 1987, Wilmington, 1991, Am. Heart Assn., Wilmington, 1991-93. Named one of Outstanding Young Women of Am., 1981. Mem. ANA, AAUW, N.C. Nurses Assn., N.C. Pub. Health Assn., Sigma Theta Tau. Home and Office: 108 Seapath Est Wrightsville Beach NC 28480-1964

MCDONNELL, ALICE ELAINE, health services administrator, educator; b. Honesdale, Pa., Oct. 6, 1933; d. Ralph Neville and Ruth Meroe (Budd) Schweighofer; m. John E. McDonnell (dec. Oct., 1988); children: Gwen E., John Jr. BS in Nursing, Columbia U., 1955, Supervision in Nursing, 1957, D. in Pub. Health, 1982; MPA, Marywood Coll., 1977; fellow, Temple U. & U. Pitts., Geriatric Edn. Ctr., 1987. RN, Pa., N.Y. Head nurse Babies Hosp., N.Y.C., 1955-56; from edn. and svc. supr. to dir. profl. svcs. VNA of Lackawanna County, Scranton, Pa., 1956-79; adminstr., mgmt. cons., dir. profl., clin and ednl. ops. Hospice of Pa., Inc., Hospice Found., Inc., 1980-86; home care cons. Interim Health Care, Home Health Svcs., 1986—; adjunct prof. Marywood Coll. Grad. Sch. Arts and Scis., Scranton, Pa., 1978-79; prof. and coord. health svcs. adminstrn. Marywood Coll. Grad. Sch. Arts and Scis., Scranton, 1980—, chair dept. pub. adminstrn., 1982—, chair gerontology inst., 1982—; charge nurse, adminstrv. cons. Ellen Meml. Nursing Ctr., Blakely Pine Health CAre Ctr., Scranton, 1986—; cons. Interim Health Care, Scranton, 1985—; mem. adv. bd. Hospice St. John, Hazelton, Pa., 1994—; bd. dirs. Hosp. Mgmt. Forum. Author: (book) Quality Hospice Care, 1985; contbr. articles to profl. jours. Bd. dirs. Alzheimers Assn., Maria Joseph Manor, Pa. Hospice Network, Am. Cancer Soc., Dunmore Sr. Citizens Ctr., Inc.; bd. dirs. and exec. com. United Way of Scranton. Named Faculty fellow Geriatric Edn. Ctr., U. Pitts. and Temple U.; recipient cert. of appreciation Sr. Care Planning Task Force of Moses Taylor Hosp., Star Achiever award, Duryea Lions Club. Mem. ANA, Nat. League for Nursing, Am. Coll. Healthcare Execs., Am. Pub. Health Assn., Am. Soc. for Pub. Adminstrn., Am. Soc. on Aging., Hosp. Mgmt. Forum of Northeastern Pa. Office: Marywood Grad Sch Dept Arts & Scis 2300 Adams Ave Scranton PA 18509

MCDONNELL, BARBARA, health facility administrator. B, Univ. Ill.; M, Univ. Iowa; JD magna cum laude, Univ. Pa. Law Sch. With Sherman & Howard, 1982-87; staff atty. Colo. Ct. Appeals, 1988-89; law clerk Phila.; legal adv. Gov. Romer, dep. dir. policy and rsch., 1989-90; exec. dir. Colo. Dept. Human Svcs., 1991—. Rep. Nursing Adv. bd., team leader Policy Acad. Team on Families & Children At Risk. Office: Dept Human Svcs 1575 Sherman St Denver CO 80203-1714*

MCDONOUGH, EUGENE FRANCIS, JR., surgeon; b. Boston, Oct. 19, 1930; s. Eugene Francis and Abigail Julia (Barry) McD.; m. Ingrid Anna Barrett, June 8, 1974; 1 child, Eugene Francis III. Student, Harvard Coll., 1952; MD, Tufts U., 1955, MS in Surgery, 1960. Resident surgery Boston City Hosp., 1955-56, 59-62, Meml. Sloan Kettering Cancer Ctr., N.Y.C., 1962-65; instr. surgery Harvard Med. Sch., Boston, 1966-72, asst. prof. clin. surgery, 1972—; mem. surg. staff Faulkner Hosp., Boston, 1966—, New Deaconess Hosp. Contbr. surg. articles to profl. jours., chpt. to book. Fellow ACS (pres. Mass. chpt. 1991), Soc. Surg. Oncology, New Eng. Surg. Soc., Boston Surg. Soc. (v.p. 1989). Home: 23 Bemis Rd Dedham MA 02026-5608 Office: 1658 Centre St West Roxbury MA 02132-1212

MC DONOUGH, JOHN RICHARD, lawyer; b. St. Paul, May 16, 1919; s. John Richard and Gena (Olson) McD.; m. Margaret Poot, Sept. 10, 1944; children—Jana Margaret, John Jacobus. Student, U. Wash., 1937-40; LL.B., Columbia U., 1946. Bar: Calif. 1949. Asst. prof. law Stanford U., 1946-49, prof., 1952-69; asso. firm Brobeck, Phleger & Harrison, San Francisco, 1949-52; asst. dep. atty. gen. U.S. Dept. Justice, Washington, 1967-68; asso. dep. atty. gen. U.S. Dept. Justice, 1968-69; of counsel and ptnr. firm Keatinge & Sterling, L.A., 1969-70; ptnr. Ball, Hunt, Hart, Brown and Baerwitz, 1970-90, Calsmith Ball Wichman Case & Ichiki, L.A., L.A., 1990—; exec. sec. Calif. Law Revision Commn., 1954-59, mem. commn., 1959-67, vice chmn., 1960-64, chmn., 1964-65; participant various continuing edn. programs. Served with U.S. Army, 1942-46. Mem. ABA, State Bar Calif., Los Angeles County Bar Assn., Am. Coll. Trial Lawyers. Democrat. Office: Carlsmith Ball Wichman Case & Ichiki 555 S Flower St Fl 25 Los Angeles CA 90071-2326

MCDONOUGH, JOHN RICHARD, cardiologist; b. Tacoma, Wash., Aug. 25, 1928; s. John Francis and Gladys Ferne (Corrington) McD.; m. Jane Loretta Landolt, Nov. 20, 1954; children: John R. Jr., Stephen G., Patrick K., Catherine A., Thomas G., James M., Mark F. BS, Seattle Coll., 1952; MS in Physiology, Creighton U., 1953, MD, 1954; MPH in Epidemiology, U. Calif., Berkeley, 1959. Diplomate Am. Bd. Preventive Medicine, Am. Bd. Internal Medicine, Am. Bd. Cardiovascular Disease. Rheumatic fever program heart disease control USPHS, Chgo., 1956-58; project dir., CY field study heart disease control USPHS, Claxton, Ga., 1959-62; asst. prof. epidemiology U. N.C., Chapel Hill, 1962-64; chief hypertension sect. USPHS, Washington, 1964-66; resident in medicine USPHS Hosp., New Orleans, 1966-68; sr. fellow cardiology U. Wash., Seattle, 1968-70, assoc. prof. med. cardiology, 1970-75, clin assoc. prof. of medicine, 1975—; pvt. practice Allenmore Med. Ctr., Tacoma, Wash., 1975—. Contbr. articles to profl. jours. Rsch. grant NIH, 1970-75. Fellow ACP, Am. Heart Assn., Am. Coll. Cardiology. Roman Catholic. Home: 702 No 6th St Tacoma WA 98403 Office: Allenmore Med Ctr B-6007 S 19th and Union Sts Tacoma WA 98405

MCDONOUGH, JOHN WILLIAM, orthopaedic surgeon; b. Youngstown, Ohio, Nov. 18, 1942; s. John Joseph McDonough and Alberta Nelson Palmer; m. Jacquelyn Augusta Sansone, Aug. 9, 1969; children: John William III, Jeffrey Keegan. BS, Kings Coll., 1964; DO, U. Osteo. Medicine & Health, Des Moines, 1968. Diplomate Am. Bd. Orthopedic Surgery. Pvt. practice orthopedic surgery Wisconsin Rapids, 1975-79; pres. McDonough Orthopaedic & Sports Medicine Ctr., Wisconsin Rapids, 1979—; sec.-treas. med. staff Riverview Hosp., Wisc. Rapids, 1995-96, pres. 1981-82. Served to capt. U.S. Army, 1970-72, Vietnam. Fellow Am. Acad. Orthopedic Surgeons; mem. Am. Coll. Sports Medicine, Am. Orthopedic Soc. Sports Medicine, Arthroscopy Assn. N.Am., Wood County Med. Soc. (v.p. 1996, pres. 1997). Home: 4540 Church Ave Wisconsin Rapids WI 54494 Office: McDonough Orthopedics 400 Dewey St Wisconsin Rapids WI 54494

MCDONOUGH, MARTHA ROSE, osteopathic physician; b. Charlemont, Mass., Oct. 16, 1944; d. Elmer and Mary (Larry) Sherman; m. John P. McDonough, Aug. 19, 1967; children: John P. IV, Brian. BA magna cum laude, Simpson Coll., Indianola, Iowa, 1985; DO, U. Osteo. Medicine-Health Sci., Des Moines, 1989. Diplomate Nat. Bd. Osteo. Med. Examiners. Chief intern Des Moines Gen. Hosp., 1989-90; resident in family practice Med. Svcs. Sunnyridge, Des Moines, 1990—. Bd. dirs. Indianola Swim Club, 1984-86. G.W. Loerke scholar, 1990. Mem. Iowa Osteo. Med. Assn. Office: 21495 Ridgetop Cir Sterling VA 20166

MCDONOUGH-MEANS, SHARON, physician, pediatric consultant; b. Dayton, Ohio, Sept. 21, 1944; d. Charles Allen and Irene Sarah (Roberts) McDonough; divorced; children: Aaron Charles, Timothy James. BA, Northwestern U., 1966; MD, Ind. U., 1970. Diplomate Am. Bd. Pediats. Resident in pediats. Riley Hosp. for Children, Indpls., 1971-73; staff pediatrician Metro Health Plan, Indpls., 1973-76; mem. pediats. faculty, assoc. dir. ambulatory care U. Ill., Park Ridge, 1976-80; mem. ambulatory care pediats. staff Blank Hosp., Des Moines, 1983; devel. disabilities fellow in pediats. U. Iowa, Iowa City, 1985-87; acute and devel. pediatrician Med. Assocs., Dubuque, Iowa, 1987-90, Child Health Specialty Clinics, Dubuque, 1987-91; physician Developmental-Behavioral Pediats., Des Moines, 1992—. Contbr. articles to profl. jours. Mem. Am. Acad. Pediats. (devel. and behavioral pediats., state commn. on child abuse), Polk County Med. Soc. (del. to Iowa Med. Soc. 1993—), Iowa Med. Soc. (maternal-child health com.), Physicians for Social Responsibility. Home and Office: 900 65th St # 28 Des Moines IA 50312-1056

MCDOUGAL, WILLIAM SCOTT, urology educator; b. Grand Rapids, Mich., 1942; s. William Julian and Verna Wilma (Pasma) McD.; m. Mary Stuart Logan, Sept. 19, 1992; 1 child, Molly Katherine. AB, Dartmouth Coll., 1964; MD, Cornell U., 1968. Intern in surgery U. Hosps., Cleve., 1968-69, resident in surgery, 1969-75, attending urologist, 1977-80; postdoctoral fellow in physiology Yale U., New Haven, 1971-72; postdoctoral fellow in surgery Case-Western Res. U., Cleve., 1972-75; chief, burn study div. Inst. Surg. Rsch. Brook Army Med. Ctr., Ft. Sam Houston, 1975-77; instr. surgery U. Tex., San Antonio, 1975-77; asst. prof. urology Case Western Res. U., Cleve., 1977-78, assoc. prof., 1978-80; assoc. prof. Dartmouth Coll., Hanover, N.H., 1980-84, chmn. dept. urology, 1982-84; prof., chmn. dept. urology Vanderbilt U., Nashville, 1984-90; prof. surgery Harvard Med. Sch., 1991—; chief urology Mass. Gen. Hosp., Boston, 1991—. Office: Mass Gen Hosp Dept Urology Fruit St Boston MA 02114

MCDOUGALL, IAIN ROSS, nuclear medicine educator; b. Glasgow, Scotland, Dec. 18, 1943; came to U.S., 1976; s. Archibald McDougall and Jean Cairns; m. Elizabeth Wilson, Sept. 6, 1968; children: Shona, Stewart. MB, ChB, U. Glasgow, 1967, PhD, 1973. Diplomate Am. Bd. Nuclear Medicine (chmn. 1985-87), Am. Bd. Internal Medicine (gov. 1984-86). Lectr. in medicine U. Glasgow, 1969-76; fellow Harkness-Stanford Med. Ctr., 1972-74; assoc. prof. radiology and medicine Stanford (Calif.) U., 1976-84, prof. radiology and medicine, 1985—. Contbr. numerous articles to sci. jours. Fellow Royal Coll. Physicians (Glasgow), Am. Coll. Physicians; mem. Am. Thyroid Assn., Soc. Nuclear Medicine, Western Assn. for Clin. Research. Office: Stanford U Med Ctr Divsn Nuclear Medicine Stanford CA 94305

MCDOWALL, ROBERT HUGH, anesthesiologist, educator; b. Akron, Ohio, May 4, 1956; s. Robert H. and Julia V. (Chuchu) McD. BA, Coll. Wooster, 1978; MD, U. Cin., 1982. Diplomate Am. Bd. Anesthesiologists, Am. Bd. Pediatrics. Clin. fellow Nat. Cancer Inst., Cin., 1979; resident pediatrics Columbia U. Coll. Physicians and Surgeons, N.Y.C., 1982-85, resident anesthesiology, 1985-87, fellow pediatric anesthesiology and critical care, 1987-88; asst. clin. mem. Meml. Sloan-Kettering Cancer Ctr., N.Y.C., 1989—, med. dir. pediatric anesthesia, 1992—; asst. prof. anesthesiology Cornell U. Med. Ctr., N.Y.C., 1989—. Contbr. articles to profl. jours., chpts. to books. Fellow Mus. Modern Art, N.Y.C., 1988—. Fellow Am. Acad. Pediatrics; mem. Am. Soc. Anesthesiologists, Internat. Anesthesia Rsch. Soc., Soc. Pediatric Anesthesia, Soc. Pediatric Critical Care Medicine, Soc. Critical Care Medicine.

MCDOWELL, BILLY M. L., rodeo clown, health facility administrator; b. Kingfisher, Okla., Jan. 10, 1935; s. Cleo M. and Elizabeth A. (McIntosh) McD.; m. Nancy H. Thomas; 1 child, Tara Brooke. BS in Edn. & Psychology, Central State Coll., Edmond, Okla., 1957; postgrad., U. Okla. Exec. dir. Tulsa Indsl. Clinic, 1980-85, Amethyst Hall Corp., Santa Fe, 1985-86; clin. coord. Mental Health Mgmt., Mukogee, Okla., 1987-88; dir. Still Regional Health Ctr., Jefferson City, Mo., 1990-91; pres. Anchorage Retarded Children's Assn., 1965, Chugach Rehab. Corp., Anchorage, 1966-70, Maine Assn. Substance Abuse Programs, Augusta, 1978-79; pres., treas. State Rehab. Assn., Anchorage, 1964-70. Performing rodeo clown since 1953; rodeo clown, dir., promoter, developer Children's Miracle Network Telethon, 1989; dir., developer, performer comedy program puppets, song & dance, 1985 stic dir. dance workshop, 1980-85; assisted in drafting fed. regulations on alcohol and drug abuse; rsched. and devel. charts on the affect of alcohol on the brain; pioneered habitation theory on alcohol drug treatment. Bd. dirs. Alaska Plan to Combat Mental Retardation, 1966, Nat. Occupational Program Cons., 1980-83; apptd. to Gov's. Blue Ribbon Panel on Alcoholism, Augusta, 1979, Colo. Health Systems Agy., Denver, 1974-75. Named Man of Yr. Rehab. Assn., Anchorage, 1967. Democrat. Home and Office: 154 S Redwood Stillwater OK 74040

MCDOWELL, DONALD ENGLAND, vascular surgeon, educator; b. Zion, Md., Oct. 23, 1924; s. Harry Clayton and Helen Clark (England) McD.; m. May Vanderpool, June 21, 1945 (div. Dec. 1974); children: Duncan Edward, Clyde Benjamin, Glenn Norris, Bruce Allen, Melody Ann McDowell Istrati; m. Amada Paredes, Dec. 21, 1974; children: Joy Lynn, Bonnie Lee. BS cum laude, Wheaton Coll., 1946; MD, Temple U., 1947. Diplomate Am. Bd. Surgery, Am. Bd. Thoracic Surgery. Surg. intern USPHS Hosp., N.Y.C., 1947-48; surg. resident VA Hosps., N.Y.C., 1947-51; sr. asst. surgeon Inst.

Interam. Affairs, USPHS, Paraguay, 1951-53; cardiothoracic resident Presbyn.-U. Pa. Hosp., Phila., 1953-54, 58-59; med. missionary So. Bapt. Fgn. Mission Bd., Asuncion, Paraguay, 1954-74; dir. physician asst. program Alderson-Broaddus Coll., Philippi, W.Va., 1973-75; chief surg. svc. VA Hosp., Clarksburg, W.Va., 1975-80; prof. surgery, chief vascular surgery sect. W.Va. U. Sch. Medicine, Morgantown, 1980—; bd. dirs. Univ. Health Assocs., Morgantown, 1987-91; mem. grievance bd., W.Va. U., Morgantown, 1986-90. Contbr. articles to profl. jours. Bd. dirs. Alliance Christian Sch., Morgantown, 1982-90; mem. internat. students com. Christian and Missionary Alliance Ch., Morgantown, 1983—. Recipient Svc. to Soc. award Wheaton Coll., 1972. Fellow ACS (pres. W.Va. chpt. 1991-92); mem. Southeastern Surg. Congress (governing coun. 1987-95), So. Thoracic Surg. Assn., Internat. Soc. Cardiovascular Surgery, Soc. for Clin. Vascular Surgery, Ea. Vascular Soc. Republican. Baptist. Home: 1204 Parkview Dr Morgantown WV 26505 Office: WV U Dept Surgery Health Scis Ctr Dept Surgery Morgantown WV 26506

MCDOWELL, DONALD L., hospital administrator; b. Indpls., June 9, 1934; married; 5 children. BS Acctg., Ohio State U., 1956; grad. Edn. Adminstrn., U. Fla. Acctg. tng. program Chevrolet divsn. Gen. Motors Corp., Toledo, Ohio, 1956-58, acctg. asst. supr. Chevrolet divsn., 1958-59; acctg. supr. Chevrolet divsn. Gen. Motors Corp., Atlanta, 1959-61; controller U. Fla., Gainesville, 1961-67; dir. mgmt. info. systems Fla. Bd. Regents, Tallahassee, 1967-68; v.p. adminstrv. affairs Fla. Internat. U., Miami, 1969-74; exec. dir. ops. Vanderbilt U., 1974-76, v.p. bus. affairs, 1976-80; exec. v.p., treas. Maine Med. Ctr., 1980-91, interim pres., 1990-91, pres., 1991—; bd. dirs. Maine Bank and Trust; com. mem. So. Assn. Colls. and Schs., program classification com. Nat. Ctr. Higher Edn. Mgmt. Systems; educator Fla. Internat. U.; city mgrs. adv. com. Portland. Mem. Bldg. com. YWCA Portland; chmn. Hosp. adv. com. Maine Health Care Fin. Commn.; at-large mem. House Dels. Am. Hosp. Assn.; Pres'. coun. visitors U. So. Maine; bd. dirs. ARC, Greater Portland United Way, Park Danforth Home for the Aged, Portland C. of C. (pres. 1990-91), Community Health Svcs., Portland Stage Co., Maine Hosp. Assn., Portland Symphony Orchestras, Voluntary Hosps. Am., New England (treas.), Regional C. of C. (chmn.), Maine Devel. Found., Ptnrs. for Progress, New England Healthcare Assembly. Office: Maine Med Ctr 22 Bramhall St Portland ME 04102-3134*

MCDOWELL, ELIZABETH MARY, retired pathology educator; b. Kew Gardens, Surrey, Eng., Mar. 30, 1940; came to U.S., 1971; d. Arthur and Peggy (Bryant) McD. B Vet. Medicine, Royal Vet. Coll., London, 1963; BA, Cambridge U., 1968, PhD, 1971. Gen. practice vet. medicine, 1964-66; Nuffield Found. tng. scholar Cambridge (Eng.) U., 1966-71; instr. dept. pathology U. Md., Balt., 1971-73, asst. prof., 1973-76, assoc. prof., 1976-80, prof., 1980-96, ret., 1996. Co-author: Biopsy Pathology of the Bronchi, 1987; editor: Lung Carcinomas, 1987; contbr. over 120 articles to sci. jours., chpts. to books. Rsch. grantee NIH, 1979-92. Fellow Royal Coll. Vet. Surgeons Gt. Britain and Ireland. Home: 606 W 37th St Baltimore MD 21211

MCDUFFIE, MARCIA JENSEN, pediatrics educator, researcher; b. Phila., Apr. 10, 1949; d. John Calvin and Agnes Margaret (Jakob) J.; children: Kathryn Steere, Joanna Steere, Michael. Student, Duke U., 1967-69; BA cum laude with honors in Biochemistry, U. Pa., 1971; MD with honors, U. N.C., 1981. Diplomate Am. Bd. Pediat. Pediat. intern U. Colo. Health Scis. Ctr., Denver, 1981-82, resident in pediat., 1982-84, asst. prof., 1987-93, rsch. mem. Barbara Davis Ctr. for Childhood Diabetes, 1989-93; postdoctoral fellow div. basic immunology dept. medicine Nat. Jewish Ctr. for Immunology and Respiratory Medicine, Denver, 1984-87; assoc. prof. U. Va. Health Scis. Ctr., Charlottesville, 1993—; reviewer Sci., Diabetes, Jour. Clin. Investigation, European Jour. Pediat., Lab. Investigation. Assoc. editor Jour. Immunology, 1992-94; contbr. articles to profl. jours. Recipient career devel. award Juvenile Diabetes Found., 1992-95; rsch. grantee Juvenile Diabetes Found., 1991-95, Am. Diabetes Assn., 1994-96. Mem. Soc. for Pediatric Rsch., Am. Assn. Immunologists. Office: U Va Health Scis Ctr MR-4 Rm 5116 Charlottesville VA 22908

MCELDOWNEY, RENE, health care educator, consultant; b. Denver, Mar. 31, 1956; d. Raymond James and Barbara Louise (McNeal) Polanis; m. George Adams McEldowney Jr., June 1, 1984. AB, Morris Harvey Coll., Charleston, W.Va., 1977; BS, W.Va. State Coll., 1983; MBA, Marshall U., 1987; PhD, Va. Tech. U., 1994. X-ray technologist Charleston Area Med. Ctr., 1977-79, nuc. medicine technologist, 1979-84; asst. to v.p. acad. affairs Marshall U., Huntington, W.Va., 1984-87, mgmt. instr., 1987-89; asst. prof. Auburn (Ala.) U., 1992—; rsch. cons. Netherland Sch. Govt., Das Hagg, Holland, 1990—; physics cons. Health Physics & Assocs., Roanoke, Va., 1991-92. Founder Food Search, Charleston, 1987-89; mem. Score, Huntington, 1988-89; literacy vol. Ala. Literacy Coun., Montgomery, Ala., 1993—; mem. Montgomery Jr. League, 1992—. Recipient scholarship Oxford U., 1991. Mem. ASPA, Am. Acad. Mgmt., Mortar Bd., Kappa Kappa Gamma. Office: Auburn U 1224 Haley Ctr Auburn AL 36849

MCELROY, EMILIE LIN, mental health professional; b. San Francisco, Jan. 10, 1954; d. Earl Edwin and Carolyn Ardell (Brickley) McE.; m. Robert Louis HItsman Jr., Feb. 25, 1984; children: Lynda Nicole, Devin Joseph, Jennifer Maighdlin, Rachel Siobhan, Ian Jeremiah, Elizabeth Ailis. Student, U. Calif., Davis, 1986, U. Louisville, 1986—; BS, NYU, 1990. Artistic dir., gen. mgr. Sunshine Children's Theatre, Davis, 1977-83; counselor Progress Ranch, Inc., Davis, 1981-83; youth worker shelter house YMCA, Louisville, 1983-84, house coord., 1984-85; house dir. Schizophrenia Found. Ky., Louisville, 1985-91; dir. Creative Cons., Lyndon, Ky., 1985—; advocate, counselor Louisville Rape Relief Ctr., 1984—. Organizer Calif. Dem. State Conf., 1982; apptd. spl. adv. Jefferson County (Ky.) Juvenile Ct. Dependency Docket; commd. layminister Ctrl. Ky. Cath. Ch., 1995. Mem. NAFE, Psi Chi. Roman Catholic. Home and Office: 9110 Farnham Dr Lyndon KY 40242-3431

MCELROY, THOMAS HEWITT, dentist; b. St. Louis, Feb. 23, 1952; s. George Laverty and Beth (Kellogg) McE.; m. Sarah Eileen Topping, Feb. 26, 1983; children: Sarah Elizabeth, Rachel Meredith, Timothy Hewitt. BA in Biology, U. Mo., St. Louis, 1974; DDS, U. Mo., Kansas City, 1978, Grad. Diploma in Prosthodontics, 1980; Cert. Maxillofacial Prosthetics, U. Tex. Cancer Ctr., 1981. Lic. dentist, Mo. Asst. clin. prof. dentistry U. Mo., Kansas City, 1978, 82—; dental oncologist/prosthodontist Ellis Fischel Cancer Ctr., Columbia, Mo., 1981-85; cons. physician Truman Meml. VA Med. Ctr., Columbia, 1984-85, acting chief dental svc., 1986, staff dentist/prosthodontist, 1985—; site visit evaluator Nat. Cancer Inst., New Orleans, 1984. Contbr. articles to profl. jours. Pres. Mo. United Meth. Men, Columbia, 1992-93. Recipient Vets. Affairs award for achievement Dept. Vets. Affairs, 1987, 92, Cert. of Recognition, ACS, 1984, Cert. of Appreciation, Am. Cancer Soc., Tex. divsn., 1980. Fellow Am. Assn. Hosp. Dentists, Am. Acad. Maxillofacial Prosthetics; mem. ADA, Internat. Soc. for Oral Oncology (founding mem.), Am. Coll. Prosthodontists, U. Tex. Cancer Ctr.-M.D. Anderson Assocs. (founding mem.). Republican. Office: Harry S Truman Meml Med Ctr 800 Hospital Dr Columbia MO 65201

MCELVAIN, MARY PARKER, nursing educator, women's health nurse; b. Oak Harbor, Wash., Sept. 26, 1956; m. George W. McElvain, Apr. 5, 1980; children: Scott William, Zachary James, Emily Brooks. BSN cum laude, U. Southwestern La., 1978. RN, Colo.; cert. in inpatient obstetric nursing. Staff nurse labor/delivery unit Lafayette (La.) Gen. Hosp.; staff nurse labor/delivery dept. U. Kans. Med. Ctr., Kansas City, Menorah Med. Ctr., Kansas City; instr. Penn Valley Community Coll., Kansas City, coord. maternal-child edn.; staff nurse labor and delivery, homecare St. Mary's Hosp. Mem. AWOHNN, Ob-GYN Assn.,P.C. (charge nurse), Mo. Nurse's Assn.

MCENTEE, MARY SUSAN, nutrition services specialist; b. Estherville, Iowa, Aug. 3, 1961; d. Melvin George and Mary Ann (Hatten) Fangman; m. Scott William McEntee, Aug. 4, 1984; children: Mathew, Zachary, Jacob. BA in Food and Nutrition in Bus., U. No. Iowa, 1983; postgrad., Drake U., 1995—. Food svc. supr., cafeteria/catering supr., purchaser Iowa Meth. Med. Ctr., Des Moines, 1983-93, asst. dir. patient svcs. and prodn., 1983-93; adminstrv. asst. Human Gene Therapy Rsch., Des Moines, 1993-94; dir. food and nutrition svcs. Ctrl. Iowa Health Sys., Des Moines, 1994—. Mem. allocations bd. United Way of Ctrl. Iowa, Des Moines, 1992-94; elder care reviewer Area Agy. on Aging, Des Moines, 1994—. Fellow ASHFSA (Iowa Hawkeye chpt. edn. chair 1986, membership chair 1988, pres.-el;ect 1991, pres. 1992-93, past pres. 1994); mem. East Des Moines C. of C. (bd. dirs. 1996). Roman Catholic. Office: Ctrl Iowa Health Sys 1200 Pleasant St Des Moines IA 50309-1453

MCENTYRE, JAMES M., ophthalmologist; b. Calhoun, Ga., May 23, 1934; s. James Ferguson and Etta (Payne) McE.; m. Carolyn Ann Shane, June 8, 1963. BS in Chemistry, U. Ga., 1955; MD, Med. Coll. Ga., Autusta, 1959. Diplomate Am. Bd. Ophthalmology. Instr. surgery U. Mo. Med. Ctr., Columbia, 1966-67; asst. prof. surgry U. Ky. Med. Ctr., Lexington, 1968-69; pvt. practice Sarasota, Fla., 1969—; clin. asst. prof. ophthalmology U. South Fla. Med. Coll., Tampa, 1972-76; med. dir. Lions Eye Bank U. Mo., 1966, U. Ky. Eye Bank, 1968-69. Contbr. articles to profl. jours. Recipient Letter of Comendation, USN Bur. of Medicine and Surgery, India, 1960; Appreciation award Mo. Lions Club, 1966, Physician's Recognition award AMA, 1974-95; Ann Winship Bates Leach scholar, 1968. Office: 2255 S Tamiami Trail Sarasota FL 34239

MCEWAN, ROBERT NEAL, molecular biologist, medical consultant; b. Washington, Sept. 6, 1949; s. Thomas Cornealius and Esther (Johnson) McE.; m. Elizabeth Mary Ross, Aug. 24,, 1973; 1 child, Amy Elizabeth; stepchildren: Gary W. Tizard, Jacqueline A. Klein. BS, Va. Mil. Inst., 1971. Med. technician USPHS, Washington, 1971-72; biologist McGuire Va. Hosp., Richmond, 1972-75; rsch. assoc. Frederick (Md.) Cancer Rsch. Facility, 1975-84, The Upjohn Co., Kalamazoo, Mich., 1984-93; crit. care cons. The Upjohn Co., Balt., 1993-95; transplant specialist Roche Labs., Inc., 1995—; adj. faculty Med. Sch. Northwestern U., Chgo., 1984-87; mem. indsl. adv. bd. Cen. Va. Gov.'s Sch., 1992-95; founder, leader Inch by Inch Bayview Med. Ctr., 1995—. Exec. prodr., creator: (video for cable TV) You Can Climb Again, The Organ Transplant Challenge, 1995; patentee in field. Leader 4-H, Kalamazoo, Mich., 1988-90; founder, mem. Adventures in Spaces, pres. 1988-90; mem. Gull Lake Middle Sch. PTA, pres. 1987-89, Gull Lake Area Community Vols., pres. 1988. Recipient Outstanding Svc. award Middle Sch. Educators Assn., 1988, STAR award Kalamazoo Gazette, Vol. Action Ctr., 1989, Svc. Leadership award Gull Lake Area Community Vols., 1990. Mem. Am. Soc. Microbiology, Nat. 4-H Sci. Tech. Design Team. Home: 402 Cypress Ct Bel Air MD 21015-6001 Office: Roche Labs Inc 340 Kingsland St Nutley NJ 07110-1199 Office: Roche Laboratories, Inc. 340 Kingsland St Nutley NJ 07110-1199

MCEWEN, GERALD NOAH, JR., bio scientist executive; b. Washington, 1943; s. Gerald Noah and Kathryn Lyle (Kimes) McE.; m. Carol Sue Edwards, Aug. 27, 1966; children: Jennifer Lyle, Kathleen Schofield. B.S. in Life Sci., Ind. State U., Terre Haute, 1966, A.M. in Life Sci., Ind. State U., 1968; Ph.D. in Physiology and Biophysics, U. Ill.-Urbana, 1973, J.D. George Wash U., 1989, Vis. lectr. U. Ill., Urbana, 1973-74; research assoc. NASA-Ames Research Ctr., Moffett Field, Calif., 1974-76; research physiologist SRI-Internat., Washington, 1976-77; mgr. Biosci. Group, SRI Internat., 1977-78, sr. bioscientist and dir. health hazard info. program, 1978-80; ingredient safety coordinator Cosmetic, Toiletry and Fragrance Assn., Washington, 1980-82, dir., 1982-86, v.p. sci., 1986—. Industry liaison representive to cosmetic ingredients review expert panel and to the US FDA dental product panel. Recipient Tech. Achievement award NASA, 1976; Superior Achievement award, SRI Internat., 1978; NRC research grantee, 1974-76. Mem. Am. Physiol. Soc., FASEB, Theta Alpha Phi., Am Acad. Dermatology, Am. Contact Dermatitis Soc. Methodist. Lodge: Masons. Contbr. Editor to several texts, frequent speaker at National and internat. seminars on personal care product safety regulation; Contbr. articles to profl. jours. Home: 2799 N Quebec St Arlington VA 22207-5212 Office: 1110 Vermont Ave NW Washington DC 20005-3522

MCFADDEN, JAMES FREDERICK, JR., surgeon; b. St. Louis, Dec. 5, 1920; s. James Frederick and Olivia Genevieve (Imbs) McF.; m. Mary Cella Switzer, Sept. 15, 1956 (div. Sept. 1969); children: James Frederick, Kenneth Michael, John Switzer, Mary Cella, Joseph Robert; m. Deanne Nemec Puls, Apr. 29, 1989. AB, St. Louis U., 1941, MD, 1944. Intern Boston City Hosp., 1944-45; ward surgeon neorsurg. and orthopedics McGuire Gen. Hosp., Richmond, Va., 1945; ward surgeon in internal medicine Regional Hosp., Fort Knox, Ky., 1946; ward surgeon plastic surgery Valley Forge Gen. Hosp., Phoenixville, Pa., 1946-47; intern St. Louis City Hosp., 1947-48; resident in surgery VA Hosp., St. Louis, 1948-52; clin. instr. surgery St. Louis U., 1952-62; gen. practice medicine specializing in surgery St. Louis, 1952—; mem. staff St. Mary's Hosp., 1952-77, St. John's Mercy Hosp., 1952-74, Desloge Hosp., 1952-62, Frisco RR Hosp., 1953-64, DePaul Hosp., 1954—, Christian Hosp., 1955-66, 83—. Mem. St. Louis Ambassadors, 1979-81; officer St. Louis County Aux. Police, 1973-75. Served to capt. AUS, 1945-47. Recipient Eagle Scout award, Order of the Arrow Honor award Boy Scouts Am. Fellow ACS, Royal Soc. Medicine, Internat. Coll. Surgeons; mem. St. Louis Med. Soc., Am. Coll. Occupl. and Environ. Medicine, Am. Soc. Clin. Hypnosis, Internat. Soc. Hypnosis, Am. Assn. RR Surgeons, St. Louis U. Student Conclave, Alpha Sigma Nu, Phi Beta Pi. Roman Catholic. Home: PO Box 411933 Saint Louis MO 63141-1933 Office: 11500 Olive Blvd Saint Louis MO 63141-7143

MCFADDEN, ROBERT STETSON, hepatologist; b. Houston, Mar. 29, 1951; s. David Barnett and Phyllis Reed (Gowell) McF.; m. Addie Elizabeth Hunt, Mar. 23, 1975; children: William Gordon, Elizabeth Stetson. BS in Biology, Baylor U., 1973; MD, U. Tex., Galveston, 1977. Diplomate Am. Bd. Internal Medicine; cert. gastroenterology Am. Bd. Internal Medicine. Intern in internal medicine La. State U. Med. Sch., New Orleans, 1977-78, resident in internal medicine, 1978-81; staff physician clinic Pub. Health Hosp., New Orleans, 1981; fellow gastroenterology U. Ala., Birmingham, 1981-83; fellow hepatology U. Miami, Fla., 1983-84; gastroenterologist Diagnostic Clinic Houston, 1984-87, Oklahoma City Clinic, 1987-92; hepatologist Okla. Transplantation Inst., Oklahoma City, 1993—; cons. gastroenterology Diagnostic Clinic of Houston, 1984-87, Oklahoma City Clinic, 1987-92; cons. liver diseases and liver transplant medicine Okla. Transplant Inst., Oklahoma City, 1993—. Contbr. articles to profl. jours. Mem. ACP, AMA, Am. Assn. for Study of Liver Diseases, Internat. Liver Transplantation Soc., Okla. State Med. Assn. Republican. Baptist. Home: 2600 Coffee Creek Edmond OK 73003 Office: Okla Transplantation Inst 3435 NW 56th St Oklahoma City OK 73112

MCFARLAND, KAY FLOWERS, medical educator; b. Daytona Beach, Fla., Jan. 27, 1942; d. Ernest Clyde and Sarah Elizabeth (Holder) Flowers; m. Dee Edward McFarland, Aug. 18, 1963; children: Grace, Joy, Eric, Sarah. BS, Wake Forest Coll., 1963; MD, Bowman Gray Sch. Medicine, 1966. Diplomate Am. Bd. Internal Medicine, Endocrinology, Geriatrics. Intern N.C. Bapt. Hosp., Winston-Salem; resident medicine Cleve. Clinic; fellow endocrinology Med. Coll. Ga., Augusta, from instr. to asst. prof. medicine, 1971-77; assoc. prof. to prof. ob-gyn. Sch. Medicine U. S.C., Columbia, 1977-86, prof. medicine Sch. Medicine, 1986—, assoc. dean continuing edn. Sch. Medicine, 1986-91. Contbr. chpts. to books and articles to profl. jours. Fellow ACP, ACE; mem. Am. Diabetes Assn. (Profl. award 1975, Woman of Valor award 1996). Office: USC Sch Medicine Ste 506 Two Medical Park Columbia SC 29203

MCFARLAND, LYNNE VERNICE, pharmaceutical executive; b. San Antonio, Tex., June 3, 1953; d. Earle Clifford and Avis Marie (Jones) Olson; m. Marcus Joseph McFarland, July 27, 1975. BS in Microbiology, Portland State U., 1975, MS, 1980; PhD in Epidemiology, U. Wash., 1988. Pub. Health Cert. Rsch. asst. U. Oreg. Health Sci. Ctr., Portland, 1977-79, lab. supr., 1980-82; intern Wash. State Pub. Health Labs, Seattle, 1983; teaching asst. Dept. Epidemiology U. Wash., Seattle, 1984, rsch. asst., 1984-88, postdoctoral researcher Dept. Med. Chemistry, 1988, lectr. Dept. Med. Chemistry, 1988, rsch. asst. prof., 1991—; dir. scientific affairs Biocodex, Inc., Seattle, 1988—; reviewer McGraw-Hill Book Co., N.Y.C., 1982; editorial reviewer Ob-Gyn, L.A., 1989—, Jour. of Infect Diseases, 1991, 95—, Vet. Adminstrn., 1991; also review for gastroenterology, 1990, clin. infectious diseases, 1995—. Reviewer Gastroenterology; contbr. articles to profl. jours. Lobbyist environ. issues Wash. State Biotech. Assn., Seattle, 1990; vol. Literacy Plus, Seattle, 1990. Recipient Poncin scholarshp, Seafirst Bank, Seattle, 1985-88. Mem. Am. Soc. Microbiology, Soc. for Epidemiol. Rsch., Soc. Microbiol. Ecology and Diseases, Wash. Assn. of Epidemiology. Office: Biocodex Inc 1910 Fairview Ave E Ste 208 Seattle WA 98102-3620

MCFARLAND, MARY ANN, nursing educator, academic administrator; b. Boston, July 19, 1939; d. Mario and Eva Mary (Luciano) Brambilla; m. Joseph Roy McFarland, Apr. 26, 1970; 1 child, Stephen Roy. Diploma, Mass. Gen. Hosp. Sch. Nursing, Boston, 1960; BS, Boston Coll., 1965; MS in Nursing, U. Pa., 1967; EdD, Portland (Oreg.) State U., 1989. Staff nurse, asst. head nurse Mass. Gen. Hosp., 1960-67; clin. nurse specialist U. Minn. Hosps., Mpls., 1967-70; asst. prof. nursing Columbus (Ga.) Coll., 1970-71, 74-75; from instr. to asst. prof. U. Hawaii, Honolulu, 1971-74; asst. prof. Oreg. Health Scis. U., Portland, 1975-77, assoc. prof., 1977-94; prof., 1994—; assoc. dean sch. Nursing Oreg. Health Scis. U., Portland, 1983—. Author: Interpreting Cardiac Arrythmias, 1975, Nursing Implications of Laboratory Tests, 1982, 87, 93; contbr. articles to profl. jours. Recipient Disting. Service award Hawaii Heart Assn., Honolulu, 1974; grantee USPHS, 1964-65, 65-67. Mem. Am. Nurses Assn., Oreg. Nurses Assn., Nat. League for Nursing, Sigma Theta Tau, Phi Kappa Phi, Kappa Delta Pi. Roman Catholic. Home: 507 Palo Alto Dr Vancouver WA 98661-6624 Office: Oreg Health Scis U 3181 SW Sam Jackson Park Rd Portland OR 97201-3011

MCFARLAND, MILES MCCAIN, pathologist; b. Ripley, Miss., Aug. 28, 1952; s. Daniel Miles and Anne (Solomon) McF.; m. Barbara Ruth Axelrod, Oct. 7, 1979; children: Graham, Danielle. BA, U. Va., 1974; MD, U. Pa., 1979. Cert. in anatomic and clin. pathology. Intern in internal medicine U. Md. Hosp., 1979-80; resident in anatomic and clin. pathology Pa. Hosp., 1980-84; fellow in surg. pathology Hosp. of U. of Pa., 1984-85; pathologist Pa. Hosp., Phila., 1985-88, Med. Coll. Pa., Phila., 1988-92, Grad. Hosp., Phila., 1992—. Fellow Coll. Am. Pathologists; mem. Am. Soc. Clin. Pathologists, Alliance for Continuing Med. Edn., U.S.-Canadian Acad. Pathology. Office: Grad Hosp Pathology Dept 1800 Lombard St Philadelphia PA 19146-1414

MCFARLAND, ROBERT BRUCE, physician; b. Ames, Iowa, Sept. 18, 1929; s. Julian Ecwart and Winnie Florence (Goering) McF.; m. Zoë Euphrosyne Bucuvalas, June 1, 1958; children: Laura Ann, Bruce Damon. BA, Kenton Coll., 1950; MD, U. Iowa, 1954. Intern San Francisco Gen. Hosp., 1955; house officer Mass. Gen. Hosp., Boston, 1957-59; asst. resident U. Colo. Med. Ctr., Denver, 1959-61; physician pvt. practice, Boulder, Colo., 1961-76, 78-93; prof. U. Mo., Kansas City, 1976-78. Contbr. articles to profl. jours. Vestryman St. John's Episcopal Ch., Boulder, 1966-69; jail physician Boulder County, Kansas City, 1972-75, 76-78; co-founder Parenting Place, Boulder, 1984-95; cons., bd. health No. Cheyenne Tribe, Lame Deer, Mont., 1976-84. Comdr. USNR-R, 1955-78. Home: 2300 Kalmia Ave Boulder CO 80304

MCFARLAND, SUSAN LOUISE, nurse, consultant; b. Reno, Aug. 10, 1958; d. William Henry and Bobbie Ann (Brown) McF. BSN, La. State U., 1981; MPH, U. Tex., Houston, 1992, postgrad., 1992—. RN, La., Tex.; registered emergency med. technician and instr., ACLS instr., BLS instr.; cert. in hyperbarics and flight nursing. Staff nurse, charge nurse, acting head nurse emergency dept. Charity Hosp. La., New Orleans, 1981-84; charge nurse, acting head nurse Ochsner Health Care Facility La. World Exposition, New Orleans, 1984; head nurse emergency dept. Ochsner Found. Hosp., New Orleans, 1984-86, spl. relief flight nurse Ochsner flight care dept., 1986-90; payment systems coord. Ochsner Med. Ctr. Fin. Adminstrn., New Orleans, 1986-89; clin. cons. to bus. office Ochsner Found. Hosp., New Orleans, 1989-90; spl. relief staff, charge nurse Ochsner Emergency Dept., 1986-93; home health/pvt. duty nurse Vis. Nurse Assn., Houston, 1992-94; staff nurse emergency dept. Westbury Hosp., Houston, 1992-94; occupational health nurse Occupational Safety and Health Cons., Houston, 1991—; indsl. hygienist hazard evaluation and tech. assistance bd. NIOSH, Cin., 1993, rsch. indsl. hygienist industry wide studies br., 1994-96; sr. rsch. asst. dept. environ. health and safety M.D. Anderson Cancer Ctr., Houston, 1993-94. Vol. ARC. Mem. Am. Conf. Govtl. Indsl. Hygienists, Am. Assn. Occupational Health Nurses, Women in Aviation-Internat., Alpha Delta Pi. Home: 7900 N Stadium Dr Unit 114 Houston TX 77030

MCFARLANE, JOE ROBERT, JR., lawyer, medical association executive, investor; b. Brownwood, Tex., Aug. 9, 1936; s. Joe Robert and Helen Virginia (Russell) M.; m. Jane Arnot, June 6, 1961; children: Elizabeth Ann, Amy Helen, Joe Robert III. Student, Stanford U., 1954-57; MD, Baylor U., 1961; JD, U. Tex. Sch. of Law, 1993. Diplomate Am. Bd. Ophthalmology. Practice medicine specializing in ophthalmology San Antonio, 1965—; pres. Ophthalmology Assocs. San Antonio, 1986-90; pvt. practice law specializing in health care law, 1993—; mem. practitioner ophthal. adv. faculty Am. Acad. Ophthalmology, San Francisco, 1975-80; clin. prof. U. Tex., San Antonio, 1983—. Contbr. articles to profl. jours. Pres. high sch. Spirit Group, Alamo Heights, Tex., 1980; treas. Parent Tchr. Student Orgn., Alamo Heights, 1981; mem. bd. control Nix Med. Ctr., San Antonio, 1984—. Maj. USAR, 1962-70. Fellow ACS; mem. Am. Acad. Ophthalmology (practitioner adv. faculty, 1975-80, com. interspecialty and allied health edn. 1985-88), Am. Eye Study Club, Am. Bd. Ophthalmology (assoc. examiner 1976-92), Am. Acad. Ophthalmology Coun. (councillor 1981-88, regional coordinator 1987-88, chmn. com. credentials 1987-88), San Antonio Soc. Ophthalmology (pres. 1975), Tex. Ophthalmology Assn. (councillor 1975-78, Ophthalmic Mut. Ins. Co. bd. dirs., underwriters and claims com.). Republican. Presbyterian. Clubs: San Antonio Country, Argyle, Giraud, Conopus, Town. Office: Cox & Smith Inc 112 E Pecan St Ste 1800 San Antonio TX 78205

MC FEE, ARTHUR STORER, physician; b. Portland, Maine, May 1, 1932; s. Arthur Stewart and Helen Knight (Dresser) McF.; m. Iris Goeschel, May 13, 1967. B.A. cum laude, Harvard U., 1953, M.D., 1957; M.S., U. Minn., 1966, Ph.D., 1967. Diplomate: Am. Bd. Surgery. Intern U. Minn. Hosp., 1957-58, resident in surgery, 1958-65; asst. prof. surgery U. Tex. Med. Sch., San Antonio, 1967-70; asso. prof. U. Tex. Med. Sch., 1970-74, prof., 1974—; co-dir. surg. ICU Med. Ctr. Hosp., San Antonio, 1968—; spl. cons. on emergency med. care text to AAOS. Contbr. articles to profl. jours. Served with USNR, 1965-67. Fellow ACS; mem. AMA, Am. Assn. History of Medicine, Assn. Acad. Surgery, Tex. Med. Assn., Bexar County Med. Soc., Tex. Surg. Soc., Western Surg. Assn., San Antonio Surg. Soc., Soc. Surgery Alimentary Tract, So. Med. Assn., N.Y. Acad. Scis., Royal Soc. Medicine, So. Surg. Assn., Internat. Surg. Soc., Halsted Soc., J. Bradley Aust Surg. Soc. Home: 131 Brittany Dr San Antonio TX 78212-1721 Office: 7703 Floyd Curl Dr San Antonio TX 78284-6200

MCGAGHIE, WILLIAM CRAIG, medical educator; b. Chgo., June 28, 1947; s. William and Vivian Iona (Skoglund) M.; m. Pamela Wall, Mar. 13, 1976; children: Michael Craig, Kathleen Ann. BA, Western Mich. U., 1969; MA, Northwestern U., 1971, PhD, 1973. Lectr., Northwestern U., Evanston, Ill., 1973-74; asst. prof. U. Ill., Chgo., 1974-78; asst. prof. U. N.C., Chapel Hill, 1978-81, assoc. prof. sch. of medicine, 1981-89, prof., 1989-92; prof. preventive medicine and prof. med. edn. Northwestern U. Med. Sch., 1992—. Author: Competency-Based Curriculum Development, 1978; editor: Handbook for the Academic Physician, 1986; cons. editor College Teaching, Review Ednl. Rsch.; mem. editl. bd. Evaluation and the Health Professions, 1981—; contbr. numerous articles to profl. jours. Lic. lay reader Episcopal Ch. Grantee USPHS, Culpepper Found., Wash. Sq. Health Found. Mem. APA (v.p.), Am. Ednl. Research Assn. Avocations: running, gourmet cooking. Home: 2153 Beechwood Ave Wilmette IL 60091-1505 Office: Northwestern U Med Sch Office Med Edn 3-130 Ward Bldg W117 303 E Chicago Ave Chicago IL 60611-3008

MCGARVEY, WILLIAM K., otolaryngologist, surgeon; b. Marion, Ind., Aug. 3, 1937; s. Eugene J. and Rosemary (Kelley) McG.; m. Janet Lee Prentice, Feb. 27, 1975; children: Erika, Kevin. AB in Anatomy and Physiology, Ind. U., 1959, MD, 1962. Diplomate Bd. Otolaryngoly and Head and Neck Surgery. Intern San. Francisco Gen. Hosp., 1962-63; resident in otolaryngology and head and neck surgery Ind. U. Med. Sch. and assoc. hosps., Indpls., 1963-67; practice medicine specializing in otolaryngology and head and neck surgery San Francisco, 1969-74, Indpls., 1974—; asst. prof. otolaryngology and head and neck surgery Ind. U. Sch. Medicine, 1974; asst. prof. otolaryngology and head and neck surgery, U. Calif. Med. Sch., San Francisco, 1969-74; chmn. dept. otolaryngology and head and neck surgery, Community Hosp., Indpls., 1976-78. Served with maj. U.S. Army, 1967-69, Vietnam. Fellow ACS, Am. Acad. Otolaryngology and Head and Neck Surgery, Am. Acad. Facial Plastic and Reconstructive Surgeons; mem. Am. Acad. Otolaryngic Allergy, Undersea Med. Soc. Hyperbaric Medicine.

Republican. Methodist. Clubs: Meridian Hills (Indpls.) Country, Skyline (Indpls.). Lodge: Masons. Home: 1816 Wood Valley Dr Carmel IN 46032-3561 Office: Ind Otolaryngology-Head and Neck Surgery 5508 E 16th St Indianapolis IN 46218

MCGAUGHEY, CHARLES GILBERT, retired research biochemist; b. San Diego, Sept. 8, 1925; s. Gilbert Arthur and Louisa Ellen (Inskeep) McG. BA, U. Calif., Berkeley, 1950; MA, U. So. Calif., 1952. Diplomate Am. Inst. Oral Biology. Scientist radiol. hazards evaluation U.S. Naval Radiol. Def. Lab., San Francisco, 1952; research biochemist VA Med. Ctr., Long Beach, Calif., 1953-81; prin. investigator studies dental caries and oral cancer Oral Diseases Research Lab., 1978-81. Contbr. articles to profl. jours. Grantee Nat. Inst. Dental Research, 1965. Mem. AAAS. Republican. Home: 337 N Winnipeg Pl Long Beach CA 90814-2564

MCGAVOCK, BRENDA WEISHAAR, clinical psychologist; b. Kansas City, Mo., Jan. 14, 1952; d. Williston Penfield and Alice (Mitchell) Bunting; m. Douglas John Weishaar, june 15, 1978 (div. Apr. 1986); children: Cara, Josephine; m. Robert Kent McGavock, Aug. 10, 1991. BA with honors in Psychology, U. Kans., 1974; MS in Clin. Psychology, U. Wyo., 1978, PhD in Clin. Psychology, 1980. Lic. psychologist, Mo. Staff psychologist Mental Hygiene Clnic, Harry S. Truman Meml. VA Hosp., Columbia, Mo., 1980-83; dir. psychology Charter Hillside Hosp., Columbia, 1984-85; pvt. practice Ctr. for Family & Individual Coun., Columbia, 1982-89; staff mem. Boone Hosp. Ctr., Columbia, 1987—; pvt. practice Fletcher & Weishaar, Columbia, 1990—; treas., bd. dirs. Mo. Behavioral and Mental Health Specialists, Columbia, 1993—; stress mgmt. cons. Boone Hosp. Ctr., Columbia, 1987—; asst. trainer Neuro-Linguistic Programming, Columbus, Ohio, 1988-89; mem. profl. rev. panel Counseling Svcs., U. Mo., Columbia, 1987—. Dir. fed. women's program Harry S. Truman Meml. VA Hosp., Columbia, 1980-83; comm.dir./chaperone Hinkson Valley Pony Club, Columbia, 1990—; vol. Sexually Abused Women, Columbia, 1995; Sunday sch. tchr. Unity Ctr. Columbia, 1987. Mem. APA, ASTD, Am. Soc. Clin. Hypnosis, Mo. Psychol. Assn., Nat. Register Health Svc. Providers in Psychology, Women's Network Columbia C. of C. Office: Fletcher & Weishaar 2716 Forum Blvd Ste 2B Columbia MO 65203

MCGEE, JAMES O'DONNELL, pathologist; b. Mossend, Lanarkshire, Scotland, July 27, 1939; s. Michael and Bridget (Gavin) McG.; m. Anne Lee, Aug. 27, 1961; children: Leeanne, Sharon, Damon. MB, ChB, Glasgow (Scotland) U., 1962, PhD, 1969, MD, 1973; MA, Oxford (Eng.) U., 1975. Jr. dept. pathology U. Glasgow, 1963-65, rsch. fellow, 1965-67, lectr., 1967-69, 71-73, sr. lectr., 1973-75; MRC fellow Roche Inst. Molecular Biology, Nutley, N.J., 1969-70, vis. scientist, 1970-71; prof., head Nuffield dept. pathology and bacteriology U. Oxford, Eng., 1975—; mem. Com. on Safety of Medicines, London, 1984-89; mem. sci. and grants coms. Cancer Rsch. Campaign, London, 1978-91; fellow Linacre Coll., Oxford, 1975; mem. sci. adv. bd. Eurocell, 1992—; head Oxford Telepathology Coordinating Centre, 1994—; guest lectr. Hellenic Pathology Soc., 1994, Telemedicine, 1995; mem. European Telepathology Com., 1995. Author: (with R.S. Patrick) Biopsy Pathology of the Liver, 1980, 2d edit., 1988; editor: In situ Hybridization, 1990, (with J.M. Polak) Oxford Textbook of Pathology, vols. 1, 2a, 2b, 1992, (with P.G. Isaacson and N.A. Wright) Diagnostic Molecular Pathology, vols. 1, 2, 1992, The Natural Immune System: The Macrophage, 1992, (with C.E. Lewis) The Natural Immune System: The NK Cell, 1992. Named Disting. Vis. Scientist, Roche Inst. Molecular Biology, Nutley, 1989. Fellow Royal Coll. Phys. and Surgs., Royal Coll. Pathologists (Kettle Meml. lectr. 1980). Office: U Oxford Nuffield Dept Pathology and Bacteriology, John Radcliffe Hosp, Oxford OX3 9DU, England

MCGEE, JOHN EDWARD, retired gynecologist; b. Granite City, Ill., Nov. 25, 1928; s. James Anthony and Anna Elizabeth McGee; m. Margaret Ann Grems, Oct. 17, 1953; children: Michael, Joseph, Ann, Jane, Brian, Robert, James, Maureen. BS, St. Louis U., 1949, MD, 1953. Cert. Am. Bd. Ob-Gyn. Intern Ancker Hosp., St. Paul, 1953-54; resident in internal medicine U. Minn., Mpls., 1954; resident in ob-gyn St. Louis U. Hosp., 1957-60; chief dept. ob/gyn Ft. Madison (Iowa) Hosp., 1965; chief dept. maternal child health Burlington (Iowa) Med. Ctr., 1983, chief of staff, 1986; pres. S.E. Iowa Health Sys. Agy., 1975, Burlington Preferred Provider Orgn., 1991-94. Pres. Ft. Madison Sch. Bd., 1969. Lt. comdr. USNR, 1955-57. Fellow Am. Coll. Ob/Gyn; Mem. AMA, Am. Urogynecological Soc., Iowa Med. Soc. Republican. Roman Catholic. Home and Office: 1005 Denmark Hilltop Fort Madison IA 52627-2749

MCGEE, MARY ALICE, health science research administrator; b. Winston-Salem, N.C., Oct. 14, 1950; d. C.L. Jr. and Mary Hilda (Shelton) McG. AB, Meredith Coll., 1972. Tchr. Augusta (Ga.) Schs., 1972-73; specialist grants Med. Sch. Brown U., Providence, R.I., 1974-76; profl. basketball player, 1975-76; dir. research adminstn. Med. Sch. Brown U., Providence, 1976-94; tchr., coach Providence Country Day Sch., East Providence, R.I., 1995—. Bd. dirs. Sojourner House, Providence, 1983—, v.p., 1986, 91, treas. 1987-89. Mem. Soc. Rsch. Adminstrs., Nat. Coun. U. Rsch. Adminstrs., R.I. Assn. Women in Edn. Home: 121 Plain St Rehoboth MA 02769-2540 Office: Providence Country Day Sch 2117 Pawtucket Ave East Providence RI 02914-1724

MCGEE, MICHAEL DAVID, physician; b. San Jose, Calif., Apr. 19, 1958; s. Daniel LaRoy and Joan Rose (Johnson) McG.; m. Shayda Majidi-Ahi, June 15, 1991; 1 child, Shayan. BS, Stanford U., 1979, MD, 1985. Diplomate Am. Bd. Neurology and Psychiatry. Assoc. med. dir. Addison Gilbert Hosp., Gloucester, Mass., 1989-91; dir. addictions svcs. New Eng. Meml. Hosp., Stoneham, Mass., 1991-94; psychiatrist-in-chief Solomon Mental Health Ctr., Lowell, Mass., 1994-95; med. dir. Merit Behavioral Care, Burlington, Mass., 1994—; med. dir., addictions svcs. Choate Health Mgmt., Lynn, Mass., 1995—; pres. Psych Solutions, Wenham, Mass., 1991—. With USAF, 1975-77. Rsch. grantee Nat. Inst. Drug Abuse, 1996, Med. Scientist Tng. Program award Fed. Govt./Stanford U., 1980. Mem. Am. Psychiat. Assn., AMA, Mass. Psychiat. Assn., Am. Soc. Addiction Medicine, Am. Coll. Physician Execs. Unitarian. Home: 41 William Fairfield Dr Wenham MA 01984 Office: MBC Ste 335 20 Mall Rd Burlington MA 01803

MC GHAN, WILLIAM FREDERICK, pharmacist, educator; b. Sacramento, July 6, 1946; s. Roy William and Nelleen (Zischang) McG.; children: Monica, Matthew, Brian, Brent; m. Marilyn Dix Smith. Community scholar, U. Calif.-San Francisco, 1966-70; Pharm.D., U. Calif., San Francisco, 1970; Ph.D., U. Minn., 1979. Clin. intern U. Calif. Med. Center, San Francisco, 1969-70; clin. resident U. Calif. Med. Center, 1970-71; pharmacy coordinator Appalachian Student Health Project, 1970; staff dir. Student Am. Pharm. Assn., Washington, 1971-74; chmn. community health Student Am. Pharm. Assn., 1969-70; staff dir. Project SPEED, nat. drug edn. program, 1971-73; assoc. dir., 1973-74; staff dir. Acad. Pharm. Scis., Washington, 1974-76; mem. pub. policy com. Acad. Pharm. Scis., 1974-78, chmn. publs. com., 1975-76; grad. fellow, instr. Coll. Pharmacy, U. Minn., 1976-78; asst. prof. Sch. Pharmacy, U. So. Calif., 1978-82; prof., coord. div. adminstrv. and behavioral scis. Coll. Pharmacy U. Ariz., Tucson, 1982-89; founder, sr. rschr. Inst. for Pharm. Econs., 1989—; prof. Phila. Coll. Pharm. & Sci., 1989—; mem. membership com. Nat. Coord. Coun. for Drug Edn., 1974-75; mem. steering com. Am. Pharm. Assn. Drug Interactions Program, 1973-76; Acad. Pharm. Scis. liaison to NAS-NRC, 1975-76. Editor Student Am. Pharm. Assn. News, 1971-74; editor Acad. Reporter, 1974-76. Recipient Archambault award Am. Soc. Cons. Pharm. Fellow Am. Found. for Pharm. Edn., Am. Assn. Pharm. Sci. (chmn. econs. sect. 1988); mem. Am. Pharmacy Assn., Acad. Pharm. Rsch. and Sci. (chmn. econ., social and adminstrv. scis. sect. 1987-88, pres. 1988), Am. Soc. Hosp. Pharmacists, Am. Assn. Colls. Pharmacy (bd. dirs. 1995-97, chmn. pharm. adminstrn. sect. 1989-90, chmn. coun. of faculties 1995-96, Lyman award), Internat. Assn. Pharmoecons. and Outcomes Rsch. (founder; pres. 1995-96), Delta Sigma Phi, Rho Chi, Phi Kappa Phi, Sigma Xi. Office: Phila Coll Pharmacy & Sci 600 S 43rd St Philadelphia PA 19104-4418

MCGILL, CHARLES MORRIS, physician, consultant; b. Seattle, Oct. 25, 1908; s. Robert Allen and Angela Folsom (Chase) McG.; m. Edith Hansen, Nov. 30, 1935; children—Charles Robert, Kenneth Chase. Student Pacific U., 1926-27; B.S., U. Wash., 1931; M.D., Vanderbilt U., 1935; M.P.H., Harvard U., 1945. Diplomate Am. Bd. Occupational Medicine. Commd. med. officer USPHS, 1935, advanced through grades to lt. col., 1947; med. dir. Tacoma Smelter Co., 1945-57; practice medicine specializing in occupational medicine, Tacoma, 1957-62; assoc. prof. occupational medicine U. Wash., Seattle, 1950-60; med. dir. Weyerhaeuser Co., Tacoma, 1960-72; regional med. dir. Western Electric Co., Kent, Wash., 1973-80; dir. employee health Consol. Hosps., Tacoma, 1959—; med. cons. Wash. Pub. Power Supply System, Richland, Wash., 1982— dir. employee health St. Joseph Hosp., Tacoma, 1976—. Contbr. articles to profl. jours. Fellow Am. Occupational Med. Assn. (bd. dirs. 1963-69), Am. Acad. Occupational Medicine, Am. Pub. Health Assn.; mem. Pierce County Med. Soc., Wash. Med. Assn., AMA. Home: 10124 36th St NW Gig Harbor WA 98335-5814

MCGILL, GRACE ANITA, occupational health nurse; b. Lawrence, Mass., Mar. 8, 1943; d. Joseph John and Tina Mary (Sicurella) Tabacco; m. Howard L. McGill, Jr., Feb. 28, 1965; children: Cynthia, Deborah, David. RN, Mass. Gen. Hosp., 1963; BS, Lesley Coll., 1987; MS in Mgmt., Lesley Grad. Sch., 1990. Cert. occupl. health nurse. Nurse Phillips Acad., Andover, Mass., 1963-65, 97th Gen. Hosp., Frankfurt, Germany, 1966, Highsmith-Rainey Hosp., Fayetteville, N.C., 1968, Lawrence (Mass.) Gen. Hosp., 1969-78, Baldpate Psychiat. Hosp., Georgetown, Mass., 1978-79; nursing staff St. Joseph's Hosp., Lowell, Mass., 1980-81; head nurse St. Joseph's Hosp., Lowell, 1981-83; occupl. health nurse Wang Labs., Inc., Lowell, 1983-87, corp. safety specialist, 1987-90; health svcs. adminstr. Loral Infrared and Imaging Sys., Inc., Lexington, Mass., 1990-93; supr. health svcs. Osram Sylvania, Inc., Danvers, Mass., 1993-95; occupl. health nurse Occupl. Health Strategies, Inc., Chelmsford, Mass., 1995—; contract instr. Sch. Pub. Health, Harvard U.; contract adminstr. occupl. health programs at Hewlett-Packard-Chelmsford, OHS, Inc., Madbury, N.H.; treas. Am. Bd. Occupational Health Nurses, 1996—. Mem. NAFE, Am. Assn. Occupl. Health Nurses, Am. Soc. Safety Engrs., Mass. Gen. Hosp. Nurses Alumnae Assn., Lesley Coll. Alumnae. Episcopalian. Home: 81 Lancaster Dr Tewksbury MA 01876-1322

MCGILL, STEPHEN ANDREW, chief operating officer medical group; b. Louisville, Sept. 10, 1957; s. Wallace C. and Marjorie R. (Wilson) McG.; m. Mary Lovell, Oct. 9, 1982; children: Cathryn Page, Philip Andrew. BA, Vanderbilt U., 1979; MPA, U. Ga., 1981. Cert. assn. exec. Planner Tenn. Dept. Econ. and Community Devel., Chattanooga, 1981-84; spl. projects advisor Chattanooga Area Regional Coun. Govt., 1984-87; exec. dir. Chattanooga and Hamilton County Med. Soc., 1987-95. Mem. exec. com. Walker County (Ga.) Dem. Party, 1987-95; grad. Walker County Leadership Program, LaFayette, Ga., 1988. Mem Medical Group Mgmt. Assn., Kiwanis (bd. dirs. Chattanooga Valley 1987-89). Democrat. Baptist. Home: 8020 Rosemere Way Chattanooga TN 37421 Office: Caduceus Medical Assocs Ste D 6028 Shallowford Rd Chattanooga TN 37422

MCGILLICUDDY, JOAN MARIE, psychotherapist, consultant; b. Chgo., June 23, 1952; d. James Neal and Muriel (Joy) McG. BA, U. Ariz., 1974, MS, 1976; PhD, Walden U., 1996. Cert. nat. counselor. Counselor ACTION, Tucson, 1976; counselor, clin. supr. Behavioral Health Agy. Cen. Ariz., Casa Grande, 1976-81; instr. psychology Cen. Ariz. Coll., Casa Grande, 1978-83; therapist, co-dir. Helping Assocs., Inc., Casa Grande, 1982—, v.p., sec., 1982—; cert. instr. Silva Method Mind Devel., Tucson, 1986—. Mem. Mayor's Com. for Handicapped, Casa Grande, 1989-90, Human Svcs. Planning, Casa Grande, 1985-95. Named Outstanding Am. Lectr. Silva Midn Internat., 1988-96. Mem. ACA. Office: Helping Assocs Inc 1901 N Trekell Rd Casa Grande AZ 85222-1706

MCGING, NOREEN MARIE, health services professional; b. Chgo.; d. John Francis and Nora Philomena (Barnicle) McG. BSN, Loyola U., Chgo., 1981. Cert. med.-surg. nurse, ANA. Staff nurse surg. unit St. Joseph Hosp. and Health Care Ctr., Chgo., 1981-86, dir. staffing support svcs., 1986-89; project dir. Cath. Health Alliance for Met. Chgo., Ill., 1989-95; dir. quality mgmt. Transitional Hosp. Corp., 1995—. Active Art Inst. Chgo., Ill., 1980—, Chgo. Coun. on Fgn. Rels., 1991—. Mem. Am. Orgn. Nurse Execs. (exec. mem.), Ill. Orgn. Nurse Execs. (exec. mem.), Nat. Assn. for Healthcare Quality (exec. mem.), Ill. Assn. for Healthcare Quality (exec. mem.).

MCGINLEY, WILLIAM HUGH, psychology educator; b. L.A., Sept. 16, 1935; s. Daniel Leo and Hazel Mae (Dailey) McG.; m. Pathy Ruth Howard, Apr. 24, 1964 (div. May 1986); children: Bryan Keith, Laura Michelle. AA, Long Beach City Coll., 1959; BA, UCLA, 1961; MA, Calif. State U., Long Beach, 1964; PhD, U. Ky., 1968. Lic. psychologist, Wyo. Co. rep. Bendix Corp., Teterboro, N.J., 1961-62; social worker Los Angeles County, Long Beach, 1964; asst. prof. psychology U. Man., Winnipeg, Can., 1968-70; prof. U. Wyo., Laramie, 1970—, dir. grad. program experimental psychology, 1988-92; cons. HM Psychol. Svcs., Laramie, 1976—. Contbr. articles to profl. jours. Vice-mayor City of Laramie, 1980-87, councilman, 1978-88, mem. land use planning commn., 1982-88; mem. goals com. Wyo. Assn. Municipalities, 1983-88. Served as sgt. USAF, 1953-56. Fellow NIH, 1964-66; grantee NIH, 1971-73, State of Wyo., 1976-78, Can. Council, 1968-70. Mem. Am. Assn. Applied and Preventive Psychology, Soc. Personality Assessment. Home: 3411 Alta Vista Dr Laramie WY 82070-5046 Office: U Wyo Dept Psychology Laramie WY 82071

MCGINLEY, WILLIAM JOHN, nursing and rehabilitation center administrator; b. Sioux City, Iowa, June 2, 1953; s. William John and Rosemary Adele (English) McG.; m. Susan Fellows, June 2, 1984; children: Sarah Ann, Marie Alyson. BS, Boston State Coll., 1978; MBA, Boston U., 1989. Adminstr. several head injury rehab. ctrs. Greenery Rehab. Group, Inc., 1980-86; v.p. ops. Greenery Rehab. Group, Inc., Newton, Mass., 1986-93; adminstr. Harrington House Nursing and Rehab. Ctr., Walpole, Mass., 1993—. Fellow Am. Coll. Healthcare Adminstrs. (cert.). Office: Harrington Nursing & Rehab Ctr 160 Main St Walpole MA 02081

MCGINN, EILEEN, public health advisor, researcher; b. Phila., Mar. 29, 1947. BA cum laude, CUNY, 1968; MPH, U. Pitts., 1974. Tchr. English Peace Corps, Dogondoutchi, Niger, 1968-70; tchr. sci. Diocese of Bklyn., 1971-72; clinic dir. Monsour Med. Ctr., Jeannette, Pa., 1974-76; grants officer Assn. for Voluntary Surg. Contraception, N.Y.C., 1976-79; program officer Planned Parenthood Fedn., N.Y.C., 1979-81; chief of party USAID/Zaire, Kinshasa, 1983-85; dep. chief of party John Snow, Inc., Nepal, Kathmandu, 1986-89; program mgr. Asia Assn. Voluntary Surg. Contraception, N.Y.C., 1989-92; cons., 1992—; cons. CEDPA, Washington, 1985, Population Svcs. Internat., Washington, 1985, Assn. Voluntary Surg. Contraception, Kenya and Tanzania, 1982, Bangladesh, 1989, USAID, Togo, 1993, John Snow/SEATS, Papua New Guinea, 1994. Author: Field Worker's Manual, 1989, Nurse's Manual, 1989; contbr. articles to profl. jours. N.Y.S. State Regents scholar, 1964-68, NYU scholar, 1982; USPHS grantee, 1972-73. Mem. APHA, Nat. Coun. for Internat. Health. Office: 210 E 15th St New York NY 10003-3936

MCGINN, FRANCIS PETER, gastroenterological and endocrine surgeon, consultant; b. Liverpool, Eng., July 28, 1940; s. Ronald and Mary Isabella (Morton) McG.; m. Drusilla Patience Grafton, Sept. 11, 1965; children—Piers Russell, Dominic Stuart, Joanna Frances Mary, Ross Andrew. M.B., B.S., London U., 1963, D. Obst., Royal Coll. Ob-Gyn, 1965, M. Phil., 1970, M.S., 1975; FRCS, Royal Coll. Surgeons Eng. 1969. Lectr. physiology Kings Coll., London U., 1965-67; sr. house officer Bristol Royal Infirmary, 1967-70; registrar Frenchay Hosp., Bristol, 1970-72; lectr. surgery Profl. Surgical Unit, Southampton U., 1972-76 cons. surgeon Southampton U. Hosp., 1976—; dir surgery Southampton U. Hosps, 1996— Surgeons, Southampton, 1983—. Mem. Surg. Research Soc., Assn. Surgeons of Gt. Britain and North Ireland. Presbyterian. Clubs: Royal Lymington Yacht, Royal Southampton Yacht. Avocations: sailing; tennis; cycling. Home: Monkswell House Palace Ln, Beaulieu, Hampshire SO42 7YG, England Office: Southampton Gen Hosp, Tremona Rd Southampton, Hampshire SO9 4XY, England

MCGINN, KERRY ANNE, clinical nurse; b. San Francisco, Sept. 12, 1942; d. Robert M. and Barbara Jean (Dorr) Mullen; m. Arthur J. McGinn, Aug. 26, 1961; children: Michael, Kathleen, John, Steven. BA, Calif. State U., Sacramento, 1973; BSN, U. Calif., San Francisco, 1976; MA, San Francisco State U., 1982; postgrad., U. Calif., San Francisco, 1996—. Cert. oncology nurse. Clin. RN USPHS, San Francisco, 1976-81, VA Med. Ctr., San Francisco, 1982-84, San Francisco Gen. Hosp., San Francisco, 1984-87; clin. nurse Planetree Model Hosp. Unit Calif. Pacific Med. Ctr., San Francisco, 1987-92; nurse coord. Breast Care Ctr. U. Calif., San Francisco/Mount Zion, 1993, coord. Cancer Resource Ctr., 1994; home care nurse U. Calif., San Francisco/Mt. Zion, 1995—. Co-author: The Ostomy Book, 1980, 2d edit., 1992, The Informed Woman's Guide to Breast Health, 1992, The Ostomy Book for Nurses, 1985; co-author: Women's Cancers, 1992. Recipient Outstanding Book award Med. Self-Care mag. Mem. United Ostomy Assn. (hon. life), Oncology Nursing Soc., Bay Area Oncology Nursing Soc., Sigma Theta Tau. Home: 217 9th Ave San Francisco CA 94118-2208

MCGINN, PATRICIA FERRIS, professional counselor; b. Riverside, Calif., July 30, 1938; d. John Mark and Kathryn (Miller) Ferris; m. Bernard John McGinn, July 10, 1971; children: Daniel Ferris, John Ferris. BA magna cum laude, St. Mary's Coll., Notre Dame, Ind., 1960; MA, U. Notre Dame, 1965, U. D.C., 1972. Lic. clin. profl. counselor. Tchr. St. Joseph's High Sch., South Bend, Ind., 1962-63; tchr. St. Cecilia's Acad., Washington, 1965-68, sch. counselor, 1969-71; tchr. St. Patrick's Acad., Washington, 1968-69; family therapist The Depot, Chgo., 1972-78; dir. counseling ctr. St. Mary's Coll., 1978-80; pvt. practice Chgo., 1980—. Mem. ACA, Am. Mental Health Counselors Assn., Ill. Counseling Assn., Ill. Mental Health Counselors Assn. (exec. dir. 1993—, co-chair govt. rels. com. 1989-93), Coalition Ill. Counseling Orgns. (exec. dir. 1994—). Democrat. Roman Catholic. Office: 5847 S Blackstone Ave Chicago IL 60637-1818

MCGINNIES, ELLIOTT MORSE, psychologist, educator; b. Buffalo, Sept. 19, 1921; s. Elliott Morse and Mabel Christina (Hussong) McG.; m. Bessie Yeh, Jan. 27, 1967; children: Michelle, Lisa, Amy. BA, SUNY-Buffalo, 1943; MA, Brown U., 1944; PhD, Harvard U., 1948. Teaching fellow Harvard U., 1944-47; asst. prof. U. Ala., 1947-52; assoc. prof., then prof. U. Md., 1952-70; prof., chmn. dept. psychology Am. U., 1970-86, prof. emeritus, 1987— ; vis. scholar U. Calif., Berkeley, 1987-88; Fulbright prof. Nat. Taiwan U. With AUS, 1943. Fellow Am. Psychol. Assn.; mem. Eastern Psychol. Assn., Psychonomic Soc., Sigma Xi. Author: Social Behavior: A Functional Analysis, 1970, The Reinforcement of Social Behavior, 1971, Attitudes, Conflict and Social Change, 1972, Perspectives on Social Behavior, 1994. Office: The Am Univ Dept of Psychology 4400 Massachusetts Ave NW Washington DC 20016-8001

MC GINNIS, JAMES MICHAEL, physician; b. Columbia, Mo., July 12, 1944; s. Leland Glenn and Lillian Ruth (Mackler) McG.; m. Patricia Anne Gwaltney, Aug. 4, 1978; children—Brian, Katherine. A.B., U. Calif., Berkeley, 1966; M.A., M.D., UCLA, 1971; M.P.P., Harvard U., 1977. House officer in internal medicine Boston City Hosp., 1971-72; internat. med. officer HEW, 1972-74; dir. Office for Asia and Western Pacific, 1974-75; state coordinator smallpox eradication program WHO, India, 1974-75; fellow Harvard Center for Community Health and Med. Care, Boston, 1976-77; cons. to sec. HEW, Washington, 1977; dep. asst. sec. for health, dir. office disease prevention HEW, 1977-95, asst. surgeon gen., 1980-95, acting dir. office of rsch. integrity, 1992-93; scholar-in-residence Nat. Acad. Scis., Washington, 1995—; instr. medicine George Washington U. Med. Sch., 1973-75; adj. prof. pub. policy Duke U., 1979-81; chair, sec. task force on smoking and health; chair exec. com. HHS Environ. Health Policy Com.; mem. U.S. Japan Leadership program; chair World Bank/European Commn. Task Force on Reconstrn. of Health Sector, Bosnia, 1996—. Mem. editl. bd. Jour. Med. Edn., 1975-78, Jour. Preventive Medicine, 1987—, Jour. Health Promotion, 1992—; editor-in-chief: Healthy People 2000, Surgeon General's Report on Nutrition and Health, Determining Risks to Health. Served with USPHS, 1972-75, 77—. Recipient Arthur S. Flemming Pub. Svc. award, 1979, USPHS Disting. Svc. medal, 1989, Surgeon Gen.'s medallion, 1995, Fed. Profile in Leadership award, 1989, Wilbur Cohen award, 1995, award for excellence APHA, 1995. Fellow Am. Coll. Epidemiology, Am. Coll. Preventive Medicine. Office: 330 C St SW Washington DC 20201-0001

MCGINNIS, MICHAEL PATRICK, psychotherapist; b. Madison, Wis., Oct. 4, 1950; s. James and Patricia Jane (Cole) McG.; m. Carol Ann Bailey, Aug. 8, 1982; children: Arielle Dominque, Chandra Eden. Student, U. Wis., 1968-69, U. Maine, 1971-73; BA, Sonoma State U., 1980, MA, 1984. Cert. marriage, family and child counselor, Calif. Offset printer Portland (Maine) Printing Co., 1970-71, Pronto Prints, Madison, 1972-74; mental health specialist Sheltered Workshop, Madison, 1975-77; mental health worker social svc. dept. Treatment Alternatives to Street Crimes, Santa Rosa, Calif., 1977-79; counselor Nat. Coun. on Alcoholism, Santa Rosa, 1978-79, exec. dir. Sonoma County, 1979-81; counselor, trainer Sonoma County Family Svc. Agy., Santa Rosa, 1981-86; pvt. practice, Healdsburg, Calif., 1985—; trainer, cons. domestic violence treatment Calif. Dept. Mental Health, 1979-84, YWCA Women's Emergency Shelter, Santa Rosa, 1980-86. Mem. Calif. Assn. Marriage and Family Therapists (clin.), Am. Profl. Soc. on Abuse on Children (clin.), Calif. Profl. Soc. on Abuse of Children (clin.). Democrat. Home and Office: 610 Alta Vista Dr Healdsburg CA 95448-4651

MCGINNIS, PATRICK BRYAN, mental health counselor; b. Bellville, Ill., June 17, 1948; s. Raymon Lee and Virginia B. (Wiggins) McG.; 1 child, Patrick Bryan II. BS, Rollins Coll., 1977, MS in Criminal Justice, 1981; MA in Counseling Psychology, Norwich U., 1996. Cert. hypnotherapist, criminal justice addictions profl., criminal justice specialist-master addictions counselor. Ct. liaison officer, probation officer, classification spec. State of Fla. Dept. Corrections, Polk County, 1975-87; victim intervention program coord./therapist Peace River Ctr. for Personal Devel., Inc., Lakeland, Fla., 1987-90; clin. social worker State of Fla. Dept. Corrections/South Fla. Reception Ctr., Miami, 1991-92; counselor CareUnit of Coral Springs' Carepsychcenter, Coral Springs, Fla., 1992-93; psychotherapist Ctr. for Human Potential, Ft. Lauderdale, Fla., 1993—; counselor Unity Counseling Ctr./Unity Ch. of Ft. Lauderdale, 1993-94; vocat. rehab. counselor Fla. Divsn. Vocat. Rehab., Ft. Lauderdale, 1995—. With USAF, 1968-69. Recipient State of Fla. Clinician of Yr. award Fla. Coun. for Cmty. Mental Health, 1990; named Clinician of Yr., Peace River Ctr. for Personal Devel., 1980 Law Enforcement Officer of Yr., Greater Lakeland Area Am. Legion. Home: 8560 NW 20th Ct Sunrise FL 33322-3802 Office: Ctr for Human Potential Ste 103 1881 NE 26th St Ste 103 Fort Lauderdale FL 33305

MCGIVERN, DIANE, nursing educator. PhD, NYU, 1972. RN. Head divsn. nursing NYU, N.Y.C. Fellow AAN. Office: New York Univ Hosp Rm 429 50 W 4th St New York NY 10012*

MC GLYNN, SEAN PATRICK, physical chemist, educator; b. Dungloe, Ireland, Mar. 8, 1931; came to U.S., 1952, naturalized, 1957; s. Daniel and Catherine (Brennan) McG.; m. Helen Magdalena Salacz-von Dohnanyi, 4Apr. 11, 1955; children: Sean Ernst, Daniel Julian, Brian Charles, Sheila Ann, Alan Patrick. B.S., Nat. U. Ireland, 1951, M.S., 1952; Ph.D., Fla. State U., 1956. Fellow Fla. State U., 1956, U. Wash., 1956-57; mem. faculty La. State U., 1957—, prof. chemistry, 1964—, Boyd prof. chemistry, 1967—, dean Grad. Sch., 1981-82, vice chancellor for research, 1981-91; asso. prof. biophysics Yale U., 1961; Humboldt prof. physics U. Bonn, W.Ger., 1979-80; cons. to pvt. cos. Author: (with others) Molecular Spectroscopy of the Triplet State, 1969, Introduction to Applied Quantum Chemistry, 1971, Photophysics and Photochemistry in the Vacuum Ultraviolet, 1985, The Geometry of Genetics, 1988; editor Wiley-Interscience Monographs in Chem. Physics; contbr. over 400 articles and chpts. to profl. pubs. Fellow Research Corp., 1960-63; Sloan fellow, 1964-68; recipient award Baton Rouge Council Engrng. and Sci. Socs., 1962-63; Sr. Scientist award Alexander von Humboldt Found., 1979; Disting. Research medal U. Bologna, Italy, 1979. Mem. Am. Chem. Soc. (S.W. regional award 1967, Fla. sect. award 1970, Coates award 1977), AAAS, Am. Phys. Soc. Home: 1056 E Lakeview Dr Baton Rouge LA 70810-4621

MCGONAGLE, DUNCAN FRANCIS, mental health nurse, substance abuse counselor; b. Brooklyn, N.Y., May 6, 1939; s. John and Kathleen (Rooney) McGonagle; m. Gloria Maria Carrubba, Dec. 5, 1987. AA, Allan Hancock, 1964; AAS in Nursing, CUNY, 1992. Substance abuse counselor Pritikin Longevity Ctr., Santa Monica, Calif., 1978-84; paramedic N.Y.C. Emergency Med. Svc., 1987-92; psychiatric nurse Bellevue Hosp. Ctr., N.Y.C., 1992—; founder Methadone Anonymous, N.Y. aux. police officer N.Y.C. Police Dept., 1985—. With USN, 1956-60, 1961-62, Vietnam. Recipient Nat. award for Clin. Excellence in Nursing, Nat. Nurses Soc. on Addictions, 1995. Mem. Blue Knights, Knights of Life, Rolls Royce Owners Club, Harley Owners Group. Roman Catholic. Home: 73 Verona St Brooklyn NY 11231-1612

MCGOVERN, JOHN HUGH, urologist, educator; b. Bayonne, N.J., Dec. 18, 1924; s. Patrick and Mary (McGovern) McG.; m. Mary Alice Cavazos, Aug. 2, 1980; children by previous marriage: John Hugh, Robert, Ward, Raymond. BS, Columbia U., 1947; MD, SUNY, Bklyn., 1952. Diplomate Am. Bd. Urology. Rotating intern Bklyn. Hosp., 1952-53; asst. resident in surgery Bklyn. VA Hosp., 1953-54; with urology N.Y. Hosp., 1954-56; exchange surg. registrar West London Hosp., Eng., 1956-57; resident in urol. surgery N.Y. Hosp., 1957-58, rsch. asst. pediatric urology, 1958-59, asst. attending surgeon James Buchanan Brady Found., 1959-61, assoc. attending surgeon, 1961-66, attending surgeon, 1966—; asst. in surgery Med. Coll. Cornell U., 1957-59, asst. prof. clin. surgery, 1959-64, assoc. prof., 1964-72, prof., 1972—; attending staff in urology Lenox Hill Hosp., 1969—, in-charge urology, 1969-83; cons. urology Rockefeller Inst., St. Vincent's Hosp., Mercy Hosp., Phelps Meml. Hosp.; chmn. coun. on urology Nat. Kidney Found., 1982. Contbr. articles to profl. jours., chpts. to books. Lt. M.C., U.S. Army, 1942-45. Recipient Conatvoy mos medal Chile, 1975, Tree of Life award Nat. Kidney Found., 1990; named Huesped de Honor, Mimunicipalidad de Guayaquil (Ecuador), 1976; award in urology Kidney Found. N.Y., 1977, Sir Peter Freyer medal, Galway, Ireland, 1980. Fellow N.Y. Acad. Medicine (exec. com. urol. sect. 1968-72, chmn. 1972), ACS (credentials com. 1991—), Am. Acad. Pediatrics (urological); mem. AMA (diagnostic and therapeutic tech. assessment bd. 1991—, diagnostic and therepautic tech. assessment program panel 1991, DATTA panel 1991—), Am. Assn. G.U. Surgeons, N.Y. State Med. Soc. (chmn. urol. sect. 1975), Med. Soc. County N.Y., Am. Urol. Assn. (hon. mem. 1994—, pres.-elect 1988-89, pres. 1989-90, pres. N.Y. sect. 1979-80, N.Y. rep. exec. com. 1982-87, socioecons. com. 1987, chmn. fiscal affairs rev. com. 1987, chmn. awards com. 1990, time and place com. 1989-90), N.Y. State Urol. Soc. (exec. com. 1982—), Pan Pacific Surg. Assn., Am. Assn. Clin. Urologists (pres.-elect 1987-88, pres. 1988-89, bd. dirs. 1984—, mem. interpersonal rels. com. 1975—, govt. rels. com. 1989-90, program com. 1989-90, nominating com. 1989-90), Assn. Am. Physicians and Surgeons, Pan Am. Med. Assn. (diplomate 1981—), Urol. Investigators Forum, Soc. Pediatric Urology (pres.-elect 1979-80, pres. 1980-81), Am. Trauma Soc., Kidney Found. (med. adv. bd. N.Y. sect., trustee, 1979) Société Internationale d'Urologie (exec. com. U.S. sect.); hon. mem. Sociedad Peruana de Urología, Sociedad Guatemale de Urología, Sociedad Ecuadorians de Urologia, Royal Coll. Surgeons (London). Home and Office: 53 E 70th St New York NY 10021-4941

MCGOVERN, THOMAS BOARDMAN, physician, pediatrician; b. St. Louis, Sept. 26, 1940; s. John Thomas and Hazel Marie (Boardman) McG.; m. Jane Emily Keyes, June 17, 1967; children: John Thomas, Erin Kathleen, Ann Michal, Robert Andrew. AB, Dartmouth Coll., Hanover, N.H., 1962; MD, U. Mo., Columbia, 1965. Diplomate Am. Bd. Pediatrics, 1976, 89. Maj. USAF, 1966-72; rotating intern M. Co. Gen. Hosp., Indpls., 1966-67; flight med. officer USAF, Kovea, Calif., 1967-69; pediatric resident USAF Hosp., K. AFB, Miss., 1969-71; pediatrician USAF, Westover AFB, Mass., 1971-72, partnership, Binghamton, N.Y., 1972-86, Assocs. in Medicine, Johnson City, N.Y., 1986-91, United Med. Assocs., Johnson City, N.Y., 1991—; pediatric dept. chmn. Binghamton Gen. Hosp., 1980-82, sec.-treas. med. staff, 1982-84; pediatric dept. chmn. Lourdes Hosp., Binghamton, 1984-86, 93-95; clin. asst. prof. pediatrics Health Science Ctr., Syracuse, N.Y., 1980—. Cons. pediatrician Handicapped Children's Assn., Johnson City, 1973-78, mem. bd. dirs. 1980-91. Fellow Am. Acad. Pediatrics; mem. N.Y. State Med. Soc., Broome County Med. Soc. (bd. dirs. 1972—). Republican. Roman Catholic. Home: 4 Cornell Ave Binghamton NY 13903 Office: United Med Assocs PC 601 Riverside Dr Johnson City NY 13790

MCGOWAN, DENNIS PATRICK, physician; b. July 17, 1956. BS in Engring. with distinction, Iowa State U., 1978; MS in Engring., U. Newcastle upon Tyne, Eng., 1980; MD, U. Iowa, 1983. Diplomate Am. Bd. Orthop. Surgery. Intern in gen. surgery SUNY, Syracuse, 1984-88, resident in orthop. surgery, 1988-89; staff orthop. surgeon Med. Svc. Ctr. Liberty Mut. Ins. Co., Boston, 1988-89; assoc. dept. orthop. surgery Beth Israel Hosp., Boston, 1988-89; asst. chief, dir., cons. Dept. Vet. Affairs Med. Ctr., Des Moines, 1989—; clin. asst. prof. dept. orthop. surgery Coll. of Medicine U. Iowa, Iowa City, 1989—, adj. asst. prof. Coll. of Engring., 1989—; orthop. surgeon Nat. Wheelchair Games, Dept. Vet. Affairs Med. Ctr., New Orleans, 1990, Miami, Fla., 1991, Dayton, Ohio, 1992, San Antonio, 1993; ops. engring. intern Quaker Oats Co., Chgo., 1977; mfg. engr. Govt. Avionics, Rockwell Internat., Cedar Rapids, Iowa, 1978; orthop. cons. Iowa Found. for Med. Care, West Des Moines, 1991—, Health Care Resources, Prin. Mut. Ins. Co., Des Moines, 1990—; lectr. in field. Contbr. articles to profl. jours. Recipient grants. Mem. AMA, Am. Acad. Orthop. Surgeons, Am. Assn. Clin. Anatomists, Paralyzed Vets. of Am. (hon.), Tau Beta Pi. Home: 4126 Ardmore Rd Des Moines IA 50310 Office: VA Med Ctr 3600 30th St Des Moines IA 50310

MCGRATH, EDMUND, podiatric surgeon; b. Bklyn., Oct. 29, 1955; s. Edmund John and Suzanne (Frawley) M. BS in Biology, U. South Fla., 1979; DPM, Calif. Coll. Podiatric Medicin, 1983. Resident L.A. Surg. Inst., 1983-84; pvt. practice San Francisco, 1980-84, L.A., 1984-91, N.Y.C., 1993—; cons. and lectr. in field, 1984-96. Contbr. articles to profl. jours. Pres. N.Y. Heart Assn., 1994; trustee Big Bros. Am., N.Y.C., 1996; pres. Parents Without Ptnrs., N.Y.C., 1994-96, Young Reps., N.Y.C., 1995-96. Mem. U.S. Kayaking Club (pres. 1987-91), Elks (v.p. 1986-89). Roman Catholic. Home and Office: 8510 Bay Pkwy Brooklyn NY 11214

MCGRATH, MARY HELENA, plastic surgeon, educator; b. N.Y.C., Apr. 12, 1945; d. Vincent J. and Mary M. (Manning) McG.; m. Richard H. Simon, Apr. 11, 1970; children: Margaret E. Simon, Richard M. Simon. BA, Coll. New Rochelle, 1966; MD, St. Louis U., 1970; MPH, George Washington U., 1994. Lic. surgeon, D.C. Resident in surg. pathology U. Colo. Med. Ctr., Denver, 1970-71, intern in gen. surgery, 1971-72, resident in gen. surgery, 1971-75, chief resident in gen. surgery, 1975-76; resident in plastic and reconstructive surgery Yale U. Sch. Medicine, New Haven, Conn., 1976-77; chief resident plastic and reconstructive surgery Yale U. Sch. Medicine, New Haven, 1977-78; fellow in hand surgery U. Conn.-Yale U., New Haven, 1978; instr. in surgery divsn. plastic and reconstructive surgery Yale U. Sch. Medicine, New Haven, 1977-78, asst. prof. plastic surgery, 1978-80; attending in plastic and reconstructive surgery Yale-New Haven Hosp., 1978-80, Columbia-Presbyn. Hosp., N.Y.C., 1980-84, George Washington U. Med. Ctr., Washington, 1984—, Children's Nat. Med. Ctr., Washington, 1985—; asst. prof. plastic surgery Columbia U., N.Y.C., 1980-84; assoc. prof. plastic surgery Sch. Medicine, George Washington U., Washington, 1984-87, prof. plastic surgery, 1987—; attending physician VA Hosp., West Haven, Conn., 1978-80; attending in surgery Hosp. Albert Schweitzer, Deschapelles, Haiti, 1980; co-investigator Charles W. Ohse Fund, Yale U. Sch. Medicine, 1979; prin. investigator various rsch. grants, 1979-89; historian, bd. dirs. Am. Bd. Plastic Surgery, 1991-95; guest examiner certifying exam., 1986-88, 95-96; specialist site visitor Residency Rev. Com. for Plastic Surgery, 1985, 87, 91, 94; presenter in field; cons. in field; senator med. faculty senate George Washington U., bd. govs. Med. Faculty Assocs. Co-editor: (with M.L. Turner) Dermatology for Plastic Surgeons, 1993; assoc. editor: The Jour. of Hand Surgery, 1984-89, Plastic and Reconstructive Surgery, 1989-95, chmn. nominating com., 1994—; contbr. book chpts.: Problems in General Surgery, 1985, Human and Ethical Issues in the Surgical Care of Patients with Life-Threatening Disease, 1986, Problems in Aesthetic Surgery, Biological Causes and Clinical Solutions, 1986; guest reviewer numerous jours.; contbr. articles, abstracts to profl. jours. Fellow ACS (bd. govs. 1995—, chmn. adv. coun. for plastic surgery 1995—); mem. AAAS, AMA, Am. Surg. Assn., Am. Assn. Hand Surgery (exec. sec. 1988-90, rsch. grants com. 1983-86, chmn. edn. com. 1983-88, 1st prize ann. resident contest 1978, numerous other c ms., D.C. chpt. program ann. meeting chmn. 1992, v.p. 1993-94, pres. 1994—), Am. Assn. Plastic Surgeons (pub. info. com. 1988-89, James Barrett Brown com. 1990-92, rsch. and edn. com. 1992-95), Am. Burn Assn., Am. Soc. for Aesthetic Plastic Surgery (FDA implant task force 1990—, pub. edn. com. 1991-92, sci. rsch. com. 1990—), Am. Soc. Maxillofacial Surgeons, Am. Soc. Plastic and Reconstructive Surgery (chmn. ethics com. 1985-87, chmn. device/tech. evaluation com. 1993-94, bd. dirs. 1994—, mem. ednl. found. bd. dirs. 1985-96, treas. 1989-92, v.p. 1992-93, pres.-elect 1993-94, pres. 1994-95), Am. Soc. Reconstructive Microsurgery (mem. edn. com. 1992-94), Am. Soc. Surgery of Hand (chmn. 1987 ann. residents' and fellows conf. 1986-87, mem. rsch. com. 1988-90), Assn. Acad. Chmn. Plastic Surgery (mem. prerequesite tng. com. 1990-92, mem. com. aesthetic surgery tng. 1992—), Assn. Acad. Surgery, D.C. Met. Area Soc. Plastic and Reconstructive Surgeons, Internat. Soc. Reconstructive Surgery, Met. D.C. Soc. Surgery Hand, N.Y. Surg. Soc., Northeastern Soc. Plastic Surgeons (chmn. sci. program com. 1991, chmn. fin. com. 1992-93, treas. 1993—), Plastic Surgery Rsch. Coun. (chmn. 1990), Surg. Biology Club III, The Wound Healing Soc., Washington Acad. Surgery, Washington Med. and Surg. Soc. Office: George Washington U # 6B-422 2150 Pennsylvania Ave NW Washington DC 20037-2396

MCGREEVY, MARY, retired psychology educator; b. Kansas City, Kans., Nov. 10, 1935; d. Donald and Emmy Lou (Neubert) McG.; m. Phillip Rosenbaum (dec.); children: David, Steve, Mariya, Chay, Allyn, Jacob, Dora. BA in English with honors, Vassar Coll., 1957; postgrad., New Sch. for Social Rsch., NYU, 1958-59, Columbia U., 1959-60, U. P.R., 1963-65, U. Mo., 1965-68, U. Kans.; PhD, U. Calif., Berkeley, 1969. Formerly exec. Doubleday & Co., N.Y.C., 1957-60; chief libr. San Juan Sch., P.R., 1962-63; NIMH drug rschr. Russell Sage Found., Clinico de los Addictos, Rio Piedras, P.R., 1963-65; psychiat. rschr. U. P.R. Med. Sch., 1963-65; psychiat. researcher U. Kans., Lawrence, 1966-68; rsch. assoc. Ednl. Rsch., 1968-69; assoc. prof. U. Calif., Berkeley, 1968-69, disting. prof., ret., 1969; yacht owner Encore; lectr. in field. Author: (poetry) To a Sailor, 1989, Dreams and Illusions, 1993, Coastings, 1996, also articles, poems, book revs. Founder, exec. dir. Dora Achenbach McGreevy Poetry Found., Inc.; active Fla. Atlantic U. Found., 1993—; vol. Broward County Hist. Commn., Friends of the Libr., Ft. Lauderdale and Main Broward County Librs., 1969—; mem. Am. Friends of Bodleian Libr., Oxford, Eng., Frances Loeb Lehman Art Gallery, Vassar Coll., Ctr. de las Artes, Miami, Fla., Friends of Modern Mus. Art, Friends of the Guggenheim, Friends of Met. Mus. Art, Nelson-Atkins Mus. Art, Friends of U. Mo. Libr., Johnson County Mental Health Assn., Ft. Lauderdale Philharm. Soc., St. Anthony's Cath. Women's Club, Women's Rsch. inst., Nova Southea. U., Davie, Fla. Recipient Cert. for Svc. Broward County Hist. Commn., 1994, Nat. Women's History Project award, 1995; Sproul fellow, Bancroft Libr. fellow, Russell Sage Found. fellow; postdoctoral grantee U. Calif. Mem. AAUW (corr. sec. 1991-95, bd. dirs. 1991—, honoree Ednl. Found. Fund 1993, Jeanne Faiks meml. scholarship fund com. 1992—, chairperson cultural events 1995—, Women of History awards), Pres.'s Coun., Broward Women's History Coalition (bd. dirs. 1991—, archivist, mem. ad hoc com.), Am. Philos. Assn., Women in Psychology, Union of Concerned Scientists, South Fla. Poetry Inst. (yearly poetry anthology 1991—), Poets of the Palm Beaches (yearly poetry anthology 1992, 93—, 1st prize free verse ann. contest), Mo. Sociol. Assn., Fla. Philosophy Assn. (spkr. 1991, 93, chairperson self in philosophy 1994), Vassar Alumni Assn. (class historian), Oxfam Am., Pem-Hill Alumni Assn., Sierra Club (newspaper reporter, mem. environ. com., archvist 1993-95, co-chairperson beach clean-up 1993), Secular Humanists (bd. dirs. 1992—, program chairperson 1995—), Fla. Women's Consortium, Vassar Club Kansas City, Vassar Alumni Assn. N.Y. Home: PO Box 900 Fort Lauderdale FL 33302-0900

MC GREGOR, DOUGLAS HUGH, pathologist, educator; b. Temple, Tex., Aug. 28, 1939; s. Harleigh Heath and Joyce Ellen (Lambert) McG.; m. Mizuki Kitani, July 6, 1969; children: Michelle Sakuya, David Kenji. BA, Duke U., 1961, MD, 1966; postgrad. U. Edinburgh, Scotland, 1961-62. Diplomate: Am. Bd. Pathology. Intern and chief resident in pathology UCLA Med. Ctr., Los Angeles, 1966-68; surgeon and lt. comdr. Atomic Bomb Casualty Commn., Hiroshima, Japan, 1968-71; chief resident in pathology Queens Med. Ctr., Honolulu, 1971-73; asst. and assoc. prof. pathology U. Kans. Med. Ctr., Kansas City, 1973-82, prof., 1982—; dir. anat. pathology VA Med. Ctr., Kansas City, Mo., 1975-94, chief pathology & lab. medicine, 1994—. Contbr. numerous articles to profl. jours., chpts. to books. Leader YMCA Indian Princess Program, Overland Park, Kans., 1977-79, Indian Guide Program, 1978-80, Cub Scouts Am., Overland Park, 1980-82, Boy Scouts Am., Leawood, Kans., 1982—. Served as lt. comdr. USPHS, 1968-71; Japan. Grantee Merck, Sharp and Dohme, 1980, NIH, 1980. Fellow Coll. Am. Pathologists, Am. Soc. Clin. Pathologists; mem. Am. Assn. Pathologists, Internat. Acad. Pathologists, Soc. Exptl. Biology and Medicine, N.Y. Acad. Scis., AAAS, Kansas City Soc. Pathologists (sec.-treas. 1982-83, pres. 1983-84). Club Leawood Country. Research in biology and pathology of parathyroid hormone secretion; platelet-leukocyte aggregation; ultrastructure and pathobiology of neoplasms; radiation carcinogenesis; morphogenesis of atherosclerosis. Home: 9400 Lee Blvd Shawnee Mission KS 66206-1826 Office: VA Med Ctr 4801 E Linwood Blvd Kansas City MO 64128-2226

MCGREGOR, VICTOR A., mental health services professional; b. Cape Town, South Africa, Nov. 1, 1956; s. Roy Cranston Campbell and Vicki Mary (Sanvido) McG. BSN, LaSalle Coll.; MSN, U. Pa.; diploma, Theol. Edn. by Extension Coll., 1982; diploma in psychiat. nursing, Midland Coll. Nursing, Pietermaritzburg, South Africa, 1985; postgrad., Union Inst. Nurse practitioner psychiat. Columbia Presbyn. Psychiat. Shelter Program; pvt. practice N.Y.C. Mem. Phila. Jungian Soc., Sigma Theta Tau.

MCGREGOR, WALTER, medical products company designer, inventor, consultant, educator; b. Kyiv, Ukraine, Nov. 2, 1937; came to U.S., 1957; s. William and Lydia (Aplass) McG.; m. Helen McGregor, July 18, 1965; children: Roxanne, Walter Jr. BS, Fairleigh Dickinson U., 1973, MBA in Pharm. Mktg., 1975. Sect. leader Ethicon Inc., Somerville, N.J., 1965-68, supr., 1968-76, mgr., 1976-83, dir. surg. products devel. and materials engring., 1983-92, dir. of tech., 1992-94; pres., CEO Biomark Tech. Inc., Flemington, N.J., 1994—; sr. v.p. Global Med. Countertrade Corp., 1994—; pres. Global Med. Countertrade Svcs., Inc., 1994—; CEO Primatech USA, Inc., 1996—; guest cons. Wilmer Inst., Johns Hopkins Hosp. Rsch. Lab., Balt., 1965-70; guest lectr. dept. plastic surgery U. Va. Med. Sch., Charlottesville, 1986—. Contbr. articles to profl. jours. Patentee surg. instruments. Life mem. Rep. Presdl. Task Force, Washington, 1984—; mem. Rep. Nat. Com., 1991. Fellow Soc. for Advancement of Med. Instrumentation; mem. Am. Med. Informatics Assn. (founding), Am. Mktg. Assn. (profl.), Med. Mktg. Assn. Home: 104 Hoffman Rd Flemington NJ 08822-7023 Office: Biomark Tech Inc 104 Hoffman Rd Flemington NJ 08822-7023

MCGUIGAN, TRACY LEIGH, geriatrics nurse; b. Meriden, Conn., Nov. 11, 1970; d. Ellsworth George and Jo-Anne (Wolfe) M. BSN, Fairfield (Conn.) U., 1992. RN, Conn.; cert. BLS. Geriatrics nurse VA Med. Ctr., West Haven, Conn., 1992—. Mem. Nat. League for Nursing. Roman Catholic. Home: 1050 Campbell Ave West Haven CT 06516 Office: VA Med Ctr 950 Campbell Ave West Haven CT 06516

MCGUINESS, CATHY LYNNE, medical records administrator; b. Norwalk, Conn., Aug. 9, 1954; d. George Perry and Fanny (Sacchitiello) Wingard; m. Brian Joseph McGuiness, Nov. 18, 1989; 1 child, Mary Ellen. AS, Post Jr. Coll., Waterbury, Conn., 1974; BS in Health Care Adminstrn., Quinnipiac Coll., Hamden, Conn., 1982. Accredited record technician. Sec. Post Jr. Coll., Waterbury, 1972-74; med. sec. Yale U. Sch. Medicine, New Haven, 1974-82; admissions coord./support svcs. asst. Yale Psychiat. Inst., New Haven, 1982-86, med. records mgr., 1987-93; corr. coord. Silver Hill Found., New Canaan, Conn., 1986-87; med. records supr. State of Conn. Dept. Mental Health, Stamford, Conn., 1993-94, State of Conn. Dept. Corrections, Cheshire, 1994—; cons. Country Place, Litchfield, Conn., 1992-93. Vol. EMT Echo Hose Ambulance Corps, Shelton, Conn., 1976-79. Mem. Am. Health Info. Mgmt. Assn., Conn. Health Info. Mgmt. Assn. Congregationalist. Home: 16 Summit Rd Naugatuck CT 06770

MCGUIRE, BRIAN LYLE, health science facility consultant, educator; b. Mobile, Ala., June 13, 1959; s. Frank Ludlow, Jr. and Mary Lyle (Davidson) McG.; m. Jean Ellen Marler, June 18, 1983. BS in Acctg., U. S. Ala., 1982, MBA, 1990; PhD, U. Cen. Fla., 1996. CPA, Ala.; cert. mgmt. acct. Staff acct. Smith, Dukes & Buckalew, CPA's, Mobile, 1983-86; corp. acct. So. Med. Health Systems, Mobile, 1986, dir. corp. ops, 1987-88; exec. dir. Med. Arts Clinic, Inc. subs. So. Med. Health Systems, Foley, Ala., 1986-88; adminstr. Mobile Heart Ctr., 1988-91; acctg. instr. U. Ctrl. Fla., Orlando, 1991-95; asst. prof. acctg. U. So. Ind., Evansville, 1995—. Jr. asst. scoutmaster Boy Scouts Am., Birmingham chpt. Recipient Eagle Scout Order of Arrow Boy Scouts Am., 1977; named one of Outstanding Young Men of Am., 1982. Mem. AICPA, Inst. Mgmt. Accts. (chpt. bd. dirs. 1983-85, pres. 1987-88, nat. bd. dirs. 1989-91, 92-93, pres. regional coun. 1992-93, nat. com. mem. 1993—, Remington Rand trophy), Med. Group Mgmt. Assn., Ala. Soc. CPAs, Mobile Jaycees (treas. 1983-84, v.p. adminstrn. 1984-85, presdl. citation 1984), Alumni Assn. U. South Ala., Hist. Mobile Preservation Soc., Lake Forest Yacht and Country Club, Athelstan Club, Pi Kappa Phi, Phi Kappa Phi, Beta Gamma Sigma. Episcopalian. Office: U So Ind Dept Acctg and Bus Law 8600 University Blvd Evansville IN 47712-3597

MCGUIRE, JAMES HORTON, physics educator; b. N.Y., June 7, 1942; s. Horton E. and Karolyn W. (Wright) McG.; m. V. Jane Rasmussen, Oct. 10, 1981; children: Carrie Marti, Bruce, Brooke. BS, Rensselaer U., 1964; PhD, Northeastern U., 1969. Asst. prof. Tex. A&M U., College Station, 1969-72; prof. Kans. State U., Manhattan, 1972-91; Murchison-Mallory prof. physics Tulane U., New Orleans, 1991—. Assoc. editor: Encyclopedia Physics; contbr. articles to profl. jours. Recipient Disting. Alumni award in edn. Northeastern U., 1995; grantee NSF, 1992, DOE, 1992. Fellow Am. Phys. Soc. (sec.-treas. divsn. atomic molecular optical physics 1989-92), Internat. Conf. on Physics of Atmoic and Elec. Collisions (sec.); mem. The Nat. Faculty, Am. Chem. Soc., Am. Assn. Physics Tchrs. Democrat. Office: Tulane U Dept Physics New Orleans LA 70118

MCGUIRE, JOHN ALBERT, dentist; b. Warren, Ohio, June 20, 1950; s. Bernard Leo and Lucille Ann (Guarnieri) McG.; m. Pamela Kay Muter, May 30, 1969; children: John, Jessica. BS, Ohio State U., 1972, DDS, 1975. Dentist, capt. USAF, Bellevue, Nebr., 1975-77; dentist pvt. practice Dayton, Tenn., 1977-83, Knoxville, Tenn., 1983—. Author: (short story) Stirs, 1990. Mem. Sertoma Club, Knoxville, 1983-86, Jaycees, Dayton, 1978-81; vol. United Meth. Ch., Tilaran, Costa Rica, 1985. Recipient Scholarship, Fred M. Roddy Found., 1990. Mem. Phi Kappa Phi. Home: 301 Grandeur Dr Knoxville TN 37920-6325 Office: 6017 Chapman Hwy Knoxville TN 37920-5932

MCGUIRE, JOHN LAWRENCE, pharmaceuticals research executive; b. Kittanning, Pa., Nov. 3, 1942; s. Lawrence F. and Florence G. (Jones) McG.; m. Pamela Hale, Aug. 2, 1969; children—Megan L., Christa H. BS, Butler U., 1965; MA, Princeton U., 1968, PhD, 1969; postgrad., Columbia Sch. Bus., 1981. Asst. in instrn. Princeton U., N.J., 1967-69; pharmacologist Ortho Pharm. Corp., Raritan, N.J., 1969-72, sect. head molecular biology, 1972-75, exec. dir. research, 1975-80, v.p. preclinical research and devel., 1980-88, bd. dirs., 1988-93; sr. v.p. rsch. and devel. worldwide, bd. dirs. R.W. Johnson Pharm. Rsch. Inst., Raritan, N.J., 1988-92; corp. v.p. bus. devel., pharm./diagnostics group Johnson & Johnson, New Brunswick, N.J., 1992—; adj. assoc. prof. dept. medicine M.S. Hershey Sch. Medicine Pa. State U., 1978—; adj. prof. dept. animal sci. Rutgers U., 1983-92; adj. prof. ob-gyn. East Va. Med. Sch., 1987—; adj. prof. ob-gyn. and reproduction endocrinology U. Medicine and Dentistry, N.J., 1995—; cons. NASA, 1985-87. Mem. editorial bd. Ullman's Ency. Indsl. Chemistry, 1987—; contbr. articles to profl. jours.; patentee in field. Mem. exec. bd. Keystone Area council Boy Scouts Am., Harrisburg, Pa., 1975-96, George Washington council, Trenton, N.J., 1980-86, 95—; trustee Raritan Valley Community Coll., N.J., 1986—, vice-chmn., 1990—, United Way of Hunterdon County, N.J., 1983—, pres., 1985-87, Hunterdon Med. Ctr., Flemington, N.J., 1978—, vice chmn., 1984-88, chmn., 1988—; trustee Hunterdon Health Care Sys. Flemington, N.J., 1986—, chmn. 1989—, Atlantic Health Systems Morristown, N.J., 1991-93, vice-chmn., 1992-93, Tri State United Way, N.Y., 1987-94; bd. dirs. Hunterdon County YMCA, N.J., 1982-87; chmn. bd. dirs. Mid Jersey Health Corp., 1986-88; trustee The Pennington (N.J.) Sch., 1995—. Recipient Silver Beaver award Boy Scouts Am., 1984; Population Council fellow, 1969. Mem. Am. Soc. Pharmacology and Exptl. Therapeutics, Soc. Exptl. Biology and Medicine, Am. Physiol. Soc., Endocrine Soc., Am. Coll. Ob-Gyn, Am. Soc. Clin. Pharmacology and Therapetics, Licensing Execs. Soc., Biochemistry Soc. Great Britain, Royal Soc. Medicine (U.K.), Am. Chem. Soc. Club: Princeton (N.Y.C.). Home: 9 Sunnyfield Dr Whitehouse Station NJ 08889-9465 Office: Johnson & Johnson New Brunswick NJ 08933

MCGUIRE, MICHAEL FRANCIS, plastic and reconstructive surgeon; b. St. Louis, Oct. 4, 1946; s. Arthur Patrick and Virginia Claribel (Gannon) McG. BA, Columbia U., 1968, MD, 1972. Diplomate Am. Bd. Surgery, Am. Bd. Plastic Surgery. Intern UCLA, 1972-73, resident in gen. surgery, 1973-77, resident in plastic surgery, 1978-80; fellow in plastic surgery rsch. Stanford (Calif.) U., 1977-78; traveling fellow in plastic surgery Gt. Britain, 1980; chief plastic surgery L.A. County-Olive View Med. Ctr., Sylmar, Calif., 1980-85; pvt. practice Santa Monica, Calif., 1980—; bd. dirs. Calif. Med. Rev., Inc.; pres. Pacific Coast Plastic Surgery Ctr., Inc., Santa Monica, 1987—; asst. clin. prof. surgery UCLA, 1980—, mem. exec. com., 1993—; vice chmn. plastic surgery St. John's Hosp., Santa Monica, 1987-91, chmn. plastic surgery, 1992—, chmn. surg. svcs. com., 1996—, dir. cleft palate team L.A. County-Olive View Med. Ctr., 1986—; mem. ops. com. Med. Profl. Group, 1995. Charter patron L.A. Music Ctr. Opera, 1983—; sponsoring patron Los Angeles County Art Mus., 1986—; patron Colleague Helpers in Philanthropic Svc., Bel Air, Calif., 1987, 93, 95; pres. Found. for Surg. Reconstrn., 1996—. Fellow ACS, Royal Soc. Medicine; mem. Am. Soc. Plastic and Reconstructive Surgeons, Am. Soc. Aesthetic Plastic Surgery, Los Angeles County Med. Assn. (v.p. 1995—), Calif. Soc. Plastic Surgery (exec. com., auditor 1988-89, program chmn. 1990, exec. coun. 1991-94, treas. 1994—), Am. Assn. Accreditation of Ambulatory Surgery (facilities ops. com. 1995-96, bd. dirs. 1996), Alpha Omega Alpha. Democrat. Episcopalian. Office: 1301 20th St Ste 460 Santa Monica CA 90404-2050

MCGUIRE, ROBERT LEE, surgeon; b. Canton, Ohio, July 14, 1934; s. James William and Zella Louise (Paroz) McG.; m. Marilyn Leio Sewell, July 4, 1968 (dec. Mar. 1995); children: Carrie Louise, Russell Andrew. BA, Coll. Wooster, Ohio, 1956; MD, N.Y. Med. Coll., N.Y.C., 1961. Diplomate Am. Bd. Surgery. Intern surgery L.I. Coll. Hosp., Bklyn., 1961-62, resident surgery, 1964-68, asst. attending surgery, 1969-71, assoc. attending surgery, 1971-73, chmn. sect. transplantation, 1969-73; fellow transplantation U. Colo., Denver, 1968-69; pvt. practice surgery Plantation, Fla., 1973—; bd. advisors Pine Crest Prep. Sch., Ft. Lauderdale, Fla., 1985-90; liaison tumor bd. ACS West Side Hosp., Plantation, 1995-96; chief surgery Plantation Gen. Hosp., 1994—. Bd. dirs., past pres. Metro unit Am. Cancer Soc., Ft. Lauderdale, 1971-96, bd. dirs., past pres., Fla. divsn., 1981-96; mem. rsch. adv. bd. Fla. Cancer Control, State of Fla., 1995—; bd. trustees Goodwin Inst. Cancer Rsch., Plantation, 1990-96. Lt. comdr. USN, 1961-64. Fellow ACS. Home: 4150 NE 22nd Ave Fort Lauderdale FL 33308 Office: 4101 NW 4th St Ste 305 Plantation FL 33317

MCGUIRE, SANDRA LYNN, nursing educator; b. Flint, Mich., Jan. 28, 1947; d. Donald Armstrong and Mary Lue (Harvey) Johnson; m. Joseph L. McGuire, Mar. 6, 1976; children: Matthew, Kelly, Kerry. BS in Nursing, U. Mich., 1969, MPH, 1973, EdD, 1988. Staff nurse Univ. Hosp., Ann Arbor, Mich., 1969; pub. health nurse Wayne County Health Dept., Eloise, Mich., 1969-72; instr. Madonna Coll., Livonia, Mich., 1973; pub. health coord. Plymouth Ctr. for Human Devel., Northville, Mich., 1974-75; asst. prof. cmty. health nursing U. Mich., Ann Arbor, 1975-83; asst. prof. U. Tenn., Knoxville, 1983-88, assoc. prof., 1990—; dir. Kids Are Tomorrow's Srs. Program, 1988—; resource person Gov.'s Com. Unification of Mental Health Services in Mich.; speaker profl. assns. and workshops; bd. dirs. Ctr. Understanding Aging, 1987-93, v.p. 1995—. Author: (with S. Clemen-Stone and D. Eigsti) Comprehensive Family and Community Health Nursing, 1981, 4th edit. 1995. Bd. dirs. Mich. chpt. ARC, 1980-83, Knoxville chpt., 1984-85; founder Knoxville Intergenerational Network, 1989. USPHS fellow, 1972-73, Robert Woodruff fellow, 1996—. Mem. APHA, ANA, Tenn. Nurses Assn., Nat. League Nursing, Tenn. League Nursing, Tenn. Pub. Health Assn., (chmn. mental health sect. 1976) Mich. Pub. Health Assn. (dir., co-chmn. residential services com. 1976-79, chmn. health services 1979-82), Nat. Coun. on Aging, Ctr. for Understanding Aging (v.p., 1994-95), Plymouth (chmn. residential services com. 1975-77) Tenn. Assn. Retarded Citizens, So. Nursing Rsch. Soc., Sigma Theta Tau, Pi Lambda Theta, Phi Kappa Phi. Home: 11008 Crosswind Dr Knoxville TN 37922-4011 Office: 1200 Volunteer Blvd Knoxville TN 37916-3806

MCGUIRE, WILLIAM F., urologist; b. Clifton Forge, Va., Apr. 22, 1924; s. Laurence Cornelius and Clara Maude (Powell) McG.; m. Florence K. Bell, June 21, 1947 (div. Feb. 1974); children: Jamie H. McGuire Kirby, William Mark; m. Etta Carolyn McGuire, Feb. 22, 1974. MD, U. Va., 1951. Diplomate Am. Bd. Urology. Intern Barnes Hosp., St. Louis, 1951-52; resident Bowman Gray Sch. Medicine, N.C. Bapt. Hosp., Winston-Salem, N.C., 1952-55; urologist Pulaski (Va.) Gen. Hosp., 1955-74, Pulaski Cmty.

Hosp., 1974—; chief of surgery Pulaski Cmty. Hosp., 1980—. With USN, 1943-46, ETO. Mem. AMA, Am. Urol. Assn. (Mid-Atlantic sect.), Med. Soc. Va. (area rep.), Va. Urol. Soc. (past pres.), S.W. Va. Med. Soc. (past pres.), Rotary (past pres.). Methodist. Office: Urol Assocs New River Valley 2460 Lee Hwy Pulaski VA 24301

MC GUIRE, WILLIAM JAMES, social psychology educator; b. N.Y.C., Feb. 17, 1925; s. James William and Anne M. (Mitchell) McG.; m. Claire Vernick, Dec. 29, 1954; children—James William, Anne Maureen, Steven Thomas. BA, Fordham U., 1949, MA, 1950; PhD, Yale U., 1954; PhD (hon.), Eötvös U., Budapest, Hungary, 1990. Postdoctoral fellow U. Minn., 1954-55; assoc. prof. psychology U. Ill., 1958-61; prof. Columbia U., 1961-67, U. Calif., San Diego, 1967-70; vis. prof. London Sch. Econs., 1970-71; asst. prof. Yale U., New Haven, 1955-58, prof., 1971—, chmn. dept. psychology, 1971-73; Mem. adv. panel for sociology and social psychology NSF, 1963-65; mem. review panel for social scis. NIMH, 1968-72, cons., 1974-85. Author: Content and Processes in the Experience of Self, 1988, A Perspectivist Approach to Strategic Planning, 1989, Structure of Attitudes and Attitude Systems, 1989, The Content, Structure, and Operation of Thought Systems, 1991; contbr. to Ency. Brit.; editor Jour. Personality and Social Psychology, 1967-70; cons. editor European Jour. Social Psychology, 1978—, Jour. Applied Social Psychology, 1983—, Jour. Exptl. Social Psychology, 1994—, Pub. Opinion Quar., 1990-95. With AUS, 1943-46. Recipient Ann. Social Psychology award AAAS, 1964, Gen. Electric Found. awards, 1963, 64, 66, Disting. Scientist award Soc. Exptl. Social Psychology, 1992; grantee NSF, 1960-79, NIH, 1979—; Fulbright fellow Louvain (Belgium) U., 1950-51, Ctr. for Advanced Study in Behavioral Scis. fellow, 1965-66, Guggenheim fellow, 1970-71, William James fellow Am. Psychol. Soc., 1989—. Fellow APA (pres. divsn. personality and social psychology 1973-74, Disting. Sci. Contbn. award 1988); mem. Am. Sociol. Assn., Am. Assn. Pub. Opinion Rsch., Sigma Xi. Home: 225 Saint Ronan St New Haven CT 06511-2313 Office: Yale U Dept Psychology Box 208205 New Haven CT 06520-8205

MCGUIRE, WILLIAM PATRICK, III, oncologist, educator; b. Columbus, Ohio, Mar. 4, 1944; s. William Patrick Jr. and Mary Lou (McMaster) McG.; m. Deborah Brosseau, Aug. 12, 1977; 1 child, William Cameron. BS in Chemistry, Emory U., 1966, BA in Russian, 1966; MS in Cell Biology, Baylor U., 1971, MD, 1971. Diplomate Am. Bd. Internal Medicine, Am. Bd. Oncology. Intern, resident Yale-New Haven Hosp., 1971-73; sr. assoc. Nat. Cancer Inst., Bethesda, Md., 1976-79; assoc. prof. medicine U. Ill., Chgo., 1979-85; assoc. prof. oncology Johns Hopkins U., Balt., 1985-93; prof. medicine Emory U., Atlanta, 1993—; mem. oncol. adv. bd. Sandoz, Newark, 1993—, Bristol-Myers, Princeton, N.J., 1990—, Smith-Kline-Beecham, Phila., 1994—, Sequus, Palo Alto, Calif., 1995—. Editor: Taxol, 1995. Comdr. USPHS, 1973-79. Home: 714 Sherwood Rd Atlanta GA 30324 Office: Emory U 1365 Clifton Rd Ste 36192 Atlanta GA 30322

MC GUIRE, WILLIAM W., health maintenance organization executive; b. Troy, N.Y., 1948. Grad., U. Tex., 1970, U. Tex., 1974. Chmn., CEO, pres., dir. United Healthcare Corp. Dir. Minn. Orch. Assn., Mpls. Office: United Healthcare Corp 300 Opus Ctr 9900 Bren Rd E Minnetonka MN 55343-9664

MCGULPIN, ELIZABETH JANE, nurse; b. Toledo, Oct. 18, 1932; d. James Orville and Leah Fayne (Helton) Welden; m. David Nelson Buster, Apr. 9, 1956 (div. Nov. 1960); children: David Hugh, James Ray, Mark Stephen; m. Fredrick Gordon McGulpin, Oct. 7, 1973. AA in Nursing, Pasadena City Coll., 1968. RN, Wash. Lic. nurse Las Encinas Hosp., Pasadena, Calif.; nurse Hopi Indian Reservation HEW, Keams Canyon, Ariz., 1969-70; nurse, enterostomal therapist Pasadena Vis. Nurse Assn., 1972-74; nurse Seattle King County Pub. Health, 1977-81; home care nurse Victorville, Calif., 1983-85; nurse Adult Family Home, Woodinville, Wash., 1986—; vol. nurse, counselor Child Protective Svcs., Victorville, 1984; realtor Century 21, Lynden, Wash., 1993—. Vol. nurse Am. Cancer Soc., Pasadena, 1973-75, United Ostomy Assn., Los Angeles, Victorville, 1973-84; RN, ARC, 1996—. Am. Cancer Soc. grantee. Mem. Nat. Assn. Realtors, Wash. Assn. Realtors, Whatcom County Assn. Realtors, Vis. Nurse Assn. (Enterostomal Therpay grantee 1973). Home: 106 Kale St Everson WA 98247-9660

MCHAN, EVA JANE, psychologist; b. Sylva, N.C., Feb. 7, 1941; d. John V. and Nancy Evelyn (Moody) McHan; m. Dale S. Dacus, Dec. 21, 1959 (div. 1979); children: Angela Carole, Christopher A., Michael R. BS, U. Tenn., 1964; MS, Memphis State U., 1968; PhD, Tulane U., 1976; MPH, Harvard U., 1983. Postdoctoral fellow Harvard Psychology & Ctr. for Internat. Affairs, 1980-81; assoc. fellow Harvard Ctr. for Internat. Affairs, 1982-83; asst. prof. Am. U., Beirut, Lebanon, 1981-82; — King Saud Med. Coll., Riyadh, Saudi Arabia, 1983-85; faculty U. Md., Ger., 1985-87; faculty devel. staff U. Md., Im Bosseldorn, W. Ger., 1987-88; dean ednl. svcs. Franklin Coll., Lugano, Switzerland, 1988-89; dir. Cen. ger. Middle East, coord. social sci. European div. U. Md., Im Bosseldorn, 1989—. Contbr. articles to profl. jours. Mem. Am. Psychol. Assn., World Psychiatric Assn. Home: Im Bosseldorn 30, Heidelberg Germany 6900

MC HENRY, MARTIN CHRISTOPHER, physician, educator; b. San Francisco, Feb. 9, 1932; s. Merl and Marcella (Bricca) McH.; m. Patricia Grace Hughes, Apr. 27, 1957; children: Michael, Christopher, Timothy, Mary Ann, Jeffrey, Paul, Kevin, William, Monica, Martin Christopher. Student, U. Santa Clara, 1950-53; MD, U. Cin., 1957; MS in Medicine, U. Minn., 1966. Intern, Highland Alameda County (Calif.) Hosp., Oakland, 1957-58; resident, internal medicine fellow Mayo Clinic, Rochester, Minn., 1958-61, spl. appointee in infectious diseases, 1963-64; staff physician infectious diseases Henry Ford Hosp., Detroit, 1964-67; staff physician Cleve. Clinic, 1967-72, chmn. dept. infectious diseases, 1972-92, sr. physician infectious diseases, 1992—. Asst. clin. prof. Case Western Res. U., 1970-77, assoc. clin. prof. medicine, 1977-91, clin. prof. medicine, 1991—; assoc. vis. physician Cleve. Met. Gen. Hosp., 1970—; cons. VA Hosp., Cleve., 1973—. Chmn. manpower com. Swine Influenza Program, Cleve., 1976. Served with USNR, 1961-63. Named Disting. Tchr. in Medicine Cleve. Clinic, 1972, 90; recipient 1st ann. Bruce Hubbard Stewart award Cleve. Clinic Found. for Humanities in Medicine, 1985, Nightingale Physician Collaboration award Cleve. Clinic Found. Divsn. Nursing, 1995. Diplomate Am. Bd. Internal Medicine. Fellow ACP, Infectious Diseases Soc. Am., Am. Coll. Chest Physicians (chmn. com. cardiopulmonary infections 1975-77, 81-83), Royal Soc. Medicine of Great Britain; mem. Am. Soc. Clin. Pharmacology and Therapeutics (chmn. sect. infectious diseases and antimicrobial agts., 1970-77, 80-85, dir.), Am. Thoracic Soc., Am. Soc. Clin. Pathologists, Am. Fedn. Clin. Rsch., Am. Soc. Tropical Medicine and Hygiene, Am. Soc. Microbiology, N.Y. Acad. Scis. Contbr. numerous articles to profl. jours., also chpts. to books. Home: 2779 Belgrave Rd Pepper Pike OH 44124-4601 Office: 9500 Euclid Ave Cleveland OH 44195-0001

MCHENRY, WILLIAM JAMES, counselor, educator; b. Houtzdale, Pa., Dec. 31, 1937; s. Kenneth and Charlotte (Couser) McH.; m. Paula Rae Jones, Sept. 2, 1961; children: Lisa Kae McHenry Walker, Linda Renee, William James II. BS, Lock Haven U., 1959; MEd, Pa. State U., 1964; EdD, George Washington U., 1969. Cert. rehab. counselor, cert. sch. counselor, Pa. Tchr. Tyrone (Pa.) Area Schs., 1959-60, Clearfield (Pa.) Area Schs., 1960-64; guidance counselor Painted Post (N.Y.) Jr. High Sch., 1964-67; prof. dept. counseling and human devel. Edinboro U. of Pa., 1969—, dir. Act 101, 1979-84, dir. rehab. counseling program, 1985-93, dir. student pers. svcs. program, 1987-89; counselor U.S. Army, Ft. Myer, Arlington, Va., 1968-69. Coach Big League Baseball, Edinboro, 1987-90. NDEA fellow, 1967-69; Employment Coun. grantee, 1987. Mem. Am. Assn. for Counseling and Devel., Masons, Phi Delta Kappa. Republican. Methodist. Home: PO Box 554 Edinboro PA 16412-0554 Office: U Pa Edinboro Dept Counseling & Human Dev Normal St Edinboro PA 16412

MCHUGH, EARL STEPHEN, dentist; b. Colorado Springs, Colo., Feb. 27, 1936; s. Earl Clifton and Margaret Mary (Higgins) M.; m. Joan Bleckwell, Aug. 24, 1957; children: Kevin, Stacey, Julie. BA, Cornell U., 1958; DDS, U. Mo., 1962. Pvt. practice, Kansas City, Mo., 1964—; lectr. U. Mo. Dental Sch., Kansas City, 1988, clin. staff, 1989, 90, 91, 92, 93, 94, 95, ethics seminar faculty staff, addiction in dentistry faculty, 1995; cons. Hallmark, Inc., Kansas City, 1988; adv. dir. Rsch. Hosp., Kansas City. Contbr. articles to profl. jours. Deacon Presbyn. Ch. Prairie Village, Kans., 1982-84; vol. Shawnee Mission Hosp. Kans., 1985-88; lectr. Drug Recovery Program, Kansas City, Kans., 1988-89, 92, 93, 94. Capt. Dental Corp, U.S. Army, 1962-64. Mem. Valley Hope Assn. (rsch. hos. adv. bd. 1995-96), Audubon Soc. (Ortnithologist of Yr. award Kansas City chpt. 1990), Kans. Ornithol. Soc. (v.p. 1989-90, pres. 1990-91), Internat. Coun. Bird Preservation (Kans. del. 1990, coord. Kans. Breeding Bird Atlas 1992, 93, 94, 95, chmn. Kans. bird records com.), Omicron Kappa Upsilon, Chi Psi.

MC HUGH, MARGARET ANN GLOE, psychologist; b. Salt Lake City, Nov. 8, 1920; d. Harold Henry and Olive (Warenski) Gloe; m. William T. McHugh, Oct. 1, 1943; children: Mary Margaret McHugh-Shuford, William Michael, Michelle McHugh Sprague. BA, U. Utah, 1942; MA in Counseling and Guidance, Idaho State U., 1964; PhD in Counseling Psychology, U. Oreg., 1970. Lic. psychologist; nat. cert. counselor . Tchr. kindergarten, Idaho Falls, Idaho, 1951-62, tchr. high sch. English, 1962-63; counselor Counseling Center, Idaho State U., Pocatello, 1964-67; instr. U. Oreg., Eugene, 1967-70; asst. prof. U. Victoria, B.C., Can., 1970-76; therapist Peninsula Counseling Center, Port Angeles and Sequim, Wash., 1976-81, McHugh & Assocs. Counseling Center, 1981—, ret. 1995. Served with WAVES, 1943-44. Mem. APA, ACA, Am. Assn. Marriage and Family Therapy, Wash. Psychol. Assn. (rsch. women issues, rels's., depression and women, sexual abuse, adults with childhood and abuse trauma). Home: 1175 Cameron Rd Sequim WA 98382-9437

MC HUGH, PAUL R., psychiatrist, neurologist, educator; b. Lawrence, Mass., May 21, 1931; s. Francis Paul and Mary Dorothea (Herlihy) McH.; m. Jean Barlow, Dec. 27, 1959; children: Clare Mary, Patrick Daniel, Denis Timothy. AB, Harvard U., 1952, MD, 1956. Diplomate: Am. Bd. Psychiatry and Neurology. Intern Peter Bent Brigham Hosp., Boston, 1956-57; resident in neurology Mass. Gen. Hosp., 1957-60, fellow in neuropathology, 1958-59; teaching fellow in neurology and neuropathology Harvard, 1957-60; clin. asst. psychiatry Maudsley Hosp., London, Eng., 1960-61; mem. neuropsychiatry div. Walter Reed Army Inst. Research, Washington, 1961-64; asst. prof. psychiatry and neurology Cornell U., N.Y.C., 1964-68; assoc. prof. Cornell U., 1968-71, prof., 1971; dir. electroencephalography N.Y. Hosp., 1964-68; founder, dir. N.Y. Hosp. Bourne Behavioral Rsch. Lab., 1967-68, clin. dir., supr. psychiat. edn., founder, dir. Weschester divsn. dept. psychiatry, 1968-73; prof., chmn. dept. psychiatry U. Oreg. Health Sci. Center, Portland, 1973-75; Henry Phipps prof. psychiatry Johns Hopkins, Balt., 1975—; chmn. dept. psychiatry Johns Hopkins, 1975—, prof. dept. mental hygiene, 1976—; psychiatrist-in-chief Johns Hopkins Hosp., 1975—; dir. Blades Ctr. for Clin. Practice and Rsch. in Alcoholism Johns Hopkins Med. Inst., 1992—; chmn. med. staff Johns Hopkins Hosp., 1983-89, trustee, 1983—; vis. prof. Guys Hosp., London, Eng., 1976; chmn. bio-psychology Study sect. NIH, 1986-89. Author: The Perspectives of Psychiatry, 1983; (with Phillip R. Slavney) Psychiatric Polarities, 1987, Genes, Brain and Behavior, 1990; contbg. author: Cecil-Loeb Textbook of Medicine; mem. editorial bd. Am. Jour. Physiology, Jour. Nervous and Mental Disease, Comprehensive Psychiatry, Medicine, Psychol. Medicine, 1976—, Am. Scholar; contbr. articles to profl. jours. Mem. Md. Gov.'s Adv. Com., 1977-80. Grantee NIH, 1964-68, 67-70, 70-74, 75—; recipient William C. Menninger award ACP, 1987. Fellow Royal Coll. Psychiatry, Am. Psychiat. Assn.; mem. Inst. Medicine-NAS, Am. Neurol. Assn., Am. Physiol. Soc., Harvey Soc., Am. Coll. Neuropsychopharmacology, Am. Psychopath. Assn., Pavlovian Soc., W Hamilton St. Club. Home: 3707 St Paul St Baltimore MD 21218-2403 Office: Johns Hopkins Med Insts 600 N Wolfe St Baltimore MD 21205-2110*

MCILVAIN, HELEN EUGENE, medical educator; b. Kansas City, Mo., Nov. 17, 1942; d. Harold Schall and Virginia Lee (Hall) Roberts; m. Robert Jeffrey McIlvain, Feb. 24, 1964 (div. 1974); 1 child, Patrick Schall. BA, Kans. State Tchrs. Coll., 1965; MS in Edn., Kans. State U., 1974, PhD, 1977. Counselor Belleville (Ill.) Area Coll., 1977-81; asst. prof. Med. Ctr. U. Nebr., Omaha, 1981-86, behavioral specialist Med. Ctr., 1986-87, instr. Med. Ctr., 1987-89, asst. prof. family practice Med. Ctr., 1989-93; assoc. prof. family practice Med. Ctr., 1993—; cons. psychologist VA, Chgo., 1977-80; stress mgmt. cons. No. Natural Gas, Omaha, 1984-85, Procter & Gamble Corp., Cin., 1987-92, Nebr. Dept. Social Svcs., 1987-93; ednl. cons. Volkswagon of Am., Troy, Mich., 1984. Contbr. articles to profl. jours. Bd. dirs. Am. Lung Assn. Nebr., 1988-93. Smoking cessation rsch. grantee Nebr. Dept. Health, 1985-87, 89, 90, 91, 95. Mem. Assn. for Behavioral Scis. and Med. Edn., Soc. Behavioral Medicine, Soc. Tchrs. of Family Medicine, Assn. Tchrs. Preventive Medicine, Phi Kappa Phi. Democrat. Office: U Nebr Med Ctr Dept Family Practice 600 S 42nd St Omaha NE 68105-1002

MCILWAIN, WILLIAM ANTHONY, orthopedic surgeon; b. Waynesboro, Miss., May 29, 1949; s. Robert Lee and Bernice Arley (Taylor) McI.; m. Dian Wymer, June 12, 1971; children: William A., Jr., Cameron Cole, Douglas Graham. BS, U. Tenn., 1970, MD, 1974. Diplomate Am. Bd. Orthopedic Surgery. Chemist Quaker Oats Chemicals, Memphis, 1970-71; intern, resident orthopedic surgery U.S. Army Brooke Army Med. Ctr., San Antonio, 1974-78; orthopedic surgeon, asst. chief orthopaedic surgery 2d Gen. Hosp., Landstuhl, Germany, 1978-80; asst. chief spinal trauma ctr. Armed Forces Europe, Landstuhl, 1979-80; pvt. practice orthopedic surgery Bristol, Tenn., 1980—; pres. Bristol Orthopedic Assocs., 1982—; med. dir. physical therapy dept. Bristol Regional Med. Ctr., 1983—, chmn. dept. surgery, 1984-85; assoc. prof. clin. medicine East Tenn. State U., Johnson City, 1984—. Fellow Am. Acad. Orthopedic Assns., Am. Coll. Surgeons, N. Am. Spine Soc., Arthroscopy Assn. N. Am.; mem. Am. Coll. Physician Execs., Diagnostic Spine Soc. (pres. 1993). Home: 7 S Briarcliff Rd Bristol TN 37620 Office: Bristol Orthopaedic Assocs Office Plz 300E 1 Medical Park Blvd Bristol TN 37620

MCINERNEY, JOHN FRANCIS, psychologist; b. Phila., Sept. 4, 1950; s. Thomas Pierce and Rosemarie (McCann) McI.; BA magna cum laude, LaSalle Coll., 1972; MA with distinction, Hofstra U., 1974, PhD, 1975; m. Barbara C. Smith, Aug. 12, 1972; children: Eridget Clair, Caitlin Marie. Sch. psychologist Wyandanch (N.Y.) Jr./Sr. H.S., 1974-75; dir. pre-sch. programs for handicapped, dir. spl. svcs., supervising psychologist Cape May County Schs. for Spl. Svcs., Cape May Court House, N.J., 1975-83, cons. pediatric psychologist for spl. svcs., 1983—; pvt. practice psychology, Cape May County, N.J., 1977—; clin. dir., CEO Cape Behavioral Health Group, Cape May Courthouse, N.J.; mem. Cmty. Team for Treatment Child Abuse, Cape May County, 1980-83; cons. Fundacion Educativa Del Sur, Spl. Edn. Found., Guatemala City, 1981; adj. faculty, cons. on alcohol and drug abuse treatment Inst. Rational-Emotive Therapy, N.Y. and Phila., 1984—; cons. clin. psychologist; mem. med. staff Burdette Tomlin Meml. Cmty. Hosp. Author: (with others) Rational-Emotive Therapy with Alcoholics and Substance Abusers, 1988; mem. editl. bd. Jour. Rational-Emotive and Cognitive-Behavioral Therapy. Past mem. bd. dirs. Cape May County Mental Health Svcs.; mem. Human Svcs. Coalition-Adolescent Task Force; past mem. alcohol, mental health and drug abuse com. Health Sys. Agy. So. N.J. Recipient award Concerned Parents, 1981; Inst. Rational-Emotive Therapy assoc. fellow, 1980, approved supr., 1982. Mem. Am. Psychol. Assn., Nat. Assn. Sch. Psychologists, N.J. Psychol. Assn., N.J. Acad. Psychology, Nat. Register Health Svc. Providers in Psychology, Am. Conf. on Irish Studies. Roman Catholic. Home: 13 Coventry Ln Ocean View NJ 08230-1443 Office: Cape Behavioral Health Group 307 Brighton Rd Ste 2 Cape May Court House NJ 08210

MCINERNEY, JOHN VINCENT, obstetrician and gynecologist; b. Evergreen Park, Ill., July 13, 1957; s. Vincent F. and Kathleen T. McI.; m. Cabrini F. Costello, July 14; children: Patrick, Meghan, Elizabeth, John, Brendan, Molly. DO, Chgo. Coll. Osteo. Medicine, 1983; BS, Loyola U. Chgo., 1979. Diplomate Am. Bd. Osteopathic Medicine, Am. Bd. Ob-Gyn. Intern Chgo. Osteo. Hosp., 1983-84, resident in ob-gyn., 1984-88; obstetrician-gynecologist Assoc. of Edward C. Ryan, Orland Park, Ill., 1988-92, Assoc. of Scott Multack, Downers Grove, Ill., 1992-93; pvt. practice Palos Heights, Ill., 1993—; sr. staff Palos Cmty. Hosp., 1988—; attending staff Christ Hosp., 1989—; coord. continuing med. edn. in ob-gyn. Christ Hosp., 1994-96, vice chmn. continuing med. edn. adv. com., 1995—; clin. isntr. Rush Med. Coll., 1990—, Finch. U., Chgo. Med. Sch., 1996—; clin. mentor Chgo. Med. Sch., 1995-96. Chmn. Brother Rice H.S. devel. coun., Chgo., 1995-96, pres. alumni assn., 1992—; leader Boy Scouts Am. Recipient Chgo. Coll. Osteo. Medicine Alumni Assn. Pres.'s citation, 1994. Fellow Am. Coll. Ob-Gyn. (steering com. on residents edn., 1995-96, Am. Soc. Colposcopy and Cervical Pathology; mem. Chgo. Gynecologic Soc., Am. Assn. Gynecol. Laparoscopists. Roman Catholic. Home: 9800 S Longwood Dr Chicago IL 60643 Office: 11824 Southwest Hwy Palos Heights IL 60463

MCINERNEY, JOSEPH JOHN, biomedical engineer, educator; b. Boston, Aug. 13, 1932; s. John Joseph and Anne (Berry) McI.; m. Suzanne Finke, Oct. 20, 1970; children by previous marriage: Joseph, Lynn, Maureen; children by present marriage: Kathleen, John. B.S. in Mech. Engring., Northeastern U., 1960; M.S. in Nuclear Engring., Pa. State U., 1962, Ph.D. in Theoretical Physics, 1964, M.S. in Human Physiology, 1980. Nuclear physicist Knolls Atomic Lab., Schenectady, 1964-76; postdoctoral fellow Sch. Medicine, Pa. State U., Hershey, 1976-79, staff rsch. scientist, 1979—; asst. prof. depts. biomed. engring. and medicine, Pa. State U., State College, 1984-90, assoc. prof., 1990—; referee Am. Nuclear Soc., Hinsdale, Ill., 1966—, Med. Biol. Engring., 1986—; cons. Whitaker Found., Harrisburg, Pa., 1981—, NIH, 1985—, mem. standard com. Am. Nuclear Soc., Hinsdale, 1966—. Patentee in field. Contbr. articles to profl. jours. Served with USN, 1951-55. NIH fellow, 1976-79; Whitaker Found. grantee, 1979-81; Am. Heart Assn. grantee, 1979-80; NIH grantee, 1976-84, 84—, Pa. Rsch. Corp. grantee, 1983-84, Applied Rsch. Labs. grantee, 1985—. Mem. Am. Nuclear Soc., Am. Heart Assn., AAAS, Am. Physiol. Soc., Am. Fedn. Clin. Rsch., Am. Assn. Physicists in Medicine, IEEE (referee 1986—), Sigma Xi, Pi Tau Sigma. Democrat. Home: 260 Quarry Rd Hummelstown PA 17036-8902 Office: Pa State U Milton S Hershey Med Ctr PO Box 850 Hershey PA 17033-0850

MCINTIRE, JON WILLIAMS, psychologist; b. Barberton, Ohio, Feb. 2, 1944; s. John Frederick and Magel Madeline (Williams) McI.; m. Louise Emily Walters, June 14, 1965 (div.); children: Kevin Jon, Brian Douglas. BS, Mich. State U., 1965; PhD, U. Tex., 1973. Lic. psychologist, clin. psychologist. Va. Practicum supr. U. Tex., Austin, 1968-69, research asst., 1969, intern, 1969-71; asst. prof. Madison Coll., Harrisonburg, Va., 1971-73; dir. and assoc. prof. James Madison U., Harrisonburg, 1973-81; pvt. practice psychology, Harrisonburg, 1981—; pres. Shenandoah Ctr. for Therapeutic Riding, 1987-88, 90—. Vice chmn. Mental Health and Retardation Bd., Harrisonburg, 1980-84, chmn., 1984-86; chmn. Va. Alcohol Safety Action Program, Harrisonburg, 1980-84; bd. dirs. Cmty. Counseling Ctr., Harrisonburg, 1973-80; mem. local Human Rights Com., 1987-93; bd. dirs. Therapeutic Riding Assn., Va., 1985—, Citizens Against Sexual Assault, 1994—, Task Force on Violence, Harrisonburg City Schs. and Cmty., 1993—. Mem. Am. Psychol. Assn., Va. Psychol. Assn. (chmn. bd. profl. affairs 1984, newsletter editor 1979-80), Am. Soc. Clin. Hypnosis. Avocation: horses. Home: RR 1 Box 957 Port Republic VA 24471-9749 Office: 356 S Main St Harrisonburg VA 22801

MCINTOSH, DIANA MARIE, mental health services professional, consultant; b. Dayton, Ky., Dec. 25, 1953; d. Frank Martin and Patricia Ann (Dabbs) Scott; m. Henley McIntosh, Aug. 12, 1972; children: Aaron Matthew, Abigail Melissa. BSN, Coll. Mt. St. Joseph, 1976; MSN, U. Cin., 1978. RN, Ohio; cert. clin. specialist. Staff nurse St. Elizabeth Hosp., Covington, Ky., 1976-78; nurse educator Coll. Mt. St. Joseph, Mt. St. Joseph, Ohio, 1978-86; psychosocial cons. Christ, Emerson and Bethesda Hosps., Cin., 1980—; dir. supportive svc. Ctrl. Clin., Cin., 1983—. Contbr. articles to profl. jours. Active parents advisory com. YMCA, Ft. Thomas, Ky., 1989-93. Recipient Elizabeth Kemble, Distinguished Alumni awards U. Cin. Mem. ANA, Am. Group Psychotherapy Assn., Tri-State Group Psychotherapy Assn. (historian), S.W. Ohio Nurses Assn. (bd. dirs.). Office: Ctrl Clin 3259 Elland Ave Cincinnati OH 45267

MCINTOSH, HENRY DEANE, cardiologist; b. Gainesville, Fla., July 19, 1921; s. Thomas Irvin and Nelle Deane (Calwell) McI.; m. Harriet Owens, Nov. 6, 1945; children: Thomas Irvin, James Owens, Willa Elizabeth. BS, Davidson Coll., 1943; MD, U. Pa., 1950; DSc (hon.), U. Francisco Martinique, Guatemala de la Asuncion, 1987; hon. prof., Kunming Med. Coll., Yunnan, People's Republic of China, 1996. Diplomate Am. Bd. Internal Medicine, subspecialty bd. cardiovascular disease. Intern medicine Duke U., Durham, N.C., 1950-51, fellow cardiology, 1952-54, instr. medicine Sch. Medicine, 1954-55, assoc., 1955-57, from asst. prof. to assoc. prof., 1957-62, prof., 1962-70, chief cardiology divsn., 1966-70; asst. resident medicine Lawson VA Hosp., Atlanta, 1951-52; chief resident medicine VA Hosp., Durham, N.C., 1954-55, asst. chief cardiovascular-renal sect., 1955-56; prof., chmn. dept. medicine Baylor Coll. Medicine, Houston, 1970-77, chief sect. cardiology, 1977, adj. prof. medicine, 1977—; chief med. svc. The Meth. Hosp., Houston, 1970-77; clin. prof. medicine U. Fla. Sch. Medicine, Gainesville, 1977—, U. South Fla. Sch. Medicine, Tampa, 1993—; cons. VA Hosp., Durham, 1956-70, Watts Hosp., Durham, 1956-79, Womack U.S. Army Hosp., Ft. Bragg, N.C., 1957-70, Portsmouth (Va.) Naval Hosp., 1957-70, VA Hosp., Hosuton, 1970-77, Harris County Dist. Hosps., Houston, 1970-77, St. Luke's Episc. Hosp., Houston, 1970-77, Hermann Hosp., Houston, 1970-77, Lakeland (Fla.) Regional Med. Ctr., 1977-92, St. Joseph's Hosp., Tampa, 1992—; med. dir. prevention and rehab. ctr. St. Joseph's Heart Inst., Tampa, 1992—. Editl. bd. Circulation, Heart and Lung, Am. Jour. Cardiology, Am. Jour. Geriatric Cardiology; asst. editor Modern Concepts in Cardiovascular Disease, 1967; editor Baylor Cardiology Series, 1975-77; contbr. 240 articles to profl. jours. Founder, bd. dirs. Heartbeat Internat., Lakeland, Fla., 1983-92, Tampa, Fla., 1992—, pres., 1993-95, chmn. bd. dirs., 1995—. Capt. U.S. Army, 1943-45. Decorated Silver Star; decorated Croix de Guerre with two bronze and one silver star; recipient Disting. Alumni award Duke U. Med. Ctr., 1972, Rotary Internat. Hon. Fellowship, 1985, Paul Harris Fellow, 1986, U.S. Presdl. Citation from Ronald Reagan, Heartbeat Internat., 1986, Disting. Kennedy Lectureship, Univ. Assn. Emergency Medicine, 1986, Disting. Alumni award Davidson Coll., 1988. Fellow Am. Coll. Cardiology (Disting. Svc. award 1996, pres. 1974-75, govt. rels. com. 1986-93, prevention com. 1986-90, chair 1987-90, rep. to pub. health svc. objectives for the yr. 2000, 1988-96, Spl. Achievement award Fla. chpt. 1994); mem. AMA, ACP (Laureate award Fla. chpt. 1994), NASPE (continuing med. edn. coun. 1988-91, bldg. com. 1992-94, Disting. Svc. award 1991), Am. Fedn. Clin. Rsch., Soc. Clin. Investigation (Founders award 1984), Assn. Univ. Cardiologists, Am. Clin. and Climatological Soc., Am. Soc. Internal Medicine, Assn. Am. Physicians, Assn. Profs. Medicine, Am. Heart Assn. (v.p. 1977-78, rsch. com. 1986-90, chair sci. sessions com. 1971-73, coun. clin. cardiology 1975-76, Disting. Achievement award coun. clni. cardiology 1986), Coun. Geriat. Cardiology (membership com. 1986—, pres. 1991-92, Disting. Svc. award 1995). Presbyterian. Home: PO Box 1788 Lakeland FL 33802-1788 Office: St Joseph's Heart Inst PO Box 4227 3003 Dr Martin Luther King Blvd Tampa FL 33677-4227

MCINTYRE, DEBORAH, psychotherapist, author; b. Pensacola, Fla., Sept. 11, 1955; d. John Joseph and Mary Cecelia (Campbell) McI.; m. Denis Miller Donovan, Sept. 6, 1985. BA in Psychology, George Mason U., 1976; MA Counseling Psychology, U. West Fla., 1980; AA in Nursing, Pensacola Jr. Coll., 1981. Diplomate Am. Bd. Med. Psychotherapists (fellow); RN, Va., Fla. Child psychotherapist Holly Hall Sch. for Exceptional Children, Vienna, Va., 1975-77; area rep. Youth For Understanding, Vienna, 1976-78; vol. child psychotherapist Children's Resource Ctr. of N.W. Fla., Pensacola, Fla., 1979-80; staff/charge nurse med. surgery Va. Beach Gen. Hosp., 1981-83; intake coord., child and family psychotherapist Psychiatric Inst., Norfolk, Va., 1982-83; head nurse, program coord., child and family therapist Children's Service, Horizon Hosp., Clearwater, Fla., 1983; child and adolescent psychotherapist The Children's Ctr. for Devel. Psychiatry, St. Petersburg, Fla., 1983—; cons., trainer Project Playpen, Juvenile Welfare Bd., St. Petersburg, 1985-87; cons. Early Childhood Coun. of Pinellas County; mem. adv. bd. New Traumatology Ann. Conf.; participant in workshops and seminars for mental health care. Author: (with Denis M. Donovan) Healing the Hurt Child: A Developmental-Contextual Approach, 1990; editl. adv. bd. The New Child Psychiatry; contbr. articles to profl. jours., chpts. to books. Fellow Am. Psychol. Soc.; mem. Am. Orthopsychiat. Assn. Roman Catholic. Office: Childrens Ctr Devel Psychiatry 6675 13th Ave N Ste 2-A Saint Petersburg FL 33710-5483

MCINTYRE, IAIN MATTHEW, toxicologist, researcher; b. Melbourne, Victoria, Australia, Aug. 18, 1956; s. John and Gwen Macmillan (Matthews) McI.; m. Sandra Sue Rossmoore, Apr. 24, 1988; children: Heather Rachel, Andrew John William. BS, Univ. Melbourne, Australia, 1978, BS with honors, 1979, MSc, 1980, PhD, 1983. Lectr. Wayne State U., Detroit, 1982-

83, asst. prof., 1983-85; rsch. fellow U. Melbourne, 1985-90; mgr. toxicology Victorian Inst. Forensic Medicine, Melbourne, 1990—; hon. sr. rsch. fellow La Trobe U., Melbourne, 1990—; hon. sr. rsch. fellow dept. forensic medicine Monash U., Melbourne, 1994—. Mem. editl. bd. Jour. Analytical Toxicology, 1993—; contbr. over 100 articles to profl. jours., numerous chpts. to books. Recipient Bursary award CIBA Found., 1985, Ann. Rsch. award for psychoneuroendocrinology Australian Soc. for Psychiat. Rsch., 1985; rsch. fellow U. Melbourne, 1985-87. Mem. Internat. Assn. Forensic Toxicologists, Melbourne Cricket Club. Office: Victorian Inst Forensic Med, Victorian Inst Forensic Pathology, 57-83 Kavanagh St, Southbank 3006, Australia

MCINTYRE, JOAN ELLEN, social worker; b. Bryn Mawr, Pa., June 7, 1933; d. Charles Joseph and Ruth Marie (Israel) M. Estudios Hispanicas, U. Madrid, 1953; AB, Rosemont (Pa.) Coll., 1954; MSW, Columbia U., 1964. Cert. clin. social worker, N.Y. Dir., program dir. Camp Jeanne d'Arc, Merrill, N.Y., 1954-67; unit coord. Fountain House Found., N.Y.C., 1967-69; sr. social worker NYU Med. Ctr., 1969-70; social work supr. Misericordia Hosp. Med. Ctr., Bronx, N.Y., 1971-83; pvt. practice Pelham, N.Y., 1979—; asst. prof. NYU, 1968-72. Reporter Nat. Election Svc., 1976-84; observer LWV, 1974-83; cons. Pelham Art Ctr., 1975; pres. Women's Rep. Club, Pelham, 1972; treas. Com. on Fair Taxes, Pelham, 1974; sec. Pelham Heights Assn., 1975. Mem. Pelham C. of C., Better Bus. Bur., Coun. Renal Social Workers (Cert. Appreciation 1983). Office: 102 3rd Ave Pelham NY 10803-1427

MCINTYRE, MILDRED JEAN, clinical psychologist, writer, neuroscientist; b. Boston; d. William James and Theodora Grace (Jackson-McCullough) McI. BA, Swarthmore Coll., 1965; MA, Clark U., 1972, PhD, 1975. Lic. psychologist, Mass., Alaska, Hawaii. Ford Found. fellow, 1972, 73. Mem. APA, Internat. Neuropsychol. Soc., Cognitive Neurosci. Soc. Office: PO Box 990124 Boston MA 02199-0124

MCISAAC, MICHAEL ANDREW, physician assistant; b. Detroit, Oct. 9, 1951; s. Francis Robert and Pauline Claire (Hasse) M.; m. Doreen Joyce Baumel, June 21, 1986; children: Molly Colleen, Duncan Michael. BS, Mercy Coll. Detroit, 1975. Cert. physician asst. Physician asst. Fairbanks (Alaska) Clinic, 1976, State of Alaska, Anchorage, 1976, BP Exploration (Alaska), Inc., Anchorage, 1976—. Fellow Am. Acad. Physician Assts., Alaska Acad. Physician Assts., Am. Acad. Physician Assts. in Occupational Medicine, NRA. Office: BP Exploration (Alaska) Inc PO Box 196612 Anchorage AK 99519

MCKAIG, CALVIN NEWTON, ophthalmologist; b. Gladewater, Tex., May 22, 1936; s. Hubert L. and Lillie Mae (Calvin) McK.; m. Mary Lou Payne, Dec. 27, 1958; children: Laura Kathryn, Clark Calvin, Martha Lu. BBA cum laude, Baylor U., 1958, MD, 1964. Diplomate Am. Bd. Ophthalmology. Intern Hermann Hosp., Houston, 1964-65, resident, 1965-68; pvt. practice Arlington, Tex., 1968—. Capt. USAFR, 1965-70. Recipient Cert. of Honor, Tex. State Bd. Med. Examiners, Austin, 1964, Disting. Svc. award Tex. Soc. Prevention of Blindness, Ft. Worth, 1977. Fellow ACS, Am. Acad. Ophthalmology, Tex. Soc. Ophthalmology and Otolaryngology; mem. AMA, Am. Soc. Cataract and Refractive Surgery, Tex. Med. Assn. (del. 1978-86), Tarrant County Ophthal. Soc. (pres. 1975-76), Arlington Downtown Rotary Club, Alpha Epsilon Delta. Baptist. Office: 707 N Fielder Rd Ste B Arlington TX 76012-4637

MCKAIN, MARK KELLY, physician; b. Indpls., Mar. 21, 1955; s. John Maurice and Barbara Ann (Jenkins) McK.; m. Margaret Domasinsky, Mar. 9, 1985; children: Patrick J., Kevin J. BA, Coll. Idaho, Caldwell, 1979; MD, Wayne State U., 1987. Diplomate Am. Bd. Surgery. Intern William Beaumont Hosp., Detroit, 1987-88, resident in surgery, 1988-92; pvt. practice Twin Falls, Idaho, 1992—. Fellow ACS. Office: 253 Martin St Twin Falls ID 83301

MCKECHNIE, ARLENE VERONICA, nursing administrator; b. Detroit, Jan. 14, 1939; d. George Anthony and Veronica Rose (Dubiel) Szymanski; m. Norval F. McKechnie, Jan. 28, 1961; children: Cheryl, Michelle, Dennis, Mark, Neil, Ronald. RN magna cum laude, Providence Hosp. Sch. Nursing, Detroit, 1959; BS in Health Care Adminstrn. with honors, St. Leo (Fla.) Coll. Coord. diplomate Am. Bd. Quality Assurance and Utilization Rev. Physicians; cert. case mg. Cert. Ins. Rehab. Specialists; cert. profl. in utilization rev. V.p. McKechnie Machinery Co., Longwood, Fla., 1972—, McKechnie Internat., Longwood, 1977—; utilization rev. nurse Medwatch Inc., Lake Mary, Fla., 1989-92, supr. nurses, 1990—, med. case mgr., 1991—; v.p Medwatch Inc., Casselberry, Fla., 1992—; med. case mgr. Eslu, Inc., Lake Mary, 1993—. Editor, author newsletter MedWatch Minutes, 1994—. Officer Home Sch. Assn., Altamonte Springs, Fla., 1980; officer, chmn. bd. Bd. of Edn., Bishop Moore H.S., 1983-84; pre-marriage counselor Ch. of Annunciation, Altamonte Springs, 1993—.

MCKECHNIE, JOHN CHARLES, gastroenterologist, educator; b. Louisville, Feb. 1, 1935; s. Albert Hay and Edna Scott (Johnson) M.; children: Steven Keith, Kevin Stuart. BA, U. Louisville, 1955; MD, Baylor Coll. Medicine, 1959. Diplomate Am. Bd. Internal Medicine, Am. Bd. Gastroenterology. Intern Jefferson Davis Hosp., Houston, 1959-60; resident in internal medicine Baylor Affiliated Program, Houston, 1960-61, 65-66; gen. practice medicine, Benham, Ky., 1964; practice medicine specializing in gastroenterology, Houston, 1966—; clin. instr. Baylor Coll. Medicine, Houston, 1966-69, asst. prof., 1969-72, assoc. prof., 1972-77, prof., 1977—; mem. staff Methodist Hosp.; cons. Ben Taub Hosp., St. Luke's Episcopal Hosp. Served to capt. USMC, 1962-64. Fellow Am. Coll. Gastroenterology (gov. Tex. 1979-80, trustee 1981-84), ACP; mem. AMA, So. Med. Assn., Tex. Med. Assn., Am. Gastroent. Assn., Digestive Disease Found., Am. Soc. Gastrointestinal Endoscopy, Tex. Soc. Gastrointestinal Endoscopy, Houston Gastroent. Soc. (pres. 1983), Alpha Omega Alpha. Republican. Baptist. Contbr. numerous articles to profl. jours. Office: 6560 Fannin St Ste 1630 Houston TX 77030-2710

MCKEE, DWIGHT LIST, physician; b. Cleve., Aug. 24, 1948; s. Richard List and Florence May (Johnson) McK.; m. Jillellen Gurney, Jan. 1, 1989; children: Micaela Rose Collins, Luke Alexander. BA cum laude, Williams Coll., 1970; student, Case Western Res. U., 1970-73; MD, U. Ky., 1975. Diplomate Am. Bd. Internal Medicine and Med. Oncology. Intern surgery Washington Hosp. Ctr., Washington, 1975-76; assoc. med. dir. Integral Health Svcs., Putnam, Conn., 1976-79; pvt. practice Boulder, Colo., 1980-84; rsch. assoc. Inst. Applied Biology, N.Y.C., 1984-86; founding ptnr., co. physician Profl. Dental Techs., Batesville, Ark., 1986-88; intern internal medicine L.A. County/ U. So. Calif. Hosp., L.A., 1988-89; resident internal medicine Santa Clara Valley Med. Ctr., San Jose, Calif., 1989-91; fellow hematology/oncology Scripps Clinic and Rsch. Found., La Jolla, Calif., 1992-95; internal medicine staff Scripps Clinic and Rsch. Found., La Jolla, 1995—; health affairs cons. Profl. Dental Techs., Batesville, 1988—; guest scientist immunology The Scripps Rsch. Inst., La Jolla, 1994-96; pvt. practice Oncology Med. Ctr. of North County Vista, Calif., 1995—. Contbr. chpt. to book and articles to profl. jours. Mem. Am. Soc. Clin. Oncology, Am. Soc. Hematology, Am. Assn. for Cancer Rsch., Phi Beta Kappa. Home: 12584 Montellano Tr San Diego CA 92130 Office: Scripps Clinic & Rsch Found 10666 N Torrey Pines Rd La Jolla CA 92037

MCKEE, FRANCIS JOHN, medical association executive, lawyer; b. Bklyn., Aug. 31, 1943; s. Francis Joseph and Catherine (Giles) McK.; m. Antoinette Mary Sancis; children: Lisa Ann, Francis Dominic, Michael Christopher, Thomas Joseph. AB, Stonehill Coll., 1965; JD, St. John's U., 1970. Bar: N.Y. 1971. Assoc. Samuel Weinberg, Esquire, Bklyn., 1970-71, Finch & Finch, Esquire, Long Island City, N.Y., 1971-72; staff atty. Med. Soc. of State of N.Y., Lake Success, N.Y., 1972-77; prin. Francis J. McKee Assocs., Clinton, N.Y., 1984—; exec. dir. Suffolk Physicians Rev. Orgn., East Islip, N.Y., 1977-81, N.Y. State Soc. Surgeons, Inc., Clinton, N.Y., 1981—, N.Y. State Soc. Orthopaedic Surgeons, Inc., Clinton, 1981—, Upstate N.Y. chpt. ACS, Inc., Clinton, 1981—, N.Y. State Ophthalmol. Soc., 1984-92, N.Y. State Soc. Obstetricians and Gynecologists, 1985—, Orthopac of N.Y., 1986—, Nat. Com. for the Preservation Orthopaedic Practice, Clinton, 1989—; L.I. Ophthalmological Soc., 1994—. With U.S. Army, 1966-68. Mem. N.Y. State Bar Assn., Oneida County Bar Assn., Am. Soc. Assn. Execs., Am. Assn. Med. Soc. Execs., Nat. Health Lawyers Assn., Skenandoa Club, Am. Legion. Republican. Roman Catholic. Home: 19 Mulberry St Clinton NY 13323-1532 Office: Box 308 40 Chenango Ave Clinton NY 13323-0308

MCKEE, JEAN MARIE, physician assistant; b. Waverly, N.Y., Dec. 29, 1926; d. Alfred John and Julia Veronica (Cain) McGrade; m. John McKee, June 14, 1941 (dec. Oct. 1993); children: Michael John, Susan Elizabeth, Timothy Daniel, Teresa Ann. AS, U. Sante Fe; BS, U. Gla. Cert. physician asst., Fla. Surg. technician OR Robert Packer Hosp., Sayre, Pa.; office nurse Dr. Eisenbaugh, Lake Black, Fla.; technician ER Sebring (Fla.) Hosp.; physician asst. Student Health U. Fla., Gainesville, 1975-90; ret., 1990. Republican. Roman Catholic. Home: 1730 Independence Ave Melbourne FL 32940

MCKEE, MARGARET CRILE, pulmonary medicine and critical care physician; b. Cleve., Jan. 12, 1945; d. Richard List and Florence Mae (Johnson) McK. BA, Coll. Wooster, 1967; M in Regional Planning, Cornell U., 1971; MD, SUNY, Stony Brook, 1976. Diplomate Am. Bd. Internal Medicine, Pulmonary Medicine and Critical Care. Social planner Model Cities, Binghamton, N.Y., 1970-71; resident internal medicine Harlem Hosp., N.Y.C., 1976-79; physician Health Ins. Plan, Bedford-Williamsburg, N.Y., 1979-80; pulmonary fellow Columbia Presbyn. Med. Ctr., N.Y.C., 1980-82; chief of medicine Phoenix Indian Med. Ctr., 1983-92; pvt. practice Ariz. Med. Clinic, Sun City, Ariz., 1992—. Mem. Am. Coll. Chest Physicians, Am. Thoracic Soc., Soc. of Critical Care Medicine, Union of Concerned Scientists, Sierra Club. Methodist. Office: Ariz Med Clinic 13640 N Plaza Del Rio Blvd Peoria AZ 85381-4848

MCKEE, WILLIAM M., medical administrator; b. Superior, Wis., June 4, 1936; s. Jay W. and Marcile V. (Heist) McK.; m. Caroline M. Stowers, June 13, 1959; children: Gregory, Sarah, David. BS, U. Wis., 1957; MD, S, 1960. Diplomate Am. Bd. Internal Medicine. Med. dir. Providence Med. Ctr., Seattle, 1967-95, Quality Providence Health Sys. Puget Sound, Seattle, 1995—; gen. internist Wenatchee (Wash.) Valley Clinic, 1967-87. Pres. Apple Valley Kidney Fund, Wenatchee, 1972; bd. dirs. Northwest Kidney Ctr., Seattle, 1988—. Fellow Am. Coll. Physicians; mem. Am. Coll. Physician Execs., Wash. State Med. Assn., King County Med. Soc. Avocations: fishing, boat building. Office: Providence Health Sys Puget Sound 1600 E Jefferson Seattle WA 98124

MCKEEN, EDWIN CLIFFORD, psychologist; b. Bend, Oreg., Jan. 31, 1939; s. Edwin Owen and Margaret Carla (Eckelman) McK.; m. Patti M. Ooley, Jan. 3, 1992; children: Rachel, Lindsey, Alexandria. BA, Portland (Oreg.) State U., 1964, MA, 1969; PhD, U. Oreg., 1973. Lic. psychologist, Oreg.; cert. sch. psychologist Tchrs. Stds. and Practices Commn. Psychol. examiner Portland Pub. Schs., 1966-69; rsch. asst. U. Oreg., Eugene, 1970-72; psychologist Josephine County Mental Health, Grants Pass, Oreg., 1972-76; dir. spl. svcs. Grants Pass Pub. Schs., 1976-78, psychologist, 1978-81; pvt. practice, Astoria, Oreg., 1981-84, Tigard, Oreg., 1986-96; counselor Am. Sch. in Japan, Tokyo, 1984-86; sch. psychologist Beaverton (Oreg.) Sch. Dist., 1986-95; advisor to adminstrv. bd. Stepping Stone House, Grants Pass, 1974-76; del. behavior therapist Person to Person Program, China, 1982; psychologist, ednl. cons. Tokyo Cmty. Counseling Svcs., 1984-86; adj. instr. Lewis and Clark Coll., Portland, 1994; guest lectr. Portland State U., 1991-94; presenter in field. Chmn. Juvenile Svcs. Commn., Grants Pass, 1980-82; mem. biomed. ethics com. Columbia Meml. Hosp., Astoria, 1983-84; vol. Head Start programs Washington County (Oreg.) Cmty. Action, 1992-94. Grantee Law Enforcement Assistance Agy., Jackson and Josephine Counties, Oreg., 1972-75. Mem. APA, NASP, Assn. for Advancement Behavior Therapy, Oreg. Psychol. Assn., Oreg. Sch. Psychologists Assn. (charter, 1st co-chmn. 1971-72). Office: Ste 195 15350 SW Sequoia Pkwy Tigard OR 97224

MCKENNA, DENNIS GARRETT, physician assistant; b. Chgo., Aug. 21, 1943; s. Garrett and Alice Elizabeth (Carr) McK.; m. Peg Ann Povolish, May 27, 1972; children: Shannon Kilree, Joseph Garrett. BS in Biology, Loyola U., 1966, MEd in Adminstrn. and Supervision, 1968; Cert. Physician Asst., St. Louis U., 1975. Asst. athletic dir., head athletic trainer Loyola U., Chgo., 1971-73; physician asst. primary care Family Med. Ctr., Nashville, Ill., 1975, C.J. Jannings III MD, Fairfield, Ill., 1975-76, Tomlinson Med. Assn., Lincoln, Ill., 1976-77; physician asst. neurol. surgery J. Cochran VA, St. Louis, 1977-89; physician asst. Clin. Inst. Neurosurgery Wash. U. Sch. Med., St. Louis, 1985-89; pvt. practice physician asst. neurosurgery Cobb Neurosurgery Assn., Marietta, Ga., 1989—. Mem. performing arts dir. search com. North Atlanta H.S., 1991-95, jazz blues com., 1994-95. Recipient Humanitarian award B'nai B'rith Soc., 1961. Fellow Am. Acad. Physician Assts., Acad. Neurosurg. Physician Assts. (founder 1990); mem. Nat. Commn. Cert. Physician Assts. (cert.), Am. Assn. Neurol. Surgeons (assoc.), Ga. Acad. Physician Assts., Alpha Delta Gamma, Blue Key Fraternity. Home: 3270 Highborne Pl Marietta GA 30066 Office: Cobb Neurosurg Assn 80 Lacy St Marietta GA 30060

MCKENNA, JOHN JOSEPH, psychology educator, clinical psychologist; b. Harrisburg, Pa., Jan. 21, 1940; s. John Joseph and Elizabeth Carmelita (Sculley) McK.; m. Jacquelyn Helen Willette, May 25, 1974. STM, Andover Newton Theol. Sch., 1972; PhD, U. Vt., 1987. Lic. clin. psychologist, Vt. Tng. coord. Alcohol & Drug Abuse Div., Waterbury, Vt., 1972-73; project dir. Alcohol & Drug Abuse Div., Montpelier, Vt., 1973-74; intern. Vt. State Hosp., Waterbury, Vt., 1979-80, Behavior Therapy & Psychotherapy Ctr., Burlington, Vt., 1980-83; intern Wright House, Colchester, Vt., 1985-88; pvt. practice Colchester, Vt., 1988—; from instr. to assoc. prof. Trinity Coll., Burlington, Vt., 1974—; coord. of assessment Trinity Coll., 1990-93; presenter conf. Vt. Psychol. Assn., Rutland, 1995; cons. Diocesan rev. bd. for Sexual Misconduct, 1995—. Recipient Sears Roebuck Found. Teaching Excellence and Campus Leadership award Trinity Coll., 1990, Wye faculty fellow Wash. U., 1989. Mem. Am. Psychol. Soc., New Eng. Psychol. Assn., Vt. Psychol. Assn. Home: 157 Rivermount Ter Burlington VT 05401-1115 Office: Trinity Coll 208 Colchester Ave Burlington VT 05401-1470

MCKENNA, JOHN RICHARD, surgeon; b. Springfield, Mo., Dec. 27, 1926; s. George Edward and Eunice Marie (Stark) McK.; m. Wilma Pearl Choate, May 10, 1951; children: Mary Kathleen, Mary Ann, John Richard Jr., James David. BA, U. Tex., 1949; MD, U. Tex. Med. Br., Galveston, 1953. Diplomate Am. Bd. Surgery. Intern USPHS, New Orleans, 1953-54; staff physician USPHS, Galveston, 1954-56; resident in gen. surgery USPHS, Balt., 1956-59; asst. chief surgery USPHS, Memphis, 1959-61; dep. chief surgery USPHS, Norfolk, Va., 1961-64; chief of surgery USPHS, Galveston, 1964-72; pvt. practice Galveston Surg. Group, 1972-94, Gulf Coast Med. Group, Galveston, 1994—; asst. prof. surgery U. Tex. Med. Br., Galveston, 1964—. Contbr. articles to profl. jours. With USN, 1944-46; capt. USPHS, 1953-72. Mem. AMA, Tex. Med. Assn. Home: 45 Adler Cir Galveston TX 77551 Office: Gulf Coast Med Group 200 University Blvd Galveston TX 77550

MCKENNA, MICHAEL J., toxicologist; b. Buffalo, Oct. 9, 1946; s. William T. and Mildred (Carey) McK.; m. Mary Radell, Aug. 16, 1969; children: Mary, Ryan. BA, St. John Fisher Coll., 1968; PhD in Toxicology, U. Rochester, 1975. Diplomate Am. Bd. Toxicology. Sr. rsch. toxicologist Toxicology Rsch. Lab. Dow Chem. U.S.A., Midland, Mich., 1975-77, rsch. specialist, 1977-79, group leader, 1979-82, rsch. mgr., 1982-84; assoc. dir. Pathology and Exptl. Toxicology Parke-Davis Rsch., Ann Arbor, Mich., 1984-89, v.p. Drup Devel., 1989-95; pres. Lab. Biopharm. Rsch. Internat., Inc., Wilmington, N.C., 1995—; bd. dirs. Am. Bd. Toxicology, 1982-86. Contbr. articles to profl. jours. Mem. AAAS, Soc. Toxicology (membership com. 1987-90), Mich. Soc. Toxicology (v.p. 1982-83, pres. 1983-84), Internat. Soc. for the Study of Xenobiotics, Drug Info. Assn., Sigma Xi. Office: Lab Biopharm Rsch Internat Inc 1410 Commonwealth Dr Wilmington NC 28403

MCKENNA, ROBERT E., JR., health marketing executive, physician assistant; b. Honolulu, Mar. 4, 1954; s. Robert E. and Alice Jeanne (Stone) McK.; m. Ruth L. Hirschfeld, Dec. 28, 1976; children: Devin S., Brandon S. BS, physician assoc., U. Okla., 1981; MPH, Portland (Oreg.) State U., 1996. Cert. Nat. Commn. Cert. Physician Assts., 1981. Physician asst. Plaza Med. Ctr., New Port Richey, Fla., 1981-84; profl. hosp. rep. Merck Human Health Divsn., Tampa, Fla., 1984-87, sr. coord. health sci. assn., 1987-90; exec. health sci. assoc. Merck Human Health Divsn., Portland, Oreg., 1990-96; mgr. cardiovascular market devel. Merck Human Health Divsn., Calif., 1996—; mem. tech. com. Oreg. Scorecard Consortium, Oreg. Health Policy Inst., Portland, 1995—; invited participant Health Cmties. 2000, Portland/Multnomah Progress Bd., 1995; adv. bd. cmty. health improvement program, Providence Health Sys., Portland, 1995; strategic planner, Oreg. Health Policy Inst., 1995, Heart Inst. Spokane, Wash., 1994-95. Lectr. in field. To E-5 hosp. corpsman, USN, 1975-79. Mem. Am. Acad. Cardiovascular and Pulmonary Rehab., Am. Acad. Physician Assts., Am. Coll. Health Care Execs., Am. Heart Assn. (coun. on clin. cardiology), Am. Soc. of Hypertension, Oreg. Pub. Health Assn. Home and Office: Merck Human Health Divsn 21264 SW 90th Ave Tualatin OR 97062

MCKENNA-CLIMES, THERESA K., family practice physician; b. Covington, Ky., May 6, 1954; d. Richard H. McKenna and Catherine A. (Menne) Ryan; m. Gary A. Climes, Oct. 6, 1990; children: Alison M., Caitlin E. BS, Mich. State U., 1976, DO, 1986. Diplomate Am. Bd. Family Practice. Intern Flint Osteopathic Hosp., 1986-87; resident Edward W. Sparrow Hosp., Lansing, Mich., 1987; physician Portland (Mich.) Family Practice, 1989-90, Eaton Rapids (Mich.) Med. Clinic, 1990-94, Okemos (Mich.) Family Practice, 1994—. Mem. AMA, Am. Acad. Family Physicians, Am. Osteo. Assn. Office: Okemos Family Practice 1600 W Grand River Ste 4 Okemos MI 48864

MCKENZIE, HARRY JAMES, surgeon, surgical researcher; b. Meyersdale, Pa., Aug. 7, 1960; s. Henry Sadrus and Betty Elaine (Reiber) McK.; m. Judith Palmieri, July 6, 1985; 1 child, Henry James. BS, Duquesne U., 1984; postgraduate, U. Pitts., 1986-87; MD, Hahnemann U., 1992. Surg. intern Temple U., Conemaugh Med. Ctr., Johnstown, Pa., 1992-93, surg. resident, 1993-97; mem. problem task force Conemaugh Med. Ctr., 1992-93. Contbr. articles to profl. jours.; presenter in field. Hosp. vol. Ctrl. Med. Pavilion, Pitts., 1981-84, Presbyn. Hosp., Pitts., 1986-87; med. exam. officer, Phila. Special Olympics, 1989-90; grad. banquet spkr. Salisbury (Pa.) H.S., 1993.. Recipient 3d place rsch. competition award, ACS Region III com. on trauma, Norfolk, Va., 1993; recipient 1st place rsch. competition award ACS-Pa. com. on trauma, Hershey, 1993. Mem. ACS, AMA, Am. Soc. Gen. Surgeons, Pa. Med. Soc., Cambria County Med. Soc. Home: 111 Curtis Dr Johnstown PA 15904

MCKENZIE, JENNIFER EULETH, nurse; b. Port Antonio, Jamaica, July 9, 1960; came to U.S., 1989; d. Dola McKenzie and Hortense (Ellis) Thomas; children: Zoya, Mikhail, Asante. BS, CCNY, 1995; Cert. in Nursing, U. Hosp. of W.I. Sch. Nursing, Kingston, Jamaica, 1983; Lab. Tech. Cert., Coll. Arts, Sci. and, Technology, Kingston, 1979. RN, N.Y.; med.-surg. nurse, crit. care nurse. Lab. technician Coll. of Arts, Sci. and Technology, Kingston, 1977-80; RN U. Hosp. of W.I., Mona, Jamaica, 1983-89; med.-surg. nurse Columbia Presbyn. Med. Ctr., N.Y.C., 1989—. Mem. N.Y. State Nurses Assn., Am. Assn. Diabetes Educators, Sigma Theta Tau, Golden Ken.

MCKENZIE, PAMELA JEAN, physician; b. Denver, Apr. 24, 1940; d. John and Vashti Keefe McK.; divorced; 1 child, Duncan. MD, U. Colo., Denver, 1965. Intern, then resident Yale New Haven (Conn.) Hosp., 1965-67; fellow in child devel. Yale Child Study Ctr., New Haven, 1967-69, from instr. to asst. prof., 1969-71; asst. prof. JFK Child Devel. Ctr., Denver, 1971-76, Kempe Child Abuse Ctr., Denver, 1976-78; dir. child devel. ctr. The Children's Hosp., Denver, 1978—. Editor: (book) The Fragile X Syndrome, 1984; contbr. articles to profl. jours. Fellow Am. Acad. Pediatrics. Democrat. Office: The Childrens Hosp 1056 E 19th Ave Denver CO 80218-1007

MCKENZIE-ANDERSON, RITA LYNN, psychologist; b. Boston, Nov. 25, 1952; d. Wallace Andrew and Angelina Rita (Bagnoli) McK; m. Brien Anderson, Oct. 22, 1994. BA, Framingham State Coll., 1974; MEd, Northeastern U., 1975; PhD, Temple U., 1983. Lic. psychologist, Mass. Pvt. practice Fairfield, Conn., 1984-86; psychologist Johnson Life Ctr., Springfield, Mass., 1986-87, dir. outpatient therapy, 1987-88; pvt. practice Springfield, 1988—; investigator Springfield Juvenile Ct., 1989—; adj. faculty Holyoke (Mass.) Community Coll., 1989-90, Springfield Tech. Community Coll., 1989-90; dir. day treatment DuBois Day Treatment Ctr., Stamford, Conn., 1982-86; cons. psychologist Community Care Mental Health Ctr., Springfield, 1989—, Spofford Hall Treatment Ctr., Ludlow, Mass., 1991-92. Trustee Northampton (Mass.) State Hosp., 1989-93; mem. organizing com. Week of Young Child, Springfield, 1988-93; bd. dirs. Stop Abuse Against Kids. Mem. Women Bus. Owners Alliance, Zonta Internat. Office: 380 Union St Ste 14 West Springfield MA 01089-4123

MCKEOWN, BARRY CLIFTON, exercise physiology educator; b. Brookings, S.D., June 13, 1943; s. Wayne D. and Evelyn A. (Erickson) McK. BS, S.D. State U., 1966, MS, 1967; PhD, U. Ill., 1979. Tchr., athletic dir. Wessington Springs (S.D.) Acad., 1967-68, Houghton (N.Y.) Acad., 1968-69; rsch. assoc. U. Ill., Urbana, 1973-77; grad. coord. health, phys. edn. and recreation S.D. State U., Brookings, 1977-83; prof. physiology of exercise U. Tex., Arlington, 1983—, chmn. dept. exercise, sport and health studies, 1995—; acad. cons. Cen. Coll., McPherson, Kans., 1984—; vis. prof. La Universidad del Zulia, Marcaibo, Venezuela, 1993. Author: (lab. manual) Physiology Exercise, 1991; also articles. With USAF, 1969-73. Fellow Human Biology Coun.; mem. AAHPERD (fellow rsch. consortium, chmn. rsch. sect. cen. dist. 1982, pres. Exercise Physiology Acad. 1991-92), Am. Coll. Sports Med. (bd. dirs. Tex. chpt. 1988-93, exec. dir. 1994—), Tex. Assn. Health, Phys. Edn., Recreation and Dance (chmn. rsch. sect. 1989, mem. editorial bd. Jour. 1989-91), Fellowship Christian Athletes. Republican. Mem. Wesleyan Ch. of Am. Office: U Tex UTA Box 19259 Arlington TX 76019

MCKINLEY, C. TIMOTHY, physician, county coroner; b. Cin., Aug. 26, 1957; s. Charles Willard and Mary Lou (Hauke) McK.; m. Shawna Lynn Anderson, June 23, 1994; children: Christopher Ryan, Marissa Christina. AS summa cum laude, So. State Coll., 1977; BS in Biology summa cum laude, U. Cin., 1979, MD, 1983. Diplomate Am. Bd. Family Practice. Resident Dept. Family Medicine, U. Cin., 1983-86; family physician Sardina (Ohio) Med. Clinic, 1986—; Brown county coroner Brown County, Georgetown, Ohio, 1989—; med. dir. Villa Georgetown Nursing Home, 1987-94, Brown County Annual Health Fair, 1987-94, Optioncare Home Infusion Svcs., Brown County Home Care Unit, 1987-94; past mng. ptnr., 1990-94; mem. quality assurance and exec. com. Clermont Mercy Hosp., Brown County Gen. Hosp.; pres. Brown County Med. Staff, 1989-91, v.p., sec., treas., 1987-89; mem. admissions com. U. Cin. Coll. of Medicine, on site instrn. med. students, family medicine residents, vol. faculty. Mem. Phi Beta Kappa, Alpha Omega Alpha. Home: 12926 St Rt 774 Bethel OH 45106 Office: Sardinia Med Ctr 151 Maple Ave Sardina OH 45171

MCKINLEY, CAMILLE DOMBROWSKI, psychologist; b. Buffalo, May 6, 1922; d. Eugene Anthony and Anne Victoria (Sliwinska) Dombrowski; m. Thomas Leroy Smith, Dec. 30, 1944 (div. 1977); children: Thomas Dan, Cynthia Camille (dec.), Pamela Susan; m. William Frank McKinley, Oct. 7, 1984 (dec. Mar. 1985). BA, Syracuse U., 1943; MA, Boston U., 1947; edn. specialist, Mich. State U., 1970, PhD, 1978. Acad. advisor Mich. State U., East Lansing, 1966-70, dir. Career Ctr., 1970-81, counseling psychologist Counseling Ctr., 1981-91; pres. Priam Pubs., 1978—; mem. Career Planning and Placement Coun. Mich. State U., 1970-91. Editor: The Mich. State Univ. Referral Directory, 1970-91, The Gracious Reader, 1970-80; editor, publisher The CAM Report, 1978—. Founding pres. Greater Lansing chpt. Planned Parenthood, Mich., 1967; v.p. Opera Co. of Mid-Mich., 1983-85; bd. dirs. Wharton Ctr. for Performing Arts and Dean's Cmty. Coun., Mich. State U., mem. Platinum Cir. Mem. Mich. State U. Pres.'s Club and Beaumont Tower Soc., Pontiac Yacht Club, Mackinac Island Yacht Club, Zonta Internat., Zeta Tau Alpha. Home: PO Box 1862 East Lansing MI 48826-1862

MCKINLEY, KEVIN L., neurologist; b. Joplin, Mo., Apr. 24, 1961; s. Galen Dean and Mary Alice (Hunt) McK.; m. Dawn Marie Sokol, May 7, 1988; children: Megan, Michael. BA, U. Mo., 1982, MD, 1985. Diplomate Am. Bd. Psychiatry & Neurology. Resident in neurology Baylor U., Houston, 1985-89, fellow in neuromuscular medicine, 1989-90; instr. Baylor Medicine, Houston, 1990-92; faculty Ochsner Clinic, New Orleans, 1992-96; asst. prof. Tulane Medicine, New Orleans, 1992—. Mem. AMA, Am. Acad.

Neurology. Office: Ochsner Clinic 1514 Jefferson Hwy New Orleans LA 70118

MCKINNEY, DAVID LEON, JR., internist, osteopath; b. Dallas, Aug. 31, 1965; s. David Leon and Camilla Elaine (Agee) McK.; m. Rebecca Ellen Barnett, July 8, 1995. BA in Biology, Baylor U., Waco, Tex., 1987; DO, U. North Tex., 1991. Diplomate Am. Bd. Internal Medicine. Intern, then intern N.E. Cmty. Hosp., Bedford, Tex., 1991-92; resident in internal medicine East Tenn. State U., Johnson City, 1992-94, chief resident, clin. instr., 1994-95; clin. dir. Fla. Cmty. Health Ctrs., Ft. Pierce, 1995; chmn. Dist. 15 HIV Entitlement Com., Ft. Pierce, 1995; mem. Nat. Health Svc. Corps, 1988—. Named Resident of Yr. in internal medicine East Tenn. State U., 1993; scholar Nat. Health Svc. Corps, 1988. Mem. AMA, ACP, Am. Osteo. Assn., So. Med. Assn., Alpha Omega Alpha. Repulican. Baptist. Home: 1306 SW Cottonwood Cove Port St Lucie FL 34986 Office: Fla Cmty Health Ctrs 609 N 7th St Fort Pierce FL 34950

MCKINNEY, JOHN MERRILL, JR., cardiothoracic surgeon; b. Gainesville, Fla., Apr. 9, 1959; s. John Merrill and Margaret Ann (Leeds) McK.; m. Michelle Ann Miller, Dec. 27, 1985; children: Lauren, Jacqueline, Caroline. BS in Chemistry, Miami U., 1982; MD, Ohio State U., 1987. chmn. quality assurance cardiac svcs. Holmes Regional Med. Ctr., Melbourne, Fla., 1995-96. Intern, resident in gen. surgery Good Samaritan Hosp., Cin., 1987-92; resident in cardiac surgery U. Louisville, 1992-94. Recipient rsch. award Good Samaritan Hosp., 1992, Tchg. award U. Louisville, 1994. Fellow ACS (assoc.); mem. Soc. Thoracic Surgery. Office: Cardiothoracic Surg Assocs 1601 S Apollo Blvd Melbourne FL 32901

MCKINNEY, RICK HAYES, optometrist; b. Wichita, Kans., Dec. 25, 1958; s. Roger Thomas McKinney and B. Joann (Hayes) Simmons; m. Chrystal Dawn Partin, June 7, 1980; children: Cole Tyler, Paige Diane. BS in Biology cum laude, Southwestern Coll., Winfield, Kans., 1981; OD magna cum laude, U. Houston, 1985. Lic. optometrist Kans., Tex. Pvt. practice Newton, Kans., 1985—; optometric chmn. liaison com. Blue Cross/Blue Shield of Kans., Topeka, 1988—. Commr. Newton Recreation Commn., 1994—, chmn., 1995-96; bd. dirs. Am. Cancer Soc., Newton, 1990-94. Mem. Am. Optometric Assn., Kans. Optometric Assn., Phi Kappa Phi, Beta Sigma Kappa. Office: 216 Meridian Rd Ste 1A Newton KS 67114-5119

MCKINNEY, WILLIAM T., psychiatrist, educator; b. Rome, Ga., Sept. 20, 1937. BA cum laude, Baylor U., 1959; MD, Vanderbilt U., 1963. Diplomate Nat. Bd. Med. Examiners (mem. psychiatry test com. 1982-87, chmn. 1984-87); cert. Am. Bd. Psychiatry and Neurology (sr. examiner 1979-90, bd. dirs. 1991—, mem. rsch. com., co-chair part I test com., chair added qualifications in geriatric psychiatry test com., mem. part II audio visual com., mem. disability accomodations com., rep. to residency rev. com.). Intern in medicine Bowman Gray Sch. Medicine, Wake Forest U., Winston-Salem, N.C., 1963-64; resident dept. psychiatry Sch. Medicine, U. N.C., Chapel Hill., 1964-66, Sch. Medicine, Stanford (Calif.) U., 1966-67; clin. assoc. psychosomatic sect. adult psychiatry br., tng. specialist, asst. br. chief NIMH, Bethesda, Md., 1967-69; asst. prof. psychiatry dept. psychiatry Sch. Medicine, U. Wis., Madison, 1969-72, assoc. prof. psychiatry, 1972-74, prof. psychiatry, 1974-93; Asher prof. of psychiatry dept. psychiatry and behavioral scis., dir. Asher Ctr. for Study and Treatment of Depressive Disorders Med. Sch., Northwestern U., Chgo., 1993—; part-time clin. pvt. practice, Bethesda, 1967-69; NIMH rsch. career investigator Sch. Medicine, U. Wis., Madison, 1970-75, rsch. psychiatrist Primate Lab., 1974-93, affiliate sci. Wis. Regional Primate Rsch. Ctr., 1974-93, affiliate prof. psychology dept. psychology, 1974-93, chmn. dept. psychiatry, 1975-80, dir. Wis. Psychiat. Rsch. Inst. Ctr. Health Scis., 1975-80; sr. staff psychiatrist William S. Middleton Meml. VA Hosp., Madison, Wis., 1974-93; rschr. sub dept. animal behaviour U. Cambridge, Eng., 1974; mem. rsch. rev. com. VA Behavioral Scis., 1976-79; Abbott Sigma XI Club lectr., 1976; Milw. Psychiat. Hosp. lectr., 1977; mem. program adv. com. and workshop chmn. Dahlem Found. Internat. Conf. on Depression, Berlin, 1982; U. Minn. lectr. at Festshrift, 1982; cons. grad. sch. U. Minn., 1982; fellow Ctr. Advanced Study in Behavioral Scis., Stanford, Calif., 1983-84; mem. external adv. bd. Clin. Rsch. Ctr. Dept. Psychiatry U. N.C., Chapel Hill, 1984—, cons., bd. advisors clin. rsch. fellow tng. program dept. psychology, 1988—; William F. Orr lectr. Vanderbilt U., 1985; vis. prof. dept. psychiatry U. Tex. Health Scis. Ctr., Dallas, 1986, U. Utah Sch. Medicine, Salt Lake City, 1987, U. Minn. Sch. Medicine, Mpls., 1988; cons. biol. scis. tng. br. divsn. manpower and tng. programs NIMH, 1975-76, mem. psychiatry spl. tng. com. 1983, plenary lectr., Clearwater, Fla., 1987, co-chairperson Workshop on Non-Human Primate Models of Psychopathology, 1987, mem. biol. psychopathology spl. rev. com., 1992—; mem. sci. core group MacArthur Found. Mental Health Rsch. Network I: The Psychobiology of Depression and Other Affective Disorders, 1988-93; vis. spkr. So. Calif. Psychiat. Soc., L.A., 1988; plenary lectr. Soc. Biol. Psychiatry ann. meeting, Montreal, 1988; vis. prof. Dalhousie U. Sch. Medicine, N.S., 1989, HCA Riveredge Hosp., Chgo., 1989, U. Pa., Phila., 1991, U. N.Mex., Albuquerque, 1992, Northwestern U., Chgo., 1992; invited spkr. Animal Models in Psychopharmacology Symposium, Duphar, Amsterdam, 1990; vis. spkr., cons. CIBA-GEIGY, Basel, Switzerland, 1990; mem. minority instns. rsch. devel. rev. com. Alcohol, Drug Abuse and Mental Health Adminstrn., 1990; guest spkr. Inst. Pa. Hosp., Phila., 1991; reviewer Human Frontier Sci. Program, 1992—; external cons. dept. psychiatry Mental Health Clin. Rsch. Ctr. U. Tex. Southwestern Med. Ctr., Dallas, 1992—; presenter in field. Author: Animal Models of Mental Disorders: A New Comparative Psychiatry, 1988; co-author: Mood Disorders: Towards a New Psychobiology, 1984; mem. editl. bd. Archives of Psychiatry and Neurol. Scis., Contemporary Psychiatry, 1981-82, Ethology and Sociobiology, Experientia, 1982-89, Trends in Neurosciences, 1982-86, Neuropsychopharmacology, 1987-90; manuscript and book reviewer numerous sci. jours.; contbr. articles to profl. jours. USHPS fellow in biostats.bilt U., 1962; recipient Beauchamp award Vanderbilt U. Med. Sch., 1963, Rsch. Career Devel. award NIMH, 1975, Rsch. Leave award U. Wis., 1983-84, Am. Acad. Pediats. award, 1991. Fellow Am. Psychiat. Assn. (cons. psychiat. edn. consultation svc. 1983—), Am. Coll. Psychiatrists, Am. Coll. Neuropsychopharmacology (mem. constn. and rules com. 1985-87, mem. ethics com. 1987-89, mem. fin. com. 1990-92, panel chair San Juan, P.R. 1992, panel presenter 1992); mem. Am. Soc. Primatologists, Am. Psychosomatic Soc. (mem. program com. 1975-76), Internat. Primatology Soc., Internat. Coll. Neurobiology, Biol. Psychiatry and Psychopharmacology (lectr. Zurich 1985), Internat. Soc. Devel. Psychobiology, Internat. Soc. Ethological and Behavioral Pharmacology (bd. advisors 1983—), Collegium Internat. Neuro-Psychopharmacologicum, Psychiat. Rsch. Soc., Soc. Neuroscience, Wis. Psychiat. Assn. (chmn. program com. 1972, co-chairperson task force on sexual misconduct and membership edn. 1986-88, pres.-elect 1989-91, pres. 1991-93). Office: Northwestern U Med Sch Dept Psychiatry and Behavioral Scis 303 E Chicago Ave Bldg 9-176 Chicago IL 60611-3008

MCKINNON, JOHN WESLEY LEANDER, JR., physician assistant; b. San Antonio, Dec. 24, 1943; s. Leander McKinnon and Leathia Adla (Callies) McK; m. Denise Murray, July 30, 1990; 1 child, Bettina Aleathia. BS, Howard U., 1985; MPH, U. D.C., 1993. Certified physician assistant, 1979. Office machine repairman Houston Sch. Dist., 1965-66; computer specialist U.S. Army, Ft. Lee, Va., 1969-72; LPN, 2290th U.S. Army Hosp., Rockville, Md., 1974-85; clin. specialist Walter Reed Army Med. Ctr., Washington, 1974-85; paramedic D.C. Fire Dept., Washington, 1983-90; physician's asst. D.C. Dept. Corrections, Washington, 1990—, mem. pharm. com., 1992—; res. officer D.C. Police Dept., 1972-80; practitioner, manager Chronic Disease Clinic, D.C. Detention Ctr., 1984; pub. health educator U. D.C., 1985; infectious disease officer NIMH, 1980-82. Author: (booklet) Guides for Computer Operators, 1972. Publ. health advisor St. Elizabeths Hosp., Washington, 1984-85. Sgt. 1st class U.S. Army, 1966-69. Recipient Clinton Thompson award Howard U., 1979, outstanding award D.C. Prisons, 1993; Presdl. scholar U. D.C., 1985. Mem. Am. Acad. Physician Assts., Am. Acad. Surgeons, Am. Assn. Phys. Edn., Therapy and Pub. Health, Fraternal Order Police (cons. 1994—). Republican. Baptist. Home: 1225 Emerson St NE Washington DC 20017 Office: DC Dept Corrections 1901 D St SE Washington DC 20003

MCKISSICK, JANET M., family practice physician; b. Rochester, N.Y., June 5, 1961; d. Dale Clay and Katie Louise (Wilson) McK. BA, U. Va., 1983, MD, 1987. Diplomate Am. Bd. Family Practice. Pvt. practice Allendale County Rural Health, Fairfax, S.C., 1991-96. Office: Allendale Co Rural Health PO Box 36 Fairfax SC 29827

MCKNIGH, MELANIE JEANNE, nephrologist; b. Denver, Mar. 6, 1961; d. George Tipton and Barbara P. (Parswell) McK.; m. Patrick Daniel Martin, Dec. 21, 1990; 1 child, Ryan Henri Martin. BS, La. State U., 1983, MD, 1985. Diplomate Am. Bd. Internal Medicine. Staff physician Tulane U., Pineville, La., 1991-92; fellow La. State U. Med. Ctr., New Orleans, 1993-95; staff physician Ochsner Clinic, Baton Rouge, 1995—. Mem. Jr. League Baton Rouge, 1994—. Home: 18732 W Piney Point Baton Rouge LA 70817 Office: 16777 Medical Center Dr Baton Rouge LA 70816

MCKNIGHT, LENORE RAVIN, child psychiatrist; b. Denver, May 15, 1943; d. Abe and Rose (Steed) Ravin; m. Robert Lee McKnight, July 22, 1967; children: Richard Rex, Janet Rose. Student, Occidental Coll., 1961-63; BA, U. Colo., 1965, postgrad. in medicine, 1965-67; MD, U. Calif., San Francisco, 1969. Diplomate Am. Bd. Psychiatry and Neurology. Cert. adult and child psychiatrist Am. Bd. Psychiatry. Intern pediatrics Children's Hosp., San Francisco, 1969-70; resident in gen. psychiatry Langley Porter Neuropsychiat. Inst., 1970-73, fellow child psychiatry, 1972-74; child psychiatrist Youth Guidance Center, San Francisco, 1974-74; pvt. practice medicine specializing in child psychiatry, Walnut Creek, Calif., 1974-93; asst. clin. prof. Langley Porter Neuropsychiat. Inst., 1974—; asst. clin. prof. psychiatry U. Calif. San Francisco Med. Ctr. Internat.; med. dir. CPC Walnut Creek (Calif.) Hosp., 1990-93. Insts. Edn. fellow U. Edinburgh, 1964; NIH grantee to study childhood nutrition, 1966. Fellow Am. Acad. Child and Adolescent Psychiatry; mem. Am. Coll. Physician Execs., Internat. Arabian Horse Assn., Diablo Arabian Horse Assn. Avocation: breeding Arabian Horses. Office: Kaiser Martinez Inpat Psych 200 Muir Rd Martinez CA 94553-4614

MCKOWN, JANE ANN, medical and surgical nurse, educator; b. Greenfield, Ohio, Dec. 18, 1924; d. Ralph Worley and Hazel Mae (Smith) Hull; m. James Williams McKown, May 1, 1948; children: James Thomas, Janet Ann. Diploma, Christ Hosp. Sch. Nursing, Cin., 1945; BSN cum laude, Ohio U., 1978. Cert. by Dept. Aging, Am. Heart Assn. Office nurse, lab trainee Cin.; staff devel. Greenfield (Ohio) Area Med. Ctr.; nursing educator Area Agy. on Aging Dist. 7, Rio Grande, Ohio; instr. So. State Community Coll., Hillsboro, Ohio. With Army Cadet Nurse Corps, 1945. Mem. ANA, Ohio Nurses Assn., Highland County Heart Assn. Home: 10935 State Route 138 SW Greenfield OH 45123-9281

MCKUSICK, VICTOR ALMON, geneticist, educator, physician; b. Parkman, Maine, Oct. 21, 1921; s. Carroll L. and Ethel M. (Buzzell) Mc K.; m. Anne Bishop, June 11, 1949; children: Carol Anne, Kenneth Andrew, Victor Wayne. Student, Tufts Coll., 1940-43; MD, Johns Hopkins U., 1946; DSc (hon.), N.Y. Med. Coll., 1974; MD (hon.), Liverpool U., 1976; DSc (hon.), U. Maine, 1978, Tufts U., 1978, U. Rochester, 1979, Meml. U., Nfld., 1979; DMCh (hon.), U. Helsinki, 1981; D Med. Sci. (hon.), Med. U. S.C., 1979; MD (hon.), Edinburgh U., 1984; DSc (hon.), Aberdeen U., 1988, Med. Coll. Ohio, 1988, Bates Coll., 1989; PhD (hon.), Tel Aviv U., 1989; MD (hon.), Zurich (Switzerland) U., 1990; DSc (hon.), Colby Coll., 1991, U. Chgo., 1991, Mt. Sinai Sch. Medicine, 1992. Diplomate Am. Bd. Internal Medicine. Tng. in clin. medicine, lab. rsch. Johns Hopkins U./USPHS, 1946-52; instr. medicine Johns Hopkins Sch. Medicine, 1952-54, asst. prof., 1954-57, assoc. prof., 1957-60, chief divsn. med. genetics, dept. medicine, 1957-73, prof. medicine, 1960-85, prof. epidemiology, biology, 1969-78, William Osler prof. medicine, 1978-85, chmn. dept. medicine, 1973-85; physician-in-chief Johns Hopkins Hosp., 1973-85, Univ. prof. medical genetics, 1985—, chief div. med. genetics, 1957-73, 85-89; mem. rsch. adv. com. Nat. Found., 1959-78, med. adv. bd. Howard Hughes Med. Inst., 1967-83, com. mapping and sequencing of human genome Nat. Acad. Sci., 1986-88; pres. Internat. Med. Congress, Ltd., 1972-78; mem. Nat. Adv. Rsch. Resources Coun., 1970-74; mem. bd. sci. advisers Roche Inst. Molecular Biology, 1967-71; trustee Jackson Lab., 1979—; founding mem. Am. Bd. Med. Genetics, 1979-82; pres. 8th Internat. Congress of Human Genetics, 1991; mem. human genome adv. com. NIH, 1988-92, NIH/DOE work group on ethical, legal and societal implications of human genome project, 1990-95; co-chmn. Centennial of Johns Hopkins Hosp., 1989-90; co-founder, co-dir. ann. short course in med. and exptl. mammalian genetics, Bar Harbor, Maine, 1960—; co-founder, co-dir. European Sch. Med. Genetics Sestri Levante, 1988—; chmn. com. on DNA tech. in forensic sci. NRC/NAS, 1989-92, adv. update com., 1993-96. Author: Heritable Disorders of Connective Tissue, 1956, 60, 66, 72, 93, Cardiovascular Sound in Health and Disease, 1958, Medical Genetics 1958-60, 1961, Human Genetics, 1964, 69, On the X Chromosome of Man, 1964, Mendelian Inheritance in Man, 1966, 68, 71, 75, 78, 83, 86, 88, 90, 92, 94, (with others) Osler's Textbook Revisited, 1967, Genetics of Hand Malformations, 1978, Medical Genetic Studies of the Amish, 1978, A Model of its Kind, 1989, Osler's Legacy, 1990, A Century of Biomedical Science at Johns Hopkins, 1993; author, editor: Online Mendelian Inheritance in Man, 1985—; editor-in-chief Medicine jour., 1985—; founding co-editor-in-chief Genomics jour. 1987—; editor med. textbook. Recipient Disting. Achievement award Modern Medicine, 1965, John Phillips award ACP, 1972, Silver medal U. Helsinki, 1974, Gairdner Internat. award, 1977, Premio Internazionale Sanremo per le Ricerche Genetiche, 1983, Col. Saunders award March of Dimes, 1988, Disting. Alumnus award Johns Hopkins U., 1983, Alumnus Svc. award Johns Hopkins Med. Sch., 1989, Passano award, 1989, Disting. Svc. award Miami Biotech. Winter Symposium, 1991, Frank Bradway Rogers Info. Advancement award Med. Libr. Assn., 1991, Silver Columbus medal Comune di Genova, 1952, Maine prize (with twin), 1993, Mendel medal Villanova U., 1995, Big "M" award Maine State Soc. Washington, D.C., 1995; named to Internat. Pediatrics Hall of Fame, 1987. Fellow AAAS (chair med. scis. sect. 1991), Am. Acad. Orthopedic Surgeons (hon.), Royal Coll. Physicians (London), Hastings Ctr., Am. Coll. Med. Genetics (hon.); mem. Nat. Acad. Sci. (James Murray Luck award 19820, Am. Philos. Soc. (v.p. 1996—, Benjamin Franklin medal for disting. achievement in scis. 1996), Am. Soc. Human Genetics (pres. 1975, Wm. A. Allan award 1977), Assn. Am. Physicians (Kober medal 1990), Am. So Investigation (v.p. 1967), The Human Genome Orgn. (founder pres. 1988-89), Am. Acad. Arts and Sci., Little People of Am. (hon. life), Acad. Nat. Medicine (France; corr.), Am. Bd. Med. Genetics (founding), Inst. Medicine, Phi Beta Kappa, Alpha Omega Alpha, Johns Hopkins Club, West Hamilton St. Club, St. Andrew's Soc. Balt. Presbyterian (elder). Home: 221 Northway Baltimore MD 21218-1141 Office: Johns Hopkins Hosp Ctr Med Geneetics-Blalock 1007 600 N Wolfe St Baltimore MD 21287-4922

MCLAIN, DAVID ANDREW, internist; b. Chgo., Aug. 16, 1948; s. William Rex and Wilma Lucille (Raschka) McL.; m. Pamela Rose Fullmer, June 15, 1974; children: Edward, Richard. BA, Northwestern U., 1970; MD with Honors, Tulane U., 1974. Diplomate Am. Bd. Internal Medicine, Am. Bd. Rheumatology. Intern Oschner Clinic, New Orleans, 1974-75; resident Barnes Hosp., St. Louis, 1975-77; fellow in rheumatology Washington U., St. Louis, 1977-79, instr. dept. medicine, 1979-81; with VA Hosp., St. Louis, 1979-81; pvt. practice Birmingham, Ala., 1981—; chief rheumatology sect. dept. internal medicine Brookwood Med. Ctr., Birmingham, 1983-87, 89-90, 91-94, med. dir. phys. therapy, 1986—; mem. staff St. Vincent's Hosp., Birmingham, 1981—, Shelby Med. Ctr., Alabaster, Ala., 1982—, Lakeshore Rehab. Hosp., Birmingham, 1983—, HealthSouth Hosp., 1989—; dir. courses continuing med. edn., 1983—. Editor: (jour. series) Internal Medicine; contbr. articles, abstracts to profl. jours. Mem. med. adv. com. Birmingham chpt. Lupus Found. Am., 1982—, co-originator Lupus Day, Brookwood Med. Ctr., 1983—; bd. dirs. north ctrl. br. Arthritis Found., 1982—, organizer, originator Benefit Horse Show and Art Fair, Birmingham, 1985, del. nat. coun., 1987, chmn. med. and sci. com. Ala. chpt., 1988-89; active Nat. Arthritis Found.; med. advisor Sjogren's Syndrome Found., 1988—. Recipient award of Appreciation Ala. Podiatry Assn., 1984, Ala. Chpt. Arthritis Found., 1986, award for Decade of Leadership in Rheumatology, 1992, Excellence in Tchg. award Med. Assn. State of Ala., 1995. Fellow ACP, Am. Coll. Rheumatology (founding mem.); mem. AMA (Physicians Recognition award 1979, 82, 85, 88, 91, 94), Am. Soc. Internal Medicine, Am. Med. Equestrian Assn. (bd. dirs. 1995—), Ala. Soc. Rheumatic Diseases (founding mem.), Ala. Soc. Internal Medicine, Med. Assn. State Ala. (Excellence in Tchg. award 1995), Jefferson County Med. Soc., Brookwood Splty. Physicians Assn. (founding incorporator, bd. dirs., pres. 1990—), U.S. Combined Tng. Assn. (area coun., editor newsletter, adult riders com., bd. govs. 1992-94, chmn. safety com. 1992—, chmn ad hoc coalition to promote equestrian helmet safety 1993-95), U.S. Dressage Fedn. (founder aux. U.S. Tes Callers Assn.), Alpha Omega Alpha. Office: Birmingham Rheumatology McLain Med Assocs 2022 Brookwood Med Ctr Dr Ste 509 Birmingham AL 35209-6807

MCLAIN, GERALD GRADY (JERRY MCLAIN), hospital executive; b. Vernon, Tex., Oct. 29, 1953; s. Clarence Grady and Ura Lee (Hays) McL.; m. Karon Sue Payton, Mar. 17, 1980; children: Christopher Grady, Jeremy Richard. AA, Vernon Regional Jr. Coll., 1972-74; BS, Ea. N.Mex. U., 1974-76; postgrad., Tex. Tech. U., 1976-77, 79. Announcer, program dir. Sta. KOLJ, Quanah, Tex., 1971-74; on-air dir. Sta. KENW-TV, Portales, N.Mex., 1974-76, news anchor, 1975-76; teaching asst. telecommunications Tex. Tech. U., Lubbock, 1976-77, on-air dir. Sta. KTXT-TV, 1976-77; instructional media specialist Vernon Regional Jr. Coll., 1977-79; ind. audio/video producer Vernon, 1977—; dir. pub. info. Vernon State Hosp., 1979-89, dir. media svcs., 1979—; cons. Rsch. and Extension Ctr. Tex. A&M U., Vernon, 1977-79, 88—. Contbr. articles on edn. and indsl. TV and computers to various mags. Dir., producer numerous video and multi-media presentations for various health sci. and charitable orgns., 1977—; v.p. Vernon chpt. Am. Diabetes Assn., 1986—; bd. dirs. Tex. Affiliate Am. Diabetes Assn., Austin, 1987-92, nat. programs com., 1991-92; bd. dirs. Wilbarger County United Way, Vernon, 1983; mem. Tex. Dept. Mental Health/Mental Retardation Media Coun., 1986—, chair, 1992—; mem. Tex. Agrl. Extension Svc. Health Adv. Com., Vernon, 1985-87; tchr. adult I Calvary Bapt. Ch., Vernon, 1989-92, deacon, sound engrng. com., chair nominating com., 1993—, sec. deacon bd., 1994—. Mem. Nat. Assn. Mental Health Info. Officers (v.p. 1984-86). Democrat. Home: 2833 Ridge Top Ln Vernon TX 76384-7566 Office: Vernon State Hosp PO Box 2231 Vernon TX 76385-2231

MCLAIN, JAMES BRUCE, orthodontist; b. Chgo., Mar. 8, 1954; s. William Rex and Wilma L. (Raschka) McL. BA, Northwestern U., Evanston, Ill., 1974; DDS, U. N.C., 1978, MPH, 1979, MS, 1981. Diplomate Am. Bd. Orthodontics. Instr. Bowman Gray Sch. Medicine, Winston-Salem, N.C., 1982-83; asst. prof. Bowman Gray Sch. Medicine, 1983-85; pvt. practice Winston-Salem, 1985-95; ptnr. McLain & Steedle, PLLC, Winston-Salem, 1995—; clin. asst. prof. U. N.C. Sch. Dentistry, Chapel Hill, 1985-88; program coord. Wake County Health Dept. Orthodontic Program, Raleigh, N.C., 1981-82; cons. dentofacial anomalies program Bowman-Gray Sch. Medicine, 1982-93, Forsyth Meml. Hosp. Oral Facial Clinic, Winston-Salem, 1992—. Contbr. articles to profl. jours., chpts. to books. Corp. sponsor Habitat for Humanity, Winston-Salem, 1995. Recipient Nat. Rsch. Svc. award Nat. Inst. Dental Rsch. NIH, 1978-81; Morehead fellow in dentistry John Motley Morehead Found., Chapel Hill, 1978-81. Mem. ADA, Am. Assn. Orthodontics (Joseph E. Johnson Table Clinic award 1982), Omicron Kappa Upsilon. Office: McLain & Steedle PLLC 1564 N Peace Haven Rd Winston Salem NC 27104

MCLAIN, MYRTLE S., emergency physician; b. Ensign, Mich., Dec. 24, 1930; d. F.I. and Marie I. (Haggblad) Sundberg; m. Ernest L. McLain, Sept. 18, 1924 (dec. Dec. 1995); hcildren: Alice, Jan, Dawn, Carol, Kenneth, Ross. BS, U. Mich., 1952, MD, 1996. Diplomate Am. Bd. Emergency Medicine. Emergency physician St. Mary's, Mercy and Hackley Hosps., Grand Rapids & Muskegon, Mich., 1967-77; family physician Grandville (Mich.) Med. Ctr., 1980-82, Creston Med. Ctr., Grand Rapids, 1990-94; chief emergency medicine St. Mary's Hosp., Grand Rapids, 1977-81; dep. med. examiner Kent County, Grand Rapids, 1982-95; emergency physician Holland (Mich.) Cmty. Hosp., 1982-90, Met. Hosp., Grand Rapids, 1984-94, Gerber Meml. Hosp., Fremont, Mich., 1984—; cons. West Mich. Comprehensive Health Planning, Grand Rapids, 1982-85; bd. mem. West Mich. Peer Rev. Orgn., Grand Rapids, 1984-88. Bd. mem. Kent County ARC, Grand Rapids, 1984-88. Fellow Am. Coll. Emergency Physicians (life); mem. AMA, Nat. Assn. Med. Examiners, Am. Med. Womens Assn., Mich. State Med. Soc., Kent County Med. Soc.

MCLAIN, ROBERT FELIX, orthopaedic surgeon; b. Agana, Guam, May 25, 1956; s. Donald Roderick and Mary Edna (Wood) McL; m. Becky Ellen Ziegler, Aug. 19, 1978; 1 child, Robert Donald. BS, U. Calif., Davis, 1978, MD, 1984. Diplomate Am. Bd. Orthop. Surgery. Resident in orthop. U. Iowa Hosps., Iowa City, 1984-89, NIH rsch. fellow, 1989-90; spine surgery fellow U. Calif., Davis, 1990-91, asst. prof., 1991-94, assoc. prof., 1994—; dir. spine rsch. Orthop. Rsch. Lab., Davis, 1992—. Assoc. editor Spine jour., 1993—; contbr. 55 articles to profl. jours. Am. Brit. Can. Traveling fellow Am. Orthop. Assn., 1995, N.Am. Traveling fellow, 1993; recipient Zimmer Rsch. award Orthop. Rsch. and Edn. Found., 1992; Morton Levitt Rsch. scholar, 1983. Fellow Internat. Soc. for Study of Lumbar Spine, Am. Acad. Orthop. Surgeons; mem. Orthop. Rsch. Soc., Scoliosis Rsch. Soc., N.Am. Spine Soc. Office: Univ of California Dept Orthop Surgery 2230 Stockton Blvd Sacramento CA 95817

MCLANAHAN, CHARLES SCOTT, neurosurgeon; b. Chgo., Sept. 23, 1946; s. Charles Jackson and Anna Martin (Findley) McL.; m. Mary Ivey, Aug. 23, 1975; children: George, Ward, Matt. BA, Yale U., 1969; MD, Columbia U., 1973. Diplomate Am. Bd. Neurol. Surgery. Resident in neurosurgery Emory U., Atlanta, 1973-78, instr. neurosurgery, 1979; asst. prof. neurosurgery La. State U. Med. Sch., New Orleans, 1979-80; neurosurgeon Charlotte (N.C.) Neurosurg. Assocs., PA, 1980—. Republican. Office: Charlotte Neurosurg Assocs 1010 Edgehill Rd N Charlotte NC 28207

MCLAUGHLIN, CARLIN J., oncologist, hematologist; b. Phila., Oct. 10, 1958; s. Joseph P. and Eileen F. (Denney) McL.; m. Lynn Schmidt; children: Carryn L., Kyle Oliver. AB in Biology, Gettysburg Coll., 1980; DO, Phila. Coll. Osteo. Medicine, 1984. Intern Delaware Valley Med. Ctr., Langhorne, Pa., 1984-85; resident internal medicine Delaware Valley Med. Ctr., Langhorne, 1985-88, chief resident, 1988; fellow hematology-oncology Thomas Jefferson U., Phila., 1988-91; pvt. practice in oncology Langhorne, 1991—; program dir. Delaware Valley med. Ctr. Internal Medicine Residency, Langhorne, 1995—. Mem. Ea. Coop. Oncology Group. Lutheran. Office: Ste 604 390 Middletown Blvd Langhorne PA 19047

MCLAUGHLIN, EDWARD DAVID, surgeon, medical educator; b. Ridley Park, Pa., Jan. 8, 1931; s. Edward D. and Catherine J. (Hilbert) McL.; m. Mary Louise Hanlon, June 20, 1959; children: Catherine, Louise, Edward, Patricia. BS magna cum laude Georgetown U., 1952; MD, Jefferson Med. Coll., 1956. Intern, Jefferson Med. Coll., Phila., 1956-57, resident in surgery, 1957-59; resident in surgery Jefferson Med. Coll. Hosp., Phila., 1962-64; practice medicine specializing in surgery; surg. asso. Nat. Cancer Inst., NIH, 1959-61, surgeon, 1961-62; teaching fellow Harvard Med. Sch., Boston and clin. research fellow Mass. Gen. Hosp., Boston, 1964-66; sr. surg. registrar Hawkmoor Chest Hosp., Devon, Eng., 1966-67; sr. surgeon Chestnut Hill Hosp., 1967-71; asst. prof. surgery Jefferson Med. Coll., 1968-72, assoc. prof., 1972—, lectr. Jefferson continuing med. edn. program, 1976-77; assoc. chmn. of surgery Mercy Cath. Med. Center, Phila., 1972-88; pres., treas. Cedar Mgmt. Corp., 1981-86; pres., treas. Garnet Moor Ltd., 1981-91, Garnetmoor Pub. Svc. Ltd., 1986-91, Garnet Valley Acad. Alliance, 1991—, Garnet Valley Academic Assn., 1995—; treas. Physicians and Surgeons Ltd., 1983-86. Chmn., Bethel Twp. Planning Study Group, 1971-72, Bethel Twp. Sewer Authority, 1972-78, Bethel Twp. Planning Commn., 1989-91; mem. bd. of sch. dirs. Garnet Vally Sch. Dist., 1990—; mem. resources com., Garnet Valley Sch. Bd., 1991-95, chmn. curriculum com., 1992-95, chmn. edn. com., 1995-96, alt. mem. fin. com., 1995-96, mem. policy com., 1995—, mem. bldg. com., 1995—, Cmty. Laison Garnet Valley Sch. bd. dirs., 1995; mem. facility com., 1995—. With USPHS, 1959-62. Recipient Mead Johnson award for research, 1962, Americus award KC, 1963, Lindback award Jefferson Med. Coll., 1974; named Outstanding Prof. of 1976-77, Phi Alpha Sigma Jefferson Med. Coll. Diplomate Am. Bd. Surgery. Fellow ACS; mem. Phila. Acad. Surgery, N.Y. Acad. Scis., Med. Soc. State Pa., AAAS, Am. Soc. Artificial Internal Organs, AMA, Pa. Thoracic Soc., Georgetown U. Alumni (bd. govs. 1970-72, senator 1972—), Nu Sigma Nu, Alpha Kappa Kappa. Contbr. articles on research in cancer to med. jours. and articles on edn. to ednl. jours. Home and Office: 3112 Garnet Mine Rd Boothwyn PA 19061-1718

MC LAUGHLIN, JERRY LOREN, pharmacognosy researcher, educator; b. Coldwater, Mich., Oct. 14, 1939; s. Ralph Todd and Rosella (Shreve) McL.; m. Frances Jeanette Whitaker, July 15, 1960 (div. Feb. 20, 1981); children: Angie Lee, Andrew Todd.; m. Elzbieta Lozinska, Nov. 28,

1981. B.S., U. Mich., 1961, M.S., 1963, Ph.D., 1965. Asst. prof. pharmacognosy U. Mich., Ann Arbor, 1965-66, Mo. U., Kansas City, 1966-67; asst. prof. U. Wash., Seattle, 1967-70; assoc. prof. U. Wash., 1970-71; asso. prof. pharmacognosy Purdue U., West Lafayette, Ind., 1971-75; prof. Purdue U., 1975—, exec. adminstrv. asst., 1975-80. Assoc. editor Jour. Natural Products, 1984-94; contbr. articles to profl. jours. Recipient Lederle Faculty Rsch. award, 1969, 73, Cancer Rsch. award Purdue U., 1987; USPHS fellow, 1961-65, rsch. grantee, 1965-66, 69-71, 74-78, 84—; NSF grantee, 1974, 75, 79. Fellow Am. Assn. Pharm. Scientists; mem. Am. Soc. Pharmacognosy (exec. com. 1974-77, v.p. 1981-82, pres. 1982-83), Am. Chem. Soc., AAAS (life), Am. Pharm. Assn. (stimulation rsch. award 1993), Acad. Pharm. Sci., Soc. Econ. Botany, Cactus and Succulent Soc., Sigma Xi, Kappa Psi, Phi Kappa Phi, Rho Chi, Phi Lambda Upsilon. Home: 2101 W 600 N West Lafayette IN 47906-9728 Office: Purdue U Sch Pharmacy Dept Med Chem & Molecular Pharmacology West Lafayette IN 47907

MCLAUGHLIN, RODNEY EUGENE, school administrator, psychologist; b. Chambersburg, Pa., Apr. 4, 1933; s. Leonard Charles and Helen Ruth (McGaughey) McL.; m. Maria Teresa Anduze, Jan. 30, 1956; children: Michael Eugene, Stephen Mark. BS, Pa. State U., 1955, MS, 1959, DEd, 1976. Sch. psychologist Clinton and Union Counties, Lock Haven, Pa., 1957-58; counseling psychologist Pa. State U., University Park, 1959-60; psychologist Rockview Correctional Institution, Bellefonte, Pa., 1960-61; adminstr. student pers. svcs. Milton Hershey (Pa.) Sch., 1961-92; bd. dirs., past chmn. George Frey Ctr. for Emotionally Disturbed Children, Harrisburg, Pa., 1971-89; vice chair Pa. State Bd. Psychology, Harrisburg, 1986—; lectr. in field. Fellow Pa. Psychol. Assn. (chmn. internal affairs bd. 1977-81, pres. 1983-84, Outstanding Svc. award 1981, 83-84); mem. Am. Psychol. Assn., Nat. Assn. Sch. Psychologists, Mental Health Assn. (chmn. edn. com.). Republican. Lutheran. Lodge: Rotary. Home: 1584 Mcintosh Way Hummelstown PA 17036-8729 Office: Milton Hershey Sch Student Pers Svcs Founders Hall Hershey PA 17033

MCLAUGHLIN, THOMAS CHRISTOPHER, urologist; b. Flushing, N.Y., Jan. 17, 1936; s. George E. and Rosemary (Deibel) McL.; m. Anne Belknap Dick, May 6, 1967; children: Catherine Hawkins, Elizbeth Deibel, Thomas Christopher Jr. BS, Georgetown U., 1958, MD, 1962. Diplomate Nat. Bd. Med. Examiners, Am. Bd. Urology. Intern gen. surgery U. Fla. Hosp., Gainesville, 1962-63, asst. resident in gen. surgery, 1963-64, asst. resident in urology, 1964-66, chief resident in urology, 1966-67; clin. assoc. dept. urology Cleve. Clinic Found., 1969-70; urologist Lakeland (Fla.) Regional Med. Ctr., 1970—; v.p. Lakeland Regional Med. Ctr., 1981, pres. elect, 1982, pres. 1983, bd. dirs. 1984-90, chmn. quality assurance com., 1984-85, strategic planning com., 1985-86, fin. and pers. com., 1986-88, vice chmn. bd., 1988-89, chmn. of bd. 1989-90; active med. staff Watson Clinic, Lakeland, 1970—, mem. fin. com. 1975-81, 1991-92, exec. com. 1976-79; chmn. dept. surgery, 1977-79, peer rev. and risk control com., 1977-79. Contbr. articles to profl. jours. Capt. USAF, 1967-70. Fellow Am. Coll. Surgeons; mem. AMA, Fla. Med. Assn., Polk County Med. Assn., Am. Urol. Assn. (mem. bylaws com. 1981-86, AUA centennial hist. com. 1992-94, AUA urology work force com. 1995-96, numerous coms. and offices in southeastern section including bd. dirs., 1981-89, 93-95, pres. 1994-95), Fla. Urol. Soc. (sec.-treas. 1979-80, pres. 1981-82, other offices and coms.), Am. Lithotripsy Soc., Am. Assn. Clin. Urologists, Urology Found. Fla., Inc. (pres. 1990-95), Am. Group Practice Assn. (bd. dirs. 1980-81, pres. southeastern region 1979-80), Lakeland Rotary Club (pres. 1978-79), Lakeland Area C. of C. (pres. 1989, chmn. of the bd. 1990), Georgetown U. Alumni Assn. (bd. govs. 1978-88), Georgetown U. Sch. Medicine Alumni Assn. (mem. dean's coun. 1978-88)), Lakeland Yacht Club (bd. dirs. 1989-92, Lone Palm Golf Club. Home: 1425 Seville Pl Lakeland FL 33803 Office: Watson Clinic 1600 Lakeland Hills Blvd Lakeland FL 33805

MCLAY, CELIA WALLACE, physician; b. Pontiac, Mich., Aug. 28, 1960; d. Wallace Daniel and Mary (Leighton) McL. BS, Mich. State U., 1990, DO, 1994. Intern Detroit Med. Ctr.-Grace Hosp., 1994-95; resident phys. medicine and rehab. Detroit Med. Ctr. Rehab. Inst. Mich., 1995—. Mem. Women's Internat. League for Peace and Freedom, 1980-96. Mem. Am. Acad. Osteopathy (nat. coord. 1990-96), The Cranial Acad., Am. Acad. Phys. Medicine and Rehab. (resident rep. 1996—). Home: 11662 Aspen Plymouth MI 48170

MCLEAN, BONNIE SHEPHERD, oriental medicine physician, nurse; b. New Orleans, Mar. 9, 1945; d. Arthur and Barbara (McCravy) Butt; m. David Speed McLean (div.); children; Arthur Cameron, Douglas Speed. MA, Pepperdine U., 1977; OMD, Calif. Acupuncture Coll., 1986; BSN, Duke U., 1987. Lic. acupuncturist, Calif. RN various cities, 1967-85; pvt. practice in oriental medicine Santa Monica, Westlake, also L.A., 1985—; cons. in pain mgmt. Woodview Calabasas (Calif.) Hosp., 1987—, Pine Grove Hosp., Canoga Park, Calif., 1989—; instr. Bresler Ctr., Santa Monica, 1986, Sch. of Inner Guidance and Knowledge, Burleigh Heads, Australia, 1993-95, Acad. Natural Therapies, Burleigh Heads, 1995. Co-author: Manual of Chinese Medicine and Massage, 1985; author: (with others) Pain Management for Anesthesiologists, 1993. Democrat. Taoist. Home: 19711 Valley View Dr Topanga CA 90290-3257 Office: Orthopaedic Surgery Midway Med Plz 5901 W Olympic Blvd # 401 Los Angeles CA 90036

MC LEAN, DONALD MILLIS, microbiology, pathology educator, physician; b. Melbourne, Australia, July 26, 1926; s. Donald and Nellie (Millis) McL.; married. B.Sc., U. Melbourne, 1947, M.B., 1950, M.D., 1954. Fellow Rockefeller Found., N.Y.C. and Hamilton, Mont., 1955; vis. instr. bacteriology U. Minn., Mpls., 1957; med. officer Commonwealth Serum Labs., Melbourne, 1957; virologist Research Inst., Hosp. for Sick Children, Toronto, Ont., Can., 1958-67; assoc. prof. microbiology, assoc. in pediatrics U. Toronto Med. Sch., 1962-67; prof. med. microbiology U. B.C. Med. Sch., Vancouver, Can., 1967-91, prof. emeritus Pathology, 1991—. Author: Virology in Health Care, 1980, Immunological Investigation of Human Virus Disease, 1982, Same-Day Virus Diagnosis, 1984, Virological Infections, 1988, Medical Microbiology Synopsis, 1991, Acute Viral Infections, 1991; contbr. articles to profl. jours. Fellow Royal Coll. Physicians (Can.), Royal Coll. Pathologists; mem. Am. Epidemiological Soc., Am. Soc. Tropical Medicine, Can. Med. Assn., Am. Soc. Microbiology, Am. Soc. Virology. Home: 6-5885 Yew Street, Vancouver, BC Canada V6M 3Y5

MCLEAN, IAN WILLLIAM, ophthalmic pathologist, researcher; b. Durham, N.C., Sept. 21, 1943; s. I. William and Brita (Rosenqvist) McL.; m. Susan R. Gabler, June 14, 1987; children: Elenor Lee, Rebecca Ann, January D. BS, U. Mich., 1965, MD, 1969. Diplomate in anatomic pathology Am. Bd. Pathology. Pathology intern U. Colo. Med. Ctr., Denver, 1969-70, resident in pathology, 1970-73; staff pathologist, dept. ophthalmic pathology Armed Forces Inst. Pathology, Washington, 1973-83, acting chmn. dept. ophthalmic pathology, 1983-86, chmn. dept., 1986—. Contbr. more than 100 articles to sci. jours. Col. U.S. Army, 1973-94. Recipient Gold medal U Sao Paulo, 1988. Mem. Assn. for Rsch. in Vision and Ophthalmology, Eastern Ophthalmic Pathology Soc., Am. Acad. Ophthalmology, Am. Assn. Ophthalmic Pathologists, Verhoeff Soc. Office: Armed Forces Inst Pathology Dept Ophthalmic Pathol Washington DC 20306

MCLEAN, MICHAEL R., orthopedist, orthopedic surgeon; b. Dallas, Mar. 6, 1948; s. William Franklin and Mary Katherine (Scofield) McL.; m. Josephine Stripling, June 3, 1979; 1 child, Morgan Elizabeth. BS in Math., U. Tex., Austin, 1970; MD, U. Tex., Galveston, 1974. Diplomate Am. Bd. Orthopedic Surgery. Surgery intern Mayo Clinic, Rochester, Minn., 1974-75; surgery resident NYU Bellevue, N.Y.C., 1975-77; orthopedic surgery resident U. Tex. Health Sci. Ctr., San Antonio, 1977-81; pvt. practice Conroe, Tex., 1981-82, Nacogdoches, Tex., 1982—. Mem. Am. Heart Assn. (pres. Nacogdoches chpt.). Republican. Methodist. Office: McLean Orthopaedics PA 1300 Mound Nacogdoches TX 75963

MCLEAN, ROBERT BRENNAN, physician; b. Hazleton, Pa., Dec. 27, 1935; s. Laird Brennan and Julia Elizabeth (Schuetrumpf) McL.; m. Jane Cecelia Altmiller, Apr. 16, 1960. BA, U. Pa., 1957, MD, 1961; MHA, Baylor U., 1974. Diplomate Am. Bd. Surgery. Med. officer, advanced through grades to col. U.S. Army, Washington, 1960-90; corp. med. dir. Nat. Passenger R.R. Corp. (AMTRAK), Washington, 1990, chief med. officer, 1990-95. Decorated Bronze Star, Legion of Merit medal 3; recipient Superior Svc. medal Dept. Def., 1986. Fellow ACS, Am. Coll. Physician Execs.; mem. Assn. Am. R.R.'s, D.C. Med. Soc. Home: 8205 Hensley Ct Alexandria VA 22308-1529

MCLEAN, RONALD WILLIAM, university administrator; b. Ilion, N.Y., Nov. 11, 1927; s. William Roberts Cuthbert and Bessie (Soutar) McL.; m. Helen Francis Finnigan, June 12, 1947; children: Eric, David, Janice, Jeffrey, Mary Ellen. BS in Pharmacy, Albany Coll. of Pharmacy, 1951; MS in Edn., SUNY, Albany, 1980; LHD (hon.), Albany Coll. Pharmacy, 1995. Staff pharmacist Fox Drug Co., Carthage, N.Y., 1951-52; owner McLean Pharmacy, Newport, N.Y., 1952-76; ptnr. Maple Dale Pharmacy, Banneveld, N.Y., 1968-73; asst. dir. div. of extension svcs. Albany Coll. of Pharmacy, Union U., 1976-78, dir. divsn. ext. svcs., 1976-93; interim pres., dean, 1994-95; assoc. dean academic affairs Albany Coll. of Pharmacy, Union U., 1994-96; cons. pharmacist St. Margarets Home for Babies, Albany, 1982-93; mem. N.Y. State Bd. Pharmacy, 1982-89, disciplinary officer, 1989—. Bd. pres. Interfaith Partnership for Homeless, Albany, 1986-88; bd. dirs. Am. Cancer Soc., Syracuse, N.Y., 1985-87. Staff sgt. U.A. Army, 1945-47. Recipient Disting. Achievement in Pharmacy award Merk Sharpe-Dohme, 1989; named Disting. Alumnus Am. Coll. Pharmacy Alumni Assn., 1983. Mem. Am. Assn. of Colls. of Pharmacy (chair sect. of continuing profl. edn. 1990-91), Pharm. Soc. State of N.Y. (ednl. cons. 1989—), Honey Hill Country Club (pres.). Office: Albany Coll Pharmacy Union U 106 New Scotland Ave Albany NY 12208-3425

MCLENDON, CINDY FARROW, health care administrator; b. Austin, Jan. 2, 1957; d. Charles Lowday and Peggy Lee (Bargsley) Farrow; m. Jim Conway McLendon,. Mar. 15, 1980; children: Austin, Travis, Cooper. Bachelor's, U. Mary Hardin-Baylor, Belton, Tex., 1979; Master's, U. Tex., 1982. RN, CRRN, Tex. Nurse mgr. VA Hosp., Temple, Tex., 1979-85; rehab. head nurse St. David's Hosp., Austin, 1985-87; dir. clin. svcs. Healthcare Rehab. Svcs., Austin, 1987-89; adminstr., exec. dir. Ramsey Pl. Rehab., Austin, 1989-93; CEO Healthcare Rehab. Ctr., Austin, 1994—; surveyor Commn. on Accreditation of Rehab. Facilities, Tucson, 1991—; guest lectr. U. Tex., 1987. Mem. editorial adv. bd. Aspen Publs., Gaithersburg, Md., 1995; spkr. in field. Vol. AIDS Svcs. of Austin, 1989—, Tex. Hosp. Assn., Austin, 1989-92. Mem. Alliance of Tex. Head Injury Facilities (chmn. 1988-93), Assn. Rehab. Nurses (pres. Ctrl. Tex. chpt. 1986-87). Office: Healthcare Rehab Ctr 1106 W Dittmar Austin TX 78745

MCLEOD, ALEXANDER REEVES, ophthalmologist; b. Enterprise, Ala., Nov. 5, 1941; s. Alexander Warthen and Annette (Coskrey) McL.; m. Ruth F. McLeod, Feb. 29, 1964; children: Alexander Meier, Brooks Anne. AA, Pensacola (Fla.) Jr. Coll., 1961; student, U. Fla., 1961-62; MD, Med. Coll. of Ala., 1966. Diplomate Am. Bd. Ophthalmology. Pvt. practice Pensacola, 1973—; clin. instr. pharmacology La. State U. Sch. of Medicine, New Orleans, 1967-69; lectr. pediatrics program Sacred Heart Hosp., Pensacola, 1973—, clin. assoc. prof. pediatric ophthalmology, 1990—; cons. dept. pediatrics Keesler AFB, Biloxi, Miss., 1986. Author: (chpt.) Deglutition-Troclear Synkinesis, 1973; contbr. articles to profl. jours. Board dirs. United Cerebral Palsy, Pensacola, 1979, Escambia County Assn. for Retarded Citizens, Pensacola, 1980. Surgeon USPHS, 1966-68. NIH fellow Bascom Palmer Eye Inst.; recipient Disting. Alumnus award Pensacola Jr. Coll., 1990. Fellow Am. Acad. Ophthalmology; mem. AMA (Physicians Recognition award 1991—), Am. Assn. Pediatric Ophthalmology and Strabismus, Am. Soc. Cataract and Refractive Surgery, N.W. Fla. Ophthalmology Soc. (sec. 1975-76, pres. 1977-78), Fla. Med. Assn., Escambia County Med. Soc. (pub. rels. com. 1980—, med. liability com., treas. med. countersuit trust fund), Bascom Palmer Eye Inst. Alumni Assn. Home: 6109 Confederate Dr Pensacola FL 32503-7512 Office: 2020 Langley Ave Pensacola FL 32504-8145

MCLEOD, JAMES GRAHAM, neuroscience educator; b. Sydney, New South Wales, Australia, Jan. 18, 1932; s. Hector Reginald and Dorothy Shirley (Craig) McL.; m. Robyn Edith Rule, Jan. 13, 1962; children: Anne, Robert, Philip, Rebecca. BSc in Medicine, U. Sydney, 1953, MB, BS, 1959; DPhil, Oxford U., 1956; D (hon.), U. Aix-Marseille. Bosch prof. medicine U. Sydney, 1972—, Bushell prof. neurology, 1978—; head. dept neurology Royal Prince Alfred Hosp., Sydney, 1978-94; chmn. inst. clin. neurosci. Royal Prince Alfred Hosp., 1990-94. Author: Physiological Approach to Clinical Neurology, 1981, Introductory Neurology, 1995, Peripheral Neuropathy of Childhood, 1991. Named Officer of Order of Australia, 1986; Rhodes scholar, 1953-56. Fellow Royal Australisian Coll. Physicians, Royal Coll. Physicians, Australian Acad. Sci., Australian Acad. Tech. Scis.; mem. Nat. Health and Med. Rsch. Coun. (med. rsch. com. 1985-93). Office: U Sydney, Dept Medicine, Sydney NSW 2006, Australia

MCLEOD, JAMES WILLIAM, orthopaedic surgeon; b. Oklahoma City, July 9, 1947; s. Joseph William and Lucille Elizabeth (True) McL.; m. Elaine Constance Fenech, July 17, 1970; children: Matthew James, Geoffrey Alexander. MD, Okla. U., Oklahoma City, 1972. Diplomate Am. Bd. Orthop. Surgery. Intern Naval Regional Med. Ctr., Portsmouth, Va., 1972-73, resident in orthop. surgery, 1974-77; staff orthop. surgeon Naval Regional Med. Ctr., Jacksonville, Fla., 1977-80; orthop. surgeon Walter Reed Hosp., Gloucester, Va., 1980-88, Lewis Gale Clinic, Ronaoke, Va., 1988—. Lt. comdr. USN, 1974-80. Fellow Am. Acad. Orthop. Surgery; mem. Va. Orthop. Soc., So. Orthop. Soc., So. Med. Assn. Republican. Office: Lewis Gale Clinic 4910 Valley View Blvd Roanoke VA 24012

MC LERAN, JAMES HERBERT, university dean emeritus, oral surgeon; b. Audubon, Iowa, Apr. 9, 1931; s. Louis D. and Alma K. (Christensen) McL.; m. Hermine Weinert Hayden, July 15, 1979; 1 children, Stephen Andrew; step children: John Wilson Hayden, Charles Matthew Hayden. BS, Simpson Coll., 1953; DDS, U. Iowa, 1957, MS, 1962. Diplomate: Am. Bd. Oral and Maxillofacial Surgeons. Instr. U. Iowa, 1959-60, asst. prof., 1963-67, assoc. prof., 1967-69, prof. oral surgery, 1972—, assoc. dean Coll. Dentistry, 1972-74, dean, 1974—; prof. and chmn. dept. oral surgery U. N.C., Chapel Hill, 1969-72. Served with Dental Corps USN, 1957-59. Recipient Finkbine Leadership award U. Iowa, 1957; named Instr. of Yr. Jr. ADA, 1964, Outstanding Instr. award, 1965. Mem. ADA, Am. Assn. Oral and Maxillofacial Surgeons, Iowa Assn. Oral and Maxillofacial Surgeons, Internat. Assn. Dental Rsch., Midwestern Assn. Oral and Maxillofacial Surgeons, N.C. Soc. Dental Surgeons, N.C. Dental Soc., Iowa Dental Assn. (Disting. Svc. award 1992), Univ. Dist. Dental Soc., Johnson County Dental Soc., Am. Coll. Dentists, Internat. Coll. Dentists, Fedn. Dentaire Internat., Am. Assn. Dental Schs. (pres. 1978-79), Psi Omega. Lodge: Rotary. Office: U Iowa Coll Dentistry Iowa City IA 52242

MCLESKEY, CHARLES HAMILTON, anesthesiology educator; b. Phila., Nov. 8, 1946; s. W. Hamilton and Marion A. (Butts) McL.; m. Nanci S. Simmons, June 3, 1972; children: Travis, Heather. BA, Susquehanna U., 1968; MD, Wake Forest U., 1972. Diplomate Am. Bd. Anesthesiology. Intern Maine Med. Ctr., Portland, 1972-73; resident in anesthesiology U. Wash. Sch. Medicine, Seattle, 1973-76, NIH rsch. trainee, 1974-75; clin. teaching assoc. dept. anesthesiology U. Calif., San Francisco, 1976-78; asst. prof. anesthesiology Wake Forest U. Bowman Gray Sch. Medicine, Winston-Salem, N.C., 1978-83, assoc. prof., 1983-84; assoc. prof. U. Tex. Med. Br., Galveston, 1985-87; assoc. prof. anesthesiology U. Colo. Health Sci. Ctr., Denver, 1987-91, prof., 1991-93, dir. acad. affairs, 1987-93; prof., chmn. dept. anesthesiology Tex. A&M U., 1993—; chmn. dept. anesthesiology, med. dir. perioperative svcs. Scott and White Clin. and Meml. Hosp., Temple, Tex., 1993—; assoc. med. dir. Scott and White Health Plan, 1995—; cons., lectr. Janssen Pharmaceutica, Piscataway, N.J., 1980—, Alza Corp., Palo Alto, Calif., 1986—; cons. Glaxo-Wellcome Co., Research Triangle Park, N.C., Abbott Labs., Chgo., Marion Merrill Dow, Kansas City, Kans., Aspect Med., Natick, Mass.; lectr. to over 500 nat. and state med. orgns., 1982—; examiner Am. Bd. Anesthesiology. Assoc. editor Anesthesiology Rev.; editor Geriatric Anesthesiology, 1996; contbr. numerous articles to med. jours. Mem. choir Friendswood (Tex.) Meth. Ch., 1985-87; mem. Friendswood Fine Arts Commn., 1985-87. Lt. comdr. M.C., USN, 1976-78. Woodruff-Fisher scholar, 1964-68. Mem. Internat. Platform Assn., Nat. Spkrs. Assn., Assn. U. Anesthetists, Am. Soc. Anesthesiologists (del. 1983-88, 88—), Soc. for Edn. in Anesthesio (past v.p., now pres.), Colo. Soc. Anesthesiologists (pres.), Internat. Anesthesia Rsch. Soc., Evergreen Newcomers, Alpha Omega Alpha. Republican. Presbyterian.

MCLINN, HARRY MARVIN, facial orthopaedic educator, consultant; b. Huntsville, Ala., Oct. 31; s. Benjamin and Clara (Derrick) McL.; m. angela Louise Jones, Aug. 1, 1944; children; Teloca, Marvin, Jenol. DDS, Howard U., 1944; cert., Columbia U., 1947. Diplomate Am. Bd. Orthodontics. Pvt. practice Pa., N.Y., 1950-73; med. officer U.S. Civil Svc., 1973-76; Louise Ball fellow Columbia U., N.Y.C., 1947; dept. head orthodontics Howard U., 1948-50; pvt. practice N.Y.C., 1950-73; assoc. prof. orthodontics U. Medicine Dentistry of N.J., Newark, 1973-85; facial orthopedic cons. Englewood, N.J., N.Y.C., 1985—; dept. head orthodontics Howard Dental, Washington, 1948-50; health cons., N.J., N.Y.C., 1975—. Contbr. articles to profl. jours. Mem. Englewood Bd. Health, N.J., 1970's; panel mem., cons. handicapped children, N.Y.C., 1955-70; planning bd. Englewood Hosp., N.J., 1976-82. Capt. U.S. Army, 1944-46. Fellow Internat. Coll. Dentists; mem. ADA, Am. Assn. Orthodontics, AAUP, Omega Kappa Upsilon, Lambda Kappa.

MCMAHON, ANITA SUE, women's health nurse; b. Elgin, Ill., Dec. 11, 1940; d. Herman Henry and Neva Imogene (Lusted) Mass; m. Daniel D. McMahon, Aug. 20, 1960; children: Daniel, Patrick, Christine, Joseph, Susanne. AAS with high honors, Elgin C.C., 1983; BS, St. Francis Coll., Joliet, Ill., 1992; student, Alverno Coll., Milw. Cert. inpatient obstet. nurse; cert. childbirth educator. Nurse preceptor, staff nurse med.-surg. Sherman Hosp., Elgin, 1983-90, ob-gyn. nurse, 1990—, childbirth instr., 1991—, charge nurse, 1992—, obstet. leadership coun., 1995—. Creator, editor quar. Nurse's Notes. Home: 617 Hawthorne Ct Carpentersville IL 60110-1970

MCMAHON, DAVID FREYVOGEL, psychiatrist; b. Hartford, Conn., Feb. 9, 1949; s. David Gue and Leona Anna (Freyvogel) McM.; m. Martha Jean Howard, July 26, 1980; children: Melissa, Bethany. B.S.E., Princeton U., 1971; MD, Stanford U., 1975. Intern Yale U., New Haven, 1975-76, resident psychiatry, 1976-78, fellow in psychiatry Sch. Medicine, 1978-79; chief psychiatry William W. Backus Hosp., Norwich, Conn., 1979-95; assoc. corp. med. dir. Choate Health Mgmt., 1995—; med. dir. Bayridge Hosp., Lynn, Mass., 1995—; clin. instr. Yale U. Sch. Medicine, New Haven, 1979-83. Mem. editorial bd. Postgrad. Medicine, 1991—; contbr. articles to med. jours. Co-host radio program Sta. WICH Radio, Norwich, 1980-95; mem. governance bd. Community Mental Health Svcs., New London County, Conn., 1981-87. Fellow Am. Psychiat. Assn.; mem. APA (com. on telemed. svcs.), Conn. Psychiat. Soc. (treas. 1987-89, pres. 1990-91, rep. to Nat. Assembly 1992-95, chair fellow selection com. 1992-95, Conn. Hosp. Assn. (chmn. psychiat. adminstrs. conv. 1986-87), Hartford Psychiat. Soc. (pres.), Ea. Conn. Yale Med. Alumni Assn., Princeton Alumni Assn. Ea. Conn. Office: Bayridge Hosp 60 Granite St Lynn MA 01904

MCMAHON, JOHN ALEXANDER, lawyer, educator; b. Monongahela, Pa., July 31, 1921; s. John Hamilton and Jean (Alexander) McM.; m. Betty Wagner, Sept. 14, 1947 (div. Mar. 1977); children: Alexander Talpey, Sarah Francis, Elizabeth Wagner, Ann Wallace; m. Anne Fountain Willets, May 1, 1977. A.B. magna cum laude, Duke U., 1942; student, Harvard U. Bus. Sch., 1942-43; J.D., Law Sch., 1948; LL.D., Wake Forest U., 1978; D.Sc. (hon.), Georgetown U. Sch. Medicine, 1985. Bar: N.C. 1950. Prof. pub. law and govt., asst. dir. Inst. Govt. U. N.C., 1948-59; gen. counsel, sec.-treas. N.C. Assn. County Commrs., Chapel Hill, 1959-65; v.p. spl. devel. Hosp. Saving Assn., Chapel Hill, N.C., 1965-67; pres. N.C. Blue Cross and Blue Shield, Inc., Chapel Hill, 1968-72, Am. Hosp. Assn., Chgo., 1972-86; chmn. dept. health adminstrn. Duke U., Durham, N.C., 1986-92, exec.-in-residence Fuqua Sch. Bus., 1992—; mem. Chapel Hill bd. N.C. Nat. Bank, 1967-72; bd. govs. Blue Cross Assn., 1969-72; mem. Orange County Welfare Bd., 1956-63; chmn. N.C. Comprehensive Health Planning Coun., 1968-72, Health Planning Coun. of Ctrl. N.C., 1963-69; mem. Pres.' Com. on Health Edn., 1971-72; mem. com. health svcs. industry and health industry adv. com. Econ. Stablzn. Program, 1971-74; mem. adv. coun. Kate Bitting Reynolds Health Care Trust, 1971-95; mem. adv. coun. Northwestern U., 1973-86; mem. med. adv. com. VA, 1975-85; bd. dirs. Eason, Earl and Assocs., Greenville, S.C., The Forest at Duke, Durham, N.C. Author: North Carolina County Government, 1959, The North Carolina Local Government Commission, 1960; editor: N.C. County Yearbook, 1959-64, Proceedings of the Annual National Forum on Hospital and Health Affairs, 1993—. Mem. Orange County Dem. Exec. Com., also chmn. Kings Mill Precinct, 1964-68; chmn. bd. trustees Duke U., 1971-83, chmn. emeritus, 1983—; bd. dirs. Rsch. Triangle Found., 1971-83, 92—, Nat. Ctr. for Health Edn., 1974-86; bd. mgrs., mem. exec. com. Internat. Hosp. Fedn., London, 1975-85, pres., 1981-83. With USAAF, 1942-46, col. Res., ret. Mem. N.C. State Bar, Inst. Medicine of NAS, Duke Alumni Assn. (pres. 1968-70), Hope Valley Country Club (Durham), Dunes Golf and Beach Club (Myrtle Beach). Presbyterian. Home: 181 Montrose Dr Durham NC 27707-3929 Office: Duke U Fuqua Sch Bus Durham NC 27708-0120

MCMAHON, MARIA O'NEIL, social work educator; b. Hartford, Conn., Jan. 2, 1937; d. John Joseph and Margaret (Galvin) O'Neil; m. Dennis Richard McMahon, June 10, 1988; stepchildren: Lezlie, Nora, Kelly, Stacie, Michael. BA, St. Joseph Coll., West Hartford, Conn., 1958; MSW, Cath. U. Am., 1964, D. Social Work, 1978. Supr., child and family therapist Highland Heights Residential Treatment Ctr., New Haven, 1964-71; chair dept. socialogy and social work St. Joseph Coll., 1971-84; prof. E. Carolina U., Greenville, N.C., 1985—, dean Sch. Social Work, 1985-91; cons. to various univs., 1970—; trainer Conn. Dept. Social Svcs., 1982-84, N.C. Dept. Social Svcs., 1987-89. Author: The General Method of Social Work Practice, 1984, 2d edit., 1990, 3d edit., 1996, Advanced Generalist Practice, With An International Perspective, 1994; editor report in field; contbr. articles, book revs. to profl. publs. Commr. Nat. Coun. Social Work Edn., Alexandria, Va., 1983-85; chair bd. dirs. Ea. N.C. Poverty Com., 1987—, Cath. Social Ministries of Archdiocese of Raleigh (N.C.), 1989-92. Recipient Outstanding Educator award AAUW, 1981, Disting. Alumnae award, Cath. U. of Am., 1994. Mem. Nat. Assn. Social Workers (Outstanding Social Worker of Yr., Conn. chpt. 1981), Acad. Cert. Social Workers, Am. Correctional Assn., Nat. Assn. Women Deans, Nat. Coun. Social Work Edn. Democrat. Roman Catholic. Office: E Carolina U Sch Social Work Ragsdale Hall Greenville NC 27858

MCMAHON, THOMAS ARTHUR, biology and applied mechanics educator; b. Dayton, Ohio, Apr. 21, 1943; s. Howard Oldford and Lucille (Nelson) McM.; m. Carol Ehlers, June 20, 1965; children: James Robert, Elizabeth Kirsten. B.S., Cornell U., 1965; S.M., MIT, 1967, Ph.D., 1970. Postdoctoral fellow Harvard U., Cambridge, Mass., 1969-70, lectr. bioengring., 1970-71, asst. prof., 1971-74, assoc. prof., 1974-77, prof. applied mechanics and biology, 1977—; cons. numerous industries, legal firms. Author: (novels), Principles of American Nuclear Chemistry, 1970, McKay's Bees, 1979, Loving Little Egypt, 1987; (non-Fiction) Muscles, Reflexes and Locomotion, 1984; (with others) On Size and Life, 1983. Grantee NIH; System Devel. Found., Sloan Found.; recipient Richard and Hinde Rosenthal award Am. Acad. and Inst. Arts and Letters, 1988. Mem. Biomed. Engring. Soc., Am. Physiol. Soc., N.Y. Acad. Scis., PEN. Home: 65 Crest Rd Wellesley MA 02181-4620 Office: Harvard U Pierce Hall Dept Applied Scis Cambridge MA 02138

MCMANIGAL, SHIRLEY ANN, university dean; b. Deering, Mo., May 4, 1938; d. Jadie C. and Willie B. (Groves) Naile. BS, Ark. State U., 1971; MS, U. Okla., 1976, PhD, 1979. Lic. med. technologist, clin. lab. dir. Med. technologist, 1958-75; chair dept. med. tech. U. So. Miss., Hattiesburg, 1979-83; chair dept. med. tech. Tex. Tech U. Health Scis. Ctr., Lubbock, 1983-87, dean Sch. Allied Health, 1987—; gov.'s appointee to statewide health coord. coun., 1994—. Leadership Tex., 1992; Lt. Alumnae Regl. dir., 1994—. Recipient Citation, State of Tex., 1988; named Woman of Yr., AAUW, Tex. div., 1990, Woman of Excellence in Edn. YWCA, Lubbock, 1990. Mem. AAUW (bd. dirs. Tex. 1990-94), Am. Coun. on Edn./Nat. Identification Program (steering com. for Tex.), Clin. Lab. Mgmt. Assn. (chair edn. com. 1989, 91), Am. Soc. Med. Tech., Nat. Assn. Women in Edn., So. Assn. Allied Health Deans at Acad. Health Ctrs., S.W. Assn. Clin. Microbiology, Tex. Soc. Allied Health Professions (pres. 1990-91), Tex. Soc. Med. Tech. (Educator of Yr. 1990), Alpha Eta, Phi Beta Delta. Home: 5003 94th St Lubbock TX 79424-4839 Office: Tex Tech U Sch Allied Health Dept Scis Ctr Lubbock TX 79430

MCMANUS, EDWARD HUBBARD, government official; b. Roxbury, Mass., Jan. 11, 1939; s. Paul Carter and Dorothy (Shaw) McM.; m. Sharon

Pickett, Feb. 10, 1968; children: Kevin, Keith, Michael. B.A., U. Mass., 1960; M.A., U. Wis., 1970. Mgmt. analyst Bur. Internat. Commerce, Dept. Commerce, Washington, 1965-66; asst. to adminstrv. officer NIMH, NIH, Bethesda, Md., 1966-68; adminstrv. officer div. research resources NIH, Bethesda, 1968-69; asst. exec. officer div. research resources NIH, Bethesda, Md., 1970-71; fin. mgmt. officer Nat. Library Medicine, NIH, Bethesda, 1971-73; exec. officer Nat. Eye Inst., Bethesda, 1973-81, dep. dir., 1981—. Served to lt. (j.g.) USN, 1961-64. Mem. Am. Mgmt. Assn., Am. Soc. Pub. Adminstrn., Internat. Agy. for Prevention of Blindness (exec. bd.). Office: Nat Eye Inst 31/6A05 31 Center Dr MSC 2510 Bethesda MD 20892-2510

MCMANUS, PATRICK JOHN, physician; b. Washington, July 13, 1959; s. Reginald Paul and Kathleen Flanagan McManus; m. Mary Elizabeth Pleasants, Sept. 27, 1986; children: Ann maitland, Elizabeth Cameron, Daniel Patrick. BA in Chemistry/Classics, Bowdoin Coll., 1981; MD, U. Va., 1985. Diplomate Am. Bd. Internal Medicine. Intern, resident U. Mass. Med. Ctr., Worcester, 1985-88; pvt. practice Fredericksburg (Va.) Internal Medicine, 1988—; med. dir. Potomac Point Adult Home, Fredericksburg, 1988—, Mary Washington Hospice, 1994—; pres. Primary Care Assocs., 1995—. Vol. Ross Free Clinic, Fredericksburg, 1994—. Mem. Phi Beta Kappa, Alpha Omega Alpha. Office: Fredericksburg Internal Med 2216 Princess Anne St Fredericksburg VA 22401

MCMEEKIN, THOMAS O., dermatologist; b. Chelby, Nebr., Apr. 17, 1945; s. Wallace Walton and Evajame (Taber) McM.; m. Susan Jo, Sept. 17, 1966; children: Michele, Sean. BA with distinction, Stanford U., 1967; MD with honors, U. Rochester, 1971. Intern Beth Israel Hosp., Boston, 1971-72; resident U. Rochester (N.Y.), 1974-76, Mass. Gen. Hosp., Boston, 1976-78; clin. assoc. prof. depts. medicine, pediatrics, dermatology U. Rochester Sch. Medicine, 1978—; dermatologist pvt. practice, Rochester, 1978—; pres. Geneese Valley Laser Ctr., Rochester, 1990—. Capt. USPHS, 1972-74. Kohn fellow U. Rochester, 1980-81; recipient Doren J. Stephens Alumni award U. Rochester, 1971, Brian Flanagan Teaching Svc. award, 1995. Fellow Am. Acad. Dermatology (Svc. award 1993), Am. Bd. Internal Medicine, Am. Soc. LAser MEdicine (co-chmn. 1993-94), Am. Soc. Dermatologic Surgery (edn. com. 1983—); mem. N.Y. State Dermatological Soc. (v.p. 1993, treas. 1992), Buffalo Rochester Dermatological Soc. (pres. 1990), Rochester Dermatological Soc. (pres. 1980-89), Alpha Omega Alpha. Office: 300 Whitespruce Blvd Rochester NY 14623

MCMENAMIN, PAUL JOHN, ophthalmologist; b. Queens, N.Y., Feb. 24, 1957; m. Gail A. Peterson, Jan. 13, 1990. BS, St. Johns U., N.Y.C., 1979, MS, 1982; MD, SUNY, Bklyn., 1987. Med. intern Yale-New Haven Hosp., 1987-88; ophthalmology resident N.Y. Eye and Ear Infirmary, N.Y.C., 1988-91; ophthalmologist Williamsburg Eye Assocs., Va., 1991-95; pvt. practice Williamsburg, Va., 1995—; Diplomate Am. Bd. Ophthalmology. Fellow Am. Acad. Ophthalmology, Am. Bd. Ophthalmology; mem. AMA, Contact Lens Assn., Med. Soc. Va., Alpha Omega Alpha. Home: 141 Hearthside Ln Williamsburg VA 23185 Office: 1315 Jamestown Rd Ste 102 Williamsburg VA 23185

MCMICHAEL, MARCIA HASTON, legal nursing consultant; b. Borger, Tex., July 26, 1945; m. Patrick McMichael, Dec. 14, 1980. ADN, Okla. State U., Oklahoma City, 1986; BS in Med. Tech., U. Okla., 1967, BS as Physician Asst., 1980. RN, Okla., Calif., Tex. Physician's asst. in plastic surgery Edward A. Shadid, MD, Oklahoma City, 1980-81; physician's asst. in internal medicine James E. Walraven, MD, Oklahoma City, 1981-87; staff nurse Downey (Calif.) Cmty. Hosp., 1987-88; nurse home healthcare Excel Health Svcs., Inc., Costa Mesa, Calif., 1988-90; owner cons. bus. Med-Law Case Rev., Dallas, 1989—. Mem. Am. Assn. Legal Nurse Cons. (founding), Phi Beta Kappa.

MCMILLAN, DONALD EDGAR, pharmacologist; b. Butler, Pa., Sept. 23, 1937; s. Chandler Burdell and Ruth Elizabeth (Beach) McM.; m. Marjorie Ann Leavitt, Feb. 4, 1963; children: David Craig, Pamela Jean. B.S., Grove City Coll., 1959; M.S., U. Pitts., 1962, Ph.D., 1965. Postdoctoral fellow Harvard U. Med. Sch., 1965-66; instr. in pharmacology SUNY Downstate Med. Ctr., N.Y.C., 1967-68, asst. prof., 1968-69; asst. prof. pharmacology U. N.C., 1969-72, asso. prof., 1972-76, prof., 1976-78; prof., chmn. dept. pharmacology U. Ark. for Med. Scis., 1978-80, prof., chmn. dept. pharmacology and toxicology, 1980—, prof. psychiatry, 1985—, Wilbur D. Mills prof. alcoholism and drug abuse prevention, 1991—; dir. Substance Abuse Treatment Ctr.; vis. lectr. U. Ctrl. Caracas, Venezuela, 1974; IRG mem. neurobiology rev. panel NSF, 1979-80; IRG mem. Nat. Inst. Drug Abuse, 1982-88, 92-95, chair 1994-95, SRC mem., 1988-95; bd. dirs. Chapel Hill (N.C.) Drug Action Com., 1977-78; cons. Health Effects Inst., 1985-87; cons. sci. adv. bd. EPA, 1985-89; spl. merit rev. bd. Armed Forces Radiobiology Rsch. Inst., 1982; mem. com. toxicity data elements NRC, 1980-83. Author: Central Nervous System Pharmacology— A Self Instruction Text, 1974, 2d, rev. edit., 1979; research, numerous publs. in behavioral pharmacology and drug abuse; bd. editors Jour. Pharmacology and Exptl. Therapeutics, 1972—, Psychopharmacology, 1973-81, Neurotoxicology, 1979-82, Toxicology and Applied Pharmacology, 1982-89, Neurobehavioral/Toxicology and Teratology, 1982-90, Behavioral Pharmacology, 1989—. Grantee NIMH, 1971-74, Nat. Inst. Environ. Health Scis., 1976-80, N.C. Alcoholism Rsch. Authority, 1975-77, EPA, 1982-85, Kellogg Found., 1987-92, U.S. Dept. Edn., 1989-91, Nat. Inst. Drug Abuse, 1976—. Mem. AAAS, Behavioral Pharmacology Soc. (pres. 1982-84), Behavioral Toxicology Soc. (pres. 1988-90), Am. Soc. Pharmacology and Exptl. Therapeutics, Am. Psychol. Soc., European Behavioral Pharmacology Soc., Soc. Toxicologists (pres. So. Cen. chpt. 1985-86), Com. on Problems of Drug Dependence. Home: 100 Longway Dr Little Rock AR 72211-9531 Office: U Ark Med Scis Sch Medicine Dept Pharmacology & Toxicol 4301 W Markham St Little Rock AR 72205-7101

MCMILLAN, JULIA A., pediatrician; b. Pinehurst, N.C., July 10, 1946. MD, SUNY, Syracuse, 1976. Intern SUNY Upstate Med. Ctr., Syracuse, 1976-77, resident in pediatrics, 1977-78, 79-80, fellow in infectious diseases, 1979-81; mem. staff Johns Hopkins U. Hosp., Balt.; assoc. prof. Johns Hopkins U., Balt. Mem. Am. Acad. Pediatrics, ASM, IDSA. OFfice: Johns Hopkins Hosp Dept Pediatrics 600 N Wolfe St Baltimore MD 21287-3224*

MCMINN, HENRY FRANCIS, medical technologist; b. Albany, N.Y., Oct. 23, 1956; s. William R. and Sarah (Grace) McM. AS, Ctrl. Tex. Coll., 1983; AAS, Austin C.C., 1991. Cert. med. tech., med. lab. tech. Med. lab. tech. Seton Med. Ctr., Austin, Tex., 1988-93; charge med. tech. J.C. Hosp., Taylor, Tex., 1993—; med. tech. oncology S.W. Cancer Rsch. Ctr., Austin, 1991—; quality control Austin Biomed. Rsch., 1990-92; med. tech. Austin Regional Clinic, 1989—; del. to Vietnam Am. Med. Technologists Citizen Amb. Program, 1996. Animal lab. tech. Am. Soc. Prevention Cruelty to Animals, Austin, 1994—; asst. troop leader Boy Scouts Am., Coppers Cove, Tex., 1988-90; vol. med. tech. Austin Health Clinic, 1995—. Served to sr. airman USAF, 1976-80. Decorated humanitarian svc. award USAF, 1977, 79, good conduct medal, 1977. Mem. Am. Med. Technologists, Am. Soc. Clin. Pathologists, Tex. State Soc. Med. Technologists. Republican. Roman Catholic. Home: 1108 Pitcairn Dr Pflugerville TX 78660 Office: JC Hosp 700 Mallard Dr Taylor TX 78412

MCMONIGLE, HUGH ANDREW, enucleator; b. Hailey, Idaho, Aug. 2, 1932; s. Hugh Bartholomew and Bernadette Eugenie (leBailly) McM.; m. Helen Marie Davis, Feb. 22, 1957; children: Marie Camille, Anne Michelle, Hugh Davis, Andrew George, Robert Eugene. BS, Idaho State Coll., 1954; postgrad., San Francisco Mortuary Coll., San Francisco, 1955; MA, San Francisco State Coll., San Francisco, 1966; postgrad., U. Calif., San Francisco, 1974. Morgue driver San Francisco Coroner's Office, San Francisco, 1955-69; tchr. San Francisco Coll. Mortuary Sci., San Francisco, 1954—; dep. curator U. Calif. Sch. Medicine, San Francisco, 1969—; enucleator U. Calif. Dept. Ophthalmology, San Francisco, 1974—, No. Calif. Transplant Bank, San Francisco, 1974—. Active Archdiocesan Pastoral Coun., San Francisco Archdiocese, 1970-74, Good Shepherd Parent Tchrs. Group, Pacifica, Calif., 1968-81. Mem. Am. Bd. Funeral Svc. Roman Catholic. Office: San Francisco Coll Mort Sci 1598 Dolores St San Francisco CA 94110-4927

MC MULLAN, DOROTHY, nurse educator; b. Bloomfield, N.J., June 19, 1911; d. Samuel H. and Anne (Gardiner) McM.; m. Bernard J. Pisani, July 10, 1982. Diploma, Cornell U.-N.Y. Hosp. Sch. Nursing, 1935; B.S., N.Y. U., 1948, M.A., 1950, Ed.D., 1962. Pub. health nurse Henry St. Vis. Nurse Service, N.Y.C., 1935-39; pvt. duty nurse N.Y.C., 1939-41; instr. N.Y. Hosp.-Cornell U. Sch. Nursing, 1947-55; supr. N.Y. Hosp.-Cornell Med. Center, 1947-50, asst. dept. head, 1950-53, adminstrv. asst. nursing services for methods improvements, 1953-55; instr. N.Y. Hosp.-Cornell Med. Center (Sch. Nursing); dir., prof. nursing Russell Sage Coll., 1955-61; dean, prof. Ind. State U. Sch. Nursing, Terre Haute, 1962-71; dir. div. nursing Nat. League for Nursing, N.Y.C., 1971-77; chmn. dept. baccalaureate and higher edn. N.Y. League, 1960-62; mem. Nat. Commn. on Allied Health Edn., 1977-80; cons. on nurse edn., 1977-80; cons. Council on Postsecondary Accreditation, 1977-78; v.p. N.Y. Nurses Assn., 1960-61; pres. Vigo County Coordinating Council, 1966-69; mem. adv. bd. Ind. Regional Med. Planning, 1966-71; sec. exec. com. Ind. Comprehensive Health Council, 1967-71; mem. adv. com. on women in services U.S. Dept. Def., 1971-73; mem. nursing adv. com. Am. Cancer Soc., 1975-77; mem. com. on health manpower Nat. Health Council, 1975-79. Author: (with Hayt, Groeschel) Law of Hospital and Nurse, 1958, The Role of the Nurse as Employee: A Case of Mutual Responsibilities, 1976, Preparation of the Nurse Specialist, 1977. Bd. dirs. Vigo County cancer Soc., Vigo County cerebral Palsy Assn., Goodwill Industries Terre Haute, Cmty. Found. Wabash Valley, 1964-71; mem. Heritage Found.; mem. coun. Citizens Against Govt. Waste. Recipient Ann. award of Vigo County Ind. Bus. and Profl. Women's Orgn., 1967, Army Nurse Corps Spl. award, 1973, Dept. of Def. cert., NYU Founders Day cert., 1963, Pres.'s award Ind. State U., 1988, Disting. Alumnus award Cornell U./N.Y. Hosp. Sch. Nursing Alumni Assn., 1990; recognized for disting. and devoted svc. as pres. Ind. League for Nursing, 1966-71; named in People of Progress in Terre Haute, 1967. Mem. APHA, Cornell U.-N.Y. Hosp. Sch. Nursing Alumnae Assn. (pres. 1950-52), Ind. League for Nursing (pres. 1966-71), So. N.Y. League for Nursing (pres. 1980-82, exec. sec. 1982-88, award 1987, Dorothy McMullan Pisani ann. award 1987), League Nursing (mem. exec. com., chmn. Gt. Lakes Regional Assembly 1969-71), Nat. League Nursing (bd. dirs. 1981-83), Assn. Higher Edn., Inst. Biomed. Edn. (bd. dirs. 1984-89), Am. Assn. for World Health (exec. com. 1980-90, exec. 1984-89), N.Y. County Med. Soc. Auxiliary (v.p. 1984-90), Kappa Delta Pi. Republican. Episcopalian. Home: 209 Sunset Ave Englewood NJ 07631-4413

MCMURRAY, JAMES G., urologist; b. Johnson City, Tex., July 2. 1940; s. Jean G. and Virginia (Wood) McM.; m. Elizabeth H. McMurray, Aug. 8, 1958 (div. Feb. 1982); children: Susan Hall, Julie, David; m. Janice Price Foley, Mar. 4, 1983; 1 child, Erin Foley. BSE, Ark. State U., Jonesboro, 1962; MD, U. Miss., 1967. Diplomate Am. Bd. Urology. Resident in urology U. Miss. Med. Sch., Jackson, 1970-74; solo practice urology Huntsville, Ala., 1974—; prin. investigator Med Affil. Rsch. Ctr., Huntsville, 1995—. Lt. USN, 1968-70. Mem. Rotary Internat. (sec. Huntsville). Republican. Presbyterian. Home: 9 Old Chimney Rd Huntsville AL 35801 Office: 303 Williams Ave Huntsville AL 35801

MCMURRY, FRED G., neurosurgeon; b. Sept. 10, 1943; m. Sep. 25, 1965. BS, Antioch Coll., Yellow Springs, Ohio, 1966; MS, Temple U., 1970. Diplomate Am. Bd. Neurological Surgery. Resident in neurosurgery Cleve. Clinic, 1974-78; staff neurosurgeon Geisinger Med. Ctr., Danville, Pa., 1978-93; pvt. practice Yellowstone Neurosurgical, Billings, Mont., 1993—. Office: Yellowstone Neurosurg Assoc 1145 N29th Ste 501 Billings MT 59102

MCMURRY, WILLIAM SCOTT, allied health educator; b. Poteau, Okla., Apr. 10, 1921; s. Ulysses Scott and Syntha Alice (McDonald) McM.; m. Kathryn Elizabeth Robison, Feb. 2, 1946. BS, N.E. U., Okla., 1942; DDS, U. Mo., 1950, MS, 1966; PhD, Columbia Pacific U., 1983. Commd. 2d lt., U.S. Air Force, 1941, advanced through grades to lt. col., 1963; ret., 1969; assoc. chief of staff edn. VA, Dayton, Ohio, 1973-79; asst. dean veterans affairs Wright State Med. Sch., 1975-79, assoc. prof. surgery and continued edn.; prof. St. Petersburg (Fla.) Jr. Coll., 1967-73; adj. prof. Ohio State U., 1973-79; assoc. prof. allied health So. Ill. U., 1979—. Fellow Am. Assn. Oral and Maxillofacial Surgeons (ret.), Internat. Assn. Oral and Maxillofacial Surgeons; mem. Council Occupational Edn.. Midwestern Oral Surgeons, Ill. Assn. Oral and Maxillo Facial Surgeons, Okla. State Dental Assn., Ill. Police Assn., Ret. Officers Assn., Assn. Mil. Surgeons, Assn. Ret. Fed. Employees, Air Force Assn. Republican. Lodges: Masons, Lions. Contbr. articles to profl. jours. Office: So Ill U Stc Building Ste 118-a Carbondale IL 62901

MC MURTRY, JAMES GILMER, III, neurosurgeon; b. Houston, June 11, 1932; s. James Gilmer and Alberta Elizabeth (Matteson) McM.; student Rice U., Houston, 1950-53; M.D. cum laude, Baylor U., Houston, 1957. Intern, Hosp. U. Pa., Phila., 1957-58; resident gen. surgery Baylor U. Affiliated Hosps., Houston, 1958-59; asst. neurol. surgery Coll. Physicians and Surgeons, Columbia U., N.Y.C., 1959-60; asst. resident neurol. surgery and neurology Neurol. Inst. N.Y., Columbia Presbyn. Med. Center, N.Y.C., 1960-62, chief resident neurol. surgery, 1962-63; Nat. Inst. Neurol. Disease and Blindness spl. fellow neurol. surgery Coll. Physicians and Surgeons, Columbia U., N.Y.C., 1963-64, instr. neurol. surgery, 1963-65, assoc., 1965-68, asst. prof. clin. neurol. surgery, 1968-73, assoc. prof., 1973-89, prof., 1989—; asst. attending neurol. surgeon Neurol. Inst. N.Y., N.Y.C., 1964-73, assoc. attending neurol. surgeon, 1973-89, attending neurol. surgeon, 1989—; chief neurol. surgery clinic Vanderbilt Clinic, Columbia Presbyn. Med. Center, N.Y.C., 1964-68; attending-in-charge neurosurgery Lenox Hill Hosp., N.Y.C., 1970-91; assoc. cons. neurol. surgery Englewood (N.J.) Hosp., 1964—; asst. cons. neurol. surgery Harlem Hosp., N.Y.C., 1964—; cons. neurol. surgery Bronx (N.Y.) VA Hosp., 1964-65; mem. NIH Parkinson Research Group, Columbia U., 1965—; mem. med. adv. bd. N.Y. State Athletic Commn. Jesse H. Jones scholar Baylor U. Coll. Medicine, 1953-57, Allen fellow dept. neurol. surgery Columbia U., 1964-65. Diplomate Am. Bd. Neurol. Surgery. Fellow ACS, Linnean Soc. (London); trustee Glimmerglass Opera, Morris-Jumel, Opera Manhattan. Mem. AAUP, AAAS, AMA, Am. Assn. Neurol. Surgeons, European Congress Pediatric Neurosurgery, Am. Soc. Stereotaxic Surgeons, Pan Am. Med. Assn., N.Y. State Soc. Surgeons, N.Y. State Neurosurgery Soc., N.Y. Acad. Sci., N.Y. Neurosurg. Soc., Med. Soc. State N.Y., N.Y. County Med. Soc., Osler Soc., Baylor U. Coll. Medicine Alumni Assn., Med. Strollers, The Med. Soc. of London, The Harveian Soc., Alpha Omega Alpha. Presbyn. Clubs: The Union (N.Y.C.), The Garrick (London), The Atheneum (London), The Met. Opera (N.Y.C.), The Norfolk Yacht and Country. Author: Medical Examination Review Book-Neurological Surgery, 1970, rev. edit., 1975; Neurological Surgery Case Histories, 1975; contbr. articles to profl. jours. Home: 1 Cobb Ln Tarrytown NY 10591-3003 Office: 710 W 168th St New York NY 10032-2603

MCMURTRY, JAMES MAURICE, urologist; b. Detroit, July 9, 1940; m. Florene Coleman, 1965; 2 children. BS, Wayne State U., 1962, MD, 1966. Diplomate Am. Bd. Urology. Intern Harper Hosp., Detroit, 1966-67, resident in gen. surgery, 1969-70, resident in urology, 1970-73; pvt. practice, Detroit, 1973-95, Taylor, Mich., 1996—. Col. M.C., U.S. Army, 1967-69, 91, Vietnam, Saudi Arabia. Mem. Nat. Med. Assn., Mich. Urol. Assn. Office: Henry Ford Med Group 24555 Haig Taylor MI 48180

MCMURTY, ROBERT Y., academic dean. Dean U. Western Ont. Faculty Medicine, Can. Office: U Western Ont, Health Sci Ctr Rm H112, London, ON Canada N6A 5CI*

MCNABB, CRAIG L., emergency room nurse; b. Atlanta, Feb. 3 1948; s. Vernon Lee an Martha B. (Branham) McN.; m. Diane E. Pennington, June 22, 1987; children: Michael Shawn, Scott Lee Pruett. AA, DeKalb Jr. Coll., Clarston, Ga., 1973; BA, Ga. State U., 1975, BSN, 1993. RN, Ga.; BCLS, ACLS. Staff nurse Grady Meml. Hosp., Atlanta, 1993-94, R.T. Jones Meml. Hosp., Canton, Ga., 1994—. Mem. Emergency Nurses Assn., Ga. State U. Sch. Nursing Alumni Assn. (dir. 1993—), Sigma Eta Tau. Republican. Methodist. Home: 908 Audrey Dr Woodstock GA 30188 Office: R T Jones Regional Hosp Hospital Rd Canton GA 30114

MCNABB, DARCY LAFOUNTAIN, medical management company executive; b. Middletown, N.J., Aug. 27, 1955; d. Donald Mark LaFountain and Suzanne (Gilman) LaFountain Westergard; m. Leland Monte McNabb, July 4, 1981 (div. Feb. 1989); 1 child, Leland Monte Jr. BBA in Internat. Fin. cum laude, U. Miami, 1977. Real estate agent, Grad. Realtor's Inst. Market rsch. asst. Burger King Corp., Miami, Fla., 1975-77; regional mktg. supr. Burger King Corp., Huntington Beach, Calif., 1977-78; mgr., restaurant planning Holiday Inns, Inc., Memphis, 1978-79, mgr., nat. promotions, 1979-83; dir., lodging and travel planning Holiday Corp., Memphis, 1983-86; affiliate broker The Hobson Co., Realtors, Memphis, 1986-88, Crye Leike, Memphis, 1988-92; v.p. comm. and planning Medshares Mgmt. Group, Inc., Memphis, 1991—. Active Friends Pink Palace Mus., Memphis, 1987-91, Family Link/Runaway, Memphis, 1980-88; chmn. Foster Care Rev. Bd., Memphis, 1988—; bd. dirs. Bethany House, Memphis, 1989—, pres., 1995; pres., bd. dirs. Am. Cancer Soc., 1994—; mktg. com. Health Industry Coun., 1994-95. Named Profl. Vol. of Yr., Friends of Pink Palace Mus., Memphis, 1989, 93, U.S. Masters Swimming All-Am., 1993, 94; grad. Leadership Memphis, 1995; named Cmty. Hero for Olympic Torch Relay, 1996. Mem. Le Bonheur Club, Memphis Runners Track Club. Republican. Episcopalian. Home: 1948 Harbert Ave Memphis TN 38104-5216 Office: Medshares Mgmt Group Inc 2714 Union Avenue Ext Memphis TN 38112-4415

MCNABB, JAMES DAVID, ophthalmologist; b. Dallas, Feb. 6, 1940; s. Gerald C. and Virginia (Horton) McN.; m. Kay Lynn Kriegel, June 21, 1969; children: Keith David, Kelsey Elaine. AB, U. Rochester, N.Y., 1962; MSc, McGill U., Montreal, Que., Can., 1964; MD, U. Tex. Med. Br., 1969. Diplomate Am. Bd. Ophthalmology. With Cataract & Eye Ctr., Austin, Tex. Lt. comdr. USPHS, 1970-73. Fellow Am. Acad. Ophthalmology; mem. AMA, Tex. Med. Assn., Am. Soc. Cataract and Refractive Surgeons, Contact Lens Soc. Am., Tex. Ophthalmol. Soc., Tex. Soc. Ophthalmology and Otolaryngology, Internat. Soc. Refractive Surgeons. Episcopalian. Home: 1411 Mohle Dr Austin TX 78703-2431 Office: Cataract & Eye Ctr 1101 W 40th St Austin TX 78756-3609

MCNABB, LEONARD MATTHEW, clinical social worker, administrator; b. Hornell, N.Y., Nov. 24, 1948; s. John Wallace and Loretta Catherine (Leonard) McN.; m. Marla Sue Krakowsky, Dec. 19, 1970; 1 child, Alissa Marie. BS, Shippensburg U., 1970; MSW, Marywood Coll., 1973; postgrad., U. Scranton. Coord. St. Michael's Sch. for Boys, Hoban Heights, Pa., 1973-74; human svc. planner Wyo. County Children and Youth, Tunkhannock, Pa., 1974-76, supr., 1976-78; social svcs. mgr. United Svcs. Agy., Wilkes-Barre, Pa., 1978-81; clinician Advanced Psychol. Svcs., Tunkannock, 1990—; mgr. Community Counseling Svcs., Tunkannock, 1981—; bd. dirs. Victims Resources Policy Bd., Tunkhannock, 1986—. Asst. patrol dir. Montage Nat. Ski Patrol, 1988. Grantee Bur. of Corrections, 1971. Mem. NASW, Acad. Cert. Social Workers (diplomate in clin. social wk.), Alpha Delta Mu. Home: 1017 Sleepy Hollow Rd Clarks Summit PA 18411-2709 Office: Community Counseling Svcs 99 Bridge St Tunkhannock PA 18657-1303

MCNAIRN, PEGGI JEAN, speech pathologist, educator; b. Dallas, Sept. 22, 1954; d. Glenn Alton Harmon and Anna Eugenia (McVay) Hicks; m. Kerry Glen McNairn, Jan. 27, 1979; children: Micah Jay, Nathan Corey. BS in Speech Pathology, Tex. Christian U., 1977, MS in Communications Pathology, 1978; PhD in Ednl. Adminstrn., Kennedy Western U., 1991. Cert. speech pathologist, mid mgmt. Staff speech pathologist, asst. dir. infant program Easter Seal Soc. for Crippled Children and Adults Tarrant County, Ft. Worth, 1978-80; staff speech pathologist, spl. edn. lead tchr. Sherrod Elem. Sch. Arlington (Tex.) Ind. Sch. Dist., 1981-84, secondary speech/lang. specialist, early childhood assessment staff Spl. Services dept., 1984-89; owner, dir. Speech Assocs., 1989-92; mem. state forms com. Arlington (Tex.) Ind. Sch. Dist., 1985-86, chairperson assessment com., 1986-87; cons. augmentative communication Prentke Romich Co., 1992—; adj. prof., clin. supr. Tex. Christian U., Ft. Worth, 1978-79; clin. speech pathologist North Tex. Home Health Assn., Ft. Worth, 1980-92. Author: Quick Tech Activities for Literacy, 1993, Readable, Repeatable Stories and Activities, 1994, Quick Tech Magic: Music-Based Literacy Activities, 1996. Chairperson United Cerebral Palsy Toy Lending Libr., 1989-90; sunday sch. tchr. 1st United Meth. Ch., Arlington, 1982-87; mem. South Arlington Homeowners Assn., Arlington, 1985-87; 3rd v.p. Bebensee Elem. PTA. Recipient Outstanding Svc. to Handicapped Am. Biog. Inst., 1989; Cert. of Achievement John Hopkins U. for computing to assist persons with disabilities, 1991. Mem. Internat. U.S. Tex. Socs. for Augmentative and Alternate Comm. (sec. Tex. branch), Neurodevelopmental Assn., Assn. for Curriculum and Supervision, Am. Speech and Hearing Assn., Tex. Speech-Lang.-Hearing Assn., Tex. Speech and Hearing Assn. (task force mem for augmentative comm.) Teaching Tex. Tots Consortium, Tex. Christian U. Speech and Hearing Alumni Assn., Kappa Delta Pi, Alpha Lambda Delta. Democrat. Home and Office: 215 Spanish Moss Dr Arlington TX 76018-1540

MCNALLY, RANDALL E., plastic surgeon; b. Chgo., Aug. 18, 1929; s. Edward and Mary Ryan McNally; m. Margaret McNally. BS, U. Notre Dame, 1951; MD, St. Louis U., 1955. John W. Curtin prof. plastic surgery Rush Med. Sch.; chmn. dept. plastic and reconstructive surgery Rush-Presbyn.-St. Luke's Med. Ctr., Chgo. Office: 1725 W Harrison Chicago IL 60612

MCNAMARA, DENNIS LOUIS, business development executive; b. Milw., June 20, 1965; s. James O'Connell and Anne Marilyn (Niebler) McN. AB, Duke U., 1987; MBA, U. Mich., 1992. Rsch. technician U. N.C., Chapel Hill, 1987-90; intern Merck Sharp & Dohme Internat., Rahway, N.J., 1991; sales rep. Abbott Labs., Abbott Park, Ill., 1992-94; mgr. bus. planning and strategic devel. Apex Biosci., Research Triangle Park, N.C., 1994-95; mgr. bus. devel. Sequana Therapeutics, La Jolla, Calif., 1995—. Contbr. articles to profl. jours. Coach Chapel Hill-carrboro Pacers, 1987-88. Dwight F. Benton scholar U. Mich., 1990; Carolina Summer fellow U. N.C., Chapel Hill., 1986, Dorot fellow Dorot Found., 1985. Office: 11099 N Torrey Pines Rd Ste 160 La Jolla CA 92037-1029

MCNAMARA, JO ANNE, nurse; b. Emmetsburg, Iowa, July 23, 1932; d. Joseph Michael and Mary Victoria (Roper) McN. BSN, Briar Cliff Coll., 1956; MA, U. Redlands, Calif., 1979. Registered nurse. Pediatric supr. St. Joseph Mercy Hosp., Sioux City, Iowa, 1955-57; staff nurse Good Samaritan Hosp., West Palm Beach, Fla., 1957-58; psychiat. supr. Glenwood Hills Hosp., Mpls., 1958-61; surg. staff nurse VA Hosp., Mpls., 1961-62; pediatric nurse Mt. Sinai Hosp., Los Angeles, 1963-64, instr. inservice, 1964-69; instr. nursing Los Angeles Unified Sch., 1970-74; edn. coordinator Century City Hosp., Los Angeles, 1975-85; coordinator quality assurance Temple Community Hosp., L.A., 1986-91, dir. edn., 1986-91; sch. nurse L.A. Unified Schs., 1991—. Vol. Crisis Intervention Ctr., Los Angeles, 1984. Mem. Quality Assurance Profls., Health Edn. Coun., Patient Care Assessment Coun., Spina Bifida Assn., Calif. Sch. Nurse Orgn., L.A. Coun. Sch. Nurses. Democrat. Roman Catholic. Home: 20130 Lorne St Canoga Park CA 91306-1842 Office: LA Unified School Dist 450 N Grand Ave Los Angeles CA 90012-2100

MCNAMARA, JOHN REGIS, psychology educator; b. Binghamton, N.Y., May 27, 1941; s. Regis Charles and Jane (Bradley) McN.; m. Lucille J. Martel, Dec. 5, 1972; children: Brian, Paul. BA, U. Notre Dame, 1963; MA, Xavier U., 1967; PhD, U. Ga., 1972. Diplomate Am. Bd. Profl. Psychology. Asst. prof. psychology and medicine U. Mo., Kansas City, 1971-72; prof. clin. psychology Ohio U., Athens, 1972—; cons. U.S. Army, Panama Canal Zone, 1972, U.S. Gen. Acctg. Office, Washington, 1977-81; trainer U.S. AID-Mideast, Athens, 1994. Author: Overcoming Dating Anxiety, 1991; editor: Behavioral Approaches to Medicine, 1979, Critical Issues, Developments and Trends in Professional Psychology, Vol. 1, 1982, Vol. 2, 1984, Vol. 3, 1987. Fellow APA, Behavior Therapy and Rsch. Soc.; mem. assn. for Advancement of Behavior Therapy, Sigma Xi. Home: 23 Coventry Ln Athens OH 45701 Office: Ohio U Porter Hall Dept Psychology Athens OH 45701

MCNAMARA, MARY ANNE, internist; b. Buffalo, July 29, 1948; d. William Leo and Dorothea Evelyn (Kuntz) Schichtel; m. Daniel Norman McNamara, July 17, 1971; children: Daniel Joseph, David Norman. BA, Canisius Coll., 1970; MEd, SUNY, Buffalo, 1976; DO, Nova/Southeastern, North Miami Beach, Fla., 1991. Diplomate Am. Bd. Internal Medicine. H.s. instr. Eden Ctrl. H.S., N.Y., 1970-71; rsch. technologist McMaster U., Hamilton, Ont., Can., 1971-72, VA Hosp., Buffalo, 1975-76; med. technologist North Ridge Hosp., Ft. Lauderdale, Fla., 1981-86; hematology supr. West Boca Med. Ctr., Boca Raton, Fla., 1986-87; internist Boca Raton Med. Group, Fla., 1996—. Mem. AMA, ACP, Am. Coll. Osteopathic Internists,

Am. Osteopathic Assn., Am. Med. Women's Assn., Am. Soc. Clin. Pathologists (cert. med. technologist), Fla. Osteopathic Med. Assn. Office: Boca Raton Med Group 2900 N Military Trail Boca Raton FL 33431

MCNAMARA, PAULA RUTH WAGNER, therapeutic recreation programs director; b. St. Louis, Feb. 23, 1925; d. Paul Brooks and Leah Ruth (Dick) Wagner; m. Raymond Edmund McNamara, May 28, 1949; children: Carol Rae, Marla Ann, Cynthia Ruth, Erin Marie, Brian Francis. BFA, Sch. of Art Inst., 1948; MA, W. Va. Grad. Coll., 1988. Cert. therapeutic recreation specialist. Supr. leisure edn. W. Va. Rehabilitaion Ctr., Institute, 1970-91; exec. dir. W. Va. Therapeutic Recreation Assn., Institute, 1992—; rep. Nat. Therapeutic Recreation Assn., Arlington, Va., 1984—. Amb. Friendship Force, 1993—; conf. del. Partners of the Americas, Washington, 1991. Mem. Nat. Therapeutic Recreation Assn., Am. Therapeutic Recreation Assn., W.Va. Therapeutic Recreation Assn. (sec. 1991). Office: WVa Therapeutic Recreation Assn PO Box 554 Institute WV 25112-0554

MCNEAL, KIMBERLY JAN, orthodontist, dentofacial orthopedist; b. Paris, Tex., Mar. 24, 1956; d. William Lloyd and Jean (Thomas) McNeal; m. Raif Poineal, Dec. 7, 1992. BS cum laude, Angelo State U., San Angelo, Tex., 1978; MS, Ea. Ky. U., Richmond, 1981; DMD with high distinction, U. Ky., 1987; postgrad., Emory U., 1987-89. Orthodontist and dentofacial orthopedist in pvt. practice Atlanta, 1989—; bd. dirs. Atlanta Women's Med. Alliance. Recipient Pierre Fauchard award U. Ky., 1987, Cert. of Merit, Am. Acad. Oral Medicine, 1987. Mem. ADA, Am. Assn. Orthodontists, Am. Cleft Palate-Craniofacial Assn., Ga. Dental Assn., No. Dist. Dental Soc., So. Assn. Orthodontists, Found. for Advancement in Craniofacial Edn. Office: 8737 Dunwoody Pl Ste 1 Atlanta GA 30350

MCNEELEY, SHERRIE LEANN, physician assistant, managed care relations analyst; b. Las Cruces, N.Mex., June 10, 1955; d. George Asa Borden and Roselee Alcie (Ruebush) Williams. BS, Alderson-Broaddus Coll., Philippi, W.Va., 1977; MHS, Johns Hopkins U. Sch. Hygiene and Pub. Health, 1984. Cert. physician asst, 1978, 84, 90, 95. Physician asst. Johns Hopkins Hosp., Balt., 1978-79, Am. U. Student Health Ctr., Washington, 1979-82, People's Commn. Health Ctr., Balt., 1985-88; Burroughs Wellcome Health Policy fellow Am. Acad. Physician Assts., Alexandria, Va., 1988-89; assoc. dir. govt. rels. Am. Rehab. Assn., Washington, 1989-96; dir. managed care rels. Am. Diabetes Assn., Alexandria, 1996—. Author, editor: Physician Assistants Professional Liability Handbook, 1989, Managing Risk Through Quality Physician Assistance Practice, 1995. Bd. dirs. Md. Women's Health Coalition, Balt., 1987-89; mem. Women's Nat. Dem. Club. Fellow Am. Acad. Physician Assts. (bd. dirs. 1991-95, pres.-elect 1995-96, pres. 1996—, del. 1985-89, task force for orgnl. efficiency 1987-88, bd. dirs. edn. and rsch. found. 1987-88, jud. affairs com. 1989-90, pres. 1996—), Md. Acad. Physician Assts. (pres. 1985-87, chmn. legis. and govt. affairs 1984-86, 87-89); mem. APHA, Women in Govt. Rels. Home: 10601 Montrose Ave Apt 103 Bethesda MD 20814-4217

MCNEELY, ALMA GRETCHEN, nurse educator, administrator and historian; b. Detroit, Mar. 29, 1941; d. Carl Bertil and Katherine Rose (Brown) Orman; m. Joseph Francis Cavon, June 26, 1962 (div. 1981); children: Leslie Muriel Cavon Contreras, Joseph Anthony; m. Richard Irving McNeely, Dec. 18, 1981. Diploma, Harper Hosp. Sch. Nursing, 1962; BSN, Biola U., 1981; MSN, Loma Linda U., 1983; D of Nursing Sci., U. San Diego, 1993. RN, Utah; cert. pediat. nurse. Staff nurse Harper Hosp., Detroit, 1962, Midway Hosp., St. Paul, 1963; pediatric charge nurse St. John Hosp., Detroit, 1963-64; staff nurse Mo. Bapt. Hosp., St. Louis, 1965-66; office nurse, mgr. pvt. practice plastic and reconstructive surgeon, Santa Ana, Calif., 1967-81; adj. asst. prof. nursing Mont. State U., 1983-86; doctoral fellow, rsch. asst. U. San Diego, 1986-88; adj. asst. prof. Mont. State U., 1988-90, asst. dean, 1990-96; dean St. Mark's-Westminster Sch. Nursing Westminster Coll., Salt Lake City, 1996—. Contbg. author: Family Health Nursing, 1989, 2d edit., 1995, American Nursing: A Biographical Dictionary, Vol. I, 1988, Vol. II, 1992. Facilitator, Parents Anonymous, Missoula, 1984-86. Mem. ANA, Utah Nurses Assn., Am. Assn. History of Nursing, Sigma Theta Tau (pres. Zeta Upsilon chpt. 1990-92, mem. Iota Iota chpt. 1996—). Republican. Presbyterian. Home: 1467 Penrose Dr Salt Lake City UT 84103 Office: Westminster College St Marks-Westminster Sch Ns 1840 S 1300 E Salt Lake City UT 84105

MCNEER, J. FREDERICK, internist, specialist in cardiovascular disease; b. Berea, Ky., Aug. 18, 1946; s. James William and Clara Mae (Maynard) McN.; m. Patricia Ann Lyons, Aug. 15, 1970; children: Trisha Christine Chilcott, Megan Catherine Amrine. BS in Chemistry, Hampden-Sydney Coll., 1969; MD, Duke U., 1972. Diplomate Am. Bd. Internal Medicine, Am. Bd. Cardiovascular Disease. Resident internal medicine Duke U., Durham, N.C., 1972-74; fellow in cardiovascular disease Duke U., Durham, 1974-77, assoc. in medicine, 1977-78; pvt. practice in cardiovascular disease St. Francis Hosp., Tulsa, Okla., 1978—; assoc. clin. prof. medicine Duke U., Durham, N.C., 1990—; chmn. credentials com. St. Francis Hosp., Tulsa, 1984-90. instnl. rev. bd., 1993-96; mem. bd. dirs., 1995—. Contbr. over 30 articles on cardiovascular disease to profl. jours. including New Eng. Jour. of Medicine, 1984—. Fellow Am. Coll. Cardiology, Am. Heart Assn. (coun. of clin. cardiology). Office: 6465 S Yale Ste 1001 Tulsa OK 74136

MCNEIL, BARBARA JOYCE, radiologist, educator; b. Cambridge, Mass., Feb. 11, 1941; d. Archibald Pius and Katherine (Joyce) McN. A.B., Emmanuel Coll., 1962; M.D., Harvard U., 1966, Ph.D., 1972. Diplomate: Am. Bd. Nuclear Medicine. Intern Mass. Gen. Hosp., Boston, 1966-67, resident in nuclear medicine, 1971-73; prof. radiology and clin. epidemiology Harvard Med. Sch. and Brigham & Women's Hosp., Boston, 1983—, dir. ctr. for cost effective care, 1980-93; chmn. dept. Ridley Watts prof. health care policy Harvard Med. Sch., 1988—; chmn. Blue Cross-Mass. Hosp. Assn. Fund for Coop. Innovation, 1981-87; mem. Prospective Payment Assessment Commn., 1983-91; mem. nat. adv. coun. Agy. for Health Care Policy, Rsch. and Evaluation, 1991—. Editor: Critical Issues in Medical Technology, 1982; contbr. articles to profl. jours. Fellow AAAS, Am. Coll. Nuclear Physicians (Presdl. award 1995); mem. Am. Acad. Arts and Scis., Inst. Medicine (coun. 1991—), Fleischner Soc., Nat. Coun. on Radiation Protection, Am. Coll. Radiology, Soc. Nuclear Medicine. Office: Harvard Med Sch Dept Health Care Policy 25 Shattuck St Boston MA 02115-6027

MCNEIL, HOYLE GRAHAM, JR., pharmacist, administrator, pharmacy management and consulting company executive; b. Knoxville, Tenn., Jan. 29, 1950; s. Hoyle Graham Sr. and Betty Sue (Stone) McN.; m. Kathryn Kimberly Bebb, Aug. 10, 1985. Student U. Tenn., 1968-72; BS in Pharmacy, Mercer U., 1975, PharmD, 1977. Lic. pharmacist, Ga., Tenn. Clin. pharmacist, drug info. coord. U. Tenn. Meml. Hosp., Knoxville, 1976-80; dir. pharmacy, purchasing and ancillary svcs. Peninsula Hosp., Louisville, Tenn., 1980-90; cons. pharmacist Corner-Stone of Recovery, Louisville, 1989-93; bd. dirs. Cornerstone of Recovery, Inc.; ptnr., pres. First Pharmacy Mgmt., Inc., Knoxville, 1985—, Home Health Care Infusion Therapy; asst. hosp. adminstr. Peninsula Hosp., Louisville, Tenn., 1986-89; pharmacy cons. Knox County Detoxification Ctr., 1991—; cons. hosps., nursing homes; bd. dirs. Knox County Bd. Health, Knoxville, 1985—; apptd. co-chmn. Knox County Community Health Agy., 1990-92, pres. elect, 1991; alt. del. Tenn. Community Health Adv. Coun. of Commr. of Human Svcs., 1990—; mem. adv. bd. Ptnrs. Home Healthcare Agy., 1992—; mem. adv. bd. Nat. Arthritis Soc. Smoky Mountain chpt., 1990—, ResCare Home Health Agy., 1991—; dir. pharmacy Oakwood Med. Ctr., 1993-95. Mem. editorial adv. panel Am. Pharmacy, 1990—, mem. adv. bd. Home Healthcare Agy., pharmacy jours. publ. coms.; mem. adv. bd. for publs. Drug Topics, 1991—; contbr. articles to Jour. Am. Pharm. Assn., Urban Health Jour., other publs. Editor newsletter: Drug Info. Update, 1977-81. Pres., 2d yr. profl. class Mercer U., 1973-74. Fellow Am. Soc. Cons. Pharmacists; mem. Knoxville Soc. Hosp. Pharmacists (pres. 1983-84), Knoxville Pharm. Assn. (pres. 1984-85), Tenn. Pharm. Assn. (del. 1983-85, co-chmn. impaired pharmacists com. 1984, Tenn. Pharmacists Assn. (chmn. peer assistance com. 1985-93), Tenn. Soc. Hosp. Pharmacists, Tenn. Hosp. Assn. (psychiat. hosp. task force), Tenn. Healthcare Assn., Am. Pharm. Assn., Am. Soc. Hosp. Pharmacists, Knox County Mental Health Assn., Am. Coll. Utilization Rev. Physicians, Am. Biog. Inst. (research bd. advisors), Nat. Assn. Quality Assurance Profls., Soc. Healthcare Adminstrs., Phi Lambda Sigma, Kappa Psi (pres. Gamma Psi chpt. 1974-75, Brother of Yr., 1975). Avocations: reading, gardening, traveling, spectator sports. Home: 5314 Stone Oak Rd Knoxville TN 37920-5024 Office: First Pharmacy Mgmt Inc PO Box 10586 Knoxville TN 37939-0586

MCNEIL, PAULINE EDITH, medical educator, veterinary pathologist; b. Cardiff, Wales, Aug. 8, 1950; d. Fred Edward George and Edith Kathleen (Hartley) Montgomery; m. Derek Bryan McNeil, Jan. 5, 1974; children: Gareth James, Catherine Alys. BVMS, U. Glasgow, Scotland, 1973, PhD, 1984. House pathologist U. Glasgow, 1975-79, lectr., 1979-92, sr. lectr., 1992—; cons. pathologist Cattle Health Project, Azores, 1995. Contbr. chpts. to books, articles to profl. jours. Rsch. grantee Guidedogs for the Blind Assn., 1994. Mem. European Soc. Vet. Dermatology (mem. bd., chmn. rsch., further edn.), Brit. Vet. Dermatology Study Group (treas. 1993-95). Anglican. Office: U Glasgow, Veterinary Sch, Glasgow G6I 1QH, Scotland

MCNEILL, GARY D., mental health clinician; b. Burlington, Vt., Nov. 9, 1952; s. George D. and Anne M. (Kupris) McN.; m. Kim M. Hammersley, Sept. 20, 1980; children: Nathaniel Louis, Tristam Daniel. BS in Natural Sci., Boston State Coll., 1974; MA in Human Psychology, Beacon Coll., 1979; BSN, U. So. Maine, 1984. RN, Maine; clin. specialist in adult psychiat./mental health nursing; lic. social worker, substance abuse counselor. Clin. specialist McLean Hosp., Belmont, Mass., 1975-77, Alcohol Edn. Svcs., Concord, Mass., 1978-80, Lowell (Mass.) Gen. Hosp., 1977-79, Middlesex Cts., Boston, 1979-80, Restitution Alternative, Springvale, Maine, 1980-81; with child and family svcs. unit Dept. Human Svcs., Portland, Maine, 1982; sr. chem. dependence therapist, sr. clinician, triage nurse Jackson Brook Inst., Portland, 1984—; bd. dirs. York County Child Abuse and Neglect Coun., Biddeford, Maine, 1983-91. Mem. Sigma Theta Tau. Home: PO Box 4670 East Waterboro ME 04030 Office: Jackson Brook Inst 175 Running Hill Rd South Portland ME 04106-3220

MCNEILY, MARY ZORA, health facility administrator; b. Hamilton, Ont., Can., Apr. 27, 1952; came to U.S.; d. Ned and Nada Maletin; m. Curtlan McNeily, Aug., 1972; children: Shannon, Colin. BSN, Columbia Union Coll., Takoma Park, Md., 1985; MHA, Cen. Mich. U., 1987. Asst. dir. nurses, head nurse Providence Hosp., Washington; exec. dir. Prince George's Found. for Med. Care, Inc., Upper Marlboro, Md.; quality assurance mgr. Jefferson Hosp., Alexandria, Va., dir quality assurance. Capt. U.S. Army, 1978-81. Mem. Am. Hosp. Assn., Am. Med. Peer Rev. Assn., Nat. Assn. Quality Assurance Profls. Home: 6104 Kennedy Dr Bethesda MD 20815-6510

MC NELLY, FREDERICK WRIGHT, JR., psychologist; b. Bangor, Maine, Apr. 14, 1947; s. Frederick Wright and E. Frances (Cutter) McN.; 1 adopted son, Roger; foster children: Joseph, Ronald, Michael, Jeffrey. BA magna cum laude, U. Minn., 1969; MA, U. Mich., 1971, PhD, 1973. Registered clin. psychologist, Ill., Wis.; lic. foster parent, Ill., 1973-86. Rsch. coord. NSF project U. Minn., Morris, 1968-69, lab. instr., 1969; trainee USPHS, 1969-70, 72; teaching fellow psychology U. Mich., Ann Arbor, 1970-72; ednl. examiner Ann Arbor Pub. Schs., 1971; dir. psychol. svcs. Children Devel. Ctr., Rockford, Ill., 1972-82, program dir., 1982-86; cons. psychologist, 1986—; lectr. Rock Valley Coll., Rockford, 1974-75; part-time pvt. practice psychology, Rockford and Belvidere, Ill., 1980-86, Beloit, Wis., 1985-86, full time 1986—; mental health cons. Rockford Head Start, 1982—, United Cerebral Palsy, Blackhawk Region, 1986—, Access Svcs., Mendota, Ill., 1992—; mem. health svcs. adv. com. human resources dept., City of Rockford, 1985—; presenter state and regional workshops and confs. Contbr. articles to profl. jours. Active Boy Scouts Am.; chmn. spl. edn. regional advisory com. Bi-County Office of Edn., Rockford, 1976-78; mem. Nat. and Ill. Com. on Child Abuse; co-chmn. Winnebago County Child Protection Assn., 1980; elder Willow Creek United Presbyn. Ch., Rockford, 1980-83; mem. stronghold renovation session com. Presbytery of Blackhawk, Oregon, Ill., 1985. Named U.S. Jaycees Outstanding Young Man of 1977. Mem. APA, Midwestern Psychol. Assn., Ill. Psychol. Assn., No. Ill. Psychol. Assn. (chmn. 1976-77), No. Ill. Pvt. Practice Mental Health Assn. (v.p. 1993-94, pres. 1994-96), Coun. for Exceptional Children, Soc. Rsch. in Child Devel., Nat. Assn. Retarded Citizens, Ill. Assn. Retarded Citizens, Am. Humane Assn. (children's div.), Nat. Register Health Svc. Providers in Psychology, Nat. Assn. of Disability Examiners. Home: 11591 Beverly Ln Belvidere IL 61008-8708 Office: Childrens Devel Ctr 650 N Main St Rockford IL 61103-6921 Office: 972 N Main St Rockford IL 61103-7061

MCNERNEY, JOHN CORNELIUS, medical consultant; b. Southington, Conn., Dec. 8, 1902; s. Cornelius and Mary M. (Martin) McN.; m. Evelyn Fay (dec. 1950); m. Katherine J. Gallagher, July 21, 1956 (dec. 1995). MD, Jefferson Med. Sch., 1927. Diplomate Am. Bd. Neurosurgery. Resident Jefferson Hosp., Phila., 1927-30; fellow Crile Clinic, Cleve., 1935-36; asst. mem. staff in neurol. surgery Jefferson Hosp., Phila., 1938-41; instr. in neurol. surgery Temple U., Phila., 1941-42; commd. lt. comdr. USNR, 1942, advance through grades to capt., 1946; ret. USN, 1951; chief neurol. surgery Nat. Naval Med. Ctr., Bethesda, Md., 1948-51; asst. prof. neurol. surgery Women's Med. Coll., Phila., 1951-52; cons. St. Joseph's Hosp., Stamford, Conn., 1953—. Fellow ACS, Internat. Coll. Surgeons; mem. AMA, Am. Assn. Neurosurgeons, Army Navy Club, Rotary Club. Home and Office: 111 Four Brooks Rd Stamford CT 06903-4629

MC NERNEY, WALTER JAMES, health policy educator, consultant; b. New Haven, June 8, 1925; s. Robert Francis and Anna Gertrude (Shanley) McN.; m. Shirley Ann Hamilton, June 26, 1948; children: Walter James, Peter Hamilton, Jennifer Allison, Daniel Martin, Richard Hamilton. B.S., Yale U., 1947; M.H.A., U. Minn., 1950. Research asst. Labor-Mgmt. Center, Yale U., 1947; instr. advanced math. Hopkins Prep. Sch., New Haven, 1947-48; adminstrv. resident R.I. Hosp., Providence, 1949-50; asst. to coordinator Hosp. and Clinics of Med. Center, U. Pitts., 1950-53; also instr., then asst. prof. hosp. adminstrn. at univ. Grad. Sch. Pub. Health, U. Pitts., 1953-55; assoc. prof., dir. program hosp. adminstrn. Sch. Bus. Adminstrn., U. Mich., 1955-58; prof., dir. Bur. Hosp. Adminstrn., 1958-61; pres. Blue Cross Assn., Chgo., 1961-77; pres., chief exec. officer Blue Cross and Blue Shield Assns., Chgo., 1977-81; Herman Smith prof. health policy Grad. Sch. Mgmt., Northwestern U., 1982—; cons. in field, 1982—; mem. Nat. Coun. on Health Planning and Devel., HEW, 1976-82; mem. bd. dirs. Nat. Health Coun., 1963-77, pres., 1972-73; mem. nat. commn. on cost of med. care AMA, 1977, mem. com. on pvt. philanthropy, 1977-78; past pres. Internat. Fedn. Vol. Health Svc. Funds; mem. devel. com. Yale U.; trustee Nat. Exec. Svc. Corps; chmn. task force on Medicaid and related progrsm HEW, 1969-70; charter mem. Inst. Medicine-NAS, chmn. bd. on health care svcs., chmn. bd. on spl. initiatives; mem. physican payment rev. commn. U.S. Congress, Dept. Vets.' Affairs; mem. Commn. on the Future Structure of Vets. Health Care; mem. coal commn. U.S. Dept. Labor; mem. coun. on performance measurement Joint Commn. on Accreditation of Healthcare Orgns.; mem. nat. adv. coun. for health care policy, rsch. and evaluation HHS; bd. dirs. Stanley Works, Medicus, Value Health Inc., Nellcor Inc., Ostel Tech., Ventritex, Inc., Hanger Orthopedics Group Inc.; chmn. bd. McNerney Heintz, Inc., Am. Health Properties Inc.; adv. coun. to dean Yale U. Med. Sch.; vis. com. U. Mich. Med. Ctr., adv. coun. chmn. Agy. for Health Care Policy and Rsch., chmn., bd. trustees Med. Outcomes Trust. Author: Hospital and Medical Economics, 1962, Regionalization and Rural Health Care, 1962; contbr. articles to profl. jours. Mem. Pres.' Com. on Health Edn., 1972-73; trustee Hosp. Research and Ednl. Trust, Inst. for Future; vis. com. Harvard Med. and Dental Schs. Served to lt. (j.g.) USNR, 1943-46. Nuffield Provincial Hosps. Trust-Kings Fund (Eng.) fellow, 1970; recipient Justin Ford Kimball award Am. Hosp. Assn., 1967; Outstanding Achievement award U. Minn., 1970, sec.'s unit citation HEW, 1970, Yale medal , 1979, award for merotorious svc. AMA, 1981, award of honor Am. Hosp. Assn., 1982, C. Rufus Rorem Health Svc. award, 1995; named 1 of 100 most important young men and women in U.S. by Life Mag., 1962; inducted into Healthcare Hall of Fame, Modern Mag., 1996. Clubs: Commonwealth, Yale (N.Y.C.). Office: Northwestern U Grad Sch Mgmt 2001 Sheridan Rd Evanston IL 60208-0814

MCNULTY, IRVING BAZIL, biology educator; b. Salt Lake City, Jan. 6, 1918; s. Irving Monroe and Svea Melvina (Lindegren) McN.; m. Elizabeth Lund, Dec. 24, 1943 (div. 1967); children: Michael, Marc, Michelle; m. Joyce Reeder, Mar. 21, 1980. BA, U. Utah, 1942, MS, 1947; PhD, Ohio State U., 1952. From instr. to prof. biology U. Utah, Salt Lake City, 1947-87. Chmn. adv. bd. State Arboretum Utah, Salt Lake City, 1981-87. Served to 2d lt. USAF, 1943-45. Mem. AAUP, AAAS, Am. Soc. Plant Physiologists, Bot. Soc. Am. Democrat. Office: U Utah Biology Dept Salt Lake City UT 84112

MCNULTY, MATTHEW FRANCIS, JR., health sciences and health services administrator, educator, university administrator, consultant, horse and cattle breeder; b. Elizabeth, N.J., Nov. 26, 1914; s. Matthew Francis and Abby Helen (Dwyer) McN.; m. Mary Nell Johnson, May 4, 1946; children: Matthew Francis III, Mary Lauren. BS, St. Peter's Coll., 1938, DHL (hon.), 1978; postgrad., Rutgers U. Law Sch., 1939-41; grad., Officer Candidate Sch., U.S. Army, 1941, U.S. Army Staff and Command Sch., Ft. Leavenworth, 1945; MHA, Northwestern U., 1949; MPH, U. N.C., 1952; ScD (hon.), U. Ala., 1969, Georgetown U., 1986. Contract writer, mgmt. trainee acturial div. Prudential Life Ins. Co., Newark, N.J., 1938-46; dir. med. adminstrn. VA, Chgo. and Washington, 1946-49; project officer to take over and operate new VA Teaching Hosps. VA, Little Rock, Birmingham, Ala. and Chgo., 1949-54; adminstr. U. Ala. Jefferson-Hillman Hosp., Birmingham, 1954-60; founding gen. dir. U. Ala. Hosps. and Clinics, 1960-66; founding prof. hosp. adminstrn. U. Ala. Grad. Sch., 1954-69, vis. prof., 1969—, founding dir. grad. program health adminstrn., 1964-69; prof. epidemiology and preventive medicine Sch. Medicine U. Ala., 1960-69; founding dean Sch. Health Adminstrn. (now Sch. Health Related Profls.), 1965-69; pres. Matthew F. McNulty, Jr. & Assocs., Inc., 1954-91; founding dir. Coun. Teaching Hosps. and assoc. dir. Assn. Am. Med. Colls., 1966-69; prof. community medicine and internat. health Georgetown U., 1969-89, prof. emeritus 1989—, v.p. med. ctr. affairs, 1969-72, exec. v.p., med. ctr. affairs, 1972-74; chancellor, dir. Georgetown U. Med. Ctr., 1974-86; chancellor emeritus Georgetown U., 1986—; chmn. acad. affairs com., trustee Hahnemann U., Phila, 1987—; trustee Fla. Found. for Active Aging, 1989—; cons. VA Adv. Com. on Geriatrics & Gerontology, 1991—; founding chmn. bd. Univ. D.C. Affiliated Health Plan, Inc., 1974-78; founding chmn. bd. trustees Georgetown U. Community Health Plan, Inc., 1972-80; vis. prof. Cen. U., Caracas, Venezuela, 1957-61; hosp. cons., 1953—; bd. dirs. Kaiser-Georgetown Community Health Plan, Inc., Washington, 1980-85, bd. dirs. Kaiser Health Plans and Hosps., Oakland, Calif., 1980-85, emeritus, 1985—; mem. Statuatory VA Spl. Med. Adv. Group, 1978-89, Higher Edn. Com. on Dental Schs. Curriculum, 1978-79; preceptor hosp. adminstrn. Northwestern U., Washington U., U. Iowa, U. Minn., 1953-69; mem. nat. adv. com. health research projects Ga. Inst. Tech., 1959-65, 73-85; nat. adv. com. health rsch. projects U. Pitts., 1956-60; adv. com. W.K. Kellogg Found., 1960-65; vis. cons., lectr. Venezuelan Ministry Health and Social Welfare, 1967-69; dir. Blue Cross-Blue Shield Ala., 1960-61, 65-68; trustee, mem. exec. com. Blue Cross and Blue Shield Nat. Capital Area, 1973-89, Washington Bd. Trade, 1972-86; mem. feasability study P.R. VA Med. Care, 1949, feasability study Ariz. Med. Edn., 1956. Bd. dirs. Greater Birmingham United Appeal, 1960-66; trustee, chmn. Jefferson County (Ala.) Tb Sanatorium, 1958-64; mem. health services research study sect. NIH, 1963-67; cons. USPHS, 1959-63; mem. White House Conf. on Health, 1965, on Medicare Implementation, 1966, NIH, USPHS and DHEW Commns., 1967-86, others; trustee Nat. Council Internat. Health, 1975-86; pres. Nat. League Nursing, 1979-81. Served to maj. USAAF, 1942-46, lt. col. USAFR, 1946-55. Recipient Disting. Alumnus award Northwestern U., 1973, Disting. Alumnus award U. N.C., John Benjamin Nichol award Med. Soc. D.C., Mayor and D.C. Coun., Matthew F. McNulty, Jr. Unanimous Recognition Resolution of 1986, Centennial award Georgetown U. Alumni Assn. award, 1982, Patrick Healy Disting. Svc. award, 1985, Alumni Life Senator Election award, 1986; named to Hon. Order Ky Cols., 1984. Fellow Am. Pub. Health Assn., Am. Coll. Healthcare Execs. (life, bd. regents and council of regents 1961-67, Disting. Health Sci. Exec. award 1976); mem AAAS, Am. Hosp. Assn. (life, Disting. Service award 1984), Ala. Hosp. Assn. (past pres.), Nat. Lr Nursing (past pres.), D.C. League Nursing (past dir.), Nat. Forum Health Planning (past pres., Disting. award, 1987), Council Med. Adminstrn., Internat. Hosp. Fedn., Jefferson County Ala. Vis. Nursing Assn. (past pres., Disting. Service award), Ala. Pub. Health Assn. (past chmn. med. care sect.), Southeastern Hosp. Conf. (past dir.), Birmingham Hosp. Council (past pres.), Hosp. Council Nat. Capital Area (pres. 1985-89, exec. com. 1989—, past pres. 1989-93, treas. 1993—), Assn. Univ. Programs in Hosp. Adminstrn. (Disting. award 1971), Greater Birmingham Area C. of C. (Merit award), Washington Acad. of Medicine, Am. Assn. Med. Colls. (founding chmn. teaching hosp. council 1964-69, Disting. Service Mem.), Royal Soc. Health, Am. Systems Mgmt. Soc. (Disting. award), Orgn. Univ. Health Ctr. Adminstrs., Santa Gertrudis Breeders Internat., Bashkir Curley Horse Breeders Assn., Med. Soc. of D.C. (John Benjamin Nichols award 1982), Univ. Club Ala., Cosmos Club, City Tavern Club, KC (3d degree, coun. 10499 Ocean Springs, 4th degree Francis Deignan Assembly), Knights of Malta, Omicron Kappa Upsilon. Home and Office: Teoc Pentref 3100 Phil Davis Rd Ocean Springs MS 39564-9076

MCNUTT, KRISTEN WALLWORK, consumer affairs executive; b. Nashville, Nov. 17, 1941; d. Gerald M. and Lee Wallwork; m. David McNutt, Sept. 13, 1969. BA in Chemistry, Duke U., 1963; MS in Nutrition, Columbia U., 1965; PhD in Biochemistry, Vanderbilt U., 1970; JD, DePaul U., 1984. Bar: N.Y. 1984, D.C. 1984. Exec. dir. Nat. Nutrition Consortium, Washington, 1979-81; asst. prof. pub. health U. Ill., Chgo., 1981-83; assoc. dir. Good Housekeeping Inst., N.Y.C., 1982-85; v.p. consumer affairs Kraft Inc., Glenview, Ill., 1985-87; pres. Consumer Choices Inc., Winfield, Ill., 1988—. Author: Nutrition and Food Choices, 1979; editor: Sugars in Nutrition, 1975, Consumer Mags. Digest, 1989—. Bd. dirs. Better Bus. Bur., Chgo. and No. Ill., 1986-88; FDA Food Adv. Com., 1992-94. Mem. N.Y. Bar Assn., D.C. Bar Assn., Fedn. Am. Socs. Exptl. Biology (Congl. Sci. fellow), Soc. for Nutrition Edn. (pres. 1983-84), Am. Inst. Nutrition, Am. Dietetics Assn. Home and Office: Consumer Choices Inc 28W176 Belleau Dr Winfield IL 60190

MCPHAIL, JASPER LEWIS, surgeon; b. Slate Spring, Miss., Dec. 30, 1930; s. James Jesse and Alberta Eudora (Windham) McP.; m. Dorothy Alyce Binford, June 30, 1957; children: John Mark, Gary Lewis, Keith Binford. BS, Miss. Coll., 1952; MD, Baylor Medical Coll., 1956; MBA, Oral Roberts Univ., 1987. Diplomate Am. Bd. Surgery, Am. Bd. Thoracic Surgery. Cardiovascular surgeon Christian Medical Coll., Vellore, India, 1962-66; assoc. prof. surgery Univ. Ark. Medical Sch., Little Rock, 1967-69; dir. sch. health scis. Univ. Cen. Ark., Little Rock, 1970-75; cardiovascular surgeon Bapt. Medical Ctr., Little Rock, 1969-75; cardiovascular surgeon, tchr. Good Samaritan and VA Hosp., Phoenix, Ariz., 1976-81; chair dept. surgery City of Faith Medical Ctr., Tulsa, Okla., 1981-88; gen. vascular and thoracic surgery Dallas, 1989-95, Demopolis, Ala., 1995—; cons., medical practice mgmt. McPhail & Assocs., Dallas, 1989-95; pres., CEO Medical Surgical Speciality Assocs., Dallas, 1990-95, Demopolis, 1995—. Author: Beneath the Himalayas, 1966, (book chpt.): National Medical School Review, 1994. Chmn. United Way, 1985-87. Recipient Outstanding Young Man of Am. award Jaycees, 1964, Svc. to Humanity award Miss. Coll., 1968, Golden Apple award Univ. Ark, 1969. Fellow Am. Coll. Surgeons, Am. Coll. Cardiology; mem. Am. Assn. Thoracic Surgery, AMA, Am. Coll. Health Care Execs., Am. Coll. Physicians Execs. Republican. Baptist. Home: 2101 Marengo Dr Demopolis AL 36732 Office: Med Surg Speciality Assocs 118 S Main # 2 Linden AL 36748

MCPHEARSON, GERALDINE JUNE, medical and surgical nurse; b. Red Bud, Ill., June 3, 1938; d. Arthur and Viola (Liefer) Althoff; children: Deborah, Michael, Belinda, Sabrina. Diploma, Evang. Deaconess Hosp. Sch. Nursing, St. Louis, 1959. RN. Sch. nurse San Antonio Ind. Sch. Dist.; head nurse Bethesda Gen. Hosp., St. Louis; supr. Am. Blood Components, Inc., St. Louis; head nurse Meml. Hosp., Belleville, Ill.; coord. arthritis svc. staff Meml. Hosp. Mem. Nat. Assn. Orthopaedic Nurses (1st pres., sec., v.p., organizer Ill. chpt.).

MCPHEE, MALCOLM CLINTON, physician; b. Tisdale, Sask., Can., July 11, 1939; came to U.S., 1973; m. Corrinne Petrusia Greschuk, July 10, 1965; children: Neil Edward, Charlene Ann, Kelly Lynn. Student, U. Sask., 1958-60, M.D., 1964. Diplomate: Am. Bd. Phys. Medicine and Rehab., Royal Coll. Physicians Can. Intern McLaren Hosp., Flint, Mich., 1964-65; resident U. Mich., Ann Arbor, 1965-69; asst. dir. Phys. medicine and rehab. dept.- Calgary Gen. Hosp., Alta., 1969-73; dir. phys. medicine and rehab. dept. Colonel Belcher Hosp., Calgary, 1970-73; cons. phys. medicine and rehab. Mayo Clinic, Rochester, Minn., 1973—; chmn. Mayo Clinic, 1981—; cons. Alta. Children's Hosp., Calgary, 1970-73; cons. psychiatrist Foothills Gen. Hosp., Calgary, 1971-73, Rochester Meth. Hosp., 1973—, St. Mary's Hosp., 1973—. Inventor nerve conduction studies, electrode placement device,

1970. Mem. AMA, Am. Acad. Phys. Medicine and Rehab., Am. Assn. Electromyography and Electrodiagnosis, Am. Spinal Injury Assn., Assn. Acad. Physiatrists. Home: 803 Sierra Ln NE Rochester MN 55906-4230 Office: Mayo Clinic Scottsdale 13400 E Shea Blvd Scottsdale AZ 85259-5404

MCPHEETERS, GEORGE OTT, surgeon, educator; b. Honolulu, Mar. 20, 1953; s. Otto Howard and Alice Muriel (Fowler) McP. BS, Stanford U., 1975; MD, U. Hawaii, 1980. Diplomate Am. Bd. Surgery. Intern in surgery U. Hawaii, Honolulu, 1980-81, asst. prof. surgery, 1985-95, assoc. prof., 1995—; resident in surgery Mass. Gen. Hosp., Boston, 1982-83; staff surgeon Straub Clinic and Hosp., Honolulu, 1985—, Queens Hosp., Honolulu, 1985—, Kapiolani Hosp., Honolulu, 1985—; fellow surg. clinic Sahlgrenska Hosp.-U. Gothenburg, Sweden, 1992-93. Fellow ACS; mem. Hawaiian Surg. Assn. (pres. 1994-96). Home: 4959-2 Maunalani Cir Honolulu HI 96816 Office: Straub Clinic and Hosp 888 S King St Honolulu HI 96813

MCPHERON-ALEX, THEDA JOHNSON, nursing consultant; b. Greenville, Ala., Sept. 22, 1954; d. Lee Aubrey and Velma Yvette (Godwin) Johnson; m. Stephen Dennis McPheron, Mar. 19, 1977 (div. June 1986); children: Stephen Aubrey, Stephanie Rebecca; m. Leonard M. Alex, July 3, 1993. LPN, Ala. Southern Coll., 1977; RN, George Wallace Coll., Selma, Ala., 1986; BA in Sociology and Psychology, Judson Coll., Marion, Ala., 1995; postgrad., U. Ariz., 1995—. RN, GA., Fla., Ala.; cert. registered rehab. nurse; lic. rehab. supplier, Ga., Fla.; lic. catastrophic rehab. case mgr., Ga., Fla., Ala.; lic. tax cons. LPN charge nurse Camden (Ala.) Nursing Facility, 1975-80; RN/LPN ICU and emergency rm. charge Perry Community Hosp., Marion, 1981-86; nurse labor and delivery, ICU Vaughn Regional Hosp., Selma, 1985-86; nurse labor and delivery supr. Bainbridge (Ga.) Health Care, 1987; DON Bainbridge Health Care, 1987; team leader Archbold Hosp., Thomasville, Ga., 1987-88; rehab. nurse Albea Rehab. Svcs., Valdosta, Ga., 1989; owner Genesis Rehab. Svcs., Bainbridge, 1990-94, Cherokee Cons. Assocs., Blackfoot, Idaho, 1992—; cons. Nat. Commn. to Prevent Infant Mortality, Washington, U.S. Office Minority Health, Rockville, Md., 1994—, U.S. Office Minority Health Resource Ctr., Silver Spring, Md., 1993—, Nat. Rural Health Assn., Kansas City, 1993—, March of Dimes Birth Defects Found., White Plains, N.Y., Nat. Cancer Inst. Spl. Populations SBIR Program, Bethesda, Md., Nat. Multiple Sclerosis Soc., N.Y.C., Pinnacle Learning Systems, Phoenix, Cultural Diversity Mag., Eden, Md.; spkr. women's and health issues numerous confs. Author Employment Skills Tng. Program, 1992, 93, The Inner Source: Native Am. Practices, Daily Living with ADA; mem. bd. advisors Women's Times, Boise, Idaho, 1994—. Rep. State of Ga. Nurse in Washington Internship, 1991; Ga. del. Gov.'s Interstate Indian Coun, 1992-93; hearing officer State of Idaho Divsn. Vocat. Rehab. Dist. 5, 1993-94; bd. dirs. Internat. Minority Affairs Coop., Silver Spring, Md., 1993—, MEA Found., Ketchum, Idaho, 1994—; active Task Force for Minority Health State of Idaho, 1994-95, Task Force on Farm Worker's Coalition State of Idaho, 1994-95. Named Woman of Month Women's Times, 1994. Mem. Cherokees of Ala. (tribal), Phi Theta Kappa. Democrat. Presbyterian. Home: 6161 E Pima Apt 1132 Tucson AZ 85712 Office: PO Box 636 Blackfoot ID 83221-0636

MCPHERRON, ANTHONY ALLAN, osteopath; b. Bremen, Ind., Oct. 6, 1967; s. Larry Lynn and Nancy Ellen (Shively) McP.; m. Kristina Ann Hodges, Dec. 22, 1990; children: Danielle Elizabeth, Amanda Michelle. BS, Ind. State U., 1990; DO, Ohio U., 1994. Diplomate Nat. Bd. Osteopathic Med. Examiners; cert. athletic trainer Nat. Athletic Trainers Assn. Rsch. asst. Ohio U., Athens, 1992; intern St. Vincent Med. Ctr., Toledo, Ohio, 1994-95, orthopaedic surgery resident, 1995—. Mem. AMA, Am. Osteopathic Assn., Nat. Athletic Trainers Assn., Ohio Osteopathic Assn., Sigma Sigma Phi. Republican. Methodist. Home: 5743 Ryewyck Apt 3 Toledo OH 43614 Office: St Vincent Med Ctr 2213 Cherry St Toledo OH 43608

MCPHILIMY, SCOTT ANTHONY, osteopath; b. Flint, Mich., June 15, 1970; s. Harry Michael and Star Marie (Royston) McP. BS, U. Mich., 1992; DO, Mich. State U., 1996. Mem. Am. Osteo. Assn., Am. Coll. Gen. Practitioners, Mich. Assn. Osteo. Physicians & Surgeons, Student Osteo. Med. Assn. Home: 102 1/2 W Henry St Flushing MI 48433

MCQUARRIE, DONALD GRAY, surgeon, educator; b. Richfield, Utah, Apr. 17, 1931; s. John Gray and LoRetta (Smith) McQ.; m. Dolores Jean Dietrich, July 16, 1956; children—William Gray, Michelle Dolores Colton. B.S., U. Utah, 1952, M.D., 1956; Ph.D., U. Minn., 1964. Diplomate Am. Bd. Surgery, Am. Bd. Thoracic and Cardiovascular Surgery. Intern U. Minn. Hosps., 1956-57; resident in surgery U. Minn., Mpls., 1957-59, resident, 1961-65, asst. prof. surgery, 1964-68, assoc. prof. surgery, 1968-72, prof. surgery, 1972—, vice chmn. dept. surgery, 1993—; mem. surg. staff Mpls. VA Hosp., 1964—, chief surgical svc., 1993—, resident in thoracic surgery, 1965-66, dir. surg. research lab., 1964-78; vis. prof. U. Tex.-San Antonio, 1974, U. Ind. and Indpls. VA, 1977, affiliated program U. Ariz., Phoenix, 1982, Case Western Res. U., 1986. Editor, contbg. author: Head and Neck Cancer, 1986, Reoperations in General Surgery, 1991, 2d edit., 1996; contbr. articles on surg. and basic med. scis. to profl. publs., 1955—. Served to lt. M.C., USN, 1959-61. USPHS postdoctoral fellow, 1962-65. Fellow ACS (commn. on cancer 1980-89, exec. council commn. on operating room environ. 1985-91, pres. Minn. chpt. 1983-84, liaison to Assn. Oper. Rm. Nurses 1985—, gov. 1990—); mem. Minn. Surg. Soc. (pres. 1980-81), Assn. Acad. Surgery, Mpls. Surg. Soc. (pres. 1978-79), Soc. Head and Neck Surgeons, Central Surg. Assn., Soc. Univ. Surgeons, Société Internationale de Chirurgie, Am. Surg. Assn., Assn. VA Surgeons (pres. 1987), Soc. Surg. Oncology, Hennepin County Med. Soc., Minn. Med. Assn., Am. Soc. Clin. Oncology, Phi Beta Kappa, Phi Kappa Phi. Clubs: Minneapolis, Interlachen Country (Mpls.). Home: 6625 Mohawk Trl Minneapolis MN 55439-1029 Office: Mpls VA Med Ctr Dept Surgery 1 Veterans Dr Minneapolis MN 55417-2300

MCQUEEN, REBECCA HODGES, health care executive, consultant; b. Dothan, Ala., July 20, 1954; d. Edward Grey and Shirley Louise (Varner) Hodges; m. David Raymond McQueen, Mar. 5, 1982; children: Matthew David, Owen Grey. BS, Emory U., 1976, MPH, 1979. Research assoc. North Cen. Ga. Health Systems Agy., Inc., Atlanta, 1979-80; assoc. dir. Health Services Analysis, Inc., Atlanta, 1980-82; med. group adminstr. Southeastern Health Services, Inc./Prucare, Atlanta, 1982-84; sr. v.p., COO SouthCare Med. Alliance, Atlanta, 1985-93; pres., CEO, PROMINA N.W. Health Network, Atlanta, 1993-96; sr. v.p. managed care PROMINA Health Sys., Atlanta, 1996—; cons. North Cen. Ga. Health Systems Agy., 1980-81, Region 4 HHS, Atlanta, 1980-82, instr. Applied Stats., Washington, 1980-82; mem. Health Data com. and Health Cost subcom. Atlanta Healthcare Alliance, 1985—; cons. Atlanta Com. for the Olympic Games, 1992. Contbr. articles to profl. jours. Adviser to med. support panel Atlanta Com. for Olympic Games; mem. Morningside/Lenox Park Civic Assn., Friends of Atlanta-Fulton Pub. Libr., Atlanta Bot. Garden, Planned Parenthood-Atlanta, Ga. Coun. on Child Abuse, Atlanta Wellness Coun. Recipient rsch. award Nat. Conf. on High Blood Pressure Control, 1981; nominee Woman of Achievement award YWCA. Mem. APHA (women's caucus com., presenter 1980, 81), ACLU, NOW, Am. Coll. Healthcare Execs. (diplomate), Women Healthcare Execs., Am. Managed Care and Rev. Orgn. (presenter nat. conf. 1989), Am. Assn. Preferred Provider Orgns., Delta Omega, Delta Delta Delta. Democrat. Methodist. Office: PROMINA Health Sys-Managed Care 2000 S Park Pl Atlanta GA 30339

MCQUIGGAN, MARK CORBEILLE, urologist; b. Detroit, May 15, 1933; s. Mark Ronald and Catherine Charlotte (Corbeille) McQ.; m. Carolyn Ann Brunk, Mar. 25, 1961. BS, U. Mich., 1954, MD, 1958. Diplomate Am. Bd. Urology. Resident in surgery and urology U. Mich., 1959-64; group practice Urology Assocs., Detroit, 1964-67; dir. med. edn. Providence Hosp., Southfield, Mich., 1967-69; clin. instr. urology U. Mich., 1969-70; pvt. practice Southfield, 1969—; pres. med. staff North Detroit Gen. Hosp., 1983-84, pres. Providence med. staff, 1995, 96. Fellow ACS; mem. AMA, Am. Urological Assn., Mich. Urological Assn. (exec. com. 1987-94, pres. 1992-93). Republican. Methodist. Home: 29653 Club House Ln Farmington Hills MI 48334 Office: 22250 Providence Dr Ste 203 Southfield MI 48075

MC QUILLEN, MICHAEL PAUL, physician; b. N.Y.C., Sept. 9, 1932; s. Paul and Dorothy Marian (Moore) McQ.; m. Louise Devlin; children: Daniel, Thomas, Patrick, Kathleen. B.A. cum laude, Georgetown U., 1953, M.D., 1957; MA, U. Va., 1994. Diplomate Am. Bd. Psychiatry and Neurology (bd. dirs. 1991-95, exec. com. 1995). Rotating intern Royal Victoria Hosp., Montreal, Que., Can., 1957-58; resident in neurology Georgetown U. Med. Center, 1958-60; fellow in physiology Johns Hopkins U. Med. Sch. and Hosp., 1960-62, instr. medicine, 1962-65; mem. faculty U. Ky. Med. Center, 1965-74, prof. neurology, 1972-74, prof., chmn. neurology, 1987-93; prof. neurology, chmn. dept. Med. Coll. Wis., Milw., 1974-87; clin. faculty mem. dept. neurology U. Va. Health Sci. Ctr., Charlottesville, 1993-94; prof. neurology U. Rochester St. Mary's Hosp., N.Y., 1995—; vis. sci. Inst. Neurophysiology U. Copenhagen, 1971-72; vis. prof. U. Ky. Med. Ctr., 1978, Royal Coll. Surgeons, Ireland, 1983. Author articles, papers in field. Mem. Cath. Commn. on Intellectual Affairs. Recipient Neurology medal Georgetown U. Med. Sch., 1957; Clin. Teaching award Med. Coll. Wis., 1976; Disting. Service award N.Y. Med. Coll., 1983; named to Johns Hopkins Soc. Scholars, 1981. Fellow Am. Acad. Neurology; mem. Royal Acad. Medicine Ireland, Nat. Myasthenia Gravis Found. (chmn. 1981-83), Am. Neurol. Assn., N.Y. Acad. Scis., Assn. U. Profs. Neurology, Am. Assn. Electromyography and Electrodiagnosis, AMA, Wis. Neurol. Assn. (pres. 81-82), Milw. Acad. Medicine, Alpha Omega Alpha. Home: 4 Bragdon Dr Rochester NY 14618 Office: St Mary's Hosp Dept Neurology Rochester NY 14611

MCREE, JOHN BROWNING, JR., physician; b. Anderson, S.C. Dec. 9, 1950; s. John Browning and Melinda Bratton (Beaty) McR.; m. Melody Lynnn Jennings, May 29, 1976; children: Ansley, Sarabeth. BS, Presbyn. Coll., Clinton, S.C., 1973; MD, Med. U. of S.C., 1977. Diplomate Am. Bd. Family Physicians. Resident Anderson (S.C.) Meml. Hosp., 1977-80; physician Family Practice Assocs., North Augusta, S.C., 1980—; asst. clin. prof. family medicine Med. Coll. Ga., 1982—. Fellow Am. Acad. Family Physicians. Presbyterian. Home: 201 Oakhurst Dr North Augusta SC 29841-9719 Office: Family Practice Assocs 509 W Martintown Rd North Augusta SC 29841-3108

MCREE, SANDRA KAY, health facility executive; b. Lawrenceburg, Tenn., Jan. 18, 1956; d. Floyd and Marvenell (Forsythe) Burgess; m. Harold Glen McRee, Feb. 8, 1974; children: Sharon, Leslie, Glynda. Student, Ind. U. Acct. supr. Giles County Hosp., Pulaski, Tenn., 1975-79, bus. office mgr., 1979-84; adminstrv. asst. Hillside Hosp., Pulaski, 1984-86; dir. bus. sys. Cmty. Health Sys., Inc., Brentwood, Tenn., 1986-94, asst. v.p. revenues and receivables, 1994-95; ops. v.p. Columbia Healthcare Corp., Nashville, 1995—; mem. monitor adv. team Health Care Mgmt. Systems, Nashville, 1989-90. Mem. Healthcare Fin. Mgmt. Assn. (matrix and com. mem. 1986—, Follmer award 1991, Cert. Mgr. Patient Acctg. 1992, Tenn. chpt. 2d v.p. 1994-95). Office: Columbia Health Care Corp 4525 Harding Rd Nashville TN 37205

MCREYNOLDS, DAVID HOBERT, hospital administrator; b. Bristol, Tenn., Dec. 28, 1953; s. Hobart Evans and Lena Mae (Brewer) McR.; m. Cynthia Carole Yambert, Sept. 6, 1974; children: Amy, Joseph, John, Rachel. MS, U. S.C., 1983. CPA, Tenn; cert. mng. care profl. Corp. acct. Gen. Care Corp., Nashville, 1975-80; controller Athens-Limestone Hosp., Athens, Ala., 1980-82; dir. fin. St. Mary's Med. ctr., Knoxville, Tenn., 1982-85; v.p. Archbishop Bergan Mercy Hosp., Omaha, 1985-87, Regional Healthcare, Inc., Brooksville, Fla., 1987-91; exec. dir. Hernando Healthcare, Inc. dba Brooksville Regional Hosp. (formerly Lykes Meml. Hosp.), 1987-91; v.p., corp. controller Peninsula Healthcare System, Knoxville, 1991-93; v.p., adminstr. Peninsula Village, Louisville, Tenn., 1993-96; COO Peninsula Healthcare, Louisville, 1996—. Pres. United Meth. Men., Brooksville, 1988-89; mem. Hernando County Health Adv. Bd., Brooksville, 1988-90; bd. dirs. United Way Hernando County, 1987-90, Hernando Cmty. Blood Bank, 1987-91; treas. Hernando Assn. for Retarded Citizens, 1990-91; mem. Knox County Com. on Spl. Edn., 1993-94. Fellow Healthcare Fin. Mgmt. Assn.; mem. Am. Coll. Healthcare Execs., Inst. Mgmt. Accts., Tenn. Assn. Child Care, Rotary (bd. dirs. Brooksville chpt. 1988-89. Presbyterian. Home: 4323 Near Shore Dr Louisville TN 37777-5231

MCREYNOLDS, RICHARD A., pathologist, researcher, educator; b. Washington, Sept. 11, 1944. BS in zoology and chemistry, George Washington U, 1966; MS in microbiology and immunology, U. Va., 1968, MD, 1971. Diplomate Am. Bd. Anatomic Pathology, Nat. Bd. Med. Examiners. Intern/resident Peter Bent Brigham Hosp., Boston, 1971-73; investigator NIH, Bethesda, Md., 1973-75; asst. prof. pathology sch. medicine U. Ala., Birmingham, 1975-77; NIH fellow immunopathol. U. Conn., Farmington, 1977-79; head pathology sect. Allied Chem. Corp. Med. Affairs, Morristown, N.J., 1979-82; prin. rsch. pathologist Lederle Labs., Pearl River, N.Y., 1982-85; asst. prof. pathology East Carolina U. Sch. Medicine, Greenville, N.C., 1985—; full grade surgeon USPHS, 1973-75, USPHS Res., 1975—. Mem. Alpha Omega Alpha. Office: Dept Pathology East Carolina U Sch Med Greenville NC 27858-4354

MCRIGHT, KENNETH LEON, health products executive; b. Wolfe City, Sept. 23, 1925; s. William Clarence and Myrtle Irene (Power) McR.; m. Clara Ann Padgett, Mar. 24, 1939. Student, Kans. City Art Inst., Mo., 1947, Okla. State Tech., 1950-53; diploma in Comml. Art, Okla. A&M Coll., 1953. Instr. comml. art, advt. Okla. State Tech. U., Okmulgee, 1953-64; pres. Ken McRight Supplies, Inc., Tulsa. Holder of 2 patents in therapeutic cusions and mattress overlays. Recipient Speedy award Paralyzed Vets. Am., 1992. Mem. (assoc.) Paralyzed Vets. Am. Home: 7456 So Sleepy Hollow Dr Tulsa OK 74136 Office: Ken McRight Supplies Inc 7456 So Oswego Tulsa OK 74136

MCSHANE, FRANKLIN JOHN, III, nurse anesthetist, army officer; b. Columbia, S.C., July 25, 1962; s. Franklin John Jr. and Helga Rita (Fischer) McS.; m. Leesa Ann West, Sept. 24, 1988; children: Amanda Nicole, Hannah Ryan. BSN, U. Mass., 1985; MSN, U. Tex., Houston, 1995. RN, Tex.; cert. RN anesthetist ANCC.; cert. ACLS instr., CPR, neonatal resuscitation program provider Am. Heart Assn. Commd. 2d lt. U.S. Army, 1985, advanced through grades to maj., 1995; clin. staff nurse oncology unit Letterman Army Med. Ctr., San Francisco, 1985-86, clin. staff nurse surg. ICU and post anesthesia care unit, 1987-90; head nurse emergency room 67th Evacuation Hosp., Würzburg, Germany, 1990-92, infection control nurse, 1992-93; staff nurse anesthetist Walter Reed Army Med. Ctr., Washington, 1996—; adj. lectr. emergency med. svcs. tract City Colls. Chgo. Europe, 1991-93; adj. clin. faculty U. Tex. Program in Anesthesia Nursing Walter Reed Army Med. Ctr., 1996—; presenter in field. Contbr. articles to nursing jours. Mem. ANA, Am. Assn. Nurse Anesthetists, Sigma Theta Tau. Office: Walter Reed Army Med Ctr Dept Anesthesia Washington DC 20307

MCSHEFFERTY, JOHN, research company executive; b. Akron, Ohio, Mar. 14, 1929; s. John and Jean (Conway) McS.; m. Glenna Gloria Childs, Apr. 18, 1959; children: John III, Amy Childs. BSc, U. Glasgow, 1953, PhD, 1957. Various rsch. positions Sterling Winthrop Rsch. Inst., Rensselaer, N.Y., 1957-62; dir. pharm. devel. Ortho Pharm. Corp. div. Johnson and Johnson, Raritan, N.J., 1962-75; dir. rsch. Janssen R & D, Inc., Piscataway, N.J., 1975-77; v.p. R & D family products Internat. Playtex, Paramus, N.J., 1977-79; pres. Gillette Rsch. Inst., Gaithersburg, Md., 1979—. Fellow Royal Pharm. Soc. of Gt. Britain; mem. Indsl. Rsch. Inst. (bd. dirs. 1988-92), Am. Acad. Dermatology, Am. Mgmt. Assn. (bd. dirs. 1994—), Am. Chem. Soc., Am. Pharm. Assn., N.Y. Acad. Scis., Soc. Cosmetic Chemists, Dirs. Indsl. Rsch., Assn. Rsch. Dirs., Sigma Xi. Office: Gillette Rsch Inst 401 Professional Dr Gaithersburg MD 20879-3432

MCSWEENEY, FRANCES KAYE, psychology educator; b. Rochester, N.Y., Feb. 6, 1948; d. Edward William and Elsie Winifred (Kingston) McS. BA, Smith Coll., 1969; MA, Harvard U., 1972, PhD, 1974. Lectr. McMaster U., Hamilton, Ont., Can., 1973-74; asst. prof. Wash. State U., Pullman, 1974-79, assoc. prof., 1979-83, prof. psychology, 1983—, chmn. dept. psychology, 1986-94; cons. in field. Contbr. articles to profl. jours. Woodrow Wilson fellow, Sloan Fellow, 1968-69; NSF fellow, 1970-72; NIMH fellow, 1973. Fellow Am. Psychol. Assn., Am. Psychol. Soc.; mem. Western Psychol. Assn., Psychonomic Soc., Assn. Behavior Analysis, Phi Kappa Phi, Phi Beta Kappa, Sigma Xi. Home: SW 860 Alcora Pullman WA 99163 Office: Wash State U Dept Psychology Pullman WA 99164-4820

MCWHINNEY, IAN RENWICK, physician, medical educator; b. Burnley, Eng., Oct. 11, 1926; emigrated to Can., 1968, naturalized, 1981; s. Archibald Renwick and Mary (Freeland) McW.; m. Betty Heap, Apr. 30; children: Heather, Julie. MB, BCh, Cambridge (Eng.) U., 1949; MD, Cambridge (Eng.) U., Eng.; MD (hon.), U. Oslo, 1991. Intern St. Bartholomews Hosp., London, 1949-50; resident (Warwick), Eng., 1953-54; pvt. practice medicine Stratford-on-Avon, Eng., 1954-68; prof. family medicine U. Western Ont., London, Can., 1968-92; prof. emeritus U. Western Ont., London, 1992—; med. dir. palliative care unit Parkwood Hosp., 1986-91. Author: The Early Signs of Illness, 1964, Introduction to Family Medicine, 1981, A Textbook of Family Medicine, 1989. Capt. Royal Army M.C., 1951-53. Recipient Excellence cert. Soc. Tchrs. Family Medicine, 1979, Curtis G. Hames Rsch. award, 1989. Fellow Coll. Family Physicians (Victor Johnston orator 1980), Royal Coll. Gen. Practitioners, Royal Coll. Physicians; mem. Inst. Medicine-Nat. Acad. Scis. (fgn. assoc.). Office: U Western Ont, Dept Family Medicine, London, ON Canada N6A 5C1

MCWHORTER, KATHLEEN, orthodontist; b. Houston, May 29, 1953; d. Archer and Lucile (Taft) McW. BA summa cum laude, U. Houston, 1986; DDS with honors, Baylor Coll., 1990. Mgr. Am. Internat. Rent-A-Car, Houston, 1974-79; mktg. researcher Concoco Oil Co., Houston, 1979-83; orthodontist Baylor Coll. Dentistry, Dallas, 1990—; presenter Am. Assn. Dental Rsch., Montreal, Que., Can., 1988, Cin., 1990; rsch. fellow Baylor Coll. Dentistry, Dallas, 1987, 88, 89. Contbr. articles to profl. jours. Mem. ADA, Am. Assn. Orthodontists, Am. Assn. Women Dentists, Am. Assn. Dentistry for Children, Internat. Assn. Dental Rsch., Am. Assn. Dental Rsch., Tex. Dental Assn., Dallas County Dental Soc., The Crescent Club. Office: Baylor U Coll Dentistry Dept Orthodontics 3302 Gaston Ave Dallas TX 75246-2013

MCWHORTER, RUTH ALICE, counselor, marriage and family therapist; b. Norfolk, Va., May 14, 1946; d. Lester Arthur and Mabel Winifred (Hopwood) Gorman; m. Dean Gundersen, Dec. 27, 1967 (div. Oct. 1971); m. R. Dale Lawhorn, Jan. 6, 1972 (div. Nov. 1979); m. Brent Wilson McWhorter, Aug. 16, 1986; stepchildren: Daniel Chastin, Kenley Reid, Scott Jason. BA in Edn., Ariz. State U., 1970, M of Counseling Psychology, 1979. Cert. profl. counselor, Ariz., cert. marriage and family therapist, Ariz. Tchr. lang. arts Globe (Ariz.) Mid. Sch., 1969-72; tchr. English Isaac Jr. High Sch., Phoenix, Ariz., 1973-74; real estate salesperson Ben Brooks & Assocs., Phoenix, 1975-76, Century 21 Metro, Phoenix, 1976-77; overnight counselor The New Found., Phoenix, 1978-80; family therapist Youth Svc. Bur., Phoenix, 1980-81; owner, corp. officer, profl. counselor/marriage & family Family Devel. Resources (now Family Psychology Assocs.), Phoenix, 1981—; cons., vol. counselor Deseret Industries, Phoenix, 1992-96. Bd. dirs. Westside Mental Health Svcs., Phoenix, 1982-87; vol. facilitator Ariz. Multiple Sclerosis Soc., Phoenix, 1988. Mem. ACA, Internat. Assn. Marriage and Family Therapists, Am. Assn. Marriage and Family Therapists, Am. Mental Health Counselors Assn., Ariz. Counselors Assn., Ariz. Mental Health Counselors Assn. (sec.-treas. ctrl. chpt. 1982, sec. ctrl. chpt. 1995), Am. Assn. Christian Counselors, Assn. Mormon Counselors and Psychotherapists (sec.-treas. 1990—). Office: Family Devel Resources PC PO Box 55291 Phoenix AZ 85078-5291

MCWILLIAMS, CONSTANCE FLORENCE, health facility manager; b. Pitts., Sept. 7, 1945; d. Bernard S. and Josephine (Mosakowski) Pawlowski; m. Frank X. McWilliams, Oct. 4, 1969. BSN summa cum laude, LaRoche Coll., Pitts., 1986, MSN, 1989; RN, St. Mary's Hosp. Sch. Nursing, Huntington, W.Va., 1966. RN, Pa., Ky., W.Va., Calif., Ohio, Mich., Ont., Can.; Registered Diagnostic Cardiac Sonographer. Charge nurse coronary care Marquette (Mich.) Gen. Hosp., 1978; charge nurse critical care North Hills Passavant Hosp., Pitts., 1979; instr. Community Coll. Allegheny County, Pitts., 1980-89; nurse adminstr. Diagnostic Cardiac Lab. Assn., Pitts., 1979-94; mgr. ancillary and clin. support svcs. Premier Med. Mgmt. Svcs., Pitts., 1994—. Mem. AACN, AAANA, NAFE, Sigma Theta Tau, Theta Mu. Home: 143 Lingay Dr Glenshaw PA 15116-1038 Office: Premier Med Mgmt Svcs 400 Penn Center Blvd Pittsburgh PA 15235-5613

MCWRIGHT, CORNELIUS GLEN, biological sciences educator; b. Sebree, Ky., Aug. 3, 1929; s. Robert Earl and Lockie Mae (Sutton) McW.; m. Carolyn Marie Martin, June 9, 1957; children: Glen Martin, Marta Lee, Michael Robert. BA, U. Evansville, 1952; MS, George Washington U., 1965, PhD, 1970. Spl. agt. FBI, Washington, 1955-57, supervisory spl. agt., 1957-73, chief biol. scis. rsch., 1973-77, chief rsch., 1977-79; adj. asst. prof. biol. scis. George Washington U., Washington, 1969, adj. assoc. prof., 1970-75, adj. prof. biol. and forensic scis., 1975—; sr. fellow Ctr. for Strategic and Internat. Studies, Georgetown U., 1982-85; cons. in forensic medicine, police sci., counter-terrorism tech. Nat. Inst. Justice, Rand Corp., 1987—; mem. tech. adv. com. biotechnology U.S. Dept. Commerce, 1990—. Served with USMC, 1946-48; to lt., USN, 1952-54. Fellow Am. Acad. Forensic Scis.; mem. Am. Soc. Microbiology, Sigma Xi. Episcopalian. Club: George Washington. Home: 7409 Estaban Pl Springfield VA 22151-2806 Office: George Washington U Dept Forensic Scis Washington DC 20052

MEACHAM, WILLIAM FELAND, neurological surgeon, educator; b. Washington, Dec. 12, 1913; s. Marion H. and Mamie (Henderson) M.; m. Alice Marie Mathews, June 14, 1944; children: William Feland, Patrick, Barbara, Robert. B.S., Western Ky. State Coll., 1936; M.D., Vanderbilt U., 1940. Diplomate: Am. Bd. Surgery, Am. Bd. Neurol. Surgery. Intern surgery Vanderbilt U. Hosp., Nashville, 1940-41; asst. resident surgery Vanderbilt U. Hosp., 1941-43, resident surgeon, 1943-44, asst. vis. surgeon, 1944; asso. vis. surgeon Out-Patient Service, 1944; asst. in surgery Vanderbilt U. Sch. Medicine, 1941-43, instr. surgery, 1943-44, William Henry Howe fellow in neurol. surgery, 1945-47, asst. clin. prof. surgery, 1947-50, assoc. clin. prof. surgery, 1950-53, assoc. prof. neurol. surgery, 1953-54, prof. neurol. surgery, 1954-59, clin. prof. neurol. surgery, 1959-85, prof. emeritus clin. neurosurgery, 1985—; vol. asst. Montreal Neurol. Inst., 1947; asst. clin. prof. neurol. surgery Meharry Med. Sch., 1947-50, clin. prof., 1950—; attending neurosurgeon Nashville Gen., St. Thomas, Mid-State Bapt. hosps., Riverside and Madison Sanitaria; cons. in neurosurgery Thayer Vets. Hosp., Murfreesboro (Tenn.) Vets. Hosp., Jr. League Home for Crippled Children.; Chmn. Study Commn. on Stroke, Tenn. Mid South Regional Med. Program, 1968. Mem. Am. Acad. Neurol. Surgery, ACS (chmn. adv. council for neurol. surgery 1959-63, bd. govs. 1964- 66, bd. regents 1966-75, 2d v.p. 1982-83), AMA, Nashville Acad. Medicine (past pres., chmn. bd. dirs.), Nashville Surg. Soc. (past pres.), Am. Surg. Assn., Neurosurg. Soc. Am. (past pres., mem. exec. council), Neurosurg. Travel Club, Soc. Neurol. Surgeons (pres. 1971), Soc. Univ. Surgeons, Southeastern Surg. Congress, So. Med. Assn., So. Neurosurg. Soc. (past pres.), Tenn. Med. Assn., Am. Assn. Neurol. Surgeons (dir., past sec., past treas., pres. 1972), Am. Cancer Soc. (dir.), Sigma Xi, Alpha Omega Alpha. Methodist. Home: 3513 Woodmont Blvd Nashville TN 37215-1427 Office: 709 St Thomas Med Pla 4230 Harding Rd Nashville TN 37205-2013

MEAD, KEVIN WILLIAM, retired radiation oncologist, oncology educator; b. Toowoomba, Queensland, Australia, Oct. 25, 1921; s. William and Elizabeth (Murphy) M.; m. Margaret Jessie Junner, 1948; children: Paul, Philip. B in Medicine and Surgery, U. Sydney, Australia, 1945. Radiation oncology registrar Queensland Radium Inst., Brisbane, Australia, 1947-51, radiation oncologist, 1954-64; dep. dir. Queensland Radium Inst., Brisbane, 1964-81; radiation oncology registrar Holt Radium Inst., Manchester, Eng., 1952, Royal Marsden Hosp., London, 1953; assoc. prof. Prince of Wales Hosp. and U. N.S.W., Sydney, 1981-88. Author chpts. in books; contbr. articles to profl. jours. Fellow Royal Australasian Coll. Radiology. Roman Catholic. Home: 71 Coverdale St, Indooroopilly Brisbane Queensland 4068, Australia

MEAD, PHILIP BARTLETT, healthcare administrator, physician; b. Poughkeepsie, N.Y., June 23, 1937; s. Ralph Allen and Altina (Gervin) M.; m. Ann Elaine Smith, June 27, 1964; children: Ralph Allen II, David Smith. BA, Hamilton Coll., 1959; MD, Cornell U., 1963. Diplomate Nat. Bd. Med. Examiners, Am. Bd. Ob-Gyn. Intern in medicine Bellevue Hosp., N.Y.C., 1963-64; resident in ob-gyn. N.Y. Hosp./Cornell Med. Ctr., N.Y.C., 1964-69; asst. prof. U. Vt. Coll. Medicine, Burlington, 1971-76, assoc. prof., 1976-81, prof., 1981—; hosp. epidemiologist Med. Ctr. Hosp. of Vt., Burlington, 1984-93; dir. clin. sys. Vt. Acad. Med. Ctr., Burlington, 1993-95; sr. v.p., med. dir. Fletcher Allen Health Care, Burlington, 1995—. Lt. comdr. M.C., USN, 1969-71. Fellow ACOG, Infectious Disease Soc. Am.; mem. Infectious Disease Soc. Ob-Gyn (pres. 1987-88), Soc. Hosp. Epidemiologists, Phi Beta Kappa, Alpha Omega Alpha. Republican. Methodist.

Home: 10 Pinehurst Dr Shelburne VT 05482-7240 Office: Fletcher Allen Health Care 111 Colchester Ave Burlington VT 05401 also: 1 S Prospect St Burlington VT 05401

MEAD, PHILOMENA, mental health nurse; b. Yonkers, N.Y., June 23, 1934; d. Alfonso F. and Jennie (Saltarelli) D'Amato; m. Kenneth Mead, Nov. 10, 1956; children: Scott Kenneth, Jeanne Bette. RN, St. Vincents Hosp., Bridgeport, Conn., 1955; BS in Psychology, Sacred Heart U., 1980; cert. in nursing mgmt., Fairfield U., 1988. Cert. psychiat. mental health nurse, nursing specialist, nat. chem. dependency nurse, CPR. Day supr.-relief, night supr. Hall Brooke Hosp., Westport, Conn., 1956-58, day supr., asst. dir. nurses, 1958-66, evening supr.-relief, 1967-68, team nurse, 1974-83, coord. nursing care, 1983-86, adminstrv. coord., 1986-87, nursing care coord. substance abuse treatment unit, 1987-91; charge evening nurse Carolton Hosp., Fairfield, Conn., 1971-73; nurse psychiat. emergency rm. and brief treatment unit West Haven (Conn.) VA, 1991—, mem. staff psychiat. emergency rm., 1995—. Roman Catholic. Home: 67 Adams Rd Fairfield CT 06430-3018

MEAD, SEDGWICK, physician; b. Guymon, Okla., July 2, 1911; s. Redmond Boyd and Bertha Mabel (Hunter) Corbett; m. Marjorie Frances Chick, Sept. 22, 1940 (dec.); children: Sedgwick Jr., Marshall; m. Mary Adelaide Abbott, May 8, 1995. Student, U. Ariz., 1930-31; SB cum laude, Harvard U., 1934, MD, 1938. Diplomate Am. Bd. Phys. Medicine and Rehab. Baruch fellow Harvard Med. Sch., Boston, 1946-47; assoc. prof. Sch. of Medicine Washington U., St. Louis, 1948-54; med. dir. Kaiser Found. Rehab. Ctr., Vallejo, Calif., 1954-69; ast. clin. prof. Sch. of Medicine Stanford (Calif.) U., 1955-60; clin. prof. U. Calif., Davis, 1969-72; chief neurology Kaiser-Permanente Med. Ctr., Vallejo, 1969-77; med. dir. Easter Seal Rehab. Ctr., Oakland, Calif., 1983-93; intern Mass. Gen. Hosp., 1938-40, resident pathology, 1940-41, resident neurology, 1941-42; cons. coun. on med. physics AMA, Chgo., 1950-54; pres. Assn. Rehab. Ctrs., 1953, Am. Acad. Cerebral Palsy, Richmond, Va., 1967. Chmn. governing bd. Retired Physicians Assn. Perm Med. Group, Oakland, 1989-90; trustee Costra Costa County Mosquito Abatement Dist., Concord, Calif., 1970-93; mem. White House Conf. on Health, Washington, 1953. With AUS, 1942-45, col. USAR, ret. 1971. Scholar Harvard Coll., 1932. Mem. AMA, World Med. Assn., Mass. Med. Soc., Am. Acad. Neurology, Am. Acad. Cerebral Palsy (pres. 1967), Faculty Club U. Calif. Berkeley, Harvard Club San Francisco. Unitarian.

MEAD, TERRY EILEEN, clinic administrator, consultant; b. Portland, Oreg., Mar. 14, 1950; d. Everett L. and Jean (Nonken) Richardson; divorced; 1 child, Sean Knute Wade Adcock. AA summa cum laude, Seattle U., 1972; postgrad., U. Wash., 1971. Project mgr. Assoc. Univ. Physician, Seattle, 1971-74; pathology supr. Swedish Hosp., Seattle, 1974-77; svcs. supr. Transamerica, Seattle, 1977-78; various mgmt. positions Providence Hosp., Seattle, 1978-83; adminstr. Evergreen Surg. Ctr., Kirkland, Wash., 1983-86; bus. mgr. Ketchikan (Alaska) Gen. Hosp., 1986—; instr. U. Alaska, Ketchikan, 1990; adminstr. Bethel (Alaska) Family Clinic, 1994—; CFO Southeast Oreg. Rural Health Network, 1996—; CEO Mead's Med. Mgmt., 1996—; sec. S.E. adv. bd. U. Alaska, Ketchikan, 1987-94; CEO Meads Med. Mgmt.; cons. to hosps. and physicians, Wash., Alaska, 1980—; mgr. Practice Mgmt. Cons., Seattle, 1982-83. Mem. City Charter Rev. Com., Ketchikan, 1990-94; High Sch. Facilities Com. Ketchikan, 1990; S.E. dir. search com. U. Alaska, Ketchikan, 1990; treas. Calvary Bible Ch., Ketchikan, 1989-91; bd. dirs. S.E. Alaska Symphony, 1992-94, Jr. Achievement, 1992-93; chmn. fin. com. City of Bethel, 1994-96. Mem. Rotary Internat. Home: PO Box 1287 Bethel AK 97624-1287 Office: PO Box 379 Chiloquin OR 97624-2580

MEADER, DARRELL LEE, psychologist, disaster health specialist; b. Ft. Wright, Ky., Oct. 21, 1941; s. Edward Ogden and Lillian (Hull) M.; m. Deloris Caudill, June 22, 1965; children: Darrell Lee, William Edward. BS, No. Ky. U., 1975, postgrad., 1975-77, AD in Nursing, 1979. RN, Ohio, Ky., Tex., N.C.; cert. scuba diver, advance, open water, search and recovery. With St. Elizabeth Hosp., Covington, Ky., 1968-70; staff Jewish Hosp., Cin., 1970-72, Lakeside Place, Cold Srpings, Ky., 1972-75, Bethesda Hosp., Cin., 1975-78, Children's Hosp., Cin., 1979; team leader Bethesda Hosp., 1979-81; charge nurse burn CCU Univ. Hosp., Cin., 1981—, chaplain critical care areas, 1989—; disaster svcs. MAT team mem. Nat. ARC, Cin., 1968—; cons. Meader Cons. Svcs., Ft. Wright, Ky., 1975—; mental health officer Hurricane Hugo, St. Croix, V.I., 1989; ARC disaster health officer Hurricane Bob, 1991; mayor for a day P.R. Flood, 1992; disaster relief worker Hurrican Andrew, 1992. Contbr. articles to profl. jours. Col. U.S. Army Spl. Forces, 1958. Mem. DAV, British Red Cross Cayman Island Br., Res. Officers Assn., Am. Def. Preparedness Assn., Vietnam Vets. Assn., Spl. Forces Assn. Democrat. Baptist. Home: 800 Kyles Ln Covington KY 41017-8122 Office: Meader Cons Svc 800A Kyles Ln Covington KY 41017-8122 also: Meader's Lung Chows Kennel 800 Kyles Ln # B Covington KY 41017-8122

MEADERS, BRIAN CHARLES, physician assistant; b. Spokane, Wash., July 3, 1958; s. Charles Clifton and Gloria Melissa (Kemberry) M. BS, U. Tex., 1984. Physician asst. Azar Eye Clinic, Lafayette, La., 1984—. Fellow Am. Acad. Physician Assts. Office: Azar Eye Clinic 516 St Landry Lafayette IN 70506

MEADERS, NOBUKO YOSHIZAWA, therapist, psychoanalyst; b. Kobe, Hyogo-ken, Japan, Mar. 2, 1942; d. Shigenobu and Ayako (Takahashi) Tsuchiya; m. Wilson E. Meaders, Apr. 2, 1976 (div. Apr. 1985); m. Takeshi Yoshizawa, June 15, 1989. AA, Seiwa Coll., Nishinomiya, Japan, 1965, Warren Wilson Coll., Swannanoa, N.C., 1967; BA, So. Meth. U., Dallas, 1969; MS in Social Work, U. Tex., Arlington, 1971; cert. psychotherapy-psychoanalysis, Postgrad. Ctr. Mental Health, N.Y.C., 1977, cert. in supervision psychotherapeutic processes, 1979. Cert. social worker, N.Y.; diplomate Am. Bd. Examiners in Clin. Social Work. Psychiat. social worker Killgore Children's Psychiat. Hosp., Amarillo, Tex., 1971-73, Jewish Child Care Assn., Childville div., N.Y.C., 1973-74; supr. social work, social work dept. Bellevue Hosp., N.Y.C., 1974-76; asst. dir. tng. Postgrad. Ctr. Mental Health, N.Y.C., 1979-82, assoc. supr., 1979-82, supr., 1982-85, sr. supr., 1985—, tng. analyst, 1989—; pvt. practice psychotherapy and psychoanalysis N.Y.C., 1976—; clin. cons. Pace U. Personal Devel. Ctr., N.Y.C., 1987—; mem. adv. bd. Japanese-Am. Cons. Ctr., N.Y.C., 1983—. Fellow N.Y. Soc. Clin. Social Work Psychotherapists; mem. NASW, Acad. Cert. Social Workers.

MEADOW, SAMUEL ROY, pediatrics educator; b. Wigan, Lancashire, Eng., June 9, 1933; s. Samuel Tickle Meadow and Doris Marion Peacock; m. Gillian Margaret MacLennan; children: Julian Robert Ian, Anna Jane; m. Marianne Jane Murrel, Aug. 7, 1979. MA BM BCH, Oxford U. FRCP, DCH. Sr. rsch. fellow Birmingham U., U.K., 1967-68; sr. lectr. U. Leeds, U.K., 1970-80; found. prof. dept. pediatrics and child health St. James U. Hosp., Leeds, 1980—; pres. BPA, 1994—; Chmn. Acad. Bd. BPA, 1989-94. Author: Lecture Notes on Paediatrics, 6th Edit., 1991, Bladder Control and Enuresis, 1973; editor: ABC of Child Abuse, 2d edit., 1993, Pediatric Kidney Disease, 1992, Archives of Disease in Childhood, 1979-87. Lt. Royal artillery, Germany, 1951-53. Named Blackwell Prof., New Zealand Paedatric Assn., Charles West Lectr., Coll. of Physicians, Lond, 1993. Mem. British Paediatric Assn. (Donald Patterson prize 1968, pres. 1994—), Assn. for Child Psychology and Psychiatry (chmn. 1983-84). Office: St James Univ Hosp, Dept Pediatric Child Health, Leeds LS9 7TF, England

MEAGHER, MICHAEL, radiologist; b. New Rochelle, N.Y., Oct. 24, 1942; s. Joseph Aloysius and Elizabeth (Ahern) M.; m. Martha Batten Mitchell, 1968; children: Kelly, Courtney. Student, Rensselaer Poly. Inst., 1960-62; AB with distinction, U. Rochester, 1964; MD, Stanford U., 1969. Diplomate Am. Bd. Radiology, Nat. Bd. Med. Examiners. Intern in medicine Cornell U., N.Y. Hosp., 1969-70; jr. asst. resident in diagnostic radiology U. Wash., Seattle, 1970-71, sr. asst. resident diagnostic radiology, 1973-74, resident diagnostic radiology, 1974-75; active staff mem. dept. radiology Queen's Med. Ctr., Honolulu, 1975—, Leahi Hosp., Honolulu, 1981—, Kahuku (Hawaii) Hosp., 1988—; pres. Radiology Assocs., Inc., 1978, 81-84, 90; chmn. dept. radiology Queen's Med. Ctr., 1979-80, 82-86, 88-90, dir. dept. radiology, 1985-91, dir. magnetic resonance imaging, 1991—, chmn. cancer com., 1980-82; mem. med. staff Hawaii Health Tech. Magnetic Resonance Imaging Facility, Honolulu, 1986—, chief of staff, 1978; clin. instr. dept. radiology U. Hawaii Sch. Medicine, 1983-89, clin. assoc. prof., 1989-93, clin. prof., 1993—, asst. rsch. prof. Cancer Rsch. Ctr. Hawaii, 1989—; clin. asst. prof. dept. radiology U. Wash. Sch. Medicine, 1980-88; presenter in fld. Contbr. articles to profl. publs. Chmn. high tech. adv. com. State Health Planning and Devel. Agy., 1983—; bd. dirs. Friends of Hawaii Pub. TV, 1979-81; pres., CEO Queen's Health Care Plan, Honolulu, 1985-89, chmn. bd. dirs., 1989-91; bd. dirs. Managed Care Mgmt., Inc., Honolulu, 1990; v.p. bd. dirs. Hawaii Opera Theatre, 1990-91, treas., 1991—. Lt. comdr. USN, 1971-73. NIH fellow, 1966; Kaiser Found. grantee, 1967. Fellow Am. Coll. Radiology; mem. AMA, Hawaii State Radiol. Soc. (sec.-treas. 1978-79, v.p. 1979-80, pres. 1980-81), Radiol. Soc. N.Am., Soc. Computer Applications in Radiology (charter), Am. Roentgen Ray Soc. Home: 1234 Maunawili Rd Kailua HI 96734-4642 Office: Queen's Med Ctr Dept Radiology Honolulu HI 96813

MEAGLIA, JAMES PAUL, urologist; b. Arcadia, Calif., Aug. 29, 1958; s. James John and Catherine Lucille (Balassi) M.; m. Diane Marie Lauracella, July 11, 1987; 1 child, Gianna Rose. BS, U. So. Calif., 1981; MD, Chgo. Med. Sch., 1985. Intern and resident U. Calif., San Diego, 1985-91; pvt. practice Orange County Urology Assocs., Inc., Mission Viejo, Calif., 1991—. Fellow ACS; mem. Am. Urologic Assn. (western sect.), Orange County Urologic Soc., K.C. Republican. Roman Catholic. Office: Orange County Urology Assoc Ste 321 26732 Crown Valley Pkwy Mission Viejo CA 92691

MEALEY, BRIAN LUKE, periodontist, air force officer; b. Houston, Sept. 20, 1959; s. George A. and Jeanne (Cavanagh) M.; m. Carla Rhea Reddy, June 18, 1983; children: Colleen Marie, Patrick Luke, Nathaniel George. DDS, U. Tex., San Antonio, 1983; MS, U. Tex., 1990. Commd. officer USAF, 1983, advanced through grades to lt. col.; gen. dentistry resident USAF Gen. Dentistry Residency, Barksdale AFB, La., 1983-84; gen. dental officer USAF Clinic, Soesterberg, The Netherlands, 1984-87; resident dept. periodontics Wilford Hall Med. Ctr., Lackland AFB, Tex., 1987-90, asst. chmn. for clin. investigation, 1990-94, dir. resident edn. and tng., 1994—; clin. asst. prof. U. Tex. Health Sci. Ctr., San Antonio, 1991—. Mem. ADA, Am. Acad. Periodontology (Balint Orban Meml. Rsch. award, 1989), S.W. Soc. Periodontists (John Prichard award for grad. rsch. 1990), Air Force Assn., Omicron Kappa Upsilon. Roman Catholic. Office: Wilford Hall Med Ctr/DST Dept Periodontics Lackland AFB TX 78236-5317

MEARS, RICHARD WALTER, clinical psychologist; b. Norfolk, Va., June 11, 1940; s. Richard Walter Mears and Mildred Anne (Bell) Cox; m. Wendy Clark Talmage, Aug. 26, 1967; 1 child, Jonathan Clark Talmage. BA, Randolph Macon Coll., 1962; MA, East Carolina U., 1965; PhD, U. Ga., 1971. Lic. clin. psychologist, Va. Dir. Springdale Schs., Inc., Camden, S.C., 1977-86; dir. psychol. svcs., forensic coord. S.W. Va. Med. Health Inst., Marion, 1986—; pvt. practice Marion, 1986—. Bd. dirs. United Way, Smyth County Cmty. Hosp. Found., vice chairperson, 1994—. Devereux fellow NIMH, Devon, 1970. Mem. APA, Masons, Rotary (lt. dist. gov. 1994—). Home: 328 Panorama Dr Marion VA 24354-4529 Office: SW Va Mental Health Inst 502 E Main St Marion VA 24354-3320

MECHANECK, RUTH SARA, clinical psychologist; b. N.Y.C., Feb. 4, 1941; d. Isidore and Anna (Nadler) M.; 1 child, Christopher. BA, Brandeis U., 1961; MA, U. Minn., 1963; PhD, CUNY, 1976. Cert. psychologist, N.Y. Jr. rsch. assoc. Inst. Devel. Studies, N.Y.C., 1963-65; rsch. assoc. William Alanson White Inst., N.Y.C., 1965-68; instr. Briarcliff Coll., Briarcliff Manor, N.Y., 1975-76; staff psychologist Met. Ctr. Mental Health, N.Y.C., 1979-81; pvt. practice N.Y.C., 1981—; adj. asst. prof. psychology Hunter Coll., N.Y.C., 1991; project dir. rsch. Single Mothers by Choice, N.Y., 1983-87; cons. Childrens Def. Fund, N.Y., 1975-77, child abuse task force N.Y. State Assembly, 1975-77. Author: (with others) Single Mothers, 1987. NICHD fellow CUNY, 1969-71. Mem. APA, N.Y. State Psychol. Assn., Nat. Register of Health Svc. Providers in Psychology, Assn. Advancement Psychology. Home and Office: 340 E 93rd St Apt 22M New York NY 10128-5555

MECHANIC, DAVID, social sciences educator; b. N.Y.C., Feb. 21, 1936; s. Louis and Tillie (Penn) M.; m. Kathleen Mars Wiltshire; children: Robert Edmund, Michael Alexander. B.A., CCNY, 1956; M.A., Stanford U., 1957, Ph.D., 1959. Faculty U. Wis., Madison, 1960-79; prof. sociology U. Wis., 1965-73, John Bascom prof., 1973-79; dir. U. Wis. (Center for Med. Sociology and Health Services Research), 1971-79, chmn. dept. sociology, 1968-70; prof. social work and sociology Rutgers U., New Brunswick, N.J., 1979—; acting dean faculty arts and scis. Rutgers U., 1980-81, Univ. prof., dean faculty arts and scis., 1981-84, Univ. prof. and Rene Dubos prof. behavioral scis., 1984—, dir. Inst. for Health, Health Care Policy and Aging Research, 1985—; mem. panel on health svcs. rsch. Pres.'s Sci. Adv. Com., 1971-72; mem. treatment com. on reduction of cancer mortality Nat. Cancer Inst., 1984; vice-chmn. com. pain, disability and chronic illness behavior Inst. Medicine-NAS, 1985-86, mem. panel on prevention of disability, 1989-90; mem. Com. on Prevention of Mental Disorder, 1992-94; coord. panel Pres.'s Commn. Mental Health, 1977-78; mem. Nat. Adv. Coun. Aging, NIH, 1982-86; expert adv. panel on mental health WHO, 1984-89; mem. health adv. bd. GAO, 1987-95; mem. panel on tech., ins. and health care sys. Office of Tech. U.S. Congress, 1992-95; mem. nat. com. on vital and health stats. HHS, 1988-92; mem. commn. on behavioral and social scis. and edn. NRC, 1992-95, commn. on med. edn. Robert Wood Johnson Found., 1990-92; mem. adv. com. Picker/Commonwealth Scholar's Program, 1992—; nat. adv. com. Robert Wood Johnson Scholars in Health Policy Rsch. Program, 1992—; mem. panel on Rethinking Disability Policy, Nat. Acad. Social Ins., 1993-96; vis. scholar Kings Fund Inst., london, 1994-95. Author: Students Under Stress, 1962, 2d edit., 1978, Medical Sociology, 1968, rev. edit., 1978, Mental Health and Social Policy, 1969, rev. edit., 1980, 89, Public Expectations and Health Care, 1972, Politics, Medicine and Social Science, 1974, (with Charles E. Lewis and Rashi Fein) A Right to Health, 1976, Growth of Bureaucratic Medicine, 1976, Future Problems in Health Care, 1979, From Advocacy to Allocation: The Evolving American Health Care System, 1986, Painful Choices: Research and Essays on Health Care, 1989, Inescapable Decisions: The Imperatives of Health Reform, 1994; author, editor: Symptoms, Illness Behavior and Help-Seeking; editor: Handbook of Health, Health Care and the Health Professions, 1983, Improving Mental Health Services: What the Social Sciences Can Tell Us, 1987; Co-editor: (with Robert Houser, Archibald Haller and Tess Hauser) Social Structure and Personality, 1982, (with Linda Aiken) Applications of Social Science to Clinical Medicine and Social Policy, 1986; Paying for Services: Promises and Pitfalls of Capitation, 1989; (with Marian Osterweis and Arthur Kleinman) Pain and Disability: Clinical Behavior and Public Policy Perspectives, 1987, (with Carl Taube and Ann Hohmann) The Future of Mental Health Services Research, 1989. Fellow Ctr. for Advanced Study in Behavioral Scis., 1974-75, NIMH rsch. fellow, 1965-66, Ford Behavioral Sci. fellow, 1956-57, Guggenheim fellow, 1977-78; recipient Ward medal CCNY, 1956, Med. Sociologists award Am. Sociol. Assn., 1983, Carl Taube award APHA, 1990, Disting. Investigator award Assn. for Health Svcs. Rsch., 1991, Disting. Contbn. award mental health sect. Soc. for Study of Social Problems, 1991, Emily Mumford medal Columbia U., 1991, Investigator award in health policy rsch. Robert Wood Johnson Found., 1995—. Fellow AAAS (chmn. sect. social, econ. and polit. scis. 1985); mem. Am. Sociol. Assn. (governing coun. 1977-78, chmn. med. sociol. sect. 1969-70, chmn. publs. com. 1989-91, chmn. mental health sect. 1992-93), Sociol. Rsch. Assn. (pres. 1991-92), Inst. Medicine-Nat. Acad. Scis. (governing coun. 1972-74), Nat. Acad. Scis., Am. Acad. Arts and Scis., Hogg Found. Mental Health (nat. adv. coun. 1987), Phi Beta Kappa. Office: Rutgers U Inst Health Policy Aging Rsch 30 College Ave New Brunswick NJ 08901-1245 Home: 14 Cameron Ct Princeton NJ 08540-3924

MECKLER, HAROLD, chemist; b. N.Y.C., Nov. 5, 1956; s. Lawrence H. and Lillian Norma (Rosenberg) M.; m. Helene Englander, Mar. 15, 1986; children: Emily Amanda, Hannah Faye. BS, U. Md., 1978; PhD, SUNY, Buffalo, 1983. Sr. chemist chem. devel. Sterling Winthrop Rsch. Inst., Rensselaer, N.Y., 1982-84; group leader, sect. head process rsch. Ciba Pharm. Divsn., Summit, N.J., 1984-94; mgr. organic chemistry Telor Ophthalmic Pharms., Wilmington, Mass., 1994-95; dir. chem. devel. Albany Molecular Rsch.

MEDALIE, JACK HARVEY, physician; b. Buhl, Minn., Jan. 8, 1922; m.; 3 children. BSc, Witwatersrand U., Johannesburg, 1941; MD, BChir, Witwatersrand U., 1945; MPH (hon.), Harvard U., 1958. Instr. dept. anatomy U. Witwatersrand, Johannesburg, 1942-43; sr. lectr. dept. social medicine Hebrew U., Hadassah, Jerusalem, 1962-66; from assoc. prof. to prof., chmn. dept. family medicine Tel-Aviv U., 1966-74; chmn. dept. family medicine Case Western Res. U., 1975-87, prof. cmty. health, 1976-87, prof. family medicine, 1976—, prof. med. and pediat., 1978—, prof. emeritus, 1992—; co-prin. investigator congenital abnormality study NIH, 1972-74, Dept. Health, Edn. and Welfare, 1976-82, Robert Wood Johnson Found., 1978-88; vis. prof., family medicine and epidemiology U. N.C., Chapel Hill, 1973-74; vis. sr. rsch. scientist, Nat. Heart, Blood and Lung Inst., Bethesda, Md., 1974, 90-91; med. coun. U. Hosps. Cleve., 1975-87, com. impaired physicians, 1980-87; med. edn. com. Case Western Res. U., 1980-85, chmn. ambulatory and primary care clerkship com., 1981-83; task force health consequences bereavement Nat. Acad. Sci., 1982-85, membership com., 1984-88; dir. dept. family practice U. Hosps., Cleve., 1982-87; rsch. cons. Mt. Sinai Med. Ctr., Cleve., 1991—. Contbr. articles to profl. jours. Fellow Am. Acad. Family Physicians, Am. Heart Assn., Royal Soc. Med. Found.; mem. Inst. Med.-Nat. Acad. Sci., Soc. Tchrs. Family Medicine (chmn. at. task force 1985-87, Curtis Hames Career Rsch. award 1988, Cert. Excellence 1988, Maurice Saltzman award 1988), Soc. Behavioral Medicine. Office: Case Western Res Univ Dept of Family Medicine 2119 Abington Rd Cleveland OH 44106-2333*

MEDEARIS, DONALD NORMAN, JR., physician, educator; b. Kansas City, Kans., Aug. 22, 1927; s. Donald Norman and Gladys (Sandford) M.; m. Mary Ellen Marble, Aug. 25, 1956; children: Donald Harrison, Ellen Sandford, John Norman, Jennifer Marble. AB, U. Kans., 1950; MD, Harvard U., 1953. Diplomate: Am. Bd. Pediatrics. Intern internal medicine Barnes Hosp., St. Louis, 1953-54; resident pediatrics Children's Hosp., Cin., 1954-56; rsch. fellow pediatrics Harvard U. rsch. div. infectious diseases Children's Med. Ctr., Boston, 1956-58; from asst. to assoc. prof. pediatrics and microbiology Johns Hopkins Sch. Medicine, Balt., 1959-65; Joseph P. Kennedy Jr. Meml. Found. Sr. Rsch. Scholar in Mental Retardation, 1960-65; prof. pediatrics U. Pitts. Sch. Medicine, 1965-74, chmn. dept., 1965-69, dean, 1969-74; med. dir. Children's Hosp., Pitts., 1965-69; prof. pediatrics Case Western Res. U., Cleve., 1974-77; dir. pediatrics Cleve. Met. Gen. Hosp., 1974-77; Charles Wilder prof. pediatrics Harvard U. Med. Sch., 1977-95, Charles Wilder disting. prof. pediatrics, 1995—; chief Children's Svc. Mass. Gen. Hosp., Boston, 1977-95; mem. Pres.'s Commn. on Study Ethical Problems in Medicine and Biomed. and Behavioral Rsch., 1979-82. Contbr. articles to profl. jours., texts. Vestry Trinity Ch., Boston, 1983-87. Served with USNR, 1945-46. Mem. Am. Acad. Pediatrics, Am. Pediatric Soc., Infectious Disease Soc. Am., Inst. Medicine/Nat. Acad. Sci., Alpha Omega Alpha. Office: Massachusetts Gen Hosp Fruit St Boston MA 02114

MEDEIROS, ALDO DA CUNHA, medical educator; b. Natal, Brazil, Jan. 5, 1948; s. Cipriano Jose and Maria (Cunha) M.; m. Vera Maria Alecio Brasil; children: Daniela, Vitor. Grad., U. Fed. do Rio Grande do Norte, Natal, 1973; MS, U. Fed. do Rio de Janeiro, Rio de Janeiro, 1978; MD, UFRJ, Rio de Janeiro, 1980. Physician UFRN, 1973, prof. surgery, rschr., 1981-96; resident in surgery Hosp. Servidores do Estado, Rio de Janeiro, 1974-75; vice dir. dept. surgery UFRN, 1991, dir. dept. surgery, 1993; dir. Rsch. Inst., Natal, 1981-96; cons. CNPq, Brasilia, Brazil, 1989-96; chief and founder postgrad. course in surgery Dept. Surgery, UFRN, 1996—. Fellow Soc. Exptl. Surgery, Gastroenterology Soc.; mem. Acad. Scis., Collegio Brasileiro Cirurgiões (vice master 1988, master 1996), Acad. Medicine. Home: Ave Miguel Alcides Araujo 1889, 59078-270 Natal RN, Brazil Office: U Fed do RN, Ave Nilo Peçanha 620, 59010 Natal RN, Brazil

MEDEIROS, M. JOYCE, community health educator; b. Boston, Feb. 17, 1954; d. Raymond A. and D. Jean (Russell) Harrington; m. Joseph A. Medeiros, July 26, 1977; children: Jessica A., Jo Ellen. Grad., Youville Hosp. Sch. Practical Nursing, 1973; BS in Cmty. Health Edn., U. Maine, Farmington, 1992. Staff nurse Goddard Meml. Hosp., Stoughton, Mass., 1973-87; dist. dir. Somerset Family YMCA, 1988-90; ITV aide Skowhegan (Maine) H.S., 1990-91; intern Somerset Residential Care Ctr., 1991-92, WARNACO, 1992; dir. edn. Sebasticook Valley Hosp., 1992-96; spl. needs edn. tech. transition III MSAD # 59 Madison H.S., 1996—; camp nurse, dir. 4-H Camp Farley, 1982-87, Camp at Eastward Starks, Maine, 1990. Mem. gov. coun. U. Maine, Farmington. Mem. AAHPERD, ASHA, MPHA, Eta Sigma Gamma, Phi Sigma Pi. Home: 241 Dill Rd Starks ME 04911

MEDH, JHEEM D., medical educator, biochemistry researcher. BS in Chemistry and Biochemistry, U. Bombay, India, 1982; MS in Biochemistry, U. Bombay, 1984; PhD in Biochemistry, U. Tex. Med. Br., Galveston, 1990. Jr. rsch. fellow, dept. physiology L.T.M. Med. Coll., Bombay, 1984-86; rsch. asst., dept. human biol. chemistry and genetics U. Tex. Med. Br., 1986-90; postgrad. rsch. biochemist, dept. medicine U. Calif., San Diego, 1991-93; asst. rsch. scientist, adj. asst. prof., dept. medicine U. Iowa Coll. Medicine, Iowa City, 1993—. Presenter in field of role of LDL receptor-related protein, receptor-associated protein and lipoprotein lipase on the regulation of lipoprotein metabolism. Juvenile Diabetes Internat. Found. fellow 1992-93; recipient nat. grand-in-aid award Am. Heart Assn., 1995-98; recipient Gip Hudson award Nat. Student Rsch. Forum, 1989, Stephen C. Silverthorne award Grad. Sch. Biomed. Scis., U. Tex. Med. Br. Mem. Am. Heart Assn. (coun. for basic science), Am. Soc. Cell Biology, Juvenile Diabetes Found. Internat. Home: 209 Woodside Dr Iowa City IA 52246*

MEDINA, SALVADOR, surgeon; b. Mexico City, Dec. 26, 1950; s. Salvador and Natalia (Gonzalez) M.; m. Emma Sanchez; children: Salvador, Juan Pablo. BA in Sci., Centro U. Mex., Mexico City, 1968; MD, UNAM, Mexico City, 1974. Diplomate Am. Bd. Surgery, Am. Bd. Colon and Rectal Surgery. Intern D.C. Gen. Hosp.; resident Charleston Area Med. Ctr.-W.Va. U., 1978-80; surgeon Hosp. Angeles, Mexico City; colon and rectal fellow U. Tex., Houston, 1981-82. Co-author: Gastroenterology, 1990; contbr. articles to profl. publs. Fellow ACS, South Eastern Surg. Congress (assoc.); mem. Am. Soc. Colon and Rectal Surgeons, World Assn. Hemato-Pancreato-Bilary Surgery, N.Y. Acad. Scis., Assn. Mex. Surg. Gen. (vocal 1987-88, treas. 1988-89, coord. 1990-91), Soc. Hosp. Angeles (vocal-sec. 1986-88, v.p. 1988-89, pres. 1989-90). Home: Ladera 76, 04500 Mexico City Mexico Office: Hosp Angeles, C A Sta Teresa 1055-503, Mexico City Mexico

MEDNICK, DAVID, clinical psychologist, clinical neuropsychologist; b. N.Y.C., Jan. 3, 1962. D of Psychology, Yeshiva U., 1990. Lic. psychologist, N.J. Affiliated practitioner Bergen Neuropsychology Group, Teaneck, N.J., 1990—; staff psychologist Wellness Ctr. Fairleigh Dickinson U., Teaneck, N.J., 1990—. Mem. APA, N.J. Psychol. Assn., Nat. Acad. Neuropsychology, Nat. Register Health Svc. Providers in Psychology. Office: Bergen Neuropsychology 121 Cedar Ln Teaneck NJ 07666

MEDVED, ARNOLD, physician, dermatologist; b. Winnipeg, Manitoba, Canada, Oct. 8, 1937; Came to the U.S., 1964; s. Hyman and Bess (Stein) M.; m. Doris Medved, Febr. 2, 1964; children: Paul N., Lyle D., Leanne R. MD, U. Manitoba, 1961. Diplomate Am. Bd. Dermatology, 1967, Am. Bd. Dermatopathology, 1975. Dermatology tchg. fellow U. Minn. Med. Sch., Mpls., 1964-67; cons. in dermatology Winnipeg Clinic, 1968-74, Health Scis. Ctr., Winnipeg, 1968-74; lectr. in medicine U. Manitoba, 1968-74; cons. in dermatology and dermatopathology Santa Barbara Cottage Hosp., 1974—; asst. clin. prof. medicine U. So. Calif., L.A., 1978—. Contbr. numerous articles to profl. jours. Fellow Am. Acad. Dermatology, Royal Coll. Physicians (Canada); mem. Calif. Med. Assn., Pacific Dermatology Assn., Tri Counties Dermatology Soc. (pres. 1989), Santa Barbara Med. Soc. Office: Sansum Med Clinic 317 W Pueblo St Santa Barbara CA 93105

MEDVED, EVA, dietitian, educator; b. Cadiz, Ohio, May 15, 1922; d. Joseph and Lucy (Truly) M. BS, Kent State U., 1943; MS, Ohio State U., 1952, PhD, 1964. Cert. tchr.; lic. dietitian. Tchr. Alliance (Ohio) High Sch., 1943-47, Lincoln High Sch., Canton, Ohio, 1947-62; asst. prof. Ohio U., Athens, 1963-65; prof. Kent (Ohio) State U., 1965-87, Ariz. State U., Sun City, 1988—; cons., speaker Prentice-Hall Pubs., 1987—. Author: World of Food, 1970, 73, 77, 80, 86, 88, 90, Food in Theory and Practice, 1978, Food Preparation and Theory, 1986. Rsch. grantee USDA 1968-70; scholarship Timken Co. 1960, 62. Mem. Am. Assn. Family and Consumer Scis. (nutrition chair 1965—), Am. Dietetic Assn., Nutrition Today Soc., Ohio Nutrition Coun. (publ. chair 1979—), Ohio Assn. Family and Consumer Scis. (exec. com. 1965—, Outstanding Home Economist award 1987), Ohio

Dietetic Assn., Stark County Home Econs. Assn. (pres. 1965—), Stark County Dietetic Assn. Republican. Roman Catholic. Home: 4885 Pond Dr NW Canton OH 44720-7434

MEDWAY, FREDERIC JEFFREY, pediatrics and psychology educator, psychologist; b. June 4, 1947; s. Irwin and Corrine (Finkel) M.; m. Marcia Fern Lutz, Aug. 13, 1977; children—Lauren, Scott. B.A., Syracuse U., 1969; M.A., Fairleigh Dickinson U., 1970; Ph.D., U. Conn., 1975. Lic. psychologist, S.C. Asst. prof. psychology U. S.C., Columbia, 1975-80, assoc. prof., 1980-86, prof., 1986—; adj. assoc. prof. pediatrics Med Sch., 1984—, dir. sch. psychology tng. program, 1993—; pvt. practice psychology, Columbia, 1980—, numerous sch. dists., justice agys., family courts. Author: (with T. Cafferty) School Psychology: A Social Psychological Perspective, 1992; editor: Psychological Services in the High School, 1982; Jour. Sch. Psychology Monograph, 1980; editorial bd. Jour. Sch. Psychology; contbr. program scripts S.C. Ednl. TV Network; contbr. articles to profl. jours. Fellow Am. Psychol. Assn. (Lightner Witmer research award 1982); mem. Nat. Assn. Sch. Psychologists, Am. Edn. Research Assn. Lodge: Rotary. Avocations: sailing, cooking, wine tasting. Home: 101 Larkspur Rd Columbia SC 29212-2047 Office: Univ SC Dept Psychology Columbia SC 29208

MEECHAN, ROBERT JOHN, medical educator; b. Newport, Wash., Aug. 25, 1926; s. Robert John Meechan and Katharine M. (Battick) Williams; m. K. Brenda Hanrahan, Dec. 27, 1952; children: Robert D., Patrick J., Peter T. BA, Oreg. State Coll., 1949; MA, MD, U. Oreg., 1953. Diplomate Am. Bd. Pediatrics. Instr. pediatrics Oreg. Health Science U., Portland, 1956-62, asst. prof., 1962-68, assoc. prof., 1968-72, prof. pediatrics, 1972-89, asst. dean admissions, 1976-86; prof. emeritus, 1989—. Served with USN, 1944-46. Recipient Disting. Service award Alumni Oreg. Health Sci. Ctr., 1986. Mem. Ambulatory Pediatric Assn., Oreg. Acad. Pediatrics, North Pacific Pediatric Soc., Portland Acad. Pediatrics (sec., treas. 1962-65, pres. 1965). Democrat. Roman Catholic. Home: 12040 SE Foster Pl Portland OR 97266-4961

MEEGAN, CIARÁN JOHN, pharmacist; b. Dundalk, Colouth, Ireland, June 1, 1960; m; s. Larry and Joan (Conlon) M.; m. Maria Adrienne Burke, July 5, 1988. BSc in Pharmacy, U. Dublin, Ireland, 1981, MSc, 1984. Cmty. pharmacy mgr. Noyek's Pharmacy, Dublin, 1984-87; sr. pharmacist Beaumont Hosp., Dublin, 1987-93; chief I pharmacist Mater Hosp., Dublin, 1993—. Mem. Pharmaceutical Soc. Ireland (mem. coun. 1994—), Hosp. Pharmacists Assn. Ireland (pres. 1995—). Home: 4 Coulson Ave, Dublin 6, Ireland Office: Mater Misericordiae Hosp, Eccles St, Dublin 7, Ireland

MEEHAN, JOHN JOSEPH, JR., hospital administrator; b. Boston, Jan. 29, 1946; s. John Joseph and Marjorie Louise (Hill) M.; m. Pamela Marshall, Mar. 25, 1973; children—Seth, Andrew, Sean. B.A., Dartmouth Coll., Hanover, N.H., 1968; M.H.A., U. Minn., Mpls., 1974. Unit mgr. Boston Hosp. Women, 1971-72; adminstrv. resident Hennepin County Gen. Hosp., Mpls., 1973-74; v.p. Putnam Meml. Hosp., Bennington, Vt., 1974-79; asst. dir. Hartford Hosp., Conn., 1979-81, assoc. exec. dir., 1981-85, exec. v.p., 1985-87, pres., chief operating officer, 1987-89; pres., chief exec. officer, 1989—; faculty Hartford Grad. Ctr., 1979-81; preceptor U. Minn., 1981—, Yale U., New Haven, 1981—; mem. New Eng. Health Care Assembly, 1975—, officer, 1982-92; pres., CEO Hartford Health Care Corp., 1989—, Conn. Health Sys., Inc., 1996—. Active Bennington Lion's Club, 1975-79, Conn. Hosp. Assn., Urban League Greater Hartford, 1979—, Greater Hartford C. of C., 1979—, also bd. dirs., 1994—; chmn. ARC, Bennington, 1978-79; bd. dirs. St. Joseph Coll., ConnectiCare IPA/HMO, 1990-95, Mech. Savs. Bank, 1993—; corporator St. Francis Hosp., 1988—, Inst. Living, 1993—; fellow Am. Leadership Forum, 1993—. Served to lt. (j.g.) USNR, 1968-70. Decorated Naval medals and ribbons, 1968-70; recipient Disting. Naval Grad. award, 1968, Stuart Thompson M.D. award U. Minn., 1974. Mem. Am. Hosp. Assn., Conn. Hosp. Assn. (bd. dirs. chmn. 1996—), Capital Area Health Consortium.

MEEHAN, PATRICK J., public health officer; b. Tulsa, Dec. 30, 1956; married; 1 child. BA in Chemistry, U. Calif., Santa Cruz, 1978; MD, Washington U., St. Louis, 1982. Diplomate Am. Bd. Family Practice; lic. physician, N.H., Ga. Resident in family practice Navidad Med. Ctr./U. Calif., Salinas, 1982-85; with Epidemic Intelligence Svc. CDC and Prevention, Ctr. Environ. Health and Injury Control, Atlanta, 1988-89, preventive medicine resident, 1989-91; family practice physician Su Clinica Familiar, Harlingen, Tex., 1985-87; med. dir. prenatal and family planning Region 8 Tex. Dept. Pub. Health, Harlingen, 1986-87; acting health officer, cons. in communicable disease Santa Cruz (Calif.) County Health Dept., 1987-88; dir. N.H. divsn. Pub. Health Svc., 1991-94; dir. Ga. divs. pub. health Dept. Human Resources, Atlanta, 1994—; family practice physician Locum Tenens, Raymondville, Tex., 1987, Salud Para La Gente, Watsonville, Calif., 1987-88; adj. asst. prof. Emory U., Atlanta; clin. assoc. prof. Morehouse Sch. Medicine; lectr. in field. Contbr. numerous articles to profl. jours. Mem. APHA, Med. Assn. Ga., Am. Acad. Family Physicians, Ga. Pub. Health Assn., Assn. of State and Territorial Health Ofcls. (chair com. on injury control, com. on tobacco or health). Office: 2 Peachtree St NW Atlanta GA 30303*

MEEKER, BRIAN WALTER, physician; b. Burlington, Iowa, Jan. 19, 1959; s. Orville Walter and Hildegarde Louise (Detjen) M.; m. Linda Kaye Ball, May 27, 1978; children: Adam Lee, Erin Louise, Georgia Kaye, Daniel Brice. BS in Biology, Northeast Missouri State U., 1981; DO, U. Osteo. Medicine/Health Sci., Des Moines, 1984. Diplomate Am. Bd. Family Practice. Staff physician Cuba City (Wis.) Doctor's Clinic, 1985-86; resident physician St. Luke's Family Practice Ctr., Milw., 1986-88; rural family physician Strawberry Point (Iowa) Med. Ctr., 1988-92; Vinton (Iowa) Family Med. Ctr., 1992—. Chmn. Iowa affil. PALS, Am. Heart Assn., Des Moines, 1994-96; med. examiner Benton County, 1994—; pres. med. staff Virginia Gay Hosp., Vinton, 1993—; expert on rural health care Subcom. of U.S. Senate, Washington, 1993. Recipient Nat. Osteo. scholarship Am. Osteo. Assn., 1980, Nat. Health Svc. Corps scholarship, 1992. Fellow Am. Bd. Family Practice; mem. AMA, Am. Acad. Family Physicians, Iowa Med. Soc., Iowa Osteo. Med. Assn. (mem. pub. rels. com. 1988-95), Lions Club. Lutheran. Home: 214 W 10th Vinton IA 52344 Office: Vinton Family Med Ctr 504 N 9th Ave Vinton IA 52349

MEELHEIM, HELEN DIANE, nursing administrator; b. Charleston, W.Va., Mar. 25, 1952; d. Richard Young and Dolores (Frick) M. BS in Nursing, U. N.C., 1974; MS in Nursing, East Carolina U., 1982; JD, U. N.C., 1992. Bar N.C. 1995. Charge nurse Pitt County Health Dept., Greenville, N.C., 1974-77; nursing adminstr. East Carolina U. Sch. of Med., Greenville, N.C., 1978-89, clin. instr., 1986-92; cons. Eastern Area Health Edn. Ctr., Greenville and Fayetteville, 1989-92; staff emergency room U. N.C. Hosps., Chapel Hill, 1989-92; dir. fin. ops., human resources N.C. Bd. Med. Examiners, 1992—. Maj. Army Nurse Corps, USAR, Oper. Desert Storm/Shield, 1990-91. Mem. ANA (cert. family nurse practitioner, 1987—), Am. Acad. Nurse Practitioners, Nat. Health Lawyers Assn., N.C. Soc. Health Care Attys, Sigma Theta Tau. Episcopalian. Avocation: painting. Home: 4622 Pine Trace Dr Raleigh NC 27613-3316 Office: NC Bd Med Examiners PO Box 20007 Raleigh NC 27619

MEENAN, ROBERT FRANCIS, academician, rheumatologist, researcher; b. Cambridge, Mass., Apr. 5, 1947; s. Paul Leo and Anna Bernadine (Curtin) M.; m. Lynda Jane Fortman, Apr. 29, 1972; children: Molly, Mark. BA, Harvard U., 1968; MD, Boston U., 1972; MPH, U. Calif., Berkeley, 1977; MBA, Boston U., 1989. Diplomate Am. Bd. Internal Medicine and Rheumatology. Asst. prof. Sch. of Medicine Boston U., 1977-82, assoc. prof. Sch. of Medicine, 1982-88, prof. Sch. of Medicine, 1988—, assoc. dir. Arthritis Ctr., 1977-88, chief arthritis sect. Sch. of Medicine, 1988-92, dir. Arthritis Ctr., 1988-92, dean and prof. Sch. Pub. Health, 1992—; mem. nat. arthritis adv. bd. NIH, Washington, 1988-92; Svartz Meml. lectr. Swedish Med. Soc., 1989. Contbr. Jour. Arthritis Impact Measurement Scales, Jour. Social Security Disability, Jour. Dictionary of Rheumatic Disease, Outcome Assessmentation Clin. Moles; contbr. over 75 articles to profl. jours. Trustee Arthritis Found., 1989—. Internat. League Against Rheumatism fellow, 1981; recipient Nat. Svc. award Arthritis Found., 1989. Fellow ACP, Am. Coll. Rheumatology (pres. 1990-91); mem. Am. Soc. for Clin. Investigation. Office: Boston U Sch Pub Health 80 E Concord St Roxbury MA 02118-2307

MEENGS, WILLIAM LLOYD, cardiologist; b. Zeeland, Mich., Dec. 23, 1942; s. Lloyd Stanley and Gertrude (Wyngarden) M.; A.B., Hope Coll., 1964; M.D., U. Mich., 1968; m. Helen Delores Van Dyke, June 10, 1964; children—Michelle Rene, William Lloyd, Lisa Ann. Intern in internal medicine Univ. Hosp., Ann Arbor, Mich., 1968-69, resident in internal medicine, 1971-73, fellow in cardiology, 1973-75; practice medicine specializing in cardiology, Petoskey, Mich., 1975—; cardiologist Burns Clinic Med. Center, Petoskey, 1975—, chmn. dept. cardiology and cardiac surgery, 1978-89; med. dir. No. Mich. Heart Center, 1989—; cardiologist Little Traverse Hosp., Petoskey, 1975—, dir. coronary care unit, 1986-89; dir. cardiac catheterization lab. No. Mich. Hosps., Petoskey, 1985-87, 92—, adult spl. care units, 1986-89; vice chmn. bd. dirs. Burns Clinic Med. Ctr. 1989-92. Contbr. med. articles to profl. jours. Trustee Mich. Heart Assn. 1979-83. Served as surgeon USPHS, 1969-71. Fellow Am. Coll. Cardiology, Soc. Cardiovascular Angiography and Interventions; mem. ACP, Am. Heart Assn. (fellow Council on Clin. Cardiology), Am. Soc. Echocardiography, Alpha Omega Alpha. Home: 1224 Autumn Ln Petoskey MI 49770 Office: Burns Clin Med Ctr 560 W Mitchell St Petoskey MI 49770-2251

MEERSCHAERT, JOSEPH RICHARD, physician; b. Detroit, Mar. 4, 1941; s. Hector Achiel and Marie Terese (Campbell) M.; m. Jeanette Marie Ancerewicz, Sept. 14, 1963; children—Eric, Amy, Adam. B.A., Wayne State U., 1965, M.D., 1967. Diplomate Am. Bd. Phys. Medicine and Rehab. Intern, Harper Hosp., Detroit, 1967-68; resident in phys. medicine and rehab. Wayne State U. Rehab. Inst., Detroit, 1968-71; chief div. phys. medicine Naval Hosp., Chelsea, Mass., 1971-73; attending physician William Beaumont Hosp., Royal Oak, Mich., 1973—, med. dir. rehab. unit, 1979—; pvt. practice medicine specializing in phys. medicine and rehab., Royal Oak, 1973—; mem. med. adv. bd. Nat. Wheelchair Athletic Assn., 1973—, examining physician Nat. Wheelchair Athletic Games, Marshall, Minn., 1982, U.S. team physician VII World Wheelchair Games, Stoke Mandeville, Eng.; clin. instr. Wayne State U., 1973-83, clin. asst. prof. phys. medicine and rehab., 1983—; mem. Mich. Dept. Licensing and Regulation State Bd. Phys. Therapy, 1978-81. Served with M.C., USN, 1971-73. Recipient John Hussey award Mich. Wheelchair Athletic Assn., 1981. Fellow Am. Coll. Pain Medicine; mem. Am. Acad. Phys. Medicine and Rehab. (reviewer, presenter), Am. Congress Rehab. Medicine, Mich. Phys. Medicine and Rehab. Soc., Am. Geriatrics Soc., Am. Assn. Electromyography and Electrodiagnosis, Mich. Rheumatism Soc., Mich. Acad. Phys. Medicine and Rehab. (chmn. program com. 1977-78, trustee 1980—, del. 1982), Oakland County Med. Soc. (alt. del. 1979-81), Met. Soc. Crippled Children and Adults (bd. dirs. 1979-82, pres. 1981-82), Alpha Omega Alpha. Roman Catholic. Contbr. articles to profl. jours. Office: 3535 W 13 Mile Rd Royal Oak MI 48073-6700

MEESE, MARK RUSSELL, surgeon; b. Kansas City, Mo., Dec. 29, 1958; s. George Clifford and Nola Mae (Robinson) M.; m. Paula Jayne Webb, Aug. 8, 1981; children: Kristin Renee, Mark Ryan, Abbe Michele. BS in Chemistry, Okla. U., 1981, MD, 1985. Diplomate Am. Bd. Surgery. Intern, resident U. Okla. Health Scis. Ctr., Tulsa, 1985-90; surgeon Surg. Assocs. Inc., Tulsa, 1990—; staff privileges St. Francis Hosp., Tulsa. Fellow ACS, Okla. Surg. Assn., Southwestern Surg. Assn. Republican. Baptist. Office: Surg Assocs Inc 6465 S Yale Tulsa OK 74136

MEESTERS, YBE, psychologist, researcher; b. Oosterwolde, Friesland, The Netherlands, Mar. 5, 1951; s. Sjoerd and Kornelia (Westerhof) M.; m. Johanna Sybrigje Borger, May 12, 1986; children: Sjoerd Ferdinand Sjieuwe, Alie Nynke Roelie. RN, Acad. Hosp., Groningen, The Netherlands, 1979; MSc, State U., Groningen, The Netherlands, 1988, PhD, 1994. Electronic engr. Tektronix Ltd., Heerenveen, The Netherlands, 1973-75; nurse Acad. Hosp., Groningen, 1975-89, psychologist, rschr., 1989—. Contbr. articles to profl. jours. Mem. Soc. Light Treatment and Biol. Rhythms, Nederlands Inst. van Psychologen, Vereniging voor Gedragstherapie. Home: Washuisterweg 7, 9791 TE Ten Boer The Netherlands Office: Acad Hosp Groningen, PO Box 30 001, 9700RB Groningen The Netherlands

MEEZAN, ELIAS, pharmacologist, educator; b. N.Y.C., Mar. 5, 1942; s. Maurice and Rachel (Epstein) M.; m. Elisabeth Gascard, May 14, 1967; children: David, Nathan, Joshua. BS in Chemistry, CCNY, 1962; PhD in Biochemistry, Duke U., 1966. Asst. prof. physiology and pharmacology Duke U., Durham, N.C., 1969-70; asst. prof. pharmacology U. Ariz., Tucson, 1970-75; assoc. prof. U. Ariz., 1975-79; prof., chmn. dept. pharmacology U. Ala., Birmingham, 1979-89, prof., dir. Metabolic Diseases Rsch. Lab., 1989-93, prof. dept. pharmacology, 1993—. Asso. editor: Life Sci, 1973-79. Helen Hay Whitney postdoctoral fellow, 1966-69; recipient NIH Research Career Devel. award, 1977-79. Mem. Am. Soc. Pharmacology and Exptl. Therapeutics, Am. Soc. Biol. Chemistry, AAUP, AAAS, N.Y. Acad. Sci., Assn. Med. Sch.Pharmacology. Democrat. Jewish. Home: 1202 Cheval Ln Birmingham AL 35216-2037 Office: U Ala Dept Pharmacology Birmingham AL 35294

MEFFERD, ROY B., JR., medical scientist, psychometrician; b. Hico, Tex., Sept. 22, 1920; s. Roy B. and Delfa (Russell) M.; m. Mary Louise Key; children—Marsha Ellen, Roy Scott. A.S., Tarleton State U., 1938; B.S., Tex. A&M U., 1940, M.S., 1940; Ph.D., U. Tex., 1951, MBA, 1992. Research scientist bacteriology U. Tex., Austin, 1947-51; dir. metabolism lab. Southwest Found. for Research and Edn., San Antonio, 1951-54; dir. mental health research lab. Biochem. Inst. U. Tex., Austin, 1954-59; dir. psychiatric and psychosomatic research lab. Houston VA Med. Ctr., 1959-80, pres. Birkman-Mefferd Rsch. Found., 1972-80; sr. cons. Birkman and Assocs., Inc., Houston, 1966—; prof. physiology Baylor Coll. of Medicine, Houston, 1949-92; adj. prof. behavioral scis. Sch. Pub. Health, U. Tex., 1976—; adj. prof. psychology U. Houston, 1972-80, assoc. edn., 1987—. Contbr. articles to profl. jours. Served to capt. U.S. Army, 1942-47. Recipient Rosalie B. Hite cancer research fellowship, 1949-51; Damon Runyon cancer research fellow, 1952-53. Mem. Am. Psychol. Assn., Am. Physiol. Soc., Am. Chem. Soc. Avocations: painting; music. Home: 823 Longview Dr Sugar Land TX 77478-3732 Office: Birkman & Assocs Inc Post Oak Blvd # 3040 Houston TX 77056

MEGEE, GERALDINE HESS, social worker; b. Newark, Ohio, June 9, 1924; d. A.P. Hess and Ethel Stoyle Luther; children: John Megee, Sarah Martens, Thomas Megee. BS, Northwestern U., 1944; MSEd, Ind. U., 1976, MSW, 1978; PhD candidate, Fielding Inst. Cert. social worker, Ill., Fla.; cert. addictions profl., Fla., criminal justice specialist; diplomate social work. Dir. Foster Care Prog., Webster-Cantrel Hall, Decatur, Ill., 1978-81; owner, dir. Family Systems Ctr., Decatur, 1981—; pvt. practice clinic and employee assistance Decatur, 1981—; dir. Charter Counseling Ctr., Charter Glade Hosp., Naples, Fla., 1985-87; owner FamilyWorks, Naples, 1991—. Mem. NASW, Am. Assn. Marriage and Family Therapists, Am. Acad. Sexologists, Sigma Pi Lambda. Home: 9856 Tonya Ct Bonita Springs FL 33923 Office: 5051 Castello Dr Ste 205 Naples FL 33940-2986

MEGOFNA-PETILLO, C(HRISTINE) GAIL, correctional health and marketing professional, administrator, medical corporation manager; b. New Britain, Conn., Aug. 12, 1949; d. Edward Lucian and Mary Dorothy (Cappello) Jacynowicz; m. Sam R. Petillo; children: William John Megofna Jr., Jeffrey Ryan, Jennifer Lynn. A in Bus. Adminstrn./Med. Scis., Briarwood Coll., Southington, Conn., 1969; R.N., Tunxis Sch. Nursing, Farmington, 1981; postgrad., 1981-86; A in Mktg., Tunxis C.C., 1984; BS in Mktg., U. Hartford. Cert. in counseling and human svcs. Kinetic therapist Kinetic Concepts, San Antonio, Tex., 1981-83; mktg. cons. JM Mktg., Rocky Hill, Conn., 1983-87; area mgr. PCS div. EMPI, Fridley, Minn., 1984-85; mktg. mgr. H.L. Moore Med. Corp., New Britain, 1985-87; adminstr. Nursefinders of Hartford, Inc., 1987-88; dir. pub. relations Conn. Peer Rev. Orgn., 1988—, Mktg. Quality Care Rev., 1988—, Correctional Health Care, Middletown, Conn., 1988—; pres., owner Petillo & Petillo Constrn. and Remodeling, Inc., New Britain, Conn., 1989—; cons., owner, pres. correctional health care. Pres. Briarwood Coll., Southington, 1967-69. Mem. NAFE, Am. Mktg. Assn., Sales and Mktg. Execs., Conn. Bus. and Industry Assn., Am. Correctional Assn., Am. Correctional Health Services Assn. (bd. dirs.), Am. Jail Assn. (chmn. profl. adv. com.), Alpha Chi. Democrat. Roman Catholic. Club: New Britain Jr. Woman Club (health chmn. 1977, treas. 1977, sec. 1978). Avocations: golf, reading music, coaching little league.

MEHBOD, HASSAN, nephrologist, internist; b. Shiraz, Iran, Sept. 10, 1933; s. Mehdi and Badrol-Sadat (Anvar) M.; m. Darlene VanPutten, June 6, 1964; children: William M., Daine H., Susan L. MD, Tehran U., 1958. Diplomate Am. Bd. Internal Medicine, Am. Bd. Nephrology. Chief nephrology VA Med. Ctr., Dayton, Ohio, 1967-76, assoc. chief of staff, 1972-76; pvt. practice Dayton, 1973—; coord. internal medicine residency program Good Samaritan Hosp., Dayton, Ohio, 1976—, dir. dialysis svcs., 1977—, chmn. internal medicine residency com., 1978-82, chmn. dept. internal medicine, 1984-87, chmn. profl. activities com., 1988-91; clin. prof. medicine Wright State U., Dayton, Ohio, 1992—; clin. assoc. prof. medicine Ohio State U., Columbus, 1974-79. Fellow ACP; mem. AMA (bd.'s com. 1984-85, rep. staff 1996—), Ohio Med. Assn., Montgomery County Med. Soc. (trustee 1978-81, chmn. credential com. 1981, bd. dirs. 1982—), Physicians for Social Responsibility (leadership cir. 1988—). Office: H Mehbod MD Inc 2200 Philadelphia Dr Dayton OH 45406

MEHENDALE, HARIHARA MAHADEVA, toxicologist, educator; b. Philya, India, Jan. 12, 1942; s. Shinginakodlu Mahadeva Bhat and Narmada M. (Tahmankar) M.; m. Rekha N. Joshi, May 10, 1968; children: Roopa, Neelesh. BSc, Karnataka U., Dharwar, India, 1963; MS in Entomology, N.C. State U., 1966, PhD in Physiology, 1969. Diplomate, Am. Bd. Toxicology (bd. dirs. 1986-90, sec. 1987-90), Acad. Toxicol. Scis. Postdoctoral fellow in toxicology U. Ky., Lexington, 1969-71; vis. fellow Nat. Inst. Environ. Health Sci., 1971-72, staff fellow, 1972-75; asst. prof. dept. pharmacology and toxicology, U. Miss. Med. Ctr., Jackson, 1975-78, assoc. prof., 1978-80, prof., 1980, dir. toxicology tng. program, 1982-92; named Prof. and Kitty DeGree endowed prof. and chair in toxicology Coll. Pharmacy and Health Scis. Northeast La. U., Monroe, 1992—; vis. prof. dept. forensic medicine, Karolinska Inst., Stockholm, 1983-84; adj. prof. Geriatric Edn. Ctr., 1986-91. Mem. editorial bds. Fundamental and Applied Toxicology, 1983-86, Jour. Toxicology and Environ. Health, 1986-93, Jour. Biochemical Toxicology, 1988-93, Toxicology and Applied Pharmacology, 1989—, Indian Jour. Environment and Toxicology, 1990-94. Overseas editor Indian Jour. Pharmacology, 1984-94. Contbr. over 230 articles to profl. jours. Past pres. India Assn. Miss.; bd. dirs. Ctr. for Toxicology, J.J. Coll. Criminal Justice, N.Y.C. Recipient Sr. Fogarty Internat. fellowship, 1983; grantee NIH, EPA, Air Force Office of Scientific Rsch., Burroughs Wellcome Fund, Dept. Energy, Agy. for Toxic Substances and Diesease Registry, Miss. Lung Assn., Miss., Heart Assn. Fellow AAAS; mem. Am. Soc. Pharmacology and Exptl. Therapeutics (chmn. divsn. toxicology 1993-96), Am. Assn. for Study of Liver Disease, Soc. Toxicology (awards com. 1996—, Burroughs Wellcome Toxicology Scholar award, 1988-92, Zeneca Internat. Travel award 1993), Am. Chem. Soc., Am. Coll. Toxicology (coun. mem. 1996—), Internat. Soc. Study Xenobiotics Am. (mem. publ. com. 1991—, chmn. 1994-96), Thoracic Soc., Am. Assn. Colls. of Pharmacy, Internat. Union Pharmacologists, South Central Soc. of Toxicology (v.p. 1986—, pres. 1987—), Assn. Scis. Indian Origin in Am. (founding pres. 1981, Disting. Svc. award 1990, Outstanding Scientist award 1992), Acad. Environ. Biology India (pres. 1990-93), Soc. Toxicology (India), Indian Pharm. Soc., Soc. Neurosci. (India), Indian Sci. Congress Assn., Entomol. Soc. of India, Miss. Acad. Sci. (Outstanding Contbns. to Sci. award 1986), Miss. Heart Assn. (Ernest G. Spirey award 1988), Hindu Temple Soc. Miss. (life, sec. bd. trustees 1991-92, chmn. bd. trustees 1992-95), Sigma Xi (chpt. v.p. 1981-82, pres. 1982-83). Home: 1030 Inabnet Blvd Apt 203 Monroe LA 71203-7104 Office: Northeast La U Coll Pharmacy and Health Scis Monroe LA 71209

MEHLHORN, GARY LEN, ophthalmologist; b. Memphis, Apr. 10, 1948; s. Roscoe Morris and Audrey June (Krauch) M.; m. Katherine Ann Fisher, Sept. 23, 1972; children: Matthew, Adam, Emily, Allison. BS in Biochemistry, Mich. State U., 1970; MD, U. Tenn., 1973. Flight surgeon tng. Naval Aerospace Med. Inst., Pensacola, Fla., 1975-76; flight surgeon NAS Oceana, Virginia Beach, Va., 1976-78; house physician Hampton (Va.) Gen. Hosp., 1976-78; resident in ophthalmology U. Tenn., 1978-81; emergency rm. physician Lauderdale County Hosp., Ripley, Tenn., 1978-80; vitreo-retinal fellow Vitreo-Retinal Rsch. Found., Memphis, 1981-82; Ophthalmologist/retina-vitreous-macula specialist Eye Surgeons of Springfield (Mo.), 1982—. Fellow Am. Acad. Ophthalmology, Mo. State Med. Assn., Mo. State Ophthal. Assn., Greene County Med. Soc. Lutheran. Office: Eye Surgeons of Springfield 3800 S National Ste 500 Springfield MO 65807-5283

MEHLMAN, EDWIN STEPHEN, endodontist; b. Hartford, Conn., Nov. 30, 1935; s. Sol Abraham and Rose (Slitt) M.; m. Lesley Judith Lunin, June 13, 1959; children: Jeffrey Cole, Brian Scott, Erik Van. BA, Wesleyan U., 1957; DDS, U. Pa., 1961; cert. endodontics, Boston U., 1965. Diplomate Am. Bd. Endodontists. Instr. oral medicine Sch. Dental Medicine Harvard U., Boston, 1965-67; clin. instr. endodontics Sch. Dental Medicine Tufts U., Boston, 1968-70; lectr. endodontics Sch. Dental Medicine, Harvard U., Boston, 1970-72, asst. clin. prof. endodontics, 1972—; staff assoc. Forsyth Dental Ctr., Boston, 1965—; asst. prof. endodontics Boston U. Sch. Dental Medicine, 1995—; pvt. practice Providence, 1965—; vis. lectr. dental hygiene U. R.I., Kingston, 1965-71, Community Coll. R.I., Lincoln, 1990—; cons. com. on accreditation of Dentists and Dental Aux. Edn. Programs, 1974-78. Contbr. articles to profl. jours. Pres. Temple Habonim, Barrington, R.I., 1968-70, Bur. Jewish Edn. of R.I., 1980-84; area v.p. Jewish Fedn. R.I., 1975-78; mem. R.I. Legis. Commn. to Study Malpractice Crisis, 1985-86; chmn. R.I. Dental Polit. Action Com., 1987-90. Capt. USAF, 1961-63. Recipient Etherington award Six N.E. Dental Assns. for Outstanding Contbns. to Dentistry. Fellow Am. Coll. Dentists, Internat. Coll. Dentists, Pierre Fauchard Acad. (Award of Merit); mem. ADA (coun. on govt. affairs and fed. dental svcs. 1988-92, vice chmn. 1991-92, 1st v.p. 1994-95), Am. Assn. Endodontists (dir. 1988-91), R.I. Dental Assn. (pres. 1986-87), N.E. Dental Assns. (Outstanding N.E. Dentist 1995). Jewish. Home: 6 Ridgeland Rd Barrington RI 02806-4028 Office: 130 Waterman St Providence RI 02906-2010 also: 1090 New London Ave Cranston RI 02920-3016

MEHRINGER, CHARLES MARK, medical educator; b. Dickinson, N.D., Nov. 21, 1945; m. Ruth Mehringer; 1 child, Sydney.; BS in Biology, Lamar U., 1966; MD, U. Tex., 1970. Diplomate Am. Bd. Radiology, Am. Bd. Neuroradiology. Intern UCLA Hosp., 1970-71; resident in diagnostic radiology Harbor-UCLA Med. Ctr., Torrance, Calif., 1971-74, fellow in neuroradiology, 1976-77; asst. prof. dept. radiology UCLA Sch. Medicine, 1977-80, dir. spl. procedures, 1980-94, assoc. prof. dept. radiology, 1986—; vice-chmn. dept. radiological scis. UCLA Sch. Medicine, Torrance, 1992—, acting chmn. dept. radiology, 1992—, chief diagnostic radiology, 1983-92; chief radiological svcs., cons. U.S. Air Force for Japan and Korea, 1974-76; cons. U. Calif./Irvine (Calif.) Med. Ctr., 1988—, St. Marys Med. Ctr., Long Beach, Calif., 1986—, Long Beach VA Hosp., 1979—, L.A. County Dept. Chief Med. Examiner-Coroner, 1977—; bd. dirs. Rsch. and Ednl. Inst.; presenter in field. Co-author: (with others) Neurological Surgery of the Ear and Skull Base, 1982, Vascular Surgery, 1984, 2d edit., 1994, Youman's Neurological Surgery, 1990, Common Problems in Infertility and Impotence, 1990, Intraluminal Imaging of Vascular and Tubular Organs: Diagnostic and Therapeutic Applications, 1993, Neuroradiology, A Study Guide, 1995; contbr. articles to profl. jours. Bd. dirs., exec. com. Med. Found. Harbor-UCLA Med. Ctr., 1992—. Recipient numerous grants for rsch., 1977—. Mem. Am. Coll. Radiology, Am. Soc. Neuroradiology (sr. mem.), Western Neuroradiologic Soc., L.A. Radiologic Soc., L.A. County Med. Assn. Home: 834 Rome Dr Los Angeles CA 90065 Office: UCLA Med Ctr Box 27 1000 W Carson St Torrance CA 90509

MEHRTENS, SUSAN EMILY, research company executive; b. Elmhurst, N.Y., Sept. 27, 1945; d. William Frederic, and Pauline (Kaufmann) M.; m. Edwin M. Davis, May 31, 1981 (div. Apr. 1984). BA, Queens Coll, 1967; MPhil, Yale U., 1969, PhD, 1973. Asst. prof. Queens Coll., Flushing, N.Y., 1971-77; assoc. prof. Coll. of Atlantic, Bar Harbor, Maine, 1977-87; pres., chief exec. officer Potlatch Group Inc., Mineola, N.Y., 1987—; cons. Family Care Am., Phoenix, 1991, F.C. Nahser Advt. Inc.; instr. Mt. Desert (Maine) Island Adult Edn., 1977-87, U.S Power Squadron-Sewanaka, Freeport, N.Y., 1975-77. Author: Earthkeeping, 1974, Being Human in the West, 1991, Ecoguide, 1991, Revisioning Science, 1991; co-author: The Fourth Wave, 1993; contbr. articles to profl. jours. Grantee Am. Philos. Soc., 1974, 86, Am. Coun. Learned Socs., 1974; Yale U. fellow, 1967-69. Mem. Phi Beta Kappa. Home and Office: 239 Barwick Blvd Mineola NY 11501-3234

MEIER, BERNHARD, cardiologist; b. Bern, Switzerland, Feb. 6, 1950; s. Hans Ulrich and Alice Frieda (Haefeli) M.; m. Monika Kamber, Apr. 28, 1981; children: Fabian, Michael, Philip. MD, U. Zurich, Switzerland, 1975. Fellow in cardiology Emory U., Atlanta, 1981-83; dir. internat. cardiology U. Geneva, 1984-85, dir. invasive cardiology, 1989-91, asst. prof., 1987; prof., head cardiology U. Bern, 1992—. Author: Coronary Angioplasty, 1987, Atlas of Coronary Balloon Angioplasty, 1994; editor: Interventional Cardiology, 1991. 1st lt. Swedish mil., 1986. Fellow Europeean Soc. Cardiology, Am. Coll. Cardiology; mem. Swiss Soc. Cardiology. Office: Univ Hosp, Cardiology, CH-3010 Bern Switzerland

MEIER, PATRICIA LYNN, occupational health nurse; b. Fargo, N.D., Mar. 22, 1947; d. Oliver Ernest and Helen June (Richards) Klauss; m. Raymond Stephen Meier, Mar. 7, 1970; children: Kari, Christopher, Timothy. RN, N.D. Staff nurse St. Luke's Hosp., Fargo, 1970, head nurse nursery, 1970-72, infection control nurse, 1974-80, emergency rm. nurse, 1974-76; infection control coord. Meritcare, Fargo, 1980-88; perinatal instr. N.D. State Dept. Health, Bismarck, N.D., 1975-80; infection control/employee health nurse Heartland Med. Ctr., Fargo, 1989-94; employee health nurse Dakota Heartland Health Sys., Fargo, 1994—; facilitator/mentor Teens Teaching AIDS, Fargo, 1993-95. Mem. Ch. of St. Anne and St. Joachim, Fargo; bd. dirs. Valley AIDS Network, 1986-95. Mem. Nat. Employee Health-Occupl. Health Assn. Office: Dakota Heartland Health Sys 1711 S University Dr Fargo ND 58103

MEIER, ROBERT M., clinical psychologist; b. N.Y.C., Jan. 3, 1947; s. Max J. and Madeline (Bentz) M.; m. Susan L. Sheffler, June 9, 1985; children: Justine, Andrew, David. BA, U. Mich., 1968; PhD, Boston U., 1975. Psychologist Lawrence (Mass.) Mental Health Ctr., 1972-75, VA, Boston, 1976-81; pvt. practice, Seattle, from 1981, Waltham, Mass. Chmn. of canvass Unitarian Universalist Ch., Arlington, Mass., 1991-92. Mem. APA, Mass. Psychol. Assn. Home: 26 Kensington Pk Arlington VA 02174

MEIGHAN, STUART SPENCE, hospital consultant, internist, writer; b. Glasgow, Scotland, Jan. 30, 1923; came to U.S., 1962; s. Stuart Spence and Annie Louise (Brown) M; m. Anne Stewart Henderson, Nov. 4, 1952 (div. 1968); children: Jane Spence, Stuart Spence; m. Louise Rhys McGregor, July 7, 1985. MB, U. Glasgow, 1945. Registrar, sr. registrar Nat. Health Svc., U.K., 1948-57; sr. staff mem. Allan Blair Meml. Clinic, Regina, Sask., Can., 1957-62; internist Cleland Clinic, Oregon City, Oreg., 1962-64; dir. med. affairs Good Samaritan Hosp., Portland, Oreg., 1964-78; pres. Spence Meighan and Assocs., Portland, 1978—; cons. several hosps. and orgns. Contbr. over 100 articles to profl. jours. Lt. Royal Navy, 1946-48. Recipient Disting. Svc. award Am. Soc. Internal Medicine. Fellow Am. Coll. Physicians, Royal Coll. Physicians. Home and Office: 408 NW Rainier Ter Portland OR 97210-3347

MEIGS, KENNETH JAMES, JR., osteopath; b. Bremerton, Wash., Jan. 24, 1964; s. Kenneth James Meigs and Linda Mae (Grace) Schultz; m. Cindi Fern Nedry, Aug. 25, 1984; children: Kolton James, Konnor James. BA, Western Wash. U., 1987; DO, Coll. Osteo. Medicine Pacific, 1992. Diplomate Nat. Bd. Osteo. Med. Examiners; bd. cert. Am. Coll. Osteopathic Family Practitioners. Intern Eastmoreland Hosp., Portland, Oreg., 1992-93, resident in family practice, 1993-95; pvt. practice Columbia Family Med., P.C., Portland, 1995—. Vol. St. Joseph Hosp., Bellingham, Wash., 1987-88, L.A. Marathon, 1989; med. vol. Montclair (Calif.) Health Clinic, 1988-89, Stengaard Clinic Outreach Program, Phoenix, 1989. Mem. Am. Osteo. Assn., N.W. Osteo. Med. Found., Multnomah County Med. Soc., Am. Coll. Osteo. Family Practitioners, Osteo. Physicians and Surgeons of Oreg. Home: 3331 SW Miller Dr Gresham OR 97080 Office: 3510 NE 122d Ste 201 Portland OR 97230

MEIJLER, FRITS LOUIS, cardiologist, educator; b. Den Ham, The Netherlands, Apr. 29, 1925; m. Annemarie P. Schendstok, Apr. 4, 1953; children: Annejet P., Gerda, Theo Dirk. HBS-B, Almelo, Eindhoven, 1947; MD, U. Amsterdam, 1957, PhD, 1960. Tng. in internal medicine and cardiology U. Amsterdam, The Netherlands, 1957-62; mem. staff Wilhelmina Gasthuis, Amsterdam, 1962-67; prof. cardiology State U. Utrecht, The Netherlands, 1968-85; prof. cardiology Interuniv. Cardiology Inst., 1973-85, chmn. sci. council, 1983—; retired, 1993. Author 4 books; contbr. articles to profl. publs., Dutch newspapers. Served with Royal Dutch Army, 1947-49. Decorated Wounded in Action Svc. decoration, House Order of Orange, Order of Dutch. Lion. Fellow Am. Coll. Cardiology, Am. Heart Assn., European Soc. Cardiology; mem. Dutch Cardiac Soc. (hon.), Royal Netherlands Acad. Arts Scis., Royal Acad. Medicine Belgium. Home: 20 G Stadhouderskade, 1054 ES Amsterdam The Netherlands Office: Interuniv Cardiology Inst Netherlands, PO Box 19258, 3501 DG Utrecht The Netherlands

MEILLER, MORRIS, physician; b. Lima, Peru, July 18, 1931; came to U.S., 1960; s. Abraham and Bertha (Pait) M.; m. Maria Elvira Santaella, Dec. 20, 1963 (div. Aug. 1991); 1 stepchild, Bryan Alan; m. Nelida Beatriz Houriet, Dec. 20, 1991; stepchildren: Andres, Martin. BS, U. San Marcos, 1952; MD, U. San Marcos Sch. Medicine, 1960. Diplomate Am. Bd. Psychiatry and Neurology. Resident Sheppard and Enoch Pratt Hosp., Towson, Md., 1963-64; asst. psychiatrist Johns Hopkins Hosp. Phipps Clinic, Balt., 1963-64; staff psychiatrist Spring Grove Hosp. Ctr., Catonsville, Md., 1970-75, St. Elizabeth's Hosp., Washington, 1979-82; chief mental hygiene clinic VA Outpatient Clinic, Orlando, Fla., 1975-77; staff psychiatrist Springfield Hosp. Ctr., Sykesville, Md., 1985-91; psychiatrist, unit dir. Walter P. Carter Ctr., Catonsville, 1991-94; psychiatrist Spring Grove Hosp. Ctr., Catonsville, Md., 1994—; cons. in field. Mem. Am. Psychiat. Assn., Md. Psychiat. Soc. Home: 16420 Old Frederick Rd Mount Airy MD 21771-3332 Office: Spring Grove Hosp Ctr 55 Wade Ave Catonsville MD 21228

MEILMAN, PHILIP WARREN, psychologist, education educator; b. N.Y.C., Jan. 9, 1951; s. Sidney and Hilda (Cohen) M.; m. Alice Dixon Wheeler, May 17, 1980; children: Anna, Laura. BA, Harvard U., 1973; PhD, U. N.C., 1977. Lic. clin. psychologist, Va. Staff psychologist counseling ctr. Coll. William and Mary, Williamsburg, Va., 1977-80, dir. counseling ctr., 1990—; asst. prof. U. Nebr. Med. Ctr., Omaha, 1980-85; asst. dir. counseling ctr. Dartmouth Coll., Hanover, N.H., 1986-90; dir. psychol. svcs. Cornell U., Ithaca, N.Y., 1996—; com. mem. drug prevention program, survey instrument com. U.S. Dept. Edn., Washington, 1987—; co-dir. Core Inst. So. Ill. U., 1990—. Contbr. articles to profl. jours. Drug Abuse Prevention grantee U.S. Dept. Edn., 1987, 90-92, 94. Office: Coll William and Mary Psychol Svcs Counseling Ctr Williamsburg VA 23187

MEINER, SUE ELLEN THOMPSON, gerontologist, nursing educator and researcher; b. Ironton, Mo., Oct. 24, 1943; d. Louis Raymond and Verna Mae (Goggin) Thompson; m. Robert Edward Meiner, Mar. 5, 1971; children: Diane Thompson Bubb, Suzanne Elaine. AAS, Meramec C.C., 1970; BSN, St. Louis U., 1978, MSN, 1983; EdD, So. Ill. U., Edwardsville, 1991. RN, Mo.; cert. med./surg. clinician; cert. gerontol. nurse practitioner; cert. clin. specialist in gerontol. nursing. Staff RN St. Joseph's Hosp., St. Charles, Mo., 1976-78; nursing supr. Bethesda Gen. Hosp., St. Louis, 1975-76, 71-74; adult med. dir. Family Care Ctr.-Carondelet, St. Louis, 1978-79; program dir., lectr. Webster Coll./Bethesda Hosp., Webster Groves, Mo., 1979-82; diabetes clin. specialist Washington U. Sch. Medicine, St. Louis, 1982; chmn. dept. nursing, asst. prof. St. Louis C.C., 1983-88, Barnes Hosp. Sch. Nursing, 1988-89; instr. U. Mo., St. Louis, 1989; assoc. prof. St. Charles County C.C., St. Peters, Mo., 1990-92, Deaconess Coll. of Nursing, 1991-93; patient care mgr. Deaconess Hosp., St. Louis, 1993-94; assoc. prof. Jewish Hosp. Coll. of Nursing and Allied Health, 1994-96; gerontol. nurse, instr. Wash. U. Sch. Med., St. Louis, 1996—; nat. dir. edn. Nat. Assn. Practical Nurse Edn. and Svc., Inc., St. Louis, 1984-86; mem. task force St. Louis Met. Hosp. Assn., 1987-88; mem. adv. com. Bd. Edn. Sch. Nursing, St. Louis, 1986-90; project dir. NIH Grant Washington U., St. Louis, 1996—. Contbr. articles to profl. jours. and books. Chmn. bd. dirs. Creve Coeur Fire Protection Dist. Mo., 1984-89; vice chmn. Bd. Cen. St. Louis County Emergency Dispatch Svc., 1985-87; asst. leader Girl Scouts U.S., St. Louis, 1975; treas. Older Women's League, St. Louis, 1992-93. Recipient Woman of Worth award Gateway chpt. Older Women's League, 1993. Mem. ANA, Am. Nurses Found., Nat. League for Nursing, Am. Soc. of Aging, Mid-Am. Congress on Aging, Creve Coeur C. of C., Order Ea. Star (chaplain 1970), Jobs Daus. (guardian 1979-80), Sigma Theta Tau (fin. chmn. 1984, archivist 1985-87), Sigma Phi Omega (pres. 1990-91), Kappa Delta Pi. Home and Office: 700 Wren Path Ct Ballwin MO 63021-4794

MEINHOLD, CHARLES BOYD, health physicist; b. Boston, Nov. 1, 1934; s. Russell and Jane (Boyd) M.; m. Anne Elizabeth DuVally, Oct. 20, 1956; children: Anne Frances, Patricia Marie, Michael John, Peter Russell, Catherine Louise. BS in Physics, Providence Coll., 1956; postgrad., U. Rochester, 1956-57. Staff scientist health physics div. Brookhaven Nat. Lab., Upton, N.Y., 1957-72, head, sr. health physicist safety and environ. div., 1972-88, sr.scientist, div. head, 1988-91; sr. scientist radiol. sci. divsn. Dept. Advanced Tech. Dept. Nuclear Energy, Upton, 1991—; pres. Nat. Coun. on Radiation Protection and Measurement, Bethesda, Md., 1991—; mem. Internat. Commn. on Radiol. Protection, 1978—; mem. Nat. Commn. on Radiol. Protection, 1977—; cons. Consol. Edison Co., 1984—. pres. South Haven Bd. Edn., Brookhaven, N.Y., 1965-87. Named Hon. Prof., China Inst. Atomic Energy. Fellow Health Physics Soc.; mem. Internat. Radiation Protection Assn. (v.p. 1988-92, pres. 1992—). Roman Catholic. Home: 41 Old South Country Rd Brookhaven NY 11719-9526 Office: Dept Nuclear Energy Radiol Sci Div Bldg 703m B Upton NY 11973

MEISEL, RICHARD LANE, JR., obstetrician-gynecologist; b. Lakin, Kans., Apr. 13, 1953; s. Richard L. and Glenda Lee Meisel; m. Penni Fincham; 1 child, Theodore Quintin. Student, USAF Acad., 1971-73; BGS, U. Kans., Lawrence, 1975; MD, U. Kans., Wichita, 1983. Diplomate Nat. Bd. Med. Examiners, Am. Bd. Obstetricians and Gynecologists. Intern St. Joseph Hosp., Denver, 1983-84; resident Sch. Medicine U. Kans., Wichita, 1984-88, asst. prof., 1990-95, assoc. prof., 1995—; fellow Mt. Sinai Med. Ctr., N.Y.C., 1988-90; attending physician Wesley Med. Ctr., Wichita, 1990—; dir. Maternal-Fetal Medicine, Wichita, 1990—; presenter in field. Contbr. sci. papers, abstracts to profl. publs. Mem. AMA, ACOG, Soc. Perinatal Obstetricians, Kans. Med. Soc., Med. Soc. Sedgwick County.

MEISKEY, SHIRLEY SUZANNE, health information administrator; b. Lancaster, Pa., Mar. 5, 1945; d. Norman Burnell and Nevo Nannette (West) Snader; m. Thomas Eugene Meiskey, Aug. 24, 1968. AAS, No. Va. Community Coll., 1974; BA in Health Info. Mgmt., Stephens Coll., 1983; MS in Health Care Adminstrn., Cen. Mich. U., 1987. Corr. sec. Greater S.E. Community Hosp., Washington, 1974-76, patient care evaluation asst., 1976-77, asst. to dir., 1977-80, assoc., mgr. record svcs., 1980-87; assoc. prof., coord. health info. technician Montgomery Coll., Takoma Park, Md., 1987—; cons. in field; mem. adv. com. med. record adminstrn. program George Washington U., Washington, 1988-89. Mem. Am. Health Info. Mgmt. Assn. (program com. 1992 assemble on edn.), D.C. Health Info. Mgmt. Assn. (pres. 1985-86, editor D.C. Current 1989, 92-93), chair tri-state spl. events 1987-88). Democrat. Lutheran. Home: 3107 Collard St Alexandria VA 22306-1419

MEISLER, DAVID M., ophthalmologist; b. Cleve., Jan. 20, 1951. BA magna cum laude, Boston U., 1973; MD, Ohio State Coll. Medicine, 1976. Diplomate Am. Bd. Ophthalmology, Nat. Bd. Med. Examiners. Intern Mt. Sinai Hosp., Cleve., 1976-77; resident Northwestern U., Chgo., 1977-80; cornea fellow U. Iowa, Iowa City, 1980-81, Proctor Found., San Francisco, 1981-82; staff ophthalmologist Cleve. Clinic Found., 1982—. Office: Cleve Clinic Found 9500 Euclid Ave Cleveland OH 44195

MEISLIK, JERRY, ophthalmologist; b. Usti-Nad-Labem, Czech Republic, Oct. 21, 1946; came to U.S., 1949; s. Sigmund and Bella Meislik; m. Rhona Abrams. BA, Bklyn. Coll., 1967; MD, Albany Med. Coll., 1971. Diplomate Am. Bd. Ophthalmology. Intern Albany (N.Y.) Med. Coll., 1971-72; gen. practitioner USPHS, Grundy, Va., 1972-74; resident ophthalmology U. Colo. Med. Ctr., Denver, 1974-77; pvt. practice Huron Ophthalmology, Ypsilanti, Mich., 1978-80; chief surgeon Beyer Hosp., Ypsilanti, 1982-84, chief ophthalmology dept. St. Joseph Mercy Hosp., Ypsilanti, 1985-86. Fellow Am. Acad. Ophthalmology.

MEISNER, JAY STEVEN, medical educator; b. Bklyn., Mar. 1, 1956; s. Aaron and Martha (Savitsky) M. B of Engring., The Cooper Union, 1977; MS, Worcester Polytech Inst., 1980; MD, PhD, MS, Albert Einstein Coll. Medicine, 1987. Diplomate Am. Bd. Internal Medicine, Am. Coll. Cardiology. Intern Bronx (N.Y.) Mcpl. Hosp. Ctr., 1987, resident, 1988-89; fellow in cardiovascular medicine Albert Einstein Coll. Medicine, Bronx, 1990-92; attending physician, dir. cardiac ultrasound lab. Jacob Med. Ctr., Bronx, 1992—; attending physician, staff echocardiographer Weiler Hosp. of Albert Einstein Coll. Medicine, Bronx, 1993—; asst. prof. internal medicine Albert Einstein Coll. Medicine, Bronx, 1993—. Co-author: (chpt.) Blood Flow in the Heart and Great Vessels, 1989; contbr. chpt. to book, articles to profl. jours.; manuscrpit reviewer Am. Jour. Physiology, 1995—. Soc. Nuclear Medicine fellow, 1986; Rudin scholar Albert Einstein Coll. Medicine, 1986. Mem. Cardiovascular System Dynamics Soc., Biomed. Engring. Soc., Alpha Omega Alpha, Tau Beta Pi, Eta Kappa Nu. Office: Albert Einstein Coll Dept Cardiology 1300 Morris Park Ave Bronx NY 10461

MEISNER, JUDITH ANNE, clinical social worker, marital and sex therapist, psychotherapist; b. Dayton, Ohio, Mar. 20, 1931; d. Lowell DeWight and Mary Elizabeth (Anderson) Richardson; m. S. Clair Varner, 1953 (div. 1964); m. Carl E. Meisner, Dec. 31, 1970; children: Christopher, Cynthia, Deborah, Catherine; stepchildren: Janet, Elizabeth, Barbara. BA, Oberlin Coll., 1952; MSW, Fla. State U., 1970; PhD, Inst. Advanced Study Human Sexuality, 1987. Cert. Acad. Cert. Social Workers; bd. cert. diplomate; lic. clin. social worker; lic. marriage and family therapist; diplomate Am. Bd. Sexology, Am. Coll. Sexologists, clin. supr. Am. Bd. Sexology. Psychiat. aide Inst. Living, Hartford, Conn., 1952-53; caseworker, supr. Div. Family Svcs., Dept. Health and Rehabilitative Svcs., St. Petersburg, Fla., 1964-66, 66-68; dir. standing com. on health and rehabilitative svcs. Fla. Ho. Reps. , Fla. State Legis., Tallahassee, 1970-72; adj. prof. grad. sch. social work Fla. State U., Tallahassee, 1972-73; family life cons. Family Counseling Ctr., St. Petersburg, 1973-75; coord. Teenage Info. Program for Students Pinellas County Sch. Bd., St. Petersburg, 1975-78, coord. Citizen's Task Force on Edn. for Family Living, 1978-80; psychotherapist Counseling & Cons. Svcs., St. Petersburg, 1975—; profl. adv. bd. Nat. Found. March of Dimes Pinellas chpt., Clearwater, Fla., 1976-85, Parents Without Ptnrs. chpt. 186, St. Petersburg, 1973—; mem. Family Life Edn. Coun. Pinellas County Sch. Bd., Clearwater, 1980-85. Bd. dirs. Neighborly Sr. Svcs., Clearwater, 1974-85, pres., bd. dirs., 1982, 83; bd. dirs. Marriage and Family Counseling of Pinellas County, Inc., 1993—. Fellow Am. Acad. Clin. Sexologists (life); mem. NASW, Am. Assn. for Marriage and Family Therapists (clin.), Pinellas Assn. for Marriage and Family Therapists (clin.), Am. Assn. Sex. Educators, Counselors and Therapists (life, cert. sex educator, sex therapist), Soc. for the Sci. Study of Sex, Fla. Soc. Clin. Social Workers, Soc. of Neuro-Linguistic Programming (cert. master practitioner), Harry Benjamin Internat. Gender Dysphoria Assn., Fla. Soc. of Clin. Hypnosis. Home: 7 Marina Ter Treasure Island FL 33706

MEISSNER, ANN LORING, psychologist, educator; b. Richland Center, Wis., Nov. 26, 1924; d. Frank Gilson Woodworth and Leona Bergman; m. Hans Meissner, July 4, 1946 (div. 1953); children: Edie, John Arthur; m. Corbin Sherwood Kidder, Oct. 28,1979. BS, U. Mich., 1953; MS, U. Wis., 1960, PhD, 1965; MPH, U. Calif., Berkeley, 1969; diploma, Gestalt Inst., Cleve., 1974, U. Minn., 1993. Lic. psychologist, Minn. Assoc. dir. Coop. Sch. Rehab. Ctr., Mpls., 1965-72; assoc. prof. W.Va. U., 1972-74; psychologist Alternative Behavior Assn., Mpls., 1974-79, Judson Family Ctr., Mpls., 1979-84; pvt. practice St. Paul, 1984—; dir. nursing Augsburg U., Mpls., 1974-76; adj. prof. St. Mary's Coll., Mpls., 1979—; mem. staff Gestalt Inst. Twin Cities, Mpls., 1978-88; dir. Today Per., Mpls., 1980-91; mem. State Bd. Psychology, Mpls., 1982-86; adv. bd. doctoral program U. St. Thomas, St. Paul, adj. faculty, 1993. Recipient Disting. Human Svc. Profl. award N. Hennepin C.C., Mpls., 1981. Mem. APA, Minn. Women Psychologists. Episcopalian. Home: 111 Kellogg Blvd E Apt 1501 Saint Paul MN 55101-1214 Office: 1360 Energy Park Dr Ste 330 Saint Paul MN 55108-5252

MEISSNER, WILLIAM WALTER, psychiatrist, clergyman; b. Buffalo, Feb. 13, 1931; s. William Walter and Mary Emma (Glauber) M. BA, St. Louis U., 1956, PhL, 1957, MA, 1957; STL, Woodstock Coll., 1962; MD, Harvard U., 1967. Diplomate Am. Bd. Psychiatry and Neurology, Bd. Psychoanalysis. Entered S.J., 1951; intern Mt. Auburn Hosp., Cambridge, Mass., 1967-68; resident Mass. Mental Health Ctr., Boston, 1968-71; mem., instr. Boston Psychoanalytic Inst., 1971—, tng. and supervising analyst, 1980—; staff psychiatrist Mass. Mental Health Ctr., 1971-87, Cambridge (Mass.) Hosp., 1971-78; asst. clin. prof. psychiatry Harvard U. Med. Sch., 1973-76, assoc. clin. prof., 1976-81, clin. prof. psychiatry, 1981-87; prof. psychoanalysis Boston Coll., 1987—. Author: Annotated Bibliography in Religion and Psychology, 1961, Group Dynamics in the Religious Life, 1965, Foundations for a Psychology of Grace, 1966, The Assault on Authority-Dialogue or Dilemma, 1971, Basic Concepts in Psychoanalytic Psychiatry, 1973, The Paranoid Process, 1978, Internationalization in Psychoanalysis, 1981, The Borderline Spectrum, 1984, Psychoanalysis and Religious Experience, 1984, Psychotherapy and the Paranoid Process, 1986, Life and Faith: Psychoanalytic Perspectives on Religious Experience, 1987, Treatment of Patients in the Borderline Spectrum, 1988, What is Effective in Psychoanalytic Therapy, 1991, Ignatius of Loyola: The Psychology of a Saint, 1992; mem. editorial bd. Psychoanalytic Inquiry, 1983—, Jour. Geriatric Psychiatry, 1980—, Rev. of Psychoanalytic Books, 1980-84, Psychoanalytic Study of Society, 1981—, Theol. Studies, 1981-91, Dynamic Psychotherapy, 1982-89, Internat. Forum for Psychoanalysis, 1983—, Internat. Jour. Psychoanalytic Psychotherapy, 1984—, Psychoanalytic Edn., 1990—, Bull. of Menninger Clinic, 1985—, Jour. Am. Psychoanalytic Assn., 1995—, Psychoanalysis and Psychotherapy, 1989—, Internat. Series in Psychology of Religion, 1990—, Am. Jour. Psychotherapy, 1993—. Recipient Deutsch prize Boston Psychoanalytic Inst., 1969. Fellow Am. Psychiat. Assn. (task force on treatments of psychiat. disorders 1989, Oskar Pfister award 1989), Mass. Psychiat. Soc., Ctr. for Advancement Psychoanalytic Studies; mem. Am. Psychoanalytic Assn. (councilor-at-large 1980-84), Internat. Psycho-Analytical Assn., Boston Psychoanalytic Inst., Am. Psychotherapy Seminar Ctr. (mem. prof. adv. com. 1991—), Sigma Chi, Psi Chi. Office: Boston College Carney Hall 420 D Chestnut Hill MA 02167-3806

MEISTAS, MARY THERESE, endocrinologist, diabetes researcher; b. Grand Rapids, Mich., July 22, 1949; d. Frank Peter and Anne Therese (Karsokas) M. MD, U. Mich., 1975. Diplomate Am. Bd. Internal Medicine, Am. Bd. Endocrinology. Intern, then resident in internal medicine Cleve. Clinic Hosp., 1975-78, endocrinology fellow, 1978-79; fellow in pediatric endocrinology Johns Hopkins Hosp., Balt., 1979-81; diabetes researcher Joslin Diabetes Ctr., Boston, 1981-86; assoc. in medicine Brigham and Women's Hosp., Boston, 1981-86; asst. in medicine, diabetes researcher Mass. Gen. Hosp., Boston, 1986-92; staff endocrinologist Emerson Hosp., Concord, Mass., 1989—. Mem. ACP, Am. Diabetes Assn., Am. Fedn. Clin. Research, Endocrine Soc. Office: Emerson Hosp 747 Main St Ste 111 Concord MA 01742-3302

MEITELES, LAWRENCE Z., otolaryngologist, educator; b. N.Y.C., Sept. 20, 1960; s. Simon Meiteles. BA cum laude, Yeshiva U., 1981; MD, Albert Einstein Coll. Medicine, 1986. Diplomate Am. Bd. Otolaryngology, Nat. Bd. Med. Examiners. Intern gen. surgery Montefiore Med. Ctr., Bronx, N.Y., 1986-87; resident, chief resident surgery otolaryngology N.Y. Eye and Ear Infirmary, N.Y.C., 1987-91; fellow otolaryngology, neurology, and skull base surgery, lectr. otolaryngology U. Mich., Ann Arbor, 1991-93; asst. prof. dept. otolaryngology N.Y. Med. Coll., Valhalla, 1993—; dir. Balance Function Ctr. St. Agnes Hosp., White Plains, N.Y., 1993—. Fellow Am. Acad. Otolaryngology Head and Neck Surgery, Am. Neurotology Soc., Am. Coll. Surgeons (assoc.); mem. AMA, Med. Soc. State N.Y. Office: Westchester Med Ctr Macy Pavilion Rm 1042-B Valhalla NY 10595

MEITIN, DEBORAH DORSKY, health care executive; b. Cleve., July 25, 1951; d. Irving and Rosalind (Lewis) D.; m. Samuel R. Meitin, Dec. 6, 1987. BS, Mich. State U., 1973; M Health Adminstrn., Ohio State U., 1981. Cert. med. technologist. Med. technologist U. Hosps., Cleve., 1974-79; adminstrv. dir. surgery and anesthesiology Cleve. Met. Gen. Hosp., 1981-86; sr. cons. Ernst & Whinney, Chgo., 1986-87; sr. v.p. Diversified Health Search, Maitland, Fla., 1988-89; pres. Health Search Cons., Altamonte Springs, Fla., 1989-91; pres. Greater Fla. Devel. Co., Altamonte Springs, 1988—; sr. cons. Ernst & Young, Orlando, 1991-92, mgr., 1992-94; sys. analyst Fla. Hosp., Orlando, 1995—. Mem. bd. profl. women's group Jewish Fedn., Chgo., 1986-87; mem. coms. Jewish Cmty. Ctr., Chgo., 1986-87, Orlando, Fla., 1990—, v.p., 1991-94; bd. dirs. Michael Reese Hosp.-Jr. Med. Rsch. Coun., Chgo., 1986-87, Temple Israel, Orlando, 1989—. Fellow Am. Coll. Healthcare Execs.; mem. Ctrl. Fla. Healthcare Exec. Group (pres. 1995-96), Ohio State U. Grad. Program in Health Adminstrn. Alumni Assn. (bd. dirs. 1982-84), Phi Kappa Phi, Beta Beta Beta. Democrat. Home: 268 Buttercup Cir Altamonte Springs FL 32714-5844 Office: 601 E Rollins St Orlando FL 32803-1248

MEJIA, ELVIRA, medical assistant; b. Zacatecas, Mexico, May 14, 1948; came to U.S., 1968; d. Ramiro and Rosa Maria (Gutierrez) M. BS, Benito Juarez Coll., Fresnilio, Mexico, 1967; grad., Laural Sch., Phoenix, 1983. Lab. tech. Scott & White Meml. Hosp., Temple, Tex.; office mgr. Raul & Alicia Lopez-Guerra M.D., P.A., Corpus Christi, Tex. Mem. NAFE, Am. Inst. for Cancer Rsch. Home: 3545 Ocean Dr Corpus Christi TX 78411-1340

MEKALANOS, JOHN J., microbiology educator. Prof. dept. microbiology and molecular genetics Harvard Med. Sch., Boston; invited spkr. Centenary Symposium of the Pasteur Inst., 1987; mem. vaccines and related biol. products adv. com. FDA, 1988. Recipient Eli Lilly & Co. Microbiology and Immunology Rsch. award Am. Soc. Microbiology, 1991, Milton Fund award, 1981, Am. Cancer Soc. Faculty Rsch. award 1986, NIH Merit award, 1989, AAAS Newcomb Cleve. Prize. Office: Harvard Med Sch Dept Microbiol Molecular Gen 200 Longwood Ave Boston MA 02115-6092

MELCHER, JERRY WILLIAM COOPER, clinical psychologist, army officer; b. Bloomington, Ill., Oct. 17, 1948; m. Margaret Frances Orban; children: Heather, Shawna, Jerry. BS, Lincoln U., Jefferson City, Mo., 1975; MS, Tex. A&I U., 1976; PhD, Tex. A&M U., 1980. Psychometrist Lamar U., Beaumont, Tex., 1978-79, psychologist, 1979-81; commd. 1st lt. U.S. Army, 1981, advanced through grades to lt. col., 1987; clin. intern William Beaumont Army Med. Ctr., 1981-82; psychologist 1st Cav. Divsn., Fort Hood, Tex., 1982-84; chief psychology svc. Darnall Army Community Hosp., Fort Hood, Tex., 1984-85, Blanchfield Army Community Hosp., Fort Campbell, Ky., 1986-87; clin. psychologist Area Counseling Assocs., Millington, Tenn., 1987—, U.S. Army Rsch., Memphis, 1988-93; 1451st Combat Stress Det., Jackson, Miss., 1993—; clin. dir. Genesis Treatment Ctr., Memphis, 1990-94; v.p., psychol. dir. Life Time Resources, 1994—; tng. coord. CETA, Beaumont, 1980-81; res. psychologist Operation Desert Storm, Fort Stewart, Ga., 1991. Bd. dirs. Family Aid Network, Killeen, Tex., 1984-85; vol. Rape Crisis Ctr., Beaumont, 1979. Decorated Bronze Star with valor device, Meritorious Svc. medal; Cross of Gallantry with palm (Vietnam). Mem. APA. Office: Area Counseling Assocs 8222 US Highway 51 N Millington TN 38053-1708

MELCHIOR, JEROME, urologic surgeon; b. Topeka, Kans., Dec. 10, 1937; s. Joseph John and Mary (Crettol) M.; m. Martha Roush, Oct. 18, 1974; children: Kiersten, Kevin. BA, U. St. Thomas, 1959, MEd, 1962; MD, U. Kans., 1967. Diplomate Am. Bd. Urology. staff Good Samaritan Hosp., Vincennes, 1974—. Fellow Am. Coll. Surgeons; mem. AMA, Ind. State Med. Assn. (pres. 1995-96). Home: 1529 Old Orchard Rd Vincennes IN 47591 Office: 200 S 6th St Vincennes IN 47591

MELE, JOANNE THERESA, dentist; b. Chgo., Dec. 5, 1943; d. Andrew and Josephine Jeanette (Calabrese) M. Diploma, St. Elizabeth's Sch. Nursing, Chgo., 1964; diploma in Dental Hygiene, Northwestern U., 1977; A.S., Triton Coll., 1979; D.D.S., Loyola U., 1983. Registered nurse, dental hygienist. Staff nurse in medicine/surgery St. Elizabeth's Hosp., Chgo., 1964-66, operating room nurse, 1966-67; head nurse operating room Cook County Hosp., Chgo., 1967-76, head nurse ICU, 1976-77; dental hygienist Mele Dental Assocs., Ltd., Oakbrook, Ill., 1977-79, practice dentistry, 1983—; clinical asst. prof. Loyola U., Chgo., 1988. Recipient Northwestern U. Dental Hygiene Clinic award, 1977; Dr. Duxler Humanitarian award scholar Loyola U., 1982. Mem. Chgo. Dental Soc., Ill. State Dental Soc., Acad. Gen. Dentistry, Am. Assn. Women Dentists, Acad. Operative Dentistry, Am. Prosthodontic Soc., Psi Omega (Kappa chpt.). Roman Catholic. Avocations: reading; music; golfing; jogging; skiing.. Office: Mele Dental Assocs Ltd 120 Center St Ste 610 Hinsdale IL 60521

MELEIS, AFAF IBRAHIM, nurse sociologist, educator, clinician, researcher; b. Alexandria, Egypt, Mar. 19, 1942; d. Abdel Baki Ibrahim and Soad Hussein Hassan; m. Mahmoud Meleis, Aug. 21, 1964; children: Waleed, Sherief. BS magna cum laude, U. Alexandria, 1961; MS, UCLA, 1964, MA, 1966, PhD, 1968; D of Pub. Svc. (hon.), U. Portland, 1989. Instr. U. Alexandria, 1961-62; acting instr. UCLA, 1966-68, asst. prof. nursing, then assoc. prof., 1968-75; assoc. prof., dean Health Inst., Kuwait, 1975-77; prof. nursing U. Calif., San Francisco, 1977—, also dir. Study Immigrant Health and Adjustment; vis. prof. colls. in Sweden, Brazil, Japan, Saudi Arabia, Kuwait, Egypt; 1st Centennial prof. Columbia U., N.Y.C., 1992-94; cons., speaker in field. author: theoretical Nursing: Development & Progress, 1985 (Book of Yr., am. Jour. Nursing, 1985), 2d edit., 1991; contbr. articles to rsch. and profl. jours. Recipient Helen Hahm award U. Calif. Sch. Nursing, San Francisco, 1981, Teaching awards U. Calif., San Francisco, 1981, 85, Pres. Hosni Mubarak medal of Excellence, 1990; Kellogg Internat. fellow, 1986-89. Fellow Am. Acad. Nursing; mem. Coun. Nurse Researchers, Western Soc. Research in Nursing, Am. Nurses Assn. Home: 39 Corte Ramon Greenbrae CA 94904-1228 Office: U Calif San Francisco Sch Nursing N511Y San Francisco CA 94143-0608

MELEN, NANCY ELLEN, medical facility administrator; b. Jersey City, N.J., July 19, 1953; d. Constantine and Nancy Joan (Muoio) Nalewaiski; divorced; children: Michelle Eileen, Robert William, Karen Marie. AS in Med. Records Tech., St. Petersburg Coll., 1990. Accredited records technician. Med. records clk. Bayonet Piont Hosp., Port Richey, Fla., 1983-84, Lake Seminole (Fla.) Hosp., 1986; med. records coord. Medfield Hosp., Largo, Fla., 1988-90; coding coord. Profl. Rev. Orgn., Tampa, Fla., 1990-91; coding supr. Suncoast Hosp., Largo, 1991-92; utilization rev. coord. Helen Ellis Hosp., Tarpon Springs, Fla., 1992-93; area mgr. Patient Document Svc./Record Copying Svc., Orlando, Fla., 1993-94; dir. med. records Majestic Towers Health Ctr., St. Petersburg, Fla., 1994—; med. records cons. Jacaranda Manor, St. Petersburg, 1991—; on-site clin. mgr. to coordinate students St. Petersburg Jr. Coll., Suncoast Hosp., 1990. Author curriculum materials in field. Mem. Am. Health Info. Mgmt. Assn., Gulfcoast Med. Record Assn. (cert. of appreciation 1991). Roman Catholic. Home: 11488 Robert Dr Largo FL 34778-3909

MELENDEZ, EDWIN MANUEL, orthopaedic hand surgeon; b. Rio Piedras, P.R., Jan. 2, 1958; s. Manuel and Olga (Martinez) M.; m. Mari Lopez, Feb. 23, 1985; children: Andre G., Gian-Franco, Stephan A. BS in Chemistry magna cum laude, U. P.R., 1978, MD, 1982, grad. in Orthop. Surgery, 1987. Diplomate Am. Bd. Orthopaedic Surgery, sub.-bd. Surgery of the Hand, also Nat. Bd. Med. Examiners. Gen. surgery intern U. P.R. Sch. Medicine, resident in orthopaedic and fracture surgery; fellowship in hand surgery Hosp. for Joint Diseases, Orthop. Inst., N.Y.C., 1988; pvt. practice hand and orthop. surgeon Tampa, Fla., 1991—; chmn. emergency/trauma liaison St. Joseph's Hosp., Tampa, 1996—. Contbr. articles to profl. jours. Maj. USAF, 1988-91. Fellow Am. Acad. Orthop. Surgeons; mem. Am. Assn. for Hand Surgery, Fla. Med. Assn., Fla. Hand Soc., Hillsborough County Med. Assn. Roman Catholic. Office: Edwin M Melendez MD PA 4602 N Armenia Ave Ste D-3 Tampa FL 33603

MELENDEZ, MICHAEL PAUL, psychotherapist, social worker, educator; b. Wichita Falls, Tex., Oct. 29, 1952; s. Carlos Saul and Alice Marion (O'Neill) M. BA, U. Ariz., 1975; MSW, Boston U., 1983. Lic. clin. social worker, Mass.; qualified in clin. social work; bd. cert. diplomate in clin. social work. Clin. coord. Ctr. for Alternative Edn., Boston, 1983-84; sr. social worker Judge Baker Children's Ctr., Boston, 1984-89; psychotherapist Assocs. for Counseling, Brookline, Mass., 1984—; clin. assoc. prof. Simmons Coll. Sch. Social Work, Boston, 1989—; pres. Latino Health Inst. Mem. NASW, Mass. Acad. Clin Social Workers, Am. Orthopsychiat. Assn., Coun. on Social Work Edn., AIDS Action Com. Democrat. Roman Catholic. Home: 14 Pond St # 3 Jamaica Plain MA 02130 Office: 51 Commonwealth Ave Boston MA 02116

MELLA, GORDON WEED, physician; b. Menlo Park, Calif., Aug. 22, 1931; s. Hugo and Pearl (Weed) M.; m. Dorothee Lusson, June 23, 1953 (div. May 1970); children: Richard, Glen, Gordon; m. Lynne Daniels Mella, Aug. 11, 1973; children: William, Cynthia, Heidi, Amanda. BS, Ursinus Coll., Collegeville, Pa., 1952; MD, Thomas Jefferson U., Phila., 1956. Fellow Am. Acad. Pediatrics, 1961. Med. officer, pediatrician USN, 1956-68, USNR, 1982-92; pvt. practice gen. pediatrics Gaithersburg, Md., 1968—. Team physician Winston Churchill H.S., Potomac, Md., 1985—. Fellow Am. Acad. Pediatrics (chmn. sch. health com. 1995—); mem. AMA, Montgomery County Med. Soc., Montgomery-Prince George's Pediatric Soc., Med. and Chirurgical Faculty of Md. Mem. Ch. of Latter Day Saints. Office: Pediatric Medicine 19251 Montgomery Village Ave Gaithersburg MD 20879

MELLBERG, JAMES RICHARD, dental research chemist; b. Manitowac, Wis., June 3, 1932; s. Millard Filmore Mellberg and Marion Eleanor (Elmer) Zimmerman; m. Gail Maureen Loehning, Sept. 26, 1956; children: Eric, Diane, Laura. BS, Wis. State U., Oshkosh, 1955; MS, Loyola U., Chgo., 1960. Head dental rsch. dept. Kendall Co., Barrington, Ill., 1958-75; assoc. dir. dental rsch. Colgate-Palmolive Co., Piscataway, N.J., 1975-94; cons. Naval Dental Rsch. Inst., Great Lakes, Ill., 1972—. Author: Fluoride in Preventive Dentistry, 1983; patentee in field; contbr. over 150 articles in field to sci. publs. Recipient 20 sci. exhibit awards ADA, 1964-87. Mem. Internat. Assn. Dental Rsch. (Disting. Scientist award), Am. Chem. Soc., European Orgn. Caries Rsch. Home: PO Box 227 Pottersville NJ 07979-0227

MELLEROWICZ, HANS HOLGER THEODOR, orthopedic surgeon, educator; b. Berlin, Aug. 3, 1951; s. Harald and Rosemarie (Kindler) M.; m. Heike B. Struve, May 29, 1950; children: Lara Marie, Leif Eric. Student, Free U., Berlin, 1977, MD, 1978. Physician Govt. Germany, Berlin, 1979; specialist orthopedic surgery, sr. surgeon Oskar-Helene-Heim, Free U. Berlin, 1980-85; specialist orthopedic surgery, sr. physician OHH-Free U. Berlin, Orthopedic Surgery Dept., 1985—; asst. prof. orthopedics and sports medicine Free U. Berlin, Germany, 1994; lectr. in ultrasound in medicine, ultrasound in sports medicine. Mem. internat. bd. Brit. Jour. Sports Medicine, 1990, Arthroscopy and Related Rsch., 1992, Deutsche Zeitschrift Sportmedizin, 1995. Mem. Berlin Sports Medicine Assn. (specialist sports medicine 1987, v.p. 1986—), Internat. Soc. Fracture Repair (founding mem.), German Pediatric Orthopedic Soc. (congress for pediatric orthopedics 1993), Internat. Soc. Orthopedics and Traumatology, German Soc. for Ultrasound in Medicine. Home: Terrassenstr 11, 14129 Berlin Germany Office: OHH, Clayallee 229, 14195 Berlin Germany

MELLIN, GILBERT WYLIE, pediatrics educator, consultant; b. Manorville, Pa., Sept. 22, 1925; s. Willard Colby and Hazel Naomi (Wylie) M.; m. Suzanne Naomi Seeds, Dec. 28, 1955; children: Deborah Louise, Sarah Agnew. BS summa cum laude, Bethany Coll., 1945; MD, Johns Hopkins U., 1949. Diplomate Am. Bd. Pediatrics. Intern in gen. medicine U. Pitts. Med. Ctr., 1949-50; jr., sr. and chief resident in pediatrics Bellevue Hosp., N.Y.C., 1950-53; instr. NYU Med. Sch., N.Y.C., 1952-53; jr. assoc. Children's Hosp., Washington, 1953-55; instr., assoc. in pediatrics Columbia U. Coll. Physicians and Surgeons, N.Y.C., 1955-58, asst. prof., 1958-67, assoc. prof., 1967—, acting chmn. dept., 1970-71; clin. instr. Georgetown U. Med. Sch., Washington, 1953-55; asst. pediatrician Babies Hosp. and Vanderbilt Clinic, Presbyn. Hosp., N.Y.C., 1955-57, asst. attending, 1957-67, assoc. attending, 1967—, acting dir. pediatric svc. 1970-71, dir. quality assurance, 1977—; mem. adv. bd. Assn. for Mentally Ill Children in Manhattan, 1961—; mem. tech. adv. com. on cleft palate N.Y.C. Dept. Health, 1961—; mem. hosp. rev. com. New York County Health Svcs. Rev. Orgn., 1977—, bd. dirs., 1982—; also others. Contbr. articles to med. jours. With USNR, 1943-46; sr. surgeon USPHS, 1948, 53-55. Fellow APHA (program area com. on drugs 1967-68); mem. AAAS, Am. Acad. Pediatrics, Am. Pediatric Soc., Harvey Soc., Soc. for Pediatric Rsch., Teratology Soc. (charter), Johns Hopkins U. Med. and Surg. Assn. Presbyterian. Home: 494 Ridgeland Ter Leonia NJ 07605-1017 Office: Columbia U Coll Phys & Surg 630 W 168th St New York NY 10032-3702

MELLINKOFF, SHERMAN MUSSOFF, medical educator; b. McKeesport, Pa., Mar. 23, 1920; s. Albert and Helen (Mussoff) M.; m. June Bernice O'Connell, Nov. 18, 1944; children: Sherrill, Albert. BA, Stanford U., 1941, MD, 1944; LHD (hon.), Wake Forest U., 1984, Hebrew Union Coll., L.A., 1988. Diplomate Am. Bd. Internal Medicine, Am. Bd. Gastroenterology, Am. Bd. Nutrition. Intern asst. resident Stanford U. Hosp., San Francisco, 1944-45; asst. resident Johns Hopkins Hosp., Balt., 1947-49, chief resident, 1950-51, instr. in medicine, 1951-53; fellow in gastroenterology Hosp. of U. Pa., Phila., 1949-50; from asst. prof. to prof. medicine UCLA Sch. of Medicine, L.A., 1962-86; dean UCLA Sch. Medicine, L.A., 1962-86, emeritus prof. of medicine, 1990—; disting. physician of VA Wadsworth VA Medical Ctr., L.A., 1990-93; mem. sci. adv. panel Rsch. to Prevent Blindness, Inc., N.Y.C., 1975-93; mem. program devel. com. Nat. Med. Fellowships, Inc., N.Y.C., 1984—. Editorial bd. The Pharos, 1986; contbr. articles to profl. jours. Apptd. by Gov. of Calif. to McCone Com., 1965. Capt. U.S. Army, 1945-47. Recipient Abraham Flexner award Assn. Am. Med. Colls., 1981, J.E. Wallace Sterling Disting. Alumnus award Stanford U. Sch. of Medicine, 1987. Master ACP; fellow Royal Coll. of Physicians; mem. Am. Gastroenterol. Assn. Assn., of Am. Physicians, Inst. of Medicine of NAS, Am. Acad. of Arts and Scis., The Johns Hopkins Soc. of Scholars. Office: UCLA Sch of Medicine Dept of Medicine 44-143 CHS Los Angeles CA 90024

MELLOR, MARJORIE JO, family practice physician; b. Schuyler, Nebr., Oct. 10, 1960; d. Charles Rodney and Patricia Joan (Teeple) Scheuneman; children: Andrew, Grant, Wendi. BA, Midland Coll., 1981; MD, U. Neb. Med. Ctr., 1986. Diplomate Am. Bd. Family Practice. Resident Lincoln (Nebr.) Family Practice, 1989; ptnr. Lone Tree Med. Assoc., Central City, Nebr., 1989-93; emergency physician Good Samaritan Hosp., Kearney, Nebr., 1993—; staff Norton (Kans.) County Hosp., 1994-96, Cozad Cmty. Hosp., 1996—; attending U. Nebr. Med. Ctr., 1989—. Bd. dirs. Ctrl. City Libr. Found., 1989-92; vol. Ctrl. City Family Support Svcs., Inc., 1990-93. Mem. AMA, Kans. Med. Assn., Nebr. Perinatal Orgn. Home: 2010 Ave C Cozad NE 69130

MELLORS, ROBERT CHARLES, physician, scientist; b. Dayton, Ohio, 1916; s. Bert S. and Clementine (Steinmetz) M.; m. Jane K. Winternitz, Mar. 25, 1944; children: Alice J., Robert C., William K., John W. Ph.D., Western Res. U., 1940; M.D., Johns Hopkins, 1944. Diplomate Am. Bd. Pathology. Intern Nat. Naval Med. Ctr., Bethesda, Md., 1944-45; rsch. fellow medicine Meml. Center Cancer and Allied Diseases, N.Y.C., 1946-50; rsch. fellow pathology Meml. Ctr. Cancer and Allied Diseases, 1950-53, asst. attending pathologist, 1953-57, assoc. attending pathologist, 1957-58; sr. fellow Am. Cancer Soc., 1947-50; sr. clin. rsch. fellow Damon Runyon Meml. Fund, 1950-53; asst. attending pathologist Meml. Hosp., N.Y.C., 1953-57, assoc. attending pathologist, 1957-58; asst. attending pathologist Ewing Hosp., N.Y.C., 1953-57, assoc. attending pathologist, 1957-58; instr. biochemistry Western Res. U., 1940-42; rsch. assoc. Poliomyelitis Rsch. Ctr. and Dept. Epidemiology Johns Hopkins U. Sch. Hygiene, 1942-44; asst. prof. biology Meml. Ctr. Cancer and Allied Diseases, N.Y.C., 1952-53; asst. prof. pathology Sloan Kettering div. Cornell U., 1953-57, assoc. prof., 1957-58; prof. pathology Cornell U. Med. Coll., 1961-90, prof. emeritus, 1990—; assoc. attending pathologist N.Y. Hosp., 1961-72, attending pathologist, 1972-86; pathologist-in-chief, dir. labs., 1958-84, emeritus, 1984-85, hon. staff, 1986—; assoc. dir. rsch. Hosp. for Spl. Surgery, N.Y.C., 1958-69, dir. rsch., 1969-84, emeritus, 1984-85, scientist emeritus, 1986—; mem. rsch. adv. com. NIH, 1962-66; adv. com. Nat. Inst. Environ. Health Sci., 1966-69; com. nomenclature and classification of disease Coll. Am. Pathologists, 1960-64. Author: Analytical Cytology, 1955, 2d edit., 1959, Analytical Pathology, 1957. Served as lt. (j.g.), M.C. USNR, 1944-46. Recipient Kappa Delta award Am. Acad. of Orthopedic Surgeons, 1962. Fellow Royal Coll. Pathologists, Molecular Medicine Soc., Am. Soc. Clin. Pathology; mem. Am. Assn. Pathologists, Am. Assn. Immunologists, Am. Soc. Biochemistry and Molecular Biology, Am. Coll. Rheumatology, Am. Orthopedic Assn. (hon.). Home: 3 Hardscrabble Cir Armonk NY 10504-2222

MELLSTEDT, HÅKAN SÖREN THURE, oncologist, hematologist, medical facility administrator; b. Lund, Sweden, Oct. 23, 1942; s. Ture and Stina (Carlstedt) M.; m. Eva Bengtsson, May 21, 1966. MD, Karolinska Inst., Stockholm, 1969, PhD, 1974. Asst. prof. medicine Karolinska Inst., Stockholm, 1975-86, assoc. prof., 1986—; sr. asst. physician Serafimer Hosp., Stockholm, 1978-80; head internal medicine, dept. oncology Karolinska Hosp. and Inst., Stockholm, 1980-85, head biotherapy and lymphoma unit, 1985-96, dep. dir., 1986-96; prof. exptl. oncology and head physician U. Uppsala and Acad. Hosp., Sweden, 1996—; sci. advisor Centoccor, Malvern, USA, 1988—, E. Merck GmbH, Darmstadt, Germany, 1990-94, Pasteur-Merieux Serum and Vaccines, Lyon, France, 1996—, Pharmacia AB, Stockholm, 1992—, Cell Rsch. Corp., Cambridge, Mass., 1994—, BioInvent AB, Lund, Sweden, 1995—, Glaxo-Wellcome, Ltd., London, 1995—. Contbr. articles to profl. jours. Recipient Alfaferone prize Istituto Immunologico Italiano, Rome, 1989; grantee Swedish Cancer Soc., 1987—. Mem. Swedish Cancer Soc. (scientific com.), European Soc. Med. Oncology (nat. rep., steering com.), Am. Assn. Cancer Rsch., N.Y. Acad. Sci., Swedish Soc. Oncology (chmn. 1993—), Soc. Biol. Ther. Office: Karolinska Hosp-Oncology, Box 100, S-171 76 Stockholm Sweden

MELMON, KENNETH LLOYD, physician, biologist, pharmacologist, consultant; b. San Francisco, July 20, 1934; s. Abe Irving and Jean (Kahn) M.; m. Elyce Edelman, June 9, 1957; children: Bradley S., Debra W. AB in Biology with honors, Stanford U., 1956; MD, U. Calif. at San Francisco, 1959. Intern, then resident in internal medicine U. Calif. Med. Ctr., San Francisco, 1959-61; clin. assoc., surgeon USPHS, Nat. Heart, Lung and Kidney Inst., NIH, 1961-64; chief resident in medicine U. Wash. Med. Ctr., Seattle, 1964-65; chief div. clin. pharmacology U. Calif. Med. Ctr., 1965-78; chief dept. medicine Stanford U. Med. Ctr., 1978-84, Arthur Bloomfield prof. medicine, prof. pharmacology, 1978-86, prof. medicine and molecular pharmacology, 1978—; assoc. dean postgrad. med. edn., 1994—; dir. tech. transfer program Stanford U. Hosp., 1986-93; mem. sr. staff Cardiovasc. Rsch. Inst.; chmn. joint commn. prescription drug use Senate Subcom. on Health, Inst. Medicine and HEW-Pharm. Mfrs. Assn.; mem. Nat. Bd. Med. Examiners, 1987-96; pres. Bio 2000, Woodside, Calif., 1983-85; co-founder Immulogic, Waltham, Mass., 1988; sci. advisor Hoffman LaRoche, Epoch, Vysis, others; cons. FDA, 1965-82, Office Tech. Assessment, 1974-75, Senate Subcom. on Health, 1975—; bd. dirs. Vysis, Chgo., Immulogic, Boston, Epoch, Seattle; cons. to govt.; founder Inst. Biol. and Clin. Investigation, Ctr. for Molecular and Genetic Medicine, Stanford Cmty. of Internists Stanford Med. Group, Intergrate Ctr. Clin. Immunology. Author articles, chpts. in books, sects. encys.; Editor: Clinical Pharmacology: Basic Principles in Therapeutics, 3d edit., 1992, Cardiovascular Therapeutics, 1974; assoc. editor: The Pharmacological Basis of Therapeutics (Goodman and Gilman), 1984; mem. editorial bd. numerous profl. jours. Surgeon USPHS, 1961-64. Burroughs Wellcome clin. pharmacology scholar, 1966-71; John Simon Guggenheim fellow Weizman Inst., Israel, 1971, NIH spl. fellow, Bethesda, 1971. Fellow AAAS (nat. coun. 1985-89); mem. Am. Fedn. Clin. Rsch. (pres. 1973-74), Am. Soc. Clin. Investigation (pres. 1978-79), Assn. Am. Physicians, Western Assn. Physicians (pres. 1983-84), Am. Soc. Pharmacology and Exptl. Therapeutics, Am. Soc. Clin. Pharmacology and Therapeutics (Oscar Hunter award in therapeutics 1994), Inst. Medicine of NAS, Am. Physiol. Soc., Calif. Acad. Medicine, Med. Friends of Wine, Phi Beta Kappa. Democrat. Jewish. Home: 51 Cragmont Way Woodside CA 94062-2307 Office: Stanford U Med Ctr Dept Medicine # S025 Stanford CA 94305

MELNICK, VIJAYA LAKSHMI, biology educator, research center director; b. Kerala, India; came to U.S., 1959; m. Daniel Melnick, June 28, 1963; 1 child, Anil D. BS, Madras Agriculture Coll., India, 1959; MS, U. Wis., 1961, PhD, 1964, postgrad., 1964-66. Asst. prof. dept. biology Fed. City Coll., Washington, 1970-74; assoc. prof. dept. biology U. D.C., Washington, 1974-77, prof. biology, 1977—; dir. Ctr. for Applied Rsch. and Urban Policy, Washington, 1992—; sr. staff assoc. Internat. Ctr. Inter-Disciplinary Studies in Immunology Georgetown U. Med. Sch., 1978-85, assoc. dir. tech. transfer, edn. and community outreach Ctr. Inter-Disciplinary Studies in Immunology, 1985—; sr. rsch. scholar Ctr. for Applied Rsch. and Urban Policy, Washington, 1984-85; spl. asst. policy and bioethics Nat. Inst. Aging/NIH, Bethesda, Md., 1980-82; vis. prof., rsch. participant Carnegie program Oak Ridge Grad. Sch. Biomed. Sci., U. Tenn., 1974-78; vis. scientist Biology and Medicine Inst., Lawrence Livermore Labs., U. Calif., 1972-73; invited del. cell biologist to People's Republic of China, 1990, to Initiave on Edn. Sci. & Tech. to Republic South Africa, 1995; mem. health edn. adv. com. Internat. Med. Svc. for Health, Washington; mem. Nestle Infant Formula Audit Commn., 1981-91; mem. Mayor's Adv. Bd. on Infant and Maternal Health, 1987—; del. 1st Asian-Pacific Orgn. for Cell Biology Congress, Shanghai, 1990; mem. nat. coun. on rsch. in child welfare Child Welfare League Am., Inc., 1992—; mem. adv. coun. D.C. family policy seminar Georgetown U. Grad. Pub. Policy Program, 1993—; mem. adv. com. tng. program for postdoctoral program in devel. immunology Internat. Ctr. Interdisciplinary Studies in Immunology, Georgetown U. Med. Ctr., 1993—; mem. steering com. Nat. Consortium for African Am. Children, Nat. Commn. to Prevent Infant Mortality, 1993—; host scientist Science in American Life exhibition Nat. Mus. Am. Hist. The Smithsonian Inst., 1994—; del. Initiative for Edn., Sci., & Tech., South Africa, 1995. Invited del. initiative on edn., sci., and tech. to Republic of South Africa, 1995. Recipient Outstanding Svc. award March of Dimes, 1987; postdoctoral fellow U. Wis. Med. Sch., 1964-66. Mem. APHA, AAAS, Am. Soc. Cell Biology, Assn. for Women in Sci., Am. Polit. Sci. Assn., Nat. Assn. Minority Med. Educators (legis. com. 1977—), Nat. Assn. for Equal Opportunities in Higher Edn. (sci. and tech. adv. com. 1982), N.Y. Acad. Sci., Sigma Xi, Sigma Delta Epsilon. Office: U DC Ctr Applied Rsch 4200 Connecticut Ave NW Washington DC 20008-1174

MELSEN, BIRTE, orthodontics educator; b. Fredericia, Denmark, June 9, 1939; d. Otto Emil and Kjerstine (Caspersen) P.; m. Flemming Melsen, Apr. 5, 1963; children: Michael, Christian. DDS, Royal Dental Coll., Aarhus, Denmark, 1964, specialist, 1971, Doctor Odont, 1974. Asst. tchr. Inst. of Cariology, Royal Dental Coll., Aarhus, 1964-65; rsch. assoc. Inst. Orthodontics, Royal Dental Coll., Aarhus, 1965-67, asst prof., 1967-72, acting head, 1971—, assoc. prof., 1972-75, prof., head, 1975—; orthodontist SCh. Dental Clinics, Silkeborg, 1965-67, cons., orthodontist, 1967-88; pvt. practice orthodontics, 1980—; vis. prof. U. Padova, Italy, 1981-84; contract prof. U. Naples, Italy, 1990—. Contbr. more than 150 articles to profl. jours. Decorated knight of Dannebrog; recipient Zendium prize, 1991, The Jarabak Mem. Orthodontic Tchrs. and Rsch. award, 1995. Mem. Scandinavian Orthodontic Soc. (pres. 1976), Danish Orthodontic Soc. (pres. 1988-90, head 1995—), European Orthodontic Soc. (v.p. 1990), Austrian Dental Soc. (hon.), Deutsche Kieferorthopädische Gesellschaft (hon. mem.), Egyptian Orthodontic Soc. (hon. mem.). Home: Elsdyrvej 28, 8270 Hoejbjerg Denmark Office: Royal Dental Coll, Vennelyst Blvd, 8000 Aarhus Denmark

MELSHEIMER, HAROLD, obstetrician, gynecologist; b. Legenfeld, Germany, June 11, 1927; came to U.S., 1955; naturalized, 1960; s. Louis and Hella Leonie (Schwehr) Peterman; m. Norma Sykes Sabrina, Nov. 27, 1967; children: Laura, Linda. BS, Marburg U., West Germany, 1951, MD, 1954. Diplomate Am. Bd. Ob-Gyn. Intern Baden County Hosp., West Germany, 1954-55, St. Mary's Hosp. Med. Ctr., Long Beach, Calif., 1955-56; resident Queens Hosp. Med. Ctr., Honolulu, 1956-57, Calif. Hosp. Med. Ctr., L.A., 1957-59; pvt. practice ob-gyn. Encino, Calif., 1959-87; ret.; former dept. chief, now hon. staff mem. Am. Med. Internat. Med. Ctr. Tarzana, Calif., Encino Hosp.; founder Technion Inst. of Tech. Contbr. articles to profl. jours. Operational mem. USCG Aux., 1971. Recipient cert. of honor Wisdom Soc.; named Hon. Citizen, Rep. of Korea, 1966. Fellow ACS (life), Am. Coll. Ob-Gyn., Internat. Coll. Surgeons; mem. AMA, Calif. Med. Assn., L.A. County Med. Assn., Am. Physicians Fellowship for Israel Med. Assn., N.Y. Acad. Scis., Braemar Country Club. Home: 25660 Deertrail Dr Tehachapi CA 93561-9140

MELTON, ARTHUR RICHARD, health care executive; b. Ysleta, Tex., Apr. 28, 1943; s. Francis Charles and Jean (Graham) M.; m. Frances Bay, Aug. 19, 1965; children—David Bay, Amy Elizabeth. B.S., U. Utah, 1969; M.P.H., U. N.C., 1974, Dr. Pub. Health, 1976. Microbiologist Utah Dept. Health, Salt Lake City, 1970-73; dir. labs. S.D. Dept. Health, Pierre, 1976-87; dir. divsn. of lab. svcs. Utah Dept. Health, Salt Lake City, 1987-92, dep. dir. 1992-96, dir. 1996—. Mem. Am. Pub. Health Assn. (governing council 1980-83), S.D. Pub. Health Assn. (pres. 1980-81). Mormon. Home: 6835 Heather Way West Jordan UT 84084-2304 Office: 288 N 1460 W Box 142802 Salt Lake City UT 84114

MELTON-SCOTT, MARY MEULI, hospital administrator, consultant, author, lecturer; b. Dec. 4, 1943; d. August Martin and Vada Irene (Matthews) Meuli; m. James Lynn Bell, May 23, 1961 (div. 1964); 1 child, James Lynn Jr.; m. Charles David Scott, Jr., Sept. 18, 1964 (div. 1969); 1 child, Charles David III; m. Charles Tabb, Jr., June 23, 1970 (div. 1973); 1 child, Erika Elizabeth; m. Johnny Wayne Scott, 1983. BA, McMurry Coll., 1971; MS, Wright State U., 1978; PhD, Columbia Pacific U., 1983; MBA, Xavier U., Cin., 1986; cert. AIDS trainer Nat. Inst. Drug Abuse. Cert. alcoholism counselor, 23 states, including Ohio; B.A.B.E.S. World prevention curriculum. High sch. tchr. Dayton pub. schs., Ohio, 1972-74; therapist Greene Hall, Greene Meml. Hosp., Xenia, Ohio, 1975-77; clin. dir. Bur. Alcoholism Svcs., Dayton, 1978-83; v.p. Dettmer Hosp./Upper Valley Med. Ctr., Troy, Ohio, 1983-86; adminstr. Valley View Hosp., Las Cruces, N.Mex., 1986-88; owner, pres. Melton-Scott Enterprises, Tipp City, Ohio, 1983-86, So. N.Mex. D.W.I. Programs, 1988-90; chief fin. officer The August Corp., 1989, bd. dirs., 1989—; owner, pres. E.T.C., Ohio, Inc., 1989—; cons. WORAC, Dayton, 1978-83; exec. dir. Miami County Mental Health, Ohio, 1984-86; chief exec. officer Alcohol Drug Abuse Treatment Svcs., Inc., 1989-91; task force chmn. Vietnam Vets. N.Mex.; grant writer. Mem. NAFE, Assn. Mental Health Adminstrs., Nat. Assn. Alcoholism Counselors, Nat. Coun. on Alcoholism (Ohio chpt.), Am. Coll. Health Care Adminstrs., Ohio Assn. Alcohol/Drug Abuse Counselors (pres.), Sigma Delta Tau. Avocations: writing, gardening, needlework, sports. Home: 51 E Burton Ave Dayton OH 45405-4130 Office: 4950 Northcutt Place Dayton OH 45414 also: The August Corp 400 N Bowman Rd Space 4A Little Rock AR 72211

MELTZER, RAE, social worker; b. Russia, Jan. 7, 1922; d. Ely and Ida (Belatzkin) Libin; m. Jack Meltzer, June 26, 1944; children: Richard, Marc, Ellen. BA, U. Chgo., 1943, MA, 1959. Cert. social worker, Tex., Ill. Pvt. practice clin. social worker Dallas, Chgo.; vis. assoc. prof. U. Tex., Dallas; field wk. assoc. prof. U. Chgo. Contbr. articles to profl. jours. founder, chmn. bd. dirs. Park Forest Family Counseling Svc.; bd. dirs. Virginia Frank Child Devel. Ctr. Mem. Am. Coun. Social Wk., Nat. Assn. Social Workers, Am. Group Psychotherapy Assn., Register of Clin. Social Workers, Acad. Cert. Social Workers. Home: 4550 N Park Ave Apt 803 Chevy Chase MD 20815

MELUGIN, MICHAEL BLAIR, oral and maxillofacial surgeon; b. Everett, Wash., Apr. 4, 1963; s. B.N. and Jane E. Melugin; m. Pamela R. Hanson, Oct. 23, 1994. DDS with honors, U. Wash., 1988; Cert. of Specialty in Oral Surgery, U. Tex./Southwestern Med. Ctr., Dallas, 1992. Diplomate Am. Bd. Oral and Maxillofacial Surgery. Clin. prof. Sch. Dentistry U. Wash., Seattle, 1992-94; pvt. practice Puget Sound Oral and Maxillofacial Surgery, Seattle, 1992-94; asst. prof. surgery Med. Coll. Wis., Milw., 1994—; instr. ACLS Lifetech, Kirkland, Wash., 1992-94. Contbr. articles to profl. jours. Grantee Med. Coll. Wis., 1995. Fellow Am. Assn. Oral and Maxillofacial Surgeons; mem. ADA, Wis. Dental Assn., Greater Milw. Dental Assn., Wis. Soc. Oral and Maxillofacial Surgeons. Office: Med Coll Wisconsin Dept Oral/Maxill Surgery 9200 W Wisconsin Ave Milwaukee WI 53226

MELVIN, DOROTHY MAE, retired microbiologist; b. Fayetteville, N.C., Jan. 27, 1923; d. Willie James and Lillie Mae (Bain) Melvin. AB, U. N.C.-Greensboro, 1942; MS, U. N.C.-Chapel Hill, 1945; PhD, Rice U., 1951. Cert. Am. Acad. Microbiology. Microbiologist parasitology trng., Ctrs. for Disease Control, Atlanta, 1945-49, 1951-61, chief parasitology tng. sect., Atlanta, 1962-85. Mem. Am. Soc. Tropical Medicine and Hygiene, Am. Soc. Parasitologists, Sigma Xi. Author manuals; contbr. articles to sci. jours. Home: 2418 Kingscliff Dr NE Atlanta GA 30345-2124

MELVIN, JOHN LEWIS, physician, medical educator, administrator; b. Columbus, Ohio, May 26, 1935; s. John Harper and Ruth Eleanor (Wertenberger) M.; m. Carol Ann Pate, Apr. 10, 1991; children from a previous marriage: Megan Marie, Beth Anne, John Patrick, Mia Michelle. BS, Ohio State U., 1955, MD, 1960, M in Med. Sci., 1966. Rotating Intern Mt. Carmel Hosp., Columbus, 1960-61; resident in phys. medicine Univ. Hosp., Columbus, 1961, 63-66; asst. prof. Ohio State U., Columbus, 1966-69, assoc. prof., 1969-73; prof., chmn. dept. Med. Coll. Wis., Milw., 1973-91; prof., dep. chmn. dept. Temple U., Phila., 1992—; cons. to numerous U.S. govtl. agys., health care insts.; lectr. in field; research assoc. Ohio State

Research Found., Columbus, 1966-68; assoc. coordinator Ohio State Regional Med. Program, Columbus, 1969-71; med. dir. Curative Rehab. Ctr., Milw., 1973-91; v.p. med. affairs Moss Rehab. Hosp., Phila., 1991—; dept. chmn. Einstein Med. Ctr., Phila., 1991—. Contbr. articles to profl. jours. Bd. dirs. Vis. Nurses Assn., Milw., 1974-83; mem. com. Mental Health Planning Council, Milw., 1974-75, Wis. Council Devel. Disabilities, Madison, 1979-80; mem. planning and evaluation com. Elizabethtown Hosp. for Children and Youth, Pa., 1977; advisor Nat. Multiple Sclerosis Soc., Milw., 1979-87; mem. Wis. Nicaragua Ptnrs., 1982-91; trustee Easter Seal Research Found., vice chmn., 1985, chmn. 1986-88. Served to capt. M.C., U.S. Army, 1961-63. Recipient cert. of appreciation Goodwill Industries, 1972, spl. recognition award Commn. Accreditation Rehab. Facilities, 1977, Performance award Wood VA Med. Ctr., 1978, Goldschmidt award Nat. Rehab. Hosp., 1990, cert. of appreciation Jour. Rehab. Adminstrn., 1982; Alumni Achievement award Ohio State U., 1985; grantee Rehab. Svcs. Adminstrn., 1979-91, Health Care Financing Adminstrn., 1984-85; Ford Found. fellow, 1951-53. Fellow Am. Acad. Cerebral Palsy and Devel. Medicine, Am. Acad. Phys. Medicine and Rehab. (sec. 1992-94, bd. dirs. 1992—, Zeiter Lectr. award 1987); mem. Am. Bd. Phys. Medicine and Rehab. (Diplomate, chmn. 1988-93, chmn. residency Rev. Com. 1985-88), Am. Bd. Med. Specialists (exec. com. 1990-92), Med. Soc. Milw., Milw. Acad. Medicine, Wis. Soc. Phys. Medicine and Rehab., Am. Assn. Electromyography and Electrodiagnosis (pres. 1979-80), Am. Congress Rehab. Medicine (pres. 1987-88, gold medal 1971, 78, Gold Key award 1988), Am. Heart Assn., Am. Hosp. Assn. (sect. rehab. hosp., chmn. 1981), AMA (cert. of appreciation 1976, 82), Am. Paraplegia Soc., Assn. Acad. Physiatrists (pres. 1985-87), Internat. Fedn. Phys. Medicine and Rehab. (exec. com. 1980—, hon. sec. 1980-88, pres. elect 1995—), Internat. Rehab. Medicine Assn., Rehab. Internat. Med. Commn., Nat. Assn. Rehab. Facilities (pres. 1981-83, bd. dirs.), Coun. of Med. Splty. Socs. (pres. 1989-90), Alpha Omega Alpha. Home: 244 Delancey St Philadelphia PA 19106-4330 Office: Moss Rehab Hospital 1200 W Tabor Rd Philadelphia PA 19141-3019

MELVIN, W. SCOTT, physician, educator; b. Toledo, Feb. 7, 1961; s. William J. and Carol Ann (Laing) M.; m. Meg Wilson, Jan. 9, 1993; children: James, Julie, Jeffrey. BS, Ohio Northern U., 1983; MD, Med. Coll. Ohio, 1987. Resident in surgery U. Md., Balt., 1987-92; surg. fellowship Grant Med. Ctr., Columbus, Ohio, 1992-93; asst. prof. surgery Ohio State U., Columbus, 1993—. Fellow Internat. Coll. Surgeons; mem. Soc. Am. Gastroentestinal & Endoscopic Surgeons, Soc. Surgery Alimentary Tract, Assn. Surg. Edn., Alpha Omega Alpha. Office: Ohio State U Dept Surgery 410 W 10th Ave Columbus OH 43210

MELZACK, RONALD, psychology educator; b. Montreal, Que., Can., July 19, 1929; s. Joseph and Annie (Mandel) M.; m. Lucy Birch, Aug. 7, 1960; children: Lauren, Joel. BSc, McGill U., Montreal, 1950, MSc, 1951, PhD, 1954; DLitt (hon.), U. Waterloo, 1992. Lectr. Univ. Coll., London, 1957-58; assoc. prof. MIT, 1959-63; lectr. psychology MdGill U., 1953-54, prof., 1963—; E.P. Taylor prof. McGill U., $D, $D, $D, 1986. Author: The Day Tuk Became a Hunter, and Other Eskimo Stories, 1967, Raven, Creator of the World, 1970, The Puzzle of Pain, 1973, Why the Man in the Moon is Happy, and Other Eskimo Creation Stories, 1977, (with P.D. Wall) The Challenge of Pain, 1982, 2nd edit., 1988, Pain Measurement and Assessment, 1983, (with P.D. Wall) Textbook of Pain, 1984, 3rd edit., 1994, (with D.C. Turk) Handbook of Pain Assessment, 1992. Decorated Officer, Order of Can., 1995; recipient Molson prize Can. Coun., 1985, Gaston Labat award Am. Soc. Regional Anesthesia, 1989, J.J. Bonica award VI World Congress on Pain, 1990, Prix du Que. Marie-Victorin, 1994; recipient Disting. Contbn. award Can. Pain Soc., 1995. Fellow APA, AAAS, Royal Soc. Can., Can. Psychol. Assn. (Disting. Contbns. to Psychol. Sci. award 1986, hon. pres. 1988-89); mem. Internat. Assn. Study of Pain (hon., past pres.), Can. Pain Soc. (Award for Disting. Contbn. to pain rsch. and mgmt. in Can. 1995). Home: 51 Banstead Rd, Montreal, PQ Canada H4X 1P1

MEMMER, MARY MARGARET, nursing educator; b. St. Paul, Apr. 23, 1936; d. Philip Loren and Georgia Mildred (Rose) Kelly; m. David Jay Memmer, June 24, 1972. B.S. in Nursing, U. Nebr., 1958; M. in Nursing Edn., U. Minn., 1960; postgrad. U. Wash., 1966-67. R.N., Calif.; cert. pub. health nurse, Calif. Staff nurse U. Nebr. Hosp., Omaha, 1958-59, U. Minn. Hosp., Mpls., 1959; instr. U. Nebr., Omaha, 1961-62; instr., then asst. prof. U. Mich., Ann Arbor, 1962-66; instr. U. Wash., Seattle, 1967-68; from asst. prof. to prof. nursing Calif. State U.-Chico, 1968-94, prof. emeritus, 1994—. Author of 5 learning modules Intercampus Nursing Project; contbr. articles to profl. jours., chpts. to Nursing Textbook, 1987. Mem. Chico Symphony Orch., 1975—. Grantee U. Mich., 1965, Calif. U. and Coll. System, 1974-75, 73-74, Calif. State U.-Chico, 1977-78, 81, 90, 91, 92; recipient several awards. Mem. U. Nebr. Sch. Nursing Alumnae Assn., Sigma Theta Tau. Democrat. Methodist. Office: Calif State U Dept of Nursing Chico CA 95929-0200

MENA, ALBERTO A., health association manager; b. San Francisco, May 19, 1964; s. Antonio and Mercedes (Fernandez) M.; m. Francisca B., Jan. 2, 1993. MD, U. Den. de la Este, San Pedro de Macoris, Dominican Republic. Cert. physician, Dominican Republic. Physician Pub. Health, Santo Domingo, 1989-90; health mgr. ABCD Head Start, Boston, 1995—; CPR/first aid instr., ARC, Boston, 1995-96; CNA/Home Aid, Mariner Health Care, Methuen, Mass., 1990-95. Home: 109 Nesmith St Apt 3 Lawrence MA 01841

MENANTEAU, BERNARD PAUL, medical educator; b. Angers, France, Apr. 24, 1939; s. Charles and Simone (Deveaux) M.; m. Marie-Therese Puig, Dec. 30, 1976. Diploma in Radiology, U. Paris, 1967; MD, U. Reims, France, 1969. Resident Univ. Hosp., Reims, 1965-69, asst., 1969-74; asst. prof. U. Sherbrooke, Can., 1974-78; prof. diagnostic radiology, chmn. dept. radiology U. Reims, 1978—; expert Supreme Ct. of Appeal, Paris, 1991—; v.p. U. Reims, 1971-74; mem. med. commn. Univ. Hosp., Reims, 1980-95. Co-author: Chest Radiology, 1989; contbr.: Vocabulary of Signs and Symptoms of the Musculo-Skeletal System, 1992. Recipient Decoration, Ministry of Edn., Reims, 1994. Mem. Radiol. Soc. N.Am., Am. Roentgen Ray Soc., French Soc. Radiology (pres. ea. sect. 1992-95). Home: 9 Rue Piper, 51100 Reims France Office: Robert Debre Hospital, Rue General Koenig, 51092 Reims France

MENCHE, DAVID SOLOMON, orthopaedic surgeon; b. Chgo., Mar. 4, 1954; s. Herman and Ann Menche; m. Paula P. Menche, July 3, 1978; children: Livia, Alexa, Julia. BA, Yeshiva U., 1975; MD, NYU, 1979. Diplomate Am. Bd. Orthopaedic Surgery. Gen. surg. intern Beth Israel Hosp., 1979-80; orthopaedic surg. resident Hosp. Joint Diseases Orthopaedic Inst., N.Y.C., 1980-84; attending orthopaedic surgeon Meth. Hosp., 1985; clin. instr. orthopaedics Mt. Sinai Sch. Medicine, 1985; attending surg. staff mem. Beth Israel Med. Ctr., 1985; asst. prof. clin. orthopeduc surgery Med. Ctr. NYU, 1990; former dir. orthopaedics Booth Meml. Med. Ctr., Flushing, N.Y., 1988, asst. dir. dept. rehab., 1989, asst. dir. Inst. Sports Medicine, 1986, chief arthroscopic surgery divsn. orthopaedics, 1987; assoc. dir. sports medicine Hosp. Joint Diseases Orthopaedic Inst., N.Y.C., 1988, med. dir. phys./occupl. therapy, 1992—; A-O Internat. Trauma fellow, Switzerland, 1983; Henry W. Frauenthal Sports Medicine travelling fellow, 1984. Reviewer CLin. Orthopaedics & Related Rsch.; assoc. editor Sports Medicine, 1992-95. Mem. Am. Acad. Orthopaedic Surgery. Office: Sport Ctr 305 2d Ave New York NY 10003-2739

MENCO, BERNARD, biologist; b. Arnhem, The Netherlands, Jan. 9, 1946; came to U.S., 1982; s. A. and A. (Hakkert) M. BSc, Agrl. U., Wageningen, The Netherlands, 1968, MSc, 1972, PhD, 1977. Rsch. officer U. Warwick, Coventry, U.K., 1972-75; sr. rsch. assoc. State U. Utrecht, The Netherlands, 1975-81, Klinikum Essen, Fed. Republic Germany, 1981-82; from rsch. assoc. to rsch. assoc. prof. Northwestern U., Evanston, Ill., 1982—. Contbr. articles to profl. jours.; editor: Microscopy Rsch. and Technique, 1990—. Recipient Takasago award European Chemoreception Orgn., 1990; finalist Hennessey-Moet-Louis Vuitton prize; Hasselblad Found. fellow, 1988. Mem. Am. Chemoreception Orgn., Soc. Neurosci., Soc. Cell Biology. Office: Northwestern U Dept Neurobiol Physiol Evanston IL 60208

MENDEL, MAURICE, audiologist, educator; b. Colorado Springs, Colo., Oct. 6, 1942; married; 3 children. BA, U. Colo., 1965; MS, Washington U., 1967; PhD in Audiology, U. Wis., 1970. Asst. prof. audiology U. Iowa Hosp., 1970-74, assoc. rsch. scientist, 1975-76; assoc. prof. U. Calif., Santa Barbara, 1976-84, prof. audiology, 1984-88; chmn. dept. audiology and speech pathology Memphis State U., 1988-92; dean Sch. Audiology and Speech-Lang. Pathology U. Memphis, 1993—; program dir. speech and hearing sci. U. Calif., Santa Barbara, 1980-82. Fellow Am. Speech-Lang.-Hearing Assn., Soc. Ear Nose and Throat Advance in Children; mem. Am. Acad. Audiology, Internat. Elec. Response Audiology Study Group, Internat. Soc. Audiology, Tenn. Assn. Audiology and Speech-Lang. Pathologists, Sigma Xi. Office: U Memphis CRISCI 807 Jefferson Ave Memphis TN 38105-5042

MENDELOW, ALEXANDER DAVID, neurosurgeon; b. London, May 19, 1946. MB, BCh, Witwatersand U., Johannesburg, S.Africa, 1969, PhD, 1978. Sr. registrar, dept. neurosurgery Gen. Hosp., Edinburgh, Scotland, 1977-80; sr. lectr., dept. neurosurgery Gen. Hosp., Glasgow, Scotland, 1980-86; reader, dept. neurosurgery Gen. Hosp., Newcastle-Upon-Tyne, Eng., 1987-92, prof. neurosurgery, 1992—. Contbr. articles to profl. jours. Fellow Royal Coll. Surgeons; mem. Soc. Brit. Neurosurgeons. Office: Newcastle Gen Hosp, Westgate Rd, Newcastle-Upon-Tyne NE4 6BE, England

MENDELOW, GARY N., physician, emergency consultant; b. Buffalo, N.Y., Sept. 4, 1940; s. Martin and Katherine (Rosenthal) M.; m. Elaine Susan Barron, Mar. 31, 1973; children: Ronald, Raquel. Attended, U. Buffalo, 1958-60; natural science cert., U. Basel, Switzerland, 1962, MD, 1970. Diplomate Am. Bd. Emergency Medicine, 1991. Intern Charity Hosp., New Orleans, La., 1970-71; resident Erie County Med. Ctr., Buffalo, 1972-74; emergency physician Am. Coll. Emergency Physicians, Dallas, 1974—. Fellow Am. Coll. Emergency Physicians; mem. AMA, N.Y. Med. Soc. Jewish. Home: 134 Brandywine Dr Buffalo NY 14221 Office: Twin Cities Physician PE 64 Cleveland Ave Buffalo NY 14222

MENDELS, JOSEPH, psychiatrist, educator; b. Cape Town, Republic of South Africa, Oct. 29, 1937; came to U.S., 1964; s. Max and Lily (Turecki) M.; m. Ora Kark, Jan. 22, 1960; children: Gilla Avril, Charles Alan, David Ralph. MB, ChB, U. Cape Town, 1960; MD, U. Witwatersrand, Johannesburg, Republic of South Africa, 1965. Asst. prof., assoc. prof. psychiatry and pharmacology U. Pa., Phila., 1967-73; prof. U. Pa. and VA Hosp., Phila., 1973-80; med. dir. Fairmount Inst., Phila., 1980-81; prof. psychiatry and human behavior Thomas Jefferson Med. Ctr., 1985—; med. dir. Therapeutics PC Phila. Med. Inst., Phila., 1981—; cons. NIMH, NIH, numerous pharm. cos., 1968—; lectr. to univs. and hosps. worldwide, 1968—. Author, editor: Concepts of Depression, 1971, Biological Psychiatry, 1973, Psychobiology of Affective Disorders, 1981; contbr. over 200 articles to med. jours. Fellow Internat. Coll. Neuropsychopharmacology, Am. Coll. Neuropsychopharmacology, Am. Coll. Clin. Pharmacology; mem. Am. Psychiat. Assn. (Lester N. Hofheimer prize 1976). Office: 9 E Laurel Rd Stratford NJ 08080

MENDELSOHN, FREDRIC ANTHONY, neurologist; b. N.Y.C., June 9, 1946; s. Fred Vincent and Phyllis (Galgano) M.; m. Sonia Maria Conza, June 20, 1971; children: Jason, Adam, Kyle. BA, Hofstra U., 1966, MA, 1970; MD, U. Louisville, 1971. Intern Nassau County Med. Ctr., East Meadow, N.Y., 1971-72, resident in neurology, 1972-75; chmn. utilization com. St. Charles Hosp., Port Jefferson, N.Y., 1976-82; med. dir. ambulatory svcs. St. Charles Hosp., Port Jefferson, 1977-93, med. dir. rehab. dept., 1987-93, pres. med. staff, 1987; chmn. med. care evaluation com. Mather Meml. Hosp., Port Jefferson, 1977-80, chmn. quality assurance com., 1980-86, pres. med. staff, 1985; med. dir. head injury unit St. Johnlands Nursing Ctr., Kings Park, N.Y., 1995—; med. advisor MS Soc., Epilepsy Soc. Bd. dirs. St. Charles Sch. and Therapeutic Ctr., Port Jefferson, 1987—. Fellow Am. Acad. Neurology. Republican. Roman Catholic. Office: 500 Portion Rd Ronkonkoma NY 11779

MENDELSOHN, IRWIN EMANNUEL, psychiatrist, psychoanalyst, educator; b. Jersey City, June 25, 1931; s. Louis and Betty (Yulinsky) M.; m. Barbara B. Berger, June 14, 1953; children—Lawrence N., Steven J., Alan P. B.S., Purdue U., 1952; M.D., SUNY-Bklyn., 1956; cert. in psychoanalysis N.Y. Sch. Psychiatry, 1967. Diplomate Am. Bd. Psychiatry and Neurology. Asst. instr. internal medicine SUNY Downstate Med. Sch., Bklyn., 1959-60; instr. psychiatry N.Y. Sch. Psychiatry, Wards Island, N.Y., 1965-67; practice medicine specializing in psychiatry and psychoanalysis, Jericho, N.Y., 1967—; bd. dir. mental hygiene clinic Nassau County Med. Ctr., East Meadow, N.Y., 1973-76, bd. dir. liaison service, 1976-81, cons. burn ctr., 1981—; asst. clin. prof. psychiatry SUNY-Stony Brook Med. Ctr., 1973—. Contbr. chpt. to book. Capt. U.S. Army, 1960-62. Fellow Acad. Psychosomatic Medicine, 1975, Nassau Acad. Medicine, 1984. Fellow Am. Acad. Psychoanalysis, (Life Fellow) Am. Psychiat. Assn.; mem. Nassau County Med. Soc., Nassau Psychiat. Soc. (bd. dirs. 1988—, chmn. ethics com. 1979-81).

MENDELSOHN, JOHN, oncologist, hematologist, educator; b. Cin., Aug. 31, 1936; s. Joe and Sarah (Feibel) M.; m. Anne Charles, June 23, 1962; children: John Andrew, Jeffrey Charles, Eric Robert. BA, Harvard U., 1958, MD, 1963. Diplomate Am. Bd. Internal Medicine, Am. Bd. Hematology, Am. Bd. Med. Oncology. Intern, resident Peter Bent Brigham Hosp., Boston, 1963-65, 67-68; fellow in hematology Washington U. Sch. Medicine, St. Louis, 1968-70; asst. prof. to prof. medicine U. Calif., La Jolla, 1970-85, Am. Cancer Soc. prof. clin. oncology, 1982-85, dir. Cancer Ctr., 1977-85; prof. medicine Cornell U. Med. Coll., N.Y.C., 1985-96; chmn. dept. medicine Meml. Sloan Kettering Cancer Ctr., N.Y.C., 1985-96; pres., prof. medicine U. Tex. M.D. Anderson Cancer Ctr., Houston, 1996—; mem. bd. sci. counselors divsn. cancer treatment Nat. Cancer Inst., 1986-90; bd. dirs. Am. Assn. Cancer Rsch.; cons. Hybritech, Genentech, Immunex, Im Clone, Prism, Bristol-Myers; founder, 1st dir. U. Calif. San Diego Cancer Ctr. Editor-in-chief: (textbook) The Molecular Basis of Cancer; mem. editl. bd. Jour. Immunology, Blood, Cancer Rsch., Jours. Clin. Oncology, Gworth Factors; editor-in-chief Clin. Cancer Rsch.; contbr. numerous articles in field of oncology to profl. jours. Mem. Gov.'s Cancer Adv. Coun., Calif., 1982-85; bd. dirs. Am. Cancer Soc., San Diego, 1981-85. Officer USPHS, 1965-67. Fulbright scholar U. Glasgow, Scotland, 1958-59; named Headliner of Yr. in Medicine, San Diego, 1985. Mem. Assn. Am. Physicians, Am. Soc. Clin. Investigation, Am. Soc. Clin. Oncology, Am. Assn. Cancer Rsch., Am. Soc. Hematology, Century Assn., Harvard Club N.Y., Phi Beta Kappa, Alpha Omega Alpha. Office: U Tex MD Anderson Cancer Ctr 1515 Holcombe Blvd Houston TX 77030

MENDENHALL, CARROL CLAY, physician; b. Missouri Valley, Iowa, July 26, 1916; s. Clay and Maude (Watts) M.; student U. So. Calif., 1942-44, Chapman Coll., 1946-47, Los Angeles City Coll., 1947-48; D.O., Coll. Osteo. Physicians and Surgeons, 1952; M.D., Calif. Coll. Medicine, 1962; m. Lucille Yvonne Bonvouloir, June 14, 1946 (div. July 1957); 1 son, Gregory Bruce; m. 2d, Barbara Marilyn Huggett-Davis, Sept. 28, 1974. Intern, Los Angeles County Osteo. Hosp., 1952-53; gen. practice medicine, 1953-82, specializing in weight control, Gardena, Calif., 1961-74, specializing in stress disorders and psychosomatic medicine, Ft. Worth, 1974-78, specializing in integral medicine and surgery, Santa Clara, Calif., 1978—; med. dir. Green's Pharms., Long Beach, Calif., 1956-64; v.p. Internat. Pharm. Mfg. Co., Inc., San Pedro, Calif., 1965-66; pres. Chemico of Gardena, Inc., 1964-69; staff Gardena Hosp.; active staff O'Connor Hosp., San Jose, Calif., 1979—; tchr., lectr. biofeedback, prevention and treatment of stress, creative thought; founder, dir. Eclectic Weight Control Workshop, 1971-74, Longevity Learning, Longevity Learning Seminars, 1980; past mem. adv. bd. dirs. L.A. Nat. Bank. Cadre med. dir. Gardena Civil Def., 1953-54, asst. to chief med. dir., 1954-60, chief med. and first aid services, 1960-64. Served as pharmacist's mate USNR, 1944-46. Fellow Royal Soc. Health, Am. Acad. Med. Preventics, Am. Acad. Homeopathic Medicine; mem. Calif. Med. Assn., Santa Clara County Med. Soc., Acupuncture Research Inst. (also alumni assn.), Los Aficionados de Los Angeles (pres. 1964-66), Am. Soc. Clin. Hypnosis. Flamenco Soc. No. Calif. (bd. dirs. 1986—). Address: 1653 Milroy Pl San Jose CA 95124-4723

MENDES, ROBERT WARNER, pharmaceutical educator and company executive; b. Fall River, Mass., Apr. 6, 1938; s. Manuel John and Ethel (Potter) M.; m. Catherine Burgess, Aug. 27, 1960; 1 child, Cheryl Ann. BS in Pharmacy, Northeastern U., 1960; MS, U. N.C., 1964, PhD, 1966. Lic. pharmacist, Mass., N.C. Prof., chair pharmaceutics and indsl. pharmacy Mass. Coll. Pharmacy, Boston, 1965-92, adj. prof., 1992—; v.p. regulatory affairs, dir. new tech. Ascent Pharms. Inc., Billerica, Mass., 1992—; cons. in field, 1971—; mem. editorial adv. bd. Pharm. Tech.; presenter in field. Contbr. articles to profl. publs., chpts. to books. Mem. Mansfield (Mass.) Planning Bd., 1967-73, chair, 1969-73; mem. Southeastern Regional Planning and Econ. Devel. Commn., Mass., 1968-73, chair, 1970; mem. Mansfield Charter Commn., 1972. Mem. Am. Assn. Pharm. Scientists, Soc. Cosmetic Chemists (chair New Eng. chpt. 1980, 93), Regulatory Affairs Profls. Soc., Food and Drug Law Inst. Office: Ascent Pharms Inc 9 Linnell Cir Billerica MA 01821-3902

MENDEZ, C. BEATRIZ, obstetrician, gynecologist; b. Guatemala, Apr. 21, 1952; d. Jose and Olga (Sobalvarro) M.; m. Mark Parshall, Dec. 12, 1986. BS in Biology and Psychology, Pa. State U., 1974; MD, Milton Hershey Coll. Medicine, 1979. Diplomate Am. Bd. Ob-gyn. Resident in ob-gyn. George Washington U., Washington, 1979-83; pvt. practice Santa Fe, 1985-95, Locum Tenens, 1996—; vol. physician Women's Health Svcs., Santa Fe, 1995—; chair perinatal com. St. Vincent's Hosp., Santa Fe, 1986-89, quality assurance mem., 1986—, chief ob-gyn., 1992-94; bd. dirs. Milton S. Hershey Coll. Medicine, Hershey, Pa., 1977-82. Vol. Women's Health Svcs., Santa Fe, 1985—. With USPHS, 1983-85. Mosby scholar Mosby-Hersey Med. Sch., Hershey, 1979. Fellow Am. Coll. Ob-Gyn. (Continuing Med. Edn. award 1986—); mem. AMA (Physician Recognition award 1986—), Am. Assn. Gynecol. Laparascopists, Internat. Soc. Gynecol. Endoscopy, Am. Fertility Soc., Am. Soc. Colposcopy and Cervical Pathology, N.Mex. Med. Soc., Santa Fe Med. Soc., Residents Assn. George Washington U. (co-founder 1981-83). Democrat.

MENDEZ, HERMANN ARMANDO, pediatrician, educator; b. Guatemala, Apr. 26, 1949; came to U.S., 1980; citizen of El Salvador; s. Hermann and Martha (Abularach) Mendez Fortun; m. Maria Elena Ortiz, Feb. 23, 1971; children: Natalia, Amalia. MD, U. El Salvador, 1977. Diplomate Am. Bd. Pediatrics, Am. Bd. Pediatric Infectious Diseases. Asst. prof. pediatrics Health Sci. Ctr. SUNY, Bklyn., 1988-91, assoc. prof., 1991—. Recipient Asst. Sec. for Health award USPHS, 1990, United U. Professions Excellence awardHealth Sci. Ctr., Bklyn., 1991. Fellow Am. Acad. Pediatrics, Infectious Disease Soc. of Am. Office: SUNY HSCB Dept Pediatrics Box 49 450 Clarkson Ave Brooklyn NY 11203-2012

MENDLOWSKI, BRONISLAW, retired pathologist; b. Tarnopol, Poland, June 28, 1914; came to U.S., 1948; s. Eugeniusz and Kazimiera (Zielinski) M.; m. Zita Pawlowski, Apr. 16, 1926 (dec. 1988); children: Jerry, Michael, Anna. DVM, U. Lwow, Poland, 1944; MRCVS, U. Edinburgh, Scotland, 1947; MS (hon.), U. Ill., Urbana, 1963. Pathologist W. Scotland Agr. Coll., 1945-46, Wis. State Diagnostic Lab., 1951-60, U. Ill., Urbana, 1960-63; sr. rsch. fellow in pathology Merck Inst. for Therapeutic Rsch., West Point, Pa., 1963-84; ret., 1984. Contbr. articles to profl. jours. Mem. N.Y. Acad. Sci. Roman Catholic. Home: 215 Cornwall Dr Chalfont PA 18914-2319

MENDOZA, HARRIET H., social worker; b. N.Y.C.; children: Alison Tave, Richard Mendoza. AB, Smith Coll., Northampton, Mass., 1943; MSW, Smith Coll., 1960. Cert. social worker, N.Y. Supr. Suffolk County Dept. Social Svcs., Hauppauge, N.Y.; intake social worker L.I. Jewish-Hillside Med. Ctr., Glen Oaks, N.Y.; sr. caseworker Jewish Community Svcs. L.I., Smithtown, N.Y.; sch. social worker BOCES III, Dix Hills, N.Y.; pvt. practice Cold Spring Harbor. Mem. Nat. Assn. Social Workers (past pres.), N.Y. State Soc. Clin. Social Wk. Psychotherapists (fellow), Acad. Cert. Social Workers, Am. Bd. Examiners Clin. Social Work (bd. cert. diplomate). Home: 10 Erick Ct Cold Spring Harbor NY 11724-1901

MENDOZA, SALLY PATRICIA, psychology educator; b. Santa Fe, Sept. 24, 1951; d. David John Rhodes and Jennifer Margaret (Fields) Peacock; m. Israel David Mendoza, June 22, 1971 (div. Feb. 1974). Student, Wash. State U., 1969-71; BA, The Evergreen State Coll., 1974; PhD with distinction, Stanford U., 1978. Research assoc. Stanford (Calif.) U., 1978, 80-81; instr. The Evergreen State Coll., Olympia, Wash., 1979-80; postdoctoral fellow U. Calif., Davis, 1981-84, asst. research scientist, 1984-90, asst. prof. psychology, 1986-90, assoc. prof. psychology, assoc. research scientist, 1990-94; prof. psychology, rsch. scientist U. Calif. Primate Rsch. Ctr., Davis, 1994—; leader behavioral & neurobiology unit Calif. Regional Primate Rsch. Ctr. U. Calif., 1996—; bd. sci. counselors Nat. Inst. Child Health & Human Devel., 1995—. Co-editor: Social Conesion: Essays Toward a Sociophysiological Perspective, Primate Social Conflict; book rev. editor Am. Jour. Primatology, 1991-93, cons. editor, 1991-92, assoc. editor, 1992—; assoc. editor Aggressive Behavior, 1993—, Jour. Comparative Psychology, 1994—; contbr. articles to jours. and chpts. to books. Organizer United Farm Workers Union, Dallas, 1971-72. Recipient Nat. Research Service award Nat. Inst. Child Health and Human Devel., 1981-84; William Caldwell Young Mem. fellow West Coast Sex Soc., 1977, Biol. Scis. Tng., NIMH, 1974-77. Fellow APA; mem. AAAS, Am. Soc. Primatologists (program chair 1986-88, chair local arrangements 1990), Animal Behavior Soc., Internat. Primatol. Soc. (sec. gen. 1992—), Psychonomic Soc., Sigma Xi. Office: U Calif Primate Rsch Ctr Davis CA 95616

MENDOZA, STANLEY ATRAN, pediatric nephrologist, educator; b. Pitts., May 7, 1940; s. Joseph William and Marian Ruth (Atran) M.; m. Carole Ann Klein, June 23, 1963; children: Daniel, Joseph. Student, Harvard U., 1957-59; B.A., Johns Hopkins U., 1961, M.D., 1964. Diplomate: Am. Bd. Pediatrics. Intern Johns Hopkins Hosp., Balt., 1964-65; jr. asst. resident dept. medicine Children's Hosp. Med. Ctr., Boston, 1965-66; asst. attending physician, dir. renal rsch. labs Children's Meml. Hosp., Chgo., 1969-71; asst. prof. pediatrics Sch. Medicine U. Calif., San Diego, 1971-73; assoc. prof. Sch. Medicine U. Calif., 1973-79, prof. pediatrics, dept. pediatrics, div. pediatric nephrology, 1979—, vice chmn. dept. pediatrics, 1986-87, chmn. dept. pediatrics, 1992—. Contbr. article in field to profl. publ. Served With USPHS, 1966-69. Fogarty Sr. Internat. fellow, 1978-79; Alan J. Wurtzburger research scholar, 1964; recipient Johns Hopkins Med. Soc. award, 1964, hon. mention Borden Undergrad. research award in medicine, 1964; Eleanor Roosevelt internat. fellow Internat. Union Against Cancer, 1984-85. Mem. Am. Fedn. Clin. Research, Am. Pediatric Soc., Am. Physiol. Soc., Am. Soc. Nephrology, Am. Soc. Pediatric Nephrology, Internat. Soc. Nephrology. Office: U Calif San Diego Dept Pediatrics 200 W Arbor Dr San Diego CA 92103-1911

MENDOZA SANTOYO, FERNANDO, research facility administrator, consultant; b. Silao, Guanajuato, Mex., July 29, 1956; arrived in Eng., 1981; s. Fernando Mendoza Morfin and Maria Teresa (Santoyo Gonzales) De M.; m. Ana Gema Guevara Aguilar, May 9, 1981; children: Fernando, Ana Sofia. BSc in Physics, Met. U., Mexico City, 1980; MSc in Applied Optics, U. London, 1982; PhD in Interferometry, Loughborough (Eng.) U., 1988. Registered profl. engr., Eng. Rsch. scientist Optical Rsch. Ctr., Leon, Mex., 1983-84; rsch. fellow Loughborough U., 1984-91; cons. CMP Tech., Wantage, Eng., 1990, Brit. Aerospace, Bristol, Eng., 1990-91, Rolls Royce Motor Cars, Crewe, Eng., 1990-91, Glaxo/Fisons, Eng., 1991. Contbr. articles to profl. jours. UNESCO scholar, 1981, Brit. Coun. scholar, 1984, Consejo Nacional Ciencia Tecnologia Optica scholar, 1984; Sci. and Engring. Rsch. Coun. grantee, 1987-91. Mem. Internat. Soc. Optical Engrs., Imperial Coll. Alumni Assn. Roman Catholic. Home: Paseo de Las Flores 141, CP 37210 Leon, Guanajuato Mexico Office: Optical Rsch Ctr, Centro Investigaciones Optica, AC Postal 948 37000 Leon Mexico

MENDUKE, HYMAN, biostatistics educator; b. Warsaw, Poland, Aug. 20, 1921; came to U.S., 1923; s. Aaron and Ethel (Fox) M.; m. Phyllis Bonow Hirsch, Apr. 14, 1946 (dec. July 1985); 1 child, Judith Menduke Schwartz; m. Clara Gochin Wolinsky, July 19, 1987. AB, U. Pa., 1943, MA, 1948, PhD, 1952. Instr. social and economic stats. U. Pa., Phila., 1947-53; from asst. to assoc. prof. biostats. Thomas Jefferson U., Phila., 1953-63, prof. community health and preventive medicine, 1963-79, prof. pharmacology (biostats.), 1978-92, hon. prof. pharmacology biostats., 1992—; dir. sponsored programs Med. Coll., 1965-83; lectr. statis. evaluation clin. data Phila. Coll. Pharmacy Sci., 1975-83, adj. prof., 1983-92; vis. prof. Phila. Coll. Osteo. Medicine, 1990—; cons. in field. Contbr. articles to profl. jours. Staff sgt. U.S. Army, 1942-46. Fellow Coll. Physicians of Phila.; mem. Am. Statis. Assn. (pres. Phila. chpt., nat. rep.), Biometric Soc., Jefferson Med. Coll. Alumni Assn. (hon. life), Pi Gamma Mu, Phi Mu Epsilon, Sigma Xi (past pres. Thomas Jefferson Univ. chpt.). Home: 460 Leonard Rd Huntingdon Valley PA 19006-2370

MENDYKA, WALTER ADAM, JR., pharmacist; b. Cleve., Mar. 22, 1955; s. Walter Adam Sr. and Frances Jean (Toth) M. BS in Zoology, Ohio State U., 1977, BS in Pharmacy, 1982. Staff pharmacist Cleve. Apothe Care, 1982-84, 88-91; mgr., pharmacist Gray Drug Fair Inc., 1984-87; staff pharmacist Gray Drug Fair Inc., Cleve., 1984-87; pharmacy mgr. Apothe-Care, Cleve., 1996—; cons. pharmacist Benedictine H.S., Cleve., 1988—, Cleve. Cavaliers NBA Team, 1989—, Balt. Ravens NFL Team, 1996—; team pharmacist Cleve. Browns NFL Team, 1988-96. Roman Catholic. Home: 6725 Bonna Ave Cleveland OH 44103-1521 Office: Apothe-Care 11201 Shaker Blvd Cleveland OH 44104

MENE, MATTHEW PUGLIESE, urologist, surgeon; b. Queens, N.Y., Feb. 19, 1965; s. Albert J. and Patrician P. (Pugliese) M.; m. Susan E. Zunitch, July 21, 1989; children: Elizabeth, Ashley. BS, N.Y. Inst. Tech., 1987; DO, N.Y. Coll. Osteo. Medicine, 1990; MSc, Phila. Coll. Osteo. Medicine, 1996. Intern Massaequa Gen. Hosp., Seaford, N.Y., 1990-91; resident Phila. Coll. Osteo. Med., 1991-96. Contbr. articles to profl. jours. Mem. Am. Coll. Osteo. Surgeons (resident achievement award 1994), Am. Osteo. Assn. (grantee 1994), Ohio Osteo. Assn. Republican. Roman Catholic. Home: 1959 Redwood Dr Defiance OH 43512 Office: Defiance Clinic 1400 E Second St Defiance OH 43512

MENEGAZ, RENÉE MARIE, anatomy educator and researcher; b. Pitts., Nov. 2, 1927; d. Peter Angelo and Pauline Rina (Scavino) M.; m. R. Darrell Bock, Sept. 27, 1952; children: Conrad Edmond, Monica Marie, Paul Sohn. MA, U. Chgo., 1956, PhD, 1968. Lectr., rsch. assoc. dept. anatomy U. Chgo., 1965—. Roman Catholic. Office: U Chgo 1027 E 57th St Chicago IL 60637-1508

MENG, HEINZ KARL, biology educator; b. Baden, Republic of Germany, Feb. 25, 1924; came to U.S., 1929; s. Richard Ludwig and Elise (Merkel) M.; m. Elizabeth Agnes Metz, June 20, 1953; children: Robin Elizabeth, Peter-Paul. BS, Cornell U., 1947, PhD, 1951. Cert. tchr. ornithology, entomology, vertebrate zoology. Biology prof. SUNY, New Paltz, 1951—; dir. No. Am. Falconers' Assn., 1967-76. Author: Falcons Return, 1975, revised edit., 1992; pioneer in field of in-captivity breeding of Peregrine falcons. Grantee SUNY, 1957, 58, 61, NSF, 1967, IBM, 1980, 82, 83, 85, 86, 87, 88, 91, 93, Eppley Found. Rsch., 1993. Fellow Explorers Club; mem. Am. Ornithologists Union, Wilson Ornithological Soc., Cooper Ornithological Soc., New Paltz Peregrine Falcon Found. (pres. 1977—), Wildlife Soc. Home: 10 Joalyn Rd New Paltz NY 12561-2115 Office: SUNY Dept Biology New Paltz NY 12561

MENGIS, CHRIS LUDWIG, retired internist; b. Monroe, La., July 6, 1924; s. Chris L. and Elizabeth Josephine (Winzerling) M.; children: Robert, Elizabeth, Miranda, Matilda, Sophie (dec.). MD, Tulane U. Rsch. asst. JTF-1, 1946; intern Madigan Army Hosp., Tacoma, Wash., 1951-52; surgeon 370th Amphibious Brigade, Ft. Sherman, Canal Zone, 1952-53; resident in internal medicine Brooke Army Hosp., Fort Sam Houston, Tex., 1953-55; asst. chief medicine Post Hosp., Fort Jay, N.Y., 1955-59; pvt. practice San Juan Clinic, Farmington, N.Mex., 1959-60, St. Vincent Hosp., Santa Fe, N.Mex., 1960-79; asst. chief internal medicine Walla Walla (Wash.) VA Hosp., 1980-93; ret., 1993—. Contbr. articles to profl. jours. Bd. dirs. N.Mex. Tuberculosis Assn., Santa Fe; active Santa Fe Vol. Fire Dept.; pres. Santa Fe Cmty. Coun., 1964. Capt. U.S. Army Med. Corps, 1956-59. Democrat. Home: PO Box 149 Athena OR 97813

MENITOFF, PAUL ALAN, psychiatrist; b. Boston, May 4, 1946; s. Ralph and Ethel (Bickoff) M.; m. Susan Mathilde Hirsch, June 8, 1980. BA cum laude, Harvard U., 1969; MD, Cornell U., 1973. Diplomate Am. Bd. Psychiatry and Neurology. Intern in surgery Univ. Hosp., Boston, 1973-74; psychiat. resident Payne Whitney Clinic N.Y. Hosp./Cornell Med. Ctr., N.Y.C., 1974-77; forensic psychiat. fellow U. So. Calif./L.A. County Med. Ctr., 1977-78; forensic psychiat. fellow Med. Sch. U. Md., Balt., 1978-79; staff psychiatrist Clifton T. Perkins Hosp., Jessup, Md., 1978-80; mem. med. staff St. John's Hosp., Lowell, Mass., 1980—, St. Joseph's Hosp., Lowell, 1980-93; mem. med. staff Lowell Gen. Hosp., 1993—, chief dept. psychiatry, 1996—; pvt. practice, Chelmsford, Mass., 1980—; clin. inst. psychiatry U. So. Calif. Med. Sch., L.A., 1977-78; clin. asst. prof. psychiatry U. Md. Med. Sch., Balt., 1979-80. Mem. Am. Psychiat. Assn., Mass. Psychiat. Assn., Acad. Psychosomatic Medicine, Am. Acad. Psychiatry and the Law, Mass. Med. Soc. Democrat. Office: Greater Lowell Psychiat Assocs 9 Acton Rd Chelmsford MA 01824-3411

MENKES, ALAN LEWIS, financial consultant; b. Bklyn., Jan. 30, 1943; s. William B. and Olga (Rapoport) M.; m. Laura Lynn Mattison, Dec. 21, 1990; 1 child, Alexandra Holden Rose; children by previous marriage: Daniel L., Adam L., Alexander L., David B., Jonathan A. DO, Phila. Coll. Osteo. Medicine, 1967; MA, Claremont (Calif.) Grad. Sch., 1989; MD, Columbia Coll. Medicine, Turks, Caicos, 1989. Diplomate Am. Bd. Internal Medicine. Intern Botsford Gen. Hosp., Farmington, Mich., 1967-68; resident in internal medicine S.E. Med. Ctr., North Miami, Fla., 1969-72; pres., CEO Inland Hypertension Med. Group, Claremont, 1977-88; prof., chmn. dept. medicine Coll. Osteo. Medicine of Pacific, Pomona, Calif., 1977-88; sr. fin. cons. Lexington Capital Mgmt., Gold River, Calif., 1995—; exec. v.p. Bowles & Assocs., Laguna Beach, Calif.; cons. Dept. Consumer Affairs, Calif., 1977—; mem. adv. bd. Vineyard Nat. Bancorp., Rancho Cucamonga, 1993—; mem. alumni coun. Claremont Grad. Sch., 1993—. Contbr. articles to profl. jours. Mediator Claremont Dispute Resolution Ctr., Glendora, Calif., 1988. Study grantee Norwich-Eaton Labs., 1966. Fellow Am. Coll. Internists. Office: Bowles & Assocs 219 Broadway Ste 514 Laguna Beach CA 92651

MENNIN, GERALD STANLEY, ophthalmologist; b. N.Y.C., Mar. 20, 1932; s. Daniel and Sadie (Krieger) M.; 1 child, Danielle. BA, NYU, 1954; MD, SUNY, N.Y.C. Intern Beth Israel Hosp., N.Y.C., 1958-59; resident Bronx Mcpl. Hosp. Ctr./Einstein Coll. Medicine, 1050-62; pvt. practice Yonkers; chief ophthalmology Yonkers Gen. Hosp., 1986—; attending ophthalmologist Montefiore Hosp., Bronx, 1962—, Bronx Mcpl. Hosp., 1962—, St. John's Hosp., Yonkers, 1981—, Yonkers Gen. Hosp., 1962—, Manhattan Eye and Ear Hosp., N.Y.C., 1990—. Fellow ACS, Am. Acad. Ophthalmologists, Nat. Arts Club. Office: 45 Ludlow St Yonkers NY 10705-1947

MENNINGER, WILLIAM WALTER, psychiatrist; b. Topeka, Oct. 23, 1931; s. William Claire and Catharine Louisa (Wright) M.; m. Constance Arnold Libbey, June 15, 1953; children: Frederick Prince, John Alexander, Eliza Wright, Marian Stuart, William Libbey, David Henry. A.B., Stanford U., 1953; M.D., Cornell U., 1957; LittD (hon.), Middlebury Coll., 1982; DSc (hon.), Washburn U., 1982; LHD (hon.), Ottawa U., 1986; LLD (hon.), Heidelberg Coll., 1993. Diplomate: Am. Bd. Psychiatry and Neurology, Am. Bd. Forensic Psychiatry. Intern Harvard Med. Service, Boston City Hosp., 1957-58; resident in psychiatry Menninger Sch. Psychiatry, 1958-61; chief med. officer, psychiatrist Fed. Reformatory, El Reno, Okla., 1961-63; assoc. psychiatrist Peace Corps, 1963-64; staff psychiatrist Menninger Found., Topeka, 1965—, coordinator for devel., 1967-69, dir. law and psychiatry, 1981-85, dir. dept. edn., dean Karl Menninger Sch. Psychiatry and Mental Health Scis., 1984-90, exec. v.p., chief of staff, 1984-93; pres., chief exec. officer Menninger Found., 1993—; clin. supr. Topeka State Hosp., 1969-70, sect. dir., 1970-72, asst. supt., clin., dir. residency tng., 1972-81; pres., chief exec. officer Menninger Clinic, Topeka, 1991—; staff Stormont-Vail Hosp., Topeka, 1984-94, assoc., 1994—; clin. prof. Kans. U. Med. Coll.; adj. prof. Washburn U., Wichita State U.; instr. Topeka Inst. for Psychoanalysis; mem. adv. bd. Nat. Inst. Corrections, 1975-88 , chmn., 1980-84; cons. U.S. Bur. Prisons; mem. Fed. Prison Facilities Planning Council, 1970-73; bd. dirs. Mercantile Bank Topeka (formerly Mchts. Nat. Bank, Topeka). Syndicated columnist: In-Sights, 1975-83; author: Happiness Without Sex and Other Things Too Good to Miss, 1976, Caution: Living May Be Hazardous, 1978, Behavioral Science and the Secret Service, 1981, Chronic Mental Patient II, 1987; editor: Psychiatry Digest, 1971-74; mem. editorial bd. Bull. Menninger Clinic, 1985—; contbr. chpts. to books, articles to profl. jours. Mem. nat. health and safety com. Boy Scouts Am., 1970-92, chmn., 1980-85, mem. nat. exec. bd., 1980-90, mem. nat. adv. coun., 1990—; mem. Kans. Gov.'s Adv. Commn. on Mental Health, Mental Retardation and Community Mental Health Svcs., 1983-90; bd. dirs. Nat. Com. for Prevention Child Abuse, 1975-83; mem. nat. adv. health coun. HEW, 1967-71; mem. Nat. Commn. Causes and Prevention Violence 1968-69, Kans. Gov.'s Penal Planning Coun., 1970; chmn. Kans. Gov.'s Criminal Justice Adv. Commn., 1991-94, rsch. adv. com. U.S. Secret Svc., 1990—; trustee Kenworthy-Swift Found., 1980—; ruling elder 1st Presbyn. Ch., Topeka, 1992-95; active Ks. Gov.'s Commn. on Crime Reduction and Prevention/ Koch Commn. 1994—; dir. Police Found., Washington, 1996—; trustee Midwest Rsch. Inst., Kansas City, Mo., 1996—. With USPHS, 1959-64. Fellow ACP, Am. Psychiat. Assn. (chmn. com. on chronically mentally ill 1984-86, chmn. Guttmacher award bd. 1990-96), Am. Coll. Psychiatrists; mem. AAAS, AMA, Group for Advancement of Psychiatry (chmn. com. mental health svcs. 1974-77, 91—), Inst. Medicine NAS, Am. Psychoanalytic Assn. (chmn. com. on psychoanalysis, community and society 1984-93), Am. Acad. Psychiatry and Law, Stanford (Univ.) Assocs. Office: Menninger Found PO Box 829 Topeka KS 66601-0829

MENNUTI, MICHAEL THOMAS, medical educator; b. Trenton, N.J., Nov. 10, 1942; m. Nancy Lee Cleary, 1965; children: Jonathan Robert, Cara Elizabeth. BS, Georgetown U., 1964, MD, 1968. Diplomate Am. Bd. Ob-Gyn (dir. divsn. maternal-fetal medicine 1991-94, bd. dirs. 1996—), Maternal Fetal Medicine, Clin. Genetics, Clin. Cytogenetics. Asst. instr. ob-gyn. Hosp. of U. Pa., Phila., 1969-73; clin. instr. ob-gyn. Wash. U. Sch. Med., Tacoma, 1974-75; asst. prof. ob-gyn. U. Pa. Sch. Medicine, Phila., 1975-81, asst. prof. human genetics, pediat., 1978-81, assoc. prof. ob-gyn. & human genetics, pediat., 1981-86, dir. residency tng., prof. ob-gyn. & human genetics, pediat., chmn. dept. ob-gyn., 1986—. Contbr. chpts. to books. Fellow Am. Coll. Ob-Gyn. (chmn., vice chmn., program chmn., sec. Dist. III 1978-95, chmn. Dist. III 1992-95, chmn. com. ob practice 1994-96), Coll. Physicians of Phila., Am. Gynecol. and Obstet. Soc.; mem. Am. Soc. Human Genetics, Am. Coll. Med. Genetics (founding), Alpha Omega Alpha. Office: U Pa Hosp Dept Ob-Gyn 3400 Spruce St Philadelphia PA 19104

MENSCER, DARLYNE, physician; b. Mooresville, N.C., Sept. 19, 1953; d. Darrell Vance and Margaret Carolyn (Westmoreland) M. BA in Biology, Wake Forest U., 1975; MD, U. N.C., 1979. Intern, resident in family practice Charlotte (N.C.) Meml. Hosp., 1982, asst. dir. family practice residency program, 1982-84, assoc. program dir., 1984-90, dir. geriatric edn., 1990—; advisor med. ethics TV program, Charlotte, 1984—; com. chmn. Caregiver Support Program of Affordable Care for Elderly, Charlotte, 1986—. Fellow Am. Acad. Family Practice; mem. AMA, N.C. Med. Soc., Mecklenburg Family Practice Assn. (pres. 1986, sec.-treas. 1987), Soc. Tchrs. Family Medicine, Mecklenburg County Med. Soc. (pres. 1996). Democrat. Presbyterian. Home: 6909 Brandenburt Ct Charlotte NC 28210 Office: Carolinas Med Ctr PO Box 32861 Charlotte NC 28232-2861

MENTA, DOMINIC, retired pediatrician; b. Phila., Oct. 2, 1923; s. Salvatore and Angelina (Buccheri) M.; m. Edith Harveson, 1954; children: Michael, Timothy. BA, U. Pa., 1948; MD, Hahnemann U., 1953. Diplomate Am. Bd. Pediatrics. Pediatric practice Drexel Hill, Pa., 1957-73; group practice Pediatric Med. Assocs., Havertown, Pa., 1973-89; bd. dirs. Delaware County Child Day Care Assn., 1970-89. Sgt. U.S. Army Air Corps, 1942-45, PTO. Mem. Am. Acad. Pediat., Phila. Pediat. Soc. (exec. bd. 1974-75). Home: 1620 Valley Dr Venice FL 34292

MENTER, M(ARTIN) ALAN, dermatologist; b. Doncaster, Eng., Oct. 30, 1941; came to U.S., 1975; s. Harry Menter and Esme (Green) Behr; m. Pamela Mary Williams, Dec. 4, 1966; children: Keith, Colin, Keith. MB Bch, U. Witwatersrand, 1966; MMed in Dermatology, U. Pretoria, 1971. Diplomate Am. Bd. Dermatology. Intern medicine then dept. surgery Johannesburg (Republic South Africa) Gen. Hosp., 1967, sr. intern medicine and dermatology, 1968; resident in dermatology U. Pretoria and Pretoria Gen. Hosp., 1968-71; sr. resident in dermatology Guy's Hosp., London, 1972; sr. resident, tutor in dermatology St. John's Hosp. for Disease of Skin, London, 1972-73; cons. dermatologist Pretoria Gen. Hosp., 1973-75; dermatologist Baylor U. Med. Ctr., Dallas, 1975—; chmn. div. dermatology Baylor U. Med. Ctr., 1992—; med. dir. Nat. Psoriasis Found. Tissue Bank, Dallas, 1993—; clin. prof. dermatology U. Tex. Southwestern Med. Sch., 1996—; fellow dept. dermatology U. Tex. Southwestern Med. Sch., Dallas, 1977-79, assoc. clin. prof. dermatology, 1977-95; med. dir. Psoriasis Ctr., Baylor U. Med. Ctr., Dallas, 1979—; clin. assoc. prof. dept. periodontics Baylor Coll. Dentistry, Dallas, 1985—; presenter local, state and nat. dermatol. orgns. and teaching programs. Editorial bd. Jour. Am. Acad. Dermatology, 1993—; contbr. numerous articles to profl. jours., chpts. to books. Coach Rugby football team U. Pretoria, 1974; represented S. Africa Nat. Rugby football team, 1968; coach. commr. Boys Under 12 Classic League Soccer, Dallas, 1978-82; active various local civic organizations and coms. Recipient Clin. Rsch. award Imperial Chem. Industries, 1972-73. Mem. AMA, Acad. Dermatology (com. on psoriasis 1988-93, chmn. 1990-93, com. on stds. care for psoriasis 1988-92, chmn. 1989-92, dir. Psoriasis Symposium 1990-93, bd. dirs. 1995—), Am. Acad. Dermatol. Surgery, Brit. Assn. Dermatology, Dallas County Med. Soc. (med. student rels. com. 1989-94), Dallas Dermatol. Soc. (sec.-treas. 1979, pres. 1980, rep. to adv. coun. Am. Acad. Dermatology 1987-89), Dermatol. Therapy Assn. (pres. 1985), Tex. Dermatol. Soc. (program coord. 1987-93, pres. 1995-96), Tex. Med. Assn. (subcom. on joint sponsorship 1992-95). Home: 5230 Royal Ln Dallas TX 75229 Office: Tex Dermatology Assocs Tullhill Office Park W 5310 Harvest Hill Ste 260 Dallas TX 75230

MENTGEN, JANET LEE, nursing educator; b. Hartford, Conn., Dec. 18, 1938; d. William E. and Bobbie Lee (Odom) Flint; m. Glen A. Mentgen, Sept. 27, 1963; children: William Paul, Lynn Allison, Lisa Christine. BSN, U. Colo., 1961. Dir. nursing Western Home Health, Arvada, Colo., 1982-85; program adminstr. Health Control Ctr., Denver, Colo., 1984-89; pres., program dir. Prin. Colo. Ctr. for Healing Touch, Inc., Lakewood, Colo., 1989-95; instr. Red Rocks C.C. Lt. j.g. USN, 1961-63. Named Nurse of Yr. Am. Holistic Nurses Assn., 1988. Mem. Am. Holistic Nurses Assn. (bd. dirs., program adminstr.), Nurse-Healers Profl. Assocs., ANA. Home: 14951 W 76th Dr Arvada CO 80007

MENTZ, HENRY A., III, plastic surgeon; b. New Orleans, Apr. 9, 1958; s. Henry A. Jr. and Ann (Lamantia) M.; m. Paula Comiskey, May 20, 1989; children: Henry A. IV, James August. BS, La. State U., 1980, MD, 1984. Diplomage Am. Bd. Facial Plastic Surgery, Otolaryngology, Plastic Surgery. Intern otolaryngology Tulane U., New Orleans, 1984-89; resident plastic surgery St. Joseph's Hosp., Houston, 1989-91; plastic surgeon Aesthetic Plastic Surgeons, Houston, 1991—; clin. assoc. prof. Baylor U., Houston, 1992—, St. Joseph U., Houston, 1992—; chief surgery Sharpstown Gen. Hosp., Houston, 1994—, chief plastic surgery, 1994—. Fellow ACS, Internat. Coll. Surgeons, Am. Acad. Otolaryngology; mem. Am. Soc. Plastic and Reconstructive Surgeons, N.Am. Liposuction Soc. Republican. Episcopalian. Home: 2611 Barbara Ln Houston TX 77005 Office: Aesthetic Plastic Surgeons 6624 Fannin 2260 Houston TX 77030

MENTZER, JUNE ANN TOWNSEND, psychologist; b. Portsmouth, Ohio, June 15, 1920; d. Robert Presley and Edna Genevieve (Korth) Townsend; m. Robert H. Brown, Dec. 20, 1946 (div. 1963); children: Robert H. Jr., Betsy Lee, Julie Ann Brown Pridgen; m. Robert Wesley Mentzer, June 18, 1966; stepchildren: Kathryn Joyce Mentzer Tatham, Kristyn Sue. Student, Goucher Coll., 1938-40; AB, Ohio State U., 1946, MA, 1961. Lic. psychologist, Ohio. Kindergarten tchr. Newark (Ohio) City Schs., 1957-58, spl. edn. tchr., 1959-60, psychologist, 1960-63; dir. spl. edn., chief sch. psychologist Licking County Schs., Newark, 1963-80; pvt. practice psychology Newark, 1980—; psychologist and parent counselor Licking County Council for Mental Retardation, Newark, 1950-63; broadcasts on spl. edn. and psychology on stas. WHTH and WNKO, 1963-68; psychologist Licking County Headstart Program, 1969, 70, Ohio State U., Newark, 1984—, Cen. Ohio Tech. Coll. Contbr. articles on psychology, spl. edn. to Newark Advocate News, 1950—. Pres. Licking County Coun. for Exceptional Children, 1959; elder Presbyn. Ch. Mem. Ohio Psycholcgists Assn., Ctrl. Ohio Psychologists Assn., Licking County Mental Health Assn. (bd. dirs. 1979-82), Ohio Sch. Psychologists Assn. (hon., life), Sch. Psychologists Ctrl. Ohio (hon., life, pres. 1973, Huelsman award 1981, treas. polit. action com. 1985-88), Monday Talks Club, Kappa Alpha Theta, Pi Lambda Theta. Republican. Home: 104 Shannon Ln Granville OH 43023-9562

MENTZER, RICHARD LYNN, JR., physician, tree farmer; b. Stillwater, Okla., May 24, 1946; s. Richard Lynn and Carrie Lucille (Dearnbarger) M.; m. Patricia Rae Hickey, Mar. 22, 1974; children: Lucas D., Silas J., Caleb M. Student, U. Conn., 1964-65; BA, Johns Hopkins U., 1968; MD, U. Calif., San Francisco, 1972. Tree farmer Greenleaf (Oreg.) Forest Products, 1973—; intern U. Oreg. Health Scis. Univ., 1972-73; emergency physician Lebanon (Oreg.) Community Hosp., 1973-84; gen. practice physician Lake Creek Med. Clinic, Blachly, Oreg., 1984—. Scoutmaster, Boy Scouts Am., Triangle Lake, Oreg., 1990—. Mem. Lane County Med. Soc., Tree Farm Assn. Home: 92285 Nelson Mountain Rd Greenleaf OR 97430-9718 Office: Lake Creek Med Clinic 20270 Blachly Grange Rd Blachly OR 97412-9714

MENZIES, WILLIAM, urologist; b. Pitts., Sept. 19, 1928; s. William and Jean M. children: Brenice, Martha. BS, U. Pitts., 1951, MD, 1954. Resident in surgery West Pa. Hosp., Pitts., 1958-60, resident in urology, 1960-63; pvt. practice Texoma Urology Ctr., Wichita Falls, Tex., 1963—; chmn. dept. surgery Wichita Gen. Hosp., Wichita Falls, Tex., 1993-95; pres. med. staff Bethania Hosp., Wichita Falls, 1982. Chmn. March of Dimes, Wichita Falls, 1982. Capt. AUS Med. Corps, 1957-58. Mem. John Hunter Surg. Soc. (v.p. 1979-80). Home: 4419 Martinique Wichita Falls TX 76308 Office: Texoma Urol Ctr Reagan Urol Group 1511 10th St Wichita Falls TX 76301-4404

MENZOIAN, JAMES OSCAR, surgeon, educator; b. Cambridge, Mass.. MD cum laude, SUNY, Bklyn., 1965-69; MA, AB in Biology, Boston U., 1959-63, MA in Biology, 1963-65. Diplomate Am. Bd. Surgery; cert. gen. vascular surgeon; lic. mass. Surg. intern Boston U. Med. Ctr., U. Hosp., 1969-70; surg. resident U. Hosp., Boston, 1970-72, 74-76; academic trainee dept. surgery Boston U. Sch. Medicine, 1972-74, from asst. to prof. surgery, 1976—; attending surgeon Boston City Hosp., U. Hosp., 1976—; from coord. to program dir. surg. tng. program div. surgery Boston U. Sch. Medicine, 1984—, chief sect. vascular surgery, 1987—, dir. vascular fellwoship tng. program div. surgery, 1988—; ad hoc faculty promotions com. Boston U. Med. Ctr., med. sch. surg. curriculum com., intern. selction com., resident evaluation com., affiliated hosps. surg. exec. com., staff exec. com.; assoc. examinter Am. Bd. Surgery, 1985, 86; scientific adv. com. Boston City Hosp., 1981—; co-dir. non-invasive vascular lab. Univ. Hosp., Boston, 1982-86; human investigation studies com. Jewish Meml. Hosp.; counselor Suffolk Dist. Med. Soc.; utilization review com. U. Hops., OR com.; guest examiner Am. Bd. Surgery Gen. Vascular Surg. Certifying Examiner, 1992; cons. Jordan Hosp., Plymouth, Pa., 1980—, Jewish Meml. Hosp., Boston, 1980—, Choate Hosp., Woburn, Mass., 1981-86. Presenter in field; contbr. articles to profl. jours., chpts. to books. Capt. USAF Reserve, 1971-77, USAR, 1989. Rsch. fellow Worcester Found. for Exptl. Biolgoy, Worcester, mass., 1965, Dept. Physiology Tufts U. Sch. Medcine, Boston, 1966; recipient 17 grants in field, 1976—. Fellow Am. Coll. Surgeons (councillor Mass. chpt.); mem. AMA (diagnostic therapeutic tech. assessement program 1992), Am. Heart Assn. (mem. stroke coun.), Am. Venous Forum (program com. 1992), Am. Fedn. Clin. Rsch., New England Soc. Vascular Surgery (profl. activities com. chmn. 1981-86, cont. edn. com., v.p. 1992), New England Surg. Soc., Mass. Med. Soc., Boston Surg. Soc., Eastern Vascular Soc., Soc. Clin. Vascular Surgery (program com.), Assn. Academic Surgery, Benjamin Waterhouse Med. Histor. Office: Univ Hosp 88 E Newton St Boston MA 02118-2308

MERAB, JACQUES P., internist, cardiologist; b. N.Y.C., Aug. 14, 1954; s. Antoine Joseph and Janine (Bussgang) M. BS, MIT, 1976; MD, Harvard U., 1980. Diplomate Am. Bd. Internal Medicine, Am. Bd. Cardiology. Asst. clin. prof. of medicine Columbia U., N.Y.C.; asst. attending physician Presbyn. Hosp., N.Y.C. Office: CPMC East Side 16 East 60th St New York NY 10021

MERCADER, JOSEP M., radiologist, educator; b. Gerona, Spain, Oct. 8, 1941; s. Roberto F. Mercader and Elvira V. Sobrequés; m. Sonia G. Gonzalez, May 29, 1977; children: Carla, Josep M. Med. Licentiate, U. Barcelona, Spain, 1965, MD, 1987. Cert. radiologist, prof. Radiologist Hosp. Clinic U. Barcelona, 1967-85, Hosp. Del Mar, Barcelona, 1970-82; head neuroradiology Hosp. Clinic U. Barcelona, 1985-92, head dept. radiology, 1992—; prof. U. Barcelona, 1988, prof., head radiology, 1996—; dir. Magnetic Resonance and Neuroradiology Ctr. Radiologico Computarizado de Barcelona, 1986—. Contbr. rsch. articles to profl. jours. 2d lt. Spanish Navy, 1965-66. Mem. Spanish Soc. Med. Radiology (cons. com. 1995), Soc. for Magnetic Resonance (corr. mem.), Radiol. Soc. N.Am. (corr.), Spanish Soc. Neuroradiology (pres. 1990—), European Soc. Neuroradiology (nat. del. Spain 1993—), World Fedn. Neuroradiol. Socs. (nat. del. Spain 1995—), Nautical Club Costa Brava-Palamós. Home: 14o-1a, Josep Tarradellas 120/ 2, Barcelona Spain Office: Centro Radiologico Comput, Tavern 82, 08006 Barcelona Spain

MERCANDO, ANTHONY DOMINIC, cardiologist; b. Yonkers, N.Y., Oct. 6, 1954; s. Dominic and Ida Mercando; m. Lee-Ann Davis, May 3, 1980; children: Michelle, Christina, Andrew, Anne Marie. BSEE, Manhattan Coll., Bronx, 1976; MD, Harvard U., 1980. Lic. physician, N.Y. Med. intern Montefiore Med. Ctr., Bronx, 1980-81, med. resident, 1981-83, cardiology fellow, 1984-86, attending arrhythmia svc., 1986-88; ptnr. Westchester Cardiology Assocs., Tuckahoe, N.Y., 1988—; founder, pres. Amadeus Multimedia Technologies, Ltd., Irvington, N.Y., 1995—; assoc. dir. ACLS Montefiore Hosp., 1991—. Contbr. articles to profl. jours., chpts. to books; computer editor Jour. Pacing and Clin. Electrophysiology, 1993—. Bd. dirs. Home Nursing Assn. Westchester, Tuckahoe, 1994—; tech. com. Irvington Sch. Bd., 1995—. R. Rosen fellow in pacing and electrophysiology N. Am. Soc. Pacing and Electrophysiology, 1986, Sable Meml. Heart fellow United Order Odd Fellows, 1985. Fellow Am. Coll. Cardiology; mem. N.Am. Soc. Pacing and Electrophysiology. Roman Catholic. Office: Westchester Cardiology 1 Elm St Tuckahoe NY 10707

MERCER, RAMONA THIEME, nursing educator; b. Ala., Oct. 4, 1929; d. William Henry and Nell Thieme; m. Lewis Pyle Mercer, Dec. 31, 1971; 1 child, Camille E. Ronay. Diploma in nursing, St. Margaret's Hosp., Montgomery, Ala., 1950; BSN, U. N.Mex., 1962; MSN, Emory U., 1964; PhD, U. Pitts., 1973. Prof. dept. family health nursing U. Calif., San Francisco, 1973-88, prof. emeritus, 1988. Author: First-Time Motherhood, 1986, Transitions in a Woman's Life, 1989, Parents at Risk, 1990, Becoming a Mother, 1995. Recipient Disting. Rsch. Lectureship award Western Inst. Nursing, 1988, Disting. Alumnus award U. Pitts., 1988, Disting. Contbn. to Nursing Sci. award Am. Nurses Found., 1990. Mem. Am. Acad. Nursing, Coun. Nurse Researchers, ANA, Sigma Theta Tau. Home: 1809 Ashton Ave Burlingame CA 94010-5712

MERCHANT, ROLAND SAMUEL, SR., hospital administrator, educator; b. N.Y.C., Apr. 18, 1929; s. Samuel and Eleta (McLymont) M.; m. Audrey Bartley, June 6, 1970; children: Orelia Eleta, Roland Samuel, Huey Bartley. BA, NYU, 1957, MA, 1960; MS, Columbia U., 1963, MSHA, 1974. Asst. statistician N.Y.C. Dept. Health, 1957-60, statistician, 1960-63; statistician N.Y. TB and Health Assn., N.Y.C., 1963-65; biostatistician, adminstrv. coord. Inst. Surg. Studies, Montefiore Hosp., Bronx, N.Y., 1965-72; resident in adminstrn. Roosevelt Hosp., N.Y.C., 1973-74; dir. health and hosp. mgmt. Dept. Health, City of N.Y., 1974-76; from asst. adminstr. to adminstr. West Adams Community Hosp., L.A., 1976; spl. asst. to assoc. v.p. for med. affairs Stanford U. Hosp., Calif., 1977-82, dir. office mgmt. and strategic planning, 1982-85, dir. mgmt. planning, 1986-90; v.p. strategic planning Cedars-Sinai Med. Ctr., L.A., 1990-94; cons. Roland Merchant & Assocs., L.A., 1994—; clin. assoc. prof. dept. family, community and preventive medicine Stanford U., 1986-88, dept. health rsch. and policy Stanford U. Med. Sch., 1988-90. Served with U.S. Army, 1951-53. USPHS fellow. Fellow Am. Coll. Healthcare Execs., Am. Pub. Health Assn.; mem. Am. Hosp. Assn., Nat. Assn. Health Services Execs., N.Y. Acad. Scis. Home: 27335 Park Vista Rd Agoura Hills CA 91301-3639 Office: Roland Merchant & Assocs 27335 Park Vista Rd Agoura Hills CA 91301-3639

MERCURI, LOUIS GERARD, oral surgeon; b. Scranton, Pa., Jan. 4, 1945; m. Joan Elizabeth Ball; children: Gregory Michael, Jeffrey Alan. BS in Biology, Georgetown U., 1966, DDS cum laude, 1970; cert. oral and maxillofacial surgery, U. Ill. Med. Ctr., Chgo., 1974, MS in Oral and Maxillofacial Surgery, 1975. Diplomate Am. Bd. Oral and Maxillofacial Surgery. Intern U. Ill. Hosp.-Divsn. Oral and Maxillofacial Surgery, Chgo., 1970-71, rsch. resident, 1971-72, jr. resident, 1972-73, sr. resident, 1973-74; asst. prof. dept. oral and maxillofacial surgery U. Ill. Med. Ctr.-Coll. Dentistry, Chgo., 1974-77; asst. clin. prof. dept. surgery U. Ill. Med. Ctr.-Coll. Medicine, Chgo., 1974-77; asst. prof. dept. oral and maxillofacial surgery Med. Coll. Va., Va.

Commonwealth U., Richmond, 1977-81, assoc. prof. dept. oral and maxillofacial surgery, 1981-86, grad. faculty, 1977-86; assoc. prof. dept. oral and maxillofacial surgery U. Ill.-Coll. Dentistry, Chgo., 1989-93; full faculty mem. Grad. Coll. U. Ill., Chgo., 1990-93; prof. dept. surgery Loyola U. Med. Ctr., Stritch Sch. Medicine, 1993—; cons. VA Med. Ctr., McGuire Vets. Hosp., Richmond, 1977-86, VA Med. Ctr., Hampton, Va., 1982-86, Portsmouth (Va.) Naval Hosp., 1985-86, VA Med. Ctr., West Side Hosp. Dental Svc., Chgo., 1989-93, VA Med. Ctr., Hines, Ill., 1993—, others; presenter in field. reviewer Jour. Oral & Maxillofacial Surgery, 1984—, Oral Surgery, Medicine, Pathology, 1993—; referee Jour. Orofacial Pain, 1992—; contbr. chpts. to books and articles to profl. jours. Scholar Internat. Coll. Dentists, 1970; fellow Internat. Coll. Dentists, 1996; grantee MCV/VCU Sch. Dentistry, Richmond, 1978, 81, NIH, 1982, 3-M Corp., 1983-84, Techmedica Corp., Camarillo, Calif., 1988-94, Osteomed, Glendale, Calif., 1990-91, Anspach, Palm Beach Gardens, Fla., 1994—. Fellow ADA, Am. Assn. Oral and Maxillofacial Surgeons, Am. Dental Soc. Anesthesiology; mem. Am. Assn. Dental Schs., Am. Assn. for Dental Rsch., Am. Pain Soc., Internat. Assn. Oral and Maxillofacial Surgeons, Internat. Assn. for the Study of Pain (charter), Internat. Assn. for Dental Rsch. (oral and maxillofacial surgery group), Southeastern Soc. Oral and Maxillofacial Surgeons (assoc.), Ill. Soc. Oral and Maxillofacial Surgeons (councilman 1988-91), Great Lakes Soc. Oral and Maxillofacial Surgeons, Chgo. Soc. Oral and Maxillofacial Surgeons, Chgo. Dental Soc. (West Surburban Br.), Ill. Dental Soc., Chgo. Dental Forum,Soc. Educators in Oral and Maxillofacial Surgery, Am. Soc. Temporomandibular Joint Surgeons, Am. Assn. Hosp. Dentists, Omicron Kappa Upsilon (Zeta chpt., Kappa chpt.). Home: 604 Bonnie Brae River Forest IL 60305 Office: Dept Surgery, Divsn Oral Loyola Univ Med Ctr 2160 S First Ave Maywood IL 60153

MERCURIO, CATHERINE GRACE, physician's assistant; b. N.Y.C., Feb. 2, 1939; d. Frank and Louise (Barile) CaLiguiri; m. Pat Anthony Mercurio, Nov. 21, 1957; children: Gregory James, Anthony James, Marisa Elena. BS, Wagner Coll., 1976. Registered physician's asst. Physician's asst. USPHS Outpatient Clinic, N.Y.C., 1978-81, HIP Med. Group, Bklyn., 1982-84; physician's asst., medico-legal cons. N.Y.C. Law Dept., 1984-88; physician's asst. L.I. Coll. Hosp., Bklyn., 1989-92, semi-ret., 1992; cons. in field, Staten Island, N.Y., 1988-89. Vol. Little Theatre, New Smyrna Beach, 1993-95. Fellow Am. Coun. Physician's Assts.; mem. Psi Chi. Democrat.

MEREDITH, LINDA JOSEPHINE, nurse; b. Cin., June 12, 1952; d. John W. and Lucille R. (Baker) McDonald; m. Arthur G. Meredith, Nov. 9, 1979; children: Andrew, Douglas. BSN, U. Cin., 1974, MS in Nursing, 1990. RN. Staff nurse U. Hosp., Cin., 1974-76; staff & charge nurse Good Samaritan Hosp., Cin., 1976-87; nurse Riverhills Healthcare, Inc., Cin., 1987-95, coord. renal transplant, 1995—; clin. pathways transplant The Christ Hosp., Cin., 1996. Mem. St. Therese Mother's Club, Southgate, Ky., 1989—, costumes, 1994—. Mem. Am. Nephrology Nurses Assn., Sigma Theta Tau. Office: Riverhills Healthcare Inc 2123 Auburn Ave #320 Cincinnati OH 45219

MERENA, LESLEY ANN, nursing home administrator; b. Hartford, Conn., Apr. 12, 1948; d. Merritt T. and Marjorie (Fairweather) Salmon Jr.; children: Claudette, Ann-Louise, J. D. Kurtis. Grad., Joseph Lawrence Sch. Nursing, New London, Conn.; BS in Healthcare Adminstrn., St. Joseph's Coll., North Windham, Maine; MBA, U. New Haven. RN, Conn. Charge and staff nurse med.-surg. ICU, St. Vincent's Med. Ctr., Bridgeport, Conn., 1969-81, quality assurance coord.-discharge planner-risk mgmt. coord., 1984-87; med. and legal cons. Day, Berry and Howard, Stamford, Conn., 1988-94; asst. dir. nursing Jewish Home for Elderly, Fairfield, Conn., 1985—; guest lectr. Sacred Heart Univ., presenter in field. Com. chair State of Conn. Pub. Health Code Nursing Task Force; mem. Program of People to People Internat., citizen amb. representing U.S.; mem. Internat. Ethics Delegation to Poland, Hungary, Czech Republic, 1996. Mem. Am. Soc. for Healthcare Risk Mgmt., Am. Soc. Law, Medicine and Ethics, Sigma Theta Tau. Home: 236-E Edgemoor Rd Bridgeport CT 06606 Office: Jewish Home for Elderly 175 Jefferson St Fairfield CT 06432-1018

MERENBLOOM, ROBERT BARRY, hospital and medical school administrator; b. Balt., July 13, 1947; Philip William and Florence Ruth (Surosky) M.; B.A., U. Md., 1969; M.S., Morgan State U., 1973; M.B.A., U. Balt., 1980. Mem. staff Mayor Balt. Office Manpower Resources, 1972-73; assoc. staff mem. Office Dean, U. Md. Med. Sch., 1976-80; adminstrv. officer rsch. and devel. Balt. VA Med. Ctr., 1974-80; assoc. adminstr. dept. medicine Sch. Medicine Johns Hopkins U., Balt., 1980-84, adminstr. dept. medicine Johns Hopkins Hosp., 1984-88, assoc. Sch. Hygiene and Pub. Health, 1984-88; lectr. dept. medicine Bowman Gray Sch. Medicine Wake Forest U., 1988-93, asst. chmn. dept. medicine, 1988-91, assoc. chmn. dept. medicine, 1991-93; vice chmn., asst. prof. medicine, clin. asst. prof. health adminstrn. & policy Med. U. S.C., Charleston, 1993—; instr. sociology U. Balt., 1973-76; adj. faculty Weekend Coll., Coll. Notre Dame, Balt., 1980—; assoc. mgmt. Babcock Grad. Sch. Bus. Wake Forest U. Exec. dir. J. Paul Sticht Ctr. on Aging. Recipient Hon. Corpsmen Leader award Office Mayor Balt., 1973; Outstanding Performance award Balt. VA Med. Ctr., 1975, Superior Performance award, 1980. Mem. Am. Gerontology Soc., So. Gerontology Soc., Soc. Rsch. Adminstrs., Nat. Coun. Univ. Rsch. Adminstrs., Adminstrs. Internal Medicine, Assn. Am. Med. Colls. (group on bus. affairs), Am. Hosp. Assn., Am. Pub. Health Assn., Am. Coll. Healthcare Adminstrs., Soc. Gen. Internal Medicine, Johns Hopkins Club, Piedmont Club, Harbour Club.

MERENDA, PETER FRANCIS, psychologist, emeritus educator; b. Everett, Mass., July 18, 1922; s. Frank and Sarah (Lino) M.; m. Rose Cafasso, Aug. 31, 1946; children—Anne, Rosemary, Pamela. B.S., Tufts U., 1947, M.A., 1948; CAS, Harvard U., 1951; Ph.D., U. Wis., 1957. Asst. prof. psychology U. R.I., Kingston, 1960-63, assoc. prof., 1963-65, assoc. dean Grad. Sch., 1965-68, univ. coord. rsch., prof., 1965-84, prof. emeritus, 1985—; sr. psychologist W.V. Clarke Assocs., Providence, 1957-88, Coauthor: Educational Measurement, 1978, Multivariate Analysis, 1980. Served to lt.j.g. USN, 1944-46. Fulbright scholar, 1967-68, 74-75; grantee NATO, 1973-76, Pacific Cultural Found., Taiwan, 1981, 83, Gulbekian Found. Portugal, 1984. Fellow AAAS, APA, Am. Psychological Soc., Soc. for Personality Assessment, SPA; mem. Internat. Assn. Applied Psychology (pres. psychol. assessment div. 1982-86, exec. com. 1986—), R.I. Psychol. Assn. (pres. 1984-86), New Eng. Psychol. Assn. (pres. 1981-82), Internat. Council Psychologists (pres. 1980-81). Roman Catholic. Office: WV Clarke Assocs Inc 75 Sockanosset Cross Rd Cranston RI 02920-5558

MERENDINO, K. ALVIN, surgical educator; b. Clarksburg, W.Va., Dec. 3, 1914; s. Biagio and Cira (Bivona) M.; m. Shirley Emojane Hill, July 6, 1943; children: Cira Anne Watts, Nancy Jane Napuunoa, Susan Hill Mitchell, Nina Merendino-Sarich, Maria King Merendino-Stillwell. BA, Ohio U., 1936, LLD (hon.), 1967; MD, Yale U., 1940; PhD, U. Minn., 1946. Diplomate Am. Bd. Surgery, Am. Bd. Thoracic Surgery. Intern Cin. Gen. Hosp., 1940-41; resident U. Minn. Hosp., Mpls., 1941-45; rsch. asst. Dr. Owen H. Wangensteen, 1942-43; trainee Nat. Cancer Inst., 1943-45; dir. program in postgrad. med. edn. in surgery Ancker Hosp., St. Paul, 1946-48; instr. dept. surgery U. Minn., Mpls., 1944-45, asst. prof. dept. surgery, 1945-48; assoc. prof. dept. surgery U. Wash., Seattle, 1949-55, dir. exptl. surgery labs., dept. surgery, 1950-72, prof. dept. surgery, 1955-81, prof. emeritus, 1981—, prof. and adminstrv. officer dept. surgery, 1957-64, prof., chmn., 1965-72; chmn. dept. surgery King Faisal Specialist and Rsch. Ctgr., Riyadh, Saudi Arabia, 1976, dir. med. affairs, 1976-79, dir. Cancer Therapy Inst., spl. cons. to Coun., supr. for exec. mgmt., assoc. dir. med. affairs, 1981-82; dir. ops. King Faisal Med. City, Riyadh, 1981-85; mem. adv. com. for med. rsch., Boeing Airplane Co., 1959-67, chmn., 1962l cons. Children's Orthopedic Hosp., Seattle, 1972-82; mem. adv. com. on heart disease and surgery for crippled children's svc., Wash. State Dept. Health and Div. Vocational Rehab., 1961; mem. surgery study sect. NIH, 1958-62, subcom. on prosthetic valves for cardiac surgery, chm. 1st Nat. Conf., 1960, mem. adv. com. 2d Nat. Conf. on Prosthetic Heart Valves, 1969, Surgery A study sect. chmn., 1970-72, Nat. Heart and Lung Inst. Tng. Com., 1965-69; cons. VA, Seattle, 1949-59, 65-81; mem. adv. com. on hosps. and clinics, USPHS, 1963-66; mem. surgery test com. Nat. Bd. Med. Examiners, 1963-67; mem. surgery resident rev. com., Conf. Com. on Grad. Edn. in Surgery, 1963-73, vice-chmn., 1972-73; chmn. 2d Saudi Arabian Med. Conf., Riyadh, 1978; mem. com. on postgrad. med. edn., Kingdom of Saudi Arabia Ministry of Health, 1978-79. Editor in chief: Prosthetic Valves for Cardiac Surgery, 1961; assoc. editor: Prosthetic Heart Valves, 1969; mem. editorial bd. Am. Jour. Surgery,. 1958—, Jour. Surg. Rsch., 1961-69, Pacific Medicine and Surgery, 1964-68, King Faisal Hosp. Medicine Jour. (renamed Annals of Saudi Medicine), 1981-85; contbr. articles to profl. jours., chpts. to books; producer movies on surgery. Recipient cert. of merit Ohio U. Alumni Assn., 1957, Outstanding W.Va. Italian-Am. award W.Va. Italian Heritage Festival Inc., Clarksburg, W.Va., 1984, Spirit of Freedom award A. James Mancin, Sec. State W.Va., 1984, Disting. W. Virginian award State of W.Va., 1984, John Baird Thomas Meml. award Ohio U.; named Surgery Alumnus of Yr., U. Minn., 1981, Disting. Citizen Wash. State, Lt. Gov. John Cherberg, 1981; NIH grantee, 1951-76. Fellow ACS (numerous coms., bds.), Soc. of Univ. Surgeons (councilman at large 3 yrs.), Internat. Soc. Surgery; mem. Am. Surg. Assn. (adv. mem. com. 1959-64, v.p. 1972-73), Am. Assn. for Thoracic Surgery, Halsted Soc., Henry N. Harkins Surg. Soc., N. Pacific Coast Surg. Assn., Seattle Surg. Soc., So. Surg. Soc. (Arthur H. Shipley award 1972), Am. Bd. Surgery 1958-64 (vice chmn. 1962-63, chmn. 1963-64, emeritus 1964—); University Club, Seattle Golf Club, Phi Beta Kappa, Sigma Xi, Beta Theta Pi (sec., pres.), Phi Beta Pi (hon.). Republican. Episcopalian. Home: The Highlands Seattle WA 98177 Office: U Wash Sch Medicine Dept Surgery Seattle WA 98195

MERIAN, HAROLD ARTHUR, neonatal nurse, anesthetist, naval reserve officer; b. Andrews AFB, Md., Nov. 18, 1959; s. Harold Holmes Merian and Peggy (Sutton) Dunn. Student, Linfield Coll., 1978-79, Wash. State U., 1979-80; BSN, SUNY, Albany, 1987; postgrad., U. New Eng., 1994—. RN, Calif., Wash., Maine, N.H.; cert. trauma nurse; cert. ACLS provider Am. Heart Assn.; cert. BCLS instr; cert. neonatal ALS provider; cert. extracorporeal membrane oxygenation nurse perfusionist; cert. pediatric ALS provider. Enlisted man USN, 1981-87, commd. ensign, 1987, advanced through grades to lt. comdr., 1995; hosp. corpsman Charleston, S.C., 1981-82; lab. technician USS Constellation, 1982-83; histopathology technician Camp Pendleton, Calif., 1984-87; nurse Navy Hosp., Naval Air Sta. Whidbey, Oak Harbor, Wash., 1987-90; staff nurse neonatal ICU Children's Hosp., L.A., 1990-92, perdiem nurse neonatal ICU; staff nurse cardiac ICU and Emergency Trauma Ctr. Desert Hosp., Palm Springs, Calif., 1992-93; evening team leader post anesthesia care unit Eisenhower Med. Ctr., Rancho Mirage, Calif., 1993-94; per diem nurse emergency dept. York (Maine) Hosp., 1994-95. Music and theatre scholar Linfield Coll., 1978-79; music scholar Eastern Wash. State U., 1978. Mem. Am. Assn. Nurse Anesthetists, New Eng. Assembly of Student RN Anesthetists (v.p.), Navy Nurse Corps., Naval Res. Assn. Democrat. Roman Catholic. Home: 65 Woodridge Rd Brewer ME 04412

MERIDEN, TERRY, physician; b. Damascus, Syria, Oct. 12, 1946; came to U.S., 1975; s. Izzat and Omayma (Aidi) M.; m. Lena Kahal, Nov. 17, 1975; children: Zina, Lana. BS, Sch. Sci., Damascus, 1968; MD, Sch. Medicine, Damascus, 1972, doctorate cum laude, 1973. Diplomate Am. Bd. Internal Medicine. Resident in infectious diseases Rush Green Hosp., Romford, Eng., 1973; house officer in internal medicine and cardiology Ashford (Eng.) Group Univ. Hosps., 1973-74; sr. house officer in internal medicine and neurology Grimsby (Eng.) Group Univ. Hosps., 1974; registrar in internal medicine and rheumatology St. Annes Hosp., London, 1974-75; jr. resident in internal medicine Shadyside Hosp., Pitts., 1975-76, sr. resident in internal medicine, 1976-77; fellow in endocrinology and metabolism Shadyside Hosp. and Grad. Inst., Pitts., 1976-77; clin. asst. prof. U. Ill., Peoria, 1979; pres. Am. Diabetes Assn., Peoria, 1982-84; dir. Proctor Diabetes Unit, Peoria, 1984—, 1984—; adviser to the Gov. of Ill. on Diabetes. Mem. editorial bd. Diabetes Forecast mag., Clin. Diabetes, 1990; contbr. articles to profl. jours. Fellow ACP, FACE, Am. Coll. Endocrinology; mem. AMA (Recognition award 1985, ADA (chmn. profl. edn. and rsch. 1980—, mem. editl. bd. and Spanish lit. bd. nat. bd. dirs. 1986—, vice chmn. nat. com. on diabetes edn. and affiliate svcs. 1986—, Outstanding Svc. award 1984, Outstanding Diabetes Educator award 1986), Am. Cancer Soc. (Life Line award 1983), Am. Assn. Clin. Endocrinology (founding), Am. Coll. Endocrinology, The Obesity Found. (Century award 1984, Recognition award 1985). Home: 115 E Coventry Ln Peoria IL 61614-2103 Office: 900 Main St Ste 300 Peoria IL 61602-1005

MERIGAN, THOMAS CHARLES, JR., physician, medical researcher, educator; b. San Francisco, Jan. 18, 1934; s. Thomas C. and Helen M. (Greeley) M.; m. Joan Mary Freeborn, Oct. 3, 1959; 1 son, Thomas Charles III. BA with honors, U. Calif., Berkeley, 1955; MD, U. Calif., San Francisco, 1958. Diplomate: Am. Bd. Internal Medicine. Intern in medicine 2d and 4th Harvard med. services Boston City Hosp., 1958-59, asst. resident medicine, 1959-60; clin. assoc. Nat. Heart Inst., NIH, Bethesda, Md., 1960-62; asso. Lab. Molecular Biology, Nat. Inst. Arthritis and Metabolic Diseases, NIH, 1962-63; practice medicine specializing in internal medicine and infectious diseases Stanford, Calif., 1963—; asst. prof. medicine Stanford U. Sch. Medicine, 1963-67, assoc. prof. medicine, 1967-72, head div. infectious diseases, 1966-92, prof. medicine, 1972—, George E. and Lucy Becker prof. medicine, 1980—; dir. Diagnostic Microbiology Lab., Univ. Hosp., 1966-72, Diagnostic Virology Lab., 1969—, Ctr. AIDS Rsch. Stanford U., 1988—; hosp. epidemiologist, 1966-88; mem. microbiology rsch. tng. grants com. NIH, 1969-73, virology study sect., 1974-78; cons. antiviral substances program Nat. Inst. Allergy and Infectious Diseases, 1970—, mem. AIDS clin. drug devel. commn., 1986-94; mem. Virology Task Force, 1976-78, bd. sci. counselors, 1980-85; mem. U.S. Hepatitis panel U.S. and Japan Coop. Med. Sci. Program, 1979-90, AIDS subcom. Nat. Adv. Allergy and Infectious Diseases Coun., 1988-89; co-chmn. interferon evaluation Group Am. Cancer Soc., 1978-81; mem. vaccines and related biol. products adv. com. Ctr. for Drugs and Biols., FDA, 1984-88; mem. internat. adv. com. on biol. sci. Sci. Council, Singapore, 1985-88; mem. adv. com. J.A. Hartford Found., 1979-84; mem. Albert Lasker awards jury, 1981-84; mem. peer review panel U.S. Army Med. Rsch. and Devel. Com., 1986-88; nat. com. to rev. current procedures for approval New Drugs for Cancer and AIDS, 1989-90; mem. Com. to Study Use of Coms. within FDA, 1991-92. Contbr. numerous articles on infectious diseases, virology and immunology to sci. jours.; editor: Antivirals with Clinical Potential, 1976, Antivirals and Virus Diseases of Man, 1979, 2d edit., 1984, 3d edit., 1990, Regulatory Functions of Interferon, 1980, Interferons, 1982, Interferons as Cell Growth Inhibitors, 1986; assoc. editor: Virology, 1975-78, Cancer Research, 1987-91; co-editor: monograph series Current Topics in Infectious Diseases, 1975—, Cytomeglovirus Infect and Ganciclovir, 1988, Focus on Didanosine (ddI), 1990, Practical Diagnosis of Viral Infection, Textbook of AIDS Medicine, 1994, Surrogate Markers for HIV Infection, 1995; editl. bd.: Archives Internal Medicine, 1971-81, Jour. Gen. Virology, 1972-77, Infection and Immunity, 1973-81, Intervirology, 1973-85, Proc. Soc. Expt. Biology and Medicine, 1978-87, Reviews of Infectious Diseases, 1979-89, Jour. Interferon Research, 1980-89, Antiviral Research, 1980-86, Jour. Antimicrobial Chemotherapy, 1981-91, Molecular and Cellular Biochemistry, 1982-89, AIDS Research and Human Retroviruses, 1983—, Jour. Virology, 1984-89, Biotechnology Therapeutics, 1988—, Jour. Infectious Diseases, 1989—, Clinical Drug Investigation, 1989—, HIV: Advances in Research and Therapy, 1990—, Internat. Jour. Antimicrobial Agts. 1990—, The AIDS Reader, 1991—, AIDS, 1993, Clinical Immunotherapeutics, 1994—, Antiviral Therapy, 1996—. Recipient Borden award for Outstanding Rsch., Am. Assn. Med. Colls., 1973, Merit award, Nat. Inst. Allergy and Infectious Diseases, 1988, Maxwell Finland award Infectious Diseases Soc. Am., 1988; Guggenheim Meml. fellow, 1972. Fellow AAAS; mem. AMA, Assn. Am. Physicians, Western Assn. Physicians, Am. Soc. Microbiology, Am. Soc. Clin. Investigation (coun. 1977-80), Am. Assn. Immunologists, Am. Fedn. Clin. Rsch., Western Soc. Clin. Rsch., Soc. Exptl. Biology and Medicine (publ. com. 1985-89), Infectious Diseases Soc. Am., Am. Soc. Virology, inst. Medicine, Pan Am. Group for Rapid Viral Diagnosis, Internat. Soron Rsch. (coun. 1983-89), Calif. Med. Assn., Santa Clara County Med. Soc., Calif. Acad. Medicine, Royal Soc. Medicine, Alpha Omega Alpha. Home: 148 Goya Rd Menlo Park CA 94028-7307 Office: Stanford U Sch Medicine Div Infectious Diseases Stanford CA 94305

MERKERT, GEORGE L., JR., orthopedic surgeon; b. Mpls., Apr. 9, 1925; s. George LeRoy and Mary Elizabeth (Craig) M.; m. Karin Inger, Sept. 16, 1979; children: George L., Craig Napier, Thomas Whitney, Jon Walter. MD, U. Louisville, 1948. Diplomate Am. Bd. Orthopaedic Surgery. Intern rotating Ancker Hosp., St. Paul, 1948-49, resident in gen. surgery, 1949-50; resident in gen. surgery Grad. Sch. Orthopaedic Surgery U. Minn., 1953-54; pres. Colorado Springs (Colo.) Orthopaedic Group, 1955—. Served to lt. USNR, 1950-57. Mem. Am. Acad. Orthopaedic Surgeons, Am. Acad. Cerebral Palsy, Am. Coll. Surgeons, Western Orthopaedic Assn., Rocky Mountain Trauma Soc., AMA, Broadmoor Golf Club, Colorado Springs Country Club. Republican. Presbyterian. Home: 3229 Leslie Dr Colorado Springs CO 80909-1039 Office: Colorado Springs Orth Grp 801 N Cascade Ave Colorado Springs CO 80903-3223

MERKIN, ALBERT CHARLES, pediatrician, allergist; b. Chgo., Sept. 4, 1924; s. Harry A. and Goldie (Lamasky) M.; m. Eunice Aprill, Aug. 22, 1948; children: Audrey, Ellen, Joseph. Student, U. Ill., 1942-44; MD, U. Ill., Chgo., 1949. Diplomate Am. Bd. Allergy and Immunology, Am. Bd. Pediatrics. Intern, resident Cook County Hosp., Chgo.; resident Children's Meml. Hosp., Chgo.; with Valley Pediatric and Allergy Clinic, Las Vegas, Nev. Capt. USAF, 1950-53. Fellow Am. Acad. Pediatrics (state chmn. Nev. 1961-64, sect. allergy and immunology), Am. Coll. Allergy; mem. Am. Acad. Allergy, Allergy Subsplty. Group of Acad. Pediatrics. Office: Valley Pediat & Allergy Ste 12 2881 S Valley View Blvd Las Vegas NV 89102

MERKIN, DONALD H., internist; b. Bronx, N.Y., Nov. 12, 1945; s. Eugene and Hortense Ruth (Erdrich) M.; m. Carol Ann Williams, July 22, 1967; children: Daniel Hansen, Andrew David. BA, Parsons Coll., 1968; MS, Colo. State U., 1972; PhD, Cornell U., 1974; MD, U. Autonoma de Ciudad, Juarez, Mexico, 1978. Asst. prof. U. So. Colo., Pueblo, 1973-74, Bethel Sch. of Nursing, Colorado Springs, 1973-74, U. Colo., Colorado Springs, 1973-74, So. Ill. U. Sch. Medicine, Springfield, Ill., 1975-76; internist Westside Med. Assocs., Bradenton, Fla., 1982-84, pvt. practice, Sarasota, Fla., 1984-88, Superior (Wis.) Clinic, Ltd., 1989-91; internist Gulf Coast Ortho. Ctr.- Inst. for Spl. Surgery, Hudson, Fla., 1991-94, dir. orthopedic medicine, 1992-94; pvt. practice Internal Medicine Assocs. of Pasco County, Hudson, Fla., 1995—; dir. Orthopedic Medicine Clinic, 1992-94. Author: Pregnancy as a Disease, 1976. Officer candidate USMC, 1969. Nat. Inst. Child Health and Human Devel. fellow Cornell U., 1970-73; Fulbright fellow Nat. Assn. Colls. for Tchr. Edn., India, 1974. Mem. AMA, Fla. Med. Soc., Pasco County Med. Soc., Am. Soc. Internal Medicine, Fla. Soc. Internal Medicine. Lutheran. Office: Internal Medicine Assocs Pasco County 13906 Lakeshore Blvd Ste 330 Hudson FL 34667

MERLINO, ANTHONY FRANK, orthopedic surgeon; b. Providence, Jan. 21, 1930; s. Anthony Frank and C. Mildred (Campagna) M.; m. Dolores Mary Aucello, Nov. 22, 1956; children: Christa Marianne, Paula Nicole. BS, Providence Coll., 1951; MS, U. Conn., 1952; MD, Jefferson Med. Coll., 1956. Diplomate Am. Bd. Orthopedic Surgery. Intern St. Joseph Hosp., Providence, 1956-57; resident orthopedic surgery VA Hosp., Phila., 1959-63; pvt. practice medicine specializing in orthopedic surgery, Phila., 1963-68, Providence, 1968—; attending orthopedic surgeon St. Joseph Hosp., Providence, pres. med. staff, 1974-75, trustee, 1973-76, med. staff/trustee joint conf. com. 1982; attending orthopedic surgeon Our Lady of Fatima Hosp., North Providence, R.I.; vis. orthopedic surgeon R.I. State Hosp., Howard, 1968-75; asst. orthopedic surgery Hahnemann Med. Coll., Phila., 1965-69; pediatric orthopedic surg. cons. Crippled Children's Program of R.I., 1968-86; cons. orthopedic surgeon Roger Williams Gen. Hosp., Providence, 1969-89; v.p. R.I. Orthopedic Group, Inc., Providence, 1969-83; pres., 1983—; team physician hockey and basketball teams Providence Coll., 1968-87; mem. R.I. Gov.'s Med. Malpractice Commn., 1975-77, R.I. Bd. Examiners in Chiropractic, 1977-80; mem. study commn. R.I. Med. Rev. Bd., 1977-85; mem. corp. Blue Cross/Shield R.I., 1976-87; physician-adv. R.I. Assn. Med. Assts., 1979-84; mem. R.I. Workers' Compensation Adv. Panel, 1978-88; mem. adv. bd. Cath. Social Svcs., 1981-84; police surgeon Am. Law Enforcement Officers' Assn., 1980; cons. orthopedic surgery Am. Assn. Medicolegal Cons., 1980-90; pres. Hindle Bldg. Assocs., 1983—. Contbr. articles to profl. jours. Mem. med. splty. adv. bd. Medical Malpractice Prevention, 1985-90. Capt., M.C., USAF, 1957-59. Recipient Dr. William McDonnell award Providence Coll. Alumni Assn., 1981. Fellow Am. Acad. Orthopedic Surgeons, ACS, (pres. R.I. chpt. 1982-84), Internat. Coll. Surgeons, Latin Am. Soc. Orthopedics and Traumatology; mem. AMA, Orthopaedic Rsch. and Edn. Found. (life), Am. Coll. Legal Medicine, Am. Fracture Assn., Pan-Pacific Surg. Assn., New Eng., R.I. (sec.-treas. 1978-80, v.p. 1980-82, pres. 1982-84), Ea. Orthopedic Socs., Jefferson Orthopaedic Soc., R.I. Med. Soc. (commr. profl. rels. 1976, ho. of dels. 1976-82, commr. internal affairs 1982), Providence Med. Assn., Am. Profl. Practice Assn., Am. Acad. Compensation Medicine, Am. Coll. Sports Medicine, Am. Orthopedic Soc. for Sports Medicine, Am. Med. Photography Assn., Internat. Soc. Orthopedics and Traumatology, Internat. Soc. Rsch. in Orthopedics and Trauma, Am. Soc. Law and Medicine, Thomistic Inst. Drs. Guild, R.I. Hist. Soc., Boston Orthopedic Club, Mal Brown Club, The 100 of R.I. Club. Roman Catholic. Home: 2 Countryside Dr North Providence RI 02904-3419 Office: 655 Broad St Providence RI 02907-1444

MERMANN, ALAN CAMERON, pediatrics educator, chaplain; b. Bklyn., June 23, 1923; s. William Joseph and Ada Fischer (McCree) M.; m. Constance Barnes, Sept. 4, 1948 (div. Mar. 1988); children: Edith, Constance, Sarah, Elizabeth; m. Cecily Allen Reynolds, Apr. 15, 1989. BA, Lehigh U., 1943; MD, Johns Hopkins U., 1947; MDiv, Yale U., 1979, MST, 1988. Diplomate Am. Bd. Pediatrics; med. license, Conn.; ordained to Christian ministry, United Ch. of Christ, 1979. Intern pediatrics Bellevue Hosp., N.Y.C., 1947-48, Johns Hopkins Hosp., Balt., 1948-49; sr. asst. resident pediatrician N.Y. Hosp., N.Y.C., 1949-50; resident pediatrician Meml. Hosp., N.Y.C., 1950-51; rsch. fellow Sloane-Kettering Inst., N.Y.C., 1953-54; pvt. practice pediatrics Guilford, Conn., 1954-82; clin. instr. pediatrics Yale Sch. Medicine, 1954-59, asst. clin. prof. pediatrics, 1959-71, assoc. clin. prof. pediatrics, 1971-79, clin. prof. pediatrics, 1979—; trustee New Eng. Coll., Henniker, N.H., 1969-91; fellow Branford Coll., Yale U., 1979—; mem. instnl. rev. bd. Union Carbide Corp., Danbury, Conn., 1991—; lectr. pastoral theology Yale Divinity Sch., 1979-82; asst. pastor First Congregational Ch., Guilford, 1979-82; assoc. pastor Ch. of Christ Congl., United Ch. of Christ, Norfolk, Conn., 1995—; chaplain Yale Sch. Medicine, 1982—, human investigation com., 1983-91, med. ctr. bioethics com., chair pediatrics ethics com., sch. medicine admissions com., com. on well-being of students. Contbr. articles to profl. jours. Lt. USNR, 1951-53. Fellow Am. Acad. Pediatrics. Democrat. Home: 36 Eld St New Haven CT 06511-3816

MEROLLA, MICHELE EDWARD, chiropractor, broadcaster; b. Providence, Feb. 20, 1940; s. Joseph and Viola (Horne) M.; m. Ednamarie H.; children: Michele Edward II, Matthew Joseph, Samantha Joan, Alexandra Marie. BSc, Bryant Coll., 1961; DC, Chiropractic Inst. N.Y., 1965; LHD, Logan Chiropractic Coll., St. Louis, 1973. Owner chiropractic clinics, New Bedford, Taunton, Somerset, Seekonk, Attleboro and Westport, Mass., 1965—. Daily Network radio talk show host Holistic Hotline; owner radio sta. WARA-AM, Attleboro, Mass. Mem. Nat. Assn. Broadcasters, New Bedford City Coun., 1969-73, Airport Commn., 1972-75, Sch. Com., 1978-83, Recreation Commn., 1983-89; pres. New Bedford Aid Ctr., 1977; bd. dirs. Your Theatre Inc. Recipient Svc. award New England Chiropractic Coun., 1973. Mem. Southeastern Mass. Chiropractic Soc. (bd. dirs.), Mass. Chiropractic Soc., Am. Chiropractic Assn., N.Y. Acad. Sci., Fla. Chiropractic Soc., New Bedford Preservation Soc. (bd. dirs.). Editor: New England Jour. Chiropractic, 1965-75. Home: 62 Rear Manhattan Ave Fairhaven MA 02719 also: 3300 NE 23d Ave Lighthouse Point FL 33064 Office: 100 Bedford St New Bedford MA 02740-4839

MERRIAM, GEORGE RENNELL, JR., ophthalmologist; b. Harrisburg, Pa., May 22, 1913; s. George Rennell and Harriet (Lombard) M.; m. Martha Hildegarde Carlson, Sept. 5, 1936; children: George, John, Charlotte, Susan. AB, Brown U., 1934; MD, Columbia U., 1941. Diplomate Am. Bd. Ophthalmology. Instr. in ophthalmology Coll. of Physician and Surgeons/Columbia U., N.Y.C., 1949-54, assoc. in ophthalmology, 1955-58, asst. prof. of clin. ophthalmology, 1959-63, assoc. prof. clin. ophthalmology, 1964-73, prof. clin. ophthalmology, 1973-78, prof. emeritus, 1978—; ophthalmologist Francis Delafield Hosp., N.Y.C., 1949-75; dir. surgical svc. Edward S. Harkness Eye Inst., N.Y.C., 1960-78; cons. ophthalmologist, Meml. Hosp., N.Y.C., 1949-69; cons. Harlem Hosp., N.Y.C., 1970-87. Contbr. articles to profl. jours. Capt. Med. Corps, 1942-45, ETO. Mem. AMA, ACS, Am. Ophthal. Soc., Am. Acad. of Ophthalmology, Am. Radium Soc., N.Y. Ophthal. Soc., N.Y. Acad. Medicine. Republican. Presbyterian.

MERRICK, DAVID KENT, internist; b. Fremont, Nebr., Sept. 26, 1937; s. Alton Joyce and Nadine Beryl (Bemis) M.; m. Mary Kay Merrick, Aug. 5, 1961; children: Dan, Sam. BA, U. Nebr., 1959; MD, U. Nebr., Omaha,

1963. Diplomate Am. Bd. Internal Medicine. Intern Bishop Clarkson Meml. Hosp., Omaha, 1963-64; resident Mayo Clinic, Rochester, Minn., 1966-70; pvt. practice Boise, Idaho, 1970—; clin. prof. medicine U. Wash., Seattle, 1976—; med. dir. Sch. Respiratory Therapy, Boise State U., 1971—. Bd. dirs. United Way, Boise, 1994—, Blue Cross/Blue Shield, Boise, 1985—, chmn. bd., 1995-96. Capt. U.S. Army, 1964-66. Fellow ACP, Am. Coll. Chest Physicians. Republican. Methodist. Home: 700 Warm Springs Boise ID 83712 Office: 425 W Bannock Boise ID 83702

MERRIFIELD, H. H., physical therapy clinician, educator; b. Syracuse, N.Y., Mar. 12, 1930; s. Homer A. Merrifield and Hazel (Hamlin) Sheedy; divorced; children: Michael, Merri. AB, Colgate U., 1952, MA, 1955; PhD, U. Iowa, 1960; BS, SUNY, Syracuse, 1975. Lic. phys. therapist, Tex. Instr. St. Lawrence U., Canton, N.Y., 1955-58; asst. prof. Ithaca (N.Y.) Coll., 1960-62, 1962-71, prof., 1972-82; prof. phys. therapy, chmn. dept. Tex. Tech U Health Scis. Ctr., Lubbock, 1982—; vis. prof. SUNY, Cortland, summers 1967, 76, U. Calif., Berkeley, 1967-68, SUNY Upstate Med. Ctr., Syracuse, spring 1973, Syracuse U., fall 1975; cons. Ithaca Pub. Sch. System, 1978, Phila. Coll. Pharmacy, 1981, West Tex. Hosp. Rehab. Ctr., Lubbock, 1986, Rehab. Hosp. of Midland/Odessa (bd. of gov's. 1993—), 1992; conf. presenter, 1986, 87, 89, 91. Cons. editor Jour. Allied Health Behavioral Scis., 1977-82; contbr. over 35 articles to profl. jours. Bd. dirs. Cen. N.Y. Arthritis Found., Syracuse, 1977-82, The Parenting Cottage, Lubbock, 1987-92; mem. Tompkins County Arthritis Action, Ithaca, 1981-82. Recipient award of merit Cen. N.Y. chpt. Arthritis Found., 1980. Fellow Am. Coll. Sports Medicine; mem. Am. Phys. Therapy Assn. (del. 1986-91, adv. coun., chmn. phys. therapy edn. com. 1986-87), Tex. Phys. Therapy Assn. (liaison polit. action com. 1985—, bd. dirs. 1989-93, bylaws com. 1989—, chmn. West Tex. dist. 1989-93), Sigma Xi, Sigma Chi, Phi Kappa Phi, Alpha Eta Soc. (Outstanding Tchr. award 1993). Home: 4609 8th St Lubbock TX 79416-4704 Office: Tex Tech U Health Scis Ctr 3601 4th St Lubbock TX 79430-0001

MERRILL, JAMES ALLEN, obstetrician, gynecologist, educator; b. Cedar City, Utah, Oct. 27, 1925; s. Arthur Lynn and Thelma (Peery) M.; m. Patricia Gallagher, June 19, 1949; children: Janet Merrill Jones, Cynthia, Elizabeth, Rebecca. AB, U. Calif., Berkeley, 1945; MD, U. Calif., San Francisco, 1948. Diplomate Am. Bd. Ob-Gyn. Intern in obstetrics and gynecology U. Calif Hosp., San Francisco, 1948-49, asst., then chief resident, 1953-57; asst. resident pathology Cleve. City Hosp., 1949-50; resident pathologist Boston Lying-In Hosp., 1950-51; asst. chief gynecology cancer svc. U. Calif. Med. Ctr., San Francisco, 1957-61; chief gynecology cancer svc. U. Okla. Hosps., Oklahoma City, 1961-82, gynecologist, obstetrician-in-chief, 1961-82; chief staff U. Hosp., Oklahoma City, 1979-81; tchng. fellow pathology Med. Sch. Harvard U., Boston, 1950-51; instr. obstetrics and gynecology U. Calif., San Francisco, 1957-58, asst. prof., 1958-61, asst. clin. prof. pathology, 1959-61, rsch. fellow Cancer Rsch. Inst., 1957-58, rsch. asst. Cancer Rsch. Inst., 1958-61; chmn. dept. obstetrics and gynecology U. Okla., Oklahoma City, 1961-82, prof. gynecology and obstetrics, 1961-84, prof. pathology, 1961-84, prof. cytotech., 1970-84; sec.-treas. Am. Bd. Ob-Gyn, Inc., 1976-84, exec. dir., 1984-94; prof. obstetrics and gynecology U. Wash., Seattle, 1984—; cons. VA Hosp., Oklahoma City, 1961-84, U.S. Army Hosp., Fort Sill, Okla., 1962-84, USAF Hosp., San Antonio, 1964-84; mem. various coms. U. Okla., 1963-83; mem. residency rev. com. 1972-93. Editor: (with others) Gynecology and Obstetrics: The Health Care of Women, 1975; contbr. chpts. to books in field, also articles to profl. jours. Pres. Okla. Ballet Soc., 1966-69. With USN, 1944-46, M.C. USAF, 1951-53. Recipient Aesculapian award U. Okla. Student Body, 1963, 69, Regents award U. Okla., 1969; Markle scholar, 1958-63. Fellow Am. Cancer Soc. (fellow com.); mem. Am. Gynecol. Soc. (treas. 1969-74), Am. Assn. Obstetricians and Gynecologists, Am. Gynecol. and Obstet. Soc., Soc. Gynecol. Investigation (council 1966-69), Assn. Profs. Gynecology and Obstetrics (pres. 1966-67), Soc. Gynecol. Oncologists, San Francisco Gynecol. Soc., Cen. Assn. Obstetricians and Gynecologists, Am. Coll. Obstetricians and Gynecologists, Paciifc Coast Ob-Gyn Soc., Internat. Soc. Gynecol. Pathologists, Internat. Soc. Advancement Humanistic Studies in Gynecology (pres. 1972-73), Am. Soc. Cytology, Am. Fertility Soc., Am. Assn. Cancer Rsch., Nat. Bd. Med. Examiners (test com.). Republican. Home: 39 Williams Dr Moraga CA 94556

MERRILL, MICHAEL H., psychologist, therapist; b. Garden City, Kans., Jan. 12, 1954; s. Michael and Cleo (Maglaras) M.; m. Stephanie Kraus, May 29, 1976. BS in Journalism, U. Kans., 1976; BS in Elem. Edn., Washburn U., 1980; MA in Human Devel., U. Kans., 1984, PhD in Devel. Psychology, 1988. Ind. farmer Garden City, 1976-79; tchr. pre-sch. Menninger Found., Topeka, 1980-81; instr. behavior analysis, child and community psychology U. Kans., Lawrence, 1981-88; instructional designer computer/info. systems Arthur Andersen & Co., St. Charles, Ill., 1988-92; mgmt. psychologist RHR Internat., Chgo., 1992-94; corp. psychologist, biofeedback & stress mgmt. therapist pvt. practice, Chgo., 1994—. Contbr. articles to profl. pubs. Organizer Sta. KANZ FM Pub. Radio, Garden City, 1977-79; vol. Community Day Care Assn., Topeka, 1979-80, The Villages, Topeka, 1979-80; mem. Sta. KANU FM Pub. Radio, Lawrence, 1980-88. Mem. APA, Assn. for Behavior Analysis, Assn. for Advancement of Behavior Therapy, Assn. for Applied Psychophysiology and Biofeedback.

MERRILL, STEPHEN ALAN, psychiatrist; b. July 22, 1941; s. Michael H. and Nanette Merrill; m. Frances Linda Merrill, July 5, 1965; children: Andrew, Beth. AB, U. Rochester, 1963; MD, SUNY, Bklyn., 1967. Diplomate Am. Bd. Psychiatry and Neurology. Med. intern L.I.C.H., Bklyn., 1967-68; resident in psychiatry SUNY-Upstate Med. Ctr., Syracuse, 1968-71; pvt. practice Syracuse, N.Y., 1973—; clin. asst. prof. dept. psychiatry SUNY, Syracuse, 1973—. Maj. USAF, 1971-73. Mem. AMA, APA, Onon County Med. Soc., Med. Soc. State N.Y. Jewish. Office: 1400 State Tower Bldg Syracuse NY 13202

MERRITT, HENRY NEYRON, SR., psychotherapist; b. Darlington, S.C., Nov. 9, 1919; s. Henry Orme and Lilllian (Parrott) M.; m. Bess Castles, Aug. 21, 1953; children: Henry Neyron Jr., JoAnn. BS, Clemson U., 1941; MD, Kansas City (Mo.) U., 1944; MEd, U. S.C.; PhD, Phiathea Coll., London, Ont., Can., 1969. Diplomate Am. Bd. Med. Psychotherapists, Fla. Psychol. Practitioners Assn. Physician Bloudias Clinic, Columbia, S.C., 1944-53; biologist Montgomery County Bd. Edn., Silver Spring, Md., 1953-64; adj. prof. U. Md., College Park, 1953-64; assoc. prof. Frostburg (Md.) State U., 1964-67, Va. Poly. Inst., Blacksburg, 1967-68; prof., chmn. dept. health U. Wis., LaCrosse, 1968-72; dir. drug ctr. U. S. Navy, Jacksonville, Fla., 1972-76; dir. Psychotherapy Ctr., Jacksonville, 1976—. Fellow Am. Orthopsychiat. Assn., Masons, Shriners. Republican. Mem. Unity Ch. Home: 135 Blake Ave Orange Park FL 32073-4136 Office: 6039 Longchamp Dr Jacksonville FL 32244-5131

MERRITT, WILLIAM THOMAS, anesthesiologist, consultant, researcher; b. Easton, Md., Aug. 12, 1946; s. William Tholmas and Marie (LaBeau) M.; m. Helen M. Bunker, Oct. 30, 1981; children: William, Ryan, Caitlin. BS in Chemistry, Biology, Mt. St. Mary's Coll., 1968; MD, U. Md., Balt., 1972. Pediatric intern U. Md. Hosp., Balt., 1972-73, pediatric resident, 1976-78; fellow pediatric infectious disease Walter Reed Army Med. Ctr., Washington, 1978-80; assoc. prof., chief liver transplant anesthesia Johns Hopkins Hosp., Balt., Calif., 1980-82; anesthesiology resident Johns Hopkins Hosp., Balt., 1982-84, critical care anesthesiology, 1984-85, chief liver transplant anesthesia, 1986—; cons. Modular Instruments, Malvern, Pa., 1987—. Contbr. articles to profl. jours. Coach Naval Acad. Sailing Squadron, Annapolis, Md., 1976—. With USN, 1978-82, 88-90. Mem. ASA, IARS, Internat. Liver Transplantation Soc. (sec./treas. 1989—). Roman Catholic. Office: Johns Hopkins Hosp Dept Anesthesiology Tower 711 600 N Wolfe St Baltimore MD 21205

MERRYMAN, HARRY MCGEE, psychologist, administrator; b. Oakland, Calif., May 9, 1949; s. Andrew Curtis and Ann (McGee) M.; m. Linda Coleman, June 27, 1981; 1 child, Rachel. BS in Psychology, U. Oreg., 1974, MS in Orgnl. Psychology, 1982, MS in Counseling Psychology, 1982, PhD in Counseling Psychology, 1985. Lic. psychologist, Mass. Counseling psychologist Univ. Counseling Ctr. U. Oreg., Eugene, 1985-86, Worcester (Mass.) Poly. Inst., 1986-88; asst. dir. Counseling Ctr. of Rochester (N.Y.) Inst. of Tech., 1988-89, acting dir., 1989-90, dir., 1990—. Mem. Am. Psychol. Assn., Am. Assn. Counseling and Devel., Am. Coll. Personnel Assn., Am. Coll. Health Assn., Assn. Univ. and Coll. Counseling Ctr. Dirs. Episcopalian. Home: 220 Linden St Rochester NY 14620-2314 Office: Rochester Inst Tech Counseling Ctr Rochester NY 14623

MERSHON, JOHN LEE, reproductive endocrinologist; b. Martinsville, Ind., Aug. 10, 1960; s. Jack Belle and Janet Maebelle (Graves) M.; m. Ann Roberta Cutler, Sept. 9, 1988; children: Erin Elizabeth, John Patrick, Jack Sebastian. BS in Biology and Chemistry, Purdue U., 1981; MD, Ind. U., Indpls., 1985. Intern and resident in ob-gyn. Ohio State Med. Ctr., Columbus, 1985-89; fellow in reproductive endocrinology and infertility U. Cin. Med. Ctr., 1989-91, asst. prof. dept. ob-gyn., 1991—. Mem. Alpha Omega Alpha. Home: 18 Trailbridge Dr Cincinnati OH 45241-3256

MERSON, MICHAEL HOWARD, public health physician, epidemiologist; b. N.Y.C., June 7, 1945; s. Leo and Paula Enid (Katz) M.; m. Claudia Regina Jupiter, Feb. 1, 1975; 1 child, Jonathan. BA, Amherst Coll., 1966; MD, SUNY, Bklyn., 1970. Commd. officer USPHS, 1972, advanced through grades to capt.; chief enteric disease br. Ctrs. for Disease Control, Atlanta, 1974-75; chief epidemiologist Cholera Rsch. Lab., Dacca, Bangladesh, 1977-78; dir. diarrheal diseases control program WHO, Geneva, 1978-90, dir. global program on AIDS, 1990—; trustee, bd. dirs. Internat. Ctr. for Diarrheal Diseases, Dacca, 1985-90. Recipient Arthur Fleming award U.S. Jaycees, 1975. Mem. Royal Soc. Tropical Medicine and Hygiene, Internat. Epidemiol. Assn., Am. Soc. for Epidemiology, Am. Soc. for Microbiology, Soc. Scholars. Office: Yale U 60 College St New Haven CT 06520-8034

MERTEN, UTZ PETER, physician; b. Cologne, Germany, July 22, 1942; m. Franie Sachs, 1973; children: Patrick Sinclair, Marc Leon. Attended, U. Berlin, 1963-69, Oxford, 1967-68; MD, Kiel, Germany, 1970. Head Lab Dr. Merten & Ptnr., Cologne, Germany, 1976; cons. MCS-AG, DELAB, OKO-Control. Office: Lab Dr Merten & Ptnr, Stadtwaldgurtel 35, 50935 Cologne Germany

MERTINS, JAMES WALTER, entomologist; b. Milw., Feb. 18, 1943; s. Walter Edwin and Harriet Ellen (Sockett) M.; m. Marilee Eloise Joeckel, Dec. 8, 1979. BS in Zoology, U. Wis., Milw., 1965; MS in Entomology, U. Wis., 1967, PhD in Entomology, 1971. Project assoc. dept. entomology U. Wis., Madison, 1971-75, rsch. assoc. dept. entomology, 1975-77; asst. prof. dept. entomology Iowa State U., Ames, 1977-84; entomol. cons. Ames, 1984-89; entomologist Nat. Vet. Svcs. Labs. USDA Animal and Plant Health Inspection Svc., Ames, 1989—. Co-author: (textbook) Biological Insect Pest Suppression, 1977, Russian edit., 1980, Chinese edit., 1988; contbr. articles to profl. jours. NSF Grad. fellow, 1970. Mem. Entomol. Soc. Am. (Insect Photgraphy award 1984, 86), Entomol. Soc. Can., Mich. Entomol. Soc., Wis. Entomol. Soc. (pres., sec., treas., bd. dirs.), Cyclone Corvettes, Inc. (cofounder, pres. 1978, 79, sec., treas., bd. dirs., Mem. of Yr. 1982), Am. Mensa. Office: Animal & Plant Health Inspection Svs USDA PO Box 844 Ames IA 50010-0844

MERVILDE, MICHAEL JOHN, clinical social worker; b. Mishawaka, Ind., Mar. 7, 1947; s. Armond Emil and Amelia (Canarecci) M.; m. Karen Sue Selig, Aug. 3, 1974; children: Lisa Marie, Michael John Jr. AB, St. Edwards U., Austin, Tex., 1969; MSW, Washington U., St. Louis, 1975. Acting exec. dir. Hotline, South Bend, Ind., 1973; clin. assoc. Drug Info. Ctr., St. Louis, 1973-74, Social Health Assn., St. Louis, 1975; mental health coord. Kewaunee County Unified Bd., Algoma, Wis., 1975-78; clin. social worker Bay Psychiat. Clinic, Green Bay, Wis., 1978-86; ptnr., clin. social worker Green Bay Wellness & Behavioral Health Clinic, 1985—. Mem. NASW (bd. dirs. Wis. chpt. 1981-85), Acad. Cert. Social Workers, Acad. Family Mediators (assoc.), Optimists (charter, sec. Green Bay). Roman Catholic. Office: Green Bay Wellness & Behavioral Hlth Clinic 125 S Jefferson St Green Bay WI 54301-4500

MERZ, FERDINAND KARL, psychology educator; b. Chgo., May 16, 1924; arrived in Fed. Republic Germany, 1927; s. Hermann Adam and Maria (Plessing) M.; m. Eva Margarethe Emde, Aug. 8, 1950; children: Stephan, Sebastian, Martina. PhD, U. Würzburg, Germany, 1951, Habilitation, 1960. Asst. U. Würzburg, 1955-60, dozent, 1960-63; dozent U. Marburg, Germany, 1963-64, prof. psychology, 1964—. Co-author: Erbpsychologie, 1977; author: Geschlechterunterschiede, 1979; contbr. articles to profl. jours. Home: Unter dem Gedanke 3 35047 Marburg Hessen, Germany Office: U Marburg, Gutenbergstr 18, 35041 Marburg Germany

MES, LOUIS GERRIT BRYANT, plastic surgeon; b. Krugersdorp, South Africa, Dec. 25, 1944; s. Frits Ferdinand and Mavis Dorothy (Parsons) M.; m. Talitha Kumi Roos, Dec. 11, 1972; children: Francçis, Esther, Nicole. MB, B of Surgery, U. Witwatersrand, South Africa, 1969. Diplomate Am. Bd. Plastic Surgery. Intern Gen. Hosp., Johannesburg, South Africa, 1970-71; instr. in anatomy U. Witwatersrand, 1971-72; surg. med. officer Anglo-Am. Corp., Welkom, South Africa, 1972-73; sr. house officer in gen. surgery Nat. Health Orgn., Mansfield, Eng., 1973-74; sr. house officer in plastic surgery Nat. Health Orgn., Bridge of Earn, Scotland, 1974-75; sr. resident in plastic surgery U. Mich., Ann Arbor, 1975-77, clin. instr. in plastic surgery, 1977-78; pvt. practice Lafayette, La., 1978—. Contbr. articles to profl. jours. Pres. Fine Arts Found., Lafayette, 1983-87; mem. numerous environ. and cultural orgns. Named Disting. Prof., U. Crete, 1995. Fellow Royal Coll. Surgeons (Scotland), Am. Coll. Surgeons (Mich. chpt. Frederick Coller award 1977); mem. Am. Soc. Plastic and Reconstructive Surgeons, Southeastern Soc. Plastic and Reconstructive Surgeons, Am. Cleft Palate Soc., La. Med. Soc., Lafayette Parish Med. Soc. Republican. Office: Plastic Surgery Assocs 1101 S College Rd Lafayette LA 70503

MESCHAN, ISADORE, radiologist, educator; b. Cleve., May 30, 1914; s. Julius and Anna (Gordon) M.; m. Rachel Farrer, Sept. 3, 1943; children: David Farrer, Eleanor Jane Meschan Foy, Rosalind Weir, Joyce Meschan Lawrence. BA, Western Res. U., 1935, MA, 1937, MD, 1939; ScD (hon.), U. Ark., 1983. Instr. Western Res. U., 1946-47; prof., head dept. radiology U. Ark., Little Rock, 1947-55; prof., dir. dept. radiology Bowman Gray Sch. Medicine, Wake Forest U., Winston-Salem, N.C., 1955-77; now prof. emeritus Bowman Gray Sch. Medicine, Wake Forest U. Author: Atlas of Normal Radiographic Anatomy, 1951, Roentgen Signs in Clinical Diagnosis, 1956, (with R. Meschan) Synopsis of Roentgen Signs, 1962, Roentgen Signs in Clinical Practice, 1966, Radiographic Positioning Related Anatomy, 1969, 2d edit., 1978, Analysis of Roentgen Signs, 3 vols, 1972, Atlas of Anatomy Basic to Radiology, 1975, Synopsis of Analysis of Roentgen Signs, 1976, Synopsis of Radiographic Anatomy, 1978, 2d rev. edit., 1980, (with B.W. Wolfman) Basic Atlas of Sectional Anatomy, 2d edit.; co-author: Atlas of Cross-Sectional Anatomy, 1980, Roentgen Signs in Diagnostic Imaging, vol. 1, 1984, vol. 2, 1985, vol. 3, 1986, vol. 4, 1987; editor: The Radiologic Clinics of North America, 1965; contbr. articles to profl. jours. Recipient Disting. Alumnus award Case-Western Res. U. Sch. Medicine, 1984, Disting. Faculty Svc. Alumni award Wake Forest U. Bowman Gray Sch. Medicine, 1989. Fellow Am. Coll. Radiology (com. chmn., Gold medal 1978, Living Legends of Radiology 1986); mem. Am. Roentgen Ray Soc., AMA, Radiology Soc. N.Am., N.C. Radiol. Soc., So. Med. Assn., Soc. Nuclear Medicine, Assn. U. Radiologists, Phi Beta Kappa, Sigma Xi, Alpha Omega Alpha. Home: 305 Weatherfield Ln Kernersville NC 27284-8337

MESCHAN, RACHEL FARRER (MRS. ISADORE MESCHAN), obstetrics and gynecology educator; b. Sydney, Australia, May 21, 1915; came to U.S., 1946, naturalized, 1950; d. John H. and Gertrude (Powell) Farrer; m. Isadore Meschan, Sept. 3, 1943; children: David Farrer-Meschan, Jane Meschan Foy, Rosalind Meschan Weir, Joyce Meschan Lawrence. MB, BS, U. Melbourne (Australia), 1940; MD, Wake Forest U., 1957. Intern Royal Melbourne Hosp., 1942; resident Women's Hosp., Melbourne, 1942-43, Bowman-Gray Sch. Medicine, Wake Forest U., Winston-Salem, N.C., 1957-73, asst. clin. prof. dept. ob-gyn, 1973—; also marriage counselor. Co-author (with I. Meschan): Atlas of Radiographic Anatomy, 1951, rev., 1959; Roentgen Signs in Clinical Diagnosis, 1956; Synopsis of Roentgen Signs, 1962; Roentgen Signs in Clinical Practice, 1966; Radiographic Positioning and Related Anatomy, 1968; Analysis of Roentgen Signs in General Radiology, 1973; Roentgen Signs in Diagnostic Imaging, Vol. III, 1936, Vol. IV, 1987. Home: 305 Weatherfield Ln Kernersville NC 27284-8337

MESEC, DONALD FRANCIS, psychiatrist; b. Waukegan, Ill., Aug. 29, 1936; s. Joseph and Johanna (Setnicar) M.; m. Francesca Auditore, June 20, 1964 (div. 1987); 1 child, Steven Francis; m. Patricia Guitteau, Mar. 27, 1988. BS cum laude, U. Notre Dame, 1958; MD, N.Y. Med. Coll., 1963. Diplomate Am. Bd. Psychiatry and Neurology. Resident in psychiatry and neurology N.Y. Med. Coll.-Manhattan State Hosp., N.Y.C., 1964-67; chief of svc. Manhattan Psychiat. Ctr., N.Y.C., 1970-76, dir. psychiat. rsch., 1974-75, dir. Meyer Manhattan Alcohol Rehab. Ctr., 1975; med. dir. Meyer Day Ctr., N.Y.C., 1976-77; staff psychiatrist Asheville VA Hosp., N.C., 1977-78; practice medicine specializing in psychiatry, Phoenix, 1978—; instr. clin. psychiatry Columbia U., N.Y.C., 1972-77; dir. psychiat. edn. St. Joseph's Hosp., Phoenix, 1982—, co-dir. pain program, 1982—, vice chmn. dept. psychiatry, 1984—, chmn. dept. psychiatry, 1987—; chief div. mental health MacDonald Meml. Hosp., Republic Palau, 1991—; with pacific ops. U.S. Dept. Health and Human Svcs., 1991—. Served with USPHS, 1963-64. Mem. New York County Med. Soc., Ariz. Med. Assn., Maricopa County Med. Soc., Ariz. Psychiat. Soc., AMA, Am. Psychiat. Assn., Am. Acad. Clin. Psychiatrists. Office: PO Box 3009 Kingman AZ 86402-3009

MESHOTO, DANIEL JOSEPH, physician; b. St. Louis, July 7, 1966; s. Carl Joseph and Ruby Meshoto. DO, Kirksville Coll. Osteo. Medicine, 1993. Intern Deaconess Med. Ctr., St. Louis, 1993-94, resident in family practice, 1994-96; pvt. pracitce Cedar Hill, Mo., 1996—. Home: 5425 Clifton Saint Louis MO 63109

MESIHA, MOUNIR SOBHY, industrial pharmacy educator; b. Alexandria, Egypt, Feb. 14, 1945; came to U.S., 1985; s. Madiha Sidhom, Sept. 4, 1972; 1 child, Mena. BS in Pharmacy with distinction, Pharmacy Coll., Alexandria, 1967; PhD in Pharmaceutics, Pharmacy Coll., Kharkov, Ukraine, 1977. Lic. pharmacist. Instr. Dept. of Pharms. U. Assiut, 1967-69, instr., 1969-72, sr. instr., 1972-77, asst. prof. indsl. pharmacy, 1978-83, assoc. prof., 1983-85; prof. indsl. pharmacy U. P.R., San Juan, 1985-89, L.I. U., Bklyn., N.Y., 1990—; sci. com. mem. Industry U. Rsch. Ctr., P.R., 1988-89; pres. rsch. com. Coll. Pharmacy, San Juan, 1988-89. Contbr. articles to Jour. Pharmacy and Pharmacology, Die Pharmazie, Drug Devel. and Indsl. Pharmacy, Internat. Jour. Pharmaceutics, others. Industry U. Rsch. Ctr. grantee, P.R., 1989. Mem. Am. Diabetes Assn., Am. Pharm. Soc., Am. Assn. Colls. Pharmacy, Am. Assn. Pharm. Scientists (chartered), Fedn. Internat. Pharmaceutique (assoc.). Christian Orthodox. Home: 239 Halsey Ave Jericho NY 11753-1625 Office: L I U Coll Pharmacy 75 Dekalb Ave Brooklyn NY 11201-5497

MESNIKOFF, ALVIN MURRAY, psychiatry educator; b. Asbury Park, N.J., Dec. 25, 1925; s. Nathan and Rachel (Feinberg) M.; m. Wendy Savin, June 15, 1952; children: Nathaniel, Rachel, Joel, Ann. A.B., Rutgers U., 1948; M.D., U. Chgo., 1954; cert. Psychoanalytic medicine, Columbia U., 1962. Diplomate: Am. Bd. Psychiatry and Neurology. Pvt. practice, 1958—; collaborating psychoanalyst Columbia U. Psychoanalytic Ctr. for Tng. and Rsch., N.Y.C., 1962—; dir. Washington Heights Community, N.Y. State Psychiat. Inst., N.Y.C., 1965-68; assoc. clin. prof. psychiatry Columbia U. Coll. Physicians and Surgeons, 1958-68; prof. psychiatry SUNY, Bklyn., 1968-81; dir. South Beach Psychiat. Ctr., S.I., N.Y., 1968-75; regional dir. N.Y. State Dept. Mental Health, N.Y.C., 1975-78, dep. commr. research, 1978-81; Marion E. Kenworthy prof. Psychiatry Columbia U. Sch. Social Work, 1981-89; lectr. Union Theol. Sem., N.Y.C., 1989-90; cons. St. Vincent's Hosp., S.I., 1970-76; attending psychiatrist S.I. Hosp., 1972-76; sr. attending psychiatrist St. Luke's/Roosevelt Hosp. Ctr., N.Y., 1987—; cons. Ford Found., N.Y.C., 1980-81. Contbr. chpts. to books, articles to profl. jours. Bd. dirs. Reality House, 1967-74; mem. task force med. sch. enrollment and physician manpower N.Y. State Bd. Regents, 1973-75; mem. task force on gen. and splty. hosp. care N.Y. State Health Planning Commn., 1973-74. Served with U.S. Army, 1943-45. Grantee Ford Found., 1982. Fellow Am. Psychiat. Assn. (life); mem. Am. Psychoanalytic Assn., Assn. Psychoanalytic Medicine, Am. Friends Tel Aviv U. (chmn. 1974-75), Phi Beta Kappa. Jewish. Office: 360 Central Park W New York NY 10025-6541

MESSAMORE, MICHAEL MILLER, pharmacist; b. Loudon, Tenn., May 27, 1955; s. John Clifford and Lillie Florence (Miller) M.; m. Laura Leigh Munsey, Oct. 19, 1985; 1 child, Sarah Beth. AA, Hiwassee Jr. Coll., Madisonville, Tenn., 1976; BA, Wabash Coll., 1978; BS in Pharmacy, Mercer U., 1981. Pharmacist Eckerd Drugs, Norton, Va., 1981-83; pharmacist, asst. mgr. Eckerd Drugs, Kingsport, Tenn., 1983-90, Super X Drugs, Bristol, Va., 1990-94; pharmacist Revco Drugs, Bristol, 1994—. Mem. 1st Dist. Pharm. Assn., Va. Pharm. Assn., Tenn. Pharm. Assn., Soc. of Pharmacists, Am. Pharm. Assn., Soc. Chain Pharmacists, Moose, Masons. Baptist. Home: 134 Deaderick Dr Kingsport TN 37663-2114 Office: Revco Drugs # 3369 2004 Lee Hwy Bristol VA 24201-1626

MESSER, BILLY FREEMAN, JR., critical care nurse; b. Dothan, Ala., Feb. 13, 1968; s. Billy Freeman and Sharlene (Williams) M. ADN, Wallace Community Coll., Dothan, 1989; BSN, U. Ala., Tuscaloosa, 1993; postgrad., Xavier U., 1995—. RN, Ala. Staff nurse DCH Regional Med. Ctr., Tuscaloosa, 1989-92, U. Ala. at Birmingham Hosp., 1992-93, Grady Meml. Hosp., Atlanta, 1993-94; nursing legal cons., Ala., 1992. Author profl. papers. Mem. AACN (cert. CCRN), Am. Assn. Nurse Anesthetists, Wallace Assn. Nursing Students. Democrat. Home: Apt D231 3901 N I 10 Service Rd W Metairie LA 70002-6836 Office: Med Ctr La at New Orleans 1532 Tulane Ave New Orleans LA 70140-1004

MESSER, STANLEY BERNARD, psychology educator; b. Montreal, Que., Can., Nov. 28, 1941; s. Nathan Harry and Sylvia (Hamovitch) M.; m. Donna Rebecca Ann Evin, Dec. 29, 1966; children: Elana, Leora, Tova. BSc, McGill U., Montreal, 1962; MA, Harvard U., 1966, PhD, 1969. Lic. psychologist, N.J. Asst. prof. Rutgers U., New Brunswick, N.J., 1968-74, assoc. prof., 1974-80, prof., 1980—, acting chair dept. clin. psychology, 1992-93, chair dept. clin. psychology, 1993—. Co-author: Models of Brief Psychodynamic Therapy: A Comparative Approach, 1995; co-editor: Psychoanalytic and Behavior Therapy: Is Integration Possible?, 1984, Hermeneutics and Psychological Theory, 1988, History of Psychotherapy: A Century of Change, 1992, Essential Psychotherapies, 1995; adv. editor Contemporary Psychology, Psychotherapy Research, Jour. Psychotherapy Integration, Clin. Psychology: Sci. and Practice, In Session, Psychotherapy. Bd. dirs. B'nai Brith Hillel Found., Rutgers U., 1980—. Grant N.J. Coun. on the Humanities, 1985. Fellow Am. Psychol. Assn.; mem. Soc. for Psychotherapy Rsch., Soc. for the Exploration of Psychotherapy Integration, Eastern Psychol. Assn. Office: Rutgers U GSAPP PO Box 819 Piscataway NJ 08855-0819

MESSER-REHAK, DABNEY LEE, physical therapist; b. Des Moines, Iowa, June 21, 1951; d. Joseph Thomas and June (Grady) Messer; m. Thomas James Rehak, June 27, 1981. BS, Chgo. Med. Sch., 1974; MS, U. Wis., 1984. Physical therapist Loyola U. Hosp., Maywood, Ill., 1974-78; faculty U. Ill. Med. Ctr., Chgo., 1978-81; physical therapist U. Wis. Hosp., Madison, 1982-84; lectr. Baxter-Travenol Labs., Deerfield, Ill., 1984—; cons. Mercy Ctr. for Health Care Services, Aurora, Ill., 1985-90, dir. physical therapy, 1986-90; dir. med.-surg./rehab. svcs. Cen. DuPage Hosp., Winfield, Ill., 1990—; cons. Edward Hosp., Naperville, 1984; mem. profl. adv. bd. for cmty. nursing svc. Midwesten U. Coll. of DuPage; vice-chmn. DuPage County Health Planning Coun. Contbr. articles to profl. jours. Mem. NAFE, Am. Phys. Therapy Assn. (chair dist. 1990—), Ill. Phys. Therapy Assn. (treas.), Bus. and Profl. Women. Presbyterian. Office: Cen DuPage Hosp 25 Winfield Rd Winfield IL 60190

MESSERSCHMIDT, GERALD LEIGH, pharmaceutical industry executive, physician; b. Vancouver, B.C., Can., Feb. 2, 1950; s. George Gus and Joan May (Chapman) M.; m. Donna Kay Mackinley, Sept. 29, 1990; children: Jacqueline Diane, Victoria Leigh, Jonathan Leigh. BS, Portland State U., 1972; MD, U. Oreg., Portland, 1976. Diplomate Am. Bd. Internal Medicine, Am. Bd. Med. Oncology, Am. Bd. Hematology. Resident in internal medicine Letterman Army Med. Ctr., San Francisco, 1976-79; fellow in oncology and hematology NIH, Bethesda, Md., 1979-82; head exptl. hematology Nat. Cancer Inst., NIH, Bethesda, Md., 1981-82; dir. bone marrow transplants for Dept. of Def. Wilford Hall Med. Ctr., San Antonio, 1982-88; dir. bone marrow transplants U. Mich. Med. Ctr., Ann Arbor, 1988-90; dir. med. affairs Ciba-Geigy Pharm., Summit, N.J., 1990-92, exec. dir. med. affairs, 1992-93; v.p. med. and regulatory affairs DNX Corp.,

Princeton, N.J., 1993-94; corp. v.p. C.R. Bard Inc., Murray Hill, N.J., 1994-95, sr. v.p., 1995-96; CEO, pres. Kimeragen, Inc., N.Y.C., 1996—. Maj. USAF, 1982-88. Fellow ACP; mem. Am. Soc. Oncology, Am. Soc. Hematology. Home: 1250 Brentford ln Tredyffrin PA Office: Kimeragen Inc 300 Pheasant Run Newtown PA 18940

MESSERSCHMIDT, WILLIAM HAMILTON, physician; b. Abington, Pa., Sept. 18, 1956; s. William Walter and Marilyn Gail (Young) M.; m. Nadine Dorothy Brennan, Oct. 7, 1989; 1 child, William Laurance. BS, Pa. State U., 1977; MD, Jefferson Med. Coll., 1979. Diplomate Am. Bd. Surgery, Am. Bd. Thoracic Surgery. Resident in surgery Thomas Jefferson U. Hosp., Phila., 1979-84, resident in cardiothoracic surgery, 1984-87; surgeon Wilkes-Barre (Pa.) Cardiothoracic Surgery Group, 1987-88; asst. prof. surgery James H. Quillen Coll. Medicine, Johnson City, Tenn., 1988-92; assoc. prof. East Tenn. State U., Johnson City, 1992—, dir. divsn. cardiovascular and thoracic surgery, 1988—; clin. rsch. dir., bd. dirs. Cardiovasc. Rsch. Inst., Johnson City, 1995-96; chmn. cardiovasc. com. Johnson City Med. Ctr. Hosp., 1993-96. Bd. dirs., past pres. Washington County divsn. Am. Heart Assn., Johnson City, 1988—. Grantee Cardiovasc. Rsch. Inst., 1995-96. Fellow ACS, Am. Coll. Chest Physicians; mem. Soc. Thoracic Surgeons, So. Thoracic Surg. Assn., Tenn. Med. Assn., Washington Johnson County Med. Assn. (treas., pres.-elect 1992-96). Republican. Lutheran. Home: 1600 Willowbrook Dr Johnson City TN 37601 Office: East Tenn State U Dept Surg James H Quillen Coll Med PO Box 70575 Johnson City TN 37614

MESSINA, LOUIS MICHAEL, vascular surgeon, educator; b. Bklyn., July 27, 1951; s. John Louis and Elizabeth Ann (Ross) M.; m. Katie Ragland, June 17, 1978; children: Julia Antoinette, Peter Louis, Katharine Elizabeth. BA, Fordham U., 1973; MD summa cum laude, SUNY Downstate Med. Ctr., Bklyn., 1978. Diplomate Nat. Bd. Med. Examiners, Am. Bd. Surgery with subspecialty in vascular surgery, Am. Bd. Critical Care. Intern U. Calif., San Francisco, 1978-79, resident, 1980-85, postdoctoral fellow, 1981-83, vascular surgery fellow, 1985-86, instr. dept. surgery, 1985-86, prof., 1995—, chief vascular surgery, 1995—; asst. prof. U. Mich., Ann Arbor, 1986-93, assoc. prof., 1993-95; vis. prof. Pacific Vascular Rsch. Found. Engel scholar, 1975. Roman Catholic. Office: U Calif San Francisco Vascular Surgery 505 Parnasus M488 Box 0222 San Francisco CA 94143-0222

MESSING, SIMON DAVID, anthropologist, retired; b. Franfurt on Main, Germany, July 13, 1922; came to U.S., 1940; s. Jacob and Helen (Friedler) M.; m. Denise Messing, July 25, 1967; 1 child, Jacqueline. BS, CCNY, 1949; PhD, U. Pa., 1957. Asst. prof. Paine Coll., Augusta, Ga., 1956-58; assoc. prof. Hiram (Ohio) Coll., 1958-60, U. So. Fla., Tampa, 1960-61, 63-64; foreign svc. USAID, Addis Ababa, Ethiopia, 1961-63, 64-67; prof. anthropology So. Conn. State U., 1968-89, emeritus, 1989—; prof. emeritus of anthropology So. Conn. State U., New Haven, 1989—; researcher pub. health USAID-Ethiopia, 1961-63, 64-67. Author: Target of Health in Ethiopia, 1972, The Story of the Falashas of Ethiopia, 1982, Highland Plateau Amhara of Ethiopia, 1985. With U.S. Army, 1943-45. Recipient Harrison fellowship, U. Pa., 1950-51, Ford Found. grant, 1954. Fellow Am. Anthrop. Assn., African Studies Soc., Soc. for Applied Anthropology, Soc. for Med. Anthropology.

MESSINGER, ARTHUR LOUIS, orthopedic surgeon; b. Chgo., Aug. 9, 1925; s. Arthur I. and Thresa (Makovsky) M.; m. H. Phyllis Boxer, June 14, 1953; children: Judith, Patricia, Michael. BS, Duke U., 1945; MD, U. Ill., Chgo., 1949. Cert. Am. Acad. Orthopedic Surgery. Intern Emanuel Hosp., Portland, Oreg., 1949-50; resident VA Hosp., Portland, 1950-55, USN-Orthopedic Svc., 1950-52, Children's Hosp., Lincoln, Nebr., 1953-54; pvt. practice Santa Clara County, 1955—; attending staff Santa Clara Valley Med. Ctr., Stanford U., 1955-65; asst. chief orthopedic svc., chief orthopedic surgeon S.C. County Cerebral Palsy Program, 1960—; med. dir. neurol. rehab. Ctr. of Cmty. Hosp., Los Gatos-Saratoga, 1978-86; ind. med. examiner State of Calif. Indsl. Accident Commn., 1983—. Exec. bd., 1st v.p. Easter Seal Soc., 1961-68; cons. paramedic tng. program Am. Heart Assn., 1972; bd. dirs., orthopedic cons. Timpany Swim Rehab. Ctr. San Jose, 1981-86. Lt. USN, 1943-45, 50-52, UNSR, 1946-50, 52-56. Recipient Outstanding Contbn. in Cmty. Svc. award, 1994. Mem. AMA, S.C. Med. Soc. (various coms. including ethics com. 1994—), Santa Clara County Med. Soc., Santa Clara Valley Orthopedic Club (past pres. 1958, 72). Jewish. Home: 2295 Gundersen Dr San Jose CA 95125 Office: 700 W Parr Ave Los Gatos CA 95030

MESSINGER, BARRY NILES, orthopedist; b. Bridgeport, Conn., Mar. 5, 1952; s. Henry Juda and Beatrice Messinger; m. Geri Lynn Messinger, June 17, 1993; 1 child, Heidi. BS in Biology, Yale U., 1974; MD, U. Conn., 1979, degree orthopedic surgery, 1984. Diplomate Am. Bd. Orthopedic Surgery. Orthopedic surgeon Sports Medicine and Orthopedic Surgery of Manchester, Conn., 1985-95; pvt. practice Manchester, 1996—; cons. U. Conn. divsn. athletics, Storrs, 1985—, Manchester Road Race, 1993—, World Games Spl. Olympics, New Haven, Conn., 1995; preceptor U. Conn. dept. family practice, Hartford, 1989—; clin. assoc. U. Conn. dept. orthopedic surgery, Farmington, 1985—. Fellow sports medicine Brookline Sports Medicine, 1984-85. Fellow Am. Acad. Orthopedic Surgery; mem. AMA, Conn. State Med. Soc. (med. aspects of sports com. 1989—), Hartford County Med. Assn. Office: 360 Tolland Turnpike # 3C Manchester CT 06040

MESSMORE, HARRY LEROY, JR., internist; b. Atkinson, Ill., Nov. 18, 1922; s. I. Harry Leroy and Ella Louise (Richter) M.; m. Marilyn Jean Anderson, Nov. 14, 1943; children: Susan, Curtis, Rex, Gary. MB, U. Ill., 1949; MD, U. Ill. Coll. Medicine, 1952. Lic. MD, Ill.; Diplomate Am. Bd. Internal Medicine; cert. in hematology and oncology. Physician pvt. practice Arthur, Ill., 1953-64; resident in internal medicine Hines (Ill.) VA Hosp., 1964-67, resident in hematology, 1967-68, staff physician, 1968-71; asst. prof. Loyola U. Stritch Sch. of Medicine, Maywood, Ill., 1969-74, assoc. prof., 1974-81, prof. medicine, 1981-95; staff physician Hines VA Hosp., 1982-95; chief sect. of hematology Loyola U. Stritch Sch. of Medicine, Maywood, 1971-81. Contbr. sci. articles to profl. jours. Capt. U.S. Army, 1941-45. Recipient Stritch medal Loyola U. of Chgo., 1994. Fellow ACP. Republican. Office: Loyola U Med Ctr 2160 S First Ave Maywood IL 60153

MESTER, ADAM, physician, educator; b. Budapest, Hungary, Mar. 13, 1950; s. Endre and Georgina Agotha (Schubert) M.; m. Judit Ortutay, Oct. 7, 1978; children: Oliver, Marton. MD, Semmelweis U., Budapest, 1974. Cert. radiologist. Resident and asst. Dept. Radiology Semmelweis U. of Medicine, 1974-80, fellow Dept. Radiology, 1980-84, attending physician Dept. Radiology, 1984-90; head Nat. Laser Therapy Lab., 1990; assoc. prof. Dept. Radiology Semmelweis U. Medicine, 1992—; divsn. leader Dept. Radiology Semmelweis U. Medicine, 1992; head Nat. Laser Therapy Lab., Budapest, 1990. Mem. editl. bd. Laser Therapy Jour., Osteologiai Kozlemenyek Jour.; contbr. chpts. to books. Mem. bd. dirs. Hungarian Med. Laser Soc., Budapest, 1993—, subcom. Med. Optics & Laser of Hungarian Acad. of Scis., 1994—, Hungarian Crohn Soc., Budapest, 1995—. Mem. World Assn. of Laser Therapy (hon.), Internat. Low Power Laser Soc. (past sec. gen. 1990, 92), Hungarian Radiologists (sec. gen. osteologic sect. 1993—). Home: Lisznyai 25/B, H-1016 Budapest Hungary Office: Dept Radiology-Semmelweis U, Ulloi UT 78/A, H-1082 Budapest Hungary

METCALF, JAMES A., neurologist. BA, Northwestern U., 1969, MD, 1973. Diplomate Am. Bd. Psychiatry & Neurology, Nat. Bd. Med. Examiners; cert. in electroencephography Am. Bd. Qualificaion. Intern Evanston (Ill.) Hosp., 1973-74; resident in neurology Harbor-UCLA, Torrence, 1974-77; fellow in EEG Neurol. Assocs. Tucson, 1977-78; pvt. practice Paducah, Ky., 1978-89; ptnr. Purchase Neurology, P.C., Paducah, 1989—; med. dir. rehab. unit Lourdes Hosp., Paducah, 1985-91; neurologist Commn. for Handicapped Svcs., Paducah, 1979-89, 91—. Mem. Am. Sleep Disorders Assn. (bd. cert.). Office: PO Box 8129 225 Med Ctr Dr Ste 402 Paducah NY 42002-8129

METCALF, JAMES MICHAEL, neonatologist; b. Covina, Calif., May 12, 1954; s. George Wilson and Andrée Marie (Renouard) M.; children: Eric, Megan, Casey, Noel. BS in Biology, U. So. Calif., 1976; MD, Univ. Centro de Estudios Tecnicos, Santo Domingo, Dominican Republic, 1982. Diplomate Am. Bd. Pediatrics. Intern, then resident pediatrics Jersey City Med. Ctr., 1982-84, chief resident pediatrics, 1984-85; neonatal fellow U. Medicine & Dentistry of N.J. UMDNJ Rutgers U., New Brunswick, 1985-87; attending neonatologist Marietta (Ga.) Neonatology, P.C., 1987—; dir. neonatology ICU, Cobb Hosp. and Med. Ctr., Austell, Ga., 1988—. Contbr. articles to profl. jours. Mem. Am. Med. Polit. Action Com., 1984—, Physicians for Social Responsibility, 1989—. Fellow Am. Acad. Pediatrics; mem. Ga. chpt. Am. Acad. Pediatrics, Cobb Area Pediatric Soc., Nat. Perinatal Assn. Home: 4120 Brigade Trail Kennesaw GA 30152 Office: Marietta Neonatology PC PO Box 4214 Marietta GA 30061-4214

METCALF, JAMES RICHARD, orthodontist; b. Troy, N.Y., Aug. 2, 1950; s. James M. and Ruth Amy (Metcalf) Sunukjian; m. Cynthia A. Komatinsky, Aug. 25, 1973; children: Jeffrey, Jennifer. BA, SUNY, Oswego, 1972; DMD, U. Pitts., 1976, M in Dental Sci., 1980. Resident Strong Meml. Hosp., Rochester, N.Y., 1977; orthodontist Northeastern Dental Assocs., Schenectady, N.Y., 1980-81, Orthodontic Assocs., Lowell, Mass., 1981—. Contbr. articles to profl. jours. Mem. Cen. Congl. Ch. (fin. com. 1988—). Mem. ADA, NRA (cert. instr. pistol, rifle, shotgun, home firearms responsibility and personal protection courses), Am. Assn. Orthodontists (award 1976), Mass. Soc. Orthodontists, Mass. Dental Soc., Greater Lowell Dental Soc. (pres. 1987-88), State Rifle and Pistol Assn. Mass., New Eng. Wood Carvers, Nat. Wood Carvers, Am. Radio Relay League, Chelmsford Rotary Club (chmn. cmty. svc. 1994—, bd. dirs.), Westford (Mass.) Sportsmens Club, Tewksbury (Mass.) Rod and Gun Club, Omicron Kappa Upsilon. Home: 63 Thomas Dr Chelmsford MA 01824-2061 Office: Orthodontic Assocs 517 Rogers St Lowell MA 01852-3826

MÉTHÉ, PIERRETTE, dietitian; b. Montreal, Can., May 5, 1933; s. Joseph-Aimé and Germaine (Brosseau) M.; m. Patrick-Reginald Hamel, Oct. 26, 1957; children: Julie, Sonia. BS in Nutrition, Laval U., Quebec City, Can., 1955; student, Montreal U., 1985. Dietetic intern Toronto (Ont., Can.) Western Hosp., 1956; clinical and teaching dietitian Hotel-Dieu Hosp., Chicoutimi, Que., 1957; clinical dietitian Ottawa (Ont.) Civic Hosp., 1957-58; dir. dietetics St. Vincent Hosp., Ottawa, 1958-61; nutritionist rsch. Nat. Health and Welfare, Ottawa, 1961-62; dir. dietetics S.M.B.D. Jewish Gen. Hosp., Montreal, 1962—. Co-author: (dictionary) Alexandre Dumas, 1990. Recipient Outstanding Performance and Leadership in Food Svc. Mgmt. award Bernard and Assocs., 1989, Exceptional Performance award Jewish Gen. Hosp., 1987-89. Mem. Profl. Corp. Dietitians (chmn. profl. inspection com. 1975-78, Am. standards com. 1986—), Canadian Dietetic Assn. (life, pres. 1978-79, strategic planning task force 1982-85, aux. edn. task force 1989-90), Am. Soc. for Food Svc. Adminstrs. Home: 219 Springdale, Pointe Claire, PQ Canada H9R 2R4

METREY, GEORGE DAVID, social work educator, academic administrator; b. Milw., July 23, 1939; s. Richard Joseph and Catherine (Evans) M.; m. Cheryl Ann Mosca, June 21, 1969; 1 child, Mary Beth. A.B., Marquette U., 1961; M.S.W., Fordham U., 1963; Ph.D., NYU, 1970. Lic. ind. clin. social worker, R.I., N.J. Social worker N.J. Diagnostic Ctr., Edison, 1963-64, asst. social work supr., 1964-66, dir. psychiat. social work, 1966-70; coordinator undergrad. social work program Kean Coll., N.J., 1970-73, assoc. prof. social work, 1970-74, prof., 1974-79, chmn. dept. sociology, anthropology and social work, 1973-77, dir. social work program, acting assoc. dean Sch. Arts and Sci., 1977-79; dean Sch. Social Work, prof. R.I. Coll., Providence, 1979—; field instr. Fordham U. Sch. Social Service, 1966-70, adj. prof., 1969-77; adj. assoc. prof. Rutgers U. Grad. Sch. Social Work, 1972-73. Mem. program com. R.I. affiliate Am. Heart Assn., 1980—, bd. dirs., 1983-89, chmn. program com., 1985-87, exec. com., 1985-87; sec. bd. dirs. Ocean State Adoption Resource Exch., 1987-89, pres. bd. dirs., 1989-92. Recipient Fordham U. Grad. Sch. Social Svc. Outstanding Alumni, 1984, Spl. award disting. award R.I. Coll. Alumni Assn., 1996. Mem. NASW (N.J. Social Worker of Yr. 1977, pres. 1978-80, parliamentarian R.I. 1981—, treas. R.I. chpt. 1986-87, mem. nat. competence cert. commn. 1989-91, nat. 2d v.p. 1978-80, chair nat. program com. 1981-83), Coun. on Social Work Edn. (bd. dirs. 1979-82, mem. commn. on accreditation 1996—), Acad. Cert. Social Workers, Nat. Assn. Deans and Dirs. Schs. Social Work (nominating com. 1993-96, program com. 1993-96), Alpha Phi Omega, Gamma Pi Mu, Alpha Delta Mu (regional v.p.). Roman Catholic. Home: 540 Waverly Rd Wyckoff NJ 07481-1229 Office: RI Coll Sch Social Work Providence RI 02908

METS, MARILYN BAIRD, pediatric ophthalmologist; b. Providence, R.I., Jan. 1, 1948; d. Russell James and Beatrice (Wentworth) Baird; m. Laurens Jan Mets, June 12, 1971. BA, Wheaton Coll., 1969; MS, Harvard Sch. Pub. Health, 1971; MD, George Washington U., 1976. Instr. Rush-Presbyn. St. Luke's Hosp., Chgo., 1981-83; asst. prof. U. Chgo., 1983-90; assoc. prof. Northwestern Hosp., Chgo., 1990—; assoc. prof. Children's Meml. Hosp., Chgo., 1990—; lectr. Rush Presbyn. St. Lukes, 1993—; staff ophthalmologist Evanston/Glenbrook Hosp., Glenview, Ill., 1993—, Michael Reese Hosp., Chgo., 1994—; bd. dirs. Toxoplasmosis Rsch. Inst., Chgo., 1991—; dir. retinal physiol. lab. Northwestern U. Med. Sch., 1990—. Sec. bd. dirs. Ill. Soc. for the Prevention of Blindness, Chgo., 1986-94. Fellow Am. Acad. Ophthalmology; mem. Am. Assn. Pediat. Ophthalmology & Strabismus, Pan Am. Assn. Ophthalmology, Costenbader Soc., Ophthalmic Genetics Study Soc., Sigma Xi. Office: Children's Meml Hosp 2300 Children's Plz Box 70 Chicago IL 60614

METTING, PATRICIA JEAN, medical physiologist, educator; b. Toledo, Jan. 21, 1954; d. J. Robert and Betty Jean (Gongwer) McDuffee; m. Michael T. Metting, Aug. 20, 1976; children: Megan Colleen, Patrick Michael. BS, U. Toledo, 1975; PhD, Med. Coll. Ohio, 1980. Instr. health tech. U. Toledo, 1975-78; instr. physiology Med. Coll. Ohio, Toledo, 1978-79, asst. prof. physiology, 1980-88, assoc. prof. physiology and molecular medicine, 1989—, pres. faculty senate, 1993-94; rsch. peer rev. com. Am. Heart Assn., Columbus, Ohio, chmn., 1993-94. Contbg. author: Reflex Control of the Circulation, 1991, 1995 Yearbook of Pulmonary Disease. Recipient Outstanding Alumnus award U. Toledo, 1978, Nat. Rsch. Svc. award NIH, 1979-82, Disting. Alumnus award Med. Coll. Ohio, 1990, Recognition award Ohio Acad. Sci., 1992. Mem. Am. Heart Assn. (fellow coun. high blood pressure rsch., pres. Lucas County divsn. 1996-98, trustee), Am. Physiol. Soc. (fellow cardiovasc. sect., long range planning com.), Ohio Physiol. Soc. (pres. 1994-95). Office: Med Coll Ohio PO Box 10008 3000 Arlington Ave Toledo OH 43614-2595

METTINGER, KARL LENNART, neurologist; b. Helsingborg, Sweden, Nov. 1, 1943; came to the U.S., 1989; s. Nils Allan and Anna Katarina (Hallberg) M.; m. Chesne Maree Ryman, Jan. 27, 1979. MD, U. Lund, 1973; PhD, Karolinska Inst., 1982. Intern Stockholm Hosps., 1973-74; resident Karolinska Hosp., Stockholm, 1974-77, clin. neurologist, 1977-85; med. dir. Kabi Hematology, Stockholm, 1985-87; dep. gen. mgr. Kabi Cardiovascular, Stockholm, 1987-89; med. dir. Ivax/Baker Norton Pharms., Miami, Fla., 1989-93, sr. clin. rsch. dir., 1993—; assoc. prof. Karolinska Inst., Stockholm, 1983-91; cons. neurologist Odenplan Med. Ctr., Stockholm, 1984-89. Author: Cerebral Thromboembolism, 1982, Refaat-Myths and Billions in Biotech, 1987; editor: Coronary Thrombolysis: Current Answers to Critical Questions, 1988, Controversies in Coronary Thrombolysis, 1989. Lt. Swedish Army, 1979. Recipient Silver award Spanish Health Ministry, 1989, Classical Langs. award King Gustav V Found., 1963. Mem. Swedish Stroke Soc. (bd. dirs. 1979-89, pres. 1984-86), Swedish Med. Soc., Swedish Christian Med. Soc. (bd. dirs. 1972-88, pres. 1983-88), Am. Heart Assn., N.Y. Acad. Scis., Nat. Found. for Advancement of Arts, Internat. Assn. Christian Physicians (exec. com. 1975-86). Home: 5401 Collins Ave Apt 1022 Miami FL 33140-2535 Office: IVAX 4400 Biscayne Blvd Miami FL 33137

METTS, BROOKS CONRAD, clinical pharmacy educator, poison information specialist; b. Oxford, Miss., July 10, 1943; s. Brooks C. and Clara Lynn (Moorman) M.; m. June Inez Kilpatrick, Oct. 7, 1972; 1 child, Jonathan Patrick. B.S. in Pharmacy, U. Tenn.-Memphis, 1967, Pharm.D., 1970. Registered pharmacist, Tenn., S.C. Asst. prof. W.Va. U., Morgantown, 1970-72, dir. Drug and Poison Info. Ctr., 1971-72; asst. prof. U. S.C., Columbia, 1972-77, assoc. prof. pharmacy, 1977—, dir. Drug and Poison Info. Ctr., 1972-84, coordinator clin. pharmacy edn., 1974-79, dir. Palmetto Poison Ctr., 1980—. Co-author: A Handbook of Information for the Pharmacy Student in the Clinical Setting, 1971; author: (with others) Other Rodenticides in Clinical Management of Poisoning and Drug Overdose, 2nd edit., 1990. Contbr. articles to profl. jours. Recipient Bristol award Bristol Labs., 1967. Mem. Am. Soc. Hosp. Pharmacists (adv. panel student membership 1976—), Am. Pharm. Assn., Am. Assn. Colls. Pharmacy (liaison rep. 1980—), Nat. Poison Ctr. Network (chmn. dept. patient info. 1982-83), Am. Assn. Poison Control Cts. Presbyterian. Lodge: Optimist (pres. 1976-77, bd. dirs. 1994-96). Avocation: Photography. Office: Palmetto Poison Ctr U SC Columbia SC 29208

METZ, CHARLES EDGAR, radiology educator; b. Bayshore, N.Y., Sept. 11, 1942; s. Clinton Edgar and Grace Muriel (Schienke) M.; m. Maryanne Theresa Bahr, July, 1967 (div. 1988); children: Rebecca, Molly. BA, Bowdoin Coll., 1964; MS, U. Pa., 1966, PhD, 1969. Instr. radiology U. Chgo., 1969-71, asst. prof., 1971-75, assoc. prof., 1976-80, dir. grad. programs in med. physics, 1979-85, prof., 1980—, prof. structural biology, 1984-86; mem. diagnostic rsch. adv. group Nat. Cancer Inst., 1980-81; mem. sci. com. Nat. Coun. on Radiation Protection and Measurements, 1982-95, Internat. Commn. on Radiation Units and Measurements, 1988-96, chmn. sci. com., 1992—; cons. and lectr. in field. Assoc. editor Radiology jour., 1986-91, Med. Physics jour., 1992-95; mem. editl. bd. Med. Decision Making, 1980-84; contbr. over 150 articles to sci. jours. and chpts. to books. Mem. Radiol. Soc. N.Am., Am. Assn. Physicists in Medicine, Soc. Med. Decision Making, Assn. Univ. Radiologists, Soc. for Health Svcs. Rsch. in Radiology, Phi Beta Kappa, Sigma Xi. Office: U Chgo Dept Radiology MC2026 5841 S Maryland Ave Chicago IL 60637-1463

METZ, EDWARD ALLEN, physician, educator; b. Phila., Nov. 30, 1936; s. George Edward and Emma May (Dolquist) M.; m. Gay C. Gilmore, Nov. 23, 1978; children: Tim, Franklin, Donna, Barbara, Joanne. BS, Drexel Inst. Tech., 1964; DO, Phila. Coll. Osteo. Medicine, 1970; degree, U.S. Army Gen. Staff Coll., 1995. Diplomate Am. Bd. Family Practice. Intern, then resident in gen. surgery Cmty. Gen. Hosp. Osteopathic Hosp., Harrisburg, Pa.; physician Port Allegany (Pa.) Cmty. Hosp., 1972-78, Morningside Clinic, Sioux City, Iowa, 1978-80, Fossil Butte Med. Clinic, Kemmerer, Wyo., 1980-85; commd. major U.S. Army Med. Corp., 1986, advanced through grades to lt. col., 1988; physician Legend Buttes Health Svc., Crawford, Nebr., 1985—; clin. instr. dept. cmty. medicine and rural health U. N.D. Sch. Medicine, 1996—; asst. prof. medicine U. Nebr. Med. Ctr., Omaha, 1995—; pres., bd. dirs. Prehistorica Prairies Discovery Ctr., Crawford, 1992—. Fellow Am. Acad. Family Physicians; mem. AMA, Assn. Mil. Surgeons of the U.S., Mineral Soc. Am., Soc. for Mining, Metallurgy and Exploration, Kemmerer Rotary Club (pres. 1983, 84), Crawford Rotary Club (pres. 1986, 87), Crawford Area C. of C. (bd. dirs., pres.). Home: PO Box 523 211E Belmont Rd Crawford NE 69339 Office: Legend Buttes Health Svcs 11 Paddock St Crawford NE 69339

METZ, KEVIN, nursing home administrator; b. Buffalo, Aug. 27, 1956; s. Jerome T. and Coletta E. (George) M.; m. Louise Robinson Russell, June 9, 1984; 1 child, John Michael. B in Profl. Studies, SUNY, Utica, 1979. Lic. nursing home adminstr., Ala., Ga. Asst. adminstr. Fairview Nursing Hom, Birmingham, Ala., 1979-82; adminstr. Warren Manor Nursing Home, Selma, Ala., 1982-87, Cedar Crest, Montgomery, Ala., 1987-89, Woodley Manor Nursing Home, Montgomery, 1989, Athens (Ga.) Heritage Home, Inc., 1989-91, 94—, St. Mary's Hosp. Long Term Care Facility, Athens, 1991-92, Lilburn (Ga.) Geriatric Ctr., Inc., 1992-94. Chmn. Pruitt Corp. Go for the Gold Com., 1993-95; bd. dirs. Selma/Dallas County Am. Heart Assn., 1985-87. Fellow Am. Coll. Health Care Adminstrs. (cert., pres. Ala. chpt.); mem. Ga. Health Care Assn. (pres. N.E. coun.), Ga. Nursing Home Assn. (bd. mem. at large 1993-94, pres. N.E. coun. 1991-93). Roman Catholic. Home: 120 Pine Tops Dr Athens GA 30606 Office: Athens Heritage Home Athens GA 30606

METZ, LAWRENCE NEALE, neurologist; b. Springfield, Mass., Aug. 1, 1933; s. John and Charlotte Lois (Katzman) M.; m. Myrna Lee Schecter, July 4, 1966; children: Jodi, Marcia, Martin. AB, Dartmouth Coll., 1955; MD, Ann Arbor, 1959. Diplomate Am. Bd. Psychiatry and Neurology. Intern King's County Hosp., Bklyn., 1959-60; resident in neurology U. Mich. Med. Ctr., Ann Arbor, 1960-63; fellow Nat. Hosp. for Nervous Diseases, London, Eng., 1963-64; pvt. practice in neurology Springfield, Mass., 1964-66; group practice Neurosurgical and Neurol. Group, Inc., Springfield, 1967—; chief of neurology Bay State Med. Ctr., Springfield, 1969-88; clin. assoc. prof. neurology Tufts Med. Sch., Springfield, 1978—. Contbr. articles to profl. jours., chpt. to book. Major U.S. Army, 1967-69. Grantee: U.S. Pub. Health Svc., 1959, 1962-63. Fellow Am. Acad. Neurology, N. Am. Neuropathology Soc.; mem. AMA, Mass. Med. Soc., Hampden Dist. Med. Soc., Mass. Neurol. Assn. (pres. 1984-85), Maimondes Med. Club (pres. 1973-74), Am. Soc. Clin. Neurophysiology. Office: Neurosurg & Neurol Group 80 Congress St Springfield MA 01104

METZ, RONALD IRWIN, retired priest, addictions counselor; b. Walthill, Nebr., Aug. 11, 1921; s. Harry Elmer and Emma Rilla (Howe) M.; m. Helen Chapin, July 14, 1951; children: Mary Selden Metz Evans, Helen Winchester Metz Ketchum, Grace Chapin. BA in Chinese and Far Ea. Studies, U. Calif., Berkeley, 1945; MA in Mid. Ea. Studies, Am. U., Beirut, 1954; M Div., Yale U., 1969, STD, 1975. Ordained priest Episcopal Ch., 1969. Intelligence officer various govtl. intelligence agys., Far East and Washington, 1944-52; exec. Arabian/Am. Oil Co., Dhahran and Riyadh, Saudi Arabia, 1954-66; deacon Grace Cathedral, San Francisco; priest St. George's Cathedral, Jerusalem, 1969; exec. asst. to archbishop Jerusalem and Mid. East Archbishopric, 1969-75; rector Ch. of the Holy Spirit, Erie, Pa., 1976-81; chaplain Brent Sch., Baguio, Philippines, 1981-82; counselor of chemically dependent Washington, 1982—; addictionologist, vol. New Beginnings Treatment Ctr., P.I.W. Hosp., Washington, 1989-90, Found. Next Step Outpatient Treatment Ctr., Washington, 1991-92; adj. clergy St. Margaret's Ch., Washington; mem. D.C. Diocesan Commn. on Alcohol and Drug Abuse, Washington, 1982-89. Bd. dirs. Mid. East Inst., Washington, 1959-60, Pub. Broadcasting System, n.w. Pa., 1976-81; mem. adv. bd. Children's Aid Internat., 1988-89. Served to col. U.S. Army, 1942-45, CBI, OSS. Decorated Bronze Star. Mem. Iran Diocesan Assn. U.S.A, Phi Beta Kappa, Sigma Chi (chaplain D.C. alumni assn. 1982—). Democrat. Home: 3001 Veazey Ter NW Apt 334 Washington DC 20008-5455

METZER, WALTER STEVEN, neurologist, educator, medical writer and editor; b. Hot Springs, Ark., Dec. 15, 1949; s. Walter Mathew and Mildred Jean Metzer; m. Teddie marie O'Kelley, Jan. 24, 1976. BS in Applied Psychology, Ga. Inst. Tech., 1972; MD, U. Ark., Little Rock, 1976. Diplomate Am. Bd. Psychiatry and Neurology. Intern U. Ark. Coll. Medicine, Little Rock, 1976-77; resident in neurology U. Ark. Coll. for Med. Scis., Little Rock, 1980-82, asst. prof. neurology, 1983-89; assoc. clin. prof. neurology U. Ark. Coll. Medicine, 1989—; asst. med. dir. East Little Rock Community Clinic, 1977-79; staff neurologist McClellan Meml. VA Hosp., Little Rock, 1986-89, chief, neurology svc., 1989-92; pvt. practice neurology North Little Rock, Ark., 1992—; med. writer and editor, owenr EDITOR, 1995—. Author book chpts. rsch. study reports, pharm. submissions, articles, abstracts and letters. Recipient Svc. award East Little Rock Cmty. Clinic, 1979, Honored Faculty award U. Ark. Coll. Medicine, 1985-86, 92; named to Outstanding Young Men of Am., 1985; Richard P. Moll scholar Ga. Tech., 1972. Fellow Am. Acad. Neurology; mem. Ark. Med. Soc., Movement Disorder Soc., Pulaski County Med. Soc., Ga. Inst. Tech. Alumni Assn., Ark. Caduceus Club, Sigma Xi. Office: Ark Headache & Neurology St Vincent North St Vincent N North Little Rock AR 72120

METZLER, DWIGHT FOX, civil engineer, retired state official; b. Kans., Mar. 25, 1916; s. Ross R. and Grace (Fox) M.; m. Lela Ross, June, 1941; children: Linda Diane, Brenda Lee, Marilyn Anne, Martha Jeanne. BSCE, Kans. U., 1940, CE, 1947; SM, Harvard U., 1948. Registered profl. engr., Kans., N.Y.; diplomate Am. Acad. Environ. Engrs. Asst. engr. Kans. Bd. Health, 1940-42, san. engr., 1946-48; chief engr. Topeka, 1948-62; assoc. prof. dept. civil engring. U. Kans., 1948-59, prof., 1959-66; exec. sec. Kans. Water Resources Bd., Topeka, 1962-66; dep. commr. N.Y. State Dept. Health, Albany, 1966-70, N.Y. State Dept. Environ. Conservation, Albany, 1970-74; sec. Kans. Dept. Health and Environment, Topeka, 1974-79, dir. water supply devel., 1979-84, retired, 1984; cons. san. engring. Fed. Pub. Housing Authority, USPHS, 1943-46; housing cons. Chgo.-Cook County Health Survey, 1946; cons. water supply and water pollution control USPHS, 1957-66; adviser Govt. of India, 1960; mem. ofcl. exchange to USSR on environ.health research and practice, 1962; adviser WHO, 1964-84; cons., expert witness Occidential Chem. Co., Love Canal, 1990-91; mem. Water Pollution Bd., Internat. Joint Commn., 1967-74, Assembly of Engring. NRC, 1977-80. Assoc. editor Internat. Jour. Water Pollution Rsch.; contbr. articles to profl. jours. Chmn. Kans. Bible Chair Bd., 1957-66; chmn. com. for new bldg. U. Kans. Sch. Religion. Recipient Disting. Service award U. Kans., 1970, Disting. Engring. Service award U. Kans., 1984. Fellow Royal Soc. Health Gt. Britain (hon.), Am. Pub. Health Assn. (former mem. governing council, exec. bd., pres., chmn. action bd., Centennial award 1972, Sedgwick medal 1981), ASCE (sec. sanitary engring. div. 1959-61, chmn. 1963); mem. Am. Water Works Assn. (Fuller award 1954, Purification div. award 1958), Water Pollution Control Fedn. (Bedell award 1963, hon. mem. 1983), Kans. Pub. Health Assn. (Crumbine award 1965), Kans. Engring. Soc. (Outstanding Engr. award 1978), Nat. Acad. Engring., Kans. Rural Water Assn. (Conger award 1990), Sigma Xi, Tau Beta Pi. Home: 900 SW 31st St Apt 325 Topeka KS 66611-2196

METZLER, JERRY DON, nursing administrator; b. Mishawaka, Ind., Mar. 6, 1935; s. Gerald Donald and Cleota Christabell (Dowell) M.; m. Dorothy J. Masters, Aug. 18, 1962. BS, Ariz. State U., 1962, MEd, 1967; BSN, San Diego State U., 1973; MS, U. Ariz., Tucson, 1980. Sci. tchr. Washington Sch., Sanger, Calif., 1963-68; tchr. biology San Jacinto (Calif.) High Sch., 1968-70; staff nurse Maricopa County Hosp., Phoenix, 1973-76; staff nurse St. Luke's Hosp., Phoenix, 1976-77; nursing instr., dept. head Gila Pueblo Coll., Globe, Ariz., 1977-78; nurse educator, asst. dir. nursing USPHS Indian Hosp., Tuba City, Ariz., 1980-84; asst. nursing svc. mgr. Phoenix Indian Med. Ctr., 1984-85; pub. health educator Phoenix Indian Med. Ctr., 1985-88; dir. nursing USPHS Indian Hosp., Owyhee, Nev., 1988-90; sr. project officer USPHS, Dallas, 1990—. With USN, 1956-60, USPHS, 1980—. Mem. Res. Officers Assn., Am. Nurses Assn., Commd. Officers Assn. of USPHS, Masons, Sigma Theta Tau. Republican. Methodist. Home: 420 Shockley Ave De Soto TX 75115-3229 Office: PHS ROVI 1200 Main St Dallas TX 75202-4348

METZLER, LINDA DIANNE, physician assistant; b. Dayton, Ohio, Oct. 20, 1952; d. Paul S. and R. Ilene Coons; m. Melvin F. Metzler, Sept. 4, 1992; children: Chris, Loren, Colin, Kylie, Andrew, Kevin, Benjamin. Student, Miami U., Oxford, Ohio, 1970-71, Wright State U., Dayton, Ohio, 1971-75; AS Physician Asst., Kettering Coll. Med. Arts, Ohio, 1977; BA in Human Svcs. Adminstrn., Antioch U., Yellow Springs, Ohio, 1996. Cert. physician asst. Pharmacy technician Kettering Meml. Hosp., 1972-79; physician asst. James Bean, M.D., Kettering, 1979-80, Dayton VA Med. Ctr, 1980-82; stencil artist, free-lance artist Springboro, Ohio, 1982-92; ophthalmic asst. John D. Bullock, M.D., Dayton, 1992-93; resch. assoc. II Wright State U., Dayton, 1993-96; physician asst. All Care Family Health Ctr., Dayton, 1996—, Swope Family Practice, Dayton, 1996—; rsch. cons. Wright State U., Dayton, 1993—. Healthcare editor weekly newspaper column Oakwood Register, 1993—; healthcare editor Winkler Pub., 1993—; contbr. articles to profl. jours. V.p. Oakwood Sister Cities Assn., Dayton, 1994-95, pres., 1995-96. Recipient Outstanding Volunteerism award Wright State U., Dayton, 1995. Mem. Am. Assn. Physician Assts., Ohio Assn. Physician Assts., Dayton Philharmonic Chorus, Friends of Smith Gardens. Office: Swope Family Practice Dayton OH 45419

MEUB, DANIEL W., neurosurgeon; b. L.A., Feb. 2, 1924; s. Albert Philip and Olga Maria (Gablowsky) M.; m. Betty May Rinehart, June 25, 1945 (div. 1984); children: Karen, Kristin, Daniel, Eric; m. Suzanne Stevens Wentworth, Oct. 1, 1984; children: James, William, Elizabeth, Jack, Geordian, Anne. AB, MD, U. Calif., San Francisco, 1947. Dep. chief dept. neurosurgery Stanford (Calif.) U. Hosp., 1978—; mem. bd. dirs., pres. Sequoia Hosp., Redwood City, Calif., 1983-93; assoc. clin. prof. surgery Stanford Med. Sch., 1958—. Capt. U.S. Army, 1953-54. Mem. Menlo Circus Club. Home: 4155 Old Adobe Rd Palo Alto CA 94306 Office: 1101 Welch Rd C-9 Palo Alto CA 94306

MEUNIER, PIERRE JEAN, medical educator; b. Miribel, France, June 5, 1936; s. Marcel Jacques and Marie Ernestine (Ballufin) M.; m. Marie Aimée Loiseleur, July 16, 1961 (div. 1984); children: Gilles, Pascal, Francois; m. Annie Bernadette Mariés, Dec. 27, 1986. B, Lycée Ampère, Lyons, France, 1953; MD, Claude Bernard U., Lyons, France, 1967. Resident Lyons Hosps., 1963-67; asst. prof. Lyons Hosps. Claude Bernard U., 1967-71, prof., head dept. rheumatology and bone disease, 1979—; head rsch. unit INSERM 234, 1979-92; v.p. Groupe de Rsch. et d'Info. Osteoporoses, Paris, 1990—; cons. WHO, Geneva; cons. in field; trustee European Found. for Osteoporosis, 1996—. Editor-in-chief Bone, 1978-89, Osteoporosis Internat., 1989—; contbr. articles to profl. jours. Served with French Navy, 1962-63. Recipient Internat. League Against Rheumatism prize 1989, prize Paget's Disease Found., 1991. Mem. European Calcified Tissue Soc. (sec. 1985-91), Nat. Sci. Commn. INSERM, Sci. Coun. Drug Agy., WHO (cons.), Ordre des Palmes Academiques (officer). Home: 4 rue des Pierres Plantees, 69001 Lyon France Office: Pavillon F Hosp, Ed Herriot Pl D'Arsonval, 69437 Lyon France

MEYER, ANN JANE, human development educator; b. N.Y.C., Mar 11, 1942; s. Louis John and Theresa M. B.A., U. Mich., 1964; M.A., U. Calif.-Berkeley, 1967, Ph.D., 1971. Asst. prof. dept. human devel. Calif. State U.-Hayward, 1972-77, assoc. prof., 1977-84, prof., chmn. dept., 1984—. Mem. Am. Psychol. Assn., Western Psychol. Assn., Am. Soc. Aging. Office: Dept Human Devel Calif State U Hayward CA 94542

MEYER, ANTHONY ANDREW, surgeon; b. Melrose, Minn., Apr. 24, 1948. MD, U. Chgo., 1977. Diplmate Am. Bd. Surgery. Intern U. Calif., San Francisco, 1977-78, resident in surgery, 1978-82; staff U. N.C. Hosps., Chapel Hill, 1982—; prof. surgery U. N.C., Chapel Hill, 1982—. Mem. ACS. Office: U NC Dept Surgery Box 7210 164 Burnett Womack Bldg Chapel Hill NC 27599*

MEYER, ARTHUR NATHANIEL, oncologist; b. Wilkes-Barre, Pa., Jan. 8, 1936; s. Max and Rose (Wruble) M.; m. Barbara Bernice Parris, Aug. 14, 1966; children: Mark, David, Rachel. AB in Biology, Wilkes Coll.; MD, Thomas Jefferson U. Diplomate Am. Bd. Internal Medicine, Am. Bd. Medical Oncology. Intern Misericordia Hosp.; resident Phila. VA Hosp.; pvt. practice oncology, 1967—. Mem. ACP, Am. Soc. of Clin. Cardiology, Alpha Omega Alpha. Republican. Jewish. Office: 401 Third Ave Kingston PA 38704

MEYER, BARRY STEVEN, osteopathic internist; b. Detroit, Jan. 7, 1965; s. Harvey Hezkel and Rosalyn Meyer. BS in Psychology, Mich. State U., 1987; DO, U. Osteo. Medicine, Des Moines, 1991. Chief med. intern Garden City Hosp., Detroit, 1991-92; internist, mem. house staff coun. Henry Ford Hosp., Detroit, 1992—, sr. staff physician, 1995-96; sr. staff physician Oakland Gen. Hosp., Madison Heights, Mich., 1996—. Trustee Zionist Orgn. Am., Southfield, Mich., 1993. Mem. ACP (assoc., abstract presenter 1994), Wayne County Med. Soc., Mich. State Med. Soc., Smithsonian Assocs. Jewish. Office: 34036 Banbury Farmington Hills MI 48331

MEYER, CAROL FRANCES, pediatrician, allergist; b. Berea, Ky., June 2, 1936; d. Harvey Kessler and Jessie Irene (Hamm) Meyer; m. Daniel Baker Cox, June 5, 1955 (div. Apr. 1962). AA, U. Fla., 1955; BA, Duke U., 1957; MD, Med. Coll. Ga., 1967. Diplomate Am. Bd. Pediatrics, Am. Bd. Allergy and Immunology. Intern in pediatrics Med. Coll. Ga., Augusta, 1967-68; resident in pediatrics Gorgas Hosp., Canal Zone, 1968-69; fellow in pediatric respiratory disease Med. Coll. Ga., 1969-71, instr. pediat., 1971-72; med. officer pediatrics Canal Zone Govt., 1972-79; med. officer pediatrics Dept. of Army, Panama, 1979-82, med. officer allergy, 1982-89, physician in charge allergy clinic, 1984-89; asst. prof. pediatrics and medicine Med. Coll. Ga., Augusta, 1990—; mem. Bd. of Canal Zone Merit System Examiners, 1976-79. Contbr. articles to profl. jours. Mem. First Bapt. Ch. Orch., 1992—; founding mem., violoncello Curundu Chamber Ensemble, 1979-89. Recipient U.S. Army Exceptional Performance awards, 1985, 86, 89, Merck award Med. Coll. Ga.,, 1967; U. Fla. J. Hillis Miller scholar, 1954. Mem. AAAS, Am. Coll. Rheumatology, Allergy and Immunology Soc. Ga., Hispanic-Am. Allergy and Immunology Assn., Ga. Pediatric Soc., Pan Am. Med. Assn., Soc. Leukocyte Biology, Am. Coll. Allergy, Asthma and Immunology, Am. Acad. Allergy, Asthma and Immunology, Am. Acad. Pediat., Am. Med. Women's Assn., Panama Canal Soc. Fla., Ga. Ornithol. Soc., Ga. Thoracic Soc., Am. Lung Assn. (Ga. East Ctrl. br. exec. bd.), Am. Assn. Ret. Persons, Nature Conservancy, Royal Soc. for Preservation Birds, Nat. Assn. Ret. Fed. Employees, Nat. Audubon Soc., Panama Audubon Soc., Willow Run Homeowner's Soc. (pres.), Alpha Omega Alpha. Office: Med Coll Ga BG 232 1120 15th St Augusta GA 30912

MEYER, FREDERICK RICHARD, physiologist, educator; b. Bklyn., May 26, 1938; s. Frederick Edward and Evelyn (Young) M.; m. Ellen B. Bierwagen, June 2, 1962; children: Laura E., Sara E. BS, Valparaiso U., 1960; MA, Ind. U., 1962, PhD, 1966. Asst. prof. biology Wilson Coll., Chambersburg, Pa., 1965-67; prof. Valparaiso (Ind.) U., 1967—; part-time instr. Ind. U. Sch. Medicine, Gary, 1980-86; dir. Valparaiso U. Overseas Study Ctr., Reutlingen, Germany, 1988-90. Dem. precinct committeeman, Valparaiso, 1972-76; pres. Valparaiso Found., 1982. NIH grad. rsch. fellow, NIH, 1964-65. Mem. Am. Physiol. Soc., Ind. Acad. Sci., Human Anatomy and Physiology Soc., Midwest Assn. Higher Edn., Sigma Xi. Office: Valparaiso U Nsc # 243 Valparaiso IN 64383-6493

MEYER, GEORGE GOTTHOLD, psychiatrist, educator; b. Frankfurt, Germany, Nov. 13, 1931; came to U.S., 1941, naturalized, 1946; s. Hans and Hilda (Lesser) M.; m. Paula Saslaw, June 17, 1953; children: Bruce Alan, Brian Lee, Barry Dale. B.A., Johns Hopkins U., 1951; M.D., U. Chgo., 1955. Diplomate: Am. Bd. Psychiatry and Neurology (asst. examiner 1979—). Intern USPHS Hosp., Staten Island, N.Y., 1955-56; resident in psychiatry U. Chgo. Hosps. and Clinics, 1958-60, chief resident, 1960-61, chief psychiat. inpatient service, 1966-69; mem. faculty U. Chgo. Med. Sch., 1961-69, assoc. prof. psychiatry, 1968-69; assoc. prof. psychiatry U. Tex. Med. Sch., San Antonio, 1969-71; prof. U. Tex. Health Sci. Ctr., San Antonio, 1971—, clin. prof., 1982—; dir. N.W. San Antonio Mental Health Ctr., 1969-74; mem. exec. bd. Crisis Ctr., San Antonio, 1971-75; cons. VA Hosp., San Antonio and Kerrville, Tex., Kerrville State Hosp., San Antonio State Hosp., Santa Rosa Hosp., Santa Rosa Children's Hosp., Jewish Family Svc., 1980-86, Cath. Family Svcs.; active staff Villa Rosa Hosp., Meth. Hosp.; courtesy staff Regional Hosp., Charter Real Hosp., Mission Fiesta Hosp., Univ. Hosp.; psychiat. cons. Dallas Office, NIMH, 1970-81; also psychiatry edn. br., 1978-82; med. dir. Mex. Am. Unity Coun., San Antonio, 1970-80; vis. lectr. psychiatry U. Edinburgh (Scotland) Med. Sch., 1966; vis. prof. psychiatry U. Man. (Can.) Winnipeg, 1977; mem. med. adv. bd. for driver licensing Tex. Dept. Health, 1973-78. Author 4 books; contbr. numerous articles to med. jours. Bd. dirs., cons. Ecumenical Ctr. Religion and Health San Antonio, 1974-86; bd. dirs. Cmty. Guidance Ctr. of Bexar County, 1979-81; bd. dirs., cons. Jewish Family Svc., San Antonio, 1980-86. Served with USPHS, 1955-58. NIMH career tchr. grantee, 1961-53; recipient Okie award Gov. Okla., 1969. Fellow APA, Am. Psychiat. Assn. (life); mem. Tex. and Bexar County Med. Assns., Tex., Bexar County and World Psychiat. Assns., Am. Coll. Psychiatrists, Biofeedback Soc. Tex (dir. 1980-82), Sigma Xi, Alpha Omega Alpha, Phi Lambda Upsilon. Home: 2907 Marlborough Dr San Antonio TX 78230-4427 Office: 4499 Medical Dr Ste 267 San Antonio TX 78229-3712

MEYER, GEORGE WILBUR, internist; b. Cleve., Apr. 30, 1941; s. George Wilbur and Emily Fuller (Campbell) M.; m. Carolyn Edwards Garrett, Apr. 8, 1967; children: Robert James, Elizabeth Jackson, Dobro Goodale. BS, MIT, 1962; MD, Tulane Med. Sch., 1966. Intern So. Pacific Hosps. Inc., San Francisco, 1966-67; resident Pacific Presbyn. Med. Ctr., San Francisco, 1969-72; commd. 1st lt. USAF, advanced through grades to col., 1980; fellow in gastroenterology David Grant USAF Med. Ctr., Travis AFB, Calif., 1974-76; asst. chair dept. medicine USAF Med. Ctr., Keesler AFB, Miss., 1976-78; asst. prof. dept. medicine Uniformed Svcs. Univ., Bethesda, Md., 1978-80; chair dept. medicine Wright Patterson AFB, Dayton, Ohio, 1980-82; chief of medicine Wilford Hall USAF Med. Ctr., Lackland AFB, Tex., 1982-86; chief clin. svcs. USAF Acad., Colo., 1986-89; comdr. 1st Med. Groups, Langley AFB, Va., Germany, 1988-89, 86th Med. Group, Ramstein AFB, Germany, 1989-92; program dir. internal medicine Ga. Bapt. Med. Ctr., Atlanta, 1993—; cons. Walter Reed Army Med. Ctr., Washington, 1978-80, Nat. Naval Med. Ctr., Bethesda, 1978-80; assoc. prof. Wright State U. Sch. Medicine, Dayton, 1980-82; cons. Dayton VA Med. Ctr., 1980-82; clin. assoc. prof. medicine U. Tex. Health Sci. Ctr., San Antonio, 1982-86, Med. Coll. Ga., Augusta, 1993—. Mem. editl. bd. Gastrointestinal Endoscopy, 1993—; contbr. articles and revs. to profl. jours. and chpts. to books. Mem. leadership com. Am. Cancer Soc., Ramstein AFB, 1989-93, bd. dirs. Atlanta City Unit, 1995—, El Paso Teller Unit, Colorado Springs, 1986-88, Bexar Metro Unit, San Antonio, 1984-86; mem. adv. com. United Health Svcs., Dayton, 1980-82. Fellow ACP, Am. Coll. Gastroenterology; mem. Am. Soc. for Gastro Endoscopy, Am. Gastrointestinal Assn., Am. Assn. for Study of Liver Diseases. Office: Ga Bapt Med Ctr 303 Parkway Dr NE Atlanta GA 30312-1212

MEYER, GLENN ARTHUR, neurosurgeon, educator; b. Baraboo, Wis., Mar. 8, 1934; m. Shirley Jean Swanson; children: Gregory Alexander, Melissa Ione, Grant Andrew. Student, U. Wis., 1951-54, U. Minn., 1954-55, U. Wis., 1955-56; BS, U. Wis., 1957, MD, 1960. Diplomate Am. Bd. Neurological Surgery; Nat. Bd. Med. Examiners. Intern Mpls. Gen. Hosp. (name now Hennepin County Gen. Hosp.), 1960-61; resident neurol surgery U. Hosp., Madison, Wis.; instr. in neurosurgery U. Wis., Madison, 1966; asst. prof. neurosurgery U. Tex. Med. Br. Hosps., Galveston, 1969-71, assoc. prof. neurosurgery, 1971-72; assoc. prof. neurosurgery Med. Coll. Wis., Milw., 1972-83, prof. neurosurgery, 1983—, prof. pediatrics, 1985—; med. advisor Social Security Adminstrn., Bur. Hearings and Appeals, 1970—; cons. staff Community Meml. Hosp., Menomonee Falls, Wis., 1972—, Good Samaritan Hosp., Milw., 1973—, St. Luke's Hosp., Milw., 1983—; courtesy staff Elmbrook Meml. Hosp., Brookfield, Wis., 1972—; attending staff Columbia Hosp., Milw., 1982—; neurosurg. staff VA Hosp., Wood, Wis., 1972—; sr. attending staff Froedtert Meml. Luth. Hosp., Milw., 1980—, also served various coms.; active staff, mem. various coms. Milw. Children's Hosp., 1973—; bd. dirs. Curative Rehab. Ctr., Milw., 1991. Assoc. editor Clin. Neurosurgery, 1971-73; continuing edn. editor Congress Neurol. Surgery Newsletter, 1974-76. Contbr. numerous articles to profl. jours. Patentee in field. Elder Presby. Ch., 1971. Served to lt. col. U.S. Army, 1967-69. Sears Roebuck, Freida Nishan, Steenbock scholar. Fellow ACS; mem. AAAS, AMA, NIH (ad. hoc com. craniofacial anomalies), Internat. Neurosurg. Forum, Internat. Soc. Pediatric Neurosurgery, Am. Assn. Neurol. Surgeons (pediatric sect. 1985), Am. Coll. Radiology, Am. Coll. Surgeons (mem. credentials com. 1988), Am. Soc. Stereotactic and Functional Neurosurgery (com. psychosurgery), Cen. Neurosurgical Soc. (sec. 1980, pres. 1982), Congress Neurol. Surgeons (asst. chmn. program com. 1976, annual meeting editorial com. 1973-75), Found. Internat. Edn. in Neurol. Surgery, Inc., Assn. Academic Surgery, Assn. Advancement Med. Instrumentation, Interurban Neurosurg. Soc., Pediatric Oncology Group, Soc. Neurosci., So. Med. Assn., So. Neurosurg. Soc., Houston Neurol. Soc., State Med. Soc. Wis. (Ho. of Dels. 1976-79), Med. Soc. Milw. County (emergency med. services com. 1977-80, vice chmn. coalition med. orgns. com. 1980-82, pub. edn. com. 1982-88), Milw. Acad. Medicine (program com. 1979-81, 85, 86, sec. 1989, pres. 1992, trustee 1995—), Milw. Neuropsychiat. Soc. (pres. 1979), Wis. Neurosurg. Soc. (pres. 1976-77, chmn. peer rev. com. 1978-81, rep. joint com. Socioecon. Affairs 1978—), U. Wis. Med. Alumni Assn. (council 1973), Phi Chi, Phi Eta Sigma, Alpha Zeta, Phi Kappa Phi. Office: 9200 W Wisconsin Ave Milwaukee WI 53226-3512

MEYER, HARRY MARTIN, JR., retired health science facility administrator; b. Palestine Tex., Nov. 25, 1928. s. Harry Martin and Marjory Isabel (Griffin) M.; m. Mary Jane Martin, Aug. 19, 1949 (div. 1966); children: Harry, Mary, David; m. Barbara Story Chalfant, Nov. 21, 1966. BS Hendrix Coll., 1949, MD U. Ark., 1953; Diplomate Am. Bd. Pediatics, 1960. instr. biology Little Rock Coll., 1949, intern. Walter Reed Army Hosp., Washington, 1953-54, med. officer dep. virus and rickettsial diseases, Walter Reed Army Inst. Rsch., 1954-57, asst. resident dep. pediatrics, N.C. Meml. Hosp., Chapel Hill, 1957-59, head virology sect. div. biologics standards, NIH, Bethesda, Md., 1959-64, chief lab. of viral immunol., div. biologics standards, NIH, 1964-72, dir. bur. biologics FDA, Bethesda, 1972-82, dir. Ctr. for Drugs & Biologics FDA, Rockville, Md., 1982-86, pres. med. research div. Am. Cyanamid Co., Pearl River, N.Y., 1986-93; retired 1993. Served to rear admiral USPHS, 1959-86, capt. U.S. Army, 1953-57. Mem. AMA, Am. Epidemiol. Soc., Am. Acad. Pediatrics, Am. Pediatric Soc. Protestant. Avocations: sailing, scuba diving, skiing, back packing. Conbr. articles to profl. jours.; patentee in field.

MEYER, JEAN-PIERRE, psychiatrist; b. Paris, Apr. 3, 1949; s. Henry Jules and Jacqueline Suzanne (Roux).; m. Marie Elisabeth Buisan, June 25, 1977; children: Arnaud Jean, Gauthier Henri. MD, Broussais U., Paris, 1975; Cert. of Maritime Medicine, 1976; Cert. of Med. Expertise, Cochin U., Paris, 1978; specialist in psychiatry, Necker U., Paris, 1978. Intern Fontainebleau (France) Hosp., 1974, Enfants Malades Hosp., 1975, Melun (France) Hosp., 1976, Mohamed V Hosp., Rabat, Morocco, 1976, Lagny (France) Hosp., 1977; intern psychiatrist infirmary of police Paris, 1977, sole practice medicine, specializing in psychiatry, 1979—; cons. Paris Hosp., 1986—; expert cons. Securite Sociale, Paris and Creil, 1984—; expert cons. Ct. of Appeals, Paris, 1988; archbishopric, Paris, 1979—. Author: Relaxation Therapeutique, 1986; co-author: Le Projet en Psychotherapie, 1983, Abrege de Neuro-Psychiatrie, Conduites Pratiques de Psychiatrie, 1994. Contbr. articles to profl. jours. V.p. Mutual Ins.'s, Paris, 1972—. Mem. Intergroupe de Formation en Relaxation, Med. Assn. Paris., Soc. Français de Relaxation (treas.). Roman Catholic. Office: 9 Rue Du Général Delestraint, 75016 Paris France

MEYER, JUDITH LOUISE, obstetrician, gynecologist; b. East Grand Rapids, Mich., Feb. 26, 1933; d. George and Evangeline (Boerma) M. AB, Calvin Coll., Grand Rapids, 1955; postgrad., Mich. State U., 1955-56; MD, Women's Med. Coll. Pa., 1961. Intern Blodgett Meml. Med. Ctr., Grand Rapids, 1961-62; resident Med. Coll. Pa., Phila., 1962065; pvt. practice Grandville, Mich., 1965—; asst. clin. prof. coll. human medicine Mich. State U., Grand Rapids, 1970—. Violinist Grand Rapids Symphony, 1961, 65-74, West Shore Symphony, Muskegon, Mich., 1976-81, Kent Philharmonic, Grand Rapids, 1989—; singer Park Congl. Choir, Grand Rapids, 1987—. Fellow Am. Coll. Ob-gyn., Am. Fertility Soc.; mem. Am. Women Surgeon's Assn., Mich. State Med. Soc., Kent County Med. Soc. (legis. com.), Woman's City Club, Ladies Literary Club. Republican. Mem. Reformed Ch. Am. Office: 3181 Prairie St SW Grandville MI 49418-2076

MEYER, KAREN ANN GRITZAN, speech/language pathologist; b. Bronx, Nov. 7, 1947; d. Stephan and Pauline Theresa (Linkiewicz) Gritzan; m. Charles J. Meyer, Oct. 17, 1970; children: Matthew, Thomas. BA cum laude, Hunter Coll., CUNY, 1969; MA (fellow), Northwestern U., 1971. Cert. speech-hearing and handicapped tchr., N.Y.; lic. speech and language pathology, N.Y. Speech and lang. pathologist Mt. St. Ursula Speech Center, Bronx, 1971; speech and lang. pathologist Westchester Assn. Retarded Children (N.Y.), 1971-72; clin. communicologist, instr. rehab. medicine Mental Retardation Inst., N.Y. Med. Coll. and Flower Fifth Ave. Hosp., N.Y.C., 1972-75; pvt. practice speech and lang. pathology for children, Brewster, N.Y., 1980—; sr. supervising speech/lang. pathologist Westchester Exceptional Children's Sch., North Salem, N.Y., 1985—; adj. lectr., clin. supr. Hunter Coll. Center for Communication Disorders, 1980-85, asst. to coordinator Inst. Lang. and Learning Disabilities, 1981; externship clin. supr. speech/lang. pathology Nat. Disting. Svc. Registry, 1990; indiv. itinerant svc. contractor speech/lang. therapy Putnam County Dept. Health Svcs. for Children with Disabilities, N.Y., 1993—. Mem. Am. Speech Lang. and Hearing Assn. (cert. speech/lang. pathologist, moderator 2 sessions 1981 conf.), N.Y. State Speech Lang. and Hearing Assn. (chmn. com. career devel/student concerns and continuing edn. conv. 1984), Autism Soc. Am., Phi Beta Kappa, Sigma Alpha Eta. Roman Catholic. Home: 59 Blackberry Dr Brewster NY 10509-1332

MEYER, LEON R., guidance counselor; b. Vienna, Austria, Jan. 1, 1935; s. George and Ethel (Porpur) M.; m. Barbara Ann Rieder, Dec. 24, 1961 (widowed Nov. 1987); children: Ethel Meyer Dotts, Debra Meyer Tolliday, Robert. BA, Bklyn. Coll., 1959, MS in Edn., 1962; Profl. Diploma, St. John's U., 1974; JD cum laude, Touro Law Sch., 1996. Cert. guidance counselor, N.Y. Tchr. N.Y.C. Bd. Edn., 1959-70, guidance counselor, 1970-91. With U.S. Army, 1954-56. Mem. ABA, United Fedn. of Tchrs./ Guidance Counselors Chpt., N.Y. State United Tchrs., Am. Fedn. Tchrs., N.Y. State Bar Assn. Jewish. Home: 264 Beach 137th St Belle Harbor NY 11694-1332

MEYER, MAURICE WESLEY, physiologist, dentist, neurologist; b. Long Prairie, Minn., Feb. 13, 1925; s. Ernest William and Augusta (Warnke) M.; m. Martha Helen Davis, Sept. 3, 1946; children—James Irvin, Thomas Orville. B.S., U. Minn., 1953, D.D.S., 1957, M.S., 1959, Ph.D., 1961. Teaching asst. U. Minn. Sch. Dentistry, 1954-55, USPHS fellow, 1955-56, rsch. fellow, 1956-57, mem. faculty, 1960—; prof. physiology, dentistry and neurology U. Minn., 1976-88, prof. emeritus, 1988—; investigator Ctr. Rsch. and Cerebral Vascular Disease, 1969—; dir. lab. Center Research and Cerebral Vascular Disease, 1975—; postdoctoral research fellow Nat. Inst. Dental Research, 1957-60, research fellow, 1958-61, mem. faculty, 1961—, asso. prof. neurology, 1974-80, mem. grad. faculty, 1973—; trainee Inst. Advanced Edn. in Dental Research, 1964—; vis. asso. prof., also vis. research fellow dept. physiology and Sch. Dentistry Cardiovascular Research Inst., U. Calif., San Francisco, 1971. Contbr. articles to profl. jours. Served to col. Dental Corps AUS, 1943-50. Decorated D.F.C., Air medal with 3 oak leaf clusters. Fellow AAAS; mem. ADA, Minn. Dental Soc., Internat. Assn. Dental Research (pres. Minn. sect. 1967-68), Soc. Exptl. Biology and Medicine, Am. Physiol. Soc., Microcirculatory Soc., Am. Assn. Dental Schs. (chmn. 1972-73), Can. Physiol. Soc., Sigma Xi, Omicron Kappa Upsilon. Club: Masons. Home: 560 Rice Creek Ter NE Minneapolis MN 55432-4472 Office: U Minn 6-255 Millard Minneapolis MN 55455

MEYER, RICHARD ALAN, pediatric cardiologist; b. Bklyn., May 1, 1938; m. Rhoda Barron, Dec. 30, 1962; children: Jennifer, Leslie. BA, Washington-Jefferson Coll., 1960; MD, U. Cin., 1964. Intern Highland Alameda County Hosp., Oakland, Calif., 1964-65; resident Children's Hosp., Cin., 1965-67, fellowship pediatric cardiology, 1969-72; instr. Coll. of Medicine U. Cin., 1972, asst. prof. pediatrics, 1972-74, assoc. prof. pediatrics, 1974-78, prof. pediatrics, 1979; cons. Good Samaritan Hosp., 1980—, The Christ Hosp., 1980—, Jewish Hosp., 1980—, Bethesda-Oak Hosp., 1980—; attending pediatrician Children's Hosp., Cin., 1972; attending cardiologist, dir. cardiac ultrasound, 1974, assoc. staff physician Univ. Hosp., Gen. Divsn., Cin., 1976. Editl. bd. Am. Jour. of Cardiology, 1984-86, Ultrasound in Medicine and Biology, 1978—, Jour. of Clinical Ultrasound, 1979-82, Jour. of Ultrasound in Medicine, 1982—, Am. Rev. of Diagnostics, 1983—, Echocardiography: A Review of Cardiovascular Ultrasound, 1983-85, Am. Jour. of Cardiac Imaging, 1987—, Am. Registry of Diagnostic Med. Sonographers, 1984-86, Am. Jour. Cardiology; assoc. editor Echocardiography: A Review of Cardiovascular Ultrasound, 1985—; cons. Jour. of Am. Soc. of Echocardiography, 1987-93; contbr. numerous articles to profl. jours. Mem. spkrs. bur. Heart Assn. S.W. Ohio, 1973—, Tax Levy, 1980, 86; adv. com. Finneytown Area Summer Theatre, 1983—; pres. Finneytown Civic Assn., 1983, 86-87; bd. dirs., charter mem. Finneytown Schs. Ednl. Found., 1983, 86-89; task force chmn. Springfield Twp. Cmty. History Panel com. for the 1988 Cin. Bicentennial Celebration, 1987; chmn. Joint Organizing com. of First Annual Finneytown Springfest. Lt. comdr. USN, 1967-69. Recipient Friends of Edn. award Ohio Edn. Assn., 1991; grantee NIH, 1987-93, 87-95. Mem. Am. Heart Assn. (program com. coun. on cardiovascular disease in the young 1980-83), Am. Soc. of Echocardiograph (long range planning com. 1980—), Am. Inst. Ultrasound in Medicine (ethics com. 1986—, FDA task force on ultrasound output intensities, 1986—, fetal doppler task force 1986—), Soc. of Pediatric Echocardiology (chmn. com. of physician tng. guidelines 1982-85), Am. Coll. Cardiology (allied health profl. com. 1986—). Office: Children's Hosp Med Ctr 3333 Burnet Ave Cincinnati OH 45229

MEYER, ROBERT, physician; b. N.Y.C., Dec. 19, 1947; s. B. Robert and Kathryn (Horrigon) M.; m. Terri G. Edersheim; children: Daniel Alan, David Steele, Kathryn Claire. AB, Brown U., 1970; MA in Religion, Yale U., 1973; MD, NYU, 1977. Diplomate Am. Bd. Internal Medicine. Dir. divsn. of clin. pharmacy North Shore U. Hosp., Manhasset, N.Y., 1983-92; assoc. dir. medicine Bronx Mcpl. Hosp. Ctr., 1992-94, dir. of medicine, 1994—. Asst. editor Clin. Pharmacology and Therapeutics, 1990—. Mem. ACP, AAAS, Am. Fed. Clin. Rsch. Office: Dept Med Jacobi Rm 314 Bronx Mcpl Hosp Ctr Bronx NY 10461

MEYER, ROGER PAUL, physician; b. Atlanta, Mar. 30, 1950; s. Leonard Arthur and Janet Elanor (Miller) M.; children: Seth E., Hilary R. BA in Psychology with honors, U. N.C., 1972; MD, Med. Coll. Ga., 1976; postgrad., U. N.Mex., 1980. Physician in pvt. practice Carson Med. Group, Carson City, Nev., 1980—; chief of staff Carson Tahoe Hosp., 1986-87, chmn. dpt. ob-gyn., 1990-91; v.p. Nev. Physicians Rev. Orgn., 1987; dir. Physicians Managed Care IPA, Nev. Physicians Resources MSO. Fellow Am. Coll. Ob.-Gyn. (Nev. legislature liaison 1991); mem. Am. Acad. Reproductive Medicine, Am. Coll. Physician Execs. Democrat. Jewish. Office: Carson Med Group 1200 N Mountain St Carson City NV 89703-3824

MEYER, WALTER H., retired food safety executive, consultant; b. Cin., Aug. 19, 1922; s. Walter R. and Daisy M. (Spaulding) M.; m. Margaret M. Motz, Sept. 30, 1944; children: Walter H. Jr., Stephen E., Elizabeth A. Meyer Smith. BSChE, Mich. State U., 1948. Assoc. dir. food product devel. Procter & Gamble, Cin., 1948-88; chmn. food industry liaison to AMA Food and Nutrition Com., Chgo., 1975-80; chmn. tech. com. Edible Oils Inst., Washington, 1960-88, Grocery Mfrs. Assn., Washington, 1978. Mem. coun. Amberley Village, Ohio, 1963-84. 1st lt. U.S. Army, 1943-46, ETO. Republican. Presbyterian. Home: 7651 Sagamore Dr Cincinnati OH 45236

MEYER-BAHLBURG, HEINO F. L., psychologist, educator; b. Hamburg, Germany, Feb. 26, 1940; came to U.S., 1969; s. Wilhelm and Marie Luise Meyer-B. Vordiplom in Psychology, U. Hamburg, 1963, Diplom Psychology, 1966; Dr.rer.nat., U. Duesseldorf, 1970. Sci. asst. U. Duesseldorf, 1970; rsch. asst., then rsch. assoc. prof. psychiatry and pediatrics SUNY Med. Sch., Buffalo, 1970-77; rsch. scientist N.Y. State Psychiat. Inst., N.Y.C., 1977—; from assoc. clin. prof. med. psychology to prof. clin. psychology in psychiatry Columbia U. Coll. Physicians and Surgeons, 1978—; pediatric behavioral endocrinologist in psychiatry svc., then full prof., psychologist Presbyn. Hosp., N.Y.C., 1978—. Contbr. numerous articles to profl. publs. Recipient Disting. Sci. Achievement award Soc. for Sci. Study of Sex, 1993; grantee NIMH. Mem. AAAS, APA, German Psychol. Soc., Soc. Pediatric Psychology, Internat. Acad. Sex Rsch., Internat. Soc. Rsch. on Agression, German Sexual Rsch. Soc., Internat. Soc. Psychoneuroendocrinology, Soc. Sci. Study Sex, Soc. Rsch. Child Devel., Soc. Sexual Therapy and Rsch., Lawson Wilkins Pediatric Endocrine Soc., Harry Benjamin Internat. Gender Dysphoria Assn., Internat. AIDS Soc. Office: Columbia U. Dept Psychiatry 722 W 168th St Unit 10 New York NY 10032-2603

MEYERHOFF, GORDON ROY, psychiatrist; b. N.Y.C., Nov. 18, 1921; s. Louis and Bessie (Feinberg) M.; m. Eleanor Steinberg, Feb. 3, 1946; children: Kathe Meyerhoff Hertzberg, Michael. BA, Bklyn. Coll., 1943; MA, Oberlin Coll., 1946; MD, Columbia U., 1950. Physician N.Y. State Dept. Edn., Albany, 1951—; pvt. practice psychiatry Bklyn. and Roslyn Heights, N.Y., 1951—; psychiat. cons. child care agys., N.Y.C., 1951—. Pres. Roslyn Synagogue, 1975-88. With U.S. Army, 1943-45, ETO. Fellow Am. Psychiat. Assn., Am. Geriatric Assn. Jewish. Home and Office: 19 Hillside Ave Roslyn Heights NY 11577-1015 also: 281 Marcy Ave Brooklyn NY 11211

MEYERS, ABBEY S., foundation administrator; b. Bklyn., Apr. 11, 1944; d. Herbert and Blossom (Ruben) Feldman; m. Jerrold B. Meyers, Oct. 23, 1966; children: David, Adam, Laura. AAS, N.Y.C. Community Coll., 1962. Comml. artist various advt. agys., N.Y.C., 1962-65; dir. patient svcs. Tourette Syndrome Assn., Bayside, N.Y., 1980-85; exec. dir., founder Nat. Org. for Rare Disorders, New Fairfield, Conn., 1985-95, pres., CEO, 1995—; U.S. commr. Nat. Commn. on Orphan Diseases, Washington, 1986-89; mem. subcom. Human Gene Therapy NIH, Bethesda, Md., 1989-92; mem. recombinant DNA adv. com. NIH, 1992-96; mem. Health Care Payor Adv. Commn. on Conn. Commn. on Hosps. and Health Care, 1992-94. Author: (with others) Orphan Drugs and Orphan Diseases: Clinical Reality and Public Policy, 1983, (with others) Cooperative Approaches to Research and Development of Orphan Drugs, 1985, (with others) Tourette Syndrome: Clinical Understanding and Treatment, 1988, (with others) Physicians Guide to Rare Diseases, 1992. Bd. dirs. Nat. Orphan Drug and Device Found., N.Y.C., 1982-85; leader Coalition to Pass Orphan Drug Act of 1983, 1979-82. Recipient Pub. Health Svc. award HHS, 1985, Commr.'s Spl. citation FDA, 1988. Mem. Nat. Health Coun. (bd. dirs. 1989-94), Alliance of Genetic Support Groups (bd. dirs. 1987-89). Office: Nat Org for Rare Disorders PO Box 8923 Fairwood Profl Bldg New Fairfield CT 06812

MEYERS, DAVID LAURENCE, emergency physician; b. Detroit, Dec. 26, 1946; s. Leon M. and Shirley (Sovel) M.; m. Roberta Strickler, Jan. 31, 1981; children: Aaron Strickler, Emily Adrienne Strickler. AB, Franklin and Marshall Coll., 1968; MD, Temple U., 1975; postrad., Harvard U. Sch. Pub. Health, 1992. Intern, resident Cook County Hosp., Chgo., 1975-79; dir. emergency medicine Resurrection Med. Ctr., Chgo., 1984-94; chief emergency medicine Sinai Hosp. of Balt., 1994—; cons. emergency medicine MMI Cos., Deerfield, Ill., 1986—; instr. Northwestern U. Med. Sch., Chgo., 1980-94. Contbr. chpt. to book. Bd. dirs., past pres. bd. dirs. Erie Family Health Ctr., Chgo., 1984-94. Fellow Am. Coll. Emergency Physicians; mem. AMA, AAAS, Am. Med. Informatics Assn., N.Y. Acad. Scis., Balt. City Med. Soc., Med. Chirurgical Faculty of Md. Home: 2301 Ken Oak Rd Baltimore MD 21209 Office: Sinai Hosp of Balt 2401 W Belvedere Ave Baltimore MD 21215

MEYERS, JAMIE FOSTER, oral and maxillofacial surgeon; b. Houston, Nov. 5, 1956; d. James Holden Foster and Willette Maxine (LaFoe) Rasure; m. Joseph Paul Meyers, Mar. 10, 1979; children: Nicholas Joseph, Zachary Holden, Alexander James. AA, Texarkana (Tex.) C.C., 1976; B.Pharmacy, U. Houston, 1979; DDS, U. Tex., Houston, 1987; MD, U. Mo., Kansas City, 1991. Pharmacist Jack Eckerd Drug Corp., Houston, 1979-84; oral and maxillofacial surgeon Kansas City, Mo., 1992-93, Palestine, Tex., 1993—. Contbr. articles to profl. jours. Mem. ADA, AMA, Tex. Dental Assn., Anderson County Dental Soc., Tex. Med. Assn., Met. Med. Soc., Am. Assn. Oral and Maxillofacial Surgery. Ch. of Christ. Office: 919 S Magnolia Palestine TX 75801

MEYERS, KAREN LORAYNE DONNELL, rehabilition counselor; b. Augusta, Ga., Aug. 11, 1952; d. James Moncie and Ruby Lorayne (Bartlett) Donnell; m. Joseph Arthur Meyers, July 2, 1982. BA in Psychology, Augusta Coll., 1974; MEd in Rehab. Counseling, U. Ga., 1991. Instr. YWCA, Augusta, 1971, asst. dir. summer camp, 1971; recreation leader II, Gracewood State Sch. and Hosp., Ga., 1972-74, work therapist, 1974-84, med. librarian, 1984, work therapist, 1984-87, rehab. counselor, 1987—; investigator EEO devel. team, 1979-84; mem. women's guild Doctors Hosp., Augusta, 1982. Jr. bd. dirs. USO, Augusta, 1971; bd. dirs. Augusta Tng. Shop for Handicapped, 1979-80. Mem. Zeta Tau Alpha (Eta Mu chpt.). Republican. Methodist. Avocations: reading, sewing, gardening. Home: 2423 Patterson Bridge Ext Hephzibah GA 30815-9205 Office: 1727 Wrights Bord Rd PO Box 12007 Augusta GA 30914-2007

MEYERS, MAY LOU, psychologist, educational consultant; b. Austin, Tex., May 21, 1930; d. Ira William and Gertrude (Tebbs) Wilke; m. Carol Hansford Meyers, Mar. 22, 1951; children: Donna Michelle Spillers, Duane Randall. BA, U. Tex., 1951, MS, 1979. Lic. assoc. psychologist, Tex. Psychol. assoc. Charles T. Fries, Tyler, Tex., 1979-88; assoc. sch. psychologist Whitehouse (Tex.) Ind. Sch. Dist., 1980-95. Mem. Am. Psychol. Assn., East Tex. Psychol. Assn., Phi Beta Kappa, Pi Lambda Theta. Presbyterian.

MEYERS, MORTON ALLEN, physician, radiology educator; b. Troy, N.Y., Oct. 1, 1933; s. David and Jeanne Sarah (Dunn) M.; m. Beatrice Applebaum, June 1, 1963; children—Richard, Amy. M.D., SUNY, Upstate Med. Coll., 1959. Diplomate: Am. Bd. Radiology. Intern Bellevue Hosp., N.Y.C., 1959-60; resident in radiology Columbia-Presbyn. Med. Ctr., N.Y.C., 1960-63; fellow Am. Cancer Soc., 1961-63; prof. dept. radiology Cornell U. Med. Center, N.Y.C., 1973-78; prof., chmn. dept. radiology SUNY Sch. Medicine, Stony Brook, 1978-91; prof. dept. radiology SUNY Sch. Medicine, 1991—; vis. investigator St. Mark's Hosp., London, 1976; spkr. Radiol. Soc. N.Am., 1986. Author: Diseases of the Adrenal Glands: Radiologic Diagnosis, 1963, Dynamic Radiology of the Abdomen: Normal and Pathologic Anatomy, 1976, 4th edit., 1994, Iatrogenic Gastrointestinal Complications, 1981; series editor: Radiology of Iatrogenic Disorders, 1981-86; editor: Computed Tomography of the Gastrointestinal Tract: Including the Peritoneal Cavity and Mesentery, 1986; founding editor in chief Abdominal Imaging, 1976—; mem. editorial bd. Iatrogenics, Surg. and Radiol. Anatomy; contbr. chpts. to med. textbooks, articles to med. jours.; speaker in field. Served to capt. M.C. U.S. Army, 1963-65. Fellow Am. Coll. Radiology; mem. AAAS, Am. Coll. Gastroenterology, Radiol. Soc. N.Am., Am. Roentgen Ray Soc., Am. Gastroenterol. Assn., Soc. Uroradiology, Soc. Gastrointestinal Radiologists, Assn. Univ. Radiologists, N.Y. Roentgen Ray Soc., N.Y. Acad. Gastroenterology, Phila. Roentgen Soc., Harvey Soc., N.Y. Acad. Scis., L.I. Radiologic Soc., Alpha Omega Alpha. Home: 14 Wainscott Ln East Setauket NY 11733-3816 Office: SUNY Health Scis Ctr Sch Medicine Dept Radiology Stony Brook NY 11794

MEYERS, WAYNE MARVIN, microbiologist; b. Huntingdon County, Pa., Aug. 28, 1924; s. John William and Carrie Venca (Weaver) M.; m. Esther Louise Kleinschmidt, Aug. 26, 1953; children: Amy, George, Daniel, Sara. BS in Chemistry, Juniata Coll., 1947; diploma, Moody Bible Inst., 1950; M.S. in Med. Microbiology, U. Wis., 1953, Ph.D. in Med. Microbiology, 1955; M.D., Baylor Coll. Medicine, 1959; DSc (hon.), Juniata Coll., 1986. Instr. Baylor Coll. Medicine, 1955-59; intern Conemaugh Valley Meml. Hosp., Johnstown, Pa., 1959-60; staff physician Berrien Gen. Hosp., Berrien Ctr., Mich., 1960-61; missionary physician Am. Leprosy Missions, Burundi and Zaire, Africa, 1961-73; prof. pathology Sch. Medicine U. Hawaii, Honolulu, 1973-75; chief microbiology divsn. Armed Forces Inst. Pathology, Washington, 1975-89, chief mycobacteriology, 1989—, registrar leprosy registry, 1975—; mem. leprosy panel U.S.-Japan Coop. Med. Sci. Program, 1976-83; mem. sci. adv. bd. Leonard Wood Meml., 1981-85, sci. cons. dir., 1985-87, sci. dir., 1987-90; cons., 1990—; rsch. affiliate Tulane U., 1981—; corp. bd. dirs. Gorgas Meml. Inst. Tropical and Preventive Medicine, Inc. Bd. dirs. Internat. Jour. Leprosy, 1978—; contbr. numerous chpts. and articles on tropical medicine to textbooks and jours. Adv. bd. Damien-Dutton Soc. for Leprosy Aid, Inc., 1983-96, corp. bd. dirs., 1996—; adv. bd. Am. Leprosy Missions, Inc., 1979-88, chmn. bd., 1985-88, program cons. to bd., mem. bd. reference, 1988—; mem. Hansen's Disease Ctr., Carville, La., 1983-85; chmn., 1985—. With U.S. Army, 1944-46. Allergy Found. Am. fellow, 1957, 58; WHO rsch. grantee, 1978-87. Mem. Internat. Leprosy Assn. (councillor 1978-88, pres. 1988-93), Internat. Acad. Pathology, Internat. Soc. Tropical Dermatology, Am. Soc. Tropical Medicine and Hygiene, Am. Soc. Microbiology, Binford-Dammin Soc. Infectious Disease Pathologists (sec.-treas. 1988-91, pres. 1995-96), Internat. Soc. Travel Medicine, Sigma Xi. Office: Armed Forces Inst Pathology Washington DC 20306-6000

MEYERSICK, SHARON KAY, nurse, insurance administrator; b. Waynesville, Mo., Mar. 19, 1945; d. James Monroe and Fannie Mae (Williams) Atkinson; m. Bernard William Meyersick Jr., July 27, 1974 (dec. May 1992). AD in Nursing, Mercamec Community Coll., St. Louis, 1970; BS in Nursing, Tarkio Coll., Mo., 1983; postgrad., Webster Coll., St. Louis, 1988. Staff nurse Normandy Osteopathic Hosp., St. Louis, 1970-76, head nurse, 1976-79, instr. nursing edn., 1979-81; quality assurance nurse Barnes Hosp., St. Louis, 1981-84; review analyst Blue Cross-Blue Shield of Mo., St. Louis, 1985-87, supr. program review, 1987-91; patient care coord. Prudential Ins. Co. Am./St. Louis Health Care Mgmt., St. Louis, 1991—. Office: Prudential Ins Co Am Saint Louis Health Care Mgmt 12312 Olive Blvd Saint Louis MO 63141-6448

MEYLER, MARK ZINOVYEVICH, dentist; b. Odessa, Ukraine, June 6, 1948; came to U.S., 1989; s. Zinoviy and Liya (Keselman) M.; m. Anna Zilberman, Feb. 19, 1955; 1 child, Zinovy. D Stomatology, Odessa Med. Inst., 1971; Stomatologist, Surgeon 1st Degree, Ukraian Inst. Doctors, Kharkov, 1984; DDS, NYU, N.Y.C., 1991. Stomatologist, surgeon Stomatology Clinic #7, Odessa, 1971-88; dentist Beach Haven Dental Office, Bklyn., 1992-94, M/M Dental, Bklyn., 1994—. Inventor New Americans collected sci. reports, 1991. Mem. ADA. Office: M/M Dental 50 Shore Blvd Brooklyn NY 11235

MEYNIER, MAURICE JOSEPH, JR., obstetrician-gynecologist, educator; b. New Orleans, Oct. 16, 1904; s. Maurice Joseph and Louise Julie (Charpantier) M.; m. Charlotte Dorothee Mosle, May 3, 1934; children: Margaret Louise, Maurice Joseph. BA, Rice U., 1927; MD, U. Tex.-Galveston, 1931. Diplomate Am. Bd. Ob-Gyn. Intern and resident Grad. Hosp. U. Pa., Phila., 1931-33; resident in ob-gyn King's County Hosp., Bklyn., 1933-35; practice medicine specializing in ob-gyn, Houston, 1935-77; past mem. staff Jefferson Davis Hosp., Hermann Hosp., Meth. Hosp.; past pres. St. Joseph Hosp., 1968 (all in Houston); assoc. clin. prof. ob-gyn Baylor Coll. Medicine, Houston, 1946-77, now emeritus prof.; assoc. clin. prof. ob-gyn U. Tex. Health Scis. Ctr., Houston, 1975-77, emeritus prof. Served to maj. USAAF, 1942-46. Contbr. numerous articles to med. jours.; patentee nipple shield for breast nursing, vaginal tampon, pivoting boat motor device unit. Fellow ACS; mem. AMA, Am. Coll. Ob-Gyn, So. Med. Assn., Tex. Med. Assn., Houston Surg. Soc., Tex. Assn. Ob-Gyn (past pres. 1960), Houston Ob-Gyn Soc. (pres. 1964), Harris County Med. Soc. (pres. 1969), Alpha Kappa Kappa. Republican. Clubs: Houston, Doctors. Home: 777 N Post Oak Rd Apt 1607 Houston TX 77024-3824

MEYSKENS, FRANK LOUIS, JR., hematologist, oncologist, educator; b. San Francisco, Sept. 3, 1945; m. Alice Covell; children: Moriah, Covell, Desiree. BS, U. San Francisco, 1967; MD, U. Calif., San Francisco, 1972. Prof. medicine and biol. chemistry U. Calif. Irvine, Orange, 1989—; chief hematology/oncology, co-dir. cancer program, dir. Clin. Cancer Ctr., U. Calif. Irvine, 1989—; co-chairperson conf. on minorities Nat. Cancer Inst., 1990; Hamilton lectr. U. Rochester Cancer Ctr., 1989; active various profl. adv. and cons. bds. Contbr. over 200 articles to sci. jours. Recipient Grace A. Goldsmith award Am. Coll. Nutrition, 1989, Yr. 2000 award Nat. Cancer Inst., 1990. Office: Univ Calif Irvine 101 The City Dr S Bldg 44 Orange CA 92668-3201*

MEZEY, JUDITH PAUL, social worker; b. N.Y.C., Nov. 14, 1946; d. Chester Eugene and Shirley (Bagley) Paul; m. Robert Joseph Mezey, Apr. 6, 1968; children: Jennifer Robin, Barry Paul. BS, Boston U., 1968; EdM, Columbia U., 1972; MSW, Barry U., 1990. Lic. social worker; RN. Pediatric staff nurse Albert Einstein Coll., N.Y.C., 1967-69; clin. instr. Morrisania-Montefiore Hosp., N.Y.C., 1969-71; grad. student nursing Tchrs. Coll., Columbia U., N.Y.C., 1971-72; clin. instr. Pace U., N.Y.C., 1972-74, U. Miami, 1976-77, Fla. Internat. U., Miami, 1978-79; clin. instr. Barry U., Miami, 1979-86, social work grad. student, 1987-90; psychotherapist A&A Profl. Assocs., South Miami, 1991-93; pvt. practice Miami, Fla., 1993—; facilitator support group Bapt. Hosp., Miami, 1991—. Bd. dirs. Dave and Mary Alper Jewish Cmty. Ctr., Miami, 1986—, chmn. spl. needs com., Miami, 1988—; founding chairperson Spl. Needs Program, 1988. Recipient Fed. Nurse Traineeship grant U.S. Govt., 1970. Mem. NASW. Democrat. Jewish. Home: 6740 SW 99th Ter Miami FL 33156-3240 Office: 9260 Sunset Dr Ste 203 Miami FL 33173

MFAREJ, BONNIE ELAINE, health services administrator; b. East Stroudsburg, Pa.; d. Robert Franklin and Ruth Evelyn (Scheller) George; m. Michael George Mfarej; 2 children. BA, Stephens Coll., 1980; MS, Temple U., 1983. Lic. nursing home adminstr., Pa. Assoc. adminstr. Good Shepherd Rehab. Hosp., Allentown, Pa., 1983-96; v.p. Good Shepherd Home, Allentown, 1996&. Mem. Am. Congress of Rehab., Am. Health Info. Mgmt. Assn., Assn. Health Care Quality Eastern Pa., Pa. Med. Record Assn., Lehigh Valley Med. Record Assn., Pa. Assn. Rehab. Facilities Med. Rehab. Coun. Office: Good Shepherd Home 501 St John St Allentown PA 18103

MICHAEL, ALFRED FREDERICK, JR., physician, medical educator; b. Phila.; s. Alfred Frederick and Emma Maude (Peters) M.; children: Mary, Susan, Carol. M.D., Temple U., 1953. Diplomate: Am. Bd. Pediatrics (founding mem. sub-bd. pediatric nephrology, pres. 1977-80). Diagnostic lab. immunology and pediatric nephrology intern Phila. Gen. Hosp., 1953-54; resident Children's Hosp. and U. Cin. Coll. Medicine, 1957-60; postdoctoral fellow dept. pediatrics Med. Sch., U. Minn., Mpls., 1960-63; asso. prof. Med. Sch., U. Minn., 1965-68, prof. pediatrics, lab. medicine and pathology, 1968—, dir. pediatric nephrology, Regents' Prof., head Dept. Pediatrics, 1986—; established investigator Am. Heart Assn., 1963-68. Mem. editorial bd. Internat. Yr. Book of Nephrology, Kidney Internat., Am. Jour. Nephrology, Kidney Internat., Am. Jour. Nephrology, Clin. Nephrology, Am. Jour. Pathology; contbr. articles to profl. jours. Served with USAF, 1955-57. Recipient Alumni Achievement award in clin. scis. Temple U. Sch. Medicine, 1988; NIH fellow, 1960-63; Guggenheim fellow, 1966-67; AAAS fellow, 1995. Mem. AAAS, AMA, Am. Acad. Pediat., Am. Soc. Clin. Investigation, Assn. Am. Physicians, Am. Pediat. Soc., Soc. for Pediat. Rsch., Am. Assn. Investigative Pathology, Am. Soc. Cell Biology, Ctrl. Soc. for Clin. Rsch., Am. Soc. Nephrology (coun., pres.-elect 1992—, pres. 1993), Internat. Soc. Nephrology, Soc. for Exptl. Biology and Medicine, Am. Fedn. Clin. Rsch., Minn. Med. Assn. Congregationalist. Office: U Minn Hosp Dept Pediatrics PO Box 391 Minneapolis MN 55455

MICHAEL, ANDREW JOSEPH, ophthalmologist; b. Dallas, Apr. 12, 1958; s. Ludwig A. and Carmen M. Michael; m. Patricia T. Michael, Aug. 8, 1982; children: Benjamin, William. BA, U. N.C., 1979; MD, U. Tex., Dallas, 1987. Intern Baylor U. Med. Ctr., Dallas, 1987-88; resident Wills Eye Hosp., Phila., 1988-91, fellow, 1991-92; instr. U. Colo. Health Sci. Ctr., Denver, 1992-95, assoc. prof., 1995—; pvt. practice Glaucoma Assocs. P.C., Denver, 1992—. Contbr. numerous articles to profl. jours. Recipient P. Russ Mcdonald award Wills Eye Hosp., 1992. McDermott scholar, 1980-87. Fellow Am. Acad. Ophthalmology. Office: Glaucoma Associates 850 E Harvard Ave #205 Denver CO 80210

MICHAEL, DOROTHY ANN, nurse, naval officer; b. Lancaster, Pa., Sept. 20, 1950; d. Richard Linus and Mary Ruth (Hahn) Michael.; m. Juan Roberto Morales, July 15, 1995. Diploma, R.N., Montgomery Hosp. Sch. Nursing, Norristown, Pa., 1971; BSN, George Mason U., 1980; MSN, U. Tex. Health Sci. Ctr., 1985. Commd. ensign USN, 1970, advanced through grades to capt. Nurse Corps, 1994; staff nurse Nat. Naval Med. Ctr., Bethesda, Md., 1971-73; charge nurse Naval Hosp., Guantanamo Bay, Cuba, 1973-74, Naval Regional Med. Ctr., Phila., 1974-76, Naval Hosp., Keflavik, Iceland, 1977, Naval Hosp., Bethesda, 1980-84, sr. nurse, asst. officer-in-charge Br. Med. Clinic, Naval Weapons Ctr., China Lake, Calif., 1986-89; coord. quality assurance Naval Hosp., Oakland, Calif., 1989-92, assoc. dir. inpatient nursing, 1992-93; divsn. officer USNS Mercy, Persian Gulf, 1990-91, assoc. dir. surg. nursing, 1993-95; dir. nursing svc. Naval Hosp., Great Lakes, Ill., 1995—; splty. advisor to dir. Navy Nurse Corp., Navy Med. Command, Washington, 1983-84. V.p. Deepwood Homeowners Assn., Reston, Va., 1978-82; advisor, com. mem. Reston Found., 1979. Recipient R.W. Bjorklund Mgmt. Innovator award Kern County, Calif., 1988, Comdr.'s Award for Outstanding Professionalism in Pub. Health Support, 1988. Mem. Vietnam Vets Am., Vets. Fgn. Wars, Orgn. Nurse Execs., Am. Nurses Assn. (cert. nursing adminstrn.), Am. Legion, Sigma Theta Tau. Roman Catholic. Home: 421 Flanders Ln Grayslake IL 60030

MICHAEL, JERROLD MARK, public health specialist, former university dean, educator; b. Richmond, Va., Aug. 3, 1927; s. Joseph Leon and Esther Leah M.; m. Lynn Y. Simon, Mar. 17, 1951; children: Scott J., Nelson L. B.C.E., George Washington U., 1949; M.S.E., Johns Hopkins U., 1950; M.P.H., U. Calif., Berkeley, 1957; Dr. P.H. (hon.), Mahidol U., 1983; Sc.D. (hon.), Tulane U., 1984. Commd. ensign USPHS, 1950, advanced through grades to rear adm., asst. surgeon gen., 1966; ret., 1970; dean Sch. Pub. Health, U. Hawaii, Honolulu, 1971-92, prof. pub. health, 1971-95; emeritus prof. pub. health U. Hawaii, Honolulu, 1995—; bd. dirs. Nat. Health Coun., 1967-78, Nat. Ctr. for Health Edn., 1977-90; mem. nat. adv. coun. on health professions edn., 1978-81; chmn. bd. dirs. Kuakini Med. Ctr., Honolulu; sec., treas. Asia-Pacific Acad. Consortium Pub. Health; vis. prof. U. Adelaide, 1993, George Washington, 1994; hon. prof. Beijing Med. U., 1994. Contbr. articles to profl. jours.; assoc. editor Jour. Environ. Health, 1958-80, Asia-Pacific Jour. of Pub. Health, 1986-95. Served with USNR, 1945-47. Decorated D.S.M., comdr. Royal Order of Elephant (Thailand); recipient Walter Mangold award, 1961, J.S. Billings award for mil. medicine, 1964, gold medal Hebrew U. Jerusalem, 1982, San Karcil gold medal Govt. of Malaysia, 1989, Disting. Svc. award Gov. of Hawaii, 1989, Assn. Schs. Pub. Health, 1992, recognition of svc. award Pacific Island Health Officers Assn., 1992, USPHS awards, also others. Fellow Am. Public Health Assn.; mem. Am. Acad. Health Adminstrn., Am. Soc. Cert. Sanitarians, Nat. Environ. Health Assn., Am. Acad. Environ. Engrs. Democrat. Jewish. Club: Masons. Home: 16736 Gooseneck Terrace Olney MD 20832

MICHAEL, MAX, III, internist; b. Atlanta, Mar. 14, 1946; s. Max, Jr., and Barbara Elizabeth (Seigel) M.; m. Marilyn Anne Losco, June 22, 1970 (dec. Nov. 1991); children—David Max, Sara Adrienne; m. Ellen Alexander, May 14, 1994. B.A. cum laude with honors in Biology, Vanderbilt U., 1968; M.D., Harvard U., 1972. Diplomate Am. Bd. Internal Medicine. Med. resident Med. Ctr., U. Ala., Birmingham, 1972-74; Robert Wood Johnson clin. scholar, Chapel Hill, N.C., 1974-76; staff physician Cooper Green Hosp., Birmingham, 1977—, dir. outpatient services, 1977-92, chief staff, 1982-86, 91-92, chmn. dept. medicine, 1983-92, CEO, med. dir., 1992—; assoc. prof. U. Ala. Birmingham; med. dir. Birmingham Health Care for the Homeless Coalition. Recipient Advanced Achievement Internal Medicine award Am. Bd. Internal Medicine, 1987. Fellow ACP; mem. Am. Pub. Health Assn., Jefferson County Med. Soc. Democrat. Jewish. Contbr. articles to sci. jours. Home: 4316 Glenwood Ave Birmingham AL 35222-4303 Office: 1515 6th Ave S Birmingham AL 35233-1601

MICHAEL, SANDRA DALE, reproductive endocrinology educator, researcher; b. Sacramento, Calif., Jan. 23, 1945; d. Gordon G. and Ruby F. (Johnson) M.; m. Dennis P. Murr, Aug. 12, 1967 (div. 1974). BA, Calif. State Coll., Sonoma, 1967; PhD, U. Calif., Davis, 1970. NIH predoctoral fellow U. Calif., Davis, 1967-70, NIH postdoctoral fellow, 1970-73, asst. rsch. geneticist, 1973-74; asst. prof. SUNY, Binghamton, 1974-81, assoc. prof., 1981-88, prof. reproductive endocrinology, 1988—, dept. chair, 1992—; adj. prof. dept. ob-gyn. SUNY Health Scis. Ctr., Syracuse; mem. NIH Reproductive Endocrinology Study Sect., 1991-95—; cons., presenter in field; grant reviewer NIH, NSF, USDA and others. Contbr. articles to profl. jours. Vice chair Tri Cities Opera Guild, Binghamton, 1987-90, chair, 1990-92; mem. Harpur Forum, Binghamton, 1987—, SUNY Found., Binghamton, 1990-96. Fulbright Sr. scholar Czech Republic, 1994; grantee NIMH, 1976-79, Nat. Cancer Inst., 1977-80, 83-87, Nat. Inst. Environ. Health Scis., 1979-80, NSF, 1981-83, NIH, 1987—. Mem. Endocrine Soc., Soc. for the Study of Reprodn., Soc. for Study of Fertility, Am. Soc. for Immunology of Reprodn., Women in Endocrinology (sec.-treas. 1992-95), Soc. for Exptl. Biology and Medicine, N.Y. Acad. Sci., Sigma Xi. Office: State Univ of NY Dept Biol Scis Binghamton NY 13902

MICHAELIDES, DOROS NIKITA, internist, medical educator; b. Nicosia, Cyprus, Jan. 7, 1936; came to U.S., 1969; s. Nikita P. and Elpinike (Taliadorou) M.; m. Eutychia J. Loizides, Feb. 27, 1965; children: Nike-Elsie, Joanna-Doris. MD cum laude (Royal Greek Govt. scholar), U. Athens, 1962; D.T.M. and H. (Greek State Scholarship Found. scholar), U. Liverpool (Eng.), 1967; MSc in Clin. Biochemistry (Greek State Scholarship Found. scholar), U. Newcastle-upon-Tyne (Eng.), 1969. Clk., intern U. Uppsala (Sweden), 1962; resident Nicosia Gen. Hosp., 1963-66; fellow U. Liverpool Hosps., 1967; fellow internal and clin. medicine Royal Infirmary, U. Edinburgh, 1967-68; research fellow Royal Victoria Infirmary, U. Newcastle-upon-Tyne, 1968-69; resident internal medicine Bapt. Meml. Hosp., Memphis, 1969-72; fellow in chest diseases Western Okla. Chest Disease Hosp., 1970-71; chief clin. immunology and respiratory care center, Erie, Pa.; chief respiratory care center VA Med. Ctr., Erie, 1972-84, acting chief dept. medicine, 1980-81; asst. clin. prof. medicine Hahnemann Univ. Sch. Medicine, Phila., 1977—; asst. clin. prof. medicine Gannon U., Erie, 1977—; mem. staff internal medicine Hamot Med. Ctr., immunology & chest diseases Metro Health Ctr., Erie; preceptor medicine St. Vincent's Health Ctr.; affiliate staff Cleveland Clinic Found; vol. physician Greek Nat. Guard, Cyprus, 1964. Recipient citation for outstanding services to vets. DAV, 1975, citation Adminstr. U.S. Vets. Affairs, 1978. Diplomate Am. Bd. Family Practice, Am. Bd. Allergy and Immunology; cert. in infectious diseases and immunochemistry, Eng. Fellow ACP (life), Am. Assn. Cert. Allergists, Am. Coll. Allergy and Immunology (com. autoimmune diseases), Am. Assn. Clin. Immunology and Allergy (pulmonary com.). Am. Coll. Chest Physicians (life; critical care com.), Royal Soc. Medicine, Am. Coll. Angiology, N.Y. Acad. Scis., Am. Coll. Clin. Pharmacology, Am. Assn. Cert. Allergists. Greek Orthodox. Author: The Occurrence of Proteolytic Inhibitors in Heart and Skeletal Muscle, 1969; Blood Gases, Acid-Base and Electrolytes Disturbances, 1980; Immediate Hypersensitivity: The Immunochemistry and Therapeutics of Reversible Airway Obstruction, 1980; The Equivalent Potency of Corticosteroid Preparations used in Reversible Airway Obstruction, 1981; contbr. articles to med. jours. Home: 4107 State St Erie PA 16508-3129 Office: Allergy Immunology & Chest Diseases 1611 Peach St Ste 220 Erie PA 16501-2121

MICHAELS, CRAIG ADAM, psychologist; b. N.Y.C., Mar. 2, 1954; s. Melvin A. and Helen (Courtney) M.; m. Susan Jane Knowles; children: Noah Lynn, Alana Rose, Esther Leor. BFA, San Francisco Art Inst., 1976; MA in Spl. Edn., NYU, 1979, ABD, 1990, PhD, 1993. Cert. rehab. counselor, 1990. Reading specialist Stephen Gaynor Sch., N.Y.C., 1978-80; vocat. program coord. Endeavor Learning Ctr., Silver Springs, Md., 1981-85; sr. learning disability specialist Nat. Ctr. on Employment and Disability, Albertson, N.Y., 1985-86, coordinator learning disability project, 1986-87, sr. coord. learning disability projects, 1987-88, sr. coord. spl. rehab. projects, 1988-94; dir. Rsch. and Tng. Inst., Nat. Ctr. for Disability Scvs., Albertson, N.Y., 1994—. Author, editor: From High School to College, 1988, How to Succeed in College, 1988, Transition Strategies for Persons with Learning Disabilities, 1994; contbr.: Dyslexia: A Neuropsychological and Learning Perspective, 1988; author, editor: Social Skills for the World of Work and Beyond, 1991, Gateways to the Working World, 1991. Mem. Nat. Rehab. Assn., Am. Ednl. Rsch. Assn., Learning Disabilities Assn. Am., Am. Assn. for Counseling and Devel., Coun. on Exceptional Children. Office: Nat Ctr For Disability Svcs 201 I U Willets Rd Albertson NY 11507-1516

MICHAK, HELEN BARBARA, educator, nurse; b. Cleve., July 31; d. Andrew and Mary (Patrick) M. Diploma Cleve. City Hosp. Sch. Nursing, 1947; BA, Miami U., Oxford, Ohio, 1951; MA, Case Western Res. U., 1960. Staff nurse Cleve. City Hosp., 1947-48; pub. health nurse Cleve. Div. Health, 1951-52; instr. Cleve. City Hosp. Sch. Nursing, 1952-56; supr. nursing Cuyahoga County Hosp., Cleve., 1956-58; pub. information dir. N.E. Ohio Am. Heart Assn., Cleve., 1960-64; dir. spl. events Higbee Co., Cleve., 1964-66; exec. dir. Cleve. Area League for Nursing, 1966-72; dir. continuing edn. nurses, adj. assoc. prof. Cleve. State U., 1972-86; asst. regional cons. Ohio Bd. Nursing, 1991—. Trustee N.E. Ohio Regional Med. Program, 1970-73; mem. adv. com. Dept. Nursing Cuyahoga C.C., 1967-87; mem. long term care com. Met. Health Planning Corp., 1974-76, plan devel. com. 1977; mem. policy bd. Ctr. Health Data N.E. Ohio, 1972-73; mem. Rep. Assembly and Health Planning and Devel. Commn., Welfare Fedn. Cleve., 1967-72, Cleve. Cmty. Health Network, 1972-73, United Appeal Films and Speakers Bur., 1967-73; mem. adv. com. Ohio Fedn. Lic. Practical Nurses, 1970-73; mem. tech. adv. com. No. Ohio Lung Assn., 1967-74, 90-93; mem. Ohio Commn. on Nursing, 1971-74; mem. citizens com. nursing homes Fedn. Community Planning, 1973-77; mem. com. on home health services Met. Health Planning Corp., 1973-75; mem. profl. adv. com. on home care Fairview Gen. Hosp., 1987-91. Mem. Nat. League Nursing (mem. com. 1970-72), Am. Nurses Assn. (accreditation visitor 1977-78, 83-88) Ohio Nurses Assn., (com. continuing edn. 1974-79, 82-87, 89-92, chmn. 1984-86), Greater Cleve. (joint practice com. 1973-74, Greater Cleve. Nurses Assn. (trustee 1975-76) , Cleve. Area Citizens League for Nursing (trustee 1976-79, v.p. 1988-90), Zeta Tau Alpha, Sigma Theta Tau. Home and Office: 4686 Oakridge Dr North Royalton OH 44133

MICHALAK, PETER PAUL, emergency room physician; b. Kingston, Pa., Mar. 21, 1950; s. Alexander J. and Dorothy (Paulik) M.; m. Carla Marie Michalak, May 20, 1987; 1 child, Peter P. Jr. BS in Biology cum laude, King's Coll., 1972; DO, Phila. Coll. Osteo. Medicine, 1976. Diplomate Am. Bd. Emergency Medicine. Intern Tresom Gen. Hosp., 1976-77; dir. emergency medicine Cobre Valley Hosp., Tucson, 1993—. Fellow Am. Coll. Emergency Physicians; mem. Am. Osteo. Assn., Pima Med. Soc. Republican. Roman Catholic. Home: 5520 N Suncrest Tucson AZ 85718

MICHALOPOULOS, CHRISTOS DEMETRIUS, cardiologist; b. Lyrkeia, Argolis, Greece, Aug. 30, 1931; s. Demetrius Christos and Angelike Sotirios (Colovos) M.; m. Vasiliki Petros Mitrakos, Feb. 21, 1965; children: Angela, Katherine. MD, U. Athens, Greece, 1969. Med. diplomate. Commd. 2d lt. Greek Army, 1956, advanced through grades to brig. gen., 1985; dir. 204-212 Med. Bn., Alexandroupolis, Greece, 1966-68; chief editor Hellenic Armed Forces Med. Rev., Athens, 1968-72; head dept. cardiology Athens Gen. Mil. Hosp., 1972-74; dir. med. dept. various mil. units, Athens, Corinth, Edessa, Greece, 1974-77; head dept. cardiology Athens Gen. Mil. Hosp., 1978-81; dir. 411th Gen. Mil. Hosp., Tripolis, Greece, 1981-82; head dept. cardiology NIMTS Hosp., Athens, 1983-87; ret., 1987, pvt. practice,, 1983—. Translator: The Heart (Hurst), 1978; translator, editor: Cardiology Clinics, 1990—; exec. editor Hellenic Jour. Cardiology, 1989-95; mem. editorial bd. European Heart Jour., 1991-95. Mem. Hellenic Cardio. Soc., Hellenic Armed Forces M.C. Sci. Assn. (bd. dirs. 198-92), Hellenic Com. Against Thromboembolic Diseases (gen. sec. 1976—), N.Y. Acad. Scis., Am. Coll. Angiology. Office: 9 Neoph Metaxa Str, 104-39 Athens Greece

MICHALSKI, CAROL ANN, medical, surgical and psychiatric nurse, writer, poet; b. Balt., Feb. 21, 1955; d. John B. Rassa and Genevieve J. Ryncewicz; m. Martin Joseph Michalski, June 21, 1976; children: Matthew, Nathan. RN, Grand View Hosp., Sellersville, Pa., 1976; BS in Health Care Adminstrn., Pacific Western U., 1986, PhD in Religious Studies/Ministry, 1987. RN; ordained to ministry Christian Ch., 1983. Staff nurse Md. Gen. Hosp., Balt., 1974-75, Union Meml. Hosp., Balt., 1975-77; head nurse Levindale Chronic Hosp., Balt., 1977-79; charge staff nurse Franklin Sq. Hosp. Ctr., Balt., 1979—, pain mgmt. liaison, 1993—; head procedure com. Levindale Chronic Hosp., Balt., 1978-79; min. Faith Seed Ministries, Balt., 1983—; Bible Coll. adminstr. L.W. Christian Ctr., Balt., 1987-89. Author: Don't Blame God-Making Sense Out of Tragedy and Suffering, 1995; contbr. articles and poetry to profl. jours. and anthologies. Asst. youth activities Ridgeleigh Cmty. Assn., Balt., 1980; block capt. Woodcroft Civic Assn., Balt.; coord. Churchville Christian Sch., 1993-94; Christian Home Educator's Network group coord. Teen Boys Group, 1995—. Recipient Nursing Achievement award Johnston Sch.-Union Meml. Hosp., 1984, Ministry Recognition Certs. Gospel Tabernacle Balt., 1990, 91, poetry awards. Mem. Md. League Nursing, Nat. Author's Registry, Internat. Soc. Poets.

MICHEL, THOMAS MARK, internal medicine educator, scientist, physician; b. Portland, Oreg., July 14, 1955. AB in Biochem. Scis., Harvard U., 1977; PhD in Biochemistry, Duke U., 1983, MD, 1984. Diplomate Am. Bd. Internal Medicine, Am. Bd. Cardiovasc. Disease. House officer, jr. and sr. resident in medicine Brigham and Women's Hosp., Boston, 1984-87, clin. and rsch. fellow in medicine cardiovasc. div., 1987-88, assoc. physician, staff physician cardiovasc. div., 1988—; clin. fellow in medicine Harvard U. Med. Sch., Boston, 1984-87, rsch. fellow dept. genetics, 1988-90, instr. medicine, 1988-89, asst. prof., 1989-95, assoc. prof., 1995—; tutor in biochem. scis. Harvard Coll., Harvard U., Cambridge, Mass., 1990—; lectr. molecular mechanisms of disease Harvard Med. Sci.-MIT health scis. and tech. program, 1990—; speaker at seminars, confs. and univs.; vis. lectr. U. Alta., U. Calgary, U. Alcala, Madrid, St. Bartholomew's Hosp., London; Cecilie Greig vis. prof. Hammersmith Hosp., Royal Postgrad. Med. Sch., London; plenary lectr., Nitric Oxide Forum, Tokyo. Contbr. articles to med. jours. Recipient John J. Abel award in Pharmacology Am. Soc. for Pharmacology Therapeutics, 1995, young scholar's award Am. Soc. Hypertension, 1991; Harvard nat. scholar Harvard U., 1973-77; fellow NIH, 1977-84. Fellow Am. Coll. Cardiology; mem. ACP, Am. Fedn. for Clin. Rsch., Henry Christian award for excellence in rsch. 1992, 93), Am. Heart Assn. (Established Investigator award 1993—, Clinican-Scientist award 1988-93), Am. Soc. for Biochemistry and Molecular Biology, Mass. Med. Soc. Office: Brigham & Women's Hosp Harvard Med Sch 75 Francis St Boston MA 02115-6110*

MICHELIS, MICHAEL FRANK, nephrologist; b. Bklyn., Dec. 11, 1938; s. Michael and Gisella (Gammer) M.; B.A., Columbia U., 1959; M.D., George Washington U., 1963; m. Mary Ann Wolak, July 28, 1973; children—Elizabeth Ann, Katherine Clare. Intern, Resident Lenox Hill Hosp., N.Y.C., 1963-65; resident Hosp. Med. Coll. Pa., Phila., 1965-67; fellow in renal disease dept. medicine U. Pitts. Sch. Medicine, 1969-70, asst. prof. medicine, 1971-75; chief renal diagnostic unit VA Hosp., Pitts., 1971-75; asst. prof. clin. medicine N.Y.U. Med. Sch., 1975-93; assoc. prof. clin. medicine N.Y. Med. Coll., 1980-87, prof., 1987-92; assoc. prof. clin. medicine Cornell U. Med. Coll., 1992-93; prof. clin. medicine N.Y.U. Med. Coll., 1993—; chief nephrology sect. Lenox Hill Hosp., N.Y.C., 1975—; spl. lectr. Georgetown U. Med. Sch., 1973—; lectr. Western Pa. Continuing Edn. for Physicians, 1972-75, vis. prof., 1976; mem. merit rev. bd. VA, 1973-76; cons. clin. fellowship rev. com. NIH, 1981—; mem. exec. com. End Stage Renal Disease Network, N.Y.C., 1981-85; mem. med. adv. bd. Nat. Kidney Found. of N.Y./N.J., 1987—. Served to maj. M.C., AUS, 1967-69. Decorated Army Commendation medal, 1969; grantee Health, Research and Services Found., 1970, 72. 74. Mem. AMA (invited lectr. 1973-75). ACP, Am. Fedn. Clin. Research, Am. Soc. Nephrology, Internat. Soc. Nephrology, Central Soc. Clin. Research. Greek Orthodox. Contbr. articles to profl. jours. and textbooks. Asst. editor Clin. Nephrology, 1979-89, Am. editor, 1989—; assoc. editor Geriatric Nephrology, 1986, Jour. of Geriatric Nephrology and Urology, 1989—. Home: 16 Woodland Park Dr Tenafly NJ 07670-3027 Office: Lenox Hill Hosp 100 E 77th St New York NY 10021-1882

MICHELS, EUGENE, physical therapist; b. Cin., May 16, 1926; s. Joseph and Anna (Bauer) M.; m. Genevieve Wilma Readinger, June 28 1947; children: Karen, Timothy, Donald, Marian, Monica, Martha, David, Ann. B.S., U. Cin., 1950; cert. phys. therapy, U. Pa., 1951, M.A., 1965; Litt.D. (hon.), Thomas Jefferson U., 1985. Phys. therapist Grad. Hosp., U. Pa., Phila., 1951-58, mem. faculty dept. phys. therapy, 1965—, asst. prof., 1969-75, asso. prof., 1975-77; dir. phys. therapy Magee Meml. Hosp., Phila., 1958-65; assoc. exec. v.p. Am. Phys. Therapy Assn., 1977-88. Served with USNR, 1944-46. Recipient Lindback Found. Disting. Tchg. award, 1972; Pa. Phys. Therapy Assn. ann. achievement award named Carlin-Michels Achievement award in honor of Eleanor J. Carlin and Eugene Michels. Mem. Pa. Phys. Therapy Assn. (past pres.), Am. Phys. Therapy Assn. (past pres., Dorothy Briggs Meml. Sci. Inquiry award 1971, Golden Pen award 1977, Mary McMillan lectr. 1984, Catherine Worthingham fellow 1986, Eugene Michels New Investigator award established in his honor 1989, John Maley award sect. rsch. 1994), World Confedn. Phys. Therapy (pres. 1974-82). Democrat. Roman Catholic. Home: 7608 Wellesley Dr College Park MD 20740-3040

MICHELS, KIM MARIE, pediatrics nurse; b. Bellevue, Iowa, July 6, 1970; d. James Richard and Kathleen Anita (Konrardy) M. BSN, U. Iowa, 1992. RN, Iowa. Staff nurse U. Iowa Hosps. and Clinics, Iowa City, 1993-95; staff nurse hematology/oncology-transplant unit Children's Hosp., Denver, 1995—. Mem. Diabetic Collaborative Practice. Roman Catholic. Home: 1225 S Bellaire # 404 Denver CO 80222

MICHELS, ROBERT, psychiatrist, educator; b. Chgo., Jan. 21, 1936; s. Samuel and Ann (Cooper) M.; m. Verena Sterba, Dec. 23, 1962; children—Katherine, James. BA, U. Chgo., 1953; MD, Northwestern U., 1958. Intern Mt. Sinai Hosp., N.Y.C., 1958-59; resident in psychiatry Columbia Presbyn.-N.Y. State Psychiat. Inst., N.Y.C., 1959-62; mem. faculty Coll. Physicians and Surgeons, Columbia U., N.Y.C., 1964-74; assoc prof. Coll. Physicians and Surgeons, Columbia U., 1971-74; psychiatrist student health service Columbia U., 1966-74; supervising and tng. analyst Columbia U. Center for Psychoanalytic Tng. and Research, 1972—; attending psychiatrist Vanderbilt Clinic, Presbyn. Hosp., N.Y.C., 1964-74; Barklie McKee Henry prof. psychiatry Cornell U. Med. Coll., N.Y.C., 1974-93, prof. psychiatry, 1993—, chmn. dept. psychiatry, 1974-91; Stephen and Suzanne Weiss dean Cornell U. Med. Coll., 1991-96; provost for med. affairs Cornell U., 1991-96, Walsh McDermott U. prof. of medicine 1996—; psychiatrist-in-chief N.Y. Hosp., 1974-91, attending psychiatist, 1991—; attending psychiatrist St. Luke's Hosp. Ctr., N.Y.C., 1966—. Co-author: The Psychiatric Interview in Clinical Practice, 1971; contbr. articles to profl. jours. Served with USPHS, 1962-64. Mem. Am. Psychiat. Assn., Am. Coll. Psychiatrists, N.Y. Psychiat. Soc., Royal Medico-Psychol. Assn., Psychiat. Rsch. Soc., Assn. Rsch. in Nervous and Mental Diseases, Assn. Acad. Psychiatry, Am. Psychoanalytic Assn., Internat. Psychoanalytic Assn., Ctr. Advanced Psychoanalytic Studies, N.Y. Acad. Scis., Alpha Omega Alpha. Office: Cornell U Med Coll 1300 York Ave New York NY 10021-4805

MICHELSEN, AXEL, biologist, educator, foundation administrator; b. Haderslev, Denmark, Mar. 1, 1940; s. Erik and Vibeke (Behrens) M.; m. Ulla West-Nielsen, Feb. 1, 1980; children: Lars, Helle, Thomas. PhD, U. Copenhagen, Denmark, 1966, DSc, 1971. Asst. prof. U. Copenhagen, 1966-72; prof. Odense (Denmark) U., 1973—; chmn. Danish Sci. Rsch. Coun., Denmark, 1975-78; dir. Carlsberg Found., Denmark, 1986—. Author: The Physiology of the Locust Ear, 1971, Sound and Life, 1975, Time Resolution in Auditory Systems, 1985, The Dance Language of the Honeybee, 1992; mem. editorial bd. several jours. Decorated Knight of the Order of Danneborg (Denmark); Alexander von Humboldt rsch. award, 1990. Mem. Acad. Wissenschaften und der Lit., Acad. of Europe, Royal Danish Acad. Scis. and Letters, Deutsche Acad. Naturforscher Leopoldina, Bayerische Acad. Wissenschaften. Home: Laessoegade 204, 5230 Odense M, Denmark Office: Odense U Biologisk Inst, Campusvej 55, DK-5230 Odense M, Denmark

MICHELSEN, CHRISTOPHER BRUCE HERMANN, surgeon; b. Boston, Aug. 18, 1940; s. Jost Joseph and Ingeborg Elizabeth (Dilthey) M.; BA, Bowdoin Coll., 1961; MD, Columbia U., 1969; m. Amy Lee; children: Heidi Elizabeth, Matthew Christopher, Joshua Jost. Intern Columbia Presbyn. Med. Center, N.Y.C., 1969-70, resident, 1970-71; orthopedic resident N.Y. Orthopedic Hosp., N.Y.C., 1971-73, jr. Anne C. Kane fellow, 1973-74, sr. Anne C. Kane fellow and hip fellow, 1974-75, traveling fellow, 1975-76; internat. A-O fellow, postgrad. fellow in biomechanics, instr. biomed. engrng. Case-Western Res. U.; prof. clin. orthopaedic surgery Columbia Coll. Physicians and Surgeons; co-dir. combined orthopaedic neuro surg. spine svc.; chief orthopaedic spine surgery svc., chief orthopaedic svc. Allen Pavillion, CPMC, 1994, attending orthopedic surgeon, CPMC; chief orthopaedic svc. Individual Mobilization Designee, Fitzsimmons Army Med. Coll., 1995—. Col. USAR, 1961—. Diplomate Am. Bd. Orthopaedic Surgery. Fellow ACS, N.Y. Acad. Medicine, Am. Assn. for Surgery of Trauma, Am. Orthopaedic Assn., N.Am. Spine Soc., Am. Acad. Orthopaedic Surgeons, Internat. Coll. Surgeons; mem. AMA, Am. Coll. Physician Execs., Am. Coll. Physician Execs., Orthopaedic Research Soc., Am. Soc. Bone & Mineral Rsch., Royal Soc. Medicine (affiliate). Home: 102-57 Shearwater Ct E Jersey City NJ 07305 Office: 5141 Broadway New York NY 10034-1159

MICHELSON, EDWARD HARLAN, retired medical educator; b. St. Louis, June 6, 1926; s. Leo and Bess (Levitt) M.; m. Carole Joy Fenias Benoit, Feb. 14, 1952 (div. 1967); children: Estelle, Sheryl, Robin; m. Louise Alice Desmond, Aug. 8, 1982. BS, U. Fla., 1949, MS, 1951; PhD, Harvard U., 1956. Instr. Cambridge (Mass.) Jr. Coll., 1951-53; rsch. assoc. to assoc. prof.Sch. Pub. Health Harvard U., Cambridge, 1953-83; prof. Uniformed Svcs. Sch. Health Scis., Bethesda, Md., 1983-95; prof. emeritus, 1995; cons. in field. Editorial bd. Malacological Rev., 1984—; contbr. articles to profl. jours., chpts. to books. With USN, 1944-46; ATO. Mem. Am. Soc. parasitologists, Am. Soc. Tropical Medicine, Malacological Soc. London, Am. Inst. Biol. Scis., Am. Malacological Union, Phi Beta Kappa, Phi Kappa Phi. Home: 9735 D SW 92nd Ct Ocala FL 34481-8635

MICHENER, JAMES LLOYD, medical educator; b. Dec. 19, 1952; m. Gwendolyn Curtis Murphy; children: Rebecca Liane, Joshua Kieran. BA, Oberlin (Ohio) Coll., 1974; MD, Harvard Med. Sch., 1978. Diplomate Am. Bd. Family Practice. Resident in family medicine Duke U. Med. Ctr., Durham, N.C., 1978-81, Kellogg fellow, 1981-82, clin. prof. dept. cmty. and family medicine, 1994—, chmn. dept. cmty. and family medicine, 1994—; v.p. Durham Health Care, Inc., 1985-86. Co-author: Nutrition in Practice, 1990, 2d edit., 1992; contbr. numerous articles to med. pubs. including Academic Medicine, The Jour. of Family Practice, Medical Care, others; mem. editl. bd. Rx Nutrition, 1989-91; presenter in field. Bd. dirs. N.C. Med. Soc. Found., 1995—; STFM rep. resource com. on nutrition edn. Am. Acad. Family Practice Found., 1987-91. Grantee The Fullerton Found., Inc., The Josiah Macy, Jr. Found., U.S. Dept. Health and Human Svcs. Mem. AMA, Assn. Tchrs. of Preventive Medicine, Am. Acad. of Family Physicians Found., Am. Heart Assn. (del. Nat. Cholesterol Edn. Program 1987), N.C. Acad. Family Physicians (bd. dirs. 1995—). Home: 4011 Duck Pond Trail Chapel Hill NC 27514 Office: Duke U Med Ctr Box 2914 Durham NC 27710

MICHENFELDER, JOHN DONAHUE, anesthesiology educator; b. St. Louis, Apr. 13, 1931; s. Albert A. and Ruth J. (Donahue) M.; m. Margaret Grey Nick, Oct. 22, 1955 (dec. Nov. 1971); children: Carol, David, Joseph, Paul, Matthew, Laura; m. Mary Monica Milroy, Aug. 11, 1972; 1 child, Patrick. BS, St. Louis U., 1951, MD, 1955. Diplomate Am. Bd. Anesthesiology. Intern Presbyn. St. Luke's Hosp., Chgo., 1955-56; resident in internal medicine Presbyn. St. Luke's Hosp., 1956; resident in anesthesiology Mayo Clinic, Rochester, Minn., 1958-61, cons. in anesthesiology, 1961-91; prof. anesthesiology Mayo Med. Sch., Rochester, 1976-93, emeritus prof., 1993—. Author: Anesthesia and the Brain, 1988, Clinical Neuroanesthesia, 1990. Lt. USN, 1956-58. NIH grantee, 1966-89, 91-95; Faculty Anaesthetists of Royal Coll. Surgeons Ireland fellow, 1982, Faculty Anaesthetists Royal Coll. Surgeons Eng. fellow, 1988. Mem. Am. Soc. Anesthesiologists (Excellence in Rsch. award 1990, Disting. Svc. award 1990), Inst. Med., Assn. Univ. Anesthetists (councilman 1975-78). Home: 325 1st Ave NW Oronoco MN 55960-1410 Office: Mayo Clinic Dept of Anesthesiology 200 1st St SW Rochester MN 55905-0001

MICHIE, SARA H., pathologist, educator; b. Tulsa, Okla., Jan. 3, 1955. BS in Biology, Stephen F. Austin U., 1977; MD, U. Tex., Houston, 1981. Diplomate Am. Bd. Pathology. Resident anatomic pathology Stanford (Calif.) U. Med. Ctr., 1981-83, postdoctoral fellow immunology dept. pathology, 1983-84, 86-87, postdoctoral fellow diagnostic immunopathology, 1984-85; resident dept. pathology U. Iowa, Iowa City, 1985-86, postdoctoral fellow, 1986; assoc. investigator lab. svc. VA Hosp., Palo Alto, Calif., 1988-89, staff physician, 1989—, assoc. investigator, 1990-91; clin. instr. pathology dept. Stanford U., 1989-92, asst. prof. pathology, 1992—. Contbr. articles to profl. jours. Recipient Rsch. award Am. Diabetes Assn., 1996. Mem. Am. Soc. Investigative Pathology, Soc. Investigative Pathology, Bay Area Flow Cytometry Group, Sigma Xi, Alpha Omega Alpha. Office: VA Hosp Palo Alto 3801 Miranda Ave Mail Stop 1545 Palo Alto CA 94304

MICKEL, SUSAN GREENE, neurologist, educator; b. Cleve., Mar. 31, 1950; d. Robert Kay Funkhouser and Suzanne Greene (Drinker) Moran; m. Steven Hayford Mickel, Apr. 10, 1976; children: Matthew, Catherine. BA, George Washington U., 1972; MD, Emory U., 1979. Diplomate Am. Bd. Psychiatry and Neurology. Resident neurology Emory U. Affiliated Hosp., Atlanta, 1980-83; instr., asst. prof. Emory U., Atlanta, 1983-85; fellow dementia Mass. Gen. Hosp., Boston, 1985-87; dir. memory disorders divsn., staff neurologist Marshfield (Wis.) Clinic, 1987—; clin. asst. prof. U. Wis., Madison, 1994—; mem. med. adv. bd. Wis. Alzheimer's Info. and Tng. Ctr., Milw., 1988-95, Profl. award, 1994; bd. dirs. Alzheimer's Assn. Wis., Marshfield Area Respite Care Ctr. Recipient Citation for Scholastic Achievement Am. Med. Women's Assn., 1979. Mem. AAAS, Am. Acad. Neurology, Soc. for Neurosci., Behavioral Neurology Soc., Movement Disorders Soc., N.Y. Acad. Scis. Office: Marshfield Clinic 1000 N Oak Ave Marshfield WI 54449

MICKEY, BRUCE EDWARD, neurosurgeon; b. New Orleans, Sept. 5, 1952; m. Barbara Ann Schultz, Jan. 23, 1988. AB, Harvard U., 1974; MD, U. Tex. Southwestern Med. Sch., 1978. Diplomate Am. Bd. Neurol. Surgery. Intern U. Tex. Southwestern Med. Sch., Dallas, 1978-79, resident in neurol. surgery, 1979-84, asst. prof., 1984-90, assoc. prof., 1990—. Mem. Am. Assn. Neurol. Surgeons, Congress Neurol. Surgeons, North Am. Skull Base Soc. Office: U Tex Southwestern Med Sch 5323 Harry Hines Dallas TX 75235-8855

MICKLEY, G. ANDREW, psychologist, neuroscientist, educator, retired air force officer; b. Pitts., Feb. 28, 1948; s. Gordon Andrew and Martha Elizabeth (Myers) M.; m. Jacqueline Ruth Mansour, Aug. 15, 1970; 1 child, Katherine Ruth. BA, Gettysburg Coll., 1970; MA, U. Va., 1972, PhD, 1978. Commd. 2d lt. USAF, 1970, advanced to maj., 1983, advanced to lt. col., 1988-93, ret., 1993; test/rev. psychologist Occupational Measurement Ctr., San Antonio, 1972-76; prin. investigator Armed Forces Radiobiology Rsch. Inst., Bethesda, Md., 1976-79, chief exptl. psychology div., 1984-89; dep. chief radiation physics br. USAF Sch. Aerospace Medicine, 1989-90; sci. dir. Radiofrequency Radiation Divsn., Armstrong Lab., 1990-93; assoc. prof. USAF Acad., Colorado Springs, 1981-83; adj. assoc. prof. Uniformed Svcs. U. of Health Scis., 1983-89, U. Colo., 1981-83, life sci. div. U. Tex., San Antonio, dept. radiology U. Tex. Health Scis. Ctr., 1989-93; assoc. prof. dept. psychology, dir. neurosci. program Baldwin-Wallace Coll., Berea, Ohio, 1993—, chmn. dept. psychology, 1996—; grant reviewer NSF, 1983—, USPHS, 1985—, NIH, 1992—. Cons. editor Science, Pharmacology, Biochemistry and Behavior, Radiation Rsch., Life Sci.; contbr. articles to profl. jours., chpts. to books. USAF Sch. Aerospace Medicine grantee, 1978-80, Def. Nuclear Agy. grantee, 1980-83, NSF grantee, 1994—; recipient Rsch. and Devel. award USAF, 1981. Mem. AAAS, Soc. for Neurosci., Radiation Rsch. Soc., Soc. Toxicology, Internat. Behavioral Neurosci. Soc., Sigma Xi, Psi Chi, Phi Sigma. Lutheran. Avocations: tennis, skiing, running, reading. Office: Baldwin-Wallace Coll Dept Psychology Carnegie Hall 275 Eastland Rd Berea OH 44017-2088

MICKLITSCH, CHRISTINE NOCCHI, health care administrator; b. Hazleton, Pa., Oct. 23, 1949; d. Nicholas Edmund and Matilda Nocchi; m. Wayne D. Micklitsch, May 20, 1972; children: Sarah N., Emily M. BS, Pa. State U., State College, 1971; MBA, Boston U., 1979. Blood bank med. technologist The Deaconess Hosp., Boston, 1971-73; sr. blood bank med. technologist Tufts New Eng. Med. Ctr., Boston, 1973-76, environ. svcs. coord., 1976-78; adminstrv. resident Joslin Diabetes Found., Boston, 1978-79; sr. analyst Analysis, Mgmt. & Planning, Inc., Cambridge, Mass., 1979-80; adminstrv. dir. Hahnemann Family Health Ctr., Worcester, Mass., 1980-84; exec. dir. Swampscott (Mass.) Treatment & Trauma Ctr., 1984-85; dir. practice mgmt., instr. U. Mass. Med. Ctr., Worcester, 1985-91; dir. adminstrv. svcs. The Fallon Clinic, Worcester, 1991-94; mgr. physician network devel. The Fallon healthcare Sys., Worcester, 1994—. Incorporator, pres. Newton (Mass.) Highlands Cmty. Devel. Corp., 1981-82; treas. Patriot's Trail coun. Girl Scouts U.S., Newton, 1993—; Christian edn. instr. Newton Highlands Congl. Ch., 1987-94. Kellogg fellow Ctr. for Rsch. in Ambulatory Health Care Adminstrn., Denver, 1979; grantee in grad. tng. in family medicine HHS, U. Mass. Med. Sch., Worcester, 1989. Fellow Am. Coll. Med. Practice Execs. (state coll. forum rep. 1989—, ea. sect. coll. forum rep. 1993—); mem. Am. Coll. Med. Practice Execs. (mem. chair 1995-96), Mass. Med. Group Mgmt. Assn. (pres. 1987-89, newsletter editor 1984—), Boston U. Health Care Mgmt. Program Alumni Assn., Alpha Omicron Pi (parlimentarian Epsilon Alpha chpt. 1969-70). Home: 320 Lake Ave Newton MA 02161-1212 Office: Fallon Healthcare Sys Chestnut Pl 10 Chestnut St Worcester MA 01608-2804

MIDDLETON, ANTHONY WAYNE, JR., urologist, educator; b. Salt Lake City, May 6, 1939; s. Anthony Wayne and Dolores Caravena (Lowry) M.; m. Carol Samuelson, Oct. 23, 1970; children: Anthony Wayne, Suzanne, Kathryn, Jane, Michelle. BS, U. Utah, 1963; MD, Cornell U., 1966. Intern, U. Utah Hosps., Salt Lake City, 1966-67; resident in urology Mass. Gen. Hosp., Boston, 1970-74; practice urology Middleton Urol. Assos., Salt Lake City, 1974—; mem. staff Primary Children's Hosp., staff pres., 1981-82; mem. staff Latter-Day Saints Hosp., Salt Lake Regional Med. Ctr.; assoc. clin. prof. surgery U. Utah Med. Coll., 1977—; vice chmn. bd. govs. Utah Med. Self-Ins. Assn., 1980-81, chmn. 1985-87; med. dir. Uroquest Co., 1996—. Bd. dirs. Utah chpt. Am. Cancer Soc., 1978-86; bishop, later stake presidency Ch. Jesus Christ Latter-day Saints; vice chmn. Utah Med. Polit. Action Com., 1978-81, chmn., 1981-83; chmn. Utah Physicians for Reagan, 1983-84; mem. U. Utah Coll. Medicine Dean's Search Com., 1983-84; bd. dirs. Utah Symphony, 1985—, Primary Children's Found., 1989—. Capt. USAF, 1968-70. Editor (monthly pub.) AACU-FAX, 1992—, Millenial Star Brit. LDS mag. 1960-61. Mem. ACS, Utah State Med. Assn. (pres. 87-88, disting. svc. award 1993), Am. Urologic Assn. (socioecons. com. 1987—, chmn. western sect. socioecons. com. 1989—, western. sect. health policy com. chmn., 1990—), AMA (alt. del. to House of Dels. 1989-92, 94, 96—), Salt Lake County Med. Assn. (sec. 1965-67, pres. liaison com. 1980-81, pres.-elect 1981-83, pres. 1984), Utah Urol. Assn. (pres. 1976-77), Salt Lake Surg. Soc. (treas. 1977-78), Am. Assn. Clin. Urologists (bd. dirs. 1989-90, nat. pres. elect 1990-91, pres. 1991-92, nat. bd. chmn. urologic polit. action com. UROPAC, 1992—), Phi Beta Kappa, Alpha Omega Alpha, Beta Theta Pi (chpt. pres. Gamma Beta 1962). Republican. Contbr. articles to profl. jours. Home: 2798 Chancellor Pl Salt Lake City UT 84108-2835 Office: 1060 E 1st St Salt Lake City UT 84102-4147

MIDDLETON, CHARLENE, retired medical and surgical nurse, educator; b. Ennis, Tex., Sept. 13, 1922; d. Charles Silvester and Harriet Eugenia (Ford) M. Diploma, Scott and White Hosp., Temple, Tex., 1945; AA, Temple Jr. Coll., 1947; BA, U. Tex., Austin, 1956. Nurse coord., ambulatory care svcs. Naval Regional Med. Ctr., Long Beach, Calif.; instr. nursing arts Scott and White Hosp., evening supr.; now ret. Lt. comdr. U.S. Navy, 1957-77. Mem. Scott and White Alumni Assn. (past pres. Dist. 7).

MIDDLETON, ELLEN LONG, family nurse practitioner, educator; b. Danville, Pa., June 14, 1954; d. Samuel Murray and Dorothy Morgan (Wasley) Long; m. Jeffrey Long Middleton, Sept. 5, 1981; children: Matthew Long, Andrew Long, Douglas Long. BS, U. Vt., 1976; MSN, U. Wash., 1982; postgrad., Boston Coll., 1995—. Cert. family nurse practitioner. Nurse practitioner emergency dept. Hosp. of U. Pa., Phila., 1985-88, nursing dir. admission evaluation ctr., 1988-90; nursing dir. Family Practice Clinic Family Health Svcs., Worcester, Mass., 1990-94; family nurse practitioner U. Mass. Med. Ctr., 1990—; instr. Boston Coll., 1994—; lectr. U. Pa., 1985-89. Mem. Sigma Theta Tau.

MIDDLETON, ELLIOTT, JR., physician; b. Glen Ridge, N.J., Dec. 15, 1925; s. Elliott and Dorothy (Thoman) M.; m. Elizabeth Blackford, Sept. 25, 1948; children: Elliott III, Ellen Alice, Blackford, James Jay. A.B., Princeton U., 1947; M.D., Columbia U., 1950. Diplomate: Am. Bd. Internal Medicine, Am. Bd. Allergy and Immunology. Intern Presbyn. Hosp., N.Y.C., 1950-51; resident in medicine Presbyn. Hosp., 1951-52; asst. in medicine immunochem. lab. Coll. Physicians and Surgeons, Columbia U., 1952-53; clin. assoc. Nat. Heart Inst., 1953-55; fellow in allergy R.A. Cooke Inst. Allergy, Roosevelt Hosp., N.Y.C., 1955-56; practice medicine Montclair, N.J., 1956-69; dir. clin. services and research Children's Asthma Research Inst. and Hosp., Denver, 1969-76; assoc. clin. prof. medicine U. Colo., 1969-76; prof. medicine and pediatrics, dir. allergy div. Sch. Medicine, SUNY, Buffalo, 1976-92; emeritus prof. medicine SUNY, Buffalo, 1995; hon. staff physician Buffalo Gen. Hosp.; prof. medicine emeritus, 1995. Editor-in-chief Allergy: Principles and Practice, 1978, 4th edit., 1993; editor Jour. Allergy and Clin. Immunology, 1983-88; contbr. numerous articles to jours. chpts. to books. Served with M.C. USNR, 1944-50; Served with M.C. USPHS, 1950-55. Fellow Am. Acad. Allergy and Immunology (pres. 1972, Disting. Svc. award 1991), Am. Coll. Physicians; mem. AAAS, Am. Assn. Immunologists. Episcopalian. Home: RR 1 Box 596 Chebeague Island ME 04017 Office: Buffalo Gen Hosp 100 High St Buffalo NY 14203-1126

MIDDLETON, GEORGE, JR., clinical child psychologist; b. Houston, Feb. 26, 1923; s. George and Bettie (McCrary) M.; m. Margaret MacLean, Nov. 17, 1953. BA in Psychology, Birmingham-Southern Coll., 1948; MA in Psychology, U. Ala., Tuscaloosa, 1951; PhD in Clin. Psychology, Pa. State U., 1958. Lic. psychologist, La. Asst. clin. psychology Med. Coll. Ala., Birmingham, 1950-52; dir. dept. psychology Bryce Hosp., Tuscaloosa, 1952-54; instr. counseling Coll. Bus. Adminstrn. Pa. State U., 1956-58; asst. prof. spl. edn. McNeese State U., 1962-65, assoc. prof. spl. edn., 1962-65; dir. La. Gov.'s Program for Gifted Children, 1963—; prof. spl. edn. McNeese State U., 1965-73, prof. psychology, 1973-74; pvt. practice clin. psychology and neuropsychology, 1974—; cons. psychologist Calcasieu Parish Sch. Bd., 1975—; cons. Charter Hosp. Adolescent Psychiat. Unit, dir. psychol. svcs., 1990-95. Mem. Am. Psychol. Assn., Nat. Acad. Neuropsychology, Internat. Neuropsychol. Soc., La. Psychol. Assn. (pres. 1973-74), La. Sch. Psychol. Assn., S.W. La. Psychol. Assn. (pres. 1965, 73, 84), La. State Bd. Examiners Psychologists (chmn. 1977-78), Coun. for Exceptional Children, Assn. for the Gifted. Episcopalian. Home and Office: 2001 Southwood Dr Ste A Lake Charles LA 70605-4139

MIDDLETON, JOHN DEFEVER, surgeon, hospital administrator; b. Galveston, Tex., Oct. 14, 1952; s. John Wright and Dorothy (Butrick) M.; m. Melinda Smith, June 7, 1975; children: Anne, David, Julia. BA in Chemistry, Colo. Coll., 1974; MD magna cum laude, U. Tex., Galveston, 1978. Diplomate Am. Bd. Surgery. Resident gen. surgery Mayo Grad. Sch. Med., Rochester, Minn., 1978-83, fellow vascular surgery, 1983-84; surgeon Physician's Plus Med. Group, Madison, Wis., 1984-88, Surg. Assocs., Billings, Mont., 1988—; dir. trauma svcs. St. Vincent's Hosp., Billings, Mont., 1993—. Chmn. state trauma task force Mont. EMS Bur., 1994—. Fellow Am. Coll. Surgeons (chmn. Mont. commn. on trauma 1994—); mem. Southwestern Surg. Soc., No. Plains Vascular Soc., Alpha Omega Alpha. Office: Surg Assocs 1230 N 30th St Billings MT 59101

MIDLARSKY, ELIZABETH RUTH, psychology educator; b. N.Y.C.; d. Abraham Allan and Frances Lucille (Wiener) Steckel; m. Manus Issachar Midlarsky, June 25, 1961; children: Susan Rachel, Miriam Joyce, Michael George. BA, CUNY, 1961; MA, Northwestern U., 1966, PhD, 1968. Lic. psychologist, N.J., Mich., Colo. Asst. prof. U. Denver, 1968-73; dir. rsch. and evaluation Malcolm X Med. Ctr. (now Park East), Denver, 1973-75; assoc. prof., dir. psychol. tng. program Met. State Coll., Denver, 1975-77; assoc. prof. psychology U. Detroit, 1977-83, prof. psychology, 1983-90, chair dept. psychology, 1978-81, dir. Ctr. Study Devel. and Aging, 1977-83; prof. clin. psychology Tchrs. Coll. Columbia U., N.Y.C., 1990—, dir. Ctr. for Lifespan and Aging Studies, 1992—; mem. initial rev. group NIMH, Bethesda, Md., 1976-82; mem. ad hoc rev. groups NHLBI, Bethesda, 1985—; mem. study sect. NIH, Bethesda, 1986-91; mem. reviewers rsch., 1991-94. Author: Altruism in Late Life, 1994; co-editor Humboldt Jour. Social Rels., 1985-86; editor Acad. Psychol. Bull., 1982-86; contbr. chpts. to books and articles to profl. jours. Mem. exec. coun. Mich. Psychol. Assn. Grantee Nat. Inst. Aging, 1982-85, 87-90, AARP, 1982-83, 88-89, 92-95; postdoctoral rsch. fellow AAUW, 1974-75. Fellow APA (publs. com. 1990-92, student award com. 1990), Am. Psychol. Soc., Am. Orthopsychiat. Assn.; mem. Gerontol. Soc. Am. (exec. com. on program com. 1983-84), Soc. Psychol. Study Social Issues. Home: 3 Falcon Rd East Brunswick NJ 08816-2716 Office: Columbia U Dept Clin Psych Box 148 525 W 120th St New York NY 10027-6625

MIELCAREK, LEON MICHAEL, JR., ophthalmologist; b. Chester, Pa., Dec. 26, 1936; s. Leon Michael and Eleanor Frances (Szczurowski) M.; m. Eileen Dickson, Mar. 9, 1974; children: Laura Maureen, Linda Michelle, Lacey Morgan. AB in Zoology, U. Pa., 1958; MD, Thomas Jefferson Med. Coll., Phila., 1962. Diplomate Am. Bd. Med. Examiners, Am. Bd. Ophthalmology. Chief resident Scheie Eye Inst. U. Pa., Phila., 1968; pres., founder Mielcarek Eye Assocs., Media, Pa., 1970—. bd. dirs. Delaware County Blind/Sight Ctr., Chester, Pa., 1976—. Lt. USNR, 1963-66. Fellow ACS; mem. AMA, Am. Acad. Ophthalmology, Am. Soc. Cataract and Refractive Surgery, Pa. State Med. Soc., Delaware County Med. Soc. Republican. Roman Catholic. Home: 2244 E Deerfield Dr Media PA 19063

MIELKE, CLARENCE HAROLD, JR., hematologist; b. Spokane, Wash., June 18, 1936; s. Clarence Harold and Marie Katherine (Gillespie) M.; m. Marcia Rae, July 5, 1964; children: Elisa, John, Kristina. BS, Wash. State U., 1959; MD, U. Louisville, 1963. Intern, San Francisco Gen. Hosp., 1963-64; resident in medicine Portland VA Hosp., 1964-65, San Francisco Gen. Hosp., 1965-67; fellow in hematology U. So. Calif., 1967-68; teaching fellow, asst. physician, instr. Tufts-New Eng. Med. Ctr. Hosps., Boston, 1968-71; sr. scientist Med. Rsch. Inst., San Francisco, 1971-90; chief hematology Presbyn. Hosp., San Francisco, 1971-82; asst. clin. prof. medicine U. Calif. Sch. Medicine, San Francisco, 1971-80, assoc. clin. prof., 1979-90, bd.92—dirs. Inst. Cancer Rsch.; trustee, bd. dirs. Med. Rsch. Inst. San Francisco, Sacred Heart Hosp. Found., 1994—. NIH grantee, 1973-88; dir. emeritus Inst. Cancer Rsch.; trustee emeritus, bd. dirs. Med. Rsch. Inst., 1988—; dir. Health Rsch. and Edn. Ctr., Wash. State U., 1989—, prof. pharmocology, 1989—, prof. vet. medicine, 1989—, assoc. dean rsch., 1992—. Fellow ACP, Internat. Acad. Clin. & Applied Thrombosis & Hemostasis, Internat. Soc. Hematology, Am. Coll. Angiology; mem. Am. Soc. Internal Medicine, Internat. Soc. Thrombosis and Hemostasis, Am. Heart Assn., N.Y. Acad. Scis., AMA, San Francisco Med. Soc., Am. Thoracic Soc., AAAS, Internat. Soc. Angiology. Editor emeritus, Jour. Clin. Apheresis, 1981; contbr. chpts. to books, articles to med. jours. Office: Wash State U Health Rsch & Edn Ctr West 601 First Ave Spokane WA 99204-0399

MIGDEL, MERYL MARLA-SHEINBERG, speech and language pathologist; b. Bklyn., Jan. 14, 1955; d. Lawrence P. and Irene Sheinberg; m. Larry H. Migdel, June 22, 1974; children: Rena Felise, Douglas Ian Phillip, Daina Lauren Samantha. BA in Speech and Hearing Scis., Bklyn. Coll., 1976, MS, 1980. Lic. speech and lang. pathologist, N.Y.; cert. clin. competency. ESL tutor City Coll. of CUNY, N.Y.C.; speech/lang. pathologist ESEA Title I Prog. Handicapped Hebrew Inst. for the Deaf, Bklyn.; speech pathologist N.Y.C. CRMD Prog., Bklyn.; speech/lang. pathologist Western Orange County Headstart; sr. speech/lang. pathologist Horton Meml. Hosp., Middletown, N.Y.; pvt. practice speech and lang. pathologist Monroe, N.Y., 1989—. Recipient Continuing Edn. award, 1988. Mem. ASCD, Am. Speech, Lang., Hearing Assn., N.Y. Speech, Lang., Hearing Assn., Am. Speech and Hearing Found., Orange County Speech, Lang., Hearing Assn. Home: 1 Placid Ln Monroe NY 10950

MIGEON, CLAUDE JEAN, pediatricics educator; b. Lievin, Pas-De-Calais, France, Dec. 22, 1923; came to U.S., 1950, naturalized, 1967; s. André and Pauline (Descamps) M.; m. Barbara Lou Ruben, Apr. 2, 1960; children: Jacques, Jean-Paul, Nicole. M.D., Sch. Medicine, U. Paris, 1950. Fellow dept. pediatrics Sch. Medicine, Johns Hopkins U., 1950-52, asst. prof., 1954-60, asso. prof., 1960-71, prof. pediatrics, 1971—; instr. biochemistry U. Utah, 1952-54; pediatrician Johns Hopkins Hosp., 1954—; mem. diabetes and metabolism tng. grants com. NIH, 1963-67, gen. clin. research centers com., 1968-71, mem. endocrinology study sect., 1974-78; cons. Med. Research Council Can., 1969-85, others; vis. prof. Maadi Armed Forces Hosp., Cairo, 1985, Guy's Hosp., London, 1986. Co-editor: (textbook) The Diagnosis and Treatment of Endocrine Disorders in Childhood and Adolescence, 4th edit., 1994; mem. editl. bd.: Johns Hopkins Med. Jour., 1970-72, Jour. Clin. Endocrinology and Metabolism, 1971-77, Hormone Rsch., 1979—; contbr. articles to profl. jours. Fulbright fellow, 1950; Am. Field Service fellow, 1950-51; Andre and Bella Meyer fellow, 1951-52; recipient research career award NIH, 1964-85. Fellow AAAS; mem. Endocrine Soc. (coun. 1971-74, chmn. pub. affairs com. 1974-91, Ayerst award, Williams award), Soc. Pediatric Rsch. (emeritus), Am. Pediatric Soc., Lawson Wilkins Pediatric Endocrine Soc. (founding pres. 1972), Am. Soc. Clin. Investigation (emeritus), Am. Physiol. Soc., Japanese Pediatric Endocrine Soc. (hon.), Found. for Am. Meml. Hosp. (bd. dirs. 1985—), Soc. Francaise d'Endocrinologie (fgn. corr. mem.). Home: 502 Somerset Rd Baltimore MD 21210-2720 Office: Johns Hopkins Hosp CMSC 3-110 Baltimore MD 21205

MIGL, DONALD RAYMOND, optometrist, pharmacist; b. Houston, Tex., Sept. 18, 1947; s. Ervin Lawrence and Adele Marie (Boenisch) M.; m. Karen S. Coale, Mar. 23, 1974; children: Christopher Brian, Derek Drew, Monica Michelle. BS in Pharmacy, U. Houston, 1970, BS, 1978, OD, 1980, postgrad., 1992; postgrad., U. Ala. Med. Ctr., Birmingham, 1974-76, Stephen F. Austin State U., Nacogdoches, Tex., 1987-88. Registered pharmacist; cert. Nat. Bds. Examiners Optometry, Treatment & Mgmt. Ocular Disease; cert. therapeutic optometrist. Pharmacist Tex. Med. Ctr., Houston, 1967-69, St. Luke's and Tex. Childrens Hosp., 1967-69, Meml. Hosp., 1969-70, Ben Taub (Harris County) Hosp., 1970-71, Shades Mountain Pharmacy, Birmingham, 1974-76, Westbury Hosp., Houston, 1976-81; instr. pharmacology lab. Coll. Optometry U. Houston, 1980; pvt. practice, Nacogdoches, Tex., 1981—; mem. interdisciplinary health teams, 1977; charter advisor publ. Contact, CIBA Vision Corp., 1988-89. Judge health sci. div. Houston Area Sci. Fair, 1970. Recipient svc. award Houston Community Interdisciplinary Health Screening Programs, 1977, Spl. Academic Achievement award in pharmacy and optometry U. Houston, 1980. Mem. Am. Optometric Assn. (Optometric recognition award 1985-96), Tex. Optometric Assn. (recognition cert. 1979), Piney Woods Optometric Soc. (pres. 1984), Am. Pharm. Assn. (recognition cert. 1970), Tex. Pharm. Assn., Am. Soc. Hosp. Pharmacists, U.S. Jaycees, Gold Key, Omicron Delta Kappa. Methodist. Lodge: Rotary (Paul Harris Fellow 1987, Pres. award Outstanding Svc., 1991-92). Home: 4122 Ridgebrook Dr Nacogdoches TX 75961 Office: Eagle Eye 20/20 Plus Vision PO Box 632730 Nacogdoches TX 75963-2730

MIGUEL DESOUSA, LINDA J., critical care nurse, nursing educator; b. Honolulu, Dec. 6, 1946; d. Gregory and Irene N. (Calasa) Furtado; children: Joseph H. Miguel Jr., Brett A. Miguel. ADN, Maui Community Coll., Kahului, Hawaii, 1980; BSN, U. Hawaii, 1987, MS, 1990. RN, Hawaii. Charge nurse ICU-CCU Maui Meml. Hosp., Wailuku; nursing instr. Maui Community Coll., Kahului; unit supr.-coronary care Straub Clinic and Hosp., Honolulu; nursing instr. Kapiolani Community Coll., Honolulu; edn. dir. Waianae Health Acad.; researcher in field. Contbr. articles to profl. jours. Outer Island Students Spl. Nursing scholar, 1988-90, Rsch. scholarship, 1989. Mem. AACN, Hawaii Nurses Assn., Hawaii Soc. for Cardiovascular and Pulmonary Rehab., Assn. Am. Women in C. C.s, Sigma Theta Tau. Home: 98-402 Koauka Loop #1202 Aiea HI 96701

MIHAN, RICHARD, retired dermatologist; b. L.A., Dec. 20, 1925; s. Arnold and Virginia Catherine (O'Reilly) M.; student U. So. Calif., 1945; MD, St. Louis U., 1949. Rotating intern Los Angeles County Gen. Hosp., 1949-51, resident in dermatology, 1954-57; practice medicine specializing in dermatology, Los Angeles, 1957-95; emeritus clin. prof. dept. medicine, dermatology and syphilology U. So. Calif. Served as lt. (j.g.) M.C., USNR, 1951-53, ret. as lt. comdr. Diplomate Am. Bd. Dermatology. Fellow ACP; mem. Internat. Soc. Dermatology, Soc. Investigative Dermatology, Pacific Dermatologic Assn. (exec. bd. 1971-74), Calif. Med. Assn. (chmn. dermatologic sect. 1973-74), AMA, Los Angeles Dermatol. Soc. (pres. 1975-76), Am. Acad. Dermatology, L.A. Acad. Medicine (pres. 1988-89), Order of St. Lazarus (comdr.); Club: Calif. Roman Catholic. Home: 3278 Wilshire Blvd Apt 503 Los Angeles CA 90010-1431

MIHM, MARTIN CHARLES, JR., pathologist, educator; b. Pitts.; s. Martin Charles and Cecilia Matilda (Hepp) M. AB, Duquesne U., 1955; MD, U. Pitts., 1961; MA (with honors), Harvard U., 1989. Diplomate Am. Bd. Dermatology, Am. Bd. Pathology. Intern Mt. Sinai Hosp., N.Y.C., 1961-62, resident in medicine, 1963-64; resident in dermatology Mass. Gen. Hosp., Boston, 1964-67, resident in Pathology, 1968-72, chief dermatopathology, 1973-94; asst. prof. pathology Harvard U. Med. Sch., Boston, 1972-75, assoc. prof., 1975-79, chief dermatopathology, 1982-93; prof. pathology Mass. Gen. Hosp.-Harvard U., Boston, 1980-93; prof., chief dermatopathology, dermatology Albany (N.Y.) Med. Coll., 1993—; adj. prof. pathology Vanderbilt U., 1989—; chmn. pathology com. Intergroup Melanoma Study, 1983—; pathologist Malignant Melanoma Coop. Group, 1972-77; chief sr. adminstr. Wellman Labs., Mass. Gen. Hosp., 1985-93; cons. WHO, 1985—, chmn. pathology standing com., 1991—; vis. prof. pathology Harvard Med. Sch. Author: Primer of Dermatopathology, 1984, 2d edit., 1992, Problematic Pigmented Lesions, 1990; editor: Lymphoproliferative Disorders of the Skin, 1986, Pathbiology and Recognition Malignant Melanoma, 1988; contbr. articles to med. jours. Served to comdr. USPHS, 1967-69. Fellow ACP, Am. Acad. Dermatology, Am. Soc. Dermatopathology; mem. AMA (Harvard Med. Sch. rep. to med. sch. sect. 1991), Harvard Dermatology House Officer's Assn. (pres. 1982), Harvard Club (Boston, N.Y.C.), Alpha Omega Alpha, Pi Gamma Mu. Democrat. Roman Catholic. Home: 100 Memorial Dr Apt 87A Cambridge MA 02142-1330 Office: Albany Med Coll 47 New Scotland Ave Albany NY 12208-3412

MIIKE, LAWRENCE HIROSHI, public health officer; m. Kiliwehi Kono, 1993; 3 stepchildren, Kapono, Nainoa, Makana. BS in Chemistry, Amherst Coll., 1962; MD, U. Calif., San Francisco, 1966; JD, UCLA, 1972. Intern Phila. Gen. Hosp., 1966-67; with Nat. Ctr. Health Svcs. Rsch. and Devel., Washington, 1972-73; faculty Health Policy Program Sch. Medicine U. Calif., San Francisco, 1973-75, Med. Sch. Georgetown U., Washington, 1977-89; sr. assoc. Office of Tech. Assessment, U.S. Congress, Washington, 1977-89; founder, exec. dir. Papa Ola Lōkahi, Hawaii, 1989-92; prof. family prace and cmty. health U. Hawaii, Honolulu, 1989-92; med. dir. Hawaii QUEST Program, Honolulu, 1993-95; dir. Dept. Health, State of Hawaii, Honolulu, 1996—. With USAF, 1967-69. Office: 1250 Punchbowl St Honolulu HI 96813

MIKAN, KATHLEEN JOYCE KEHRER, medical/surgical nurse, educator; b. Galion, Ohio. BSN cum laude, Ohio State U., Columbus, 1961; MSN, U. Colo., Denver, 1963; PhD, Mich. State U., East Lansing, 1972; postdoctoral, U. Utah, Salt Lake City, 1991. Staff nurse Ohio State U. U. Hosp., Columbus, 1961; asst. instr. Ohio State U., Columbus, 1961-62, instr. med.-surg. nursing, team nursing and fundamentals of nursing, 1963-65; asst. prof. Mich. State U., East Lansing, 1965-67, co-dir. multi-media project, 1967-69; asst. prof. Case Western Res. U., Cleve., 1970-72, assoc. in nursing, 1970-74, program dir. Health Sci. Communications Ctr., 1971-74, ednl. specialist primary health practitioner program, 1972-74, assoc. prof., 1972-74, adminstrv. officer, 1973-74; dir. learning resources U. Ala., Birmingham, 1974-91, prof., 1974—, mem. faculty post master fellowship program in oncology nursing edn., 1980-83, media dir., 1984-87, 1985-89, project faculty, cost mgmt. edn. for nurses contract, 1986-88, media expert, 1988-91, prof., 1974—; nurse Camp Taconic, Pittsfield, Mass., summers, 1961, 62; mem. planning com. 5th Nat. Learning Resources Conf. U. Tex., San Antonio, 1994; SCAMC referee for paper selection Ann. Symposium on Computer Applications in Med. Care, 1985—; out of state expert rsch. proposal reviewer La. Edn. Quality Support Fund State of La. Bd. Regents, 1990; cons. expansion of learning resource capacity and computer utilization to various schs. nursing; mem. spl. project review panel divsn. of Nursing HEW, 1989—; mem. adv. bd. dirs. The Soc. Nursing Profls., 1991—; speaker, presenter in field; cons. WHO, Indonesia, 1995; sec. Univ. Ala. Birmingham Faculty Senate, 1995—. Manuscript reviewer FOCUS, 1984—; author (with Eula Aiken) In Computer Applications in Nursing Education and Practice, 1992; contbr. articles to profl. jours. Mem. Lung Resource Ctr. Com. Ala. Lung Assn., 1980-90, community health and program support com., 1990—. Recipient Red Ribbon award Am. Film Festival Case Western Res. U., 1972, Bronze award Internat. Film and TV Festival Case Western Res. U., 1972. Fellow Am. Acad. Nursing (Svc. cert. 1990); mem. ANA (coun. on computer applications in nursing), Assn. for Ednl. Communications and Tech., Nat. League for Nursing (nat. forum on computers in health care and nursing, coun. on nursing informatics), Ala. Instrl. Media Assn., Ala. Lung Assn., Ala. State Nurses Assn., Am. Acad. of Nursing (pub. rels. com. 1987-90), Ohio State U. Nursing Alumnae Assn., U. Colo. Alumni Assn., U. Colo. Sch. of Nursing Alumni, Lambda Alpha Delta, Sigma Theta Tau (Internat. Officer award 1985-91, heritage com. 1985-91, sec. 1985-91, publ. com. 1987-91, Internat. Heritage award, chair 1991, co-chair resolutions com. biennial conv. 1991, co-chair voting com. biennial conv. 1991, libr. sci. com. 1991—, evaluation visitor 1991, installing officer 1992), Phi Kappa Phi, Am. Nurses Found. Century Club.

MIKAWA, KATSUYA, anesthesiology educator; b. Matsuyama, Ehime, Japan, May 23, 1960; s. Katsumi and Ichiko Mikawa; m. Mako Inoue, Oct. 1987; 1 child, Lisa. MD, Kobe (Japan) U., 1985, PhD, 1990. Med. diplomate. Instr. Kobe U. Hosp., 1990-92, asst. prof., 1992—. Contbr. articles to profl. jours. Office: Kobe U Sch Medicine, Dept Anesthesiology, Kusunoki-cho 7 Chuo-ku, Kobe 650, Japan

MIKE-NARD, BEVERLY JEAN, nurse; b. Youngstown, Ohio, Nov. 3, 1957; d. Michael Ablen and Marion Charlotte (Saba) Mike; children: Stacy Nicole, Kenneth Robert Jr. Nursing diploma, St. Elizabeth Hosp. Med. Ctr., 1978; student, Youngstown State U., 1988-89; BSN, Pa. State U., 1991; MSN, Case Western Res. U., 1993. RN, Ohio; cert. hosp. based neonatal resuscitation program instr., cert. CPR instr., cert. neonatal nurse practitioner. Nurse asst. St. Elizabeth Hosp. Med. Ctr., Youngstown, 1977-78, nurse orthopaedic dept., 1978-81, nurse neonatal ICU, 1982-93, neonatal nurse, CPR instr., asst. apnea home monitor program, 1993—; sec. Color My World Day Care Ctr., 1986-92; first neonatal nurse practitioner in Mahoning, Trumbull, Columbiana, Mercer and Lawrence County. Active PTA, Austintown, Ohio, 1985-89, Poland, Ohio, 1989—; mem. parish coun. St. Maron Ch., 1994—, CCD tchr., 1994-95. Mem. ANA, NAACOG (cert.), NCC (cert.), Ohio Nurses Assn., Nat. Assn. Neonatal Nurses, Nat. Apostolate Maronites. Democrat. Maronite Catholic. Home: 3330 Partridge Park Dr Poland OH 44514-2807 Office: St Elizabeth Hosp Med Ctr 1044 Belmont Ave Youngstown OH 44504-1006

MIKHAIL, BLANCHE ISKANDER, community health nursing educator; b. Bassion, Egypt, June 1, 1945; came to U.S., 1976; d. Iskander Mikhail and Malaka Tadros; m. Michael Galiouby, May 9, 1976. BSN, Alexandria U., 1965, MPH, 1974; DNSc, Boston U., 1984. Supr. med./surgical unit Ahmed Maher Hosp., 1965-69; instr. Higher Inst. of Nursing/Cairo U., 1969-77; charge nurse Resthaven Corp., Boston, 1979-80; staff nurse Staff Builders Health Care Svcs., Boston, 1979-83; teaching asst. Boston U. Sch. of Nursing, 1979-82; staff nurse St. John of God Hosp., Brighton, Mass., 1983-84; lectr. of nursing Higher Inst. Nursing, Alexandria (Egypt)U., 1978-84, assoc. prof. nursing, 1984-89; asst. prof. nursing U. Tex., Houston, 1990-91; assoc. prof. nursing Calif. State U., Bakersfield, 1991-95, prof., asst. chair dept. nursing, 1995—; chair. grad. curriculum com., 1993—, STT rsch. com., 1994—, promotion and tenure com., 1995—; mem. grad. admissions and progression com., 1992—, dept. nursing adv. bd., 1993—, search and screening com., 1995—; mem. Kern County Nurse Adminstr.'s Coun., 1991—; participant numerous workshops in field. Contbr. articles to profl. jours. and publs. Mem. adv. bd. Planned Parenthood. Doctoral study scholar Egyptian govt., 1977, AAUW, 1979; grantee P.E.O., Internat. Peace Scholarship Fund, 1980, 81. Mem. APHA, Kern RN Soc., Sigma Theta Tau, Xi Epsilon (chpt. faculty counselor 1993-95, mem. exec. bd. 1993—). Coptic (Egyptian) Orthodox Christian. Office: Calif State Univ Dept of Nursing 9001 Stockdale Hwy Bakersfield CA 93311

MIKKELSEN, ERICH OLAF, pharmacologist; b. Varde, Jylland, Denmark, Oct. 19, 1933; s. Kaj and Elna Kristine (Madsen) M.; m. Gertrud Ester Fleissig Hammelsvang, Mar. 31, 1958 (div. Jan. 7, 1972); 1 child, Frank; m. Inge Jensen Gade, June 21, 1973; 1 child, Anders. MD, U. Aarhus, Denmark, 1966, DMSc, 1980. Surgeon dept. surgery and internal medicine Esbjerg Hosp., Denmark, 1966-68; physician dept. internal medicine Viborg Hosp., Denmark, 1968-69, sr. physician, 1969-70; cardiologist dept. cardiology Aarhus Kommunehospital, U. Aarhus, Denmark, 1970-73; psychiatrist dept. psychiatry Statshospital, Viborg, 1970-73; asst. prof. clin. pharmacology U. Aarhus, Denmark, 1973-80, assoc. prof. pharmacology, 1979—; examiner in pharmacology U. Copenhagen, 1988—, in med. rsch., 1992—; rschr. Cardiovascular Rsch. Ctr., Denmark, 1991—. Referee to med. jours. Blood Pressure, 1992, Ethnopharmacology, 1991—, Pharmacology and Toxicology, 1980—, Pharmacy and Pharmacology, 1993—; contbr. chpt. to med. book. Lt. Danish armed forces, 1967-68. Grantee Danish Med. Rsch. coun., 1978-88, Lundbeck Fonden, 1989. Mem. Danish Med. Assn., Danish Soc. Pharmacology and Toxicology, Danish Soc. Clin. Pharmacology. Home: Fritz Sybergsvej 16, 8270 Højbjerg Jylland Denmark Office: U Aarhus, Dept Pharmacology, 8000 Aarhus C Jylland Denmark

MIKKONEN, RAIJA HELMI MARIA, radiologist, researcher; b. Kuhmoinen, Finland, Mar. 24, 1955; d. Sulo Armas and Kerttu Eeva Maria (Simola) Nieminen; m. Atso Juhani Mikkonen, Febr. 7, 1981; children: Petri Juhani, Niina Maria. MD, U. Tampere, 1987; specialist of radiology, U. Helsinki, 1994. Mcpl. officer of health Järvenpää, Finland, 1981-88; resident of surgery and gynecology Hyvinkää, Finland, 1988-90; resident of radiology Jorui Hosp., Espoo, Finland, 1990-91; resident of radiology Helsinki U. Hosp., Finland, 1991-94, specialist in radiology, 1994—; sr. resident Helsinki U. Hosp., Finland, 1993-94. doctor mem. Nat. Pensions Inst., Järvenpää, 1987-89. Recipient Rsch. grantee State Subsidy for Univ. Hosps., Helsinki, 1995; Radiological Soc. of Finland award, 1995, Finnish Cultural Found. award, 1996. Office: Helsinki U Hosp, Haartmaninkatu 4, 00290 Helsinki Finland

MIKLUSAK, THOMAS ALAN, psychiatrist, psychoanalyst; b. Cherry Point, N.C., Mar. 25, 1946; s. Alex Frank and Betty Ann (Baker) M.; m. Chris G. Wolski, June 21, 1969; children: Courtney, Ryan. BA, U. Notre Dame, 1968; MD, Ind. U., Indpls., 1972; PhD in Adult Psychoanalysis, So. Calif. Psychoanalytic Inst, Beverly Hills, 1990. Intern Santa Barbara (Calif.) Cottage and Gen. Hosps., 1972-73; resident adult psychiatry UCLA/Brentwood VA, Westwood, Calif., 1973-76; fellow child psychiatry UCLA, Westwood, Calif., 1975-77; adult psychoanalysis clin. assoc. So. Calif. Psychoanalytic Inst., Beverly Hills, Calif., 1982-90; child psychoanalysis clin. assoc. So. Calif. Psychoanalytic Inst., Beverly Hills, 1985-91; pvt. practice child and adult psychiatry and psychoanalysis Pasadena, Calif., 1977—; asst. prof. child psychiatry U. So. Calif. Med. Sch., L.A., 1984—; instr. So. Calif. Psychoanalytic Inst. Mem. Am. Psychoanalytic Assn., Am. Psychiat. Assn., So. Calif. Psychoanalytic Soc., Soc. Calif. Psychiat. Soc. Office: 180 S Lake Ave Ste 255 Pasadena CA 91101-2619

MIKULOWSKI, PAWEL, pathologist; b. Cracow, Poland, Apr. 27, 1930; arrived in Sweden, 1966; s. Jan and Olga (Lobaczewska) M.; m. Maria Jakubowska, Jan. 16, 1954; children: Maria A., Stanislaw. PhD, Jagellonian U., Poland, 1954. Asst. prof. dept. pathology Med. Acad., Carcow, Poland, 1954-64, assoc. prof., 1964-66; asst. pathologist Mas Malmo, Sweden, 1966-68, chief physician, 1968-73, chief physician dept. pathology, 1974—, dir. dept. pathology, 1974-88; assoc. prof Dalhousie U., Halifax, N.S., Can., 1973. Contbr. articles to profl. jours. Mem. Internat. Soc. Gynecol. Pathology, Internat. Soc. Urologic Pathology, Internat. Acad. Pathology. Roman Catholic. Home: Högestadscatan 30, 21622 Malmoe Sweden Office: U Hosp Mas, Dept Pathology, 21401 Malmoe Sweden

MILACK, GARY PAUL, podiatric physician and surgeon; b. Floral Park, N.Y., May 7, 1949; s. Paul Philip and Ruth (Fogelson) M.; BS, Coll. Emporia, 1971; DPM, Ohio Coll. Podiatric Medicine, 1975; m. Deborah A. Stitz, May 25, 1980; children: Justin Paul, Tiffany Joy, Bradley Ray. Diplomate Am. Inst. Foot Medicine, Am. Acad. Pain Mgmt.; cert. in foot surgery. Resident in foor surgery Md. Podiatry Residency Program, Balt., 1975-76; pvt. practice podiatric medicine, Shoreham, N.Y., 1978—; staff Kings Park Psychiat. Hosp. Ctr., 1978—, Cen. Suffolk Hosp., Riverhead, N.Y., 1982; outpatient advisor Podiatric Products, 1989; podiatric med. advisor Matrx Med. Co.; lectr. on sedation, emergency care and surgical monitoring of ambulatory surgery cases.; dir. Shorehans Foot surgery Complex; mem. med. bd. Matrix Med, Co. Mem. editorial bd. Jour. Pain Mgmt.; editor-in-chief Contemporary Podiatric Physician. Recipient Salvation Army Outstanding Svc. in Clinic award, 1975; March of Dimes award for service, 1979; Presdl. award for fitness walking, 1977. Fellow Suffolk Acad. Medicine, Am. Soc. Podiatric Dermatology, Acad. Ambulatory Foot Surgeons, Nat. Soc. Conscious Sedation in Podiatric Med. (founder, exec. dir., instr. conscious sedation techniques), Am. Soc. Podiatric Medicine, Am. Assn. Hosp. Podiatrists; mem. Am. Podiatric Med. Writers Assn. (trustee), Am. Coll. Podiatric Physicians (v.p., pres.), Am. Bd. Podiatric Med. Specialties (bd. dirs.), Am. Inst. Foot Medicine (bd. dirs.), Am. Med. Writers Assn., Am. Acad. Administrn., Soc. Dental Anesthesiology (affiliate), Internat. Soc. Dental Anesthesiology. Contbg. editor Current Podiatry Dermatology Sect; editor-in-chief Jour. Current Podiatric Medicine, Derma-Prints newsletter; contbg. editor Podiatry Products Report; mem. editorial rev. bd. to sci. jours.; contbr. articles to profl. jours. Office: 45 Route 25A Ste 1D Shoreham NY 11786-1389

MILAD, MOHEB FAWZY, consultant, urologist; b. Cairo, Arab Republic Egypt, Mar. 16, 1945; s. Fawzy Milad and Basima Helmi; m. Dalal Kamal; children: Nadine Moheb, Michael Moheb. MB. BCh., Ain Shams U., Cairo, 1969; diploma in urology, Inst. of Urology and U. London, 1985. Intern Ain Shams U. Hosp., Cairo, 1969-70; med. officer Amoco Oil Co., Cairo, 1970-71; sr. house officer Newcastle Area Health Authority, Newcastle, Eng., 1971-73; sr. house officer, jr. registrar Coventry (Eng.) Health Authority, 1974-76; registrar East Sussex Health Authority, Eastbourne, Brighton, Eng., 1976-78; asst. surgeon, urologist Internat. Hosp., Bahrain, 1978-80, chief of staff, 1978-80, cons. in charge, 1978-80; chmn. jour. club Dhahran (Saudi Arabia) Health Ctr. (Aramco), 1982-86, chmn. urology meeting, 1990—. Contbr. articles to profl. jours. Fellow Royal Coll. Surgeons Edinburgh, Internat. Coll. Surgeons; mem. Royal Coll. Surgeons Eng., Brit. Assn. Urol. Surgeons. Home: Saudi Aramco, Box 10005, Dhahran 31311, Saudi Arabia Office: Dhahran Health Ctr Saudi, Aramco Box 76, Dhahran 31311, Saudi Arabia

MILAM, JOHN BENJAMIN, ophthalmologist; b. Bay Springs, Miss., Sept. 7, 1947; s. John Thomas and Helen Carolyn (Graham) M.; m. Sherry Lilette Edwards, Aug. 1, 1970; 1 child, Mary Amanda. BA, U. Miss., Oxford, 1969; MD, U. Miss., Jackson, 1973. Diplomate Am. Bd. Ophthalmology. Straight med. intern Bapt. Meml. Hosp., Memphis, 1973-74; resident in ophthalmology U. Miss. Med. Ctr., Jackson, 1975-78; fellow in pediatric ophthalmology Baylor Coll. Medicine, Houston, 1978-79, fellow in cornea and external disease, 1979-80; pvt. practice, Jackson, 1980—. Fellow ACS, Am. Acad. Ophthalmology (councillor 1989-94); mem. AMA, Am. Assn. Pediatric Ophthalmology and Strabismus, Miss. Med. Assn., Miss. Eye, Ear, Nose and Throat Assn. (exec. com. 1989—). Episcopalian. Office: 1421 N State St Ste 301 Jackson MS 39202

MILAM, JOHN DANIEL, pathologist, educator; b. Kilgore, Tex., May 22, 1933; s. Ott G. and Effie (White) M.; m. Carol Jones Milam, Aug. 1, 1959; children: Kay, Beth, John Jr., Julie. BS, La. State U., 1955, MS, 1957, MD, 1960. Attending pathologist St. Luke's Episcopal Hosp., Houston, 1967-89; cons. in pathology Tex. Children's Hosp., Houston, 1979—; prof. lab. medicine M.D. Anderson Cancer Ctr., U. Tex., Houston, 1990—; prof. pathology and lab. medicine U. Tex. Med. Sch., Houston, 1989—; chief pathology Lyndon B. Johnson Gen. Hosp., Houston, 1995—. Contbr. numerous articles to profl. jours., chpts., abstracts to books. Trustee Am. Bd. Pathology, 1985—, pres., 1995; bd. dirs. Harris County chpt. ARC, 1978—. Mem. Am. Assn. Blood Banks (pres. 1984, Disting. Svc. award 1988), Tex. Soc. Pathologists (George T. Caldwell award 1981). Republican. Baptist. Home: 11927 Arbordale Ln Houston TX 77024-5001 Office: U Tex Houston Med Sch Dept Pathology 6431 Fannin St Rm 2022 Houston TX 77030-1501

MILAN, RICHARD JOSEPH, JR., clinical psychologist; b. Roanoke, Va., July 9, 1959; s. Richard J. Sr. and Elsie T. (Howell) M.; m. Diane Kluge, July 18, 1981; children: Kerry Richard, Laura Elise, Emily Lynn. BA, Roanoke Coll., 1981; PhD, U. S.C., 1986. Lic. clin. psychologist, Va., practicing psychologist, N.C. Assoc. dir. human sexuality project U. S.C., Columbia, 1982-85; staff psychologist Alamance County Mental Health Ctr., Burlington, N.C., 1986-90, Ctr. for Behavioral and Rehab. Medicine, Roanoke, Va., 1990; pvt. practice psychologist The Manassas Group, Roanoke, 1990—; cons. psychologist Lewis-Gale Psychiat. Ctr. (name changed to Ctr. Behavioral Health and Rehab., Lewis-Gale Med. Ctr.), Salem, Va., 1990—, psychology dept. Roanoke Meml. Hosp. Rehab. Ctr., 1990—, Disability Determination Svcs., 1992—. Contbr. articles to profl. jours. Mem. APA, Va. Psychol. Assn., Va. Acad. Clin. Psychologists, Blue Ridge Acad. Clin. Psychologists. Office: The Manassas Group 3635 Manassas Dr Roanoke VA 24018-4053

MILANE, RICHARD JOHN, physician assistant; b. Zuni, N.Mex., Oct. 20, 1949; s. Oscar and Lolita (Coonsis) M.; m. Priscilla, Aug. 28, 1970; children: Shelley, Richelle, Richard Jr. AS, U. N.Mex., 1977; AA, South Seattle Coll., 1981. Radiology tech. Gallup (N.Mex.) Hosp., 1972-74; physician asst. Taholah (Wash.) I.H.S. Clin., 1976-78, Seattle Health Bd., 1978-83, Tuba City (Ariz.) P.H.S. Hosp., 1984-86; from radiology tech. to physician asst. Zuni P.H.S. Hosp., 1986-88; physician asst., surg. asst. Gallup Med. Group, 1989-90; physician asst. Santa Fe Indian Sch., 1994-95; physician asst. in family medicine and urgent care dept. No. Navajo Med. Ctr., Shiprock, N.Mex., 1996—. Home: No Navajo Med Ctr PO Box 1117 Tree Nos Pos AZ 86514

MILDENBERGER, BRETT G., optometrist; b. Hamilton, Mont., May 24, 1962; m. Kellie Mildenberger, Aug. 30, 1984; children: Chase, Chance. OD, Pacific U. Optometrist Big Sky Eye Care Clinic & Optical, Hamilton. Office: Big Sky Eye Care Clinic & Optical PO Box 707 Hamilton MT 59840

MILDER, PETER, physician; b. Aug. 5, 1948; cmae to U.S., 1994; m. Joanna K. Milder; 1 son, Geoffrey. BSc in Psychology with honors, McGill U., 1969; MD, McMaster U., 1972. Resident in family practice McMaster U., Hamilton, Ont., Can., 1997-74; family practice physician CCH Mgmt. Solutions, Alexandria, La., 1994—. Office: Family Medicine Ctr 3311 Prescott Rd # 410 Alexandria LA 71301

MILDVAN, DONNA, infectious diseases physician; b. Phila., June 20, 1942; d. Carl David and Gertrude M.; m. Rolf Dirk Hamann; 1 child, Gabriella Kay. AB magna cum laude, Bryn Mawr Coll., 1963; MD, Johns Hopkins U., 1967. Diplomate Am. Bd. Internal Medicine and Infectious Diseases. Intern, resident Mt. Sinai Hosp., N.Y.C., 1967-70, fellow, infectious diseases, 1970-72; asst., assoc. prof. clin. medicine Mt. Sinai Sch. Medicine, N.Y.C., 1972-87; prof. clinical medicine Dept. Medicine, Mt. Sinai Sch. Medicine, N.Y.C., 1987-88, prof. medicine, 1988-94; physician-in-charge infectious diseases Beth Israel Med. Ctr., N.Y.C., 1972-79, chief, div. infectious diseases, 1980—; prof. medicine Albert Einstein Coll. of Medicine, N.Y.C., 1994—; mem. AIDS charter rev. com., NIH/Nat. Inst. Allergy and Infectious Diseases, Bethesda, 1987—; cons. FDA, Rockville, 1987—, Ctrs. for Disease Control, Atlanta, 1985-86; among first to describe AIDS, "Pre-AIDS", AIDS Dementia, 1982, among first to study AZT, 1986; Keynote speaker, II Internat. Conf. on AIDS, Paris, 1986 and other achievements in field; Sophie Jones Meml. lectr. in infectious diseases U. Mich. Hosps., 1984. Contbr. numerous articles to profl. jours; co-editor two books, several book chpts. and abstracts on infectious diseases and AIDS. Grantee N.Y. State AIDS Inst., 1986-87; Henry Strong Denison scholar Johns Hopkins U. Sch. Medicine, 1967; recipient Woman of Achievement award AAUW, 1987; contract for antiviral therapy in AIDS, Nat. Cancer Inst./Nat. Inst. Allergy and Infectious Diseases, 1985-86, subcontract Nat. Inst. Allergy and Infectious Diseases, ACTU, 1987—. Fellow Infectious Diseases Soc. Am.; mem. Am. Soc. Microbiology, AAAS, Harvey Soc., Internat. AIDS Soc. Democrat. Jewish. Office: Beth Israel Med Ctr 1st Ave New York NY 10003-7903

MILES, DONALD ORVAL, clinical microbiologist; b. Callaway, Nebr., May 29, 1939; s. Kermit Lester and Pearl Merna (Johnson) M. m. Paula Dee Ragsdale, June 12, 1960 (div. Nov. 1982); 1 child, Jennifer Lynne; m. Vicki Dee Dillow, Nov. 23, 1988; stepchildren: Denise Rene Chamness Steck Vargas, Ricky Lee Chamness, Rhonda Len Chamness. BA, Hastings (Nebr.) Coll., 1964; student, U. Nebr., 1957-60, MS, 1967, PhD, 1972. Cert. specialist in pub. health and med. microbiology. Instr. dept. microbiology U. Nebr., Lincoln, 1972; postdoctoral fellow dept. oral biology Coll. Dentistry, U. Nebr., 1973; asst. prof. Sch. Health Scis. Grand Valley Colls., Allendale, Mich., 1973-76; chief sect. microbiology and immunology, dept. pathology St. Mary's Hosp., Grand Rapids, Mich., 1976-81; clin. microbiologist, sect. supr. lab. dept. St. Francis Med. Ctr., Cape Girardeau, Mo., 1981—; adj. faculty dept. biology S.E. Mo. U., Cape Girardeau, 1983—; researcher S.E. Mo. Coop. Lyme Disease Rsch. Group, 1989-95. Editorial cons Biol. Abstracts, RRM Med. and Clin. Microbiology, Phila., 1984—; contbr. articles to profl. jours. Bd. dirs. West YMCA, Grand Rapids, 1981; bd. dirs., vol. ARC, Cape Girardeau, 1982-89; mem. choir St. Mary's Ch., Anna, Ill., 1988-94. Comdr. USNR, 1956-92, ret. Nat. Inst. Dental Rsch. fellow, 1973. Mem. Am. Soc. for Microbiology, Nebr. Acad. Sci. (emeritus), Am. Soc. Clin. Pathologists, South Central Assn. Clin. Microbiology, So. Assn. Clin. Microbiology, Southwestern Assn. Clin. Microbiology (area dir 1986-90), Am. Herbalist Guild, Sigma Xi. Home: 350 State Hwy Y JAckson MO 63755 Office: Lab Dept St Francis Med Ctr 211 Saint Francis Dr Cape Girardeau MO 63703-5049

MILES, MICHAEL VAN, clinical researcher, educator, pharmacologist, consultant; b. Springfield, Mo., Oct. 5, 1944; s. Benny Leroy and Betty Jean (White) M.; children: Michelle, Mela.ie, Matthew, Mark. B.S., U. Okla., 1976; Dr. Pharmacy, U. Tex., 1979. Registered pharmacist. Asst. prof. Samford U., Birmingham, Ala., 1979, U. N.C., Chapel Hill, 1985-93; assoc. prof. pediatrics Eastern Va. Med. Sch., 1993—; asst. pharmacy dir. Children's Hosp., Birmingham, 1979-85; dir. pediatric applied pharmacology rsch. program Ctr. Pediatric Rsch., Norfolk, 1993—; cons. Comprehensive Epilepsy Ctr. for Children, Birmingham, 1983-85. Contbr. author: Applied Clinical Pharmacokinetics, 1984, also articles. Office: Ctr Pediatric Rsch 855 W Brambleton Ave Norfolk VA 23510-1005

MILES, RICHARD JOHN, osteopath; b. Milw., Sept. 7, 1965; s. Clinton John and Susan Theresa (Turner) M.; m. Trayce Ann Burns, May 23, 1995; 1 child, Andrew Steven. BS in Biology, Mich. Tech. U., 1987; DO, U. Osteo. Medicine/Health Sci., 1992. Commd. 2d lt. U.S. Army, 1988, advanced through grades to capt.; chief aviation medicine Lyster Army Hosp., Ft. Rucker, Ala., 1993-94, chief outpatient svcs., 1994, chief emergency med. svcs., 1994—. Mem. AMA, Am. Osteo. Assn., Am. Coll. Emergency Physicians, Soc. U.S. Army Flight Surgeons (sec. 1995—). Republican. Roman Catholic. Home: # 3 Stratford Ln Enterprise AL 36330 Office: USAAMC Emergency Dept Fort Rucker AL 36362

MILES, SAMUEL ISRAEL, psychiatrist, educator; b. Munich, Mar. 4, 1949; came to U.S., 1949; s. Henry and Renee (Ringel) M.; m. Denise Marie Robey, June 26, 1977; children: Jonathan David, Justin Alexander. BS, CCNY, 1970; MD, N.Y. Med. Coll., 1974; PhD, So. Calif. Psychoanalytic Inst., 1986. Diplomate Am. Bd. Psychiatry and Neurology with added qualifications in forensic psychiatry. Intern D.C. Gen. Hosp., Washington, 1974-75; resident in psychiatry Cedars-Sinai Med. Ctr., Los Angeles, 1975-78; practice medicine specializing in psychiatry Los Angeles, 1978—; ind. med. examiner Calif. Dept. Indsl. Relations, 1984-91, qualified med. examiner, 1991—; asst. clin. prof. psychiatry UCLA Sch. Medicine, 1978—; attending psychiatrist Cedars-Sinai Med. Ctr., 1978—; attending psychiatrist Brotman Med. Ctr., Culver City, Calif., 1978—; mem. faculty So. Calif. Psychoanalytic Inst., 1986—; mem. psychiat. panel Superior Ct. Los Angeles County, 1990—, Fed. Ct., 1990—. Fellow Am. Acad. Psychoanalysis, Am. Orthopsychiat. Assn.; mem. Acad. Psychiatry and the Law, Am. Coll. Legal Medicine, Calif. Psychiat. Assn. (mem. managed care com. 1991—), So. Calif. Psychiat. Soc. (coun. rep. 1985-88, 92-95, chairperson pvt. practice com. 1988-92, sec. 1991-92, mem. worker's compensation com. 1992—, trea.-elect 1996), So. Calif. Psychoanalytic Inst. (pres. clin. assocs. orgn. 1981-82, mem. admissions com. 1988—, mem. ethics stds. com. 1991-92, chairperson ethics stds. com. 1993—, mem. exec. com. 1993—). Jewish. Office: 8631 W 3rd St Ste 425E Los Angeles CA 90048-5908

MILEWSKI, BARBARA ANNE, pediatrics nurse, neonatal intensive care nurse; b. Chgo., Sept. 11, 1934; d. Anthony and LaVerne (Sepp) Witt; m. Leonard A. Milewski, Feb. 23, 1952; children: Pamela, Robert, Diane, Timothy. ADN, Harper Coll., Palatine, Ill, 1982; BS, Northern Ill. U., 1992; postgrad., North Park Coll. RN, Ill.; cert. CPR instr. Staff nurse Northwest Community Hosp., Arlington Heights, Ill., Resurrection Hosp., Chgo.; nurse neonatal ICU Children's Meml. Hosp., Chgo.; day care cons. Cook County Dept. Pub. Health; CPR instr. Stewart Oxygen Svcs., Chgo.; instr., organizer parenting and well baby classes and clinics; vol Children's Meml. Hosp.; health coord. CEDA Head Start; cons. day care Cook County Dept. Pub. Health. Vol. first aid instr. Boy Scouts Am.; CPR instr. Harper Coll., Children's Meml. Hosp.; dir. Albany Park Cmty. Ctr. Head Start, Chgo.; day care cons. Cook County Dept. Pub. Health. Mem. Am. Mortar Bd., Sigma Theta Tau.

MILEWSKI, STANISLAW ANTONI, ophthalmologist, educator; b. Bagrowo, Poland, June 16, 1930; s. Alfred and Sabina (Sicinska) M.; came to U.S., 1959, naturalized, 1967; BA, Trinity Coll., U. Dublin (Ireland), 1954, MA, 1959, B. Chir., M.B., B.A.O., 1956; m. Anita Dobiecka, July 11, 1959; children: Andrew, Teresa, Mark. House surgeon Hammersmith Hosp. Postgrad. Sch. London, 1958; intern St. Raffael Hosp., New Haven, 1960-61; resident in ophthalmology Gill Meml. Hosp., Roanoke, Va., 1961-64; practice medicine specializing in surgery and diseases of the retina and vitreous; mem. staff Manchester (Conn.) Meml. Hosp., 1964-71, chief of ophthalmology, sr. attending physician St. Francis Hosp., Hartford, Conn., 1971—; asst. clin. prof. ophthalmology U. Conn., 1972—. Clin. fellow Montreal (Que., Can.) Gen Hosp., McGill U., 1971-72, Mass. Eye and Ear Infirmary, Harvard Med. Sch., Boston, 1974; diplomate Am. Bd. Ophthalmology. Fellow ACS; mem. AMA, New England Ophthal. Soc., Conn. Soc. Eye Physicians, Vitreous Soc. Republican. Roman Catholic. Home: 127 Lakewood Cir S Manchester CT 06040-7086 Office: 191 Main St Manchester CT 06040-3556 also: 43 Woodland St Ste 100 Hartford CT 06105-2339

MILFORD, ALBERT FINDLEY, surgeon; b. Ann Arbor, Mich., Jan. 9, 1943; s. Albert Findley II and Beth (Wharton) M.; m. Lisa, June 17, 1972; children: Amy Elizabeth, Albert Findley IV. BA, Northern Mich. U., 1966; MS, Eastern Mich. U., 1968; DO, Chgo. Coll. Osteo. Medicine, 1972. Asst. prof. Midwestern U., Downers Grove, Ill., 1977-84, assoc. prof., 1984-91, prof. surgery, 1991—; dir. trauma svcs. Olympia Fields (Ill.) Osteo. Hosp. & Med. Ctr., 1988-90, assoc. chmn. dept. surgery, 1995—; chmn. dept. surgery St. Margaret Mercy Hosp., Dyer, Ind., 1966—. Republican. Roman Catholic. Office: Surg Assocs Osteo Ltd 20303 S Crawford Ste 210 Olympia Fields IL 60461

MILGRAM, GAIL GLEASON, alcohol and drug abuse education professional; b. South Amboy, N.J., June 14, 1942; d. John Thomas and Evelyn (Lynch) Gleason; m. William H. Milgram, Aug. 6, 1966; children: Lynn Patricia, Anne Melissa. BS, Georgian Court Coll., Lakewood, N.J., 1963; MEd, Rutgers U., 1965, EdD, 1969. Assoc. prof. Ctr. Alcohol Studies Rutgers U., New Brunswick, N.J., 1971-82, prof., dir. edn. and tng., 1982—; adj. faculty U. Medicine and Dentistry N.J., 1980—; bd. dirs. North Conway Inst., Alcohol and Drug Counselor Cert. Bd. of N.J., Inc., Freedom House, Alcohol Rsch. Documentation, Inc. Mem. editl. bd. Alcoholism Treatment Quar., 1983—, Jour. Chem. Dependency Treatment, 1987—, Jour. Studies on Alcohol, 1989; author: Facts About Drinking: Guide to Coping With Alcohol and Alcohol Problems, 1990, Coping With Alcohol, 1987, What, When and How to Talk to Students About Alcohol and Other Drugs: A Guide for Teachers, 1986, What, When and How to Talk to Your Children About Alcohol and Other Drugs: A Guide for Parents, 1983. Recipient Disting. Svc. award N.J. Dept. Health, 1989, Middlesex County Alcohol Assn., 1983. Office: Rutgers U Ctr Alcohol Studies Busch Campus Smithers Hall New Brunswick NJ 08903

MILHAUD, GUY EMILE, toxicology educator, consultant; b. Garac, France, Jan. 8, 1934; s. Joseph Victor and Anna Marie (Lannes) M.; m. Ginette Alberta Fabre, Apr. 27, 1959; 1 child, Dorothee. DVM, U. Toulouse, France, 1957; agregation, U. Paris, 1963, lic. in scis., 1965. Sr. asst. Nat. Vet. Sch., Toulouse, 1959-64; prof. toxicology Nat. Vet. Sch., Alfort, France, 1964—; expert Higher Pub. Hygiene Coun. France, Coun. European, Commn. on Toxics in Agr., Commn. Autorisation de Mise sur le Marché des Medicaments Vétérinaires. Contbr. articles on fluorides, lead, zinc, and cadmium poisoning to sci. jour. Decorated officier Ordre Nat. du Merite, officier Merite Agricole, Palmes Académiques (France). Mem. Confrerie des Chevaliers du Tastevin. Home: 68 Rue de Rendez-Vous, 75012 Paris France Office: Nat Vet Sch Alfort, 7 Ave du General De Gaulle, 94704 Maisons Alfort France

MILHORAT, THOMAS HERRICK, neurosurgeon; b. N.Y.C., Apr. 5, 1936; s. Ade Thomas and Edith Caulkins (Herrick) M.; children: John Thomas, Robert Herrick. BA, Cornell U., 1957, MD, 1961. Intern, asst. resident in gen. surgery N.Y. Hosp.-Cornell Med. Ctr., 1961-63; clin. assoc., dept. surg. neurology Nat. Inst. Neurol. Diseases and Blindness, Bethesda, 1963-65; asst. resident, chief resident in neurosurgery N.Y. Hosp.-Cornell Med. Ctr., 1965-68, asst. neurosurgeon NIH, 1968-71; assoc. prof. neurol. surgery, assoc. prof. child health and devel. George Washington U. Sch. Medicine, Washington, 1971-74; prof. child health and devel. George Washington U., Washington, 1974-81, prof. neurol. surgery, 1974-81; chmn. dept. neurosurgery Children's Hosp. Nat. Med. Ctr., Washington, 1971-81; prof. neurol. surgery, dept. chmn. SUNY Health Sci. Ctr., Bklyn., 1982—; neurosurgeon-in-chief Kings County Hosp. Ctr.; regional chmn. neurol. surgery L.I. Coll. Hosp., 1986—, Coney Island Hosp., 1986—; program dir. Neurosurgery Rsch. Tng. Program, 1982—; mem. Nat. Coun. Scientists, NIH, 1969-82. Author: Hydrocephalus and Cerebrospinal Fluid, 1972, Pediatric Neurosurgery, 1978, Cerebrospinal Fluid and the Brain Edemas, 1987 (with M.K. Hammock) Cranial Computed Tomography in Infancy and Childhood, 1981; contbr. 220 articles to sci. publs. and chpts. to books. Chmn. bd. Internat. Neurosci. Found., pres. 1086—; chmn. med. adv. bd. Am. Spingomyelia Alliance Project, 1996—. Lt. commdr. USPHS, 1963-65. Recipient 1st prize in pathology, Cornell U. Med. Sch. Dept. Ob-Gyn., 1960, Charles L. Horn prize Cornell Med. Sch., 1961, Best Paper award ann. combined meeting N.Y. Acad. Medicine/N.Y. Neurosurg. Soc., 1965, Pudenz award for Excellence in CSF Physiology, 1994; named one of N.Y.'s Best Doctors, N.Y. Mag., 1992. Mem. AAAS, Internat. Soc. Pediat. Neurosurgery, Am. Assn. Neurol. Surgery (pediat. sect.), Am. Syringomiglia Alliance Project (chmn. med. adv. bd. 1996—), Am. Acad. Pediat. (surg. sect.), Soc. Pediat. Rsch., N.Y. Acad. Medicine, N.Y. Soc. Neurosurgery (pres. 1988-90), Bklyn. Neurologic Soc. (pres. 1988-95), Soc. Neurosci., Internat. Soc. Neurosci., Soc. Neurol. Surgeons, Med. Club Bklyn., Sigma Xi. Office: SUNY Health Sci Ctr Bklyn 450 Clarkson Ave PO Box 1189 Brooklyn NY 11203

MILICEVIC, JELENA, health science specialist; b. Skopje, Macedonia, Yugoslavia, Jan. 1, 1939; came to U.S., 1972; d. Miladin and Hedy (Hem) M.; m. Ernst Anzbock, Dec. 14, 1959 (div. 1971); children: Harald, Evelyn; m. Ranko Caric, Nov. 3, 1973 (div. 1980); 1 child, Peter. Student, Molloy Coll., 1979-81, L.I. U., 1981-82, Rockland C.C., 1985, Vt. Coll., 1985-86, Orange County C.C., 1988, Empire State Coll., 1990—. Ordained to ministry Universal Spiritualist Assn. U.S.A., 1985; lic., real estate agt., N.Y.; registered and cert. reflexologist, N.Y. Owner Walter's Bake Shop, 1973-79; nurse's aide Hillside Manor, 1980; clerical worker Molloy Coll., 1980-81, L.I. U., 1981-82; chiropractor asst. Steven R. Siegel D.C., 1982; owner Linden Motel, 1983; lectr. on Shiatsu and reflexology New Age Ctr., 1985-86; v.p., min. Universal Ctr. New Age Consciousness, Inc., Milford, Pa., 1985—; with Abatelli Realty, 1988; gen. agt. Intern Cons. Exchange, San Diego, Calif., 1986; spa and skincare therapist, 1993. Mem. Am. Message Therapy Assn., Alliance of Message Therapists, Inc., Universal Spiritualist Assn., N.Y. State Soc. Med. Massage Therapists, Internat. Platform Assn., Assoc. Bodywork and Massage Profls., Carmel Art Assn. Home: 25930 Colt Ln Carmel Valley CA 95924 Office: 15-71 208th St Bayside NY 11360

MILKE, DENIS JEROME, psychiatrist; b. Cleve., Nov. 2, 1938; s. Merle J. and Kathleen R. (Schaeffer) M.; B.S., Pa. State U., 1960; M.D., Hahnemann Med. Coll., 1965; children—Dana Lynne, Christopher Denis. Intern, Harrisburg Hosp., 1965-66; resident in psychiatry Western Inst. and Clinic, U. Pitts., 1966-69; pvt. practice medicine specializing in psychiatry, Wormleysburg, Pa., 1972—; med. dir. Office of Mental Health, Pa. Dept. Pub. Welfare, Harrisburg, Edgewater Psychiat. Ctr., Harrisburg, Pa. With U.S. Army, 1969-72. Diplomate Am. Bd. Psychiatry and Neurology. Fellow Am. Orthopsychiat. Assn, Am. Psychiat. Assn.; mem. Psychiat. Physicians of Pa., Pa. State Med. Soc., Dauphin County Med. Soc., AMA, Soc. Clin. and Exptl. Hypnosis. Club: West Shore Country. Office: 1013 Mumma Rd Ste 203 Lemoyne PA 17043-1144

MILKS, SALLY ANN, food service manager, dietitian; b. Bradford, Pa., Nov. 29, 1949; d. John David and Pearl Marie (Meier) Morrison; m. Frank Elmer Milks, Aug. 18, 1973 (div. 1978); 1 child, Jason Michael. B.S. in Edn., Mansfield State Coll., 1971; student Indiana U. of Pa., 1969-71. Registered dietitian. Clin. dietitian St. Vincent Med. Ctr., Erie, Pa., 1971-72, 73-74; dietetic intern Shadyside Hosp., Pitts., 1972-73; cons. dietitian Sheridan Manor Nursing Home, Buffalo, 1975-77; nutrition instr. E.J. Meyer Sch. Nursing, Buffalo, 1975-77, chief clin. dietitian, 1977-78; asst. dir. food services ARA Services, Erie County Med. Ctr., 1978-79, dir. food services, 1979-82, dist. mgr., Phila., 1982-94; dir. programs and standards Compass Group USA, Inc., Secaucus, N.J., 1995—; mem. adv. council Buffalo State U., 1985—; guest lectr. food and nutrition dept., 1980—. Ho. of dels. United Way of Buffalo and Erie County, 1983—. Mem. Am. Dietetic Assn., Erie County Assn. for Retarded Children (2d v.p. 1983-85, chmn. residential services com. 1981-87). Home: 17 Apollo Dr Buffalo NY 14228-1823 Office: Compass Group USA Inc Basteman Divsn One Harmon Plz Secaucus NJ 07094

MILLARD, RONALD WESLEY, physiologist; b. Bridgeport, Conn., Sept. 10, 1941; s. Wesley Leon and Vivian (Blakeman) M.; m. Christine Ann Berg, Nov. 30, 1968; children: Jacob Christian, Lucas Wesley. BS, Tufts U., 1963; PhD, Boston U., 1969. Asst. prof. Harvard U., Boston, 1974-75, Brown U., Providence, 1975-78; assoc. prof. U. Cin., 1978-87, prof. Coll. Medicine, 1987—. Contbr. over 100 articles to profl. publs. Mem. Am. Heart Assn., Am. Physiol. Soc., Am. Soc. Pharmacology and Exptl. Therapeutics, Internat. Soc. for Heart Rsch., Biomed. Engring. Soc.

MILLER, AILEEN ETTA MARTHA, medical association administrator, consultant, metabolic nutritionist; b. Sullivan, Ind., Oct. 4, 1924; d. Arthur Henry and Alice Maria (Michael) Dettmer; m. Robert Charles Miller, Sept. 1, 1945; children: Robert Conrad, Debra Carol, Theresa Marie. D of Chiropractic, Palmer Coll. Chiropractic, 1945. Sec. Soroptimist Internat., East Detroit, Mich., 1951-52, Mich. State Chiropractic Assn. Dist. 1, East Detroit, 1957-58, Macomb County Chiropractic Assn., East Detroit, 1982-86; pres. Macomb County Chiropractic Assn., Warren, Mich., 1986-87; cons. Chiropractic Physicians, Warren, 1986—. Recipient Humanitarian and Svc. award Palmer Coll., 1995. Mem. Internat. Chiropractic Assn., Mich. State Chiropractic Assn., Roy Sweat Rsch. and Edn. Found., Found. Chiropractic Edn. and Rsch., Palmer Coll. Alumni Assn., Atlas Orthogonal Chiropractic Assn. (humanitarian and svc. award 1995), Assn. for Rsch. and Enlightenment (assoc. licentiate of United Metaphysical Chs., East Pointe, Mich. divsn.). Office: Chiropractic Physicians 30020 Schoenherr Rd Warren MI 48093-3100

MILLER, ARTHUR JOSEPH, neurophysiology and craniofacial biology researcher; b. San Francisco, Jan. 18, 1943; s. Arthur Joseph and Theresa (Walczak) M.; m. Marilyn Loushin, Aug. 21, 1965; children: Garreth, Ashleigh, Heath. BA, San Jose State U., 1965; postgrad., Brain Research Inst., 1966-70; PhD, UCLA, 1970. Asst. prof. U. Ill., Chgo., 1970-75; asst. prof. growth, devel., physiology U. Calif., San Francisco, 1975-78, assoc. prof., 1978-84, prof., 1984—. Author: Craniomandibular Muscles: Their Role in Form and Function; mem. editorial bd. Dysphagia; reviewer for

Brain Rsch., Exptl. Neurology, Archives Oral Biology, Am. Jour. Orthodontics, Jour. Orofacial Pain, others; ad hoc reviewer NIH, Can. Med. Rsch. Coun., NSF; contbr. articles to profl. jours. Mem. ADA, Neurosci. Soc., Internat. Assn. for Dental Research, Internat. Brain Research Assn., Dysphagia Rsch. Soc., Omicron Rho Upsilon. Democrat. Roman Catholic. Home: 160 Leslie Dr San Carlos CA 94070-3461 Office: U Calif Dept Growth & Devel San Francisco CA 94143

MILLER, BARBARA JUNE, physician assistant; b. Elgin, Ill.; d. Warren Calvin and Nora (Kirchman) M.; m. Michael J. Muszynski, June 17, 1980. BS in biology, chem., Valparaiso Univ., 1975; cert. physician asst., U.S. Pub. Health Svc. Hosp., 1980; MS in indsl. safety, Northern Ill. Univ., 1989. Physician asst. Columbus Hosp., Chgo., 1980-83; social svc. specialist Winnebago County Dept. Pub. Health, Rockford, Ill., 1983-84; physician asst. student health Northern Ill. Univ., Dekalb, Ill., 1984-90; physician asst. family medicine Chgo. Osteopathic Acad. Medical Practice, Olympia Fields, Ill., 1990-92; physician asst. occupational health Meth. Hosp., Gary, Ind., 1993-95, Corp. Health Dimensions, Gary, Ind., 1995—; asst. prof. Finch Univ. Chgo. Medical Sch., Chgo., 1994—. Recipient Safety award Northern Ill. Univ., 1988. Fellow Ill. Acad. Physicians Assts. (v.p. 1996, sec. 1992-95, v.p. 1993), Am. Acad. Physicians Assts, Am. Acad. Physicians Assts. in Occupational Medicine, Am. Assn. Univ. Women, Am. Youth Hostels (bd. dirs.). Methodist. Office: Finch Univ 3333 Green Bay Rd North Chicago IL 60064

MILLER, BARRY, research administrator, psychologist; b. N.Y.C., Dec. 25, 1942; s. Jack and Ida (Kaplan) M.; m. Susan Hallermeier; children: Eric, Arianne, Kristina, Barrie. BS in Psychology, Bklyn. Coll., 1965; MS in Psychology, Villanova U., 1967; PhD in Psychiatry, Med. Coll. Pa., 1971. Instr. psychology Villanova (Pa.) U., 1971-73; asst. dir. dept. behavioral sci., med. rsch. scientist Ea. Pa. Psychiatric Inst., Phila., 1971-73, sr. med. rsch. scientist, 1973-80; dir. Pa. Bur. Rsch. and Tng., Harrisburg, 1973-81; asst. prof. psychology U. Pa. Med. Sch., Phila., 1975-78, clin. prof. psychology, 1978—; assoc. prof. psychiatry Med. Coll. Pa., Phila., 1981-90, rsch. assoc. prof. medicine, 1983-90, assoc. dean for rsch., 1981-90; dir. for rsch. devel. Albert Einstein Healthcare Network, Phila., 1990-95; dir. The Permanente Med. Group Rsch. Inst., Oakland, Calif., 1995—; adj. assoc. prof. psychiatry Med. Coll. Pa., Phila., 1990—; rsch. assoc. prof. psychiatry Temple U. Sch. Med., Phila., 1990—; mem. sci. and tech. task force Pa. Econ. Devel. Partnership, Harrisburg, 1987-88, adv. com. Clin. Rsch. Ctr. Psychopathology of Elderly, Phila., 1985-88; mem. cancer control prgram Pa. Dept. Health, 1994; vis. rsch. assoc. prof. Med. Coll. Pa., Phila., 1991—. Contbr. articles to profl. jours.; mem. editorial bd. Jour. Mental Health Adminstrn., 1988—, assoc. editor, 1989—. Bd. dirs. Community Mental Health Ctr. 6A, Phila., 1969-73, Northwest Jewish Youth Ctrs., Phila., 1974-75; mem. Lafayette Hill Civic Assn., 1973-86, Citizens Coun. Whitemarsh (Pa.) Twp., 1975-86. Grantee HHS, NIH. Fellow Pa. Psychol. Assn.; mem. AAAS, Am. Psychol. Assn., Assn. Mental Health Adminstrs., Assn. Univ. Tech. Mgrs., Soc. Rsch. Adminstrs. Office: The Permanente Med Group 1800 Harrison St Oakland CA 94612-3429

MILLER, C. ARDEN, physician, educator; b. Shelby, Ohio, Sept. 19, 1924; s. Harley H. and Mary (Thuma) M.; m. Helen Meihack, June 26, 1948; children—John Lewis, Thomas Meihack, Helen Lewis, Benjamin Lewis. Student, Oberlin Coll., 1942-44; M.D. cum laude, Yale, 1948. Intern, then asst. resident pediatrics Grace-New Haven Community Hosp., 1948-51; faculty U. Kans. Med. Center, 1951-66, dir. childrens rehab. unit, 1957-60, dean Med. Sch., dir., 1960-66; prof. pediatrics and maternal and child health U. N.C., Chapel Hill, 1966—, vice chancellor health scis., 1966-71, chmn. dept. maternal and child health, 1977-87; chmn. exec. com. Citizens Bd. Inquiry into Health Services for Am., 1968-71. Mem. editorial bd.: Jour. Med. Edn, 1960-66; Author numerous articles in field. Trustee Appalachian Regional Hosps., 1974-84, Alan Guttmacher Inst., Planned Parenthood Fedn. Am. Markle scholar in med. scis., 1955-60; recipient Robert H. Felix Distinguished Service award St. Louis U., 1977, Martha Mae Eliot award in pub. health, 1984, Sedgewick Meml. medal Am. Pub. Health Assn., 1986, O. Max Gardner award U. N.C., 1987. Fellow Royal Soc. Health (hon.), Clare Hall Cambridge (Eng.) U. (life); mem. Am. Pub. Health Assn. (chmn. action bd. 1972-75, pres. 1974-75), Soc. Pediatric Research, Assn. Am. Med. Colls. (v.p. 1965-66), Inst. of Medicine of Nat. Acad. Sci., Sigma Xi, Alpha Omega Alpha, Delta Omega. Home: 908 Greenwood Rd Chapel Hill NC 27514-3910

MILLER, CHARLES JAY, dentist; b. Pitts., Nov. 10, 1924; s. I. Franklin and Ella (Abrams) M.; m. Barbara Thorpe, May 30, 1975; children: Sandi, Wayne, Wendy, John Thorpe. BS, U. Pitts., 1948, DDS, 1950. Diplomate Am. Acad. Osseointegration. Dentist Miller, Werrin, Gruendel, P.A., Pitts., 1950—; chmn. Council Dental Health, Odontological Soc. Wester Pa., Pitts., 1974; clin. prof. fixed partial prosthodontics Grad. Sch. Dental Medicine, U. Pitts., 1981—. Author: Inlays, Crowns and Bridges, 1962 (translated into German, Portuguese and Spanish, 1965-67); editor: Restorative Dentistry, 1972, (with others) Electrosurgery, 1989, Cosmetic Dentistry, 1987. Bd. dirs. United Jewish Fedn., Pitts., 1981-83; chmn. alumni giving fund U. Pitts., 1990—. 1st lt. USAAF, 1944-45, ETO. Decorated Air medal with 5 silver oak leaf clusters, Presdl. Citation, European campaign ribbon, Victory ribbon; recipient Disting. Alumnus award U. Pitts., 1988. Fellow Am. Coll. Dentists, Internat. Coll. Dentists; mem. Greater N.Y. Acad. Prosthodontics, Internat. Congress Oral Implantologists, Am. Acad. Esthetic Dentistry (charter), Concordia Club (pres. 1984-86), Kiwanis (pres. Pitts. 1965). Democrat. Office: 3506 Fifth Ave Pittsburgh PA 15213-3310

MILLER, CHARLINE ZIMMERMAN, psychotherapist, consultant; b. Cleve., Feb. 3, 1954; d. Mike and Lucy J. (Schade) Zimmerman; m. William S. Miller III, July 29, 1983; children: Elizabeth, Rebecca. BA, MA, Case Western Res. U., 1975; MA in Clin. and Community Psychology, Cleve. State U., 1979. Lic. profl. and clin. counselor, Ohio. Dir. drug and alcohol treatment svcs. Ravenwood Ctr., Chardon, Ohio, 1982-87; pvt. practice, cons. Cleveland Heights, Ohio, 1985—. Mem. Ohio Assn. Children of Alcoholics (founding bd. mem., sec. bd. dirs., 1987—). Office: 1991 Lee Rd #104 Cleveland Heights OH 44118

MILLER, CONSTANCE J. ERRICKSON, cardiology nurse, military officer; b. Stratford, N.J., Oct. 7, 1970; d. Willard Joseph and Susan Virginia (Webb) E. BSN, Widener U., 1993. RN; CCRN. Commd. 1st lt. U.S. Army Nurse Corps, 1993; cardiology staff nurse Walter Reed Army Med. Ctr., Washington, 1993-95, staff nurse med. MICU/PICU, 1995—. Softball coach, Little League, Montgomery County Recreation, Gaithersburg, Md., 1995. Mem. AACCN, Sigma Theta Tau. Republican. Office: Walter Reed Army Med Ctr Ward 45B Washington DC 20307

MILLER, DANIEL WEISS, psychologist; b. N.Y.C., Sept. 14, 1924; s. Paul and Helen (Weiss) M.; children: Sarah, David, Larissa. BA, New Sch. Social Research, 1952; MA in Psychology, CUNY, 1955; postgrad. Yeshiva U., 1957-58, N.Y.U., 1956-57, Humanistic Psychology Inst., 1978-81; PhD in Psychology, Internat. Inst. for Advanced Studies, 1989. Psychology intern N.J. State Psychologists Tng. Program, Trenton State Hosp., 1953-55; probation officer N.Y.C. Surrogate Ct., 1955-57; sr. psychologist Central Islip State Hosp., N.Y., 1957-58; chief psychologist Kings Park N.Y., State Hosp., 1958-62; research psychologist Elmhurst Gen. Hosp., Queens, N.Y., 1962-63, Rockland State Hosp., N.J., 1964; pvt. practice psychoanalytic psychotherapy, N.Y.C., 1972—; dir. organic process therapy Primal-Gestalt; lectr.; tng. therapist centers in Paris, Greece, Frankfurt, Ger., and Brazil and Montreal, Que., Can. Author: The Unseen Universe of Mind and Matter, 1993; science editor: To Your Health; editor newsletter; contbr. articles to profl. jours. Lic. psychologist, N.Y. Mem. ISSEEEM, Am. Psychol. Soc., Assn. for Past Life Rsch. & Therapy, Am. Soc. for Psychic. Research, U.S. Psychotronics Assn. (N.Y. chpt.), N.Y. Acad. Sci., Internat. Primal Assn. (bd. dirs.), Lyceum Club. Home and Office: 106 Saint Marks Ave Brooklyn NY 11217-2412

MILLER, DAVID BENNETT, psychology educator, animal behavior researcher; b. Cleve., Sept. 21, 1948; s. Joseph and May (Eglin) M.; m. Linda Lach, July 31, 1976. B.A., U. Fla., 1970; M.S. U. Miami, Fla., 1972, Ph.D., 1973. Postdoctoral fellow N.C. Div. Mental Health, Raleigh, 1973-77, research assoc., 1978-80; Alexander von Humboldt fellow U. Bielefeld, Fed. Republic Germany, 1977-78; asst. prof. psychology U. Conn., Storrs, 1980-82, assoc. prof., 1982-88, prof., 1988—. Editor Bird Behavior, 1995—, contbr. articles to profl. jours. Mem. Am. Psychol. Assn. (chmn. program com. 1983), Animal Behavior Soc. (chmn. policy and planning com. 1985—), Psychonomic Soc., Internat. Soc. for Devel. Psychobiology, Am. Ornithol. Union. Office: Conn U U-20 Conn Dept Psychology Storrs CT 06269-1020

MILLER, DAVID EARL, biological sciences educator; b. Platteville, Wis., Feb. 2, 1950; s. Clement Earl and Viola Mary Anna (Johnsen) M. BS in Biol. Scis. magna cum laude, U. Wis., Platteville, 1972, MA in Teaching, 1974, MEd in Sci. summa cum laude, 1987; MA in Biol. Scis. summa cum laude, Ball State U., Muncie, Ind., 1984, DEd in Sci., 1985. Cert. tchr., Ill., Iowa, W.Va., Wis. Tchr. U. Wis., Platteville, 1972-74, Horizon Campus Z.B.T.H.S., Zion, Ill., 1974-79; doctoral fellow Ball State U., Muncie, 1979-80; tchr. Pearce Campus of Z.B.T.H.S., Zion, 1980-84, Denison U., Granville, Ohio, 1984-85, Hazard (Ky.) Community Coll., 1985-86, McMurry Coll., Abilene, Tex., 1986-87; substitute tchr. Southwestern Community Sch. Dist., Hazel Green, Wis., 1987—; assoc. prof. biol. scis. Alderson-Broaddus Coll., Philippi, W.Va., 1988-95; sci. tchr. River Valley Sch. Dist., Spring Green, Wis., 1996—. Mem. post com. Explorer Post 93, Zion, 1976-84, chair, 1979; sec. W.Va. Day for the Homeless, Philippi chpt., 1989-91; asst. prin. bass sect. Abilene Philharmonic Orch., 1986-87; prin. bass sect. Dubuque Symphony Orch., 1971-74, Dubuque Chorale Orch., 1971-74, Licking County Symphony Orch., 1984-85; with Kenosha Civic Symphony Orch., 1974-84, Messiah Orchs., 1969—; prin. bass Buckhannon Chamber Orch., 1991-92. Recipient Thomas A. Edison Sci. Educator's award, 1976, Cert. of Recognition for excellence in performance of Mus. Theater, 1978; Ball State U. doctoral fellow, 1979-80, NSF project fellow, 1981, 89. Mem. ABATE of Wis./W.Va., Assn. Southeastern Biologists, East-Central Ind. Audubon Soc., Faculty Scholars Program Coun., League of Herpetologists, Nat. Rifle Assn., Nat. Speleological Soc., Nature Conservancy, Southwestern Wis. Speleological Soc. (sec. 1971-72), Wis. Acad. Scis., Arts and Letters, Phi Delta Kappa, Phi Kappa Phi. Office: 1070 N Water St Platteville WI 53818

MILLER, DAVID EDMOND, physician; b. Biscoe, N.C., June 6, 1930; s. James Herbert and Elsie Dale (McGlaughon) M.; m. Marjorie Willard Penton, June 4, 1960; children: Marjorie Dale, David Edmond. AB, Duke U., 1952, MD, 1956. Diplomate Am. Bd. Internal Medicine (subspecialty bd. cardiovasular disease). Internmed. ctr. Duke U., Durham, N.C., 1956-57, resident in internal medicine, 1957-58, 59, 60, research fellow cardiovascular disease, 1958-59, 61, assoc. internal medicine and cardiology, 1963-79, clin. asst., prof. medicine cardiology, 1979—; practice medicine specialising in internal medicine Durham, 1964—; attending physician internal medicine div. cardiology Watts Hosp., Durham, 1964-76, chief medicine, 1975-76; attending physician cardiology divsn. internal medicine Durham Regional Hosp. (formerly Durham County Gen. Hosp.), 1976—, chmn. dept. internal medicine, 1976-82, pres. med. staff, 1980-81; adv. com. Duke Med. Ctr. Contbr. articles to profl. jours. Council clin. cardiology N.C. chpt. Am. Heart Assn., 1963—. Served to lt. comdr. USNR, 1961-63. Fellow ACP, Am. Coll. Cardiology, Royal Soc. Medicine, Royal Soc. Health; mem. AMA, So. Med. Assn., N.C. Med. Soc. (del. ho. of dels. 1981, 82, 83), N.C. Durham-Orange County Med. Soc., Am. Soc. Internal Medicine, N.C. Soc. Internal Medicine (exec. coun. 1984-92), Am. Fedn. Clin. Rsch. Methodist. Clubs: Capitol, Hope Valley Country, Univ., Duke Faculty, Carolina Yacht. Home: 1544 Hermitage Ct Durham NC 27707-1680 Office: 2609 N Duke St Ste 403 Durham NC 27704-3048

MILLER, DAVID JOHN, psychologist, education administrator; b. St. Louis, Aug. 22, 1956. BA in Psychology, U. Mo., 1978, MA in Psychology, 1980, PhD in Psychology, 1983. Lic. psychologist, Pa. Intern VA Med. Ctr., Palo Alto, Calif., 1983; coord. psychiatry VA Med. Ctr., Pitts., 1984-87, dir. clin. tng., 1987-91, chief psychology svc., 1993—, assoc. chief staff/edn., 1995—; assoc. prof. Sch. Medicine U. Pitts., 1989—. Editor: Research Fraud, 1990; contbr. articles to profl. jours. Mem. APA, Pa. Psychol. Assn., Am. Assn. Preventive Psychology. Office: VA Medical Ctr University Dr # 11B Pittsburgh PA 15240

MILLER, DONALD ANGUS, physician assistant; b. Buffalo, Nov. 12, 1941; s. Ralph Harold Miller and Catherine (Montgomery) McFate; m. Shirley Anne Swanson, Mar. 14, 1970; children: Breyana Gwendolyn, Erik Swanson. BA in English and Psychology, So. Ill. U., 1972; BS in Health Scis., SUNY at Stony Brook, 1974; postgrad., Ball State U., 1988-90. Cert. physician asst. Physician asst. Algoma (Wis.) Clinic, 1974-75; sr. field physician asst. supr. Aleyeska Pipeline Co., Fairbanks, Alaska, 1975-76; regional clin. coord. NHSC, Region V, USPHS, Chgo., 1976-80; CWO, OIC, battalion aid sta. 123 Field Artillery Army Nat. Guard, Rock Island, Ill., 1976-79; capt., family practice staff physician asst. USAF Residency Program, Eglin AFB, Fla., 1980-84; capt., officer in clin. svc. Hessisch-Oldendorf Med. Sta., Hessisch-Oldendorf, Germany, 1984-87; maj., asst. chief profl. svc. 305th Strategic Clinic, Grissom AFB, Ind., 1987-90; majr., asst. chief clin. svc. 17th Med. Squadron, Goodfellow AFB, Tex., 1990-94; physician asst., clinic dir. Allison (Iowa) Med. Ctr., 1994—; physician asst. rep. Nat. Task Force for Mid-Level Practitioners, USPHS, Bethesda, Md., 1978-80; founder, 1st pres. Pub. Health Svc. Acad. of Physician Assts., Chgo., 1978-80. Author: NP/PA Patient Care Guidelines, 1978; mng. editor newspaper Chgo. Loopline News, 1967-69; editor-in-chief mag. Garland Ct. Rev., 1967-69, Squadron Officer Sch. Classbook, 1981. Bd. dirs. Okaloosa County Concert Bd., 1981-84, Adult Day Care Inc., 1991-94; organizer recycling San Angelo (Tex.) Friends of the Environment, 1991-94; pres., organizer Tour de Clinics 100 Mile Ann. Bike Ride, San Angelo, 1992-94; founder Butler County (Iowa) Germanfest, 1994-95. Decorated Army Commendation medal, Meritorious Svc. medal, Air Force Commendation medal with oak leaf cluster; recipient Humanitarian Svc. award USAF, 1983, Chief Biomed. Scientist award, 1989, others. Fellow Am. Acad. Physician Assts. (del. 1976-79, 91-92, 95-96, reference com.), Iowa Physician Asst. Soc. (chief del. 1995-96), Air force Soc. of Physician Assts. (teller comml. del. 1980-84); mem. Lions Club Internat., Allison Comml. Club (chmn. 1994-96). Home: 20382 Spring Ave Clarksville IA 50619 Office: Allison Med Ctr PO Box 623 502 Locust St Allison IA 50602

MILLER, DONALD NEAL, psychologist; b. N.Y.C., July 15, 1944; s. Philip B. and Yetta (Berkman) M.; m. Regina Kahn, Nov. 23, 1967; 1 child, Perchik Solomon. AAS in Engring. Sci., Westchester Community Coll., 1964; BA in Econs., U. Kans., 1970, MA in Human Devel., 1972, PhD in Child and Devel. Psycholgy, 1974. Psychologist Conn. Dept. Mental Retardation/Southbury Tng. Sch., Southbury, 1974-76; psychologist, dir. psychology Conn. Dept. Mental Retardation/North Cen. Regional Ctr., Bloomfield, 1976-78; psychologist, dir. clin. svcs. Conn. Dept. Mental Retardation/N. Cen. Reg. Ctr., Bloomfield, 1978-86, Conn. Dept. Mental Retardation Region 2, Newington, 1986-87; psychologist, dir. staff devel. Conn. Dept. Mental Retardation Region 2, Farmington, 1987-91; psychologist, dir. mgmt. info. systems Conn. Dept. Mental Retardation/N. Cen. Region, Farmington, 1991—. Sgt. USAF, 1965-69. Mem. Am. Assn. on Mental Retardation (sec.-treas. northeast region 1990—, treas. Conn. chpt. 1982—, pres. Conn. chpt. 1979-81), Probus Club of Hartford (pres. 1985-86), Emmanuel Synagogue (pres. 1994-96). Office: Dept Mental Retardation/N Cen Region 270 Farmington Ave Ste 245 Farmington CT 06032-1909

MILLER, DWIGHT RICHARD, cosmetologist, corporate executive, hair designer; b. Johnstown, Pa., Jan. 24, 1943. Grad., Comer & Doran Sch., San Diego; DSci. (hon.), London Inst. for Applied Rsch., 1973. Cert. aromatherapist; lic. cosmetologist., instr.; Brit. Mastercraftsman. Styles dir. Marinello-Comer, Hollywood, Calif., 1965-67; expert Pivot Point Internat., Chgo., 1967-68; styles dir. Lapins, L.A., 1969; dir. Redken, L.A., 1970, Vidal Sassoon, London, 1971-74; world amb. Pivot Point, New Zealand and Australia, 1974-75; internat. artistic dir. Pivot Point, Chgo., 1975-78; internat. dir., co-founder Hair Artists Inst. & Registry, 1978-81; internat. artistic dir. Zotos Internat., Darien, Conn., 1981-87, Matrix Essentials, Inc., Solon, Ohio, 1987-92; bd. dirs., v.p. creative, internat. artistic dir. Anasazi Exclusive Salon Products, Inc., Dubuque, Iowa, 1992—; judge hairdressing competitions including Norwegian Masters, Australian Nat. Championships; pres. Intercrimpers, London, 1974-75. Author: Sculptic Cutting Pivot Point 75, Prismatics, 1983; prod., dir. 15 documentaries, numerous tech. and industry videos; contbr. articles, photographs to popular mags.; developer several profl. product lines including Vidal Sassoon-London, Design Freedom, Bain de Terre, Ultra Bond, Vavoom!, Systeme Biolage, Anasazi. With USMC, 1960-64. Named Artistic Dir. Yr. Am. Salon mag.; presented with Order of White Elephant, 1976; recipient London Gold Cup for Best Presentation London Beauty Festival, 1982, Dr. Everett G. McDonough award for Excellence in Permanent Waving, World Master award Art and Fashion Group, 1992. Mem. Cercle des Arts et Techniques de la Coiffure, Intercoiffure, Haute Coiffure Franchaise, Soc. Cosmetic Chemists, Hair Artists Great Britain, Internat. Assn. Trichogists, Nat. Cosmetologists Assn. (HairAmerica), Am. Soc. Phytotherapy and Aromatherapy, HairChicago (hon.), Art and Fashion Group (pres. 1993), 'Dressers MC (pres. 1990—), London's Alternative Hair Club (patron). Address: 13900 Watt Rd Novelty OH 44072-9741

MILLER, EDWARD DORING, JR., anesthesiologist; b. Rochester, N.Y., Feb. 1, 1943; s. Edward D. and Natalie (Sidam) M.; m. Leslie Coombs, June 15, 1968 (dec. Apr. 1987); children: Sara Davenport, Katherine Coombs; m. Lynne Perkins, Apr. 30, 1988. AB, Ohio Wesleyan U., 1964; MD, U. Rochester, 1968. Diplomate Am. Bd. Anesthesiology, Am. Coll. Anesthesiology; cert. critical care medicine. Surg. intern University Hosp., Boston, 1968-69; anesthesia resident Peter Bent Brigham Hosp., Boston, 1969-71; fellow in physiology Harvard Med. Sch., Boston, 1971-73; dir. anesthesia research Brooke Army Med. Ctr., Ft. Sam Houston, Tex., 1973-75; asst. prof. anesthesiology U. Va. Med. Ctr., Charlottesville, Va., 1975-79, assoc. prof. anesthesiology, 1979-82, prof. anesthesiology, 1982-83, prof. anesthesiology, surgery, 1983-86; E.M. Papper prof. anesthesiology, chmn. dept. Columbia U. Coll. Physicians and Surgeons, N.Y.C., 1986-94; Mark C. Rogers prof., chmn. dept. anesthesiology Johns Hopkins U., Balt., 1994—, interim dean med. faculty, v.p. medicine Sch. Medicine, 1996—; sr. scientist physiology, pharmacology Hosp. Necker, Paris, 1981-82; examiner Am. Bd. Anesthesiology; v.p. clin. faculty U. Va., 1983-85, pres. 1985-86. Editor Anesthesia and Analgesia, 1982-92; contbr. numerous articles to profl. jours. Pres. Barracks-Rugby-Preston Neighborhoods, Va., 1977-79; vestry Christ Episc. Ch., Va., 1985-86. Served to maj. M.C., U.S. Army, 1973-75. Recipient Research Career Devel. award Nat. Inst. Gen. Med. Scis., 1978-83; NIH grantee, 1977-87, Inst. Nat. de la Sante et de la Recherche Medicale grantee, 1981-82. Mem. Assn. U. Anesthetists (sec. 1984-87), Am. Soc. Anesthesiologists, Am. Physiol. Soc., Internat. Anesthesia Research Soc. (trustee 1988—), Soc. Critical Care Medicine, Soc. Cardiovascular Anesthesiologists, Assn. Univ. Anesthesiologists (pres. 1990-92), Found. for Anesthesia Edn. and Rsch. (bd. dirs. 1986—), Up Med. Bd. Presbyn. Hosp. Home: 15 Meadow Rd Baltimore MD 21212-1022 Office: Johns Hopkins U Sch Med Blalock #1415 600 N Wolfe St Baltimore MD 21287-4965

MILLER, EDWARD GODFREY, JR., biomedical sciences educator, researcher; b. Pitts., Feb. 16, 1941; s. Edward G. and Helen J. (Yuhas) M.; m. Brenda Dianne Halyard, Sept. 5, 1964; 1 child, Elizabeth Venia. BS in Chemistry, U. Tex., 1963, PhD in Biochemistry, 1969. Postdoctoral U. Wis., Madison, 1969-72; asst. prof. dept. biochemistry Baylor Coll. Dentistry, Dallas, 1972-75, assoc. prof. dept. biochemistry, 1975-88, prof., chair dept. biochemistry, 1988-92, prof. dept. biomed. scis., 1992—. Contbg. author: ADP-Ribosylation of Proteins, 1985, ADP-Ribose Transfer Reactions. Mechanisms and Biological Significance, 1989, 14th International Scientific Colloquium on Coffee, 1992, 15th International Scientific Colloquium on Coffee, 1993, Food Phytochemicals for Cancer Prevention I. Fruits and Vegetables, 1994. Precinct chair Dem. Party, Richardson, Tex., 1978-82. Mem. Am. Inst. Nutrition, Am. Soc. Cell Biology, Am. Chem. Soc., Am. Assn. Dental Rsch., Soc. Exptl. Biology and Medicine, Sigma Xi, Phi Beta Kappa, Phi Lambda Upsilon. Presbyterian. Home: 1820 Blake Dr Richardson TX 75081-2656 Office: Baylor Coll Dentistry 3302 Gaston Ave Dallas TX 75246-2013

MILLER, EDWARD HENDERSON, orthopaedic surgeon; b. Ft. Worth, Sept. 16, 1935; s. Harry Jackson and Mary Elizabeth (Henderson) M.; m. Carol Kay Roach, Sept. 7, 1957; children: Pamela, Steven, Edward, Matthew. BSME, Purdue U., 1957; MD, U. Cin., 1961. Intern in surgery U. Calif., San Francisco, 1961-62, fellow, 1964-65, resident, 1965-68; asst. prof. surgery U. Cin., 1968-70, assoc. prof., 1971-76, prof., dir. dept. orthopaedic surgery, 1976-81; assoc. orthopaedic surgeon Orthopaedic Cons. of Cin., 1981—; assoc. dir. Bone and Joint Inst. of The Christ Hosp., Cin., 1985—; mem. attending staff Christian R. Holmes div. U. Hosp. U. Cin. Med. Ctr., The Children's Hosp. Med. Ctr., Cin., Deaconess Hosp.; cons. staff The Shriners Hosp. Cin. Burn Unit, The Good Samaritan Hosp.; mem. courtesy staff Bethesda Base Hosp., Bethesda North Hosp., Our Lady of Mercy Hosp.; various com. and adminstrv. positions with The Christ Hosp., U. Cin., Christian R. Holmes Hosp.; vis. prof. orthopaedic surgery U. Louisville, 1971, Howard U., Washington, 1971, U. Mexico City and Shriner's Crippled Children's Hosp., Mexico City, 1971; vis. prof. traumatology Munich Inst. of Tech. Med. Sch., 1972; vis. prof. Coll. Medicine and Dentistry of N.J., 1979, Orthopaedic Residents' Program, Memphis, 1982, Copenhagen Orthopaedic Assn.; Leroy Abbott lectr. U. Calif. San Francisco, 1980; guest faculty mem. U. Wash., 1982, Lenzerheide, Switzerland, 1983-87; guest lectr. Norwegian Soc. Surgery of Rheumatoid Arthritis; vis. lectr. U. Umea, Sweden, 1988; vis. surgeon Örnsköldsvik (Sweden) Regional Hosp.; presenter and speaker numerous seminars, confs., etc. to profl. orgns., hosps. and univs. Editor orthopaedic words Gould Medical Dictionary, 4th edit.; contbr. numerous articles to profl. jours. Capt. USAFR, 1962-64, col., 1964—. Fellow Am. Bd. Orthopaedic Surgery (examiner 1984-88), Am. Acad. Orthopaedic Surgeons (chmn. region 6 admissions com. 1980); mem. AMA, Ohio Med. Assn., Cin. Med. Assn., Ohio Orthopaedic Soc. (exec. com. 1973-88, sec., treas. 1986-87, pres.-elect 1987—), Cin. Orthopaedic Soc. (sec. 1974-75, pres. 1976-77), Tri-State Orthopaedic Soc., Clin. Orthopaedic Soc. (chmn. membership com. 1981-82, gen. chmn. 1988), Am. Orthopaedic Assn., Am. Soc. for Surgery of Trauma, ASTME, Am. Soc. for Metals, Orthopaedic Research Soc., LeRoy Abbott Orthopaedic Soc., Russell Hibbs Orthopaedic Soc., Societé Internationale de Chirurgie Orthopaedique et de Traumatologie. Clubs: Zanesfield Rod and Gun; Sugar Hill Gun (Cin.). Lodges: Masons, Shriners. Home: 12337 Bluff Rd N Traverse City MI 49686-8535 Office: Orthopedic Cons of Cin Inc 111 Wellington Pl Cincinnati OH 45219-1758

MILLER, ERIC RANDALL, optometrist; b. Wilmington, Del., June 29, 1970; s. Warren Keene and Ruth Elaine (Hummel) M. BS, Pa. Coll. Optometry, 1992, OD, 1995; BA, W.Va. U., 1993. Resident in primary care/ocular disease Eye Inst., Phila., 1995-96. Mem. Am. Optometric Assn., Pa. Optometric Assn., Am. Acad. Optometry.

MILLER, GARY EVAN, psychiatrist, mental health services administrator; b. Cleve., Aug. 19, 1935; s. Henry M. and Mollie (Price) M.; m. Karen Ann Marie Barrett, Sept. 16, 1972; children: Anna Charis, Rebecca Elizabeth. MD, U. Tex., Galveston, 1960. Diplomate in psychiatry, addiction psychiatry, and geriatric psychiatry Am. Bd. Psychiatry and Neurology. Intern Montefiore Hosp., N.Y.C., 1960-61; resident in psychiatry Univ. Hosps. Cleve., 1961-62, Austin (Tex.) State Hosp., 1963-65; dep. commr. mental health services Tex. Dept. Mental Health and Mental Retardation, 1967-70; dir. Rio Grande State Center for Mental Health and Mental Retardation, Tex. Dept. Mental Health, Harlingen, 1966-67; asst. commr., dir. Rochester regional office N.Y. State Dept. Mental Hygiene, 1970-72; clin. asst. prof. psychiatry U. Rochester Sch. Medicine and Dentistry, 1970-72; asst. clin. prof. psychiatry SUNY, Buffalo, 1970-72; cons. mental health Ga. Dept. Human Resources, Atlanta, 1972; dir. div. mental health Ga. Dept. Human Resources, 1972-74; clin. prof. psychiatry Emory U. Sch. Medicine, Atlanta, 1972-74; vice chmn. Ga. State Planning and Adv. Council for Devel. Disabilities Services and Constrn., 1972-73; cons. mental health services orgn. and adminstrn., 1974-76; dir. mental health and devel. services State of N.H. Concord, 1976-82; commr. Tex. Dept. Mental Health and Mental Retardation Austin, 1982-88; clin. prof. psychiatry U. Tex. Health Sci. Ctr., Houston; adj. assoc. prof. psychiatry U. Tex. Health Sci. Ctr., San Antonio, 1984-95; dir. profl. svcs. HCA Gulf Pines Hosp., Houston, 1988-94, chief of staff, 1993; clin. dir. adult psychiatry Cypress Creek Hosp., Houston, 1994—, pres. med. staff, 1996; assoc. clin. psychiatry Post Oak Psychiatry Assocs., Houston, 1988-90; pres. Alternative Svcs. Network, Houston, 1990—; clin. dir. adult psychiatry Cypress Creek Hosp., Houston, 1994—, pres.-elect med. staff, 1995, pres., 1996—; dir. state alcoholism program in Ga., 1972-74, also, South Tex. region, 1966-67; mem. faculty U. S.C. Sch. Alcohol and Drug Studies, 1972-76; bd. dirs. nat. patient rights policy research project NIMH, 1981; Bd. dirs. Genessee Regional Health Planning Council, Rochester, 1970-72. Contbr. articles to profl. jours. Served as capt. M.C., U.S. Army, 1962-63. Recipient Cert. of Recognition, Ga. Psychol.

Assn., 1973. Fellow Am. Psychiat. Assn. (cert. in adminstrv. psychiatry 1983); mem. AMA, Am. Soc. Addiction Medicine (cert. alcoholism and other drug dependencies 1993), N.H. Psychiat. Soc. (pres. 1981-82), Nat. Assn. State Mental Health Program Dirs. (bd. dirs. 1984-88, sec. 1986-88), N.H. Med. Soc., Am. Acad. Psychiatry and the Law, Am. Assn. Psychiat. Adminstrs. (pres. Tex. chpt.), Tex. Med. Assn., Tex. Soc. Psychiat. Physicians, Mental Health Assn. Houston and Harris County (bd. dirs. 1989-95, v.p. advocacy 1990-95), Alpha Omega Alpha. Home: 5314 Westminister Ct Houston TX 77069-3338 Office: 530 Wells Fargo Dr Ste 110 Houston TX 77090-4026

MILLER, GEORGE ARMITAGE, psychologist, educator; b. Charleston, W.Va., Feb. 3, 1920; s. George E. and Florence (Armitage) M.; m. Katherine James, Nov. 29, 1939; children: Nancy, Donnally James. BA, U. Ala., 1940, MA, 1941; AM, Harvard U., 1944, PhD, 1946; Doctorat honoris causa, U. Louvain, 1976; D Social Sci. (hon.), Yale U., 1979; DSc honoris causa, Columbia U., 1980; DSc (hon.), U. Sussex, 1984, New Sch. Social Rsch., 1993; LittD (hon.), Charleston U., 1992. Instr. psychology U. Ala., 1941-43; research fellow Harvard Psycho-Acoustic Lab., 1944-48; asst. prof. psychology Harvard U., 1948-51, assoc. prof., 1955-58, prof., 1958-68, chmn. dept psychology, 1964-67, co-dir. Ctr. for Cognitive Studies, 1960-67; prof. Rockefeller U., N.Y.C., 1968-79; adj. prof. Rockefeller U., 1979-82; prof. psychology Princeton U., 1979-90, James S. McDonnell Disting. Univ. prof. psychology, 1982-90, James S. McDonnell Disting. Univ. prof. psychology emeritus, 1990—, program dir. McDonnell-Pew Program in Cognitive Neurosci., 1989-94; assoc. prof. MIT, 1951-55; vis. Inst. for Advanced Study, Princeton, 1972-76, 82-83, mem., 1950, 70-72; vis. prof. Rockefeller U., 1967-68; vis. prof. MIT, 1976-79, group leader Lincoln Lab., 1953-55; fellow Ctr. Advanced Study in Behavioral Scis., Stanford U., 1958-59; Fulbright research prof. Oxford (Eng.) U., 1963-64; Sesquicentennial prof. U. Ala., 1981. Author: Language and Communication, 1951, (with Galanter and Pribram) Plans and the Structure of Behavior, 1960, Psychology, 1962, (with Johnson-Laird) Language and Perception, 1976, Spontaneous Apprentices, 1977, Language and Speech, 1981, The Science of Words, 1991; editor Psychol. Bulletin, 1981-82. Recipient Disting. Service award Am. Speech and Hearing Assn., 1976, award in behavioral scis. N.Y. Acad. Scis., 1982, Hermann von Helmholtz award Cognitive Neurosci. Inst., 1989, Nat. Medal Sci. NSF, 1991, Gold Medal Am. Psychological Found. 1990, Nat. Medal of Sci. 1991, Louis E. Levy medal Franklin Inst., 1991; Guggenheim fellow, 1986, William James fellow Am. Psychological Soc., 1989; Fondation Fyssen Priz Internat. for cognitive sci., 1992. Fellow Brit. Psychol. Assn. (hon.); mem. NAS, AAAS (chmn. sect. J 1981), Am. Psychol. Assn. (pres. 1968-69, Disting. Scientific Contbn. award 1963, William James Book award divsn. gen. psychology 1993), Eastern Psychol. Assn. (pres. 1961-62), Acoustical Soc. Am., Linguistic Soc. Am., Am. Statis. Assn., Am. Philos. Soc., Am. Physiol. Soc., Psychometric Soc., Soc. Exptl. Psychologists (Warren medal 1972), Am. Acad. Arts and Scis., Psychonomic Soc., Royal Netherlands Acad. Arts and Scis. (fgn.), Sigma Xi. Home: 753 Prospect Ave Princeton NJ 08540-4080 Office: Princeton Univ Dept Psychology Green Hall Princeton NJ 08544

MILLER, GEORGE GIVENS, cardiologist; b. Snyder, Tex., Aug. 30, 1958; s. Frank Maynor and Carol Dean (Westbrook) M.; m. Lisan Jean Faust, June 7, 1986; children: Geroge Givens II, Austin Daniel. BS in Zoology, Tex. A&M U., 1980; MD, U. Tex. Med. Sch., Houston, 1984. Diplomate Am. Bd. Internal Medicine, Am. Bd. Cardiovascular Diseases. Internal medicine resident U. Fla., Gainesville, 1984-87; cardiology fellow U. Tex. Med. Sch., Houston, 1990-93; internat. cardiology fellow William Beaumont Hosp., Royal Oak, Mich., 1993-94; pvt. practice cardiologist Fayetteville, Ark., 1994—; med. dir. Sisters of Charity Indigent Health Care Clinic, St. Elizabeth's Hosp., Beaumont, Tex., 1987-90. Recipient Joe G. Wood award for excellence in medicine, 1993. Fellow Am. Coll. Cardiology; mem. AMA, ACP. Home: 2497 E Oaks Dr Fayetteville AR 72703 Office: Fayetteville Diagnostic Clinic 3344 N Futrall Fayetteville AR 72703

MILLER, GERALD CECIL, immunologist, laboratory administrator, educator; b. Wichita, Kans., Dec. 20, 1944; s. Cecil William and Mildred Ester (Carlisle) M.; m. Josephine Buller, June 1, 1968; children: Nathan Gerald, Natalie Buller. BA, Emporia (Kans.) State U., 1967, MS, 1969; PhD, Kans. State U., 1972. Diplomate Am. Bd. Med. Lab. Immunology. Rsch. fellow Mayo Med. Sch. and Mayo Found., Rochester, Minn., 1972-75; sr. scientist Health Cen. Rsch. Found., Mpls., 1975-77; grad. teaching and rsch. asst. Emporia State U., 1967-69; grad. teaching and rsch. asst. Kans. State U., Manhattan, 1969-70, NIH predoctoral fellow, 1970-72; ast. prof. microbiology and immunology Oral Roberts U. Sch. Medicine, Tulsa, 1977-82; owner, dir. Immuno-Diagnostics Lab. Inc., Tulsa, 1982-94; adj. assoc. prof. Oral Roberts U. Sch. Medicine, Tulsa, 1986-90; mem. ancillary med. staff Children's Med. Ctr., Tulsa, 1979—; chief immunology, microbiology and flow cytometry Regional Med. Lab., Tulsa, 1994—; clin. lab. immunologist Pathology Lab. Assocs., Tulsa, 1994—; adj. asst. prof. U. Okla. Med. Coll., Tulsa, 1986—. Mem. editl. bd. Jour. Clin. Lab. Analysis; contbr. articles and abstracts to sci. jours. Trustee 1st United Meth. Ch., 1994—, mem. adminstrv. bd., 1978—; bd. dirs. Brush Creek Boys Ranch, 1996—; cert. ofcl. USA Track and Field, 1986—. Named Outstanding Faculty Mem., Oral Roberts U. Sch. Medicine, 1982. Mem. AAAS, Am. Soc. Microbiology, Assn. Med. Lab. Immunologists (treas.-elect), Clin. Immunology Soc., N.Y. Acad. Scis., Sigma Xi. Office: Regional Med Lab 1923 S Utica Ave Tulsa OK 74104-6520

MILLER, G(ERSON) H(ARRY), research institute director, mathematician, computer scientist, chemist; b. Phila., Mar. 2, 1924; m. Mary Alexa Heath, Jan. 28, 1961; children: Byron, Alexandra. BA, Pomona Coll., 1949; MEd in Counseling and Pers., Temple U., 1951; PhD. in Ednl. Psychology, U. So. Calif., 1957; MS in Math., U. Ill., 1982, postgrad., 1963-65. Jr. high sch. and jr. coll. instr. math. L.A. Sch. Dist., 1953-57; assoc. prof. Western Ill. U., Macomb, 1957-60; prof. Towson State U., Balt., Md., 1960-61; prof. math. and edn. Parsons Coll., Fairfield, Iowa, 1961-65; prof. Tenn. Technol. U., Cookeville, 1966-89; prof. math. and computer sci. Edinboro (Pa.) U., 1968-71, 81-89, asst. dir. Institutional Rsch., 1972-80; dir. Studies On Smoking, Inc and SOS Stop Smoking Clinic, Edinboro, 1972—; spkr. state, nat. and internat. profl. meetings; condr. seminars on smoking and health London, Fed. Republic Germany, Alaska, New Brunswick, N.J., Chgo., Costa Rica; dir. Nat. Study Math. Requirements for Scientists and Engrs., 1966-73. Contbr. numerous articles to profl. jours. Pres. Edinboro YMCA, 1972-83; bd. dirs. Common Cause, Harrisburg, Pa., 1975-80; Sgt. USAAF, 1943-46, PTO. Grantee U.S. Office Edn., 1968, 70, No Other World, 1973, NAS, 1980, ITT Life Ins. Corp., 1983, Erie Community Found., 1987. Fellow Am. Inst. Chemists (cert. profl. chemist); mem. AAAS, APHA, Am. Assn. World Health, Am. Chem. Soc., Am. Soc. Engring. Edn., Internat. Assn. Pure and Applied Chemists, Internat. Soc. for Preventive Oncology, Math. Assn. Am., Am. Diabetes Assn., Nat. Coun. Tchrs. Math., Sch. Sci. and Math. Assn., N.Y. Acad. Scis. (hon.), Acad. Sr. Profls. (hon.). Home and Office: Studies on Smoking Inc 125 High St Edinboro PA 16412-2552 also: 25 Crescent Pl S Saint Petersburg FL 33711

MILLER, GLENN HOWARD, psychiatrist, educator; b. Chgo., Jan. 8, 1942; s. Hymen D. and Mildred Miller; m. Michele Paula Prochep, Dec. 26, 1964; children: Erika Julie, Jason Adam. MD, U. Chgo., 1966; cert. in Psychiatry, Yale U., 1970; certs. in Adult and Child Psychoanalysis, Wash. Psychoanalytic Inst., 1984. Diplomate Am. Bd. Psychiatry and Neurology. Intern Jackson Meml. Hosp., 1966-67; resident in psychiatry Yale U., New Haven, Conn., 1967-70; pvt. practice Bethesda, Md., 1973—; mem. staff George Washington U. Hosp., Washington; clin. prof. psychiatry George Washington U., 1974—; mem. faculty Washington Psychoanalytic Inst., 1984—, Washington Sch. Psychiatry, 1978—; adj. prof. law Georgetown U., Washington, 1981—; cons. Bethesda Naval Hosp., 1976—, Walter Reed Army Hosp., 1979—, Forensic Programs Div. St. Elizabeths Hosp., 1973—; asst. clin. prof. psychiatry Uniformed Svcs. U. Health Scis., 1985—. Contbr. numerous articles profl. jours.; frequent speaker various orgs. Major U.S. Army, 1970-73. Recipient fellowship U. Chgo., 1965, Yale U., 1967-70. Fellow Am. Psychiat. Assn.; mem. Washington Psychiat. Assn., Am. Acad. Psychiatry and the Law, Washington Coun. Child Psychiatry, Washington Psychoanalytic Soc., Am. Acad. Child Psychiatry. Home and Office: 8213 Tomlinson Ave Bethesda MD 20817-4413

MILLER, HAROLD I., surgeon; b. Boston, Mar. 25, 1916; s. Abraham and Annie Catherine (Knopf) M.; m. Maida Rosenberg, Jan. 26, 1947; children: Jonathan L., Jacqueline A., Jeremy M. AB, Harvard U., 1937; MD, Boston U., 1941. Diplomate Am. Bd. Surgery. Faculty Boston U. Sch. Medicine, 1946—, assoc. clin. prof. surgery. Contbr. articles to profl. jours. Capt. M.C. U.S. Army, 1942-46. Fellow ACS; mem. Boston Surg. Soc., Internat. Cardiovascular Soc. Home: 21 Princeton Rd Chestnut Hill MA 02167 Office: 720 Harrison Ave Ste 202 Boston MA 02118-2334

MILLER, HARRY CHARLES, JR., physician, urologist, educator; b. Ridgewood, N.J., Sept. 22, 1928; s. Harry Charles and Ruth G (McDermott) M.; m. Kari L. Palmer, June 14, 1969; children: Harry C., Carolynn A., Barbara J., Janet E., Jennifer T., Sandra L. AB, Amherst Coll., 1950; MD, Yale U., 1954. Intern Duke U. Hosp., Durham, N.C., 1954-55; resident U. Rochester Med. Ctr., N.Y., 1959-62; pvt. practice specializing in urology Washington, 1973—; asst. prof. urology U. Rochester Health Sci. Ctr., 1962-71; assoc. prof. U. Okla. Health Sci. Ctr., Oklahoma City, 1971-73; prof., chmn. dept. urology George Washington U. Med. Ctr., Washington, 1973—. Served with U.S. Army, 1955-57. Mem. AMA, ACS, Am. urol. Assn. (exec. com., pres. Mid-Atlantic sect., bd. dirs. 1989—), Am. Acad. Pediat., Societe Internationale d'Urologie, Soc. Pediat. Urology, Soc. Univ. Urologists, Am. Assn. Clin. Urologists (sec.-treas., pres.-elect., pres. 1993-94), Beekeepers Assn. No. Va. (treas. 1976-79), Great Falls Grange, River Bend Golf and Country Club, Urology Polit. Action Com. (treas. 1992—). Office: George Washington U Med Ctr 2150 Pennsylvania Ave NW Washington DC 20037-2396*

MILLER, HARRY JOHNSON, hematology educator, oncologist; b. Miles City, Mont., Feb. 19, 1926; s. Harry G. and Harriet R. (Wildish) M.; m. Lucia Taylor, Dec. 31, 1947; children: Sally, Elizabeth, Katherine, Patricia, Blair. BS, Northwestern U., 1950, MD, 1952. Diplomate Am. Bd. Internal Medicine Hematology and Med. Oncology. Instr. Med. Sch. Northwestern U., Chgo., 1959-62, assoc. Med. Sch., 1962-70, asst. prof. Med. Sch., 1970-76, assoc. prof. Med. Sch., 1976-94; attending physician Evanston (Ill.) Hosp., 1959—, head hematology div., 1965-94, pres. profl. staff, 1974-75. Contbr.: (book) Fundamentals of Cancer Management, 1982. Chmn. bd. Unitarian Ch., Evanston, 1976; pres. bd. Hospice of the North Shore, Evanston, 1988-90. Sgt. USAAF, 1944-46. Named Physician of the Yr., Evanston Hosp., 1978, Vol. of the Yr., Northshore mag., 1990. Recipient Henry P. Russe Citation for Exemplary Compassion in Healthcare, Inst. of Med. of Chicago, 1993. Fellow ACP; mem. Am. Soc. Hematology, Am. Fedn. Clin. Rsch., Am. Soc. Clin. Oncology, Internat. Soc. Hematology, Eastern Coop. Oncology Group.

MILLER, HEIDI BETH, physician assistant; b. Pitts., Jan. 12, 1961; d. Robert Leroy and Marjorie Sloan (Shaner) M. BS in Med. Sci., Alderson-Broaddus Coll., 1983. Cert. physician asst. Physician asst. Dr. Bakshy Chhibber, Pt. Pleasant, W.Va., 1983-84; emergency medicine/physician asst. resident L.A. Coll.-U. So. Calif. Med. Ctr., 1984-85; physician asst. Yale New Haven Hosp., 1985-87, Rochester (N.Y.) Gen. Hosp., 1987—; lectr. ACLS Am. Heart Assn., Rochester, 1988—. Fellow Am. Acad. Physician Assts.; mem. Soc. Emergency Medicine Physician Assts. (bd. dirs. 1988—), Red Blanket Soc., N.Y. State Soc. Physician Assts., Rochester Soc. Physician Assts., Rochester Gen. Hosp. Soc. Physician Assts., Yale Soc. Physician Assts., Conn. Acad. Physician Assts. (chmn. pub. edn. com. 1986-87), Commn. of 100s Alumni. Lutheran. Office: Rochester Gen Hosp 1425 Portland Ave Rochester NY 14621-3001

MILLER, HENRY ISAAC, biotechnology specialist, federal official; b. Phila., July 1, 1947; s. Milton and Sadie (Feldman) M.; m. Geraldine Pearl Goldstein, Dec. 27, 1970 (div.). BSc, MIT, 1969; MS, MD, U. Calif., San Diego, 1975. Clin. fellow in medicine Harvard U. Med. Sch., Boston, 1975-77; rsch. assoc. NIH, Bethesda, Md., 1977-79; med. officer Ctr. for Drugs and Biologics FDA, Rockville, Md., 1979-83, Office of Biologics FDA, Rockville, 1983-85; spl. asst to FDA commr. FDA, Rockville, 1985-89, dir. office of biotech., 1989-94; Wesson fellow sci. philosophy and pub. policy Hoover Inst., 1994-96, sr. rsch. fellow, 1996—; cons. prof. Stanford U., 1994—; mem. Def. Tech. Forecast Panel, CIA, Langley, Va., 1983, Nat. Biotech. Policy Bd., Bethesda, Md., 1989—; FDA rep. on NIH/DNA Adv. Com., 1980—; editorial bd. Bio Essays, 1984-89, Advanced Drug Delivery Revs., 1987—, Clin. Rsch. Practices and Drug Regulatory Affairs, 1990—, Human Gene Therapy, 1991. Editor: Insulins, Growth Hormones and DNA Technology, 1981; contbr. articles to Nature, Sci., Jour. Biol. Chemistry, Jour. AMA, Wall St. Jour. Recipient award for Internat. Reg. activities, Assn. of Biotech. Cos., 1988. Mem. AAAS, Am. Soc. for Clin. Pharmacology and Therapeutics, N.Y. Acad. Sci. Office: Hoover Inst Stanford U Stanford CA 94305-6010

MILLER, HOWARD, physician; b. Bklyn., July 3, 1928; s. Samuel Carl and Cele (Goldstein) M.; m. Mary Caroline Thrift, May 8, 1967; children: Henry Carl, Terri Ann, Steven Wayne, Cynthia Kay. BA, Alfred (N.Y.) U., 1949; MA, Washington U., St. Louis, 1950; MD, SUNY, Bklyn., 1955. Intern and resident in internal medicine various hosps., Denver, 1955-58; pvt. practice internal medicine St. Thomas More Hosp., Canon City, Colo., 1960-67, Northridge (Calif.) Hosp., 1969-76; assoc. dir. clin. investigation Riker Labs., Inc., 1967-69, med. cons., 1967-76; dir. clin. rsch. Riker Labs., Inc., Brussels, St. Paul, 1976-78, Mead Johnson & Co., Evansville, Ind., 1978-81; dir. to v.p. med. rsch. Sandoz Pharm. Corp., E. Hanover, N.J., 1981-90; sr. v.p. R & D Family Health Internat., Durham, N.C., 1990-94, ret., 1994. Contbr. articles to profl. jours. Mem. rev. com. N.J. Heart Assn., Edison, 1986. Capt. U.S. Army, 1958-60. Mem. AMA, ACP, Am. Heart Assn. (hypertension coun.), N.Y. Acad. Scis., Inter-Am. Soc. Hypertension. Home: 275 Lake Point Sanford NC 27330

MILLER, I. GEORGE, physician, educator, researcher; b. Chgo., Apr. 18, 1937; s. Irving George and Florence (Levy) M.; m. Arlette Goldmuntz, Mar. 25, 1962; children: Lisa, John, David. A.B., Harvard U., 1958, M.D., 1962. Intern Univ. Hosp., Western Res, U., Cleve., 1962-63; resident Univ. Hosp., Western Res., U., Cleve., 1963-64; epidemiology intelligence officer Communicable Disease Ctr. USPHS, Atlanta, 1964-66; research fellow in medicine Harvard U. Med. Sch., Boston, 1966-69; asst. prof. pediatrics, epidemiology, biophysics and biochemistry Yale Sch. Medicine, New Haven, 1969-72, J.F. Enders prof., 1979—; mem. exptl. virology study sect. NIH, 1974-77; mem. sci. adv. com. damon Runyon Fund, 1979-85, dir., 1985-94; Leukemia Soc. Am., 1976-81. Contbr. numerous articles, chpts. to profl. publs.; editl. bd. Jour. Virology, 1981-87, Virology, 1982-86. Recipient epidemic Intelligence Service Alumni Assn. prize, 1967; Macy faculty scholar, 1977, Am. Cancer Soc. scholar, 1990; Howard Hughes Med. Inst. investigatorship, 1972-80. Fellow Infectious Diseases Soc. (Squibb award 1982, Enders award 1989); mem. Am. soc. Clin. Investigation, Am. Pediatric Soc., Am. Soc. Virology, Assn. Am. Physicians. Jewish. Home: 95 Alden Ave New Haven CT 06515-2718 Office: Yale U Sch Medicine Pediatrics Infectious Diseases PO Box 208064 New Haven CT 06520-8064*

MILLER, JACK DAVID R., radiologist, physician, educator; b. Johannesburg, South Africa, Apr. 15, 1930; s. Harold Lewis and Inez (Behrman) M.; m. Miriam Sheckter, Dec., 1988. B.Sc., M.B., Ch.B., U. Witwatersrand, Johannesburg, 1956. Diplomate: Am. Bd. Radiology. Intern Coronation Hosp., Johannesburg, 1957-58; resident in radiology Passavant Meml. Hosp., Chgo., 1959-62, Wesley Meml. Hosp., Chgo., 1959-62; fellow in radiology Northwestern U. Med. Sch., 1962-63; chmn. dept. radiology U. Hosp., Edmonton, Alta., Can., 1971-83; clin. prof. radiology U. Alta., 1971—. Fellow Royal Coll. Physicians Can., Am. Coll. Radiology. Office: U Alberta Dept Radiology, Edmonton, AB Canada

MILLER, JACKIE SUE, physician; b. St. Joseph, Mo., Sept. 3, 1965; d. Walter Robert and Marcella Earleen (Sisk) M. BS in Biology, Northeast Mo. State U., Kirksville; DO, Kirksville Coll. Osteo., Medicine. Intern Dallas Meml. Hosp., 1992-93; chief resident Capital Region Med. Ctr., Jefferson City, Mo., 1994-95; family practice physician Gentry County Meml. Hosp., Albany, Mo., 1995—. Mem. Mt. Moriah Bapt. Ch., Berlin, Mo., 1983—. Mem. Am. Osteo. Assn., AMA, Am. Coll. Family Practitioners, Am. Quarter Horse Assn. Home: Rte 1 Box 117 King City MO 64463 Office: Gentry County Meml Hosp 606 N College Albany MO 64402

MILLER, JAMES, surgeon; b. Denver, Aug. 2, 1948; s. Ivan E. and Carolyn Elizabeth (Lunn) M.; m. Sandra Fett, May 25, 1974 (div. Dec. 1978); children: Jennifer, Ashley, Brian. BS, N.E. Mo. State U., 1970; DO, Kirksville Coll. Osteo. Med., 1974. Diplomate Am. Osteo. Bd. Surgery, Am. Bd. Surgery. Surgeon Detroit Surg. Assocs., 1979-82, Parkview Surgeons, Toledo, 1982-88; vascular fellow Ariz. Heart Inst., Phoenix, 1988-89; pvt. practice Phoenix, 1989—. Contbr. articles to profl. jours. Mem. Am. Osteo. Assn. Republican. Home: PO Box 55556 Phoenix AZ 85078-5556 Office: 6707 N 19th Ave Phoenix AZ 85015

MILLER, JAMES MCCALMONT, pediatrician; b. Springfield, Mass., Sept. 25, 1938; s. John Haynes and Josephine (Darrah) M.; m. Jane Rose, July 7, 1975; children: John, Charlotte, Willard. AB, Hamilton Coll., 1960; MD, Cornell U., 1964. Resident U. Colo. Med. Ctr., Denver, 1964-67; staff pediatrician Kaiser Permanente Med. Ctr., Walnut Creek, Calif., 1969-87, chief pediatrician, 1971-82; chief pediatrician Kaiser Permanente Med. Ctr., Pleasanton, Calif., 1982-87; staff pediatrician Appalachian Regional Health, Hazard, Ky., 1987-92, Northwest Pediatric Ctr., Centralia, Wash., 1992—; clin. assoc. U. N.Mex., Albuquerque, 1967-69; instr. U. Calif., San Francisco, 1969-87, U. Ky., Lexington, 1988-92. With U.S. Army, 1967-69. Fellow Am. Acad. Pediatrics; mem. Wash. State Med. Assn. Office: Northwest Pediatric Ctr 908 S Scheuber Rd Centralia WA 98531

MILLER, JANEL HOWELL, psychologist; b. Boone, N.C., May 18, 1947; d. John Estle and Grace Louise (Hemberger) Howell; BA, DePauw U., 1969; postgrad. Rice U., 1969; MA, U. Houston, 1972; PhD, Tex. A&M U., 1979; m. C. Rick Miller, Nov. 24, 1968; children: Kimberly, Brian, Audrey, Rachel. Asso. sch. psychologist Houston Ind. Sch. Dist., 1971-74; research psychologist VA Hosp., Houston, 1972; asso. sch. psychologist Clear Creek Ind. Sch. Dist., Tex., 1974-76; instr. psychology, counseling psychology intern Tex. A. and M. U., 1976-77; clin. psychology intern VA Hosp., Houston, 1977-78; coordinator psychol. services Clear Creek Ind. Sch. Dist., 1978-81, assoc. dir. psychol. services, 1981-82; pvt. practice, Houston, 1982—; faculty U. Houston-Clear Lake, 1984—; adolescent suicide cons., 1984—. DePauw U. Alumni scholar, 1965-69; NIMH fellow U. Houston, 1970-71; lic. clin. psychologist, sch. psychologist, Tex. Mem. APA, Tex. Psychol. Assn., Houston Psychol. Assn. (media rep. 1984-85), Am. Assn. Marriage and Family Therapists, Tex. Assn. Marriage and Family Therapists, Houston Assn. Marriage and Family Therapists, Soc. for Personality Assessment. Home: 806 Walbrook Dr Houston TX 77062-4030 Office: Southpoint Psychol Svcs 11550 Fuqua St Ste 450 Houston TX 77034-4537

MILLER, JASON, psychiatrist, consultant; b. N.Y.C., Dec. 26, 1913; s. Samuel and Cecelia (Keshin) M. BS, Columbia U., 1935; MD, Edinburgh U., Scotland, 1940. Clin. instr. psychiatry NYU, 1952-72; asst. clin. prof. psychiatry Albert Einstein Coll. Medicine, N.Y.C., 1972-74; sr. lectr. Am. Inst. Psychoanalysis, N.Y.C., 1965—; dir. psychiatry Prison Health System, N.Y.C., 1974-83; psychiatric cons. L.I. Coll. Hosp., 1980—. Contbr. articles to profl. jours. Served to sr. asst. surgeon USPHS, 1942-46. Fellow Am. Psychiatric Assn. (life), Am. Acad. Psychoanalysis (life); mem. AMA, N.Y. State Med. Soc., N.Y. County Med. Soc. Club: Atrium, East River Tennis (N.Y.C.). Home: 435 E 65th St Apt 10F New York NY 10021-6972 Office: 1065 Lexington Ave New York NY 10021-3274

MILLER, JEFFREY DAVID, allergist; b. N.Y.C., Oct. 19, 1947; s. Leonard and Ruth Miller; m. Annette Krieger, Dec. 22, 1968; children: Andrew, Amy. BA, CUNY, 1967; MD, NYU, 1971. Diplomate Am. Bd. Allergy and Immunology, Am. Bd. Pediat. Pvt. practice, Danbury, Conn., 1976—. Contbr. articles to med. jours.; patentee in field. Fellow Am. Acad. Allergy, Am. Acad. Pediat.; mem. New Eng. Soc. Allergy, Conn. Allergy Soc. (pres. 1995-96), N.Y. Allergy Soc. (sec. 1992-94). Office: Allergy and Asthma Assocs 107 Newtown Rd Danbury CT 06810

MILLER, JERRY ALLAN, JR., pediatrician; b. Abingdon, Va., May 31, 1951. MD, Med. Coll. Ga., Augusta, 1976. Diplomate Am. Bd. Pediat. Intern in family practice U. Tex. Med. Sch., Houston, 1976-77, resident in pediatrics, 1977-80; with Nat. Health Svc. Corps, Thomson, Ga., 1980-82; pvt. practice Augusta (Ga.) Pediatric Assocs., 1982—; chmn. bd. dirs. Summer Med. Inst., Phila., Augusta, 1992—. Fellow Am. Acad. Pediat.; mem. Phi Beta Kappa, Alpha Omega Alpha. Presbyterian. Office: Augusta Pediatric Assocs PC 1230 Augusta West Pkwy Augusta GA 30909

MILLER, JO CAROLYN DENDY, family and marriage counselor, educator; b. Gorman, Tex., Sept. 16, 1942; d. Leonard Lee and Vera Vertie (Robison) Dendy; m. Douglas Terry Barnes, June 1, 1963 (div. June 1975); children: Douglas Alan, Bradley Jason; m. Walton Sansom Miller, Sept. 19, 1982. BA, Tarleton State U., 1964; MEd, U. North State, 1977; PhD, Tex. Women's U., 1993. Tchr., Mineral Wells (Tex.) High Sch., 1964-65, Weatherford (Tex.) Middle Sch., 1969-74; counselor, instr. psychology Tarrant County Jr. Coll., Hurst, Tex., 1977-82; pvt. practice family and marriage counseling, Dallas, 1982—. Author: (with Velma Walker, Jeannene Ward) Becoming: A Human Relations Workbook, 1981. Mem. ACA, Tex. State Bd. Examiners Profl. Counselors, Tex. State Bd. Marriage and Family Therapists, Tex. Counseling Assn., Am. Mental Health Counselors Assn., North Ctrl. Tex. Counseling Assn., Dallas Symphony Orch. League, Nat. Coun. Family Rels., Tex. Mental Health Counselors Assn., Internat. Assn. for Marriage & Family Counselors. Methodist. Office: Counseling & Consulting of North Dallas 8222 Douglas Ave Ste 777 Dallas TX 75225-5938

MILLER, JON PHILIP, research and development organization executive; b. Moline, Ill., Mar. 30, 1944; s. Clyde Sheldon and Alice Mae (Taes) M.; m. Shirley Ann Hymes, Aug. 21, 1965; children: Melissa, Elizabeth. AB, Augustana Coll., 1966; PhD, St. Louis U., 1970; MBA, Pepperdine U., 1983. Rsch. assoc. to sr. biochemist ICN Pharm., Inc., Irvine, Calif., 1970-72, leader molecular pharmacology group, 1972-73, head molecular pharmacology/drug metabolism dept., 1973-76, dir. biology div., 1975-76; dir. SRI-NCI liaison group SRI Internat. (formally Stanford Rsch. Inst.), Menlo Park, Calif., 1976-78, sr. bioorganic chemist, 1978-80, head medicinal biochemistry program, 1980-84, dir. biotech. rsch. dept., 1982-85, dir. biotech. and biomed. rsch. lab., 1985-92, assoc. dir. life scis. div., 1989-92; dir. bus. devel. Panlabs, Inc., Bothell, Wash., 1992—. Office: Panlabs West Coast Office Ste 205 1191 Chess Dr Foster City CA 94404-1110

MILLER, JON WILLIAM, emergency physician; b. Louisville, Aug. 7, 1949; s. John William and Anne Woodroof (Trosper) M.; m. Sandra Leigh Merzweiler; children: John William, Jeremy Brian. BS in Chemistry, U. Louisville, 1971, MD, 1975; degree in risk mgmt., U. South Fla., 1995. Asst. prof. U. Louisville, 1978-80; asst. prof. U. Ky., Lexington, 1978-80, 90-95, assoc. prof., 1996—; instr., paramedic Rowan County Emergency Med. Svc., Morehead, Ky., 1990—; med. dir. Polk County Rescue and Assocs., Lakeland, Fla., 1984-90; paramedic instr. Louisville/Jefferson County Emergency Med. Svc., Louisville, 1976-80; medico-legal reviewer for various contracts, New Port Richy, Fla., 1987-90. Author: (textbook chpt.) Emergency Medicine, 1994; contbr. articles to profl. jours. Fellow Am. Coll. Emergency Physicians, Am. Coll. Emergency Medicine, Am. Assn. Emergency Physicians, Am. Bd. Quality Assurance (utilization rev. physician 1990—). Office: St Claire Med Ctr 222 Medical Cir Morehead KY 40351

MILLER, JOSEF M., otolaryngologist, educator; b. Phila., Nov. 29, 1937; married, 1960; 3 children. BA in Psychology, U. Calif., Berkeley, 1961; PhD in Physiology and Psychology, U. Wash., 1965; MD (hon.), U. Göteborg, Sweden, 1987; MD (h.c.), U. Turku, Finland, 1995. USPHS fellow U. Mich., 1965-67; rsch. assoc., asst. prof. dept. Psychology U. Mich., Ann Arbor, 1967-68, prof., dir. rsch. dept. Otolaryngology, dir. Kresge Hearing Rsch. Inst., 1984—; asst. prof. depts. Otolaryngology, Physiology and Biophysics U. Wash., Seattle, 1968-72, rsch. affiliate Regional Primate Rsch. Ctr, 1968-84, assoc. prof., 1972-76, acting chmn. dept. Otolaryngology, 1975-76, prof., 1976-84; mem. study sect. Nat. Inst. Neurol. and Communicative Disorders and Stroke, NIH, 1978-84, ad hoc bd. dirs. sci. counselors, 1988; sci. rev. com. Deafness Rsch. Found., 1978-83, chair, 1983—; mem. faculty Nat. Conf. Rsch. Goals and Methods in Otolaryngology, 1982; adv. com. hearing, bio-acoustics and biomechanics Commn. Behavioral and Social Scis. and Edn., Nat. Rsch. Coun., 1983—; hon. com. Orgn. Nobel Symposium 63, Cellular Mechanisms in Hearing, Karlskoga, Sweden, 1985; cons. Otitis Media Rsch. Ctr., 1985-89, Pfizer Corp., 1988; faculty opponent U. Göteborg, Sweden, 1987; rsch. adv. com. Gallaudet Coll., 1987; chair external sci. adv. com. House Ear Inst., 1988-91; author authorizing legis. Nat. Inst. Deafness and Other Comm. Disorders, NIH, 1988, co-chair adv. bd. rsch. priorities com., bd. dirs. Friends adv. coun., 1989—, chair rsch. subcom., 1990-93, treas., bd. dirs., 1996—; grant reviewer Mich. State Rsch. Fund, NSF, VA; reviewer numerous jours. including Acta Otolaryngologica, Jour. Otology, Physiology and Behavior, Science. Mem. editorial bd. Am. Jour. Otolaryngology, 1981—, AMA, Am. Physiology Soc., Annals of Otology, Rhinology and Laryngology, 1980—, Archives of Oto-Rhino-Laryngology, 1985-93, Hearing Rsch., Jour. Am. Acad. Otolaryngology-Head and Neck Surgery, 1990—. Bd. dirs. Internat. Hearing Found., 1985—. Fellow U. Wash., 1962-65, Kresge Hearing Rsch. Inst., U. Mich., 1965-67; recipient award Am. Acad. Otolaryngology; grantee Deafness Rsch. Found., U. Wash., 1969-71; rsch. grantee NIH, 1969-73. Mem. AAAS, Am. Acad. Otolaryngology and Head and Neck Surgery (com. rsch. in otolaryngology 1971-82, continuing edn. com. 1975-79, NIH liaison com. 1988—, program steering com. jour. 1990), Am. Auditory Soc., Am. Otclogical Soc., Am. Neurotological Soc., Am. Otologic Honor Soc., Acoustical Soc. Am. (com. rsch. psychol., physiol. acoustics 1969-78), Fedn. Am. Physiological Soc., Fedn. Am. Socs. Experimental Biology, Soc. Neurosci., Assn. Rsch. Otolaryngology (sec.-treas. 1979-80, pres. elect 1981, pres. 1982. program dir. mtg. 1983, award of merit com. 1985, 95-96, chair 1988, program dir., pres. symposium homeostatic mech. of inner ear 1993), Sigma Xi. Office: U Mich Kresge Hearing Rsch Inst 1301 E Ann St # R5032 Ann Arbor MI 48109-0500

MILLER, JOSEPH KEITH, neurologist; b. Buffalo, June 5, 1957; s. Daniel Jerome and Jeannette June (Eberl) M.; m. Ellen Marie Oberacker, May 26, 1984; children: Bradley Daniel, Jessica Marie. BA in biology and psychology, U. Rochester, 1979; MD, SUNY, Buffalo, 1983. Diplomate Am. Bd. Psychiatry and Neurology, Am. Bd. Electroencephalography and Neurophysiology. Intern in internal medicine dept. medicine Millard Fillmore Hosp., Buffalo, 1983-84, resident, chief resident in neurology Dent Neurologic Inst., 1984-87; neurologist, med. dir. Neurophysiology Dept. and EEG sch. Johnson Neurol. Clinic, High Point, N.C., 1988—; clin. asst. instr. neurology Sch. Medicine SUNY, Buffalo, 1984-87; asst. in neurology Coll. Medicine U. Ill., Chgo., 1987-88; clin. instr. neurology Bowman Gray Sch. Medicine, Winston-Salem, N.C., 1988—. Contbr. articles to profl. jours. Bd. dirs. Triad N.C. chpt. Alzheimer's Assn., Piedmont Epilepsy Assn. Fellowship in electroencephalography and epilepsy dept. neurology U. Ill., Chgo., 1987-88. Mem. AMA, Am. Epilepsy Soc., Am. Acad. Neurology. Home: 1236 Sturbridge Ave High Point NC 27262-7334 Office: Johnson Neurol Clinic 606 N Elm St High Point NC 27262-4336

MILLER, JOSEPH MORTON, internist; b. Boston, Nov. 9, 1921; s. Benjamin and Esther (Sugar) M.; m. Betty Jean Harris, Sept. 17, 1976; children: Gregory, Coralia. AB, Harvard Coll., 1942; MD, Harvard Med. Sch., 1945; MPH, Harvard Sch. Pub. Health, 1960. Diplomate Am. Bd. Internal Medicine, Preventive Medicine. Cons. occupl. health Plymouth, N.H., 1960—; cons. environ. and toxicology. Capt. U.S. Army, 1946-48. Mem. APHA, Am. Coll. Environ. and Occupl. Medicine. Home and Office: New Hebron Rd Plymouth NH 03264

MILLER, KAREN SEIFERT, health facility administrator; b. Plainfield, N.J., Feb. 18, 1959; d. William A. and Victoria M. (Dziedzic) Seifert; m. Karl E. Miller, June 18, 1983; children: Colin James, Evan Alexander. BA, Rutgers U., 1981; M in Healthcare Adminstrn., U. Md., 1988. Legis. asst. Acad. Gen. Dentistry Tucker, Roberts & Co., Inc., Washington, 1981; asst. dir. fundraising Am. Cancer Soc., Washington, 1981-84; govt. liaison, legis. asst. Am. Osteopathic Hosp. Assn., Alexandria, Va., 1984-86, 86-87, asst. v.p. profl. affairs, 1987-90; found. dir. The Found. for Osteopathic Health Svcs., Washington, 1987-90; asst. v.p. Coll. Osteopathic Healthcare Execs., Washington, 1989-90; asst. adminstr. Levindale Hebrew Geriatric Ctr. & Hosp. Inc., Balt., 1990—. Mem. Am. Coll. Health Care Execs. (assoc.), Md. Assn. Health Care Execs. Office: Levindale Hebrew Geriatric Hosp 2434 W Belvedere Ave Baltimore MD 21215

MILLER, LAURA JEAN, medical center director; b. Louisville, Nov. 11, 1946; d. Arthur and Marion (Adams) M.; m. Garrett Van Koughnett; children: Michael J. Uhlik, Caroline E. Uhlik. BA, U. Mo., Columbia, 1970; MPA, U. Mo., Kansas City, 1978. Presdl. mgmt. intern U.S. Dept. Vets. Affairs, Topeka, 1978-79; Presdl. mgmt. intern U.S. Dept. Vets. Affairs, Kansas City, Mo., 1979-80, asst. to chief of staff, 1980-86; regional quality assurance mgr. U.S. Dept. Vets. Affairs, Grand Prairie, Tex., 1986-89; assoc. dir. trainee U.S. Dept. Vets. Affairs, Dallas, 1989-90, asst. med. ctr. dir., 1990-91; assoc. med. ctr. dir. U.S. Dept. Vets. Affairs, Salem, Va., 1991-94; med. ctr. dir. U.S. Dept. Vets. Affairs, Pitts., 1994—; mem. exec. planning coun. U. Pitts., Western Psychiat. Inst. and Clinic, 1995—; mem.adv. bd. Vietnam Vets. Leadership Program Western Pa., Pitts., 1995—. Mem. Am. Coll. Healthcare Execs., Health Exec. Forum of Southwestern Pa., Interagy. Healthcare Inst. Alumnni. Office: VA Med Ctr 7180 Highland Dr Pittsburgh PA 15206

MILLER, LEE CLYDE, psychiatrist; b. Norristown, Pa., Sept. 29, 1943; s. Clyde Smith and Evelyn Elizabeth (Stephens) M.; m. Joanne Faul Brandt, July 1, 1967; children: Christopher Rushton, Jason Faul. BS, Ursinus Coll., Collegeville, Pa., 1965; MD, Temple U., 1969. Diplomate Am. Bd. Psychiatry and Neurology. Intern Polyclinic Med. Ctr., Harrisburg, Pa., 1969-70, dir. psychiatry, 1975-86; resident in psychiatry Norristown State Hosp., 1970-71, Inst. of Living, Hartford, Conn., 1973-75; pvt. practice Harrisburg, 1986—; psychiat. cons. Community Counseling Assocs., Harrisburg, 1985—. Contbr. articles to med. jours. Mem. Lower Paxton Twp. Energy Adv. Com., 1978. Lt. comdr. M.C., USN, 1971-73. Fellow Am. Psychiat. Assn.; mem. AMA, Pa. Med. Soc., Pa. Psychiat. Soc. (treas. 1995-96, 96-97), Ctrl. Pa. Psychiat. Soc. (pres. 1983-84). Office: 2201 Forest Hills Dr Ste 9 Harrisburg PA 17112-1089

MILLER, LEONARD DAVID, surgeon; b. Jersey City, July 8, 1930; s. Louis Abner and Esther (Levy) M.; children—Steven Lawrence, Jason Lloyd. A.B., Yale U., 1951; M.D., U. Pa., 1955. Intern Hosp. of U. Pa., Phila., 1955-56; resident Hosp. of U. Pa., 1956-57, 59-65; practice medicine, specializing in surgery Phila., 1965—; vice chmn. dept. research and surgery U. Pa., 1972-75, acting chmn., 1975-78, John Rhea Barton prof., 1978-83, chmn. dept. surgery, 1978-83; dir. Harrison Dept. Surgery. Mem. editorial bd.: Annals of Surgery, 1973—. Served to capt., M.C. USAF, 1957-59. Recipient Lindback award for disting. teaching, 1969, Student award for clin. teaching, 1965. Mem. Am. Surg. Assn., AAAS, Soc. for Surgery of Alimentary Tract, Nat. Soc. Med. Research (rep.), Soc. Univ. Surgeons, Am. Soc. Surgery of Trauma, Coll. Physicians of Phila., N.Y. Acad. Sci., Sigma Xi, Alpha Omega Alpha. Office: Univ Pa Hosp Dept Surgery 4 Silverstein 3400 Spruce St Philadelphia PA 19104

MILLER, LINDA J., healthcare consultant; b. Orange County, Ind., July 12, 1942; d. John E. and Geraldine B. (Turner) M. BA, Anderson U., 1964; MSSW, U. Louisville, 1967; Cert. in Health Adminstrn., U. Calif., 1972. Dir. family care Ind. Dept. Mental Health, Madison, 1964-69; dir. patient svcs. Meml. Med. Ctr., Long Beach, Calif., 1969-74; v.p., corp. svcs. Mem. Med. Ctr., Long Beach, 1979-83; CEO Community Hosp., Anderson, Ind., 1974-79; cons. First Cons. Group, Long Beach, 1983-86, v.p., mgmt. cons., 1986-89; chief op. officer First Cons. Group, Indpls., 1989-93; healthcare cons. Anderson, 1993—; active numerous healthcare bds., task forces and coms.; lectr. and presenter in field. Mem. Am. Coll. Healthcare Execs., Healthcare Fin. Mgmt. Assn., Am. Hosp. Assn. Home: 1015 S Layton Rd Anderson IN 46011

MILLER, LOUIS HOWARD, biologist, researcher; b. Balt., Feb. 4, 1935; s. David and Daisy (Arenson) M.; m. Nancy Jo Harned, Sept. 26, 1959; 1 child, Jennifer. BS, Haverford Coll., 1956; MD, Washington U., St. Louis, 1960; MS in Parasitology, Columbia U., 1964. Asst. prof. then assoc. prof. Coll. of P & S, Columbia U., N.Y.C., 1967-71; head malaria sect. NIAID, NIH, Bethesda, Md., 1971-92, chief lab. parasitic diseases, 1992—. Contbr. articles to profl. jours. Capt. U.S. Army, 1965-67. Recipient Paul Ehrlich/Ludwig Darmstaedter prize, 1989. Fellow Royal Soc. Tropical Med. Hygiene, Queensland Inst. Med. Rsch., ACP; mem. Am. Soc. Tropical Medicine & Hygiene (pres. 1988), NAS, Inst. of Medicine, Assn. Am. Physicians. Office: NIH Building 4 Rm 126 Bethesda MD 20892*

MILLER, MARGARET JOANNE, pediatrics nurse; b. Rolette, N.D., Apr. 12, 1939; d. William J. and Nora (Slaubaugh) Graber; m. Ervin S. Miller, June 16, 1962; children: Charlene, Angela, Lisa. ASN, Vincennes U., 1960; student, St. Mary's-of-the-Woods Coll., Terre Haute, Ind., 1986-87, Ind. U., South Bend, 1989, Regents Coll., 1995-96. RN, Ind., Tex. Head nurse St. Joseph Mem. Hosp., Kokomo, Ind., 1975-77; asst. dir. Mennonite Mutul Aid, 1982-84; staff nurse Meml. Hosp., South Bend, Ind., 1984-87, asst. head nurse, 1987-89, asst. unit dir., 1989-91; unit dir. for pediatrics Med. Ctr. Hosp., Odessa, Tex., 1992—. Mem. Soc Pediatric Nurses. Home: 3411 Rocky Lane Rd Odessa TX 79762-5046

MILLER, MELANIE KAY, critical care nurse; b. Lebanon, Pa., Nov. 10, 1963; d. Harold John and Phyllis Annette (De Pugh) Caskie; m. Kenneth Robert Miller, Feb. 3, 1990. Nursing diploma, Reading Hosp. and Med. Ctr., Reading, Pa., 1984. RN, Pa; CCRN, cert. CPR instr., ACLS instr., EMT, pre-hospital trauma life support. Staff nurse Reading Hosp. and Med. Ctr., 1984-86; nurse clinician M.S. Hershey Med. Ctr., Hershey, Pa., 1986-91; advanced life support coord., staff nurse Community Gen. Osteo. Hosp., Harrisburg, 1988—; rep. adv. com. Dauphin County Emergency Med. Svcs., Harrisburg, 1990-94, rep/pres. coun., 1991-94. EMT class coord. Lebanon County, 1987-90; EMT, Annville (Pa.) Union Hose Fire Co., 1986-89; health profl. Western Dist., Palmyra, Pa., 1985—. Home: 5600 Chambers Hill Rd Harrisburg PA 17111-3301

MILLER, MICHAEL STEPHEN, neurologist; b. Sacramento, Calif., Jan. 29, 1945; s. Jacob Irving and Hannah (Glaser) M.; m. Barbara Kersh, June 30, 1968; children: Jonathan Lewis, Sara Anne. BS, U. Md., 1966; PhD, Northwestern U., 1971; MD, U. Md., 1976. Diplomate Am. Bd. Psychiatry & Neurology. Rsch. fellow Calif. Inst. Tech., Pasadena, 1970-71; tchg. staff St. Agnes Hosp., Balt., 1983-86; chemist Dept. Interior, College Park, Md., 1966. Mem. AMA, Am. Acad. Neurology, Sigma Xi. Avocations: music, dogs. Office: 3455 Wilkens Ave Baltimore MD 21225

MILLER, MILTON HOWARD, psychiatrist; b. Indpls., Sept. 1, 1927; came to Can., 1971; s. William and Helen L. (Lefkovits) M.; m. Harriet Sanders, June 27, 1948; children—Bruce, Jeffrey, Marcie. B.S., Ind. U., 1946, M.D., 1950; diploma in psychiatry, Menninger Sch., Topeka, 1953. Intern Indpls. Gen. Hosp., 1950-51; resident Menninger Sch. Psychiatry, Topeka, 1951-53; with dept. psychiatry Univ. Hosps., U. Wis., Madison, 1955-71; prof. Univ. Hosps., U. Wis., 1961-71, chmn., 1962-71; dir. Wis. Psychiat. Inst., 1962-71; vis. prof. Nat. Taiwan U., Taipei, 1969-70; prof. psychiatry U. B.C., Vancouver, 1972-78; head dept. psychiatry U. B.C., 1972-78; dir. WHO-U. B.C. Mental Health Tng. Centre, Vancouver, 1974-78; dep. dir coastal region Dept. of Mental Health, L.A. County, 1978-86; chmn. dept. psychiatry Harbor-UCLA Med. Ctr., Torrance, Calif., 1978—; prof., vice chmn. dept. psychiatry UCLA, 1978—; dep. med. dir. Dept. of Mental Health, L.A., 1986—; cons. in field. Author: Psychiatry: A Personal View, 1981; Contbr. articles to profl. jours. Fellow Am. Psychiat. Assn., Royal Coll. Psychiatry; mem. Can. Psychiat. Assn., Royal Coll. Physicians and Surgeons (examiner 1973—), Can. Med. Assn., World Fedn. for Mental Health (mem. exec. bd. 1973—). Home: 1321 Paseo Del Mar San Pedro CA 90731 Office: Harbor-UCLA Med Ctr Dept Psychiatry Torrance CA 90509-2910

MILLER, MORTON G., psychiatrist; b. Phila., Mar. 8, 1935; s. Philip and Rose (Staff) M.; Ruth Perloff, June 23, 1957; children: Jonathan, Joanna, Jessica. BA, U. Pa., 1956; MD, Albert Einstein Coll. Medicine, 1960. Cert. Nat. Bd. Med. Examiners, 1961, Am. Bd. Psychiatry and Neurology, 1968. Rotating intern U.S. Pub. Health Svcs. Hosp., San Francisco, 1961; resident psychiatry Yale U. New Haven (Conn.) Hosp., 1961-64; staff psychiatrist Community Mental Health Ctrs. Br. NIMH, 1964-65; dir. spl. mental health programs NIMH, 1967-71, assoc. dir. spl. and collaborative programs, 1969-71; assoc. prof. psychiatry SUNY-Stony Brook Sch. Medicine, 1972-78, prof. clin. psychiatry, 1978-85; chmn. dept. psychiatry and behavioral medicine Lahey Clinic Med. Ctr., Burlington, Mass., 1985—. Contbr. articles to profl. jours. Co-chmn. Harvard (Mass.) Housing Partnership, 1988-89. Fellow Am. Psychiat. Assn.; mem. Phi Beta Kappa. Office: Lahey Clinic Found 41 Mall Rd Burlington MA 01805-0001

MILLER, NANCY A., nursing administrator; b. Lehighton, Pa., Apr. 6, 1942; d. Calvin Erck and Mabel Rosetta (Burkett) Geiger; children: Michael Todd Miller, Nicole Ann Miller. Diploma, St. Luke's Sch. Nursing, Bethlehem, Pa., 1962. RN, Pa. Staff nurse Vis. Nurse Assn., Stroudsburg, 1981-89; dir. community health svcs. Home Health Schs., Stroudsburg, Pa.; adminstr. Home Care Affiliates, Stroudsburg; DON Stroud Manor, East Stroudsburg, Pa., 1989-91, Brookmont Health Care Ctr. Inc., Effort, Pa., 1991—. Office: Brookmont Health Care Ctr Box 50 Effort PA 18330

MILLER, NANCY ELLEN, health research administrator, educator; b. Long Beach, N.Y., Aug. 20, 1947; d. Jerome H. and Kathy P. M. BA, NYU, 1969; MA, Harvard U., 1970; PhD, U. Chgo., 1978; cert. Washington Sch. Psychiatry, 1981; postgrad. Washington Psychoanalytic Inst., 1981. Clin. psychologist City of Chgo. Dept. Mental Health, 1971-77; research asst. dept. psychiatry U. Chgo., 1972-75, research asso., 1975-77; exec. sec. Sci. Rev. Group NIMH, 1977-79, chief clin. research program Center for Studies of Mental Health Aging, 1977-86, chief clin. research program Mental Disorders Aging Research Br., 1986-93; chief clin. and exptl. rsch. program, br. schizophrenia rsch. br. divsn. clin. and treatment rsch. NIMH, NIH, 1993-96; sr. sci. policy analyst Office of Sci. Policy, Office of Dir. NIH, 1996—; instr. clin. geriatric psychiatry Georgetown U. Sch. Medicine; clin. faculty psychiatry dept., Navy Med. Command, Nat. Capital Region; clin. prof. dept. psychiatry Uniformed Services U. Health Scis.; del. White House Conf. on Aging, 1981. Author: (with Gene Cohen) Clinical Aspects of Alzheimer's Disease and Senile Dementia, 1981, Schizophrenia and Aging: Schizophrenia, Paranoia and Schizophreniform Disorders in Late Life, 1988, (with E. Erlenmeyer-Kimling) Life-Span Research on the Prediction of Psychopathology, 1986, (with Lester Luborsky, Jaques Barber and John Docherty) Psychodynamic Treatment Research, 1993; mem. editorial bd. Jour. Ednl. Gerontology, 1976-80, Neurobiology of Aging, 1980-86, Profl. Psychology, 1980-85, Psychoanalytic Psychology, 1983-88, Clin. Gerontologist, 1983—, Am. Jour. Orthopsychiatry, 1985-90, Internat. Psychogeriatrics, 1989—, Am. Jour. Geriatric Psychiatry, 1992—; contbr. numerous articles in field. USPHS fellow, 1972-76; HEW fellow, 1975-77; recipient Alcohol, Drug Abuse and Mental Health Adminstrn. Honor award, U.S. Pub. Health Service Spl. Recognition award. Mem. AAAS, Am. Orthopsychiat. Assn., Am. Psychoanalytic Assn., Am. Psychol. Assn., Boston Soc. Gerontologic Psychiatry, D.C. Psychol. Assn., Washington Psychoanalytic Soc., Gerontol. Soc. Am., Internat. Assn. Gerontology, Internat. Brain Research Orgn., Internat. Neuropsychol. Soc., Internat. Psychogeriatric Assn., Soc. Neurosci., Soc. Psychotherapy Research, Phi Delta Kappa, Pi Lambda Theta. Home: 3617 Newark St NW Washington DC 20016-3179 Office: NIH Office Sci Policy Office of the Dir 9000 Rockville Pike Bldg 1 Rm 218 Rockville MD 20892-0001

MILLER, NEAL ELGAR, psychologist, emeritus educator; b. Milw., Aug. 3, 1909; s. Irving E. and Lily R. (Fuenfstueck) M.; m. Marion E. Edwards, June 30, 1948; children: York, Sara. B.S., U. Wash., 1931; M.S., Stanford U., 1932; Ph.D., Yale U., 1935; D.Sc., U. Mich., 1965, U. Pa., 1968, St. Lawrence U., 1973, U. Uppsala, Sweden, 1977, LaSalle Coll., 1979, Rutgers U., 1985. Social sci. research fellow Inst. Psychoanalysis, Vienna, Austria, 1935-36; asst. research psychologist Yale U., 1933-35; instr., asst. prof., research asst. psychol. Inst. Human Relations, 1936-41, assoc. prof., research assoc., 1941-42, 46-50, prof. psychology, 1950-52, James Rowland Angell prof. psychology, 1952-66; fellow Berkeley Coll., 1955—; prof. Rockefeller U., N.Y.C., 1966-81; prof. emeritus Rockefeller U., 1981—; research affiliate Yale U., 1985—; expert cons. Am. Inst. Research, 1946-62; spl. cons. com. human resources Research and Devel. Bd., Office Sec. Def., 1951-53; mem. tech. adv. panel Office Asst. Sec. Def., 1954-57; expert cons. Ops. Research Office and Human Resources Research Office, 1951-54; bd. of sci. counsellors Nat. Inst. of Aging, 1987-90; bd. gov.s and mem. of exec. com. N.Y. Acad. of Scis., 1987. Author: (with J. Dollard et al) Frustration and Aggression, 1939, (with Dollard) Social Learning and Imitation, 1941, Personality and Psychotherapy, 1950, Graphic Communication and the Crisis in Education, 1957, N.E. Miller: Selected Papers, 1971; contbr. chpts. to psychol. handbooks; editor: Psychological Research on Pilot Tng., 1947. Chmn. bd. sci. dirs. Roscoe B. Jackson Meml. Lab., Bar Harbor, Maine, 1962-76, hon. trustee, 1980—; bd. sci. counsellors NIMH, 1957-61; fellowship com. Founds. Fund for Research in Psychiatry, 1956-61; mem. central council Internat. Brain Research Orgn., 1964; v.p. bd. dirs. Foote Sch., 1964-65; chmn. NAS/NRC Com. on Brain Scis., 1969-71; bd. sci. counsellors Nat. Inst. Child Health and Human Devel., 1969-72; v.p. Inst. for Advancement of Health, 1982-90. Maj. USAAC., 1942-46; officer in charge research, Psychol. Research Unit 1, Nashville 1942-44; dir. psychol. research project Hdqrs. Flying Tng. Command, Randolph Field, Tex. 1944-46. Recipient Warren medal for exptl. psychology, 1954, Newcomb Cleveland prize, 1956, Nat. medal of sci., 1964, Kenneth Craik Rsch. award U. Cambridge, 1966, Wilbur Cross medal Yale U., 1966, Alumnus Summa Laude Dignitatus U. Wash., 1967, Disting. Alumnus award Western Wash. State Coll., Gold medal award Am. Psychol. Found., 1975, Mental Health Assn. rsch. achievement award, 1978, Inst. for Advancement of Health Sci. and Art of Health award, 1988, Disting. Scholar award Internat. Soc. for Behavioral Medicine, 1990. Fellow Am. Acad. Arts and Scis. (coun. 1979-83), Brit. Psychol. Soc. (hon. fgn.), Internat. Soc. Rsch. on Aggression (life); mem. Am. Philos. Soc., N.Y. Acad. Scis. (hon. life), Spanish Soc. Psychology (hon.), APA (coun. reps. 1954-58, pres. exptl. divsn. 1952-53, pres. 1960-61, pres. divsn. health psychology 1980-81, Disting. Sci. Contbn. award 1959, award for Disting. Contbns. to Knowledge 1983, citation for Outstanding Lifetime Contbn. to Psychology, 1991, establishment of Neal E. Miller Disting. Lectr. in Neurosci. 1995—, Divsn. Health Psychology Centennial award for outstanding achievement 1992), Eastern Psychol. Assn. (pres. 1952-53), NRC (divsn. anthropology and psychology 1950-53, chmn. 1958-60), Nat. Acad. Sci. (chmn. sect. psychology 1965-67, chmn. com. brain sci. 1969-71, sr. fellow Inst. of Medicine 1983—, bd. mental health and behavioral medicine 1980-85), German Soc. Behavioral Medicine and Behavior Modification (hon.), Soc. Exptl. Psychologists, AAAS, Soc. Neurosci. (pres. 1971-72, pres. award for Career of Outstanding Neurosci. Rsch. Teaching and Svc. 1994), Biofeedback Soc. Am. (pres.-elect 1983, pres. 1984, Outstanding Rsch. award 1987, Disting. Rsch. award 1995), Acad. Behavioral Medicine Rsch. (pres. 1978-79, Neal E. Miller New Investigator award establish 1989), Mory's Grad. Club (New Haven), Grad. Club Assn., Sigma Xi (pres. Rockefeller U. chpt. 1968-69), Phi Beta Kappa. Office: Yale U Dept Psychology PO Box 208-205 New Haven CT 06520-8205

MILLER, PATRICIA ANNE, speech and language pathologist; b. Lamesa, Tex., Aug. 19, 1957; d. Warren Layton and Evelyn Joyce (Pearson) Oliver; m. John Ernest Roberts, May 25, 1979 (div.); 1 child, Jason Aaron; m. Michael David Miller, Nov. 30, 1984; children: Jennifer Anne, Catherine Denise. BS, Howard Payne Coll., 1979; postgrad., Baylor U., 1983. Cert. tchr., Tex.; lic. speech-lang. pathologist, Tex. Speech therapist Crosbyton (Tex.) Cen. Ind. Sch. Dist., 1980-81; speech therapist Hillsboro (Tex.) Spl. Edn. Coop., 1981, speech therapy cons., 1982-83; speech therapist Cleburne (Tex.) Ind. Sch. Dist., 1987-89, Levelland (Tex.) Ind. Sch. Dist. Coop., 1989; speech therapist Speech, Lang. and Hearing Ctr. Lamesa Ind. Sch. Dist., Lubbock, Tex., 1990-95; speech-lang. pathologist Sundance Rehab. Corp., Lamesa, Tex., 1995—. Mem. Tex. Speech and Hearing Assn. Baptist. Office: 703 S 1st St Lamesa TX 79331-6249

MILLER, PATRICIA LOUISE, state legislator, nurse; b. Bellefontaine, Ohio, July 4, 1936; d. Richard William and Rachel Orpha (Williams) Miller; m. Kenneth Orlan Miller, July 3, 1960; children: Tamara Sue, Matthew Ivan. RN, Meth. Hosp. Sch. Nursing-Indpls., 1957; BS, Ind. U., 1960. Office nurse A.D. Dennison, MD, 1960-61; staff nurse Meth. Hosp., Indpls., 1959, Community Hosp., Indpls., 1958; representative, State of Ind., Dist. 50, Indpls., 1982-83, senator, State of Ind., Dist. 32, Indpls., 1983—, mem. edn. com., 1984-90, health welfare and aging com. 1983-90, labor and pension com. 1983-94, legis. apportionment and elections coms., chmn. interim study com. pub. health and mental health Ind. Gen. Assembly, 1986; chair Senate Environ. Affairs, 1990-92, Health and Environ. Affairs, 1992—; mem. election com., 1992—; mem. budget subcom. Senate Fin. Com., 1995— . Mem. Bd. Edn., Met. Sch. Dist. Warren Twp., 1974-82, pres., 1979-80, 80-81; mem. Warren Twp. Citizens Screening Com. for Sch. Bd. Candidates, 1972-74, 84, Met. Zoning Bd. Appeals, Div. I, appointed mem. City-County Council, 1972-76; bd. dirs. Central Ind. Council on Aging, Indpls., 1977-80; mem. State Bd. of Voc. and Tech. Edn., 1978-82, sec., 1980-82; mem. Gov.'s Select Adv. Commn. for Primary and Secondary Edn., 1983; precinct committeeman Republican Party, 1968-74, ward vice chmn., 1975-78, ward chmn., 1978-85, twp. chmn., 1985-87; vice chmn. Marion County Rep., 1986—; del. Rep. State Conv., 1968, 74, 76, 80, 84, 86, 88, 90, 92, 94, sgt. at arms, 1982, mem. platform com., 1984, 88, 90, 92, co-chmn. Ind. Rep. Platform Com., 1992; del. Rep. Nat. Conv., 1984, alternate del., 1988, Rep. Presdl. Elector Alternate, 1992; active various polit. campaigns; bd. dirs. PTA, 1967-81; pres. Grassy Creek PTA, 1971-72; state del. Ind. PTA, 1978; mem. child care adv. com. Walker Career Center, 1976-80, others; bd. dirs. Ch. Fedn. Greater Indpls., 1979-82, Christian Justice Center, Inc., 1983-85, Gideon Internat. Aux., 1977—; mem. United Meth. Bd. Missions Aux. of Indpls., 1974-80, v.p., 1974-76; bd. dirs. Lucille Raines Residence, Inc., 1977-80; exec. com. S. Ind. Conf. United Meth. Women, 1977-80, lay del. S. Ind. Conf. United Meth. Ch., 1977—, fin. and adminstrn. com., 1979-88, planning and research com., 1980-88, co-chmn. law adv. com., chmn. health and welfare, conf. council ministries, also mem. task force, bd. ordained ministry, also panel, chmn. com. on dist. superintendency, dist. council on ministries; sec. Indpls. S.E. Dist. Council on Ministries, 1977-78, pres., 1982; chmn. council on ministries Cumberland United Meth. Ch., 1969-76; chmn. stewardship com. Old Bethel United Meth. Ch., 1982-85, fin. com., 1982-85, adminstrv. bd., mem. council on ministries, 1981-85; co-chair Evangelism Com., 1994—; jurisdictional del. United Meth. Ch., 1988, 92; alternate del. United Meth. Ch. Gen. Conf., 1988, delegate, 1992; mem. health and human svcs. com. Midwest Legis. Conf., 1995. Recipient Phi Lambda Theta Honor for outstanding contbr. in field of edn., 1976; Woman of the Year, Cumberland Bus. and Profl. Women, 1979; Ind. Voc. Assn. citation award, 1984, others. Mem. Indpls. Dist. Dental Soc. Women's Aux., Ind. Dental Assn. Women's Aux., Am. Dental Assn. Women's Aux., Council State Govt. (intergovtl. affairs com.), Nat. Conf. State Legislatures (health com. vice chmn. 1994—), Warren Twp. Rep. Franklin Rep., Lawrence Rep., Center Twp. Rep., Fall Creek Valley Rep., Marion County Council Rep. Women, Ind. Women's Rep., Indpls. Women's Rep., Ind. Fedn. Rep. Women, Nat. Fedn. Rep. Women, Beech Grove Rep., Perry Twp. Rep. Home: 1041 Muessing Rd Indianapolis IN 46239-9614

MILLER, PAUL RICHARD, orthopaedic surgeon; b. Louisville, Jan. 20, 1959; s. Arthur Taggart and Marion Adams Miller; m. Anne Katherine Schmank; children: Douglas Paul, Andrew David. BS, Marquette U., 1981; MD, U. Chgo., 1986. Diplomat Am. Bd. Orthopedic Surgery. Intern Loyola U. Med. Ctr., 1986-87, resident, 1987-91; fellow Cin. Sports Medicine, 1994-95; staff Falls Med. Group, Monomonee Falls, Wis., 1995—. Maj. U.S. Army, 1991-94. Fellow Am. Acad. Orthopaedic Surgeons, Arthroscopy Assn. of N.Am.; mem. AMA. Office: Falls Med Group N84W16889 Menomonee Ave Menomonee Falls WI 53045

MILLER, RANDAL HOWARD, health science association administrator; b. Fostoria, Ohio, Apr. 11, 1947; s. Richard Paul and Michaline (Tinkovicz) M.; m. Patricia June Smith, May 29, 1970 (div. Apr. 1978); 1 child, Rhett Howard; m. Angel Jo Belfiore, May 27, 1978; 1 child, Shea Michal. BS, Bowling Green (Ohio) U., 1970. Chief labs. dept. health City of Cleve., 1975-78; coordinator lab. projects St. Vincent Charity Hosp., Cleve., 1980-83; pres. Trace Elements Analysis, Inc., Richfield, Ohio, 1979-88; asst. dir. clin. pathology Univ. Hosps., Cleve., 1988-92; adminstr. and mktg. dir. Univ. Med. Labs., Cleve., 1992-96; exec. dir. Howard Miller Assocs., Cleve., 1995—; corp. sec. Midwest LabLink, Ltd., Ohio, 1995—. Served to sgt. U.S. Army, 1970-76. Mem. Clin. Lab. Mgmt. Assn., Am. Soc. Clin. Pathologists, Med. Group Mgmt. Assn., Ohio Pub. Lab. Dirs., Greater Cleve. Hosp. Assn. (vice-chmn. lab. com. 1986-89, chmn. lab. com. 1989-90), Alpha Sigma Phi. Roman Catholic. Office: Howard Miller Assocs PO Box 31011 Cleveland OH 44131

MILLER, RICHARD KERMIT, biologist, professor; b. Scranton, Pa., Oct. 17, 1946; s. Roland Kermit and Vera (Edwards) M.; m. Judith Ann Berens. AB in Biology, Dartmouth Coll., 1968; PhD in Pharmacology, Toxicology, Dartmouth Med. Sch., 1973; postgrad., Jefferson Med. Coll., Phila., 1972-74. Asst. prof. sch. medicine and dentistry U. Rochester, N.Y., 1974-80, assoc. prof., 1980-88, prof. ob.-gyn., toxicology, 1988—; dir. divsn. rsch. U. Rochester, 1978—, dir. PEDECS, 1987—; prof. reproductive biology U. Paris VI, 1983; mem. bd. sci. counselors Nat. Toxicology Program NIH,

1988-92; chair panel on pregnancy biomarkers nat. rsch. coun. Nat. Acad. Medicine; mem. sci. rev. bd. NIH/TERIS, 1988—; mem. com. teratology Nat. Libr., 1987-93; cons. FDA, Nat. Inst. Environ. Health Sci., EPA, 1988—; advisor WHO program rsch. devel. in human reproduction, 1990-94. Editor-in-chief Trophoblast Research, 1982—; editorial bd. Teratology, 1979-87, Placenta, 1980—, Reproductive Toxicology, 1986—, Procs. of Soc. for Exptl. Biology and Medicine, 1991—, Early Pregnancy, 1996—. Sr. internat. fellow NIH/Fogarty, 1983, fellow Smith Kline and French, 1972-74, NIH, 1968-74; named Disting. Prof. Fulbright Program, 1988. Mem. Am. Soc. for Pharmacology and Exptl. Therapeutics, European Teratology Soc., Internat. Fedn. of Placental Assns. (sec. gen. 1993—), Neurobehavioral Teratology Soc. (councilor 1986-89), Soc. for Gynecologic Investigation, Teratology Soc. (pres. 1991-92, chair pub. affairs 1985-88), Sigma Xi. Office: U Rochester Med Ctr Dept Ob-Gyn 601 Elmwood Ave Rochester NY 14642-8668

MILLER, RICHARD LAWRENCE, dermatologist; b. Toledo, Jan. 6, 1944; s. William and Ernestine (Neulicht) M.; m. Joyce Margaret Karsh, Dec. 17, 1967; children: Jennafer Lynn, Aaron Mark, Stephanie Michelle. AB, Franklin and Marshall U., 1965; MD, Duke U., 1968. Intern Maimonides Med. Ctr., Bklyn., 1968-69; pvt. practice Setauket, N.Y., 1975—; chief dermatology J.T. Mather Meml. Hosp., Port Jefferson, N.Y.; asst. prof. dermatology SUNY Hosp., Stony Brook. Lt. comdr. USNR, 1969-71. Fellow L.I. Dermatology Soc., N.Y. State Dermatology Soc., Am. Acad. Dermatology, AMA, Suffolk Dermatology Soc. (pres. 1981-82). Office: 200 Main St Setauket NY 11733

MILLER, RICHARD LYNN, pharmaceutical company executive; b. Stevens Point, Wis., Sept. 27, 1945; s. Gordon L. and Jean Ellen (Leary) M.; m. Lisa L. Palmer, Sept. 15, 1973; children: Analiese, Colin, Autumn. BS in Biology, U. Wis., Stevens Point, 1967; PhD in Microbiology, U. Minn., 1974. Rsch. asst. microbiology U. Minn., Mpls., 1970-74; postdoctoral fellow Pa. State U., Hershey, 1975-77; sr. microbiologist 3M Riker, St. Paul, 1977-79, rsch. specialist, 1979-86, sr. rsch. specialist, 1986-87; mgr. pharmacology 3M Pharms., St. Paul, 1987—. Contbr. articles and abstracts to profl. jours. With U.S. Army, 1968-70. NIH postdoctoral fellow, 1970, 75. Mem. AAAS, N.Y. Acad. Sci., Internat. Soc. Antiviral Rsch., Inflammation Rsch. Assn. Office: 3M Pharmaceuticals 270-25-06 3M Ctr Saint Paul MN 55144

MILLER, ROBERT A., health facility administrator; b. Ottumwa, Iowa, Dec. 15, 1949; s. Carl Robert and Margaret Irene (Allen) M.; m. Connie Lynn Lindsey (div. Feb. 1988); children: Destin Robert, Kiley Allen. AA in System Analysis, Indian Hills, Ottumwa, 1970; ISP in Health Care Adminstrn., U. Minn., 1982; BSBA, Iowa Wesleyan Coll., 1983. Bus. mgr. Henry County Health Ctr., Mt. Pleasant, Iowa, 1970-72; asst. adminstr. Henry County Health Ctr., Mt. Pleasant, 1972-74, adminstr., 1974-80, CEO, 1980—; owner, chmn. Health Software, Inc., Mt. Pleasant, 1979-95; trustee Iowa Hosp. Assn., Des Moines, 1980-95; bd. dels. Am. Hosp. Assn., Washington, 1992-95; chmn. bd. dirs. VHA-IA, HEC, Cedar Raids, Iowa; adj. faculty U. Iowa, 1991—. Bd. dirs., pres. C. of C., Mt. Pleasant, 1986; trustee Iowa Wesleyan Coll., Mt. Pleasant, 1990—. Named Young Adminstr. of the Yr., Iowa Hosp. Assn., Des Moines, 1984, recipient Ships Wheel award, 1990. Republican. Office: Henry County Health Ctr Saunders Park Mount Pleasant IA 52641

MILLER, ROBERT HAROLD, otolaryngologist, educator; b. Columbia, Mo., July 2, 1947; s. Harold Oswald and Ruth Nadine (Ballew) M.; m. Martha Guillory, Apr. 18, 1981; children: Morgan Guillory, Reed Thurston. BS in Biology, Tulane U., 1969, MD, 1973; cert. in otolaryngology-head/neck surg., UCLA Med. Ctr., 1978; MBA, Tulane U., 1996. Diplomate Am. Bd. Otolaryngology. From asst. prof. to assoc. prof. otolaryngology-HNS Baylor Coll. Medicine, Houston, 1978-87; prof., chmn. otolaryngology-HNS Tulane Sch. Medicine, New Orleans, 1987—; bd. dirs. Am. Bd. Otolaryngology; chief of staff Tulane Hosp., 1995—. Mem. editl. bd. Archives of Otolaryngology, 1986—, Head & Neck Surgery, 1987—. Named Outstanding Young Man, Houston C. of C., 1980; Robert Wood Johnson Health Policy fellow, 1996—. Fellow ACS, Am. Soc. Head & Neck Surgery, Am. Acad. Oto-Head & Neck Surgery (Disting. Svc. award 1994, Honor award 1991), Triological Soc. (exec. sec. 1992—). Home: 205 Brockenbraugh Ct Metairie LA 70005-3319 Office: Tulane U Sch Medicine 1430 Tulane Ave New Orleans LA 70112-2699

MILLER, ROBERT HENRY, internist; b. Providence, R.I., Mar. 3, 1942; s. Himon and Florence (Koppelman) M.; m. Diana Lillian Mordokovich; children: David, Daniel, Georgi. BA, U. Wash., 1963; MD, U. Tenn., 1967. Diplomate Am. Bd. Internal Medicine. Intern USPHS Hosp., Seattle, 1968-69; resident in internal medicine U. Wash. Affilited Hosps., Seattle, 1969-72; instr. in medicine U. Wash., Seattle, 1972; asst. prof. medicine, chief divsn. emergency medicine So. Ill. Sch. Medicine, Springfield, 1972-76, assoc. prof. medicine, chief divsn. emergency medicine, 1976-77; physician emergency dept. Glynn Brunswick (Ga.) Meml. Hosp., 1977-82; physician Glynn Immediate Care P.C., Brunswick, 1982—; med. dir. King's Bay Emergency Med. Svcs., St. Mary's, Ga., 1983—; clin. prof. family practice and cmty. medicine Mercer U. Sch. Medicine, Macon, Ga., 1993—. Author: Textbook of Basic Emergency Medicine, 1975, 2d edit., 1980, Manual of Pre-hospital Emergency Medicine, 1992. Ill. Dept. Pub. Health critical care fellow, 1973-74. Fellow Am. Coll. Physicians; mem. Am. Coll. Emergency Physicians, Nat. Assn. Emergency Med. Svc. Physicians. Home: 16 Tanglewood Rd Saint Simons Island GA 31522 Office: Glynn Immediate Care PC 3400 Parkwood Dr Brunswick GA 31520

MILLER, ROBERT JOHN, anesthesiologist, osteopathic physician, research; b. Wheeling, W.Va., Dec. 27, 1957; s. Joseph Edward and Dolores Josephine (Dewey) M. BS in Agr., Ohio State U., 1980; MD, Spartan Health Scis. U., Vieux Fort, St. Lucia, 1986; DO, U. Health Scis., Kansas City, Mo., 1991. Diplomate Nat. Bd. Osteo. Med. Examiners; cert. BCLS, ACLS, ACLS instr., pediatric advanced life support, advanced trauma life support, neonatal advanced life support; cert. lab. animal technician. Rotating intern Clarion (Pa.) Hosp., 1991-92; resident in anesthesia Med. Coll. Ohio, Toledo, 1992-95; fellow in ob-gyn. anesthesia N.C. Bapt. Hosp.-Wake Forest U. Bowman Gray Sch. Medicine, Winston-Salem, 1995-96; assoc. prof. anesthesia Med. Coll. Ohio, 1996—; dir. high risk obstet. anesthesia Flower Hosp./Med. Coll. Ohio, 1996—. Mem. Am. Soc. Anesthesiology, Am. Osteo. Assn., Soc. Obstetric Anesthesia and Perinatology, Soc. for Ambulatory Anesthesia, Internat. Anesthesia Rsch. Soc., Pa. Osteo. Med. Assn. Office: Wake Forest U Bowman Gray Sch Medicine Medical Center Blvd Winston Salem NC 27157

MILLER, ROBERT SCOTT, mental health administrator, social worker; b. Seattle, Dec. 12, 1947; s. Bert Lester and Carol Theresa (Gustafson) M.; m. Karen Ann Staake, Nov. 12, 1977; children: Sarah, Megan, Emily. BA in Sociology cum laude, Seattle Pacific U., 1970; AM in Social Work, U. Chgo., 1972; MA in Human Resources Mgmt., Pepperdine U., 1977. Cert. social worker, Wash. Br. supr. Wash. State Dept. Social and Health Svcs., Oak Harbor and Anacortes, 1975-78; supr. casework Wash. State Dept. Social and Health Svcs., Everett, 1973-75; lectr., coord. rural community mental health project U. Wash., Seattle, 1978-83; exec. dir. Armed Svcs. YMCA, Oak Harbor, 1984-86; area dir. United Way of Island County, Oak Harbor, 1986-88, exec. dir., 1988-92; exec. dir. Saratoga Community Mental Health, Coupeville, Wash., 1992-93; outpatient therapist, attention-deficit/hyperactivity disorder mental health specialist Cath. Cmty. Svcs. Northwest, Oak Harbor, Wash., 1993-96, dir., 1996—; dir. Island and Skagit Counties; part-time instr. sociology Chapman U., Orange, Calif., 1988-95; mem. adv. bd. Island Family Health Ctr., Oak Harbor, 1990-91. Contbr. articles to profl. jours. Bd. dirs. Puget Sound chpt. Huntington's Disease Soc. Am., 1989-93, pres., 1991, fundraising chmn., 1989-91, v.p., 1990; mem. adv. bd. United Ways Wash., 1991-92; chmn. Island County bd. emergency food and shelter program Fed. Emergency Mgmt. Agy.; vice chmn. Cmty. Resource Network, Oak Harbor, 1991; mem. steering com. Grater Oak Harbor Econ. Summit, 1991; mem. strategic planning com. Whidbey Gen. Hosp., Coupeville, 1992-93; mem. exec. com. Mt. Baker coun. Boy Scouts Am., 1993; bd. dirs. Opportunity Coun., Bellingham, 1993-94; bd. dirs. Concerts on the Cove, Coupeville, 1993-96, v.p., 1994-95; mem. Oak Harbor Citizen's Comprehensive Plan Task Force, 1994. Recipient outstanding svc. award Armed Svcs. YMCA of U.S., Dallas, 1985, two program merit awards McDonald's Corp., Oak Harbor, 1986; named Alumni of a Growing Vision, Seattle Pacific U., 1991, Diplomat of Yr. Greater Oak Harbor C. of C., 1991. Mem. NASW (bd. dirs. Wash. chpt. 1982-85), Wash. Assn. Social Welfare (pres 1975-76), Acad. Cert. Social Workers. Lutheran. Home: 2450 S Rocky Way Coupeville WA 98239-9610 Office: Cath Community Svcs NW 1121 SE Dock St Oak Harbor WA 98277-4021

MILLER, ROY RAYMOND, optician, ocularist; b. Delta, Ohio, Sept. 20, 1929; s. Roy Draton and Ethel Bernice (Shaffer) M.; m. Evelyn Frances Birsen, Jan. 16, 1954; children: Stephanie, Christopher, Neil Benjamin. Student, Burnham High Sch., Sylvania, Ohio. Lic. Optician. Optician Miller Opticians Inc., Lima, Ohio, 1961-88; pres. Miller Opticians and Miller, Lima, 1961-88, Artificial Eye Lab., Toledo, 1961-88; lic. ocularist Miller Artificial Eye Lab., Toledo; appointed to Ohio Optician and Oculorist Bd., Gov. Vonivoich. Lectr. Nat. Convention, 1978, 1987. Candidate U.S. Congress, Lima 1984, zoning appeals bd. Shawnee Twp., 1980-88, lic. bd. Ohio Optical Dispensing Bd., 1979-85. Cpl. US Army, 1951-52. Fellow Nat. Acad. Opticianry (Contbn. to Edn. of Opticianry award 1995); mem. Am. Soc. Ocularists, Opticians Assn. Am. (past bd. dirs., Optician of Yr. 1995), Guild Prescription Opticians of Am. (bd. dirs.), Optician Assn. Ohio (past pres.), Sertoma (pres. 1983-84), Kiwanis (pres. 1973-74). Republican. Roman Catholic. Office: Miller Opticians Inc 825 W Market St Lima OH 45805-2742

MILLER, SCOTT WILSON MATTHEW, nurse informaticist, administrator; b. Quebec, Que., Can., July 6, 1952; s. Robert Louis and Frances (Wilson) M. Diploma, St. Elizabeth Hosp. Sch. Nursing, 1977; BSN magna cum laude, Bethel Coll., 1986; MS in Nursing Adminstrn., Calif State U., Fresno, 1991; postgrad., U. Calif., San Francisco, 1995—. RN, Calif., Ind., Wash.; cert. post anesthesia nurse, ACLS, informatics nurse specialist. Staff nurse St. Joseph's Med. Ctr., South Bend, Ind., 1977-86; adminstrv. dir. St. Agnes Med. Ctr., Fresno, 1986-88, staff nurse PACU, 1988-90, mgr. nursing informatics, 1990-95; dept. cmty. health systems, Sch. Nursing U. Calif., San Francisco, 1995—; presenter in field. Contbg. author: Transcultural Nursing, Assessment and Invervention, 1994; contbr. articles on transcultural nursing to profl. jours. Mem. ANA, Calif. Nurses Assn., Am. Soc. Post Anesthesia Nurses, Post Anesthesia Nurses Assn. Calif., Nursing Adminstrs. Coun., Bay Area Men in Nursing, Orgn. Nurse Execs. (scholar 1990), Am. Assembly Men in Nursing, Assn. Nurses in AIDS Care, No. Calif. Nursing Informatics Assn., Tech. and Info. Mgmt. Edn. Soc., Sigma Theta Tau. Home: 1556 W Heshdon Ave #105 Fresno CA 93711 Office: Dept Cmty Health Systems Sch of Nursing U Calif San Francisco San Francisco CA

MILLER, SHEILA D. P., medical and surgical nurse; b. Moncks Corner, S.C., Aug. 11, 1959; d. Isaac and Susan Victoria (Williams) Perkins; m. Joseph Miller, Jr., Aug. 17, 1981; 1 child, Brandon Jorell. BSN, Med. U. S.C., 1980; MSA, Cen. Mich. U., 1993. Staff nurse North Trident Regional Hosp., Charleston, S.C.; staff clin. nurse Womack Army Community Hosp., Ft. Bragg, N.C.; staff clin. nurse emergency rm. Bamberg (Fed Republic Germany) Army Health Clinic; staff clin nurse sICU, Winn Army Community Hosp., Ft. Stewart, Ga., head nurse Day Surg. Ctr.; nurse cons. Child Devel. Svcs., Baumholder, Germany, 1993-95; bed ctrl. clin. coord. Ralph H. Johnson VA Med. Ctr., Charleston, S.C., 1995—. Virginia L. Agpar meml. scholar, 1979. Mem. Am. Nurse's Assn. Home: 731 Jorell Ln Saint Stephen SC 29479-9106

MILLER, SHELDON IRVIN, psychiatrist, educator; b. Cleve., June 29, 1938; s. Edward A. and Evelyn Miller; m. Sarah Johnston, June 18, 1861; children: Lynne, David. AB, Oberlin Coll., 1960; MD, Tufts U., 1964. Diplomate Am. Bd. Psychiatry and Neurology. Prof. psychiatry Case Western Res. U. Sch. Medicine, Cleve., 1979-81; clin. prof. psychiatry U. Calif., Irvine, 1982-84; dir. acute inpatient svc. Sheppard & Enoch Pratt Hosp., Towson, Md., 1983-86; clin. prof. psychiatry U. Md., Balt., 1984-86; prof., chmn. of psychiatry U. Medicine and Dentistry, N.J. U. Hosp., Newark, 1986-91; chief of svc. psychiatry St. Barnabas Med. Ctr., Livingston, N.J., 1987-91; dir. Stone Inst. Psychiatry Northwestern Meml. Hosp., Chgo., 1991—; prof., chmn. psychiatry Northwestern U. Med. Sch., Chgo., 1991—; mem. psychiatry residency rev. com. Editor: Clinical Text Addictive Disorders, 1991, (jour.) Am. Jour. Addictions, 1990—; contbr. articles to sci. and psychiat. jours. Bd. dirs. Mental Health Assn., Ill., 1992—; advisor Abraham Low Inst., Ill., 1990-91; pres., bd. trustees Essex County Nat. Coun. Alcoholism, N.J., 1990-91. Lt. commdr. USPHS, 1968-70. Alcohol dependence grantee NIMH, 1990; fetal alcohol syndrome grantee Nat. Inst. on Alcohol Abuse and Alcoholism, 1983. Fellow ACP, Am. Psychiat. Assn. (com. mem. practice guidelines com.); mem. The Am. Acad. of Psychiat. on Alcohol and Addictions (exec. com., pres. 1987-89), Assn. Acad. Psychiatrists, Rsch. Soc. on Alcoholism, Am. Assn. Chairs. Depts. of Psychiatry, Am. Bd. Psychiatry & Neurology (bd. dirs. 1991—), Sigma Xi. Office: Northwestern U Med Sch 303 E Superior #561 Chicago IL 60611

MILLER, STEPHEN BRYAN, social worker, marriage counselor; b. Clare, Mich., Aug. 1, 1951; s. Bryan David and Shirley Jean (Dull) M.; m. Nancy Marie Brandau, Aug. 24, 1974; children: Jennifer Marie, Adam Bryan. AA, Ferris State U., Big Rapids, Mich., 1972; BS, Western Mich. U., 1974, MSW, 1978. Lic. marriage counselor. Social worker Ionia (Mich.) Intermediate Schs., 1974-76, Sanilac County Dept. Social Svcs., Sandusky, Mich., 1976; clin. social worker Caro (Mich.) Regional Mental Health Ctr., 1978; sch. social worker Tuscola Intermediate Schs. Caro, 1978-81, Allegan (Mich.) County Schs., 1981-83, Thornapple-Kellogg Pub. Schs., Middleville, Mich., 1983—; field instr. Western Mich. U., Kalamazoo, 1988—; pvt. marriage counselor, Kentwood, Mich., 1989—; family and marriage cons. John Knox Presbyn. Ch., Grand Rapids, Mich., 1989—. Chairperson Kentwood Activities Com., 1988-89; deacon John Knox Presbyn. Ch., Grand Rapids, 1987-90. Mem. NASW, Acad. Cert. Social Workers (cert.), Mich. Nat. Edn. Assn. (region IX del. 1986-88), Mich. Assn. Tchrs. of Emotionally Disturbed Children. Democrat. Home: 5642 Juanita Dr SE Grand Rapids MI 49508-6427 Office: Thornapple-Kellogg Schs 509 W Main St Middleville MI 49333-9772

MILLER, STEPHEN DONALD, ophthalmologist; b. Santa Monica, Calif., Oct. 14, 1945; s. Mark Ronald and Corrinne Maroe (Yelton) M.; m. Linda Mae Choppman, Dec 21, 1969; children: Alexandra, Stephanie. AB in Physics, Occidental Coll., 1967; MD, Stanford U., 1972. Intern U. Rochester (N.Y.), 1972-73; resident U. Iowa, Iowa City, 1975-79; instr. U. Iowa Hosps., Iowa City, 1978-79; chief ophthalmology Kaiser Permanente, Honolulu, 1979-94, chief surgery, 1980-87; v.p. Hawaii Permanente Med. Group, Honolulu, 1990—; presenter and cons. in field. Contbr. articles to profl. jours. Pres., bd. trustees Honolulu Waldorf Sch., 1986—; chair artistic com. Honolulu Symphony Soc., 1994—; bus. action group Seva Found., San Rafael, Calif., 1985—. Lt. comdr. USPHS, 1972-75. Nat. Merit scholar, 1967. Fellow Am. Acad. Ophthalmology; mem. Vitreous Soc., Nepal Ophthalmic Soc. (hon.). Lutheran. Office: Hawaii Permanente Med Group 1010 Pensacola St Honolulu HI 96814

MILLER, TAMARA DEDRA, psychologist; b. Cleve., Jan. 13, 1961; d. Taswill Taylor and Ethel (Midgett) M.; stepd. Gwendolyn (Hicks) M. BA in Psychology, Wittenberg U., 1982; D in Psychology, Wright State U., 1987. Lic. clin. psychologist, Ohio. Chief psychol. svc. USAF, Altus, Okla., 1987-89; chief psychol. testing USAF, Dayton, Ohio, 1989-92; dir. PTSD program Dept. VA, Dayton, 1992—; clin. prof. Wright State U., Dayton, 1992—; cons. Jackson County Youth, Altus, 1987-89, Ctr. for Retardation, Altus, 1987-89; adj. prof. Ctrl. State U., Wilberforce, 1991—; mem. panel Women's Fed. Program, Dayton, 1991; clin. advisor Les Femmes Concerned Citizens for Cancer, Dayton, 1992—. Consulting editor: Professional Psychology: Research and Practice, 1994. Capt. USAF, 1986-89. Mem. Nat. Coun. Negro Women Inc., VA Psychologists, Delta Sigma Theta. Home: 5670 Olive Tree Dr Dayton OH 45426-1313 Office: Dept VA Affairs Med Ctr 4100 E 3rd St Dayton OH 45403-2244

MILLER, TEERAPORN, nurse; b. Bangkok, Thailand, June 22, 1970; d. Richard Henry and Suporn (Sangvanboon) Terry; m. John Michael Miller, Aug. 8, 1992. BSN, U. Fla., 1992. RN; cert. in chemotherapy. Gen. nurse Shands Hosp., U. Fla., Gainesville, 1992 nurse, case mgr. Broward Gen. Med. Ctr., Ft. Lauderdale, Fla., 1992—.

MILLER, TERRY W., academic adminstrator, legal consultant; b. Clinton, Okla., July 7, 1948; s. Gerald and Bess Miller; m. Julie Randolph, May 5, 1979; children: Celeste, Cody, Haley, Harrison. BS, U. Okla., 1971, BSN, 1974; MSN, U. Tex., 1977, PhD, 1991. Mem. faculty East Ctrl. Okla. State U., 1975-79; prof. San Jose (Calif.) State U., 1980—; dir. adult health NCLEX-RN, CTB/MGraw-Hill, Monterey, Calif., 1987-88;, 1991—; owner, cons. Miller-Randolph & Assocs., Okla., Tex., Calif.; mem. exec. adv. bd. Calif. Nursing/NURSEweek; cons. HCOP grant. Author: Clinical Nursing Skills, 1985, Community Health Nursing, 1995; (with others) Community Health Nursing: Concepts and Practice, 3d edit., 1990. Mem. statewide acad. senate Calif. State Univ. System. Post-baccalaureate fellow, 1989-91; Shirley C. Titus scholar, 1988. Mem. ANA (del. biennial conv. 1980, chair med.-surg. div. on practice for Okla. 1978-80).

MILLER, THERESA VALENTINI, social worker, psychotherapist; b. N.Y.C., Nov. 23, 1951; d. Fermin George and Dorothy (Lindeborg) Valentini; m. Matthew Neil Miller, Oct. 25, 1981; children: Marisa, Elisabeth. BS, SUNY, Stony Brook, 1973; MSW, SUNY, Albany, 1975. Bd. certified diplomate clin. social work, N.Y. Med. social worker Nursing Sisters Home Vis. Svc., Bklyn., 1975-78, Meth. Hosp., Bklyn., 1978-82; psychotherapist 5th Ave. Ctr. for Counselling and Psychotherapy, N.Y.C., 1978-80; social work supr. Meth. Hosp., N.Y.C., 1982-88; dir. social work Coney Island Hosp., Bklyn., 1988-92; pvt. practice psychotherapy Bklyn., 1980—. Bd. dirs. Park Slope Geriatric Day Ctr., Bklyn., 1988—. Mem. NASW, Acad. Cert. Social Workers (cert. diplomate in clin. social work). Home: 100-02 160th Ave Howard Beach NY 11414-3833 Office: 7111 Fifth Ave Brooklyn NY 11209-1608

MILLER, TIMOTHY ALDEN, plastic and reconstructive surgeon; b. Inglewood, Calif., Dec. 11, 1938; s. Henry Bernard and Florence Algena (Maddock) M.; 1 child, Matthew Christopher. Student, U. Calif., Berkeley; MD, UCLA, 1963. Diplomate Am. Bd. Surgery, Am. Bd. Plastic Surgery (bd. dirs. 1991—). Intern Vanderbilt U. Hosp., Nashville, 1963-64; resident in surgery, dept. surg. pathology UCLA, 1966-67, resident, then chief resident gen. and thoracics sugery, 1967-69, acting asst. prof., 1969-70, prof. surgery, 1981—; asst. surg. resident John Hopkins Hosp., 1967; fellow plastic and reconstructive surgery U. Pitts., 1970-72; chief plastic surgery West L.A. VA Med. Ctr., 1973—; dir. Am. Bd. Plastic Surgery, 1991—. Author: (novel) Practice to Deceive, 1991; assoc. editor Jour. Plastic & Reconstructive Surgery, 1987-93, co-editor, 1994—. Trustee Children's Inst. Internat., 1995—. Capt. U.S. Army, 1964-66, Vietnam. Decorated Bronze Star; recipient Thomas Symington award Pitts. Acad. Medicine, 1971. Mem. Am. Soc. for Plastic Surgery (co-editor Jour. Plastic and Reconstructive Surgery), Am. Soc. for Aesthetic Plastic Surgery (bd. dirs. 1990-95), Plastic Surgery Ednl. Found. (bd. dirs. 1991—); trustee Children's Inst. Internat. Office: UCLA Med Ctr 200 Medical Plz Ste 669 Los Angeles CA 90095-6960

MILLER, TODD DONALDSON, medical education consultant; b. Charleston, W.Va., Mar. 28, 1953; s. George Lynn and Virginia DeLaine (Lindberg) M.; m. Cynthia Louise Linden, June 21, 1980; children: Sam, Jill, Gabe, Mitch. BA, Northwestern U., 1975; MD, U. Ill., 1979. Sr. assoc. cons. Mayo Clinic, Rochester, Minn., 1986-89; asst. prof. medicine Mayo Med. Sch., Rochester, Minn., 1988-94; cons. Mayo Clinic, Rochester, Minn., 1989—; assoc. prof. medicine Mayo Med. Sch., 1994—. Contbr. chpts. to books. Fellow ACP, Am. Coll. Cardiology, Am. Heart Assn., Am. Running & Fitness Assn. (editl. bd. 1988—). Office: Mayo Clinic East 16A 200 1st St SW Rochester MN 55905

MILLER, WAYNE DUNBAR, speech pathologist, audiologist; b. Brockton, Mass., Dec. 26, 1934; s. Wilford Eugene and Doris Mae (Dunbar) M.; m. Helen Louise Grant; children: Valerie-Gail, Wilford Gordon. BA in Speech Pathology, Staley Coll., Brookline, Mass., 1958; ME in Counseling, Psychotherapy, Suffolk U., 1971. Certs. in clin. competence speech pathology, lang. pathology and audiology; lic. speech pathologist, audiologist, Mass. Tchr. English Mendon (Mass.) High Sch., 1958-59; acad. clin. practicum in aphasiology Holy Ghost Hosp., Cambridge, Mass., 1959-61; pvt. practice speech pathology, 1961—; supr. speech therapy and hearing Paul A. Dever State Sch., Taunton, Mass., 1961-70; neuro-audiology and aphasiology specialist Goddard Meml. Hosp., Stoughton, Mass., 1966-93; mem. allied med. staff Sturdy Meml. Hosp., Attleboro, Mass., 1970—; mem. allied med. staff, audiologist-speech pathologist Good Samaritan Med. Ctr., Brockton/Stoughton, Mass., 1993—; speech pathologist Attleboro Pub. Schs., 1970—; founder Speech, Lang. and Hearing Clinic Morton Hosp., 1968. Deacon Covenant Congl. Ch., North Easton, Mass., 1979-81, 87; mem. profl. adv. bd. and utilization rev. com. Stoughton Pub. Health Com., 1980—; sustaining mem. Rep. Nat. Com., 1981-95. With Army N.G., 1953-61. Clin. fellow Parson (Kans.) State Hosp., 1964. Fellow Am. Acad. Audiology; mem. NEA, Am. Speech-Lang.-Hearing Assn. (pres.'s coun., Cert. of Excellence), Am. Audiology Soc., Mass. Speech and Hearing Assn., Mass. Edn. Assn., Attleboro Edn. Assn., U.S. Naval Inst., Am. Legion, Sons of Union Vets. of the Civil War, Masons, Shriners, DeMolay (chpt. adv. coun. 1980-89, rainbow adv. bd. 1987-89). Home and Office: 76 Short St South Easton MA 02375-1019 also: Good Samaritan Med Ctr Cushing Campus Brockton MA 02072

MILLER, WAYNE E., pediatrician, internist; b. Ipswich, S.D., Mar. 27, 1957; s. Fred W. and Margaret (Lacher) M. BS, No. State U., 1978; MD, Am. U. Caribbean, 1991. Med. technologist BioSci. Labs., Van Nuys, Calif., 1978-89; resident St. Joseph Mercy Hosp., Pontiac, Mich., 1991-95; physician Mercy Med. Group, Rochester Hills, Mich., 1995—. Mem. ACP, Am. Acad. Pediatrics, Am. Soc. Clin. Pathologists (cert.). Lutheran. Office: Mercy Med Group 1812 S Rochester Rd Rochester Hills MI 48307

MILLER, WILLIAM LESLIE, pathologist, laboratory administrator; b. Louisville, May 10, 1934; s. Leslie and Lillie Mae (Parson) M.; m. Hilda Fae Cook, Sept. 3, 1956; children: William Marcus, Leslie Scott, Jennifer Carson, Leslyn Fae. BS, U. Louisville, 1956, MD cum laude, 1959. Diplomate Am. Bd. Pathology; lic. physician, Ky., Ind., Ariz., Tenn., Ill., Mo. Intern Mallory Inst. Pathology, Boston, 1960; resident Mass. Gen. Hosp., Boston, 1961; resident Louisville Gen. Hosp., 1962-63, staff pathologist, 1963-66; staff pathologist Ft. Walton Beach, Fla., 1968-70; staff pathologist, chief hematopathology Ariz. Med. Ctr., Tucson, 1970-72; staff pathologist, acting chief pathology svc. VA Hosp., Tucson, 1971; vice chmn. and chief clin. pathology U. Tenn. Med. Units, Memphis, 1972-73; dir. hematopathology, dep. dir. clin. lab. City of Memphis Hosps., 1972-73; chief pathologist, dir. labs. Muhlenberg Cmty. Hosp., Greenville, Ky., 1973—; chmn. tumor bd. Muhlenberg Cmty. Hosp., Greenville, 1989—. Contbr. articles to profl. jours. Capt. M.C. U.S. Army, lt. col. USAR, 1966—. Recipient Mosby Book Co. awards, 1957, 59; NIH Cancer Rsch. fellow, 1961-63; U. Louisville Flexner scholar, 1952-55. Fellow Am. Soc. Clin. Pathologists, Coll. Am. Pathologists, Internat. Assn. Pathologists; mem. AMA, Am. Soc. Hematology, Ky. Soc. Pathology, (pres.), Ky. Med. Assn. (trustee 1989-92), Greenville-Muhlenberg C. of C. (pres.), Kiwanis (chpt. pres.), Alpha Omega Alpha, Phi Kappa Kappa. Republican. Baptist. Office: 508 Hopkinsville St Greenville KY 42345

MILLEY, JOHN ROSS, neonatologist, educator; b. Hartford, Conn., Oct. 10, 1946; s. Chesley Ross and Muriel Frances (Potter) M.; m. Donna Beatrice Scholts, June 11, 1968; 1 child, Jeffrey Ross. BA in Chemistry, Ill. Wesleyan U., 1967; PhD in Chemistry, U. Chgo., 1974, MD, 1975. Diplomate Am. Bd. Pediats., Neonatal Perinatal Medicine, Nat. Bd. Med. Examiners; lic. physician, Md., Pa., Utah. Intern in pediats. Johns Hopkins U., Balt., 1975-76, resident in pediats., 1976-78, fellow in perinatal medicine, 1978-80, asst. in pediats., 1979-80; from asst. prof. to assoc. prof. ob-gyn. U. Pitts. Sch. Medicine, 1980-88; mem. med. staff Primary Children's Med. Ctr., Salt Lake City, 1988—, U. Utah Med. Ctr., Salt Lake City, 1988—; assoc. prof. pediats. U. Utah Sch. Medicine, Salt Lake City, 1988—; dir. neonatal fellowship program U. Pitts., 1987-88, U. Utah, Salt Lake City, 1988—; mem. med. staff Johns Hopkins Hosp., Balt., 1979-80, Children's Hosp. Pitts., 1980-88, Children's Home of Pitts., 1985-88, LDS Hosp., Salt Lake City, 1988—, Magee-Womens Hosp., Pitts., 1980-88, mem. quality assurance com., 1985-88, perinatal morbidity and mortality com., 1984-88; vis. prof. dept. pediatrics U. Cin. Sch. Medicine, 1987; mem. instnl. rev. bd. Primary Children's Med. Ctr., Salt Lake City, 1989—, chmn. instnl. rev. bd., 1991—; mem. ad hoc subcom. for decentralized lab. testing U. Utah Sch. Medicine,

Salt Lake City, 1990—; prin. investigator numerous grants, programs Nat. Inst. Child Health and Human Devel. Ad hoc reviewer: Pediats. Rsch., Diabetes, Am. Jour. Physiology; contbr. articles to profl. publs. Mem. med. adv. com. Pitts. Planned Parenthood, 1982-86. Rsch. grantee Children's Hosp. Pitts., 1980-85, Magee-Womens Hosp. Rsch. Fund, 1980-81, 81-84, 82-85, 84-85, 86-87, Ann Ricketson Loftberg Fund, 1981-85, Western Pa. Heart Assn., Inc., 1981-82, Ross Labs., 1984-86, 84-88, U. Utah Sch. Medicine, 1988-89. Fellow Am. Acad. Pediats. (dist. VIII perinatal sect. 1988—), Am. Physiol. Soc., Intermountain Pediat. Soc., Soc. for Pediat. Rsch., Perinatal Rsch. Soc., Utah Perinatal Assn., Study Group for Complications of Perinatal Care. Office: Univ Utah Sch Medicine 50 N Medical Dr Salt Lake City UT 84132-0001

MILLIARD, ALINE, social worker; b. Portage, Maine, Nov. 18, 1937; d. Alderic and Ida (Dionne) M. MSW, Adelphi U., 1976; diploma social work supervision, Hunter Coll., 1986. Bd. cert. diplomate, clin. cert. social worker. Nurses' aide Good Samaritan Hosp., West Islip, N.Y., 1964-65, admitting office clk., 1965-70, social svc. asst.; intake worker Maryhaven Diagnostic & Guidance Ctr., Port Jefferson, N.Y., 1972-74; coord. marriage counseling program Diocesan Human Rels. Svcs., Portland, Maine, 1977, family svc. worker, 1977-79; sch. social worker Sanford (Maine) Pub. Sch. Dept., 1979-81; campus social worker Green Chimneys Childrne Svcs., Brewster, N.Y., 1982-85, dir. group homes, 1985-88; social worker Med. Ctr. Hosp. Vt., Burlington, 1989—. Mem. Acad. Cert. Social Workers, NASW. Home: 64 1/2 Howard St Burlington VT 05401-4814 Office: MCHV Colchester Ave Burlington VT 05401

MILLIGAN, GLENN ELLIS, psychologist; b. Emporia, Kans., Nov. 12, 1919; s. Ellis S. and Clara (Kriete) M.; m. Phyllis Eaton, Aug. 26, 1945 (div.); children: Douglas, Gregory, David; m. Janice Barron Dawes, Oct. 10, 1970; 1 step-dau., Virginia. BS, Kans. State Tchrs. Coll., 1941, MS, 1942; postgrad., U. Chgo., 1943-44; Ed.D., Colo. State Coll., 1951. Head dept. edn. Findlay (Ohio) Coll., 1946-55; psychologist Columbus (Ohio) Pub. Schs., 1955-56; asso. prof. edn. Ohio Wesleyan U., Delaware, 1956-60; exec. dir. Am. Assn. Mental Deficiency, Columbus, 1960-65; cons. mental retardation Vocat. Rehab. Adminstrn., HEW, 1965-67; psychologist spl. edn. Montgomery County Pub. Schs., Rockville, Md., 1967—; Lectr. Catholic U. Am. Editor: (1st) Mental Retardation, 1963-64, (with others) Directory of Residential Facilities for the Mentally Retarded, 1965. Fellow Am. Assn. Mental Deficiency; mem. Am. Psychol. Assn., NEA (life). Home: 5208 Elsmere Ave Bethesda MD 20814-5731 Office: Montgomery County Pub Schs Spring Mill Field Office 11721 Kemp Mill Rd Silver Spring MD 20902-1722

MILLIGAN, MICHAEL LEE, dentist; b. Kenton, Ohio, Sept. 5, 1952; s. Robert L. and Lena R. (Chiesa) M.; m. Karen S. Nice, Sept. 20, 1975; children: Kristen, Patrick, Lyndsey, Marisa. BS, U. Houston, 1975; DMD, So. Ill. U., 1978. Gen. practice dentistry Bloomington, Ill., 1978—; co-developer Eastland Profl. Bldg., Bloomington, 1987-88. Ill. Men's Golf Champion, 1974, Ill. Men's Match Play Golf Champion, 1977, Chgo. Dist. Golf. Champion, 1973, 74, 77, Butler Nat. Amateur Golf Champion, 1994. Mem. ADA, Ill. Dental Soc., McLean County Dental Soc. (pres. 1987-88). Lodges: K.C. Home: 208 Grandview Dr Normal IL 61761-3135 Office: 1404 Eastland Dr Ste 101 Bloomington IL 61701-3517

MILLION, RODNEY REIFF, radiologist; b. Idaville, Ind., 1929. MD, Ind. U., 1954. Diplomate Am. Bd. Radiology. Intern Harbor Gen. Hosp., Torrance, 1954-55; resident in radiology Ind. U., 1958-60; resident in radiol. therapy MD Anderson Hosp., Houston, 1960-62; mem. staff Shands Tchg. Hosp., Gainesville, Fla.; prof. radiol. oncology U. Fla., Gainesville. Mem. ARS, ASTRO, Am. Coll. Radiology. Office: Shands Tchg Hosp Dept Radiology Gainesville FL 32602-0385*

MILLMAN, ARTHUR LANCE, ophthalmologist, surgeon; b. N.Y.C., Feb. 8, 1958; s. Harry H. and Susan Z. M.; m. Sandra L. Millman; children: Suzanne, Alana. BSN, Northwestern U., Evanston, Ill., MD. Diplomate Am. Bd. Ophthalmology and Eye Plastic Surgery. Dir. Manhattan Ctr. Facial Plastic Surgery; asst. prof. N.Y. Eye and Ear Infirmary; fellow Heed & Knapp Found. Author: (textbook) Facial Plastic Surgery; contbr. articles to profl. jours. Mem. N.Y. Acad. Medicine (William Warner Happin award), N.Y. Facial Plastic Soc. (founding mem.).

MILLMAN, JEROME ISRAEL, anesthesiologist; b. Detroit, Apr. 19, 1934; s. Sara (Michaels) M.; m. Audrey Lois Sinclair, Aug. 23, 1955 (div. 1965); children: Elissa Sheryl, Martin Neil; m. Felicitas Aquirre dela Cruz, Oct. 6, 1976. BS, U. Mich., 1955, MD, 1960. Intern Detroit Receiving Hosp., 1960-61; resident in anesthesiology U. Mich. Med. Ctr., Ann Arbor, 1961-63; practice medicine specializing in anesthesiology Centinela Hosp., Inglewood, Calif., 1977—. Home: 1625 Indiana Ave South Pasadena CA 91030-4113

MILLON, DELECTA GAY, nursing educator; b. Flint, Mich., Aug. 4, 1943; d. Rudolph Albert Spaleny and Odessa Mae (Bergeron) Kelley; divorced; children: Daniel Lawrence, Christopher Matthew. ADN, Flint Community Jr. Coll., 1963; BS in Edn. and Human Svcs., U. Detroit, 1981; MA in Classroom Teaching, Mich. State U., 1986, cert. in vocat. edn., 1986; postgrad., Mary Grove Coll. RN, Mich.; lic. emergency med. tech.; cert. emergency med. technician instr.-coord., firefighter I. Nurse McLaren Gen. Hosp., Flint, 1963-64, Flint Osteo. Hosp., 1974-76; tchr. Mott Adult High Sch., 1971-75, Flint Comm. Schs., 1974—; occupational nurse GM, 1986—; evaluator emergency med. tech. practical exam. State of Mich., nurse's assisting cert. exam. Vol. tchr. Mundy Twp. Fire Dept., Swartz Creek, Mich., 1986—. Mem. Soc. Mich. Emergency Med. Technician Instrs. and Coords. (sec. 1980-87, outstanding contbn. award 1987). Roman Catholic. Office: Genesee Area Skill Ctr G-5081 Torrey Rd Flint MI 48507

MILLOY, FRANK JOSEPH, JR., surgeon; b. Phoenix, June 26, 1924; s. Frank Joseph and Ola (McCabe) M.; BS, Notre Dame U., 1946; MS, Northwestern U., 1949, M.D., 1947. Intern, Cook County Hosp., Chgo., 1947-49, resident, 1953-57; practice medicine, specializing in surgery, Lake Forest, Ill., 1958—; asso. attending staff Presbyn.-St. Lukes Hosp.; attending staff Cook County Hosp.; mem. staff U. Ill. Rsch. Hosp.; clin. asso. prof. surgery, U. Ill. Med. Sch.; asso. prof. surgery Rush Med. Sch. Cons. West Side Vet. Hosp. Served as apprentice seaman USNR, 1943-45; lt. M.C., USNR, 1950-52; PTO. Diplomate Am. Bd. Surgery and Thoracic Surgery. Mem. A.C.S., Chgo. Surg. Soc., Internat. Soc. Surgery, Am. Coll. Chest Physicians, Soc. Thoracic Surgeons, Phi Beta Pi. Clubs: Metropolitan, University (Chgo.). Home: 574 Jackson Ave Glencoe IL 60022-2036

MILLS, CELESTE LOUISE, hypnotherapist, professional magician; b. L.A., May 16, 1952; d. Emery John and Helen Louise (Bradbury) W.; m. Robert Richardson Feigel, Apr. 11, 1971 (div. 1973); m. Peter Alexander Mills, June 12, 1991. (div. 1992). BBA, Western State U., Doniphan, Mo., 1987; PhD in Religion, Universal Life Ch. Univ., 1987; grad., Hypnotism Tng. Inst., Glendale, Calif., 1990. Cert. hypnotherapist. Credit mgr. accounts receivable Gensler-Lee Diamonds, Santa Barbara, Calif., 1973-74, Terry Hinge and Hardware, Van Nuys, Calif., 1975-78; credit mgr., fin. analyst Peanut Butter Fashions, Chatsworth, Calif., 1978-82; personal mgr. Charter Mgmt. Co., Beverly Hills, Calif., 1982-83; co-owner, v.p. Noreen Jenney Communicates, Beverly Hills, 1983-85; corp. credit mgr., fin. analyst Cen. Diagnostic Lab., Tarzana, Calif., 1985-89; credit mgr., fin. analyst Metwest Clin. Lab., Inc., Tarzana, Calif., 1989-90; pvt. practice, 1990—; cons. Results Now, Inc., Tarzana, 1986-87. Prodr., host (TV) Brainstorm, 1993—. Media spokesperson Am. Cancer Soc., 1990—. Mem. NAFE, NOW, Nat. Humane Ednl. Found., Credit Mgrs. Assn. Trade Groups (bd. govs. 1988-89), Nat. Clin. Lab. Trade Group (chmn. 1988-89), Med. and Surg. Suppliers Trade Group (vice chmn. 1988-89, chmn. 1989-90), Soc. Am. Magicians, Acad. Magical Arts, Internat. Brotherhood of Magicians, Assn. Advanced Ethical Hypnosis, Am. Coun. Hypnotist Examiners.

MILLS, JOHN GERALD, physician; b. Lansing, Mich., Mar. 13, 1948; s. Francis Joseph Jr. and Melva Irene (Bedell) M.; 1 child, Jeremiah Garret. BS with honors, Mich. State U., 1974, MS, 1976, DO, 1979; MPH, U. Mich., 1982. Diplomate Am. Bd. Preventive Medicine, Am. Osteo. Bd. Preventive Medicine. Chief profl. edn. U.S. Army Sch. Aviation Medicine, Ft. Rucker, Ala., 1980-81, chief edn. and tng., 1983-84; chief aeromed. cons. svc. U.S. Army Aeromed. Activity, Ft. Rucker, 1984-85; asst. prof. preventive medicine Kirksville (Mo.) Coll. Osteo. Medicine, 1985-86, assoc. prof., 1986-87; surgeon 18th aviation XVIII Airborne Corps., Ft. Bragg, N.C., 1988-89; assoc. prof., chmn. dept. preventive medicine/pub. health U. North Tex. Health Sci. Ctr., Ft. Worth, 1989-92, 95-96, assoc. dean clin. affairs, 1992-94; clin. dir. hyperbaric medicine/wound U. North Tex. Health Sci. Ctr. and Osteo. Med. Ctr. Tex., Ft. Worth, 1992—. Contbr. articles to profl. publs. Maj. U.S. Army, 1988-89. Fellow Am. Osteo. Coll. Preventive Medicine (trustee 1990—), Am. Coll. Preventive Medicine (pres. 1994-95); mem. Am. Osteo. Assn. (chmn. osteo. bd. 1987-88), Soc. USA Flight Surgeons (sec. 1983-84, aerospace med. specialist 1989), Tex. Osteo. Med. Assn., Undersea and Hyperbaric Med. Assn., Mich. State U. Alumni Assn. (life). Office: U North Tex Health Sci Ctr 3500 Camp Bowie Blvd Fort Worth TX 76107-2644

MILLS, RICHARD PENCE, ophthalmologist; b. Evanston, Ill., Sept. 13, 1943; s. Glen Earl and Ruth Arlene (Pence) M.; m. Catherine Louise Baily, June 1, 1966 (div. Sept. 1975); 1 child, Lianne Louise; m. Karen Elisabeth, Aug. 1, 1976; children: Elisabeth Ruth, Emily Carole. BA magna cum laude, Yale U., 1964, MD cum laude, 1968. Clin. instr. dept. ophthalmology U. Wash., Seattle, 1972-75, clin. asst. prof., 1975-80, clin. assoc. prof. depts. ophthalmology, medicine, 1980-84, assoc. prof. dept. ophthalmology, 1984-87, prof., vice-chmn. dept. ophthalmology, 1987—; adj. prof. depts. medicine and neurol. surgery, U. Wash., 1987—; pres. St. Peter Hosp. Med. Staff, Olympia, Wash., 1982; trustee Bishop Found., Seattle, 1996. Author: (books) Glaucoma Surgical Techniques, 1991, Perimetry Update: 1990-91, 1991, Perimetry Update: 1992-93, 1993, 94-95, 95. Surgeon USPHS, 1969-73. Recipient Optic Neuritis Treatment Trial award Nat. Eye Inst., Washington, 1988-91, Collaborative Initial Glaucoma Treatment Study, 1993-96, Collaborative Normal Tension Glaucoma Study award Glaucoma Rsch. Found., San Francisco, 1988-96. Fellow Am. Acad. Ophthalmology (pres. 1995, Honor award 1989, Sr. Honor award 1996), Wash. Acad. Eye Physicians and Surgeons (pres. 1983, Spl. Honor 1993), Wash. State Med. Assn. (trustee 1996), Am. Glaucoma Soc. (dir. 1993-94), No. Am. Neuro-Ophth. Soc., Internat. Perimetric Soc. (sec. 1988-94). Office: Univ Wash Dept Ophthalmology Box 356485 1959 NE Pacific Seattle WA 98195

MILLS, ROGER MARION, cardiologist; b. Athens, Ohio, Jan. 23, 1943; s. Roger Marion Sr. and Adrienne Ellen (McGuire) M.; m. Susan Brownell (div. Sept. 1987); children: David McGuire, Andrew Loomis; m. Diane Evans, Dec. 19, 1987. BA, Amherst (Mass.) Coll., 1964; MD, U. Pa., 1968. Diplomate Am. Bd. Internal Medicine; lic. pilot. Intern, then resident in internal medicine Hosp. U. of Pa., Phila., 1968-71; rsch. fellow in cardiology Harvard Med. Sch. Peter Bent Brigham Hosp., Boston, 1973-75; cardiologist, dir. coronary care unit Worcester (Mass.) Meml. Hosp., 1975-87, dir. catherization lab., acting chief of cardiology, 1985-87; assoc. prof. U. Mass. Med. Sch., Worcester, 1975-87; dir. clin. cardiology, assoc. prof. medicine Boston U. Hosp., 1987-90; med. dir. cardiac transplant program, dir. clin. cardiology Shands Hosp. at U. Fla., Gainesville, 1990—, co-chair Transplant Ctr., 1992—; assoc. prof. Coll. Medicine U. Fla., Gainesville, 1990-95, prof., 1995—; treas. med. staff Worcester Meml. Hosp., 1978-82; pres. med. staff U. Mass. Med. Ctr., Worcester, 1983-84; contbr. articles to profl. jours. Bd. dirs. Home for Aged Women, Worcester, 1980-87. Lt. comdr. USNR, 1971-73. Fellow ACP, Am. Coll. Cardiology, Coun. on Clin. Cardiology, Am. Heart Assn. (bd. dirs. Fla. affiliate), Soc. for Cardiac Angiography and Intervention. Republican. Episcopalian. Office: U Fla Coll Medicine Box 100277 JHMHSC 1600 SW Archer Rd Gainesville FL 32610

MILLS, THOMAS COOKE, psychiatrist; b. San Francisco, Nov. 24, 1955; s. Willard Cooke and Billie Dee (Hunt) M. BS, MIT, 1977; MD, U. Ill., Chgo., 1981; MPH, U. Calif., Berkeley, 1991. Diplomate Am. Bd. Psychiatry and Neurology. Resident in psychiatry U. Calif., San Francisco, 1981-85, asst. clin. prof., 1985-91, assoc. clin. prof., 1991—; med. dir. Jail Psychiat. Svcs., San Francisco, 1985-88; pvt. practice San Francisco, 1985-88; staff psychiatrist Dept. Vets. Affairs, San Francisco, 1988-93, psychiat. authorizing physician, 1991-93; postdoctoral fellow U. Calif., Berkeley, 1990-91. Fellow NIMH, 1990-91. Mem. Am. Psychiat. Assn., No. Calif. Psychiat. Soc. Office: PO Box 460520 San Francisco CA 94146-0520

MILMAN, DOUGLAS SCOTT, psychologist; b. Balt., July 12, 1953; s. Donald Stuart and Marilyn Martha (Holstein) M. BA, Bard Coll., 1976; MA, Adelphi U., 1978, PhD, 1983, cert. in psychotherapy & psychoanalysis, 1994. Lic. psychologist, N.Y.; cert. substance abuse counselor, N.Y. Psychologist SUNY, Farmingdale, 1980—, Baldwin (N.Y.) Coun. Against Drug Abuse, 1981—; pvt. practice Baldwin, 1987—; adj. clin. supr. Adelphi U., 1994. Author: Are You Normal?, 1983. Mem. APA (cert. proficiency in the treatment of alcohol and substance abuse 1996), Adelphi Soc. for Psychotherapy and Psychoanalysis, United U. Profls., Nassau County Psychol. Assn., N.Y. State Psychol. Assn., Nat. Register Health Svc. Providers. Office: 1914 Grand Ave Baldwin NY 11510-2454

MILNE, EDWARD LAWRENCE, biomedical engineer; b. Ottawa, Ont., Can., June 20, 1948; came to U.S., 1985; s. Roderick Francis and Mary Angela (Massiah) M.; m. Pamela Mary Sklenka, Aug. 23, 1975; children: Marc Aaron, Adam Daniel. BSc, Dalhousie U., 1971. Rsrch. asst. Tech. U. N.S., Halifax, Can., 1973-76; technologist Dalhousie U., Halifax, 1976-85; biomed. engr. Mt. Sinai Med. Ctr., Miami Beach, Fla., 1986—. Contbr. articles to profl. jours. Office: Mt Sinai Med Ctr 4300 Alton Rd Miami FL 33140-2849

MILNER, BRENDA ATKINSON LANGFORD, neuropsychologist; b. Manchester, Eng., July 15, 1918; emigrated to Can., 1944; d. Samuel and Leslie (Doig) Langford. BA, Cambridge (Eng.) U., 1939, MA, 1949, ScD, 1972; PhD, McGill U., 1952; DSc (hon.), 1991;, LLD (hon.), Queen's U., 1980; ScD (hon.) U. Manitoba, 1982, U. Lethbridge, 1986, Mt. Holyoke Coll., 1986, U. Laval, 1987, U. Toronto, 1987; LHD (hon.), Mt. St. Vincent U., 1988; Hon. D. U. de Montréal, 1988; DSc (hon.) Wesleyan U., 1991, Acadia U., 1991, U. St. Andrews, 1992. Exptl. officer U.K. Ministry of Supply, 1941-44; prof. agrégé Institut de Psychologie, Université de Montréal, 1944-52; rsch. assoc. psychology dept. McGill U., Montreal, 1952-53, lectr. dept. neurology and neurosurgery, 1953-60, asst. prof., 1960-64, assoc. prof., 1964-70, prof. psychology, 1970-93; Dorothy J. Killam prof. Montreal Neurological Inst., 1993—; head neuropsychology rsch. unit Montreal Neurol. Inst., 1953-90; Clothworkers fellow Girton Coll., Cambridge, 1972-73. Mem. editorial bd. Neuropsychologia, 1973-93, Behavioral Brain Rsch., 1980-88, Hippocampus, 1990—. Decorated officer Order of Can., officier l'Ordre Nat. du Que., 1985; Career investigator Med. Rsch. Coun. Can., 1964—; recipient Kathleen Stott prize Newnham Coll., 1971, Karl Spencer Lashley award Am. Philos. Soc., 1979, Izaak Walton Killam Meml. prize Can. Coun., 1983, Hermann Von Helmholtz prize Cognitive Neuroscience Inst., 1984, Penfield award Can. league Against Epilepsy, 1984, William James fellow Am. Psychol. Soc., 1989, Wilder Penfield prize Province of Quebec, 1993, Neural Plasticity prize Fondation IPSEN, Paris; named Great Montrealer, 1987. Fellow APA (Disting. Contbn. award 1973), AAAS, Royal Soc. London, Royal Soc. Can. (McLaughlin medal 1995), Can. Psychol. Assn.; mem. NAS (fgn. assoc.), Am. Epilepsy Soc. (William G. Lennox award 1974, 95), Am. Neurol. Assn., Association de Psychologie Scientifique de Langue Française, Brit. Soc. Exptl. Psychology, Exptl. Psychol. Soc., Psychonomic Soc., Eastern Psychol. Assn., Internat. Neuropsychology Symposium, Internat. Brain Rsch. Orgn. (exec. sec. 1993—), Soc. Neurosci. (Ralph W. Gerard prize 1987), Am. Acad. Neurology (assoc.), Assn. Rsch. in Nervous and Mental Diseases (assoc.), Royal Soc. Medicine (affiliate), Sigma Xi. Office: Montreal Neurol Inst, 3801 University St, Montreal, PQ Canada H3A 2B4

MILNOR, WILLIAM ROBERT, physician; b. Wilmington, Del., May 4, 1920; s. William Robert and Virginia (Sterling) M.; m. Gabriella Mahaffy, Aug. 19, 1944; children—Katherine Alexander, William Henry. A.B., Princeton U., 1941; M.D., Johns Hopkins U., 1944. Diplomate: Am. Bd. Internal Medicine. Intern, resident Johns Hopkins Hosp., 1944-46; research fellow Nat. Heart Inst., 1949-51; physician-in-charge heart sta. Johns Hopkins Hosp., 1951-60, physician, 1952—; mem. faculty Johns Hopkins Med. Sch., 1951—, prof. physiology, 1969—; vis. fellow St. Catherine's Coll., Oxford (Eng.) U., 1968; mem. med. adv. panel Am. Inst. Biol. Scis., 1971—; assessor Nat. Med. Research Council of Australia, 1976—. Author: Hemodynamics, 2d edit., 1989, Cardio-vascular Physiology, 1990; contbr. articles to med. textbooks, med. jours. Served to capt. M.C. USAAF, 1946-48. Fellow A.C.P.; mem. Am. Physiol. Soc., Am. Fedn. Clin. Research, Biomed. Engring. Soc., Am. Heart Assn. (chmn. research com. 1966), Heart Assn. Md. (past pres.). Clubs: L'Hirondelle, Princeton, 14 W Hamilton St. Office: Johns Hopkins Med Sch 725 N Wolfe St Baltimore MD 21205-2105

MILOWE, IRVIN D., psychiatrist, psychoanalyst; b. Bklyn., Dec. 27, 1931. BA, Columbia U., 1953; MD, Cornell U., 1957. Cert. in psychiatry, psychoanalysis, child analysis. Intern U. Wash., Seattle, 1957-58; fellow psychiatry U. Cin., 1958-60, fellow child psychiatry, 1958-61; chief psychiatry USPHS Hosp., Seattle, 1961-63; fellow in child psychiatry NIMH, Children's Hosp. Nat. Med. Ctr., Washington, 1963-64; chief of psychiatry Health, Edn., Welfare Mental Health Ctr., Washington, 1964-65; dir. Community Psychiat. Ctr., Bethesda, 1965-68; teaching analyst Balt.-Washington Psychoanalytic Inst., Washington, 1969—; clin. prof. pediatrics and child psychiatry Childrens' Hosp. Nat. Med. Ctr., Washington, 1969—; clin. prof. psychiatry George Washington U., 1969—. Contbr. various articles to profl. jours. Fellow Am. Psychiat. Assn. (assembly rep. 1988—); mem. Internat. Psychoanalytic Assn., Washington Psychiat. Soc. (pres. 1987-88), Ctr. for Advanced Psychoanalytic Studies, Am. Psychoanalytic Assn., N.Y. Freudian Soc. (tng. & supervising analyst 1991—). Office: Irvin D Milowe MD PC 1006 23rd St NW Washington DC 20037-1421

MILSOM, IAN, gynecologist, lecturer, consultant; b. Yorkshire, England, June 4, 1950; arrived in Sweden, 1974; s. George Smith and Elsie May (Lear) M.; m. Karin Inger Johanisson, June 15, 1991. MBChB, Liverpool U., 1973; PhD, Göteborg U., Sweden, 1984. Specialist in ob-gyn. House officer Broadgreen Hosp., Liverpool, 1973-74; registrar dept. ob-gyn. East Hosp., Göteborg, Sweden, 1974-80; jr. lectr. dept. ob-gyn. U. Göteborg, Sweden, 1981-90, sr. lectr. dept. ob-gyn., cons. gynecologist, 1990—. Contbr. chpts. to books. Mem. Swedish Soc. Ob-Gyn. (head postgrad. edn.). Home: Bjorndammusterrassen 35, S-43342 Partille Sweden Office: East HospU, Dept Ob-Gyn, S-41685 Göteborg Sweden

MILSTED, AMY, medical educator. BSEd, Ohio State U., 1967; PhD, CUNY, 1977. Lectr. Hunter Coll./CUNY, 1970-76; instr. Carnegie-Mellon U., Pitts., 1976-77; postdoctoral fellow Muscular Dystrophy Assn./Carnegie-Mellon U., Pitts., 1978-79; rsch. assoc. Case Western Res. U., Cleve., 1979-82; rsch. chemist VA Med. Ctr., Cleve., 1982-87; project staff The Cleve. Clin. Found., 1987-89; asst. staff dept. brain and vascular rsch. Cleve. Clinic Found., 1989-93; grad. faculty Sch. Biomed. Scis. Kent (Ohio) State U., 1995—; assoc. prof. dept. biology U. Akron, Ohio, 1993—; adj. faculty biology dept. Cleve. State U., 1991—. Contbr. articles to profl. jours. Mem. Am. Heart Assn., Am. Soc. Cell Biology, Am. Chem. Soc., Endocrine Soc., AAAS. Office: University of Akron Dept of Biology ASEC 279 Akron OH 44325-3908

MILSTEIN, CÉSAR, molecular biologist; b. Oct. 8, 1927; s. Lázaro and Máxima Milstein; m. Celia Prilleltensky, 1953. Ed., Colegio Nacional De Bahia Blanca, U. Nacional de Buenos Aires, Fitzwilliam Coll., Cambridge. Brit. Council fellow, 1958-60; staff Instituto Nacional de Microbiologia, Buenos Aires, 1957-63; head Div. de Biologia Molecular, 1961-63; mem. staff Lab. Molecular Biology, Med. Rsch. Coun., Cambridge, Eng., 1963-95, dep. dir., 1988-95. Contbr. articles to profl. jours. Decorated Companion of Honour to the Queen; recipient Rozenberg prize, 1979, Mattia award, 1979, Gross Howit prize, 1980, Koch prize, 1980, Wolf prize in medicine, 1980, medal Wellcome Found., 1980, Gimenez Diaz medal, 1981, Sloan prize GM Cancer Rsch. Found., 1981, Gardner award Gardner Found., 1981, Nobel prize for medicine, 1984. Fellow Royal Coll. Physicians (hon.), Royal Soc. (Royal medal 1982, Copley medal 1989), Royal Coll. Pathologists (hon.); mem. NAS (fgn. assoc.). Office: Med Rsch Coun Lab Mol Biol, Hills Rd, Cambridge CB2 2QH, England

MILSTEIN, JERROLD MARSHALL, child neurologist, educator; b. Mpls., Apr. 21, 1939; s. Joe and Minnie (Nolman) M., m. Leslie Joan Howard, Aug. 8. 1962; children: David S., Jonathan W. BA, U. Minn., 1960, BS, MD, 1964. Diplomate Am. Bd. Pediatrics, Am. Bd. Psychiatry and Neurology. Intern U. Calif. Affiliated Hosps., Los Angeles, 1964-65; resident in pediatrics and neurology U. Minn., 1965-68; clin. instr. U. Calif., Davis, 1968-70; spl. fellow in neurology U. Minn., 1970-71; asst. prof. U. Minn. Med. Sch., Mpls., 1971-77; assoc. prof. neurology U. Wash. Med. Sch., Seattle, 1977—; dir. child neurology Children's Orthopedic Hosp. and Med. Ctr., Seattle, 1977—. Bd. dirs. Jewish Community Ctr., Mpls., 1974-77. Served to capt. USAF, 1968-70. USPHS fellow 1970-71. Fellow Am. Acad. Neurology; mem. Profs. Child Neurology (sec.-treas. 1982-86), Child Neurology Soc., Internat. Neurochemistry Soc., Am. Epilepsy Soc. Home & Office: Children's Orthopedic Hosp Med Ctr 4800 Sand Point Way NE Seattle WA 98105-3901

MILSTEN, RICHARD, urologist; b. Tulsa, Jan. 9, 1940; m. Nancy Ellen Feuerstein, June 16, 1963. BA, Yale U., 1967; MA, Columbia U., 1968. Diplomate Am. Bd. Urology. Intern in gen. surgery Dartmouth Hitchcock Hosp., Hanover, N.H., 1968-70; resident in urology Med. Coll. Va., Richmond, 1970-73; urologist Ctr. for Urol. Care, Voorhees, N.J., 1975—. Author: Male Sexual Function, Myth, Fantasy and Reality, 1978. Lt. comdr. USN, 1973-75. Fellow Acad. Medicine N.J.; mem. AMA, ACS, Med. Soc. N.J., Phila. Urol. Assn., Soc. for Sex Therapy and Rsch., Am. Inst. Ultrasound in Medicine, Am. Assn. Clin. Urologists, Am. Lithotripsy Soc., Internat. Soc. for Impotence Rsch., Endourological Soc., Urology Soc. N.J., Am. Soc. Sex Educators, Counselors and Therapists, Camden County Med. Soc., Glouster County Med. Soc. (assoc.). Office: Ctr for Urol Care 100 Carnie Blvd Ste A-3 Voorhees NJ 08057

MILTON, WAYNE ALVIN, human services administrator; b. Lingle, Wyo., Apr. 28, 1945; s. Gale E. and Lodisa E. (Haines) M.; m. Linda Jo Rowley, Apr. 1963 (div.); 1 child, Jodi L.; m. Patricia Ann McClure, Jan. 6, 1968; children: Troy M., Tamara M. AA, Goshen County Community Coll., Torrington, Wyo., 1967; BS, U. Wyo., 1970, MBA, 1982. Adminstrv. acct., supr. U. Wyo., Laramie, 1970-73; acct., auditor Fed. Hwy. Adminstrn., Helena, Mont., 1973-75, Sacramento, 1975; dep. dir. fin. and acctg. Dept. Health & Social Svcs., Cheyenne, Wyo., 1976-84, mgmt. svcs. adminstr., 1985—. Tchr. Sunday sch., deacon, ch. moderator North Cheyenne Bapt. Ch., 1975—. With U.S. Army, 1963-64. Recipient Edn. Achievement award Nat. Observer, 1965. Mem. DAV (life), Nat. Human Svcs. Fin. Officers Orgn. Democrat. Home: PO Box 853 Cheyenne WY 82003 Office: Wyo Dept Health 2300 Capital Ave Hathaway Bldg Cheyenne WY 82002

MILUTINOVIĆ, ZORAN SPASOJE, physician, otorhinolaryngologist; b. Belgrade, Serbia, Yugoslavia, May 5, 1951; s. Spasoje Ranko and Milica Trajko (Petrović) M.; m. Violeta Vaso Sladoje, June 13, 1994. MD, Belgrade U., 1976, MS, 1980, PhD, 1983. Bd. cert. otorhinolaryngologist, phoniatrician. Staff mem. Clinic Otolaryngology Clin. Ctr. Serbia, Belgrade, 1978-87; head dept. phoniatrics Clinic Otolaryngology Zvezdara Clin. Ctr., Belgrade, 1987-94; head. dept. phoniatrics Zemun Clin. Ctr., Belgrade, 1994—; asst. prof. otorhinolaryngology Sch. Medicine Belgrade U., 1989-96, assoc. prof., 1996—; vis. prof. pro tempore Cleve. Clinic Found., 1992. Editor: Phonosurgery, 1990 (Zvezdara Univ. Hosp. award 1990); mem. editl. bd. Serbian Archives Medicine, 1995—; contbr. articles to profl. jours. V.p. City Coun. Belgrade Serbian Renewal Movement, 1991-92, Ind. Syndicate Physicians, Belgrade, 1992-93. Recipient Profl. Contbn. award Serbian Med. Soc., 1992. Mem. Internat. Assn. Phonosurgeons (founder, pres. 1990—, gen. sec. 1990-96, bd. dirs. 1996—), Union European Phoniatricians (liaison officer 1990—), Yugoslav Soc. Audiology & Phoniatrics (v.p. 1989-90, 91-92, pres. 1988-89, 90-91, Profl. & Sci. Contbn. award 1986), Internat. Assn. Logopedics & Phoniatrics. Home: 70 G Zdanova St, 11000 Belgrade Serbia Office: Zemun Clin Hosp Ctr, 9 Vukova St, 11080 Belgrade Serbia

MIMURA, YOSHIKAZU, endocrinologist, educator; b. Tokyo, Mar. 2, 1950; s. Kesayoshi Takizawa and Tatsu Mimura; m. Kyoko Yokota, Nov. 28, 1980; children: Azusa, Shin-ei, Yoko. MD, Shinshu U., 1977; PhD, U. Tokyo, 1988; postgrad., Mayo Grad. Sch. Medicine, 1993. Diplomate Japan Surg. Soc., Japanese Soc. Gastroenterol. Surgery. Resident Tsukuba (Japan) U. Hosp., 1977-79, Tokyo U. Hosp., 1979-80; chief Ome (Japan) Gen. Hosp., 1981-83; instr. U. Tokyo, 1984-91, 93—; rsch. fellow Mayo Clinic, Rochester, Minn., 1991-93. Contbr. articles to profl. jours. Mem. Japan

Surg. Soc., Japan Endocrine Soc., Japanese Soc. for Surg. Metabolism and Nutrition (councilor 1993—). Home: 4-2-C-807 Koyodai, Inagi Tokyo 206, Japan Office: U Tokyo, 3d Dept Surgery, 3-28-6 Mejirodai Bunkyo-ku, Tokyo 112, Japan

MINCKLEY, BARBARA B., nurse, educator, retired; b. Boston, Feb. 25, 1925; d. Kenneth Cotton and Dorothy (Riley) Brown; children: Alison, Barbara, Carrie, Gregory. BSN, Stanford U., 1960; MSN, U. Calif., San Francisco, 1967, D Nursing Sci., 1972; cert. adult nurse practitioner, Stanford U., 1975. Assoc. dean grad. divsn. U. Utah Coll. Nursing, Salt Lake City, 1975-78; project dir. nursing rsch. div. U. Ill. Coll. Nursing, Chgo., 1978-80; exec. dir. Midwest Alliance in Nursing, Indpls., 1980-85; project coord. nursing rsch. Ariz. State U. Coll. Nursing, Tempe; dir. dept. nursing Calif. State U., Long Beach, 1988-93; lectr. in field. Contbr. articles to profl. publs. Fellow Am. Acad. Nursing, Sigma Xi, Sigma Theta Tau. Home: 22 Ocean Woods Dr W Saint Augustine FL 32084

MINCY, JEROME WAYNE, research scientist; b. Indpls., Oct. 10, 1950; s. John Radford and Mae Eloise (McElwain) M.; m. Lisa Joellen Thornbury, Aug. 13, 1978; children: Lauren Michell, Jerilyn Renee. BS in pharmacy, Purdue U., 1973, MS in indsl. & physical pharmacy, 1982. Registered pharmacist, Ind. Pharmacist, mgr. Hook's Drugs, Batesville, Ind., 1977-81; pharmacist AARP, Indpls., 1981-83; prodn., asst. mgr. Ctrl. Pharm., Seymour, Ind., 1983-85, dir. capsule and bead prodn., 1985-93, sr. rsch. scientist, 1993—; speaker in field. Mem. Lions Club (v.p. 1995), Purdue Club (pres. 1994—). Republican. Presbyterian. Home: 433 Mutton Circle Dr Seymour IN 47274 Office: Ctrl Pharm 1101 C Ave West Freeman Field IN 47274

MINDELL, DAVID PAUL, biologist, educator; b. Buffalo, Mar. 4, 1953; s. Eugene Robert and June Alice (Abrams) M.; m. Margaret Alice Heasley, Dec. 9, 1978; children: Loren David, Ilana Jean. MS, W.Va. U., 1978; PhD, Brigham Young U., 1986. George S. Wise postdoctoral fellow Tel Aviv U., 1986-87; postdoctoral fellow Harvard U., Cambridge, Mass., 1987-88; vis. asst. prof. of biology Tex. Tech U., Lubbock, 1988-89; asst. prof. U. Cin., 1989-94, U. Mich., 1994—. Home: 2520 Victoria Ave Ann Arbor MI 48104-6315 Office: Univ of Michigan Biology Dept and Mus of Zoology Ann Arbor MI 48109

MINDELL, EARL LAWRENCE, nutritionist, author; b. St. Boniface, Man., Can., Jan. 20, 1940; s. William and Minerva Sybil (Galsky) M.; came to U.S., 1965, naturalized, 1972; BS in Pharmacy, N.D. State U., 1963; PhD in Nutrition, Pacific We. U., 1985; masner herbalist Dominion Herbal Coll., 1995; m. Gail Andrea Jaffe, May 16, 1971; children: Evan Louis-Ashley, Alanna Dayan. Pres. Adanac Mgmt. Inc., 1979—; instr. Dale Carnegie course; lectr. on nutrition, radio and TV. Mem. Beverly Hills, Rancho Park, Western Los Angeles (dir.) regional chambers commerce, Calif., Am. pharm. assns., Am. Acad. Gen. Pharm. Practice, Am. Inst. for History of Pharmacy, Am. Nutrition Soc., Internat. Coll. Applied Nutrition, Nutrition Found., Nat. Health Fedn., Am. Dieticians Assn., Orthomolecular Med. Assn., Internat. Acad. Preventive Medicine. Clubs: City of Hope, Beverly Hills Rotary, Masons, Shriners. Author: Earl Mindell's Vitamin Bible, Parents Nutrition Bible, Earl Mindell's Quick and Easy Guide to Better Health, Earl Mindell's Pill Bible, Earl Mindell's Shaping Up with Vitamins, Earl Mindell's Safe Eating, Earl Mindell's Herb Bible, Newsletter The Mindell Letter, Mindell's Food as Medicine, Earl Mindell's Soy Miracle, 1995, Anti-Aging Bible, 1996; columnist Let's Live mag., The Vitamin Supplement (Can.), The Vitamin Connection (U.K.), Healthy N' Fit; contbr. articles on nutrition to profl. jours. Home: 244 S El Camino Dr Beverly Hills CA 90212-3809 Office: 107 S Beverly Dr Beverly Hills CA 90212-3020

MINDELL, EUGENE ROBERT, surgeon, educator; b. Chgo., Feb. 24, 1922; s. Leon and Tillie (Rosenthal) M.; m. June A. Abrams, Sept. 19, 1945; children: Barbara, Ruth, David, Douglas. BS, U. Chgo., 1943, MD, 1945. Diplomate Am. Bd. Orthopaedic Surgery (bd. dirs. 1977-84, pres. 1983-84). Resident in orthopaedic surgery U. Chgo. Clinics, 1948-52; instr. U. Chgo., 1952; mem. faculty dept. orthopaedic surgery Sch. Medicine SUNY, Buffalo, 1953—, prof. Sch. Medicine, 1964—; chmn. dept. SUNY Sch. Medicine, Buffalo, 1964-88, dir. orthopaedic oncology Sch. Medicine, 1988—; mem. bd. mgrs. Erie County Med. Ctr., 1990-96. Assoc. editor Jour. Bone and Joint Surgery, 1984-88, trustee, 1991—; contbr. articles to profl. jours. Lt. (j.g.) M.C. USNR, 1946-48. Eugene R. Mindell Chair of Orthopaedic Surgery established in his honor SUNY, Buffalo, 1996; recipient Disting. Svc. award Alumni U. Chgo. Sch. Medicine, 1990; NRC fellow, 1949-50/. Fellow ACS; mem. Am. Acad. Orthopaedic Surgeons (bd. dirs. 1991), Am. Orthopaedic Assn. (v.p. 1990-91), Assn. Orthopaedic Chmn., Am. Assn. Surgery of Trauma, Am. Orthopaedic Rsch. Soc. (pres. 1972-73, residency rev. com. 1985-91), Musculoskeletal Tumor Soc. (pres. 1989-90), Coun. Musculoskeletal Specialty Socs. (chmn. elect 1991, chmn. 1992). Jewish. Home: 85 Depew Ave Buffalo NY 14214-1509 Office: 100 High St Buffalo NY 14203-1126

MINEKA, SUSAN, psychology educator; b. Ithaca, N.Y., June 2, 1948; d. Francis Edward and Muriel Leota (McGregor) M. BA in Psychology magna cum laude, Cornell U., 1970; PhD, U. Pa., 1974. Lic. psychologist, Ill. Prof. psychology U. Wis., Madison, 1974-85, U. Tex., Austin, 1986-87; prof. Northwestern U., Evanston, Ill., 1987—; co-dir. Panic Treatment Ctr., EvanstonHosp., 1988—; mem. NIH Panic Consensus Panel, 1991. Editor Jour. Abnormal Psychology, 1990-94; contbr. articles to profl. jours. Grantee NSF and NIMH, 1977-89. Fellow APA (bd. sci. affairs 1992-94, chair 1994, pres. divsn. 12, sect. 3 1995), Am. Psychol. Soc.; mem. Psychonomic Soc., Assn. for Advancement Behavior Therapy, Midwestern Psychol. Assn. (pres.-elect 1995-96, pres. 1996—), Internat. Primatol. Soc., Internat. Soc. for Rsch. on Emotion, Soc. for Rsch. in Psychopathology (mem. exec. bd. 1992-94), Phi Beta Kappa, Sigma Xi. Democrat. Home: 1825 N Lincoln Plz Apt 1609 Chicago IL 60614-5337 Office: Northwestern U Psychology Dept Evanston IL 60208

MINER, MICHAEL E., neurosurgery educator; b. Louisville, July 25, 1943; s. Gerald Lamont and Alice Mae (Murphy) M.; m. Mildred Elizabeth Kennedy, 1972 (dec. July, 1978); children: Caroline, Matthew, Amanda, Nicholas; m. Mary Ann Bruton, 1980 (dec. Dec., 1992). BS, U. Kans., Lawrence, 1965; MD, U. Kans., Kansas City, 1969, PhD, 1975. Diplomate in neurological surgery Am. Bd. Psychiatry and Neurology. Prof. U. Tex. Med. Sch., Houston, 1975—, dir. divsn. neurosurgery, 1984—; neurosurg. dir. Por Cristo, Boston, 1983—. Author: Neurotrauma, 1986; contbr. articles on neurosurg. disorders to profl. jours. Chmn. Houston Child-Safe Com., 1986—. Served to capt. U.S. Army, 1965-75. Grantee NIH, 1983-87; named Outstanding Tchr., U. Tex., 1984. Mem. Peruvian Surg. Soc., Am. Assn. Neurol. Surgeons (cert.), Soc. Neurol. Surgeons, Ohio State Neurosurg. Soc. (pres. 1995-96). Office: Univ of Tex Med Sch at Houston Dept of Immunology & Organ Transplant 6431 Fannin St # 148 Houston TX 77030-1501 also: Ohio State Univ Hosps Neurol Dept Columbus OH 43210

MINER, PHILIP BARTON, JR., gastroenterologist, educator; b. Worcester, Mass., July 13, 1946. MD, U. Colo., 1971. Asst. prof. U. Kans., Kansas City, 1977-82, assoc. prof. medicine, 1982-90, prof. medicine, 1990—, divsn. dir. gastroenterology, 1987—. Contbr. over 65 articles to profl. jours. Diplomate Am. Bd. Internal Medicine, Am. Bd. Gastroenterology. Office: Univ Kans Med Ctr 3901 Rainbow Blvd Kansas City KS 66103

MING, SI-CHUN, pathologist, educator; b. Shanghai, China, Nov. 10, 1922; came to U.S., 1949, naturalized, 1964; s. Sian-Fan and Jan-Teh (Kuo) M.; m. Pen-Ming Lee, Aug. 17, 1957; children—Carol, Ruby, Stephanie, Michael, Jeffrey, Eileen. M.D., Nat. Central U. Coll. Medicine, China, 1947. Resident in pathology Mass. Gen. Hosp., Boston, 1952-56; assoc. pathologist Beth Israel Hosp., Boston, 1956-67; asst. prof. pathology Harvard U. Med. Sch., 1965-67; assoc. prof. U. Md., 1967-71; prof. Temple U., Phila., 1971-93, prof. emeritus, 1993—, acting chmn. dept. pathology, 1978-80, dep. chmn. dept. path., 1980-86; mem. Internat. Study Group on Gastric Cancer; mem. coun. Internat. Gastric Cancer Assn.; U.S. rep. WHO Collaborating Ctr. for Primary Prevention, Diagnosis and Treatment of Gastric Cancer; hon. prof. Tianjin Med. Coll., Shanghai Second Med. U., Fourth Mil. Med. U., China, 1988—. Author: Tumors of the Esophagus and Stomach, 1973, supplement, 1985, Precursors of Gastric Cancer, 1984, Pathology of the Gastrointestinal Tract, 1992. Nat. Cancer Inst. sr. fellow Karolinska Inst. Stockholm, 1964-65; named hon. prof. Tianjin Med. U., Shanghai Second Med. U. and Fourth Mil. Med. U., China, 1988—. Mem. AAAS, U.S. Canadian Acad. Pathology, Am. Soc. Investigative Pathology, Am. Gastroenterol. Assn., N.Y. Acad. Scis. Office: 3400 N Broad St Philadelphia PA 19140-5196

MINKIN, ROBERT ALAN, health facility administrator; b. San Francisco, Aug. 7, 1952; s. Louis Wilson Minkin and Juliette (Dayan) Silver; m. Patricia Minkin, June 4, 1978; children: Jonathan Ryan, Sarah Lynn. AA, Coll. San Mateo, Calif., 1972; BA, Calif. State U., Rohnert Park, 1976; MBA, Calif. State U., San Francisco, 1978. Cert. health care exec. Am. Coll. Healthcare Execs. Adminstrv. asst. and resident Cmty. Hosp. Sonoma County, Santa Rosa, Calif., 1975-78; v.p. Garden Sullivan PMC, San Francisco, 1978-80; sr. v.p., adminstr. Meml. Hosp. Assocs., Modesto, Calif., 1980-87; COO Riverside (Calif.) Cmty. Hosp., 1987-89; pres. Riverside Cmty. Ventures Corp., 1989-90; sr. mgmt. cons. The Hunter Group, Pt. Viera, Fla., 1990-92; exec. v.p. Desert Hosp., Palm Springs, Calif., 1992-95, pres., CEO, 1995—; cons. in field. Office: Desert Hosp 1150 N Indian Canyon Dr Palm Springs CA 92263

MINKOFF, KENNETH MARK, psychiatrist; b. Bklyn., Dec. 26, 1948; s. Arnold and Phyllis Betty (Filzer) M.; m. Maxine Linda Roth, Dec. 12, 1971 (div. Jan. 1988); children: Alison, Rebecca, Michael; m. Linda Mary Swain, July 24, 1988; children: Alexander, Sarah. BA, Harvard U., 1968; MD, U. Pa., 1973. Diplomate Am. Bd. Psychiatry and Neurology. Intern Grad. Hosp., Phila., 1973; resident in psychiatry U. Calif., San Diego, 1973-76; faculty dept. psychiatry Cambridge Hosp., Harvard Med. Sch., 1976—, asst. clin. prof., 1994—; med. dir. day treatment Somerville (Mass.) Mental Health Clinic, 1976-78, clinic dir., 1978-84; pvt. practice Woburn, Mass., 1984—; chief psychiatry Choate-Symmes Health Svcs., Woburn, 1984-90, Choate Health Systems, Woburn, 1990—; cons., tchr., 1987—. Co-editor: Dual Diagnosis of Serious Mental Illness and Substance Disorder, 1991, Public Sector Managed Health Care: A Survival Manual, 1996; contbr. articles to med. jours., chpt. to book. Recipient clin. excellence award Mass. Alliance for Mentally Ill, 1988. Mem. Am. Psychiat. Assn., Group for Advancement Psychiatry (chmn. com. on psychiatry and community 1986-93), Am. Acad. Psychiatrists in Alcoholism and Addiction, Am. Coll. Psychiatrists, Am. Heart Assn. (gov. coun. sect. on psych. and substance abuse 1993-94). Jewish. Home: 12 Jefferson Dr Acton MA 01720-3104 Office: Choate Health Systems 23 Warren Ave Woburn MA 01801-4979

MINNERS, HOWARD ALYN, physician, research administrator; b. Rockville Center, N.Y., Sept. 1, 1931; s. Howard A. and Marie Henriette (Soberski) M.; m. Gretchen Paffenbarger, Oct. 25, 1958; children: Todd, Bradford. AB, Princeton U., 1953; MD, Yale U., 1957; MPH, Harvard U., 1960. Diplomate Am. Bd. of Preventive Medicine; cert. Nat. Bd. of Med. Examiners. Commd. 2d. lt. USAF, 1956; intern Wilford Hall USAF Hosp., San Antonio, 1957-58; resident Sch. of Aerospace Medicine, USAF, Brooks AFB, Tex., 1960-62; advanced through grades to maj. USAF, 1966; advanced through grades to rear adm. USPHS, ret., 1987; dir. office rsch. promotion and devel. WHO, Geneva, Switzerland, 1977-80; dir. Office of Sci. Advisor Agy. Internat. Devel., Washington, 1981-91; assoc. dir. NIH Nat. Inst. of Allergy and Infectious Diseases, 1966-77. Fellow World Acad. Art and Sci., Am. Coll. Preventive Medicine; mem. AAAS, Internat. Found. Sci. Stockholm (pres., chmn. bd. trustees 1991—).

MINNIE, MARY VIRGINIA, social worker, educator; b. Eau Claire, Wis., Feb. 16, 1922; d. Herman Joseph and Virginia Martha (Strong) M. BA, U. Wis., 1944; MA, U. Chgo., 1949, Case Western Reserve U., 1956. Lic. clin. social worker, Calif. Supr. day care Wis. Children Youth, Madison, 1949-57; coordinator child study project Child Guidance Clinic, Grand Rapids, Mich., 1957-60; faculty, community services Pacific Oaks Coll., Pasadena, Calif., 1960-70; pvt. practice specializing in social work various cities, Calif., 1970-78; ednl. cons. So. Calif. Health Care, North Hollywood, Calif., 1978—; med. social worker Kaiser Permanente Home Health, Downey, Calif., 1985-87; assoc. Baby Sitters Guild, Inc., 1987-94; cons. Home Health, 1987-90; pres. Midwest Assn. Nursery Edn., Grand Rapids, 1958-60; bd. dirs., sec. So. Calif. Health Care, North Hollywood; bd. dirs., v.p. Baby Sitters Guild Inc., South Pasadena, 1986-94; cons. project Head Start Office Econ. Opportunity, Washington, 1965-70. Mem. Soc. Clin. Social Workers, Nat. Assn. Social Workers, Nat. Assn. Edn. Young Children (1960-62). Democrat. Club: Altrusa (Laguna Beach, Calif.) (pres. 1984-87). Home and Office: 2225 Silver Oak Way Hemet CA 92545-8126

MINNING, CARL AUGUSTINE, JR., ophthalmologist; b. Mariemont, Ohio, Sept. 27, 1955; s. Carl Augustine and Evelyn Grace Minning; m. Joan Lynn Hannon, Nov. 3, 1979; children: Christopher, Abigail. BA, Ohio State U., 1979, MD, 1979. Diplomate Am. Bd. Ophthalmology. Intern Riverside Meth. Hosp., Columbus, Ohio, 1979-80; resident in ophthalmology Ohio State U., Columbus, 1980-82, chief resident, 1982-83; pvt. practice, Zanesville, Ohio, 1983—. Contbr. articles to med. jours. Mem. AMA, Am. Soc. Cataract and Refractive Surgery, Ohio Med. Assn., Ohio Ophthal. Soc., Muskingum County Acad. Medicine, Franklin County Eye, Ear, Nose and Throat Soc., Alpha Omega Alpha, Phi Eta Sigma. Office: Eye Surg Assocs Zanesville Inc 2935 Maple Ave Zanesville OH 43701

MINOCHA, ANIL, physician, educator, researcher; b. India, Feb. 4, 1957; Came to U.S., 1982; s. Ram Saroop and Kamla Devi M. Pre-med. diploma, Punjab U., India, 1974; MD, Med. Coll., Rohtak, India, 1980; postgrad. studies in pharmacology, Baylor Coll. Medicine, 1982-84. Diplomate Am. Bd. Internal Medicine, Am. Bd. Gastroenterology, Am. Bd. Forensic Medicine, Am. Bd. Geriatric Medicine. House officer depts. ophthalmology and dermatology Med. Coll. Hosp., Rohtak, India, 1980-81; med. officer State Health Svcs. Govts. of Punjab and Haryana, India, 1981-82; rsch. asst. Baylor Coll. Med., Houston, 1982-84; fellow clin. pharmacology U. Va., Charlottesville, 1984-86; resident physician Franklin Square Hosp., Balt., 1986-89; fellow gastroenterology Mich. State U., East Lansing, 1989-91; asst. prof. U. Louisville, 1991-95; assoc. prof. medicine U. Okla., Oklahoma City, 1995—; instr. dept. medicine Mich. State U., 1989-91; staff physician dept. medicine VAA Med. Ctr., Louisville, 1991-95; mem. credentials com. Humana Hosp., U. Louisville, 1992, other coms., 1992-94; mem. R&D com. VA Hosp., 1992-95; presenter in field. Contbr. numerous articles to profl. jours. Prin. investigator Gulf Biosystems, Charlottesville, 1985; biomed. rsch. grantee Mich. State U., 1990; sch. medicine rsch. grantee U. Louisville, 1993. Fellow ACP, Am. Coll. Gastroenterology, Am. Coll. Forensic Examiners; mem. Am. Gastroenterol. Assn., Am. Assn. for Study of Liver Disease.

MINTZ, A. AARON, pediatrician; b. Houston, July 29, 1922; s. Morris and Rebecca M.; children: Steven Jay, Richard Alan, Beverly Ann; m. Jo Miller, July 16, 1989. BA, Rice U., Houston, 1943; MD, U. Tex. Med. Br., Galveston, 1948. Diplomate Am. Bd. Pediatrics. Intern U. Iowa Hosp., Iowa City, 1948-49; resident internal medicine VA Hosp., Houston, 1949-50; resident in pediatrics Baylor Affiliated Hosps., Houston, 1950-52; asst. prof. pediatrics to prof. pediatrics Baylor Coll. Medicine, Houston, 1952—; mem. staff, chief dept. pediat. Ben Taub Gen. Hosp.; mem. staff Tex. Children's Hosp., Meth. Hosp.; lectr. in field. Contbr. numerous articles to profl. jours. Recipient Baylor Pediatric Housestaff award for teaching, 1973; grantee Lakeside Labs., 1960-61, E.R. Squibb & Sons, 1961, Am. Petroleum Inst., 1961-63, Plough Inc., 1961, McNeil Labs., 1963, Bristol Lab., 1964-65, E.I. DuPont De Nemours, 1966-67, Johnson & Johnson, 1965, 70, 71, Eaton Labs., 1963, Hoffman-LaRoche, 1963-64, 65, 73-74, 77-78, 82-83, 83-84, 84-85, Ayerst Labs., 1967, 67-68, Eli Lilly Labs., 1969-70, 77-78, Wyeth Labs., 1970-72, Endo Labs., 1977-78, 83. Mem. Soc. Adolescent Medicine, Ambulatory Pediatric Soc., Am. Acad. Pediatrics, So. Soc. for Pediatric Rsch., Houston Pediatric Soc., Harris County Med. Soc., Alpha Omega Alpha. Office: Baylor Coll Medicine Houston TX 77030-3498

MINTZ, DENA MARLENE, optometrist; b. Aug. 29, 1957. Student, Calif. State U., Fullerton, 1980-83; BS in Visual Sci. cum laude, So. Calif. Coll. Optometry, 1985, OD, 1987. Ind. contractor Sun City (Calif.) Vision Clinic, 1987-89; sole propr. optometric practice Corona, Calif., 1988—; asst. prof. Optometric Ctr. So. Calif. Coll. Optometry, Fullerton, 1987—, lab. instr., 1989; supr. optometric interns Baldwin Park Optometric Ctr., 1987; instr. Calif. State U., Fullerton, 1991; rschr. in field. Vol. career conf. YWCA, 1991, 92, Women's Wellness Cay, Circle City Hosp./Charter Hosp. of Corona, 1991, Kids' Care Fair, 1994. Fellow Am. Acad. Optometry (diplomate candidate cornea and contact lens sect.); mem. Am. Acad. Optometry (Calif. chpt., trustee 1993, sec. 1994, pres.-elect 1996), Orange County Optometric Soc. (trustee 1989-90), Calif. Optometric Assn. (ocular disease symposium com. 1995—), Am. Optometric Assn. (contact lens sect.), Assn. Optometric Educators, Corona C. of C., Am. Bus. Women's Assn. (v.p. 1991-92, chmn. scholarship com. 1991-92, chmn. membership com. 1992-93, Woman of Yr. 1993), Rotary. Office: 800 Magnolia Ave Ste 113 Corona CA 91719

MIOSSEC, PIERRE JEAN, immunologist, rheumatologist; b. Quimper, France, Sept. 27, 1955; s. Herve and Yvonne (Diraison) M.; m. Marie Coatalem, June 26, 1982; children: Vincent, Philippe. MD, U. Brest, France, 1983; PhD in Immunology, U. Marseille, France, 1987. Rsch. fellow U. Tex., Dallas, 1983-85; asst. in rheumatology U. Montpellier, France, 1985-89; assoc. in clin. immunology U. Lyon, France, 1989—; rschr. Nat. Inst. Med. Rsch., Lyon, 1989—. Contbr. articles to profl. jours. Mem. Am. Coll. Rheumatology, N.Y. Acad. Scis., French Soc. Rheumatology, French Soc. Immunology (Alessandro Robecchi prize 1995). Home: 173 Ave Franklin Roosevelt, 69500 Bron France Office: Dept Immunology and Rheumatology, Hosp Edouard Herriot, 69437 Lyon France

MIR, M(OHAMMAD) AFZAL, physician; b. Trehgam, Kashmir, May 6, 1936; came to U.K., 1964, naturalized, 1972; s. M. Abdullah and Taja (Bhutt) M.; m. Zarifa War, Jan. 8, 1962 (div. 1970); 1 child, Farooq; m. Lynda Green, Mar. 7, 1977; children: Deborah Tabassum, Joanne Taj. FSc, Sri Pratap Coll., Srinagar, 1956; MB, BChir, Ujjain, India, 1962. Med. officer Agy. Hosp. Gilgit, Kashmir, 1962-64; sr. house officer Alderhey Children's Hosp., Liverpool, Eng., 1964-65; med. registrar Withington Hosp., Manchester North Hosp., Queen Mary Hosp., Middlesborough, 1965-74; sr. med. registrar Manchester (Eng.) Royal Infirmary, 1974-77; sr. lectr., cons. physician U. Wales Coll. of Cardiff, 1978—. Mem. Med. Rsch. Soc., Brit. Diabetic Assn., Brit. Cardiac Soc., Am. Hypertension Soc., Assn. Physicians in Wales, Welsh Diabetic Group Cardiff. Home: Isoced Old Mill Rd Lisvane, Cardiff CF4 5XP, Wales Office: U Wales Coll Medicine, Heath Park, Cardiff CF4 4XN, Wales

MIRAGLIO, ANGELA MARIA, dietitian; b. Chgo., Sept. 12, 1944; d. Charles A. and Rose C. (Moles) M.; m. Robert S. Schwartz, Oct. 22, 1983. BS, Mundelein Coll., 1966; MS, U. Chgo., 1975. Registered dietitian. Clin. nutrition dir. West Suburban Kidney Ctr., Oak Park, Ill., 1974-78; clin. nutritionist Pediatric Outpatient Clinics U. Chgo., 1978-83; owner AMM Nutrition Services, Chgo., 1984—; treas. Cons. Nutritionist Dietetic Practice Group, 1989-91; part-time instr. Chgo. City-Wide Coll., 1979-81; lectr. De Paul U. Sch. Nursing, Chgo., 1978-80. Author: Food Composition Tables for Renal Diets, 1978; contbr. articles to profl. jours. Bd. dirs. Dorridge Condominium Assn., Chgo. Mem. Am. Dietetic Assn., Am. Assn. Diabetes Educators, Soc. for Nutrition Edn., Chgo. Dietetic Assn. (sec. 1969-71), Chgo. Nutrition Assn. Roman Catholic. Home and Office: 290 King Ln Des Plaines IL 60016-5976

MIRANDA, ABRAHAM G., physician; b. San Juan, P.R., June 19, 1961; s. Manuel S. and Margarita (Ruiz) M.; m. Gloria Garcia, July 7, 1984; children: Max, Katarina. BS cum laude, U. Tex. Pan Am., 1982; ME, U. Tex., Houston, 1986. Diplomate in internal medicine and infectious disease Am. Bd. Internal Medicine; lic. physician, Tex.; cert. in hyperbaric medicine. Intern, resident in internal medicine U. Tex. Med. Sch., Houston, 1986-89, fellow in infectious diseases, 1989-92, instr. clin. medicine, 1989-92; med. dir. Valley AIDS Coun., 1993-94; mem. staff Valley Bapt. Med. Ctr., Harlingen, Tex., 1993—. Contbr. articles to profl. jours. Mem. ACP, AMA, Tex. Med. Assn., Am. Soc. for Microbiology. Office: 2121 Pease St Ste 1-G Harlingen TX 78550

MIRANDA, CHARLES ALAN, optometrist; b. Teaneck, N.J., Jan. 7, 1952; s. Charles Robert and Jane Evelyn (Larson) M.; m. Teresa Parthenia Gurganious, June 25, 1977; children: Alyssa Ann, Kelsey Larson, Kristin Elise. BS in Biology, Villanova U., 1973; DO, Penn. Coll. Optometry, 1979. Pvt. practice Burlington, Vt., 1979-85, Georgia, Vt., 1985—. Mem. Am. Optometric Assn., Vt. Optometric Assn. (treas. 1989—), New Eng. Coun. Optometry, Lions Club. Home: RD 2 Box 1305 Fairfax VT 05454 Office: RD 2 Box 1158 Fairfax VT 05454

MIRANDA, MICHELE RENEE, optometrist; b. Springfield, Mass., Jan. 6, 1960; d. Vincent Michael and Lucy Theresa (Scibelli) M. BS, Springfield Coll., 1982; DO, New Eng. Coll. Optometry, 1986. Diplomate Internat. Assn. Bd. Examiners in Optometry. Resident VA Med. Ctr., Roxbury/Brockton, Mass., 1988; optometrist Med. Eye Care Assoc., Norwood, Mass., 1987-95, Bassett Healthcare, Cooperston, N.Y., 1995-96, Baystate Eye Care, Springfield, Mass., 1996—; liaison New Eng. Coun. Optometrists, Boston, 1989-91, bd. corporators, 1991-93; spkr. in field. Recipient Alumni Assn. award New Eng. Coll. Optometry, 1986, Barnes Hind Student Recognition award New Eng. Coll. Optometry, 1986. Mem. Am. Optometric Assn., N.Y. State Optometric Assn., Mass. Soc. Optometrists (pres. 1990-91), Beta Sigma Kappa. Roman Catholic. Office: Baystate Eye Care 275 Bicentennial Hwy Springfield MA 01108

MIRMADJLESSI, SEID HOSSEIN, physician; b. Lahijan, Guilan, Iran, Sept. 20, 1940; s. Mirabdullah and Tuba (Islami) M.; m. Fatemeh Tavaftchian, Mar. 21, 1967; children: Nima, Mitra. Faculty of medicine, U. Rome, Italy, 1965. Cert. Am. Bd. Internal Medicine, 1970, Am. Bd. Gastroenterology, 1972, Italian State Bd., 1966, Iranian State Bd., 1972, Washington State Bd., Ohio State Bd. Residency in gastroenterology Faculty of Medicine, Rome, 1965-67; intern St. Francis Gen. Hosp., Pitts., 1967-68; med. residency Washington Hosp. Ctr., 1968-70; fellow in gastroenterology Cleve. Clinic, 1970-72; attending physician Firouzgar Hosp., Tehran, Iran, 1972-74; asst. prof. medicine Faculty of Medicine, Tehran, 1974-76, assoc. prof. medicine, 1976-82; attending physician Iranian Med. Inst., Tehran, 1972—, Sassan Hosp., Tehran, 1974—. Contbr. numerous articles to profl. jours. Lt. Imperial Iranian Army, 1973-74. Recipient Peskind award Cleve. Clinic, 1972. Fellow Am. Coll. Physicians; mem. Am. Gastroenterological Assn., Iranian Soc. Gastroenterology and Hepatology (pres. 1992—). Home: Africa Ave Morvarid Koutcheh, Shemiran Towers Tehran Iran Office: Iranian Med Inst, 315 N Nejatu Llahi Ave, 19158 Tehran Iran

MIRRA, CATHERINE M., social worker; b. N.Y.C., Jan 30, 1952. AA, Rockland Community Coll., 1975; BS, Dominican Coll., 1981; MSW, Columbia U., 1982. Lic. social worker, N.J. Sr. program devel. specialist State of N.J.-Judiciary, Bergen County; adminstr. County of Bergen-Youth Svcs. Commn., Hackensack. Mem. Nat. Assn. Social Workers, Acad. Cert. Social Workers.

MIRRA, SUZANNE SAMUELS, neuropathologist, researcher; b. N.Y.C., Feb. 16, 1943. BA, Hunter Coll., 1962; MD, SUNY, Bklyn., 1967. Instr. pathology Yale U. Sch. Medicine, New Haven, 1971-73; staff pathologist Atlanta VA Med. Ctr., Decatur, Ga., 1973—; asst. prof. pathology Emory U. Sch. Medicine, Atlanta, 1973-80, assoc. prof. pathology, 1981-93, prof. pathology, 1993—; dir., prin. investor Emory Alzheimer's Disease Ctr., Atlanta, 1991—. Mem. editl. bd. Arch Pathol. Lab. Med., 1988—, Jour. Neuropathology Exptl. Neurology, 1991-95, Brain Pathology, 1995—, Alzheimer's Disease Reviews, 1995—. Recipient Albert E. Levy Sci. Faculty Rsch. award Emory U., 1987, Disting. Alumnus Achievement award SUNY, 1992; named to Hunter Coll. Hall of Fame, 1996. Fellow Coll. Am. Pathologists (Presdl. award 1987,89, Herbert Lansky award 1990, chair neuropathology commn. 1992-95); mem. Am. Assn. Neuropathologists (v.p. profl. affairs 1992—), Alzheimer's Assn. (bd. dirs. Atlanta chpt. 1987—). Office: VA Med Ctr 113 Emory U 1670 Clairmont Rd Decatur GA 30033-4004

MIRSEN, THOMAS ROBERT, neurology educator; b. Buenos Aires, Argentina, May 14, 1957; came to U.S., 1965; s. Stefan and Maria (Kunowski) M. AB in Biochemistry cum laude, Princeton U., 1978; MD cum laude, SUNY, Bklyn., 1982. Diplomate Am. Bd. Psychiatry and Neurology. Intern Albert Einstein & Jacobi Hosps., Bronx, N.Y., 1982-83; resident in neurology NYU-Bellevue Med. Ctr., 1983-86; clin. rsch. fellow U. Western Ont., London, Can., 1986-89; neurol. coord. N.Am. Symptomatic Carotid

Endarterectomy Robarts Rsch. Inst., London, Can., 1989-90; assoc. prof. neurology Cooper Hosp., U. Medicine and Dentistry of N.J., Camden, 1990—. Author: (with others) Epidemiology and Classification of Vascular and Multi-Infarct Dementia, 1988, Changing Concepts of Vascular Dementia, 1988; contbr. articles to profl. jours. Chmn. Stroke Awareness Task Force N.J. affiliate Am. Heart Assn., 1993-96, mem. stroke coun., 1989; mem. Phila. Coun. for Stroke Treatment. Grantee Alzheimer's Disease and Related Disorders Assn., 1990-91. Mem. Soc. for Clin. Trials, Alpha Omega Alpha. Home: 3102B Ramsberry Ct Mount Laurel NJ 08054 Office: Cooper Hosp/Univ Med Ctr 3 Cooper Plz Camden NJ 08103-1438

MIRTALLO, JAY MATTHEW, pharmacist, educator; b. Stamford, N.Y., Oct. 29, 1953; s. Leonard and Betty Louise (Clapper) M.; children: Karissa Wesley, Taylor Jay. BS in Pharmacy cum laude, U. Toledo, 1976; MS in Hosp. Pharmacy, Ohio State U., 1978. Resident in hosp. pharmacy Ohio State U. Hosps., Columbus, 1978, clin. pharmacist, 1978—, clin. assoc. prof. coll. pharmacy, 1985—; grad. faculty Coll. Pharmacy Ohio State U., 1983, adj. asst. prof. dept. surgery, 1984; lectr. rsch. ednl. audiences; cert. nutrition support pharmacist, 1994—; chmn. Clin. Nutrition Panel. Mem. editl. bd. Ann Pharmacother, 1982—, Clin. Pharmacy, 1983-95, Nutrition in Clin. Practice, 1986-90; contbr. articles to profl. jours. Fellow Am. Soc. Hosp. Pharmacists; mem. Am. Soc. Parenteral and Enteral Nutrition (Disting. Pharmacist award 1993), Ohio Soc. Hosp. Pharmacists (Hosp. Pharmacist of Yr. 1985), Ctrl. Ohio Soc. Hosp. Pharmacists (Outstanding Svc. award 1983). Roman Catholic. Office: Ohio State U Med Ctr Dept Pharmacy DN 368 410 W 10th Ave Columbus OH 43210-1240

MIRVIS, DAVID MARC, health administrator, cardiologist, educator; b. Hampton, Va., Dec. 20, 1945; s. Allan and Lena (Sear) M.; m. Arlynn Shara Katz, June 30, 1968; children: Simcha Zev, Tova Aliza, Shoshana Fruma. Student, Yeshiva Coll., N.Y.C., 1966, MD, 1970. Diplomate Am. Bd. Internal Medicine. Intern U. Tenn., Memphis, 1970-71, fellow, resident, 1973-75, asst., assoc. prof., 1973-83, prof., 1983—; assoc. dean U. Tenn., Memphis, 1987—; fellow, cardiovascular physiology NIH, Bethesda, Md., 1971-73; chief of cardiology Memphis VA Med. Ctr., 1983-87, chief of staff, 1987—; pres. Rsch., Inc., 1990—; dir. Health Svcs. Rsch. Divsn., The Univs. Prevention Ctr. Author, editor: Body Surface Electrocardiographic Mapping, 1988; author: Electrocardiography: A Physiologic Approach; contbg. editor Jour. Electrocardiology, 1984—, Am. Jour. Noninvasive Cardiology, 1986—. Com. chair Anshei Sphard Synagogue, Memphis, 1987—. Grantee NIH, 1975-89. Fellow Am. Heart Assn. (coun. on circulation), Am. Coll. Cardiology; mem. Am. Soc. Clin. Investigation, Am. Acad. Med. Dirs., Internat. Soc. Computerized Electrocardiography, So. Soc. Clin. Rsch. Democrat. Home: 5676 Redding Ave Memphis TN 38120-1848 Office: U Tenn 956 Court Ave Memphis TN 38103-2814

MISIEK, DALE JOSEPH, oral and maxillofacial surgeon; b. Hartford, Conn., Dec. 10, 1952; s. Joseph John and Jadwiga Magdelena (Wojtowicz) M.; m. Patricia Ann Munson, June 28, 1975; children: Matthew Bryan, Stacy Lynne, Michael Stephen. BA magna cum laude, U. Conn., Storrs, 1974; DMD, U. Conn., Farmington, 1978; cert. advanced tng. oral and maxillofacial surgery, La. State U., 1982. Diplomate Am. Bd. Oral and Maxillofacial Surgery. Resident oral surgery Charity Hosp. of La., New Orleans, 1978-82, mem. clin. surgery com., 1984-86, mem. surgery com., 1986—, mem. credentials com., 1988—; asst. prof. dept. oral and maxillofacial surgery Sch. Dentistry, La. State U., New Orleans, 1984-87, assoc. prof., 1987-94; prof. dept. oral and maxillofacial surgery Sch. Dentistry La. State U., New Orleans, 1994—; also mem. various coms. Sch. Dentistry, La. State U., New Orleans; practice dentistry specializing in oral surgery New Orleans, 1982-84; mem. staff Ear, Eye, Nose and Throat Hosp., New Orleans, 1982—, chmn. dental dept., also mem. exec. com., credentials com. and instrument com., 1983-84; mem. staff East Jefferson Gen. Hosp., Metairie, 1982, chmn. dental dept., 1990-94, med. records com., 1983-85, credentials com., 1994—; mem. staff Univ. Hosp., New Orleans, 1982—; courtesy staff Children's Hosp., New Orleans, 1982—, Mercy Hosp., New Orleans, 1982—, So. Bapt. Hosp., New Orleans, 1983—, Our Lady of the Lake Regional Med. Ctr., Baton Rouge, 1985, Kenner (La.) Regional Med. Ctr., 1986—, Dr.'s Hosp., Metairie, 1986—; cons. VA Med. Ctr., New Orleans, 1984—; lectr. in field. Contbr. articles and abstracts to profl. jours. Recipient C.V. Mosby Book award. Fellow Am. Assn. Oral and Maxillofacial Surgeons (mem. spl. com. for devel. stds. and criteria for care 1986—, spl. com. on oral and maxillofacial surgery self-assessment program 1990), Am. Coll. Oral and Maxillofacial Surgeons; mem. ADA (cons. commn. on dental accreditation 1986—), Am. Bd. Oral and Maxillofacial Surgery (adv. com. 1990-95), La. Dental Assn., New Orleans Dental Assn. (mem. sci. program com. 1983-84), La. Soc. Oral and Maxillofacial Surgeons (mem. anesthesia com. 1983-85, mem. advanced cardiac life support com. 1986-88, sec./treas. 1991-95, v.p. 1996—), Internat. Assn. Oral and Maxillofacial Surgery, Acad. Osseointegration, Internat. Assn. Dental Rsch., Am. Assn. Dental Rsch., Orleans Parish Med. Soc., Am. Heart Assn. (instr.), Phi Beta Kappa, Phi Kappa Phi, Omicron Kappa Upsilon. Republican. Roman Catholic. Office: La State U Med Ctr Sch Dentistry Dept Oral Surgery 1100 Florida Ave # 220 New Orleans LA 70119-2714

MISIOREK, MARY MADELYN, social worker; b. Mt. Holly, N.J., Sept. 7, 1950; d. Frank and Anna (Dudek) M. BA, Trenton (N.J.) State Coll., 1972; MSW, Rutgers U., 1993. Social worker State of N.J., Pemberton, 1973-79; psychiat./med. social worker Rancocas Hosp., Willingboro, N.J., 1980-95; clin. mgr. The Counseling Program, Marlton, N.J., 1995—. Mem. NASW, LCSW, ACSW, Alpha Beta Mu. Office: The Counseling Program Clinical Dept Marlton NJ 08053

MISKOFF, ALVIN RICHARD, physician; b. Bklyn., Jan. 7, 1942; s. Irving Louis Miskoff and Mollie Ethel (Nesenman) Epstein; m. Cheryl Ann Bachman, Aug. 25, 1965 (div. Jan. 1992); children: Barbara, Cary, Jeffrey; m. Barbara Jean Florentino, Sept. 19, 1992; 1 child, Kristy. AB, Rutgers U., 1963; DO, U. Health Scis., Kansas City, Mo., 1968. Diplomate Am. Bd. Internal Medicine; medical oncology, 1975; hematology, 1982. Pvt. practice in hematology, oncology Menlo Park Med. Group, Ediston, N.J., 1976-78, A. Richard Miskoff, DO PA, Ediston, N.J., 1978—; bd. dirs. Woodbridge (N.J.) Dept. of Health, 1980-86. Author: Guide to Therapeutic Oncology, 1979. Maj. U.S. Army, 1970-76. Mem. Am. Osteo. Assn., Am. Coll. Physicians, Am. Soc. Clin. Oncology, Am. Soc. Hematology, Middlesex County Osteo. Assn. (pres. 1992—). Home: 15 Glynn Ct Parlin NJ 08859 Office: 1032 New Durham Rd Edison NJ 08817

MISNER, LORRAINE, laboratory technologist; b. Fitchburg, Mass., June 24, 1948; d. Cedric Winfield and Pearl Erma (Hallisey) M. BA in Biology, Fitchburg State Coll., 1971; MS in Med. Technology, Anna Maria Coll., 1983. Lab. technologist Leominster (Mass.) Hosp., 1971-87; research asst. U. Lowell Rsch. Found. (now U. Mass. Lowell Rsch. Found.), 1987—. Piccolo Townsend (Mass.) Mil. Band, 1964-93; mem. choir United Ch. of Christ, 1961—. Mem. Am. Soc. Clin. Pathologists (assoc., registrant), Am. Soc. for Clin. Lab. Sci., Mass. Soc. for Med. Tech., Am. Assn. Clin. Chemistry.

MISONO, KUNIO, medical educator; b. Hiroshima, Japan, Nov. 21, 1946; married; 2 children. BS in Chemistry, Saitama U., Urawa, Japan, 1969; MS in Biochemistry, Osaka State U., Sakai, Japan, 1971; PhD in Biochemistry, Vanderbilt U., 1978; postdoctoral tng. in microbiology, Duke U., 1978-80. Chemist Ministry of Welfare, Tokyo, 1971-72; rsch. asst. in biochemistry Vanderbilt U. Sch. Medicine, Nashville, 1972-74; rsch. assoc. in microbiology Duke U. Sch. Medicine, Durham, N.C., 1978-80; rsch. instr. in biochemistry Vanderbilt U. Sch. Medicine, 1981-82, rsch. asst. prof. biochemistry, 1983-86; prin. scientist, group leader, rsch. divsn. Schering-Plough Corp., 1986-87; assoc. staff Cleve. Clinic Found. Rsch. Inc., 1987—, dir. protein and peptide chemistry core facility, 1988—; adj. assoc. prof. dept. biology Case Western Reserve U., Cleve., 1992—. Contbr. numerous articles to profl. jours. Recipient NIH nat. rsch. svc. award 1979-80. Mem. Am. Chem. Soc., Am. Peptide Soc., Endocrine Soc., Protein Soc., Am. Heart Assn. (High Blood Pressure Rsch. Coun. fellow 1989, Tenn. affiliate rsch. fellow 1980-81, Investigatorship award 1982-84), Am. Soc. Biochemistry and Molecular Biology, Sigma Xi. Office: Cleveland Clinic Found Dept Molecular Cardiology 9500 Euclid Ave FF3-02 Cleveland OH 44195-5071*

MISRA, RAGHUNATH PRASAD, physician, educator; b. Calcutta, W. Bengal, India, Feb. 1, 1928; came to U.S., 1964; s. Guru Prasad and Anandi M.; m. Therese Rettenmund, Sept. 13, 1963; children: Sima, Joya, Maya, Tara. BSc with honors, Calcutta U., 1948; MBBS, Med. Coll., Calcutta, 1953; PhD, McGill U., Montreal, Que., 1965. Diplomate Am. Bd. Anatomical and Clin. Pathology. Asst. prof., dir. kidney lab. U. Louisville Sch. Medicine, 1964-68; asso. investigator and dir. kidney lab Mt. Sinai Hosp., Cleve., 1968-73; asst. prof. Case Western Reserve Med. Sch., Cleve., 1973-76; asst. prof., dir. kidney lab. La. State U., Sch. Medicine, Shreveport, 1976-80, assoc. prof., 1980-86; prof. La. State U., Sch. of Medicine, Shreveport, 1986—, dir. Ocular Pathology Lab., 1988—; cons. VA Med. Ctr., Shreveport, 1977—, EA Conway Meml. Hosp., Monroe, La., 1980—. Author: Atlas of Skin Biopsy, 1983. Pres. India Assn. of Shreveport, 1979, 81. Recipient Tallisman Fellowship, Mt. Sinai Hosp., 1970-73. Fellow Am. Coll. Pathologists, Am. Soc. Clin. Pathologists, U. Calcutta Med. Alumni Assn. Am. (pres. 1992-93), Sigma Xi (pres. 1987-89). Democrat. Hindu. Office: La State U Sch Medicine 1501 Kings Hwy Shreveport LA 71130-3932

MISULIS, KARL EDWARD, physician; b. Saranac Lake, N.Y., Aug. 6, 1953; s. Edward Victor and Ruth Aileen (Miller) M.; m. Christa Margaret Stoscheck, June 14, 1980; children: Edward Nicholas, Karl Christian. BS with honors, Queens U., 1975; PhD, SUNY, Syracuse, 1980; MD, Vanderbilt U., 1982. Diplomate Am. Bd. Psychiatry and Neurology. Chief resident, neurology Vanderbilt U., Nashville, 1984-85, resident, neurology, 1982-86, asst. prof. neurology, 1986-90, assoc. prof. neurology, 1990—; neurologist Semmes-Murphey Clinic, Jackson, 1991—; mem. nat. speaker's bur. Parke-Davis, Ann Arbor, Mich., 1993—, others. Author: (books) Essentials of Clinical Neurophysiology, 1993, Spehlmann's Evoked Potential Primer, 1994, Neurologic Localization and Diagnosis, 1996; editor: Scientific Foundations of Neurology, 1996; contbr. articles to profl. publs. Recipient CIDA award NIH. Mem. So. Clin. Neurol. Soc. (v.p. 1994—), AAN (mem. com. on crit. care), Am. Acad. Neurology (Saul Korey award), Am. Acad. Clin. Neurophysiology, Alpha Omega Alpha. Office: Semmes-Murphey Clin 614 Skyline Dr Jackson TN 38301

MITCH, WILLIAM EVANS, nephrologist; b. Birmingham, Ala., July 22, 1941; s. William Evans and Mary Elizabeth (Ackerman) M.; m. Frances Alexandra Fisher, Aug. 21, 1965; children: Eleanor Baylor, William Armistead. BA, Harvard Coll., 1963; MD, Harvard Med. Sch., 1967. Intern Brigham & Women's Hosp., Boston, 1967-68; resident Brigham & Women's Hosp., 1968-69; clin. assoc. Nat. Inst. Health, Bethesda, Md., 1969-72; resident Johns Hopkins Hosp., Balt., 1972-73, Brigham & Women's Hosp., 1973-74; asst. prof., assoc. prof. Johns Hopkins U. Dept. Pharm., Balt., 1974-78; assoc. prof. medicine Harvard Med. Sch., Boston, 1978-87; prof. medicine Emory U. Sch. Medicine, Atlanta, 1987—; pres. region II Nat. Kidney Found., 1990-92; sec., treas. Internat. Soc. Metabolism, 1988—; study sect. NIH, 1988-92; chmn. Am. Heart Assn., 1992-94. Editor: The Progressive Nature of Renal Disease, 1986, 2d edit., 1992, Nutrition and the Kidney, 1988, 2d edit., 1993. With USPHS, 1969-72. Grantee NIH, 1979—. Mem. Am. Soc. Clin. Investigation, Assn. Am. Physicians. Office: Emory U Sch Medicine 1364 Clifton Rd NE Atlanta GA 30322-1059

MITCHELL, CAROL ANN, nursing educator; b. Portsmouth, Va., Aug. 31, 1942; d. William Howell and Eleanor Bertha (Wesarg) M.; m. David Alan Friedman, June 17, 1971 (div. 1988). Diploma, NYU, 1963; BS, Columbia U., 1968, MA, 1971, EdM, 1974, EdD, 1980; MS, SUNY, Stony Brook, 1990. Charge nurse Nassau County Med. Ctr., East Meadow, N.Y., 1963-65; staff nurse Meml. Hosp., N.Y.C., 1965-68; head nurse, supr. Community Hosp. at Glen Cove (N.Y.), 1969-71; assoc. prof. dept. nursing Queensborough Community Coll. CUNY, Bayside, 1971-80; assoc. prof. Marion A. Buckley Sch. Nursing Adelphi U., Garden City, N.Y., 1981-88; edn. cons. Nat. League for Nursing, N.Y.C., 1980-81; prof. sch. nursing SUNY, Stony Brook, 1988-92, chmn. adult nursing, 1988-92; prof. chair Coll. Nursing East Tenn. State U., 1992-95, mem faculty, 1995—; mem. faculty Regents Coll. degrees in nursing program USNY, Albany, 1978-91, cons., 1978—; faculty cons. geriatrics Montefiore Med. Ctr., 1991-93. Editor emeritus: Scholarly Inquiry in Nursing Practice, 1983—; contbr. articles to profl. jours. Robert Wood Johnson clin. nurse scholar postdoctoral fellow U. Rochester (N.Y.), 1983-85. Mem. Am. Nurses Assn., Nat. League for Nursing, Gerontol. Soc. Am., N.Am. Nursing Diagnosis Assn., Soc. for Research in Nursing Edn.

MITCHELL, DAVID CRERAR, orthopedist; b. Detroit, Mar. 22, 1930; s. C. Leslie and Irene (Tennant) M.; children: Peyton Leslie, David C. Jr., Timothy. MD, Duke U., 1955. Intern U. Mich., Ann Arbor, 1955-57; resident in orthopedics Mass. Gen. Hosp./Children's Hosp., Boston, 1959-63; sr. staff physician Henry Ford Hosp., Detroit, 1963—. Served to capt. U.S. Army, 1957-59. Mem. AMA, Mich. Med. Soc., Am. Acad. Orthopedic Surgeons, Clin. Orthopedic Soc., Mid-Am. Orthopedic Assn., Mich. Orthopedic Soc., Internat. Soc. Orthopedics and Traumatology, Detroit Acad. Orthopedic Surgeons. Club: Country Club of Detroit (Grosse Pointe Farms, Mich.). Home: 271 Hillcrest Ave Grosse Pointe MI 48236-3122 Office: Henry Ford Hosp/Lakeside 14500 Hall Rd Sterling Heights MI 48313

MITCHELL, DONALD E., rehabilitation counselor, transition counselor; b. Kansas City, Mo., Jan. 19, 1948; s. Rosa E. Mitchell. BA, Southwestern Coll., 1970; MS in Community Counseling, Emporia State U., 1983, MS in Vocat. Rehab. Counseling, 1986; postgrad., U. Kans., Pitts. State U., Emory U. Svc. technician, sales and sheet metal installer Lee's Cooling and Heating, Independence, Kans., 1976-82; dir. partial hosp. facility, case mgr. Iroquis Ctr. for Human Devel., Greensburg, Kans., 1983-85; job coach Kans. Social Rehab. Svc., Topeka, 1985-86; title IV counselor Independence Community Coll., 1986-87; vocat., rehab. counselor II, transition counselor Kans. Rehab. Svcs., Chanute, 1988—; program dir. Magdeline Group Home, Kans. City, 1995—. Bd. dirs. Helping Hearts Heal. Mem. Nat. Eagle Scout Assn., Helping Hearts Heal (bd. dirs.), Kans. Vocat. Evaluator and Assessment Assn. (membership chmn., pres.), Nat. Rehab. Assn., Kans. Rehab. Assn., Chi Sigma Iota.

MITCHELL, EDWIN HARRIS, JR., physician assistant; b. Colombia, S.C., Apr. 22, 1954; s. Edwin Harris and Noella Maria Teres (Pajaud) M.; m. Lindajean Parisi, July 14, 1991; children: Lyndsey Noelle, Crystaljean Parisi, Scott Phillip Harris. BA in Biology, Fisk U., Nashville, 1977; Cert. of Paralegal Studies, Queens Coll., Jamaica, N.Y., 1989; BS, cert. in allied health and physician asst., CCNY/Harlem Hosp., 1994. Nursing technician Parkview Hosp., Nashville, 1972-77; mortuary technician Queens Hosp. Ctr./Queens Med. Examiner, Jamaica, 1982—; physician asst. radiology LaGuardia Hosp., Forest Hills, N.Y., 1995—. Mem. Am. Acad. Physician Assts., N.Y. State Soc. Physician Assts. Home: 46-01 Hendrickson Ave Valley Stream NY 11580

MITCHELL, ELLISON CAPERS, JR., psychologist; b. Greenville, S.C., July 18, 1941; s. Ellison Capers and Sara Kathryn (Brown) M.; m. Lucy Oakley, May 7, 1977; 1 child, Kristine Marie Sumner. BA, Duke U., 1963; PhD, U. Tenn., 1974. Lic. clin. psychologist. Clin. intern San Fernando Valley Guidance Clinic, Van Nuys, Calif., 1970-71; Gestalt therapy trainee Gestalt Therapy Inst. L.A., 1970-71; dir. Quiet Thunder Camp, Starke, Fla., 1976; co-founder, sr. ptnr. Ctr. for Psychology and Counseling, Knoxville, Tenn., 1976—; psychotherapist St. Mary's Med. Ctr., Knoxville, 1984-85; founding dir. Gestalt Ctr. South, Knoxville, 1974—; dir. co-dependency program U. Tenn. Med. Ctr., Knoxville, 1988-90; cons. Vietnam Vets. Ctr., Knoxville, 1986-87; adj. prof. U. Tenn. 1974-81; founder Soc. for Creative Expression, Inc., 1987. Bd. dirs. Tenn. Children's Dance Ensemble, Knoxville, 1983-85. Lt. USNR, 1963-66. Mem. Health Confs. Assn., Inc. (pres. 1988, bd. dirs. 1987—), Am. Psychol. Assn., Tenn. Psychol. Assn. Episcopalian. Office: Chambliss Place 4877 Chambliss Ave Knoxville TN 37919-5122

MITCHELL, GARY SCOT, hospital administrator; b. Ft. Bragg, N.C., Dec. 23, 1962; s. Gary Anderson and Peggy Lou (Cole) M.; m. Tina Marie Massini, May 21, 1987 (div. Nov. 1991); 1 child, Gary Scot; m. Bonnie Lynn Ramsey, Dec. 4, 1992. BS, Concord Coll., Athens, W.Va., 1985; M Health Svcs. Adminstrn., Med. U. S.C., Charleston, 1991. Diplomate Am. Coll. Healthcare Execs. Adminstrv. fellow Appalachian Regional Healthcare, Hinton, W.Va., 1991-92, adminstr., 1992—; bd. mem. Upsate EMS Coun., Greenville, S.C., 1990-91; coun. mem. Summers County E911 Adv. Coun., Hinton, 1995. Submitting author: Case Studies in Health Management, 1991. Bd. dirs. Summers County (W.Va.) Family Resource Network, 1994—; chmn. Partners in Health Network Cmty. Needs Assessment/Health Promotion Com., 1995—. Mem. Am. Coll. Healthcare Exxecs. (assoc.), Summers County C. of C. (bd. mem. 1992—), Hinton Ruritan Club (bd. mem. 1993—), Kiwanis Club Hinton (pres. 1994-95). Office: Summers County Appalachian Regional Healthcare Hosp Terrace St Hinton WV 25951

MITCHELL, GEOFFREY CHRISTOPHER, physician, software developer, financial consultant; b. Columbus, Ohio, May 27, 1953; s. Earnest Edward Mitchell and Martha Joan (Kellough) Mitchell-Noe; m. Margaret Mary Zuber, Sept. 12, 1972; children: Matthew, Andrew, Kevin. BS, Ohio State U., 1974; MD, Med. Coll. Ohio, 1981. Diplomate Am. Bd. Emergency Medicine. Intern, resident Riverside Meth. Hosp., Columbus, 1981-84; attending physician St. Ann's Hosp., Westerville, Ohio, 1984-91; founding ptnr. IHA Inc., St. Ann's, Westerville, 1987-91; attending physician Riverside Meth. Hosp., 1991—; founder, pres. Smart Chart (med. software), Columbus, 1994—; course dir. Emergency Medicine Rev., Columbus, 1993; portfolio mgr. for pvt. clients, 1994; mem. faculty 1st Internat. Conf. on Emergency Medicine, Tegucigalpa, Honduras, 1993. Contbg. author: Photo and Xray Stimuli in Emergency Medicine, 1994; author/developer med. software, computerized stock and mut. fund selection; author suture technique Vertical Figure 8, 1987. Mem. short-term med. missions Christian Med. Soc., Honduras, 1981, 84, 89, Project Amazon, Manaus, Brazil, 1993. Recipient 2d Place award U.S. Investing Championship, L.A., 1991, 6th Place, 1993. Fellow Am. Coll. Emergency Physicians; mem. Ohio State Med. Assn., Christian Med. Soc. Home: 3847 Olentangy Blvd Columbus OH 43214-3533 Office: Riverside Meth Hosp Dept Emergency Medicine 3535 Olentangy River Rd Columbus OH 43214-3925

MITCHELL, GEORGE TRICE, physician; b. Marshall, Ill., Jan. 20, 1914; s. Roscoe Addison and Alma (Trice) M.; m. Mildred Aletha Miller, June 21, 1941; children: Linda Sue, Mary Kathryn. BS, Purdue U., 1935; MD, George Washington U., 1940. Intern Meth. Hosp., Indpls., 1940-41; gen. practice medicine Marshall, 1946—; mem. courtesy staff Union and Regional Hosps., Terre Haute, Ind.; clin. assoc. Sch. Basic Medicine U. Ill.; chmn. bd. dirs. First Nat. Bank, Marshall. Author: Dr. George-An Account of the Life of a Country Doctor, 1993. Mem. adv. coun. premedicine Eastern Ill. U., 1965-69; alt. del. Rep. Conv., 1968, del., 1972; trustee Lakeland Jr. Coll., 1978-92. Lt. col. USAAF, 1941-45. Named Health Practitioner of Yr. Ill. Rural Health Assn., 1993, Nat. Health Practioner of Yr. Nat. Rural Health Assn., 1995; recipient Purdue Alumni Assn. Citizenship award, 1996. Fellow Am. Acad. Family Physicians (Family Physician of Yr. 1993); mem. AMA, Ill. med. Soc. (2d v.p. 1980-81), Clark County Med. Soc. (pres.), Aesculapian Soc. of Wabash Valley (pres. 1965), Nat. Rural Health Assn. (Practitioner of Yr. 1995), Clark County Hist. Soc. (pres. 1968-70), Masons (32 degree), Shriners. Methodist. Home: RR 2 Marshall IL 62441-9802 Office: 410 N 2nd St Marshall IL 62441-1010

MITCHELL, IAN MOORHOUSE, consultant cardiac surgeon; b. Guildford, Surrey, Eng., Feb. 25, 1957; s. R. G. Bruce and Sheila M. (Dean) M.; m. Johanna Elizabeth Allflatt, Aug. 7, 1982; children: James, Annelies, David. BSc with honours, Leeds (Eng.) U., 1979, MB ChB, 1979, MD with distinction, 1994. Rsch. fellow Royal Hosp. for Sick Children, Glasgow, Scotland, 1989-91; sr. registrar Yorkshire Regional Health Authority, Leeds, 1991-95; cons. cardiac surgeon Nottingham (Eng.) City Hosp., 1995—. Rsch. grantee Tenovus-Scotland, 1990, Assn. for Children with Heart Diseases, 1990. Fellow Royal Coll. Surgeons Glasgow; mem. Soc. Cardiothoracic Surgeons. Office: Nottingham City Hosp, Dept Cardiothoracic Surgery, Hucknall Rd, Nottingham NG5 1PB, England

MITCHELL, JANET BREW, health services researcher; b. N.Y.C., Oct. 20, 1949; d. Robert Moscrip Mitchell and Dorothy Brennan; m. Jerry Lee Cromwell, June 15, 1980; children: Alexander, Genevieve. BA with highest honors, U. Calif., San Diego, 1971; MSW, UCLA, 1973; PhD, Brandeis U., 1976. Rsch. asst. Brandeis U./Worcester Tng. Program in Social Rsch. & Psych., Waltham, Mass., 1973-75; sr. analyst Abt Assocs., Cambridge, Mass., 1975-77; asst. prof. Boston U. Sch. Medicine, 1977-80; pres. Ctr. for Health Econs. Rsch., Waltham, Mass., 1980—; mem. com. on monitoring access to health care svcs. Inst. Medicine, 1989-92; mem. nat. adv. com. Robert Wood Johnson Health Care Fin. Fellows, 1988-93; cons. VA, 1982-85, NIH, 1983-85, Health Care Financing Adminstrn., 1979—; advisor Physician Reimbursement Study, Congl. Budget Office, 1984-85; mem. adv. panel on physicians & med. tech. Office of Tech. Assessment, 1984-85; mem. health care tech. study sect. Nat. Ctr. for Health Svcs. Rsch., 1984-88; psychiat. social worker UCLA Med. Ctr., 1971-72; med. social worker U. So. Calif., 1972-73, Univ. Hosp. San Diego, 1973. Author (with F.A. Sloan & J. Cromwell) Private Physicians and Public Programs, 1978; contbr. chpts. to 8 books; contbr. numerous articles to profl. jours. Thesis grantee VA, 1976-77. Office: Ctr for Hlth Econ Rsch 300 Fifth Ave Waltham MA 02154-8705

MITCHELL, JEFFREY THOMAS, health science facility administrator; b. Columbus, Ohio, Aug. 9, 1946; s. Roger Lyman and Virginia Claire (Sands); children: Lauren Claire, Spencer Thomas. BS, Wright State U., 1976; Masters in Hosp. Adminstr, Xavier U., 1978. Asst. v.p. Grandview Hosp., Dayton, Ohio, 1977-81; v.p. Wyandotte (Mich.) Gen. Hosp., 1981-85; assoc. prof. Mercy Coll. Detroit, 1981-85; v.p. Aultman Hosp., Canton, Ohio, 1985-91; adminstr., chief exec. officer The Shriner's Children's Hosp., Lexington, Ky., 1992-93; v.p. Innovative Med. Svcs., Inc., Bradenton, Fla., 1994—; bd. dirs. Erie Shores Health Services Inc., Monroe, mem. ambulatory surgery S. Mich. Program Afford. Health, 1980-85, adminstrv. mem. S. Detroit Ongoing Med. System Council, 1981-85, ambulatory task force mem. Miami Valley Health Systems Agy., Dayton 1977-81; instr. grad. program health adminstrn. Cen. Mich. U., Mt. Clemens. Mem. United Arts Found. Stark County, Stark County Cancer Com. Mem. Am. Coll. Health Care Execs. Republican. Episcopalian. Home: 7001 20th Ave W Bradenton FL 34209 Office: CompCare USA 5534 Cortez Rd W Bradenton FL 34210-2817

MITCHELL, JO KATHRYN, hospital technical supervisor; b. Clarksville, Ark., Dec. 1, 1934; d. Vintris Franklin and Melissa Lucile (Edwards) Clark; m. James M. Mitchell, June 4, 1955 (dec. Feb. 1973); children: James, Karen Ann, Leslie Kay, Vicki Lynn. Student, U. Ark., Fayetteville, 1952-53; student, Coll. Ozarks, 1953-54, U. Ark., 1954-55, Little Rock U., 1958. Technologist clin. chemistry U. Hosp., Little Rock, 1956-57, asst. supr., 1957-59, rsch. technologist, 1960-62, asst. supr. clin. chemistry, 1979-82, supr. clin. chemistry, 1982—; technologist Conway County Hosp., Morrilton, Ark., 1959; office mgr., co-owner Medic Pharmacy, Little Rock, 1962-71; owner The Cheese Shop, Little Rock, 1977-80. Adult advisor Order Rainbow Girls local, Little Rock, 1970-84, state, Ark., 1977-84. Mem. Pharmacy Aux. (pres. 1967-69), Order Eastern Star. Methodist. Home: 6908 Lucerne Dr Little Rock AR 72205-5029

MITCHELL, JOHN CHARLES, III, nephrologist; b. Tulsa, Jan. 19, 1940; s. John Charles and Bernita Maxine (Breon) M.; m. Ann Bell, Aug. 27, 1960; children: Andrea, Elizabeth, Martha, John. BA, U. Kans., Lawrence, 1962; MD, U. Kans., Kansas City, 1966. Diplomate Am. Bd. Internal Medicine, Am. Bd. Nephrology. Cons. internal medicine and nephrology Mayo Clinic, Rochester, Minn., 1971—; dir. continuint med. edn. Mayo Found., Rochester, 1983-89, dir. biostudies unit, 1994—; assoc. prof. medicine Mayo Med. Sch., Rochester, 1985—; mem. med. adv. bd. Upper Midwest chpt. Nat. Kidney Found., Mpls., 1971-85. Contbr. papers to profl. pubs. Maj. USAF, 1971-73. Fellow ACS; mem. AMA, Nat. Assn. Nephrology, Rotary Internat., Phi Beta Kappa, Alpha Omega Alpha, Omicron Delta Kappa. Home: 920 SW 10th St Rochester MN 55902

MITCHELL, JOHN DAVID, ophthalmologist; b. Arlington, Va., Nov. 13, 1958; s. Joseph David and Janice Lynn (Funkhouser) M.; m. Mary Bell McPherson, Oct. 29, 1983; children: John David Fontaine, Thomas Barrick, Lewis Hopkins. BS in Biochemistry, Va. Tech., 1980; U. Va., 1985. Cert. Am. Bd. Emergency Medicine. Intern Med. Ctr. Del., Wilmington, 1985-86, resident, 1986-88; emergency medicine attending CMty. Hosp., Roanoke, Va., 1988-91, Emergency Rm. Assocs., Roanoke, Va., 1991-94; clin. asst.

prof. U. Va., Roanoke, 1992-94; resident Washington Hosp. Ctr., 1994—; mem. adv. bd. Coll. Health Scis., Roanoke, 1989-91. Recipient Western Va. EMS Coun. Recognition award, 1989, 90, 91, Davis Cup award Washington Hosp. Ctr. Dept. Ophthalmology, 1996. Mem. Am. Acad. Ophthalmology. Republican. Episcopalian. Home: 10907 Fox Sparrow Ct Fairfax VA 22032 Office: Washington Hosp Ctr 110 Irving St NW Washington DC 20010

MITCHELL, JOHN DOUGLAS, clinical neurologist, educator; b. Amersham, Buckinghamshire, England, June 30, 1951; s. Thomas and Constance M.; m. Christine Elizabeth Aitken, June 25, 1983; children: Susan Helen Mary, Catriona Jane. MB, ChB, U. Aberdeen, Scotland, 1975; MRCP, Royal Coll. Physicians, 1978; FRCP, Royal Coll. of Physicians and Surgeons, 1989; MD, U. Aberdeen, Scotland, 1991; FRCP, Royal Coll. Physicians, Edinburgh, 1992, Royal Coll. Physicians, London, 1993. Registrar in neurology Addenbrooks Hosp. Cambridge, 1979-80; sr. registrar in neurology No. Gen. Hosp., Edinburgh, 1980-84; sr. lectr. in med. neurology U. Edinburgh, Scotland, 1984; cons. neurologist Royal Preston Hosp., 1986; hon. prof. clin. neurology U. Cen. Lancashire, 1993; mem. motor neurone disease subcom. World Fedn. of Neurology, 1990—; vice-chmn. Lancashire Ctr. for Med. Studies, 1992—; med. adv. com. Migraine Trust, 1993—; chmn. rsch. adv. panel Motor Neuron Disease Assn., 1994—. Contbr. chpt. to books. Office: Royal Preston Hosp, Sharoe Green Ln, PR2 9HT Fulwood Preston Lancashire England

MITCHELL, KENNETH D., physiologist, medical educator; b. Musselburgh, Scotland, Mar. 5, 1959; m. Maria Heavens, Sept. 30, 1995. BSc with upper 2d class honors, U. Edinburgh, Scotland, 1981, PhD in Physiology, 1986. Physiology tutor Univ. Med. Sch., Edinburgh, 1981-84; rsch. assoc. Dept. Physiology and Biophysics Nephrology Rsch. and Tng. Ctr. U. Ala., Birmingham, 1984-86, postdoctoral rsch. fellow, 1986-87, rsch. instr., 1987-88, scientist I, 1987-88; asst. prof. Dept. Physiology Tulane U. Sch. Medicine, New Orleans, 1988-95, assoc. prof., 1995—. Contbr. articles to profl. jours. Nat. Heart, Lung and Blood Inst. grantee, 1995—. Mem. Am. Physiological Soc., Am. Soc. Nephrology, Am. Heart Assn. (fellow Coun. High Blood Pressure Rsch. 1993—, Established Investigator award 1995—), Internat. Soc. Nephrology. Office: Dept Physiology SL39 1430 Tulane Ave New Orleans LA 70112*

MITCHELL, LAURA ANNE GILBERT, critical care nurse; b. Anniston, Ala., Oct. 13, 1957; d. Leonard A. and Betty Joyce (Wilkinson) Gilbert; m. Lee H. Mitchell, June 20, 1981; 1 child, Joseph L. ADN, DeKalb Coll., 1987; BSN magna cum laude, Med. Coll. Ga., 1993. CCRN. Staff nurse, preceptor ICU and CCU Gwinnett Med. Ctr., Lawrenceville, Ga., 1987-89, charge nurse cardiac catheterization lab., 1989—. Mem. AACN, Phi Theta Kappa (internat.), Sigma Theta Tau. Home: 435 Clark Lake Estate Dr Grayson GA 30221-1234

MITCHELL, MADELEINE ENID, nutritionist, educator; b. Jamaica, W.I., Dec. 14, 1941; came to U.S., 1963, naturalized, 1974; d. William Keith and Doris Christine (Levy) M. B.Sc. in Home Econs., McGill U., Montreal, Que., Can., 1963; M.S., Cornell U., 1965, Ph.D., 1968. Asst. prof. Wash. State U., Pullman, 1969-77, assoc. prof., 1978—, acting chmn. home econs. research ctr., 1981-83, asst. dir. Agri Research Ctr., Coll. Agr. and Home Econs., 1984-86; nutrition scientist U.S. Dept. Agr., Washington, 1980-81. Mem. Am. Dietetics Assn., Am. Soc. Clin. Nutrition, Am. Inst. Nutrition, Assn. Faculty Women, Sigma Xi, Phi Kappa Phi, Omicron Nu. Episcopalian. Avocations: genealogy, music. Office: Wash State U Human Nutrition Dept Food Sci Pullman WA 99164-6376

MITCHELL, MARK ALLAN, pharmacology educator; b. Compton, Calif., May 1, 1950; s. Vernon Raymond and Nina Joune (Strickler) M.; m. Mary Patricia McGuire, Nov. 25, 1990. BS in Biology, Baylor U., 1973; MS in Physiology, Zoology, Idaho State U., 1976; PhD in Physiology, Pharmacology, U. N.D., 1980; postgrad., Univ Ctr. at Tulsa, 1987; JD, U. Tulsa, 1995. Postgrad. rsch. assoc. dept. pharmacology U. Mo., 1981-82; postdoctoral fellow NIH, 1982-83; v.p., co-founder CARE Diagnostics, Inc., 1983-84; rsch. assoc. cardiovascular pharmacology U. Mo. Coll. Vet. Medicine Dept. Biomed. Scis., 1984-85; asst. prof. pharmacology Okla. Coll. Osteo Medicine and Surgery, Tulsa, 1985-88; asst. prof. pharmacology Okla. State U. Coll. Osteo. Medicine, Tulsa, 1988-91, assoc. prof. pharmacology, 1991-95; corp. trainer/cons OSHA Am. Mgmt. Assn.; founder, pres. Legal-Forensics, Ltd., 1991—. Contbr. articles, abstracts to profl. publs. Bd. dirs. Star Mental Health, Inc., 1993—, Street Sch. Tulsa, 1986-91, Call Rape, Inc., Tulsa, 1987-91, Bohemian Soc.-Fund Raising Support Group for Multiple Sclerosis Soc. Tulsa, 1989-91; mem. Leadership Tulsa, 1990—; mem. adv. bd. Tulsa Area United Way, 1989-90; bd. dirs., vice chmn. Am. Theater Co., Tulsa, 1986-88; mem. adv. coun. Cmty. Alcohol Programs, Inc., Kansas City, Mo., 1984-85, Nat. Coun. on Alcoholism, Kansas City, 1984-85. Rsch. fellow Nat. Inst. Alcoholism and Alcohol Abuse, NIH. Mem. ABA, AAUP, Okla. Trial Lawyers Assn., Soc. for Exptl. Biology and Medicine, Okla. Soc. Physiologists, Okla. Acad. Sci., Sigma Xi. Office: Northcutt Clark Gardnenr Hron & Powell Dept Physiology & Pharmacology PO 1669 Ponca City OK 74602-1669

MITCHELL, MARK W., oral and maxillifacial surgeon; b. Wheeling, W.Va., Dec. 13, 1956; s. John A. and Gwen M. (Braun) M.; m. Susan Denise Williams, Aug. 4, 1979; children: Nicole Denise, Jaclyn Vanessa. DDS, W.Va. U., 1981. Dental resident W.Va. U. Med. Ctr., Morgantown, 1982; oral & maxillofacial resident La. State U., New Orleans, 1982-86; oral & maxillofacial surgeon Coastal Jaw Surgery, Palm Harbor, Fla., 1986—; spkr. Tampa Bay Profls., Clearwater, Fla., 1995—; internat. lectr. El Salvador Nat. Dental Congress, San Salvador, 1994; lectr. Pinellas County Dental Assn., Clearwater, Tampa Bay Acad. Gen. Dentistry, Tampa, 1995, others. Vol. overseas dental mission Mexican Med. Presbyn. Ch. Bd. U.S.A., 1989, Guatemala, 1989. Mem. Am. Assn. Oral & Maxillofacial Surgeons, Am. Dental Soc. Anesthesiology, Am. Dental Assn., Fla. Soc. Oral & Maxillofacial Surgeons, Fla. Dental Soc. Anesthesiology, Fla. Dental Assn., Internat. Congress Oral Implantologists, Acad. Osseointegration, West Coast Dental Assn., Upper Pinellas County Dental Assn. (treas.), West Pasco Dental Soc., Dunedin C. of C., Pinellas/Pasco County Christian Dental Assn. (pres.), Pasco County Children's Dental Health Assn. (chmn.), Rotary (motivation spkr. 1995), Delta Sigma Delta, Omicron Kappa Upsilon. Republican. Office: Coastal Jaw Surgery 2711 Tampa Rd Palm Harbor FL 34684

MITCHELL, PAMELA HOLSCLAW, nursing educator, researcher; b. Denver, June 27, 1940; d. Harold Leslie and Maurine Agnes (Boatman) Holsclaw; m. Donald Waldo Mitchell, Sept. 17, 1966; children: Robert Edward, Kenneth Pearce, Andrew David. BS in Nursing, U. Wash., 1962; MS, U. Calif., 1965; PhD, U. Wash., 1991. Diplomate Am. Bd. Neurosci. Nurses. Asst. head nurse Mass. Gen. Hosp., Boston, 1962-64; pub. health nurse II Dane County Health Dept., Madison, Wis., 1966-67; nursing instr. Emory U., Atlanta, 1967-68; asst. prof. U. Wash., Seattle, 1970-71, 72-78, assoc. prof., 1977-82, prof. physiol. nursing, 1982—, specialist div. neurology, 1978-93, acting chmn. physiologic nursing, 1984-85, prin. investigator critical care nursing sys. and patient outcome, 1991-96, assoc. dean acad. programs, 1993-96, prin. investigator transcranial doppler ultra sonic infra-cranial pressure waveform and nursing care, 1993—, Elizabeth Soule disting. prof. health promotion, 1996—, prof. biobehavioral nursing & health, 1996—, core investigator for cost & outcomes rsch., 1996—; rsch. affiliate Wash. Regional Primate Ctr., Seattle, 1978-92; project dir. AACN, Newport Beach, Calif., 1986-91; mem. expert panel on quality of care Am. Acad. Nursing, 1994—; rev. panelist biomed. and behavioral labs. NIH, 1994—; Virginia Franklin lectr. U. Md., 1995. Co-author: Neurological Assessment for Nursing Practice, 1984 (Book of Yr. award Am. Jour. Nursing 1984); author: Concept Basic to Nursing, 1973, 77, 81, translated to Norwegian, Danish, Spanish; editor, author Am. Assn. Neurosci. Nurses Clin. Reference Text (AANN's Neurosci. Nursing Book of Yr. Award 1989); contbr. articles to jours. and nursing textbooks. Mem. adv. bd. local chpt. Nat. Multiple Sclerosis Soc., Seattle, 1977—, ARC, 1979-87, Alzheimer's Disease Rsch. Ctr. U. Wash. Recipient disting. writing award Wash. and Am. jours. nursing, 1983, Disting. Tchg. award U. Wash. Sch. Nursing, 1986, Jennifer Davis award for leadership in neurosci. nursing, 1995; fellow Am. Acad. Nursing, 1980. Mem. ANA, AACN, APHA, Am. Assn. Neurosci. Nurses (chmn. clin. reference 1983-88, bd. dirs. 1989-93, editor Neurosci.), Western Inst. Nursing (bd. govs. 1996—), Coun. Nurse Researchers, Nurses in Advanced Practice, Soc. Critical Care Medicine, Assn. for Health Svcs. Rsch. Democrat. Congregationalist. Home: 6016 Upland Ter S Seattle WA 98118-2928 Office: U Wash Acad Programs in Nursing Box 357260 Seattle WA 98195

MITCHELL, PAULA RAE, nursing educator; b. Independence, Mo., Jan. 10, 1951; d. Millard Henry and E. Lorene (Denton) Gates; m. Ralph William Mitchell, May 24, 1975. BS in Nursing, Graceland Coll., 1973; MS in Nursing, U. Tex., 1976; EdD in Ednl. Adminstrn., N.Mex. State U., 1996. RN, Tex., Mo.; cert. childbirth educator. Commd. capt. U.S. Army, 1972; ob-gyn. nurse practitioner U.S. Army, Seoul, Korea, 1977-78; resigned, 1978; instr. nursing El Paso (Tex.) C.C., 1979-85, dir. nursing, 1985—, acting div. chmn. health occupations, 1985-86, div. chmn., 1986—, curriculum facilitator, 1984-86; ob-gyn. nurse practitioner Planned Parenthood, El Paso, 1981-86, mem. med. com., 1986—; cons. in field. Author: (with Grippando) Nursing Perspectives and Issues, 1989, 93; contbr. articles to profl. jours. Founder, bd. dirs. Health-C.R.E.S.T., El Paso, 1981-85; mem. pub. edn. com. Am. Cancer Soc., El Paso, 1983-84, mem. profl. activities com., 1992-93; mem. El Paso City-County Bd. Health, 1989-91; mem. Govt. Applications Rev. Com., Rio Grande Coun. Govts., 1989-91; mem. collaborative coun. El Paso Magnet H.S. for Health Care Professions, 1992-94. Decorated Army Commendation medal, Meritorious Svc. medal. Mem. Nat. League Nursing (mem. resolutions com. Assocs. Degree coun. 1987-89, accreditation site visitor, AD coun. 1990—, mem. Tex. edn. com. 1991-92, Tex. 3rd v.p. 1992-93), Am. Soc. Psychoprophylaxis Obstetrics, Nurses Assn. Am. Coll. Obstetricians & Gynecologists (cert. in ambulatory women's health care; chpt. coord. 1979-83, nat. program rev. com. 1984-86, corr. 1987-89), Advanced Nurse Practitioner Group El Paso (coord. 1980-83 legis. committee 1984), Am. Phys. Therapist Assn. (commn. on accreditation, site visitor for phys. therapist assistant programs 1991—), Orgn. Assoc. Degree Nursing (Tex. membership chmn. 1985-89, chmn. goals com. 1989—, mem nat. by-laws com., 1990—), Am. Vocat. Assn., Am. Assn. Women Community & Jr. Colls., Tex. Orgn. Nurse Execs., Nat. Coun. Occupational Edn. (mem. articulation task force 1986-89, program standards task force 1991-93), Nat. Coun. Instructional Adminstrs., Tex. Soc. Allied Health Profls., Tex. Nurses Assn., Nat. Soc. Allied Health Profls. (mem. edn. com. 1993—), Sigma Theta Tau, Phi Kappa Phi. Mem. Christian Ch. (Disciples of Christ). Home: 4616 Cupid Dr El Paso TX 79924-1726 Office: El Paso C C PO Box 20500 El Paso TX 79998-0500

MITCHELL, PETER WILLIAM, addictions counselor; b. Queens, N.Y., Sept. 2, 1950; s. James Francis and Margaret (Tiernan) M.; m. Mary Elizabeth Brett, May 15, 1976; children: Bryan Scott, Shannon Marie, Kevin James, Michael Ryan. BS in Mktg., Fordham U., 1972; MBA, Calif. Coast U., 1984. Cert. criminal justice specialist, master addictions counselor. Spl. agt. FBI, Washington, 1972-77; store co-mgr. First Nat. Stores, Inc., Somerville, Mass., 1977-78; area sales mgr. H.J. Heinz Co., Indpls., 1978-83; exec. sales rep. Sandoz Nutrition Corp., Mpls., 1983-91; regional sales mgr. Fresenius Pharma USA, Inc., New Brunswick, N.J., 1991-92; sales cons. Cardinal Health/Marmac Div., East Windsor, Conn., 1992-93; primary counselor, case mgr. Sunrise House Found., Lafayette, N.J., 1993—. Bd. mem. Vernon (N.J.) Twp. Little League, 1985-89, Vernon (N.J.) Bd. Ethics, 1991—. Recipient Capitol award Nat. Leadership Coun., Washington, 1991. Mem. Nat. Assn. Alcoholism & Drug Abuse Counselors, Am. Assn. Compulsive Gambling Counselors. Republican. Roman Catholic. Home: 101 Greenhill Rd Hamburg NJ 07419 Office: Sunrise House Found PO Box 600 Lafayette NJ 07848-0600

MITCHELL, RIE ROGERS, psychologist, counseling educator; b. Tucson, Feb. 1, 1940; d. Martin Smith and Lavaun (Peterson) Rogers; student Mills Coll., 1958-59; BS, U. Utah, 1962, MS, 1963; postgrad. San Diego State U., 1965-66; MA, UCLA, 1969, PhD, 1969. Registered play therapist, supr.; cert. sandplay therapist; diplomate Am. Bd. Psychology, 1992; m. Rex C. Mitchell, Mar. 16, 1961; 1 child, Scott Rogers. Tchr., Coronado (Calif.) Unified Sch. Dist., 1964-65; sch. psychologist Glendale (Calif.) Unified Sch. Dist., 1968-70; psychologist Glendale Guidance Clinic, 1970-77; asst. prof. ednl. psychology Calif. State U., Northridge, 1970-74, asso. prof., 1974-78, prof., 1978—, chmn. dept. ednl. psychology, 1976-80, acting exec. asst. to pres., 1981-82; acting exec. asst. to pres. Calif. State U., Dominguez Hills, 1978-79; cons. to various Calif. sch. dists.; pvt. practice psychology, Calabasas, Calif. Recipient Outstanding Educator award Maharishi Soc., 1978; Woman of Yr. award U. Utah, 1962, Profl. Leadership award Western Assn. Counselor Edn., 1990. Mem. Calif. Assn. Counselor Edn., Supervision and Adminstrn. (dir. 1976-77), Western Assn. Counselor Edn. and Supervision (officer 1978-82, pres. 1980-81, profl. leadership award, 1990), Assn. Counselor Edn. and Supervision (dir. 1980-81, program chmn. 1981-82, treas. 1983-86, Presdl. award 1986, Leadership award 1987), UCLA Doctoral Alumni Assn. (pres. 1974-76), Am. Psychol. Assn., Am. Ednl. Research Assn., Calif. Women in Higher Edn. (pres. chpt. 1977-78), Calif. Concerns (treas. 1984-86), Sandplay Therapists Am. (bylaws chmn. 1995—, exceptions chmn. 1995-96, fin. officer 1996—), Pi Lambda Theta (pres. chpt. 1970-71, chairwoman nat. resolutions 1971-73). Author: Sandplay: Past Present & Future, 1994; contbr. numerous articles on group process, sandplay, counselor edn. to profl. jours. Home: 4503 Alta Tupelo Dr Calabasas CA 91302-2516 Office: Calif State U Counselor Edn Dept Northridge CA 91330

MITCHELL, ROSS GALBRAITH, pediatrics educator; b. Nov. 18, 1920; s. Richard Galbraith and Ishobel Mark (Ross) M.; m. June Phylis Butcher, Sept. 16, 1950; children: Andrew, Lindsay, Alison, Christine. B in Medicine and Surgery, U. Edinburgh, Scotland, 1944, MD, 1954. House physician Hosp. for Sick Children, London, 1949-50; pediatric registrar Royal Hosp. for Sick Children, Edinburgh, 1950-51; Rockefeller fellow Mayo Clinic, Rochester, Minn., 1952-53; lectr. in child health U. St. Andrews, Scotland, 1952-55; cons. pediatrician Dundee (Scotland) Royal Inf., 1955-63; prof. child health U. Aberdeen, Scotland, 1963-72; prof. child health U. Dundee, 1973-85, prof. emeritus, 1985—; mem. Gen. Med. Coun., U.K., 1983-86; dean faculty of medicine U. Dundee, 1978-81; chmn. editorial bd. Mac Keith Press, London, 1980-95. Author: Disease in Infancy and Childhood, 1973; editor: Child Health in the Community, 1977; contbr. chpts. in books and profl. jours. Surgeon lt. Royal Navy, 1944-47. Decorated Burma Star (U.K.), 1945. Fellow Royal Coll. Physicians; mem. Assn. Physicians Gt. Britain, Am. Acad. Cerebral Palsy and Devel. Medicine (fgn. corr.), Internat. Cerebral Palsy Soc. (hon.), Brit. Pediat. Assn. Mem. Ch. of Scotland. Home: 4 Abertay Gardens, Dundee DD5 2RR, Scotland

MITCHELL, RUSSELL HARRY, dermatologist; b. Erie, N.D., Oct. 19, 1925; s. William John and Anna Lillian (Sogge) M.; B.S., B.A., U. Minn., Mpls., 1947, B.M., M.D., 1951; postgrad. U. Pa. Med. Sch., 1968-69; m. Judith Lawes Douvarjo, May 24, 1968; children: Kathy Ellen, Gregory Alan, Jill Elaine, Crystal Anne. Intern, Gorgas Hosp., C.Z., 1951-52; resident in dermatology U.S. Naval Hosp., Phila., 1967-70; asst. chief out-patient dept. Gorgas Hosp., 1955-64; chief med. and surg. wards Ariz. State Hosp., Phoenix, 1965; commd. lt. (j.g.) M.C., U.S. Navy, 1953, advanced through grades to capt., 1968; svc. in Vietnam; ret., 1981; pvt. practice specializing in dermatology, Leesburg, Va., 1978—; mem. staff Loudoun Meml. Hosp., 1975—; dermatologist Nat. Naval Med. Center, Bethesda, Md., 1973-81; asst. prof. Georgetown U. Med. Sch., 1975-85. Pres. Archaeol. Soc. Panama, 1962-64. Decorated Bronze Star with combat V; Vietnam Gallantry Cross with palm and clasp; Condecoración Vasco Nuñez de Balboa in orden de Caballero (Panama); diplomate Am. Bd. Dermatology. Fellow Am. Acad. Dermatology, Am. Acad. Physicians, Explorers Club; mem. AMA, Assn. Mil. Surgeons, Assn. Mil. Dermatologists (life), Am. Soc. Contemporary Medicine and Surgery, Soc. Am. Archaeology, Royal Soc. Medicine, Pan Am. Med. Assn., Loudoun County Med. Soc., Dermatology Found., Marine's Meml. Club (assoc.), Internat. Platform Assn., Phi Chi. Contbr. articles to med. and archaeol. publs. Home: 18685 Woodburn Rd Leesburg VA 20175-9008 Office: 823J S King St Leesburg VA 20175-3910

MITCHELL, TEDDY LEE, physician; b. Columbia, La., Feb. 24, 1962; s. Oliver Clayton nad Mary Elizabeth (Johnston) M.; m. Janet Luisa Tornelli, Apr. 9, 1988; children: Mary Katherine, Oliver Charles. BS in Biology, Stephen F. Austin State U., 1983; MD, U. Tex. Med. Br., 1987. Diplomate Am. Bd. Internal Medicine, Cert. of Added Qualification-Sports Medicine. Intern U. Tex. Med. Br., Galveston, 1987-88, resident, 1988-90, 90-91; staff physician Cooper Aerobics Ctr., Dallas, 1991—, med. dir. wellness program, 1991—. Mem. Rep. Sen. Inner Cir., Washington, 1993, Heritage Found., Washington, 1993. Mem. AMA, Am. Coll. Sports Medicine, Am. Coll. Physicians (cert Merit 1990), Tex. Med. Assn., Dallas County Med. Soc. Methodist. Home: 3224 Lovers Ln Dallas TX 75225-7626

MITCHELL, THOMAS N., lab administrator; b. Balt., Jan. 19, 1959; s. Braxton Dallam and Elizabeth S. T. (Byrd) M.; m. Rebecca S. Thomas, Aug. 25, 1985; children: Corbin T., Sarah E. BA, Western Md. Coll., 1985. Quality control engr. Pharmatopes Inc. (now Syncor), Timonium, Md., 1980-81; ophthalmic technician Johns Hopkins U., Balt., 1981-83, sr. programmer, 1985-92, sr. rsch. asst., 1992—, DNA lab. adminstr., 1993—. Contbr. articles to profl. jours. Mem. parks bd. Westminster City Govt., 1991-94. Mem. Seven Seas Cruising Assn. Home: 8305 Alston Rd Baltimore MD 21204 Office: Johns Hopkins Ctr for Hereditary Eye Diseases 600 N Wolfe St Baltimore MD 21287-9237

MITCHELL, THOMAS SOREN, urologist; b. Santa Monica, Calif., Feb. 15, 1941; s. Cyril Louis and Florence Jeanette (Mortensen) M.; m. Michal Jane Lawrence, June 19, 1963; children: Thomas Soren Jr., Lee Delphine. BA, Loma Linda U., 1962, MD, 1966. Diplomate Am. Bd. Urology. Resident U. Wash. Hosp., Seattle, 1966-67, Loma Linda (Calif.) Univ. Hosp., 1967-68; resident in urology U. Calif. Hosp., San Diego, 1970-74; pvt. practice urology Santa Monica, Monterey, Calif., 1974-96; chief urology St. John's Hosp., Santa Monica, 1990-94; asst. clin. prof. urology UCLA Med. Sch., 1976—. Capt. USAF, 1968-70, Vietnam. Mem. Pacific Oncology Soc. (exec. bd. dirs., sec. 1994—), Am. Urol. Assn., Bay Surg. Soc., Santa Monica C. of C. Office: 2021 Santa Monica Blvd 510E Santa Monica CA 90404

MITCHELL, TOM HERRON, retired physician; b. West Point, Miss., Sept. 11, 1924; m. Agnes Herlong, Feb. 17, 1979; children: Emily Mitchell Sutphin, Kathleen Mitchell Haskins, Charles D., John H. Med. cert., U. Miss., 1943; BS, Miss. State Coll., 1944; MD, Tulane U., 1947. Gen. rotating intern So. Bapt. Hosp., New Orleans, 1947-48; resident in gen. practice Mercy Hosp.-Street Meml., Vicksburg, Miss., 1948-50; pvt. practice, Vicksburg, 1953-87; ret., 1987; mem. staff, chmn. Street Clinic, Vicksburg, 1953-75, bd. dirs., 1968-70, med. dir., 1970-75; mem. staff Mercy Regional Med. Ctr., Vicksburg, 1948-50, 53-75, 78-87, mem. hon. med. staff, 1987—, chmn. dept. family practice, 1953-75, past instr. Sch. Nursing, bd. dirs. 1986-90; mem. Miss. Bd. Nursing, 1965-70; mem. nurse edn. adv com. Miss. Bd. Trustees of Instns. Higher Learning, 1968-72; bd. dirs., chmn. exec. com. Miss. Found. for Med. Care, 1974-75, exec. dir., 1975-78. Mem. projects rev. com. Ctrl. Miss. Planning Coun., 1972-74, bd. dirs., 1972-75, vice chmn., 1974-75; former supt. Sunday sch., elder and tchr. men's Bible class First Presbyn. Ch., Vicksburg. Served with M.C., USNR, 1950-52. Mem. AMA (vol. physician for Vietnam 1968), Am. Acad. Family Physicians, Miss. Med. Assn. (past v.p.), West Miss. Med. Soc. (past pres. and del.), Miss. Acad. Family Physicians (past pres., past mem. bd. dirs., Family Practitioner of Yr. award 1988). Home: 304 Montaign Dr Vicksburg MS 39180-5742

MITCHELL, VERNICE VIRGINIA, nurse, poet, author; b. Scott, Miss., Mar. 11, 1921; d. Isaiah and Martha Magdalene (Edwards) Smith; m. Willis Mitchell, Aug. 17, 1940; children: Elaine, Kenneth, Liethia, John, Ransom, Paul. Diploma, Princeton Continuation Coll., 1955. Nurse Cook County Sch. Nursing, Chgo., 1951-59, U. Ill. Hosp., Chgo., 1959-67, Grant Hosp., Chgo., 1967-78, Northwestern Meml. Hosp., Chgo., 1979-84; with U. Ill. Hosp. Aetna Nurse's Registry, Chgo., 1984—. Author: The Book Success Through Spiritual Truths, 1987, Details Through Rose-Colored Glasses, 1995, (poems) A Woman, chicago, The 12 Months; also numerous poetry and musical lyrics; poems submitted to Dial-A-Poem, Chgo., 1988-89. Chmn. cookbook project 1988-89. Recipient merit cert. Am. Poetry Assn., 1982, merit cert. World of Poetry, 1983, 85, Golden Poet award 1986, 87, 88, Silver Poet award, 1989, 90; inducted into the Hall of Fame for Sr. Citizens, Chgo., 1991. Mem. 6700 Emerald Ave. Block Club (pres. 1971-92).

MITCHELL, WAYNE LEE, health care administrator; b. Rapid City, S.D., Mar. 25, 1937; s. Albert C. and Elizabeth Isabelle (Nagel) M.; m. Marie Galletti; BA, U. Redlands (Calif.), 1959; MSW, Ariz. State U., 1970, EdD, 1979. Profl. social worker various county, state, and fed. agys., 1962-70, Bur. Indian Affairs, Phoenix, 1970-77, USPHS, 1977-79; asst. prof. Ariz. State U., 1979-84; with USPHS, Phoenix, 1984—. Bd. dirs. Phoenix Indian Cmty. Sch., 1973-75, ATLATL, 1995; bd. dirs. Phoenix Indian Ctr., 1974-79, Cmty. Svc. award, 1977; mem. Phoenix Area Health Adv. Bd., 1975; mem. Community Behavioral Mental Health Bd., 1976-80; mem. bd. trustees Heard Mus. of Anthropology, Phoenix, Ariz., 1996; mem. bd. dirs. Partnership for Cmty. Devel. Ariz. State U.-West, 1996—; lectr. in field. Bd. dirs. Cen. Ariz. Health Systems Agy.; mem. Fgn. Rels. Com. Phoenix. Served with USCG, 1960-62. Recipient Cmty. Svc. award Ariz. Temple of Islam, 1980, Ariz. State U., 1996, Dir. Excellence award Phoenix Area IHS Dir., 1992, 93. Mem. NASW, UN Assn., Am. Hosp. Assn., Am. Orthopsychiat. Assn., NAACP, Internat. Platform Assn., Asia Soc., U.S.-China Assn., Kappa Delta Pi, Phi Delta Kappa, Chi Sigma Chi, Nucleus Club. Congregationalist. Democrat. Contbr. articles to publs. Home: PO Box 9592 Phoenix AZ 85068-9592 Office: 3738 N 16th St Phoenix AZ 85016-5947

MITCHELL, WILLIAM AVERY, JR., orthodontist; b. Greenville, S.C., Apr. 26, 1933; s. William Avery and Eva (Rigdon) M.; m. Patricia Ann Scott, June 26, 1965; 1 child, William Avery III. BS, Furman U., 1955; DDS, Emory U., 1959; MS in Dentistry, 1967. Diplomate Am. Bd. Orthodontics. Pvt. practice Decatur, Ga., 1963-67, Greenville, 1967—; instr. Emory U. Dental Sch., Atlanta, 1965-66, instr. dept. orthodontics, 1966-68; guest lectr. Greenville Tech. Coll., 1979—; councilor Coll. Diplomates of Am. Bd. Orthodontics, 1988-91, treas., 1991-92, sec., 1992-93, pres.-elect, 1993-94, pres., 1994-95, 95-96. Bd. dirs. United Speech and Hearing, Greenville, 1972-75; chmn. dental divsn. United Way, Greenville, 1983, 84; fund raiser Roper Mt. Sci. Ctr., 1985; mem. adv. bd. Greenville Tech. Coll., 1985-88; pres. Booster Club Christ Ch. Episc. Ch., 1987-88, mem. bd. visitors, 1990—; deacon 1st Bapt. Ch. Lt., capt. U.S. Army, 1959-61. Recipient Emil Eisenberg Scholarship, Ga. Dental Assn., Atlanta, 1958-59. Fellow Am. Coll. Dentists, Internat. Coll. Dentists; mem. ADA, Am. Assn. Orthodontists (del. 1985-91, 93—), S.C. Dental Assn. (gen. chmn. ann. meeting, 1996, George P. Hoffmann Disting. Dentist award 1996), So. Assn. Orthodontists (pres. 1993-94, trustee 1983, 84, 85, sr. dir. 1989-92), S.C. Orthodontic Assn. (pres. 1978), Piedmont Dist. Dental Soc. (bd. dirs. 1972, Greenville County Dental Soc. (pres. 1972, Outstanding Svc. award 1994), S.C. Acad. Dental Practice Adminstrn., Emory Orthodontic Assn. (pres. 1972), Furman Paladin Club (bd. dirs. 1980-84), Commerce Club (bd. dirs. Greenville chpt. 1983—), Rotary, Greenville Country Club. Office: 10 Cleveland Ct Greenville SC 29607-2414

MITCHELL, WILLIAM MARVIN, pathology educator; b. Atlanta, Mar. 3, 1935; s. William Joseph and Marvin Eugenia (Peavy) M.; m. Shirley Ann Crowell, Dec. 22, 1959; children: Alexander James, Keith Townsend, Derek Loren. AS, Vanderbilt U., 1957, MD, 1960; PhD, Johns Hopkins U., 1966. Diplomate Am. Bd. Pathology. Asst. prof. microbiology and medicine Vanderbilt U., Nashville, 1966-70, assoc. prof. pathology, 1970-78, prof., 1978—; med. dir. Specialized Assays, Nashville, 1981-91; med. dir. Vanderbilt Pathology Lab. Svcs., 1994—; cons. NIH, DuPont Co., Smith Kline, others. Patentee in field; contbr. articles to profl. jours. Bd. dirs. St. Augustine's Chapel, Nashville, 1981-86; judge Regional Sci. and Engring. Fair, Nashville, 1985, 88; judge Internat. Sci. Engring. Fair, Nashville, 1992, Birmingham, 1994. Eleanor Roosevelt Internat. Cancer fellow Internat. Union Against Cancer, 1976-77; grantee NIH. Mem. AAAS, Am. Assn. Pathology, Am. Chem. Soc., Am. Soc. Biol. Chemists, Am. Soc. Microbiology, Internat. Acad. Pathology, Am. Soc. Interferon Rsch., Am. AIDS Soc., Sigma Xi. Episcopalian. Office: Vanderbilt U Dept Pathology Nashville TN 37232

MITNICK, HAL, rheumatologist. BA, Lafayette Univ., 1968; MD, N.Y. Univ. Sch. Medicine, 1972. Diplomate Am. Bd. Internal Medicine, Am. Bd. Rheumatology. Mem. staff dept. rheumatology N.Y. Univ., 1978, mem. staff dept. internal medicine, 1976, clinical prof. medicine, 1995—. Fellow Am. Coll. Rheumatology. Office: 333 E 34th St New York NY 10016

MITRE, BLIMA KIRMAYER, pathologist; b. Romania, Aug. 15, 1942; came to U.S., 1968, naturalized, 1978; d. Moses and Regina Kirmayer; m. Ricardo J. Mitre, Oct. 7, 1967; children—Edward, Sandra, Marcie, Richard

James. Grad. Universidad Mayor de San Simon, 1967. Intern Viedma Hosp., Cochabamba, Bolivia, 1967-68; resident in pathology Bapt. Meml. Hosp., Jacksonville, Fla., 1968-70; with Presbyn. Hosp., Pitts., 1970-72, Children's Hosp., Pitts., 1972-73; staff pathologist Passavant Hosp., 1990—; clin. asst. prof. pathology U. Pitts. Med. Sch., 1970—. Mem. AMA, ACMS, PMS, Internat. Acad. Pathology, Am. Soc. Clin. Pathologists, Coll. Am. Pathologists, Pa. Assn. Clin. Pathologists. Office: Passavant Hosp 9100 Babcock Blvd Pittsburgh PA 15237

MITSUYASU, RONALD T., physician, researcher, medical educator; b. Berkeley, Calif., Feb. 12, 1952; s. Kiyoshi and Hisako (Sato) M.; m. Sharon R., June 23, 1984. BA in Biochemistry, U. Calif., 1973; MD, UCLA, 1978. Diplomate Am. Bd. Internal Medicine. Intern internal medicine Rush-Presbyn.-St. Luke's, Chgo., 1978, resident internal medicine, 1878-81; fellow in hematology, oncology Sch. Medicine UCLA, 1981-84, asst. prof. medicine Sch. Medicine, 1984-90, assoc. prof. medicine Sch. Medicine, 1990—, dir. CARE Ctr. Sch. Medicine, 1991—; Mem. exec. com. AIDS Clin. Trials Group, 1995—, adv. bd. vaccines and related biologics FDA, Rockville, Md., 1989-92. Contbr. over 100 articles to profl. jours., chpts. to books. Fellow Am. Coll. Physicians; mem. Am. Assn. Cancer Rsch., Am. Soc. Clin. Oncology, Am. Soc. Hematology, Am. Fed. Clin. Rsch., Internat. AIDS Soc. Office: UCLA CARE Ctr. 10833 Le Conte Ave BH-412 CHS Los Angeles CA 90095-1793

MITTAL, SITA RAM, cardiologist; b. Ajmer, Rajasthan, India, Jan. 29, 1949; s. Gouri Shankar and Ratan Devi (Garg) M.; m. Shakuntla Kamdar, May 8, 1970; children: Sunil, Sankulp, Sarveshwar. MB BS, Rajasthan U., 1970, MD, 1974; MAMS, Nat. Acad., 1976; DM in Cardiology, PGI Chandigarh, 1979. Tutor forensic medicine Med. Coll., Ajmer, India, 1973-75, tutor medicine, 1975-76, asst. prof. medicine, 1976-89, assoc. prof. medicine, 1989-92, prof. medicine, 1992-95, prof. cardiology, 1995—; head dept. of cardiology JLN Med. Coll., Ajmer, 1989—; mem. subspeciality coun. on cardiac muscle disease, 1994; lectr. in field. Editl. mem. Internat. Jour. of Cardiology, Amsterdam, 1994—, Indian Heart Jour., 1991—; contbr. articles to profl. jours. Recipient DP Basu award, Cardiol. Soc. India, 1986, VV Shah oration, 1995, Coelho Meml. lectureship, Assn. Physicians India, 1989, JR Vakil lectureship, 1992, SV Singh professorship, 1993, Searl Oration, 1995, Farooq Abdulla Oration, 1996. Fellow Indian Soc. Electrocardiology (RS Rajagopalan award 1985, 87), Indian Coll Physicians. Home: XI/101 Brahampuri, Ajmer 305001, India Office: Heart Disease Inst, JLN Med Coll Campus, Ajmer 305001, India

MITTELMAN, MICHAEL H., optometrist, researcher; b. N.Y.C., Apr. 21, 1953; s. Harry and Elise (Brown) M.; m. Tanis M. Nerenhausen, Nov. 29, 1980; children: Laurel, Emily, Tori. BA, Jacksonville U., 1975; OD, Pa. Coll. Optometry, 1980; MPH, U. Ala., Birmingham, 1990; diploma, U.S. Naval War Coll., 1993. Diplomate Am. Acad. Optometry. Commd. officer USN, 1980, advanced through grades to comdr.; head optometry dept. Naval Hosp., Cherry Point, N.C., 1980-84, U.S. Naval Hosp., Rota, Spain, 1984-87; head optometry divsn. Naval Aerospace and Operational Med. Inst., Pensacola, Fla., 1987-93; dep. dir. rsch. Naval Aerospace Med. Rsch. Lab., Pensacola, 1993—. Inventor in field. Sec. Multidisciplinary Practice Sect., Pensacola, 1993—; chmn. Elem. Sch. Adv. Coun., Pensacola, 1994-95. Recipient Ashton Greybeil award Soc. U.S. Navy Flight Surgeons, 1994, Best Newsletter Editorial, Soc. Optometric Editors, 1994. Mem. Am. Optometric Assn. (editor MPS Horizon newsletter 1992—), Aerospace Med. Assn., Assn. Med. Surgeons of the U.S., Armed Forces Optometric Soc. (pres. 1993-94, Optometrist of Yr. 1995). Office: Naval Aerospace Med Rsch 51 Hovey Rd Pensacola FL 32508

MITTERMEYER, BERNHARD T., dean. Interim dean Tex. Tech. U. Health Sci. Ctr., Lubbock. Office: Tex Tech U Health Sci Ctr 3601 4th St Lubbock TX 79430*

MITTL, RAINER N., ophthalmologist; b. Munich, W.Ger., Mar. 19, 1939; s. Joseph and Maria (Schwickert) M.; came to U.S., 1965; M.D., U. Munich, 1964; m. Janice J. Janoski, June 28, 1970. Intern, E. Orange (N.J.) Gen. Hosp., 1966; resident in ophthalmology N.Y. Med. Coll., 1967-70; fellow Johns Hopkins Hosp., 1972-73; practice medicine, specializing in ophthalmology, N.Y.C., 1973—; mem. staff Columbia-Presbyn. Med. Ctr. Mem. AMA, Am. Acad. Ophthalmology, Am. Coll. Surgeons, Internat. Coll. of Surgeons, Vitreous Soc., Assn. for Rsch. in Vision and Ophthalmology. Clubs: N.Y. Athletic, University. Office: Suite 314 Edward S Harkness Eye Inst Columbia-Presbyn Med Center 635 W 165th St New York NY 10032

MITTLEMAN, DAVID AARON, ophthalmologist; b. N.Y.C., Dec. 11, 1962; s. Bernard H. and Doris (Freedman) M. BS, Yale U., 1984; MD, Johns Hopkins U., 1988. Diplomate Am. Bd. Ophthalmology. Resident in ophthalmology Wills Eye Hosp., Phila., 1989-92; pres. Mittleman Eye Ctr., West Palm Beach, Fla., 1992—; chief of ophthalmology SurgiCtr. of the Palm Beaches, West Palm Beach, 1992-94; bd. dirs. Bear Island Devel., West Palm Beach, 1995—. Mem. Am. Acad. Ophthalmology, Am. Soc. Cataract and Refractive Surgeons, Treasure Coast Ophthalmology Soc., Palm Beach Ophthalmology Soc. Office: Mittleman Eye Ctr 2601 N Flagler Dr # 106 West Palm Beach FL 33407

MITZ, VLADIMIR, plastic surgeon; b. Vielikoie Selo, USSR, Mar. 3, 1943; came to France, 1949, naturalized, 1957; s. Hersz Jumen and Maria (Mincberg) M.; 1 child, Illitch. M.D., 1973. Intern, Lariboisiere Hosp., Paris, 1967; resident Jackson Meml. Hosp., Miami, Fla., 1975; chief clinic Assistance Publique, Paris, 1973-78, mem. staff, 1980—; prof. anatomy Faculty Medicine, Paris, 1970-74; dir. micro vascular lab. Boucicaut Hosp., Paris, 1980—. Author: Operation Beaute, 1984, Lambeaux Musculo Cutanes, 1984, Plaies et Bosses, 1988, Les Dessous de la Peau, 1990, le Choix d'être belle, 1992, La Chirurgie Esthetique, Manuel de Chirurgie du Sein; producer movie Operation Verite, 1982, the SMAS Biplane Face Lift. Pres. Mouvement de Recherche en Plastique Humaine, Paris, 1972. Mem. French Acad. Surgery, Brazilian Soc. Plastic Surgery (assoc.), French Soc. Plastic Reconstructive Aesthetic Surgery, Assn. des Chirurgiens Esthetiques et Plastiques au l'Hosp. Boucicaut. Avocation: painting, Sculpture. Home: 12 Rue du Renard, 75004 Paris France Office: 176 Blvd St Germain, 75006 Paris France

MIXSON, WILLIAM TUNNO, retired gynecologist; b. Gainesville, Fla., May 22, 1924; s. William Tunno and Mabel Gray (Currell) M.; m. Katherine Louise Hoffman, June, 1948 (div. 1977); children: William T. III, Richard Allyn, Robert David; m. Beverly Jean Armstrong, 1977. BS, U. Miami, Coral Gables, Fla., 1946; MD, Temple U., 1948, MSc in Ob-gyn., 1953. Diplomate Am. Bd. Ob-gyn. Intern Phila. Gen. Hosp., 1948-50; residency Temple U. Hosp., Phila., 1950-53; pvt. practice ob-gyn. Coral Gables, 1953-72, pvt. practice gynecology, 1972-89; pvt. practice gynecology South Miami, Fla., 1989-96; retired, 1996; clin. assoc. prof. ob-gyn. Sch. Medicine, U. Miami, 1954-95; chief staff Dr.'s Hosp., Coral Gables, 1968-69; exec. com. Nat. Practitioner Data Bank, Rockville, Md., 1990—. Contbr. articles to profl. jours. Exec. bd., Planned Parenthood Greater Miami, 1989—. Fellow Am. Coll. Obstetricians and Gynecologists (bd. govs. 1977-87, pres. 1985-86, Miles lectr. 1985, Dist. Svc. award 1985), ACS (bd. govs. 1979-84); mem. South Atlantic Assn. Obstetricians and Gynecologists (pres. 1984-85), Fla. Obstet. and Gynecol. Soc. (pres. 1985). Republican. Home: 8820 SW 67th Ct Miami FL 33156-1700

MIYAIRI, TAKESHI, cardiovascular surgeon; b. Matsumoto-shi, Nagano, Japan, Aug. 23, 1958; s. Akira and Akiko (Harada) M.; m. Harumi Yoshida, Apr. 17, 1994; 1 child, Imo. MD, Tokyo U., 1996. Chief surgeon Asahi Gen. Hosp., Chiba, Japan, 1993—. Office: Asahi Gen Hosp, Dept Cardiac Surgery I-1326, Chiba Asahi 289-25, Japan

MIYAKE, AKIO, biologist, educator; b. Kyoto, Japan, June 29, 1931; s. Yoshikazu and Yukie (Yamazaki) M.; m. Sadako Harada, Mar. 15, 1965 (dec. June 1986); children: Akiko, Toshio; m. Terue Harumoto, Dec. 30, 1988; 1 child, Yuka. BS, Kyoto U., 1953, D of Science, 1959. Asst. Osaka (Japan) City U., 1953-63; visiting scholar Ind. U., Bloomington, 1959-61; lectr. Kyoto (Japan) U., 1963-70; group leader Max-Planck Inst. for Molecular Genetics, West Berlin, 1970-74; visiting scholar U. Pisa, Italy, 1975-77, U. Münster, West Germany, 1978-83; prof. U. Camerino, Italy, 1983—. Contbr. articles on sexual reprodn. in microorganisms to profl. jours. and books. Recipient Zool. Soc. of Japan Prize, 1981. Mem. Zool. Soc. Japan, Genetics Soc. of Japan, AAAS, Soc. Protozoologists. Home: Corso Italia 150, I-62022 Castelraimondo Italy Office: U Camerino Dept Cell Biol, Via F Camerini 2, I-62032 Camerino Italy

MIYAMOTO, MISAKO, psychology educator; b. Bangkok, Thailand, Feb. 25, 1928; d. Kenji and Sumi (Kakiuchi) M. BA in Home Econs., Japan Women's U., Tokyo, 1954; MA in Psychology, Brandeis U., 1959; PhD in Edn., U. Tokyo, Japan, 1980. Asst. Japan Women's U., Tokyo, 1949-56, instr., 1956-57, 60-67, assoc. prof., 1967-75; prin. Jr. High, Japan Women's U., Tokyo, 1967-70; prof. Japan Women's U., Tokyo, 1975-96, prof. emeritus, 1996—, pres., 1993—; instr. U. Tokyo, 1984, Nagoya U., 1984, Kumamoto U., 1985, U. Tsukuba, 1985, Hiroshima U., 1986, Waseda U., Tokorozawa, Japan, 1988-90, Shirayuri Women's Coll. Tokyo, 1988-85. Editor: Psychology of Achievement Motive, 1979, Educational Psychology, 1988, Development of Emotion and Motivation, 1991; author: Psychology of Achievement Motivation, 1981. Recipient Fulbright Travel grant, 1957-60, Omicron Nu award Am. Home Econs. Assn., 1957-58. Fellow Japanese Assn. Applied Psychology, Japanese Psychol. Assn., Japanese Assn. Ednl. Psychology, Japanese Assn. Humanistic Psychology, Japanese Assn. Family Psychology, Japanese Assn. Health Psychology, Japanese Assn. Devel. Psychology. Home: 3-26-5 Higashi-Oizumi, Nerima-ku, Tokyo 178, Japan Office: Japan Women's U, 2-8-1 Mejirodai Bunkyo-ku, Tokyo 112, Japan

MIZRAHI, ABRAHAM MORDECHAY, retired cosmetics and health care company executive, physician; b. Jerusalem, Apr. 16, 1929; came to U.S., 1952, naturalized, 1960; s. Solomon R. and Rachel (Haliwa) M.; m. Suzanne Eve Glasser, Mar. 15, 1956; children: Debra, Judith, Karen. B.S., Manchester Coll., 1955; M.D., Albert Einstein Coll. Medicine, 1960. Diplomate: Am. Bd. Pediatrics, Nat. Bd. Med. Examiners. Intern U. N.C., 1960-61; pediatric resident Columbia-Presbyn. Med. Center, N.Y.C., 1961-63; NIH fellow in neonatology Columbia-Presbyn. Med. Center, 1963-65; assoc. dir. Newborn Service Mt. Sinai Hosp., N.Y.C.; also dir. Newborn Service Elmhurst Med. Center, 1965-67; staff physician Geigy Pharm. Corp., N.Y.C., 1967-69; head cardio-pulmonary sect. Geigy Pharm. Corp., 1969-71; sr. v.p. corp. med. affairs USV Pharm. Corp., Tuckahoe, N.Y., 1971-76; v.p. health and safety Revlon, Inc., N.Y.C., 1976-89, sr. v.p. human resources, 1989-94; ret., 1994; assoc. in pediatrics Columbia U., 1963-67; cons. in neonatology Misericordia-Fordham Med. Ctr., 1967-89; clin. affiliate N.Y. Hosp.; clin. asst. prof. Cornell U. Med. Coll., 1982—. Contbr. articles to profl. jours. Trustee Westchester (N.Y.) Jewish Center. Mem. AMA, N.Y. State and County Med. Soc., Am., N.Y. acads. medicine, Am. Soc. Clin. Pharmacology and Therapeutics, Am. Pub. Health Assn., Am. Occupational Med. Assn. Home: 7 Jason Ln Mamaroneck NY 10543-2108

MLAKAR, JOSEPH M., plastic surgeon; b. Columbus, Ohio, Oct. 21, 1961; s. Joseph J. and Maryann (Recznik) M.; m. Lorraine Annette Smith, Oct. 26, 1986; 1 child, Luke Clement. BS, Kent State U., 1985; MD, Northeastern Ohio U., 1985. Diplomate Am. Bd. Plastic Surgery. Resident in gen. surgery and plastic surgery Butterworth Hosp./Mich. State U./GRAMEC, Grand Rapids, 1985-90; fellow in burns, pediatric dept. Shriners Burns Inst./U. Tex. Med. Br., Galveston, 1990-91; fellow in pediatric craniofacial surgery L.A. Med. Ctr./U. So. Calif., 1991-92; pvt. practice Plastic Surg. Assocs., Grand Rapids, 1992-94; dir. cleft palate program Shriners Burns Inst., 1994—; asst. prof. plastic surgery U. Tex. Med. Br., 1994—; cons. Health Vols. Overseas, Washington, 1995—. Contbr. articles to profl. publs., chpt. to book. Team mem. Heal the Children, Guatemala, 1989, 93; team mem., co-leader burn care workshop Health Vols. Overseas, Hanoi, Vietnam, 1995. Recipient Best Clin. Study award Midwest Assn. Plastic Surgery, 1990, So. Calif. chpt. ACS, 1992, GRAMEC Rsch. Day, 1994. Mem. Am. Burn Assn., Am. Soc. Plastic and Reconstructive Surgeons, Am. Cleft Palate/Craniofacial Assn., Soc. Critical Care Medicine. Roman Catholic. Office: Shriners Burns Inst 815 Market St Galveston TX 77550

MOAWAD, ATEF, obstetrician, gynecologist, educator; b. Beni Suef, Egypt, Dec. 2, 1935; came to U.S., 1959; s. Hanna and Baheya (Hunein) M.; m. Ferial Fouad Abdel Malek, Aug. 22, 1966; children: John, Joseph, James. Student, Cairo U. Sch. Sci., 1951-52; MB, BCh, Cairo U. Sch. Medicine, 1957; MS in Pharmacology, Jefferson Med. Coll., 1963. Diplomate Am. Bd. Ob-Gyn; licentiate Med. Coun Can. Rotating intern Cairo U. Hosp., 1958-59, Elizabeth (N.J.) Gen. Hosp., 1959-60; resident in ob-gyn. Jefferson Med. Coll. Hosp., Phila., 1961-64; lect. dept. pharmacology U. Alta., Can., 1966; asst. prof. dept. ob-gyn. and pharmacology U. Alta., Can., 1967-70, assoc. prof., 1970-72; assoc. prof. dept. ob-gyn. and pharmacology U. Chgo., 1972-75, prof. dept. ob-gyn. and pediatrics, 1975—, co-dir. perinatal ctr., 1974-80; obstetrician-gynecologist, chief obstetrics, co-dir. perinatal ctr. The Chgo. Lying-in Hosp. U. Chgo., 1980—; vis. investigator dept. ob-gyn. U. Lund, Sweden, 1969. Co-author book chpts., jour. articles. Mem. perinatal adv. com. Chgo. March of Dimes, 1977—, health profl. adv. com., 1983—; mem. perinatal adv. bd. com. State of Ill., 1978—; mem. Chgo. Maternal Child Health Adv. Com., chmn., 1991—; mem. Mayor's Adv. Com. on Infant Mortality, 1991—. Fellow Jefferson Med. Coll., 1960-61, Case Western Reserve U., 1964-65; grantee Brush Found., 1966-67, Maternal Fetal Medicine Unites Network NIH, 1994; recipient award Phila. Obstet. Soc., 1964, Disting. Teaching award Am. Profs. Gynecology and Obstetrics, 1993. Fellow Am. Coll. Ob-Gyn. (Purdue-Frederick award 1978), Royal Coll. Surgeons (Can.); mem. Soc. for Gynecol Investigation, Pharmacol. Soc. Can., Am. Gynecol. and Obstet. Soc., Soc. Perinatal Obstetricians, N.Y. Acad. Scis., Chgo. Gynecol. Soc., Can. Med. Assn., Christian Med. Soc., Edmonton Obstetrics Soc. Office: U Chgo Dept Ob-Gyn 5841 S Maryland Ave Chicago IL 60637-1463

MOCCIA, MARY KATHRYN, social worker; b. Harrisburg, Pa.; d. John Joseph and Winifred Louise Trephan. BEd, U. Hawaii, 1978, MSW with distinction, 1980; postgrad., Fuller Theol. Sem., 1987. Diplomate clin. social work. Intern Koko Head Mental Health Clinic, Honolulu, 1978-79, Dept. Social Services and Housing, Honolulu, 1979-80; vol. worker, group co-leader Waikiki Mental Health Ctr., Honolulu, 1979, social worker, 1980; workshop facilitator St. Louis-Chaminade Edn. Ctr. Dept. Insts. and Workshops, Honolulu, 1980-83; founding mem. Anorexia and Bulimia Ctr. Hawaii, Honolulu, 1983, pvt. practice psychotherapy and cons., 1983—; personal counselor Chaminade U. Honolulu, 1980-88; clin. social worker Queen's Med. Ctr., 1988—; practicum instr. U. Hawaii, 1992—; guest lectr. U. Hawaii Sch. Social Work, Honolulu, 1980-81; vol. telephone specialist Suicide and Crisis Ctr. and Info. and Referral Service, Honolulu, 1981-83; group leader obesity program Honolulu Med. Group, 1988—; mem. Hawaii Coun. Self Esteem, 1993; condr. various workshops on anorexia and bulimia. Guest appearances on local tv and radio programs. Mem. Manoa Valley Ch. Mem. NASW, Nat. Assn. Christians in Social Work, Acad. Cert. Social Workers, Registry Clin. Social Workers, Mortar Bd. (pres., nat. del. 1978), Phi Kappa Phi, Pi Lambda Theta, Alpha Tau Delta (pres. 1970). Office: Queens Med Ctr Dept Social Work 1301 Punchbowl St Honolulu HI 96813-2413

MOCHARLA, RAMAN, physician, radiologist, microbiologist, researcher; b. Mattigiri, Karnataka, India; naturalized citizen; s. V. Krishnarao and Savithramma Mocharla; m. Hanna Tialowska; children: Robert Michael, Christopher Paul, Michael John. BS in Biology, Agra U., India; MS in Microbiology, G.B.P. Univ., India; PhD in Microbiology, U. Kurukshetra, India; MD, Ind. U.; cert. in microbiology UNESCO/WHO and Czechoslavak Acad. Sci., Prague. Intern St. Vincent's Hosp., Indpls.;resident diagnostic Radiology U. Ark., rsch. asst. G.B.P. Univ.; scientist S-1 Indian Coun. Agr. Rsch., New Delhi; UNESCO/WHO fellow Czechoslovak Acad. Sci., Prague; postdoctoral fellow U. Okla., Norman; assoc. rsch. scientist Okla. Med. Rsch. Found., Oklahoma City, S.R. Noble Found., Ardmore, Okla.; rsch. assoc. Ind. U. Sch. Medicine, Indpls. Contbr. articles to profl. jours. Fellow Coun. Sci. and Indsl. Rsch. New Delhi, Nat. Inst. Gen. Med. Sci., Nat. Dental Rsch. Inst. Mem. AMA, Radiol. Soc. N.Am., Am. Roentgen Ray Soc., Am. Coll. Radiology, Ark. Med. Soc., Inst. Biology London, N.Y. Acad. Scis. (life), Sigma Xi (life), Phi Lambda Upsilon (life). Avocations: music, travel, cooking, outdoor games. Home: 915 Cartier Ln Little Rock AR 72211-5516 Office: Dept Diagnostic Radiology U Ark Med Scis 4301 W Markham Slot #556 Little Rock AR 72205-7199

MOCK, DAVID CLINTON, JR., internist; b. Redlands, Calif., May 6, 1922; s. David Clinton and Eithel (Benson) M.; m. Marcella Enriqueta Fellin, Nov. 13, 1952. A.B., U. So. Calif., 1944; M.D., M.H.D., Hahnemann Med. Coll., 1948. Intern Hahnemann Hosp., Phila., 1948-49; resident San Mateo (Calif.) County Hosp., 1949-51, 54, VA Hosp., Oklahoma City, 1954-55; research fellow in exptl. therapeutics U. Okla., Oklahoma City, 1956-57, L.N. Upjohn fellow, 1958, dir. exptl. therapeutics unit, 1959-62; dir., preceptorship program, 1968-76; assoc. prof. medicine U. Okla., Oklahoma City, 1963-72, prof., 1972-84, emeritus prof. medicine, 1984—, assoc. dean med. student affairs, 1970-76, assoc. dean postdoctoral edn., 1976-82, dir. continuing med. edn., 1980-83, dir. Transitional Yr. program, 1980-84, dir. History of Medicine program, 1982-84; assoc. mem. Faculty of Homeopathy Royal London Homeopathic Hosp., Eng.; pres., dir. Coachella Valley Fruit Co., Inc., Indio, Calif. Lt. comdr. USPHS, 1951-53; now capt. Res. Fellow ACP; mem. Am. Fedn. Clin. Research, N.Y. Acad. Scis. Unitarian. Home: 570 Alameda Blvd Coronado CA 92118-1617

MOCK, MELINDA SMITH, orthopedic nurse specialist, consultant; b. Austell, Ga., Nov. 15, 1947; d. Robert Jehu and Emily Dorris (Smith) Smith; m. David Thomas Mock, Oct. 20, 1969. AS in Nursing, DeKalb Coll., 1972. RN, Ga.; cert. orthopedic nurse specialist, orthopedic nurse. Nursing technician Ga. Baptist Hosp., Atlanta, 1967, staff nurse, 1979; asst. corr. Harcourt, Brace & World Pub. Co., Atlanta, 1968-69; receptionist-sec. Goodbody & Co., Atlanta, 1969-70; nursing asst. DeKalb Gen. Hosp., Decatur, Ga., 1970-71; staff nurse Doctor's Meml. Hosp., Atlanta, 1972-73; staff nurse Shallowford Cmty. Hosp., Atlanta, 1973, relief charge nurse, 1973, charge nurse, 1973-76, head nurse, 1976-79, orthopedic nurse specialist emergency room, 1979; rehab. specialist Internat. Rehab. Assocs., Inc., Norcross, Ga., 1981, sr. rehab. specialist, 1981, rehab. supr., 1981-82; cons., founder, propr. Healthcare Cost Cons., Alpharetta, Ga., 1982-83; cons., founder, pres. Healthcare Cost Cons., Inc., Alpharetta, 1983—; mem. legis. com. of adv. coun. Ga. Bd. Nursing, Atlanta, 1984-85; mem. adv. coun. Milton H.S. Coop. Bus. Edn., 1986-89; mem. Congressman Patrick Swindall Sr. Citizen Adv. Coun., 1988, Congressman Ben Jones Vets. Affairs Adv. Com., 1989-92, White House Conf. on Small Bus. (appointed by Newt Gingrich 1995), Nat. Fedn. Specialty Nursing Orgns. Task Force on Profl. Liability Ins., 1987-89, Dep. voter registrar Fulton County, Ga., 1983-87; Rep. treas. 23d house dist., mem. Fulton County Rep. Com., 1989—, nominating com., 1991, 92, 93, 95, 96, chmn. polit action com., 1993-95, asst. treas., 1994-95, sec., 1995—; treas. 41st House Dist. Rep. Party, 1993—; 1st vice chairwoman 6th Congl. Dist. Rep. Party, 1993—; mem. State Com. Ga. Rep. Party, 1993—; del. Fulton County Rep. Conv., 1991, 92, 94, 95, 96, del. Ga. 4th Congrl. Dist., 1991, 92, parliamentarian, 1992, credentials com., 1992, Ga. Rep. Conv., 1991, 92, 93, 95, 96, del. Ga. 6th Congrl. Dist. Rep. Party Convention, 1993, 95, 96; alt. del.-at-large Nat. Rep. Conv., 1996; mem. Chattahoochee Rep. Women, 1989—, chmn. campaign com., 1992-94, rec. sec., 1995—; chmn. nominating com. House Dist. 23, 1990; mem. steering com. to re-elect state rep. Tom Campbell, 1990; mem. campaign staff to re-elect state senator Sallie Newbill, 1990, 92, 94; health advisor campaign to elect Matt Towery for lt. gov., 1990, health adv. compaign to elect Bob Barr U.S. Senate, 1991-92; mem. election com. Mark Burkhalter for State Rep.; vol. campaign staff to re-elect Congressman Newt Gingrich, 1992, 94, 96; mem. campaign staff to elect Jim Hunt as state rep., 1996; vol. campaign to elect Tom Price to state senate, 1996. Recipient Nat. Disting. Service Registry award, 1987; named one of Outstanding Young Women Am., 1984. Mem. NAFE, Nat. Assn. Orthopedic Nurses (nat. policies com. 1981-82, chmn. govt. rels. com. 1987-90, nat. treas. 1991-95, nurse Washington intern 1987, legis. contbr. editor news 1989, chmn. legis. workshop, 1989, co-chmn. legis. workshop, 1990, guest editl. Orthopaedic Nursing Jour. 1988, spkr. 1990, 92, 93, 94, Ann. Congress, del. 1982, 91, 92, 93, 94, 96, Pres.'s award 1992, chmn. budget and fin. com. 1991-95, nat. bylaws and policies com. 1995—, bylaws and policies com. Altanta chpt. 1994—, pres.-elect Atlanta chpt. 1996—), Orthopedic Nurses Assn. (nat. bd. dirs. 1977-79, nat. treas. 1979-81, Coun. Splty. Nursing Orgns. Ga. (nominating com. 1976-77), Ga. Med. Auditors Assn., Nat. Nurses in Bus. Assn., Assn. Rehab. Nurses (bd. dirs. Ga. chpt. 1980-81, del. people-to-people program to China 1981), Nat. Fed. Ind. Bus. (guardian 1988—, adv. coun. 1990—, healthcare task force chmn. 1992—, vice-chmn./fed. liaison Ga. adv. coun. 1995—), Am. Bd. Nursing Specialities (chmn. nominating com. 1993-94, 94-95, chmn. com. on specialty bd. rev. 1993-95), Ga. Jaycees (dist. 4C rep. Ga. Jaycee Legis. 1984, 85), Ga. seatbelt coalition, Orthopaedic Nurses Cert. Bd. (bd. dir. 1991-96, pres. 1992-93, task force on advancedfication 1991-92), North Fulton C. of C. (vice chmn. health service effectiveness alliance 1984-85, chmn. 1985-86, co-chmn./editor periodical 1985, 3rd Quarter Workhorse award 1985), Alpharetta Jaycees (adminstrv. v.p. 1984-85, internal v.p. 1985-86), Alpharetta Jaycee Women (bd. dirs. 1983). Baptist. Avocations: reading, boating, cmty. svc. activities. Home: 424 Michael Dr Alpharetta GA 30201 Office: Healthcare Cost Cons Inc PO Box 466 St Alpharetta GA 30239

MOCZYDLOWSKI, EDWARD GERARD, biologist, researcher; b. Pitts., Sept. 18, 1953; s. Edward J. and Adele (Shumovich) M.; m. Stephenie K. Lemmon, June 27, 1981; children: Seth R. and Laurel A. BA summa cum laude, Cornell U., 1975; PhD, U. Calif., San Diego, 1980. Asst. prof. physiology U. Cin., 1984-86; asst. prof. pharmacology Yale U. Sch. Medicine, New Haven, Conn., 1986-89; assoc. prof. pharmacology Yale U. Sch. Medicine, New Haven, 1989—; mem. editorial bd. Jour. of Gen., Physiology, 1989—. Named Searle scholar, 1985. Mem. Biophysical Soc., Soc. for Neuroscience, Soc. Gen. Physiologists, Internat. Soc. on Toxinology, Phi Beta Kappa. Unitarian. Office: Yale U Sch Medicine Dept Pharmacology PO Box 208066 New Haven CT 06520-8066

MOCZYGEMBA, JACKIE A., health information manager, educator; b. San Antonio, Mar. 29, 1959; d. Johnnie J. and Dorothy M. (Gawlik) Moy; m. Ross D. Moczygemba, July 21, 1984; children: Stephen and Shannon. AAS in Med. Assisting, San Antonio Jr. Coll., 1980; BS in Med. Records Adminstrn., S.W. Tex. State U., 1982, MBA, 1995. Registered records adminstr. Dir. health info. Guadalupe Valley Hosp., Seguin, Tex., 1983-95; asst. prof. S.W. Tex. State U., San Marcos, 1995—; cons. Seguin Convalescent Home, Nesbit Nursing Home, Seguin, 1990-94, Kingsland (Tex.) Hills Care Ctr., 1990—. Bd. dirs. Am. Cancer Soc. local chpt., Seguin, 1990-91; v.p. St. James Parish Coun., 1993. Mem. Am. Health Info. Mgmt. Assn., Tex. Health Info. Mgmt. Assn., Alamo Area Health Info. Mgmt. Assn. Republican. Catholic. Home: 159 High Country Seguin TX 78155

MODELL, ARNOLD H., psychiatrist, educator; b. N.Y.C., July 12, 1924; s. Julius and Selma (Klar) M.; m. Miriam Kennedy, Aug. 31, 1950 (dec. 1972); children: Ellen, Eric; m. Penelope Wells, May 17, 1972 (dec. 1996). AB, Columbia U., 1944; MD, SUNY, Bklyn., 1947. Intern Kings County Hosp., Brookly, N.Y., 1947-48; resident Worcester (N.Y.) State Hosp., 1948-49, Yale U., New Haven, Conn., 1949-51; clin. prof. psychiatry Harvard Med. Sch., Boston, 1982—; tng. and supervisory analyst Boston Psychoanalytic Soc. & Inst., 1971—; psychiatrist Beth Israel Hosp., Boston, 1954—. Author: Object Love and Reality, 1968, Psychoanalysis in a New Context, 1984, Other Times, Other Realities: The Private Self, 1990; contbr. articles to profl. jours. Lt. USN, 1951-53. Fellow Am. Psychiat. Assn.; mem. Am. Psychoanalytic Assn. Democrat. Home and Office: 82 Kirkstall Rd Newtonville MA 02160-2246

MODELL, JACK GARY, psychiatrist; b. St. Paul, Minn., June 3, 1956; s. Jerome H. and Marilyn J. (Singer) M.; m. Judith D. Lindross, June 22, 1980; 1 child, Jason I. BA, U. Colo., Boulder, 1978; MD, U. Colo., Denver, 1982. Resident in psychiatry U. Vt., Burlington, 1982-86; pvt. practice Mass., 1986-87; fellowship in neurosci. U. Mich., Ann Arbor, 1987-88, asst. prof. psychiatry, 1988-91; assoc. prof. psychiatry U. Ala., Birmingham, 1991—. Mem. AMA, N.Y. Acad. Scis., Phi Beta Kappa.

MODLIN, CHARLES STANLEY, urologist; b. New Castle, Ind., Mar. 10, 1961; s. Charles Stanley and Grace (Hampton) M.; m. Sheryl Fridie Modlin, Sept. 22, 1987; children: Charles Stanley III, Sarah Elizabeth. BA in Chemistry, Northwestern U., 1983, MD, 1987. Diplomate Am. Bd. Med. Examiners. Urology resident NYU Med. Ctr., 1987-93; kidney transplantation fellowship Cleve. Clinic Found., 1993-96, transplantation rschr., 1993-96, staff dept. urology, 1996—. Contbr. articles to profl. jours. Mem. Am. Urol. Assn., Urol. Soc. Transplantation and Vascular Surgery, Am. Soc. of

Minority Health and Transplant Profls., Am. Soc. of Transplant Physicians. Methodist. Home: 18601 Shaker Blvd Shaker Heights IL 44122 Office: Cleve Clinic Found Desk A110 9500 Euclid Ave Dept Urology Cleveland OH 44195

MODLY, DORIS MATHERNY, nursing educator and administrator; b. Belgrad, Yugoslavia, Jan. 20, 1933; came to U.S., 1952; d. Otto Conrad and Mira (Bertani) Matherny; m. Zoltan M. Modly, June 15, 1957; children: Charlotte, Thomas, Dora-Maria, Suzanne, Mira. BSN, Western Reserve U., 1957; MSN, Case Western Reserve U., 1977, Ma in Anthropology, 1983, PhD in Nursing, 1987. Staff nurse U. Hosp. Cleve., 1957-58; instr. St. Luke's Hosp. Sch. Nursing, Cleve., 1958-59; supr. Fairhill Mental Health Ctr., Cleve., 1967-73; sr. instr. Sch. Nursing Luth. Hosp., 1973-75; supr. U. Hosp. Cleve., 1984-85; instr. F.P. Bolton Sch. Nursing, Cleve., 1977-79, asst. prof., 1979-85; dir. profl. nursing affairs Cleve. Clinic Found., 1985-88; from asst. prof. to assoc. prof. F.P. Bolton Sch. Nursing, Cleve., 1988-96, prof., 1996—; dir. BSN program F. P. Bolton Sch. Nursing, Cleve., 1988-90; dir. Doctor of Nursing Program F. P. Bolton Sch. Nursing, 1990-92, dir. internat. nursing programs, 1993—; dir. WHO Collaborating Ctr., Cleve., 1993—; sr. nursing fellow Project Hope, Budapest, Hungary, 1991-95; cons. in field. Contbr. chpts. to books and articles to profl. jours. NEH fellow, 1982, 89; Fulbright scholar, 1996—. Fellow Am. Acad. Nursing; mem. ANA, Nat. League Nursing, Ohio Nurses Assn., Greater Cleve. Nurses Assn. (bd. dirs.), Sigma Theta Tau (bd. dirs., Alpha Mu chpt.). Office: Case Western Reserve U Sch Nursing 2121 Abington Rd Cleveland OH 44106-2333

MODRICH, PAUL L., biochemistry educator; b. Raton, N.Mex., June 13, 1946. BS in Biology, MIT, 1968; PhD in Biochemistry, Stanford U., 1973; postgrad., Harvard U., 1973-74. Asst. prof. chemistry U. Calif., Berkeley, 1974; asst. prof. biochemistry Duke U., 1976, assoc. prof. biochemistry, 1980, prof. biochemistry, 1984, dir. program in genetics, 1989-92, investigator Howard Hughes Med. Inst., 1994. Contbr. articles to profl. jours.; assoc. editor: Biochemistry, 1992-94, mem. editl. adv. bd., 1986-91, 95—; mem. editl. bd. Nucleic Acids Rsch., 1980-82, Jour. Biol. Chemistry, 1982-83. Recipient award in enzyme chemistry Pfizer, 1983, award NAS, 1993, Mott prize in cancer rsch. GM, 1996. Mem. NIH (mem. biochemistry study sect. 1980-84, NIH NIGMS merit award 1986), Am. Soc. Biochemistry and Molecular Biology (councillor 1989-92, mem. publs. com. 1995—). Office: Duke U Howard Hughes Med Inst Dept Biochemistry Duke U Med Ctr Durham NC 27710*

MOE, PAUL G., physician; b. Granite Falls, Minn., Feb. 19, 1931; m. Barbar Raidt. BA, U. Minn., 1953, MD, 1956; MS, Ohio State U., 1962. Prof. pediatric neurology U. Colo. Med. Ctr. and Children's Hosp., Denver, 1967—. Capt. USAF, 1957-59. Fellow Am. Acad. Pediatrics, Am. Acad. Neurology; mem. Child Neurol. Soc., Am. Epilepsy Soc., Phi Beta Kappa, Alpha Omega Alpha. Office: Childrens Hosp 19th and Downing Denver CO 80218

MOE, SCOTT THOMAS, chemist; b. Webster City, Iowa, Dec. 14, 1964; s. John Harry and Betty Ann Moe; m. Veronica Vovides, May 17, 1990. BS in Chemistry, Winona State U., 1986; PhD of Pharmacy, U. Iowa, 1990. Rsch. fellow Nat. Inst. Drug Abuse, Mpls., 1990-91, U. Minn., Mpls., 1992; asst. rsch. scientist, assoc. Medicinal Chemistry NPS Pharm., Inc., Salt Lake City, 1993—. Patentee in field; contbr. articles to profl. jours. Recipient Hon. Sci. award Bausch & Lomb Pharms., 1983. Mem. Am. Chem. Soc. (divsn. Medicinal Chemistry, Organic Chemistry, Outstanding Undergrad. Achievement award 1986). Methodist. Office: NPS Pharms Inc 420 Chipeta Way Salt Lake City UT 84108-1256

MOEHRING, THOMAS JOHN, microbiology educator, researcher; b. N.Y.C., Aug. 15, 1936; s. Gustave Thomas and Margaret A. (Maloney) M.; m. Joan Marie Marquart, June 6, 1964. B.S. cum laude, Fairleigh Dickinson U., 1961; M.S., Rutgers U., 1963, Ph.D., 1965. Postdoctoral fellow Stanford U., Palo Alto, Calif., 1965-68; asst. prof. med. microbiology U. Vt., Burlington, 1968-72, assoc. prof., 1972-76, prof., 1976-87, prof. microbiology, 1987-89, prof. microbiology and molecular genetics, 1989—, faculty grad. coll., 1968—, faculty cell and molecular biology program, 1976—; mem. Vt. Cancer Ctr., 1980—. Contbr. articles to profl. jours. Rutgers U. Fellow, 1964; U. Vt. Scholar, 1982; biomedical research grantee NIH, 1969—. Mem. Am. Soc. Microbiology, AAAS, Soc. for In Vitro Biology, Sigma Xi. Home: 296 S Cove Rd Burlington VT 05401-5444 Office: U Vt Dept Microbiology & Molecular Genetics Burlington VT 05405

MOELLERING, ROBERT CHARLES, JR., internist, educator; b. Lafayette, Ind., June 9, 1936; s. Robert Charles and Irene Pauline (Nolde) M.; children: Anne Elizabeth, Robert Charles, Catherine Irene; m. Mary Jane Ferraro, July 11, 1987. BA, Valparaiso U., 1958, DSc, 1980; MD cum laude, Harvard U., 1962. Diplomate: Am. Bd. Internal Medicine. Intern Mass. Gen. Hosp., Boston, 1962-63, resident, 1963-64, postdoctoral fellow in infectious diseases, 1967-70, resident, 1966-67, mem. infectious disease unit and asst. physician, 1970-76, assoc. physician, 1976-83, hon. physician, 1983—, cons. bacteriology, 1972-87; instr. medicine Harvard U. Med. Sch., Boston, 1970-72, asst. prof., 1972-76, assoc. prof., 1976-80, prof., 1980—; chmn. dept. medicine, physician-in-chief New Eng. Deaconess Hosp., 1981—; pres., CEO Deaconess Profl. Practice Group, 1995—; Shields Warren-Mallinckrodt prof. clin. rsch. Harvard U. Med. Sch., Boston, 1981-89, Shields Warren-Mallinckrodt prof. med. rsch., 1989—; mem. subcom. on susceptibility testing Nat. Com. for CLin. Lab. Standards, 1976-88; mem. subcom. on antimicrobial agts. and chemotherapy, 1978-80; subcom. on antimicrobiol disc. diffusion suceptibility testing, 1980-88. Mem. editl. bd. Antimicrobial Agts. and Chemotherapy, 1977-81, editor, 1981-85, editor-in-chief, 1985-95; editor European Jour. Clin. Microbial Infectious Diseases, 1990—; consulting. editor Infectious Disease Clinics N.Am., 1986—; editor Les Infections, 1983; editl. bd. New Eng. Jour. Medicine, 1977-81, European Jour.Clin. Microbiology, 1981—, Jour. Infectious Diseases, 1981-85, 89-93, Infectious Disease Alert, 1981-92, Pharmacotherapy, 1982—, Antimicrobial Agts. Ann., 1984-87, Zentralblatt Fur Bacteriologie, Microbiologie and Hygience, 1984—, Jour. of Infection, 1986—, Innovations, 1986-90, Residents Forum in Internal Medicine, 1988-90, Diagnostic Microbiology and Infectious Disease, 1989-90, Internat. Jour. Antimicrobial Agts., 1990—, Infectious Diseases in Clin. Practice, 1991-92, Jour. Infection and Chemotherapy, 1995—. Served with USPHS, 1964-66. Grantee USPHS, NIH. Fellow ACP, Am. Acad. Microbiology, Infectious Diseases Soc. Am. (v.p. 1988-89, pres. elect 1989-90, pres. 1990-91, past pres. 1991-92); mem. Am. Soc. Microbiology, Am. Clin. and Climatol. Assn., Internat. Soc. Chemotherapy, Am. Soc. Clin. Investigation, Assn. Am. Physicians, European Soc. Clin. Microbiology, Am. Fedn. Clin. Rsch., Assn. Profs. Medicine, Roxbury Clin. Records Club, Mass. Med. Soc. (councilor), Brit. Soc. Antimicrobial Chemotherapy, Coun. Biology Editors, Alpha Omega Alpha, Phi Kappa Psi. Home: 49 Longfellow Rd Wellesley MA 02181-5220 Office: New Eng Deaconess Hosp Dept Medicine 110 Francis St Boston MA 02215-5501

MOERSCH, GARY ROBERT, physician assistant; b. Escanaba, Mich., Feb. 20, 1952. BS Physician Asst., Mercy Coll. of Detroit, 1980. Physician asst. urgent care Casa Blanca Clinics Ltd., Gilbert, Ariz.; physician asst. emergency rm. Pinnacle Emergency Svc., Mesa, Ariz., Ariz. Physicians, Inc., Mesa, Santa Cruz Emergency Svcs., Payson, Ariz. Fellow Am. Acad. of Physician Assts., Ariz. Acad. of Physician Assts., Soc. of Emergency Rm. Physician Assts.; mem. Casa Blanc Med. Group (chmn.), ARRT. Republican. Lutheran. Office: Casa Blanca Clinics Ltd 4001 E Baseline Rd Gilbert AZ 48234

MOESCHLER, JOHN BOYER, physician, educator; b. Omaha, Mar. 14, 1950; s. William Joseph and Norma Rose (Boyer) M.; children: Kate, Emily. BS, Creighton U., 1972; MD, U. Nebr., 1975. Bd. cert. Am. Bd. Pediatrics, Am. Bd. Med. Genetics. Intern Univ. Nebr. Med. Ctr., Omaha, 1975-76, resident, 1976-78; fellow Univ. Wash., Seattle, 1978-80; asst. prof., dept. pediatrics Univ. Nebr. Med. Ctr., Meyer Children's Rehab. Inst., Omaha, 1980-83; asst. prof., dept. pediatrics, sect. med. genetics W.Va. Univ. Med. Sch., Morgantown, 1983-85; asst. prof., dept. maternal and child health Dartmouth Med. Sch., Dartmouth-Hitchcock Med. Ctr., Hanover, N.H., 1985-88; assoc. prof., dept. maternal and child health Dartmouth Med. Sch., Dartmouth-Hitchcock Med. Ctr., Hanover, 1988—; dir. Clin. Genetics & Child Devel. Ctr. Dartmouth-Hitchcock Med. Ctr., Hanover, 1988—; med. dir., Clinic for Children with Neuromotor Disabilities Dept. Health & Human Svcs., Bur. Spl. Med. Svcs., N.H., 1985—; med. dir. Genetic Svcs. Program Dept. Health & Human Svcs., Bus. of Spl. Med. Svcs., N.H., 1988—; bd. dirs. Planned Parenthood of No. New England; attending physician Children's Orthopedic Hosp., Seattle, 1978-80; assoc. dir. Birth Defects Clinic, Children's Meml. Hosp., Omaha, 1982-83; cons. Nebr. State Svcs. for Crippled Children, 1980-83; dir. pediatric rehab. MCRI and Univ. Nebr. Hosp., Omaha, 1982-83; steering com. New England Regional Genetics Group, 1988—; presenter in field. Contbr. articles to Jour. Pediatrics, Am. Jour. Med. Genetics, Am. Jour. Disabled Child, Jour. Ment. Def. Rsch., Jour. Ultrasound Med., Dysmorphology and Clin. Genetics, Jour. Clin. Dysmorphology, Prenatal Diagnosis, Am. Jour. Diseases Children, Devel. Medicine and Child Neurology, Clin. Genetics, and others. Fellow Am. Acad. Pediatrics, Am. Acad. Cerebral Palsy & Devel. Medicine; mem. Soc. for Devel. Pediatrics, Am. Soc. Human Genetics (info. and edn. com. 1990—), Am. Assn. on Mental Retardation, N.H. State Med. Soc., Grafton County Med. Soc. Home: 9 Woodside Rd Durham NH 03824-2120 Office: Clin Genetics Dartmouth-Hitchcock Med Ctr Child Development Ctr Hanover NH 03756

MOESTRUP, SØREN KRAGH, scientist, educator; b. Vejle, Denmark, Sept. 1, 1961; s. Jens Kragh and Bodil Marie Moestrup; m. Mette Sommerlund, Aug. 13, 1988; children: Kasper, Jakob. MA, U. Aarhus, Denmark, 1988, MD, 1988, Dr in Med. Sci., 1994. Rsch. asst. dept. physiology U. Aarhus, 1988-90; sr. rsch. asst. Aarhus U., 1990-91 sr. rsch. fellow dept. med. biochemistry, 1991-92, asst. prof. dept. med. biochemistry, 1992-96; $D; assoc. prof. Aarhus U., 1996—; vis. scientist dept. biochemistry Oxford (Eng.) U., 1994-95. Contbr. more than 50 articles to profl. jours. Recipient Gold Medal, U. Aarhus, 1988. Mem. N.Y. Acad. Sci. Office: U Aarhus Dept Med Biochem, Bldg 170 Ole Worms Alle, 8000 DK Aarhus Denmark

MOFENSON, HOWARD C., pediatrician, toxicologist; b. N.Y.C., Jan. 26, 1925; s. Jack L. and Theresa (Cohen) M.; m. Lois Stugart July 26, 1947; children: Lynne, Jeffrey, Dayna. MD, Jefferson Med. Coll. Attending Winthrop U. Hosp., Mineola, N.Y., Nassau County Med. Ctr., East Meadow, N.Y.; prof. pediatrics SUNY, Stony Brook, N.Y., prof. emergency medicine; prof. clin. pharmacy St. John's Sch. Pharmacy, Queens, N.Y.; prof. of toxicology N.Y. Coll. Osteo.; Acting dean SUNY. Contbr. articles to profl. jours. With U.S. Army, 1942-46. Decorated Purple Heart (2), Bronze Star (2). Mem. Am. Assn. Poison Control (pres.), Am. Acad. Pediatrics, Am. Diabetes Assn. Home: 160 Emory Rd Mineola NY 11501

MOFFATT, MICHAEL DENNIS, health facility administrator; b. Detroit, Aug. 28, 1949; s. Norman A. and Esther Moffatt; m. Cathy Elizabeth Dittrick June 8, 1985. BA in Comms., U. Mich., 1971, MA in Edn., 1982; AS in Radiologic Tech., Washtenaw C.C., Ann Arbor, Mich., 1976. Cert. ultrasound tech. Staff sonographer, lectr. divsn. diagnostic ultrasound Henry Ford Hosp., Detroit, 1979-83, program coord. diagnostic med. sonography program, 1983—; instr. diagnostic med. sonography program Oakland C.C., Southfield, Mich., 1980-81; adj. faculty ultrasound physics Ferris State Coll., Big Rapids, Mich.,1980-82, co-dir. ultrasound physics rev. course, 1983; course dir., lectr. intensive sonographic physics rev. Bay Med. Edn., Bay City, Mich., 1983. Mem. JRC-DMS/CAHEA (site vis., chmn. 1982, 84, 87), ARDMS (organizer 1980, 82, 84, examiner 1979-81), SDMS (chairperson econ. status com. 1981-82), AIUM, Mich. Sonographers Soc. (econ. com. 1979-80, v.p. 1981-82, pres. 1982-83). Office: Radiology Dept Henry Ford Hosp 2799 W Grand Blvd Detroit MI 48202

MOFFET, HUGH LAMSON, pediatrician; b. Monmouth, Ill., Jan. 6, 1932; s. Victor Logue and Helen (Sipfle) M.; m. Donna Mae Pierschke, Sept. 20, 1984; children: Cynthia, Sandra, Douglas. AB, Harvard U., 1953; MD, Yale U., 1957. Instr. Bowman Gray Sch. Medicine, Winston-Salem, N.C., 1957-60; asst. prof. Northwestern U., Chgo., 1960-68, assoc. prof., 1968-71; assoc. prof. U. Wis., Madison, 1971-75, prof., 1975—; head div. infectious diseases Children's Meml. Hosp., Chgo., 1960-71. Author: (book) Clinical Microbiology, 1975, 2d rev. edit., 1980, Pediatric Infectious Diseases, 1975, 3d rev. edit., 1989. Capt. USAR, 1953-68.

MOFFITT, TONY LEE, emergency nurse; b. Vincennes, Ind., Nov. 7, 1961; s. Larry Richard Moffitt and Bonita Jean (Burrell) Shidler; m. Susan Raye Holsen, June 4, 1991; children: Sarah Ann, Alexander Lee. ADN, Olney Coll., 1987. RN, Fla.; cert. ACLS provider, emergency nurse, pediatric emergency nurse, PALS. Staff nurse Lawrence County Meml., Lawrenceville, Ill., 1987; staff nurse Lakeland (Fla.) Regional Med. Ctr., 1987-90, mem. recruitment and retention, 1988-90, asst. charge nurse, 1990-93; emergency nurse South Fla. Bapt., Plant City, 1991—, charge nurse, 1993-94; team leader Cardiac Interventional Unit, 1994-95. Emergency med. tech. and paramedic clin. instr. Polk Community Coll., Lakeland, 1990-92. Republican. Home: 1522 Sherwood Lakes Blvd Lakeland FL 33809-6800 Office: Lakeland Regional Med Ctr Lakeland Hills Blvd Lakeland FL 33802

MOGABGAB, WILLIAM JOSEPH, epidemiologist, educator; b. Durant, Okla., Nov. 2, 1921; s. Anees and Maude (Jopes) M.; m. Joy Roddy, Dec. 24, 1948 (div. July 1988); children: Robert (dec.), Ann, Kay, Edward R., Jean, Robert M. Berryman, William J.M. Berryman; m. Rose Warren Berryman, July 18, 1988. B.S., Tulane U., 1942, M.D., 1944. Diplomate Am. Bd. Internal Medicine, Am. Bd. Microbiology. Intern Charity Hosp. La., New Orleans, 1944-45, resident, 1946-49, vis. physician, 1949-51, sr. vis. physician, 1971-75; cons., 1976—; mem. faculty Tulane U. Sch. Medicine, 1948—, prof. medicine, 1962-92; cons. infectious diseases, epidemiology, internal medicine New Orleans Dept. Health, 1992—; vis. investigator, asst. physician Hosp. Rockefeller Inst. Med. Research, N.Y.C., 1951-52; chief infectious disease VA Hosp., Houston, 1952-53; asst. prof. medicine Baylor U. Coll. Medicine, 1952-53; head virology div. NAMRU 4, USNTC, Great Lakes, Ill., 1953-55; cons. infectious disease VA Hosp., New Orleans, 1956—; cons. FDA Orphan Products Devel. Grants Program, 1984—. Assoc. mem. commn. influenza Armed Forces Epidemiological Bd., 1959-71; mem. New Orleans Mayor's Health Adv. Com., 1983—. With UNS, 1945-46; comdr. USNR, ret. 1981. Fellow Nat. Found. Infantile Paralysis, 1951-52. Fellow ACP, Am. Acad. Microbiology, Infectious Disease Soc. Am., Am. Coll. Epidemiology; mem. Soc. Exptl. Biology and Medicine, So., Central socs. clin. research, Am. Fedn. Clin. Research, Am. Soc. Cell Biology, Am. Soc. Microbiology, Am. Soc. Clin. Investigation, Tissue Culture Assn., Am. Pub. Health Assn., Am. Soc. Internal Medicine, Am. Soc. Clin. Pharmacology and Therapeutics, So. Med. Soc., AMA, AAAS, Am. Soc. Internal Medicine, Southwestern Assn. Clin. Biology, Soc. Epideniol. Research, Am. Soc. Virology. Home: 3 Fortress Rd New Orleans LA 70122-1336

MOGAN, GLEN RAYMOND, gastroenterologist; b. N.Y.C., Oct. 1, 1949; s. Harry H. and Elsie (Beck) M.; m. Diane Susan Hoberman, Jan. 22, 1972; children: Grant, Craig, Douglas. BA, Case Western Res. U., 1971; MD, Upstate Med. Sch., 1975. Diplomate Am. Bd. Internal Medicine, sub-bd. gastroenterology. Intern, resident, fellow Mt. Sinai Hosp., N.Y.C., 1975-80; pvt. practice West Orange, N.J., 1980—; chief sect. gastroenterology St. Barnabas Med. Ctr., West Orange, N.J., 1980—. Author: Digestive Disease, Constipation-Elderly, 1990. Fellow Am. Coll. Physicians; mem. Am. Gastroent. Assn., Am. Soc. Gastrointestinal Endoscopy, Alpha Omega Alpha. Jewish. Office: 741 Northfield Ave Ste 204 West Orange NJ 07052

MOGENSEN, FINN, physician, consultant; b. Frederikshavn, Denmark, Sept. 19, 1934; s. Aksel Christian and Meta Marie (Gregersen) M.; m. Jane Voss Frank; children: Hanne Vita, Henrik, Palle. Student, Acad. Coll., Copenhagen, 1960; Med. grad., Arhus (Denmark) U., 1969; ENT Specialist, Arhus Hosp., 1976; Audiologist, Odense (Denmark) Hosp., 1978. Sr. resident Kalundborg (Denmark) Hosp., 1969-70, Hobro (Denmark) Hosp., 1970-71, Randers (Denmark) Hosp., 1971-72, Arhus (Denmark) Hosp., 1972-74, Vejle (Denmark) Hosp., 1974-76, Odense (Denmark) Hosp., 1976-78, Holstebro (Denmark) Hosp., 1979—; chief physician ENT Dept. and Audiological Clinic, Holstebro, 1981—; cons. in audiology, Greenland, 1978, 80, 81, 84, Nepal, 1994, Assn. for Better Hearing, Scandinavia, 1985, 87; chmn. Scandinavian expert panel on risk of damage at different levels of noise, 1987 (award 1987); mem. group evaluation of low-cost hearing aids in support of people with hearing disability WHO, 1991. Internat. cons. The Assn. for Better Hearing, Denmark, 1977-94, v.p., 1988-93. Mem. Tech. Audiological Lab. (bd. dirs.), European Cooperation Sci. and Tech. Rsch. Office: Holstebro Cen Hosp, Lagardsvej, 7500 Holstebro Denmark

MOGHISSI, KAMRAN S., obstetrician, gynecologist, educator; b. Tehran, Iran, Sept. 11, 1925; came to U.S., 1959, naturalized, 1965; s. Ahmad and Monireh (Rohani) M.; m. Ida Laura Tedeschi, Jan. 2, 1952; children: Diana J., Soraya R. ChB, MB, U. Geneva, 1951, MD, 1952. Diplomate Am. Bd. Ob-Gyn., Am. Bd. Reproductive Endocrinology. Intern, Univ. Hosp., Geneva, 1951-52, Horton Gen. Hosp., United Oxford Hosps., Banbury, Eng., 1952-53; resident in ob-gyn. Gloucestershire Royal Hosp., Eng., 1953-54, St. Helier Hosp., London, 1954-55, Leeds Regional Hosp. Bd., Yorkshire, Eng., 1955-56, Detroit Receiving Hosp., 1961, attending gynecologist, 1962; assoc. prof. ob-gyn. U. Shiraz Med. Sch., Iran, 1957-59; rsch. assoc. ob-gyn. and physiol. chemistry, Wayne State U., Detroit, 1959-61, asst. prof., 1962-66, assoc. prof., 1966-70, prof., 1970—, dir. div. reproductive endocrinology and infertility, 1970-94; vice chmn., 1983-88, chmn. dept. ob-gyn., 1988-91; sr. attending physician ob-gyn. Hutzel Hosp., Detroit, 1963, vice chief, 1978-82, 83-89, chief, 1982-83, 88-91, chief of staff, 1991-93, attending surgeon, chief ob-gyn. Harper-Grace Hosp., 1983-84, attending surgeon, emeritus, chief ob-gyn. emeritus, 1991—; obstetrician, gynecologist, chief, Detroit Med. Ctr., 1988-91; cons. and lectr. in field. Contbr. chpts. to books, articles to profl. jours. Developer exhibits in medicine, movies and teaching prodns.; mem. numerous editorial bds.; cons. in field. Fellow ACS, Am. Coll. Ob-Gyn. Am. Gynecol. and Obstetric Soc.; mem. AMA (ho. of dels. 1992—), AAAS, Am. Soc. Reprodn. Medicine (formerly Am. Fertility Soc., pres. 1990-91), Soc. Study Reprodn., Am. Soc. Andrology, Wayne County Med. Soc., Mich. Soc. Ob-Gyn, Central Assn. Ob-Gyn., N.Y. Acad. Scis., Soc. Reproductive Endocrinologists (charter mem., pres. 1990), Soc. Reproductive Surgeons (charter mem.), Soc. for Assisted Reproductive Tech. (charter mem.), Lochmoor Club (Grosse Pointe), Renaissance Club (Detroit). Home: 56 Moorland Dr Grosse Pointe Shores MI 48236-1112 Office: Hutzel Hosp 4707 Saint Antoine Blvd Detroit MI 48201-1427

MOGLIA, PAUL LOUIS, psychologist; b. N.Y.C., Oct. 16, 1954; s. John Joseph and Frances Bernadette (McLarnon) M.; m. Jean Ann Busi, Nov. 25, 1988; children: Eugenia, Michael, Briana. BA, Cathedral Coll., Douglaston, N.Y., 1976; MA, Fordham U., 1980, Boston Coll., Chestnut Hill, Mass., 1984; PhD, Boston Coll., Chestnut Hill, Mass., 1988. Lic. psychologist, N.Y. Tchr. Cathedral Prep. Sem., N.Y.C., 1977-79, Loyola Sch., N.Y.C., 1979-80; lectr. religious studies Mercy Coll., Dobbs Ferry, N.Y., 1980-82; lectr. English Regis Coll., Weston, Mass., 1984-86; teaching fellow Boston Coll., 1984-88; clin. fellow Harvard Med. Sch., Cambridge, Mass., 1988; pvt. practice Yonkers and Glen Cove, N.Y., 1991—; faculty devel. fellow Albert Einstein Coll. Medicine, Bronx, N.Y., 1992-94; asst. dir. dept. family practice St. Joseph's Hosp. Med. Ctr., Paterson, N.J., 1996—; cons. psychologist St. Joseph's Sem., Yonkers, 1989—; cons. to pvt. med. and mental health practitioners, N.Y.C., 1988—, to legal firms, 1990—; coord. behavioral medicine, dir. 5th pathway program, chair faculty evaluation com. St. Joseph's Med. Ctr., Yonkers, 1988-95; reviewer profl. jours., books, 1990—; clin. instr. dept. psychiatry, dept. family medicine N.Y. Med. Coll., Valhalla; mem. faculty Inst. Urban Family Medicine, N.Y.C.; lectr. psychosocial and family sys. medicine, psychology and religion. Author: John: Apostle and Friend, 1980; also articles. Recipient rsch. award Fordham U., 1980, study grant, 1979, Teaching award Am. Acad. Family Physicians, 1992, 93, 94; teaching fellow Boston U., 1982-86. Mem. APA, Soc. Behavioral Medicine, Soc. Tchrs. Family Medicine, Nat. Register Health Svc. Providers, Cath. Bibl. Soc., N.Y. State Psychol. Assn. (regional rep.), Westchester Psychol. Assn., Phi Delta Kappa, Alpha Sigma Nu. Home & Office: 73 Hitching Post Ln Glen Cove NY 11542-1625

MOHAIDEEN, A. HASSAN, surgeon, healthcare executive; b. Ramanathapuram, India, Aug. 14, 1940; s. Abdul and Mariam (Pitchai) Kader; m. Zarina M. Meera, May 30, 1965 (dec. July 1986); children: Ahamed, Mariam, Najeeba, Azeema; m. Laurie J. Kucich, June 23, 1989; children: Yasmin Sara, Leila Jahan. MD, U. Madras, India, 1965; MBA, Wagner Coll., 1996. Diplomate Am. Bd. Surgery, Am. Bd. Quality Assurance and Utilization. Intern Govt. Stanley Hosp., Madras, 1965-66, Good Samaritan Hosp., West Islip, N.Y., 1967-68; resident in gen. and vascular surgery L.I. Coll. Hosp., Bklyn., 1968-73, asst. attending surgeon, 1973-76, assoc. attending surgeon, 1976-78, attending surgeon, 1978—, chief divsn. vascular surgery, 1980-93; sr v.p., 1995—; dir. vascular lab. L.I. Coll. Hosp., Bklyn., 1981-93; sr. v.p., managed care and exec. vice-chmn. dept. surgery The Bklyn.-Caledonian Hosp. Ctr. (affiliate of NYU), 1995—; sr. v.p. Bklyn.-Caledonian Hosp. Ctr. (affiliate of NYU), 1995—; asst. surgeon G.H.Q. Hosp., Ramnad, India, 1966-67; assoc. attending surgeon Meth. Hosp., Bklyn., 1982-90, attending surgeon, 1991; asst. attending surgeon Bklyn. Caledonian Med. Ctr., 1973-85, mem. courtesy staff, 1985-94, attending surgeon, 1994—; attending physician Victory Meml. Hosp., Bklyn., 1982-95; vis. physician Kings County Hosp. Ctr., Bklyn., 1973—; clin. instr. in surgery Downstate Med. Ctr., SUNY, Bklyn., 1973-78, clin. asst. prof. surgery, 1978—; mem. exec. com. of med. staff L.I. Coll. Hosp., Bklyn., 1979-93, treas. med. staff, 1982-85, pres., 1985-87, med. chmn. Guild Ball com., 1981, mem. quality assurance com. dept. surgery, 1988-94, chmn. credentials com., 1990-93, quality assurance and risk mgmt. com., 1990-93; bd. dirs. Aetna Health Plans of N.Y., AIDS adv. com., 1987—, stds. com., 1986-94, quality assurance com.; mem. credentials com. Prucare, 1988-92; sr. v.p. managed care Bklyn. Hosp., 1995—; mem. quality mgmt. com. Oxford Health Plans, 1995—; mem. quality improvement com. Chubb Health, N.Y., 1994—. Contbr. articles to med. jours. Fellow ACS (com. on Long Island dist. applicants, 1988—), Royal Coll. Physicians and Surgeons Can. (cert.), Internat. Coll. Surgeons; mem. AMA (Physician's Recognition award), AAAS, Am. Coll. Physician Execs., Med. Soc. of State of N.Y., N.Y. State Soc. of Surgeons, N.Y. Acad. of Scis., Med. Soc. of County of Kings (medication com., 1979-85), Bklyn. Surg. Soc., Soc. for Non-Invasive Vascular Technicians, Kings Physicians I.P.A. (pres./med. dir., 1985-95), Bklyn. Physicians I.P.A. (v.p., 1985-96, pres.). Office: 705 86th St Brooklyn NY 11228-3219

MOHAMED, DONNA FAHIMAH, counselor; b. Chapel Hill, N.C., Oct. 19, 1959; d. Thomas Lloyd and Helen Eleanor (Helms) Pendergraft; m. Dilip Gandhi, Aug. 19, 1978; 1 child, Sundeep; m. Mustafa Hussein Al-Bar, Apr. 15, 1991; 1 child, Maidah Nasreen. BA in Religious Studies with high honors and distinction, U. N.C., 1994. Rehab. therapist John Umstead Hosp. Continuing Treatment, Butner, N.C., 1985-86; immigration paralegal Law Offices of Douglas Holmes, Durham, N.C., 1986-87; immigration specialist Law Offices of Manlin Chee, Greensboro, N.C., 1987-92; program dir., accredited counselor Immigration & Minority Assistance Network, Durham, 1992—; pro bono project rep. Lawyers Com. for Human Rights, Fredericksburg, Va., 1987-88; minority devel. counselor, Ibad Ar-Rahman Sch., Durham, 1990-91; immigration cons. to bd. dirs. Jamaat Ibad Ar-Rahman, Inc., Durham, 1990-94; dir. cmty. counseling IMAN, Durham, 1991—; speaker N.Am. Coun. for Muslim Women, Chgo., 1994; panelist on cultural awareness, Dept. Edn. and Counseling, U. N.C., Chapel Hill, 1994; organizer, presenter ann. workshops Coll. Bound Program for Youth, Chapel Hill, 1992—. Recipient 1st prize ann. cooking contest Triangle Muslim Women's Group, 1992. Mem. Am. Muslim Coun., Am. Immigration Lawyers Assn. (pro bono affiliation), Muslim Women's Orgn. (pres. Chapel Hill, N.C. chpt. 1991-93), Muslim Student's Assn. (exec. dir. Chapel Hill chpt. 1992-93), Islamic Soc. N.Am., Social Scientists Am., Golden Key Nat. Honor Soc. Democrat.

MOHAMMED, RIAZ, surgeon, consultant; b. Gujrat, Pakistan, Mar. 17, 1950; arrived in Scotland, 1957; s. Bashire and Bagum (Din) Hussain; m. Janet McLean, July 17, 1974; children: Mark, Sylvia. MB BChir, Glasgow (Scotland) U., 1974, MD, 1978. Cert. creditation in gen. surgery Creditation Com. in Surgery, London. House physician Nat. Health Svc., East Kilbride, Scotland, 1974-75; house surgeon NHS, Glasgow, 1975; anatomy demonstrator Glasgow U., 1975-76; sr. house surgeon Stobhill Hosp., NHS, Glasgow, 1976-77; registrar surgeon Falkirk (Scotland) Royal Infirmary, NHS, 1977-78, Stobhill Hosp., NHS, Glasgow, 1978-79; rsch. gastroenterologist dept. surgery Sir. Andrew Watt-Kay's Unit, Glasgow, 1979-81; sr. registrar gen. surgery Greater Glasgow Health Bd., 1981-88; cons. gen., gastrointestinal surgeon Queen Margaret Hosp., NHS-Trust, Dunfermline, Fife, Scotland, 1988—; chmn. minimally invasive surgery Queen Margaret Hosp., Nat. Health Svc., Dunfermline, 1994—; vice-chmn. Local Negotiation Com. (Queen Margaret Hosp.) for British Med. Assn., Dunfermline, 1994—.

Contbr. papers to profl. jours. Fellow Royal Coll. Surgeons (Edinburgh, examiner Royal Coll. Physicians and Surgeons Glasgow 1990—), Assn. Surgeons of Gt. Britain and Ireland; mem. Assn. Endoscopic Surgeons of Gt. Britain and Ireland. Office: Queen Margaret Hosp Nat Health Svc, Whitefield Rd, Fife Dunfermline KY12 OSU, Scotland

MOHAN, CHANDRA, research biochemistry educator; b. Lucknow, India, Aug. 3, 1950; came to U.S., 1977; s. Prithivi Nath and Tara Rani (Sharma) Shastri; m. Nirmala Devi Sharma, July 23, 1978; children: Deepak, Naveen. BS, Bangalore (India) U., 1970, MS, 1972, PhD, 1976. Research assoc. U. So. Calif. Med. Sch., Los Angeles, 1977-83, asst. prof., 1983-93; dir. tech. svc., sr. tech. writer CalBioChem Corp., San Diego, 1993—. Assoc. editor Biochem. Medicine, Los Angeles, 1986—; contbr. articles to profl. jours. Recipient BRSG award U. So. Calif., 1983. Mem. AAAS, Am. Diabetes Assn., N.Y. Acad. Scis., Soc. Exptl. Biology and Medicine, Am. Inst. Nutrition. Hindu. Home: 13638 Dicky St Whittier CA 90605-2949 Office: CalBioChem Corp 10394 Pacific Center Ct San Diego CA 92121-4340

MOHAN-ROBERTS, VEENA, ophthalmologist; b. Delhi, India, Oct. 1, 1939; arrived in U.K., 1970; d. Shyam and Sushila (Lal) Nath; m. Ravinder Mohan, Mar. 1, 1964 (div. 1972); m. Frederick Charles Roberts, Jan. 21, 1984. MB, BS, Lady Harding Coll., Delhi, 1963; DO, Royal Coll. Surgeons, London, 1971. Sr. house officer St. Woolos Hosp., Newport, U.K., 1970-72; registrar Chelmsford (U.K.) and Essex Hosp., 1973-74, West of Eng. Eye Infirmary, Exeter, Devon, U.K., 1974-76; sr. registrar Birmingham ((U.K.) Midland Eye Hosp., 1976-79; cons. West Midlands Regional Health Authority, Birmingham, 1980—. Contbr. articles to profl. jours. Fellow Royal Coll. Surgeons, Royal Coll. Ophthalmologists; mem. Brit. Med. Assn., Oxford Ophthalmological Soc., Hosp. Cons. and Specialist Assn., Overseas Drs. Assn., Midland Ophthalmological Soc. (sec. 1989—). Hindu.

MOHENO, PHILLIP BERTRAND BERKEY, science educator, biomedical researcher; b. Los Angeles, Sept. 16, 1952; s. Bernard and Flora (Moheno) Berkey; m. Yolanda Peraza, Aug. 30, 1980; children: Karla Rose, Daniel Phillip. BS, UCLA, 1974, postgrad., 1976; PhD, U. Calif., Santa Barbara, 1985. Cert. community coll. instr. Research asst. Salk Inst. Biol. Studies, La Jolla, Calif., 1970-73; grad. researcher, dept. chemistry UCLA, 1975-78; research asst. La Jolla Cancer Research Found., 1979; instr. biology Oxnard (Calif.) Coll. and Santa Barbara (Calif.) City Coll., 1980-85; supr. tchr. edn. U. Calif., Santa Barbara, 1982-85; asst. dir. MESA program Calif. State Coll., Bakersfield, 1985-87, asst. prof. Physical Sci. Edn., 1987-90; asst. prof. multicultural sci. edn. dept. policy studies coll. edn. San Diego State U., 1990—. Fellow Ford Found. UCLA, 1974-78; Am. Cancer Soc. grantee, Cancer Fedn. grantee. Mem. Nat. Sci. Tchrs. Assn., Am. Chem. Soc., Sigma Xi. Democrat. Mem. Soc. Friends. Home: 603 Colima St La Jolla CA 92037 Office: San Diego State U San Diego CA 92182-0415

MOHL, ALLAN S., social worker; b. Passaic, N.J., Feb. 10, 1933; s. Milton and Ruth (Meisler) M.; m. Judith Klein, Dec. 21, 1958; children: Barbara, Eric, Adam. BA, NYU, 1954, MA, 1956, MSS, 1960; PhD, Columbia Pacific U., 1991. Diplomate Clin. Social Work. Dir. resdl. social svcs. Queens Soc. for Prevention of Cruelty of Children, Queens, N.Y., supvr. of incest; psychotherapist in pvt. practice Ardsley, N.Y.; cons. Tip Neighborhood House, Bronx; dir. family svcs. Tip Neighborhood House; sch. social worker Com. on Spl. Edn., Dist. 28, N.Y.C.; condr. workshop on incestuous families and child sexual abuse; unit dir. Children's Village, Dobbs Ferry, N.Y.; cons. Parents Anonymous, South Bronx, N.Y. Contbr. articles to profl. jours. Former chmn. Gen. Social Svcs. Adv. Coun. # 6; active participant Bronx Task Force on Child Abuse and Neglect; group leader Project Enable, South Bronx, N.Y.; sponsor Parents' Anonymous group, Bronx. With U.S. Army, 1956-58. NIMH grantee. Mem. NASW, Am. Assn. Marriage and Family Therapy, Am. Orthopsychiat. Assn., N.Y. State Soc. Clin. Social Wk. Psychotherapists, Internat. Assn. Counselors and Therapists, Am. Group Psychotherapy Assn. (assoc. clin. mem.). Home: 8 Shorthill Rd Ardsley NY 10502-2020

MOHL, NORMAN DAVID, dental educator; b. Paterson, N.J., May 15, 1931; s. Irving and Fannie (Weiss) M.; m. Eldene Jaffe, Dec. 27, 1953; children: Ilana, Lawrence, Daniel, Steven. DDS, U. Buffalo, 1956; MA, SUNY, Buffalo, 1968, PhD, 1971. Dentist, pvt. practice Buffalo, 1958-67; prof. SUNY, 1971—; assoc. dean acad. affairs SUNY, Buffalo, 1972-87, dir. oral sci. grad. program, 1977-94; coun. mem. on dental materials, instruments and equipment ADA, Chgo., 1987-92; cons. NIH, Washington, 1988—, FDA, Washington, 1989—; chmn. dept. oral diagnostic scis., SUNY, Buffalo, 1994—. Author, editor: A Textbook of Occulsion, 1988, TMJ and Masticatory Muscle Disorders, 1995; contbr. articles to profl. jours. Lt. USNR, 1956-58. Mem. Internat. Assn. for Dental Rsch., Neuroscis. TMJ-Orofacial Pain Programs (pres. 1991-92), Am. Coun. on Edn. (fellow Acad. Adminstrn., spl. asst. v.p. for health scis. 1975-76). Home: 242 Wedgewood Dr Buffalo NY 14221-1401 Office: SUNY 3435 Main St Buffalo NY 14214-3001

MOHLER, TERENCE JOHN, psychologist; s. Edward F. and Gertrude A. (Aylward) M.; m. Carol B. Kulczak; children: Renee, John, Timothy. BE, ME, EdS, Toledo U.; PhD, Walden U., Union Inst., 1979. Psychologist, Toledo Bd. Edn., 1969-89; sr. ptnr. Psychol. Assocs., Maumee, Ohio, 1970—; assoc. fellow Inst. for Advanced Study in Rational Psychotherapy, N.Y.C. Served with U.S. Army, 1951-53; Korea. Lic. psychologist, Ohio. Mem. Am., Ohio, Northwestern Ohio, Maumee Valley Psychol. Assns., Soc. Behaviorists, Toledo Acad. Profl. Psychology, Nat. Registry Mental Health Providers, Am. Pers. and Guidance Assn., Ohio Pers. and Guidance Assn., Coun. for Exceptional Children, Rotary (Paul Harris Fellow), Kappa Delta Phi. Home: 1904 Glen Ellyn Dr Toledo OH 43614-3256 Office: 5757 Monclova Rd Maumee OH 43537-1837

MOHN, MICHAEL R., optometrist; b. West Reading, Pa., Jan. 23, 1952; s. Stanley Raymond and Marian Ruth (Hamaker) M.; m. Enid Michelle Kline, Aug. 16, 1975 (div. Mar. 1976); m. Cynthia Lee Kochel, May 31, 1980; children: Mallory Kae, Alison Leigh. BS in Biology, Kutztown (Pa.) State U.; BS in Gen. Sci., Pa. Coll. Optometry, OD. Pvt. practice, Shillington, Pa., 1984—. Trustee Calvary UM Ch., Mohaton, Pa., 1995—; trustee Pa. Coll. Optometry, 1996. Officer U.S. Army, 1980-83; lt. col. USAR, 1983—. Health profl. scholar U.S. Army, 1979. Fellow Am. Acad. Optometry (cert.), Am. Coll. Optometric Physicians; mem. Am. Optometric Assn., Pa. Optometric Assn. (trustee), Berks County Optometric Soc. (sec.-treas., pres., trustee). Republican. Roman Catholic. Home: 259 Church Rd Mohonton PA 19540 Office: Shillington Eye Assocs 453 E Lancaster Ave Shillington PA 19607

MOHR, GARY ALAN, physician; b. Erie, Pa., Aug. 17, 1952; s. Arthur John and Sue (Richardson) M.; children: Benjamin, Nathan, Elizabeth, Katelyn, Eric. BS, Pa. State U., 1979; MD, Jefferson Med. Coll., 1979. Pvt. practice Canon City, Colo., 1982—. Founder, treas. Jefferson Soc., Fremont County, Colo., 1991. Mem. Mensa. Lutheran. Office: 730 Macon Ave Canon City CO 81212-3314

MOHR, JOHN LUTHER, biologist, environmental consultant; b. Reading, Pa., Dec. 1, 1911; s. Luther Seth and Anna Elizabeth (Davis) M.; m. Frances Edith Christensen, Nov. 23, 1939; children: Jeremy John, Christopher Charles. AB in Biology, Bucknell U., 1933; student, Oberlin Coll., 1933-34; PhD in Zoology, U. Calif., Berkeley, 1939. Research asso. Pacific Islands Research, Stanford, 1942-44; rsch. assoc. Allan Hancock Found., U. So. Calif., 1944-46, asst. prof., 1946-47, asst. prof. dept. biology, 1947-54, asso. prof., 1954-57, prof., 1957-77; chmn. dept., 1960-62, prof. emeritus, 1977—; vis. prof. summers U. Wash. Friday Harbor Labs., 1956, '57; marine borer and pollution surveys harbors So. Calif., 1948-51, arctic marine biol. research, 1952-71; chief marine zool. group U.S. Antarctic research ship Eltanin in Drake Passage, 1962, in South Pacific sector, 1965; research deontology in sci. and academia; researcher on parasitic protozoans of anurans, crustaceans, elephants; analysis of agy. and industry documents, ethics and derelictions of steward agy., sci. and tech. orgns. as they relate to offshore and coastal onshore oil activities, environ. effects of oil spill dispersants and offshore oil industry discharges and naturally occurring radioactive material NORMs. Active People for the Am. Way; mem. Biol. Stain Commn., 1948-80, trustee, 1971-80, emeritus trustee, 1981—, v.p., 1976-80. Recipient Guggenheim fellowship, 1957-58. Fellow AAAS (coun. 1964-73), So. Calif. Acad. Scis., Sigma Xi (exec. com. 1964-67, 68, 69, chpt.-at-large bd. 1968-69); mem. Am. Micros. Soc., Marine Biol. Assn. U.K. (life), Am. Soc. Parasitologists, Western Soc. Naturalists (pres. 1960-61), Soc. Protozoologists, Soc. Integrative and Comparative Biology, Ecol. Soc. Am., Planning and Conservation League, Calif. Native Plant Soc., Save San Francisco Bay Assn., Ecology Ctr. So. Calif., Assn. Forest Svc. Employees Environ. Ethics, Common Cause, Huxleyan, Sierra Club, Phi Sigma, Theta Upsilon Omega. Home: 3819 Chanson Dr Los Angeles CA 90043-1601

MOHR, LAWRENCE CHARLES, physician; b. S.I., N.Y., July 8, 1947; s. Lawrence Charles Sr. and Mary Estelle (Dawsey) M.; m. Linda Johnson, June 14, 1970; 1 child, Andrea Marie. AB, U. N.C., 1975, MD, 1979. Diplomate Am. Bd. Internal Medicine. Commd. 2d lt. U.S. Army, 1967, advanced through grades to col., 1989; med. intern Walter Reed Army Med. Ctr., Washington, 1979-80, resident in medicine, 1980-82, chief resident, 1982-83, attending physician, 1984-86, pulmonary fellow, 1986-87; command surgeon 9th Inf. Div., Ft. Lewis, Wash., 1983-84; med. cons. Madigan Army Med. Ctr., Tacoma, 1983-84; White House physician Washington, 1987-93; asst. prof. medicine Uniformed Svcs. U. of the Health Scis., Bethesda, Md., 1984-91; assoc. prof. medicine Uniformed Svcs. U. Health Scis., Bethesda, Md., 1991-94; assoc. clin. prof. medicine George Washington U., Washington, 1990-94; prof. medicine Med. U. S.C., Charleston, 1994—, dir. environ. hazards assessment program, 1995—; mem. Working Group on Disability in U.S. Presidents, 1995—. Bd. dirs. Internat. Lung Found., Washington; mem. adv. bd. Nat. Mus. Health and Medicine, Washington. Decorated Silver Star, Bronze Star with 2 V devices and 3 oak leaf clusters, Purple Heart, Meritorious Svc. medal with oak leaf cluster, Air medal, Army Commendation medal with oak leaf cluster; recipient Erskine award Walter Reed Army Med. Ctr., 1982; named Outstanding Med. Resident, 1982. Fellow ACP, Am. Coll. Chest Physicians; mem. AMA, Army and Navy Club, Order Mil. Med. Merit, Harbour Club, Phi Beta Kappa. Episcopalian. Home: Ste 11-R 310 Broad St Charleston SC 29401 Office: Med U S C Environ Hazards Assess Prgm 171 Ashley Ave Charleston SC 29425

MOHR, MYRON GEORGE, psychologist; b. Van Wert, Ohio, Nov. 25, 1942; s. Paul George and Ellen Elizabeth (McClain) M. BA, Kent (Ohio) State U., 1964; MA, La. State U., 1967, PhD, 1971. Lic. clin. psychologist, La. Project dir. The Phone, La. State U., Baton Rouge, 1970-74; exec. dir. Baton Rouge Crisis Intervention Ctr., 1975-88; project dir. Baton Rouge Intervention Ctr., 1988-89; pvt. practice Baton Rouge, 1989—; APA-HOPE (HIV Office for Psychologist Edn.) trainer, 1993. Author: (with others) Experienced Resident Assistant, 1989. Mem. APA, La. Psychol. Assn., Baton Rouge Area Soc. Psychology, Am. Assn. Suicidology (bd. dirs. 1979-87, chief cert. examiner 1988-89), Coun. for the Nat. Register. Democrat. Office: 1200 S Acadian Thrway Ste 206 Baton Rouge LA 70806

MOHR, SELBY, retired ophthalmologist; b. San Francisco, Mar. 11, 1918; s. Selby and Henrietta (Foorman) M.; AB, Stanford U., 1938, MD, 1942; m. Marian Buckley, June 10, 1950; children—Selby, John Vincent, Adrianne E., Gregory P. Asst. resident in ophthalmology U. Calif. Hosp., 1942-43; pvt. practice ophthalmology, San Francisco, 1947-88; mem. past pres. med. staff Marshall Hale Meml. Hosp.; mem. staff Mt. Zion Hosp., St Francis Meml. Hosp. Dir. Sweet Water Co., Mound Farms, Inc., Mound Farms Oil & Gas, Inc. Lt. (j.g.) USNR, 1943-46; PTO. Diplomate Am. Bd. Ophthalmology. Fellow Am. Acad. Ophthalmology; mem. AMA, Calif., San Francisco Med. Socs., Pan-Pacific Surg. Soc., Pan-Am. Assn. Ophthalmology. Home: 160 Sea Cliff Ave San Francisco CA 94121-1125

MOHRDICK, EUNICE MARIE, nurse, consultant, health educator; b. Alameda, Calif.; d. Walter William and Eunice Marie (Connors) M. BS in Nursing Edn., U. San Francisco, 1955; MA in Edn. spl interest, San Francisco State Coll., 1967; Pub. Health Cert., U. Calif., San Francisco, 1968; EdD, Western Colo. U., 1977. RN, Calif. Supr. oper. rm. St. John's Hosp., Oxnard, Calif., 1947-50, supr. maternity, delivery and nursery rms., 1950-53; nurse, supr. St. Mary's Hosp., San Francisco, 1943-45, supr., instr., 1955-60, 62-65; asst. dir. nursing, tchr. nursing history St Mary's Coll. of Nursing, San Francisco, 1953-55; tchr. home nursing Mercy High Sch., San Francisco, 1960-61; tchr. Health, Family Life San Francisco Unified Schs., 1968-83; tchr. holistic health Contra Costa Coll., 1981-86; cons. pvt. practice Albany, Calif., 1986—; tchr. El Cerrito (Calif.) Senior Ctr., 1986-88. Author: Elementary Teacher Handbook, How to Teach Sex Education, Grades, 4,5,6, 1977. Mem. Madonna Guild, San Francisco, 1986—, v.p., 1989—; mem. Half Notes' Singing Club to Sick and Spl. Needy, 1970—. Recipient Title I Grant U. Calif. San Francisco, 1968, Workshop Grant for Culture Inter-relationship Study, Singapore, UNESCO, Washington U., St. Louis, 1973. Mem. AAUW, San Francisco State U. Alumna, U. San Francisco Nursing Alumni (charter mem., bd. dirs. 1974-88), Mensa. Republican. Roman Catholic. Home & Office: 555 Pierce St Apt 129 Albany CA 94706-1011

MOHRI, HIDEO, biology educator; b. Tokyo, June 6, 1930; s. Keishiro and Yaeko (Amano) M.; m. Toshiko Fujita, Nov. 3, 1959; children: Kensuke, Kohei, Yucca. BS, U. Tokyo, 1953, DSC, 1961. Rsch. assoc. Misaki (Japan) Marine Biol. Sta., U. Tokyo, 1954-59, rsch. assoc. Coll. Arts. and Scis., 1959-65, assoc. prof. biology, 1965-76, prof., 1976-91, dean Coll. Arts and Scis., 1987-89; prof. U. of Air, Chiba, Japan, 1991-92, v.p., 1992-95; dir.-gen. Nat. Inst. for Basic Biology, Okazaki, Japan, 1995—. Editor, author: Biological Functions of Microtubules and Related Structures, 1982, New Horizons in Sperm Cell Research, 1987, Biology of the Germ Line in Animals and Man, 1993. Recipient award Mainichi Shinbunsha, 1972. Mem. Zool. Soc. Japan (prize 1974), Japanese Soc. Devel. Biologists, Internat. Soc. Devel. Biologists, Japanese Biochem. Soc., Japanese Soc. Andrology. Shinto. Office: Nat Inst for Basic Biology, Nishigonaka 38, Myodaiji, Okazaki 444, Japan

MOISES, HANS WERNER, psychiatrist; b. Celle, Germany, July 3, 1948; s. Hans and Sophia (Schorler) M.; m. Claude Soulie, Apr. 18, 1975; children: Miriam, Maurice. MD, U. Heidelberg, 1980. Rsch. asst. Ctrl. Inst. Mental Health, Mannheim, Germany, 1978-86; fellow in molecular genetics Stanford U. Sch. Medicine, Calif., 1987-89; cons. psychiatry Univ. Hosp., Kiel, Germany, 1989—; lectr. U. Kiel, 1994—, dir. molecular genetics lab., 1989—. Mem. German Soc. Biol. Psychiatry, Soc. Biol. Psychiatry. Office: Kiel Univ Hosp Dept Psych, Niemannsweg 147, 24105 Kiel Germany

MOK, PETER PUI KWAN, clinical pharmacist; b. Burma, May 30, 1938; came to U.S., 1961, naturalized, 1974; s. Chi-Wing Mok; BA in Zoology, UCLA, 1966; BSc in Pharmacy, Phila. Coll. Pharmacy and Sci., 1969; Pharm.D., U. Mich., 1971; m. Drosa Chang, Jan. 4, 1969; children: Mimi Elizabeth, Oliver Jacob. Clin. pharmacy resident U. Mich. Hosps. and Med. Ctr., 1970-71; instr. preventive and community medicine Albany Med. Coll. (N.Y.), 1971-76, clin. asst. prof., 1976—; dir. pharm. care, chmn. quality assurance, dir. pharm. care Whitney Young Health Ctr., Albany, 1971—; clin. prof. Albany Coll. Pharmacy, 1971—. Bd. dirs. Chinese Community Ctr. of Albany-Schenectady, Rensselaer areas 1979-82. Cited for excellence of clin. practice Pharmacy Practice Inst., Albany Coll. Pharmacy, Union U., 1978, Excellence of Practice, Dept. Health & Human Svcs., 1988. Mem. Am. Soc. Health Sys. Pharmacists, Am. Chinese Pharm. Assn., Am. Pharm. Assn., Pharm. Soc. of N.Y. Contbr. articles to profl. jours., papers to confs. Address: PO Box 1315 Guilderland NY 12084-1315 Office: Whitney Young Health Ctr Lark Dr Albany NY 12210

MOL, BEN W., epidemiologist, consultant; b. Laren, The Netherlands, Sept. 21, 1965; s. Ben C. Mol and J. A. Albers. Cons. Acad. Med. Ctr., Amsterdam, The Netherlands, 1993—. Office: Acad Med Ctr, Dept Clin Epidemiology, PO Box 22700, 1100 NE Amsterdam The Netherlands

MOLIERE, JEFFREY MICHAEL, cardiopulmonary administrator; b. San Pedro, Calif., Nov. 22, 1948; s. Dwight Hedrick and Geraldine Stabile. AA, L.A. Harbor Coll., 1968; postgrad., Calif. State U., Long Beach, 1968-69; cert. in respiratory care, Calif. Coll. for Health Sci., 1982, Biosystems Inst., 1984; assoc. degree, Ind. U., Indpls., 1987, B in Gen. Studies, 1990; MS in Cmty. Health Adminstrn., Calif. Coll. for Health Sci., 1994. Registered respiratory therapist, respiratory care practitioner; cert. pulmonary tech. Alt. supr. Good Samaritan Hosp., Vincennes, Ind., 1976-79; critical care technician Winona Meml. Hosp., Indpls., 1979-80; neonatal ICU-critical care technician Mercy Hosp., Urbana, Ill., 1980-82; cardio-pulmonary supr. Winona Meml. Hosp., Indpls., 1982-92; dir. pulmonary svcs. MidWest Med. Ctr., Indpls., 1992-93; mgr., bronchoscopy, pulmonary function testing, respiratory care VA Med. Ctr., Indpls., 1993—, ednl. coord., EEO counselor, 1993—; mem. adj. faculty Ind. Vocat.-Tech. Coll., 1993—; adv. bd. Allied Health Ind. U., 1995—. Mem. adv. bd. allied health Ind. U., 1996—, Ind. Vocat. Tech. Coll., 1987—. Mem. Nat. Bd. Respiratory Care, Am. Assn. for Respiratory Care (clin. practice guideline rev. bd.), Ind. Soc. for Respiratory Care, Nat. Bd. for Respiratory Care, Alpha Sigma Lambda (charter, Membership award 1990).

MOLINA, JOSEPH MARIO, medical administrator; b. Long Beach, Calif., May 16, 1958; s. C. David and Mary R. (Salandini) M.; m. Therese Ann Flynn; children: Carley, Colleen, David, Mary Clare. BA, Calif. State U., Long Beach, 1980; MD, U. So. Calif., 1984. Diplomate Am. Bd. Internal Medicine. Assoc. investigator VA, San Diego, 1988-90; asst. clin. prof. U. So. Calif., L.A., 1990-91; med. dir. Molina Med. Ctrs., Long Beach, 1991-94, v.p. HMO, 1994—. Mem. Am. Coll. Physician Execs., Am. Coll. Physicians, Am. Diabetes Assn., Endocrine Soc. Office: Molina Med Ctrs Inc 1 Golden Shore Dr Long Beach CA 90802

MOLINA MARTÍNEZ, FRANCISCO JOSÉ, neurologist; b. Valencia, Spain, July 31, 1964; s. Ángel Molina and Amparo Martínez; m. Marta De La Llave, Sept. 15, 1990; children: Sergio, Raquel. MD, U. Complutense de Madrid, 1988; degree in neurology, U. Autónoma de Madrid, 1992. House officer dept. neurology Hosp. Puerta de Hierro, Madrid, 1989-92; neurologist cons. Hosp. Son Dureta, Palma de Mallorca, Spain, 1993—, botulinum toxin therapist dept. neurology, 1993—, house officer's tchg. tutor dept. neurology, 1996—; lectr. Balearic Ofcl. Med. Coll., Spain, 1993—, Balearic Isles U., Spain, 1993—. Contbr. articles to profl. jours. Fellow Balearic Neurol. Soc.; mem. Spanish Neurol. Soc., European Fedn. Neurol. Socs. Roman Catholic. Office: Hosp Son Dureta, C/Andrea Doria No 55, 07014 Palma de Mallorca Spain

MOLINARI, JOSEPH FRANCIS, optometrist; b. Worcester, Mass.; s. Wallace F. and Antoinette M. (Tortora) M. AA, Cen. New Eng. Coll., 1972; BS, New Eng. Coll., 1973, OD, 1974; MEd, Mercer U., 1979. Staff optometrist Lahey Clin. Med. Ctr., 1977-79; asst. prof. U. Ala., 1979-82; gen. practice optometry, Panama City Beach, Fla., 1982—; cons. USAF, Tyndall AFB, 1980-83, chief DS & M Vet. Affairs, Tallahassee, 1994—. Contbr. articles to profl. jours.; item writer Nat. Bd. Optometry, Washington, 1980-83. Pres. Harbour Villas Assn., Inc., 1985-86, Gulf of Mex. Optics Inc., Panama City Beach, 1984-96; chmn. Bay Point Anterior Segment Symposium Inc., 1984-95. Lt. col. USAFR, 1974—. Recipient Spurgeon Eure award Am. Optometric Found., 1978, 81-82, Dallos Contact Lens Research award Brit. Contact Lens Assn., 1984, Outstanding Svc. and Recognition award Assn. Milit. Surgeons of U.S., 1996, 20 Yr. Recognition Armed Forces Optometric Soc. Fellow Am. Acad. Optometry, Am. Coll. Optometric Physicians (diplomate); mem. Fla. Optometric Assn. (del. 1984-85), Neuro-optometry Soc. (chmn. 1985-88), Am. Coll. Optometry Physicians. Lodge: Am. Legion. Office: 10010 Middle Beach Rd Panama City Beach FL 32407

MOLINE, HAROLD EMIL, research plant pathologist; b. Frederic, Wis., Nov. 13, 1939; s. Thorsten and Agnes Virginia (Johnson) M.; m. Bonnie Gay Larson, Mar. 6, 1965; children: Jenel, Christopher. BS, U. Wis., 1967; PhD, Iowa State U., 1972. Plant pathologist USDA-Agrl. Rsch. Svc., Brookings, S.D., 1972-73; rsch. plant pathologist USDA-Agrl. Rsch. Svc., Beltsville, Md., 1974—; adj. prof. George Washington U., 1981-85, Howard U., Washington, 1977-91. Co-author: Postharvest Phsyiology of Vegetable, 1987; editor: Postharvest Pathology of Fruits and Vegatables, 1984; contbr. articles to profl. jours. Founder Bowie-Croften (Md.) Garden Club, 1980—. With USN, 1958-62. Mem. Am. Phytopathol. Soc., Sigma Xi. Lutheran. Office: USDA-ARS Barc W # 002 Beltsville MD 20705

MOLINOFF, PERRY BROWN, biologist, science administrator; b. Smithtown, N.Y., June 3, 1940; s. Henry Charles and Thelma (Brown) M.; m. Marlene Sirota, 1963; children: Jeffrey, Sharon. BS, Harvard U., 1962, MD, 1967. Intern U. Chgo. Hosp. & Clinics, 1967-68; research assoc. NIMH, Bethesda, Md., 1968-70; vis. fellow Univ. Coll., London, 1970-72; asst. prof. U. Colo. Health Sci., Denver, 1972-76; assoc. prof. U. Colo. Health Sci., 1976-80, prof., 1980-81; prof., chmn. U. Pa., Phila., 1981-94; v.p. C.N.S. Drug Discovery Bristol-Myers Squibb, Wallingford, Conn., 1995—. Editor: Basic Neurochemistry, 1989, Biology of Normal and Abnormal Brain Function, 1990, Goodman and Gilman: The Pharmacological Basis of Therapeutics, 1996; editl. adv. bd. Molecular Pharmacology, 1976—. Med. adv. bd. Dysautonomia Found., 1977—. Lt. comdr. USPHS, 1968-70. Mem. Soc. Neurosci. (membership com., treas.), Am. Heart Assn. (rsch. com.), John Morgan Soc. (sec.-treas. 1988—), Pa. Heart Assn. Home: 10 Broad St Weston CT 06883 Office: Bristol-Myers Squibb 5 Research Pkwy PO Box 5100 Wallingford CT 06492-7600

MOLITORIS, BRUCE ALBERT, nephrologist, educator; b. Springfield, Ill., June 26, 1951; s. Edward and Joyce (Tomasko) M.; m. Karen Lynn Wichterman, June 16, 1973; children: Jason, Jared, Julie. BS, U. Ill., 1973, MS in Nutrition, 1975; MD, Wash. U., 1979. Resident Sch. Medicine U. Colo., Denver, 1979-81, nephrology fellow, 1981-84, asst. prof. medicine, 1984-88, assoc. prof. medicine, 1988-93, prof., 1993; dir. nephrology Ind. U. Med. Sch., Indpls., 1993—; vis. scientist U. Colo., MCDB, Boulder, 1989-90, Max Planck Inst., Federal Republic of Germany, 1984-85; NIH reviewer, 1991-94; dir. home dialysis Denver VA Ctr., 1984-93. Mem. editl. bd. Am. Jour. Physiology, 1989—, Am. Jour. Kidney Diseases, 1991, Am. Jour. Kidney Disease, 1996; assoc. editor Jour. Ivnestigative Medicine, 1994—; contbr. articles to profl. jours. Pres. Cherry Creek Village South Homeowners Assn., 1989-90; v.p. Our Father Luth. Ch., Denver, 1989-90; coach Cherry Creek Soccer Assn., Greenwood Village, 1988-91, Centennial little league Titans Basketball; bd. dirs. CSSA, 1993. Recipient Upjohn Achievement award, 1979, Liberty Hyde Bailey award, 1973. Mem. Am. Soc. Nephrology, Internat. Soc. Nephrology, N.Y. Acad. Sci., Am. Soc. Clin. Investigation, Am. Fedn. for Clin. Rsch. (nat. counselor 1991-94), Western Assn. Physicians. Office: Indiana Univ Med Ctr Fesler Hall 115 1120 South Dr Indianapolis IN 46202-5135

MOLL, M. CHARLES, oral and macillofacial surgeon; b. Grand Rapids, Mich., Sept. 27, 1942; s. Melvin C. and Isabel Rita (Droski) M.; m. Helen M. Long, Dec. 26, 1966; children: Matthew Charles, Cynthia Ann. AB in Dental Scis., Ind. U., 1964; DDS, Ind. U., Indpls., 1967, postgrad., 1967-70. Diplomate Am. Bd. Oral and Maxillofacial Surgeons. Oral and maxillofacial surgeon in pvt. practice Indpls., 1970—; clin. instr. oral and maxillofacial surgery dept. Ind. U. Dental Sch., Indpls., 1971—. Recipient various awards. Mem. ADA, Am. Assn. Oral and Maxillofacial Surgeons, Ind. Dental Assn., Ind. Oral and Maxillofacial Surgeons, Gt. Lakes Soc. Oral and Maxillofacial Surgeons, Am. Acad. Osseointegration, Sertoma of East Indpls., Omicron Kappa Upsilon. Office: 125 N Shortridge Rd Indianapolis IN 46219-4908

MOLLE, WILLIAM E., retired internal medicine educator; b. Toledo, Sept. 13, 1915; s. Hyman and Sadie (Levinson) M.; m. Leah White, Jan. 8, 1944. BSc, U. Toledo, 1936; MB, U. Cin., 1939, MD, 1940. Diplomate in internal medicine and gastroenterology Am. Bd. Internal Medicine. Resident in medicine Cin. Gen. Hosp., 1940-42, fellow in gastroenterology, 1946-47; attending physician Cedars-Sinai Med. Ctr., L.A., 1947-92, emeritus physician, 1992—; assoc. prof. medicine UCLA Med. Ctr., 1955-92, emeritus prof., 1992—. Vol. physician Venice (Calif.) Family Clinic, 1992—. Capt. M.C., USAAF, 1942-46, ETO.

MOLLEN, EDWARD LEIGH, pediatrician, allergist and immunologist; b. Richmond, Va., May 13, 1946; s. Irving Roth and Ruth (Damsky) M.; m. Mary Viola Jeffrey, Dec. 14, 1975; children: Shawn, Michael, Eric, Christopher. BS in Chemistry, Coll. William and Mary, 1968; MD, Med. Coll. Va., 1972. Diplomate Am. Bd. Pediatrics, Am. Bd. Allergy and Immunology. Resident in pediatrics Med. Coll. Va., Richmond, 1972-75, fellow in allergy and immunology, 1975-77; practice allergy and pediatric allergy and clin. immunology Allergy Assocs. of Richmond, 1977-85; pvt. practice allergy/pediatric allergy and clin. immunology Richmond, 1985—. Fellow Am. Acad. Allergy and Immunology, Am. Acad. Pediatrics; mem. Med. Soc. Va., Richmond Acad. Medicine, Am. Thoracic Soc., Va. Allergy Soc. Office: 5855 Bremo Rd Ste 702 Richmond VA 23226-1926

MOLLER, AAGE RICHARD, physiologist; b. Finderup, Denmark, Apr. 16, 1932; s. Jens and Kristine Marie (Pedersen) M.; m. Margareta Bjuro, July 26, 1977; children: Peter, Jan. Cand. med., Karolinska Inst., Stockholm, 1975, PhD, 1965. Research assoc., asst. prof., research fellow Swedish Med. Research Council, Karolinska Inst., 1966-77; assoc. prof. otolaryngology U. Gothenburg, Sweden, 1977-78; research prof. otolaryngology and physiology U. Pitts. Sch. Medicine, 1978-83, research prof. neurol. surgery, 1983-88, prof. neurol. surgery, 1988—; sr. lectr. Carnegie Mellon U., Pitts., 1980-86; dir. rsch. Internat. Ctr. Insect Physiology and Ecology, Nairobi, Kenya, 1970-76. Author of profl. books; contbr. articles to profl. jours.; editor-in-chief Hearing Research, Elsevier, Holland, 1977—. Served as cpl. Danish Army, 1951-53. Fellow Acoustical Soc. Am.; mem. AAAS, Am. Soc. Intraoperative Monitoring (pres. 1991-92), Soc. Occupational and Environ. Health, Soc. Neurosci., N.Y. Acad. Sci., Assn. Rsch. in Otolaryngology, Am. Physiol. Soc., Am. Acad. Clin. Neuro-Physiology. Home: 5427 Northumberland St Pittsburgh PA 15217-1128 Office: U Pitts Med Ctr 200 Lothrop St Ste B-400 Pittsburgh PA 15213-2546

MOLLOFF, FLORENCE JEANINE, speech and language therapist; b. St. Louis, Aug. 28, 1959; d. Lawrence Allan and Rietta Gertrude (Fiegenbaum) M. BS, Fontbonne Coll., St. Louis, 1983; MEd summa cum laude, Nat. Louis U., St. Louis, 1989; student, Project ACCESS Inst., 1992, Judevine Ctr. Autistic Children Tng., 1992. Cert. speech correctionist, Mo. Intern St. Louis State Sch. for Profoundly Retarded, 1983-84; speech therapist St. Louis Pub. Schs., 1984—; Judvine Ctr. for Autistic Children Tng., 1992; speech/lang. therapist St. Louis Pub. Schs./Autism Program, 1992-93; speech/lang. therapist Michael Sch. Medically Fragile and Multiply Handicapped St. Louis Pub. Schs., 1993—; speech, lang. therapist St. Louis Pub. Schs./Michael Sch. for Medically Fragile and Multiply Handicapped, 1993—; ednl. cons. program devel. Mo. Coalition for Environ., St. Louis, Columbia, Kansas City, 1990—; cons., trainer in puppetry Kids on the Block, St. Louis Pub. Schs., 1988—; vol. grant writer West End Restoration Corp. Author, creator transition curriculum: Consultative Resource Program, 1989; creator puppet program: Save Our Astonishing Plantet, 1990; ednl. cons. program devel. young St. Louis audiences (adapted program for severe to profoundly handicapped children "Arabian Nights", 1994; contbr. artist St. Louis Internat. Jazz Mus.; vol. grant writer West End Restoration Corp. Educator, lobbyist Coalition for the Environ., St. Louis, 1990; activist, lobbyist Housing Now, St. Louis, 1989; foster paranet Christian Children's Fund, 1986—; activist Habitat for Humanity Internat., 1994—; mem., fundraiser Gateway I Have a Dream Found., 1995—; mem. nat. steering com. (hon.) Pres. Clinton's Re-election, 1995; vol. grant writer West End Restoration Corp.; mem. Emily's List. Mem. AAUW, Coun. Exceptional Children (state rep. Mo. divsn. for children with communicative disorders 1988-89, presenter nat. conv. 1989), Internat. Platform Assn., Am. Fedn. Tchrs. (bldg. rep. 1992), Nat. Arbor Day Found., Nat. Parks and Conservation Assn., Nat. Women's Polit. Caucus, Mo. Assn. for Augmentative Comm. Systems, Met. St. Louis Women's Polit. Caucus, Emily's List, Am. Med. Writers Assn., Soc. for Technical Communication. Democrat. Home: 9823 Lullaby Ln Saint Louis MO 63114-2510

MOLLOY, CHRISTOPHER JOHN, molecular cell biologist, pharmacist; b. N.Y.C., Feb. 18, 1954; s. James Francis and Dorothy Jean (Russell) M. BS in Pharmacy, Rutgers U., 1977, PhD in Pharmacology-Toxicology, 1987. Registered pharmacist, N.J. Pharmacist W.M. Weinstein Prescriptions, Livingston, N.J., 1977-81; teaching asst. Rutgers Coll. of Pharmacy, Piscataway, N.J., 1982-85; grad. asst. Rutgers U., Piscataway, 1985-86; postdoctoral fellow Nat. Cancer Inst., NIH, Bethesda, Md., 1986-90; sr. rsch. investigator Bristol-Myers Squibb Pharm. Rsch. Inst., Princeton, N.J., 1990—; adj. asst. prof. Univ. Med. and Dentistry N.J.-Robert Wood Johnson Med. Sch., Piscataway, N.J., 1992—; Please note that we do not give dates in CER section. Reviewer Cancer Rsch., 1987—, Carcinogenesis, 1988—, Jour. Molecular Cell Cardiology, 1995—, Molecular Pharmacology, 1994—; contbr. articles to Nature, Molecular and Cellular Biology, Proc. NAS, Jour. Biol. Chemistry, Jour. Clin. Investigation. Recipient Grad. fellowship award Soc. of Cosmetic Chemists, 1983, Biotech. fellowship Nat. Cancer Inst., Bethesda, Md., 1986, Visiting fellowship, Spanish Health Ministry, Madrid, 1990, Selected Reference (Hot Paper) The Scientist Newspaper, Phila., 1991. Mem. AAAS, Am. Heart Assn., Am. Soc. Biochem. and Molecular Biology, N.Y. Acad. Scis. Am. Assn. Cancer Rsch. N.Am. Vascular Biology Orgn., Sigma Xi. Office: Bristol Myers Squibb PO Box 4000 Princeton NJ 08543-4000

MOLNAR, ALBERT C., physician; b. Budapest, Hungary, Oct. 15, 1942. BA, Western Res. U., 1965; MD, Ohio State U., 1969. Diplomate Am. Bd. Phys. Medicine and Rehab. Commd. 2d lt. U.S. Army, 1968, advanced through grades to col., 1993, ret., 1995; pvt. practice phys. medicine and rehab. Austin, Tex., 1995—. Fellow Fed. Health Care Execs.; mem. Am. Acad. Phys. Medicine and Rehab., Am. Assn. Electrodiagnostic Medicine. Home: Rte 1 Box 141D Elgin TX 78621 Office: Plaza St David Ste 411 1015 E 32d St Austin TX 78705-2701

MOLOFF, ALAN LAWRENCE, army officer, physician; b. Bklyn., Sept. 29, 1954; s. Louis Rubin and Muriel (Trabeck) M. BS, U. Vt., 1976; DO, U. N.J., 1983; MPH, Harvard U., 1988; student, U.S. Army Command/Gen. Staff Course, 1994-95. Diplomate Am. Bd. Preventive Medicine; bd. cert. aerospace medicine, undersea medicine. Commd. platoon leader U.S. Army, 1976, advanced through grades to lt. col., 1993; intern Fitzsimons Army Med. Ctr., Aurora, Colo., 1983-84; med. officer 1st Battalion 10th Spl. Forces Group, Bad Tolz, Fed. Republic of Germany, 1984-87; resident in aerospace medicine Harvard U., Boston, 1987-89; Chief Spl. Ops. Forces Divsn. Acad. Health Scis., San Antonio, 1989-92; Command Surgeon Spl. Forces Command, Ft. Bragg, N.C., 1992-93, Dep. Surgeon, 1993-94; with Command and Gen. Staff Coll. U.S. Army, 1994-95; Dep. Surgeon 30th Med. Brigade, Heidelberg, Germany, 1995-96; USAREUR FWO surgeon 30th Med. Brigade, Heidleberg, Germany, 1996—; lectr. advanced trauma life support NOAA, Aerospace Med. Assn. Contbr. articles to profl. jours. Active in civic activities. Decorated Meritorious Svc. medal with 2 oak leaf clusters, Joint Svc. Commendation medal, S.W. Asian Svc. medal, Army Commendation medal with oak leaf cluster, Armed Forces Svc. medal, NATO medal, German Paratrooper badge, Pathfinder badge, Expert Field Med. badge, Order of Mil. Med. Merit, Master Parachutist award. Fellow Am. Coll. Preventive Medicine, Aerospace Med. Assn. (assoc.); mem. Am. Osteo. Assn., Aerospace Med. Assn., Assn. Mil. Surgeons of U.S., Assn. Mil. Osteo Physicians and Surgeons, Soc. U.S. Army Flight Surgeons (life). Home: 67 Im Emmertsgrund, Emmertsgrund Germany Office: HHC 30th Med BDE Dep Surgeon Unit 29218 Box 246 APO AE 09102

MOLONEY, THOMAS WALTER, consulting firm executive; b. N.Y.C., Feb. 8, 1946; s. Thomas Walter and Anne (Heney) M. BA, Colgate U., 1967; MA, Columbia U., 1970, MPH, 1973, MBA, 1975. Program dir. Nat. Ctr. for Deaf-Blind, New Hyde Park, N.Y., 1971-72; spl. asst. to dir. and dean N.Y. Hosp., N.Y.C., 1973-74; asst. v.p. Robert Wood Johnson Found., 1975-80; sr. v.p. The Commonwealth Fund, N.Y.C., 1980-92; dir. pub. policy and health programs The Inst. for Future, 1992—; vis. lectr. Princeton (N.J.) U., 1975-80; bd. dirs. Grantmakers in Health, N.Y.C., 1984—, chmn. bd., 1984-88; mem. health adv. com. GAO, 1987—; mem. health adv. coun. Johns Hopkins U. Sch., Hygiene and Pub. Health, Balt., 1989-91; bd. dirs. Found. Health Svcs. Rsch., Washington, 1985-92; mem. bd. visitors Med. Sch., U. Calif. at Davis, 1988—; mem. vis. com. Grad. Sch. Mgmt. and Urban Policy New Sch. for Social Rsch., N.Y.C., 1988-92; mem. Nat. Bd. Examiners, 1986-90; mem. sr. adv. bd. global leadership program U. Mich. Grad. Sch. Bus., Ann Arbor, 1988—; mem. pres. com. The N.Y. Acad. Scis., 1987-90; policy scholar The Eisenhower Ctr. Columbia U., N.Y.C., 1992—, Inst. Health Policy Studies U. Calif., San Francisco, 1992—. Author books; editor: New Approaches to the Medicaid Crisis, 1983; contbr. articles to profl. jours. bd. dirs. New Eng. Med. Ctr., Boston, 1982-89. Policy scholar Inst. Health Policy Studies U. Calif., San Francisco, 1992—, Eisenhower Ctr. Columbia U., 1992—. Fellow AAAS; mem. Inst. Medicine, Nat. Acad. Scis., Nat. Acad. Social Ins., N.Y. Acad. Medicine, N.Y. Acad. Scis. (pres'. com. 1987-90). Home: 72 Norwood Ave Montclair NJ 07043-1935 Office: Inst for the Future Fl 8 111 Fifth Ave New York NY 10003

MOMTAHENI, DAVID M., oral and maxillofacial surgeon, academician, clinician; b. Tehran, Iran, Dec. 1, 1950; came to U.S., 1975; m. Esther Marry Michael, May 15, 1982; children: Adam, Ashley. DMD, Nat. U. Iran, Tehran, 1975; cert. in pathology, Harvard U., 1978; cert. in maxillofacial surgery, Albert Einstein Coll. Medicine, 1982. Diplomate Am. Bd. Oral Maxillofacial Surgery. Asst. prof. Albert Einstein Coll. of Medicine, N.Y.C., 1983-86; chief resident Montefiore Hosp. and Med. Ctr., N.Y.C., 1980-81; mem. surg. team Cranio Facial Ctr., asst. attending Albert Einstein Coll. of Medicine, N.Y.C., 1983—; dir. Temporomandibular Joint Clinic, TMJ Montefiore Med. Ctr., N.Y.C., 1984-90; assoc. clin. prof. Columbia U., N.Y.C., 1986—; pvt. practice N.Y.C., 1986—; affiliate Albert Einstein Coll. Hosp., Montefiore Hosp. and Med. Ctr., Columbia Presbyn. Med. Ctr., Beth Israel, Cabrini Hosp.; surg. cons. Profl. Dental Reviewer, 1988-91;. Coauthor: (chpt.) Gastrointestinal Disorders of the Elderly, 1984; contbr. articles to profl. jours. Mem. Rep., 1986. Nat. U. of Iran scholar, 1975-78. Fellow Am. Assn. Oral and Maxillofacial Surgeons; mem. ADA, Internat. Soc. Plastic and Reconstructive Surgery, N.Y. Acad. Dentistry, Am. Soc. Laser in Dentistry (founder, past pres.), Acad. of Osseointegration, Am. Soc. Dental Anesthesillogy, 1st Dental Soc., Ea. Dental Soc. N.Y. (v.p.), Montefiore Med. Ctr. Alumni Assn., Harvard U. Dental Alumni Assn., Tufts U. Dental Alumni Assn. Republican. Roman Catholic. Office: 630 Fifth Ave New York NY 10111-0001

MONAGHAN, MICHAEL SEAN, pharmacist. PharmD, Creighton Univ., 1989. Diplomate Am. Bd. Pharmacy, Pharmacotherapy Specialist. Asst. prof. pharmacy Univ. Ark. Medical Scis., Little Rock, Ark., 1990-96, assoc. prof. pharmacy practice, 1996; assoc. prof. pharmacy Creighton Univ., Omaha, Nebr., 1996—; cons., mem. Pharmacy & Therapeutics com. Pharmacy Assoc., Inc., Litte Rock, 1994—. Contbr. articles to profl. jours. Bd. dirs. Ark. Affiliate of Am. Diabetes Assn., 1995—. Recipient numerous grants. Mem. Ark Assn. Hosp. Pharmacists, Ark. Pharmacists Assn., Am. Assn. Coll. Pharmacy, Am. Coll. Clinical Pharmacy (assoc.), Ohio Pharmacists Assn., Am. Soc. Health-System Pharmacists, Kappa Psi. Office: Creighton Univ Sch of Pharm and Health 2500 California Plz Omaha NE 68178

MONAGHAN, W(ILLIAM) PATRICK, immunohematologist, retired naval officer, health educator, consultant; b. Ashtabula, Ohio, June 24, 1944; s. Paul E. and June E. (Sober) M. m. Mary Lou Gustafson, Mar. 15, 1976; children: Ian Patrick, Erin Kelly. BS, Old Dominion U., Va., 1963; MS in Biology, Bowling Green State U., Va., 1972, PhD, 1975. Enlisted U.S. Navy, 1961, commd. ensign Med. Service Corps, 1969, advanced through grades to comdr., 1983; staff med. technologist officer Nat. Naval Med. Ctr., Bethesda, Md., 1969; clin. lab. and blood bank officer USS Sanctuary (AH-17), S. Vietnam, 1969-70; clin. lab. officer Naval Med. Ctr., Charleston, S.C., 1970-72; blood bank fellow U.S. Army Med. Rsch. Lab., Ft. Knox, Ky., 1972-73; head blood bank Nat. Naval Med. Ctr., 1975-85, faculty and course dir. for immunohematology med. tech., 1976-84, dir. blood bank, 1976-84; asst. prof. pathology George Washington U. Sch. Medicine, Washington, 1976-83, assoc. prof., 1983-88; mem. faculty Walter Reed Army Med. Ctr., Washington, 1976-88; dep. asst. dean grad. and continuing edn. Uniformed Svcs. U. of Health Sci., Washington, 1984-88, ret., 1988; prof. Grad. Sch. Nursing Uniformed Svcs. U. of Health Sci., Washington; v.p. Met. Washington Blood Banks, 1976-81, ex officio mem. bd. dirs. 1981-87; cons. D.C. chpt. Hemophiliac Found., 1977-78; spl. USN rep. Am. Soc. Med. Tech., 1976-88; dir. N.E. area blood system Navy Blood Program, 1978-88; mem. tri-service blood bank com. Dept. Def. Blood Program, 1978-88; faculty and program adv. com. ARC, Washington, 1978-84, Johns Hopkins Med. Sch., Balt., 1978-85; faculty U. Tenn. Center for Health Scis., Memphis, 1978, U. Ill. Sch. Medicine, Peoria, 1978-79, Grad. Sch. Nursing Uniformed Svcs. U. of Health Scis., Bethesda, Md.; guest lectr. NIH Blood Bank, 1978-90; adj. assoc. prof. Bowling Green State U., Ohio, 1981-89; bd. dirs. Exam, Inc., Rockville, Md. Navy editor Procs. Armed Forces Med. Lab. Scientists, 1976, 79. 80, editor-in-chief, 1982-85; assoc. editor Am. Jour. Med. Tech., 1978-88, Jour. Allied Health; Navy editor History of the Blood Program of the U.S. Mil. Svcs. in Vietnam and S.E. Asisa, 1976; contbr. articles to profl. jours.. Active, Big Bros., 1976-85. Decorated numerous combat and svc. medals; USN grantee, 1977-79. Mem. Am. Soc. Med. Technologists (chmn. immunohematology task group 1976), Am. Blood Commn. (task force 1976, regionalization), Am. Assn. Blood Banks (sci. assembly 1976—, adminstrv. sect. 1976—, blood component therapy com. 1977-79, edn. com. 1976-83), AAAS, Am. Soc. Clin. Pathologists, Soc. Mil. Surgeons, Naval Inst., Sigma Xi, others. Home: 14116 Parkvale Rd Rockville MD 20853-2526 Office: Uniformed Svcs U Health Sci Grad Sch Nursing 11426 Rockville Pike #400B Rockville MD 20852

MONAHAN, EDWARD JOSEPH, III, orthodontist; b. Great Falls, Mont., July 31, 1942; s. Edward Joseph and Helen Jeanette (Winter) M.; m. Saundra Louise Yost, June 17, 1967; children: Heather Kataryn, Shannon Kelly. DDS, U. of Minn., Mpls., 1967; MSD, U. of Minn., 1972. Dentist USAF, Ankara, Turkey, 1968-70; orthodontic resident U. of Minn., Mpls., 1970-72; orthodontist Alexandria, Minn., 1972—. Ch. coun. pres. First Luth. Ch., 1979-82. With USAF, 1967-70. Mem. Hon. Dental Soc., W. Cent. Dist. Soc., Minn. Dental Assn., ADA. Minn. Assn. of Orthodontists, Midwestern Soc. of Orthodontists, Am. Assn. of Orthodontists, Rotary. Home: 1724 E Lake Geneva Rd NE Alexandria MN 56308-7965 Office: 1106 Broadway St Alexandria MN 56308-2530

MONAHAN, GERGORY ROBERT, human services administrator; b. N.Y.C., Apr. 25, 1952; s. James Vincent and Julia Marie (Myles) M. BS, Iona Coll., 1987; MA, St. Joseph's Sem., 1992. Counselor Transport Worker's Union H.B.T., N.Y.C., 1989—. Home: 13 Bolton Gardens Bronxville NY 10708

MONCHER, DANIEL JOSEPH, hospital executive, accountant; b. Detroit, Nov. 3, 1960; s. James Charles and Elizabeth Ann (Smilnak) M.; m. Mary Kathryn Kasten, June 2, 1984; children: Nicholas Daniel, Benjamin Charles. BS in Bus., Miami U., Oxford, Ohio, 1982; MBA, Tiffin (Ohio) U., 1994. CPA, Ohio. Mgr. audit staff Ernst & Whinney, Toledo, 1982-86; dir. fin. Mercy Hosp., Toledo, 1986-88; v.p. fin., chief fin. officer Mercy Hosps., Tiffin and Willard, Ohio, 1988—, interim pres., CEO, 1993. Trustee Dental Dispensary N.W. Ohio, 1987-88, Tiffin Health Found., 1989—, Am. Heart Assn., Seneca County Div., 1991—, Mercy Tiffin Physician Hosp. Orgn., 1993—. Mem. AICPAs, Ohio Soc. CPAs, Healthcare Execs., Soc. for Healthcare Planning and Mktg. (sect. for managed care), Healthcare Execs. of N.W. Ohio, Am. Acad. Med. Adminstrs., Healthcare Fin. Mgmt. Assn., Am. Coll. Healthcare Execs., Evans Scholars Found. (par Club 1982—). Roman Catholic. Office: Mercy Hosp 485 W Market St Tiffin OH 44883-2611

MONCMAN, MICHAEL-GERARD JOSEPH, neurosurgeon; b. Allentown, Pa., Oct. 25, 1952; s. Anna Marie Moncman; m. Patricia A. Tribeck, Sept. 5, 1993; children: Alexis, Ryan. BS in Biology, Allentown Coll. St. Francis, 1974; MS in Biology, Cath. U. Am., 1977; DO, Phila. Coll. Osteo. Medicine, 1981, MS in Neurosurgery, 1987. Tchg. asst., tchg. fellow Cath. U. Am., Washington, 1974-77; intern, adminstrv. intern Allentown Osteo. Med. Ctr., 1981-82, mem. nursing insvc. staff, 1981-82; resident in gen. surgery Dr.'s Hosp., Columbus, Ohio, 1982-83; resident in neurologic surgery Met. Hosp., Phila., 1983-87, chief house officer, chief resident neurosurgery, 1986-87; dir. med. staff edn. Rehab. Hosp. of Altoona, Pa., 1988—; chmn. adj. faculty mem. neurosurgery Ohio U. Coll. Osteo. Medicine, Athens, 1983-87; mem. utilization rev. com., Altoona Hosp., 1994, chmn., 1994—, mem. exec. com., 1994, chmn. utilization osteopathic concepts com. 1990-94; mem. courtesy staff HealthSouth Rehab. Hosp. Mercy Hosp., Clearfield Hosp., Nason Hosp., Meml. Hosp. of Bedford County. Contbr. articles to profl. publs. Fellow Am. Coll. Osteo. Surgeons (sec.-treas. neurologic surgeons sect. 1990-92, mem. ethics com. 1990-91, mem. ednl. com. 1992-93, chmn. neurologic surgeons sect. 1994); mem. AMA, Am. Osteo. Assn., Pa. Osteo. Med. Assn., Pa. Med. Soc., Cleve. Clinic Found. (affiliate physician), Blair County Med. Soc., Am. Acad. Pain Mgmt., Phila. Coll. Osteo. Medicine Alumni Assn. (life), Phi Sigma Gamma. Office: 1701 12th Ave Ste F Altoona PA 16601

MONDEN, MORITO, surgeon, educator; b. Fukuyama, Hiroshima-Ken, Japan, Aug. 8, 1945; s. Kazuo and Ayako Monden; m. Yasuko Matsumoto, Apr. 12, 1975; children: Masayuki, Kazuyuki. MD, Osaka (Japan) U., 1970, PhD, 1979. Mem. surg. staff Osaka U. Hosp., 1973-79, lectr., 1979-87, asst. prof., 1987-90, assoc. prof., vice chmn. dept. surgery, 1990-94, prof., chmn. dept. surgery, 1994—; vis. fellow Meml. Sloan-Kettering, N.Y.C., 1979-81. Contbr. articles to profl. jours. Mem. Internat. Soc. Surgery, N.Y. Acad. Scis., Transplantation Soc. Home: 4-3-4 Midoricho, Ashiya Hyogo 659, Japan Office: Osaka U Med Sch Dept Surgery, 2-2 Yamadaoka, Suita Osaka 565, Japan

MONDSCHEIN, LAWRENCE GEOFFREY, medical products executive; b. New Brunswick, N.J., Nov. 3, 1957; s. Harold and Florence (Kaplovsky) M.; m. Ellen Laurie Hirschhorn, Aug. 17, 1995. BS, Rutgers U., 1980, MLS, 1985, PhD, 1988. Regulatory asst. Janssen Pharmaceutica, Piscataway, N.J., 1983-84, database adminstr., 1984-86; rsch. adminstr. Janssen Rsch. Found., Piscataway, 1986-89; mgr. chem. info. Johnson & Johnson World Hdqrs., New Brunswick, N.J., 1989—; mem. planning panel on toxicology & environ. health Nat. Libr. Medicine, Bethesda, Md., 1992. Contbr. articles to profl. jours. Trustee Essex Skating Club of N.J., sec., 1984-88, v.p., 1988-90, pres., 1990-93. Mem. U.S. Figure Skating Assn. (nat. juege 1992—, sectional vice chmn. for judges 1993-95, bd. dirs. 1995—), Am. Soc. for Info. Sci. Office: Johnson & Johnson 1 Johnson & Johnson New Brunswick NJ 08933

MONEK, DONNA MARIE, pharmacist; b. New Brunswick, N.J., Aug. 9, 1947; d. James Frank and Angeline Eleanor (Marzella) M. BS, Phila. Coll. of Pharmacy, 1970; MBA, Fairleigh Dickinson U., East Rutherford, N.J., 1976. Reg. pharmacist, N.J. Staff pharmacist Freehold (N.J.) Area Hosp., 1971-72, dir. pharmacy, 1972-76; dir. pharmacy Rahway (N.J.) Hosp., 1976—; cons. home health care intravenous therapy, Rahway, N.J., 1985. Rep. committeewoman Middlesex County, 1972-86, 92—; mem. Bd. Health, Metuchen, N.J., 1987—. Mem. Am. Soc. Hosp. Pharmacists, N.J. Soc. Hosp. Pharmacists, N.J. Hosp. Assn. (group purchasing 1980, chairperson profl. stds. 1989-90, vice chairperson state pharmacy com. 1990-91, chairperson 1992), Am. Pharm. Assn., N.J. Pharm. Assn., Metuchen Rep. Club, Cranford Dramatic Club, Kappa Epsilon. Roman Catholic. Office: Rahway Hosp 865 Stone St Rahway NJ 07065-2797

MONETA, GIOVANNI BATTISTA, research educator; b. Genoa, Italy, Oct. 4, 1958; s. Umberto and Agnese Moneta; m. Satu Synnöve Keskonen. Degree, U. Padua, 1983; MA, U. Chgo., 1990, PhD, 1990. Assoc. rschr. Northwestern U., Chgo., 1987-88; rsch. fellow U. Helsinki, 1989; rschr. Finnish Inst. Occupational Health, Helsinki, 1989-93, INSERM, Paris, 1993-94, EHESS, Paris, 1994-96; assoc. prof. U. Padua, Italy, 1996—; cons. in edn. and tng. NIVA, Helsinki, 1989-93. Recipient Volvo award in clin. scis. ISSLS, 1991. Home: 7 Rue du Banquier, 75013 Paris France

MONEY, JOHN WILLIAM, psychologist; b. Morrinsville, N.Z., July 8, 1921; came to U.S., 1947, naturalized, 1962; s. Frank and Ruth (Read) M. MA with honors, Victoria U. Coll., N.Z., 1943; postgrad., U. Pitts., 1947; PhD, Harvard U., 1952; DHL (hon.), Hofstra U., 1992. Jr. lectr. philosophy and psychology U. Otago, N.Z., 1945-47; part-time vis. lectr. Bryn Mawr Coll., Pa., 1952-53; mem. faculty Johns Hopkins U., 1951—, prof. med. psychology, 1972-86, assoc. prof. pediatrics, 1959-86, prof. emeritus med. psychology and pediatrics, 1986—; psychologist Johns Hopkins Hosp., 1955—, founder psychohormonal research unit, 1951, founding mem. gender identity com., 1966—; vis. prof. pediats. Albert Einstein Coll. Medicine, 1969, U. Nebr. Coll. Medicine, 1972; vis. prof. endocrinology Harvard U., 1970; vis. prof. ob-gyn. U. Conn., 1975; Rachford lectr. Children's Hosp., Cin., 1969; bd. dirs. Sex Info. and Edn. Coun. U.S., 1965-68, Neighborhood Family Planning Ctr., 1970-82; mem. task force homosexuality NIMH, 1967-69; mem. study sect. devel. and behavioral scis. NIH, 1970-74; mem. task force on nomenclature Am. Psychiat. Assn., 1977-79, 85-87; pres. Am. Found. Gender and Genital Medicine and Sci., 1978—; bd. advisors Elysium Inst., 1980—; mem. adv. bd. Internat. Coun. Sex. Edn. and Parenthood, 1981—; mem. external com. for rev. of Inst. for Sex Rsch., Ind. U., 1980; mem. sci. adv. bd. The Kinsey Inst. for Rsch. in Sex, Gender and Reprodn., 1982—; hon. chmn. internat. adv. bd. Nat. Inst. Rsch. in Sex Edn., Counseling and Therapy, 1991; Kan Tongpo vis. prof. dept. psychiatry U. Hong Kong, 1994. Mem. editl. bd. numerous jours.; field editor Medicine and Law: an Internat. Jour., 1982—. Recipient Hofheimer prize Am. Psychiat. Assn., 1956, Gold medal Children's Hosp., Phila., 1966, citation Am. Urol. Assn., 1975, Harry Benjamin medal of honor Erickson Ednl. Found., 1976, Outstanding Contbn. award Md. Psychol. Assn., 1976, Lindemann lectr. pediatrics Cornell U., 1983, Bernadine Disting. lectr. U. Mo., 1985, Maurice W. Laufer Meml. lectr. Bradley Hosp. and Brown U., 1986, Disting. Scholar award Harry Benjamin Internat. Gender Dysphoria Assn., 1987, Outstanding Rsch. Accomplishments award Nat. Inst. Child Health and Human Devel., 1987, Gloria Scientae award, 1991, Lifetime Outstanding Sci. Contbn. award Internat. Cmty. Profls. for Treatment of Sex Offenders, 1991, Richard J. Cross award Robert Wood Johnson Med. Sch., 1992, Career Achievement award N.Y. Soc. Forensic Scis., 1994, Coun. of Sex Edn. and Parenthood Internat. award, 1994; named Sexologist of Yr. Polish Acad. Sex. Sci., 1988; James McKeen Cattell fellow Am. Psychol. Soc., 1993; subject of book John Money: A Tribute (E. Coleman, editor), 1991. Fellow AAAS (life), Soc. Sci. Study Sex (charter, pres. 1974-76, award 1976, Past Pres. award 1987, Kinsey award western regional chpt. 1996), Harriet Lane Alumni Soc., Nat. Inst. Rsch. Sex Edn., Counseling and Therapy (hon.); mem. APA (master lectr. 1975, Disting. Sci. award 1985), Deutsche Gesellschaft für Sexualforschung, Internat. Orgn. Study Human Devel., Soc. Pediat. Psychology, Lawson Wilkins Pediat. Endocrine Soc. (founder), Am. Assn. Sex Educators, Counselors and Therapists (hon. mem., awards 1976, 85), European Soc. Pediat. Endocrinology (corr.), Internat. Acad. Sex Rsch. (charter, award 1991), Assn. Sexologists (life), Columbian Sexol. Soc. (hon.), Internat. Soc. Psychoneuroendocrinology, N.Y. Acad. Scis., Md. Soc. Med. Rsch., Internat. Coll. Pediats., Czechoslovak Sexology Soc. (hon., mem. internat. adv. bd. 1995), New Zealand Soc. on Sexology (hon., life), Sociedad Brasileira de Sexologia (hon.), Sociedad Andaluza de Sexologia (hon.), Can. Sex Rsch. Forum (hon.), Asian Fedn. for Sexology (hon.), Assn. de Especialistas en Sexologia (hon.). Home: 2104 E Madison St Baltimore MD 21205-2337 Office: Johns Hopkins Hosp Baltimore MD 21205

MONGAN, JAMES JOHN, physician, hospital administrator; b. San Francisco, Ca., Apr. 10, 1942; s. Martin and Audrey Vera (Cunningham) M.; m. Jean Trotter Holmes, Apr. 22, 1972; children—John Holmes, Sarah Holmes. Student, U. Calif., Berkeley, 1959-62; BA, Stanford U., 1963, MD, 1967. Intern Kaiser Found. Hosp., San Francisco, 1967-68; med. officer USPHS, Denver, 1968-70; profl. staff mem. U.S. Senate Fin. Com., Washington, 1970-77; dep. asst. sec. for health HEW, Washington, 1977-79; assoc. dir. human resources Domestic Policy Staff, White House, 1979-81; asst. surgeon gen. USPHS, 1979-81; exec. dir. Truman Med. Center, U. Mo., Kansas City, 1981—; dean sch. medicine U. Mo., Kansas City, 1987-96; pres., COO Mass. Gen. Hosp., 1996—; prof. medicine Kansas City Sch. Medicine U. Mo.; prof. in healthcare adminstrn. Kansas City Sch. Bus. and Pub. Adminstrn. U. Mo.; mem. health adv. com. GAO. Commr. Dept. Vets. Affairs Commn. on Future Structure of Vets. Health Care, 1990-91; mem. Pew Health Profesions Commn., Kaiser commn. on Future of Medicaid, Joint Commn. Users Adv. Group; trustee Pembroke Hills Sch., Kansas City, Mo.; bd. dirs. Midwest Rsch. Ins., Kansas City, Mo. Med. officer USPHS, 1968-70, asst. surgeon gen., 1979-81; trustee Kaiser Family Found.; chmn. Commonwealth Fund Health Adv. Com. Mem. NAS (Inst. Medicine), Am. Hosp. Assn. (trustee 1988-91), Am. Assn. Teaching Hosps. (bd. dirs. coun. teaching hosps. 1984-90). Home: 831 Westover Rd Kansas City MO 64113-1121 Office: Massachusetts General Hospital 32 Fruit St Boston MA 02114*

MONHEIT, ALAN GOODMAN, obstetrician, gynecologist; b. Phila., Apr. 5, 1949; s. Richard S. and Jane G. Monheit; m. Deborah Monheit; children: Robin, Jeffrey, Daniel. BSc, Muhlenberg Coll., 1971; MD, U. Pa., 1975. Intern U. Calif., San Diego, 1975-76, resident physician dept. ob-gyn., 1975-79, fellow maternal/fetal medicine, 1979-81; attending physician/clin. assoc. prof. SUNY, Stony Brook, 1981—; tchr. medicine, specialist in high risk pregnancy SUNY, Stony Brook, 1981—. Contbr. articles to profl. jours. Asst. coach Three Village Soccer Club, Stony Brook, 1991. Recipient Faculty Teaching award Dept. Ob-Gyn., SUNY, Stony Brook, 1982, 88. Mem. Am. Coll. Ob-Gyn., Assn. Profs. Ob-Gyn., Soc. Perinatal Obstetricians (poster prize 1987), L.I. Perinatal Soc., Suffolk County Ob-Gyn. Soc., Phi Beta Kappa. Office: SUNY Dept Ob-Gyn HSC T-9 Stony Brook NY 11794

MONISTERE, CAROLYN ALLEN, medical technologist; b. Jackson, Miss., June 9, 1967; d. Billy Benson and Viola Bernice (Oliver) Allen; m. Timothy Wayne Monistere, Aug. 7, 1993. AAS, Miss. Delta C.C., 1989. Lab. generalist Delta Regional Med. Ctr., Greenville, Miss., 1989-93, 93—, Terrebonne Gen. Med. Ctr., Houma, La., 1992, Chicot Meml. Hosp., Lake Village, Ark., 1992—, Crittenden Meml. Hosp., West Memphis, Ark., 1993; paramed. examiner EMSI, Jackson, Miss., 1995—. Republican. Mem. Assembly of God Ch. Home: 194 Primrose St Greenville MS 38701

MONJAN, ANDREW ARTHUR, health science administrator; b. N.Y.C., Feb. 9, 1935; s. Victor Momjian and Sonia (Sherinian) Dardarian; m. Susan Vollenweider, July 1961 (div. Nov. 1965); m. Usha Bose, Aug. 14, 1969; children: Matthew, Vanessa. BSc, Rensselaer Poly. Inst., 1960; PhD, U. Rochester, 1965; MPH, Johns Hopkins U., 1970. Rsch. asst. Sterling-Winthrop Rsch. Inst., Rensselaer, N.Y., 1960; USPHS rsch. fellow Ctr. for Brain Rsch. U. Rochester, N.Y., 1964-66; asst. prof. depts. psychology and physiology U. Western Ont., London, Can., 1966-69; from asst. prof. to assoc. prof. dept. epidemiology Sch. Hygiene and Pub. Health Johns Hopkins U., Balt., 1971-83; expert epidemiology extramural programs br. NIH, Bethesda, Md., 1983-85; chief neurobiology/immunology programs physiology aging br. NIH, Bethesda, 1985-87, acting assoc. dir., 1987, chief neurobiology, acting chief neuropsychology brs., 1987—; exec. sec. Nat. Commn. on Sleep Disorders Rsch., 1990-92; presenter in field. Contbr. articles to profl. jours. N.Y. State Regents scholar, 1955-59; N.Y. State Regents Grad. Tchg. fellow, 1960-62, USPHS rsch. fellow, 1962-64, 64-66. Mem. Soc. for Neurosci., Sigma Xi. Office: Nat Inst Aging Ste 30307 7201 Wisconsin Ave MSC 9205 Bethesda MD 20892-9205

MONLUX, ANDREW W., educator, veterinarian; b. Algona, Iowa, Jan. 29, 1920; s. Delos David and Elvira Ulrica (Seastream) M.; m. Jean Eleanor Hauser, Aug. 20, 1950; children—Roy David, Laura Joan. D.V.M., Iowa State U., 1942, M.S., 1947; Ph.D., George Washington U., 1951. Pvt. practice Woden, Iowa, 1942; asst. vet. hygiene Iowa State U., 1946-48; Am. Vet. Med. Assn. fellow Armed Forces Inst. Pathology, Washington, 1948-51; veterinarian USDA, 1951-56; prof. vet. pathology, chmn. dept. Coll. Vet. Medicine, Okla. State U., Stillwater, 1956-72, Regents prof. vet. pathology, 1972-85, prof. emeritus, 1985—; pres. Southwest Vet. Labs., Stillwater, 1985—. Co-author: Principles of Veterinary Pathology, 7th edit, 1965, Atlas of Meat Inspection Pathology, 1972. Served to maj. AUS, 1942-46. Mem. Am., Okla. vet. med. assns., Research Workers in Animal Diseases in N.Am., Animal Disease Research Workers So. States, Vet. Cancer Soc., Sigma Xi, Phi Zeta, Phi Kappa Phi, Gamma Sigma Delta. Home: 2202 Black Oak Dr Stillwater OK 74074-2124

MONNIER, VINCENT MICHAEL, pathology educator, consultant, researcher; b. Zurich, Switzerland, Nov. 16, 1945; came to U.S., 1977; s. Marcel M. and Gilberte Monnier; m. Adele M. Marihatt, 1969; children: Gilliane, Stephanie, Camille. MD, U. Basel, Switzerland, 1972, diploma in chemistry, 1975. Diplomate Am. Bd. Clin. Pathology. Postdoctoral rsch. assoc., dept. biochemistry U. Geneva, Switzerland, 1976-77; postdoctoral rsch. assoc. Rockefeller U., N.Y.C., 1977-80, asst. prof., 1980-82; resident in clin. pathology Case Western Reserve U., Cleve., 1982-85; sr. instr. Univ. Hosps. of Cleve., 1982-85; asst. prof. pathology Case Western Reserve U., 1985-89, assoc. prof. pathology, 1989-93, prof. pathology, 1993—; mem. biol. and clin. subcom. A, Nat. Inst. on Aging, Washington, 1990-94, rsch. rev. com., Juvenile Diabetes Assn., N.Y.C., 1990-94. Author, co-author various books, contbr. articles to profl. jours. on the role of the Maillard/Glycosylation reaction in aging, diabetes, and endstage renal disease; editl. bds. Amino Acids, 1990—, Jour. Biochemistry, 1994—. Recipient Paul E. Lacy award Nat. Disease Rsch. Interchange, Phila., 1990, Nathan Shock award Nat. Inst. on Aging, Balt., 1996; recipient rsch. grants Nat. Inst. on Aging, Bethesda, Md., 1983—, Nat. Eye Inst., Bethesda, 1985—. Mem. Diabetes Assn. Greater Cleve. (trustee 1990—). Office: Case Western Reserve Univ Institute of Pathology Cleveland OH 44106

MONNINGER, ROBERT HAROLD GEORGE, ophthalmologist, educator; b. Chgo., Nov. 5, 1918; s. Louis Robert and Katherine (Lechner) M.; m. Anna Evelyn Turnen, Sept. 1, 1944; children—Carl John William, Peter Louis Philip. A.A., North Park Coll., 1939; B.S., Northwestern U., 1941, M.A., 1945; M.D., Loyola U., Chgo., 1953, Sc.D. (hon.), 1968. Diplomate Am. Bd. Cosmetic Plastic Surgery. Intern St. Francis Hosp., Evanston, Ill., 1953-54; resident Presbyterian-St. Luke's, U. Ill. Research and Eye, Va. hosps., 1954-57; mem. leadership council Ravenswood Hosp. Med. Ctr.; instr. chemistry Lake Forest Coll., Ill., 1946-47; instr. biochemistry, physiology Loyola U. Dental Sch., 1948-49; clin. assoc. prof. ophthalmology Stritch Sch. Medicine, Loyola U., Maywood, Ill., 1957-72; practice medicine specializing in ophthalmology Lake Forest, 1957—; clin. prof. ophthalmology Finch U. Health Scis./Chgo. Med. Sch.; guest lectr. numerous univs. med. ctrs. U.S., Can., Europe, Central and S.Am., Orient; resident lectr. Klinikum der Goethe-Universitat, Fed. Republic Germany, 1981; mem. panel Nat. Disease and Therapeutic Index; cons. Draize eye toxicity test revision HEW, cons. research pharm. cos. Nat. Assoc. Smithsonian Instn.; bd. dirs. Eye Rehab. and Research Found.; postgrad. faculty Internat. Glaucoma Congress; lectr. Hopital Dieu, Paris; lectr. postgrad. courses for developing nations physicians WHO; life mem. Postgrad. Sch. Medicine U. Vienna; cons. Nat. Acad. Sci.; adv. bd. Madera Del Rio Found. Cons. author Textbook of Endocrinology. Editorial bd. Clin. Medicine, 1958—, EENT Digest, 1958—, Internat. Surgery, 1972—, profl. jours. Served with USMCR, 1941-44. Recipient citation Gov. Bahamas, 1960, Ophthalmic Found. award, 1963, Sci. Exhibit award Ill. State Med. Soc., 1966, Franco-Am. Meritorious citation, 1967, Paris Post No. 1 Am. Legion award, 1967, citation Pres. Mexico, 1968, Sightsaving award Bausch & Lomb, 1968, exhibit award Western Hemisphere Congress Internat. Surgeons, 1968, Research citation Japanese Soc. Ophthalmology, 1969; Barraquer Gold Medallion; Physician's Recognition award AMA, Bicentennial citation Library of Congress Registration Book; Pres.'s medal of merit; meritorious citation Gov. Ill., citation and medal Lord Mayor of Rome, also Pres. of Italy, 1981, Civic Ctr. of Evanston, Ill., 1981, commendation and citation Ill. Gen. Assembly, 1982, cert. of accomplishment Loyola U. Alumni Assn., Chgo., 1983; Catherine White Scholarship fellow, 1945-46. Fellow Internat. Coll. Surgeons (postgrad. faculty continuing edn.), Am. Coll. Angiology, Oxford Ophthal. Congress and Soc. (lectr. 1960-61), Royal Soc. Health, Internat. Acad. Cosmetic Surgery (editorial bd.), Sociedad Mexicana Ortopedia (hon.), C. Puestow Surg. Soc.; mem. AAAs, Internat. Soc. Geog. Ophthalmology (program course coordinator, lectr. ocular electrophysiology VI Internat. Congress, Rio de Janiero), Pan Am. Assn. Ophthalmology, Assn. for Research Ophthalmology, Am. Assn. Ophthalmology, Am. Soc. Contemporary Ophthalmology, Internat. Glaucoma Soc., Ill. Soc. for Med. Research, Ill. Assn. Ophthalmology, Internat. Soc. clin. electrophysiology of Vision (hon., lectr. 1978), Brazilian Soc. Ophthalmology (hon. corr.), German Ophthal. Soc., Internat. Fedn. Clin. Chemists (lectr.), Primum Forum Ophthalmologicum (lectr.), European Ophthal. Soc. (lectr.), Internat. Congress Anatomists (lectr.), Assn. des Diabetologues Francise (lectr.), German Soc. for Internal Medicine (lectr.), Met. Opera Guild, Fedn. Am. Scientists, N.Y. Acad. Scis., Ill. Acad. Scis., AAUP, Nat. Soc. Lit. and Arts, Nat. Hist. Soc., Rush Med. Sch.-Presbyn. St. Luke's Alumni Assn., Sociedad Poblana Oftalmologia (hon, silver placue, commemorative prestige lectr. 1982) (Mex.), Internat. Platform Assn., Cousteau Soc., Sigma Xi, Sigma Alpha Epsilon, Phi Beta Pi, Theta Kappa Psi.

MONOS, DIMITRIOS, medical educator, researcher. BS in Biology, U. Patras, Greece, 1975; PhD in Biochemistry and Immunology, Georgetown U., 1981. Vis. fellow lab. tumor immunology & biology Nat. Cancer Inst. NIH, Bethesda, Md., 1982-84; immunopathology fellow dept. pathology & lab. medicine U. Pa., Phila., 1984-86, rsch. assoc. immunology, 1986-88, asst. prof., 1990-96, assoc. prof., 1996—; vis. scholar dept. biochemistry & molecular biology Harvard U., 1988-90; dir. immunogenetics lab. dept. pathology Children's Hosp. Phila., 1996; lectr. in field. Editl. bd. CLin. and Diagnostic Lab. Immunology; ad hoc reviewer Cancer Rsch., Diabetes, Human Immunology, Jour. Immunology, New Eng. Jour. Medicine; contbr. articles to profl. jours. With Greek Army, 1988. Recipient New Investigator Rsch. award NIH, 1986, Rsch. award Am. Diabetes Assn., 1995; grantee NIH, 1986—, U. Pa., 1987-88, 95, Diabetes Rsch. & Edn. Found., 1990, Juvenile Diabetes Found., 1990-92, Nat. Marrow Donor Program, 1992-94, ADA, 1995-96; Fogarty Internat. fellow NIH, 1982. Mem. Am. Assn. Immunologists, Am. Soc. Histocompatibility & Immunogenetics, Acad. Clin. Lab. Physicians & Scientists, Sigma Xi. Office: Children's Hosp Phila Dept Pediats Abramson Rsch Bldg 1208B 34th St & Civic Ctr Blvd Philadelphia PA 19104

MONRO, JAMES LAWRENCE, cardiac surgeon; b. Singapore, Nov. 17, 1939; s. John Kirkpatrick and Landon Carter (Reed) M.; m. Caroline Jane Dunlop, Sept. 29, 1973; children: Charles, Rosanne, Andrew. MB BS, London Hosp. Med. Coll., 1964. Sr. house officer St. James' Hosp., London, 1966-67; registrar surg. unit London Hosp., 1967-69, sr. registrar cardiothoracic surgery, 1972-73; resident surg. officer Brompton Hosp., London, 1969; sr. registrar Green Ln Hosp., Auckland, New Zealand, 1970-72; cons. cardiac surgeon Gen. Hosp., Southampton, Eng., 1973—. Author: A Colour Atlas of Cardiac Surgery: Acquired Heart Disease, 1982, A Colour Atlas of Cardiac Surgery: Congenital Heart Disease, 1984; contbr. numerous articles to profl. pubis. Fellow Royal Coll. Surgeons; mem. European Assn. Cardiothoracic Surgery, Soc. Cardiothoracic Surgeons of Gt. Britain and Ireland, Brit. Cardiac Soc. Office: Gen Hosp, Dept Cardiac Surgery, Southampton SO16 6YD, England

MONROCHE, ANDRÉ VICTOR JACQUES, physician; b. Saumur, France, May 31, 1941; s. Maurice and Thérèse (Chevreau-Rocheron) M.; m. Bodet-Pasquier, July 8, 1966; children: Benoît, Sabine, Hélène, Matthieu. MD, Faculté de Médecine, Angers, France, 1970; Degree in Rheumatology, Faculté de Médecine, Paris, 1972. Gen practice spa medicine Villa Forestier, Aix-les-Bains, France, 1970-72; gen. practice rheumatology and sports medicine Cabinet Med., Angers, 1973—. Author: Eléments de Rheumatologie, 1975, Eau et Sport pour votre Santé, 1988, L'eau et la Forme, 1995; editor Chiron-Paris; editor-in-chief Cinésiologie, 1980, Internat. Sport Médecine Rev. Mem. Panathlon Club d'Angers (internat., founder, pres. 1990), Club of Paris (v.p. 1986, 89). Office: Cabinet Medical, 1 rue d'Alsace, 49100 Angers France

MONROE, DAVID JOHN, optometrist; b. Pitts., Nov. 29, 1962; s. Robert Joseph and Theresa Ann (Drost) M.; m. Beth Ann, Toth, Monroe, June 25, 1994. BS in Biology, U. Pitts., Johnstown, Pa., 1984; BS in Visual Scis., Pa. Coll. Optometry, 1987, D Optometry, 1989. Optometrist Sterling Vision, Pitts., 1989-92, Profl. Eyecare Assocs., Tarentum, Pa., 1992—. Mem. Nat. Fedn. for the Blind; mem. fundraising com. U. Pitts. Johnstown Alumni Assn., 1994—. Mem. Am. Optometric Assn., Pa. Optometric Assn. (active lobbyist 1994-95), Western Pa. Optometric Assn., Moose. Democrat. Roman Catholic. Home: 670 Regency Dr Pittsburgh PA 15239 Office: Profl Eyecare Assocs 214 Corbbbet St Tarentum PA 15084

MONROE, PAULA RUTH, psychologist; b. Worcester, Mass., Dec. 23, 1951; d. Dudley Benson and Gladys Elinor (Norbery) Sherry; m. David Michael Monroe, Feb. 19, 1977; 1 child, Allison. BA, U. North Tex., 1974; MA, U. Tulsa, 1980, PhD, 1990. Lic. psychologist, Okla. Asst. dean Coll. Arts and Scis. U. Tulsa, 1983-85; staff psychologist, mgr. psychol. testing ctr. Children's Med. Ctr., Tulsa, 1990-95; pvt. practice Psychosocial Enhancement Svcs., Inc., Tulsa, 1995—. Contbr. articles to profl. jours. Mem. APA.

MONTANO, GARY LYNN, emergency medicine physician; b. Denver, July 2, 1951; s. Frank E. and Suzanne M. (McLean) M.; m. Cindy K. Kam, Apr. 10, 1976; children: Matthew, Lauren, Ross. BS with honors, U. Tex., Galveston, 1976; BA, U. Tex., Austin, 1980; MD, U. N.Mex., 1993. Physician asst. Centro Familiar de Salud, Albuquerque, 1976-89, U. N.Mex., Albuquerque, 1982-93, Lovelace Med. Ctr., Albuquerque, 1986-93; med. resident Baystate Med. Ctr., Springfield, Mass., 1993—. Mem. legis. com. N.Mex. Acad. Physician Assts., Albuquerque, 1980-86; bd. dirs. Diabetes Assn. of Albuquerque, 1982; coach City League Softball, Albuquerque, 1982; chmn. Homeowners Assn., Albuquerque, 1990-93. Mem. Emergency Medicine Residents Assn., Acad. Emergency Medicine Assn., Alpha Epsilon, Alpha Omega Alpha. Roman Catholic. Office: Baystate Med Ctr Dept Emergency Medicine 759 Chestnut St Springfield MA 01199

MONTAQUILA, STEPHEN MICHAEL, optometrist; b. Providence, R.I., Sept. 11, 1969; s. Robert Frank and Madeline Ann (saccoccio) M.; m. Manuela Margrete Mauss, May 26, 1996. BS, U. R.I., 1990, The New Eng. Coll. Optometry, Boston, 1992; D Optometry, The New Eng. Coll. Optometry, Boston, 1994. Lic. optometrist, R.I., Mass. Optometrist Drs. Ferris and Assoc., Inc., Warwick, R.I., 1994—, The R.I. Eye Inst., Providence, 1994-95. Mem. Am. Optometric Assn., R.I. Optometric Assn., New Eng. Coun. of Optometrists, New Eng. Coll. Optometry Alumni Assn. Home: 39 Hamden Rd Cranston RI 02920 Office: Drs Ferris and Assoc Inc 615 Jefferson Blvd Warwick RI 02886

MONTELEONE, PATRICIA, academic dean. Dean. assoc. v.p. St. Louis u. Sch. Medicine. Office: St Louis U Sch Medicine 1402 S Grand Blvd Saint Louis MO 63104

MONTEMAYOR, JESUS SAMSON, physician; b. La Carlota City, The Philippines, May 17, 1939; came to U.S., 1972; s. Jesus Cavada and Elena Poticar (Samson) M.; m. Catalina Abellana, Sept. 26, 1971; children: Grace, Gail, Jennifer, Jessica. AA, U. San Carlos, Cebu City, The Philippines, 1958; MD, Southwestern U., Cebu City, Philippines, 1969. Adj. physician C.L. Montelibano Meml. Hosp., Bacolod City, The Philippines, 1969-70; resident physician Drs. Hosp., Bacolod City, 1970-72; resident in pathology Wyckoff Heights Hosp., Bklyn., 1975-80, emergency rm. physician, 1984-88; fellow in medicine NYU Med. Ctr.-Goldwater Meml. Hosp., Roosevelt Island, 1980-84, attending physician, 1984-95; emergency rm. physician Astoria (N.Y.) Hosp., 1983-84. Fellow Am. Coll. Internat. Physicians; mem. AAAS, Am. Geriatric Soc., Assn. Philippine Physicians in Am., Am. Acad. Home Care Physicians, Am. Med. Dirs. Assn., N.Y. Acad. Scis. Republican. Roman Catholic. Home: 1073 Hart St Brooklyn NY 11237-3405

MONTERO, CARLOS F., orthopedic surgeon; b. Buenos Aires, Argentina, Apr. 21, 1944; s. Aristides Carlos and Juana Beatriz (Chichisola) M. MD, U. Buenos Aires, 1968. Diplomate Am. Bd. Orthopedic Surgeons. Intern Nassau Hosp., Mineola, N.Y., 1968-69; resident in surgery Bronx VA Hosp., City Hosp., N.Y.C., 1969-70; resident in orthopedics Nassau County Med. Ctr., East Meadow, N.Y., 1970-73, fellow in hand surgery, 1973-74; pvt. practice hand surgery Levittown, N.Y., 1974—. Office: Nassau Orthopedic Surgeons 2920 Hempstead Tpke Levittown NY 11756

MONTES, SALLY, medical record administrator, consultant; b. Bronk, N.Y., Oct. 8, 1959; d. José and Emma (Colón) M.; m. Pablo Monserrate, June 4, 1989 (div. Dec. 1995); children: David, Eric. BS, P.R. U., 1982, postgrad. cert., 1983, MPH, 1984. Registered record adminstr. Med. record asst. Ctr. Areawide de Health, Naranjito, P.R., 1983-87; med. record dir. Pediatric Univ. Hosp., Pio Piedras, P.R., 1987-94, Correctional Health Program, Hato Rey, P.R., 1994—. Mem. AHIMA, Quality Assn. P.R., P.R. Med. Record Assn. Evangelistic. Home: Apt 905 Condo Med Ctr Plz Rio Piedras PR 00921 Office: Correctional Health Program PO Box 70184 San Juan PR 00936

MONTEVERDE, JOHN PASCUAL, internist, cardiologist; b. Manila, Mar. 8, 1948; came to U.S., 1972; s. Policarpio and Jovita Monteverde; m. Cynthia Yap, Nov. 4, 1976; children: Jay, Jon. BS, U. Santo Tomas, Manila, 1967, MD magna cum laude, 1972. Diplomate Am. Bd. Internal Medicine, Am. Bd. Cardiovasc. Disease. Resident in medicine Northwestern U., Chgo., 1973-75, fellow in cardiology, 1975-76; fellow in cardiology Cleve. Clinic, 1976-78; pvt. practice, Chgo., 1978—; chmn. cardiac rehab. St. Mary of Nazareth Hosp., Chgo., 1982-83, sr. antioplaster, 1987—, dir. cardiac catheterization lab., 1989-92, assoc. dir. critical care unit, 1993—, pres.-elect med. staff, 1991, pres. med. staff, 1992; chmn. medicine, dir. critical care Sacred Heart Hosp., Chgo., 1989; dir. ICU, dir. cardiology Norwegian Am. Hosp., Chgo., 1989—. Named Top Cardiology, ABC-TV, Chgo., 1993, award Fraternal Order Eagles, 1995; disting. fellow Northwestern U. Med. Sch. Alumni Assn., 1991. Fellow Am. Coll. Cardiology, Am. Heart Assn. (fellow coun. clin. cardiology); mem. Soc. Cardiac Angiographers, Physician Orgn. Am. (founder, pres. 1995—). Home: PO Box 4685 Oak Brook IL 60522-4685 Office: St John Heart Clinic SC 2222 W Division St Chicago IL 60622

MONTGOMERY, GARY, dentist; b. Buffalo, Oct. 14, 1957; s. Roderick Frederick and Agnes H. (Debolock) M.; m. Annegret Susanne Herrmann, Nov. 2, 1985 (div. July 17, 1994); children: Robert Frederick, Peter Erich. BSChemE cum laude, Washington U., St. Louis, 1979; DMD, Harvard U., 1984. Gen. dentist lic. practitoner clinic Sch. Dental Medicine Harvard U., Boston, 1983-84; resident in gen. dentistry U. Md. Hosp., Balt., 1984-85; pvt. practice Cleve., 1985—; mem. courtesy staff Fairview Gen. Hosp., Cleve., 1990-92; mem. courtesy staff St. Vincent Charity Hosp. and Health Ctr., Cleve., 1991-93, mem. assoc. ative staff in oral surgery, 1993-95, active med. staff in dentistry, 1995—. Recipient Community Svc. award HELP Found., 1992. Mem. ADA, Ohio Dental Assn., Cleve. Dental Soc., Alpha Lambda Delta, Tau Beta Pi. Lutheran. Home: 3900 Spencer Rd Rocky River OH 44116-3866 Office: 1148 Euclid Ave Ste 317 Cleveland OH 44115-1604

MONTGOMERY, JOHN ATTERBURY, research chemist, consultant; b. Greenville, Miss., Mar. 29, 1924; s. Daniel Cameron and Ruth (Atterbury) M.; m. Jean Kirkman, July 19, 1947; children: John Jr., Elaine Porter, Kirkman, Ruth Adrianne. AB cum laude, Vanderbilt U., 1946, MS in Organic Chemistry, 1947; PhD in Organic Chemistry, U. N.C., Chapel Hill, 1951. Research chemist So. Research Inst., Birmingham, Ala., 1952-56; dir. organic chemistry So. Research Inst., 1956-74, v.p., 1974-81, sr. v.p., dir. Kettering Meyer Lab., 1981-90, disting. scientist rsch., 1990—; exec. v.p., dir. rsch., chief exec. officer Biocryst, 1990—; adj. prof. Birmingham So. Coll., 1957-62; adj. sr. scientist U. Ala., Birmingham, 1978—; bd. dirs. Am. Assn. Cancer Research, Assn. Am. Cancer Insts.; mem. Pres. Reagan's Cancer Panel. Author over 600 rsch. papers; editor profl. books; mem. editl. bd. numerous profl. jours. Recipient T.O. Soine Meml. award U. Minn., 1979. Fellow N.Y. Acad. Scis.; mem. Am. Chem. Soc. (councilor 1971-86, recipient Herty medal 1974, So. Chemist award 1980, Burger award 1986, Edward E. Smissman Bristol-Myers Squibb Award, 1995), Am. Assn. Cancer Research (Cain Meml. award 1982), Am. Soc. Pharmacology and Exptl. Therapeutics, Internat. Soc. Heterocyclic Chemistry (adv. bd. 1982-83), Sigma Xi, Alpha Chi Sigma. Republican. Episcopalian. Clubs: Country of Birmingham, The Club (Birmingham) Lodge: Rotary. Home: 3596 Springhill Rd Birmingham AL 35223-2032 Office: So Research Inst PO Box 55305 Birmingham AL 35255-5305 also: BioCryst Pharmaceuticals 2190 Parkway Lake Dr Birmingham AL 35244-2812

MONTGOMERY, JOHN RICHARD, pediatrician, educator; b. Burnsville, Miss., Oct. 24, 1934; s. Guy Austin and Harriet Pauline (Owens) M.; m. Dottye Ann Newell, June 26, 1965; children: John Newell, Michelle Elizabeth. BS, U. Ala., 1955, MD, 1958. Intern U. Miss., Jackson, 1958-59, resident in pediatrics, 1959-60; resident in pediatrics Baylor Coll. Medicine, Houston, 1960-61, 63-64, fellow in pediatric infectious diseases and immunology, 1964-66, asst. prof. pediatrics, 1966-70, assoc. prof. pediatrics, 1970-75, prof. pediats., 1975—, chief pediatric programs U. Ala. Sch. Medicine, Huntsville, 1975-95. Served with AUS, 1961-62; Korea. Mem. Soc. Pediatric Rsch., Am. Assn. Immunologists, Infectious Diseases Soc. Am., N.Y. Acad. Scis., Am. Acad. Pediatrics (pres. Ala. chpt. 1991-93), Sigma Xi, Phi Beta Kappa. Contbr. articles to profl. jours.; assisted in devel. of germ-free environ. bubble to protect patient with no natural immunity (patient later subject of movie The Boy in The Bubble).

MONTGOMERY, PHILIP O'BRYAN, JR., pathologist; b. Dallas, Aug. 16, 1921. BS, So. Meth. U., 1942; MD, Columbia U., 1945. Diplomate Am. Bd. Pathology, Am. Bd. Clin. Pathology and Forensic Pathology. Intern Mary Imogene Bassett Hosp., Cooperstown, N.Y., 1945-46; fellow in pathology Southwestern Med. Sch., Dallas, 1950-51, asst. prof. pathology, 1953-55, assoc. prof., 1955-61, prof., 1961—, assoc. dean, 1968-70, Ashbel Smith prof. pathology, 1991—; rsch. asst. pathology and cancer rsch. Cancer Rsch. Inst. New Eng. Deaconess Hosp., Boston, 1951-52; spl. asst. to chancellor U. Tex. System, 1971-75; exec. dir. Cancer Ctr. U. Tex. Health Sci. Ctr. Dallas, 1975-89; pathologist Parkland Meml. Hosp., Dallas, 1952—, Dallas City Zoo, 1955-68; med. examiner DallasCounty, 1955-58; cons. Navarro County Meml. Hosp., Corsicana, Tex., 1952-53, McKinney (Tex.) Vets. Hosp., 1952-65, Lisbons Vets. Hosp., Dallas, 1953—, St. Paul Hosp., Dallas, 1958—, Flow Meml. Hosp., Denton, Tex., 1958-65; pathologist Tex. Children's Hosp., Dallas, 1954-55. Contbr. numerous articles to profl. jours., sci. abstracts, jours. Bd. dirs. Planned Parenthood of Dallas, 1958-63, pres., 1958-60; trustee St. Mark's Sch. Tex., 1958—, v.p., chmn. exec. com. bd. trustee, 1966-68, v.p., 1968-69, pres. 1974-76; trustee Lamplighter Sch., 1967-70; chmn. Dallas Area Libr. Planning Coun., 1970-72, Goals for Dallas Health Task Force com., 1975-76, Fleet Adm. Nimitz Mus. commn., 1979-81; mem. adv. bd. Dallas Citizens coun., chmn. health com. 1988-89; bd. dirs. Met. YMCA, 1960-63, Dallas Coun. on World Affairs, 1962-65; pres., bd. dirs. Damon Runyon, Walter Winchell Cancer Fund, 1974-79; cord. Dallas Arts Dist., 1982-95. Fellow Am. Soc. Clin. Pathologists; mem. Am. Assn. Pathologists and Bacteriologists, Am. Assn. Cancer Rsch., Internat. Acad. Pathology, Am. Acad. Forensic Scis., Soc. Exptl. Biology and Medicine, Internat. Soc. Cell Biology, Biophys. Soc., Am. Soc. Cell Biology, Am. soc. Exptl. Pathology, Tissue Culture Assn., Internat. Fedn. Med. Electronics, Profl. Group Med. Electronics of Inst. Radio Engrs., AAAS, Optical Soc. Tex. (founding), Pan-Am. Med. Assn., AMA, So. Med. Assn., Tex. Med. Assn., AAUP. Office: 5323 Harry Hines Blvd Dallas TX 75235-7200

MONTGOMERY, ROBERT RAYNOR, pharmaceutical company executive; b. Sydney, Australia, July 6, 1943; s. Robert John and Gillian Eileen (Raynor) M.; children: Natasha, Karyn. Matriculation, St. Patrick Coll., Goulburn, Australia, 1962. Chartered acct. Sr. Peat Marwick Mitchell & Co., Sydney, 1967; supervising sr. Peat Marwick Mitchell & Co., London, 1967-68; supr. Peat Marwick Mitchell & Co., N.Y.C. and Rome, 1968-69; mgr. Peat Marwick Mitchell & Co., Athens, Greece, 1969-74; sr. mgr. Peat Marwick Mitchell & Co., Brussels, 1974-77; area dir. Alcon Labs., Inc., Brussels, 1977-78; dir. internat. fin. and adminstrn. Alcon Labs., Inc., Ft. Worth, 1978-81; v.p. corp. fin. Alcon Labs., Inc., 1981-82, v.p., chief fin. officer, dir., 1982-83, sr. v.p. fin. and adminstrn., 1983-89, exec. v.p., 1990—; bd. dirs. Visx, Ryder Internat., Alcon Labs., Inc. Commonwealth scholar U. NSW, Stanford Bus. Sch. Office: Alcon Labs Inc 6201 South Fwy Fort Worth TX 76134-2001

MONTGOMERY, THEODORE ASHTON, physician; b. Los Angeles, Oct. 27, 1923; s. Wayne A. and Hazel (Osmer) M. MD, U. So. Calif., 1947; MPH cum laude, Harvard U., 1955. Diplomate: Am. Bd. Preventive Medicine, Am. Bd. Pediatrics. Intern Los Angeles County Gen. Hosp., 1946-48; intern Los Angeles Children's Hosp., 1948; resident Los Angeles Childrens' Hosp., 1950-51, St. Louis Childrens' Hosp., 1951-52; asst. in pediatrics Washington U., St. Louis, 1951-52; instr. pediatrics U. So. Calif., 1952-55; practice medicine specializing in pediatrics Los Angeles, 1952-54; lectr. pub. health U. Calif., Berkeley, 1960-83; cons. child health Calif. Dept. Pub. Health, 1954-60, chief maternal and perinatal health, 1960-61, acting chief bur. maternal and child health, 1961-63, asst. chief div. preventive med. services, 1963-66, chief, 1966-68, chief preventive medicine program, 1968-69, dep. dir. of Dept., 1969-73; chief div. disease control Alameda County Health Care Services Agy., 1973-74; cons. maternal and child health Calif. Dept. Health, Berkeley, 1974-78; chief maternal and child health br. No. Calif. Regional Office, Calif. Dept. Health Services, 1978-83; WHO fellow med. care adminstrn., Europe, 1966; co-chmn. Calif. Inter-agy. Council on Tb, 1966-72; vice chmn. Calif. Drug Research Adv. Panel, 1969-70; White House Conf. Mental Retardation, 1963; Gov's. chmn. Calif. Regional Hemodialysis Rev. Com., 1968-73; exec. sec. Gov.'s Population Study Commn., 1966; mem. com. on Tb, Calif. Lung Assn., 1973-74. Author: (with others) Standards and Recommendations for Public Prenatal Care, 1960, Guide to Hearing Testing of School Children, 1961; contbr. articles to med. jours. Bd. dirs. Calif. Interagy. Coun. on Family Planning, 1970-73; chmn. Calif. State Interdepartmental Com. on Food and Nutrition, 1977-79, pres. Clan Montgomery Soc. Internat., 1981-84, regional commr., 1985-91. With M.C. AUS, 1948-50. Fellow Am. Acad. Pediatrics (chmn. Calif. com. Indian health 1973-76, mem. nat. com. on Indian health 1963-79, vice chmn. 1977-79), Am. Pub. Health Assn. (chmn. task force on population policy 1971-72); mem. Alpha Epsilon Delta, Delta Omega. Home: 85 Wildwood Gdns Piedmont CA 94611-3831

MONTGOMERY-DAVIS, JOSEPH, osteopathic physician; b. Annapolis, Md., Aug. 27, 1940; s. John and Flonila Alice (Sutphin) Swontek. Student,

U. Wis., Milw., 1967-70; DO, Chgo. Coll. Osteo. Medicine, 1974. Diplomate Nat. Bd. Examiners for Osteo. Physicians and Surgeons. Chief technologist nuclear medicine dept. Columbia Hosp., Milw., 1964-70; intern Richmond Heights (Ohio) Gen. Hosp., 1974-75; pvt. practice Raymondville, Tex., 1975—; med. care adv. com. Tex. Dept. Human Svcs., Austin, 1983-86, 90-94, physician payment adv. com., 1991—; cons. health care issues Tex. Osteo. Med. Assn., 1991—; health officer Willacy County Bd., Raymondville, 1984—. Contbr. articles to profl. jours. With USAF, 1959-63. Mem. Am. Osteo. Assn., Am. Coll. Osteo. Family Physiaicns (spl. Recognition award 1995), Tex. Soc. Am. Coll. Osteo. Family Physicians (pres. 1985-86, Physician of Yr. award 1989), Tex. Med. Found., Tex. Osteo. Med. Assn. (pres. 1989-90), Tex. Coll. Osteo. Medicine Alumni Assn., Phi Eta Sigma, Sigma Sigma Phi. Office: Raymondville Med Clinic 525 S 10th St Raymondville TX 78580

MONTI, JOSEPH, JR., pharmacist; b. Huntington, W.Va., Dec. 9, 1937; s. Joseph Sr. and Mary (Bonel) M.; m. Janet Smithberger, June 22, 1963; children: John Joseph, Steven Michael. BS in Pharmacy, W.Va. U., 1959. Registered pharmacist, W. Va. 1st lt. U.S. Army, 1960-62. Recipient Bowl of Hygeia award A.H. Robins Co., 1981, Most Outstanding Alumnus Sch. of Pharmacy, W. Va. U., 1983. Mem. Am. Legion, 40 + 8 Orgn. Democrat. Roman Catholic. Home: 1040 Riverside Dr Welch WV 24801-2614

MONTICELLI, GIANLUIGI, physiology educator; b. Milan, Lombardia, Italy, Oct. 12, 1946; s. Antonio and Rosa (Pisoni) M. PhD, State U., Milan, 1970. Asst. prof. State U., Milan, 1970-83; prof. State U., Turin, Italy, 1978-88, Milan, 1977-78, 83—, Novara, 1992-94; del. of asst. profs. sci. faculty State U., Milan, 1981-83, mgmt. coun. mem., 1987-90, cons. TV ctr., 1985-88, mgmt. coun. mem. TV ctr., 1987-90; mgmt. coun. mem. Istituto peril Diritto allo Studio Universitario State U., 1993—, chmn., 1994—. Author: Introduzione alle Misure con Elettrodi Selettivi (pH e p(ione)), 1977, Elettricita' e Magnetismo, 1978, 86, Fenomeni di Trasporto ed Elettrici in Membrane Biologiche, 1990; contbr. articles to profl. jours. Recipient Rsch. Prize Cuore, Nutrition Found. of Italy and Quaker-Chiari Forti, 1986. Mem. Soc. Italiana di Fisiologia, Soc. Italiana di Biofisica Pura e Applicata, Internat. Union of Pure and Applied Biophysics (commn. on edn. and devel. in biophysics 1981—). Home: Via Marcona 90, 20129 Milan Italy Office: Universita' Degli Studi, Via Trentacoste 2, 20134 Milan Italy

MONTION, ROBERT MATTHEW, health system administrator; b. Visalia, Calif., Sept. 21, 1936; s. Louis and Ruth (Iterrera) M.; m. Sylvia Ann Vaca, Oct. 24, 1992; children: Robert, Eric, Matthew, Olivia. BA in Pub. Adminstrn., Calif. State U., Fresno, 1978. Asst. adminstr. Tulare (Calif.) County Gen. Hosp., 1978-80; CEO North Kern Hosp., Wasco, Calif., 1980-83, Oak Valley Dist. Hosp., Oakdale, Calif., 1983-87; rural health adminstr. St. Agnes Med. Ctr., Fresno, Calif., 1987-89; program mgr. Tulare County Health Svcs., 1989-92; CEO Alta Healthcare Dist., Dinuba, Calif., 1992—; treas., dir. Medi County Cmty. Health (HMO), Tulare, 1992—; sec. Ctrl. Valley Health Alliance, Visalia, Calif., 1993; dir. Key Health Sys. (HMO), Visalia, 1994, Integrated Health Svcs., Porterville, Calif., 1995. Pres., founder Tulane-Kings Hispanic C. of C., Visalia, 1993; pres. Coll. Sequoias Affirmative Action Com., 1993. Recipient At the Helm award Assn. Calif. Hosp. Dist., Sacramento, 1994. Democrat. Roman Catholic. Home: 3145 W Beech St Visalia CA 93277

MONTO, ARNOLD SIMON, epidemiology educator; b. Bklyn., Mar. 22, 1933; s. Jacob and Mildred (Kaplan) M.; m. Ellyne Gay Polsky, June 15, 1958; children: Sarah D. Monto Maniaci, Jane E., Richard L., Stephen A. BA in Zoology, Cornell U., Ithaca, N.Y., 1954; MD, Cornell U., N.Y.C., 1958. Diplomate Am. Coll. Epidemiology. Intern, asst. resident in medicine Vanderbilt U. Hosp., Nashville, 1958-60; USPHS postdoctoral fellow in infectious disease Stanford U. Med. Ctr., Palo Alto, Calif., 1960-62; mem. staff virus diseases sect. mid. Am. rsch. unit Nat. Inst. Allergy and Infectious Disease, Panama Canal Zone, 1962-65; from asst. prof. to prof. epidemiology U. Mich. Sch. Pub. Health, Ann Arbor, 1965—, chmn. dept. population planning and internat. health, 1993—, dir. Ctr. for Population Planning, 1993—; vis. scientist Clin. Rsch. Ctr., Northwick Park Hosp., Harrow, Eng., 1976; scholar-in-residence bd. on sci. and tech. for internat. devel. NAS and Inst. Medicine, Washington, 1983-84; vis. scientist div. communicable diseases WHO, Geneva, 1986-87; mem. pulmonary diseases adv. com. Nat. Heart, Lung and Blood Inst., Bethesda, Md., 1979-83; mem. nat. adv. coun. Nat. Inst. Allergy and Infectious Diseases, Bethesda, 1989-93,. Contbr. articles to med. jours. Recipient career devel. award NIH. Fellow Am. Coll. Epidemiology, Infectious Diseases Soc. Am.; mem. APHA (governing coun. 1978-80), Am. Epidemiol. Soc. Office: U Mich Sch Pub Health 109 S Observatory Ann Arbor MI 48109

MONTONE, FRANCIS JOHN, pediatrician; b. Phila., Sept. 1, 1953; s. Frank James and Josephine Ann (Terroni) M.; m. Rita Ann Marzen, Oct. 23, 1976; children: Anna Maria, Livia Marie, Francis James. BS in Pharmacy, Phila. Coll. Pharmacy and Sci., 1976; DO, Phila. Coll. Osteo. Medicine, 1984. Diplomate Am. Bd. Pediatrics. Rotating intern Springfield (Pa.) divsn. Met. Hosp., 1984-85; pediatrics resident Geisinger Med. Ctr., Danville, Pa., 1985-88; pvt. practice Agarwal, Clendenen & Assocs., Salisbury, Md., 1988-90; hosp.-based physician Peninsula Gen. Hosp., Salisbury, 1990-91, Kent Gen. Hosp., Dover, Del., 1991-93; pediatrician A.I. duPont Children's Clinic, Dover, 1993—. Bd. dirs. Thomas More Acad., Magnolia, Del., 1995. Fellow Am. Acad. Pediatrics, Am. Coll. Osteo. Pediatricians (sr.). Roman Catholic. Office: A I duPont Children's Clin 1726 S Governors Ave Dover DE 19904

MONTOYA, JOSE GILBERTO, infectious diseases physician; b. Barranquilla, Atlantico, Colombia, Sept. 3, 1960; came to U.S., 1987; s. Elvira (Gonzalez) Bolanos. MD, U. del Valle Sch. Medicine, 1985. Diplomate Am. Bd. Internal Medicine, Infectious Diseases. Intern, resident internal medicine Tulane U., New Orleans, 1987-90; postdoctoral fellow infectious diseases Stanford (Calif.) U., 1990-94; attending physician Stanford (Calif.) U. Med. Ctr., Menlo Park, Calif., 1994—, Veterans Affairs Palo Alto (Calif.) Health Cove Sys., 1994—. Contbr. articles to profl. jours. Attending physician Arbortree Clinic, Menlo Park, Calif., 1995—. Mem. AAAS, ACP, Am. Soc. Microbiology, Infectious Diseases Soc. Am. Home: 586 Lagunita Dr #40 Stanford CA 94305 Office: Stanford U Sch Medicine 300 Pasteur Dr Stanford CA 94305

MONTREY, JILL SUZANNE, general surgeon; b. St. Louis, May 25, 1954; d. James Ted and Laverne Anne (Milzark) M.; m. Robert William Enzenauer, Mar. 30, 1979; children: Katherine Elizabeth, William Joseph. BA, St. Louis U., 1975; MD, U. Mo., 1979. Diplomate Am. Bd. Surgery. Gen. surgeon U.S. Army Blanchfield Army Hosp., Ft. Campbell, Ky., 1984-86; gen. surgeon, pvt. practice Western Surg. Care, Denver, 1986-94; asst. prof. So. Ill. U. Sch. of Medicine, Springfield, 1994—. Maj. U.S. Army, 1979-86. Recipient Sue Miller award Nancy Gosellin Found., Denver, 1994. Fellow Am. Coll. Surgeons, Assn. Women Surgeons.

MONTRONE, PAUL MICHAEL, scientific instruments company executive; b. Scranton, Pa., May 8, 1941; s. Angelo H. and Beatrice M. (Giancini) M.; m. Sandra R. Gaudenzi, May 30, 1963; children: Michele Marie Cogan, Angelo Henry, Jerome Lawrence. B.S. in Accounting magna cum laude, U. Scranton, 1962; Ph.D. in Fin., Econs. and Ops. Research, Columbia U., 1965. Ops. analyst Office Sec. Def., Washington, 1965-67; exec. v.p., chief fin. officer Wheelabrator-Frye Inc., Hampton, N.H., 1970-83; exec. v.p. Signal Cos., Inc., La Jolla, Calif., 1983-85; pres. Engineered Products Group Signal Cos., Inc., Hampton, N.H., 1983-85; exec. v.p. fin. and adminstrn. AlliedSignal Inc., Morristown, N.J., 1985-86; pres. The Henley Group Inc., Hampton, N.H., 1986-92, bd. dirs.; chmn., CEO Wheelabrator Techs. Inc., Hampton, N.H., 1987-90; pres., co-owner The Gen. Chem. Group Inc., 1989-94, chmn. bd., 1994—; pres., CEO, bd. dirs. Fisher Sci. Internat., Inc., Hampton, 1991—; vice chmn. Abex Inc., Hampton, 1992-95; bd. dirs. Wheelabrator Techs.; adv. bd. ICI, Inc., Zeneca Inc., Sintokagio, Ltd. Mng. dir. Met. Opera Assn.; mem. dean's adv. coun. The Bus. Roundtable, Bus. Sch. Columbia U., N.Y.C. Capt. U.S. Army, 1965-67. Roman Catholic. Clubs: Brook, University (N.Y.C.); Bald Peak Colony (Melvin Village, N.H.); Lyford Cay (Nassau, Bahamas). Office: Fisher Sci Internat Inc Liberty Ln Hampton NH 03842-1808

MONTZ, LINDA ANN, nurse; b. Chgo., Oct. 20, 1950; d. Anton Frank and Ann Theresa (Roland) Mikota; m. Keith Eugene Montz, Sept. 6, 1969; children: Robert David, Jeffrey Glen, Jennifer Lynn. AA in Psychology, Southwestern Coll., 1976; BSN, U. Hawaii, 1979; MGA in Health Care Adminstrn., U. Md., 1990, MS in Psychiat. Nursing, 1991. Nurse Tripler Army Med. Ctr., Honolulu, 1979-83; head nurse, outpatient clinic Carlisle (Pa.) Barracks Health Clinic, 1983-85; chief nurse U.S. Army Health Clinic, Ft. Ritchie, Md., 1985-89; chief nursing edn., staff devel. svcs. Army Cmty. Hosp., Bremerhaven, Germany, 1991-92; chief nurse edn. and staff devel. svcs. Army Med. Ctr., Frankfurt, Germany, 1992-93; dir. hosp. quality improvement Weed Army Cmty. Hosp., Ft. Irwin, Calif., 1993-96; asst. chief dept. nursing Dwight David Eisenhower Army Med. Ctr., Fort Gordon, Ga., 1996—; cons. Army Community Svc., Ft. Ritchie, 1985-89, Child Spouse/Abuse Team, Ft. Ritchie, 1985-89. Vol. Boy Scouts Am., Honolulu, 1980-83, Girl Scouts U.S., Honolulu, 1977-83, Camp Fire Girls, Honolulu, 1976-83. Mem. Soc. for Edn. Rsch. Psychology/Mental Health Nursing, Nat. Assn. for Healthcare Quality, Am. Soc. Healthcare Risk Mgrs., Am. Assn. Utilization Mgmt. Nurses, Sigma Theta Tau, Phi Kappa Phi. Lutheran. Home: 571 W 5 Notch Rd North Augusta SC 29841 Office: DDEAMC Dept of Nursing Fort Gordon GA 30905

MONYAK, WENDELL PETER, pharmacist; b. Chgo., Sept. 14, 1931; s. Wendell and Mary Elizabeth M.; m. Lorraine Mostek, Aug. 29, 1964. BS in Chemistry, Roosevelt U., 1957; BS in Pharmacy, St. Louis Coll. Pharmacy, 1961. Asst. chief pharmacist Little Co. of Mary Hosp., Chgo., 1961-66; chief pharmacist MacNeal Meml. Hosp., Berwyn, Ill., 1966-72; dir. pharmacy Ill. Masonic Med. Ctr., Chgo., 1972, dir. pharm. services, 1972-87; dir. pharmacy services St. Anne's Hosp., Chgo., 1987-88; adminstr., 1989—; teaching assoc. U. Ill., 1972-87. Author: Hospital Formulary and Therapeutic Guide for Residents and Interns, 1974, 3d edit. 1986. Pres., chmn. bd. dirs. Bohemian Home for Aged, 1986—. With M.C., AUS, 1955-57. Mem. Am. Pharm. Assn., Am. Soc. Hosp. Pharmacists, Ill. Pharm. Assn. (Spl. Recignition award), No. Ill. Soc. Hosp. Pharmacists, Chgo. Hosp. Coun. Club: Oakbrook Exec. Home: 19 W 059 Chateau N Oak Brook IL 60521 Office: 1347 Crystal Naperville IL 60563

MONZINGO, AGNES YVONNE, veterinary technician; b. Mangum, Okla., July 16, 1942; d. Ira Lee and Opal Alice (McAlexander) Mayfield; m. Monty Brent Monzingo, Dec. 19, 1959; children: Tara, Dawn, Michael, Kermit. AS, San Antonio Coll., 1969. Mgr. Tupperware Corp., Wichita Falls, Tex., 1966-69; with La Louisiane, San Antonio, 1974-79; counselor Diet Ctr., Duncanville, Tex., 1984-87; vet. technician DeSoto (Tex.) Animal Hosp., 1985—. Author: (weekly column) Happy Tracks, 1981. Pres. Dallas Stake Primary, 1983-88; commr. Boy Scouts Am., 1988-93. Recipient Wood badge Boy Scouts Am., 1987, Wisdom Trail Dist. award of merit, 1990, Silver Beaver award Boy Scouts Am., 1993. Mem. Tex. Assn. Registered Vet. Technicians (v.p. 1991), Tex. Assn. Animal Technicians (pres. 1988, com. chair 1990-92), Tex. Assn. Registered Technicians (pres. 1992), Am. Boxer Club, Dallas Boxers Club (sec. 1982-92), Metroplex Vet. Hosp. Mgrs. Assn. Mem. LDS Ch.

MOOD, ROCHELLA RABON, critical care nurse; b. Camden, S.C., Oct. 17, 1964; d. Clarence Howard Rabon and Mary Frances (Lambert) Black; m. William Jervey Mood Jr., May 20, 1995. BSN, Med. U. S.C., 1986; MSN, Ga. State U., 1994. CCRN, ACLS, BCLS. Staff nurse Crawford Long Hosp., Atlanta, 1986-87; staff nurse/charge nurse Ga. Baptist Med. Ctr., Atlanta, 1987-96, asst. nurse mgr., 1996—; preceptor Ga. Baptist Hosp., 1990—, student preceptorship coord., 1994—; mem. Resource Utilization Team, Atlanta, 1994—. Mem. AACN, ANA, Ga. Nurses Assn. Home: 1046 Sasha Ln Roswell GA 30075 Office: Ga Baptist Med Ctr 303 Parkway Dr NE Atlanta GA 30312

MOODY, A. RANDALL, II, neurologist; b. Jackson, Miss., Jan. 1, 1957; s. Austin Randall Moody and Thelma Wade; m. Sharon Kaye, July 28, 1984; children: Nicole, Danielle. MD, U. Tex. Health Sci. Ctr., San Antonio, 1982. Diplomate Am. Bd. Psychiatry and Neurology, Am. Bd. Ind. Med. Examiners; cert. ind. med. examiner in neurology. Intern U. So. Calif., L.A., 1982-83; resident U. Tex. Health Sci. Ctr., San Antonio, 1983-86; pvt. practice Kerrville, Tex., 1986-92, Las Vegas, Nev., 1993—; v.p. DeltaVox, Inc., Las Vegas, 1992-96. Mem. Am. Acad. Neurology, Tex. Med. Assn., Clark County Med. Soc. Office: Ste 202 2080 E Flamingo Las Vegas NV 89119

MOODY, CHERYL ANNE, social services administrator, social worker, educator; b. Winston-Salem, N.C., July 31, 1953; d. Fred Bertram and Mary Edna (Weekley) M. BSW with honors, Va. Commonwealth U., 1975; MSW, U. Mich., 1979. Social worker Family Svcs., Inc., Winston-Salem, 1974-77; sch. social work intern Huron Valley Jr. H.S., Milford, Mich., 1977-78; children's social work intern Downriver Child Guidance Clinic, Allen Park, Mich., 1978-79; children's svcs. specialist Calhoun County Dept. Social Svcs., Battle Creek, Mich., 1979-81; children's psychiat. social worker Eastern Maine Med. Ctr., Bangor, 1981-82, sr. med. social worker, 1982-85; clin. social worker Ctr. for Family Svcs. in Palm Beach County, Inc., West Palm Beach, Fla., 1988-89, Jupiter, Fla., 1989-91; dir. children's programs Children's Home Soc. of Fla., West Palm Beach, 1985—; asst. prof. social work Fla. Atlantic U., Boca Raton, 1993—. Vol. group leader Lupus Found., Boca Raton, 1994—. Mem. NASW, Acad. Cert. Social Workers. Democrat. Methodist. Home: 6212 62nd Way West Palm Beach FL 33409-7130 Office: Children's Home Soc of Fla 3600 Broadway West Palm Beach FL 33407-4844

MOODY, EDWARD BRIDGES, physician, biomedical engineer; b. Omaha, Apr. 2, 1954; s. Edson Bridges and Sara Jane (Sears) M.; m. Virginia Jane Welch, Mar. 18, 1978; 1 child, Alexander. BA in Chemistry, Knox Coll., 1976; MD, Rush Med. Coll., 1980; MS, Rutgers U., 1987. Diplomate Am. Bd. Nuclear Medicine. Intern in diagnostic radiology W.Va. U. Med. Ctr., Morgantown, 1980-81; rsch. fellow in neurophysiology Lyons (N.J.) VA Med. Ctr., 1987-89; resident physician in nuclear medicine Vanderbilt U. Med. Ctr., Nashville, 1989-92; asst. prof. diagnostic radiology U. Ky. Coll. Medicine, Lexington, 1992—. Contbr. articles to profl. jours. Capt. U.S. Army, 1980-83. Mem. IEEE, Soc. Nuclear Medicine, Am. Coll. Nuclear Physicians. Office: Univ Ky Med Ctr Nuclear Medicine Rm N-3 800 Rose St Lexington KY 40536

MOODY, MAXWELL, JR., retired physician; b. Tuscaloosa, Ala., Aug. 7, 1921; s. Maxwell and Jean Kilroy (Lahey) M.; m. Betty Alice Morrissey, May 10, 1946 (dec. Feb. 1994); children: Maxwell III, Susan, Elizabeth Sims; m. Barbara Loftis, Mar. 4, 1995. BA, U. Ala., 1941; MD, U. Pa., 1944. Diplomate Am. Bd. Internal Medicine. Intern Gorgas Hosp., Ancon, C.Z., 1944-45, Ancon, 1944-45; resident Grad. Sch. Medicine, U. Pa., Phila., 1947-48, Univ. Hosp., Birmingham, Ala., 1948-50; jr. and sr. resident in medicine U. Ala. Hosp., Birmingham, 1948-50; pvt. practice Tuscaloosa, 1950-87, ret., 1987; pres. Tuscaloosa County Med. Soc., Ala. Soc. Internal Medicine; pres., chn. bd. Ala. Heart Assn. Former state chmn., nat. trustee Ducks Unltd. Capt. U.S. Army, 1945-47. Fellow Am. Coll. Physicians. Republican. Episcopalian. Home: 7604 Mountbatten Rd NE Tuscaloosa AL 35406-1110

MOODY, PATRICIA ANN, psychiatric nurse, artist; b. Oceana County, Mich., Dec. 16, 1939; d. Herbert Ernest and Dorothy Marie (Allen) Baesch; m. Robert Edward Murray, Sept. 3, 1960 (div. Jan. 1992); children: Deanna Lee Cañas, Adam James Murray, Tara Michelle Murray, Danielle Marie Murray; m. Frank Alan Moody, Sept. 26, 1992. BSN, U. Mich., 1961; MSN, Washington U., St. Louis, 1966; student, Acad. of Art, San Francisco, 1975-78. RN; lic. coast guard, ocean operator. Psychiat. staff nurse U. Mich., Ann Arbor, 1961-62, Langley-Porter Neuro-Psychiat. Inst., San Francisco, 1962-63; instr. nursing Barnes Hosp. Sch. Nursing, St. Louis, 1963; psychiat. nursing instr. Washington U., St. Louis, 1966-68; psychiat. nurse instr. St. Francis Sch. Nursing, San Francisco, 1970-71; psychiat. staff nurse Calif. Pacific Med. Ctr., San Francisco, 1991—; psychiat. staff nurse Charter Heights Behavioral Health Sys., Albuquerque, 1996—; owner, cruise cons. Cruise Holidays Albuquerque, 1995—. Oil and watercolors included in various group exhbns., 1982-93. V.p. Belles-Fundraising Orgn., St. Mary's Hosp., San Francisco, 1974; pres. PTO, Commodore Sloat Sch. 1982. Recipient Honor award Danforth Found., 1954, Freshman award Oreon Scott Found., 1958; merit scholar U. Mich., 1957. Mem. San Francisco Women Artists (Merit award for oil painting 1989), Artist's Equity (bd. dirs. No. Calif. chpt. 1987-89, pres. No. Calif. chpt. 1990), Met. Club. Republican. Lutheran. Home: 219 Spring Creek Ln NE Albuquerque NM 87122 Office: Cruise Holidays Albuquerque 11032 Montgomery Blvd NE Albuquerque NM 87111

MOOIJ, JAN J. A., academic neurosurgeon; b. Zutphen, The Netherlands, Oct. 11, 1945; s. Anne L. A. and Willy J. (Kruys Voorberge) M.; m. Lillian M. L. Stiller, Nov. 11, 1971; children: Ilja, Harald, Matthias, Hans. MD, U. Groningen, The Netherlands, 1971, PhD, 1976. Asst. scientist U. Groningen, 1971-76, trainee in neurosurgery, 1976-81, staff neurosurgeon, 1983-88, chef de clinique, 1989-93; trainee in neurosurgery Zürich, Switzerland, 1982; neurosurgeon Amsterdam, The Netherlands, 1982—; prof., chmn. dept. neurosurgery Univ. Hosp., 1993—. Contbr. articles to profl. jours. Prin. oboist Orchestra "De Harmonie", Groningen, 1973—. Mem. Dutch Neurosurgery Soc., French Neurosurgery Soc. Home: Boterdiep Wz 38, 9781 EK Bedum The Netherlands Office: Univ Hosp, PO Box 30001, 9700 RB Groningen The Netherlands

MOON, HARRY KYLE, plastic and reconstructive surgeon; b. Birmingham, Ala., Jan. 14, 1950; s. Kyle Boak and Mary (Lindon) M.; m. Ann Marie Daunt, June 25, 1983; children: Savannah, Lauren, Kyle, Hunter. BA in English, Tulane U., 1972; MD, U. South Ala., 1978. Diplomate Am. Bd. Plastic Surgery, Nat. Bd. Med. Examiners. Resident in gen. surgery U. Hawaii, Honolulu, 1978-79, 80-81, Med. U. S.C., Charleston, 1979-80; resident in plastic surgery Cleve. Clinic Found., 1981-83, staff physician, 1984-88; overseas fellow U. Melbourne, Australia, 1983-84; chief staff Cleve. Clinic Fla., Ft. Lauderdale, 1988—, vice chmn. bd. govs., 1991; bd. dirs. Cleve. Clinic Fla. Health Plan, 1992-96, Barnett Bank South Fla. N.A., Ft. Lauderdale; trustee Cleve. Clinic Hosp., Ft. Lauderdale, 1992-96. Contbr. articles to med. jours. Bd. dirs. Broward County coun. Girl Scouts U.S.A., 1989-95; trustee CarQuest Bowl, Joe Robbie Stadium, 1993—, Mus. Art, Ft. Lauderdale, 1994—. Fellow ACS, Am. Soc. Aesthetic Plastic Surgery, Am. Coll. Physician Execs.; mem. AMA, Am. Soc. Plastic and Reconstructive Surgeons, Am. Assn. Plastic Surgeons (James Barnett Brown award 1988), Fla. Med. Assn., Lauderdale Yacht Club (bd. govs. 1994—). Methodist. Office: Cleve Clinic Fla 3000 W Cypress Creek Rd Fort Lauderdale FL 33309

MOON, LINDA ELLEN, medical center researcher; b. Corpus Christi, June 10, 1946; d. Troy William and Beatrice Claire (Cryer) Moon; m. Jerry Preston Reid, Oct. 29, 1965 (div. 1971); 1 son, James Troy; m. Jack James Flagg, Feb. 6, 1986. BA, U. Tex., 1969. Research asst. Tex. A&M U. Research and Extension, Overton, 1969; lab. technician East Tex. Chest Hosp., Tyler, 1970-73; med. tech. James M. Gray & Assocs., Houston, 1974, Motley Clin. Labs., Inc., Houston, 1974-75; med. technician III, U. Tex. Cancer Ctr., M.D. Anderson Hosp., Houston, 1976-84; sr. research asst. dept. surgery/organ transplant U. Tex. Health Sci. Ctr., 1984-87; gen. supr. flow cytometry labs. Cytology Tech., Inc., Houston, 1987-88; tech. dir. Diagnostic Genetics, Inc., Houston, 1988—; med. lab. specialist cytogenetics prenatal diagnostic group Labs. Genetic Svcs., Inc., Houston, 1990-93, 95—; cons. Moon Svcs., 1993—. Republican. Methodist. Home and Office: 3203 S Braeswood Blvd Houston TX 77025-2502

MOON, MARLA LYNN, optometrist; b. Connellsville, Pa., July 31, 1956; d. George Donnelly and Pauline Harriet (Hough) M. BS, Pa. State U., 1978, Pa. Coll. Optometry, Phila., 1980; OD, Pa. Coll. Optometry, 1982. Cert. Nat. Bd. Examiners, Pa., N.J. Bds. of Optometric Examiners. Intern Gesell Inst. for Human Devel., New Haven, 1981, U.S. Mil. Acad., West Point, N.Y., 1981, Dr. William Moskowitz, Somerville, N.J., 1981-82, Elwyn Ins., Feinbloom Ctr., Phila., 1982; resident, pediatrics unit The Eye Inst., Phila., 1982-83; ptnr. Drs. Carlin and Moon, State College, Pa., 1983—; vis. lectr. Dominican Coll., Orangeburg, N.Y., 1985, Pa. State U., University Park, 1985-89, 91-92, 95; faculty Pa. Coun. Horseback Riding for Handicapped, State College, 1988-96; cons. JMS Mobility Assocs., Inc., Exton, Pa., 1983-89, Univ.Hosp. and Rehab. Ctr., Hershey, Pa., 1988-93, John Heinz Rehab. and Med. Ctr., Wilkes-Barre, Pa., 1990—. Adv. bd., v.p. Learning Disabilities Assn., State College, 1983-92; com. chmn. Local Children's Team, State College, 1985-89; pres., bd. dirs. Cen.-Clear Child Svcs., Phila., 1984—; active Task Force Project Self Sufficiency, Bellefonte, Pa., 1988—; bd. dirs. Pa.-Del. Assn. for Educators and Rehab. Blind and Visually Impaired, Harrisburg, 1988-95. Recipient Phila. County Optometric Soc. award, 1982, Knight-Henry Meml. award Optometric Ext. Program, Phila., 1982, Disting. Svc. award Assn. Educators and Rehab. of Blind and Visually Impaired (Pa.-Del. chpt.), 1992, Woman of Distinction award Soroptimist Club of Centre County, 1996. Fellow Am. Acad. Optometry; mem. Am. Optometric Assn. (Optometric Recognition awawrd 1985-96), Pa. Optometric Assn. (chmn. 1989-91), Mid-Counties Optometric Soc. (pres. 1992-94), Pa. State Alumni Assn. (life), Altrusa Club (sec., v.p., pres. 1987—), Omega Epsilon Phi. Office: 423 S Pugh St State College PA 16801-5308

MOON, SAMUEL DAVID, medical educator; b. Westminster, S.C., June 14, 1949; s. David Smithson and Beverly Baines (Cook) M.; m. Jean Gibert, Aug. 10, 1971 (div. 1974); m. Robin Allene Dennett, Dec. 22, 1979; children: Mirial Michael Teeter, Ezra Smithson. BS, Wofford Coll., 1971; MD, Med. Coll. Va., 1975; MPH, U. N.C., 1990. Diplomate Am. Bd. Preventive Medicine, Am. Bd. Pain Medicine. mem. adv. bd. N.C. Ergonomics Resource Ctr., Raleigh, 1995—; mem. clin. faculty scis. coun. Duke U., Durham, N.C., 1995—. Editor: Beyond Biomechanics, 1995. Fellow Am. Acad. Family Physicians. Office: Duke U Med Ctr Box 2914 Durham NC 27710

MOON, TIMOTHY D., urologist, educator; b. Edinburgh, Scotland, June 11, 1949; s. Francis Eric and Kathleen Joyce Moon; m. Heather May Moon, Mar. 11, 1976; children: Stephanie, Laura. BSc in Med. Scis., U. Edinburgh, 1969, MB, ChB, 1972. Diplomate Am. Bd. Urology. Asst. prof. U. Minn. Hosps., Mpls., 1983-84, Tulane U. Sch. Medicine, New Orleans, 1984-90; chief sect. urology VA Med. Ctr., New Orleans, 1986-90; assoc. prof. div. urology U. Wis. Sch. Medicine, Wisconsin, 1990—; chief sect. urology William S. Middleton VA Med. Ctr., Wisconsin, 1990—, asst. chief surgery, 1995; reviewer Urology, 1994—. Contbg. author: Problems in Geriatric Endocrinology, 1992; contbr. articles to med. jours. Fellow Royal Coll. Physicians and Surgeons Can.; mem. Am. Urol. Assn., Soc. Univ. Urologists, Soc. Urologic Oncology, Internat. Soc. Urology, Am. Assn. for Cancer Rsch., Can. Urol. Assn. Office: U Wis Sch Medicine 600 Highland Ave G5/341 Madison WI 53792

MOONEY, ROBERT MICHAEL, ophthalmologist; b. Mt. Vernon, N.Y., July 25, 1945; s. Robert Michael and Marie Evelyn (sabatini) M.; m. Dorothy May Kazmaier, Feb. 21, 1981. BS in Biology, Fordham U., 1966; MD, U. Bologna, Italy, 1972. Diplomate Am. Bd. Ophthalmology. Intern Grasslands Hosp., Valhalla, N.Y., 1972-73; resident in surgery Grasslands Hosp., 1973-74; resident in ophthalmology N.Y. Med. Coll., Valhalla, 1974-76; chief resident ophthalmology N.Y. Med. Coll., 1976-77; acting dir. dept. ophthalmology Westchester County Med. Ctr., Valhalla, 1980-86; pvt. practice Katonah-Mt. Kisco, N.Y., 1979—; asst. clin. prof. ophthalmology N.Y. Med. Coll., Valhalla, 1982—. Fellow Am. Acad. Ophthalmology, Am. Coll. Surgeons; mem. Med. Soc. State of N.Y., Westchester County Med. Soc., Westchester Acad. Medicine (chmn. sect. ophthalmology 1987-89), MENSA. Republican. Roman Catholic. Office: 51 Bedford Rd Katonah NY 10536-2135

MOONIS, MARY CHARLENE, long-term care nurse, medical/surgical nurse; b. Cottonwood, Ariz., Jan. 2, 1948; d. Jesse Charles and Lillian Clara (O'Brien) Brewer; m. Donald M. Moonis Jr., Feb. 6, 1980; children: Brenda, Heather, Steven. ADN, CCAC South Campus, 1986. EMT, asst. chief, training officer McKeesport EMS, 1977-80; staff nurse Presbyn. U. Hosp., Pitts., 1986-87; asst. dir. nursing, risk mgr. Kane Regional Ctr., McKeesport, Pa., 1986—; part-time faculty allied health Cmty. Coll. Allegheny County, West Mifflin, Pa., 1989-90; mem. infection control com., quality control com., safety com. Kane Regional Ctr., McKeesport. Mem. APIC, ASCP, MEMS, Nat. Safety Coun., Phi Theta Kappa. Office: Kane Regional Mc Keesport 100 9th St Mc Keesport PA 15132-3952

MOORADIAN, ARSHAG DERTAD, physician, educator; b. Aleppo, Syria, Aug. 20, 1953; came to U.S., 1981; s. Dertad and Araxie (Halajian) M.; m. Deborah Lynn Miles, June 25, 1985; children: Arshag Dertad Jr., Ariana Araxie. BS, Am. U., Beirut, 1976, MD, 1980. Diplomate Am. Bd. Internal

Medicine. Asst. prof. medicine UCLA, 1985-88; assoc. prof. U. Ariz., Tucson, 1988-91; prof. St. Louis U., 1991. Contbr. articles to Jour. Endocrinology, Diabetes, Jour. Gerontology, Neurochemistry Rsch. VA grantee, 1985—. Mem. Am. Fedn. Clin. Rsch., Gerontol. Soc. Am., Endocrine Soc., Am. Diabetes Assn. (chmn. task force on micronutreints 1990-91). Mem. Armenian Orthodox Ch. Office: Saint Louis U Med Sch 1402 S Grand Blvd Saint Louis MO 63104-1004

MOORE, AUSTEN PETER, neurologist, educator; b. Hull, Yorkshire, Eng., Dec. 4, 1952; s. Austen Joseph and Patricia Theresa (Ferraro) M.; m. Julia Kay Wadham, June 20, 1981; children: Gregory, Ursula. MB ChB, Birmingham (Eng.) U., 1975, MD, 1987. House officer Birmingham Hosp., 1975-76; sr. house officer gen. medicine Leeds (Eng.) Hosp., 1977-79; registrar in gen. medicine Hallamshire Hosp., Sheffield, Eng., 1979-81; registrar in neurology Queen Elizabeth Hosp., Birmingham, 1981-83, Inst. Neurol. Scis., Glasgow, Scotland, 1983-87; lectr. in neurology Walton Ctr. for Neurology and Neurosurgery, Liverpool, Eng., 1987-94, assoc. specialist in neurology, 1994—. Editor: Handbook of Botulinum Toxin Treatment, 1995; contbr. articles to profl. jours., chpt. to book. Mem. Royal Coll. Physicians, Assn. Brit. Neurologists, Movement Disorder Soc. Office: Walton Ctr Neurology, Rice Ln, Liverpool L9 1AE, England

MOORE, CHARLES AUGUST, JR., psychologist; b. Medford, Oreg., Feb. 22, 1944; s. Charles August and Bernadine (Newlun) M. BS, Lewis and Clark Coll., 1965; MA, U. Colo., 1967, PhD, 1972. Lic. psychologist, Calif., Oreg. Teaching asst. U. Colo., Boulder, 1965-66, 70-71, rsch. asst., counselor, practicum supr., 1966-67, 71-72; asst. psychologist State Home and Tng. Sch., Grand Junction, Colo., 1967; intern in psychology Camarillo (Calif.) State Hosp., 1968-69; psychology assoc., program psychologist Camarillo Drug Abuse Program (The Family), 1969-70; intern in psychology Oxnard (Calif.) Mental Health Ctr., 1969; clin. psychologist, dir. intern tng. Rural Clinics, Reno, 1972; clin. psychologist Kern County Mental Health Svcs., Bakersfield, Calif., 1972-74; clin., cons. psychologist San Diego County Mental Health Svcs., 1974-88; pvt. practice La Jolla (Calif.) Clinic, 1976-78; August Ctr., Chula Vista, Calif., 1978-85; staff psychologist Dept. Vet.'s Affairs Domiciliary, White City, Oreg., 1988—; guest lectr. Calif. State Coll., Bakersfield, 1973-74; mem. Health Systems Agy. Mental Health Task Force, 1979; mem. doctoral dissertation com. U.S. Internat. U., 1975-76; mem. mental health task force San Diego County Bd. Suprs., 1979. Contbr. articles to profl. jours. Mem. Univ. City Community Coun., San Diego, 1976-78; bd. dirs. Pub. Employees Assn., 1976-77. Recipient Experiment in Internat. Living European Study award Lewis and Clark Coll., 1962; USPHS fellow, 1967-68; U. Colo. Grad. Sch. Rsch. grantee, 1971; recipient Hands and Heart award Dept. Vets. Affairs, 1989-90, Domiciliary Spl. Contbn. and Outstanding Performance awards, 1990, 91. Mem. APA, Am. Psychology and Law Soc., Calif. Psychol. Assn., Western Psychol. Assn., San Diego County Psychol. Assn., Assn. County Clin. Psychologists San Diego, San Diego Psychology and Law Soc., San Diego Soc. Clin. Psychologists. Office: Dept VA Domiciliary Psychology Svc 8495 Crater Lake Hwy White City OR 97503-3011

MOORE, CHARLOTTE ELEANOR, nutritional counselor; b. Denver, Nov. 15, 1923; d. Charles Mayo and Sylvia (Barnett) Witt; m. William P. Moore, Mar. 28, 1987; children: Julie Ann Gilliam, Mary Lisa Zuchegno. Student, U. Northern Colo., 1940-42; BA, Rockmont Coll., 1981. Cert. live cell technician. Tchr. Englewood (Colo.) Schs., 1943-45; sec. to supr. of schs. and sch. bd. Town of Truth or Consequences, N.Mex., 1945-47; office mgr. Crusader Oil Corp., Denver, 1947-49; ind. nutritional counselor Englewood, Colo., 1983—. Sec. libr. bd. Colo. Women's Coll., Denver, 1963-65; deacon Wellshire Presbyn. Ch., Denver, 1984-87; mem. various coms. Salvation Army, United Way, Planned Parenthood. Republican. Home: 4060 S Bellaire St Englewood CO 80110-5028

MOORE, DANIEL EDMUND, psychologist, educator, retired educational administrator; b. Pitts., Dec. 31, 1926; s. John Daniel and Alma Helen (Goehring) M.; m. Rose Marie Blunkosky, Nov. 11, 1949; children: Catherine Chiodo, Claire Marie Moore Caveney, Mary Moore Brilmyer, Suzanne Moore Gray, Elizabeth Moore Sullivan. BSEd, Duquesne U., 1949, MEd, 1952; postgrad., California (Pa.) State Coll., 1954-56, U. Pitts., 1958-59, Mt. Mercy Coll., 1959-60, Cath. U. Am., 1966, W.Va. U., 1970-72. Lic. psychologist; cert. sch. psychologist. Tchr. math. Cecil Twp. Sch. Dist., McDonald, Pa., 1949-52, Pitts. Public Schs., 1952-53; with Mt. Lebanon Twp. (Pa.) Sch. Dist., 1953-88, psychologist, 1954-71, dir. pupil personnel svcs., 1988; psychol cons. Peters Twp. Sch. Dist., McMurray, Pa., 1961-88, Blackhawk Sch. Dist., Beaver, Pa., 1989—, Quaker Valley Sch. Dist., Sewickley, Pa., 1989-90; lectr., supr. Grad. and Undergrad. Sch. Edn. Duquesne U.; psychologist DePaul Inst., Pitts., 1992—; lectr. ednl. psychology Grad. Sch. Edn., Duquesne U., 1957-92, supr. student tchrs., 1989-92; ednl. cons. St. Francis Schs. Nursing, New Castle and Pitts., 1959-91; mem. test adv. bd. Ednl. Records Bur., 1976-86; hearing officer Right to Edn. Office, Dept. Edn., Harrisburg, Pa., 1975—; in-svc. adv. bd. Pa. Dept. Edn. Hearing Officers. Mem. Chartiers Valley Sch. Dist. Bd., 1963-94, pres., 1971, v.p., 1991; mem. Pkwy. West Tech. Sch. Bd. 1965-67; bd. dirs. secondary sch. rsch. program Ednl. Testing Svc., Princeton, 1971-85; bd. dirs. Robert E. Ward Home for Children, 1975-87, St. Agatha Parish Coun., 1988—, Pathfinder Sch., 1989, v.p., 1990-94, pres. sch. bd., 1991-92; vol. Bridgeville Area Food Bank, 1988—; chairperson Parish 100 Jubilee Ceremony, Goodwill Villa Bd., Goodwill Plaza, Inc., Goodwill Villa Bd. of Incorporators, 1992—; pres. bd. dirs. Goodwill Plaza, 1992—; jubilee chairperson St. Agatha's, Bridgeville, Pa. With USNR, 1945-48. Henry C. Frick grantee, 1970, 73; named Jaycee Educator of Yr. for South Hills Area, Ward Home Outstanding Community Leader, 1984. Mem. Am., Pa. psychol. assns., Coun. Exceptional Children (pres. 1957), Phi Delta Kappa (pres. chpt. 1974-75, chmn. lay awards com. 1979—, Svc. Key award 1985). Roman Catholic. Home: 213 Station St Bridgeville PA 15017-1806 Office: 428 Forbes Ave Pittsburgh PA 15219-1603

MOORE, DAVID MAX, internist; b. Decatur, Ill., Oct. 25, 1949; s. Max E. and Jean E. (Funk) M. BA, So. Ill. U., 1971; DO, Chgo. Coll. Osteo. Medicine, 1975. Diplomate Am. Bd. Internal Medicine. Resident in internal medicine Cook County Hosp., Chgo., 1975-78; ptnr. Assoc. Internists, Chgo., 1978-80; pvt. practice Chgo., 1980-93; cons. Nat. Inst. Health Risk Project, 1985-87; mem. Ill. State AIDS Adv. Coun., 1985-88; co-dir. AIDS Svc., Ill. Masonic Med. Ctr., 1985-95, dir. HIV/AIDS program, 1994—; co-chair Chgo. Area AIDS Caregivers Retreat, 1990; clin. asst. prof. medicine U. Ill., Chgo., 1987-94; asst. prof. medicine Rush Med. Coll., 1994—; bd. dirs. Chgo. Cmty. Physicians Consortium for Rsch. on AIDS, 1990—; field investigator AIDS Rsch. Alliance, 1990—; med. dir. Strong Spirit Wellness Ctr., 1995—. Bd. dirs. AIDS Pastoral Care Network, 1992-95. Mem. Am. Coll. Physicians. Home: 2426 W Foster Ave Chicago IL 60625-2519 Office: 938 W Nelson Chicago IL 60657

MOORE, EMILY ALLYN, pharmacologist; b. Evansville, Ind., Apr. 3, 1950; d. Otis Barton and Helen Louise (Felker) Allyn; m. Robert Alan Yount, Nov. 25, 1972 (div. Feb. 1986); 1 child, Joseph Taylor; m. Robert E. Moore Jr., Aug. 11, 1990; 1 child, Alexander Allyn. AB in Chem. Biology, Ind. U., Bloomington, 1971; MS in Applied Computer Sci., Purdue U., Indpls., 1985; PhD in Pharmacology, Ind. U., Indpls., 1976. Vis. asst. prof. biology Ind. U., Bloomington, 1979; rsch. assoc. in biochemistry Ind. U., Indpls., 1979-81, rsch. assoc., 1982-83, computer programmer for med. genetics, 1983-85, asst. scientist. med. genetics, 1985-87; tech. assessment specialist Boehringer Mannheim Corp., Indpls., 1987, mgr. sci. info., 1987-89; mgr. Tech. Assess, Indpls., 1989-93, quality process analyst, 1993-94. Contbr. articles to profl. jours. Officer or bd. dirs. LWV, Hendricks County, Ind., 1977-84; elder St. Luke's United Ch. of Christ, Speedway, Ind., 1983-85; mem. adv. bd. Operation SMART, Indpls., 1989-90.

MOORE, EMILY C., nurse, nursing administrator, research coordinator; b. Rochester, N.Y., Oct. 4, 1964; d. William L., Jr. and Elizabeth L. (Tuttle) Clay. m. Richard G. Moore Aug. 12, 1989. BSN magna cum laude, Keuka Coll., 1988. RN, N.Y., Va., Alta., Can.; cert. oncology nurse. Staff nurse Strong Meml. Hosp., Rochester, 1988-89, 93, U. Alberta Hosps., Edmonton, Alberta, 1990-93, Sentara Cancer Inst., Norfolk, Va., 1993—; clin. mgr. Sentara Norfolk Gen. Hosp., 1994-95; coord. collection ctr. Nat. Marrow Donor Program, 1994-95, clin. rsch. coord., 1996—. Mem. Oncology Nurses Assn. (S.W. Va. chpt.). Home: 302 Honey Locust Way Chesapeake VA 23320 Office: Sentara Norfolk Gen Hosp 600 Gresham Dr Norfolk VA 23507

MOORE, ERNEST EUGENE, JR., surgeon, educator; b. Pitts., June 18, 1946; s. Ernest Eugene Sr. and Mary Ann (Burroughs) M.; m. Sarah Van Duzer, Sept. 2, 1978; children: Hunter Burroughs, Peter Kitrick. BS in Chemistry, Allegheny Coll., 1968; MD, U. Pitts., 1972. Surg. resident U. Vt., Burlington, 1972-76; chief of trauma Denver Gen. Hosp., 1976—, chief dept. surgery, 1984—; chief div. of emergency med. svcs. U. Colo., Denver, 1984—, prof. surgery, vice chmn. dept., 1985—; dir. rsch. Colo. Trauma Inst., Denver, 1984—. Editor: Critical Decisions in Trauma, 1987, Trauma, 1988, rev. edits., 1991, 96, Early Care of the Injured, 1989; assoc. editor Jour. Trauma, Am. Jour. Surgery, Surgery-Problem Solving Approach, 2d edit., 1994, others; patentee retrohepatic vena cava shunt. Fellow ACS (com. on trauma, vice chair 1990), Soc. Univ. Surgeons (pres. 1989), am. Assn. Surgery of Trauma (pres. 1993), Internat. Assn. Surgery of Trauma and Surg. Intensive Care (pres.-elect 1995), Pan Am. Trauma Assn. (pres. 1991), Southwestern Surg. Congress (v.p. 1996), Western Trauma Assn. (pres. 1989). Republican. Home: 2909 E 7th Avenue Pky Denver CO 80206-3839 Office: Denver Gen Hosp Dept Surgery Denver CO 80204

MOORE, HAROLD BEVERIDGE, retired microbiology educator; b. Alix, Arkansas, Sept. 11, 1928; s. Harold Moore and Irene (Beveridge) Pherson; m. Marion Elizabeth Tanner, Aug. 26, 1950; children: Diane Marie, Linda Jean. AB in Zoology, San Diego State U., 1951; MA in Microbiology, UCLA, 1955, PhD in Microbiology, 1958. Med. microbiologist Sharp Meml. Hosp., San Diego, 1957-60, microbiology cons., 1960-86; asst. prof. San Diego State U., 1960-64, assoc. prof., 1964-67, prof. microbiology, 1967—; cons. Palomar Hosp., Escondido, Calif., 1964—, Mercy Hosp., San Diego, 1976-84, Pomerado Hosp., Poway, Calif., 1980-94. Co-author Lab Manual for Medical Bacteriology, 1971; contbr. articles to profl. jours. Fellow Am. Acad. Microbiology; mem. Am. Soc. Microbiology, So. Calif. Am. Soc. Microbiology, Sigma Xi. Democrat. Presbyterian. Home: 1776 Avenida Cherylita El Cajon CA 92020-7701

MOORE, JAMES BILL, nephrologist; b. Tupelo, Miss., Aug. 30, 1952; s. James William and Sarah Ann (Whitten) M.; m. Kelsey Anne Green, June 3, 1989; children: James William, Eleanor Gibson, Martha Carolyn, Anne Kunton. BS, U. Miss., 1973, MD, 1977. Diplomate Am. Bd. Internal Medicine in Nephrology. Instr. U. Tenn., Memphis, 1983-86; clin. asst. prof. medicine U. Miss., Jackson, 1987—; private practice nephrology Jackson, 1988—. Office: Jackson Nephrology Assocs 768 Lakeland Dr Jackson MS 39216

MOORE, JANET RUTH, nurse, educator; b. Bridgeport, Conn., Sept. 19, 1949; d. Robert Hartland and Florence (Merritt) Bessom; m. William James Moore, Sept. 5, 1971; children: Jeffrey, Gregory. AA, Green Mountain Coll., 1969; diploma, Mass. Gen. Hosp., 1974; BS in Nursing, Am. Internat. Coll., 1980; MS in Nursing, U. Mass., 1993. RN, Mass.; cert. gerontol. nurse, gerontol. clin. nurse specialist ANCC. Nurse's aide Lynn (Mass.) Hosp., 1967-69, staff nurse, 1972-73; nursing asst. U.S. Army Hosp., Ft. Polk, La., 1971-72; staff nurse Ludlow (Mass.) Hosp., 1980-85; staff edn. instr. Springfield (Mass.) Mcpl. Hosp., 1985-88; dir. staff edn. Jewish Nursing Home, Longmeadow, Mass., 1988-93; instr. Baystate Med. Ctr. Sch. Nursing, Springfield, Mass., 1993—; nurse Camp Wilder, Springfield, 1981-84; clin. instr. Holyoke (Mass.) Community Coll., 1990. Mem. Jr. League of Springfield, 1981-88, Community Health Edn. Council for Children and Adolescents; bd. dirs. Mass. Soc. for Prevention of Cruelty to Children, Springfield, 1985-90, Coun. of Chs., chairperson, Div. on Aging, 1989-90. Mem. ANA, Wilbraham Jr. Women's Club, Sigma Theta Tau, Alpha Chi. Home: 104 Burleigh Rd Wilbraham MA 01095-2620 Office: Baystate Med Ctr Sch of Nursing Springfield MA 01199

MOORE, JAY WINSTON, director cytogenetics laboratory; b. Madison, Wis., Apr. 20, 1942; s. Millard Harold and Leona J. (Miller) M.; m. Nancy E. Shimits; children: Meredith, Steven. BS, Cedarville Coll., 1964; MS, U. Nebr., 1966; PhD, U. Mass., 1970. Diplomate Am. Bd. Med. Genetics. From asst. prof. to prof. Eastern Coll., St. David's, Pa., 1970-84; fellow pediatric genetics Johns Hopkins Sch. of Medicine, Balt., 1984-86; asst. dirs. cytogenetics U. Iowa, Iowa City, 1986-90; dir. cytogenetics lab. Children's Hosp., Columbus, Ohio, 1990—; asst. clin. prof. Ohio State U., Columbus, 1991—. Fellow Am. Coll. Med. Genetics; mem. Am. Soc. Human Genetics. Office: Childens Hosp Cytogenetics Lab 700 Childrens Dr Columbus OH 43205

MOORE, JOHN MALCOLM, JR., urologist, surgeon; b. Arkadelphia, Ark., Oct. 14, 1937; s. John Malcolm and Evelyn Jewell (Kinard) M.; m. Barbara Ann Goad, Dec. 19, 1966; children: John Malcolm III, Michael Warren. BA, U. Ark., 1959, BS, 1961, MD, 1963. Diplomate Am. Bd. Urology. Intern U. Miami(Fla.)/Jackson Meml. Hosp., 1963-64; flight surgeon USAF, Little Rock, 1964-66; resident in surgery and urology U. Ark. Med. Sch., Fayetteville, 1966-67; ptnr. Urology Assocs., Little Rock, 1970—. Contbr. articles to profl. jours. Past chmn. Ark. State Crime Lab. Bd., Little Rock; bd. dirs. Ark. State Health Coordinating Coun., Little Rock; mem. State Racing Commn., Nat. Assn. State Racing Commrs.; commr. Ark. Health Bldg. Commn.; past bd. dirs. Pulaski Heights Meth. Ch. Capt. USAF, 1964-66. Fellow ACS; mem. AMA, Am. Assn. Clin. Urologists, Air Space Med. Assn., Urology Assn., Southwestern Med. Assn., Ark. State Med. Soc., Ark. Urology Soc. Home: 2317 N Beechwood Rd Little Rock AR 72207 Office: Ark Urology Assocs 500 S University Ste 512 Little Rock AR 72205

MOORE, JUDY L., psychologist; b. Kansas City, Mo., Oct. 1, 1940; d. Kenneth Gerald and Dorothy May (Coffman) Friend; m. George V. Czaplinski; children: Michelle Moore, Elizabeth Moore, Lane Czaplinski. BS, Cen. Mo. State U., 1972; MA, U. Mo., 1975, PhD, 1979. Lic. psychologist. Sch. psychologist Belton (Mo.) Pub. Schs., 1972-77; pres. Moore-Markus, Kansas City, 1977—; guest speaker U. Leningrad, 1990. Mem. APA, Mo. Psychol. Assn., Greater Kansas City Psychol. Assn., Internat. Soc. for the Study Multiple Personality and Dissociative States, Midwest Bioethics Com., Noetic Soc., The Establishment. Office: Moore-Markus 411 Nichols Rd Ste 238 Kansas City MO 64112-2015

MOORE, KENNETH L., physician; b. Norris, Tenn., Dec. 17, 1943. BS, Tenn. Tech. U., 1964; MD, U. Tenn., 1967. Diplomate Am. Orthopedic Surgery. Orthopedic surgeon Mid-Tenn. Bone and Joint, Columbia, 1976—. Mem. AMA, Tenn. Med. Assn., Am. Assn. Hand Surgery, Tenn. Orthopedic Soc. (pres.-elect 1995-96, sec.-treas. 1994-95), Campbell Club. Office: Mid-Tenn Bone and Joint Clinic 1223 Haft Trotwood Ave Columbia TN 38401

MOORE, MARY ANN, chiropractor; b. St. Paul, May 29, 1953; d. Lyman Maurice and Louise Elizabeth (Braymen) M.; m. Stephen Michael Batson, June 21, 1981; children: Michael Stephen, Fauna Louise. Degree summa cum laude, Life Chiropractic Coll., Marietta, Ga., 1981. Nurse's aide Highland Park Nursing Home, St. Paul, 1971; phys. therapy asst. U. Minn. Hosp., Mpls., 1973-74; nurse's aide Pleasant Hill Nursing Home, St. Paul, 1975; sales clk. Dayton's Dept. Store, St. Paul, 1976; waitress, gift shop clk. Yellowstone Nat. Park, Wyo., 1976-77; asst. mgr. Shangri-La Health Resort, Bonita Springs, Fla., 1977-78; nurse's aide Marietta Nursing Home, 1979-80; pvt. practice Chesterfield, S.C., 1986—. Contbr. articles to newspapers. Mem. Chesterfield C. of C. Jehovah's Witness. Home: RR 1 Box 245A Ruby SC 29741-9797 Office: Moore Chiropractic Ctr 102 Marshal St Chesterfield SC 29709-1618

MOORE, MELINDA, health science association administrator. MD, MPH, Harvard U., 1975. Diplomate Am. Bd. Pediatrics, Am. Bd. Preventive Medicine. With divsn. viral diseases Ctr. Disease Control, 1978; dep. dir. Internat. Health Program Office Ctr. Disease Control, Atlanta, 1991-96, acting dir., 1996—; cons. African Child Survival Initiative-Combating Childhood Communicable Diseases Project, Atlanta and Zaire; acting team leader New Ind. States project team Internat. Health Program Office. Office: Ctr Disease Control & Prevention Internat Health Program Office 4770 Buford Hwy NE Atlanta GA 30341-3724

MOORE, RICHARD ALAN, optometrist; b. La Harpe, Ill., Jan. 6, 1948; s. Emory Royal and Betty Jane (Baldwin) M.; divorced; children: Shannon Louise, David Matthew. BA in Philosophy, Drake U., 1970; BS in Optometry, Pacific U., 1972, OD, 1974. Lic. optometrist Ill., Oreg., Calif. Pvt. practice optometry Portland, Oreg., 1974-79, Carthage, Ill., 1980—; mem. clin. faculty Pacific U., Forest Grove, Oreg., 1978-79; lectr. Ill. Paraoptometric Soc. State Seminar, 1984. Editor: (newsletter) Southwester (Service Above Self award 1978-79). Mem. planning commn. City of Carthage, 1982-90; bd. dirs. Hancock Ctrl. Sch. Dist., Carthage, 1985-90, pres., 1987-90; v.p. Coll. Edn. Found., Inc., 1989—, Carthage Pk. Dist., 1982-88; organizer, pres. Hancock Transp. Coalition, 1990-92; organizer, pres. protem Hancock County Sch. Bd. Assn., 1990; Rep. candidate for state rep. from 95th dist., 1990, Hancock County Bd., 1990-94, chmn. legis. com., 1993; mem. Hancock County Rep. Ctrl. Com., 1990-92; precinct committeeman Hancock Twp., 1990-92. Mem. Am. Optometric Assn. (Best Non-Tech. Article award 1988, Recognition award 1989, Best Guest Editorial award 1991), Ill. Optometric Assn. (exec. coun. 1985-91, organizer, 1st chmn. soc. pres.'s coun. 1987, v.p. govtl. rels. 1987-91, chmn. polit. action com. 1987-91, mem. pres.'s cabinet 1987-91, chmn. resolutions com. 1991), West Ctrl. Ill. Optometric Soc. (pres. 1985-87), Carthage C. of C. (pres. 1983-84), Kiwanis (pres. Carthage chpt. 1981-82). Republican. Home: 517 W Adams St Macomb IL 61455-1323 Office: Carthage Optometric Office PO Box 457 Carthage IL 62321-0457

MOORE, RICHARD CARROLL, JR., family physician; b. Balt., Nov. 24, 1946; s. Richard Carroll and Virginia Mae (Clark) M.; m. Jeremy Pierson, Jan. 27, 1973; children: Peter Gregory, Laura Alexandra. BA, Johns Hopkins U., 1968, MPH, 1981; MD, UCLA, 1972. Diplomate Am. Bd. Family Practice. Intern South Balt. Gen. Hosp., 1972-73; commd. med. officer USPHS, 1976; chief med. div. USCG Aviation Tng. Ctr., Mobile, Ala., 1976-80; chief med. ops. USCG, Washington, 1981-86; sr. med. officer USCG Yard, Curtis Bay, Md., 1986-88; dir. Health Unit # 1, USPHS, 1988—; mem. exec. bd. Emergency Med. Svcs. Coun., Mobile County, 1979, Med. and Chirurg. Faculty Md. Mem. editorial bd. MD Med. Jour., 1995—. Bd. dirs. Midway Fed. Credit Union, 1989—, pres., 1991—. With USN, 1973-76. Mem. Aerospace Med. Assn., So. Med. Assn, Assn. Naval Aviation, Soc. U.S. Naval Flight Surgeons, Johns Hopkins U. Alumni Assn., Commd. Officers Assn. USPHS, UCLA Alumni Assn., Alpha Omega Alpha, Sigma Phi Epsilon,. Republican. Home: 3223 Browntown Rd Front Royal VA 22630-9705 Office: USPHS Health Unit 1 19844 Blue Ridge Mt Rd Bluemont VA 20135-0129

MOORE, STEPHEN ALAN, ophthalmologist; b. N.Y.C., Nov. 29, 1941; s. Jerry and Mildred (Fagan) M.; m. Kimberly Culver, Aug. 31, 1982. BA, Lafayette Coll., 1963; MD, Chgo. Med. Sch., 1968. Intern Michael Reese Hosp., Chgo., 1964-68; ophthalmology resident Jefferson Hosp., Phila., 1971-74; pvt. practice ophthalmology Great Barrington, Mass., 1974—. Capt. USAF, 1969-71. Fellow Am. Acad. Ophthalmology; mem. New Eng. Ophthalmol. Soc. Office: 140 West Ave Great Barrington MA 01230

MOORE, STEVEN RANDAL, mental health facility administrator, psychologist; b. Arkansas City, Kans., Mar. 31, 1952; s. Jack E. and Lucille (Suttle) M.; m. Sharon Moore, Aug. 16, 1974; children: Ashley, Christopher. BA, Wichita (Kans.) State U., 1975, MA, 1978; PhD, U. Kans., 1982. Lic. psychologist, Kans. Psychologist Cath. Charities, Kansas City, Mo., 1978-79; rsch. asst. U. Kans., Kansas City, 1978-79, instr., 1981; instr. Avilla Coll., Kansas City, Mo., 1985; adminstr., psychologist Rainbow Mental Health Facility, Kansas City, 1980—; rsch. cons. Kans. State Dept. of Edn., Topeka, 1978-79; cons. Severe Personal Adjustment Project, Kansas City, Kans., 1978; guest reviewer Jour. Rsch. in Childhood Edn., 1989. Author: (chpt.) Autism Teacher Training Program, 1982. U.S. Dept. Edn. grantee, 1981. Mem. Coun. for Exceptional Children, Coun. for Children with Behavior Disorders, Nat. Assn. Sch. Psychologists, FJGKC (commr. 1984—). Office: Rainbow Mental Health Facility PO Box 3208 Kansas City KS 66103-0208

MOORE, THOMAS KENT, chiropractor; b. Kansas City, Kans., Oct. 20, 1950; s. William Isaac Walton and Betty Lue (Lawrence) M.; m. Diane Noriega, Dec. 28, 1977; children: Frank Esquivel, Debbie Rayes, Sammy Esquivel. BA in Biology, U. Tex., 1972; D Chiropractic cum laude, Parker Coll. Chiropractic, 1989. Lic. Tex. Bd. Chiropractic Examiners. Dr. Back Pain Chiropractic, Irving, Tex., 1989-90; dr., owner The Back Clinic, Ft. Worth, 1990—. Roman Catholic. Home: 229 Heather ln Fort Worth TX 76140 Office: The Back Clinic 6631 McCart Ave Fort Worth TX 76133

MOORE, VERNON JOHN, JR., pediatrician, lawyer, medical consultant; b. Chgo., Mar. 18, 1942; s. Vernon John Moore; m. Rutheva deVera Dizon, Feb. 27, 1979; children: Christopher, Joseph. BS, Loyola U., Chgo., 1964, JD, 1986; MD, U. Ill.-Chgo., 1968. Bar: Ill. 1986, U.S. Dist. Ct. (no. dist.) Ill. 1986. Intern St. Joseph Health Care Ctrs. and Hosp., Chgo., 1968-69, resident in pediatrics, 1971-74, chief resident, 1972-74; pvt. practice Chgo., 1974-76; ped. med. cons. Hartgrove Hosp., Chgo., 1996—; asst. dir. pediat. edn. St. Joseph Health Care Ctrs. and Hosp., 1974-76, co-dir., 1978-86, acting chmn. dept. pediats., 1985-86; clin. assoc. prof. Pediats. Loyola U., Maywood, Ill., 1981-87; med. cons. CNA Ins. Cos., Chgo., 1987-94. Part-time staff Chgo. office Sen. Everett M. Dirksen, 1961-64. With USN, 1969-71, 76-78; capt. USNR, 1983—. Fellow Am. Acad. Pediat., Am. Coll. Legal Medicine; mem. Ill. Bar Assn. (chmn. standing com. on interprofl. coop. 1991-92), U. Ill. Alumni Assn. (bd. dirs. 1983-89), Alumni Assn. Coll. Medicine U. Ill. (alumni councillor 1989—), U. Ill. Pres. Coun. Republican. Roman Catholic. Home: 146 Park Ave River Forest IL 60305-2040 Office: Hartgrove Hosp 520 N Ridgeway Ave Chicago IL 60624

MOORE, WARREN HAMILTON, nuclear medicine specialist, educator; b. Charlotte, N.C., Nov. 12, 1950. BA in Chemistry and Biology, U. N.C., 1973, MD, 1977. Diplomate Am. Bd. Internal Medicine, Am. Bd. Nuclear Medicine. Resident in internal medicine Med. U. S.C., Charleston, 1977-80; resident in nuclear medicine Baylor Coll. Medicine, Houston, 1980-82, asst. prof. radiology, 1982-95, assoc. prof., 1995—; chief nuclear medicine svc. St. Luke's Episc. Hosp./Tex. Heart Inst., Houston, 1989—, Tex. Children's Hosp., Houston, 1988—; chief nuclear medicine sect. Baylor Coll. Medicine, 1995—; pres. S.W. Imaging Assocs., Houston, 1990—. Contbr. articles to profl. jours. and chpts. to books. Fellow ACP, Am. Coll. Cardiology, Am. Coll. Nuclear Medicine, Am. Coll. Nuclear Physicians (chmn. bylaws com. 1993—); mem. Tex. Assn. Physicians in Nuclear Medicine (pres. 1989-90), Soc. Nuclear Medicine (pres. southwestern chpt. 1992-93, chmn. edn.-tng. com. 1992-96), Phi Beta Kappa, Alpha Epsilon Delta. Office: Saint Lukes Episc Hosp 6720 Bertner Ave MC3-261 Houston TX 77030

MOORE-RIESBECK, SUSAN, osteopathic physician; b. Joliet, Ill., Jan. 23, 1963; d. Roy W. and Rita M. (Gondek) Moore; m. David E. Riesbeck. BS in Chemistry, Loyola U., Chgo., 1984; DO, Kirksville Coll. Osteo. Med., 1990. Diplomate Am. Bd. Family Practice. Chief resident in family practice Michiana Cmty. Hosp., South Bend, Ind., 1990-92, asst. residency dir., 1993—; med. dir. Transitional Health Svcs. Shamrock Gardens, South Bend, Ind., 1994—, Healthwin Nursing Home, South Bend, Ind., 1995—; Healthwin, South Bend; chair family practice dept. St. Mary Cmty. Hosp., South Bend, Ind., 1994—; med. advisor House Call, Mishawaka, Ind. Ann Wright Hazen scholar, 1987-90, Quad City Osteo. Assn. scholar, 1987; recipient Janet M. Glasgow Meml. Achievement citation AMA, 1990. Mem. Am. Osteo. Assn., Ind. Assn. Osteo Physicians and Surgeons (mem. organizational affairs com. 1996—), Am. Coll. Family Practitioners in Osteo. Medicine and Surgery, Phi Sigma Alpha. Office: 2515 E Jefferson Blvd South Bend IN 46615-2635 also: 150 W Angela South Bend IN 46617-1101

MOORMAN, WARREN LODOWICK, JR., plastic and reconstructive surgeon; b. Salem, Va., July 25, 1919; s. Warren Lodowick and Bunah Fay (LeFew) M.; m. Elizabeth Churchill Peters, Jan. 14, 1950; children: Virginia, Elizabeth, Grace, Warren III, Sarah. BS, Roanoke Coll., Salem, Va., 1940; MD, Med. Coll. Va., 1943. Diplomate Am. Bd. Surgery, Am. Bd. Plastic and Reconstructive Surgery. Staff surgeon Roanoke VA Hosp., Salem, 1950-55; fellow Mayo Clinic, Rochester, Minn., 1955-57; staff plastic and reconstructive surgeon Lewis-Gale Clinic, Salem, 1957-90; ret., pres., 1970-72. Contbr. articles to profl. jours. Mem. Roanoke Bicentennial Commn., 1976; pres. Salem Hist. Soc., 1988-90; bd. dirs. Roanoke Valley Preservation Found., 1988-96. Capt. M.C. U.S. Army, 1945-47. Fellow ACS; mem. SAR

(Fincastle Resolutions chpt.), Rotary Man of the Yr. 1977). Home: 39 Hawthorne Rd Salem VA 24153-2723

MOORS, LINDA DENISE, physician assistant; b. Balt., July 3, 1962; d. Ronald Eugene and Mary Ethel (Bledsoe) Bacon; m. Jody Cleaon Henderson, Aug. 4, 1984 (div. Mar. 1986); m. Steven John Moors, July 4, 1986. BS, PA, Trevecca Nazarene Coll., 1984, BS, 1984. Cert. CPR, ACLS, ARC, 1985—; cert. Nat. Commn. on Cert. of Physician Assts., 1985, 91. Pvt. practice physician asst. Dr. Carolyn Ross, College Station, Tex., 1985; prison physician asst. Fed. Bur. Prisons, Bastrop, Tex., 1985; clin. physician asst. Horizon Med. Ctr., Kingman, Ariz., 1985-86; prison physician asst. Ariz. Dept. Corrections, Tucson, 1986-88; vocat. sch. physician asst., health svcs. supr. Tucson Job Corps, 1988-90; physician asst. Talbert Med. Group, Tucson, 1990-92, Green Valley, Ariz., 1992—. Fellow Am. Acad. Physician Assts., Ariz. State Assn. Physician Assts. Democrat. Office: Talberg Med Group 275 W Continental Green Valley AZ 85614

MOORTHY, AROUR VISHNU, pathologist; b. Madras, India, Jan. 15, 1945; s. Arror Srinivas and Arour Yeshoda Rao; m. Indira Rao, May 13, 1968; children: Priya, Poornima, Prathima. MBBS, Stanley Med. Coll., 1966; MD, Mysore Univ. Coll. India, 1971. Diplomate Am. Bd. Internal Medicine & Nephrology. Assoc. prof. pathology U. Wis., Madison, 1977—. Office: VA Hosp 2500 Overlook Terr Madison WI 53705

MOOSBURNER, NANCY, nutritionist; b. Houston, Tex., Apr. 6, 1943; d. Henry Fenno and Shirley Louise (McCandless) Laughton; m. Stephen Weinert, Nov. 1964 (div. Nov. 1974); children: Catherine, Jeffery; m. Otto Moosburner, Feb. 7, 1976; 1 child, Brian. BS, U. Nevada Reno, 1979, MS, 1982. Edn. specialist Nev. Dept. of Edn., Carson City, 1980-83, state dir., 1983-84; sch. nutrition program supr. Douglas Co. Sch. Dist., Minden, Nev., 1987-93; dir. sch. nutrition St. Helens (Oreg.) Sch. Dist., 1993-94; instr. Truckee Meadows C.C., Reno, Nev., 1982-83, Portland C.C., St. Helens, 1993-94; child nutrition program supr. Auburn (Wash.) Sch. Dist., 1994—; state pres Nev. Sch. Food Svc. Assn., Minden, 1992-93. Contbr. articles to profl. jours. Recipient Excellence in Food Svc. award U.S. Dept. Agri., 1989; named Outstanding Women of Am., 1977. Mem. Am. Dietetic Assn., Am. Sch. Food Svc. Assn. (dir. West region 1991-93, mem. exec. bd.), Soc. for Nutrition Edn., Am. Family and Consumer Svcs. Assn. (formerly Am. Home Econs. Assn.), Oreg. Sch. Food Svc. Assn. (pub. communication 1993-94). Democrat. Home: PO Box 2628 Longview WA 98632-8665

MOOSSA, A. R., surgery educator; b. Port Louis, Mauritius, Oct. 10, 1939; s. Yacoob and Maude (Rochecoute) M.; m. Denise Willoughby, Dec. 28, 1973; children: Pierre, Noel, Claude, Valentine. BS, U. Liverpool, Eng., 1962, MD (hon.), 1965; postgrad., Johns Hopkins U., 1972-73, U. Chgo., 1973-74. Intern Liverpool Royal Infirmary, 1965-66; resident United Liverpool Hosps. and Alder Hey Children's Hosp., 1966-72; from asst. prof. surgery to assoc. prof. U. Chgo., 1975-77, prof., dir. surg. rsch., chief gen. surgery svc., vice chmn. dept., 1977-83; chmn. dept. surgery U. Calif.-San Diego Med. Ctr., 1983—; Litchfield lectr. U., Oxford, Eng., 1978; praelector in surgery U. Dundee, Scotland, 1979; Hampson Trust vis. prof. U. Liverpool, Eng., 1992, G.B. Ong. vis. prof. U. Hong Kong, 1993, Philip Sandblon vis. prof. U. Lund, Sweden. Editor: Tumors of the Pancreas, 1982, Essential Surgical Practice, 1983, 3d edit., 1995, Comprehensive Textbook of Oncology, 1985, 2d edit., 1991, Gastrointestinal Emergencies, 1985, Problems in General Surgery, 1989, Operative Colorectal Surgery, 1993. Fellow Royal Coll. Surgeons (Hunterian prof. 1977); mem. ACS, Am. Surg. Assn., Soc. Univ. Surgeons, Am. Soc. Clin. Oncology. Office: U Calif San Diego Med Ctr 200 W Arbor Dr San Diego CA 92103-1911

MORABITO, ROCCO ANTHONY, urologist; b. Huntington, W.Va., Nov. 23, 1950; s. Nicola F. and Theresa M. (Lobaldo) M.; m. Deborah Gayle Hall, 1973 (div. 1986); m. Brenda Kay Lyons, June 14, 1991; children: Shawn, Chris, Rocco Jr., Justin. BA, W.Va. U., 1972, MD, 1976. Diplomate Am. Bd. Urology, Nat. Bd. Med. Examiners. Surg. residency W.Va. U. Hosp., Morgantown, 1976-78, urol. residency, 1978-81; pres. Huntington (W.Va.) Urol. Assn., 1981—, Midwest Mobile Lithotripsy, Huntington, 1989—, Tri-State Health Ptnrs., Huntington, 1994—; pres., med. staff Cabell Huntington Hosp., Huntington, 1991-93; clin. asst. prof. urology, W.Va. U. Sch. Medicine, 1981—, Marshall U. Sch. Medicine, Huntington, 1981—. Fellow ACS; mem. AMA, Am. Urol. Assn., So. Med. Assn., W.Va. State Med. Assn., Cabell County Med. Soc., W.Va. U. Sch. Medicine Alumni Assn. (chmn. 1989-94). Republican. Roman Catholic. Home: 20 Kensington Lane Huntington WV 25705 Office: Huntington Urological Assn 2828 First Ave Ste 305 Huntington WV 25702

MORAFKA, DAVID JOSEPH, biology educator; b. San Francisco, Sept. 18, 1945; s. Aaron and Dorothy (Warner) M.; m. Sylvia Sarantis. BA in Zoology, U. Calif., Berkeley, 1967; PhD in Biology, U. So. Calif., 1974. Prof. biology Calif. State U.-Dominguez Hills, Carson, 1972—; mem. nat. coll. bd. Edn. Testing Svc., Princeton, N.J., 1978-80; mem. Desert Tortoise Recovery Team, U.S. Fish and Wildlife Svc. Author: Biogeographical Analysis of Chihuahuan Desert, 1977; editl. bd. Chelonian Biology and Conservation, Biology Conservation, 1987-93; contbr. articles to profl. jours. Advisor Friend of Madrona Marsh, Torrance, Calif., 1973—. Grantee NIH, 1985-91, NSF, 1980, 82, 85, World Wildlife Fund, Office of Endangered Species. Fellow Inst. de Ecologia de Mexico (editor 1978—), Royal Ont. Mus. Democrat. Home: 3255 Glendon Ave Los Angeles CA 90034-4405 Office: Calif State U-Dominguez Hills 1000 E Victoria St Carson CA 90747-0001

MORAHAN-MARTIN, JANET MAY, psychologist, educator; b. N.Y.C., Jan. 13, 1944; d. William Timothy and May Rosalind (Tarangelo) Morahan; m. Curtis Harmon Martin, June 2, 1979; 1 child, Gwendolyn May. AB, Rosemont (Pa.) Coll., 1965; MEd, Tufts U., 1968; PhD, Boston Coll., 1978. Asst. mkt. rsch. analyst Compton Advt. Co., N.Y.C., 1965-67; mkt. rsch. analyst Ogilvy & Mather Advt., N.Y.C., 1967; ednl. rsch. asst. Tufts U., Medford, Mass., 1968-69; counselor Psychol. Inst. Bentley Coll., Waltham, Mass., 1971-72; dir. counseling svcs. Bryant Coll., Smithfield, R.I., 1972-75, psychology instr., 1972-76, asst. prof. psychology, 1976-81, assoc. prof. psychology, 1981-91, prof. psychology, 1991—; bd. dirs. Multi-Svc. Ctr., Newton, Mass., 1980-82. Contbr. articles to profl. jours., chpts. to books; reviewer APA Conv., 1985—, Teaching of Psychology Jour., 1988—, Collegiate Micro-Computer Jour., 1991, 93, Nat. Soc. Sci. Jour., 1991. Bd. dirs. Wellesley (Mass.) Community Children's Ctr., 1986-90, Coun. for Children, Newton, Mass., 1984-86. NIMH fellow, 1967-68; NSF grantee, 1974-76, U.S. Office Edn. grantee, 1980. Mem. Am. Psychol. Assn., Mass. Audubon Soc., Nat. Social Sci. Assn., Mass. Hort. Soc., N.E. Soc. for Behavioral Analysis and Therapy. Home: 17 Fuller Brook Rd Wellesley MA 02181-7108 Office: Bryant Coll 1150 Douglas Pike Smithfield RI 02917-1291

MORAIN, WILLIAM DOUGLAS, surgeon, educator; b. Jefferson, Iowa, June 17, 1942; s. Frederick Elwyn and Lois (Garver) M.; m. Dagmar Ristic, Sept. 6, 1969; children: Anne, Peter William. AA, Graceland Coll., 1962; BA, Grinnell Coll., 1964; MD, Harvard, 1968. Diplomate Am. Bd. Plastic Surgery (bd. dirs. 1992—, sec.-treas. 1994—). Intern, resident in surgery Peter Bent Brigham and Children's Hosp., Boston, 1968-71; resident, chief resident in plastic surgery Stanford Med. Ctr., Calif., 1973-76; prof. surgery Dartmouth Med. Sch., Hanover, N.H., 1987—; staff surgeon Dartmouth-Hitchcock Med. Ctr., Hanover, 1976—; chief plastic surgery VA Hosp., White River Junction, Vt., 1976—; pres. Plastic Surgery Ednl. Found., 1991. Author: The Cutaneous Arteries of the Human Body (Webster Soc. prize 1982), 1983. Assoc. editor: Advances in Plastic Surgery, 1983—; editor-in-chief Annals of Plastic Surgery, 1992—; Medical Heritage, 1985—; Dartmouth Medical Alumni Bulletin, 1984-93. Assoc. producer EF Teleplast, 1984-87. Producer videoteleconf. series, 1985. Contbr. articles to profl. jours. Bd. dirs. Bel Canto Chamber Singers, Hanover, 1984. Served to maj. U.S. Army, 1971-73. Recipient Disting. Service award Plastic Surgery Ednl. Found., 1985. Fellow ACS (v.p. N.H. chpt. 1985-87, pres. 1987-89); mem. Am. Soc. Plastic and Reconstructive Surgeons (bd. dirs. 1984-91, Presdl. Appreciation award 1981), Am. Assn. Plastic Surgeons, Northeastern Soc. Plastic Surgeons (pres. 1992), Soc. Head and Neck Surgeons, New Eng. Surg. Soc. Mem. United Ch. of Christ. Avocations: singing; antiquarian book collecting. Home: 6 Wheelock Wood Hanover NH 03755-1558 Office: Dartmouth-Hitchcock Med Ctr One Medical Center Dr Lebanon NH 03756

MORALES, LOUIS, JR., plastic surgeon; b. Nara, Japan, Sept 1, 1949; came to U.S., 1953; s. Louis and Masano (Yasui) M.; m. Candace Joy Chapin, Nov. 22, 1980 (div.); children: Louis Chapin, Jonathan Leigh, Nicholas Ryan; m. Susan Marie Peterson, Feb. 14, 1992. BS, U Tex., El Paso, 1971; MD, U. Tex., San Antonio, 1975. Diplomate Am. Bd. Gen. Surgery, Am. Bd. Plastic Surgery. Resident in gen. surgery Emory U., Atlanta, 1975-80, resident in plastic surgery, 1980-82; fellow in craniofacial surgery U. Pa., Phila., 1982-83; asst. prof. surgery U. Utah, Salt Lake City, 1983-89, assoc. prof., 1989—, chief plastic surgery, 1987-89; dir. pediatric plastic and craniofacial surgery Primary Children's Med. Ctr., Salt Lake City, 1989-95, chmn. dept. surgery, 1994-95. Fellow ACS, Am. Acad. Pediatrics; mem. Am. Assn. Plastic Surgeons, Am. Soc. Plastic Surgeons, Am. Cleft Palate Assn., Internat. Soc. Craniofacial Surgery. Republican. Roman Catholic. Home: 5005 S Fairbrook Ln Salt Lake City UT 84117 Office: 100 N Medical Dr # 3600 Salt Lake City UT 84113

MORALES-GALARRETA, JULIO, psychiatrist, child psychoanalyst; b. Trujillo, Peru, Dec. 1, 1936; came to U.S., 1973; s. Julio Morales-Fernandez and Lidia (Galarreta) Morales; (div.); children: Lourdes Lydia, Julio Fernando. MD, U. Trujillo, 1966; grad., St. Louis Psychoanalytic Inst., 1984, grad. in child psychoanalysis, 1985. Diplomate Am. Bd. Psychiatry and Neurology; cert. psychoanalyst.; cert. child psychoanalyst. Resident in psychiatry Ministry of Pub. Health, Peru, 1965-68; supr. psychiat. tng. program Ministry Pub. Health, Peru, 1970-72; physician and surgeon U. Trujillo, 1966; instr. psychaitry St. Marcos U., Peru, 1968-72; resident in psychiatry Fairfield Hills Hosp., Newtown, Conn., 1972-74; fellow in child psychiatry Washington U., St. Louis, 1974-76, instr. child psychiatry, 1976-82; dir. child devel. project St. Louis Psychoanalytic Inst., 1982-94, dir. child and adolescent psychotherapy program, 1993—, dir. child psychoanalysis, 1996—; assoc. clin. prof. psychiatry and pediatrics St. Louis U., 1983-96, clin. prof. psychiatry and pediatrics, 1996—; faculty psychoanalysis and child analysis St. Louis Psychoanalytic Inst., 1984—, supervising analyst in child analyst, 1988, tng. and supervising analyst in adult and child psychoanalysis, 1991—. Fellow Peruvian Psychiat. Assn., Am. Psychiat. Assn., Am. Psychol. Assn.; mem. St. Louis Met. Med. Soc., Am. Acad. Child Psychiatry, Am. Psychoanalytic Assn., Am. Soc. Adolescent Psychiatry, Assn. Child Psychoanalysis. Home: 665 S Skinker Blvd Saint Louis MO 63105-2300 Office: 141 N Meramec Ave Saint Louis MO 63105-3750

MORAN, JAMES M., respiratory therapist; b. Springfield, Mass. May 15, 1956; s. James M. Moran and Veronica (Deegan) Glouster; m. Pauline Ann Hoare; children: Seamus M., Brian C. Assoc. degree, STCC, Springfield, Mass., 1981. Transport aide Mercy Hosp., Springfield, 1974-78, equipment technician, 1978-80, respiratory therapist, 1980-90; respiratory therapist Protocare of Mass., Springfield, 1990-92, clin. mgr., 1992-95; clin. mgr. Abbey Home Health Care, Springfield, 1994-95; lead respiratory therapist Apria Health Care, Springfield, 1995—. chmn. Am. Lung Assn., Springfield, 1995-96, Dan Tatro Meml. Fund, Springfield, 1994-96, coach, asst. coach Agawan (Mass.) Athletic Assn., 1993-96, resource A.W.A.K.E., Springfield, 1993, HIV-related info., 1990—. Mem. Am. Assn. Respiratory Care. Office: Protocare 338 Birnie Ave Springfield MA 01107-1104

MORAN, MANUEL, general and colon and rectal surgeon, educator; b. Salamanca, Spain, May 6, 1958; came to U.S., 1987; s. Joaquin and Encarnacion Moran; m. Cynthia Rae Dieterick, Dec. 15, 1992. MD, U. Salamanca, 1981, PhD cum laude, 1986. Diplomate Am. Bd. Surgery, Am. Bd. Colon and Rectal Surgery. Intern in gen. surgery U. Clin. Hosp., Salamanca, Spain, 1981-86; resident in gen. surgery U. N.D., 1987-92; fellow in colon and rectal surgery Alton Ochsner Med. Found., New Orleans, 1992-93; staff surgeon VA Hosp., Amarillo, Tex., 1994—; asst. prof. Tex. Tech U. Med. Sch., Amarillo, 1994—. Fellow ACS (assoc.); mem. AMA, Am. Soc. Colon and Rectal Surgeons. Home: Apt 322 1550 Bell St Amarillo TX 79106-4494

MORAN, MICHAEL LEE, physical therapist, computer consultant; b. Batavia, N.Y., Sept. 26, 1955; s. John Henry and Jane Miriam (Daly) M.; m. Jeanne Marie Grunau, Oct. 14, 1978; children: Katie, Michael L. BS, SUNY, Stony Brook, 1978; MS, U. Scranton, Pa., 1983; ScD, Nova U., Ft. Lauderdale, 1990. Staff/chief phys. therapist Allied Svcs. for the Handicapped, Scranton, Pa., 1978-81; chief phys. therapist Mercy Hosp., Wilkes-Barre, Pa., 1981-83; staff phys. therapist Spinks & Violand, Monticello, N.Y., 1983-84; dir. phys. therapy Moran Phys. Therapy, Scranton, 1984-88, Manor Health Care, Inc., Kingston, Pa., 1988-92, Coll. Misericordia, Dallas, Pa., 1992—; cons. Phys. Therapy Online Network, Shawnee Mission, Kans., 1989-92; article abstractor Jour. Am. Phys Therapy Assn., 1983—. Assoc. editor Issues on Aging, 1992-94, editor, 1994-96; contbr. articles to profl. jours. Mem. Nat. Eagle Scout Assn. Office: Coll Misericordia Dept Phys Therapy 301 Lake St Dallas PA 18612-1008

MORAND, JACQUES, obstetrician and gynecologist; b. Sallanches, Haute-Savoie, France, Mar. 22, 1949; s. Michel and Josette (Amour) M.; m. Chantal Charnay, Feb. 27, 1971; children: Pierre, Annabelle, Pauline. Cert. ob/gyn. Intern Ctr. Hosp. de Roanne, France, 1975-81; head ob/gyn. divsn. Ctr. Hosp. de St.-Vallier, France, 1981—. Home: les Marettes, 26140 Andancette France Office: Ctr Hospitalier de Saint Vallier, 26240 Saint Vallier France

MORANT, RICARDO BERNARDINO, psychology educator; b. New Britain, Conn., Feb. 13, 1926; s. J. Ramon and Rosario (Ciscar) M.; m. G. Francisca Giner, Dec. 26, 1955; children—Ramon, Francisca, Dclores, Ricardo. A.B., Harvard, 1948; postgrad., Wesleyan Coll., Middletown, Conn., 1948-49; M.A., Clark U., 1950, Ph.D., 1952. Faculty Brandeis U., Waltham, Mass., 1952—; prof. psychology Brandeis U., 1965—, Fierman prof. psychology, 1968—, chmn. dept., 1962-73; chmn. Sch. Social Scis. 1982-86, 94-96; chmn. Latin Am. Studies Brandeis U., 1984-91; Prin. investigator NIMH, Spencer Found., Rothman Found. 1960—; spl. research space perception, body orientation. Bd. dirs. Coun. Pub. Schs., 1970-73; mem. steering com. Sensory Aid Eval. and Devel. Ctr., MIT, 1963-67; chmn. bd. trustees Hiatt Ednl. Programs, 1982-94. Served with USNR, 1946-48. Fellow APA; mem. Ea. New Eng. Psychol. Assn., Psychonomic Soc. Home: 35 Cliff Rd Wellesley MA 02181-3001 Office: Brandeis Univ Waltham MA 02154

MORAVEC, CHRISTINE D. SCHOMIS, medical educator; b. L.A., Apr. 26, 1957. BA, John Carroll U., 1978, MS, 1984; PhD, Cleve. State U., 1988. Tchr. Trinity H.S., Garfield Heights, Ohio, 1978-80; grad. teaching asst. dept. biology John Carroll U., Cleve., 1982-84; rsch. assoc. dept. cardiovascular biology Cleve. Clinic Found., 1990-93, project scientist dept. cardiovascular biology, 1990-93, asst. staff dept. cardiovascular biology, 1993-94; asst. prof. dept. physiology & biophys. Case Western Res. U. Sch. Medicine, Cleve., 1993—; adj. asst. prof. Cleve. State U., 1994—; asst. staff Ctr. Anesthesiology Rsch. Cleve. Clinic Found., 1994—. Contbr. articles to profl. jours. Grad. fellow Cleve. Clinic Found., 1984-88, Postdoctoral fellow, 1988-89, recipient Tarazi fellow, 1989. Mem. Am. Physiol. Soc., Am. Heart Assn. (basic sci. coun. 1990—; Established Investigatorship award 1995), Ohio Physiol. Soc., Electron Microscopy Soc. Northeastern Ohio, Cardiac Muscle Soc. Office: Cleve Clin Found Ctr Anesthesiology Found 9500 Euclid Ave FF40 Cleveland OH 44195*

MORAWETZ, RICHARD BACON, neurosurgeon; b. Marietta, Ga., Nov. 27, 1944; s. Richard J. and Mary B. (Bacon) M.; m. Mary Jean Middlebrooks, May 31, 1968. Diploma, Emory U., 1965; MD, Duke U., 1969. Diplomate Am. Bd. Neurol. Surgery. Sr. scientist Comprehensive Cancer Inst. U. Ala., Birmingham, 1986—, dir. divsn. neurosurgery, 1988—, J.G. Galbraith prof. neurosurgery, 1993—; chmn. med. records com U. Ala., Birmingham, mem. cost containment com., grad. med. edn. com. Co-contbr. articles to profl. jours. Mem. Am. Heart Assn., Stroke Coun. Mem. Am. Acad. Neurol. Surgery, Neurosurg. Soc. Am., Congress Neurol. Surgeons, Neurosurg. Soc. Ala. (pres. 1994-96, exec. coun. joint sec. cerebrovascular surgery 1995-96), So. Neurosurg. Soc. (pres. 1994-95). Office: U Ala Birmingham Divsn Neurosurgery 1813 6th Ave S MEB 512 Birmingham AL 35294

MORBIDI, MARIO, orthopaedic surgeon; b. Monterotondo, Rome, Italy, Sept. 12, 1953; s. Gino and Fernanda (Zappelli) M. MD, U. La Sapienza, Rome, 1978. Cons. Ospedale S. Pietro, Rome, 1981—; specialist orthopaedic surgery U. La Sapienza, Rome, 1981; visitor surgeon U. Toronto, 1982-83, 85—. Contbr. articles to profl. jours. Mem. Societa Italiana Ortopedia e Traumatologia, Internat. Arthroscopy Assn., Associazione Laziale Ortopedici Traumatologi Ospedalieri, Gruppo Italiano Artoscopia, Tennis Club Parioli, Rotary. Home: Via Taro 3, 00199 Rome Italy Office: Casa Di Cura Nostra Signora Della Mercede, Via Tagliamento 25, 00199 Rome Italy

MORDOCK, JOHN BAYLEY, JR., psychologist, mental health center administrator; b. Cumberland, Md., Aug. 2, 1938; s. John Bayley and Nancy Douglas (James) M.; m. Melody Robitaille, Nov. 30, 1991; children: Kalay D., Kaylin M., Marten, Massen. BS, Springfield Coll., 1960; MA, U. Ill., 1961; PhD, U. Hawaii, 1967; CAS, SUNY, New Paltz, 1989. Diplomate Am. Bd. Profl. Psychology. Coordinator research Dereeux Found., 1966-69, sr./chief psychologist, 1969-77, clin. dir., 1977-80, program dir., 1980-83; asst. exec. dir. Astor Home and Child Guidance Ctrs., Poughkeepsie, N.Y., 1983—. Author: The Other Children, 1975; Ego-Impaired Children Grow Up, 1978; Crisis Counseling, 1983, 2nd edit., 1991, Counseling Defiant Children, 1994, Selecting Treatment Interventions, 1996. Contbr. numerous articles to profl. jours. Rehab. Services Adminstrn. fellow, 1961; NSF fellow, 1964; NIMH fellow, 1966. Fellow Am. Psychol. Assn.; mem. Assn. Mental Health Adminstrs. Club: Trout Unlimited. Avocations: skiing, fly fishing. Home: 52 Old Farms Rd Poughkeepsie NY 12603-5037 Office: Astor Community Med Health Programs 13 Mt Carmel Pl Poughkeepsie NY 12601-2006

MOREDOCK, GERALD MICHAEL, physician, educator; b. Lebanon, Ind., July 19, 1948; s. Gilbert Burns and Dolores Eleanor (Millikan) M.; m. Naomi Ruth Sloan, June 8, 1968; children: Janine, Aaron, Karrie. BS in chemistry, Ind. U., 1970; MD, Ind. U., Indpls., 1974. Physician McDonald & Ballhagen, PC, Ronan, Mont., 1977-78; pvt. practice Watford City, N.D., 1978-86; prof. Trevecca Nazarene Univ., Nashville, 1986—, now also dean div. natural and applied scis.; pres. bd. dirs. Middle Tenn. Area Health Edn. Corp., Murfreesboro, 1989-91. Fellow Nazarene Med., Wesleyan Med., Free Meth. Med.; mem. AMA, Am. Acad. Family Physicians, Tenn. Acad. Family Physicians, Tenn. Acad. Physician Assts., Tenn. Med. Assn. Republican. Office: Trevecca Nazarene U 333 Murfreesboro Rd Nashville TN 37210-2834

MOREHOUSE, LAWRENCE GLEN, veterinarian, emeritus professor; b. Manchester, Kans., July 21, 1925; s. Edwy Owen and Ethel Merle (Glenn) M.; m. Georgia Ann Lewis, Oct. 6, 1956; children: Timothy Lawrence, Glenn Ellen. BS in Biol. Sci., Kans. State U., 1952, DVM, 1952; MS in Animal Pathology, Purdue U., 1956, PhD, 1960. Lic. vet. medicine. Veterinarian County Animal Hosp., Des Peres, Mo., 1952-53; supr. Brucellosis labs. Purdue U., West Lafayette, Ind., 1953-60; staff veterinarian lab. svcs. USDA, Washington, 1960-61; discipline leader in pathology and toxicology, animal health divsn. USDA Nat. Animal Disease Lab., Ames, Iowa, 1961-64; prof., chmn. dept. veterinary pathology Coll. Vet. Medicine U. Mo., Columbia, 1964-67, 84-86; dir. Vet. Med. Diagnostic Lab., 1968-88; prof. emeritus Coll. Vet. Medicine U. Mo., Columbia, 1986—; cons. USDA, to comdg. gen. U.S. Army R & D Command, Am. Inst. Biol. Scis., NAS, Miss. State U., St. Louis Zoo Residency Tng. Program, Miss. Vet. Med. Assn., Okla. State U., Pa. Dept. Agr., Ohio Dept. Agr. Co-editor: Mycotoxic Fungi, Mycotoxins, Mycotoxicoses: An Encyclopedic Handbook , 3 vols., 1977; contbr. numerous articles on diseases of animals to profl. jours. Active Trinity Presbyn. Ch., Columbia, 1989-92; bd. dirs. Mo. Symphony Soc., Columbia, 1989-92. With USN, 1943-46, PTO, U.S. Army, 1952-56. Recipient Outstanding Svc. award U.S Dept Agr., 1959, Merit Cert., 1963, 64, Disting. Svc. award Coll. Vet. Medicine U. Mo., 1987. Fellow Royal Soc. Health London; mem. Am. Assn. Vet. Lab. Diagnosticians (E.P. Pope award 1976, chmn. lab. accreditation bd. 1972-79, 87-90, pres. 1979-80, sec.-treas. 1983-87), World Assn. Vet. Lab. Diagnosticians (bd. dirs. 1984—), N.Y. Acad. Sci., U. S. Animal Health Assn., Am. Assn. Lab. Animal Sci., Mo. Soc. Microbiology, Am. Assn. Avian Pathologists, N.Am. Conf. Rsch. Workers in Animal Diseases, Mo. Univ. Retirees Assn. (v.p. 1996—). Presbyterian. Home: 916 Danforth Dr Columbia MO 65201-6164 Office: U Mo Vet Med Diagnostic Lab PO Box 6023 Columbia MO 65201

MOREIN, JOAN ZARET, psychologist; b. Phila., Jan. 12, 1942; d. Paul and Pearl (Weinroth) Zaret; m. Barry A. Morein, Aug. 21, 1963; 1 child, Jonathan Roger. BA, Temple U., 1963, MA, 1969; postgrad., Inst. for Psychoanalytic Psychotherapies, 1975-85. Lic. psychologist, Pa.; cert. addictions counselor, Pa. Social worker Phila. State Hosp., 1965-68; psychologist Oak Lane Day Sch., Blue Bell, Pa., 1969-74, The Woods Schs., Langhorne, Pa., 1969-74, Green Tree Sch., Phila., 1973-74; dir. STEP program Centralized Comprehensive Human Svcs., Inc., Phila., 1975-84, dir. therapeutic work program, 1980-84, dir. rehab. mental health, 1984-86; dir. men's outpatient Diagnostic & Rehab. Ctr., Phila., 1990-91; dir. MICA Partial Hosp., 1987-90; psychologist MCC, Wilmington, Del., 1991; psychologist Western Psychol. Cons., Wynnewood, Pa., 1978—, Penn Recovery Systems, 1991-92, Comprehensive Psychol. Svcs., 1991-92, Charter Fairmount Inst., 1991-92; psychologist, site dir. PsychResource Assocs., 1991—; sr. adj. instr. Hahnemann U., Phila., 1974—; preceptor Lincoln U., 1989-91; tng. cons. Outley Profl. Svcs., 1993-95. Mem. Del. Valley Partial Hospitalization Assn. (bd. dirs. 1989-91), The MICA Coalition (bd. dirs. 1990-92), Nat. Assn. for Advancement Psychoanalysis, APA, Pa. Psychol. Assn., Del. Valley Group Psychotherapy Assn. Office: Western Psychol Consultants 60 Rock Glen Rd Wynnewood PA 19096-3828

MOREIRA, ALLAN, urologist; b. Managua, Nicaragua, Sept. 30, 1937; came to U.S., 1955; s. Gilberto and Esther (Conrado) M.; m. Laila I.B. Olsson, Oct. 15, 1960; children: Ingrid, Linda, Kerstin, Alan. AA, U. Calif., Berkeley, 1957; MD, Creighton U., 1962. Intern Mercy Hosp., Des Moines, 1962-63; gen. practice Cogley Clinic, Council Bluffs, Iowa, 1963-64; resident Mt. Zion Hosp., San Francisco, 1966-67, U. Calif., San Francisco, 1967-70; urologist pvt. practice, Fremont & San Francisco, Calif., 1970-76; urologist Kaiser Permanente, Honolulu, 1984-94, chief dept. urology, 1994—. Col. U.S. Army, 1964-84. Mem. AMA, Calif. Med. Assn., Hawaii Urological Soc., Assn. Mil. Surgeons U.S., Soc. Govt. Svc. Urologists. Republican. Roman Catholic. Office: Kaiser Permanente 3288 Moanalua Rd Honolulu HI 96819

MORELAND, FERRIN BATES, retired toxicologist, actor; b. Portland, Oreg., Aug. 12, 1909; s. Eldon W. and Lavisa M.; m. Hazel Munn Brookshire, 1938; children: Margaret, Howard. BS, Oreg. State U., 1930; MA, Rice U., 1932; PhD, Vanderbilt U., 1936. Diplomate Am. Bd. Clin. Chemistry, Am. Bd. Forensic Toxicology. Instr. State U. of Iowa, 1936-42; assoc. prof. Baylor Med. Coll., Houston, 1947-65; lab. dir. Tex. Inst. for Rehab. and Rsch., 1959-65; mgr. biomed. labs. Brown and Root-Northrop, NASA, Houston, 1965-68; chief chemist Metabolic Rsch., Houston, 1968-70; chief toxicologist Harris County Med. Examiner, Houston, 1970-79, ret., 1979; clin. chemistry cons. The Meth. Hosp., Tex. Children's Hosp., Jefferson Davis Hosp., VA Hosp. Ex-chief Southside Place Fire Dept.; book reader Houston Taping for the Blind; actor many theater prodns., movies, and TV and print commls. Capt. USAAC, 1942-45. Mem. Am. Chem. Soc. (officer, com. mem.), Am. Assn. Clin. Chemists (pres. 1958-59, com. mem.).

MORELLI, ANTHONY FRANK, pediatric dentist; b. Chgo., Aug. 10, 1956; s. Frank A. and Josephine M. (Cerniglia) M.; m. Tina Makris, July 24, 1982; children: Deanna Nicole, Michelle Tina. BS, Loyola U., Chgo., 1976; DDS, Loyola U., Maywood, Ill., 1984, postgrad., 1986. Cert. specialist pediatric dentistry, Ill; Diplomate Am. Bd. Pediatric Dentistry. Pediatric dentist Infant Welfare Soc. Chgo., 1984-90; chief resident dept. pediatric dentistry sch. dentistry Loyola U., Maywood, 1985-86, assoc. prof. pediatric dentistry, 1986-91; pvt. practice La Grange, Ill., 1988—; mem. staff Children's Meml. Hosp., Chgo. and Westchester, Ill., Mt. Sinai Hosp., Chgo., MacNeal Hosp., Chgo. Mem. ADA, Chgo. Dental Soc., Am. Soc. Dentistry Children, Am. Acad. Pediatric Dentistry, Am. Bd. Pediatric Dentistry (diplomate), Ill. Soc. Pediatric Dentistry. Home: 6448 Cambridge Rd Willowbrook IL 60521 Office: 4727 S Willow Springs Rd La Grange IL 60525

MORELLO, ROBERT FRANK, physician; b. New Rochelle, N.Y., May 8, 1947; s. Joseph Frank and Felicia (Gargiulo) M.; m. Nordeen Michelle Squilla, July 31, 1976; children: Samantha, Scott, Sabrina. BS in Biology, St. John's U., 1969; MD, Autonomous U. Guadalajara, Mex., 1976. Diplomate Am. Bd. Ophthalmology. Resident in internal medicine Bronx Lebanon

Hosp. Ctr./Albert Einstein Coll. Medicine, 1977-78, resident in ophthalmology, 1978-79; attending ophthalmologist New Rochelle Hosp. Med. Ctr., 1981—; cons. ophthalmologist Calvary Hosp., Bronx, N.Y., 1983—. Participating physician Vol. Healthy Program. Fellow Am. Coll. Surgeons, Internat. Coll. Surgeons, Am. Acad. Ophthalmology. Office: 120 Warren St New Rochelle NY 10801

MORENO, EDUARDO CARLOS, urologist; b. Guayaquil, Ecuador, Oct. 9, 1941; Came to U.S., 1972; m. Martha Molicia; children: Clara, Eddie, Steve. MD, U. Guayaquil, 1968. Diplomate Am. Bd. Urology. Intern St. Francis U., Evanston, Ill., 1972-73; resident Luis Veranza Hosp., Guayquil, Ecuador, 1969-72, U. Ill., Chgo., 1973-75, U. Miami (Fla.), 1975-78; urologist pvt. practice, Lakeland, Fla., 1978—. Fellow Am. Coll. Surgeons; mem. AMA, Am. Urological Assn., Am. Lithotripsy Soc., Interamerican Coll. Physicians and Surgeons, Fla. Med. Assn., Fla. Urological Soc., Polk County Med. Soc. Office: 4435 Florida Nat Dr Lakeland FL 33813

MORENO, JOSE GUILLERMO, psychiatrist; b. Bogota, Colombia, Sept. 6, 1951; came to U.S., 1976; s. Guillermo and Olga (Herrera) M.; m. Anne Dorothea Novitt, Dec. 17, 1978; children: Christina, Andrew, Michael. MD, Javeriana U., Bogota, 1973. Intern Javeriana U., Bogota, 1973-74; asst. dir. Mental Health Hosp., Armero, Colombia, 1975-76; resident psychiatry N.J. Med. Sch., Newark, 1976-79; attending psychiatrist St. Joseph's Hosp., Paterson, N.J., 1979—, St. Michael's Hosp., Newark, 1979—, Chilton Meml. Hosp., Pompton Plains, N.J., 1980—; chief psychiat. inpatient unit St. Joseph's Hosp. and Med. Ctr., Paterson, 1981-85, chmn. dept. psychiatry, 1985—; pres. Jose G. Moreno, MD, P.A., Chester, N.J.; chief resident dept. psychiatry N.J. Med. Sch., Newark, 1978-79; assoc. prof. sch. grad. med. edn. Seton Hall U., 1989—. Mem. AMA, Am. Psychiat. Assn., N.J. Psychiat. Assn., U.S. Naval Inst. Republican. Roman Catholic. Office: 205 Ridgedale Ave Florham Park NJ 07932-1349

MORENO, MANUEL, chiropractor; b. Aguascalientes, Mex., July 1, 1942; came to U.S., 1956; s. Pablo and Matilda (Gonzalez) M.; m. Narcy Rodriguez, Apr. 8, 1991; children: Henry E., Pablo M. BS, U. Tex., El Paso, 1971; D Chiropractic, Tex. Chiropractic Coll., 1982. Diplomate Am. Bd. Chiropractic. Rehab. counselor State Commn. for the Bind, El Paso; pvt. practice chiropractic physician El Paso. With USN, 1961-65. Fellow Am. Back Soc., Internat. Acad. Clin. Acupuncture; mem. Hispanic C. of C. Democrat. Roman Catholic. Home: 2109 Woodfin El Paso TX 79925 Office: Bassett Chiropractic Ctr 5901 Gateway West El Paso TX 79925

MORENO-CABRAL, CARLOS EDUARDO, cardiac surgeon; b. Zacatecas, Mex., Nov. 4, 1951; s. Manuel Julio Moreno and Dominga Cabral; children: Rodrigo, Iza, Daniel. MD, Nat. U. Mex., 1976. Diplomate Am. Bd. Surgery, Am. Bd. Thoracic Surgery. Resident in gen. surgery U. Hawaii, 1977-80, Mich. State U., 1980-82; fellow in cardiac surgery Stanford (Calif.) U., 1982-84, 86-88; tng. in thoracic surgery SUNY, Bklyn., 1984-86; dir. cardiac transplant program St. Francis Hosp., Honolulu, 1989—. Author: Postoperative Management in Adult Cardiac Surgery, 1988. Fellow ACS; mem. Soc. Thoracic Surgeons. Office: 1380 Lusitana 912 Honolulu HI 96813

MORETTA, ANA E., medical records administrator; b. Dominican Republic, Oct. 2, 1934; d. Guillermo A. and Juana E. (Diaz) Villalona; m. Carlos S. Moretta Cabrera, July 26, 1959; children: Carlos Enrique, Carlos Samuel, Carlos Alberto. AA, Coll. Las Antillas, 1959; BS, Adventist U., 1976. Tchr. sci. Dominican Acad., Santo Domingo, 1959-65; from med. records clk. to med. records tech. Bella Vista Hosp., Mayaguez, P.R., 1965-78; med. record adminstr. San Antonio Mcpl. Hosp., Mayaguez, 1979-81; sr. med. record tech. Meml. Hosp., Chattanooga, 1981-83; from sr. med. record tech. to supervisor med. record office George Washington U., Washington, 1983-90; med. record analyst Altamonte Hosp., Orlando, 1990-91; med. record adminstr. Hosp. Clin. Espanola, Mayaguez, 1992—. Mem. Am. Health Info. Mgmt. Assn. Mem. 7th Day Adventist Ch. Home: H-27 Almirante St Mayaguez PR 00680

MORETTO, JANE ANN, nurse, public health officer; b. Belgium, Ill., Apr. 9, 1934; d. Bernard James and Mildred Bertha (Sutton) Moretto; RN, Mercy Hosp. Sch. Nursing, Urbana, Ill., 1955; B.S. in Nursing, St. Joseph Coll., Emmitsburg, Md., 1969. Relief head nurse, staff nurse Mercy Hosp., Urbana, Ill., 1955-57; staff nurse in psychiatry VA Hosp., Danville, Ill., 1957-59; staff nurse pulmonary disease VA Hosp., Long Beach, Calif., 1959-60, staff nurse surg. unit, L.A., 1960-61, staff nurse oper. rm., 1961-64; commd. lt. comdr. USPHS, 1969, advanced through grades to capt., 1975—; staff nurse USPHS Hosp., Galveston, Tex., 1964-66, staff nurse tumor ICU, Balt., 1967, asst. oper. rm. supr., New Orleans, 1969-71, oper. rm. supr., Brighton, Mass., 1971-78, dep. dir. nursing, dir. insvc. edn. Carville, La., 1978-80, dir. nurses Gillis W. Long Hansen's Disease Ctr., 1980-91, clin. nurse cons. lower extremity amputation prevention program Carville Diabetic Foot Program, 1991-95; cons. in field; lectr. in field. Inventor teaching foot model. Recipient Superior Performance award, USPHS Hosp., Galveston, 1966, Outstanding Svc. medal for exemplary performance of duty Dept. Health Human Svcs.-Pub. Health Svc., 1986 (citation, 1990, Unit Commendation award USPHS, 1981, Isolated Hardship award USPHS, 1981, Hazardous Duty award USPHS, 1992, Commendation medal USPHS, 1993); named Nurse of Yr., Baton Rouge Dist. Nurses Assn., 1991. Mem. Am. Nurses Assn., La. Nurses Assn., La. Hosp. Assn., La. Soc. Nursing Svc. Adminstrs., Nat. Assn. for Uniformed Svcs., Assn. Mil. Surgeons of U.S., Assn. Oper. Rm. Nurses, Alumnae Assn. of Schlarman High Sch., Alumnae Assn. of St. Joseph Coll., Commd. Officers Assn. USPHS. Roman Catholic. Home: 1741 Cobble Ln Mount Dora FL 32757

MORETTO, THOMAS J., physician; b. Bremen, Ind., Mar. 12, 1944; s. James and Margaret E. (Huff) M.; m. Louise Ann Moretto, June 19, 1986; children: Christopher Todd, Natalie, Colby, Catherine. BA, Hanover Coll., 1966; MD, Ind. Med. Sch., Indpls., 1970. Diplomate Am. Bd. Family Practice. Resident St. Vincent Hosp., Indpls., 1973; pvt. practice Northwest Family Physician, 1973-93; physician, pres. Group One Family Physician, Indpls., 1993-94, Am. Health Network, Indpls., 1994—; state med. dir. Health Plus HMO, Indpls., 1990-95; med. dir. Prin. Health Ins., Fort Wayne, Ind., 1990—; chair dept. family practice St. Vincent Hosp., Indpls., 1980—. Mem. Ind. Acad. Family Practice, Marion County Med. Soc. Methodist. Office: Group One 3400 Lafayette Rd Indianapolis IN 46222

MORETZ, ROGER CLARK, cell biologist; b. Warren, Ohio, July 4, 1942; s. Rodney Russell and Ruth Elizabeth (Gurganious) M.; m. Carol Marilynn Taylor, Aug. 12, 1967; children: Brenda Lynn, Heather Dawn. BA in Physics, Greenville Coll., 1964; MS in Radiol. Health, Rutgers U., 1965; PhD in Biophys Sci., SUNY, Buffalo, 1973. Rsch. asst. Tam div. Nat. Lead Co., Niagara Falls, N.Y., 1966-67; rsch. scientist Roswell Pk. Meml. Inst., Buffalo, 1967-72; postdoctoral fellow U. Colo., Boulder, 1972-74; rsch. assoc. Peter B. Brigham Hosp., Boston, 1974-76; rsch. scientist N.Y. State Inst. for basi Rsch., S.I., 1976-89; sr. prin. scientist Boehringer Ingelheim Pharms., Ridgefield, Conn., 1989—; lectr. Coll. Med. and Dentistry N.J., Piscataway, 1978-80. Contbr. chpts. to books and articles to profl. jours. Elder, music dir. New Durham Chapel, Piscataway, N.J., 1978-89; v.p. PTO Arbor Sch., Piscataway, 1979-80; pres. Parent-Tchr. Fellowship Timothy Chrsitan Sch., Piscataway, 1984-86. NIH fellow, 1972. Mem. AAAS, Electron Microscopy Soc. Am., Conn. Electron Microscopy Soc., Microbeam Analysis Soc. (met. sect., sec.-treas. 1988-89). Office: Boehringer Ingelheim Pharms 900 Ridgebury Rd Ridgefield CT 06877

MORGAN, ALAN, surgeon; b. Newport, Gwent, U.K., June 27, 1931; came to U.S., 1966; s. Reginald John and Mary Ann (Evans) M.; m. J. Mary Braund, Feb. 14, 1959; children: Richard John Charles, Charlotte Mary, Rowland William Philip. MB Ch.B., U. Bristol, Eng., 1957. Attending surgeon Children's Hosp., Seattle, 1969—; attending surgeon Northwest Hosp., Seattle, 1969—, assoc. in pediatric surgery, 1975—; clin. prof. surgery U. Wash., Seattle, 1988—; adj. prof. biol. structure U. Wash., Seattle, 1988—; staff sec. Children's Hosp., Seattle, 1976-77. Contbr. 27 articles to profl. jours. Bd. dirs. King County Med. Blue Shield, Seattle, 1977-82; pres. Seattle Chamber Music Festival, Seattle, 1992-93. C. Fellow ACS, Royal Coll. Surgeons (Eng.); mem. Pacific Coast Surg. Assn. (v.p. 1994-95), Seattle Tennis Club, Sand Point Golf Club, Chartwell Stable (ptnr. 1978—). Democrat. Anglican. Home: 3877 45th Ave NE Seattle WA 98105 Office: 1560 N 115th St Ste 102 Seattle WA 98133

MORGAN, ALEXANDER CHARLES, psychiatrist, educator; b. Orange, N.J., Nov. 9, 1941; s. Alexander and Jean (Grey) M.; m. Donna Dee Donegan, Apr. 29, 1967; children: Ian Clerihew, Elise Kinsella. BS cum laude, Davidson (N.C.) Coll., 1963; MD, Columbia U., 1967. Diplomate Am. Bd. Psychiatry and Neurology, Am. Bd. Geriatric Psychiatry; cert. in psychoanalysis. Intern Cambridge (Mass.) Hosp., 1967-68; resident in medicine Boston City Hosp., 1968-69; resident in psychiatry Univ. Hosp./Boston U. Med. Ctr., 1971-74; cons. home med. svc. Univ. Hosp., Boston, 1974-75; instr. psychiatry Med. Sch. Boston U., 1974—; dir. geriatric team of ambulatory community svc. Cambridge (Mass.) Hosp., 1975-79; med. dir. geriatric svc. dept. psychiatry Cambridge (Mass.) Hosp., Cambridge Hosp., 1979-84; preceptor for residents dept. psychiatry Cambridge (Mass.) Hosp., 1983-87, dir. geriatric tng. dept. psychiatry, 1984-87, dir. geriatric psychiatry, 1987—; instr. in psychiatry Harvard U. Med. Sch., 1975-94; asst. clin. prof. psychiatry Harvard U., Boston, 1994—; cons. Neville manor Nursing Home, Cambridge, 1975-79. Coach Newton (Mass.) Soccer Assn., 1979-89; mem. Newton Community Chorus, 1982—. Lt. comdr. USN, 1969-71. NIMH grantee, 1983-89. Mem. Boston Psychoanalytic Soc. and Inst. (instr. inst. and extension div.), Newton Squash and Tennis Club. Democrat. Office: Cambridge Hosp 1493 Cambridge St Cambridge MA 02139-1047

MORGAN, ANDREW LANE, urologist; b. Honolulu May 13, 1920; s. James Albert and Elsie Edna (Johnson) M.; BA, Dartmouth Coll., 1942; MD, Cornell U., 1945; m. Miriam Cleary, June 9, 1951; children: Andrew Lane, Christine, Martha, James. Diplomate Am. Bd. Urology. Intern, Lenox Hill Hosp., N.Y.C., 1945-46; resident, Queen's Med. Ctr., Honolulu, 1948-50, Yale U., 1950-52; practice medicine, specializing in urology, Honolulu, 1952-87; ret., 1987; chmn. dept. surgery Queen's Med. Ctr., 1979; clin. prof. urology John Burns Sch. Medicine, U. Hawaii; mem. renal transplant team St. Francis Med. Ctr. Past pres. Hawaii Med. Libr., 1957-58. Served to capt., AUS, 1946-48. Fellow ACS; mem. AMA, Am. Urol. Assn. (past pres. Western sect.), Hawaii Med. Assn., Societe Internationale d'Urologie, Honolulu County Med. Soc. (bd. govs. 1970-76, treas. 1978-79), Pacific Club (Honolulu). Episcopalian. Home: 44 Puako Beach Dr Kamuela HI 96743-9707

MORGAN, AVANELLE PROCTOR, physician; b. Yonkers, N.Y., Mar. 26, 1945; d. Egbert Purdy and Avanelle Major (Proctor) M. AB cum laude, Cornell U., Ithaca, 1967; MD, SUNY, 1971; AAS in Family Med. Practice, Cayuga C.C., Auburn, N.Y., 1996. Bd. cert. family practice. R-2 intern Cleve. Metro Gen. Hosp., 1971-72; resident family practice Resident-Maine Med. Ctr., Portland, 1972-75; pvt. practice Union Springs, N.Y., 1978-89; physician Health Svcs. of Ctrl. N.Y., Lafayette, 1989-95, Finger Lakes Family Medicine, Scipio, N.Y., 1996—; dept. head Auburn (N.Y.) Meml. Hosp., 1980-82, bd. trustees, 1985-89. Contbr. article to profl. jour. Physician USPHS, 1975-78. Recipient Commendation medal USPHS-Nat. Health Svc. Corps, 1978. Fellow Am. Acad. Family Physicians; mem. Cayuga County Med. Soc. (sec. 1985-86), Am. Acad. Family Practice. Presbyterian. Home: 5207 Ridge Rd Union Springs NY 13160 Office: Finger Lakes Family Medicine Center Rd Scipio Center NY 13147

MORGAN, CATHERINE MARIE, psychologist, writer; b. Duluth, Minn., Mar. 27, 1947; 1 child, Andrew. BS, U. Nebr., 1968; MEd, U. Okla., 1973; PhD Okla. State U., 1987; postgrad., Menninger Found. Psychotherapy Tng. Program, 1987-89. Child devel. specialist Southwest Guidance Ctr., Wheatland, Okla., 1973-74; pvt. practice Family Counseling Assocs., San Antonio, 1974-75; psychol. asst. Edmond Guidance Ctr., Okla., 1975-82; psychol. asst. supr. Southeast Guidance Ctr., Del City, Okla., 1982-86; psychol. intern Cleve. County Health Dept., Moore, Okla., 1986-87; psychologist Cen. State Hosp., Norman, Okla., 1987-89; pvt. practice assocs. in pschology, Edmond, Okla.; v.p. Behavior Mgmt. Specialists, Oklahoma City, 1983—; pres. Assocs. in Psychology, 1988—. Mem. AAUW, APA, Okla. Psychol. Assn., Southwestern Psychol. Assn., Am. Pers. and Guidance Assn., Am. Bus. Women's Assn., P.E.O., Kappa Delta Pi. Avocations: writing, reading, knitting, racquetball. Office: 5400 NW Grand Blvd Oklahoma City OK 73112

MORGAN, CHARLES HERMANN, JR., clinical psychologist; b. N.Y.C., Mar. 14, 1949; s. Charles Hermann and Miriam Hudson (Wagner) M.; m. Ruth-Anne Hein, Aug. 16, 1969; children: Jennifer Susan, Benjamin Charles. BA, Columbia U., 1971; MA, New Sch. for Social Rsch., 1974; PhD, U. Fla., 1979. Licensed clin. psychologist, Ky. Asst. prof. Morehead (Ky.) St. U., 1979-84, assoc. prof., 1984-89, prof., 1989—; pvt. practitioner Morehead, 1980—; mem. Ky. State Bd. of Psychology, Frankfort, Ky., 1988-96; cons. C.D. Perkins Rehab. Ctr., Thelma, Ky., 1979-82. Contbr. articles to profl. jours. Chief ofcl. Dist. Gov.'s Cup Competition, Morehead, Ky., 1992. Recipient Outstanding Young Men of Am. award U.S. Jaycees, 1981, Sch. Community award Montgomery County Sch. Bd., 1986. Mem. APA, Assn. State and Provincial Psychology Bds., Ea. Psychol. Assn., Southeastern Psychol. Assn., Soc. for Personality Assessment, Ky. Psychol. Assn. (ethics com. 1982-85, 87-90, Disting. Psychologist award 1995). Presbyterian. Office: Morehead State U Upo # 1336 Morehead KY 40351

MORGAN, CLYDE NATHANIEL, dermatologist; b. Bell County, Tex., Nov. 2, 1923; s. Xenophen William and Rhoda Ella (Deck) M.; m. Birdie Joyce Rich, Mar. 3, 1951; children: Clyde Nathaniel Jr., Reinette Jean, Nancy Elaine. BS, Abilene Christian Coll., 1948; MD, U. Tex. Galveston, 1953. Assoc. prof. biology Abilene (Tex.) Christian Coll., 1954-56; pvt. practice Abilene, 1954-67, dermatologist, 1969—. Contbr. articles to profl. jours. Mem. AMA, SAR (v.p. 1995-96, award 1995), Am. Coll. Cryosurgery, Internat. Soc. Cryosurgery, Tex. Med. Assn., Tex. Dermatologic Soc., Taylor-Jones-Haskell County Med. Soc. Republican. Mem. Ch. of Christ. Home: 1718 Cedar Crest Dr Abilene TX 79601-3228 Office: 1166 Merchant St Abilene TX 79603-5014

MORGAN, CRAIG D., orthopaedic surgeon; b. Olean, N.Y., Oct. 2, 1950; s. James Franklin Jr. and Helen Aileen (Dawson) M.; m. Natalie Jean Holt, July 9, 1975; children: Craig Drewry, Holt Franklin. BA in Chemistry and Biology cum laude, Hope Coll., Holland, Mich., 1972; MD cum laude, Emory U., 1977. Diplomate Am. Bd. Orthopaedic Surgery. Resident U. Mich., Ann Arbor, 1982; pres., founding mem. Del. Orthopaedic Ctr., Wilmington, 1986—; dir. sports medicine Alfred I. duPont Inst., Wilmington, 1988—; clin. instr. orthopaedic surgery Thomas Jefferson U., Phila., 1989-94, assoc. prof., 1994—; bd. dirs. Arthrex, Inc., Naples, Fla.; cons. Bowen, Inc., Rockville, Md., 1982—. Assoc. editor Jour. Arthroscopy, 1990—; contbr. chpts. to books and articles to profl. jours.; patentee in field. Mem. Am. Orthopaedic Soc. Sports Medicine, Am. Acad. Orthopaedic Surgeons, Internat. Arthroscopy Assn. (bd. dirs. 1990-95, sec.), Internant. Knee Soc. (bd. dirs. 1993-95, sec.), Internat. Arthroscopy, Knee and Sport Medicine Soc. (bd. dirs. 1995—, sec.), Alpha Omega Alpha. Office: Del Orthopaedic Ctr 2501 Silverside Rd Wilmington DE 19810

MORGAN, CRYSTAL FAYE, health services administrator; b. Amarillo, Tex., Jan. 31, 1967; d. Larry Cleveland Bowerman and Loretta Faye (Blackburn) Jordan; m. David James Morgan, Sept. 1, 1986; children: David James Jr., Andrea Faye. AS in Aerospace Group Equipment Tech., C.C. of Air Force, Ft. Lauderdale, Fla., 1989, AS in Health Svcs. Adminstrn., 1995; BS in Bus. Mgmt., Nova U., 1992; MS in Human Resources Mgmt., Wilmington Coll., 1995. Receptionist, ins. clk. Atoka (Okla.) Chiropractic, 1984-85; enlisted woman USAF, 1985, advanced through grades to staff sgt., 1993; aerospace ground equipment mechanic USAF, Panama City, Panama, from 1985; aerospace ground equipment mechanic USAF, Cannon AFB, N.Mex., until 1991, supr. med. records 27th med. group, 1991-92, asst. supr. managed care, 1992-93; supr. med. records 436th med. group USAF, Dover AB, Del., 1993, supr. quality improvement, quality cons., 1994-95, supr. managed care, 1995—; examiner Del. Quality Award, Dover, 1994-95. Mem. Am. Soc. Quality Control, Nat. Assn. for Healthcare Quality. Republican. Baptist. Office: 436th Med Group/SGST 307 Tuskegee Blvd Dover AFB DE 19902

MORGAN, CYNTHIA PHILLIPS, paramedic educator; b. Houston, Sept. 16, 1958; d. Frank Gilbert and Joanna (Kountz) Phillips; m. Randall James Morgan, May 28, 1994. BS, U. Southwestern La., 1985, AS in paramedicine, 1987. Lic. Nat. Registered EMT-Paramedic, La. Field paramedic Acadian Ambulance Svc., Lafayette, La., 1986-87, East Baton Rouge Emergency Med. Svc., 1988-90; hyperbaric technician Our Lady of the Lake Hosp., Baton Rouge, 1990-91; instr. U. Southwestern La., Lafayette, 1991—. Assisted revisions: Prehospital Drug Therapy, 1994. Mem. La. Assn. Emergency Med. Svc. Instrs./Coords. (sec./treas. 1994—), La. Assn. nationally Registered EMT's, Kappa Delta (alumni adv. bd., pledge advisor 1994—). Roman Catholic. Home: 835 Canberra Rd Lafayette LA 70503 Office: Univ Southwestern La 104 University Cir Lafayette LA 70504

MORGAN, DANIEL DAVIES, surgeon; b. New Haven, June 8, 1939; s. Daniel Davies Sr. and Rose Marie (Martinoles) M.; m. Katharine Lyle MacKinnon, Nov. 11, 1966; children: Daniel McBurney, Preston Lindsay. BA, Yale U., 1959; MD, Columbia U., N.Y.C., 1963. Diplomate Am. Bd. Orthopaedic Surgery. Resident in orthopaedic surgery Walter Reed Army Med. Ctr., Washington, 1966-70; pvt. practice Fremont, Calif., 1971—; mem., orthopaedic surgeon Fremont Orthopaedic Med. Group, 1972—; chief med. staff Washington Hosp., Fremont, 1989-90. Chmn. Yale U. Alumni Schs. Com., S.E. San Francisco, 1983—. Maj. U.S. Army, 1964-71. Decorated Bronze Star, Army Commdendation medal with Oak Leaf Cluster. Fellow Am. Acad. Orthopaedic Surgeons; mem. AMA, Calif. Med. Assn., Western Orthopaedic Assn., Alameda Contra Costa Med. Soc. Democrat. Home: 256 Segovia Pl Fremont CA 94539-3046 Office: Fremont Orthopaedic Med Group 38690 Stivers St Fremont CA 94536-5336

MORGAN, ELMER ALLEN, JR., physician associate; b. Salisbury, N.C., Aug. 4, 1949; s. Elmer Allen Sr. and Hazel Ruth (Jackson) M.; m. Kim Loraine Canady, May 29, 1989; 1 child, Stephani Lea. Grad. in Med. Sci., Emory U., 1975. Cert. physician assoc., Ga. Physician assoc. Emory U. Clinic, Atlanta, Ga., 1975-82, Peachtree Cardiovascular, Atlanta, Ga., 1982—. With U.S. Army, 1968-71. Fellow Am. Assn. Physician Assts. Office: Peachtree Cardiovascular Assocs Ste 390 5669 Peachtree Dunwoody Rd Atlanta GA 30342

MORGAN, EVELYN BUCK, nursing educator; b. Phila., Nov. 3, 1931; d. Kenneth Edward and Evelyn Louise (Rhineberg) Buck; m. John Allen McGeary, Aug. 15, 1958 (div. 1964); children—John Andrew, Jacquelyn Ann McGeary Keplinger; m. Kenneth Dean Morgan, June 26, 1965 (dec. 1975). R.N., Muhlenberg Hosp. Sch. Nursing, 1955; B.S. in Nursing summa cum laude, Ohio State U., 1972, M.S., 1973; Ed.D., Nova. U., 1978. R.N., N.J., Ohio, Fla., Calif.; cert. clin. specialist Am. Nurses Assn. Psychiat.-Mental Health Clin. Specialists; advanced R.N. practitioner Fla. Bd. Nursing. Staff nurse Muhlenburg Hosp., Plainfield, N.J., 1955-57; indsl. nurse Western Electric Co., Columbus, Ohio, 1957-59; supr. Mt. Carmel Hosp., Columbus, 1960-65; instr. Grant Hosp. Sch. Nursing, 1965-72; cons. Ohio Dept. Health, 1972-74; prof. nursing Miami (Fla.)-Dade Community Coll., 1974-96, ret., 1996; family therapist Hollywood Pavilion Hosp., 1977-82; pvt. practice family therapy, Ft. Lauderdale, Fla., 1982—. Sustaining mem. Democratic Nat. Com., 1975—. Mem. Am. Nurses Assn., Fla. Council Psychiat.-Mental Health Clin. Specialists, Nat. Guild Hypnotists, Am. Nurses Found., Am. Holistic Nurses Assn., Sigma Theta Tau. Democrat. Roman Catholic.

MORGAN, HOWARD EDWIN, physiologist; b. Bloomington, Ill., Oct. 8, 1927; s. Lyle V. and Ethel E. (Bailey) M. Student, Ill. Wesleyan U., 1944-45; MD, Johns Hopkins U., 1949. Intern Vanderbilt U., Nashville, 1949-51; resident in ob-gyn. Vanderbilt U., 1951-53, instr., 1953-55, instr. physiology, 1957-59, asst. prof. physiology, 1959-62, assoc. prof., 1962-65, prof. physiology, 1965-67; Evan Pugh prof., chmn. physiology Pa. State U., Hershey, 1967-87; sr. v.p. rsch. Geisinger Clinic, Danville, Pa., 1987—; v.p. rsch. Am. Heart Assn., 1977-79; mem. Nat. Heart, Lung and Blood Adv. Coun., 1979-83. Editor: Physiol. Revs, 1973-79, Am. Jour. Physiology: Cell Physiology, 1981-84. With U.S. Army, 1955-57. Recipient award of Merit Am. Heart Assn., 1979, Carl Wiggers award, 1984; Howard Hughes scholar, 1982. Mem. Am. Physiol. Soc. (pres., Daggs award 1992), Am. Heart Assn. (pres., Disting. Achievement award 1988, Gold Heart award 1994), Am. Soc. Biol. Chemists, Biochem. Soc., Biophys. Soc., Internat. Soc. Heart Rsch. (pres., Peter Harris award 1995), Inst. Medicine of NAS. Office: Geisinger Clinic Weis Ctr for Rsch 100 N Academy St Danville PA 17822

MORGAN, JACOB RICHARD, cardiologist; b. East St. Louis, Ill., Oct. 10, 1925; s. Clyde Adolphus and Jennie Ella Henrietta (Van Ramshorst) M.; m. Alta Eloise Ruthruff, Aug. 1, 1953; children: Elaine, Stephen Richard. BA in Physics, BBA, U. Tex., 1953; MD, U. Tex., Galveston, 1957. Diplomate Am. Bd. Internal Medicine, Am. Bd. Cardiology. Ensign USN, 1944, advanced through grades to capt., 1969; intern U.S. Naval Hosp., Oakland, Calif., 1957-58; chief medicine U.S. Naval Hosp., Taipei, Republic of China, 1962-64; internal medicine staff San Diego, 1964-67, chief cardiology, 1969-73; ret., 1973; dir. medicine R.E. Thomas Gen. Hosp., El Paso, Tex., 1973-75; asst. clin. prof. medicine U. Calif., San Diego, 1970-73; prof. medicine, assoc. chmn. dep. Tex. Tech U. Sch. Medicine, Lubbock and El Paso, 1973-75; pvt. practice National City, Calif., 1976—; dir. cardiology Paradise Valley Hosp., National City, 1976-88; presenter in field. Contbr. articles on cardiology to sci. jours. Recipient Casmir Funk award, 1972. Fellow ACP, Am. Coll. Cardiology, Am. Coll. Chest Physicians, Am. Heart Assn. (coun. on clin. cardiology). Home: 9881 Edgar Pl La Mesa CA 91941-6833 Office: 2409 E Plaza Blvd National City CA 91950-5101

MORGAN, JAMES DAYLE, dermatologist, military officer; b. Nevada, Iowa, June 9, 1976; s. James Alford and Clara (Williams) M.; m. Glenda Gay Stevens, Aug. 11, 1961; children; Michael B., Lori D., Zack R., Leah U. BS, Okla. U., 1958, MD, 1961. Diplomate Am. Bd. Dermatology. Commd. ensign U.S. Navy, 1960, advanced through grades to capt., 1976, resigned, 1980; intern U.S. Navy, Camp Pendleton, Calif., 1961-62; flight tng. U.S. Navy, Pensacola, Fla., 1962-63; flight surgeon U.S. Navy, Key West, Fla., 1963-67; resident in dermatology U.S. Navy, San Diego, Calif., 1967-70; dermatologist U.S. Navy, Norfolk, Va., 1970-80; pvt. practice dermatology Lake Wales, Fla., 1980—. Med. editor Spray Water Ski Mag., 1981-84. Republican. Office: 1109 Bryn Mawr Ave Lake Wales FL 33853-4333

MORGAN, MARK ALLEN, obstetrician, gynecologist; b. Enid, Okla., June 17, 1957; s. Wayne Thomas and Della Mae (Goodhue) M.; m. Sharyl Jaleen Scharn, June 7, 1980; children: Robert Wayne, Jamie Lynn. BS, So. Nazarene U., 1979; MD, Okla. U., 1983. Diplomate Am. Bd. Obstetrics and Gynecology. Intern, then resident obstetrics & gynecology, chief adminstrv. resident Okla. U. Health Scis. Ctr., Oklahoma City, 1983-87, fellow maternal fetal medicine, 1987-89, asst. prof., dir. primate colony, 1989-91; asst. prof. obstetrics-gynecology Irvine Med. Ctr. U. Calif., Orange, 1991-94; assoc. prof., dir. obstetrics and maternal-fetal medicine U. Pa. Sch. Medicine, Phila., 1994—; med. cons. Emerson Teen Parent Program, Oklahoma City, 1987-91, adv. bd., 1988-91. Reviewer Am. Jour. Obstetrics and Gynecology, 1991—. Fellow Am. Coll. Obstetricians and Gynecologists; mem. AMA, So. Med. Assn., Soc. Perinatal Obstetricians (assoc.), Phi Delta Lambda. Republican. Nazarene. Office: U Pa Med Ctr Hosp of U Pa 3400 Spruce St Philadelphia PA 19104

MORGAN, RAYMOND F., plastic surgeon; b. Pitts., Apr. 24, 1948; s. Edwin J. and Alberta (Hirt) M.; m. Sue Ann; children: Ryan Frederic, Alexander Evan, Elizabeth Anne. BS, U. Pitts., 1969, MEd, 1972, DMD, 1972; MD, W.Va. U., 1976. Diplomate Am. Bd. Plastic Surgery, Am. Bd. Hand Surgery. Intern Johns Hopkins U. Hosp., Balt., 1976-77, resident surgery, 1977-80, resident plastic surgery, 1980-82; resident hand surgery Union Meml. Hosp., Balt.; staff U. Va. Health Scis. Ctr., Charlottesville, M.T. Edgerton prof., chmn. dept. plastic surgery, 1988—. Mem. ACS, Soc. Univ. Surgeons, So. Surg. Assn., Am. Soc. for Surgery of the Hand, Am. Assn. Plastic Surgeons. Office: U of Va Dept of Plastic Surgery Charlottesville VA 22908

MORGAN, ROBERT C., physical therapist; b. Pitts., July 28, 1947; s. Eugene Francis and Genevieve Nora (Lynn) M.; m. Carol Ann Howarth, Nov. 17, 1979; children: Emily Elizabeth, Alice Ann. BS, U. Pitts., 1974, MS, 1978, PhD, 1985. Millwright US Steel Corp., McKeesport, Pa., 1966-71; cardio pulmonary tech. West Penn Hosp., Pitts., 1972-74; staff phys. therapist Montefiore Hosp., Pitts., 1974-78, asst. chief phys. therapist, 1978-81, chief phys. therapist, 1981-85; chief phys. therapy Maxicare-Health Am., Pitts., 1985-87; asst. adminstr. Gtr. Pitts. Rehab. Hosp., Monroevill, Pa., 1987-89; assoc. prof. Slippery Rock (Pa.) U., 1989-91; chmn. dept. phys. therapy Duquesne U., Pitts., 1991—; cons. Wheeling (W. Va.) Jesuit Coll.,

1994, Clarkson U., Potsdam, N.Y., 1996. Author (instructional unit on world wide web) Rheumatoid Arthritis, 1995. Grantee Sch. Health Related Professions U. Pitts., 1977. Mem. Am. Phys. Therapy Assn., Pa. Phys. Therapy Assn. (del. 1991-94), Rehab. Enring. Soc. N.Am. Office: Duquesne U Dept Phys Therapy 109 Health Scis Bldg Pittsburgh PA 15282

MORGAN, ROSE MARIE, biology educator; b. Minot, N.D., Nov. 17, 1935; d. Clinton Edward and Clara Adlyn (Fedje) M.; m. J.L. Parsons, Sept. 23, 1967 (div. 1970). BS, Minot (N.D.) State U., 1963; MS, N.D. State U., 1968; PhD, Tex. Woman's U., 1981. Rsch. microbiologist N.D. State U., Fargo, 1965-75; teaching asst. Tex. Woman's U., Denton, 1977-81; prof. Minot State U., 1983—; bench med. technologist Trinity Med. Ctr., 1960-65, adj. prof. clin. lab. sci., 1989-90; extension lectr. in anatomy, physiology, microbiology and biochemistry Minot State U., 1981-83; adj. prof. clin. lab. sci. St. Josephs Hosp., Minot, 1989—, Trinity Med. Ctr., Minot, 1989—. Contbr. articles to profl. jours. including Jour. Environ. Sci. Health, Tex. Jour. Sci., Am. Jour. Med. Tech., Jour. Am. Sci. Pollution (London), The Am. Biology Tchr.; textbook reviewer Times Mirror Mosby, 1985, West Pub. Co., 1990, Prentice-Hall, 1993, William C. Brown, 1993-95, Macmillan, 1993, Saunder, 1995. Mem. Mayor's Coun. for traffic safety; active various community coms. Recipient numerous grants. Mem. AAUW (internat. fellowship panel 1993-95), NEA, Am. Soc. Clin. Pathologists (assoc.), Am. Soc. Med. Technologists, N.W. Dakota Sci. Tchrs. Assn., N.D. Acad. Sci. (chairperson Dennison com. 1988-89), N.Y. Acad. Sci., N.D. Higher Edn. Assn., N.D. Edn. Assn., Minot State U. Edn. Assn., Sigma Xi, Phi Delta Kappa, Phi Delta Gamma (Alpha Theta chpt.), Delta Kappa Gamma (Gamma chpt.). Lutheran. Home: 823 6th St SW Minot ND 58701-4581 Office: Minot State U 8500 University Ave Minot ND 58701

MORGAN, STANLEY CHARLES, plastic and reconstructive surgeon; b. Phoenix, July 23, 1935; s. Fred Charles and Hazel (King) M.; m. Doris Anne Duke, Sept. 8, 1956; children: Pamela Anne, Cheryl Lynn, Mark Thomas. BS, U. Ariz.; MD, St. Louis Sch. Medicine. Diplomate Am. Bd. Plastic Surgery. Intern UCLA Ctr. Health Svcs., 1961-62, resident plastic surgery, 1966-68; resident gen. surgery Wadsworth Vets. Hosp., L.A., 1962-66; practice medicine specializing in plastic surgery Pasadena, Calif., 1970—; asst. clin. prof. U. So. Calif. Sch. Medicine, Los Angeles, 1981—, UCLA Ctr. Health Scis., 1970-81. Lt. col. U.S. Army, 1968-70. Fellow ACS, Am. Soc. Plastic and Reconstructive Surgeons, Am. Soc. Aesthetic Plastic Surgery, Calif. Soc. Plastic Surgeons. Office: 10 Congress St Ste 407 Pasadena CA 91105-3023

MORGAN, TIMOTHY JOE, dentist; b. St. Charles, Mo., Aug. 10, 1953; s. Gerald Kreon and Edith Emma Francis (Knoernschild) M.; m. Jan Denise Naughton, Nov. 18, 1978; children: Rebecca Lynn, Jennifer Ann, Michelle Kay. BS in Biology, Cen. Mo. State U., 1975; DDS, U. Mo., Kansas City, 1979; Grad., U.S. Dental Inst., Chgo., 1986. Assoc. G. Neubauer and R. Prine, DDS, Blue Springs, Mo., 1979-80; gen. practice dentistry Quincy, Ill., 1980—; asst. prof. operative dentistry U. Mo., Kansas City, 1979-80; vol. Nat. Children's Dental Health Month, Quincy, 1981-92. Patentee orthodontic appliance. Elder Our Redeemer Luth. Ch., Quincy, 1984-86; mem. Parent Tchrs. League, Quincy. Mem. ADA, Internat. Assn. Orthodontics, T.L. Gilmer Dental Soc. (pres. 1986-87). Republican. Office: 3011 Maine St Quincy IL 62301-4400

MORGAN, WILLIAM DOUGLAS, mental health counselor, consultant; b. Cleve., Apr. 22, 1956; s. William Wallace and Joan L. Morgan; m. Dale Jayne Tredinnick, June 2, 1979; children: Amy, Elizabeth, Catherine. BA, Pa. State U., 1978; MA, MDiv, Trinity Div. Sch., Deerfield, Ill., 1988; MA, Internat. Christian Grad. U., San Bernardino, Calif., 1989, Widener U., 1995; postgrad., Widener U. Campus min. Blacksburg, Va., 1978-81; campus min. Campus Crusade for Christ, Richmond, Ky., 1981-85, Vernon Hills, Ill., 1985-88; dir. human resource devel. Here's Life, Conn., Hartford, 1988-92; pvt. practice as mental health counselor West Hartford, Conn., 1988-92, Paoli, Pa., 1992—; mem. adv. bd. Children With Attention Deficit Disorder, Enfield, Conn., 1990-92. Named Outstanding Young Man in Am., 1984. Mem. ASTD, ACA, Am. Mental Health Counselors Assn. Presbyterian. Home: 1435 Sunnyhill Ln Havertown PA 19083-2921 Office: 63 Chestnut Rd Paoli PA 19301-1535

MORGAN, WINFIELD SCOTT, III, pathologist, educator; b. Takoma Park, Md., Jan. 9, 1921; s. Winfield and Viola (Williams) M.; m. Catherine Lillian Robb, May 29, 1948; children: Deborah Sue, Kenneth, Lyndon, Janet, Robert. B.S., Albright Coll., Reading, Pa., 1942; M.D., Temple U., 1945. Intern Robert Packer Hosp., Sayre, Pa., 1945-46; fellow medicine Guthrie Clinic and Robert Packer Hosp., 1946; resident physician Mass. Gen. Hosp., Boston, 1948-51; staff pathologist Mass. Gen. Hosp., 1952-62; instr. pathology Tufts U. Sch. Medicine, 1952-58; instr., then assoc. pathology Harvard Med. Sch., 1960-62; prof. pathology Case-Western Res. U. Sch. Medicine, 1962-67; dir. pathology Met. Gen. Hosp., Cleve., 1962-67; dir. labs. Aultman Hosp., Canton, Ohio, 1967-74; prof. pathology, interim chmn. W.Va. U. Med. Ctr., Morgantown, 1989-91, prof., chmn. dept. pathology, 1992-94, dir. surg. pathology, 1974-94; Cons. health research facilities br. NIH, 1964-67; Brit. Am. exchange fellow cancer research Oxford, Eng., 1951-52; spl. research fellow Nat. Cancer inst., Wenner-Grens Inst., Stockholm, Sweden, 1958-60. Mem. editorial bd. Jour. Exptl. and Molecular Pathology, 1964-73. Served with USAAF, 1946-48. Mem. Am. Soc. Exptl. Pathology, Am. Assn. Pathologists and Bacteriologists, AAAS, Internat. Acad. Pathologists. Office: W Va U Med Center Morgantown WV 26506

MORGANROTH, JOEL, cardiologist, educator; b. Detroit, Oct. 29, 1945; m. Gail Morrison, June 25, 1972. BS, U. Mich., 1967, MD, 1970. Diplomate Am. Bd. Cardiology, Am. Bd. Internal Medicine. Intern, asst. resident Beth Israel Hosp., Boston, 1970-72; resident, fellow Nat. Heart and Lung Inst., NIH, Bethesda, 1972-74, U. Pa. Med. Sch., Phila., 1974-75; asst. prof. medicine U. Pa., Phila., 1975-78; assoc. prof. Jefferson Med. Sch., Phila., 1978-82; prof. medicine and pharmacology Hahnemann U., Phila., 1982-89; dir. Nat. Cardiovasc. Rsch. Ctr., Haddonfield, N.J., 1982-89, sudden death prevention program Likoff Cardiovasc. Inst., Phila., 1982-88, cardiac R&D The Grad. Hosp., Phila., 1987-92; dir. edn., rsch. Presbyn. Med. Ctr., 1992-94, Phila. Heart Inst., 1992-94; pres. Premier Rsch. Worldwide, Phila., 1994—. Author/editor 25 books; contbr. over 300 articles to med. jours. Mem. editl. bd. Am. Jour. Cardiology, Jour. Am. Coll. Cardiology, Circulation, others. Fellow Am. Coll. Cardiology, ACP, Am. Coll. Chest Physicians, Am. Coll. Clin. Pharmacology; mem. Phila. Acad. Cardiology (pres. 1985), S.E. Pa. Heart Assn. (pres. 1986). Home: 1040 Stony Ln Gladwyne PA 19035-1136 Office: Premier Rsch Worldwide 124 S 15th St Philadelphia PA 19102-3002

MORGART, MICHELE, psychologist, consultant; b. Phila., July 2, 1947; d. Robert Paul and Elizabeth (Byrne) M.; divorced; 1 child, Michael Paul. BA in Psychology and English, U. Akron, Ohio, 1981, MA in Psychology, 1984. Cert. tchr., Ohio; lic. profl. clin. counselor; cert. employee assistance profl. Counselor and edn. specialist Columbia Mercy Med. Ctr., Canton, Ohio, 1984—; dir. concern: Employee Assistance Program Columbia Mercy Med. Ctr., Canton, 1992—; cons. Summit County Adolescent Task Force Svcs. Network, Akron, 1988—; cons. C.A.R.E. Cmty. Drug Edn., Cuy Falls, Ohio, 1984; cons., chmn. City Ethics Adv. Bd., 1994. Vol. Summit County Drug Bd., Akron, 1978-81. Mem. APA (cert.), Employee Asst. Profl. Assn., Psi Chi, Phi Sigma Alpha. Office: Columbia Mercy Med Ctr 1320 Mercy Dr NW Canton OH 44708-2614

MORGENSTERN, LEON, surgeon; b. Pitts., July 14, 1919; s. Max Samuel and Sarah (Master) M.; m. Laurie Mattlin, Nov. 27, 1967; 1 son, David Ethan. Student, CCNY, 1936-37; B.A. magna cum laude, Bklyn. Coll., 1940; M.D., N.Y. U., 1943. Diplomate: Am. Bd. Surgery. Intern Queens Gen. Hosp., Jamaica, N.Y., 1943-44; fellow, asst. resident in pathology Queens Gen. Hosp., 1947-48, resident in surgery, 1948-52; practice medicine, specializing in surgery Los Angeles, 1953-59, 60—, Bronx, N.Y., 1959-60; dir. surgery Cedars of Lebanon Hosp., Los Angeles, 1960-73; dir. surgery Cedars-Sinai Med. Center, Los Angeles, 1973-88, emeritus dir. surgery, 1989—; dir. Bioethics Program Cedars-Sinai Med. Ctr., L.A., 1995—; clin. prof. surgery UCLA Sch. Medicine, 1973-85, prof. in residence, 1985—; dir. bioethics program Cedars-Sinai Med. Ctr., 1995—; asst. prof. surgery Albert Einstein Coll. Medicine, N.Y.C., 1959-60. Assoc. editor Mount Sinai Jour. Medicine, 1984-88; contbr. articles to profl. publs. Served to capt. M.C. U.S. Army, 1944-46. Mem. Soc. for Surgery Alimentary Tract, Soc. Am. Gastrointestinal Endoscopic Surgeons (hon.), Am. Gastroent. Assn., L.A. Surg. Soc. (pres. 1977), ACS (sec.-treas. 1976-77, pres. 1978, bd. dirs. So. Calif. chpt. 1976-78, gov.-at-large), Internat. Soc. Surgery, Western Surg. Assn., Pacific Coast Surg. Assn., AMA, Calif. Med. Assn., Los Angeles County Med. Assn., Am. Surg. Assn., others. Home: 5694 Calpine Dr Malibu CA 90265-3812

MORGENSTERN, LEWIS B., medical educator. Grad., U. Mich.; postgrad., U. Tex. Resident in neurology Johns Hopkins Hosp., Balt.; asst. prof. neurology U. Tex. Med. Sch., Houston, 1994—. Recipient Clinician Scientist award Am. Heart Assn., 1996. Mem. Alpha Omega. Office: U Tex Health Sci Ctr PO Box 20036 Houston TX 77225

MORGENSTERN, MICHAEL ALEX, osteopath physician; b. N.Y.C., Mar. 17, 1949; s. Sol and Betty (Podberesky) M.; m. Linda Sue Olszewski, June 20, 1970; children: David J., Adam R., Rachel S. BA in Psychology, SUNY, Buffalo, 1971, MA in Microbiology, 1973, PhD in Microbiology, 1976; DO in Osteopath, Kirkville Coll. of Osteopath., 1981. Diplomate Am. Bd. Family Practice, Nat. Bd. Med. Examiners; cert. ACLS instr., ATLS instr. Med. dir., emergency physician Blanchard Valley Hosp., Findlay, Ohio, 1986-87; emergency physician emergency dept. Lima (Ohio) Meml. Hosp., 1987-89, med. dir. of emergency dept., 1989-92; EMS med. dir., emergency physician Elyria (Ohio) Meml. Hosp. and Med. Ctr., 1992-93; emergency physician Deaconess Hosp. of Cin., 1994—; med. dir. Sharonville (Ohio) Fire Dept.; ATLS faculty U. Cin. Med. Ctr., Good Samaritan Hosp., Cin.; ACLS instr. Deaconess Hosp., Cin.; med. dir. Loraine C.C. Paramedic and Emergency Med. Technician Program, Loraine, Ohio, LifeCare Ambulance Svc., Elyria, Amberleigh (Ohio) Fire and Rescue, Carlisle (Ohio) Fire Dept., Elyria Twp., Grafton, Ohio, Sheffield (Ohio) Twp., Lima Tech. Coll., Paramedic and Emergency Med. Technician Program, 1989-92, Appollo Joint Vocat. Schs., Emergency Technician Program, 1990-92, Perry Fire and Rescue Dept. Perry, Ohio, 1988-92, Lafeyeete (Ohio) Fire Dept., 1989-92, Wayne (Ohio) Fire Dept., 1989-92, Harrod Fire Dept., 1990-92. Contbr. articles to profl. jours. Counselor Boy Scouts Am. With U.S. Army Res., 1977-81. Mem. Am. Osteopathic Assn., Am. Coll. Osteopathic Emergency Physicians, Am. Coll. of Emergency Physicians, Am. Coll. of Osteopathic Family Physicians, Ohio Osteopathic Med. Assn., Ohio Osteopathic Med. Acad., Berlin Internat. Med. Soc., Ohio Acad. of Osteopathic Family Physicians. Office: Deaconess Hosp 411 Straight St Cincinnati OH 45219

MORGENSTERN, STEPHEN, developmental optometrist; b. Bklyn., Mar. 2, 1940; s. Abraham and Yetta (Steiger) M.; B.S. in Pharmacy, Bklyn. Coll. Pharmacy, 1961; B.S., Pa. Coll. Optometry, 1969, O.D., 1970; m. Marcia Mandel, Oct. 11, 1970; children: Andrew Seth, Rebecca Jill, Lauren Dayna. Instr., Bklyn. Coll. Pharmacy, 1961; registered pharmacist, 1961-62; resident orthoptics and vision tng. Optometric Center N.Y., 1970, engaged in myopia research project, 1970; developmental optometrist N.Y. Center Learning Disorders, 1970-71; pvt. practice developmental optometry, East Northport, Coram, N.Y., 1970—; dep. examiner N.Y. State Bd. Optometry, 1985-90; examiner N.E. Regional Clin. Optometric Assessment Testing Svc., 1990—; pres. Visicare Internat. Corp.; rsch. dir. The Vet. Nutrition Rsch. Inst.; optometrist staff mem. Suffolk County Assn. Retarded Children, 1973-80; cons. in field. Author manual, Handwriting Skills for Left Handed Children. Served to 1st lt. USAF, 1962-65. Fellow Coll. Optometrists in Vision Devel.; mem. Am., N.Y. State, Suffolk County optometric assns., Optometric Extension Program (clin. asso.), Internat. Myopia Prevention Assn., Assn. Children with Learning Disorders, Coun. Exceptional Children, N.Y. Assn. Brain Injured Children, Suffolk County Mental Health Assn., KP. Home: 6 Norman Ct Huntington Station NY 11746-5812 Office: 554 Larkfield Rd East Northport NY 11731-4205 also: 248 Middle Country Rd Coram NY 11727-4423

MORGENTALER, ABRAHAM, urologist, researcher; b. Montreal, Quebec, Can., May 14, 1956; came to U.S., 1974; s. Henry Morgentaler and Chawa Rosenfarb; m. Susan Deborah Edbril, June 12, 1982; children: Maya Edbril, Hannah Edbril. AB, Harvard U., 1978, MD, 1982. Diplomate Am. Bd. Urology. Intern Harvard Surg. Svc.-N.E. Deaconess Hosp., Boston, 1982-83; resident Harvard Program in Urology, Boston, 1984-88; instr. surgery Harvard Med. Sch., Boston, 1988-92, asst. prof. surgery (urology), 1993—; staff urologist, dir. male infertility program and impotency Beth Israel Hosp., Boston, 1988—; dir. andrology lab. Beth Israel Hosp., 1990—. Author: The Male Body, 1993. Mem. AMA, Am. Urologic Assn., Am. Fertility Soc., Am. Soc. Andrology, Boston Fertility Soc., Am. Assn. Clin. Urologists. Office: Beth Israel Hosp 330 Brookline Ave Boston MA 02215-5400

MORI, PAUL ALBERT, nuclear radiologist; b. Amherst, Ohio, May 5, 1925; s. Paul Albert and Mattie Melissa (Cummings) M.; m. Minna Conn, Aug. 30, 1947; children: Mark, Kurt, Thorpe, Meredith. BA, Ohio State U., 1947, MD, 1948. Diplomate Am. Bd. Radiologists, Am. Bd. Nuclear Medicine. Resident radiology U. Mich., Ann Arbor, 1952-55, Am. Cancer Soc. fellow, 1955-56, sr. clin. instr., 1955-56; dir. radiology Bapt. Med. Ctr., Jacksonville, Fla., 1956-70; founding ptnr. Drs. Mori, Bean & Brocks, P.A., Jacksonville, 1968—; nuclear radiologist Bapt. Med. Ctr./Meml. Med. Ctr., Jacksonville, 1968—; pres. med. staff Meml. Med. Ctr., Jacksonville, 1978; med. bd. Bapt. Med. Ctr., Jacksonville, 1956-76, governing bd., 1986—; exec. com. Health Systems Agy. N.E. Fla., Jacksonville, Am. Bicentennial Commn., Jacksonville; hon. cons. Brit. Health Svc., London, 1980. Author: Where There's Smoke, 1958 (Am. Cancer Soc. Cert. of Merit 1960); contbg. editor: Radiology for the Emergency Physician, 1981, 2nd edit., 1989; contbr. articles to profl. jours. Dir. Fla. chpt. Am. Cancer Soc.; v.p. Fla. Com. on Smoking and Health; med. missionary Meth. Ch., Zimbabwe, Africa; found. lectr. Joe Berg Ednl. Foun., Jacksonville. Lt. USNR, 1950-52. Fellow Am. Coll. Radiology (councilor Fla.), Am. Coll. Nuclear Physicians; mem. AMA, Radiol. Soc. N.Am. (councilor Fla.), Fla. Med. Assn., Fla. Radiol. Soc. (Gold medal 1991), Duval County Med. Soc. (chmn. hosp. affairs com., Beall's award for med. rsch. 1982). Presbyterian. Home: 4836 Yacht Club Rd Jacksonville FL 32210 Office: DRS Mori Bean & Brooks PA 3599 University Blvd D #10 Jacksonville FL 32216

MORI, TAKAHISA, neuroradiologist, cardiologist; b. Yao, Osaka, Japan, Dec. 18, 1959; s. Kimiaki and Ryouko (Tsujimoto) M.; m. Yumiko Yukawa, Jan. 24, 1988; 2 children. MD, U. Kyoto, 1986; DMS, Kochi Med. Sch., Japan, 1996. Resident Kyoto (Japan) U. Med. Sch., 1986-87; resident Kokura Meml. Hosp., Kitakyushu, Japan, 1987-88, staff, 1988-90; staff Kochi Med. Sch., Nankoku, Japan, 1990—; Mem. com. Chugoku-Shikoku Intravascular Neurosurgery Conf., Tokushima, Japan, 1993—. Contbr. articles to profl. jours. Grantee Ministry Edn., Scu. & Culture, 1995. Office: Kochi Med Sch, Okoh-cho Kohasu, 783 Nankoku Kochi, Japan

MORIGUCHI, IKUO, pharmaceutical science educator; b. Pusan, Japan, Oct. 10, 1928; s. Noboru and Chiyoko (Kokubu) M.; m. Yoshiko Muraga, Apr. 29, 1961; children: Nobuko, Tetsuo, Takao. BS, U. Tokyo, 1957, PhD, 1966. Rschr. Chugai Pharm. Co., Ltd., Tokyo, 1957-66; asst. prof. Showa U., Tokyo, 1966-67, assoc. prof., 1967-71; prof. Kitasato U., Tokyo, 1972-94, prof. emeritus, 1994—; dean Sch. Pharm. Scis. Kitasato U., 1988-92. Editor: Lead Generation of New Drugs, 1987; author computer programs. Mem. Pharm. Soc. of Japan, Acad. Pharm. Sci. and Tech. Japan, Internat. QSAR Soc. Home: 29 Shimizugaoka, Minami-ku, Yokohama 232, Japan Office: Kitasato U, 5-9-1 Shirokane, Minato-ku, Tokyo 108, Japan

MORIO, MICHIO, anesthesiology educator; b. Onomichi, Hiroshima, Japan, Apr. 19, 1931; s. Ryoichi and Yasuko (Sakihara) M.; m. Akiko Nakatani, Oct. 21, 1957; 1 child, Tomoko. MD, Hiroshima U., 1956; PhD, Kyoto U., 1961. Diplomate Japanese Bd. Anesthesiology. Instr., Kyoto U. Hosp., 1961-62; asst. prof. anesthesiology Hiroshima U. Hosp., 1962-65, assoc. prof., 1965-66, prof., chmn. dept. anesthesiology, 1967—, councilor, 1979-84, 88—, dir. Univ. Hosp., 1980-84; dean Sch. Med. Hiroshima U., 1988—; vis. prof. anesthesiology Albert Einstein Coll. Medicine, 1971-72. Editor-in-chief Hiroshima Jour. Anesthesia, 1965—; Jour. Hiroshima Med. Assn., 1982—. Examinar, Japanese Ministry of Health and Welfare, 1979-81; head bd. Japanese Ministry of Prefectural Govt., 1979-82; councilor Radiation Effect Found., Hiroshima; 1980-83. Japanese Ministry of Edn. grantee, 1974-76, 77-78, 78-80, 79-83, 84-86, 87—. Named hon. citizen Karl-Franzens Graz U. Fellow Japan Soc. Promotion of Sci. (vis. grantee 1981), Japanese Ministry of Edn., Sci. and Culture (vis. grantee 1971-72); mem. Japanese Soc. Anesthesiology, Japanese Assn. Acute Medicine, Japanese Med. Assn.; hon. mem. Yugoslavian Soc. Anesthetists, Bulgarian Soc. Anesthesiology Resuscitation (hon.). Clubs: Numata Tennis, Prince, Rotary. Home: Midori 2-27-34, Minami-ku, Hiroshima 734, Japan Office: Hiroshima U Sch Med, Dept Anesthesiology Kasumi 1-2-3, Minami-ku Hiroshima 734, Japan

MORISHIGE, FUKUMI, surgeon; b. Fukuoka, Japan, Oct. 24, 1925; s. Fukumatsu and Teruko M.; m. Fumie Osada, Apr. 18, 1954; children: Kyoko, Hisakazu, Noritsugu. MD, Kurume U., 1952, DMS, 1962; PhD, Fukuoka U., 1983. Intern Kurume U., 1951-52; asst. Kurume (Japan) U., Dept. Pathology, 1952-55, Kyoto (Japan) U. Inst. Chest Disease, 1955-58; v.p. Tachiarai Hosp., Fukuoka, Japan, 1959-67, Torikai Hosp., Fukuoka, Japan, 1968-80; chmn. Tachiarai Hosp., Fukuoka, Japan, 1980-84; dir. Nakamura Hosp., Fukuoka, Japan, 1984-86, supreme advisor, 1987—; dir. Morishige Cancer Clinic, Chiba, Japan, 1992—; resident fellow Linus Pauling Inst. of Sci. and Medicine, Palo Alto, Calif., 1976—; chemistry advisor Nissan Chem. Industries Ltd., Tokyo, 1983—. Author: Nutrition of Nucleic Acid, 1983, Brain Blood Circulation, 1986; contbr. articles to profl. jours. Fellow Linus Pauling Inst. Sci. and Medicine; mem. Japan Soc. Magnetic Resonance (founder, bd. dirs. 1978—, exec. sec. 1979—), Internat. Assn. for Vitamin & Nutritional Oncology (exec. com. 1983—), Japanese Cancer Assn., Japanese Assn. for Thoracic Surgery, Japan Surg. Soc. Democrat. Buddhist. Home and Office: Miyakono 2-10-13, Ooami-Shirasato-Machi, Sambu Chiba 299-32, Japan Office: Sta Pla Hotel 1401, 2-1-1 Hakata-Eki-Mae, Hakata Fukuoka, Japan

MORISSETTE, CAROL LYNNE, healthcare consultant; b. Connellsville, Pa., Apr. 26, 1941; d. Charles Lynn and Iola Grace (Sembower) Sliger; m. George Van Barriger, May 27, 1966 (div. Feb. 1972); m. Richard W. Morissette, Oct. 25, 1991. RN, Montefiore Hosp., 1962; BS, Coll. St. Francis, 1985; MA in Mgmt., Nat. Louis U., 1988. Cert. case mgr. Pub. health nurse Kendall County Health Dept., Yorkville, Ill., 1970-72; team leader Edward Hosp., Naperville, Ill., 1972-73; emergency nurse Cen. Dupage Hosp., Winfield, Ill., 1973-74; staff nurse and head nurse Palos Community Hosp., Palos Heights, Ill., 1974-77, surg. nurse, 1977-82; auditor Med-Charge Analysis, Chgo., 1982-83; mgr. Intracorp CIGNA, Glen Ellyn, Ill., 1983-86, Metlife Healthcare Network, Schaumburg, Ill., 1986; project mgr. Healthcare Intermediaries, Lombard, Ill., 1986-88; dir., provider services Multicare HMO, Chgo., 1988-89; ptnr. Greenberg Assocs., 1989-91; nurse cons. Office Workers' Compensation Programs, U.S. Dept. Labor, Chgo., 1993—; mem. group comparison studies healthcare delivery/costs USSR, 1981, China, 1982, England, 1985, Egypt, 1992. V.p. Indian Oak Condominium Assn., Bolingrook, Ill., 1972-76; treas. Hickory Heights Condominium Assn., Hickory Hills, Ill., 1978-83, bd. dirs., 1983-95. Mem. NAFE, Women's Health Exec. Network, Am. Coll. Healthcare Execs., Chgo. Health Exec. Forum, Am. Assn. Occupational Health Nurses, Individual Case Mgmt. Assn. (cert. case mgr.). Home: 14136 S Kilpatrick Ave Crestwood IL 60445-2221

MORITA, RICHARD YUKIO, microbiology and oceanography educator; b. Pasadena, Calif., Mar. 27, 1923; s. Jiro and Reiko (Yamamoto) M.; m. Toshiko Nishihara, May 29, 1926; children—Sally Jean, Ellen Jane, Peter Wayne. B.S., U. Nebr., 1947; M.S., U. So. Calif., 1949; Ph.D., U. Calif., 1954. Microbiologist Mid-Pacific Expdn., 1950, Danish Galathea Deep-Sea Expdn., 1952, Trans-Pacific Expdn.; Postdoctoral fellow U. Calif., Scripps Inst. Oceanography, 1954-55; asst. prof. U. Houston, 1955-58; asst. prof., assoc. prof. U. Neb., 1958-62; prof. microbiology and oceanography Oreg. State U., Corvallis, 1962—; prog. dir. biochemistry NSF, 1968-69; Disting. vis. prof. Kyoto Univ.; cons. NIH, 1968-70; researcher in field. Contbr. articles to sci. lit. Patentee in field. Served with U.S. Army, 1944-46. Grantee NSF, 1962—, NIH, 1960-68, NASA, 1967-72, Office Naval Research, 1966-70, Dept. Interior, 1968-72, NOAA, 1975-82, Bur. Land Mgmt., 1982, EPA, 1986—; recipient awards including King Fredericus IX Medal and Ribbon, 1954, Sr. Queen Elizabeth II Fellowship, 1973-74, Hotpack lectr. and award Can. Soc. Fellow Japan Soc. for Promotion Sci.; mem. Am. Soc. Microbiology (Fisher award). Office: Oreg State U Dept Microbiology Corvallis OR 97331

MORITA, YOKO, neurologist, researcher; b. Takasaki, Japan, May 22, 1955; s. Hiroshi and Toshiko (Fukushima) M.; m. Shigeru Tsuzuki, Sept. 24, 1985 (div. June 1993); 1 child, Itaru. MD, Keio U., Tokyo, 1980; DMS, Keio U., 1985. Diplomate Japanese Bd. Internal Medicine, Japanese Bd. Neurology. Resident in medicine and neurology Keio U. Hosp., Tokyo, 1980-84; instr. dept. neurology Keio U., Tokyo, 1984-87, fellow in neurology, 1987-90; vis. rschr. dept. med. cell rsch. U. Lund, Sweden, 1990-92; med. staff in neurology Second Tokyo Nat. Hosp., 1992—; vis. prof. Keio U., 1996—. Contbr. articles to profl. jours. Mem. Japanese Soc. Neurology, Japanese Soc. Internal Medicine, Internat. Soc. Cerebral Blood Flow and Metabolism, Japanese Soc. Stroke, Japanese Soc. Cerebral Blood Flow and Metabolism (councilor 1996—). Home: 2-5-27 Tachibanadai, Aoba-ku Yokohama, Kanagawa 227, Japan Office: Second Tokyo Nat Hosp Dept Neurology, 2-5-1 Higashigaoka, Tokyo 152, Japan

MORITSUGU, KENNETH PAUL, physician, government official; b. Honolulu, Mar. 5, 1945; s. Richard Yutaka and Hisayo Joan (Nishikawa) M.; children: Erika Lizabeth, Vikki Lianne. Student, Chaminade Coll. Honolulu, 1963-65; BA in Classical Langs. with honors, U. Hawaii, 1967; MD, George Washington U., 1971; MPH, U. Calif., Berkeley, 1975; DSc (hon.), Coll. Osteopathic Medicine, U. New Eng., 1988, Midwestern U., 1993; D Pub. Svc. (hon.), U. North Tex., 1994. Diplomate Am. Bd. Preventive Medicine (fellow); cert. correctional health profl. Intern USPHS Hosp., San Francisco, 1971-72, resident, 1972-75; commd. USPHS, 1968, advanced through grades to med. dir., 1979; promoted to rank of rear adm., asst. surgeon gen., 1988; staff med. officer USPHS Hosp., San Francisco, 1972-73; regional cons. med. manpower planning and devel. HEW, San Francisco, 1976-78; chief internat. edn. programs br. HEW, Washington, 1978; dep. dir. div. medicine HEW, 1978; dir. Bur. Health Professions, div. medicine HHS, Rockville, Md., 1978-83, dir. Nat. Health Service Corps, 1983-87, dep. dir. Bur. Health Professions, 1987; med. dir. Fed. Bur. Prisons Dept. Justice, Washington, 1987—. Decorated D.S.M.; recipient Commendation medal, Meritorious Svc. medal, Outstanding Svc. medal, Surgeon Gen.'s medallion, Surgeon Gen.'s medal, Dirs. award for Exceptional Svc., U.S. Marshal's Svcs., John D. Chase award for outstanding physician adminstrn., AMSUS, Nathan Davies award AMA, others. Fellow Am. Coll. Preventive Medicine, Royal Soc. Health, Royal Soc. Medicine; mem. APHA, Assn. Tchrs. Preventive Medicine, Assn. Mil. Surgeons U.S., Res. Officers Assn., Mensa, Am. Guild Organists. Home: 726 Sonata Way Silver Spring MD 20901-5063 Office: US Dept Justice Fed Bur Prisons 320 1st St NW Ste 1000 Washington DC 20534-0002

MORITZ, DENNIS MICHAEL, cardiothoracic surgeon; b. Chgo., July 3, 1943; s. Michael George and Mary Ellen (Doyle) M.; m. Pamela Jane Conerty, Nov. 12, 1966; 1 child, Christopher Michael. BS with honors, U.S. Naval Acad., 1965; MS with distinction, U.S. Naval Postgrad. Sch., Monterey, Calif., 1970; MD with honors, U. Ill., Chgo., 1981. Diplomate Am. Bd. Surgery, Am. Bd. Thoracic Surgery; lic. physician, Ill. Commd. 2d lt. U.S. Navy, 1965, advanced through grades to col., 1977, served on nuclear submarines and in med. ctrs., to 1977; served in U.S. Army, 1981—; asst. chief cardiac surgery Brooke Army Med. Ctr., San Antonio, 1989-92; asst. chief cardiothoracic surgery Walter Reed Army Med. Ctr., Washington, 1993-95, program dir., chief cardiothoracic surgery, 1995—; cons. to Surgeon Gen., U.S. Army, 1995—; asst. prof. surgery Uniformed Svcs. U. Health Scis., Bethesda, Md., 1989—. Contbr. articles to profl. jours. Fellow ACS, Am. Coll. Cardiology, Am. Coll. Chest Physicians; mem. Soc. Thoracic Surgeons, Uniformed Svcs. U. Surg. Assocs., Assn. Mil. Surgeons, Alpha Omega Alpha. Roman Catholic. Home: 7680-301 Woodpark Ln Columbia MD 21046 Office: Walter Reed Army Med Ctr Dept Cardiothoracic Surgery Washington DC 20307-5001

MORITZ, TIMOTHY BOVIE, psychiatrist; b. Portsmouth, Ohio, July 26, 1936; s. Charles Raymond and Elisabeth Bovie (Morgan) M.; m. Joyce Elizabeth Rasmussen, Oct. 13, 1962 (div. Sept. 1969); children: Elizabeth Wynne, Laura Morgan; m. Antoinette Tanasichuk, Oct. 31, 1981; children: David Michael, Stephanie Lysbeth. BA, Ohio State U., 1959; MD, Cornell

U., 1963. Diplomate Am. Bd. Psychiatry and Neurology. Intern in medicine N.Y. Hosp., N.Y.C., 1963-64, resident in psychiatry, 1964-67; spl. asst. to dir. NIMH, Bethesda, Md., 1967-69; dir. Community Mental Health Ctr., Rockland County, N.Y., 1970-74, Ohio Dept. Mental Health, Columbus, Ohio, 1975-81; med. dir. psychiatry Miami Valley Hosp., Dayton, Ohio, 1981-82; med. dir. N.E. Ga. Community Mental Health Ctr., Athens, Ga., 1982-83, Charter Vista Hosp., Fayetteville, Ark., 1983-87; clin. dir. adult psychiatry Charter Hosp., Las Vegas, Nev., 1987-94; pvt. practice psychiatry Las Vegas, Nev., 1987—; prof. Wright State U., Dayton, Ohio, 1981-82; asst. prof. Cornell U., N.Y.C., 1970-73; cons. NIMH, Rockville, Md., 1973-83. Author: (chpt.) Rehabilitation Medicine and Psychiatry, 1976; mem. editorial bd. Directions in Psychiatry, 1981—. Dir. dept. mental health and mental retardation Gov.'s Cabinet, State of Ohio, Columbus, 1975-81. Recipient Svc. award Ohio Senate, 1981, Svc. Achievement award Ohio Gov., 1981. Fellow Am. Psychiat. Assn. (Disting. Svc. award 1981); mem. AMA, Nev. Assn. Psychiat. Physicians, Nev. State Med. Assn., Clark County Med. Soc., Cornell U. Med. Coll. Alumni Assn. Office: Timothy B Moritz MD 3815 S Jones Blvd # 7 Las Vegas NV 89103-2289

MORIURA, SHIGEAKI, surgeon; b. Nagoya, Japan, Mar. 4, 1955; s. Showzabro and Miwako (Tanaka) M.; m. Yuko Hayashi, Mar. 16, 1980; 2 children. MD, Nagoya (Japan) U., 1979, DMS, 1990. Surgeon Toyohashi (Japan) Mcpl. Hosp., 1979-84; resident Nat. Cancer Ctr. Hosp., Tokyo, 1984-87; surgeon, rschr. surgery 1 Nagoya U., 1987-89; surgeon Aichi Prefectural Owari Hosp., Ichinomiya, Japan, 1989-94, Nagoya Posts and Telecomms. Hosp., 1995—. Contbr. papers to profl. jours. Mem., mgr. Fushimi Classical Music Assn., Nagoya, 1995. Mem. Japanese Soc. Gastroenterol. Surgery, Japanese Surg. Soc., Japanese Assn. for Thoracic Surgery. Home: 3-32 Hakuryu-cho Mizuho-ku, Nagoya 467, Japan Office: Nagoya Posts/Telecomms Hosp, 2-2-5 Izumi Higashi-ku, Nagoya 467, Japan

MORMANDO, ROBERT MICHAEL, internist; b. Poughkeepsie, N.Y., July 22, 1965; s. Leonard John and Ruth (Kvinge) M.; m. Joyce Mary Bakewicz, Apr. 24, 1992. BS in Biology, Siena Coll., 1987; DO, N.Y. Coll. Osteo. Medicine, 1991. Rotating intern Luth. Med. Ctr., Bklyn., N.Y., z, 1991-92; resident St. Vincents Hosp. and Med. Ctr., N.Y.C., 1992-95, chief med. resident, 1995-96; clin. inst. medicine U. Hosp., Stony Brook, 1996—. Mem. AMA (assoc.), ACP (assoc.), Am. Osteo. Assn., Squires and Femmes Bowling League (pres. 1993-96). Home: 7 Bonnie Ln Stony Brook NY 11790

MORMON, DARWIN LEIGH, optometrist, educator; b. Peru, Ill., May 19, 1945; s. Darwin and Jean Mae (Cobleigh) M.; m. Brenda Paulette Harwell, Mar. 6, 1971; children: Lisa Leigh, Paul Darwin. BS in Optometry, Ind. U., 1967, OD, 1969; MEd, Memphis State U., 1973. Prof. optometry So. Coll. of Optometry, Memphis, 1969—; pvt. practice Germantown, Tenn., 1986—; cons. So. Eye Assocs., Memphis, Nat. Bd. Examiners in Optometry, Washington, Stereo Optical Co., Chgo., 1989—, Ocular Scis., San Francisco. Deacon Trinity Bapt. Ch., Memphis, 1977—; active Briarcrest Devel. Coun., 1982-84; bd. dirs. Boy Scout Troup 245, 1983-90. Named Oustanding Young Man of Am. Jaycees, 1978, Outstanding Lectr. Am. Optometric Found., 1975. Mem. Am. Optometric Assn. (Optometric Recognition award 1988-96), Tenn. State Optometric Assn., Internat. Acad. Sports Vision (editl. bd.), Omega Delta (grand nat. pres.).

MOROZ, GEORGES, psychiatrist; b. Nice, France, Nov. 7, 1949; s. Alexandre and Rosine (Grass) M.; m. Beverly Horowitz, Apr. 20, 1983; children: Sarah, Erica. MD, U. Paris, 1979. Diplomate Am. Bd. Psychiatry and Neurology. Rsch. fellow downstate med. ctr. SUNY, Bklyn., N.Y., 1983-84; physician med. ctr. Cornell U., N.Y.C., 1984-85, Albert Einstein Coll. Medicine, Bronx, N.Y., 1985-86; asst. med. dir. Ciba-Geigy Pharm., Summit, N.J., 1986-89; internat. project leader Ciba-Geigy AG, Basel, Switzerland, 1989-91; assoc. dir. dept. therapeutic rsch. Hoffmann-La Roche, Inc., Nutley, N.J., 1991—. Mem. Am. Psychiatric Assn. Office: Hoffmann La Roche Inc 340 Kingsland St Nutley NJ 07110-1199

MORRÉ, DOROTHY MARIE, nutrition educator, researcher; b. Bonnets Hill, Mo., Jan. 18, 1935; d. Conrad and Marie (Huesgen) Wibberg; m. D. James Morré, Aug. 25, 1956; children: Connie, Jeffrey, Suzanne. BS, U. Mo., 1958; PhD, Purdue U., 1977. Asst. prof. Purdue U., West Lafayette, Ind., 1978-83, assoc. prof., 1983-89, prof., 1989—. Author: (chpt.) Role of the Golgi Apparatus in Cellular Biology, 1991; contbr. articles to profl. jours. including Jour. Biol. Chemistry, Biochimica et Biophysica Acta, Protoplasma. Mem. Am. Soc. Cell Biologists, Am. Inst. of Nutrition, Sigma Xi.

MORRELL, ROCCO L., osteopath; b. Port Arthur, Tex., June 12, 1948; s. Peter Lee and Marylou (Tritico) M.; m. Marilyn Kay Rogers, May 29, 1976; children: Peter, John, Christopher, Matthew. BS in Pharmacy, U. Houston, 1971; BS in Biology, Lamar U., 1973; DO, Tex. Coll. Osteo. Medicine, 1979. Intern and resident USPHS, New Orleans, 1979-82, Tulane U. Med. Ctr., 1979-82; chief of medicine Doctors Hosp., 1983-92, vice chief of staff, 1984, chief of staff, 1985-86, dir. med. edn., 1990—; dir. med. edn. U. North Tex. Health Sci. Ctr./FP Residency, 1990—; dir. ICU Doctors Hosp., 1986-93, dir. cardiology dept., 1986-93, dir. pulmonary dept., 1990-93, intern tng. com. 1983—; utilization reviewer St. Mary's Hosp., 1986; clinician Bishop Byrne Regional Wellness Ctr., 1983-93; physician reviewer Tex. Med. Found., 1985—, regional quality assurance com. Mem. ACP, Osteo. Med. Soc. (dist. XII), Jefferson County Med. Soc., Am. Osteo. Assn., Tex. Osteo. Assn., Tex. Med. Assn., Tex. Med. Found., Tex. Coll. of Osteo. Medicine (Atlas Shenoid chpt.), Tex. Coll. Osteo. Medicine Alumni Assn. (life mem.), Am. Heart Assn. (mid and south Jefferson County divsn.). Home: 450 Kings Row Port Neches TX 77651 Office: 5500 39th St Groves TX 77619

MORRIS, ALBERT JEFF, pharmaceutical company official; b. Memphis, May 29, 1945; s. Arthur and Idella (Carter) M.; m. Sylvianne Odetta Griffin, July 2, 1972; children: Walter, Teresa, Michael, Christina, Sabrina. BS, LeMoyne-Owen Coll., 1972; MA, Webster U., St. Louis, 1982, MBA, 1988. Profl. rep. Burroughs Wellcome Co., St. Louis, 1972-77, spl. rep. trainer, 1977-84, Towne-Oller rep., 1981-82, field mgmt. trainee, 1984—, sr. profl. rep., antiviral liaison rep., 1988-91; exec. rep., 1991-92; sr. exec. rep. Glaxowellcome, 1992—. Asst. scout master Boy Scout. With USN, 1967-70, Vietnam. Decorated Bronze Star with combat V, Purple Heart; Cross of Gallantry with palm (Vietnam). Mem. K.C. (grand knight 1985-86, trustee 1986-89). Roman Catholic.

MORRIS, ALVIN LEONARD, dentist, educational administrator; b. Detroit, July 2, 1927; s. Frank and Lulu (Cornett) M.; m. Arlene Teschler, Feb. 1, 1947 (dec. Apr. 1974); children: Jeffry, Gregg, Beth; m. Beverly Hackman, 1975. Student, U. Ill., 1944-45; D.D.S., U. Mich., 1951; Ph.D., U. Rochester, 1957; D.Sc. (hon.), U. Md., 1983. Intern Letterman Army Hosp., San Francisco, 1951-52; postdoctoral research fellow NIH, 1954-57; head dept. oral diagnosis U. Pa. Sch. Dentistry, 1957-61; dean U. Ky. Coll. Dentistry, Lexington, 1961-68; asst. v.p. U. Ky. Coll. Dentistry (Med. Center), 1968-69, v.p. adminstrn. univ., 1970-75; exec. dir. Assn. for Acad. Health Centers, Washington, 1975-79; prof. dental care systems Sch. Dental Medicine, asso. v.p. health affairs U. Pa., 1979-87, sr. assoc. Leonard Davis Inst. Health Econs., Wharton Grad. Sch., 1980-87, prof. emeritus, 1987—; research prof. Health Services Research Ctr./Sch. of Dentistry, U. N.C., Chapel Hill, 1987-89; cons. Dental Corps, U.S. Army, 1960-70, VA, 1962-75, U.S. Dept. Def., 1969-72; pub. health service cons. dental study sect. USPHS, 1963-67; also chmn.; cons., lectr. USN Dental Sch.; cons. Army Med. Service Adv. Com. Preventive Dentistry, 1967-71; mem. Nat. Adv. Council Edn. Health Professions, 1968-72; bd. dirs. Nat. Center Health Edn., 1977-84; adv. com. Ednl. Testing Service, 1977-82; chmn. adv. com. Nat. Preventive Dental Demonstration Program, 1976-83. Served with inf. AUS, 1944-46; to 1st lt. Dental Corps 1951-54. Recipient Pierre Fauchard medal, 1974, Henry Spenadel medal, 1982, Callahan medal, 1991. Fellow Internat., Am. colls. dentists; mem. ADA (Disting. Svc. award 1985), Inst. Medicine of NAS, AAAS, Internat. Assn. Dental Rsch., So. Conf. Dental Deans and Examiners (pres. 1964-65), Sigma Xi. Presbyterian (deacon, trustee). *

MORRIS, ELIZABETH TREAT, physical therapist; b. Hartford, Conn., Feb. 20, 1936; d. Charles Wells and Marion Louise (Case) Treat; BS in Phys. Therapy, U. Conn., 1960; m. David Breck Morris, July 10, 1961; children: Russell Charles, Jeffrey David. Phys. therapist Crippled Children's Clinic No. Va., Arlington, 1960-62, Shriners Hosp. Crippled Children, Salt Lake City, 1967-69, Holy Cross Hosp., Salt Lake City, 1970-74; pvt. practice phys. therapy, Salt Lake City, 1975—. Mem. nominating com. YWCA, Salt Lake City. Mem. Am. Phys. Therapy Assn., Am. Congress Rehab. Medicine, Am. Alliance for Health Phys. Edn. Recreation & Dance, Nat. Speakers Assn., Utah Speakers Assn., Salt Lake Area C. of C., Friendship Force Utah, U.S. Figure Skating Assn., Toastmasters Internat., Internat. Assn. for the Study Pain, Internat. Platform Assn., World Confederation Phys. Therapy, Medart Internat. Home: 4177 Mathews Way Salt Lake City UT 84124-4021 Office: PO Box 526186 Salt Lake City UT 84152-6186

MORRIS, GEORGE THOMAS ARNOLD, internist; b. Raleigh, N.C., Mar. 29, 1934; s. George T. and Jessie M. (Arnold) M.; m. Mary Lide, Mar. 17, 1956; children: G. Thomas, Robert W., Francis L., David S. BS, Wake Forest U., 1955; MD, Bowman Gray Sch. Medicine, 1959. Diplomate Am. Bd. Internal Medicine. Resident N.C. Bapt. Hosp., Winston-Salem, 1963-66; physician Alamance Health Svcs., Burlington, N.C., 1966—. Capt. M.C., U.S. Army, 1960-63. Mem. AMA, ACP, Am. Soc. Internal Medicine. Republican. Baptist. Home: 440 Cedarwood Dr Burlington NC 27215-4810 Office: 711 Hermitage Rd Burlington NC 27215-3511

MORRIS, JAMES BRUCE, internist; b. Rochester, N.Y., May 13, 1943; s. Max G. and Beatrice Ruth (Becker) M.; B.A., U. Rochester, 1964; M.D., Yale U., 1968; m. Susan Carol Shencup, July 31, 1966; children: Carrie, Douglas, Deborah, Rebecca. Intern, SUNY, Buffalo, 1968-69, resident, 1969-70, 72-73, chief resident, 1973; fellow U. Miami, 1974; pvt. practice medicine specializing in internal medicine and infectious diseases, Plantation, Fla., 1974—; chmn. infection control com. Lauderdale Lakes Gen. Hosp., 1974-76; chmn. infection control com. Plantation Gen. Hosp., 1976-80, 83-85, chmn. pharmacy com., 1980-81, chmn. tissue com., 1982; sec., program chmn. dept. medicine Bennett Community Hosp., 1978-80, chmn. dept. medicine, 1980-81, vice chief staff, 1981-83; chmn. infection control com. Fla. Med. Center, 1980-82; chief staff Humana Hosp. Bennett, 1983-85, trustee, 1983-88, chmn. infection control com., 1985-87 ; clin. assoc. prof. U. Miami Med. Sch., 1975—. Served with USAR, 1970-72. Diplomate Am. Bd. Internal Medicine, Am. Bd. Infectious Diseases. Fellow ACP; mem. AMA, Am. Soc. Microbiology, Infectious Diseases Soc. Am., Am. Soc. Internal Medicine, Fla. Med. Assn., Broward County Med. Assn. Office: Sachs Morris & Sklaver 7353 NW 4th St Fort Lauderdale FL 33317-2202

MORRIS, JAMES CULVIN, III, plastic surgeon; b. Louisville, Mar. 21, 1937. BS, Davidson (N.C.) Coll., 1958; MD, Duke U., 1962. Diplomate Am. Bd. Surgery, Am. Bd. Plastic Surgery. Resident Barnes Hosp., Washington U., St. Louis, 1962-70, U. Va. Med. Ctr., Charlottesville, 1970-71; pvt. practice Roanoke, 1971—; assoc. clin. prof. U. Va., Charlottesville, 1975—. Fellow ACS. Office: 2233 Sanford Ave SW Roanoke VA 24014

MORRIS, JEFFREY SELMAN, orthopedic surgeon; b. Johannesburg, South Africa, June 26, 1948; arrived in Can., 1979; came to U.S., 1990; s. Israel and Anna Riva (Belikoff) M.; m. Carol Parker, Jan. 21, 1973 (div. 1986); children: Amit, Leora. BSc, U. Witwatersrand, Johannesburg, 1970, B of Medicine, B of Surgery, 1973. Rotating intern Natalspruit Hosp., South Africa, 1974, surg. resident, 1975-76; resident in orthopedic surgery Cen. Emek Hosp., Afula, Israel, 1977-79, Queen's U., Kingston, Ont., Can., 1979-82; orthopedic surgeon Port Arthur Clinic, Thunder Bay, Ont., 1983-86, Joseph Brant Meml. Hosp., Burlington, Ont., 1986-90, Beachwood (Ohio) Orthopedic Assocs., 1990—; mem. staff Meridia South Pointe Hosp., Cleve.; assoc. staff Meridia Hillcrest Hosp., Cleve. Contbr. articles to profl. jours., chpt. to book. Med. advisor Arthritis Soc., Thunder Bay, 1983-86. Mem. ACS, Can. Med. Assn., Ont. Med. Assn., Can. Orthopedic Assn., Ont. Orthopedic Assn., Ohio Orthopedic Soc., Cleve. Orthopedic Soc., Cleve. Acad. Medicine, Royal Coll. Physicians and Surgeons (Can.), Can. Soc. Surgery of the Hand, Ohio Med. Assn. Jewish. Office: Beachwood Orthopedic Assocs 23250 Mercantile Rd Beachwood OH 44122-5928

MORRIS, JOSEPH ANTHONY, health science association administrator; b. nr. Marboro, Md., Sept. 6, 1918; s. Charles Lafayette and Essie (Stokes) M.; BS, Cath. U. Am., 1940, MS, 1942, PhD, 1947; m. Ruth Savoy, Nov. 1, 1942; children: Carol Ann, Marilyn T., Joseph A., Larry A. Asst. scientist Josiah Macy, Jr. Found., N.Y.C., 1943-44; virologist, Depts. Agr., Interior, Laurel, Md., 1944-47; virologist, chief hepatitis virus research Walter Reed Army Inst. Research, Washington, 1947-56; virologist, asst. chief, dept. virus and rickettsial diseases U.S. Army Med. Command, Japan, 1956-59; virologist chief sect. respiratory viruses, div. biologics standards NIH, Bethesda, Md., 1959—, dir. slow, latent and temperate virus br. FDA, Bethesda, 1972-76; lectr. dept. microbiology U. Md., College Park, 1977-79; vice-chmn. Bell of Atri, Inc., College Park, 1979-82, chmn., 1983; cons. Commn. on Influenza, Armed Forces Epidemiologic Bd., 1960—, Nat. Inst. Neurol. Diseases and Blindness, 1962—. Mem. Soc. Tropical Medicine and Hygiene, Soc. Am. Microbiologists, Soc. Exptl. Biology and Medicine, Am. Assn. Immunologists, N.Y. Acad. Sci. Discoverer of respiratory sycytial virus; research on infectious hepatitis, respiratory diseases of virus etiology and zoonosis. Home: 23E Ridge Rd Greenbelt MD 20770-0714

MORRIS, KATHERINE LANG, counseling psychologist; b. Benson, Minn., Jan. 22, 1947; d. Howard James and Barbara Anne (Bennett) L. BA in Art History, Smith Coll., Northampton, Mass., 1969; MA, Bethel Theol. Sem., St. Paul, 1973; MEd, U. Mo.-Columbia, 1978, Ph.D., 1982. Lic. psychologist, Calif. Tchr., Am. Sch., Barcelona, Spain, 1970-71; campus ministry Univ. Reformed Ch., East Lansing, Mich., 1973-76; counselor Univ. Counseling Ctr., U. Mo., Rolla, 1978-79; coordinator Ctr. for Student Vols. Action, 1979-81; counseling psychologist U. Calif., Davis, 1982-94; pvt. practice counseling psychologist, Sacramento, Calif., 1986-92; dir. counseling dept. health svcs. U. Minn., Duluth, 1994—; cons. in field. Mem. APA. Avocations: skiing, racquetball, writing. Office: U Minn Health Svcs Duluth MN 55811

MORRIS, KENNETH WAYNE, dentist; b. Lynchburg, Va., Mar. 12, 1939; s. Ulysses Bernice and Elvira (Adams) M.; m. Judy A. Morris (widowed Dec. 1976); m. Robin C. Morris, June 19, 1977; children: Jeff, Chris, Kendall, Cory. BA, U. Va., 1961; DDS, Med. Coll. Va., 1965. Gen. dentistry South Hill, Va., 1967—; staff Community Meml. Hosp., South Hill, Va., 1967—. Composer Gospel Record, 1978. Mem. ADA, Gideons Internat. (state chaplain, state faith fund coord., state v.p., state pres.), Va. Dental Soc., Southside Component, South Hill C. of C., Woodfield CLub, Tanglewood Shores Golf and Country Club. Republican. Baptist. Home: 509 Raleigh Ave PO Box 599 South Hill VA 23970 Office: 604 N Thomas St South Hill VA 23970-1422

MORRIS, LEIGH EDWARD, hospital executive officer; b. Hartford City, Ind., Dec. 26, 1934; s. Fredus Orlando and Martha (Malott) M.; m. Marcia Renee Meredith, Oct. 7, 1967; children: Meredith Anne, Curtis Paul. BS in Commerce, Internat. Coll., 1954; BSBA, Ball State U., 1958; M in Health Adminstrn., U. Minn., 1972. Mem. labor relations staff Borg-Warner Corp., Muncie, Ind., 1961-64; various positions then personnel mgr. Internat. Harvester Co., Ft. Wayne, Ind., 1964-70; pres. Huntington (Ind.) Meml. Hosp., 1972-78, La Porte (Ind.) Hosp., 1978—; bd. dirs. First of Am. Bank of Ind., Am. Hosp. Svcs., Inc.; chmn., bd. dirs. Am. Hosp. Pub. Co.; chmn. La Porte Devel. Corp., 1980-81. Chmn. La Porte chpt. ARC, 1984-86. With U.S. Army, 1958-60. Recipient Disting. Alumni award Ball State U., Muncie, Ind., 1968, James A. Hamilton award U. Minn., Mpls., 1972, Trustees award Am. Hosp. Assn., 1996. Fellow Am. Coll. Healthcare Adminstrn., Health Care Fin. Mgmt. Assn.; mem. APHA, Am. Hosp. Assn. (trustee, regional chmn. 1985-89), Soc. for Healthcare Planning and Mktg. (bd. dirs.), Ind. Hosp. Assn. (chmn. 1980-81), La Porte C. of C. (chmn. 1981-82), Constantian Soc., Masons. Republican. Presbyterian. Home: 1519 Indiana Ave La Porte IN 46350-5105 Office: La Porte Hosp Inc PO Box 250 La Porte IN 46352-0250

MORRIS, LOREE, registered nurse; b. Salt Lake City, July 13, 1954; d. Elliot Cobia and Margaret (Derbyshire) M.; 1 child, Jasmin Loree. BSN, Brigham Young U., 1976. RN, Utah, Ariz. ICU staff nurse, night supervisor Flagstaff (Ariz.) Hosp., 1976-78; health missionary Ch. Jesus Christ of the Latter-Day Saints, Hong Kong, 1978-80; charge nurse ICU Flagstaff Hosp., 1980-81; charge nurse coronary ICU LDS Hosp., Salt Lake City, 1981-87; from utilization mgmt. nurse to med. claims rev. specialist Intermountain Health Care-Health Plans, Salt Lake City, 1987—. Merit badge counselor Boy Scouts Am., Flagstaff, 1976-78; troop leader Girl Scouts U.S., Salt Lake City, 1986-87. Mem. Singles for Transracial Adoption. Republican. Home: 1542 Baroness St Salt Lake City UT 84116

MORRIS, LYNNE LOUISE, psychotherapist; b. Youngstown, Ohio, Nov. 5, 1946; d. Richard Davies and Elsie Margaret Raymond) B.A., Westminster Coll., Pa., 1969; MSW, NYU, 1971. Cert. clin. social worker. Social worker Community Service Soc., N.Y.C., 1971-74, Altro Health and Rehab. Services, Inc., N.Y.C., 1974-79; field instr. Hunter Coll. Sch. Social Work, NYU Grad Sch. Social Work, 1974-79; clin. coordinator Montefiore Hosp. and Med. Center, Bronx, N.Y., 1979-81; asst. dir. II, social service dept. Montefiore Hosp., Bronx, 1981-83; pvt. practice psychotherapy, N.Y.C., 1976—; sr. staff therapist Counseling and Human Devel. Center, N.Y.C., 1979—. Contbr. articles of profl. jours. including Jour. Geriatric Psychiatry, 1975; abstractor Abstracts for Social Workers, 1975. Fellow N.Y. State Soc. Clin. Social Work Psychotherapists; mem. Nat. Assn. Social Workers (clin. diplomate), Acad. Cert. Social Workers, Am. Assn. Pastoral Counselors (profl. affiliate). Home and office: 161 W 75th St Apt 2C New York NY 10023-1802

MORRIS, MELANIE MARIE, nurse; b. Lima, Ohio, Aug. 3, 1963; d. Andrew J. and Helen (Kaniclides) Menegos. BS in Nursing, U. Akron, 1986, MBA in Mgmt., 1993. RN, Ohio. Home health aid Nurses' Ho. Calls, Akron, Ohio, 1985, Portamedic, Akron, 1985; intravenous technician Akron City Hosp., 1985-86, nurse, 1987-88; nurse Vis. Nurse Svc., Akron, 1988-89; nurse Akron Gen. Med. Ctr., 1989—, clin. mgr. SICU/MICU, 1994—. Mem. Young Adult League, Akron; mem. Annunciation Ch. Choir, Akron, sec. 1989-90, 92-94, pres. 1995—. Mem. Daus. of Penelope (treas. 1988-90). Republican. Greek Orthodox.

MORRIS, PAULA DOROTHEA, chiropractor; b. N.Y.C., Aug. 6, 1921; d. Samuel and Fanny (Spindel) Reif; m. Michael Kendrick, May 28, 1984 (div. May, 1987); m. Cristopher Morris. DO, Balcombe U., Sussex, Eng., 1962; D in Chiropractic, Chiropractic Inst. N.Y., 1967. Diplomte Am. Chiropractic Bd., English Bd. Osteopathic Medicine. Chiropractor pvt. practice N.Y.C., 1968-79; chiropractor, nutritionist, physical therapist Centro Medico, Calpe, Alicante, Spain, 1979—; doctor-trainer Javea (Alicante) Cricket Team; exercise cons. Marcia's Dance Studio, Calpe, Alicante; nutrition cons. Centro Medico, Calpe, Alicante. Columnist Costa Blanca Jour., Spain. Mem. Am. Chiropractic Assn., Am. Back Assn. Republican. Pentecostal. Home: 6805 Fulton Ave Ventnor NJ 08406 Office: Centro Medico, Avda Gabriel Miro 15, 33410 Calpe Alicante, Spain

MORRIS, PETER WILLIAM, internist; b. Birmingham, Ala., Feb. 20, 1930; s. William Konstantine and Maria (Chronis) M.; m. Diane Michael Leontis, June 21, 1964; children: William, Adrianne. BS, U. Ala., 1952; MD, Med. Coll. Ala., 1956. Diplomate Am. Bd. Internal Medicine. Intern Univ. Hosp., Birmingham, Ala., 1956-57, resident, 1959-61; fellow in hematology Duke U., Durham, N.C., 1961-63; pvt. practice medicine Birmingham, 1963—; clin. asst. prof. medicine U. Ala. Sch. Medicine, Birmingham, 1968—; pres., chmn. bd. dirs. Ala. Quality Assurance Found., Birmingham, 1991-92. Lt. U.S. Navy, 1957-59. Fellow ACP; mem. AMA, Am. Soc. Internal Medicine, So. med. Assn., Med. Assn. State Ala. (prs. 1992-93), Ala. Soc. Internal Medicine (pres. 1995-96, Internist of Yr. 1993). Greek Orthodox. Home: 3050 Westmoreland Dr Birmingham AL 35223 Office: 2660 10th Ave S #630 Birmingham AL 35205

MORRIS, RICHARD LOUIS, healthcare company executive; b. Piits., Apr. 15, 1940; s. Robert Edwin and Marina (Hegeman) M.; m. Roberta Christine Pavlik, Jan. 26, 1963; children: Richard Jr. Tracy, Anne, John. Student, Duquesne U., Pitts., U. Md. Sales rep. Procter and Gamble, Washington D.C., 1976-70, Nat. Chemsearch Corp., Washington, 1970-71, Sherwood Med., Washington D.C., 1971-72; v.p. LaBarge Inc., St. Louis, 1972-81, Mon-A-Therm, Inc., St. Louis, 1981-; founder, pres., bd. dirs. Innovation Med. Techs., Inc., St. Louis, 1990—; founder, dir. Mon-A-Therm, Inc., St. Louis, 1981-88; dir. sales Mallinckrodt Anesthesia Products, Mallinckrodt, Inc., 1988-90. Mem. Lions Club Internat. Republican. Roman Catholic. Home: 1751 Baxter Forest Ct Chesterfield MO 63005-4659 Office: 750 Goddard Ave Chesterfield MO 63005-1100

MORRIS, ROBERT D., JR., physician; b. Akron, Ohio, Aug. 28, 1952; s. Robert D. and Kathleen (Mason) M.; m. Marcia J. Goss, June 28, 1975; 1 child, Sarah K. BS, W.Va. U., 1975; DO, W.Va. Sch. Osteopathic Med., 1980. Diplomate Am. Bd. Internal Medicine. Pharmacist Wheeling (W.Va.) Hosp., 1975—; intern Cuyahoga Falls (Ohio) Gen. Hosp., 1980-81; resident in internal medicine Ohio Valley Med. Ctr., Wheeling, 1981-84; internist Wheeling Clinic, New Martinsville, W.Va., 1984-91; emergency room physician Ohio Valley Med. Ctr., 1991-93, Wetzel County Hosp., New Martinsville, 1994—. Mem. Am. Coll. Physicians, Am. Coll. Emergency Physicians, W.Va. Soc. Osteopathic Medicine, Rotary New Martinsville (pres. 1993-94, sec. 1995-96). Home: 250 Virginia St New Martinsville WV 26155 Office: Wetzel County Hosp 3 E Benjamin Dr New Martinsville WV 26155

MORRIS, ROBERT DARRELL, life energy research director; b. Beaver, Pa., Sept. 3, 1914; s. David Earl and Marguerite (Krepps) M.; m. Ina Logan, Apr. 30, 1953 (div. July 26, 1976); children: Heather, Tamara; m. Berniece Henderson; children: R. Jeffrey, Stephen H. BA, Mount Union Coll., 1935; STD, Sch. Theology, Boston, 1938; MPH Sch. Pub. Health, U. Pitts., 1960. Dir. clin. tng. Pa. Hosp., Phila., 1939-40; chaplain, dir. clin. tng. Episcopal Hosp., Phila., 1940-53; lectr. clin. theology Temple U., Phila., 1948-52; intern social biology Pioneer Health Ctr., Peckham, London, 1949; family therapist Craig House for Children, Pitts., 1954-64; dir. social rsch. U. Miami Med. Sch. Family Medicine, Fla., 1966-68; pvt. practice Miami, 1969-89, life energy researcher, 1980—; co-dir. Orgone Biophys. Rsch. Lab., San Francisco, 1984-88. Recipient Jacob Sleeper fellowship Boston U., 1938-39, Doehla fellowship Rust Grant Rust Found., 1963, Durlach Grant Durlach Found., 1953. Mem. AAAS, Occidental Research Found., Upledger Inst. for Cranio-Sacral Therapy, N.Y. Acad. Sci., Coral Reef Yacht. Republican. Episcopalian. Home and Office: Life Energy Rsch 402 Pioneer Dr Prescott AZ 86303-4110

MORRIS, ROBERT WARREN, physician assistant; b. Oakland, Calif., Mar. 28, 1948; s. Warren and Javine (Don Carlos) M.; children: Rebecca Lynn, Daniel Robert. BS, Old Dominion U., 1971; BS with honors, George Washington U., 1976; postgrad., N.Y. Med. Coll. Diplomate Nat. Bd. Med. Examiners; registered, N.Y. Physician asst. internal medicine Group Health Assn., Washington, 1976-81; physician asst. family practice Waddington (N.Y.) Med. Clinic, 1981-83; physician asst. internal medicine Northeast Permanente Med. Group, White Plains, N.Y., 1983—; mem. pharmacy and therapeutics com. Kaiser Health Plan, White Plains, 1986—, AIDS task force mem., 1989—, quality care com., 1986-90, health ctr. adminstr., Tarrytown, Yonkers, N.Y., 1985-90. Mem. Am. Assn. Physician Assts. Home: 2 Scenic Cir Croton on Hudson NY 10520 Office: Kaiser Found Health Plan 210 Westchester Ave White Plains NY 10604

MORRIS, SAMUEL CARY, environmental scientist, consultant, educator; b. Summit, N.J., Dec. 16, 1942; s. Samuel Cary Jr. and Roberta Ann (Griffiths) M.; m. Stephanie Margaret Rose, Aug. 13, 1966; children: Jennifer, Daniel, Laura. BSCE, Va. Mil. Inst., 1965; MS in Sanitary Engring., Rutgers U., 1966; ScD in Environ. Health, U. Pitts., 1973. Asst. prof. environ. sci. Ill. State U., Normal, 1971-72; rsch. assoc. U. Pitts., 1972-73; asst. scientist, then assoc. scientist Brookhaven Nat. Lab., Upton, N.Y., 1973-77, scientist, 1977—, dep. head div. analytic scis., 1990—; head Biomed. and Environ. Assessment Group, 1994—; adj. prof. Carnegie Mellon U., Pitts., 1976—; editl. bd. Environ. Internat., 1983—; lectr. SUNY-Stony Brook, 1992—. Author: Cancer Risk Assessment, 1990; mem. editl. bd. Environ. Modeling and Assessment, 1995—; contbr. chpts. to books, articles to profl. jours. Capt. U.S. Army, 1966-68. Mem. ASCE, Inst. for Ops. Rsch. and the Mgmt. Scis., Air and Waste Mgmt. Assn., Soc. Risk Analysis (coun. mem. 1984-86), Delta Omega. Office: Brookhaven Nat Lab Dept Analytic Sciences Upton NY 11973

MORRIS, STEPHEN EUGENE, surgery educator; b. Murray, Utah, May 18, 1955; s. Douglas and Marilyn Morris; m. Marie Kuhni. BA in

Chemistry magna cum laude, U. Utah, 1978, MD, 1982. Diplomate Am. Bd. Surgery, Am. Bd. Surg. Critical Care. Burn fellow Shriner's Burns Inst., Galveston, Tex., 1987-89; resident in surgery U. Utah, Salt Lake City, 1982-87, asst. prof. surgery, 1989-96, assoc. prof. surggery, 1996—; assoc. dir. Intermountain Burn Ctr., Salt Lake City, 1989—; med. dir. Intermountain Tissue Ctr., Salt Lake City, 1994—. Recipient Meritorious Rsch. award AMA, 1980; Winthrop rsch. fellow Am. Assn. Surgery for Trauma, 1988. Fellow ACS; mem. Am. Burn Assn. (rehab. com. 1993-95), Assn. Acad. Surgeons, Surg. Infection Soc., Am. Assn. Tissue Banks, Southwestern Surg. Congress, Alpha Omega Alpha. Office: Univ Hosp Dept Surgery 50 N Medical Dr Rm 3B-316 Salt Lake City UT 84132

MORRIS, UNA LORRAINE, physician; b. Kingston, Jamaica, W.I., Jan. 17, 1949; came to U.S., 1965; d. Arthur Samuel and Lydia (Reid) Morris; m. Charles Cecil Chong, Mar. 27, 1981; children—Keone Tremaine, Cheynne Jehon, Wei-Lin Lorraine Chong. M.D., U. Calif.-San Francisco, 1974. Diplomate Am. Bd. Radiology. Intern, Kaiser Permanente Hosp., Oakland, Calif., 1974; resident in radiology Martin Luther King Jr. Gen. Hosp, Los Angeles, 1975-79; fellow U. Calif.-Irvine; practice medicine specializing in radiology, Los Angeles, 1980—; asst. prof. radiology U. So. Calif., Los Angeles, 1984—; program coordinator San Gabriel Women Physicians Assn., 1982—; organizer, liaison Jamaican Med. Airlift, Los Angeles, 1982—. Contbr. articles to profl. jours. V.P Jamaica Project Health, Inc., Pasadena. Named Sportswoman of Yr. for Jamaica, Jamaica Amateur Athletic Assn., 1964, 65, 66; mem. Olympic team 1964, 68, 72. Mem. Radiol. Soc. N.Am. Baptist. Address: 1617 Homewood Dr Altadena CA 91001-2608

MORRISON, ASHTON BYROM, pathologist, medical school official; b. Northern Ireland, Oct. 13, 1922; came to U.S., 1955; s. Samuel and Henrietta (Good) M.; m. Claire Morris, M.D.; 1 dau., Mary Claire. MB, Queen's U, Belfast, No. Ireland, 1946; PhD, Queens U., Belfast, No. Ireland, 1950, MD (hon.), 1988; MD, Duke U., 1946. Intern Royal Victoria Hosp., Belfast, 1947; asst. lectr. Queens U., 1947-52; registrar dept. exptl. medicine Cambridge U., 1952-55, dir. med. studies Corpus Christi Coll., 1954-55; assoc. Duke U., N.C., 1955-58; asst. prof. pathology U. Pa. Sch. Medicine, 1958-61; assoc. prof. U. Rochester Sch. Medicine, 1961-65; prof. pathology, chmn. dept. Rutgers U. Med. Sch., 1965-80; v.p. acad. affairs Eastern Va. Med. Authority, 1980-83; dean Eastern Va. Med. Sch., 1980-83; prof. pathology Robert Wood Johnson Med. Sch.-U. Medicine and Dentistry N.J., Camden, 1983-93; assoc. dean in charge Robert Wood Johnson Med Sch.-U. Medicine and Dentistry N.J., Camden, 1983-89, prof. pathology emeritus, 1994—; prof. pathology Ea. Va. Med. Sch., 1994—; 22nd Scott Heron lectr. Royal Victoria Hosp., Belfast, No. Ireland, 1978. Recipient Disting. Alumnus award Duke U. Med. Sch., 1987. Mem. Am. Assn. Investigative Pathologists (emeritus), Am. Physiol. Soc. (emeritus), Soc. Exptl. Biology and Medicine (emeritus), Am. Soc. Nephrology (emeritus). Home: 315 Brooke Ave Apt 306 Norfolk VA 23510 Office: Eastern Va Med Sch 358 Mowbray Arch Ste 108 Norfolk VA 23507

MORRISON, D. BARRY, optometrist; b. Montgomery, W.Va., June 28, 1958; s. David Thomas and Nancy Lee (Bennett) M.; m. Rebecca Gayle Palmer, Aug. 23, 1986. BA in Biology, W.Va. U., 1979; BS in Optometric Sci., New Eng. Coll. Optometry, 1981, OD, 1983. Diplomate Nat. Bd. Examiners Optometry; lic. optometrist W.Va., Ga. Intern and clin. teaching asst. Boston Eye Clinic, 1980-83; extern Dorchester (Mass.) House Multi-Svc. Ctr., 1982; resident in optometric medicine and primary care So. Coll. Optometry, Memphis, 1983-84; pvt. practice Martinsburg, W.Va., 1984-92, 95—; assoc. Jerry Fogle, M.D., Martinsburg, 1992-94. P.A.S.S. vol. Musselman H.S., 1993-96. Lt. col. W.Va. Air N.G., 1985—. Mem. Am. Optometric Assn. (contact lens sect., low vision sect.), W.Va. Optometric Assn. (area chmn. 1996), So. Coun. Optometry, Air Nat. Guard Optometric Soc., Assn. Mil. Surgeons of U.S., Beta Sigma Kappa. Republican. Methodist. Office: 2604 Aikens Ctr Martinsburg WV 25401

MORRISON, DONALD WILSON, psychologist; b. Roseville, Mich., Sept. 6, 1932; s. Leonard Lester and Leona (Holland) M.; children: Dawn Marie. James Charles, Dena Jean. BD, Concordia Sem. Springfield, Ill., 1958; BS, Concordia Tchrs. Coll., River Forest, Ill., 1961; MS (univ. fellow 1961-63), Wayne State U., 1963, PhD, 1967 Ordained to ministry Lutheran Ch., Mo. Synod, 1958; asst. pastor Trinity Luth. Ch., Lansing, Mich., 1958-63; dean Mich. Lutheran Coll., Detroit, 1963-67; asst. prof. Miami U., Oxford, Ohio, 1967-71; asso. prof. Temple U., Phila., 1971-73; pvt. practice psychology, King of Prussia, Pa., 1973—; owner, Morrison Assos., 1981—; cons. psychologist suburban Phila. police depts., 1973—; lectr., instr. Pa. Dept. Community Affairs, 1982—; dir. clin. services Divorce Trauma Ctr., 1987-93. Mem. APA, Pa. Psychol. Assn. Author: Personal Problem Solving in the Classroom, 1977; contbr. articles in field to profl. jours. Office: 600 Crossfield Rd King Of Prussia PA 19406

MORRISON, GILBERT CAFFALL, psychiatrist; b. Beaumont, Tex., Feb. 28, 1931; s. Frank William and Ardis Emma (Caffall) M.; m. Betty Joyce Neville, June 28, 1952; children: Kay Morrison Mammen, Keith Neville, Kimberly Sue Morrison Pelz, Christopher Gilbert. Student, Southwestern U., 1948-50; B.S., Tulane U., 1952, M.D., 1957; Ph.D., So. Calif. Psychoanalytic Inst., 1978. Intern Touro Infirmary, New Orleans, 1957-58; resident in psychiatry Cin. Gen. Hosp. U. Cin., 1958-60; fellow in child psychiatry Children's Psychiat. Center, U. Cin., 1960-62, asst. prof. child psychiatry, 1964-68; with So. Calif. Psychoanalytic Inst., 1968-73; clin. prof. psychiatry and child psychiatry dept. psychiatry and human behavior U. Calif., Irvine, 1968—; practice medicine specializing in psychiatry, child psychiatry, psychoanalysis and family psychiatry Newport Beach, Irvine, Calif., 1973—; supervising and tng. psychoanalyst So. Calif. Psychoanalytic Inst., Los Angeles, 1978. Author, editor: Emergencies in Child Psychiatry, 1975. Served to lt. comdr. M.C. USNR, 1962-64. Fellow Am. Psychiat. Assn. (life), Am. Orthopsychiat. Assn., Am. Acad. Child Psychiatry, Am. Psychoanalytic Assn.; mem. Orange County Coun. Child Psychiatry (pres. 1975-76). Home: 22382 Valdemosa Mission Viejo CA 92692-1194 Office: 7700 Irvine Center Dr Ste 210 Irvine CA 92718-2924

MORRISON, GLENN, neurosurgeon; b. Phila., June 16, 1940; married, 3 children. AB, Colgate U., 1962; MD, Case Western Reserve U., 1967; postgrad., Nat. Comm. Disease Ctr., 1968. Diplomate Am. Bd. Neurological Surgery. Intern Cleve. Met. Hosp., 1968; resident in neurosurgery Univ. Hosps. Cleve., 1970-74; with Neurosurg. Assocs., Coral Gables, Fla., 1974-85, Baptist Hosp., Miami, 1974—; pvt. prac. Coral Gables, 1985—; chief pediatric neurological surgery Miami Children's Hosp., 1986—; asst. clinical prof. dept. neurological surgery, U. Miami Sch. Med.; cons. divsn. children's med. svcs. state of Fla. Lt. Cmdr. USPHS, 1968-70. Recipient Nat. Found. Rsch. award, 1967. Fellow ACS (sec., treas. greater Miami chpt. 1979-83, pres. 1983-85, interview com. 1980—); mem. AMA, Am. Assn. Neurol. Surgeons, Congress Neurol. Surgeons, Am. Acad. Pediats., Am. Heart Assn., Neurol. Soc. Am., Internat. Soc. Pediat. Neurosurgery, So. Neurosurg. Soc. (v.p. 1989-90, treas. 1992-95, pres. 1996-97), Fla. Neurosurg. Soc. (pres. 1982), Greater Miami Neurosurg. Soc. (pres. 1978), numerous others. Office: Med Arts Bldg Ste 301 Miami Children's Hosp 3200 SW 60th Ct Miami FL 33155 also: 4685 Ponce De Leon Blvd Miami FL 33146

MORRISON, IAN ALASTAIR, foundation executive; b. Glasgow, Scotland, Apr. 22, 1924; came to U.S., 1932, naturalized, 1937; s. William John and Alexandrina (Smith) M.; m. Naida Brown, Apr. 19, 1946; children: Craig William, Sheila Elise. BA, Wagner Coll., S.I., N.Y., 1948, LHD, 1968; MA, Columbia U., 1950, MS, 1958, EdD, 1961; LHD, Bard Coll., 1968. Assoc. prof. history, dean students Wagner Coll., 1949-56; exec. Inter Royal Corp., N.Y.C., 1956-57; exec. sec. Greer Sch., Millbrook, N.Y., 1958-61; exec. dir. Greer Sch., Millbrook, 1961-72; pres. Greer-Woodycrest Children's Found., N.Y.C., 1972-89, The Greer Inst. of Group Care Cons., 1979-90; pres. Greer Crest retirement community, N.Y.C., 1984-89, pres. emeritus, 1989-95. Author: Higher Education in World War II, 1950, American Political Parties, Political Science Handbook, 1953, Foster Care in the United States, 1975; editor NAHC Pub. Affairs Bull., 1975-87, Continuing Care Retirement Communities: Social, Political and Financial Issues; pub. Resdl. Group Care quar.; contbr. articles to profl. jurs.; author pub. affairs newsletter. Pres. Eastchester (N.Y.) Bd. Edn., 1962-66, Unionvale (N.Y.) Bd. Edn., 1969-87; mem. adv. coun. Dutchess C.C.; mem. long-range com. Columbia U. Divsn. Geriatrics and Gerontology; trustee emeritus St. Francis Hosp., Poughkeepsie, N.Y., 1981-90, chmn., 1990; bd. dirs. Palma Sola Bot. Park, Bradenton, Fla., 1994; elder Palma Sola Presbyn. Ch., 1996. With AUS, WWII, ETO, POW, Germany. Decorated Purple Heart with oak leaf cluster, Prisoner of War medal, Bronze Star; Grad. fellow 1948 Wagner Coll., 1948. Mem. N.Y. State Assn. Child Care Agencies (pres. 1969), N.Y. State Assn. Children's Inst. (chmn. edn. com. 1961-68, pres. 1968), Nat. Assn. Homes for Children (hon. life mem., dir. 1975-89, pres. 1977-79, chmn. pub. affairs com. 1975-87, bd. dir. 1975-87, author code of ethics, 1976), Nat. Assn. Sr. Living Industry (founding mem.), Child Welfare League Am., Fgn. Policy Assn., St. Andrews Soc., Caledonia Soc. (bd. dirs. Sarasota), Nat. Assn. Homes for Children, Am. Assn. Homes for Aged, Nat. Assn. Fundraising Execs., Union League Club (N.Y.C.), Milbrook (N.Y.) Golf and Tennis Club, Columbia U. Club (N.Y.C.), Bradenton Country Club.

MORRISON, JACQUELYN LARSON, gerontologist; b. Palo Alto, Calif., Oct. 28, 1945; d. John Monroe and Glendora Drusilla (Sampson) Larson; m. Stephen Earl Kelley, Dec. 24, 1963 (div. 1994); children: Kristina Leona Jane, Stephenie Victoria; m. Malcolm H. Morrison, May 7, 1995. AA, Coll. San Mateo, 1974; BS summa cum laude, Coll. Notre Dame, Belmont, Calif., 1980; postgrad., San Francisco State U., 1980-82, Coll. Notre Dame, 1992-94, Pa. State U., 1996—. ESL aide Cabrillo Unified Sch. Dist., Half Moon Bay, Calif., 1975-76; community services specialist Ret. Sr. Vol. Program, Menlo Park, Calif., 1980-82, dir., 1982-83; dir. vol. services Vis. Nurse Assn. San Francisco, 1983-85; gerontology specialist San Jose (Calif.) Office on Aging, 1986-90, gerontology supr., 1990-92; analyst San Jose Dept. Human Resources, Retirement Benefits, 1992-94, v.p. counseling and corp. programs York County (Pa.) Family Svc. Assn., 1994—; lectr. San Jose State U., 1991-93. Founder Ocean Shore Residents Assn., Half Moon Bay, 1975; founder Friends of RSVP Inc., Redwood City, Calif., 1983; adv. coun. York Vol. Ctr., tech. resource trainer, 1995—. Mem. Internat. Soc. for Retirement Planning (chpt. pres., bd. dirs. 1985—, v.p. 1991-96, pres. 1995—), Nat. Coun. Aging, Am. Soc. Aging (com. chmn. 1984-87, chmn. retirement program planning com. 1988-90, 95—, chair recreation and leisure planning com, 1990-96, bd. dirs. 1996—, trainer/cons. 1996), Assn. Profl. Vol. Mgrs. (founder, chmn. 1984-87, trainer), Nat. Recreation and Pk. Assn. (task force on aging 1989-91, founding pres. aging and leisure sect. 1991-94), Calif. Pk. and Recreation Soc. (bd. dirs., founder, pres. sect. aging 1988-90), Alpha Gamma Sigma, Delta Epsilon Sigma, Kappa Gamma Pi. Democrat. Lutheran. Home: 6060 Gensemer Ln Harrisburg PA 17111-3832 Office: York County Family Svc Assn 1 W Market St York PA 17401-1231

MORRISON, JOHN TAYLOR, occupational medicine physician; b. Madison, Wis., Apr. 23, 1934; s. John Taylor and Eleanor Constance (Goodnight) M.; m. Barbara Stephany Wallace, Aug. 24, 1957; children: Stephany Taylor Morrison Price, Nancy Hamilton, Elizabeth Wallace, John Andrew. BS, U. Wis., 1956; MD, U. Pa., 1960. Diplomate Am. Bd. Preventive Medicine. Rotating intern U. Chgo., 1960-61, resident in internal medicine, 1961-63; fellow in gastroenterology U. Cin., 1966-68, chief resident in internal medicine, 1968-69; pvt. practice Boulder, Colo., 1969-78; sr. staff specialist IBM, Purchase, N.Y., 1978-81, sr. mng. physician, 1981-84, mgr. med. programs, 1984-85, group med. dir., 1985-88; asst. v.p. health and safety svcs., med. dir. BellSouth Telecom., Atlanta, 1988-94; corp med. dir. Gates Corp., Denver, 1994—; mem. drug utilization rev. com. divsn. med. assistance Colo. Dept. Social Svcs., 1975-77; chmn. utilization rev. com. Boulder County Hospice, Inc., 1979-82; mem. Boulder County Bd. Health, 1979-84, pres., 1982-84; ; mem. med. adv bd. The Medical Disability Advisor (Presley Reed), 1991; presenter in field; asst. prof. div. environ. and occupl. health Emory U. Sch. Pub. Health, Atlanta, 1992-94. Contbr. articles to med. jours. Surgeon USPHS, 1963-66. Fellow Am. Coll. Occupl. and Environ. Medicine (chpt. program chmn. 1980-81, chpt. pres. 1982-83); mem. AMA, Colo. Med. Soc. (state conv. del. 1976-82), Rocky Mountain Acad. Occupl. Medicine (program chmn. 1980-81, pres. 1982-83). Republican. Episcopalian. Home: 1065 S High St Denver CO 80209-4552 Office: Gates Clinic 1000 S Broadway Denver CO 80217

MORRISON, MALCOLM HAROLD, health care executive; b. Cambridge, Mass., Aug. 5, 1943; s. Theodore and Elizabeth (Shelman) M.; m. Judith Louise Parker, Aug. 20, 1967 (div. May 1995); children: Andrew David, Seth Gabriel; m. Jacquelyn Larson Kelley, May 7, 1995. BSc, McGill U., Montreal, Can., 1965; MA, Boston U., 1967; MPA, U. Mich., 1968; PhD, Brandeis U., 1974. Social sci. rsch. analyst, economist U.S. Social Security Adminstrn., Balt., 1973-77; grant/contract officer U.S. Social Security Adminstrn., Washington, 1977-79; dir. disability studies U.S. Social Security Adminstrn., Washington, Balt., 1986-90; chief rsch. support staff U.S. Dept. Labor, Washington, 1979-83; faculty rsch. assoc. Wharton Sch., Phila., 1983-85; dir. rsch. Nat. Assn. Rehab. Facilities, Washington, 1990-92; v.p. Continental Med. Systems, Mechanicsburg, Pa., 1993-95; pres. Morrison Informatics, Harrisburg, Pa., 1996—; bd. dirs. Am. Soc. Aging, San Francisco, Com. Accreditation Rehab. Facilities, Tucson, Fedn. Am. Health Systems, Washington. Author: Economics of Aging: The Future of Retirement, 1982; contbr. articles to profl. jours. Co-chair Aging Disability and Rehab. Network Am. Soc. Aging, San Francisco, 1993—; mem. sci. adv. bd. Henry H. Kessler Found., West Orange, N.J., 1995—; bd. dirs. Recreation and Revitalization Connection, Inc., Chevy Chase, Md., 1989—. Mary E. Switzer fellow Nat. Rehab. Assn., 1986, 91, Interovernmental fellow U. Pa., 1983-85; Comp Health scholar Kenan-Flagler Bus. Sch. U. N.C., 1995. Fellow Gerontol. Soc. Am. Home and Office: Morrison Informatics Inc 1150 Lancaster Blvd Mechanicsburg PA 17055

MORRISON, MICHELLE WILLIAMS, nursing educator, administrator, author; b. Reno, Nev., Feb. 12, 1947; d. Robert James and Dolores Jane (Barnard) Williams; m. Harrison Russell Morrison, Dec. 29, 1974. BSN, U. Nev., Reno, 1973; M Health Svc., U. Calif., Davis, 1977. RN, Oreg. Staff nurse VA Hosp., Reno, 1973-77; family nurse practitioner Tri-County Indian Health Svc., Bishop, Calif., 1977-78; instr. nursing Roque C.C., Grants Pass, Oreg., 1978-82; psychiat. nurse VA Hosp., Roseburg, Oreg., 1982; dir. edn. Josephine Meml. Hosp., Grants Pass, 1983-84; geriatric nurse practitioner Hearthstone Manor, Medford, Oreg., 1984-86; chmn. nursing dept. Roque Community Coll., Grants Pass, Oreg., 1986-89; prin. Health and Ednl. Cons., Grants Pass, 1989—; dir. nursing Highland House Nursing Ctr., Grants Pass, 1990; bd. dirs. Tri-County Indian Health Svc.; cons. for nursing svcs. in long term care facilities. Author: Professional Skills for Leadership; contbr.: Fundamental Nursing: Concepts and Skills. Mem. Josephine County Coalition for AIDS, Grants Pass, 1990. With USN, 1965-69. Mem. NAFE, Nat. League Nursing, Oreg. Ednl. Assn., Oreg. State Bd. Nursing (re-entry nursing com. 1992-93). Office: PO Box 89 Williams OR 97544-0089

MORRISON, MURRAY ALLAN, orthopaedic surgeon; b. Columbus, Ohio, Dec. 6, 1939; s. Benjamin Gerald and Mildred (Jacobs) M.; m. Susan Gail Kobren, July 30, 1967; children: Jennifer Anne, Sarah Elise. AB, Harvard U., 1961; MD, NYU, 1965. Diplomate Am. Bd. Orthopaedic Surgery. Surg. intern U. Mich. Med. Ctr., Ann Arbor, 1965-66, asst. resident surgery, 1966-67; orthodaedic resident Hosp. of U. of Pa., Phila., 1967-70; attending surgeon Bridgeport (Conn.) Hosp., 1970—; sr. attending surgeon Bridgeport Hosp., 1980—, chief sect. of orthopedic surgery, 1992—; clin. instr. Yale U. Sch. of Medicine, New Haven, 1985—; dir. Ralston Orthopedic Libr., U. Pa. Dept. of Ortho-surgery, Phila., 1984—. Fellow Am. Coll. Surgeons, Am. Acad. Orthopaedic Surgeons, Eastern Orthopaedic Assn., Conn. State Med. Soc. Office: Orthopedic Specialty Group 325 Reef Rd Fairfield CT 06430-6537

MORRISON, ROBERT TOWNSEND, nephrologist; b. Boston, Dec. 26, 1951; s. Robert Stier and Marie Day (Townsend) M.; m. Margaret Lou Dougherty, July 10, 1976; children: Sarah Marie, Samuel Thomas. BS, Rensselaer Poly. Inst., 1976; student, Columbia U., 1981; MD, Albany Med. Coll., 1985. Assoc. Herbert F. Gold and Assocs., Brookline, Mass., 1976; ins. claims adjuster GAB Adjustment Corp., Boston, 1976-78; lab. technician Rockefeller U., N.Y.C., 1980-81; resident in internal medicine USAF Med. Ctr., Wright-Patterson AFB, Ohio, 1985-88; fellow in nephrology Wilford Hall USAF Med. Ctr., Lackland AFB, Tex., 1988-90; chief nephrology svc. 13th Air Force Med. Ctr., Republic of Philippines, 1990-91, David Grant USAF Med. ctr., Travis AFB, Calif., 1991-94; med. dir., CEO, chief nephrology GMH Dialysis Ctr., Xenia, Ohio, 1994—; nephrologist, internist Med. Svc. Assocs., Xenio, Ohio, 1994—; asst. clin. prof. medicine U. Calif. at Davis, Sacramento, 1991-94, Wright State U. Sch. Medicine, Dayton, Ohio, 1995—; nephrology cons. Pacific Air Command, USAF, Clark AB, The Philippines, 1990-91; instr. Uniformed Svcs. U. Health Scis., 1988-90. Author jour. articles and abstracts. Co-chair combined fed. campaign United Way of Solano County, 1993-94; chmn. drives ARC, Albany, N.Y., 1982-83; chmn. Hunger Task Force of Riverside Ch., 1979-81. Maj. USAF, 1985-94, Res., 1994—. Mem. ACP, Nat. Kidney Found., Soc. Air Force Physicians, Am. Soc. Nephrology, Greene County Med. Soc. (bd. dirs.), Ohio Med. Assn., Sigma Chi (pres. chpt. 1975-76). Democrat. Home: 126 W North College St Yellow Springs OH 45387-1563 Office: Med Svc Assocs 386 N Detroit St Xenia OH 45385

MORRISON, SCOTT IRA, optometrist; b. Bklyn., Apr. 22, 1959; s. Herbert Irving and Iris (Weinstein) M.; m. Jacki Fay Posner, Aug. 4, 1985; children: Jacob, Ben. BA, Queens Coll., 1981; OD, SUNY, N.Y.C., 1985. Optometric technician DC 37, N.Y.C., 1983-85, cons., 1985-88; pvt. practice New Paltz, N.Y., 1985—; asst. clin. prof. SUNY State Coll. Optometry, Walden, N.Y., 1985—; cons. Early Edn. Ctr., Highland, N.Y., 1985—, Divsn. for Youth, Highland, 1986—, New Paltz (N.Y.) Nursing Home, 1987—. Author posters. Fellow Am. Acad. Optometry; mem. APHA, Am. Optometric Assn., Am. Diabetes Assn., Hudson Valley Optometric Soc. (pres. 1995—), Coll. Optometrists In Vision Devel., Rotary (sec. 1985-95), Lions. Office: 243 Main St Ste 120 New Paltz NY 12561

MORRISON, WILLARD LANGDON, JR., environmental services executive, consultant; b. Melrose, Mass., Aug. 22, 1918; s. Willard L. and Ruth (Ansell) M.; m. Joy Overall; children: Leland, Marjorie; m. Janis Marshall; 1 child, Phillip. BS, MIT, 1940; diploma, Inst. Design, Chgo., 1946. Dir. product devel. West Bend (Wis.) Co., 1940-47; coord. indsl. design Montgomery & Ward Co., Chgo., 1948-50; sr. tech. advisor aluminum divsn. Olin Mathieson Chem. Co., Chgo., 1951-54; pres. Morrison and Co, Engrs., Lake Forest, Ill., 1955-60; dir. comml. devel. Archer divsn. R.J. Reynolds Industries, Winston-Salem, N.C., 1961-69; pres. Med. Plastics Corp., Greensboro, N.C., 1969-73; dir. rsch. and engring. Washington Group, Inc., Winston-Salem, 1973-75; dir. mkt. devel. Amerimex Corp., Charlotte, N.C., 1976-79; pres. Microban Products Co. divsn. Tultex Corp., Winston-Salem, 1980-84; pres., owner Advanced Environ. Systems, Inc., Winston-Salem, 1980—; pres. Antimicrobial Products Sales Co., Winston-Salem, 1968—; ptnr. Profl. Execs. Cons., Charlotte, 1970-75. Mem. Delta Kappa Epsilon. Republican. Home: 1896 Meadowbrook Dr Winston Salem NC 27104 Office: Advanced Environ Systems 304 Harvey St Winston Salem NC 27103

MORRISS, FRANK HOWARD, JR., pediatrics educator; b. Birmingham, Ala., Apr. 20, 1940; s. Frank Howard Sr. and Rochelle (Snow) M.; m. Mary J. Hagan, June 29, 1968; children: John Hagan, Matthew Snow. BA, U. Va., 1962; MD, Duke U., 1966. Diplomate Am. Bd. Pediatrics, Am. Bd. Perinatal and Neonatal Medicine. Intern Duke U. Med. Ctr., Durham, N.C., 1966-67, resident in pediatrics, 1967-68, fellow in neonatology, 1970-71; fellow in neonatology U. Colo., Denver, 1971-73; asst. prof. to prof. U. Tex. Med. Sch., Houston, 1973-86; prof. U. Iowa Coll. Medicine, Iowa City, 1987—, chmn. dept., 1987—. Editor: Role of Human Milk in Infant Nutrition and Health, 1986; contbr. numerous articles to profl. jours, chpts. to books. Lt. comdr. USN, 1968-70. NIH grantee, 77-87, 90—. Mem. Am. Pediatric Soc., Soc. Pediatric Rsch., Am. Acad. Pediatrics, Soc. Gynecol. Investigation, Midwest Soc. Pediatric Rsch., Assn. Med. Sch. Pediatric Dept. Chmn. Methodist. Office: U Iowa Hosps & Clinics Dept Pediatrics Iowa City IA 52242

MORRISSETTE, PAUL EDMOND, psychologist; b. Berlin, N.H., Dec. 9, 1930; s. Henri and Mina (Bergeron) M.; m. Judith Ann Toomey, Nov. 20, 1983. BA, St. Mary's U. Sem., Balt., 1953; MEd, Rivier Coll., 1970; DMin, Boston U., 1976. Lic. psychologist, Mass.; ordained priest Episcopal Ch. Psychotherapist House of Affirmation, Whitinsville, Mass., 1979-82; psychotherapist Worcester (Mass.) Pastoral Counseling Ctr., 1982-85, exec. dir., 1985-88; psychotherapist Chandler St. Assocs., Worcester, 1988—. Fellow Am. Assn. Pastoral Counselors; mem. Am. Psychol. Assn., Mass. Psychol. Assn., Assn. Marriage and Family Therapy, Am. Group Psychotherapy Assn. Home: 3 Westport Rd Worcester MA 01605-1043 Office: Chandler Street Assocs 467 Chandler St Worcester MA 01602-2529 also: Med Arts Ctr 52 Boyden Rd Ste 201 Holden MA 01520

MORRISSEY, HELEN M., medical and surgical nurse, administrator; b. Troy, N.Y., Sept. 27, 1939; d. Arthur M. and Anna (Gennamore) M. Diploma, St. Luke's Hosp. Sch. Nursing, Pittsfield, Mass.; BSN, Russell Sage Coll., Troy, 1976. Cert. cmty. health nurse. Health care surveyor, patient abuse investigator N.Y. State Dept. Health, Albany; assoc. dir. Albany Meml. Hosp.; nursing cons. Hosp. Assn. N.Y. State, Inc., Albany; cmty. health nurse Leonard Hosp. Home Care, Troy; cmty. health nurse Seton Home Healthcare, intake coord. Mem. ANA, N.Y. State Nurses Assn.

MORRITT, GRAHAM NATHANIEL, cardiothoracic surgeon; b. Kolar, Karnataka, India, Dec. 7, 1942; arrived in Eng., 1971; s. Charles Thomas and Georgina (D'Rosario) M.; m. Jennifer Audrey, Dec. 17, 1967; children: Andrew Nathaniel, Daniel Graham. MB, BS, Christian Med. Coll., Vellore, India, 1967. Med. officer Mission Hosp., Ikkadu, Madras, India, 1969-70; demonstrator in anatomy Christian Med. Coll., Vellore, India, 1970-71; sr. house officer Westcumberland Hosp., Whitehaven, Eng., 1971-73; rotation registrar Newcastle Area Health Authority, Eng., 1973-76; career registrar Lothian Health Bd., Edinburgh, Scotland, 1976-78; sr. registrar Newcastle Area Health Authority, 1978-81, cons., 1981-85; cons. Newcastle on Tyne, cardiothoracic surgery, thoracic laser surgery, oesophageal investigative lab., 1981—; cons. cardiothoracic surgeon, South Cleveland Hosp., Middlesborough, 1995—. Contbr. articles to profl. jours., 1978—. Fellow Royal Coll. of Surgeons of Edinburgh; mem. Soc. of Thoracic & Cardiovascular Surgeons of Great Britain (overseas travelling fellow 1979, 1983), British Med. Laser Assn., European Assn. for Cardiovascular Surgery, Closehouse Golf Club. Methodist. Office: Freeman Hosp, South Cleveland Hosp, Middlesborough England

MORROW, GEORGE TELFORD, II, health care executive, lawyer; b. Oakland, Calif., Aug. 25, 1943; s. George Telford and Sterling Elizabeth (Hirschboeck) M.; m. Joan Helen Schieferstein, Apr. 7, 1971. BA with honors, Rutgers U., 1965; MA, Brown U., 1967; JD cum laude, William Mitchell Coll. Law, 1977. Bar: Minn. 1977. Trial lawyer Mpls., 1977-84; gen. counsel Physician's Healthplan, Minnetonka, Minn., 1984-85; sec., v.p., gen. counsel United Healthcare Corp., Minnetonka, 1985-87; pres., chief exec. officer Physician's Healthplan, Minnetonka, Minn., 1987-88; prin. and regional practice leader Wm. Merceu, Inc., 1991-93; pres. Health Ventures, Inc., 1993-95; CEO Family First Health Care, 1996—. Contbr. articles to newspapers and mags. Minn. Humanities Commn. grantee, 1978. Mem. ABA, Minn. Bar Assn., Am. Soc. Corp. Secs., KitchiGammi Club, Hazeltine Nat. Golf. Club. Office: Health Ventures Ltd 1050 Carlson Ctr 601 Lakeshore Parkway Minnetonka MN 55305

MORROW, JASON DREW, medical and pharmacology educator; b. St. Louis, Mar. 30, 1957; s. Ralph Ernest and Vera Rowena (Cummings) M.; m. Lisa Lee Hyman, Mar. 26, 1983; children: Jeremy Nash, Stephanie Rose. BA magna cum laude, Vanderbilt U., 1979; MD, Washington U., St. Louis, 1983. Diplomate Am. Bd. Internal Medicine, Am. Bd. Infectious Diseases. Med. intern, resident Vanderbilt U. Hosp., Nashville, 1983-86, Hugh J. Morgan chief med. resident, 1987-88, rsch. fellow in clin. pharmacology, 1988-91; sr. rsch. fellow dept. pharmacology Vanderbilt U., Sch. Medicine, Nashville, 1991-94, asst. prof. pharmacology and medicine, 1994-95; assoc. prof. Vanderbilt U., Nashville, 1995—, dir. Eicosanoid Core Lab. dept. pharmacology, 1992—; clin. fellow in infectious diseases Barnes Hosp./Washington U., 1986-87; staff physician in medicine and infectious diseases VA Med. Ctr., Nashville, 1991—; mem. internat. adv. com. 9th Internat. Conf. on Prostglandins and RElated Compounds, Florence, Italy, 1994, 10th Conf., Vienna, Austria, 1996. Ad hoc reviewer Jour. Biol. Chemistry, Prostglandins, numerous other sci. publs.; contbr. over 140 articles, abstracts, revs. and papers to sci. jours., chpt. to book. Physician Nashville Union Rescue Mission, 1988—. Recipient Physician-Scientist award NIH, 1990-91, grantee; recipient Rsch. Found. Devel. award Internat. Life Scis. Inst., 1992—; Centennial Clin. Pharmacology fellow Boehringer-Ingelheim, 1990-91, Howard Hughes Med. Inst. Physician rsch. fellow, 1991-94. Mem. AMA, ACP, AAAS, Am. Fedn. Clin. Rsch., So. Soc. Clin.

Investigation, Infectious Diseases Soc. Am., Am. Soc. Pharmacology Exptl. Therapeutics, Phi Beta Kappa. Home: 6129 Montcrest Dr Nashville TN 37215-5621 Office: Vanderbilt U Dept Pharmacology 23rd and Pierce Aves Nashville TN 37232-6602

MORROW, JAY S., physician, endocrinologist; b. Cleve., Nov. 5, 1948; s. Morty S. Morrow and Bernice (Bruss) Burstein; m. Cheryl L. Hall Banks, June 24, 1972 (div. Oct. 1989); children: Jeffrey L., Jonathan L.; m. Daphne B. Warman Selsky, June 22, 1993; stepchildren: Daniel S. Selsky, Claire F. Selsky. BA in Biology, Case Western Res. U., 1970; MD, Pa. State U., 1976. Diplomat Am. Bd. Med. Examiners, Am. Bd. Internal Medicine, Am. Bd. Endocrinology and Metabolism. Intern, jr. to sr. resident R.I. Hosp., Providence, 1976-79; tchg. fellow in medicine Brown U. Sch. of Medicine, R.I., 1978-79; med. staff fellow, clin. endocrinology br. NIH, Bethesda, Md., 1979-82; med. officer Divsn. Metabolic/Endocrine Drug Products FDA, Rockville, Md., 1982-85; pvt. practice endocrinology, internal medicine Gaithersburg, Md., 1983-93; sr. clin. instr. Case Western Res. U., Cleve., 1993-95; clin. asst. prof. Case Western Res. U., 1995—; pvt. practice endocrinology and internal medicine Cleve., 1993—. Contbr. articles to profl. jours. Lt. col. USPHS, 1979-84. Recipient Merck award, 1976. Fellow Am. Coll. Endocrinology, Am. Coll. Physicians; mem. The Endocrine Soc., Am. Diabetes Assn., Am. Assn. Clin. Endocrinologists, Diabetes Assn. of Greater Cleveland (bd. trustees). Office: # 305 29001 Cedar Rd Lyndhurst OH 44124

MORROW, JON STANLEY, pathology educator, medical scientist; b. Ft. Wayne, Ind., BS, Ind. U., 1969, PhD, 1974; MD, Yale U., 1976. Prof. pathology Yale Med. Sch., New Haven, Conn., 1989—; chmn. pathology dept. Yale Med. Sch., New Haven, 1990—; chief pathology Yale-New Haven (Conn.) Hosp., 1990—. Office: Yale U Sch Medicine Dept Pathology 333 Cedar St New Haven CT 06510-3206

MORSE, BRAD STERLING, hospital administrator; b. San Angelo, Tex., May 18, 1965; s. Carl and Verna (Dalager) M.; m. Jacque Roach, Apr. 11, 1992; 1 child, Brad Jr. BBA, Tex. Christian U., 1988; MBA, M in Health Adminstrn., U. Houston, Clear Lake, Tex., 1991. Resident Cooke/Ft. Worth Med. Ctr., 1989-90; chief ops. officer Rio Grande Regional Hosp., McAllen, Tex., 1992-95; CEO CHS Randolph County Med. Ctr., Pocahontas, Ark., 1995—. Mem. Ark. Hosp. Assn., Am. Coll. Healthcare Execs., Rotary. Presbyn. Office: Randolph County Med Ctr 2801 Medical Center Dr Pocahontas AR 72455

MORSE, EDWARD EVERET, hematologist; b. Gardner, Mass., June 7, 1932; s. Lucius Victor and Lillian May (Wiley) M.; m. Janet Marilyn Jillson, Aug. 14, 1954; children: Deborah Faith Callahan, Sandra Louise, David Victor, Timothy Alan. AB, Harvard U., 1954, MD, 1958. Diplomate Am. Bd. Pathology, Hematology. Asst. prof. medicine, Dir. Blood Bank The Johns Hopkins Hosp. and Univ., Batl., 1963-68; assoc. to prof. U. of Conn. Health Ctr., Farmington, 1968—; med. dir. Balt. Red Cross Blood Ctr., 1962-68, Conn. Red Cross Blood Ctr., Hartford, 1961-73, cons., 1973—. Sr. asst. surgeon, USPHS, 1958-60. Fellow Assn. Clin. Scientists (Clin. Scientist of Yr. 1986, v.p. 1978, pres. 1979). Home: 41 Smallwood Rd West Hartford CT 06107 Office: U Conn Health Ctr MC222 Lab Med Farmington CT 06030

MORSE, F. D., JR., dentist; b. Glen Lyn, Va., Apr. 5, 1928; s. Frank D. and Ida Estell (Davis) M.; B.S., Concord Coll., 1951; DDS, Med. Coll. Va., 1955; m. Patsy Lee Apple, Feb. 4, 1967; 1 child, Fortis Davis; m. Nancy Zink: 1 child, Pamela Marie. Free lance photographer, 1950-56; practice dentistry, Pearisburg, Va., 1958—; mem. staff Giles Hosp., Pearisburg, 1958-86. Served from asst. dental surgeon to sr. asst. dental surgeon USPHS, 1955-57; assigned to USCG, 1957-58. Mem. Am., S.W. Va. dental assns., Assn. Mil. Surgeons, AAAS Nat. Assn. Advancement Sci., Fedn. Dentaire Internat., Internat. Platform Assn., W.Va. Collegiate Acad. Sci., Beta Phi. Kiwanian. Achievements include research in dental ceramics and roof coatings. Home: Bicuspid Acr Pearisburg VA 24134 Office: Giles Profl Bldg Pearisburg VA 24134

MORSE, FRANCIS FREDERICK EDGAR, dentist; b. N.Y.C., Dec. 23, 1921; s. Robert John and Frances Elizabeth (Moulton) M.; m. Dorothea Marie Hespe, Mar. 16, 1946 (div.); children—Francis Frederick Edward, Marianne Elizabeth, Robert John, Christopher George; m. Margaret Amelia Livengood, May, 1975 (dec. Feb. 1987). Student Hobart Coll., 1939-42; D.O.S., U. Pa., 1945. Practice dentistry, Durham, N.C., 1977—; guest lectr. Columbia U., N.Y.C., 1960-70, U. Pa., Phila., 1965-68, Seton Hall U., Jersey City, 1962-65. Alumni exec. com. mem. U. Pa. Sch. Dental Medicine, 1962-67. Served to lt. USNR, 1945-47, China. Recipient Alumni award of Merit, U. Pa., 1971. Fellow N.Y. Acad. Dentistry, Greater N.Y. Acad. Prosthodontics (life), Am. Acad. Restorative Dentistry; mem. ADA, Durham-Orange County Dental Soc., Treyburn Country Club, Hope Valley Country Club. Republican. Episcopalian. Avocations: architecture; boating; skiing. Home: 207 Johnstone Ct Durham NC 27712-9454 Office: 3001 Academy Rd Durham NC 27707-2653

MORSE, JOYCE SOLOMON, nursing administrator; b. Bklyn., July 20, 1945; d. Leonard E. and Julia E. (Crystal) Solomon; m. Mark Schuman, Oct. 26, 1988; 1 child, Sharon E. Morse. BSN, Hunter Coll., N.Y.C., 1966; MA, NYU, 1971; PNP, Seton Hall U., 1974. RN, N.Y., N.J.; cert. PNP. Staff nurse emergency rm. Coney Island Hosp., Bklyn., 1966-67; pediatric nursing faculty St. John's Episcopal Hosp. Sch. Nursing, Bklyn., 1967-69; faculty Coll. of Nursing, Seton Hall U., South Orange, N.J., 1971-74; dir. in-svc. edn. and staff devel. Clove Lakes Nursing Home, Staten Island, 1974-76; asst. to med. dir. United Cerebral Palsy N.Y. State, N.Y.C., 1976-84; dir. nursing Matheny Sch./Hosp., Peapack, N.J., 1984-92, dir. children svcs. divsn., 1992—; adj. asst. prof. nursing Coll. St. Elizabeth, Convent Station, N.J., 1992—. Editor: A Life-Span Approach to Nursing Care for Individuals with Developmental Disabilities, 1994. Maj. USAR ret. Fellow Nat. Assn. Pediat. Nurses and Practitioners, Am. Assn. Mental Retardation (pres. nursing divsn. 1994-96); mem. ANA, Nurses of the Developmentally Disabled (v.p.), Developmental Disabilities Nurses Assn., N.J. State Nurses Assn., Sigma Theta Tau. Home: 4-B Leva Dr Morristown NJ 07960-6386 Office: Matheny Sch/Hosp 244 Main St Peapack NJ 07977

MORSE, KENNETH KARL, optometrist; b. Sheridan, Wyo., May 30, 1968; s. Kenneth R. Morse and Donna M. (Near) Dexter; m. Crystal Rice, Jan. 6, 1989; children: Nathan Paul, Adam Kendall. AS, Sheridan (Wyo.) Coll., 1987; B in Visual Sci., Pacific U., 1991, D in Optometry, 1993. Optometrist pvt. practice Billings, Mont., 1993-94; optometrist Eye Care Assocs., Lewistown, Mont., 1994—; cons. Mont. Low Vision Clinic, Billings, 1994—. Mem. Am. Optometric Assn., Mont. Optometric Assn., Elks, Beta Sigma Kappa. Republican. Mem. First Christian Ch. Office: Eye Care Assocs 821 W Main St Lewistown MT 59457

MORSE, MARTIN A., surgeon; b. Louisville, June 25, 1957; s. Marvin Henry and Betty Anne (Hess) M. BS in Zoology with distinction, Duke U., 1979, MD, 1983. Diplomate Nat. Bd. Med. Examiners. Intern, jr. resident dept. surgery Barnes Hosp./Washington U., St. Louis, 1983-85; rsch. fellow dept. pediatric surgery Children's Hosp./Harvard Med. Sch., Boston, 1985-87; sr. resident dept. of surgery U. Rochester, N.Y., 1987-89, chief resident, 1989-90; rsch./clin. fellow in transplantation dept. pediatric surg. Children's Hosp. Med. Ctr., Cin., 1990-92; clin. fellow hand and upper extremity surgery dept. orthopedic surgery U. Pitts. Med. Ctr., 1992-93; fellow in plastic and reconstructive surgery, dept. surgery U. Fla. Coll. Medicine, Gainesville, 1993-95; clin. staff Georgetown U., Washington, 1995—; pvt. practice plastic and reconstructive surgery McLean, Va., 1995—; lab. investigator Lab. Exptl. Pathology div. cancer cause and prevention Nat. Cancer Inst./NIH, Rockville, Md., summers 1974-80; invited prof. dept. grad. nursing Simmons Coll., Boston, 1986-87; NASA flight surgeon. Contbr. articles to profl. jours. Vol. Cystic Fibrosis, Am. Cancer Soc., Am. Heart Assn., March of Dimes, Am. Lung Soc.; founding mem. Statue of Liberty/Ellis Isle Found., N.Y.C., 1985, JFK Libr. Found., Boston, 1987, Challenger Ctr. for Space Sci. Edn., Washington, 1987, U.S. Naval Meml. Found., Washington, 1990; active Friends Nat. Libr. Medicine, Col. Williamsburg Found., Met. Mus. Art, Boston Mus. Fine Arts, Carnegie Mellon Mus.; patron The John F. Kennedy Ctr. for the Performing Arts, Friends of the Nat. Zoo, Nat. Audobon Soc., World Wildlife Fund. Farley Found. fellow Children's Hosp., Harvard Med. Sch., 1986; recipient Outstanding Svc. award Nat. Cancer Inst., NIH, 1977, Nat. Def. medal. Fellow ACS (assoc.); mem. AMA, AAAS, Soc. Laparoendoscopic Surgeons, Am. Soc. Artificial Internal Organs, Am. Trauma Soc., Fla. State Med. Soc., Assn. for Acad. Surgery, Surg. Infection Soc., Aerospace Med. Assn., Assn. Mil. Surgeons U.S., Am. Soc. Cell Biology and Tissue Culture Assn., So. Med. Assn., Physicians for Social Responsibility, Rochester Surg. Soc., N.Y. Acad. Scis., Fairfax County Med. Soc., Fla. State Med. Soc., Fla. Hand Soc., Va. State Med. Soc., Am. Legion, Naval Res. Assn., Res. Officers Assn., Phi Beta Kappa, Alpha Omega Alpha, Phi Lambda Epsilon.

MORSE, STEPHEN SCOTT, virologist, immunologist; b. N.Y.C., Nov. 22, 1951; s. Murray H. and Phyllis Morse; m. Marilyn Gewirtz, Feb. 1991. BS, CCNY, 1971; MS, U. Wis., 1974, PhD, 1977. NSF trainee dept. bacteriology U. Wis., Madison, 1971-72, rsch. asst., 1972-77; rsch. fellow Nat. Cancer Inst.-Med. Coll. Va./Va. Commonwealth U., Richmond, 1977-80, instr., 1980-81; asst. prof. microbiology Rutgers U., New Brunswick, N.J., 1981-85; rsch. assoc. Rockefeller U., N.Y.C., 1985-88, asst. prof., 1988-96; asst. prof. Sch. Pub. Health Columbia U., 1996—; cons. U.S. Congress Office Tech. Assessment, Washington, 1989; chair conf. on emerging viruses NIH, 1989; cons. Inst. Medicine-NAS, mem. com. microbial threats to health, chair subcom. on viruses, 1990-92; chair Fedn. Am. Scientists (FAS) program for monitoring emerging diseases (ProMED), 1993—; program mgr. Def. Advanced Rsch. Projects Agy., 1996—. Editor: Emerging Viruses, 1993, Evolutionary Biology of Viruses, 1994; sect. editor Ctr. for Disease Control and Prevention Emerging Infectious Diseases. Mem. Am. Soc. Microbiology, Am. Assn. Pathologists, Am. Assn. Immunologists, N.Y. Acad. Scis. (vice chair microbiology sect. 1994-96, chair 1996—), Marine Biology Lab., Sigma Xi. Office: Columbia Ur U Sch Pub Health Divsn Epidemiology 600 W 168th St New York NY 10032

MORSIANI, MARIO, diabetologist, educator; b. Ferrara, Emilia Romagna, Italy, Mar. 31, 1926; s. Francesco and Bruna (Donini) M.; m. Carla Bonsetti, Dec. 31, 1950; children: Vittorio, Eugenio, Beatrice. MD, PhD, U. Ferrara, Italy, 1950, degree in medicine and pharmacy, 1957; specialist in cardiology and metabolic diseases, U. Turin, Italy, 1965. Asst. U. Ferrara Med. Sch., 1950-68; head dept. for diabetes and metabolic diseases Servizio di Diabetologia Unita Sanitaria Locale, Ferrara, 1968-92; tchr. postgrad. sch. endocrinology and metabolic diseases U. Ferrara, 1981-92. Author: Nail Diseases, 1974, Epidemiology and Screening of Diabetes, 1989. Provincial counsellor Ferrara, 1960-75, communal counsellor, 1975-90; pres. Italian Red Cross Provincial Com., 1992-94, nat. pres., 1974-89. Mem. Assn. Medici Diabetologi, Acad. della Sci. di Ferrara, Assn. Nat. Famiglie Caduti e Dispersi in Guerra (regonal pres. 1991—). Democrat. Home: XX Settembre 64, 44100 Ferrara Emilia Romagna, Italy

MORSTYN, GEORGE, medical investigator, oncologist; b. Siemanowice, Poland, Dec. 28, 1950; came to U.S., 1991; s. Karol and Stephanie (Greenberg) M.; m. Rosa Berta Popp; children: Lisa, Thomas. B of Med. Sci., Monash U., Victoria, Australia, 1973, MB BS, 1975; PhD, Melbourne U., Victoria, Australia, 1983; FRACP, Coll. of Physicians, Australia, 1983. Intern then resident Alfred Hosp., Victoria, 1976-78; rsch. scholar Walter Eliza Hall Inst., Melbourne, 1979-81; clin. assoc. Nat. Cancer Inst., Bethesda, Md., 1981-83; prin. rsch. fellow Ludwig Inst. for Cancer Rsch., Victoria, 1983-91; v.p. Amgen, Thousand Oaks, Calif., 1991—. Editor: Phototherapy, 1990; contbr. articles to profl. jours. Mem. Med. Oncology Group (Australia), Am. Soc. Hematology, Am. Soc. Clin. Oncology. Office: Amgen 1840 De Havilland Dr Thousand Oaks CA 91320-1701

MORTARA, RONALD WILLIAM, physician, neurosurgeon; b. N.Y.C., Feb. 7, 1946; m. Marianne Mortara, 1969. AB, Dartmouth Coll., 1967; MD, SUNY, Bklyn., 1972. Diplomate Am. Bd. Neurol. Surgery. Intern in surgery Med. Ctr. Hosp., Burlington, Vt., 1973-78, resident in neurology and neurosurgery, 1978; fellowship in neurosurgery U. Western Ont., Can., 1978, U. Zurich, Switzerland, 1979; asst. prof. neurosurgery Boston U. Med. Ctr., 1980-86, assoc. prof. neurosurgery, 1986—; chief neurosurgery Metro West Med. Ctr., Framingham, Mass., 1993—. Office: Neurosurgical Care Inc 463 Worcester Rd Framingham MA 01701

MÖRTBERG, ANDERS MATHIAS, anesthesiologist; b. Hudiksvall, Sweden, July 20, 1943; m. Eva Britt Holmkvist, Nov. 21, 1968; children: Lisa, Erik, Sara. Med. Lic., Karolinska Inst., Stockholm, 1971. Cert. specialist in anesthesiology. Resident St. Eriks Hosp., Stockholm, 1968-70, Sundsvall (Sweden) Hosp., 1970-75; cons. Örnsköldsviks (Sweden) Hosp., 1975-79, head clinic, head of anesthesiology, 1979—. Home: Svanägen 48, S-89100 Örnsköldsvik Sweden Office: Örnsköldsviks Sjukhus, IVA, S-89189 Örnsköldsvik Sweden

MORTE, PAUL DAVID, physician; b. Boston, May 6, 1943; m. Valerie Paulsen, Dec. 27, 1992 (div.); 1 child, Allison Ellen. AB, Georgetown Univ., 1966; DO, Phila. Coll. Osteopathic Med., 1974. Diplomate Am. Bd. Psychiatry and Neurology, Am. Bd. Electrodiagnostic Medicine. Intern internal medicine Phila. Naval Hosp., Phila., 1974-75; residency neurology Bethesda Naval Hosp., Bethesda, Md., 1975-78; fellowship clinical neurophysiology Univ. Calif., San Diego, 1991-92; staff neurologist Naval Hosp., San Diego, 1978-81; clinical dir. physician asst. program Naval Sch. Health Scis., San Diego, 1981-82; chief of neurology Portsmouth (Va.) Naval Hosp., 1982-91; staff neurologist and head neurophysiology lab. Naval Hosp., San Diego, 1992-96; neurol. pvt. practice Lawrence, Kans., 1996—; asst. clin. prof. neurology U. Calif., San Diego, 1980-82, asst. clin. prof. George Washington U., Washington, 1982-83, adj. asst. prof., 1985-87, asst. prof. clin. neurology Ea. Va. Med. Sch., 1983-91. Contbr. articles to profl. jours. With U.S. Navy, 1966-69; medical officer 1974-96. Mem. Kans. Med. Soc.

MORTENSEN, MARY ELLEN, pediatrician, educator, medical administrator; b. Austin, Minn., Oct. 9, 1951; d. Jerry Sheehan and Mary Jean (Daugherty) Lund; m. Brian Kim Mortensen, Mar. 15, 1980; children: Lindsey, Brian. BA, Smith Coll., 1974; MD, Emory U., 1978; MS, U. Ariz., 1983. Diplomate Am. Bd. Med. Toxicology, Am. Bd. Pediatrics. Resident in pediatrics U. Ariz., Tucson, 1978-81, fellow in clin. pharmacology, 1981-83; with epidemiology intelligence svc. Ctrs. for Disease Control, Atlanta, 1983-85; clin. asst. prof. dept. pediatrics Emory U., Atlanta, 1984-87; med. epidemiologist Agy. for Toxic Substance and Disease Registry, Atlanta, 1985-87; med. dir. Cen. Ohio Poison Ctr., Columbus, 1987-92; med. dir. Ohio health ops. Nationwide Life Ins. Co., 1995—; asst. prof. pediats. Ohio State U., Columbus, 1987-92, assoc. prof., 1992-95, clin. assoc. prof., 1995—; cons. Nat. Libr. Medicine, Washington, 1990-95; dir. Ctrl. Ohio Lead Clinic, Columbus, 1989-95, mem. med. toxicology sub-bd., 1992-95; reviewer U.S. Pharmacopid Drug Info., Washington, 1989—. Contbr. articles and revs. to profl. jours. and chpts. to books. Lt. comdr. USPHS, 1983-87. Fellow Am. Acad. Clin. Toxicology, Am. Acad. Pediatrics (cons. com. on drugs 1987-92, chmn. exec. com. sect. on clin. pharmacology and therapeutics 1990-93, com. on environ. health 1990-92, chmn. com. on environ. health Ohio chpt. 1990-95); mem. Am. Assn. Poison Control Ctrs. (bd. dirs. 1987-92). Office: Nationwide Health Plans 200 E Campus View Blvd Ste 300 Columbus OH 43235-4678

MORTIMER, ANN MARGARET, psychiatrist, educator, consultant; b. Batley, Yorkshire, Eng., Nov. 5, 1957; d. Harry and Muriel (Wood) M.; m. Edward John Turner, Jan. 5, 1985. BSc, U. Leicester, 1978, MB ChB, 1981; M in Med. Sci., U. Leeds, 1987. Lectr. U. Leeds, 1986-88; cons. psychiatrist Huddersfield Health Authority, 1988-91; sr. lectr. psychiatry Charing Cross and Westminster Med. Sch., London, 1991-95; prof., found. chair psychiatry U. Hull, 1995—; mem. Sandoz U.K. Adv. Bd., Frimley, Surrey, 1993—; examiner in medicine U. London, 1993—. Author: Ctrl. Nervous System Drugs, 1994; editor Psychopathology, 1991. Recipient faculty award U. Leicester, 1980, Young Investigator award Internat. Congress on Schizophrenia, 1992. Mem. Royal Coll. Psychiatrists (media experts 1991—, examiner 1995—), Vibram Mountaineering Club. Office: De La Pole Hosp, Willerby, Hull HU10 6ED, England

MORTON, JAMES IRWIN, hospital administrator; b. Chulumani, Sud Yungas, Bolivia, Feb. 28, 1935; came to U.S., 1952; s. Harrison Cecil and Flossie Mae (Irwin); m. Beverly Jean Nash, June 9, 1957; c1 child, Linda Kathleen. BA, Andrews U., 1957; MHA, U. Mich., 1959. Commd. 2nd lt. USAF, 1959, advanced through grades to col., 1988.; adminstr. Whitfield (Miss.) Med. Surg. Hosp., 1988—; pres. coun. Jackson-Vicksburg Hosp., 1992-93; cons. to surgeon gen. USAF, Washington, 1980-88. Charter mem. The Miss. Chorus, 1989—, bd. dirs., treas., 1990-93. Decorated Legion of Merit. Fellow Am. Coll. Healthcare Execs. (pres. Miss. affiliates 1991-92, Miss. Regent 1994-99). Office: Whitfield Med Surg Hosp Whitfield MS 39193

MORTON, JEROME HOLDREN, school psychologist; b. Duluth, Minn., July 30, 1942; s. Jerome Raefield and Svea (Holdren) M.; m. Anna Mary Moore, June 9, 1964; children: Scot, Jeanette. BA, Centre Coll., 1964; MS, Miami U., Oxford, Ohio, 1966; PhD, U. Tenn., 1973. Psychologist Pinellas County Sch. System, Clearwater, Fla., 1969-71; dir. psychol. and spl. edn. svcs. Little Tenn. Valley Ednl. Coop., Lenoir City, Tenn., 1973-76, exec. dir., 1977—; pres. and bd. dirs. Psychol. and Ednl. Cons., P.C., Knoxville, Tenn., 1985—; dir. Knoxville Alternative Ct. for Learning, 1985-91; rsch. assoc. spl. svcs. dept. Coll. Edn. U. Tenn., Knoxville, 1991-93; due process hearing officer State Tenn. Dept. Edn., Nashville, 1974-85; hon. asst. prof. psychology dept. U. Tenn., Knoxville, 1978—; mem. bd. advisors Big South Fork Regional Assn., Outdoor Adventure and Rsch. Ctr., 1991-93; bd. dirs. Mental Health Assn. Knox County, 1990-92, v.p. pub. policy, 1991-92; bd. dirs. East Tenn. Spl. Tech. Access Ctr, 1989-96, chmn. bd. dirs., 1993-95. Co-author: Students at risk and intervention strategies, 1989; contbr. author Dropouts: Who Drops Out and Why-And The Recommended Action, 1990; contbr. articles to profl. jours. Co-chmn. East Tenn. Coalition for Children, 1983-84, chmn., 1984-85. Served with U.S. Army, 1966-69. Recipient Best Principal/Best School award Knoxville C. of C., 1989. Mem. APA, Tenn. Assn. Psychology in Schs. (pres. 1976-77), Tenn. Psychol. Assn. (v.p. 1976-77), Nat. Assn. Sch. Psychology, Internat. Speakers Network, Inc. Office: 1432 E Lee Hwy Loudon TN 37774-6440

MORTON, KAREN C., dietitian; b. Hartford, Conn., Mar. 11, 1954; d. Arthur Carl and Elsie Rita (Gryguv) Camilli; m. David M. Morton, July 25, 1976 (div.); children: Katy Jean, Allison Marie. BS in Nutrition, U. N.H., 1976. Mgr., cons. Oakridge Convalescent Ctr., Bloomfield, Conn., 1983-87; dir. corp. dining svcs., quality mgmt. Apple Health Care, Avon, Conn., 1987—; sec.-treas. Conn. Cons. Dietitians in Health Care Facilities, 1990-92. Capt. U.S. Army, 1978-81, chief nutrition care divsn. USAR, 1981—. Mem. Am. Dietetic Assn. (cert.), Nat. Assn. Healthcare Quality, Conn. Dietetic Assn. Home: 1576 Boulevard West Hartford CT 06107 Office: Apple Health Care 21 Waterville Rd Avon CT 06001

MORTON, PAULA GALE, nursing educator, psychiatric mental health nurse; b. Redmond, Oreg., June 22, 1946; d. Victor L. and Zella (Scharick) M. Diploma, O'Connor Hosp. Sch. Nursing, San Jose, Calif., 1967; BSN, Ea. Wash. U., 1973; M.Nursing, Oreg. Health Scis. U., 1974; EdD, Portland State U., 1982. RN, Ill., Oreg. Staff-charge nurse Mercy Hosp., Champaign, Ill., 1967-68, Holladay Park Hosp., Portland, Oreg., 1968-71; dir. nursing insvc. program, instr. Dammasch State Hosp., Wilsonville, Oreg., 1975-82; assoc. chief nurse for edn. VA Med. Ctr., Roseburg, Oreg., 1982—. Contbr. articles to nursing jours. Mem. ANA (coun. advanced practitioners in psychiatry-mental health nursing), Sigma Theta Tau, Phi Kappa Phi. Home: 158 Beech St Roseburg OR 97470

MORTON, RICHARD ALBERT DUNLAP, physician; b. El Paso, Tex., Sept. 6, 1932; s. Richard Albert Dunlap and Julie Ann (More) M.; children: Priscilla, Richard Albert Dunlap III, Maria, Margaret, Andrew, Arthur. Student, Tex. Western Coll., 1950-53, U. Colo., 1953; MD, Tulane U., 1957. Diplomate Am. Bd. Otolaryngology. Physician Drs. Morton, Blumenfeld & Charbonneau, PA, El Paso; pvt. practice of Otolaryngoloby, 1963—; bd. mem. Tex. Liability Trust, Austin, 1981-87, 91—, Tex. State Bd. Med. Examiners, Austin, 1988-91; pres. Tex. State Bd. Med. Examiners, Austin, 1990-91. Bd. mem. El Paso (Tex.) Ind. Sch. Dist., 1970-76. Capt. USAF, 1961-63. Fellow Am. Coll. Surgeons, Am. Acad. Otolaryngology; mem. AMA (del. 1980—), Tex. Med. Assn. (del. 1970-80), Tex. Surg. Soc., Tex. Otolaryngological Assn. (pres. 1980-81), Sierra Med. Ctr. Hosp. (governing bd. 1981-82), Rotary Club El Paso. Republican. Office: Drs Morton Blumenfeld & Charbonneau 1733 Curie Dr Ste 100 El Paso TX 79902-2909

MOSACK, MARGUERITE ANN, psychologist, educator; b. Garfield Heights, Ohio, May 14, 1951; d. Anthony Joseph and Christine Clarice Mosack. BA, U. Dallas, 1973; MA in Psychology, Duquesne U., 1984. Lic. psychologist, Pa. Psychotherapist Duquesne U. Counseling & Testing Ctr., Pitts., 1985-87; psychol. evaluator Pitts. Assessment and Consultation Ctr., 1985-87; psychology intern Staunton Clinic at Sewickley (Pa.) Valley Hosp., 1987-88; psychologist Northeastern Pa. Counseling Ctr., Kingston, 1988-91; pvt. practice Wilkes-Barre, Pa., 1991—; instr. psychology Community Coll. Allegheny County, Pitts., 1986, Pa. State U., Lehman; grad. instr. mental health referral Inst. Formative Spirituality, Duquesne U., Pitts., 1988; instr. grad. mgmt. Misericordia Coll., Dallas, Pa., 1990; lectr., cons. We Are Remembered Ministry Diocese of Pitts., 1986-87; presenter women's spirituality Luzerne County Women's Conf., Wilkes-Barre, 1989-90, Luzerne County Women's Conf., Wilkes-Barre, 1989-90, 92-93; presenter psychol. issues of elderly Misericordia Coll. Conf., 1989; presenter stress mgmt. ARC, Persian Gulf Support Groups, 1991, breast cancer support group Nesbitt Hosp., 1994; presenter wellness Campus Compact, 1994; instr. assertiveness tng. for educators Pa. State U., 1991. Instr. bereavement issues SHARE Nesbitt Hosp., Kingston, 1995. Mem. APA, Northeastern Pa. Psychol. Assn., Pa. Psychol. Assn., Luzerne County Women's Network, NE Pa. Behavioral Health Care Network (pres.-elect bd. dirs. 1994).

MOSCA, ANTHONY JOHN, substance abuse professional; b. Cambridge, Mass., June 28, 1944; s. Anthony Mosca and Margaret Mary Kelleher; m. Sheryl Lyn Everett, July 12, 1986. BA in Psychology, U. N.H., 1978; MA in Psychology, Assumption Coll., Worcester, Mass., 1984; postgrad., Rivier Coll., Nashua, N.H., 1990. Lic. mental health counselor, Mass.; cert. addictions specialist, Am. Acad. Health Care Providers in the Addictive Disorders. Psychiat. counselor, milieu coord. New England Meml. Hosp., Stoneham, Mass., 1979-80; alcoholism counselor Nor Cap Lodge, Foxboro, Mass., 1980-82; alcohol and drug counselor Bournwood Hosp., Brookline, Mass., 1982-83; coord. of vocat. evaluation unit Project Hire, Norwood, Mass., 1983-85; rehab. counselor Driving Under the Influence program, Tewksbury, Mass., 1985-86; clin. dir./substance abuse counselor New Beginnings Counseling, Inc., Lowell, Mass., 1986-88; substance abuse specialist Human Resource Inst., Lowell, Mass., 1986-94; coord. Structured Outpatient Addictions Program Behavioral Health Consortium No. Mass., Lawrence, 1994—; pvt. practice A.S.M. Counseling, Dracut, Mass., 1988—; guest speaker Sharsheen Vocat. Tech. High Sch., Billerica, Mass., 1986. Campaign cons., Seabrook, N.H., 1975; handicap access advocate, Lowell, Dracut, 1990—; guest speaker disabled students group., Middlesex C.C., Lowell, 1993, Ctr. Ind. Living, Lawrence, 1995. Recipient letter of commendation from Nancy Reagan. Mem. Internat. Assn. of Addictions and Offender Counselors, Am. Counseling Assn., Am. Acad. of Health Care Providers in the Addictive Disorders, Am. Mental Health Counselors Assn., Mass. Mental Health Counselors Assn. Home: 59 Mill St Unit 106 Dracut MA 01826-3248 Office: Behavioral Health Consortium No Mass 30 General St Lawrence MA 01841-2961

MOSCHELLA, SAMUEL L., dermatology educator; b. East Boston, Mass., Apr. 22, 1921. BS, Tufts U., 1943, MD cum laude, 1946. Diplomate Am. Bd. Dermatology. Intern in medicine Boston City Hosp., 1946-47; resident in dermatology U.S. Naval Hosp., Phila., 1948, St. Albans, 1951; postgrad. in skin and cancer Bellevue Hosp., N.Y.C., 1952-53; chief dermatology U.S. Naval Hosp., Phila., 1953-54, chief dermatology, asst. chief medicine, Guantanamo Bay, Cuba, 1948-51, chief dermatology, Chelsea, Mass., 1956-62, chmn. dept. dermatology, Phila., 1962-67; chmn. dept. dermatology Lahey Clinic Med. Ctr., Burlington, Mass., 1969-82; clin. prof. dermatology Harvard U. Med. Sch., Boston, 1980-91, prof. emeritus, 1991—; cons. U.S. Pub. Health Leprasorium, Carville, La., 1968—, U.S. Naval Hosp., Phila., 1967-72, Bethesda, Md., 1976—; guest lectr. U. Pa. Grad. Sch., 1962-67, Harvard Sch. Tropical Medicine, 1975—. Author/editor: (with otherw) Dermatology, 3d edit., 1992; contbr. articles to profl. jours.; also papers, book chpts. Fellow ACP; mem. AMA, Am. Acad. Dermatology, Am. Dermatol. Assn., Am. Soc. Dermapathology, Internat. Leprosy Assn., Internat. Soc. Dermatology, New Eng. Dermatologic Soc., Mass. Acad.

Dermatology, Boston Dermatology Soc., Mass. Med. Soc., soc. Investigative Dermatology. Home: 887 Commonwealth Ave Newton MA 02159-1036 Office: Lahey Clinic Med Ctr 41 Mall Rd Box 541 Burlington MA 01805

MOSELEY, SUSAN CALLOW, psychologist; b. Boston, Mar. 6, 1949; d. Allan Dana and Eleanor May (Magee) Callow; m. John Travis Moseley, Aug. 5, 1979; children: Stephanie Marie, Shannon Eleanor. BA, Tufts U., 1971; BSN, N.Y. Med. Coll., 1973; MS, U. Oreg., 1983, PhD, 1986. RN, Mass., Calif., Oreg.; lic. psychologist, Oreg. Staff nurse Pacific Med. Presbyn. Hosp., San Francisco, 1974-75; co-program dir. inpatient drug and alcohol unit Palo Alto VA Hosp., Menlo Park, Calif.; grad. tchg. fellow student counseling ctr. U. Oreg., Eugene, 1975-79; staff nurse inpatient psychiat. unit Sacred Heart Hosp., Eugene, 1979-83; psychol. resident Office of Dr. Susanne Schumann, Eugene, 1986-88; pvt. practice psychology Eugene, 1988—. Trustee, deacon 1st Congl. Ch., Eugene, 1992—; bd. dirs. Birth to Three, Eugene; mem. Friends of U. Oreg. Art Mus., Eugene; vol. Edison Elem. Sch., Roosevelt Mid. Sch., Eugene; vol. counselor Ctr. for Cmty. Counseling, Eugene, 1992—. Mem. APA, Oreg. Psychol. Assn. (ethics com. 1992—), Lane County Psychologists Assn., Lane Ind. Practitioner's Assn., Assn. for Advancement of Psychotherapy, Am. Orthopsychiat. Assn. Democrat. Home: 2140 Essex Ln Eugene OR 97403 Office: 3003 Willamette St Ste C Eugene OR 97405

MOSER, DEBRA KAY, medical educator. BS in Nursing magna cum laude, Humboldt State U., Arcata, Calif., 1977; M Nursing, UCLA, 1988, D Nursing Sci., 1992. RN, Calif., Ohio; cert. pub. health nurse, Calif. Staff nurse, relief supr. med.-surg. fl. Mad River Cmty. Hosp., Arcata, 1977-78, staff/charge nurse intensive care/cardiac care unit, 1978-86; clin. nursing instr. Humboldt State U., Arcata, 1985-86; staff/charge nurse surg. ICU Santa Monica (Calif.) Hosp., 1987-88; spl. reader UCLA Sch. Nursing, 1990-91, rsch. assoc., 1986-91, clin. rsch. nurse, 1988-92, project dir., 1991-92, asst. prof., 1992-94; asst. prof. dept. adult health and illness Ohio State U. Coll. Nursing, Columbus, 1994—; interviewer and study sponsor Modifiers of Myocardial Infraction Onset Study, Ohio State U., 1994—; mem. working group on ednl. strategies to Prevent Prehosp. Delay in Patients at High Risk for Acute Myocardial Infraction, Nat. Heart Attack Alert Program, NIH, Nat. Heart, Lung and Blood Inst., 1993-95; abstract grader sci. sessions program Am. Heart Assn., 66th Sci. Sessions, 1993; grad. advisor Sigma Theta Tau-Gamma Tau chpt., 1993-94; mem. med. adv. com. Westside YMCA Cardiac Rehab. Program, 1993-94; mem. Task Force on Women, Behavior and Cardiovascular Disease NIH, Nat. Heart, Lung and Blood Inst., 1991. Reviewer Am. Jour. Critical Care, 1992—, Heart and Lung, 1991—, Progress in Cardiovascular Nursing, 1993—, Heart Failure: Evaluation and Care of Patients With Left-Ventricular Systolic Function, 1993, Intensive Coronary Care, 5th edit., 1994, Rsch. in Nursing & Health, 1995—, Jour. Am. Coll. Cardiology, 1995; mem. editl. bd. Am. Jour. Critical Care, 1994—, Jour. Cardiovascular Nursing, 1995—; ad hoc reviewer Western Jour. Nursing Rsch., 1991; contbr. articles to profl. jours., chpts. to books. Recipient scholarship UCLA, 1988-90, scholarship Kaiser Permanente Affiliate Schs., 1990, Ednl. Achievement award LA-AACN, 1990, Alumni rsch. award UCLA, 1990, rsch. abstract award AACN-IVAC, 1993; grantee Sigma Theta Tau-Gamma Tau chpt., 1989-90, AACCN, 1989-90, 92-93, NIH, Nat. Ctr. Nursing Rsch., 1990-92, UCLA Program in Psychneuroimmunology, 1992-93, UCLA Sch. Nursing, 1993, UCLA Acad. Senate, 1993-94, AACCN/Sigma Theta Tau Internat., 1994-95, NIH, Nat. Inst. Nursing Rsch., 1991-96, Sigma Theta Tau Epsilon chpt., 1995, Ohio State U., 1995, Nat. Am. Heart Assn., 1995—. Mem. AACCN, Am. Heart Assn. Coun. Cardiovascular Nursing (New Investigator award 1995, Heart Failure Rsch. prize 1995), Sigma Theta Tau (rsch. com. 1990-94, excellence in rsch. award Gamma Tau chpt. 1993). Home: 6871 Meadow Oak Dr Columbus OH 43235 Office: Ohio State U Coll Nursing Dept Adult Health & Illness 1585 Neil Ave Columbus OH 43210*

MOSER, KENNETH MILES, physician, educator; b. Balt., Apr. 12, 1929; s. Simon and Helene Joyce M.; m. Sara Falk, June 17, 1951; children—Gregory, Kathleen, Margot, Diana. B.A., Haverford Coll., 1950; M.D., Johns Hopkins U., 1954. Diplomate: Am. Bd. Internal Medicine. Intern, resident in medicine D.C. Gen. Hosp., Georgetown Hosp., 1954-59; chief pulmonary and infectious disease service Nat. Naval Med. Center, Bethesda, Md., 1959-61; dir. pulmonary div. Georgetown U. Med. Center, Washington, 1961-68; prof. medicine, dir. pulmonary and critical care med. div. U. Calif., San Diego Sch. Medicine, 1968—; dir. Specialized Ctr. Rsch. U. Calif.-San Diego/Nat. Heart Lund and Blood Inst., 1978—. Author 10 books in field of pulmonary medicine and thrombosis.; Contbr. articles to med. jours. Bd. dirs. Am. Lung Assn. of San Diego and Imperial Counties, 1969-76, Am. Lung Assn. of Calif., 1976-80; mem. manpower com. Nat. Heart, Lung and Blood Inst., bd. dirs. 1978—. Served with U.S. Navy, 1959-61. Fellow ACP, AAAS, Am. Coll. Chest Physicians; mem. Am. Thoracic Soc. (exec. bd., pres. 1985-86), Am. Heart Assn. Coun. on Thrombosis, Am. Physiol. Soc. Office: U Calif San Diego Med Ctr 200 W Arbor Dr San Diego CA 92103

MOSER, NORMAN O., physician; b. Ft. Wayne, Ind., Aug. 30, 1951; s. Earl Rudolph and Iva Burel (Uran) M.; m. Pamela Kay Brown-Moser, Aug. 13, 1982 (div.); m. Vicki Jean Brown (div. Aug. 1979); 1 child, Misty. DO, Kirksville Coll. Osteo., Medicine, 1990; PharmD, Purdue U., 1982, RPh, 1982. Nephrologist Lima (Ohio) Internal Medicine, 1995—; fellow in nephrology Kidney Disease Program, Louisville, 1993-95; resident in medicine Doctors Hosp., Columbus, Ohio, 1990-93. Named to Outstanding Young Men of Am., 1984; recipient Silver Knight award for Outstanding Pub. Svc., Hook Drug Co., 1986. Office: Lima Internal Medicine Dept Nephrology Ste 106 1220 East Elm St Lima OH 45804

MOSER, ROBERT GARY, dentist; b. Dyersburg, Tenn., Nov. 17, 1945; s. William Robert and Bernice (Parmenter) M.; m. Betty Ann Bridgewater, Jan. 30, 1966; children: Ashley Sussanne, Andrea Leigh, Bradley Bridgewater, Alison Elisabeth, Jonathan Joseph. BS in Chemistry, Union U., Jackson, Tenn., 1967; DDS, U. Tenn., 1974; Cert. Comp. Dentistry, U. Fla., 1983. Grad. teaching instr. Memphis State U., 1967-69; dir. sci. instrn. Haywood County High Sch., Brownsville, Tenn., 1969-71; pvt. practice dentistry Union City, Tenn., 1974-81, Bartow, Fla., 1981—; pres. Turning Point Seminars, Inc., Lakeland, Fla., 1986-89; area cons. L.D. Pankey Inst., Miami, 1979—. Editorial writer, cons. Modern Dentalab, 1984-87. Bd. dirs. N.W. Tenn. Mental Health Ctr., Martin, 1977-80; trustee Bartow Meml. Hosp., 1994—. Fellow Acad. Gen. Dentistry (master), Acad. Dentistry Internat.; mem. ADA, Fla. Dental Assn., West Coast Dental Assn., Polk County Dental Assn., Fla. Acad. Dental Practice Adminstrn., Acad. Operative Dentistry, Am. Equilibration Soc., Fla. Soc. Comprehensive Dentistry, Fla. Acad. Gen. Dentistry (editor assn. jour.), Imperial Ridge Acad. Gen. Dentistry, L.D. Pankey Inst. Alumni Assn., Masons, Shriners, Alpha Tau Omega. Republican. Baptist. Home: 5625 Lakeland Highlands Rd Lakeland FL 33813-3266 Office: Turning Point Dental Assocs 2090 Flamingo Dr Bartow FL 33830-4262 Also: PO Box 579 Highland City FL 33846-0579

MOSER, ROBERT HARLAN, physician, educator, writer; b. Trenton, N.J., June 16, 1923; s. Simon and Helena (Silvers) M.; m. Linda Mae Salsinger, Mar. 18, 1989; children from previous marriage: Steven Michael, Jonathan Evan. BS, Loyola U., Balt., 1944; MD, Georgetown U., 1948. Diplomate Am. Bd. Internal Medicine. Commd. 1st lt. U.S. Army, 1948, advanced through grades to col., 1966, intern D.C. Gen. Hosp., 1948-49, fellow pulmonary disease D.C. Gen. Hosp., 1949-50; bn. surgeon U.S. Army, Korea, 1950-51; asst. resident Georgetown U. Hosp., 1951-52; chief resident Georgetown U. Hosp. U.S. Army, 1952-53; chief med. service U.S. Army Hosp. U.S. Army, Salzburg, Austria, 1953-55, Wurzburg, Fed. Republic Germany, 1955-56; resident in cardiology Brooke Gen. Hosp. U.S. Army, 1956-57, asst. chief dept. medicine Brooke Gen. Hosp., 1957-59, chief Brooke Gen. Hosp., 1967-68, fellow hematology U. Utah Coll. Medicine, 1959-60, asst. chief U.S. Army Tripler Gen. Hosp., 1960-64, chief William Beaumont Gen. Hosp., 1965-67, chief Walter Reed Gen. Hosp., 1968-69, ret., 1969; chief of staff Maui (Hawaii) Meml. Hosp., 1969-73, chief dept. medicine, 1975-77; exec. v.p. Am. Coll. Physicians, Phila., 1977-86; v.p. med. affairs The NutraSweet Co., Deerfield, Ill., 1986-91; assoc. prof. medicine Baylor U., 1958-59; clin. prof. medicine Hawaii U., 1969-77, Washington U., 1970-77, Abraham Lincoln Sch. Medicine, 1974-75; adj. prof. medicine U. Pa., 1977-86, Northwestern U., 1987-91; adj. prof. Uniformed Svcs. U. Health Scis., 1979—; clin. prof. medicine U. N.Mex. Coll. Medicine, 1992-96, emeritus, 1996—; flight contr. Project Mercury, 1959-62; cons. mem. med. evaluation team Project Gemini, 1962-66; cons. Project Apollo, 1967-73, Tripler Gen. Hosp., 1970-77, Walter Reed Army Med. Ctr., 1974-86; sr. med. cons. Canyon Cons. Corp., 1991—; mem. cardiovasc. and renal adv. com. FDA, 1978-82; chmn. life scis. adv. com. NASA, 1984-87, mem. NASA adv. coun., 1983-88, chmn. gen. med. panel Hosp. Satellite Network, 1984-86; mem. adv. com. NASA Space Sta., 1988-93; mem. Dept. Def. Com. on Grad. Med. Edn., 1986-87; mem. Life Scis. Strategic Planning Study Group, 1986-88; mem. space studies bd. NRC, 1988-93, space exploration initiation study, 1990, NASA Space Sta. Commn., 1992-93, mem. com. adv. tech. human supp. space, 1996—. Author: Diseases of Medical Progress, 1955, rev. edit., 1969, House Officer Training, 1970; co-author: Adventures in Medical Writing, 1970, Decade of Decision, 1992; editor, chief div. sci. publs. Jour. AMA, Chgo., 1973-75; contbg. editor Med. Opinion and Rev., 1966-75; chmn. editorial bd. Diagnosis mag., 1986-89; mem. editorial bd. Hawaii Med. Jour., Family Physicians, Archives of Internal Medicine, 1967-73, Western Jour. Medicine, 1975-87, Chest, 1975-80, Med. Times, 1977-84, Quality Rev. Bull., 1979-91, The Pharos, 1991—, Emergency Med., 1993—, Travel Medicine, 1994—; contbr. over 200 articles to med. sci. jours and med. books. Master ACP (exec. v.p. 1977-86); fellow Am. Coll. Cardiology, Royal Coll. Physicians and Surgeons Can. (hon.), Am. Clin. and Climatol. Assn.; mem. AMA (adv. panel registry of adverse drug reactions 1960-67, coun. on drugs 1967-73),), Am. Med. Writers Assn., Am. Therapeutic Soc., Am. Osler Soc., Inst. Med., Nat. Assn. Phys. Broadcasters, Chgo. Soc. Internal Medicine, Coll. Physicians Phila., Soc. Med. Cons. to Armed Forces, Alpha Sigma Nu, Alpha Omega Alpha. Democrat. Jewish. Home and Office: Canones Rd # 616 Chama NM 87520

MOSER, ROSEMARIE SCOLARO, psychologist; b. Hackensack, N.J., June 16, 1954; d. Giovanni Natale and Mary (Bellaera) Scolaro; m. Robert Lawrence Moser, June 4, 1978; children: Rachel Ann, Alexander Robert. Student, Lafayette Coll., 1972-74; BA, U. Pa., 1976, MS, 1977, PhD with honors in psychology, 1981. Diplomate Am. Bd. Med. Psychotherapists, Am. Bd. Forensic Examiners; lic. psychologist, N.J., Pa., Md.; cert. sch. psychologist, N.J., Pa., Del., Md. Doctoral intern Towson (Md.) State U. Counseling Ctr., 1979-80; counseling psychologist U. Md., Balt., 1980-84; sch. psychologist Lawrence Pub. Schs., Lawrenceville, N.J., 1984-85, Mercer County Non-Pub. Schs., Hamilton Square, N.J., 1985; pvt. practice psychology Morrisville, Pa. and Lawrenceville, N.J., 1985—; dir. RSM Psychology Ctr., Lawrenceville, 1995—; lectr. U. Pa., Phila., 1985-87; staff psychologist Helene Fuld Med. Ctr., Trenton, N.J., 1986—; mem. cmty. faculty Trenton Psychiat. Hosp., 1989-90. Contbr. articles on psychology in profl. jours. Mem. Mercer County Med. Soc. Aux., N.J., 1987—, pres., 1990-91. Named one of Outstanding Young Women Am., 1980, Act-Discover grantee, 1986-87, Am. Assn. Counseling & Devel. Profl. Enhancement research grantee, 1986-87. Fellow Am. Bd. Med. Psychotherapists, Am. Bd. Forensic Examiners, Pa. Psychology Assn.; mem. Am. Psychology Assn. Divsns. 1, 17, 22, 29, 40, Am. Mental Health Counselors, N.J. Psychology Assn., N.J. Acad. Psychology (Psychologist Recognition award 1987-94), Ea. Psychol. Assn., Am. Assn. for Counseling and Devel. (project dir., grant recipient, 1987-88), Nat. Bd. Cert. Clin. Hypnotherapists, Am. Soc. Clin. Hypnosis, Nat. Register Health Svcs. Providers in Psychology, Nat. Acad. Neuropsychology, N.J. Neuropsychology Soc., Phila. Neuropsychology Soc. Office: 3131 Princeton Pike Bldg 5 Lawrenceville NJ 08648

MOSER, ROYCE, JR., physician, medical educator; b. Versailles, Mo., Aug. 21, 1935; s. Royce and Russie Frances (Stringer) M.; m. Lois Anne Hunter, June 14, 1958; children: Beth Anne Moser McLean, Donald Royce. BA, Harvard U., 1957, MD, 1961; MPH, Harvard Sch. Pub. Health, Boston, 1965. Diplomate Am. Bd. Preventive Medicine (trustee), Am. Bd. Family Practice. Commd. officer USAF, 1962, advanced through grades to col., 1974; resident in aerospace medicine USAF Sch. Aerospace Medicine, Brooks AFB, Tex., 1965-67; chief aerospace medicine Aerospace Def. Command, Colorado Springs, Colo., 1967-70; comdr. 35th USAF Dispensary Phan Rang, Vietnam, 1970-71; chief aerospace medicine br. USAF Sch. Aerospace Medicine, Brooks AFB, 1971-77; comdr. USAF Hosp., Tyndall AFB, Fla., 1977-79; chief clin. scis. div. USAF Sch. Aerospace Medicine, Brooks AFB, 1979-81, chief edn. div., 1981-83, sch. comdr., 1983-85; ret., 1985; prof. dept. family and preventive medicine U. Utah Sch. Medicine, Salt Lake City, 1985—, vice chmn. dept., 1985-95; dir. Rocky Mountain Ctr. for Occupl. and Environ. Health, Salt Lake City, 1987—; cons. in occupational, environ. and aerospace medicine, Salt Lake City, 1985—; presenter nat. and internat. med. meetings. Author: Effective Management of Occupational and Environmental Health and Safety Programs, 1992; contbr. book chpts. and articles to profl. jours. Mem., past pres. 1st Bapt. Ch. Found., Salt Lake City, 1987-89; mem., chmn. numerous univ. coms., Salt Lake City, 1985—; bd. dirs. Hanford Environ. Health Found., 1990-92; mem. preventive medicine residency rev. com. Accreditation Coun. Grad. Med. Edn., 1991—; mem. ednl. adv. bd. USAF Human Sys. Ctr., 1991—; chmn. long-range planning com. Am. Bd. Preventive Medicine, 1992-95. Decorated Legion of Merit (2). Fellow Aerospace Med. Assn. (pres. 1989-90, chair fellows group 1994—, Harry G. Mosely award 1988), Am. Coll. Preventive Medicine (regent 1981-82), Am. Coll. Occupl. and Environ. Medicine (v.p. med. affairs 1995—, Robert A. Kehoe award 1996), Am. Acad. Family Physicians; mem. Internat. Acad. Aviation and Space Medicine (selector 1989-94, chancellor 1994—), Soc. of USAF Flight Surgeons (pres. 1978-79, George E. Schafer award 1982), Phi Beta Kappa. Home: 664 Aloha Rd Salt Lake City UT 84103-3329 Office: Dept Family & Preventive Med 50 N Medical Dr Salt Lake City UT 84132-0001

MOSES, DONALD ALLEN, psychiatrist; b. Bklyn., Feb. 8, 1938; s. Edward and Evelyn (Roberts) M.; m. Sarah Moseley Dean, Dec. 6, 1957; children: Richard David, Erik Alan. BS, Bates Coll., 1958; MD, N.Y. Med. Coll., 1962. Intern Queen's Hosp., Honolulu, 1962-63; clin. instr. Columbia U. Med. Sch., N.Y.C., 1964-65; resident Hillside Hosp., Glen Oaks, N.Y., 1965-68, fellow in psychoanalytic psychotherapy, 1968-70; cons. psychiatrist Manhasset (N.Y.) Community Day Care Ctr., 1968-76; clin. instr. Cornell U. Med. Sch., N.Y.C., 1976—; pvt. practice Greenvale, N.Y., 1968—; psychiatric cons. Nassau Soc. for Prevention of Cruelty to Children, Nassau County, N.Y., 1982—. Author: Are You Driving Your Children to Drink, 1975. Mem. AMA, Am. Psychiatric Assn., Nassau County Psychiatric Soc., Am. Assn. Clin. Psychiatrists, Am. Soc. Adolescent Psychiatrists, Am. Acad. Psychoanalysis, Lotos Club. Office: 90 Glen Cove Rd Greenvale NY 11548-1009

MOSES, ELBERT RAYMOND, JR., speech and dramatic arts educator; b. New Concord, Ohio, Mar. 31, 1908; s. Elbert Raymond Sr. and Helen Martha (Miller) M.; m. Mary Miller Sterrett, Sept. 21, 1933 (dec. Sept. 1984); 1 child, James Elbert (dec.); m. Caroline Mae Entenman, June 19, 1985. AB, U. Pitts., 1932; MS, U. Mich., 1934, PhD, 1936. Instr. U. N.C., Greensboro, 1936-38; asst. prof. Ohio State U., Columbus, 1938-46; assoc. prof. Ea. Ill. State U., Charleston, 1946-56; asst. prof. Mich. State U., E. Lansing, Mich., 1956-59; prof. Clarion (Pa.) State Coll., 1959-71, chmn. dept. speech and dramatic arts, 1959—, emeritus prof., 1971—; Fulbright lectr. State Dept. U.S. Cebu Normal Sch., Cebu City, Philippine Islands, 1955-56; vis. prof. phonetics U. Mo., summer 1968; hon. sec.'s advocate dept. of aging State of Pa., Harrisburg, 1980-81. Author: Guide to Effective Speaking, 1957, Phonetics: A History and Interpretation, 1964, Three Attributes of God, 1983, Adventure in Reasoning, 1988, Beating the Odds, 1992, In Pursuit of Life, 1996; poems included in Best Poems of the 90s, 1992; contbr. articles to profl. jours.. Del. 3d World Congress Phoneticians, Tokyo, 1976; mem. nat. adv. com. fng. students and tchrs. HEW del. to Internat. Congress Soc. Logopedics and Phoniatre, Vienna, 1965; liaison rep. to Peace Corps; pres. County Libr. Bd.; past exec. dir. Clarion County United Way; commr. Boy Scouts Am., 1976-77; pres. Venango County Adv. Coun. for Aging, 1978-79. Maj. AUS, 1942-46, lt. col. AUS, ret. Recipient Ret. Sr. Vol. Program Vol. of Yr. award No. Ariz. Coun. Govts., 1989, Spl. award Speech Comm. Assn., 1989, Endowment Benefactor award, 1991; 6 Diamong Pin of Melvin Jones Found., Internat. Lions, Best Male Songwriter, Poet of Yr. awards Entertainer Network Nashville, 1994, Listing Achievement in Entertainer-Indi-Assn. as Most Consistent Golden Poet of Nashville, 1995, EIA Platinum Poet, 1995. Fellow United Writers Assn.; mem. Ariz. Comm. Support System, Quarter Century Wireless Assn., Soc. Wireless Pioneers, Mil. Affiliate Radio System, Hospitalier Order of St. John of Jerusalem, Knights Hospitalier, Knightly and Mil. Order of St. Eugene of Trebizond (chevalier), Soverign and Mil. Order of St. Stephen the Matyr (comdr.), Knightly Assn. of St. George the Matyr, Ordre Chevaliers du Sinai, Hist. File, VFW (comdr.), Am. Legion (comdr.), Rotary (pres. 1966-67, dist. gov. 1973-74), Order of White Shrine of Jerusalem, Niadh Nask (Marshall of Kilbonane), Internat. Chivalric Inst., Confedn. of Chivalry (life, mem. grand coun.), Ordre Souverain et Militaire de la Milice du Saint Sepulcre (chevalier grand cross), Sovereign World Order of White Cross (lord of knights, dist. commdr. Ariz.), Prescott High Twelve Club (pres. 1990), Morse Telegraph Club, Inc., Phi Delta Kappa (Svc. Key 1978). Republican. Methodist. Home: 2001 Rocky Dells Dr Prescott AZ 86303-5685

MOSES, HAMILTON, III, neurology educator, hospital executive, management consultant; b. Chgo., Apr. 29, 1950; s. Hamilton Jr. and Betty Anne (Theurer) M.; m. Elizabeth Lawrence Hormel, 1977 (dec. 1988); m. Alexandra McCullough Gibson, 1992. BA in Psychology, U. Pa., 1972; MD, Rush Med. Coll., Chgo., 1975. Intern in medicine Johns Hopkins Hosp., Balt., 1976-77, resident in neurology, 1977-79, chief resident, 1979-80, assoc. prof. neurology, 1986-94, vice chmn. neurology and neurosurgery, 1980-86, v.p., 1988-94, dir. Parkinson's Ctr., 1984-94; dir. neurol. inst., prof. neurology and neurosurgery and mgmt. U. Va., Charlottesville, 1994—; sr. advisor Boston Cons. Group, 1995—; sr. advisor The Boston Cons. Group, 1996; founder several tech. bus. Editor, major author: Principles of Medicine, 1985-96; editor newsletter Johns Hopkins Health, 1988—; contbr. numerous articles to med. jours. Mem. com. on med. ministries Episcopal Diocese Md., Balt., 1987; bd. dirs. Valleys Planning Ct. Mem. Am. Acad. Neurology (sec. 1989-91), Am. Neurol. Assn., Md. Neurol. Soc. (pres. 1984-86), Movement Disorders Soc., Md. Club, Green Spring Valley Hunt Club (Garrison, Md.). Republican.

MOSES, LINCOLN E., statistician, educator; b. Kansas City, Mo., Dec. 21, 1921; s. Edward Walter and Virginia (Holmes) M.; m. Jean Runnels, Dec. 26, 1942; children—Katherine, James O'D., William C., Margaret, Elizabeth; m. Mary Louise Coale, 1968. A.B., Stanford, 1941, Ph.D., 1950. Asst. prof. edn. Columbia Tchrs. Coll., 1950-52; faculty Stanford U., 1952—, prof. stats., 1959—, exec. head dept., 1964-68; assoc. dean Stanford U. (Sch. Humanities and Scis.), 1965-68, 85-86, dean grad. studies, 1969-75; faculty Stanford U. (Med. Sch.), 1952—; adminstr. Energy Info. Adminstrn., Dept. of Energy, 1978-80; L.L. Thurstone disting. fellow U. N.C., 1968-69; com. mem. Am. Friends Svc. Com., intermittently 1954—, chmn. No. Calif. chpt., 1972-76, 84-88. Guggenheim fellow, 1960-61; fellow Ctr. for Advanced Study in Behavioral Scis., 1975. Fellow Am. Acad. Arts and Scis., Inst. Math. Statistics (council 1969-72); mem. Inst. of Medicine of Nat. Acad. Scis., Am. Statis. Assn. (council 1966-67), Biometric Soc. (pres. Western N. Am. region 1969), Internat. Statis. Inst. Office: Stanford U Dept Health Rsch and Policy Stanford CA 94305

MOSES, MARION, preventive medicine physician; b. Wheeling, W.Va., Jan. 24, 1936; d. Maron and Mary (Wakim) M. BSN, Georgetown U., 1957; MA in Edn., Columbia U., 1960; MD, Temple U., 1976. Diplomate Am. Bd. Preventive Medicine with subspecialty in pub. health and occupl. medicine. Resident in internal medicine U. Colo., Denver, 1976-77; resident in occupl. medicine Mt. Sinai Med. Ctr., N.Y.C., 1977-80, instr. occupl. medicine, 1980-81; med. dir. Nat. Farm Workers Health Group, Keene, Calif., 1983-86; asst. clin. prof. U. Calif., San Francisco, 1984-92; pres., founder Pesticide Edn. Ctr., San Francisco, 1988—; adj. faculty Sch. Pub. Health, San Diego State U., 1989-94; chmn. pesticide exposure workshop U.S. EPA/NIEHS/ATSDR, Arlington, Va., 1994; mem. nat. adv. com. First People of Color Environ. Summit, Washington, 1991, Pesticide Farm Safety Ctr., U. Calif., Davis, 1986-90, Health Effects of Herbicides, VA, Washington, 1981-84; cons. editor Am. Jour. Indsl. Medicine, Archives Environ. Health, 1986—; pesticide expert TV shows, radio and talk shows, cmty. meetings. Author: Designer Poisons, 1995; author/prodr. (video): Harvest of Sorrow, 1992 (Gold Apple award 1993); newsletter editl. bd. Citizens Clearinghouse for Hazardous Waste, Arlington, 1988—. Mem. adv. com. Bay Area Breast Cancer Project, San Francisco, 1995—; pro bono cons. United Farm Workers of Am., AFL-CIO, Keene, 1986—. Grantee various founds. including Rockefeller Found., Henry Kaiser Found., others, 1989-90, 93-95, EPA, 1990-92, Wonder Woman Found., 1984. Home and Office: Pesticide Education Ctr PO Box 420870 San Francisco CA 94142

MOSES, STEPHEN JAY, physician; b. Bklyn., Apr. 19, 1948; s. Otto G. and Isabelle B. M.; m. Marlene E., Aug. 3, 1975; children: Robyn, Amy. AB in Biology, Franklin and Marshall Coll., 1969; MD, SUNY, Syracuse, 1973. Diplomate Am. Bd. Internal Medicine, Am. Bd. in Rheumatology. Attending physician Valley Med. Assocs., P.C., Ansonia, Conn., 1978—; chief of rheumatology Griffin Hosp., Derby, Conn.; assoc. clin. prof. medicine Yale U. Sch. Medicine, 1981—. Bd. dirs. New Haven IPA, 1991-96, Congregation or Shalom, Orange, Conn., 1992-94. Fellow Am. Coll. Physicians, Am. Coll. Rheumatology. Office: Valley Med Assocs PC 135 Division St Ansonia CT 06401

MOSESSON, MICHAEL WILLIAM, physician; b. N.Y.C., Dec. 31, 1934; s. Benjamin D. and Esther F. (Weisenfeld) M.; m. Shirley A. McDowell, July 23, 1967; children: Matthew, Marni, Aimee. BS, Bklyn. Coll., 1955; MD, SUNY, Bklyn., 1959. Intern Harvard Med. Svcs. Boston City Hosp., 1959-60; resident Barnes Hosp. Wash. U., St. Louis, 1963-64, instr. dept. medicine, 1965-67; asst. prof. medicine SUNY, Bklyn., 1967-71, assoc. prof. medicine, 1971-75, prof. medicine, 1975-81; prof. medicine U. Wis., Madison, 1981—; vis. prof. Coll. de France, Paris, 1985; rsch. com. Am. Heart Assn., 1976-82; blood products adv. com. FDA-HHS, 1988-92. Contbr. articles to profl. jours. Sr. asst. surgeon USPHS, 1960-63. Recipient NIH Rsch. Career Devel. award, 1967-72, Josiah Macy Jr. Found. Faculty scholar award, 1977-78. Mem. Internat. Soc. on Thrombosis and Haemostasis (mem. sci. and standardization com. 1989-94), Internat. Fibrinogen Rsch. Soc. (chmn. exec. com. 1990—).

MOSHE, SOLOMON L., neurology and pediatrics educator; b. Athens, Greece, May 8, 1949; came to U.S., 1973; s. Leon and Sarina Moshe; m. Nancy Cornblath, June 26, 1977; 1 child, Jared. MD, Nat. U. Athens, 1972. Diplomate Am. Bd. Pediat., Am. Bd. Psychiatry and Neurology, Am. Bd. Clin. Neurophysiology. Inter, then resident in pediat. U. Md. Hosp., Balt., 1973-75; fellow in pediatric neurology Albert Einstein Coll. Medicine, Bronx, N.Y., 1975-78, rsch. fellow in neurology and neurosci., 1978-79, asst. prof. neurology, 1979-84, assoc. prof., 1984-89, prof., 1989—, asst. prof. pediatrics, 1979-85, assoc. prof., 1985-91, prof., 1991—, prof. neurosci., 1989—; mem. sci. adv. bd. Charles U. 3d Sch. Medicine, Prague, Czechoslovakia, 1990—; chmn. profl. adv. bd. Epilepsy Soc., Inc., Pearl River, N.Y., 1991—; Hans Berger lectr., 1995. Author: (with Pellock and Salon) The Parke-Davis Manual on Epilepsy, 1992, (with Schwartzkroin, Noebels and Swann) Brain Development and Epilepsy, 1995; co-inventor computer software Spike Simulator. Coach East Hudson Youth Soccer League, 1989—. Recipient Michael prize, 1984, rsch. recognition award Am. Epilepsy Soc., 1990; Jacob K. Javits neurosci. grantee, 1995—. Mem. Am. EEG Soc. (pres.-elect 1996-97), Ea. Assn. Electroencephalographers (pres. 1992-94). Office: Albert Einstein Coll Med Kennedy Bldg Rm 316 1410 Pelham Pky S Bronx NY 10461

MOSHER, LOREN RICHARD, psychiatrist; b. Monterey, Calif., Sept. 3, 1933; s. Harold and Anne (O'Brien) M.; m. Irene Carleton, May 26,1 961 (div. 1972); children: Hal, Tim, Missy; m. Judy Schreiber, Apr. 10, 1988. AB, Stanford U., 1956, postgrad., 1956-58; MD, Harvard U., 1961. Diplomate Am. Bd. Psychiatry and Neurology, Nat. Bd. Med. Examiners. Asst. prof. psychiatry Yale U., New Haven, 1967-68; chief Ctr. Studies of Schizophrenia, div. extramural rsch. NIMH, Rockville, Md., 1968-80; prof. psychiatry U.S. U. Health Sci., Bethesda, Md., 1981-88; chief med. dir. dept. health and human svcs. County of Montgomery, Rockville, Md., 1988-96; clin. prof. U.S. U. Health Sci., Bethesda, Md., 1988—; clin. dir. mental health svcs. San Diego County, Calif., 1996—; cons. Swedish, German and Italian Health Depts., 1989-96. Co-author: Community Mental Health Principles and Practice, 1989, Community Mental Health: a Practical Guide, 1994; editor books; editorial adv. bd. Contemporary Family Therapy, Internat. Jour. Therapeutic Communities, Schizophrenia Bull., Psychosocial Rehab. Jour.; contbr. articles to profl. jours. Capt. USPHS, 1974-88. Mem. APA, Am. Family Therapy Acad., Am. Assn. Marriage and Family Therapy, Am. Orthopsychiat. Assn. Home: 2616 Angell Ave San Diego CA 92122 Office: County of San Diego Health Svcs Complex Box 85524 San Diego CA 92186-5524

MOSHER, PAUL RAYMOND, social worker; b. Rochester, N.Y., Feb. 23, 1959; s. Robert F. Mosher and Pauline L. (Raucher) Allman. AAS in Human Svcs., Monroe Community Coll., Rochester, N.Y., 1982; BS in Social Work, SUNY, Brockport, 1984; MS in Social Work, U. Louisville, 1986. Cert. social worker; credentialed alcoholism counselor; master addiction counselor. Resident counselor Heritage Christian Home, Henrietta, N.Y., 1984-86; team leader Daybreak Alcoholism Treatment Facility, Rochester, 1986-89; social worker Wayne County Mental Health, Newark, 1989-90; substance abuse program dir. Huther-Doyle/Discovery, Webster, N.Y., 1990—. Mem. ACSW (cert.), Nat. Assn. Social Workers. Home: 1929 Clifford Ave Rochester NY 14609-3631 Office: Huther Doyle/Discovery 360 East Ave Rochester NY 14604

MOSIER, CURTIS LEE, surgeon; b. Ames, Iowa, May 21, 1952; s. C.C. and Barbara Helen (Hostetter) M.; m. Susan Kay Shroder, May 8, 1982; children: Sara, Tate. BS, Iowa State U., 1974; MD, U. Iowa, 1978. Diplomate Am. Bd. Surgery. Resident gen. surgery Iowa Meth. Med. Ctr., Des Moines, 1978-83; pvt. practice Denton, Tex., 1984—. Fellow ACS; mem. AMA, Tex. Med. Assn., Denton County Med. Soc. Office: 1300 Fulton #203 Denton TX 76201

MOSKAL, JOSEPH TUVIA, orthopaedic surgeon; b. Haifa, Israel, June 4, 1955; came to U.S., 1960; m. Pamela Swertfeger, June 4, 1988; children: Nani Estelle, Morgan Bailey. BA, SUNY, Binghamtom, 1977; MD, Wash. U., 1981. Diplomate Am. Bd. Orthopaedic Surgery, Nat. Bd. Med. Examiners. Intern gen. surgery Barnes Hosp., St. Louis, 1981-82; resident orthopaedics U. Va. Med. Ctr., Charlottesville, 1982-86; spl. fellow adult reconstruction & total joint replacement The Cleve. Clinic Found., 1986-87; fellow orthopaedic traumatology Md. Inst. Emergency Med. Svc. Sys., Balt., 1987; clin. asst. prof. orthopaedics U. Va. Health Scis. Ctr.; cons. staff Va. Med. Ctr., Salem; dir. Bone Bank, Roanoke Meml. Hosps., 1988—; mem. exec. com. Cmty. Hosp. Roanoke Valley; speaker in field. Contbr. articles to profl. jours. Fellow Am. Coll. Surgeons, Am. Acad. Orthopaedic Surgeons; mem. AMA,So. Orthopaedic Assn., Ea. Orthopaedic Assn., Va. Orthopaedic Assn., Med. Soc. Va., Roanoke Acad. Medicine, Assn. Arthritic Hip and Knee Surgery. Office: Roanoke Orthopaedic Ctr 4064 Postal Dr SW Roanoke VA 24018

MOSKOWITZ, MILDRED ROSE, psychotherapist, educator; b. Phila., Apr. 16, 1922; d. Nathan and Gertrude (Pollet) Reback; m. Sidney M. Moskowitz, Feb. 9, 1946 (dec. Feb. 1988); children: Michael, Naomi. BA, Bklyn. Coll., 1943; MS, Columbia U., 1945. Diplomate clin. social worker; cert. Nat. Registry Cert. Group Psychotherapists. Child therapist, caseworker Jewish Bd. Guardians, N.Y.C., 1945-57; supr., bd. dirs. Manhattan Office, N.Y.C., 1952-57; dir. Riverdale office Jewish Bd. Guardians, N.Y.C., 1970-73; dir. Boro Hall Office, N.Y.C., 1973-78; pvt. practice psychotherapy N.Y.C., 1978—; adj. prof. sch. social work NYU, 1978—; mem. summer faculty Sch. Social Work Smith Coll., N.Y.C., 1979-94. Fellow Am. Orthopsychiat. Assn., N.Y. State Soc. Clin. Social Work Psychotherapists, Am. Acad. Cert. Social Workers (cert., diplomate); mem. Am. Assn. Marriage and Family Therapy, Am. Group Psychotherapy Assn., Eastern Group Psychotherapy Assn., Assn. for Self Psychology. Home: 145 W 86th St New York NY 10024-3406 Office: 40 W 86th St New York NY 10024-3605

MOSKOWITZ, RANDI ZUCKER, nurse; b. N.Y.C., Oct. 19, 1948; d. Seymour and Gertrude (Levy) Zucker; R.N., Jewish Hosp. & Med. Center Sch. Nursing, 1969; BA, Marymount Manhattan Coll., 1975; MS, Hunter Coll., 1979; MBA, Columbia U., 1990; m. Marc N. Moskowitz, July 11, 1976. Gen. staff nurse neurosurgery unit, N.Y. Hosp., N.Y.C., 1969-71, sr. staff nurse Recovery Room, 1971-76, nurse coordinator utilization rev., 1976-79; health educator Office of Cancer Communications, Meml. Sloan-Kettering Cancer Center, 1979-81; adminstrv. nurse oncologist Bklyn. Community Hosp. Oncology Program, Meth. Hosp., 1981-83, grants coordinator radiotherapy dept., 1983-86; adminstr. Ambulatory Oncology Ctr., Columbia-Presbyn. Med. Ctr., N.Y.C., 1986-89; adminstr. Surg. Day Hosp., Meml. Sloan-Kettering Cancer Ctr., 1990—; Masters prof. oncology Columbia U. Sch. Nursing. Co-editor Oncology Nursing: Advances, Treatments and Trends into the Twenty-first Century; contbr. articles to profl. jours. Mem. Soc. Ambulatory Care Profl., Oncology Nursing Soc. (sec. N.Y.C. chpt. 1983-87, pres. 1988-89). Home: 446 E 86th St Apt 5-f New York NY 10028-6466 Office: Meml Sloan-Kettering Cancer Ctr 1275 York Ave New York NY 10021-6007

MOSKOWITZ, RICHARD LEE, surgeon; b. N.Y.C., Jan. 28, 1953; s. Norman David and Rosalind (Shapiro) M. BA in Biology, Alfred U., 1974; MD, Pa. State U., 1978. Bd. cert. gen. surgery; recert. gen. surgery; bd. cert. colon and rectal surgery. Resident L.I. Jewish Hosp., New Hyde Park, N.Y., 1978-82, chief resident, 1982-83; attending surgeon Manhattan Med. Group, N.Y.C., 1985-86, Colon Surgery & Proctology Assocs., Morristown, N.J., 1986—. Contbr. articles to profl. jours. Colon/Rectal Surgery fellow Greater Balt. Med. Ctr., 1983-84. Fellow Am. Coll. Surgeons, Am. Soc. Colon & Rectal Surgeons; mem. St. Marks Assn. Office: Colon Surgery & Proctology Assocs 130 Speedwell Ave Morris Plains NJ 07950

MOSKOWITZ, ROLAND WALLACE, internist; b. Shamokin, Pa., Nov. 3, 1929. MD, Temple U., 1953. Intern Temple U. Hosp., Phila., 1953-54; fellow in internal medicine Mayo Clinic, Rochester, Minn., 1954-55, 57-60; mem. staff U. Hosps. Cleve.; prof. medicine Case Western Res. U. Sch. Medicine, Cleve. Mem. ACR, Alpha Omega Alpha. Office: U Hosps Cleve Divsn Rheum Diseases 11100 Euclid Ave Cleveland OH 44106

MOSLEY, CYNTHIA LISA, marketing professional; b. Culver City, Calif.; d. Robert Eugene and Elizabeth Jane (Jeffers) Haynie; m. James David Mosley. BA cum laude, U. Portland, 1987; MBA, Calif. State U., Fullerton, 1992; advanced mgmt. cert., U. Calif., Riverside, 1995, exec. mgmt. cert., 1996. Intern YWCA, Portland, Oreg., 1986-87; cons. Comprehensive Care Corp., Orange, Calif., 1987-89; referral coord. Corona (Calif.) Cmty. Hosp., 1989-92; dir. cmty. programs Valley Health Sys., Hemet, Calif., 1992—; bd. dirs. Valley Youth Found., Hemet; mem. Valley Health Mag., Hemet, 1995—. Mem. ways and means com. First Congl. Ch., Corona, 1996—. Mem. Corvettes of So. Calif. (hospitality com. 1989-90). Home: 960 Sapphire Ln Corona CA 91720 Office: Valley Health Sys 1117 E Devonshire Hemet CA 92543

MOSS, ARTHUR JAY, physician; b. White Plains, N.Y., June 21, 1931; s. Abraham Loeb and Ida (Bank) M.; m. Joy Folkman, June 23, 1957; children: Katherine, Deborah, David. BA, Yale U., 1953; MD, Harvard U., 1957. Resident Mass. Gen. Hosp., 1957-58, 60-61; fellow in cardiology med. ctr. U. Rochester, N.Y., 1961-65, from asst. to assoc. prof. sch. medicine and dentistry, 1966-71, clin. assoc. prof., 1971-82, clin. prof., 1982-91, prof. medicine, 1991—, dir. heart rsch. follow-up program med. ctr., 1971—; mem. cardiology adv. com. Nat. Heart, Lung, and Blood Inst., NIH, 1980-82, chmn., 1982-84. Author: Antiarrhythmic Agents, 1973; editor: Clinical Aspects of Life-threatening Arrhythmias, 1984, QT Prolongation and Ventricular Arrhythmias, 1992, Noninvasive Electrocardiology, 1995; editor-in-chief Ann. Noninvasive Electrocardiology, 1996—; editl. bd. Am. Jour. Cardiology, 1988—. Lt. USNR, 1958-60. Mem. Alpha Omega Alpha. Home: 581 Claybourne Rd Rochester NY 14618-1224 Office: Univ Rochester Med Ctr PO Box 653 Rochester NY 14642-8653

MOSS, BARRY MICHAEL, physician; b. Detroit, Dec. 27, 1948. BS, Wayne State U., 1970, MD, 1974. Diplomate Am. Bd. Internal Medicine. Intern Wayne State U., 1974-75; resident Boston City Hosp., 1975-77; physician Franklin Med. Cons., Southfield, Mich., 1979—; clin. asst. prof. Wayne State U., Detroit, 1988—. Mem. Am. Coll. Physicians, Mich. State Med. Soc. Office: Franklin Med Cons 29275 Northwestern Southfield MI 48034

MOSS, BETTY SMITH, social worker; b. Fairfield, Ala., Dec. 8, 1931; d. James William Clarke and Helen Sarah (McKelduff) Smith; m. Cameron Gresham, Nov. 1, 1952; children: James Michael, David Patrick, Catherine Alice Moss Hodges, Nancy Carol Moss Weaks. BSSW, U. Ala., Birmingham, 1983. Lic. social worker, Ala.; cert. AIDS counselor, Fla. Staff Cooper Green Hosp., Birmingham, Ala., 1983-86; vol. Medicare, Medicaid Advocacy prog. counselor AARP, Panama City, Fla., 1987; vol. chmn. of hosp. vols. ARC, Tyndall AFB, Panama City, Fla., 1987-88; case mgr. Bay County Coun. on Aging, 1988; discharge planner Bay Med. Ctr., Panama City, Fla., 1988-94; ret., 1994. Bd. dirs. Western Mental Health Clinic; com. mem. AIDS Task Force, Birmingham, 1985-86. Mem. Nat. Assn. Social Workers, Acad. of Cert. Baccalarate Social Workers, Omicron Delta Kappa, Phi Kappa Phi, Alpha Lambda Delta. Home: 3007 Whispering Pines Ln Fultondale AL 35068

MOSS, DEBRA LYNNE, physician, executive; b. St. Louis, Feb. 14, 1955; d. Morris and Sylvia (Richman) M.; m. Joseph Howell Ingram, Jan. 7, 1984; children: Tracy, Robert. BA in Chemistry, U. Mo., Kansas City, 1976; MD, Tufts U., 1980; M of Mgmt.-Health and Hosp. Svcs., Northwestern U., 1989. Diplomate Nat. Bd. Med. Examiners. Adminstrv. ptnr. Doctors Officenter Med. Group, Mt. Prospect, S.C., 1984-86; pres. Dr. Debra Moss and Assocs., Highland Park, S.C., 1986—; pres. Doctors Officenter of Ill. and Univ. Med. Group, Bannockburn, 1991-95; nat. dir. managed care and network devel. Avanti Health Svcs., Bannockburn, 1992-95; med. dir. Sanus Health Plan of Ill., Oakbrook, 1993-95; nat. med. dir. Avanti Health Svcs., Bannockburn, 1994-95; sr. v.p. managed care and network devel. Paidos Health Mgmt. Svcs., Inc., Deerfield, Ill., 1995—. Fellow Am. Acad. Pediat., Am. Coll. Quality Assurance and Utilization Review; mem. AMA, Am. Med. Women's Assn., Am. Coll. Physician Execs., Am. Coll. Med. Adminstrs., Am. Occupl. Medicine Soc. Office: Paidos Health Mgmt Svcs 102 Wilmot Ste # 300 Deerfield IL 60015

MOSS, GERALD S., dean, medical educator; b. Cleve., Mar. 4, 1935; s. Harry and Lillian (Alter) M.; m. Wilma Jaback, Sept. 1, 1957; children: William Alan, Robert Daniel, Sharon Lynn. BA, Ohio State U., 1956, MD cum laude, 1960. Diplomate Am. Bd. Surgery (apptd. assoc. examiner com. 1989); lic. Ill. Intern Mass. Gen. Hosp., Boston, 1960-61, resident, 1961-65; from asst. prof. to assoc. prof. dept. surgery Coll. Medicine U. Ill., Chgo., 1968-72, prof., 1973-77, 89—, head dept. surgery, 1989, dean, 1989—; prof. dept. surgery Pritzker Sch. Medicine U. Chgo., 1977-89; prof. dept. surgery U. Ill., Coll. of Medicine, 1989—; tutor in surgery Manchester (Eng.) Royal Infirmary, 1964; asst. chief surgical svcs. VA West Side Hosp., Chgo., 1968-70; attending surgeon dept. surgery Cook County Hosp., Chgo. 1970-72, chmn. 1972-77; dir. surgical rsch. Hektoen Inst. for Med. Rsch., Cook County Hosp., 1972-77, Micheal Reese Hosp. and Med. Ctr., Chgo., 1977-89, chmn. dept. surgery, 1977-89, chief svc. 1989, trustee, 1981, and numerou coms.; appointed to Nat. Rsch. Coun., NAS, 1966-68, Ad Hoc Subcom., NAE, 1970, Ad Hoc Study Sect., 1970, del. to Third Joint U.S-USSR Symposium, 1983, Blood Diseases and Resources Adv. Com., 1984-88, Planning Com. for discussing key blood problems, Nat. Heart and Lung Inst., 1987, chmn. Plasma and Plasma Products Com., 1979, bd. dirs., 1983, v.p., 1985, Ad Hoc Transition Com., Am. Blood Commn., 1989, Panel on Rsch. Opportunities, Office Naval Rsch. Program, 1987, exec. com., coord. com., Nat. Blood Edn. Program, 1988, Tech. Adv. Task Force Am. Hosp. Assn., 1988, chmn. review panel contract proposals, NIH, 1975, program project site visit, 1976, chmn. site-visit review group, 1977, adv. com. Blood Resources Work group, 1978, Planning Com. for Consensus, 1987, Small Bus. Innovation Rsch., 1988, Med. Rsch. Scv. Merit Review Bd. VA, 1978-81, Liaison Com. Graduate Med. Edn. AMA, 1979, and numerous other coms. for various med. organizations; cons. Nat. Heart and Lung Inst., Transfusion Medicine Acad. Awardees Program; vis. prof. Montefiore Med. Ctr. Bronx, N.Y., 1986, Ohio State U., 1988, U. N.Mex., Albuquerque, 1989, Seton Med. Ctr., Austin, Tex., 1990, U. Ill. Coll. Medicine, Peoria, 1991; guest lectr., participant numerous meetings, symposiums; cons. in field. Contbr. numerous articles to profl. jours., chpts. to books.. With U.S. Army, 1965-68, Vietnam. Teaching fellow Harvard Med. Sch., 1962; receipient Stitt Lectr. award Assn. Mil. Surgeons U.S.A., 1981; grantee U.S. Navy, 1969-84, U.S. Army, 1971-74, 75-78, NIH, 1969, 83-84, Dept. Pub. Health, 1973, HEW, 1974-77, UpJohn, 1974, Northfield Labs. 1985-89. Fellow ACS (pre and postoperative care com. 1975-83, rep. Am. blood commn. 1977—, mem. various coms., speaker various symposiums), Am. Soc. Surgery Trauma; mem. Am. Surgical Assn. (rep. Nat. Soc. Med. Rsch. 1984-88), Am. Trauma Soc., Am. Physicians Fellowship (rep. Israel Med. Assn.), Assn. Acad. Surgery (chmn. membership selection com. 1973-75, pres. elect 1974-75, pres. 1975-76, exec. coun. 1977-79), Soc. Univ. Surgeons (rep. Nat. Soc. Med. Rsch. 1973-77, com. Surgical Edn. 1979-81), Ctrl. Surgical Soc. (rep. Nat. Soc. Med. Rsch. 1973-77), Shock Soc. (chmn. planning com. 1986, chmn. program com. 1986, pres. elect 1986-87, pres. 1987-88), Soc. for Surgery Alimentary Tract (mem. com. west north ctrl. region 1978-82), Internat. Soc. Blood Transfusion, SurgicalBiology Club II, Nat. Soc. for Med. Rsch., Collegium Internationale Chirugiae Digestivae, Societe Internationale de Chirugie, Sigma XI, Alpha Omega Alpha (faculty advisor 1972-73). Office: U Ill Coll Medicine 1853 W Polk St # C 784 Chicago IL 60612-4316

MOSS, RICHARD B., pediatrician; b. N.Y.C., Oct. 30, 1949. MD, SUNY, Downstate, 1975. Intern Children's Meml. Hosp., Chgo., 1975-76, resident, 1976-77; fellow Stanford (Calif.) U. Med. Sch., 1977-79, 80-81; now pediatrician Lucile Salter Packard Children's Hosp., Palo Alto, Calif.; prof. pediats. Stanford U. Med. Sch. Office: Stanford U Sch Med Ctr Dept Pediats Stanford CA 94305-5119

MOSS, WILLIAM WALLACE, physician; b. Charlottesville, Va., Feb. 23, 1948; s. James Mercer and Rachel Scott (Bybee) M.; m. S. Lynn Smith, Aug. 19, 1969; children: David Aubrey, Alicia Ellen. BS, Eckerd Coll., 1969; MD, U. Va., 1973. Diplomate Am. Bd. Internal Medicine, Am. Bd. Med. Oncology. Med. resident U. Mich., Ann Arbor, 1973-75; clin. assoc. Nat. Cancer Inst., Bethesda, Md., 1975-78; med. oncology practice Bradenton, Fla., 1978—; chief of medicine L.W. Blake Hosp., Bradenton, 1982, vice chief of staff, 1983-84, chief of staff, 1984-86. Fellow ACP. Office: Bradenton Oncology Ctr 6001 21st Ave W Bradenton FL 34209-7847

MOSSER, DONN GORDON, radiologist; b. Topeka, Jan. 17, 1921; s. Lloyd Henry and Emma Rebecca (Pyle) M.; m. Alice Myra Harrington, Aug. 21, 1943 (dec. Sept. 1993); children: Donn Gordon Jr., Dana Myra, Gregory Leonard; m. Janet Hale Havard, June 24, 1995. AB in Chemistry, U. Kans., 1942, MD, 1946; MS in Radiology, U. Mpls., 1954. Diplomate Am. Bd. Radiology. Dir. divsn. radiation therapy U. Minn. Med. Sch., Mpls., 1952-63; med. dir. radiation oncology Abbott Northwestern Hosp., Mpls., 1963-90; locum tenens in various states Mpls., 1990—; bd. dirs., pres. Minn. Med. Found., Mpls., 1968-82, Am. Cancer Soc., Mpls., 1952-75. Sr. asst. surgeon USPHS, 1947-49. Fellow Am. Coll. Radiology; mem. Radiol. Soc. North Am., Am. Radium Soc., Am. Roentgen Ray Soc., Am. Soc. Clin. Oncology, Am. Soc. Radiology and Oncology. Congregational. Home and Office: 3200 W Calhoun Rd Minneapolis MN 55416

MÖSSNER, JOACHIM, internist, gastroenterologist; b. Würzburg, Bavaria, Fed. Republic Germany, Nov. 17, 1950; s. Franz Emil and Ursula Amalie (Gunder) M.; m. Karin Sigrid Neidhardt, July 22, 1978; children: Felix Oskar, Lone Dorothea, Flora Eleonore. Student, U. Würzburg, Fed. Republic Germany, 1970-76, MD, 1978, Habilitation, 1987. Intern Dept. of Surgery, Tauberbischofsheim, Fed. Republic Germany, 1977, Medizinische Poliklinik, U. Würburg, 1978; resident Med. Poliklinik, U. Würburg, 1978-82, 85-86, chief gastroenterology unit, 1986-93; rsch. assoc. dept. physiology U. Calif., San Francisco, 1983-85; chief dept. internal medicine, gastroenterology U. Leipzig, 1993—; full prof. medicine U. Würzburg, 1989—. Assoc. editor Internat. Jour. Pancreatology, Jour. Gastroenterology. Grantee Deutsche Forschungsgemeinschaft, 1982—. Mem. German Soc. Internal Medicine, Am. Soc. Gastroenterology, German Soc. Gastroenterology, Internat. Soc. Pancreatology, Am. Soc. Pancreatology, N.Y. Acad. Scis., Internat. Gastro Surg. Club. Home: Guttenbergerstr 20, 97082 Würzburg Germany Office: U Leipzig Medizinische Klinik II, Philipp Rosenthal Str 27, 04103 Leipzig Germany

MOSS-SALENTIJN, LETTY (ALEIDA MOSS-SALENTIJN), anatomist; b. Amsterdam, The Netherlands, Apr. 14, 1943; came to U.S., 1968; d. Ewoud and Johanna Maria (Schoonhoven) Salentijn; m. Melvin Lionel Moss, Apr. 17, 1970. DDS, State U., Utrecht, The Netherlands, 1967, PhD, 1976. Asst. prof. histology, State U., Utrecht, 1967-68; asst. prof. Columbia U., 1968-74, assoc. prof., 1974-86, prof., 1986—, dir. dental radiology, 1980-86, dir. grad. program dental sci., 1986—, dir. postdoctoral affairs, 1987-90, asst. dean postdoctoral programs, 1990-94, assoc. dean acad. affairs, 1995—. Author: Orofacial Histology & Embryology, 1972; Dental and Oral Tissues, 1980, 2d edit., 1984, 3d edit. 1990; contbr. chpts. to books, articles to profl. jours. Fellow Royal Microscopical Soc.; mem. Am. Assn. Anatomists, Internat. Assn. Dental Rsch., Am. Soc. Biomechanics, Sigma Xi. (chpt. sec. 1980-87, pres. 1987-89), Omicron Kappa Upsilon (pres. local chpt. 1987). Avocation: stained glass art. Home: 560 Riverside Dr Apt 20K New York NY 10027-3242 Office: Columbia U Assoc Dean Academic Affairs 630 W 168th St New York NY 10032-3702

MOST, JOHN ANTHONY, nursing educator, consultant, physician; b. Dubuque, Iowa, Aug. 12, 1928; s. George Henry and Mary Caroline (Fay) M.; children: John George, Wiliam Andrew, Sara Ann, Gregory Patrick Joseph, Ann Caroline. Student, Loras Coll., Dubuque, 1946-49; MD, St. Louis U., 1953. Diplomate Nat. Bd. Med. Examiners, Am. Bd. Family Practice. Surg. intern Univ. Hosp., Little Rock, 1953-54; resident surgery U.S. Naval Hosp., Chelsea, Mass., 1960-61; pvt. practice Carlsbad, N.Mex., 1961—; mem. staff Guadalupe Med. Ctr., Carlsbad; mem. assoc. faculty N.Mex. State U., Carlsbad. Bd. dirs. N.Mex. Lung Assn., Albuquerque; past pres. Boys' Club, Carlsbad; past chmn. bd. trustees Guadalupe Med. Ctr., Carlsbad. Lt. comdr. USNR, 1954-61. Fellow AMA, Am. Acad. Family Physicians (past state pres.); mem. Am. Soc. Law and Medicine, Hasting Ctr. (assoc.), Thoracic Soc. (past v.p.). Republican. Roman Catholic. Home: 1133 Tracy Pl Carlsbad NM 88220-5270 Office: Medical Arts Bldg Carlsbad NM 88220

MOSTER-STEIN, DEBBIE G., nursing educator; b. San Francisco, June 20, 1955; d. Jerry and Ann (Moskowitz) Moster; m. Evan Stein, Nov. 7, 1982; 1 child, Sarah June. BSN, UCLA, 1977, MSN, FNP, 1980. Cert. family nurse practitioner ANA, med.-surg. ANA. Clin. nurse UCLA; family nurse practitioner Calif. Pediatric Ctr., L.A.; nursing instr. Wadsworth div. VA West Los Angeles, L.A.; cons. in field. Recipient VA Adminstr.'s award. Mem. NANDA, Sigma Theta Tau.

MOSTILLO, RALPH, medical association executive; b. Newark, Apr. 11, 1944; s. Joseph and Antoinette (Cipriano) M. BA in Chemistry magna cum laude, Rutgers U., Newark, 1972; MA in Biochemistry, Princeton U., 1974, PhD in Biochemistry, 1978. NIH rsch. fellow Princeton (N.J.) U., 1972-78; sr. scientist drug regulatory affairs Hoffmann-La Roche, Inc., Nutley, N.J., 1979-85; founder, chmn., chief exec. officer Am. Cancer Assn., Nutley, 1986—. Assoc. editor U.S. Pharmacopoeia XX-Nat. Formulary XV, 1980-85. With USN, 1962-66, Vietnam. Mem. Am. Chem. Soc., Am. Mgmt. Assn., Am. Mktg. Assn., N.Y. Acad. Scis., Am. Legion, Vietnam Vets. of Am., Phi Beta Kappa. Home: PO Box 505 Nutley NJ 07110-0505 Office: Am Cancer Assn PO Box 87 Nutley NJ 07110-0087

MOSTOFI, FATHOLLAH KESHVAR, pathologist, educator, consultant; b. Teheran, Iran, Aug. 10, 1911; came to U.S., 1931; s. Farajullah Khan and Kursum (Khanum) M.; m. Dorothy Ida Krock, June 20, 1940; 1 child, Keith. AB, BSc, U. Nebr., 1935; MD, Harvard U., 1939, grad. Kennedy Sch. Govt., 1982. Diplomate Am. Bd. Pathology. Intern St. Luke's Hosp., Bethlehem, Pa., 1939-40; house officer Peter Bent Brigham Hosp., Boston, 1940-41; resident in pathology Boston Lying-In Hosp. and Free Hosp. for Women, 1941-42, Children's Hosp., Boston, 1942-43; asst. pathologist Mass. Gen. Hosp., Boston, 1943-44; rsch. fellow Nat. Cancer Inst., Bethesda, Md., 1947-48; pathologist, spl. asst. VA Cen. Lab. Anat. Pathology Armed Forces Inst. Path., Washington, 1948-62; chmn. dept. genitourinary pathology Armed Forces Inst. Pathology, Washington, 1962—; sci. dir. Am. Registry Pathology, 1957-59; clin. assoc. prof. pathology Johns Hopkins U., Balt., 1960—; clin. prof. pathology Georgetown U., 1961—, U. Md., 1968—, Uniformed Svcs. U. Health Scis., Bethesda, Md., 1970—; head Collaborating Ctr. for Urologic Tumors, WHO, Geneva, 1963—; hon. prof. Chinese Peoples Liberation Army Gen. Hosp. Postgrad. Med. Sch., Beijing, 1988—; registrar Am. Urol. Assn., Washington, 1949—; hon fellow Royal Coll. Pathologists, 1990. Co-author: Tumors of the Male Genital System, 1973, International Histological Classification of Bladder Tumors, 1974, of Testes Tumors, 1977, of Prostatic Tumore, 1980, of Kidney Tumors, 1981, Atlas of Kidney Biopsies, 1980; four books transl. into Russian, French, Spanish; editor: Bilharziasis Proc., 1976; co-editor: The Kidney, 1966, The Skin, 1971, The Platelet, 1972, The Liver, 1973, Striated Muscle, 1973, Kidney Disease: Present Status, 1979. Maj. M.C., U.S. Army, 1944-47. Recipient Presdl. Rank of Disting. Exec. Svc., 1982, Ferdinand C. Valentine award N.Y. Acad. Medicine, John Shaw Billings Lifetime Achievement award DOD-AFIP, ARP, 1995; 2 books dedicated to him. Mem. Internat. Acad. Pathology (sec.-treas. 1952-70, pres. 1972-76), Internat. Soc. Pathology, U.S.-Can. Acad. Pathology (pres. 1972-73, gold medal 1974, ann. F.K. Mostofi award for disting. svc. to pathology established in his name), Internat. Coun. Socs. Pathology (sec.-treas. 1970—), Acad. Medicine (pres. 1992—), Cosmos Club, Harvard Club. Republican. Islam. Home: 7001 Georgia St Chevy Chase MD 20815 Office: Armed Forces Inst Pathology 147th and Alaska Ave NW Washington DC 20306-6000

MOTE, GORDON EDWARD, health facility administrator; b. Chlumonie, Bolivia, Dec. 5, 1943; came to U.S., 1944; s. Robert Grant and Caroline Elizabeth (Heubach) M.; m. Patricia Louise Hoss, June 18, 1968 (div. July 1984); 1 child, Gregory Edward; m. Raylene Louise Parrett, Oct. 13, 1985. BA in Biology, Loma Linda U., 1968; MBA, Century U., 1988, PhD, 1995. Field dir., staff biologist World Life Rsch. Inst., Colton, Calif., 1967-68; dept. mgr., instr. biology Loma Linda U., Riverside, Calif., 1970-73; dir. ops. Versitron Industries, Riverside, 1973-78; asst. to v.p. Zee Med. Products, Irvine, Calif., 1978-80; adminstr. Bio-Labs., Colton, 1980, Stout & Perkins Acctg. Corp., Redlands, Calif., 1981-84; contr. Riverside-San Bernadino County Indian Health, Banning, Calif., 1987-88; mgmt. and health care cons. Profl. Mgmt. Solutions, Grand Terrace, Calif., 1984—; pres., exec. dir. Integrated Life Style Mgmt., Grand Terrace, 1993—; bd. dirs. Cyric Software, San Diego, 1991—, Pac-Tech Sys. Inc., Calimesa, Calif., 1994—; instr. Nat. Assn. Underwater Instructors, 1971—. Mem. Am. Mgmt. Assn. Home and Office: 22833 Finch St Grand Terrace CA 92313-5556

MOTHKUR, SRIDHAR RAO, radiologist; b. Mothkur, India, Oct. 5, 1950; came to U.S., 1975; s. Venkat Rao and Laxmi Bai (Gundepally) M.; m. Sheila Rama Rao Paga, Nov. 30, 1973; children: Swathi, Preethi, Venkat Krishna. Student, Coll. Arts and Sci. Osmania U., Siddipet, India, 1966; MB, BS, Osmania U., Hyderabad, India, 1972, DPH, 1974. Diplomate Am. Bd. Radiology. Rotating intern Osmania Gen. Hosp., Hyderabad, 1972-73, internal medicine intern, 1973, resident in surgery, 1974-75; resident Resurrection Hosp., Chgo., 1975-76; resident in radiology Luth. Gen. Hosp., Park Ridge, Ill., 1976-79, chief resident radiology, 1978-79; with rotations in nuclear medicine, angiography and neuroradiology Rush-Presbyn. St. Luke's Med. Ctr., Chgo., 1978; chmn. and med. dir. dept. radiology Louise Burg Hosp., Chgo., 1979-85, Shriner's Hosp., Chgo., 1986-88; fellow in ultrasound and computered tomography U. Ill., Chgo., 1988-89, fellow in magnetic resonance imaging, 1988-89; staff radiologist St. Anthony and Meml. Hosp., Michigan City, Ind., 1989—, Kingwood Hosp., Michigan City, 1989-94, Charter Hosp., Behavioral Health Sys. Ind., Michigan City, 1994—; spl. staff radiologist Christ Hosp. Med. Ctr., Oaklawn, Ill., 1988-89; med. dir. interventional radiology St. Anthony and Meml. Hosp., Michigan City, 1989-93, MRI Ctr., 1989—, med. dir. diagnostic imaging Meml. Hosp., Michigan City, 1994—; clin. asst. prof. in radiology U. Ill., Chgo., 1990—. Fellow Am. Coll. Internat. Physicians, Am. Coll. Angiology, Internat. Coll. Angiology; mem. AMA, Internat. Soc. Krishna Consciousness, Radiol. Soc. N.Am., Telugu Assn. N.Am., Am. Roentgen Ray Soc., Am. Assn. Physicians from India, Am. Diabetes Assn., Am. Coll. Emergency Physicians, Am. Soc. Head and Neck Radiology, Am. Telugu Assn., Am. Coll. Radiology, Soc. Magnetic Resonance Imaging, Soc. Cardiovascular and Interventional Radiology, Soc. Magnetic Resonance in Medicine, Indian Radiol. and Imaging Assn., Tristate Telugu Assn., Ind. Interventional Radiol. Assn., India Med. Assn. N.W. Ind., Ill. State Med. Soc., Chgo. Med. Soc., Telugu Assn. Greater Chgo. Republican. Hindu-Brahmin. Home: 1457 Sand Creek Dr S Chesterton IN 46304-2268 Office: Michigan City Radiologists Inc 916 Washington St Michigan City IN 46360-3518

MOTLAGH, MOJTABA RASTGAR, psychiatrist; b. Tehran, Iran, May 22, 1940; came to U.S., 1971; s. Mehdi Rastgar Motlagh; m. Corazon Cadiz Hobbs, Aug. 1988 (div.); children: James Pakpaz Rastgar, Pooya R. Motlagh. MD, U. Tehran, 1966. Diplomate Am. Bd. Psychiatry and

Neurology. Intern Morristown (N.J.) Meml. Hosp., 1972-73; resident in pediatrics Brookdale Hosp. Med. Ctr., Bklyn., 1973; resident in adult psychiatry Trenton (N.J.) Psychiat. Hosp., 1973-75; fellow in child psychiatry Rutgers Med. Sch., Piscataway, N.J., 1975-77; pvt. practice adult and child psychiatry Las Vegas, Nev.; asst. prof. psychiatry U.N.R. Med. Sch.

MOTLEY, JOHN PAUL, psychiatrist, consultant; b. Carbondale, Pa., July 5, 1927; s. Joseph Adrian and Lillian (McCormick) M.; BS, Georgetown U., 1951; MD, Hahnemann Med. Coll., Phila., 1955; children: Marianne, Patricia, Kathleen, John Paul, Elizabeth, Joseph A. III, Grace, Michael. Intern, Hahnemann Med. Coll. Hosp., Phila., 1955-56; resident in psychiatry Inst. of Living, Hartford, Conn., 1956-59; practice medicine specializing in psychiatry, Point Pleasant, N.J., 1961—; mem. staff Jersey Shore Med. Ctr., 1961-72, chief of psychiatry, 1970-72; mem. staff Point Pleasant Hosp., 1961—, chief of psychiatry, 1961—; cons. in forensic psychiatry to various cts. and agys. Served with U.S. Army, 1944-46, ETO. Diplomate Am. Bd. Psychiatry and Neurology. Fellow Am. Psychiat. Assn.; mem. AMA, Royal Coll. Psychiatry, Am. Coll. Psychiatry, N.J. Psychiat. Assn. (past pres.). Clubs: Springlake Golf. Republican. Roman Catholic. Office: 3822 River Rd Point Pleasant Beach NJ 08742-2067

MOTLEY, MONA EVETTE, health services administrator; b. Dayton, Ohio, July 30, 1970; d. Marvin Edward and Myrtle Olivia (Wilkinson) Miliner; m. Alonzo Vester Motley Jr., Aug. 14, 1993; children: Lauren Alexis, Alonna Vante. BS in Health, Ohio U., 1992, M of Health Adminstrn., 1994. Lic. nursing home adminstr., Ohio. Adminstrv. intern Miami Valley Hosp., Dayton, 1992, O'Bleness Meml. Hosp., Athens, Ohio, 1992; grad. adminstr. Parks Hall Med. Ctr., Athens, 1992-93; adminstrv. intern Dept. of Vets. Affairs Med. Ctr., Dayton, 1993; adminstr.-in-tng. Hickory Career Nursing Home, The Plains, Ohio, 1993-94; dir. edn. and cmty. programs Am. Heart Assn., Dayton, 1995; asst. to the divsn. dir. Montgomery County Combined Health Dist., Dayton, 1995—; mem. Child and Family Health Svs., Dayton, 1995—; mem. Montgomery County Early Intervention Consortium, Dayton, 1995—. Mem. Homeless Shelter Adv. Bd., Dayton, 1995—. Mem. Am. Coll. of Healthcare Execs., Am. Coll. of Health Care Adminstrs., Nat. Assn. of Health Svcs. Execs., Alpha Kappa Alpha. Home: 203C Outer Belle Rd Dayton OH 45426 Office: Combined Health Dist. Montgomery County 451 W Third St Dayton OH 45422-1280

MOTT, THURMAN, psychiatrist; b. Ft. Wayne, Ind., Nov. 15, 1927; s. Thurman and Letha Faye (Johnson) M.; m. Lorraine Elizabeth Droneburg; children: Keith Alan, Teresa Lynn, Geoffrey Kendall. Student, Purdue U., 1944-46; BS, MD, Northwestern U., Chgo., 1952. Resident Menninger Sch. Psychiatry, Topeka, Kans., 1953-58; psychiatrist Rip Van Winkle Clinic, Hudson, N.Y., 1958-59; dir. psychiatric edn. Dept. Mental Hygiene, Balt., 1959-61; asst. commr. Md. Dept. Mental Hygiene, Balt., 1961-63; pvt. practice psychiatry Frederick, Md., 1963-70; dir. campus counseling U. Md., Balt., 1970-89; assoc. prof. psychiatry U. Md., 1970-91; pvt. practice psychiatry Ijamsville, Md., 1989-92. Editor Am. Jour. Clin. Hypnosis, 1984-95. Fellow Am. Soc. Clin. Hypnosis (life, sec. 1983-84), Soc. for Clin. and Exptl. Hypnosis, Am. Psychiatric Assn.; mem. Md. Psychiatric Soc. Methodist. Address: 5384 Beulah Dr Ijamsville MD 21754-9604

MOTTER, THOMAS FRANKLIN, medical products executive; b. Modesto, Calif., June 27, 1948; s. Thomas Dean and Beverley June (Mosier) M.; m. Wanda Lenice Parker, Feb. 9, 1968 (div. Jan. 1972); children: Eric Franklin, Katrine Lenice; m. Jerry Ann Averill, Oct. 24, 1976; children: Heidi Marika, Courtney Averill. AA, Cabrillo Jr. Coll., Santa Cruz, Calif., 1968; BA, Stephens Coll., 1970; MBA, Pepperdine U., 1975. Social worker County of Santa Cruz and Amador, 1970-77; nat. dir. mktg. Humphrey Instruments/SmithKline, San Leandro, Calif., 1978-88; internat. gen. mgr. HGM Med. Lasers, Salt Lake City, 1988-89; pres., CEO Paradigm Med. Industries Inc., Salt Lake City, 1989—. V.p. Sandy (Utah) Pony Baseball, 1994-95; coach Kearns (Utah) Am. Legion Basketball, 1995-96. Capt. U.S. Army, 1970-76. Named. Mem. NABA, Am. Legion. Episcopalian. Office: Paradigm Med Industries Inc 1772 W 2300 S Salt Lake City UT 84119

MOTTO, JEROME ARTHUR, psychiatry educator; b. Kansas City, Mo., Oct. 16, 1921. MD, U. Calif., San Francisco, 1951. Diplomate Am. Bd. Neurology and Psychiatry. Intern San Francisco Gen. Hosp., 1951-52; resident Johns Hopkins Hosp., Balt., 1952-55; sr. resident U. Calif., San Francisco, 1955-56, from asst. prof. to prof. emeritus., 1956—. Contbr. articles to profl. jours. With AUS, 1942-46; ETO. Fellow Am. Psychiatric Assn. (life).

MOTULSKY, ARNO GUNTHER, geneticist, physician, educator; b. Fischhausen, Germany, July 5, 1923; came to U.S., 1941; s. Herman and Rena (Sass) Molton; m. Gretel C. Stern, Mar. 22, 1945; children: Judy, Harvey, Arlene. Student, Cen. YMCA Coll., Chgo., 1941-43, Yale U., 1943-44; BS, U. Ill., 1945, MD, 1947, DSc (hon.), 1982, MD (hon.), 1991. Diplomate Am. Bd. Internal Medicine, Am. Bd. Med. Genetics. Intern, fellow, resident Michael Reese Hosp., Chgo., 1947-51; staff mem. charge clin. investigation dept. hematology Army Med. Service Grad. Sch., Walter Reed Army Med. Ctr., Washington, 1952-53; research assoc. internal medicine George Washington U. Sch. Medicine, 1952-53; from instr. to assoc. prof. dept. medicine U. Wash. Sch. Medicine, Seattle, 1953-61, prof. medicine, prof. genetics, 1961—; head div. med. genetics, dir. genetics clinic Univ. Hosp., Seattle, 1959-89; dir. Ctr. for Inherited Diseases, Seattle, 1972-90; attending physician Univ. Hosp., Seattle; cons. Pres.'s Commn. for Study of Ethical Problems in Medicine and Biomed. and Behavioral Research, 1979-83; cons. various coms. NRC, NIH, WHO, others. Editor Am. Jour. Human Genetics, 1969-75, Human Genetics, 1969—. Commonwealth Fund fellow in human genetics Univ. Coll., London, 1957-58; John and Mary Markle scholar in med. sci., 1957-62; fellow Ctr. Advanced Study in Behavioral Scis., Stanford U., 1976-77, Inst. Advanced Study, Berlin, 1984. Fellow ACP, AAAS; mem. NAS, Internat. Soc. Hematology, Am. Fedn. Clin. Research, Genetics Soc. Am., Western Soc. Clin. Research, Am. Soc. Human Genetics, Am. Soc. Clin. Investigation, Am. Assn. Physicians, Inst. of Medicine, Am. Acad. Arts and Scis. Home: 4347 53rd Ave NE Seattle WA 98105-4938 Office: U Wash Divsn Med Genetics Box 356423 Seattle WA 98195-6423

MOTYL, TOMASZ KAZIMIERZ, physiologist, researcher, educator; b. Sobienie Jeziory, Warsaw, Poland, Mar. 4, 1950; s. Henryk and Barbara Jadwiga (Świetochowska) M.; m. Małgorzata Helena Sasinowska-Motyl, Jan. 17, 1976 (div. 1993); 1 child, Marta-Anna. DVM, Vet. Faculty, Warsaw, Poland, 1973, PhD, 1978, habilitation, 1988. Asst. Vet. Faculty Agrl. U., Warsaw, Poland, 1974-78, asst. prof., 1978-88, assoc. prof., 1989-92, prof., 1992—; cons. Nat. Com. for Scientific Rsch., Warsaw, 1994—. Contbr. articles to profl. jours. Served with nat. milit. svc. Recipient group award Acad. Scis., Czechoslovakia, 1981, group award U.S. Detp. Agrl., 1982, Golden Merit cross, 1994. Mem. Polish Hunting Assn., Club of Colectioner & Culture of Hunting. Roman Catholic. Home: Polinezyjska 4/41, 02-777 Warsaw Poland Office: Dep Animal Physiology, Nowoursynowska 166, 02-787 Warsaw Poland

MOTZKIN, DONALD, urologist; b. N.Y.C., Nov. 15, 1932; s. Sam and Shirley (Horowitz) M.; m. Evelyn Herszkorn, Dec. 17, 1955; children: Patricia G., Linda J., Neil E., Nancy E., Richard L., Lisa R. Student, NYU, 1946-49; MD, SUNY, 1956. Intern Mt. Sinai Hosp., N.Y.C., 1956-57; resident in surgery Baylor U., Houston, 1960-61, resident in urology, 1961-64; staff urologist Ross Lars Med. Group, 1964-66; pvt. practice Van Nuys, Calif., 1966—. Flight surgeon USAF, 1957-60. Office: 15211 Vanowen St #208 Van Nuys CA 91405

MOUCHIZADEH, JOSEPH, urologist; b. London, Dec. 19, 1955; s. David and Bertha (Horesh) M. MB BS, U. London, 1979. Diplomate Am. Bd. Urology. Resident in urology U. N.Mex. Albuquerque, 1987-91; urologist Cigna Health Plans (now Friendly Hills Healthcare Network), L.A., 1991-95; clin. attending urologist L.A. County Hosp./U. So. Calif., 1992-95; urologist Friendly Hills Hosp., L.A., 1996—. Office: Friendly Hills Clinic 450 E Huntington Dr Arcadia CA 91024

MOULDER, PETER VINCENT, cardiovascular surgeon, educator; b. Jackson, Mich., Jan. 26, 1921; s. Peter Vincent and Marcella (McDonald) M.; m. Jane Eleanor Lyons, Feb. 9, 1946; children: Mary E. Moulder Jaeger, Peter Vincent III, James T., Jane A. Moulder Kauzlarich. BS magna cum laude, U. Notre Dame, 1942; MD with honors, U. Chgo., 1945; MA (hon.), U. Pa., 1971. Diplomate Am. Bd. Surgery, Am. Bd. Thoracic Surgery. Intern U. Chgo., 1945-46, resident in surgery, 1946-52, 52-53, chief resident in gen. surgery, 1953-54, chief resident thoracic surgery, 1954-55, from instr. to prof. dept. surgery, 1952-68; resident in surgery U. Ill. Rsch. and Ednl. Hosp., Chgo., 1952; prof. dept. surgery U. Pa., Phila., 1968-73, U. Fla., Gainesville, 1973-79; prof. dept. surgery Sch. Medicine, Tulane U., New Orleans, 1980-92, adj. prof. dept. biomed. engring., 1984—; emeritus prof. Tulane U., New Orleans, 1992—; clin. prof. La. State U. Sch. Medicine, 1992—; med. dir. Biosouth Rsch. Labs., 1992—; thoracic surgeon New Orleans Vets. Adminstrn. Hosp., 1992—; cons. cardiovascular surgery Naval Hosp., Great Lakes, Ill., 1955-58; cons. thoracic surgery Cook County Hosp., Chgo., 1966-68, Naval Hosp., Phila., 1969-73; dir. surgery Pa. Hosp., Phila., 1968-72; chief thoracic and cardiovascular surgery VA Hosp., Gainesville, 1973-79; med. investigator VA, 1973-80; mem. editorial bd. Annals of Thoracic Surgery, 1965-68, Chest, 1968-73. Mem. editorial bd. Annals Thoracic Surgery, 1965-68, Surg. Clinics N.Am. New Operations, 1966, Chest, 1968-73; contbr. articles to profl. publs. Lt. (j.g.) USNR, 1942-57, active duty, 1943-48. Recipient Alexander Vishnevsky medal USSR, 1966, Centennial Sci. Honor award U. Notre Dame, 1965, Gold medal Law Sci. Acad., 1968; named to Mil and Hospitaller Order of St. Lazarus, 1990. Mem. AMA, ACS, IEEE, IEEE Soc. Acoustics, Speech and Signal Processing, IEEE Computer Soc., Am. Physiol. Soc., Am. Assn. Thoracic Surgery, Am. Surg. Assn., Am. Soc. Clin. Surgery, Am. Soc. Artificial Internal Organs, Internat. Soc. Artificial Organs, Am. Math. Assn., Am. Coll. Chest Physicians, Am. Coll. Cardiology, Am. Heart Assn., Cen. Surg. Assn., Soc. Clin. Surgery, Soc. Univ. Surgeons, Soc. Thoracic Surgeons, Soc. for Vascular Surgery, Internat. Cardiovascular Soc., So. Thoracic Surg. Assn., Assn. for Computing Machinery and SigBio, Assn. for Advancement Med. Instrumentation, Soc. Critical Care Medicine, Orleans Parish Med. Soc., La. State Med. Soc., Alton Ochsner Surg. Soc., New Orleans Surg. Soc., Surg. Soc. La., Chgo. Surg. Soc., Tulane Surg. Soc. (founder), Chest Club (midwest chpt.), Cardiovascular Surgeons Club, Coll. Physicians Phila., Alpha Omega Alpha. Roman Catholic. Home: 2734 Saint Charles Ave New Orleans LA 70130-5930 also: La State U Sch Medicine Dept Surgery 1542 Tulane Ave New Orleans LA 70112-2822

MOULTON, PAUL RUSH, ophthalmologist; b. Bangor, Maine, May 30, 1958; s. Gardner Nelson and Bonnie Dale (Rush) M.; m. Gabrielle Helen Strunc, May 26, 1984; children: Amanda, Alexander, Julianna. BS in Engring., Duke U., 1980; MD, Tufts U., 1984. Diplomate Am. Bd. Ophthalmology. Intern Meml. Med. Ctr., Corpus Christi, Tex., 1984-85; resident in ophthalmology Greater Balt. Med. Ctr., 1985-88; pvt. practice, Bangor, 1988—. Fellow Am. Acad. Ophthalmology; mem. AMA, New Eng. Ophthal. Soc., Maine Med. Assn., Maine Soc. Eye Physicians and Surgeons, Penobscot County Med. Soc. Office: 5 Grove St Bangor ME 04401-5394

MOUNTAIN, CLIFTON FLETCHER, surgeon, educator; b. Toledo, Apr. 15, 1924; s. Ira Fletcher and Mary (Stone) M.; children: Karen Lockerby, Clifton Fletcher, Jeffrey Richardson. AB, Harvard U., 1947; MD, Boston U., 1954. Diplomate Am. Bd. Surgery. Dir. dept. statis. rsch. Boston U., 1947-50; cons. rsch. analyst Mass. Dept. Pub. Health, 1951-53; intern U. Chgo. Clinics, 1954, resident, 1955-58, instr. surgery, 1958-59; sr. fellow thoracic surgery Houston, 1959; mem. staff M.D. Anderson Hosp. and Tumor Rsch. Inst.; asst. prof. thoracic surgery U. Tex., 1960-63, assoc. prof surgery, 1973-76, prof., 1976-94, prof. emeritus, 1995—, prof. surgery Sch. Medicine, 1987—, chief sect. thoracic surgery, 1970-79, chmn. thoracic oncology, 1979-84, chmn. dept. thoracic surgery, 1980-85, chmn. program in biomath. and computer sci., 1962-64, Mike Hogg vis. lectr. in S.Am., 1967; mem. sci. mission on cancer USSR, 1970-78, and Japan, 1976-84; mem. com. health, rsch. and edn. facilities Houston Cmty. Coun., 1964-78; cons. Am. Joint Com. on Cancer Staging and End Result Reporting, 1964-74, Tex. Heart Inst., 1994—; mem. Am. Joint Com. on Cancer, 1974-86, chmn. lung and esophagus task force; mem. working party on lung cancer and chmn. com. on surgery Nat. Clin. Trials Lung Cancer Study Group, NIH, 1971-76; mem. plans and scope com. cancer therapy Nat. Cancer Inst., 1972-75, mem. lung cancer study group, 1977-89, chmn. steering com., 1973-75, mem. bd. sci. counselors divsn. cancer treatment, 1972-75; hon. cons. Shanghai Chest Hosp. and Lung Cancer Ctr., Nat. Cancer Inst. of Brazil; sr. cons. Houston Thorax Inst., 1994—. Editor The New Physician, 1955-59; mem. editorial bd. Yearbook of Cancer, 1960-88, Internat. Trends in Gen. Thoracic Surgery, 1984-91; contbr. articles to profl. jours., chpts. to textbooks. Chmn. profl. adv. com. Harris County Mental Health Assn.; bd. dirs. Harris County chpt. Am. Cancer Soc. Lt. USNR, 1942-46. Recipient award Soviet Acad. Sci., 1977, Garcia Meml. medal Philippine Coll. Surgeons, 1982, Disting. Alumni award Boston U., 1988, Disting. Achievement U. Tex. M.D. Anderson Cancer Ctr., 1990, Disting. Svc. award Internat. Assn. for the Study of Lung Cancer, 1991, Disting. Alumnus award Boston U. Sch. of Medicine, 1992. Fellow ACS, Am. Coll. Chest Physicians (chmn. com. cancer 1967-75), Am. Assn. Thoracic Surgery, Inst. Environ. Scis., N.Y. Acad. Sci., Assn. Thoracic and Cardiovascular Surgeons of Asia (hon.), Hellenic Cancer Soc. (hon.), Chilean Soc. Respiratory Diseases (hon., hon. pres. 1982); mem. AAAS, Am. Assn. Cancer Rsch., AMA, So. Med. Assn., Am. Thoracic Soc., Soc. Thoracic Surgeons, Soc. Biomed. Computing, Am. Fedn. Clin. Rsch., Internat. Assn. Study Lung Cancer (pres. 1976-78), Am. Radium Soc., Pan-Am. Med. Assn., Houston Surg. Soc., Soc. Surg. Oncology, James Ewing Soc., Sigma Xi. Home: 7932 Prospect Pl La Jolla CA 92037 Office: U Calif Med Ctr Divsn Cardiothoracic Surg 200 W Arbor Dr San Diego CA 92103-8892

MOVAHED, SHAVIAT PANAH, cardiologist; b. Shiraz, Iran, Nov. 15, 1961; came to U.S., 1991; s. Asgary and Narjes (Binesh) Movahed Shavirat Panahi. Degree with honors, Johannes Gutenberg U., Mainz, Germany, 1982; MD with highest honors, Hannover (Germany) Med. Sch., 1989; diploma cmty. health/tropical medicine, Berlin, 1990. Resident in medicine Siloah Hosp., Hannover, 1989, Weser Hosp., Hannover, 1991; resident in pathology U. Rochester (N.Y.) Med. Ctr., 1992, resident in medicine, 1993—; rschr. in field; tchg. asst. Hannover Med. Sch., 1985-88, Siloah and Hameln Nursing Schs., 1988, 89; tchg. asst. in pathology U. Rochester, Strong Meml. Hosp., 1992. Wind surfing instr., Italy. Recipient Internat. Exch. award Ulster County C.C., 1992; scholar, Innsbruck, Austria, 1985, Tufts Med. Sch., 1986, Plymouth, Eng., 1987, Berlin, 1990. Mem. ACP, AAAS, Am. Coll. Clin. Pathology. Office: U SC Sch of Medicine Dept of Medicine 2 Medical Pk Ste 501 Columbia SC 29203

MOWBRAY, CAROL BEATRICE THIESSEN, mental health researcher, social work educator; b. Boston, Aug. 20, 1948; d. Peter Isaac and Jessamine Beatrice (Olpin) Thiessen; m. Charles Sherman Mowbray, June 1, 1970; children: Orion, Nicholas. BS, Tufts U., 1970, MS, 1971; PhD, U. Mich., 1975. Lectr. dept. psychology Mich. State U., East Lansing, 1974-75; social rsch. analyst Mich. Dept. Mental Health, Lansing, 1975-76, dir. spl. analytical studies, 1976-77, exec. asst. to dir., 1977-78, dir., program and grants coord., 1978-80, dir. rsch., evaluation and demonstration, 1980-90; assoc. prof. social work Wayne State U., Detroit, 1990-94; assoc. prof. social work U. Mich., Ann Arbor, 1994—, assoc. dir. Risk Poverty and Mental Health Rsch. Ctr., 1995—, assoc. dean rsch., 1996—; cons. grant rev. NIMH, Rockville, Md., 1981—. Author: Women and Mental Health, 1984; mem. editorial bd. Evaluation and Program Planning, Psychiat. Rehab. Jour.; consulting editor: SW Rsch.; contbr. articles to profl. jours. Rsch. grantee dual diagnosis NIMH, 1989-95, supported edn. grantee Substance Abuse-Mental Health Svcs. Adminstrn., 1992—, mentally ill mothers grantee NIMH, 1994—. Fellow APA (sect. chmn. 1990-92, Disting. Svc. award div. 18 1988); mem. NASW, Internat. Assn. Psychosocial Rehab. Svcs. (rsch. com. 1994—), Am. Evaluation Assn., Midwest Psychol. Assn. Home: 5460 Prairie Vw Brighton MI 48116-7715 Office: U Mich Sch Social Work 1065 Frieze Bldg Ann Arbor MI 48109-1285

MOWRY, ROBERT WILBUR, pathologist, educator; b. Griffin, Ga., Jan. 10, 1923; s. Roy Burnell and Mary Frances (Swilling) M.; m. Margaret Neilson Black, June 11, 1949; children: Janet Lee, Robert Gordon, Barbara Ann. B.S., Birmingham So. Coll., 1944; M.D., Johns Hopkins U., 1946. Rotating intern U. Ala. Med. Coll., 1946-47, resident pathology, 1947-48; sr. asst. surgeon USPHS-NIH, Bethesda, Md., 1948-52; fellow pathology Boston City Hosp., 1949-50; asst. prof. pathology Washington U., St. Louis, 1952-53; asst. prof. pathology U. Ala. Med. Ctr., Birmingham, 1953-54, assoc. prof. pathology, 1954-57; prof. U. Ala. Med. Center, Birmingham, 1958-89, prof. emeritus, 1989—, prof. health svcs. adminstrn., 1976-84, dir. Anat. Pathology Lab., 1960-64, dir. grad. programs in pathology, 1964-72; sr. scientist U. Ala. Inst. Dental Research, 1967-72, dir. autopsy services, 1975-79; vis. scholar dept. pathology U. Cambridge, Eng., 1972-73; cons. FDA, 1975-81. Author: (with J.F.A. McManus) Staining Methods: Histologic and Histochemical, 1960; mem. editorial bd. Jour. Histochemistry and Cytochemistry, 1960-75, Stain Tech., 1965-90, AMA Archives of Pathology, 1967-76, Biotechnics and Histochemistry, 1991—. Served with USPHS, 1948-52. Mem. Am. Soc. Investigative Pathology, Internat. Acad. Pathology, Biol. Stain Commn. (v.p. 1974-76, pres. 1976-81, trustee 1966—), Soc. for Glycobiology, Am. Assn. Univ. Profs. Pathology, Phi Beta Kappa, Sigma Xi, Delta Sigma Phi, Alpha Kappa Kappa. Presbyterian. Home: 4165 Sharpsburg Dr Birmingham AL 35213-3234

MOXLEY, JOHN HOWARD, III, physician; b. Elizabeth, N.J., Jan. 10, 1935; s. John Howard, Jr. and Cleopatra (Mundy) M.; m. Doris Banchik; children: John Howard IV, Brook, Mark. BA, Williams Coll., 1957; MD, U. Colo., 1961; DSc (hon.), Sch. Medicine Hannemann U. Bar: Diplomate Am. Bd. Internal Medicine. Intern Peter Bent Brigham Hosp., Boston, 1961-62, resident in internal medicine, 1962-66; with Nat. Cancer Inst., USPHS, 1963-65; asst. to dean, instr. medicine Harvard Med. Sch., Boston, 1966-69; dean Sch. Medicine, U. Md., 1969-73; vice chancellor health scis., dean Med. Sch., U. Calif.-San Diego, 1973-79; asst. sec. for health affairs Dept. Def., Washington, 1979-81; sr. v.p. Am. Med. Internat., Beverly Hills, Calif., 1981-87; pres. MetaMed. Inc., Playa Del Rey, Calif., 1987-89; mgr. dir. Korn/Ferry Internat., L.A., 1989—; cons. FDA, NIH; dir. Nat. Fund for Med. Edn., 1986—, chmn., 1993—; dir. Henry M. Jackson Found. for Adv. Mil. Medicine. Contbr. articles to profl. jours. Dir. Polyclinic Health Svcs. Games of XXIII Olympiad. Recipient gold and silver award U. Colo. Med. Sch., 1974, commr.'s citation for outstanding svc. to over-the-counter drug study FDA, 1977, spl. achievement citation Am. Hosp. Assn., 1983, Sec. of Def. medal for disting. pub. svc., 1981. Fellow ACP, Am. Coll. Physicians Execs. (Disting.); mem. Inst. Medicine NAS, AMA (chmn. coun. sci. affairs 1985), Calif. Med. Assn. (chmn. sci. bd. 1978-83, councilor), San Diego C. of C., Soc. Med. Adminstrs., Am. Hosp. Assn. (trustee 1979-81), Alpha Omega Alpha. Rotary. Office: Korn/Ferry Internat 1800 Century Park E Ste 900 Los Angeles CA 90067-1512

MOY, SAMUEL YEW, psychologist; b. N.Y.C., July 27, 1959; s. Danny Ging Yui and Yen Hay (Eng) M.; m. Shirley Eng, May 24, 1980; children: Lauren, Karyn, Daniel, Katherine. BA, King's Coll., 1980; MA, Fuller Sem., 1986, PhD, 1987. Lic. psychologist, N.Y., Conn. Staff psychologist Klingberg Family Ctrs., New Britain, Conn., 1987-90; v.p. PATH, P.C., West Hartford, Conn., 1990-94, pres., 1995—; v.p. Pathwise Behavioral Health, Farmington, Conn., 1993—; cons. Dept. Children and Family, Hartford, Conn., 1989-91, New Opportunities of Waterbury, Conn., 1989-93. Pres. bd. dirs. Covenant to Care, Bloomfield, Conn., 1990-93. Mem. Am. Psychol. Assn., Conn. Psychol. Assn. Office: PATH, PC 970 Farmington Ave West Hartford CT 06107

MOYER, DONALD ANTHONY, physician assistant; b. Lebanon, Pa., Jan. 20, 1954; s. Myles Victor and Beatrice Sevilla (Artz) M.; m. Aleta Ann Lynch, Nov. 28, 1980; 1 child, Heather Ann. Assocs. in Clin. Health Scis., Pa. State U./Hershey Med. Ctr., 1981. Cert. physician asst., Pa. Physician asst. Fredericksburg (Pa.) Comm. Health Ctr., 1981-82, Charles Schlaher MD and Assocs., York, Pa., 1983, Harrisburg (Pa.)Reproductive Health Svcs., 1984, Lebanon (Pa.) Surg. Assocs., 1984—. Councilman Cornwall (Pa.) Borough Coun., 1994—; mem. Cornwall Borough Bd. of Health, 1992—; mem., past pres. Ind. First Aid Unit, Lebanon, 1969-79. With USN, 1971-75. Fellow Am. Acad. Physician Assts., Pa. Acad. Physician Assts. Republican. Methodist. Home: 125 Hillside St Lebanon PA 17042 Office: Lebanon Surgical Assocs South 4th at Hathaway Pk Lebanon PA 17042

MOYER, JOHN HENRY, III, physician, educator; b. Hershey, Pa., Apr. 1, 1917; s. John Henry and Anna Mae (Gruber) M.; m. Mary Elizabeth Hughes; children: John Henry IV, Michael, Carl, Anna Mary, Nancy Elizabeth, Mary Louise, Matthew Timothy. BS, Lebanon Valley Coll., 1939, DSc (hon.), 1968; MD, U. Pa., 1943. Diplomate Am. Bd. Internal Medicine, Nat. Bd. Med. Examiners; lic. physician Mass., Pa., Tex. Intern Pa. Hosp., Phila., 1943; resident in Tb and contagious diseases Belmont Hosp., Worcester, Mass., 1944-45; asst. instr. Tb and contagious diseases U. Vt., 1944-45; chief resident in medicine Brooke Gen. Hosp., San Antonio, 1947; fellow in pharmacology and medicine Sch. Medicine, U. Pa., Phila., 1948-50; attending physician, then. sr. attending physician Jefferson Davis Hosp., Houston, 1950-57, Meth. Hosp., Houston, 1950-57; from asst. prof. to prof. internal medicine and pharmacology Coll. Medicine, Baylor U., Houston, 1950-56, prof., 1956-57; prof., chmn. dept. medicine Hahnemann Med. Coll. and Hosp., Phila., 1957-74, exec. v.p. acad. affairs, 1971-73; sr. v.p., dir. profl. and ednl. affairs Conemaugh Valley Meml. Hosp., Johnstown, Pa., 1974-88; emeritus dir. profl. and ednl. affairs Conemaugh Valley Meml. Hosp., Johnstown, 1988—; prof. Temple U., 1977—; dir. regional affairs Sch. Medicine Temple U., 1977-88; clin. prof. Coll. Medicine Pa. State U., Hershey, 1976—; adj. prof. natural scis. U. Pitts., Johnstown, 1982-88; adj. prof. physician asst. sci. St. Francis Coll., 1983-88, sr. cons. physician asst. program adv. com., 1985-88; vis. prof., lectr. various ednl. instns.; mem. Pa. State Bd. Med. Edn. and Licensure, 1977-86, sec. to bd., 1982-86; mem. task force on profl. edn., mem. hypertension info. and edn. adv. com. U.S. HEW, 1972-75; chmn. high blood pressure control adv. bd. to sec. health State of Pa., 1980-86; cons. numerous profl. orgns. Editorial cons. Am. Jour. Cardiology, 1960-72; editor-in-chief Cyclopedia of Medicine, Surgery and Specialties, 1963-65; mem. editorial adv. bd. Internal Medicine News, 1969-92; editor 16 multi-authored textbooks; contbr. more than 600 articles to profl. jours. Mem. bd. trustees Pa. Heart Assn., 1959-65, v.p. bd. trustees, 1965; mem. bd. govs. Heart Assn. Southeastern Pa., 1958-64, 67-72; bd. dirs. Houston Heart Assn., 1952-57; mem., then emeritus fellow med. adv. bd. coun. for high blood pressure Am. Heart Assn., 1954—, chmn., 1964-65, mem., then emeritus fellow cen. adv. bd. coun. on circulation; deacon, Salem United Ch. of Christ. Maj. U.S. Army, 1945-48. Recipient Susan and Theodora R. Cummings Humanitarian award, 1962, 65, 66, Presdl. citation Cultural Exchg. Program, U.S. State Dept., 1964, Honors Achievement award Angiology Rsch. Found., 1965; named Alumni of Yr., Lebanon Valley Coll., Annville, Pa., 1967. Fellow ACP (Laureate award for Western Pa. 1986), Am. Coll. Cardiology (trustee 1961-68), N.Y. Acad. Scis. (emeritus), Am. Coll. Chest Physicians (emeritus); mem. AMA (emeritus, mem. ho. dels. 1966-72, cons. coun. on drugs 1968-72, mem. sect. coun. on clin. pharmacology and therapeutics), AAAS (emeritus), Am. Soc. Clin. Pharmacology and Therapeutics (emeritus dir., hon. dir.), Am. Fedn. Clin. Rsch. (emeritus), Am. Soc. Pharmacology and Exptl. Therapeutics (emeritus), Assn. Am. Med. Colls., Am. Acad. Med. Dirs., Am. Soc. Internal Medicine, Pa. Soc. Internal Medicine (pres. 1992-94, Pressman award for lifetime of contbns. and commitment to internal medicine 1996), Sems. and Symposia (pres.), Assn. Hosp. Med. Edn., Assn. Former Chmn. Medicine, U.S. Pharmacopaeia Convention (pres. 1970-75, bd. trustees 1970-80), Sigma Xi, many others. Republican. Address: 1090 Miller Rd Palmyra PA 17078-9602

MOYERS, SYLVIA DEAN, retired medical record librarian; b. Independence, W.Va., Oct. 22, 1936; d. Wilkie Russell and Ina Laura (Watkins) Collins; m. Paul Franklin Moyers, June 29, 1957; children: Tammy Jeanne, Thomas Paul, Tara Sue. Student, Am. Med. Record Assn., 1977-79. Sec., Teets Lumber Co., Terra Alta, W.Va., 1954-58, Preston County News, Terra Alta, 1958-60; med. record clk. med. record dept. Hopemont (W.Va.) Hosp., 1960-75, dir., 1975-88; sec. The Terra Alta Bank, W.Va., 1990-95; ret., 1995. Charter mem., past mother advisor Terra Alta Assembly No. 26, Order of Rainbow for Girls, past grand editor Mountain Echoes. Republican. Methodist. Home: RR 2 Box 273-e Albright WV 26519-9753

MOYLAN, DAVID JOHN, III, radiation oncologist, educator; b. Phila., Nov. 28, 1951; s. David John Jr. and Virginia (Hippenstiel) M.; children: Matthew, Elizabeth Anne, Tara Patricia, Lauren Victoria. SB, MIT, 1973; MD, Georgetown U., 1977. Intern Bryn Mawr (Pa.) Hosp., 1977-78, resident in internal medicine, 1978-79; resident in radiation oncology Thomas Jefferson U. Hosp., Phila., 1979-82; asst. prof. Jefferson Med. Coll., Phila., 1982-85, Pa. State Hershey Med. Sch., 1986—; med. dir. Schuylkill Cancer

Treatment Ctr., Pottsville, Pa., 1985—, Mahoning Valley Cancer Ctr., Lehighton, Pa., 1988—. Mem. Am. Soc. Therapeutic Radiology and Oncology (mem.-at-large, bd. dirs. 1991-94), Am. Soc. Clin. Oncology, Radiation Rsch. Soc. Office: Schuylkill Cancer Treatment Ctr One Norwegian Plz Pottsville PA 17901-3056

MOYLAN, JAY RICHARD, medical products executive; b. Greenfield, Mass., Dec. 20, 1950; s. Richard J. and Margaret M. (McCarthy) M.; m. Sharon J. Slater, June 18, 1976; children: Jaimee, Shauna. AA in Liberal Arts, Greenfield Community Coll., 1972; AS in Respiratory Therapy, Springfield Tech. Community C., 1975; BS in Health Care Mgmt., U. Mass., 1983. Staff respiratory therapist Mercy Hosp., Springfield, Mass., 1973-74; respiratory therapy supr. Brattleboro (Vt.) Meml. Hosp., 1974-75; dir. cardiopulmonary svc. Farren Meml. Hosp., Turners Falls, Mass., 1975-83; cardiopulmonary sales rep. Erich Jeager, Inc., Rockford, Ill., 1983-85; cardiovascular sales rep. Electro Catheter Corp., Rahway, N.J., 1985-86; cardiopulmonary sales specialist Sensor Medics Corp., Yorba Linda, Calif., 1986-95; regional sales mgr. OmniCell Technologies, Inc., Palo Alto, Calif., 1995—; chmn. Coun. Pulmonary Svc. Mgrs., Springfield, 1980-81. Chmn. Cath. Stewardship Appeal Holy Trinity Parish, Greenfield, 1989; bd. dirs. cen. Mass. chpt. Am. Lung Assn., 1981-83; treas. FMH Credit Union, 1980-83; councilor Mass. Thoracic Soc., 1995—. Recipient Achievement award Mass. Soc. Respiratory Care, 1989. Mem. Coun. Pulmonary Svc. Mgrs. (Lifetime Mem. award), Am. Coll. Sports Medicine, Am. Assn. Respiratory Care (registered, rev. com. 1991), Am. Registry Diagnostic Med. Sonographers (registered), Nat. Bd. Respiratory Care (cert.), Nat. Soc. Cardiopulmonary Tech. (cert.), Mass. Thoracic Soc., Mass. Lung Assn., New Eng. Soc. for Healthcare Materials Mgmt. Home: 53 Meadow Ln Greenfield MA 01301-9703

MOZEN, PAUL H., internist; b. Cleve., May 29, 1954; s. Herschel E. and Eleanor (Roth) M.; 1 child, Elena. BS with honors, Grand Valley State U., Allendale, Mich., 1978; DO, U. Health Scis., Kansas City, Mo., 1982. Diplomate Am. Bd. Internal Medicine; lic. physician, Mich., Nev. Intern Botsford Gen. Hosp., Farmington Hills, Mich., 1984-87; internal medicine resident U. Nev., Reno, 1987; pvt. practice Sparks, Nev., 1987—; staff Washoe Med. Ctr., Sparks Family Hosp., chmn. dept. medicine; staff St. Mary's Hosp.; adj. clin. instr. U. Nev., 1985; med. dir. Vital Care of Nev. Mem. AMA, ACP, Am. Osteo. Assn., Washoe County Med. Soc., Nev. Med. Assn. Office: 2385 E Prater Way #309 Sparks NV 89434

MOZENA, JOHN DANIEL, podiatrist; b. Salem, Oreg., June 9, 1956; s. Joseph Iner and Mary Teresa (Delaney) M.; m. Elizabeth Ann Hintz, June 2, 1979; children: Christine Hintz, Michelle Delaney. Student, U. Oreg., 1974-79; B in Basic Med. Scis., Calif. Coll. Podiatric Medicine, D in Podiatric Medicine, 1983. Diplomate Am. Bd. Podiatric Surgery. Resident in surg. podiatry Hillside Hosp., San Diego, 1983-84; pvt. practice podiatry Portland, Oreg., 1984—; dir. residency Med. Ctr. Hosp., Portland, 1985-91; lectr. Nat. Podiatric Assn. Seminar, 1990, Am. Coll. Gen. Practitioners, 1991, Am. Coll. Family Physician, 1995. Cons. editor Podiatry Mgmt. mag., 1994—; contbr. articles to profl. jours.; patentee sports shoe cleat design, 1985. Podiatric adv. coun. Oreg. Bd. Med. Examiners. Fellow Am Coll. Ambulatory Foot Surgeons, Am. Coll. Foot Surgeons. Republican. Roman Catholic. Office: Town Ctr Foot Clinic 8305 SE Monterey Ave Ste 101 Portland OR 97266-7728

MOZES, MARTIN FRED, surgeon; b. Warsaw, Poland, Oct. 22, 1939; came to U.S., 1968; s. Mark and Anna (Engel) M.; m. Chava Faibish, Dec. 16, 1968; children: Jonathan, Karee. MD, Hebrew U., Jerusalem, 1966. Diplomate Am. Bd. Surgery. Intern Tel Hashomer Hosp., Israel, 1964-65; resident U. Minn. Hosp., Mpls., 1968-74; prof. surgery U. Ill., Chgo., 1988; dir. Multiorgan Transplant Ctr., Henry Ford Hosp., Detroit, 1988—. Contbr. over 100 articles to med. jours. Lt. M.C., Israeli Def. Forces, 1964-67. Jewish.

MOZLEY, P(AUL) DAVID, JR., neuropsychiatrist, educator; b. Calif., Mar. 5, 1957; s. Paul D. and Doris (Neill) M.; m. Lyn Harper, Feb. 25, 1989. BS in Phys. Chemistry, Coll. William and Mary, 1980; MD, East Carolina U., 1984. Diplomate Am. Bd. Nuclear Medicine. Intern Jefferson Med. Coll., Thomas Jefferson U., Phila., 1984-85; resident in psychiatry U. Pa., Phila., 1985-88; rsch. fellow in neuropsychiatry U. Pa., 1987-89, rsch. fellow in nuclear medicine, 1989-91. Mem. AMA, Am. Psychiat. Assn., Soc. Nuclear Medicine. Mem. Ch. of Christ. Office: Hosp Univ Pa 110 Donner Bldg Philadelphia PA 19104-4211

MOZO, WILLIAM BRANTLY, JR., dentist; b. Cheyenne, Wyo., Jan. 9, 1950; s. William Brantly and Naomi Ruth (Berry) M.; D.D.S., U. Mo., 1975; m. Elizabeth Faria, June 27, 1976; children—Adam, Jason, Rebecca. Resident, Englewood (N.J.) Hosp., 1975-76; pvt. practice dentistry, South Plainfield, N.J., 1976—; mem. staff Muhlenberg Hosp., Rahway Hosp.; pres. Mozo Enterprises; instr. oral pathology Middlesex County Coll., 1978. Chmn. dental div. United Way, 1977-81. Mem. Am., N.J., Central dental socs., Acad. Gen. Dentistry, Warren Jaycees. Methodist. Club: South Plainfield Rotary. Home: 9 Claire Dr Warren NJ 07059-6805 Office: 1550 Park Ave S Plainfield NJ 07080

MOZZONE, KEITH CHARLES, chemist; b. Springfield, Pa., Aug. 31, 1962; s. Charles John and Barbara Jane (Heller) M.; m. Karen Louise Heimbach, June 14, 1986; children: Kristina Marie, Kurt Charles. BS in Chemistry magna cum laude, West Chester U., 1994. Lab. asst. Wyeth Labs., Radnor, Pa., 1986-87; lab. technician Rorer Ctrl. Rsch., Ft. Washington, Pa., 1987-88, sr. lab. technician, 1988-94; asst. scientist Rhone-Poulenc Rorer Pharm., Collegeville, Pa., 1994—. Co-patentee in field. Mem. Internat. Soc. for Pharm. Engring., Parenteral Drug Assn., Pi Gamma Mu. Methodist. Home: 160 Bayberry Dr Limerick PA 19468

MRAK, ROBERT EMIL, neuropathologist, educator, electron microscopist; b. Oakland, Calif., Dec. 18, 1948; s. Emil Marcel and Vera Dudley (Greaves) M.; m. Paula Elizabeth North, Oct. 18, 1980; children: Lara North, Eric North, Ian North. BS in Math., U. Calif., Davis, 1970, MD, 1975, PhD in Zoology, 1976. Diplomate Am. Bd. Pathology, Am. Bd. Neuropathology. Resident in pathology Vanderbilt U. Hosp., Nashville, 1976-78, fellow in molecular biology, 1978-80; asst. prof. pathology Vanderbilt U., 1980-84; asst. prof. pathology U. Ark. for Med. Scis., Little Rock, 1984-87, assoc. prof. pathology and anatomy, 1987-93, prof. pathology and anatomy, 1993—; chief electron microscopy VA Hosp., Little Rock, 1984—; cons. in neuropathology Ark. Children's Hosp., Little Rock, 1984—. Editor, author: Muscle Membranes in Diseases of Muscle, 1985; contbr. articles and abstracts to profl. jours. Rsch. grantee VA, 1980-83, Muscular Dystrophy Assn., 1981-85, NIH, 1986-90, 95—. Mem. Am. Assn. Neuropathologists, Soc. for Neurosci., U.S. and Can. Acad. Pathology. Office: U Ark for Med Scis 4301 W Markham St Little Rock AR 72205-7101

MRAZEK, DAVID ALLEN, pediatric psychiatrist; b. Ft. Riley, Kans., Oct. 1, 1947; s. Rudolph George and Hazel Ruth (Schayes) M.; m. Patricia Jean, Sept. 2, 1978; children: Nicola, Matthew, Michael, Alissa. AB in Genetics, Cornell U., 1969; MD, Bowman Gray Sch. Medicine, 1973. Lic. psychiatrist, child psychiatrist, N.C., Ohio, Colo., D.C., Va., Md.; med. lic. N.C., Ohio, D.C., Va., Md. Lectr. child psychiatry Inst. of Psychiatry, London, 1977-79; dir. pediatric psychiatry Nat. Jewish Ctr. for Immunology and Respiratory Medicine, Denver, 1979-91; chmn. psychiatry Childrens Nat. Med. Ctr., Washington, 1991—; acting chair psychiatry and behavioral scis. George Washington U. Sch. medicine, 1996—; dir. Children's Rsch. Inst. Neurosci., 1995—; asst. prof. psychiatry U. Colo. Sch. Medicine, 1979-83, assoc. prof. psychiatry and pediatrics, 1984-89, prof., 1990-91; prof. psychiatry and pediatrics George Washington U. Sch. Medicine, 1991—. Contbr. articles and book chpts. on child devel. and asthma to profl. publs. Recipient Rsch. Scientist Devel. awards NIMH, 1983-88, 88-91. Fellow Am. Acad. Child Psychiatry, Royal Soc. Medicine, Am. Psychiat. Assn. (Blanche F. Ittleson award 1996), Royal Coll. Psychiatrists; mem. Am. Coll. Psychiatrists, Group for the Advancement of Psychiatry, Colo. Child and Adolescent Psychiatry Soc. (pres. 1984). Office: Childrens Nat Med Ctr Psychiatry Dept 111 Michigan Ave NW Washington DC 20010-2970

MROCZEK, WILLIAM JOSEPH, research physician; b. N.Y.C., Aug. 9, 1940; s. William and Helena (Federowicz) M.; B.A., Seton Hall U., 1962; M.D., N.J. Coll. Medicine, 1966; m. Christine Landegger, Apr. 7, 1979; children: Ashley Elizabeth, Natasha Elena, Phoebe Victoria, Matthew Alexander; children by previous marriage—Michelle Anne, Melissa Lynn. Intern, St. Michael Hosp., Newark, 1966-67; resident Georgetown U. med. div. D.C. Gen. Hosp., 1967-69; fellow in cardiovascular disease Georgetown U. Sch. Medicine, 1969-70, asst. prof. medicine, 1972-77; chief dept. hosp. clinics Ft. Campbell, Ky., 1970-72; assoc. prof. medicine Howard U., Washington, 1977-82; dir. hypertension and hemodynamics lab. D.C. Gen. Hosp., 1972-82. Pres. No. Va. chpt. Am. Heart Assn., 1983-84; dir. Cardiovascular Ctr. No. Va., 1983—; mem. exec. com. Jefferson Hosp., Alexandria, Va. Served to maj. U.S. Army, 1970-72. Diplomate Am. Bd. Internal Medicine. Fellow Am. Coll. Cardiology, Am. Coll. Clin. Pharmacology, Am. Coll. Angiology, Am. Coll. Geriatrics, Am. Coll. Clin. Pharmacology (bd. regents); mem. Internat. Soc. Hypertension, Am. Soc. Hypertension, Am. Fedn. Clin. Research, Am. Soc. Nephrology, Am. Soc. Clin. Pharmacology and Therapeutics, Nat. Kidney Found., N.Y. Acad. Scis., AMA. Contbr. numerous articles to med. jours. Office: 6043 Arlington Blvd Falls Church VA 22044-2721

MUCHMORE, JOHN STEPHEN, endocrinologist; b. L.A., Jan. 1, 1945; s. Allan Winner and Lyntha Carol (Weed) M.; m. Susan Jill Crawford, June 13, 1968; children: Adam Ian, Rachel Kathleen. AB, Knox Coll., 1967; MD, U. Okla., 1975; PhD in Pharm. and Toxicology, U. Rochester, 1976. Diplomate AM. Bd. Internal Medicine in endocrinology and metabolism. Intern U. Okla. Health Sci. Ctr., 1975-76, resident in medicine, 1976-78, fellow endocrinology, metabolism and hypertension, 1978-80; Pvt. practice Oklahoma City, 1980—; cardiac transplant physician Okla. Transplantation Inst., Bapt. Med. Ctr. of Okla., Oklahoma City, 1989-93; med. dir. Info. Sys. Integris Health, Oklahoma City, 1993—. Recipient Nat. Rsch. Svc. award Nat. Heart, Lung and Blood Inst., Bethesda, Md., 1978. Mem. AMA, AAAS, Am. Coll. Physicians, Alpha Omega Alpha. Office: Plaza Med Assocs 3433 NW 56th St Oklahoma City OK 73112-4444

MUCHNICK, RICHARD STUART, ophthalmologist; b. Bklyn., June 21, 1942; s. Max and Rae (Kozinsky) M.; BA with honors. Cornell U., 1963, MD, 1967; m. Felice Dee Greenberg, Oct. 29, 1978; 1 child, Amanda Michelle. Intern in medicine N.Y. Hosp., N.Y.C., 1967-68, now assoc. attending ophthalmologist, chief Pediatric Ophthalmology Clinic; resident in ophthalmology, 1970-73; practice medicine, specializing in ophthalmology, notably strabismus and ophthalmic plastic surgery N.Y.C., 1974—; attending surgeon, chief Ocular Motility Clinic, Manhattan Eye, Ear and Throat Hosp., N.Y.C.; clin. assoc. prof. ophthalmology Cornell U., N.Y.C., 1984—. Served with USPHS, 1968-70. Recipient Coryell Prize Surgery Cornell U. Med. Coll., 1967. Diplomate Am. Bd. Ophthalmology, Nat. Bd. Med. Examiners. Fellow A.C.S., Am. Acad. Ophthalmology; mem. Am. Soc. Ophthalmic Plastic and Reconstructive Surgery, Am. Assn. Pediatric Ophthalmology and Strabismus, Internat. Strabismological Assn., N.Y. Soc. Clin. Ophthalmology, AMA, N.Y. Acad. Medicine, Manhattan Ophthal. Soc., N.Y. Soc. Pediatric Ophthalmology and Strabismus, Alpha Omega Alpha, Alpha Epsilon Delta. Clubs: Lotos, 7th Regt. Tennis. Clin. researcher strabismus, ophthalmic plastic surgery, 1973—. Office: 69 E 71st St New York NY 10021-4213

MUCKER, MICHAEL PAUL, optometrist; b. Windber, Pa., Feb. 11, 1959; s. Paul James and Carole Lena (Franchic) M. BS, U. Pitts. at Johnstown, 1981; BS, OD, Pa. Coll., 1985; OD. Optometrist Sears Optical, Johnstown, Pa., 1986-91; optometrist, owner Johnstown Family Vision, 1991—. Mem. Am. Optometric Assn., Pa. Optometic Assn., Southwestern Pa. Optometric Soc. (v.p. 1989-91, pres. 1991-93). Office: Johnstown Family Vision 1513 Scalp Ave Johnstown PA 15904

MUCKLE, DAVID SUTHERLAND, surgeon, educator; b. Weardale, Durham, Eng., Aug. 30, 1939; s. John L. and Ruth J. (Sutherland) M.; m. Christine Haymonds; children: Carolyn Jane, Deborah Christine. B.Med., U. Durham, 1963, B.Surgery, 1963, M.D., 1981, M.Surgery, 1971. Surgeon, Oxford, 1970-77, South Cleveland Hosp., 1977—; cons. orthopedic surgeon, 1977—; med. advisor Fédération Internationale de Football Assn., Switzerland, 1977—; surgeon, dep. chmn. med. com. Football Assn., 1983—; surgeon Nuffield Hosp., Cleveland, 1981—; med. com. Union Des Assns. Européennes de Football, 1990—, Switzerland; vis. prof. U. Teesside, 1994—. Author: Femoral Neck Fracture, 1977; Injuries in Sport, 1982; An Outline of Fractures, 1985; An Outline of Orthopaedic Practice, 1986. Recipient Championship medal European Nations Cup Final, 1992. Fellow Brit. Orthopedic Assn. (rsch. scholarship com. 1990—), Brit. Orthopedic Rsch. (com. mem. 1979, Pres. Orthopedic Rsch. prize 1973), Royal Coll. Surgeons (Eng. and Edinburgh). Avocations: writing, natural history, poetry, all sports. Home: Redcroft 72 The Grove, Marton Middlesbrough TS7 8AJ, England Office: Middlesbrough Gen Hosp, Ward 14, Middlesbrough TS5 5AZ, England

MUDER, ROBERT RICHARD, physician, epidemiologist; b. Pitts., June 11, 1951; s. Richard Edward and Gemma (Lombardi) M.; m. Janet D. Vlha, June 4, 1977 (div. 1993); children: Jane Elizabeth, Michael Richard. BA, Oberlin (Ohio) Coll., 1973; MD, U. Pitts., 1977. Diplomate Am. Bd. Internal Medicine. Intern, then resident in medicine Mercy Hosp., Pitts., 1977-81, asst. coord. med. edn., 1983-84, coord. med. edn., 1984-86, assoc. program dir., 1986-89, fellow in infectious disease, 1981-83; asst. prof. medicine U. Pitts., 1989-94, assoc. prof., 1994—; chief infection control Pitts. VA Med. Ctr., 1986—. Sect. editor Infectious Disease Alert; contbr. articles to profl. jours. Mem. ACP, Am. Soc. for Microbiology, Infectious Diseases Soc. Am., Soc. for Hosp. Epidemiology Am., Phi Beta Kappa, Alpha Omega Alpha. Office: Pitts VA Med Ctr University Dr # C Pittsburgh PA 15213

MUEHLBAUER, PETER FRANKLIN, cardiologist, composer; b. N.Y.C., Aug. 14, 1939; s. Mendel Aaron and Shela (Klusner) M.; m. Barbara Lee Freedman, June 30, 1962 (div. May 1983); children: Matthew Steven, Lauren Suzanne; m. Judith Dorothy Silver, June 5, 1983; 1 step-child, Lisa Philippa Orazietti. AB, Columbia U., 1959, MD, 1963. Diplomate Am. Bd. Internal Medicine, Am. Bd. Cardiovascular Disease. Intern, Jewish Hosp. and Med. Ctr. Bklyn., 1963-64, resident in medicine, 1964-65; resident in medicine and cardiology Montefiore Hosp. and Med. Ctr., Bronx, N.Y., 1967-70; pvt. practice medicine specializing in cardiology, Bronx, 1970-71, White Plains, N.Y., 1971—; chief cardiology Lincoln Hosp., Bronx, 1970-71; mem. staff White Plains Hosp. and Med. Ctr., N.Y., Montefiore Hosp. and Med. Ctr., Bronx, 1970-92; clin. instr. medicine Albert Einstein Coll. Medicine, Bronx, 1970-75. Contbr. articles to med. jours., 1965, 67. Composer: Toccata for Piano, 1981; Pentatoot, 1981; String Quartet #1, 1982; Piano Fantasie, 1984. Served as capt. USAF, 1965-67. Fellow Council Clin. Cardiology of Am. Heart Assn., Am. Coll. Cardiology; mem. ASCAP, N.Y. State Med. Soc., Westchester County Med. Soc. Jewish. Home: 95 Marcourt Dr Chappaqua NY 10514-2506 Office: 44 N Broadway White Plains NY 10603-3736

MUELLEGGER, ROBERT RUDOLF, dermatologist, researcher; b. Graz, Styria, Austria, May 22, 1962; s. Robert and Erika (Picili) M.; m. Andrea Irene Sticher, July 1, 1995; 1 child, Antonia. MD, Karl-Franzens-U., Graz, 1989. Cert. clin. examiner for medications. Intern ear nose throat ward Hosp. Krankenhaus der Elisabethinen, Graz, 1990; intern internal medicine ward, neurologic ward Hosp. Krankenhaus der Barmherzigen Brüder, Graz, 1991-92; intern dept. ob-gyn. surg. ward Provincial Hosp. Graz, 1992-93; resident Dept. Dermatology, Graz, 1993—; MD ind. rsch. work Dept. Pediats., Graz, 1989-93, MD lectrs. on borreliosis and bacterial diseases of the skin, 1993—; mastership, MD Austrian Army Med. Corps, Graz and Götzendorf, Austria, 1990, Styrian Nursing Sch., Graz, 1994—; head Leadership Sci. Events. Recipient Karl H. Spitzy award Sci. Soc. Physicians in Vienna, 1991, Hans Weitgasser award Sci. Soc. Styrian Dermatologists, 1995. Mem. Styrian Sci. Soc. Dermatologists (sec. 1996—), Soc. for Investigative Dermatology, Internat. Soc. Cutaneous Lymphomas, European Acad. Dermatology and Venerology, European Soc. Chemotherapy & Infectious Diseases. Office: Dept Dermatology, Auenbruggerplatz 8, A-8036 Graz Austria

MUELLEMAN, ROBERT LEO, medical educator; b. Omaha, July 4, 1957; s. Joseph John and Virginia Lee (Fromm) M.; m. Diane Marie Schekirke, June 18, 1982; children: Therese, Thomas, Daniel, Robert. BS cum laude, U. Nebr., Omaha, 1979, MD with honors, 1984. Diplomate Am. Bd. Emergency Medicine. Asst. prof. U. Nebr. Med. Ctr., Omaha, 1988-93; assoc. prof. U. Mo., Kansas City, 1993—; mem. injury control adv. com. Mo. Dept. Health, Jefferson City, Mo., 1994—. Contbr. chpt. to book and articles to profl. jours. Mem. Health Care Coalition Against Family Violence, Kansas City, Mo., 1993—. Fellow Am. Coll. Emergency Physicians (pres. Nebr. chpt. 1992-93, bd. mem. Mo. chpt. 1993—); mem. Soc. Acad. Emergency Medicine (pub. health and edn. com. chair 1984—), Alpha Omega Alpha. Democrat. Roman Catholic. Office: Truman Med Ctr 2301 Holmes Kansas City MO 64108-2640

MUELLER, BRUCE ALLEN, pharmacist, educator; b. Racine, Wis., May 2, 1961; s. Robert Charles and Margaret Mary (Defries) M.; m. Laurie Lynn LaRose, Oct. 11, 1986; children: Christine, Brian, Rebecca. Student, U. Wis. Milw., 1979-81; BS in Pharmacy, U. Wis. Madison, 1984; D of Pharmacy, U. Tex. Health Sci. Ctr., 1988. Intern pharmacy St. Luke's Meml. Hosp., Racine, Wis., 1984-85; pharmacist Med. Ctr. Hosp., San Antonio, 1985-88; asst. prof. clin. pharmacy Purdue U., Indpls., 1988-93, assoc. prof. clin. pharmacy, 1993—; adj. asst. prof. medicine Ind. U., Indpls., 1990—; mem. planning com. Great Lakes Residency Conf., Indpls., 1996. Mem. Editor Rev. Panel Medi Span, Indpls., 1991—; nephrology editl. panel mem. Annals of Pharmacotherapy, Cin., 1995—; contbr. articles to profl. jours. Fellow Am. Coll. Clin. Pharmacy (sec. 1996—), Am. Soc. Health Sys. Pharmacists, Ind. Soc. Health Sys. Pharmacists, Ind. Coll. Clin. Pharmacists. Office: Purdue Univ OPW U2005 1001 W 10th Indianapolis IN 46202

MUELLER, CHARLES FREDERICK, radiologist, educator; b. Dayton, Ohio, May 26, 1936; s. Susan Elizabeth (Wine) W.; m. Kathe Louise Lutterbei, May 28, 1966; children: Charles Jeffrey, Theodore Martin, Kathryn Suzanne. BA in English, U. Cin., 1958, MD, 1962. Diplomate Am. Bd. Radiology, Am. Bd. Nuclear Medicine. Asst. prof. radiology U. N.Mex., Albuquerque, 1968-72, assoc. prof. radiology, 1972-74; assoc. prof. radiology Ohio State U., Columbus, 1974-79, acting chmn. dept. radiology, 1975, prof. radiology, 1979—, prof. radiology, dir. post grad. program radiology, 1980—; bd. dirs. Univ. Radiologists, Inc., Columbus, v.p., 1980-86; pres., founder Ambulatory Imaging, Inc., Columbus, 1985—; founder Am. Soc. Emergency Radiology, 1988, pres., 1993-94. Author: Emergency Radiology, 1982; contbr. articles to profl. jours. Com. chmn. Boy Scouts of Am., Columbus, 1980-84. Served to capt. USAF, 1966-68. Research grantee Ohio State U. 1975, Gen. Electric Co., 1986-88. Fellow Am. Coll. Radiologists; mem. Assn. Univ. Radiologists, Am. Roentgen Ray Soc., Radiol. Soc. N.Am., AMA, N.Mex. Soc. Radiologists (pres. 1973-74), Ohio State Radiol. Soc. (pres. 1986-87). Republican. Presbyterian. Lodges: Commandery #6, Consistory. Office: Ohio State Univ Hosps Dept Radiology 410 W 10th Ave Columbus OH 43210-1240

MUELLER, DALE MARSHA, nursing educator; b. L.A., Oct. 25, 1947; d. Harry and Ethel Jovie (Frumkin) Struman; 1 child, Tanya Helene. AA magna cum laude, L.A. City Coll., 1978; BA summa cum laude, UCLA, 1971; MS in Clin. Psychology, Calif. State U., Long Beach, 1977; doctoral studies, Pepperdine U., 1995—. Subacute adminstr. Continental Med. Systems, 1990-93; rehab. adminstr. Casa Colina, 1986-90; with Oneline Campus U. Phoenix, San Francisco; instr. Chapman U., Orange, Calif.; pvt. practice Sightline-Health Sys. Mgmt., Diamond Bar, Calif.; expert witness in field; cons., nat. seminar presenter The Polaris Group, Hingham, Mass.; lectr. statewide nursing program Calif. State U. Contbr. articles to profl. jours. Mem. Am. Heart Assn., Calif. Assn. Health Facilities, Calif. Nurses Assn. (bd. dirs., commr. nursing edn.), Phi Beta Kappa. Home: 3015 La Paz Ln Apt C Diamond Bar CA 91765-3850

MUELLER, GARY LOUIS, endocrinologist; b. Montgomery, Ala., July 26, 1946; s. Delbert Louis and Mary Rose (Kirby) M.; m. Carolyn Regena Mooneyham, Sept. 23, 1978. BA with honors, U. Mo., 1968, MD, 1972. Diplomate Nat. Bd. Med. Examiners, Am. Bd. Internal Medicine. Commd. 2d lt. USAF, 1968, advanced through grades to col.; chief internal med. clinic USAF Med. Ctr.-Keesler, Biloxi, Miss., 1977-81; chief endocrine svcs. and fellowship program Wilford Hall Med. Ctr., San Antonio, 1981-85; chmn. dept. medicine USAF Med. Ctr.-Scott, Belleville, Ill., 1985-86; chief clin. medicine Mil. Airlift Command, Belleville, 1986-87; chief hosp. svcs., dep. comdr. Malcolm Grow Med. Ctr., Andrews AFB, Md., 1987-89; comdr. 509th strategic hosp. Pease AFB, Portsmouth, N.H., 1989-90; comdr. 92 med. group Fairchild AFB, Spokane, Wash., 1990-93; team chief med. inspection Kirtland AFB, Albuquerque, 1993-96; ret. USAF, 1996; endocrinologist Summit Endocrinology, Hermitage, Tenn., 1996—. Contbr. articles to sci. jours., chpts. to textbooks. Bd. dirs., v.p. Inland Empire coun. Girl Scouts U.S., Spokane, 1991-93, bd. dirs. Chapparal coun., Albuquerque, 1994-95; unit commr. Mid. Tenn. coun. Boy Scouts Am., 1995—. Recipient Outstanding Vol. award Inland Empire coun. Girl Scouts U.S., 1993, wood Badge, Inland N.W. coun. Boy Scouts Am., 1993; James West fellow Inland N.W. coun. Boy Scouts Am., 1994. Fellow ACP; mem. Am. Diabetes Assn., Am. Assn. Clin. Endocrinologists, The Endocrine Soc. Office: Summit Endocrinology 5651 Frist Blvd Ste 608 Hermitage TN 37076

MUELLER, HILTRUD S., cardiologist; b. Amorbach, Germany, July 4, 1926; d. Rudolf and Elisabeth (Hess) M. MD magna cum laude, U. Heidelberg, 1951. Faculty USPHS tng. program St. Vincent's Hosp. and Med. Ctr., N.Y.C., 1967-68, clin. asst. physician, 1968-69, asst. attending/dir. CICU, 1970-72, assoc. attending, cons., 1973—; attending, dir. cardiology St. Vincent's Hosp. and Med. Ctr., Worcester, Mass., 1973-75; asst. attending dept. medicine St. Mary's Hosp., Bklyn., 1969-72; attending, dir. cardiology St. Louis U. Hosp., 1976-81; attending, assoc. dir. cardiology Montefiore Med. Ctr., Bronx, 1981—; prof. medicine Albert Einstein Coll. Medicine, Bronx, 1981—. Author: (with others) Cardiology: A Clinicophysiologic Approach, 1971, Myocardial Blood Flow in Man, Shock in Myocardial Infarction, 1974, Care of the Critically Ill, 1974, Controversies in Cardiology, 1977, The Patient in Shock, 1977, The Organ in Shock, 1977, Intraaortale Balloongegen-Pulsation, 1977, Assisted Circulation, 1979, Radioimmunoassay of Drugs and Hormones in Cardiovascular Medicine, 1979; contbr. numerous articles to profl. jours. Recipient numerous grants. Fellow ACP, Am. Coll. Cardiology, N.Y. Cardiologic Soc.; mem. Am. Heart Assn., Assn. of Univ. Cardiologists. Office: Montefiore Med Ctr 111 E 210th St Bronx NY 10467

MUELLER, JEAN MARGARET, nursing consultant; b. Huntington, N.Y., June 3, 1951. Diploma in Nursing, Pilgrim State Hosp., 1973; BSN, SUNY, Stony Brook, 1979; M in Profl. Studies, New Sch. for Social Rsch., 1986. RN, N.Y. Nurses aide Huntington Hosp., N.Y., 1971, LPN, 1972, RN, charge ICU/CCU, MICU/SICU, telemetry, 1973-77; charge nurse, MICU North Shore U. Hosp, Manhasset, N.Y., 1977-78; private duty cases, Holter monitor scanning, 1978-84; dir. nursing svcs., assoc. dir. nursing svcs. Nesconset (N.Y.) Nursing Ctr., 1984-86; nursing edn. instr. St. Charles Hosp., Port Jefferson, N.Y.; labor and delivery nurse SUNY, Stony Brook; teaching and rsch. nurse II Diabetes Ctr., SUNY, Stony Brook; tchg. hosp. insvc. educator I SUNY, Stony Brook, 1990-94; hosp. nursing svcs. cons. Office Health Sys. Mgmt., N.Y. State Dept. Health, Hauppauge, N.Y., 1994—; mem. adj. faculty Sch. of Nursing SUNY, Stony Brook, 1992—, St. Joseph's Coll., 1994; rsch. com. dept. family medicine with E. Stark, E.A.P.; hosp. nursing svcs. cons. office health sys. mgmt. N.Y. State Dept. Health, 1994—; lectr. Med., Emotional and Psychol. Indicators of Family Violence. Contbr. articles to profl. jours. Active Mothers Against Drunk Driving; mem. Suffolk County Family Violence Task Force. Recipient President's award for leadership tng. programs SUNY, 1993, for spl. needs of elderly tng. programs and humanistic approach to health care tng. programs, 1994. Mem. Nat. Nurses Assn., Sigma Theta Tau. Home: 234 Hallock Rd Stony Brook NY 11790-3026

MUELLER, PAUL, physiologist, educator; b. Olten, Switzerland, Apr. 17, 1925; s. Gustav and Elise (Bartschi) M.; m. Gertrud Elsbeth Reinhart, Apr. 25, 1951; children: Barbara-Anne, Martin Thomas, Christoph Paul. MD, U. Zurich, Switzerland, 1950. Postdoctoral fellow cardiology N.Y. Med. Coll., N.Y.C., 1951-52; resident internal medicine U. Bern, 1952-56, vice dir. clinic internal medicine, 1956-60, resident asst. physiologist, 1961-64, assoc. prof., 1966-68, prof., 1969-90. With Swiss Med. Army Corps, 1967-90. Grantee Swiss Nat. Sci. Found.; rsch. fellow U. Coll., London, 1965-66. Mem. Swiss Soc. Internal Medicine, Swiss Physiol. Soc. (pres. 1985-86). Home: Stalden

29, CH-4500 Solothurn Switzerland Office: U Bern Physiol Inst, Buehlplatz 5, CH 3012 Bern Switzerland

MUELLER, RUDHARD KLAUS, toxicologist; b. Glauchau, Saxony, Fed. Republic Germany, Aug. 20, 1936; s. Rudhard Otto and Hildegard Dora (Krasselt) M.; m. Ursula Hanni Rossberg, May 5, 1961; children: Cornelia, Beatrix, Mildred. Diploma in chemistry, U. Leipzig, German Dem. Republic, 1960, D in Nat. Scis., 1965, D habil., 1977. Mem. staff forensic medicine U. Leipzig, German Dem. Republic, 1960-75, venia legendi toxicological chemistry, 1975, assoc. prof. forensic toxicology, 1982—, head postgrad. study program toxicology faculty of medicine, 1987, prof., 1989—; head Inst. Doping Analysis Kreischa near Dresden, Germany, 1992—. Author, editor: (book) Toxicological Analysis, (German) 1976, (English) 2d edit. 1991. Recipient Rudolf Virchow award Min. Pub. Health, Berlin, 1977, Gottfried Wilhelm Leibniz award U. Leipzig, 1979. Mem. Internat. Assn. Forensic Toxicologists (co-found., mem. com. Systematic Toxicological Analysis, 1978—, chmn. 1991—), Soc. Legal Medicine, Soc. Toxicol. and Forensic Chem. Home: 92 Kurt Eisner St, D-04275 Leipzig Germany Office: U Forensic Medicine, 28 Johannisallee, D-04103 Leipzig Germany

MUELLER, WILLYS FRANCIS, JR., pathologist; b. Detroit, July 15, 1934; s. Willys Francis and Antoinette Frances (Stimac) M.; M.D., U. Mich., 1959; m. Dolores Mae Vella, Aug. 25, 1956; children: Renee Ann, Willys Francis, Paul E., Mark A., Maria D., Beth M., Matthew P. Intern, Providence Hosp., Detroit, 1959-60, resident, 1960-62; resident Wayne County Gen. Hosp., Eloise, Mich., 1962-64; asst. pathologist Grace Hosp., Detroit, 1964; asso. pathologist Hurley Hosp., Flint, Mich., 1964-66; asso. pathologist Hurley Med. Ctr., Flint, 1968—, dir. lab., 1981—; chief dep. med. examiner Genesee County, Mich., 1971—; pres. Pathology Assos. Inc.; assoc. clin. prof. Coll. Human Medicine, Mich. State U.; med. dir. blood svcs. Wolverine region/ Grant Lakes region ARC, 1981-96. Served with M.C., U.S. Army, 1966-68. Fellow Am. Soc. Clin. Pathologists, Coll. Am. Pathologists, Am. Acad. Forensic Scis.; mem. AMA (Physician's Recognition award 1974-77, 78-81, 81-84, 85-87, 87-90, 91, 93-96, 96—), Mich State Med. Soc., Mich. Soc. Pathologists (sec.-treas. 1981-83, pres. elect 1984, pres. 1985), Genesee County Med. Soc. (pres. 1987), Mich. Assn. Blood Banks (bd. dirs., pres. 1992), Nat. Assn. Med. Examiners. Republican. Roman Catholic. Club: K.C. Editor: Bull. of Genesee County Med. Soc. Home: 13335 Pomona Dr Fenton MI 48430-1223 Office: Hurley Med Ctr Dept Pathology Flint MI 48502

MUELLER-HEUBACH, EBERHARD AUGUST, medical educator, obstetrician-gynecologist; b. Berlin, Feb. 24, 1942; U.S., 1968; s. Heinrich G. and Elisabeth (Heubach) Mueller; m. Cornelia R. Uffmann, Feb. 6, 1968; 1 child, Oliver Maximilian. Abitur, Lichtenbergschule, Darmstadt, W.Ger., 1961; M.D., U. Cologne (W.Ger.), 1966. Diplomate Am. Bd. Ob-Gyn.. Intern U. Cologne, 1967-68, Middlesex Gen. Hosp., New Brunswick, N.J., 1968-69; rsch. fellow Columbia U., N.Y.C., 1969-71; resident and chief resident Sloane Hosp. for Women, N.Y.C., 1971-75; asst. prof. U. Pitts. Sch. Medicine/Magee-Women's Hosp., 1975-81, assoc. prof., 1981-89; prof., chmn. dept. Ob-Gyn., Bowman Gray Sch. Medicine, Wake Forest U., Winston-Salem, N.C., 1989—. Reviewer Am. Jour. Ob-Gyn, 1978—, Obstetrics and Gynecology, 1979—; contbr. chpts. to books, articles to profl. jours. Fellow Am. Coll. Obstetricians and Gynecologists (Hoechst award 1972); mem. Tri-State Perinatal Orgn. (v.p. 1981), Pa. Perinatal Assn. (pres.-elect 1982-84, pres. 1984-86), Soc. Gynecologic Investigation, Soc. Perinatal Obstetricians, Am. Fedn. Clin. Rsch., Pitts. Ob-Gyn. Soc. (v.p. 1985-86, pres. 1986-87), Am. Gynecol. and Obstet. Soc., Perinatal Rsch. Soc., Coun. Univ. Chairs Obstetrics and Gynecology (sec.-treas. 1995-96, pres.-elect 1996—). Research on animal studies in fetal and maternal physiology; diabetes mellitus in pregnancy, high risk obstetrics. Office: Bowman Gray Sch Med Dept Ob-Gyn Medical Center Blvd Winston Salem NC 27157

MUFSON, MAURICE ALBERT, physician, educator; b. N.Y.C., July 7, 1932; s. Max and Faye M.; m. Diane Cecile Weiss, Apr. 1, 1962; children: Michael Jeffrey, Karen Andrea, Pamela Beth. A.B., Bucknell U., 1953; M.D., NYU, 1957. Intern Bellevue Hosp., N.Y.C., 1957-58; resident Bellevue Hosp., 1958-59; chief resident Cook County Hosp., Chgo., 1965-66; sr. surgeon USPHS Lab. Infectious Diseases, NIH, 1961-65; asst. prof. medicine U. Ill., 1965-69, assoc. prof., 1969-73, prof., 1973-76; prof., chmn. dept. medicine Marshall U., 1976—; vis. scientist Karolinska Inst., 1984-85. Contbr. articles to profl. jours. Served with U.S. Navy, 1959-61. WHO grantee, 1967; recipient Meet-the-Scholar award Marshall U., 1986, REsearcher of Yr. award Sigmz Xi, Marshall U., 1989; co-recipient Louis Weinstein award Jour. Clin. Infectious Diseases, 1994. Fellow ACP (traveling scholar 1987, Laureate award W.Va. chpt.), Infectious Diseases Soc. Am.; mem. AMA, Soc. Exptl. Biology and Medicine, Ctrl. Soc. Clin. Rsch., So. Soc. Clin. Investigation, W.Va. State Med. Assn., Assn. Profs. Medicine (counselor 1992-95, pres.-elect 1995-96, pres. 1996-97), Alpha Omega Alpha. Office: Marshall U Sch Medicine Dept Medicine Huntington WV 25701

MUFTI, SIRAJ ISLAM, biologist, researcher; b. Bedadi, Hazara, Pakistan, May 10, 1938; came to U.S., 1967; s. Sultan M. and Saeeda M. (Khan) M.; m. Bebe Z. Khan, Jan. 10, 1965; children: Sheereen, Shaheen. BSc, U. Peshawar, Pakistan, 1955; MSc, Am. U., Beirut, 1963; PhD, U. Ariz., 1973. Rsch. asst. Argl. Rsch. Inst., Peshawar, 1955-59, asst. botanist, 1959-61; agr. officer, dir. Ministry of Agr./North Nigeria Devel. Corp., Kaduna, Nigeria, 1963-67; rsch. assoc. in molecular biology Vanderbilt U., Nashville, 1973-75; asst. prof. Pahlavi U., Shiraz, Iran, 1975-77; rsch. asst. prof. Mt. Sinai Med. Ctr., N.Y.C., 1979-81; adj. asst. prof. U. Ariz., Tucson, 1977-79, 198189, assoc. rsch. prof., 1989—. Contbr. numerous articles to profl. jours. Student mentor U. Ariz., Tucson, 1985—; councilor Ariz. State Prison Complex, Tucson, 198—; bd. dirs., sec. Asian-Am. Assn., Tucson, 1988-90. Am. U. scholar, 1961; NIH grantee, 1979, 81, 89, 90, 92. Mem. AAAS, Am. Assn. for Cancer Rsch., AAUP. Democrat. Islam. Home: 7458 E Princeton Dr Tucson AZ 85710-4932 Office: U Ariz Health Science Ctr Tucson AZ 85721

MÜGGE, ANDREAS, cardiologist; b. Uelzen, Germany, Sept. 8, 1956; m. Dorothea Schmiade, June 15, 1988. MD, Hannover (Germany) Med. Sch., 1981. Rsch. assoc. in pharmacology U. Hamburg, Germany, 1983-85; fellow in cardiology Hannover Med. Sch., 1985-89, assoc. in cardiology, 1991-95, prof. medicine, 1996—; rsch. assoc. cardiovascular div. U. Iowa, Iowa City, 1989-90. Fellow Am. Coll. Cardiology, European Soc. Cardiology, Am. Heart Assn.; mem. German Soc. Cardiology, German Soc. Pharmacology. Office: Hannover Med Sch Cardiology, 30625 Hannover Germany

MÜHE, ERICH, surgical educator; b. Bad Windsheim, Bavaria, Germany, May 23, 1938; s. Karl and Friedel (Schmidt) M.; m. Hannelore Strebel, Oct. 6, 1952; children: Christian, Michael. MD, U. Erlangen, Fed. Republic Germany, 1966. Diplomate in surgery, Fed. Republic Germany. First resident Surg. Clinic, U. Erlangen, 1973-82, lectr., 1973-79, prof., 1979—; chief surg. clinic Kreiskrankenhaus, Böblingen, Fed. Republic Germany, 1982—; prof. surgery U. Tübingen (Fed. Republic Germany), 1982—. Contbr. over 250 articles to med. jour., chpts. to books; inventor bed bicycle for prevention thrombosis and pulmonary embolism, 1971, 1st laparoscopic cholecystectomy in the world (with-and without pneumoperitoneum), 1985. Recipient L. Rehn prize Mittelrheinische Chirurgen, 1974. Fellow ACS; mem. Deutsche Gesellschaft für Chirurgie (Jubilee prize 1992), Bayerische Gesellschaft für Chirurgie (J.H. Nussbaum prize 1965), Deutsche Krebsgesellschaft, N.Y. Acad. Scis. Office: Kreiskrankenhaus, Bunsenstrasse 120, D-7030 Böblingen Germany

MUICO-MERCURIO, LUISA, critical care nurse; b. Caloocan, Manila, Philippines, Nov. 17, 1955; d. Amado B. and Eustaquia (Buenavista) Muico; m. Wilfred Tongson Mercurio, Dec. 28, 1974; children: Elyjah Matthew, Kristoffer Ross, Mercurio. ADN, Harbor City Coll., 1978; BSN, Calif. State U., 1990, postgrad., 1992—. Cert. ACLS instr., BLS instr; CCRN; cert. pub. health nurse. Staff nurse ICU Long Beach (Calif.) Meml. Med. Ctr., 1978-80; staff nurse CVT/ICU Cedar Sinai Med. Ctr., L.A., 1980-84; staff nurse ICU, critical care unit, emergency rm., cath. lab. Long Beach Community Hosp., 1982-86; ICU, CCU coord. Pioneer Hosp., Artesia, Calif., 1986-87; staff nurse CSU Kaiser-Permanente, L.A., 1988-90, pub. health nurse, 1990, asst. dept. adminstr., 1990-92; asst. dept. adminstr. Kaiser-Permanente, Sunset and Bellflower, Calif.; cardiovascular/thoracic surgery nurse coord. Kay Med. Group/Hosp. Good Samaritan, L.A., 1992—; staff nurse critical care unit UCLA, 1994—; nursing faculty Pacific Coast Coll., 1994—. Named to Dean's list Harbor City Coll, 1976-78, Dean's list Calif. State U., 1988-90. Mem. AACN (cert.), Nat. Golden Key Honor Soc., Nursing Honor Soc., Sigma Theta Tau (Nu Mu chpt). Republican.

MUILENBURG, ROBERT HENRY, hospital administrator; b. Orange City, Iowa, Apr. 29, 1941; s. Henry W. and Anna (Vander Zwaag) M.; m. Judith Ann Gebauer, Jan. 1, 1959; children: Ronald, Eric, Matthew. B.A., U. Iowa, 1964, M.A., 1966. Adminstrv. asst. Ill. Masonic Med. Ctr., Chgo., Ill., 1966-67; asst. adminstr. Ill. Masonic Med. Ctr., Chgo., Ill, 1967-68; assoc. adminstr. Ill. Masonic Med. Ctr., Chgo., Ill., 1968-71; assoc adminstr. U. Utah Hosp., Salt Lake City, 1971-75, adminstr., 1975-78; adminstr. U. Wash. Med. Ctr., Seattle, 1978-84; clin. assoc. prof. health services adminstrn. and planning U. Wash., Seattle, 1978—; exec. dir. U. Wash. Med. Ctr., 1984—. USPHS trainee, 1966. Fellow Am. Coll. Hosp. Adminstrs.; mem. Am. Hosp. Assn. (del. 1984-88, chmn. metro. hosp. sect. 1987, bd. dirs. 1992-94), Wash. State Hosp. Assn. (bd. dirs. 1982-84, 89-54), Seattle Area Hosp. Coun. (pres. 1983), Univ. Health System Consortium (bd. dirs. 1994—), Seattle C. of C. (bd. dirs. 1994—). Home: 10019 49th Ave NE Seattle WA 98125-8131 Office: U Wash Med Ctr RC-35 1959 NE Pacific St Seattle WA 98195-0004

MUIR, JOHN ROBERT, cardiologist; b. London, July 30, 1936; s. Edward Grainger and Estelle (Russell) M.; m. Susan Mary Rudland, 1965 (div. 1982); children: Edward Robert, Elizabeth. BA with honors, Oxford U., 1958, MB BCh, 1961, D.M., 1968. House surgeon surg. unit Middlesex Hosp., 1961-62; house physician Leicester Royal Infirmary, 1962, London Chest Hosp., 1962-63; sr. house officer Cen. Middlesex Hosp., 1963; med. registrar profl. med. unit U. Birmingham, Birmingham, Eng., 1964-66; sr. registrar Nat. Heart Hosp., London, 1966-70; USPHS postdoctoral rsch. fellow dept. biochemistry, St. Louis U., 1968; prof., chmn. dept. cardiology Welsh Nat. Sch. Medicine, Cardiff, 1970-78; med. dir. Allied Med. Group, Riyadh, Saudi Arabia, 1978-80; chmn. cardiac dept. Armed Forces Hosp., Riyadh, 1980-83; pvt. practice London, 1983—; Editor: Advanced Medicine, 1979; editor Saudi Med. Jour., 1980-83; contbr. articles and chapts. to med. publs. Fellow Royal Soc. Medicine, Royal Coll. Physicians London, Assn. Physicians Gt. Britain and Ireland; mem. Brit. Cardiac Soc., Med. Rsch. Soc., Naval and Mil. Club London. Mem. Ch. of Scotland. Office: 21 Devonshire Pl, London W1N 1PD, England

MUKAI, CECILIA PUI SHUEN, nurse educator; b. Hong Kong, Sept. 20, 1950; d. Shun Kam and Wai Yu (Lee) Wong; m. Leonard Mukai, July 14, 1974; children: Eric, Aaron. BS, U. Hawaii, 1973; MS in Nursing, Yale U., 1976; PhD, U. Hawaii, 1991. Cert. family nurse practitioner, instr. CPR. Staff nurse Victoria Gen. Hosp., Halifax, Nova Scotia, 1978-80; nurse practitioner Kaiser Permanente, Honolulu, 1981-86; asst. prof. U. Hawaii Manoa, Honolulu, 1981-87; instr. U. Hawaii and Hawaii Community Coll., Hilo, 1987-91; assoc. prof. U. Hawaii Hilo, 1991—; item writer NCLEX, 1993, 96. Recipient Hawaii Heart Assn. Project Grant; Sigma Theta Tau grantee. Mem. AAUP, ANA, NEA, HERA.

MUKAWA, AKIO, pathology educator; b. Kanazawa, Ishikawa, Japan, June 10, 1928; s. Tatsuchiyo and Moto (Ohtsuka) M.; m. Hiroko Matsuo, May 5, 1968; children: Chisui, Yasutake. MD, U. Kanazawa, Japan, 1954, PhD, 1959. Diplomate Am. Bd. Pathology. Resident pathology Queens Hosp. Ctr., N.Y.C., 1959-63; lectr. pathology U. Kanazawa Med. Sch., 1963-67; neuropathology fellow Albert Einstein Coll. Medicine, N.Y.C., 1966-67; dir. pathology Nat. Hosp. Kanazawa, 1967-72; prof. pathology Kanazawa Med. U., Uchinada, Japan, 1972-96, emeritus prof. pathology, 1995—; cons. Mukawa Inst. Pathology, Uchinada, 1996—. Author: Autopsy Technique, 1988. Mem. Japanese Path. Soc. (trustee 1971—), Am. Soc. Clin Pathologists (fgn. fellow 1989—). Home and Office: Taiseidai 55 Uchinada, Ishikawa 920-02, Japan

MULCAHY, JOHN JOSEPH, medical educator; b. N.Y.C., Jan. 7, 1941; m. Rae Anne Snyder, Aug. 8, 1970; children: Lori, Maureen, Michael, Mark. BA, Holy Cross Coll., 1962; MD, Georgetown U., 1966; PhD in Physiology, U. Mich., 1972; MS in Urology, U. Minn., Rochester, 1974. Diplomate Am. Bd. Urology. Asst. prof. urol. surgery U. Ky., Lexington, 1974-78; assoc. prof. urology Ind. U., Indpls., 1978-90; prof. urology Ind. U., 1990—. Recipient Cristol award Mayo Urol. Alumni Assn., Rochester, Minn., 1993. Mem. AMA, ACS, Am. Urol. Assn., Soc. Univ. Urologists, Soc. for Study of Impotence, Internat. Soc. Impotence Rsch. Roman Catholic. Office: Ind U Med Ctr Wishard Hosp 1001 W 10th St Indianapolis IN 46202

MULCAHY, ROBERT THOMAS, physician; b. East Cleve., May 8, 1948; s. George Thomas and Marilyn Jean (Peck) M.; m. Candace Ann Clair, Sept. 8, 1970 (div. Sept. 1979); m. Diane Marie Rasicci, May 3, 1985. AA, Lakeland C.C., Kirtland, Ohio, 1970; BS in Edn., Bowling Green State U., 1972; cert. urologic physician asst., U. Cin., 1975; MD, Med. Coll. Ohio, 1982. Diplomate Am. Bd. Internal Medicine. Biology and chemistry tchr. Wickliffe (Ohio) H.S., 1972-73; physician asst. Drs. Silverman and Leonard, New Orleans, 1975-77, Huron Rd. Hosp., East Cleve., 1977-79; intern internal medicine Akron (Ohio) City Hosp., 1982-83, resident in internal medicine, 1983-85; pvt. practice Willoughby, Ohio, 1985-91; physician Kaiser-Permanente, Willoughby, Ohio, 1991-93, chief of internal medicine, 1993—; chmn. drug utilization rev. Lake Hosp. Sys., Willoughby, 1994—. Mem. ACP, Ohio State Med. Assn. Home: 6777 Rolling Acres Ct Concord OH 44077 Office: Kaiser-Permanente 5105 Som Center Rd Willoughby OH 44094

MULCH, ROBERT F., JR., physician; b. Quincy, Ill., June 21, 1951; s. Robert Franklin and Martha Jo (Nisi) M.; m. Barbara Ann Best, Apr. 5, 1975; children: Matthew, Luke. BS, U. Ill., 1973; MD, Rush Med. Coll., Chgo., 1977. Diplomate Am. Bd. Family Practice; cert. in geriatrics. Intern Riverside Meth. Hosp., Columbus, Ohio, 1977-78; resident in family practice Riverside Meth. Hosp., Columbus, 1978-80; family practice medicine Hillsboro, Ill., 1980—; ptnr. Springfield Clin.; asst. clin. prof. family medicine So. Ill. U., Springfield, 1981—; advisor Montgomery County Counseling Ctr.; reviewer Cen. Ill. Peer Rev. Orgn.; chmn. pharmacy and therapeutics com. Hillsboro Hosp. Sec. Hillsboro Sports Assn. Fellow Am. Acad. Family Practice; mem. Am. Geriatric Soc., Am. Heart Assn., Montgomery County unit Am. Cancer Soc. (pres.). Lutheran. Office: Hillsboro Med Ctr SC 1250 E Tremont St Hillsboro IL 62049-1912

MULDARY, THOMAS WILLIAM, psychologist; b. Lackawanna, N.Y., Apr. 20, 1949; s. Charles Gallagher and Winifred Ann (Ebbitt) M.; m. Patricia Mary Spezeski, Sept. 20, 1980. BS, Eastern Mich. U., 1971, MS, 1973; PhD, U.S. Internat. U., 1979. Lic. psychologist, Mich. Instr. Siena Heights Coll., Adrian, Mich., 1974-76; clin. intern USN Alcoholism Rehab. Ctr., San Diego, 1977, 78-79; instr. U. Calif., San Diego, 1980; adj. prof. Nat. U., San Diego, 1978-80; pvt. practice psychology Ann Arbor, Mich., 1980-82; lectr. dept. psychology Eastern Mich. U., Ypsilanti, 1980—; psychologist Warwick Assocs., Adrian, 1982-93, Muldary and Muldary, P.C., 1993—; cons. Jackson (Mich.) Police Dept., 1981—, Vocat. Rehab. Svcs., Mich. Dept. Edn., 1981-84, Bridgeway Ctr., Jackson, 1982, Probate Ct. Lenawee County, 1992-94; adj. instr. Jackson C.C. at Mich. State Prison, 1973-76; pres. bd. dirs. Family Awareness Ctr., Adrian, Mich. Author: Interpersonal Relations for Health Professionals, 1983 (Book of Yr. 1984), Burnout and Health Professionals, 1983; contbg. author: Management of the Physically and Emotionally Abused, 1983. Mem. Lenawee County Sexual Abuse Task Force. Mem. APA, Mich. Psychol. Assn., Mich. Soc. Forensic Psychologists, Am. Psychology Law Soc., Profl. Acad. Custody Evaluators (diplomate). Roman Catholic.

MULDER, DONALD GERRIT, surgeon, educator; b. Hospers, Iowa, 1924. M.D., Johns Hopkins U., 1952. Diplomate Am. Bd. Surgery, Am. Bd. Thoracic Surgery (chmn. 1983-85). Intern Johns Hopkins Hosp., Balt., 1952-53, resident, 1953-55; resident Calif. Med. Ctr., Los Angeles, 1955-57; instr. surgery U. Calif, Los Angeles, 1957-58, asst. prof., 1958-64, assoc. prof., 1964-69, prof., 1969—. Fellow ACS; mem. AMA. Office: Univ Calif Sch Medicine Los Angeles CA 90024

MULFORD, RAND PERRY, medical products executive; b. Denver, Sept. 30, 1943; s. Roger Wayne and Ann Louise (Perry) M.; 1 child, Conrad Perry; m. Paula Marie Skelley, 1987. BS in Basic Engring., Princeton U., 1965; MBA, Harvard U., 1972. Mgmt. cons. McKinsey & Co. Inc., Chgo., 1972-80; v.p. planning and control splty. chem. group Occidental Chem. Co., Houston, 1980-82; pres. Technivest Inc., Houston, 1982-85; exec. dir. corp. planning Merck & Co., Inc., Rahway, N.J., 1985-88; v.p. fin. Advanced Tissue Scis., Inc., La Jolla, Calif., 1989-90; CEO Chiron Mimotopes Peptide Systems, San Diego, Calif., 1991-94; COO Xytronyx, Inc., San Diego, 1994-95; chmn. of bd. Medication Delivery Devices, San Diego, 1991-95; mem. adv. bd. L. Karp & Sons, Inc., Elk Grove Village, Ill., 1980—. Lt. USN, 1965-70. Home: 2178 Caminito Del Barco Del Mar CA 92014-3619

MULGREW, JOHN, human development and psychology educator, psychotherapist; b. N.Y.C., Jan. 12, 1936; s. James Francis and Stella Elizabeth (Deserosurs) M.; m., Aug. 10, 1963; children: Catherine, John. BS, Fordham U., 1963; MS, St. John's U., 1967; PhD, Fla. State U., 1971. Asst. dir. counseling ctr. Appalachian State U., Boone, N.C., 1971-73, dir. counseling ctr., 1973-82, prof. human devel. and psychology counseling dept., 1982—; dir. Gestalt Tng. Ctr., Boone, 1974—. Mem. Am. Acad. Psychotherapists, Am. Group Psychotherapy Assn. Home: 21904 Hillandale Dr Boone NC 28607-4658 Office: Appalachian State U Human Devel & Psychol Counseling Boone NC 28608

MULHOLLAN, MICHELLE MARY BESS, medical and surgical nurse; b. Clearfield, Pa., June 3, 1971; m. Dennis N. Mulhollan Jr., June 22, 1991. AD, Lock Haven U., Clearfield. RN, Pa. Dietary worker Clearfield Hosp., 1987-89, nurse, 1994—. Home: PO Box 65 Bigler PA 16825

MULICK, EDWARD JAMES, orthodontist; b. Missoula, Mont., June 2, 1938; s. Edward Claude Mulick and Neta I. (McFadden) Marolich; m. Jeanne Mae Christison, Aug. 13, 1960; children: Edward Michael, Susan Marie, Michelle Ann, Michael John, Patrick Sean. BS, Gonzaga U., 1960; DDS, Creighton U., 1963; MS, U. Nebr., 1970. Gen. practice dentistry Priest River, Idaho, 1963-68; practice dentistry specializing in orthodontics Boise, Idaho, 1970—; cons. Boise State U. Vocat. Sch., 1978—, Am. Inst. Health, Boise, 1986—. Fellow Internat. Coll. Dentists; mem. ADA, Am. Assn. Orthodontists, Idaho Dental Assn. (pres. 1986), SW Idaho Dist. Dental Assn. (pres. 1982-83), Idaho State Orthodontic Assn. Republican. Roman Catholic. Lodge: Kiwanis (pres. 1976). Home: 4001 Delmonte Dr Boise ID 83704-3514 Office: Boise Orthodontic Assocs 7373 Emerald St Boise ID 83704-8624

MULINOS, MICHAEL GEORGE, retired research physician; b. Kefalonia, Kefaloma, Greece, Nov. 24, 1897; came to U.S., 1908; s. George Gerassimos and Helen (Couros) M.; m. Joyce Leora Stevens; 1 child, Stephen Michael. AB, Columbia U., 1921, MA, 1922, MD, 1924, PhD, 1927. Intern St. Vincent's Hosp., Erie, Pa., 1924-25; from asst. prof. to assoc. prof. pharmacology Coll. Physicians and Surgeons, Columbia U., 1929-44; assoc. prof. physiology and pharmacology N.Y. Med. Coll., N.Y.C., 1944-58; med. rsch. dir. Interchem. Corp., N.Y.C., 1945-47; med. dir. Comml. Slvents Corp., N.Y.C., 1953-62; pres. Med. Execs., N.Y.C., 1969-70, sec.-treas., 1970-85; assoc. med. dir. Life Extension Inst., N.Y.C., 1977-85; med. dir., dir. rsch. Unimed, Inc., Somerville, N.J., 1977-87; cons. med. rsch. to the chem. and pharm. industry, 1947-53, to pharm. and advt. industries, 1963-77; rsch. cons. Schmid Labs., Little Falls, N.J., 1977-80. Pres. Hellenic Med. Soc., N.Y., 1924, Assn. Med. Dirs., N.Y., 1956. Sterling Drug Inc. honoree Coll. Physicians and Surgeons, Columbia U., 1985; recipient Cert. of Recognition, Columbia Univ. Fellow AAAS. Republican. Orthodox. Home: 42 Marion Ter Easton MD 21601-3830

MULKEY, DAVID ALLEN, pathologist; b. Bonne Terre, Mo., Mar. 17, 1939; s. James Robert and Helen Elizabeth (Eydmann) M.; B.S., U. Ark., 1964, M.D., 1964; m. Sandra Lee Seward, June 21, 1969; children: John David, Christopher Lee. Intern, U. Ark. Med. Center, Little Rock, 1964-65; resident in pathology U. Colo. Med. Center, Denver, 1965-69; cons. pathology Webb-Waring Inst. Pulmonary Research, Denver, 1965-69; asso. pathologist Hosp. of the Good Samaritan, Los Angeles, 1969-72; asso., dep. dir. Valley Clin. Lab., Palm Desert, Calif., 1972-74; asso. Associated Pathologists Lab., Las Vegas, Nev., 1974—; asst. clin. prof. U. So. Calif. Sch. Medicine, Los Angeles, 1970—; dir. sci. adv. com. Community Blood Bank, Palm Springs, Calif., 1973-74; co-investigator, exec. mem. pathology com., chmn. lung pathology subcom. S.W. Oncology Group, 1976-77; chmn. Las Vegas Com. for Fluoride, 1976—; med. dir. Nev. Blood Services, 1979—. Served with USAR, 1956. Diplomate Am. Bd. Pathology. Mem. AMA, Nev. Med. Assn. (chmn. allied health commn. 1979—), Am. Soc. Clin. Pathologists, Coll. Am. Pathologists, Am. Soc. Cytology, Nev. Soc. Pathologists, Nev. Lung Soc., Clark County Med. Soc. (council 1979—, sec. 1984-85). Home: 1064 Pinehurst Dr Las Vegas NV 89109 Office: 4230 Burnham Ave Las Vegas NV 89119-5410

MULKS, MARTHA HUARD, microbiologist, educator; b. Waterville, Maine, June 9, 1950; d. Leslie John and Ethelyn L. (King) Huard; m. Charles Franklin Mulks Jr., May 30, 1970; 1 child, Carclyn Leslie. BA, Cornell U., 1971; PhD, Rensselaer Poly. Inst., 1977. Postdoctoral fellow Tufts-New England Med. Ctr., Boston, 1977-80, rsch. asst. prof., 1981-83; asst. prof. Mich. State U., East Lansing, 1983-88, assoc. prof., 1988-96, prof., 1996—. Editl. bd. Infection and Immunity, 1990-95; contbr. 40 articles to profl. jours. Med. Found. Inc. rsch. fellow, 1981-83; NIH rsch. grantee, 1985-92, USDA rsch. grantee, 1985-88. Mem. AAAS, Am. Soc. Microbiology, Sigma Xi, Phi Zeta. Office: Mich State U Dept Microbiology East Lansing MI 48824

MULLAN, FITZHUGH, public health physician; b. Tampa, Fla., July 22, 1942; s. Hugh and Mariquita (Macmanus) M.; m. Judith Wentworth, June 9, 1968; children: Meghan Elizabeth, Jason Michael, Caitlin Patricia. BA, Harvard U., 1964; MD, U. Chgo., 1968; DSc, U. Osteo. Medicine, 1993; LHD, Coll. Osteo. Medicine Pacific, 1993. Intern Jacobi Hosp., Bronx, 1968-70; resident Lincoln Hosp., Bronx, 1970-72; physician Nat. Health Svc. Corps., Santa Fe, N.Mex., 1972-75; dir. Nat. Health Svc. Corps, Rockville, Md., 1977-81; scholar-in-residence Inst. Medicine, Washington, 1981-82; sr. med. officer NIH, Bethesda, Md., 1982-84; sec. for health and environment State of N.Mex., Santa Fe, 1984-85; assoc. prof. Johns Hopkins Sch. Hygiene and Pub. Health, Balt., 1986-88; dir. pub. health history project Office of Surgeon Gen., Rockville, 1988-90; dir. bur. health professions USPHS, Rockville, 1990-96; contbr. editor Health Affairs, Bethesda, 1996—. Author: White Coat, Clenched Fist: The Political Education of an American Physician, 1976, Vital Signs: A Young Doctor's Struggle With Cancer, 1983, Plagues and Politics: The Story of the United States Public Health Service, 1989; contbr. articles to profl. jours. Fellow Am. Acad. Pediatrics; mem. AMA, Am. Pub. Health Assn., Am. Assn. for History of Medicine, Inst. of Medicine of the Nat. Acad. of Sci. Office: Health Affairs Ste 600 7500 Old Georgetown Rd Bethesda MD 20814

MULLANE, JOHN FRANCIS, pharmaceutical company executive; b. N.Y.C., Mar. 10, 1937; s. John Gerard and Rita Ann (Hoben) M.; m. Ruth Ann Cecka, Nov. 17, 1962; children—Rosemarie, Michael, Kathleen, Therese, Thomas. M.D., SUNY, 1963, Ph.D., 1968; J.D., Fordham U., 1977. Bar: N.Y. 1978, D.C. 1979. Assoc. med. dir. Ayerst Labs. div. Am. Home Products Corp., N.Y.C., 1973-75, dir. clin. research, 1975-76, v.p. clin., 1977, v.p. sci., 1978-82, sr. v.p., 1982, exec. v.p., 1983-88; pres. Mullane Health Care Cons., N.Y.C., 1989—; dir. drug devel. DuPont Med. Products, Wilmington, Del., 1990; sr. v.p. DuPont-Merck, Wilmington, 1991-94; exec. v.p. Amylin Pharms., 1994—. Contbr. articles to profl. jours. Served to lt. col. U.S. Army, 1970-73. Recipient Upjohn Achievement award, 1970; N.Y. Heart Assn. Crawford-Maynard fellow, 1966-68. Fellow Am. Coll. Clin. Pharmacology; mem. ABA, Am. Soc. Clin. Pharmacology and Therapeutics, Am. Assn. Study of Liver Diseases, Pelham Country Club, Lomas Sante Fe Country Club, Tara Golf and Country Club. Roman Catholic. Home: 1137 Via Mil Cumbres Solana Beach CA 92075 Office: Amylin Pharms 9373 Towne Centre Dr San Diego CA 92121-3027

MULLEEDY, JOYCE ELAINE, nursing service administrator, educator; b. Paterson, N.J., Aug. 30, 1948; d. Edward and Jane (Van De Weert) Schuurman; m. Philip Anthony Mulleedy, May 14, 1982. BS, Paterson State Coll., 1970. RN, cert. emergency nurse, emergency med. technician, paramedic. Pub. health nurse Vis. Nurse Assn. of No. Bergen County, Ramsey, N.J., 1970-72; health dir. Camp Fowler Assn., Speculator, N.Y., 1973-76; exec. dir. Am. Cancer Soc., Speculator, 1976-77; pub. health nurse Hamilton County Nursing Service, Lake Pleasant, N.Y., 1977-80, supervising pub. health nurse, 1980-82, dir. patient svcs., 1982-86; quality improvement coord. Susquehanna-Adirondack Regional Emergency Med. Svcs. Program, 1986-96; dir. ednl. svcs. Adirondack Appalachian Regional Emergency Med. Svcs. program, 1996—. mem. profl. adv. com. Hamilton County Nursing Svc., Indian Lake, N.Y., 1992—. Author instructional booklet: Assessing Your Patients, 1983, (pamphlet) A Note to Parents, 1985, Advanved Assessment and Treatment of Life Threatening Pediatric Emergencies, 1995. Bd. dirs. Am. Cancer Soc.-Hamilton County Unit, Speculator, 1972-76, Speculator Vol. Ambulance Corps, Inc., 1974—, ARC-Hamilton County chpt., Lake Pleasant, N.Y., 1981-88; mem. adminstrv. bd. dirs. Grace United Meth. Ch., Speculator, 1982—, Rainbow Christian Children's Ctr., 1992—. Martha Hazen Scholar Am. Legion, 1966; recipient Svcs. award Am. Legion, 1977. Mem. N.Y. State Assn. County Health Ofcls., Adirondack-Appalachian Regional Emergency Med. Svcs. Coun. (chmn. 1982-87, chmn. tng. com. 1982—), Emergency Nurses Assn., Hamilton County Emergency Med. Svcs. Coun. (sec.-treas. 1974-90, instr. 1974—). Republican. Home: PO Box 203 Speculator NY 12164-0203 Office: Susquehanna Adirondack Regional Emergency Med Svcs Prog PO Box 212 Speculator NY 12164-0212

MULLEN, ANDREW JUDSON, physician; b. Selma, Ala., June 23, 1923; s. Andrew J. and Helen (Johnson) M.; A.B., Vanderbilt U., 1948; M.D., Jefferson Med. Coll., 1952; children: J. Thomas, Debbie, Gail, Andrea, Shawn, Connie, Beth. Intern, U.S. Marine Hosp., Galveston, Tex., 1952-53; resident Tex. Med. Center, Houston, 1954-57; chief neurology and psychiatry service VA Hosp., Jackson, Miss., 1957; dir. Mobile (Ala.) Mental Health Center, 1957-58; practice medicine, specializing in psychiatry and neurology, Shreveport, La., 1958—; chief female service Confederate Meml. Med. Center, 1959-63, bd. dirs., chmn. pub. rels. com., 1964-72; med. dir. Shreveport Child Guidance Center, 1961-64; mem. med. adv. bd. Humana Corp.; cons. psychiatry and neurology Barksdale AFB, VA Hosp.; chief staff Brentwood Neuro-Psychiat. Hosp., Shreveport, 1970-73; clin. prof. psychiatry La. State U. Sch. Medicine, 1975—. Dep. coroner, cons., Caddo Parish, La., 1964; chmn. mental health com. Community Council, 1964—; chmn. bd. dirs. Brentwood Hosp., Shreveport, 1982-84, chief med. staff, 1985-86; bd. dirs. Humana, Brentwood hosps., 1986—; psychiat. dir. Charter Outreach Program, Shreveport, 1987—; chief of staff, med. dir. Charter Forest Hosp, 1988—, Caddo Oaks Hosp., 1993—; charter Forest Hosp, 1988-94. With RCAF, 1941-42, Sgt. AUS, 1942-45. Decorated Purple Heart with oak leaf cluster, Bronze Star. Diplomate Am. Bd. Psychiatry and Neurology (asso. examiner). Fellow Am., So. psychiat. assns., Am. Coll. Psychiatrists; mem. AMA, So. Med. Assn., Shreveport Med. Soc. (dir. 1971-72), Am. Soc. Psychol Analytical Physicians, Flying Physicians Assn., Alpha Tau Omega, Nu Sigma Nu. Episcopalian. Home: 241 Symphony Ln Shreveport LA 71105-4143 Office: 745 Olive St Ste 203 Shreveport LA 71104-2246

MULLEN, CHARLES FREDERICK, health services administrator; b. Washington, June 14, 1938; s. DeWitt Cliffton and Annabelle (Fischer) M.; m. Mary Elizabeth Turrisi, Sept. 11, 1964 (div. Mar. 1975); children: Henry John, Elizabeth Mary. BA, U. Va., 1962; BS, New England Coll. Optometry, 1969, OD, 1970; D of Ocular Sci., So. Coll. Optometry, 1994. Dir. clinics New England Coll. Optometry, Boston, 1970-76; exec. dir. The Eye Inst., Pa. Coll. Optometry, Phila., 1976-90; dir. optometry svc. Dept. VA, Washington, 1990—; adj. clin. prof. SUNY, N.Y.C., 1990—; mem. Dept. VA Spl. Subcom. Eye Care, Washington, 1991—; observer Eye Coun., Nat. Eye Inst., Bethesda, Md., 1990—, del. ANSI, 1990—. Contbr. articles to profl. jours. Host parent Overbrook Sch. Blind, Phila., 1985-86; vol. Big. Bro., West Chester, Pa., 1988-89; bd. dirs. Clavary Schlter, Washington, 1990-92. Lt. (j.g.) USNR. Mem. Am. Acad. Optometry, Am. Pub. Health Assn., Am. Optometric Assn., NAt. Assn. VA Ops., Assn. Mil. Surgeons U.S. (chmn. optometric sect. 1991, 95), Assn. Schs. & Colls. Optometry (affiliate). Democrat. Episcopalian. Home: 4796 W Braddock Rd Alexandria VA 22311 Office: Dept VA 810 Vermont Ave NW Washington DC 20420

MULLER, EUGENE WILLIAM, psychologist; b. Teaneck, N.J., Oct. 23, 1956; s. Eugene Harry and Emily M.; m. Ju-Nie Shen, Mar. 26, 1984. BS in Psychology, Ramapo Coll., 1978; MA in Psychology, Columbia U., 1982, MA in Computing in Edn., 1984, EdD in Psychology, 1985. Lic. psychologist, N.Y. Data mgr. Tchrs. Coll. Columbia U., N.Y.C., 1983-85; test specialist N.Y.C. Bd. Edn., 1985-86; sr. psychometrician N.Y. Stock Exch., N.Y.C., 1987-88; pres. Indsl. and Ednl. Measurement, Montvale, N.J., 1988—; adj. prof. CUNY, Queens, 1985-87; cons. Nat. Assn. Purchasing Mgmt., Tempe, Ariz., 1987—; dir. assessment Bloomfield (N.J.) Coll., 1992—. Author: (with others) Changes in Science Education, 1990, Handbook of Test Validity, 1991; editor: CPM Diagnostic Kit, 1988. Mem. APA, Am. Ednl. Rsch. Assn., Nat. Coun. on Measurement in Edn., Met. Assn. Applied Psychologists, Kappa Delta Pi, Phi Delta Kappa. Office: 7 Terkuile Rd Montvale NJ 07645-1213

MULLER, FREDERICA DANIELA, psychology educator; d. Leopold and Elena; m. Dr. L. Muller; children: Daniela, Adrian. Grad., Med. Inst. Radiology, Romania, 1962, PsyD in Clin. Psychology, 1965, M in Internat. Law and Bus., 1966; specialization courses in Psychodrama, Moreno Inst., Vienna, 1969; grad., Inst. Rsch. in Aging, Rome, 1970, Miami Inst. Psychology, 1987. Diplomate Am. Bd. Forensic Medicine, Am. Bd. Forensic Examiners; lic. psychologist, Pa.; lic. psychotherapist, Fla.; cert. family mediator, Fla. Supreme Ct. continuing edn. units provider psych. Prof. Sch. Continuing Edn. Barry U., North Miami, Fla.; instr. advanced courses in psychology, psychodrama, med. ethics, social manners; guest speaker Colloque Internat., Bucharest, Romania, 1989-93; guest lectr. U. Arboga, Sweden 1968-72; founder Internat. Studies for Biopsychosocial Issues, 1991; cons. dept. of marriage, family and child devel. systemic studies, Nova U., 1992; founder Euro Am. Exch. Co., 1980; with Santé Internat., Switzerland, 1982-85; dir. Ctr. Biopsychosocial Medicine, 1995. Conducted rsch. on stress and aging with Dr. Anna Aslan, world renowned author; developed 45 minute stress reduction program for use in the work place. Author: The Management of Occupational Stress and Its Linkage to Social Pressures; contbr. articles to profl. jours. Mem. APA, Medicins du Monde (hon.), Am. Soc. Group Psychotherapy and Psychodrama, Soc. Psychol., Studies Social of Issues, World Fedn. for Mental Health.

MULLER, GREGORY ALAN, health facilities administrator, mayor; b. Newark, Feb. 11, 1947; s. Richard Mapes and Doris J. (Morgan) M.; m. Geraldine A. Bleach, May 1, 1976; children: Laura M., Gregory P. AS in Psychology, Union Coll.; BSBA, S.W. U. La.; MBA, Can. Sch. Mgmt., Toronto, 1994. Sr. br. mgr. fin. divsn. Household Internat., Inc., 1972-84, ops. mgr. retail svcs. divsn., 1984-87, mgr. legal svcs., 1987-89; v.p., chief loan officer Lehigh Savs. Bank, Union Twp., N.J., 1989-91; program dir., bus. mgr., lectr., fin. counselor St. Barnabas Behavioral Health Hosp., Union, N.J., 1991—; dir. administrative ops. behavioral health Union (N.J.) Hosp., 1991—. Mem. Union Twp. Com., 1987-90, 90-93, commr. fire dept., mcpl. drug alliance, Union ctr. spl. improvement dist., mayor Union Twp., 1995; sec. Union Count y Planning Bd., 1993—; mem. Union Twp. Bd. Edn., chmn. fin., 1985-87; active Regular Rep. Club Union, bd. dirs.; mem. N.J. Coun. on affordable housing. Mem. DAV, VFW, Union County Coll. Alumni, Rutgers Sch. Drug & Alcohol Studies Alumni,Am. Soc. Profl. Appraisers, Union County Assn. Realtors, Am. Soc. Notary Pubs., Vietnam Vets. Am., Am. Legion, Masons, Shriners, Elks, Optimists. Home: 1675 Kenneth Ave Union NJ 07083-5115

MÜLLER, KARSTEN ERASMÚS, retired obstetrician and gynecologist; b. Odense, Denmark, Oct. 21, 1926; s. Sven and Karen Harriet (Lützhöft) M.; m. Kirsten Henriette Jensen, Oct. 2, 1953; children: Lise, Klaus. Degree, Kathedral Sch., Odense, 1945, Med. Sch. U. Copenhagen, 1953. Young assisting dr. various hosps., 1953-60; elder assisting dr. Dept. of Surgery, U. Hosp. of Århus, Denmark, 1960-62; elder assiting dr. Dept. Ob-Gyn., Univ. Hosp. of Copenhagen, 1962-63, 64-65; younger asst. dr. Danish Red Cross Hosp., Kinshasa, 1963-64; elder asst. dr. Dept. of Ob-Gyn., Frederiksberg Hosp., Copenhagen, 1965-69; chief of dept. Dept. Ob-Gyn., Ctrl. Hosp. of Senderborg, 1969-94; mem. exec. com. Union of Younger Surgeons in Denmark, 1962-63; mem. coun. Union of Jr. Drs., Denmark, 1961-62; chmn. local com. Danish Soc. for Fight Against Cancer, Sønderburg, 1974-81; chmn. subcom. for history Union of Drs. in County of South Jutland, Denmark, 1985-89. Contbr. numerous articles to various Scandinavian med. jours. Lt. Med. Corps. Danish Army, 1953. Mem. Rotary Club of Sonderborg (pres. 1982-83). Home: 10 Skovbrinken, 6400 Sonderborg Denmark

MULLER, NORMA E., social worker; b. Stuttgart, Ark., Aug. 29, 1939; d. Lloyd T. and Beryl (Wiest) Estes; m. Richard L. Muller, Aug. 7, 1960; 1 child, Richard Jr. BS, U. Cen. Ark., 1961; MSW, U. Md., 1965. Lic. social worker, Md. Work cons. Charles County Nursing Home, La Plata, Md.; emergency rm. social worker (part-time) Physicians Meml. Hosp., La Plata; chief social worker Charles County Health Dept., La Plata, chief devel. disabilites programs. Mem. NASW, Acad. Cert. Social Workers, So. Md. Social Workers Assn. Home: 3153 Eutaw Forest Dr Waldorf MD 20603-4070

MULLER, REID THOMAS, physician; b. N.Y.C., Aug. 17, 1960; s. Charles William and Patricia Jane (Sheridan) M.; m. Shelley Ann Gilroy, Sept. 19, 1987; children: Aislinn Patricia, Reid Charles. BS, Rensselaer Polytechnic Inst., 1980; MD, Ross U. Sch. Medicine, 1984. Diplomate Am. Bd. Internal Medicine. Resident Meth. Hosp., Bklyn., 1984-87, fellow in cardiology, 1987-89; mem. staff Cmty. Meml. Hosp., Hamilton, N.Y., 1989—, Crouse-Irvine Meml. Hosp., Syracuse, N.Y., 1990—, Oneida (N.Y.) City Hosp., 1991—; dir. cardio lab. Cmty. Meml. Hosp., 1989—, dir. ICU, 1989-91; dir. cardiac lab. Oneida City Hosp., 1991—. Contbr. articles to profl. jours. Fellow ACP, Am. Coll. Chest Physicians, Am. Coll. Cardiology. Office: 150 Broad St Hamilton NY 13346

MULLER, ROBERT JOSEPH, gynecologist; b. New Orleans, Dec. 5, 1946; s. Robert Harry and Camille (Eckert) M.; m. Susan Philipsen, Aug. 22, 1974; children: Ryan, Matt. BS, St. Louis U., 1968; BS, MSc, Emory U., 1976; MD, La. State U., New Orleans, 1981. Intern Charity Hosp., New Orleans, 1981-82; resident La. State U. Affiliate Hosp., 1982-85; resident staff physician La. State U. Med. Ctr., New Orleans, 1981-85; pvt. practice Camellia Women's Ctr., Slidell, La., 1985—; staff physician Tulane Med. Ctr., New Orleans, 1986—; med. dir. Northshore Regional Med. Ctr., Slidell, 1987—, New Orleans Police Dept., 1981-95, S.W. La. Search and Rescue, Covington, La., 1986—, St. Tammany Parish Sheriff Dept., Covington, 1989—, commdr., 1990—, Camellia City Classic, Slidell, 1989—, Crawfishman Triathalon, Mandeville, La., 1988—, Res-Q-Med Laser Team, 1984—. Contbr. articles to profl. jours. Recipient Commendation Medal New Orleans Police Dept., 1986, 87, 89, Medal Valor St. Tammany Parish Sheriff Office, Covington, 1990, Cert. Valor S.E. La. Search and Rescue, Mandeville, 1990; named one of Outstanding Young Men of Am., 1984. Mem. Am. Coll. Ob-Gyn., La. State Med. Soc., Profl. Assn. Diving Instrs. (divemaster 1991, asst. instr. 1995), So. Offshore Racing Assn. (med. dir. 1982—), Offshore Profl. Racing Tour (med. dir. staff 1990—), Am. Power Boat Assn. (med. staff 1984-89). Roman Catholic. Home: 128 Golden Pheasant Dr Slidell LA 70461-3007 Office: Camellia Womens Ctr 105 Smart Pl Slidell LA 70458-2039

MÜLLER-ISBERNER, JOACHIM RÜDIGER, psychiatrist, educator; b. Leipzig, Saxon, Germany, Mar. 25, 1952; s. Joachim Roland and Ursula (Köhler) M.; m. Petra Isberner, Sept. 28, 1984; 1 child, Nora Isberner. MD, Liebig U., Giessen, Germany, 1976. Intern Univ. Hospital, Giessen, Germany, 1976-77; resident Psychiat. Hospital Giessen, 1979-83; med. dir. Forensic Hospital, Haina, Germany, 1987—; instr. Justus Liebig U., 1988—. Contbr. articles to med. jours. Capt. German Army, 1977-78. Mem. Internat. Acad. Law and Mental Health, German Soc. for Psychiat. and Nerve Medicine. Home: Professorenweg 18, D-35394 Giessen Hessen, Germany Office: Forensic Psychiat Hospital, Landgraf-Philip-Platz, D-35114 Haina Hessen, Germany

MULLIGAN, MICHAEL EUGENE, physician, radiologist; b. Troy, N.Y., Feb. 26, 1954; s. Eugene Lawrence and Carolyn Anne (Roeck) M.; m. Frances Anne Came, May 11, 1974; 1 child, Matthew Michael. BA summa cum laude, St. Anselm Coll., Manchester, N.H., 1976; MD, Tufts U., 1980. Diplomate Am. Bd. Radiology, Nat. Bd. Med. Examiners. Intern Tripler Army Med. Ctr., Honolulu, 1980-81, resident in diagnostic radiology, 1981-84, chief uroradiology sect., 1987, chief skeletal radiology sect., 1987-90, chief diagnostic radiology svc., 1989-90; officer in charge skeletal radiology sect. Walter Reed Army Med. Ctr., Washington, 1991-93; from asst. prof. to assoc. prof. clin. radiology Uniformed Svcs. U. Health Scis., Bethesda, Md., 1990—; asst. prof. diagnostic radiology U. Md. Med. Ctr., Balt., 1993—. Author: Classic Radiologic Signs, 1996. Asst. coach Montgomery Youth Hockey Assn., 1994—, Good Counsel H.S. Hockey Team, 1994—; trustee Bel Pre Homeowners Assn., 1995—. Lt. col. U.S. Army, 1974—. Decorated Joint Svcs. Commendation medal, Meritorius Svc. medal with 2 oak leaf clusters, others. Mem. AMA, Radiol. Soc. N.Am., Am. Roentgen Ray Soc., Am. Acad. Forensic Scis., Soc. Skeletal Radiology, Am. Coll. Radiology, Soc. Magnetic Resonance Imaging, Delta Epsilon Sigma. Office: U Md Med System Dept Diagnostic Radiology 22 S Greene St Baltimore MD 21201

MULLIKIN, CATHERINE MARY, critical care nurse; b. Hornell, N.Y., Mar. 2, 1959; d. Douglas Milton Wise and Sandra Louise Amidon Woodworth; m. Dennis Paul Mullikin, Dec. 15, 1979; children: Jessica Lynn, Jonathan Ryan. Diploma, St. James Mercy Hosp., Hornell, 1991. RN, N.Y.; cert. critical care nurse; cert. ACLS. Staff nurse St. James Mercy Hosp., Hornell, 1992—, preceptor ICU/CCU, 1992-94; surg. intensive care staff nurse Strong Meml. Hosp., Rochester, N.Y.; lectr. St. James Sch. Nursing, Hornell, 1993, 94, preceptor to staff nurses in EKG interpretation, 1993-94; health care reform contractor Ho. of Reps., Washington, 1994. Fellow Critical Care Nurse Assn., New Eng. Hist. and Geneal. Soc. Democrat. Episcopalian. Home: 28 E Van Scoter St Hornell NY 14843

MULLIN, WALTER R., plastic surgeon, educator; b. Columbus, Ga., May 10, 1943; s. Cecil Walter and Frances E. (Monroe) M.; m. Patricia Mullin; children: Scott, Crista. BS, U. Fla., 1965; MD, U. Miami, 1969. Diplomate Am. Bd. Plastic Surgery. Pvt. practice Plastic Surgery Ctr., Miami, 1976—; acting chief plastic surgery VA Hosp., Miami, 1978-83; assoc. prof. plastic surgery U. Miami Sch. Medicine, 1976—. Contbr. articles to profl. jours. 1st lt. USAR, 1975-77. Fellow Am. Coll. Surgeons; mem. Am. Bd. Plastic Surgery. Home: 4995 Hammock Lake Dr Miami FL 33156 Office: Plastic Surgery Ctr 1444 NW 14th Ave Miami FL 33125

MULLINS, CHARLES BROWN, physician, academic administrator; b. Rochester, Ind., July 29, 1934; s. Charles E. and Mary Ruth B. (Bamberger) M.; B.A., N. Tex. State U., 1954; M.D., U. Tex., 1958; m. Stella Churchill, Dec. 27, 1955; children—Holly, David. Intern, U. Colo. Med. Center, Denver, 1958-59; resident medicine Parkland Meml. Hosp., Dallas, 1962-64; USPHS rsch. fellow U. Tex. Southwestern Med. Sch., Dallas, 1964-65; chief resident medicine Parkland Meml. Hosp., 1965-66; USPHS spl. rsch. fellow cardiology br. Nat. Heart Inst., Bethesda, Md., 1967-68; practice medicine specializing in cardiology, Dallas, 1966—; mem. sr. attending staff Parkland Meml. Hosp., dir. med. affairs, 1977-79; mem. cons. staff Presbyn. Hosp., VA Hosp.; asst. prof. medicine U. Tex. Southwestern Med. Sch., Dallas, 1968-71, asso. prof., 1971-75, dir. clin. cardiology, 1971-77, prof., 1975-79, clin. prof. medicine, 1979-81, prof., 1981—; prof. medicine U. Tex. Health Sci. Center, Dallas, 1979-81; exec. vice-chancellor health affairs U. Tex. System, 1981—; chief exec. officer Dallas County Hosp. Dist., 1979-81. Served with M.C., USAF, 1959-62. Diplomate Am. Bd. Internal Medicine. Fellow ACP, Am. Coll. Cardiology (Tex. gov. 1974-77, chmn. bd. govs. 1976), Am. Heart Assn. Council on Clin. Cardiology; mem. Am. Fedn. Clin. Rsch., Assn. Acad. Health Ctrs., Assn. Univ. Cardiologists, Laennec Soc., AMA, Alpha Omega Alpha. Contbr. articles on cardiology to med. jours. Office: 601 Colorado St Austin TX 78701-2904

MULLINS, JAMES I., virologist, educator; b. Miami, May 25, 1952; s. James I. Mullins and Evelyn Lelia (Bailey) Meier; m. Barbara J. Sina, Aug. 8, 1978 (div. Feb. 1984). BA, U. So. Fla., 1974; PhD, U. Minn., 1978. Postdoctoral fellow Calif. Inst. Technology, Pasadena, 1978-82; asst. prof. Harvard U., Sch. Pub. Health, Boston, 1982-86; assoc. prof. Harvard U., Dept. Cancer Biology, Boston, 1987-89, adj. prof., 1989—; acting prof. Stanford (Calif.) U. Sch. Medicine, 1989-90; prof. Stanford U., Dept. Immunology, 1990—, prof., chmn., 1991—; cons. in field. Contbr. over 60 articles to profl. jours. Recipient Gov.'s Recognition award for AIDS Rsch., 1986.

MULLINS, RUTH GLADYS, nurse; b. Westville, N.S., Can., Aug. 25, 1943; d. William G. and Gladys H.; came to U.S., 1949, naturalized, 1955; student Tex. Womans U., 1961-64; BS in Nursing, Calif. State U.-Long Beach, 1966; MNursing, UCLA, 1973; m. Leonard E. Mullins, Aug. 27, 1963; children: Deborah R., Catherine M., Leonard III. Pub. health nurse, L.A. County Health Dept., 1967-68; nurse Meml. Hosp. Med. Center, Long Beach, 1968-72; dir. pediatric nurse practitioner program Calif. State U., Long Beach, 1973—, asst. prof., 1975-80, assoc. prof., 1980-85, prof., 1985—; health svc. credential coord. Sch. Nursing Calif. State U., Long Beach, Calif., chmn., 1979-81, coord. grad. programs, 1985-92; mem. Calif. Maternal, Child and Adolescent Health Bd., 1977-84; vice chair Long Beach/Orange County Health Consortium, 1984-85, chair 1985-86. Tng. grantee HHS, Divsn. Nursing Calif. Dept. Health; cert. pediatric nurse practitioner. Fellow Nat. Assn. Pediatric Nurse Assocs. and Practitioners (exec. bd., pres. 1990-91), Nat. Fedn. Nursing Specialty Orgns. (sec. 1991-93); mem. Am. Pub. Health Assn., Nat. Alliance Nurse Practitioners (governing body 1990-92), Assn. Faculties Pediatric Nurse Practitioner Programs, L.A. and Orange County Assn. Pediatric Nurse Practitioners and Assocs., Am. Assn. U. Faculty, Ambulatory Pediatric Assn. Democrat. Methodist. Author: (with B. Nelms) Growth and Development: A Primary Health Care Approach; contbg. author: Quick Reference to Pediatric Nursing, 1984; asst. editor Jour. Pediatric Health Care. Home: 6382 Heil Ave Huntington Beach CA 92647-4232 Office: Calif State U Dept Nursing 1250 N Bellflower Blvd Long Beach CA 90840-0006

MULLINS, WAYMAN C., psychologist, educator, consultant; b. Little Rock, Nov. 10, 1951; s. William Wayman and Mary Anna (Beall) M.; m. Louise C. Casey, Aug. 2, 1976; children: Ruth, Rachael. BA, U. Ark., 1978, MA, 1979, PhD in Psychology, 1983. Diplomate in police psychology. Teaching and rsch. asst. U. Ark., Fayetteville, 1977-82; asst. prof. psychology Hofstra U., Hempstead, N.Y., 1982-84; asst. prof. criminal justice S.W. Tex. State U., San Marcos, 1984-87, assoc. prof., 1987-93, prof., 1993—; cons. San Antonio Police Dept., 1984—, U.S. Govt., 1987—. Author: Terrorist Organizations in the U.S., 1988, 1942: Issue in Doubt, 1994, Crisis Management, 1996; editor Jour. Police and Criminal Psychology, 1984-95; contbr. articles to profl. jours. and books. Pres. N.W. Ark. Vets. Assn., Fayetteville, 1975-77, San Marcos Little League, 1989-94; mem. exec. coun. San Marcos Explorer Post, 1988-93; advisor Criminal Justice Explorer Post #120; res. police officer San Marcos Police Dept., 1987-95; res. deputy with Hays County Sheriff's Dept. Recipient grants. Mem. Soc. Police and Criminal Psychology (pres. 1984-85), Acad. Criminal Justice Scis., Am. Psychol. Assn., Human Factors Soc., Internat. Assn. Chiefs of Police, N.Y. Acad. Scis., Internat. Narcotic Enforcement Officers Assn. Office: SW Tex State U Dept Criminal Justice San Marcos TX 78666

MULROW, PATRICK JOSEPH, medical educator; s. Patrick J. and Delia (O'Keefe) M.; m. Jacquelyn Pinover, Aug. 8, 1953; children: Deborah, Nancy, Robert, Catherine. AB, Colgate U., 1947; MD, Cornell U., 1951; MSc (hon.), Yale U., 1969. Intern N.Y. Hosp., 1951-52, resident, 1952-54; instr. physiology Med. Coll. Cornell U., 1954-55; research fellow Stanford U., 1955-57; instr. medicine Yale U., 1957-60, asst. prof., 1960-66, assoc. prof., 1966-69, prof. medicine, 1969-75; chmn. dept. medicine Med. Coll. Ohio, Toledo, 1975-95, prof. medicine, 1975—; chmn. ednl. com. Council for high blood pressure rsch. Am. Heart Assn., 1968-70, mem. exec. com., 1986—, vice-chmn. of coun., 1990-92, chmn. 1992-94, past chmn., 1995—; mem. study sect. NIH, 1970-74. Editorial bd. Jour. Clin. Endocrinology and Metabolism, 1966-70, 75-79, Endocrine Rsch., 1974—, Jour. Exptl. Biology and Medicine, Hypertension, 1994—; contbr. articles to profl. jours. With USNR, 1944-46. Mem. ACP, Am. Soc. Clin. Investigation, Assn. Am. Physicians, Am. Physiol. Soc., Endocrine Soc., Am. Fedn. Clin. Rsch., Am. Clin. and Climatol. Assn., Am. Heart Assn. (nat. rsch. com., chmn. cardiovasc. regulation rsch. study com. 1986-91), Assn. Profs. Medicine, Assn. Program Dirs. in Internal Medicine, Cen. Soc. Clin. Rsch. (pres. 1988-89), Internat. Soc. Hypertension, World Hypertension League (sec.-gen. 1995—), Inter-Am. Soc. Hypertension, Sigma Xi (pres. Yale chpt. 1965-66), Alpha Omega Alpha. Home: 9526 Carnoustie Rd Perrysburg OH 43551-3501 Office: Med Coll of Ohio Dept of Medicine PO Box 10008 Toledo OH 43699-0008

MULTACH, MARK, physician, educator; b. Miami Beach, Fla., May 20, 1956; s. David and Roberta Rosalie (Cohen) M.; 1 child, Matthew Daniel. BS, Northwestern U., 1978; MD, U. Miami, 1982. Asst. prof. U. Miami Sch. Medicine, Coral Gables, Fla., 1985-91, assoc. prof., dir. clin. programs/acting chief gen. medicine, 1991—. Author (with others): Streptoccal Pharyngitis, 1986. Mem. Am. Geriatrics Soc., Am. Coll. Physicians, Soc. Gen. Internal Medicine. Home: 12545 SW 68th Ct Miami FL 33156-6211 Office: U Miami Sch Medicine PO Box 016960 R-103A Miami FL 33101-6960

MULVEY, LAURI DIANE, pediatric ophthalmologist; b. Bronxville, N.Y., Jan. 2, 1952; d. Lawrence Mance and Dorothy Eve (Quash) Ervin; m. John Michael Mulvey, Sept. 28, 1982; children: Claire Kristen, John Michael, Elizabeth Shannon. BA, Sarah Lawrence Coll., 1972; MD, Harvard U., 1977. Diplomate Am. Bd. Ophthalmology. Attending surgeon Med. Ctr. Princeton, N.J., 1972; courtesy staff, surgery Wills Eye Hosp., Phila., 1982—. Contbr. articles to profl. jours. Mem. Am. Acad. Ophthalmology, Am. Soc. Pediatric Ophthalmologists and Strabismologists, N.J. Acad. Ophthalmology, Mercer County Med. Soc., Delaware Valley Pediatric Ophthalmology Assn., Harvard Club of Princeton. Protestant. Office: 213 Nassau St Princeton NJ 08540

MULVEY, MARY C., retired adult education director, gerontologist; b. Bangor, Maine, Aug. 17, 1909; d. Michael J. and Ann Loretta (Higgins) Crowley; m. Gordon F. Mulvey, Jan. 25, 1940. BA, U. Maine, 1930; MA, Brown U., 1953; EdD, Harvard U., 1961; LHD (hon.), U. Maine, 1991. Dir. adminstrn. on aging State of R.I., $S, R.I., 1960-63; co-founder Nat. Coun. Sr. Citizens, 1961; pres. Nat. Sr. Citizens Edn. and Rsch. Ctr., Washington, 1963—; 1st v.p. Nat. Coun. Sr. Citizens, 1976—; guidance counselor Providence Sch. Dept., 1963-65; dir. adult edn. City of Providence Sch. Dept., 1965-79; reg. prog. rep. Title V, Older Ams. Act, Nat. Coun. Sr. Citizens, Washington, 1980-94; major role in enactment of Medicare and Older Americans Act, 1950-65; del., adv. com. White House Conf. on Aging, 1961, 71, 81, 95; cons. Fed. Housing for the Aging, Washington, 1963-65, mem. tech. rev. com. Older Ams. Act Title IV, 1966-70; instr. preparing retirement, developer women's program U. R.I., 1963-80; appt. by Pres. Carter to Fed. Coun. Aging, 1979, by Pres. Clinton, 1995; pres. R.I. State Coun. Sr. Citizens, 1982—; charter mem. adv. bd. Coll. Arts, Humanities, U. Maine, 1992—; mem. various coms. state and nat. level. Publs. and contbr. articles to profl. jours. Recipient Soroptomists fellow award in rsch. in gerontology Harvard U., 1955, 57, 59, Cert. of award as Project Dir. of Sr. AIDES Employment Program, 1968-79, Medicare award R.I. State Coun. Sr. Citizens and Nat. Coun. Sr. Citizens, 1985, Disting. Achievement award U. Maine, 1980, Disting. Achievement award Berwick Acad., 1981, Justice for All award R.I. Bar Assn., 1981, Woman of Yr. award Nat. Sr. Pageant, 1982, R.I. Women 1st R.I. Sec. of State, 1991, citation Syracuse U., 1991, R.I. Dept. Elderly Affairs, 1993, 25th Anniversary Title V Sr. Employment award Nat. Coun. Sr. Citizens, 1993, Lifetime Achievement award Nat. Coun. Sr. Citizens, 1994, Co-Founder and Continuing Bd. Mem. award Nat. Coun. Sr. Citizens, 1995, Svcs. for St. Citizens award, 1995; inducted into R.I. Heritage Hall of Fame, 1993. Fellow Gerontol. Soc. Am.; mem. ACA, AAUW, Am. Assn. Adult and Continuing Edn., Harvard U. Alumni Assn. (Alumni award R.I. chpt. 1986), U. Maine Alumni Assn., Brown U. Alumni Assn., Pi Lambda Theta, Delta Delta Delta. Home: 95 Plymouth Rd East Providence RI 02914-1943

MUMFORD, ROBERT SUTTON, psychiatrist; b. Seattle, July 23, 1918; s. Maurice Clearance and Ione (Sutton) M.; m. Emily Hamilton, July 1950 (div. 1969); m. Beverly Hess Hamilton, 1975; children: Bonnie McIlhenny, Betsy Cohen, Nancy Pierce. MD, McGill U., 1943. Diplomate Am. Bd. Psychiatry and Neurology; cert. Nat. Bd. Medicine. Intern Montreal Gen. Hosp., Can., 1943, L.A. County Hosp., 1944; resident in psychiatry N.Y. Psychiat. Inst., 1947-48, Bellevue Psychiat. Hosp., 1948-50; pvt. practice N.Y.C., 1950—, Old Greenwich, Conn., 1975—; assoc. editor N.Y. State

Psychiat. Assn. Bull., 1950—; cons. in psychiatry Presbyn. Hosp., N.Y.C. Capt. USAF, 1944-47. Fellow Am. Psychiat. Assn. (life), Am. Coll. Psychiatrists, Am. Coll. Psychoanalysts (pres. 1987), N.Y. Acad. Medicine (life); mem. AMA (life), Univ. Club, Innis Arden Country Club. Republican. Mem. Christian Ch. Home and Office: 14 Grimes Rd Old Greenwich CT 06870-2019 Office: 90 Park Ave Ste 1600 New York NY 10016

MUNCH, LARRY C., physician; b. Kansas City, Mo., June 5, 1956; s. Kenneth C. and Elinore V. (Cello) M.; m. Rita K. Munn, July 29, 1982. BS, U. Ky., 1979, MD, 1983. Diplomate Am. Bd. Urology. Asst. prof. surgery U. Ky. Medicine, Lexington, 1988—; staff urologist Lexington Clinic, 1996—. Fellow Am. Coll. Surgeons. Office: Lexington Clinic 1221 S Broadway Lexington KY 40504

MUNCY, ESTLE PERSHING, physician; b. Tazewell, Tenn., Apr. 9, 1918; s. William Loyd and Flora Media (Monday) M.; m. Dorothy Davis, Dec. 31, 1946 (div. Apr. 1980); children: Robert H., Teresa A., Dorothy J., Estle II, James; m. Jean Marie Hayter, Mar. 19, 1985. AB, Lincoln Meml. U., 1939; MD, U. Tenn., 1943. Resident Dallas Meth. Hosp., 1948; tchg. resident Tufts Med. Sch., Boston, 1949-50; physician Jefferson City, Tenn., 1950-96. Author: The Muncys in the New World, 1988, People and Places in Jefferson County, Tennessee, 1994. Alderman Jefferson City, 1974-77; chmn. Jefferson City Planning Commn., 1976-79. Capt. M.C., U.S. Army, 1944-46. Mem. Tenn. Heart Assn. (pres. 1966-67), Hamblen County Med. Soc. (pres. 1960-61), Jefferson County Hist. Soc. (pres. 1993-94, historian 1995—). Republican. Baptist. Home: 1428 Russell Ave Jefferson City TN 37760-2529

MUNDINGER, MARY O'NEIL, nursing educator; b. Fredonia, N.Y., Apr. 27, 1937; d. Thomas Lewis and Dorothy (Hanselman) O'Neil; m. Paul C. Mundinger, Aug. 23, 1958; children: Paul Jr., Ann Mundinger Schimenti, Thomas, Elizabeth. BS, U. Mich., 1959; MA, Columbia U., 1974, PhD, 1981. Administr., instr. Tchrs. Coll. Columbia U., N.Y.C., 1975; adj. instr. Pace U., N.Y.C., 1975-77, asst. prof., 1977-82; asst. prof. nursing, dir. grad. program Columbia U. Sch. Nursing, N.Y.C., 1982-83, assoc. prof. nursing, dir. grad. program, 1983-84, assoc. prof., assoc. dean adminstrv. affairs, 1984-85, assoc. prof., asst. dean faculty of medicine, 1986—, dean, prof., 1986—; bd. dirs. Conn. Hospice, Branford; adv. group steering com. N.Y. Acad. Medicine, N.Y.C., 1992—; regional adv. com. Nat. Network Librs. of Medicine, N.Y.C., 1992—; Robert Wood Johnson health policy fellows bd. Inst. Medicine, Washington, 1990—, Health Svcs. Improvement Fund, N.Y.C., 1992—, health policy adv. com. Sen. Edward Kennedy, Washington, 1985—, med. adv. bd. Walt Disney Imagineering (Wonders of Life), Orlando, Fla., 1988-89; charter mem. health care tech., Inst. Medicine, NAS, 1985—. Author: Home Care Controversy: Too Little, Too Late, Too Costly, 1983 (Book of Yr. 1984), Autonomy in Nursing, 1980 (Book of Yr. 1981). Recipient grant W.K. Kellogg Found., 1989, grant Katzenbach Found., 1986. Office: 630 W 168th St New York NY 10032-3702 office: Office of Dean of Nursing Columbia Univ 116 Street and Broadway New York NY 10027*

MUNDORFF SHRESTHA, SHEILA ANN, cariologist; b. Rochester, N.Y., Dec. 14, 1945; d. Karl Mundorff and Elizabeth Mary (Braun) Ross; m. Buddhi Man Shrestha, June 18, 1988. BS in Biology, Nazareth Coll., Rochester, 1967; MS in Microbiology, U. Rochester, 1984. Lab. technician Eastman Dental Ctr., Rochester, 1967-69, rsch. asst., 1969-71, rsch. assoc., 1971-92, small animal expt. coord., 1984-92, sect. head animal/microbiol. rsch., 1987—, chmn. Instl. Animal Care and Use Com., 1990—, vivarium dir., 1990—, med. emergency program dir., 1991-92, asst. prof., 1992—; mem. animal resource group ADA Health Found., Chgo., 1981-83; cons. working group Sci. Consensus Conf.-Assessment Cariogenic Potential of Foods, San Antonio, 1985; participant, reactor, co-chair animal caries models working groups Conf. on Clin. Aspects of Demineralization of Teeth, Rochester, N.Y., 1994. Patentee in field. CPR instr. ARC, Rochester, 1978-94, cert. 1st responder, N.Y.S., 1992-95. NIH, Nat. Inst. Dental Rsch. grantee, 1986, 87, 88. Mem. Am. Assn. Dental Rsch. (sec.-treas. Rochester sect. 1977-92). Roman Catholic. Office: Eastman Dental Ctr 625 Elmwood Ave Rochester NY 14620-2913

MUNIC, RACHELLE ETHEL, health services administrator; b. Hartford, Conn., Apr. 15, 1953; d. Abe and Sara (Levenberg) M. BS in Med. Tech. summa cum laude, U. Bridgeport, 1975; physician asst. cert., Yale U., 1979; MBA in Health & Med. Svcs. Adminstrn., Widener U., 1991. Med. technologist St. Francis Hosp., Hartford, 1975-77; physician asst. Fox Chase Cancer Ctr., Phila., 1979-85; clin. dir. Fox Chase Network, Phila., 1986-92; adminstrv. dir., oncology Cooper Hosp., U. Med. Ctr., Camden, N.J., 1992-96, healthcare cons., 1996—; corp. mgr. cancer svcs. Grad. Health Sys., Phila., 1996—; mem. Cancer Prevention and Control Adv. Group to N.J. Commn. on Cancer Rsch., New Brunswick, N.J., 1993-96; presenter in field. Dana scholar U. Bridgeport, 1972; recipient Foster G. McGaw Scholarship award Assn. Univ. Programs in Health Adminstrn., 1990, Student award Hosp. Assn. Pa., 1992; Breast Cancer project grantee The Susan G. Komen Breast Cancer Found., Dallas, 1995. Mem. Am. Hosp. Assn., Am. Cancer Soc. (Camden County), Assn. Cancer Execs., Soc. Radiation Oncology Adminstrs., Assn. Cmty. Cancer Ctrs. (del.), Widener Alumni Assn. (pres. 1995).

MUNIER, WILLIAM BOSS, medical service executive; b. Corning, N.Y., Dec. 8, 1942; s. John Hammond and Marguerite (Boss) M.; m. Sandra Lorraine Koerber, 1965 (div. 1976); m. Ann Elizabeth Wessel, 1980; children: Michael, Andrew, Laura. BA, U. Pa., 1964; MD, Columbia U., 1968; MBA, Harvard U., 1973. Diplomate Nat. Bd. Med. Examiners; lic. physician, surgeon, N.Y. Surg. intern Roosevelt Hosp., N.Y.C., 1968-69; profl. staff HEW, Washington, 1969-71, 73-75, dir. Office Quality Standards, 1975-77, dir. Office Health Practice Assessment, 1977-79; exec. v.p. Mass. Med. Soc., Boston, 1979-84; prin. Ernst & Whinney, Boston, 1984-85; pvt. practice mgmt. cons. Wellesley, Mass., 1985-86; pres. Quality Standards in Medicine, Inc., Boston, 1986—; vis. prof. Harvard Sch. Pub. Health, Boston, 1980-90. Contbr. articles to profl. jours. Mem. human services com. Town of Wellesley, 1984-85. Served with USPHS, 1969-79. Mem. AMA, Mass. Med. Soc., St. Botolph Club, Capitol Hill Club. Republican. Episcopalian.

MUNK, ZEV MOSHE, allergist, researcher; b. Stockholm, July 14, 1950; m. Susan Deitcher; 4 children. BS, McGill U., 1972; MD, C.M., 1974. Licentiate Med. Council Can.; diplomate Am. Bd. Internal Medicine, Am. Bd. Allergy and Clin. Immunology. Intern Royal Victoria Hosp., Montreal, 1974-75, resident, 1975-76; resident in clin. immunology and allergy Montreal Gen. Hosp., 1976-78; practice medicine specializing in allergy and clin. immunology, Houston, 1978—; mem. staff Meml. City Med. Ctr., Meml. S.W., Meth., Spring Branch Meml., West Houston Med. Ctr, Cy-Fair hosps. (all Houston); clin. instr. allergy and clin. immunology Baylor Coll. Medicine, 1979—, U. Tex.-Houston, 1979—; pres. Breco Rsch., Pharm-Olam Internat. Clin. Rsch. Orgn., 1994—. Pres. Young Israel Synagogue of Houston, 1994-96; founder Allergy Ctr., Inc., Houston, Clin. Rsch. Ctr., Houston. McGill U. scholar, 1968-74. Fellow Am. Acad. Allergy, Am. Coll. Allergy and Immunology, Royal Coll. Physicians (Can.); mem. ACP, Tex. Med. Assn., Que. Med. Assn., Am. Fedn. Clin. Research, Am. Acad. Allergy, Tex. Allergy Soc., Harris County Med. Soc., Houston Allergy Soc. Contbr. articles to med. jours. Office: 902 Frostwood Dr Ste 222 Houston TX 77024-2402

MUNN, STEPHEN RICHARD, transplant surgeon; b. Masterton, New Zealand, Oct. 29, 1954; came to U.S., 1986; s. Murray Albert and Patricia (Mason) M.; m. Glenys Anne Hooper, Feb. 12, 1977; children: Luke, Daniel, Seth, Joshua, Caleb. MB ChB, Otago MEd. Sch., 1978. House surgeon Christchurch (New Zeland) Hosp., 1978-79, resident, 1980-85; lectr. surgery Otago Med. Sch., Dunedon, New Zealand, 1985-86; sr. lectr. surgery U. Auckland (New Zealand), 1989-91; transplant surgeon Mayo Clinic, Rochester, Minn., 1991—; bd. dirs. LifeSource, Mpls.; mem. med. adv. bd. Region II Renal Rev. Com., Mpls., 1993-95. Contbr. articles to profl. jours. Bd. dir. Schaeffer Acad., Rochester, 1992—; bd. elders 1st Bapt. Ch., Rochester, 1996—. Surgery fellow Mayo Clinic, 1986-87, Transplant Surgery fellow, 1988-89, Fogarty fellow U. Minn., Mpls., 1987-88. Mem. Am. Soc. Transplant Surgeons (edn. com. 1994—, post-grad. com. 1995—), Internat. Pancreas & Islet Transplant Soc., Assn. Acad. Surgeons, Transplnatation Soc. Office: Mayo Clinic 200 1st St SW Rochester MN 55905

MUNN, WILLIAM CHARLES, II, psychiatrist; b. Flint, Mich., Aug. 9, 1938; s. Elton Albert and Rita May (Coykendall) M.; student Flint Jr. Coll., 1958-59, U. Detroit, 1959-61; M.D., Wayne State U., 1965; children by previous marriage—Jude Michael, Rachel Marie, Alexander Winston. Intern David Grant USAF Med. Center, Travis AFB, Calif., 1965-66; resident in psychiatry Letterman Army Hosp., San Francisco, 1967-70; practice medicine, specializing in psychiatry, Fairfield, Calif., 1972—; chief in-patient psychiatry David Grant Med. Center, 1970-71, chmn. dept. mental health, 1971-72; psychiat. cons. Fairfield-Suisun Unified Sch. Dist., 1971—, Fairfield Hosp. and Clinic, 1971, N. Bay Med. Ctr.(formerly Intercommunity Hosp.), Fairfield, 1971—, Casey Family Program, 1980—, Solano County Coroner's Office, 1981; asst. clin. prof. psychiatry U. Calif., San Francisco, 1976—; cons. Vaca Valley Hosp., Vacaville, Calif., 1988—, VA Hosp., San Francisco, 1976, David Grant USAF Hosp., 1976. Served to maj., M.C., USAF, 1964-72, flight surgeon, chief public health, chief phys. exam. center McGuire AFB, N.J., 1966-67. Diplomate Am. Bd. Psychiatry and Neurology (examiner). Mem. Am. Psychiat. Assn., No. Calif. Psychiat. Soc., E. Bay Psychiat. Assn. Office: 1245 Travis Blvd Ste E Fairfield CA 94533-4842

MUNNA, JOHN CHARLES, plastic surgeon; b. Oceanside, N.Y., Jan. 5, 1934; s. Joseph Rocco and Therese Helen (Marano) M.; m. Rana Kay Djuvstad, Sept. 16, 1973; children: Gian Carlo, Christian Andrea. BS, Fordham U.; MD, N.Y. Med. Coll., N.Y.C., 1962. Diplomate Am. Bd. Surgery, Am. Bd. Plastic Surgery. Intern Kings County Hosp., Bklyn., 1962-63; gen. surgery resident N.Y. Med. Coll., Flower & Fifth Ave. and Met. Hosp., 1963-67; plastic surgery resident We. Pa. Hosp. & Allegheny Gen. Hosp., Pitts., 1969-71; pvt. practice specializing in plastic surgery Atlanta, 1972—. Contbr. articles to profl. jours.; developer ARIOSO skin care system. With USN/USMC, 1967-69. Fellow ACS; mem. Am. Soc. Plastic and Reconstructive Surgeons, Am. Soc. Aesthetic Plastic Surgery. Roman Catholic. Home: 505 Hollydale Ct NW Atlanta GA 30342-3633

MUÑOZ, RICARDO FELIPE, psychology educator; b. Lima, Peru, Apr. 30, 1950; came to U.S., 1961; s. Luis Alberto and Clara Luz (Valdivia) M.; m. Pat Marine, Mar. 31, 1979; children: Rodrigo Alberto, Aubrey Elizabeth Luz. AB, Stanford U., 1972; MA, U. Oreg., 1975, PhD, 1977. Asst. prof. psychology U. Calif., San Francisco, 1977-83, assoc. prof., 1983-89, prof., 1989—; dir. depression clinic San Francisco Gen. Hosp., 1985-90, chief psychologist, 1987—, deputy chief acad. affairs, 1991—; dir. UCSF Clin. Psychology Tng. Program, 1992—; bd. dirs. div. health promotion and disease prevention, Inst. Medicine, NAS, Washington. Co-author: Control Your Depression, 1986, How to Control Your Drinking, 1982, Prevention of Depression: Research and Practice, 1993; editor: Depression Prevention: Research Directions, 1987; co-editor; Social and Psychological Research in Community Settings, 1979. Recipient Health Promotion award Nat. Coalition Hispanic Mental Health and HumanSvcs. Orgn., 1984, Dr. Martin Luther King Jr. award U. Calif., San Francisco, 1991, Lela Rowland Prevention award Nat. Mental Health Assn., 1994. Fellow Am. Psychol. Assn.; mem. AAAS, Nat. Hispanic Psychol. Assn., Am. Assn. for Artificial Intelligence, Phi Beta Kappa. Office: U Calif 1001 Potrero Ave Ste 7M San Francisco CA 94110-3518

MUNOZ, STEVEN MICHAEL, physician associate; b. Dallas, Aug. 7, 1952; s. Joseph Paul and Connie Rae (Coffman) M.; m. Paula Lou Marchant, Dec. 12, 1974 (div. 1983); 1 child, Kimberly Rene; m. Maureen Geneva Flowers, Aug. 12, 1984; children: Danielle Geneva, Sean Michael. B Med. Sci., Emory U., 1977. Physician assoc. Med. Ctr. Cen. Ga., Macon, 1977-79. William B. Martin M.D., P.C., Loganville, Ga., 1979-80, Howell Indsl. Clinic, Atlanta, 1980-81, Stanley Fineman M.D., P.C., Marietta, Ga., 1981-82; physician assoc., dir. sales and adminstrn. Family Practice Ctr./ Atlanta Occupational Medicine, 1982-85; physician assoc., dir. mktg. Gwinnette Ctr. med. Clinic, Norcross, Ga., 1985-89; physician assoc. So. Orthopedic Clinic, Atlanta, 1989-90, North Fulton Health Care Assoc., Roswell, Ga., 1990-96; physician assoc. adult & pediatric care Kaiser Permanente Internal Medicine Clinic, Atlanta, 1996—; asst. clin. prof. Emory U. Sch. Medicine, Atlanta, 1981—; dir. patient edn. com. Ga. Lung Assn., 1981-82; med. adviser ARC, Atlanta, 1980-83, Ga. Statewide Hypertension Task Force, 1981-82. With U.S. Army, 1972-75, Res., 1975-94. Mem. Am. Acad. Physician Assts., Ga. Assn. Physician Assts. (bd. dirs., pub. edn. com. chair 1984), Soc. Army Physician Assts. Republican. Home: 5785 Stonehaven Dr Kennesaw GA 80152-3759 Office: Kaiser Permanente 20 Glenlake Pky Atlanta GA 30328

MUNRO, BARBARA HAZARD, nursing educator, college dean, researcher; b. Wakefield, R.I., Nov. 28, 1938; d. Robert J. and Honore (Egan) Hazard; m. Bruce Munro, June 1, 1961; children: Karen Aimee, Craig Michael, Stephanie Anne. BS, MS, U. R.I., Kingston; PhD, U. Conn. RN, Conn. Asst. prof. U. of R.I. Coll. of Nursing, Kingston; assoc. prof., chmn. program in nursing rsch. Yale U., New Haven, Conn.; assoc. prof., asst. dir. Ctr. for Nursing Rsch. U. Pa., Phila.; dean, prof. Boston Coll. Sch. Nursing, 1990—; presenter and workshop leader various nursing confs. and seminars in U.S. Contbr. articles and rsch. to profl. pubs. Trustee St. Elizabeth's Med. Ctr. Boston, 1994—. Recipient Nat. Rsch. Svc. award. Fellow Am. Acad. Nursing; mem. ANA, Nat. League for Nursing, Sigma Theta Tau, Pi Lambda Theta, Phi Kappa Phi.

MUNRO, MALCOLM GORDON, obstetrician/gynecologist, educator; b. Woodstock, Ont., Can., Mar. 22, 1952; came to U.S., 1991; s. Charles Gordon and Maribelle (Logie) M.; m. Sandra June Brander-Smith, Nov. 17, 1990; children: Tyler Gordon, Megan Danielle. MD, U. Western Ont., London, 1975. Diplomate Am. Bd. Ob-Gyn. Intern Royal Columbian Hosp., New Westminster, B.C., 1975-76; resident ob.-gyn, U. Western Ont., London, 1976-77; resident U. B.C., Vancouver, 1978-80, clin. fellow gyneolgic. oncology, 1980-81, clin. instr. ob-gyn., 1981-83; asst. clin. prof. UCLA, Vancouver, 1983-89; assoc. clin. prof. U. B.C., Vancouver, 1983-92; assoc. prof. UCLA, 1991-95, prof., 1995—, assoc. chmn. dept. ob/gyn., 1994-95; chmn. ob/gyn dept. B.C. Med. Assn., Vancouver, 1984-88, Rsch. Coordinating Com. Grace Hosp., Vancouver; founding co-chair gynecologic studies group, Washington, 1993—; cons. Cancer Control Agy., B.C., 1981-91, Ethicon Endosuture Core Cons. Group, 1992—. Author: (book) Gynecology, A Practical Approach, 1990; contbr. articles to profl. jours., chpts. to books; inventor, patentee laparoscopic loop electrodes, 1993; mem. editl. bd. Treating the Female Patient, 1988-94, Jour. of Gynecologic Technique, 1993—; reviewer Obstetrics and Gynecology, 1990—, Fertil Steril, 1993—; mem. ad hoc rev. com. Jour. Am. Assn. Gynecologic Laparoscopists, 1994—. Med. dir. Planned Parenthood, Vancouver, 1980-85; founding dir. U. B.C. Coop. Osteoporosis Program, 1987-91, Multidisciplinary Osteoporosis Clinic, U. Hosp., Vancouver, 1987-91. Recipient Appreciation cert. Planned Parenthood of B.C., 1991; grantee Vancouver Found., 1988, P.W. Woodward Found., 1988, Ethicon Endosurgery, 1992, NIH/NIAID AIDS and Cervical Neoplasia co-investigator, 1992-94. Fellow Royal Coll. Surgeons Can., Soc. Obstetricians and Gynecologists Can.; mem. Can. Fertility and Andrology Soc., Am. Fertility Soc., Am. Assn. Gynecologic Laparoscopists, Am. Coll. Obstetricians and Gynecologists (vice-chair B.C. section VIII 1987-90). Office: UCLA 22-262 CHS Los Angeles CA 90095-1740

MUNROE, SHIRLEY ANN, retired hospital association executive, health care consultant; b. Mpls., Mar. 31, 1924; d. Laurence John and Esther (Tuttle) M.; pre-nursing cert. La Sierra Coll., Arlington, Calif., 1943; R.N., Glendale Sanitarium and Hosp. Sch. Nursing, 1946; postgrad. UCLA Extension, 1953-55, Los Angeles City Coll., 1948-51; cert. U. Calif. at Santa Cruz extension, 1971; m. Stanley G. Fjelstrom, Dec. 26, 1954 (div. June 1957). Chief nurse, office mgr. for pvt. practice physicians, Los Angeles, 1946-51; bus. mgr. Bolander Clinic and Emergency Hosp., Van Nuys, Calif., 1951-56, Mendocino Med. Ctr., Ukiah, Calif., 1956; adminstr. Hillside Community Hosp., Ukiah, 1956-78, sec., 1956-78; dir. Ctr. for Small or Rural Hosps., Am. Hosp. Assn., Chgo., 1978-79, dir. constituency programs, 1979-83, exec. dir. constituency sects., 1984-85, v.p., 1985-88 healthcare cons., 1989—; mem. adv. and eval. com. Ukiah Dist. Sch. Vocat. Nursing, 1965-78; faculty U. Calif. extension at Berkeley, Basic Adminstrn. Hosp. Adminstrs. Program, 1966-70; dir., sec. Obs. Investment Co., Ukiah, 1957-67. Asst. dir. pub. relations alumni postgrad. assembly Loma Linda U., Los Angeles, 1949-55; dir. pub. relations world meeting Aerospace Med. Assn., Los Angeles, 1953; chmn. re-edn. nursing com. Calif. Dept. Employment, 1962; cons. lectr. nurse aide edn., adult edn. Willits, Ukiah high schs., 1962; chmn. Career Project for Sr. High Sch. Girls, 1962-64; mem. Mendocino-Lake adv. com. Regional Med. Program, 1969-73; mem. vocat. edn. adv. com. Ukiah Unified Sch. Dist., 1970-73. Soloist, Presbyn. Ch., Ukiah, 1956-69, Ukiah Oratorio Soc., 1958-65; supt. children's edn. Seventh-day Adventist Ch., 1961-64, dir. pub. relations, 1967-78, chmn. ch. bd., 1967-78, soloist, 1958-78; mem. ch. bd., 1967-78, mem. exec. com. Ill. conf., 1983-89; mem. ch. bd. Seventh-day Adventist Ch., Elmhurst, 1979-89, dir. music, mem. ch. bd., Roswell, N.Mex., 1989—, dir. ch. ministries, 1990-93, Ch. Elder, 1992—; mem. exec. com. Seventh Day Adventist Ch. Southwestern Union Conf., 1991—; N.Am. divsn. del. to 56th World Session of the Gen. Conf. Seventh Day Adventists, Utrecht, The Netherlands, 1995; Choir dir, Westminster Presbyn. Ch., Roswell, 1993—; co-chmn. edn. com. Mendocino County br. Am. Cancer Soc., 1961-62, bd. dirs., 1961-76, pres., 1963-65; mem. steering com. Am. Heart Assn., Mendocino County br. Calif. Heart Assn.; chmn. trustees Tri-County Pre-Payment Medi-Cal Pilot Project, State of Calif., 1969-71; trustee Nor Coa Health, 1967-76, 1st v.p. 1969-71, pres., 1971-72, chmn. South Planning council, 1972-74; mem. Mendocino-Lake counties council, 1966-76; bd. dirs. Mendocino County chpt. ARC, 1968-70; bd. dirs. Blue Cross No. Calif., 1971-78, exec. bd., 1973-78, hosp. provider rep., 1970-78; leader del. People to People Internat. U.S. Citizen Ambassador Program, 1981; mem. bd. Adventist Health System/North, 1981-87, chmn. strategic planning com., 1983-87; mem. bd. Hinsdale Hosp., 1979-94, mem. joint conf. com., 1980-89, chmn. strategic planning com., 1983-88, bd. dirs. fin. com., 1989-94; bd. dirs. Broadview Acad., Lafox, Ill., 1983-86, Roswell Symphony Orch., 1990—, sec.-treas., 1991-93, 2d v.p., 1992-93, 1st v.p. 1993-95, pres., chmn. bd. dirs., 1995—; 2d v.p. Roswell Symphony Guild, 1993-95. Named Trustee of the Year Hinsdale Health System, 1991; recipient Civic Participation award, Outstanding Women in Professions award Calif. Fedn. Bus. and Profl. Women's Clubs, 1965; Outstanding Service award Mendocino-Lake br. Am. Cancer Soc., 1963, 64, 65, Notable Service award, 1968; Walker fellow, 1973; The Ann. Shirley Ann Munroe Leadership Devel. Award named in her honor by Sect. for Small or Rural Hosps. and The Hosp. Rsch. and Ednl. Trust of Am. Hosp. Assn. Mem. Am. Hosp. Assn. (ho. of dels. 1974-78, regional adv. bd. 1974-78, rural resource com. 1976-78, v.p.), Calif. Hosp. Assn. (membership com. 1960-61; legis. liaison 1960, panel hosp. peer rev. adminstrs. 1968-78; mem. ins. com. 1971-78), REmpire Hosp. Conf. (ins. com. 1957-59, exec. com. 1968-71, 1st v.p. 1968, pres. 1969), Hosp. Council No. Calif. (bd. dirs. 1968-77, pres. 1975-76, chmn. com. on program and edn. 1968-70), Assn. Western Hosps. (edn. research found. council 1963-65), Glendale Sanitarium and Hosp. Sch. Nursing Alumni Assn. (pres. Glendale 1947-48), Bus. and Profl. Women's Club (exec. bd. 1957-61, pres. 1959-60, 3d v.p. 1960-61, career advancement com. 1961-62, chmn. personal devel. com. 1962-64, mem. bd. 1962-65, music chmn. Redwood Empire dist. 1960-61), Republican. Club: Soroptimist (pres. Ukiah 1971-72, music chmn. 1962-63, service com. 1961-78, editor bull. 1965-66, Woman of Achievement award 1965, dir. 1970-73). Address: 2614 N Pennsylvania Ave Roswell NM 88201-5871

MUNSHOWER, JOHN CARL, family physician; b. Abington, Pa., May 30, 1965; s. Ronald Forrest and Nancy Ann (Pecsi) M.; m. Shauna Ann Lydon, Sept. 12, 1992; 1 child, Amanda Marie. BS, U. Scranton, 1987; DO, Phila. Coll. Osteo. Medicine, 1991. Diplomate Am. Bd. Family Medicine. Intern Phila. Coll. Osteo. Medicine, 1991-92; resident Grad. Hosp. Health Sys., Phila., 1992-94; family physician Family Care Assocs., Media, Pa., 1994—; physician advisor managed care negotiations Crozer Keystone Health Sy., Media, 1994—, physician advisor angioplasty, 1994—. Mem. AMA (Physician's Recognition award 1994—), Pa. Med. Soc., Am. Coll. Family Physicians, Am. Osteo. Assn., Pa. Osteo. Med. Assn. (alt. del. 1994—, del. com. on young physicians 1994—), Pa. Osteo. Family Practitioners Soc. Republican. Roman Catholic. Office: Family Care Assocs 280 N Prividence Rd Media PA 19063

MUNSON, ERIC BRUCE, hospital administrator; b. Elmhurst, Ill., Mar. 11, 1943; married. B, Wabash Coll., 1965; MHA, U. Chgo., 1967. Asst. to adminstr. Swedish Covenant Hosp., Chgo., 1966-67; asst. dir. U. Chgo. Hosps., 1970-73; assoc. adminstr. U. Hosp., Denver, 1973-77, adminstr., 1977-80; exec. dir. U. N.C. Hosp., Chapel Hill, 1980—. Home: 119 Black Oak Pl Chapel Hill NC 27514-6502 Office: Univ N C Hosps 101 Manning Dr Chapel Hill NC 27514-4220*

MUNSON, NORMA FRANCES, biologist, ecologist, nutritionist, educator; b. Stockport, Iowa, Sept. 22, 1923; d. Glenn Edwards and Frances Emma (Wilson) M.; BA, Concordia Coll., 1946; MA, U. Mo., 1955; PhD (NSF fellow 1957-58, Chgo. Heart Assn. fellow 1959), Pa. State U., 1962; postgrad. Ind. U., 1957, Western Mich. U., 1967, Lake Forest Coll., 1971, 72, 78; student various fgn. univs., 1964-71. Tchr., Aitkin (Minn.) H.S., 1946-48, Detroit Lakes (Minn.) H.S., 1948-54, Libertyville (Ill.) H.S., 1955-79; rschr. Nutrition, Arthritis, Alzheimer's, Hypoglycemia and Multiple Sclerosis, Libertyville, 1965—; lectr. counseling and nutrition. Author biology lab. manual; contbr. articles to profl. jours. Ruling elder 1st Presbyn. Ch., Libertyville, 1971-77; pres. Lake County Audubon Soc., 1975-79, 82-86, 88-89, treas., 1990—; pres. Libertyville Edn. Assn., 1964-67, news editor Lake County Audubon Newsletter, 1972-96; active Rep. Party Ill., Citizens to Save Butler Lake, Citizens Choice, Defenders; mem. U.S. Congl. Adv. Bd., 1985—; bd. dirs. Holy Land Christian Mission Internat.; mem. Heritage Found., Citizens Lake County for Environ. Action Reform, Wilderness Soc. Recipient Hilda Mahling award, 1967, C. of C. award, 1971, Ill. Best Tchr. award, 1974; Biology Tchr. of Yr. award, 1971; NSF fellow, 1957, 58, 60-62, 70-71. Fellow Am. Biog. Inst. Rsch., Internat. Biog. Assn.; mem. Nat. Biology Tchrs. Assn. (rsch. in degenerate diseases, award 1971), AAAS, Am. Inst. Biol. Sci., Ill. Environ. Coun., Nat. Audubon Soc., Ill. Audubon Coun., Nat. Health Fedn., Internat. Platform Assn., Internat. Profl. and Bus. Women, Nat. Wildlife Fedn., N.Y. Acad. Scis., Chgo. Acad. Sci., Parks and Conservation Assn., Concerned Women for Am. Nature Conservation, Evanston North Shore Bird Club, Delta Kappa Gamma. Home and Office: 206 W Maple Ave Libertyville IL 60048-2174

MUNSON, PAUL LEWIS, pharmacologist; b. Washta, Iowa, Aug. 21, 1910; s. Lewis Sylvester and Alice E. (Orser) M.; m. Aileen Geisinger, Mar. 7, 1931 (div. 1948); 1 dau., Abigail (Mrs. Mark Krumel); m. Mary Ellen Jones, Aug. 15, 1948 (div. 1971); children: Ethan Vincent, Catherine Laura; m. Yu Chen, Feb. 27, 1987; 1 stepchild, Ming An Chen. B.A., Antioch Coll., 1933; M.A., U. Wis., 1937; Ph.D., U. Chgo., 1942; M.A. (hon.), Harvard, 1955. Fellow, asst. biochemistry U. Chgo., 1939-42; research biochemist William S. Merrell Co., Cin., 1942-43; research biochemist, head endocrinology research Armour Labs., Chgo., 1943-48; research asst., then research asso. Yale Sch. Medicine, 1948-50; asst. prof., asso. prof. pharmacology, then prof. Harvard Sch. Dental Medicine, 1950-65; prof. pharmacology, chmn. dept. U. N.C. Sch. Medicine, 1965-77, Sarah Graham Kenan prof., 1970—; Mem. U.S. Pharmacopeia Panel on Corticotropin, 1951-55; mem. pharmacology test com. Nat. Bd. Med. Examiners, 1966-71; mem. gen. medicine B study section NIH, 1966-70, chmn., 1969-70, mem. pharmacology-toxicology rev. com., 1972-76. Author numerous articles on hormones; co-editor: Vitamins and Hormones, 1968-82; editl. bd. Endocrinology, 1957-63, Jour. Pharmacology and Exptl. Therapeutics, 1959-65, Jour. Dental Rsch., 1962-64, Biochem. Medicine, 1967-84, Am. Jour. Chinese Medicine, 1973-79, Pharmacol. Revs., 1967-70, editor-in-chief, 1977-81; editor-in-chief: Principles of Pharmacology, 1981-94. Fellow AAAS, Am. Acad. Arts and Scis.; mem. Am. Soc. Pharmacology and Exptl. Therapeutics (council 1970-73, sec.-treas. 1971-72), Am. Soc. Biol. Chemists, Endocrine Soc. (council 1963-65, Fred Conrad Koch award 1976), Am. Soc. Bone and Mineral Research (William F. Neuman award 1982), Am. Chem. Soc., Biometrics Soc., Internat. Assn. Dental Research (councillor 1957-59), AAUP, ACLU (mem. internat. confs. on calcium regulating hormones, Elsevier Sci. Pubs. award 1989), Assn. Med. Sch. Pharmacology (council 1971-73, sec. 1972-73, pres. 1974-76), Am. Thyroid Assn. (nominating com. 1973), Sigma Xi. Dem. Socialist. Unitarian. Home and Office: 1520 Taylor Ave Parkville MD 21234-5241

MUNSTER, ANDREW MICHAEL, medical educator, surgeon; b. Budapest, Hungary, Dec. 10, 1935; came to U.S., 1965; s. Leopold S. and Marianne (Barcza) M.; m. Joy O'Sullivan, Dec. 7, 1963; children: Andrea, Tara, Alexandra. MD, U. Sydney (Australia), 1959. Diplomate Am. Bd. Surgery. Research fellow Harvard U. Med. Sch., Boston, 1966-67; asst. prof. surgery U. Tex.-San Antonio, 1968-71, assoc. prof. surgery Med. U. S.C., Charleston, 1971-76; assoc. prof. Johns Hopkins U., Balt., 1976-85, prof. surgery, 1985—; dir. burn ctr. Balt. City Hosp., 1976—; v.p. Chesapeake

Physicians, Balt., 1978-84. Author: Surgical Anatomy, 1971; Surgical Immunology, 1976; Burn Care for House Officers, 1980; contbr. numerous articles to med. jours. Pres., Chesapeake Ednl. Research Trust, Balt., 1980-84, Charleston Symphony, 1974-75, Charleston TriCounty Arts Council, 1975-76. Served to lt. col. U.S. Army, 1968-71. Recipient John Hunter prize U. Sydney, 1959; named Hunterian prof. Royal Coll. Surgeons, 1974. Fellow Royal Coll. Surgeons of Eng., Royal Coll. Surgeons of Edinburgh (Scotland), Am. Assn. Surgeons of Trauma, Colombian Coll. Surgeons (hon.); mem. Am. Burn Assn. (sec. 1990-93, 1st v.p. 1993-94, pres.-elect 1994-95, pres. 1995), Soc. Surg. Assn., Soc. Univ. Surgeons, Am. Surg. Assn. Office: Balt Reg Burn Ctr 4940 Eastern Ave Baltimore MD 21224-2735

MUNSTERTEIGER, KAY DIANE, speech and language pathologist; b. Newcastle, Wyo., June 2, 1956; d. Donald Francis and Janice Mathilda (Emerson) M. BS, U. Wyo., 1978; MS, U. Nev., Reno, 1980. Speech lang. pathologist No. Nev. Speech lang. Clinic, Reno, 1980-82, Washakie County Sch. Dist. 1, Worland, Wyo., 1982—; pvt. practice speech pathologist Worland, 1982—; speech lang. pathologist, cons. Washakie County Sch. Dist. 2, Tensleep, Wyo., 1984-85; speech lang. pathologist Spl. Touch Presch., Worland, 1985-86, 89-93, Rehab Visions, 1995—; pres. bd. examiners Speech Pathology and Audiology, 1988-93. Mem. Pub. Sch. Caucus. Mem. NEA, State Edn. Assn., Am. Speech Lang. Hearing Assn., Wyo. Speech Lang. Hearing Assn., Nat. Stuttering Project, Pub. Sch. Caucus, Assn. Childhood Edn. Internat., Phi Kappa Phi. Democrat. Roman Catholic. Office: Washakie County Sch Dist # 1 1200 Culbertson Ave Worland WY 82401-3520

MUNZER, ALFRED, internist; b. The Hague, The Netherlands, Nov. 23, 1941; came to U.S., 1958; s. Simcha and Gisele Munzer.. BA, CUNY-Bklyn. Coll., 1963; MD, SUNY, Bklyn., 1968. Intern in internal medicine State U.-Kings County Med. Ctr., Bklyn., 1968-69, resident in internal medicine, 1969-70; resident in internal medicine U. Rochester (N.Y.)/Strong Meml. Hosp., 1970-71; fellow in pulmonary medicine Johns Hopkins U., Balt., 1971-72; chief pulmonary and infectious disease Malcolm Grow USAF Med. Ctr., Suitland, Md., 1972-74; co-dir. pulmonary medicine Washington Adventist Hosp., Takoma Park, Md., 1974—. Contbr. chpt. to: Lippincott Manual of Nursing PRactice, 1982, Textbook of Internal Medicine, 1996. Pres. Am. Lung Assn., N.Y.C., 1993-94. Maj. USAF, 1972-74. Fellow Am. Coll. Chest Physicians (chpt. pres. 1976-77); mem. ACP, Am. Thoracic Soc. (bd. dirs. 1981-83, 92-95), Dramatists Guild (assoc.). Democrat. Jewish. Home: 2939 Van Ness St NW Washington DC 20008 Office: Washington Adventist Hosp 7600 Carroll Ave Takoma Park MD 20912

MURAI, NORIMOTO, plant molecular biologist, educator; b. Sapporo, Japan, Mar. 4, 1944; came to U.S., 1968; s. Nobuo and Hideko (Odagiri) M.; m. Andreana Lisca, Nov. 14, 1977; 1 child, Naoki. BS, Hokkaido U., 1966, MS, 1968; PhD, U. Wis., 1973. Rsch. assoc. dept. botany U. Wis., Madison, 1974-78, project assoc. dept. bacteriology, 1979, postdoctoral fellow dept. plant pathology, 1980-82; lab. head dept. molecular biology Nat. Inst. Agrobiol. Resources, Tsukuba, Japan, 1983-84; assoc. prof. plant pathology and crop physiology La. State U., Baton Rouge, 1985-92, prof., 1992—; adj. prof. biochemistry, full mem. grad. faculty and interdept. studies in plant physiology and genetics La. State U.; mem. study sect. on minority biomed. rsch. support program NIH, 1993; grant reviewer USDA, NSF, NIH. Reviewer manuscripts Genome, Protein Engring., Plant Cell, Plant Physiol., Planta, Plant Molecular Biology, Plant Cell Report, Australia Jour. Plant Physiol. Named Honors Rschr., Phi Delta Kappa, 1989; grantee Fulbright Found., 1968, Sci. and Tech. Agy., Tokyo, 1984, La. Edn. Quality Support Fund, 1988, 89, 91, 94, 95, Monsanto Co. Fund, 1992, 93, U.S. Dept. Agr., 1995. Mem. AAAS, Am. Soc. Plant Physiologists, Internat. Soc. Plant Molecular Biology, Japan Molecular Biology Assn., Crop Sci. Soc. Am., Fulbright Assn., Sigma Xi, Gamma Sigma Delta, Phi Delta Kappa. Office: La State U Dept Plant Path Crop P Baton Rouge LA 70803

MURAKAMI, HARUO, internist; b. Sapporo, Japan, June 16, 1930; s. Teikichi and Shizue Kuranami; m. Hiroko Murakami, May 27, 1959; children: Keiko, Tomoko, Chiharu. MD, Tokyo Med. and Dental U., 1957. Fellow 1st Clinic of Internal Medicine, Tokyo Med. and Dental U., 1957-67; chief Ichikawa Daiichi Hosp., Tokyo, 1967-77; dir. Murakami Clinic, Tokyo, 1977—. Contbr. articles to med. jours. Mem. Japanese Soc. Internal Medicine, Japan Med. Assn., Den-en-Chofu Med. Assn. (dir. 1980—). Liberal Democrat. Bhuddist. Home: 5-11-7 Minami-Yukigaya, Ohta-ku, Tokyo 145, Japan Office: Murakami Clinic, 5-11-7 Minami-Yukigaya, Ohta Ku Tokyo 145, Japan

MURCH, SIMON HARRY, pediatric gastroenterologist; b. Liverpool, Eng., June 29, 1956; s. Henry Osborne and Anne Margaret (Godfrey) M.; m. Fiona Margaret King, July 12, 1980; 1 child, Rosalind. MBBS, U. London, 1980, PhD, 1995. Lectr. child health St. Bartholomew's Hosp., London, 1988-91; sr. lectr. Royal Free Hosp., London, 1995—; action rsch. fellow St. Bartholomew's Hosp., London, 1992-93, lectr. pediatric gastroenterology, 1993-94, sr. lectr., 1995; sr. lectr. Royal Free Hosp., London, 1995—; Mem. Royal Coll. Physicians, U.K., 1984. Contbr. articles to profl. jours. Project grantee Action Rsch., Eng., 1992-93. Fellow Royal Soc. Medicine; mem. Royal Coll. Physicians, Brit. Soc. Immunology, The Neonatal Soc., Brit. Soc. for Pediatric Gastroenterology and Nutrition, European Soc. Pediatric Gastroenterology and Nutrition. Office: Univ Dept Pediat Gastroenterology, Royal Free Hosp Bond St, London NW3 2QG, England

MURDOCH, BERNARD CONSTANTINE, psychology educator; b. Greensboro, N.C., Dec. 5, 1917; s. Homer Odell and Hilma Caroline (Lang) M.; m. Martha Grace Hood, June 29, 1946; children: Norma, Constance, Joyce, Diana. B.S., Appalachian State Tchrs. Coll., 1938; Ed.M., U. of Cincinnati, 1939; Ph.D., Duke, 1942; postgrad., N.Y. U., 1942-43. Licensed applied psychologist, Ga. Math. critic tchr. Appalachian State Tchrs. Coll. demonstration sch., 1938; math. and sci. tchr. Lexington (N.C.) High Sch., 1939-40; sci. tchr. Harding High Sch., Charlotte, N.C., 1945-46; also dir. Guidance and Testing Bur., Vets. Info. Center, Charlotte; prof. edn. and psychology Presbyn. Coll., Clinton, S.C., 1946-48; acad. dean Presbyn. Coll., 1947-48; also extension prof. edn. U. S.C., 1946-48; mem. research staff Am. Council on Edn., Office of Naval Rsch., Washington, 1948-50; dean Muskingum Coll., New Concord, Ohio, 1950-54; prof., head psychology dept. Wesleyan Coll., Macon, Ga., 1954-82, prof. emeritus, 1982—; chmn. dept. behavioral scis. Wesleyan Coll., 1973-82, also dir. testing.; pres. Fore(In)Sight Found. Inc., 1991—. Author: Consistency of Test Responses, 1942, Love and Problems of Living, 1992; co-author: The Decrease of Doctorates in the Sciences, 1936-48; contbr. to sci., ednl. and religious publs. Served to capt. USAAF, 1942-45. Fellow AAAS; mem. Am. Psychol. Assn. (life), Southeastern Psychol. Assn., Ga. Psychol. Assn. (dir., pres. 1969-70), Ga. Mental Health Assn. (dir.), NEA, Ga. Mental Health Council (psychology rep. 1973-74), Ga. State Bd. Examiners Psychologists (pres. 1974-75), Am. Ednl. Research Assn., Phi Kappa Phi (past pres.), Phi Delta Kappa, Kappa Delta Pi, Pi Gamma Mu. Presbyn. Club: Mason. Home: 4966 Iebulon Rd Macon GA 31210-4405

MURDOCH-KITT, NORMA HOOD, clinical psychologist; b. Clinton, S.C., May 16, 1947; d. Bernard Constantine and Martha Grace (Hood) Murdoch; m. Jonathan Michael Murdoch-Kitt, Mar. 23, 1974; children: Kelly Michelle, Mark Jason, Sabrina Brittany, Laura Kristina. BA, Wake Forest U., 1969; MS, U. Pitts., 1971, PhD, 1975 . Psychology intern Eastern Pa. Psychiat. Inst., 1972-73; asst. prof., therapist campus counseling center Coll. William and Mary, Williamsburg, Va., 1973-74; staff psychologist child psychiatry dept. Med. Coll. Va., 1974-75; pvt. practice individual psychotherapy and family and marital therapy, Richmond, Va., 1975—; clin. prof. psychiatry Med. Coll. Va., 1995—. Mem. Richmond Dem. Com., 1976-79, 82-85, 88-89, 91—; v.p. govtl. relations com. Ginter Park Residents Assn., 1987, pres., 1988, 89; mem. Richmond Human Rels. Adv. Commn., 1976-80, Richmond Mayor's Com. on Concerns of Women, 1987—, chair, 1989-93; mem. Richmond Citizens Crime Commn., 1985-83, co-chair police chief sect. com. 1994-95; founder, 1st state chmn. polit. action com. ERA, 1977-78; chief lobbyist ERA Ratification Council, 1977-79; mem. long range planning com. Bapt. Theol. Sch., Richmond, 1993—; long range planning com. Bapt. Theol. Seminary, Richmond, 1993—; v.p. The Women's Ctr., Inc. 1996—. USPHS fellow, 1969-72. Mem. APA (steering com. State Leadership Conf. 1986-91, chair 1991, Richmond area chair Red Cross/Am. Psychol. Assn. Disaster Mental Health Network 1993—), Va. Psychol. Assn. (state legis. lobbyist 1978-79, chmn. legis. com. 1981-83, bd. profl. affairs 1981-85, pres. 1986), Va. Acad. Clin. Psychologists (chmn. profl. affairs com. 1982-84), Va. Breast Cancer Found. (rsch. chair 1992—), Richmond Area Psychol. Assn. (pres. elect 1994, pres. 1995), Chronic Fatigue Assn. (Va chpt.), Internat. Soc. for Study Multiple Personality and Dissociation, LWV, ACLU. Presbyterian. Club: Richmond First (chmn. edn. com. 1979-80, dir. 1980-81). Office: Murdoch-Kitt Profl Bldg 3217 Chamberlayne Ave Richmond VA 23227-4806

MURDOCK, MONI (MARY MARGARET MURDOCK), marriage and family therapist; b. Mishawaka, Ind., Jan. 19, 1938; d. Joseph Weldon and Evelyn Mary (Diroll) Hennessy; m. Charles William Murdock, May 25, 1963; children: Kathleen Tracy, Michael Hennessy, Kevin Charles, Sean Joseph. BS cum laude, Marquette U., 1959; MSW, Loyola U., Chgo., 1961; postgrad., The Family Inst., Ill., 1975-77. Caseworker Ill. Children's Home and Aid Soc., Chgo., 1961-64; clin. social worker Logan Ctr., South Bend, Ind., 1973, St. Joseph County Mental Health Ctr., South Bend, 1974-75; clin. social worker Doyle Ctr. Loyola U., Chgo., 1975-77, clin. supr., 1977-87; pvt. practice psychotherapy The Family Ctr., Evanston, 1979—; family bus. cons. Murdock & Murdock, 1979—; co-founder, exec. com. Loyola U. Family Bus. Ctr., 1990—. Prodr. videotape Family Assessment, 1992. Bd. dirs., co-founder Little Flower Montessori Sch., South Bend, 1969-74; pres. alumni Family Inst., 1980-83, bd. dirs., 1987-91, chmn., 1987-89. Grantee HEW, 1959-60; stipentee VA, 1960-61. Mem. Am. Family Therapy Assn. (charter), Am. Assn. Marriage and Family Therapy (clin., approved supr.), NASW (cert., clin.), Registry Clin. Social Workers (clin. diplomate), Family Firm Inst., Midwest Family Bus. Study Group. Home: 2126 Thornwood Wilmette IL 60091 Office: The Family Ctr 2530 Crawford Ave Evanston IL 60201-3798

MURER, HEINI ULLRICH PAUL, physiology educator; b. Beckenried, Switzerland, Aug. 6, 1944; s. Franz Vital and Ida Franziska Murer; m. Verena Maria Barmettler, Jan. 19, 1980; children: Carla, Livia, Anita. MSc in Biology, U. Fribourg, Switzerland, 1969, PhD in Biochemistry, 1971; privatdozent, U. Frankfurt, Fed. Repbulic Germany, 1978. Postdoctoral fellow dept. biochemistry ETH, Zürich, Switzerland, 1972-75; sr. researcher Max Planck Inst. Biophysics, Frankfurt, Fed. Republic Germany, 1975-79; assoc. prof. dept. biochemistry U. Fribourg, 1979-80; prof. physiology U. Zürich, 1980—, full prof., 1996—. Editor: Pflügers Archiv, Heidelberg, 1980—, Jour. Membrane Biology, N.Y., Miami, 1986—, Physiol. Revs., Bethesda, Md., 1988—, Am. Jour. Physiology, Jou. Molec. Physiology, 1980-86, Jour. Renal Physiology, 1984, Cellular Physiology and Biochemistry, 1991; contbr. over 200 articles, 64 revs. to profl. jours. Maj. Swiss Army Inf., 1965-96. Recipient Cloëtta award Cloëtta Found., Zurich, 1989, Adolf Fick award, 1994, Peter F. Curran Meml. award, 1995, Homer W. Smith award, 1991. Mem. Swiss Soc. Biochemistry, Swiss Soc. Physiology, Am. Soc. Physiology, German Soc. Physiology, N.Y. Acad. Scis., Soc. Gen. Physiology, Am. Soc. Nephrology (Homer Smith award 1991), Internat. Soc. Nephrology, Am. soc. Cell Biology, The Phsyiol. Soc. Roman Catholic. Office: Dept Physiology Universitat, Winterthuerstrasse 190, CH-8057 Zürich Switzerland

MURILLO, VELDA JEAN, social worker, counselor; b. Miller, S.D., Dec. 8, 1943; d. Royal Gerald and Marion Elizabeth (Porter) Matson; m. Daniel John Murillo, June 25, 1967 (div. Dec. 1987); 1 child, Damon Michael. BS, S.D. State U., 1965; MA, Calif. State U., Bakersfield, 1980. Cert. marriage, family and child counselor. Social worker adult svcs. Kern County Dept. Welfare, Bakersfield, 1965-78, social worker child protective svcs., 1978-84; asst. coord. sexual abuse program Kern County Dist. Atty., Bakersfield, 1985-91, coord. sexual abuse program, 1991—; Mem. Calif. Sexual Assault Investigators, 1982-84, Kern Child Abuse Prevention Coun., Bakersfield, 1982-84; co-developer, presenter Children's Self Help Project, Bakersfield, 1982-87; cons. mem. Sexual Assault Adv. Com., Bakersfield, 1991—. Democrat. Office: Kern County Dist Atty 1215 Truxtun Ave Bakersfield CA 93301

MURILLO-ROHDE, ILDAURA MARIA, marriage and family therapist, consultant, educator, dean; b. Garachine, Panama; came to U.S., 1945; d. Amalio Murillo and Ana E. (Diaz) de Murillo; m. Erling Rohde, Sept. 19, 1959. BS, Columbia U., 1951, MA, 1953, MEd, 1969; PhD, NYU, 1971; hon. diploma, Escuela Nat. de Enfermeria, Guatemala, 1964; diploma naturopatia, Centro Estudios Naturista, Barcelona, Spain, 1992. RN; lic. marriage and family therapist, N.J.; cert. mental health-psychiat. nursing, ANA; lic. sex. therapist, N.J. Instr., supr. Bellevue Psychiat. Hosp., N.Y.C., 1950-54; asst. dir., dir. psychiat. div. Wayne County Gen. Hosp., Eloise, Mich., 1954-56; chief nurse psychiat. div. Elmhurst Gen. Hosp., Queens, N.Y., 1956-58, Met. Hosp. Med. Ctr., N.Y.C., 1961-63; psychiat. cons. to govt. of Guatemala WHO, UN, Guatemala, 1963-64; assoc. prof., chmn. psychiat. dept. N.Y. Med. Coll. Grad. Sch. Nursing, N.Y.C., 1964-69; dir. mental health-psychiatry, asst. prof. NYU, N.Y.C., 1970-72; assoc. prof. Hostos Coll., CUNY, N.Y.C., 1972-76; assoc. dean acad. affairs U. Wash., Seattle, 1976-81; prof., dean Coll. of Nursing SUNY, Downstate Med. Ctr., Bklyn., 1981-85; dean and prof. emeritus SUNY, Bklyn., 1985—; bd. dirs. Puerto Rican Family Inst., N.Y.C., 1983—; dir. Latin Am. Oncological Nurses Fuld Fellowships, 1989-90; psychiat. cons. Sch. Nursing, U. Antioquia, Medellin, Colombia, 1972-73, WHO; psychiat./rsch. cons. for master program Sch. Nursing, U. Panama, Project Hope, 1986. Editor: National Directory of Hispanic Nurses, 1981, 2d edit., 1986, 3d edit., 1994; contbr. numerous articles to profl. nat. and internat. jours., chpts. to books in field. Mem. Wash. State adv. com. U.S. Commn. on Civil Rights, Seattle, 1971-81; nat. adv. com. White House Conf. on Families, Washington, 1979-81; pres. King County Health Planning Council, Seattle, 1979-81; exec. com. Puget Sound Health Systems Agy., Seattle, 1979-81. Univ. Honors scholar NYU, 1972; named Citizen of the Day, Radio Sta. KIXI and N.W. Airlines, Seattle, 1979, Disting. lectr. Sigma Theta Tau, 1988-89, Woman of Yr., N.Y. Gotham Club Bus. and Profl. Women, 1989; recipient 1st Nat. Intercultural Nursing award Coun. of Intercultural Nursing, ANA, New Orleans, 1984, Women's Honors in Pub. Svc. award Minority Fellowship Programs and Cabinet Human Rights, ANA, 1986, Disting. Alumna award Divsn. Nursing, NYU Alumni Assn., 1989, 1st Nat. Dr. Hildegard Peplau award Las Vegas conv. ANA, 1992, Practice award Tchrs. Coll., Columbia U. Nursing Edn. Alumni, 1994; designated Living Legend for leadership in practice, edn. and rsch. Am. Acad. Nursing, 1994. Fellow Am. Assn. Marriage and Family Therapy; mem. ANA (affirmative action task force 1974-84, commn. human rights, cabinet human rights, rep. ANA at ICN Cong. Tokyo 1977, spokesperson Nat. Health Ins., conceived and designed Coun. Intercultural Nursing), Am. Orthopsychiat. Assn. (bd. dirs. 1976-79, treas. 1986-89), N.Y. Ass. Marriage and Family Therapy (pres. 1973-76), Nat. Assn. Hispanic Nurses (founder, 1st pres. 1976-80), Internat. Fedn. Bus. and Profl. Women (UN rep. to UNICEF London 1987—, del. to World UN Summit for Children N.Y.C. 1990, UN N.Y. Com. for Internat. Yr. of Family 1994), Am. Rsch. Inst. (dep. govt. 1987), NYU Club, Gotham Bus. and Profl. Women's Club. Democrat. Home: 300 W 108th St Apt 12A New York NY 10025-2704 Office: SUNY Bklyn Coll Nursing Box 22 450 Clarkson Ave Brooklyn NY 11203-2012

MUROFF, LAWRENCE ROSS, nuclear medicine physician; b. Phila., Dec. 26, 1942; s. John M. and Carolyn (Kramer) M.; m. Carol R. Savoy, July 12, 1969; children: Michael Bruce, Julie Anne. AB cum laude, Dartmouth Coll., 1964, B of Med. Sci., 1965; MD cum laude, Harvard U., 1967. Diplomate Am. Bd. Radiology, Am. Bd. Nuclear Medicine. Intern Boston City Hosp., Harvard, 1968; resident in radiology Columbia Presbyn. Med. Ctr., N.Y.C., 1970-73, chief resident, 1973; instr. dept. radiology, asst. radiologist Columbia U. Med. Ctr., N.Y.C., 1973-74; dir. dept. nuc. medicine, computed tomography and MRI Univ. Cmty. Hosp., Tampa, Fla., 1974-94, H. Lee Moffitt Cancer Hosp., Tampa, 1994—; pres. Imaging Cons. Inc., Tampa, 1994—; clin. asst. prof. radiology U. South Fla., 1974-78, clin. assoc. prof., 1978-82, clin. prof., 1982—; clin. prof. U. Fla., 1988—. Contbr. articles to profl. jours. Pres. Ednl. Symposia, Inc., 1975—. Lt. comdr. USPHS, 1968-70. Fellow Am. Coll. Nuclear Medicine (disting. fellow., Fla. del.), Am. Coll. Nuclear Physicians (regents 1976-78, pres.-elect 1978, pres. 1979, fellow 1980), Am. Coll. Radiology (councilor 1979-80, 91—, chancellor 1981-87, chmn. commn. on nuclear medicine 1981-87, fellow 1981); mem. Am. Assn. Acad. Chief Residents Radiology (chmn. 1973), AMA, Boylston Soc., Fla. Assn. Nuclear Physician (pres. 1976), Fla. Med. Assn., Hillsborough County Med. Assn., Radiol. Soc. N.Am., Soc. Nuclear Medicine (coun. 1975-90, trustee 1980-84, 86-89, pres. Southeastern chpt. 1983, vice chmn. correlative imaging coun. 1983), Fla. Radiol. Soc. (exec. com. 1976-91, treas. 1984, sec. 1985, v.p. 1986, pres. elect 1987, pres. 1988-89, gold medal 1995), West Coast Radiol. Soc., Soc. Mag. resonance Imaging (bd. dirs. 1988-91, chmn. edinl. program 1989, chmn. membership com. 1989-93), Clinical Magnetic Resonance Soc. (pres. elect 1995—), Phi Beta Kappa, Alpha Omega Alpha. Office: 1527 S Dale Mabry Hwy Tampa FL 33629-5808

MURPHEY, MARGARET JANICE, marriage and family therapist; b. Taft, Calif., July 24, 1939; d. Glen Roosevelt Wurster and Lucile Mildred (Holt) Lopez; m. Russell Warren Murphey, June 20, 1959; children: Lucinda Kalbfleisch, Rochelle Murphey, Janice Sorenson. BA in Social Sci., Calif. State U., Chico, 1986, MA in Psychology, 1989; postgrad., La Salle U. Sec. Folson State Prison, Calif., 1963-66; tchr. Desert Sands Unified Schs., Indio, Calif., 1969-72; claims determiner Employment Development Dept., Redding, Calif., 1976-78; sec. Shasta County Pers., Redding, 1978-79; welfare worker Shasta County Welfare Office, Redding, 1979-85; therapy intern Counseling Ctr. Calif. State U., Chico, 1989-90; therapist Family Svc. Assn., Chico, 1987-90, Butte County Drug and Alcohol Abuse Ctr., Chico, 1989-90; mental halth counselor Cibecue (Ariz.) Indian Health Clinic, 1990—; mem. Kinisba Child Abuse Com., 1994—. Vol. Pacheco Sch., Redding, 1972-76; Sunday sch. tchr., dir. vacation Bible sch. Nazarene Ch., Sacramento, Indio and Redding, 1958-85. Recipient Sch. Bell award Pacheco Sch. Mem. APA, ACA, Am. Assn. Christian Counselors, Am. Assn. Multi-Cultural Counselors, Psi Chi. Home: PO Box 1114 Show Low AZ 85901-1114 Office: Cibecue Health Ctr Apache Behavioral Health PO Box 1089 Whiteriver AZ 85941-1089

MURPHEY, ROBERT STAFFORD, pharmaceutical company executive; b. Littleton, N.C., Oct. 29, 1921; married; 2 children. B.S., U. Richmond, 1942; M.S., U. Va., 1947, Ph.D. in Organic Chemistry, 1949. Research chemist in medicinal chemistry A.H. Robins & Co. Inc., Richmond, Va., 1948-53, dir. chemistry research, 1953-55, assoc. dir., 1955-57, dir. research, 1957-60, dir. internat. research, 1960-66, dir. sci. devel., 1966-82, asst. v.p., 1967-73, dir. sci. devel., v.p., 1973-82, v.p. sci. affairs and corp. devel., 1982-83, sr. v.p. sci. affairs and corp. devel., 1983-87, sr. v.p., dir. new bus. devel., 1983-90; sr. v.p., dir. bus. devel. E.C. Robins Internat., Inc., Glen Allen, Va., 1990—. Mem. AAAS, Am. Chem. Soc. Office: E C Robins Internat Inc 11064 Staples Mill Rd Glen Allen VA 23060-2404

MURPHREE, HENRY BERNARD SCOTT, psychiatry and pharmacology educator, consultant; b. Decatur, Ala., Aug. 11, 1927; s. Henry Bernard and Nancy Mae (Burrus) M.; m. Dorothy Elaine Simmons, Nov. 14, 1953 (dec.); children: Julie Elizabeth, Susan Louise, Jefferson Van; m. Dorothy Elizabeth Olson, Sept. 23, 1993. Student, MIT, 1944-45; BA, Yale U., 1950; MD, Emory U., 1959. Intern internal medicine, fellow clin. pharmacology, instr. Emory U., 1959-61; resident psychiatry Med. Sch. Rutgers U., 1972-76, mem. grad. faculty psychology, 1972—; rsch. asst. Johns Hopkins U., Balt., 1950; asst. chief neuropharmacology Bur. Rsch., Princeton, N.J., 1961-68; from assoc prof. to prof. Univ. of Medicine and Dentistry Robert Wood Johnson Med. Sch., Piscataway, N.J., 1968—, assoc. dean acad. affairs Univ. Medicine and Dentistry, 1977-81, chmn. psychiatry Univ. Medicine and Dentistry, 1977-91; cons. medicinal chemistry and pharmacology FMC Chem. R&D Ctr., Princeton, N.J., 1962-68, Hoffman-LaRoche, Nutley and Verona, N.J., 1968-77. Contbr. articles to profl. jours. Founding mem. Somerset Coun. Alcoholism, Somerville, N.J., 1974-77; mem. Sci. Adv. Com., State of N.J., 1981—; bd. trustees Carrier Found., Belle Mead, N.J., 1981-95, vice chmn. bd., chmn. exec. com., 1989-95. Lt. MSC USN, 1951-55. Mem. Am. Soc. for Pharmacology and Exptl. Therapeutics, Am. Psychiat. Assn., Soc. Biol. Psychiatry, Am. Coll. Neuropsychopharmacology, Sigma Xi, Alpha Omega Alpha. Home: 757 Route 518 Skillman NJ 08558-2513 Office: U Med & Dentistry NJ Robert Wood Johnson Med Sch 675 Hoes Ln Piscataway NJ 08854-5635

MURPHREE, JAMES WALLACE, retired radiologist; b. Pratt, Kans., Jan. 26, 1924; s. Charles Otto and Beatrice Lottie (Durham) M.; m. Melrose Kelly, Oct. 10, 1948 (div. Oct. 1976); children: Paula, Kathy, Jim, Melanie; m. Barbara Battye Walker Kelham, Mar. 18, 1989. Student, Northeastern State U., 1941-43, Emory U., 1943, U. Okla., 1943; MD, U. Okla., Oklahoma City, 1947. Diplomate Am. Bd. Radiology, Am. Bd. Nuclear Medicine. Intern and resident St. Joseph's Hosp., St. Paul, 1947-49; fellow in radiology Cleve. Clinic, 1951-53; locum tenens Lockard & Wallingford Radiology, Bartlesville, Okla., 1953; radiologist St. Joseph Med. Ctr., Ponca City, Okla., 1954-76, Meml. Hosp., Clovis, N.mex., 1976-77, Hendricks Med. Ctr., Abilene, Tex., 1977-78, Jackson Meml. Hosp., Lexington, Va., 1978; locum tenens various hosps., 1978-95; radiologist Tahlequah (Okla.) City Hosp., 1990-95; ret., 1995; vis. lectr. in radiology Coll. Medicine U. Okla., Oklahoma City, 1971, mem. admissions com., 1974-75. Pres. Rotary Internat., Ponca City, 1963, Ponca City Country Club, 1962; elder first Presbyn. Ch., Ponca City, 1956-76; chmn. edn. com. Ponca City C. of C., 1962-65. Lt. USNR, 1949-51. Fellow Am. Coll. Radiology (pres. Okla. chpt. 1962); mem. AMA, Okla. State Med. Assn. (trustee 1957-60, contbg. editor 1962-65), Northeastern Okla. Radiol. Soc., Radiol. Soc. N.Am., Soc. Nuc. Medicine, Cookson Hills Med. Soc. Republican. Home: Rt 2 Box 44 Pryor OK 74361

MURPHREE, TAMMY MARIE, clinical manager; b. Jackson, Tenn., May 1, 1964; d. Talmage Herman and Hazel Marie (Morris) Evans; m. Paul Michael Murphree, Dec. 22, 1984; children: Mitzi Marie, Andrew Taylor. RN, Meth. Hosp., Memphis, 1984; BSN, Union U., Jackson, Tenn., 1989. Staff nurse med./surg. floor Jackson-Madison County Gen. Hosp., 1985-88; asst. head nurse med./surg. floor Jackson-Madison County Gen. Hosp., Jackson, 1988-89; 1st surg. asst. Jackson Clinic, 1989-93; clin. mgr. med. fl. Jackson-Madison County Gen. Hosp., 1993—. Mem. Assn. Oper. Rm. Nurses, Sigma Theta Tau, Alpha Chi, Pi Epsilon Iota (treas. 1983-84).

MURPHY, ALBERT THOMAS, psychologist, educator; b. Boston, Jan. 21, 1924; s. Albert Thomas and Elizabeth (Green) M.; m. Therese Ann Landry, July 16, 1949; children: Mark T., Steven N., Scott R. A.B., Emerson Coll., 1949; M.A., U. So. Calif., 1950, Ph.D., 1952. Asst. prof. Boston U., 1952-55, assoc. prof., 1955-58, prof. spl. edn. and allied health professions, 1958—, dir. Communicative Disorders Clinic, 1952-63, dir. Psychoednl. Clinic, 1963-69, chmn. dept. spl. edn., 1969-72, 80-82; cons. United Cerebral Palsy, U.S. Office Edn., R.I., Mass. depts. mental health, Mass. State Dept. Edn. Author: Functional Voice Disorders, 1964, Stuttering: Training the Therapist, 1966, (with others) Stuttering: Treatment of the Young Stutterer in the Schools, 1964, Stuttering and Personality Dynamics, 1960, Stuttering: Its Prevention, 1962, Stuttering and the Reinforcement Therapies, 1970, The Families of Hearing Impaired Children, 1979, Special Children, Special Parents, 1981; others. Served with USMCR, 1942-46. Decorated D.F.C., Air medal. Fellow Am. Speech and Hearing Assn., Am. Psychol. Assn., others. Unitarian-Universalist. Home: 500 Ocean St Apt 44 Hyannis MA 02601-4759 Office: 605 Commonwealth Ave Boston MA 02215-1605

MURPHY, BARBARA ANNE, emergency physician, surgery educator; b. Cin., Oct. 20, 1937; d. Harold August and Lorna Louise (Gabbard) Tiemeyer; m. D. Michael Murphy, Feb. 5, 1960; children: Michael Patrick, Douglas Andrew. BS cum laude, Ohio State U., 1959; MD magna cum laude, Med. Coll. Pa., 1975. Diplomate Am. Bd. Emergency Medicine. Resident in emergency medicine Geisinger Med. Ctr., Danville, Pa., 1978; staff physician Albemarle Hosp., Elizabeth City, N.C., 1978-79, Durham County Hosp., Durham, N.C., 1979-87; asst. prof. emergency medicine East Carolina U., Greenville, N.C., 1987-90; asst. prof. surgery-emergency medicine Duke U., Durham, 1990—; dir. propsed residency emergency medicine Duke U., Durham, 1994—. Author: (book chpt.) Pediatric Emergency Medicine, rev. edit., 1992; editor: Emergency Med. Abstracts, 1988—; book reviewer: Annals of Emergency Medicine, 1995—; contbr. articles to profl. jours. Fellow Am. Coll. Emergency Physicians (mem. clin. policies com. 1991—); mem. Soc. for Acad. Emergency Medicine, Alpha Omega Alpha, Phi Beta Kappa. Home: PO Box 837 Hillsborough NC 27278 Office: Duke U Med Ctr Box 3096 Durham NC 27710

MURPHY, DOUGLAS CRAIG, psychotherapist; b. Balt., Jan. 20, 1943; s. Eugene Henry Murphy and Mildred Lee (Amoss) Miller; m. Nancy Katherine Assero, Mar. 10, 1978; 1 dau., Meghan Aubra. B.A., Antioch U., Balt., 1973, M.A., 1975; postgrad. Georgetown U., 1977-81. Cert. Nat.

Acad. Cert. Clin. Mental Health Counselors, Md. Chief counselor Balt. City Hosp., 1972-74; instr. U. Md. Med. Sch., Balt., 1975-77; adminstr. Families and Children's Service, Balt., 1974-77; pvt. practice family psychotherapy, Balt., 1977—; clin. dir. Family Crisis Ctr., Balt., 1979—; clin. intern Georgetown U., Washington, 1982-84, clin. staff, 1984—; fac. Essex Cmty. Coll., Balt., 1993—, Md. Inst. Coll. of Art, Balt., 1994; trainer Brotherhood of Man, Towson, Md., 1978-79; clin. supr. Johns Hopkins U., Balt., 1980-84; cons. Bolton Hill Counseling Ctr., Balt., 1979, Mem. Interagy. Com. on Abuse and Neglect, Towson, Md.; mem. Domestic Violence Coordinating Com., Balt. Mem. Am. Personnel and Guidance Assn., Am. Orthopsychiat. Assn. Home: 3606 Crossland Ave Baltimore MD 21213-1007 Office: Family Health Services 1010 St Paul St Baltimore MD 21202-2661

MURPHY, EDRIE LEE, hospital laboratory administrator; b. Redwood Falls, Minn., Dec. 4, 1953; d. Melvin Arthur and Betty Lou (Wenholz) Timm; m. David Joseph Murphy, July 28, 1984; children: Michael David, Scott Christopher. BS in Med. Tech. summa cum laude, Mankato State U., 1976; MBA, U. St. Thomas, 1984. Registered med. technologist. Med. technologist Children's Health Care, St. Paul, 1976-81, chemistry supr., 1981-85, lab. mgr., 1985-95, dir. lab. systems, Mpls., St. Paul's Campus, 1995—. Contbr. articles to profl. jours. Charles H. Cooper scholar, 1975. Mem. Am. Soc. Clin. Lab. Scis., Minn. Soc. Clin. Lab. Scis., Am. Assn. Clin. Chemists, Clin. Lab. Mgmt. Assn. (sec./treas. Minn. chpt. 1994-96, bd. dirs. 1996—), Phi Kappa Phi. Club: Elan Vital Ski (v.p. membership 1981-82) (Mpls.). Avocations: photography, sailing, skiing, tennis, travel. Office: Children's Health Care 345 Smith Ave N Saint Paul MN 55102-2369

MURPHY, JAMES C., rehabilitation services professional; b. Cedar Rapids, Iowa, Sept. 29, 1953; s. James J. Murphy and Eva J. (Vernon) Jones; m. Priscilla Kay Dennie, June 15, 1973; children: Joshua James, Elijah Curtis. Cert. substance abuse counselor; nat. cert. chem. dependency counselor. Psychiat. aide Iowa State Mental Health Inst., Independence, 1973-75, adolescent counselor, 1975-76, counselor trainee, 1975-76; outpatient substance abuse counselor Northeast Coun. on Substance Abuse, Waterloo, Iowa, 1976-77, supr. minority alcohol prog., 1978-79, case mgmt. cons., 1977-79, residential counselor, 1978-80, dir. residential facility, 1980-84; prog. dir. Adolescent Treatment Ctr. of Winnebago, Minn., 1984—; CEO Addiction Recovery Techs., Inc., 1991—; provider rep. Faribault/Martin County DHS Adv. Com., Fairmont, Minn., 1987—; cons. Pharm. Mgmt. Systems, St. Louis, 1988-92; CEO, pres. Addiction Recovery Techs., 1991—. Sect. leader 4-H, Winnebago, 1985-87. With USMC, 1970-72, Vietnam. Mem. So. Minn. Assn. Alcohol/Drug Abuse Counselors (pres.-elect 1990-92), So. Minn. Regional Coalition of C.D. Profls. (steering com. 1990-93), Nat. Assn. Alcohol/Drug Abuse Counselors (Minn. del. 1990), Minn. Chem. Dependency Assn. (region 10 bd. dirs.), Minn. Assn. Resources for Recovery (v.p. charter bd. 1995, gov. region 9 1995—). Mem. Christian Ch. Home: 31453 240th St Winnebago MN 56098-9748

MURPHY, JOSEPH JAMES, chiropractic physician; b. Newark, N.J., July 30, 1956; s. Joseph P. and Roberta (Nittolo) M.; m. Rebecca Lynn Swanson, June 21, 1986; children: Joseph Raymond, Alexandra Renee. BA in Biology, Rider Coll., 1978; D in Chiropractic Medicine, Palmer Coll., 1984. Diplomate Nat. Bd. Chiropractic Examiners; cert. N.J. State Bd. Med. Examiners. Rsch. chemist Mallinkrodt, Inc., Englewood, N.J., 1979-81; staff physician Mid-Island Chiropractic, Levittown, N.Y., 1984; dir., chief exec. officer Suburban Chiropractic Ctr., Chatham, N.J., 1984—. Advisor Chatham High Sch. Key Club, 1986-87. D. D. Palmer scholar, 1981, 82, 83. Mem. APHA, AAAS, Am. Assn. Cereal Chemists, Am. Chiropractic Assn., N.J. Chiropractic Soc. (bd. dirs. 1987—, chmn. inter profl. rels. com. 1989—, 1st v.p. 1992-95, pres. 1995—, editor-in-chief Jersey Jour. 1986—, Meritorious Svc. award 1986, Disting. Svc. award 1987, 88, 89, 90), N.Y. Acad. Sci., Internat. Soc. Food Technologists, Morris County Chiropractic Soc. (pres. 1987—), Chatham C. of C. (chmn. profl. rels. com. 1988-92, pres. 1989-92), Kiwanis (bd. dirs. Chatham club 1986-89, Disting. Svc. award 1995), Kiwanis (bd. dirs. Chatham club 1986-89), Tri Beta. Republican. Presbyterian. Home: 139 Woods End Dr Basking Ridge NJ 07920-1970 Office: Suburban Chiropractic Ctr 301 Main St Chatham NJ 07928-2410

MURPHY, JOSEPH L., internist; b. Chgo.. BS, Loyola U., Chgo., 1957; MD, Loyola U., 1965. Diplomate Am. Bd. Internal Medicine. Intern and resident in internal medicine St. Joseph Hosp., Chgo., 1965-69; pvt. practice Chgo.; asst. prof. Stritch Loyola, 1974-77; asst. prof. clin. medicine Northwestern U., 1977—; pres. med. staff St. Joseph Hosp., 1981-84, med. staff sect. rep., 1983—, mem. physician exec. com., 1972-93, 95—; bd. dirs., treas. CRIS Radio Med. Show for Print Handicapped, 1986-92. Bd. dirs. Chgo. Access Cable TV, 1989-92; exec. adv. bd. St. Joseph Hosp., 1981-87; mem. Ill. coalition Against Tobacco; mem. Blue Cross/Blue Shield Physician Adv. Com., 1992—. Recipient Outreach award AMA, 1991, 92, 93, 94, 95. Fellow ACP, Am. Geriatric Soc., Chgo. Inst. Medicine (bd. dirs. 1995—), Am. Coll. Med. Quality; mem. Ill. Soc. Internal Medicine (coun. mem. 1986—, chmn. membership com. 1992—, pres. 1995-96, Disting. Internist award 1990, 93), Ill. Hosp. Assn. (med. staff coun. 1986-90), Am. Bd. Quality Assurance and Utilization Rev. Physicians (pres. and chmn. bd. 1992—, chmn. continuing med. edn. com. 1992—, Openshaw Leadership award), Am. Coll. Physician Execs., Am. Soc. Internal Medicine, Nat. Bd. Med. Broadcasters, Am. Found. for Edn. in Health Care Quality (pres. 1996—), Ill. Med. Soc. (allt. del. or del. to ho. of dels. 1985—, coun. on pub. rels. and membership svcs. 1992—), Chgo. Med. Soc. (bd. trustees 1992-95, vice chmn. 1994, cons. 1990—, mem. profl. liability com. 1990—, Midwest clin. conf. com. 1993—, North Shore br. pres. 1986-87, treas. 1988—, Photography Award 3d pl. 1991, Poetry award 1st pl. 1992, 93, 94, 95). Office: Ste 260 4890 W Kennedy Blvd Tampa FL 33609

MURPHY, JUDITH L., nursing administrator, gerontology nurse; b. Cleve., June 11, 1945; d. Chester and Winona (Addis) Noel; children: Sean, Lisa. Diploma, Mercy Sch. Nursing, Toledo, 1966; student, Spokane Falls Community Coll., Graceland Coll., Lamoni, Iowa. RN, Ohio; cert. in gerontology.

MURPHY, KATHLEEN ANN, optometrist; b. Newark, Ohio, July 3, 1956; d. Herbert James and Patricia Ann (Roney) M. BA in Zoology, Miami U., Oxford, Ohio, 1978; OD, Ohio State U., 1982. Lic. optmetrist. Pvt. practice optometrist Dublin, Ohio, 1982—; part-time clinic instr. Ohio State U. Coll. Optometry, Columbus, 1982-85; part-time tchr. Columbus (Ohio) State C.C., 1984-89; adv. bd. Columbus State Optometric Technician Program, Columbus, 1987-89; cons. Metatec Corp., Dublin, 1995. Named Outstanding Young Women of Am., 1982. Mem. Am. Optometric Assn., Ohio Optometric Assn., Ctrl. Ohio Optometric Assn. (sec., treas., trustee), Dublin Women in Bus. and Professions (trustee 1982—), Moundbuilders Country Club. Republican. Roman Catholic. Office: 5194 Blazer Pkwy Dublin OH 43017

MURPHY, MARGARET A., nursing educator, adult nurse practitioner; b. N.Y.C., Apr. 4, 1934; d. William J. and Margaret (Burchill) Allen; m. Raymond L.H. Murphy, Jr., July 12, 1958; children: Raymond L.H. III, Michael W., Ann Murphy Postell, Maureen D. Murphy Olsen, Alice M., Matthew D. BSN, St. Joseph Coll., West Hartford, Conn., 1955; MS, NYU, 1957; PhD, Boston Coll., Chestnut Hill, Mass., 1987. RN, Mass.; cert. adult nurse practitioner. Instr. Boston U. Sch. Nursing, 1971-72; pulmonary clin. nurse specialist Pulmonary Assocs., Boston, 1972-73; pulmonary nurse clinician Tufts U., Medford, Mass., 1973-76; instr. Boston Coll., 1976-82, asst. prof., 1982-87, instr. prof. nursing, 1976-82, asst. prof., 1982-87, assoc. prof. nursing, 1987—, chmn. adult health nursing, 1988-92, dir. adult nurse practitioners program, 1987—, dir. Kennedy Audio Visual Resource Ctr., 1991-95, coord. MBA-MSN program, 1993-96; rschr. lung sound patterns in health and disease funded by Uniformed Svcs., 1995-96. Contbr. to nursing publs. Fellow USPHS, 1957-58. Fellow Am. Coll. Nurse Practitioners; mem. ANA, Mass. Nurses Assn. (co-chmn. cabinet on legis.), Am. Thoracic Soc., Mass. Thoracic Soc. (chmn. com. on nursing practice, counselor 1989-91), Sigma Theta Tau (chmn. awards and scholarships com. 1994-96, pres. 1996—).

MURPHY, MARY KATHLEEN, nursing educator; b. Elkins, W.Va., Jan. 27, 1953; d. Wyatt W. and Emma Loretta (Bohan) M.; children: Bridget Allyn, Kelley M. Poling. Diploma, Upshur County Sch. Nursing, Buckhannon, W.Va., 1982; ADN, Davis and Elkins Coll., 1984, BSN magna cum laude, 1986; MSN, W.Va. U. Cert. correctional health profl., substitute vocat. tchr. practical nursing, W.Va. Nurse. asst head nurse in ob-gyn. Meml. Gen. Hosp., Elkins, W.Va.; staff nurse, resource pool in ob-gyn. W.Va. U., Morgantown; DON Correctional Med. Systems, Huttonsville, W.Va.; instr. in nursing Davis and Elkins Coll.; nurse mgr. Elkins Mountain Sch. Randolph County Bd. Edn. Reviewer nursing texts Lippincott-Raven Pub. Mem. ANA, W.Va. Nursing Assn. (reviewer approval unit com. edn.), Inst. Noetic Scis., So. States Correctional Assn., Alpha Chi, Sigma Theta Tau.

MURPHY, MARY KATHRYN, industrial hygienist; b. Kansas City, Mo., Apr. 16, 1941; d. Arthur Charles and Mary Agnes (Fitzgerald) Wahlstedt; m. Thomas E. Murphy Jr., Aug. 26, 1963; children: Thomas E. III, David W. BA, Avila Coll., Kansas City, 1962; MS, Cen. Mo. State U., 1975. Cert. in comprehensive practice of indsl. hygiene. Indsl. hygienist Kansas City area office Occupational Safety and Health Adminstrn., 1975-78, regional indsl. hygienist, 1979-86; dir. indsl. hygiene Chart Svcs., Shawnee, Kans., 1986-87; dir. indsl. hygiene and hazardous substance control Hall-Kimbrell Environ. Mgmt. and Pollution Control, Lawrence, Kans., 1987-88, mgr. dept. indsl. hygiene div. environ. mgmt. and program control, 1988-89; dir. indsl. hygiene Hazardous Waste divsn. Burns & McDonnell, Engrs., Architects, Kansas City, Mo., 1989-93; mgr. health & safety dept. Burns & McDonnell Waste Cons., Inc., Overland Park, Kansas, 1990-93, dir. indsl. hygiene U.S. Army Corps Engrs., Kansas City, 1993; regional program mgr. environ. & safety ctrl. region FAA, Kansas City, 1993—; asst. dir. safety office U. Kans. Med. Ctr., 1978-79; adj. prof. continuing edn. divsn. U. Kans.; adj. lectr. Ctrl. Mo. State U. Summer talent fellow Kaw Valley Heart Assn., 1961. Mem. AAAS, Am. Indsl. Hygiene Assn. (sec.-treas. Mid-Am. sect. 1978-79, bd. dirs. 1981, mem. auditcom.), Am. Chem. Soc., Am. Conf. Govt. Indsl. Hygienists (mem. chem. agts. threshold limit value com.), Am. Acad. Indsl. Hygiene, Air and Waste Mgmt. Assn., Environ. Audit Roundtable, N.Y. Acad. Scis., Internat. Soc. Environ. Toxicology and Cancer, Am. Coll. Toxicology, Am. Conf. on Chem. Labeling. Home: 10616 W 123rd St Shawnee Mission KS 66213-1952 Office: FAA-ACE 473 601E 12th St Kansas City MO 64106

MURPHY, MARYLIN ANN, nurse manager; b. Lawrence, Mass., July 18, 1951; d. John R. and Christina A. (Igo) Donahue; m. Colin Thomas Murphy, Sept. 3, 1972; children: Meaghann C., Brendan R. Diploma, NE Deaconess Hosp., 1972; BS, New England Coll., 1990. Staff nurse NE Deaconess Hosp., Boston, 1972-80, 84-86, Strong Meml. Hosp., Rochester, N.Y., 1981-83; vis. staff VNA Home Care, Andover, Mass., 1990-92; discharge planner Beverly (Mass.) Hosp., 1992-93; from quality assurance specialist to area clin. nurse mgr. Home Health VNA, Haverhill, Mass., 1993—; practice com. Health Pathways of New England, Wellesley, Mass., 1994—. Roman Catholic. Home: 4 Blackberry Ln Methuen MA 01844

MURPHY, MICHAEL KENNETH, osteopathic physician, navy officer; b. Bklyn., Aug. 26, 1947; s. James Michael and Elizabeth May (Kirkpatrick) M.; m. Deborah Sue Wood, Oct. 14, 1972; children: Elizabeth W., Kathleen Anne. BS, King's Coll., Wilkes-Barre, Pa., 1969; DO, Kirksville (Mo.) Coll. Osteo., 1973. Diplomate Am. Bd. Family Practice, Am. Bd. Osteopathic Family Physicians; lic. physician, Ariz., Del., Fla. Commd. ensign USN, 1970, advanced through grades to capt., 1991; intern then resident Navy Hsop., Camp Pendelton, Calif., 1973-76; chief svc. Navy Hsop., Patuxent River, Md., 1976-80, Orlando, Fla., 1980-82; officer in charge T.A.D. to MMART # 14, USS Peleliu, 1983; asst. dir., head clin. divsn. Naval Hosp., Pensacola, Fla., 1984-86, head emergency med. dept., dir. med. svc., 1986-87; exec. officer Naval Hosp., Phila., 1989-91; commanding officer Naval Hosp., Oak Harbor, Wash., 1991-93; instr., cons., master tng. specialist Naval Med. Quality Inst., Bethesda, Md., 1993—; assoc. prof. U. Health Care Scis., Washingotn, 1986, U. Medicine and Dentistry, Camden, N.J., 1990, Osteo. Med. Ctr. Phila., 1990, Coll. Osteo. Medicine of the Pacific, Pomona, Calif., 1991; lectr. and speaker in field. Contbr. articles to profl. jours. Vol. Boy Scouts Am., Nat. Youth Sports Program, Spl. Olympics. Decroated Meritorious Svc. medal (3), Navy Commendation (2), Navy Meritorious Unit Commendation, Nat. Def., Coast Guard Spl. Operation Svc. ribbon, Navy Overseas Svc. ribbon, Humanitarian Svc. award. Mem. Assn. Mil. Surgeons U.S., Am. Osteo. Assn. (trustee 1991), Am. Coll. Osteo. Family Physicians, Am. Acad. Family Physicians, U.S. Naval Inst., Fla. Osteo. Med. Assn., Md. Osteo. Assn., Osteo. Assn. D.C., Washingotn Osteo. Med. Assn., Uniformed Svcs. Acad. Family Physicians. Office: Navy Med Quality Inst 8901 Wisconsin Ave Bethesda MD 20889-5611

MURPHY, MICHAEL OWEN, dermatologist; b. Des Moines, Aug. 20, 1937; s. James Howard and Esther Cornelia (Ross) M.; m. Olivia Eleanor Granillo, Nov. 30, 1963; children: Thomas, Ann Marie, Timothy. BA, St. Ambrose Coll., Davenport, Iowa, 1959; MD, Med. Coll. Wis., Milw., 1963. Diplomate Am. Bd. Dermatology. Rotating intern St. Joseph's Hosp., Phoenix, 1963-64; commd. USN, advanced through grades to capt.; med. officer USS Hector, FPO San Francisco, 1964-66; resident dermatology Naval Hosp., San Diego, 1966-69; dermatologist Naval Hosp., Camp Pendleton, Calif., 1969-77; chief dermatology dept. Naval Hosp., Portsmouth, Va., 1977-85. Fellow Am. Acad. Dermatology, Pacific Dermatol. Assn.; mem. San Diego Dermatol. Soc. Roman Catholic. Home: 2920 Levante St Carlsbad CA 92009 Office: KaiserPermanente 780 Shadowridge Dr Vista CA 92083

MURPHY, RAMON J.C., physician, pediatrician; b. N.Y.C., Feb. 12, 1944; s. William J. and Angelines (Castroviejo) M.; m. Lila J. Kalinich, Sept. 2, 1971; children: Jessica, David. BA, U. Notre Dame, 1965; MD, Northwestern U., 1969; MPH, Columbia U., 1974. Diplomate Am. Bd. Pediats. Intern in medicine Cook County Hosp., Chgo., 1969-70; resident in pediats. Children's Meml. Hosp., Chgo., 1970-71, Babies Hosp.-Columbia-Presbyn. Med. Ctr., N.Y.C., 1971-73; resident in cmty. medicine Mt. Sinai Hosp., N.Y.C., 1973-74, clin. asst. pediatrician, 1974-75, asst. attending pediatrician, 1975-83, assoc. attending pediatrician, 1983—, assoc. instr. cmty. medicine, 1974-75, asst. prof. clin. pediats., asst. prof. cmty. medicine, 1975-83, assoc. prof. clin. pediats., 1983—; pediatrician Uptown Pediats., P.C., N.Y.C., 1976—; vis. clin. fellow pediats. Columbia U., Coll. Physicians and Surgeons, N.Y.C., 1971-73; pediats. cons. Oxford Health Plan, 1990-94. Contbr. articles to profl. jours. Co-med. dir. Benito Juarez People's Health Ctr., Chgo., 1970-71; dep. co-dir. Wagner Child Health Project, N.Y.C., 1973-75; sch. physician The Day Sch., 1984—, The Trinity Sch., 1992—, trustee, 1993—. Fellow Am. Acad. Pediats; mem. N.Y. Pediat. Soc. (program chmn. 1986-89, pres. 1989-90), Soc. for Adolescent Medicine, Mt. Sinai Alumni Assn. Office: 1175 Park Ave New York NY 10128

MURPHY, RICHARD EDWARD, physician assistant; b. N.Y.C., Feb. 3, 1949; s. Daniel Joseph and Evelyn Marie (Dorsey) M.; m. Barbara Jean Hohl, July 21, 1973; 1 child, Ryan Lewis. AB, Fairfield U., 1971; cert. physician asst., Northeastern U., 1975, MBA, 1987; cert. advanced mgmt. studies, European Inst. Bus. Adminstrn., Fontainbleau, France, 1987. Cert. physician asst. Nat. Bd. Med. Examiners. Chief physician asst. dept. surgery New Eng. Med. Ctr., Boston, 1975—; asst. dir. Kiwanis Pediatric Trauma Inst., Boston, 1981-95; instr. in surgery Sch. Medicine Tufts U., Boston, 1983-88, asst. prof. surgery Sch. Medicine, 1988—; cons. Boston Med Flight, 1984-85; lectr. in mktg. Grad. Sch. Bus. Northeastern U., 1990-91, clin. instr. Coll. Pharmacy and Allied Health, 1978-85; lectr. program in cardiovascular perfusion New Eng. Med. Ctr., Boston, 1985-92. Co-author: Perioperative Care in Cardiothoracic Surgery, 1st edit., 1988; editl. bd. Physician Asst. Jour., 1985-88, Clin. Revs., 1990—; contbr. articles to profl. publs. Mem. Acad. Physician Assts., Mass. Assn. Physician Assts. Office: New Eng Med Ctr Box 133 750 Washington St Boston MA 02111

MURPHY, ROBERT FRANCIS, biology educator and researcher; b. Bklyn., Aug. 25, 1953; s. Robert Francis and Marguerite Ann (McClean) M.; m. Vivian Mathilde Grosswald, Aug. 15, 1981 (div. May 1990); children: Robert Emile, Charles Francis; m. Cynthia Ann Miller, Nov. 23, 1991; 1 child, Michael James. BA, Columbia U., 1974; PhD, Calif. Inst. Tech., 1979. Rsch. assoc. Columbia U., N.Y.C., 1979-83; asst. prof. dept. biol. sci. Carnegie Mellon U., Pitts., 1983-89, assoc. prof., 1989—; cons. Becton Dickinson Immunocytometry Systems, San Jose, Calif., 1982-92; assoc. Pitts. Cancer Inst., 1986—; mem. cell biology study panel NSF, Washington, 1989-92, biol. scis. study sect. NIH, 1993—. Co-editor: Applications of Fluorescence in the Biomedical Sciences, 1986, Endosomes and Lysosomes: A Dynamic Relationship, 1993; contbr. over 50 articles to profl. publs. Recipient Presdl. Young Investigator award NSF, 1984; Damon Runyon-Walter Winchell Cancer Found. postdoctoral fellow, 1979; grantee NIH, NSF, Am. Cancer Soc., 1995, Am. Heart Assn., 1995. Mem. AAAS, Internat. Soc. Analytical Cytology, Am. Soc. Cell Biology, Sigma Xi. Home: 2537 Club House Dr Wexford PA 15090-7956 Office: Carnegie Mellon U 4400 5th Ave Pittsburgh PA 15213-2617

MURPHY, ROBERT P., physician; b. Aug. 11, 1943; m. Emily Ying Chew, Oct. 11, 1986; children: Alison Anne Chew Murphy, Emma Elizabeth Ying Murphy, Erica Lynn Chew Murphy. BS, St. Louis U., 1965; MD, Northwestern U., 1969. Intern Milw. County Gen. Hosp., 1969-70; resident internal medicine U. Calif., Irvine, 1972-75; resident ophthalmology Stanford (Calif.) U. Med. Ctr., 1975-78; assoc. prof. Sch. of Medicine Johns Hopkins U., Balt., 1984-91; pvt. practice Retina Ctr. St. Joseph Hosp., Towson, Md., 1991—. Mem. Am. Acad. Ophthalmology, Assn. Rsch. in Vision and Ophthalmology, Macula Soc., Retina Soc., Pan-Am. Assn. Ophthalmology, Md. Soc. Eye Physicians and Surgeons. Office: Retina Inst Md O'Dea Med Arts Bldg 7505 Osler Dr Ste 103 Baltimore MD 21204-7737

MURPHY, RUTH MARKMANN, psychiatrist; b. Phila., Mar. 12, 1922; d. M. Jacob and Helen (Goodman) Markmann; m. William F. Murphy, Dec. 23, 1950; children: Jean, Stephen. BA, Radcliffe Coll., 1943; MD, Columbia U., 1948. Resident in psychiatry Boston VA Hosp., Framingham, Mass., 1949-51, McLean Hosp., Belmont, Mass., 1956-59, Mass. Mental Health Hosp., Boston, 1959-60; pvt. practice Lincoln, Mass., 1960-96; retired, 1996.

MURRAY, DAVID ROBERT, internist, cardiology; b. San Antonio, May 14, 1960; s. Robert George and Joan Alice (Petersen) M.; m. Natalie Scott Callander, Sept. 5, 1992; children: Jason Patrick, Danielle Callander. BA in Biochemistry highest distinction, Northwestern U., 1982; MD with honors, U. Ill., Chgo., 1986. Diplomate Am. Bd. Internal Medicine with subspecialty in cardiovascular disease. Intern U. Calif., San Diego, 1986-87, resident in internal medicine, 1987-89, rsch. fellow cardiology, 1989-90; clin. fellow cardiology U. Calif., 1990-92; asst. prof. medicine U. Tex. Health Sci. Ctr., San Antonio, 1992—. Contbr. articles to profl. jours. Fellow Am. Coll. Cardiology, Am. Heart Assn. (coun. on clin. cardiology); mem. ACP, Phi Beta Kappa, Alpha Omega Alpha. Home: 9223 St Ives San Antonio TX 78250 Office: Univ Tex Health Sci Ctr 7703 Floyd Curl Dr San Antonio TX 78284

MURRAY, HAROLD DIXON, biological educator, malacologist; b. Neodesha, Kans., May 25, 1931; s. Claude Allen and Beulah Augusta (Dixon) M.; m. Beverly Frances Martindale, Oct. 3, 1954; 1 child, Stephen Weston. BS, Ottawa U., 1952; MSc, Kans. State Coll., 1953; PhD, U. Kans., 1960. Instr. U. Kans., Lawrence, 1960-61; asst. prof. Trinity U., San Antonio, 1961-66, assoc. prof., 1966-73, chmn. biology, 1975-84, acting dean, 1979-80, 87-88, prof. biology, 1973—. Author: Unionid Mussels in Kansas, 1962. Author booklet Premedical Advising in Texas, 1981. Served to cpl. U.S. Army, 1953-54. Fellow Tex. Acad. Sci.; mem. Am. Malacological Union (pres. 1974-75), Am. Soc. Parasitologists, Southeastern Assn. Advisors for Health Professions (chair 1989-91), Tex. Assn. Advisors for Health Professions (chair 1981), Sigma Xi. Home: 247 Pinewood Ln San Antonio TX 78216-6722 Office: Trinity U 715 Stadium Dr San Antonio TX 78212-7200

MURRAY, HENRY WILKE, physician, educator; b. Washington, Oct. 28, 1946; s. Albert Francis and Elizabeth (Wilke) M.; m. Diana Telling, June 14, 1969; children: Kathryn Elizabeth, John Henry. BA, Cornell U., 1968, MD, 1972. Diplomate Am. Bd. Internal Medicine, Am. Bd. Infectious Diseases. Intern, then resident N.Y. Hosp., N.Y.C., 1972-74, chief med. resident, 1976-77, attending physician, 1988—; resident Johns Hopkins Hosp., Balt., 1974-75; fellow Rockefeller U., N.Y.C., 1977-80; asst. prof. Cornell U. Med. Coll., N.Y.C., 1979-83, assoc. prof., 1983-87, chief infectious diseases, 1983—, prof. medicine, 1988—. Contbr. article to profl. jours. Trustee Nightingale-Bamford Sch., N.Y.C., 1989—. Recipient Tchr.-Scientist award Mellon Found., 1980, Career Devel. award, Rockefeller Found., 1981; NIH, WHO, Rockefeller Found. grantee, 1980—. Fellow Infectious Diseases Soc. Am. (Squibb award 1989); mem. Am. Soc. for Clin. Investigation, Am. Soc. for Microbiology. Office: Cornell U Med Coll 1300 York Ave New York NY 10021-4805*

MURRAY, JOHN JOSEPH, physician, researcher; b. Boston, Apr. 19, 1951; s. John Joseph and Elizabeth Mary (Tierney) M.; m. Katherine Thompson Murray, Oct. 6, 1984; children: Katherine Tierney, John Joseph VI. AB, Harvard U., 1973; MD, Vanderbilt U., 1979, PhD, 1979. Diplomate Am. Bd. Internal Medicine, Am. Bd. Allergy and Immunology. Resident in internal medicine Vanderbilt Med. Ctr., Nashville, 1979-82, chief resident in medicine, 1982-83, fellow in clin. pharmacology, 1983-85; fellow in allergy/rheumatology/immunology Duke Med. Ctr., Durham, N.C., 1985-86; asst. prof. Duke U., 1986-88; asst. prof. Vanderbilt Med. Ctr., 1988-94, assoc. prof., 1994—; cons. Searle Pharms., Skokie, Ill., 1993—, Abbott Pharms., Chgo., 1992—, Marion-Merrell Dow Pharms., Kansas City, Mo., 1993, Greer, Inc., Wilmington, N.C., 1992—. Contbr. articles to profl. jours. Pfizer fellow, 1983-87; grantee RJR Nabisco, 1987-90, NIH, 1988—. Mem. ACP, Am. Acad. Allergy/Immunology/Asthma, S.E. Allergy Assn. Home: 921 Calloway Dr Brentwood TN 37027 Office: Vanderbilt Med Ctr 843 Light Hall Nashville TN 37232-0111

MURRAY, JOSEPH EDWARD, plastic surgeon; b. Milford, Mass., Apr. 1, 1919; s. William Andrew and Mary (DePasquale) M.; m. Virginia Link, June 2, 1945; children: Virginia, Margaret, Joseph Link, Katharine, Thomas, Richard. A.B., Holy Cross Coll., 1940, D.Sc., 1965; M.D., Harvard, 1943; D.Sc., Rockford (Ill.) Coll., 1966, Roger Williams Coll., 1986; hon. degree, Anna Marie Coll., 1993, SUNY, Albany, 1993, U. Suffolk, 1993. Diplomate: Am. Bd. Surgery, Am. Bd. Plastic Surgery (chmn. 1969). Chief plastic surgeon Peter Bent Brigham Hosp., Boston, 1951-86, chief plastic surgeon emeritus, 1986—; chief plastic surgeon Children's Hosp. Med. Center, Boston, 1972-85, emeritus, 1985; prof. surgery Harvard Med. Sch., 1970—. Served to maj. M.C. AUS, 1944-47. Recipient Gold medal Internat. Soc. Surgeons, 1963, hon. award Am. Acad. Arts and Sci., 1962, Nobel prize for medicine or physiology, 1990, Sabin award 1994. Fellow AAAS (hon.), AMA, Royal Australasian Coll. Surgeons, Royal Coll. Surgeons of Eng., Royal Coll. Surgeons Ireland, Royal Coll. Surgeons Edinburgh; mem. ACS (regent 1970-79, v.p. 1983), NAS, Am. Surg. Assn. (v.p. 1979), New Eng. Surg. Assn. (pres. 1986-87), Boston Surg. Soc. (pres. 1975), Soc. U. Surgeons, Am. Assn. Plastic Surgeons (hon. award 1969, pres. 1964-65), Am. Acad. Arts and Sci., Harvard Med. Sch. Alumni Coun. (pres. 1984), Alpha Omega Alpha. Clubs: Badminton and Tennis, Wellesley Country. Home: 108 Abbott Rd Wellesley MA 02181-6104

MURRAY, JULIA KAORU (MRS. JOSEPH E. MURRAY), occupational therapist; b. Wahiawa, Oahu, Hawaii, 1934; d. Gijun and Edna Tsuruko (Taba) Funakoshi; m. Joseph Edward Murray, 1961; children: Michael, Susan, Leslie. BA, U. Hawaii, 1956; cert. occupational therapy U. Puget Sound, 1958. Therapist, Inst. Logopedics, Wichita, Kans., 1958; sr. therapist Hawaii State Hosp., Kaneohe, 1959; part-time therapist Centre County Ctr. for Crippled Children and Adults, State College, Pa., 1965; vice chmn. adv. bd. Hosp. Improvement Program, East Oreg. State Hosp., Pendleton, 1974; v.p. Ind. Living, Inc., 1976-79; job search instr.; mem. adv. com. Oreg. Ednl. Coordinating Commn., 1979-82; mem. Oreg. Bd. Engring. Examiners, 1979-87; supr., occupational therapist Fairview Tng. Ctr., Salem, Oreg., 1984-94; occupational therapist U.S. Naval Hosp., Okinawa, Japan, 1994—. Rep. from Umatilla County Commrs. to Blue Mountain Econ. Devel. Council, 1976-78; mem. Ashland Park and Recreation Bd., 1972-73; vice chmn. adv. bd. LINC, 1978; mem. exec. bd. Liberty-Boone Neighborhood Assn., 1979-83. Mem. Am. Occupational Therapy Assn., Oreg. Occupational Therapy Assn., Hawaii Occupational Therapy Assn. (sec. 1960) Occupational Therapy Assn., LWV (bd. dirs. Pendleton 1974, 77-78, pres. 1975-77; bd. dirs. Oreg. 1979-81, Ashland, Wis., 1967-71, Wis. v.p. 1970). Office: Medically Related Svcs US Naval Hosp Okinawa Japan Psc 482 FPO AP 96362-1600

MURRAY, MARY BETH, respiratory therapist, educator; b. Bellaire, Ohio, Dec. 2, 1962; d. John William and Pauline Ann (Buzek) M. BS, Wheeling (W. Va.) Coll., 1985; MS, U. Pitts., 1992. Reg. Respiratory Therapist, Nat. Bd. Respiratory Care. Staff technician Wheeling Hosp., 1984-85; staff therapist, lead therapist Mercy Hosp., Pitts., 1985-89; asst. prof., clin. coord.

Wheeling Jesuit Coll., 1989—; practitioner rep. TB Assn. Ohio County, Wheeling, 1991—. Mem. Chartier Guild (treas. 1993—). Office: Wheeling Jesuit Coll 316 Washington Ave Wheeling WV 26003

MURRAY, ROBERT FULTON, JR., physician; b. Newburgh, N.Y., Oct. 19, 1931; s. Robert Fulton and Henrietta Frances (Judd) M.; m. Isobel Ann Parks, Aug. 26, 1956; children: Colin Charles (dec.), Robert Fulton III, Suzanne Frances, Dianne Akwe. B.S., Union Coll., Schenectady, 1953; M.D., U. Rochester, N.Y., 1958; M.S., U. Wash., Seattle, 1968. Diplomate Am. Bd. Internal Medicine, Am. Bd. Med. Genetics. Rotating intern Denver Gen. Hosp., 1958-59; resident in internal medicine U. Colo. Med. Center, 1959-62; staff investigator (service with USPHS) Nat. Inst. Arthritis and Metabolic Diseases, NIH, Bethesda, Md., 1962-65; NIH spl. fellow med. genetics U. Wash., 1965-67; mem. faculty Howard U. Coll. Medicine, Washington, 1967—; prof. pediatrics and medicine Howard U. Coll. Medicine, 1974—, grad. prof., 1976, prof. oncology, 1976, chief div. med. genetics, 1968—, chmn. dept. genetics and human genetics Grad. Sch., 1976—; nat. adv. gen. med. scis. coun. NIH, 1971-75, recombinant DNA adv. com., 1988-92; sci. adv. bd. Nat. Sickle Cell Anemia Found.; ethics adv. bd. to sec. HEW, 1978-80; chmn. Washington Mayor's Adv. Com. on Metabolic Disorders, 1980-89; active Med. Com. Human Rights. Co-author: Genetic Variation and Disorders in Peoples of African Origin, 1990; co-editor: Genetic, Metabolic and Developmental Aspects of Mental Retardation, 1972, Genetic Counseling: Facts, Values and Norms, 1979; assoc. editor Am. Jour. Clin. Genetics, 1977-93; mem. editorial adv. bd. Ency. Bioethics, 1975-77, 93-95; mem. editorial bd. Jour. Clin. Ethics, 1990. Trustee Union Coll., 1972-80. Rotary Found. fellow, 1955-56; research grantee NIH, 1969-75. Fellow ACP, AAAS, Inst. Medicine (coun. mem. 1983-85), Inst. Soc., Ethics and Life Scis. (bd. dirs.), Am. Coll. Med. Genetics; mem. AAUP, Assn. Acad. Minority Physicians, Am. Soc. Human Genetics, Genetics Soc. Am., Acad. Medicine Washington, Neighbors Inc. D.C., Sigma Xi, Alpha Omega Alpha. Unitarian. Home: 510 Aspen St NW Washington DC 20012-2740 Office: Coll Medicine Box 75 Howard Univ Washington DC 20059

MURRAY, TIMOTHY GARRETT, ophthalmologist; b. Biloxi, Miss., Sept. 19, 1959; s. Robert Maurice and Lynn (Lindner) M. BA, Johns Hopkins U., 1981, MD, 1985. Diplomate Am. Bd. Ophthalmology. Intern Union Meml. Hosp., Balt., 1985-86; resident ophthalmology U. Calif., San Francisco, 1986-89, chief resident ophthalmology, 1988-89; fellow ophthalmology Med. Coll. Wis., Milw., 1989-90, fellow vitreoretinal surgery, 1990-91; asst. prof. ophthalmology Bascom Palmer Eye Inst., Miami, Fla., 1991—. Contbr. chpt. to book and articles to profl. jours. Guest spkr. Mus. of Discovery and Sci., Miami, 1994; chmn. bd. Nat. Retinoblastoma Rsch. and Support Found., Miami, 1996. Grantee NIH, 1991—, 92—, Stanley J. Glaser Found., 1992-93, Am. Cancer Soc., 1993-94, Fight for Sight, Inc., 1994-95. Mem. AMA, Am. Acad. Ophthalmology, Am. Assn. for Cancer Rsch., Am. Diabetes Assn., Assn. for Rsch. in Vision & Ophthalmology, N.Am. Hyperthermia Soc. Office: Bascom Palmer Eye Inst 900 NW 17 St Rm 254 Miami FL 33136

MURRAY-LYON, IAIN MALCOLM, gastroenterologist; b. Edinburgh, Scotland, U.K., Aug. 28, 1940; s. Ranald Malcolm and Jennipher Helen (Dryburgh) Murray-L.; m. Teresa Elvira Gonzalez Montero, Nov. 7, 1981; children: Caroline Claire, Andrew Malcolm. BSc, U. Edinburgh, 1962, MBChB, 1964, MD, 1973. Med. registrar Royal Infirmary, Edinburgh, 1967-68; sr. med. registrar liver unit Kings Coll. Hosp., London, 1968-72; hon. sr. lectr. liver unit Kings Coll. Hosp., 1972-74; gastroenterologist Charing Cross Hosp., London, 1974—; cons. physician Hosp. St. John & Elizabeth, London, 1976—, King Edward VII Hosp. for Officers, London, 1991—. NIH fellow, 1972. Fellow Royal Coll. Physicians (London), Royal Coll. Physicians (Edinburgh); mem. British Assn. for Study of Liver (sec. 1985-86), British Soc. Gastroenterology (chmn. liver sect. 1989-90). Mem. Ch. Scotland. Home: 12 St James Gardens, London W11 4RD, England Office: 149 Harley St, London WIN 2DE, England

MURRELL, HUGH JERRY, physician, radiologist; b. Tyler, Tex., Oct. 20, 1937; s. Hugh Jackson and Oman (Hudson) M.; m. Beverly Ann Robertson, July 6, 1963; children: Hugh Robertson, Heather Margaret, Hudson Gaines. Student, Rice U., 1955-58; MD, U. Tex., Galveston, 1962; MD (hon.), U. Mo., 1995. Diplomate Am. Bd. Radiology. Dir., clin. prof. U. Mo. Hosp. and Clinics, Columbia, 1985—; dir. radiation oncology Boone Hosp. Ctr., Columbia, Mo., 1984—. Lt. comdr. USN, 1963-65. Fellow Am. Coll. Radiology; mem. AMA, Mo. State Med. Assn. (pres. 1994-95, chmn. legis. com. 1989-96). Office: Boone Hosp Ctr 1600 E Broadway Columbia MO 65201

MURRELL, RICHARD ALLEN, cardiac surgeon, consultant; b. Ft. Wayne, Ind., Sept. 8, 1947; s. Elmo and Lena Mae (Stephans) M.; m. Kathy Sue Grant, Nov. 11, 1979; children: Lauren Ann, Sarah Allison. AB in Zoology, Ind. U., 1969, MD, 1972. Diplomate Am. Bd. Surgery, diplomate Am. Bd. Thoracic Surgery. Resident surgeon Ind. U. Hosps., Indpls., 1972-78, active staff surgeon, 1978-80; active staff surgeon Ball Meml. Hosp., Muncie, Ind., 1980-85, Deaconess, Welborn, St. Mary's Hosps., Evansville, Ind., 1985—; rep. bd. mem. Am. Heart Assn., Ind., 1980-84, coun. on cardiovascular surgery, 1980—. Capt. U.S. Air Force, 1972-78. Fellow ACS; mem. Ind. Med. Assn., N.Y. Acad. Scis., Vanderburg County Med. Soc., Soc. Thoracic Surgeons, Alpha Tau Omega. Republican. Methodist. Office: 350 W Columbia St Ste 350 Evansville IN 47710-1782

MURSTEIN, BERNARD IRVING, psychology educator, psychotherapist; b. Vilna, Poland, Apr. 29, 1929; came to U.S., 1930; s. Leon and Martha (Schalachman) M.; m. Nelly Kashy, Aug. 27, 1954; children: Danielle, Colette. B Social Sci., CCNY, 1950; MS, U. Miami, 1951; PhD, U. Tex., 1955. Diplomate Am. Bd. Profl. Psychology. Psychotherapy intern Louisville Child Guidance Ctr., 1953-54; Hogg Found. rsch. fellow in pediatrics U. Tex. and M.D. Anderson Hosp., Houston, 1955-56; asst. prof. psychology, dir. psychol. clinic La. State U., 1956-58; assoc. prof., coord. rsch. U. Portland, Oreg., 1958-60; dir. rsch., psychotherapist Interfaith Counseling Ctr., Portland, 1960-62; assoc. prof. family relations U. Conn., 1962-63; Fulbright prof. Inst. de Psychologie U. de Louvain, Belgium, 1968-69; assoc. prof. dept. psychology Conn. Coll., New London, 1963-65, prof., 1965—, chmn. dept. psychology, 1976-79, 90-91; pvt. practice Waterford, Conn., 1979—; cons. Psychol. Clinic, Southeastern La. Coll., 1957; ind. counselor and psychol. evaluator, Baton Rouge, 1957-58; grant cons. NSF; editorial cons. numerous profl. jours. including Jour. Abnormal Psychology, Internat. Jour. Psychology, Jour. Social and Personal Relationships. Author: Theory and Research in Projective Techniques, 1963, Handbook of Projective Techniques, 1965, Theories of Attraction and Love, 1971, Love, Sex, and Marriage Through the Ages, 1974, Who Will Marry Whom? Theories and Research in Marital Choice, 1976, Exploring Intimate Life Styles, 1978, Paths to Marriage, 1986; contbr. chpt. to Contemporary Issues in Thematic Apperceptive Methods, 1961, Projective Techniques, 1964; cons. editor Jour. Projective Techniques and Personality Assessment, 1963-70; assoc. editor Jour. Marriage and the Family, 1975-80. Grantee NIMH, 1960-62, 64-68, NSF, 1970-71, Mellon Found, 1978, 80, George I. Alden Trust Acad. Bus. Integration Program, 1982; U.S. Pub. Health Fellowship stipend recipient, 1954-55; named May Buckley Sadowski prof., 1994. Fellow APA (clin. div., personality and social psychology div., family psychology div., div. chmn. membership com. 1973-75, div. chmn. subcom. on fellows 1973-75); mem. Soc. Personality Assessment (pres. 1973-74), Nat. Coun. Family Rels. (mem. nominations com. 1975-76), Internat. Coun. Psychologists. Democrat. Jewish. Home: 46 Beacon Hill Dr Waterford CT 06385-4110 Office: Conn Coll Box 5581 270 Mohegan Ave New London CT 06320-4196

MURTAGH, FREDERICK REED, neuroradiologist, educator; b. Phila., Nov. 20, 1944; s. Frederick and Mary (Shaner) M.; (div.); children: Ryan David, Kevin Reed; m. Dorothy Rossi. BA, William and Mary Coll., 1966; MD, Temple U., 1971. Prof., dir. neuroradiology U. S. Fla., Tampa, 1978—. Author: Imaging Anatomy of Head & Spine, 1991. Lt. USNR, 1972-74. Mem. Am. Coll. Radiology (cert. added qualification in neuroradiology 1995), Assn. Univ. Radiologists, Am. Soc. Neuroradiology (sr. mem.), Radiol. Soc. N.Am., Southeastern Neuroradiology Soc. Office: U South Fla 3301 Alumni Dr Tampa FL 33612-9413

MURTAUGH, MAUREEN ANN, nutrition educator; b. Lower Marion, Pa., July 26, 1961; d. James Leo Jr. and Margaret Anne (Dreisbach) M. BS in Clin. Nutrition, Syracuse U., 1983; PhD in Nutritional Sci., U. Conn., 1991. Registered dietitian, Ill. Clin. dietitian Marriott Corp., Easton, Md., 1983-84, Arlington, Va., 1984-86; rsch. asst. U. Conn., Storrs, 1986-91; asst. prof. Rush U., Chgo., 1991—. Mem. Am. Inst. Nutrition, Am. Dietetic Assn. (chair-elect perinatal nutrition practice group 1996—), No. Ill. Diabetes Assn. (mem. nutrition com. 1992—, bd. dirs. 1996—). Roman Catholic. Office: Rush U 1653 W Congress Pky Chicago IL 60612-3833

MUSA, MAHMOUD NIMIR, psychiatry educator; b. Arraba, Jenin, Palestine, Mar. 22, 1943; came to U.S., 1964; s. Nimir A. and Zarifa (Haseeb) M.; m. Wafaa M. Arafat, Mar. 24, 1991. BS, Am. U. Beirut, 1964; MS, U. Wis., 1966, PhD, 1972; MD, Med. Coll. Wis., 1979. Diplomate Am. Bd. Psychiatry. Rsch. assoc. U. Wis., Madison, 1972-75; asst. prof. Idaho State U., Pocatello, 1975-76; resident Ill. State Psychiat. Inst., Chgo., 1979-83; assoc. prof. psychiatry Chgo. Med. Sch., North Chicago, Ill., 1987-90; prof. psychiatry Loyola U., Maywood, Ill., 1990—; cons. Mus. Sci. & Industry, Chgo., 1985-90; editl. bd. Jour. Clin. Pharmacology. Editor: Pharmacikinetics and Monitoring Psychiatry Drugs, 1992; mem. editl. bd. Jour. Clin. Pharmacology. Cons. Kovler Ctr. for Treatment of Survivors of Torture, CHgo., 1989-92. Recipient Scientific Achievement award Ill. Psychiat. Soc., Chgo., 1982. Fellow Am. Coll. Clin. Pharmacology, Great Lakes Soc. Clin. Pharmacology (pres. 1991-92); mem. AAAS, Am. Psychiat. Assn. Home: 1115 S Plymouth Ct Apt 102 Chicago IL 60605-2027

MUSANTE, GERARD JOHN, clinical psychologist; b. N.Y.C., Apr. 3, 1943; s. Victor John Joseph and Dorothy Alice (Rosasco) M.; m. Rita Rea Glasser, June 9, 1965; children: David, Jason, Michael. BS in Indsl. Rels., NYU, 1965; PhD in Clin. Psychology, U. Tenn., 1971. Lic. psychologist, N.Y., N.C.; diplomate in clin. psychology Am. Bd. Profl. Psychology. Staff clin. psychologist Oak Ridge (Tenn.) Community Mental Health Ctr., 1969-70; asst. prof. med. psychology dept. community health scis. Duke U. Med. Ctr., Durham, N.C., 1971-77, staff psychologist Student Health Clinic, 1971-77, dir. behavioral program Dietary Rehab. Clinic, 1971-77; dir. Structure House, weight control ctr. and lifestyle changes, Durham, 1977—; cons. psychologist dept. social rehab. and control N.C. Office Correction, 1971-73; cons. medicaid psychiat. utilization rev. com. State of N.C., 1973-74, Nat. Bd. Med. Examiners, 1974-78; bd. dirs. Ctrl. Carolina Bank, Durham. Mem. editorial bd. Addictive Behaviors, 1975-78; contbr. articles to profl. jours., chpts. to books. Trustee Durham Acad.; mem. bd. N.C. Mus. Life and Sci., United Way, mem. Durham Leadership Coun. Mem. APA, Assn. for Advancement Behavioral Therapy, N.C. Psychol. Assn. (chmn. com. on health ins. 1973-75), N.C. Assn. for Advancement Psychology (adv. bd. 1983), Hollow Rock Swim and Racquet Club, Hope Valley Country Club, Rotary, Farmington Country Club. Home: 3101 Cornwall Rd Durham NC 27707-5101 Office: Structure House 3017 Pickett Rd Durham NC 27705-6005

MUSCARELLA, VINCENT JOSEPH, podiatrist, educator; b. Norristown, Pa., Nov. 21, 1953; s. Armelio Salvatore and Marie (Bellitta) M.; m. Margaret Rose Cesare, June 22, 1974; children: Erica Ann, Rosemarie. BS in Biology, Widener U., 1975; D Podiatric Medicine, Pa. Coll. Podiatric Medicine, 1981. Diplomate Am. Bd. Podiatric Surgery (oral examiner 1991—), Am. Bd. Podiatric Orthopadics and Medicine. Resident in surgery Met. Hosp., Phila., 1981-83; pvt. practice, Norristown, 1983—; mem. surg. faculty Pa. Coll. Podiatric Medicine, Phila., 1983—, mem. orthopedic faculty, 1995—; chmn. pediatric surg. divsn. Suburban Gen. Hosp., Norristown, 1989—. Author: Hallux Valgus, 1993. Mem. Am. Podiatric Medicine Assn., Pa. Podiatric Med. Assn., Sons of Italy. Democrat. Roman Catholic. Home: 2561 Betzwood Dr Norristown PA 19403 Office: 190 W Germantown Pike Norristown PA 19401

MUSCH, DAVID CHARLES, epidemiologist; b. Aug. 11, 1954. BS, Calvin Coll., 1976; MPH, U. Mich., 1978, PhD, 1981. Rsch. investigator with dept. ophthalmology U. Mich., Ann Arbor, 1981-86, asst. rsch. scientist, 1986-89, assoc. rsch. scientist, 1989—, assoc. rsch. scientist dept. epidemiology, 1991—; nat. res. reviewer NIH, Bethesda, Md., 1990-94; cons. Chiron Vision, Inc., Claremont, Calif., 1990—. Mem. editorial bd. Ophthalmology, 1987—; contbr. articles to profl. jours. Mem. deacon bd. Ann Arbor Christian Reformed Ch., 1983-86, mem. elder bd., 1991-94; sec., pres., bd. dirs. Christian Sch. Assn. Ann Arbor, 1986-89. Rsch. grantee Mich. Eye Bank, Ann Arbor, 1983-88, 92—, Nat. Eye Inst., NIH, Bethesda, 1986-87, 93—, Pharmacia Inc., Piscataway, N.J., 1986-89, Chiron IntraOptics, Inc., Irvine, Calif., 1988-91. Mem. AAAS, Am. Coll. Epidemiology, Am. Acad. Ophthalmology (Honor award 1992), Assn. for Rsch. in Vision and Ophthalmology. Office: U Mich Kellogg Eye Ctr 1000 Wall St Ann Arbor MI 48105-1912

MUSCHENHEIM, FREDERICK, pathologist; b. N.Y.C., July 9, 1932; s. Carl and Haroldine (Humphreys) M.; m. Linda Alexander, Mar. 29, 1958; children: Alexandra Lydia, Carl William, David Henry. AB, Harvard U., 1953; MDCM, McGill U., Montreal, Can., 1963. Intern Santa Clara County Hosp., San Jose, Calif., 1963-64; resident pathology U. Colo. Med. Ctr., Denver, 1964-68, chief resident clin. pathology, 1968-69; pathologist Freeman, Hanske, Munkittrick & Foley PA, Mpls., 1969-77; clin. pathologist Union-Truesdale Hosp., Fall River, Mass., 1977-78; chief pathologist St. Clare's Hosp., Denville, N.J., 1978-83, Oneida Healthcare Ctr., 1984—; clin. asst. prof. SUNY Health Sci. Ctr., Syracuse, 1984-90, clin. assoc. prof., 1990—; chief med. staff Oneida City Hosps., 1991; pres. Sunderman Fund, Bermuda Biol. Sta. for Rsch., v.p. Madison County (N.Y.) bd. health, 1995-96. Choir 1st Presbyn. Ch. of Cazenovia, N.Y., 1984—, trustee, 1985-89. Mem. Assn. Clin. Scientists (v.p. 1989, pres. 1990, rec. sec. 1995—, Diploma of Honor 1991), Coll. Am. Pathologists (mem. govt. affairs com. 1994—, nominating com. 1995), Med. Soc. State of N.Y. (mem. legis. com. 1991—), Med. Soc. Madison County (v.p. 1990-91, pres. 1991-93), N.Y. State Assn. Pub. Health Labs. (v.p. 1992-93, pres. 1993-94, edn. chmn. 1994-95), N.Y. Soc. Pathologists (councilor 2nd dist. 1991—), ARC Blood Svcs. (chmn. med. adv. coun. 1995—). Home: 5257 Owera Point Rd Cazenovia NY 13035-9340 Office: Oneida Healthcare Ctr 321 Genesee St Oneida NY 13421-2611

MUSCHIO, HENRY MICHAEL, JR., biology educator; b. N.Y.C., Apr. 25, 1931; s. Henry M. and Katherine (Diorio) M.; m. Lucy DeRea, Sept. 14, 1957; children: Henry M. III, Joseph P., Edward C., Laura M. AB in Biology, Syracuse U., 1952; MS in Biology, Fordham U., 1957, PhD in Biology, 1963. Instr. Fairleigh Dickinson U., Madison, N.J., 1958-62; asst. prof. Montclair State Coll., Upper Montclair, N.J., 1962-66; prof., dept. head allied health and biol. scis. Dutchess Community Coll., Poughkeepsie, N.Y., 1966-93; prof. emeritus, 1993—; cons. Choice, publ. of Assn. of Coll. & Rsch. Librs., 1967—; accreditation evaluator Mid. States Assn. Colls. and Schs., 1992-96. Bd. dirs. Anderson Sch., Hyde Park, N.Y., 1980-89; bd. dirs. Rehab. Programs, Inc., Poughkeepsie, N.Y., 1971-81, 2d v.p., 1974-78. HEW grantee 1985-88, NSF grantee 1979-82, March of Dimes grantee, 1975-80. Mem. N.Y. State Assn. two Yr. Colls. (pres. 1987-89, named Outstanding Mem. 1986), Rotary (bd. dirs. 1988-89). Republican.

MUSICK, WILLIAM DANIEL ANDERSON, psychologist; b. Galveston, Tex., Aug. 17, 1943; s. John Edward and Stella (Mazo) M.; m. Mary Nolan, Nov. 25, 1977; 1 dau., Natalie. BS, Tex. A&M U., 1974, MS, 1976, PhD, 1979. Pvt. practice psychology, Columbia, Md., 1981—. Served to lt. col. inf. U.S. Army, 1963-69. Decorated Bronze Star. Fellow APA; mem. Md. Psychol. Assn. (pres. 1988—). Office: 10796 Hickory Ridge Rd Columbia MD 21044-3246

MUSIL, FRANTIŠEK, clinical chemist; b. Plzeň, Czech Republic, July 28, 1957; s. František and Žofie (Nejmanová) M.; m. Jana Járová, Dec. 18, 1982; children: František, Jiří. MD, Charles U., Prague, Czech Republic, 1982, Anesthesiology, 1986, Clin. Chemistry, 1991. Lic. physician. Resident in anesthesiology Dist. Hosp., Klatovy, 1986-88, resident in clin. chemistry, 1991; anesthesiologist U. Hosp., Plzeň, Czech Republic, 1982-83; anesthesiologist Dist. Hosp., Klatovy, Czech Republic, 1983-86, cons. anesthesiologist, 1986-88, clin. chemist, 1988-91, dep. cons. clin. chemist, 1991-92, cons. clin. chemist, 1991—; head pvt. med. lab. BioLab Ltd, Klatovy, 1992—. Mem. Czech Anesthesiology and Critical Care Assn., Czech Clin. Chemistry Assn., Czech Parenteral and Enteral Nutrition Assn., Czech Med. Chamber. Home: Purkyňova 740/II, 339 01 Klatovy Czech Republic Office: BioLab Ltd Pvt Med Lab, Purkyňova 740/II, 339 01 Klatovy Czech Republic

MUSK, ARTHUR WILLIAM, physician, researcher; b. Kalgoorlie, W. Australia, Aug. 12, 1943; s. Arthur Thomas and Jean Mary (Scott) M.; m. Jacqueline Gay Cruttenden, May 15, 1971; children: Gabrielle, Michael. MB, BS, U. W. Australia, 1967; MSc, Harvard Sch. Pub. Health, Boston, 1977; MD, U. New S. Wales, Sydney, 1987. Resident med. officer Royal Perth Hosp., Perth, W. Australia, 1966-67, Sir Charles Gaironer Hosp., Perth, W. Australia, 1967; med. registrar Sir Charles Gairoder Hosp., Perth, W. Australia, 1968, Royal Perth Hosp., Perth, W. Australia, 1969, Sir Charles Gairdner, Perth, W. Australia, 1970-71; rsch. fellow Prince Henry Hosp., Sydney, Australia, 1972-74, Harvard Sch. Pub. Health, Boston, 1975-77, Med. Rsch. Coun. Pneumoconiosis Rsch. Unit, Penarth, Wales, 1977-78; physician, clin. prof. Head Dept. Respiratory Med., Perth, W. Australia, 1978—; sec., pres. Thoracic Soc. Australia (Western Australia Br.), Perth, West Australia, 1981—; pres. Australian Coun. on Smoking and Health, 1991—. Contbr. articles to profl. jours. Pres. TCC Emergency Welfare Found., Perth, W. Australia, 1981-84, U. Camp for Children,, 1965-66. Decorated Order of Australia; recipient Wunderly Medal, Thoracic Soc. ANZ, 1991. Fellow Australasian Coll. Physicians, Australasian Faculty of Occupl. Medicine, Am. Coll. Chest Physicians, Royal Australian Coll. Physicians, Am. Coll. Physicians; mem. faculty of Occupl. Medicine Royal Coll. Physicians. Office: Sir Charles Gairdner Hosp, Verdun St, Nedlands 6009, Australia

MUSKIN, PHILIP, psychiatrist; b. Bklyn., Dec. 23, 1948. AB Neurobiology/Behavior, Cornell U., 1969; MA in Exptl. Psychology, New Sch. for Social Research, 1970; MD, N.Y. Med. Coll., 1974; cert. psychoanalysis, Columbia U., 1983. Med. intern Met. Hosp., N.Y.C., 1974-75; psychiat. resident N.Y. State Psychiat. Inst., N.Y.C., 1975-78; NIMH fellow Columbia-Presbyn. Me. Ctr., N.Y.C., 1978-79; asst. clin. prof. Columbia U./Coll. Physicians and Surgeons, N.Y.C., 1980-87; assoc. clin. prof. psychiatry Columbia U./Coll. Physicians and Surgeons, 1987—, assoc. prof. clin. psychiatry, 1991—; assoc. chief svcs. consultation-liaison psychiatry Columbia-Presbyn. Med. Ctr., N.Y.C., 1984—; mem. med. bd. Presbyn. Hosp., N.Y.C., 1983—. Contbr. articles to profl. jours.; co-author several book chpts.; producer, dir. (videotape movie) Three Faces of Aids, 1988. Cons. First Step Widows Program, ARC, Mineola, N.Y., 1978-80. Grandstreet Boys scholar, N.Y.C., 1973; named for excellence in medicine Merck Manual award, 1974; Tchr. of Yr. N.Y. State Psychiat. Inst., 1985, 90, 94. Fellow Am. Psychiat. Assn., Am. Coll. Psychoanalysis, Acad. Psychosomatic Medicine; mem. Soc. Liaison Psychiatry (pres. 1990), Am. Soc. Psychiat. Oncology/AIDS (treas. 1988-90), Assn. Acad. Psychiatry, Am. Psychoanalytic Assn. Office: 1700 York Ave New York NY 10128-7814

MUSLIN, ALICE THOMPSON, clinical social worker, consultant; b. Berwyn, Ill., Oct. 22, 1942; d. LaRue Gayle and Jessie Dorothy (Hofstra) Thompson; m. Bernard J. Muslin, Oct. 1, 1972 (dec. June 1991); 1 child, Jennifer Lynn. AB, Ind. U., 1964; MA, U. Chgo., 1966. Cert. social worker; lic. clin. social worker, Ill. Caseworker United Charities, Chgo., 1966-68; asst. prof. med. social work U. Ill. Coll. Medicine, Chgo., 1968-77; social worker in pvt. practice Evanston, Ill., 1977—; cons. Perspectives, Oak Brook Terrace, Ill., 1985-88. Trustee Evanston Hist. Soc., 1995—. Mem. Coterie (pres., historian). Democrat. Jewish. Home: 730 Michigan Evanston IL 60202

MUSSENDEN, GEORG ANTONIO, electronics engineer; b. San Juan, P.R., Aug. 25, 1959; s. Gustavo Adolfo and Christa-Maria (Gotsch) M. Student U. P.R.-Rio Piedras, 1977-79; B.S. in E.E. with honors, U. Fla.-Gainesville, 1982, postgrad. in elec. engring. Electronics technician Radiotelephone Communicators of P.R. (Motorola), 1976; computer systems programmer and operator U. P.R., Rio Piedras, 1978-79, research asst. dept. physics, 1978-79; computer programmer Regional Electrocardiogram Analysis Ctr., J. Hillis Miller Health Ctr., U. Fla., Gainesville, 1981; pre-profl. engr. IBM Corp. Devel. Lab., Endicott, N.Y., 1981, sr. assoc. engr./scientist entry systems tech. SPD, CPD and ESD design and devel. labs., Boca Raton, Fla., 1982-93; elec. hardware devel. engr. sci. Core Internat. Rsch. and Devel. Corp., Boca Raton, 1993—. Contbr. articles to profl. jours. Scholar San Jose Alumni, 1973-77, Fonalledas Found., 1977-79, Procter and Gamble, 1980; U.F. Sr. Honors scholar, 1980; scholar Nat. Fund Minority Engring., 1980, Du Pont, 1981; Nat. Consortium for Grad. Degrees for Minorities in Engring. fellow, 1981. Mem. N.Y. Acad. Scis., IEEE, SMPTE, AES, Golden Key, Eta Kappa Nu, Tau Beta Pi, Phi Kappa Phi. Roman Catholic. Clubs: Audio-Visual, Amateur Radio. Achievements include 9 technological invention disclosures. Office: Core Internat Rsch & Devel Corp 6500 E Rogers Cir Boca Raton FL 33487-2655

MUSSENDEN, GERALD, psychologist; b. N.Y.C., June 1, 1941; s. Geraldo and Adele (Gimenez) M.; m. Iris Manuela Prado, Aug. 11, 1967; children: Gerald, Ricardo-Antonio, Gina. BA, Tarkio Coll., 1968; MS, Brigham Young U., 1971, PhD, 1974. Diplomate Am. Bd. Profl. Disability Cons., Am. Bd. Forensic Examiners. Dir. child program Albert Einstein Coll. Medicine, N.Y.C., 1974-76; psychologist Mental Health Ctr., Bartow, Fla., 1976-77, Norside Community Mentala Health Ctr., Tampa, Fla., 1977-80; pvt. practice Brandon (Fla.) Counseling Ctr., 1980—; criminal ct. psychologist Fla. Cts., Hillsborough, Fla., 1978—; with children's svcs. State Rehab., Hillsborough, 1977—; rehab. psychologist Vocat. Rehab., Hillsborough; psychologist Div. Blind Svcs., Hillsborough. Fellow Ford Found., 1972-73. Mem. APA, Fla. Psychol. Assn., Bay Area Psychol. Assn., Soc. Personality Assessment. Home: 317 Cactus Rd Seffner FL 33584-6105 Office: Brandon Counseling Ctr 134 N Moon Ave Brandon FL 33510-4420

MUSSENDEN, MARIA ELISABETH, psychologist, substance abuse counselor; b. San Juan, P.R., Oct. 4, 1949; came to U.S., 1979; d. Gustavo Adolfo and Christa-Maria (Gotsch) M. BA in Music magna cum laude, U. P.R., Rio Piedras, 1971, MA in Gen. Exptl. Psychology, 1978; MS in Counseling Psychology, U. Fla., 1989, postgrad. in counseling psychology, 1979-89. Cert. tchr., P.R. Counselor alcohol dependency treatment program VA Hosp., Gainesville, Fla., fall 1980, counselor cardiac rehab. unit, fall 1981; counseling psychology intern Psychol. & Vocat. Counseling U. Fla., Gainesville, 1982-83; alcohol specialist Alcothon House, Gainesville, 1983-84, counselor I, 1984—; rehab. therapist North Fla. Evaluation and Treatment Ctr., Gainesville, 1985, human svcs. counselor III, 1985-89; substance abuse counselor Vista Pavilion, Gainesville, 1987—; psychol. specialist Marion Correctional Instn., Lowell, Fla., 1989—; pvt. practice tchr., 1966-79; part-time lectr. Inter-Am. U., Hato Rey, P.R., 1971-78; part-time music tchr. Music Acad., 1972-78; part-time music therapist Centro Didactico del Lenguaje, Hato Rey, 1978-79; tchr. music P.R. Dept. of Edn., San Juan, 1974-79; presenter in field. Ford Found. fellow, 1972-73, 74-75, Angel Ramos Found. fellow, 1973-74, Fonalledas Found. fellow, 1982-83; recipient Presdl. award U. Fla., 1985. Mem. APA, Fla. Assn. for Behavior Analysis, Mental Health Assn., Nat. Alliance for the Mentally Ill, Puerto Rican Music Therapy Assn. (co-founder), Mu Alpha Phi (hon. Gold medal 1967). Roman Catholic. Home: 125 SW 40th Ter Gainesville FL 32607-2754

MUSSHOFF, KARL ALBERT, radiation oncologist; b. Wuppertal, Germany, June 11, 1910; s. Gustav and Amalie (Kauls) M.; m. Margarethe Herbst, Aug. 25, 1951; children: Stephan, Renate. MD, U. Munich, 1936. Univ. lectr. medicine and radiology U. Freiburg, Germany, 1960; prof., 1977—, emeritus dir. sect. radiotherapy Radiol. Centre Albert-Ludwigs-U., Freiburg, 1977—. Recipient W.C. Röntgen Plakette of Remscheid-Lennep, Birth-town of Röntgen, 1983; Leopold Freund Medaille of Österreichische Gesellschaft für Radiologie, Radiobiologie, Medizinische Radiophysik, 1985. Mem. Group European Radiotherapists (hon., pres. 1973), European Soc. Therapeutic Radiology and Oncology, German Cancer Soc. (hon.), German Soc. Radiation-Oncology, German Radiation Soc., S.W. German Radiation Soc. (pres. 1972), German Soc. Internal Medicine, German Soc. Radiooncology, German Soc. Hematology and Oncology, German Soc. Radiooncology, Soc. German Physicists and Doctors, Am. Coll. Radiology (hon. fellow), Beirat der Deutschen Krebshilfe. Co-editor Jour. Cancer Rsch. Clin. Oncology, Strahlentherapie, Jour. Radiation Oncology Biol. Physics, Pneumonologie-Pneumonology, Kösener Senioren Convent. Home: 33 Eichenweg, 76547 Sinzheim-Vormberg Baden, Germany

MUSTACCHI, PIERO, physician, educator; b. Cairo, May 29, 1920; came to U.S., 1947; naturalized, 1962; s. Gino and Gilda (Rieti) M.; m. Dora Lisa Ancona, Sept. 26, 1948; children: Roberto, Michael. BS in Humanities, U. Florence, Italy, 1938; postgrad. in anatomy, Eleve Interne, U. Lausanne,

Switzerland, 1938-39; MB, ChB, Fouad I U., Cairo, Egypt, 1944, grad. in Arabic lang. and lit., 1946; D Medicine and Surgery, U. Pisa, 1986; D Honoris Causa, U. Aix-Marseilles, France, 1988; hon. degree, U. Alexandria, Egypt, 1985. Qualified Med. Examiner, Calif. Indsl. Med. Coun., 1994. House officer English Hosp., Ch. Missionary Soc., Cairo, Egypt, 1945-47; clin. affiliate U. Calif., San Francisco, 1947-48; intern Franklin Hosp., San Francisco, 1948-49; resident in pathology U. Calif., San Francisco, 1949-51; resident in medicine Meml. Ctr. Cancer and Allied Diseases, N.Y.C., 1951-53; rsch. epidemiologist Dept. HEW, Nat. Cancer Inst., Bethesda, Md., 1955-57; cons. allergy clinic U. Calif., San Francisco, 1957-70, clin. prof. medicine and preventive medicine, 1970-90, clin. prof. medicine and epidemiology, 1990—, head occupl. epidemiology, 1975-90, head divsn. internat. health edn. dept. epidemiology and internat. health, 1985-90; médecin agréé, official physician Consulate Gen. of France, San Fransisco, 1995—; med. cons., vis. prof. numerous edn. and profl. instns., including U. Marseilles, 1981, 82, U. Pisa, Italy, 1983, U. Gabon, 1984, U. Siena, Italy, 1985, work clinic U. Calif., 1975-84, Ctr for Rehab. and Occupl. Health U. Calif., San Francisco, 1984-93; cons. numerous worldwide govtl. agys.; ofcl. physician French Consulate Gen., San Francisco, 1995. Contbr. chpts. to books, articles to profl. jours. Editorial bd. Medecine d'Afrique Noire, Ospedali d'Italia. Served with USN, USPHS, 1953-55. Decorated Order of Merit (Commander) (Italy), Ordre de la Legion d'Honneur (France), Medal of St. John of Jerusalem, Sovereign Order of Malta, Order of the Republic (Egypt); Scroll, Leonardo da Vinci Soc., San Francisco, 1965; award Internat. Inst. Oakland, 1964; Hon. Vice Consul. Italy, 1971-90. Fellow ACP, Am. Soc. Environ. and Occupational Health; mem. AAAS, Am. Assn. Cancer Rsch., Calif. Soc. Allergy and Immunology, Calif. Med. Assn., San Francisco Med. Soc., West Coast Allergy Soc. (founding), Mex. Congress on Hypertension (corr.), Internat. Assn. Med. Rsch. and Continuing Edn. (U.S. rep.), Villa Taverna Club, Acad. Italiana della Cucina. Democrat. Home: 3344 Laguna St San Francisco CA 94123-2208 Office: U Calif Parnassus Ave San Francisco CA 94143

MUSTALISH, ANTHONY CHARLES, physician, educator; b. Newark, Oct. 28, 1940; s. Anthony William and Wanda Helen (Macknowski) M.; m. Elayne Harriet Klarsfeld, June 11, 1967; children: Rachel, David, Peter. BA, NYU, 1962, MD, 1966, MPH, Harvard U., 1971. Diplomate Am. Bd. Preventive Medicine, Am. Bd. Emergency Medicine, Nat. Bd. Med. Examiners. Health officer N.Y.C. Dept. Health, 1971-74, dep. commr., 1974-77; chief emergency services Brookdale Hosp., Bklyn., 1977-78, Lenox Hill Hosp., N.Y.C., 1978-90, COO, 1988-90; attending emergency physician N.Y. Hosp., 1990—; asst. prof. emergency medicine and pub. health Cornell U. Med. Coll., 1990—; med. dir. occupl. health svcs. Rockefeller Group, Inc., 1990-95; instr. Mt. Sinai Sch. Med., N.Y.C., 1971-74; assoc. prof. med. N.Y. Med. Coll., N.Y.C., 1971 74, 81-88; adj. prof. Hunter Coll., N.Y.C., 1972-82; lectr. Columbia U. Sch. Pub. Health, N.Y.C., 1971—. Contbr. articles to profl. jours., chpts. to books. Served to capt. U.S. Army, 1968-70, Vietnam. Fellow Am. Coll. Preventive Medicine, N.Y. Acad. Medicine; mem. Am. Coll. Emergency Physicians, ACP, Am. Pub. Health Assn., Am. Bd. Occupl. Medicine and Environ. Health. Home: 170 E 83rd St New York NY 10028-1920 Office: Lenox Hill Hosp 292 Madison Ave New York NY 10021

MUSTAPHA, TAMTON, gastroenterologist; b. Calicut, Kerala, India, Oct. 17, 1941; s. Mahamood and Asmabi (Tamton) Thoosikannan; student Malabar Christian Coll., India, 1958; M.D., Calicut Med. Coll., 1963; m. Rahma Marikar, June 15, 1969; children: Monisha, Mumtaz, Nigel. Resident in internal medicine VA Hosp., Bklyn., 1967-68, Grasslands Hosp., Valhalla, N.Y., 1968-70; resident in gastroenterology Montefiore Hosp., Bronx, 1970-72; practice medicine, specializing in gastroenterology, Hudson, N.Y., 1972—; attending physician Columbia Meml. Hosp., Hudson, 1972—, Columbia Greene Med. Ctr., chief dept. medicine, 1989-91; instr. medicine Albany Med. Center, 1972—; bd. dirs., chmn. auditing assurance Hudson Valley PSRO; pres. No. Columbia Assocs., Columbia Greene Med. Assocs.; chmn. bd. Greene Health Care Assocs.; bd. dirs. regional heart assn. Paul Harris fellow, Rotary Internat., 1979—; mem. town planning bd. Kinderhook, 1987—; chmn. bd. trustees Columbia Green C.C.; pres. Prime Med. Assocs.; diplomate Am. Bd. Internal Medicine, Am. Bd. Gastroenterology. Fellow Am. Coll. Gastroenterologists; mem. Columbia County Med. Soc., N.Y. State Med. Soc., AMA, Am. Gastroent. Assn., ACP, Am. Soc. Internal Medicine, Acad. Scis., Am. Heart Assn. (bd. dirs.), Am. Coll. Physician Execs., Columbia and Dutches Lung Assn., Assn. for Mentally Retarded, Am. Assn. Physicians and Dentists of India (pres. Capital dist. 1986). Republican. Lodge: Rotary (dir. 1976-78, pres.-elect 1986-87, pres. 1987—), Mason (master), Shriners, Cypres Temple. Home: Brindhaven Rd # 1 Valatie NY 12184 Office: 848 Columbia St Hudson NY 12534-2339

MUSTIAN, MIDDLETON TRUETT, hospital administrator; b. Texarkana, Tex., Mar. 27, 1921; s. Thomas William and Hattie (Cornelius) M.; m. Jackie Cain, Dec. 3, 1955; children—Mark Thomas, John Perry, Janet Louise. B.B.A., Baylor U., 1949. Asst. adminstr. Bapt. Hosp., Alexandria, La., 1950-54; asst. adminstr. Miss. Bapt. Hosp., Jackson, 1954-55; adminstr. Meml. Hosp., Panama City, Fla., 1955-60, Alachua Gen. Hosp., Gainesville, Fla., 1960-64, Cen. Unit Meml. Bapt. Hosp., Houston, 1964; asst. dir. Meml. Bapt. Hosp. System, Houston, 1964; pres., chief exec. officer Tallahassee Meml. Regional Med. Center Hosp., 1964-89, pres. emeritus, 1990—; pres., CEO TMH Reg. Med. Ctr. Found., Inc., 1976-89; clin. instr. dept. health adminstrn. U. Gainesville; mem. Hosp. Cost Containment Bd., State of Fla. Contbr. articles to hosp. jours. Bd. dirs. Blue Cross of Fla.; mem. Fla. Statewide Health Coordinating Council. Served to capt. Med. Adminstrv. Corps U.S. Army, 1940-45. Decorated Purple Heart. Fellow Am. Coll. Hosp. Adminstrs. (regent); mem. Am. Hosp. Assn., Fla. Hosp. Assn. (past pres.). Democrat. Baptist. Clubs: Kiwanis, Masons. Home: 6325 Velda Dairy Rd Tallahassee FL 32308-6308

MUSTION, ALAN LEE, pharmacist; b. Oklahoma City, Feb. 6, 1947; s. Granville E. and Iris E. (Graham) M.; children: Jeffrey Alan, Jennifer Chere; m. Mary Jane Bozek, Dec. 4, 1982. BS in Pharmacy, Southwestern Okla. State U., 1970. Staff pharmacist VA Med. Ctr., Oklahoma City, 1970-74, dir. pharmacy, Saginaw, Mich., 1974-76, asst. dir. pharmacy, Richmond, Va., 1976-77, dir. pharmacy, Iowa City, Iowa, 1977-90; dir. pharmacy svcs. VA Hosp., Houston, 1990—; clin. instr. clin./hosp. div. U. Iowa, 1977-90; adj. asst. prof. pharmacy practice U. Houston, 1990—. Contbr. articles to profl. jours. Served to lt. col. USAR. Recipient VA Spl. Achievement awards, 1973, 77, 86, 87, 88, 89, 92, 93, 94, VA Suggestion awards, 1979, 81, 83, VA Cost Reduction award, 1983, VA Contbr. award, 1987; rsch. grantee Travenol Labs., 1980-87, VA HSR&D grantee, 1984, 88. Mem. Am. Soc. Hosp. Pharmacists, Tex. Soc. Hosp. Pharmacists, Houston-Galveston Soc. Hosp. Pharmacists, Assn. Mil. Surgeons of U.S., Am. Assn. Colls. Pharmacy, Res. Officers Assn., Kappa Psi. Methodist. Home: 4111 Island Hills Dr Houston TX 77059-5539 Office: VA Med Ctr 2002 Holcombe Blvd Houston TX 77030-4211

MUSTOE, THOMAS ANTHONY, physician, plastic surgeon; b. Columbia, Mo., June 29, 1951; s. Robert Moore and Carolyn (Swett) M.; m. Kathryn Claire Stallcup, Aug. 13, 1977; children: Anthony, Lisa. BA cum laude in biology, Harvard Coll., 1973, MD cum laude, 1978. Diplomate Am. Bd. Otolaryngology, Am. Bd. Plastic Surgery. Rsch. assoc. dept. microbiology Harvard Med. Sch., Cambridge, Mass., 1976-77; intern in medicine Mass. Gen. Hosp., Boston, 1978-79; resident in surgery Peter Bent Brigham Hosp., Boston, 1979-80; resident in otolaryngology Mass. Eye and Ear Infirmary, Boston, 1980-82, chief resident, 1982-83; resident in plastic surgery Brigham and Women;s Hosp., Children's Hosp., Boston, 1983-84, chief resident, 1984-85; asst. prof. in surgery Wash. U. Sch. Medicine, St. Louis, 1985-89, assoc. prof., 1989-91; prof., chief divsn. plastic surgery Northwestern U. Med. Sch., Chgo., 1991—; plastic surgeon Northwestern Meml. Hosp., 1991—, Evanston Hosp., 1991—, Children's Meml. Hosp., 1992—, Shriner's Hosp. Chgo., 1994—; co-chmn. Gorden Rsch. Conf., 1995; spl. cons. Fed. Drug Adminstrn., 1994-95. Editl. bd. Archives of Surgery, 1992—, Plastic and Reconstructive Surgery, 1993—, Wound Repair and Regeneration, 1992—; contbr. articles to profl. jours., more than 125 publs., book chpts.; book reviewer. Harvard Nat. scholar, 1969-73; Rhodes scholar candidate, Harvard Coll., 1973. Fellow Am. Coll. Surgeons (surg. biology club III); mem. AMA, Am. Soc. Plastic and Reconstructive Surgery (rsch. fund proposal com. 1987-92, sci. program com. 1993-95, co-chmn. gen. reconstruction subcom. 1995, plastic surgery device com. 1989-93, resource book for plastic surgery residents com. 1991-93, chmn. resource book com., socioecon., 1992-94, chmn. device and technique assessment com. 1994, domestic clin. symposia com. 1992-95, edn. tech. com. 1994—, adv. implant group 1994-96, task force for outcomes and guidelines 1995-96, ultrasonic lipectomy task force 1995-96), Am. Assn. Plastic Surgery (rsch and edn. com. 1994-96), Midwest Assn. Plastic Surgeons, Plastic Surgery Rsch. Coun. (com. indsl. rels. 1992, judge Snyder and Crikelair awards 1991, rep. Coun. Acad. Surgeons 1991-94, program com. 1992-94, 95), Soc. Head and Neck Surgeons (membership com. 1993-95), Soc. Univ. Surgeons, Assn. Acad. Chmn. Plastic Surgery (matching program and ctrl. application svc. com. 1994), Wound Healing Soc. (audit com. 1992, program com. 1990, 92, 94, 97, bd. dirs. 1993-96, fin. com. 1994-96), Chgo. Plastic Surg. Soc., Chgo. Surg. Soc., Double Boarded Soc. (pres. 1995—), Sigma Xi, Aesculapian Club. Home: 144 Greenwood Evanston IL 60201 Office: Northwestern U Med Sch 707 N Fairbanks Ct Ste 811 Chicago IL 60611

MUSTON, LINDA SUE, medical and surgical nurse; b. Long Beach, Calif., Jan. 12, 1952; d. Thaine W. and Mildred (Lomax) Ristine; m. Joe S. Muston, May 15, 1974; 1 child, Carrie. AA, York Jr. Coll., 1972; BS, Abilene U., 1974, Langston U., 1992. RN, Okla. Sub-assembly Timex, Abilene, Tex., 1974-75; nurse aide Abilene State Sch., 1975-86; cashier Tye (Tex.) Truck Stop, 1986; bus driver Pub. Sch., Stillwater, Okla., 1986-87; mgr. Hardee's, Stillwater, 1987-89; nurse aide Masonic Charity Found., Guthrie, Okla., 1989-91; nurse tech. St. Anthony's Hosp., Oklahoma City, 1991—. 1st lt. USAF, 1991—. Mem. Nat. Student Nurse Assn. Home: 126 E Perimeter Dr San Antonio TX 78227-4913

MUSUMECI, SALVATORE, optometric physician; b. Bklyn., Feb. 9, 1960; s. Salvatore and Anna (Conigliaro) M.; 1 child, Nicholas Salvatore; m. Stephanie Lynn Giglio, May 30, 1992; children: Stephen Sebastian, Michael Vincent. BA in Chemistry, U. South Fla., 1983; OD, New England Coll. Optometry, 1987. Bd. cert. Fla. Bd. Optometry. Staff optometrist Eye Inst. West Fla., Largo, 1987, Ctr. for Sight, Venice, Fla., 1988-90; pvt. practice Sarasota, Fla., 1990-91; staff optometrist, dept. chair Cigna Healthcare, Tampa, Fla., 1991-92; dir. optometric svcs. Guggino Family Eye Ctr., Tampa, 1992-95; ctr. dir. Omega Eye Assocs., Clearwater, Fla., 1996—; clin. assoc. prof. Nova Southeastern U., Miami, 1993—; lectr. Pilkinston Barnes Hind, Sunnyvale, Calif., 1994—, Vistakon, 1995—; clin. instr U. Ala., Birmingham, 1996—. Fellow Am. Acad. Optometry; mem. Am. Optometric Assn., Fla. Optometric Assn., So. Coun. Optometrists, Hillsborough County Soc. Optometrists (sec. 1991—). Republican. Roman Catholic. Office: Omega Eye Assocs 1840 N Highland Ave Clearwater FL 34615

MUTH, ERIC ANTHONY, pharmacologist; b. Bethesda, Md., July 23, 1948; s. Frank Julius and Irene (Early) M.; m. Kathleen Jo Griffin, Oct. 25, 1974; children: Elizabeth Helen, Marianne Irene. BA, Cornell U., 1973; PhD, George Washington U., 1981. Biologist Lab. Clin. Sci., NIMH, Bethesda, 1973-80; supr., neurochemistry Wyeth Labs., Phila., 1981-84; mgr. cen. nervous system pharmacology Wyeth-Ayerst Rsch., Phila., 1984-86; assoc. dir., CNS Wyeth-Ayerst Rsch., Princeton, N.J., 1987-89, dir. cen. nervous system pharmacology div., 1989—; lectr. in psychopharmacology Villanova (Pa.) Univ., 1984. Contbr. articles to profl. jours. Interviewer Cornell Alumni Secondary Sch. Com., West Chester, Pa., 1983-85. With U.S. Army, 1968-71. Mem. AAAS, N.Y. Acad. Sci., Soc. Neurosci. Office: Wyeth-Ayerst Rsch CN # 8000 Princeton NJ 08543

MUTH, ERIC PETER, ophthalmic optician; b. Munich, Germany, July 25, 1940; s. Erich Walter and Anna Lisa (Pentenrieder) M.; came to U.S., 1948, naturalized, 1955; BS, Charter Oak Coll., 1978; MBA, PhD in Mgmt., Columbia Pacific U., 1983; degree (hon.) Anoka-Hannipen Tech. Coll., 1995; m. Rachel Hubbard, Apr. 4, 1971; children: Eric Van, Karl George, Ellen Anna. Lic. optician, Conn. Pres. Park Lane Opticians, Inc., Milford, Conn., 1968—; cons. Nat. Acad. Ophthalmology Found. Mus., San Francisco, 1982-88, Nat. Mus. Hist., Smithsonian Inst., 1983-94, Gesell Inst. Human Devel., 1984, 89; mem. adv. com. South Cen. Community Coll., Seattle, 1984; mem. adv. bd. Internat. Scientific Inst., P.R., 1989, adv. bd. Middlesex C.C., 1989 (vice chmn.). Mem. editorial rev. bd. (U.S.A.) Dispensing Optician mag., 1984—; author: Management for Opticians, Butterworths Textbook, 1983; contbr. The Social History of Eyeglasses in Japan, 1991, die Brille, Leipzig, 1989, Thinking on the Edge, Agamennon, 1993; pub. over 200 papers in 6 langs.; contbg. editor Optical Mgmt., 1979-80, OpticScan Canada, 1981-82, Indian Optician, 1982, Prism Mag., Can., 1988; tech. editor Optical Index, 1980-82; reviewer optical books. Presdl. appointment U.S. Selective Svc. Sys., 1991-92; Scoutmaster Boy Scouts Am., 1960-62; bd. dirs. ARC, Conn. chpt., 1988; advisor Tri Hi-Y YMCA, 1964; chmn. Korea-Vietnam Meml. com., Milford, 1985-86; organizer WWII Monument Com. 1991; trustee Conn. Visual Health Ctr., 1982-84; mem. Soc. 3d U.S. INf. Div., 1987. Served with AUS, 1957-59, Conn. Army N.G., 1960-69. Recipient Eng. Nelson/Wingate prize, 1983, Service Above Self award Rotary, 1986, Optician of the Yr. Guild of Prescription Opticians Am., 1991. Fellow Nat. Acad. Opticianry (regional membership chmn., faculty speakers bur., citation 1988), Internat. Acad. Opticianry, Opticians Assn. Am. (historian citation 1993, diploma in refractometry 1995); mem. Conn. Opticians Assn. (pres. 1974, chmn. membership and ethics coms., Optician of Yr 1975), Conn. Guild Prescription Opticians (pres. 1980, Man of Yr 1981), Assn. Dispensing Opticians Eng., Nat. Commn. on Opticianry Accreditation (commr. 1989-93), Brit. Guild Dispensing Opticians, Ednl. Found. in Ophamalic Optics, Calif. Soc. Dispensing Opticians (hon.), Ariz. Soc. Dispensing Opticians (hon.), Am. Legion (citation 1986), Milford C. of C. (chmn. law and safety com. 1975, Community Service award 1986), Internat. Platform Assn., Am. Bd. of Opticianry and Nat. Contact Lens Examiners (cert.), Am. Bd. of Opticianry Master of Ophthalmic Optics, Charter Oak Coll. Alumni Assn. (bd. dirs. 1987, alumni citation 1995). Recipient Senate Citation State of Conn., 1993, German-Am. Friendship award, Germany, 1995, State of Conn. Justice of the Peace, 1995; sr. rsch. fellow Internat. Soc. for Philosophical Inquiry, 1991—, pers. cons., 1996. Lodges: Lions, Rotary. Avocations: skydiving, ballooning, motorcycling, Tae Kwan Do (presdl. sports award, 1973). Home: 25 Parkland Pl Milford CT 06460-7723 Office: Park Lane Opticians Inc 50 Broad St Milford CT 06460-3358

MUTHUKUMAR, GANAPATHY, biochemist; b. Namakkal, Tamilnadu, India, Feb. 17, 1955; came to U.S., 1982; s. Ganapathy and Sethurama Lakshmi (Arumugam) G.; m. Alahari Arunakumari, Apr. 17, 1982; children: Madhukiran, Manoja. BSc, Madurai-Kamaraj U., Tamilnadu, India, 1974; MSc, Andhra U., Guntur, A.P., India, 1976; PhD, U. Madras, India, 1981. Postdoctoral fellow U. Nebr., Lincoln, 1982-85; vis. scientist Mich. State U., East Lansing, 1986-88; instr. R.W.J. Med. Sch., Piscataway, N.J., 1988-91; scientist I Enzon, Inc., Piscataway, 1992-93, scientist II, 1993-94, assoc. dir., head bioprocess devel., 1995—. Contbr. articles to profl. jours. Mem. AAAS, Am. Soc. Microbiology (referee 1986-88). Democrat. Hindu. Home: 38 Vliet Dr Belle Mead NJ 08502 Office: Enzon Inc 20 Kingsbridge Rd Piscataway NJ 08854

MUTZIGER, JOHN CHARLES, physician; b. Natchez, Miss., June 23, 1949; s. Dudley Henson and Marie Louise (Eyrich) M.; m. Sarah Edwards Meyer, Nov. 17, 1973 (div. Apr. 1979); m. Janis Merle Averyt, Sept. 13, 1980 (div. Apr. 1979, remarried Oct. 1995); m. Janis Merle Averyt, Sept. 13, 1990 (div. Apr. 1995)children: John Charles Jr., William Westley. BS in Anthropology with honors, Tulane U., 1971; DO, U. Health and Sci., 1982. Diplomate Am. Bd. Family Practitioners. Owner Family Med. Clinic of Philadelphia, Miss., 1983-90, Family Med. Clinic of Decatur, Miss., 1990-91, Poplar Springs Family Med. Clinic, 1992—; emergency room dir. Laird Hosp., Union, 1990-92. Mem. Rotary, Phila., 1983-89; bd. dirs. Meridian Symphony Orch., 1992. Mem. AMA (Phys. recognition award 1991), Am. Coll. Family Practitioners, Am. Acad. Family Practitioners, Am. Osteo. Assn., Am. Osteo. Acad. Addictionology (charter mem. 1986—), Miss. State Med. Assn., Miss. Osteo. Med. Assn. (pres. 1986-87, program chmn. ann. coast conv. 1986-95), So. Med. Assn. Republican. Presbyterian. Home: 5503 13th Pl Meridian MS 39305-1446 Office: Poplar Springs Family Med Ctr PO Box 3730 Meridian MS 39303-3730

MUUSS, ROLF EDUARD, retired psychologist, educator; b. Tating, Germany, Sept. 26, 1924; came to U.S., 1953, naturalized, 1992; s. Rudolf A. and Else (Osterwald) M.; m. Gertrude Louise Kremser, Dec. 22, 1953; children: Michael John, Gretchen Elise. Diploma, Tchr. Coll., Flensburg, Germany, 1951; student, U. Hamburg, Germany, 1951, Ctrl. Mo. State Coll., 1951-52, Columbia Tchrs. Coll., 1952; MEd, Western Md. Coll., 1954; PhD, U. Ill., 1957. Tchr. pub. sch. Germany, 1945-46, 51, 52-53, substitute prin., 1952-53; tchr. trainee U.S. Office Edn., 1951-52; houseparent Child Study Ctr., Balt., 1953; grad. asst. U. Ill., 1954-57; rsch. assoc. prof. Iowa Child Welfare Rsch. Sta., State U. Iowa, 1957-59; rsch. cons., 1960, 61; mem. faculty Goucher Coll., 1959-95, prof. edn., 1964-95, chmn. dept., 1972-75, dir. spl. edn., 1977-92, Elizabeth C. Todd disting. prof., 1980-85, chmn. dept. sociology and anthropology, 1983-85, prof. emeritus, 1995—; rsch. assoc. edn. Johns Hopkins, 1962-63; part-time or summer tchr. U. B.C., 1962, Johns Hopkins U., 1962, 65, U. Del., 1965, Towson U., 1967, U. Ill., 1967; tchg. assoc. Sheppard and Enoch Pratt Hosp., 1969-80; guest lectr. Tchrs. Coll., Kiel, Fed. Republic Germany, 1977-78; hearing officer spl. edn. cases State of Md., 1980-96. Author: First-Aid for Classroom Discipline Problems, 1962, Theories of Adolescence, 1962, 5th edit., 1988, 6th edit., 1996, Grundlagen der Jugendpsychologie, 1982; also numerous articles; editor: Adolescent Behavior and Society: A Book of Readings, 1971, 4th edit., 1990. Served with German Air Force, 1942-45. Recipient award for disting. scholarship Goucher Coll., 1979; grantee Andrew W. Mellon Found., 1976-77. Fellow Am. Psychol. Soc., Am. Psychol. Assn., Md. Psychol. Assn. (treas. 1971-73); mem. Balt. Psychol. Assn. (chmn. membership com. 1966, v.p. 1970-71), Soc. Rsch. Child Devel., Soc. Rsch. on Adolescence, Kappa Delta Pi (v.p. Alpha chpt. 1956-57), Phi Delta Kappa. Home: 1540 Pickett Rd Lutherville Timonium MD 21093-5822

MUZYKANTOV, VLADIMIR RURICK, immunochemist, researcher; b. Moscow, Nov. 23, 1957; came to U.S., 1993; s. Rurick Vladimir and Olga Victor Muzykantov; m. Irina Vladimirovna Gorokhovskaia, Feb. 13, 1991. MD, First Med. Sch., Moscow, 1980; PhD, Nat. Cardiology Rsch. Ctr., Moscow, 1985. Lab. asst. Cardiology Rsch. Ctr., Moscow, 1980-84, jr. rsch. assoc., 1984-87, rsch. assoc., 1987-90, sr. rsch. assoc., 1990-92; sr. rsch. assoc. U. Pa., Phila., 1993—; mem. internat. adv. com. 2d Conf. on Eicosanoid, Berlin, 1991; mem. young scientist com. Inst. Exptl. Cardiology, Moscow, 1984-86, chmn., 1986-90. Contbr. articles to profl. jours. including Blood, Jour. Nuclear Medicine, Laboratory Investigations; author: Dances on the Flame, 1992. Named Internat. Young Investigator, 16th Gray Conf., Manchester, Eng., 1991, World Congress Angiology, Rome, 1989, Wood/Whelan award Internat. Biochemistry Union, 1992. Fellow Will Rogers Pulmonology Fellowship; mem. Russian Immunology Soc., Russian Biochemistry Soc., Inflammation Rsch. Assn., N.Y. Acad. Sci. Office: Univ of Pa Med Ctr IFEM 1 John Morgan 36th St Philadelphia PA 19104

MYATT, SUE HENSHAW, nursing home administrator; b. Little Rock, Aug. 16, 1956; d. Bobby Eugene and Janett Lanell (Ahart) Henshaw; m. Tommy Wayne Myatt; children: James Andrew, Thomas Ryan. BS in Psychology, Old Dominion U., 1978, MS in Ednl. Counseling, 1982. Cert. activity cons. Nat. Cert. Coun. of Activity Profls., gerontol. activity therapy cons., Va. Dir. activity Manning Convalescent, Portsmouth, Va., 1983-84, Camelot Hall, Norfolk, Va., 1984-86; coord. activities Beverly Manor, Portsmouth, 1986-87, Gerogian Manor Assisted Living Facility, 1989-90; dir. activities Huntington Convalescent Ctr., Newport News, Va., 1990-91; nursing home adminstr.-in-tng. Bayview Healthcare Ctr., Newport News, 1991-92; adminstr. Evangeline of Gates, Gatesville, N.C., 1992-95, Mary Washington Health Ctr., Colonial Beach, Va., 1993-95, Brian Ctr. Health & Rehab., Lawrenceville, Va., 1995—; instr. Tidewater Community Coll., 1990. Mem. Nat. Assn. Activity Profl. (cert. legis. com.), Va. Assn. Activity Profl. (v.p. 1986-87, creator logo), Hampton Roads Activity Profls. Assn. (sec. 1985-86, pres. 1986-87, v.p. 1987-88). Home: 518 Tanglewood Dr Bracey VA 23919

MYER, EDWIN CHARLES, neurologist; b. Johannesburg, June 10, 1929; came to the U.S., 1970; s. Bernard and Emily Myer; m. Helga Myer, 1965 (div. 1967); children: Jonathon, Steven; m. Ann F. Farren, Apr. 2, 1970; children: Jennifer, B. Landon. MBBCh, U. Witwatersrand, 1956, diploma in pediatrics, 1968. Intern Johannesburg Hosp., 1957-59; pvt. practice Rudolph Bros., Johannesburg, 1960-65; resident in pediatrics Childrens Hosp., Johannesburg, 1966-69; resident in neurology Johns Hopkins Hosp., Balt., 1970-73; neurology/pediatric faculty Med. Coll. Va., Richmond, 1973—; chmn. divsn. child neurology Med. Coll. Va., 1978-95, vice chmn. dept. neurology, 1988—. Co-editor: Neurologic Emergencies in Infants and Childhood. Mem. Am. Acad. Neurology, Am. Acad. Pediatrics (chmn. sect. neurology 1995—), Am. Neurol. Assn., Am. Epilepsy Soc., Child Neurology Soc. (tng. com., exec. com. 1991). Office: Med Coll Va PO Box 980 211 MCV Richmond VA 23298-0211

MYEROWITZ, P. DAVID, cardiologist, surgeon, educator; b. Balt., Jan. 18, 1947; s. Joseph Robert and Merry (Brown) M.; B.S., U. Md., 1966, M.D., 1970; M.S., U. Minn., 1977; m. Susan Karen Macks, June 18, 1967 (div.); children—Morris Brown, Elissa Suzanne, Ian Matthew. Intern in surgery U. Minn., Mpls., 1970-71, resident in surgery, 1971-72, 74-77; resident in cardiothoracic surgery U. Chgo., 1977-79; practice medicine, specializing in cardiovascular surgery, Madison, Wis., 1979—; asst. prof. thoracic and cardiovascular surgery U. Wis., Madison, 1979-85, assoc. prof., 1985, chief sect. cardiac transplantation, 1984-85, Karl P. Klassen prof., chief thoracic and cardiovascular surgeon Ohio State Univ. and Hosps., Columbus, 1985—. Served with USPHS, 1972-74. Mem. ACS, Am. Coll. Cardiology, Assn. for Acad. Surgery, Soc. Univ. Surgeons, Soc. Thoracic Surgeons, Am. Soc. Artificial Internal Organs, Am. Coll. Chest Physicians, Am. Heart Assn., Internat. Soc. Heart Transplantation, Internat. Soc. Cardiovascular Surgery, Am. Assn. Thoracic Surgeons. Jewish. Author: Heart Transplantation; contbr. articles to profl. jours. Office: Ohio State Univ Hosps Doan N # 825 Columbus OH 43210

MYERS, ALLEN RICHARD, rheumatologist; b. Balt., Jan. 14, 1935; s. Ellis Benjamin and Rosina (Blumberg) M.; m. Ellen Patz, Nov. 26, 1960; children: David Joseph, Robert Todd, Scott Patz. BA, U. Pa., 1956; MD, U. Md., 1960. Diplomate Am. Bd. Internal Medicine, Am. Bd. Rheumatology. Intern Univ. Hosp., Balt., 1960-61; resident in medicine Univ. Hosp., Ann Arbor, Mich., 1961-64; fellow in rheumatology Mass. Gen. Hosp. and Harvard Med. Sch., Boston, 1966-69; dir. clin. tng. rheumatology U. Pa. Sch. Medicine, Phila., 1969-72, chief rheumatology sect., 1972-78; dep. chair medicine Temple U. Sch. Medicine, Phila., 1978-84, acting chmn. medicine, 1984-86, dean, 1991-95, prof. medicine, 1978—, assoc. v.p. Health Scis. Ctr., 1988-95; vis. prof. Cardiothoracic Inst., U. London, 1988; mem. med. adv. bd. Scleroderma Rsch. Found., Santa Barbara, Calif., 1986. Mem. editl. bd. Arthritis & Rheumatism, 1985-90, Brit. Jour. Rheumatology, 1989-94; editor: Systemic Scleroderma, 1985, Medicine, 1986, 93, 96. Pres. Phila. Health Care Congress, 1994—; mem. adv. com. Pa. Lupus Found., 1976—. With USPHS, 1964-66. Recipient Margaret Whitaker prize U. Md. Sch. Medicine, 1960, Lindback Found. award Temple, 1981; named Physician of Yr. Temple U. Hosp., 1986. Fellow Phila. Coll. Physicians (councillor 1994—), ACP, Am. Coll. Rheumatology; mem. Phila. Rheumatism Soc., Am. Fedn. Clin. Rsch., N.Y. Acad. Scis., Brit. Soc. Rheumatology. Office: Temple U Sch Medicine 3400 N Broad St Philadelphia PA 19140-5196

MYERS, DANNY KEITH, medical technologist; b. Oklahoma City, Aug. 25, 1945; s. Harold K. and Lois B. (Richardson) M.; m. Margaret A. Little, Dec. 16, 1967; children: Lisa R., David R. BS, Cen. Okla. State U., 1967; M in Med. Technol., St. Anthony Sch. Med. Tech., 1968; MA, Cen. Mich. U., 1981. Med. technologist St. Anthony Hosp., Oklahoma City, 1968-77; program dir. Rose State Coll., Midwest City, Okla., 1970-82; lab. adminstrv. dir. Southwest Med. Ctr. Okla., Oklahoma City, 1982-96. Southwest Med. Ctr.-Moore, Okla., 1990-93; chief oper. officer toxicology div. Med Arts Lab., Oklahoma City, 1987-90; lab dir. Norman Reg. Hosp., Norman, Okla., 1996—; cons. Interagy. Task Force on Manpower Data, Oklahoma City, 1975-76. Contbr. articles to profl. jours. Mem. adv. com. Assn. Cen. Okla. Govts., Oklahoma City, 1981-82. Mem. Am. Soc. Med. Technology, Okla., Okla. Soc. Med. Technology (pres. 1975-76, Mem. of Yr. 1976, 87), Clin. Lab. Mgmt. Assn. (pres. Okla. chpt. 1991-93), Oklahoma County Soc. Med. Tech. (pres. 1973-74), Omicron Sigma, Alpha Mu Tau. Office: Norman Reegional Hops PO Box 1308 901 N Porter St Norman OK 73070-1308

MYERS, ELMER, psychiatric social worker; b. Blackwell, Ark., Nov. 12, 1926; s. Chester Elmer Myers and Irene (Davenport) Lewis; widowed; children: Elmer Jr., Keith, Kevin. BA, U. Kans., 1951, MA, 1962; student, U. Calif., Santa Barbara, 1977-78. Psychiat. social worker Hastings (Nebr.) State Hosp., 1960-62; psychiat. social worker State of Calif., Sacramento, 1962-75, supr. psychiat. social worker, 1975-80; supr. psychiat. social worker Alta Calif. Regional Ctr., Sacramento, 1980-85; exec. dir. Tri-County Family

Services, Yuba City, Calif., 1966-69; cons. to 3 convalescent Hosps., Marysville, Calif., 1969-71; lectr. Yuba Coll., Marysville, 1971-76; assoc. prof. Calif. State U., Chico, 1972-73; cons. in field, Marysville, 1985—; group therapist Depot Homeless Shelter, 1996—. Juror Yuba County Grand Jury, Marysville, 1965, 87-88; sec. Y's Men's Club, Yuba City, 1964-65; chmn. Tri-County Home Health Agy., Yuba City, 1974-76; vice-chmn. Gateway Projects, Inc., Yuba City, 1974-75; bd. dirs. Christian Assistance Network, 1993, Habitat for Humanity, 1993, Yuba County Truancy Bd., Marysville, 1964-67, Golden Empire Health Sys. Agy., Sacramento, 1972-76, Youth Svcs. Bur., Yuba City, 1967, Bi-County Mental Retardation Planning Bd., Yuba City, 1972, Yuba County Juvenile Justice Commn., Marysville, 1982-90, Am. Cancer Soc., Marysville, 1985-92, Yuba County Rep. Ctrl. Com., 1983-90, Salvation Army, 1990, facilitator care project, 1992; asst. dir. Marysville Adult Activity Ctr., 1990; active Yuba-Sutter United Way, 1971-73, 91—, Tri-County Ethnic Forum, sec., 1991—; mem. steering com. Marysville Sr. Ctr. Assn., 1992, 95—; mem. Yuba County Cmty. Svcs. Commn., 1994; v.p. Yuba-Sutter Gleaners, 1995—. Recipient Cert. Spl. Recognition Calif. Rehab. Planning Project, 1969, Cert. Spl. Recognition State of Calif., 1967; Cert. Spl. Recognition Alta Calif. Regional Ctrs., 1985. Mem. Nat. Assn. Social Workers (cert.), Kern County Mental Health Assn. (chmn. 1978-79). Lodge: Rotary (bd. dirs. Marysville club 1975-76). Home and Office: 3920 State Highway 20 Marysville CA 95901-9003

MYERS, ERNEST M., otolaryngologist, head and neck surgeon; b. Pitts., July 9, 1945; s. Ernest H. and Ruth M. (Johnson) M.; children: Erica, Stacey, Candice, Mia; m. Patricia L. Randolph. BA, U. Pitts., 1966, MD, 1970. Diplomate Am. Bd. Otolaryngology, Head and Neck Surgery (guest examiner 1992-93). Assoc. prof. surgery Howard U. Sch. Medicine, Washington, 1979-86. Editor: (textbook) Head and Neck Oncology: Diagnosis, Treatment and Rehabilitation, 1991. Mentor, Mentors of D.C., 1989; pres. bd. dirs. Riverdance, Reston, Va., 1994. Capt. U.S. Army, 1970-74. Named one of Outstanding Otolaryngologists in The Washingtonian Mag., 1993, 95. Mem. ACS, Wash. Acad. of Surgeons, Nat. Med. Assn. (past sec. and past pres. otolaryngology sect.). Office: Howard U Hosp 2041 Georgia Ave Washington DC 20060

MYERS, EUGENE NICHOLAS, otolaryngologist, otolaryngology educator; b. Phila., Nov. 27, 1933; s. David and Rosalind (Nicholas) M.; m. Barbara Labov, June 10, 1956; children: Marjorie Rose, Jeffrey N. BS in Econs., U. Pa., 1954; MD, Temple U., 1960. Diplomate Am. Bd. Otolaryngology. Intern Mt. Sinai Hosp., N.Y.C., 1960-61; resident Mass. Eye and Ear Infirmary, Boston, 1963-65; asst. prof. clin. otolaryngology U. Pa., 1968-72; prof. clin. oncology dept. oral pathology U. Pitts. Sch. Dental Medicine, Pitts., 1975-82, prof. dept. diagnostic services, 1982—; prof., chmn. dept. otolaryngology U. Pitts. Sch. Medicine, 1972—; chief dept. otolaryngology U. Pitts. Med. Ctr., 1972—; cons. VA Med. Ctr., Pitts., 1972—, Children's Hosp., Pitts., 1972—. Editor: Cancer of the Head and Neck, 1981, 2d edit., 1989, 3d edit., 1996, Tracheotomy, 1985; mem. editorial bd. Laryngoscope, 1973—, Jour. Head and Neck Surgery, 1978-92, AMA Archives of Otolaryngology, 1983-91, Annals of Otology Rhinology and Laryngology, 1984—, Oncology, 1986—, European Archives of Oto-Rhino-Laryngology, 1990—; editor-in-chief Advances in Orolaryngology, Yr. Book Med. Pubs., 1985—; co-editor Butterworth's Intern Med. Revs., Eng., 1981. Mem. adv. bd. Pa. Lion Hearing Research Found., Pitts., 1983—. Served to capt. M.C., U.S. Army, 1965-67. Recipient Cert of Merit Com. Research, Am. Acad. Otolaryngology-Salicylate Otoxicity, 1965; recipient Award of Merit Am. Acad. Otolaryngology-Head and Neck Surgery Inc., 1978, Robert E. Shoemaker Research award Pa. Acad. Ophthalmology and Otolaryngology, 1979. Fellow ACS (mem. bd. govs. 1981-87, mem. adv. coun. 1985-87), Am. Laryngol. Assn. (sec. 1982-88, pres. 1989-90, mem. coun. 1990-93, James Newcomb award 1993), Am. Acad. Otolaryngology (chmn. com. on head and neck surgery 1981-83, bd. dirs. 1985-88, 90—, pres. 1994-95); mem. Am. Bd. Otolaryngology (bd. dirs 1981—, pres.-elect 1994-96, pres. 1996—), Assn. Acad. Depts. Otolaryngology (mem. coun. 1978-80), Nat. Cancer Inst. (chmn. upper aerodigestive tract working group 1986-89), am. Soc. Head and Neck Surgery (mem. coun. 1977-93, pres. 1988-90), Triological Soc. (mem. coun. 1989-92, v.p. Ea. sect. 1994-95), Pitts. Athletic Assn. Republican. Jewish. Office: U Pitts Sch Med Eye & Ear Inst Ste 500 200 Lothrop St Pittsburgh PA 15213-2588

MYERS, FRANK JAY, orthopedist, surgeon; b. Johnstown, Pa., Nov. 6, 1953; s. Frank and Laurine Esther (Johnson) M.; m. Denise Marie Michaud, Sept. 3, 1982; children: Alex, Erik. BS, U. Pitts., 1975; DO, Kirksville Coll., 1981. Intern Richmond Heights Gen. Hosp., Cleve., 1981-82; resident in orthops. Brentwood Hosp., Cleve., 1982-86; pvt. practice Seminole, Fla., 1989-90, Madison, Ohio, 1990—; chief surgery USAF Hosp., Ellsworth AFB, S.D., 1987-89; med. staff Meml Hosp., Geneva, Ohio, 1990-96, chief surgery, 1995-96; med. staff Ashtabula Coutny Med. Ctr., 1990-96, Lake Hosp. Sys., 1991-96, Richmond Heights Gen. Hosp., 1992-96. Maj. USAF, 1986-89. Republican. Office: Frank J. Myers DO 6550 N Ridge Rd # 201 Madison OH 44057

MYERS, GARRY LYNN, chemist, researcher; b. Kingsport, Tenn., Mar. 3, 1950; s. William J. and Ruby L. (Cox) M.; m. Nina G. Alderson, June 14, 1975. BS in Chemistry, East Tenn. State U., 1985. Chemist Eastman Chem. Co., Kingsport, 1969-75, advanced chemist, 1975-88, adv. tech. rep., 1988-92; v.p. R & D, Fuisz Tech. Ltd., Chantilly, Va., 1992—; bd. dirs., mem. adv. bd. Air Trol Chem. Co., Johnson City, Tenn., 1992-94. Numerous patents in field. Mem. Am. Chem. Soc., Internat. for Pharm. Engring., Am. Assn. Pharm. Scientists. Republican. Methodist. Office: Fuisz Tech Ltd 3810 Concorde Pky Ste 100 Chantilly VA 22021-1128

MYERS, HOWARD MILTON, pharmacologist, educator; b. Bklyn., Dec. 12, 1923; s. Charles and Rose (Nassberg) M.; m. Louise Perry, Mar. 14, 1972; children by previous marriage: Clifford Raymond, Nancy Rose, Stephen Andrew. D.D.S., Western Res. U., 1949; Ph.D., U. Rochester, 1958; M.A. (hon.), U. Pa., 1974; M.A., San Francisco State U., 1964. Prof. oral biology U. Calif., San Francisco, 1965-71; prof. biochemistry U. Pacific Sch. Dentistry, San Francisco, 1971-74; dir. Center for Oral Health Research, U. Pa., Phila., 1974-78; prof. pharmacology Sch. of Dental Medicine, 1974-86; dir. research/tchr. tng. grant U. Calif., San Francisco, 1965-71; prof. emeritus pharmacology U. Pa.; adj. prof. pharmacology U. Calif.-San Francisco Sch. Medicine, Calif. Coll. Podiatric Medicine; adj. prof. oral biology U. Calif.-San Francisco Sch. Dentistry, 1987-95; pharmacology cons. Nat. Bd. Podiatric Examiners, 1992-95; reviewer U.S.-Israel Binat. Sci. Found., 1982-95. Contbr. articles to profl. jours.; editor: Monographs in Oral Science, 1972-95. Served with U.S. Army, 1942-45. NIH fellow Karolinska Inst., Stockholm, 1964-65; Fogarty Sr. Internat. Research fellow U. Geneva, 1980-81. Mem. AAAS (chmn. sect. dentistry 1974), Am. Assn. Dental Research (pres. 1973-75), Council Biology Editors., Am. Chem. Soc. Home and Office: 3649 Market St Apt 601 San Francisco CA 94131-1307

MYERS, JACK DUANE, physician; b. New Brighton, Pa., May 24, 1913; s. Louis Albert and Esther Fern (McCabe) M.; m. Jessica Helen Lewis, Aug. 31, 1946; children: Judith (dec.), John, Jessica, Elizabeth, Margaret. AB, Stanford, 1933, MD, 1937. Residency tng. medicine Stanford U. Hosps., Peter Bent Brigham Hosp., Boston, 1937-42; asst. prof. medicine Emory U., 1946-47; from instr. to asso. prof. medicine Duke, 1947-55; prof. medicine, chmn. dept. U. Pitts., 1955-70, univ. prof., 1970-85, univ. prof. emeritus, 1985—; Sec.-treas. Am. Bd. Internal Medicine, 1964-67, chmn., 1967-70; chmn. Nat. Bd. Med. Examiners, 1971-75; chmn. gen. medicine study sect. Nat. Inst. Arthritis and Metabolic Diseases, 1963-65, research career program com., 1966-69, mem. nat. adv. council, 1970-74. Served from capt. to lt. col. M.C. AUS, 1942-46. Mem. Assn. Am. Physicians, Am. Physiol. Soc., Am. Soc. Clin. Investigation (sec. 1954-57), A.C.P. (regent 1971-78, pres. 1976-77), Inst. Medicine of Nat. Acad. Scis. Home: 220 N Dithridge St Pittsburgh PA 15213

MYERS, JACOB MARTIN, psychiatrist; b. Mercersburg, Pa., Aug. 16, 1919; s. Jacob Martin and Winifred Mabel (Kendall) M.; m. Marjorie Ann Grand Girard; children: Carol Ann, Susan Jean. AB, Princeton U., 1940; MD, Johns Hopkins U., 1943. Diplomate Am. Bd. Psychiatry and Neurology. Intern in internal medicine Meml. Hosps., Boston, 1944; resident in psychiatry Johns Hopkins Hosp., Balt., 1944-48, sr. asst. resident in psychiatry, 1948-50, chief resident in psychiatry, 1950-51; assoc. in psychiatry, from asst. prof. to prof. psychiatry Sch. Medicine U. Pa., 1951-70, prof. psychiatry, 1970-77, clin. prof. psychiatry, 1977-85, prof. emeritus, 1985—; emeritus psychiatrist-in-chief Pa. Hosp., Phila., 1985—; mem. ethics com. Pa. Hosp., 1983—, hon. mem. profl. staff, 1988—; cons. healthcare fin. adminstrn. U.S. HHS, 1985-90. Editor: Cures by Psychotherapy, 1984; editorial Bd. Diseases of the Nervous Systems, 1971-77, Weekly Psychiatry Update, 1977-78, Jour. of Clin. Psychiatry, 1978-80. Mem. Citizens Commn. Phila. Task Force, 1980-81; com. on ministry Presbytery of Phila., 1981-86, com. on candidates, 1987-93, Zubrow lectureship com., 1988—; bd. trustees Presbyn. Med. Ctr., Phila., 1993-95. Fellow ACP (life), Am. Psychiat. Assn., Am. Coll. Psychiatrists (pres. 1971-72, Bowis award 1974), Phila. Psychiat. Soc. (pres. 1968), Phila. Psychoanalytic Soc., Coll. Physicians Phila.; mem. AMA, Am. Psychopath. Assn., Pa. Psychiat. Soc. (pres. 1964), Phi Beta Kappa, Alpha Omega Alpha. Home: 966 Kennett Way West Chester PA 19380-5723

MYERS, KATHLEEN ANNE, pediatrics nurse; b. Tacoma, Wash., July 23, 1970; d. David Arthur and Carol Susan (Frederick) M. Student, N.W. Nazarene Coll., Nampa, Idaho, 1988-89; BSN, Seattle Pacific U., 1993. Cert. pediatric nurse; cert. BLS, PALS. Mem. nursing staff pediat. Yakima (Wash.) Valley Meml. Hosp., 1993—. Mem. Assembly of God Ch.

MYERS, LAWRENCE STANLEY, JR., radiation biologist; b. Memphis, Apr. 29, 1919; s. Lawrence Stanley and Jane Myers; m. Janet Vanderwalker, June 13, 1942; children: David Lee, Frederick Lawrence, Lee Scott. BS, U. Chgo., 1941, PhD, 1949. Jr. chemist Metall. Lab. of Manhattan Engring. Dist., U. Chgo., 1942-44; asst. chemist Clinton Labs. of Manhattan Engring. Dist., Oak Ridge, Tenn., 1944-46; chemist Inst. for Nuclear Studies, U. Chgo., 1947-48; assoc. chemist Argonne (Ill.) Nat. Lab., 1948-52; asst. prof. radiology UCLA, 1953-70, assoc. rsch. phys. chemist Atomic Energy project, 1952-59, lectr. in radiol. scis., 1970-76, adj. prof. radiol. scis., 1976-82; rsch. radiobiologist, chief radiobiology div. UCLA Lab. Nuclear Medicine and Radiation Biology, 1959-76; prof. radiology and nuclear medicine Uniformed Svcs. Univ. of Health Scis., 1982-88; sci. advisor Armed Forces Radiobiology Rsch. Inst., 1982-87; cons. Oak Ridge Assoc. Univs., 1987-94; vis. scientist AFRRI, 1987-93; adj. biophysicist Radiation Biology Br. Nat. Cancer Inst. NIH, 1993—; co-organizer UCLA Internat. Conf. on Radiation Biology, 1957, 59; participant in three major Fed. Govt. planning exercises related to energy rsch. and devel. in U.S., 1973-74; mem. adv. com. Ctr. for Fast Kinetic Rsch. U. Tex., Austin, 1975-81, chmn., 1977-81; mem. adv. bd. Radiation Chemistry Data Ctr., U. Notre Dame, 1976-84, sec. 1979-81, chmn. 1981-83; chmn. Long Range Planning Com., Radiation Rsch. Soc., 1976-78; dir. Issues and Requirements Workshop for Analysis of the 1976 "Inventory of Fed. Energy Related Environ. and Safety Rsch.", 1977. Contbr. more than 100 sci. articles and abstracts to profl. jours. Com. mem. Boy Scouts of Am., Pacific Palisades and Malibu, Calif., 1956-67. Fellow AAAS; mem. Radiation Rsch. Soc., Biophys. Soc., N.Y. Acad. Sci., Am. Inst. Biol. Scis., Am. Soc. for Photobiology, Soc. for Free Radical Rsch., European Soc. for Photobiology, Sigma Xi. Home: 11810 Coldstream Dr Potomac MD 20854-3612 Office: NIH Nat Cancer Inst Radiation Biology Br Bethesda MD 20892-1002

MYERS, MARILYN GLADYS, pediatric hematologist and oncologist; b. Lyons, Nebr., July 17, 1930; d. Leonard Clarence and Marian N. (Manning) M.; m. Paul Frederick Motzkus, July 24, 1957 (dec. Aug. 1982). BA cum laude, U. Omaha, 1954; MD, U. Nebr., 1959. Diplomate Am. Bd. Pediatrics. Intern Orange County Gen. Hosp., Orange, Calif., 1959-60, resident, 1960-62; fellow in hematology/oncology Orange County Gen. Hosp./Children's Hosp. L.A., 1962-64; assoc. in rsch., chief dept. hematology/oncology Children's Hosp., Orange, 1964-80, dir. outpatient dept., 1964-73, assoc. dir. leukapheresis unit, 1971-80; clin. practice hematology, oncology, rheumatology Orange, 1964-80; instr. Coll. Medicine U. Calif., Irvine, 1968-71, asst. clin. prof. pediatrics, 1971—; pvt. practice hematology, oncology, rheumatology Santa Ana, Calif., 1980—; clin. rschr. exptl. drugs. Contbr. articles to med. jours. Mem. med. adv. com. Orange County Blood Bank Hemophiliac Found. Grantee Am. Leukemia Soc., 1963, Am. Heart Assn., 1964. Fellow Am. Acad. Pediatrics; mem. AMA, Calif. Med. Assn., L.A. County Med. Assn., Orange County Med. Assn., Orange County Pediatric Soc., Southwestern Pediatric Soc., L.A. Pediatric Soc., Internat. Coll. Pediatrics, Orange County Oncologic Soc., Am. Heart Assn. (Cardiopulmonary Coun.). Republican. Methodist. Office: 2220 E Fruit St Ste 217 Santa Ana CA 92701

MYERS, RICHARD LEE, microbiology and immunology educator; b. Crystal Springs, Miss., July 18, 1939; s. Charles Raymond and Billie Myers; m. Mary Kathleen Feagan, Jan. 3, 1980; children: Barbra Leigh, Ashley Nichole. BS, Delta State U., 1961; MS, Memphis State U., 1965; PhD, Okla. U., 1972. Home: 4406 Congressional Cir Nixa MO 65714-8726 Office: Southwest Mo State U 901 S National Ave Springfield MO 65804-0027

MYERS, ROBERT EUGENE, health facility administrator; b. West Branch, Mich., Aug. 4, 1953; s. George Joseph and Eunice Irene (Atherton) M.; m. Victoria Ann Boyce, Sept. 27, 1983. BSN, Graceland Coll., Lamoni, Iowa, 1975; MPA, U. Mo., Kansas City, 1987. RN, Mo., Iowa. Staff nurse VA Hosp., Kansas City, Mo., 1975, head nurse, 1975-78; instr. Graceland Coll., Lamoni, Iowa, 1978-80; staff exec. Reorganized Ch. Jesus Christ of Latter Day Saints, Independence, Mo., 1981; dir. shift ops. Truman Med. Ctr., Kansas City, 1981-82, patient care supr., 1983-87, dir. health svcs., 1987-95, asst. adminstr., 1995—; v.p. Internat. Mktg. Assoc., Inc., Overland Park, Kans., 1982-83; researcher in field. Contbr. articles to profl. jours. Mem. Am. Coll. Healthcare Execs., Am. Orgn. Nurse Execs., Am. Correctional Health Svcs. Assn., Am. Jail Assn., Am. Correctional Assn., Mo. Nurses Assn., Kans. Nurses Assn., Sigma Theta Tau.

MYERS, SANDRA JOY, nursing educator; b. Newark, Jan. 26, 1936; d. Layton Dennis and Naomi Belle (Hardman) Stirrat; m. Joseph Peterman; 1 child, Regina; m. Jon Adolph Myers, July 22, 1978; children: Jon Adolph II, Michael, Tracy Myers Anderson. Diploma in nursing, Hartford (Conn.) Hosp., 1957; AA, Golden West Coll., Huntington Beach, Calif., 1976; BSN, Calif. State U., Long Beach, 1979. RN, Calif.; lic. pub. health nurse, Calif.; community coll. instr. credential, Calif. Staff nurse med.-surg. acute care facilities, Conn., Fla., Calif., 1957-71; office mgr. Martin E. Hansen, MD, Newport Beach, Calif., 1972-76; staff nurse, weekend supr. Vis. Nurse Assn. Orange County, Irvine, Calif., 1976-81; instr. nursing Golden West Coll., 1981; dir. nursing, adminstr. Superior Care, Inc., home health agy., Irvine, 1981-83; dir. nursing ops. PEI HomeCare subs. Pharmacy Enterprises, Inc., Orange, Calif., 1983-85; dir. nursing resources HealthCare Network, Tustin, Calif., 1985-92; exec. dir. Community Hospice Care Orange County, Orange, Calif., 1992-94; ind. homehealth cons., 1994-95; dir. quality assurance/edn. Skilled Care Pharmacy, Yorba Linda, Calif., 1995—; pres., v.p., sec., fin. chair Continuity of Care Coun. Orange County; bd. dirs. Vis. Nurses Assn. Orange County Hospice; mem. speaker's bur. Purdue Frederick Co.; presenter in field. Mem. Calif. Assn. for Health Svcs. at Home, Calif. State Hospice Assn., Orange County Bio Ethics Network-Long Term Care, Profl. Advs. Long Term Care, Continuity of Care Assn. of Calif. (fin. chair).

MYERS, WILLIAM JENNINGS, orthopedic and hand surgeon; b. Washington, Feb. 25, 1956; s. William Jennings and Barbara Lee (Sayers) M.; m. Kathleen Mary Scheewe, Sept. 7, 1985. BA cum laude, Franklin and Marshall Coll., 1978; MD, Georgetown U., 1982. Diplomate Am. Bd. Orthopedic Surgery. Surg. intern Presbyn.-U. Pa. Med. Ctr., Phila., 1982-83; resident in orthopaedic surgery Bronx-Lebanon Hosp. Ctr., N.Y., 1983-87; fellow in hand surgery U. Miami, 1987-88; pvt. practice Daytona Orthopaedic Ctr., Daytona Beach, Fla., 1988—. Contbr. articles to profl. jours. Recipient McCarthy award, Halifax Med. Ctr., Daytona Beach, 1983, 84. Fellow ACS, Am. Acad. Orthopaedic Surgeons; mem. AMA, Am. Soc. Surgery of Hand, Soc. Mil. Orthopaedic Surgeons, So. Orthopaedic Assn., Eastern Orthopaedic Assn., Assn. Mil. Surgeons U.S., Fla. Hand Soc., Fla. Med. Assn., Fla. Orthopaedic Soc., So. Med. Assn., Volusia County Med. Soc. Office: Daytona Orthopaedic Ctr 330 N Clyde Morris Blvd Daytona Beach FL 32114

MYERS, WILLIAM STEPHEN, physician; b. Phila., Oct. 4, 1937; s. Edward L. and Carolyn R. (Mason) M.; m. Barbara Ellen Myers; children: Robert Scott, Richard Scott. BS, Temple U., 1959; DO, Phila. Coll. Osteo. Medicine, 1964. Diplomate Am. Bd. Family Practice. Inern Met. Hosp.; pres. med. staff Mercy Haverford Hosp., Havertown, Pa., 1978; treas. Bryn Mawr (Pa.) Physicians IPA, 1989-90, pres., 1991-93; chief svc. of family practice Bryn Mawr (Pa.) Hosp., 1991-94; med. dir. IHS of Pa. at Broomall, Pa., 1993—. Fellow Am. Acad. Family Practice; mem. AMA, Am. Osteo. Assn., Pa. Med. Osteo. Assn., Pa. Acad. Family Practice, Coll. Physicians of Phila., Med. Club Phila. Republican. Episcopalian. Office: 912 Hagys Ford Rd Penn Valley PA 19072

MYERSON, DAVID HENRY, pathologist; b. N.Y.C., Oct. 4, 1948; s. Philip and Margery Hazel M. AB, Brown U., 1970; MD, Albert Einstein Coll. Medicine, 1979, PhD in Molecular Biology, 1979. Diplomate Am. Bd. Pathology. Resident in anatomic pathology Coll. of Physicians and Surgeons, Columbia/Presbyn. Med. Ctr, N.Y.C., 1979-81; fellow Tumor Biology Prog. Fred Hutchinson Cancer Rsch. Ctr., Seattle, 1981-83, assoc. clin. rsch., 1984-86, asst. mem. Div. Clin. Rsch., 1986-92, assoc. mem., 1992—; asst. prof. dept. pathology U. Wash., 1985-91, assoc. prof., 1991—; staff Swediah Hosp., Seattle, 1987—; co-dir. molecular cytogenetics Fred Hutchinson Cancer Rsch. Ctr., 1989—. Contbg. author books in field. Recipient fellowship Damon Runyon-Walter Winchell Found., N.Y.C., 1981-83. Mem. AAAS, Internat. Acad. Pathology, Pan Am. Soc. for Clin. Virology, Binford-Dammin Soc. Infectious Disease Pathologists. Office: Fred Hutchinson Cancer Rsch Ctr 1124 Columbia St Seattle WA 98104-2015

MYERSON, RALPH MAYER, physician; b. New Britain, Conn., July 21, 1918; s. Benjamin and Idah Sarah (Fineberg) M.; m. Loretta Francis Walsh, Aug. 7, 1943; children: Patricia Ann Huntington, Paul Andrew. BS summa cum laude, Tufts Coll., Medford, Mass., 1938; MD cum laude, Tufts Med. Coll., Boston, 1942. Diplomate Am. Bd. Internal Medicine. Intern Boston City Hosp., 1942-43, resident, 1946-48; staff physician VA Hosp., Wilmington, Del., 1948-53; asst. chief medicine VA Hosp., Phila., 1953-58, chief med. svc., 1958-72, chief of staff, 1972-75; group dir. Smithkline & French Labs., Phila., 1975-80, cons., 1980-85; freelance writer Phila., 1985-90; assoc. dean grad. med. edn. Med. Coll. Pa., Phila., 1990-92; v.p. Dickson Rsch. Group, Berwyn, Pa., 1990-94; Medex, Ardmore, Pa., 1994—. Contbr. 150 articles to profl. jours.; author 7 textbooks on medicine. Capt. U.S. Army Med. Corps, 1943-46. Fellow ACP, Am. Gastroenterology Assn., Am. Coll. Gastroenterology; mem. AMA, Pa. Soc. Medicine, Phi Beta Kappa, Alpha Omega Alpha. Home: 310 Maplewood Rd Merion Station PA 19066-1031 Office: Medex 10 E Athens Ave Ardmore PA 19003-1413

MYHRE, BYRON ARNOLD, pathologist, educator; b. Fargo, N.D., Oct. 22, 1928; s. Ben Arnold and Amy Lillian (Gilbertson) M.; m. Eileen Marguerite Scherling, June 16, 1953; children: Patricia Ann, Bruce Allen. B.S., U. Ill., 1950; M.S., Northwestern U., 1952, M.D., 1953; Ph.D., U. Wis., 1962. Intern Evanston (Ill.) Hosp., 1953-54; resident Children's Meml. Hosp., Chgo., 1956-57, U. Wis. Hosp., Madison, 1957-60; assoc. med. dir. Milw. Blood Center, 1962-66; sci. dir. Los Angeles Red Cross Blood Center, 1966-72; dir. Blood Bank Harbor-UCLA Med. Center, Torrance, 1972-85; chief clin. pathology Harbor-UCLA Med. Center, 1985—; prof. pathology UCLA, 1972—. Author: Quality Control on Blood Banking, 1974, (with others) Textbook of Clinical Pathology, 1972, Paternity Testing, 1975; editor seminar procs.; contbr. articles to med. jours., chpts. to books. Served with USAF, 1954-56. Mem. AMA, Am. Soc. Clin. Pathology (dep. commr. commn. on continuing edn.), Am. Assn. Blood Banks (pres. 1978-79), Coll. Am. Pathologists (chmn. blood bank survey com.), Assn. Clin. Scientists (pres. 1993), Calif. Med. Assn., Calif. Blood Bank Systems (past pres.), Wis. Blood Bank Assn. (past pres.), L.A. Acad. Medicine (past pres.), Harbor-UCLA Faculty Soc. (past pres.), Palos Verdes Breadfast Club (v.p. 1995). Home: 4004 Via Larga Vis Pls Vrds Est CA 90274-1122 Office: Harbor-UCLA Med Center 1000 W Carson St Torrance CA 90509-2910

MYLLYLÄ, VALTTERI, physician; b. Oulu, Finland, Sept. 17, 1936; s. Leevi Bejamin and Siiri Ellen (Toivonen) M.; m. Marjatta Keskuoja, May 25, 1948; children: Karoliina, Ulriika, Hannele, Juliaana, Birgitta, Henriika, Charlotta, Angelika. Lic. in medicine, U. Helsinki, Finland, 1963; specialist in radiology, U. Oulu, Finland, 1974, D Med. Science and Surgery, 1980, Docent in Radiology, 1984; competant as prof., U. Kuopio, Finland, 1989, U. Tampere, Finland, 1991. Mcpl., city physician Haapajärvi, Lahti, Kuhmalahti, Finland, 1963-67; gen. practitioner Oulu, 1968-70; house officer U. Cen. Hosp., Oulu, 1970-73, specialist, 1974-90, asst. sr. physician, 1990-95, sr. physician, 1995—; cons. radiologist Pub. Health Care, Hyrynsalmi, Finland, 1977—, Suomussalmi, Finland, 1983—, Doctor Centrum Plasma, Raahe, Finland, 1990—. Author: (textbook) Radiologia, 1991; contbr. numerous articles to sci. jours. Elected employees' rep. Oulu U. Cen. Hosp., 1986—; city councilman City of Oulu, 1969-72; mem. parish coun. Evangelical Lutheran Ch., Oulu-Karjasilta, 1995—. Med. sr. lt. Army of Finland, 1975. Mem. Evangelical Lutheran Ch. Home: Solkitie 3, 90250 Oulu Finland

MYNATT, WILLIAM ATCHLEY, retired dentist; b. Knoxville, Tenn., Apr. 7, 1927; s. William Howard and Anna (Sumter) M.; m. Lee Tickle, June 29, 1950; children: Rebecca Judson Mynatt George, William Atchley Jr., Anne Elizabeth Mynatt Neikirk. DDS, U. Tenn., 1953. Pvt. practice dentistry Asheville, N.C., 1954-95; ret. Fellow Internat. Coll. Dentists (dep. regent 1981-85), Am. Coll. Dentists (chmn. N.C. and S.C. 1986), Coll. Acad. Dentists Internat.; mem. ADA, N.C. Dental Assn., Perire Fauchard Acad., Acad. Operative Dentistry, Biltmore Forest Country Club. Presbyterian.

MYRE, STEVEN ALAN, clinical pharmacy educator; b. Albert Lea, Minn., Sept. 3, 1948; s. Herman T. and Irene A. Myre; m. Susan Elizabeth Gordon, July 24, 1976; children: Elizabeth A., Laura C. BS, U. Minn., 1972, PharmD, 1975. Registered pharmacist, Ohio, Minn. Pharmacy intern Mt. Sinai Hosp., Mpls., 1972-73; pharmacy resident U. Minn., Mpls., 1973-74; pharmacist United Hosps., St. Paul, 1974-75; asst. prof. pharmacy U. Cin., 1975-80, assoc. prof. pharmacy, 1980—, asst. prof. medicine, 1986—; cons. Hennepin County Welfare Dept., Mpls., 1973, Pharm. Cons. Svcs. Inc., Mpls., 1974, various pharm. corps., U.S., 1975—. Contbr. articles to profl. jours. Mem. faculty senate U. Cin., budget chmn., 1983-84. Mem. Am. Coll. Clin. Pharmacy, Am. Assn. Colls. Pharmacy, Ohio Conf. Clin. Pharmacy (chmn. 1984), AAUP (chpt. sec. 1982),, U. Cin. Found. (trustee, faculty rep. 1986-90), Rho Chi. Office: U Cin Dept Medicine Pharmacy Cincinnati OH 45267-0004

MYSKO, WILLIAM K., emergency physician, educator; b. Orange, N.J., Nov. 7, 1943; s. William J. and June O. (Kiefer) M.; m. Madeleine R. Seipp, June 16, 1969; children: Claire, Joseph, Luke, Martha. BS, Rutgers U., 1966; DO, Phila. Coll. Osteo. Medicine, 1975. Bd. cert. diplomate Am. Bd. Emergency Medicine. Intern Walter Reed Army Med. Ctr., Washington, 1975-76; gen. med. officer U.S. Army Health Clinic, Ft. Monroe, Va., 1976-78; emergency physician St. Joseph Hosp., Towson, Md., 1979-83; dir. emergency medicine Mercy Hosp., Balt., 1983-89, Church Hosp., Balt., 1989-90; emergency physician John Hopkins Bayview Med. Ctr., Balt., 1990-91; asst. prof., clin. dir. Johns Hopkins Hosp., Balt., 1991—. Contbr. articles to profl. jours. Capt. U.S. Army, 1975-78. Fellow Am. Coll. Emergency Physicians. Office: Johns Hopkins Hosp Dept Emergency Medicine Baltimore MD 21287-2080

MYSLINSKI, NORBERT RAYMOND, medical educator; b. Buffalo, Apr. 14, 1947; s. Bernard and Amelia Joan (Lesniak) M.; m. Patricia Ann Byrne, June 19, 1970 (dec. 1980); m. René Carter, Nov. 21, 1993; 1 child, Matthew Ryan. BS in Biology, Canisius Coll., Buffalo, 1965-69; PhD in Pharmacology, U. Ill., Chgo., 1973. Research assoc. Tufts U., Boston, 1973-75; asst. prof. U. Md., Balt., 1975-80; assoc. prof. physiology U. Md., 1980—, co-dir. Facial Pain Clinic, 1980-84, instr. nursing, 1982-84; research fellow U. Bristol, Eng., 1984-85; instr. C.C. Balt., 1980-82; dir. grad program dept. physiology U. Md., 1981—; founder, dir. Patricia Byrne Nursing Scholarship Fund Trocaire Coll., Buffalo, 1980—; dir. NIH Minority Rsch. Apprentice Program Balt. Coll. Dental Surgery, 1988—; faculty Marine-Estuarine Environ. Scis. grad program U. Md., 1988—; grant rev. com. Nat. Inst. Nursing Rsch., 1993—; grant reviewer Dept. of Health and Human Svcs.; cons. in field. Editor newsletter Med. Soc. Med. Rsch., 1977-82; author 23 book chpts., 9 revs. and numerous abstracts on pharmacology and neurosci.; inventor in field; reviewer 7 jours. Rep. task force on aging U. Md., 1979-84; instr. Am. Heart Assn., Balt., 1978—, ARC, Balt., 1977-83; eucharistic minister, pastoral visitor Catholic Ch., 1983-93. Capt U.S. Army 1969-77. Grantee NIH, various drug cos. and founds.; USPHS fellow, 1969-73; recipient Alumni of Yr. award St. Mary's H.S., Lancaster, N.Y., 1996.

Mem. Europena Brain and Behavior Soc. (hon.), Internat. Brain Rsch. Orgn., Md. Soc. Med. Rsch. (exec. com., bd. dirs. 1978-86), Internat. Assn. Dental Rsch. (advisor 1980-81), Am. Physiol. Soc., Soc. for Neurosci. (pres. Balt. chpt. 1990-92, editor newsletter 1990—), Am. Soc. Pharmacology & Exptl. Therapeutics. Republican. Home: 9395 Carrie Way Ellicott City MD 21042-1701 Office: U Md OCBS Dept 666 W Baltimore St Baltimore MD 21201-1510

NABATOFF, ROBERT ALLAN, vascular surgeon, educator; b. N.Y.C., Nov. 19, 1918; s. Abraham Louis and Emma (Goldin) N.; m. Joan Herman, Sept. 11, 1955; children: Diane, Richard, Ross. BA, U. Mich., 1939; MD, SUNY, N.Y.C., 1943. Intern Mt. Sinai Hosp., N.Y.C., 1943-44, resident in surgery, 1945-46, Dazian Found. pathology fellow, 1944-45; Rosenstock Found. fellow in cardiovascular surgery Presbyn. Hosp., N.Y.C., 1948-49; asst. clin. prof. in vascular surgery Mt. Sinai Hosp., N.Y.C., 1972-74, assoc. clin. prof. in vascular surgery, 1974-79, clin. prof. vascular surgery, 1978—, attending vascular surgeon, 1979—, dir. ambulatory surg. svc., 1982—; cons. vascular surgeon Jewish Hosp. and Home for Aged, N.Y.C., 1978—. Author 3 book chpts.; contbr. over 60 articles to profl. jours.; inventor 6 surg. devices. Recipient Hon. Medallion, Keio Sch. Medicine, Japan, 1962, Medallion of Honor, Mt. Sinai Alumni Assn., 1965. Fellow AMA, ACS, N.Y. Acad. Medicine; mem. N.Y. State Med. Soc., N.Y. County Med. Soc., N.Y. Soc. for Cardiovascular Surgery, N.Y. Surg. Soc., Pan Am. Med. Assn. (pres. vascular surgery sect.). Office: Medical Office 1020 Park Ave New York NY 10028-0913

NABRIT, SAMUEL MILTON, retired embryologist; b. Macon, Ga., Feb. 21, 1905. BS, Morehouse Coll., 1925; MS, Brown U., 1928; 13 hon. degrees, various U.S. univs. Instr. zoology Morehouse Coll., 1925-27, prof., 1928-31; prof. Atlanta U., 1932-55; pres. Tex. So. U., 1955-66; commr. US AEC, 1966-67; exec. dir. So. Fellows Fund, 1967-81; exch. prof. Atlanta U., 1930, dean Grad. Sch.; gen. edn. bd. fellow Columbia U., 1943; rsch. fellow U. Brussels, 1950; coord. Carnegie Exp. Grant-in-Aid Rsch. Program; mem. sci. bd. NSF, 1956-60; mem. corp. Marine Biol. Lab., Woods Hole; mem. Marine Biol. Labs., AEC, 1966-67; exec. dir. Nat. Fellows Fund, 1967-81; interim dir. Atlanta U. Ctr., 1989-91. Fellow AAAS; mem. Inst. Medicine-NAS, Soc. Devel. Biology, Nat. Assn. Rsch. Sci. Tchg., Nat. Inst. Sci. (pres. 1945), Am. Soc. Zoology, Sigma Xi.

NACHMAN, RALPH LOUIS, physician, educator; b. Bayonne, N.J., June 29, 1931; s. Samuel Nachman and Ethel Nelson; m. Nancy Rubin; children: Susan, Steve. BA, Vanderbilt U., 1953, MD, 1956. Lic. physician N.Y.; diplomate Am. Bd. Internal Medicine; subsplty. hematology, med. oncology. Intern in medicine Vanderbilt U. Hosp., 1956-57; asst. resident in medicine Montefiore Hosp., 1960-62; asst. resident in pathology N.Y. Hosp.-Cornell U. Med. Ctr., N.Y.C., 1957-58, rsch. fellow in medicine, 1962-63; dir. labs. for clin. pathology N.Y. Hosp., 1963-69, assoc. attending physician, 1968-72, attending physician, 1972—; from instr. to asst. prof. to assoc. prof. medicine Cornell Med. Ctr., 1963-72, chief divns. hematology, 1968-93, prof. medicine, 1972—; vice chmn. dept. medicine Cornell U. Med. Coll., 1974-78, acting chmn. dept. medicine, 1974-75, dir. Specialized Ctr. Rsch. in Thrombosis, 1976—, acting co-chmn. dept. medicine, 1980-81, bd. overseers, 1987-89, chmn. Dept. of Med., 1990; physician-in-chief New York Hospital, 1990; guest investigator Rockefeller U., 1969-70; Wiessberg lectr. Case Western Res. U., 1978; Aggeler lectr. U. Calif., San Francisco, 1981; Patek lectr. Boston U., 1981; Rosenthal lectr. Mt. Sinai, 1982; Beaumont lectr. Wash. U., 1983; Wiener lectr. N.Y. Blood Ctr., 1983; chmn. Gordon Conf. on Hemostasis, 1984; Alpha Omega Alpha lectr. N.Y. Med. Coll., 1985; Sharp lectr. Wayne State U., 1986; Roon lectr. Scripps Rsch. Inst., 1987; Johnson lectr. Internat. Soc. on Thrombosis, 1987; Merck lectr. Cleve. Clinic, 1987; vis. prof. Harvard U., 1991; E. Stanley Emery Jr. Meml. lectr, physician-in-chief pro tempore, 1991; chief resident's vis. prof. Baylor Coll. Medicine, 1991; Samuel S. Riven vis. prof. Vanderbilt U., 1992; Hymie Nossel Meml. lectr. Columbia U., 1992; Pfizer vis. prof. Royal Soc. Medicine, 1992; disting. lectr. Am. Heart Assn., 1994; Seckler lectr. Mt. Sinai Med. Ctr., 1994; Runme Shaw Meml. lectr. Acad. Medicine, Singapore, 1994; chmn. hematology study panel Health Rsch. Coun., N.Y.C., 1973-75; mem. NIH-Program Project Com., Heart and Lung Inst., 1975-79; bd. govs. Am. Bd. Internal Medicine, 1985-88; cons. Manhattan VA Hosp.; vis. physician Rockefeller U. Hosp. Author: Genetics of Coronary Heart Disease, 1992, Systemic Lupus Erythematosus, 1993, (jours.) Blood, 1994, Ann. Internal Medicine, 1993; assoc. editor: Beeson McDermott Textbook of Medicine, XIV edit., 1975, XV edit., 1979, Blood, 1976-82, Am. Jour. Medicine, 1978; adv. editor: Jour. Exptl. Medicine, 1976; editl. bd. Arteriosclerosis, 1983; contbr. articles to med. jours. With USN, 1958-60. Fellow ACP; mem. AAAS, Assn. Am. Physicians, Am. Soc. Clin. Investigation, Am. Fedn. Clin. Rsch., Am. Clin. and Climatol. Assn., N.Y. Acad. Sci., N.Y. Soc. for Study of Blood (pres. 1975), Am. Soc. Hematology (exec. coun. 1978-79), Harvey Soc. (coun. 1980), Am. Physiol. Assn., Internat. Soc. Thrombosis and Hemostasis (coun. 1986-92), Soc. Exptl. Biology and Medicine, Am. Soc. Biol. Chemists, Inst. Medicine of NAS, N.Y. Acad. Medicine, Cornell Med. Alumni (hon.), Nat. Blood Club (pres. 1981-82), Peripatetic Club, Alpha Omega Alpha, Phi Beta Kappa. Home: 657 Floyd St Englewd Clfs NJ 07632-2049 Office: NY Hosp-Cornell Med Ctr F-433 525 E 68th St # F-433 New York NY 10021-4873*

NACLERIO, ROBERT M., otolaryngologist, educator; b. N.Y.C., Mar. 30, 1950; s. Albert Paul and Lee Ann (Rabinowitz) N.; m. Sharon Ann Silhan, Mar. 30, 1983; children: Jessica, Daniel. BA, Cornell U., 1972; MD with honors, Baylor U., 1976. Diplomate Am. Bd. Otolaryngology. Intern in surgery Johns Hopkins Hosp., Balt., 1976-77, resident in surgery, 1977-78; resident in otolaryngology Baylor Coll. Medicine, Houston, 1978-80, chief resident in otolaryngology, 1982-83; fellow in clin. immunology divsn. Johns Hopkins U. Sch. Medicine, Balt., 1980-82, asst. prof. medicine and otolaryngology, 1983-87, asst. prof. pediatrics, 1986-87, dir. divsn. pediatric otolaryngology, 1986-94, assoc. prof. otolargyngology, medicine and pediatrics, 1987-92, prof. otolaryngology, medicine and pediatrics, 1992-94; chief of otolaryngology, head and neck surgery U. Chgo., Chgo., 1994—; cons. Richardson-Vicks Inc., 1986-89, 90, NIH, 1987, Proctor & Gamble, 1987, 94, Sandoz Rsch. Inst., 1988, Schering Rsch., 1988, Wallace Labs., 1989, Joint Rhinologic Conf., 1989, Internat. Congress Rhinology, 1991, Norwich-Eaton Pharm. Inc., 1991-92, Ciba-Geigy Corp., 1991-92, Mktg. Corp. Am., 1993—, others; mem. med. bd. Children's Ctr., 1991-94, other local comms.; reviewer Am. Jour. Rhinology, others; lectr. in field. Editor: Rhinoconjunctivitis: New Perspectives in Topical Treatment, 1988; asst. editor: Am. Jour. Rhinology, 1986—, Rhinology, 1988—; mem. editorial bd. Otolaryngology-Head and Neck Surgery, 1990—, Laryngoscope, 1990—, Jour. Allergy and Clin. Immunology, 1992-97; contbr. numerous chpts. to books, papers and abstracts to profl. jours. and procs. Fellow ACS, Am. Acad. Otolaryngology-Head and Neck Surgery (mem. com. 1985-90, 90-92, subcom. 1987-92), Am. Laryngol., Rhinol. and Otol. Soc., Inc.; mem. Am. Acad. Allergy and Immunology (mem. com. 1983-88, 88-89, 88-95, chmn. com. 1990-91, 91—, Jerome Glazer Meml. lectureship), Am. Fedn. Clin. Rsch., Am. Soc. Pediatric Otolaryngology (rsch. com. 1990-94, chmn. subcom. 1990), Md. Soc. Otolaryngology-Head and Neck Surgery, Soc. Univ. Otolaryngologists-Head and Neck Surgeons, Pan-Am. Assn. Otorhinolaryngology, Internat. Symposium on Infection and Allergy of the Nose (v.p.). Office: U Chgo MC1035 5841 S Maryland Ave MC 1035 Chicago IL 60637

NADAS, JOHN ADALBERT, psychiatrist; b. Innsbruck, Austria, Mar. 14, 1949; came to U.S., 1950; s. Julius Zoltan and Ibolya Erzsebet (Szöllösy) N.; m. Gabriella Ilona Ormay, Apr. 11, 1981; children: János, Miklós, István. BA, Case Western Res. U., Cleve., 1970; MD, Duke U., Durham, N.C., 1974. Diplomate Am. Bd. Psychiatry and Neurology. Resident in psychiatry U. Chgo., 1974-77; pvt. practice Munster, Ind., 1977-84, Canton, 1984—; instr. psychiatry Northeastern Ohio U. Coll. Medicine, Rootstown, 1985-86; coord. psychiat. edn. Timken Mercy Med. Ctr., Canton, Ohio, 1985-87, clin. dir. psychiat. svcs., 1990-91; asst. prof. Northeast Ohio U. Coll. Medicine, Rootstown, 1986—; cons. Crisis Ctr., Canton, 1985-92. Author: Philosophical Basis of Depth Psychotherapy, 1983, Journey Toward Energy, 1995. Mem. AMA, Am. Psychiat. Assn. Roman Catholic. Office: 1330 Timken Mercy Dr NW Ste 320 Canton OH 44708-2624

NADE, SYDNEY M., orthopedic surgeon, educator; b. Sydney, NSW, Australia, June 7, 1939; s. Louis and Ludwika Nade; m. Sally Pitman; 3 children. BSc in Medicine, U. Sydney, 1960, MB BS with 1st class honors, 1963, MD, 1975; DSc, U. Western Australia, 1989. House physician Australian and U.K. hosps., 1963-69; sr. registrar Radcliffe Infirmary, Oxford, Eng., 1970-71; Lord Nuffield scholar in orthopedic surgery Nuffield Orthopaedic Ctr., Oxford, 1971-72; assoc. prof. orthopedic and traumatic surgery U. Sydney, 1972-78, clin. prof., 1986—; prof. orthopedic surgery U. Western Australia, 1978-86; sr. staff specialist, orthopedic surgeon Westmead Hosp., Sydney, 1986—. Co-author: Musculo-Skeletal Infections, 1987, Infections in Bones and Joints, 1994; contbr. over 100 articles to profl. jours. Fellow Royal Coll. Surgeons, Royal Australasian Coll. Surgeons, Australian Orthopedic Assn.; mem. Royal Coll. Physicians U.K.

NADEL, ALAN MARC, neurologist; b. Pitts., July 19, 1942; s. Leonard and Annabel (Sternberg) N.; m. Zoe Nadel, Dec. 26, 1967; 1 child, Craig Ellis. BA, Dartmouth Coll., 1964; MD, U. Pitts., 1968. Diplomate Am. Bd. Internal Medicine, Am. Bd. Qualification in Electroencephalography, Am. Bd. Psychiatry and Neurology; lic. physician, Pa., Mass., Tenn., Ark. Intern U. Pitts., 1968-69, resident, 1969-70; chief resident Duke U., Durham, N.C., 1974-75; pvt. practice Memphis, 1975—. Contbr. articles to profl. jours. Tchr. Memphis Literary Coun., 1990-92. Lt. comdr. USN, 1970-72. Fellow ACP, Am. Acad. Neurology, Am. Electroencephalographic Soc.; mem. Am. Soc. Neuroimaging (exec. com. 1980-83), Am. Soc. Internal Medicine, Tenn. Med. Soc., Memphis Acad. Neurology, So. EEG Soc. (coun.), Memphis and Shelby County Med. Soc. Office: 6005 Park Ave # 626B Memphis TN 38115

NADELL, ANDREW THOMAS, psychiatrist; b. N.Y.C., Nov. 3, 1946; s. Samuel Tyler and Bertha Elaine (Trupine) N.; m. Eleanore Edwards Ramsey, July 24, 1993. MA, Columbia U., 1968; MSc, U. London, 1973; MD, Duke U., 1974. Diplomate Am. Bd. Psychiatry and Neurology. Resident in psychiatry U. Calif., Davis, 1974-77; clin. instr. psychiatry Stanford (Calif.) U. Sch. Medicine, 1979-84, clin. asst. prof. psychiatry, 1984-93. Trustee Calif. Hist. Soc., 1989-95. Fellow Royal Soc. Medicine; mem. Am. Psychiat. Assn., Am. Assn. History Medicine, Am. Osler Soc., Calif. Med. Assn., Bay Area History Medicine Soc. (sec. 1984-88, v.p. 1988-90, pres. 1990-92, bd. govs. 1992—), Soc. Social History Medicine, Assn. Internat. de Bibliophilie, Soc. Internat. d'Histoire de la Medicine, Stanford Univ. Librs. Assocs. (adv. coun. 1988-94), Univ. Club, Olympic Club, Grolier Club, Roxburghe Club, Colophon Club, Book Club of Calif. Office: 1515 Trousdale Dr Burlingame CA 94010

NADELSON, CAROL COOPERMAN, psychiatrist, educator; b. Bklyn., Oct. 13, 1936; m. Theodore Nadelson, July 16, 1965; children: Robert, Jennifer. B.A. magna cum laude, Bklyn. Coll., 1957; M.D. with honors, U. Rochester, N.Y., 1961. Dir. med. student edn. Beth Israel Hosp., Boston, 1974-79, psychiatrist, 1977; assoc. prof. psychiatry Harvard U. Med. Sch., Boston, 1976-79; research scholar Radcliffe Coll., Cambridge, Mass., 1979-80; prof. psychiatry Tufts Med. Sch., Boston, 1979-95; vice chmn., dir. tng. and edn. dept. psychiatry Tufts-New Eng. Med. Ctr., Boston, 1979-93; clin. prof. psychiatry Harvard Med. Sch., Boston, 1995—. Editor: The Woman Patient, Vols. 1, 2 and 3, 1978, 82; Treatment Interventions in Human Sexuality, 1983; Marriage and Divorce: A Contemporary Perspective, 1984, Women Physicians in Leadership Roles, 1986, Training Psychiatrists for the '90s, 1987, Treating Chronically Mentally Ill Women, 1988, Family Violence, 1988, Women and Men: New Perspectives on Gender Differences, 1990, International Review of Psychiatry Vols. 1 & 2, 1993, 96, Major Psychiatric Disorders, 1982, The CHallenge of Change: Perspectives on Family, Work and Education, 1983; editor-in-chief Am. Psychiatric Press, Inc., 1986—, pres., CEO, 1995—; contbr. over 200 articles to profl. jours. Trustee Menninger Found., 1988—. Recipient Gold Medal award Mt. Airy Psychiat. Ctr., 1981, award Case Western Res. U., 1983, Elizabeth Blackwell award Am. Med. Women's Assn., 1985; Picker Found. grantee, 1982-83. Fellow Ctr. for Advanced Study in the Behavioral Scis., Am. Psychiat. Assn. (pres. 1985-86, Seymour D. Vestermark award 1992, Disting. Svc. award 1995); mem. Am. Coll. Psychiatrists (bd. regents 1991-94, Disting. Svc. award 1989), AMA (impaired physicians com. 1984, Sidney Cohen award 1988), Group for Advancement of Psychiatry (bd. dirs. 1984). Office: 30 Amory St Brookline MA 02146-3909

NADJARI, HOWARD I., surgeon; b. Jamaica, N.Y., June 5, 1955; m. Patricia Howe Nadjari, Aug. 29, 1995. BA, Johns Hopkins U., 1977; MD, Temple U., 1984. Diplomate Am. Bd. Gen. Surgery. Staff surgeon Nassau County Med. Ctr., East Meadow, N.Y., 1991—, dir. hyperbaric medicine. Office: Nassau County Med Ctr 2201 Hempstead Tpke East Meadow NY 11554

NADLER, CHARLES FENGER, internist, educator; b. Chgo., Nov. 8, 1929; s. Walter H. and Augusta M. (Fenger) N.; m. Nancy Butler Waller, June 23, 1953; children: Charles Fenger Jr., Caroline Nadler Healy, Robert Brewster. AB, Dartmouth Coll., 1951; MD, Northwestern U., Chgo., 1955. Diplomate Am. Bd. Internal Medicine. Intern in medicine Barnes Hosp., St. Louis, 1955-56, asst. resident in medicine, 1956-57, 59-60; clin. assoc. Nat. Cancer Inst., NIH, Bethesda, Md., 1957-59; fellow in hematology U. Colo. Med. Ctr., Denver, 1960-61; attending physician Northwestern Meml. Hosp., Chgo., 1961—; assoc. prof. medicine Northwestern U. Med. Sch., 1961—; bd. dirs. Northwestern Healthcare Corp., Chgo., 1994—. Contbr. over 75 articles on cytogenetics and biochem. genetics to sci. jours. Rsch. assoc. Field Mus., Chgo., 1970—. Sr. asst. surgeon USPHS, 1957-59. Fellow ACP; mem. Ctrl. Soc. Clin. Rsch., Soc. for Exptl. Biology and Medicine, Am. Soc. Mammalogists. Home: 399 W Fullerton Ave Chicago IL 60614 Office: Northwestern Meml Hosp 707 Fairbanks Ct Chicago IL 60611

NADLER, HENRY LOUIS, pediatrician, geneticist, medical educator; b. N.Y.C., Apr. 15, 1936; s. Herbert and Mary (Kartiganer) N.; m. Benita Weinhard, June 16, 1957; children: Karen, Gary, Debra, Amy. A.B., Colgate U., 1957; M.D., Northwestern U., 1961; M.S., U. Wis., 1965. Diplomate: Am. Bd. Pediatrics, Am. Bd. Med. Genetics. Intern NYU Med. Ctr., 1961-62, sr. resident pediatrics, 1962-63, chief resident, 1963-64, teaching asst. NYU Sch. Medicine, 1962-63, clin. instr., 1963-64; clin. instr. U. Wis. Sch. Medicine, 1964-65; practice medicine specializing in pediatrics Chgo., 1965—; fellow Children's Meml. Hosp. dept. pediatrics Northwestern U., 1964-65; assoc. in pediatrics Northwestern U. Med. Sch., 1965-66, asst. prof., 1967-68, assoc. prof., 1968-70, prof., 1970-81, chmn. dept. pediatrics, 1970-81; prof. Northwestern U. Med. Sch. (Grad. Sch.), 1971-80; mem. staff Children's Meml. Hosp., 1965-81, head div. genetics, 1969-81, chief of staff, 1970-81; dean, prof. pediatrics, ob-gyn Wayne State U. Med. Sch., Detroit, 1981-88; prof. U. Chgo., 1988-89, U. Ill., 1989—; pres. Michael Reese Hosp. and Med. Ctr., Chgo., 1988-91; market med. dir. Aetna Health Plans, Phoenix, 1993-94, mktg. v.p., CEO, 1994-95; v.p. managed care/physician integration, med. dir. Am. Healthcare Sys., San Diego, 1995; mem. vis. staff, div. medicine Northwestern Meml. Hosp., 1972-81; staff Children's Hosp. of Mich., 1981-88. Mem. editorial bd. Comprehensive Therapy, 1973-84, Am. Jour. Human Genetics, 1979-83, Pediatrics in Rev., 1980-83, Am. Jour. Diseases of Children, 1983-91; contbr. articles to profl. jours. Recipient E. Mead Johnson award for pediatric rsch., 1973, Meyer O. Cantor award for Disting. Svc. Internat. Coll. Surgeons, 1987; Irene Heinz Given and John La Porte Given rsch. prof. pediatrics, 1970-81. Fellow Am. Acad. Pediatrics; mem. Am. Soc. for Clin. Investigation, Am. Soc. Human Genetics, Am. Pediatric Soc., Soc. for Pediatric Rsch., Midwest Soc. for Pediatric Rsch., Pan Am. Med. Assn., Alpha Omega Alpha. Home & Office: 25150 N Windy Walk Dr # 23 Scottsdale AZ 85255

NADOL, JOSEPH B., JR., otolaryngologist, educator; b. Cambridge, Mass., 1943. MD, Johns Hopkins U., 1970. Surg. intern Beth Israel Hosp., Boston, 1970-71, resident in surgery, 1971-72; resident in otolaryngology Mass. Ear and Eye Infirmary, Boston, 1972-75, asst. on otolaryngology, 1975-80, assoc. surgeon, 1980—, chief otolaryngologist, 1985; asst. prof. otolaryngology Harvard U., Cambridge, Mass., 1976-80, assoc. prof., 1981-85, Walter Augustus Le Compte prof., 1987—, chmn. otolaryngology dept., 1985—. Mem. ACS, AMA, Am. Assn. Ophthalmology and Otolarygology, Soc. Univ. Otolaryngologists, Soc. Head and Neck Surgeons, Am. Neurolog. Assn. Office: Mass Eye and Ear Infirmary 243 Charles St Boston MA 02114-3002*

NAFTOLIN, FREDERICK, physician, reproductive biologist educator; b. Bronx, N.Y., Apr. 7, 1936; s. Nathan and Jean (Pesacov) N.; children: Michael Eugene, Joshua Joseph; m. Marcie Myerson, Nov. 1, 1987. A.A., UCLA, 1957; B.A. with honors, U. Calif., Berkeley, 1958; M.D. with honors, U. Calif., San Francisco, 1961; D.Phil., U. Oxford, 1970. Intern King County Hosp., Seattle, 1961-62; resident in ob-gyn UCLA, 1962-66; asst. chief gynecology, endocrine fellow USPHS, Seattle, 1966-68; NIH fellow Oxford (Eng.) U., 1968-70; asst. prof. ob-gyn U. Calif., San Diego Sch. Medicine, 1970-73; asso. prof. ob-gyn Harvard Med. Sch., 1973-75; prof., chmn. ob-gyn dept. McGill Faculty Medicine, Montreal, 1975-78; prof., chmn. dept. ob-gyn Yale Med. Sch., New Haven, Conn., 1978—, prof. dept. biology, 1983—; dir. Yale U. Ctr. for Research in Reproductive Biology, 1986—; vis. prof. U. Geneva, 1982-83, Weizmann Inst., 1991-92. Author 15 books including: Subcellular Mechanisms in Reproductive Neuroendocrinology, 1976, Abnormal Fetal Growth, 1978, Clinical Neuroendocrinology, 1979, Dilatation of the Uterine Cervix, 1980; 2-vol. series Basic Reproductive Medicine, Vol. I, Basis of Normal Reproduction, Vol. II, 1981, Male Reproduction, Vol. III, Metabolism of Steroids by Neuroendocrine Tissues, Follicle Stimulation and Ovulation Induction, 1986; mem. editorial bd. Jour. Soc. Gynecologic Investigation, Menopause, Endocrine Revs.; contbr. over 400 papers, articles to med. jours. Fogarty Internat. fellow, 1982, John Simon Guggenheim fellow, 1983; Berlex Internat. scholar, 1991. Mem. Am. Gynecol. and Obstet. Soc., Soc. Gynecol. Investigation (pres. 1991-92), Endocrine Soc., Internat. Soc. Neuroendocrinology, New Haven Ob-Gyn. Soc., Can. Fertility Soc., Soc. for Neurosci., N.Am. Menopause Soc., Pituitary Soc. Office: Yale Med Sch Dept Ob-Gyn 333 Cedar St New Haven CT 06520-8063

NAGASE, HIROSHI, pharmaceutical company executive, chemist; b. Toki, Gifu, Japan, Aug. 8, 1947; s. Kumao and Aki Nagase; m. Machiko Kawano, Oct. 1, 1977; children: Yukari, Misa. B, Nagoya U., 1971, M, 1973, D, 1977. Rsch. chemist Basic Rsch. Lab., Toray Industries, Inc., Kamakura, Japan, 1976-79, sr. rsch. chemist, 1978-85, sr. med. chemist, 1987-95; dir. rsch. Basic Rsch. Lab., Toray Industries, Inc., Kamakura, 1995—; vis. scientist dept. medicinal chemistry U. Minn., Mpls., 1985-87. Home: 2-10-4 Kajiwara, Kamakura 247, Japan Office: Basic Rsch Lab Toray Industries Inc, 1111 Tebiro, Kamakura 248, Japan

NAGEL, JOACHIM HANS, biomedical engineer, educator; b. Haustadt, Saarland, Feb. 22, 1948; came to U.S., 1986; s. Emil and Margarethe Nagel; m. Monika Behrens. MS, U. Saarbruecken, Fed. Republic Germany, 1973; DSc, U. Erlangen, Fed. Republic Germany, 1979. Rsch. assoc., lectr., instr. U. Saarbruecken, 1973-74; rsch. assoc., lectr., instr. Dept. Biomed. Engring., U. Erlangen-Nuernberg, 1974-75, asst. prof., 1975-79, dir. med. electronics and computer div., 1976-85, assoc. prof., 1980-86; assoc. prof. radiology Med. Sch. U. Miami, Coral Gables, Fla., 1990-91, assoc. prof. psychology Sch. Arts and Scis., 1988-91, assoc. prof. biomed. engring. Coll. Engring., 1986-91, prof. biomed. engring, radiology and psychology, 1991—; dir. Inst. Biomed. Engring. U. Stuttgart, 1996—. Editor Annals of Biomedical Engineering, Section Instrumentation, 1989-94, Inst. of Physics Physiological Measurement, 1994—; contbr. articles numerous articles to profl. jours. NIH grantee since 1986. Mem. IEEE (sr.), IEEE/Engring. in Medicine and Biology Soc. (chmn. Internat. Conf. 1991, chmn. Internat. Progr. Com. Conf. 1989, 90, 92), IEEE/Acoustics, Speech, and Signal Processing Soc., Biomed. Engring. Soc. (sr.), N.Y. Acad. Scis., Internat. Soc. Optical Engring., Romanian Soc. for Clin. Engring. and Med. Computing (hon.), Sigma Xi. Roman Catholic. Office: U Miami PO Box 248294 Miami FL 33124-0621

NAGEM, EDMUND, JR., cardiovascular and thoracic surgeon; b. New Orleans, May 9, 1947; s. Edmund Sr. and Helen Jean (Bishir) N.; m. Catherine Lea Rouch, Aug. 23, 1969 (div. Mar. 1991); children: Melissa Lea, Melanie Lea; m. Catherine B. Lamy, Apr. 28, 1992. Student, McNeese State Coll., 1968; MD, La. State U., 1972. Diplomate Am. Bd. Surgery, Am. Bd. Thoracic Surgery. Intern, then resident Confederate Meml. Med. Ctr., Simetuefort, La., 1972-77; resident cardiothoracid Ochsner Found. Hosp., New Orleans, 1977-79; pvt. practice Lafayette, La., 1979—. Alexis De Toqueville mem. United Way. Fellow ACS, Am. Coll. Cardiology. Office: 155 Hospital Dr Ste 301 Lafayette LA 70503

NAGEY, DAVID AUGUSTUS, physician, researcher; b. Cleve., Oct. 14, 1950; s. Tibor Franz and Patricia Ann (Griffin) N.; m. Elaine Traicoff, Aug. 7, 1971; children: Stefan Anastas, Nicholas Tibor. Student Cornell U., 1966-67; BS with distinction, Purdue U., 1969; PhD in Bioengring., Duke U., 1974, MD, 1975. Diplomate Am. Bd. Obstetrics and Gynecology, Am. Bd. Maternal-Fetal Medicine; registered profl. engr., Md. Resident in ob/gyn., Duke U. Sch. Medicine, Durham, N.C., 1975-79, fellow in maternal-fetal medicine, 1979-81; asst. prof. U. Md. Sch. Medicine, Balt., 1981-84, assoc. prof., 1984-95, prof., 1995—, asst. dir., divsn. maternal-fetal medicine, 1981-85, dir. divsn. maternal-fetal medicine, 1985-96, rsch. assoc. prof. Dept. of Epidemiology and Preventive Medicine, 1992-96; adj. assoc. prof. dept. elec. engring. U. Md., 1986-92; assoc. prof., dir. maternal transport program Johns Hopkins Hosp. and Sch. Medicine, 1996—; adj. assoc. prof. dept. maternal and child health Sch. of Hygiene and Pub. Health, Johns Hopkins U., 1986—; rsch. assoc. Nat. Inst. Child Health & Human Devel., 1991-92; assoc. examiner Am. Bd. Obstetrics and Gynecology, 1991-92, examiner, 1993—, mem. editl. bd. 1985—; examiner Am. Bd. Maternal-Fetal Medicine, 1996—. Assoc. editor: Computers in Medicine and Biology, 1984—; mem. editl. bd. Jour. Maternal-Fetal Investigation, 1991—, Ob/Gyn., 1995—; contbr. articles to med. jours. ACOG/Syntex grantee, 1987. Fellow Am. Coll. Obstetricians and Gynecologists (com. sci. program 1988-95, mem. com. tech. Bulletins-Obstetrics, 1994—); mem. AAAS, IEEE (healthcare engring. policy com. 1987-91), So. Perinatal Assn. (pres. 1987), Nat. Perinatal Assn. (bd. dirs. 1986-90), Bayard Carter Assn. Ob-Gyn., Md. Ob-Gyn. Soc. (pres. 1990-91, exec. com. 1987—). Avocation: sailing. Office: Johns Hopkins Hosp Dept Ob/Gyn Divsn Maternal Fetal Medicine 600 N Wolfe St Houck 204 Baltimore MD 21224

NAGINO, MASATO, surgery educator; b. Nagoya, Japan, Oct. 1, 1954; s. Shotaro and Takako (Suzuki) N.; m. Noriko Tate, Oct. 1, 1983; 2 children. MD, Nagoya U., 1979, PhD, 1989. Resident Yachiyo Hosp., Anjo, Japan, 1979-82; mem. surg. staff Daido Hosp., Nagoya, Japan, 1983-86; chief dept. surgery Tohkai Hosp., Nagoya, Japan, 1988-90; asst. prof. dept. surgery Nagoya U. Sch. Medicine, 1991-96, assoc. prof. dept. surgery, 1996—. Contbr. articles to profl. jours. Rsch. fellow Cancer Inst. Hosp., Tokyo, 1982-83, Nagoya U. Sch. Medicine, 1986-88, vis. rsch. fellow Lahey Clinic Med. Ctr., Boston, 1993-94. Mem. Japanese Soc. Gastroenterology, Japanese Soc. Hepato-Biliary-Pancreatic Surgery, N.Y. Acad. Scis. Office: Nagoya U Sch Medicine, 65 Tsurumaoi-cho Showa-ku, Nagoya 466, Japan

NAGLER, ARNOLD LEON, pathologist, scientist, educator; b. N.Y.C., 1935; s. Max and Esther (Finkel) N.; m. Rosalie Groden, Feb. 18, 1961; children: Stephen Marc, Melissa Sue. B.S., CCNY, 1953; M.D., NYU, 1958, Ph.D., 1960. Lic. dir. labs., N.Y. Postgrad. tng. NYU-Bellevue Med. Ctr., 1958-61; research assoc. Mt. Sinai Hosp., N.Y.C., 1960-61; mem. faculty Albert Einstein Coll. Medicine, Bronx, N.Y., 1961—, assoc. prof. pathology, surgery, 1975—; cons., prof., chmn. pathology dept., dean pre-clin. medicine N.Y. Coll. Osteo Medicine, 1978—; trustee Robert Chambers Microsurgery Research Labs., 1978—; founder, trustee Esther Nagler Dystrophy Research Fund, N.Y. Coll. Osteo. Medicine. Mem. editorial bd.: Circulatory Shock; contbr. articles to profl. jours. Chmn. Jericho council Boy Scouts Am., 1971-73; mem. Pres.'s Task Force, 1981—, Nat. Republican Congressional Com., U.S. Senatorial Club; trustee Liberal Jewish Day Sch., N.Y.C.; corp. mem. Nassau-Suffolk Health Systems Agy., mem. Primary Care Task Force. Served with U.S. Army, 1953-55. NIH grantee, 1961—. Fellow Am. Soc. Clin. Pathologists; mem. N.Y. Acad. Sci., N.Y. Acad. Medicine, AAAS, Am. Trauma Soc. (founder), Sigma Xi. Jewish. Home: 72 Hazelwood Dr Jericho NY 11753-1704 Office: Albert Einstein Coll Medicine 1300 Morris Park Ave Bronx NY 10461-1926

NAGLER, MELVIN, psychologist. BA in Psychology, Adelphi U., 1972, MA in Clin. Psychology, 1974, PhD in Clin. Psychology, 1978. Lic. psychologist, Mass., N.H., sch. psychologist, Mass., N.Y. Staff psychologist Newton Guidance Clinic, Newton, Mass., 1976-77, Cable Memorial Hosp., Ipswich, Mass., 1977-79, North Shore Children's Hosp., Salem, Mass., 1977-82; pvt. practice Newburyport, Mass., 1978—; clin. dir. Port. Psychol. Assocs., 1994—; clin. fellow Harvard Med. Sch., Dept. Psychiatry, Boston, 1975-76; tng. Family Inst. Cambridge, 1977-78. Mem. Am. Psychol. Assn., Mass. Psychol. Assn. Office: 3 Market St Newburyport MA 01950-2505

NAGOSHI, CRAIG TETSUO, psychology researcher; b. Honolulu, Mar. 9, 1956; s. Kunio and Tokiko (Nonaga) N.; m. Deborah Sparrow, Oct. 26, 1991 (div. Mar. 1994); m. Jennifer Krull, Feb. 4, 1996. BA in Psychology, U. Hawaii, 1978, MA in Psychology, 1980, PhD in Psychology, 1984. Researcher Inst. Behavioral Genetics U. Colo., Boulder, 1984-87; staff fellow Nat. Inst. on Drug Abuse Addiction Rsch. Ctr., Balt., 1987-89; asst. prof. dept. psychology Ariz. State U., Tempe, 1989-93, assoc. prof. dept. psychology, 1993—; statis. cons., Honolulu, 1980-84. Contbr. articles to profl. jours. Mem. Howard County SANE/FREEZE, 1987-89. Drug Abuse Tng. grantee Nat. Inst. Drug Abuse, 1984-86. Mem. Behavior Genetics Assn., Internat. Soc. Biomed. Research on Alcoholism, Internat. Soc. Study of Individual Differences, Research Soc. on Alcoholism, Sigma Xi. Democrat. Home: 1127 E Carson Dr Tempe AZ 85282-1521 Office: Ariz State U Dept Psychology Tempe AZ 85287

NAGOSHI, MICHAEL HISASHI, internist, educator; b. Honolulu, Sept. 21, 1957; s. Jack Takuro and Elsie (Takita) N.; m. Lea Asano; children: Erin, Eric. BA in Chemistry, U. Hawaii, 1979, MD, 1983. Diplomate Am. Bd. Internal Medicine. Intern integrated transitional residency program U. Hawaii, Honolulu, 1983-84, resident, 1984-86, asst. prof. medicine, 1986—, dir. standardized patient project Office of Med. Edn., 1989—. Vol. attending physician Inst. of Human Svcs., Honolulu, 1987-88. Fellow ACP; mem. AMA, Hawaii Med. Assn. Office: Central Medical Clinic 321 N Kuakini St #201 Honolulu HI 69817

NAGUIB, MOHAMED, anesthesiologist; b. Cairo, Nov. 14, 1952; s. Mohamed Ezzat and F. (Khalil) Ibrahim; m. Mona Sabry Abdulmeguid; children: Yoma, Mai, Yussr. MB, BCh, Faculty Medicine, Cairo, 1976, MSc, 1980, MD, 1987. Intern Cairo U. Tchg. Hosps., 1978-79, resident, 1979-81; asst. prof. King Saud U., Riyadh, Saudi Arabia, 1986-90, assoc. prof., 1990-95, prof. dept. anesthesia, 1995—; postdoctoral fellow U. Calif., San Diego, 1992, 93; coord. rsch. Faculty Medicine, Riyadh, 1987—. Author: Evolution of the Concept From Fick to the Present Day, 1993; reviewer editl. bd. Can. Jour. Anaesthesia, 1986-88, Anesthesiology, 1994—, Drugs, Netherlands, 1995—; contbr. articles to profl. jours. Recipient Clin. Med. Scis. award Abdel Hameed Sherman Found., 1992, several grants King Abdulaziz Sci. & Tech., Riyadh, 1995-96. Fellow Royal Coll. Surgeons Ireland; mem. Internat. Anesthesia Rsch. Soc. Office: King Saud U, Dept Anesthesia PO Box 7805, Riyadh 11472, Saudi Arabia

NAGY, CHRISTA FIEDLER, biochemist; b. Marienbad, Czech Republic, July 8, 1943; d. Herbert A. Fiedler and Anna C. (Gluth) Rathmann; m. Bela Imre Nagy, Aug. 22, 1969; 1 child, Byron. BS in Biology, Fairleigh Dickinson U., 1967, MS in Biochemistry, 1974; PhD in Biochemistry, Rutgers U., 1981. Assoc. scientist Hoffmann-La Roche Inc., Nutley, N.J., 1975-80, sr. scientist, 1981-88, assoc. rsch. investigator, 1988-95; contract med. writer Nutley, 1996—. Mem. AAAS, N.Y. Acad. Scis., Am. Soc. Biol. Chemists, Am. Med. Writers Assn. Roman Catholic. Office: Hoffmann LaRoche Inc 340 Kingsland St Nutley NJ 07110-1150

NAGY, CHRISTINE LEE, rehabilitation, home care and geriatrics nurse, nursing educator; b. N.Y.C., July 11, 1961; d. Augustus Richard Monturo and Martha Kay Childress Ferris; m. William John Nagy, Aug. 19, 1989; 1 child, Alexander Christopher; 1 stepchild, Angeline Nicole. BA in Communications, BSN, Cleve. State U., 1990. Cert. in gerontology, rehab. and nursing adminstrn. Staff/charge nurse Metrohealth Med. Ctr., Cleve., 1988-90; charge nurse Jackson Meml. Hosp., Miami, Fla., 1990-92; unit mgr. geriatric rehab. and long term care Saginaw (Mich.) Community Hosp., 1992; charge nurse, nursing home care and rehab. unit Saginaw VA Hosp., 1992-93; unit mgr. geriatric rehab. unit Mt. Sinai Med. Ctr., Miami Beach, Fla., 1993-94; home care rehab. coord. Marymount Hosp., Garfield Heights, Ohio, 1994—; mem. policy, procedure, nurses wk., long term care coms. and behavior modification team Saginaw Community Hosp., 1992—. BLS instr. ARC/Am. Heart Assn., Cleve., Miami, 1990, 91, continuing edn./insvc. educator, 1990—; active Broward County Schs. PTA, 1993, 94, Garfield Heights Schs. PTA, 1994, Black River Schs. PTA; cub scout den leader, coach Seminole Dist. and Greater Cleve. Dist. Boy Scouts Am.; vol. Lakewood Meals on Wheels, Ohio, 1987-90, Garfield Heights Meals on Wheels; mem. St. Stephen's Ch. Ladies Guild, West Salem, Ohio; coaching asst. youth/boys divsn. Ashland Soccer Assn. Mem. ANA, Nat. League for Nursing, Assn. Rehab. Nurses, Mich. Nurses Assn., Fla. Nurses Assn., Ohio Nurses Assn., Nat. Spinal Cord Nurses. Republican. Roman Catholic.

NAHAS, GABRIEL GEORGES, pharmacologist, educator; b. Alexandria, Egypt, Mar. 4, 1920; came to U.S., 1947, naturalized, 1962; s. Bishara and Gabrielle (Wolff) N.; m. Marilyn Cashman, Feb. 13, 1954; children: Michele, Anthony, Christiane. BA, U. Toulouse, France, 1937, MD, 1944; MS, U. Rochester, 1949; PhD, U. Minn., 1953; DSc (hon.), U. Uppsala, 1988. Rockefeller Found. fellow U. Rochester, 1947-48; Mayo Found. fellow Mayo Clinic, 1949-50; rsch. fellow U. Minn., 1950-53, mem. faculty, 1955-57; mem. staff Walter Reed Army Inst. Rsch., 1957-59; faculty George Washington U. Med. Sch., 1957-59; mem. faculty Columbia U. Coll. Physicians and Surgeons, N.Y.C., 1959-92, prof. anesthesiology, 1962-92; rsch. prof. anesthesiology NYU Med. Sch., N.Y.C., 1992—; disting. vis. scientist Addiction Rsch. Ctr., NIDA, 1987; adj. rsch. prof. anesthesiology U. Paris, 1968-71; fellow Coun. Circulation and Basic Sci., Am. Heart Assn., 1961—; mem. com. on trauma NRC, 1964-66; mem. adv. bd. Cousteau Soc.; cons. commn. on narcotics, drug control program UN. Author 700 sci. publs. and 30 books and monographs in English and French. Decorated Presdl. Medal of Freedom with gold palm Govt. of U.S.; comdr. Legion of Honor, Croix de Guerre with 3 palms (France), Order Brit. Empire, Order Orange Nassau Netherlands, Silver medal City of Paris; recipient Medal of Honor, Statue of Liberty Centennial, 1986; Fulbright scholar, 1966. Fellow AAAS, N.Y. Acad. Sci.; mem. Am. Physiol. Soc., Harvey Soc., Am. Soc. Pharmacology and Exptl. Therapeutics, Am. Soc. Clin. Pharmacology, Soc. Physiol. Langue Française, French Acad. Medicine (laureate), Brit. Pharm. Soc., Sigma Xi. Home: 40 E 74th St New York City NY 10021-2732 Office: NYU Med Ctr Dept Anesthesiology 550 1st Ave New York NY 10016-6481

NAHMAN, N. STANLEY, JR., medical educator, researcher; b. Ft. Belvoir, Va., Aug. 24, 1954; m. Beverly Johnson, 1979. Student, U. Colo., 1973; grad., U. Toledo, 1976, Med. Coll. Ohio, 1979. Diplomate Am. Bd. Internal Medicine, Am. Bd. Nephrology. Med. intern Presbyn. Med. Ctr., Denver, 1979-80; med. dir. TriCounty Med. Ctr. Nat. Health Svc. Corp. USPS, Bulls Gap, Tenn., 1980-82; med. resident Mt. Carmel Med. Ctr., Columbus, 1982-84, chief resident in internal medicine, 1983-84; fellow divsn. renal diseases Ohio State U., Columbus, 1984-87, asst. prof. medicine dept. internal medicine divsn. nephrology, 1987-94, assoc. prof. medicine dept. internal medicine divsn. nephrology, 1994—. Contbr. articles to profl. jours. Recipient Rsch. award Am. Diabetes Assn., 1995. Mem. ACP, Am. Soc. Nephrology, Am. Fedn. Clin. Rsch., Kidney Coun. Am. Heart Assn., Internat. Soc. Nephrology, Ctrl. Soc. Clin. Rsch. Office: Ohio State U N210 Means Hall 1654 Upham Dr Columbus OH 43210*

NAHRWOLD, DAVID LANGE, surgeon, educator; b. St. Louis, Dec. 21, 1935; s. Elmer William and Magdalen Louise (Lange) N.; m. Carolyn Louise Hoffman, June 14, 1958; children: Stephen Michael, Susan Alane, Thomas James, Anne Elizabeth. AB, Ind. U., 1957, MD, 1960. Diplomate Am. Bd. Surgery, Am. Bd. Thoracic Surgery. Intern, then resident in surgery Ind. U. Med. Ctr., Indpls., 1960-65; postdoctoral scholar in gastrointestinal physiology VA Ctr., UCLA, 1965; asst. prof. surgery Med. Sch. Ind. U., 1968-70; assoc. prof. Coll. Medicine Pa. State U., 1970-73; vice chmn. dept. surgery Pa. STate U., 1971-82, assoc. provost, dean health affairs, 1981-82, prof., chief divsn. gen. surgery, 1974-82; Loyal and Edith Davis prof., chmn. dept. surgery Med. Sch. Northwestern U., Chgo., 1982—; surgeon-in-chief Northwestern Meml. Hosp., Chgo., 1982—; pres., CEO Northwestern Med. Faculty Found., Inc., 1996—; mem. Nat. Digestive Disease Adv. Bd., 1985-89; bd. dirs. Am. Bd. Surgery; vice chmn. 1994-95, chmn. 1995-96. Editor-in-chief Jour. Laparoendoscopic Surgery, 1993—; mem. editl. bd. Surgery, 1981-94, Archives of Surgery, 1983-93, Digestive Surgery, 1986—, Am. Jour. Surgery, 1994—, Current Opinion in Gen. Surgery, Jour. Lithotripsy and Stone Disease, 1988-92; contbr. articles to profl. jours. With M.C., U.S. Army, 1966-68. Fellow ACS (bd. govs. 1992—, vice-chmn. bd. govs. exec. com. 1994—); mem. AMA, Am. Bd. Med. Specialties, Accreditation Coun. for Grad. Med. Edn., Am. Phys. Soc., Am. Surg. Assn. (2d v.p. 1993-94), Assn. Acad. Surgery, Assn. for Surg. Edn., Ctrl. Surg. Assn. (sec. 1994—), Chgo. Med. Soc., Chgo. Surg. Soc. (pres. 1993-94), Collegium Internat. Chirurgiae Digestive (pres. U.S. chpt. 1988-90), Gastroenterology Rsch. Group, Ill. State Med. Soc., Ill. Surg. Soc., Internat. Biliary Assn., Soc. Clin. Surgery (sec. 1984-88), Soc. Surgery Alimentary Tract (pres. 1989-90, trustee), Soc. Univ. Surgeons, Soc. Surg. Chairmen, We. Surg. Assn., Sigma Xi, Alpha Omega Alpha. Office: Northwestern U Med Sch Dept Surgery 250 E Superior St Ste 201 Chicago IL 60611-2914

NAIMI, SHAPUR, cardiologist; b. Tehran, Iran, Mar. 28, 1928; s. Mohsen and Mahbuba (Naim) N.; came to U.S., 1959; MB, ChB, Birmingham (Eng.) U., 1953; m. Amy Cabot Simonds, May 11, 1963; children: Timothy Simonds, Susan Lyman, Cameron Lowell. House physician Royal Postgrad Med. Sch. London, 1955; sr. house officer Inst. Diseases of the Chest, London, 1956; fellow in grad. tng. New Eng. Med. Center and Mass. Inst. Tech., 1961-64; cardiologist Tufts New Eng. Med. Center, Boston, 1966—, dir. intensive cardiac care unit, 1973—, assoc. prof. 1970-93, prof. 1993—. Recipient Distinguished Instr. award, 1972, Teaching citation, 1976, Excellence in Teaching award, 1982 (all Tufts Med. Sch.); diplomate Royal Coll. Physicians London, Royal Coll. Physicians Edinburgh, Am. Bd. Internal Medicine (subsplty. bd. cardiovascular disease). Fellow Royal Coll. Physicians (Edinburgh), A.C.P., Am. Coll. Cardiology; mem. Am. Soc. Exptl. Biology and Medicine, Am. Heart Assn., Mass. Med. Soc. Clubs: Country Brookline; Cohasset Yacht. Contbr. to profl. jours. Home: 265 Woodland Rd Chestnut Hill MA 02167-2204 Also: 55 Lothrop Ln Cohasset MA 02025 Office: 750 Washington St Boston MA 02111-1533

NAIR, VELAYUDHAN, pharmacologist, medical educator; b. India, Dec. 29, 1928; came to U.S., 1956, naturalized, 1963; s. Parameswaran and Ammini N.; m. Jo Ann Burke, Nov. 30, 1957; children: David, Larry, Sharon. Ph.D. in Medicine, U. London, 1956, D.Sc., 1976. Research assoc. U. Ill. Coll. Medicine, 1956-58; asst. prof. U. Chgo. Sch. Medicine, 1958-63; dir. lab. neuropharmacology and biochemistry Michael Reese Hosp. and Med. Center, Chgo., 1963-68; dir. therapeutic research Michael Reese Hosp. and Med. Center, 1968-71; vis. assoc. prof. pharmacology FUHS/Chgo. Med. Sch., 1963-68, vis. prof., 1968-71, prof. pharmacology, 1971—, vice chmn. dept. pharmacology and therapeutics, 1971-76, dean Sch. Grad. and Postdoctoral Studies, 1976—. Contbr. articles to profl. publs. Recipient Morris Parker award U. Health Scis./Chgo. Med. Sch., 1972. Fellow AAAS, N.Y. Acad. Scis., Am. Coll. Clin. Pharmacology; mem. AAUP, Internat. Brain Rsch. Orgn., Internat. Soc. Biochem. Pharmacology, Am. Soc. Pharmacology & Exptl. Therapeutics, Am. Soc. Clin. Pharmacology & Therapeutics, Radiation Rsch. Soc., Soc. Toxicology, Am. Chem. Soc., Brit. Chem. Soc., Royal Inst. Chemistry (London), Pan Am. Med. Assn. (council on toxicology), Soc. Exptl. Biology & Medicine, Soc. Neurosci., Internat. Soc. Chronobiology, Am. Coll. Toxicology, Internat. Soc. Developmental Neurosci., Sigma Xi, Alpha Omega Alpha. Club: Cosmos (Washington). Office: FUHS/Chgo Med Sch 3333 Green Bay Rd North Chicago IL 60064-3037

NAIR, VELUPILLAI KRISHNAN, cardiologist; b. Kerala, India, Dec. 30, 1941; came to U.S., 1973; s. Veupillai and Bharathy Nair; m. Sathy C. Nair, Apr. 22, 1971; children: Parvathy, Pradeep. BSc, Kerala U., Trivandum, India, 1961, MB BS, 1965, MD, 1971. Diplomate Am. Bd. Internal Medicine, Am. Bd. Cardiology. Intern, resident, fellow in cardiology Bergen Pines County Hosp., Paramus, N.J.; asst. prof. N.Y. Med. Coll. Lincoln Hosp., Bronx, 1979-80; cardiologist, dir. cardiology svc. Somerset (Pa.) Hosp., 1980—, chief of med. dental staff, 1990-93; v.p., bd. dirs. Somerset Hosp. Former pres. Somerset County divsn. Am. Heart Assn. Fellow ACP, Am. Coll. Cardiology; mem. AMA, Pa. Med. Soc., Somerset County Med. Soc. (former pres.), Soc. Hypertension, Soc. Echocardiography, Cardiac Club (advisor). Office: 223 S Pleasant Ave Somerset PA 15501-2902

NAIRN, RODERICK, immunologist, biochemist, educator; b. Dumbarton, Scotland, Mar. 25, 1951; came to U.S., 1976; s. James Bell and Muriel Elizabeth (Hyde) N.; m. Morag Gilhooly, Dec. 29, 1971; 1 child, Carolyn Mhairi. BS, U. Strathclyde, Glasgow, Scotland, 1973; PhD, U. London, 1976. Postdoctoral fellow Albert Einstein Sch. Medicine, N.Y.C., 1976-81; asst. prof. U. Mich. Med. Sch., Ann Arbor, 1981-87, assoc. prof., 1987-95, dir. student biomed. rsch. programs, 1989-92, dir. med. scientist tng. program, 1992-95; prof., chair dept. med. microbiology and immunology Sch. Medicine, Creighton U., Omaha, 1995—. Contbr. chpts. to books, articles to profl. jours. Grantee NIH, Am. Cancer Soc. Mem. AAAS, Am. Che. Soc., Soc. for Microbiology, Am. Assn. Immunologists. Presbyterian. Office: Creighton U Sch Medicine Dept Med Microbiology & Immunology Omaha NE 68178

NAITO, JUSHICHIRO, pediatrician; b. Oct. 23, 1906; s. Keiichi Naito; m. Tatsuko Fujikawa, Oct. 17, 1933; children: Hiroko Misono, Nobuko Sakaki, Kazuo Naito. DMS, Tokyo Imperial U., Japan, 1931. Pediatrician Aiiku Hosp., Tokyo, Japan, hon. dir., 1977—; pediatrician Japan Red Cross Hosp., Tokyo, Japan. Author: To Young Parents, The Child Care of Love. Recipient Albert Schweitzer Humanitarian prize St. Bartholomew's Ch., N.Y.C., 1992. Mem. Tokyo Rotary. Home: 1-15-11 Oyamadai, Setagaya Tokyo 158, Japan

NAJARIAN, HAIG HAGOP, biology educator, parasitologist; b. Nashua, N.H., Jan. 5, 1925; s. Hagop M. and Antaram (Shamlyian) N.; m. Mary Been, May 26, 1957; children—Andrea, John, Steven. B.S., U. Mass., 1948; M.A., Boston U., 1949; Ph.D., U. Mich., 1953. Asst. prof. biology Northeastern U., Boston, 1953-55; asst. prof. microbiology U. Tex., Galveston, 1960-66; prof. biology U. So. Maine, Portland, 1966—; parasitologist Parke Davis Co., Detroit, 1955-57, WHO, Baghdad, Iraq, 1957-59; prof. Wayne State U., 1955-57, Boston U., 1962-65. Author: Medical Parasitology, 1967, Sex Lives of Animals Without Backbones, 1976. Contbr. articles to profl. jours. Served with U.S. Army, 1944-46. Fellow AAAS; mem. Am. Soc. Parasitologists, Am. Soc. Tropical Medicine and Hygiene, Am. Microscopical Soc., Sigma Xi. Democrat. Avocation: reading history. Home: 173 Pleasant Ave Portland ME 04103-3203 Office: U So Maine Portland ME 04103

NAJARIAN, JOHN SARKIS, surgeon, educator; b. Oakland, Calif., Dec. 22, 1927; s. Garabed L. and Siranoush T. (Demirjian) N.; m. Arlys Viola Mignette Anderson, Apr. 27, 1952; children: Jon, David, Paul, Peter. AB with honors, U. Calif., Berkeley, 1948; MD, U. Calif., San Francisco, 1952; LHD (hon.), Univ. Athens, 1980; DSc (hon.), Gustavus Adolphus Coll., 1981; LHD (hon.), Calif. Luth. Coll., 1983. Diplomate Am. Bd. Surgery. Surg. intern U. Calif., San Francisco, 1952-53, surg. resident, 1955-60, asst. prof. surgery, dir. surg. research labs., chief transplant service dept. surgery, 1963-66, prof., vice chmn., 1966-67; spl. research fellow in immunopathology U. Pitts. Med. Sch., 1960-61; NIH sr. fellow and assoc. in tissue transplantation immunology Scripps Clinic and Research Found., La Jolla, Calif., 1961-63; Markle scholar Acad. Medicine, 1964-69; prof., chmn. dept. surgery U. Minn. Hosp., Mpls., 1967-93; med. dir. Transplant Ctr., clin. chief surgery Univ. Hosp., 1967-94; chief hosp. staff U. Minn. Hosp., Mpls., 1970-71, Regents' prof., 1985-95, Jay Phillips Disting. Chair in Surgery, 1986-95; prof. emeritus, clin. prof. surgery, 1995—; spl. cons. USPHS, NIH Clin. Rsch. Tng. Com., Inst. Gen. Med. Scis., 1965-69; cons. U.S. Bur. Budget, 1966-68; mem. sci. adv. bd. Nat. Kidney Found., 1968; mem. surg. study sect. A div. rsch. grants NIH, 1970; chmn. renal transplant adv. group VA Hosps., 1971; mem. bd. sci. cons. Sloan-Kettering Inst. Cancer Rsch., 1971-78; mem. screening com. Dernham Postdoctoral Fellowships in Oncology, Calif. div. Am. Cancer Soc. Editor: (with Richard L. Simmons) Transplantation, 1972; co-editor: Manual of Vascular Access, Organ Donation, and Transplantation, 1984; mem. editorial bd. Jour. Surg. Rsch., 1968—, Minn. Medicine, 1968—, Jour. Surg. Oncology, 1968—, Am. Jour. Surgery, 1967—, assoc. editor, 1982—; mem. editorial bd. Year Book of Surgery, 1970-85, Transplantation, 1970—, Transplantation Procs, 1970—, Bd. Clin. Editors, 1981-84, Annals of Surgery, 1972—, World Jour. Surgery, 1976—, Hippocrates, 1986—, Jour. Transplant Coordination, 1990—; assoc. editor: Surgery, 1971; editor-in-chief: Clin. Transplantation, 1986—. Bd. dirs., v.p. Variety Club Heart Hosp., U. Minn.; trustee, v.p. Minn. Med. Found. Served with USAF, 1953-55. Hon. fellow Royal Coll. Surgeons of Eng., 1987; hon. prof. U. Madrid, 1990; named Alumnus of Yr., U. Calif. Med. Sch., San Francisco, 1977; recipient award Calif. Trudeau Soc., 1962, Ann. Brotherhood award NCCJ, 1978, Disting. Achievement award Modern Medicine, 1978, Internat. Gt. Am. award B'nai B'rith Found., 1982, Uncommon Citizen award, 1985, Sir James Carreras award Variety Clubs Internat., 1987, Silver medal IXth Centenary, U. Bologna, 1988, Humanitarian of Yr. award, U. Minn., 1992, Najarian Festschrift award Am. Jour. Surgery, 1993, Jubilee medal Swedish Soc. Medicine, 1994. Fellow ACS; mem. Soc. Univ. Surgeons, Soc. Exptl. Biology and Medicine, AAAS, Am. Soc. Exptl. Pathology, Am. Surg. Assn. (pres. 1988-89), Am. Assn. Immunologists, AMA, Transplantation Soc. (v.p. western hemisphere 1984-86, pres. 1994-96), Am. Soc. Nephrology, Internat. Soc. Nephrology, Am. Assn. Lab. Animal Sci., Assn. Acad. Surgery (pres. 1969), Internat Soc. Surgery, Soc. Surg. Chairmen, Soc. Clin. Surgery, Central Surg. Assn., Minn., Hennepin County med. socs., Mpls., St. Paul, Minn., Howard C. Naffziger, Portland, Halsted surg. socs., Am. Heart Assn., Am. Soc. Transplant Surgeons (pres. 1977-78), Council on Kidney in Cardiovascular Disease, Hagfish Soc., Italian Research Soc., Minn. Acad. Medicine, Minn. Med. Assn., Minn. Med. Found., Surg. Biology Club, Sigma Xi, Alpha Omega Alpha, others. Office: U Minn Surgery Dept Mayo Meml Bldg Box 195 420 Delaware St SE Minneapolis MN 55455-0374

NAJERA, RAFAEL, virologist; b. Córdoba, Spain, Feb. 19, 1938; s. Luis and María (Morrondo) N.; m. Margarita Vazquez de Parga, July 1, 1965; children: Isabel, Gonzalo. M.B., Madrid U., 1962, M.D., 1967; M.Sci., Birmingham (Eng.) Med. Sch., 1967, postgrad., 1967-68; D.P.H., Sch. Public Health Madrid, 1965. Assoc. chief, service respiratory and exanthematic viruses Nat. Center for Virology, Majadahonda, Madrid, 1963-72, chief service, 1972-80; med. officer virus diseases unit WHO, Geneva, 1980-81; assoc. prof. virology Madrid Faculty Medicine, 1970-73; dir. Nat. Center Microbiology, 1982-86; dir. gen. NIH, Ministry of Health, Madrid, 1986-92; dir. Dept. Retrovirus Rsch. Instituto de Salud Carlos III, Madrid, Spain, 1992—. Contbr. articles to profl. jours. Dir. WHO Collaborating Ctr. for AIDS; pres. Spanish Soc. AIDS, 1989—. Decorated knight comdr. Civil Order Sanidad. Mem. Spanish Soc. Microbiology (sec., pres. virology group 1970—), Spanish Soc. Virology (pres. 1988—), Soc. Gen. Microbiology, Am. Soc. Microbiology, Internat. Assn. Biol. Standardization, European Teratology Soc., Internat. Epidemiol. Assn., Am. Public Health Assn., others. Office: Instituto de Salud Carlos III, Majadahonda, 28220 Madrid Spain

NAJŽAR-FLEGER, DORA, dentist, consultant, educator; b. Sv. Petar Orehovec, Croatia, Oct. 10, 1931; d. Antun and Marija (Planinc) N.; m. Branko Fleger, Sept. 13, 1958; children: Pek Dubravka, Marko. DDS, Sch. Medicine, Zagreb, Croatia, 1957; MD, U. Zagreb, 1971, cert., 1974, PhD, 1978. Cert. univ. full prof. Dentist Med. Heald Ctr., Daruvar, Croatia, 1957-60; asst. Dental Sch., Zagreb, 1960-72, from asst. prof. to assoc. prof., 1972-87; cons. Clin. Hosp. Ctr., Zagreb, 1984—; prof. Dental Sch. U. Zagreb, 1987—; head dental dept. Med. Heald Ctr., Daruvar, 1959-60; head dental pathology dept. Dental Sch., Zagreb, 1980-92; head dental disease dept. Clin. Hosp. Ctr., Zagreb, 1980-92; pres. Soc. Dental Pathology, Zagreb, 1984-87. Co-author: Dental Dictionary, 1994, Pathology and Therapy of Hard Tooth Tissue, 1994; author: (lit. jour.) Vrijesak, 1996; author, co-author: (periodical) Acta Stomatologica Croatica, 1960—. Recipient Postdoctoral rsch. award Can. Govt., 1983; grantee Ministry of Sci., U. Zagreb, 1991. Mem. ESE, Croatian Endodontic Assn. (v.p. 1993—), Croatian Med. Assn. Home: Novomarofska 37, 10000 Zagreb Croatia Office: U Zagreb Dental Sch, Gundulićeva 5, 10000 Zagreb Croatia

NAKAGAWA, ALLEN DONALD, radiologic technologist; b. N.Y.C., Mar. 14, 1955; s. Walter Tsunehiko and Alyce Tsuneko (Kinoshita) N. BS in Environ. Studies, St. John's U., Jamaica, N.Y., 1977; MS in Marine Biology, C.W. Post Coll., 1980. Cert. radiologic technologist, in fluoroscopy, Calif.; cert. Am. Registry Radiol. Technologists. Research asst. environ. studies St. John's U., 1976-78; lab. asst. Bur. Water Surveillance, Nassau Co. of Health Dept., Wantaugh, N.Y., 1978; clin. endocrinology asst. U. Calif. VA Hosp., San Francisco, 1981-83; student technologist St. Mary's Hosp., San Francisco, 1985-86; radiologic technologist Mt. Zion Hosp., San Francisco, 1986-88; sr. radiologic technologist U. Calif., San Francisco, 1989—, urosurg. radiologic technologists, 1988-89; attendee U. Calif. San Francisco Trauma and Emergency Radiology Conf., 1995, U. Calif. San Francisco Musculoskeletal MRI Conf., 1996. Mem. AAAS, ACLU, Calif. Soc. Radiologic Technologists, Marine Mammal Ctr., Calif. Acad. Scis., Japanese-Am. Nat. Mus., World Affairs Coun., San Francisco, Sigma Xi. Democrat. Methodist.

NAKAMOTO, FAYE, public health officer. Asst. to dir. Dept. of Health State of Hawaii, Honolulu. Office: Health Dept State of Hawaii 1250 Punchbowl St Honolulu HI 96813*

NAKAMURA, HARRIET TOSHIKO, health facility administrator; b. Honolulu, Dec. 30, 1927; d. Hoyu and Kame (Ajifu) Ginoza; m. Mitsuo Nakamura, Oct. 3, 1953; children: Alan Asao, Scott Jun. RN, Queens Hosp. Sch. Nursing, Honolulu, 1949; Nurse Anesthetist, Queens Hosp. Sch. Nursing, 1953. Cert. registered nurse anesthetist, RN, Hawaii. Nurse anesthetist The Queens Med. Ctr., Honolulu, 1960-75; patient care coord. The Queens Med. Ctr., 1975-91; retired, 1991. Mem. Am. Assn. Nurse Anesthetists.

NAKAMURA, HIROSHI, urology educator; b. Tokyo, Mar. 22, 1933; s. Yataroh and Hideko (Tanaka) N.; m. Miyoko Kodachi, Aug. 13, 1966. MD, Keio U., Tokyo, 1960; PhD, Grad. Sch. Medicine, Keio U., 1966. Med. diplomate. Asst. resident Mt. Sinai Hosp., N.Y.C., 1962-63; rsch. fellow Cornell U. Med. Coll., N.Y.C., 1966-68; asst. Sch. Medicine Keio U., Tokyo, 1968-70; chmn. urology dept. Tokyo Elec. Power Hosp., 1970-73; vis. asst. prof. surgery Cornell U. Med. Coll., N.Y.C., 1973; chmn. urology Kitasato Inst. Hosp., Tokyo, 1973-77; chmn. dept., prof. urology Nat. Def. Med. Coll., Tokorozawa, Saitama, Japan, 1977—, dir. dept. acad. affairs, 1994—. Author: New Clin. Urology, 1982, Practice of Renal Transplantation, 1985, Bedside Urology, 1991; editor: Up-to-date Urology, 1983. Recipient Tamura award Keio U. Sch. Medicine, 1967, All-around Med. award, Igaku-Shoin, Ltd., Tokyo, 1967. Buddhist. Home: 4-403 Boei Idai 3-2 Namiki, Tokorozawa 359 Saitama, Japan Office: Nat Def Med Coll Dept Urol, 3-2 Namiki, Tokorozawa 359 Saitama, Japan

NAKAMURA, NORI, radiobiologist; b. Kokura, Japan, Sept. 26, 1946; s. Sadame and Fumie (Numasaki) N.; m. Ruriko Kuze, July 14, 1973; children: Hisashi, Atsushi. BSE, Osaka U., Japan, 1968; D d'U., Paris-Sud U., 1973; M in Biology, Hiroshima U., Japan, 1974; PhD in Biology, Hiroshima U., 1979. Cert. radioisotope facility supr. Rsch. assoc., lectr. Tokyo U., 1974-84; from investigator to sr. investigator Radiation Effects Rsch. Found., Hiroshima, 1984-89, asst. dept. chief, 1989—; cons. Nat. Inst. Genetics, Mishima, 1983-84, Rsch. Inst. Nuclear Med. Biology, Hiroshima, 1985—; lectr. Yasuda Women's Coll., Hiroshima, 1991—. Mem. editorial bd. Internat. Jour. Radiation Biology, 1991-95, Jour. Radiation Rsch., 1993—; contbr. articles to profl. jours. Mem. Japan Radiation Rsch. Soc., Japan Environ. Mutagen Soc., Japan Tissue Culture Soc., Japan Cancer Rsch. Soc. Office: Radiation Effects Rsch Found, 5-2 Hijiyama Pk Minami-ku, Hiroshima 732, Japan

NAKANISHI, SHIGETADA, immunology educator; b. Ogaki, Gifu, Japan, Jan. 7, 1942; s. Tadayoshi and Ayako (Inagaki) N.; m. Chieko Ikeda, Oct. 15, 1970 (dec. Dec. 1981); children: Atsuko, Jun-ichi; m. Masako Kinoshita, Mar. 30, 1985; 1 child, Hiroto. MD, Kyoto (Japan) U., 1962, PhD of Med. Scis., 1974. Vis. assoc. Lab. Molecular Biology Nat. Cancer Inst./NIH, 1971-74; assoc. prof. dept. chemistry Kyoto U. Faculty of Medicine, 1974-81, prof. Inst. for Immunology, 1981—. Contbr. articles to sci. jours. Recipient Asahi award Asahi Shinbun, 1982, Takeda Med. award Takeda Sci. Found., 1987, Erwin von Baelz prize Boehringer Ingelheim, 1991, Uehara award Uehara Meml. Found., 1992, Bristol-Myers Squibb award for disting. achievement in neuroscience rsch., 1995. Office: Kyoto U Inst Immunology, Yoshida Sakyo-ku, Kyoto 606, Japan

NAKANO, EIZO, biology educator; b. Nagoya, Aichi, Japan, July 20, 1922; s. Yasutaro and Shin (Kobayashi) N.; m. Nobuko Kato, Jan. 8, 1949; 1 child, Sahoko Yokota. BA in Sci., Nagoya U., 1946, DSc, 1956. Asst. prof. biology Nagoya U., 1950-73, prof. bilogy, 1973-86, prof. emeritus, 1986, dir. Radioisotpe Ctr., 1976-82, dir. Exptl. Sta. Freshwater Fish, 1980-86, dir. Gene Rsch. Ctr., 1985-86; prof. biology Tokai Gakuen Womans Coll., Nagoya, 1986-93; dir. Inst. Human Cultures Tokai Gakuen Womans Coll., 1987-92; dir. Biosci. Rsch. Lab., 1993—; vis. prof. lab. molecular embryology

Cosiglio Nazionale delle Richerche, Naples, Italy, 1974-75, U. Palermo, Italy, 1987; adv. bd., cons. Stazione Zoologica Anton Dohn, Naples, 1988—; mem. sci. com. Internat. Marine Ctr., Oristano, Italy, 1988—. Author: Biochemistry of Development, 1979, Developmental Biology, 1986; assoc. editor jour. Cell Differentiation, 1979-90, Roux's Arch. Devel. Biology, 1979-91. Decorated Ufficiale Italian Republic, Rome, 1978; recipient Anton Dohrn medal Stazione Zooligca, 1991. Mem. Italian-Japanese Soc. Biol. (pres. 1978-93), Zool. Soc. Japan (councillor 1975-84), Japan Radioisotope Assn. (trustee, cons. 1976—). Home: Nijigaoka 1-7 Meito, Iwasakidai 2-706, Nisshin Nissin 470-01, Japan

NAKAYAMA, HIROAKI, microbiologist, educator; b. Fukuoka, Japan, May 22, 1935; s. Hiroo and Mitsuko (Kunika) N.; m. Yasuko Inoue, Mar. 25, 1963; children: Mikiko, Mioko, Hanako Anne. MD, Kyushu U., 1960, PhD, 1967. Rsch. assoc. Kyushu U., Fukuoka, 1965-69, dentistry prof., 1977—, dean Faculty Dentistry, 1991-95; rsch. assoc. Stanford (Calif.) U., 1969-73; prof. Kyushu Dental Coll., Kitakyushu, 1973-77; Lic. physician. Mem. Am. Soc. Microbiology, Japanese Soc. Bacteriology. Home: 4395 Midori-machi, Fukuma, Fukuoka-ken 811-32, Japan Office: Kyushu U Faculty Dentistry, Maidashi 3-1-1 Higashi-ku, Fukuoka 812, Japan

NAKAZATO, HIROSHI, molecular biologist; b. Osaka, Japan, July 25, 1941; s. Goro and Yaye (Kijima) N.; m. Michiyo Matsuda; children: Mari, Yuri. BS, Tokyo U., 1965, MS, 1967, PhD, 1970. Postdoctoral fellow U. Pitts., 1970-74, rsch. assoc., 1974-76; cancer expert NCI, Bethesda, Md., 1976-80; molecular biologist Suntory Inst. for Biomed. Rsch., Osaka, Japan, 1981—. Contbr. articles to profl. jours. Mem. AAAS, N.Y. Acad. Scis., Metastasis Rsch. Soc., Japanese Cancer Assn., Japanese Soc. Immunology, Molecular Biology Soc. Japan, Japanese Biochem. Soc., Japanese Soc. for Bone and Mineral Rsch. Home: G306 3-9 Higashinara, Ibaraki Osaka 567, Japan Office: Suntory Inst Biomed Rsch, 1-1-1 Wakayamadai Shimamoto-cho, Mishimia Osaka 618, Japan

NAKAZAWA, MITSURU, ophthalmologist, educator; b. Hakodate, Hokkaido, Japan, Jan. 20, 1956; s. Mitsutake and Chie (Kanazawa) N.; m. Junko Oizumi, Apr. 8, 1980; 1 child, Yuki. MD, Tohoku U., Sendai, Japan, 1980, MSD, 1989. Diplomate Japanese Bd. Ophthalmology. Resident in ophthalmology Tohoku Univ. Hosp., Sendai, 1980-82, fellow in ophthalmology, 1982-85, mem. ophthalmology staff, 1985, 88-89, asst. prof. ophthalmology, 1989-95, assoc. prof. ophthalmology, 1995—; postdoctoral asst. ophthalmology U. Cin., 1985-88; bd. dirs. Tohoku U. Eye Bank, Japanese Soc. Ophthalmic Diabetology. Contbr. articles to profl. jours. Grantee Ministry of Edn., 1989, 91, 93, Japan Eye Bank Assn., 1989, Japan Soc. for Prevention of Blindness, 1993, Nanbyo Igaku Kenkyu Zaidan, 1996. Mem. Japanese Soc. Ophthalmology (Acad. award 1996), Japan Ophthalmologists Assn., Assn. Rsch. in Vision and Ophthalmology, Japanese Soc. Ophthalmic Surgeons. Office: Dept Ophthal Tohoku U Sch Med, 1-1 Seiryo-machi Aoba-ku, Sendai Miyagi 980-77, Japan

NAKDIMEN, KENNETH ALAN, psychiatrist; b. Bklyn., Jan. 20, 1947; s. Marcus and Gilda (Turin) N. BA, Boston U., 1967; MD, Med. Coll. Va., 1972. Diplomate Am. Bd. Psychiatry and Neurology. Resident in psychiatry Brookdale Hosp. Med. Ctr., Bklyn., 1972-75; outpatient clinic psychiatrist Queens Hosp. Ctr., Jamaica, N.Y., 1975—; clin. asst. prof. psychiatry Mount Sinai Sch. Medicine, 1996—. Contbr. articles to med. jours. Mem. Am. Psychiat. Assn. Home: One Lincoln Plz (12M) New York NY 10023 Office: Queens Hosp Ctr Adult Psychiatric Clinic Jamaica NY 11432

NALCIOGLU, ORHAN, physics educator, radiological science educator; b. Istanbul, Feb. 2, 1944; U.S., 1966, naturalized, 1974; s. Mustafa and Meliha N. BS, Robert Coll., Istanbul, 1966; MS, Case Western Res. U., 1968; PhD, U. Ore., 1970. Postdoctoral fellow dept. physics U. Calif.-Davis, 1970-71; Rsch. assoc. dept. physics U. Rochester, N.Y., 1971-74, U. Wis., Madison, 1974-76; sr. physicist EMI Med. Inc., Northbrook, Ill., 1976-77; prof. depts. radiol. scis., elec. engring., medicine and physics U. Calif.-Irvine, 1977—, head divsn. physics and engring., 1985—; dir. Biomedical Magnetic Resonance Rsch., 1987—, dir. Rsch. Imaging Ctr., 1992—; cons. UN, 1980-86. Editor several books; contbr. articles to profl. jours. Mobil scholar, 1961-66. Fellow IEEE (pres. NPSS, 1993-94), Am. Assn. Physicists in Medicine; mem. Internat. Soc. Magnetic Resonance. Republican. Subspecialty: medical physics. Office: U Calif Irvine Coll Medicine Dept Radiol Sci Irvine CA 92697-5020

NAMBA, TATSUJI, physician, medical researcher; b. Changchun, China, Jan. 29, 1927; came to U.S., 1959, naturalized, 1968; s. Yosuke and Michino (Hinata) N. MD, Okayama U., Japan, 1950, PhD, 1955. Asst., lectr. medicine Okayama U. Med. Sch. and Hosp., 1955-62; rsch. assoc. Maimonides Med. Ctr., Bklyn., 1959-66; dir. neuromuscular labs. Maimonides Med. Ctr., 1966-70, dir. neuromuscular disease div., head electromyography clinic, 1966—; instr., asst. prof., assoc. prof. medicine SUNY, Bklyn., 1959-76, prof., 1976—; mem. med. adv. bd. Myasthenia Gravis Found., 1968—. Recipient commendation for rsch. and clin. activities on insecticide poisoning Minister Health and Welfare, Japanese Govt., 1958; Fulbright scholar, 1959-62. Fellow ACP, Royal Soc. Medicine; mem. AMA, Am. Acad. Neurology, Am. Soc. Pharmacology and Exptl. Therapeutics, Am. Soc. Clin. Pharmacology and Therapeutics, Am. Assn. Electrodiagnostic Medicine. Home: 4114 9th Ave Brooklyn NY 11232 Office: 4802 10th Ave Brooklyn NY 11219-2916

NAMEROW, DAVID MARK, pediatrician; b. N.Y.C., Dec. 12, 1947; s. Nathan and Claire (Goodstein) N.; m. Pearila Brickner, June 14, 1981; children: Jordan Ilana, Evan Gabrielle, Zoe Alexandra. BS, CCNY, 1968; MD, U. Louisville, 1972. Pediatric intern Children's Hosp. Med. Ctr., Cin., 1972-73, resident in pediatrics, 1973-75; fellow in adolescent medicine U. Md. Hosps., Balt., 1975-77; pediatrician Plaza Med. Assocs., Flanders, N.J., 1977-79; dir. adolescent medicine St. Joseph's Hosp. Med. Ctr., Paterson, N.J., 1977-81; founder, pediatrician PediatriCare Assocs., Fair Lawn, N.J., 1979—; attending pediatrician Valley Hosp., Ridgewood, N.J., 1979—; adj. asst. clin. prof. pediatrics N.Y. Hosp.-Cornell Med. Ctr., N.Y.C., 1979—. Fellow Am. Acad. Pediatrics; mem. Soc. for Adolescent Medicine, Ambulatory Pediatric Assn. Office: PediatriCare Assocs 2020 Fair Lawn Ave Fair Lawn NJ 07410-2319

NANA, AHMED ABDULLAH, hospital administrator; b. Roodepoort, Gautang, South Africa, Feb. 17, 1960; s. Abdullah Mohammed and Fatima (Patel) N.; m. Shahida Essop Cassim, Jan. 12, 1986; children: Maryam, Muhammad, Umar, Abu Bakr. B in Acctg. Sci. with honors, U. South Africa, South Africa, 1984. Audit mgr. Levitt Kirson, South Africa, 1981-86; hosp. mgr. Lenmed Clinic, Lenasia, South Africa, 1986—; dir. Nat. Assn. Pvt. Hosps., South Africa, 1985-86. Mem. South African Inst. Chartered Accts. Islam. Home: 99 Bdshani Dr Azaadville, Gautang 1750, South Africa Office: Lenmed Clinic Ltd, PO Box 855, Lenasia 1820, South Africa

NANCE, FRANCIS CARTER, health facility administrator, educator, surgeon; b. Manila, Jan. 1, 1932; s. Dana Wilson and Anna (Boatner) N.; m. Patricia L. Terry, Feb. 14, 1959; children: Ellen, Michael, Catherine, John. Pre-med, Vanderbilt U., 1949-52, U. Tenn., 1952-53; MD and MS in Physiology, U. Tenn., 1959. Diplomate Am. Bd. Surgery, Nat. Bd. Med. Examiners. Intern U. Chgo. Clinics, 1959-60; asst. resident Hosp. of U. of Pa., 1960-64, chief resident in surgery, 1964-65; Harrison fellow dept. surg. rsch. U. Pa., 1960-65; instr. La. State U., New Orleans, 1965-67, asst. prof., 1967-69, assoc. prof. surgery and physiology, 1969-73; prof. surgery and physiology La. State U. Med. Ctr., New Orleans, 1973-85; chief burn svc. La. State U. Surg. Svc. Charity Hosp. of La., New Orleans; chmn. dept. surgery St. Barnabas Med. Ctr., Livingston, N.J.; prof. surgery U. Medicine & Dentistry N.J., N.J. Med. Sch., Newark; prof. emeritus La. State U. Med. Ctr.; rschr. in field. Contbr. numerous articles to profl. jours. Am. Cancer Soc. fellow, 1962-63, 63-64; grantee NSF, 1957-59, USPHS, 1964, Edward G. Schleider Edn. Found., 1967, 68, Parke-Davis Co., 1968, 69, Marion Labs., 1970, Eaton Labs., 1970, NIH, 1972, 74, Upjohn Co., 1974, 78, Lilly Co., 1976, McGraw Labs., 1977, Ethicon Co., 1979, Davis and Geck, 1985, 86, Johnson and Johnson, 1987. Mem. AAAS, ACS, Am. Assn. for Surgery of Trauma, Am. Burn Assn., Am. Coll. Emergency Physicians, Am. Gastroent. Assn., Am. Surg. Assn., Assn. Acad. Surgery, Assn. for Gnotobiotics, Assn. Program Dirs. in Surgery, Soc. Internat. Chirurgiae Digestivae, Soc. Surgery of the Alimentary Tract, Soc. Univ. Surgeons, Southern Med. Assn., Southern Soc. Clin. Surgeons, Southern Surg. Assn., Southeastern Surg. Congress, Surg. Assn. La., Surg. Infection Soc., N.J. Acad. Medicine, N.J. Gastroenterology Soc., N.J. Med. Soc., New Orleans Surg. Soc., Orleans Parish Med. Soc., Ravdin-Rhoads Surg. Soc., Soc. Internat. de Chirurgiae Digestivae, Soc. for Surgery of Alimentary Tract, Soc. for Univ. Surgeons, Southeastern Surg. Congress, So. Med. Assn., So. Soc. Clin. Surgeons, So. Surg. Assn., Surg. Assn. La., Surg. Infection Soc. Office: St Barnabas Med Ctr 94 Old Short Hills Rd Livingston NJ 07039-5672

NANCE, MARTHA MCGHEE, rehabilitation nurse; b. Huntington, W.Va., Jan. 24, 1944; d. Orme Winford and Sadie Mae (Dudley) McGhee; m. John Edgar Nance, Mar. 17, 1990; children: Laura Beckner, Suzie Brickey. RN, St. Mary's Sch. Nursing, Huntington, W.Va., 1980; student, Marshall U., Huntington, W.Va., 1978-88. Cert. rehab. nurse, cert. case mgr. Surg. head nurse Huntington Hosp. Inc., nursing supr.; quality assurance dir. Am. Hosp. for Rehab., Huntington, 1988-89, DON, 1989-90; rehab. charge nurse Am. Putnam Nursing and Rehab. Ctr., Hurricane, W.Va., 1990—; mgr. health svcs. Mountain State Blue Cross/Blue Shield, Charleston, W.Va., 1995—, mgr. precert., case mgmt. and med. rev., 1995—. Mem. Assn. for Practitioners in Infection Control. Home: RR 4 Box 100 Hurricane WV 25526-9351

NANKIN, HOWARD RONALD, endocrinologist, educator; b. Bklyn., May 25, 1936; m. Judith B. Okun, June 1, 1960; children: Kenneth, Stephanie, Matthew. Student, Ohio State U., 1954-57; MD, SUNY, Syracuse, 1961. Diplomate Am. Bd. Internal Medicine with subspecialty in endocrinology and metabolism. Resident/fellow Upstate Med. Ctr., Syracuse, 1961-64, U. Utah, Salt Lake City, 1964-66; from instr. to assoc. prof. U. Pitts., 1968-77; prof. medicine U. S.C., Columbia, 1977—, dir. medicine II incl. phys. diagnosis II, 1979-80, dir. phys. diagnosis II, 1980-82, co-dir. phys diagnosis II, 1982-84. Contbr. articles to profl. jours.; editor: The Andrology Report, 1991-93; editl. bd. Jour. Andrology, 1983-86, Jour. Clin. Endocrinology and Metabolism, 1976-80; ad hoc reviewer Jour. Clin. Endocrinology Metabolism, Fertility Sterility, Jour. Andrology, others. Mem. numerous coms. WJB Dorn Vets. Hosp., Columbia, 1977-93. Fellow Am. Coll. Endocrinology; mem. S.C. Med. Assn. (Thomas A. and Shirley W. Roe award 1986), Am. Soc. Andrology (chmn. nominating com. 1979-80, sec. 1980-83, v.p. 1989-90, pres. 1990-91), Soc. for Study of Reprodn., Endocrine Soc. (mem. pubs. com. 1987-90, co-chmn. clin. pub. com. 1989), So. Soc. for Clin. Investigation, Am. Soc. Clin. Investigation, Columbia Med. Soc. (pub. rels. com. 1984-85, program and sci. work com. 1989-90, health access com. 1992-93), Am. Assn. Clin. Endocrinologists (bd. dirs. 1993—, steering com. 1991). Office: Univ of South Carolina Dept Medicine Med Library Bldg #318 Columbia SC 29208

NANKIN, PABLO, surgeon; b. Mexico City, Sept. 4, 1944; came to U.S., 1976; s. Abraham and Sara (Brener) N.; m. Jan. 7, 1967; children: Jody, Stephanie, Jenifer, Tamara. BS, Colegio Cristobal, Mexico, 1960; MD, U. Mexico, 1967. Intern Reddy Meml. Hosp., Montreal, Que., Can., 1965-66; resident in surgery Jewish Gen. Hosp., Montreal, Que., Can., 1968-69, Mt. Sinai Hosp., Chgo., 1969-71; chief resident Michael Reese Hosp., Chgo., 1971-72; fellow in cardiovascular surgery Tex. Heart Inst., Houston, 1972; surgeon specializing in vascular diseases L.A., 1976—. Contbr. articles to profl. jours. Mem. Calif. Med. Assn., Denton Cooley Cardiovascular Soc., Soc. Clin. Vascular Surgery, L.A. County Med. Soc. Address: 21870 Cartagena Dr Boca Raton FL 33428

NANNA, MICHELE, cardiologist, educator; b. Mola di Bari, Puglia, Italy, Mar. 21, 1953; came to U.S., 1981; naturalized, 1985; s. Giovanni and Maria (Francese) N.; m. Barbara Luise McKnight, Aug. 5, 1981 (div. Feb. 1991); children: Michael Giovanni Jr., Anna Maria; m. Nancy J. Konovalov, Nov. 14, 1991; 1 child Giovanni Jacob Michele. MD summa cum laude, U. Bari, Italy, 1978. Lic. physician, Italy, Calif., N.Y. Intern Ospedale Conzorziale, Bari, 1978-81; clin. clerkship U. Soc. Calif. Med. Ctr., L.A., 1982-83; instr. medicine, fellow in cardiovascular disease U. So. Calif., 1983-86; asst. prof. medicine U. Rochester, N.Y., 1986-88, Albert Einstein Coll. Medicine, Bronx, N.Y., 1988-94; assoc. prof. of med., 1994—; dir. care unit Bronx Mcpl. Hosp. Ctr., 1988-92; dir. lab. Montefiore Med. Ctr., Bronx, N.Y., 1988—; cardiology cons. Monroe Community Hosp., Rochester, 1987-88; mem. coms. Bronx Mcpl. Hosp. Ctr., 1988—, chmn. com., 1990-92. Editor jour. Ultrasound in Medicine and Biology, 1986—; editor-in-chief Jour. Cardiovascular Diagnosis and Procedures, 1993—; contbr. chpts. to books and articles to profl. jours. Grantee NIH, 1987, Whitaker Found., Genetech Inc., Bristol-Myers Squibb, Inc. Mem. AMA, Am. Heart Assn., Am. Coll. Cardiology, N.Y. Athletic Club. Republican. Roman Catholic. Office: Albert Einstein Coll Med Montefiore Med Ctr 111 E 210th St Bronx NY 10467-2490

NANTZ, WILLIAM C., hospital administrator; b. Mannford, Okla., Dec. 11, 1935; s. Floyd and Evelyn (Roop) N.; m. Nellieree Knowles, Jan. 23, 1960. BS, Okla. State U., 1959; MS, U. Ark., 1975. Commd. 2d lt. USAF, 1959, advanced through grades to lt. col., 1981; hosp. adminstr. AFB Hosp. Athens, Greece, 1972-75; asst. dir. medicine and edn. Hdqrs. Aero Med. div. Brooks AFB, San Antonio, 1975-79; comdr. 2d aero. med. sq. Hdqrs., Frankfurt, Fed. Republic Germany, 1979-83; dir. edn. and health care support Hdqr. Areo Med. div. Brooks AFB, San Antonio, 1983-85; med. plans officer Hdqr., Seoul, South Korea, 1985-87; retired USAF, 1987; med. cons. San Antonio, 1987-89; exec. v.p. Neurology Svcs. Inc./Neurentox Internat. Inc., 1989-92; adminstr. Selma Med. Assocs., Miami, Fla., 1992-93; COO Comty. Health of South Dade, Inc., Miami, 1993—. Contbr. articles to med. publs. Named to Outstanding Young Am., 1970, Notable Am. of Bicentennial Era, 1976. Mem. Am. Coll. Health Care Execs. Republican. Methodist. Home: 5178 NW 103rd Ave Miami FL 33178-3202

NAPARSTEK, NATHAN, school psychologist; b. Forest Hills, N.Y., Aug. 1, 1956; s. Chaim and Chana N.; m. Denise Kerman, May 1, 1983; children: Eli, Rachel, Joseph. PhD, SUNY, Albany, 1988. Lic. psychologist. Sch. psychologist Beacon City Schs., N.Y., 1981-83, Schenectady City schs., 1984—; adj. prof. Coll. St. Rose, 1989-92; pvt. practice, Latham, 1991—. Author: The Learning Solution: What To Do If Your Child Has Trouble with Schoolwork, 1995. Mem. APA, NASP. Home: 906 Northumberland Dr Niskayuna NY 12309

NAPARSTEK, YAAKOV, physician, researcher; b. Ramat-Gan, Israel, Sept. 27, 1948; s. Shmuel and Chana (Moussak) N.; m. Ella Srebnik; children: Daphna, Sharon. MD, Hebrew U., Jerusalem, 1972. Diplomate Israel Bd. Internal Medicine, Israel Bd. Clin. Immunology and Allergy, Israel Bd. Rheumatology. Leiferman chair rheumatology, 1988—; prof. medicine Hadassah U. Hosp., Jerusalem, 1993—, head clin. immunology and allergy unit, 1995—, head Clin. Immunology and Rheumatology Ctr.; rsch. fellow Weizmann Inst., Rehovot, Israel, 1981, Tufts U., Boston, 1983-85; vis. prof. NIH, Bethesda, Md., 1991-92. Contbr. articles to profl. jours. Maj. Israel Def. Forces. Recipient Internat. Rsch. fellowship Fogarty Internat. Ctr., NIH, 1983-85, Outstanding Physician award 40th Anniversary of State of Israel, 1988, Fogarty award for vis. scientist, NIH, 1991. Teva award for rsch. in life scis., 1993, numerous sci. rsch. grants. Office: Hadassah Univ Hosp, PO Box 12000, Jerusalem Israel

NAPIER, SANDRA LYNN, medical and surgical nurse; b. Seco, Ky., Apr. 14, 1954; d. Luther and Edna (Frazier) Joseph; m. Clifton Jerome Napier; children: Brian Jerome, Jimmy Ray. LPN, Letcher County Area Vocat. Tech., 1985; attended, Hazard and Southeast C.C., 1991-94. LPN Whitesburg (Ky.) Med. Clinic, 1986—, dept. head internal medicine, 1993—, LPN, dept. head, mid-level practitioner, 1994—. Home: HC8S Box 2208 Premium KY 41845 Office: Whitesburg Med Clinic 107 E Main St Whitesburg KY 41858

NAPIONTEK, MAREK MAKSYMILIAN, orthopedic surgeon; b. Poznań, Poland, Jan. 6, 1955; s. Maksymilian and Urszula Halina (Ziórkowska) N.; m. Emilia Stella Szumińska, June 1, 1985; children: Maria, Barbara, Wojciech. MD, Karol Marcinkowski U. Med. Sci, Poznań, 1980, PhD, 1988. Intern K. Marcinkowski U. Med. Scis., Poznan; resident dept. ortho. Inst. Ortho. & Rehab., Poznan, asst. lectr., 1980-89, lectr., head pediat. ortho. ward, 1989—. Contbr. articles to profl. publs. Recipient Sci. award Polish Min. of Health, 1990. Mem. Polish Soc. Orthopedics and Traumatology, European Pediatric Orthopedic Soc., Lions. Roman Catholic.

NAPLES, JOHN DANIEL, gynecologist, educator; b. Buffalo, Aug. 23, 1934; s. John Dominic and Anne Gabrielle (Sorgi) N.; A.B., Canisius Coll., 1955; M.D., Georgetown U., 1959; m. Jeanne Migliore, June 28, 1958; children: Maria, Christopher, Jill. Intern, Buffalo Gen. Hosp., 1959-60; resident in ob-gyn SUNY, Buffalo, 1960-64; practice medicine specializing in gynecology, infertility and microsurgery, Buffalo, 1964-66, 68—; mem. staff Erie County Med. Center, Kenmore Mercy, Sisters of Charity, Children's hosps.; assoc. prof. SUNY Med. Sch. at Buffalo. Mem. bd. regents Canisius Coll. Served with M.C. USN, 1966-68. Recipient Pediatric medal Georgetown U., 1959, Physician Recognition award AMA, 1970, 84, 87, 90, 93; diplomate Am. Bd. Ob-Gyn. Mem. Am., N.Y. State, Erie County (N.Y.) med. socs., Am. Coll. Obstetricians and Gynecologists, ACS, Am. Cancer Soc., Western N.Y. Obstetrical-Gynecol. Soc., Am. Soc. Gynecol. Laparoscopists, Soc. Reproductive Surgeons. Roman Catholic. Contbr. articles to med. publs. Home: 173 Hidden Ridge Common Williamsville NY 14221 Office: 1000 Youngs Rd Williamsville NY 14221

NAPOLI, PETER JOSEPH, cardiothoracic surgeon; b. Ft. Smith, Ark., Nov. 16, 1955; s. Joseph Francis and Lucy Patricia (Rinaldo) N. MD, Georgetown U., 1985. Diplomate Am. Bd. Surgery, Am. Bd. Thoracic Surgery. Rose through ranks to lt. col. U. S. Army; resident in gen. surgery Tripler Army Med. Ctr., Honolulu, 1985-90; from fellow in cardiothoracic surgery to staff cardiothoracic surgeon Brooke Army Med. Ctr., San Antonio, 1991-96. Fellow Am. Coll. Surgeons. Office: Dept Cardiothoracic Surgery Brooke Army Med Ctr Fort Sam Houston TX 78234-6200 and: Shannon Clinic Dept Cardiothoracic Surgery San Angelo TX 76902

NAPOLIELLO, DANIEL ANDREW, nursing administrator; b. Omaha, Sept. 27, 1944; Ceasare Dan and Therese Mary (Sierszynski) N.; m. Sally Ann Rodak, Jan. 7, 1967; children: John, Ann Marie, Michael. Diploma in nursing, St. Joseph Hosp., Omaha, 1965; BS in Nursing, U. S.C., 1975; MEd, Chapman Coll., 1977. Commd. 2nd lt. U.S. Army, 1964; advanced through grades to commdr. Nurse Corps U.S. Army, 1994; chief nurse 8th combat support hosp. Nurse Corps U.S. Army, Fort Ord, Calif., 1975-77, resigned, 1977; commd. officer USPHS, 1977-94; retired, 1994; advanced through grades to comdr. USPHS, 1988; dir. nursing Indian Hosp. USPHS, Rosebud, S.D., 1977-78, Winnebago, Nebr., 1984-87; assoc. hosp. dir. nursing edn. USPHS, Balt., 1978-81, evening supr. nursing, coord. quality assurance, 1981-84; retired, 1994; area hosp. nursing cons. Phoenix Area Indian Health Svc., 1987-94; nurse cons. Glendale, 1994—; quality mgmt. specialist Intergroup of Ariz., Peoria, 1996—; mem. USPHS Nursing Continuing Edn. Rev. Com., Rockville, Md., 1979-81, 88-92, Indian Health Svc. Nursing Profl. Splty. Group, Rockville, 1984-90, Ind. Health Svc. Coun. of Nursing Svcs., 1987-94, chmn., 1988-92. Contbr. articles to profl. jours. Asst. scoutmaster Sioux coun. Boy Scouts Am., 1977-78, scoutmaster Balt. coun., 1978-81, asst. dist. commr. Prairie Gold area coun. 1982-87, Theodore Roosevelt coun., 1987-93, chmn. dist. health and safety com., 1978-81, mem. health careers subcom. nat. exploring com., 1989-94, dist. commr. Grand Canyon coun., 1993—; instr. CPR, ARC, 1982-87; mem. Hebr. Hist. Soc., Union Pacific R.R. Hist. Soc. Recipient citation USPHS, 1987, commendation medal, 1989, Chief Nurse Office award, 1991, Outstanding Svc. medal, 1992, Nursing Excellence award for Nursing Practice, 1991, Wood Badge Boy Scouts Am., 1981, St. George Emblem, 1982, 3 Bead Wood Badge, 1989, Disting. Commr. award, 1991, Silver Beaver award, 1992, Surgeon Gen.'s Exemplary Svc. medal USPHS, 1993, Dirs. award for Excellence and EEO Excellence award, Indian Health Svc., Phoenix, 1994. Mem. ANA, Nebr. Nurses Assn., Balt. Chpt. Commd. Officers Assn. of USPHS (nurse officers rep. 1980, v.p. 1981), Aberdeen Area Coun. on Nursing (pres. 1986-87), Nat. Model Railroaders Assn., Nat. Scout Collectors Soc., Camerail Club, Commd. Officers Assn. (sec.-treas. Phoenix chpt. 188-89, v.p. Phoenix chpt. 1990-91, pres. 1991-92, nat. del. 1987, 88, 92). Democrat. Roman Catholic. Home: 8880 West X Christopher Michael Lane Peoria AZ 85345

NAPOLITANO, LENA MARIE, surgeon, educator; b. Waterbury, Conn., Oct. 31, 1957; d. Carmine and Mary (Dell'Anno) N. BA, Boston U., 1979; MD, George Washington U., 1984. Diplomate Nat. Bd. Med. Examiners, Am. Bd. Surgery. Rsch. asst. dept. surgery Yale U. Med. Ctr., New Haven, 1979-80; resident in gen. surgery George Washington U. Med. Ctr., Washington, 1984-87, sr. resident in gen. surgery, asst. in surgery, 1988-89, chief resident in gen. surgery, clin. instr. in surgery, 1989-90; clin. and rsch. fellow dept. anesthesia and surgery Mass. Gen. Hosp./Harvard Med. Sch., Boston, 1987-88; instr., fellow in surg. critical care and trauma U. N.C. Hosps., Chapel Hill, 1990-91; trauma rsch. fellow dept. surgery U. N.C., Chapel Hill, 1991-92, attending in surgery, trauma and critical care, 1991-92; asst. prof. surgery and anesthesia U. Mass. Med. Ctr., Boston, 1992-95, dir. surg. critical care, co-dir. surg. ICU, trauma svcs., 1992-95; asst. prof. surgery U. Md. Med. Ctr. and Balt. VA Med. Ctr., 1995—; dir. surg. critical care, nutrition support svcs. U. Md. Med. Ctr. and Balt. VA Med. Ctr., 1995—; mem. med. adv. bd. Innova Home Therapies, Worcester, Mass., 1992-95; mem. med. svcs. com. Ctrl. Mass.EMS Corp., Worcester, 1992-95; mem. disaster med. assistance team Internat. Inst. for Disaster and Emergency Medicine, U. Mass. Med. Ctr., 1993—; rschr., lectr. in field. Contbr. articles to profl. publs., chpts. to books; reviewer Critical Care Medicine, Jour. Intensive Care Medicine. Conn. State scholar, 1975-79, Davis & Geck scholar, 1991; recipient Outstanding Resident award Holy Cross Hosp., 1988, Surg. Resident award Alpha Omega Alpha, 1989; grantee U. Mass. Med. Ctr., 1993, Burroughs Wellcome, Sterling Winthrop Inc., Soc. Critical Care Medicine, Cetus Corp., Alpha-Beta Tech., Inc., Healthcare Innovation. Fellow ACS (Harry Zehner Jr. Meml. Travelling Fellowship award Wash. chpt. 1989), Am. Coll. Chest Physicians; mem. AMA, Assn. for Acad. Surgery (mem. exec. coun. 1993—, mem. nominations com. 1994—), Surg. Infection Soc. (mem. edn. and fellowship com. 1995—), Assn. Women Surgeons (specialty rep. for trauma and critical care), Nathan Womack Surg. Soc., Soc. Critical Care Medicine, Worcester Med. Soc., Am. Med. Women's Assn., Ea. Assn. for Surgery of Trauma, Am. Soc. Parenteral and Enteral Nutrition, Am. Burn Assn., Shock Soc., Assn. VA Surgeons, Phi Beta Kappa. Office: Balt VA Med Ctr/ U Md Med Ctr 10 N Greene St Baltimore MD 21201

NARA, BONNIE A., psychologist; b. Connellsville, Pa., Jan. 29, 1949; d. Edward G. and Edith R. (Fasson) N.; m. James V. Morley, Oct. 28, 1989. BA with honors, Seton Hill Coll., 1970; MEd, Calif. U. Pa., 1971, MS with highest honors, 1980; PhD, U. W.Va., 1981. Cert. sch. psychologist, Pa. Counselor Uniontown (Pa.) Area Sch. Dist., 1974-86; psychologist Ctr. for Motivation and Achievement, Pitts., 1986—. Chair pers. com. Twin Trees, Inc., Connellsville, 1979-85, chair, 1982-83; mem. Westmoreland County Prevention of Child Abuse, Greensburg, Pa., 1983-86; mem. Immaculate conception Ch., Connellsville. Mem. NEA, AAUW, Am. Counseling and Psychology Assn., Pa. Edn. Assn., Pa. Psychol. Assn., Greater Uniontown Area C. of C. (edn. coun.), Our Lady of Mt. Carmel Club (Connellsville), Lionness Lodge. Republican. Roman Catholic.

NARAD, JOAN STERN, psychiatrist; b. N.Y.C., June 21, 1943; d. Victor and Grete (Metzger) S.; m. Richard M. Narad; children: Christine, Laurie, Michael. BA, NYU, 1964; MD, Woman's Med. Coll., Pa., 1968. Diplomate Am. Bd. Psychiatry, Am. Bd Child Psychiatry. Intern pediatrics Stanford (Calif.) U. Hosp., 1968-69; resident adult psychiat. Med. Coll., Phila., 1969-71, chief resident in child psychiatry, 1971-73; grad. in psychoanalysis and child psychoanalysis Phila. Psychoanalytic Inst., 1978; practice medicine specializing in child and adolescent psychiatry Westport, Conn., 1979—; chief Adolescent and Young Adult Svc., Silver Hill Found., New Canaan, Conn., 1980-84, 89-93, sr. adolescent cons., 1993-94; unit chief Riverview Hosp. for Children and Youth, Middletown, Conn., 1994—; cons. Cath. Home Girls, Phila., 1971-78, Germantown Friends Sch., 1973-79; asst. prof. Child Psychiat. Med. Coll. Pa., 1975-79; asst. clin. prof. Yale Child Study Ctr., 1979-92, assoc. clin. prof., 1992—. Fellow NIMH, 1968. Fellow Am. Acad. Child and Adolescent Psychiat.; mem. Am. Psychiat. Assn., AMA, Alumnae Assn. Med. Coll. Pa., Am. Psychoanalytic Assn., Western New Eng. Psychoanalytic Soc., Conn. Coun. Child Psychiatry. Home and Office: 3 Colony Rd Westport CT 06880-3703

NARAMORE, JAMES JOSEPH, family practice physician, educator; b. Gillette, Wyo., Nov. 29, 1949; s. Kenneth Chester and Joan (Biggerstaff) N.; m. Karen Rae Buttermore, July 9, 1972; children: Lindsay, Marissa, Jessica, Marcus. BA with highest achievement in Biology, John Brown U., Siloam Springs, Ark., 1972; MD with family practice honors, U. Utah, 1977.

Diplomate Am. Bd. Family Practice. Resident in family practice U. Nebr., Omaha, 1977-80, chief resident; pvt. practice, Gillette, 1981—; mem. staff Campbell County Meml. Hosp., Gillette, 1980—, chief staff, 1986, chief dept. family practice, 1990-91; instr. dept. human medicine U. Wyo., 1983-86, clin. assoc. prof. family practice, 1986—; ptnr., co-founder Med. Arts Lab., Gillette, 1981—; med. dir. Campbell County Detention Ctr., 1988—; med. dir. Pioneer Manor Nursing Home, Gillette, 1989—; aviation med. examiner FAA, Oklahoma City, 1986—; cons. on occupational medicine to numerous industries, Campbell County, 1986—. Charter mem. Gillette Area Leadership Inst., 1986-87; chmn. missions com. Grace Bible Ch., Gillette, 1983—, chmn. bd. elders, 1989—. Mem. Am. Acad. Family Physicians, Wyo. Med. Soc., Campbell County Med. Soc. (pres. 1983-84), Gillette C. of C. (bd. dirs. 1987-90), Toastmasters (pres. Gillette 1992, Competent Toastmaster award 1986—). Republican. Home: 1214 Hilltop Ct Gillette WY 82718-5625 Office: Family Health 407 S Medical Arts Ct Ste D Gillette WY 82716-3372

NARANG, RAVINDER M., physician; b. Oct. 11, 1938; arrived in U.S., 1967; s. Des Raj and Krishna Wati (Sethi) N.; m. Sudershan Choudhry, Mar. 11, 1966; children: Malini, Vandna. MBBS, Amritsar Medical Coll., Amritsar, India, 1960; MD, Delhi Univ., Delhi, India, 1967. Diplomate Am. Bd. Internal Medicine, Am. Bd. Cardiovascular Diseases. Intern Medical Coll., Amritsar, India, 1960-61; resident Irwin Hosp., New Delhi, 1960; resident surgeon Safdarjang Hosp., New Delhi, 1961-62, registrar, 1962-65; registrar G.B. Pant Hosp. Maulana-Azad Medical Coll., New Delhi, 1965-67; resident Beekman Downtown Hosp., N.Y.C., 1967-68; sr. resident medicine Coney Island Hosp., Bklyn., 1968-69; chief resident Coney Island Hosp., 1969-70; fellow in medicine Coll. Medicine N.J., Newark, 1970-72; chief sect. cardiology Gen. Hosp. Ctr. Passaic, 1984-86, Beth Israel Hosp., 1985-87; chief cardiac catheterization lab. Gen. Hosp. Ctr. Passaic, 1987-88, 1991—; instr. in internal medicine Albert Einstein Coll. Medicine, N.Y., 1972-75, asst. prof. medicine, 1975-78; attending internal medicine, Passaic Gen. Hosp., 1978, Beth Israel Hosp., 1978, St. Mary's Hosp., 1978, St. Joseph's Hosp., 1979; assoc. internal medicine, Hackensack Medical Ctr., 1994; chairperson of exec. com., v.p. medical staff Gen. Hosp. Ctr. Passaic, 1993, 94, pres. medical staff, 1995, 96. Contbr. numerous articles to profl. jours. Active Arya Samaj Bergan Passaic County, 1985—. Recipient Man of Yr. award Passaic Heart Found., 1986. Fellow Soc. Cardiac Angiography and Interventions, Am. Coll. Chest Physicians, Am. Coll. Angiology, Am. Coll. Cardiology, Am. Heart Assn. (coun. on clinical cardiology), Acad. Medicine N.J.; mem. Am. Fedn. Clinical Rsch., Am. Soc. Echocardiography, Passaic and N.Y. Heart Assn., Passaic County Medical Soc., N.J. Medical Soc., N.J. Soc. Interventional Cardiology. Office: Ravinder M Narang MD 721 Clifton Ave Clifton NJ 07013

NARDI, THOMAS JAMES, psychologist; b. N.Y.C., Feb. 27, 1949. BA, Manhattan Coll., 1970; MS, St. John's U., 1972, PhD, 1977. Lic. psychologist, N.Y., N.J. Psychologist Bronx (N.Y.) Children's Psychiat. Ctr., 1973-80, Rockland County Bd. Coop. Edn. Svcs., N.Y.C., 1980-81, St. Dominic's Home, Blauvelt, N.Y., 1981-82; clin. dir. N.Y. Ctr. for Eclectic Cognitive Behavior Therapy, Nanuet, N.Y., 1982—; adj. prof. Pace U., Pleasantville, N.Y., 1979—, L.I. U. Mercy Coll., Dobbs Ferry, N.Y., 1978—. Co-author: (play) Somethings You Remember, 1986. Recipient Gran Croce al Merito del Lavoro Italian Acad. for Social and Econ. Improvement, 1985, George Stewart Meml. award for Literary Contbns. to Field of Hypnosis Assn. to Advance Ethic Hypnosis, 1982. Mem. Internat. Acad. Eclectic Psychotherapy, Am. Bd. Sexology, Am. Acad. Behavioral Medicine.

NASH, BARRY E., ophthalmologist, physician; b. N.Y., Apr. 11, 1940; s. Marcus and Martha (Cooper); m. Murial Ellen Munson, Oct. 17, 1968; children: Eric, Michael, Eileen, Heather. BS, George Wash. Univ., D.C., 1958-62; MD, N.Y. Med. Coll., N.Y., 1962-65. Diplomate Am. Bd. Ophthalmology, Am. Bd. Surgery. Mem. staff Fawcett Meml. Hosp., Port Charlotte, Fla., 1975—, St. Joseph Hosp., Port Charlotte, Fla., 1975—, Charlotte Regional Hosp., Punta Gorda, Fla., 1975—; bd. dirs. Fawcett, Columbia, HCA, Port Charlotte, Fla., 1975—, chmn. Physician Hosp. Orgn., 1993—. Maj. USAF, 1991-93, AK. Fellow ACS; mem. Am. Bd. Opthalmology, Fla. Soc. Opthalmology. Republican. Office: Eye Assocs Charlotte County 2595 Harbor Blvd Port Charlotte FL 33952

NASH, DAVID, physician; b. Syracuse, N.Y., Oct. 15, 1929; s. Sam and Pearl Nash; m. Ellen C. Nash, Sept. 2, 1956; children: Stephen, Robert. BA magna cum laude, NYU, 1950, MD, 1953. Diplomate Am. Bd. Internal Medicine. Intern Mt. Sinai, N.Y.C., 1953; asst. resident in medicine Univ. Hosp., Syracuse; resident in medicine Mt. Sinai, N.Y.C.; med. rsch. fellow in cardiology Beth Israel Hosp. and Harvard Med. Sch., Boston, 1959; clin. prof. medicine Upstate Med. Ctr., Syracuse, 1985; mem. staff St. Joseph's Hosp., Syracuse; pres. DTN Clin. Rsch. Lab. Ltd., Syracuse, 1975—; manuscript reviewer JAMA, Annals of Internal Medicine, Am. Jour. Cardiology, Jour. of the Am. Coll. of Cardiology, Postgrad. Medicine, Geriatrics, 1980-94; presenter Am. Heart Assn., Am. Coll. Cardiology, N.Y. Acad. Medicine, Hugh Lofland Ann. Conf. on Arterial Wall Metabolism, Cardiovascular Risk Factor Internat. Meeting. Contbr. over 150 articles to profl. jours. Maj. USAF, 1955-57. Fellow ACP, Am. Coll. Cardiology, Am. Coll. Nutrition, Am. Heart Assn. (coun. on arteriosclerosis, coun. on epidemiology), Onondaga County Med. Soc. Office: 600 E Genesee St Syracuse NY 13202-3108

NASH, DAVID BRET, physician; b. N.Y.C., Nov. 15, 1955; s. Albert J. and Charlotte Nash; m. Esther Jean Nash; children: Rachel and Leah (twins), Jacob. BA, Vassar Coll., 1977; MD, U. Rochester, 1981; MBA, U. Pa., 1986. Internship The Graduate Hosp., U. Pa., 1981-82, residency, 1982-84; med. dir. Health Evaluation Ctr., Hosp. U. Pa., Phila., 1988-90; dir. health policy and clin. outcomes Thomas Jefferson U. Hosp., Phila., 1990—. Editor: Future Practice Alternatives, 1987, Providing Quality Care, 1989. Bd. dirs. Delaware Valley Child Care Coun., Phila., 1988—. Fellow ACP; mem. Phi Beta Kappa. Office: Thomas Jefferson U 621 Curtis Bldg 1015 Walnut St Philadelphia PA 19107-5005

NASH, J. FRANK, pharmacologist, toxicologist; b. Indpls., July 11, 1958; s. J. Frank and Arlene Jean (Kandel) N.; m. Patricia Marie Anselmo, June 15, 1991. BS, Purdue U., 1981, MS, 1984, PhD, 1986. Postdoctoral fellow Case Western Res. U., Cleve., 1986-88, asst. prof. psychiatry and neurosci., 1988-92; toxicologist Procter & Gamble Co., Cin., 1992—. Contbr. articles to profl. jours. Recipient Young Investigators award, Nat. Alliance for Rsch. on Schizophrenia and Depression, 1988, 90. Mem. Am. Soc. Pharmacology and Exptl. Therapeutics, Soc. for Neurosci., Sigma Xi, Rho Chi. Presbyterian. Office: Procter & Gamble Co Sharon Woods HB Bldg 11511 Reed Hartman Hwy Cincinnati OH 45241-2421

NASH, JOYCE DONOVAN, psychologist, health educator, author; b. Carnegie, Pa., Aug. 2, 1940; d. James Stanley and Eleanor M. (Schafer) Donovan; m. John Nash, Sept. 10, 1960 (div. 1964); m. Morgan W. White, Feb. 6, 1983. BS, So. Ill. U., 1972; MA, Stanford U., 1975, PhD, 1977, Pacific Grad. Sch. of Psychology, 1993. Dir. tng. Weight Watchers, San Francisco, 1979-81; health educator Carmel Profl. Assocs., Calif., 1983-85; cons. in field. Author: Taking Charge of Your Weight and Well Being, 1978, Taking Charge of Your Smoking, 1981; (audiocassette album) Taking Charge of Health, 1984, Maximize Your Body Potential, 1986, Now That You've Lost It, 1992, What Your Doctor Can't Tell You About Cosmetic Surgery, 1995. Recipient Nat. Research Service award Dept. Health and Human Services, 1978-79. Mem. Am. Psychol. Assn., Soc. Behavioral Medicine, Assn. Advancement of Behavioral Medicine, Calif. Psychol. Assn. Republican. Office: 770 Welch Rd # 161 Palo Alto CA 94304 also: 999 sutter St San Francisco CA 94109

NASH, PEGGY BRICKSON, social worker; b. St. Louis, Aug. 28, 1947; d. Clyde Wilbur and Pauline Josephine (McGennis) Brickson; m. Gary Stephen Nash, Sept. 4, 1971; children: Stephen Joseph, John Andrew. BA, Baylor U., 1969; MSW, Smith Coll., 1971. Lic. master social worker; advanced clin. practitioner, Tex.; ACSW. Social worker Meth. Home Child Guidance Ctr., Waco, Tex., 1971-73; social worker Timberlawn Psychiatry Hosp., Dallas, 1973-82, asst. dir. of social work dept., 1975-82; pvt. practice in psychotherapy Dallas, 1975—; exec. com., bd. dirs. Herrin House, Dallas; clin. instr. Smith Coll. Sch. for Social Work, Northampton, Mass., 1979-80. Bd. dirs. Dallas Assn. for Parent Edn., 1978-79, adv. bd., 1979-81; chair family life com. 1st Bapt. Ch., Richardson, Tex., 1988. Mem. NASW (state rep. 1978-79, chair Dallas unit 1978-79, chair pvt. practice com. of Tex. 1992-93), Am. Assn. of Marriage and Family Therapists (clin. mem.). Home: 9307 Faircrest Dallas TX 75238 Office: 7557 Rambler Rd Ste 750 Dallas TX 75231

NASH, ROBERT ARNOLD, pharmaceutical engineering educator, consultant; b. Bklyn., July 6, 1930; s. Sol and Anne (Finkel) N.; m. Joan Brill, Dec. 21, 1952; children: Kevin J., Ellen G., Michael B. BS in Pharmacy, L.I. U., 1952; MS in Pharm. Chemistry, Rutgers U., 1954; PhD in Pharmaceutics, U. Conn., 1958. Rsch. assoc. Merck Sharpe & Dohme, Westpoint, Pa., 1957-60; project leader Lederle Labs., Pearl River, N.Y., 1960-67, mgr. pharm. R & D, 1967-76; dir. pharm. devel. Purdue Frederick Co., Norwalk, Conn., 1976-81; assoc. prof. pharm. engrng. St. John's U., Jamaica, N.Y., 1981—; cons. Orentreich Found., N.Y.C., 1981—. Co-editor: Pharmaceutical Process Validation, 1984, 93; mem. editl. bd. Jour. Validation Technology; contbr. chpts. to books and articles to profl. jours. Mem. Ramapo (N.Y.) Zoning Bd. Appeals, 1967-90, chmn., 1990-91. Mem. Am. Chem. Soc., Am. Assn. Pharm. Scientists, Acad. Pharm. Scis., Internat. Soc. Pharm. Engrng. Home: 249 Westervelt Ln Mahwah NJ 07430-3229 Office: St John's U Grand Central And Utopia Pky Jamaica NY 11439-0002

NASRALLAH, HENRY ATA, psychiatry researcher, educator; b. Apr. 30, 1947; came to U.S., 1972; s. Ata George and Rose G. (Yameen) N.; m. Amelia C. Tebsherani, June 6, 1972; children: Ramzy George, Rima Alice. BS in Biology, Am. U. of Beirut, 1967; MD, Am. U Coll Medicine, Beirut-Lebanon, 1971. Intern Am. U. Med. Ctr., Beirut, Lebanon, 1972; resident in psychiatry U. Rochester, N.Y., 1975; rsch. assoc. NIMH, Washington, 1975-77; asst. prof. psychiatry U. Calif., San Diego, 1977-79; from assoc. prof. to prof. psychiatry U. Iowa, Iowa City, 1979-85; prof., chmn. dept. psychiatry Ohio State U., Columbus, 1985—; staff psychiatrist VA Med. Ctr., La Jolla, Calif., 1977-79; chief psychiatry svc. VA Med. Ctr., Iowa City, 1979-85. Editor: (5 vol. book series) Handbook of Schizophrenia, 1986-90; co-editor: NMR Spectroscopy in Psychiatric Brain Disorders, 1995; editor-in-chief Schizophrenia Rsch., 1987—, Psychiatry Watch, 1996—; author and co-author over 200 published articles, 1976—. Pres. Psychiat. Rsch. Found. of Columbus, 1985—; mem. Alliance for the Mentally Ill, Columbus, 1987—. Recipient VA grants, 1979-84, NIMH, 1983—. Fellow Am. Psychiat. Assn. (coun. on rsch.), Am. Coll. Neuropsychopharmacology (chmn. pubs. com. 1992-95), Am. Coll. Psychiatrists (Deans Award com. 1996—), Am. Acad. Clin. Psychiatrists (pres. 1989-90), Soc. Biol. Psychiatry (awards com. 1988-90). Office: Ohio State U Dept Psychiatry 1670 Upham Dr Columbus OH 43210-1252

NASS, DEANNA ROSE, counselor, professor; b. N.Y.C., June 30, 1939; d. Nat. and Jean (Mark) Spitzer. BFA, U. Chgo., 1961, MFA, 1964; MA, NYU, 1969; MPhil, PhD, Columbia U., 1979. Art tchr. N.Y.C. Bd. Edn., 1964-68; assoc. prof., counselor Dept. Student Svcs., CUNY, 1968—; dir. counseling svcs. Coll. of S.I./CUNY, 1992—. Editor: The Rape Victim, 1977; contbr. articles to profl. jours. Recipient Full Tuition Scholarship U. Chgo., 1964; Grantee Drug Edn. Program, 1970-71; recipient Cert. Recognition U.S. Dept. Labor, 1976. Mem. Am. Assn. U. Profs., Phi Delta Kappa, CUNY Acad. for Humanities & Scis. Home: 225 E 73rd St New York NY 10021-3654

NASS, JACK, psychiatrist; b. Paris, Jan. 7, 1948; came to U.S., 1953; s. Joseph and Rose (Mauer) N.; m. Marsha Harriette Weiner, Dec. 17, 1973; children: Rachel Lynn, Evan Holland. BS, CCNY, 1969; MD, Free U. Brussels, 1975. Diplomate Am. Bd. Forensic Examiners, Am. Bd. psychiatry and Neurology with added qualifications in geriatric psychiatry. Sub-intern Maimonides Med. Ctr., Bklyn., 1974; rotating intern. L.I. Jewish Hosp., 1975; resident in psychiatry Hillside Med. Ctr., New Hyde, N.Y., 1976-79; Lectr. psychiatry L.I. Jewsih Hosp. Liaison and Consultation Div., New Hyde Park, N.Y., 1969—; attending psychiatrist Wintrhop-U. Hosp., Mineola, N.Y., 1969-86; adj. prof. psychiatry Stony Brook Med. Sch., Stony Brook, N.Y., 1981—; cons. psychiatrist Franklin Gen. Hosp., Valley Stream, N.Y., 1982-94; chmn. dept. psychiatry Hempstead Gen. Hosp., Hempstead, N.Y., 1989-93; pres.-elect med. staff Hempstead (N.Y.) Gen. Hosp., 1987-89, pres. contitution and bylaws com., 1987-93; psychiatric cons. sleep disorder clinic Winthrop-Univ. Hosp., 1988—; med. svc. dir. geriatrics South Oaks Hosp., 1994-95. Bd. dirs. Hebrew Acad. of Nassau County, 1992—. Mem. Am. Psychiat. Assn., Nassau County Psychiat. Soc. (bd. dirs. 1991-93), Am. Psychosomatic Soc., Am. Assn. for Geriatric Psychiatry, N.Y. Acad. Scis. Fellow APA; mem. Am. Psychiat. Assn., Nassau County Psychiat. Soc. (bd. dirs. 1991-93), Am. Psychosomatic Soc., Am. Assn. for Geriatric Psychiatry, N.Y. Acad. Scis., Am. Acad. psychiatry & the Law. Office: 350 W Main St Babylon NY 11702-3417

NASSER, MOES ROSHANALI, optometrist; b. Sumve, Mwanza, Tanzania, Jan. 20, 1956; came to U.S., 1976; s. Roshanali Hassanali and Rehmat (Kara) N.; m. Anar Hemnani, Dec. 20, 1979; children: Faria, Sarah. BS in Optometry, U. Houston, 1980, OD, 1982. Cons., mgr. optometric practice Houston, 1984—; mem. adv. bd. Houston Eye Assocs.; cons. in field. Vol. Agakhan Ch., Tanzania, 1966-71; sec. Agakhan Ch. health com., 1976-82, mem. ch. coun., Houston, 1981-82, mem. coun. for S.W., 1987-90, chmn. edn. bd. for Southwest, 1987-90, Agakhan Found.; hon. sec. Shia Imami Ismaili Tarigah and Religious Edn. Bd. U.S., 1990-93; convenor S.W. U.S.A. for Inst. of Ismaili Studies, London. Mem. Harris County Optometric Soc., Tex. Optometric Assn., Tex. Assn. for Optometrists, Am. Optometric Assn., Alta. Optometric Assn., Can. Assn. Optometrists. Office: 1524 Willowbrook Mall Houston TX 77070-5715

NASSER, WILLIAM KALEEL, cardiologist; b. Terre Haute, Ind., June 3, 1933; s. T.K. and Maude Nasser; m. Wanda Hurst, Dec. 23, 1958; children: Teresa, Tom, Tony. BS, Ind. State U., 1957; MD, Ind. U., Indpls., 1961. Intern Ind. U. Sch. Medicine, Indpls., 1962-63, resident, 1962-64, USPHS trainee in cardiology, 1964-66, from instr. to clin. assoc. prof. medicine, 1966-84, clin. prof. medicine, 1984—; dir. cardiac catheterization lab. St. Vincent Hosp., Indpls., 1973-79, also cons. cardiologist; cons. cardiologist Community Hosp., Indpls.; mem. Indpls. bd. assocs. Rose-Hulman Inst. Tech., 1986—. Contbr. chpts. to books, articles to profl. jours. Bd. dirs. Ind. Pub. Health Found., 1985-89, Ind. Heart Inst., 1986—; trustee Ind. State U., 1983-87. Cpl., U.S. Army, 1953-55, Korea. Recipient Vital award Marion County chpt. Am. Heart Assn., 1980, others. Fellow ACP, Am. Coll. Cardiology, Am. Heart Assn. (coun. on clin. cardiology); mem. AMA, Am. Soc. Echocardiography, Ind. State Med. Assn., Ind. Heart Assn. (bd. dirs.), Marion County Med. Soc., Marion County Heart Assn. Republican. Roman Catholic. Home: 10662 Winterwood Carmel IN 46032-9688 Office: Nasser Smith & Pinkerton 8333 Naab Rd Ste 400 Indianapolis IN 46260

NAST, EDWARD PAUL, cardiac surgeon; b. Balt., Dec. 13, 1958; s. Richard Cecil and Lenora (Heilig) N.; m. Sandye Hammerman, June 3, 1984; 1 child, Bennett Ross. BS, Emory U., 1979; MD, U. Md., 1984. Diplomate Am. Bd. Thoracic Surgery, Am. Bd. Surgery. Intern Georgetown U. Med. Ctr., Washington, 1984-85, resident in gen. surgery, 1985-86, 88-91; resident in thoracic and cardiovascular surgery U. Md. Med. Sys., Balt., 1991-93; fellow in cardiac surgery NIH, Bethesda, Md., 1986-88; cardiac surgeon St. Joseph's Cardiac Surgery Assocs., P.C., Syracuse, N.Y., 1993—. Contbr. articles to profl. jours. Fellow Am. Coll. Cardiology, Am. Coll. Chest Physicians; mem. AMA, ACS, Med. Soc. of State of N.Y., Soc. Thoracic Surgeons, Phi Beta Kappa. Office: St Josephs Cardiac Surgery 101 Union Ave #813 Syracuse NY 13203

NATALE, STUART WADE, optometrist; b. Berwyn, Ill., Dec. 21, 1965; s. Ronald P. and Mary Jane (Links) N.; m. Tammy Ann Burgin, Oct. 1, 1994. BS in Biology, Ill. State U., 1988; OD, Ill. Coll. Optometry, 1992. Pvt. practice, Schaumburg, Ill., 1991—. Home: 6313 S Lakeshore Dr Oakwood Hills IL 60013 Office: Hoffing's Eye Clinic 1760 Wise Rd Schaumburg IL 60193

NATELLO, GREGORY WILLIAM, cardiologist, educator; b. Phila., Mar. 30, 1954; s. Americo Vespucci and Catherine (Logan) N.; m. Judy Marie Cutcliffe; children: Logan Angelina, Connolly Claire. AB in Biology, Gettysburg COll., 1976; DO, Phila. Coll. Osteo. Medicine, 1980. Diplomate Nat. Bd. Examiners, in internal medicine, geriatric medicine, cardiovascular disease Am. Bd. Internal Medicine. Intern Detroit Osteo. Hosp., 1980-81; gen. practice medicine Pennsauken, N.J., 1981-82; resident in internal medicine Cleve. Clinic Found., 1982-85; fellow in geriatrics Case Western Res. U., Cleve., 1985-86; assoc. in cardiovascular disease U. Ala., Birmingham, 1986-89; fellow in interventional cardiology Thomas Jefferson U., Phila., 1989-91; asst. prof. medicine, dir. labs. cardiac cattheterization U. Mo., Columbia, 1991-93; asst. prof. medicine U. Tenn., Chattanooga, 1993-96; instr. phys. diagnosis Case Western Res. U., 1984-85, U. Ala., 1988-89; cardiology cons. Dept. athletics U. Mo.-Columbia, 1991-93, U. Tenn., Chattanooga, 1993-96, co-leader heart failure continuous quality improvement team, 1995-96; assoc. West Fla. Med. Ctr. Clinic, P.A., 1996—. Contbr. articles to profl. jours. Recipient award of Merit for Outstanding Achievement, Detroit Osteo. Hosp., 1981, Disting. Sr. Resident award Cleve. Clinic Found., 1985. Mem. AMA, ACP, Am. Coll. Chest Physicians, Am. Coll. Cardiology, Am. Heart Assn., Phila. Coll. Osteo. Medicine Alumni Assn. (life), Eisenhower Soc. Gettysburg, Tenn. Osteo. Med. Assn., Am. Geriatric Soc., Jefferson Med. Coll. Alumni Assn., Phi Kappa Psi. Republican. Roman Catholic. Office: West Fla Med Ctr Clinic PA Dept Cardiology 8333 N Davis Hwy Pensacola FL 32514

NATH, JOGINDER, genetics and biology educator, researcher; b. Joginder Nagar, Panjab, India, May 12, 1932; came to U.S. 1957; s. Moti Ram and Vira Wali (Khorana) N.; m. Charlotte Lynn Reese, Apr. 5, 1969; children—Pravene, Brian. B.S. with honors, Panjab U, Amritsar, India, 1953; M.S. with honors, Panjab U, 1955; Ph.D., U. Wis., 1960. Research assoc. Am. Inst. Biol. Research, Madison, Wis., 1960-63; asst. prof. So. Ill. U., Carbondale, Ill., 1964-66; from asst. to assoc. prof. W.Va. U., Morgantown, 1966-72, prof., chmn. dept. genetics and devel. biology, 1972—. Contbr. articles on cytogenetics, mutagenesis, biochem. genetics and cryobiology to profl. jours. Chmn. bd. Morgantown Day Sch., 1977-79. Grantee NSF, 1967-68, DOE, 1992-95, Nat. Inst. Occupational Safety & Health, 1985-95. Mem. Soc. Cryobiology, Environ. Mutagen Soc., Electron Microscopy Soc., Sigma Xi. Office: WVa U Coll Agr Dept Genetics & Devel Biology Morgantown WV 26506

NATHAN, DAVID GORDON, physician, educator; b. Boston, May 25, 1929; s. E. Geoffrey and Ruth (Gordon) N.; m. Jean Louise Friedman, Sept. 1, 1951; children: Deborah, Linda, Geoffrey. BA, Harvard U., 1951; MD, Harvard Med. Sch., 1955. Diplomate Am. Bd. Internal Medicine, Am. Bd. Pediatrics. Intern dept. medicine Peter Bent Brigham Hosp., Boston, 1955-56, sr. resident, 1958-59; jr. assoc. in medicine Brigham and Women's Hosp., Boston, 1961-67, sr. assoc. in medicine, 1967—; assoc. in medicine, hematology Childrens Hosp., Boston, 1963-68, chief, div. hematology, 1968-73, chief div. hematology and oncology, 1974-84; pediatrician-in-chief Dana Farber Cancer Inst., Boston, 1974-85; Robert A. Stranahan prof. pediatrics Harvard Med. Sch., Boston, 1977-95; physician-in-chief Childrens Hosp., Boston, 1985-95; pres. Dana-Farber Cancer Inst., Boston, 1995—; Richard and Susan Smith prof. medicine Harvard Med. Sch., Boston, 1996—, prof. of pediatrics, 1996—. Author: Genes, Blood and Courage, 1994; editor: Hematology in Infancy and Childhood, 4th edit., 1993. With USMC, 1948-49. Recipient Nat. Medal Sci. NSF, 1990. Fellow AAAS; mem. Inst. of Medicine of NAS, Am. Acad. Arts & Scis., Am. Pediatric Soc., Soc. Pediatric Rsch., Assn. Am. Physicians, Am. Soc. Clin. Investigators, Am. Soc. Hematology (pres. 1986), Phi Beta Kappa (hon.). Office: Dana-Farber Cancer Inst 44 Binney St Boston MA 02115

NATHAN, RONALD GENE, medical educator, writer, researcher, consultant; b. Paterson, N.J., Feb. 22, 1951; s. Kurt Caesar and Hinda (Kremer) N.; children: Jennifer Rose, William Miles. BA with distinction, Cornell U., 1973; MA, U. Houston, 1975, PhD, 1978. Teaching fellow U. Houston, 1974-76, teaching asst., 1976, 78, instr. child devel., 1977-78; part time psychometrician, U. Tex., Houston, 1978; intern Tex. Rsch. Inst. of Mental Scis., Tex. Med. Ctr., Houston, 1977-78; clin. asst. prof. dept. psychology, U. N.C., Chapel Hill, 1978-79, asst. prof. depts. psychiatry and family medicine, La. State U. Sch. Medicine, Shreveport, 1979-83, assoc. prof., dir. med. psychology, 1983-86, assoc. prof., dir. behavioral scis., 1986-87; assoc. prof. depts. family practice and psychiatry Albany (N.Y.) Med. Coll., 1987-92; prof. 1992—; mem. adv. bd. for mental health/psychiat. nursing, Coll. Nursing Northwestern State U. La., 1983-87, Mid-Atlantic Ednl. Inst., 1991—, The Ctr. for Corp. Health, 1993—; cons. Merrill Lynch Pierce Fenner & Smith, Ruston and Shreveport, 1983, Libbey Glass, Shreveport, 1983-84, AT&T, Shreveport, 1985, Blue Cross/Blue Shield, Baton Rouge, 1985, Fleet-Norstar Bank, Albany, 1988, behavioral sci. curriculum com. Med. Sch. U. Mo., Kansas City. Co-author: Stress Management: A Conceptual and Procedural Guide, 1980; Stress Management: A Comprehensive Guide to Wellness, 1982, 84, 86, The Doctors' Guide to Instant Stress Relief, 1987, 89; Coping with the Stressed-Out People in Your Life, 1994; contbr. chpts., monographs, articles to profl. publs. in field, papers to profl. confs.; guest reviewer Focus on Critical Care, 1984, Am. Psychologist, 1984, Jour. Rsch. in Childhood Edn., 1989; assoc. editor Am. Jour. Health Promotion. Prin. investigator NIH rsch. grant, 1981-83; named Outstanding Faculty Mem. Family Practice Sr. Residents, 1990. Fellow Am. Inst. of Stress; mem. APA (divs. 2, 12, 38, 46, pub. info. rep. 1980—), Soc. Tchrs. Family Medicine, Soc. Behavioral Medicine, Nat. Ctr. for Health Edn. (charter assoc.), Phi Beta Kappa, Phi Kappa Phi. Office: Albany Med Coll A-21 Dept Family Practice 1 Clara Barton Dr Albany NY 12208-3401

NATHAN, SWAMI, psychiatrist; b. Tirukovilur, Tamil Nadu, India, Nov. 9, 1942; came to U.S., 1973; s. Rajagopalan and Vijaya N.; m. Girija Devi, Nov. 24, 1969; children: Chitra, Mahender. Premed. degree, U. Madras, India, 1961, MB, BS, 1969. Diplomate Am. Bd. Psychiatry and Neurology. Asst. prof. clin. psychiatry Columbia U., Coll. Physicians and Surgeons, N.Y.C., 1979-80; from asst. prof. to assoc. prof. in psychiatry U. Pitts., 1980-89; med. dir., dir. rsch. clin. rsch. unit Western Psychiatric Inst., U. Pitts., 1985-89; vice chmn. dept. psychiatry Allegheny Gen. Hosp., Pitts., 1989—, dir. inpatient svcs., dept. psychiatry, 1989-95; prof. psychiatry Med. Coll. Pa. and Hahnemann U., Allegheny Campus, 1989—; cons. VA Hosp., Pitts., 1981-85. Contbr. articles to profl. jours.; author numerous chpts. in books; reviewer for numerous jours. Recipient Andrew K. Bernath award for Outstanding Resident Physician in Psychiatry, Manhattan Psychiatric Ctr., N.Y.C., 1975, 76. Mem. Am. Psychiatric Assn., Internat. Soc. Psychoneuroendocrinology, Internat. Soc. Chronobiology, AAAS, N.Y. Acad. Scis. Office: Allegheny Gen Hosp 320 E North Ave Pittsburgh PA 15212-4772

NATHAN, VINCENT R., toxicologist; b. Mobile, Ala.; s. Lorenzo G. Jr. and Rose Marie (Butler) N.; m. Juanita Coats, July 21, 1990. BS, Tenn. State U., 1972; MPH, U. Tex., Houston, 1983; PhD, Mich. State U., 1992. Rsch. analyst SRI Internat., Arlington, Va., 1976-78; rsch. scientist Rice U., Houston, 1979-83; cons. Mich. Hosp. Assn., Lansing, Mich., 1986-88; sr. toxicologist, mgr. Environ. Sci. & Engring., Inc., Williamston, Mich., 1990-93. Dir. Christian edn. Mask Meml. CME Ch., Lansing, 1992; vol. scientist McKinley Mus. History, Canton, Ohio, 1991. Mem. APHA, Am. Soc. Hosp. Engrs., Mich. Safety Conf. (co-chair healthcare 1987-88). Methodist. Home: PO Box 80364 Nashville TN 37208-0364 Office: Meharry Med Coll Divsn Environ Health Dept Family and Preventive Medicine Nashville TN 37208

NATHANS, DANIEL, molecular biology and genetics educator; b. Wilmington, Del., Oct. 30, 1928; s. Samuel and Sarah (Levitan) N.; m. Joanne E. Gomberg, Mar. 4, 1956; children: Eli, Jeremy, Benjamin. B.S., U. Del., 1950; M.D., Washington U., 1954. Intern Presbyn. Hosp., N.Y.C., 1954-55, resident in medicine, 1957-59; clin. assoc. Nat. Cancer Inst., 1955-57; guest investigator Rockefeller U., N.Y.C., 1959-62; prof. microbiology Sch. Medicine Johns Hopkins, 1962-72, prof., dir. dept. microbiology, 1972-82, Univ. prof. molecular biology and genetics, 1982—; mem. Pres. Coun. Advisers on Sci. & Tech., 1990-93; sr. investigator Howard Hughes Med. Inst., 1982—. Recipient Nobel prize in physiology or medicine, 1978, Nat. Medal of Sci., 1993. Fellow Am. Acad. Arts and Scis.; mem. NAS. Office: Johns Hopkins U-Sch Med Dept Molecular Biology & Genetics 725 N Wolfe St Baltimore MD 21205-2105*

NATHANSON, DONALD LAWRENCE, psychiatrist; b. N.Y.C., June 3, 1936; s. Nathaniel and Florence (Stoneberg) N.; m. Carolyn Diane Pries, Oct. 25, 1970 (div. 1975); 1 child, Julie Ann; m. Rosalind Helene Race, May 21, 1978. BA cum laude, Amherst Coll., 1956; MD, SUNY, Syracuse, 1960. Diplomate Am. Bd. Psychiatry and Neurology. Intern Albert Einstein Med. Ctr., Phila., 1960-61; resident in internal medicine Hahneman Med. Coll. and

Hosp., Phila., 1961-64; staff endocrinologist U.S. Naval Hosp., Phila., 1964-66; resident in psychiatry Inst. Pa. Hosp., Phila., 1966-67, Hahneman U., Phila., 1967-69; pvt. practice Phila., 1969—; teaching fellow internal medicine Hahnemann U., Phila., 1963-64, clin. instr. psychiatry, 1969-71, clin. asst. prof., 1971-85, clin. assoc. prof., 1985-93; clin. prof. psychiatry and human behavior Jefferson Med. Coll., Phila.; mem. staff Inst. Pa. Hosp., Phila., 1969—, sr. attending psychiatrist, 1986—; pres. Medigraphic Systems, Inc., N.Y.C., 1963-66; exec. dir. Silvan S. Tomkins Inst. Author, editor: The Many Faces of Shame, 1987, Denial: A Clarification of Concepts and Research, 1989; author: Shame and Pride: Affect, Sex, and the Birth of the Self, 1992, Knowing Feeling: Affect, Scripts and Psychotherapy, 1996; contbr. articles to med. publs. Bd. dirs., co-chmn. membership com. Le Coin d'Or, Phila., 1964-70; mem. gov.'s ball com. We the People 200, Phila., 1988; bd. dirs. Concerto Soloists Chamber Orch., Phila., 1983-88, Pa. Opera Theater Co., 1988-91. Fellow Am. Psychiat. Assn., Royal Soc. Medicine, Coll. Physicians Phila., Phila. Psychiat. Soc., Am. Orthopsychiat. Assn.; mem. Nat. Assn. Watch and Clock Collectors, Antiquarian Horological Soc. Gt. Britain. Republican. Jewish. Office: 2403 Med Tower Bldg 255 S 17th St Philadelphia PA 19103-6231

NATHANSON, MORTON, neurologist, educator; b. N.Y.C., May 31, 1918; s. Nathan and Celia N.; m. Margret Regina Maier, Dec. 16, 1948; children—David, Madlyn, Laura. AB, U. Mich., 1939; MD, La. State U., New Orleans, 1943. Diplomate Am. Bd. Neurology. Resident NYU, Bellevue, 1946-49, dir. multiple sclerosis rsch. program, 1950-54, asst. prof., 1954-60, assoc. prof., 1960-67; resident in neuropathology Columbia Coll. Physicians & Surgeons, 1967; clin. prof. neurology Mt. Sinai Sch. Medicine, N.Y.C., 1967-72, profl. lectr., 1973—: prof. neurology Sch. Medicine SUNY-Stony Brook, 1972-89; prof. emeritus, 1989—; prof. neurology Albert Einstein Coll. Medicine, 1990—; adj. prof. neuropsychology Queens Coll., City U. N.Y., 1978—; doctoral faculty CUNY Grad. Sch., 1979—; chief neurology L.I. Jewish Med. Ctr., New Hyde Park, N.Y., 1972—, chmn. emeritus, 1985—. Contbr. chpts. to books, numerous articles to profl. jours. With M.C. U.S. Army, 1944-46. Recipient NIH contract award, 1978-82. Fellow Am. Acad. Neurology; mem. Am. Neurol. Assn., Assn., Am. Fedn. Clin. Rsch., Am. Assn. History Medicine, Soc. Neuroscience N.Y. Acad. Sci., N.Y. Acad. Medicine, Brit. Brain Rsch. Assn., European Brain and Behavior Soc., Assn. Reserved Nerve Mental Disease, Internat. Soc. for History Medicine, Soc. Neurosci., Harvey Soc., Sigma Xi. Home: 1 Pebble Ln Roslyn Heights NY 11577-2711 Office: Albert Einstein Coll of Medicine Chmn Emergency Neurology Long Island Jewish Med Ctr New Hyde Park NY 11040

NATHANSON, RICHARD PAUL, physician; b. N.Y., May 24, 1956; s. Morton Gilbert and Estella Judith (Velasquez) N.; m. Catalina Huerta, Feb. 11, 1983. BA in Chemistry, U. South Fla., 1978; MD, U. Miami, 1986. Intern, resident U. Tex. Health Sci. Ctr., San Antonio, 1986-89; physician Internal Medicine Group, Beaumont, Tex., 1989-91, Arden Hill Internists, Orlando, Fla., 1991—; chief of internal medicine Princeton Hosp., Orlando, 1994-96. Mem. AMA, ACP. Office: Arden Hill Internists 6388 Silverstar Rd Ste 1C Orlando FL 32818

NATHIN, DONALD MARVIN, nephrologist; b. N.Y.C., Apr. 8, 1937; s. Louis Thomas and Pauline (Kessler) N.; m. Myrna Chervin, June 15, 1958; children: Debra, Robert, Steven. BA, NYU, 1957; MD, Chgo. Med. Sch., 1961. Diplomate Am. Bd. Internal Medicine. Intern, 1st yr. resident Brookdale Hosp., Bklyn., 1961-63; resident Montefiore Hosp., Bronx, N.Y., 1965-67; attending physician Pascack Valley Hosp., Westwood, N.J., 1967—, chief dept. nephrology, 1975—, asst. dir. divsn. medicine, 1992—, med. dir., 1995—. Capt. USAF, 1963-65. Mem. ACP, Am. Soc. Internal Medicine, Am. Soc. Nephrology, Internat. Soc. Nephrology, Nat. Kidney Found. Jewish. Home: 24 Old Farms Rd Woodcliff Lake NJ 07675 Office: 150 Washington Ave Dumont NJ 07628

NATHWANI, BHARAT NAROTTAM, pathologist, consultant; b. Bombay, Jan. 20, 1945; came to U.S., 1972; s. Narottam Pragji and Bharati N. (Lakhani) N. MBBS, Grant Med. Coll., Bombay, 1969, MD in Pathology, 1972. Intern Grant Med. Coll., Bombay U., 1968-69; asst. prof. pathology Grant Med. Coll., 1972; fellow in hematology Cook County Hosp., Chgo., 1972-73; resident in pathology Rush U., Chgo., 1973-74; fellow in hematopathology City of Hope Med. Ctr., Duarte, Calif., 1975-76, pathologist, 1977-84; prof. pathology, chief hematopathology U. So. Calif., L.A., 1984—. Contbr. numerous articles to profl. jours. Recipient Grant awards Nat. Libr. Medicine, Bethesda, Md., Nat. Cancer Inst., 1991. Mem. AAAS, Internat. Acad. Pathology, Am. Soc. Clin. Pathology, Am. Soc. Hematology, Am. Soc. Oncology. Office: U So Calif Sch Medicine HMR 209 2011 Zonal Ave Los Angeles CA 90033-4526

NATSUKARI, NAOKI, psychiatrist, neurochemist; b. Tokyo, July 16, 1952; came to U.S., 1991; s. Masao and Hideko (Kobayashi) N.; m. Ikuko Ueno, May 28, 1989; children: Shunya, Ryota. BS, Waseda U., Tokyo, 1976, MS, 1978; MD, Hamamatsu (Japan) U., 1986, PhD, 1991. Researcher Nikkiso Corp., Shizuoka, Japan, 1978-79; resident Hamamatsu U. Hosp., 1986, Okada Hosp., Okazaki, Japan, 1986-87; rsch. assoc. Nat. Inst. Physiol. Scis., Okazaki, 1991-92; postdoctoral fellow Med. Coll. Pa., Phila., 1991-92; vis. fellow NIMH, Washington, 1992—. Recipient award Ichiro Kanehara Found., Tokyo, 1991. Mem. AAAS, Soc. Neurosci., Japanese Neurochem. Soc., Japanese Biol. Soc., Japanese Neurology and Psychiatry Soc., N.Y. Acad. Sci. Office: NIMH at St Elizabeth Hosp Neuropsychiatry Br 2700 Martin Luther King Jr Washington DC 20032

NAU, CHARLES J., government affairs director, lawyer; b. Chgo., Mar. 12, 1947; s. Charles J. and Roma (Murphy) N. BA maxima cum laude, U. Notre Dame, 1969, LLD cum laude, 1974. Bar: N.Y. 1975, Calif. 1983, France, 1979. Gen. counsel Syntex Labs., Inc., Palo Alto, Calif., 1983-94; dir. govt. affairs ALZA Corp., Palo Alto, Calif., 1995—; cons. Nat. Inst. Drug Abuse CDC, Washington, 1990, leadership advisor Nat. Leadership Coalition on AIDS, Washington, 1990—; del. EEC-UNESCO Internat. Conf. AIDS in the Workplace, Paris, 1992. Chair SYNPAC, Palo Alto, 1986-94; del. Dem. Nat. Convention, N.Y., 1980; exec. dir. Dems. Abroad, 1984. Mem. Nat. Health Care Attorneys. Office: ALZA Corp 950 Page Mill Rd Box 10950 Palo Alto CA 94303-0802

NAUERT, ROGER CHARLES, healthcare executive; b. St. Louis, Jan. 6, 1943; s. Charles Henry and Vilma Amelia (Schneider) N.; B.S., Mich. State U., 1965; J.D., Northwestern U., 1969; M.B.A., U. Chgo., 1979; m. Elaine Louise Harrison, Feb. 18, 1967; children: Paul, Christina. Bar: Ill. 1969. Asst. atty. gen. State of Ill., 1969-71; chief counsel Ill. Legis. Investigating Commn., 1971-73; asst. state comptroller State of Ill., 1973-75; dir. adminstrn. and fin. Health and Hosps. Governing Commn. Cook County, Chgo., 1975-79; nat. dir. health care services Grant Thornton, Chgo., 1979-88; exec. v.p. Detroit Med. Ctr., 1988-91; exec. v.p. Columbia-Presbyn. Med. Ctr., N.Y.C., 1991-93; sr. v.p. Mt. Sinai Med. Ctr., N.Y.C., 1993-96; pres., CEO Radius Health Sys., Garden City, N.Y., 1996—; vis. lectr. healthcare mgmt. & fin. Columbia U., Vanderbilt U., U. Chgo., 1978—; preceptor Wharton Sch., U. Pa. Ford Found. grantee, 1968-69. Mem. Am. Hosp. Assn., Am. Public Health Assn., Am. Coll. Healthcare Execs., Nat. Health Lawyers Assn., Health Care Fin. Mgmt. Assn. (faculty mem.), Alpha Phi Sigma, Phi Delta Phi, Delta Upsilon. Clubs: N.Y. Athletic, Mt. Kisco Country. Author: A Sociology of Health, 1977; The Demography of Illness, 1978; Proposal for a National Health Policy, 1979; Health Care Feasibility Studies, 1980; Health Care Planning Guide, 1981; Health Care Strategic Planning, 1982; Overcoming the Obstacles to Planning, 1983; Principles of Hospital Cash Management, 1984; Healthcare Networking Arrangements, 1985; Strategic Planning for Physicians, 1986; HMO's: A Once and Future Strategy, 1987, Mergers, Acquisitions and Divestitures, 1988, Tax Exempt Status Under Seige, 1989, Governance in Multi-Hospital Systems, 1990, Planning Alternative Delivery Systems, 1991, Direct Contracting: The Future is Now, 1992, The Rise and Fall of the U.S. Healthcare System, 1993, A Proposal for National Healthcare Reform, 1994, Academic Medical Centers and the New Age of Managed Care, 1995, The Quest For Value in Healthcare, 1996. Home: 461 Haines Rd Bedford Corners NY 10549 Office: Radius Health Sys 765 Stewart Ave Garden City NY 11530

NAUGHTEN, ROBERT NORMAN, pediatrician; b. Stockton, Calif., Oct. 13, 1928; s. Norman Stafford and Junetta (Doherty) N.; m. Ann Louise Charkins, June 26, 1954; children: Robert James, Annette Marie Naughten-Dessel, Patricia Louise Schoof. AA, San Jose City Coll., San Jose, Calif., 1948; BA, U. Calif., Berkeley, 1950; MA, Stanford U., 1955; MD, Hahnemann U., 1959. Lic. physician and surgeon, Calif. Intern Highland-Alameda County Hosp., Oakland, Calif., 1959-60; rsch. fellow Nat. Cancer Inst., Stanford, Calif., 1960-61; resident pediat. Stanford Med. Ctr., 1961-63; pvt. practice specializing in pediat. Los Gatos, Calif., 1963—; instr. Santa Clara Valley Med. Ctr., San Jose, 1963—, Dept. of Pediat., Stanford, 1963-73; cons. drug abuse San Jose Police Dept., 1963-68; cons. child abuse Dist. Atty., San Jose, 1984—; cons. dept. social svcs. State of Calif., 1989—. Contbr. articles to profl. jours. Bd. dirs., v.p. Outreach and Escort, Inc., San Jose, 1985-88. Named Alumnus of Yr. San Jose City Coll., 1967, Chef of the West Sunset Mag., 1989; fellow Coll. of Physicians, Phila., 1986. Mem. AMA, Calif. Assn., Santa Clara Med. Assn. (v.p. 1986-88), Am. Acad. Pediatrics, Am. Acad. Allergy and Clin. Immunology, Calif. Alumni Assn. (Berkeley), Stanford Alumni Assn., Commonwealth Club (San Francisco), Soc. of the Sigma Xi. Democrat. Roman Catholic. Home: 13601 Riverdale Dr Saratoga CA 95070-5229 Office: 777 Knowles Dr Ste 14 Los Gatos CA 95030-1417

NAUGHTON, JAMES LEE, internist; b. 1946. AB, Dartmouth Coll., 1968; MD, Harvard U., 1972. Intern U. Calif. Moffitt Hosp., San Francisco, 1972-73; resident in medicine U. Calif. Affiliated Hosps., San Francisco, 1973-75, San Francisco Gen. Hosp., 1975-76; fellow in nephrology U. Calif., San Francisco, 1976-77, assoc. clin. prof. medicine, 1982—; pvt. practice, ptnr. Pinole Med. Group, Pinole, Calif. Office: Pinole Med Group 2160 Appian Way Pinole CA 94564

NAUGHTON, JOHN PATRICK, cardiologist, medical school administrator; b. West Nanticoke, Pa., May 20, 1933; s. John Patrick and Anne Frances (McCormick) N.; children: Bruce, Marcia, Lisa, George, Michael, Thomas. AA, Cameron State Coll., Lawton, Okla., 1952; BS, St. Louis U., 1954; MD, Okla. U., 1958; MD (hon.), Kosin U., 1995. Intern George Washington U. Hosp., Washington, 1958-59; resident U. Okla. Med. Center, 1959-64; asst. prof. medicine U. Okla., 1966-68; assoc. prof. medicine U. Ill., 1968-70; prof. medicine George Washington U., 1970-75, dean acad. affairs, 1973-75, dir. div. rehab. medicine and Regional Rehab. Research and Tng. Center, 1970-75; dean Sch. Medicine, SUNY, Buffalo, 1975—; prof. medicine and physiology Sch. Medicine, SUNY, 1975—, lectr. in rehab. medicine, 1975; acting v.p. for health scis. SUNY, 1983-84, v.p. clin. affairs, 1984—; dir. Nat. Exercise and Heart Disease Project, 1972—; chmn. policy adv. bd. Beta-blocker Heart Attack Trial Nat. Heart, Lung and Blood Inst., 1977-82; pres. Western N.Y. chpt. Am. Heart Assn., 1983-85, v.p. N.Y. State affiliate, 1985, pres. N.Y. State affiliate, 1988-90; chmn. clin. applications and preventions adv. com. Nat. Heart, Lung and Blood Inst., 1984; mem. Fed. COGME working group on consortia, 1996, N.Y. Gov.'s Commn. on Grad. Med. Edn., 1985, N.Y. State Coun. on Grad. Med. Edn., 1988-90, chmn. 1996—; pres. Assoc. Med. Schs. N.Y., 1982-84, mem. adminstrv. com. Coun. of Deans, 1983-89; mem. N.Y. State Dept. of Health Adv. Com. on Physician Recredentialing; mem. exec. coun. Nat. Inst. on Disability and Rehab. Rsch. 1991-92. Author: Exercise Testing and Exercise Training in Coronary Heart Disease, 1973, Exercise Testing: Physiological, Biomechanical, and Clinical Principles, 1988. Career devel. awardee Nat. Heart Inst., 1966-71; recipient Brotherhood-Sisterhood award in medicine NCCJ, N.E. Minority Educators award, 1990, Acad. Alumnus of Yr. award Okla. U., 1990, award for svc. to minorities in med. edn., 1991, Honorary Doctor of Medicine award, Kosin U., 1995, Frank Sindelar award N.Y. State Am. Heart Assn., 1995, James Platt White Soc. award, 1995, Outstanding Contbns. in the field of Health Care award Sheehan Meml. Hosp., 1995. Fellow ACP, Am. Coll. Cardiology, Am. Coll. Sports Medicine (pres. 1970-71), Am. Coll. Chest Physicians; mem. N.Y. State Heart Assn. (pres.), Am. Coll. Cardiology (coun. N.Y. chpt.). Office: SUNY Buffalo Sch Medicine Biomed Scis 3435 Main St Buffalo NY 14214-3001

NAUGLE, JEAN MARIE, legal nurse consultant; b. Huron, S.D., Aug. 11, 1955; d. Duane Burton and Dorothy Ann (Davies) Carson; m. Duane Douglas Naugle, June 15, 1985. AA in Nursing, L.A. City Coll., 1979; diploma, Calif. Hosp., 1979. RN, Calif.; cert. gastrointestinal clinician. Clin. nurse Sharp Meml. Hosp., San Diego, 1982-87; clin. head nurse endoscopy U. Calif. San Diego Med. Ctr., 1983-93; coord. endoscopy svcs. Children's Hosp., San Diego, 1993-95; ind. legal nurse cons., 1995—. Editor: Medi-Link. Mem. Soc. Gastroenterology Nurses and Assocs. (pediatric spl. interest group chmn.), So. Calif. Soc. Gastroenterology Nurses and Assocs. (edn. chmn. 1991-96, pres.-elect 1996), Am. Assn. Legal Nurse Cons. (edn. com. San Diego chpt. 1996—).

NAUGLE, ROBERT PAUL, dentist; b. Cleve., May 3, 1951; s. Paul Franklin Albert and Olga (Bigadza) N.; m. Nancy Elaine Baker, June 14, 1975; 1 child, Jennifer Elaine. BS, Heidelberg Coll., Tiffin, Ohio, 1973; DDS, Case Western Res. U., 1977. Pvt. practice Uniontown, Ohio, 1980—. Capt. USAF, 1977-80. Mem. ADA, Ohio Dental Assn., Acad. Gen. Dentistry, Stark County Dental Soc., Akron Dental Soc., Air Force Assn., Rotary (past program chmn. Uniontown, Student of Month chmn., past pres., past v.p., past treas., Paul Harris fellow, sgt.-at-arms). Republican. Mem. United Church of Christ. Office: 13027 Cleveland Ave NW Uniontown OH 44685

NAUM, CHRIS C., pulmonologist; b. Gary, Ind., July 10, 1957; s. Carl C. and Virginia (Cumbaroff) N.; m. Shelley Ann Clark, June 23, 1984; children: Katelyn, Allison, Nicholas. BA, Ind. U., 1979, MD, 1983. Diplomate Am. Bd. Internal Medicine. Intern, resident internal medicine Ind U., Indianapolis, 1983-86, lectr., 1986-87; pulmonary fellow U. Pitts., 1987-90; staff Methodist Hosp. Ind., Indpls., 1990—; adj. prof. Ball State U., Indpls., 1994—, Butler U., Indpls., 1994—. Fellow Am. Coll. Chest Physicians; mem. AMA, Am. Thoracic Soc., Ind. Thoracic Soc., Ind. State Med. Assn., Ind. U. Alumni Assn. Presbyn. Office: Respiratory Cons Ind 1801 N Senate Blvd Ste 400 Indianapolis IN 46202

NAUMBURG, GEORGE WASHINGTON, JR., retired psychiatrist; b. N.Y.C., June 21, 1918; s. George Washington and Ruth (Morgenthau) N.; m. Michelle Rosenthal, Mar. 18, 1961; children by previous marriage: Peter Henry, Eric George, Janet Lucile (dec.), Elizabeth Harriet. BS, Harvard U., 1940; MD, Yale U., 1945; cert. in Psychoanalysis, Psychoanalytic Clinic, 1955. Diplomate Am. Bd. Psychiatry and Neurology. Chief resident psychiatry Mt. Sinai Hosp., N.Y.C., 1948-49; pvt. practice medicine specializing in psychiatry N.Y.C., 1950-88; asst. prof. psychiatry Downstate Med. Sch., Bklyn., 1957-58; clin. assoc. prof. psychiatry Mt. Sinai Sch. Medicine, 1968-96; pres., winemaker N. Salem Vineyard, Inc., North Salem, N.Y., 1979—. Pres. The Baron de Hirch Fund, N.Y.C., 1967—; mem. Dean's coun. Yale Sch. of Medicine, 1989-93. Fellow Am. Psychiatric Assn.; mem. Assn. for Psychoanalytic Medicine, Am. Psychoanalytic Assn., AMA, N.Y. State Medicine Soc., N.Y. Co. Med. Soc. Democrat. Jewish. Club: Harvard. Office: North Salem Vineyard 441 Hardscrabble Rd North Salem NY 10560

NAUNHEIM, KEITH S., thoracic surgeon; b. Alexandria, La., Oct. 2, 1952; s. Alfred Roberts and Suzanne (Leschen) N.; m. Rosanne Fae Suchomal, June 3, 1978; children: Katherine, Theodore, Matthew, Margaret. BA cum laude, Johns Hopkins U., 1974; MD cum laude, U. Chgo., 1978. Diplomate Am. Bd. Surgery, Am. Bd. Thoracic Surgery. Asst. prof. St. Louis U. Sch. Medicine, 1985-88, assoc. prof., 1988-94, prof., 1994—. Author, editor: Glenn's Textbook of Thoracic and Cardiovascular Surgery, 1995; mem. edit. bd. Annals of Thoracic Surgery, 1995; contbr. articles to profl. publs. Mem. ACS, Am. Assn. Thoracic Surgeons, Soc. Thoracic Surgeons, St. Louis Thoracic Surg. Soc. (pres. 1994-96), Thoracic Surgery Dirs. Assn., European Assn. for Cardiothoracic Surgery, Alpha Omega Alpha. Roman Catholic. Office: St Louis U Health Scis Ctr 3635 Vista at Grand Saint Louis MO 63110

NAVAR, LUIS GABRIEL, physiology educator, researcher; b. El Paso, Tex., Mar. 24, 1941; s. Luis and Concepcion (Najera) N.; m. Randa Ann Bumgarner, Oct. 15, 1965; children: Tonia, Tess, Gabriel, Daniel. BS, Tex. A&M U., 1962; PhD, U. Miss., 1966, postdoctoral study, 1966-69. Instr. dept. physiology/biophysics U. Miss., Jackson, 1966-67, asst. prof., 1967-71, assoc. prof., 1971-74; assoc. prof. U. Ala., Birmingham, 1974-76, prof., 1976-88, assoc. prof. Nephrology Rsch. and Tng. Ctr., 1979-83, prof., 1983-88; prof., chmn. dept. physiology Tulane U. Med. Sch., New Orleans, 1988—; vis. scientist Duke U. Med. Ctr., Durham, N.C., 1972-73. Assoc. editor: News in Physiol. Scis., 1994—, Am. Jour. Physiology, 1983-89, mem. editorial bd., 1982-83; assoc. editor Hypertension, 1993—; mem. editorial bd. Kidney Internat., 1976-87, Hypertension, 1980-83, assoc. editor, 1993—; editorial bd. Kidney, 1992—, Clinical Science, 1994—; contbr. sci. papers, book chpts., slides and tapes to profl. publs. Chmn. cardiorenal rsch. study com. Am. Heart Assn., 1994-95, mem. nat. rsch. com. 1994-99. Recipient Rsch. Career Devel. award Nat. Heart, Lung and Blood Inst., 1974-79, Merit award, 1988. Mem. AAAS, Am. Physiol. Soc. (coun. 1991-94), Am. heart Assn. (kidney, high blood pressure couns., nat. rsch. com. 1994—), N.Y. Acad. Sci., Am. Soc. Nephrology, Internat. Soc. Nephrology, Am. Soc. Hypertension (coun. 1992-94), Internat. Soc. Hypertension, Assn. Chmn. Depts. Physiology (councillor 1993-95, pres.-elect 1995-96, pres. 1996-97). Democrat. Roman Catholic. Home: 10020 Hyde Pl River Ridge LA 70123-1522 Office: Tulane U Med Sch Dept Physiology 1430 Tulane Ave New Orleans LA 70112-2699

NAVEJA-ELLIS, FRANCESCA ANGELA, mental health clinic administrator; b. N.Y.C., June 23, 1939; d. Antonio and Jeannette Marie (Thomas) Naveja; m. David H. Ellis, Oct. 21, 1957; children: Theresa Fae Ann Zendejas, David Cary Ellis. AA with Honors, Allan Hancock Coll., 1985; BS, Columbia Pacific U., 1988; MA, U. San Francisco, 1989. Adminstr. Community Ministry Ctr., Chino, Calif., 1977-79; bus. mgr. Humanistic Mental Health, Santa Maria, Calif., 1984-85; med. sec. A. Edward Hoctor, MD., Santa Maria, 1985; bus. mgr. Affiliated Psychotherapist, Santa Maria, 1985-87; founder, exec. dir., psychotherapist, C.E.O. AP Inst., Inc. Community Counseling Ctr., Santa Maria, 1988—; program dir. Safe Interventions, Santa Maria, Case Mgmt. and Consulting Assocs., Santa Maria; mem. adj. faculty Columbia Pacific U., Sierra U.; founder, dir. Trias Inst., Santa Maria, 1984—, AP Inst., Santa Maria, 1986-87, AP Inst. Valley Counseling Ctr., 1986-95; bd. dirs. Friends of Ruth Women's Shelter, Santa Maria, 1985; cons. St. Joseph's High Sch., 1990; CEO Cen. Coast Cons. Assocs., 1991—. Editor, author quar. newsletter Pride, 1990—. Vol. Dem. Women's Caucus 1986; mem. Women's Network, Santa Maria, 1986-89; mental health adv. coun. Santa Barbara County, 1990, with Domestic violence Edn./Elimination Svcs., 1992-95. Mem. Am. Mental Health Counseling Assn., Assn. Christian Therapists (regional coord., 1988-90), Calif. Assn. Marriage Family Therapists, Cen. Coast Jung Soc., Western Assn. Spiritual Dirs., Cen. Coast Hypnosis Soc. Mem. Am. Assn. Prof. Hypnotherapists. Office: Lovelock Mental Health PO Box 1046 Lovelock NV 89419

NAVIA, JUAN MARCELO, biologist, educator; b. Havana, Jan. 16, 1927; came to U.S., 1961; s. Juan and Hortensia (DeLaCampa) N.; m. Josefina Blanca Bonich, Aug. 20, 1950; children: Juan, Carlos, Ana, Beatriz. BS, MIT, 1950, MS, 1951, PhD, 1965; DDSc (hon.), Chiang Mai U., Thailand, 1996. Sr. scientist Inst. Dental Rsch. U. Ala., Birmingham, 1969-88; dir. nutrition and oral health tng. program U. Ala., Birmingham, 1986-88, dir. rsch. tng. Sch. Dentistry, 1971-81, dir. clin. rsch. tng. program - MD, PhD, 1972-75, dir Sparkman Ctr., 1981-94, prof. comparative medicine, 1973-94, prof. biochemistry, 1976-86, prof. nutrition scis., 1977-94; ret., prof. emeritus, 1994—; adv. bd. mem. Fogarty Internat. Ctr., Bethesda, Md., 1985-88, Princeton (N.J.) Dental Resource Ctr., 1987-90; dean U. Ala. Sch. Pub. Health, 1989-92. Author: Animal Models in Dental Research, 1977; editor: The Biologic Basis of Dental Caries, 1980; contbr. Encyclopedia Americana, 1968. Am. Inst. Nutrition fellow, 1995, Sr. Internat. Fogarty fellow, 1979, AAAS fellow, 1982; recipient H. Trendley Dean Meml. award Internat. Assn. Dental Rsch., 1990, U. Ala. Birmingham's Pres.'s medal, 1992. Mem. Internat. Assn. Dental Rsch. (pres. cariology 1983-84), Am. Assn. Dental Rsch., Am. Chem. Soc., European Orgn. Caries Rsch., Inst. Food Technologists, Nat. Coun. Internat. Health, Sociedad Latinoamericana de Nutricion, N.Y. Acad. Scis., Internat. Serra Club, Sigma Xi, Sigma Delta Pi. Republican. Roman Catholic. Office: U Ala at Birmingham Dept Comparative Medicine Volker Hall 403 Birmingham AL 35294

NAYAK, DEBI PROSAD, microbiology and immunology educator; b. Eadpore, India, Apr. 1, 1937; came to U.S., 1961; s. Sarat Chandra and Durga Rani (Mandal) N.; m. Abantika Datta Nayak, June 18, 1965; children: Prasun, Dipak. B in Vet. Sci., U. Calcutta, India, 1957; MS, U. Nebr., 1963, PhD, 1965. Acting asst. prof. UCLA Sch. Medicine, 1965-66, asst. research virologist, 1966-68, asst. prof., 1968-71, assoc. prof., 1971-77, prof., 1977—; mem. study sect. NIH, 1986-90, mem. microbiology and infectious diseases rsch. com. NIAID/NIH, 1989-94. Author, editor: The Molecular Biology of Animal Viruses, vols. I and II, 1977, Genetic Variation Among Influenza Viruses, 1981; mem. editorial bd. Virus Rsch., 1984-91; patentee in field. NIH grantee, 1973—; Sr. Dernham fellow Am. Cancer Soc., 1969-74. Mem. AAAS, Am. Soc. Virologists, Am. Soc. Microbiology, NIH (study sect., research grantee 1973—). Office: UCLA Dept Microbiology & Immunology 10833 Le Conte Ave Los Angeles CA 90024-1747

NAYERAHMADI, HABIB, psychologist; b. Tehran, Iran, Apr. 4, 1949; came to U.S., 1975; s. Younes Nayerahmadi and Nasimeh (Sheikhzadeh) Tavassoli; m. Mitra Farzaneh, Aug. 6, 1979; children: Kooshan, Poorya. BA in Psychology, Pars Coll., Tehran, 1973; MA in Clin. Psychology, Ball State U., 1978; PhD, U. Pa., 1989. Psychologist, counselor Imperial Iranian Air Force, Tehran, 1973-75; rsch. asst. U. Pa., Phila., 1980-82; assoc. Uni-Marts, Inc., Phila., 1981-88; rsch. cons. CON-RAIL, Phila., 1986-87; sr. clin. psychologist North Princeton (N.J.) Devel. Ctr., 1988—. Author: Development of a Homesickness Scale for Iranian Population, 1989; contbr. articles to profl. jours., U.S. and Iran. Mem. Am. Psychol. Assn., Am. Ednl. Rsch. Assn. Home: 3521 Hale Rd Huntingdon Valley PA 19006-3230 Office: North Princeton Devel Ctr PO Box 1000 Princeton NJ 08543-1000

NAYFA, TERRY M., podiatrist; b. Oklahoma City, Oct. 30, 1953; s. Henry and Blanch May (Shadid) N.; m. Paula Miller, June 8, 1985; 1 child, Jennifer. BS in Biol. Scis., Ctrl. State U., Edmond, Okla., 1975; B in Basic Med. Scis., DPM, Calif. Coll. Podiatric Medicin, San Francisco, 1978. Diplomate Am. Bd. Podiatric Orthopedics and Primary Podiatric Medicine, Am. Bd. Podiatric Surgery, Am. Acad. Pain Mgmt. Resident in podiatric surgery Northlake (Ill.) Cmty. Hosp., 1978-79; pvt. practice Oklahoma City and Duncan, Okla., 1980—; mem. faculty surg. dissertation seminar Ill. Coll. Podiatric Medicine, 1979, mem. podiatric residency com., 1980—; mem. med. staff Bapt. Med. Ctr. Okla., Oklahoma City, Deaconess Hosp., Oklahoma City, Duncan Regional Med. Ctr., Edmond Regional Med. Ctr., Hillcrest Health Ctr., Oklahoma City, Okla. Surgicare, Oklahoma City, mem. profl. activities com., 1987—; mem. med. staff Parkview Hosp., El Reno, Okla., Presbyn. Hosp., Oklahoma City, St. Anthony Hosp., Oklahoma City, Surgery Ctr. Okla., Oklahoma City, mem. profl. activites com., 1992—. Contbr. papers to profl. jours. Fellow Am. Coll. Foot and Ankle Orthopedics and Medicine, Am. Coll. Foot and Ankle Surgeons; mem. Am. Podiatric Circulatory Soc., Am. Podiatric Med. Assn., Okla. Podiatric Med. Assn. (bd. govs. 1984-85), Alpha Chi, Alpha Gamma Kappa, Pi Delta. Office: 3726 NW 50th Oklahoma City OK 73112 also: 2025 Elk Ave Duncan OK 73533

NAZAIRE, MICHEL HARRY, physician; b. Jérémie, Haiti, Sept. 29, 1939; s. Joseph and Hermance N.; m. Nicole N., Dec. 28, 1968 (div.); children: Hanick and Carline (twins). Grad., Coll. St. Louis de Gonzague, 1959; MD Faculty of Medicine and Pharmacology, State U. Haiti, 1966. Intern, State U. Hosp., Port-Au-Prince, Haiti, 1965-66; resident physician Sanitarium, Port-Au-Prince, Haiti, 1966-68; practice medicine specializing in pneumophysiology, Port-Au-Prince, 1966—; physician fellow Klinik Havelhohe, West Berlin, 1969-70, 89-91; attending physician Sanitarium, Port-Au-Prince, 1976-91. Dep. mem. Internat. Parliament for Safety and Peace; envoy-at-large Internat. State Parliament; mem. global environ. technol. network Who. Contbr. articles to Jour. Indsl. Hygiene, Pneumology and Respiratory Protection. Fellow Internat. Soc. for Respiratory Protection, Am. Coll. Chest Physicians (assoc.); mem. Am. Pub. Health Assn., Am. Conf. Govtl. Indsl. Hygienists, Internat. Union Against Tuberculosis. Address: 6407 S 12th St Apt 1711 Tacoma WA 98465

NAZARIAN, LAWRENCE FRED, pediatrician; b. N.Y.C., May 17, 1940; s. Samuel George and Winifred Lucia (Zotian) N.; m. Sharon Louise Carlson, June 22, 1963; children: Douglas, Stephen, Sarah. BA, Yale U., 1960; MD, U. Rochester, 1964. Pediatrician Panorama Pediatric Group, Rochester, N.Y., 1969—; clin. prof. pediatrics U. Rochester (N.Y.) Sch.

Medicine and Dentistry, 1969—; mem. physician adv. bd. Equifax Health Ctr., Fairport, N.Y., 1991—; bd. dirs. James P. Wilmot Fedn., Rochester. Contbr. articles to profl. jours.; assoc. editor PEdiatrics in Rev. Jour., 1990—. Mem. troop com. Boy Scouts Am., Pemfield, N.Y., 1978-88; mem. coun. com. Luth. Ch. of Reformation, Rochester, 1969—. Maj. USAR, 1967-69. Fellow Am. Acad. Pediatrics; mem. Med. Soc. State of N.Y., Ctrl. N.Y. Pediatric Club, Monroe County Med. Soc., Rochester Acad. Medicine, Rochester Pediatric Soc. Office: Panorama Pediatric Group 220 Linden Oaks Rochester NY 14625

NEAL, ANTHONY JAMES, oncologist; b. London, Oct. 18, 1961. MB, BS, St. Thomas' Hosp., London, 1985; MD, Inst. Cancer Rsch., Sutton, Eng., 1995. Registrar Royal London Hosp., 1988-92; clin. rsch. fellow Inst. Cancer Rsch., Sutton, 1993-94; sr. registrar Royal Marsden Nat. Health Svc. Trust, London and Sutton, 1994-95; cons. oncologist Royal Marsden NHS Trust, Sutton, 1996—. author: Clinical Oncology: A Textbook for Students, 1994; contbr. articles to profl. jours. Recognised Tchr. and Hon. Sr. Lectr., U. London/Inst. Cancer Rsch., 1996. Fellow Royal Coll. Radiologists; mem. Royal Coll. Physicians (U.K.), Brit. Med. Assn., Brit. Oncol. Assn. (Amgen-Roche Jr. Investigator award 1994), European Soc. Therapeutic Radiology (Estro-Varian Physics Rsch. award 1994, Estro-Philips Traveling fellow 1994). Office: Royal Marsden NHS Trust, Downs Rd, Sutton SM2 5PT, England

NEAL-BARNETT, ANGELA MARIE, psychology educator; b. Youngstown, Ohio, Feb. 13, 1960; d. Andrew Lee and Doris Lucille Neal; m. Edgar J. Barnett Jr., July 17, 1995. BA, Mt. Union Coll., 1982; MA, DePaul U., 1985, PhD, 1988. Lic. psychologist, Ohio. Clin. therapist ECHO Community Health Orgn., Chgo., 1985-87; post-doctoral fellow U. Pitts. (Pa.), Western Psychiat. Inst., 1988-89; asst. prof. Kent (Ohio) State U., 1989—, 1989-95, assoc. prof., 1995—; bd. dirs. King-Kennedy Ctr., Ravenna, Ohio, 1989-95; rsch. fellow Inst. African Am. Affairs, Kent, 1991—; co-chair Allied Health Edn. Com., 1994—; mem. NIMH Child Psychopathology and Treatment Rev. Panel. Contbr. articles to profl. jours. Mem. alumni coun. Mt. Union Coll. Urban Rsch. grantee Ohio Bd. Regents, 1990, biomed. support grantee NIH, 1991, small grantee NIMH, 1994-96. Mem. APA, Ohio Pscyhol. Assn., Assn. Advancement Behavior Therapy, Assn. Black Psychologists, African Am. Lit. Guild Kent. Methodist. Office: Kent State U Dept Psychology 118 Kent Hall Kent OH 44242-0001

NEALE, HENRY WHITEHEAD, plastic surgery educator; b. Richmond, Va., July 18, 1940; s. Richard C. and Eva W. Neale; m. Margaret C. Neale, June 20, 1964; children: Leigh, Jennifer, Henry Whitehead Jr., William. BS, Davidson Coll., 1960; MD, Med. Coll. Va., 1964. Diplomte Am. Bd. Surgery, Am. Bd. Plastic Surgery (guest examiner 1986-90, dir. 1990-96, mem. com. on plans and qualifying exam. com. 1993-96, exec. com. 1993—, chmn. certifying examing com. 1993-95, mem. ethics com. 1993, liaison to Am. Bd. Surgery 1993-96, pres.-elect 1995—). Rotating intern Mercy Med. Ctr., Springfield, Ohio, 1964-65; resident in gen. surgery U. Cin. Med. Ctr., 1965-71, dir. div. plastic, reconstructive and hand surgery, 1974—; resident in plastic surgery Duke U. Med. Ctr., Durham, N.C., 1971-74; fellow in hand surgery, Christine Kleinert hand fellow U. Louisville, 1973; asst. prof. surgery U. Cin. Coll. Medicine, 1974-77, assoc. prof., 1977-82, prof., 1982—; active staff, dir. hand surgery and plastic surgery clinics U. Cin. Med. Ctr. Hosp. Group, 1974—; dir. burn reconstructive and plastic surgery, co-dir. hand surgery svc. Shriners Burns Inst., Cin., 1983—; dir. div. plastic, reconstructive and hand surgery and plastic surgery clinic Childrens Hosp. Med. Ctr., Cin., 1983—; assoc. attending staff Good Samaritan Hosp.; courtesy staff Christ Hosp., Jewish Hosp.; numerous presentations in field. Mem. editl. bd. Jour. Plastic and Reconstructive Surgery, 1989—; contbr. numerous articles to med. jours. Capt. M.C., USAF, 1965-70. Rsch. grantee Eli Lilly Co., 1979-91. Fellow ACS; mem. AMA, Am. Assn. Plastic Surgeons, Am. Burn Assn., Am. Cleft Palate Assn., Am. Soc. for Aesthetic Plastic Surgery, Am. Soc. Plastic and Reconstructive Surgeons, Am. Soc. for Surgery of Hand, Acad. Medicine Cin., Assn. Acad. Chairmen in Plastic Surgery, Cin. Surg. Soc., Grad. Surg. Soc. Cin., Greater Cin. Soc. Plastic and Reconstructive Surgeons (pres. 1988-89), Ohio Med. Assn., Ohio Valley Soc. Plaastic and Reconstructive Surgery (pres. 1985-86), Plastic Surgery Rsch. Coun. Home: 2970 Alpine Ter Cincinnati OH 45208-3408 Office: U Cin Coll Medicine Div Pl Reconst Hand Surgery 231 Bethesda Ave Cincinnati OH 45229-2827

NEASE, BETH ELLEN, physician assistant; b. Washington, Mar. 3, 1951; d. Betty Ellen Nease Harden; m. David Thompson, Apr. 17, 1996. BS in Med. Sci., Alderson-Broaddus Coll., 1984. Health care adminstr., physician asst. Huttonsville (W.Va.) Corr. Ctr., 1984-85; physician asst. Stateville Corr. Ctr., Joliet, Ill., 1985; dir. black lung clinic Cmty. Health Found., Man, W.Va., 1985-86; physician asst., interim exec. dir. Family Health Care, Spencer, W.Va., 1986-91; physician asst. Marmet (W.Va.) Med. Ctr., 1991-92, Minnie Hamilton Health Care, Grantsville, W.Va., 1992-93; cons. to USPHS Bluestone Health Ctr., Matoaka, W.Va., 1993-94; physician asst., office mgr. Wedgewood Family Practice and Psychiatry Assocs., Morgantown, W.Va., 1994—; mem. adv. bd. USPHS, Phila., 1988-92, conf. spkr., 1990-94; clin. chairperson W.Va. Primary Care Assn., 1990-94; clin. dir. Bluestone Health Ctr., Matoaka, 1993-94. Active Roane County Drug Task Force, Spencer, 1988-91. Fellow Am. Assn. Physician Assts., W.Va. Assn. Physician Assts. (chair membership 1988-89, sec. 1989-93, dir.-at-large 1993-95, pres.-elect 1994-96, pres. 1995—, conf. spker.). Home: Rt 10 Box 401 Morgantown WV 26505

NEASE, JUDITH ALLGOOD, marriage and family therapist; b. Arlington, Mass., Nov. 15, 1930; d. Dwight Maurice Allgood and Sophie (Wolf) Allgood Morris; student Rockford Coll., 1949-50; BA, NYU, 1953, MA, 1954; MS, Columbia U. Sch. Social Work, 1956; m. Theron Stanford Nease, Sept. 1, 1962; children: Susan Elizabeth, Alison Allgood. Social worker, psychiatric social worker Bellevue Psychiat. Hosp., N.Y.C., 1956-59; psychiat. social worker St. Luke's Hosp., N.Y.C., 1959-62; asst. psychiat. social work supr. N.J. Neuropsychiat. Inst., Princeton, 1962-64; group co-leader Ctr. for Advancement of Personal and Social Growth, Atlanta, 1973-76, asst. dir., social work supr., group co-leader Dixon Hills Counseling Ctr., Columbia Theol. Sem., 1973-82; marriage and family therapist Cath. Social Svcs., Atlanta, 1978-87; chief Cmty. Mental Health Svc., Ft. McPherson, Atlanta, Ga., 1987-92; master's level clinician Ctr. for Psychiatry, Smyrna, Ga., 1990-92; pvt. practice marriage and family therapy. Mem. NASW, Acad. Cert. Social Workers, Am. Assn. Marriage and Family Therapy, Am. Group Psychotherapy Assn. Republican. Episcopalian. Home: 4678 Cedar Park Way Stone Mountain GA 30083-1887

NEATHERY, PATRICIA SUE, dietitian, consultant; b. Dothan, Ala., Apr. 18, 1934; d. John Joseph and Sue (Latil) Astleford; m. Thornton Lee Neathery, Aug. 25, 1956; children: Susan, David, Leanne. BS, U. Ala., 1956, grad., 1970-73. Dietitian Bryce Hosp., Tuscaloosa, Ala., 1963-65; pvt. practice cons. West Ala., 1970-86; dietitian Brewer-Porch Children's Ctr. U. Ala., Tuscaloosa, 1982—. Am. Heart Assn. scholar, 1964. Mem. AAUW (1st v.p. 1980-82), Am. Dietetic Assn., Ala. Dietetic Assn., Tuscaloosa Dietetic Assn. (chmn. legis. com. 1979, pres. 1990-91), Ala. Home Econs. Assn. (treas. 1974, pres. 1990-91), Civitan Internat. (bd. mem.), Alpha Delta Pi (alumnae pres. 1986-87). Republican. Episcopalian. Home: 3032 Firethorn Dr Tuscaloosa AL 35405-2747 Office: U Ala Dept Psychology Brewer-Porch Children's Ctr PO Box 870156 Tuscaloosa AL 35487-0156

NEAVES, WILLIAM BARLOW, cell biologist, educator; b. Spur, Tex., Dec. 25, 1943; s. William Fred and Revvie Lee (Hefner) N.; m. Priscilla Wood, Jan. 28, 1965; children: William Barlow, Clarissa D'laine. AB magna cum laude, Harvard U., 1966; postgrad., Med. Sch., 1966-67, PhD, 1969. Lectr. vet. anatomy U. Nairobi, 1970-71, vis. prof., 1978; lectr. anatomy Harvard U., 1972; asst. prof. cell biology U. Tex. Health Sci. Ctr., Dallas, 1972-74; assoc. prof. U. Tex. Health Sci. Ctr., 1974-77, prof., 1977—, Doris and Brian Wildenthal Prof. of Biomed. Sci., 1993—, dean Grad. Sch. Biomed. Scis., 1980-88, interim dean Southwestern Med. Sch., 1986-88, dean Southwestern Med. Sch., 1989—; rsch. assoc. herpetology Los Angeles County Mus., 1970-73; vis. lectr. U. Chgo., 1976-77. Assoc. editor Anat. Record, 1975-87; mem. editl. bd. Biology of Reprodn., 1983-86, Jour. Andrology, 1987-89; contbr. chpts. to books, articles to profl. jours. Bd. dirs. Dallas Zool. Soc., 1989-94, Dallas Mus. Natural History, 1993—, Damon Runyan-Walter Winchell Cancer Fund, 1986-92, v.p., 1990-92. Rockefeller Found. fellow, 1970-71; Milton Fund grantee, 1970-71; Population Council grantee, 1973-75; NIH grantee, 1973-89; Ford. Found. grantee, 1976-78. Fellow AAAS; mem. Am. Assn. Anatomists, Am. Soc. Andrology (Young Andrologist award 1983), Dallas Assembly, N.Y. Acad. Scis., Soc. Study of Reprodn., Liaison Com. on Med. Edn. (joint com. of AMA and Assn. Am. Med. Colls.), Sigma Xi, Alpha Omega Alpha. Methodist. Office: 5323 Harry Hines Blvd Dallas TX 75235-7200

NEBEL, BERNARD JAMES, biology educator; b. Geneva, N.Y., June 5, 1934; s. Bernard Rudolf and Mabel (Ruttle) Nebel; m. Jean Elizabeth Inglis, Sept. 9, 1961 (div. 1987); children: Tamra, Christopher; m. Janet Rose Lowenstein, Aug. 4, 1990 (dec. 1994). BA, Earlham Coll., 1960; PhD, Duke U., 1965. Postdoctoral fellow Smithsonian Instn., Washington, 1965-68; asst. prof. U. Md., Balt., 1968-70; prof. Catonsville (Md.) County Community Coll., 1970-95; retired, 1995. Author: Environmental Science, 1980, 5th edit., 1996. Mem. AAAS, Am. Inst. Biol. Sci., Wilderness Soc., Sierra. Democrat. Home: 122 N Beechwood Ave Baltimore MD 21228-4927

NEBEL, WILLIAM ARTHUR, obstetrician, gynecologist; b. Charlotte, N.C., Dec. 23, 1936; s. Arthur Ernest and Marie (Hunter) N.; m. Ann Elizabeth Bonner, June 20, 1959; children: Ann Marie Nebel, William Arthur Jr. AB in History, U. N.C., 1958, MD, 1962. Diplomate Am. Bd. Ob-Gyn. Intern Duke Univ. Med. Ctr., Durham, N.C., 1962-63; asst. clin. prof. ob-gyn Duke Univ. Med. Ctr., Durham, 1973—; resident in ob-gyn U. N.C., Chapel Hill, 1963-67, clin. instr. Sch. Med., 1969-70, clin. prof., 1989—; pvt. practice medicine specializing in ob-gyn Chapel Hill, 1970—; chmn. ob-gyn dept. Durham County Gen. Hosp., 1978-80, pres. med. staff, 1988-89, cons. staff, 1992—; mem. Steering Com. Chapel Hill Health Maintenance Orgn. Planning Project, 1973; mem. Orange County Health Bd., 1977, 80; mem. Birth, Neonatal Task Force, State of N.C. Dept. Human Resources, 1985; mem. organizing com. Coordinated Med. Svcs. N.C., 1985; bd. dirs. N.C. Blue Cross/Blue Shield, 1985-87; bd. dirs. Cen. Carolina Physicians Health, Village Bank, chmn. bd. 1987-89. Contbr. numerous articles to profl. jours.; author numerous presentations to profl. assns. Chmn. troop com. Boy Scouts Am., Troop 39, 1975-78; basketball coach Chapel Hill Recreation Dept., 1975-79; mem. Orange County Com. of N.C. 2000; bd. dirs. U. N.C. Ednl. Found.; vestryman Ch. of the Holy Family, 1973-76; pres. orange County unit Am. Cancer Soc., 1975-76, N.C. divsn. bd. dirs. 1977-78; bd. dirs. N.C. Blue CrossBlue Shield Personal Care Plan, 1985, Ctrl. Carolina Physicians Health, 1985-88, Found. for Better Health of Durham, 1988-89. Recognized by Am. Acad. Family Physicians, 1976-80; named Chapel Hill-Carrboro Father of Yr., 1977; United Cerebral Palsy Med. student fellow, 1960-61, Am. Cancer Soc. fellow, 1965-66. Mem. Internat. Corr. Soc. of Obstetricians and Gynocologists, Am. Fertility Soc., Am. Cancer Soc., S. Cen. Ob-Gyn. Soc. (pres. 1984-85), N.C. Med. Soc. (sect. chmn. 1983-84), N.C. Ob-Gyn. Soc. (pres. 1982-83), Piedmont Ob-Gyn. Soc., Durham-Orange County Med. Soc., Robert A. Ross Ob-Gyn. Soc. (pres. 1976), Village Med. Soc. (pres. 1970-80), Rotary (past pres., Paul Harris fellow), Alpha Omega Alpha, Phi Alpha Theta, Phi Chi, Pi Kappa Alpha. Democrat. Episcopalian. Office: Chapel Hill Ob-Gyn PO Box 3317 Chapel Hill NC 27515-3317

NEBELKOPF, ETHAN, psychologist; b. N.Y.C., June 13, 1946; s. Jacob and Fannie (Carver) N.; m. Karen Horrocks, July 27, 1976; children: Demian David, Sarah Dawn. BA, CCNY, 1966; MA, U. Mich., 1969; PhD, Summit U., 1989. Social worker Project Headstart, N.Y.C., 1965; coord. Project Outreach, Ann Arbor, 1968-69; program dir. White Bird Clinic, Eugene, Oreg., 1971-75; counseling supr. Teledyne Econ. Devel. Corp., San Diego, 1976-79; dir. planning and edn. Walden House, San Francisco, 1979-89, dir. tng., 1990-93; program evaluator United Indian Nations, Oakland, Calif., 1994—; adj. prof. Dept. Social Work, San Francisco State U., 1982-87; cons. Berkeley Holistic Health Ctr., Berkeley, 1979-84, Medicine Wheel Healing Co-op, San Diego, 1976-79; alternate del. Nat. Free Clinic Coun., Eugene, Oreg., 1972-74. Author: White Bird Flies to Phoenix, 1973, The New Herbalism, 1980, The Herbal Connection, 1981, Hope Not Dope, 1990. Mem. Mayor's Task Force on Drugs, San Francisco, 1988; mem. treatment com. Gov.'s Policy Coun. on Drugs, Sacramento, 1989; task force Human Svcs. Tng., Salem, Oreg., 1972; organizer West Eugene Bozo Assn., 1973; founder Green Psychology, 1993. Named Outstanding Young Man of Am., U.S. Jaycees, 1980; recipient Silver Key, House Plan Assn., 1966. Fellow Am. Orthopsychiat. Assn.; mem. Calif. Assn. Family Therapists, World Fedn. of Therapeutic Communities, Nat. Writer's Club, N.Y. Acad. Scis., Internat. Assn. for Human Rels. Lab. Tng., Calif. Assn. of Drug Programs and Profls. (pres. 1988-90), Phi Beta Kappa. Office: 6641 Simson St Oakland CA 94605-2220

NEBERGALL, ROBERT WILLIAM, orthopedic surgeon, educator; b. Des Moines, Dec. 31, 1954; s. Donald Charles and Shirley (Williams) N.; m. Teresa Rae Fawell, May 27, 1978; children: Nathaniel Robert Baird, Bartholomew William Campbell. BS in Biology, Luther Coll., 1977; DO, U. Osteo. Health Scis., 1981. Intern Des Moines Gen. Hosp., 1981-82; resident orthopedic surgery Tulsa Regional Med. Ctr., 1982-86; trauma fellow Assn. Osteosynthesis/Assn. Study of Internal Fixation Fellowship Program, Stuttgart and Mainz, West Germany, 1986; sports medicine fellow U. Oreg. Orthopedic and Fracture Clinic, Eugene, 1986; orthopedic surgeon Tulsa Orthopedic Surgeons, 1987—; team physician Tulsa Ballet Theatre, 1987—, Internat. Pro Rodeo Assn., Oklahoma City, 1987—, Nathan Hale H.S. Football, 1992—, Ctrl. H.S., 1993—, Tulsa Roughnecks Soccer, 1993—, Okla. All State Games, 1994—; clin. asst. prof. surgery Okla. State U. Coll. Osteo. Medicine; chmn. dept. orthopedic surgery Tulsa Regional Med. Ctr.; pres. Green Country Ind. Practice Assn. Mem. Okla. Found. for Peer Rev., Oklahoma City, 1988—; past pres. Culver (Ind.) Summer Sch. Alumni Assn., 1991; trustee Culver Ednl. Found. of Culver Mil. Acad., 1991-93. Recipient Vol. award Tulsa Ballet Theatre, 1990, Physicians Recognition award AMA, 1990; named Outstanding Young Man in Am., U.S. Jaycees, 1983. Mem. Am. Osteo. Acad. Orthopedics, Am. Coll. Sports Medicine, Am. Osteo. Orthopedic Soc. Sports Medicine (past pres.), N.Y. Acad. Scis., Assn. Osteosynthesis Fellowship Alumni Orgn., Sigma Sigma Phi. Methodist. Home: 2116 S Detroit Ave Tulsa OK 74114-1208 Office: Tulsa Orthopedic Surgeons 802 S Jackson Ave Ste 130 Tulsa OK 74127-9010

NECCO, E(DNA) JOANNE, school psychologist; b. Klamath Falls, Oreg., June 23, 1941; d. Joseph Rogers and Lillian Laura (Owings) Painter; m. Jon F. Puryear, Aug. 25, 1963 (div. Oct. 1987); children: Laura L., Douglas F.; m. A. David Necco, July 1, 1989. BS, Cen. State U., 1978, MEd, 1985; PhD in Applied Behavioral Studies, Okla. State U., 1993. Med.-surg. asst. Oklahoma City Clinic, 1961-68; spl. edn. tchr. Oklahoma City Pub. Schs., 1978-79, Edmond (Okla.) Pub. Schs., 1979-83; co-founder, owner Learning Devel. Clinic, Edmond, 1983-93; asst. prof. profl. tchr. edn. U. Ctrl. Okla., Edmond, 1993—; adj. instr. Ctrl. State U., Edmond, 1989-93, Oklahoma City U., 1991-93; mem. rsch. group Okla. State U., Stillwater, 1991-93; presenter in field. Contbr. articles to profl. jours. Com. Boy Scouts of Am., SCUBA Post 604, Oklahoma City, 1981-86; mem. Edmond Task Force for Youth, 1983-87, Edmond C. of C., 1984-87; active Okla. Ctr. for Neurosci., 1991; evaluator for Even Start Literacy Program, 1994—. Mem. ASCD, Nat. Assn. for Sch. Psychologists, Am. Bus Women's Assn., Coun. for Exceptional Children, Learning Disabilities Assn., Am. Assn. for Gifted Underachieving Students, Okla. Learning Disabilities Assn., Okla. Assn. for Counseling and Devel., Golden Key Nat. Honor Soc., Internat. Soc. for Scientific Study of Subjectivity, Am. Coun. on Rural Spl. Edn., Ctrl State U. (Okla., life), Phi Delta Kappa. Republican. Home: 17509 Woodsorrel Rd Edmond OK 73003-6951 Office: U Ctrl Okla Coll Edn 100 N University Dr Edmond OK 73034

NECHES, RICHARD BROOKS, cardiologist, educator; b. Long Branch, N.J., Nov. 22, 1955; s. Jacob and Evelyn (Brooks) N. BS summa cum laude, Wofford Coll., 1976; MD, Med. U. S.C., Charleston, 1979. Diplomate Am. Bd. Internal Medicine, cardiovascular diseases; lic. physician, N.Y., N.J. Resident internal medicine Brookdale Hosp. Med. Ctr., Bklyn., 1979-82; fellow cardiovascular diseases Beth Israel Med. Ctr., N.Y.C., 1982-84, chief fellow cardiology, 1984; pvt. practice cardiology, 1984—; co-chief div. cardiology dept. medicine St. John's Episcopal Hosp., Far Rockaway, N.Y., 1990—; clin. instr. medicine SUNY, Stony Brook, 1987-88; clin. asst. prof. medicine U. Medicine and Dentistry N.J., Robert Wood Johnson Med. Sch., New Brunswick, 1989-91, SUNY Health Sci. Ctr., Bklyn., 1991—; participant internat. cardiology studies. Contbr. articles to profl. jours. Mem. Am. Heart Assn. Fellow Am. Coll. Cardiology, Am. Coll. Angiology, N.Y. Cardiological Soc.; mem. Phi Beta Kappa. Office: St John's Episcopal Hosp Dept Medicine 327 Beach 19th St Far Rockaway NY 11691-4423

NECHES, WILLIAM HAROLD, pediatrics educator; b. Bklyn., June 11, 1940; s. Abraham B. and Rose B. Neches; m. Ellen Diane Alster, June 14, 1962; children: Stuart, Barbara. BA, Syracuse U., 1961; MD, SUNY, Bklyn., 1965. Diplomate Am. Bd. Pediats., sub-bd. pediat. cardiology. Resident Maimonides Med. Ctr., Bklyn., 1965-68; fellow Tex. Children's Hosp., Houston, 1970-72; prof. U. Pitts., 1972—. Author: Pediatric Cardiac Catheterization, 1991; editor: Perspectives in Pediatric Cardiology, 1988. Bd. dirs. Pa. affiliate Am. Heart Assn., Harrisburg, 1980—. Maj. U.S. Army, 1968-70. Recipient Disting. Achievement award Pa. affiliate Am. Heart Assn., 1988, Disting. Svc. award, 1991; tchg. scholar Am. Heart Assn., 1975-80. Office: Children's Hosp 3705 Fifth Ave Pittsburgh PA 15213

NEEDHAM, CHARLES WILLIAM, neurosurgeon; b. Bklyn., Oct. 14, 1936; s. William and Jeanne (Studioso) N.; m. Constance Taft, June 15, 1958; children: Susan, Andrew, Jennifer, Sarah, Benjamin. B.S. cum laude Wagner Coll., 1957; M.D., Albany Med. Coll., 1961; M.Sc., McGill U., 1969. Cert. Am. Bd. Neurol. Surgery; lic. physician Conn. Asst. prof. neurol. surgery UCLA Sch. Medicine, 1969-71; clin. assoc. prof. neurol. surgery U. Ariz., Tucson, 1971-84; staff neurosurgeon Norwalk (Conn.) Hosp., Bridgeport (Conn.) Hosp., 1996—; clin. instr. neurosurgery Yale U. Sch. Medicine, 1989—; postdoctoral fellow Nat. Inst. Neurol. Diseases & Blindness, 1967-69. Author: Neurosurgical Syndromes of the Brain, 1973, Cerebral Logic, 1978, Principles of Cerebral Dominance, 1982, Neurosurgical Signs, 1986; contbr. articles to profl. jours. Served to capt. USAF MC, 1963-65. Recipient numerous awards for excellence in medicine including AMA Continuing Edn. awards, 1978—, Yale U. Sch. Medicine award, 1986. Fellow ACS; mem. AAAS, Am. Assn. Neurol. Surgeons, Congress Neurol. Surgeons, Brain and Behavioral Scis. Assn., N.Y. Acad. Scis., New Eng. Neurosurg. Soc., Conn. State Neurosurg. Soc. (pres. 1992—), Fairfield (Conn.) County Med. Soc. Avocations: philosophy, physics, anthropology, writing. Home: 1 Sipperleys Hill Rd Westport CT 06880-1245 Office: 5 Elmcrest Ter Norwalk CT 06850-3938

NEEDHAM, GLEN RAY, entology and acarology educator; b. Lamar, Colo., Dec. 25, 1951; s. Robert Lee and Evor Elaine (Kern) N.; m. Karla Marie Lohr, May 28, 1983; children: Kathleen Marie, John Harrison, Elizabeth Anne. BS, S.W. Okla. State U., 1973; MS, Okla. State U., 1975, PhD, 1978. Grad. rsch. asst. Okla. State U., Stillwater, 1974-78; asst. prof. Ohio State U., Columbus, 1978-84, assoc. prof., 1984—, co-organizer and coord. acarology summer program. Co-editor: Africanized Honey Bees and Bee Mites, 1988, Acarology IX: Proceedings and Symposia. Donor ARC, Columbus. Recipient Dist. Alumnus award Okla. State U., 1992. Mem. Acarology Soc. Am. (pres. 1994), Entomol. Soc. Am., Ohio State Beekeepers Assn., Soc. Vector Ecology, Gamma Sigma Delta, Sigma Xi. Methodist. Office: Ohio State U 484 W 12th Ave Columbus OH 43210-1214

NEEDHAM, THOMAS EDWARD, pharmacy educator; b. Newton, N.J., Apr. 12, 1942; s. Thomas E. and Elenora (Chretien) N.; married, Nov. 22, 1973; children: James, David. BS, U. R.I., 1965, MS, 1967, PhD, 1970. Registered pharmacist, R.I. From asst. prof. to assoc. prof. U. Ga. Sch. Pharmacy, Athens, 1970-79; assoc. dir. pharm. devel. Travenol Labs., Morton Grove, Ill., 1979-82, dir. new product devel., 1982-87; sect. head drug delivery Searle, Skokie, Ill., 1987-89; prof., chmn. pharmaceutics, dir. drug delivery R&D lab. U. R.I. Coll. Pharmacy, Kingston, 1989—; cons. pharm. cos., 1989—. Contbr. articles to profl. jours. Drug Delivery Rsch. grantee 4 pharm. cos. U. R.I., 1989-90. Mem. Am. Assn. Pharm. Scientists (various coms. 1986-90), Controlled Release Soc. (various coms. 1985-90). Office: U RI Coll Pharmacy Fogarty Hall Kingston RI 02881

NEEDLEMAN, HERBERT LEROY, psychiatrist, pediatrician; b. Phila., Dec. 13, 1927; s. J. Joseph and Sonia Rita (Shupak) N.; m. Shirley Weinstein, Sept. 12, 1948 (div. 1957); 1 child, Samuel; m. Roberta Pizor, June 2, 1963; children Joshua, Sara. BS, Muhlenberg Coll., Allentown, Pa., 1948; MD, U. Pa., 1952. Intern Phila. Gen. Hosp., 1952-54; resident in pediatrics Children's Hosp. of Phila., 1957-58, chief resident in pediatrics, 1958-59; resident in psychiatry Temple U. Med. Ctr., Phila., 1962-65, asst. prof. psychiatry, 1967-71; spl. fellow in psychiatry NIMH, Bethesda, Md., 1965-67; assoc. prof. psychiatry Harvard Med. Sch., Boston, 1971-81; prof. psychiatry and pediatrics U. Pitts. Sch. Medicine, 1981—; cons. air lead criteria document EPA, Washington, 1977; editor Ctrs. for Disease Control, Atlanta, 1978; mem. adv. com. on childhood lead poisoning prevention, 1990; chmn. devel. toxicology subpanel NAS, 1986. Editor: Low Level Lead Exposure: The Clinical Implications of Current Research, 1980, contbr. articles to profl. jours. Chmn. Com. of Responsibility, Boston, 1966-75, Alliance to End Childhood Lead Poisoning, Washington, 1991-92; bd. dirs. Mass. Advocacy Ctr., Boston, 1972-80. Capt. U.S. Army, 1955-57. Recipient Sarah L. Poiley Meml. award N.Y. Acad. Scis., 1985, The Charles A. Dana award, 1989; NAS IOM, 1990, H. John Heinz award, 1995. Fellow Am. Acad. Pediatrics; mem. Soc. of Toxicology, Am. Pediatric Soc., Am. Acad. of Child and Adolescent Psychiatry, Am. Acad. of Pediatrics Com. on Environ. Hazards, Phi Beta Kappa, Sigma Xi. Democrat. Jewish. Home: 5734 Aylesboro Ave Pittsburgh PA 15217-1412 Office: Univ Pitts Sch Medicine 305 Iroquois Ave Pittsburgh PA 15237-4724

NEEDLEMAN, PHILIP, cardiologist, pharmacologist; b. Bklyn., Feb. 10, 1939. BS, Phila. Coll. Pharm. & Sci., 1960; MS, U. Md. Med. Sch., 1962, PhD in Pharmacology, 1964. Fellow Sch. Medicine Washington U., St. Louis, 1965-67, from asst. prof. to prof. Sch. Medicine, 1967-75, prof. Sch. Medicine, 1975—, with dept. pharmacology, 1976—, corp. v.p. R&D, chief scientist, 1991—. Contbr. numerous articles to profl. jours. Recipient Rsch. Career Devel. award NIH, 1974, 76, Wellcome Creesy award in clin. pharmacology, 1977, 78, 80, 87, Cochems Thrombosis Rsch. prize, 1980. *

NEEL, HARRY BRYAN, III, surgeon, scientist, educator; b. Rochester, Minn., Oct. 28, 1939; s. Harry Bryan and May Birgitta (Bjornsson) N.; m. Ingrid Helene Vaga, Aug. 29, 1964; children: Carlton Bryan, Harry Bryan IV, Roger Clifton. BS, Cornell U., 1962; MD, SUNY-Bklyn., 1966; PhD, U. Minn., 1976. Diplomate Am. Bd. Otolaryngology. Intern Kings County Hosp., Bklyn., 1966-67; resident in gen. surgery U. Minn. Hosps., Mpls., 1967-68; resident in otolaryngology Mayo Grad. Sch. Medicine Mayo Clinic, Rochester, Minn., 1970-74, cons. in otohinolaryngology, 1974—, cons. in cell biology, 1981—, assoc. prof. otolaryngology and microbiology Med. Sch., 1979-84, prof., 1984—, also chmn. dept. otolaryngology. Author: Cryosurgery for Cancer, 1976; contbr. chpts. to books, articles to profl. jours. V.p. bd. dirs. Minn. Orch. in Rochester, Inc., 1982, pres., chmn., 1983-84; mem. devel. com. Minn. Orchestral Assn., 1983, Mayo Found. bd. devel., 1983-86; bd. dirs. Mayo Health Plan, 1986-92, chmn., 1990-92; mem. bd. Mayo Mgmt. Svcs., Inc., 1992—; mem. bd. regents U. Minn., 1991—, chair faculty staff, student affairs com., 1993-95, vice chmn. bd., 1995—; bd. dirs. Greater Rochester Area Univ. Ctr., 1993—. With USPHS, 1968-70. Recipient travel award Soc. Acad. Chmn. Otolaryngology, 1974, Ira J. Tresley rsch. award Am. Acad. Facial and Reconstructive Surgery, 1982, Notable award Nat. Assn. Collegiate Women Athletic Admisntrs., 1992, The Best Doctors in Am. award Woodward/White, 1992-93, 94-95. Mem. AMA, ACS (bd. govs. 1985-90, devel. bd. 1988—, treas. 1990—, sec.-treas. Minn. chpt. 1983-85, pres. 1988-89), Am. Acad. Otolaryngology-Head and Neck Surgery (prize for basic rsch. in otolaryngology 1972, bd. dirs. 1988-91, established Neel Disting. Rsch. Lectureship Endowment Fund 1994), Minn. Med. Assn., Zumbro Valley Med. Soc., Am. Broncho-Esophagological Assn. (pres.-elect 1988, pres. 1989-90), Am. Laryngological, Rhinological and Oto. Sco. (Mosher award 1980, pres.-elect 1995—), Am. Laryngological Assn. (Casselberry award 1985, sec. 1988-93, v.p. 1994, pres. 1994—, Newcomb award 1996), Assn. for Rsch. in Otolaryngology, Assn. Acad. Depts. in Otolaryngology (sec.-treas. 1984-86, pres.-elect 1986, pres. 1988-9), Alumni Assn. Cornell U. (Outstanding Alumni award 1985, Collegium ORL Amicitiae Sacrum 1990—), Am. Bd. Otolaryngology (bd. dirs. 1986—, most admired man of decade 1992). Republican. Presbyterian. Club: Rochester Golf and Country. Home: 828 8th St SW Rochester MN 55902-6310 Office: Mayo Clinic 200 1st St SW Rochester MN 55905-0001

NEEL, JAMES W., biology educator; b. Turlock, Calif., July 20, 1925; s. Lloyd Earl and Margaret Noble (Bevans) N.; m. Frances Arlene Miller, Sept. 22, 1956. BS, U. Calif., Berkeley, 1949; PhD, UCLA, 1964. From lab. tech. to prin. lab. tech. UCLA Atomic Energy Project, 1949-59; rsch. asst. UCLA Dept. Irrigation & Soilsci., 1959-63; asst. prof., assoc. prof. biology San Diego State U., 1963-69, prof. biology, 1969-93, assoc. dean coll. scis., 1976-93, prof. emeritus, 1993—, dir. coll. scis. grad. access office, 1995—; cons. Rand Corp., Santa Monica, Calif., 1963-71. Contbr. articles to profl. jours. Sgt. U.S. Army, 1943-45. Mem. AAAS, Am. Inst. Biol. Scis., Am. Soc. Agronomy, Soil Sci. Soc. Am., Sigma Xi. Office: San Diego State U Dept Biology San Diego CA 92182

NEELY, ROBERT ALLEN, ophthalmologist; b. Temple, Tex., Mar. 1, 1921; s. Jubal A. and Almeida (Fordtran) N.; BA, U. Tex., 1942, MD, 1944; postgrad. Washington U., 1951-52; m. Eleanor V. Stein, June 29, 1944 (dec.); m. Joy S. Brown, Aug. 24, 1990; children: Byron D., Warren F. Intern, also resident Hermann Hosp., Houston, 1944-45, 55-57; gen. practice medicine, 1946-51, specializing in ophthalmology, Bellville, Tex., 1955—, ret.1992; trustee, staff mem. Bellville Hosp., Inc.; pres. Mid-Tex. Nursing Homes, Inc.; ret., 1992; chmn. bd. dirs. 1st Nat. Bank of Bellville. Mem. Bellville Ind. Sch. Dist. Sch. Bd., 1948-53; past pres. Bellville Area United Fund; adv. bd. mem. Sam Houston Area coun. Boy Scouts Am., past mem. nat. council; mem. chancellor's coun. U. Tex. System. Served with USNR, 1943-46, 53-55. Recipient Silver Beaver award Boy Scouts Am. Fellow Am. Acad. Ophthalmology; mem. AMA, Austin-Grimes-Waller Counties (past pres.), Ninth Dist. (past pres.) med. soc., Tex. Med. Assn., Tex. Ophthal. Assn., Houston Ophthal. Soc., Tex. Soc. Opthalmology and Otolaryngology, Bellville C. of C., VFW (life), Bellville Golf Club (past pres.), Doctors Club, Lions (past pres.). Republican. Lutheran. Home: 105 E Hacienda St Bellville TX 77418-3103

NEER, CHARLES SUMNER, II, orthopedic surgeon, educator; b. Vinita, Okla., Nov. 10, 1917; s. Charles Sumner and Pearl Victoria (Brooke) N.; m. Eileen Meyer, June 12, 1990; children: Charlotte Marguerite, Sydney Victoria, Charles Henry. BA, Dartmouth Coll., 1939; MD, U. Pa., 1942. Diplomate Am. Bd. Orthopaedic Surgery (bd. dirs. 1970-75). Intern U. Pa. Hosp., Phila., 1942-43; asso. in surgery N.Y. Orthopedic-Columbia-Presbyn. Med. Center, N.Y.C., 1943-44; instr. in surgery Coll. Physicians and Surgeons, Columbia U., N.Y.C., 1946-47; instr. orthopaedic surgery Coll. Physicians and Surgeons, Columbia U., 1947-57, asst. prof. clin. orthopaedic surgery, 1957-64, asso. prof., 1964-68, prof. clin. orthopaedic surgery, 1968-90, prof. clin. orthopaedic surgery emeritus, spl. lectr. orthopaedic surgery, 1990—; attending orthopaedic surgeon Columbia-Presbyn. Med. Ctr., N.Y.C.; chief adult reconstructive svc. N.Y. Orthopaedic Hosp.; chief shoulder and elbow clinic Presbyn. Hosp.; cons. orthopaedic surgeon emeritus N.Y. Orthopaedic-Columbia-Presbyn. Med. Ctr., 1991—; chmn. 4th Internat. Congress Shoulder Surgeons; chmn. Internat. Bd. Shoulder Surgery, 1992—. Founder, chmn. bd. trustees Jour. Shoulder and Elbow Surgery, 1990—; contbr. articles to books, tech. films, sound slides. Served with U.S. Army, 1944-46. Recipient Disting. Svc. award Am. Bd. Orthopaedic Surgeons 1975. Fellow ACS (sr. mem. nat. com. on trauma), Am. Acad. Orthop. Surgeons (com. on upper extremity, shoulder com.); mem. AMA, ACS (mem. com. trauma), Am. Bd. Orthop. Surgeons (bd. dirs. 1970-75, Disting. Svc. award 1975), Am. Shoulder and Elbow Surgeons (inaugural pres.), Am. Assn. Surgery Trauma, Am. Orthop. Assn., Mid-Am. Orthop. Assn. (hon.), N.Y. Acad. Medicine, Allen O. Whipple Surg. Soc., N.Y. State Med. Soc., N.Y. County Med. Soc., Pan Am. Med. Assn., Am. Trauma Soc., Soc. Latino Am. Orthop. y Traumatology, Internat. Soc. Orthop. Surgery and Traumatology, Va. Orthop. Soc. (hon.), Carolina Orthop. Alumni Assn. (hon.), Conn. Orthop. Club (hon.), Houston Orthop. Assn. (hon.), Soc. Française de Chirurgie Orthop. et Traumatology (hon.), Soc. Italiana Orthop. Etravmatologia; patron, Shoulder and Elbow Soc. Australia, South African Shoulder Soc., Giraffe Club, Internat. Bd. Shoulder Surgery (chmn. 1992—), Alpha Omega Alpha, Phi Chi. Home and Office: 231 S Miller St Vinita OK 74301-3625

NEER, HOWARD LESTER, physician, educator; b. Dayton, Ohio, Mar. 16, 1929; s. Lester Cook and Katherine (Zwaster) N.; m. Gloria Pyle, Sept. 7, 1952; children: Cynthia Neer Burkey, Barbara Neer Heyward. BA, Miami U., Oxford, Ohio, 1946; DO, Chgo. Coll. Osteo. Medicine, 1954. Diplomate Am. Bd. Quality Assurance and Utilization Rev. Physicians, Am. Bd. Osteopathic Gen. Practice; lic. real estate broker. Intern Grand View Hosp., Dayton, 1954-55; pvt. practice family medicine Lutz, Fla., 1955-56, Plantation, Fla., 1956—; assoc. dean clin. affairs, prof. gen. practice Southeastern U. Health Scis., Miami, Fla., 1991—; chmn. bd. dirs. Fla. Physicians Ins. Trust, 1976-91, Gulf Atlantic Ins. Co., Tallahassee, 1980-94, Fla. Med. Ctr. South; mem. Broward Collier Profl. Rev. Bd., Ft. Lauderdale, 1980-82; mem. Broward Area Health Planning Coun., Ft. Lauderdale, 1982-84, Broward County Health Svcs. Coun., Ft. Lauderdale, 1986; sec. osteo. sect. Mut. Ins. Co., Nashville, 1988-91; founder, chmn. bd. dirs. Doctor's Hosp. Plantation, Fla.; chmn. bd. Universal Med. Ctr. Hosp., Plantation, Fla. Recipient Disting. Svc. award Chgo. Coll. Osteo. Medicine, 1982. Fellow Am. Coll. Osteo. Family Practice (cert.); mem. Am. Osteo. Assn. (chmn. bur. ins. 1988-91, trustee 1986—, chair dept. govtl. affairs 1988-89, dept. bus. affairs 1989-90, pres.-elect 1994, pres. 1995-96), Fla. Osteo. Med. Assn. (pres. 1960-91, trustee 1976-77), Broward County Osteo. Med. Assn. (past pres.). Presbyterian. Office: Southeastern U Health Scis 5757 N Dixie Hwy Fort Lauderdale FL 33334-4135

NEFF, MARTIN SYLVAN, physician; b. Phila., Oct. 28, 1937; s. Albert Louis and Pearl (Turk) N.; m. Jeanne Moliver, June 9, 1963; children: Roni, Debra, Sally. BA, U. Pa., 1959; MD, N.Y. Med. Coll., 1963. Diplomate Am. Bd. Internal Medicine; subspecialty in Nephrology. Intern Phila. Gen. Hosp., 1963-64; resident Hahnemann Hosp., Phila., 1966-68, fellow in nephrology, 1968-70; attending chief of nephrology Elmhurst (N.Y.) Hosp. Ctr., 1970—; prof. medicine Mt. Sinai Sch. Medicine, N.Y.C., 1970—; pres. End Stage Renal Disease Network N.Y. State, 1989-92, chmn. med. rev. bd., 1992-96. Chmn. med. adv. bd. Nat. Kidney Found., N.Y., N.J., 1994-96. Fellow Am. Coll. Physicians. Democrat. Jewish. Office: Elmhurst Hosp Ctr 7901 Broadway Elmhurst NY 11373

NEFF, P. SHERRILL, health care executive; b. Balt., Dec. 18, 1951; s. Paul Heston and Mary (Poulnot) N.; m. Sarah B. Barrett, June 20, 1976 (div. 1985); 1 child, Jacob Colin; m. Alicia Phyll Felton, May 26, 1988; 1 child, Michael Felton. BA, Wesleyan U., 1974; JD magna cum laude, U. Mich., 1980. Bar: Pa. 1980. Atty. Morgan Lewis & Bockius, Phila., 1980-84; investment banker Alex Brown & Sons, Inc., Balt., 1984-93, mng. dir., 1992-93; sr. v.p. corp. devel. U.S. Healthcare, Blue Bell, Pa., 1993-94; pres., CFO Neose Techs., Inc., Horsham, Pa., 1994—, also bd. dirs.; bd. dirs. Jeff Banks, Inc., Phila. Trustee Zero Moving Dance Co., Phila., 1984-93. Mem. Pa. Biotech. Assn. (bd. dirs. 1996—). Democrat. Jewish. Home: 619 Revere Rd Merion Station PA 19066-1007 Office: Neose Techs. Inc PO Box 1109 102 Witmer Rd Horsham PA 19044

NEGOVSKY, VLADIMIR ALEXANDROVICH, resuscitation researcher; b. Kozelets, Chernigov, Ukraine, Mar. 19, 1909; s. Alexander Timofeevich and Varvara Semenovna (Gulanitskaya) N.; m. Praskovia Snezhkina, 1930 (div. 1954); 1 child, Alla Alexandrovna. Candidate med. sci., Moscow State Med. Inst., 1942, D in Med. Sci., 1943; Doctorate (hon.), Med. Acad. Poznan, Poland, 1973. Founder, dir. Rsch. of Lab. of Gen. Reanimatology, Moscow, 1936-85; dir. Inst. for Gen. Reanimatology, Moscow, 1985-88, sci. adviser, 1988—. Mem. USSR Acad. Med. Sci., European Resuscitation Coun. (hon. life). Office: Inst Gen Reanimatology, 25 Petrovka Str Bldg 2, 103031 Moscow Russia

NEGRI, EVA VANNA, epidemiologist; b. Milan, Lombardy, Italy, Feb. 9, 1959; d. Guido Negri and Flora Tedeschi; m. Carlo La Vecchia, July 24, 1987; children: Irene, Adriano. DSc in Math., U. Milan, 1985, postgrad., 1985-88. Rsch. fellow Inst. Rsch. Pharmacology Mario Negri, Milan, 1984-90, mem. rsch. staff, 1990-92, chief epidemiological methodology unit, 1992—; analyst Inter-U. Consortium Lombardy Automatic Data Processing, Milan, 1986-90; referee Am. Jour. Epidemiology, Cancer, Causes and Control, European Jour. Cancer, Internat. Jour. Epidemiology, Revue d'Epidemiologie et de la Sante Publique. Mem. editl. bd. Advances in Therapy, Jour. Epidemiology and Biostatistics; contbr. articles to profl. jours. Rsch. fellow EEC, 1988. Office: Inst Rsch Pharmacology Mario Negri, Via Eritrea 62, 20157 Milan Italy

NEHER, ERWIN, biophysicist; b. Landsberg, Bavaria, Germany, Mar. 20, 1944; s. Franz Xaver and Elisabeth (Pfeiffer) N.; m. Eva-Maria Ruhr, Dec. 26, 1978; children: Richard, Benjamin, Carola, Sigmund, Margret. MS, U. Wis., 1967; Dr. rer. nat., Tech. U., Munich, 1970. Rsch. assoc. Max Planck Inst. for Psychiatry, Munich, 1970-72; rsch. assoc. Max Planck Inst. for Biophys. Chemistry, Göttingen, 1972-75, 1976-83, rsch. dir., 1983—; rsch. assoc. Yale Univ., 1975-76; Fairchild Scholar, Calif. Inst. of Tech., 1988-89. Author: Elektronische Messtechnik, 1974; editor: Single Channel Recording, 1983; contbr. numerous articles to profl. jours. Co-recipient Nobel Prize physiology or medicine, 1991; recipient Louisa Gross-Horwitz award Columbia U., N.Y.C., 1986, Leibniz award Deutsche Forschungsgemeinschaft, Bonn, 1986, Gairdner Found. award, 1989. Mem. AAAS (fgn. assoc.), NAS (fgn. assoc.), Royal Soc. (fgn. mem.), Bavarian Acad. Scis. (corr.), Academia Europea, Akademie d. Wissensch. zu Goettingen. Roman Catholic. Office: Max Planck Inst Biophys Chemistry, Am Fassberg Pf 2841, 37077 Göttingen Germany

NEHER, ROBERT TROSTLE, biology educator; b. Mt. Morris, Ill., Nov. 1, 1930; s. Oscar Warner and Etha Mae (Trostle) N.; m. Mary Rebecca Timmons, June 12, 1954; children: Kenneth, Jon, Daniel. B.A. in Sci., Manchester Coll., Ind., 1953; M.A.T. in Biology, Ind. U., 1955, Ph.D. in Botany, 1963; M.R.E. in Counseling, Bethany Sem., Chgo., 1957. Assoc. Christian edn. Ch. of Brethren, Elgin, Ill., 1956; asst. prof., then assoc. prof. biology U. LaVerne, Calif., 1958-62, prof. biology, 1966—, chmn. nat. sci. div., 1978—, dep. dir. Nat. Energy Research and Info. Inst., 1982-88, chair pre-health sci. com., 1985—; aquaculture cons. Bolsa Aquaculture Consortium, 1973-76, AM China Corp., 1981; cons. devel. of in-service tchr. tng. in environ. edn. Los Angeles Pub. Schs.; dir. coll. level curriculum program Montclair High Sch., Van Nuys, Calif. Co-editor: Energy from Biomass, 1979. Contbr. articles to profl. jours. City councilman LaVerne City Council, 1976-84, mayor pro tem, 1980-84; commr. Los Angeles County Watershed Commn., 1976-91; bd. dirs. Pomona Valley Youth Svcs. juvenile div. chmn., 1978-79; chmn. San Gabriel Valley Get-About Transp. Bd., 1980-84; mem. Los Angeles County Solid Waste Curbside Recycling Task Force, 1980-82; chmn. La Verne City Commn. on Environ. Quality, 1972-75; mem. La Verne City Planning Commn., 1966-72; moderator La Verne Ch. of Brethren, 1966-75, chmn. bd., 1977-80, mem. ch. bd. dirs., 1966-84; trustee San Gabriel Valley Mosquito Abatement Dist., 1991—. Named Outstanding Tchr. of Yr., La Verne Coll., 1969-70. NSF grantee, 1960-61; NSF faculty fellow Ind. U., Bloomington, 1961-62; Mem. AAAS (life mem.), Am. Soc. Plant Taxonomists, Calif. Bot. Soc., San Bernardino County Mus. Assn., Audubon Soc., Sierra Club, Friends of the Earth, Nat. Geog. Soc., Mother Earth (life mem.), Sigma Xi. Home: 2373 Bonita Ave La Verne CA 91750-4932 Office: U La Verne 2373 Bonita Ave La Verne CA 91750-4932

NEHLIN, JAN O., medical biologist; b. Caracas, Venezuela, May 7, 1964; s. Sven O. and Jacqueline (Kordeuter) N. BSc, U. Simon Bolivar, 1986; D in Med. Scis., Uppsala U., 1992. Grad. fellow Uppsala U., Sweden, 1986-92; postdoctoral fellow Ludwig Inst. Cancer Rsch., Uppsala, 1992-94, U. Calif., Berkeley, 1994—. Mem. Am. Soc. Cell & Molecular Biology. Office: Berkeley Nat Lab 1 Cyclotron Rd 70A-1118 Berkeley CA 94720

NEIBEL, OLIVER JOSEPH, JR., medical services executive; b. Kansas City, Mo., Apr. 17, 1927; s. Oliver Joseph and Eula Lee (Durham) N.; m. Patricia Helen O'Keefe, June 24, 1950 (div. 1971); children: Oliver Joseph III, Deborah Sue; m. Diane Bachus Nelson, Apr. 11, 1981. BS U. Ariz., 1949; JD U. Va., 1952. Bar: Wash. 1952, Ill. 1961, Nebr. 1973. Instr., U. Washington, 1952-53; practiced in Seattle, 1953-57; asst. atty. gen. State of Wash., 1957-61; legislative atty. AMA, Chgo., 1961-63; exec. dir., gen. counsel Coll. Am. Pathologists, Chgo., 1963-72; v.p., gen. mgr. Physicians Lab., Omaha, 1973—. Justice of peace, Mountlake Terrace, Wash., 1955-57. Served with USNR, 1945. Mem. Wash. Bar Assn., Nebr. Bar Assn., Ill. Bar Assn., Nat. Health Lawyers Assn., Med. Group Mgmt. Assn., Phi Kappa Psi (chpt. pres. 1948-49), Delta Theta Phi, Alpha Kappa Psi, Delta Sigma Rho. Mason, Elk, Rotarian, Shriners. Clubs: Wash. Athletic (Seattle); Tavern (Chgo.); Omaha Press. Home: 7918 Potter Plz Omaha NE 68122-1449 Office: 4840 F St Omaha NE 68117-1407

NEIBERGER, RICHARD EUGENE, pediatrician, nephrologist, educator; b. Onaga, Kans., Nov. 16, 1947; s. Earl Edward and Margaret Bell (Grim) N.; m. Mary June Chamberlin, Oct. 31, 1971; children: Ami, Eric, Chris, Robert. BS in Physics, U. Ctrl. Fla., 1971; PhD, U. Louisville, 1979, MD, 1982. Diplomate Am. Bd. Pediat., Nat. Bd. Med. Examiners. Intern, then resident in pediat. Albert Einstein Coll. Med., Bronx, N.Y., 1982-85; fellow in pediat. nephrology Albert Einstein Coll. Med., Bronx, 1985-88; asst. prof. U. Fla. Coll. Med., Gainesville, 1988-93, assoc. prof., 1993—; assoc. med. dir. Children's Kidney Ctr., Gainesville, 1989—; rsch. peer rev. com. Fla. affiliate Am. Heart Assn., 1993—; physician advisor Fla. Med. Quality Assurance, Tampa, 1994—. Contbr. articles to profl. jours. Sunday Sch. Tchr. Trinity United Meth. Ch., Gainesville, 1992—; Bd. dirs. Children's Home Soc., Gainesville, 1994—; troop com. mem. Boy Scouts Am. Trinity Ch., Gainesville, 1994—. Grantee CoInvest, Bethesda, Md., 1995. Mem. AMA, Fla. Med. Assn., So. Med. Assn., Am. Soc. Nephrology, Internat. Pediat. Nephrology Assn., Am. Soc. Pediat. Nephrology. Republican. Methodist. Office: Dept Pediat Univ Fla 1600 Archer Rd Gainesville FL 32610-0296

NEILSON, ERIC GRANT, physician, educator, health facility administrator; b. Bklyn., Sept. 14, 1949; s. Jack Drew and Lynette Elsie (Lundquist) N.; m. Linda Rae Apolzon, May 27, 1972; children: Tinsley, Sigrid. BS magna cum laude, Denison U., 1971; MD magna cum laude, U. Ala., 1975; MD (hon.), U. Pa., 1987. Asst. prof. U. Pa., Phila., 1980-87, assoc. prof., 1987-91, prof., 1991—, C. Mahlon Kline prof., 1993—, chief renal-electrolyte & hypertension divsn. dept. medicine, 1988—; attending physician Hosp. of U. Pa., 1980—; cons. in field. Med. editorial bds. on sci. jours.; contbr. numerous articles to profl. jours. Chmn. med. adv. bd. Lupus Found. of Phila., 1985-95; chmn. pathology A study sect. NIH, Bethesda, Md., 1990-92; chmn. grant rev. com. Nat. Kidney Found. of Delaware Valley. Recipient Clin. Scientist award Am. Heart Assn., 1980, Young Investigator award Am. Soc. Nephrology/Am. Heart Assn., 1985, Established Investigator award Am. Heart Assn., President's medal Am. Soc. Nephrology, 1994. Fellow ACP; mem. Am. Soc. Clin. Investigation, Assn. Am. Physicians, Am. Soc. Nephrology, Am. Assn. Immunologists, Am. Fedn. Clin. Rsch., Assn. Subsplty. Profs. (pres. 1994-96). Mem. Soc. of Friends. Office: U Pa Renal Electrolyte Sect 700 Clin Rsch Bldg 415 Curie Blvd Philadelphia PA 19104-6140

NEILSON, THOMAS DAVID, psychologist, consultant; b. Syracuse, N.Y., Mar. 19, 1959; s. Roger Dale and Nancy (Porter) N. BA, Wake Forest U., 1981; MA, Appalachian State U., 1985; PsyD, Fla. Inst. Tech., 1987. Lic. psychologist, Tenn. Clin. psychologist Luton Mental Health Ctr., Nashville, 1987-89; dir. tng., sr. clin. psychologist Cumberland Psychology Internship Consortium/Luton Health Ctr, Nashville, 1989—; psychol. cons. determination sect. Tenn. Medicaid/Disability Program, Nashville, 1988—. Mem. APA, Tenn. Psychol. Assn., Nashville Area Psychol. Assn., Psi Chi. Home: 732 Branch Creek Rd Nashville TN 37209 Office: Luton Mental Health Ctr 1921 Ransom Pl Nashville TN 37217

NEIMS, ALLEN HOWARD, univeristy dean, medical scientist; b. Chgo., Oct. 24, 1938; s. Irving Morris and Ruth (Geller) N.; m. Myrna Gay Robins, June 18, 1961; children: Daniel Mark, Susan Roberta, Nancy Elizabeth. B.A., B.S., U. Chgo., 1957; M.D., Johns Hopkins U., 1961, Ph.D., 1966. Intern, resident in pediatrics Johns Hopkins Hosp., 1961-62, 66-68; research assoc. Lab. Neurochemistry, NIH, 1968-70; asst. prof. physiol. chemistry and pediatrics Johns Hopkins Med. Sch., 70-72; assoc. prof. McGill U., 1972-77, prof. pharmacology and pediatrics, 1977-78; dir. Roche developmental pharmacology unit, 1972-78; prof., chmn. dept. pharmacology and therapeutics, prof. pediatrics U. Fla., Gainesville, 1978-89, dean Coll. Medicine, 1989—; Fulton Bequest prof. U. Melbourne, Australia, 1974; mem. human embryology and devel. study sect. NIH, 1979-83; sci. cons. Can. Found. for Study of Sudden Infant Death, 1974-77, Nat. Soft Drink Assn., 1976-78, Internat. Life Scis. Inst., 1978-89; bd. sci. counsellors Nat. Inst. Child Health and Human Devel., 1984-89. Contbr. chpts. to books, articles to med. jours. Served to comdr. USPHS, 1968-70. NIH, Can. Med. Research Council grantee. Mem. Can. Assn. Research in Toxicology (pres. 1976-78), Am. Soc. Pharmacology and Exptl. Therapeutics (past mem. exec. coms. clin. pharmacology and drug metabolism), Pediatric Research Soc., Am. Soc. Clin. Pharmacology and Therapeutics, Assn. Am. Med. Colls, Coun. of Deans, Am. Pediatric Soc., Am. Acad. Pediatrics. Office: U Fla Coll Medicine PO Box 100215 Gainesville FL 32610-0215

NEINSTEIN, LAWRENCE STEVEN, physician, educator; b. L.A., Dec. 26, 1949; s. Shirley Neinsteon; m. Debra Barak, Dec. 17, 1972; children: Yael, Aaron, David. BS, U. Calif., L.A., 1971, MD, 1974. Diplomate Am. Bd. Internal Medicine, Am. Bd. Adolscent Medicine. Resident Cedars Sinai Med. Ctr., L.A., 1974-78; asst. prof. clin. pediatrics and medicine U. So. Calif., L.A., 1979-84, assoc. prof. clin. pediatrics and medicine, 1984-89, tenure assoc. prof. pediatrics and medicine, 1989—; assoc. dir. dovsn. adolscent medicine Children Hosp. L.A., 1988-95, mem. med. exec. com., 1994—; exec. dir. U. So. Calif. Univ. Park Health and Counseling Ctr., 1995—. Author: Adolescent Health Care Practical Guide, 3rd edit., 1996, Issues in Reproductive Health, 1994. Bd. dirs. L.A. Hebrew H.S., 1994—, Temple Ari El, North Hollywood, Calif., 1994—. Adolscent Med fellow Childrens Hosp. L.A., 1978-79; Regents scholar, 1972. Fellow ACP; mem. AMA, Soc. Adolescent Medicine (exec. bd. 1990-93, Jefferson abstract selection com. 1994—), Phi Beta Kappa. Office: Children Hosp LA 4650 Sunset Blvd Los Angeles CA 90027

NEIS, ARNOLD HAYWARD, pharmaceutical company executive; b. N.Y.C., Feb. 13, 1938; s. Harry H. and Mary Ruth (Bishop) N.; m. Lucy de Puig, Dec. 8, 1989; children by previous marriage: Nancy R., Robert C. B.S. cum laude, Columbia U., 1959; M.B.A., N.Y.U., 1967. With Scott Chem. Co., 1959-64; v.p. mktg., then v.p. Odell, Inc., N.Y.C., 1964-71, pres. Knomark div., 1969-71; pres., chief exec. officer E.T. Browne Drug Co., Inc., Englewood Cliffs, N.J., 1971—; dir. Esquire A.B. Stockholm, Knomark Can. Ltd., E.T. Browne Internat. Fellow Royal Soc. Chemists, Royal Geog. Soc., Am. Inst. Chemists, N.Y. Acad. Scis.; mem. AAAS, Am. Chem. Soc., Am. Pharm. Assn., New Eng. Soc. (bd. dirs.), Explorers Club (v.p., bd. dirs.), Chemists Club, Lotos Club, Soldiers, Sailors and Airmans Club (bd. dirs.), St. Georges Soc. Episcopalian. Home: 898 Park Ave New York NY 10021-0234 Office: PO Box 1613 140 Sylvan Ave Englewood NJ 07632-2502

NEIS, ARTHUR VERAL, healthcare and development company executive; b. Lawrence, Kans., May 30, 1940; s. Veral Herbert and Louise (Schlegel) N.; m. Fleeta Weigel, Apr. 12, 1969; children: Frederich Arthur, Benjamin Jason, Sarah Louise. BS in Bus., U. Kans., 1962, MS in Acctg., 1963. CPA, Kans., Iowa. Mgmt. cons. Arthur Andersen & Co., Kansas City, Mo. and Mpls., 1963-74; chief corp. acctg. Carlson Co., Mpls., 1974-76; controller The Fullerton Cos., Mpls., 1976-78; asst. treas. Fru-Con Corp., St. Louis, 1978-80, asst. controller, 1981, controller, 1982-86; corp. contr. LCS Holdings, Inc. (Weitz Corp. and Subsideries), Des Moines, 1986-87; treas., chief fin. officer The Weitz Corp., Des Moines, 1987—; treas., CFO Weitz Co., Des Moines, 1987-93, Life Care Services Corp., Des Moines, 1987—; bd. dirs. LCS Holdings, Inc. (Weitz Corp.); mem. adv. group NAIC, 1990-93. Bd. dirs. Inst. Humane Studies George Mason U., Fairfax, Va., 1973—, exec. com., 1975-83, chmn., 1978-83; bd. dirs. Lake Country Sch., Mpls., 1973-78; treas. Villa de Maria Montessori Sch., St. Louis, 1982-86, bd. dirs.; trustee Crossroads Sch., St. Louis, 1984-86, exec. com. bd., 1984-86; vice chair, bd. dirs. Alliance for Arts and Understanding, 1993—, co-chair, 1993—; trustee Fin. Execs. Rsch. Found., 1994—; trustee Plymouth Congrl. United Ch. of Christ, 1993—. Mem. AICPA, Kans. Soc. CPAs, Iowa Soc. CPAs, Fin. Execs. Inst. (bd. dirs. Iowa chpt. 1986, 88-94, sec. 1988-90, v.p. 1990-91, pres. 1991-92). Home: 1575 NW 106th St Clive IA 50325-6604 Office: Life Care Svcs Corp 800 2nd Ave Des Moines IA 50309-1328

NELDNER, KENNETH H., dermatologist, educator; b. Lewiston, Minn., Feb. 15, 1927; s. Herbert F. and Anna E. (Stein) N.; m. Lillian L. Neldner, Feb. 4, 1950; children: Katherine, Marabeth, Linda. BA, U. Minn., 1949; MA, U. Colo., 1950; MD, U. Minn., 1955, MS, 1963. Diplomate Am. Bd. Dermatology. Intern Ancker Hosp., St. Paul; resident Mayo Clinic, Rochester, Minn., 1960-63, fellow in dermatology, 1960-63; prof. dept. dermatology U. Colo., Denver, 1964-83; pvt. practice, Denver, 1964-83; prof. and chmn. dept. dermatology Tex. Tech. U., Lubbock, 1983-94; cons. VA, Lubbock, 1983—. Author: Pseudoxanthoma Elasticum, 1988; contbr. over 100 articles to profl. jours. Sgt. USAF, 1944-46. Fellow Am. Acad. Dermatology; mem. AMA, Soc. for Investigative Dermatology, Am. Soc. for Clin. Nutrition, Tex. Med. Assn., Assn. Profs. Dermatology, Pacific Dermatology Assn., Space Dermatol. Soc., Noah Worcester Dermatol. Soc., Tex. Dermatologic Soc., Royal Soc. Medicine (London), Am. Dermatologic Assn. Republican. Office: Dept Dermatology Tex Tech U Health Sci Ctr 3601 4th St Lubbock TX 79430-0001

NELKIN, DOROTHY, sociology and science policy educator; b. Boston, July 30, 1933; d. Henry and Helen (Fine) Wolfers; m. Mark Nelkin, Aug. 31, 1952; children: Lisa, Laurie. B.A., Cornell U., 1954. Research assoc. Cornell U., Ithaca, N.Y., 1963-69, sr. research assoc., 1970-72, assoc. prof., 1972-76, prof. sci. tech. sociology program, 1976-90, prof. sociology, 1977-90; univ. prof., prof. sociology, affiliate prof. law NYU, 1990—, Clare Boothe Luce vis. prof., 1988-90; cons. OECD, Paris, 1975-76, Inst. Environ., Berlin, 1978-79; maitre de conference U. Paris, 1975-76; maitre de recherche Ecole Polytechnique, Paris, 1980-81. Author: The Atom Besieged, 1981, The Creation Controversy, 1982, Science as Intellectual Property, 1983, Workers at Risk, 1984, Selling Science: How the Press Covers Science and Technology, 1987, 2d edit., 1995, Dangerous Diagnostics: The Social Power of Biological Information, 1989, 2d edit., 1994, A Disease of Society: Cultural Impact ofAIDS, 1991, The Animal Rights Crusade, 1991, Controversy: Politics of Technical Decision, 3d edit., 1992, The DNA Mystique: The Gene as Cultural Icon, 1995. Adviser Office Tech. Assessment, 1977-79, 82-83; expert witness ACLU, Ark., 1982; mem. Nat. Adv. Coun. to NIH Human Genome Project, 1991-95. Vis. scholar Resources for the Futures, 1980-81; vis. scholar Russell Sage Found., N.Y.C., 1983; Guggenheim fellow, 1983-84. Fellow AAAS (bd. dirs.), Hastings Inst. Soc. Ethics and Life Scis.; mem. NAS Inst. of Medicine, Soc. for Social Studies Sci. (pres. 1978-79). Home: 3 Washington Square Vlg New York NY 10012-1836 Office: NYU Dept Sociology 269 Mercer St New York NY 10003-6633

NELSON, ALAN RAY, internist, medical assocation executive; b. Logan, Utah, June 11, 1933; s. Ray J. and Leah B. (Olson) N.; m. Gwen L. Sparrow, Jan. 2, 1959; children: John R., Shannon, Alan L. Student, Utah State U., 1951-54; MD, Northwestern U., 1958. Diplomate Am. Bd. Internal Medicine, Am. Bd. Endocrinology and Metabolism. Intern Highland Alameda County Hosp., Oakland, Calif., 1958-59; resident in internal medicine U. Utah, Salt Lake City, 1959-62, assoc. clin. prof., 1964-89; clin. prof. U. Utah, 1989-92; practice medicine specializing in internal medicine and endocrinology Salt Lake City, 1964-91; assoc. Meml. Med. Ctr., Salt Lake City, 1964-91; exec. v.p. Am. Soc. Internal Medicine, Washington, 1992—; mem. Nat. Profl. Standard Rev. Coun., 1973-77; pres. Utah Profl. Rev. Orgn., 1971-75; mem. AMA Coun. on Legis., 1977-80, trustee 1980—, chmn. 1986-88, pres.-elect 1988-89, pres. 1989-90; commr. Joint Commn. on Accreditation of Hosps., 1982-86, sec.-treas., 1985-86. Chair Health Care Quality Alliance, 1992-96. With M.C. USAF, 1962-64. Recipient Spl. Recognition award Am. Soc. Internal Medicine, 1973, Disting. Internist award, 1989. Fellow ACP; mem. Utah Med. Assn. (pres. from 1976, award 1973, 79), Inst. Medicine of NAS, (governing coun. 1984-87), World Med. Assn. (pres.-elect 1990-91, pres. 1992-92). Home: 11905 Parkside Dr Fairfax VA 22033-2648 Office: ASIM 2011 Pennsylvania Ave NW Washington DC 20006-1813

NELSON, BERNARD WILLIAM, foundation executive, educator, physician; b. San Diego, Sept. 15, 1935; s. Arnold B. and Helene Christina (Falck) N.; m. Frances Davison, Aug. 9, 1958; children—Harry, Kate, Anne, Daniel. A.B., Stanford U., 1957, M.D., 1961. Asst. prof., asst. dean medicine Stanford U., Palo Alto, Calif., 1965-67, assoc. dean medicine, 1968-71, cons. assoc. prof., 1980-86; assoc. dean U. Wis., Madison, 1974-77, acting vice chancellor, 1978-79; exec. v.p. Kaiser Family Found., Menlo Park, Calif., 1979-81, 1981-86; chancellor U. Colo. Health Sci. Ctr., Denver, 1986—; mem., v.p., pres. Nat. Med. Fellowships, 1969-77. Trustee Morehouse Med. Sch., 1981-83. Fellow Inst. Medicine; mem. Calif. Acad. Sci., Alpha Omega Alpha (bd. dirs. 1978—). Office: U Colo Health Sci Ctr Box 6245 4200 E 9th Ave Denver CO 80262*

NELSON, CARNOT EDWARD, psychology educator; b. Milw., Feb. 20, 1941; s. Max T. and Marion Beatrice (Roth) N.; m. Alice E. Katz, Sept. 1, 1963; children: Jeremy H., Seth R. BS, U. Wis., 1963; PhD, Columbia U., 1966. Asst. prof. sociology Emory U., Atlanta, 1966-67; asst. prof. psychology The Johns Hopkins U., Balt., 1967-71; assoc. prof. U. South Fla., Tampa, 1971-77, prof. psychology, 1977—; acting assoc. dean U. South Fla., Fort Myers, 1985-86, assoc. chair psychology. Editor: Communication Among Scientists and Engineers, 1970; guest editor Am. Behavioral Scientist, 1987; contbr. articles to profl. jours. Bd. dirs. Congregation Rodeph Sholom, Tampa, 1988-94, pres.-elect, 1994-95, pres., 1995—. Nat. Inst. Edn. fellow, Washington, 1976-78. Fellow APA, Am. Psychol. Soc., Soc. for Personality and Social Psychology; mem. Soc. Exptl. Social Psychology, Soc. Indsl. and Organizational Psychology. Office: U South Fla Dept Psychology Tampa FL 33620

NELSON, CHARLES LANSING, physician; b. Walla Walla, Wash., Nov. 18, 1945; s. Gerald Kenneth Nelson and Lorraine L. (Lansing) Dummler; m. Joan Ardell Hatley, Dec. 18, 1965 (div. Dec. 1980); children: Nichole, Charles, Jonathan, Michael. BS, Walla Walla Coll., 1972; DO, U. Health Scis., 1976. Diplomate Nat. Bd. Med. Examiners. Gen. practice osteo. medicine Sunnyside, Wash., 1977-83, Pasco, Wash., 1983—; med. dir. restorative care unit Our Lady of Lourdes Hosp., 1991—. Vol. physician Shriner's, Pasco, 1991—. Named Disting. Citizen by Lt. Gov. of State of Wash., 1983. Mem. Am. Coll. Gen. Practitioners in Osteo. Medicine and Surgery, Am. Assn. Physicians and Surgeons, DAV (Gold Leader), U. Health Scis.-Coll. Alumni Assn. (life), Non-Commd. Officers Assn. Am. (life), Rho Sigma Chi. Seventh-day Adventist. Office: 810 S 10th St Pasco WA 99301

NELSON, CHRISTOPHER GRANT, dermatologist; b. Peoria, Ill., Feb. 11, 1946; s. Grant Leonard and Shirlee Ann (Brunnenmeyer) N.; m. Mary Jo Donnelly, June 30, 1972; children: Christopher Jr., Andrew Anthony. BS, U. Iowa, 1968, MD, 1971. Diplomate Am. Bd. Dermatology. Intern Ball Meml. Hosp., Muncie, Ind., 1971-72; resident in dermatology U. Tex. Med. Br., Galveston, 1974-77; mem. staff Bayfront Med. Ctr., St. Petersburg, 1977—, Edward H. White II Meml. Hosp., St. Petersburg, 1977—, All Children's Hosp., St. Petersburg, 1977—, Palms of Pasadena Hosp., St. Petersburg, 1977—, St. Anthony's Hosp., St. Petersburg, 1977—, Humana Hosp. Sun Bay, St. Petersburg, 1977—; tchr. Bayfront Med. Ctr., 1977—; clin. asst. prof. U. South Fla. Coll. Medicine, 1977—. Contbr. articles to profl. jours. Vol. Am. Cancer Soc. Mem. AMA, So. Med. Assn., Fla. Med. Assn., Am. Acad. Dermatology, Am. Soc. Dermatologic Surgery, Pinellas County Med. Soc., Fla. West Coast Soc. Dermatology (sec.-treas. 1982-84, pres. 1984-87), Fla. Soc. Dermatologic Surgery, St. Petersburg Yacht Club (bd. dirs. 1989-95, entertainment chmn. 1989-92, house and grounds com. 1987-95), Dragon Club, Masons, Royal Order of Jesters. Presbyterian.

NELSON, CONNIE GAYLE, social worker; b. Little Rock, Oct. 17, 1945; d. Albert and Dorothy George; m. Mark H. Nelson, Nov. 11, 1974; 1 child, Carly. BA, U. Ark., 1967; MSW, Wash. U., St. Louis, 1969. Lic. ind. clin. social worker, R.I. Psychiat. social worker S.W. Ind. Mental Health Ctr., Evansville, 1969-74; supr. sch. social work program Bismarck (N.D.) Pub. Schs., 1974-79; med. social worker St. Alexius Hosp. Med. Ctr., Bismarck, 1979-80; clin. social worker United Hosp. Med. Ctr., Grand Forks, N.D., 1980-82; social worker supr. Benton (Ark.) Svcs. Ctr., 1982-83; coord. spl. child programs Luton Cmty. Mental Health Ctr., Nashville, 1983-86; sch. social worker Nashville Pub. Sch. Sys., 1986-87; dir. Family and Child Devel. Ctr., Delray Beach, Fla., 1987-89; clin. coord. Family Resources, Inc., Woonsocket, R.I., 1989-95; care mgr. Greenspring Health Svcs., West Warwick, R.I., 1995-96; pvt. practice Johnston, R.I., 1996—; field instr. U. Tenn., Nashville, 1985-86, Barry U., Miami, 1987-89, R.I. Coll., Providence, 1991-95; instr. N.D. State U., Bismarck, 1976-77. Mem. Acad. Cert. Social Workers. Home: 8 Danecroft Ave Greenville RI 02828-2318

NELSON, DARWIN BRUCE, psychologist; b. Luling, Tex., Dec. 29, 1942; s. Renold S. Nelson and Laverne M. Baker; m. Kaye Welch, July 6, 1962; children: Michael Scott, John Ashley. BS, U. Corpus Christi, 1964; MS, East Tex. State U., 1966, PhD, 1968. Lic. psychologist, Tex. Asst. prof. ednl. psychology Miss. State U., Starkville, 1968-69; prof. psychology Tex. A&I U., Kingsville, 1969-86; dir. counseling Tex. A&M U., Corpus Christi, 1987—; cons. psychologist Nueces County Adult Probation, Corpus Christi, 1985—, Charter Hosp., Corpus Christi, 1987—. Mem. Am. Counseling Assn., Am. Assn. Marriage and Family Therapists. Home: 6050 Rio Vista Dr Corpus Christi TX 78412-2860

NELSON, DAVID JEROME, optometrist; b. Altoona, Penn., June 27, 1948; s. Donald Jerome and Ruth Rosella (Long) N.; m. Pamela Ann Jemison, June 24, 1972; children: Melinda, Abigail, Felicia. BS in Premedicine, Pa. State U., 1970; BS, Pa. Coll. Optometry, 1972, OD, 1974; MS in Edn., U. So. Calif., Seoul, 1987. Lic. optometrist, Pa. Commd. 2d. lt. U.S. Army, 1973, advanced through grades to maj., 1984; clinic chief, optometrist 196th Sta. Hosp., SHAPE, Belgium, 1974-79, Kenner Army Cmty. Hosp., Ft. Lee, Va., 1980-84; clinic chief, optometrist, cons. 121 EVAC Hosp., Seoul, 1984-87, Neurnberg Area Comm. Hosp., 1987-91; optometrist Kimbrough Army Cmty. Hosp., Ft. Meade, Md., 1991-93; ret., 1993; pvt. practice, Hanover, Pa., 1993—. Pres., treas. Neurnberg H.S. Parent Tchr. Student Orgn., 1988-91. Mem. Am. Optometric Assn., Ctrl. Pa. Optometric Soc., Pa. Optometric Assn., Christian Businessmen's Com., Hanover C. of C., Rotary. Republican. Office: Stonegate Optical Inc 1010 Eichelberger St Hanover PA 17331

NELSON, DEWEY ALLEN, neurologist, educator; b. Eldrado, Ark., Dec. 2, 1927; s. Herman Eugene and Pearl Estelle (Shirley) N.; m. E. Jem Nolt, Oct. 7, 1951; children: Allen, Stephen, Jean, John, Daniel. BS, Cornell U., 1948, MD, 1951. Diplomate Am. Bd. Psychiatry and Neurology, Am. Bd. Neurophysiology. Resident Bellevue Hosp., N.Y.C., 1951-52, 54-57; chief neurology Med. Ctr. Del., Wilmington, 1957-83, sr. neurology, 1983-88, hon. sr. neurology, 1988—; chief neurology St. Francis Hosp., Wilmington, 1957-83; founder, neurologist Neurology Assocs., Wilmington, 1957-85; assoc. clin. prof. neurology Thomas Jefferson U. Med. Ctr., Phila., 1971-75, prof. neurology, 1975—; med. expert, advisor to ct. Social Security Adminstrn., 1982—. Contbr. 70 articles to profl. jours., poetry to periodicals. 1st lt. U.S. Army, 1952-54, Korea. Decorated Bronze Star, United Nations Svc. medal with 2 battle stars, Nat. Def. Svc. medal; recipient Bronze Hope Chest award Nat. Multiple Sclerosis Soc., 1960, Plaque award Multiple Sclerosis Clinic, 1979; Teagle Found. scholar, 1946-51. Republican. Presbyterian (ruling elder). Home: 206 N Spring Valley Rd Wilmington DE 19807-2427

NELSON, DON GAYLORD, physician; b. Moline, Ill., Nov. 16, 1938; s. Einer Nels and Mildred Christine (Olson) N.; m. Nancy Elaine Breece, June 13, 1964; children: Christine Ann, Jeffrey Brian, Susan Beth. MD, U. Ill., Chgo., 1965. Intern U. Ill., Chgo., 1965-66; resident in internal medicine U. Cinn., 1968-70, 71-72, fellow in pulmonary disease, 1970-71, 72-73; physician Springer Clinic, Tulsa, 1973—; clin. asst. prof. U. Okla., Tulsa, 1977-91, clin. assoc. prof., 1991—. Contbr. articles to profl. jours. Lt. Comdr. USPHS, 1966-68. Fellow Am. Coll. Chest Physicians; mem. AMA, Am. Coll. Physicians, Am. Thoracic Soc, Okla. Thoracic Soc. (rpes. 1980). Home: 2605 E 66th Pl Tulsa OK 74136-1241 Office: Springer Clinic 6160 S Yale Ave Tulsa OK 74136-1930

NELSON, DONALD ANDERS FULLER, physician, educator, health facility administrator; b. Kenmare, N.D., Mar. 14, 1949; s. Daniel Anders and Ruth Elizabeth (Fuller) N.; m. Mary Anne Hull, Mar. 6, 1976. BS, Dana Coll., 1971; MD, U. Iowa, 1975. Diplomate Am. Bd. Family Practice. Resident Cedar Rapids Family Practice Residency, 1975-78, mem. faculty, dir. ob.-gyn., 1984—; pvt. practice Cedar Rapids, 1978-84; mem. adv. com. med. asst. program Kirkwood Coll., Cedar Rapids, 1983—; chmn. ASTM com. E31 on Healthcare Imformatics, 1994—. Mem. editorial adv. bd. Computer News for Physicians, 1988-90. Fellow Am. Acad. Family Physicians; mem. Christian Med. and Dental Soc. (nat. bd. trustees 1981-84), COSTAR Users Group (bd. dirs. 1990—), Alpha Omega Alpha. Office: Family Health Ctr 855 A Ave NE Cedar Rapids IA 52402-5064

NELSON, EDITH ELLEN, dietitian; b. Vicksburg, Mich., Sept. 26, 1940; d. Edward Kenneth and Anna (McManus) Rolffs; m. Douglas Keith Nelson; children: Daniel Lee, Jennifer Lynn. BS, Mich. State U., 1962; MEd in Applied Nutrition, U. Cin., 1979. Lic. dietitian, Fla. Clin. dietitian Macon (Ga.) Gen. Hosp., Blodgett Meml. Hosp., Grand Rapids, Mich.; grad. teaching asst. U. Cin., 1978-79; dir. nutrition svcs. Dialysis Clinic, Inc., Cin., 1979-88; cons. dietitian Panama City Devel. Ctr., Ft. Walton Beach Devel. Ctr., Fla., 1988-94, N.W. Fla. Community Hosp., Chipley, Fla., 1993-94, Beverly Enterprises, Panama City Beach, 1994—; renal dietitian Dialysis Svcs. Fla., Ft. Walton Beach, 1989-92. Mich. Edn. Assn. scholar, 1958; Nat. Kidney Found. grantee, 1986. Mem. Am. Dietetic Assn., Fla. Dietetic Assn., Panhandle Dist. Dietetic Assn., Nat. Kidney Found. (coun. on renal nutrition, Fla. coun. on renal nutrition), Omicron Nu. Home: 150 Grand Lagoon Shores Dr Panama City FL 32408

NELSON, GAYLE VANCE, pediatric dentist; b. Sidney, Nebr., Sept. 26, 1946; d. H.C.Q. and Dorothy Olive (Roberts) N.; m. Angeline Marie Nelson, Mar. 29, 1969; children: Kristen Kay, Deanna Lynn, Elaine Marie. DDS, U. Nebr., 1971; MS in Dentistry, Ind. U., 1983. Pvt. practice pediatric dentistry Sioux Falls, S.D., 1976—; asst. prof. pediatrics U. Nebr. Med. Ctr., Omaha, 1976-82, mem. dental rsch. bd. dirs., 1996—; asst. prof. pediatrics U. S.D., Sioux Falls, 1976-96; chief med. staff Sioux Falls Surg. Ctr., 1985-88; examiner Am. Bd. Pediatric Dentistry, 1983-90, chmn., 1990, cons., 1990—. Patentee in field; author: Posterior Composites in Primary Teeth, 1983; contbr. numerous articles to profl. jours. Bd. dirs. McKennan Hosp. Found., 1996—. With Spl. Forces, U.S. Army, 1971-74. R.E. McDonald scholar, 1976. Fellow Am. Acad. Pediatric Dentistry, Acad. Gen. Dentistry, Am. Bd. Pediatric Dentistry, Southeastern Dist. Dental Soc. (chair for programs 1976-91). Presbyterian. Office: Spectrum Profl Ctr 2900 E 26th St Ste 200 Sioux Falls SD 57103-4060

NELSON, JAMES HAROLD, health sciences administrator; b. Gosnell, Ark., Apr. 26, 1936; s. J.D. and Louise (Gann) N.; m. Betty Sue Leonard, Sept. 21, 1974; children: Amelia Rebecca, Rachel Louise. BS, Ark. State U., 1961, MS, 1969; PhD, Okla. State U., 1972. Br. chief U.S. Army Environ. Hygiene Agy., Edgewood, Md., 1972-76; from rsch. area mgr. to div. chief U.S. Army Biomed. R & D Lab., Frederick, Md., 1976-92; project mgr. applied med. systems U.S. Army Med. Materiel Devel. Activity, Fort Detrick, Md., 1992—; mem. Fed. Work Group Pest Mgmt., Washington, 1977-81; chmn. equipment com. Armed Forces Pest Mgmt. Bd., Washington, 1979-83; cons. dir. engrs. Ft. Detrick, Frederick, 1976—; guest lectr. Acad. Health Scis., U.S. Army, Ft. Sam Houston, Tex., 1986-88. Contbr. articles to profl. jours.; assoc. editor: Jour. Am. Mosquito Control Assn., 1982-88; chmn. editorial bd.: Equipment & Insecticides-Mosquito Control, 1989. With USN, 1954-58. Recipient numerous commendations U.S. Army, Ft. Detrick, 1981-93, R&D Achievement award Asst. Sec. of the Army, 1988, Order of Mil. Med. Merit, 1992. Mem. AAAS, Am. Pub. Health Assn., Entomol. Soc. Am., Assn. Mil. Surgeons U.S., N.Y. Acad. Scis., Internat. Platform Assn., AMVETS, Am. Legion, Sigma Xi (pres. 1987-88). Republican. Episcopalian. Home: 2419 Tabor Dr Middletown MD 21769-9006 Office: US Army Med Materiel Devel Activity Fort Detrick Frederick MD 21702

NELSON, JANICE MARIAN, pathologist, educator; b. Jamestown, N.Y., Nov. 1, 1951; d. Donald L. and Marian M. Nelson. BS in Biology, Syracuse U., 1973; MD, SUNY, Syracuse, 1976. Diplomate Am. Bd. Pathology, Am. Bd. Blood Banking. Resident in anatomic pathology U. Fla. Med. Ctr., Gainesville, 1976-78; resident and fellow in clin. pathlogy Los Angeles County-U. So. Calif. Med. Ctr., L.A., 1978-81, med. dir. blood bank, tissue and transfusion med. svcs., 1981—; asst. prof. pathology U. So. Calif. Sch. Medicine, L.A., 1982-88, assoc. prof. pathology, 1988-93, prof. pathology. Fellow Am. Soc. Clin. Pathologists (dep. commr. commn. on continuing edn. 1984-90, commr. 1995—, mem. rsch. devel. and strategic planning com. 1986-89, bd. dirs. 1989—), Coll. Am. Pathologists; mem. Acad. Clin. Lab. Physicians and Scientists, Am. Assn. Blood Banks, Internat. Soc. Blood Transfusion. Democrat. Office: LA Co-U So Calif Med Ctr 1200 N State St # 771 Los Angeles CA 90033-4525

NELSON, JANIE RISH, hospital executive; b. Gloster, Miss., Mar. 1, 1941; d. William Hubert and Essie Dell (Davis) Rish; m. John Preston Nelson, Jr., Aug. 19, 1984. Student S.W. Miss. Jr. Coll., 1959-61, Stephens Coll., 1981—. Accredited record technician. Admissions clk. Field Hosp., Centreville, Miss., 1963-68, asst. dir. med. records, 1968-73; dir. med. records West Feliciana Parish Hosp., St. Francisville, La., 1976—. Med. records cons. Beverly Enterprises & Centreville Health Care, 1983-84. Mem. nat. adv. bd. Am. Security Council, 1984-85; mem. U.S. Congl. Adv. Bd. for La., 1985; fund raiser Republican Com., 1984. Mem. Am. Med. Records Assn., La. Med. Records Assn., Nat. Assn. Female Execs., Tumor Registration Assn. La., Miss. Sheriffs Assn. (hon.). Republican. Presbyterian. Club: Civic. Avocations: Reading; public speaking; gardening. Home: PO Box 374 Centreville MS 39631-0374

NELSON, JENNIFER KAY, dietitian; b. St. Paul, Apr. 13, 1953; d. John Merlyn and Elizabeth Ann (Atkinson) N.; m. Peter Charles O'Brien, Nov. 13, 1982; 1 stepchild, Louise Catherine. BS, U. Minn., 1975; MS, U. Wis., Menomonie, 1981. Registered dietitian; cert. nutrition support dietitian. Chief clin. dietetics Scott USAF Med. Ctr., Scott A.F.B., Ill., 1975-78; clin. dietitian Rochester (Minn.) Meth. Hosp., 1978-83; home enteral nutrition coord. Mayo Clinic, Rochester, 1983—, coord. clin. dietetics, 1986-94, asst. prof. nutrition, 1990-94, assoc. prof. nutrition, 1994—; project mgr. clin. dietetics, Mayo Clinic, Rochester, 1994—, On-Line Nutrition Editor, 1996—. Editor: Mayo Clinic Diet Manual, 1988, 94; co-editor: Mayo Clinic Family Health Book, 1990 (Book of Month 1990), Mayo Clinic Heart Book, 1993, Mayo Clinic Complete Book of Pregnancy and Baby's First Year, 1994; mem. editl. bd. Nutrition in Clinical Practice, 1994—; contbr. articles to profl. jours. 1st lt. USAF, 1975-78. Recipient Meritorious Svc. award USAF. Mem. Am. Dietetic Assn., Am. Soc. Parenteral and Enteral Nutrition (dietitians com. 1985-91, 94—, founding mem. Minn. chpt., sec. 1989-91, tech. advisor on enteral nutrition 1990-94, membership chair 1992-94,. Office: Mayo Clinic 200 1st St SW Rochester MN 55905-0001

NELSON, JOHN BROCKWAY, III, psychiatrist; b. Princeton, N.J., Jan. 25, 1928; s. John B. and Mary G. Nelson; m. Marianne Nelson, 1953; 4 children. AB, Earlham Coll., 1950; MD, Jefferson Med. Coll., 1954. Diplomate in psychiatry and child psychiatry Am. Bd. Psychiatry and Neurology. Resident in psychiatry Boston VA Hosp., 1955-56, 58-59; fellow in child psychiatry DA Thom Clinic for Children, Boston, 1959-61, staff psychiatrist, 1961-65, dir., 1965-70; staff psychiatrist South Shore Mental Health Ctr., 1961-64, 70-76, dir. psychiat. tng., 1970-76; dir. Brookline (Mass.) Mental Health Clinic, 1976-83; med. dir. Metrowest Mental Health Ctr., 1983-91, staff psychiatrist, 1991—; chmn. New Eng. child mental health task force, Boston, 1979; instr. Boston U. Sch. Medicine, 1968-71, Tufts Sch. Medicine, 1970-80, Harvard U., 1978-94. Lt. USN, 1957-59. Mem. Am. Assn. Child and Adolescent Psychiatry (pres. New Eng. chpt. 1991-93), Mass. Med. Soc. Home: 17 Prospect Ave Newton MA 02160 Office: Metrowest Mental Health Assn 88 Lincoln St Framingham MA 01701

NELSON, JOHN MARSHALL, medical information services company executive; b. Madison, Wis., Oct. 28, 1941; s. Russell Arthur and Dorothea (Smith) N.; m. Linda Taylor, Oct. 13, 1962 (div. June 1968); children: Ann, David; m. Katherine Dianne Hoagland, Sept. 24, 1972; children: James, George. AB, Harvard Coll., 1963; MD, Case Western Reserve U., 1967; MBA, U. Chgo., 1983. Diplomate Am. Bd. Internal Medicine. Staff assoc. NIH, Bethesda, Md., 1968-71; rsch. assoc., asst. prof. medicine Promis Lab. Med. Sch. Univ. Vt., 1973-76; med. dir. Madison Gen. Hosp., 1976-84; assoc. clin. prof. Med. Sch. U. Wis., 1976-84; v.p. corp. med. affairs Gen. Health Mgmt. Co., Madison, 1984-86; dir. med. and ednl. affairs Washington Hosp. Ctr., 1986-87; pres. Nelson Info. Systems, Bethesda, Md., 1987—; cons. Med. Sch. U. Utah, Salt Lake City, 1985-86; med. reviewer FDA, 1990-91. Contbr. articles to profl. jour. Coach youth soccer, 1984-85; merit badge counselor Boy Scouts Am., 1987; mem. Harvard Schs. Com., Md., 1988-91; vestry St. John's Episcopal Ch., Bethesda, 1988-91. Harvard Hon. Nat. Scholar, 1959-62; recipient Steuer Meml. award Case Western Reserve U., Cleve., 1967. Fellow ACP, Am. Coll. Physician Execs.; mem. AMA, Univ. Club Chgo., Harvard Club (Washington), Alpha Omega Alpha. Republican. Episcopalian. Home: 6616 Millwood Rd Bethesda MD 20817-6058 Office: 4740 Chevy Chase Dr Chevy Chase MD 20815-6461

NELSON, KAREN ANNE, speech and language specialist; b. Newton, N.J., Mar. 7, 1960; d. Charles R. and Ethel (Swenson) N. BS, East Stroudsburg (Pa.) U., 1982. Speech correctionist Hackettstown (N.J.) Pub. Schs., 1983; speech therapist Sussex County Ednl. Svcs. Commn., Newton, N.J., 1983-84; speech-lang. specialist Byram Twp. Sch. Dist., Stanhope, N.J., 1984—. Mem. NEA, N.J. Edn. Assn., Byram Twp. Edn. Assn., Sussex County Speech-Lang.-Hearing Assn., N.J. Speech-Lang.-Hearing Assn. Office: Byram Twp Schs 12 Mansfield Dr Stanhope NJ 07874-3123

NELSON, KAY ELLEN, speech and language pathologist; b. Milw., Apr. 14, 1947; d. John A. and Margaret B. (Janke) Strobel; m. Kuglitsch Dale, Mar. 2, 1974 (div. Dec. 1981); 1 child, Ashley Lara. BA with distinction, U. Wis., Madison, 1969; MA, U. Wis., Milw., 1972. Speech and lang. pathologist Sch. Dist. 146, Dolton, Ill., 1970-71, Waukesha County Handicapped Children's Edn. Bd., Waukesha, Wis., 1972-77, 79-80, Kettle Moraine Area Schs., Wales, Wis., 1980-94; dir. speech/lang. pathology MJ Care, Inc., Fond du Lac, Wis., 1994-96; speech-lang. pathologist, clin. specialist NovaCare, Inc., New Berlin, Wis., 1996—; pvt. practice Dousman, Wis., summers 1991-93. Fellow Herb Kohl Found., 1993. Mem. Am. Speech, Lang. and Hearing Assn. (cert. of clin. competence, ACE awards 1990, 91, 92, 94, 95), Wis. Speech., Lang. and Hearing Assn. (sch. rep. dist VII 1991—, chmn. sch. svcs. com. 1992-94, v.p. sch. svcs. 1994-95, rep.-at-large 1995-96), Internat. Soc. for Augumentive and Alternative Comm., U.S. Soc. for Augumentive and Alternative Comm., Wis. Soc. for Augumentive and Alternative Comm. (sec. 1990-92, membership chmn. 1990-93, v.p. profl. affairs 1993). Unitarian. Office: NovaCare Inc 13700 W National Ave New Berlin WI 53151

NELSON, LINDA SHEARER, child development and family relations educator; b. New Kensington, Pa., Dec. 8, 1944; d. Walter M. and Jean M. (Black) Shearer; m. Alan Edward Nelson, Dec. 29, 1973; children: Amelia (Amy), Emily. BS in Home Econs. Edn., Pa. State U., 1966; MS in Child Devel. and Family Rels., Cornell U., 1968; PhD in Higher Edn. and Child Devel., U. Pitts., 1982. Head tchr.-lab. nursery sch. Dept. of Psychology, Vassar Coll., Poughkeepsie, N.Y., 1968-69; instr. child devel. dept. home econs. edn. Indiana U. Pa., 1969-72, asst. prof., 1972-77, assoc. prof., 1977-84, prof. child devel. and family rels. Coll. Health/Human Svcs., 1984—, dept. chair, 1991-93; prof. child devel. and family rels. Indiana U. Pa. Coll. Health and Human Svcs., 1993—; mem. values task force Indian U. Pa. Coll. Health and Human Svcs., 1995-96; mem. refocusing II com. Indiana U. Pa., 1994-95, strategic planning com. mem. values task force, 1995-96; ind. cons., trainer Head Start Programs, Pa., 1970—, Child Care Programs and Agys., Pa., 1970—; child devel. assoc. rep. Coun. for Early Childhood Profl. Recognition, Washington, 1989-91; field rep. Keyston U. Rsch. Corp., Erie, 1990-91; keynote/guest spkr. child devel./child care and home econs. confs., Pa. and nat., 1985—. Mem. adv. bd. Early Childhood Edn., Annual Edits., 1985—; mem. adv. bd. Interface: Home Economics and Technology Newsletter, 1993-96; contbr. articles to profl. jours. Bd. dirs. Indiana County Child Care Program, 1970-92; guest spkr. Delta Kappa Gamma, Indiana, 1990, Bus. and Profl. Women, Indiana, 1991, IUP's The Marriage Project, 1996. Grantee in field, 1985—. Mem. AAUW (guest spkr. 1996), Nat. Assn. for Edn. Young Children, Pitts. Assn. for Edn. Young Children (conf. co-chair 1983-85, in-svc. tng. spkr. 1995), Assn. Pa. State Coll. and Univ. Faculties, Kappa Omicron Nu. Democrat. Presbyterian. Office: Indiana U of Pa Human Devel and Environ Studies Dept 207 Ackerman Hall Indiana PA 15705

NELSON, MARITA LEE, anatomist; b. Torrance, Calif., Aug. 8, 1934; d. Lee George and Marie Blanche (Waples) N.; BS, UCLA, 1957, MS, 1959; PhD in Anatomy (Univ. fellow), U. Calif., Berkeley, 1968. Instr., Ill. State U., 1960-64; assoc. U. Calif., Berkeley, 1965-68, instr., 1968-69, acting asst. prof., 1969, asst. prof., 1972-74; asst. prof. Georgetown U. Schs. Medicine-Dentistry, 1969-72; assoc. prof. anatomy and reproductive biology John A. Burns Sch. Medicine, U. Hawaii, 1974-82, prof., 1982-96, prof. anatomy and pathology, 1996—. Recipient Teaching award Kaiser Found., 1977, Golden Pineapple award John A. Burns Sch. Medicine, 1979, Basic Sci. Tchr. Yr., 1986, 1988, 1992, Excellence in Teaching award, 1984; Disting. Teaching award U. Calif.-Berkeley, 1983, Regents medal U. Hawaii, 1984. Mem. Am. Assn. Anatomists, Am. Assn. Clin. Anatomists, AAAS, AAUP, Assn. Women in Sci., Hawaiian Assn. Women in Sci., Hawaiian Acad. Sci., Sigma Xi, Pi Lambda Theta. Research on environ. endocrinology, effects of high altitude on maturation and pituitary function, multimedia edn. in anatomy, and on plastination of biol. specimens. Office: 1960 E West Rd Honolulu HI 96822-2319

NELSON, NANCY ELEANOR, pediatrician, educator; b. El Paso, Apr. 4, 1933; d. Harry Hamilton and Helen Maude (Murphy) N. BA magna cum laude, U. Colo., 1955, MD, 1959. Intern, Case Western Res. U. Hosp., 1959-60, resident, 1960-63; pvt. practice medicine specializing in pediats., Denver, 1963-70; clin. prof. U. Colo. Sch. Medicine, Denver, 1988—, asst. dean Sch. Medicine, 1982-88, assoc. dean, 1988—. Mem. Am. Acad. Pediats., AMA (sect. med. schs. governing coun. 1994—), Denver Med. Soc. (pres. 1983-84), Colo. Med. Soc. (bd. dirs. 1985-88, judicial coun. 1992—). Home: 1265 Elizabeth St Denver CO 80206-3241 Office: 4200 E 9th Ave Denver CO 80262

NELSON, PAUL WILLIAM, surgeon; b. Kansas City, Mo., Aug. 29, 1952; s. Radford Kibble and Margaret Ruth (Burns) N.; m. Diane Jeanne Carr, Nov. 27, 1991; children: Andrew, Erin, Kenneth, Jennifer, Amy, Sarah. AB, Dartmouth Coll., 1974; MD, U. Kans., 1977. Diplomate Am. Bd. Surgery. Intern, resident in surgery U. Tex., Galveston, 1977-82; fellow in transplant surgery Mass. Gen. Hosp., Boston, 1982-84; asst. prof. surgery U. Mo., Kansas City, 1984-92; assoc. prof. surgery U. Mo., 1992—; chair dept. surgery St. Luke's Hosp., Kansas City, 1995—. Fellow Am. Coll. Surgeons; mem. Am. Soc. Transplant Surgeons, Southwestern Surg. Conf., Western Surgical Assn., The Transplantation Soc. Office: 4320 Wornall Rd Ste 308 Kansas City MO 64111

NELSON, RICHARD PHILIP, medical educator, dean; b. Bloomington, Ill., Dec. 28, 1946; s. Edward Philip and Dorothy Emma (Bergquist) N.; m. Phyllis Nelson, June 22, 1969; children: Elyse, Emily. BA, Northwestern U., Evanston, Ill., 1968; MD, Northwestern U., Chgo., 1972. Diplomate Am. Bd. Pediatrics. Resident pediat. Children's Meml. Hosp., Chgo., 1972-75, chief resident, 1975-76; clin. fellow pediatrics Harvard U., Boston, 1976-78; dir. Minn. Svcs. for Children with Handicaps/Minn. Dept. Health, Mpls., 1978-82; asst. prof. U. Minn. Med. Sch., Mpls., 1982-87; dir. developmental disabilities Gillette Children's Hosp., St. Paul, 1982-87; assoc. prof. pediatrics U. Iowa, Iowa City, 1987-94, prof. pediatrics, 1994—, dir. Child Health Specialty Clinics, 1987—, assoc. dean, 1992—. Editor: Maternal and Child Health Practices, 1994; co-author chpts. in books. Mem. Iowa Health Care Reform Coun., 1993; bd. dirs. Health Policy Corp. of Iowa, 1993; mem. Inst. of Medicine, Nat. Forum on Future of Children and Families, MCH Health Care Reform, 1991. James Patton scholar Northwestern U. Med. Sch., 1968-72. Mem. Am. Acad. Pediatrics (com. on child health care financing 1992—), Beta Beta Beta. Office: Child Health Specialty Clin 247 Hospital School Iowa City IA 52242-1011

NELSON, ROBERT PAUL, JR., lawyer; b. Oakland, Calif., Feb. 28, 1934; s. Robert Paul and Clara Mae (Sauter) N.; m. Ann Mae Perine; children: Robert Paul III, Melissa Ann, Christine Perine. AB, U. Calif., Berkeley, 1956, LLB, 1961. Bar: Calif. 1962. Ptnr. Cooley, Godward, Castro, Huddleson & Tatum, San Francisco, 1962-85, Orrick, Herrington & Sutcliffe, Sacramento, 1985—. Bd. dirs. Sacramento Symphony Assn., 1987—. Mem. ABA, Calif. Bar Assn. (chmn. com. on corps. 1982-83, chmn. exec. com. Bus. Law sect. 1985-86, advisor 1986-87), San Francisco County Bar Assn., Sacramento County Bar Assn., Sacramento C. of C., Sacramento Valley Venture Capital Forum, U.S. Conf. of Mayors/Nat. Resource Recovery Assn., U. Calif. Alumni Assn., Phi Kappa Sigma. Clubs: Merchants Exchange, University (San Francisco); Berkely Tennis; Commanderie de Bordeaux of San Francisco. Lodge: Masons.

NELSON, RONALD ANDREW, flight surgeon, occupational health consultant; b. Spokane, Wash., May 29, 1964; s. Marvin Eugene and Shirley Mae (Farrell) N. BS in Chemistry with honors, Stanford U., 1986; MD, Vanderbilt U., 1990. Intern in internal medicine Keesler Med. Ctr., Keesler AFB, Miss., 1990-91; flight surgeon USAF 3rd Med Ctr., Elmendorf AFB, Ark., 1991-95; occupl. health cons. USAF 3rd Med. Ctr., Elmendorf AFB, Alaska, 1992-95; flight surgeon USAF 33rd Fighter Wing, Eglin AFB, Fla.,

1995—. Maj. USAF, 1996—. Mem. Soc. USAF Flight Surgeons (Flight Surgeon of the Yr. 1994), Aerospace Med. Assn. Presbyterian. Office: 96th AMDS/SGPF 307 Boatner Rd Ste 114 Eglin AFB FL 32542

NELSON, RONALD JOHN, cardiothoracic surgeon, educator; b. St. Paul, Nov. 20, 1934; s. Clarence Oscar and Magnhild Marie (Anderson) N.; m. L. Ruth Needels, June 10, 1961; children: Daniel G., Peter J., Kristen A. B.A. magna cum laude, U. Minn., 1956, B.S., 1957, M.D., 1959. Diplomate Am. Bd. Surgery, Am. Bd. Thoracic Surgery. Intern King County Hosp., Seattle, 1959-60; resident in surgery U. Wash., Seattle, 1961-68, instr. dept. surgery, 1967-68; asst. chief cardiovascular surgery Harbor/UCLA Med. Ctr., Torrance, 1968-73, chief cardiovascular surgery, 1973-76, chief div. thoracic and cardiovascular surgery, 1976-89; chief cardiac surgery St. John's Heart Inst., 1989-93, cardiac surgeon, 1989—; dir. Research and Edn. Inst., 1981-82; asst. prof., assoc. prof. surgery UCLA Sch. Medicine, 1970-80, prof. surgery, 1981-89, clin. prof. surgery, 1989—; mem. staff UCLA Med. Ctr., Santa Monica. Contbr. chpts. to books, articles to sci. jours. Chmn., Rolling Hills Covenant Ch., Rolling Hills Estates, Calif., 1975-77; mem. bd. reference Fuller Theol. Sem. Extension, Pasadena, Calif., 1978-83. Postdoctoral fellow NIH, 1964-65, research grantee, 1978—. Fellow ACS, Council of Cardiovascular Surgery of Am. Heart Assn.; mem. Pacific Coast Surg. Assn., Am. Assn. Thoracic Surgery, Soc. Thoracic Surgeons, other profl. orgns., Phi Beta Kappa, Alpha Omega Alpha. Home: 13969 Marquesas Way # B219 Marina Dl Rey CA 90292-6040 Office: St Johns Place 1301-20th St Ste # 590 Santa Monica CA 90404

NELSON, SCOTT RUSSELL, osteopath; b. Luverne, Minn., Jan. 28, 1954; s. John Eugene and Phyllis Adeline (Bauer) N.; m. Donna Marie McGorty, June 2, 1979; children: Jennifer Elizabeth, Melissa Rachael, Shawn Michael Thomas, Erik Daniel Thomas, Breanna Ariel Nelson. BS magna cum laude, Tex. A&M U., 1978; DO, North Tex. State U., 1982. Cert. advanced cardiac/trauma life support. Intern Dallas-Ft. Worth Med. Ctr., 1983; osteo. physician, dir. Theodosia (Mo.) Med. Clinic, 1983-84; emergency osteo. physician Ozarks Med. Ctr., West Plains, Mo., 1984—, cons. osteo. physician, 1986—; dir. osteo. biomechanical evaluation and treatment service Ozarks Med. Ctr., West Plains, 1987; staff osteo. physician Baxter County Regional Hosp., Mountain Home, Ark., 1984-87; emergency physician Amarillo Emergency Receiving Ctr. N.W. Tex. Hosp., Amarillo, Tex., 1987—; assoc. clin. prof. dept. surgery and internal medicine Tex. Tech. U. Health Scis. Ctr. Sch. Medicine; staff physician Seton Med. Ctr., Austin, Tex., 1991—, Bapt. Meml. Hosp. System, San Antonio, 1991-92; mng. ptnr. Amarillo Emergency Physicians. Deacon Emmanuel Ch., Mountain Home, 1986. Fellow Am. Coll. Emergency Physicians; mem. Beta Beta Beta, Phi Kappa Phi, Sigma Sigma Phi. Republican. Office: NW Tex Hosp Amarillo Emergency Receiving Ctr 1501 Coulter Dr Amarillo TX 79106-1770

NELSON, STEVEN FRANK, social services administrator; b. Kansas City, Mo., Mar. 12, 1949; s. Vernon Rex and Verna Ruth (Martens) N.; m. Connie Lee Trammel, 1974 (div. 1979); children: Erica L., Crystal A.; m. Rebecca L. Boltin, Sept. 7, 1983; children: Steven F. Jr., James V. Student, Dodge City Community Coll., 1972-73, 75, Wichita State U., 1984, Butler County Community Coll., El Dorado, Kans., 1988. Outreach counselor outpatient program St. John's Hosp., Wichita, Kans., 1985-87; asst. dir. Keystone, Riverside Hosp., Wichita, 1987-89; exec. dir. Keystone, Geary Community Hosp., Junction City, Kans., 1989-90, dir. chem. dependency unit, 1990—; mem. Kans. Alcohol Safety Action Project; mem. task force alcohol and drug svcs. Kans. Hosp. Assn., 1988-90; cons. peer counseling Geary County Health Dept., Junction City; bd. dirs. Substance Abuse Among Youth Prevention, Junction City, 1989-92. With USN, 1968-70, Vietnam. Recipient Crossroads of Leadership award Junction City C. of C., 1990. Mem. Nat. Assn. Alcohol and Drug Abuse Counselors, Kans. Alcohol and Drug Abuse Counselors, Assn. U.S. Army, Amateur Trap Assn., Kans. trap Assn., Kiwanis. Office: Geary Community Hosp CDU 1102 St Mary's Rd PO Box 490 Junction City KS 66441

NELSON, STUART JAMES, internist, educator; b. Santa Monica, Calif., Apr. 25, 1947; s. Clair Edmund and Ruth (Gibson) N.; m. Linda K. F. Mui, June 18, 1978; children: Victoria, Mark, Elizabeth. AB in Math., U. Calif., Berkeley, 1970; MD, SUNY, Bklyn., 1975. Diplomate Nat. Bd. Med. Examiners, Am. Bd. Internal Medicine. Intern Phila. Gen. Hosp., 1975-76; resident Met. Hosp., N.Y.C., 1976-78; instr. medicine SUNY, Stony Brook, 1978-82, asst. prof. clin. medicine, 1982-86, clin. assoc. prof. medicine, preventive medicine, 1986-91; assoc. prof. medicine Med. Coll. Ga., Augusta, 1991—; assoc. head divsn. gen. internal medicine SUNY, Stony Brook, 1985-90; reviewer for profl. jours.; con. Nat. Libr. Medicine, Bethesda, 1988—. Contbr. articles to profl. jours. Fellow Am. Coll. Physicians; mem. AAAS, Am. Med. Informatics Assn., Soc. Gen. Internal Medicine, Med. Libr. Assn. Presbyterian. Office: Med Coll of Ga Hb # 2010 Augusta GA 30912

NELSON, THOMAS ERL, orthopedic surgeon, educator; b. St. Paul, July 31, 1959; s. Erling Emil and Gladys Ethel (Kirchoff) N.; m. Kathryn Loretta Pyzdrowski, June 27, 1987; children: Molly, Thomas II. BSChE, U. Minn., 1981, MD, 1986. Diplomate Am. Bd. Orthop. Surgery. Asst. prof. U. Fla., Gainesville, 1992-94; orthop. surgeon Marshfield (Wis.) Clinic, 1994—. Contbr. articles to profl. jours. Fellow Am. Acad. Orthop. Surgeons; mem. Internat. Soc. Limb Salvage, Alpha Omega Alpha, Tau Beta Pi. Office: Marshfield Clinic 1000 N Oak Ave Marshfield WI 54449

NELSON, WILLIAM JOHN, oral and maxillofacial surgeon; b. Joliet, Ill., Apr. 7, 1955; s. Herbert F. and Marjorie A. (Anson) N.; m. Michelle M. Jones; children: Matthew, Colleen, Caitlin. BS, Creighton U., 1977, DDS, 1981. Diplomate Am. Bd. Oral and Maxillofacial Surgeons (bd. examiner 1991—). Resident Gundersen Clinic, LaCrosse (Wis.) Luth. Hosp., 1981-84; surgeon Oral and Maxillofacial Surgery Assocs., S.C., Green Bay, Wis., 1984—; med. staff Green Bay Packers, 1992—. Surgeon vol. St. Jude Hosp., St. Lucia, W.I., 1986, Health Vol. Overseas, Bogota, Colombia, 1995; dir. Am. Cancer Soc., Green Bay, 1987-94; dir., trustee Gundersen Med. Found., LaCrosse, Wis., 1995—. Fellow Am. Acad. Cosmetic Surgery, Am. Coll. Oral and Maxillofacial Surgeons, Am. Assn. Oral and Maxillofacial Surgeons. Office: Oral & Maxillofacial Surg 704 S Webster Green Bay WI 54301

NELSON, WILLIAM RANKIN, surgeon, educator; b. Charlottesville, Va., Dec. 12, 1921; s. Hugh Thomas and Edith (Rankin) N.; m. Nancy Laidley, Mar. 17, 1956 (div. 1979); children: Robin Page Nelson Russel, Susan Kimberly Nelson Wright, Anne Rankin Nelson Cron; m. Pamela Morgan Phelps, July 5, 1984. BA, U. Va., 1943, MD, 1945. Diplomate Am. Bd. Surgery. Intern Vanderbilt U. Hosp., Nashille, 1945-46; resident in surgery U. Va. Hosp., Charlottesville, 1949-51; fellow surg. oncology Meml. Sloan Kettering Cancer Ctr., N.Y.C., 1951-55; instr. U. Colo. Sch. Medicine, Denver, 1955-57; asst. clin. prof. U. Colo. Sch. Medicine, 1962-87, clin. prof. surgery, 1987—; asst. prof. Med. Coll. Va., Richmond, 1957-62; mem. exec. com. U. Colo. Cancer Ctr.; mem. nat. bd., nat. exec. com. Am. Cancer Soc. Contbr. articles to profl. jours. and chpts. to textbooks. Capt. USAAF, 1946-48. Recipient Nat. Div. award Am. Cancer Soc., 1979. Fellow Am. Coll. Surgeons (bd. govs. 1984-89); mem. AMA, Internat. Soc. Surgery, Brit. Assn. Surg. Oncology, Royal Soc. Medicine (U.K.), Soc. Surg. Oncology (pres. 1975-76), Soc. Head and Neck Surgeons (pres. 1986-87), Am. Cancer Soc. (pres. Colo. div. 1975-77, exec. com., nat. bd. dirs., del. dir. from Colo. div. 1975—), Am. Soc. Clin. Oncology, Western Surg. Assn. Colo. Med. Soc., Denver Med. Soc., Denver Acad. Surgery, Rocky Mt. Oncology Soc., Univ. Club, Rotary. Republican. Episcopalian.

NEMEC, JOSEF, organic chemist, researcher; b. Ostresany, Czechoslovakia, Sept. 7, 1929; came to U.S., 1969; s. Josef Nemec and Marie (Joskova) Nemcova; m. Anna Pastush, Aug. 29, 1975; 1 child, Marketa. MS, Inst. Chem. Tech., Prague, Czechoslovakia, 1954; PhD, Czechoslovak Acad. Scis., Prague, 1958. Organic chemist Inst. Chem. Tech., Prague, 1954-61; sr. rsch. chemist Czechoslovak Acad. Scis., Prague, 1961-69; rsch. fellow in organic chemistry Wayne State U., Detroit, 1969-70; sr. rsch. scientist Squibb Inst. Med. Rsch., New Brunswick, N.J., 1970-75; staff mem. St. Jude Children's Rsch. Hosp., Memphis, 1975-84; sr. scientist Nat. Cancer Inst.-Program Resources, Inc. Cancer R&D Ctr., Frederick, Md., 1984-95; adj. prof. med. chemistry U. Tenn., Memphis, 1970-91; external examiner U. Zimbabwe, Harare, 1994—; cons. in field. Contbr. articles to scholarly and profl. jours. Grantee Nat. Cancer Inst., 1975-85. Mem. AAAS, Am. Chem. Soc., Royal Soc. Chemistry, Czechoslovak Soc. Arts and Scis.

NEMEROFF, CHARLES BARNET, neurobiology and psychiatry educator; b. Bronx, N.Y., Sept. 7, 1949; s. Philip Peace and Sarah (Greenberg) N.; m. Melissa Ann Pilkington, May 24, 1980; children: Matthew P., Amanda P., Sarah-Frances P. B.S., CCNY, 1970; M.S., Northeastern U., 1973; Ph.D., U. N.C., 1976, M.D., 1981. Diplomate Am. Bd. Psychiatry and Neurology; lic. physician, N.C., Ga. Research asst. ichthyology Am. Mus. Natural History, N.Y.C., 1968-71, neurochemistry lab. McLean Hosp., Belmont, Mass., 1971-72; research assoc. surgery Beth Israel Hosp., Boston, 1972-73; teaching asst. biology Northeastern U., 1972-73; postdoctoral fellow Biol. Scis. Research Ctr., U. N.C., Chapel Hill, 1976-77, research fellow, 1977-83, clin. instr. psychiatry, 1983; resident in psychiatry N.C. Meml. Hosp., Chapel Hill, 1981-83; asst. prof. dept. psychiatry and pharmacology Duke U., Durham, N.C., 1983-85, assoc. prof. psychiatry, 1985-89, assoc. prof. pharmacology, 1986-89, prof. depts. psychiatry and pharmacology, 1989-91; chief div. biological psychiatry, 1988-91, prof., chmn. dept. psychiatry and behavioral scis. Emory U. Sch. Medicine, 1991—, Reunette W. Harris prof. psychiatry and behavioral scis., 1994—; vis. prof. physiology Cath. U., Santiago, Chile, 1978. Predoctoral fellow Schizophrenia Research Found., Soc. Scottish Rite, Lexington, Mass., 1975-76; postdoctoral fellow Nat. Inst. Neurol., Communicative Disorders and Stroke, 1977; recipient Michiko Kuno award U. N.C., 1978, 79, Merck award for acad. excellence, 1981; grantee Nat. Inst. Aging, 1982-83, NIMH, 1983—; Merck award for young investigators Am. Geriatrics Soc., 1985, 2d prize Anna Monica Found. for Research in Endogenous Depression, 1987, Merit award NIMH, 1987; Nanaline Duke fellow Duke U. Med. Ctr., 1985-87; Rsch. prize World Fedn. Societies of Biol. Psychiatry, 1991; recipient Edward J. Sachar award Columbia U., 1993, Edward A. Strecker prize Instl. Pa. Hosp., 1993, Outstanding Alumni award in health scis. Northeastern U., 1995. Fellow Am. Coll. Neuropsychopharmacology (Mead Johnson travel award 1982, coun. 1993—), Am. Coll. Psychiatrists (chmn. contbns. com. 1991-93, edn. com. 1993—, bd. regents 1994—); mem. Soc. Neurosci. (program com. 1993-95), AAAS, N.Y. Acad. Scis., Internat. Soc. Psychoneuroendocrinology (pres. 1993—, Curt P. Richter award 1985), Internat. Soc. Neurochemistry, Am. Soc. Neurochemistry (Jordi-Folch-Pi award 1987), Endocrine Soc. Internat. Soc. Neuroendocrinology, Soc. Biol. Psychiatry (A.E. Bennett award 1979, gold medal award 1996), Am. Fedn. Clin. Research, AMA, Am. Pain Soc., Am. Psychiat. Assn. (Kempf award 1989, Samuel Hibbs award 1991, coun. rsch. 1993—, chmn. 1994-95, rsch. prize 1996), Argentine Assn. Psychoneuroendocrinology (sci. council), Sigma Xi. Democrat. Jewish. Editor: (with A.J. Prange, Jr.) Neurotensin, a Brain and Gastrointestinal Peptide, 1982, (with A.J. Dunn) Peptides, Hormones and Behavior, 1984, (with P.T. Loosen) Handbook of Clinical Psychoneuroendocrinology, Neuropeptides in Psychiatric and Neurological Disorders, 1987, Neuropeptides in Psychiatric Disorders, 1991, Neuroendocrinology, 1992, (with P. Kitabgi) The Neurobiology of Neurotensin, 1992, (with A.F. Schatzberg) Textbook of Psychopharmacology, 1995; editor-in-chief: Depression, 1993—; co-editor-in-chief: Critical Revs. in Neurobiology, 1992—; contbr. numerous articles and abstracts to profl. jours., chpts. in books. Office: Emory U Sch Medicine Dept Psychiatry 1639 Pierce Dr Atlanta GA 30322

NEMICKAS, RIMGAUDAS, cardiologist, educator; b. Kaunas, Lithuania, Mar. 10, 1938; came to U.S., 1949; s. Romualdas and Elena (Saulyte) N.; m. Joan A. McLee, Feb. 16, 1965; children: Rimas Jonas, Kristina Nemickas Tomlinson, Thomas Edward, Nikolas. Student, Ind. U., 1954-57; MD magna cum laude, Loyola U., 1961; MD (hon.), Kaunas Med. Acad., 1993. Diplomate in internal medicine and cardiovascular diseases Am. Bd. Internal Medicine; lic. physician, Ill., Ind. Intern U. Chgo. Clinics, 1961-62; resident inmedicine U. Ill. Rsch. and Edn. Hosps., 1966-67; fellow in cardiology Cook County Hosp., Chgo., 1962-63, U. Chgo. Hosp., 1967-69; asst. prof. medicine Loyola U., Maywood, Ill., 1969-73, dir. cardiac care unit, 1969-77, assoc. chief cardiology, 1972-77, assoc. prof. medicine, 1973-79, clin. prof. medicine, 1979—; dir. cardiology Ill. Masonic Med. Ctr., Chgo. 1980—; chmn. Loyola Med. Practice Plan, Maywood, 1972-77; mem. Ill. Med. Soc. Ins. Svcs. Physician Rev. Com., Chgo., 1977-95. Mem. Task Force for Health Care Reform, Vilnius, Lithuania, 1994, Lithuanian Ministry of Health. Capt. USAF, 1963-66. Fellow ACP, Am. Coll. Cardiology, Am. Coll. Chest Physicians; mem. AMA, Am. Heart Assn., Chgo. Soc. Internal Medicine, Chgo. Cardiology Group (sec.-treas. 1992-93). Republican. Roman Catholic. Office: Ill Masonic Med Offices 3000 N Halsted St Chicago IL 60657

NEMOTO, TAKUMA, physician; b. Japan, Apr. 10, 1930; came to U.S., 1955; m. Susan M. Mackey, June 18, 1960; children: Carol Ann, Patricia Lynn, david Takuma, Peter Allen. MD, Keiou Sch. Medicine, Tokyo, 1954. Physician Roswell Pk. Cancer Inst., Buffalo, 1962-88, Breast Care Ctr., Buffalo, 1988—. Fellow ACS, Soc. Surg. Oncology. Office: 55 Spindrift Dr Ste 104 Williamsville NY 14221-7800

NEMOY, NORMAN J., urologist; b. Chgo., Apr. 21, 1939; s. David and Ida (Toppel) N.; m. Carol Ruskind, 1963 (div. 1986); m. Carole Curb, Mar. 23, 1991; children: John, Laura, Caroline. Student, U. Ill., 1957-59; MD, U. Ill., Chgo., 1963. Diplomate Nat. Bd. Med. Examiners, Am. Bd. Urology. Rotating intern UCLA Affiliated Hosps., 1963-64; internal medicine resident Mt. Zion Med. Ctr., San Francisco, 1964-65; urology resident Stanford Med. Ctr., Palo Alto, Calif., 1965-69, U.S. Pub. Health fellow, 1966-67; attending staff mem. Cedars-Sinai Med. Ctr., L.A., 1969—; clin. instr. in urology UCLA; attending staff mem. Midway Hosp., Century City Hosp. Contbr. numerous articles to profl. publs. Fellow ACS; mem. AMA, Am. Soc. Nephrology, Am. Urol. Assn., Calif. Med. Assn., Los Angeles County Med. Assn. (pres. Beverly Hills dist. 1985-88). Office: 8631 W 3d St Ste 915 E Los Angeles CA 90048-5912

NEPPE, VERNON MICHAEL, neuropsychiatrist, author, educator; b. Johannesburg, Transvaal, Rep. South Africa, Apr. 16, 1951; came to U.S., 1986; s. Solly Louis and Molly (Hesselsohn) N.; m. Elisabeth Selima Schachter, May 29, 1977; children: Jonathan, Shari. BA, U. South Africa, 1976; MB, BCh, U. Witwatersrand, Johannesburg, 1973, diploma in psychol., medicine, 1976, M in Medicine, 1979, PhD in Medicine, 1981; MD, U.S., 1982. Diplomate Am. Bd. Psychiatry and Neurology, Am. Bd. Geriatric Psychiatry, Am. Bd. Forensic Psychiatry, Am. Bd. Forensic Examiners, Am. Bd. Forensic Medicine; registered psychiatry specialist U.S., Republic of South Africa, Can. Specialist in tng. dept. psychiatry U. Witwatersrand, Johannesburg, 1974-80; sr. cons. U. Witwatersrand Med. Sch., Johannesburg, 1980-82, 83-85; neuropsychiatry fellow Cornell U., N.Y.C., 1982-83; div. dir. U. Wash. Med. Sch., Seattle, 1986-92; dir. Pacific Neuropsychiat. Inst., Seattle, 1992—; mem. clin. faculty dept. psychiatry and behavioral scis. U. Wash. Med. Sch., 1992—; adj. prof. psychiatry St. Louis U. Sch. of Medicine, dept. psychiatry and human behavior, 1994—; attending physician N.W. Hosp., 1992—; neuropsychiatry cons. South African Brain Rsch. Inst., Johannesburg, 1985—; chief rsch. cons. Epilepsy Inst., N.Y.C., 1989; mem. faculty lectr. Epilepsy: Refining Med. treatment, 1993-94. Author: The Psychology of Déjà, 1983, Innovative Psychopharmacotherapy, 1990, (text) BROCAS SCAN, 1992, (with others) 31 book chpts.; editor 14 jours. issues; contbr. articles to profl. jours. Recipient Rupert Sheldrake prize for rsch. design (2d prize) award New Scientist, 1983, Marius Valkhoff medal South African Soc. for Psychical Rsch., 1982, George Elkin Bequest for Med. Rsch., U. Witwatersrand, 1980; named Overseas Travelling fellow, 1982-83. Fellow Psychiatry Coll. South Africa (faculty), Royal Coll. Physicians of Can., North Pacific Soc. for Neurology, Neurosurgery and Psychiatry, Coll. Internat. Neuropharmacologicum, Am. Coll. Forensic Examiners; mem. AMA, Parapsychologic Assn., Am. Psychiat. Assn. (U.S. transcultural collaborator diagnostic and statis. manual 1985-86, cons. organic brain disorders 1988—), Am. Epilepsy Soc., Soc. Biol. Psychiatry, Can. Psychiat. Assn., Soc. Sci. Exploration, Am. soc. Clin. Psychopharmacology. Jewish. Office: Pacific Neuropsychiat Inst 10330 Meridian Ave N Ste 380 Seattle WA 98133-9463

NEPPER RASMUSSEN, JØRGEN, neuroradiologist, consultant; b. Dianalund, Denmark, Nov. 7, 1944. MD, Aarhus (Denmark) U., 1977. Cert. neuroradiologist; specialist in diagnostic radiology. Resident Aalborg Hosp., Denmark, 1977-83, fellow dept. radiology, 1983-85; registrar dept. neuroradiology Aarhus U. Hosp., Denmark, 1985-88; cons. dept. neuroradiology Odense U. Hsop., Denmark, 1988—; asst. prof. Odense U., Denmark, 1989—; chmn. Scandinavian Soc. Neuroradiology, 1994-95. Contbr. chpts. to books in field. Recipient Travel grantee Danish Soc. Radiology, 1995. Mem. European Soc. Neuroradiology, Scandinavian Soc. Neuroradiology. Office: Dept Radiology Neuroradiology Sect, Odense U Hosp-SDR Blvd, DK-5000 Odense Denmark

NEREM, ROBERT MICHAEL, engineering educator, consultant; b. Chgo., July 20, 1937; s. Robert and Borghild Guneva (Bakken) N.; m. Jill Ann Thomson, Dec. 21, 1958 (div. 1977); children: Robert Steven, Nancy Ann Nerem Chambers; m. Marilyn Reed, Oct. 7, 1978; stepchildren: Christina Lynn Maser, Carol Marie Maser. BS, U. Okla., 1959; MS, Ohio State U., 1961, PhD, 1964; D (honoris causa), U. Paris, 1990. Asst. prof. Ohio State U., Columbus, 1964-68, assoc. prof., 1968-72, prof., 1972-79, assoc. dean Grad. Sch., 1975-79; prof. mech. engring., chmn. dept. U. Houston, 1979-86; Parker H. Petit prof. Ga. Inst. Tech., Atlanta, 1987—, Inst. prof., 1991—, dir. Inst. for Bioengring. and Biosci., 1995—; mem. Ga. Gov.'s Adv. Coun. on Sci. and Tech. Devel., Atlanta, 1992-95; ALZA disting. lectr. Biomed. Engring. Soc., 1991, ASME Thurston lectr., 1994. Contbr. over 100 articles to profl. jours. Fellow Am. Inst. Med. and Biol. Engring. (founding pres. 1992-94), ASME, AAAS; mem. NAE, Biomed. Engring. Soc., Inst. Medicine, Internat. Union for Phys. and Engring. Scis. in Medicine (pres. 1991-94), Internat. Fedn. for Med. and Biol. Engring. (pres. 1988-91), U.S. Nat. Com. on Biomechanics (1988-91 chmn.), Polish Acad. Scis. Home: 2950 Waverly Ct NW Atlanta GA 30339-4200 Office: Ga Inst Tech Inst Bioentring & Biosci 281 Ferst Dr Atlanta GA 33032-0363

NERSESSIAN, EDWARD, psychiatrist, psychoanalyst, educator; b. Nov. 28, 1944. GCE A'level, Leeds Coll. Tech., Leeds, Eng., 1964; MD, U. Louvain, Belgium, 1970. Intern Hotel Dieu de Montreal, Montreal, Can., 1969-70; resident in psychiatry Hillside Hosp., Glen Oaks, N.Y., 1970-72, N.Y. Hosp. Payne Whitney Clinic, N.Y.C., 1972-73; pvt. practice N.Y.C., 1973—; asst. clin. prof. psychiatry Cornell U., 1975, clin. assoc. prof., 1990; asst. attending psychiatrist N.Y. Hosp., 1975, clin. assoc. attending psychiatrist N.Y. Hosp. PWC, 1990, Payne Whitney Clinic. Editor: (with R. Kopff) Textbook of Psychoanalysis. Fellow Am. Psychiatric Assn.; mem. N.Y. Psychoanalytic Soc. (cert. tng. supr. psychoanalyst, pres. 1991—), Am. Psychoanalytic Assn., Internat. Psychoanalytic Assn. Office: 72 E 91st St New York NY 10128-1321

NERY, FLORES, urologist; b. Guatemala City, Guatemala, May 26, 1948; M. Beatrice Flores; children: Diego, Gabriel. MD, U. San Carlos, Guatemala, 1973. Diplomate Am. Bd. Urology. Instr. Baylor Coll. Medicine, Houston, 1981-84, asst. prof., 1984—. Mem. AMA, Urol. Assn. (Houston chpt.), Michael DeBakey Surg. Soc., Houston Pediatric Soc., Col Medicos y Curjanos Guatemala, Harris County Med. Soc. Christian. Office: Baylor College of Medicine 6624 Fannin Ste 1280 Houston TX 77030

NESBITT, CAROL KELLEY, health services administrator; b. Panama City, Fla., Sept. 27, 1963; d. Bobby G. Kelley and Peggy (Spears) Barnett; m. Curtis R. Nesbitt, Feb. 22, 1992; 1 chld, Jacob Randal. Diploma, St. Vincent Sch. Nursing, Birmingham, Ala., 1984; student, U. Ala., Birmingham, 1981, Wallace State C.C., Hanceville, Ala., 1983-85. RN, Ala.; diplomate Am. Bd. Quality Assurance and Utilization Rev. Physicians. Staff and charge nurse St. Vincent's Hosp., Birmingham, 1984-90, staff nurse, flex pool, 1990-94; instr. St. Vincent's Hosp. Good Health Sch., Birmingham, 1988-91; patient care coord. S.E. HealthPlan, Birmingham, 1988-91, med. rev. analyst, 1990-91; utilization rev. quality assurance mgr. Health Choice, Birmingham, 1993-94; health svcs. dir. Advance HealthLink, Birmingham, 1994-96; med. svcs. dir. GuideStar Health Systems, Birmingham, Ala., 1996—. Mem. Nat. Assn. Healthcare Quallity, Ala. Assn. Healthcare Quality. Home: 1080 Manual Hill Rd Cordova AL 35550 Office: GuideStar Health Systems 1000 Urban Ctr Dr Ste 460 Birmingham AL 35242

NESBITT, JOHN ARTHUR, leisure studies educator; b. Detroit, Mar. 29, 1933; s. John Jackson and Anna Maye (Hartley) N.; m. Dolores Antonia Gutierrez, Apr. 8, 1961; children: John Arthur, Victoria Bowen. Student, Olivet Coll., 1952-53; BA, Mich. State U., 1955; MA, Columbia U., 1961, EdD, 1968. Registered hosp. recreation dir.; cert. therapeutic recreation specialist. Dir. program Jaycees Internat., Miami, Fla., 1957-60; recreation leader Inst. Rehab. Medicine, NYU-Bellevue Med. Center, 1960-61; dir. World Commn. on Vocat. Rehab., Internat. Soc. Rehab. of Disabled, N.Y.C., 1961-63; dep. dir. gen. Internat. Recreation Assn., N.Y.C., 1964-65; asst. sec. gen. Internat. Soc. for Rehab. of Disabled, N.Y.C., 1966-68; asst. prof., coordinator rehab. services San Jose State U., 1968-69; assoc. prof., dir. Inst. Interdisciplinary Studies, 1969-72; assoc. prof., chmn. dept. leisure studies U. Iowa, Iowa City, 1972-76; prof. recreation edn. program U. Iowa, 1976-85, prof., chmn. dept. leisure studies, 1986-87; pres. Spl. Recreation, Inc., 1978—; dir. Com. for Handicapped People of U.S. People Program, 1964—; chmn. com. recreation and leisure U.S. Pres.'s Com. on Employment of Handicapped, 1972-81; dir. Internat. Ctr. on Spl. Recreation, 1988—. Author, editor books in field; editor: Alert Mag., 1956, Jaycees Internat. World, 1957-60, Internat. Rehab. of Disabled Rev., 1965-68, Therapeutic Recreation Jour, 1968-70, Jour. Iowa Parks and Recreation, 1974-76, Play, Recreation and Leisure for People Who Are Disabled, 1977, Fed. Funding for Spl. Recreation, 1978, New Concepts and New Processes in Spl. Recreation, 1978, New Horizons in Profl. Tng. in Recreation Service for Handicapped Children and Youth, 1983, Nisbet/Nesbitt Family Surname Assn. Newsletter, 1983-86, Spl. Recreation Digest, 1984—, Spl. Recreation Compendium, 1986; sr. editor Recreation and Leisure Service for Disadvantaged, 1969; editor, compiler Spl. Recreation Compendium of 1,500 Resources for Disabled People, 3d edit., 1989. Bd. dirs., treas. United Cerebral Palsy Assn., San Mateo and Santa Clara County, 1970-72; bd. dirs. Harold Russell Found., 1971-73, Goodwill Industries Santa Clara County, 1969-72, rehab. counselor, master therapeutic recreation specialist. Served with USAF, 1955-57; maj. Ret. Recipient numerous awards and citations for work with handicapped. Mem. Nat. Therapeutic Recreation Soc. (pres. 1970-71), Nat. Rehab. Assn., Am. Assn. Leisure and Recreation (bd. dirs. 1977-80), Nat. Consortium on Phys. Edn. and Recreation for Handicapped (pres. 1976-77), Nat. Forum Comml. Recreation and Handicapped (chmn. 1979), AAHPER, Iowa Parks and Recreation Assn. (bd.dirs. 1973-75, 89-90), Nat. Rehab. Counseling Assn., Council Exceptional Children, Pi Sigma Epsilon. Presbyterian. Office: Office Special Recreation 363 Koser Ave Iowa City IA 52246-3038

NESBITT, LEE TERRELL, JR., dermatologist; b. Gaffney, S.C., May 2, 1941. MD, Tulane U., 1966. Intern Charity Hosp., Tulane U., New Orleans, 1966-67, resident in dermatology, 1969-72; prof., head dept. dermatology La. State U. Sch. Medicine, New Orleans; attending physician Univ. Hosp., New Orleans. Fellow ACP; mem. Am. Acad. Dermatology, Am. Dermatology Assn. Office: La State U Med Ctr 1542 Tulane Ave New Orleans LA 70112-2825*

NESBITT, LLOYD IVAN, podiatrist; b. Toronto, Ont., Can., Sept. 24, 1951; s. Allan Jay and Rose (Shuster) N.; m. Marlene Cindy Weigler, May 13, 1984; children: Hilary Liza, Andrea Eve, Jeffrey Ryan. D in Podiatric Medicine, Calif. Coll. Podiatric Medicine, San Francisco, 1975. Diplomate Internat. Soc. Podiatric Laser Surgery. Residency program Vancouver (B.C.) Gen. Hosp., Can., 1975-76; pvt. practice podiatric medicine Toronto; cons. podiatry Alan Eagleson Sports Medicine Clinic, Toronto, 1979—; lectr. numerous colls., fitness ctrs. and sports medicine confs., Ont., 1979—. Contbr. numerous articles to sports medicine books and jours; editor Canadian Podiatrist Jour., 1979-88. Fellow Can. Podiatric Sports Medicine Acad. (pres. 1979-89, editor newsletter 1977-89), Am. Acad. Podiatric Sports Medicine; mem. Internat. Soc. Podiatric Laser Surgery (diplomate), Am. Podiatric Med. Assn., Sierra Club. Home: 122 Argonne Crescent, Willowdale, ON Canada M2K 2K1 Office: Madison Ctr Office Tower, 4950 Yonge St Ste 2414, Toronto, ON Canada M2N 6K1

NESHEIM, ROBERT OLAF, food products executive; b. Monroe Center, Ill., Sept. 13, 1921; s. Olaf M. and Sena M. (Willms) N.; m. Emogene P. Sullivan, July 13, 1946 (divorced); children: Barbara Mowry, Susan Yost (dec.), Sandra Rankin; m. doris Howes Calloway, July 4, 1981. BS, U. Ill., 1943, MS, 1950, PhD, 1951; postgrad. in advanced mgmt. program, Harvard U., 1971. Farm mgr. Halderman Farm Mgmt. Svc., Wabash, Ind., 1946-48; instr. U. Ill., 1951; mgr. feed rsch. The Quaker Oats Co., Barrington, Ill., 1952-64; prof., head of dept. animal sci. U. Ill., 1964-67; dir. nutrition rsch. The Quaker Oats Co., Barrington, Ill., 1967-69, v.p. R & D, 1969-78; v.p. sci. & tech. The Quaker Oats Co., Chgo., 1978-83; sr. v.p. sci. & tech. Avadyne, Inc., Monterey, Calif., 1983-85; pres. Advanced Healthcare,

Monterey, 1985-91; ret., 1991. Capt. U.S. Army, 1943-46, South Pacific. Fellow Am. Inst. Nutrition (treas. 1983-86), AAAS; mem. Inst. Food Technologists, Fed. Socs. Exptl. Biologists (treas. 1973-79), APHA, Corral de Tierra Club (Salinas, Calif.).

NESSEL, EDWARD HARRY, swimming coach; b. Roselle, N.J., 1945; s. Irving Meyer Nessel and Ruth Eliott; m. Eileen Robin Berstein, 1973; children: Lee Allyson, Jason Eric, Matthew Scott (dec.). BS in Chemistry, Rutgers U., 1967, degree in pharmacy chemistry, 1968, postgrad., 1971; postgrad., Jersey City State, 1970; MS in Bacteriology, Wagner Coll., 1978, MPH, 1978. Registered pharmacist, Calif., N.J., Fla.; cert. U.S. Swimming Coach. Researcher, product developer Mennen Cos., Morrisplains, N.J., 1967; pharmacist supr. Pathmark Pharmacies, N.J., 1968-79; pharmacist, mgr. Roxy Drug Co., Inc., Irvington, N.J., 1979-90; diet and nutrition cons. Fanwood Scotch Plaines YMCA, 1985—, masters swim coach, 1984—, swimming and racing cons., head age group coach, asst. sr. coach, 1989-91; head swim coach Jewish Cmty. Ctr. Metrowest, West Orange, 1991—, Maccabi, 1990-91, 92, 93, 94; coach N.J. Masters Swimming, 1985—; physiology and sports medicine cons. Nat. Health and Fitness; health and fitness chmn. N.J. Masters Swimming; nat. masters swimming coaches com. Nat. Com. for Sports Medicine; chair N.J. Masters Swimming; pres. Jersey Masters Swimming Inc.; sports chair age group and masters swimming Garden State Games; summer coord. long-course 50 meter swim season Rayway YMCA, 1987—. Contbr. articles on swimming, self def. and physiology to profl. jours. Athletic and swimming cons. N.J. Spl. Olympics, 1986; cons. Essex County Narcotic Strike Force, Garden State Games ofcl.; chairperson govs. coun. phys. fitness for swimming events Garden State Games, 1989, 90. Recipient Presdl. Series award 1986; winner N.J. State Pentathlon champion Masters Swimming, 1986, 87, YMCA Masters Nat. Swim champion, 1988, 91, 95; apptd. head swim coach U.S. Jr. Nat. Swim Team, World Maccabi Games, Israel, 1997. Mem. NRA (disting. expert rating in pistol shooting), Am. Assn. Microbiologists, N.J. Pharm. Assn., N.J. Guild Pharmacists, Internat. Practical Shooters Confedn. (N.J. State Champion 1982, 83), Am. Swimming Coaches Assn. (master level), U.S. Swimming Coaches Assn. (cert. level 5), Master Swim Coaches Assn. Am., Rutgers Coll. Alumni Assn., Am. Med. Athletic Assn. (life, contbg. editor quar. 1993—), Willow Grove Swim Club (bd. dirs. 1986—), South River Pistol Club. Home: 10 Irene Ct Edison NJ 08820-1024 Office: JCC Metrowest 760 Northfield Ave West Orange NJ 07052-1102

NESSMITH, H(ERBERT) ALVA, dentist; b. Miami, Fla., Nov. 27, 1935; s. William Boyd and Florence Editha (Lowe) N.; m. Paula Ann Fox, Oct. 1, 1960 (div. 1984); children: Amy Susan, Lynn Margaret, Mark Alva. Student, U. Miami, Fla., 1953-56; DDS, Northwestern U., 1960. Gen. practice dentistry Tequesta, Fla., 1963—; dental cons. Palm Beach-Martin County Med. Ctr., Jupiter, Fla., 1970—. Mem. advminstrv. bd. United Meth. Ch. Tequesta, Jupiter, 1970—, chmn., 1988-90; pres. Meth. Men, 1982; chmn. Coun. on Ministries, 1992-94; pres. Jupiter Elem. PTO, 1972; clarinetist Symphonic Band of Palm Beaches, Fla. Concert Band; pianist and clarinetist United Meth. Ch.; mem. adminstrv. com. Christian Dental Soc., 1994—; active Village of Tequesta Hist. Commn., 1992—, Jupiter (Fla.) Cmty. Resource Ctr., 1994—; mem. adminstrv. bd. Christian Dental Soc., 1994—. Mem. ADA, North Palm Beach County Dental Soc., Fla. Dental Assn., Jupiter-Tequesta-Juno Beach C. of C. Democrat. Lodge: Kiwanis (pres. Jupiter/Tequesta chpt. 1980-81). Home: 196 River Dr Tequesta FL 33469-1934 Office: Inlet Profl Bldg 175 Tequesta Dr Jupiter FL 33469-2733

NESTER, EUGENE WILLIAM, microbiology educator; b. Johnson City, N.Y., Sept. 15, 1930; married, 1959; 2 children. BS, Cornell U., 1952; PhD, Western Reserve U., 1959. Am. Cancer Soc. rsch. fellow genetics Stanford U., 1959-62, instr. microbiology, 1962-63, from asst. to assoc. prof. microbiology and genetics, 1963-72; prof. microbiology U. Wash., Seattle, 1972—, chmn. microbiology, 1982-96. Recipient Chiron Corp. Biotechnology Rsch. award, Australia prize, 1990. Fellow NAS, AAAS, Am. Acad. Microbiology; mem. Am. Soc. Microbiology. Office: Univ Wash Microbiology Dept Box 357242 Seattle WA 98195-7242

NESTIANU, VALERIU S., physiology educator; b. Bucharest, Romania, Dec. 3, 1926; s. Simion Gh. and Alexandrina D. (Nedelcu) N.; m. Maria-Margareta V. Enea, Sept. 16, 1960; 1 child, Adrian V. MD, Faculty of Medicine, Bucharest, Romania, 1951; PhD in Medicine, Faculty of Medicine, 1972. Demonstrator dept. physiology Faculty of Medicine, Bucharest, Romania, 1949-50, asst. dept. physiology, 1953-61, lectr. dept. physiology, 1961-70; rschr. Inst. Neurology Romanian Acad., Bucharest, 1951-53; sr. lectr., chmn. dept. physiology Faculty of Medicine U. Craiova (Romania), 1970-79, prof., chmn. dept. physiology, 1979—; rschr. Inst. Neurology Romanian Acad., 1953-55, prin. rschr., 1955-56, chief lab., 1956-59; chancellor Nat. Coun. Sci. Rsch., Bucharest, 1966-68; dean Faculty of Medicine U. Craiova, 1970-73, 90, sci. sec. faculty, 1975-89, chmn. dept. physicology, physiopathology & med. informatics, 1973-75, 91—. Author: The Reticular Formation of The Brain, 1965, The Physiology of Sportsmen High Altitude Acclimatisation, 1968, (with others) Visual Physiology, 1989; contbr. articles to profl. jours. Mem. Romanian Soc. Physiol. Scis. (pres.), Romanian Soc. Neuronal Networks,. Christian Orthodox. Home: Calea Bucuresti Bloc C8, Sci Apt 8, Ro-1100 Craiova Dolj, Romania Office: U Craiova Faculty Medicine, Str Petru Rares # 4, Ro-1100 Craiova Dolj, Romania

NESTOR, JOHN JOSEPH, JR., pharmaceutical executive; b. Miami, Fla., Jan. 21, 1945; s. John J. and Marion (Sexton) N.; m. Janet Francis, Aug. 14, 1976; 1 child, James. BS in Chemistry, Poly. Inst. Bklyn., 1966; PhD in Organic Chemistry, U. Ariz., 1971; postgrad. in peptide chemistry, Cornell U., Ithaca, N.Y., 1972-74. Staff rschr. I/II/sr. Syntex Rsch., Palo Alto, Calif., 1974-83, dept. head, 1983-85, asst. dir. Inst. Bioorganic Chemistry, 1985-87, v.p., inst. dir., 1987-94, disting. scientist, v.p., 1994—. Editor: LHRH and Its Analogs, part I, 1984, part II, 1987. Mem. indsl. adv. bd. U. Calif.-San Diego, 1990—. Mem. AAAS, Internat. Soc. Quantum Biology, Am. Peptide Soc., Am. Chem. Soc.

NETSCHER, DAVID TERENCE, surgeon; b. South Africa, Sept. 5, 1953; m. Ruth Evans, 1978; children: Francis Douglas, George Michael. BS cum laude, U. Witwatersrand, 1973, MBBCh cum laude, 1977. Diplomate Am. Bd. Surgery, Am. Bd. Plastic Surgery. Intern Johannesburg Gen. Hosp., 1978; sr. house office rotation in gen. surgery Beckenham and Bromley Hosps., London, 1979-80; sr. house officer Whipps Cross Hosp., London, 1980-81; fellow in hand surgery Hand Surgery Assocs., Louisville, 1983; resident in gen. surgery U. Louisville, 1981-85; resident in plastic surgery Baylor Coll. Medicine, 1986-88; Christine Kleinert hand and microsurgery fellow Louisville Hand Surgery, 1988-89; asst. prof. divsn. plastic surgery Baylor U., Houston, 1989-94, asst. prof. dept. otorhinolaryngology & communicative scis., 1993—, assoc. prof. plastic surgery, 1994—; chief plastic surgery sect. VA Med. Ctr., Houston, 1994—, attending surgeon, 1989—, Meth. Hosp., Houston, 1989—, St. Luke's Episc. Hosp., Houston, 1989—. Contbr. articles to profl. jours. and chpts. to books. Recipient Outstanding Med. Svc. award Tex. Breast Implant Info. Found., 1994. Fellow ACS; mem. Am. Soc. for Reconstructive Microsurgery, Am. Soc. for Aesthetic Plastic Surgery, Am. Soc. for Surgery of Hand, Am. Assn. for Hand Surgery, Plastic Surgery Rsch. Coun. Office: Baylor Coll Medicine Divsn Plastic Surgery 6560 Fannin # 800 Houston TX 77030

NEUBAUER, PETER BELA, psychoanalyst; b. Krems, Austria, July 5, 1913; came to U.S., 1941, naturalized, 1946; s. Samuel and Rose (Blau) N.; m. Susan Rachlin, Nov. 25, 1953 (dec.); children—Joshua Rachlin, Alexander Lewis. M.D., U. Berne, 1938. Intern Lawrence Meml. Hosp., New London, Conn., 1941, Beth-El Hosp., Bklyn., 1942; resident in psychiatry Bellevue Hosp., N.Y.C., 1943-45; dir. Child Devel. Ctr., Jewish Bd. Family and Children's Services, N.Y.C., 1951-83; clin. prof. psychiatry Psychoanalytic Inst., N.Y. U., 1979—; lectr. child psychoanalysis Psychoanalytic Inst. for Tng. and Research Columbia U., 1973. Author: Children in Collectives: Child Rearing Aims and Practices in Kibbutzim, 1965, Early Child Day Car, 1974, Process of Child Development, 1976, (with Alexander Neubauer) Nature's Thumbprint, 1990; contbg. author: Fathers and Their Families, 1989; mem. editorial bd. Psychoanalytic Study of the Child, 1978. Recipient Hulse award N.Y. Council Child Psychiatry, 1975, Heinz Hartmann award N.Y. Psychoanalytic Soc., 1981, Mary S. Sigourney award, 1994. Mem. Am. Psychoanalytic Assn., Am. Acad. Child Psychiatry, Assn. Child Psychoanalysis, Internat. Assn. Child and Adolescent Psychiatry, Assn. for Child Psychoanalysis (pres. 1974-76). Office: 33 E 70th St New York NY 10021-4946

NEUBERG, HANS W., physician; b. Hanover, Germany, Mar. 26, 1921; s. George and Gertrude (Dux) N.; came to U.S., 1937, naturalized, 1943; BS, Wagner Coll., 1941; MD, Columbia, 1950; m. Birgit Aron, Apr. 8, 1949; children: Peter G., Gerald W. Intern Presbyn. Hosp., N.Y.C., 1950-53, asst. resident, NRC fellow in medicine, 1953-54, asst. attending physician, 1966-80, assoc. attending physician, 1980-91, attending physician, 1992—; instr. medicine Columbia Coll. Phys. and Surg., 1954-63, assoc. in medicine, 1963-67, asst. prof. clin. medicine, 1967-80, assoc. clin. prof. medicine, 1980-91, clin. prof. medicine, 1992—. Served with AUS, 1943-46. Fellow ACP; mem. Alpha Omega Alpha. Home: 85 Erledon Rd Tenafly NJ 07670-2503 Office: 620 W 168th St New York NY 10032

NEUBERGER, JOHN STEPHEN, preventive medicine and epidemiology educator; b. N.Y.C., June 29, 1938; s. Seymour Neuberger and Norma (Endel) Greenspan; m. Geri Cox, July 13, 1980; 1 child. BME, Cornell U., 1961; MBA, Columbia U., 1967; MPH, Johns Hopkins U., 1974, DrPH, 1977. Asst. prof. U. Kans. Sch. Medicine, Kansas City, 1978-84, assoc. prof., 1984—; cons. region VII, EPA, Kansas City, 1979-81; mem. toxicology adv. com. Kans. Dept. Health and Environ., Topeka, 1982-86. Contbr. articles to profl. jours. Bd. dirs. Coalition for Engironment, Kansas City, 1987-91, pres., 1990-91; mem. adv. bd. Kansas City Earth Week, 1990; mem. Cherokee County Task Force, 1986-94, Oak Grove Sch. Task Force, Kansas City, 1989-90; mem. air quality forum, 1991-93; mem. Kansas City Pub. TV Cmty. Adv. Bd., 1991-92. 1st lt. U.S. Army, 1961-63. Grantee EPA, 1979-80, Kans. Dept. Health and Environ., 1982-83, 84-86, U.S. Dept. Energy, 1988-89. Mem. AAAS, Am. Assn. Cancer Rsch., Am. Coll. Epidemiology, Am. Coun. on Sci. and Health (scientific bd., policy advisor 1986—), Am. Pub. Health Assn. (epidemiology and environ. health sects.). Office: U Kans Sch Medicine Rainbow Blvd at 39th Kansas City KS 66103-2070

NEUFANG, KARL FRIEDRICH RUDOLF, radiologist; b. Cologne, Germany, Nov. 21, 1953; s. Karl Friedrich and Hedwig Johanna (Kopp) N.; m. Ursula Anna Mueller Neufang, Oct. 18, 1985; 1 child, Benedikt Johannes Cornelius. MD, U. Sch. Medicine, Cologne, Germany, 1978. Med. diplomate. Asst. U. Hosp. Radiology, Cologne, Germany, 1979; med. officer Ctrl. Army Hosp. Koblenz, Germany, 1979-80; asst. U. Hosp. Radiology, Cologne, Germany, 1981-85; sr. officer, 1985-92; pvt. practice Inst. for Diagnostic Radiology and Nuclear Medicine, Euskirchen, Germany, 1992—; chmn. Dept. Diagnostic Radiology, Central Clinic, Augsburg, Germany, 1992. Co-author: Digital Subtraction Angiography, 1988, Degenerative Vascular Disease, 1992; co-editor: Vascular Stenting/Magnetic Resonance Angiography, 1991; assoc. editor: Aktuelle Radilogie, 1991-93. Med. Capt. Ctrl. Army Hosp., 1979-80, Koblenz. Mem. RSNA, ESMRMB, Deutsche Rontgengesellschaft. Roman Catholic. Office: Praxis Radiologie, Nuklearmedizin, D-53879 Euskirchen Germany

NEUFELD, ELIZABETH FONDAL, biochemist, educator; b. Paris, Sept. 27, 1928; U.S. citizen; m. 1951. Ph.D., U. Calif., Berkeley, 1956; D.H.C. (hon.), U. Rene Descartes, Paris, 1978; D.Sc. (hon.), Russell Sage Coll., Troy, N.Y., 1981, Hahnemann U. Sch. Medicine, 1984. Asst. research biochemist U. Calif., Berkeley, 1957-63; with Nat. Inst. Arthritis, Metabolism and Digestive Diseases, Bethesda, Md., 1963-84, research biochemist, 1963-73, chief sect. human biochem. genetics, 1973-79, chief genetics and biochem. br., 1979-84; prof., chmn. dept. biol. chemistry UCLA Sch. Medicine, 1984—. Passano Found. sr. laureate, 1982; named Calif. Scientist of Yr., 1990; recipient Dickson prize U. Pitts., 1974, Hillenbrand award, 1975, Gairdner Found. award, 1981, Albert Lasker Clin. Med. Rsch. award, 1982, William Allan award, 1982, Elliott Cresson medal, 1984, Wolf Found. prize, 1988, Christopher Columbus Discovery award for biomed. rsch., 1992, Nat. Medal of Sci., 1994. Fellow AAAS; mem. NAS, Inst. Medicine of NAS, Am. Acad. Arts and Scis., Am. Soc. Human Genetics, Am. Chem. Soc., Am. Soc. Biochemistry and Molecular Biology (pres. 1992-93), Am. Soc. Cell Biology, Am. Soc. Clin. Investigation. Office: UCLA Sch Medicine Dept Biol Chemistry Los Angeles CA 90024-1737

NEUFELD, NAOMI DAS, pediatric endocrinologist; b. Butte, Mont., June 13, 1947; d. Dilip Kumar and Maya (Chaliha) Das; m. Timothy Lee Neufeld, Nov. 27, 1971; children: Pamela Anne, Katherine Louise. AB, Pembroke Coll., 1969; M. in Med. Sci., Brown U., 1971; MD, Tufts U., 1973. Diplomate Am. Bd. Pediatrics, Am. Bd. Endocrinology. Intern R.I. Hosp., Providence, 1973-74, resident in pediatrics, 1974-75; fellow in pediatric endocrinology UCLA, 1975-78; staff endocrinologist Cedars-Sinai Med. Ctr., Los Angeles, 1978-79, chief pediatric endocrinology sect., 1979-85, dir. pediatric endocrinology, 1985—; asst. research pediatrician UCLA, 1978-79, asst. prof.-in-residence pediatrics, 1979-85, assoc. prof.-in-residence, 1985—; med. dir. Kidshape Program Children's Weight Control, 1986—; pres. Pediat. Endocrine & Diabetes Specialists, Inc., 1996—; consulting physician Ventura County Med. Ctr., 1989—. Contbr. articles to profl. jours. Mem. bd. deacons Pacific Palisades Presbyn. ch. 1988—. Named Clin. Investigator, NIH, 1978; grantee United Cerebral Palsy Soc., 1979, March of Dimes, 1981, NIH, 1983-88. Mem. Am. Diabetes Assn., Soc. Pediatric Research, Endocrine Soc., Juvenile Diabetes Found. (research grantee 1980). Presbyterian. Home: 16821 Charmel Ln Pacific Palisades CA 90272-2218 Office: 8635 W Third St #295 Los Angeles CA 90048

NEUFELD, ORVILLE GLENN, emergency physician; b. Fairview, Okla., Nov. 8, 1937; s. Harry C. and Anna (Toews) N.; m. Ida P. Penner; children: Phillip W., Charles W. BS, Southwestern State U., Weatherford, Okla., 1959; MS, Ark. State U., 1965, PhD, 1968; DO, U. Health Scis., 1973. Diplomate Am. Bd. Family Physicians. Intern Univ. Health Scis. Ctr., Kansas City, Mo., 1973-74; asst. prof. in pharmacology U. Calif., San Francisco, 1967-68; assoc. prof., acting chmn. dept. pharmacology and physiology Kansas City (Mo.) Coll. Osteo. Medicine, 1968-72; pvt. practice Fairview, Okla., 1974-91; emergency medicine physician Spectrum Emergency Care, Colorado Springs, Colo., 1992—; med. officer, pharmacy and therapeutics commr. Colo. State Dept. Corrections, Canon City, 1993—; chief of staff Fairview Mcpl. Hosp., dir. med. edn., 1980-91. Bd. evangelism Mennonite Brethren U.S. Conf., Hillsboro, Kans., 1988-94; trustee Tabor Coll., Hillsboro, 1988—. NIH fellow, 1964-68. Mem. Am. Coll. Family Physicians (cert.), Am. Osteo. Assn. Home: 18335 Sloan Ln Monument CO 80132

NEUFFER, MYRON GERALD, genetics educator; b. Preston, Idaho, Mar. 4, 1922; s. Myron David and Camille (Cole) N.; m. Margaret McGregor, Mar. 18, 1943; children: David, John, Gregory, Dale, Barbara, Peggy Neuffer Hendrix, Linda Neuffer Chaston. BS, U. Idaho, 1947; MS, U. Mo., 1948, PhD, 1952. Asst. prof. dept. field crops U. Mo., Columbia, 1951-56, assoc. prof. dept. field crops, 1956-66, prof. dept. field crops, 1966-67, prof. dept. genetics, chmn. dept., 1967-69, prof. biol. scis., 1970-76, prof. agronomy, 1976-92, prof. agronomy emeritus, 1992—. Author: Mutants of Maize, 1968. With U.S. Army, 1943. Fellow AAAS; mem. Genetics Soc. Am., Am. Genetics Assn., Am. Soc. Agronomy. Home: 2003 Valleyview Dr Columbia MO 65201-6020 Office: U Mo Dept Agronomy 109 Curtis Hall Columbia MO 65211

NEUGARTEN, BERNICE LEVIN, social scientist; b. Norfolk, Nebr., Feb. 11, 1916; d. David L. and Sadie (Segall) Levin; m. Fritz Neugarten, July 1, 1940; children: Dail Ann, Jerrold. B.A., U. Chgo., 1936, Ph.D., 1943; D.Sc. (hon.), U. So. Calif., 1980; PhD (hon.), Cath. U., Nijmegen, 1988. Rsch. assoc. Com. on Human Devel., U. Chgo., 1948-50; asst. prof. U. Chgo., 1951-60, assoc. prof., 1960-64, prof., 1964-80, chmn., 1969-73, prof. social svc. adminstrn., 1978-80, mem. com. on policy studies, 1979-80, Rothschild disting. scholar, prof. emeritus, 1988—; prof. emerita Northwestern U., 1980-88; mem. council U. Chgo. Senate, 1968-71, 72-75, 78-80, chmn. council com. on univ. women, 1969-70; nat. adv. council Nat. Inst. on Aging, 1975-76, 78-81, Fed. Council on Aging, 1978-81; dep. chmn. White House Conf. on Aging, 1980-81. Author: (with R.J. Havighurst) American Indian and White Children: A Social-Psychological Investigation, 1955, reprint, 1969, (with R.J. Havighurst) Society and Education, 1957, rev., 1962, 67, 75, (with Assocs.) Personality in Middle and Late Life, 1964, reprint, 1980, (with J.M.A. Munnichs et al) Adjustment to Retirement, 1969, (with R.P. Coleman) Social Status in the City, 1971, Middle Age and Aging, 1968; co-editor: (with H. Eglit) Age Discrimination, 1981, Age or Need? Public Policies for Older People, 1982; assoc. editor Jour. Gerontology, 1958-61, Human Devel., 1962-68; adv. or cons. editor other profl. jours., 1959—; author monographs, research papers and reports. mem. various adv. bodies. Recipient Am. Psychol. Found. Disting. Tchg. award, 1975, Disting. Psychologist award Ill. Psychol. Assn., 1979, Sandoz Internat. Prize for Gerontol. Rsch., 1987, Ollie Randall award Nat. Coun. on Aging, 1993, Gold Medal award for lifetime contbn. as a psychologist in the public interest Am. Psychol. Found., 1994. Fellow AAAS, Am. Psychol. Assn. (coun. rep. 1967-69, 73-76, Disting. Sci. Contbn. award 1980, honoree Women's Heritage Exhibit 1992, Gold Medal award 1994), Am. Sociol. Assn., Gerontol. Soc. Am. (pres. 1968-69, Kleemeier award 1971, Brookdale award 1982, Disting. Mentor award 1988), Am. Acad. Arts and Scis., Internat. Assn. Gerontology (governing coun. 1975-78, chmn. N.Am. exec. com. 1983-85, disting. creative contrbn. to gerontology award); mem. Inst. Medicine of NAS. Home: # 1202 1551 Larimer St Denver CO 80202

NEUGER, SANFORD, orthodontics educator; b. Cleve., Aug. 17, 1925; s. Samuel and Ethel (Manheim) N.; m. Marjorie Odess, Sept. 8, 1963; 1 child, Howard Michael. BS, Western Res. U., 1947, DDS, 1953; MS in Orthodontics, Ind. U., 1957. Diplomate Am. Bd. Orthodontics. Orthodontics demonstrator Western Res. U., Cleve., 1957-58; asst. prof., assoc. prof. orthodontics Western Res. U./Case Western Res. U., Cleve., 1958-75; clin. prof. orthodontics Case Western Res. U., Cleve., 1975—, acting chmn. Orthodontics Dept., 1969-71; asst. dental surgeon U. Hosp., Cleve., 1967—. Author: (syllabus) Contemporary Edgewise Mechanics-Sliding Mechanics, 1973, Limited Tooth Movement, 1970; author-presenter: (videotape) Orthodontics Soldering, 1970. Vol. United Way, 1988, Case Western Res. U. Alumni Assn., Jewish Nat. Fund. Comdr. USNR (ret. 1972). Named Man of Yr. Case Western Res. U. Orthodontics alumni, 1982. Fellow Am. Coll. Dentists; mem. Am. Dental Soc., Cleve. Dental Soc. (bd. dirs. 11965-90), Cleve. Soc. Orthodontists (pres. 1969)., Great Lakes Assn. Orthodontists Assn., Am. Assn. Orthodontists, Pierre Fauchard Soc., Alpha Omega (pres. Cleve. chpt. 1984-85), Omicron Kappa Upsilon. Jewish. Home: 24850 Hilltop Dr Cleveland OH 44122-1350 Office: 1500 S Green Rd Cleveland OH 44121-4040

NEUHARTH, DANIEL J., II, psychotherapist; b. Sioux Falls, S.D., Nov. 10, 1953; s. Allen Harold and Loretta Faye (Helgeland) N. BA, Duke U., 1975; MS in Journalism, Northwestern U., 1978; MA, John F. Kennedy U., 1988; PhD in Clin. Psychology, Calif. Sch. Profl. Psychology, 1992. Lic. marriage, family and child counselor. Reporter USA Today, Washington, 1982-83; lectr. San Diego State U., 1983-84; talk show host KSDO-AM, San Diego, 1983-84; pres. Dialogues, San Francisco, 1987—; psychotherapist pvt. practice, San Francisco, 1992—; vis. prof. U. Fla., Gainesville, 1980-81, U. Hawaii, Honolulu, 1981-82; adj. faculty U. San Francisco, 1989—; nat. adv. com. Freedom Forum Media Studies Ctr. Columbia U. Host, producer radio talk show Saturday Night People, 1984; contbg. author: Confessions of an S.O.B., 1989. Office: Dialogues PO Box 1022 Fairfax CA 94978-1022

NEUHAUS, KONSTANTIN, internist; b. Basel, Switzerland, July 10, 1940; s. F. M. Konstantin and Raissa (Erni) N.; m. Sylvia Meier, Jan. 13, 1967; children: Sibylle, Michael. MD, Medizinische Univ. Clinic, Basel, Switzerland, 1968. Head physician Medizinische Univ. Clinic, Basel, 1971-78; pvt. practice internal medicine Olten, Switzerland, 1978—. Co-editor (with F. Duckert) Blutgerinnung und Antikoagulation, 1976, (with F. Koller) Internistische Notfallsituationen, 5th edit., 1992. Maj. Swiss Army Med. Corps. Mem. Internat. Soc. of Nephrology, Gesellschaft für Nephrologie. Christkatholic. Home: Terrassenweg 33, CH-4600 Olten Switzerland Office: Baslerstrasse 30, CH-4600 Olten Switzerland

NEUHAUSER, DUNCAN VON BRIESEN, health services educator; b. Phila., June 20, 1939; s. Edward Blaine Duncan and Gernda (von Briesen) N.; m. Elinor Toaz, Mar. 6, 1965; children: Steven, Ann. B.A., Harvard U., 1961; M.H.A., U. Mich., 1963; M.B.A., U. Chgo., 1966, Ph.D., 1971. Research assoc. U. Chgo., 1965-70; asst. prof. Sch. Pub. Health, Harvard U., Boston, 1970-74; assoc. prof. Sch. Pub. Health, Harvard U., 1974-79; cons. in medicine Mass. Gen. Hosp., Boston, 1975-80; assoc. dir. Health Systems Mgmt. Ctr. Case Western Res. U., Cleve., 1979-85, prof. epidemiology, biostats. and orgnl. behavior, 1979—, prof. medicine, 1981—, prof. family medicine, 1990—, Charles Elton Blanchard prof. health mgmt., 1995—, co-dir. Health Systems Mgmt. Ctr., 1985—; cons. in medicine Cleve. Met. Gen. Hosp., 1981—; adj. mem. med. staff Cleve. Clinic Found., 1984—. Author numerous books, sci. papers; editor: jours. Health Matrix, 1982-90, Med. Care, 1983—. Vice chmn. bd. dirs. Vis. Nurse Assn. Greater Cleve., 1983-84, chmn., 1984-85; bd. dirs. New Eng. Grenfell Assn., Boston, 1972—, Braintree (Mass.) Hosp., 1975-86; trustee Internat. Grenfell Assn., St. Anthony, Nfld., Can., 1975-83, Blue Hill (Maine) Hosp., 1983-89; trustee Hough Norwood Health Ctr., 1983-94, chmn., 1993-94. Recipient E.F. Meyers Trustee award Cleve. Hosp. Assn., 1987, Hope award Nat. Multiple Sclerosis Soc., 1992; Kellogg fellow, 1963-65; Keck Found. scholar, 1982—; Neuhauser lectr. Soc. Pediatric Radiology, 1982; Freedlander lectr. Ohio Permanente Med. Group, 1986. Mem. Inst. Medicine of NAS, Soc. for Clin. Decision Making, Cleve. Skating Club, St. Botolph Club (Boston), Kollegewidgwok Yacht Club (Blue Hill, Maine, commodore 1991-93), Beta Gamma Sigma. Home: 2655 N Park Blvd Cleveland Heights OH 44106-3622 Office: Case Western Reserve U Med Sch 10900 Euclid Ave Cleveland OH 44106-4945

NEUHOFF, KATHLEEN TOEPP, veterinarian, podiatrist; b. South Bend, Ind., Nov. 2, 1953; d. Frank Conrad and Rosemary (Williams) Toepp; m. Kenneth Leo Neuhoff, June 27, 1953; children: Carolyn, Patricia, Michael, Matthew. BS in Agr., Purdue U., 1976, DVM, 1979; D of Podiatric Medicine, Scholl Coll., 1993. Diplomate Am. Bd. Veterinary Practitioners, Am. Bd. Podiatric Surgery. Assoc. Magrane Animal Hosp., Mishawaka, Ind., 1979-83; dir. Magrane Animal Hosp., South Bend, Ind., 1983—; surg. residency Mich. Community Hosp., 1993-94; owner Family Foot Care Clinic, South Bend, 1994—; pres., bd. dirs. Animal Emergency Clinic, South Bend, 1988-92, St. Michael's Eme. Sch., 1989-91; cons. on animal control South Bend City Coun., 1987; mem. pres.'s coun. Purdue U., 1989—. Contbr. articles to profl. jours and book revs. to popular mags. Bd. dirs. St. Michael's Elem. Sch., Plymouth, Ind., 1989-92; bd. dirs. Holy Cross Sch., 1993—. Recipient Humanitarin Svc. award Humane Soc. St. Joseph County, 1985, Woman Veterinarian of Yr. award, also Pub. Rels. award Ind. Vet. Med. Assn., 1991. Mem. AVMA (mem. alternative and complementary therapy com. 1996—), Am. Animal Hosp. Assn. (area dir. 1988-90, regional coord. 1990-93, regional bd. dirs. 1994—, chmn. student com. 1990-91), Am. Assn. Avian Vets., Ind. Vet Med. Assn. (pub. rels., ethics and animal welfare coms. 1984—), Michiana Vet. Med. Assn. (sec. 1986-87, treas. 1987-88, v.p. 1988-90, pres. 1990-91), Am. Horse Show Assn., Lake Michigan Hunter-Jumper Assn., Mishawaka C. of C. (Svc. award 1990), Am. Podiatric Med. Assn., Am. Bd. of Foot and Ankle Surgery, Stickle Soc., Scholl. Coll. of Podiatric Medicine. Republican. Roman Catholic. Office: Magrane Animal Hosp 2324 Grape Rd Mishawaka IN 46545-3006 also: Family Foot Care Clinic 727 E Jefferson Blvd South Bend IN 46617-2902

NEUMAN, FREDRIC JAY, psychiatrist; b. N.Y.C., Aug. 1, 1934; s. Henry and Eva (Rabinowitz) N.; m. Susan Kley, Aug. 10, 1958; children: Eve, James, Michael. AB, Princeton U., 1955; MD, NYU, 1959. Cert. Am. Bd. Psychiatry and Neurology; lic. medicine, N.Y. Rotating intern St. Vincent's Hosp., N.Y.C., 1959-60; resident psychiatry Albert Einstein Coll. Medicine, N.Y.C., 1960-62, 64-65; asst. chief neuro-psychiatry 20 Stat Hosp., Nurnberg, Fed. Republic of Germany, 1962-64; post-doctoral fellow, child fellow, research fellow Albert Einstein Coll. Medicine, 1964-66; ward psychiatrist Soundview Community Ctr. project Bronx State Hosp., N.Y., 1968-69; chief admitting Grasslands Hosp., 1969-71, dir. in charge research and tng., 1971-74; dir. liaison svcs. Westchester County Med. Ctr., 1974-77; assoc. dir. phobia clinic White Plains Hosp., White Plains, N.Y., 1978-93; dir. anxiety and phobia clinic White Plains Hosp., 1993—; cons. psychiatrist St. Patrick's Home for the Aged, Bronx, N.Y., 1967-71; instr. psychiatry N.Y. Med. Coll., 1971-73; asst. prof. psychiatry, 1973-78; mem. statutory profl. adv. com. Pub. Health Nurses, Westchester County, 1971-79; dir. psychiatry Westchester Community Health Plan, 1977-78. Author: The Seclusion Room, 1978, Caring: Home Treatment for the Emotionally Disturbed, 1980, Maneuvers, 1983, Fighting Fear: An 8 Week Guide to Treating

Your Own Phobias, 1985. Capt. U.S. Army, 1962-64. NIMH student fellow, 1957-58. Mem. Am. Psychiat. Assn., AAAS, N.Y. Acad. Sci. Democrat. Jewish. Office: 170 Maple Ave White Plains NY 10601-4710

NEUMAN, RICHARD STEPHEN, pharmacology educator; b. San Francisco, June 12, 1945; arrived in Can., 1968; s. Voy Louis and Dorothy Elizabeth (Dobler) N.; m. Judith Anne Costello, Feb. 26, 1969; children: Keir Cajal, Adah Liana. AA, City Coll. San Francisco, 1965; BA, San Francisco State Coll., 1968; PhD, U. Alta., Edmonton, 1973. Asst. prof. pharmacology Meml. U. Nfld., St. John's, 1974-79, assoc. prof. pharmacology, 1979-88, dir. computing svcs. faculty of medicine, 1981-91, prof. pharmacology, 1988—, assoc. dean basic med. scis., 1991—; vis. scientist Institut Nat. de la Sante et de la Recherche Medicale, Paris, France, 1986-87. Fellow Institut Nat. de la Sante et de la Recherche Medicale, 1987, Med. Rsch. Coun. fellow, 1973-74, traveling scientist award, 1986-87. Mem. Can. Assn. Neurosci., Soc. Neurosci., Pharmacological Soc. Can., N.Y. Acad. Scis., Assn. Med. Sch. Pharmacology, Serotonin Club. Office: Meml U Faculty Medicine, Health Scis Ctr, Saint John's, NF Canada A1B 3V6

NEUMAN, TOM S., emergency medical physician, educator; b. N.Y.C., July 23, 1946; s. Otto and Susan Ann (Baltaxe) N.; m. Doris Rubin, Aug. 24, 1969; children: Allison Rachel, Russell Solomon. AB, Cornell U., 1967; MD, NYU, 1971. Diplomate Nat. Bd. Med. Examiners, Am. Bd. Internal Medicine, Am. Bd. Preventative Medicine, Am. Bd. Emergency Medicine. Intern Bellevue Hosp., N.Y.C., 1971-72, resident, 1972-73; commd. med. officer USN, 1973; advanced through grades to capt. USNR, 1990; instr. Naval Undersea Med. Inst., New London, Conn., 1973-74; staff med. officer Submarine Devel. Group One, San Diego, 1974-76, 78-80; emergency room physician Chula Vista (Calif.) Community Hosp., 1975-80; attending physician VA Med. Ctr., La Jolla, Calif., 1976-78; fellow in pulmonary medicine and physiology U. Calif. Sch. Medicine at San Diego, 1976-78, clin. instr., 1978-80, asst. clin. prof., 1980-84, flight physician Life Flight Aeromed. Program, 1980-86, asst. dir. dept. emergency medicine, 1980-94; assoc. dir. dept. emergency medicine, 1994—; attending physician pulmonary divsn. U. Calif. Sch. Medicine at San Diego, 1980—, assoc. clin. prof. medicine and surgery, 1984-87, base hosp. physician, 1984—, dir. Hyperbaric Med. Ctr., 1984—; med. officer UDT/SEAL Res. Unit 119, San Diego, 1980-84, Mobile Diving and Salvage Unit One, USNR, San Diego, 1984-86, PRIMUS Unit 1942-A, U. Calif. at San Diego, 1988-90; sr. med. officer Seal Teams 1/3/5, USNR, Coronado, Calif., 1986-87; asst. officer in charge Med. Unit 1942-A U. Calif. Sch. Medicine, San Diego, 1990-95, prof. clin. medicine, 1996—; mem. med. adv. bd. western regional underwater lab. program U. So. Calif. Marine Sci. Ctr., Catalina, 1982-85; assoc. adj. prof. medicine and surgery U. Calif. Sch. Medicine at San Diego, 1987-96, adj. prof. surgery, 1987—; mem. San Diego Coroner's com. for investigation of diving fatalities, 1974—; mem. diving cons. Vocat. Diver Tng. Facility, Calif. Inst. Med., Chino, Calif., 1967; mem. task force City Mgr. on Carbon Monoxide Poisoning, San Diego, 1991; active Am. Nat. Stds. Inst. com. for minimal course content for recreational scuba instr. cert., 1992-94; chmn. emergency med. physician quality improvement com., 1992-94; spkr. in field. Author book chpts.; contbr. articles to profl. jours. Fellow ACP, Am. Coll. Preventive Medicine; mem. Am. Thoracic Soc., Am. Lung Assn., Undersea and Huperbaric Med. Soc. (program com. 1981-82, nominations com. 1982-83, chmn. 1988-89, mem. edn. com. 1982-87, chmn. awards com. 1983-84, v.p. exec. com. 1983-84, co-chmn. credentials com. 1984-85, editor-in-chief Undersea and Hyperbaric Medicine 1995—), Profl. Assn. Diving Instrs. (emeritus). Office: Dept Emergency Medicine UCSD Med Ctr 200 W Arbor Dr Bldg 8676 San Diego CA 92103-1911

NEUMANN, PETER R., physician; b. N.Y.C., Jan. 18, 1949; s. Norbert and Ingeborg (Blumenrath) N.; m. Marcy L. Schmittendorf, Sept. 4, 1977; children: Jeffrey, Rachael, Bradley, Jacob. BS, U. Wis., 1971; MD, SUNY, Buffalo, 1975. Diplomate Am. Bd. Surgery, Am. Bd. Plastic Surgery. Resident in surgery Buffalo Gen. Hosp., 1975-79; resident in oncologic surgery Roswell Park Meml. Hosp., 1978-79; resident in plastic surgery Nassau County Med. Ctr., East Meadow, N.Y., 1979-81; clin. asst. instr. in surgery SUNY/Buffalo Sch. of Medicine, 1975-79; clin. instr. in surgery Cornell Med. Ctr., '1984—; chief, Divsn. Plastic Surgery Franklin Hosp. Med. Ctr., N.Y., 1990—; presenter in field. Contbr. articles to profl. jours. Fellow ACS; mem. AMA, Am. Soc. Plastic and Reconstructive Surgeons, Nat. Assn. Interns and Residents, Nassau County Med. Soc., Nassau Acad. Medicine, N.Y. Regional Plastic Surg. Soc., Nassau Surg. Soc. (pres. 1996—), Am. Cancer Soc. (bd. dirs. L.I. chpt.). Home: 4 Woodland Dr Woodbury NY Office: Nassau Plastic Surg Assocs 935 Northern Blvd Great Neck NY 11021

NEUMEISTER, BIRGID VANADIS, medical microbiologist, researcher; b. Leipzig, Saxonia, Germany, July 31, 1956; d. Heinz Richard and Charlotte Elisabeth (Garich) N. MD, U. Leipzig, 1982. Resident dept. immunology U. Leipzig, 1982-86; resident Med. Clinic, Leipzig, 1986-88; resident dept. transfusion medicine U. Heidelberg-Mannheim, Germany, 1988-90; resident dept. med. microbiology U. Ulm, Germany, 1990-94; asst. med. dir. dept. transfusion medicine U. Tübingen, Germany, 1994—. Author: Mikrobiologie in Frage und Antwort-Lehrbuch zur Vorbereitung auf die Mündliche, 1994; contbr. articles to profl. jours. Recipient Pomblitz prize U. Leipzig, 1987; rsch. grantee Karl-Thomae GmbH, 1995. Mem. German Soc. Med. Microbiology, Union German Med. Microbiologists. Lutheran. Office: U Tubingen Dept Transfusion Medicine, Hoppe-Seyter Str 3, 72076 Tübingen Germany

NEURATH, HANS, biochemist, educator; b. Vienna, Austria, Oct. 29, 1909; came to U.S., 1935; s. Rudolf and Hedda (Samek) N.; m. Hilde Bial, June, 1935 (div. 1960); 1 child, Peter Francis; m. Susi Ruth Spitzer, Oct. 11, 1960. PhD, U. Vienna, Austria, 1933; DSc (hon.), U. Geneva, Switzerland, 1970, U. Tokushima, Japan, 1977, Med. Coll. Ohio, 1989, U. Montpellier, France, 1989, Kyoto U., Japan, 1990. George Fisher Baker fellow Cornell U., Ithaca, N.Y., 1936-38; prof. biochemistry Duke U., Durham, N.C., 1938-50; prof. biochemistry U. Wash., Seattle, 1950—, chmn. dept. biochemistry, 1950-75, prof. emeritus biochemistry, 1980—; sci. dir. Fred Hutchinson Cancer Rsch. Inst., Seattle, 1976-80; dir. German Cancer Research Ctr., Heidelberg, Fed. Republic Germany, 1980-81; hon. prof. U. Heidelberg, 1980—; fgn. sci. mem. Max Planck Inst. for Exptl. Medicine, Goettingen, Fed. Republic Germany, 1982—; cons. Battelle Meml. Inst., Columbus, 1970-75. Editor: (compendium) The Proteins (3 edits.), 1953-79; editor Biochemistry Jour., 1962-91, Protein Sci., 1991—; contbr. numerous articles to sci. publs. Advisor NIH, Bethesda, Md., 1954-70; mem. med. adv. bd. Howard Hughes Med. Inst., Miami, Fla., 1969-79, Virginia Mason Rsch. Ctr., Seattle, 1982—. Guggenheim fellow, 1955; named hon. mem. Japanese Biochem. Soc., 1977; recipient Disting. Alumnus award Duke U. Med. Sch., 1970, Stein and Moore award Protein Soc., 1989. Fellow AAAS; mem. NAS (nat. bd. grad. edn. 1971-75); sr. mem. Inst. of Medicine . Home: 5752 60th Ave NE Seattle WA 98105-2036 Office: U Wash Dept Biochemistry Seattle WA 98195

NEUROHR, FERDINAND GUSTAV, III, dentist; b. Queens Village, N.Y., Nov. 26, 1952; s. Ferdinand Gustav and Barbara Conant (Blomquist) N.; m. Laura Christine Gottcent, Aug. 21, 1977; children: Peter F., Kristin G. BA, Colgate U., 1974; DMD, Fairleigh Dickinson U., 1979. Asst. attending St. Luke's/Roosevelt Hosp., N.Y.C., 1979-80; pvt. practice N.Y.C., 1979—; clin. instr. Fairleigh Dickinson U., Hackensack, N.J., 1982-86; asst. clin. prof. NYU, 1991, 95—. Bd. edn. Our Redeemer Lutheran Ch., Seaford, N.Y., 1992-95; coun. Epiphany Lutheran Ch., Hempstead, N.Y., 1984-87, chmn. stewardship com., 1986-88. Fellow N.Y. Acad. Dentistry; mem. Am. Dental Assn., Am. Prosthodontic Soc., Am. Coll. Prosthodontists, Am. Acad. Restorative Dentisty. Lutheran. Office: 509 Madison Ave Ste 1704 New York NY 10022

NEUSE, EBERHARD WILHELM, macromolecular chemistry educator, researcher; b. Berlin, Mar. 7, 1925; arrived in Republic of South Africa, 1971; s. Eberhard O. and Felizitas H. (Winde) N.; m. Hildegard Berger, Oct. 25, 1963; children: Christian W., Kenneth D. BSc, Tech. Univ., Hannover, Germany, 1948, MSc magna cum laude, 1951, PhD magna cum laude, 1953; DSc, U. Witwatersrand, Johannesburg, South Africa, 1976. Devel. chemist Neynaber & Co AG, Bremerhaven, Germany, 1954-57; rsch. assoc. Princeton (N.J.) Univ., 1957-59; sr. R&D specialist, prin. investigator, sect. chief McDonnell Douglas Astronautics Co., Santa Monica, Calif., 1960-70; sr. lectr. then reader, prof. macromolecular chemistry U. Witwatersrand, Johannesburg, 1971—; cons. Chemi industry and legal profession, Johannesburg, 1975—. Author: Nordlicht uber der Finmark, 1955, Metallocene Polymers, 1970; author 10 book and ency. chpts., 1966-96; inventor in field; contbr. articles to profl. jours. Mem. N.Y. Acad. Sci., Am. Chem. Soc. (chair program com., polymer divsn. South Calif. sect. 1967-69), Controlled Release Soc., South African Chem. Inst. Office: Dept Chemistry, U Witwatersrand, Wits 2050, South Africa

NEUSPIEL, DANIEL ROBERT, pediatrician, epidemiologist; b. Haifa, Israel, May 15, 1952; came to U.S., 1953; s. William and Miriam (Schwerstein) N.; m. Cathy Canepa, Apr. 12, 1987; children: Juliana, Samuel. BA, Rutgers U., 1975; MD, N.J. Med. Sch., 1979; MPH, U. Pitts., 1984. Diplomate Nat. Bd. Med. Examiners, Am. Bd. Pediatrics, Am. Bd. Preventive Medicine; cert. Am. Soc. Addiction Medicine. Resident in pediatrics Children's Hosp., Pitts., 1979-82; fellow in epidemiology U. Pitts., 1982-84; asst. prof. Albert Einstein Coll. of Medicine, Bronx, 1984-90, assoc. prof., 1990—; med. dir. U. Avenue Family Practice, 1995—; founding dir. early family outreach program North Cen. Bronx Hosp. Contbr. articles to Jour. AMA, Am. Jour. Pub. Health, Neurotoxicol. Teratol, Devel. Behavior Pediatrics. Office: Univ Ave Family Practice 105 W 188th St Bronx NY 10458

NEUSTADT, JEFFREY B., orthopaedic surgeon; b. Louisville, May 4, 1956; s. David H. and Carolyn (Jacobson) N.; m. Susan A. Harris, Apr. 1, 1989; children: Gabriel Sam, Sydney Leah Ruth. BA, Amherst Coll., 1978; MD, Emory U., 1983. Diplomate Am. Bd. Orthopedic Surgery. Instr. dept. orthopedic surgery Georgetown U., Washington, 1990-91; clin. asst. prof. U. So. Fla., Tampa, 1991—; chief div. orthopedic surgery All Children's Hosp., St. Petersburg, Fla., 1991—; cons. Children's Med. Svcs., St. Petersburg, 1991—. Fellow Am. Acad. Orthopedic Surgery, Scoliosis Rsch. Soc.; mem. Pediat. Orthopedic Soc. N.Am., Fla. Orthopaedic Soc., Fla. Med. Assn., Pinellas County Med. Soc. Office: Childrens Ortho/Scoliosis 880 6th St S Ste 310 Saint Petersburg FL 33701 also: 2727 W MLK Jr Blvd Ste 720 Tampa FL 33607

NEUSTROM, MARK R., allergist, immunologist; b. Cedar Rapids, Iowa, Mar. 21, 1957; m. Mary B., Mar. 10, 1994. BS in Zoology, Iowa State U., 1979; DO, U. Osteo. Medicine & Health, 1987. Diplomate Am. Bd. Immunology, Am. Bd. Allergy and Immunology. Resident U. S.D., Sioux Falls, 1987-90; allergist, immunologist Kansas City Allergy & Asthma Assocs., 1994—. Allergy & Immunology fellow Med. Coll. Wis., Milw., 1992-94. Mem. Asthma & Allergy Found. Am. (bd. dirs. Kansas City chpt. 1995-96), Am. Acad. Allergy, Asthma & Immunology, Am. Coll. Asthma, Allergy & Immunology (latex com. 1995-96), Greater Kansas City Allergy Soc., Joint Coun. Allergy & Immunology. Office: Kansas City Allergy & Asthma Assocs 4500 College Blvd Ste 200 Kansas City KS 66211

NEUTZLING, VIRGINIA RUTH, healthcare company executive; b. Canton, Ohio, Dec. 10, 1942; d. James F. and Ruth E. (Swank) Roush; m. Homer S. Neutzling, Sept. 26, 1964 (dec. July 1976); children: Melanie L., Kimberly L., H. Lee. Grad., Mercy Profl. Sch. Nursing, 1963; BS, Walsh Coll., 1982; MEd, Kent State U., 1985. RN, Ohio. From staff nurse to head nurse Timken Mercy Med. Ctr., Canton, Ohio, 1963-77; staff nurse UpJohn Healthcare Svcs., Canton, 1979-83; health educator Stark County Health Dept., Canton, 1983-87; exec. dir. Stark County Health Care Coalition, Inc., Canton, 1987-94; pres., owner Health & Wellness Concepts, Inc., Canton, Ohio, 1994; trustee Drs. Hosp. Inc. of Stark County. Mem. adv. com. YMCA Big Bros.-Big Sisters Greater Canton, 1986—, Rotary, 1989—; chmn. Health Care for Uninsured, Canton, 1988—; chair steering com. Hall of Fame Regional Sr. Olympics, 1994—. Mem. Nat. Wellness Assn., Nat. Assn. for Female Execs., Ohio Pub. Health Assn., Northeastern Ohio Wellness Com. (chair 1987—). Avocations: family, reading, needlework, gardening, travel, music. Home and Office: 2223 45th St NE Canton OH 44705-2922

NEUWIRTH, ROBERT SAMUEL, obstetrician, gynecologist; b. N.Y.C., July 11, 1933; s. Abraham Alexander and Phyllis Neuwirth; children from previous marriage: Susan, Jessica, Laura, Michael, Alexander. BS, Yale U., 1954, MD, 1958. Intern Presbyn. Hosp., N.Y.C., 1958-59, resident, 1959-64; asst. prof. ob-gyn. Columbia U., 1964-68, assoc. prof., 1968-71, prof., 1972—, Babcock prof., 1977—; dir. ob-gyn. Bronx Lebanon Hosp., N.Y.C., 1967-72, Woman's Hosp., N.Y.C., St. Luke's Hosp. Ctr., 1974—; prof. Albert Einstein Coll. Medicine, 1971-72; cons. WHO, NIH, AID, FDA. Author: Hysteroscopy, 1975; contbr. articles to profl. jours. Mem. Am. Coll. Obstetricians and Gynecologists, Soc. Gynecologic Investigation, N.Y. Obstet. Soc., Am. Assn. Profs. Ob-Gyn., Assn. Vol. Sterilization (chmn. biomed. com. 1971—). Office: 425 W 59th St Fl 5 New York NY 10025-8107

NEVANS-PALMER, LAUREL SUZANNE, rehabilitation counselor; b. N.Y.C., Aug. 1, 1964; d. Roy N. and Virginia (Place) Nevans; m. Russell Baird Palmer III, Oct. 12, 1991. BA in English, Secondary Edn. cum laude, U. Richmond, 1986, postgrad., 1989-92; MA in Edn. and Human Devel., George Washington U., 1991, cert. in job devel. and placement, 1992. Group leader S.E. Consortium for Spl. Svcs., Larchmont, N.Y., 1980-85; vocat. instr. Assn. for Retarded Citizens Montgomery County, Rockville, Md., 1986-89; edn. specialist George Washington U. Out of Sch. Work Experience Program, Washington, 1989-90; rsch. asst. George Washington U. Dept. Tchr. Prep. & Spl. Edn., Washington, 1989-91; employability skills tchr., rsch. intern Nat. Rehab. Hosp. Rehab. Engring. Dept., Washington, 1991; vocat./ind. living skills specialist The Independence Ctr., Rockville, Md., 1991-93; leadership team mgr. Career Choice project The Endependence Ctr. of No. Va., Arlington, 1993-94; program dir. United Cerebral Palsy of D.C. and No. Va., Washington, 1994—; teaching asst. Rehab. Counseling Program, George Washington U., 1991. Recipient traineeship GWU Counseling Dept., 1990, 91. Mem. Nat. Rehab. Assn., Nat. Rehab. Counselors Assn., D.C. Met. Area Assn. Person's in Supported Employment (editor newsletter 1995—), Nat. Career Devel. Assn., Nat. Employment Counseling Assn., Nat. Assn. Ind. Living, Am. Assn. Counseling and Devel., Am. Rehab. Counseling Assn. Democrat. Home: 611 Woodside Pky Silver Spring MD 20910 Office: United Cerebral Palsy 3135 8th St NE Washington DC 20017

NEVIASER, ROBERT JON, orthopedic surgeon, educator; b. Washington, Nov. 21, 1936; s. Julius Salem and Jane Frances (Gibbons) N.; m. Anne Maclean Shedden, Dec. 3, 1966; children: Jeanne Nicole, Robert Jon Jr., Ian Maclean, Andrew Shedden. Grad., Phillips Acad., Andover, Mass., 1954; AB, Princeton U., 1958; MD, Jefferson Med. Coll., 1962. Diplomate Am. Bd. Orthop. Surgery with cert. of added qualification in surgery of hand. Intern N.Y. Hosp., Cornell Med. Ctr., N.Y.C., 1962-63, asst. resident, 1963-64; asst. resident in orthopaedic surgery N.Y. Orthop. Hosp., Columbia-Presbyn. Med. Ctr., N.Y.C., 1964-66, jr. Annie C. Kane fellow, 1966-67; fellow in surgery of the hand Orthop. Hosp., L.A., 1969-70; asst. prof. divsn. orthop. and hand surgery, chmn. dept. U. Conn., Hartford, 1970-71; assoc. prof. orthop. surgery George Washington U., Washington, 1971-76, prof., 1976—, dir. orthop. edn., assoc. chmn. dept. orthop. surgery, 1984-87, chmn. dept. orthop. surgery, 1987—; chmn. governing bd. Med. Faculty Assocs. George Washington U. Med. Ctr., 1995—. Contbr. articles in field to profl. jours. Lt. comdr. USNR, 1967-69. Fellow Am. Soc. Surgery of the Hand, Am. Acad. Orthop. Surgeons, Ea. Orthop. Assn., Am. Shoulder and Elbow Surgeons, Am. Orthop. Assn.; mem. Alpha Kappa Kappa. Republican. Clubs: Princeton (N.Y. and Washington); Darnestown Swim and Racquet, Cosmos. Office: 2150 Pennsylvania Ave NW Washington DC 20037-2396

NEVILLE, ALEXANDER MUNRO, pathologist; b. Glasgow, Scotland, Mar. 24, 1935; s. Alexander Munro and Georgina Neville; m. Anne Margaret Stroyan Black, Sept. 5, 1961; children: Judeth Anne, Alexander Munro. M.B. Ch.B, U. Glasgow, 1959, PhD, 1965, MD, 1969, DSc, 1985. Sr. lectr. pathology U. Glasgow, 1967-70; hon. cons. in pathology Royal Marsden Hosp., London, 1970-85; prof. pathology U. London, 1972-85; dir. Ludwig Inst. Cancer Rsch., London, 1975-85; assoc. dir., sci. sec. Ludwig Inst. Cancer Rsch., N.Y., London and Zurich, 1985—; prof. pathology Royal Postgrad. Med. Sch., London, 1992—. Author: the Human Adrenal Cortex, 1982; editor: Biopsy Pathology, 1975 (award); editor jour. Tumor Biology, 1978 (award). Fellow Royal Coll. Pathologists (hon. treas. 1993—); mem. Athenaeum Club. Home: 6 Woodlands Park, Tadworth Surrey KT20 7JL, England Office: Ludwig Inst Cancer Rsch, Glen House Stag Pl Sixth Fl, London SW1E 5AG, England also: 1345 Avenue Of The Americas New York NY 10105

NEVINS, JOSEPH R., medical educator; b. June 21, 1947. BS, U. Okla., 1970, MS, 1972; PhD, Duke U., 1976. Asst. prof. molecular cell biology Rockefeller U., 1979-82, assoc. prof., 1982-87, investigator Howard Hughes Med. Inst., 1986-87; prof. microbiology Duke U. Med. Ctr., 1987—, investigator Howard Hughes Med. Inst., 1987—, prof. genetics and head, sect. genetics, 1990-94, chmn. dept. genetics, 1994—; lectr. in field. Dept. Microbiology and Immunology fellow Duke U. Med. Ctr., 1972-76, Postdoctoral fellow Rockefeller U., 1976-79; guest scholar Inst. Virus Rsch., Kyoto U., 1986. Mem. Am. Soc. Microbiology, Am. Soc. Virology, Am. Assn. Cancer Rsch. Office: Howard Hughes Med Inst Duke U Med Ctr Dept Genetics Durham NC 27710*

NEVINS, THOMAS ERNEST, pediatrician, educator; b. Rockford, Ill., Apr. 28, 1943; s. Joseph Gerald and Mary Anne Nevins; m. Joyce Elaine Christiansen, Nov. 4, 1967; children: Gerald, Mary, Teresa, Kathleen, Andrea, Sarah, Margaret. BA, Rockhurst Coll., 1965; MD, Washington U., 1969. Diplomate Am. Bd. Pediatrics-Pediat. Nephrology. Fellow pediat. nephrology U. Minn., Mpls., instr., 1978-79, asst. prof., 1979-85, assoc. prof., 1985-93, prof., 1993—. Lt. comdr. USN Med. Corp, 1972-74. Mem. Am. Bd. Pediat. (assoc.). Office: U Minn Hosp 420 Delaware SE Box 491 Minneapolis MN 55455

NEW, PAMELA ZYMAN, neurologist; b. Chgo., Jan. 24, 1953; d. Hillard Anthony and Virginia Lillian (Drechsler) Zyman; m. Joseph Keith New, Sept. 12, 1982; children: Matthew, Anneliese, Theresa. BS in Medicine, Northwestern U., 1973, MD, 1976. Resident in internal medicine Baylor Affiliated Hosps., Houston, 1977-80, resident in neurology, 1983-85; mem. staff dept. medicine VA Hosp., Houston, 1980-81; resident in gen. surgery N.Y. Hosp., Cornell Med. Ctr., N.Y.C., 1981, resident in neurosurgery, 1981-83; fellow neuro-oncology M.D. Anderson Hosp. and Tumor Inst., Houston, 1985-87; asst. prof. divsn. neurology dept. medicine U. Tex. Health Sci. Ctr., San Antonio, 1987—; staff physician Audie L. Murphy Meml. VA Hosp., San Antonio, 1987—; lectr., researcher in field. Contbr. articles to profl. publs., chpts. to books. Mem. ACP, S.W. Oncology Group, Assn. VA Investigators and Rsch. Adminstrs., Am. Acad. Neurology, Am. Parkinson's Disease Assn. (co-dir. Parkinson's Disease Info. Referral Ctr.), Movement Disorders Soc., Soc. of Neuro-Oncology. Roman Catholic. Office: U Tex Health Sci Ctr 7703 Floyd Curl Dr San Antonio TX 78284-6200

NEWBERGER, CAROLYN MOORE, clinical and developmental psychologist; b. Milw., Mar. 11, 1941; d. Joseph E. and Mary (Tavss) Moore; m. Eli H. Newberger, May 31, 1962; 1 child, Mary Helen. BA, Sarah Lawrence Coll., 1963; EdM, Harvard U., 1972, EdD, 1977. Lic. clin. psychologist, Mass. Staff psychologist Judge Baker Children's Ctr., Boston, 1977-83; sr. psychologist Children's Hosp./Judge Baker Children's Ctr., Boston, 1983—; dir. victim recovery study Children's Hosp., Boston, 1985-92, rsch. dir. clin. rsch. tng. program on family violence, 1993—; asst. prof. Harvard Med. Sch., Boston, 1990—; Bunting fellow Radcliffe Coll., 1991; cons. and lectr. in field. Contbr. articles to profl. jours., chpts. to books. Bd. dirs. Parents Anonymous of Mass. Recipient Humanitarian award Mass. Psychol. Assn., 1988. Fellow Am. Orthopsychiat. Assn.; mem. Soc. for Rsch. in Child Devel., Am. Psychol. Assn. Office: Children's Hosp Family Devel 300 Longwood Ave Boston MA 02115-5724

NEWBERGER, ELI, pediatrician; b. N.Y.C., Dec. 26, 1940; m. Carolyn Moore, May 31, 1962; 1 child, Mary Helen. BA, Yale Coll., 1962, MD, 1966; MS, Harvard U., 1972. Intern Yale-New Haven Hosp, 1966-67; resident Children's Hosp., Boston, 1969-72, dir. family devel. program, 1972—. Pres. Mass. Community Children and Youth, Boston, 1977—. Recipient Hmanitarian award Mass. Psychol. Assn., 1988. Fellow Am. Acad. Pediatricians; mem. Am. Orthopsychiatric Assn. (pres. 1990-92). Office: Children s Hosp 300 Longwood Ave Boston MA 02115-5724

NEWBRUN, ERNEST, oral biology and periodontology educator; b. Vienna, Austria, Dec. 1, 1932; came to U.S., 1955; s. Victor and Elizabeth (Reichl) N; m. Eva Miriam, June 17, 1956; children: Deborah Anne, Daniel Eric, Karen Ruth. BDS, U. Sydney (New South Wales), 1954; MS, U. Rochester, 1957; DMD, U. Ala., 1959; PhD, U. Calif., San Francisco, 1965; Odont. Dr. (hon.), U. Lund, Sweden, 1988. Cert. periodontology, 1983. Rsch. assoc. Eastern Dental Ctr., Rochester, N.Y., 1955-57, U. Ala. Med. Ctr., Birmingham, 1957-59; rsch. fellow Inst. Dental Rsch., Sydney, Australia, 1960-61; rsch. tchr. trainee U. Calif., San Francisco, 1961-63, postdoctoral fellow, 1963-65, assoc. prof., prof., 1965-70, prof. oral biology, 1970-83, prof. oral biology and periodontology, 1983-94, prof. emeritus, 1994—; cons. FDA, 1983—. Author: Cariology, 1989, Pharmacology and Therapeutic Dentistry, 1989, (with others) Pediatrics, 1991; editor: Fluorides and Dental Caries, 1986; mem. editorial bd. Jour. Periodontal Rsch., 1985-90, Jour. Peridontology, 1990—. Bd. dirs. Raoul Wallenberg Dem. Club, San Francisco, 1987-92. Mem. AAAS (chmn. dental section, 1988-89), Internat. Assn. Dental Rsch. (pres. 1989-90), Dental Health Foun. (chmn. bd. dirs., 1985-92). Jewish.

NEWBURGE, IDELLE BLOCK, psychotherapist; b. Bklyn.; m. Lawrence G. Newburge; children: Geri, Scott. AB magna cum laude, U. Miami, 1972, MEd, 1973. Lic. mental health counselor; nat. cert. counselor. Acting supr., lead counselor Office Vocat. Rehab., Miami, 1973-79, supr. mental health unit, 1985-87; vocat., edn. specialist Spectrum Programs, Inc., Miami, 1979-81, outpatient supr., 1981-85; psychotherapist Alan Jaffe, PhD and Assoc., Lauderhill, Fla., 1985-88, A.C.S. Pvt. Counseling, Plantation, Fla., 1988-91, KPK Counseling Svcs., Plantation, 1992—; community adv. bd. Fellowship House, Miami, 1985-87; chmn., com. mem. Parent Resource Ctr., Miami, 1979-82. Active Nat. Mus. for Women in the Arts (charter), Washington, 1991—, U.S. Holocaust Meml. Mus. (charter), Washington, 1991—, Greenpeace, Humane Soc., Nat. Wildlife Fedn., NOW, N.Am. Vegetarian Soc. Fellow Am. Bd. Cert. Managed Care Providers (cert. rehab. counselor, master addiction counselor, cert. criminal justice specialist); mem. NASW, ACA, Am. Mental Health Counselors Assn., Fla. Alcohol and Drug Abuse Assn., Fla. Mental Health Counselors Assn., , Mental Health Assn. Broward County (Listen to Children Programs cons. 1988—), Mental Health Assn. Broward County (profl. mem., bd. dirs., chair), Fla. Soc. Clin. Hypnosis, Lauderhill C. of C. (charter), Plantation C. of C., Women's Forum (charter). Office: KPK Counseling Services 8030 Peters Rd # D106 Plantation FL 33324-4038

NEWCOMBE, DAVID SUGDEN, physician; b. Boston, June 28, 1929; s. Walter White and Catherine Naomi (Sugden) N.; m. Sissel Margrethe Ostgard, June 26, 1965; children: Catherine, Kirsten, Sarah. BA, Amherst (Mass.) Coll., 1952; MD, McGill U., 1956. Diplomate Am. Bd. Rhematology; lic. physician, Mass. Intern Boston City Hosp., Boston, 1956-57, fellow, 1962-63; resident in medicine Duke U., Durham, N.C., 1959-60; fellow Boston U., Boston, 1960-61; fellow in biochemistry, asst. in medicine Harvard Med. Sch., Boston, 1963-65; mem. med. staff U. Va. Hosp., Charlottesville, 1965-67; assoc. prof. medicine, mem. attending staff, dir. rheumatology unit Med. Ctr. Hosp. Vt., Burlington, 1967-77; assoc. prof. environ. health scis., assoc. prof. medicine Johns Hopkins Med. Instns., Balt., 1977-82; dir. divsn. exptl. pathology and toxicology Johns Hopkins Med. Instns., 1983-87, prof. medicine, 1983-92; assoc. chief staff Bedford (Mass.) VA Hosp., 1993—, chief phys. medicine and rehab. svcs., 1993-95; cons. and speaker in field. Contbr. chpts. to books and articles to profl. jours. Capt. Med. Corps., 1957-79, Korea. Recipient NIH trainee; fellow New England Rheumatism Soc., NIH, Am. Cancer Soc; named Am. Men of Sci. Fellow Am. Coll. Clin. Pharmacology, Am. Rheumatism Soc. (founder); mem. Sigma Xi. Office: Bedford VA Hosp 200 Springs Rd Bedford MA 01730

NEWCOMER, DARRELL RAY, pharmacy executive; b. Quinter, Kans., Mar. 16, 1948; s. Raymond Dean and Alberta Louella (Riggs) N.; m. Shirley Ann Lefler, Aug. 2, 1969; children: Amy Rebecca, Mindy Noel. BS in Pharmacy, U. Kans., 1971; MS in Clin. Hosp. Pharmacy, Ohio State U., 1973. Resident pharmacy Grant Hosp., Columbus, Ohio, 1971-73; asst. dir. pharmacy Henry Ford Hosp., Detroit, 1973-82; dir. pharmacy The Meth. Hosp., Houston, 1982-92; pharmacy mgmt. cons. Tex. So. U., Houston,

1993; clin. pharmacy adminstr. Aetna Pharmacy Mgmt., Houston, 1993-94; divisional pharmacy dir. Integrated Pharmacy Solutions, Inc., Houston, 1994-95; dir. pharmacy ops. Integrated Pharmacy Solutions Inc., Houston, 1995—; adj. asst. prof. Coll. Pharmacy, Wayne State U., Detroit, 1978-82, U. Houston, 1983—. Contbr. articles to profl. jours. Bd. dirs. Christian Family Svcs., Southfield, Mich., 1980-82, New Life Farms Found., Southfield, 1980-82. Mem. Acad. Managed Care Pharmacy, Am. Soc. Health-Sys. Pharmacists, Tex. Soc. Health-Sys. Pharmacists, Houston-Galveston Area Soc. Hosp. Pharmacists (Outstanding Pharmacist award 1986, pres. 1989-90), Rho Chi. Republican. Office: Prudential Health Care Plan MS301 One Prudential Circle Sugar Land TX 77478

NEWCOMER, DAVID L., surgeon, consultant; b. Lancaster, Pa., Dec. 3, 1947; s. Warren L. and Ruth R. (Hackman) N.; m. Susan M. Barr, Dec. 27, 1969; children: Scott, Andrew, Betsy. BS, Juniata Coll., 1969; MD, Temple U., 1973. Diplomate Nat. Bd. Medical Examiners; cert. Am. Bd. Surgery. Gen. surgeon Mid Atlantic Surg. Svcs., Lancaster, Pa., 1977—; cons. Mid Atlantic Cons. Svcs., Lancaster, 1991—. Author: (manual) Medical Practice Marketing, 1993; author: (with others) Sciarra's Textbook of Gynecology and Obstetrics, 1977. Med. dir. Emergency Med. Svcs. Coun., Lancaster, 1981. Recipient Wilbur Oakes award Juniata Coll., Huntingdon, Pa., 1969. Mem. AMA, Soc. Laparoendoscopic Surgeons, Pa. Oncologic Soc., Pa. State Med. Soc., Lancaster City/County Med. Soc. Office: Mid Atlantic Surg Svcs Inc 217 Harrisburg Ave Ste 201 Lancaster PA 17603-2900

NEWELL, DONALD CLIFFORD, JR., physician; b. Oak Hill, W.Va., Feb. 5, 1947; s. Donald Clifford and Lucille Maude (Newman) N.; m. Darlene Loretta Knuchel, Aug. 8, 1970; children: Ryan, Lee. BS, Bethany Coll., 1969; DO, Kirksville Coll., 1973. Staff physician Fayette Clinic, Lochgelly, W.Va., 1975—, Oak Hill Hosp., 1975—, Raleigh Gen. Hosp., Beckley, W.Va., 1984—; health officer Fayette County Health Dept., Fayetteville, W.Va., 1984—; county med. examiner W.Va. Med. Examiners System, Oak Hill, 1982—; med. dir. Hilltop (W.Va.) Health Care Ctr., 1984—, Fayette Continuous Care Ctr., Fayetteville, 1988—; pilot examiner FAA, Oklahoma City, 1975—; adj. faculty W.Va. Sch. Osteo. Medicine, Lewisburg, 1982—; prof. respiratory therapy Beckley Coll., 1985—; bd. dirs. Valley Bank. Pres. Oak Hill High Sch. Bd. boosters, 1991, Region IV Emergency Med. Bd., 1978; pres. clinic bd. dirs. W.Va. Sch. Osteo. Medicine, mem. pres. adv. bd, 1985—. Recipinet Cert. Appreciation, Oak Hill High Sch. Mem. W.Va. Soc. Osteo. Medicine (pres. 1988-89, trustee 1984—), Am. Radio Relay League, Aircraft Owners & Pilots Assn., Exptl. Aircraft Assn. Episcopalian. Home: 1 Main St Lochgelly WV 25866

NEWELL, FRANK WILLIAM, ophthalmologist, educator; b. St. Paul, Jan. 14, 1916; s. Frank John and Hilda (Turnquist) N.; m. Marian Glennon, Sept. 12, 1942; children: Frank William, Mary Susan Newell O'Connell, Elizabeth Glennon Newell Murphy, David Andrew Newell. M.D., Loyola U., Chgo., 1939; M.Sc., U. Minn., 1942. Diplomate Am. Bd. Ophthalmology (chmn. bd. 1967-69). James and Anna Raymond prof. dept. ophthalmology U. Chgo., 1953—; prof. extraordinario Autonomous U. Barcelona, Spain, 1972—; hon. prof. Tech. U., Japan, 1986—; sci. counselor Nat. Inst. Neurol. Diseases and Blindness, 1959-62, chmn., 1961-62; mem. nat. adv. eye coun. NIH, 1972-75; mem. Internat. Council Ophthalmology, 1977-85; bd. dirs. Heed Ophthalmic Found., 1965-93, chmn., 1975-90; dir. Ophthalmic Pub. Co., 1962—, sec., treas., 1971-95. Author: Ophthalmology: Principles and Concepts, 1965, 8th edit., 1996, The American Ophthalmological Society 1864-89, 1989; also articles; editor in chief Am. Jour. Ophthalmology, 1965-91, pub., 1972-95; editor: Trans Glaucoma Conf., Vols. 1-5, 1955-61, Amblyopia and Strabismus, 1975, Hereditary Diseases of the Eye, 1980, Stedman's Medical Dictionary, 25th edit., 1990, Documenta Ophthalmologica Historia, 1996—. Trustee Loyola U., Chgo., 1977-81. Served from 1st lt. to maj. M.C. AUS, 1942-46. Recipient Alumni Citation award Loyola U., 1962, Stritch medal, 1966, Outstanding Achievement award U. Minn., 1975, 92, Gold Key U. Chgo., 1981, Lang medal Royal Soc. Medicine, London, 1974, medal honor Soc. Eye Surgeons, 1975, Vail medal Internat. Eye Found., 1986, medalla André Bello U. Chile, 1977, medalla de Oro Instituto Barraquer, Barcelona, Spain, 1982; Disting. Svc. award Physicians Edn. Network, 1983; decorated knight Order of St. John. Mem. Nat. Soc. Prevention Blindness (dir., v.p. 1970-81, pres. 1981-83, chmn. bd. 1983-85, Dunnington medal 1976), AMA (chmn. sect. ophthalmology 1964-65, Howe prize 1968), Am. Acad. Ophthalmology and Otolaryngology (pres. 1975), Inst. Barraguer (pres. 1970-88, hon. pres. 1988—), Assn. Univ. Profs. Ophthalmology (trustee 1966-69, pres. 1968-69), Assn. Research Ophthal. (chmn. bd. trustees 1967-68), Pan-Am. Assn. Ophthalmology (dir. 1969—, pres. 1981-83), Am. Ophthal. Soc. (pres. 1986-87, Howe medal 1979), Chgo. Ophthal. Soc. (pres. 1957-58), Oxford (Eng.) Ophthal. Congress (hon. mem., dep. master 1980), Hellenic Ophthal. Soc. (hon.), Royal Soc. Medicine (hon.), Academia Ophthalmologica Internationalis (pres. 1980-84), Columbia Ophthal. Soc. (hon.), Sigma Xi, Alpha Omega Alpha. Roman Catholic. Clubs: Literary (Chgo.), Quadrangle (Chgo.). Home: 4500 N Mozart St Chicago IL 60625-3817 Office: 939 W 57th St Chicago IL 60637

NEWELL, MARIE-LOUISE, epidemiologist, educator; b. s'-Hertogenbosch, The Netherlands, Mar. 21, 1955; arrived in Eng., 1980; d. Ferdinand and Jo (van Erp) Van den Eerenbeemt; m. Colin Newell, Apr. 14, 1984; children: Anna, Nicolas. Doctoral degree, Geneeskunde, Groningen, The Netherlands, 1980; MS, LSHTM, London, 1981, PhD, 1991. MFPHM. Rsch. fellow LSHTM, London, 1982-87; lectr., sr. lectr. Inst. Child Health, London, 1987—; participant expert meetings, WHO, CDC. Editor, author: HIV Infection in Children, 1995; contbr. articles to profl. jours. Office: Inst Child Health, 30 Guilford St, London WC1M 1EH, England

NEWFELD, EDGAR ALLEN, pediatric cardiologist; b. N.Y.C., May 22, 1934; s. Benjamin and Diane (Cohen) N.; m. Myra Kay Finder, Aug. 25, 1963; children: Amy, Ellen, David. BA, Rutgers U., 1958; MD, Northwestern U., 1962. Diplomate Am. Bd. Pediatrics. Asst. prof. pediatrics SUNY, Bklyn., 1967-68, Albert Einstein Coll. Medicine, Bronx, N.Y., 1968-71, Northwestern Univ. Medicine, Chgo., 1971-75; assoc. prof. pediatrics Northwestern Univ. Medicine, 1975-77; assoc. prof. Southwestern Med. Sch., Dallas, 1977-82; clin. assoc. prof. pediatrics Southwestern Med. Sch., 1982—; pvt. practice pediatric cardiology, Dallas, 1982—. Assoc. editor Jour. Perinatology, 1992—. Served in U.S. Army, 1954-56. Fellow Am. Acad. Pediatrics, Am. Coll. Cardiology; mem. Am. Acad. Pediatrics (cardiology sect.), Coun. on Pediatric Disease in the Young, Am. Heart Assn. Office: Pediatric Cardio Assocs 8230 Walnut Hill Ln Ste 800 Dallas TX 75231

NEWHOUSE, JOSEPH PAUL, economics educator; b. Waterloo, Iowa, Feb. 24, 1942; s. Joseph Alexander and Ruth Linnea (Johnson) N.; m. Margaret Louise Locke, June 22, 1968; children: Eric Joseph, David Locke. BA, Harvard U., 1963, PhD, 1969; postgrad (Fulbright scholar), Goethe U., Frankfort, Germany, 1963-64. Staff economist Rand Corp., Santa Monica, Calif., 1968-72, dep. program mgr., health and biosci. rsch., 1971-88, sr. staff economist, 1972-81, head econs. dept., 1981-85, sr. corp. fellow, 1985—; John D. MacArthur prof. health policy and mgmt., dir. div. Health Policy Rsch. and Edn., Harvard U., 1988—; lectr. UCLA, 1970-83, adj. prof., 1983-88; mem. faculty Rand Grad. Sch., 1972-88; dir. Rand-UCLA Ctr. for Study Health Care Fin. Policy, 1984-88, co-dir., 1988-92; prin. investigator health ins. study grant HHS, 1971-86; chmn. health svcs. rsch. study sect. HHS-Agy. for Health Care Policy and Rsch., 1989-93; mem. Nat. Commn. Cost Med. Care, 1976-77; mem. health svcs. devel. grants study sect. HEW, 1978-82, Inst. Medicine of NAS, 1978—, mem. coun., 1991-97; mem. Physician Payment Rev. Commn., 1993-96, chmn. Prospective Payment Assessment Com., 1996—. Author: The Economics of Medical Care, 1978, The Cost of Poor Health Habits, 1991, A Measure of Malpractice, 1993, Free for All?, 1993; editor Jour. Health Econs., 1981—; assoc. editor Jour. Econ. Perspectives, 1992—; contbr. articles to profl. jours. Recipient David Kershaw award and prize Assn. Pub. Policy and Mgmt., 1983, Baxter Am. Found. prize, 1988, Adminstr.'s citation Health Care Fin. Adminstrn., 1988, Hans Sigrist Found. prize, 1995, Elizur Wright award, 1995. Fellow Am. Acad. Arts and Scis.; mem. Assn. for Health Svcs. Rsch. (Article of Yr. award 1989, bd. dirs. 1991—, pres. 1993-94), Am. Econ. Assn., Royal Econ. soc., Econometric Soc., Phi Beta Kappa. Office: Harvard U Health Policy Rsch and Edn 25 Shattuck St Fl 1 Boston MA 02115-6027

NEWLAND, HILLARY REID, pathologist; b. Wilmington, N.C., July 3, 1940; s. Hillery Reid and Annie Mae (Bowden) N.; m. Eleanor Milner, Aug. 25, 1963; children: Benjamin Reid, Sarah O'Beirne, Emily Cobb. BS, Davidson (N.C.) Coll., 1962; MD, Med. Coll. Ga., 1968. Diplomate Am. Bd. Pathology. Intern in internal medicine New Eng. Med. Ctr. Hosps., Boston, 1968-69; resident in pathology Med. Coll. Ga. Hosps., Augusta, 1969-70, Madigan Army Med. Ctr., Tacoma, 1970-72; asst. prof. medicine U. Alta., Edmonton, Can., 1974-75; clin. instr. U. Vt. Med. Sch., Burlington, 1975-77; pathologist diagnostic svcs. Lancaster, N.H., 1975-77; pathologist Athens (Ga.) Regional Med. Ctr., 1977-78, 79—, Wentworth-Douglass Hosp., Dover, N.H., 1978-79; pres. Athens Rsch. and Tech., Inc., 1985—; adj. faculty mem. dept. cell biology U. Ga., Athens, 1988—. Contbr. articles to profl. publs. Maj. USAR, 1970-74. Fellow ACP, Coll. Am. Pathologists, Am. Soc. Clin. Pathologists, Am. Coll. Quality Assurance Physicians; mem. Athens C. of C. (bd. dirs. 1990-92), Med. Assn. Ga. (chmn. continuing med. edn. 1989). Democrat. Office: Athens Regional Med Ctr 1199 Prince Ave Athens GA 30606-2767

NEWMAN, ANDREW, physician; b. Phila., Mar. 29, 1938; s. Louis M. and Ruth (Averbach) N.; m. Sandra S. Mislove, June 18, 1960; children: Kenneth T., Marjorie F., Pamela B. BA summa cum laude, Temple U., 1959, MD, 1963; JD, Rutgers U., 1987. Bar: Pa. 1987, N.J. 1987, D.C. 1988; bd. cert. Am. Bd. Legal Medicine, 1988, bd. cert. Am. Acad. Pain Mgmt., 1989, bd. cert. Am. Bd. Orthopedic Surgery, 1971, recert., 1995. Intern Lower Bucks County Hosp., Bristol, Pa., 1963-64; resident East Orange (N.J.) V.A. Hosp., 1964-65, Phila. (Pa.) Gen. Hosp., 1967-69, Shriners Hosp., Phila., 1969-70; pvt. practice in orthopedic surgery Phila., 1970—; clin. asst. prof. Hahnemann Med. Univ., Dept. Orthopedics, 1970—; attending physician, Dept. Orthopedics Rolling Hill Hosp., Elkins Park, Pa., 1970-84, Parkview Div. of Met. Hosp., 1971—; prof. of medicine Pa. Coll. Podiatric Medicine, Phila.; adj. prof. med. ethics Beaver Coll., Glenridge, Pa., 1996; cons. in orthopedics to Pa. Blue Shield; MD mem. Osteopathic Med. Bd., Pa.; team physician Lower Moreland High Sch. Football Team, Huntingdon Valley, Pa.; cons. Liberty Mutual Ins. Co., Bd. Med. Licensure and Discipline, R.I.; prof. legal medicine Pa. Coll. Podiatric Medicine. Contbg. editor (textbook) Legal Medicine Update, 1988-89; asst. editor Legal Aspects Medical Practice; assoc. editor Bulletin of the Am. Acad. of Orthopedic Surgery; contbr. articles to profl. jours. Lt. col. USAFR. Named Man of Yr., Am. Podiatry Assn., Chgo., 1982; recipient pres.'achievement award Am. Coll. Legal Medicine, Palm Springs, Colo. 1988. Fellow Am. Acad. Orthopedic Surgery, Am. Coll. Legal Medicine; mem. AMA, Internat. Coll. Surgeons, Am. Assn. Hand Surgery (assoc.), Am. Soc. Law and Medicine, Pa. Med. Soc., Phila. County Med. Soc., Am. Orthopedic Foot Soc., Phila. Orthopedic Soc., Soc. Mil. Orthopedic Surgeons, Nat. Bd. Podiatric Med. Examiners. Office: 300 City Ave Bala Cynwyd PA 19004

NEWMAN, ANITA NADINE, surgeon; b. Honolulu, June 13, 1949; d. William Reece Elton and Margie Ruth (Pollard) Newman; m. Frank E.X. Ward, Sept. 9, 1995; children: Justin Ellis, Chelsea Newman, Andrew Frank, Tyler William. AB, Stanford U., 1971; MD, Dartmouth Coll., 1975. Diplomate Am. Bd. Otolaryngology. Intern, then resident in gen. surgery Northwestern Meml. Hosp., Chgo., 1975-77, resident in otolaryngology, 1977-78; resident UCLA Hosp. and Clinics, 1979-82, assoc. prof., 1982—; staff surgeon Wadsworth VA Hosp., L.A., 1982-84; rsch. fellow in neurotology UCLA, 1984-88. Contbr. articles to med. jours. Mem. alumni admissions support com. Darmouth Med. Sch. Alumni Coun., 1983-87. Fellow ACS; mem. Am. Acad. Otolaryngology, Am. Med. Women's Assn., Los Angeles County Med. Women's Assn., Assn. Rsch. in Otolaryngology, Stanford Women's Honor Soc. Democrat. Office: UCLA Hosp and Clinics Div Head And Neck Surg Ucla CA 90095

NEWMAN, BARBARA DIANE, nurse; b. Winnsboro, La., Oct. 14, 1955; d. Margaret Louella (Magee) Griffing; m. Fred O. Newman, Dec. 20, 1966 (div.); children: Byron O., W. Kyle. Student, N.E. La. State U., Monroe, 1962; diploma, Warner Brown Sch. Nursing, El Dorado, Ark., 1966. RN, Tex., Ark.; cert. CPR, ACLS. Staff nurse surg. svc. Garland (Tex.) Cmty. Hosp., 1978-79, clin. coord. med./surg. nursing, 1979-80, head nurse surg. svc., 1980-84, spl. procedures coord., 1984-86, head nurse Horizon Recovery, 1986-88; shift supr. Charter suburgan Hosp., Mesquite, Tex., 1988-90; utilization mgmt. nurse Mid Tex. PCA Health Plans, Austin, 1990-92; resource mgmt. coord. Jefferson Regional Med. Ctr., Pine Bluff, Ark., 1992-94; quality mgmt. coord. PHP Healthcare at Ark. Dept. Correction, Pine Bluff, 1994—; peer adv. Tex. Peer Asst. Program for Nurses, Austin, 1987-93. Mem. Ark. Nurses Assn., Nat. Assn. Healthcare Quality, Ark. Assn. Healthcare Quality, Gastrointestinal Assts. Assn. Jehova's Witness. Home: 2100 W 40th St # 23 Pine Bluff AR 71603 : PHP Healthcare Corp 8001 W 7th St Pine Bluff AR 71603

NEWMAN, BARNEY DAVID, medical administrator, internist; b. East Liverpool, Ohio, July 27, 1950; s. Maurice J. and Esther G. (Solomon) N.; m. Jean M. Wester, Aug. 5, 1973; children: Jeremy, Gabriel, Caitlin. BA, U. Pa., 1972; MD, Pa. State U., 1977. Diplomate Am. Bd. Internists. Resident internal medicine Montefiore Hosp., Bronk, N.Y., 1977-80; staff internist Westchester Cmty. Health Plan, White Plains, N.Y., 1980-83, chief medicine, 1983-85; physician-in-chief Kaiser Permanente, White Plains, 1985-88, group med. dir., 1988-94, assoc. regional med. dir., 1994—; pres., bd. dirs. Northeast Permanente Med. Group, White Plains, 1986—; bd. dirs. Northeats Permanente Mgmt. Corp., Farmington, Conn., 1988—; clin. asst. prof. medicine N.Y. Med. Coll. Managed care editor Medscape. Bd. dirs. The Lord's Pantry, White Plains, 1992—; active Midnight Run, Inc., Dobbs Ferry, N.Y., 1989—. Mem. Am. Coll. Physicians, Am. Coll. Physician Execs. Office: Kaiser Permanente 210 Westchester Ave White Plains NY 10604

NEWMAN, BARRY MARC, pediatric surgeon; b. N.Y.C., Dec. 13, 1951; s. Sheldon and Miriam (Jasphy) N.; m. Jane Post, July 2, 1989; 1 child, Alexander Ross. BA, U. Pa., 1973; MD, SUNY, Stony Brook, 1976. Diplomate Nat. Bd. Med. Examiners, Am. Bd. Surgery, Am. Bd. Pediatric Surgery. Resident in surgery N.Y. Med. Coll., N.Y.C., 1976-78; sr. resident in surgery SUNY, Stony Brook, 1978-81; chief resident pediatric surgery Childrens Hosp. of Buffalo, 1981-83, fellow pediatric surgery and gastroenterology, 1983-84; asst. prof. surgery U. Va., Charlottesville, 1984-88, U. Ill., Chgo., 1988-93; dir. pediatric surgery Luth. Gen. Children's Hosp., Park Ridge, Ill., 1991-96; clin. assoc. prof. surgery U. Chgo., 1993-95; dir. pediatric surg. svcs. Loyola U. Med. Ctr., Maywood, Ill., 1996—, co-dir. surg. laparoscopy lab., 1996—, assoc. prof. surgery and pediatrics, 1996—; instr. Adv. Trauma and Life Support, ACS, Chgo., 1984—. Contbr. articles to profl. jours., chpts. to books. NIH grantee, 1982-83, 87-88. Fellow Am. Acad. Pediatrics, ACS; mem. Am. Gastroenterol. Assn., Am. Pediatric Surg. Assn. Democrat. Jewish. Office: Loyola U Med Ctr Dept Surgery 2160 S First Ave Maywood IL 60153

NEWMAN, BRIAN KEVIN, psychotherapist; b. Birmingham, Ala., Jan. 26, 1961; s. Danny Lee and Jerry (Bellenger) N.; m. Deborah Rae Bowles, Jan. 5, 1985; children: Rachel Mae, Benjamin Kevin. BA in Psychology, U. Ala., 1983; MA in Counseling, cert. in bibl. studies, Grace Theol. Sem., 1985; DPhil, Oxford Grad. Sch., Dayton, Tenn., 1991. Pastor Sellers Lake Bapt. Mission, Warsaw, Ind., 1984-85; dir. clin. svcs. Minirth-Meier Clinic, P.A., Richardson, Tex., 1985—. Co-author: Day by Day Love is a Choice, 1991, Passages of Marriage, 1991, Love is a Choice Workbook, 1991, The Man Within, 1991, The Father Book, 1992, Steps to a New Beginning, 1992, What They Didn't Teach You in Seminary, 1993, Receiving Love, 1996. Mem. Assn. for Couples in Marriage Enrichment, Am. Assn. Marriage and Family Therapists. Republican. Baptist. Home: 640 Meadowbrook St Allen TX 75002-4799 Office: Minirth Meier Clinic PA 2100 N Collins Blvd Richardson TX 75080-2661

NEWMAN, CAROL ANN, psychologist; b. N.Y.C., Apr. 9, 1938; d. Joyce N. and Elizabeth Feldman; m. Stanley L. Newman, July 4, 1958; children: Jordana L., Robert S. BA, Barnard Coll., N.Y.C., 1958; MA, CCNY, 1960; PhD, U. Md., 1965. Lic. psychologist, Washington, Md. Psychology intern St. Elizabeth's Hosp., Washington, 1961-62; rsch. asst. NIMH, Bethesda, Md., 1962-63; pub. health fellow U. Md., College Park, 1963-65; vis. psychologist Tavistock & Hampstead Clinic, London, 1965; psychologist Area C Community Mental Health Ctr., Washington, 1967-70, Community Psychiat. Clinic, Bethesda, 1971-87; pvt. practice, Washington, 1971—; seminar leader Washington Sch. Psychiatry, 1968-69. Mem. APA, D.C. Psychol. Assn., Washington Soc. for Study Eating Disorders, Washington Soc. Clin. Hypnosis (pres. 1984-87, treas. 1980—), Assn. for Mental Health Affiliation with Israel (pres. 1990-92), Am. Soc. Clin. Hypnosis, Register Health Svc. Providers in Psychology, Sigma Xi. Home and Office: 5739 Moreland St NW Washington DC 20015-1117

NEWMAN, CORY FRANK, clinical psychologist; b. Phila., Jan. 20, 1960; s. Norman Jerome and Phyllis (Stutman) N.; m. Jane Evans, June 24, 1990; 1 child, Lindsey Diana. BA, U. Pa., 1981; MA, SUNY, Stony Brook, 1983, PhD, 1987. Lic. psychologist, Pa. Postdoctoral fellow Ctr. for Cognitive Therapy, Phila., 1987-88, assoc. dir. edn., 1988-90, clin. dir., 1990—, asst. prof. psychology, 1991—; lectr. in field. Composer: Rhapsody on a Thematic Mirage, chamber music, 1981; co-author: Cognitive Therapy of Borderline Personality Disorder, 1993, Cognitive Therapy of Substance Abuse, 1993, Choosing To Live: How To Defeat Suicide Through Cognitive Therapy, 1996; contbr. articles to profl. jours. Grad. Coun. fellow SUNY, 1981; rsch. grantee Sigma Xi, 1985. Mem. APA, Assn. for Advancement Behavior Therapy, Soc. for Exploration Psychotherapy Integration, Phi Beta Kappa. Office: U Pa Ctr for Cognitive Therapy 3600 Market St Ste 754 Philadelphia PA 19104-2648

NEWMAN, FREDERICK L., psychologist, educator; b. N.Y.C., Dec. 15, 1938; s. David A. and Helen (Gotterer) N.; m. Sharon K. Grosshart; children: Andrew David, Adam Richard, Robert Berbiglia. BA, Allegheney Coll., 1961; MA, Kent (Ohio) State U., 1963; PhD, U. Mass., 1966. Lic. psychologist, Pa. Asst. prof. N.Mex. State U., Las Cruces, 1966-69; assoc. prof. U. Miami, Fla., 1969-72; asst. prof. U. Pa., Phila., 1972-81; assoc. prof. Med. Coll. Pa., Phila., 1980-83, Northwestern U., Chgo., 1983-86, Sch. Pub. Health U. Ill., Chgo., 1986-90; prof. health svcs. adminstrn. Fla. Internat. U., North Miami, 1990—; adj. prof. psychiatry U. Miami, 1994—; advisor to mental health dir., acting chief info. systems and evaluation Pa. Office Mental Health, Harrisburg, 1972-79; cons. Ill. Dept. Mental Health and Devel. Disabilities, Springfield, Ill. and Chgo., 1984-90, Peat, Marwick, Main, Salt Lake, Utah, 1985-86. Author: Integrated Clinical and Fiscal Management in MH, 1985, Client Oriented Cost Outcome Systems 2d Ed., 1980; contbr. numerous articles to profl. jours.; assoc. editor Jour. of Consulting and Clin. Psychology. Served with USMCR. Fellow Ctr. Advanced Study Behavioral Scis., 1971-72. Fellow AAAS, APA, Am. Psychol. Soc.; mem. APHA, Psychonomics Soc., Soc. Psychotherapy Rsch., Am. Evaluation Assn., Sigma Xi. Democrat. Unitarian-Universalist. Home: 9212 NE 10th Ave Miami Shores FL 33138 Office: Health Svcs Adminstrn N Miami Campus 3000 NE 145th St N Miami FL 33181-3612

NEWMAN, FREDRIC ALAN, plastic surgeon, educator; b. Bklyn., Aug. 16, 1948; s. Harold Louis and Isabel (Seltzer) N.; m. Stacey Hope Clarfield, Nov. 27, 1983; children: Benjamin, Marissa, Alexandra. BA, Yale Coll., 1970; MD summa cum laude, SUNY Downstate, Bklyn., 1974. Bd. cert. Am. Bd. Plastic Surgery, Am. Bd. Surgery. Resident gen. surgery Beth Israel Hosp., Boston, 1974-77; resident and chief gen. surgery SUNY Downstate, Bklyn., 1977-79; fellow plastic surgery NYU/Inst. Reconstrv. Plastic Surgery, N.Y.C., 1979-81; fellow facial reconstruction Jackson Meml. Hosp., Miami, Fla., 1981-82; asst. clin. prof. dept. plastic surgery N.Y. Med. Coll., West, 1984-95, Columbia Coll. Physicians and Surgeons, N.Y.C., 1995—; chmn. bd. Cutting Edge Techs., Inc., N.Y.C., 1994—. Author: Aesthetic Plastic Surgery, 1984, Plastic Surgery, 1985; contbr. articles to profl. jours. Fellow ACS, Internat. Coll. Surgeons (regent 1990—); mem. Am. Soc. Plastic and Reconstructive Surgeons, Am. Soc. Aesthetic Plastic Surgery, Am. Cleft Palate Assn., N.Y. State Med. Soc. Office: Two Overhill Rd Scarsdale NY 10583

NEWMAN, HARRY RUDOLPH, urologist, educator; b. Russia, Sept. 10, 1909; naturalized, 1919, came to U.S., 1935, naturalized, 1944; s. Abraham and Mary (Rudolph) N.; m. Lillian Lear, Aug. 18, 1942; children: Nancy Ellen, Robert Lear, Suzanne Mary. M.D., U. Toronto, 1935; M.S., U. Pa., 1940. Diplomate: Am. Bd. Urology. Resident urology U. Minn. Hosps., 1936-37, All Saints Hosp., London, Eng., 1937-38; sr. resident urology N.Y. Postgrad. Med. Sch. and Hosp., 1939-40, Boston Long Island Hosp., 1941-42; resident surgery N.Y. Postgrad. Hosp., 1942; resident gen. surgery Prince of Wales Hosp., Plymouth, Eng.; asst. clin. prof. urology N.Y. Postgrad. Med. Sch. & Hosp., 1946-54; sr. attending urologist Bellevue Hosp., N.Y.C., 1946-54; attending urologist Yale New-Haven Hosp.; attending univ. service Yale U., asst. clin. prof. urology, 1949—; dir. urology Albert Einstein Coll. Medicine, also clin. prof. surgery, chief urology, 1957—, clin. prof. urology, 1957-62, prof. urology, 1963-65, 66-80, emeritus chmn. and prof. urology, 1980—, chmn. dept., 1966-80; prof. history; chief urology Bronx Mcpl. Hosp., 1966—; chief urology community div. Grace New Haven Hosp., 1965-66; cons. urologist Stamford (Conn.) Hosp., St. Joseph Hosp., Stamford, 1965—; former asst. clin. prof. urology NYU; dir. urology City N.Y. Bronx Mcpl. Med. Center, 1954-65; chief urology Regional Hosp., Hunter Field, Savannah, Ga. Served from capt. to maj. USAAF, 1942-46. Fellow ACS, N.Y. Acad. Medicine, Royal So. of Health (Great Britian); mem. AMA, Physicians and Surgeons of Ont., Soc. Univ. Urologists, Masons (32 deg.), Shriners, Yale Club (N.Y.), Sigma Xi. Home: 95 Broadfield Rd Hamden CT 06517-1543 Office: 2 Church St S New Haven CT 06519-1717

NEWMAN, JOSEPH THEODORE, podiatrist; b. Munsan, Korea, July 1, 1962; s. Jimmy L. and Myung J. (Kim) N.; m. Soyong M. Pak, Mar. 30, 1990; children: Jeremy A., Brian J. AA, U. HAwaii, 1984; BS, U. Osteo. Medicine, 1987, DPM, 1989. Diplomate Am. Bd. Podiatric Orthopedics. Resident U. Osteo. Medicine, Des Moines, 1989-90; podiatrist pvt. practice, Alea, Hawaii, 1990-91, The Foot Ctr./Iowa Foot Care Ctrs., West Des Moines, 1992—; lectr., speaker in field. Contbr. articles to profl. jours. Recipient Rsch. Excellence award U. Osteo. Medicine, 1989. Fellow Am. Coll. Foot & Ankle Orthopaedics & Medicine, Internat. Acad. Podiatric Medicine; mem. Am. Diabetes Assn., Am. Podiatric Med. Assn., Iowa Podiatric Med. Soc. Republican. Roman Catholic. Office: The Foot Ctr 2700 Univ Ave #212 West Des Moines IA 50266

NEWMAN, LAWRENCE CRAIG, physician, clinical researcher; b. Bklyn., Jan. 10, 1958; s. Kenneth Jerry and Elinore (Miller) N.; m. Leslie Brooke Paris, Apr. 13, 1986; children: Daniel Grey, Eric Bryce. BA, Clark U., 1979; MD, U. Autonoma de Guadalajara, Mex., 1983. Diplomate Am. Bd. Psychiatry and Neurology. Resident in internal medicine Elmhurst (N.Y.) Hosp. Ctr., 1985-86; resident in neurology Albert Einstein Coll. Medicine, Bronx, N.Y., 1986-88, chief resident neurology, 1988-89; headache fellow Montefiore Med. Ctr., Bronx, N.Y., 1989-90, attending physician, 1990—, dep. dir. neurology, 1990-92; co-dir. Headache Unit Montefiore Med. Ctr., N.Y.C., 1990—; asst. prof. neurology Albert Einstein Coll. Medicine, Bronx, 1992—; lectr. in field. Co-author: Migraine: Beating the Odds, 1992; co-editor abstract section Headache jour., 1992-95; ad hoc reviewer Neurology jour., Headache jour., Cephalalgia jour., 1990—; contbr. articles to profl. jours. Mem. AMA, Am. Acad. Neurology, Am. Assn. for Study of Headache (ethich ad hoc com. 1993—), Nat. Headache Found., Internat. Headache Soc. Office: Montefiore Headache Unit 111 E 210 St Bronx NY 10467 also: 11 E 68th St New York NY 10021

NEWMAN, MARJORIE YOSPIN, psychiatrist; b. Bklyn., July 8, 1945; d. Toby and Audrey (Kreinik) Yospin; children: Eric, David. Student, Smith Coll., 1963-64; AB, Barnard Coll., 1967; MD, Med. Coll. Pa., 1971. Diplomate Am. Bd. Psychiatry and Neurology. Psychiatry intern, resident Albert Einstein Coll. Medicine, N.Y.C., 1971-75; asst. prof. psychiatry U. Tex. Health Sci. Ctr., San Antonio, 1975-77; asst. prof. psychiatry Sch. Medicine UCLA, 1977-79, 1977-79, asst. clin. prof. Sch. Medicine, 1979—; dir. residency tng. in psychiatry Med. Ctr. Harbor-UCLA Med. Ctr., 1977-79; pvt. practice Pasadena, Calif., 1983—. Grantee NSF, 1969; Am. Field Svc. Internat. scholar, 1963. Mem. Am. Psychiat. Assn., So. Calif. Psychiat. Soc., Smith Coll. Alumna Assn., Barnard Coll. Alumna Assn., Columbia U. Alumna Assn., Ivy League Assn. So. Calif. Office: Cotton Med Ctr South 50 Alessandro Pl Ste 340 Pasadena CA 91105-3149

NEWMAN, PHILIP ROBERT, psychologist; b. Utica, N.Y., Dec. 17, 1942; s. Samuel M. and Sara Rose (Dumain) N.; A.B. with high distinction, U. Mich., 1964, Ph.D. (Woodrow Wilson fellow 1964, Univ. fellow 1964-66, Horace H. Rackham Research scholar 1969-71), 1971; m. Barbara Miller, June 12, 1966; children: Samuel Asher, Abraham Levy, Rachel Florence. Asst. prof. psychology U. Mich., Ann Arbor, 1971-72; asst. prof.

psychology Union Coll., Schenectady, 1972-76; dir. human behavior curriculum project Am. Psychol. Assn., Washington, 1977-81; pvt. practice psychology, Columbus, Ohio, 1978—; adj. prof., sr. researcher young scholars program Ohio State U., 1990; cons. Agy. Instructional TV, 1979. Mem. APA, Internat. Assn. Applied Psychology, Internat. Sociol. Assn., Soc. Psychol. Study Social Issues, Am. Sociol. Assn., Nat. Council Family Relations, Groves Conf. Marriage and Family, Eastern Psychol. Assn., Midwestern Psychol. Assn., Western Psychol. Assn., Am. Pub. Health Assn., N.Y. Acad. Sci., Gerontol. Soc. Am., Am. Orthopsychiat. Assn., Am. Statis. Assn., Phi Beta Kappa, Sigma Xi, Phi Kappa Phi. Author: (with B. Newman) Development through Life: A Psychosocial Approach, 1975, 6th edit., 1995; Infancy and Childhood Development and Its Contexts, 1978; An Introduction to the Psychology of Adolescence, 1979; Personality Development through the Life Span, 1980; Living: The Process of Adjustment, 1981; Understanding Adulthood, 1983; Principles of Psychology, 1983; Adolescent Development, 1986, When Kids Go to College: A Parents Guide to Changing Relationships, 1992; editor: (with B. Newman) Development Through Life: A Case Study Approach, 1976. Home and Office: 1969 Chatfield Rd Columbus OH 43221-3703

NEWMAN, RICHARD AUGUST, psychiatrist, educator; b. Oak Park, Ill., May 27, 1931; s. Henry Adolph and Mildred Kathryn (Haaker) N.; BS, U. Ill., 1953, MD, 1956; m. Nancy Jane Werdelin, Aug. 28, 1954; children: John Henry, Kurt Alan, Richard Steven, Scott David. Intern, Swedish-Am. Hosp., Rockford, Ill., 1956-57; resident in psychiatry Walter Reed Gen. Hosp., Washington, 1958-61; research Walter Reed Army Inst., 1961; chief psychiatric service Valley Forge Gen. Hosp., Phoenixville, Pa., 1962-64, also asst. chief dept. psychiatry and neurology, 1962-64; practice medicine, specializing in psychiatry, Paoli, Pa., 1962-96; dir. milieu therapy Phila. Gen. Hosp., 1968-69; dir. residency tng., dept. mental health scis. Hahnemann Med. Coll., 1969-73, asso. prof., 1970-79; prof. psychiatry Med. Coll. Pa., Phila., 1979—, prof. psychiatry, 1995—, dir. continuing mental health edn., 1983-87, dir. continuing med. edn., 1985-87; regional med. dir. for mental health Intracorp/Cigna, 1989-93; assoc. med. dir. for mental health U.S. Healthcare, 1993-95; prof. psychiat. Hahnemann U., Phila., 1995—; vis. prof. psychiatry U. Alta., 1975; chief cons. psychotherapy Chester County Cmty. Mental Health Clinic, 1967-68; psychiatrist Chester County Commr.'s Bd. for Mental Health/Mental Retardation, 1971-77; instr. Phila. Psychoanalytic Soc. Extension Sch., 1972-90, mem. faculty Inst., of Phila. Psychoanalytic Soc.; chmn. psychiatric sect. Paoli Meml. Hosp., 1974-83, med. dir. psychiatry service, 1977-83; psychiat. cons. St. Judes Hosp., St. Lucia, WI, 1983-89; interim med. dir. Connections CSP, Wilmington, Del., 1995-96; staff psychiatrist Philhaven Hosp., Mt. Gretna, Pa., 1996. Served to maj. M.C., AUS, 1958-64. Diplomate Am. Bd. Psychiatry and Neurology. Fellow APA, Pa. Psychiat. Assn. (chmn. ethics com.); mem. AMA, Phila. Psychoanalytic Soc., Am. Psychoanalytic Assn. (cert. psychoanalyst), Christian Med. Soc., Soc. Med. Coll. Dirs. Continuing Med. Edn., Pa., Chester County Med. Socs., Dirs. of Residency Tng. in Psychiatry of Del. Valley (past pres.). Lutheran. Contbr. articles to profl. jours. Home: PO Box 174 Lionville PA 19353-0174 Office: Philhaven Hosp PO Box 550 Mount Gretna PA 17064

NEWMAN, ROBERT C., urologist, educator; b. Shattuck, Okla., Mar. 7, 1950; s. Floyd Smith and Erwina (Schollenbarger) N.; m. Lynn Schneider, Aug. 8, 1981. BS, Okla. U., 1972, MD, 1976; MS in Health Adminstrn., U. Colo., 1990. Resident in urology Okla. U., Okla. City, 1976-81; staff urologist Newman Med. Ctr., Shattuck, Okla., 1981-84; fellow in urology U. Fla., Gainesville, 1984-85, asst. prof., 1985-88, assoc.prof. urology/surgery Coll. of Medicine, 1988—. Contbr. articles to profl. jours. Mem. AMA, Am. Urol. Assn., Endourology Soc. Home: 214 NE 9th Ave Gainesville FL 32601-4377 Office: U Fla Box 100247 JHMHC 1000 Archer Rd Gainesville FL 32610

NEWMAN, STUART J., ophthalmologist; b. Bklyn., Oct. 4, 1955. BA summa cum laude, SUNY, Albany, 1977; postgrad., Autonomous U. Guadalajara, 1977-79; MD, U. Rochester, 1981. Diplomate Am. Bd. Ophthalmology, Nat. Bd. Med. Examiners. Intern Nassau County Med. Ctr., East Meadow, N.Y., 1981-82; physician Lydia Hall Hosp., Freeport, N.Y., 1982-83; resident ophthalmology Nassau County Med. Ctr., East Meadow, 1983-86; ophthalmologist Riverhead, N.Y., 1986-87, Thomas Eye Group P.C., Atlanta, 1988—. Mem. AMA, Am. Acad. Ophthalmology, Am. Intra-Ocular Implant Soc., Contact Lens Assn. Ophthalmologists, N.Y. State Med. Soc., N.Y. State Ophthalmol. Soc., Phi Beta Kappa, Beta Beta Beta. Office: Thomas Eye Group PC 11930 Hwy 9 S Alpharetta GA 30201-2020

NEWMARK, EMANUEL, ophthalmologist; b. Newark, May 25, 1936; s. Charles Meyer and Bella (Yoskowitz) N.; m. Tina Steinberg, Aug. 25, 1957; children: Karen Beth, Heidi Ellen, Stuart Jeffry. BS in Pharmacy, Rutgers U., 1959; postgrad., U. Amsterdam, The Netherlands, 1960-63, Armed Forces Inst. Pathology, Washington, 1971; MD, Duke U., 1966; Lancaster course in ophthalmology, Harvard U., 1967. Diplomate Am. Bd. Ophthalmology. Intern George Washington U. Hosp., Washington, 1966; trainee NIH rsch. Univ. Fla., Gainesville, 1967-70; resident ophthalmology U. Fla. Hosp., 1967-70; instr. dept. ophthalmology Univ. Fla., 1970; cons. ophthalmology Gainesville VA Hosp., 1970; clin. instr. ophthalmology U. Tex. Med. Sch., San Antonio, 1971-72; cons. ophthalmology Kerrville (Tex.) VA Hosp., 1971-72; asst. chief ophthalmology svc. Brooke Army Gen. Hosp., Fort Sam, Tex., 1971-72; clin. prof. Bascom Palmer Eye Inst., Miami, Fla., 1995—; clin. asst. prof. ophthalmology Bexar County Hosp. and Clinics, San Antonio, 1971-72; tchg. faculty Joint Com. Allied Health Pers. Ophthalmology, St. Paul, 1981—; chief ophthalmology svc. JFK Med. Ctr., Atlantis, Fla., 1982; cons. Bascom Palmer Eye Inst., 1983—; dir., sec., treas. Palm Beach Eye Assocs., Atlantis, 1973—; mem. pharm. adv. com. Agy. for Health Care Adminstrn. Bd. Optometry, 1991; mem. med. adv. bd. Fla. east coast chpt. Nat. Sjorgren's Syndrome Assn., 1990—; bd. dirs. Fla. Eye Injury and Disease Registry. Contbr. chpts. to 4 textbooks, over 12 articles to med. jours. Alumni assoc. Rutgers Coll. Pharmacy, 1960—; chmn. reunion 1986 Duke U. Med. Alumni Assn., N.C., 1967—; centurian Davison Club-Duke U. Med. Sch., N.C., 1982—; campaign chmn., nat. vice chmn. Israel Bonds, Palm Beach County, Fla., 1988—; participant charitable orgns.; v.p. Palm Beach Liturgical Culture Found., 1987-94, treas., trustee, 1987-94. Decorated Lion of Judea State of Israel, 1984; recipient Gates of Jerusalem medal, 1991, Jerusalem 3000 medal, 1996. Fellow ACS, Am. Acad. Ophthalmology (del. coun., Fla. state chmn. ednl. trust), Am. Castroveiejo Cornea Soc.; mem. AMA, Internat. Platform Assn., Assn. for Rsch. in Vision and Ophthalmology, Am. Orgn. for Rehab. Through Tng. Fedn. (nat. exec. com.-campaign cabinet 1987, pres. 1990—, Palm Beach Men's Achievement award 1988, Pres. award 1989), Fla. Med. Assn. (ho. dels. 1993-96), Palm Beach County Ophthal. Soc. (pres. 1984-85), Fla. Soc. Ophthalmology (ethics chmn. 1985-90, pres. 1990-91, James. W. Clower Jr. Cmty. Svc. award 1995), Founder's Soc. Duke U. Jewish. Home: 335 Glenbrook Dr Atlantis FL 33462-1009 Office: Palm Beach Eye Assocs 140 JFK Dr Atlantis FL 33462-1159

NEWMARK, HAROLD LEON, biochemist; b. N.Y.C., July 21, 1918; s. Abraham and Mollie W. (Wolf) N.; m. Helen Rosenberg, Mar. 13, 1949 (dec. Aug. 1985); children: Jonathan, Robin L.; m. Phyllis Klein, Sept. 6, 1987. BS, CCNY, 1939; MS, N.Y. Poly. U., 1950. Chemist Chem. Spec. of N.J.-Syntex, Newark, 1939-41, Intramed Co., N.Y.C., 1946-49, Chase Chem. Co., Newark, 1949-50, Vitarine Co., N.Y.C., 1950-59; chemist Hoffmann LaRoche, Inc., Nutley, N.J., 1966-81, dir. food, agrl. products, 1959-81; chemist Ludwig Inst. for Cancer Rsch., Toronto, Ont., Can., 1981-84; biochem. rschr. Sloan-Kettering Inst., N.Y.C., 1984-95; rsch. scientist Strang Cancer Prevention Ctr. Rockefeller U., N.Y.C., 1996—; adj. prof. Coll. Pharmacy, Rutgers U., Piscataway, N.J., 1987—. Author, editor: Calcium, Vitamin D and Colon Cancer, 1991; contbr. numerous articles to sci. publs. Cpl. USAAF, 1942-46. Mem. AAAS, Am. Chem. Soc., Am. Assn. Cancer Rsch., N.Y. Acad. Sci., N.J. Cancer Inst. Home: 11 Claremont Dr Maplewood NJ 07040-2119

NEWMARK, LAURIE JO, nurse; b. Cedar Falls, Iowa, Mar. 21, 1956; d. Curtis W. and Ann (Schlitter) Olsen; 1 child, Kristin Ann. RN, Rochester Community Coll., 1976; postgrad., Mayo Clinic, 1980. RN, Nev.; cert. BLS and ACLS instr. Physician extender Mayo Clinic, Rochester, Minn.; clin. nurse specialist Heart Inst. of Desert, Rancho Mirage, Calif.; clin. coord. Sierra Nevada Cardiology, Reno; ARN Washoe Med. Ctr., Reno. Author: Before and After Your Heart Attack, 1994. Mem. Critical Care Nurses (local chpt.). Home: 3160 Marthiam Ave Reno NV 89509-5000

NEWPORT, L. JOAN, clinical social worker, psychotherapist; b. Ponca City, Okla., July 5, 1932; d. Crawford Earl and Lillian Pearl (Peden) Irvine; m. Don E. Newport, July 9, 1954 (div. July 1971); children: Alan Keith, Lili Kim. BA cum laude, Wichita State U., 1955; MSW, U. Okla., 1977. Bd. cert. diplomate in clin. social work Acad. Cert. Social Workers; lic. social worker, Okla. Dir. children's work Wesley United Meth. Ch., Oklahoma City, 1969-71; social worker Dept. Human Svcs., Newkirk, Okla., 1972-77; in-sch. suspension counselor Kay County Youth Svcs., Ponca City, Okla., 1977; med. social worker St. Joseph Med. Ctr., Ponca City, 1977-78, dir. social work, 1978-83; pvt. practice Ponca City, 1979—; med. social worker Healthcare Svcs., Ponca City, 1983-84; cons. Blackwell, Perry, Fawhuska, O'Keene Hosps., 1978-85; cons. social work Bass Meml. Hosp., Enid, Okla., 1985; sponsor, organizer Kay County Parents Anonymous, Ponca City, 1976-83; vice chair Okla. State Bd. Lic. Social Workers, Oklahoma City, 1988-90; presentor, lectr. in field; supr. students Okla. U. Sch. Social Work. Mem. Okla. Women's Network, 1989—; mem. adv. bd. Displaced Homemakers, Ponca City, 1985-89; mem. adv. bd. Kay County Home Health, 1979-83, chair, 1979-81. Named Hon. State Life Mem. Burbank PTA, Oklahoma City, 1971; scholar Wichita (Kans.) Press and Radio Women, 1953, Conoco, Inc., Houston, 1951-54. Mem. NASW (Okla. del. Del. Assembly Washington 1987, chmn. vendorship com. 1985-87, pres. Okla. chpt. 1988-90, Social Worker of Yr. 1987), Child Abuse Prevention Task Force (pres. dist. 17 1986-88, mem. grant evaluation com. 1986-96), Zeta Phi Eta. Democrat. Methodist. Home: 109 N Walnut Ave Newkirk OK 74647-2036 Office: 619 E Brookfield Ave Ponca City OK 74601-2804

NEWSOM, BARRY DOUGLAS, cardiovascular and thoracic surgeon; b. Tucson, Ariz., Sept. 27, 1953; s. Douglas Lee and Annie Laura (Tribble) N.; m. Nancy Macfarlan Irby, Feb. 11, 1978; children: Lori Anne, Julia Caroline, Ellen Brown, Jonathan David. MD, U. Miss., Jackson, 1978. Diplomate Am. Bd. Surgery, Am. Bd. Thoracic Surgery. Intern in gen. surgery U. Miss., 1978-79, resident in gen. surgery, 1979-83, fellow in vascular surgery, 1983-84, resident thoracic surgery, 1984-86; pvt. practice, Tuscaloosa, Ala., 1986—. Contbr. articles to profl. jours. Fellow ACS; mem. AMA, Soc. Thoracic Surgeons, So. Thoracic Surg. Assn., Alpha Omega Alpha. Office: Thoracic and Cv Assocs 701 University Blvd E Tuscaloosa AL 35401-2086

NEWSOM, SANDRA K., speech and language pathologist; b. Paintsville, Ky., June 1, 1950; d. George and Ida Mae (Bentley) N.; m. Burton M. Rudolph, Aug. 30, 1991. BS, Eastern N.Mex. U., 1970; MS, Vanderbilt U., 1971; PhD, U. Tenn., 1980. Speech lang. pathologist Mtn. Comprehensive Care Orgn., Paintsville, Ky., 1971-73, VA Med. Ctr., Johnson City, Tenn., 1973-74; dir. speech and hearing clinic Appalachian State U., Boone, N.C., 1974-77; clin. supervisor U. Tenn., Knoxville, 1977-80; dir. speech pathology dept. Ft. Sanders Regional Med. Ctr., Knoxville, 1980-89; program dir. Meadowbrook Rehab. Group, Atlanta, 1989-91; from clin. supervisor to asst. prof. U. Tenn., Knoxville, 1991—; speech-lang. pathologist Ther X, Knoxville, 1991-93, Hill Haven Corp., Knoxville, 1995—, In-House Rehab., Knoxville, 1995—. Bd. dirs. Am. Cancer Soc., Knoxville, 1982. Names woman of yr. Knoxville Bus. & Profl. Women, 1986, 94. Mem. Am. Speech-Lang.-Hearing Assn., Am. Heart Assn., Brain Injury Assn. Tenn. (bd. dirs. 1995),Tenn. Assn. Audiologists & Speech Lang. Pathologists. Home: 925 Highland Point Dr Knoxville TN 37919

NEWSOME, FREDERICK V., medical educator; b. Charleston, W.Va., July 7, 1946; s. Moses and Ruth (Bass) N.; m. Osila Chindo, Mar. 23, 1974; children: Akasemi, Imhotep, Nubia, Hatshepsut. BA in Chemistry, Harvard U., 1968; MD, W.Va. U., 1972; MSc in Tropical Medicine, London Sch. Hygiene & Tropical Medicine, 1981. Diplomate Am. Bd. Internal Medicine. Instr. in medicine Coll. of Physicians and Surgeons Columbia U., N.Y.C., 1975-76; instr. in medicine Albert Einstein Med. Sch., Bronx, 1979-80; sr. lectr. in medicine U. Jos, Nigeria, 1981-88; clin. prof., head dept. of medicine Coll. of Health Scis. Usmanu Danfodio U., Sokoto, Nigeria, 1988-90; chief ambulatory medicine The Meth. Hosp., Bklyn., 1991-92; asst. prof. medicine Columbia U. Coll. Physicians & Surgeons, N.Y.C., 1992—. Contbr. articles to profl. jours. Fellow ACP, West African Coll. Physicians, Royal Soc. Tropical Medicine and Hygiene; mem. AAAS, Am. Soc. Tropical Medicine & Hygiene, Nat. Med. Assn., Assn. for Study Afro-Am. Life and History. Office: Harlem Hosp Dept Medicine Rm 14131 135th St & Malcolm X Ave New York NY 10037

NEWSOME, THOMAS WILLINGHAM, physician; b. Dallas, Nov. 3, 1940; s. William Barnes and Frances (Dyckman) N.; m. Januren Martindale, July 25, 1964; children: William Bruce, Stuart Januren. BA, Princeton U., 1963; MD, Johns Hopkins U., 1967. Diplomate Am. Bd. Surgery. Resident in surgery U. Hosp. Cleve., 1967-69, Parkland Meml. Hosp., Dallas, 1972-76; surgeon Thomas W. Newsome, MD, PA, Dallas, 1976—; pres. Gaston Episcopal Hosp., Dallas, 1988. Maj. U.S. Army, 1969-72. Fellow Am. Coll. Surgeons; mem. Southwest Physicians Assn. (bd. dirs. 1986—). Home: 6515 Orchid Ln Dallas TX 75230 Office: Thomas W Newsome MD PA 3600 Gaston # 904 Dallas TX 75246

NEWSTEAD, ROBERT RICHARD, urologist; b. Detroit, Sept. 16, 1935; s. Oran Henry and Agnes Audery (Lewandowski) N.; m. Marie Carmela LiPuma, Aug. 5, 1961; children: Elizabeth Marie, Peter Joseph, Angela Agnes, Paul Michael. Student, Coll. Idaho, 1955-57, Quincy Coll., 1957-58; MD, Loyola U., Chgo., 1963. Intern Walter Reed Gen. Hosp., Washington, 1963-64; resident U. Iowa, Iowa City, 1967-71; urologist Urology Clinic Yakima, Wash., 1971-84, pres., 1984—; chief of staff Yakima Valley Meml. Hosp., 1995—; chief of surgery St. Elizabeth Med. Ctr., Yakima, 1980-81, Yakima Valley Hosp., 1978-79. Bd. dirs. St. Elizabeth Found., Yakima, 1983-93, The Capital Theater, 1987-93, Boy Scouts Am., Yakima, 1982-86. Capt. U.S. Army, 1962-67. Fellow Am. Cancer Soc., Iowa City, 1969-70, Am. Cancer Soc., 1961; named one of Outstanding Young Men Am., 1968. Fellow Am. Bd. Urology, ACS, Am. Urol. Assn., Wash. State Urol. Bd. (mem. at large exec. com.); mem. AMA, Rubin Flocks Soc. (pres. 1985-86), Yakima Surgical Soc. (pres. 1982-83), Yakima County Med. Soc. (pres. 1989-90), Rotary. Roman Catholic. Home: 814 Conestoga Blvd Yakima WA 98908-2419 Office: Urology Clinic Yakima 206 S 11th Ave Yakima WA 98902-3205

NEWSTEAD, STEPHEN EDWARD, psychology educator; b. Scunthorpe, Lincolnshire, Eng., Dec. 27, 1946; s. Henry and Maria (Hookham) N.; m. Jane, Elizabeth Smith, July 31, 1970; children: Beth Ann, Amy Jane. B.A., Oxford U., 1969; Ph.D., Nottingham U., 1972. Lectr. psychology Bolton Inst. Higher Edn., Eng., 1972-73; sr. lectr. psychology U. Plymouth, 1973-83, head dept. psychology, 1983—, full prof., 1988—; course tutor Open U., Exeter, Eng., 1977-80; vis. prof. U. Fla., Gainesville, 1980-81. Contbr. articles to profl. jours.; editor acad. books. Bd. govs. Ivybridge Comprehensive Sch., Devon, Eng., 1981-85; councillor Ivybridge Town Council, 1983-86. Fellow Brit. Psychol. Soc. (dep. pres.); mem. Exptl. Psychology Soc., Assn. Heads of Psychology Depts. (vice-chair 1988-91), Council for Nat. Acad. Awards, Brit. Psychol. Soc. (dep. pres. 1991-94, pres. 1995-96). Club: Ivybridge Constitutional (Devon). Avocations: bridge, walking. Home: Ermeleigh Erme Rd, Ivybridge, Devon PL21 0AB, England Office: U Plymouth Dept Psychology, Drake Circus, Plymouth PL4 8AA, England

NEWTON, JAMES BRYON, physician associate; b. Kalamazoo, July 27, 1957; s. Roger Beck and Lenna Leora (Kern) N.; m. Roxanne Sue Telfer, Dec. 11, 1957; children: Rebekah Sue, Krystine Lynn. AAS in Law Enforcement, Kalamazoo U. C.C., 1985; B of Medicine, We. Mich. U., 1995. Cert. physician assoc. Paramedic Mall City Ambulance, Kalamazoo, 1977-80, 84-87, Mercy Ambulance, Kalamazoo, 1980-81; police officer Augusta (Mich.) Police, 1983-87, Sturgis (Mich.) Police, 1987-90; physician assoc. Bronson Physcian Svcs., Kalamazoo, 1994—. Recipient various police svc. awards. Mem. Am. Assn. Physician Associates, Mich. Assn. Physician Associates. Office: Bronson Physician Svcs 2121 Hudson Kalamazoo MI 49008

NEWTON, KATHY SUE, nursing educator; b. Grand Rapids, Mich., Aug. 29, 1956; d. Albert George and Irene Avis (Swain) Smith; m. Darrell Clayton Newton, July 3, 1981; children: Torri, Arminda, Samantha. Diploma in Nursing, Butterworth Hosp. Sch. Nursing, Grand Rapids, Mich., 1979; BS in Nursing, U. Mich., 1982; MS in Nursing, Wayne State U., Detroit, 1988. RN, Mich. Staff nurse Sparrow Hosp., Lansing, Mich., 1979-82; house supr. Hoyes Green Beach Hosp., Charlotte, Mich., 1983-84; nursing faculty Kellogg C.C., Battle Creek, Mich., 1984—; mem. adv. bd. So. Mich. Diabetes Outreach Network, Coldwater, 1996—; book reviewer J.B. Lippincott, 1993-95. Item writer NCLEX-PN, 1993, 95. Sunday Sch. tchr. Peace United Meth. Ch., Nashville, 1985—; vol. ARC, Grand Rapids area, 1979. Mem. NEA, Sigma Theta Tau. Home: 6324 Lawrence Rd Nashville MI 49073 Office: Kellogg CC 450 North Ave Battle Creek MI 49017

NEWTON, PYNKERTON DION, chiropractor; b. Marion, Ind., Nov. 9, 1960; s. John Walter Newton and Olivia (Taylor) McNair. BA, Ball State U., 1983, MA, 1986; D of Chiropractic, Logan Coll., 1992. Substitute tchr. Marion (Ind.) Community Schs., 1983-86; group leader Ops. Crossroads Africa, Kenya, 1986; acting asst. dir. admissions Ball State U., Muncie, Ind., 1986; corp. analyst Marine Midland Bank, N.Y.C., 1986-87, ops. mgr., 1987-89; admissions coord. Logan Coll. Chiropractic, St. Louis, 1989-92; chiropractic physician Pynkerton Chiropractic Group, P.C., Indpls., 1992—; cons. Logan Coll. Chiropractic, 1993-95. Grad. fellow Ball State U., 1984, 85, 4 Yr. Football scholar, 1979-83. Mem. NAACP, Am. Chiropractic Assn., Nat. Assn. Med. Minority Educators (cons. 1990-91), Ind. State Chiropractic Assn., Am. Black Chiropractic Assn. (exec. dir. 1995—), Schomburg Ctr. Rsch. Black Culture, Ball State U. Alumni Assn., Pi Kappa Chi. Democrat. Baptist. Office: 2102 E 52nd St Ste E Indianapolis IN 46205-1408

NEWTON, ROBERT DALLAS, JR., physician; b. N.Y.C., Aug. 7, 1957; s. Robert Dallas and Gloria Ann (Masselle) N.; m. Jane Cecilia Kolodzeki, Mar. 14, 1987; children: Marissa Anne, Robert Dallas III. BS, Pa. State U., 1979; MBA, Salisbury State U., 1984; DO, Kirksville Coll. Osteopath. Medicine, 1995; internship, So. Ill. U. Family Practice Meml. Hosp., Carbondale, Ill., 1995-96. Mgr. info. ctr. Perdue Farms Inc., Salisbury, Md., 1979-85; mgr. end user computing GTE Telenet, Reston, Va., 1985-86; mgr. office automation Martin Marietta Data Syss., Orlando, Fla., 1986-91; resident physician So. Ill. U. Family Practice, Carbondale, Ill., 1995—, chief resident, 1996. Mem. AMA, Am. Osteopathic Assn., Am. Acad. Family Physicians, Am. Coll. Osteopathic Family Physicians, Jackson County Med. Soc., Siverwood Cmty. Assn. (pres. 1987-88). Home: 601 W Walnut St Carbondale IL 62901 Office: SIU Family Practice 305 W Jackson St Ste 200 Carbondale IL 62901

NEWTON, SARAH ELIZABETH, clinical nurse, researcher and educator; b. Ann Arbor, Mich., Aug. 31, 1960; d. Maynard A. and Margery (Kenvin) N.; m. David Howard Maas. BSN, U. Mich., 1982, MS Med.-Surg. Nursing (Transplantation), 1987; PhC, 1994. RN, Mich. Clin. nurse U. Mich. Hosp., Ann Arbor, 1982—; clin. instr. U. Mich. Sch. Nursing, Ann Arbor, 1987-91, instr., 1992—; rsch. asst. U. Mich. Sch. Nursing, Ann Arbor, 1993; U.S. govt. profl. nurse trainee, 1985-86, 91-92. Mem. ANA, Mich. Nurses Assn., U. Mich. Alumni Assn., U. Mich. Nurses Alumni Assn., Sigma Theta Tau, Alpha Gamma Delta. Republican.

NEWTON, V. MILLER, medical psychotherapist, neuropsychologist, writer; b. Tampa, Fla., Sept. 6, 1938; s. Virgil M. Jr. and Louisa (Verri) N.; m. Ruth Ann Klink, Nov. 9, 1957; children: Johanna, Miller, Mark. BA, U. Fla., 1960; MDiv, Princeton Theol. Sem., 1963; postgrad., U. Geneva, Switzerland, 1962; PhD in Med. Anthropology, The Union Inst., 1981, PhD in Clin. Neuropsychology, 1993. Min. dir. Fletcher Pl. Urban Social Ministry, Indpls., 1963-65; coord. staff tng. and community rels. Breckinridge Job Corps Ctr., Ky., 1965-66; asst. prof., program dir. social scis. Webster Coll., St. Louis, 1966-69; assoc. prof., program dir. edn. U. South Fla., Tampa, 1969-73; clk. of the cir. ct. Pasco County, Fla., 1973-76; exec. dir. Fla. Alcohol Coalition, Inc., 1979-80; program and nat. clin. dir. Straight, Inc., St. Petersburg, Fla., 1980-83; dir. KIDS of North Jersey, Inc., 1983—; mem. Sec. Task Force Confidentiality and Client Info. System, Fla. Dept. of Health and Rehab. Svcs., 1979-80; chmn. pres.'s adv. Coun. Webster Coll., 1968-69; guest lectr. at the Grad. Inst. of Community Devel. So. Ill. U., 1968-69; cons. Tampa Model Cities Program, 1969-70; chmn. planning com. Tchr. Corps. Nat. Conf.; faculty mem. Internat. U. for Pres., Munich; co-chmn. Mayor's com. on Pre-sch. Edn., Indpls., 1964-65; speaker in field. Author: Gone Way Done: Teenage Drug-Use is a Disease, 1981, Kids, Drugs, and Sex, 1986, Adolescence: Guiding Youth Through the Perilous Ordeal, 1995; co-author: Not My Kid: A Parent's Guide to Kids and Drugs, 1984; appeared on TV programs NBC Mag., 1982, 1986 NBC, 1986, Drugs: A Plague upon America with Peter Jennings ABC, 1988; contbr. articles to profl. jours. Member drug abuse adv. coun. State of N.J., 1985-91; chmn., bd. dirs. Adjustment Madeira Beach, Fla., 1981—, Alcohol Community Treatment Svcs., Inc., Tampa, 1979; pres. Pasco County Coun. on Aging, 1977-79; chmn. bd. San Antonio Boys Village, 1975-76; chmn. Pasco County Data Ctr. Bd., 1973-75, Cen. Pasco Urban Planning Commn., 1972-73; adult del. White House Conf. on Youth, 1971; chmn. Nat. Tchr. Corps Field Coun., 1970-71; pres. Christian Inner City Assn., Indpls., 1964-65; mem. Gov. Ashew's Adv. Com., Pasco County, 1974-76. Aldersgate fellow, 1962; recipient Honor award Nat. LWV, 1963, Cert. Appreciation Pinellas County Bd. of County Commrs., 1982; named Outstanding Young Man of Yr., Indpls. Jaycees, 1965, Outstanding Govt. Leader, Dade City Jaycees, Fla., 1973-74. Mem. ACA, APHA, APA, Am. Bd. Med. Psychotherapists, Am. Anthrop. Assn., Nat. Acad. Neuropsychology (assoc.), Soc. Med. Anthropology, Ea. Psychol. Assn., Psychol. Anthropology, Soc. Behavioral Medicine, Soc. Adolescent Medicine, Phi Delta Theta, Rotary Internat., Order of DeMolay (state master counselor 1957). Democrat. Methodist. Office: KIDS of North Jersey PO Box 2455 Secaucus NJ 07096-2455

NEY, CHARLES, urologist; b. Harrisonburg, Va., June 20, 1912; s. Henry Ney and Julia Salamon; m. Doris Unger, Jan. 28, 1943; children: Alvin Henry, Steven Roger. BA, Johns Hopkins U., 1933, MD, 1937. Diplomate Am. Bd. Urology. Intern surgery Sinai Hosp., Balt., 1937-39; resident surgery Montefiore Hosp., N.Y.C., 1939-40, intern pathology, 1940-41; resident urology Morrisania City Hosp., N.Y.C., 1941-42; cons. urologist Einstein Sch. Medicine, N.Y.C., 1986—, Montefiore Hosp. and Med. Ctr., N.Y.C., 1986—, Bronx Lebanon Hosp. Ctr., N.Y.C., 1986—. Author: Radiographic Atlas G.U. System, 1966, 2d edit., 1981; contbr. articles to profl. jours. Lt. comdr. USN, 1942-46. Fellow ACS; mem. Am. Urol. Assn. Home: 340 Sugar Hill Rd Franconia NH 03580-5500

NEYLAN, JOHN FRANCIS, III, nephrologist, educator; b. Chgo., Feb. 20, 1953; s. John Francis and Mary Alice (Coogan) N.; m. Cynthia Barnes, May 17, 1980; children: John Francis IV, Elizabeth Marie. BS, Duke U., 1975; MD, Rush Med. Coll., Chgo., 1979. Intern in medicine Vanderbilt U., Nashville, 1979-80, resident, 1980-82; fellow in nephrology Brigham and Women's Hosp., Boston, 1983-84; fellow in immunogenetics Harvard U. Med. Sch., Boston, 1984-86, clin. preceptor, 1986; asst. prof. medicine U. Calif., Davis, 1986-88; asst. prof. medicine Emory U., Atlanta, 1988-93, assoc. prof., 1993—, med. dir. renal transplantation, 1988—; vis. cons. Wanless Hosp., Miraj, India, 1982-83; assoc. med. dir. Lifelink of Ga. Organ Procurement Orgn., Atlanta, 1989—; bd. govs. Lifelink Found., Tampa, Fla., 1988—. Editor: American Society of Transplant Physicians Newsletter, 1994—; contbr. articles and abstracts to med. jours., chpts. to books. Vol. Nat. Kidney Found., N.Y.C., 1990—, ARC, Atlanta, 1991, Spl. Olympics, Atlanta, 1991—, Habitat for Humanity, 1993—; chmn. Nat. Kidney Found. Coun. on Transplantation, 1995—. Recipient Physician's Recognition award AMA, 1989. Mem. ACP, Am. Fedn. Clin. Rsch. (councillor 1988), Am. Soc. Transplant Physicians (co-chmn. patient care com. 1988-90, chmn. 1991-93, councillor-at-large exec. coun. 1993-96, sec.-treas. 1996—, newsletter editor), Am. Soc. Nephrology, Internat. Soc. Nephrology, Transplantation Soc., United Network for Organ Sharing, Circumnavigator Club, Alpha Omega Alpha. Office: Emory U Hosp D240 1364 Clifton Rd NE Atlanta GA 30322

NEYMEYER, GARY DAVID, optometrist; b. Grundy Center, Iowa, Aug. 9, 1952; s. Allan Edwin and Janice (Van Heiden) N.; m. Linda Dykstra, Dec. 26, 1975. BS, U. Iowa, 1974; OD, Pacific Univ., Forest Grove, Oreg., 1978; Diagnostic/Therapeutic Degrees, U. Mo., St. Louis, 1990-92. Cert. optometrist, Mo., Oreg. Optometrist pvt. practice, Joplin, Mo., 1978—; Pacific U.

S.W. Mo. Optometric Soc. Office: Gary D Neymeyer OD PC 101 N Rangeline Ste 342 Joplin MO 64801

NEZIROGLU, FUGEN AYSE, psychologist; b. Istanbul, Turkey, Jan. 6, 1953; came to U.S. 1959; s. Cevat and Nezahat (Sehmen) N.; m. Jose Anibal Yaryura-Tobias, Oct. 21, 1978. BA in Psychology magna cum laude, Hofstra U., 1974, PhD, 1977; postgrad., Temple U., Phila., 1978, 79. Diplomate in clin. psychology Am. Bd. Profl. Psychology, in behavioral psychology Am. Bd. Behavioral Psychology; lic., psychologist, N.Y. Counselor Nassau County Children's Shelter, 1970-72; sch. psychology intern Farmingdale (N.Y.) Sch. Dist., 1975-76; intake examiner, counselor N. Nassau Mental Health Ctr., Manhasset, N.Y., 1972-76; counselor Nassau County Jail, East Meadow, N.Y., 1976-77; asst. psychologist North Nassau Mental Health Ctr., 1972-79, asst. rsch. psychologist, 1971-79, chief dept. exptl. psychology, 1977-79; rsch. assoc. NIMH, Hofstra U., Hempstead, N.Y., 1985-86; clin. dir., rsch. assoc., supr. clin. interns Bio-Behavior Psychiatry, Great Neck, N.Y., 1979—; staff psychologist Brunswick Psychiat. Hosp., Amityville, N.Y., 1986—; adj. courtesy staff Winthrop U. Hosp., Mineola, N.Y., 1983-92; adj. asst. prof. psychology Hofstra U., 1979-91, assoc. prof., 1991—; sr. cons. obsessive-compulsive disorder and anxiety disorders program South Oaks Hosp., 1992—, North Shore Hosp., 1996—. Author: Obsessive Compulsive Disorder: Pathogenesis, Diagnosis and Treatment, 1983, Over and Over Again: Understanding Obsessive Compulsive Disorder, 1991, others; editor Jour. Urban Psychiatry, 1980; contbr. many chpts. to books, articles to profl. jours. Grantee, Pfizer Co., Wyeth-Ayerst, Ciba-Geigy Corp., Eli Lilly Corp., others. Mem. APA, Anxiety Disorders Assn. Am., N.Y. State Psychol. Assn., Nassau County Psychol. Assn., Assn. for Advancement of Behavior Therapy, Nat. Register of Health Svc. Providers in Psychology, Internat. Soc. Rsch. on Aggression, Obsessive-Compulsive Found. (sci. adv. bd.), Phi Beta Kappa, Psi Chi. Office: Inst for Bio-Behavioral Therapy and Rsch 935 Northern Blvd Great Neck NY 11021-5309

NG, KHENG SIANG, cardiologist, educator, researcher; b. Singapore, Apr. 5, 1960; s. Siak Jinng and Wang Hong (Tan) N.; m. Lau Yung Sang, Oct. 24, 1991; children: Alyssa, Bertrand. MBBS, Nat. U. Singapore, 1984. House officer Ministry Health, Singapore, 1984-85; med. officer Ministry Defense, Artillery, Singapore, 1985-87; med. trainee Singapore Gen. Hosp. and Tan Tock Seng Hosp., Singapore, 1987-89; registrar Singapore Gen. Hosp., 1989-92; registrar Nat. U. Hosp., 1992-93, sr. registrar, 1993-95, cons., 1995—; clin. tutor Nat. U. of Singapore, 1989—; vis. cardiologist Med. Classification Ctr., Ctrl. Manpower Base, 1990—; vis. scientist Chang Gung Meml. Hosp., Taiwan, 1993; vis. fellow Stanford, Calif., 1994-95. Contbr. articles to profl. jours. Vol. Community Health Svc., Singapore, 1985-90, Singapore Coronary Club, 1992—. Recipient Pub. Svc. Commn. Local Merit award, 1979, Human Manpower Devel. Program award, 1993, Singapore Cardiac Soc. Young Investigators award, 1994. Fellow Singapore Acad. Medicine; mem. N.Am. Soc. Pacing and Electrophysiology, Royal Coll. Physicians and Surgeons (Glasgow), Singapore Cardiac Soc., Singapore Nat. Heart Assn. Office: Nat U Hosp, 5 Lower Kent Ridge Rd, Singapore 119074, Singapore

NG, LAWRENCE MING-LOY, pediatric cardiologist; b. Hong Kong, Mar. 21, 1940; came to U.S., 1967, naturalized, 1977; s. John Iu-cheung and Mary Wing (Wong) N.; m. Bella May Ha Kan, June 25, 1971; children: Jennifer Wing-mui, Jessica Wing-yee. B in Medicine, U. Hong Kong, 1965, B in Surgery, 1965. House physician Queen Elizabeth Hosp., Hong Kong, 1965-66, med. officer, 1966-67; resident physician Children's Hosp. of Los Angeles, 1967-68; resident physician Children's Hosp. Med. Center, Oakland, Calif., 1968-70, fellow in pediatric cardiology, 1970-72, now mem. teaching staff; practice medicine, specializing in pediatrics and pediatric cardiology, San Leandro, Calif., 1972—, Oakland, Calif., 1982—; mng. ptnr. Pediatric Med. Assocs. of East Bay, 1990—; chief of pediatrics Oakland Hosp., 1974-77; chief of pediatrics Vesper Meml. Hosp., 1977-79, sec. staff, 1984, v.p. staff, 1985; chief pediatrics Meml. Hosp., San Leandro, 1986-88; founder Pediatric Assocs. of East Bay, 1990. Active Republican Party. Diplomate Am. Bd. Pediatrics. Fellow Am. Acad. Pediatrics; mem. AMA, Calif. Med. Assn., Am. Heart Assn., Alameda County Assn. Primary Care Practitioners (membership chmn. 1993—, sec. treas 1994—), Los Angeles Pediatric Soc., East Bay Pediatric Soc., Smithsonian Assocs., Nat. Geog. Soc., Orgn. Chinese Ams. (chpt. pres. 1984), Chinese-Am. Physicians Soc. (co-founder, sec. 1980, pres. 1983), Chinese-Am. Polit. Assn. (life), Oakland Mus. Assns., Oakland Chinatown C. of C. (bd. dirs. 1986-91); Oakland Asian Cultural Cntr. (dir. 1996—), Hong Kong U. Alumni Assn. (sec. No. Calif. chpt. 1992—), Stanford U. Alumni Assn. (life), Chancellor's Assocs. U. Calif. at Berkeley, Commonwealth Club, Consumers' Union (life); Chinese Am. Golf Club. Buddhist. Office: 345 9th St Ste 204 Oakland CA 94607-4206 also: 101 Callan Ave Ste 401 San Leandro CA 94577-4519

NG, LORENZ K., neurologist, educator; b. Singapore, Aug. 6, 1940; came to U.S., 1958; s. Seak and Poh (Tan) N.; m. Roberta Melia, Dec. 7, 1981. BA, Stanford U., 1961; MD, Columbia U., 1965. Diplomate Am. Bd. Psychiatry and Neurology. Resident neurology U. Pa. Hosp., Phila., 1966-69; rsch. fellow NIMH, Bethesda, Md., 1969-72; spl. asst. to dir., chief rsch. lab., chief pain studies Nat. Inst. on Drug Abuse, Rockville, Md., 1972-81; dir. Washington Pain Ctr., 1982-86; med. dir. Chronic Pain program Nat. Rehab. Hosp., Washington, 1991—; pres., med. dir. Washington Pain and Rehab. Ctr., Inc., 1982-86; clin. prof. dept. neurology George Washington U., Washington, 1995—; vis. lectr. dept. neurosurgery Johns Hopkins Med. Sch.; mem. adv. coun. Alternative Medicine Program NIH, Bethesda, 1996—; spl. cons. Tan Tock Seng Hosp., Singapore, 1995—; bd. dirs. Am. Acad. Pain Medicine, Chgo., 1990-93, Reflex Sympathetic Dystrophy Syndrome Assn., N.J.; cons. Eli Lilly & Co. Author: (with S. Liao and M. Lee) Principles and Practice of Contemporary Acupuncture, 1994; editor: Alternatives to Violence, 1968, (with D. Davis) Strategies for Public Health, 1981, (with J. Bonica) Pain, Discomfort and Humanitarian Care, 1980, (with S. Mudd) Population Crisis: Implications and Plans for Action, 1965. Mem. bd. trustees Cosmos Club Found., Washington, 1993—; mem. adv. coun. Third World Found., Md., 1994; pres. Am. divsn. World Acad. Art and Sci., Mpls., 1982-93. Recipient S. Weir Mitchell award Am. Acad. Neurology, 1971, A.E. Bennett award Soc. Biol. Psychiatry, 1972, Commendation medal USPHS, 1981. Fellow Coll. of Physicians Phila., Am. Coll. Pain Medicine Chgo.; mem. Cosmos Club Washington. Home: 2026 R St NW Washington DC 20009 Office: Nat Rehab Hosp 3 Bethesda Metro Ctr # 950 Bethesda MD 20814

NG, REBECCA, optometrist; b. Oakland, Calif., Feb. 3, 1947; d. Kwong J. and Lena (Lum) N.; m. Dennis Henry Leroy, Feb. 27, 1983; children: Tamara Kim, Ailissa Nicole. BS, U. Calif. Berkeley, 1968, OD, 1970. Lic. Calif. Optometrist McLean Eye Clinic, Vicksburg, Miss., 1970-72, Kaiser Permanente, Fontana, Calif., 1972-74, Eye Ctr. Orange County, Laguna Hills, Calif., 1974—. Mem. Am. Optometry Assn., Calif. Optometry Assn. Office: Eye Ctr Orange County 24022 Calle dela Plata Laguna Hills CA 92653

NG, SOON-CHYE, gynecologist, scientist, educator; b. Singapore, Feb. 17, 1950; s. James Teng Su and Helen Gek Luang (Tan) N.; m. Kiat-Piah Tan, May 4, 1979; children: Yifan. MB, BS, U. Singapore, 1974; M in Medicine, Nat. U. Singapore, 1980, MD, 1989. Trainee U. Singapore, 1977-80; lectr. gynecology Nat. U. Singapore, 1980-83, sr. lectr., 1984-89, assoc. prof., 1990-93, prof., 1993—; head divsn. reproductive endocrinology Nat. U. Hosp., Singapore, 1995—. Developed micro-injection technique (subzonal sperm injection) and delivery. Fellow Acad. Medicine Singapore, Royal Coll. Obstetricians and Gynecologists (London, William Blair Bell meml. lectr. 1990); mem. AAAS, Ob-Gyn. Soc. Singapore (8th Henry Benjamin Sheares meml. lectr. 1989), Am. Fertility Soc., European Soc. Human Reproduction and Embryology, Soc. for Study Reproduction, Smithsonian Instn., N.Y. Acad. Sci., Nature Soc. Singapore (pres. 1995—). Office: Nat Univ Hosp Dept Ob-Gyn, Lower Kent Ridge Rd, Singapore 119074, Singapore

NGUYEN, THINH VAN, physician; b. Vietnam, Apr. 16, 1948; came to U.S., 1971; s. Thao Van and Phuong Thi (Tran) N.; m. Phi Thi Ho, Jan. 2, 1973; children: Anh-Quan, Andrew. BS, U. Saigon, 1970; MS, U. Mo., 1973; MD, U. Tex., 1982. Diplomate Am. Bd. Internal Medicine, Am. Acad. Pain Mgmt., Fed. Lic. Examination. Rsch. asst. U. Tex. Med. Sch., Dallas, 1974-78; intern U. Tex. Med. Br., Galveston, 1982-83, resident, 1983-85; internist Family Health Plan, Inc., Long Beach, Calif., 1985-88, internist, area chief, 1988-89; pvt. practice San Jose, Calif., 1990—; chmn. interdisciplinary com. Charter Cmty. Hosp., Hawaiian Gardens, Calif., 1988-89, San Jose Med. Ctr., 1993—. Fellow Am. Acad. Otolaryngic Allergy; mem. ACP, AMA, Am. Acad. Pain Mgmt., Calif. Assn. Med. Dirs. (bd. dirs. 1988-92). Office: 2470 Alvin Ave Ste 5 San Jose CA 95121-1664

NGUYEN-DINH, THANH, internist, geriatrician; b. Saigon, Vietnam; s. Bam and Chanh Thi (Duong) Nguyen-Dinh; m. Kim-Chi Nguyen-Dinh; children: Trung, Kim-Trang, Kim-Trinh, Trong. MD, Free U. Brussels, 1974; Tropical MD, Antwerp Tropical Med. Inst., 1975. Diplomate Am. Bd. Internal Medicine, Am. Bd. Geriatric Medicine. Asst. prof. medicine Howard Med. Svc., Washington, 1981-93; physician dir. St. Elizabeth Unit, D.C. Gen. Hosp., Washington, 1983-94; co-dir. Howard U. Md. Clinics, D.C. Gen. Hosp., 1990-96. Contbr. articles to profl. jours. Fellow ACP. Office: 611 S Carlin Springs Rd Ste 21 Arlington VA 22204-1061

NGUYEN-TRONG, HOANG, physician, consultant; b. Hue, Republic of Vietnam, Sept. 4, 1936; s. Nguyen-Trong Hiep and Nguyen-Phuoc Ton-nu-Thi Sung. B in Math., Lycée d'Etat Michel Montaigne, Bordeaux, 1956; state diploma of medicine, Sch. Medicine, Paris, 1966, also cert. aeronautical medicine and health and sanitation, 1965, diploma Health and Smoking, 1993; diploma post traumatic stress disorder, crises and disasters, The Am. U. and Centre Internat. de Scis. Criminelles de Paris, Washington, 1995. Resident surgeon Compiegne State Hosp., 1963-64, Meaux State Hosp., 1964-66, Lagny State Hosp., 1966; specialist in health and sanitation Paris Sch. Medicine, 1965—; specialist in family planning French Action of Family Planning, Paris, 1968—; practice medicine, Nanterre, France, 1969—; cons. physician various pharm. labs., Paris, 1987; investigator physician WHO regional office for Europe, 1991. Contbr. articles to profl. jours. Active mem. task force on tobacco dependency Biomed. Saints Péres Rsch. Unit, Paris, 1993, AIDS treatment assn. Le Val de Seine, 1993. Recipient World Decoration of Excellence, 1990, Commemorative Medal of Honor, 1990, Internat. Order of Merit, 1990. Mem. French Soc. Aviation and Space Physiology and Medicine (titulary, specialist in aviation medicine), Assn. Nanterre Physicians, Assn. Vietnamese Practitioners in France, Assn. Le Val de Seine, Chambre Syndicale des Medecins des Hauts de Seine, Ordre des Medecins des Hauts de Seine, Les Ex du XIV Shooting Club. Home: 3 Rue Gazan, 75014 Paris France Office: Cabinet Med Privé, 38 Rue des Fontenelles, 92000 Nanterre France

NICE, CHARLES MONROE, JR., physician, educator; b. Parsons, Kans., Dec. 21, 1919; s. Charles Monroe and Margaret (McClenahan) N.; m. Mary Ellen Cranmer, Dec. 21, 1940; children: Norma Jane Nice Murphy, Pamela, Deborah, Julianne, Charles Monroe III, Thomas, Mary Ellen, Rebecca. AB, U. Kans., MD, 1943; MSc in Medicine, U. Colo., 1948; PhD, U. Minn., 1956. Intern Grasslands Hosp., 1943-44; resident in radiology U. Minn. Hosp., 1948-50; mem. faculty U. Minn. Hosp., Mpls., 1951-58; prof. radiology Tulane U. Sch. Medicine, New Orlens, 1958—; chmn. dept. Tulane U. Sch. Medicine, 1960-85; mem. staff Charity Hosp., New Orleans, 1958—; mem. tng. com.investigative radiology NIH, 1967-69, mem. subcom. Sickle Cell, heart, lung, blood com., 1982-83; mem. com. on radiology NRC, 1965-67; chmn. tng. adv. com. Bur. Radiol. Health, 1970-72; guest lectr. Congress of Radiology, Japan, Colombian Radiol. Soc.; U.S. counselor Inter Am. Coll. Radiology, 1985-90. Author: Roentgen Diagnosis of Abdominal Tumors in Childhood, 1957, Clinical Roentgenology of Collagen Disease, 1966, Differential Diagnosis of Cardiovascular Disease by X-ray, 1966, Cardiovascular Roentgenology; a validated program, 1967, Cerebral Computed Tomography; contbr. articles to profl. jours. Served with AUS, 1944-46, PTO. Fellow Am. Coll. Chest Physicians (bd. gov's 1975-81), Am. Coll. Radiologists. Home: 508 Millaudon St New Orleans LA 70118-3805 Office: 1415 Tulane Ave New Orleans LA 70112-2699

NICE, RICHARD FAY, orthopedic surgeon; b. Sterling, Ill., Mar. 8, 1937; s. Fay Anthony and Gladys Marie (Clark) N.; m. Phyllis Jean Gleason, June 12, 1960; children: Christopher, Kyle. BA, Northwestern U., 1959, MD, 1962. Diplomate Am. Bd. Ortho. Surgery. Capt. U.S. Army, 1966-68, Vietnam. Office: Ortho Assn Ltd 1200 S Euclid Sioux Falls SD 57105

NICHOLAS, JAMES A., surgeon, consultant, educator; b. Portsmouth, Va., Apr. 15, 1921; s. Harry and Julia N.; m. Kiki Chris, June 14, 1952; children: Philip Duncan, Stephen James, Nicole Hambro. B.A., NYU, 1942; M.D., Downstate Med. Ctr., 1945. Diplomate Am. Bd. Orthopedic Surgery. Resident, various hosps. especially Hosp. Spl. Surgery, N.Y.C., 1946-52, asst. dir. research, 1952-60; dir. dept. orthopedic surgery Lenox Hill Hosp., N.Y.C., 1970—, dir. emeritus, 1995—, Nicholas Inst., dir. Inst. Sports Medicine and Athletic Trauma, 1973—, founding dir. Nicholas Inst. Sports Medicine, 1973—; dir. Gulf & Western Corp., N.Y.C., 1983—, Nat. Paramount Communications Inc.; cons. U.S. Army Hosp., West Point, N.Y., 1960-86, Bert Bell Retirement Plan, N.Y.C., 1984-88; orthopedic cons. NFL, N.Y.C., 1968—; mem. Presdl. Council Phys. Fitness in Sports, Washington, 1979-82, cons., 1983—; prof. orthopedic surgery Cornell Med. Coll., N.Y.C., 1970-95. Editor 15 books including: Injuries to the Spine and Lower Extremity in Sports Medicine, 1986, 2d edit., 1995, The Upper Extremity in Sports Medicine, 1990, 2d edit., 1996; patentee manual muscle tester. Trustee ctr. council Cornell U. Med. Ctr. N.Y. Hosp., 1986—; trustee Am. Jour. and Sports Medicine, 1980—. Served to capt. M.C. U.S. Army, 1945-46, 50-51, Korea. Spingold Found. grantee in sports medicine, 1976—; recipient Frank Babbott Disting. Alumnus award, 1985, Royal Order of Phoenix, Greek Govt. Service, 1970; named Health Am. Fitness Leader, Jaycees, 1982. Fellow ACS, Am. Orthopedic Assn.; mem. AOA, Orthopedic Research Soc. (sec. treas. 1968-69), Am. Orthopedic Soc. for Sports Medicine (pres. 1980, named Mr. Sports Medicine 1986), N.Y. Acad. Medicine (pres. 1974), Acad. Orthopaedic Soc. Greek Orthodox. Clubs: Mill Reef (Antigua, West Indies), Hellenic Univ., Westchester Country. Avocations: astronomy, golf, piano, synthesizer. Home: 22 Cayuga Rd Scarsdale NY 10583-6940 Office: 130 E 77th St New York NY 10021-1803

NICHOLAS, JOHN JEFFREY, physiatrist, educator; b. Murphysboro, Ill., Jan. 15, 1933; s. Charles Albert and Ethel Martha Elizabeth (Seaton) N.; m. Barbara Ann Knauff, Mar. 2, 1957; children: Sara Jeffrey, John Jeremiah, Matthew Calvin. AB, Harvard Coll., 1955; MD, Case Western Res. U., 1959. Intern SUNY, Syracuse, 1959-61, resident, 1963-65; instr. Syracuse Upstate N.Y. Med. Ctr., 1959-61, 63-69; from asst. to assoc. prof. Rehab. Inst. Chgo., 1969-72; from assoc. prof. to prof. U. Pitts., 1972-90; chmn., prof. Rush Presbyn. St. Luke's Med. Ctr., Chgo., 1990—. Capt. U.S. Army, 1961-63. Democrat. Episcopalian. Office: Rush Presbyn St Lukes Med Ctr 1725 W Harrison St Chicago IL 60612

NICHOLAS, NICKIE LEE, industrial hygienist; b. Lake Charles, La., Jan. 19, 1938; d. Clyde Lee and Jessie Mae (Lyons) N.; B.S., U. Houston, 1960, M.S., 1966. Tchr. sci. Pasadena (Tex.) Ind. Sch. Dist., 1960-61; chemist FDA, Dallas, 1961-62, VA Hosp., Houston, 1962-66; chief biochemist Baylor U. Coll. Medicine, 1966-68; chemist NASA, Johnson Spacecraft Center, 1968-73; analytical chemist TVA, Muscle Shoals, Ala., 1973-75; indsl. hygienist, compliance officer OSHA, Dept. Labor, Houston, 1975-79, area dir., Tulsa, 1979-82, mgr., Austin, 1982—; mem. faculty VA Sch. Med. Tech., Houston, 1963-66. Recipient award for outstanding achievement German embassy, 1958, Suggestion award VA, 1963, Group Achievement award Skylab Med. Team, NASA, 1974, Personal Achievement award Dept. Labor Fed. Women's Program, 1984, Career Achievement award Federally Employed Women, Inc., 1988, Meritorious Performance award DOL-OSHA, 1990, Disting. Career Svc. award Dept. Labor, 1991, Sec.'s Exceptional Achievement award Dept. Labor, 1991, Cert. Appreciation, OSHA, 1991, Asst. Sec.'s Leadership award DOL-OSHA, 1992. Mem. Am. Chem. Soc. (dir. analytical group Southeastern Tex. and Brazosport sects. 1971, chmn. elect 1973), Am. Assn. Clin. Chemists, Am. Conf. Govtl. Indsl. Hygienists, Am. Ind. Hygiene Assn., Am. Soc. Safety Engrs., Am. Harp Soc., Fed. Exec. Assn. (pres. 1984-85), Kappa Epsilon. Home: 1002 Sundance Ridge Rd Dripping Springs TX 78620-9501 Office: 903 San Jacinto Blvd Ste 319 Austin TX 78701-2450

NICHOLLS, DANNY WAYNE, orthopedic surgeon; b. Corpus Christi, Tex., Sept. 24, 1953; s. Ralph Wayne and Billie Louise (McMillen) N.; m. Carynn Elizabeth Cave, May 11, 1985 (div. 1995). BA in Biology, Ctrl. Wash. State Coll., 1976; BA in Sci. Edn., Ctrl. Wash. U., 1978; OD, Kirksville Coll. Osteo., 1982. Intern Sun Coast Hosp., Largo, Fla., 1983; flight surgeon USAF Clinic, Vance AFB, Okla., 1983-84, chief aeromed. svcs., 1984-85; chief orthopedic resident Dallas/Ft. Worth Med. Ctr., Grand Prairie, Tex., 1988-89, resident in orthopedics, 1989; chief orthopedic surgery 51st Tactical Hosp., Osan AB, Korea, 1989-90; staff orthopedic surgery 56th Tactical Hosp., MacDill AFB, Fla., 1990-91, chief orthopedic surgery, 1992-94; staff orthopedic surgery Sun Coast/Mofton Plant Hosps., Largo, Clearwater, Fla., 1991-92; surg. svcs. flight chief 6th Med. Group Hosp., MacDill AFB, 1994—. Lt. col. USAF, 1994—. Decorated USAF Commendation medal. Mem. Am. Osteo. Assn., Soc. Mil. Osteo. Surgeons, Am. Oste. Acad. Orthopedics, Assn. Mil. Osteo. Physicians and Surgeons. Home: PO Box 6133 MacDill AFB FL 33608 Office: 6th MDOSI SGOS 8421 Bayshore Blvd MacDill AFB FL 33621

NICHOLLS, RICHARD AURELIUS, obstetrician, gynecologist; b. Norfolk, Va., Aug. 12, 1941; s. Richard Beddoe and Aurelia (Gill) N.; m. Geri Bowden, Feb. 24, 1986. BS in Biology, Stetson U., 1963; MD, Med. Coll. Va., 1967. Diplomate Am. Bd. Ob-Gyn. Intern, Charity Hosp., Tulane div., New Orleans, 1967-68, resident in ob-gyn, 1968-71; asst. prof. ob-gyn Tulane Med. Sch., New Orleans, 1973-74, clin. asst. prof., 1974-83; practice medicine specializing in ob-gyn, Pascagoula, Miss., 1974-89; pvt. practice medicine, Ocean Spring, Miss., 1989—; mem. staff Singing River Hosp., chmn. surg. and ob-gyn depts., 1979-80, chmn. Ob-Gyn Dept., 1984, mem. staff Ocean Springs Hosp., laser com., pharmacy com., and theraputics com., chmn. OB-Gyn dept., mem. exec. bd., 1990-91; sec., treas. staff Ocean Springs Hosp., 1991-92, exec. bd., 1991-92, chief of staff elect, 1992-93, chief of staff, 1993-94; bd. dirs. Singing River Hosp. System, 1993-94. Bd. dirs. Miss. Racing Assn. Maj. US. Army, 1971-73. Fellow Am. Coll. Ob-Gyn, ACS; mem. Miss. State Med. Soc., Singing River Med. Soc., Am. Fertility Soc., Am. Assn. Gynecol. Laparoscopists, Am. Med. Soc., So. Med. Soc., New Orleans Grad. Med. Assembly, New Orleans Ob-Gyn Soc., Gulf Coast Ob-Gyn Soc., Conrad Collins Ob-Gyn Soc., Am. Venereal Disease Soc., Am. Cancer Soc. (bd. dirs Jackson County Br.). Contbr. articles to med. jours.

NICHOLS, BRENDA SUE, nursing educator; b. Henderson, Ky., Dec. 6, 1950; d. Marvin Elam and Cleona Jane (Bentley) Ashby; m. Harry David Nichols, Nov. 13, 1967; children: David Allen, Christopher Lynn, Thomas Andrew. AS in Nursing, U. Evansville, 1972, BSN, 1976, MA, 1978; DSc in Nursing, Ind. U., 1983. Staff nurse Community Meth. Hosp., Henderson, 1972-76, 81, 83; sch. nurse Evansville (Ind.)-Vandeburg Sch. Corp., 1977-78; nursing instr. Ky. Wesleyan Coll., Owensboro, 1978; asst. prof. U. Evansville, Ind., 1978-84; assoc. prof., dir. rsch. U. So. Miss., Hattiesburg, 1984-87; prof. nursing, dean sch. health sci. U. New Eng., N.Rivers, Lismore, Australia, 1987-90; assoc. prof., chair sch. nursing Old Dominion U., Norfolk, Va., 1990—; statis. cons. Dr. James Crumbaugh and R. Henrion, Biloxi, Miss., 1984-85; cons. Gold Coast Coll., Queensland, Australia, 1988-89, Mitchell Coll., Bathurst, Australia, 1988, Children's Hosp. of the Kings Daus., 1990-94; WHO cons. to U. Indonesia, 1995. Author: Nursing Theories, 1989; contbr. chpts. to book, articles to profl. jours.; NCLEX item writer, 1993—. Vol. Am. Cancer Soc., 1983—, Drug and Alcohol Prevention, Virginia Beach, Va., 1990-92. Fellow Am. Pain Soc., Royal Coll. Nursing; mem. ANA, Nat. League for Nursing (accreditation site visitor 1977—, program evaluator 1991—), Va. Assn. Colls. Nursing (sec. 1991), Va. League for Nursing (bd. dirs. 1996—). Democrat. Episcopalian. Home: 4620 Schooner Blvd Suffolk VA 23435 Office: Old Dominion U Sch Nursing Norfolk VA 23529-0500

NICHOLS, DAVID EARL, pharmacy educator, researcher, consultant; b. Covington, Ky., Dec. 23, 1944; s. Earl and Edythe Lee (Brooker) N.; m. Kathy J. Nichols; children: Charles D., Daniel P. BS, U. Cin., 1969; PhD, U. Iowa, 1973. Asst. prof. medicinal chemistry Purdue U., West Lafayette, Ind., 1974-79, assoc. prof., 1979-85, prof., 1985—; founder, pres. Heffter Rsch. Inst. Contbr. over 170 articles to sci. jours.; patentee in field. Grantee Nat. Inst. on Drug Abuse, 1978—, NIMH, 1978—. Fellow Am. Pharm. Assn., Am. Assn. Pharm. Scientists. Office: Purdue U Sch Pharmacy West Lafayette IN 47907

NICHOLS, DAVID HARRY, gynecologic surgeon, obstetrics and gynecology educator, author; b. Utica, N.Y., July 30, 1925; s. Harry Harrison and Katherine Valentine (Belknap) N.; m. Lorraine Elizabeth Landel, June 23, 1948; children: David L., Laurie L., Nancie L., Daniel A., Julie L. MD, U. Buffalo, 1947; MA (hon.), Brown U., 1982. Diplomate Am. Bd. Ob-Gyn. Intern E.J. Meyer Meml. Hosp., Buffalo, 1947-48; resident in ob-gyn Millard Fillmore Hosp., Buffalo, 1948-51; assoc. cancer rsch. gynecologist Roswell Pk. Meml. Inst., Buffalo, 1953-60; asst. clin. prof. ob-gyn SUNY, Buffalo, 1958-68, clin. prof., 1968-75, prof., 1975-80; prof. Brown U., Providence, 1980-92, chmn. dept. ob-gyn., 1980-91, dir. Ctr. for Women's Surgery, 1990-91; chief of pelvic reconstructive surgery Mass. Gen. Hosp., Boston, 1991—; pres. Erie County unit Am. Cancer Soc., 1962-68, Buffalo Ob/Gyn Soc., 1975-76; vis. prof. ob-gyn., reproductive biology Harvard U. Sch. Med., 1991—. Author: Atlas of Gynecological Pathology, 1951, Vaginal Surgery, 1976, 4th edit., 1996; author, editor: (med. monograph) Clinical Problems, Injuries, and Complications of GYN Surgery, 1983, 3d edit., 1995, Ambulatory Gynecology, 1985, 2d edit., 1995, Reoperative Gynecologic Surgery, 1991, Gynecologic and Obstetric Surgery, 1993. Maj. M.C., USAF, 1949-53. Fellow ACS, Am. Coll. Ob-Gyn., Internat. Coll. Surgeons, Boston Obstet. Soc.; mem. Soc. Pelvic Surgeons, Soc. Gynecol. Surgeons (nat. pres. 1984-85), N.E. Obstet. Soc., Boston Obstet. Soc., Am. Gyn. Club (pres. 1993-94), Harvard Club. Republican. Roman Catholic. Office: Mass Gen Hosp Vincent 1 Boston MA 02114 Address: 101 Prospect St Providence RI 02906-1440

NICHOLS, ELIZABETH GRACE, nursing educator, administrator; b. Tehran, Iran, Feb. 1, 1943; came to U.S., 1964; d. Terence and Eleanor Denny (Payne) Quilliam; m. Gerald Ray Nichols, Nov. 20, 1965; children: Tina Lynn, Jeffrey David. BSN, San Francisco State U., 1969; MS, U. Calif.-San Francisco, 1970, Dr. Nursing Sci., 1974, MA Idaho State U., 1989. Staff nurse Peninsula Hosp., Burlingame, Calif., 1966-72; asst. prof. U. Calif.-San Francisco Sch. Nursing, 1974-82; chmn. dept. nursing Idaho State U., Pocatello, 1982-85; assoc. dean Coll. Health Scis. Sch. Nursing U. Wyo., Laramie, 1985-91, asst. to pres. for program reviews, 1991-95, dean Coll. Nursing, U. N.D., 1995—; cons. U. Rochester, N.Y., 1979, Carroll Coll., Mont., 1980, div. Nursing Dept. HHS, Washington, 1980, 84, 85, 86, 87, Stanford Hosp. Nursing Service, Calif., 1981-82, Ea. N.Mex. U., 1988. Contbr. articles on nursing to profl. jours. Mem. adv. bd. dirs. Ombudsman Service of Contra Costa Calif., 1979-82, U. Calif. Home Care Service, San Francisco, 1975-82, Free Clinic of Pocatello, 1984. ACE fellow U. Maine system 1990-91. Fellow ACE, Gerontol. Soc. Am., Am. Acad. Nursing; mem. Gerontol. Soc. Am. (chmn. clin. medicine section 1987, sec. 1990-93), Am. Nurses Assn., Wyo. Nurses Assn., Idaho Nurses Assn. (dist. 51 adv. bd. dirs. 1982-84), Western Inst. Nursing (chair, 1990-92, bd. govs.). Club: Oakland Ski (1st v.p. 1981-82). (Calif.).

NICHOLS, FENWICK TATTNALL, III, neurology educator; b. Jacksonville, Fla., Oct. 26, 1950; s. Fenwick Tattnall Jr. and Jean Caroline (Williams) N.; m. Martha Easler, Mar. 21, 1992. BA in Chemistry, Duke U., 1972; MD, Med. Coll. Ga., 1976. Intern in pediatric medicine Grady Meml. Hosp., Atlanta, 1976-77; resident in internal medicine U. South Ala. Med. Ctr., Mobile, 1977-79; resident in neurology Med. Coll. Ga., Augusta, 1979-82, asst. prof. neurology, 1982-83, 85-89, assoc. prof., 1989-96, prof., 1996—; fellow in cerebrovascular disease Columbia-Presbyn. Neurol. Inst., N.Y.C., 1983-85. Fellow ACP; mem. AMA, Am. Acad. Neurology, Am. Soc. Neuroimaging, Am. Soc. Internal Medicine, Am. Inst. Ultrasound in Medicine, Am. Coll. Clin. Pharmacology, So Med. Assn. Office: Med Coll Ga Dept Neurology Augusta GA 30912

NICHOLS, JEFFREY NORMAN, internist; b. Ithaca, N.Y., Aug. 22, 1947; s. Benjamin and Ethel G. Nichols; m. Arlene Ellen Katz, June 4, 1967; children: Daniel, Sara, Gabriel. BA, Columbia U., 1968; MD, Cornell U., 1976. Diplomate Am. Bd. Internal Medicine with subspecialty in geriatrics. Dir. profl. affairs Elderplan, Bklyn., 1986-87; med. dir. Frances Sclervior Home and Hosp., Bronx, 1987-94, Cabrini Hursing Home, N.Y.C., 1994—; chief geriatrics Cabrini Med. Ctr., N.Y.C., 1994—; cons. med. affairs Franciscan Sisters of the Poor Found., N.Y.C., 1989—; chmn. ethics com. Cabrini Nursing Home, 1995—. Fres. Svc. Program for Older People, N.Y.C., 1991—; bd. dirs. N.Y. Coalition Against Hunger, N.Y.C., 1993—; bd. dirs., co-chair social action com. Congregation Ansche Chesed, N.Y.C., 1990—. Fellow N.Y. Acad. Medicine; mem. N.Y. Med. Dirs. Assn. (bd.

dirs. 1988—), Met. ARea Geriatrics Soc. (bd. dirs. 1988-92, 95—). Democrat. Jewish. Office: Cabrini Medical Center 227 E 19th St Rm 431 New York NY 10003

NICHOLS, JOSEPH, implant technology executive; b. N.Y.C., July 9, 1917; s. Nathan and Minnie (Minken) N.; m. Sylvia Dickler, July 13, 1951; children: Peter, Robert. BS, CCNY, 1938, MS, 1942; PhD, U. Minn., 1943; postgrad., Fed. Inst. Tech., Zurich, Switzerland, 1950-51. Sr. chemist Interchen. Corp., N.Y.C., 1943-49; from chief organic chemistry to dir. rsch. Ethicon, Inc., New Brunswick, N.J., 1951-68; pres. Princeton (N.J.) Biomedix Inc., 1968-76, Helitrex Inc., Princeton, 1976-85; v.p. rsch. and devel. Am. Biomaterials Corp., Plainsboro, N.J., 1985-86; pres. Prodex Inc., Princeton, 1986—. Patentee in field; contbr. articles to profl. jours. Recipient Johnson medal, Johnson & Johnson Co., 1965. Mem. Am. Chem. Soc., AAAS, Soc. Biomaterials, Am. Assn. Artificial Internal Organs, N.Y. Acad. Scis. Home: 28 Longview Dr Princeton NJ 08540-5637 Office: Prodex Inc 3490 Us Highway 1 Princeton NJ 08540-5920

NICHOLS, RONALD LEE, surgeon, educator; b. Chgo., June 25, 1941; s. Peter Raymond and Jane Eleanor (Johnson) N.; m. Elsa Elaine Johnson, Dec. 4, 1964; children: Kimberly Jane, Matthew Bennett. MD, U. Ill., 1966, MS, 1970. Diplomate: Am. Bd. Surgery (assoc. cert. examiner, New Orleans, 1991), Nat. Bd. Med. Examiners. Intern U. Ill. Hosp., Chgo., 1966-67, resident in surgery, 1967-72, instr. surgery, 1970-72, asst. prof. surgery, 1972-74; assoc. prof. surgery U. Health Scis. Chgo. Med. Sch., 1975-77, dir. surg. edn., 1975-77; William Henderson prof. surgery Tulane U. Sch. Medicine, New Orleans, 1977—, vice chmn. dept. surgery, 1982-91, staff surgeon, 1977—, prof. microbiology, immunology and surgery, 1979—; cons. surgeon VA Hosp., Alexandria, La., 1978-93, Huey P. Long Hosp., Pineville, La., 1978—, Lallie Kemp Charity Hosp., Independence, La., 1977-85, Touro Infirmary, New Orleans, Monmouth Med. Ctr., Long Branch, N.J., 1979-88; mem. VA Coop. Study Rev. Bd., 1978-81, VA Merit Rev. Bd. in Surgery, 1979-82; mem. sci. program com. 3d Internat. Conf. Nosocomial Infections, Ctr. Disease Control, mem. sci. program and fundraising com. 4th Internat. Conf.; bd. dirs. Nat. Found. Infectious Diseases, 1989—, v.p., 1994—; hon. fellow faculty Kasr El Aini Cairo U. Sch. Medicine, 1989; mem. adv. com. on infection control Ctrs. for Disease Control, 1991-95; disting. guest, vis. prof. Royal Coll. Surgeons Thailand 14th Ann. Clin. Congress, 1989, 17th Ann. Clin. Congress, 1992; mem. infectious diseases adv. bd. Roche Labs., 1988-95, Abbott Labs., 1990-92, Kimberly Clark Corp., 1990—, SmithKline Beecham Labs., 1990-95, Fujisawa Pharm., chmn., 1990—, Bayer Pharm., 1994—, Merck Sharpe Dohme, 1996, Depotech, 1996; mem. study group Prophylaxis Antibiotic Project La. Health Care Rev., Inc., 1995—; mem. adv. panel Gen. Drug Info. Divsn. of U.S. Pharmacopeia, 1995—. Author: (with Gorbach, Bartlett and Nichols) Manual of Surgical Infection, 1984; author, guest editor: (with Nichols, Hyslop Jr. and Bartlett) Decision Mking in Surgical Sepsis, 1991; guest editor, author: Surgical Sepsis and Beyond, 1993; mem. editl. bd. Current Surgery, 1977—, Hosp. Physician, 1980—, Infection Control, 1980-86, Guidelines to Antibiotic Therapy, 1976-81, Am. Jour. Infection Control, 1981—, Internat. Medicine, 1983—, Confronting Infection, 1983-86, Current Concepts in Clin. Surgery, 1984—, Fact Line, 1984-91, Host/Pathogen News, 1984—, Infectious Diseases in Clin. Practice, 1991—, surg. sect. editor, 1992—, Surg. Infections: Index and Revs., 1991—, So. Med. Jour., 1992—, ANAEROBE, 1994—; mem. adv. bd. Physician News Network, 1991-95; patentee (with S.G. schoenberger and W.R. Rank) Helical-Tipped Lesion Localization Needle Device. Elected faculty sponsor graduating class Tulane Med. Sch., 1979-80, 83, 85, 87, 88, 91-92. Served to major USAR, 1972-75. Recipient House Staff teaching award U. Ill. Coll. Medicine, 1973, Rsch. award Bd. Trustees U. Health Scis.-Chgo. Med. Sch., 1977, Owl Club Teaching award, 1980-86, 90; named Clin. Prof. of Yr. U. Health Scis., Chgo. Med. Sch., 1977, Clin. Prof. of Yr., Tulane U. Sch. Medicine, 1979; Douglas Stubbs Lectr. award Surg. Sect. Nat. Med. Assn., 1987, Prix d'Elegance award Men of Fashion, New Orleans, 1993. Fellow Infectious Disease Soc. Am. (mem. FDA subcom. to develop guidelines in surg. prophylaxis 1989-93, co-recipient Joseph Susman Meml. award 1990), Am. Acad. Microbiology, Internat. Soc. Univ. Colon and Rectal Surgeons, ACS (bd. dirs. 1978-80, vice chair 1981-83, chmn. operating room environment com. 1981-83, internat. relations com. 1987-93, sr. mem. 1983-87, 94—); mem. AMA, Nat. Found. for Infectious Diseases (bd. dirs. 1988—, v.p. 1994—), Joint Commn. on Accreditation of Health Care Orgn. (Infection Control adv. group, 1988—, sci. program com. 3d internat. conf. nosocomial infections CDC/Nat. Found. Infectious Diseases 1990, FDA Subcom. to Develop Guidelines in Surg. Prophylaxis, prophylactic antibiotic study groc. 1996—, AIDS commr. State of La. 1992-94), 5th Nat. Forum on AIDS (sci. program com.), U.S. Pharmacopeial Convention Inc. (adv. panel gen. drug info. divsn., surg. drugs and devices 1995—), Assn. Practitioners in Infection Control (physician adv. coun. 1991—), Internat. Soc. Anaerobic Bacteria, So. Med. Assn. (vice chmn. sect. surgery 1980-81, chmn. 1982-83), Assn. Acad. Surgery, N.Y. Acad. Sci., Warren H. Cole Soc. (pres.-elect 1988, pres. 1989-90), Assn. VA Surgeons, Soc. Surgery Alimentary Tract, Inst. Medicine Chgo., Midwest Surg. Assn., Cen. Surg. Assn., Ill. Surg. Soc., European Soc. Surg. Rsch., Collegium Internationale Chirugiae Digestivae, Chgo. Surg. Soc. (hon.), New Orleans Surg. Soc. (bd. dirs. 1983-87), Soc. Univ. Surgeons, Surg. Soc. La., Southeastern Surg. Soc., Phoenix Surg. Soc. (hon.), Hellenic Surg. Soc. (hon.), Cen. N.Y. Surg. Soc. (hon.), Tulane Surg. Soc., Alton Ochsner Surg. Soc., Am. Soc. Microbiology, Soc. Internat. de Chirugie, Surg. Infection Soc. (sci. study com. 1982-83, fellowship com. 1985-87, ad hoc sci. liaison com. 1986-89, program com. 1986-87, chmn. ad hoc com. rels. with industry 1990-93, mem. sci. liaison com. 1995-96), Soc. for Intestinal Microbial Ecology and Disease, Soc. Critical Care Medicine, Am. Surg. Assn., Kansas City Surg. Soc., Bay Surg. Soc. (hon.), Cuban Surg. Soc. (hon.), Panhellenic Surg. Soc. (hon.), Sigma Xi, Alpha Omega Alpha. Episcopalian. Home: 1521 7th St New Orleans LA 70115-3322 Office: 1430 Tulane Ave New Orleans LA 70112-2699

NICHOLS, SANDRA B., public health service officer; b. Little Rock, Mar. 27, 1958; m. Ronnie A. Nichols, 1985; 1 child, Marquise. BA in Chemistry, Columbia Coll., Mo., 1980; student, Meharry Med. Coll., 1979-80; MS in Biology, Tenn. State U., 1982; MD, U. Ark., 1988. With dept. physiology U. Ark. Med. Scis., Little Rock, 1984-85, with microbiology lab., 1985-88, resident dept. family and community medicine, 1988-91, chief resident dept. family and community medicine, 1990-91, fellow dept. family and community medicine, occupational and environ. medicine, 1991-92; dir. Ark. Dept. of Health, Little Rock, 1994—; physician Mid Delta Health Clinic, 1992—, interim med. dir., 1993-94; med. educator Delta Area Health Agy., U. Ark. Med. Scis., 1992—. Author: (with others) Family Practice textbook. Officer HHS, FDA; co-chair Pine Bluff Arsenal Citizen's Adv. Com.; mem. Gov.'s Partnership Coun. for Children and Families, Women Execs. in State Govt.; conf. participant Am. Swiss Found. Young Leaders Conf., 1995; mem. Ark. chpt. Internat. Women's Forum; mem. Ark. Arts Ctr.; spkr. Career Day, local schs.; vol. physician high schs. Recipient Nat. FBI Comty. Leadership award, 1996; named one of Ark. Bus. Top 100 Women in Ark., 1996, Top 10 Women in Ark., 1995, one of Outstanding Young Women in Am., 1981; Nat. Med. fellow, 1984-85; Pub. Health Leadership Inst. scholar, 1996, scholar Columbia Coll., 1976-80. Office: Ark Dept of Health Ste 39 4815 Markham St Little Rock AR 72205-3867

NICHOLS, TERRI DAWN MORRIS, nurse; b. Torrington, Wyo., May 17, 1958; d. Donald C. and Jackie (Steben) Morris; m. Lee Fredrick Nichols III, May 19, 1984. Diploma, Sch. Nursing, West Nebr. Gen. Hosp., 1979. RN, Wyo., Wis., Ga. Staff nurse, office mgr. to pvt. practice physician Laramie, Wyo., 1979-81; staff nurse, then nurse mgr. Meml. Hosp. Carbon County, Rawlins, Wyo., 1981-84; nurse mgr. Mercy Med. Ctr., Oshkosh, Wis., 1984-87, Med. Ctr. Cen. Ga., Macon, 1987-89; nursing adminstr. Bolingreen Care Ctr., Macon, Ga., 1989-90; nurse mgr. ortho., social svcs., past care and util. mgmt. Ivinson Meml. Hosp., Laramie, Wyo., 1990-96; asst. adminstr. quality Parkview Regional Hosp., Mexia, Tex., 1996—; cons. Internat. Childbirth Edn. Assn., 1983-84, Childbirth Educators, Oshkosh, 1984; cons. in collaborative practice; presenter seminars and ednl. programs. Bd. dirs. Carbon County Juvenile Planning Com., 1983, Carbon County Child Protection Team, 1983; bd. dirs. profl. edn. com. Am. Cancer Soc., Oshkosh, 1985; assoc. Sisters of Sorrowful Mother, Milw., 1985; vol. coord. Nurses' Day, Habitat for Humanity, 1993, 94, bd. dirs. Albany, 1995; chair Albany County/Laramie Environ. Com., 1994. Mem. Nat. Assn. Healthcare Quality, Wyo. Dist. Nurses Assn. (sec., bd. dirs. 1983), Wis. Polit. Action Com. (bd. dirs. 1986), Wis. Nurses Assn. (bd. dirs.), Wis. Dist. Nurses Assn. (pres. 1986), Am. Orgn. Nurse Execs. Affiliate. Office: Parkview Regional Hosp 312 Glendale Mexia TX 76667

NICHOLSON, CHARLES HENRY, surgeon; b. Harlan, Ky., Feb. 20, 1931; s. Esther Charles and Nola Nicholson; m. Jacqueline R. Cornett; children: Beth, George, David. BA, Vanderbilt U., 1951, MD, 1955. Diplomate Am. Bd. Surgery, Am. Bd. Thoracic Surgery. Intern Strong Meml. Hosp. Univ. Rochester, N.Y., 1956-59, chief resident, 1959-60, instr. in surgery, 1963; sr. instr. Univ. Rochester, 1963; fellow cardiac surgery Univ. Fla., 1964; gen. and thoracic surgeon Lexington (Ky.) Clinic, 1964-96, chief dept. surgery, 1973-78, 90—; chief thoracic surgery St. Joseph Hosp., 1972-77, chief gen. surgery, 1973-80; clin. prof. U. Ky. Med. Ctr.; courtesy staff Ctrl. Bapt. Hosp., Lexington, Good Samaritan Hosp., Lexington; spkr. in field. Contbr. articles to profl. jours. Treas. Ky. Blood Ctr., 1980. Capt. USAF, 1960-63. Mem. AMA, Am. Coll. Surgeons (pres. Ky. chpt. 1982, chmn. credentials com. Ky. dist. 1988-92, membership com. 1980), Ky. Surg. Soc., Ky. Med. Assn. (del. Fayette County 1978-85), Lexington Surg. Soc. (pres. 1980, v.p. 1979, sec.-treas. 1976-78) Fayette County Med. Soc. (v.p. 1981, mem. adminstrv. coun. 1980), So. Vascular Soc., So. Surg. Assn. Methodist. Office: Lexington Clinic 12215 Broadway Lexington KY 40501

NICHOLSON, CHARLES PRESTON, JR., surgeon; b. Rome, Ga., Feb. 24, 1934; s. Charles Preston and Lois (Pettit) N.; m. Mary Jo, Dec. 12, 1959; children: Charles Preston III, John Michael, Daniel Lamar. BA, Vanderbilt U., 1955; MD, U. Tenn., 1958. Diplomate Am. Bd. Surgery. Intern Grady Meml. Hosp., Atlanta, 1959-60; resident N.C. Meml. Hosp., Chapel Hill, 1960-65; chief resident, 1964-65; pvt. practice Morehead City, N.C., 1965-95; sr. aviation med. examiner, aviation safety counselor FAA. Organizer, pres. Mothers Against Drunk Driving, Carteret County, N.C., 1988; trustee N.C. Bapt. Hosp., Winston-Salem. Fellow ACS, Am. Assn. Surgery of Trauma, Southeastern Surg. Congress, So. Med. Assn., Soc. Am. Gastrointestinal Endoscopic Surgeons, Aeromed, Adv. Coun., Exptl. Aircraft Assn. Republican. Baptist. Home: 5936 Londonderry Ct NW Concord NC 28027 Office: Concord Regional Airport 9000 Aviation Blvd Concord NC 28027

NICHOLSON, ELLEN ELLIS, clinical social worker; b. Boston, Apr. 1, 1940; d. George Letham and Mary Stirling (Money) McIver; divorced; 1 child, Matthew Norman Ellis. Dental Hygienist, Forsyth Coll., 1959; BS, Northeastern U., 1973, MEd in Counseling, 1974; MSW, Boston U., 1984. Registered dental hygienist, Mass. Dental hygienist, 1959-66; clin. coord., pvt. dental practice Forsyth Dental Ctr., Boston, 1966-70; dir. vol. counseling Solomon Mental Health Ctr., Lowell, Mass., 1974-75; social worker East Boston Social Ctrs., Inc., 1976-77, dir. youth family counseling, 1977-79; supr. family svc. Boston Housing Authority, 1979-81; social worker Mass. Soc. Prevention Cruelty to Children, Hyannis, 1984-86, supr., 1986-93, clinic dir., 1993-95; dir. profl. svcs. Child and Family Svc. of Cape Cod, Hyannis, 1995—; dir. Abuse Prevention Svcs. Child and Family Svc. of Cape Cod, 1995—; psychotherapist Riverview Sch., Sandwich, Mass., 1989-93. Advisor youth group Christ Episcopal Ch., Needham, Mass., 1960-64, St. Paul's Ch., Newburyport, Mass., 1964-65; vol. counselor Solomon Mental Health Ctr., Lowell, 1972-74; chair Barnstable County Children's Task Force; chair adv. com. Carnstable County Sexual Abuse Intervention Network; mem. Barnstable County Juvenile Firesetters Task Force. Mem. ANASW, Am. Profl. Soc. on Abuse of Children, Assn. for Treatment of Sexual Abusers, Sigma Phi Alpha, Sigma Epsilon Rho, Kappa Delta Pi. Office: Child & Family Svc of Cape Cod 1019 Rte 132 Hyannis MA 02601

NICHOLSON, GERALD LEE, medical facilities administrator; b. Belleville, Ill., Dec. 30, 1944; s. Chester Lee and Bette Joan (Tarr) N.; m. Cathy Ann Sammons, May 3, 1975; children: Laura, Brianna. BA in Sociology, So. Ill. U., 1974, BS in Math., 1976, MBA, 1976. Bus. mgr. Northland Orthopedic Group, St. Louis, 1976-78; cons. AMA, Chgo., 1978-80; cons. pvt. practice Evansville, Ind., 1981-85; adminstr. Mo. Eye Inst., St. Louis, 1985-91; regional v.p. Co-Care Eye Ctrs., St. Louis, 1985-91; adminstr. Orthopaedic Assoc., P.C., Cape Girardeau, Mo., 1992—; tax preparer Nicholson Cons., St. Louis, 1990-92. Mem. Citizen Interaction Com., Chesterfield, Mo., 1989, Leadership Cape, 1992. Capt. USMC, 1966-72, Vietnam. Mem. Marine Corps Res. Officers Assn., Am. Coll. Med. Practice Execs., Med. Group Mgrs. Assn., S.E. Mo. Med. Mgrs. (pres.), Aircraft Owners and Pilots Assn., Rotary Internat. (pres. club). Home: 3010 Melrose St Cape Girardeau MO 63703-2200 Office: Orthopedic Assocs of SE Mo PC 48 Doctors Park Cape Girardeau MO 63703

NICKEL, HORST WILHELM, psychology educator; b. Spangenberg, Hessen, Germany, Sept. 30, 1929; s. Konrad and Marie Nickel; m. Irmtraud Ulm, Sept. 26, 1959; children: Wolfram, Cordula. Tchr. exam., Tchrs. Coll., Weilburg/Lahn, Fed. Republic Germany, 1953; diploma in psychology, U. Marburg/Lahn, Fed. Republic Germany, 1961; PhD, U. Erlangen-Nuernberg, Fed. Republic Germany, 1965. Tchr. primary sch., Hessen, 1953-57; lectr. Tchrs. Coll., Weilburg, Lahn, 1957-62, U. Bayreuth, Fed. Republic Germany, 1962-65; sr. lectr. U. Hamburg, Fed. Republic Germany, 1965-67; prof. Tchrs. Coll., Flensburg, Fed. Republic Germany, 1967-69, Bonn, Fed. Republic Germany, 1969-72; prof. psychology, chmn. dept. U. Düsseldorf, Fed. Republic Germany, 1972-94, emeritus prof., 1994—; cons. prof. dept. psychology U. Ga., Athens, 1987-91. Author 27 books including Entwicklunspsychologie des Kindes-und Jugendalters, vol. 2, 3d edit., 1981, vol. 1, 4th edit., 1982, Psychologie des Lehrerverhaltens, 2d edit., 1978, Begriffsbildung im Kindesalter, 1984, Sozialisation im Vorschulalter, 1985, Psychologie der Entwicklung und Erziehung, 1993, Eltern-Kind-Spielgruppen, 1996; co-author: Psychologie in der Erziehungswissenschaft 4 Vol., 1976-78, Erzieher-und Elternverhalten im Vorschulbereich, 1980, Sozialverhalten von Vorschulkindern, 1980, Modelle und Fallstudien der Schul-und Erziehungsberatung, 1982, Oekopsychologie der Entwicklung im fruhen Kindesalter, 1987, Vom Kleinkind zum Schulkind, 5th edit., 1995, Begabung und Hochbegabung, 1992, Leben, Lernen und Lehren in der Grundschule, 1996; editor Psychologie in Erziehung und Unterricht, also over 200 articles, 15 tests and questionnaires. Mem. German Soc. for Psychology, Internat. Soc. Pre- and Perinatal Psychology and Medicine, Internat. Soc. for Study Behavioural Devel. Home: Berliner Strasse 25, D-53340 Meckenheim Germany Office: Heinrich-Heine U, Universtiätsstrasse 1, D-40225 Düsseldorf Germany

NICKEL, JANET MARLENE MILTON, geriatrics nurse; b. Manitowoc, Wis., June 9, 1940; d. Ashley and Pearl (Kerr) Milton; m. Curtis A. Nickel, July 29, 1961; children: Cassie, Debra, Susan. Diploma, Milw. Inst., 1961; ADN, N.D. State U., 1988. Nurse Milw. VA, Wood, Wis., 1961-62; supervising nurse Park Lawn Convalescent Hosp., Manitowoc, 1964-65; newsletter editor Fargo (N.D.) Model Cities Program, 1970-73; supervising night nurse Rosewood on Broadway, Luth. Hosps. and Homes, Fargo, 1973-92; assoc. dir. nursing Elim Nursing Home, Fargo, 1992-94, night nurse, 1994—. Mem. Phi Eta Sigma. Home: 225 19th Ave N Fargo ND 58102-2352 Office: 3534 S University Dr Fargo ND 58104-6228

NICKELSON, KIM RENÉ, internist; b. Chgo., Feb. 13, 1956; d. Robert William and Carolynn Lucille (Marts) N.; m. Louis Peter Sguros; children: Brian Louis, Justin Robert Peter. BS in Chemistry, U. Ill., 1978; MD, Loyola U., Maywood, Ill., 1981. Diplomate Am. Bd. Internal Medicine. Intern and resident in internal medicine Luth. Gen. Hosp., Park Ridge, Ill., 1981-84; pvt. practice Oakbrook, Ill., 1984-87, Plantation, Fla., 1987—; adj. attending staff Rush-Presbyn. St. Luke's Med. Ctr., Chgo., 1984-87; assoc. attending staff Hinsdale (Ill.) Hosp., 1984-87, Westside Regional Med. Ctr., Plantation, Plantation Gen. Hosp., Fla. Med. Ctr. South, Plantation. Musician Elk Grove (Ill.) Community Band, 1978-87, Hollywood (Fla.) Symphony Orch., 1987—, Sunrise (Fla.) Pops Symphony, 1987—, Deerfield (Fla.) Community Band, 1987—. Mem. ACP, Internat. Horn Soc. Office: Internal Medicine Assocs 499 NW 70th Ave Ste 200 Plantation FL 33317-7573

NICKERSON, PETER AYERS, pathology educator; b. Hyannis, Mass., Feb. 19, 1941; s. Norman O. and Ruth (Ayers) N. AB, Brown U., 1963; MA, Clark U., 1965, PhD, 1968. Teaching asst. Clark U., Worcester, Mass., 1963-66, NASA predoctoral fellow, 1966, USPHS predoctoral fellow, 1966-67; rsch. instr. SUNY, Buffalo, 1967-69, asst. prof., then assoc. prof., 1969-80, prof. dept. pathology, 1980—, dir. grad. studies, 1974—; corp. mem. Marine Biol. Lab., Woods Hole, Mass., 1990. Contbr. over 100 articles to refereed jours. Bd. dirs., v.p. Alzheimer's Assn., Buffalo, 1986—. Mem. Am. Assn. Anatomists, Endocrine Soc., Am. Soc. Cell Biology, Am. Soc. Zoologists, Am. Soc. Investigative Pathology, Microscopy Soc. Am., Sigma Xi, Omicron Kappa Epsilon. Office: SUNY Buffalo Dept Pathology Buffalo NY 14214

NICKLE, CARROLL JOHN, preventive medicine physician; b. Brush, Colo., Oct. 7, 1949; s. Carroll J. and Vivian J. N.; m. Sharon Kay Schulke, July 11, 1970; children: Eric, Tyler. Student, Colo. State U., 1967-70; DO, Chgo. Coll. Osteo. Medicine, 1974; MPH, Johns Hopkins U., 1987. Diplomate Am. Bd. Preventive Medicine, Am. Osteo. Bd. of Family Practice. Family practice physician Lee Clinic, P.C., Greeley, Colo., 1975-84; commd. USN, 1984—, advanced through grades to capt.; student flight surgeon Naval Aerospace Med. Inst., Pensacola, Fla., 1984; squadron flight surgeon HMM-263, New River, N.C., 1984-86; resident in aerospace medicine Naval Aerospace and Operational Med. Inst., Pensacola, 1987-89; sr. med. officer USS John F. Kennedy, Norfolk, Va., 1989-91; dir. aerospace phys. qualifications Naval Aerospace and Operational Med. Inst., Pensacola, 1991-94; wing surgeon 2d Marine Aircraft Wing, Cherry Point, N.C., 1994—; chief of staff Meml. Hosp., Greeley, 1979-81. Recipient Surgeon Gen.'s award for student excellence Bur. Medicine and Surgery, Washington, 1984. Fellow Aerospace Med. Assn. (assoc.); mem. Soc. U.S. Naval Flight Surgeons (sec.-treas. 1988-89), Colo. Soc. Osteo. Medicine (pres. 1982-83), Am. Osteo. Assn., Am. Coll. Osteo. Family Physicians, Assn. Mil. Surgeons of U.S., Assn. Mil. Osteo. Physicians and Surgeons. Home: 1117 Selwood Dr Virginia Beach VA 23464 Office: Ofc of Wing Surgeon 2d Marine Aircraft Wing PSC 2d Marien Aircraft Wing PSC Box 8050 Cherry Point NC 28533

NICKLIN, GEORGE LESLIE, JR., psychoanalyst, educator, physician; b. Franklin, Pa., July 25, 1925; s. George Leslie and Emma (Reed) N.; m. Katherine Mildred Aronson, Sept. 30, 1950. B.A., Haverford Coll., 1949; M.D., Columbia U., 1951; cert. in psychoanalysis, William A. White Inst., N.Y.C., 1962. Diplomate Am. Bd. Psychiatry and Neurology. Resident, then chief resident Bellevue Psychiat. Hosp., N.Y.C., 1953-56; pvt. practice specializing in psychoanalytic psychiatry, 1956—; staff Bellevue Hosp., 1956—; asst. clin. prof. psychiatry NYU Med. Sch., 1962-70, assoc. clin. prof. psychiatry, 1970—, dir. L.I. Inst. Psychoanalysis, 1978-88, dir. emeritus, 1988—; attending psychiatrist Nassau County Med. Center Clin. Campus; assoc. clin. prof. psychiatry SUNY-Stony Brook Health Sci. Ctr., 1976—; mem. Com. to Award Martin Luther King Peace Prize. Founder Friends World Coll., 1958, trustee, 1968-89. Served with AUS, 1943-46, ETO. Decorated Purple Heart with oak leaf cluster, Bronze Star with oak leaf cluster and three battle stars. Fellow Am. Acad. Psychoanalysis, Am. Psychiat. Assn.; mem. AAAS, NAACP, Soc. Med. Psychoanalysts (pres. 1986-87), White Psychoanalytic Soc., Assn. for World Edn. (charter trustee, treas. 1970-78), 9th Inf. Divsn. Assn., Vets. of the Bulge, Mil. Order of the Purple Heart. Mem. Soc. of Friends. Clubs: Gardiner's Bay Country (Shelter Island, N.Y.); Penn (London). Home and Office: 6 Butler Pl Garden City NY 11530-4603

NICKSICH, PAUL NICK, mental health therapist; b. Helena, Mont., Nov. 7, 1951; s. Paul Nick and Lois J. (Collins) N.; m. Judy Ann Slafter, Aug. 17, 1974; children: Paul Nick Jr., Anne Elizabeth. BA, U. Wyo., 1975, MPA, 1994; MS, U. Utah, 1977. Lic. prof. counselor; lic. addictions therapist; nat. cert. counselor; cert. mental health counselor. Mental health therapist, unit coord. Southwest Counseling Svc., Rock Springs, Wyo., 1977-92, outpatient mental health therapist, 1994—; devel., supr. first day treatment program in Wyo. Mem. quality assurance team Sweetwater County Hospice, 1991; owner, operator White Mountain Consulting, 1993—. Mem. Inst. Rational-Emotive Therapy (cert.). Democrat. Unitarian. Avocations: reading, music, martial arts (Kenpo karate). Home: 813 Chestnut St Rock Springs WY 82901-4805 Office: Southwest Counseling Svc 1124 College Dr Rock Springs WY 82901-5863

NICOL, KLAUS, biomechanics educator; b. Mindelheim, Germany, May 27, 1939; s. Ernst and Carola (Bannick) N.; m. Uth Waltraud, May 30, 1961; children—Natascha Birgit, Sven-Boris, Cornelia Martina Yvonne. Abitur, Liebig-Gymnasium, Frankfurt, W.Ger., 1959; diploma of physics, Goethe U., Frankfurt, 1967, Ph.D. in Physics, 1971. Wissenschaftlicher Mitarbeiter, Inst. for sport and sport scis. Goethe U., 1972-73, Akademischer Rat, 1973-79; prof. dept. sport scis. Wilhelms U., Munster, W.Ger., 1979—, mem. and chmn. 10 univ. commns., 1979—; dir. Inst. Phys. Edn., 1982, vice dean dept. sports scis., 1982-85, 90-91, dean dept. sports sci., 1987-90. Patentee in field of measuring techniques; contbr. articles to profl. jours. Mem. Internat. Soc. Biomechanics, Deutscher Verband fur Sportwissenschaft. Mem. Free Democratic Party. Lutheran. Home: Adelheidstrasse 13, 6000 Frankfurt 50, Germany Office: FB 20 der Universitat, Horstmarer Landweg 62 B, 4400 Muenster Germany

NICOL, MARJORIE CARMICHAEL, research psychologist; b. Orange, N.J., Jan. 6, 1929; d. Norman Carmichael and Ethel Sarah (Siviter) N. BA, Upsala Coll., MS, 1978; MPh, PhD, CUNY, 1988. Mgr. advt. prodn. RCA, Harrison, N.J., 1950-58; advt. mgr., writer NPS Advt., East Orange, N.J., 1960-67; pres. measurement and eval., chief exec. officer, psychol. evaluator Nicol Evaluation System, Millburn, N.J., 1967—; CEO Rafiki, Essex County, N.J., 1965—. Author: Nicol Index, Nicol Evaluation System, 1991. Officer Montclair Rehab. Orgn., 1981—; founder, patron Met. Opera at Lincoln Ctr. Republican. Presbyterian. Home: 85 Linden St Millburn NJ 07041-2160 Office: PO Box 111 Millburn NJ 07041-0111

NICOLETTE, LILLIAN H., nursing administrator, consultant, educator; b. Phila., July 3, 1954; d. Edward C. and Louise B. (Turco) N. (dec.); m. A.C. Delia, Jr. AAS in Nursing, C.C. of Phila., 1974; BSN, Gwynedd-Mercy Coll., 1976; MSN in Nursing Adminstrn., Widener U., 1983, postgrad., 1984-88, 94—. Staff and charge nurse Grad. Health Sys., Parkview, Pa., 1974-84; faculty Meth. Hosp. Sch. Nursing, Phila., 1978-84; clin. dir. surg. svcs. Albert Einstein Med. Ctr., Phila., 1985-86; clin. dir. perioperative nursing Hahnemann U. Hosp., Phila., 1986-87; staff nurse oper. rm. Crozer Chester Med. Ctr., Upland, Pa., 1987-91; v.p., perioperative nurse Surg. Staff, Inc., Phila., 1987-91; nurse cons. Johnson & Johnson Corp., Horsham, Pa., 1991-93; cons., sterilization specialist Johnson & Johnson Med., 1993—; pres. nat. cert. bd. Nat. Certification Bd. Perioperative Nursing, Inc., 1995-96; bd. dirs. NCB PNI. Contbr. articles to profl. jours. Named Perioperative Clin. Nurse educator of Yr., 1994-95; recipient Outstanding Achievement award. Mem. ANA, Assn. Oper. Rm. Nurses (bd. dirs. Phila. chpt. 1986-88, v.p. 1989-91, pres. 1992-93, treas. 1994—), Pa. Coun. Oper. Rm. Nurses, Gwynedd-Mercy Coll. Alumni, Sigma Theta Tau.

NICOLINI, FRANCESCA ANTONIA, health science association administrator; b. Imola, Italy, Jan. 3, 1961; came to U.S., 1989; d. Roberto and Maria Luisa (Barbieri) N. BA, Liceoclassico Statale, 1979; MD, U. Bologna, 1986; PhD, U. Uppsala, 1993. Resident U. Bologna (Italy), 1985-86; dir. exptl. thrombosis program The Cleve. Clinic Found., 1992—; cons. in field. Cardiology fellow U. Bologna, 1987-89. Fellow Am. Coll. Cardiology, European Soc. Cardiology; mem. Am. Heart Assn. (coun. curiculation 1992—, rsch. fellow 1990-92). Office: The Cleve Clinic Found 9500 Euclid Ave Cleveland OH 44195

NICOLOSI, ALFRED CARL, surgery educator; b. Passaic, N.J., May 21, 1958; s. Carmen and Marian N.; m. Eileen C. Brigaitis, July 31, 1982; children: Michael B., Matthew P., Marybeth S. BS, Muhlenberg Coll., 1980; MD, U. Medicine and Dentistry N.J., 1984. Diplomate Am. Bd. Surgery, Am. Bd. Thoracic Surgery. Rsch. fellow Columbia U., N.Y.C., 1987-89; intern in surgery Med. Coll. Wis., Milw., 1984-85, resident in surgery, 1985-91, resident in cardiothoracic surgery, 1991-93, asst. prof. surgery, 1993—. Contbr. articles to med. jours. Recipient Nat. Rsch. Svc. award Nat. Heart, Lung and Blood Inst.; rsch. fellow NIH, 1988-89. Fellow Am. Coll. Chest Physicians; mem. ACS (candidate). Office: Med Coll Wis 9200 W Wisconsin Ave Milwaukee WI 53226

NICOLOSI, FRANCIS JOSEPH, physician; b. Rockford, Ill., Oct. 13, 1955; s. Philip Angelo and Rosemary (Licari) N. BS, U. Ill., 1977; MD, U. Bologna, Italy, 1985. Resident So. Ill. U. Sch. Medicine, 1987-90; physician Rockford (Ill.) Health Sys., 1990—. Fellow Am. Acad. Family Physicians; mem. AMA, Ill. State Med. Soc., Winnebago County Med. Soc. Office: Rockford Health Sys Rockford IL 61103

NIDETZ, MYRON PHILIP, health care delivery systems consultant, medical administrator ; b. Chgo., Dec. 29, 1935; s. David J. and Rose Y. (Yudell) N.; BS, U. Ill., 1958; MBC, Hamilton Inst., Phila., 1972; MPA, Roosevelt U., 1981. Diplomate Am. Acad. Med. Adminstrs.; m. Linda Freeman, Dec. 18, 1960; children: Julia, Allison. Dir., Union Coop. Eye Care Ctr., Chgo., 1961-65; dir. med. adminstrv. svcs. Michael Reese Hosp. and Med. Ctr., Chgo., 1966-75; assoc. dir. program to improve med. care and health svcs. in correctional instns. AMA, 1975-79; exec. dir. North Cen. Dialysis Ctrs., Chgo., 1979-92; pres. Myron P. Nidetz & Assocs., Inc., 1992—; adj. prof. health care adminstrn. Roosevelt U., Chgo., Calumet Coll., St. Joseph U., Whiting, Ind., 1987—; mem., bd. dirs. Renal Network of Ill.; NIC tech. cons. U.S. Dept. Justice, 1978—; bd. govs. Roosevelt Univ., pres. Pub. Adminstrn. Coun., mem. Curriculum Rev. com. Pub. Adminstrn. Active Health Planning Facilities Bd., Ill., Ill. Dept. Pub. Aid, Ill. Dept. Aging; mem. adv. bd. Am. Kidney Fund, chmn. Midwest Core Group, Nat. Kidney Found., Inst. of Medicine, Am. Assn. Retired Persons (Met. Area Satellite Group, State Legis. com., community coord.); sec. bd. dirs. Suburban Area Agy. on Aging. Served with U.S. Army, 1959-60. Fellow Am. Public Health Assn., Royal Soc. Health, Am. Acad. Med. Adminstrs.; mem. AMA, Assn. Hosp. Med. Edn., Nat. Dialysis Assn. (sec.), Am. Assn. Kidney Patients, Nat. Renal Adminstrs. Assn. (govt. affairs com.), Am. Acad. Polit. and Social Sci., Am. Geriatrics Soc., Am. Hosp. Assn., Am. Mgmt. Assn., Inst. of Soc. Ethics and Life Scis., Gerontol. Soc., Assn. Univ. Programs Health Adminstrn., Am. Mgmt. Assn. Home and Office: 14800 Minerva Ave Dolton IL 60419-2321

NIEBAUER, JOHN JOSEPH, JR., physician, educator; b. San Francisco, July 7, 1914; s. John Joseph and Frieda E. (Sauer) N.; m. Jean A. Mackay, Jan. 9, 1943; children—John S., Patricia A., Douglas W., Peter B. B.A., Stanford, 1937, M.D., 1942. Diplomate: Am. Bd. Orthopedic Surgery. Intern Stanford U. Hosp., San Francisco, 1941-42; asst. resident Stanford U. Hosp., 1942-44, resident orthopedic surgery, 1944-45; Gibney fellow orthopedic surgery Hosp. for Spl. Surgery, N.Y.C., 1945-46; asst. clin. prof. orthopedic surgery Stanford Sch. Medicine, 1946-51, asso. clin. prof., 1951-57, adj. clin. prof., 1957; clin. prof. orthopedic surgery U. Calif. Sch. Medicine, 1965—; chief staff Presbyn. Hosp., San Francisco, 1975-76; chmn. dept. hand surgery Pacific Presbyn. Med. Ctr., 1962-85; trustee Pacific Med. Ctr.; pres. Sterling Bunnell Found., Pacific Presbyn. Med. Ctr., 1982. Trustee Coll. of Marin Found., Kentfield, Calif., 1994—. Mem. AMA, Calif., San Francisco County med. socs., Am. Western orthopedic assns., Am. Acad. Orthopedic Surgery, Internat. Soc. Orthopedic Surgery and Traumatology, Am. Soc. for Surgery of Hand (pres.), Alumni Assn. Coll. of Marin.

NIEBLER, GWENDOLYN E., neurologist; b. Glen Ridge, N.J., July 23, 1962; d. Frank Karl and Elfriede Teresa (Goetzinger) N.; m. James Patrick Harris, Oct. 3, 1992. BA in Biology, Case Western Res. U., 1984; DO, Ohio U., 1988. Diplomate in neurology Am. Bd. Psychiatry and Neurology. Resident in neurology Ind. U. Med. Ctr., Indpls., 1990-93, epilepsy/EEG/evoked potential fellow, 1993-94; neurologist Ind. Neurology Assocs., Indpls., 1994—; asst. clin. prof. neurology Ind. U., Indpls., 1994—; mem. various speakers burs.; drug investigator Park-Davis, Burroughs-Wellcome, 1995—; rschr. in Huntington's disease. Author articles. Mentor for Future Physicians program Girl Scouts U.S., Indpls., 1995—. Recipient Alexander Ross award Ind. U. Sch. Medicine, 1993. Mem. AMA, Am. Osteo. Assn., Am. Epilepsy Soc., Ind. Neurology Soc., Am. Med. Women's Assn. (Janet M. Glasgow achievement citation 1988), Am. Acad. Neurology. Office: Ind Neurology Assocs 8402 Harcourt Rd Ste 603 Indianapolis IN

NIEDERAU, CLAUS ULRICH, physician, educator; b. Essen, Germany, Sept. 18, 1954; s. Kurt and Elisabeth (Ermeling) N.; m. Vera Stöcker, Aug. 22, 1991; children: Carolin, Matthias. MD, U. Düsseldorf, Germany, 1979, PhD, 1979. Intern then resident U. Düsseldorf, 1979-83, jr. faculty, 1986-92, prof. medicine, 1992—; fellow U. Calif., San Francisco, 1983-85. Editor: Pancreatic Ultrasound, 1991, Pancreatic Diseases, 1992, Yearbook of Gastroenterology, 1993, Hepato-gastroenterology, 1994. Mem. Civil Def., Wuppertal, 1973-90. Mem. Am. Gastroent. Assn., Am. Pancreatic Assn., Iron Overlaod Diseases Assn. (bd. dirs. Fla. chpt. 1985—), German Gastroent. Assn. (Clin. Rsch. award 1990), German Pancreatic Club (pres. 1991), Gastro-Surg. Club. Office: U Düsseldorf, Mooren St 5, 40225 Düsseldorf Germany

NIEDERHUBER, JOHN EDWARD, surgical oncologist and molecular immunologist, university educator and administrator; b. Steubenville, Ohio, June 21, 1938; s. William Henry and Helen (Smittle) N.; m. Tracey J. Williamson; children: Elizabeth Ann, Matthew John. B.S., Bethany Coll., 1960; M.D., Ohio State U., 1964. Diplomate Am. Bd. Surgery. Internship, surgery Ohio State U. Hosp., Columbus, 1964-65; resident, surgery U. Mich. Med. Ctr., Ann Arbor, 1967-69, NIH acad. trainee in surgery, 1969-71, resident, surgery, 1971-72, chief resident surgery, 1972-73, asst. prof. surgery and asst. prof. microbiology, 1973-77, dir. transplantation program, 1975-76, assoc. prof. surgery and assoc. prof. microbiology, 1977-80, chief divsn. surg. oncology and transplantation, sect. gen. surgery, 1979-82, sr. assoc. dean med. sch., 1983-86, assoc. dean research, 1982-86, chief divsn. surg. oncology sect. gen. surgery, 1982-86, prof. surgery, prof. microbiology and immunology, 1980-87; cons. Wayne County Gen. Hosp. Mich., 1973-84; cons. surgery Ann Arbor VA Hosp., 1973-87; prof. surgery, oncology, molecular biology and genetics The Johns Hopkins U. Sch. Med., Baltimore, 1987-91; Emile Holman prof. surgery, chair, dept. surgery, head sect. surgical scis. Stanford (Calif.) U. Sch. Medicine., 1991—, prof. microbiology and immunology, 1991—; chief of surgery Stanford (Calif.) U. Hosp., 1991—; dir. Comp. Cancer Ctr. Stanford (Calif.) Med. Ctr., 1991—; vis. prof. Howard Hughes Med. Inst. Dept. Molecular Biology and Genetics The Johns Hopkins U. Sch. Medicine, Baltimore, 1986-87. Authored books on cancer; mem. editorial bd. Jour. Immunology, 1981-85, Jour. Surg. Res., 1989—, Current Opinion in Oncology, 1989—, Annals of Surgery, 1991—, Surg. Oncology, 1991—, Cancer, 1992—, Jour. Clin. Oncology, 1993, Annals of Surg. Oncology, 1993—, Jour. Am. Coll. Surgeons, 1994—; contbr. articles to profl. jours. Active NCI divsn. Cancer Treatment Bd. Scientific Councilors, 1986-91, chmn., 1987-91, Gen. Motors Cancer Rsch. Found. Awards Assembly, 1988-92. Served to capt. U.S. Army, 1965-67. Recipient USPHS Rsch. Career Devel. award Nat. Inst. Allergy and Infectious Disease, 1974-79, Disting. Faculty Svc. award U. Mich., 1978, Alumni Achievement award Ohio State U. Coll. Medicine, 1989, Alumni Achievement award in Medicine Bethany Coll., 1995; vis. rsch. fellow divsn. immunobiology Karolinska Inst., Stockholm, 1970-71, Am. Cancer Soc. Jr. Faculty Clin. fellow, 1977-79. Fellow ACS; mem. Am. Soc. Transplant Surgeons, Transplantation Soc., Am. Surg. Assn., Am. Assn. Immunologists, Coller Surg. Soc., Soc. Univ. Surgeons, Assn. Acad. Surgeons, Soc. Surg. Oncology, Ctrl. Surg. Soc., Am. Assn. Cancer Rsch., Am. Soc. Clin. Oncology, Soc. Clin. Surgery, Biology Club II, Robert M. Zollinger-Ohio State U. Surg. Soc., Pacific Coast Surg. Assn. Office: Stanford Univ Sch Medicine Dept of Surgery MSOB X300 Stanford CA 94304-5408

NIEDERMAN, JAMES CORSON, physician, educator; b. Hamilton, Ohio, Nov. 27, 1924; s. Clifford Frederick and Henrietta (Corson) N.; m. Miriam Camp, Dec. 12, 1951; children—Timothy Porter, Derrick Corson, Eliza Orton, Caroline Noble. Student, Kenyon Coll., 1942-45, D.Sc. (hon.), 1981; M.D., Johns Hopkins U., 1949. Intern Johns Hopkins Hosp., Balt., 1949-50; asst. resident in medicine Yale-New Haven Med. Center, 1950-51, assoc. resident, 1953-55; med. ctr. practice specializing in internal medicine, infectious disease and clin. epidemiology New Haven, 1955—; instr. Yale U., 1955-58, asst. prof., 1958-66, assoc. prof., 1966-76, clin. prof. medicine and epidemiology, 1976—; mem. Nat. Coun. for Johns Hopkins Medicine. Trustee Kenyon Coll.; bd. counselors Smith Coll., 1970-77; mem. Alumni Coun. Johns Hopkins U.; mem. Conn. Soc. of Arts and Scis. Served to 1st lt. M.C. U.S. Army, 1951-53. Fellow Silliman Coll., Yale U. Fellow Am. Coll. Epidemiology; mem. Infectious Diseases Soc. Am., Am. Epidemiol. Soc., Johns Hopkins Med. and Surg. Assn.,. Democrat. Episcopalian. Clubs: Yale (N.Y.C.); New Haven Lawn. Home: 429 Sperry Rd Bethany CT 06524-3544 Office: 60 College St New Haven CT 06510-3210

NIEDERMEIER, MARY B., retired nutrition educator; b. Webster Groves, Mo., Oct. 20, 1914; d. Albertus and Daisey May (Christman) Wickersham; m. Walter H. Niedermeier, Sept. 9, 1939; children: Gail Santarelli, Bart Niedermeier. BS, Mich. State U., 1937; MA, Columbia U., 1957, profl. diploma, 1959. Cert. in dietetics, Miami Valley Hosp., Dayton, Ohio, 1938. Dist. nutritionist N.J. State Dept. of Health, Newark; instr. nutrition edn. Sch. of Dentistry Fairleigh Dickinson U., Teaneck, N.J.; instr. nutrition edn. Sch. of Nursing St. Louis U. Pres. PTA, Oradell (N.J.) Pub. Sch., 1954-57; bd. dirs. Rancho Bernardo (Calif.) Oaks North Community Ctr., 1974-76; bd. deacons Rancho Bernardo Presbyn. Ch., 1975-77; treas. PEO-TV chpt., Rancho Bernardo, 1990. Grace McCloud fellow 1957-59 Columbia U. Mem. AAUW, AAUP, Am. Dietetic Assn., Calif. Dietetic Assn., N.J. Dietetic Assn., Alpha Omicron Pi. Republican. Home: 17411 Plaza De La Rosa San Diego CA 92128-2223

NIEDERPRUEM, MARK LAURENCE, health services administrator; b. Buffalo, Jan. 5, 1956; s. Ellery J. and Virginia A. (Paul) N.; m. Christine L. Henneman, Sept. 18, 1982; children: Adam T., Clare C., Luke W. BA, SUNY, Brockport, 1978, MA, 1986. Diplomate Am. Coll. Health Care Execs. Rehab. counselor Cantalician Ctr., Buffalo, 1978-83; dir. program svcs. Orleans County chpt. Assn. Retarded Children, Medina, N.Y., 1983-86; asst. v.p. Children's Hosp., Buffalo, 1986-93; adminstr. Shriner's Hosp., Springfield, Mass., 1993—. Sec. Profl. Bus. Coun., Buffalo, 1989-93; bd. dirs. Ronald McDonald House, Springfield, Mass., 1994—. Mem. Western Mass. Hosp. Assn., Western N.Y. Health Care Exec. Mgmt. Forum (sec. 1988-93). Roman Catholic. Home: 6 Fox Hill Dr Wilbraham MA 01095 Office: Shriners Hospital 516 Carew St Springfield MA 01104

NIELSEN, GAIL ANN, radiologic technologist; b. Waterloo, Iowa, Mar. 30, 1947; d. Raymond Zack and Marlys Leota (Timmerman) Eikenberry; m. David Harry Nielsen, June 8, 1968; children: Jennifer Lyn, Kristen Michelle. BS Health Care Adminstrn., St. Joseph's Coll., Windham, Maine, 1989. Staff technologist Allen Meml. Hosp., Waterloo, 1967-69, 72-75, supr. vascular imaging, 1973-80, asst. dir. radiology, 1975-84, adminstrv. dir. radiology svcs., 1984-95, adminstrv. coord. radiology, adminstr. managed care, 1995—, mgr. health info. svcs., managed care & quality improvement, 1996—; vol. technologist U.S. Army Hosp., Bremerhaven, Fed. Republic Germany, 1970-71; instr. radiologic tech. edn., Waterloo, 1975—. Vol. ARC, Waterloo, 1986-88, United Way Black Hawk County, 1987-89, Cedar Valley Breast Cancer Awareness Task Force, Waterloo, 1988—. Recipient letter of commendation U.S. Army, 1971. Mem. Am. Soc. Radiologic Technologists (registeres AART 1967, Matt Keilley Meml. award 1990), Am. Healthcare Radiology Adminstrs. (sec. 1988-90, lectr. 1989, nat. stats. chmn. 1989-91, elected chmn. summit on manpower 1992-93, v.p. nat. and midwest region 1991-92, nat. pres. 1994-95, pres. edn. found. 1995-96, fellow 1991—), Health Professions Network (team leader 1995-96), Iowa Soc. Radiologic Technologists (sec. lectr. 1985, pres. N.E. dist. 1976-77, 81-82), Toastmasters (edn. com. Waterloo 1987-88). Lutheran. Office: Allen Meml Hosp 1825 Logan Ave Waterloo IA 50703-1916

NIELSEN, KARSTEN, pathologist; b. Maribo, Lolland, Denmark, June 4, 1952; s. Poul Sofus Christen and Gerda (Hansen) N.; m. Inger Mellerup, Oct. 26, 1977; children: Niels Mellerup, Viggo Mellerup, Laust Mellerup. MD, Aarhus (Denmark) U., 1977, D. in Med. Sci., 1991. Cert. specialist in pathology, Danish Govt., 1986. Registrar Aarhus Kommunehosp., 1977-78, Holstebro (Denmark) Sygehus, 1978-80, Aalborg (Denmark) Sygehus, 1980-82; sr. registrar Gentofte (Denmark) Hosp., 1982-87, Rigshospitalet, Copenhagen, 1987-88; chief pathologist Aalborg Sygehus, 1988—. Editor books of congresses, Danish Soc. Pathology, 1982-87. Grantee Danish Cancer Soc., 1980-91. Mem. Internat. Acad. Pathology (pres. 1990—), Danish Soc. Path. Anatomy and Cytology (sec. 1982-87), Danish Soc. Pathology (sec. 1987-92). Lutheran. Office: Aalborg Hosp, Inst of Pathology, DK 9000 Aalborg Denmark

NIELSEN, LEONARD MAURICE, physician assistant; b. Bklyn., June 6, 1949; s. Leonard Maurice Nielsen and Alma Dorothy (Weber) Sherman; m. Therese Marie Wright, Aug. 4, 1979; children: Daniel Weber, Carolyn Wright. AA, Allan Hancock Coll., Santa Maria, Calif., 1969; BS in Zoology, U. Ga., 1972; BS in Medicine/Physician Asst. Cert., Emory U., 1977; MPH, U. Ala., Birmingham, 1987. Nat. bd. cert. physician asst. Rsch. asst. and asst. instr. Physiology dept. Emory U., Atlanta, 1972-75; physician asst. Neurology-P.A.C., St. Petersburg, Fla., 1977-79; sr. physician asst. VA, Birmingham, 1979-88; med. regional clin. evaluator Dept. Vets. Affairs, Tuscaloosa, Ala., 1988-90; adminstrv. assoc. to chief staff Dept. Vets. Affairs, Tuskegee, Ala., 1990-91; dir. quality mgmt. and utilization rev. The Children's Hosp. of Ala., Birmingham, 1991-93; physician asst. U. Ala.-Birmingham Hosps., 1993-95, Walker Bapt. Regional Med. Ctr., Jasper, Ala., 1995—, Internal Medicine West, Bessemer, Ala., 1995—; cons. in quality improvement, Birmingham, 1988—; lectr. in field; adj. prof. Tuskegee Inst., 1990. Co-author: Catastrophic State of Catastrophic Health Care (in the United States), 1987; editor newsletter Ala. Soc. Physician Assts., 1990-91. Advisor EPIC Sch. fundraiser, 1985-91; active participant Birmingham Regional Healthcare Execs., 1990-95; co-chair Forest Park Neighborhood Crimefighters, Birmingham, 1980-84, Putnam Middle Sch. fundraiser, Birmingham, 1991-93; founding mem. Ala. Sch. Fine Arts Music Support Group, 1995—. With USNR, 1971-77. Recipient VA Suggestion award, 1981; Optimist Club scholar, 1967. Fellow Am. Acad. Physician Assts. (del. 1977—), Ala. Soc. Physician Assts. (sec., del. 1979—, bd. dirs. 1982-85); mem. Am. Mensa (award 1980), Nat. Assn. Quality Assurance Professions, Alumni Assn. U. Ala.-Birmingham (bd. dirs. 1992-94). Home: 4736 Vermont Ave Birmingham AL 35210

NIELSEN, NIELS STIG MØLLER, radiology consultant; b. Dronninglund, Denmark, June 5, 1951; s. Niels Møller and Lillian Vibeke (Abildgaard) N.; m. Else Marie Kristensen, Aug. 7, 1971; children: Mai Marie, Hans Henrik. MD, U. Aarhus, Denmark, 1977, specialist in diagnostic radiology, 1987. Registrar Hjørring (Denmark) Sygehus, 1977-82, Aalborg (Denmark) Sygehus, 1982-83; sr. registrar Aarhus (Denmark) Kommunehospital, 1983-85, Aalborg (Denmark) Sygehus, 1985-87, Aarhus (Denmark) U. Hosp., 1987-88; cons. radiologist Esbjerg (Denmark) Centralsygehus, 1988-90, head radiology dept., 1990—. Inventor in field. Chmn. Viking Archery Club, Esbjerg, 1993—. Mem. Assn. Radiologists in Ribe County (chmn. 1990—), Assn. Cons. in Ctrl. Hosp., Danish Soc. Diagnostic Radiology, Danish Soc. Diagnostic Ultrasound, Lions Club Internat. Home: Amigovej 11, DK 6710 Esbjerg Denmark Office: Ctrl Hosp, Østergade, DK 6700 Esbjerg Denmark

NIELSEN, SVEND, general practitioner; b. Hobro, Denmark, June 1, 1937; s. Anton and Erika N.; m. Illa Krause, Jan. 6, 1958 (div. 1971); m. Bente Ragnhild Overgård, Jan. 18, 1975; children: Morten, Mette, Jakob, Karin, Malin, Frithioff. Cand. med., U. Copenhagen Med. Sch., 1963. Staff dept. ob-gyn Rigshospitalet, 1963; staff dept. medicine and surgery Kommunehospitalet Copenhagen, 1963-64; staff dept. gynecology Sonderbro Hosp., 1965; asst. dist. physician Umanak, Greenland, 1966; staff dept. psychiatry Bispebjerg Hosp., Copenhagen, 1967-68; staff dept. medicine Hobro, 1968-69, pvt. practice gen. medicine, 1969—; chmn. com. occupational health, Danish Med. Assn., 1977-80; bd. dirs. Orgn. Gen. Practitioners, 1977-85, chmn. 1979-85. Author: Art in Hobro, DK, 1995; contbr. articles to profl. jours. Town councillor Town of Hobro, 1974-90; chmn. Town Coun. Dept. Technics and Environ., 1985-90; mem. com. econ. Town Coun., 1978-90, edn. com., 1970-78; chmn. Assn. Sports, 1978-80; chmn. Mcpl. Collection Contemporary Art, 1975—. Recipient MEFA prize, Danish Med. Assn., 1990. Mem. Danish Med. Assn. (chmn. County of No. Jutland 1995—). Lutheran. Office: Lagehuset, Korsgade 9, 9500 Hobro Denmark

NIELSON, CONSTANCE JO, psychologist, educator; b. Kansas City, Mo., Oct. 21, 1950; d. Elrod Pierce and Emily Jorene (Bullock) Wilson; m. Dennis Thomas Joe, Aug. 5, 1972 (div. 1982); m. Gary Francis Nielson, Aug. 17, 1984; 1 child, Garrett Joseph; stepchildren: Heather Marie, Adam Stevens. BS, U. Houston, 1972, MEd, 1978; postgrad., U. Mo., 1982-93, Cen. Mo. State U., 1968-70. Cert. elem. edn. and kindergarten tchr.; cert. in mental retardation all level, generic spl. edn., Mo., Tex. Resource tchr. Houston Ind. Sch. Dist., 1972-78, spl. edn. supr., 1978-79, staff devel., 1979-81; sch. psychol. examiner North Kansas City (Mo.) Schs., Kansas City, 1981—; mem. faculty, prof. Avila Coll., Kansas City, 1983-85. Coord. North Kansas City Kids on the Block Troupe, 1982—. Named Vol. of the Yr., Easter Seals Soc., 1984, Puppetter of the Yr., 1984. Mem. Coun. for Exceptional Children, Coun. for Edn. Diagnostic Svcs. Home: 3504 NE 56th Ter Kansas City MO 64119-2341 Office: North Kansas City Schs 2000 NE 46th St Kansas City MO 64116-2042

NIEMAN, GARY F., research scientist, educator; b. Buffalo, Aug. 30, 1950; s. Warren Fredrick and Betty Jane (Seufert) N.; m. Pamela Lee Kirchoff, Mar. 9, 1974; 1 child, Erich Warren. BA, SUNY, Geneseo, 1972. Technician SUNY Health Sci. Ctr., Syracuse, 1975-79, tech. specialist, 1980-88, rsch. scientist, 1989—, asst. prof. cardiorespiratory sci., 1995—. Reviewer Jour. Applied Physiology, Pediat. Rsch., Am. Jour. Respiratory and Critical Care Medicine, Am. Inst. Bio Sci.; contbr. articles to profl. jours. Coach Youth Basketball, Monlius, N.Y., 1984-89, Pop Warner Football, Monlius, 1984-91; mem. Athletic Booster Club, Monlius, 1992-94. Grantee Am. Respiratory Care Found., 1990-92, 93-94, ONY Inc., 1994-96. Mem. Am. Physiology Soc., Am. Thoracic Soc., Am. Assn. Respiratory Care, Soc. Critical Care Medicine, N.Y. Trudeau Soc., N.Y. Acad. Sci. Office: SUNY Health Sci Ctr Dept Surgery 750 E Adams St Syracuse NY 13201

NIEMI, BEATRICE NEAL, social services professional; b. Fitchburg, Mass., July 23, 1923; d. Albert G. and Florence E. (Copeland) Neal; m. Walter V. Niemi, Oct. 21, 1944 (div. 1970); children: Karen Smith-Gary, Gail Niemi Shaw. AS, Colby-Sawyer Coll., 1942; BS in Psychology, Northeastern U., 1972; MA in Counseling Psychology, Assumption Coll., 1974. Dir. homemaker svcs. Children's Aid and Family Svcs., Inc., Fitchburg, 1965-73; founder, exec. dir. Home Health Aide Svc. of North Cen. Mass., Inc., Fitchburg, 1973-85, Ctr. for Well Being, Inc., Fitchburg, 1985—; instr. Touch for Health Found., Pasadena, Calif., 1977—; tchr. The Radiance Technique Assn. Internat., St. Petersburg, Fla., 1986—; Outreach trainer The Monroe Inst., Faber, Va., 1990—; v.p. Mass. Coun. for Homemaker-Home Health Aide Svcs., Inc., 1973-81. Pres. Children's Aid and Family Svcs., Inc., Fitchburg, 1964-65; bd. dirs. United Way of Greater Fitchburg, Inc., 1964-70, Leominster (Mass.) Vis. Nursing Assn, 1972-78; chmn. adv. bd. Salvation Army, Fitchburg, 1970-72; v.p. Fitchburg Coun. of Girl Scouts. Fellow Acad. Holistic Health Practitioners; mem. ACA, Am. Mental Health Counselors Assn., Am. Holistic Health Assn., Am. Holistic Med. Found., Mass. Assn. Cmty. Health Agys. (bd. dirs. 1970-83), Mass. Mental Health Counselors Assn., Assn. for Transpersonal Psychology, Nat. Guild Hypnotists, N.E. Holistic Counselors Assn., others. Office: Ctr for Well Being Inc 70 Bond St Fitchburg MA 01420-2251

NIEMI, WILLIAM DONALD, neuroscience educator; b. Peterborough, N.H., Apr. 6, 1942; s. Veikko William and Rita Eva (Soucy) N.; m. Elizabeth Irene Turgeon, July 4, 1967; children: Erik William, Maila Lizabeth. AB, Northeastern U., 1965; MS, U. N.H., 1967; PhD, U. Vt., 1972. NIH fellow in neurochemistry Columbia U., N.Y.C., 1972-74; rsch. assoc., 1974-76, Osserman fellow in neurology, 1976, rsch. assoc. physiology, 1976-80; asst. prof. physiology Russell Sage Coll., Troy, N.Y., 1980-85, assoc. prof., 1986—;rsch. scientist Wadsworth Ctr., N.Y. State Dept. Health, 1992—. Contbr. articles to profl. jours. Mem. Brunswick Conservation Adv. Coun., 1984—. Mem. N.Y. Acad. Scis., Hudson-Berkshire Neurosci. Soc., Sigma Xi. Home: 166 Tamarac Rd Troy NY 12180-9999 Office: Russell Sage Coll Dept Physiology Troy NY 12180

NIENABER, CHRISTOPH ANTHONY, cardiologist; b. Hamm, Westphalia, Fed. Republic of Germany, Sept. 13, 1955; arrived in U.S.A., 1986; s. Wilhelm Joseph and Marie Louise (Hinkelmann) N. Student, Heinrich Heine U., Duesseldorf, Fed. Republic of Germany, 1974-75; MD, Westfälische Wilhelms U., Muenster, Fed. Republic of Germany, 1980; postgrad., Yale U., 1980. Intern Detmold, 1979; rsch. fellow Max-Planck Soc., Bad Naüheim, Fed. Republic of Germany, 1980-82; resident in internal medicine U. Hosp. Eppendorf, Hamburg, Fed. Republic of Germany, 1982-85; cardiology fellow U. Hosp. Eppendorf, Hamburg, 1985-86, instr. cardiology, 1988-89, asst. prof., 1990-91; cardiology and nuclear medicine fellow UCLA, 1986-88; assoc. prof. div. cardiology, co-dir. cardio-vascular positron emission tomography program U. Hosp. Eppendorf, Hamburg, 1991—. Contbr. articles to profl. jours. Internat. Coll. Angiology fellow, 1987. Fellow Am. Coll. Cardiology; mem. German Soc. Cardiology, German Soc. Nuclear Medicine, Am. Soc. Angiologie, Am. Heart Assn. (coun. mem.). Office: U Hosp Eppendorf Cardiology, Martini Strasse 52 2000, Hamburg 20, Germany

NIENHIUS-HORNER, CAROLYN JOANNE, educator, counselor, consultant; b. Akron, Ohio, Oct. 26, 1948; d. James Patrick and Pauline Elizabeth (Beretics) Kintz; m. Ronald Jay Nienhius, Aug. 23, 1970 (div. Dec. 1979); children: Nathan Jeremy, Seth Michael; m. Karl Ford Horner, Jr., Nov. 3, 1983. BS, Ohio State U., 1972; M in Tech. Edn. Guidance, U. Akron, 1988, M in Counseling, 1990. Lic. social worker, Ohio; cert. employee assistance profl.; trained in divorce mediation. Employee devel. trainer Sum County Dept. Human Svcs., Akron, 1984-90; employee assistance counselor Tri-County Employee Assistance Progam, Akron, 1989-90; intrvention program coord. Community Drug Bd., Akron, 1990-91; counselor, consultant, trainer Hop To It (pvt. practice), Hartville, Ohio, 1991—; instr., trainer, practicum supr., program developer, writer Stark Tech. Coll., Canton, Ohio, 1990—; cons. Child Support Enforcement Agy. Akron, 1989—; in-svc. trainer Wadsworth (Ohio) City Schs.; presenter Ohio Welfare Conf., Toledo, 1989, Ohio Counselors Conf., Columbus, 1990; curriculum writer Case Western Res. U. Mandel Sch. Applied Social Scis. Vol. ARC, Akron, 1967-88, Risk Reduction Health Promotion Task Force, Akron, 1984-89, Side Stream Smoke Task Force, 1984-89; coord. Tri County Disabled Citizens Activities, Akron, 1988-89; recorder Stark Tech. Coll. Adv. Bd., 1990—; mem. citizen ambassador program mgmt. Tng. and Incentive Delegation to Russia and Ukraine, 1992. Mem. AACD, ASTD, Ohio Coun. for Self Esteem, Internat. Assn. for Addictions and Offender Counselors, Toastmasters Internat., Chi Sigma Iota (program chmn. Alpha Upsilon chpt. 1989-90, Pres. award, Akron, 1990). Home and Office: Hop To It Counseling Svcs 7052 Pinedale St NE Hartville OH 44632-9392

NIERENBERG, DAVID WERBLIN, clinical pharmacologist, educator; b. N.Y.C., Apr. 4, 1950; s. David E. and Joan W. (Werblin) N.; m. Joan Rice, May 31, 1980; children: David, Kristin. BA, Harvard Coll., 1971, Oxford U., 1972; MD, Harvard Med. Sch., 1976. Diplomate Am. Bd. Internal Medicine, Am. Bd. Clin. Pharmacology. Resident in internal medicine Beth Israel Hosp., Boston, 1976-78; fellow in clin. pharmacology U. Calif., San Francisco, 1978-80; chief resident Stanford (Calif.) U., 1980-81; from asst. prof. to prof. medicine and pharmacology Dartmouth Med. Sch., Hanover, N.H., 1981-93, prof. medicine and pharmacology, 1993—, assoc. dean med. edn., 1993-95, Edward Tullol Krumm '43 prof., 1995—. Author: Clinical Problems in Basic Pharmacology, 1986; editor: Clinical Pharmacology, 3d edit., 1993; assoc. editor: Clinical Pharmacology and Therapeutics, 1994—. Recipient Young Investigator award Am. Coll. Clin. Pharmacology, 1992. Office: Dartmouth Hitchcock Med Ctr Hinman Box 7506 Lebanon NH 03756

NIESLUCHOWSKI, WITOLD S., cardiovascular and thoracic surgeon; b. Warsaw, Poland, Mar. 2, 1944; came to U.S., 1975; s. Stanislaw Leon and Izabela Anna (Swierczynska) N.; m. Bonnie Jean Thomas, Apr. 15, 1978; children: Jason Brian, Christopher Thomas, Megan Jean, Jennifer Anne. MD, Warsaw Med. Sch., 1967. With Akademicki Zwiazek Sportowy, Warsaw, 1961-75; cardiovascular surgeon Oxnard (Calif.) Hosp., 1975—. Mem. Oxnard Humanitarians, 1987—; bd. dirs. Am. Heart Assn., Camarillo, Calif., 1988—. Fellow ACS, Am. Coll. Cardiologists; mem. Soc. for Thoracic Surgeons. Club: Cabrillo Tennis (Camarillo). Office: 1700 N Rose # 420 Oxnard CA 93030

NIETO, JUAN MANUEL, emergency medicine physician; b. Alpine, Tex., Sept. 24, 1949; s. Edmundo Miguel and Socorro (Herrera) N.; BS, U. Notre Dame, 1970; MD, U. Colo., 1974; children: Ana Raquel, Cristina Marie. Intern, Los Angeles County, U. So. Calif. Med. Ctr., 1974-75; physician Community Health Found., Los Angeles, 1975-77, Emergency Dept. Physicians Med. Group, Marina Del Ray, Calif., 1977-78; resident in emergency medicine Denver Gen.-St. Anthony Hosp. Systems, 1978-80; mem. staff North Colo. Med. Center, Greeley, Colo., 1980-83; emergency physician, med. dir. emergency dept. Brackenridge Hosp., Austin, Tex., 1984-85; practice medicine, Austin, 1983—; emergency physician Emergency Physicians Affiliates, 1986-89; clin. asst. prof. U. Tex. Health Sci. Ctr., San Antonio, 1994—; mem. planning com. Starflight Helicopter Air Transport, 1985; instr. advanced cardiac life support, 1977; bd. dirs. Nat. Chicano Health Orgn., 1971-74; adv. E. Los Angeles Hypertension Screening Program, 1978; med. adv. Weld County Ambulance Service, 1980-83; med.

dir. Air Life, 1980-83; med. dir. Alamo Heights Emergency Med. Svc., 1988-90. del. Colo. Med. Soc., 1983. Fellow Am. Coll. Emergency Physicians; mem. Am. Coll. Emergency Physicians, Am. Public Health Assn., Tex. Med. Assn., Travis County Med. Soc., Acad. Polit. Sci., Amnesty Internat., Physicians for a Nat. Healthcare Program.

NIEWEG, OMGO EDO, surgical oncologist; b. Groningen, The Netherlands, Oct. 15, 1952; s. Hendrik Omgo and Hiltje (Brouwer) N.; m. Jantje Kroes, Feb. 7, 1989; 1 child, Hendrik Omgo. MD, U. Groningen, 1977, PhD, 1983. Intern St. Elisabeth Hosp., Curacao, Netherlands Antilles, 1976-78; fellow M.D. Anderson Cancer Ctr. U. Tex., Houston, 1990-91; resident in nuclear medicine Univ. Hosp., Groningen, 1978-83, resident in surgery, 1983-90, fellow, 1991-92; mem. staff The Netherlands Cancer Inst., Amsterdam, 1992—; cons. Amsterdam Comprehensive Cancer Ctr., 1993—. Mem. Soc. Surg. Oncology. Office: The Netherlands Cancer Inst, Plesmanlaan 121, 1066 CX Amsterdam Holland, The Netherlands

NIEWIAROWSKI, STEFAN, physiology educator, biomedical research scientist; b. Warsaw, Poland, Dec. 4, 1926; came to U.S., 1972, naturalized, 1978; s. Marian and Janina (Sledzinska) N.; m. Marta Ciswicka (div. 1974); children: Agata, Tomasz. MD, Warsaw U., 1952, PhD, 1960, Dozent, 1961. Lic. physician, Pa.; cert. Ednl. Coun. Fgn. Med. Grads. Intern, med. resident Inst. Hematology, Warsaw, 1951-54; rsch. fellow, rsch. assoc. dept. physiol. chemistry Warsaw U. Med. Sch., 1948-54; rsch. assoc., sr. rsch. assoc. Lab. Clin. Biochemistry, Inst. Hematology, Warsaw, 1951-61; physician in charge Outpatient Dept. for Hemophiliacs, Warsaw, 1957-61; head dept., prof. physiol. chemistry Med. Sch., Bialystok, Poland, 1961-68; assoc. prof. pahtology dept. pathology McMaster U., Hamilton, Ont., Can., 1970-72; rsch. prof. medicine, head coagulation sect. Specialized Ctr. Thrombosis Rsch., Temple U. Sch. Medicine, Phila., 1972-78; prof. physiology Temple U. Sch. Medicine, Phila., 1975—, prof. physiology Thrombosis Rsch. Ctr., 1978—; cons. dept. infectious diseases Warsaw U. Med. Sch., 1954-60; vis. scientist Centre Nat. de Transfusion Sanguine, Paris, 1959; cons. dept. pediatrics Warsaw U. Med. Sch., 1961-65; vis. scientist Vascular Lab., Lemeul Shattuck Hosp., Boston, 1965, 68-70; vis. prof. medicine Tufts U. Sch. Medicine, Boston, 1968-70; dir. Blood Components Devel. Lab., Hamilton Red Cross and McMaster U., 1971-72; mem. sr. coun. Internat. Com. on Haemostatis and Thrombosis, 1973—; mem. NIH rsch. rev. coms., 1975—. Editor Thrombosis Rsch., 1972-80; mem. editorial com. Procs. of Soc. of Exptl. Biology and Medicine, 1980-82, mem. editorial bd., 1980—; reviewer Jour. Clin. Investigation, Jour. Lab. and Clin. Medicine, Blood, Biochimica et Biophysica Acta, Archives of Biochemistry and Biophysics, Jour. Biol. Chemistry, Am. Jour. Physiology; author, co-author 250 articles in the field of blood coagulation, platelet physiology and cell adhesion; contbr. articles to profl. jours. Ont. Heart Found. fellow, 1970-71; recipient Jurzykowski Found. award, 1990, rsch. awards NIH, 1972—. Mem. Internat. Soc. Hematology, Internat. Soc. Thrombosis and Hemostasis, Am. Physiology Soc., Am. Soc. Hematology, Coun. of Thrombosis of Am. Heart Assn., Soc. Exptl. Biology and Medicine, Polish Inst. Arts and Scis. in Am., Am. Soc. Exptl. Pathology, Polish Am. Med. Soc. (hon.). Home: 445 S Woodbine Ave Narberth PA 19072-2027 Office: Temple U Sch Medicine 3400 N Broad St Philadelphia PA 19140-5196

NIGHTINGALE, EDMUND JOSEPH, clinical psychologist, educator; b. St. Paul, Jan. 10, 1941; s. Edmund Anthony and Lauretta Alexandria (Horejs) N.; m. Marie Arcara, Apr. 9, 1978 (dec. April 1992); 1 child, Edmund Bernard. Student, Nazareth Hall Prep. Sem., 1959-61; AB, St. Paul Sem., 1963; AB magna cum laude, Catholic U. of Louvain (Belgium), 1965, MA, 1967, S.T.B. cum laude, 1967; postgrad. U. Minn., 1971; MA, Loyola U., Chgo., 1973, PhD in Clin. Psychology, 1975. Lic. clin. psychologist, Ill., Minn.; cert. Nat. Registry of Health Svc. Providers in Psychology. With Cath. Archdiocese of St. Paul and Mpls., 1967-73; intern in clin. psychology Michael Reese Hosp. and Med. Ctr., Chgo., 1973-74, W. Side VA Hosp., Chgo., 1974-75; staff psychologist, student counseling ctr., Loyola U., Chgo., 1975; staff psychologist and clin. coordinator of inpatient unit, drug dependency treatment ctr. Hines (Ill.) VA Hosp., 1975-79, acting chief drug dependency treatment ctr., 1979-80; chief psychology VA Med. Ctr., Danville, Ill., 1980-86; chief psychology VA Med. Ctr. Mpls., 1986—; mem. personnel bd. Archdiocese of St. Paul and Mpls., 1968-70; lectr. psychology, Loyola U., Chgo., 1975; asst. professorial lectr. psychology, St. Xavier Coll., Chgo., 1975-78; adj. asst. prof. psychology in psychiatry, Abraham Lincoln Sch. Medicine, Med. Ctr. U. Ill., Chgo., 1977-82; adj. prof. psychology Purdue U., 1981-87; asst. prof. psychiatry Med. Sch., U. Minn., 1987—, clin. assoc. prof. psycholgy Coll. Liberal Arts, 1986-90, adj. asst. prof., 1990—; clin. asst. prof. U. Ill. Sch. Medicine, Urbana/Champaign, 1982-87; mem. grad. faculty in counseling psychology Ind. State U., Terre Haute, 1983-86. Bd. dirs. Inst. Postgrad. Studies, Ill. Psychol. Assn. Mem. APA (clin. psychology, pub. svc., psychol. hypnosis, sec. treas. pub. svc. 1990-91), Ill. Psychol. Assn. (clin. psychology and acad. sects.; sec. 1982-83, pres.-elect 1983-84, pres. 1984-85), AAAS, Am. Group Psychotherapy Assn., Am. Soc. Clin. Hypnosis, Minn. Psychol. Assn., Am. Evaluation Assn., Am. Assn. Univ. Profs., Assn. VA chief Psychologists (sec., treas. 1987-90, pres.-elect 1990-91, pres. 1991-92, past pres. 1992-93). Founding editor: Louvain Studies, 1966; editor: VA Directory of Psychology Staffing and Services, 1982, 83, 84, 85, 87. Recipient Outstanding Leadership award Ass. VA Chief Psychologists, 1992. Home: 2281 Ocala Ct Mendota Hts MN 55120-1646 Office: VA Med Ctr Minneapolis MN 55417

NIGHTINGALE, ELENA OTTOLENGHI, geneticist, physician, administrator; b. Livorno, Italy, Nov. 1, 1932; came to U.S., 1939; d. Mario Lazzaro and Elisa Vittoria (Levi) Ottolenghi; m. Stuart L. Nightingale, July 1, 1965; children—Elizabeth, Marisa. A.B. summa cum laude, Barnard Coll., 1954; Ph.D., Rockefeller U., 1961; M.D., NYU, 1964. Asst. prof. Cornell U. Med. Coll., N.Y.C., 1965-70, Johns Hopkins U., Balt., 1970-73; fellow in clin. genetics and pediatrics Georgetown U. Hosp., Washington, 1973-74; sr. staff officer NAS, Washington, 1975-79, sr. program officer Inst. Medicine, 1979-82, sr. scholar in residence, 1982-83; spl. advisor to pres. Carnegie Corp. N.Y., N.Y.C., 1983-94, sr. program officer, 1989-94; scholar-in-residence Nat. Acad. Scis., Washington, 1995—; vis. assoc. prof. Harvard U. Med. Sch., Boston, 1980-84, vis. lectr., 1984-95; adj. prof. pediatrics Georgetown U. Med. Ctr., 1984—, George Washington U. Med. Ctr., 1994—; mem. recombinant DNA adv. com. NIH, Bethesda, Md., 1979-83. Editor: The Breaking of Bodies and Minds: Torture, Psychiatric Abuse and the Health Professions, 1985, Prenatal Screening, Policies and Values: The Example of Neural Tube Defects, 1987; co-author: Before Birth: Prenatal Screening for Genetic Disease, 1990, Promoting the Health of Adolescents: New Directions for the 21st Century, 1993; contbr. numerous sci. articles to profl. publs. Bd. dirs. Ctr. for Youth Svcs., Washington, 1980-84, Sci. Svc. Inc., Washington, 1985-96, Amnesty Internat., U.S.A., 1989-91. Sloan Found. fellow, 1974-75. Fellow AAAS (chmn. com. on sci. freedom and responsibility 1985-88), N.Y. Acad. Scis., Royal Soc. Medicine; mem. Harvey Soc., Am. Soc. Microbiology, Am. Soc. Human Genetics (social issues com. 1982-85), Genetics Soc. Am., Inst. Medicine of NAS (chmn. com. on health and human rights 1987-90), Phi Beta Kappa, Sigma Xi. Office: Nat Acad Scis 2101 Constitution Ave NW Washington DC 20418-0007

NIGRO, ALDO, physiology and psychology educator; b. Scigliano, Italy, Mar. 27, 1927; s. Francesco and Mariannina (Pagliuso) N.; m. Rosa Siss Merro, Sept. 8, 1969; 1 child, Francesco. MD, U. Messina, Italy, 1950. Pvt. dozent physiology U. Messina, 1959, prof. psychology, 1969; dir., mgr. Polidadattico, Messina, 1990—. Author: Dialogo proteico, 1974, Modello Psicolinguistico, 1988, Human Light: A Cybernetic Theory of Consciousness, 1992, Informatic Circulation for the Biopsychological Evolution, 1993. Pres. Universita Tempo Libero, Messina, 1990. Mem. Accademia Peloritana Pericolanti. Roman Catholic. Home: N Panoramica 1330, Messina Italy 98168 Office: Cattedra Psychology, T Cannizzaro 278, Messina Italy 98100

NIHILL, KAREN BAILEY, nursing home executive, nurse clinician; b. Erie, Pa., Mar. 15, 1947; d. William C. and Eleanor (Danielson) Bailey; 1 son, Liam H. R.N., Hamot Med. Center, Erie, 1968; postgrad. SUNY, Gannon U., U. S.C., U. Pa., 1974—. RN, Pa. Critical care nurse Hamot Med. Center, 1968-71, VA Hosp., Phila., 1974-77; dir. nursing Chapel Manor and Nursing Home, Phila., 1977—, also Phila. Protestant Home and Elmira Jeffries Nursing Home; critical care nurse coord., supr. Millcreek Community Hosp., Erie, Pa., 1991—. Active Lutheran Ch. Women's Orgn. Served to lt. Nurse Corps, U.S. Navy, 1971-73. VA grantee, 1974. Mem. ACLS, Am. Assn. Critical Care Nurses, Pa. Nurses Assn. Republican. Home: 5316 Bryant St Erie PA 16509-2404

NIITU, YASUTAKA, pediatrician, educator; b. Nagano Prefecture, Japan, Aug. 3, 1920; s. Shusuke and Tsuruji N.; m. Tokiko Komuro, Dec. 8, 1952; children: Hidetaka, Iwayasu, Munetaka. Igakushi, Tohoku Imperial U., 1943, MD (Igakuhakase), 1949. Rsch. fellow Research Inst. for TB and Leprosy, Tohoku U., Sendai, Japan, 1943-54, asst. prof. dept. pediatrics, 1954-63, Univ. prof. pediatrics Research Inst. for TB and Cancer, 1964-84, prof. emeritus, 1984—; dr. Miyagi br. Japan Anti TB Assn., 1984—; pres. Sendai Kosei Hosp., 1973-80, 86-89; adviser Japan Sarcoidosis Com., Soc. Paediatrica Japonica, Japan Soc. Pediat. Pulmonology (pres. 1980-88), Japan Soc. Pediat. Infectious Diseases; tech. adviser Shenyang First Tuberculosis Hosp., Shenyang Anti-tuberculosis Ctr., Shenyang Chest Hosp., People's Republic of China. Capt. M.C., Japanese Army, 1943-45. Named to Third Order Merit Mid. Rising Sun Emperor of Japan, 1994. Mem. Internat. Orgn. Mycoplasmology, World Assn. Sarcoidosis and Other Granulomatous Diseases, Japan Soc. Chest Diseases, Soc. Japanese Virologists, Japanese Soc. TB, Am. Soc. Microbiology, Internat. Union Against TB and Lung Disease, Japan Soc. Internat. Medicine, Japan Assn. Infectious Diseases, Japanese Assn. Child Health. Co-author books in Japanese, including: Virus and Diseases, 1969; Routine Pediatric Diagnosis and Treatment, 1971; New Virology, 1972; Pediatric X-Ray Diagnosis, 1972; Handbook of Clinical Pneumology, 1977; Present Pediatrics, 1978; Clinical Virology, 1978; Sarcoidosis, 1979; Practice of Pediatric Infections, 1980; Mycoplasma, 1981; Illustrations of Mycoplasma, 1981; Illustrations of Pediatric Diagnosis and Treatment, 1981; Illustrated Pediatric Chart 1982; Topics of Infections, 1983. Mem. editl. bd. Pediatric Pulmonology, 1985—. Contbr. 300 articles to profl. jours. Home: Higashikatsuyama 1-5-6, Aobaku Sendai 981, Japan Office: Japan Anti TB Assn, Miyagi Br Miyamachi 1-1-5, Aobaku Sendai 980, Japan

NIKOLIC, GEORGE, cardiologist, consultant; b. Belgrade, Yugoslavia, Feb. 7, 1945; came to Australia, 1964; s. Ilija and Sofija (Rajic) N.; m. Annette Courtney Smith, Feb. 7, 1978; children: Alexandra Courtney, John George. MB, BS with honors, Sydney U., 1971. Diplomate Am. Bd. Internal Medicine, Am. Bd. Cardiovascular Med., Critical Care Medicine resident St. Vincent's Hosp., Sydney, Australia, 1971-72, med. registrar, 1973-74, cardiology registrar, 1975; med. and cardiology registrar Woden Valley, Canberra, Australia, 1976-77, dir. intensive care, 1978, 1982-91, sr. specialist, 1991—; cardiology fellow St. Vincent Hosps., S.I., Worcester, 1979-82; asst. prof. medicine U. Mass., Worcester, 1981-82.Contbr. articles in field to med. jours. Fellow Royal Australasian Coll. Physicians (sec. Australian capital Territory br., Canberra 1983), Am. Coll. Cardiology, Am. Coll. Chest Physicians; mem. Australia-N.Z. Intensive Care Soc., Critical Care Soc., Cardiac Soc. Australia and New Zealand. Office: Woden Valley Hosp, PO Box 11, Woden ACT 2606, Australia

NILES, BARBARA ELLIOTT, psyanalyst; b. Boston, Jan. 31, 1939; d. Byron Kauffman and Helen Alice (Heissler) Elliott; m. John Denison, June 25, 1960 (div. 1981); children: Catherine, Andrew. AA, Briarcliff Coll., 1958; BA, SUNY, 1984; MSW, Hunter Coll., 1986. Cert. social worker; cert. in psychotherapy and psychoanalysis Inst. Contemporary Psychotherapy and Psychoanalysis, 1990. Exec. com. Legal Aid Soc. Women's Aux., N.Y.C., 1965-67; sec. Water Quality Task Force Scientists' Com. for Pub. Info., N.Y.C., 1973-74; founding dir., sec. Consumer Action Now Inc., N.Y.C., 1970-77; dir. devel. Consumer Action Now's Council Environ., N.Y.C., 1976-77; dir. 170 Tenants Corp., N.Y.C., 1979-81; mem. pub. interest com. Cosmopolitan Club, N.Y.C., 1979-82; dir. INFORM Inc., N.Y.C., 1978-84; pvt. practice psychotherapy and psychoanalysis N.Y.C., 1986—; mem. faculty metro ctr. Empire State Coll., N.Y.C., 1987—. Editor: biography: Off the Beaten Track, 1984. Mem. Nat. Assn. Social Workers. Clubs: Cosmopolitan (N.Y.C.), The Vincent (Boston). Office: 230 Central Park W New York NY 10024-6029

NILSON, PATRICIA, clinical psychologist; b. Boulder, Colo., Oct. 22, 1929; d. James William and Vera Maude (Peacock) Broxon; m. Eric Walter Nilson, Dec. 23, 1950; children: Stephen Daniel, Eric Jon, Christopher Lawrence. BA, U. Colo.; RPT, Med. Coll. Va., 1951; MA in Clin. Psychology, L.I. U., 1972, PhD, 1973. Lic. psychologist, N.Y.; registered phys. therapist. Clin. psychologist Court Cons. Unit, Hauppauge, N.Y., 1972-92, Three Village Counseling Svc., Setauket, N.Y., 1974-75, Farmingville (N.Y.) Mental Health Ctr., N.Y., 1992-95; pvt. practice Commack, N.Y., 1972—; adj. asst. prof. C.W. Post Coll., Brookdale, 1974-80; cons., supr. psychologist Wayside Sch. for Girls, Valley Stream, 1975-85; cons. L.I. Lighting Co., 1980; lectr. in field. Author children's therapeutic stories; author therapeutic games: The Road to Problem Mastery; contbr. articles to profl. jours. Mem. APA, Suffolk County Psychol. Assn., Nat. Register Health Svc. Providers in Psychology, Soc. for Clin. and Exptl. Hypnosis (life), Am. Soc. Clin. Hypnosis (cert. and approved cons. in hypnosis). Office: 11 Montrose Dr Commack NY 11725-1312

NILSON, RICHARD EDWIN, psychiatrist; b. Hartford, Conn., Mar. 11, 1948; s. Edwin Norman and Edith N.; m. Susan Grace Haines, July 21, 1973. BA, Bowdoin Coll., 1970; MS, Worcester Poly. Inst., 1974; MD, U. Conn., 1977. Diplomate Am. Bd. Psychiatry and Neurology. Intern Inst. Living, Hartford Hosp., 1977-78, resident, 1978-81; staff psychiatrist Inst. of Living, Hartford, Conn., 1981-86; unit chief Inst. of Living, Hartford, 1986-88; pvt. practice Farmington, Conn., 1988—; cons. Wheeler Clinic, Plainville, Conn., 1988—. Mem. Am. Psychiat. Assn. Home: 24 Northfield West Hartford CT 06107-3321 Office: 316 Main St Farmington CT 06032-2961

NILSSON, BO ERIK, orthopedic surgeon, educator; b. Kristinhamm, Sweden, Mar. 13, 1933; s. Ragnar E. and Ragna A. (Vallerius) N.; m. Margareta A. Gustafsson, Dec. 7, 1956; children: Johan, Anders, Fredrik, Brita. MD, Karolinska Inst., Stockholm, 1958; PhD, Lund U., 1967. Lic. physician Bd. Orthopedic Surgery. Resident Soc. Relief of Crippled, Hämösand, 1958-60, Orthopedics Dept., Malmö, Sweden, 1960-64; fellow Hosp. Spl. Surgery, N.Y.C., 1964-66; lectr. Lund U., Malmö, 1966-80, prof., 1981—; chmn. dept. orthopedics Lund U., Malmö, 1981—; mem. Swedish Med. Rsch. Coun., Stockholm, 1982-88, Swedish Work Life Coun., Stockholm, 1992—; counselor Sci. Nat. Bd. Health Sci. Coun., Stockholm, 1981—. Contbr. numerous articles to profl. publs. Mem. Scandinavian Orthopedic Assn. (pres. 1990-92), Nordic Orthopedic Fedn. (pres. 1996-98). Mem. Ch. of Sweden. Office: Malmö Univ Hosp, Dept Orthopedics, Malmo Sweden

NILSSON, BO INGVAR, hematologist; b. Helsingborg, Sweden, Sept. 15, 1947; s. Jonny Ingvar and Sonja Eugenia (Akesson) N.; m. Elsa Sigbritt Warkander, Aug. 20, 1971; children: Victoria, Philip, Sofia. MD, U. Gothenburg, 1973; PhD, U. Lund, 1985. Lic. physician, 1973. Resident Dept. Radiology, Univ. Hosp., Gothenburg, 1973-74, Dept. Internal Medicine, County Hosp., Angelholm, 1974-76; resident Dept. Internal Medicine, Univ. Hosp. Lund, 1976-78, amanuensis, 1978-83; sr. house officer Dept. Internal Medicine, County Hosp., Helsingborg, 1983-86; med. dir. oncology Pharmacia Leo Therapeutics, Helsingborg, 1986-88; rsch. dir. oncology Pharmacia Leo Therapeutics, 1989-90; rsch. dir. oncology Kabi Pharmacia Therapeutics, 1991-92, dir. med. affairs, 1992-93; dir. oncology Pharmacia, Inc., 1993-95, med. dir. hematology, 1995—. Contbr. articles to profl. jours. U. Lund, Segerfalk Found. grantee, 1978-86. Mem. Am. Soc. Clin. Oncology, Am. Soc. Hematology, Internat. Soc. Regional Chemotherapy, Swedish Soc. Medicine, Swedish Soc. Hematology-Oncology (edn. com. 1985-89), N.Y. Acad. Scis., European Soc. Med. Oncology, Oncology of So. Sweden (bd. dirs. 1980-83), Wig. Home: Kristinehamnsg 12, S-25661 Helsingborg Sweden Office: 7001 Post Rd Dublin OH 43017

NILSSON, ERIK KARL, medical educator, consulting surgeon; b. Uppsala, Sweden, Sept. 4, 1939; s. Sture and Edit N.; m. Birgit Olsson, Feb. 28, 1970; children: Lisa, Olof, Asa, Hanna. PhD, U. Lund, 1972, MD, 1974 Surgeon U. Hosp., Linkoping, Sweden, 1975-82; cons. surgeon Motala (Sweden) Hosp., 1982—; assoc. prof. surgery Linkoping U., 1990—. contbr. articles to profl. jours. Mem. AAAS, European Soc. Surg. Oncology, Soc. Internat. Chirurgie. Home: Brastorpsvegen 6, S-59150 Motala Sweden Office: Dept Surgery Motala Hosp, S-59185 Motala Sweden

NILSSON, KURT GÖSTA INGEMAR, biotechnology and enzyme technology scientist; b. Göteryd, Kronberg, Sweden, June 25, 1953; s. Sven Gösta and Ebba Birgit (Karlsson) N.; m. Pia Ingrid Elisabeth, July 30, 1983; children: Jenny Ingrid Maria, Johan Martin Ingemar. MSci. in Chemistry, U. Lund, Sweden, 1976, DrSci. in Applied Chemistry, 1984, postgrad., 1977-84. Sr. scientist Swedish Sugar Co., Ltd., Malmö, Arlöv, Sweden, 1985-87; mgr. biotech. Carbohydrate Internat., Arlöv, 1987-88; assoc. prof. Chem. Ctr. U. Lund, 1989—, docent Chem. Ctr., 1991; pres., CEO Glycorex AB, Lund, 1992—; cons. in field, 1988—. Contbr. articles and revs. to profl. jours. and books. Mem. Swedish Chem. Soc., Am. Chem. Soc., Biotransformation Club, N.Y. Acad. Scis. Office: Glycorex AB, Ideon Sci Park Sölveg 41, S-22370 Lund Sweden

NIMOITYN, PHILIP, cardiologist; b. Phila., Mar. 6, 1951; s. Benjamin Solomon and Edith (Ornstein) N.; m. Hillary Rachel Saul, June 11, 1989. BS in Biology with distinction, Phila. Coll. Pharmacy and Sci., 1972; MD, Thomas Jefferson U., 1976. Cert. Nat. Bd. Med. Examiners, Am. Bd. Internal Medicine, Am. Bd. Cardiovascular Disease. Intern Hahnemann U. Hosp., Phila., 1976-77; resident in internal medicine Thomas Jefferson U. Hosp., Phila., 1977-79, cardiovascular disease fellow, 1979-81, instr. medicine, 1981-90, clin. asst. prof., 1990—; attending physician Pa. Hosp., Phila., 1995—; cons. physician Wills Eye Hosp., Phila., 1981—; attending physician Penn. Hosp., Phila., 1995—. Author: (with others) Artificial Cardiac Pacing, 1984, Quick Reference to Cardiovascular Disease, 1987, Cardiac Emergency Care, 1991; contbr. articles to profl. jours. Recipient Cert. of Merit for Sci. Exhibits AMA, 1974, 2d prize for sci. exhibits Ind. State Med. Assn., 1974. Fellow Am. Coll. Cardiology; mem. AMA, Pa. Med. Soc., Phila. County Med. Soc. Office: 1128 Walnut St Ste 401 Philadelphia PA 19107-5568

NINE, JOHN EDWARD, pharmaceutical company executive; b. Warsaw, Ind., Apr. 22, 1936; s. Ira Cecil and Mary (Bidelman) N.; m. Janet Elizabeth Allen, Aug. 8, 1966; children: Jenna Elizabeth, Janelle Elise. BS in Pharmacy, Purdue U., W. Lafayette, Ind., 1963; DSc (hon.), Purdue U., 1983; DSc (hon.) Pharmacy, L.I. U., 1993. Registered pharmacist. Dir. prodn. Ciba Geigy, Union, N.J., 1968-76; v.p. mfg. Schering-Plough, Kenilworth, N.J., 1976-80; sr. v.p. tech. Schering-Plough, 1980-86, pres. tech. ops., 1985-86; pres. SPKK Schering-Plough, Osaka, Japan, 1986—; sr. v.p. group C Schering-Plough, Kenilworth, 1988-90, pres. tech. ops. U.S., 1990-96, corp. v.p., pres. tech. ops., 1996—. Pres. bd. health, Pompton Lakes, N.J., 1965. With U.S. Army, 1959-62. Republican.

NING, XUE-HAN (HSUEH-HAN NING), physiologist, researcher; b. Peng-Lai, Shandong, People's Republic of China, Apr. 15, 1936; came to U.S., 1984; s. Yi-Xing and Liu Ning; m. Jian-Xin Fan, May 28, 1967; 1 child, Di Fan. MD, Shanghai 1st Med. Coll., People's Republic of China, 1960. Rsch. fellow Shanghai Inst. Physiology, 1960-72, leader cardiovasc. rsch. group, 1973-83, head, assoc. prof. cardiovasc. rsch. unit, 1984-87, prof. and chair hypoxia dept., 1988-90, vice chairperson academic com., 1988-90; NIH internat. rsch. fellow U. Mich., Ann Arbor, 1984-87, vis. prof., hon. prof., rsch. investigator, 1990-95; prof. and dir. Hypoxia Physiology Lab. Academia Sinica, Shanghai, 1989—; acting leader, High Altitude Physiology Group, Chinese mountaineering and sci. expdn. team to Mt. Everest, 1975; leader High Altitude Physiology Group, Dept. Metall. Industry of China and Ry. Engring. Corps, 1979; vis. prof. dept. physiology Mich. State U., East Lansing, 1989-90; vis. prof. dept. pediat. U. Wash., Seattle, 1994—. Author: High Altitude Physiology and Medicine, 1981, Reports on Scientific Expedition to Mt. Qomolungma, High Altitude Physiology, 1980, Environment and Ecology of Qinghai-Xizong (Tibet) Plateau, 1982; mem. editl. bd. Chinese Jour. Applied Physiology, 1984—, Acta Physiologica, 1988—; contbr. articles to profl. jours. Recipient Merit award Shanghai Sci. Congress, 1977, All-China Sci. Congress, Beijing, 1978, Super Class award Academia Sinica, Beijing, 1986, 1st Class award Nat. Natural Scis., Beijing, 1987, # 1 Best Article award Tzu-Chi Med. Jour., Taiwan, 1995. Mem. Am. Physiol. Soc., Internat. Soc. Heart Rsch., Royal Soc. Medicine, Shanghai Assn. Physiol. (bd. dirs. 1988—), Chinese Assn. Physiol. (com. applied physiology 1984—, com. blood, cardiovascular, respiratory and renal physiology 1988—), Chinese Soc. Medicine, Chinese Soc. Biomed. Engring. Home: 7033 43rd Ave NE Seattle WA 98115-6015 Office: U Wash Dept Pediatrics Box 356320 1959 NE Pacific St Seattle WA 98195

NININGER, JAMES EDWARD, psychiatrist; b. Ft. Worth, Oct. 31, 1948; s. Eugene Victor and Ona Fern (Stranathan) N.; m. Margarethe Von der Meden, May 13, 1989; children: Victor James, Erika Cody, Patrick William. BA, Kenyon Coll., 1970; MD, U. Cin., 1974. Diplomate Am. Bd. Psychiatry and Neurology. Resident psychiatry Mt. Sinai Hosp., N.Y.C., 1974-76, chief resident psychiatry, 1976-77; mem. faculty dept. psychiatry Cornell U. Med. Coll., N.Y.C., 1977, clin. assoc. prof. psychiatry, 1989—; pvt. practice N.Y.C., 1977—. Contbr. articles to profl. jours., chpts. to books. Vol. psychiatrist Project Reach-Out, 1986-90. Fellow Am. Psychiat. Assn. (chmn. com. on aging N.Y. br. 1988—, rep. to nat. assembly 1988-94), N.Y. State Psychiat. Assn. (v.p. 1994—); mem. Am. Assn. Geriatric Psychiatry, Kenyon Coll. Alumni Coun. (pres. 1989-90, trustee 1991—). Office: 17 E 76th St New York NY 10021-1720

NIPPER, HENRY CARMACK, toxicologist, educator; b. Alexander City, Ala., Mar. 31, 1940; s. Henry Lee and Zackie Irene (Carmack) N.; m. Margaret Anne Gilbreth, June 10, 1966; children: Zachary Gilbreth, Gregory Lee Gilbreth. AB, Emory U., 1960; MS, Purdue U., 1966; PhD, U. Md., 1971. Diplomate Am. Bd. Clin. Chemistry. Analytical chemist E.I. DuPont de Nemours Co., Wilmington, Del., 1960-63; instr. pathology U. Md. Sch. Medicine, Balt., 1973-74, asst. prof., 1974-83; dir. chemistry VA Med Ctr., Balt., 1973-83; instr. pathology Harvard Med. Sch., Boston, 1983-86; sci. dir. clin. chemistry Beth Israel Hosp., Boston, 1983-86; assoc. prof. Creighton U., Omaha, 1986—; dir. St. Joseph Hosp. Clin. Chemistry and Forensic Toxicology Labs., 1986-96, dir. Creighton Forensic Lab. 1996—; mem. clin. adv. bd. Beckman Inst., Brea, Calif., 1982-83; mem. panel on clinchem. and toxicology FDA Ctr. for Devices and Radiologic Health, 1989-92, cons., 1992—. Editor: Clinician and Chemist, 1979; Selected Papers on Clinical Chemistry Instrumentation, 1985; chair editorial bd. Forensic Urine Drug Testing, 1993—; contbr. articles to profl. jours. Soccer coach Wellesley Soccer, Mass., 1984; scout leader Boy Scouts Am., Cub Scouts, Omaha, Wellesley, also Balt., 1982-93; bd. dirs. Ruxton-Riderwood Community Assn., Balt., 1983, Omaha Morning Rotary, 1987—; pres. Nat. Registry Clin. Chemistry, 1982-93. VA rsch. grantee, 1979; Gillette-Harris rsch. fellow U. Md., 1968-69. Fellow Nat. Acad. Clin. Biochemistry; mem. Am. Assn. for Clin. Chemistry (Roe award 1978), Am. Acad. Forensic Scis., Assn. Clin. Biochemists (U.K.), Alpha Tau Omega. Democrat. Congregationalist. Club: Nantucket Yacht. Avocations: gardening, collector old toy trains. Office: Creighton U Dept Pathology 2500 California Plaza Omaha NE 68178-0222

NIR, YEHUDA, psychiatrist, educator; b. Stanislawow, Poland, Mar. 31, 1930; came to U.S., 1959; s. Samuel and Sidia (Hager) Grunfeld; m. Eva Roos, June 3, 1957; children: Daniel, Aaron; m. Bonnie Maslin, Nov. 4, 1973; children: David, Sarah. MD, Hebrew U., Jerusalem, 1958. Internship Hadassah Hosp., Jerusalem, 1958-59; residency in psychiatry Phila. Psychiat. Ctr., Phila., 1959-61, Mt. Sinai Hosp., N.Y.C., 1961-62, fellow in child psychiatry Jewish Bd. of Guardians, N.Y.C., 1962-64; Asst. prof. psychiatry Mt. Sinai Med. Sch., N.Y.C., 1973-79, NYU, N.Y.C., 1975—; Assoc. prof. psychiatry Cornell U. Med. Coll., N.Y.C., 1979—. Author: Loving Men for the Right Reasons, 1983, Not Quite Paradise, 1987, Lost Childhood, a Memoir, 1989. Bd. dirs. Am. Gathering of Jewish Holocaust Survivors. Mem. Am. Psychiat. Assn. (human rights com. 1988). Jewish. Office: 903 Park Ave New York NY 10021-0338

NIRENBERG, MARSHALL WARREN, biochemist; b. N.Y.C., N.Y., Apr. 10, 1927; s. Harry Edward and Minerva (Bykowsky) N.; m. Perola Zaltzman, July 14, 1961. B.S. in Zoology, U. Fla., 1948, M.S., 1952; Ph.D. in Biochemistry, U. Mich., 1957. Postdoctoral fellow Am. Cancer Soc. at NIH, 1957-59; postdoctoral fellow USPHS at NIH, 1959-60; mem. staff NIH, 1960—; research biochemist, chief lab. biochem. genetics Nat. Heart, Lung and Blood Inst., 1962—; researcher mechanism protein synthesis, genetic code, nucleic acids, regulatory mechanisms in synthesis macromolecules, and neurobiology. Recipient Molecular Biology award Nat. Acad. Scis., 1962, award in biol. scis. Washington Acad. Scis., 1962, medal HEW, 1964, Modern Medicine award, 1963, Harrison Howe award Am.

Chem. Soc., 1964, Nat. Medal Sci. Pres. Johnson, 1965, Hildebrand award Am. Chem. Soc., 1966, Research Corp. award, 1966, A.C.P. award, 1967, Gairdner Found. award merit Can., 1967, Prix Charles Leopold Meyer French Acad. Scis., 1967, Franklin medal Franklin Inst., 1968, Albert Lasker Med. Research award, 1968, Priestly award, 1968; co-recipient Louisa Gross Horowitz prize Columbia, 1968, Nobel prize in medicine and physiology, 1968. Fellow AAAS, N.Y. Acad. Scis.; mem. Am. Soc. Biol. Chemists, Am. Chem. Soc. (Paul Lewis award enzyme chemistry 1964), Am. Acad. Arts and Scis., Biophys. Soc., Nat. Acad. Scis., Washington Acad. Scis., Soc. for Study Devel. and Growth, Soc. Devel. Biology, Harvey Soc. (hon.), Leopoldina Deutsche Akademie der Naturforscher, Pontificial Acad. Scis. Office: NIH Lab Biochemical Genetics Bldg 36 Rm 1C06 Bethesda MD 20892*

NISBET, TOMA ALGER-SCHAUFFELE, public health service officer. Diploma, St. Mark's Hosp. Sch. Nursing, Salt Lake City, 1967; BSN, No. Ill. U., 1969, MSN, 1973. Mem. night nursing staff Sycamore (Ill.) Mcpl. Hosp., 1967-68; supr. evening relief/charge nurse DeKalb County (Ill.) Nursing Home, 1969; pub. health nurse DeKalb County Health Dept., 1969-71; project coord. health svcs. No. Ill. U. Coll. Continuing Edn., DeKalb, 1973-74; lectr. No. Ill. U. Sch. Nursing, 1979-84; divsn. dir. nursing svcs. Winnebago County Dept. Pub. Health, Rockford, Ill., 1974-84; pub. health nursing state program mgr. State of Wyo. Divsn. Health and Med. Svcs., Cheyenne, 1985-87, policy devel. and spl. projects state program mgr., 1987-88; exec. State of Wyo. Bd. Nursing, Cheyenne, 1988—; spokesperson NIX, D-A-Y Pub. Rels. for Burroughs Welcome, N.Y.C., 1987; presenter profl. confs. Bd. dirs. YWCA, Rockford, Ill., 1984-85, Winnebago County Child Protection Assn., 1975-79, Greater Rockford Chtp. Nat. SIDS, 1979-85, treas., 1981-82; mem. LWV, 1969-90, Wyo. Task Force Gov.'s Mental Health Cmty. Support Programs, 1985-87, Wyo. Commn. Nursing and Nursing Edn., 1988-95; mem. Com. for Prevention Sexually Transmitted Diseases Human Svc. Network DeKalb County, 1970-72; mem. and chief staffer Wyo.'s Long Term Care Task Force, 1987-88; sec. Wyo. State Bd. Nursing Home Adminstrs., 1988-89, vice chmn., 1990-95; del. Nat. Coun. State Bds. Nursing, 1988-95, mem. AEC com., 1990-94, mem. nomination com., 1991-92, mem. ednl. program task force, 1994-95, alt. mem. examination com., 1994-95. Recipient Pub. Health Svc. award Dept. Health and Human Svcs. Region VIII, 1986. Mem. ANA, Wyo. Orgn. Nurse Execs., Wyo. Advanced Practitioner Nursing Orgn. Home: 322 W 6th Ave Cheyenne WY 82001 Office: Wyo State Bd Nursing Barrett Bldg 2d Fl 2301 Central Ave Cheyenne WY 82002

NISENHOLTZ, FREDERICK, pharmacist; b. Phila., Oct. 20, 1929; s. Samuel and Sophie (Kaprow) N.; m. Rhoda Annette Altus, Apr. 20, 1958; children: Tina F., Hollie S. BS in Pharmacy, Temple U., 1953. Lic. pharmacist, Pa. Pharmacist Sun Ray Drug, Phila., 1955-56, Davis Pharmacy, Elkins Park, Pa., 1956-57, Levin Pharmacy, Phila., 1957-59; pharmacist, owner Nisenholtz Pharmacy, Phila., 1959-92, ret., 1992. With U.S. Army, 1953-55, Korea. Mem. Steuben Lodge 113. Office: Nisenholtz Pharmacy 7624 Castor Ave Philadelphia PA 19152-3623

NISHI, OKIHIRO, ophthalmologist, surgeon; b. Osaka, Japan, Nov. 20, 1940; s. Taseki and Sono (Shiraishi) N.; m. Kayo Nakagawa, Nov. 22, 1975; children: Jinyu, Yutaro, Hiroyuki. B Culture, U. Tokyo, 1961; MD, U. Freiburg, Germany, 1967. Asst. physician in ophthalmology U. Tokyo, 1967-70; vice dir. Nishi Eye Hosp., Osaka, 1970-86, dir., 1986—; surgeon faculty eye camp Indo-Japan Ophthalmol. Found., Madras, India, 1987, bd. dirs., 1987—; tchr. in tng. of many Indian physicians for cataract surgery, 1986—; mem. faculty Congress of European Soc. of Cataract and Refractive Surgeons, Dublin, 1987—; alt. dir. Highlights of Ophthalmology, Panama, 1994—. Author: (with others) Techniques of Phacoemulsification & IOL Implantation, 1992; translator: Pathologie des Auges (Naumann & Apple) 1987; inventor surgical instrument for cataract surgery and restoration of accommodation by lens refilling using inflatable endocap balloon; editor Japanese Jour. Cataract and Refractive Surgery, 1986—, Japanese Jour. Ophthalmic Surgery, 1988; contbr. more than 120 articles to profl. jours. including Cataract Surgery. Mem. Japan Soc. Cataract and Refractive Surgery (bd. dirs. 1986—), Internat. Intraocular Implant Club, Internat. Ophthalmic Microsurg. Study Group. Office: Nishi Eye Hosp, Higashinari-ku Nakamachi 4-14-26, Osaka 537, Japan

NISHIMOTO, WARREN SADAMU, physician; b. Honolulu, June 11, 1961; s. Herbert Sadamu and Jessie Yoshiye (Moriyasu) N.; m. Michele Leslie Jones, July 2, 1994; 1 child, Ryan Sadamu. BA in Biology, U. Hawaii, 1984; DO, Southeastern U. Health Scis., North Miami Beach, Fla., 1991. Intern Pacific Hosp of Long Beach, Calif., 1991-92, resident family practice, 1992-94; pvt. practice Salins Valley Med. Group, Salinas, Calif., 1994—. Mem. Am. Coll. Osteo. Family Physicians, Am. Acad. Osteopathy, Monterey County Med. Assn., Am. Osteo. Assn. Home & Office: Salinas Valley Med Group 212 San Jose St Ste 101 Salinas CA 93901

NISHIMURA, MANABU, nephrologist; b. Kitakyusyu, Fukuoka, Japan, Aug. 20, 1950; s. Noboru N. and Fujiko K. Nishimura; m. Hitomi Nishimura, Sept. 15, 1980; children: Sayaka, Misaki, Megumi, Takashi. MD, Kurume U. Sch. Medicine, Japan, 1977. Med. diplomate. Resident Kokura Nat. Hosp., Kitakyusyu, 1977-79; physician dept. internal medicine Asou Iizuka Hosp., Iizuka City, Japan, 1979-82, dir. dept. Kidney Ctr., 1982-85, dir. dept. nephrology, 1985—. Patentee in field. Mem. Soc. Japanese Internal Medicine, Japanese Soc. Dialysis Therapy (coun. mem. 1989—), Soc. Nephrology, Soc. Transplantation. Mem. Am. Soc. Nephrology, Internat. Soc. Peritoneal Dialysis, European Dialysis and Transplantation Assn. Office: Asou Iizuka Hosp-Nephrology, 3-83 Yoshiomachi, Iizuka City Fukuoka 820, Japan

NISHIMURA, SUSUMU, biologist; b. Taito-ku, Tokyo, Japan, Apr. 7, 1931; s. Kiyoshi and Chie (Watabe) N.; m. Michiko Uzawa, Nov. 14, 1961; children: Tomoo, Kazuo. BSc in Chemistry, U. Tokyo, 1955, PhD in Biochemistry and Biophysics, 1960. Rsch. assoc. Cancer Inst., Tokyo, 1960-62; postdoctoral fellow Biol. Div. Oak Ridge (Tenn.) Nat. Lab., 1961-63; rsch. assoc. Inst. for Enzyme Rsch. U. Wis., Madison, 1963-65; sect. chief Virology Div. Nat. Cancer Ctr. Rsch. Inst., Tokyo, 1965-68, div. chief Biology Div., 1968-92; exec. dir. Banyu Tsukuba Rsch. Inst., Banyu Pharm. Co., Ltd., Japan, 1992-95; sr. exec. dir. Banyu Tsukuba Rsch. Inst., Banyu Pharm. Co., Ltd., 1995—. Recipient Naito Sci. award Naito Found., 1980, Acad. and Imperial prize, Japan Acad., 1988, Princess Takamatsu Cancer Rsch. prize, 1988, Fujiwara Found. prize, 1990. Mem. Am. Soc. for Biochemistry and Molecular Biology (hon.), N.Y. Acad. Sci. Home: 3-10-7 Hanbaktake, Tsukuba-City Ibaraki 300-32, Japan Office: Banyu Tsukuba Rsch Inst, Okubo 3 Tsukuba, Ibaraki 300-33, Japan

NISHIOKA, GARY JIM, facial plastic surgeon; b. Hood River, Oreg., Oct. 23, 1955; s. Jim Zenshi and Michi (Miwa) N.; m. Linda Thornton, May 22, 1982; 1 child, Ryder. BS in Biology, U. Oreg., 1978; DMD, Oreg. Health Sci. U., 1982; MD, U. Tex. Health Sci. Ctr., 1990. Diplomate Am. Bd. Oral and Maxillofacial Surgery. Resident in hosp. dentistry Oreg. Health Svc. U., Portland, 1982-83; intern in anesthesiology U. Tex. Health Sci. Ctr., San Antonio, 1982-86, resident, 1984-87; intern in gen. surgery U. Mo., Columbia, 1990-91, resident in otolaryngology, 1991-95; fellow in facial plastic and reconstructive surgery Seattle, 1995—. Contbr. articles to profl. jours. Fellow Am. Bd. Otolaryngology; mem. Am. Acad. Facial Plastic and Reconstructive Surgery, Am. Acad. Otolaryngology-Head and Neck Surgery. Roman Catholic. Office: 600 Broadway Ste 280 Seattle WA 98122

NISHIOKA, KIYOSHI, dermatologist, educator; b. Osaka, Japan, Dec. 22, 1939; s. Sueo and Asako (Kashii) N.; m. Kyoko Ishiwatari, June 22, 1968; children: Chisato, Ely. MD, Osaka U., 1964, PhD, 1969. Intern Hokushin Gen. Hosp., Japan, 1964-65; rsch. fellow Inst. Dermatology, London, 1970-72; lectr. Kansai Med. Coll., Osaka, 1972-76; demonstrator Osaka U., 1969-70, 76-78, lectr., 1978-86; assoc. prof. Kitasato U., Sagamiliara, Japan, 1986-90; prof., chmn. Tokyo Med. and Dental U., 1990—. Author: How to Choose Topical Ointment, 1989, Textbook of Atopic Dermatitis, 1994; contbr. articles to profl. jours. Mem. Japanese Dermatol. Assn. (com. mem. 1990), Japanese Soc. Allergology (editor jour. 1992—, com. mem. 1976—). Home: 1-25-6 Kasugadenaka, Konohanaku, Osaka 554, Japan Office: Tokyo Med/Dental U Dermatol, 1-5-45 Yushima, Bunkyoku, Tokyo 113, Japan

NISSEL, MARTIN, radiologist, consultant; b. N.Y.C., July 29, 1921; s. Samuel David and Etta Rebecca (Ostrie) N.; m. Beatrice Goldberg, Dec. 26, 1943; children: Philippa Lyn, Jeremy Michael. BA, NYU, 1941; MD, N.Y. Med. Coll., 1944. Diplomate Am. Bd. Radiology. Intern Met. Hosp., N.Y.C., 1944-45, Lincoln Hosp., N.Y.C., 1947-48; resident in radiology Bronx Hosp., 1948-50, attending radiologist, 1952-54; resident in radiotherapy Montefiore Hosp., Bronx, 1950-51, attending radiotherapist, 1954-65; attending radiologist Buffalo (N.Y.) VA Hosp., 1951-52; attending radiotherapist Univ. Hosp. Boston City Hosp., 1965-69; asst. prof. radiology Boston U. Sch. of Medicine, 1965-69; chief radiotherapist,dir. radiation ctr. Brookside Hosp., San Pablo, Calif., 1969-77; group leader, radiopharm. drugs FDA, Rockville, Md., 1977-86; pvt. cons. radiopharm. drug devel., 1986—. Contbr. articles to profl. jours. Lectr. Am. Cancer Soc., Contra Costa County, Calif., 1973-76. Capt. MC AUS, 1945-47, Korea. Recipient Contra Costa County Speakers Bur. award Am. Cancer Soc., 1973, 76, Responsible Person for Radiol. Health Program for Radiopharm. Drugs award FDA, 1980-86. Mem. Am. Coll. Radiology, Radiol. Soc. N.Am. Office: PO Box 5537 Eugene OR 97405-0537

NISSENBAUM, GERALD, physician; b. Jersey City, Feb. 5, 1932; m. Sylvia Sinakin, Sept. 4, 1957; children: Gary David, Eliot Mark, Robert Samuel. BA, Yeshiva U., 1954; MD, SUNY, 1958. Resident Jersey City Med. Ctr., 1959-60, sr. resident, 1960-61; rsch. fellow in gastroenterology Nat. Cancer Inst., 1962-63; asst. med. dir. Hebrew Hosp., Jersey City, 1962-73; clin. instr. medicine N.J. Coll. Medicine, 1963-72; asst. attending dept. medicine Jersey City Med. Ctr., 1963-68, assoc. attending, 1968-69, attending, 1970—, dir. gastroenterology, 1973-76; clin. asst. prof. medicine N.J. Coll. medicine, 1972—; pvt. practice internal medicine and gastroenterology Jersey City. Contbr. articles to profl. jours.; developed classic cytol. reagt. used in med. and microbiology, Nissenbaum's Fixative; patentee device for localizing gastrointestinal bleeding. Capt. M.C., U.S. Army. Recipient Bernard Revel Meml. award Yeshiva U., 1972. Mem. AMA, Soc. Protozoologists, N.J. Med. Soc., NRA, Phi Lambda Kappa.

NISSENSON, ALLEN RICHARD, physician, educator; b. Chgo., Dec. 10, 1946; s. Harry and Sylvia Lillian (Chapnitzsky) N.; m. Charna A. Karp, May 28, 1978; 1 child, Ariel Rose. BS in Medicine, Northwestern U., 1967, MD, 1971. Diplomate Am. Bd. Internal Medicine, bd. cert. internal medicine and nephrology. Intern in medicine Michael Reese Hosp. and Med. Ctr., Chgo., 1971-72, resident in internal medicine, 1972-74; fellowship in nephrology Northwestern U., Chgo., 1974-76; assoc. medicine Northwestern U. Med. Sch., Chgo., 1976-77; asst. prof. medicine UCLA Sch. Medicine, 1977-82, assoc. prof. medicine, 1982-88, prof. medicine, 1988—; dir. dialysis program UCLA Ctr. for the Health Scis., 1977—; adj. attending physician Northwestern Meml. Hosp., Chgo., 1976-77; asst. attending physician UCLA Ctr. for Health Scis., 1977-82, assoc. attending physician, 1988—; attending physician nephrology Wadsworth VA Hosp., 1978—; cons. on peritoneal dialysis Baxter-Travenol Labs., 1981—; mem. nephrology adv. com. Nephrology Nursing Edn. Grant, Calif. State U., 1983-90; vice chmn. Forum of End Stage Renal Disease Networks, 1988-91; mem. sci. adv. bd. Nat. Kidney Found., 1989-91, chmn. coun. on clin. nephrology, dialysis and transplantation, 1989-91; cons. on End Stage Renal Disease reimbursement Rand Corp., 1990—, others. Editor-in-chief Advances in Renal Replacement Therapy, 1993—; mem. editl. bd. Dialysis and Transplantation, 1978—, UCLA Health Insights, 1981-89, Perspectives in Peritoneal Dialysis, 1983—, Internat. Jour. Artificial Organs, 1984—, Seminars in Dialysis, 1987—, Am. Jour. Nephrology, 1989—, Am. Jour. Kidney Diseases, 1989—, Geriat. Nephrology and Urology Jour., 1989—; mem. editl. adv. bd. Contemporary Dialysis, 1983—, Nephrology Practice Today, 1989—, Hematopoietic Therapy Index and Revs., 1993—, Primary Care Reports, 1994—; editl. cons. Am. Jour. Nephrology, 1981-88; contbr. chpts. to books, abstracts and articles to profl. publs. Recipient Nat. Kidney Found. So. Calif. Cmty. Svc. award, 1981; Robert Wood Johnson policy fellow Office of Sen. Paul Wellstone, 1994-95. Fellow ACP; mem. Am. Soc. for Artifical Internal Organs, Am. Fedn. for Clin. Rsch., Am. Soc. Nephrology, Internat. Soc. Nephrology, Internat. Soc. Artificial Organs, Western Soc. for Clin. Investigation, European Dialysis and Transplant Assn., N.Am. Soc. for Dialysis and Transplantation, Renal Physicians' Assn. (bd. dirs. 1993—, sec. bd. dirs. 1994—), Calif. Renal Physicians (bd. dirs. 1987—). Office: UCLA Med Ctr Dialysis Ctr Ste 565-59 200 Medical Plaza Los Angeles CA 90024-6945

NISTRI, ANDREA, pharmacology educator; b. Florence, Italy, Jan. 15, 1947; s. Carlo and Anna (Baroncelli) N.; m. Sandra Breckon, Aug. 4, 1972; children: Giampaolo, Christian. MD, U. Florence, 1971. Registered physician, Eng., Italy. Intern, hon. registrar in clin. toxicology St. Maria Nuova Hosp., Florence, 1972-73; resident, hon. registrar in clin. pharmacology St. Bartholomew's Hosp., London, 1973-75; asst. prof. U. Florence, 1975-76, assoc. prof., 1983-91; rsch. fellow Med. Rsch. Coun. McGill U., Montreal, Que., Can., 1977-78; lectr. St. Bartholomew's Hosp. Med. Coll., London, 1979-84, sr. lectr., 1985-87, reader, 1987-90; reader Queen Mary and Westfield Coll., London, 1990-92; prof. cellular and molecular pharmacology Internat. Sch. Advanced Studies, Trieste, Italy, 1992—; prof. pharmacology U. Pavia, Italy, 1994—. Contbr. numerous articles to profl. jours. Lt. Italian mil., 1972-74. Fellow Royal Soc. Medicine, Ciba Found., London, 1974-75; rsch. fellow NATO, Montreal, 1976. Mem. Internat. Brain Rsch. Orgn., Internat. Soc. Neurochemistry, European Soc. Neurochemistry, European Neuropeptide Club, Physiol. Soc., Soc. Neurosci., Brit. Pharm. Assn., Brit. Med. Assn. Office: Internat Sch Advanced, Via Beirut 2, 34013 Trieste Italy

NIXON, BARRY GORDON, critical care nurse; b. Vincentown, N.J., Oct. 27, 1955; s. Raymond Clair and Marjorie Jane (Michell) N. BS in Nursing cum laude, Thomas Jefferson U., 1993. RN, Pa. Nurse extern, med./respiratory ICU Thomas Jefferson U. Hosp., Phila., 1992-93, staff nurse, acute rehab. unit, 1993-95; staff nurse Intermediate Surg. ICU, 1995—. Mem. Pa. Nurses Assn., Alpha Eta Honor Soc. Allied Health Sci. Professions, Sigma Theta Tau. Home: 2001 Hamilton St P104 Philadelphia PA 19130

NIXON, CHARLES WILLIAM, bioacoustician; b. Wellsburg, W.Va., Aug. 15, 1929; s. William E. and Lenora S. (Treiber) N.; m. Barbara Irene Hunter, May 19, 1956; children: Timothy C., Tracy Scott. BS, Ohio State U., 1952, MS, 1953, PhD, 1960. Tchr. spl. edn. Ohio and W.Va. Pub. Schs., Wheeling, 1954-56; rsch. audiologist Aeromed Lab., Wright Patterson AFB, Ohio, 1956-67; supervisory rsch. audiologist Armstrong Lab., Wright Patterson AFB, 1967—; chair W4 Am. Nat. Stds. Inst., N.Y.C., 1968—; U.S. rep. hearing protection Internat. Stds. Orgn., Geneva, 1968—; USAF rep. NRC-NAS Hearing Com., Washington, 1976—; chair robotics panel Joint Dirs. Labs., Washington, 1987-88. Author reports and book chpts. Cpl. U.S. Army, 1953-55. Recipient Meritorious Svc. medal U.S. Dept. Def., Dayton, Ohio, 1986. Fellow Acoustical Soc. Am.; mem. Rsch. Soc. Am. Home: 4316 Sillman Pl Dayton OH 45440-1141

NIXON, DEBORAH, mental health and substance abuse nurse; b. Westwood, N.J., Nov. 9, 1956; d. Arthur Theodore and Ruth Tabitha (Brown) Busby; m. Maxie Nixon Jr., Apr. 17, 1993. BSN, Seton Hall U., 1982; postgrad., San Diego State U., 1986-87; postgrad. in Environ. and Occupational Health Scis., N.Y. Medical Coll. Nursing coord. managed care program mental health/substance abuse Nat. Benefit Fund., N.Y.C.; grad. research asst. San Diego State U. Grad. Sch. Pub. Health. Lt. USN, 1982-86; capt. U.S. Army, 1990—. Home: 39 Westwood Blvd Westwood NJ 07675-2520

NIZZE, JUDITH ANNE, physician assistant; b. L.A., Nov. 1, 1942; d. Robert George and Charlotte Ann (Wise) Swan; m. Norbert Adolph Otto Paul Nizze, Dec. 31, 1966. BA, UCLA, 1966, postgrad., 1966-76; grad. physician asst. tng. program, Charles R. Drew Sch. Postgrad., L.A., 1979; BS, Calif. State U., Dominguez, 1980. Cert. physician asst., Calif. Staff rsch. assoc. I-II Wadsworth Vet. Hosp., L.A., 1965-71; staff rsch. assoc. III-IV John Wayne Clinic Jonsson Comprehensive Cancer Ctr., UCLA, 1971-78; clin. asst. Robert S. Ozeran, Gardena, Calif., 1978; physician asst. family practice Fred Chasan, Torrance, Calif., 1980-82; sr. physician asst. Donald L. Morton prof., chief surg. oncology Jonsson Comprehensive Cancer Ctr., UCLA, 1983-91; administrv. dir. clin. rsch. John Wayne Cancer Inst., Santa Monica, Calif., 1991—. Contbr. articles to profl. jours. Fellow Am. Acad. Physician Assts., Am. Assn. Surgeons Assts., Calif. Acad. Physician Assts.; mem. Assn. Physician Assts. in Oncology, Am. Sailing Assn. Republican. Presbyterian. Home: 13243 Fiji Way Unit J Marina Dl Rey CA 90292-7079 Office: John Wayne Cancer Inst St John's Hosp & Health Ctr 1328 22d St 2 West Santa Monica CA 90404-2032

NOAM, GIL GABRIEL, psychologist, educator; b. Tel-Aviv, Israel, Apr. 25, 1950; came to U.S., 1975; permanent resident; s. Ernst M. and Lotte R. (Dahn) N.; B.A. in Psychology, Free U. of Berlin, Germany, 1972, dipl. psych., 1975, Ed.D Harvard U. 1984. Psychotherapist, University Psychol. Services, Tech. U., Berlin, Germany, 1973-75; with family therapy and research unit Judge Baker Guidance Center, Boston, 1975-77; clin. intern in psychology McLean Hosp., Belmont, Mass., 1975-77, asst. psychologist adult services, 1980—, assoc. child psychologist, 1982—; co-founder, co-dir. Clin. Developmental Inst., Belmont, 1982—; dir. evaluative services Hall-Mercer Children's Ctr., McLean Hosp., 1983-89, dir. Hall-Mercer Lab. Devel. Psychology and Devel. Psychopathology, 1989—; assoc. dir. adolescent and family devel. project Harvard Med. Sch., Boston, 1978—, dir. Risk and Prevention program, Harvard Med. Sch., Boston, lectr. psychology, 1980—, asst prof., 1989; instr. clin./developmental psychology Harvard U., instr. Mass. Sch. of Profl. Psychology, 1980-83, dir. risk and prevention program, 1995—; research cons. to Max-Planck Inst. for Human Devel. and Edn., Berlin, 1981—. Bd. dirs. psychology dept. Freie Universitat, Berlin, Germany, 1972-73, Mass. Com. for Children and Youth, 1980-82, Cambridgeport Problem Ctr., 1977-79. Recipient Kuhmerker Prize, 1985; German acad. fellow, 1976-78; Holzer fellow Harvard U., 1977-79; Studienstiftung fellow, 1979-81, Inst. Advanced Study-Berlin fellow, 1992-93; lic. psychologist. Fellow Mass. Psychol. Assn.; mem. Am. Psychol. Assn., German Psychol. Assn., Internat. Soc. Behavioral Devel. Contbr. articles on psychopathology, psychoanalysis, family therapy and developmental psychology to profl. jours.; and books; editor: Developmental Approaches to the Self, 1982. Home: 21 Lancaster St Cambridge MA 02140-2806 Office: Harvard Med Sch McLean Hosp 115 Mill St Belmont MA 02178-1041

NOAR, MARK DAVID, internist, gastroenterologist, therapeutic endoscopist, consultant, inventor; b. Boston, Sept. 10, 1953; s. Myron Theodore and Phyllis (Krinsky) N.; m. Martine Denise Motard, May 15, 1983; children: Emmanuelle, Ariane, Jean-Claude. BS in Biology, Ursinus Coll., Collegeville, Pa., 1975; MPH in Internat. Health, Tulane U., 1977; MD, U. Cen. del Este, Dominican Republic, 1980. Intern 5th Pathway program Coll. Medicine and Dentistry N.J.-Newark Beth Israel Hosp., 1980-81; resident in internal medicine U. Nebr. Med. Ctr., Omaha, 1981-84; fellow in gastroenterology SUNY Downstate Med. Ctr., Bklyn., 1984-86; fellow in therapeutic and surg. endoscopy, vis. staff Univ. Hosp. Hamburg, Germany, 1986-87; pvt. practice, Balt., 1988—; CEO Chesapeake Bay Brewing Co., Balt., 1992—; pres., CEO Md. Gastrenterology Network, Inc., 1993—; clin. cons. in therapeutic endoscopy Bklyn. VA Med. Ctr., 1987; dir. project devel., v.p. med. devel. Ixion, Inc., Seattle, 1987—; staff physician dept. gastroenterology St. Joseph Hosp., Balt., Franklin Square Hosp., Balt.; bd. dirs., dir. ops. Disaster Support Network, Balt., 1990—; session co-chmn. World Congress Gastroenterology Sydney, Australia, 1990, IX European Workshop on Therapeutic Digestive Endoscopy, Brussels, 1991; CEO, med. dir. The Endoscopy Ctr., Inc., Balt., 1990—; CEO, bd. dirs. Md. Gastroenterology Network, Inc., The Endoscopy Ctr.; course dir. internat. hands-on ERCP Conf., Balt., 1994, 95; founder, dir. Internat. ERCP Edn. Found., 1994—; bd. dirs. Wiltek, Inc. Author: (with N. Soehendra and H. Grimm) A Compendium of Therapeutic Endoscopy for the General Practitioner, 1991; editor-in-chief Internat. Video Jour. Therapeutic and Diagnostic Endoscopy; assoc. editor Endoscopy Rev.; contbr. articles and abstracts to med. jours., chpts. to books; inventor robotic interactive endoscopy simulation, precurved papillotome and ERCP catheters, "Noar pump" for disinfection and cleaning of endoscopes. Pub. lectr. Am. Cancer Soc., Balt., 1988—; physician educator Doctor and Lawyer Coalition Against Drugs, Balt., 1991-92. Fellow Royal Soc. Tropical Medicine and Hygiene; mem. ACP, AMA, Am. Coll. Gastroenterology, Am. Soc. Gastrointestinal Endoscopy (instr. regional advanced endoscopy 1993—, award for achievement and edn. in diagnostic/therapeutic biliary and pancreatic endoscopy 1992), Baltimore County Med. Soc., Sigma Xi. Office: Endoscopic Microsurgery Assocs 7402 York Rd Ste 100 Baltimore MD 21204-7532

NOBACK, CHARLES ROBERT, anatomist, educator; b. N.Y.C., Feb. 15, 1916; s. Charles Victor and Beatrice (Cerny) N.; m. Eleanor Louise Loomis, Nov. 23, 1938 (dec. Mar. 24, 1981); children: Charles Victor, Margaret Beatrice, Ralph Theodore, Elizabeth Louise. BS, Cornell U., 1936; MS, NYU, 1938; postgrad., Columbia U., 1936-38; PhD, U. Minn., 1942. Asst. prof. anatomy U. Ga., 1941-44; faculty L.I. Coll. Medicine, 1944-49, asso. prof., 1948-49; mem. faculty Columbia Coll. Phys. and Surg., 1949—, assoc. prof. anatomy, 1953-68, prof., 1968-86, prof. emeritus, 1986—, spl. lectr., 1986-92, acting chmn. dept., 1974-75, lectr., 1996—. Author: The Human Nervous System, 1967, 75, 81, Spinal Cord, 1971, The Nervous System Introduction and Review, 1982, 77, 86, 91, (with R. Demarest) Human Anatomy and Physiology, 1990, 2d edit., 1992, 3d edit., 1995, (with D. Van Wyseberghe and R. Carola) Human Anatomy, 1992, (with N. Strominger and R. Demarest) The Human Nervous System, Structure and Function, 1996; editor: with R. Carola and H. Harley) The Primate Brain, 1970, Sensory Systems of Primates, 1978; sr. editor: Advances in Primatology: series editor: Contbns. to Primatology; contbr. articles to profl. jours., sects. to Ency. Britannica, McGraw Hill Ency. Sci. and Tech., Collier's Ency. Fellow N.Y. Acad. Scis. (past rec. sec.), AAAS; mem. Am. Assn. Anatomists, Histochem. Soc., Internat. Primatological Soc., Am. Soc. Naturalists, Cajal Club Am. (past pres.), Assn. Phys. Anthropologists, Harvey Soc., Am. Acad. Neurology, Soc. Neurosci., Sigma Xi. Home: 116 7th St Cresskill NJ 07626-2005 Office: Columbia U Anatomy And Cell Dept New York NY 10032

NOBACK, RICHARDSON KILBOURNE, medical educator; b. Richmond, Va., Nov. 7, 1923; s. Gustav Joseph and Hazel (Kilborn) N.; m. Nan Jean Gates, Apr. 5, 1947; children: Carl R., Robert K., Catherine E. MD, Cornell U., 1947; BA, Columbia U., 1993. Diplomate Am. Bd. Internal Medicine. Intern N.Y. Hosp., 1947-48; asst. resident Cornell Med. div. Bellevue Hosp., N.Y.C., 1958-50, chief resident, 1950-52; instr. medicine Cornell U., N.Y.C., 1950-53; asst. prof. medicine SUNY Upstate Med. Ctr., Syracuse, 1955-56; assoc. prof. medicine U. Ky. Med. Ctr., Lexington, 1956-64; exec. dir. Kansas City (Mo.) Gen. Hosp. and Med. Ctr., 1964-69; assoc. dean, prof. medicine U. Mo. Sch. Medicine, Columbia, 1964-69; founding dean U. Mo. Sch. Medicine, Kansas City, 1969-78, prof. medicine, 1969-90, prof. and dean emeritus, 1990—; cons. U. Tenn., U. Mich., U. Del., Northeastern Ohio Group, U. Mo., Eastern Va. Med. Sch., Tex. Tech. U. Contbr. numerous articles to profl. jours. Bd. dirs. Kansas City Gen. Hosp., Truman Med. Ctr., Wayne Miner Health Ctr., Jackson County Med. Soc., The Shepherd's Ctr., Am. Fedn. Aging Rsch., Mo. Gerontol. Inst., The Shepherd's Ctrs. of Am.; dir. Mo. Geriatric Edn. Ctr., 1985-88. Capt. USAF Med. Svcs. 1953-55. Recipient medal of honor Avila Coll., Kansas City, 1968, merit award Met. Med. Soc., 1991, recognition award Mo. Soc. Internal Medicine, 1993. Mem. AMA, Mo. Med. Assn. (former mem. ho. of dels., v.p. 1992), Am. Geriatric Soc., Alpha Omega Alpha, Phi Kappa Phi. Home: 2912 Abercorn Dr Las Vegas NV 89134-7440 Office: U Mo-Kansas City Sch Medicine Sch Medicine 2411 Holmes St Kansas City MO 64108-2741

NOBLE, ROBERT CUTLER, medical educator; b. Raleigh, Feb. 19, 1938; s. Roy Fred and Mamie Eugenia (Cutler) N.; m. Audrey Joyce Melman, May 8, 1965; children: Lisa Meredith, Amy Brooke. Student, George August U., Gottingen, Ger., 1958-59; BA, U. N.C., 1960; MD, Duke U., 1964. Diplomate Am. Bd. Internal Medicine and Infectious Diseases. Intern, resident in medicine Duke U., Durham, N.C., 1964-66; sr. resident in medicine Stanford (Calif.) U., 1968-69, fellow in infectious diseases, 1969-71; asst. prof. medicine U. Ky., Lexington, 1971-77, assoc. prof., 1977-82, prof. medicine, 1982—. Author: Sexually Transmitted Diseases, 1985; contbr. over 82 articles to profl. jours. With USPHS, 1966-68. Fellow Infectious Disease Soc. Am.; mem. AAUP, Am. Soc. Microbiology. Office: U Ky Coll Medicine 800 Rose St Lexington KY 40536

NOBLE, RONALD MARK, sports medicine facility administrator; b. Atlanta, Dec. 28, 1950; s. Dexter Ron and Judy (Puckett) N.; m. Teresa Lowder, Sept. 20, 1975; children: Kimberly, Heather, James, Ashlee. AS, Ricks Coll., 1974; BS cum laude, Troy State U., 1976; MS, U. Tenn., 1977.

Grad. asst. U. Tenn., Knoxville, 1976-77; lectr. Tex. A&M U., College Station, 1977-79; asst. prof. U.S. Mil. Acad., West Point, N.Y., 1979-80; dir. clin. phys. NASA Med. Ctr., MSFC, 1980-85; exec. dir. Total Wellness Ctr., Huntsville, Ala., 1986-90, Preventive and Rehab. Sports Medicine Assocs., Huntsville, 1990—; clin. advisor Huntsville Med. Sch., U. Ala., 1990—, exec. dir. preventive and clin. advisor, preceptor, 1992—; adj. prof. U. Ala., Huntsville, 1982-85; sports medicine cons. Mex. Olympic Com., San Luis Potosi, 1980, Duke U. Basketball, Durham, N.C., 1987—, U.S. Olympic Team, 1994—; coord. U.S. Olympic Com. Nat. Rehab. Network; cons. USAF Dept. Manned Space Flight Ops., L.A., 1983-84, athletic dept. Ala. A&M U., 1994—; asst. coach U.S. Olympic Com., Colorado Springs, 1979-83; spl. advisor Pres. Coun. on Phys. Fitness and Sports, Huntsville, 1991; clin. advisor, preceptor U. Ala. Huntsville Med. Sch. Developer computer software in field; contbr. articles to profl. jours., also to USAF manual. Campaign mgr. Brooks for State Legislature, Huntsville, 1992; bd. dirs. Huntsville Boys Club, 1988-89, Big Bros./Sisters of No. Ala., Huntsville, 1988-89, Ala. affiliate Am. Heart Assn., Huntsville, 1980-88; commr. Ala. Gov.'s Com. on Phys. Fitness, 1991-94; mem. U.S. Olympic Com. Spkrs. Bur., 1978-80; U.S. Olympic Com., Nat. Rehab. Network for Elite Athletes. With U.S. Army, 1970-73, Vietnam. Named Outstanding Leader Jaycees of Ala., 1983; Paul Harris fellow Huntsville Rotary Club, 1987—. Mem. Huntsville Rotary (Paul Harris fellow), Kappa Delta Pi. Mem. LDS Ch. Office: PRSM Assocs 1015 Airport Rd SW Ste 203 Huntsville AL 35802-1394

NOBLES, LORI ANGELA, health information management consultant; b. Augusta, Ga., Aug. 20, 1965; d. Robert Clyde and Joanne (Ness) Mashburn; m. Raymond Hugh Nobles, Jr., June 10, 1989. BS in Med. Record Adminstrn., Med. Coll. Ga., Augusta, 1987. Registered record adminstr. Asst. dir. med. records Smyrna (Ga.) Hosp., 1987-88, med. staff coord., 1988-89; asst. dir. med. records U. Hosp., Augusta, 1989-92; health info. specialist Westinghouse Savannah River Co., Aiken, S.C., 1993-94; dir. health info. svc. McDuffie County Hosp., Thomson, Ga., 1994—; cons. Smyrna Hosp., 1989-92, Lakeside Cmty. Hosp., Cumming, Ga., 1989-92, Wilson Cunningham Kerr Assoc., 1995—. Mem. Ga. Health Info. Mgmt. (meeting strategy mgr. 1994-96), Augusta Area Health Info. Mgmt. (edn. chmn. 1989-90, v.p. 1990-91, pres. 1991-92). Home: 1417 Heard Ave Augusta GA 30904 Office: 521 Hill St SW Thomson GA 30824

NOBLETT, RUSSELL DON, medical and computer consultant; b. Lubbock, Tex., Oct. 25, 1957; s. Clois and Margaret (Scott) N. BA in Philosophy, North Tex. U., 1982; MD, U. Tex., Dallas, 1989. Resident internal medicine U. Va., Roanoke, 1992; cons.-liaison attending in internal medicine residency U. Va. Sch. Medicine, Roanoke, 1993-94, clin. instr. in internal medicine residency, 1994-95; chief emergency medicine VA Med. Ctr., Salem, Va., 1994-95; pres., owner, chief med. cons. in clin. software design Deming Internat. Cons.: Computer Cons. to Physicians, Roanoke, 1995—. Vol. physician Bradley Free Clinic, Roanoke, 1992—. Recipient Extra-Mile award for vol. work as a resident Bradley Free Clinic, Roanoke, 1992. Mem. ACP, Roanoke Acad. Medicine. Home: PO Box 21561 Roanoke VA 24018 Office: Deming Internat Cons PO Box 20371 Roanoke VA 24018

NOBLIN, CHARLES DONALD, clinical psychologist, educator; b. Jackson, Miss., Dec. 16, 1933; s. Charles Thomas and Margaret (Byrne) N.; m. Patsy Ann Beard, Aug. 12, 1989. BA, Miss. Coll., 1955; MS, Va. Commonwealth U., 1957; PhD, La. State U., 1962. Lic. psychologist, Miss., N.J., N.C. Instr. to asst. prof. La. State U., Baton Rouge, 1961-63; asst. to assoc. prof. U. N.C., Greensboro, 1963-66; assoc. prof. Rutgers Med. Sch., New Brunswick, N.J., 1966-69; dir. clin. training Va. Commonwealth U., Richmond, 1969-72; chmn. dept. psychology Va. Tech., Blacksburg, 1972-82; dir. clin. training U. So. Miss., Hattiesburg, 1982-85, chmn. dept. psychology, 1985-91, prof., 1991-93, dir. clin. tng., 1993—. Contbr. over 60 articles and presentations. Recipient Clin. Tng. grant NIMH, 1983-86, Victim Behavior & Personal Space rsch. grant U.S. Dept. Justice, 1970-71, Trubeck Found. Rsch. award, 1968-69. Baptist. Home: 7 Cane Cv Hattiesburg MS 39402-8716 also: PO Box 10036 Hattiesburg MS 39406-0036 Office: U So Miss Dept Psychology Hattiesburg MS 39406

NOCE, WALTER W., JR., hospital administrator; b. Neptune, N.J., Sept. 27, 1945; s. Walter William and Louise Marie (Jenkins) N.; m. Linda Miller, Apr. 15, 1967; children: Krista Suzanne, David Michael. BA, LaSalle U., 1967; MPH, UCLA, 1969. Diplomate Am. Coll. Healthcare Execs. Regional coord. Cmty. Health Svc., USPHS, Rockville, Md., 1969-71; v.p. Hollywood Presbyn. Med. Ctr., L.A., 1971-76, sr. v.p., 1976-77; v.p. Huntington Meml. Hosp., Pasadena, 1977-83; pres., CEO St. Joseph Hosp., Orange, Calif., 1983-90; pres. so. Calif. region St. Joseph Health Sys., Orange, 1987-90, exec. v.p., 1990-94; pres., CEO Children Hosp. of L.A., 1995—. Bd. dirs. St. Joseph Ballet, Santa Ana, Calif., 1994—. Named Alumnus of the Yr. UCLA Hosp. Adminstrn. Alumni Assn., 1987; Walker fellow, 1992. Mem. Am. Hosp. Assn. (del. ho. of dels. 1995—, alt. del. 1994), Calif. Healthcare Assn. (bd. trustees 1996), Hosp. Assn. So. Calif. (area chmn. 1996), Calif. Assn. of Hosps. and Health Sys. (chmn. 1992). Office: Childrens Hospital LA 4650 Sunset Blvd Los Angeles CA 90027

NOEL, LARRY KENNETH, family physician; b. Kirksville, Mo., Oct. 9, 1939; s. Kenneth Carl and Marietta (Waddill) N.; m. Mary Lee Green, Oct. 26, 1963; children: Kent, Lance. BS, No. Mo. State U., 1965; DO, Kirksville Coll. Osteo. Med., 1969. Diplomate Am. Bd. Family Practice. Intern Normandy (Mo.) Osteo. Hosp., 1969-70; active staff Moberly (Mo.) Regional Med. Ctr., 1970—; pvt. practice Moberly, Mo., 1970—. Mayor City of Moberly, 1988—, mem. city coun., 1978—. With USN, 1957-60. Roman Catholic. Home: 419 Greenbrier Rd Moberly MO 65270 Office: 1145 S Morley St Moberly MO 65270-1948

NOEL, TALLULAH ANN, healthcare industry executive; b. Detroit, Oct. 21, 1945; d. Harry Carababas and Ruby Dimple (Gentry) Caruso; m. Vernon E. Noel (div. 1965); children: Cynthia L. Robbins, Kimberly J. Wise. AA in Nursing, Morton Coll., Cicero, Ill., 1976; BS, Coll. St. Francis, Joliet, Ill., 1983; MS in Mgmt., Nat.-Louis U., Evanston, Ill., 1990. RN. Staff nurse Mt. Sinai Hosp., Chgo., 1976-78, head nurse, 1978-79, critical care nurse, 1979-80, oncology clinician, 1980-82; head nurse McNeal Hosp., Berwyn, Ill., 1982-84; dir. nursing Nursefinders of Elmwood Park (Ill.), 1984-86; dir. profl. svcs. Nursefinders of Chgo., Elmwood Park, 1986-87, v.p. profl. svcs., 1987-88, v.p. ops., chief oper. officer, 1988-90; area v.p. Nursefinders, Inc., Hillside, Ill., 1990-91; v.p. Amserv Healthcare, Inc., Riverside, Ill., 1992-94; pres., owner Staffing Team Internat., Inc., Oak Brook, Ill., 1994—. Bd. dirs. Morton Coll. Found., 1987-88, Chgo. Heart Assn., 1985—, Grant Works Children's Ctr., Cicero, 1982-85. Mem. Women's Health Exec. Network, Nat. League Nursing, Oncology Nursing Soc., Am. Fedn. Home Health Agys., Assn. Critical Care Nurses, others. Democrat. Roman Catholic. Office: Staffing Team Internat Inc 1100 Jorie Blvd Ste 234 Oak Brook IL 60521-2244

NOELKEN, MILTON EDWARD, biochemistry educator, researcher; b. St. Louis, Dec. 5, 1935; s. William Henry Noelken and Agnes (Westbrook) Burkemper; m. Carol Ann Agne, June 9, 1962. BA in Chemistry, Washington U., St. Louis, 1957, PhD in Chemistry, 1962. Rsch. chemist Ea. Regional Rsch., Dept. Agr., Phila., 1964-67; asst. prof. dept. biochemistry U. Kans. Med. Ctr., Kansas City, 1967-71, assoc. prof., 1971-81, acting chmn., 1973-74, prof., 1981—, interim chmn., 1993-94; vis. prof. Fed. U. Minas Gerais, Brazil, 1978; mem. rsch. proposal rev. panel Am. Heart Assn. Kans. Affiliate, Inc., 1989-93. Contbr. articles to profl. jours. Recipient Scholastic Achievement award Am. Inst. Chemists, Washington U., 1957; NSF fellow, Washington U., 1959. Mem. Am. Chem. Soc., Am. Soc. for Biochemistry and Molecular Biology, Biophys. Soc., Sigma Xi. Office: U Kans Med Ctr Dept Biochemistry 39th and Rainbow Kansas City KS 66160-7421

NOETH, CAROLYN FRANCES, speech and language pathologist; b. Cleve., July 21, 1924; d. Sam Falco and Barbara Serafina (Loparo) Armaro; m. Lawrence Andrew Noeth Sr., June 29, 1946; children: Lawrence Andrew Jr. (dec.), Barbara Marie. AB magna cum laude, Case Western Res. U., 1963; MEd, U. Ill., 1972; postgrad., Nat. Coll. Edn., 1975—. Lic. speech and lang. pathologist, Ill. Speech therapist Chgo. Pub. Schs., 1965; speech, lang. and hearing clinician J. Sterling Morton High Schs., Cicero and Berwyn, Ill., 1965-82, tchr. learning disabilities/behavior disorders, 1982, dist. ednl. diagnostician, 1982-84; Title I Project tchr., summers 1966-67, lang. disabilities cons., summers 1968-69, in-service tng. cons., summer 1970, dir. Title I Project, summers 1973-74, learning disabilities tchr. W. Campus of Morton, 1971-75, chmn. Educable-Mentally Handicapped-Opportunities Tchrs. Com., 1967-68, spl. edn. area and in-sch. tchrs. workshops, 1967—. Precinct elections judge, 1953-55; block capt. Mothers March of Dimes and Heart Fund, 1949-60; St. Agatha's rep. Nat. Catholic Women's League, 1952-53; collector various charities, 1967, 93-94; mem. exec. bd. Morton Scholarship League, 1981-84, corr. sec., 1981-83; vol. Am. Cancer Soc., 1985—; vol. judge Ill. Acad. Decathlon, 1988—. First recipient Virda L. Stewart award for Speech, Western Res. U., 1963, recipient Outstanding Sr. award, 1963. Mem. Am. (life, cert.), Ill. Speech, Language, and Hearing Assns. (life mem.), Council Exceptional Children (divsn. for learning disabilities, pioneers divsn., chpt. spl. projects chmn., exec. bd. 1976-81, chpt. pres. 1979-80), Council for Learning Disabilities, Profls. in Learning Disabilities, Internat. Platform Assn., Kappa Delta Pi, Delta Kappa Gamma (chmn., co-chmn. chpt. music com. 1979—, mem. state program com. 1981-83, chpt. music rep. to state 1982—, chmn. chpt. promotion com. 1993-94, 96—). Roman Catholic. Clubs: St. Norbert's Women's (Northbrook, Ill.), Case-Western Res. U., U. Ill. Alumni Assns., Lions (vol. Northbrook, 1966—). Chmn. in compiling and publishing Student Handbook, Cleve. Coll., 1962; contbr. lyric parodies and musical programs J. Sterling Morton High Sch. West Retirement Teas, 1972-83. Home and Office: 1849 Walnut Cir Northbrook IL 60062-1245

NOFFSINGER, ANNE-RUSSELL L., former nursing administrator, educator; b. Frankfort, Ky., Feb. 4, 1932; d. Charles Russell and Hettie Lee (Ward) Lillis; m. J. Philip Noffsinger, July 1, 1964; children: Ward, Gretchen, Hans. Diploma, Good Samaritan Hosp., Lexington, Ky., 1952; BA in English, U. Ky., 1966, MA in Counseling, 1968, EdD in Psychology, 1979; MSN, U. Tenn., 1986. Instr. fundamentals of nursing Good Samaritan Hosp., Lexington, 1955-56; assoc. dir. nursing St. Joseph Hosp., Lexington, 1958-61; instr. pediatric nursing Good Samaritan Hosp. Sch. Nursing, Lexington, 1961-68; prof., chmn. nursing Lexington Community Coll., 1968-94; asst. to pres. for instnl. advancement and rsch., 1994—. Co-author: Counseling: An Introduction for Health and Human Services, 1983. Recipient U. Ky. Alumni Great Teaching award; Helene Fuld grantee. Mem. ANA (del.), KNA (former pres.), Nat. League for Nursing, KLN (former pres.), ODK, KCADN, Sigma Theta Tau, Omicron Delta Kappa, Phi Delta Kappa.

NOLAN, JAMES PAUL, medical educator, scientist; b. Buffalo, June 21, 1929; s. James Paul and Isabel (Curry) N.; m. Christa Paul, July 23, 1956; children—Lisa, James, Christopher, Thomas. B.A., Yale U., 1951, M.D. cum laude, 1955. Diplomate Am. Bd. Internal Medicine. Instr. in medicine Yale U., New Haven, 1961-63; intern Grace-New Haven Hosp., 1955-56, resident, 1958-60, chief med. resident, 1961-62, asso. physician, 1962-63; asst. prof. medicine SUNY, Buffalo, 1963-67; asso. prof. SUNY, 1967-69, prof., 1969—, vice-chmn. dept. medicine, 1973-77, acting chmn. dept. 1978-79; chmn. dept., 1979-95; chief of medicine Buffalo Gen. Hosp., 1969-80, attending, 1969—; asso. attending Edward J. Meyer Meml. Hosp., Buffalo, 1963-68; attending Edward J. Meyer Meml. Hosp., 1968-71, cons., 1971—; cons. physician Millard Fillmore Hosp., 1981—, Deaconess Hosp., 1973—; attending Buffalo VA Hosp., Children's Hosp. Buffalo; cons. Roswell Park Meml. Inst., 1970—; acting dir. dept. medicine Erie County Med. Center, 1978-80, dir. dept., 1980—; Trustee Buffalo Gen. Hosp., 1974—. Editorial adv. bd. Jour. Medicine Exptl. and Clin, 1971—; reviewer: Gastroenterology, 1973—; contbr. numerous articles to med. and sci. jours. Served to lt. comdr., M.C. USN, 1956-58. NIH grantee, 1979-86; Hartford Found. grantee, 1981. Mem. ACP (master, chair bd. regents 1994-95), Am. Fedn. Clin. Rsch., AAAS, Am. Gastroent. Assn. (procedures com.), Am. Assn. Study of Liver Disease, Reticuloendothelial Soc., N.Y. Acad. Sci., Am. Clin. and Climatol. Assn., Interurban Club, Ctrl. Soc. Clin. Rsch., Internat. Assn. Study of Liver, Assn. Am. Physicians, Assn. Profs. Medicine (pres. 1993-94), Phi Beta Kappa, Alpha Omega Alpha. Home: 213 Burbank Dr Buffalo NY 14226-3938 Office: 462 Grider St Buffalo NY 14215-3075

NOLAN, JOHN ANDREW, physician assistant; b. Kings Mountain, N.C., Aug. 31, 1955; s. Paul Vernon and Beatrice Anne (Lewis) N.; m. Kathryn Johanna Sharbaugh, June 3, 1978; children: Brett, Ashley, Keith. BS in Biology, Mercer U., 1977; Physician Asst., Wake Forest U., 1979. Cert. physician asst. Physician asst. emergency rm. Valentine Shults Hosp., Newport, Tenn., 1979-80; dir. plant site med. unit E.I. DuPont de Nemours & Co., Inc., Brevard, N.C., 1980-88; physician asst. cardiovascular surgery Watson Clinic, Lakeland, Fla., 1988-89; physician asst. emergency rm. Lakeland (Fla.) Regional Hosp., 1989-90; dir. Happy Valley Med. Ctr./West Caldwell Health Coun., Lenoir, N.C., 1990—; physician asst. emergency rm. Caldwell Meml. Hosp., Lenoir, 1990—. Bd. dirs. Hendersonville (N.C.) Mental Health, 1986-88, Am. Cancer Soc., Brevard, N.C., 1986-88; pres. United Way, Brevard, 1989, campaign chmn., 1985; scoutleader Boy Scouts Am. Fellow Am. Acad. Physician Assts., N.C. Acad. Physician Assts.; mem. KC (v.p. 1987). Roman Catholic. Home: 118 Yadkin Ln Lenoir NC 28645 Office: Happy Valley Medical Ctr Box 296 Hwy 268 Patterson NC 28661

NOLAN, PATRICIA A., public health officer. MD, McGill U., Montreal, Que., Can., 1969; MPH, Columbia U., 1973. Cert. in pub. health Am. Bd. Prevention Medicine. Local pub. health adminstr. N.Y.C., Tucson, Ariz.; med. adminstr. Ariz. Health Care Cost Containment Sys.; state pub. health adminstr. Ill.; exec. dir. Colo. Dept. Pub. Health and Environ.; dir. R.I. Health Dept., 1995—; adj. prof. several med. schs. Mem. APHA. Office: RI Health Dept 3 Capitol Hill Providence RI 02908-5097*

NOLAN, STANTON PEELLE, surgeon, educator; b. Washington, May 29, 1933; s. James Parker and Ellen Dubose (Peelle) N.; m. Marion Faro, June 16, 1955; children—Stanton Peelle Jr., Tiphanie Ravenel. B.A., Princeton U., 1955; M.D., U. Va., 1959, M.S., 1962. Cert. Am. Bd. Surgery, Am. Bd. Thoracic Surgery. Intern U. Va. Med. Ctr., Charlottesville, 1959-60, asst. resident gen. surgery, 1960-61, research fellow surgery, 1961-62, sr. asst. resident gen. surgery, 1962-64, chief resident gen surgery, 1964-65, chief resident thoracic cardiovascular surgery, 1965-66; sr. rsch. assoc. Clinic of Surgery Nat. Heart Inst., NIH, Bethesda, Md., 1966-68; asst. prof. surgery U. Va. Med. Ctr., Charlottesville, 1968-70, assoc. prof. surgery, 1970-74, surgeon in charge div. thoracic cardiovascular surgery, 1970-93, prof. surgery, 1974—, Claude A. Jessup prof. surgery, 1981—, med. dir. Thoracic Cardiovascular post-operative unit, 1989-93; established investigator Am. Heart Assn., 1969-74; mem. surgery A study sect. NIH, Washington, 1972-76, surgery and bioengring. study sect. 1984-87, chmn. 1985-87; cons. thoracic cardiovascular surgery VA Hosp., Salem, Va., 1968—, Am. Bd. Surgery to qualifying examination com., 1988-91; surg. cons. Bur. Crippled Children, Charlottesville, 1968—; vis. cons. cardiothoracic surgery Aga Khan U., Karachi, Pakistan, 1995. Mem. editl. bd. Jour. Surg. Rsch., 1973-79, Annals of Thoracic Surgery, 1979-88; mem. sci. adv. bd. Jour. for Heart Valve Disease, 1993-94; mem. editl. adv. bd. ECRI Operating Rm. Risk Mgmt., 1992—; co-editor: Comprehensive Thoracic Surgery Curriculum, TSDA, 1995; contbr. numerous articles to profl. jours., chpts. to books. Recipient John Horsley Meml. prize U. Va. Med. Sch., 1962; Merit award Research Forum of Am. Coll. Chest Physicians, 1968; research fellow Va. Heart Assn., 1961-62, Am. Cancer Soc., 1963-64; grantee NIH, 1968-84, Am. Heart Assn., 1970-73, Medtronic Corp., 1975-81. Fellow ACS, Am. Coll. Cardiology, Am. Surg. Assn.; mem. Am. Assn. Thoracic Surgery (rep. to Assn. Am. Med. Colls., Am. Bd. Cardiovascular Perfusion, Am. Soc. Extracorporeal Tech., others), Am. Heart Assn. (coun. on cardiovascular surgery 1969—, anesthesiology, radiology and surgery study com. 1991-94), Andrew G. Morrow Soc., Assn. Acad. Surgery, Assn. Advancement of Med. Instrumentation (chair-elect 1996, co-chmn. cardiac valve prostheses stds. com. 1974—, mem. internat. stds. com. 1989—, bd. dirs. 1990—, stds. bd. 1991-94, edn. com. 1992-93), Internat. Stds. Orgn. (chmn. subcom. on cardiovascular surg. implants 1982—), Assn. Clin. Cardiac Surgeons, Halsted Soc. (exec. com. 1985-89), Coord. Com. on Perfusion Affairs (chmn. 1990—), Internat. Assn. Cardiac Biol. Implants (sci. com. 1994), Internat. Cardiovascular Soc., Muller Surg. Soc. (pres. 1979), Soc. Internat. de Cirurgie, Soc. Vascular Surgery, Soc. Thoracic Surgeons (ad hoc com. on industry rels. 1992—, stds. and ethics com. 1993-95, edn. and resources com. 1996—), Soc. Univ. Surgeons, Southeastern Surg. Congress, So. Surg. Assn. (2d v.p. 1982), Va. Surg. Soc. (v.p. 1980-83, pres. 1984), Va. Vascular Soc. (exec. coun. 1985-86), Soc. Critical Care Medicine, Raven Soc., Assn. Am. Med. Colls. (rep. coun. acad. socs. 1992—), Alpha Omega Alpha, Omicron Delta Kappa. Clubs: Chevy Chase (Md.); Farmington Country (Va.); Princeton (N.Y.C.). Office: U Va Dept Surgery Box 181-6 Charlottesville VA 22908

NOLAN, THOMAS JAMES, clinical social worker; b. Corona, N.Y., Mar. 9, 1946; s. Thomas J. Sr. and Theresa Mary (Cassell) N.; m. Margaret Mary Purcell, May 21, 1977; children: Thomas Matthew, Jaclyn Elizabeth. BA in Biology, Marist Coll., 1968; MS in Edn., Iona Coll., 1973; MSW, SUNY, Stony Brook, 1978. Cert. social worker, N.Y.; cert. marriage counselor, N.J.; lic. clin. social worker, N.J. Tchr. St. Helena High Sch., Bronx, N.Y., 1968-73; clin. interventionist Archdioscesan Drug Program, N.Y.C., 1973-78; adminstrv. supr. St. Dominic's Home, Blauvelt, N.Y., 1979-90; pvt. practice River Edge, N.J., 1990—, Rye Brook, N.Y., 1990—; faculty, staff Ctr. for Family Learning, Rye Brook, 1984—. Cons. St. Peter's Ch., River Edge, 1988—. Mem. Nat. Assn. of Social Workers, Acad. Cert. Social Workers, Am. Assn. of Marriage and Family Therapists. Home: 586 Center Ave River Edge NJ 07661-2127 Office: 28 Rye Ridge Plz Port Chester NY 10573-2820

NOLAND, TRACY KELLY, mental health nurse; b. Ft. Worth, Tex., Apr. 24, 1958; d. Herbert C. and Bettye (Murphy) Kelly; m. Horace Noland, Aug. 24, 1985; children: Kaitlyn Nicole, Trevor Kelly. BSN, U. Tex., Houston, 1983; BS in Health Edn., Tex. A&M U. Cert. CPR instr. trainer. Staff nurse VA Hosp., Houston, 1984-86; mental health nurse The Meth. Hosp., Houston, 1986-88, Tucson Psychiat. Inst., 1988-94; Charter Behavioral Health Sys., 1994—. Bible study fellowship, children's leader. Mem. Tex. Assn. for Health, Phys. Edn. Recreation and Dance, Houston Livestock Show and Rodeo (life), Sigma Theta Tau, Eta Sigma Gamma. Home: 8430 E Albion Pl Tucson AZ 85715-4403

NOLLEN, PAUL MARION, science educator; b. Lafayette, Ind., Feb. 24, 1934; s. Marion and Dorothy (VanArsdale) N.; m. Sheila Louise Hunt, Aug. 20, 1966; children: Marie, Nathan. BS, Carroll Coll., 1956; MS, U. Wis., 1957; PhD, Purdue U., 1967. Asst. prof. Western Ill. U., Macomb, 1967-69, assoc. prof., 1969-74, prof., 1974—; vis. prof. U. Iowa, Iowa City, 1979-80, BGU Disting. prof., 1991—. Contbr. over 70 articles to profl. jours. Bd. dirs. United Fund, Macomb, 1969-71; trustee, deacon, elder Presbyn. Ch., Macomb; chair com. Boy Scouts Am. Troop, Macomb, 1987-91. With U.S. Army, 1957-60, CBI. Recipient Outstanding Rsch. award Coll. of Arts and Scis., 1987. Mem. AAAS, Am. Soc. Parasitologists, Ann. Midwest Conf. of Parasitologists (presiding officer 1986-87), Phi Kappa Phi (pres. 1987-88, sec./treas. 1994—), Sigma Xi (rsch. award 1974). Home: 7835 E 1000th St Macomb IL 61455 Office: Dept Biol Scis Western Ill U Macomb IL 61455

NOLTING, EARL, academic administrator; b. Columbus, Ind., July 24, 1937; s. Earl Seeger and Gladys Marie (Veale) N.; m. Judith Lynn Tegeler, June 18, 1961; children: Susan, Matthew, David. BSBA, Ind. U., 1959, MS in Edn., 1961; PhD in Psychology, U. Minn., 1967. Lic. psychologist, Wis., Minn. Counselor, asst. prof. U. Minn., Mpls., 1966-68; assoc. dir. U. Wis., Madison, 1968-72, assoc. dean, assoc. vice-chancellor, 1970-74; assoc. prof. edn. Kans. State U., Manhattan, 1974-86, dean of students, 1974-86; dir. dept. counseling, Univ. Coll. U. Minn., Mpls., 1986—; cons. psychologist Alberg and Assocs., Shoreview, Minn., 1989—. Contbr. articles to profl. publs. Exec. bd. Adult Learner Svcs. Network, St. Paul, 1989-90. 1st lt. U.S. Army, 1961-62. Mem. AACD, APA, Minn. Psychol. Assn., Am. Coll. Pers. Assn. (news editor 1977-82, sen. 1982-85, Presdl. award 1982), Am. Counseling Assn., Am. Coll. Counseling Assn., Acad. of Family Mediators. Home: 3336 Lake Johanna Blvd Saint Paul MN 55112-7942 Office: Univ Coll U Minn 315 Pillsbury Dr SE Minneapolis MN 55455-0139

NOMIKOS, IAKOVOS NICOLAS, surgeon; b. Syros, Cyclades, Greece, Oct. 1, 1951; s. Nicolas Nomikos and Sofia Baila-Nomikos; m. Anastasia Koutsouveli, Sept. 30, 1978; children: Nicolas, George, Thalassini. MD, PhD, Med. Sch. Athens (Greece) U., 1975. Med. diplomate; bd. cert. gen. surgery. Resident gen. surgery Evangelismos Med. Ctr., Athens, 1975-80, registrar, 1984-85; registrar Larisa (Greece) Gen. Hosp., 1981-83; fellow U. Colo. Health Scis. Ctr., Denver, 1985-86, N.Y. Med. Coll., Valhalla, 1986-87; fellow liver unit Queen Elizabeth Hosp., Birmingham, Eng., 1991; lectr. Athens U. Evgenidion Hosp., 1990—; asst. prof. surgery Athens U., 1994; cons. Nat. Health System Tzanion Hosp., Piraeus, Greece, 1987—. Author: Diagnostic and Therapeutic Approach of Critically Ill Surgical Patient, 1993; contbr. articles to profl. jours. Fellow Am. Coll. Surgeons; mem. Assn. Clin. Anatomists, Hellenic Surg. Soc., Gen. Med. Coun. Eng., N.Y. Acad. Scis.

NONAKA, MAKOTO, health science and educational organization executive; b. Yokohama, Kanagawa, Japan, Dec. 9, 1948; s. Tadao and Hisako Nonaka; m. Mariko Nonaka. MD, Jikei U., Tokyo, 1975; PhD in Immunology, U. Tokyo, 1983. Asst. prof. U. Tokyo Faculty Medicine, 1981-83, Jikei U. Sch. Medicine, 1983—; asst. mem. Med. Biology Inst., La Jolla, Calif., 1983-88; pres. Nonaka Internat. Corp., La Jolla, 1983—; mem. and head div. clin. immunology La Jolla Inst. For Allergy and Immunology, 1988-90, founder, pres., chief exec. officer, 1988—, chmn. bd., 1988-91; founder, chief exec. officer, chmn. bd. Found. for Internat. Sci. Advancement, San Diego, 1991—; v.p. health affairs Univ. of the World, La Jolla, 1991—; founder, chmn. CEO Med. Techs. Applications, Inc., San Diego, 1992—; CEO Pangenix Corp., San Diego, 1995—; bd. dirs., mem. exec. com. Cancer Ctr. U. Calif.-San Diego, La Jolla, 1990—; bd. dirs., vice chmn. Japan Am. Soc. So. Calif., San Diego, 1990, Internat. Forum for Corp. Dirs., 1991—. Author: Cell Biology and Immunology of Leurocyte Function, 1978; inventor anti-human monoclonal IgE receptor antibody, human T-cell IgE receptor. Mem. adv. com. U. Calif. at San Diego, 1989—. Mem. Nat. Assn. Corp. Dirs., AAAS, Am. Acad. Allergy and Immunology, Assn. U. Tech. Transfer Mgrs., N.Y. Acad. Scis., Licensine Execs. Soc. Office: Nonaka Internat Corp 2745 Castebelle Dr Ste B La Jolla CA 92037

NONAS, CONSTANTINE JAMES, general surgeon; b. Jersey City, N.J., May 19, 1934; s. Demetrios P. and Ariadne (Marcopul) N.; m. Francis Tsistinas, Nov. 15, 1970; children: Stephanie Anne, Demetri K. BS in Biology, Coll. of Holy Cross, 1955; M.D., Tufts U., 1959. Diplomate Am. Bd. Surgery. Intern Mountainside Gen. Hosp., Montclair, N.J., 1959-60; resident in gen. surgery, 1960-61, Letterman Gen. Hosp., San Fransisco, 1963-67; resident in gen. and perivascular surgery Bronx (N.Y.) Lebannon Hosp., 1969-70; chief profl. svcs. Malcolm Grow Med. Ctr., Andrews AFB, 1980-82; chief gen. surgery dept. Kaiser-Permanento, Va., 1988—. Col. USAFMC, 1974. Fellow ACS (Washington, D.C. and Va. chpts.); mem. Chesapeake Vascular Soc., Assn. of Mil. Surgeons, Air Force Assn. of Surgeons. Republican. Greek Orthodox. Office: Kaiser Permanente Permanente Rd 12255 Fair Lakes Pky Fairfax VA 22033-3952

NOONAN, JAMES ROTHWELL, internist; b. Jackson, Tenn., Dec. 13, 1931; s. James Melton and Martha Janet (Williams) N.; m. Oct. 18, 1954; children: James Reece, Sallye Anne Noonan O'Rourke, Debbie Lou Noonan Henson, Timothy Scott. BA, Harding U., 1952, MA, 1953; BS in Edn., Bethel Coll., 1955; MD, U. Tenn., Memphis, 1964. Diplomate, cert. geriatrics Am. Bd. Internal Medicine. Tchr. Dyer County Schs., Dyersburg, Tenn., 1954-55; intern U.S. Pub. Health Hosp., New Orleans, 1964-65, resident in internal medicine, 1965-66; resident in internal medicine VA Hosp., Memphis, 1966-68; physician Dyersburg Med. Group, Dyersburg, 1964—; chief staff Meth. Hosp. Dyersburg, 1987, bd. dirs., 1989-90. Pres. West Tenn. Heart Assn., Jackson, 1970; preacher Ch. Christ, Dyersburg, 1954-55. Officer USN, 1955-61, lt. comdr. USPHS, 1964-66. Recipient Honoree for promoting and living health lifestyle Am. Heart Assn., 1994. Mem. ACP, Am. Soc. Internal Medicine, N.W. Tenn. Acad. Medicine (pres. 1971), Tenn. Med. Assn., Alpha Omega Alpha. Home: 719 Wade Hampton Rd Dyersburg TN 38024-2945 Office: Dyersburg Med Group Divsn Dyersburgg Med Group 1700 Woodlawn Ave Dyersburg TN 38024-2028

NOONAN, MELINDA DUNHAM, women's health nurse, educator; b. Peoria, Ill., Feb. 19, 1954; d. Emmett Maxwell Dunham and Dixie Maurine (DeCounter) Widner; m. Robert Joseph Noonan; children: Alissa, Meris. Diploma, Ravenswood Hosp. Sch. Nursing, 1977; BSN cum laude, U. Ill., Chgo., 1989; MS, North Park Coll., 1995. Med. asst. James J. Hines, M.D., S.C., Chgo., 1973-76; staff nurse Northwestern Meml. Hosp., Chgo., 1978-79, asst. head nurse, 1979-80, staff nurse, 1980-86, perinatal and women's health educator, 1983—, coord. Health Learning Ctr., 1989-92; coord. Women's Ctr., Prentice Women's Hosp., Chgo., 1992-94; dir. women's programs Columbus Hosp., Chgo., 1994-96; dir. women's and family svcs. Swedish Convenant Hosp., Chgo., 1996—; founder, bd. dirs. Mothers Organized for Mut. Support, Chgo., 1981-89; creator, coord. Beyond The Birth Experience Program, Chgo., 1983-91. Contbg. author: Drugs, Alcohol, Pregnancy and Parenting, 1988, Clinical Issues of Perinatal and Women's Health Nursing, 1991, Jour. Obstetrical, Gynecological and Neonatal Nursing, 1996. Bd. dirs. Mothers Organized for mut. Support, 1981-88; troop leader Girl Scouts U.S., Chgo., 1991-93. Mem. Assn. Women's Health, Obstetrics and Neonatal Nurses (consumer edn. com. 1992-93, edn. com. 1994-95), Nat. Assn. Women's Health Profls., Am. Orgn. Nurse Execs., Rebekah (vice grand 1981-82, noble grand 1982-83), Sigma Theta Tau. Democrat. Roman Catholic. Home: 3414 W Glenlake Ave Chicago IL 60659-3420 Office: Swedish Covenant Hosp 5145 N California Ave Chicago IL 60625

NOORDSIJ, ARIE JOHAN, psychiatrist; b. Rotterdam, The Netherlands, July 26, 1927; s. Arie and Cornelia Jacoba (van Verseveld) N.; m. Elize van Eijbergen, Sept. 3, 1951 (div. 1974); children: Patricia Pepita, Barbara Elize, Peter Gregory; m. Katherine Measamer, Aug. 9, 1982. MD, U. Leiden, The Netherlands, 1951. Diplomate Am. Bd. Psychiatry and Neurology; cert. in psychoanalysis WAW Inst. Asst. in pathology U. Leiden, 1950-52, intern, 1952-54, resident in psychiatry, 1954-55; resident in psychiatry U. Nebr., 1955-58; chief psychiatrist Hastings State Hosp., Ingleside, Nebr., 1958-60; asst. instr. neuropsychiatry U. Nebr., Omaha, 1958-60; staff psychiatrist VA Regional Office, Newark, 1960-61; cons. Bd. Edn., Summit, N.J., 1960-81; asst. attending Overlook Hosp., Summit, 1960-71; pvt. practice psychiatry Chatham, N.J., 1960—; adj. prof. psychiatry Drew U., Madison, N.J., 1968—; assoc. attending Morristown Meml. Hosp., Morristown, N.J., 1984—; med. dir. Family Svc. Assn., Summit, 1963-79, Clergy Cons., Flanders, N.J., 1972—, Grace Counseling Ctr., Madison, 1984-94, Hilltop Counseling Ctr., Mendham, N.J., 1994—. Officer candidate Dutch Army, 1947-48. Fellow Am. Acad. Psychoanalysis; mem. AMA, Am. Psychiat. Assn., Am. Group Psychotherapy Assn., Am. Acad. Child Psychiatry, The Netherland Club N.Y. Episcopalian. Home: 44 Park Ln Madison NJ 07940-2714 Office: 9 Tulip St Summit NJ 07901-2404

NORA, AUDREY HART, physician; b. Picayune, Miss., Dec. 5, 1936; d. Allen Joshua and Vera Lee (Ballard) H.; m. James Jackson Nora, Apr. 9, 1966; children: James Jackson Jr., Elizabeth Hart. BS, U. Miss., 1958, MD, 1961; MPH, U. Calif., 1978. Diplomate Am. Bd. Pediatrics, Am. Bd. Hematology and Oncology. Resident in pediatrics U. Wis. Hosp., Madison, 1961-64; fellow in hematology/oncology Baylor U., Tex. Childrens Hosp., Houston, 1964-66, asst. prof. pediatrics, 1966-70; assoc. clin. prof. pediatrics U. Colo. Sch. Medicine, Denver, 1970—; dir. genetics Denver Childrens Hosp., 1970-78; cons. maternal and child health USPHS, Denver, 1978-83, asst. surgeon gen. regional health adminstr., 1983-92; dir. maternal & child health bur., health resources and svc. adminstrn. USPHS, commd. med. officer, 1978, advanced through grades to asst. surgeon gen., 1983; adv. com. NIH, Bethesda, 1975-77; adv. bd. Metronet Health, Inc., Denver, 1986—, Colo. Assn. Commerce and Industry, Denver, 1985—. Author: (with J.J. Nora) Genetics and Counseling in Cardiovascular Diseases, 1978, (with others) Blakiston's Medical Dictionary, 1980, Birth Defects Encyclopedia, 1990, (with J.J. Nora and K. Berg) Cardiovascular Diseases: Genetics, Epidemiology and Prevention, 1991; contbr. articles to profl. jours. Recipient Virginia Apgar award Nat. Found., 1976. Fellow Am. Acad. Pediatrics; mem. Am. Pub. Health Assn. (governing coun. 1990-92, coun. mem. maternal and child health 1990—), Commd. Officers Assn., Am. Soc. Human Genetics, Teratology Soc., Western Soc. Pediatric Rsch. Presbyterian. Office: USPHS Room 18-05 Parklawn Bldg 5600 Fishers Ln Rockville MD 20857-0001

NORA, JAMES JACKSON, physician, author, educator; b. Chgo., June 26, 1928; s. Joseph James and May Henrietta (Jackson) N.; m. Barbara June Fluhrer, Sept. 7, 1949 (div. 1963); children: Wendy Alison, Penelope Welbon, Marianne Leslie; m. Audrey Faye Hart, Apr. 9, 1966; children: James Jackson Jr., Elizabeth Hart Nora. AB, Harvard U., 1950; MD, Yale U., 1954; MPH, U. Calif., Berkeley, 1978. Intern Detroit Receiving Hosp., 1954-55; resident in pediatrics U. Wis. Hosps., Madison, 1959-61, fellow in cardiology, 1962-64; fellow in genetics McGill U. Children's Hosp., Montreal, Can., 1964-65; assoc. prof. pediatrics Baylor Coll. Medicine, Houston, 1965-71; prof. genetics, preventive medicine and pediatrics U. Colo. Med. Sch., Denver, 1971—; dir. genetics Rose Med. Ctr., Denver, 1980—; dir. pediatric cardiology and cardiovascular tng. U. Colo. Sch. Medicine, 1971-78; mem. task force Nat. Heart and Lung Program, Bethesda, Md., 1973; cons. WHO, Geneva, 1983—; mem. U.S.-U.S.S.R. Exchange Program on Heart Disease, Moscow and Leningrad, 1975. Author: The Whole Heart Book, 1980, 2d rev. edit., 1989; (with F.C. Fraser) Medical Genetics, 4th rev. edit., 1994, Genetics of Man, 2d rev. edit., 1986, Cardiovascular Diseases: Genetics, Epidemiology and Prevention, 1991; (novels) The Upstart Spring, 1989, The Psi Delegation, 1989, The Hemingway Sabbatical, 1996. Com. mem. March of Dimes, Am. Heart Assn., Boy Scouts Am. Served to lt. USAAC, 1945-47. Grantee Nat. Heart, Lung and Blood Inst., Nat. Inst. Child Health and Human Devel., Am. Heart Assn., NIH; recipient Virginia Apgar Meml. award. Fellow Am. Coll. Cardiology, Am. Acad. Pediatrics, Am. Coll. Med. Genetics; mem. Am. Pediatric Soc., Soc. Pediatric Rsch., Am. Heart Assn., Teratology Soc., Transplantation Soc., Am. Soc. Human Genetics, Authors Guild, Authors League, Acad. Am. Poets, Mystery Writers Am., Rocky Mountain Harvard Club. Democrat. Presbyterian. Home: 3110 Fairweather Ct Olney MD 20832-3021 Office: Parklawn Bldg 5600 Fishers Ln Rm 18-05 Rockville MD 20857-0001

NORBECK, JANE S., nursing educator; b. Redfield, S.D., Feb. 20, 1942; d. Sterling M. and Helen L. (Williamson) N.; m. Paul J. Gorman, June 28, 1970; 1 child Sara J. Gorman. BA in Psychology, U. Minn., 1965, BSN, 1965; MS, U. Calif., San Francisco, 1971, DNSc, 1975. Psychiat. nurse Colo. Psychiat. Hosp., Denver, 1965-66, Langley Porter Hosp., San Francisco, 1966-67; pub. health nurse San Francisco Health Dept., 1968-69; prof. U. Calif. (San Francisco) Sch. of Nursing, 1975—, dept. chair, 1984-89, dean, 1989—; chair study sect. Nat. Inst. of Nursing Rsch., 1990-93, mem. editl. bd. Archives of Psychiat. Nursing, 1985-95, Rsch. in Nursing and Health, 1987—. Co-editor: Annual Review of Nursing Research, 1996-97; contbr. articles to profl. jours. Mem. ANA, Am. Acad. Nursing, Am. Orgn. Nursing Exec., Am. Assn. Coll. Nursing, Inst. of Medicine, Sigma Theta Tau. Office: U Calif Sch Nursing 501 Parnassus Ave San Francisco CA 94143

NORBECK, TIMOTHY BURNS, medical association executive; b. Buffalo, N.Y., June 29, 1938; s. Carl Francis N. and Helene Smith (Comstock) Browne; children: Carl, Kim, Karin; m. Michèle R. Mathieu, Mar. 24, 1990. BA, Hamilton Coll., 1960. Sales rep. Nat. Steel Corp., Detroit, Milw., Chgo., 1960-67; regional dir. AMA, Chgo., St. Louis, Chgo., 1967-73; exec. dir. R.I. Med. Soc., Providence, 1973-77, Conn. State Med. Soc., New Haven, 1977—; bd. dirs., treas. Conn. Med. Mgmt., Inc., Wallingford, 1984—; asst. treas. Conn. Med. Ins. Co., Wallingford, 1984—; cons. Vt. State Med. Soc., Montpelier, 1987; cons. R.I. Med. Soc., Providence, 1986. Contbr. articles profl. jours. chmn. bd. dirs. Am. Cancer Soc. Conn. Div., Wallingford, 1985-87, mem. nat. com. on field svcs., 1989—, bd. dirs. Conn. div.; bd. dirs. St. Louis County Narcotics Commn., 1967-70; bd. dirs. New Haven Regional Mental Health Assn., 1980-83; pres. Conn. Physicians Guild. Recipient Nat. Bronze medal Am. Cancer Soc., 1987, hon. MD, Conn. State Med. Soc. Mem. Am. Soc. Assn. Execs., Am. Assn. Med. Soc. Execs. (bd. dirs., pres.), Rotary. Democrat. Presbyterian. Home: 7 Canterbury Way North Haven CT 06473-1018 Office: Conn State Med Soc 160 Saint Ronan St New Haven CT 06511-2312

NORCROSS, JOHN C(ONNER), psychologist, educator; b. Camden, N.J., Aug. 13, 1957; s. George E. and Carol C.; m. Nancy A. Caldwell, June 25, 1981; children: Rebecca, Jonathan. BA, Rutgers U., 1980; MA, U. R.I., 1981, PhD, 1984. Lic. psychologist, Pa. Psychology intern Brown U. Sch. Medicine, 1984-85; rsch. fellow Self-Change Lab. U. R.I., 1982-86; pvt. practice clin. psychologist, 1986—; prof. psychology U. Scranton, Pa., 1985—; chmn. dept. U. Scranton, 1987-93; vis. prof. U. Guadalajara, 1990; vis. fellow U. London, 1990. Author: Toward Integration: John Norcross in a Dialogue with Windy Dryden, 1991, Changing for Good, 1994; co-author: Insider's Guide to Graduate Programs in Clinical Psychology, 1996, Systems of Psychotherapy - A Transtheoretical Analysis, 1993; editor: Therapy Wars, 1990; co-editor: Handbook of Psychotherapy Integration, 1992, APA Psychotherapy Videotape Series, 1994—; assoc. editor Jour. Psychotherapy Integration, 1990—; mem. editl. bd. 10 jours.; contbr. over 100 articles to profl. jours. Recipient Pa. Prof. Yr., 1992. Fellow APA (Jack Krasner award 1992), Internat. Acad. Eclectic Psychotherapists, Pa. Psychol. Assn.; mem. Assn. for Advancement of Psychology, Ea. Psychol. Assn., Soc. for Psychotherapy Rsch., Soc. for Applied and Preventive Psychology, Am. Evaluation Assn., Soc. for Exploration of Psychotherapy Integration. Home: RD 3 Box 463F Lake Ariel PA 18436 Office: U Scranton Dept Psychology Scranton PA 18510-4596

NORD, RANDALL LEE, physician's assistant; b. New Castle, Pa., Dec. 26, 1954; s. Carl Benjamin and Agnes (Icenhour) N. B in Allied Health Sci., U. Ala., Birmingham, 1984. Cert. Nat. Certifying Coun. for Physician Assts.; physician asst. certified. Surg. physician's asst. U. Ala., Birmingham, 1984-95, Meml. Hosp., Colorado Springs, Colo., 1995—; clin. prof. Surgeon's Asst. Program, Birmingham, 1986-95. With U.S. Army, 1976-80. Fellow Acad. Physician's Assts., Assn. Physician's Assts. in Cardiovascular Surgery, Colo. Assn. Physicians Assts. Home: 14 W Columbia St Colorado Springs CO 80907

NORDBY, EUGENE JORGEN, orthopedic surgeon; b. Abbotsford, Wis., Apr. 30, 1918; s. Herman Preus and Lucille Violet (Korsrud) N.; m. Olive Marie Jensen, June 21, 1941; 1 child, Jon Jorgen. B.A., Luther Coll., Decorah, Iowa, 1939; M.D., U. Wis., 1943. Intern Madison Gen. Hosp., Wis., 1943-44, asst. in orthopedic surgery, 1944-48; practice medicine specializing in orthopedic surgery Madison, Wis., 1948—; pres. Bone and Joint Surgery Assocs., S.C. 1969-91; chief staff Madison Gen. Hosp., 1957-63; assoc. clin. prof. U. Wis. Med. Sch., 1961—; chmn. Wis. Physicians Svcs., 1979—; dir. Wis. Regional Med. Program, Chgo. Madison and No. RR; bd. govs. Wis. Health Care Liability Ins. Plan; chmn. trustees S.M.S. Realty Corp.; mem. bd. attys. Profl. Responsibility of Wis. Supreme Ct., 1992—. Assoc. editor Clin. Orthopaedics and Related Research, 1964—. Pres. Vesterheim Norwegian Am. Mus., Decorah, Iowa, 1968—. Served to capt. M.C., AUS, 1944-46. Decorated Knight 1st class Royal Norwegian Order St. Olav; named Notable Norwegian Dane County Norwegian-Am. Fest, 1995; recipient Disting. Svc. award Internat. Rotary,1 987, Den Hoyeste Aere award Vesterheim, 1993. Mem. Acad. Orthopaedic Surgeons (bd. dirs. 1972-73), Clin. Orthopaedic Soc., Assn. Bone and Joint Surgeons (pres. 1973), Internat. Soc. Study Lumbar Spine, State Med. Soc. Wis. (chmn. 1968-76, treas. 1976—, Coun. award 1976), Am. Orthopaedic Assn., N.Am. Spine Soc., Internat. Intradiscal Therapy Soc. (sec. 1987—), Wis. Orthopaedic Soc., Dane County Med. Soc. (pres. 1957), Nat. Exch. Club, Madison Torske Klubben (founder, pres. 1978—), Norwegian-Am. Orthopaedic Soc., Phi Chi. Lutheran. Home: 6234 S Highlands Ave Madison WI 53705-1115 Office: 2704 Marshall Ct Madison WI 53705-2256

NORDHEIM, ALFRED ERNST, biology educator, biomedical researcher; b. Philippsthal, Germany, Dec. 1, 1951; s. Karl and Berta (Eiring) N. Diploma in Biology, Free U. Berlin, 1976, PhD, 1979. Rsch. assoc. MIT, Cambridge, Mass., 1980-83; leader rsch. group ZMBH, U. Heidelberg, Germany, 1984-89; dir. Inst. for Molecular Biology, Hannover (Germany) Med. Sch., 1990—. With German Air Force, 1970-71. Mem. European Molecular Biology Orgn. Office: Hannover Med Sch MHH, Inst Molecular Biology, 30623 Hannover Germany

NORDSHUS, TORE, pediatric radiologist; b. Oslo, June 12, 1946. MD, U. Oslo, 1971. Intern med. dept. Trondheim, Norway, 1969; intern surg. dept. Trondheim, 1970; resident dept. radiology Ullevail, Oslo, 1972-77; fellow dept. pediatric radiology Nat. Hosp., Oslo, 1977-82; cons. dept. pediatric radiology Ulleval U. Hosp., Oslo, 1982—. Capt. Royal Norwegian Air Force, 1971. Mem. Norwegian Ultrasound Assn. (pres. 1983-86), European Fedn. Ultrasound (sec. 1981-85), Scandinavian Assn. Pediatric Radiology (leader 1991-96).

NORDSTROM, KURT, microbiologist; b. Stockholm, Nov. 3, 1935; s. Gustaf and Anna Elisabeth (Petterson) N.; m. Ulla Birgitta Elgbrink, Dec. 27, 1959 (div. Jan. 1970); children: Cornelia, Erica, Malin; m. Ulla Marie Henriksson, Mar. 20, 1970 (div. Dec. 1985); children: Karin, Johanna; m. Sylvi Anita Gunnarson, July 1, 1989. Chem. Engr., Royal Inst. Tech., Stockholm, 1958, PhD, 1962, D Tech., 1964; Docent, U. Stockholm, U. Umea, Sweden, 1965, 66. Asst. prof. U. Umea, 1966-71, assoc. prof., 1971-75; prof. Odense U., Denmark, 1976-82; prof. Uppsala (Sweden) U., 1982—, dean biology sect./sci. faculty, 1988-92; prodean faculty sci. Uppsala U., Sweden, 1992-93. Editor: Plasmid Jour., 1981-89; contbr. articles to profl. jours. Recipient Price award Lilli Kjaers Cancer Found., Denmark, 1980. Fellow Royal Acad. Scis. at Uppsala, Royal Swedish Acad. Scis.; mem. European Molecular Biology Orgn., Swedish Soc. Microbiology (pres. 1984-88), Am. Soc. Microbiology, N.Y. Acad. Scis. Home: Linnegatan 18B, 7-53-32 Uppsala Sweden Office: Uppsala Univ, Biomedical Centre, PO Box 581, S-751 23 Uppsala Sweden

NOREIKA, JOSEPH CASIMIR, ophthalmologist; b. Scranton, Pa., Aug. 21, 1950; s. Joseph C. and Joan (Stirna) N.; m. Joanne Elizabeth Keane, May 14, 1977; children: Sarah, Michael, Katya, Mathew. BS, U. Scranton, 1972; MD, Jefferson Med. Coll., 1976; MBA, Case Western Res. U., 1988. Diplomate Am. Bd. of Opthalmology. Intern Dartmouth Hosps., Hanover, N.H., 1976-77; resident in ophthalmology U. Pitts., 1977-80, assoc. clin. prof., 1981-83; fellow U. Calif., San Francisco, 1980-81; pvt. practice Medina, Ohio, 1983—; bd. dirs. Physician Resource Group; adj. clin. staff Cleve. Clinic Found., 1980-92. Editl. advisor The Argus; sect. contbr.: Ocular Surgery News, editl. bd., Adminstrv. Ophthalmology; editl. bd. Eye World News Svc.; contbr. articles to profl. jours. Bd. dirs. Physician Resource Group. Recipient Shoemaker award Pa. Acad. Ophthalmology, 1979; Heed Found. fellow, 1980. Mem. AMA (Physician Recognition award 1984-96), Am. Acad. Ophthalmology (chmn. computerized patient record task force, practice mgmt. com., managed care adv. com., Honor award 1996), Am. Soc. Cataract and Refractive Surgeons (scientific adv. bd. rep., rep. to AMA CPT adv. com., govt. rels. com.), Am. Soc. Ophthalmology Adminstrs. (editl. bd.), Ohio State Med. Assn., Ohio Ophthalmology Soc. (editor Managed Care-In Focus, chmn. managed care com.), Medina County Med. Soc. (past pres., program chmn.), Cleve. Ophthalmology Soc. (past pres.), Alpha Sigma Nu, Beta Gamma Sigma. Office: Eye Care Medina Inc 3637 Medina Rd Ste 70 Medina OH 44256-8154

NORENBERG, RICHARD GEORGE, surgeon; b. Lincoln, Nebr., Sept. 17, 1933; s. Hugo Amos Norenberg and Mildred Floy (Fosler) Barnes; m. Ruth Arlene Lindquist, July 5, 1958; children: Lynn Ann, Eric Jon, Leif Richard, Kris Matthew. BA, North Ctrl. Coll., 1955; MD, U. Ill., 1959. Diplomate Am. Bd. Thoracic Surgery, Am. Bd. Surgery. Intern Tampa (Fla.) Gen. Hosp., 1959-60; surg. resident Bayfront Med. Ctr., St. Petersburg, Fla., 1962-63; family practitioner St. Petersburg, Fla., 1963-69; surg. resident U. Hawaii, Honolulu, 1969-72, Duke U., Oteen, N.C., 1972-74; surgeon St. Petersburg, 1974—; chmn. dept. surgery Bayfront Med. Ctr., 1977-83, chief of staff, 1986-87; clin. asst. prof. U. So. Fla., Tampa, 1983—. Trustee North Ctrl. Coll., 1984—, Bayfront Med. Ctr., 1993-96. With USAF, 1960-62. Recipient Outstanding Alumnus award North Ctrl. Coll., 1989. Fellow ACS; mem. So. Thoracic Surgery Assn., Pinellas County Med. Soc. (bd. govs. 1991-94). Methodist. Office: Ste 340 603-7th St S Saint Petersburg FL 33701

NORIN, ALLEN J., scientist; b. Chgo., July 30, 1944; s. Nathan and Ada (Axelrod) N.; children: Lary, Andy. Student, Wright Jr. Coll., 1963-65; BS, Roosevelt U., 1965-67; MS, U. Houston, 1967-69, PhD, 1969-72. Rsch. assoc. microbiology dept. U. Chgo., 1972-75; asst. prof. Montefiore Med. Ctr. Albert Einstein Coll. Medicine, Bronx, N.Y., 1976-84, assoc. prof., 1985-88; assoc. prof. SUNY Health Sci. Ctr., Bklyn., 1988-90; prof. medicine, anatomy and cell biology Health Sci. Ctr. SUNY, Bklyn., 1990—, dir. transplantation immunology and immunogenetics, 1990—; mem. histocompatibility com. N.Y. Regional Transplant Program, N.Y.C., 1990—, stds. com., 1990-94, kidney/pancreas com. 1994—; prof. SUNY Health Sci. Ctr. at Bklyn. Contbr. numerous articles to profl. jours. NIH grantee, 1977—. Mem. AAAS, Am. Assn. Immunologists, Am. Soc. Microbiology, N.Y. Acad. Sci., Am. Soc. Histocompatibility and Immunogenetics. Office: SUNY Health Sci Ctr 450 Clarkson Ave # 1197 Brooklyn NY 11203-2012

NORK, T. MICHAEL, ophthalmologist, researcher; b. Washington, Mar. 28, 1948; s. Thomas P. and Nettie (Johnson) N. BS, U. Md., 1970, U. Md., 1974; MS, Ga. Inst. Tech., 1972; MD, U. Tex., San Antonio, 1980. Diplomate Am. Bd. Ophthalmology. Rsch. asst. U. Tex. Med. Sch., San Antonio, 1974-76; internal medicine intern Sinai Hosp. of Balt., 1980-81; resident in ophthalmology Tex. Tech U., Lubbock, 1981-84; fellow in ophthalmic pathology U. Ill. Eye and Ear Infirmary, Chgo., 1984-85; retina fellow U. Wis. Med. Sch., Madison, 1985-86; from asst. prof. to assoc. prof. W.Va. U. Sch. Medicine, Morgantown, 1987-93; asst. prof. ophthalmology U. Wis., Madison, 1993-95, assoc. prof., 1995—; cons. Freeport (Ill.) Meml. Hosp., 1993—, VA Hosp., Madison, 1994—. Contbr. articles to profl. jours. Rsch. grantee NIH, 1990-96, U. Wis., 1993, 96. Fellow Am. Acad. Ophthalmology; mem. Assn. for Rsch. in Vision and Ophthalmology, The Retina Soc. Home: 17 Hickory Hollow Dr Madison WI 53705-1071 Office: U Wis Sch Medicine 600 Highland Ave F4/3 Madison WI 53792-3220

NORKIN, CYNTHIA CLAIR, physical therapist; b. Boston, May 6, 1932; d. Miles Nelson and Carolyn (Green) Clair; m. Stanislav A. Norkin, Feb. 19, 1955 (dec. 1970); 1 child, Alexandra. BS in Edn., Tufts U., 1954; cert. phys. therapy Bouve Boston Coll., 1954; MS, Boston U., 1973, EdD, 1984. Instr. Bouve-Boston Coll., 1954-55; staff phys. therapist New Eng. Med. Center, Boston, 1954-55; staff phys. therapist Abington Meml. Hosp., Abington, Pa., 1965-70, Eastern Montgomery County Vis. Nurse Assn., 1970-72; asst. prof. phys. therapy Sargent Coll., Boston U., 1973-84; assoc. prof. phys. therapy, dir., founder Sch. Phys. Therapy, Ohio U., Athens, 1984-95; cons. Boston Center Ind. Living, Cambridge Vis. Nurse Assn., Mass. Medicaid Cost Effectiveness Project, 1978; sec. Health Planning Council Greater Boston, 1976-78; book, manuscript reviewer F.A. Davis Co., 1986—; mem. arthritis adv. com. Ohio Dept. Health. Trustee Brimmer and May Sch., 1980. Mem. AAAS, Am. Phys. Therapy Assn. (on site evaluator commn. on accreditation 1986—), Mass. Phys. Therapy Assn. (chmn. Mass. quality assurance com. 1980-83), Am. Public Health Assn., Mass. Assn. Mental Health, Athens County Vi. Nurse Assn. (sec. adv. coun. 1984-95). Episcopalian. Author: (with P. Levangie) Joint Structure and Function: A Comprehensive Analysis, 1983, 2d edit., 1992; (with D.J. White) Joint Measurement: A Guide to Goniometry, 1985, 2d edit., 1995.

NORMAN, DEBRA DEON, gerontologist researcher; b. Aberdeen, S.D., Sept. 14, 1954; d. Gordon Albert and Loraine Ires (Beck) Diedtrich; (div. Feb. 1983); children: Shawn G., Stacey R. BS, U. Mary, Bismarck, N.D., 1982; MS, U. Minn., 1990, PhD, 1995. Cert. med. technologist. Clin. supr. Presentation Coll., Aberdeen, S.D., 1982-84; rsch. assoc. Dept. Pediatrics U. Minn., Mpls., 1987-88, lab. teaching specialist Med. Sch., 1984-90; med. technologist critical chemistry U. Minn. Hosps., Mpls., 1989-92; rsch. assoc. Dept. of Pharmacy Practice U. Minn., Mpls., 1992-94; fellowship Pharm. Care Inst., Mpls., 1995—; exec. bd. student rep. Minn. Gerontol. Assn., Mpls., 1994-95. Contbr. articles to profl. jours. Legis. liaison Grad. and Profl. Student Assembly, U. Minn., Mpls., 1994-95. Recipient Dept. Study Grant award U. Minn., 1987-89. Mem. Am. Assn. Coll. Pharmacy, Am. Pharm. Assn., Minn. Gerontol. Soc., Minn. Chromatography Forum. Home: 135 Nathan Ln N Plymouth MN 55441 Office: U Minn Dept Pharmacy Practice Minneapolis MN 55455

NORMAN, EDWARD COBB, psychiatrist, educator; b. Prince George, B.C., Can., Oct. 5, 1913; s. Arthur J. and Lilla E. (Cobb) N.; m. June Marie Morris, Sept. 24, 1949; children: Donald, Cornelia, Sharon. BS, U. Wash., 1935; MD, U. Pa., 1940; MPH, Tulane U., 1965. Intern, Phila. Gen. Hosp., 1940-42; resident, Pa. Hosp., 1942-43; resident Michael Reese Hosp., 1946-49; asst. surgeon, USPHS, 1943-46; pvt. practice psychiatry, Chgo., 1949-53, New Orleans, 1953—; clin. instr. psychiatry U. Ill., Chgo., 1949-53; asst. prof. clin. psychiatry Tulane U., New Orleans, 1953-60, assoc. prof., 1960-64, prof., 1964-79; emeritus, 1979—; dir. community mental health sect. Tulane U. Sch. Pub. Health Tropical medicine, 1967-79; assoc. dir. Pain Rehab. Unit Hotel Dieu Hosp., 1978—; adminstr. Learning Procedures, Inc., New Orleans, 1977-78, v.p., 1978—; cons. to govt. agys. Fellow Am. Psychiat. Assn. (life), Am. Acad. Psychoanalysis Am. Pub. Health Assn.; mem. N.Y. Acad. Sci., Forum for Improvement of Quality of Life (sec.); Delta Omega (pres. Eta chpt.). Contbr. numerous articles to profl. jours. Home: 1209 Washington Ave New Orleans LA 70130-5747

NORMAN, JACK DAVIS, plastic surgeon; b. Nashville, May 20, 1936; s. Ely and Ruby (Levein) N.; m. Ann Susan Kaplon, Oct. 29, 1976; 1 child, Mindie Elyse. BA, Vanderbilt U., 1958, MA, 1961; MD, N.Y. Med. Coll., 1963. Diplomate Am. Bd. Surgery, Am. Bd. Plastic Surgery. Intern U. Miami, Fla., 1963-64; resident surgery U. Miami, 1964-68; resident plastic surgery NYU, N.Y.C., 1970-72; pvt. practice plastic surgery Miami, 1972—; clin. instr. dept. plastic surgery U. Miami, 1972—; pres. Fla. Soc. Plastic Surgeons, 1980-81, Greater Miami Soc. Plastic Surgeons, 1985-86. Maj. USAF, 1968-70. Republican. Jewish. Office: 848 Brickell Ave #940 Miami FL 33131

NORMAN, MARY MARSHALL, counselor, therapist; b. Auburn, N.Y., Jan. 10, 1937; d. Anthony John and Zita Norman. BS cum laude, LeMoyne Coll., 1958; MA, Marquette, U., 1960; EdD, Pa. State U., 1971. Cert. Alcoholism Counselor. Tchr., St. Cecilia's Elem. Sch., Theinsville, Wis., 1959-60; vocat. counselor Marquette U., Milw., 1959-60; dir. testing and counseling U. Rochester (N.Y.), 1960-62; dir. testing and counseling, dean women, asso. dean coll., asst. dean students, dir. student activities, asst. prof. psychology Corning (N.Y.) C.C., 1962-68; rsch. asst. Center for Study Higher Edn., Pa. State U., University Park, 1969-71; dean faculty South Campus, C.C. Allegheny County, West Mifflin, Pa., 1971-72, exec. dean, coll. v.p., 1972-82; pres. Orange County C.C., 1982-90; sr. counselor The Horton Family Program, 1990—. cons. Boricua Coll., N.Y.C., 1976-77; reader NSF, 1977-78; mem. govtl. commn. com. Am. Assn. Cmty. and Jr. Colls., 1976-79, bd. dirs., 1982—; mem. and chmn. various middle state accreditation teams. Bd. dirs. Orange County United Way; bd. dirs. Orange County Alcoholism and Drug Abuse Coun., 1993—. Mem. Am. Assn. Higher Edn., Nat. Assn. Women Deans Counselors, Am. Assn. Women in Community and Jr. Colls. (charter, Woman of Yr. 1981), Pa. Assn. Two-Yr. Colls., Pa. Assn. Acad. Deans, Pitts. Council Women Execs. (charter), Am. Council on Edn. (Pa. rep. identification women for adminstrn. 1978—), Pa. Council on Higher Edn., Orange County C. of C., Gamma Pi Epsilon. Contbr. articles to profl. jours. Home: 8 Crabapple Ln Middletown NY 10940-1006 Office: 406 E Main St Middletown NY 10940

NORMAN, RICHARD DAVIESS, dental educator; b. Franklin, Ind., Feb. 7, 1927; s. William Byron and Edith May (Grubb) N.; m. Joan May Roler, July 15, 1951; children: Beverly Joan, Elizabeth Jane. AB, Franklin Coll., 1950; DDS, Ind. U., Indpls., 1958, MS, 1964. Analytical chemist Eli Lilly & Co., Indpls., 1950-54; research assoc. Ind. U., Indpls., 1955-58, instr., 1958-64, asst. prof., 1964-69, assoc. prof., 1969-73, prof., 1973-76; dir. dental clin. rsch. Johnson & Johnson Dental Products Co., Heightstown, N.J., 1976-79; cons. Colts Neck, N.J., 1979-80; clin. prof. Fairleigh Dickinson U., 1979-80; prof., chmn. restorative dentistry So. Ill. U. Sch. Dental Medicine, Alton, 1980-85, dir. rsch., 1985-93, rsch. prof. emeritus, 1993—; cons. in field. Contbr. articles to profl. jours. Pres. sch. bd. Greenwood, Ind., 1968-70. With AUS, 1945-47. Rsch. grantee NIH, 1983—, Clopper Found., 1983. Mem. ADA, Am. Assn. Dental Rsch., Internat. Assn. Dental Rsch., Am. Coll. Dentists, Masons, Omicron Kappa Upsilon, Sigma Phi Alpha. Republican. Presbyterian. Home: 5 Monterey Pl Alton IL 62002-6740 Office: 2800 College Ave Alton IL 62002-4742

NORMAN, ROBERT JOHN, obstetrics and gynecology educator; b. Woking, U.K., June 19, 1949; arrived in Australia, 1988; s. John P. and Mary N.; m. Susan Gay Tracey, June 24, 1972; children: Michael, David, Rachel. BSc with honors, U. Birmingham, Eng., 1972, MB ChB with honors, 1974. Intern Harare Hosp., Zimbabwe, 1974; resident Harare Hosp., Rhodesia, 1978-79, 1975-79; resident U. Natal, South Africa, 1979-83, sr. lectr., 1983-86, assoc. prof., 1986-88; sr. lectr., assoc. prof. U. Adelaide, Australia, 1988—; dir. Reproductive Endocrine Labs., 1988—, Repromed, Adelaide, 1993—. Contbr. articles to profl. publs. Parish councillor Trinity Ch., Adelaide, 1994. ICI clin. scholar, South Africa, 1984. Mem. Australian Soc. Reproductive Biology, Australian Menopause Soc. (sec. 1995—). Mem. Anglican Ch. Home: 39 Brookside Ave, Tranmere 5073, Australia Office: U Adelaide, TQEH, Woodville 5011, Australia

NORONHA, JOAQUIM L., physician; b. Bombay, May 25, 1950; came to U.S., 1976; s. Ligorio N. and Melba (D'Cunha) N.; m. Lynne Ellen Doherty, May 9, 1980; children: Jennifer, Brian. MB, BS, Bombay, 1973, MD, 1975. Diplomate Am. Bd. Internal Medicine. Pvt. practice Somerset, N.J., 1980—; clin. asst. prof. medicine U. Medicine and Dentistry of N.J., New Brunswick, 1980—. Fellow Am. Coll. Endocrinology; mem. AMA, Am. Mensa, Med. Soc. N.J., Middlesex County Med. Soc., Am. Diabetes Assn. (chair patient edn. 1993). Roman Catholic. Office: Joaquim L Noronha MD 1553 Hwy 27 Somerset NJ 08873

NORRBY, ERLING CARL JACOB, virology educator; b. Stockholm, Sweden, Aug. 28, 1937; s. Carl Tore Nikolaus and Anna Gertrud (Lofgren) N.; m. Margareta Norrby; children: Jacob, Lars, Christina. MD, Karolinska Inst., Stockholm, 1963, PhD, 1964. Prof. Karolinska Inst., 1972-90, prof., dean, 1990-96. Author: Allmanna Forlaget, 1987; editor: (textbook) Almqvist & Wiksell, 2d edit. 1981; contbr. numerous articles to profl. jours. Mem. Royal Swedish Acad. Scis. (v.p. 1995-97). Home: Tykovagen 21, Lidingo S-181 61, Sweden Office: Karolinska Inst MTC, Stockholm S-17177, Sweden

NORRELL, MARK AVERY, health services administrator; b. New Orleans, June 28, 1958; s. Horace Avery Norrell and Martha Lane (Williams) Hartle; m. Susan April McConnell, Dec. 22, 1988; 1 child, Logan Rarick. BS in Zoology, U. Fla., 1979, BS in Med. Tech., 1983, M of Health Sci. in Hosp. Adminstrn., 1987, MBA, 1987. Resident in hosp. adminstrn. Sarasota (Fla.) Meml. Hosp., 1986-87; asst. dir. planning South Miami (Fla.) Hosp., 1987-89, dir. planning, 1989-92; asst. adminstr. Bannock Regional Med. Ctr., Pocatello, Idaho, 1993—. Bd. dirs. United Way S.E. Idaho, 1994-95. Mem. Am. Coll. Healthcare Execs. (diplomate), Am. Soc. Clin. Pathologists (registered med. technologist). Home: 6178 Old Ranch Rd Pocatello ID 83204 Office: Bannock Regional Med Ctr 651 Memorial Dr Pocatello ID 83204

NORRELL, MARY PATRICIA, nursing educator; b. Seymour, Ind., Jan. 3; d. William C. and Mary Elizabeth (Elkins) Ulrey; m. Robert Gerald Norrell, Aug. 17, 1974; children: Shannan, Richard, Trisha. BSN, Ball State U., 1971; postgrad., Ind. U. Cert. inpatient obstetrics. Team leader Mt. Sinai Med. Ctr., Miami Beach, Fla., 1971-73; charge nurse Jackson County Schneck Meml. Hosp., Seymour, 1971, 73-74; nurse Camp Matoaka, Oakland, Maine, 1973; master instr. Ivy Tech. State Coll., Columbus, Ind., 1974—; item writer Nat. Coun. Licensure Exam. for Practical Nurses, 1992. Mem. Assn. of Women's Health, Obstetric and Neonatal Nurses, Ind. Soc. for Healthcare Edn. and Tng. Home: 572 Shawnee Ct Seymour IN 47274-1956

NORRID, HENRY GAIL, osteopath, surgeon, researcher; b. Amarillo, Tex., June 4, 1940; s. Henry Horatio and Johnnie Belle (Combs, Cummins) N.; m. Andreia Maybeth Hudson, Jan. 29, 1966 (dec. 1988); children: Joshua Andrew, Noah Adam; m. Cheryll Diane Payne, Mar. 19, 1989; stepchildren: Kim Sheri Payne, Matthew Dominic Payne. AA, Amarillo Coll., 1963; BA, U. Tex., 1966; MS, West Tex. State U., 1967; DO, Kirksville Coll. Osteo. Medicine, 1973. Diplomate Bd. Osteo. Physicians and Surgeons, Nat. Bd. Examiners Osteo. Physicians and Surgeons; cert. basic sci. tchr. Iowa, Tex., Colo. Intern Interboro Gen. Hosp., Bklyn., 1973-74; attending physician dept. gen. practice Osteo. Hosp. and Clinic N.Y., N.Y.C., 1974-77; gen. practice medicine specializing in osteo., Amarillo, Tex., 1978—; emergency care physician Amarillo Emergency Receiving Ctr. Amarillo Hosp. Dist., Tex., 1978-79, Ready Care Emergency Center, Arlington and Bedford, Tex., 1990-92; emergency room physician St. Anthony Hosp., Amarillo, Tex., 1992; emeritus mem. consulting staff physician dept. family practice Northwest Tex. Hosp., Amarillo, 1995; emergency/trauma physician Tex. EM Care, 1995—; mem. mass casualty nat. disaster response team ARC, 1995; contract staff physician Tex. Tech Univ. Sch. Medicine and Health Scis. Ctr., med. dept. and infirmary Tex. Dept. Corrections, Tex. Dept. Criminal Justice; med. cons. rehab. medicine vocat. rehab. divsn Tex. Rehab. Commn., Plano; cattleman, ranch owner, Van Zandt County, Tex.; lectr. osteo. prins. and practice, The Osteo. Hosp. and Clinic N.Y., 1974-77, mem. credentials com., 1975-76; mem. exec. com. Southwest Osteo. Hosp., Amarillo, 1983-84, chief of staff, 1984-85; sec. dept. family practice Northwest Tex. Hosp., Amarillo, 1981-82, mem. credentials com., 1984-85, joint practice com. dept. family practice, 1986-87; mem. orgnl. com. for devel. of dept. osteo. prins. and practices, chmn. N.Y.C. group N.Y. Coll. Osteo. Med., 1977; mem. North Tex. Amputee Support Group, Dallas. Contbr. articles to Tex. Jour. Sci., other publs. Scout physician Llano Estecato council Boy Scouts Am., Texas, 1978-85. Served to E-4 U.S. Army, 1956-63. Recipient William M. Giltner Meml. Fund award 1972, Humanitarian award Am. Cath. Conf., 1979, Century award Boy Scouts Am., 1982; Maxwell D. Warmer Meml. scholar 1973; scholar Kirksville Coll. Osteo. Medicine, 1970, Tex. Legislature, 1969-73, Pfizer, 1973; named to Eminent Soc. Border Legionaires, 11th Armored Cavalry Regiment, Germany, 1958. Mem. Am. Coll. Gen. Practitioners, Tex. Osteo. Med. Assn. (pres. dist. I, mem. ho. of dels. 1981-82, 95), Sons of Am. Revolution, The Sons of Republic of Tex., Am. Congress Rehab. Medicine, Am. Osteo. Assn., World Future Soc. (profl.), Gen. Soc. War of 1812, Tex. & Southwest Cattle Raisers Assn., N.Y. Acad. Scis., Ex-Student's Assn. of The Univ. Tex. (life), 11th Armored Cavalry Regiment Assn., 36th (Tex.) Inf. Divsn. Assn. (life), Baron of the Magna Charta (Sommerset chpt. 1994—), Masons, Am. Legion, Trinity Fellowship, Beta Beta Beta, Sigma Sigma Phi (pres. 1972), Alpha Phi Omega, Psi Sigma Alpha, Theta Psi, Theta Psi Clowns (1969-73). Avocations: astronomy, short wave listening, camping, fishing, anthropology. Office: 1422 S Tyler St Ste 102 Amarillo TX 79101-4238

NORRIS, ALBERT STANLEY, psychiatrist, educator; b. Sudbury, Ont., Can., July 14, 1926; s. William and Mary (Zell) N.; m. Dorothy James, Sept. 2, 1950; children: Barbara Ellen, Robert Edward, Kimberly Ann. M.D., U. Western Ont., 1951. Intern Ottawa (Ont.) Civic Hosp., 1951-52; resident in psychiatry U. Iowa, Psychopathic Hosp., Iowa City, 1953-55, Boston City Hosp., 1955-56; practice medicine Kingston, Ont., Can., 1956-57; instr. Queen's U., Kingston, 1956-57; asst. prof. psychiatry U. Iowa, 1957-62, asso. prof., 1962-64, 1965-66, prof., 1966-72; asso. prof. U. Oreg., 1964-65; prof. So. Ill. U. Sch. Medicine, Springfield, 1972-84, chmn. dept. psychiatry, 1972-82; prof. emeritus, 1984—; practice medicine specializing in psychiatry Cedar Rapids, Iowa, 1984—; vis. prof. U. Auckland, N.Z., U. Otago, New Zealand, U. Liverpool. Contbr. chpts. to books, articles to med. jours. Fellow Am. Psychiat. Soc. (life); mem. AMA, Am. Psychopath. Assn., Soc. Biol. Psychiatry, Can. Psychiat. Soc., Am. Soc. Psychosomatic Ob-Gyn, Royal Soc. Medicine. Republican. Presbyterian. Home: 5 Penfro Dr Iowa City IA 52246-4927 Office: 1730 1st Ave NE Ste 133 Cedar Rapids IA 52402-5433

NORRIS, CHARLEY WILLIAM, otolaryngologist, educator; b. Morganville, Kans., Jan. 3, 1933; s. George P. and Mary (Kaiser) N.; m. Linda Larson, Nov. 30, 1963; children: Andrew William, Erik Christopher. BA, U. Kans., 1960, MD, 1964. Intern Latter Day Saints Hosp., Salt Lake City, 1964-65, resident gen. surgery, 1965-66; ear, nose and throat resident Tufts Univ., Boston, 1966-69; jr. mem. staff Tufts U. Med. Sch., Boston, 1968-69; attending staff physician Boston City Hosp., 1969-71; asst. prof. U. Kans., Kans. City, 1971-75; assoc. prof. U. Kans., 1975-81, prof., chmn., 1981-90; chief of staff U. Kans. Hosp., 1989-92; prof. otolaryngology U. Kans., 1992—; instr. Tufts U., Boston, 1969-71; cons. Vets. Hosp., Kans. City, Mo., 1971—. Contbr. chpt. to book and articles to profl. jours. With USN, 1951-56. Fellow ACS, Am. Soc. for Head and Neck Surgery, Am. Laryngol., Rhinological and Otological Soc., Am. Acad. Otolaryngic Allergy, Am. Soc. Head and Neck Surgery, Am. Acad. Otolaryngology, N.Y. Acad. Scis. Office: U Kans Med Ctr 39th and Rainbow Blvd Kansas City KS 66160-7380

NORRIS, FRANKLIN GRAY, surgeon; b. Washington, June 30, 1923; s. Franklin Gray and Ellie Narcissus (Story) N.; m. Sara Kathryn Green, Aug. 12, 1945; children: Gloria Norris Sales, F. Gray III. BS, Duke U., 1947; MD, Harvard U., 1951. Resident, Peter Bent Brigham Hosp., Boston, 1951-54, Bowman Gray Sch. Medicine, 1954-57; practice medicine specializing in thoracic and cardiovascular surgery, 1957—; prof. anatomy and physiology, Valencia C.C., Orlando, Fla., 1995—; pres. Norris Assocs., Orlando, 1985—; mem. staff Brevard Meml. Hosp., Melbourne, Fla., Waterman Meml. Hosp., Eustis, Fla., West Orange Meml. Hosp., Winter Garden, Fla., Orlando Regional Med. Ctr., Fla. Hosp., Lucerne Hosp., Arnold Palmer Children Hosp., Princeton, Fla. Hosp. N.E. and South (all Orlando). Bd. dirs. Orange County Cancer Soc., 1958-64, Ctrl. Fla. Respiratory Disease Assn., 1958-65. Served to capt. USAAF, 1943-45. Decorated Air medal with 3 oak leaf clusters. Diplomate Am. Bd. Surgery, Am. Bd. Thoracic and Cardiovasc. Surgery, Am. Bd. Gen. Vascular Surgery. Mem. Fla. Heart Assn. (dir. 1958—), Orange County Med. Soc. (exec. com. 1964-75, pres. 1971-75), Cen. Fla. Hosp. Assn. (bd. dirs., 1980-85), ACS, Soc. Thoracic Surgeons, So. Thoracic Surg. Assn., Am. Coll. Chest Physicians, Fla. Soc. Thoracic Surgeons (pres. 1981-82), Am. Coll. Cardiology, So. Assn. Vascular Surgeons, Fla. Vascular Soc., Phi Kappa Psi. Presbyterian (elder). Clubs: Citrus, Orlando Country. Home: 1801 Bimini Dr Orlando FL 32806-1515 Office: Norris Assocs 1801 Bimini Dr Orlando FL 32806-1515

NORRIS, H. THOMAS, pathologist, academic administrator; b. Johnson City, Tenn., Nov. 24, 1934; s. Herbert Thomas and Ruth M. (Church) N.; m. Patricia Henry, June 19, 1956; children: Ruth Eileen, Margaret Ann, Edward Robert. BS with honors, Wash. State U., 1956; MD, U. So. Calif., 1959. Diplomate Am. Bd. Anatomic and Clin. Pathology. Resident pathology Mallory Inst. Pathology, Boston, 1960-62, 64-65; instr. Tufts U. Sch. Medicine, Boston, 1964-66; fellow Harvard Med. Sch., Cambridge, Mass., 1966-67; from asst. prof. to prof. U. Wash. Sch. Med., 1967-83; prof., chmn. East Carolina U. Sch. Medicine, Greenville, N.C., 1983—; asst. pathologist Mallory Inst. Pathology, Boston, 1965-66; asst. chief lab svc. VA Hosp., Seattle, 1967-74; dir. hosp. pathology U. Hosp., Seattle, 1974-83; chief pathology Pitt County Meml. Hosp., Greenville, 1983—. Editor: Contemporary Issues in Surgical Pathology, 1983, Pathology of the Colon, Small Intestine and Anus, 1991; contbr. articles to profl. jours. Bd. dirs. Am. Cancer Soc., Greenville, 1984—. Capt. USAR, 1962-64. Recipient Cert. Outstanding Achievement with Honorarium U.S. Army Sci. Conf., West Point, N.Y., 1964. Fellow ACP, Am. Soc. Clin. Pathologists, Coll. Am. Pathologists, Am. Pathology Found.; mem. AAAS, AMA, Am. Gastroent. Assn., Internat. Acad. Pathology, U.S. and Can. Acad. Pathology, Am. Assn. Pathologists, Arthur Purdy Stout Soc. Surg. Pathologists, Acad. Clin. Lab. Physicians and Scientists, Assn. Pathology Chmn., Am. Men and Women Sci., N.Y. Acad. Scis., Mass. Med. Soc., N.C. Med. Assn., N.C. Soc. Pathologists, Pitt County Med. Soc., Gastrointestinal Pathology Club (charter), Alpha Omega Alpha, Sigma Xi. Office: East Carolina U Sch Medicine Dept Pathology Lab Medicine Greenville NC 27858-4354

NORRIS, JOHN ANTHONY, health sciences executive, lawyer, educator; b. Buffalo, Dec. 27, 1946; s. Joseph D. and Maria L. (Suite) N.; m. Kathleen E. Mullen, July 13, 1969; children: Patricia Marie, John Anthony II, Joseph Mullen, Mary Kathleen, Elizabeth Mary. BA, U. Rochester, 1968; JD, MBA with honors, Cornell U., 1973; cert., Harvard U. Sch. Govt., 1986. Bar: Mass. 1973. Assoc. Peabody, Brown, Boston, 1973-75; assoc. Powers Hall, Boston, 1975-76, ptnr., mem. exec. com., 1976-80, v.p., dir., 1979-80, chmn. adminstrv. com., 1976-79, chmn. hiring com., 1979-80; chmn. bd., pres., chief exec. officer, founder Norris & Norris, Boston, 1980-85; dep. commr. and chief operating officer FDA, Washington, 1985-88, chmn. action planning and cap coms., 1985-88, chmn. reye syndrome com., 1985-87, chmn. trade legis. com., 1987-88; corporate exec. v.p. Hill & Knowlton, Inc., N.Y.C., 1988-93; worldwide dir. Health Scis. Cons. Group., 1988-93, chmn. health scis. policy coun., 1989-93; chmn. bd., pres., CEO, founder John A. Norris, Esq., P.C., Boston, 1993—; pres., CEO Nat. Pharm. Coun., Reston, Va., 1995-96; mem. faculty Tufts Dental Sch., 1974-79, Boston Coll. Law Sch., 1976-80, Boston U. Law Sch., 1979-83, Harvard U. Pub. Health Sch., 1988—; mem. bd. editors FDA Drug Bull. and FDA Consumer Report, 1985-88; bd. dirs. Summit Tech., Inc., Cytologics, Inc., Horus Therapeutics Inc., Nat. Applied Scis. Founder, faculty editor-in-chief Am. Jour. Law and Medicine, 1973-81, emeritus 1981—; editor-in-chief Cornell Internat. Law Jour., 1971-73; reviewer New Eng. Jour. Medicine Law-Medicine Notes, 1980-81; assoc. editor Medicolegal News, 1973-75. Mem. U.S. Del. to Japan (chmn.), Austria, Saudi Arabia, 1987, mem., chmn. Finland, Denmark, Italy, 1986; chmn. Mass. Statuatory Adv. Com. on Regulation of Clin. Labs., 1977-83; chmn. Boston Alumni and Scholarship Com., U. Rochester, 1979-85; mem. trustees coun. U. Rochester, 1979-85; mem. exec. com. Cornell Law Sch. Assn., 1982-85; mem. Mass. Gov.'s Blue Ribbon Task Force on DON, 1979-80, bd. trustees Jordan Hosp., 1978-80, mem. exec. com., 1979-80, chmn., chief exec. officer search com., 1980; chmn. Joseph D. Norris, Esq. Health Law and Pub. Policy Fund., 1979—; chmn. bd. Boston Holiday Project, 1981-83; mem. U.S. Pres. Chernobyl Task Force, 1986, vice-chmn. health affects sub.-com.; mem. U.S. Intra-Govtl. AIDS Task Force, 1987; mem. IOM Drug Devel. Forum, 1986-88, co-chmn. end points sub-com., 1987-88, Fed. Pain Commn., 1984-85. With U.S. Army, 1972-73. Fed. Comprehensive Health Planning fellow, 1970-73; recipient Kansas City Hon. Key award, 1988, Nat. Health Fraud Conf. award, 1988, TOYL award, 1982, FDA Award of Merit, 1987, 88, PHS award, 1987, HHS Sec. award, 1988. Mem. ABA (vice chmn. medicine and law com. 1977-80), Mass. Bar Assn., Am. Soc. Hosp. Attys., Nat. Health Lawyers, Am. Soc. Law and Medicine (1st v.p. 1975-80, chmn. bd. 1981-84, life mem. award 1981), Soc. Computer Applications to Med. Care (bd. dirs. 1984-85), Internat. Coun. for Global Health Progress (bd. dirs. 1989-95), Phi Kappa Phi. Home: 531 W Washington St Hanson MA 02341-1067 also: 2209 Burgee Ct Reston VA 22091

NORRIS, JOHN STEVEN, healthcare company executive; b. Chgo., Apr. 25, 1943; s. Norris Dale and Olive (Grissinger) N. BA, U. Ariz., 1967; B in Fgn. Trade, Am. Grad. Sch. Internat. Mgmt., 1968; MPH, U. Ariz., 1995; diplomate Am. Coll. Healthcare Execs.; lic. nursing home adminstr.; m. Susan Jean Armstrong, May 3, 1975; children: Lindsey Jean, Whitney Ann, John Scott. Inspection officer Citicorp, Brazil, Colombia, Mex., 1968-72, asst. cashier, N.Y.C., 1972-74; pres., gen. mgr. Phoenix Athletic Club, 1974-76; bus. mgr. Phoenix Pub. Inc., 1976-77; project mgr. Environ. Constrn. Co., Phoenix, 1977-79; pres. AGN Devel. Corp., Phoenix, 1979—, Valley View Realty, Inc., 1981-87; exec. v.p., sec., pres. RGW Constrn. Co., Inc.; pres. Norris/Roberts Group, Inc., Phoenix, 1987-90; CEO Christian Care Cos., Inc., Phoenix, 1990—. Bd. dirs. Christian Care Inc.; deacon christian ch.; adv. bd. dirs. Area Agy. Aging; treas. Phoenix Rotary. Fellow Am. Assn. Home Svcs. Aging; mem. Am. Coll. Healthcare Adminstrs, Phi Delta Theta. Republican. Avocations: golf, skiing, racquetball. Home: 111 W Tam O'Shanter Dr Phoenix AZ 85023-6241 Office: Christian Care Cos 2002 W Sunnyside Dr Phoenix AZ 85029

NORRIS, PETER JUSTIN, industrial hygienist; b. Ludlow, Mass., Nov. 17, 1954; s. Kenneth Richard and Santa Cecilia Elizabeth (Liantonio) N.; m. Kathleen Wilson, May 23, 1987; children: Melanie Laurence Ernould, Andrew James, Justin Patrick. BA, Cen. Conn. State U., 1976; MS, Temple U., 1981. Diplomate Am. Bd. Indsl. Hygiene. Corp. indsl. hygienist Certainteed Corp., Valley Forge, Pa., 1981-86; sr. indsl. hygienist Smith Kline & French Labs., Phila., 1986-88; mgr., environ., occupational health and safety Smith Kline Beecham Pharms., Phila., 1988-91; dir. health, safety and environ svcs. Fisons Corp., Rochester, N.Y., 1991-96; mgr. occupl. health, safety & environ. svcs. Astra Arcus USA, Rochester, N.Y., 1996—. Lt. (j.g.) USN, 1977-80, comdr., USNR, 1991—. Recipient grant Nat. Inst. for Occupational Safety and Health, Temple U., Phila., 1980-81. Mem. Am. Indsl. Hygiene Assn. (sec. WNY chpt. 1991—), Am. Soc. Safety Engrs., Air and Waste Mgmt. Assn. Republican. Office: AStra Arcus USA PO Box 20890 Rochester NY 14602

NORRIS, SUSAN ELIZABETH, social worker; b. Lubbock, Tex., Oct. 8, 1952; d. William Oxford and Katherine Burton (Sydnor) N. BA, U. Tex., Arlington, 1974; MSW, U. Conn., 1987. Child protective svcs. social worker Tex. Dept. Human resources, Ft. Worth, 1978-82; temp. word processor various cos., 1983-85; rsch. cons. Hartford, Conn., 1986-89; dir. child care svcs. United Way Conn., Hartford, 1987-92, dir. program svcs., 1992-93; faculty/assoc. dir. child and family studies, pediatrics U. Conn. Health Ctr., Farmington, 1993-94; dir. Americorps CARE, Nat. Assn. of Childcare Resource & Referral Agy's., 1994-96; program mgr. Work/Family Directions, Boston, 1996—. Bd. dirs., sec. Hartford Interval House, 1989-93; pres. bd. dirs. Hartford Area Child Collaborative, 1992-94. Democrat. Office: Work/Family Directions 930 Commonwealth Ave Boston MA 02215-1212

NORRVING, BO GUNNAR WILLIAM, neurologist, educator; b. Falköping, Sweden, Feb. 23, 1951; s. Knut and Rut (Williamson) N.; m. Lena Arrestig, June 5, 1976; three children. MD, Lund U., 1975, PhD, 1981. Intern, resident dept. neurology U. Hosp., Lund, Sweden, 1975-77, neurologist dept. neurology, 1977-87, assoc. prof. dept. neurology, 1987—, chief clin. stroke unit dept. neurology, 1991—; sci. sec. Swedish Neurol. Assn., 1981-85. Editor: Lacunar and Other Subcortical Infarcts, 1995; editl. bd. Cerebrovascular Diseases, 1991—; contbr. chpts. to books and articles to profl. jours. Chmn. Stroke Assn., Malmöhus County, 1985-87. Mem. Nat. Stroke Assn. (hon.), European Stroke Coun. (founding mem. 1989—). Office: Dept Neurology, Univ Hosp, S-22185 Lund Sweden

NORSTRAND, IRIS FLETCHER, psychiatrist, neurologist, educator; b. Bklyn., Nov. 21, 1915; d. Matthew Emerson and Violet Marie (Anderson) Fletcher; m. Severin Anton Norstrand, May 20, 1941; children: Virginia Helene Norstrand Villano, Thomas Fletcher, Lucille Joyce. BA, Bklyn. Coll., 1937, MA, 1965, PhD, 1972; MD, L.I. Coll. Medicine, 1941. Diplomate Am. Bd. Psychiatry and Neurology with supplementary cert. in geriatric psychiatry. Med. intern Montefiore Hosp., Bronx, N.Y., 1941-42; asst. resident in neurology N.Y. Neurol. Inst.-Columbia-Presbyn. Med. Ctr., N.Y.C., 1944-45; pvt. practice Bklyn., 1947-52; resident in psychiatry Bklyn. VA Med. Ctr., 1952-54, resident in neurology, 1954-55, staff neurologist, 1955-81, asst. chief neurol. svc., 1981-91, staff psychiatrist, 1991-95; neurol. cons. Indsl. Home for Blind, Bklyn., 1948-51; clin. prof. neurology SUNY Health Sci. Ctr., Bklyn., 1981—; attending neurologist Kings County Hosp., Bklyn., State U. Hosp., Bklyn. Contbr. articles to med. jours. Recipient spl. plaque Mil. Order Purple Heart, 1986, Spl. Achievement award PhD Alumni Assn. of CUNY, 1993, Lifetime Achievement award Bklyn. Coll., 1995, and others. Fellow Am. Psychiat. Assn., Am. Acad. Neurology, Internat. Soc. Neurochemistry, Am. Assn. U. Profs. Neurology, Am. Med. EEG Soc. (pres. 1987-88), Nat. Assn. VA Physicians (pres. 1989-91, James O'Connor award 1987), N.Y. Acad. Scis., Sigma Xi. Democrat. Presbyterian. Home: 7624 10th Ave Brooklyn NY 11228

NORTH, CAROL SUE, psychiatrist, educator; b. Keokuk, Iowa, May 6, 1954; d. Ray Stemen and Doris Ethelyn (Wood) N. BS in Gen. Sci., U. Iowa, 1976; MD, Wash. U., St. Louis, 1983, M in Psychiatric Epidemiology, 1993. Resident in psychiatry Barnes Hosp., Washington U. Med. Sch., St. Louis, 1983-87; rsch. fellow dept psychiatry Washington U., St. Louis, 1987-90, instr. dept. psychiatry, 1987-89, asst. prof. dept. psychiatry, 1989—; staff psychiatrist Grace Hill Neighborhood Health Ctr., St. Louis, 1987—, Midwest Psychiatry, 1993-95, Adapt of Am., 1995—. Author: Welcome, Silence, 1987, Multiple Personalities, Multiple Disorders: Psychiatric Classification and Media Influence, 1993; contbr. articles to profl. jours. Bd. Dirs. St. Louis Met. Alliance for the Mentally Ill, 1992—; trustee Rosati Stblzn. Ctr. for Homeless and Mentally Ill, 1992-94. Nat. Inst. Alcoholism and Alcohol Abuse grantee, 1988-93, Nat. Hazards Rsch. Applications Info. Ctr. grantee, 1987-88, NIMH grantee, 1991-95. Mem. Am. Psychiat. Assn., Life History Rsch. Soc., Ea. Mo. Psychiat. Soc. (exec. coun. and pres. 1996—), Am. Psychopathol. Assn., Am. Acad. Clin. Psychiatrists, Nat. Alliance for Mentally Ill, Am. Assn. Cmty. Psychiatrists, St. Louis Track Club. Presbyterian. Office: Washington U Sch Medicine Dept Psychiatry 4940 Childrens Pl Saint Louis MO 63110-1002

NORTH, LARRY WILLIAM, nursing educator; b. Hastings, Nebr., Mar. 7, 1941; s. Benton Thomas and Rosemarie (Frisch) N.; m. Kathleen Ann Graham, Dec. 31, 1967; children: Nataska Leslie, Eric William. BA, Hastings Coll., 1964; MS, U. Colo., Boulder, 1966; PhD, U. Ariz., Tucson, 1975. Nurse Mary Lanning Meml. Hosp., Hastings, 1962-63, instr., 1963-65; instr. U. Ariz., Tucson, 1966-69; assoc. prof. Idaho State U., Pcatello, 1975-80, Ariz. State U., Tempe, 1980—. Mem. Nat. League Nursing (bd. of baccalaureate and higher degree programs 1984-87, nominating com. for baccalaureate and higher degree programs 1990-93), Idaho Nurses Assn. (v.p. 1989-90), Am. Nurses Assn. Democrat. Episcopalian. Lodge: Elks. Home: 1898 E Watson Dr Tempe AZ 85283-3260 Office: Ariz State U Coll Nursing Tempe AZ 85827

NORTH, LEON LEVI, retired psychiatrist; b. East Stroudsburg, Pa., Sept. 21, 1920; s. Leon Levi and Mabel (Meeker) N.; m. Margaret Grater Brunner, Mar. 16, 1946; children: David Lee, Barbara Jane, Carole Anne, James Lawrence. BS, Ursinus Coll., Collegeville, Pa., 1943; MD, U. Pa., 1946. Diplomate Am. Bd. Psychiatry and Neurology. Intern Phila. Gen. Hosp., 1946-47; resident U.S. Naval Hosp., Phila., 1947-48, VA Hosp., Coatesville, Pa., 1949-51, Norristown (Pa.) State Hosp., 1951-54; pvt. practice Bala-Cynwyd, Pa., 1954-88; asst. clin. prof. psychiatry Hahnemann Med. Coll., Phila., 1956-66; assoc. clin. prof. psychiatry Jefferson Med. Coll., Phila., 1979-83; instr. Inst. Phila. Assn. for Psychoanalysis, Bala-Cynwyd, 1968-83; child psychiatrist Ea. State Sch. and Hosp., Trevose, Pa., 1981-85; psychiat. cons. Sch. Dist. of Phila., 1985-89. Lt. USN, 1943-49. Fellow Am. Psychiat. Assn., Am. Acad. Child and Adolescent Psychiatry (mem. of coun. 1981-83); mem. Am. Psychoanalytic Assn., Assn. for Child Psychoanalysis, Phila. Assn. for Psychoanalysis. Democrat. Unitarian. Home and Office: 515 Great Springs Rd Bryn Mawr PA 19010-1717

NORTH, RICHARD RALPH, neurologist; b. Hamilton, Ont., Can., Aug. 8, 1934; came to U.S., 1960; s. Ralph Edward and Dorothea Bernice (Pilton) N.; m. Lois Joan Wessler, Aug. 27, 1955; children: Elizabeth Ann, Amy Jo, Julie Lynn, Kristin Lee. MD, Queen's U., Can., 1959. Diplomate Am. Bd. Psychiatry and Neurology, Am. Bd. Clin. Neurophysiology. Intern Hotel Dieu Hosp., Kingston, Ont., Can., 1959-60; neurology resident Baylor U., Houston, 1960-63, fellow in neurology, 1963-64, 1964-66, asst. prof., 1966-67; asst. prof. U. Tex., Dallas, 1967-69, assoc. prof., 1969-82, clin. prof., 1982—; pvt. practice Neurologic Clinic of Tex., Dallas, 1984—. Med. advisor Dallas Epilepsy Assn., Dallas area Parkinson's Soc., Tex. Neurofibromasis Found. Recipient Prof.'s Prize in Ophthalmology award Queen's U., 1959. Fellow EEG Soc.; mem. Am. Acad. Neurology, Am. Epilepsy Soc., So. EEG Soc. Home: 7106 Highland Heather Ln Dallas TX 75248-7502 Office: Neurologic Clinic of Tex 7777 Forest Ln Ste 410 Dallas TX 75230-2505

NORTHINGTON, JAMES WRIGHT, reconstructive plastic surgeon; b. Florence, Ala., Dec. 13, 1944; s. Allen Merrill and Audrey (Johnson) N.; m. Jeanne Cuquet, June 15, 1968; children: Anna Cathryn, Marian Elizabeth. BA, Tulane U., New Orleans, 1967; MD, Tulane U., 1971. Diplomate Am. Bd. Surgery, Am. Bd. Plastic Surgery. Surg. intern William Beaumont Army Med. ctr., El Paso, Tex., 1971-72, surg. resident, 1972-76, fellow plastic surgery, 1978-80; asst. clin. prof. surgery Emory U., Atlanta, 1977-78; chief plastic surgery Madigan Army Med. Ctr., Tacoma, Wash., 1980-82; chmn. bd. Hamana Hosp., Florence, Ala., 1990-93; moderator bd. dirs. Florence Hosp., 1993—; regional adv. bd. Mut. Assurance, Birmingham, Ala., 1990—; cons. Workman's Compensation Bd., Montgomery, 1996; inspector Am. Assn. Accreditation of Surg. Facilities, Mundelien, Ill., 1982—. Contbr. articles to profl. jours. Lt. comdr. U.S. Army, 1970-82. Fellow ACS, Internat. Coll. Surgeons; mem. Ala. Soc. Plastic Surgeons (sec.-treas. 1994, pres. 1996), U. North Ala. Presidents Cabinet, Assn. State Socs., Rotary. Episcopalian. Home: Rt 7 Box 354 A Florence AL 35630 Office: Northington Clinic PC 1945 Florence Blvd Florence AL 35630

NORTON, JOHN HARRY, psychophysiologist, consultant; b. Berlin, July 2, 1929; came to U.S., 1948; s. Jacues and Ruth Frances (Schutz) N.; m. Eva Gloria Miller, Dec. 29, 1956; children: Gregory, Mike, Loraine. BSEE, U. Zurich, Switzerland, 1948; MBA, Sussex (Eng.) Coll. Tech., 1969, PhD in Behavioral Orgn., 1971. Diplomate Am. Bd. Med. Psychotherapists (fellow); cert. in applied psychophysiology Biofeedback Cert. Inst. Am. V.p. for ea. U.S. and Can., Sci. Mgmt. Corp., Morristown, N.J., 1969-71; pres. Norton Systems, Boston and Spring, Tex., 1971-87; pvt. practice Behavior Mgmt. Assocs., Springs, 1987—; mgmt. cons. Textron, Timex, Rockwell Internat., also others, 1969-71; adj. prof. St. Edward's U., Austin, Tex., 1977-79, U. Houston, 1985. Author: Performance Evaluation, 1981, Business Planning, 1986, Stress Control, 1988. Capt. U.S. Army, 1950-53, Korea. Mem. AACD, Assn. for Applied Psychophysiology and Biofeedback, Tex. Biofeedback Soc., Biofeedback Soc. Harris County, N.Y. Acad. Scis. Office: Behavior Mgmt Assocs PO Box 11010 Spring TX 77391-1010

NORTON, JOSEPH LOUIS, retired psychology educator; b. Albany, N.Y., Sept. 6, 1918; s. Arden L. and Jessie (Van Schaick) N.; m. Ruth P. McCarthy, Apr. 5, 1947 (div. 1971); 1 child, Deborah Judith. BA, St. Lawrence U., Canton, N.Y., 1940; MA, St. Lawrence U., 1941; PhD, Syracuse U., 1950. Lic. psychologist, N.Y. Counselor Mich. State U., E. Lansing, 1949-51; prof., counselor Knox Coll., Galesburg, Ill., 1951-53; assoc. prof. edn. Alfred (N.Y.) U., 1953-63; prof. ednl. psychology SUNY, Albany, 1963-83; part-time therapist Albany, 1963—. Contbr. articles to profl. jours.; editor: On the Job. Fellow APA. Democrat. Unitarian Universalist. Home and Office: 418 Elk St Albany NY 12206-2703

NORTON, LOUIS ARTHUR, dental educator; b. Gloucester, Mass., Jan. 12, 1937; s. Morris Harry and Mamie (Pett) N.; m. Elinor Sue Glaser, July 7, 1963; children: Mark Douglas, Lauren Elyse. AB, Bowdoin Coll., 1958; DMD, Harvard U., 1962, Cert. orthodontist, 1964. Prof. U. Ky., Lexington, 1966-74; prof. dental medicine U. Conn. Health Ctr., Farmington, 1974—; vis. prof. Hadassah Sch. Dental Medicine, Hebrew U., Jerusalem, 1972-73, Royal Dental Coll., U. Aarhus, Denmark, 1988-89; vis scientist Strangeways Rsch. Lab., Cambridge U., Eng., 1980-81; cons. NIMH, 1970-74, Nat. Inst. Dental Rsch., 1974—. Co-author: Education for Orthodontics, 1967; author: Biology of Tooth Movement Sailors Folk Art Underglass Biology of Tooth Movement and Cranfacial Anaptation, 1989. Capt. U.S. Army, 1964-66. Fulbright rsch. fellow Internat. Exchange of Scholars, 1972-73; Fogarty fellow NIH, 1980-81; NATO Sr Guest fellow, 1988-89. Fellow AAAS, Am. Coll. Dent.; mem. Biologic Repair and Growth Soc. (pres. 1987-88, Kappa Delta Rsch. award 1989), Conn. State Orthodontic Soc. (pres. 1987-89), Northeastern Soc. of Orthodontists (dir. 1987). Office: Univ Conn Health Ctr 263 Farmington Ave Farmington CT 06030-0001

NORTON, MARY EILEEN, international nursing educator, consultant; b. Kearny, N.J., Jan. 30, 1939; d. Peter J. and Mary (Fitzsimmons) N. Diploma, St. Mary Hosp. Sch. Nursing, 1962; BA, Jersey City State Coll., 1965; MA, Columbia U., 1970, EdM, 1973, EdD, 1985. Asst. prof. Felician Coll., Lodi, N.J., 1971-77, assoc. prof. BSN program, 1981-88, assoc. prof. MSN program, 1995—; assoc. rsch. prof. George Mason U., Fairfax, Va., 1989, 93-94; lectr. Calif. State U., Dominguez Hills, 1990—; cons. Cathedral Health Care System, Inc., Newark, Pakistan, 1992-93; assoc. prof., program dir. B.SC.N. Aga Khan U. of Health Scis., Karachi, Pakistan; postdoctoral fellow in biomed. ethics Coll. Phys. & Surgeons Columbia U., N.Y.C., 1996—; cons. WHO/PAHO, Caracas, Venezuela, 1974, Cath. Health Care System, Newark, 1991-92, 95; asst. prof. Cath. U. Am., at Imperial Med. Ctr., Teheran, Iran, 1977-79, Cornell Med. Sch., N.Y., 1980, internat. rescue com. Thailand Refugee Camps, Aga Khan U. of Health Scis., Karachi, Pakistan, 1981-83, Beijing (People's Republic China), 1988, 89; field rschr. NIMH, 1979; clin. specialist psych./mental health Cath. Community Svcs., 1986, 89, 90, 94; advisor Model United Nations Program, 1983-89; acad. specialist U. Jordan, 1988, 89; clin. specialist- clin. cons., 1975-77, 85-92; adminstr. Cath. Community Svcs., 1973-74, 82-83, 90-91; presenter in field. Producer history tape Cambodian Refugee Camps, 1981; contbg. author: Culture and Health Care. Mem. N.J. Symphony Orch. Grantee NIMH, 1972-73, U.S. Agy. for Internat. Devel., 1987, 89, U.S. Info. Svc., Jordan, 1988-89; sr. Fulbright researcher, lectr., Jordan, 1986-87, Woodrow Wilson Found. fellow, 1986. Mem. AAUW, ANA, Nat. League Nursing, Global Studies Consortium of N.J., Columbia U. Alumni Assn., Fulbright Assn. N.J., Transcultural Nursing Soc., Assn. for Practical and Profl. Ethics, Friends of Erin, Aga Khan U. Health Scis. Alumni, Sigma Theta Tau.

NORTON, ROBYN LYNN, nurse; b. Phoenix, May 19, 1963; d. Kenneth Arthur and Marjorie (Egan) N. ADN, Glendale Community Coll., 1990. RN, Ariz. Group facilitator St. Luke's Behavioral Health Ctr., Phoenix, 1987, milieu technician, 1987, counselor, 1987-90, charge nurse, 1990-92; charge nurse CPC Belmont Hills Hosp., Belmont, Calif., 1992—; staff nurse Oak Creek Hosp., San Jose, Calif., 1993—, San Jose Med. Ctr., 1993—. Recipient award Sun City Rotary, 1989; Betty Gerhardt scholar, 1988. Mem. Glendale Assn. of Student Nurses. Democrat.

NORWOOD, GEORGE JOSEPH, pharmacy educator; b. Clover, Va., Oct. 7, 1938; s. George Washington and Sara (Bailey) N.; m. Elaine Preece, Aug. 20, 1960; children: Joseph Derrick, Kevin Todd. Student, Randolph Macon Coll., 1957-58; B.S., Med. Coll. Va., 1962; Ph.D., U. Miss., 1970. Registered pharmacist. Va., N.D. Asst. prof. pharmacy adminstrn. U. Iowa, Iowa City, 1969-72, assoc. prof., 1972-74, assoc. prof. pharm. socioecons., 1974-77, prof., 1977-78, head dept. pharm. socioecons., 1974-78, dir. health services Research Ctr., 1978-81; dean Coll. Pharmacy N.D. State U., Fargo, 1981-86; dean Southeastern U. Coll. Pharm., North Miami Beach, Fla., 1986-90; prof., chmn. pharm. adminstrn. Sch. Pharmacy, U. N.C., Chapel Hill, 1990—; cons. in field. Author: Capitation for Pharmacy Services, 1982; contbr. articles to profl. jours. Mem. health manpower com. Iowa Office for Programming and Planning, Des Moines, 1975-76, mem. health personnel info. services bd., 1975-76. HEW grantee, 1976; Nat. Ctr. for Health Services Research grantee, 1978, 79, 80. Fellow Acad. Pharm. Scis. (chmn. econ. and adminstrv. scis. 1976-77); mem. Am. Pharm. Assn. (del. 1976-81), Am. Assn. Pharm. Scis. (chmn. econ. mktg. & mgmt. scis. sect. 1991-92), Am. Assn. Colls. Pharmacy (del. 1974-76), Sigma XI, Rho Chi, Kappa Psi. Home: 321 Azalea Dr Chapel Hill NC 27514-9120 Office: U NC Sch Pharmacy Beard Hall A 7360 Chapel Hill NC 27599

NORWOOD, PAUL CARLTON, endocrinologist; b. San Francisco, July 12, 1952; s. Paul C. and Deirdre N. Norwood; m. Monica C. Norwood, May 8, 1982; children: Tara, Lauren. BA, U. Calif., Santa Barbara, 1979; MD, U. Guadalahara/Loma Linda U., 1980. Intern, resident U. Calif., Long Beach (Calif.) VA Hosp., Irvine, 1981-84; fellow in endocrinology U. Calif., Davis, 1984-86; pvt. practice Sacramento, Calif., 1986—; med. dir. Hilltop Rsch., Fresno, Calif., 1996—; assoc. clin. prof. medicine U. Calif., Santa Barbara, 1991—. Author: The Vector, 1996. Pres. Am. Diabetes Assn., Fresno, 1993, bd. dirs., 1986-93. Fellow ACP; mem. Fresno-Madera Med. Soc., Calif. Med. Assn. Office: Peachwood Med Group 275 W Herndon Ave Clovis CA 93720

NORWOOD, PAULA KAY, medical and surgical nurse; b. LaCrosse, Wis., Nov. 22, 1949; d. Edward Coleman and Beverly Jane (Toske) Wheeler; m. Robert Norwood, Apr. 3, 1975; children: Rob, Jimmy. Diploma, Good Samaritan Hosp., 1970. RN, Oreg., Wash. Staff nurse orthopedics, plastic surgery Good Samaritan Hosp., Portland, Oreg.; oper. rm. nurse Mary Bridge Children's Hosp., Tacoma, Wash., Plastic Surgeons NW, Tacoma, Tacoma Ambulatory Surgery Ctr. Home: 207 Tulalip Dr NE Tacoma WA 98422-1644

NORWOOD, PAULA KING, medical biostatistics professional; b. Coco Solo, Panama, Aug. 28, 1946; came to U.S., 1946; d. Paul Alfred and Laura Merle (Smith) King; m. Thomas Edward Norwood, Mar. 13, 1972 (div. Aug. 1990); 1 child, David Thomas. BA in Math., Hendrix Coll., 1968; MS in Biometrics, U. Ark., 1970; PhD in Stats., Va. Polytechnic Inst./State U., 1974. Instr. Va. Polytechnic Inst./State U., 1973-74; sr. biometrician Norwich (N.Y.) Pharm. Corp., 1974-77; sr. biometrician Ortho Pharm. Corp., Raritan, N.J., 1977-78, mgr., med. biostats., 1978-81, dir., med. biostats. and data ops., 1981-88, exec. dir., med. biostats. and data ops., 1988-90; v.p., med. biostats. and data ops. worldwide RWJ Pharm. Rsch. Inst., Raritan, 1990-92, v.p. biostatistics and rsch. data svcs., 1992-96, v.p. global stats. and clin. data processing, 1996—. Fellow Am. Statis. Assn.; mem. Biometric Soc., Internat. Biometric Soc. (coun. mem.), Drug Info. Assn., Caucus for Women in Stats., Am. Statis. Assn., Sigma Xi. Home: 106 Moore St Princeton NJ 08540-9999 Office: RWJ Pharm Rsch Inst PO Box 300 Raritan NJ 08869-0602

NOSKO, MICHAEL GERRIK, neurosurgeon; b. Montreal, Que., Can., Feb. 24, 1957; came to U.S., 1991; s. Joseph John and June Elizabeth (Salter) N.; m. Deborah Anne Branciere, May 23, 1981; children: Douglas Joseph, Denise Elizabeth, Keith Michael. BS, McMaster U., 1978; MD, U. Toronto, 1982; PhD, U. Alberta, 1986. Intern U. Toronto (Ont., Can.) Gen. Hosp., 1982-83; resident U. Alberta Hosps., Edmonton, Can., 1986-91; asst. prof. neurosurgery Robert Wood Johnson Med. Sch., New Brunswick, N.J., 1991—; cons. and presenter in field. Contbr. articles to profl. jours., chpts. to books. Rsch. fellow Alberta Heritage Found., 1983-86; Chancellor' scholar McMaster U., 1975, Univ. scholar, 1976, Edwin Marwin Dalley Meml. scholar, 1977; recipient Acad. award Am. Acad. Neurological Surgery, 1986. Fellow Am. Coll. Surgeons (Resident Rsch. award 1986), Royal Coll. Surgeons Can., Acad. Medicine N.J.; mem. AMA, Am. Assn. Neurol. Surgeons, Can. Neurosurg. Soc., N.J. Neurosurg. Soc., N.Y. Acad. Scis., Middlesex County Med. Soc., Soc. Critical Care Medicine, Congress Neurol. Surgeons, Alpha Omega Alpha. Anglican. Office: Divsn Neurosurgery 125 Paterson St Ste 2100 New Brunswick NJ 08901-1977

NOTH, ROBERT HENRY, physician, educator, endocrinologist; b. Detroit, May 10, 1940; s. Paul Henry and Dorothy-Ann (Erehart) N.; m. Mary-Jo Cone, June 8, 1968; children: Robert Joseph, Elizabeth Marianne. BS, Stanford U., 1963; MD, Yale U., 1967. Intern Temple U. Hosp., Phila., 1967-68; resident in medicine Yale U.-New Haven Hosp., 1970-72; fellow in endocrinology Yale U., New Haven, 1972-74, asst. prof. medicine, 1974-80; chief endocrinology VA Med. Ctr., West Haven, Conn., 1977-80; assoc. prof. medicine U. Calif., Davis, 1980—; chief endocrinology unit VA Med. Ctr., Martinez, Calif., 1980—. Contbr. articles to profl. jours. Served with USPHS, 1968-70. Fellow ACP; mem. AAAS, Am. Fedn. Cin. Rsch., Endocrine Soc., Sigma Xi. Office: VA Outpatient Clinic 150 Muir Rd Martinez CA 94553-4612

NOTTINGHAM, EDGAR JAMESON, IV, clinical psychologist; b. Richmond, Va., Nov. 11, 1951; s. Edgar Jameson, III and Anna Sue (Springfield) N.; B.A., Randolph-Macon Coll., 1974; M.S. in Clin. Psychology, Va. Poly. Inst. and State U., 1976, Ph.D., 1979. Diplomate Am. Bd. Profl. Psychology. Approved supr. rational-emotive therapy. Staff psychologist, coordinator treatment, acting dir. forensic unit Southwestern State Hosp., Marion, Va., 1977-78; intern clin. psychology U. Tenn. Center Health Scis., Memphis, 1978-79; clin. psychologist, dir. and coordinator tng. in psychology Memphis Mental Health Inst., 1979-81; cons. psychologist Lakeside Hosp., 1981-86; partner East Memphis Psychol. Assocs., 1979—, Germantown Psychol. Assocs., 1984—; clin. exec. dir. Germantown Psychol. Assocs., 1986-93, dir. psychol. services Parkwood Hosp., 1987—; clin. asst. prof. U. Tenn. Ctr. Health Scis., 1981—; mem. adj. faculty Memphis State U., 1980—. Fellow Acad. Clin. Psychology; mem. APA, Inst. Advanced Study in Rational Psychotherapy (profl. mem.), Southeastern Psychol. Assn., Tenn. Psychol. Assn., Memphis Area Psychol. Assn., Assn. Advancement in Behavior Therapy, Am. Assn. Marriage and Family Therapy (clin. mem.), Am. Group Psychotherapy Assn. (clin. mem.), Phi Kappa Phi, Psi Chi, Omicron Delta Kappa, Pi Gamma Mu, Sigma Phi Epsilon. Co-author manual; contbr. articles profl. jours. Office: 7516 Enterprise Ave Ste 1 Germantown TN 38138

NOVAES, ARTHUR BELEM, JR., dental surgeon, educator, researcher; b. Pontal, Sao Paulo, Brazil, Apr. 6, 1955; s. Arthur Belem Novaes and Maria Aparecida S. Novaes; m. Maria Beatriz Moreira Bezerra, Sept. 6, 1977 (div. 1985); 1 child, Bianka B.; m. Cristiana Fernandes da Silva Evangelista, Apr. 12, 1990; 1 child, Laura Fernandes da S. Nomes. DDS, Cath. U. Campinas, Brazil, 1976; CAGS i Periodontology, Boston U., 1979, MSc, 1980; DSc, Fed. U. Rio de Janeiro, 1991. Asst. prof. Sch. Dentistry Fed. U. Rio de Janeiro, 1983-91, assoc. prof., 1991—, chmn. grad. periodontology, 1989—, dir. grad. studies, 1994—; cons. Nat. Found. Rsch., Brazil, 1995—; rschr. Nat. Coun. Rsch., 1995—. Editl. bd. Sao Paulo U. Dental Jour., 1990—, Annals Fed. U. Rio de Janeiro, 1989—. Mem. Am. Acad. Periodontology, Acad. Osseointegration (internat. rels. com. 1996—), Brazilian Soc. Periodontology (v.p. 1983-85, Jose Cassio M. Carvalho medal 1995). Home: Jorn Henrique Cordeiro 120 1806, 22631-040 Rio de Janeiro Brazil Office: Av Das Americas 1155 of 1002, 22631-000 Rio de Janeiro Brazil

NOVAK, ALAN LEE, retired pharmaceutical company executive; b. Chgo., Oct. 25, 1928; s. Samuel Adolph and Tina Lillian (Oris) N.; m. Delores Jane Tonkel, Dec. 17, 1950; children: Shaya Ray, G. Alexander, Cheryl Lynn. BS, Fla. So. Coll., 1951. Cert. purchasing mgr. Police officer Lakeland (Fla.) Police Dept., 1952-53; sales rep. Sinclair Refining Co., Tampa, Fla., 1954-58; prin. Novak's Texaco s/s and Fuel Co., Tampa, 1958-62; sales rep. Burroughs Wellcome Co., Columbus, Ohio, 1962-70; purchasing agt. Burroughs Wellcome Co., Research Triangle Park, N.C., 1970-74, dir. purchasing, 1974-94; bd. dirs. Eastern N.C. Better Bus. Bur., 1989-96. Mem. area contact Am. Israel Polit. Affairs Com., Raleigh, 1984-86; fin. sec. Temple Beth Or, Raleigh, 1975-77, treas., 1996—; mem. N.C. Coun. on the Holocaust, 1991-94. With U.S. Army, 1946-47, Japan. Mem. Am. Legion Jewish War Vets. 1st Cav. Divsn. Assn., Drug, Chem., and Allied Trades Assn. (area rep. 1975-78, bd. dirs. 1978-84, treas. 1985, v.p. 1986, pres. 1987-88), Nat. Assn. Purchasing Mgmt., Purchasing Mgmt. Assn. Carolinas-Va., Triangle Purchasing Assn., Raleigh C. of C. Republican. Jewish. Lodge: B'nai B'rith (Double Chai award 1985-87), AMRAN Shrine Temple (charter).

NOVAK, DENNIS E., family practice physician; b. East Liverpool, Ohio, Jan. 5, 1946. BA, Bklyn. Coll., 1966; Lic. in Med. Scis., U. Brussels, 1972; MD, Rutgers U., 1974. Diplomate Am. Bd. Family Practice, Nat. Bd. Med. Examiners. Resident in family practice Monmouth Med. Ctr., Long Branch, N.J., 1974-77; clin. instr. to clin. assoc. prof. Robert Wood Johnson Med. Sch., 1977—, chmn. dept. family practice; pvt. practice specializing in family medicine, 1977—; attending physician utilization rev. com. Comty. Meml. Hosp., 1987-88, quality assurance com., 1988, dept. family practice quality assurance com.; physician reviewer, quality assurance Garden State Rehab. Hosp. Mem. exec. bd. Ocean County coun. Boy Scouts Am.; bd. trustees United Way Ocean County., Area VII Physician Rev. Org., 1983-86. Fellow Am. Acad. Family Practice; mem. Ocean County Acad. Family Practice (v.p. 1983), Ocean County Med. Soc. (bd. trustees 1983-87). Address: PO Box 780 1001 Lacey Rd Forked River NJ 08731

NOVAK, GERALD PAUL, neurologist, educator; b. Cleve., Mar. 25, 1951; s. Paul B. and Ann D. (Sedlecki) N.; m. Laurie M. Tesser, July 23, 1978; children: Alicia, Adam, Craig. AB, John Carroll U., 1973; MD, Albert Einstein Coll. Medicine, 1977. Diplomate Am. Bd. Pediats., Am. Bd. Neurology and Psychiatry, Am. Bd. Clin. Neurophysiology. Pediat. resident Childrens Hosp. Phila., 1977-80; child neurology fellow Albert Einstein Coll. Medicine, Bronx, N.Y., 1980-83; clin. neurophysiology fellow Albert Einstein Coll. Medicine, Bronx, 1983-85, asst. prof. neurology, 1983-88; asst. prof. neurology L.I. Jewish Med. Ctr. Albert Einstein Coll. Medicine, New Hyde Park, N.Y., 1988—. Mem. Am. Acad. Neurology, Am. EEG Soc., Am. Epilepsy Soc., Child Neurology Soc. Office: Schneider Childrens Hosp Rm 267 Divsn Neurology New Hyde Park NY 11042

NOVAK, JAMES F., physician; b. Portland, May 5, 1944; s. John Martin and Mary Ruth Novak; m. Marilynn L. Grosso, July 10, 1971; children: Vincent, Mark. BS, U. San Francisco, 1966; MD, Oreg. Health Science U., Portland, 1970. Diplomate ABFP; cert. Md. Physician emergency room Merle West Med. Ctr., Klamath Falls, Oreg., 1991-92; physician and ptnr. Klamath (Oreg.) Med. Clinic, 1992—; clin. instr. Cascade East Family Practice Residency, Klamath Falls, 1994—; chief of staff Merle West Meml. Ctr., Klamath Falls, 1978-79; pres. elect, past bd. mem. Oreg. Acad. Family Practice, 1975—; past pres., mem. bd. dirs. Klamath Youth Devel. Ctr., Klamath Falls, 1980—. Pres. Klamath County Rotary Club, 1995-96. Fellow Am. Acad. Family Practice; mem. AMA, Oreg. Med. Assn., Klamath County Med. Soc. (pres.). Roman Catholic. Office: Klamath Med Clinic 1905 Main St Klamath Falls OR 97601

NOVICK, ANDREW CARL, urologist; b. Montreal, Apr. 5, 1948; came to U.S., 1974; s. David and Rose (Ortenberg) N.; m. Thelma Silver, June 29, 1969 (div. Dec. 1983); 1 child, Lorne J.; m. Linda Friedman, May 24, 1992; children: Rachel H., Eric D. BSc, McGill U., Montreal, 1968, MD, CM, 1972. Diplomate Am. Bd. Urology. Resident in surgery Royal Victoria Hosp., Montreal, 1972-74; resident in urology Cleve. Clinic Found., 1974-77, staff dept. urology, 1977—, head sect. renal transplant, 1977—, chmn. dept. urology, 1985—, chmn. Organ Transplant Ctr., 1985—; trustee Am. Bd. Urology, 1995—. Editor: Vascular Problems in Urology, 1982, Stewart's Operative Urology, 1989, Renal Vascular Disease, 1995; contbr. over 400 articles to profl. jours. Fellow ACS, Med. Coun. Can.; mem. Am. Urol. Assn., Am. Assn. Genito-Urinary Surgeons, Clin. Soc. Genito-Urinary Surgeons. Home: 22325 Canterbury Ln Cleveland OH 44122-3901 Office: Cleve Clinic Found 9500 Euclid Ave Cleveland OH 44195-0001

NOVICK, NELSON LEE, dermatologist, internist, writer; b. Bklyn., June 27, 1949; s. Benjamin and Vivian (Meltzer) N.; m. Meryl Sohnis, June 20, 1971; children: Yonatan, Yoel, Ariel, Daniel, Avraham. BA in Biology magna cum laude, Bklyn. Coll., 1971; MD, Mt. Sinai Sch. Medicine, 1975. Diplomate Am. Bd. Internal Medicine, Am. Bd. Dermatology, Am. Bd. Med. Examiners. Resident in internal medicine Mt. Sinai Med. Ctr., N.Y.C., 1975-78, assoc. attending, 1980—, postgrad. preceptee, 1980-83, outpatient dept. clinic chief, dermatology svc., 1983; resident Skin and Cancer Unit NYU Med. Ctr., N.Y.C., 1978-80; assoc. clin. prof. Mt. Sinai Sch. Medicine, N.Y.C., 1980—; cons. Westwood-Squibb Skin Care Info. Ctr., Vaseline Intensive Care Rsch., Bausch & Lomb, Schering-Plough, Sandoz Internat., Procter & Gamble, Lever-2000, Inst. for Med. Info. Author: Saving Face, Skin Care for Teens, Super Skin, Baby Skin, You Can Do Something About Your Allergies, You Can Look Younger at Any Age, Diseases of the Mucus Membranes, (novel) In the Path of the Wolf; co-author: The External Ear; reviewer Annals Internal Medicine, Jour. Am. Acad. Dermatology, Jour. Dermatol. Surgery and Oncology, Internat. Jour. Dermatology; editl. advisor Exec. Health's Good Health Report, Snyder Comm., Your Baby Wallboard Program; former med. editor Current Podiatric Medicine, Jour. Am. Analgesia Soc.; contbr. articles to profl. publs. Regent's Coll. scholar, 1971, Max and Leah Strauss Fund scholar, 1971, Grand St. Found. scholar, 1971. Fellow ACP (direct election), Am. Acad. Dermatology, Am. Soc. Dermatol. Surgery, Am. Acad. Cosmetic Surgery, Skin Cancer Found. (hon.); mem. AMA, AAAS, Soc. Investigative Dermatology, Skin Phototrauma Found., Internat. Soc. for Androgenic Disorders, Skin Cancer Found. (charter), N.Y. Acad. Scis., N.Y. County Med. Soc., Am. Soc. Dermatologic Surgery, Am. Analgesia Soc. (past bd. dirs.), Nature Conservancy, Audubon Soc., Nat. Geog. Found., N.Y. Zool. Soc., Am. Mus. Natural History, Smithsonian Instn., Nat. Wildlife Fedn., The Wilderness Soc., Author's Guild, Author's League Am., Phi Beta Kappa. Jewish. Office: 328 E 75th St New York NY 10021-3305

NOVITSKI, CHARLES EDWARD, biology educator; b. Rochester, N.Y., Oct. 3, 1946; s. Edward and Esther Ellen (Rudkin) N.; m. Margaret Thornton Sime, June 15, 1968; children: Nancy Ellen, Linda Nicole, Elise Michelle. BA in Biology, Columbia Coll., 1969; PhD in Biophysics, Calif. Inst. Tech., 1979. Rsch. fellow and assoc. City of Hope Nat. Med. Ctr., Duarte, Calif., 1977-80; sr. tutor in biochemistry Monash U., Victoria, Australia, 1980-82, lectr. in biochemistry, 1982-84; program leader and rsch. scientist in nematode control Agrigenetics Advanced Sci. Co., Madison, Wis., 1985-88; assoc. prof. molecular biology Cen. Mich. U., Mt. Pleasant, 1989—. Assoc. editor Jour. Nematology, 1994—; contbr. articles to various profl. jours. Mem. Soc. of Nematologists, Internat. Soc. of Plant Molecular Biology. Home: 1208 E Preston Rd Mount Pleasant MI 48858-3927 Office: Cen Mich U Dept Biology Mount Pleasant MI 48859

NOWAK, JUDITH ANN, psychiatrist; b. Albany, N.Y., Feb. 18, 1948; d. Jacob Frank and Anne Patricia (Romanowski) N. BA, Cornell U., Ithaca, N.Y., 1970, MD, 1974. Bd. cert. Psychiatry. Resident Univ. Va. Hosp., Charlottesville, 1974-77; fellow in psychiatry Cornell U. Med. Coll. Westchester Div., White Plains, N.Y., 1977-78, clin. affiliate, 1k978-79; staff psychiatrist Chestnut Lodge Hosp., Rockville, Md., 1979-81; med. officer psychiatry St. Elizabeth's Hosp., Washington, 1981; pvt. practice Washington, 1981—; clin. asst. prof. of psychiatry, George Washington U., Washington, 1981-89; clin. assoc. prof. psychiatry, George Washington U. 1989-94, clin. prof. psychiatry, 1994—. Mem. Am. Psychiat. Soc. (pub. affairs rep. 1995), Am. Psychoanalytic Soc., Washington Psychiat. Soc. (sec. 1989-90, pres. 1991-92),. Office: 908 New Hampshire Ave NW Washington DC 20037-2346

NOWELL, PETER CAREY, pathologist, educator; b. Phila., Feb. 8, 1928; s. Foster and Margaret (Matlack) N.; m. Helen Worst, Sept. 9, 1950; children: Sharon, Timothy, Karen, Kristin, Michael. B.A., Wesleyan U., Middletown, Conn., 1948; M.D., U. Pa., 1952. Intern Phila. Gen. Hosp., 1952-53; resident pathology Presbyn. Hosp., Phila., 1953-54; med.-teaching, research specializing in cancer Phila., 1956—; from instr. to prof. pathology Sch. Medicine U. Pa., 1956—, chmn. dept. pathology, 1967-73; dir. (Cancer Center), 1973-75. Served to lt., M.C. USNR, 1954-56. Recipient Research Career award USPHS, 1964-67, Parke-Davis award, 1965, Lindback Disting. Teaching award, 1967, Passano award, 1984, Rous-Whipple award Am. Assn. Pathology, 1986, de Villers award Leukemia Soc. Am., 1987, Mott prize GM Cancer Rsch. Found., 1989, 3M award, FASEB, 1993. Home: 345 Mt Alverno Rd Media PA 19063-5313 Office: U Pa Sch Medicine Dept Pathology & Lab Medicine Philadelphia PA 19104-6082

NOYES, RUSSELL, JR., psychiatrist; b. Indpls., Dec. 25, 1934; s. Russell and Margaret (Greenleaf) N.; m. Martha H. Carl, Nov. 13, 1960; children: Marjorie Noyes-Aamot, Nancy Heifner, James R. BS, DePauw U., 1956; MD, Ind. U., 1959. Diplomate Am. Bd. Psychiatry and Neurology. Intern Phila. Gen. Hosp., 1959-60; residency U. Iowa, Iowa City, 1961-63; asst. prof. psychiatry U. Iowa, 1966-71, assoc. prof., 1971-78, prof., 1978—. Editor: Handbook of Anxiety, 1988-91; contbr. articles to profl. jours. With USN, 1963-65. Fellow Am. Psychiat. Assn., Acad. Psychosomatic Medicine (pres. 1990-91); mem. Iowa Psychiat. Soc. (pres. 1986-87). Republican. Lutheran. Home: 326 Macbride Dr Iowa City IA 52246-1716 Office: Psychiatry Rsch Med Edn Bldg Iowa City IA 52242-1009

NOZAKI, ERIKO SATO, nurse; b. Yokohama, Japan, Nov. 1, 1956; came to U.S., 1959; d. Isamu and Yoko Jane (Watanabe) Sato; m. Ken Andrew Nozaki, Mar. 27, 1983; children: Matthew, Akira, Jeffrey Minoru. Assoc. Sci. in Nursing, Pacific Union Coll., 1978; BS in Pub. Health, Loma Linda U., 1980, BS in Nursing, 1982. RN, Calif. Health educator Loma Linda (Calif.) Community Hosp., 1979; ICU nurse Loma Linda U., 1979-83, Glendale (Calif.) Adventist Med. Ctr., 1983; ICU nurse Mercy Gen. Hosp., Sacramento, 1984—, admiting discharge planning, 1988—, case mgmt., 1995. Mem. Am. Assn. Critical Care Nurses.

NRIAGU, JEROME OKON, environmental geochemist; b. Ora-eri Town, Anambra, Nigeria, Oct. 24, 1942; came to U.S., 1993; s. Martin and Helena (Anaekwe) N.; children: Chinedu Delbert, Uzoma Vivian, Osita Jide. BSc with honors, U. Ibadan, Nigeria, 1965, DSc, 1987; MS, U. Wis., 1967; PhD, U. Toronto, Ont., 1970. Rsch. scientist Environment Can., Burlington, Ont., 1970-93; prof. environ. chem. sch. of pub. health U. Mich., Ann Arbor, 1993—; dir. environ. health scis. program, 1996-99; adj. prof. U. Waterloo, Ont., 1985—; vis. scientist NOAA, Ann Arbor, 1992. Author: Lead and Lead Poisoning in Antiquity, 1983; editor book series: Advances in Environmental Science and Technology, 1982—; editor 24 books on various environ. topics, 1979—; editor Sci. of the Total Environment, 1983—; contbr. articles to profl. jours.; editl. bd. 9 jours. Recipient Rigler medal Can. Soc. Limnologists, 1988. Fellow Royal Soc. Can.; mem. Geochem. Soc. Roman Catholic. Office: Univ of Michigan Environ/Indsl Health 109 Observatory St Ann Arbor MI 48109-2029

NSOULI, TALAL MOUNIR, physician, allergist, immunologist; b. Mexico City, Feb. 21, 1952; s. Mounir Saleh and Suad (Murebey) N.; m. Susan Lynn Dandy, Sept. 19, 1982; children: Mounir, Suad. Brevet diploma, Lycee Francais, Brussels, 1968; BS, Lycee Francais, 1973; MD, U. Brussels, 1981; MD in Allergy and Immunology, Georgetown U., 1985. Research fellow Georgetown Sch. Medicine, Washington, 1983—; clin. fellow Georgetown Hosp., Washington, 1983-85; attending physician Georgetown U. Hosp., Washington, 1985—, clin. assoc. prof., 1986—; med. dir. Watergate Asthma and Allergy Ctr., Washington, 1985—; rschr. ICISI Georgetown U. Hosp., 1984—; assoc. prof. Internat. Ctr. Interdisciplinary Studies of Immunology, Washington, 1986—. Contbr. articles to profl. jours. Active mem. Am. Med. Polit. Action, Washington, 1983—. Fellow Am. Coll. Allergy and Immunology; mem. Am. Coll. Allergists, AMA (Physician award 1986), Am. Thoracic Soc., N.Y. Acad. Sci., AAAS, Med. Soc. D.C. (bd. communicable diseases 1986—), Smithsonian Club, Desiree Club (Washington). Home: 8924 Holly Leaf Ln at Avenel Bethesda MD 20817 Office: Watergate Astham & Allergy Ctr/Ste 216 2600 Virginia Ave NW Washington DC 20037-1905

NUCKLOS, SHIRLEY, medical administrator, consultant; b. Canton, Ohio, Aug. 30, 1949; D. Boyd Alexander and Julia Lillian (Hood) Curtis; m. William W. Nucklos, Mar. 11, 1972; children: Túere Tené, Tiombé Nigina, Khari Oji-Lee. BS in Edn., Cen. State U., Wilberforce, Ohio, 1970; MA, Ohio State U., 1971. Cert. elem. tchr., guidance counselor. Guidance counselor Scioto Village High Sch., Powell, Ohio, 1973-78; acad. advisor Franklin U., Columbus, Ohio, 1980-82, acting asst. dir. records, 1982-83, asst. registrar, 1983-90; registrar Ohio Dominican Coll., Columbus, 1990-93; dir. human resources Mid-Am. Phys. Medicine & Exec. Med., Inc., Columbus, Ohio, 1994—; adminstrv. advisor to Black Student Union,

Franklin U., 1982-85; human resource cons. Mid-Am. Phys. Medicine, Exec. Med., Inc., Westerville, Ohio, 1989-93, dir. human resources/bus. mgr., 1993—. Vol. tchr. Umoja Sasa Shule, Columbus, 1971-74; booster Mid-west Gymnastic and Cheerleading, Dublin, Ohio, 1988-93; active various com. for minority concerns. Mem. Ohio Assn. Collegiate Registrars and Admissions Officers (sec. 1991-93, Cert. Appreciation 1985, 93), Am. Assn. Collegiate Registrars and Admissions Officers, Nat. Assn. Coll. Deans, Registrars and Admissions Officers, Ohio Assn. Women Deans, Adminstrs. and Counselors, Nat. Assn. Women Deans, Adminstrs. and Counselors, Am. Assn. Univ. Adminstrn., Va. Admissions Counselors for Black Concerns, Ohio Health Info. Mgmt. Assn. Democrat. Mem. Church of God in Christ. Office: Mid Am Phys Medicine & Exec Med Inc 254 Woodland Ave Ste 105 Columbus OH 43203-1782

NUCKOLS, FRANK JOSEPH, psychiatrist; b. Akron, Ohio, Apr. 7, 1926; s. William Alexander Jr. and Jean (Harrison) N.; m. Jane Fleetwood McIntosh, June 16, 1948; children: Claud Alexander, John Andrew. BA, U. Louisville, 1946; MD, U. Ala., 1951. Diplomate Am. Bd. Psychiatry and Neurology. Intern Holy Name Jesus Hosp., Gadsden, Ala., 1951; ward physician Ala. State Hosp., Tuscaloosa, 1951-52; resident U. Louisville, USPHS Hosp., Lexington, Ky., 1953-56; mem. faculty dept. psychiatry U. Ala. Med. Ctr., Birmingham, 1958-68, dir. tng. psychiat. residents, 1964-68, head div. community psychiatry, 1964-68, head continuing psychiat. edn. for physicians, 1964-68; chief psychiat. staff in-patient svc. U. Hosp., Birmingham, 1966-68; dir. tng. Hill Crest Hosp., Birmingham, 1975-79; pvt. practice Birmingham, 1968-93; cons. Ala. Div. Disability Determinations, Birmingham, 1993—; staff Med. Ctr. East Hosp., Birmingham, Bapt. Med. Ctr. Montclair, Birmingham; cons. staff St. Vincent's Hosp., Birmingham, Lloyd Noland Hosp., Birmingham, South Highland Hosp., Birmingham; vis. faculty, mem. interuniv. forum in cmty. psychiatry Harvard U., Boston, 1963-66; vis. faculty Baylor U. Med. Sch., Houston, 1967-71. Ensign USNR, 1941-43; sr. surgeon USPHS, 1956—. Fellow Am. Psychiat. Assn. (life), So. Psychiat. Assn.; mem. Med. Assn. Ala., So. Med. Assn., Jefferson County Mental Health Assn. (v.p. 1960), Jefferson County Med. Soc., Mental Health Assn. State Ala. (chmn. profl. adv. com. 1961), Nat. Assn. Disability Examiners, Phi Beta Pi, Tau Kappa Epsilon. Home and Office: 3741 River Oaks Cir Birmingham AL 35223-2117

NUFRIO, ELIZABETH ANNE, health facility administrator; b. Phila., Mar. 1, 1955; d. Stephen Arthur and Frances Margaret (Sieling) Davis; m. Richard Michael Nufrio, June 19, 1976; children: Michael Paul, Dana Lynn. Dipl. nursing, Thomas Jefferson U., 1976. Staff nurse Athens (Ga.) Gen. Hosp., 1976-84; staff nurse, med. auditor Athens Regional Med. Ctr., 1987-93, dir. resource utilization, 1993—; cons., presenter in field. Mem. Am. Assn. Utilization Mgmt. Nurses, Nat. Assn. Healthcare Quality, Ga. Hosp. Assn. Office: Athens Regional Med Ctr 1199 Prince Ave Athens GA 30606

NUGENT, DENISE SMITH, holistic nurse; b. Winston Salem, N.C., July 27, 1959; d. Richard Delane and Betty Jean (Williams) Smith; m. Francis William Nugent Jr., Sept. 19, 1980. RN, Cabarrus Hosp. Sch. Nursing, Concord, N.C., 1980; cert., Internat. Inst. Reflexology, St. Petersburg, Fla., 1990, cert. in reflexology, 1996. RN, N.C., Va., Pa., Mass., Ariz., Calif. Staff nurse oncology dept. Bapt. Hosp., Winston Salem, 1980-82; staff nurse diabetes dept. Lehigh Valley Hosp., Allentown, Pa., 1982-83; staff nurse home health Berks Vis. Nurse Assn., Reading, Pa., 1983-85; staff nurse diabetic educator Moses Taylor Hosp., Scranton, Pa., 1990-93; staff nurse, supr. In Home Health, San Mateo, Calif., 1993-94; holistic nurse, cons. in pvt. practice Foster City, Calif., 1995—; dir. profl. svcs. Olsten Health Care, Scranton, 1992-93; cons., 1995—; tchg. Reiki, 1995—. Mem. Am. Holistic Nurses Assn. (cert. program holistic nursing, bd. cert. holistic nurse), Inst. Noetic Sci., Calif. Connection-Holistic Nurses, Foster City C. of C. Home: 44 Rock Harbor Ln Foster City CA 94404 Office: 969-G Edgewater Blvd # 764 Foster City CA 94404

NUKI, KLAUS, dental educator, researcher; b. Vienna, May 5, 1931; came to U.S., 1957; s. Walter and Regina (Heiber) N.; m. Elizabeth Jill Hollis, Feb. 2, 1963; children: Guy, Keith, Max. BDS, U. London, 1955; MS in Pathology, U. Ill., Chgo., 1960; PhD, U. London, 1967. Lic. dental surgeon, Conn., U.K. House surgeon Queen Victoria Hosp., Esat Grinstead, Surrey, Eng., 1954-56; rsch. asst. dept. oral pathology U. Ill., Chgo., 1957-60, Royal Dental Coll., Aarhus, Denmark, 1963-64; practice gen. dentistry London, 1956-57; lectr. in pathology and periodontics U. London, 1961-67; head dept. oral biology U. Iowa Coll. Dentistry, 1967-75; prof., assoc. dean U. Conn. Health Ctr., Farmington, 1975-88; prof. oral diagnosis U. Conn. Sch. Dental Medicine, Farmington, 1988—. Assoc. editor Jour. Periodontal Rsch., 1975-91; contbr. numerous articles to sci. publs. Office: U Conn Health Ctr Farmington Ave Farmington CT 06032-1709

NULAND, SHERWIN, surgeon, author; b. N.Y.C., Dec. 8, 1930; s. Meyer and Violet (Lutsky) N.; m. Sarah Peterson, May 29, 1977; children: Victoria Jane, Andrew Meyer, William Peterson, Amelia Rose. BA, NYU, 1951; MD, Yale U., 1955. Surgeon Yale-New Haven Hosp. (Conn.), 1962-91; clin. prof. surgery Yale Sch. Medicine, New Haven, 1962—. Author: The Origins of Anesthesia, 1983, Doctors: The Biography of Medicine, 1988, Medicine: The Art of Healing, 1991, The Face of Mercy, 1993, How We Die: Reflections on Life's Final Chapter, 1994 (Nat. Book award for non-fiction 1994, Pulitzer prize finalist 1995). Pres. med. com. Jewish Home Aged, New Haven, 1985-87; v.p. Conn. Hospice, New Haven, 1978-80. Fellow ACS; mem. New Eng. Surg. Soc., Assocs. of Yale Med. Sch. Libr. (chmn. 1982-94), Yale-China Assn. (chmn. med. 1988-93). Democrat. Jewish. Home: 29 Old Hartford Tpke Hamden CT 06517-3523 Office: PO Box 6356 Hamden CT 06517-0356

NUMANN, PATRICIA JOY, surgeon, educator; b. Bronx, N.Y., Apr. 6, 1941. BA, U. Rochester, 1962; MD, SUNY Health Sci. Ctr., Syracuse, 1965. Intern, resident SUNY Health Sci. Ctr., Syracuse, 1970, from asst. prof. to assoc. prof. surgery, 1970-89, assoc. dean Coll. Medicine, 1978-84, assoc. dean Coll. Medicine Clin. Affairs, prof. surgery, 1989—; dir. breast care program SUNY Health Sci. Ctr., Syracuse, 1986—; presenter in field. Contbr. chpts. to books, articles to profl. jours. Found. bd. dirs. Vera House, Syracuse, 1993-94; hon. bd. dirs. F.A.C.T., Syracuse, 1994. Named one of Women of Distinction, N.Y. State Gov. Mario Cuomo, 1994, Disting. Tchg. Prof. SUNY, 1994; recipient Disting. Surgeon award Assn. Women Surgeons, 1991. Mem. AMA (coun. sci. affairs), ACS (com. on cancer grad. med. edn. com.), Am. Bd. Surgeons (bd. dirs. 1994—), Am. Assn. Endocrine Surgeons (v.p. 1992, pres. 1985), Assn. for Surg. Edn., Corinthian Club. Office: SUNY Health Sci Ctr 750 E Adams St Syracuse NY 13210-2306

NUNAN, FRANCIS A., obstetrician-gynecologist; b. Bryn Mawr, Pa., Feb. 6, 1932; s. Francis Anthony and Mary Kathryn (McCallion) N.; m. Shirley Anne Slater, June 21, 1958; children: Francis A. III, Michael C., James P., Nancy E., Barbara J., Joseph P., Kathryn M. BA, Harvard U., 1954; MD, Temple U., 1958. Diplomate Am. Bd. Ob-gyn. Intern Butterworth Hosp., Grand Rapids, 1958-59; resident Albany (N.Y.C.) Med. Ctr., 1962-65; asst. prof. medicine Albany Med. Coll., 1965—; pvt. practice Albany, 1965—; med. bd. dirs. Cerebral Palsy Soc., Albany, 1970—. Sec. Boys Baseball, Albany, 1960-75; cubmaster Boy Scouts Am., Albany, 1969-74, scoutmaster, 1970-80, bd. dirs., 1974—. Capt. USAF, 1959-62. Fellow Phila. Coll. Physicians; mem. Welferts Roost Country Club. Republican. Roman Catholic. Home: 23 De Lucia Ter Albany NY 12211-2005 Office: 319 S Manning Blvd Albany NY 12208-1738

NUNAN, PATRICK JOSEPH, podiatrist; b. Huntington, W.Va., Sept. 6, 1958; s. Dennis Joseph Jr. and Doris Louise (Snyder) N.; m. Sandra Marie Frajter, Aug. 20, 1983; children: Amanda, Megan, Timothy. BA in Biology, W.Va. U., 1980; DPM, Ohio Coll. Podiatric Medicine, 1984. Diplomate Am. Bd. Podiatric Surgery, Am. Bd. Podiatric Orthopedics and Primary Podiatric Medicine. Resident Foot Clinic of Youngstown, Ohio, 1984-85; assoc. Raystown Podiatry Assocs., Huntingdon, Pa., 1985-87; pres. Foot and Ankle Physicians, Westchester, Ohio, 1987—; creditials com. Jewish Hosp., Cin., 1990-94; cons. Midwest Orthotics Lab, Wilmington Coll. Sports Teams; clinic advisor Am. Running and Fitness Assn. Newsletter; tchg. staff Jewish Hosp. Podiatric Residency Program. Contbr. articles to profl. jours. Fellow Am. Coll. of Foot Surgeons, Am. Coll. of Foot Surgeons, Am. Acad. of Podiatric Sports Medicine; mem. Ohio Podiatric Med. Assn. (v.p. 1994—), Kiwanis, Am. Podiatric Med. Assn., Am. Coll. of Sports Medicine, Am. Coll. of Podopediatrics, Am. Diabetes Assn., Am. Running and Fitness Assn. Home: 5840 Winged Foot Dr Westchester OH 45069 Office: Foot & Ankle Physicians Westchester 9615 Cincinnati Columbus Rd Cincinnati OH 45241

NUNES, EDWARD VERNON, JR., psychiatrist; b. N.Y.C., Nov. 1, 1955; s. Edward Vernon Sr. and Grace (Maynard) N.; m. Katharine Helen Stiassni; 1 child, Sanford MacKenzie. BA, Dartmouth Coll., 1977; MD, U. Conn., 1981. Diplomate Am. Bd. Psychiatry and Neurology. Resident in psychiatry Columbia Presbyn. Med. Ctr./N.Y. State Psychiat. Inst., N.Y.C., 1982-85, fellow in psychiatry rsch., 1985-88, asst. attending psychiatrist, 1985—; instr. clin. psychiatry Coll. Physicians and Surgeons Columbia U., N.Y.C., 1985-88, asst. clin. prof. psychiatry Coll. Physicians and Surgeons, 1988-90, asst. prof. clin. psychiatry, 1990—; coord. substance abuse rsch. efforts Depression Evaluation Svc., N.Y. State Psychiat. Inst., N.Y.C., 1985—. Recipient Sandoz prize U. Conn., 1981, Cammer award N.Y. State Psychiat. Inst., 1985, Taylor Manor Hosp. Psychiat. Essay prize, 1985. Mem. Am. Psychiat. Assn., Am. Psychosomatic Soc., Am. Assn. Psychiatrists in Alcoholism and the Addictions, Amateur Ski Club (gov. N.Y.C. chpt. 1986—). Office: NY State Psychiat Inst 722 W 168th St New York NY 10032-2603

NUNEZ, DESMOND ANTONIO, otolaryngologist; b. Port of Spain, Trinidad, June 13, 1959; arrived in U.K., 1983; s. Vernon Lennox and Naomi Ann (Roberts) N. M.B.,B.S., U. W.I., Kingston, Jamaica, 1982. Registrar Greater Glasgow (Scotland) Health Bd., 1987-89; rsch. registrar North Riding Infirmary, Middlesborough, Eng., 1989-90; tutor U. Leeds, Eng., 1990-92; sr. registrar Leicester (Eng.) Royal Infirmary, 1992-94, Univ. Hosp., Nottingham, Eng., 1994-95; cons. otolaryngologist Royal Infirmary, Aberdeen, Scotland, 1995—; cons. Royal Aberdeen Children's Hosp., 1995—, Albyn Hosp., Aberdeen, 1995—; sr. lectr. U. Aberdeen, 1995—. Contbr. articles to profl. jours. Recipient Aaron Matalon prize U. W.I., 1982, Intern's Rsch. prize Princess Margaret Hosp., Bahamas, 1983; TWJ Found. Travel grantee, 1995. Fellow Royal Coll. Surgeons; mem. Brit. Med. Assn. (hon. divsnl. sec. 1994-95), N.Y. Acad. Scis., Brit. Skull Base Soc., Brit. Assn. Paediatric Otolaryngologists. Home: 8 Beechgrove Ter, Aberdeen AB2 4ED, Scotland Office: Aberdeen Royal Infirmary, Foresterhill, Aberdeen AB9 2ZB, Scotland

NUÑEZ, PERCY, cardiologist; b. Panama City, Panama, Nov. 4, 1943; s. Pedro V. and Isabel E. (Jaurequi) N.; m. Miriam Cecilia Emiliani, Nov. 29, 1969; children: Percy J., Mariana C., Juan F., Luis E. MD, Universidad del Valle, Cali, Colombia, 1967. Diplomate Internal Medicine, Cardiovascular Disease. Resident internal medicine Gorpes Hosp., Panama, 1969-72, med. officer cardiology, 1976-77; med. officer internal medicine Coco Solo Hosp., Panama, 1972-74; cardiology fellow St. Luke's Hosp., Houston, 1974-76; staff cardiologist Social Security Hosp., Panama, 1977-83, Paitilla Hosp., Panama, 1983—. Fellow ACP, Am. Coll. Cardiology; mem. Lions. Roman Catholic. Home: PO Box 8002, Panama City 7, Panama

NUNGESSER, DONNA KAY, nurse consultant; b. Hutchinson, Kans., Sept. 17, 1958; d. Richard Lyle and Beulah Lee (King) Rathbun; m. Billy Ray Nungesser, May 12, 1980; children: Shannon Renee Reed, Kayla Marie. AA in Nursing, Butler County C.C., El Dorado, Kans., 1988. RN, Kans. ADN Cedar View Nursing Home, Wellington, Kans., 1988-90; staff nurse/relief charge nurse St. Joseph Med. Ctr., Wichita, Kans., 1988-91; home care coord. Kimberly Quality Care, Wichita, 1990-93; clin. supr. Olsten-Kimberly Quality Care, Wichita, 1993-95; nurse cons. Insite Care, Inc., Wichita, 1995—; sec. bd. dirs. Care Coordination Team, Wichita, 1993. Chair patient care com. Episcopal AIDS Task Force, Wichita, 1993—; bd. dirs. Wichita Cmty. Clin. AIDS Program, 1994; adv. com. AIDS Fund of Wichita/Sedgwick County, 1994; AIDS educator ARC, 1991—, Kans. AIDS Edn. and Tng. Ctr., 1991—. Named Home Health Nurse of Mo., Kans. Home Care Assn., 1992; Wesley Found. scholar, 1991, 92. Mem. Assn. of Nurses in AIDS Care (co-founder Wichita area chpt., pres. 1993—), Intravenous Nurses Soc. Home: 607 Charles St Mulvane KS 67110 Office: Insite Care Inc 6611 E Central Ste F Wichita KS 67206

NUNN, JENNY WREN, pharmacist; b. Atlanta, May 5, 1944; d. Joshua Hugh and Jenny Wren (Scott) N. Student, Gulf Park Coll.; BS, U. Tenn., 1967; AS, Dyersburg State Community Coll., 1975; BS in Law Enforcement, Samford U., 1980, BS in Pharmacy, 1981. Registered pharmacist, Tenn. Pvt. practice Ripley, Tenn., 1981—; planter, land owner Wren's Flight Plantation, Chestnut Bluff, Tenn., 1980—, Scottlawn Plantation, Ripley, 1980—. Founder, bd. dirs. Mid South chpt. Greyhound Pets of Am., Memphis, 1985—; pres. Lauderdale County Humane Soc., bd. dirs 1981—; bd. dirs. Nostalgia U.S.A. Fellow Internat. Inst. History of Pharmacy Assn.; mem. NRA (life), DAR, Am. Soc. Hosp. Pharmacists, Christian Med. Soc., Bus. and Profl. Women's Assn., Dames ofCt. of Honor, Am. Horse Protection Assn. (life), Ducks Unltd., Nat. Wild Turkey Fedn., Zeta Tau Alpha. Methodist. Home and Office: RR 1 Box 1 Scottlawn Plantation Ripley TN 38063-9709

NURCOMBE, BARRY, director psychiatry, educator; b. Brisbane, Queensland, Australia, Jan. 11, 1933; came to U.S., 1976; s. Arthur Cyril and Alice Ursula (O'Gorman) N.; m. Alison Carson Thatcher, Dec. 7, 1956; children: Victor, Stephen, Lisa. MB, BS, U. Queensland, Brisbane, 1956; DPM, U. Melbourne, Victoria, Australia, 1959, MD, 1973. Diplomate Am. Bd. Psychiatry and Neurology. Med. dir. Australia Div. Youth Welfare & Guidance, Brisbane, 1960-67; assoc. prof. child psychiatry U. New South Wales, Sydney, Australia, 1967-76; dir. child psychiatry, prof. U. Vt., Burlington, 1976-84; prof. psychiatry and human behavior Brown U., Providence, 1984-89; dir. child and adolescent psychiatry, prof. Med. Sch. Vanderbilt U., Nashville, 1989—. Author: Children of the Dispossessed, 1976, The Clinical Process in Psychiatry, 1986, Child Mental Health and the Law, 1994. Capt. Australian Army, 1956-70, Res. Fellow Am. Psychiat. Assn., Am. Coll. Psychiatrists, Am. Acad. Child and Adolescent Psychiatry. Home: 110 Lynwood Ter Nashville TN 37205-2912 Office: Vanderbilt U Dept Child Psychiatry 1601 23rd Ave S Nashville TN 37212-3133

NURDEN, ALAN THOMAS, medical research scientist; b. Dumbleton, Eng., May 30, 1944; arrived in France, 1976; s. Nurden Paquita. Dir. UMR 5533 CNRS, Pessac, France, 1990—. Contbr. articles to sci. jours. Recipient Grand prix de la Fondation de la Recherche Medicale, France, 1986, prix Odette Lemonon de l'Academie des Sci., France, 1977. Mem. Internat. Soc. Thrombosis and Haemostais (coun. mem. 1986-93). Office: Hosp Cardiologique, UMR 5533 CNRS, 33604 Pessac France

NUSBAUM, GEOFFREY DEAN, psychotherapist; b. Berkeley, Calif., Apr. 1, 1946; s. Wayne Dale and Jeanne (Hankins) N.; m. Barbara Ann Pierfy, July 12, 1986; 1 child, Michael Wayne. BA, Washington U., St. Louis, 1967; MA, Hartford Sem. Fdn. Consortium, 1971, PhD, 1978. Diplomate Am. Bd. Med. Psychotherapy; cert. therapist Am. Assn. for Marriage and Family Therapy; lic. therapist, N.J. Pvt. practice Marlton, N.J. and Phila., 1972—; cons. N.Y. Fertility Rsch. Found., N.Y.C., 1978-83, Bancroft Sch., Haddonfield, N.J., 1983-87; fellow Internat. coun. Sex. Edn. and Parenthood Am. U. Author: Community, Self Identity, 1978; peer manuscript reviewer to sci. jours. Bd. dirs. Calcutta House AIDS Hospice. Mem. Am. Soc. for Reproductive Medicine, Am. Soc. for Psychosomatic Ob-Gyn., N.Y. Acad. Scis. Office: PO Box 256 Mount Ephraim NJ 08059-0256

NUSSBAUM, ARNOLD, pediatrician; b. N.Y.C., Dec. 20, 1925; s. Jack and Clara (Gewirtz) N.; m. Helen P. Coble, June 30, 1951; children: Andrea, Jack, Paul, Robert. BS, Bklyn. Coll., 1949; MD, SUNY, Downstate Med. Ctr., Bklyn., 1954. Diplomate Am. Bd. Pediatrics. Intern USPHS, S.I., N.Y.; resident in pediats. Jewish Hosp. Med. Ctr., Bklyn. With U.S. Navy, 1943-46, PTO. Mem. AMA, Kings County Med. Soc. Democrat. Jewish. Home: 67 Barlow Dr N Brooklyn NY 11234

NUSSBAUM, MICHEL ERNEST, physician; b. L.A., Nov. 7, 1947; s. Schymen and Jeannette Eleanor (Pequignot) N.; m. Joyce Wendy Laudon, Nov. 11, 1981; children: Eleanor, Anna. BA, Cornell U., 1969; MD, Free U. Brussels, 1977. Attending physician N.Y. Hosp. Med. Ctr. of Queens, Flushing, N.Y., 1982—; physician pvt. practice, Flushing, N.Y., 1982—; attending physician Flushing Hosp. Med. Ctr., 1987—; clin. instr. medicine Cornell U. Med. Coll., N.Y.C., 1994—; med. dir. Franklin Nursing Home, Flushing, 1995—; physician in charge endoscopic svcs. N.Y. Hosp. Med. Ctr., 1990—; pres. med. staff soc. N.Y. Hosp., 1992-96, vice chmn. med. bd., 1994-96. Fellow Am. Coll. Physicians, Am. Coll. Gastroenterology. Office: 142-43 Booth Meml Ave Flushing NY 11355

NUSSBAUM, MOSES, surgeon, educator; b. N.Y.C., Feb. 28, 1931; s. Ben and Gussie (Brod) N.; m. Esther Auster, Nov. 24, 1954; children: Judith, Gabriel, Tamara. AB, NYU, 1951, MD, 1955. Intern, surg. residency Beth Israel Med. Ctr., Bellevue Hosp., N.Y.C., 1955-62; attending staff Beth Israel Med. Ctr., N.Y.C., 1962—, chief, divsn. head & neck surgery, 1973—, chmn. dept. surgery, 1993—; prof. surgery Mt. Sinai Sch. Medicine, N.Y.C., 1980-94, Albert Einstein Coll. Medicine, N.Y.C., 1994—. Editor Head & Neck Surgery, 1981, 84, 88; contbr. articles to profl. jours. Capt. USAF, 1957-59. Mem. AMA, Am. Coll. Surgeons, Am. Soc. Head & Neck Surgeons, N.Y. Cancer Soc., N.Y. Surg. Soc., N.Y. Head & Neck Soc. (founding mem.), Soc. Head & Neck Surgeo ns, Internat. Bronco-Esophagological Soc., Soc. Am. Gastrointestinal Endoscopic Surgeons. Jewish. Office: Beth Israel Med Ctr 16th St and 1st Ave New York NY 10003

NUSSENZVEIG, ISRAEL, physician; b. Sao Paulo, Brazil, Feb. 25, 1923; s. Michel and Regina (Kupferblum) N.; m. Monique Ronsse, Jan. 23, 1955; children: Daniel, Tomaz, Cecilia, Paula. Grad., U. Sao Paulo, 1942, U. Sao Paulo, 1948. Resident Hosp. Clinicas, Faculty Medicine, Sao Paulo U., 1949-50, mem. emergency svc. staff, 1951-52, asst. prof., 1955-86; assoc. prof., nephrology Faculty Medicine, Sao Paulo U., 1987-91; assoc. prof. nephrology, then prof. Faculty Medicine, OSEC Found., Sao Paulo, 1991—; physician-in-chief Ipiranga Mcpl. Hosp., Sao Paulo, 1968-78. Co-author: Hydro-Electrolytic Disturbances, 1959, Nephrotic Syndrome, 1973; contbr. to books and articles to profl. jours. Nephrology fellow, Hosp. Necker, Paris, Brussels, 1953-54; recipient Diogo De Faria award, Sao Paulo Med. Assn., 1952, Clemente Ferreira award, 1952, Oswaldo Cruz award, 1959. Mem. Internat. Soc. Nephrology (mem. exec. com. 1960-69), Brazilian Soc. Nephrology (sec. gen. 1960-62). Home: Rua Mario Gonçalves Oliveira 299, 05656-030 Sao Paulo Brazil Office: Rua Itacolomi 601-Conj 51, 01239-020 Sao Paulo Brazil

NÜSSLEIN-VOLHARD, CHRISTIANE, medical researcher; b. Magdeburg, Germany, Oct. 20, 1942; d. Rolf Volhard and Brigitte (Haas) Volhard. Diploma in Biochemistry, U. Tübingen, 1968, PhD, 1973; ScD (hon.), Yale U. Rsch. assoc. lab. of Dr. Schaller Max-Planck Inst. for Devel. Biology, Tübingen, 1972-74; postdoctoral fellow lab. of Dr. W. Gehring, Biozentrum, Basel, Switzerland, 1975-76; postdoctoral fellow lab of Dr. K. Sander U. Freiburg, 1977; head rsch. group European Molecular Biology Lab., Heidelberg, 1978-80; rsch. group leader Friedrich-Miescher Laboratorium Max-Planck-Gesellschaft, Tübingen, 1981-85; sci. mem. Max-Planck-Gesellschaft, dir. Max-Planck Inst. for Devel. Biology, Tübingen, 1985-90, dir. genetics dept., 1990—; hon. prof. U. Tübingen. Contbr. numerous articles to profl. jours. Recipient Albert Lasker Basic Med. Rsch. award Albert and Mary Lasker Found., 1991, Louisa Gross Horowitz prize Columbia U., 1992, Forderpreis award Deutschen Forschungsgemeinschaft, 1986, Leibnizpreis der Deutschen Forschungsgemeinschaft, Franz Vogt prize U. Giessen, 1986, Carus prize City of Schweinfurth, 1989, Rosenstiel medal Brandeis U., Nobel Prize in Medicine, 1995; Brooks lecturer Harvard Med. Sch., 1988, Stilliman lecturer Yale U., 1989. Mem. European Molecular Biology Orgn., Deutsche Gesellschaft fur Entwicklungsbiologie, Academia Europeaea. Office: Max Planck Inst, Spemannstr 35 Postfach 2109, D-72076 Tübingen Germany

NUTH, MICHAEL D., school psychologist; b. Balt., Jan. 23, 1956; s. Joseph Andrew Jr. and Assunda Maria (Baglioni) N.; m. Barbara Marie Savatgy, June 23, 1978; children: William, John, Amanda. BA, Loyola Coll., Balt., 1978, MA in Psychology, 1980; Advanced Grad. Specialist in Human Devel., U. Md., 1988. Cert. sch. psychologist, Md., nationally cert. sch. psychologist. Sch. psychologist Balt. City Pub. Schs., 1980-90, Anne Arundel County Pub. Schs., Annapolis, Md., 1990—. Mem. Harbel Ednl. Task Force, Balt., 1988-89, Sons of the Am. Legion, Balt., 1956—. Mem. Nat. Assn. Sch. Psychologists, Md. Sch. Psychologist Assn. (treas. 1992-94, 95—). Democrat. Home: 2500 Ailsa Ave Baltimore MD 21214-2515 Office: Anne Arundel County Schs 1681 Millersville Rd Millersville MD 21108

NUTSCH, BARBARA ANN, nursing administrator; b. Akron, Ohio, Oct. 18, 1951; d. James Robert and Evelyn June (Franks) McCune; m. Robert Gerald Nutsch, Aug. 9, 1980; children: Jon, Jason, Laura, Ben. BS in Nursing, Teikyo Marycrest U., 1993. RN, Iowa. Regional facilities dir. Creative Resources & Mgmt., Cedar Rapids, Iowa, 1993—. Mem. Am. Coll. Health Adminstrs. (voting mem., v.p. state chpt. 1995—). Home: 13937 Hwy 64 Maquoketa IA 52060 Office: Creative Resources & Mgmt 5300 N Park Place NE #108 Cedar Rapids IA 52402

NUTT, REX LYNN, physical therapist; b. Tipton, Okla., June 30, 1933; s. Lacy Brackston and Nell (Smith) N.; children: Robert Lynn, Ronald Lee. BS, Abilene Christian U., 1956; MS Tex. Woman's U., 1988. Lic. phys. therapist. Staff phys. therapist Gonzales Warm Springs Found., Tex., 1955-57, 59; asst. edn. adminstr. Hermann Sch. Phys. Therapy, Houston, 1959-61, edn. adminstr., 1962-65; dir. phys. therapy dept. Spring Br. Meml. Hosp., Houston, 1964-84; pres. Rex Nutt and Assocs., Inc. (formerly Houston Phys. Therapy Svc.), 1969—; habilitation specialist Abilene (Tex.) State Sch., 1989—; acad. coord. clin. edn. Hardin-Simmons U., Abilene, 1995—; mem. Tex. State Bd. Phys. Therapy Examiners, 1979-85. Contbr. articles to Clin. Mgmt. Mag. Bd. dirs. Herod Sch. PTO, Houston, 1967-69; mem. edn. of schs. and orgns.; bd. dirs. Disability Resources, Abilene, Tex., chmn., 1993—; elder Highland Ch. Christ, Abilene, 1992—. Mem. Am. Assn. Mental Retardation, Abilene Christian U. Alumni Assn. (Citation award 1976), Tex. Phys. Therapy Assn. (Outstanding award 1974, Smyth award 1990). Avocations: photography.

NUTTER, JOHN LEMUEL, medical technologist; b. Balt., Mar. 30, 1956; s. Albert James and Lila Mae (Duncan) N.; m. Velma Gaye Viers, Aug. 16, 1980; children: Christy Nichole, Jacob Scott. Student, W.Va. Inst. Tech., 1974-75; Regents BA in Med. Tech., Bluefield State Coll., 1991. Cert. lab. asst., Vets. Hosp., Beckley, W.Va., 1977. M.L.T. Sacred Heart Hosp., Richwood, W.Va., 1978, Summers County Hosp., Hinton, W.Va., 1978-80, SWVRHC, Beckley, 1980-82, Greenbriar Physicians, Inc., Lewisburg, W.Va., 1982-88; med. lab. technician/med. technologist Greenbrier Valley Med. Ctr. Hosp., Lewisburg, 1988-92; med. technologist, lab. mgr. W.Va. Sch. of Osteo. Medicine Clinic, Inc., Lewisburg, 1992—; phlebotomist Lab. Corp. of Am., Beckley, 1992—; prof. W.Va. Sch. Osteo. Medicine, Lewisburg, 1992—; instr. Greenbrier C.C. Ctr./Bluefield State Coll., Lewisburg, spring 1996. Fellow Am. Soc. Clin. Pathology, Clin. Lab. Mgrs. Assn., Am. Med. Tech. Assn.; mem. Jaycees (pres. 1983-94, Jaycee of Yr.). Democrat. Baptist. Home: Rt 2 Box 37-A Rupert WV 25984

NWOSU, CALEB CHINEDU, osteopath; b. Port Harcourt, Nigeria, Mar. 9, 1954; came to U.S., 1982; s. Hezekiah and Rhoda (Echefu) N.; m. Cordelia Udoadi Iwunze, Dec. 6, 1981; children: Nneka, Obinna, Chinwe, Chimdi, Emeka. BA, Cheyney U., 1986; DO, Ohio U. Coll. Osteopathic Med., 1994. Intern Springfield (Pa.) Hosp., 1994-95; resident Cmty. Hosp. Lancaster (Pa.), 1995—. Mem. Am. Osteopathic Assn., Am. Acad. Family Physicians, Pa. Osteopathic Med. Assn., Ohio Acad. Family Physicians. Episcopal. Home: 527 Merioneth Dr Exton PA 19341

NYE, GARY ALAN, physician assistant, aeromedical consultant; b. Evanston, Ill., Oct. 17, 1956; s. Louis H. Jr. and Marylinn (Ellis) N.; m. Darlene C. Dow, July 11, 1992; children: Seth, Andrea, Sierra. BS in Human Biology, U. Wis., Stevens Point, 1978; BS in Med., Baylor Coll. Medicine, Houston, 1982. Cert. physician asst.; cert. ACLS instr., ATLS, PALS, EMS instr. Emergency dept. physician asst. Calais (Maine) Regional Hosp., 1983-86, E.J. Noble Hosp., Gouverneur, N.Y., 1986-87, Mayo Regional Hosp., Dover-Foxcroft, Maine, 1987—; dir./coord. Calais Life Flight, 1983-86. Author articles, abstract, presentation. Firefighter, capt. Cambridge (Maine) Fire Dept. Mem. Am. Acad. Physician Assts., Down East Assn. Physician Assts., Nat. Flight Paramedic Assn., Soc. Emergency Medicine Physician Assts. Home: RR 1 Box 117 Parkman ME 04443 Office: Mayo Regional Hosp 75 W Main St Dover Foxcroft ME 04426

NYE, WILLIAM ROGER, psychologist; b. Haverhill, Mass., Oct. 23, 1940; s. Kenneth Enoch and Virginia Pauline (Cook) N.; m. Marian Barbara Abowitz, June 30, 1970 (div. 1983); children: Michael Shepherd Abowitz Nye; 1 stepson, Christopher J. Wells. BA, Yale U., 1962; MDiv, Union Theol. Sem., N.Y.C., 1965; PhD, Adelphi U., Garden City, N.Y., 1981. Lic. psychologist, N.Y. Pastor Ch. of the Evangel, Bklyn., 1965-77; asst. minister Plymouth Ch. of the Pilgrims, Bklyn., 1977-82; pastor All Souls Universalist Ch., Bklyn., 1983—; exec. dir. Blanton-Peale Counseling Ctrs., Forest Hills, N.Y., 1983—; pres. bd. Met. Assn. of N.Y. Conf. of United Ch. of Christ, 1969-73, moderator, 1982-83. Del. Dem. Nat. Conv., Miami, 1972; pres. Pastoral and Ednl. Svcs., Brklyn., 1983-87, The Vinmont Found., N.Y.C., 1988—; sec. N.Y. Congl. Home for Aged, Bklyn., 1980-88. Mem. Am. Psychol. Assn. Democrat. United Ch. of Christ. Home: 888 East 19th St Brooklyn NY 11230-3108

NYGAARD, BJØRN, hospital administrator; b. Oslo, July 26, 1944; s. Bjarne and Ella (Fosserud) N.; m. Brith-Evy Holmen, June 10, 1967; children: Eli Bente Holmen, Kai Holmen. BA in Social Scis., U. Oslo, 1971; Diploma of Pub. Health, The Nordic Sch. Pub. Health, Gothenburg, Sweden, 1992; postgrad., NKI, Baerum, Norway, 1994. Faculty U. Tromsø, Norway, 1972-74; staff Akershus County, Oslo, 1974-80; dir. Tynset (Norway) Hosp., 1980-82, Kongsberg (Norway) Hosp., 1982-91; dir. health care and social svcs. Municipality of Sortland, Norway, 1991-92; dir. Harstad (Norway) Hosp., 1992—; lectr. health adminstrn. and health planning, 1978—. Author: Personal Administration, 1982, Helsevesenets Oppbygging Og Organisasion, 1979, 5th edit., 1989, Statistikk og Planlegging Helsesektoren, 1989, 3d edit., 1993. Sgt. Norwegian Air Force, 1965-66. Home: Grønnebakkan 56, 9400 Harstad Norway Office: Harstad Hospital, St Olavsgt 70, 9400 Harstad Norway

NYGAARD, LANCE COREY, nurse, data processing consultant; b. Casper, Wyo., June 21, 1952; s. Miles Adolph and Jenile Hansine (Mosman) N.; m. Susan Leigh Wilson, May 8, 1995; 1 child from previous marriage, Kari Melissa. AA in Nursing, U. S.D., 1980; BS in Chemistry, 1974; MLS, U. Ill., 1975. Libr. asst. Brookings Pub. Libr., S.D., 1971-75, asst. dir., 1975-77; emergency med. technician Brookings Hosp., 1976-78; sr. emergency med. technician Vermillion Ambulance, S.D., 1978-80; nurse McKennan Hosp., Sioux Falls, S.D., 1980-91, VA Hosp., 1991-96, Sioux Valley Hosp., 1996—; owner operator Data Processing Svcs., Sioux Falls, 1983—; applications cons. Computer Dimensions, Sioux Falls, 1984-85. Fin. sec., mem. ch. coun. Holy Cross Luth. Ch., Sioux Falls, S.D., 1986-91, info. resources coord., 1991-92; troop leader Minn-Ia-Kota coun. Girl Scouts U.S., 1989—, region troop supr., 1991-95. Mem. Vermillion Chemistry Club (pres. 1973-74), Sioux Valley Rose Soc. (v.p. 1988-89, pres. 1989-90), Sons of Norway (guard 1976-77). Republican. Lutheran. Avocations: World War II military history, rose gardening, photography, amateur radio. Home: 3500 S Grace Cir Sioux Falls SD 57103-7226 Office: Sioux Valley Hosp 1100 S Euclid Sioux Falls SD 57105

NYGAARD, THOMAS WILLIAM, cardiologist; b. Stavanger, Norway, Jan. 23, 1952; s. Isak and Bernice (Thomas) N.; m. Ellen Gebhardt, Aug. 9, 1980; children: Anna K., Gretchen E., Erik T. BS in Chemistry, Vanderbilt U., 1974, MD, 1978. Diplomate Nat. Bd. Med. Examiners, Am. Bd. Internal Medicine, Cardiovascular Disease. Intern in internal medicine Johns Hopkins Hosp., Balt., 1978-79, resdient in internal medicine, 1979-81; fellow in cardiovascular diseases U. Va. Hosp., Charlottesville, 1981-83, asst. prof., internal medicine, 1983-86; dir. cardiac cath. lab. Lynchburg (Va.) Gen. Hosp., 1986—; chief of staff Cen. Health/Lynchburg Gen. and VA Hosp., 1992, also bd. dirs. Contbr. articles to profl. jours. and pubis. Recipient Weinstein prize in medicine, Vanderbilt U., 1978, Amos Christie prize in pediatrics, 1978, others. Fellow Am. Coll. Cardiology, Am. Coll. Physicians, Am. Heart Assn.; mem. John Hopkins Med. and Surg. Assn., Phi Beta Kappa, Alpha Omega Alpha. Office: Med Assocs of Cen Va Cardiology Divsn 2215 Landover Pl Lynchburg VA 24501

NYHAN, WILLIAM LEO, pediatrician, educator; b. Boston, Mar. 13, 1926; s. W. Leo and Mary (Cleary) N.; m. Christine Murphy, Nov. 20, 1948; children: Christopher, Abigail. Student, Harvard U., 1943-45; M.D., Columbia U., 1949; M.S., U. Ill., 1956, Ph.D., 1958; hon. doctorate, Tokushima U., Japan, 1981. Intern Yale U.-Grace-New Haven Hosp., 1949-50, resident, 1950-51, 53-55; asst. prof. pediatrics Johns Hopkins U., 1958-61, assoc. prof., 1961-63; prof. pediatrics, biochemistry U. Miami, 1963-69, chmn. dept. pediatrics, 1963-69; prof. U. Calif., San Diego, 1969—; chmn. dept. pediatrics U. Calif., 1969-86; mem. FDA adv. com. on Teratogenic Effects of Certain Drugs, 1964-70; mem. pediatric panel AMA Council on Drugs, 1964-70; mem. Nat. Adv. Child Health and Human Devel. Council, 1967-71; mem. research adv. com. Calif. Dept. Mental Hygiene, 1969-72; mem. med. and sci. adv. com. Leukemia Soc. Am., Inc., 1968-72; mem. basic adv. com. Nat. Found. March of Dimes, 1973-81; mem. Basil O'Connor Starter grants com., 1973-93; mem. clin. cancer program project rev. com. Nat. Cancer Inst., 1977-81; vis. prof. extraordinario U. del Salvador (Argentina), 1982. Author: (with E. Edelson) The Heredity Factor, Genes, Chromosomes and You, 1976,Genetic & Malformation Syndromes in Clinical Medicine, 1976, Abnormalities in Amino Acid Metabolism in Clinical Medicine, 1984, Diagnostic Recognition of Genetic Disease, 1987; editor: Amino Acid Metabolism and Genetic Variation, 1967, Heritable Disorders of Amino Acid Metabolism, 1974; mem. editorial bd. Jour. Pediatrics, 1964-78, King Faisal Hosp. Med. Jour., 1981-85, Western Jour. Medicine, 1974-86, Annals of Saudi Medicine, 1985-87, mem. editorial com. Ann. Rev. Nutrition, 1982-86; mem. editorial staff Med. and Pediatric Oncology, 1975-83. Served with U.S. Navy, 1944-46; U.S. Army, 1951-53. Nat. Found. Infantile Paralysis fellow, 1955-58; recipient Commemorative medallion Columbia U. Coll. Physicians and Surgeons, 1967. Mem. AAAS, Am. Fedn. Clin. Rsch., Am. Chem. Soc., Soc. Pediatric Rsch. (pres. 1970-71), Am. Assn. Cancer Rsch., Am. Soc. Pharmacology and Exptl. Therapeutics, Western Soc. Pediatric Rsch. (pres. 1976-77), N.Y. Acad. Sci., Am. Acad. Pediatrics (Borden award 1980), Am. Pediatric Soc., Am. Inst. Biol. Scis., Soc. Exptl. Biology and Medicine, Am. Soc. Clin. Investigation, Am. Soc. Human Genetics (dir. 1978-81), Inst. Investigaciones Citologicas (Spain, corr.), Biochem. Soc., Société Française de Pediatrie (corr.), South African Human Genetics (hon.), Sigma Xi, Alpha Omega Alpha. Office: U Calif San Diego Dept Pediatrics # 0609A La Jolla CA 92093

NYHUS, LLOYD MILTON, surgeon, educator; b. Mt. Vernon, Wash., June 24, 1923; s. Lewis Guttorm and Mary (Shervem) N.; m. Margaret Goldie Sheldon, Nov. 25, 1949; children: Sheila Margaret, Leif Torger. B.S., Pacific Luth. Coll., 1945; M.D., Med. Coll. Ala., 1947; Honoris Doctoris Causa, Aristotelian U., Thessalonika, Greece, 1968, Uppsala U., Sweden, 1974, U. Chihuahua, Mex., 1975, Jagallonian U., Cracow, Poland, 1980, U. Gama Filho, Rio de Janeiro, 1983, U. Louis Pasteur, Strasbourg, France, 1984, U. Athens, 1989. Diplomate Am. Bd. Surgery (chmn. 1974-76). Intern King County Hosp., Seattle, 1947-48; resident in surgery King County Hosp., 1948-55; practice medicine specializing in surgery Seattle, 1956-67, Chgo., 1967—; instr. surgery U. Wash., Seattle, 1954-56; asst. prof. U. Wash., 1956-59, assoc. prof., 1959-64, prof., 1964-67; Warren H. Cole prof., head dept. surgery U. Ill. Coll. Medicine, 1967-89, emeritus head, 1989—, prof. emeritus, 1993; emeritus surgeon-in-chief U. Ill. Hosp.; sr. cons. surgeon Cook County, West Side VA, Hines (Ill.) VA hosps.; cons. to Surgeon Gen. NIH, 1965-69. Author: Surgery of the Stomach and Duodenum, 1962, 4th edit., 1986, named changed to Surgery of the Esophagus, Stomach and Small Intestine, 5th edit., 1995, Hernia, 1964, 4th edit., 1995, Abdominal Pain: A Guide to Rapid Diagnosis, 1969, 95, Manual of Surgical Therapeutics, 1969, latest rev. edit., 1996, Mastery of Surgery, 1984, 2d edit., 1992, Surgery Ann., 1970-95, Treatment of Shock, 1970, 2d rev. edit., 1986, Surgery of the Small Intestine, 1987; editor-in-chief Rev. of Surgery, 1967-77, Current Surgery, 1978-90, emeritus editor, 1991—; assoc. editor Quar. Rev. Surgery, 1958-61; editl. bd. Am. Jour. Digestive Diseases, 1961-67, Scandinavian Jour. Gastroenterology, 1966—, Am. Surgeon, 1967-89, Jour. Surg. Oncology, 1969—, Archives of Surgery, 1977-86, World Jour. Surgery; contbr. articles to profl. jours. Served to lt. M.C. USNR, 1943-46, 50-52. Decorated Order of Merit (Poland); postdoctoral fellow USPHS, 1952-53; recipient M. Shipley award So. Surg. Assn., 1967, Rovsing medal Danish Surg. Soc., 1973; Disting. Faculty award U. Ill Coll. Medicine, 1983, Disting. Alumnus award Med. Coll. Ala., 1984, Disting. Alumnus award U. Wash., 1993; Guggenheim fellow, 1955-56. Fellow ACS (1st v.p. 1987-88), Assn. Surgeons Gt. Brit. and Ireland (hon.), Royal Coll. Surgeons Eng. (hon.), Royal Coll. Surgeons Ireland (hon.), Royal Coll. Surgeons Edinburgh (hon.), Royal Coll. Physicians and Surgeons Glasgow (hon.); mem. Am. Gastroent. Assn., Am. Physiol. Soc., Pacific Coast Surg. Assn., Am. Surg. Assn. (recorder 1976-81, 1st v.p. 1989-90), Western Surg. Assn., Ctrl. Soc. Clin. Rsch., Chgo. Surg. Soc. (pres. 1974), Ctrl. Surg. Assn. (pres. 1984), Seattle Surg. Soc., St. Paul Surg. Soc. (hon.), Kansas City Surg. Soc. (hon.), Inst. Medicine Chgo., Internat. Soc. Surgery (pres. U.S. sect. 1986-88, pres. 34th World Congress 1991, internat. pres. 1991-93), Internat. Soc. Surgery Found. (sec. treas. 1992—), Collegium Internat. Chirurgiae Digestivae (pres III world congress Chgo. 1974, internat. pres. 1978-84), Soc. for Surgery Alimentary Tract (sec. 1969-73, pres. 1974), Soc. Clin. Surgery, Soc. Surg. Chmn., Soc. U. Surgeons (pres. 1967), Duetschen Gesellschaft für Chirurgie (corr.), Polish Assn. Surgeons (hon.), L'Academie de Chirurgie (France) (corr.), Swiss Surg. Soc. (hon.), Brazilian Coll. Surgeons (hon.), Surg. Biology Club, Warren H. Cole Soc. (pres. 1981), Japan Surg. Soc. (hon.), Assn. Gen. Surgeons of Mex. (hon.), Columbian Surg. Soc. (hon.), Internat. Fedn. Surg. Colls. (hon. treas. 1992—), Sigma Xi, Alpha Omega Alpha, Phi Beta Phi. Home: 310 Maple Row Winnetka IL 60093-1036 Office: M/C 958 840 S Wood St Chicago IL 60612-7317

NYLANDER, ULF MAGNUS YNGVE, ophthalmologist, educator; b. Stockholm, Apr. 17, 1931; s. Yngve and Ebba (Negri) N.; m. Marietta Juslin; children: Magnus, Richard. MD, Karolinska Inst., Stockholm, 1960. Resident in ophthalmology Karolinska Hosp., 1961-68; sr. physician Eye Clinic, Gävle (Sweden) Hosp., 1968-96, head of clinic, 1972-91; asst. prof. Karolinska Inst., Stockholm, 1968—; cons. physician St Göran Hosp., Stockholm, 1962-67. Author: Ocular Damage in Chloroquine Therapy, 1967; inventor in field. Mem. Entomologiska Föreningen, Stockholm, 1946—, Entomogisk Forening, Copenhagen. Mem. Svenska Läkareförbundet, Svenska Läkaresällskapet, Svenska Ögonläkarföreningen, Brazilian Soc. Entomology, Wiener Coleopterologen Verein. Home: Åsvägen 15, S-81833 Valbo Sweden Office: Valbo Eye Clinic, Asvegen 15, 81833 Valbo Sweden

NYLUND, LARS ERIK, obstetrician, gynecologist; b. Sundsvall, Sweden, Aug. 14, 1949; s. Joel Emanuel and Birgit (Angergardh) N.; m. Ulla Birgitta Backe, June 17, 1972; children: Kristofer, Patrik. MD, Karolinska Inst., Stockholm, 1976, PhD, 1982. Assoc. prof. Karolinska Inst., 1986—; head diagnostic ultrasound group, dept. ob-gyn. Huddinge U. Hosp., Stockholm, 1987-92, head in vitro fertilization group, dept. ob-gyn., 1987-92; with in vitro fertilization unit Sophiahemmet Hosp., Stockholm, 1992—. Author papers on utero-placental blood flow, doppler sonography blood velocity measurement, in vitro fertilization. Home: Myrmarksvägen 13, S-14143 Huddinge Sweden Office: Sophiahemmet IVF Unit, Valhallavagen 91, S-11427 Stockholm Sweden

OAK, RONALD STUART, health and safety administrator; b. Fargo, N.D., Dec. 20, 1956; s. Duane Lyle and Beverly Alice (Anderson) O. BS in Environ. Health, Colo. State U., 1979. Cert. indsl. hygienist Am. Bd. Indsl. Hygiene, cert. hazardous materials mgr. Inst. Hazardous Materials Mgmt. Compliance officer Wyo. Occupational Health and Safety Dept., Cheyenne, 1980-82, OSHA consultation program cons., 1982-84; indsl. hygienist Hager Labs., Inc., Denver, 1984-86; from assoc. to sr. indsl. hygienist Ecology and Environment, Inc., Denver, 1987-91; sr. indsl. hygienist Harding Lawson Assocs., Inc., Santa Ana, Calif., 1991-92; health and safety mgr. IT Corp., San Jose, Calif., 1993—. Mem. adv. com. Wyo. Gov.'s Com. on Hazardous Materials Response, Cheyenne, 1983-84; nat. mem. Smithsonian Assocs., Washington, 1990—, contbg. mem., 1995—. Mem. AAAS, N.Y. Acad. Scis., Am. Indsl. Hygiene Assn. Office: IT Corp 2055 Junction Ave San Jose CA 95131-2105

OAKES, ELLEN RUTH, psychotherapist, health institute administrator; b. Bartlesville, Okla., Aug. 19, 1919; d. John Isaac and Eva Ruth (Engle) Harboldt; m. Paul Otis Oakes Sr., June 12, 1937 (dic. April 1974); children: Paul Otis Jr., Deborah Ellen, Nancy Elaine Masters; m. Siegmar Johann Knopp, Nov. 24, 1975. BA in Sociology, Psychology summa cum laude, Oklahoma City U., 1961; MS in Clin. Psychology, U. Okla., 1963, PhD, 1967. Lic. clin. psychologist, Okla. Chief psychometrist Okla. U. Guidance Ctr., Norman, 1962; psychology trainee VA Hosp., Oklahoma City, 1962-64, Cerebral Palsy Ctr., Norman, Okla., 1964-65; psychology intern Guidance Service, Norman, 1965-66, staff psychologist, 1966-67; asst. prof. psychology Okla. U. Med. Sch., Oklahoma City, 1967-70; supr. psychology interns Okla. Univ. Health Scis. Ctr., 1967-80; founder, dir. Timberridge Inst., Oklahoma City, 1970-90, pres., 1980-90; pvt. practice clin. psychologist Oklahoma City, 1970-92; instr. Okla. U. extension course, Tinker AFB, Oklahoma City, 1963, U. Okla., 1965-66; discussion leader Inst. for Tchrs. of Disadvantaged Child Oklahoma City Sch. System, 1966; leader group therapy sessions Asbury Meth. and Westminster Presbyn. Chs., Oklahoma City, 1966; mem. psychology team confs. for hearing disorders, Okla. U. Med. Sch., 1967-70; cons. Oklahoma City Pub. Schs., 1970-72; cons., group leader halfway house, 1972; lectr. chs., PTAs, hosps.; reviewer Am. Psychol. Assn. Civilian Health and Med. Program of the Uniformed Svcs., 1978-89. Workshop conductor on Shame & Sexuality, Zurick Jungian Inst. winter seminar, 1992; attended Européen Congrès de Gestalt Thérapie in Paris, 1992; contbr. articles to profl. jours. Speaker Okla. County Mental Health Assn. Annual Worry Clinic, St. Luke's Ch., Oklahoma City, 1968-92, psychology dept. Sorosis Club, St. Luke's Ch.. Mem. Am. Psychol. Assn. (peer rev. project with CHAMPUS, 1978-89), Okla. Psychol. Assn. (pres. 1975-76). Address: 18 Basore Dr Bella Vista AR 72714-5544

OAKFORD, LAWRENCE XAVIER, electron microscopist, laboratory administrator; b. Cleve., Jan. 6, 1953; s. Gerald Frederick and Mary Elizabeth (Pestak) O.; m. Dorothy Jean Savage, Aug. 18, 1985; children: Tony, Jamil. MS, Calif. State Poly. U., 1977; PhD, Wash. State U., 1986. Teaching asst., technician Calif. State Poly. U., Pomona, 1975-77; rsch. asst. Wash. State U., Pullman, 1977-79, teaching asst., 1977-82; lab. dir. U. North Tex. Health Sci. Ctr., Ft. Worth, 1982—. Contbr. 21 articles to profl. jours. Com. chmn. Cowtown Marathon and 10k Run, Ft. Worth, 1984-96; mentor, judge Ft. Worth Ind. Sch. Dist. Adopt-a-Sch. Program, 1984-93; mem. pastoral coun. St. Andrews Cath. Ch., 1993-95. Mem. AAAS, Electron Microscopy Soc. Am., Societé de Microscopie du Can., Tex. Soc. for Electron Microscopy. Office: UNT Health Sci Ctr Dept Anatomy & Cell Biology 3500 Camp Bowie Blvd Fort Worth TX 76107-2644

OAKLEY, GODFREY PORTER, JR., health facility administrator, medical educator; b. Greenville, N.C., June 1, 1940; s. Godfrey Porter and Carrie O.; m. Mary Ann Bryant, Sept. 2, 1961; children: Martha Gray, Susan Herndon, Robert Bryant. Student, Duke U., 1958-61; MD, Bowman Gray Sch. of Medicine, 1965; MS in Preventive Medicine, U. Washington, 1972. Diplomate Am. Bd. Pediatrics, Nat. Bd. Med. Examiners, Am. Bd. Preventive Medicine, Am. Bd. Med. Genetics. Intern in straight pediatrics Cleve. Met. Gen. Hosp., 1965-66, resident in pediatrics, 1966-68; sr. fellow in teratology and human embryology U. Washington Sch. of Medicine, Ctrl. Lab. Human Embryology, Dept. of Pediatrics, Seattle, 1970-72; sr. fellow U. Washington Sch. Pub. Health and Community Medicine, Seattle, 1971-72; EIS officer leukemia sect. Ctrs. Disease Control and Prevention (CDC), Atlanta, 1968-70, chief etiology studies sect., bur. epidemiology, cancer and birth defects, 1972-81; chief birth defects br., choronic diseases divisn. Nat. Ctr. Environ. Health, Ctrs. Disease Control and Prevention, Atlanta, 1981-85, dir. divsn. birth defects and devel. disabilities, 1985—; clin. asst. prof. pediatrics divsn. med. genetics Emory U., Atlanta, 1968-70, 72—, clin. asst. prof. gynecology-obstetrics divsn. med. genetics, 1981—; mem. visiting med. staff Grady Meml. Hosp., Atlanta, 1974—; med. adv. bd. Ctrs. Disease Control & Prevention (CDC); mem. task force on predictors of hereditary disease or congenital defects NIH Consensus Conf., 1979; mem. genetics coordinating com. NIH/CDC; mem. adv. com. biometric and epidemiological methodology FDA/CDC; cons. bur. med. svcs. FDA; mem. Chronic Diseases Surveillance Working Group; mem. patient registry com. Cystic Fibrosis Found., med. adv. coun., 1978—; mem. drug experience coordinating com. Dept. Health, Edn. and Welfare; mem. genetics com. Ga. Dept. Human Resources, 1980—; ex-officio mem. genetic diseases rev. and adv. com. Health Svcs. Adminstrn., 1981; mem. master community health program, interdisciplinary faculty com., curriculum com. Emory U.; mem. working group on heart disease epidemiology Nat. Heart, Lung and Blood Insts., 1978; mem. ad hoc com. on Alpha-fetoprotein Pub. Health Svc.; mem. profl. adv. coun. Spina Bifida Assn. Am., 1981—; mem. WHO EURO-China Consultation, Beijing, China, 1983; lectr. in field. Mem. editorial bd. Pediatric & Perinatal Epidemiology, 1987-89; contbr. articles to profl. jours., chpts. to books. Nancy Lybrook Lasater scholar 1961-67; recipient Physician's Recognition award AMA, 1973-76, Outstanding Svc. medal Pub. Health Svc., 1981, Meritorious Svc. award, 1988, Spl. Recognition award, 1993, President's Excellence award Spina Bifida Assn. Am., 1988-89, Disting. Alumnus award U. Washington Sch. Pub. Health, 1990. Mem. Am. Acad. Pediatrics (past com. drugs/CDC liaison, com. genetics 1990, exec. com. 1990—, CDC rep. Ga. chpt. 1993), Am. Soc. Human Genetics, Am. Coll. Epidemiology, Am. Coll. Med. Genetics, Atlanta Genetics Soc., Greater Atlanta Pediatric Soc., Atlanta Obstetrical and Gynecological Soc. (assoc.), Soc. Epidemiologic Rsch., Soc. Pediatric Rsch., Teratology Soc. (pres. elect 1983-84, pres. 1984-85, editorial bd. Teratology 1978-83, edn. com. 1988), Internat. Clearinghouse Birth Defects Monitoring Systems (chmn. 1981-82, vice chmn. 1982-83, chmn. 1983-84), Alpha Omega Alpha. Home: 2224 Kodiak Dr NE Atlanta GA 30345-4152 Office: CDC NCEH BDDD 4770 Buford Hwy NE # F34 Atlanta GA 30341-3724

OAKS, JOHN ADAMS, cell biologist, parasitologist; b. Alma, Mich., Apr. 8, 1942; s. L. Robert and Mathilda R. (Vaschak) O.; m. Rebecca Neese; children: Jeffrey, Timothy. BA, Colby Coll., 1964; MS, Tulane U., 1968, PhD, 1970. Asst. professor parasitology Sch. Pub. Health Tulane U., New Orleans, 1970-73; from asst. to assoc. prof. Sch. Medicine U. Iowa, Iowa City, 1973-82; assoc. prof. Sch. Vet. Medicine U. Wis., Madison, 1982—; coord. Ctr. Rsch. and Tng. in Parasitic Diseases, U. Wis., 1984-95; cons. Am. Med. Womens Hosp. Svc. com. Contbr. articles to profl. jours. Mem. Am. Soc. Parasitologists (coun. mem. 1990-93, v.p. 1995-96, pres-elect 1996—), Am. Soc. Cell Biologists, Southwestern Assn. Parasitologists, Am. Soc. Tropical Medicine Hygiene. Office: U Wis Dept Comp Biosci Sch Vet Medicine 2015 Linden Dr W Madison WI 53706-1102

OAKS, MAURICE DAVID, retired pharmaceutical company executive; b. Everett, Pa., Jan. 22, 1934; s. Jacob Garvin and Hannah Alma (Young) O.; m. Judith Ann Rayne; 1 child, Kimberly. BS in Biology, Franklin and Marshall Coll., 1956. Sales rep. Squibb Pharm, Salisbury and Balt., Md., 1959-69; div. sales mgr. Squibb Pharm., Columbus, Ohio, 1969-71; product mgr. Squibb Pharm., Princeton, N.J., 1971-76, group product dir. antibiotics, cardiovasculars, and insulin, 1976-78, dir. product planning, U.S., 1979-80, v.p. world wide mktg. devel., 1980-82, v.p. mktg. svcs., 1983-85, pres. Princeton Pharm. Products, 1985-89; exec. v.p. Squibb Pharm. Group U.S., Princeton, N.J., 1989-90; v.p. worldwide ops. planning Bristol-Myers Squibb Pharms. Ops., Princeton, 1990-92; bd. dirs. Nat. Pharm. Coun., McLean, Va., 1985-90, mem. exec. com., 1988-90; bd. dirs., mem. audit com. Penn Engring. Mfg., Danboro, Pa. Mem. coun. Franklin and Marshall Coll. Commn. on Found. and Corp. Support, Lancaster, Pa., 1987-90, ann. fund class capt., 1991-96; mem., pres. Mid-Atlantic regional adv. coun. Franklin and Marshall Coll.; bd. dirs. Surf's Edge Condo Assn., Ocean City, Md., 1995—; active YMCA, Doylestown, Pa. With U.S. Army, 1956-58. Mem. Doylestown Country Club (Pa.). Republican. Methodist.

OATES, GEOFFREY DONALD, surgeon, consultant; b. Wolsingham, Durham, England, May 16, 1929; s. Thomas and Dorothy Verne (Jones) O.; m. Mollie Parfitt Edwards, June, 1954 (dec. Dec. 1972); children: John, Susan; m. Elizabeth Anne Wife, Mar. 31st, 1973. BSc with honors, U. Birmingham, England, 1950, MB Ch.B, 1953; MS in Surgery, U. Ill., 1964. Lectr. in anatomy U. Birmingham, England, 1954-55; with surg. tng. program U. Birmingham Hosps., West Midlands Health Authority, England, 1957-66; cons. surgeon U. Birmingham Hosps., 1966-94, emeritus, 1994—; instr. surgery, rsch. fellow U. Ill., Chgo., 1963-64, vis. prof., Thomas Bombek lectr., 1994; vis. rsch. fellow U. Wis., Madison, 1966; Frickman lectr. U. Minn., Mpls., 1989. Author: (with others) The Pathological Basis of Medicine, 1972, Clinical Trials, 1977; editor Updates in Colo-Proctology, 1992; contbr. articles to profl. jours. Capt. Royal Army MC, 1955-57. Exch. Travel Fulbright fellow, 1963-64. Fellow Royal Coll. Surgeons, Royal Soc. Medicine (pres. oncology sect. 1980-81, pres. coloproctology sect. 1989-90); mem. Assn. Coloproctology Great Britain and Ireland (pres. 1990-91), Internat. Soc. Surgery, Internat. Assn. Endocrine Surgeons. Home: 14 Hintlesham Ave, Birmingham West Midlands, England B15 2PH Office: 81 Harborne Rd, Birmingham West Midlands, England B15 3HG

OATES, JOHN ALEXANDER, III, medical educator; b. Fayetteville, N.C., Apr. 23, 1932; s. John Alexander and Isabelle (Crowder) O.; m. Meredith Stringfield, June 12, 1956; children: David Alexander, Christine Larkin, James Caldwell. BS magna cum laude, Wake Forest Coll., 1953; MD, Bowman Gray Sch. Medicine, 1956. Intern, then asst. resident medicine N.Y. Hosp.-Cornell U. Med. Center, N.Y.C., 1956-58, 61-62; clin. assoc., then sr. investigator Nat. Heart Inst., 1958-63; mem. faculty Vanderbilt U. Sch. Medicine, 1963—, prof. medicine and pharmacology, 1969—, Werthan prof. investigative medicine, 1974-84, chmn. dept. medicine, 1983—; mem. drug research bd. Nat. Acad. Scis.-NRC, 1967-71; chmn. pharmacology and toxicology tng. com. Nat. Inst. Gen. Med. Scis., 1969-70; mem . adv. coun. Nat. Heart, Lung and Blood Inst., 1985-89. Fellow ACP, Am. Acad. Arts & Scis.; mem. Am. Fedn. Clin. Rsch. (pres. 1970-71), Am. Soc. Clin. Investigation (v.p. 1976-77), Assn. Am. Physicians (pres. 1981-82), Am. Soc. Pharmacology and Exptl. Therapeutics (chmn. exec. com. divsn. clin. pharmacology 1967-69), Inst. of Medicine. Home: 6440 Brownlee Dr Nashville TN 37205-3162 Office: Vanderbilt U Med Ctr Dept Internal Medicine D3100 MCN Nashville TN 37232-2358

OATES, JOYCE MARIE, psychiatrist; b. Salt Lake City, Mar. 31, 1948; d. Douglas Francis and Lois Joy (Allgaier) O. BS, U. Utah, 1970, MD, 1974. Diplomate Am. Bd. Psychiatry and Neurology. Intern Pa. Hosp., Phila., 1974-75; resident in psychiatry Inst. of Pa. Hosp., Phila., 1975-78; physician Intensive Treatment unit Copper Mountain Community Mental Health Ctr., Salt Lake City, 1978-79; pvt. practice psychiatry Salt Lake City, 1980-88; med. dir. psychiatry Yuma (Ariz.) Reg. Med. Ctr., 1988-90; psychiatrist locum tenens CompHealth, Salt Lake City, 1990; pvt. practice psychiatrist Las Vegas, 1990—; med. dir. Cinnamon Hills residential treatment, 1993—; med. dir., part owner Vista Treatment Ctr., St. George, Utah, 1995—. Mem. Latter Day Saints.

OATES, MARY ELIZABETH, radiologist; b. Boston, June 20, 1954; d. Robert George Oates and Joan Marie (Artesani) Snelling; m. Donald Edloe Winfrey, Sept. 13, 1981; children: Victoria Joan, Olivia Kathryn, Cecilia Jeanne. AB summa cum laude, Smith Coll., 1976; MD, Boston U., 1981. Diplomate Am. Bd. Radiology. Chief div. nuclear medicine New England Med. Ctr., Boston, 1986—; assoc. prof. radiology Tufts U. Sch. Medicine, Boston, 1986—; examiner Am. Bd. Radiology, Louisville, 1995—. Mem. Am. Assn. Women Radiologists, Radiol. Soc. N.Am., Soc. Nuclear Medicine. Office: NEMC #228 750 Washington St Boston MA 02111

O'BANNION, MINDY MARTHA MARTIN, nurse; b. Cushing, Okla., Aug. 19, 1953; d. John William and Martha Florence (Vineyard) Martin; student Okla. State U., 1971-73, Oscar Rose Jr. Coll., 1973; grad. St. Anthony Sch. Nursing, 1975; RN, Tex.; m. William Neal O'Bannion, Oct. 9, 1976; children: Mindi Martha Mae, William Neale Aaron. Med. clk. Martin Clinic, Cushing, Okla., 1968-72; nursing asst. Cushing Mcpl. Hosp., 1973-75, head nurse surg. fl., 1975-76, charge nurse med. unit, 1978-79, 82-83; staff nurse Met. Hosp., Dallas, 1985; staff nurse med. unit Mesquite (Tex.) Community Hosp., 1985-87; nurse post partum unit and discharge edn. post partum unit Trinity Med. Ctr., Carrollton, Tex., 1987—. ind. beauty cons. Mary Kay Cosmetics, Dallas, Tex., 1993—. Mem. social com. Royal Haven Bapt. Ch. Women's Missionary Union, Dallas, 1977-78; mem. extension dept. nursery First Bapt. Ch., Cushing, 1979-82, extension dept. presch., 1982-84; mem. extension dept presch. Royal Haven Bapt. Ch., Dallas, 1986-87; mem. Montgomery Elem. Sch. PTA, Farmers Branch, Tex., 1986-94, Vivian Field Jr. H.S. PTA, Farmers Branch, 1993—, R.L. Turner High Sch. PTA, Farmers Branch/Carrollton, 1995—; treas., mem. nominating com. Joyce Harms group Women's Missionary Union; clk., charter mem. Brookhaven Bapt. Ch., Farmers Br., 1989-92; mem. Valwood Park Baptist Ch., Farmers Br., 1994—. Mem. Am., Tex., Okla. State Nurses Assns., St. Anthony Hosp. Sch. Nursing Alumnae, Bluebonnet Shelties (founder), Tau Beta Sigma, Alpha Xi Delta (corr. sec. 1973). Baptist. Home: 13505 Onyx Ln Dallas TX 75234-4912

O'BARA, KENNETH J., physician; b. Detroit, Feb. 27, 1947; s. John Joseph and Catherine (Levens) O'Bara; m. Marianne Schwartz, July 29, 1972; children: Thomas, Mickel. BSE, U. Mich., Ann Arbor, 1969, MD,

1976. Diplomate Am. Bd. Emergency Medicine. Resident Truman Med. Ctr., Kansas City, Mo., 1976-79; mem. staff St. Joseph Mercy Hosp., Ann Arbor, 1979-80, Centralia (Wash.) Gen. Hosp., 1980-81, St. Helen's Hosp., Chehalis, Wash., 1980-81, Valley Med. Ctr., Renton, Wash., 1981—; ACLS affiliate faculty Am. Heart Assn., Seattle, 1982-86; co-dir. Assn. Emergency Physicians, Seattle, 1983-85. Fellow Am. Coll. Emergency Physicians, Wash. State Med. Soc., King County Med. Soc. Office: 8009 S 180th St Ste 103 Kent WA 98032

OBARSKI, TIMOTHY PAUL, cardiologist; b. Chgo., Jan. 17, 1956; s. Paul Peter and Elizabeth Geraldine (Ostrowski) O.; m. Catherine Marie Berkowicz, Mar. 26, 1983; children: Corinne Patricia, Kevin Timothy. BS, U. Ill., 1979; DO, Chgo. Coll. Osteo. Medicine, 1983. Intern Chgo. Osteo. Hosps., 1983-84; resident in internal medicine Cleve. Clinic Found., 1984-87; fellow in cardiology Cleve. Clinic, 1987-90; staff cardiologist Riverside Meth. Hosps., Columbus, Ohio, 1990—, dir. echocardiography, 1994—; pvt. practice, Columbus, 1996—. Contbr. articles to profl. jours. Fellow ACP, Am. Coll. Cardiology; mem. Am. Soc. Echocardiography, Am. Osteo. Assn., AMA. Roman Catholic. Office: Heart Specialists Ohio 500 Thomas Ln Columbus OH 43214

O'BENAR, JOHN DEMARION, neurophysiologist; b. Chgo., Apr. 10, 1943; s. Jack Jay and Geraldine Agnes (Light) O'B.; m. Mary Caroline Teal, June 18, 1970. BA, Cornell Coll., 1964; MS, U. Ill., 1968, PhD, 1971; postdoctoral study, U. Calif., Berkeley, 1972; postgrad., U. Wis., 1973. Surg. rsch. tech. Billings Hosp. U. Chgo., 1958-61; teaching asst. U. Ill., Urbana, 1968-69; rsch. physiologist Naval Weapons Ctr., Crane, Ind., 1972-75, Naval Aerospace Med. Rsch. Lab., Pensacola, Fla., 1975-78; analytical chemist Army Aviation Ctr., Ft. Rucker, Ala., 1978-80; rsch. physiologist Letterman Army Inst. Rsch., San Francisco, 1980-93, Inst. Surg. Rsch., San Antonio, 1993—; railroad lighting cons. U.S. Dept. Transp., Washington, 1973-74; battlefield target acquisition cons. U.S. Dept. Navy, Washington, 1972-74, cons. Project Sanguine, 1976-78; contracting officers rep. Army Med. R&D Command, 1983-93. Author: Advances in Blood Substitute Research, 1983; contbr. chpts. to books and articles to profl. jours. Co-founder Innerarity Inst., Pensacola, 1976. Fellow NIH, 1967-71, Nat. Eye Inst., 1971-72, Marine Biol. Lab., 1967-68. Mem. Am. Physiol. Soc., Shock Soc., Phi Sigma. Home: 127 Downing Dr San Antonio TX 78209 Office: Inst Surg Rsch 3400 Rawley E Chambers Ave Fort Sam Houston TX 78234-6315

OBERDORSTER, GUNTER, toxicology educator and researcher; b. Cologne, Germany, Feb. 27, 1939; came to U.S., 1979; s. Ewald and Liesel (Selbach) O.; m. Ingeborg Gerda Karden, Mar. 22, 1968; children—Jan, Eva, Uta. D.V.M., U. Giessen, 1964, Ph.D. (Dr. Med. Vet.), 1966. Diplomate in pharmacology and toxicology. Scientist Pharm. Industry, Cologne, Fed. Republic Germany, 1965-67; asst. prof. U. Cologne, 1968-71; mem. sci. staff Fraunhofer Inst., Grafschaft, Fed. Republic Germany, 1971-79; assoc. prof. toxicology U. Rochester, N.Y., 1979-89, full prof., 1989—, head divsn. respiratory biology and toxicology; mem. contact group heavy metals European Commn., Brussels, 1977-79; cons. WHO, Geneva, 1983—, sci. adv. bd. EPA, Washington, 1984—, UNEP, Geneva, 1985, N.Y. State Health Dept., 1987. Contbr. articles to profl. jours.; editorial bd. Jour. Aerosols in Medicine, Inhalation Toxicology. Recipient Joseph von Fraunhofer prize, 1982; grantee EPA-Dept. Energy, 1979-81, NIH, 1982—. Mem. Am. Thoracic Soc., Soc. Toxicology (career achievement award inhalation specialty sect. 1996), Am. Conf. of Govtl. and Indsl. Hygienists, Internat. Soc. Aerosols in Medicine. Avocations: literature, skiing, rowing. Home: 121 Southern Pky Rochester NY 14618-1052 Office: U Rochester Dept Environ Medicine Rochester NY 14642

OBERHEIM, WILLIAM STEVEN, urologist; b. Flushing, N.Y., June 16, 1942; s. Arthur Joseph and Pauline (Ziembo) O.; m. Nancy Elizabeth Boeckeler, July 2, 1966; children: Christopher Marc, David Michael, Eric Martin, Nancy Ann. BA, Iona Coll., 1963, BS, 1964; MD, Albany Med. Coll., 1968. Diplomate Am. Bd. Urology. Intern Albany (N.Y.) Med. Ctr. Hosp., 1968-69, resident in urology, 1971-74, chief resident urology, 1974-75; urologist Childs Hosp., Albany, 1975—; asst. prof. surgery Albany Med. Coll., 1975—; urologist Albany Meml. Hosp., 1975—; assoc. urologist St. Peter's Hosp., Albany, 1975—; cons. Albany VA Hosp., 1975—; pres. Albany Urology Test Ctr., 1975—; mem. exec. com. Child's Hosp., Albany, 1990-92, St. Peter's Hosp., Albany, 1988-90; mem. profl. adv. bd. Albany Med. Ctr. Hosp., 1980. Author: Urologic Clinics of N.A., 1975, Urologic Oncology, 1977. Mem. adv. bd. MS Soc., Albany, 1996. Lt. Comdr. USNR, 1969-71. Mem. N.Y. State Med. Soc., Albany County Med. Soc., Lake George Yacht Club. Roman Catholic. Home: Upper Font Grove Rd Slingerlands NY 12159 Office: 317 S Manning Blvd Albany NY 12208

OBERHELMAN, HARRY ALVIN, JR., surgeon, educator; b. Chgo., Nov. 15, 1923; s. Harry Alvin and Beatrice (Babel) O.; m. Betty Jane Porter, June 12, 1946; children: Harry Alvin III, James I., Robert P., Thomas L., Nancy L. Student, Yale U., 1942-43; B.S., U. Chgo., 1946, M.D., 1947. Diplomate: Am. Bd. Surgery. Intern U. Chgo. Clinics, 1947-48, resident in surgery, 1948-51, 52-57; asst. prof., then assoc. prof. surgery U. Chgo. Sch. Medicine, 1957-60; mem. faculty Stanford (Calif.) Sch. Medicine, 1960—, prof. surgery, 1964-95, prof. emeritus, 1995—; mem. div. licensing Calif. Bd. Med. Quality Assurance, 1970-82. Author papers in field. Served with USAF, 1951-53. Mem. AMA, Calif. Med. Assn., Soc. Univ. Surgeons, Am., Western, Pacific Coast surg. assns., Soc. Alimentary Tract, Halsted Soc., Fedn. State Med. Bds. U.S. (bd. dirs. 1979-82). Home: 668 Cabrillo St Stanford CA 94305-8404

OBERSTEIN, MARYDALE, geriatric specialist; b. Red Wing, Minn., Dec. 30; d. Dale Robert and Jean Ebba-Marie (Holmquist) Johnson; children: Kirk Robert, Mark Paul, MaryJean. Student, U. Oreg., 1961-62, Portland State U., 1962-64, Long Beach State U., 1974-76. Cert. geriatric specialist, Calif. Florist, owner Sunshine Flowers, Santa Ana, Calif., 1982—; pvt. duty nurse Aides in Action, Costa Mesa, Calif., 1985-87; owner, activity dir., adminstr. Lovelight Christian Home for the Elderly, Santa Ana, 1987—; activity dir. Bristol Care Nursing Home, Santa Ana, 1985-88; evangelist, speaker radio show Sta. KPRZ-FM, Anaheim, Calif., 1985-88; adminstr. Leisure Lodge Resort Care for Elderly in Lake Forest, Lake Forest; nursing home activist in reforming laws to eliminate bad homes, 1984-90; founder, tchr. hugging classes/laughter therapy terminally ill patients, 1987—; founder healing and touch therapy laughter Therapy, 1991-93; bd. dirs. Performing Arts Ctr.; speaker for enlightenment and healing. Author (rewrite) Title 22 Nursing Home Reform Law, Little Hoover Commn.; model, actress and voiceovers. Bd. dirs. Orange County Coun. on Aging, 1984—; chairperson Helping Hands, 1985—, Pat Robertson Com., 1988, George Bush Presdl. Campaign, Orange County, 1988; bd. dirs., v.p. Women Aglow Orange County, 1985—; evanglist, pub. spkr., v.p. Women Aglow Huntington Beach; active with laughter therapy and hugging classes for terminally ill. Recipient Carnation Silver Bowl, Carnation Svc. Co., 1984-85, Gold medal Pres. Clinton; named Woman of Yr., Kiwanis, 1985, ABI, 1990, Am. Biog. Soc., Woman of Decade; honored AM L.A. TV Show, Lt. Gov. McCarthy, 1984. Mem. Calif. Assn. Residential Care Homes, Orange County Epilepsy Soc. (bd. dirs. 1986—), Calif. Assn. Long Term Facilities. Home: 2722 S Diamond St Santa Ana CA 92704-6013

OBERT, JESSIE CRAIG, nutritionist, consultant; b. Port Byron, Ill., Mar. 26, 1911; d. Walter Thomas and Clara D.C. Craig; m. Carl B. Obert, Dec. 7, 1935 (dec. 1943). BA, Park Coll., Parkville, Mo., 1931; SM, U. Chgo., 1943; PhD, Ohio State U., 1951. Nutritionist Chgo. Welfare Dept., 1937-42; dir. nutrition ARC, Phoenix, 1943-47; instr. Ohio State U., Columbus, 1947-51, UCLA, 1952-53; chief div. nutrition L.A. County Health Dept., L.A., 1953-76; ind. nutrition cons. L.A., 1976—. Author college textbook: Community Nutrition, 1986. Named Disting. Alumna, Ohio State U., 1976, Park Coll., 1978; recipient recognition for svc. Am. Home Econs. Assn., 1970. Mem. APHA, Am. Dietetic Assn. (del. 1965-71), Calif. Dietetic Assn. (outstanding mem. award 1977, Dolores Nyhus award 1989). Home: 2400 S Fremont Ave Alhambra CA 91803-4319

O'BOYLE, LOUIS JOHN, physician; b. Scranton, Pa., Oct. 20, 1964; s. John Martin and Phyllis A. (Iannuzzo) O'B.; m. Julianne Jean Lesko, Sept. 11, 1993. BS, U. Scranton, 1986; DO, Phila. Coll. Osteo. Medicine, 1990. Diplomate Am. Bd. Internal Medicine. Intern Community Gen. Hosp., Reading, Pa., 1990-91; internal medicine resident Hershey (Pa.) Med. Ctr., 1991-94, chief resident and instr., 1994-95; program coord. Scranton (Pa.)-Temple U., 1995-96; assoc. dir. Scranton-Temple Residency Program, 1996—; utilization rev. mem., Mercy Hosp., Scranton, 1995—, recruitment coord., 1995—. Mem. AMA, Am. Osteo. Assn., Am. Coll. Physicians, Pa. Med. Soc., Pa. Osteo. Med. Assn., Lackawanna County Med. Soc. Republican. Roman Catholic. Home: 555 Winter St Old Forge PA 18518 Office: Scranton Temple Residency Program 746 Jefferson Ave Scranton PA 18510

OBRAMS, GUNTA IRIS, research administrator; b. Düsseldorf, Germany, Sept. 2, 1953; came to U.S., 1961; d. Robert and Olga (Baltins) O.; m. Malcolm DeWitt Patterson, Dec. 22, 1975; 1 child, Andrew McDougal Patterson. BS in Biology cum laude, Rensselaer Poly. Inst., 1977; MD, Union U., Albany, N.Y., 1977; MPH, Johns Hopkins U., 1982, PhD, 1988. Resident in obstetrics and gynecology Ea. Va. Grad. Sch. Medicine, Norfolk, 1977-78; community physician Southampton Meml. Hosp., Franklin, Va., 1978-81; resident in gen. preventive medicine sch. hygiene and pub. health Johns Hopkins U., Balt., 1981-84, project dir., 1983-85, med. dir., 1985-86; med. officer divsn. cancer etiology Nat. Cancer Inst., Bethesda, Md., 1986-89, dep. chief, 1989-90, chief, 1990—. Editor: (with M. Potter): The Epidemiology and Biology of Multiple Myeloma, 1991; contbr. articles to profl. jours. With USPHS, 1987—. Recipient Nat. Cancer Inst. Nat. Rsch. Svc. award, 1981, Rsch. Career award Nat. Inst. Occupational Safety & Health; scholar Am. Med. Women's Assn., 1977. Mem. Phi Beta Kappa, Delta Omega, Alpha Omega Alpha. Office: National Cancer Institute 6130 Executive Blvd Ste 535 Bethesda MD 20892

O'BRIEN, CHARLES P., psychiatrist, educator. BA, Tulane U., 1960, MS, 1964, MD, 1966, PhD in Neurophysiology, 1964. Resident in internal medicine Mass. Gen. Hosp., 1964-65; neurologist, psychiatrist Tulane U., 1965-67, Nat. Hosp. Nervous Disorders, 1967-68; psychiatrist U. Pa., Phila., 1968-69, from instr. to asst. prof. to assoc. prof., 1969-78, prof. psychiatry, 1978—, vice chmn., 1986—; tchg. asst. neurophysiology Tulane Med. Sch., 1965-66, instr., 1966-67; vis. prof. Sch. Medicine Hahnemann U., 1980; Pfizer vis.prof. Albert Einstein Coll. Medicine, 1990. Fellow APA, Am. Coll. Neuropsychopharmacology; mem. Psychiat. Rsch. Soc., Am. Acad. Neurol., Soc. Psychotherapy Rsch., Am. Psychosomatic Soc., Inst. Medicine NAS, Coll. on Problems of Drug Dependence, Soc. Neurosci., Assn. Rsch. Nervous and Mental Dis. (pres. 1989-90). Office: U Pa VA Med Ctr 3900 Chestnut St Philadelphia PA 19104

O'BRIEN, DANA ELIZABETH, psychologist; b. Cape Canaveral, Fla., Dec. 20, 1952; d. Joseph Francis and Elizabeth (Brown) O'B.; m. John Joseph O'Shea Jr., Aug. 22, 1981; children: Brendan Seth, Colin John. BS, Trinity Coll., 1974; MS, Syracuse U., 1977, PhD, 1980. Diplomate Am. Bd. Forensic Examiners (bd. cert. forensic examiner); lic. psychologist, Md. Asst. coord. Child and Adolescent Svc., Syracuse (N.Y.) U., 1979-80; asst. prof. and clin. psychologist Hobart and William Smith Coll., Geneva, N.Y., 1980-81; dir., health ctr. Hood Coll., Frederick, Md., 1981-82; psychologist Walter P. Carter Ctr., Carruthers, Balt., 1983-84; clin. psychologist Annapolis, Silver Spring, Md., 1982—. Mem. APA., Md. Psychol. Assn., Nat. Register of Health Svc. Providers in Psychology, Acad. Family Mediators, Phi Beta Kappa. Office: 200 Forbes St Ste 303 Annapolis MD 21401-1538 also: 11161 New Hampshire Ave Silver Spring MD 20904-2606

O'BRIEN, DANIEL JOSEPH, pharmacologist, toxicologist; b. Chgo., Aug. 23, 1931; s. Daniel Joseph and Mary Isabelle (Horan) O'B.; m. Ruth Marilyn Glass, May 4, 1957; children: Mary Kathleen, Kevin Daniel. BS, Loras Coll., 1953; MS, So. Ill. U., 1960; PhD, Ind. U., 1964. Cert. in regulatory affairs by Regulatory Affairs Certification Bd., forensic examiner, forensic medicine Am. Bd. Forensic Medicine. Assoc. dir. Gillette Co., Rockville, Md., 1963-70; dir. Lakeside Labs., Milw., 1970-75; corp. mgr. Mobay Chem. Corp., Stilwell, Kans., 1976-83; pres. D.J. O'Brien & Assocs. Inc., Olathe, Kans., 1983—. Sgt. U.S. Army, 1956-57. Fellow, So. Ill. U., 1958-59, NIH, 1962-63. Mem. Am. Soc. Pharm. and Exptl. Therapeutics, Soc. Toxicology, Regulatory Affairs Profls. Soc. (cert.), Internat. Soc. Occupl. Medicine and Toxicology, Am. Coll. Toxicology, Am. Coll. Forensic Examiners. Home and Office: 1953 E Frontier Ln Olathe KS 66062-2344

O'BRIEN, GEORGE EDWARD, biology educator; b. Lawrence, Mass., Aug. 5, 1952; s. Frank Alton and Margaret Ester (Wright) O'B.; m. I. Barbara Lydon, Jan. 19, 1987; children: Michael Patrick, Bridget Shea. BS in Biol. Sci., Lowell (Mass.) Tech. Inst., 1974; MA in Internat. Edn. Devel., Columbia U., 1979; PhD in Sci. Edn., U. Iowa, 1985. Sci. chmn., tchr. U.S. Peace Corps/Mater Spei Coll., Francistown, Botswana, Africa, 1975-78; edn. cons. Ednl. Svcs., Inc., Frankfort, Ill., 1979; sci. chmn., tchr. Berkeley Prep. Sch., Tampa, Fla., 1979-80; tchr. Lawrence (Mass.) High Sch., 1980-81; rsch. coord., instr. U. Iowa, Sec. Student Tng. Prog., Iowa City, 1981-84; instr., coord. NSF, U. Iowa, 1984-85; asst. prof. sci. edn. U. Pitts., 1985-88; asst. prof. sci. edn. Fla. Internat. U., Miami, 1988-92, assoc. prof. sci. edn., 1993—, chairperson elem. edn. dept., 1993—; cons. in field; rsch. assoc. Carnegie Mus. Natural History, Pitts., 1987-90; coord. IBM funded Higher Edn. Grant, Miami, 1990—; mem. editorial review bd. Jour. Elem. Sci. Edn., 1993—. Contbr. articles to profl. jours. Fla. Dept. Edn. grantee, 1990—, Fla. Internat. U. grantee, 1990, 92, Dept. Edn. Pal. Title II grantee, 1986-88, NSF grantee, 1995—, NASA grantee, 1995—; gran; Internat. Edn. Ctr. fellow, 1975, others. Mem. AAAS, Nat. Sci. Tchrs. Assn., Sch. Sci. adn Math. Assn. (policy com. 1987-90), Nat. Assn. Rsch. in Sci. Teaching, Assn. for Edn. of Tchrs. in Sci. (membership com. 1992-95, technology com. 1995—), Assn. for Supervision and Curriculum Devel., Friends of Botswana, Returned Peace Corps Vols. Nat. Group, Pi Lambda Theta. Presbyterian. Office: Fla Internat U Dm # 283 Miami FL 33199

O'BRIEN, JOHN DALE, ophthalmologist; b. Hartford, Conn., Oct. 24, 1932; s. John Bernard and Charlotte Mary O'B.; m. Mary Louise Linthwaite, Dec. 16, 1961; children: David, Michael, James. BS, Trinity Coll., Hartford, 1956; MD, N.Y. Med. Coll., 1960. Diplomate Am. Bd. Opthalmology. Med. staff Southside Hosp., Bayshore, N.Y., 1964—, Good Samaritan Hosp., West Islip, N.Y., 1964—. Contbr. articles to profl. jours. Fellow ACS, Am. Acad. Ophthalmology; mem. Suffolk County Ophthalmology Soc., L.I. Ophthalmology Soc. Republican. Roman Catholic. Office: 375 E Main St Bay Shore NY 11706

O'BRIEN, JOHN DANIEL, psychiatrist; b. Bayonne, N.J., Feb. 25, 1939. BS, St. Peter's Coll., Jersey City, N.J., 1960; MD, Seton Hall Coll., Jersey City, N.J., 1964; cert. in psychoanalysis, William Alanson White Inst., 1977. Diplomate Am. Bd. Psychiatry in Adult, Child and Adolescent Psychiatry. Intern Kansas U. Med. Ctr., Kansas City, 1964-65; resident St. Vincent's Hosp., N.Y.C., 1965-67; child and adolescent psychiatry fellow Columbia Presbyn. Hosp./N.Y. State Psychiat. Inst., 1967-69; dir. child and adolescent psychiatry St. Vincent's Hosp. and Med. Ctr., N.Y.C., 1972-83; dir. training, assoc. dir. child and adolescent psychiatry Mt. Sinai Sch. Med., N.Y.C., 1983-88, NYU Sch. Med., N.Y.C., 1988-90; dir. child and adolescent psychiatry Elmhurst (N.Y.) Hosp. Ctr., N.Y.C., 1990—; pvt. practice adult psychoanalysis, child/adolescent psychiatry N.Y.C., 1977—; supr., tng. analyst William Alanson White Inst., N.Y.C., 1987—; assoc. prof. psychiatry Mt. Sinai Sch. Medicine, 1990—. Maj. USAF, 1969-71, Washington. Recipient training grant for Child and Adolescent Psychiatry St. Vincent's Hosp., Nat. Inst. for Mental Health, 1978. Fellow Am. Psychiatric Assn., Am. Acad. Child and Adolescent Psychiatry (pres. assembly of regional orgns. 1996—), Am. Acad. Psychoanalysis; mem. N.Y. Coun. on Child and Adolescent Psychiatry (pres. 1983), N.Y. Soc. for Adolescent Psychiatry (pres. 1990). Office: 117 E 37th St Ste 1CC New York NY 10016

O'BRIEN, JOHN STEININGER, clinical psychologist; b. Lewisburg, Pa., June 3, 1936; s. Peck Zanders and Esther (Steininger) O'B.; m. Joan Irene Romanos, Nov. 1, 1976; children: Peck David, Timothy. AB, Pa. State U., 1967; MA, So. Ill. U., 1969; PhD, Boston U., 1980. Diplomate Internat. Acad. Profl. Psychotherapists, Internat. Acad. Behavioral Medicine/Psychotherapy. Asst. tchr. educable retarded children Selin's Grove (Pa.) State Sch., 1964-66; clin. rsch. asst. Pa. State U., State Coll., 1966-67; rsch. technician Anna (Ill.) State Hosp., 1968; intern Boston City Hosp., 1968-69, from coord. alcohol study unit to psychologist, 1969-73; clin. instr. psychiatry Sch. Medicine Tufts U., St. Elizabeth's Hosp., Brighton, Mass., 1973-81; dir. psychol. svcs. Baldpate Hosp., Georgetown, Mass., 1981—, dir. outpatient substance abuse rehab. program, 1991—; bio-behavioral cons. Behavioral Medicine Inst., Quincy, Mass., 1985-88; clin. dir. Social Learning Ctr., Quincy, 1971—; behavioral therapist, clin. coord. TAP Boston Childrens Svc., 1973-76. Author: Moments with Peck, 1982; contbr. 45 articles to profl. jours. Mem. Am. Psychol. Assn., Nat. Register Health Svcs. in Psychology, Soc. Study of Addiction, Assn. Advancement Behavioral Therapy, Am. Assn. Clin. Counselors, Biofeedback Soc. Am., Internat. Acad. Profl. Counselors and Psychotherapists. Home and Office: 250 Copeland St Quincy MA 02169-4073

O'BRIEN, MARGARET JOSEPHINE, retired community health nurse; b. N.Y.C., Dec. 5, 1918; d. John J. and Nellie (Coyle) O'B. BS, St.John's U., 1954, MS, 1962; MPH, Columbia U., 1964. With Health Dept., City of New York, 1943-81, assoc. dir. Bur. Pub. Health Nursing, dir. Pub. Health Nursing Svc., asst. commr. pub. health nursing; retired. Contbr. articles to profl. jours. Recipient Outstanding Alumnus of Columbia U. Sch. of Pub. Health award, 1994. Mem. ANA, APHA, NLN, N.Y. State Nurses Assn., N.Y.C. Pub. Health Assn. Home: 11055 72nd Rd Forest Hills NY 11375-5472

O'BRIEN, MARK STEPHEN, pediatric neurosurgeon; b. West New York, N.J., Jan. 2, 1933; s. Mark Peter and Hannah (Dempsey) O'B.; m. Mary Morris Johnson, June 3, 1961 (div.); children: David, Derek, Marcia; m. Karen-Marie Sampson, June 1, 1984; children: Blythe, Blake, Lauren-Blair, Connor. A.B. cum laude, Seton Hall U., 1955; M.D., St. Louis U., 1959. Intern St. John's Hosp., St. Louis, 1959-60; resident in surgery St. John's Hosp., 1960; resident in neurology Charity Hosp., New Orleans, 1962-63; resident in neurosurgery St. Vincent's Hosp., N.Y.C., 1963-64; resident in surgery St. Vincent's Hosp., 1965; sr. resident, chief resident Cin. Children's Hosp., U. Cin., 1965-68, research fellow in neurosurgery, 1966-67, 67-68; NIH spl. fellow in neuroradiology Albert Einstein Coll. Medicine, N.Y.C., 1968-69; mem. faculty dept. surgery Emory U. Sch. Medicine, Atlanta, 1969—; prof. surgery, assoc. prof. pediatrics Emory U. Sch. Medicine, 1979—; chief neurosurgery Henrietta Egleston Hosp. for Children, Atlanta, 1971—; trustee Elaine Clark Center for Exceptional Children; mem. med. adv. bd. Nat. Found., March of Dimes; trustee Henrietta Egleston Hosp. for Children; mem. profl. adv. panel Spina Bifida Assn. Am. Editorial bd. Pediatric Neurosurgery; contbr. chpts. to books, articles to med. jours. Served with USNR, 1960-62. Mem. Am. Assn. Neurol. Surgeons, Soc. Neurol. Surgeons, Congress Neurol. Surgeons, Internat. Soc. Pediatric Neurosurgery, Greater Atlanta Pediatric Soc., Med. Soc. Atlanta, AMA, ACS, Ga. Neurosurg. Soc., Am. Acad. Pediatrics, Am. Soc. Pediatric Neurosurgery, Pediatric Oncology Group, Am. Bd. Pediatric Neurol. Surgery (sec.), Acad. Pediatric Neurosurgeons. Home: 82 Huntington Rd Atlanta GA 30309 Office: 1900 Century Blvd NE Ste 4 Atlanta GA 30345-3304

O'BRIEN, MARY, health services administrator; b. Spokane, Wash., Dec. 1, 1942; d. Robert McCarthy and Eunice (Phillips) O'B.' m. Warren M. Gilligan, June 7, 1988; 1 child, Kelley Theresa. BS, Gonzaga U., 1964; M of Mgmt., Northwestern U., 1987. Dir. chemistry dept. Sherman Hosp., Elgin, Ill., 1965; office mgr. Charles Carroll MD, Elgin, Ill., 1965-82; particle mgr. Northwest Hhealthcare, Hoffman Estates, Ill., 1982-85; healthcare administrator Fox Valley Orthopaedic Inst., Geneva, Ill., 1985—; cons. MKO Cons. Inc., Geneva, 1991—; mem. adv. bd. Bus. Dept. Elgin C.C., 1990—. Mem. BONES, MGMA, ACMPE, Tri-City Family Svcs. (dir. 1991-94), Rotary (pres. 1991-92), Eatlebrook Country Club (social chmn. 1995—). Republican. Roman Catholic. Office: Fox Valley Orthopaedic Inst 2525 Kaneville Rd Geneva IL 60134

O'BRIEN, MAUREEN, nurse case manager; b. Phila., Dec. 5, 1961; d. John Hugh and Margaret Sarah (Filoon) O'B.; m. William Joseph Gallagher, Feb. 10, 1996. Diploma in nursing, Roxborough Meml. Hosp., 1982; BS in Health Svcs. Adminstrn., Phila. Coll. Textiles Sci., 1994. RN, 1982. Staff nurse Doylestown (Pa.) Hosp., 1982-85, Abington (Pa.) Meml. Hosp., 1985-90; utilization rev. specialist/case mgr. Intracorp, Plymouth Meeting, Pa., 1990—. Republican. Roman Catholic. Home: 18 Ivy Meadows Ivyland PA 18974 Office: Intracorp 523 Plymouth Rd Plymouth Meeting PA 19462

O'BYRNE, ELIZABETH MILIKIN, pharmacologist, researcher, endocrinologist; b. Miami, Fla., May 19, 1944; d. Richard Mershon and Anne (Smith) Milikin; m. Brian Kenneth O'Byrne, July 1, 1972; children: Lucy Milikin, Kenneth Daniel. AB in Chemistry, Emory U., 1965, MS in Biochemistry, 1968; PhD in Biochemistry, N.Y. Med. Coll., 1985. Assoc. scientist Eli Lilly Rsch. Labs., Indpls., 1968-70; sr. rsch. scientist CIBA-GEIGY Pharms., Summit, N.J., 1970—. Contbr. articles to profl. jours. Mem. AAAS, N.Y. Acad. Sci., Inflammation Rsch. Assn., Osteoarthritis Rsch. Soc. Home: 234 Sagamore Rd Millburn NJ 07041-2136 Office: CIBA-GEIGY Morris Ave Summit NJ 07901

O'CALLAGHAN, ROBERT MICHAEL, physician assistant; b. Dayton, Ohio, Nov. 28, 1947; s. William Goreham and Mary Ellen (Dagg) O'C.; m. Linda Frances Weed, Aug. 3, 1978; 1 child, Matthew Robert. BS, Ohio U., 1970; Assoc. in Physician Asst., Kettering Coll. Med. Arts, 1979. Cert. physician asst., registered Pa. Environ. safety cons. Ohio Dept. Health, Columbus, 1974-77; physician asst. Vandalia (Ohio) Med. Ctr., 1979—. Coun. City on Union, Ohio, 1989—, pres. bd. park trustees, 1983—; com. Troop 246 Boy Scouts Am., Englewood, Ohio, 1994—; precinct capt. Northmont Bd. Edn., Englewood, 1992—. Fellow Am. Acad. Physician Assts., Ohio Assn. Physician Asst. Home: 106 Tall Timbers Rd Union OH 45322

OCAMPO, TERESITO NARAS, psychiatrist; b. Panpanga, The Philippines, Sept. 30, 1942; s. Lazaro A. and Marcelina (Jaras) O.; m. Marilou Sandico Ocampo; 1 child, Theresa. MD, U. of the Philippines, 1967. Diplomate Am. Bd. Psychiatry and Neurology. Resident in psychiatry William S. Hall Psychiat. Inst., Columbia, S.C.; chmn. dept. psychiatry Med. City Hosp., Pasig, The Philippines; prof., chief of psychiatry Fatima Coll. Medicine. Home: 99 Sampaguita St, Pasig The Philippines Office: Med Bldg, San Miguel Ave Rm 515, Pasig The Philippines

OCH, MOHAMAD RACHID, psychiatrist, consultant; b. Damascus, Syria, Apr. 1, 1956; came to U.S., 1981; s. Seifeddine and Souad (Oubari) O.; m. Marianne Noonan, July 24, 1960; children: Seifeddine, Adam. MD, Aleppo (Syria) U., 1980. Psychiat. cons. Human Resource Inst., Brookline, Mass., 1985; med. dir. Spectrum House, Westboro, Mass., 1986-87; assoc. med. dir. Boston Rd. Clinic, Shrewsbury, Mass., 1985—, v.p., 1989—; med. dir. mental health unit Holden (Mass.) Hosp., 1988-90; med. dir. Basic Health Mgmt., Worcester, Mass., 1988-90; asst. med. dir. Boston Rd. Clinic, Shrewsbury, 1986—, Holden Hosp., 1988—, Basic Health Mgmt., Worcester, 1988—; attending psychiatrist, asst. prof. U. Mass. Med. Ctr., Worcester; dir. mental health unit Milford Whitinsville Hosp., 1990—, chmn. dept. psychiatry, 1991-92; med. dir. Seven Hills Intensive Residential Treatment Program, 1990—; asst. chief psychiatry St. Vincent's Hosp., 1996—; mem. adv. bd. Pfeizer, 1996—; med. dir. HMA behaviral health, 1995—. Mem. Am. Psychiat. Assn., AMA. Moslem. Office: Boston Road Clinic 108 Belmont St Worcester MA 01605-2937

OCHSNER, JOHN LOCKWOOD, thoracic-cardiovascular surgeon; b. Madison, Wis., Feb. 10, 1927; s. Edward William Alton and Isabel (Lockwood) O.; m. Mary Lou Hannon, Mar. 20, 1954; children: John L., Joby Hannon, Katherine Lockwood, Frank Hannon. MD, Tulane U., 1952. Diplomate Am. Bd. Thoracic Surgery (chmn.), Am. Bd. Surgery, Am. Bd. Vascular Surgery. Intern Univ. Mich. Hosp., Ann Arbor, 1952-53, resident, 1953-54; resident Baylor U. Affiliated Hosp., Houston, 1956-58, 1958-59; chief surg. resident Tex. Children's Hosp., 1959-60; instr. Baylor U., Houston, 1960-61; mem. staff Ochsner Clinic, New Orleans, 1961-66, chmn. dept. surgery, 1966-87, chmn. emeritus dept surgery, 1987—; clin. asst. prof. Tulane U., New Orleans, 1961-65, clin. assoc. prof., 1965-70, clin. prof., 1970—. Author: (with others) Coronary Artery Surgery, 1978. Pres. Tennis Patrons Assn. New Orleans, 1972; image amb. City of New Orleans, 1982; bd. dirs. Internat. Trade Mart, New Orleans, 1983. Capt. USAF, 1954-56. Recipient award Life Mag., 1961, Golden Plate Acad. Achievement award, 1962, medal of honor, Ecuador, 1981. Mem. Internat. Soc. Cardiovascular Surgery (pres. N.Am. chpt. 1983-84, internat. pres. 1989-91), Am. Assn. Thoracic Surgery (sec. 1979-83, pres. 1992-93), New Orleans Surg. Soc. (pres. 1977-78), So. Surg. Assn. (pres. 1991), So. Assn. for Vascular Surgery (pres. 1983), Boston Club, La. Club, New Orleans Country Club, City Club, Alpha Omega Alpha. Republican. Home: 84 Audubon Blvd New Orleans LA

70118-5540 Office: Ochsner Clinic & Hosp 1514 Jefferson Hwy New Orleans LA 70121-2429

OCKNER, STEPHEN ALLAN, internist; b. New Kensington, Pa., June 10, 1931; s. Lee and Sara Elinor (Weis) O.; m. Paula Diane Seltzer, June 17, 1955; children: Lee, Samuel A., Benjamin J., Daniel M. MD, U. Pa., 1955. Diplomate Am. Bd. Internal Medicine, Nephrology. Commd. officer USAF, 1955, advanced through grades to col., 1955-75; staff physician Cleve. Clinic Found., 1975—, chmn. dept. gen. internal medicine, 1989-92; assoc. clin. prof. Hershey (Pa.) Med. Sch., 1989—; assoc. prof. Coll. Medicine Ohio State U., Columbus, 1993—. Contbr. articles to profl. jours. Fellow ACP; mem. AMA, Alpha Omega Alpha. Democrat. Office: Cleveland Clinic Found 9500 Euclid Ave Cleveland OH 44195

O'CONNELL, ANNA PORRECA, biologist; b. Phila., Apr. 26, 1937; d. Francis Paul and Anna Agnes (Donatucci) Porreca; AB, Temple U., 1959. Mem. staff Fox Chase Cancer Ctr., Phila., 1959—, research assoc., 1972-81, sr. research assoc., 1981—. Mem. Am. Soc. Microbiology, Pa. Soc. Microbiology, N.Y. Acad. Scis. Author papers in field. Office: 7701 Burholme Ave Philadelphia PA 19111-2412

O'CONNELL, BARBARA EUSTACE, psychiatrist; b. Boston, June 25, 1926; d. William Elliot Whitney and Rosalie (Jones) Ziegler; m. Richard L. O'Connell, Dec. 27, 1947 (div. Apr. 1960); children: Elizabeth W., Abigail L.; m. Arthur E. Gillman, June 27, 1961 (div. Dec. 1980); children: Theodore J., Sarah A.; m. George J. Halpern, Dec. 19, 1981. BA, Cornell U., 1947; MD, Columbia U., 1951. Diplomate Am. Bd. Psychiatry and Neurology. Rotating intern Strong Meml. Hosp., Rochester, N.Y., 1951-53; pvt. practice Bergenfield and Cresskill, N.J., 1953-56; vis. physician Englewood (N.J.) Hosp., 1954-56; resident psychiatry Bronx (N.Y.) Mcpl. Hosp. Ctr., 1958-61, asst. vis. psychiatrist, 1961-66; clin. instr. Albert Einstein Coll. Medicine, Bronx, 1961-66; vis. physician United Hosp., Port Chester, N.Y., 1966-75; pvt. practice Mamaroneck, N.Y., 1961-79, Rye, N.Y., 1979—; clin. asst. prof. psychiatry Cornell U. Med. Coll., N.Y.C., 1976—; asst. attending psychiatrist N.Y. Hosp. and Cornell Med. Ctr., White Plains, N.Y., 1976—. Reviewer Jour. Neuropsychiatry and Neuroscis., 1995—. Mem. Mamaroneck Doctors Com., 1970-79; bd. dirs. Larchmont-Mamaroneck Guidance Ctr., 1971-75; warden St. Thomas's Ch., Mamaroneck, 1979-80; mem. Westchester County Women's Adv. Bd., White Plains, 1984-86. Fellow APA (life), Am. Orthopsychiat. Assn. (life), Am. Assn. Psychoanalytic Physicians; mem. AMA, Am. Med. Women's Assn. (sec. 1980), Am. Acad. Psychiatry and Law, Med. Soc. N.Y., Med. Soc. County of Westchester (bd. dirs. 1988-91), Am. Coll. Forensic Psychiatry, Brevoort Lakeshore Assn. (pres. 1995—), Greenhaven Yacht Club (vice commodore 1988). Episcopalian. Office: 240 Brevoort Ln Rye NY 10580-1012

O'CONNELL, MICHAEL LEONARD, psychologist; b. Waco, Tex., July 25, 1935; s. Harvey Leonard and Frances Pauline (Voelkle) O'C.; m. Mildred Thelma Bartlett, Nov. 10, 1956 (div. 1965); children: Stephen, Timothy, Colleen. Student, Rice U., 1952-53; EdM, Harvard U., 1983, EdD, 1992; DD (hon.), Ch. of Modern Apostles, Miami, Fla., 1982. Ordained minister, Ch. of Modern Apostles. Data ctr. mgr. U.S. Steel, L.A., 1956-62; systems programmer U.S. Steel, San Francisco, 1962-68; systems mgr. Sanders Assocs., Nashua, N.H., 1968-72; programming mgr. Rockwell Internat., L.A., 1972-73; engring. mgr. Digital Equipment Corp., Maynard, Mass., 1973-75, product planning mgr., 1975-82, organizational cons., 1982-84, career counselor, 1984-92; prin. Excalibur Cons. & Counseling, Cambridge, Mass., 1991—; mem. faculty grad. counseling psychology/expressive therapy Lesley Coll., Cambridge, 1994—; mem. Codasyl Exec. Com., Washington, 1975—; chmn. Codasyl Data Description Com., Washington, 1979-82; cons. in field. Author: Data Bases: What's It All About, 1975, Toward An Understanding of The Psychology of Careers, 1991; editorial advisor jour. Info. Systems, London, 1983—; publ., editor Personality and Careers. Counselor So. N.H. Crisis Hot Line, Nashua, 1980-82; mem. adv. bd. Boston AIDS Consortium SPIN, Harvard AIDS Inst. Cpl. USMC, 1953-56. Tex. Dow Inst. scholar, 1952. Mem. APA, Collaboration in Social Architecture, Marine Corps Assn., Mensa (N.H. proctor 1981-84). Home: 8 Newport Rd Cambridge MA 02140-1528

O'CONNELL, PHILIP JOHN, renal physician, researcher; b. Sydney, NSW, Australia, July 27, 1955; s. Patrick Brian and Joanna June (Ryan) O.; m. Belinda Anne Hing, Apr. 26, 1986; children: John Ryan, Georgia Kate. BSc in Medicine, U. NSW, Sydney, 1978, MB BS, 1980; PhD, U. Melbourne, Australia, 1989. Intern, resident med. officer St. Vincent's Hosp., Sydney, 1980-83, renal registrar, 1984; renal registrar Royal North Shore Hosp., Sydney, 1985; vis. assoc., rsch. fellow Royal Melbourne Hosp., 1986-89; postdoctoral fellow Beth Israel Hosp./Harvard Med. Sch., Boston, 1989-92; clin. sr. lectr. Westmead Hosp./U. Sydney, 1992—. Grantee Baxter Healthcare, 1993—, Nat. Health and Med. Rsch. Coun. Australia, 1995-96, Juvenile Diabetes Found. Internat. Program, 1995—. Fellow Royal Australian Coll. Physicians; mem. Internat. Transplantation Soc., Transplantation Soc. of Australia and New Zealand, Australia and New Zealand Soc. of Nephrology. Office: Westmead Hosp, Renal Unit, Westmead NSW 2145, Australia

O'CONNELL, RALPH ANTHONY, psychiatrist, educator; b. N.Y.C., Jan. 26, 1938; s. Ralph E. and Agnes H. (O'Connell) O'C.; m. Jane Burke, June 15, 1963; children: Ralph E. III, Ellen C., John B. A.B. cum laude, Coll. of Holy Cross, Worcester, Mass., 1959; M.D., Cornell U., 1963. Diplomate Am. Bd. Psychiatry and Neurology. Intern, St. Vincent's Hosp. and Med. Ctr. N.Y., N.Y.C., 1963-64, resident, 1964, 67-69, research psychiatrist, 1969-71, chief, inpatient, dept. psychiatry, 1971-76, clin. dir. and vice chmn. psychiatry, 1974-95; prof. psychiatry N.Y. Med. Coll., Valhalla, 1984—, dean and provost N.Y. Med. Coll., 1996—. Editor-in-chief Comprehensive Psychiatry, 1983—. Served as capt. U.S. Army, 1965-66. Fellow Am. Psychiat. Assn., N.Y. Acad. Medicine (trustee 1989—). Roman Catholic. Clubs: University (N.Y.C.). Office: NY Med Coll Valhalla NY 10595

O'CONNELL-GOODFELLOW, EILEEN, speech pathologist; b. Northampton, Mass., Mar. 23, 1958; d. Richard A. and Nancy Jean (Keating) O'Connell; m. N. Kim Goodfellow, Sept. 8, 1979. BS, U. Oreg., 1981; MS, Boston U., 1983. Cert. speech hearing specialist, Mass. Clin. coor. Greenery Rehab. Ctr., Boston; speech lang., pathology dept. supr. Marlborough (Mass.) Hosp.; clin. coord. NovaCare, Inc.; rehab. mgr. Mt. Auburn Home Care, Belmont, Mass.; dir. rehab. svcs. Maine Coast Meml. Hosp., Ellsworth, 1995—. Contbr. articles to profl. jours.; co-author: Group Treatment for Head Injury: A Linguistic and Cognitive Approach, 1988. Mem. Am. Speech Lang. Hearing Assn. Home: RR 4 Box 7 Pickard Rd Ellsworth ME 04605

O'CONNOR, CHRISTOPHER J., health services administrator; b. Rochester, N.Y., July 18, 1968; s. J. Patrick and Nelly (Callens) O'C.; m. Colleen Walsh, Aug. 3, 1991; children: Mark, Timothy. BA, Iona Coll., 1989, MBA, 1992, Post Masters Cert., 1994. Asst. to the dir. grants Iona Coll., New Rochelle, N.Y., 1989-90; spl. edn. tchr., articulation coord. N.Y.C. Bd. Edn., 1990-92; inventory control specialist Mount Vernon (N.Y.) Hosp., 1992-93, asst. dir. materials mgmt., 1993-95, adminstr. for outpatient clinics/managed care, 1995—; adj. prof. Berkeley Coll., 1992-94. Mem. Am. Coll. Healthcare Execs. (assoc.), Met. Health Adminstrs. Assn., Rotary Club Mt. Vernon, Sigma Tau Delta (v.p. 1988), Delta Epsilon Sigma (v.p. 1988). Roman Catholic. Home: 2 Lockwood Ave Apt 3F Bronxville NY 10708

O'CONNOR, DANIEL JOSEPH, ophthalmologist; b. Buffalo, June 21, 1961; s. Cornelius Jude and Rosemary (Robben) O'C.; m. Amy Chadwick Smithies, June 25, 1994. BS, Boston Coll., Chestnut Hill, Mass., 1983; MD, Tulane U., New Orleans, 1987. Intern internal medicine Alton Ochsner Hosp., New Orleans, 1987-88; resident ophthalmology U. Pitts., 1988-91; fellow ophthalmology Yale U., New Haven, 1991-92; ophthalmologist No. Va. Ophthalmology, Falls Church, 1992-94, Post Eye Ctr., Plymouth, Mass., 1994—; mem. steering com. Eye Corp., Memphis, 1995—. Recipient travel scholarship Assn. Rsch. in Vision and Ophthalmology. Fellow Am. Acad. Ophthalmology, Am. Bd. Ophthalmology; mem. AMA, Am. Soc. Cataract and Refractive Surgery. Office: Post Eye Ctr 40 Industrial Park Rd Plymouth MA 02360

O'CONNOR, GINGER HOBBA, speech pathologist; b. Poynette, Wis., Apr. 20, 1951; d. Walter Leslie and Mary Elizabeth (Krause) Hobba; m. William Scott Elliott, Dec. 27, 1973 (div. 1984); children: Todd C., William Trent, Tiffany Paige; m. Michael Robert O'Connor, Aug. 11, 1990; 1 child, Tanner Michael O'Connor. BA, Marietta Coll., 1973; MA, Ohio State U., 1974. Speech pathologist Del. (Ohio) Speech/Hearing Ctr., 1974-75; speech pathologist Washington County Bd. Mental Retardation Devel. Disabilities, Marietta, Ohio, 1975—, supr. dept. communications, 1985—; speech pathologist ancillary staff Marietta Hosp., 1975—; cons., lectr. Ohio U., Athens, 1980—; lectr. South Eastern Ohio Spl. Edn. Resource Ctr., Athens, 1975—; pres., co-founder MR/DD Speech-Lang.-Hearing Network of Ohio, 1992-94. Bd. dirs. Child Devel. Ctr., Marietta, 1977-80, Washington County ARC; mem. med. adv. bd. Headstart, Marietta, 1984—; dist. program chairperson Boy Scouts Am., Parkersburg, W.Va., 1989-92; mem. Ohio Safe Kids Coalition; speech pathologist Operation Smile mission to Russia, 1995, 96; co-chair YMCA com. for Internat. Awareness, 1992—. Mem. Am. Speech Lang. Hearing Assn. (spkr. 1979—), Ohio Speech Lang. Hearing Assn. (legis. coun. rep. 1990-94, pres.-elect 1996-97), Southeastern Ohio Speech Hearing Assn. (v.p. 1982-83, pres. 1983-84), Profl. Assn. for Retarded Adults, Southeastern Ohio Soc. for Augmentative and Alternative Communication. Methodist. Home: 124 Keyser St Marietta OH 45750-1019 Office: Wash Cty Bd Men Ret Devel PO Box 702 Marietta OH 45750-0702

O'CONNOR, MICHELE, health services professional; b. Jersey City, Sept. 7, 1957; d. Joseph and Catherine (Lorgan) O'C. AAS in Med. Records Tech., Hudson County C.C., Jersey City, 1986; BS in Allied Health, Montclair State U., 1992; MPA in Health Svcs. Adminstrn., Fairleigh Dickinson U., 1995. Asst. dir. med. records Gen. Hosp. Ctr., Passaic, N.J., 1988-89; dir. med. records Gen. Hosp. Ctr., Passaic, 1989-95, dir. patient flow, 1995—. Mem. Am. Coll. Health Care Execs. (assoc., accredited record technician), Am. Health Info. Mgmt. Assn., N.J. Health Info. Mgmt. Assn. Office: Gen Hosp Ctr Passaic 350 Boulevard Passaic NJ 07055

O'CONNOR, ROBERT JAMES, gynecologist, consultant; b. S.I., N.Y., Dec. 11, 1919; s. Robert and Anna (Lindsey) O'C.; B.S., Wagner Coll., 1941; M.A., Columbia U., 1947; M.D., SUNY, 1951; m. Olive Errington, Feb. 21, 1943; children: Robert, Carol, Richard. Intern, S.I. Hosp., 1951-53; resident in ob-gyn, Woman's Hosp. N.Y., 1955-58; practice medicine specializing in ob-gyn, N.Y.C. and S.I., 1958—; attending physician in gynecology Sea View Hosp. and Home, S.I., 1958—; attending physician in gynecology S.I. Hosp., 1951—, chief of staff, 1976-78; dir. quality assurance S.I. Univ. Hosp., 1989—; cons. in gynecology USPHS Hosp., 1958—; mem. med. appeals unit N.Y. State Worker's Compensation Bd; mem. N.Y. State Bd. Profl. Med. Conduct, 1991—. Bd. dirs. S.I. chpt. ARC, 1974—, Health Systems Agy., N.Y.C. 1982—, Meals on Wheels, S.I., 1980—, N.Y.C., 1982—; trustee S.I. Hosp., 1979-93, sr. trustee, 1993—; elder Calvary Presbyn. Ch., 1958—; trustee and sec. of bd. Wagner Coll., S.I., 1985-92; chmn. bd. trustees S.I. Inst. Arts & Scis., 1989-94. Served to lt. USN, 1942-46. Diplomate Am. Bd. Ob-Gyn. Fellow Am. Coll. Ob-Gyn, Internat. Coll. Surgeons, Am. Soc. Abdominal Surgeons, N.Y. Micros. Soc.; mem. Med. Soc. N.Y. State (chmn. coordinating coun. 1st dist. br. 1977—, dir. div. med. svcs. 1979-84, dep. exec. v.p. 1984-87), Richmond County Med. Soc. (pres. 1972), AMA, S.I. Inst. Arts and Scis. (chmn. bd., 1989-94), S.I. C. of C. (dir. 1964-66). Republican. Club: Kiwanis (pres. 1968). Home: 33 Valencia Ave Staten Island NY 10301-2023 Office: SI Univ Hosp Sea View Ave Staten Island NY 10305

O'DAY, DENIS MICHAEL, ophthalmologist, educator; b. Melbourne, Victoria, Australia, Dec. 10, 1935; came to U.S., 1967; s. Kevin John and Bernadette John (Hay) O'D.; m. Ann Georgina Despard, May 28, 1966; children: Luke Gerard, Simon Patrick, Edward Daniel. Diploma, Xavier Coll., 1953; MBBS, Melbourne U., 1960. Diplomate Am. Bd. Ophthalmology. Intern St. Vincent's Hosp./U. Melbourne, 1961; resident in internal medicine St. Vincent's Hosp., 1962-64, chief resident dept. medicine, 1964, clin. asst. medicine, 1965-66; 3d asst., mem. asst. Royal Victoria Eye & Ear Hosp., Melbourne, 1967-70; resident in ophthalmology U. Calif., San Francisco, 1970; Wellcome rsch. fellow in corneal disease Inst. Opthalmology, London, 1970-72; asst. prof. ophthalmology Vanderbilt U. Sch. Medicine, Nashville, 1972-74, assoc. prof. ophthalmology, 1974-77; prof. ophthalmology, now chmn. Vanderbilt U. Sch. Medicine, 1977; cons. ophthalmologist Royal Commonwealth Soc. of Blind, Nigeria, 1972; cons. VA Hosp., 1973-74, active staff, 74; mem. active staff Nashville Gen. Hosp., 1974, Park View Hosp., 1980, Vanderbilt Hosp., 1972; mem. cons. staff St. Thomas Hosp.; bd. dirs. Am. Bd. Ophthalmology, Phila., 1988—; proctor lectr. U. Calif., San Francisco, 1993; co-med. dir. Lions Eye Bank and Sight Svc., 1973-86, med. dir. 1986—; bd. dirs. Lions Eye Bank Mid. Tenn., 1987—; ad-hoc mem. NIH Visual Sci. Study Sect., 1977. Author: Management of Functional Impairment due to Cataract, 1993; contbr. numerous articles, abstracts to profl. publs., chpts. to books. Chair ethics com. Cath. Pub. Policy Commn., Nashville, 1991—. Joyn Hayden rsch. fellow, 1965; recipient Felton Bequest and Potter Found. awards, 1967, recognition award Alcon Rsch. Inst., 1983, Sr. Sci. Investigator award Rsch. to Prevent Blindness, 1987, Health Profl. of Yr. award Tenn. chpt. Assn. for Edn. and Rehab. of Blind and Visually Impaired, 1990. Fellow ACS, Royal Australia Coll. Physicians, Royal Soc. Medicine, Am. Acad. Ophthalmology (sec. quality of care com. 1993—, Honor award for Ednl. Contbns. 1981-85, dir. clin. alert program, pub. health com. 1985-88); mem. AMA, AAUP, Am. Ophthalmol. Soc., Assn. for Rsch. in Vision and Ophthalmology, Nashville Acad. Medicine, Nashville Acad. Ophthalmology (v.p. 1980-81), Oxford Ophthalmol. Soc., Royal Australasian Coll. Physicians, Tenn. Acad. Medicine, Tenn. Acad. Ophthalmology. Roman Catholic. Office: Vanderbilt U Med Ctr East Dept Ophthal and Vis Scis Fl 8 Nashville TN 37232-8808*

ODEGAARD, CHARLES EDWIN, history educator; b. Chicago Heights, Ill., Jan. 10, 1911; s. Charles Alfred and Mary (Cord) O.; m. Elizabeth Jane Ketchum, Apr. 12, 1941 (dec. 1980); 1 child, Mary Ann Quarton. AB, Dartmouth Coll., 1932; M.A., Harvard U., 1933, Ph.D., 1937; L.H.D., Lawrence Coll., 1951; LL.D., Miami U., Oxford, Ohio,, 1955, U. B.C., Can., 1959, Gonzaga U., 1962, UCLA, 1962, Seattle U., 1965, U. Mich., 1969; Litt.D., U. Puget Sound, 1963. Asst. in history Radcliffe Coll., 1935-37; from instr. to prof. U. Ill., 1937-48; exec. dir. Am. Council Learned Soc., Washington, 1948-52; prof. history, dean Coll. Lit. Sci. and Arts U. Mich., Ann Arbor, 1952-58; pres. U. Wash., Seattle, 1958-73; pres. emeritus, prof. higher edn. U. Wash., 1974—, prof. biomed. history, 1975—; mem. U.S. Nat. Commn. UNESCO, 1949-55, advisor U.S. del. 5th Gen. Conf., Florence, Italy, 1950; chmn. Commn. Human Resources and Advanced Tng., 1949-53, pres. Internat. Council of Philosophy and Humanistic Studies, 1959-65; mem. adv. com. cultural info. USIA, 1955-62, Western Interstate Com. on Higher Edn., 1959-70, Citizens Com. on Grad. Med. Edn., 1963-66, Nat. Adv. Health Counci USPHS, 1964-68, Nat. Adv. Health Manpower, 1965-67, NEH, 1966-72, Study Commn. Pharmacy, 1973-75; mem. Macy Study Commn. on Acad. Psychiatry, 1978-79. Author: Fideles and Vassi in the Carolingian Empire, 1945; Minorities in Medicine, 1977, Area Health Education Centers, 1979, Dear Doctor: A Personal Letter to a Physician, 1986; contbr. articles on mediaeval history and higher edn. to profl. jours. bd. regents Uniformed U. Health Scis., 1973-80; chmn. Wash. State Bd. Continuing Legal Edn., 1976-79. Served from lt. (j.g.) to lt. comdr. USNR, 1942-46. Recipient Medal of Merit State of Wash., 1989. Mem. Am. Coun. on Edn. (dir., chmn. 1962-63), Am. Hist. Assn., NAS, Medieval Acad. Am., Tchrs. Ins. and Annuity Assn. (dir. 1963-69, trustee 1970-86, coll. retirement equity fund 1970-86), Inst. Medicine, Phi Beta Kappa, Phi Eta Sigma, Beta Theta Pi, Seattle Yacht Club, Univ. Club (Seattle), Cosmos Club (Washington), Bohemian Club (San Francisco), Rotary. Office: U Wash 222 Miller Hall Box 353600 Seattle WA 98195-3600

ODELL, WILLIAM DOUGLAS, physician, scientist, educator; b. Oakland, Calif., June 11, 1929; s. Ernest A. and Emma L. (Mayer) O.; m. Margaret F. Reilly, Aug. 19, 1950; children: Michael, Timothy, John D., Debbie, Charles. AB, U. Calif., Berkeley, 1952; MD, MS in Physiology, U. Chgo., 1956; PhD in Biochemistry and Physiology, George Washington U., 1965. Intern, resident, chief resident in medicine U. Wash., 1956-60, postdoctoral fellow in endocrinology and metabolism, 1957-58; sr. investigator Nat. Cancer Inst., Bethesda, Md., 1960-65; chief endocrine service NICHD, 1965-66; chief endocrinology Harbor-UCLA Med. Center, Torrance, Calif., 1966-72; chmn. dept. medicine Harbor-UCLA Med. Center, 1972-79; vis. prof. medicine Auckland Sch. Medicine, New Zealand, 1979-80; prof. medicine and physiology U. Utah Sch. Medicine, Salt Lake City, 1980—, chmn. dept. medicine, 1980-96. Mem. editorial bds. med. jours.; author 6 books in field; contbr. over 300 artilces to med. jours. Served with USPHS, 1960-66. Recipient Disting. Svc. award U. Chgo., 1973, Pharmacia award for outstanding contbns. to clin. chemistry, 1977, Gov.'s award State of Utah Sci. and Tech., 1988, also rsch. awards, Mastership award ACP, 1987. Mem. Am. Soc. Clin. Investigation, Am. Physiol. Soc., Assn. Am. Physicians, Am. Soc. Andrology (pres.), Endocrine Soc. (v.p., Robert Williams award 1991), Soc. Study of Reprodn. (bd. dirs.), Pacific Coast Fertility Soc. (pres.), Western Assn. Physicians (pres.), Western Soc. Clin. Rsch. (Mayo Soley award), Soc. Pediatric Rsch., Alpha Omega Alpha. Office: U of Utah Med Ctr 50 N Medical Dr Salt Lake City UT 84132-0001

ODEN, ROBERT RUDOLPH, surgeon; b. Chgo., Dec. 2, 1922; s. Rudolph J.E. and Olga H. (Wahlquist) O.; m. Nancy Clow; children: Louise, Boyd, Beach, Lisbeth. BS, U. Ill., 1943; MD, Northwestern U., 1947, MS in Anatomy, 1947. Intern Augustana Hosp., Chgo., 1947-48, resident in surgery, 1948-49; resident in orthopaedics Hines Vets. Hosp., Chgo., 1949-51; resident in children's orthopaedics Shriner's Hosp., 1953-54; pvt. practice Chgo., 1954-57, Aspen, Colo., 1957—; clin. assoc. prof. in orthopaedics U. Colo.; orthopaedic surgeon U.S. Olympic Com., 1960, 72, 76, 80. Assoc. editor: Clin. Orthopaedics and Related Rsch. Trustee U.S. Ski Ednl. Found., 1967-82, Aspen Valley Hosp., 1978-86; founder Aspen Orthopaedic and Sports Medicine Pub. Found., 1985, Aspen Inst. for Theol. Futures, 1978, Great Tchrs. and Preachers Series Christ Episc. Ch., 1989; mem. organizing com. Aspen World Cup, 1976-92; founder, trustee Pitkin County Bank, 1983—; founder Aspen Pitkin Employee Housing, 1975. Recipient Blegan award for most outstanding svc. to U.S. skiing, 1985, Halsted award U.S. Ski Assn., 1987, inducted into Aspen Hall of Fame, 1996. Mem. Am. Acad. Orthopaedic Surgeons, ACS, Internat. Coll. Surgeons, Western Orthopaedic Assn., SICOT, Am. Assn. Bone & Joint Surgeons, Rocky Mountain Traumatologic Soc., Canadian Orthopaedic Assn., Am. Orthopaedic Soc. for Sports Medicine, Internat. Ski Safety Soc., ACL Study Group, Internat. Soc. Knee, Internat. Knee Inst., Phi Beta Kappa. Home: PO Box 660 Aspen CO 81612-0660 Office: 100 E Main St Aspen CO 81611-1778

ODLING-SMEE, WILLIAM, surgeon; b. London, Sept. 21, 1935; s. Charles William and Katharine Hamilton (Aitcheson) O.-S.; m. Anne Marie Thacker, July 30, 1959; children: Margaret Emma, Katharine Anne, Patrick William, James Louis, Elizabeth Mary, Hugh Hamilton. MB BS, U. Durham, Eng., 1959. Sr. lectr. in surgery Queen's U., Belfast, Northern Ireland, 1973—; cons., dir. The Breast Clinic, Royal Victoria Hosp., Belfast, 1979—. Fellow RCSI, Royal Coll. Surgeons Eng. Office: Inst Clin Sci Dept Surgery, Grosvenor Rd, Belfast BT12 6BJ, Northern Ireland

ODOGUARDI, LUIGI, radiologist; b. Trebisacce, Cosemza/Calabria, Italy, May 7, 1951; s. Francesco and Rosa (Assi) O.; m. Caterina Rago, Apr. 30, 1981; children: Rosalba, Francesco. Degree in medicine, U. Pisa, Italy, 1978, cert. in radiology, 1982. Asst. radiologist USSL 17, Soveria Mannelli, Italy, 1979-83; asst. radiologist USSL 3, Trebisacce, Italy, 1983-85, vice mgr. radiology, 1985-88, offl. in territorial medicine, 1988-91, chief radiologist, 1988—; offl. in territorial medicine ASL3, Rossaho, Italy, 1995—. Coauthor: Alto Jomio Clabrese, 1983. Active Pro-Loco, Trebisacce, 1985, Circolo "G. La Pira", Trebisacce, 1988, Distretto Scolastico, Trebisacce, 1991. With Italian Army, 1980. Mem. SIRM. Roman Catholic. Home: A Manzobi 25, 87075 Trebisacce Cosenza/Calabria, Italy Office: ASL3, Via Della Repubblica, 87068 Rossano Cosenza/Calabria, Italy

ODOM, GUY LEARY, retired physician; b. New Orleans, May 20, 1911; s. Guy Leroy and Marion (Brown) O.; m. Suzanne Price, Aug. 19, 1933 (dec. Nov. 1965); children—Guy Leary, Linda P. (Mrs. Wesley Cook), Carolyn (Mrs. Terry H. Little); m. Mataline Nye, Dec. 29, 1968. M.D., Tulane U., 1933. Diplomate: Am. Bd. Neurol. Surgery (sec.-treas. 1964-70, chmn. 1970-72). Intern, resident E. La. State Hosp., Jackson, 1933-37; practice medicine, specializing in neurol. surgery Montreal, Que., Can., 1937-42, New Orleans, 1942-43, Durham, N.C., 1943-81; instr. Montreal Neurol. Inst., 1937-42; assoc. surgery La. State U., 1942-43; faculty Duke Med. Sch., 1943-81, prof. neurosurgery, 1950-81, chmn. dept., 1960-75, James B. Duke prof. neurol. surgery, 1974; cons. VA Hosp., Durham; cons. neurosurgery Watts Hosp. Durham, Womack Army Hosp., Ft. Bragg, N.C.; Mem. Adv. Bd. Med. Specialists. Mem. A.M.A., Pan Am. Med. Assn., N.C., Durham-Orange County med. socs., World Fedn. Neurol. Surgery, Internat. Soc. Neurol. Surgery, Am. Acad. Neurol. Surgeons (pres. 1967), Soc. Neurol. Surgeons (pres. 1970-71), Am. Surg. Assn., So. Neurol. Soc. (pres. 1968), Am. Assn. Neurol. Surgeons (pres. 1972). Home: 2812 Chelsea Cir Durham NC 27707-5133

ODOM, LORRIE FURMAN, oncologist, educator; b. N.Y.C., June 14, 1943; d. Samuel Paul and Sylvia Furman; m. John Albert Odom Jr., May 4, 1976; children: Devin, Nathan. BA in Zoology and Chemistry, Pomona Coll., 1965; MD, U. Colo., 1969. Staff oncologist The Children's Hosp., Denver, 1975—; prof. of pediatrics U. Colo., Denver, 1992—, dir. oncology and hematology, 1984-90, clin. dir., co-acting sect. head, 1990-93, dir. clin. oncology, 1993—; mem. extramural rev. bd. Nat. Cancer Inst., Bethesda, Md., 1991—. Author: (chpt.) Acute Myeloid Leukemia of Childhood; contbr. articles to profl. jours. Mem. Am. Soc. Clin. Oncology, Assn. Pediatric Hematology and Oncology, Am. Acad. Pediatrics, Childrens Cancer Group. Office: The Childrens Hosp 1056 E 19th Ave # B115 Denver CO 80218-1007

ODOM, TERRY DAVID, ophthalmologist; b. Robbinsville, N.C., Oct. 5, 1953; s. Harvey J. and Blanch (Orr) O.; m. Susan Beshears; children: Dana, Kelly, Allison. BA in Biology, U. Tenn., 1975; MD, Wake Forest U., 1979. Diplomate Am. Bd. Ophthalmology; lic. S.C., N.C., Va. Intern internal medicine U. South Fla. Sch. Medicine, 1979-80; rsch. asst. ophthalmology William Jennings Bryan Dorn VA Hosp., Columbia, S.C., 1980-81; resident ophthalmology U. S.C., 1981-84; pvt. practice Danville, Va., 1984—. Presenter in field. Mem. AMA, Am. Acad. Ophthalmology, Christian Med. Soc., Phi Beta Kappa. Home: 4007 Hazel Ln Greensboro NC 27408 Office: 125 Watson St Danville VA 24541

O'DONNELL, JAMES FRANCIS, health science administrator; b. Cleve., July 22, 1928; s. John Michael and Mary Louise (Hayes) O'D.; m. Winifred Locke, Sept. 10, 1955; children—Anne Catherine, Patrick John, Mary Elizabeth. B.S. in Biology, St. Louis U., 1949; Ph.D. in Biochemistry, U. Chgo., 1957. Asst., then. assoc. prof. biol. chemistry and exptl. medicine Coll. Medicine, U. Cin., 1957-68; grants assoc., div. research grants NIH, Bethesda, Md., 1968-69; program dir. population and reprodn. grants br. Ctr. for Population Research, Nat. Inst. Child Health and Human Devel., NIH, 1969-71; asst. dir. div. research resources NIH, Bethesda, 1971-76, dep. dir. div. research resources, 1976-90, acting dir. div. research resources, 1981-82, dir. Office of Extramural Programs, Office of the Dir., 1990—. Served with U.S. Army, 1950-52. Home: 11601 Bunnell Ct S Rockville MD 20854-3603 Office: NIH Rm 6182 6701 Rockledge Dr Bethesda MD 20892-7910

O'DONNELL, JOHN JOSEPH, JR., optometrist; b. Phila., Oct. 26, 1956; s. John Joseph and Mary Agnes (Hungrige) O'D.; m. Jane Susan Betz, June 28, 1980; children: Kathryn Marie, John Joseph III, Michael Charles. BS in Biology, St. Joseph U., 1978; BS in Ocular Sci., Pa. Coll. Optometry, 1981, OD with honors, 1983. Cardio-pulmonary perfusionist Hosp. U. Pa., Phila., 1978-80; staff optometrist Pa. Eye Assocs., Harrisburg, 1983-85; staff chief optometric svcs. Meml. Eye Inst., Harrisburg, 1986-93; optometrist, ptnr. Premier Eye Care Group, Harrisburg, 1994—; trustee Optometric Svc. Corp. Pa., Harrisburg, 1989. Contbr. articles to profl. jours. Fellow Am. Acad. Optometry; mem. Am. Optometric Assn., Pa. Optometric Assn. (trustee 1987-94, pres. 1994), Ctrl. Pa. Optometric Soc. (pres. 1985-86). Republican. Roman Catholic. Office: Premier Eye Care Group Inc 92 Tuscarora St Harrisburg PA 17104

O'DONNELL, MARY MURPHY, nurse epidemiologist, consultant; b. Lincoln, Ill., Feb. 21, 1918; d. Thomas Edward and Frances Ward (Hayes) Murphy; m. Maurice A. O'Donnell, Jan. 29, 1942. Diploma St. John's Sch. Nursing, Springfield, Ill., 1939. Registered nurse, Ill., Fla. Asst. to ear, nose and throat specialist, 1939-42; nurse U.S. Govt. Hosp., 1942-43; asst. to gen. practitioner, Springfield, 1943-55; staff nurse City Health Dept., Springfield,

1955-65; dir. tng. and edn. Springfield and Sangamon County Civil Def. Agy., 1965-66; exec., cons. in charge med. self-help Ill. Dept. Pub. Health, 1966-74; nurse epidemiologist St. Joseph Hosp., Port Charlotte, Fla., 1975-91, part-time epidemiologist, 1992-93, retired, 1993, cons. epidemiologist, 1993—. mem. Aids Task Force Charlotte County Dept. Pub. Health, Fla., pres. Charlotte County epidemiology group, 1991; instr. AIDS Program, 1987-93. V.p. S. Central area Ill. Women's Civil Def. Council; mem. Ill. Civil Def. Council; chmn. civil def. activities ARC; v.p., mem. health services adv. com. U.S. Civil Defense Council; ofcl. vol. rep. Am. Social Health Assn. Recipient Spl. award State Dept. of Am. Legion Aux., 1954, Cert. of Honor, hon. life membership U.S. Air Force Air Def. Team, 1959, Silver Wing Bracelet, Ground Observer Corps, 1959, Cert. of Honor, Mayor of City of Springfield, 1966, Pfizer award of merit U.S. Civil Def. Council, 1969, Presidential citation U.S. Civil Def. Council, 1972. Mem. Assn. for Practitioners in Infection Control, SW Regional Infection Control. Republican. Roman Catholic. Avocations: boating; swimming; clog dancing; golf; horses. Home: 819 Napoli Ln Punta Gorda FL 33950-6525

O'DONOGHUE, JOHN LIPOMI, toxicologist; b. Lowell, Mass., Apr. 12, 1947; s. James Gregory and Sarafina Frances (LiPomi) O'D.; m. Sandra Gail Piekos, June 24, 1967; children: Shawn Michael, Bevin Ruth. Student, U. Mass., 1964-66; VMD, U. Pa., 1970, PhD, 1979. Diplomate Am. Bd. Toxicology. Pathologist Eastman Kodak Co., Rochester, N.Y., 1974-79, pathology group leader, 1979-86, dir. toxicology, 1986-91, dir. health and environment labs., 1991—; adj. assoc. prof. lab. animal medicine and toxicology U. Rochester, 1988-93, adj. assoc. prof. environ. medicine, 1993—; ad hoc neurotoxicology advisor Sci. USEPA, Washingotn, 1987-89. Author: Neurotoxicology of Industrial and Commercial Chemicals, 1985; contbr. articles to profl. jours. and others. Recipient Sigma Xi award, 1980; USPHS postdoctoral fellow, 1970. Mem. AVMA, Am. Indsl. Health Coun. (chmn. neurotoxicology subcom. 1986-89), Soc. Toxi cology (exec. com. neurotoxicology specialty 1990). Democrat. Roman Catholic. Home: 3915 Clover St Honeoye Falls NY 14472-9319 Office: Eastman Kodak Co 1100 Ridgeway Ave B-320 Kodak Park Rochester NY 14652-6256

O'DONOHUE, WALTER JOHN, JR., medical educator; b. Washington, Sept. 23, 1934; s. Walter John and Mavis Leota (Terry) O'D.; m. Cynthia Ann Halmintoller, Aug. 10, 1957 (div. 1978); 1 child, Diane Louise; m. Maria Theresa Sauer, Nov. 27, 1978; children: Walter John III, Mary Theresa. BA, Va. Mil. Inst., 1957; MD, Med. Coll. Va., 1961. Diplomate Am. Bd. Internal Medicine, Am. Bd. Pulmonary Medicine. Resident internal medicine Med. Coll. Va., Richmond, 1961-63, 65-66, chief med. resident, 1966-67, cardio-pulmonary fellow, 1967-69, asst. prof. medicine, 1968-73, assoc. prof., 1973-77; prof. Creighton U., Omaha, Nebr., 1977—, chief pulmonary medicine div., 1977—, chmn. dept. medicine, 1985—. Editor: Current Advances in Respiratory Care, 1984, Long-term Oxygen Therapy: Scientific Basis and Clinical Application, 1995; contbr. over 100 articles to med. jours., chpts. to books. Served to capt. M.C., U.S. Army, 1963-65. Fellow ACP, Am. Coll. Chest PHysicians (regent 1986-88, gov. for Nebr. 1982-88); mem. AMA (CPT adv. com. 1992—), Am. Lung Assn. (bd. dirs. 1981-87), Nebr. Lung Assn. (bd. dirs., pres. 1979-81), Am. Assn. Respiratory Care (chmn. bd. med. advisors 1986-87), Assn. Profs. Medicine, Nat. Assn. Med. Dirs. on Respiratory Care (pres. 1995-97). Republican. Roman Catholic. Home: 12773 Izard St Omaha NE 68154-1243 Office: Creighton U Sch Medicine 601 N 30th St Omaha NE 68131-2137

O'DONOVAN, SR. MARY MAGDALEN, nursing administrator; b. County Cork, Ireland, Dec. 20, 1919; came to U.S., 1948; d. James Patrick and Margaret P. (Poole) O'D. RN cert., Our Lady of the Lake Hosp., Baton Rouge, La., 1954; BS in Nursing, Natchitoches (La.) State U., 1959; MS in Hosp. Adminstrn., Trinity U., San Antonio, 1977. Nursing supr. Our Lady of Lourdes Med. Ctr., Lafayette, La., 1954-56, St. Francis Hosp., Monroe, La., 1956-60; operating room supr. Our Lady of the Lake Hosp., Baton Rouge, 1961-67; hosp. adminstr. St. Francis Med. Ctr., Monroe, 1968-78; materials mgmt. Our Lady of the Lake Regional Med. Ctr., Baton Rouge, 1978-85, adminstr. skilled nursing, 1985—. Democrat. Roman Catholic.

O'DORISIO, THOMAS MICHAEL, internal medicine educator, researcher; b. Denver, May 29, 1943; s. Angelo Benedict and Olga Ester (Zarlengo) O'D.; m. M. Sue Wedemeyer; children: Joel, Rachelle, Nathan. BS, Regis Coll., 1965; MS in Anatomy, Creighton U., 1967, MD, 1971. Diplomate Am. Bd. Internal Medicine, Nat. Bd. Med. Examiners. Intern Creighton U., Omaha, 1971-72; resident Ohio State U., Columbus, 1972-74, fellow, 1974-77, asst. prof., 1977-79, assoc. prof., 1979-84, asst. program dir. clin. research ctr., 1984—, prof. medicine, 1984—, prof. physiology, 1985—, prof. pathology, 1993—, prof. human nutrition, 1993—, dir. div. endocrinology, diabetes and metabolism, 1989—; chmn. human subjects rev. bd. Ohio State U., 1987-89. Recipient Prof. of Yr. award Ohio State U. Class of 1983, tchg. awards from sr. class of 1981, 82, 84, 85, 89, 90, Alumni Tchg. award, 1995; grantee NIH, 1987—, Nat. Cancer Inst., 1974-77, 91, 92. Fellow Am. Assn. Clin. Endocrinology; mem. ACP, Am. Fedn. Clin. Rsch., Am. Gastroenterology Assn., Ctrl. Soc. Clin. Rsch., Endocrinology Soc. Democrat. Roman Catholic. Club: St. Thomas Moore (Newman Ctr.). Office: Ohio State U Hosp 1581 Dodd Dr Columbus OH 43210-1228

ODRICH, MARC GEOFFREY, ophthalmologist, consultant; b. Flushing, N.Y., Sept. 15, 1958; s. Ronald Basil and Johanna (Dornbush) O.; m. Susan E. Sidd. AB, Columbia U., 1980, MD, 1984. Diplomate Am. Bd. Ophthalmology. Intern Danbury (Conn.) Hosp./Yale U., 1984-85; resident Columbia Presbyn. Hosp., N.Y.C., 1985-88; cornea fellow Mass. Eye and Ear Hosp./Harvard U., Boston, 1988-90; pvt. practice ophthalmology Columbia-Presbyn. Hosp., 1990—; med. monitor Visx, Inc., Santa Clara, Calif., 1995—. Office: 3765 Riverdale Ave # 5 Riverdale NY 10463

OEHLERT, WILLIAM HERBERT, JR., cardiologist, administrator, educator; b. Murphysboro, Ill., Sept. 11, 1942; s. William Herbert Sr. and Geneva Mae (Roberts) O.; m. L. Keith Brown, Mar. 14, 1976; children: Emily Jane, Amanda Elizabeth. BA, So. Ill. U., 1967; MD, Washington U., St. Louis, 1967. Diplomate Nat. Bd. Med. Examiners, Am. Bd. Internal Medicine, Am. Bd. Cardiovascular Disease, North Am. Soc. Pacing and Electrophysiology. Intern Union Meml. Hosp., Balt., 1967-68, resident, 1968-69; resident U. Iowa, Iowa City, 1969-70, cardiology fellow, 1970-72; asst. prof. medicine, dir. coronary care units U. Okla. Health Sci. Ctr., Oklahoma City, 1972-74, asst. clin. prof. medicine, 1974-82, assoc. clin. prof. medicine, 1982-88, clin. prof. medicine, 1988—; chmn. dept. cardiology Bapt. Med. Ctr., 1992-95; pvt. practice Oklahoma City, 1974—; med. dir. cardiovascular svcs. Integris Bapt. Med. Ctr., 1993—; pres. Cardiovascular Clinic, Oklahoma City, 1987-91, chmn. exec. com., 1987-91; pres. med. dir. Cardiovascular Imaging Svcs. Corp., Oklahoma City, 1987-92; v.p. Plaza Med. Group, 1992-93; CEO W.H. Oehlert, MD, P.C., 1993—. Author: Arrhythmias, 1973, Cardiovascular Drugs, 1976; contbr. articles to profl. jours. Fellow Am. Heart Assn. (nat. program com. 1979-82, pres. Okla. affiliate 1985-86, bd. dirs. 1974-88, ACLS nat. affiliate faculty 1987-90), Am. Coll. Cardiology; mem. AMA, ACP, Nat. Assn. Residents and Interns, Am. Soc. Internal Medicine, Am. Coll. Physician Execs., Okla. County Med. Assn. (chmn. quality of care com. 1990-91), Okla. State Med. Assn., Okla. City Clin. Soc., Okla. Cardiac Soc. (pres. 1978-79), Osler Soc., Soc. Nuclear Medicine, Wilderness Med. Soc., Stewart Wolf Soc., Phi Eta Sigma, Phi Kappa Phi. Home and Office: 3017 Rock Ridge Pl Oklahoma City OK 73120-5713

OEHME, FREDERICK WOLFGANG, medical researcher and educator; b. Leipzig, Germany, Oct. 14, 1933; came to U.S., 1934; s. Friedrich Oswald and Frieda Betha (Wohlgamuth) O.; m. Nancy Beth MacAdam, Aug. 6, 1960 (div. June 1981); children: Stephen Frederick, Susan Lynn, Deborah Ann, Heidi Beth; m. Pamela Sheryl Ford, Oct. 2, 1981; 1 child, April Virginia. BS in Biol. Sci., Cornell U., 1957, DVM, 1958; MS in Toxicology and Medicine, Kans. State U., 1962; DMV in Pathology, Justus Liebig U., Giessen, Germany, 1964; PhD in Toxicology, U. Mo., 1969. Diplomate Am. Bd. Toxicology, Am. Bd. Vet. Toxicology, Acad. Toxicological Scis. Resident intern, Large Animal and Ambulatory Clinic Cornell U., 1957-58; gen. practice vet. medicine, 1958-59; from asst. to assoc. prof. medicine Coll. Vet. Medicine Kans. State U., 1959-66, 69-73, dir. comparative toxicology labs., 1969—, prof. toxicology, medicine and physiology Coll. Vet. Medicine, 1974-96, prof. toxicology, pathology, medicine and physiology, 1996—; postdoctoral research fellow in toxicology, NIH U. Mo., 1966-69; cons. FDA, Washington, Ctr. for Vet. Medicine, Rockville, Md., Animal Care com. U. Kans., Lawrence, 1969-76, Syntex Corp., Palo Alto, Calif., 1976-77; mem. sci. adv. panel on PBB Gov.'s Office, State of Mich., 1976-77, Coun. for Agrl. Sci. and Tech. Task Force on Toxicity, Toxicology and Environ. Hazard, 1976-83; cons., mem. adv. group on pesticides EPA, Cin., 1977—; expert state and fed. witness; advisor WHO, Geneva; presenter more than 580 papers to profl. meetings; numerous other activities. Author over 680 books and articles on toxicology and vet. medicine; editor, pub. Vet. Toxicology, 1970-76, Vet. and Human Toxicology, 1977—; assoc. editor Toxicology Letters; mem. editl. bd. Am. Jour. Vet. Rsch., 1975-83, Toxicology, 1979-85, Clin. Toxicology, Jour. Toxicologie Medicale, Toxicology and Indsl. Health, Poisindex, Jour. Analytical Toxicology, Companion Animal Practice; reviewer Toxicology and Applied Pharmacology, Jour. Agrl. and Food Chemistry, Spectroscopy, numerous others. Mem. council Luth. Ch. Am., sr. choir, numerous coms., adv. council Cub Scouts Am., Eagle Scouts, mgr., coach Little League Baseball; council rep., treas. area council, various coms. PTA; mem. Manhattan Civic Theatre; bd. trustees Manhattan Marlin Swim Team; dir. meet Little Apple Invitational Swim Meet, 1984. Recipient Disting. Grad. Faculty award Kans. State U., 1977-79, Dir.'s Letter of Commendation, FDA, 1983, Kenneth P. DuBois award Midwest Soc. Toxicology, 1991, Kenneth F. Lampe award Am. Acad. Clin. Toxicology, 1993, John Doull award Ctrl. States Soc. Toxicology, 1994, medal Azabu U., 1994, Silver award Aristotelian U., 1995, others; project fellow Morris Animal Found., 1967-69. Fellow Am. Acad. Clin. Toxicology (charter, past pres., numerous coms.), Am. Acad. Vet. and Comparative Toxicology (past sec.-treas., numerous coms.); mem. Soc. Toxicology (past pres., numerous coms.), World Fedn. Clin. Toxicology Ctrs. and Poison Control Ctrs. (past pres.), Soc. Toxicologic Pathologists, N.Y. Acad. Scis., Am. Vet. Med. Assn. (com. on environmentology 1971-73, adv. com. council on biol. and therapeutic agts. 1971-74, various others), Nat. Ctr. Toxicological Rsch. (vet. toxicology rep. sci. adv. bd.), Nat. Rsch. Coun. (subcom. on organic contaminants in drinking water, safe drinking water com., adv. ctr. on toxicology assembly life scis. 1976-77, panel on toxicology marine bd., assembly of engring. 1976-79, com. on vet. med. scis. assembly life scis. 1976-78), Nat. Ctr. for Toxicological Rsch. (grad. edn. subcom., sci. adv. bd. 1974-77), Cornell U. Athletic Assn, Omega Tau Sigma, Phi Zeta, Sigma Xi, numerous others. Republican. Clubs: Cornell U. Crew; Manhattan Square Dance. Home: 148 S Dartmouth Dr Manhattan KS 66502 Office: Kans U Comparative Toxicology Labs Manhattan KS 66506

OELBERG, DAVID GEORGE, neonatologist, educator, researcher; b. Waukon, Iowa, May 26, 1952; s. George Robert and Elizabeth Abigail (Kepler) O.; m. Debra Penuel, Aug. 4, 1979; 1 child, Benjamin George. BS with highest honors, Coll. William and Mary, 1974; MD, U. Md., 1978. Diplomate Am. Bd. Pediatrics, Am. Bd. Neonatal-Perinatal Medicine. Intern U. Tex. Med. Br., Galveston, 1978-79, resident, 1979-81, pediatric house staff, 1978-81; postdoctoral fellow in neonatal medicine U. Tex. Med. Sch., Houston, 1981-84, asst. prof. dept. pediatrics, 1984-90, assoc. prof., 1990-93; assoc. prof. dept. pediatrics, head perinatal rsch. Ctr. Pediatric Rsch., Ea. Va. Med. Sch., 1993—; mem. hosp. staff Hermann Hosp., Houston, 1983-93; physician Crippled Children's Services Program, Houston, 1985-93; mem. hosp. staff Lyndon B. Johnson County Hosp., 1990-93; visiting prof. Wyeth-Ayerst Labs., 1992; med. dir. Office Rsch. Children's Hosp. King's Daughter, Sentara Norfolk Gen. Hosp., 1993—. Mem. editorial adv. bd. jour. Neonatal Intensive Care; contbr. articles to profl. jours; ad hoc reviewer profl. jours.; patentee in field. Physician cons. Parents of Victims of Sudden Infant Death Syndrome, Houston, 1984. Recipient award in analytical chemistry Am. Chem. Soc., 1974, NIH Clin. Investigator award Nat. Heart, Lung and Blood Inst., 1989-94; rsch. grantee Am. Lung Assn., 1989-90, NIH, 1989-94. Fellow Am. Acad. Pediatrics, N.Y. Acad. Scis.; mem. AMA, NAS, Soc. Exptl. Biology and Medicine, So. Soc. Pediatric Rsch. (councilor), Soc. Pediatric Rsch. Achievements include a method for optical measurement of bilirubin in tissue. Avocations: sailing, gardening. Home: 1624 W Little Neck Rd Virginia Beach VA 23452-4720 Office: Ea Va Med Sch Ctr Pediatric Rsch 855 W Brambleton Ave Norfolk VA 23510-1005

OERMANN, MARILYN HAAG, nursing educator; b. Reading, Pa., Jan. 28, 1950; d. Laurence and Dorothy (Printz) Haag; m. David Henry Oermann; children: Eric, Ross. BSN, Pa. State U., 1970; M in Nursing Edn., U. Pitts., 1975, PhD, 1980. Instr. Reading (Pa.) Hosp., 1970-72, St. Margaret's Hosp., Pitts., 1972-76, U. Pitts., 1976-78; assoc. prof. Wayne State U., Detroit, 1978—; cons. on curriculum and teaching to schs. of nursing. Author: Professional Nursing Practice, 1991, co-author: Behavioral Objectives, 1991, Clinical Teaching in Nursing Education, 1992; contbr. articles to profl. jours. Fellow Am. Acad. Nursing; mem. Soc. for Rsch. in Nursing Edn., Midwest Nursing Rsch. Soc., NLN, AAUP, ANA, Sigma Theta Tau (pres. Lambda chpt.). Office: Wayne State U Coll Nursing 5557 Cass Ave Rm 360 Detroit MI 48202-3615

OERTEL, YOLANDA CASTILLO, pathologist, educator, diagnostician; b. Lima, Peru, Dec. 14, 1938; came to U.S., 1966; d. Leonardo A. and Dalila (Ramirez) C.; m. James E. Oertel, Sept. 24, 1969. MD, Cayetano Heredia, Lima, 1964. Diplomate Am. Bd. Pathology (mem. test com. for cytopathology 1988-94). Internat. postdoctoral fellowship NIH, Bethesda, Md., 1966-68; asst. prof. pathology Sch. Medicine George Washington U., Washington, 1975-78, assoc. prof., 1978-84, prof., 1984—; cons. Registry Cytology Armed Forces Inst. Pathology, Washington, 1981—. Author: Fine Needle Aspiration of the Breast, 1987; contbr. chpts. to books and articles to profl. jours. Recipient Francisco A. Carnino prize Peruvian Med. Assn., 1965, cert. Meritorious Svc. Armed Forces Inst. Pathology, 1974; named Disting. Alumna Cayetano Heredia Med. Sch., 1989. Mem. Internat. Acad. Cytology, Assn. Mil. Surgeons (hon), Colombian Soc. Pathology (hon.), Argentinian Soc. Pathology (hon.), Peruvian Soc. Pathologists (hon.), Argentinian Soc. Cytology, (hon.), Am. Soc. Cytology, Internat. Acad. Pathology, Soc. Latinoamericana Patologia, Am. Soc. Clin. Pathologists (coun. on cytopathology 1982-88). Office: George Washington U Med Ctr 901 23rd St NW Washington DC 20037-2377

OESTERLING, JOSEPH EDWIN, urologic surgeon; b. Greensburg, Ind., May 28, 1956; s. Walter Bernard and Leona Martha (Muckerheide) O.; m. Carmen Teresa Noguera, June 9, 1984; children: Christopher Charles, Jennifer Marie. BA, Columbia Coll., 1978; MD, Columbia U., 1982. Diplomate Nat. Bd. Med. Examiners, Am. Bd. Urology; lic. in Md., Fla., Ariz., Minn., Mich. Intern, dept. gen. surgery Johns Hopkins U. Sch. of Med., Balt., 1982-83, resident, dept. gen. surgery, 1983-84, resident, dept. urology, 1984-87, chief resident, dept. urology, 1988, instr., dept. urology 1988-89; cons. dept. urology Mayo Clinic, Rochester, Minn., 1989-94; asst. prof. urology Mayo Med. Sch., Rochester, 1989-93; assoc. prof. urology Mayo Clinic, Rochester, 1993-94; prof., urologist-in-chief, dir. Mich. Prostate Inst., U. Mich., Ann Arbor, 1994—; dir. Mich. Prostate Inst., U. Mich. Med. Ctr., Ann Arbor, 1994—; cons./researcher in field. Author: The ABCs of Prostate Cancer: The Book That Could Save Your Life; cons. The Jour. of Urology, Balt., 1988—, The Prostate, 1990, Cancer, 1990, Cancer Rsch., 1990; editor-in-chief Urology; book editor Urologic Oncology. Recipient Emil T. Hofman Chemistry award Univ. Notre Dame, 1975, Albert B. Schweitzer award for Acad. Excellence, Columbia Coll., 1978, Salutatorian, Columbia Coll., 1978, Samuel W. Rover and Lewis C. Rover Biochemistry award Coll. of Physicians and Surgeons of Columbia U., 1982, Valedictorian, 1982, Am. Soc. Clin. Oncology Rsch. award 1987, Devel. award Am. Cancer Soc., 1988, others in field. Fellow ACS; mem. AMA, Am. Urol. Assn. (voting mem., Grand Champion prize 1991 Western sect., Prostate Educator of Yr. 1995), N.Y. Acad. Sci., Sci. Rsch. Soc., Nat. Assn. Residents and Interns, Minn. State Med. Assn., Minn. Urol. Soc., Zumbro Valley Med. Soc., So. Minn. Med. Assn., Mich. Urol. Soc., Am. Soc. Andrology, Am. Assn. Clin. Urologists, Am. Geriatrics Soc., Am. Soc. Clin. Oncology, Can. Urol. Assn., European Assn. Urology, Endourol. Soc., Pan-Pacific Surg. Assn., Soc. for Basic Urologic Rsch., Soc. Internat. Urology, Johns Hopkins Med. and Surg. Assn., Soc. Univ. Urologists, North Cen. Sect. Am. Urologic Assn. (1st prize Clin. Rsch. 1986, 87, 1st prize Lab. Rsch. 1987), Mayo Alumni Assn., Sigma Xi. Home: 3622 Lamplighter Dr Ann Arbor MI 48103-1713

OESTERLING, THOMAS OVID, pharmaceutical company executive; b. Butler, Pa., Mar. 6, 1938; s. Victor Kenneth and Marjorie Gertrude (Oswald) O.; m. Janet Westrick, Dec. 30, 1960 (div. 1983); children: Thomas Jennifer, Daniel; m. Cynthia Adler, 1984 (div. 1987). B.S., Ohio State U., 1962, M.S., 1964, Ph.D., 1966. Research asso., research head Upjohn Co., Kalamazoo, 1966-76; dir. research and devel., dermatol. div. Johnson & Johnson Corp., New Brunswick, N.J., 1976-78; dir. pharm. research and devel. Johnson & Johnson Corp., 1978-79; v.p. med. products research and devel. Mallinckrodt, Inc., St. Louis, 1979-83; sr. v.p. research and devel. Collaborative Research Inc., Bedford, Mass., 1984-86; pres. Collaborative Research Inc., 1986-89; pres., chief exec. officer Gliatech, Inc., Cleve., 1989—; faculty mem. Arden House Conf. on Stability Evaluation Pharm. Dosage Forms, 1979. Contbr. numerous sci. articles to profl. jours. Recipient Disting. Alumni award Ohio State U. Coll. Pharmacy, 1982; Parke Davis research grantee, 1962-64; Am. Found. for Pharm. Edn. fellow, 1964-66. Mem. Am. Chem. Soc., Soc. Nuclear Medicine, Acad. Pharm. Scis., Soc. for Neurosci. Office: Gliatech Inc 23420 Commerce Park Cleveland OH 44122-5813

OETTGEN, HERBERT FRIEDRICH, physician; b. Cologne, Germany, Nov. 22, 1923; came to U.S., 1958; s. Peter and Minna (Kaul) O.; m. Trudi Hesberg, Feb. 16, 1957; children: Hans Christoph, Joerg Peter, Anne Barbara. MD, U. Cologne, 1951. Diplomate Bd. Internal Medicine, Fed. Republic of Germany. Resident in pathology City Hosp., Cologne, 1952-54, resident in medicine, 1955-58; fellow Meml. Sloan-Kettering Cancer Ctr., N.Y.C., 1958-62, assoc. to assoc. mem., 1963-69, mem., 1972—, attending physician, 1971—; prof. medicine Cornell U. Med. Coll., N.Y.C., 1972—; assoc. dir. Cancer Rsch. Inst., N.Y.C., 1985—. Author over 350 publs. in hematology, cancer rsch., immunology and clin. oncology. Recipient award for cancer rsch. Wilhelm Warner Found., Hamburg, Fed. Republic Germany, 1970, Lisec-Artz award for cancer rsch. Friedrich Wilhelm U., Bonn, Fed. Republic of Germany, 1982. Presbyterian. Home: 48 Overlook Dr New Canaan CT 06840-6825 Office: Meml Sloan-Kettering Cancer Ctr 1275 York Ave New York NY 10021-6007

O'FARRELL, TIMOTHY JAMES, clinical psychologist; b. Lancaster, Ohio, Apr. 22, 1946; s. Robert James and Helen Loretta (Tooill) O'F.; BA, U. Notre Dame, 1968; PhD in Psychology, Boston U., 1975; m. Jayne Sara Talmage, May 19, 1973; 1 child, Colin. Instr. Harvard U. Med. Sch., Boston, 1977-82, asst. prof., 1982-86, assoc. prof., 1986—, chief Harvard Families and Addiction Program, 1991—; staff psychologist VA Med. Ctr., Brockton, Mass., 1975-78, dir. Alcoholism Clinic, 1978-83, dir. Counseling for Alcoholics' Marriages Project, 1978—, chief Alcohol and Family Studies Lab., 1981—, assoc. chief psychology svc., 1988—. VA predoctoral grantee, 1969-72; rsch. grantee VA, 1978—, Nat. Inst. on Alcohol Abuse and Alcoholism, 1991—, Smithers Found., 1991—, Guggenheim Found., 1993-94; fellow Behavior Therapy and Research Soc., APA. Mem. NIAAA (psychosocial rsch. rev. group, 1989-93), Am. Psychol. Assn., Assn. for Advancement Behavior Therapy, Eastern Psychol. Assn. Author: Alcohol and Sexuality, 1983, Treating Alcohol Problems: Marital and Family Interventions, 1993; mem. editorial bd. Jour. Family Psychology, Family Dynamics Addiction Quarterly, Behavior Therapy, Clinical Psychology Rev., Psychology of Addictive Behavior; contbr. over 130 articles on families and addiction to profl. publs. Home: 260 High St Duxbury MA 02332-3406 Office: VA Med Center 116B1 Brockton MA 02401

OGDEN, LOUANN MARIE, dietitian, consultant; b. Enid, Okla., Dec. 16, 1952; d. Raymond Michael Schiltz and Donna Mae Stuever; m. Wendell Edwin Ogden, Jan. 5, 1979; 1 child, Gregory Jacob Jeremiah. BS in Home Econs., Okla. State U., 1974, MS, 1977. Registered dietitian; lic. dietitian, Tex. Dietetic intern Ind. U. Med. Ctr., Indpls., 1974; therapeutic dietitian-clin. svcs. and trayline ops. Bapt. Med. Ctr. Okla., Oklahoma City, 1975-76; grad. teaching asst. lower and upper level food preparation Okla. State U., Stillwater, 1976-77, teaching assoc. lower and upper level food preparation, 1977; chief clin. dietitian adminstrv. and clin. coordination Borgess Hosp., Kalamazoo, 1978; dietary cons. nutrition program Iowa Commn. on Aging, Des Moines, 1979-80; asst. food svc. dir., adminstrv. dietitian Timberlawn Psych. Hosp., Dallas, 1980-92; rep. group one purchasing program, mem. student tng. program Zale Lipshy U. Hosp., Dallas, 1992-93, food svc. cons., 1993—. Mem. Am. Dietetic Assn., Am. Soc. Hosp. Food Svc. Adminstrn. (nat. nominating com. 1990-91, Disting. Health Care Food Svc. Adminstr. 1992, North ctrl. Tex. chpt.: corr. sec. 1985-86, comms. chair 1986-87, rec. sec. 1987-89, pres.-elect 1989-90, pres. 1990-91, nominating com. chair, health care food svc. week com. chair 1991-92, Outstanding Mem. award 1992), Tex. Dietetic Assn., Dallas Dietetic Assn. Democrat. Roman Catholic. Home and Office: 3302 Oxford Dr Rowlett TX 75088-5936

OGESEN, ROBERT BRUCE, dentist; b. Council Bluffs, Iowa, Aug. 26, 1934; s. Ever Julius and Agnes Elizabeth (Treptow) O.; m. Suzanne Jones, June 19, 1954; children: Cindy Sue, Robert B. II, Ann Elizabeth. DDS, U. Iowa, 1958. Gen. practice dentistry Iowa City, Iowa, 1961-73; with Towncrest Dental Offices, PC, Iowa City, 1973—; adj. faculty dentistry U. Iowa, 1965-85; mem. adv. com. Lab Tech Program, Kirkwood Community Coll., Iowa, 1992—. Co-author: Hypnosis in Dentistry, 1985; contbr. articles to profl. jours. Mem. Iowa City Planning and Zoning Commn., 1971-81. Served to capt. USAF, 1958-61. Mem. ADA, Iowa Dental Assn. (coun. dental care programs 1976-80, coun. ethics, intraprofl. and pub. rels. 1985-91), Pierre Fauchard Acad., Univ. Dist. Dental Soc., Johnson County Dental Soc., Omicron Kappa Upsilon, Delta Sigma Delta. Presbyterian. Home: 305 Woodridge Ave Iowa City IA 52245-6055 Office: Towncrest Dental Offices PC 1039 Arthur St Iowa City IA 52240-6629

OGIELA, DENNIS MICHAEL, orthopaedic surgeon; b. Buffalo, July 16, 1951; m. Gloria Ann Jozwiak; children: Teegan Anne, Ryan Michael. BA, Brown U., 1973; MD, SUNY, Buffalo. Diplomate Am. Acad. Orthop. Surgeons. Resident in orthop. surgery SUNY, Buffalo; pvt. practice, bd. dirs. Danbury Orthop. Assocs., Danbury, Conn., 1983—; attending orthop. surgeon Danbury Hosp., 1983—; spine fellow U. Rochester, 1983; bd. dirs. Worklab Inc., Danbury. Contbr. articles to profl. jours. Mem. ACP. Office: Danbury Orthopedic Assocs 226 White St Danbury CT 06810

OGO, KEN, plastic surgeon, educator; b. Takikawa, Hokkaido, Japan, Oct. 28, 1939; s. Hajime and Kaoru (Ando) O.; m. Setuko Hashida, Nov. 23, 1974; 1 child, Shun. MD, Hokkaido U., Sapporo, Japan, 1964; PhD, Nihon Med. Coll., Tokyo, 1981. Diplomate Japan Soc. Plastic and Reconstructive Surgery, Japan Soc. Aesthetic Plastic Surgery; fgn. bd. cert. Am. Soc. Plastic Surgery. Attending plastic surgeon Tokyo Met. Police Hosp., chief plastic surgeon, 1974; from asst. prof. to assoc. prof. Kyorin U. Sch. Medicine, Tokyo, 1974-90, prof. dept. plastic surgery, 1990—. Home: 1-9-17-401 Kamiigusa, 167 Suginamiku Tokyo, Japan Office: Kyorin Univ Hosp, 6-20-2 Shinkawa, 181 Mitaka Tokyo, Japan

O'GRADY, CATHERINE ANN, geriatrics nurse; b. Madison, Wis., Apr. 6, 1951; d. Francis Lester and Josephine Barbara (Schwarz) Palm; m. Richard Joseph O'Grady, Dec. 29, 1962; children: Michael, Jim, Jeff, Lynn. Diploma, Mercy Hosp., Denver, 1962; BSN, Metro State Coll., Denver, 1975, postgrad., 1977; MSN, U. No. Colo., Greeley, 1982. RN, Colo.; cert. adult nurse practitioner. Office nurse Denver, 1962-63; staff nurse various hosps., Denver, 1963-73; pub. health nurse Tri-County Health Dept., Denver, 1978-81; occupational health nurse Denver Post Newspaper, 1982—, Keebler Cookie, 1982—; nurse mgr. Vis. Nurse Assn., Denver, 1982—; bd. dirs. Cath. Archdiocese Housing Authority, Denver, 1991—; bd. dirs. Am. Cancer Soc., 1993—, Adams County Social Svcs. Contbr. articles to profl. jours. Mres. govtl. affairs Am. Cancer Soc., Denver, 1995, bd. dirs., 1993—, mem. breast cancer task force, 1994-95; vol. Samaritan Homeless Shelter, 1990—; pres. Northglenn (Colo.) Garden Club, 1988; parish nurse Parish Ministry, 1992—. Recipient Vol. of Yr. award Am. Cancer Soc., 1991, Fundraising award, 1990, Outstanding Achievement award Nat. Vis. Nurse Assn., 1993, Excellence award Denver Vis. Nurse Assn., 1992. Mem. Am. Heart Assn. (chmn. edn. com. 1995-96), Am. Diabetes Assn. (minority outreach com. 1995-96), Colo. Occupational Health Nurses (chair legis. pub. issues). Democrat. Roman Catholic. Home: 730 W 100th Pl Denver CO 80221 Office: Vis Nurse Assn # 800 3801 E Florida Denver CO 80210

O'GRADY, KEVIN EDWARD, psychologist, educator; b. Washington, Feb. 26, 1949; s. Gerald P. and Mary (McDuffie) O'G.; m. Susan F. Zlotlow, Sept. 2, 1979; children: Megan Leah, Caitlin Alyce. BA, Washington & Lee U., 1972; MS, Old Dominion U., 1976; PhD, U. Conn., 1980. Lic. psychotherapist. Asst. prof. psychology U. N.Mex., Albuquerque, 1980-83; asst. prof. psychology U. Md., College Park, 1983-89; assoc. prof.

psychology U. Md., 1989—. Contbr. articles to profl. jours. Mem. Am. Psychol. Assn., Am. Stat. Assn., Psychometric Soc. Office: U Md Dept Psychology College Park MD 20742

O'GRADY, RICHARD T., human services administrator, educator; b. N.Y.C., May 1, 1937; s. Richard and Beatrice (Jordan) O'G.; m. Joan Barbara Posz, May 15, 1965; children: Barbara, Thomas. BSS, Fordham U., 1959, MSW, 1963. Social worker N.J. State Bd. Child Welfare, Jersey City, 1959-61; supr. N.J. State Bur. Children's Svcs., Jersey City, 1961-66; supr. staff devel. N.J. State Bd. Child Welfare, Trenton, 1966-68, regional supr.; regional supr. N.J. State Bur. Children's Svcs., Trenton, 1968-72; chief N.J. Bur. Family Svcs., Trenton, 1972-75; regional adminstr. N.J. Divsn. Youth and Family Svcs., Trenton, 1975-78, dep. dir., 1978-82, adminstr. regional ops., 1983-87, adminstr. Office Adult and Child Social Svcs., 1987-92, adminstr. statewide ops., 1992-95, asst. dir. Office Policy and Planning, 1995—; adj. prof. Rutgers U., New Brunswick, N.J., 1976-81, 90—. Mem. N.J. Gov.'s Task Force on Elder Abuse, 1986; mem. N.J. Gov.'s Mgmt. Improvement Program, 1985. Capt. U.S. Army, 1960-68. Mem. Am. Pub. Welfare Assn. (adminstr. child welfare 1983, adminstr. adult Protective Svcs. 1988). Home: 26 Yorkshire Rd Trenton NJ 08610-1327 Office: NJ State Div Youth & Fam Svc 1 S Montgomery St Trenton NJ 08608-2203

OGREN, CARROLL WOODROW, retired hospital administrator; b. Mpls., Mar. 22, 1927; s. Peter L. and Mabel (Wohleen) O.; m. Patricia Ann Sweeney. B.A., U. Minn., 1952; M.Hosp. Adminstrn., Washington U., St. Louis, 1958. Asst. adminstr. Washoe Med. Center, Reno, 1958-59; adminstr. Washoe Med. Center, 1959-80, Jean Hannah Clark Rehab. Center, Las Vegas, Nev., 1980-92. Served with USNR, 1944-46, 50-54, PTO. Mem. Am. Coll. Hosp. Adminstrs., Am. Hosp. Assn. (nat. com. state hosp. assn. 1967—), Nev. Hosp. Assn. (pres. 1961-62, sec. 1961-66). Club: Gourmet Toastmasters (Reno) (pres. 1960). Home: 5860 Via Manigua Las Vegas NV 89120-2348

OGURA, BRADLEY CHARLES, medical services executive; b. Oreg., Feb. 20, 1963; s. Henry Fordyce and Mary T. (Shigeno) O. BA, U. Puget Sound, 1985. Mgr. investor rels. Immunex Corp., Seattle, 1991—. Mem. Nat. Investor Rels. Inst. (pres. Seattle chpt. 1995-96). Home: 420 Vine St Seattle WA 98121 Office: Immunex Corp 51 University St Seattle WA 98101

OH, TAEHO, pharmacist manager; b. Seoul, Jan. 18, 1958; s. Whatak and Bocknim Oh. BS in Biochemistry, Juniata Coll., 1980; BS in Pharmacy, Ohio State U., 1983, MS, 1986. Registered pharmacists, Fla., Ohio. Asst. prof. Southeastern U. Health Scis., Miami Beach, Fla., 1989—; hosp. pharmacy adminstr., 1986-94; clin. pharmacist InPhyNet Med. Mgmt. Inc., Ft. Lauderdale, 1995—. Contbr. articles to profl. jours. Rsch. award Cen. Ohio Soc. Hosp. Pharmacists, 1986. Mem. Am. Soc. Hosp. Pharmacists, South Fla. Soc. Hosp. Pharmacists (pres. 1992, publ. award 1989, 90). Republican. Presbyterian. Office: InPhyNet Med Mgmt Inc Ste 600 1200 S Pine Island Ft Lauderdale FL 33324

O'HARA, JOHN PAUL, III, orthopaedic surgeon; b. Detroit, June 10, 1946; m. Randy Baird, Mar. 11, 1987; children: Riley Anne, Nolan Baird, Evan John. BA, U. Mich., 1968, MD, 1972. Resident U. Va. Med. Ctr., Charlottesville, 1973-77; fellow Nuffield Orthopaedic Ctr., Oxford, Eng., 1977; practice medicine specializing in orthopaedic surgery Southfield, 1978—; staff Providence Hosp., Southfield, Mich., 1978—, pres. elect med. staff, 1990, pres. med. staff, 1991; sect. chief orthopedics; pres. Providence Hosp. Med. Staff Research Found., 1984-85, bd. dirs., 1982—; bd. dirs. Mich. Master Health Plan, Southfield, 1982. Contbr. articles to profl. jours. Recipient Disting. Alumni award Brother Rice High Sch., 1986. Fellow Am. Acad. Orthopaedic Surgery, Mid Am. Orthopaedic Soc.; mem. Detroit Orthopaedic Soc., Mich. Orthopaedic Soc., Detroit Acad. Orthopaedic Surgeons (past pres.), Oakland Hills Country Club (Birmingham, Mich.), Beverly Hills (Mich.) Club. Home: 627 Waddington St Bloomfield Hills MI 48301-2346 Office: Porretta & O'Hara Orthopaedic Surgeons PC 22250 Providence Dr Ste 401 Southfield MI 48075-6212

O'HARA, MARTIN JAMES, cardiologist; b. Dublin, Ireland, Sept. 15, 1951; came to the U.S., 1987; s. Leopold Noel and Mary (Lochrin) O'H.; m. Mary Rachel Lee, Sept. 19, 1993. MB, BChir, BAO, U. Coll., Dublin, 1976, DCH, 1977, MD, 1987. Diplomate in internal medicine and cardiovasc. disease Am. Bd. Internal Medicine; diplomate in internal medicine Royal Coll. Physicians Ireland. Intern medicine and surgery Mater Hosp., Dublin, 1976-77; med. sr. house officer Cork (Ireland) Regional Hosp., 1978-79; med. registrar St. Lawrences Hosp., Dublin, 1979-81; cardiology rsch. registrar Northwick Park Hosp., Harrow, U.K., 1981-84; sr. med. registrar St. Vincent's Hosp., Dublin, 1984-87; cardiology fellow Mount Sinai Med. Ctr., N.Y.C., 1987-88, Columbia-Presbyn. Med. Ctr., N.Y.C., 1988-91; attending cardiologist VA Med. Ctr., Northport, N.Y., 1992-93, Fairfax Hosp., Falls Church, Va., 1993—; sec. Assn. Med. Sr. Registrars of Ireland, 1985-87; asst. prof. clin. medicine SUNY, Stony Brook, 1992-93. Contbr. articles to profl. jours. Scholar, Univ. Coll., Dublin, 1969. Mem. Am. Heart Assn., N.Y. Celtic Med. Soc. Office: 2946 Sleepy Hollow Rd Falls Church VA 22044

O'HARA, TAMARA LYNN, public health nurse, consultant; b. Cleve., Apr. 30, 1963; d. Ronald Charles and Sally Ann (Wilson) Marsho; m. Michael Tracy O'Hara, July 14, 1984; children: Ryan Michael, Megan Marie, Matthew Charles. BSN, Ursuline Coll., 1986. Staff nurse Fairview Gen. Hosp., Cleve., 1986-92; pub. health nurse Lakewood (Ohio) Divsn. Health, 1992—; nurse coord. Bur.Children with Med. Handicaps, Lakewood, 1992—; family chair Cuyahoga County Early Intervention Local Collaborative Group, 1994-95, family, clin. faculty Case Western Res. U., Cleve., 1994-96. Contbr. articles to newsletter. Recipient Collaboration award Cuyahoga County Early Intervention Local Collaborative Group, 1994-95. Office: Lakewood Divsn Health 14400 Detroit Rd Lakewood OH 44107

O'HARA, WILLIAM JAMES, retired drug company executive; b. Bklyn., Dec. 2, 1930; s. John Joseph and Mary (Quinn) O'H.; m. Marilyn Mulcahy, July 7, 1956 (dec.); children: Lynn Patricia, Kevin Joseph, Eileen, Gail Elizabeth, Nancy (dec.). B.S., Fordham U., 1952; M.B.A., NYU, 1956. With Equitable Life Assurance Soc. U.S., N.Y.C., 1954-55; with Continental Can Co., N.Y.C., 1955-56; several fin. positions with Gen. Foods Corp., White Plains, N.Y., 1956-69; controller Gen. Foods Corp. (Maxwell House div.), 1966-69; corporate controller Schering Corp., Bloomfield, N.J., 1969-72, Schering Corp. (Schering-Plough Corp.), 1972-73; v.p. finance Schering Corp., 1973-74; v.p. adminstrn. Schering Corp. (Schering div.), 1975-80; v.p., asst. treas. Schering-Plough Corp., 1981-88, ret., 1988. Served with AUS, 1952- 54. Mem. Fin. Execs. Inst. Home: 14 Crestwood Dr Suffern NY 10901-7608

O'HARE, PETER MELVILLE, plastic surgeon; b. Penrith, Cumbria, U.K., June 8, 1949. BSc in Biochemistry with honors, U. Bristol, Eng., 1970, MB ChB, 1973. Registrar Norwich (U.K.) Hosps., 1977-79; sr. registrar Belfast (Northern Ireland) Hosps., 1979-82; cons. plastic surgeon Royal Hull (U.K.) Hosps., 1982—. Contbr. articles to profl. publs. Recipient Merit award for outstanding clin. svc. Nat. Health Svc. Fellow Royal Coll. Surgeons (assessor, cons. to appointment bds. 1994, mem. spl. adv. com. 1995); mem. Brit. Assn. Plastic Surgeons, mem. career structure com. 1993), Brit. Assn. Aesthetic Plastic Surgeons (mem. coun. 1994), Brit. Assn. Surgeons of the Hand. Office: Kingston Gen Hosp, Beverley Rd, East Yorkshire HU3 1UR, England

O'HARE-VANMEERBEKE, ANNE MARIE, dietitian; b. S.I., N.Y., Jan. 5, 1960; d. Robert and Ellen O'Hare. BS in Human Ecology, Marywood Coll., Scranton, Pa., 1982. Registered dietitian. Clin. dietitian Custom Mgmt. Corp., Somerset, N.J., 1982-84; food svc. dir. Custom Mgmt. Corp., Westfield, N.J., 1984-86; cons. Anne O'Hare Cons. Svcs. (Cen. N.J.), 1986; asst. food svc. Marriott Corp., Nyack, N.Y., 1986-87; food svc. dir. Marriott Corp., Secaucus, N.J., 1987-88; dist. dietitian Marriott Corp., N.J. and N.Y. area, 1988-90; dir. food svc. Marriott Corp., Camden, N.J., 1990-92; dir. ctrl. food svc. Columbia-Presbyn. Med. Ctr., N.Y.C., 1992—; tng. mgr. area 1, Mariott Health Care Svcs., Avon, Conn., 1993—; nutrition cons. LEAP and Ocean Inc., Ocean County, N.J., 1995—. Mem. Am. Cancer Soc., Am. Heart Assn. Mem. Am. Dietetic Assn. Roman Catholic. Office: Marriott Health Car Svcs 100 Avon Meadow Ln Avon CT 06001-3774

O'HERN, JANE SUSAN, psychologist, educator; b. Winthrop, Mass., Mar. 21, 1933; d. Joseph Francis and Mona (Garvey) O'H. BS, Boston U., 1954, EdD, 1962; MA, Mich. State U., 1956. Instr. Mercyhurst Coll., 1954-55, Hofstra Coll., 1956-57, State Coll., Salem and Boston, 1957-60; asst. prof. Boston U., 1962-67, assoc. prof., 1967-75, prof. edn. and psychiat. (psychology), 1975-95, prof. emeritus, 1995—; chmn. dept. counseling psychology, 1972-75, 88-89, dir. mental health edn. program, 1975-81, dir. internat. edn., 1978-81, asst. v.p. internat. edn., 1981; pres. ASSIST Internat., Inc., 1989—; adv. bd. Internat. Study Cons., 1994—. Contbr. articles to profl. jours. Trustee Boston Ctr. Modern Psychoanalytic Studies, 1980-92. Recipient grants U.S. Office Edn., NIMH, Dept. of Def. Mem. Assn. Counselor Edn. and Suprs., Am. Counseling Assn., North Atlantic Assn. Counselor Edn. and Supervision (past pres.), Mass. Psychol. Assn., Am. Psychol. Assn., Mortar Bd., Pi Lamda Theta, Sigma Kappa, Phi Delta Kappa, Phi Beta Delta. Home: 111 Perkins St Apt 287 Boston MA 02130-4324

OHL, DEBORAH LEA, long term care consultant; b. Cin., Mar. 9, 1948; d. Edward Adrian and Anna Mae (Knierimn) Clark; m. Daniel Allen Franklin, Jan. 1, 1988 (div.); children: Jennifer Ann, David William, Kathryn Isabel. AS, Raymond Walters Coll., 1972; BA, Coll. Mt. St. Joseph, 1983. RN Ohio. Urology technician Christ Hosp., Cin., 1970-71; charge nurse Children's Hosp., Cin., 1972-76; dir. nursing Quality Health Care, Cin., 1976-78; gen. mgr. Kimberly Nurses, Cin., 1978-79; dir. nursing East Galbraith HCC & NH, Cin., 1979-80; ling term care cons. Ohl & Assocs., Cin., 1980—; cons. and speaker in field. Author of tng. materials. Named Internat. Archery Champ, Nat. Archery Assn., 1962, State, City and Nat. champ, 1961, 62, 63. Mem. Am. Coll. Health Adminstrs. Home & Office: 613 Compton Rd Cincinnati OH 45231

OILER, PEGGY ANN, medical technologist; b. Dayton, Ohio, June 27, 1948; d. Robert R. and Marilyn H. (Kearney-Wilson) O. Cert. med. technologist, High Forest Acad., 1968; AS, Gainesville Coll., 1974; BS, Brenau Coll., 1985. Staff med. technologist Gwinnett Hosp. Sys., Lawrenceville, Ga., 1968-84; lead technologist Gwinnett Med. Ctr., Lawrenceville, 1984—; asst. chem. lab. coord. Brenau Coll., Gainesville, Ga., 1985-90. Vol. ARC, Gwinnett County, Ga., 1970-84, Gwinnett Cmty. Clinic, Lawrenceville, 1989-93, Muscular Dystrophy Assn., Atlanta, 1985-88. Named Vol. of Yr., Gwinnett County chpt. ARC, 1974. Mem. Am. Med. Technologists (cert., chair resolution com. 1993, Disting. Achievement award 1990, Merit award 1993), Ga. State Soc. Am. Med. Technologists (sec.-treas. 1988-90, pres. 1990-94, Tech. of Yr. 1989). Episcopalian. Home: 268 Pine Valley Cir Lawrenceville GA 30245 Office: Gwinnett Med Ctr 1000 Medical Ctr Blvd Lawrenceville GA 30245

O'JACK, HELEN MARGARET, clinical social worker; b. Denver, Jan. 31, 1951; d. Herbert Henry and Lillian Anna (Meyer) Thimm; m. William Allan Schmeling, Jr., July 24, 1982 (div. Dec. 1992); children: Dustin William, Alexander Thimm; m. Stanislav G. O'Jack, June 16, 1995. BA in Psychology, U. Colo., 1973; MSW, U. Denver, 1982. Lic. profl. social worker, Wyo. Peer counselor Met. Community Coll., Omaha, 1975-76; outreach worker South Omaha Crisis Ctr., 1976-77; child care worker Mt. St. Vincent's Youth Home, Denver, 1978-81; social work intern health scis. ctr. U. Colo., Denver, 1981-82; coord. crisis line Vol. Info. Referral Service, Rock Springs, Wyo., 1983-85; clin. social worker, coord. elderly svcs. S.W. Counseling Svc., Rock Springs, 1985-92; med. social worker Wyo. Home Health Care, Rock Springs, 1986-95; pvt. practice, 1992—; facilitator Alzheimer's Family Support Group, Rock Springs, 1983-92; social work cons. Castle Rock Convalescent Ctr., Green River, Wyo., 1990, Sage View Care Ctr., 1992-95; sch. counselor Desert View Sch., 1992—. Mem. NEA, NASW (regional rep. on bd. dirs. Wyo. chpt. 1991-92). Democrat. Office: Desert View Elem Sweetwater Sch Dist # 1 PO Box 1089 Rock Springs WY 82902-1089

OKA, TETSUO, medical educator; b. Okayama, Japan, Jan. 9, 1938; s. Hiroshi and Naoko (Takai) O.; m. Yasuko Otsuka, Mar. 24, 1964; children: Keiko, Taro. MD, Keio U., Tokyo, 1963, PhD, 1970. Instr. dept. pharmacology Sch. Medicine, Keio U., 1964-71, asst. prof., 1972-74, assoc. prof., 1974; prof., chmn. dept. pharmacology Sch. Medicine, Toaki U., Isehara, Japan, 1974—; lectr. Keio U., 1974—, Yamanashi Med. Coll., Kofu, Japan, 1988—, U. Nagoya, Japan, 1990—. Author: Essentials of Pharmacology, 1988. Mem. N.Y. Acad. Scis., Japanese Pharm. Soc. (trustee 1989-92, 96-98). Liberal Democrat. Buddhist. Home: 46-16 Yùhigaoka, Hiratsuka 254, Japan Office: Tokai U Sch of Medicine, Dept Pharmacology, Isehara 259-11, Japan

OKADA, FUMIHIKO, psychiatrist; b. Obihiro, Hokkaido, Japan, Nov. 6, 1940; s. Michimaro and Chieko (Saida) O.; m. Junko Takeda, Apr. 28, 1978; children: Takabumi, Mona. MD, Hokkaido U., Sapporo, 1964, postgrad., 1965-73. Intern Hokkaido U. Hosp., 1964-65, asst. prof. Health Adminstrn. Ctr., 1976-81, assoc. prof. Health Adminstrn. Ctr., 1981-95; vice-dir. Tomita Hosp., Hakodate, Japan, 1995—; dir. Neuro-psychiatric Clinic/Okada Rsch. Inst., Sapporo, Japan, 1996—. Contbr. articles to profl. jours. Research fellow Vanderbilt U., 1981-82. Mem. N.Y. Acad. Scis. Home: Chuo-ku S 10 W 17 2-5, Sapporo Hokkaido 064, Japan Office: Tomita Hosp, 9-18 Komaba-cho, Hakodate 042, Japan

OKADA, MASAYOSHI, neurobiologist, researcher; b. Osaka, Japan, Sept. 5, 1963; s. Hirotsugu and Setsuko (Matsui) O.; m. Naomi Yoshimatsu, June 30, 1991; 1 child, Chihiro. B of Biology, Kyushu U., Fukuoka, Japan, 1986, MS in Biology, 1988, PhD in Biology, 1995. Rsch. scientist Shionogi Rsch. Lab., Osaka, 1988—. Mem. Japanese Biochem. Soc., Japanese Neurosci. Soc. Office: Shionogi Rsch Labs, 3-1-1 Futaba, 561 Toyonaka Osaka, Japan

OKADA, RYOZO, medical educator, clinician and researcher; b. Kiryu, Gummaken, Japan, July 20, 1931; s. Kenji and Sachi (Ishihara) O.; m. Shigeko Shindo, May 25, 1958; children: Kyoko, Taro. MD, Tokyo U., 1956, PhD, 1961. Intern then resident; asst. Sch. Med. Tokyo U., 1962-63; research fellow Hektoen Inst. Cook County Hosp., Chgo., 1963-66; attending physician Yoikuin Hosp., Tokyo, 1966-68; assoc. prof. Sch. Med. Juntendo U., Tokyo, 1968-83, prof., 1983—, dir. cardiovascular lab., 1985—; cons. Migita Hosp., Tokyo, 1968—; councilor Cardiovascular Inst. Roppongi, Tokyo, 1990—, Indsl. Medicine Found., 1995—. Contbr. articles to med. jours. and books. Active group study specific intractable diseases Met. Office of Tokyo, 1972—, cardiomyopathies Ministry of Health and Welfare, Japan, 1974—, occupational diseases Ministry of Labor, Japan, 1987—; bd. dirs. Shirane Kaizen Sch., Gumma, Japan. Fellow Am. Geriatrics Soc., Coun. Prevention Heart Disease, Japanese Circulation Soc. (councilor), Japanese Angiology Soc., Japanese Geriatrics Soc.; mem. Japanese Soc. Medicine. Home: 53 Asahigoaka, Kanagawa-ku, Yokohama 221, Japan Office: Juntendo U Sch Medicine, 2-1-1 Hongo, Bunkyoku, Tokyo 113, Japan

OKAJIMA, MITSUHARU, internist; b. Nagoya, Japan, Nov. 2, 1929; s. Goro and Chiyo (Fukuoka) O.; m. Sachiyo Hadano, May 7, 1966; children: Ken, Jun. Diploma, Nagoya U., Japan, 1950, MD, 1954, DMS, 1959. Cert. internist. Rsch. fellow U. Minn./Lab. of Physiol. Hygiene, Mpls., 1959-61, Boston U. Sch. Medicine, 1961-62; assoc. prof. Nagoya U. Rsch. Inst. Environ. Medicine, Aichi, 1967-73; prof. Fujita Health U. Sch. Medicine, Tokyoake/Aichi, Japan, 1973—; vis. scientist MIT Rsch. Lab, Cambridge, 1961-62; vis. prof. Dalhousie U./Lab Biophysics and Physiology, Halifax, Can., 1968-69. Home: 11-18 Hanazono-cho, Toyota 473, Japan Office: Fujita Health U, Sch Medicine, Toyoake, Nagoya Area 470-11, Japan

OKAMOTO, JEFFREY AKIRA, psychiatrist; b. Abington, Pa., July 18, 1954; s. Allen H. and Yone (Watanabe) O.; m. Christina Royer Neff, Aug. 11, 1985; 1 child, Stephen Andrew. BS/Biology with honors, Ursinus Coll., 1976; MD, Pa. State Coll. Medicine, 1980. Diplomate Am. Bd. Psychiatry and Neurology. Resident in psychiatry U. N.C., Chapel Hill, 1984; staff psychiatrist Philhaven Hosp., Mt. Gretna, Pa., 1986—; clin. asst. prof. Dept. Family and Community Medicine Pa. State U., 1991—; cons. staff Good Samaritan Hosp., Lebanon, 1986—; clin. instr. U. N.C. Psychiatry Dept., Chapel Hill, 1985-87. Named Chpt. Scholar Ursinus Coll., Collegeville, Pa., 1976. Mem. Am. Psychiatric Assn., Pa. Psychiatric Assn., Christian Med. Soc. Republican. Mennonite. Home: 551 Hemlock Ln Lebanon PA 17042-9017 Office: Philhaven Hosp 283 S Butler Rd Mount Gretna PA 17064

O'KANE, HUGH OLIVER, cardiac surgeon; b. Belfast, No. Ireland, Nov. 21, 1935; s. Felix Thomas and Margaret Mary (McKeever) Kane; married; children: Aisling, Hugh, Garrett, Anna. BSc in Physiology with honors, Queens U., Belfast, 1957, MB, B of Surgery, BAO, 1960, M of Surgery, 1969. House officer Mater Hosp., Belfast, 1960-61; physiology demonstrator Queens U., 1961-62; sr. house officer City Hosp., Belfast, 1962-64; surg. registrar Hosps. Authority, No. Ireland, 1964-65, sr. surg. registrar, 1965-67; surg. research fellow Mayo Clinic, Rochester, Minn., 1967-69, resident in cardiothoracic surgery, 1969-71; asst. prof. surgery, mem. staff Washington U./Jewish Hosp., St. Louis, 1971-73; cons. cardiac surgeon Royal Victoria Hosp., Belfast, 1973—. Contbr. numerous articles to profl. jours. Mem. British Cardiac Soc., Irish Cardiac Soc., Soc. Cardiothoracic Surgeons of Gt. Britain and Ireland, European Assn. Cardiothoracic Surgeons, Mayo Clinic Alumni Assn. Roman Catholic. Office: Royal Victoria Hosp, Grosvenor Rd, Belfast Ireland

OKASHIMA, MARK ALLEN, healthcare executive, financial planner; b. San Jose, Calif., Oct. 25, 1951; s. John S. and Sumi (Inouye) O. BS, U. Calif., Berkeley, 1973; MBA, U. Santa Clara, 1975. Vol. V.I.S.T.A., Carson City, Nev., 1976-78; health adminstr. Fallon (Nev.) Tribes, 1978-80; sr. project planner Gov.'s Future Commn., Carson City, 1980-81; data analyst Greater Nev. Health Agy., Reno, 1981-82; dir. rsch. market St. Mary's Regional Med. Ctr., Reno, 1982-92; dir. fin. planning Seton Med. Ctr., Daly City, Calif., 1992—; cons. Reno Philharm., 1988, 90, Reno Little Theater, 1988. Bd. dir. Internat. Visitor Coun., Reno, 1988, 91, v.p., 1989, pres., 1990. Named Outstanding Young Man of Am., 1987, Internat. Man of Achievement Internat. Biographers, 1989. Mem. Healthcare Fin. Mgmt. Assn., Am. Mktg. Assn., Calif. Berkeley Alumni Assn., U. Santa Clara Alumni Assn. Home: 220 Greenview Dr Daly City CA 94014-3457 Office: Seton Med Ctr 1900 Sullivan Ave Daly City CA 94015-2200

O'KEEFE, JOSEPH THOMAS, bishop; b. N.Y.C., Mar. 12, 1919. Ed. Cathedral Coll., N.Y.C., St. Joseph's Sem., Yonkers, N.Y., Cath. U., Washington. Ordained Roman Catholic priest, 1948; ordained titular bishop of Tre Taverse and aux. bishop of N.Y., 1982-87; apptd. and installed bishop of Syracuse, 1987. Office: PO Box 511 240 E Onondaga St Syracuse NY 13202-2608*

O'KEEFFE, DANIEL FRANCIS, physician; b. Garden City, N.Y., Oct. 13, 1947; s. Daniel Francis and Kathryn (Gregory) O'K.; m. Mary Helen Aspland, Aug. 21, 1971; children: Tara, Marin, Chandra. AB, Holy Cross Coll., Worcester, Mass., 1969; MD, U. Autonoma of Guadalagara, Mex., 1974. Diplomate Am. Bd. Ob-Gyn, Am. Bd. Ob-Gyn Maternal-Fetal Medicine. Resident, fellow U. Calif., Irving, 1980; dir. maternal-fetal medicine Good Samaritan Med. Ctr., Phoenix, 1980—; ptnr. Phoenix Perinatal Assocs., 1980—; pres. United Genetics, Phoenix, 1980—; cons. Matryx Health Ptnrs., Santa Ana, Calif., 1980—. Contbg. author: Principles and Practice of Perinatal Medicine, 1983, others; contbr. articles to profl. jours. Mem. Ariz. Perinatal Trust Edn. Team, Southwest Regional Outreach Program. Fellow Am. Coll. Ob-Gyn; mem. Roger K. Freeman Perinatal Soc., Soc. Perinatal Obstetricians, Am. Coll. Physician Execs., Ariz. Diabetes Assn., Ariz. Med. Assn., Ariz. Perinatal Soc., Arizona Perinatal Trust (bd. dirs.), Fetal Medicine and Surgery Soc., Maricopa County Med Soc., Phoenix Ob-Gyn Soc., others. Home: 5862 E Bernice Ln Paradise Valley AZ 85253 Office: 1111 E McDowell Rd Phoenix AZ 85006

OKEH, SAMSON EWRUJE, psychiatric nurse; b. Abraka, Nigeria, Nov. 5, 1943; s. Ovaguono Okeh; m. Pauline Okeh, Dec., 1969; children: Helen, Sunday, Debra, Abraka, John, Amber. Diploma, Bapt. Sch. Nursing, Eku Sapele, Nigeria, 1967; BA, U. Ill., Chgo., 1979; MA in Pub. Adminstrn., Northeastern Ill. U., 1981. RN, Ill., Md., Calif. Asst. head nurse Loretto Hosp., Chgo.; nursing supr. Greater Laurel (Md.) and Beltsville Hosp.; charge nurse, part time supr. South Wood Hosp., Chula Vista, Calif.; asst. nurse mgr. Cedars Sinai Med. Ctr., L.A., 1991—. Mem. L.A. World Affairs Coun., 1994—. Mem. United Nurses Assn. Calif., Nigerian Assn. San Diego (pres. 1990-91), URHOBO Assn. So. Calif. (pres. 1992-93), Acad. Polit. Sci., L.A. World Affairs Coun. Home: PO Box 48151 Los Angeles CA 90048-0151 Office: Cedars Sinai Med Ctr 8700 Beverly Blvd Los Angeles CA 90048-1804

OKEN, DONALD, psychiatrist, educator, health facility administrator, consultant; b. N.Y.C., Jan. 21, 1928; m. Linda R. Oken, 1966; children: J. Todd, Emily. MD, Harvard U., 1949. Diplomate Am. Bd. Psychiatry and Neurology; lic. psychiatrist, Ill., N.Y., N.C., Pa. Asst. dir. Inst. of Psychosomatic & Psychiat. Rsch. & Tng. Michael Reese Hosp., Chgo., 1958-61, adminstrv. dir. liaison psychiatry svc., 1958-65, assoc. dir. Inst. of Psychosomatic & Psychiat. Rsch. & Tng., 1961-65; acting dir. divsn. extramural rsch. programs NIMH, 1966-67, chief clin. rsch. br., 1966-68; cons. Nat. Heart Inst., 1968; chair dept. psychiatry Upstate Med. Ctr. SUNY, Syracuse, 1968-82; dir. cons./liaison svc. dept. psychiatry Pa. Hosp., 1983—; intern in medicine Boston City Hosp., 1949-50, asst. resident in medicine, 1950-51; Bertha Hochstetter Buswell fellow in medicine/psychiatry U. Rochester, N.Y., 1951-52; clin. prof. psychiatry Thomas Jefferson U. Coll. Medicine, 1995—; teaching fellow in medicine Harvard U. Med. Sch., Boston, 1950-51; clin. asst. prof. dept. psychiatry U. Ill., Chgo., 1961-65; prof. dept. psychiatry SUNY Upstate Med. Ctr., Syracuse, 1968-83; vis. prof. dept. psychiatry U. N.C., Chapel Hill, 1977-78; clin. prof. psychiatry U. Pa. Sch. of Medicine, 1984-95; mem. N.Y. State Health Rsch. Coun., 1975-80; mem. behavioral medicine study sect. NIMH, 1978-80; mem. Flex exam. task force Nat. Bd. Med. Examiners, 1982-94, chair Flex-2 MCQ test devel. com. With USAR. Home: 159 Summit Ln Bala Cynwyd PA 19004-2918 Office: Pa Hosp Dept Psychiatry 800 Spruce St Philadelphia PA 19107-6192

OKEYA, EPHRAIM NKEM, biomedical engineer; b. Ndoni Rivers, Onelga, Nigeria, Oct. 5, 1956; s. Ambrose B.C. and Theresa (Nwachi) O.; m. Laura Okeya, 1990. BA, 1975, PhD, 1976, DSc, 1990. Audtior Tourism Industry, Ndoni, Nigeria, 1970-71; editor, pub. Tourist Mag., Ndoni, Nigeria, 1972-75; engr. Nipsset/Unesco, Ndoni, Nigeria, 1975-77; med. dr. Magdalene Hosp., Ndoni, Nigeria, 1978-83; sch. dir. Space U.-Ndoni-Unesco, Ndoni, Nigeria, 1986—; Nipsset sec. gen. Unesco Biotech/Engring., France, 1976—; mem. remote sensing program Nat. Space U. Editor: Toursit Mag.-Nigeria, 1974-79; contbr. articles to profl. jours. Presdl. aspirant Nat. Rep. Conv., Nigeria, 1992. UN Family scholar, 1992—; Unesco fellow, 1976-77, 92-93. Mem. World Parliament (knight comdr. 1991), Internat. Parliament (knight templar 1992), Maison Internat. Conferation of Chivalry. Roman Catholic. Home: 149 Hospital Rd, Aba Nigeria Office: Space U Ndoni Unesco, 149 Hospital Rd, Aba Nigeria

OKOLSKI, CYNTHIA ANTONIA, psychotherapist, social worker; b. N.Y.C., July 26, 1954; d. Augusto and Valerie (Toffolo) Zaccari; m. Andrzej L. Okolski, Jan. 8, 1983; children: Gabriel, Christian. BA, Hofstra U., 1976; MA, Columbia U., 1978, MSW, 1983; cert. psychoanalytic psychotherapy, Advanced Ctr. Analytic Therapy, 1986. Counselor, instr. Hofstra U., Hempstead, N.Y., 1975-76; recreational dir. Residence for Young Adults Hostel, Hempstead, 1976-78; rsch. asst. Ctr. Policy Rsch., N.Y.C., 1978-79, Ctr. Psychosocial Studies, N.Y.C., 1979-81; group leader Fidel Sch., Glen Cove, N.Y., 1981; rsch. asst. Assn. of Jr. League, N.Y.C., 1982; social worker Children's Aid Soc., N.Y.C., 1983-84, Manhattan Psychiat. Ctr., N.Y.C., 1984-85; psychotherapist Advanced Inst. Analytic Psychotherapy, Jamaica, N.Y., 1986—; supervising psychotherapist in therapeutic foster care program St. Christopher-Ottillie, 1994—. Mem. NASW, Acad. Cert. Social Workers, Alpha Kappa Delta.

OKONIEWSKI, LISA ANNE, psychologist. BA in Psychology and Studio Art, Coll. William and Mary, 1975; MS in Clin. Psychology, Hahnemann U., 1978; PhD in Counseling Psychology, Temple U., 1984. Lic. psychologist. Counselor Eastern State Hosp., Va., 1974-75; staff psychologist Main Line Day Sch., Pa., 1978-79, Jewish Employment Vocat. Svc., Pa., 1981-82; rsch. asst. Dr. Zygmunt Piotrowski, Pa., 1980-85; staff psychologist Plymouth Healthcare Assocs., Pa., 1984-87; pvt. practice Phila., 1987—. Home: 4953 Mckean Ave Philadelphia PA 19144-4160 Office: 4951 Mckean Ave Philadelphia PA 19144-4160

OKSMAN, HENRY CHAIM, opthalmologist, researcher; b. Verocolow, Poland, Sept. 13, 1946; came to U.S., 1962; s. Jacob and Rachel Oksman; m. Zipporah Leah Oksman, Nov. 5; children: Toby, Benjamin, Tahneer, Jacob,

Maurice. BSEE, CCNY, 1969; MSEE, Poly. Inst. N.Y., 1971, PhD, 1976; MD, Albert Einstein Coll. Medicine, 1981. Diplomate Am. Bd. Ophthalmology. Internal medicine intern Montefiore Hosp., Bronx, N.Y., 1981-82; resident Mt. Sinai Hosp., N.Y.C., 1982-85; pres. rsch. and development Internat. Innovations, Inc., White Plains, N.Y., 1986-94; pvt. practice, ophthalmology Maple Eye Surg. Pc., White Plains, N.Y., 1985—; pres., dir. rsch. and development Namsko R&D Inc., White Plains, N.Y., 1994—. Holder multiple U.S. and internat. patents in biomedicine. Office: Maple Eye Surgical Pc 61 Maple Ave White Plains NY 10601

OKUI, KAZUMITSU, biology educator; b. Ohta, Japan, July 8, 1933; s. Sadajiroh and Ume (Tanaka) O.; m. Mizue Aoki Okui, May 6, 1961; children: Teiichiroh, Ari. B Agr., Tokyo U. Agr., 1962, M Agr., 1964, D Agr., 1967. Lectr. biology Denki-Tsushin U., Tokyo, 1968-70; lectr. biology Kitasato U., Sagamihara, Japan, 1970-73, asst. prof. biology, 1973-82, prof. ethology, 1982—, dean Ednl. Ctr. of Liberal Arts and Sci., 1995—, councilor, 1995—; v.p. Internat. Centre of Wild Silkworm, 1990—; vis. rsch. prof. Waikato U., New Zealand, 1991; mem. book rev. com. Yomiuri Shimbun, Tokyo, 1981-85, Sankei Shimbun, Tokyo, 1990—. Author: Entomology, 1976, Ethology, 1976, General Zoology, 1984, General Zoology, 1985, General Entomology, 1992, Human Ethology, 1992, Essay of Insects, 1993, Textbook For Ethology, 1994. Mem. Internat. Soc. Wild Silkworm (sec. 1988—, v.p. 1990—), Japan Cosmo-Biol. Soc. (councilor 1987-89), Japan Wild Silkworm Soc. (v.p. 1994—), Sci. Coun. of Japan (mem. rsch. com. 1994—). Home: 972-7 Yumoto-machi, Kanagawa-ken 250-03, Japan Office: Ednl Ctr Liberal Arts/Sci, 1-15-1 Kitasato, Sagamihara, Kanagawa 228, Japan

OKUN, NEIL JEFFREY, vitreoretinal surgeon; b. St. Louis, Nov. 21, 1957; s. Edward and Barbara J. (Braham) O.; m. Joan A. Sosnoff, May 19, 1984; children: David E., Sarah E. AB, Dartmouth Coll., 1980; MD, Washington U., 1984. Diplomate Am. Bd. Ophthalmology. Intern internal medicine Jewish Hosp. at Washington U., St. Louis, 1984-85; resident ophthalmology Washington U. Med. Ctr., St. Louis, 1985-88; fellow vitreoretinal Retina Cons., Ltd., Washington U., St. Louis, 1988-89; vitreoretinal surgeon Fla. Retina Inst., Jacksonville, Fla., 1990-91, Retina Assocs. Ctrl. Fla., Orlando, 1991—; instr. dept. ophthalmology Washington U. Sch. Medicine, St. Louis, 1988-89; clin. asst. prof. dept. ophthalmology U. South Fla., Tampa, 1992—; chmn. dept. ophthalmology Fla. Hosp. Orlando, 1996—. Recipient Upjohn Achievement award for endocrinology and metabolism Washington U. Sch. Medicine, St. Louis, 1984. Fellow ACS, Am. Acad. Ophthalmology; mem. AMA (Physicians's Recognition award for continuing med. edn. 1992—), Assn. for Rsch. in Vision and Ophthalmology, Fla. Med. Assn., Fla. Soc. Ophthalmology, Ctrl. Fla. Soc. Ophthalmology, Orange County Med. Soc., Vitreous Soc., Paul Cibis Club. Office: Retina Assocs Ctrl Fla 2501 N Orange Ave #401 Orlando FL 32804

OLANSKY, SIDNEY, dermatologist; b. Boston, Jan. 11, 1914; s. Samuel and Anna Olansky; m. Marian Elizabeth Freehafer, June 30, 1945; children: Leann, Alan, David. BS, NYU, 1934; MD, Glasgow (Scotland) U., 1940. Diplomate Am. Bd. Dermatology. Intern. Met. Hosp., N.Y.C., 1940-42; commd. USPHS, 1942, advanced through grades to; med. officer in charge Rapid Treatment Ctr., Washington, 1943-46; resident dept. dermatology Duke U. Hosp., 1946-48; pvt. practice dermatology Washington, 1948-50; dir. V.D. Rsch. Lab., Chamblee, Ga., 1950-55; assoc. prof. dermatology Duke U. Med. Ctr., 1955-59; prof. medicine, chief divsn. dermatology Emory U. Sch. Medicine, Atlanta, 1959-81, emeritus prof., 1981—; rschr. USPHS, Gallinger Meml. Hosp., 1948-50; mem. nat. serology adv. com. to SurgeonGen. of Pub. Health Svc.; cons. 3rd Army Hdqs.; mem. med. sci. com. Dermatology Found. Contbr. articles to profl. jours. Fellow ACP; mem. AMA, Am. Acad. Dermatology and Syphilology (bd. dirs.), Am. Dermatol. Assn., Am. Venereal Disease Assn. (pres. 1971-72), Am. Fedn. Clin. Rsch., Med. Assn. Ga., Med. Assn. Atlanta, Southeastern Dermatol. Assn. (sec., pres. 1971-73), Atlanta Dermatology Assn. (pres. 1971-72). Office: Ste 800 2045 Peachtree St NE Atlanta GA 30309-1412

OLBE, LARS CHRISTER, surgeon; b. Stockholm, June 1, 1931; s. Bertil and Inga Olbe; m. Kerstin Birgitta Olbe, Sept. 14, 1974; children: Anna Lena Stina, Richard, Robert. Cand. medicine, Karolinska Inst. Stockholm, 1952, lic. medicine, 1956, PhD, 1964. Demonstrator pharmacology, clin. tchr. Karolinska Inst. Stockholm, 1957-64; asst. surgeon U. Goteborg, Sweden, 1965-72; assoc. prof. surgery U. Goteborg, 1973—. Editl. bd. mem. 3 med. jours.; referee 9 internat. med. jours.; contbr. chpts. in books and numerous articles to profl. jours. Recipient Karl Henrik Koster prize, 1971, Ernst Reuterskiold prize, 1983, Thureus prize, 1991. Mem. Internat. Gastroenter. Surg. Club, European Gastroenter. Club, Brit. Soc. Gastroenterologists, Coll. Internat. Chir. Dig., Soc. Surg. Alimentary Tract, Prout Club U.K. Office: Dept Surgery, Sahlgren Hospital, 41345 Goteborg Sweden

OLD, LLOYD JOHN, cancer biologist; b. San Francisco, Sept. 23, 1933; s. John H. and Edna A. (Marks) O.;. BA, U. Calif., Berkeley, 1955; MD, U. Calif., San Francisco, 1958; MD (hon.), Karolinska Inst., 1994, U. Lausanne, Switzerland, 1995. Rsch. fellow Sloan-Kettering Inst. Cancer Rsch., N.Y.C., 1958-59, rsch. assoc., 1959-60, assoc., 1960-64, assoc. mem., 1964-67, mem., 1967—; rsch. assoc. biology Sloan-Kettering div. grad. sch. Med. Scis., Cornell U., N.Y.C., 1960-62, asst. prof. biology, 1962-66, assoc. prof. biology, 1966-69, prof. biology, 1969-81, prof. immunology, 1981—; acting assoc. dir. research planning Sloan-Kettering Inst. Cancer Rsch., N.Y.C., 1972, v.p., assoc. dir., 1973-76, v.p., assoc. dir. for sci. devel., 1976-83; assoc. dir. for research Meml. Sloan-Kettering Cancer Ctr. and Meml. Hosp., N.Y.C., 1973-83, William E. Snee Chair cancer immunology, 1983—; Harvey Soc. lectr., 1972, G.H.A. Clowes Meml. lectr., 1980; assoc. med. dir. N.Y. Cancer Rsch. Inst. Inc., 1970; med. dir. Cancer Rsch. Inst., Inc., 1971-74, dir. sci. adv. coun., 1974—; vis. prof. clin. investigation GM Cancer Rsch. Found., Dana-Farber Cancer Inst.; vis. prof. pathology Harvard U., 1986; fgn. adj. prof. med. faculty Karolinska Inst., 1994—; cons. in field. Adv. editor: Jour. Exptl. Medicine, 1971-76, 90—; Progress in Surface and Membrane Sci., 1972-74; assoc. editor: Virology, 1972-74; editl. adv. bd.: Cancer Rsch., 1967-70, Cancer, 1968-71, Recent Results in Cancer Rsch., 1972, editl. bd. Immunobiology, 1987—. Contbr. articles to profl. jours. Sci. dir., mem. Emeritus Sci. Com., Ludwig Inst. Cancer Rsch., 1971-86, chmn. sci. com. 1988—, bd. dirs. 1989—, CEO, 1995, dir. N.Y. unit, 1990; mem. rsch. coun. Pub. Health Rsch. Inst. City N.Y., 1977-80, bd. dirs., 1979-89, vice chmn. exec. com. 1984-89; adv. bd. biology div. N.Y. Hall of Sci., 1985—; mem. med. and sci. adv. bd., trustee Leukemia Soc. Am. Inc., 1970-73; mem. sci. adv. bd. Jane Coffin Childs Meml. Fund for Med. Rsch., 1970-75. Recipient Roche award, 1957; Alfred P. Sloan award cancer research, 1962, Lucy Wortham James award James Ewing Soc., 1970, Louis Gross award, 1972, Founders Tumor Immunology award Cancer Research Inst., 1975, Rabbi Shai Shacknai Meml. award, 1976; Research Recognition award Noble Found., 1978; Robert Roesler de Villiers award, 1981; N.Y. Acad. Medicine medal, 1985, Robert Koch prize, 1990. Mem. NAS, AAAS, N.Y. Acad. Scis., Harvey Soc., Am. Acad. Arts and Scis., Am. Assn. Cancer Research (bd. dirs. 1980-83), Am. Assn. Immunologists, Inst. Medicine of Nat. Acad. Scis., Phi Beta Kappa, Sigma Xi, Alpha Omega Alpha. Office: Ludwig Inst Cancer Rsch 1345 Avenue Of The Americas New York NY 10105

OLDEN, KENNETH, science administrator, researcher; b. Parrottsville, Tenn., July 22, 1938; s. Mack L. and Augusta (Christmas) O.; m. Sandra L. White; children: Rosalind, Kenneth, Stephen, Heather. BS, Knoxville Coll., 1960; MS, U. Mich., 1964; PhD, Temple U., 1970. Rsch. fellow, physiology instr. Harvard U., Cambridge, Mass., 1970-74; sr. staff fellow NIH, Nat. Cancer Inst., Bethesda, Md., 1974-77, biochemistry expert, 1977-78, rsch. biologist, 1978-79; assoc. dir. rsch. Howard U. Med. Sch. Cancer Ctr., Washington, 1979-82, dep. dir., 1982-85, dir., 1985-91; dir. Nat. Inst. Environ. Health Scis. and Nat. Toxicology Program NIH, Rsch. Triangle Park, N.C., 1991—. Author numerous books; assoc. editor Cancer Rsch., 1990—, Jour. Nat. Cancer Inst., 1990—, Molecular Biology of the Cell, 1991-93, Environ. Health Perspectives, 1992—; contbr. articles to profl. jours. Mem. awards bd. Gen. Motors Cancer Rsch. Found., Detroit, 1992—. Porter Devel. Postdoctoral fellow Am. Physiol. Soc., 1970, Postdoctoral fellow NIH, 1970-73, Macy Faculty fellow Macy Found., 1973-74. Mem. Am. Soc. Cell Biology, Am. Soc. Biol. Chemistry, So. Biol. Response Modifiers, Metastasis Rsch. Soc., Inst. Medicine, Internat. Soc. Study Comparative Oncology. Baptist. Home: 19 Quail Ridge Rd Durham NC 27705-1870 Office: Nat Inst Environ Health Scis & Nat Toxicology Prog PO Box 12233 Research Triangle Park NC 27709-2233

OLDENHOF, JAN, anesthesiologist; b. Rotterdam, The Netherlands, July 3, 1948; s. Jan and Alice (Stessingers) O.; m. Janneke Schiereck, Aug. 24, 1977; children: Maaike, Sjoerd, Freya. MD, Erasmus U., Rotterdam, 1973; anesthesiologist, Acad. Hosp., Rotterdam, 1977. Lic. comml. pilot, The Netherlands. Trainee anesthesiology Acad. Hosp., Rotterdam, 1973-77, staff mem., 1977; staff anesthesiologist Elisabeth Hosp., Tilburg, The Netherlands, 1977—; automation cons. Elisabeth Hosp., Tilburg, 1988-93. Contbr. articles to profl. jours. Mem. Dutch Acupuncture Soc. (cert. acupuncturist), Royal Dutch Med. Assn. (specialist registration com.), Dutch Med. Soc., Dutch Anesthesiol. Soc., Eindhoven Aeroclub (bd. dirs. 1992-95). Home: Eikenven 41, 5062 AD Oisterwyk The Netherlands Office: St Elisabeth Hosp, Hilvarenbeekseweg 60, 5000 LC Tilburg The Netherlands

OLDER, JAY JUSTIN, ophthalmic plastic surgeon; b. Jersey City, N.J., Feb. 7, 1940; m. Lois Rosner; children: Benjamin, Jessica. AB, Rutgers U., 1961; MD, Stanford U., 1966. Diplomate Am. Bd. Ophthalmology. Intern, resident in internal medicine Cornell U./Bellevue Hosp. Ctr., N.Y.C., 1968; resident in ophthalmology Stanford (Calif.) U., 1973; fellow in ophthalmic plastic and reconstructive surgery Stanford U., San Francisco, 1974; pvt. practice Tampa, Fla., 1974—; clin. prof. ophthalmology U. South Fla. Coll. Medicine, Tampa, 1975—, dir. oculoplastic svc., 1974-89, 90—. Author: Eyelid Tumors: Clinical Diagnosis and Surgical Treatment, 1987. Fellow Am. Acad. Ophthalmology (Sr. Honor award 1995), Am. Soc. Ophthalmic Plastic and Reconstructive Surgery (pres. 1987, sec. 1983-84), ACS; mem. Phi Beta Kappa (v.p. Greater Tampa Bay Assn. 1995-96). Office: Ophthalmic Plastic Surgery Assocs Ste 210 13601 Bruce B Downs Blvd Tampa FL 33613

OLDERMAN, GERALD, retired medical device company executive; b. N.Y.C., July 16, 1933; s. Cass and Hilda (Klein) O.; m. Myrna Ruth Schwartz, Aug. 3, 1958; children: Sharon, Neil, Lisa. BS in Chemistry, Rensselaer Poly Inst., 1958; MS Phys. Chemistry, Seton Hall U., 1971, PhD, 1972. Research chemist Nat. Cash Register, Dayton, Ohio, 1958-61; tech. mgmt. positions Johnson & Johnson, New Brunswick, N.J., 1961-75; dir. R&D, bd. dirs. surg. products hosp. divsn. Johnson & Johnson, New Brunswick, N.J., 1972-75; v.p. rsch. and devel. Surgikos div. Johnson & Johnson, New Brunswick, N.J., 1975-78; v.p. rsch. and devel.; bd. dirs. Am. Convertors divsn. Am. Hosp. Supply corp., Evanston, Ill., 1978-85; bd. dirs. Surgikos divsn. Johnson & Johnson, New Brunswick, 1975-78; v.p. internat. rsch. and devel. Pharmaseal div. Baxter Healthcare Corp., Valencia, Calif., 1985-91; v.p. R & D, bd. dirs. cardiopulmonary divsn. C.R. Bard, 1991-96, ret., 1996; cons. R.F. Caffrey Assocs., Brownsville, Vt., 1995—; con. RF Caffrey & Assoc., 1996—. Served with USMC, 1954-56. Recipient Robert Wood Johnson medal, Johnson & Johnson, 1969. Fellow Am. Inst. Chemists; mem. Assn. Advancement Med. Instrumentation, INDA, Assn. Nonwovens Industry (bd. dirs., corp. rep. 1986, 87), Nat. Fire Protection Assn. (industry rep.), Am. Soc. Artificial Internat. Organs. Home: 17 Pickman Dr Bedford MA 01730-1009 Office: RF Caffrey Assocs PO Box 319 Brownsville VT 05037

OLDS, JACQUELINE, psychiatrist, educator; b. Springfield, Mass., Jan. 4, 1947; d. James and Marianne (Ejier) O.; m. Richard Stanton Schwartz, Aug. 26, 1978; children: Nathaniel Leland, Sarah Elizabeth. BA, Radcliffe Coll., 1967; MD, Tufts U., 1971. Diplomate Am. Bd. Psychiatry and Neurology. Resident in adult psychiatry Mass. Mental Health Ctr., Boston, 1974; resident in child psychiatry McLean Hosp., Belmont, Mass., 1976, asst. attending child psychiatrist, 1979—; psychiatrist-in-charge inpatient unit McLean Hall-Mercer Children's Ctr., Belmont, 1976-79; assoc. child psychiatry Beth Israel Hosp., Boston, 1979—; cons. in child psychiatry Mass. Gen. Hosp., Boston, 1994—; instr. psychiatry Harvard U. Med. Sch, Boston, 1976-86; asst. prof. clin. psychiatry, 1986—; cons. North Shore Mental Health Ctr., Salem, 1981-82. Contbr. articles to profl. jours. Sec. Cambridge (Mass.) Nursery Sch. Bd., 1982-84. Fellow Am. Psychiat. Assn.; mem. Mass. Psychiat. Soc. (ethics com. 1988-93, mem. pub. affairs com. 1992—), Am. Acad. Child Psychiatry, Am. Psychoanalytic Assn., New England Coun. Child and Adolescent Psychiatry (bd. dirs.), Cambridge Skating Club (bd. dirs. 1989). Democrat.

O'LEARY, DENNIS PATRICK, biophysicist; b. Dec. 24, 1939; married, 1964; 2 children. BS, U. Chgo., 1962; PhD, U. Iowa, 1969. Asst. prof. surg. and anatomy UCLA, 1971-74; rsch. assoc. prof. otolaryngology and pharmacology U. Pitts., 1974-78, assoc. prof. otolaryngology and physiology, 1978-84; prof. depts. otolaryngology, physiology, biomed. enging. U. So. Calif., 1984—; USPHS rsch. fellow UCLA, 1969-70. Mem. AAAS, Inst. Medicine-Nat. acad. Sci., Am. Physiol. Soc., Soc. Neurosci., Internat. Brain Rsch. Orgn. Office: U So Calif Parkview Med Bldg C103 1420 San Pablo St Los Angeles CA 90033

O'LEARY, MICHAEL PHILIP, urologic surgeon; b. Framingham, Mass., May 10, 1952; s. James Joseph and Jacqueline Anne (Hope) O'L.; m. Kathleen J. Welch, Sept. 17, 1983; children: Jacqueline Grace, James Joseph. AB, Harvard U., 1974, MPH, 1980; MD, George Washington, 1980. Diplomate Am. Bd. Urology. Surg. resident New England Med. Ctr., Boston, 1980-82; urology resident Mass. Gen. Hosp., Boston, 1982-87; asst. prof. urology Sch. Medicine Tufts U., Boston, 1989-93; asst. prof. surgery Harvard Med. Sch., Boston, 1993—; vis. scholar Bus. Sch. Stanford (Calif.) U., 1987-89; presenter in field. Contbr. numerous articles to profl. jours. Mem. Bd. Health, Dedham, Mass., 1994. Robert Wood Johnson scholar U. Calif., San Francisco, 1987-89. Fellow ACS; mem. AMA, AAAS, Am. Urol. Assn. (exec. com. New England sect.), Am. Fertility Soc., Mass. Med. Soc. (house dels. 1995). Home: 62 Channing Rd Dedham MA 02026 Office: Brigham & Women's Hosp 45 Francis St Boston MA 02115

OLECKNO, WILLIAM ANTON, medical educator; b. St. Charles, Ill., Dec. 16, 1948; s. Adolph B. and Barbara (Walrod) O.; m. Karen Marie Guzauskas, Dec. 27, 1975. BS, Ind. U., Indpls., 1971; MPH, U. Pitts., 1973; HSD, Ind. U., 1980. Diplomate Am. Acad. Sanitarians; registered environ. health specialist, Ind. Sanitarian, DuPage County Health Dept., Wheaton, Ill., 1970-71, Ill. Dept. Pub. Health, Aurora, Ill., 1972; research assoc. Consad Research Corp., Pitts., 1973; instr., coordinator environ. health scis. program Ind. U. Med. Sch., Indpls., 1973-76; asst. prof., coordinator environ. health scis., 1976-80; assoc. prof., coord. community health program No. Ill. U., DeKalb, 1980-89, prof. cmty. health program, 1990-94, prof., coord. pub. & cmty. health programs, 1994—; pub. health and safety cons. Nat. Automatic Merchandising Assn., Chgo., 1975-80, 88—; vis. lectr. Ind. U., Bloomington, 1977-78; mem. health manpower adv. council Ind. Health Careers, Inc., 1976-80; v.p. bd. dirs. Am. Heart Assn., DeKalb County, 1981-83; chmn. DeKalb County Health Planning com., 1982-83. Recipient A. Harry Bliss editorial award Jour. Environ. Health, 1984; Ill. State Merit scholar, 1967; USPHS traineeship, 1972; grantee USPHS, 1973-78, Regional Ind. Med. Program, 1975-76, HHS,1981, Ill. Environ. Health Assn., 1986, Nat. Environ. Health Assn., 1991. Fellow The Royal Soc. Health (London); mem. Nat. Environ. Health Assn. (chmn. individual and community water supply com. 1983-85, chmn. publs. com. 1985-87, mem. Jour. Adv. Com. 1986-87; grantee Ill. assn., 1986, presdl. citation 1984, rep. Nat. Sanitation Found. internat. joint com. drinking water additives 1989—), Am. Pub. Health Assn., Ill. Environ. Health Assn. (bd. dirs. 1987-89, chmn. grant & rsch. fellow review com. 1988-89), Ill. Pub. Health Assn., Eta Sigma Gamma, Phi Delta Kappa. Author: Water Quality Parameters, 1982, 91; Alternative Methods of Centralized Wastewater Treatment, 1982; mem. editorial bd Hoosier Sanitarian, 1977-78, editor, 1978-80; contbr. articles on environ. and pub. health to profl. jours.

OLEEN-BURKEY, MERRIKAY ADELLE, research epidemiologist, educator, pharmacist; b. Princeton, Minn., Oct. 30, 1949; d. Walter Burdette and Virginia Emelia (Carlson) Oleen; m. Jeff Ray Burkey, July 7, 1990. BS in Pharmacy, N.D. State U., 1972, MS in Pharmacy, 1975; PhD in Social and Adminstrv. Pharmacy, U. Minn., 1985. Registered pharmacist, N.D., Minn. Pharmacist intern Mora (Minn.) Drug Co., 1972-73; pharmacy resident VA Med. Ctr., Fargo, N.D., 1973-75; asst. dir. clin. pharmacy svcs. Brokaw Hosp., Normal, Ill., 1976-79; dir. drug info. Wash. State U., Pullman, 1979-81; Kellogg Found. fellow U. Minn., Mpls., 1981-84; research epidemiologist Upjohn Co., Kalamazoo, 1985-90, health econs. scientist, 1990—; adj. prof. epidemiology Western Mich. U., Kalamazoo, 1988-91. Contbr. articles to profl. jours. Vol. CROP Walk, 1987-95, Planned Parenthood, 1986-90; chair adult edn. com. Prince of Peace Luth. Ch., Portage, Mich., 1992-93. Named Hosp. Pharmacist of Yr., Ill. Coun. Hosp. Pharmacists, 1979; Kellogg Found. fellow U. Minn., 1981-84; recipient Upjohn Mktg. Excellence award, 1994. Mem. APHA, LWV, Internat. Soc. Pharmacoepidemiology (membership chair 1995-96), Soc. Epidemiologic Rsch., Am. Pharm. Assn., Drug Info. Assn., Vasa. Home: 4441 Frontier Ave Kalamazoo MI 49024 Office: Pharmacia & Upjohn Inc 7000 Portage Rd Kalamazoo MI 49001-0102

OLENGINSKI, JAN ANTHONY, surgeon; b. West Point, N.Y., May 29, 1964; s. Jan Anthony and Patricia Ann (Grabowski) O. BS, U. Scranton, 1986; DO, U. Health Scis., 1990. Intern Suburban Gen. Hosp., Norristown, Pa., 1990-91; resident Phila. Coll. Osteo. Medicine, 1991-95, chief resident, 1994-95; surgeon Grad. Hosp., Phila., 1995—. Vascular surgery fellow Phila. Coll. Osteo. Medicine, 1995-96. Mem. Am. Osteo. Assn., Am. Coll. Osteo. Surgeons, Am. Assn. Osteo. Postgrad. Physicians. Pa. Osteo. Med. Assn., Pa. Med. Soc. Republican. Roman Catholic. Home: 349 Peachtree Dr Jenkintown PA 19046 Office: Ste 2110 1331 E Wyoming Ave Philadelphia PA 19124

OLER, WESLEY MARION, III, physician, educator; b. N.Y.C., Mar. 8, 1918; s. Wesley Marion Jr. and Imogene (Rubel) O.; m. Virginia Carolyn Craemer, Dec. 8, 1951; children: Helen Louise (dec.), Wesley Marion IV, Stephen Scott. Grad., Phillips Andover Acad., 1936; AB, Yale U., 1940; MD, Columbia U., 1943. Intern Bellevue Hosp., N.Y.C., 1944; resident Bellevue Hosp., 1948-50; fellow Hosp. U. Pa., 1951; practice medicine specializing in internal medicine Washington, 1952-93; mem. emeritus staff, vice chmn. dept. medicine Washington Hosp. Ctr., 1962-64; v.p. med. bd. Washington Hosp. Center, 1971-72, trustee, 1973-81, emeritus, 1994; clin. prof. medicine emeritus Med. Sch. Georgetown U. Contbr. articles on old musical instruments to jours. Founder, past pres. Washington Recorder Soc.; bd. dirs. Am. Recorder Soc. Maj. M.C. U.S. Army (paratroops), 1944-47. Fellow ACP (gov. 1980-84); mem. SAR, Mensa, Osler Soc. Washington (past pres.), Met. Club, Cosmos Club, Chevy Chase Club. Republican. Episcopalian. Home: Apt 612N 8101 Connecticut Ave Chevy Chase MD 20815-2805

OLESKOWICZ, JEANETTE, physician; b. N.Y.C., Oct. 10, 1956; d. John Francis and Helen (Zielinski) O. BA, NYU, 1977; D of Chiropractic, N.Y. Chiropractic Coll., 1982; MS, U. Bridgeport, 1984; MD, U. Medicine & Dentistry N.J., 1990. U.S. immigration officer U.S. Dept. Justice, N.Y.C., 1977; commd. med. officer USAR, 1983; advanced through grades to maj. HPSP, 1990; resident and intern Eisenhower Army Med. Ctr., Ft. Gordon, Ga., 1990-94; chief psychiatry U.S. Army Hosp., Vicenza, Italy, 1994-95; cons.- liaison psychiatrist Brooke Army Med. Ctr., Tex., 1995—. Am. sponsor for a cripples child's health care in Mid. East. Mem. AMA, Am. Psychiat. Assn. Home: 4000 Horizon Hill # 607 San Antonio TX 78229

OLINGER, GORDON NORDELL, surgeon; b. Denver, 1942. MD, U. Rochester, 1968. Intern UCLA, 1968-69, resident, 1969-70, 72-74; resident in surgery NIH Clinic, Bethesda, Md., 1970-72; with Milw. County Med. Complex; prof., chmn. Med. Coll. Wis. Mem. ACS, STS, SUS. Office: Acad Faculty 8700 W Wisconsin Ave Milwaukee WI 53226-3512*

OLINICK, STANLEY L., psychiatrist, psychoanalyst, educator; b. Boston, May 1, 1915; s. Maury S. and Etta S. (Markell) O.; m. Yvonne van der Reyden (dec. Mar. 1963); 1 child, Philip Andries; m. Vida Brown, June 26, 1964. SB magna cum laude, Harvard U., 1936; MD, SUNY, Buffalo, 1940. Diplomate Nat. Bd. Med. Examiners, Am. Bd. Psychiatry and Neurology. Med. officer St. Elizabeths Hosp., Washington, 1940-42, 46-47; student and rsch. assoc. Washington Sch. Psychiatry, Washington, 1946-49; clin. prof. psychiatry Sch. Medicine Georgetown U., Washington, 1947—; tng. & supervising analyst Washington Psychoanalytic Inst., 1954-79; cons., Washington, 1947—. Author: The Psychotherapeutic Instrument, 1980; contbr. articles to profl. jours. Major Med. Corp., U.S. Army, 1942-46. Fellow Am. Psychiat. Assn.; mem. Am. Psychoanalytic Assn. (life, councilor, com. mem.), Washington Psychoanalytic Soc. (com. mem. 1947—, pres. 1959-61), Washington Psychoanalytic Inst., Washington Psychiat. Soc. (com. mem.), Kenwood Country Club. Office: 2819 Ellicott St NW Washington DC 20008-1020

OLINS, ERIC WAYNE, osteopath; b. L.A., May 6, 1965; s. Michael Allan and Sauna Marlene (Finkelburg) O. BS, U. Calif., Riverside, 1987; MS, Calif. State U., 1989; DO, Coll. Osteo. Medicine Pacific, 1993. Lic. Colo. Intern Fitzsimons Army Med. Ctr., Aurora, Colo., 1993-94; brigade surgeon HHC 2d Brigade, Korea, 1994-95, HHC/MMC Discom, Fort Carson, Colo., 1995-96; flight surgeon 413 ACR, Fort Carson, Colo., 1996—. Mem. Am. Osteopathic Assn., Am. Osteopathic Mil. Physicians & Surgeons, Assn. Mil. Surgeons, Sigma Sigma Phi, Phi Gamma Delta. Home: 3415 Hideaway Pl Colorado Springs CO 80918 Office: HHT 413 ACR Fort Carson CO 80913-5000

OLIPHANT, CHARLES ROMIG, physician; b. Waukegan, Ill., Sept. 10, 1917; s. Charles L. and Mary (Goss) R.; student St. Louis U., 1936-40; m. Claire E. Canavan, Nov. 7, 1942; children: James R., Cathy Rose, Mary G., William D. Student, St. Louis U., 1936-40, MD, 1943; postgrad. Naval Med. Sch., 1946. Intern, Nat. Naval Med. Ctr., Bethesda, Md., 1943; pvt. practice medicine and surgery, San Diego, 1947—; pres., CEO Midway Med. Enterprises; former chief staff Balboa Hosp., Doctors Hosp., Cabrillo Med. Ctr.; chief staff emeritus Sharp Cabrillo Hosp.; mem. staff Mercy Hosp., Children's Hosp., Paradise Valley Hosp., Sharp Meml. Hosp.; sec. Sharp Sr. Health Care, S.D.; mem. exec. bd., program chmn. San Diego Power Squadron, 1985-93, 95. Charter mem. Am. Bd. Family Practice. Served with M.C., USN, 1943-47. Recipient Golden Staff award Sharp Cabrillo Hosp. Med. Staff, 1990. Fellow Am. Geriatrics Soc. (emeritus), Am. Acad. Family Practice, Am. Assn. Abdominal Surgeons; mem. AMA, Calif. Med. Assn., Am. Acad. Family Physicians (past pres. San Diego chpt., del. Calif. chpt.), San Diego Med. Soc., Public Health League, Navy League, San Diego Power Squadron (past comdr.), SAR. Clubs: San Diego Yacht, Cameron Highlanders. Home: 4310 Trias St San Diego CA 92103-1127

OLIVEIRA, JOÃO PAULO FERREIRA, nephrologist, geneticist; b. Coimbra, Portugal, Feb. 7, 1957; s. Alexandrino Beato and Maria Cristina C.M.F. (Silva) O.; m. Maria Manuela Alves Fontoura, May 16, 1982; children: João, Mariana, Inês, Nuno. MD, Faculty Medicine, Porto, Portugal, 1981, MS in Genetics, 1990; postgrad. in Nephrology, Sackler Sch. Medicine, Tel-Aviv, 1990. Cert. nephrologist, med. geneticist. Gen med. intern Hosp. São João, Porto, 1982-85, nephrology resident, 1985-91, provisional nephrologist, 1991-95, staff nephrologist, 1995—; lectr. genetics Faculty Medicine, Porto, 1985—; cons. nephrologist NMC, Feira, Portugal, 1991—, DRD, Riba de Ave, Portugal, 1991—; physician-in-charge Genetics Clinic, Hosp. São João, Porto, 1992—, Peritoneal Dialysis Program Nephrology Svc., 1994—. Assoc. editor Perspectivas em Prática Médica, 1995. Cofounder Centro de Atletismo do Porto, 1974. Mem. Internat. Soc. Nephrology, European Dialysis and Transplant Assn., European Soc. Human Genetics, Nat. Assn. Young Physicians (co-founder 1988). Roman Catholic. Office: Servico de Genética, Médica, Faculty Medicine, Porto 4200, Portugal

OLIVENCIA-YURVATI, ALBERT HENRY, surgeon; b. Allentown, Pa., Mar. 29, 1955; s. Albert Stephen and Ivelise Amalie (Olivencia) Y.; m. Sharon Anne Donelan, Aug. 31, 1974. BS in health sci., Calif. State Univ., 1981; DO, Univ. North Tex., 1986. Intern Tulsa Regional Medical Ctr., Tulsa, Okla., 1986-87; resident in gen. surgery Okla. State, Tulsa, 1987-91; resident in cardiac surgery Deborah Heart Ctr., Browns Mills, N.J., 1991-94; asst. clinical prof. surgery Mich. State Univ., East Lansing, 1994-96, Univ. N. Tex., Ft. Worth, 1996—; dir. mech. heart support Sparrow Heart Ctr., Lansing, 1994-96. Contbr. articles to profl. jours. With USAR. Recipient Resident Achievement award Am. Coll. Osteopathic Surgeons, 1989-93, Robert Irwin Literary award Am. Coll. Osteopathic Surgeons, 1988, 89, 90. Fellow Internat. Coll. Surgeons; mem. Am. Osteopathic Assn., Am. Coll. Osteopathic Surgeons, Am. Coll. Chest Physicians. Home and Office: 1002 Montgomery Ste 210 Fort Worth TX 76107

OLIVER, EARL PORTER, family physician; b. Lamasco, Ky., Apr. 26, 1918; s. Earl F. and Beatrice B. (Burns) O.; m. Margurette C. Fultz, Mar. 20, 1943; 1 chil, Margurette Jr. BS, U. Ky., 1940; MD, U. Louisville, 1943. Diplomate Am. Bd. Family Practice. Ptnr., physician Halcomis & Oliver Clinic, Scottsville, Ky., 1946-85; med. cons. GE Co., Scottsville, 1980—; edn. dir. Ky. Peer Rev. Orgn., Louisville, 1983-88; preceptor U. Louisville Coll. Medicine, 1987-94, asst. clin. prof. medicine, 1983-85. Mem., past pres. Scottsville Sch. Bd., 1963-74; mem. Consumer Adv. Com. Blue Cross, Ky., 1975—; past pres. Govs. Commn. on Aging, Ky., 1961-71, Allen County Hist. Soc., Scottsville, 1984—. Fellow Am. Acad. Family Practice; mem. AMA, Ky. Med. Assn. (trustee, vice chair 1980), Rotary Club, Masons, Shriners. Republican. Baptist. Home: 822 Gallatin Rd Scottsville KY 42164

OLIVER, EUGENE ALEX, speech and language pathologist; b. East Palatka, Fla., Apr. 18, 1938; s. John T. and Ida (McBride) O.; m. Barbara Ann Gainer, Apr. 20, 1963; 1 child, Zulika Bonita. BA, Fla. A&M Univ., 1962; MA (equiv.), Southern Conn. State Univ., 1983; cert. advanced studies (equiv.), Fairfield Univ., 1989. Cert. speech and language pathology, Conn., lic. speech pathologist, Conn. Speech and lang. pathologist Florence (S.C.) Pub. Schs., 1962-63, Baltimore Pub. Schs., 1963-66, Imperial County Supt.'s Office, El Centro, Calif., 1967-69, Danbury (Conn.) Pub. Schs., 1969-80, Albuquerque Pub. Schs., 1980-81, Monzano H.S., Albuquerque, 1980-81; speech and lang. pathologist & coord. Cuba (N.Mex.) Pub. Schs., 1981-84; speech and lang. pathologist Waterbury (Conn.) Pub. Schs., 1985—; specialist comm. disorders on H.S. level Crosby H.S., Waterbury, 1986—, specialist Wilson Learning Ctr., Waterbury, 1985—. Founding mem. Black Congress, New Milford Conn., 1969; cons. Kwanzaa Celebrations, Conn., 1993; mem. Greater Bridgeport, Conn. chpt. NAACP, 1994—. Recipient Spl. Recognition, speech dept. Waterbury Pub. Sch., 1993, Wilson Learning Ctr., 1991. Mem. NEA, Conn. Speech Lang. Hearing Assn., Conn. Edn. Assn., Waterbury Tchrs. Assn. Home: 289 Fan Hill Rd Monroe CT 06468 Office: Waterbury Pub Schs 236 Grand St Waterbury CT 06702-1930

OLIVER, GREGORY CHET, colorectal surgeon; b. Newark, June 2, 1949; s. Chester Henry and Marybelle (Littell) O.; m. Ellen Elizabeth Fowle, June 17, 1972; children: Margaret Katharine, Andrea Lee, Michael Gregory. BA, Colgate U., 1972; MD, George Washington U., 1976. Diplomate Am. Bd. Surgery, Am. Bd. Colon & Rectal Surgery. Clin. ass. prof. surgery Robert Wood Johnson Sch. Medicine; attending surgeon Muhlenberg Regional Med. Ctr., Plainfield, N.J., 1988—; attending surgeon J.F. Kennedy Hosp., Edison, N.J., 1988—; chief dept. surgery Muhlenberg Regional Med. Ctr., 1995—, trustee, 1992—. Served in USPHS, 1978-80. Fellow Am. Coll. Surgeons, Am. Soc. Colon & Rectal Surgery (nat. program dir. 1994). Republican. Presbyn. Office: Assoc Colon & Rectal Surg 1010 Park Ave Plainfield NJ 07060

OLIVER, HERMAN, psychiatrist; b. N.Y.C., June 24, 1929. BA, NYU, 1951; MD, U. Amsterdam, 1957. Intern Kings County Hosp., Bklyn., 1958; resident Bellevue Hosp., N.Y.C., 1959; resident Hillside Hosp., Queens, N.Y., 1960-61, fellow psychotherapy, 1962-63; asst. prof. psychiatry Albert Einstein Coll. Medicine, N.Y.C., 1963—; med. dir. JCS, N.Y.C. Contbr. articles to profl. jours. Fellow Am. Psychiat. Assn.; mem. Am. Community Psychiatry Assn., Nassau Psychiat. Soc., N.Y. State Med. Assn. Home and Office: 6 Sussex Rd Great Neck NY 11020-1829 Office: LIJMC New Hyde Park New York NY 11020

OLIVER, JAMES WALTER, health facility executive; b. Somerville, Mass., June 27, 1955; s. Earl Gorden and Ethel (Turner) O.; m. Deborah Day, Sept. 1, 1989; children: Ashley Elizabeth, Joshua James. AS in Building Constrn., Wentworth Inst., 1975, BS in Mgmt. Engring., 1979; MBA, Suffolk U., 1983. Staff assoc. Mass. Hosp. Assoc., Burlington, 1979-81; mgmt. engr. Univ. Hosp., Boston, 1981-82, dir. material mgmt., 1982-87; dir. materials mgmt. Miriam Hosp., Providence, 1987-89; dir. material svcs. Yankee Alliance, Andover, Mass., 1989-91, sr. v.p., 1991—. Mem. Healthcare Materials Mgmt. Soc. (pres. 1990—. v.p. edn. 1988-90, mem.-at-large 1988, Materials Mgr. of Yr. 1990). Office: Yankee Alliance 300 Brickstone Sq Andover MA 01810-1429

OLIVER, JANICE CAROLINE YEE, dentist; b. Castro Valley, Calif., Nov. 25, 1961; d. Kenneth Kwock Sang and Vicenta Chan She (Leong) Yee; m. Richard N. Oliver III, June 23, 1985. BS in Dental Sci., DDS, U. Calif., San Francisco, 1986. Assoc. Donald R. Call DDS, Sunnyvale, Calif., 1990—. Mem. ADA, Calif. Dental Assn., Santa Clara County Dental Soc., U. Calif.-San Francisco Alumni Assn., Psi Omega Beta. Democrat. Office: 990 W Fremont Ste E Sunnyvale CA 94087

OLIVER, ROSE WARSHAW, psychologist, psychotherapist; b. Poland, Mar. 9, 1910; d. Nathan and Celia (Cohn) Warshaw; came to U.S., 1914, naturalized, 1926; B.A., Barnard Coll., 1931; M.A., Queens Coll., City U. N.Y., 1967, Ph.D., Grad. Center, 1973; postgrad. fellow Inst. Rational Emotive Therapy, 1975; m. Juan Oliver, Sept. 1937; children: Teressa, John. Adj. asst. prof. psychology City U. N.Y., 1969-75; staff psychotherapist, mem. supervisory faculty Inst. Rational Emotive Therapy, N.Y.C., 1975; pvt. practice psychology and psychotherapy, Queens, N.Y.C., 1975—; workshop leader; lectr. in field; bd. profl. advisors Inst. Rational Emotive Therapy. Cert. psychologist, N.Y. Co-author: (with Frances Bock) Coping with Alzheimer's: A Caregiver's Emotional Survival Guide, 1987; contbr. articles to profl. jours. Mem. Am. Psychol. Assn., N.Y. State Psychol. Assn., Nassau County Psychol. Assn., N.Y. Soc. Clin. Psychologists. Home: 161 W 61st St New York NY 10023-7400

OLIVER, THOMAS K., JR., pediatrician; b. Hobart Mills, Calif., Dec. 21, 1925; married, 1949; two children. MD, Harvard U., 1949. Diplomate Am. Bd. Pediats. Pediats. instr. Med. Coll. Cornell U., N.Y.C., 1953-55; from asst. to assoc. prof. Ohio State U., N.Y.C., 1955-63; from assoc. prof. to prof. pediats. U. Wash., Stockholm, 1963-70; prof. pediats., chmn. dept. Sch. Med. U. Pitts., 1970-87; v.p. Am. Bd. Pediats., 1987—; prof. pediatrics Duke U., U. N.C.; spl. fellow neonatal physiol. Karolinska Inst., Sweden, 1960-61; med. dir. Children's Hosp., Pitts., 1971-78. Cons. editor Monographs Neonatology, 1975—; co-editor Seminars Perinatology, 1975-85. Mem. Soc. Pediat. Rsch., Am. Pediat. Soc., Assn. Am. Med. Colls., Am. Acad. Pediat., Inst. Med. Rsch. *

OLIVERIO, ALBERTO, psychobiology educator, researcher; b. Catania, Italy, Dec. 1, 1938; s. Aleardo and Giovanna (Picciau) O.; m. Anna Ferraris, Oct. 3, 1970; 1 child, Albertina. MD, U. Rome, 1962. Rsch. fellow NIH, Rome, 1963-64, Karolinska Inst., Stockholm, Sweden, 1964-65; asst. rsch. pharmacologist Sch. of Medicine UCLA, 1965-66; rsch. dir. Inst. Psychobiology NRC, Rome, 1971-75; prof. U. Rome, 1975—, dean Sch. Biol. Scis., 1985-86, chmn. dept. genetics and molecular biology, 1988-90; dir. Inst. Psychobiology and Psychopharmacology, NRC, 1977—. Author: Biology and Behavior, 1982, Psychobiology of Stress, 1990; editor: Behavior of Human Infants, 1983. Mem. AAAS, Internat. Brain Rsch. Orgn., European Neurosci. Assn. Home: 72 Via Nemoremse, 00199 Rome Italy Office: U Rome Inst Psychobiology, 1 Via Reno, 00198 Rome Italy

OLIVIER, PAUL NORMAND, healthcare administrator; b. New Bedford, Mass., July 7, 1967; s. Normand Edward and Norma Marie Olivier. BS, Providence Coll., 1989; M of Health Svcs. Adminstrn., George Washington U., 1992. Gen. mgr. Rohnert Park (Calif.) Healthcare Corp., 1992-93; adminstrv. dir. Santa Rosa (Calif.) Meml. Hosp., 1993-95; dir. Regional Continuum of Care, 1995—; chair Breast Cancer Detection Partnership, Santa Rosa, 1994—; loaned exec. United Way, Santa Rosa, 1992. Mem. Rohnert Park Healthy Cities, 1992, Rohnert Park Bus. Devel., 1992, Leadership Rohnert Park, 1992. Home: PO Box 2532 Santa Rosa CA 95405 Office: Santa Rosa Meml Hosp 1165 Montgomery Dr Santa Rosa CA 95402

OLLIKAINEN, JUKKA MARTI, pediatrician, researcher; b. Kuopio, Finland, Jan. 11, 1960; s. Martti Johannes and Katri Marjatta (Jokela) O.; m. Marja Helena Nurmela, Dec. 21, 1985; children: Tommi, Ville. MD, Kuopio U., 1984, specialty in pediats., 1990. Asst. pediatrician Kuopio Univ. Hosp., 1985-90, cons. pediatrician, 1990-91; leading physician Varkaus (Finland) Dist. Hosp., 1991—. Contbr. med. studies to profl. jours. With Finnish M.C., 1986. Grantee Sohlberg's Found., 1990, Maud Kuistila's Found., 1994. Office: Varkaus Dist Hosp, Savontie 55, 78300 Varkaus Finland

OLLSTEIN, RONALD NEIL, plastic surgeon; b. N.Y.C., Apr. 14, 1934; s. Philip and Miriam (Middleman) O.; children: Bruce W., Mark E., David L. (dec.); m. Louise A. Restak, Aug. 17, 1995. AB, Cornell U., 1955, MD, 1958. Diplomate Am. Bd. Plastic Surgery. Chief Burn Ctr. Harlem Hosp., N.Y.C., 1965-70; chief plastic and reconstructive surgeon Jewish Meml. Hosp., N.Y.C., 1966-80; chief plastic and reconstructive surgery, hand surgery St. Vincent's Hosp., N.Y.C., 1968—; asst. attending surgeon The Presbyn. Hosp., N.Y.C., 1988—; lectr. in surgery Columbia U. Phys./Surgery, N.Y.C., 1988—; clin. assoc. prof. surgery, NYU Sch. Med., 1971—, clin. prof. surgery, N.Y. Med. Coll., Valhalla, 1980—. Contbr. articles to profl. jours., book chpts. Fellow Am. Coll. Surgeons; mem. Am. Assn. Hand Surgery, Am. Soc. Plastic Reconstructive Surgeons, Am. Assn. Plastic Surgeons (chmn. ethics com. 1976-77). Jewish. Home: 4601 Henry Hudson Pkwy Riverdale NY 10471-3801 Office: St Vincents Hosp 153 W 11th St New York NY 10011

OLMO, JAIME ALBERTO, physician; b. Barceloneta, P.R., Aug. 28, 1930; d. Juan and Emilia (Gonzalez) O.; m. Joaquina Rivas, June 24, 1954; children: Jaime A., Carlos A., Rosa I., Javier A., Ruth de Lourdes (dec.). BS, U. P.R., 1950; MD, Santiago de Compostela, Spain, 1956. Diplomate Am. Bd. Utilization Rev. Physicians. Intern Auxillo Mutuo Hosp., Hato Rey, P.R., 1956-57; med. dir. Mcpl. Hosp., Aibonito, P.R., 1957-58; resident Doctors Hosp., Santurce, P.R., 1958-59; practice family medicine Rio Piedras, P.R., 1959-88; dir. mktg. and utilization Cardiovascular Surgery of Tex., 1988-90; dir. mktg.-latin Am. St. Joseph Hosp., Houston, 1990—; mem. staff Doctors Hosp., Hosp. San Carlos, Auxilio Mutuo, Tchrs. Hosp., San Martin Hosp.; med. dir. Blue Cross P.R., 1977-88. Treas. Assn. Antituberculosa San Juan, 1958-68, v.p., 1968-69; mem. Instituto Cultura Hispanica, Madrid, 1963—, treas., 1972-78, pres. 1978-82; pres. dist. 2 Boy Scouts Am., 1971-75, mem. P.R. Council, 1965-75; pres. Consuelo Escalona Sch. PTA, Carolina, P.R., 1969-71, also bd. dirs. Decorated Knight Corpus Christi, Toledo, Spain, 1970; recipient Scouters Key, Boy Scouts Am., 1967, Pelican award, 1968, Guajataka award, 1969, 70, Silver Beaver award, 1971; awards Instituto de Cultura Hispanica in Madrid, 1963, 70; medalia al Merito Civil Govt. of Spain, 1977. Fellow Internat. Assn. Physicians and Surgeons, Royal Acad. Medicine (London), Royal Acad. Health (London); mem. AMA, Pan Am. Med. Assn. (sec. 1973-77), P.R. Med. Assn. (ho. of dels. 1958—61, 77, 83, pres. eastern dist. 1970, treas. 1969, vice speaker ho. of dels. 1973, pres. jud. coun., pres. med. services coun., pres. 1976, numerous awards, now dir.), Assn. Physicians and Surgeons, Assn. Profl. of P.r., Ateneo de P.R., Am. Acad. Family Medicine, Am. Assn. Med. Dirs., Asociacion Puertoriquena Graduados Universidades Españolas (pres. 1968, 87), Comandante Exch. Club (pres. 1962-64), P.R. Exch. Club (dir. 1964), Lions (v.p. Aibonito 1987). Roman Catholic. Home: 13410 Rosstown Ct Sugar Land TX 77478-6047

OLNESS, KAREN NORMA, pediatrics and international health educator; b. Rushford, Minn., Aug. 28, 1936; d. Norman Theodore and Karen Agnes (Gunderson) O.; m. Hakon Daniel Torjesen, 1962. BA, U. Minn., 1958, BS, MD, 1961. Diplomate Am. Bd. Pediatrics, Am. Bd. Med. Hypnosis. Intern Harbor Gen. Hosp., Torrance, Calif.; resident Nat. Children's Hosp. Med. Ctr., Washington; asst. prof. George Washington U., Washington, 1970-74; assoc. prof. U. Minn., Mpls., 1974-87; prof. pediatrics, family medicine and internat. health Case Western Res. U., Cleve., 1987—. Named Outstanding Woman Physician, Minn. Assn. Women Physicians, 1987. Fellow Am. Acad. Pediatrics, Am. Acad. Family Physicians, Am. Soc. Clin. Hypnosis (pres. 1984-86), Soc. Clin. and Exptl. Hypnosis (pres. 1991-93); mem. Soc. for Behavioral Pediatrics (pres. 1991-92), Northwestern Pediatric Soc. (pres. 1977). Office: Case Western Res U 11100 Euclid Ave Cleveland OH 44106-1736

OLOFF, JOAN, podiatrist; b. N.Y.C., Nov. 18, 1957; d. Joseph and Gisela (Fleischman) O.; m. Murray Arthur Solomon; children: Daniel, Matthew, Jamie. BS, NYU, 1976; D in Podiatric Medicine, PCPM, 1981; MS, CCPM, 1984. Bd. cert. ABPS. Asst. prof. CCPM, San Francisco, 1983-85; pvt. practice podiatrist Los Gatos, Calif., 1985—; med. examiner Podiatric Med. Bd., Sacramento, 1984-95, cons., 1995—. Editor: Radiology of the Foot, 1985; contbr. articles to profl. jours. Fellow ACFAS; mem. CPMA, APMA. Office: Los Gatos Foot & Ankle Ctr 14601 S Bascom Ave #240 Los Gatos CA 95032-2043

O'LOONEY, PATRICIA ANNE, medical program administrator; b. Bridgeport, Conn., Dec. 2, 1954; d. John Joseph and Marjorie Ellen (Curran) O'L. BA in Molecular Biology, Regis Coll., 1976; MS in Biochemistry, George Washington U., 1978, PhD in Biochemistry, 1982. Rsch. asst. biochemistry dept. George Washington Med. Sch., Washington, 1976-82, teaching asst., 1978-81, rsch. assoc., 1982-84, sr. rsch. scientist, 1984-86, asst. prof. medicine and biochemistry, 1986-88; asst. dir. The Nat. Multiple Sclerosis Soc., N.Y.C., 1988-90, assoc. dir. rsch. and med. programs, 1990-91, dir. rsch. and med. programs, 1991—; vis. lectr. George Washington Med. Sch., 1988—. Author: Lipoprotein Lipase, 1987; contbr. articles to profl. jours. Recipient New Investigator Rsch. award NIH, 1985. Mem. Am. Soc. for Biochemistry and Molecular Biology, N.Y. Acad. Scis., Assn. for Women in Sci., The Mid-Atlantic Lipid Soc., Sigma Xi, Beta Beta Beta. Republican. Roman Catholic. Office: Nat Multiple Sclerosis Soc 733 3rd Ave New York NY 10017-3204

OLSEN, GREG SCOTT, chiropractor; b. Anaheim, Calif., June 28, 1968; s. John Carlos and Gloria (Brownmiller) Frazier. D Chiropractic, L.A. Coll. Chiropractic, Whittier, Calif., 1994. Pvt. practice, Huntington Beach, Calif., 1994; postgrad. tchg. asst. Internat. Coll. Applied Kinesiology, L.A., 1995—. Mem. Am. Chiropractic Assn., Internat. Chiropractic Assn., Internat. Coll. Applied Kinesiology, Calif. Chiropractic Assn. Office: GO Chiropractic! # 135 16168 Beach Blvd Huntington Beach CA 92647

OLSEN, INGER ANNA, psychologist; b. Copper Mountain, B.C, Can., Dec. 25, 1926; d. Dagmar O.; B.S., Wash. State U., 1954, M.S., 1956, Ph.D., 1962. Psychiat. nurse Provincial Mental Health Services B.C., 1947-51, psychologist, 1956-58; psychologist Vancouver (B.C.) City Met. Health Services, 1958-60, Wash. State U. Student Counseling Center, Pullman, 1960-62; sr. psychologist Met. Health Services, Vancouver, 1962-66; instr. psychology Vancouver Community Coll., 1966-87; docent Vancouver Aquarium Assn. Bd. dirs. Second Mile Soc., 1975-89. Contbr. articles to profl. jours. Mem. Am. Psychol. Assn., Gerontol. Soc. Am., Can. Assn. Gerontology, Phi Beta Kappa, Sigma Xi, Alpha Kappa Delta. Home: 1255 Bidwell St Apt 1910, Vancouver, BC Canada V6G 2K8

OLSEN, RICHARD GALEN, biomedical engineer, researcher; b. Colorado Springs, Colo., Aug. 10, 1945; s. Floyd Edwin and Ruth Elizabeth (Robinson) O.; m. Karen Fidler Brubaker, June 17, 1973; children: Kathryn Elizabeth, Nickolas Robert. BSEE, U. Mo., Rolla, 1968; MS, U. Utah, 1970, PhD, 1975. Registered profl. engr., Fla. Engr. Bendix Corp., Kansas City, Mo., 1966-69; elec. engr. Naval Aerospace Med. Rsch. Lab., Pensacola, Fla., 1975-79, chief engring. systems div., 1979-82, head bioengring. divsn., 1982-94; head bioengring. dept. Naval Med. Rsch. Inst. Detachment, Brooks AFB, Tex., 1994—; tech. cons. Armstrong Lab., USAF, 1991—, German Ministry of Def., Munster, 1994, Naval Surface Warfare Ctr., Dahlgren, Va., 1989-95, Naval Sea Sys. Command, Arlington, Va., 1989-91. Contbr. articles to profl. jours. and books. With U.S. Army, 1970-72. Recipient NDEA fellowship U. Utah, 1969, Fred A. Hitchcock award Aerospace Physiologist Soc. of Aerospace Med., 1987; named Engr. of the Yr., N.W. Fla. Engrs. Coun., 1991. Mem. IEEE (sr., chmn. Pensacola sect. 1982-83, radio frequency and microwave measuring methods com. 1982—, nonionizing radiation hazards com. 1983—, SCC-28 com., Cert. of Appreciation 1983), Bioelectromagnetics Soc. (charter, editl. bd. 1990-96), Aerospace Med. Assn. (editl. cons. 1986—), Rotary (bd. dirs. Suburban West 1980-81), Sigma Xi, Eta Kappa Nu, Tau Beta Pi, Phi Kappa Phi. Republican. Adventist. Home: 1503 N Baylen St Pensacola FL 32501-2101 Office: Naval Med Rsch Inst Detach 8308 Hawks Rd Brooks AFB TX 78235-5423

OLSHANSKY, DONALD H., dermatologist; b. Detroit, Oct. 20, 1931; s. Isadore Sam and Ida (Gevercer) O; m. Ruth Ann Epstein, June 23, 1957; children: Donna F., Daniel I., Janet C. BA with distinction, U. Mich., 1955, MD, 1957. Intern Hurley Hosp., Flint, Mich., 1957-58; resident dermatology Grad. Hosp., U. Pa., Phila., 1958-60, Wayne State U. Receiving Hosp., Detroit, 1960-61; pvt. practice Red Bank, N.J., 1961—; asst. attending physician Monmouth Med. Ctr., Long Branch, N.J., 1961-71; attending physician Jersey Shore Med. Ctr., Neptune, N.J., 1962-72; attending physician, dir. dermatology div. Riverview Med. Ctr., Red Bank, 1962—. Pres. Friends of the N.J. State Orch., Long Branch, 1974-76. Fellow Am. Acad. Dermatology; mem. Phila. Dermatol. Soc., Monmouth County Med. Soc. Jewish. Office: 206 Broad St Red Bank NJ 07701-2002

OLSNES, SJUR, biochemistry educator; b. Bergen, Norway, Aug. 23, 1939; s. Sigvald and Maria (Berge) O.; m. Barbara Tubylewicz Kwiatkowska, Jan. 5, 1971; 1 child, Astrid Marta. MD, U. Bonn, Germany, 1964; PhD, U. Oslo, 1972. Intern Hammerfest/Vadsø/Sjøholt, Norway, 1965-66; rsch. fellow Bergen U., Norway, 1966-68; vis. scientist Acad. Scis., Moscow, 1968; rsch. fellow Norwegian Radium Hosp., Oslo, 1969-73, sr. scientist, 1974-89, prof., 1989—; dir. U. Oslo Centre Med. Studies, Moscow, 1993—. Contbr. articles to profl. jours. Recipient Anders Fahres Med. prize for younger scientist U. Oslo, 1979, Shipley award Harvard U., Boston, 1986, Schunk award Giessen U., 1988. Mem. European Molecular Biology Orgn. (life), Academia Europaea (life), Det Norske Videnskaps-Akademi (life). Home: Vestveien 8, 0284 Oslo Norway Office: Inst Cancer Rsch, Norwegian Radium Hosp Montebello, 0310 Oslo Norway

OLSON, BARBARA FORD, physician; b. Iowa City, June 15, 1935; d. Leonard A. and Anne (Swanson) Ford; m. Robert Eric Olson, 1959 (div. 1973); children: Katherine Gee, Eric Ford, Julie Marie. BA, Gustavus Adolphus Coll., 1956; MD, U. Minn., 1960. Diplomate Am. Bd. Family Practice (cert. added qualifications geriatric medicine). Intern St. Paul-Ramsy Med. Ctr., 1960-61; resident in anesthesiology U. Hosp. Cleve., 1961-62, U. Minn. Hosp., Mpls., 1962-63; pvt. practice anesthesiology St. Johns Hosp. and Devine Redeemer Hosp., St. Paul, 1963-67, Mercy Hosp., Coon Rapids, Minn., 1967-74; staff physician Oak Terrace Nursing Home, Minnetonka, Minn., 1974-88; med. dir. nursing home care unit VA Med. Ctr., St. Cloud, Minn., 1988—. Pres., bd. dirs. Alpha Epsilon Iota Med. Found., Mpls., 1980-86. Mem. Minn. Med. Assn., Minn. Women Physicians (pres. 1981-82), Minn. Nursing Home Med. Dirs. Home: PO Box 7306 Saint Cloud MN 56302-7306 Office: VA Med Ctr 4801 8th St N Saint Cloud MN 56303-2014

OLSON, GARY WAYNE, cardiologist; b. Kirksville, Mo., Sept. 21, 1952; s. Harold Gene and Vivian Angela (Menke) O.; children: Jeffrey Taylor, Kristen Elise. BS in Biophysics, Pacific Union Coll., 1974; MD, Loma Linda U., 1977. Resident in internal medicine U. Ala., Birmingham, 1978-81, cardiology fellow, 1981-83; cardiologist Dalton (Ga.) Cardiology, 1983—. Fellow Am. Coll. Physicians, Am. Coll. Cardiology; mem. AHA, AMA. Home: 1523 Thornebrooke Cir Dalton GA 30720 Office: Dalton Cardiology 1436 Broaderick Dr Dalton GA 30720

OLSON, HOWARD CHARLES, retired psychologist; b. Glenwood, Minn., Mar. 20, 1918; s. Willie Ernest and Gertrude (Bowen) O.; m. Helen Mae Anderson Tetle, Dec. 12, 1941 (div. 1957); children: Cheryl Starr Olson, Penelle Jane Olson Chase, Karl Howard Olson; m. Virginia Pauline Thompson, Oct. 10, 1957; children: David Thompson Olson, Virginia Anne Olson Richardson. BS in Agr., N.D. State U., 1941; MS in Indsl. Psychology, N.C. State U., 1949; postgrad., U. N.C., Chapel Hill, 1948-50. Lic. psychologist, D.C. Instr. N.C. State U., Raleigh, 1950-52; sr. rsch. scientist Human Resources Rsch. Office, Washington, 1952-62; mem. tech. staff Rsch. Analysis Corp., McLean, Va., 1962-72, Gen. Rsch. Corp., McLean, 1972-75; rsch. scientist Planning Rsch. Corp., McLean, 1975-77, Advanced Rsch. Resources Orgn., Bethesda, Md., 1977-80; cons. Internat. Union Operating Engrs., Washington, 1980-82; ret., 1980—; rep. Armed Forces NRC Vision Com., Washington, 1953-58. Contbr. articles to profl. jours. Chmn. Polk County (N.C.) unit Am. Cancer Soc., 1982-84, Constrn. Bicentennial Com., Polk County, 1987-89; trustee Isothermal C.C., Spindale, N.C., 1989—; bd. dirs. N.C. divsn. Am. Cancer Soc., Raleigh, 1984-89; bd. dirs. N.C. Art Soc., Raleigh, 1989—; pres. Polk County Campus ICC Found., 1993—; sec.-treas. Health Rsch. Found., 1994—. With U.S. Army, 1942-46, lt. col. USAR, ret. Recipient Nat. award for Excellence U.S. Constn. Bicentennial Commn., 1989. Mem. Am. Psychol. Assn., Am. Psychol. Soc., Ops. Rsch. Soc. Am. (assoc. editor 1972-74), Sigma Xi. Democrat. Unitarian. Home: 417 Melrose Ave Tryon NC 28782-3332

OLSON, JOHN HARRISON, physician's assistant; b. Mason City, Iowa, Jan. 25, 1948; s. Palmer John and Vera Carmen (Hedgecock) O.; m. Jackie Sue Leach, Sept. 27, 1977 (dec. May 1983); 1 child, Eric Matthew; m. Roberta Jean Allison, Dec. 22, 1984. BS, N.Y. State U., Albany, 1984. Cert. physician asst. Physician asst. Park Clinic, Mason City, 1973-74, to pvt. physician, Beaver Dam, Ky., 1974-77, Nat. Health Svc. Corps, Salyersville, Ky., 1977-79, Iowa Vets. Home, Marshalltown, 1979-94, McFarland Clinic, Marshalltown, 1994—. Served with USN, 1966-70, Vietnam. Mem. Am. Assn. Physician Assts., Iowa Physician Assts. Soc. Home: 1803 W State St Marshalltown IA 50158 Office: McFarland Clinic 312 E Main St Marshalltown IA 50158

OLSON, LLOYD CLARENCE, physician, administrator; b. Spokane, Wash., Jan. 30, 1935; s. Clarence Florin and Ruth Mary (McCollum) O.; m. Irene Gertrude Frisen, Nov. 29, 1979; children: Kristen, Inger, Erik. BA, Reed Coll., 1957; MD, Harvard, 1961. Diplomate Am. Bd. Pediatrics, Am. Bd. Pediatric Infectious Disease. Intern Strong Meml. Hosp., Rochester, N.Y.; resident U. Wash., Seattle; spl. staff Rockerfeller Found., Bangkok, Thailand, 1970-73; assoc. prof. Ind. Univ., Indpls., 1973-76; assoc. dean, prof., chmn. pediatrics Univ. Mo., Kans. City, 1976—; pediatrician-in-chief The Children's Mercy Hosp., Kans. City, 1982—; cons. U.S. Army, Washington, 1979-82, Vietnam Med. Project Saigon, 1975-76, China Med. Bd., 1995. Author: Virus Infections, 1982. Served to lt. col. U.S. Army, 1964-70. Fellow Am. Acad. Pediatrics; mem. Am. Pediatrics Soc., Infectious Diseases Soc., Soc. for Pediatrics Research, Am. Soc. for Microbiology, Phi Beta Kappa. Republican. Methodist. Home: 5703 Woodland Pt Kansas City MO 64152-4329 Office: The Children's Mercy Hosp 24th at Gillham Rd Kansas City MO 64108

OLSON, MARIAN EDNA, nursing consultant, social psychologist; b. Newman Grove, Nebr., July 20, 1923; d. Edward and Ethel Thelma (Hougland) Olson; diploma U. Nebr., 1944, BS in Nursing, 1953; MA, State U. Iowa, 1961, MA in Psychology, 1962; PhD in Psychology, UCLA, 1966. Staff nurse, supr. U. Tex. Med. Br., Galveston, 1944-49; with U. Iowa, Iowa City, 1949-59, supr. 1953-55, asst. dir. 1955-59; asst. prof. nursing UCLA, 1965-67; prof. nursing U. Hawaii, 1967-70, 78-82; dir. nursing Wilcox Hosp. and Health Center, Lihue, 1970-77; chmn. Hawaii Bd. Nursing, 1974-80; prof. nursing No. Mich. U., 1984-88; cons., ind. nursing svcs. adminstr. practice & curriculum, 1988—. Bd. trustees Bay de Noc C.C., 1988—. Mem. Am. Nurses Assn. (mem. nat. accreditation bd. continuing edn. 1975-78), Nat. League Nursing, Am. Hosp. Assn., Am. Public Health Assn., LWV. Democrat. Roman Catholic. Home and Office: 6223 County 513 T Rd Rapid River MI 49878-9595

OLSON, MELODIE ANN, nursing educator; b. Chicago Heights, Ill., Dec. 5, 1941; d. Melvin Richard and Gwenyth (Hills) Olson. Diploma in nursing, Ill. Masonic Hosp., 1963; BSN, U. Ill.-Chgo., 1966; M.S. N., DePaul U., 1970; Ph.D., U. Tex., 1982. R.N., Ill. Staff nurse Ill. Masonic Hosp., Chgo., 1963-65, instr., 1965-69; staff nurse VA Research Hosp., Chgo., 1965-66; nursing educator Luth. Sch. Nursing, Madang, Papua-New Guinea, 1969-75; assoc. prof. nursing San Antonio Coll., 1975-83; assoc. prof. nursing Med. U. S.C., Charleston, 1983. Contbr. chpts. to one book, 10 articles to jours. Coordinator inservice edn. for home health Aides Sr. Citizens Ctr., 1984—. Mem. Am. Nurses Assn. (del. Nat. Conv. Ho. of Dels., 1988-92), S.C. Nurses Assn. (bd. dirs., chmn. cabinet on nursing edn. 1987-90, chmn. council continuing edn. 1986), State Bd. Nursing for S.C. (sec. 1993-94, del. nat. coun. 1993), Sigma Theta Tau Gamma Omicron (research com. 1987, nominating com. chair 1989). Lutheran. Office: Med U SC Coll Nursing Grad Program Charleston SC 29425

OLSON, RICHARD DAVID, psychology educator; b. Reading, Pa., Oct. 10, 1944; s. Milton Stuart and Sarah Ellen (Moyer) O.; m. M. Gayle Augustine, Aug. 26, 1967. B.A., U. Redlands, 1966; M.S., St. Louis U., 1968,

Ph.D., 1970. Lic. psychologist, La. Asst. prof. psychology U. New Orleans, 1970-74, assoc. prof., chmn. dept. psychology, 1974-79, prof., chmn. dept., 1979-81, assoc. dean Grad. Sch., 1981-82, dean, 1982-88, vice chancellor, 1984-88, rsch. prof., 1988—; chmn. dept. psychology, 1995—; cons. psychologist, New Orleans, 1973—; pres. Statis. Cons. of New Orleans, 1977-82. Editor: Learning in the Classroom, 1971, The Comma After Love, The Selected Poems of Raeburn Miller, 1994; contbr. articles to profl. jours. Grantee HEW, 1976-81. Fellow APA, Am. Psychol. Soc.; mem. Soc. for Neurosci., Animal Behavior Soc., Am. Statis. Assn. Home: 103 Doubloon Dr Slidell LA 70461-2715 Office: U New Orleans Dept Psychology Lake Front New Orleans LA 70148

OLSON, ROBERT EUGENE, physician, biochemist, educator; b. Minn., Jan. 23, 1919; s. Ralph William and Minnie (Holtin) O.; m. Catherine Silvoso, Oct. 21, 1944; children: Barbara Lynn, Robert E., Mark Alan, Mary Ellen, Carol Louise. A.B., Gustavus Adolphus Coll., 1938; Ph.D., St. Louis U., 1944; M.D., Harvard, 1951; M.D. (hon.), Chiang Mai U., Thailand, 1983. Diplomate: Nat. Bd. Med. Examiners, Am. Bd. Nutrition (pres. 1962-63). Postgrad. research asst. biochemistry St. Louis U. Sch. Medicine, 1938-43, asst. biochemistry, 1943-44, Alice A. Doisy prof. biochemistry, chmn. dept. biochemistry, 1965-82, asso. prof. medicine, 1966-72, prof. medicine, 1972-82; vis. prof. (sabbatical) dept. biochemistry U. Freiburg, Breisgau, West Germany, 1970-71; also Hoffman-La Roche Co., Basel, Switzerland, 1970-71; instr. biochemistry and nutrition Harvard Sch. Pub. Health, 1946-47; research fellow Nutrition Found., 1947-49; research fellow Am. Heart Assn., 1949-51, established investigator, 1951-52; house officer Peter Bent Brigham Hosp., Boston, 1951-52; prof., head dept. biochemistry and nutrition Grad. Sch. Pub. Health U. Pitts.; lectr. medicine Sch. Medicine, 1952-65; mem. panel malnutrition Japan-U.S. Med. Scis. Program, 1965-69; dir. Nutrition Clinic, Falk Clinic, 1953-65; mem. sr. staff Presbyn. Hosp., dir. metabolic unit, 1960-65; mem. staff St. Louis U. Hosp., 1965-81; prof. biochemistry, prof. medicine, assoc. dean acad. affairs U. Pitts. Sch. Medicine, 1982-84; prof. medicine, prof. pharm. scis. SUNY-Stony Brook, 1984-90, prof. emeritus, 1990-94; prof. pediatrics U. South Fla., Tampa, 1994—; cons. Mercy Hosp., U. Pitts. Med. Center; assoc. in medicine St. Margaret's Meml. Hosp., Pitts., dir. metabolic unit, 1954-60; cons. div. research grants USPHS, 1954-69, 72-76; dir. Anemia and Malnutrition Center, Chiang Mai, Thailand, 1967-77; vis. scholar dept. biochemistry Oxford (Eng.) U., 1961-62; vis. prof. dept. biochemistry U. Freiburg, West Germany, 1970-71; mem. food and nutrition bd. NRC, 1977-83; mem. adv. council Nat. Inst. Arthritis, Diabetes, Digestive and Kidney Diseases, 1981-85; William A. Noyes lectr. U. Ill., Urbana, 1980. Assoc. editor Nutrition Revs., 1954-56, editor, 1978-88; assoc. editor Am. Jour. Medicine, 1956-65, Circulation Rsch., 1956-76, Am. Heart Jour., 1958-65, Am. Jour. Clin. Nutrition, 1960-66, Methods in Med. Rsch., 1963-70, Biochem. Medicine, 1967-90, Molecular and Cellular Cardiology, 1967-78; assoc. editor Ann. Rev. Nutrition, 1979-84, editor, 1984-94; co-editor: Vitamins and Hormones, 1975-81. Bd. dirs. Nat. Nutrition Consortium, 1977-81, Am. Council on Sci. and Health, 1984-91. Served as lt. (j.g.) USNR, 1944-46. Recipient Fulbright award, 1961-62; Guggenheim Found. award, 1961-62, 70-71; McCollum award, 1965; Joseph Goldberger award, 1974; Atwater Meml. lectr., 1978; Geiger Meml. lectr., 1979, William A. Noyes lectr. U. Ill., 1980, H. Brooks James lectr. N.C. State U., 1981, Virginia Beal lectr. U. Mass., 1990. Fellow ACP, Am. Pub. Health Assn. (chmn. food and nutrition sect. 1960-61), Am. Inst. Nutrition (Pres. 1981-82), Assn. Am. Physicians; mem. AAAS (sec. med. scis. N. sect. 1965-67), Am. Assn. Cancer Research, Am. Heart Assn., AMA (mem. council food and nutrition 1959-67, vice chmn. 1962-67), Royal Soc. Health (London), N.Y. Acad. Scis., Am. Fedn. Clin. Research, Am. Soc. Clin. Investigation, Boyleston Med. Soc., Am. Chem. Soc. (pres. biochemistry group Pitts. sect. 1960-61), Am. Soc. Biol. Chemists, Soc. Exptl. Biology and Medicine, Am. Soc. Clin. Nutrition (pres. 1961-62, McCollum award 1965), Assn. Med. Sch. Depts. Biochemistry (pres. 1979-80), Pa., St. Louis, Allegheny County med. socs., Am. Soc. Study Liver Diseases, Phi Beta Kappa, Sigma Xi, Phi Lambda Upsilon, Alpha Omega Alpha, Alpha Sigma Nu. Clubs: Cosmos (Washington), Countryside Country Club (Tampa). Home: 2673 Camille Dr Palm Harbor FL 34684-2217 Office: U South Fla Dept Pediatrics 1 Davis Blvd Ste 307 Tampa FL 33606-3422

OLSON, SANDRA DITTMAN, medical and surgical nurse; b. Duluth, Minn., Mar. 27, 1953; d. Donald Gene and Evelyn Mae (Wilson) Dittman; m. Douglas Bruce Olson, Aug. 10, 1974; 1 child, Perryn Douglas. BSN, S.D. State U., 1974. Cert ACLS; cert. PALS. Staff nurse U.S. Army Hosp., Nurnberg, Fed. Republic Germany, 1975-79; dir. staff devel. Oak Ridge Care Ctr., Mpls., 1979-81; staff nurse med.-surg. Profl. Nursing, Metairie, La., 1982-83; staff nurse, weekend spl. Tulane Med. Ctr., New Orleans, 1982-83; charge nurse Meadowcrest Hosp., Gretna, La., 1983, house supr., 1983-95; utilization rev. and infection control nurse Advance Care Ctr., Marrero, La., 1995—; employee activity com. bd. mem. Pharmacy-Nursing Task Force; active numerous workshops on edn., staff devel., coronary and intensive care, infection control, long term care, mgmt. Bd. dirs., sec. Bon Temps Homeowners Assn.; chair ct. of honor Boy Scout Troop #378. Named Spink County Wheat Queen; recipient 1989 LA Great 100 Nurses award; S.D. Gov.'s scholar. Mem. Assn. of Women's Students (chmn. social-publicity), U. Women's Svc. Orgn. (Guidon historian), Sigma Theta Tau, Alpha Xi Delta (chmn. philathropy). Home: 2144 Lasalle Ave Terrytown LA 70056-4515

OLSON, WALTER STEVEN, psychologist, educator; b. Chgo., July 1, 1941; s. Walter and Ann (Ward) O. m. Susan Zigann, Aug. 1967 (div. 1977); children: James, David; m. Karen Rosenstein, Apr. 15, 1984 (div. 1993); m. Ivette Ramos, Aug. 22, 1993; 1 child, Andres. BS, No. Ill. U., 1965; MS, Chgo. State U., 1968; PhD, Calif. Western U., 1981. Lic. sch. psychologist, Ill.; nat. cert. sch. psychologist. Counselor Chgo. Bd. Edn., 1968-69, psychologist, 1969—; psychologist, therapist Family Counseling Svc., Chgo., 1969-91; adj. faculty U. Sarasota, Fla., 1991—; practicum supv. Gov. State U., 1991—; cons. Dept. Corrections and Criminal Justice, Chgo. State U., 1969-90; adv. bd. Chgo. Metro Wk. Release Program, 1988-89, Chgo. State U. Dept. Criminal Justice, 1988-90. Co-author: Children, Psychology and the Schools, 1970; author TV study gude for ednl. psychology, 1972; co-author internship guide for coorections and criminal justice, 1988. Mem. nat. Assn. Sch. Psychologists, Ill. Sch. Psychologists Assn., Chgo. Assn. Sch. Psychologists, Learning Disability Assn. Am., Coun. for Exceptional Children (mental retardation div.). Office: Piccolo Middle Sch 1040 N Keeler Ave Chicago IL 60651-3507

OLSON, WILLIAM HENRY, neurology educator, administrator; b. Haxtun, Colo., Sept. 2, 1936; s. William Henry and Burdene (Anderson) O.; m. Shirley Gorden, July 24, 1967; children: Erik, Marnie. B.A., Wesleyan U., 1959; M.D., Harvard U., 1963. Diplomate: Am. Bd. Psychiatry and Neurology. Intern Beth Israel Hosp., Boston, 1963-65; resident Children's Hosp. Med. Ctr., Boston, 1965-67; staff assoc. NIH, Bethesda, Md., 1969-70; asst. prof. neurology and anatomy Vanderbilt U., Nashville, 1970-73, assoc. prof. neurology and anatomy, 1973-75; prof., chmn. dept. adult neurology U. N.D., Fargo, 1975-80; chmn., prof. dept. neurology U. Louisville, 1980—. Co-author: Practical Neurology and the Primary Care Physician, 1981, Symptom Oriented Neurology, 1994. Fulbright scholar Tubingen, Germany, 1958-59. Fellow Am. Acad. Neurology; mem. Phi Beta Kappa. Home: 331 Zorn Ave # 1 Louisville KY 40206-1542 Office: Univ Louisville Dept Neurology Louisville KY 40292

OLSSON, CARL ALFRED, urologist; b. Boston, Nov. 29, 1938; s. Charles Rudolph and Ruth Marion (Bostrom) O.; m. Mary DeVore, Nov. 4, 1962; children: Ingrid, Leif Eric. Grad., Bowdoin Coll., 1959; MD, Boston U., 1963. Diplomate Am. Bd. Urology (trustee 1988-94, pres. 1993-94). Asst. prof. urology Boston U. Sch. Medicine, 1971-72, assoc. prof., 1972-74, prof., chmn. dept., 1974-80; dir. urology dept. Boston City Hosp., 1974-77; chief urology dept. Boston VA Med. Ctr., 1971-75; urologist-in-chief Univ. Hosp., Boston, 1971-80; John K. Lattimer prof., chmn. dept. urology Coll. Phys. and Surgs., Columbia U., N.Y.C., 1980—; dir. Squier Urol. Clinic, urology service Presbyn. Hosp., N.Y.C.; lectr. surgery Tufts U. Sch. Medicine. Boston Interhosp. Organ Bank, 1976-79; mem. working cadre Nat. Prostate Cancer Project, Nat. Cancer Inst., 1979-84; mem. adv. coun. Nat. Inst. Diabetes, Digestive Disease and Kidney. Editl. bd. Jour. Prostate, World Jour. Urology, Jour. Urodynamics and Neurourology, Jour. Urology; asst. editor Jour. Urology, 1978-89; contbr. chpts. to books, articles to med. jours. Recipient Disting. Alumnus award Boston U., 1985. Fellow ACS; mem. Am. Urol. Assn. (coord. continuing med. edn. New Eng. sect. 1977-80, del. rsch. com., Gold Cystoscope award 1979, Grayson-Carroll award 1971, 73), Boston Surg. Soc. (exec. com. 1976-80), Am. Assn. Clin. Urologists, Am. Surg. Assn., Am. Assn. Genitourinary Surgeons, Clin. Soc. Genitourinary Surgeons, Transplantation Soc., Soc. Urologic Oncology (pres. 1993), Soc. Univ. Urologists (pres. 1990), N.Y. Sect. Am. Urol. Assn., Am. Fertility Soc., AMA, Assn. Acad. Surgery, Am. Soc. Artificial Internal Organs, Am. Soc. Transplant Surgeons, Assn. Med. Colls., Can. Urol. Assn., Societe Internationale d'Urologie, Internat. Urodynamics Soc., Mass. Med. Soc., Soc. Govt. Urologists, Australasian Urol. Soc. (hon.), New Eng. Handicapped Sportsmen's Assn. (exec. com. 1977-81), U.S. Yacht Racing Union, Yacht Racing Union L.I. Sound Club, N.Y. Yacht Club, Cottage Park Yacht Club, Larchmont Yacht Club, Storm Trysail Club, Alpha Omega Alpha. Episcopalian. Home: 18 Elm Ave Larchmont NY 10538-3649 Office: Columbia-Presbyn Hosp P&S Box 44 630 W 168th St New York NY 10032-3702

OLSTER, STEVEN, physician assistant; b. N.Y.C., June 21, 1946; s. David and Frances Olster; m. Rachelle Olster, Aug. 28, 1971; 3 children. BS cum laude, CUNY, 1972; BS, Touro Coll., 1974. Cert. physician asst. N.Y.; LPN, N.Y. Physician asst. emergency rm./primary care Hosp. for Joint Diseases, N.Y.C., 1974-75; physician asst. emergency medicine Mary Immaculate Hosp., Jamaica, N.Y., 1975-79; physician asst. rehab. medicine dept. Dept. Vets. Affairs Med. Ctr., Bronx, N.Y., 1979-80; physician asst. orthopedics dept. Dept. Vets. Affairs Med. Ctr., Northport, N.Y., 1980—, med. pain adv. bd., 1993-95. With U.S. Army, 1966-69. Fellow Am. Acad. Physician Assts. (peer reviewer jour. 1991-95); mem. Vets. Affairs Assn. Physician Assts. (bd. dirs. 1992-94). Office: Dept Vets Affairs Med Ctr Dept Orthopedics 79 Middleville Rd Northport NY 11768

OLSTON, MARY KAY, school psychologist; b. Milw., Oct. 27, 1949; d. Gordon Rhodes and Mary Anne (Popp) O. BA, Carroll Coll., Waukesha, Wis., 1970; MS, U. Wis., 1971. Assoc. sch. psychologist Milw. Pub. Sch., 1971-74, sch. psychologist, 1974—; cons. U. Wis., 1973-76. Amb. Children's Hosp. of Wis., 1990-92. Mem. APA, Milw. Area Psychol. Assoc. (treas. 1982-84), Alliance Française de Milw. (libr. 1980-82), Double Click, Milw. Webmasters. Home: 10541 W Woodward Ave Wauwatosa WI 53222-2365 Office: EESS Ctr 6620 W Capitol Dr Milwaukee WI 53216-2040

OLUBADEWO, JOSEPH OLANREWAJU, pharmacologist, educator; b. Oroago, Kwara, Nigeria, Apr. 16, 1945; came to U.S., 1980; s. Solomon Akanbi and Leah Ifanike (Omodara) O.; m. Victoria Ibidunni Balogun, Aug. 20, 1972; children: Oludele, Oluseyi, Olubunmi, Oluwole. BSc with honors, Ahmadu Bello U., Zaria, Nigeria, 1970; PhD, Vanderbilt U., 1976. Asst. lectr. Ahmadu Bello U., 1970-75, lectr. II to lectr. I, 1975-80, sr. lectr., 1980; rsch. scientist U. Tenn. Ctr. Health Scis., Memphis, 1980-84, asst. prof., 1984-85; assoc. prof. Xavier U., New Orleans, 1985-91, prof., 1991—; spl. reviewer NIH, 1989-92. Mem. editorial bd. Jour. Nat. Pharm. Assn., 1989; reviewer Annals of Pharmacotherapy, Cellular and Molecular Biology; contbr. articles to profl. jours. Fellow African-American Inst. Grad. Program, 1971-75, Am. Heart Assn., 1983, 84, NIH, 1987, 88. Mem. AAUP, Am. Soc. for Pharmacology and Exptl. Therapeutics, Southeastern Pharmacology Soc. (life), Am. Assn. Colls. Pharmacy, N.Y. Acad. Scis. Baptist. Home: 13510 Dwyer Blvd New Orleans LA 70129-1530 Office: Xavier U La 7325 Palmetto St New Orleans LA 70125-1056

OLVER, IAN NORMAN, medical oncologist; b. Melbourne, Victoria, Australia, May 10, 1953; s. Norman Henry and Rebie Alison (Reid) O.; m. Jennifer Robyn Turner, Jan. 14, 1978; children: Scott, Christopher, Robert. MBBS, U. Melbourne, 1976, MD, 1991. Fellow in med. oncology Cancer Ctr. U. Md., Balt., 1983-85; clin. asst. dept. cancer medicine Peter McCallum Cancer Inst., Melbourne, 1985-93, head med. oncology, 1990-91; dir. med. oncology Royal Adelaide Hosp., 1991—, clin. dir., 1993—; clin. assoc. prof. U. Adelaide, 1993—; assoc. mem. Australian Drug Evaluation Com., 1995—. Author chpts. to books; contbr. more than 50 articles to profl. jours. Fellow Royal Australasian Coll. Physicians; mem. Clin. Oncol. Soc. Australia, Am. Soc. Clin. Oncology, European Soc. Med. Oncology. Home: 1 Mountainview Pl, Mount Osmond SA 5064, Australia Office: Royal Adelaide Hosp, North Terrace, Adelaide SA 5000, Australia

OLYMPIA, JOSIE LIM, psychiatrist; b. Or. Mindoro, Philippines, Feb. 9, 1944; came to U.S., 1967; B.S., U. Philippines, 1962, M.D., 1967. Rotating intern Mt. Sinai Hosp., Milw., 1968; resident in psychiatry Buffalo Psychiat. Center, 1968-71, psychiatrist I, II, III, 1971-77, dir. med. edn., 1977—; asst. chief psychiatry service Buffalo VA Med. Center, 1981—; assoc. clin. prof. psychiatry SUNY, Buffalo; cons. Niagara Falls Meml. Med. Center, N.Y. Bur. of Disability. Served to col. USAR. NEH grantee, 1979. Fellow Am. Psychiat. Assn., Am. Orthopsychiat. Assn. Roman Catholic. Office: VA Med Center 3495 Bailey Ave Buffalo NY 14215-3843

O'MALLEY, BERT WILLIAM, cell biologist, educator, physician; b. Pitts., Dec. 19, 1936; s. Bert Alloysius O'M.; m. Sally Ann Johnson; children: Sally Ann, Bert A., Rebecca, Erin K. BS, U. Pitts., 1959, MD summa cum laude, 1963; DSc (hon.), N.Y. Med. Coll., 1979, Nat. U. Ireland, 1985; MD (hon.), Karolinska Inst., Stockholm, 1984. Intern, resident Duke U., Durham, N.C., 1963-65; clin. assoc. Nat. Cancer Inst., NIH, Bethesda, Md., 1965-67, head molecular biology sect., endocrine br., 1967-69; Lucius Birch prof., dir. Reproductive Biology Ctr. Vanderbilt U. Sch. Medicine, Nashville, 1969-73; Tom Thompson prof., chmn. dept. cell biology Baylor Coll Medicine, Houston, 1973—, Disting. Svc. prof., 1985, dir. Baylor Ctr. for Reproductive Biology, 1973—; mem. endocrine study sect., NIH, 1970-73, chmn., 1973-74; chmn. CETUS-UCLA Symposium on Gene Expression, 1982; coun., mem. coun. rsch. and clin. investigation awards Am. Cancer Soc., 1985-87. Author: (with A.R. Means) Receptors for Reproductive Hormones, 1973, (with L. Birnbaumer) Hormone Action, vols. I and II, 1977, vol. III, 1978, (with A.M. Gotto) The Role of Receptors in Biology and Medicine, 1986; co-author: Methods in Enzymology: Hormone Action: Calmodulin and Calcium-Binding Proteins, 1983, Mechanism of Steriod Hormone Regulation of Gene Transcription, 1994; editor: Gene Regulation: UCLA Symposium on Molecular Cellular Biology, 1982; contbg. author to over 400 publs. Lt. comdr. USPHS, 1965-69. Recipient Ernst Oppenheimer award Am. Endocrine Soc., 1975, Gregory Pincus medal, 1975, Lila Gruber Cancer award, 1977, Disting. Achievement in Modern Medicine award, 1978, Borden award Assn. Am. Med. Colls., 1978, Dickson prize for Basic Med. Rsch., 1979, Philip S. Hench award U. Pitts., 1981, Axel Munthe Reproductive Biology award, Capri, Italy, 1982, Bicentennial Medallion of Distincton U. Pitts., 1987. Mem. AAAS, NAS, Inst. Med. NAS, Am. Soc. Biol Chemists, Endocrine Soc. (pres. 1985, Fred Conrad Koch medal 1988), Am. Soc. Clin. Investigation, Am. Inst. Chemists, Fedn. Clin. Rsch., Harvey Soc., Alpha Epsilon Delta, Phi Beta Kappa, Alpha Omega Alpha. Democrat. Roman Catholic. Office: Baylor Coll Medicine Dept Neuroscience One Baylor Pla Houston TX 77030-3411

O'MALLEY, EDWARD, physician, consultant; b. Hudson, N.Y., May 30, 1926; s. Thomas Patrick and Helen Mary (Cornell) O. BS, St. John's U., Bklyn., N.Y., 1949; MS, Loyola U., Chgo., 1952, PhD, 1954; MD, SUNY, Bklyn., 1958. Psychiat. cons. dept. of corrections N.Y.C., 1962-68; psychiatrist Cath. Charities, N.Y.C., 1963-68; dir. of mental health Suffolk County Govt., Hauppauge, N.Y., 1968-70; commr. of mental health Orange County, Goshen, N.Y., 1970-72; dir. drug abuse services State of N.Y., Bronx, 1972-78; lic. sch. psychiatrist N.Y.C. Bd. of Edn., 1962-82; chief psychiatry services VA, Huntington, W.Va., 1982-86; med. cons. State of Calif., San Diego, 1986—, psychiat. cons. dept. of corrections, 1987—; asst. prof. psychiatry N.J. Med. Sch., Newark, 1975—; examiner Am. Bd. of Psychiatry and Neurology, Los Angeles, 1980; assoc. prof. psychiatry U. Calif., San Diego, 1980—; prof. psychiatry Marshall U. Sch. of Medicine, Huntington, 1982-86; dir. com. on sea cadets Navy League, San Diego, 1937—; cons. HHS, Social Security Adminstrn., Office of Hearings and Appeals, 1989—. Contbr. articles to profl. jours. Bd. dirs. Suffolk Community Council, Hauppauge, 1968-70, United Fund of Long Island, Huntington, 1968-70. Served to capt. USN, 1978-81. Scholar N. Y. State Coll., 1946-49, SUNY Joseph Collins Med. Sch., 1955-58; Teaching and Research fellow Loyola U., 1952-54. Fellow Am. Psychiat. Assn.; mem. San Diego Psychiat. Soc., Soc. of Med. Cons. to the Armed Forces, Soc. of Mil. Surgeons of U.S.A., N.Y. Celtic Med. Soc., Union Am. Physicians and Dentists (steward 1990—), State Employed Physicians Assn. (bd. dirs. 1993—). Roman Catholic. Home: 3711 Alcott St San Diego CA 92106-1212

O'MALLEY, PATRICIA, critical care nurse; b. Boston, May 13, 1955; d. Peter and Catherine (Dwyer) O'M. BSN, Coll. Mt. St. Joseph, Cin., 1977; MS, Ohio State U., 1984, postgrad., 1990—. Cert. critical care nurse. Primary nurse critical care unit Miami Valley Hosp., Dayton, Ohio, nurse educator, clin. nurse specialist, cons.; adj. faculty Wright State U., Dayton. Contbr. articles to profl. jours., textbooks. Recipient honors Dayton Area Heart Assn., Ohio Ho. of Reps., 1994, Ohio Dept. Health, 1996. Mem. AACN (bd. dirs. Dayton-Miami Valley), Soc. Critical Care Medicine, Sigma Theta Tau. Office: Miami Valley Hosp 1 Wyoming St Dayton OH 45409-2722

O'MALLEY, THOMAS ANTHONY, gastroenterologist, internist; b. St. Helens, Lancashire, Eng., Jan. 21, 1932; s. Michael and Margaret (Melia) O'M.; m. Margaret Mary O'Kane, Apr. 7, 1958 (dec. Apr. 1985); m. Marianne Rapier, Jan. 23, 1988; children: Anne, Patricia, Katherine, Jane, Margaret. MBChB, U. Liverpool, Eng., 1956; Lic. Medicine, U. State N.Y., 1964. Diplomate Am. Bd. Internal Medicine, State Bd. Med. Examiners Fla. House physician Royal Infirmary, Liverpool, 1956-57; house surgeon Royal Liverpool Children's Hosp., 1957; resident in medicine C.S. Wilson Meml. Hosp., Johnson City, N.Y., 1957-58; fellow internal medicine Lahey Clinic, Boston, 1958-59; USPHS trainee in gastroenterology U. Rochester (N.Y.), Strong Meml. Hosp., 1959-60; chief resident medicine/Segal Watson fellow gastroenterology Genesee Hosp., Rochester, 1960-61; gastroenterologist Cancer Clinic, Regina, Sask., Can., 1963; asst. dir. med. edn. Genesee Hosp., U. Rochester, 1967-72; clin. assoc. prof. medicine U. South Fla., Tampa, 1973—; chief medicine Sarasota (Fla.) Meml. Hosp., 1973, Doctors Hosp., Sarasota, 1985. With RAF, 1961-62. Recipient Physician of Yr. award Doctors Hosp. Sarasota, 1985. Fellow ACP, Am. Coll. Gastroenterology, Chevalier du Tastevin (comdr. 1985—), Cavalieri del Vini Nobili (amb. 1989—). Office: O'Malley & Hall MD PA 2650 Bahia Vista Sarasota FL 34239

OMAN, DEBORAH SUE, health science facility administrator; b. North Platte, Nebr., Aug. 26, 1948; d. Rex Ardell and Opale Louise (Smith) O. BS, Kearney State Coll., 1970; MA in Journalism and Mass Comm., U. Nebr., 1993. Med. technologist Physicians Pathology Labs., Lincoln, Nebr., 1970-71; med. technologist student health Colo. State U., Ft. Collins, 1971-72; supr. hematology lab. Bryan Meml. Hosp., Lincoln, 1972-76; sect. supr. hematology, hemostasis Lincoln N.E. br. Corning Clin. Labs., divsn. Corning Life Scis., 1976—; hemostasis cons. Dade Diagnostics Internat., Inc., Miami Fla., 1991—; clin. cons. Med. Lab. Automation, Inc., Pleasantville, N.Y., 1990—; adj. prof. Sch. Med. Tech., Nebr. Wesleyan U., Lincoln, 1979-85; clin. instr. Sch. Med. Tech., U. Nebr. Med. Ctr., Omaha, 1990-95. Contbr. articles to profl. jours. Mem. Am. Soc. Clin. Pathologists (cert., affiliate, recognition award 1986), Lancaster Soc. Med. Technologists, Fastbreaker's for Nebr. Women's Basketball (sec. 1995—), Cornhusker Ski Club (pres. 1982-83), Kappa Tau Alpha. Republican. Mem. Christian Ch. Office: Corning Clin Labs Plz Mall South 1919 S 40th St Ste 333 Lincoln NE 68506-5243

O'MEARA, THOMAS FRANCIS, gastroenterologist; b. Takoma Park, Md., Sept. 30, 1948; s. Thomas Francis and Mary Veronica (Meehan) O'M.; m. Sally Peterson; children: Katherine Mary, Collin Farrell. BS, U.S. Mil. Acad., 1970; MD, Baylor Coll. Medicine, 1975. Commd. 2d lt. U.S. Army, 1970, advanced through grades to col.; resident in internal medicine U.S. Army, Tacoma, Wash., 1975-78; fellow in gastroenterology U.S. Army, San Antonio, 1978-80; chief gastroenterology U.S. Army, Tacoma, 1988; bd. dirs. Pro Health Alliance, Olympia, Wash.; expert cons. Madigan Army Med. Ctr., Tacoma, 1988—; mem. clin. faculty U. Wash., Seattle, 1985—. Fellow ACP, ACG, Am. Coll. Gastroenterology; mem. Order of Mil. Med. Merit, 1982. Roman Catholic. Office: 406 A Black Hills Ln SW Olympia WA 78502

OMENN, GILBERT STANLEY, university dean, physician; b. Chester, Pa., Aug. 30, 1941; s. Leonard and Leah (Miller) O.; m. Martha Darling; children: Rachel Andrea, Jason Montgomery, David Matthew. AB, Princeton U., 1961; MD, Harvard U., 1965; PhD in Genetics, U. Wash., 1972. Intern Mass. Gen. Hosp., Boston, 1965-66; asst. resident in medicine Mass. Gen. Hosp., 1966-67; research assoc. NIH, Bethesda, Md., 1967-69; fellow U. Wash., 1969-71, asst. prof. medicine, 1971-74, assoc. prof., 1974-79, investigator Howard Hughes Med. Inst., 1976-77, prof., 1979—, prof. environ. health, 1981—, chmn. dept., 1981-83, dean Sch. Pub. Health and Community Medicine, 1982—; bd. dirs. Rohm & Haas Co., Amgen, BioTechniques Labs. Inc., Immune Response Corp., Clean Sites, Inc., Population Svcs. Internat., Pacific N.W. Pollution Prevention Rsch. Ctr.; White House fellow/spl. asst. to chmn. AEC, 1973-74; assoc. dir. Office Sci. and Tech. Policy, The White House, 1977-80; assoc. dir. human resources Office Mgmt. and Budget, 1980-81; vis. sr. fellow Wilson Sch. Pub. and Internat. Affairs, Princeton U., 1981; sci. and pub. policy fellow Brookings Instn., Washington, 1981-82; cons. govt. agys., Lifetime Cable Network; mem. Nat. Com. on the Environment, environ. adv. com. Rohm & Haas, Rene Dubos Ctr. for Human Environments, AFL-CIO Workplace Health Fund., Electric Power Rsch. Inst., Carnegie Commn. Task Force on Sci. and Tech. in Jud. and Regulatory Decision Making, adv. com. to dir., Ctrs. Disease Control, 1992—, adv. com. Critical Technologies Inst., RAND; mem. Pres.'s Coun., U. Calif., 1992—. Co-author: Clearing the Air, Reforming the Clean Air Act, 1981. Editor: (with others) Genetics, Environment and Behavior: Implications for Educational Policy, 1972; Genetic Control of Environmental Pollutants, 1984; Genetic Variability in Responses to Chemical Exposure, 1984, Environmental Biotechnology: Reducing Risks from Environmental Chemicals through Biotechnology, 1988, Biotechnology in Biodegradation, 1990, Biotechnology and Human Genetic Predisposition to Disease, 1990, Annual Review of Public Health, 1991, 92, 93, 94, Clinics in Geriatric Medicine, 1992; assoc. editor Cancer Rsch., Cancer Epidemiology, Biomarkers and Prevention, Environ. Rsch., Am. Jour. Med. Genetics, Am. Jour. Preventive Medicine; contbr. articles on cancer prevention, human biochem. genetics, prenatal diagnosis of inherited disorders, susceptibility to environ. agts., clin. medicine and health policy to profl. publs. Mem. President's Council on Spinal Cord Injury; mem. Nat. Cancer Adv. Bd., Nat. Heart, Lung and Blood Adv. Council, Wash. State Gov.'s Commn. on Social and Health Services, Ctr. for Excellence in Govt.; chmn. awards panel Gen. Motors Cancer Research Found., 1985-86; chmn. bd. Environ. Studies and Toxicology, Nat. Rsch. Coun., 1988-91; mem. Bd. Health Promotion and Disease Prevention, Inst. Medicine; mem. adv. com. Woodrow Wilson Sch., Princeton U., 1978-84; bd. dirs. Inst. for Sci. in Society; trustee Pacific Sci. Ctr., Fred Hutchinson Cancer Research Ctr., Seattle Symphony Orch., Seattle Youth Symphony Orch., Seattle Chamber Music Festival, Santa Fe Chamber Music Festival; mem. Citizens for a Hunger-Free Washington; chmn. rules com. Democratic Conv., King County, Wash., 1972. Served with USPHS, 1967-69. Recipient Research Career Devel. award USPHS, 1972; White House fellow, 1973-74. Fellow ACP, AAAS, Nat. Acad. Social Ins., Western Assn. Physicians, Hastings Ctr., Collegium Ramazzini; mem. Inst. Medicine of NAS, White House Fellows Assn., Am. Soc. Human Genetics, Western Soc. Clin. Rsch. Jewish. Home: 5100 NE 55th St Seattle WA 98105-2821 Office: U Wash Dean Sch Pub Health Box 357230 Seattle WA 98195-7230

OMER, GEORGE ELBERT, JR., orthopedic surgeon, hand surgeon, educator; b. Kansas City, Kans., Dec. 23, 1922; s. George Elbert and Edith May (Hines) O.; m. Wendie Vilven, Nov. 6, 1949; children: George Eric, Michael Lee. B.A., Ft. Hays State U., 1944; M.D., Kans. U., 1950; M.Sc. in Orthopaedic Surgery, Baylor U., 1955. Diplomate Am Bd. Orthopaedic Surgery, 1959, re-cert. orthopaedics and hand surgery, 1983 (bd. dirs. 1983-92, pres. 1987-88), cert. surgery of the hand, 1989. Commd. 1st lt. U.S. Army, 1949; advanced through grades to col., 1967; ret. U.S. Army, 1970; rotating intern Bethany Hosp., Kansas City, 1950-51; resident in orthopaedic surgery Brooke Gen. Hosp., San Antonio, 1952-55, William Beaumont Gen. Hosp., El Paso, Tex., 1955-56; chief surgery Irwin Army Hosp., Ft. Riley, Kans., 1957-59; cons. in orthopaedic surgery 8th Army Korea, 1959-60; asst. chief orthopaedic surgery, chief hand surgeon Fitzsimons Army Med. Center, Denver, 1960-63; dir. orthopaedic residency tng. Armed Forces Inst. Pathology, Washington, 1963-65; chief orthopaedic surgery and chief Army Hand Surg. Center, Brooke Army Med. Center, 1965-70; cons. in orthopaedic and hand surgery Surgeon Gen. Army, 1967-70; prof. orthopaedics, surgery, and anatomy, chmn. dept. orthopaedic surgery, chief div. hand surgery U. N.Mex., 1970-90, med. dir. phys. therapy, 1972-90, acting asst. dean grad. edn. Sch. Medicine, 1980-81; mem. active staff U.

N.Mex. Hosp., Albuquerque, chief of med. staff, 1984-86; cons. staff other Albuquerque hosps.; cons. orthopedic surgery USPHS, 1966-85, U.S. Army, 1970-92, USAF, 1970-78, VA, 1970—; cons. Carrier Tingley Hosp. for Crippled Children, 1970—, interim med. dir., 1970-72, 86-87, mem. bd. advisors, 1972—, chair, 1994-96. Mem. bd. editors Clin. Orthopaedics, 1973-90, Jour. AMA, 1973-74, Jour. Hand Surgery, 1976-81; trustee Jour. Bone and Joint Surgery, 1993—, sec., 1993—; contbr. more than 200 articles to profl. jours., numerous chpts. to books. Decorated Legion of Merit, Army Commendation medal with 2 oak leaf clusters; recipient Alumni Achievement award Ft. Hays State U., 1973, Recognition plaque Am. Soc. Surgery Hand, 1989, Recognition plaque N.Mex. Orthopaedic Assn., 1991; recognized with Endowed Professorship U. N.Mex. Sch. Medicine, 1995. Fellow ACS, Am. Orthopaedic Assn. (pres. 1988-89, exec. dir. 1989-93), Am. Acad. Orthopaedic Surgeons, Assn. Orthopaedic Chmn., N.Mex. Orthopaedic Assn. (pres. 1979-81), La. Orthopaedic Assn. (hon.), Korean Orthopaedic Assn. (hon.), Peru Orthopaedic Soc. (hon.), Caribbean Hand Soc., Am. Soc. Surgery Hand (pres. 1978-79), Am. Assn. Surgery of Trauma, Assn. Bone and Joint Surgeons, Assn. Mil. Surgeons U.S., Riordan Hand Soc. (pres. 1967-68), Sunderland Soc. (pres. 1981-83), Soc. Mil. Orthopaedic Surgeons, Brazilian Hand Soc. (hon.), S.Am. Hand Soc. (hon.), Groupe D'Etude de la Main, Brit. Hand Soc., Venezuela Hand Soc. (hon.), South African Hand Soc. (hon.), Western Orthopaedic Assn. (pres. 1981-82), AAAS, Russell A. Hibbs Soc. (pres. 1977-78), 38th Parallel Med. Soc. (Korea) (sec. 1959-60); mem. AMA, Phi Kappa Phi, Phi Sigma, Alpha Omega Alpha, Phi Beta Pi. Home: 316 Big Horn Ridge Rd NE Sandia Heights Albuquerque NM 87122 Office: U N Mex Dept Orthopaedic Surgery 2211 Lomas Blvd NE Albuquerque NM 87106-2745

OMER, ROBERT WENDELL, hospital administrator; b. Salt Lake City, Feb. 10, 1948; s. Wayne Albert and Melva Bernice (Thunell) O.; m. Deborah Jackson, May 4, 1972;children: Melinda, Carmen, Creighton, Preston, Allison. BS in Biology, U. Utah, 1972; MHA, Washington U., St. Louis, 1975. V.p. St. Luke's Hosp., Cedar Rapids, Iowa, 1974-80; asst. adminstr. Franciscan Med. Ctr., Rock Island, Ill., 1980-82, Latter Day Saints Hosp., Salt Lake City, 1982-85; asst. adminstr. Clarkson Hosp., Omaha, 1985-93, v.p., COO, 1993—; bd. dirs. ARC, Heartland chpt. Omaha; bd. dirs. Nebr. Scanning Svcs. Lt. col. USAR, 1972. Fellow Am. Coll. of Healthcare Execs. 1975; mem. Nebr. Hosp. Assn., Omaha C. of C. (leadership Omaha award 1978), Omaha Healthcare Execs. Group (pres. 1989-90), Rotary (bd. dirs. 1990). Republican. Mem. LDS Ch. Home: 14111 Cedar Cir Omaha NE 68144-2120

OMIROS, GEORGE JAMES, medical foundation executive; b. Uniontown, Pa., Oct. 26, 1956; s. Chris George and Alice (Zervoudi) O.; m. Sophia Florent, June 28, 1980; children: Christopher George, Alicia Helene. BS in Polit. and Philosophy, U. Pitts., 1978; M, Cen. Mich. U., 1982. Campaign coordinator, program assoc. SW Pa. chpt. Am. Heart Assn., Greensburg, 1979, fundraising dir., 1979-80, dir. devel., 1980-84; v.p. devel., ops. Western Pa. chpt. Am. Heart Assn., Pitts., 1984-85, dep. exec. v.p., 1985-87, exec. v.p., 1987-88; exec. dir. Leukemia Soc. Am., Pitts., 1988—, nat. mktg. rep., 1988—, asst. v.p. nat. office, 1991-93; sr. exec. dir., nat. dir. Don Devel., Pitts., 1993-95, sr. exec. dir., group dir., nat. dir. comm. camp., 1995—. Cons. devel. Greek Orthodox Archdiocese, Pitts., 1982—, v.p. 1987—; chair Pitts. Metro. Com. Internat. Orthodox Christian Charities, Balt., 1993—; mem. coun., rev. com. Health Sys. Agy. Southwest Pa., Pitts., 1983-87; mem. parish coun. St. Spyridon Greek Orthodox Ch., Monessen, Pa., 1982—; met. chmn. Internat. Orthdox Christian Charities; devel. com. Persad Ctr. Mem. Nat. Soc. Fundraising Execs. (cert., founder 1980, pres. 1985-87, Outstanding Fundraising Exec. 1990), Pitts. Planned Giving Coun. (founding com. 1983—), Friends of George C. Marshall (steering com. 1990-92), Uniontown Country Club, Uniontown Rotary (local treas. 1985, sec. 1986, v.p. 1987, pres. 1988), Pitts. Rotary, Masons. Republican. Greek Orthodox. Office: Leukemia Soc Am 13 North 2 Gateway Ctr Pittsburgh PA 15222

OMMAYA, AYUB KHAN, neurosurgeon; b. Pakistan, Apr. 14, 1930; came to U.S., 1961, naturalized, 1968; s. Sultan Nadir and Ida (Counil) Khan; children: David, Alexander, Shana, Aisha, Iman, Sinan. M.D., U. Punjab, Pakistan, 1953; M.A., Oxford U., Eng., 1956. Diplomate Am. Bd. Neurological Surgery. Intern Mayo Hosp., Lahore, Pakistan, 1953-54; resident in neurosurgery Radcliffe Infirmary, Oxford, Eng., 1954-61; vis. scientist NIH, Bethesda, Md., 1963-63, assoc. neurosurgeon, 1963-68, head sect. applied rsch., 1968-74, chief neurosurgery, 1974-79; clin. prof. George Washington U. Med. Sch., 1970—; cons. VA Armed Forces Radiobiology Rsch. Inst.; chmn. Inter-Agy. Com. for Protection Human Rsch. Subjects of Fed. Coordinating Coun. for Sci., Engring. and Tech., NAS; chmn. biomechanics adv. com. com. Nat. Hwy. Traffic Safety Adminstrn.; mem. adv. com. Nat. Ctr. Injury Control & Prevention, Atlanta; inaugural Lewin Meml. lectr. U. Cambridge, Eng., 1983; mem. adv. coun. CDC; Shively lectr. Am. Assn. Auto. Medicine, 1988; Ibn-Sina lectr. Islamic Med. Assn. N.Am. Contbr. articles to profl. jours.; inventor, patentee spinal fluid flow driven artificial organs for diabetes and degenerative diseases of the nervous system. Pres. Found. for Fundamental and Applied Neurosci., Bethesda; v.p., dir. rsch. Cyborgan, Inc., Bethesda. Recipient J. W. Kirkdaldy prize Oxford U., 1956, Lifetime Achievement award Internat. Coll. Surgeons, 1996; recipient Sitara-i-Imtiaz for Achievements in Neurosurgery Govt. Pakistan, 1981; Hunterian prof. Royal Coll. Surgeons, 1968; Rhodes scholar, 1954-60. Fellow ACS, Third World Acad. Scis. (assoc., med. scis. com.), Royal Coll. Surgeons Eng.; mem. ASME (exec. affiliate), Soc. for Neurosci., Am. Assn. Neurol. Surgeons, Rsch. Soc. Neurosurgeons, Brit. Soc. Neurol. Surgeons, Am. Assn. Pakistani Physicians (pres.), Internat. Brain Rsch. Orgn. (life), Pan-Am. Med. Assn. Home: 8901 Burning Tree Rd Bethesda MD 20817-3007 Office: 8006 Glenbrook Rd Bethesda MD 20814-2608

O'MORCHOE, PATRICIA JEAN, pathologist, educator; b. Halifax, Eng., Sept. 15, 1930; came to U.S., 1968; d. Alfred Eric and Florence Patricia (Pearson) Richardson; m. Charles Christopher Creagh O'Morchoe, Sept. 15, 1955; children: Charles E.C., David J.C. BA, Dublin U., Ireland, 1953, MB, Bch., BAO, 1955, MA, 1966, MD. Intern Halifax (Yorkshire) Gen. Hosp., Eng., 1955-57; instr., lectr. physiology Dublin U., 1957-61, 63-68; instr. pathology Johns Hopkins U., Balt., 1961-62, 68-72, asst. prof. pathology, 1972-74; rsch. assoc. surgery, pathology Harvard U., Boston, 1962-63; asst. prof. anatomy U. Md., 1970-74; assoc.prof., prof. pathology, anatomy Loyola U. Chgo., 1974-84; prof. pathology, cell and structural biology U. Ill., Urbana, 1984—; head dept. pathology coll. medicine U. Ill., Urbana-Champaign, 1994—; staff pathologist VA Hosp., Danville, Ill., 1989—; assoc. head dept. pathology U. Ill., 1991-95; courtesy staff pathologist Covenant Hosp., Urbana, 1984—, Carle Clinic, Urbana, 1990—. Contbr. numerous articles to profl. jours. Recipient Excellence in Teaching award U. Ill., 1996. Mem. Internat. Acad. Cytology, Internat. Soc. Lymphology (auditor 1989-91, exec. com. 1991-93), N.Am. Soc. Lymphology (sec. 1988-90, treas. 1990-92, v.p. 1992-94, pres. 1994—), Am. Soc. Cytology, Am. Assn. Anatomists, Ill. Soc. Cytology. Home: 2709 Holcomb Dr Urbana IL 61801-7724 Office: U Ill Coll Med 506 S Mathews Ave Urbana IL 61801-3618

OMURA, TSUNEO, medical educator; b. Shizuoka, Japan, July 29, 1930; s. Bunzo and Yasu Omura; m. Yone Tominaga, Nov. 16, 1957; children: Shigeru, Minoru, Kaoru. BS, U. Tokyo, 1953, DSc, 1962. Instr. Shizuoka U., 1953-60; asst. prof. Osaka (Japan) U., 1960-70; prof. Kyushu U., Fukuoka, Japan, 1970-94, prof. emeritus, 1994—. Editor, author: Cytochrome P-450, 1978, 2d edit., 1993. Mem. Japanese Biochem. Soc., Am. Soc. Biochemistry and Molecular Biology (hon.). Home: 7-17-7 Hinosato, Munakata Fukuoka 811-34, Japan Office: Kyushu U Med Sch, Maidashi 3-1-1, Fukuoka 812, Japan

ONAKA, LESLIE ISAO, medical technologist; b. Holualoa, Hawaii, Sept. 13, 1951; s. Albert K. and Doris Y. (Ihara) O.; m. Amy H.L. Mok, July 6, 1985; 2 children: Iris L.X. and Perry H.Y. BA in Biology, U. Calif., San Diego, 1972; BS in Med. Tech., U. Hawaii-Manoa, 1979, MBA, 1992. Chemistry supr. Hilo (Hawaii) Hosp., 1980-84; med. technologist Tripler Army Med. Ctr., Honolulu, 1984-89; lectr. John A. Burns Sch. Medicine, Honolulu, 1984—; chemistry supr. Clin. Labs. Hawaii, Honolulu, 1991—; observer Nat. Com. for Clin. Lab. Standards, Wayne, Pa., 1992—. Contbr.: Clinical Chemistry: Concepts and Applications, 1993. Home: 1515 Pele St Unit B Honolulu HI 96813 Office: U Hawaii at Manoa John A Burns Sch Medicine 1960 E West Rd Honolulu HI 96822-2319

ONCINS, JOSE RAMON, physician, consultant; b. Zaragoza, Aragon, Spain, Oct. 15, 1944; s. Ramon Oncins and Maria De Frutos; m. Gemma Domenech; children: Meritxell, Olga. Bachillerato Elemental, INEM, Lleida, 1959, Bachillerato Superior, 1963; MD, Univ., Barcelona, 1970, speciality in cardiology, 1972. Resident Hosp. Belluitge, Barcelona, 1972-75, staff intensive care unit, 1975-77, head intensive care unit, 1977—. Contbr. articles to profl. jours.; patentee in field. Gen. sec. Catalogne Med. Assn., Barcelona, 1996. Lt. Military Health Svc., 1970-71. Home: Pza Garrigo 7, 08016 Barcelona Spain

ONDERKO, GREGORY JOHN, psychiatrist; b. Belle Vernon, Pa., Dec. 8, 1958; s. Stephen Edward and Julia Ann (Urchick) O.; m. Denise Joy Calvello. BA, Pa. State U., 1980; DO, U. Osteopathic Medicine & Surgery, Des Moines, 1986. Psychiatric resident Med. Coll. Pa., Phila., 1990; staff psychiatrist Manatee Glens/Glen Oaks Hosp., Bradenton, Fla., 1990—; forensic psychiatrist Manatee County Jail, Bradenton, Fla., 1990—; staff psychiatrist Coastal Recovery Ctr., Sarasota, Fla., 1991—, Manatee Meml. Hosp., Bradenton, Fla., 1996—; med. lectr. Sandoz Pharms., 1990—; psychiatric cons. Freedom Care Nursing Ctr., Bradenton, 1995—. Author: Treatment Outcomes in Schizophrenia, 1996. Spkr. Fla. Alliance for Mentally Ill, 1995, 96. Clin. scholar Janssen Pharms., 1995. Mem. AMA, Am. Osteopathic Med. Assn., Am. Polit. Med. Assn., Fla. Osteopathic Med. Assn. Office: Glen Oaks Hosp 2020 26th Ave E Bradenton FL 34208

ONDRA, STEPHEN LOUIS, neurosurgeon; b. Belleville, Ill., Mar. 23, 1957; s. Duane Thomas and Shirly Mae (Etling) O.; m. Cynthia Ann Rochon, Sept. 2, 1993; children: Stephanie Lynn, Katherine Maria, Marissa Rose. BA, Ill. Wesleyan U., 1980; MD, Rush Med. Coll., 1984. Diplomate Am. Bd. Neurologic Surgery. Staff surgeon, neurosurgeon William Beaumont Hosp., El Paso, Tex., 1990-91; neurosurgeon, dir. complex spine and skull base surgery Walter Reed Hosp., Washington, 1991-94; neurosurgeon Mich. Brain and Spine Inst., Ann Arbor, Mich., 1994—; asst. prof. neurosurgery Uniformed Svcs. U., Bethesda, Md., 1991—; clin. asst. prof. neurosurgery U. Mich., Ann Arbor, 1995—. Contbr. chpt. to book and articles to profl. jours. Maj. U.S. Army, 1984-94. Decorated Bronze star U.S. Army, Saudi Arabia, 1991. Mem. AMA, Am. Assn. Neurol. Surgeons, Congress Neurol. Surgery, Mich. Assn. Neurol. Surgeons, Alpha Omega Alpha. Office: Mich Brain & Spine Inst Ste 3112 5333 McAuley Dr Ypsilanti MI 48197

ONDRUSEK, DAVID FRANCIS, pharmaceutical company specialist; b. Johnson City, N.Y., Aug. 8, 1955; s. Frank Joseph and Juanita Elizabeth (Seeley) O.; m. Tina G. Papapavlos, July 11, 1981; children: Stephanie Ann Albina, Michael David. BA, St. Michael's Coll., Winooski, Vt., 1977; BS, Idaho State U., Pocatello, 1980. Asst. mgr. Osco Drugs, Wenatachee, Wash., 1980, Richland, Wash., 1981-83; asst. mgr. Thrift Drug, Williamsport, Pa., 1983; mgr. Revco Drug, Williamsport, 1983-88; dist. mgr. Revco Drug, Morgantown, W.Va., 1988-92, pharmacy supr., 1992; pharmacy mgr. Wal-Mart, Salisbury, Md., 1992-94; dist. mgr. Wal-Mart, Lewisburg, Pa., 1994—. Head coach Lycoming Coll. Lacrosse Team, Williamsport, 1983-88. Mem. Am. Pharm. Assn., Nat. Assn. Retail Druggists, Wash. State Pharm. Assn. Home: 157 Ridgeway Dr Lewisburg PA 17837-9235 Office: 125 Rt 15 N Lewisburg PA 17837

O'NEAL, HARRIET ROBERTS, psychologist, psycholegal consultant; b. Covington, Ky., Dec. 28, 1952; d. Nelson E. and Georgia H. (Roberts) O'N. Student, U. Paris Sorbonne, 1972; BA in Psychology, Hollins Coll., 1974; JD, U. Nebr., 1978, MA in Psychology, 1980, PhD in Psychology, 1982. Program dir., therapist Richmond Maxi Ctr., San Francisco, 1979-81; clin. coord., therapist Pacifica (Calif.) Youth Svc. Bur., 1981-83; staff psychologist Kaiser Permanente Med. Ctr., Walnut Creek, Calif., 1983-91; pvt. practice psychotherapy Pleasant Hill, Calif., 1985—, San Francisco, 1995—; psycholegal cons., Nebr., 1975-79, Calif., 1979—; oral exam commr. Calif. Bd. Behavioral Sci. Examiners, Sacramento, 1982—; pvt. practice psychotherapy, Pleasant Hill, Calif., 1985—; psycholegal cons., presenter San Francisco State U., 1980, U. Calif., San Francisco, 1980, VA Med. Ctr., San Francisco, 1983. Cons. Nebr. Gov.'s Commn. on Status of Women, 1975, 78; vol. Make-A-Wish Found., 1992—. NIMH fellow, 1974-79. Mem. APA, Employed Assistance Profls. Assn., Phi Beta Kappa, Psi Chi.

O'NEILL, JAMES PAUL, psychiatrist; b. Elizabeth, N.J., Sept. 3, 1958; s. Paul James and Dorothy (Semansky) O'N.; m. Patricia Anne Scott, Aug. 1989. BS in Biology, Niagara U., 1980; MD, U. N.E., Mexico, 1984; MD Fifth Pathway, U Medicine & Dentistry, N.J., 1985. Diplomate Am. Bd. Psychiatry and Neurology. Intern Jersey Shore Med. Ctr., Neptune, N.J., 1985-86; resident in psychiatry U. Medicine & Dentistry, Robert Wood Johnson Med. Sch., Piscataway, N.J., 1986-89, chief resident in psychiatry, 1988-89; pvt. practice, Avon By The Sea, N.J., 1989—; attending psychiatrist Monmouth Med. Ctr., Long Branch, N.J.; subcom. on intensive outpatient addiction treatment N.J. Dept. Health, 1994-95; Monmouth Ocean County chpt. rep. to Governing Coun. of N.J. Psychiat. Assn. Contbr. articles to profl. jours. Me. com. Gov.'s Coun. on Addictions Managed Care Round Table, 1992-93; mem. adv. bd. Cath. Charities, Monmouth County, N.J. NIMH fellow, 1988. Mem. AMA (N.J. del. to resident physician sect. 1987-89, Physician Recognition award 1991, 94), Am. Psychiat. Assn., N.J. Psychiat. Assn. (founding pres. resident physician sect. 1987-88, co-chmn. addictive disorders treatment com.), Am. Soc. Internal Medicine, U.S. Life Saving Assn., Med. Soc. N.J. (del. Monmouth County 1990—), Med. Soc. N.J. Residents Assn. (chmn. 1987-89). Republican. Home: 107 Lincoln Ave Avon By The Sea NJ 07717-1310 Office: 813 Main St Avon By The Sea NJ 07717-1023

O'NEILL, MARGARET E., psychological counselor; b. Youngstown, Ohio, Jan. 23, 1935; d. Julius and Anna (Zakel) Huegel; children: Paul McCann, Kathleen McCann, Kevin McCann; m. Thomas B. O'Neill, Oct. 21, 1971 (div. 1979). BSN, UCLA, 1961, MS in Nursing, 1963; MA in Counseling, Calif. Luth. Coll., Thousand Oaks, 1974; PhD in Psychology, U.S. Internat. U., San Diego, 1986. Cert. hypnotherapist, Calif. Instr. Ventura Coll., Calif., 1965-69, dept. chair, 1969-74, coordinator Women's Ctr., 1974-79, counselor, 1979-91; marriage, family and child psychologist, Ventura, 1981-92, Morro Bay and San Luis Obispo, 1992—; trainer, cons. County of Ventura, 1984-90, County of San Luis Obispo, 1991—. Mem. NAFE, San Luis Obispo Psychol. Assn., Rotary Morro Bay, New Comers Club San Luis Obispo. Democrat. Avocations: reading, dancing, hiking, walking, travel. Office: 895 Napa Ave Ste A4 Morro Bay CA 93442-1945

O'NEILL, MARY JANE, health agency executive; b. Detroit, Feb. 24, 1923; d. Frank Roger and Kathryn (Rice) Kilcoyne; Ph.B. summa cum laude, U. Detroit, 1944; postgrad. U. Wis., 1949-50; m. Michael James O'Neill, May 31, 1948; children: Michael, Maureen, Kevin, John (dec.), Kathryn. Editor, East Side Shopper, Detroit, 1939-45; club editor Detroit Free Press, 1945-48; reporter UP, Milw. and Madison, Wis., 1949; dir. public relations Fairfax-Falls Church (Va.) Community Chest, 1955-60; copy editor Falls Ch. Sun-Echo, 1958-60; free-lance writer, Washington, 1960-63; assoc. editor Med. World News, Washington, 1963-66; dir. public relations Westchester Lighthouse, N.Y. Assn. for Blind, 1967-71; dir. public edn. The Lighthouse, N.Y.C., 1971-73, dir. public relations, 1973-80; exec. dir. Eye-Bank for Sight Restoration, Inc., 1980—. Mem. N.Y. State Transplant Coun., 1991—; bd. dirs. N.Y. Regional Transplant Program, 1987-91, 94—. Mem. Women in Communications (pres. N.Y. chpt. 1980-81), Eye Bank Assn. Am. (lay adv. bd. 1981-83, dir. 1983-86, pres. N.E. Region, 1993-96, exec. com. 1994-96), Pub. Rels. Soc. Am., Women Execs. in Pub. Rels. (dir. 1982-88, pres. 1986-87), N.Y. Acad. Scis., Cosmopolitan Club. Office: Eye-Bank for Sight Restoration 210 E 64th St New York NY 10021-7480

O'NEILL, PAUL JOHN, retired psychology educator; b. Taunton, Mass., Apr. 12, 1936; s. Clarence Bernard and Edna Mary (Burke) O'N.; 1 child, Maureen Kelly O'Neill. BA, St. Bonaventure (N.Y.) U., 1960; MA, Boston U., 1961; EdD, U. Ga., 1973. Lic. psychologist. Prof. psychology Jackson (Miss.) State U., 1972—, 1972-93; dir. critical thinking and outcome measures program Jackson (Miss.) State U., 1987-93. Contbr. articles to profl. jours. With U.S. Army, 1954-56, Germany. Office: Jackson State U Dept Psychology Jackson MS 39217

ONESTI, SILVIO JOSEPH, psychiatrist; b. San Francisco, Jan. 3, 1926; s. Silvio Joseph and Johanna (Kristoffy) O.; m. Jean Thomas, May 12, 1956; children: Sally Joanna, Stephen Thomas. BS, Stanford U., 1947; MD, McGill U., 1951. Diplomate Am. Bd. Psychiatry and Neurology. Instr. pediatrics Yale Med. Sch., New Haven, 1956-58; career tchr. psychiatry NIMH, Harvard Med. Sch., Beth Israel Hosp., Boston, 1963-65; head child psychiatry unit Beth Israel Hosp., Boston, 1965-73; dir. child and adolescent psychiatry McLean Hosp., Belmont, Mass., 1973-91; dir. Hall-Mercer Ctr. for children and adolescents McLean Hosp., Belmont, 1973-91; dir. child and adolescent psychiat. tng., 1973-92; dir. clin. svcs. McLean Hosp., Belmont, 1981-83; asst. prof. psychiatry Harvard Med. Sch., Boston, 1969—; faculty Boston Psychoanalytic Soc. and Inst. Inc., Boston, 1971-81. Contbr. articles to profl. jours. With USN, 1944-46. Fellow Am. Psychiat. Assn., Am. Acad. Child and Adolescent Psychiatry, Am. Coll. Psychiatrists; mem. Group for Advancement of Psychiatry (fellow 1959-61, bd. dirs. 1987-89), Boston Psychoanalytic Soc. and Inst. Inc., Mass. Med. Soc., Alpha Omega Alpha. Home: 4 Gray Gdns W Cambridge MA 02138-2312 Office: McLean Hosp 115 Mill St Belmont MA 02178-1041

ONKEN, HENRY DRALLE, plastic surgeon; b. St.Louis, Feb. 22, 1932; s. John Werner and Clara Ruth (Dralle) O.; m. Deborah Dorsett Smith, June 3, 1961; children: John D., Michael D., Katherine Minna. AB, Princeton U., 1953; MD, Harvard U., 1957. Diplomate Am. Bd. Plastic Surgery. Resident in gen. and plastic surgery Barnes Hosp., St. Louis, 1957-66; practice medicine specializing in plastic surgery St. Louis, 1966—; pres. staff Deaconess Hosp., St. Louis, 1986-89. Bd. dirs. English Lang. Sch., 1987—; St. Louis Christmas Carolers, 1981—; co-chmn. Theater Factory of St. Louis, Webster Groves, Mo., 1984-88. Capt. USMC, 1962-64. Mem. AFTRA, Am. Soc. Plastic and Reconstructive Surgeons, Mo. State Med. Assn., Midwestern Assn. Plastic Surgeons (pres. 1996—), St. Louis Area Soc. Plastic Surgeons (treas. 1984—), St. Louis Med. Soc. (councilor 1996—), Univ. Club, Princeton Club, Aesculapian Club (Boston). Democrat. Office: 1034 S Brentwood Blvd Ste 750 Saint Louis MO 63117-1207

ONO, RICHARD DANA, biotechnology executive; b. Bridgeton, N.J., Jan. 16, 1953; s. Frank Hitoshi and Fumi (Yokoyama) O.; m. Anne Wagner, Oct. 10, 1981; children: Alison Celia, Maxwell Wagner. AB, Johns Hopkins U., 1975; AM, Harvard U., 1978, PhD, 1981. Rsch. assoc. U. Mass. Med. Sch., Worcester, 1981-83; dir. bus. devel. Damon Biotech, Inc., Needham Heights, Mass., 1983-86; gen. mgr. Regis McKenna, Inc., Cambridge, Mass., 1986-87; dir. bus. devel. Integrated Genetics, Inc., Framingham, Mass., 1987-89; v.p. bus. devel. Enzytech, Inc., Cambridge, Mass., 1989-91; chief exec. officer, pres. Arcturus Pharm. Corp., Cambridge, Mass., 1991-92; industry analyst Aberlyn Capital Mgmt. Co., Waltham, Mass., 1992-94; founder ARC Assocs., Concord, Mass., 1994—; co-foundr, bd. dirs. Mass. Biotechnology Coun., Inc., Cambridge, 1984-86; co-founder several biotechnology start-up cos. Author: Vanishing Fishes of North America, 1983; editor: The Business of Biotechnology from the Bench to the Street, 1991. Affiliate Dunster Ho., Cambridge, Mass., 1990. Recipient Raney award Soc. Ichthyologists and Herpetologists, Washington, 1979. Home: 18 Spring Rd Concord MA 01742-4730 Office: ARC Assocs PO Box 1419 Concord MA 01742-4730

ONOFRIO, BURTON M., neurosurgeon; b. New Milford, Conn., Jan. 1, 1933. MD, Cornell U., 1957. Diplomate Am. Bd. Neurol. Surgery. Intern N.Y. Hosp. Med. Ctr., N.Y.C., 1957, resident, 1958; fellow Mayo Clinic, Rochester, N.Y., 1960-64; neurol. surgeon St. Mary's Hosp., Rochester, Minn.; faculty neurosurg. dept. Mass. Gen. Hosp., Boston; cons. neurosurgeon Mayo Clinic, Rochester, Minn. Mem. AMA, Coll. Neurol. Surgeons, Minn. Neurol. Surgery Soc. Office: Mayo Clinic E-68 200 First St SW Rochester MN 55905-0001*

ONUFROCK, RICHARD SHADE, pharmacist, researcher; b. Colorado Springs, Colo., July 5, 1934; s. Frank and Mildred Joy (Overstreet) O.; m. Karen Faye Larson, June 15, 1958 (div. 1980); children: Richard Alan (dec.), Amy Mildred. BS in Pharmacy, U. Colo., 1961; diploma, Famous Artists Schs., 1963. Registered pharmacist, Colo., Ariz., South Africa. Pharmacist Aley Drug Co., Colorado Springs, 1961-75, St. Joseph Hosp., Denver, 1976-77, Navajo Nation Health Found., Ganado, Ariz., 1977-81, Kearny (Ariz.) Kennecott-Samaritan Hosp., 1984-85, NIH, Warren G. Magnuson Clin. Ctr., Bethesda, Md., 1988—; dir. pharmacy, chief pharmacist Tintswalo Hosp., South Africa, 1981-84; pharmacist, chief pharmacist Miami (Ariz.)-Inspiration Hosp., 1985-88; instr. Coll. of Ganado, 1979-80; asst. in textbook revision and illustration U. Colo., 1961; cons. Heritage Health Care Ctr., Globe, Ariz., 1988. Illustrator Pharmacy for Nurses, 1961, Colo. Jour. of Pharmacy, 1962-64; illustrations exhibited Colo. Springs Fine Art Ctr., 1964-66, Gilpin County Art Assn., Central City, Colo., 1968-74, 1st Nat. Space Art Show, Denver, 1969. dem. precinct committeeman, 1974-76; den leader Boy Scouts Am., com. mem., 1975-76; fireman, lt. Ganado Vol. Fire Dept., 1977-81; compassionate med. missionary Nazarene Ch., Tintswalo Hosp. Gazankulu, South Africa, 1981-84;bd. dirs. Friends of Libr., Kearny, 1985-87; active Grace Episcopal Ch. Mem. Am. Pharm. Assn., Am. Soc. Health Sys. Pharmacists, Washington Met. Soc. Health Sys. Pharmacists, Phi Delta Chi, Delta Sigma Phi. Home: 4831 36th St NW Apt 202 Washington DC 20008-4917 Office: NIH Clin Ctr 9000 Rockville Pike Bethesda MD 20892-0001

OOGHE, ROBERT BARKSDALE, internist; b. Richmond, Va., May 25, 1927; s. Arthur Edward and Frances Evans (Barksdale) O. Student, U. Richmond, 1944-45; BS, U.S. Naval Acad., 1949; MD, U. Va., 1957. Diplomate Am. Bd. Internal Medicine. Intern U. Va., Charlottesville, 1957-58; resident U. Va., 1959-61; pvt. practice Charlottesville, 1961—. Lt. (j.g.) USN, 1949-53. Home: 655 Ivy Farm Dr Charlottesville VA 22901 Office: 505 Faulconer Dr Ste 1A Charlottesville VA 22903-4981

OOMMEN, SAMUEL C., surgeon; b. Honavar, India, Sept. 17, 1951; came to U.S., 1976; s. Cherukara Samuel and Aley (Joshua) O.; m. Mary Samuel Oommen, Jan. 15, 1976; children: Santosh, Philip. MD, Karnatak Med. Coll., Hubli, India, 1974. Diplomate Am. Bd. Surgery, Am. Bd. Colon-Rectal Surgery. Gen. surg. resident Brookdale Hosp. Med. Ctr., 1978-82; surgeon USAF, 1982-87; colon and rectal surgery fellow U. Tex., Houston, 1984-85; pvt. practice Mt. Diablo Med. Ctr., Concord, Calif., 1987—, chmn. dept. surgery, 1990-91. Maj. USAF, 1982-87. Fellow ACS, Am. Soc. Colon Rectal Surgeons; mem. No. Calif. Soc. Colon-Rectal Surgeons (pres. 1996—). Office: Bay Area Colon Rectal Surg 2700 Grant St No 306 Concord CA 64520

OPARIL, SUZANNE, cardiologist, educator, researcher; b. Elmira, N.Y., Apr. 10, 1941; d. Stanley and Anna (Penkova) O. AB, Cornell U., 1961; MD, Columbia U., 1965. Diplomate Am. Bd. Internal Medicine. Intern in medicine Presbyn. Hosp., N.Y.C., 1965-66; sr. asst. resident in medicine Mass. Gen. Hosp., Boston, 1967-68, clin. and rsch. fellow in medicine, cardiac unit, 1968-71; asst. prof. medicine Med. Sch., U. Chgo., 1971-75, assoc. prof., 1975-77; assoc. prof. dept. medicine U. Ala., Birmingham, 1977-81, asst. prof. physiology and biophysics, 1980-81, assoc. prof., 1981—, prof. medicine, 1981—, dir. vascular biology and hypertension program, 1985—; mem. vis. faculty Nat. High Blood Pressure Edn. Program, 1974—, Joint Nat. Com. on Detection, Evaluation and Treatment High Blood Pressure, 1991; mem. bd. sci. advisors Sterling Drug, Inc., 1988-91; lectr. in field; Selkurt lectr. Ind. U. Sch. Medicine, 1994; hon. prof. Peking Union Med. Coll., 1994. Author books on hypertension; editor Am. Jour. Med. Scis., 1984-94; assoc. editor Hypertension, 1979-83, mem. editl. bd., 1984—; assoc. editor Am. Jour. Physiology-Renal, 1989-91; mem. editl. bd. Jour. Hypertensioin, 1989—; contbr. over 300 articles to profl. jours., chpts. to books. Recipient Young Investigator award Internat. Soc. Hypertension, 1979, ann. award Med. Coll. Pa., 1984; fellow Am. Coll. Cardiology, 1992. Fellow Am. Coll. Cardiology; mem. Inst. Medicine of NAS (corr. com. on human rights 1992, chmn. com. advise Dept. Def. 1993 Breast Cancer Rsch. Program), AAAS, Endocrine Soc., Inter-Am. Soc. Hypertension, Am. Soc. Hypertension (pub. policy com. 1990—, sci. program com. 1990-92), Assn. for Women in Sci., Am. Heart Assn. (coun. for high blood pressure rsch., 1973—, exec. com. 1985-90, vice chmn. 1986, coun. on basic scis. 1978—, mem.-at-large, exec. com. 1979-81, mem.-at-large bd. dirs. 1992, chmn. Louis B. Katz Prize com. 1984-86, chmn., 1988-90, chmn. budget com. 1990-91, v.p. Ala. affiliate 1986-87, pres.-elect Ala. affiliate 1987-88, 93-94, pres. Ala. affiliate 1988-89, nat. pres.-elect 1993-94, nat. pres. 1994—, Lewis K. Dahl Meml. Lectr. 1993), Am. Physiol. Soc. (clin. physiology adv. com. 1992—), Am. Soc. for Clin. Investigation (sec.-treas. 1983-86), Soc. Exptl. Biology and Medicine (councillor 1993—), So. Soc. for Clin. Investigation (Founder's award 1995), Assn. Am. Physicians, Am. Fedn. for Clin. Rsch. (midwest councillor 1974-75, nat. councillor 1975-78, sec.-treas. 1978-80, pres. 1981-82), Phi Beta Kappa, Sigma Xi, Alpha Omega Alpha (mem. nat. bd. dirs., dir.-at-large 1991, treas. 1993). Office: U Ala Sch Medicine 1034 Zeigler Research Bldg Birmingham AL 35294*

OPITZ, JOHN MARIUS, clinical geneticist, pediatrician; b. Hamburg, Germany, Aug. 15, 1935; came to U.S., 1950, naturalized, 1957; s. Friedrich and Erica Maria (Quadt) O.; m. Susan O. Lewin; children: Leigh, Teresa, John, Chrisanthi, Emma. BA, State U. Iowa, 1956, MD, 1959; DSc (hon.), Mont. State U., 1983; MD (hon.), U. Kiel, Germany, 1986. Diplomate Am. Bd. Pediatrics, Am. Bd. Med. Genetics. Intern, State U. Iowa Hosp., 1959-60, resident in pediatrics, 1960-61; resident and chief resident in pediatrics U. Wis. Hosp., Madison, 1961-62; fellow in pediatrics and med. genetics U. Wis., 1962-64, asst. prof. med. genetics and pediatrics, 1964-69, assoc. prof., 1969-72, prof., 1972-79; dir. Wis. Clin. Genetics Ctr., 1974-79; clin. prof. med. genetics and pediatrics U. Wash., Seattle, 1979—; adj. prof. medicine, biology, history and philosophy, vet. rsch. and vet. sci. Mont. State U., Bozeman, 1979-94, McKay lectr., 1992, Univ. prof. med. humanities MSU. Bozeman, 1994—; adj. prof. pediatrics, med. genetics U. Wis., Madison, 1979—, Class of 1947 Disting. prof., U. of Wis., 1992; coordinator Shodair Mont. Regional Genetic Svcs. Program, Helena, 1979-82; chmn. dept. med. genetics Shodair Children's Hosp., Helena, 1983-94; dir. Found. Devel. and Med. Genetics, Helena, Mont.; Farber lectr. Soc. Pediatric Pathology, 1987; Joseph Garfunkel lectr. So. Ill. U., Springfield, 1987, McKay lectr. Mont. State U., 1992; Warren Wheeler vis. prof. Columbus (Ohio) Children's Hospital, 1987; Bea Fowlow lectr. in med. genet. U. Calgary, 1996. Editor, author 13 books; founder, editor in chief Am. Jour. Med. Genetics, 1977—; mng. editor European Jour. Pediatrics, 1977-85; contbr. numerous articles on clin. genetics. Chair Mont. Com. for Humanities, 1991. Recipient Pool of Bethesda award for excellence in mental retardation rsch. Bethesda Luth. Home, 1988, Med. Alumni Citation U. Wis., 1989, Col. Harlan Sanders Lifetime Achievement award for work in the field of genetic scis. March of Dimes, Purkinje medal Czech Soc. Medicine, Mendel medal Czech Soc. Med. Genetics, 1996. Fellow AAAS, Am. Coll. Med. Genetics (founder); mem. German Acad. Scientists Leopoldina, Am. Soc. Human Genetics, Am. Pediatric Soc., Soc. Pediatric Rsch., Am. Bd. Med. Genetics, Birth Defects Clin. Genetic Soc., Am. Inst. Biol. Scis., Am. Soc. Zoologists, Teratology Soc., Genetic Soc. Am., European Soc. Human Genetics, Soc. Study Social Biology, Am. Acad. Pediatrics, German Soc. Pediatrics (hon.), Western Soc. Pediatrics Rsch. (emeritus), Italian Soc. Med. Genetics (hon.), Israel Soc. Genetics (hon.), Russian Soc. Med. Genetics (hon.), So. Africa Soc. Med. Genetics (hon.), Japanese Soc. Human Genetics (hon.), Sigma Xi. Democrat. Roman Catholic. Home: 2180 Lime Kiln St Helena MT 59601-5871 Office: FRB Ste 229 100 Neill Ave Helena MT 59601

OPLER, LEWIS ALAN, psychiatrist, educator, researcher; b. L.A., Apr. 16, 1948; s. Marvin Kaufman and Charlotte (Fox) D.; m. Annette Arcario; children: Mark, Daniel, Michelle, Douglas. BA magna cum laude, Harvard U., 1969; PhD in Pharmacology, Albert Einstein Coll. Medicine, 1975, MD, 1976. Diplomate Am. Bd. Psychiatry and Neurology. Asst. prof. dept. psychiatry Albert Einstein Coll. of Medicine, Bronx, 1979-85, assoc. clin. prof., 1985-87; clin. dir. Bronx Psychiat. Ctr., Bronx, 1985-87; assoc. clin. prof. dept. psychiatry Coll. Physicians Columbia U., N.Y.C., 1987-91, clin. prof. Coll. Physicians, 1991—; unit chief Presbyn. Hosp., N.Y.C., 1987-90, dir. psychiat. rsch., 1987-94; med. dir. N.Y.C. regional office N.Y. State Office Mental Health, 1994-95, med. dir. N.Y.C. region, 1995—; psychopharmacology cons. Columbia U., 1987—. Contbr. articles to profl. jours. Nat. Merit scholar, 1965; recipient Spl. Achievement award N.Y. State Office Mental Health, 1987, Exemplary Psychiatrist award Nat. Alliance for Mentally Ill, 1992, 93. Mem. Alliance for the Mentally Ill of N.Y. State (hon., bd. dirs. 1991—), Am. Psychiat. Assn., N.Y. Acad. Scis. Democrat. Office: Columbia Presbyn Med Ctr 161 Ft Washington Ave New York NY 10032-3713

OPLINGER, BONNIE M., human services professional; b. Reading, Pa., Dec. 21, 1942; d. Coster Carroll and Mary Elizabeth (Moyer) Scholder; m. Earl St. Clair Oplinger Jr., Aug. 27, 1966; children: Kurt Alan, Susan Mary, Cameron Myles, Hans Eric. BA, Albright Coll., 1965; MSW, Temple U., 1985. Cert. elem. tchr., Pa.; lic. social worker, Pa.; diplomate in clin. social work. Organist, choir dir. St. Paul's Luth. Ch., Adamstown, Pa.; tchr. Reading Sch. Dist.; adj. prof. Alvernia Coll., Reading; dir. mktg. edn. Family Guidance Ctr., Reading, 1985-88; dir. counseling svcs. CONCERN Profl. Svcs. for Children, Youth & Families, 1988—; adj. prof. Pa. State U., 1991-95, Albright Coll., 1994. Mem. NEA, NASW, PROKIDS, Berks County C. of C., Berks Teen Inst., Drug Free Schs. Adv. Com. Home: 327 E Walnut St Shillington PA 19607-2625

OPP, CURTIS, optometrist; b. Pierre, S.D., Nov. 5, 1965; m. Gayle Lynette Breukelman, July 29, 1989; children: Derek Nicholas, Connor Dwayne. BS in Biology, U. S.D., 1988; OD, Pacific U., Forest Grove, Oreg., 1993. Optometrist Wagner (S.D.) Vision Clinic, 1993—; mem. allied health pers. Wagner Cmty. Meml. Hosp., 1993—. Mem. Am. Optometric Assn., S.D. Optometric Soc., Rotary Internat. (bd. dirs. 1993-95), C. of C. (retail promotions com. 1995—), Beta Sigma Kappa. Office: Wagner Vision Clinic 121 S Main St Wagner SD 57380

OPPENHEIMER, BERTRAM JAY, retired hospital administrator; b. N.Y.C., Mar. 10, 1922; s. Joseph Loeb and Kate Blanche (Rosenwasser) O.; married. BA, Cornell U., 1943; BS, NYU, 1944; MD, Washington U., 1950. Diplomate Am. Bd. Med. Examiners, Am. Bd. Internal Medicine. Pvt. practice Yonkers, N.Y., 1954-76; adminstr., chief exec. officer Yonkers Gen. Hosp., 1976-95, ret., 1995. Capt. U.S. Army, 1943-46. Mem. Rotary.

OPPENHEIMER, STEVEN BERNARD, biology educator; b. Bklyn., Mar. 23, 1944; s. Hugo and Irma (Schellenberg) O.; m. Carolyn Roberta Weisenberg, May 23, 1971; 1 child, Mark. BS magna cum laude, Bklyn. Coll., 1965; PhD, Johns Hopkins U., 1969. Am. Cancer Soc. postdoctoral fellow U. Calif., San Diego, 1969-71; asst. prof. biology Calif. State U., Northridge, 1971-74, assoc. prof., 1974-77, prof., 1977—, dir. Sch. Sci. and Math. Ctr. for Cancer and Devel. Biology; panel mem. NSF, Washington, 1985, NIH, 1987, 94; cons. Northridge Hosp., 1984-92. Author: Introduction to Embryonic Development, 1980, 2d rev. edit., 1984, 3d rev. edit., 1989, Cancer Biological and Clinical Introduction, 1982, 2d rev. edit., 1985, 3d rev. edit., 1995, Cancer Prevention Guidebook, 1984, 2d rev. edit., 1991, Atlas of Embryonic Development, 1984; editor Cancer, Longevity Letter, 1984-85; editor Jour. of Student Rsch. Abstracts, 1995—; writer (film) Cancer Prevention, A Way of Life, 1986; contbr. articles to profl. jours. Recipient Disting. Prof. award Calif. State U., 1977, Statewide Outstanding Prof. award Bd. Trustees of 19 Campuses, 1984, Excellence in Sci. Edn. award Calif. Sci. Tchrs. Assn., 1988; grantee Nat. Cancer Inst., 1972-84, NSF, 1981—, NICHHD, 1986-88, NIH, 1993—, Joseph Drown Found., 1988—, NASA, 1988-95, Urban Cmty. Svc. Program, 1992-95, Eisenhower Program, 1990-96, others; Exxon fellow, 1982, Thomas Eckstrom Trust fellow, 1982—. Fellow AAAS; mem. Am. Soc. Zoologists (nat. program chmn., devel. biology and nat. membership chmn. 198-85), Am. Soc. Cell Biology, Soc. Devel. Biology, Am. Cancer Soc. (bd. dirs. San Fernando Valley chpt. 1985-89, Pub. Edn. award 1985, grantee 1977-86), Sigma Xi (Disting. Rsch. award 1984), Phi Kappa Phi. Home: 8933 Darby Ave Northridge CA 91325-2706 Office: Calif State U Dept Biology 18111 Nordhoff St Northridge CA 91330-8303

OPPIDO, PIERO ANDREA, neurosurgeon; b. Rome, Feb. 4, 1959; s. Giuseppe Antonio and Giuliana (Valentini) O. MD, U. Rome, 1983, PhD, 1991. Resident in neurosurgery U. Rome, 1983-88; neurotraumatology rsch. fellow U. Pa., Phila., 1988-89; clin. fellow U. Rome, 1989-92; clin. fellow neurosurgery Inst. Regine Elene, Rome, 1992—. Mem. Med. Bd. of Rome, Italian Neurosurg. Soc. Office: Viale Ippocrate 104, Rome Italy 00161

OPPLIGER, PEARL LAVIOLETTE, alcohol and drug abuse services professional; b. Barre, Vt., Aug. 16, 1942; d. Roland Bernard Sr. and Mae C. (Bouley) Laviolette; m. William Gregory Wotschak, Sept. 8, 1962 (div. Feb. 1983); children: Robin Lee Hillier, Rene Beth Greff, Rana Mae Wotschak; m. Edward Lee Oppliger, Aug. 16, 1988. BSW, Bowling Green State U., 1986; MSW, Ohio State U., 1995, Ohio State U., 1995. Lic. social worker, Ohio, CCDC III, Ohio. Sec. Ohio State U., Columbus, 1964-66; hostess Welcome Wagon, Bowling Green, Ohio, 1975-76; owner, mgr. children's clothing store Rhymes 'n' Reasons, Bowling Green, 1976-84; bookkeeper Friendly Ice Cream Inc., Bowling Green, 1979-80; sales clk. Wilson's Shoe Store, Bowling Green, 1984-85; alcoholism counselor Wood County Coun. on Alcoholism and Drug Abuse, Inc., Bowling Green, 1985-86, family counselor, 1986, supr., 1986-90, dir. recovery svcs., 1990—; adj. instr. in social work Bowling Green State U., 1988—; co-facilitator Parents Helping Parents, Bowling Green, 1990-95. Coun. mem.-at-large City of Bowling Green, 1990-93, mem. planning commn., 1988-89, asst. chmn. Bowling Green Rep. Club, 1989-91, chmn. 1991-92; co-founder Downtown Bus. Assn., Bowling Green, 1980-82; sec. Bowling Green Housing Agy., 1994—. Am. Bus. Women's Assn. scholar. Mem. AAUW (v.p. mem. com. Bowling Green br. 1991-93, Outstanding Woman in Cmty. Work 1990, 96), NASW, Phi Kappa Phi. Roman Catholic. Home: 505 Donbar Bowling Green OH 43402-1819 Office: Wood County Coun Alcoholism 320 W Gypsy Lane Rd Bowling Green OH 43402-4506

OPRITZA, GREGORY DEAN, internist; b. Akron, Ohio, Jan. 26, 1955; s. Andrew and Janice Lucille (Adams) O.; m. Roberta Kay Conflenti, May 22, 1976; children: Jaclyn Nicole, Bryan Gregory. BA, U. Pitts., 1976; MA, U. Ariz., 1979; MD, Med. Coll. Ohio, 1986. Diplomate Am. Bd. Internal Medicine. Intern, resident Georgetown U. Hosp., Washington, 1986-89; internist Med. Group of Manchester, N.H., 1989—; bd. dirs. N.H. Physicians Orgn., Manchester. Mem. Alpha Omega Alpha. Home: 14 Farmhouse Rd Bedford NH 03110 Office: Med Group of Manchester 7695 Main St Ste 300 Manchester NH 03102

O'QUINN, APRIL GALE, physician, educator; b. Columbia, Miss., Apr. 21, 1936; d. R.V. and Anna Pauline (Cook) O'Q.; diploma Scott and White Hosp. Sch. Nursing, 1965; A.A., Temple Jr. Coll., 1965; B.S. with honors, Baylor U., 1968; M.D., U. Tex. Med. Br., 1971. Intern, U. Tex. Med. Br., Galveston, 1971-72, resident ob-gyn., 1972-75; fellow in oncology M.D. Anderson Hosp., Houston, Tex., 1976-78; practice medicine specializing in ob-gyn., Galveston, 1978-81; asst. prof. dept. ob-gyn. U. Tex. Med. Br., Galveston, 1975-81; practice medicine specializing in ob-gyn, New Orleans, 1981—; mem. staff John Sealy Hosp., St. Mary's Hosp., Galveston, Tulane Med. Center, New Orleans Charity Hosp., So. Baptist Hosp. and Touro Infirmary, New Orleans; assoc. prof., dir. div. gynecol. oncology dept. ob-gyn Tulane U. Sch. Medicine, New Orleans, 1981-85, prof., 1985-89, prof., chair dept. ob.-gyn., 1989—. Diplomate Am. Bd. Ob-Gyn. Fellow Willard R. Cooke Obstet. and Gynecol. Soc., Am. Coll. Ob-Gyn.; mem. Soc. Gynecologic Oncologists, Western Assn. Gynecol. Oncologists, Tex. Assn. Obstetricians and Gynecologists, Houston Gynecol. and Obstetrical Soc., Tex. Med. Assn., Galveston County Med. Soc., Felix Rutledge Soc. Republican. Baptist. Home: 5100 Bancroft Dr New Orleans LA 70122-2801 Office: Tulane U Sch Medicine Ob Gyn Dept New Orleans LA 70112

ORBISON, DAVID VAILLANT, clinical psychologist, consultant; b. Hartford, Conn., Apr. 2, 1952; s. Theodore Tucker and Edith Vaillant (Julier) O.; m. Beth Lynne Fruendt, June 19, 1981; children: Henry Douglas, Charles Vaillant, Samuel Tucker. BA, Yale U., 1974; MA in Psychology, Duquesne U., 1976, PhD in Clin. Psychology, 1986. Bd. cert. Am. Bd. Forensic Examiners. Psychologist Harmarville Rehab. Ctr., Pitts., 1975-84; pvt. practice Pitts., 1981—; mem. adj. profl. staff Shadyside Hosp., Pitts., 1981—. Fellow Pa. Psychol. Assn. (chmn. program and edn. bd. 1988-92); mem. APA, Am. Psychoanalytic Assn. (chmn. affiliate coun. steering com. 1993-94, pres. affiliate coun. 1994-95), Greater Pitts. Psychol. Assn. (treas. 1984-86, chmn. bd. dirs. 1986-88), Pitts. Psychoanalytic Inst. (chmn. candidates' orgn. 1994—), Pitts. Psychoanalytic Soc. Office: 401 Shady Ave Ste 102C Pittsburgh PA 15206-4409

ORCUTT, JAMES CRAIG, ophthalmologist; b. Holyoke, Colo., July 22, 1946; s. John Potter and Irene M. (Falk) O.; m. Barbara McCallum, Feb. 9, 1974; children: John, Gale. BPh in Pharmacy, U. Colo., Boulder, 1969; PhD in Pharmacology, U. Colo., Denver, 1976, MD, 1977. Diplomate Am. Bd. Ophthalmology. Intern U. Wash., Seattle, 1977-78, resident, 1978-81; fellow in orbital disease Moorfields Eye Hosp., London, 1981-82; fellow in neuro-ophthalmology Hosp. for Nervous Diseases and Great Ormond St. Hosp., London, 1982; asst. prof. ophthalmology U. Wash., Seattle, 1983-88, adj. prof. otolaryngology, 1987-88, assoc. prof. ophthalmology/adj. assoc. prof. otolargyngology, 1988-95, prof. ophthalmology, 1995—; chief ophthalmology Seattle Vets. Affairs Ctr., 1983—; ophthalmology cons. Vets. Affairs Ctrl. Office, Washington, 1993—. Pres. bd. trustees Northwest Sch., Seattle, 1996—. Office: U Wash Dept Ophthalmology Box 356485 Seattle WA 98195

ORDA, RUBEN, surgeon; b. Buenos Aires, Argentina, Dec. 22, 1935; s. Moshe and Esther (Oiberman) O.; m. Sara Grossberg, Mar. 12, 1960; children—Ariel, Ruth Miriam. M.D. with honors, Buenos Aires U., 1959; Master in Surgery, Tel-Aviv U., 1975. Resident Fiorito Hosp., Buenos Aires, Argentina, 1959-64; sr. surgeon Rawson Hosp., Buenos Aires, 1964-67, Tel-Aviv Med. Center (Israel), 1968-83; head surgery Assaf Harofe Hosp., Zerifin, Israel, 1983—; chmn. divsn. surgery Tel Aviv U., 1991-95; clin. and research fellow Westminster Hosp., London, 1976-77; lectr. surgery Buenos Aires U., 1964-67; lectr. anatomy Tel Aviv U., 1967-73; assoc. prof. surgery Tel Aviv U., 1983-92, prof. surgery, 1992—; examiner gen. surgery Israel Bd. Examinations, 1983—; mem. adv. com. for surgery Ministry of Health, Israel, 1986-93. Sec. gen. of the 9th World Congress of the Collegium Internat. Chirurgiae Digestivae, Jerusalem, Israel, 1986-93, nat. del., chmn. of the Israeli chpt., 1988—. Grantee Gordon Research Found., 1978; Tel Aviv U., 1978, 80, 81, 82, 85; chmn. Coun. Chmn. Israel Surg. Soc., 1990-94, Israel Surg. Soc., 1994—. Fellow Am. Coll. Surgeons, Govenor Am. Coll Surgeons. 1995, Royal Soc. Medicine (Eng.); mem. Societe Internationale de Chirurgie, Collegium Internationale Chirurgiae Digestivae, European Soc. Surg. Research, N.Y. Acad. Scis., Israel Surg. Soc., World Assn. of Hepato-Pancreato-Biliary Surgery, Asian Surg. Assn., Internat. Gastro-Surg. Club. Home: Keren Hayesod 3/27, Ramat Ilan Givat Shmuel 54051, Israel Office: Assaf Harofe Hosp Surgery A, Tel Aviv U, Zerifin 70300, Israel

ORDAHL, JOHN NICOLAI, orthodontist; b. Colorado Springs, July 10, 1953. BA, Colo. Coll., 1975; MS, Colo. State U., 1982; DDS, U. Colo., 1983; MS, U. Iowa, 1989. Lectr. U. Colo. Sch. Dentistry, Denver, 1982-83; gen. practice resident Womack Army Hosp., Ft. Bragg, N.C., 1983-84; capt. USAR, Bad Caustatt, West Germany, 1984-87; tchg. asst. U. Iowa, Iowa City, 1987-89; pvt. practice orthodontics Colorado Springs, 1989—; asst. clin. prof. U. Colo., 1990-96. Mem. Am. Assn. Orthodontists, Am. Dental Assn., Colorado Springs Dental Soc., Colo. Dental Soc., Omicron Kappa Upsilon, Phi Kappa Phi. Office: 1711 N Murray Blvd Colorado Springs CO 80915

ORDON, ANDREW PAUL, plastic surgeon; b. Chgo., Dec. 9, 1950; s. V. Anthony and Jay Mary (Lacka) O.; m. Robyn Lee, July 20, 1985; children: Matthew, Shannon. BS in Biol. Scis., U. Calif., 1972; MD, U. So. Calif., 1979. Gen. surgery resident U. So. Calif., L.A., 1979-80; head and neck surgery resident Loma Linda-White Meml., L.A., 1980-82, head and neck surgery chief resident, 1982-83; plastic surgery resident Lenox Hill Hosp., N.Y.C., 1983-84, plastic surgery chief resident, 1984-85; asst. prof. head and neck N.Y. Med. Coll., 1987-90; asst. prof. plastic surgery U. Conn., Farmington, 1990—; fellow aesthetic surgery Beverly Hills Med. Ctr., 1983; chief plastic surgery Med. Arts Ctr. Hosp., N.Y.C., 1985-90; attending surgeon Lenox Hill Hosp., N.Y.C., 1987—, N.Y. Eye and Ear Infirmary, N.Y.C., 1987—, Beth Israel North Med. Ctr., N.Y.C., 1987—; guest appearances on 20/20, 48 Hours, CNN, Sally Jesse Raphael, Phil Donahue, Maury Povitch, Entertainment Tonight. Author: Revealing the New York, A Guide to Plastic Surgery, 1994, Everything You Wanted to Know About Plastic Surgery, 1988. Grantee NSF, 1972. Fellow ACS, Am. Acad. Facial Plastic Surgery, Liposuction Soc. Am., mem. Am. Soc. Plastic/Reconstructive Surgeons, Am. Soc. Aesthetic Plastic Surgery, Phi Beta Kappa. Republican. Episcopalian. Office: 38 E 72nd St New York NY 10021

ORDONEZ, NELSON GONZALO, pathologist; b. Bucaramanga, Santander, Colombia, July 20, 1944; came to U.S., 1972; s. Gonzalo and Itsmenia Ordonez; m. Miranda Lee Ferrell, Dec. 18, 1976 (div. June 1983); 1 child, Nelson Adrian; m. Catherine Marie Newton, Nov. 6, 1987; 1 child, Sara Catherine Itsmenia. BA and Sci., Instituto Daza Dangond, Bogota, Colombia, 1962; MD, Nat. U. Colombia, Bogota, 1970. Resident pathology U. N.C., Chapel Hill, 1972-73; resident pathology U. Chgo., 1974-76, asst. prof. pathology, 1977-78; asst. prof. pathology U. Tex. M.D. Anderson Cancer Ctr., Houston, 1978-82, assoc. prof., 1983-85, prof., 1985—, dir. immunocytochemistry sect., 1981—. Author: (with others) Renal Biopsy Pathology and Diagnostic and Therapeutic Implications, 1980, Tumors of the Lung, 1991; contbr. chpts. to books, numerous articles to med. jours. Nat. Kidney Found. fellow, 1977-78. Mem. AMA, Am. Assn. Pathologists, Internat. Acad. Pathology, Am. Soc. Clin. Pathologists, Am. Soc. Sytology, Am. Soc. Investigative Pathology, Internat. Acad. Cytology, Arthur Purdy Stout Soc. Surg. Pathologists, Latin-Am. Soc. Pathology. Office: U Tex MD Anderson Cancer Ctr 1515 Holcombe Blvd Houston TX 77030-4009

ORDORICA, STEVEN ANTHONY, obstetrician, gynecologist, educator; b. N.Y.C., Jan. 4, 1957; s. Vincent and Rose (Goiricelaya) O. BA magna cum laude, NYU, 1979; MD, Stony Brook U., 1983. Diplomate Am. Coll. Obstetrics and Gynecology, speciality cert. maternal-fetal medicine; lic. Nat. Bd. Med. Examiners. Resident obstetrics and gynecology NYU-Bellevue Hosp. Ctr., 1983-87, fellow maternal-fetal medicine, 1987-89, instr. obstetrics-gynecology, 1989-91; clin. instr. obstetrics-gynecology NYU, 1986-89, asst. prof. ob/gyn., 1991-93; dir. perinatal clinics and prenatal diagnostic unit Gouverneur Hosp., N.Y.C., 1989-94; perinatal cons. Bellevue Hosp. Ctr., N.Y.C., 1989—; faculty mem. perinatal div. NYU Med. Ctr., 1989—; presenter in field. Contbr. articles to Surgery, Am. Jour. Obstetrics and Gynecology, Am. Jour. Perinatal, Surgery, Obstetrics and Gynecology, Jour. Reproductive Medicine, Acta Geneticae Medicae et Gemellologiae, Jour. Rheumatology. Mem. Am. Coll. Obstetrics and Gynecology, Soc. Perinatal Obstetricians, N.Y. Acad. Scis., N.Y. State Perinatal Soc., AMA, Phi Beta Kappa, Beta Lambda Sigma. Office: NYU Med Ctr Ste 10Q 530 1st Ave New York NY 10016-6402

O'REILLY, RICHARD JOHN, pediatrician; b. Bklyn., Apr. 29, 1943; s. John Russell and Margaret (Cronin) O'R.; m. E. Jean Capitano, Nov. 1984; children from previous marriage: John, Steven. B.S., Coll. Holy Cross, 1964; M.D., U. Rochester, 1968. Diplomate Am. Bd. Pediatrics. Intern U. Minn. Hosp., Mpls., 1968-69; resident in pediatrics Children's Hosp. Med. Ctr. and Beth Israel Hosp., Boston, 1971-72; with dept. pediatrics Meml. Sloan Kettering Cancer Ctr., N.Y.C., 1973—; attending pediatrician, chmn. dept. pediatrics Meml. Hosp., N.Y.C., 1986—; mem. dept. immunology Sloan-Kettering Inst. Cancer Research; prof. pediatrics Cornell U. Med. Coll., 1980, Lila Acheson Wallace prof. pediatric research, 1980, Vincent Astor prof. clin. research, 1984; chief marrow transplantation svc. Meml. Sloan-Kettering Cancer Ctr., 1981—; councillor Internat. Bone Marrow Transplant Registry; pres. Damon Runyon-Walter Winchell Cancer Fund, 1991—. Editor-in-chief BBMT; assoc. editor Cancer Rsch., Clin. Cancer Rsch., Bone marrow Transplantation, NCI Study Sect. D. Served with USPHS, 1969-71. Recipient Louise and Allston Boyer-Young Investigator award for clin. research, 1980. Mem. AAAS, Am. Pediatric Soc., Am. Assn. Immunologists, Am. Acad. Pediatrics, Am. Assn. Pathologists, Soc. Pediatric Rsch., N.Y. Transplantation Soc., N.Y. Acad. Scis., Am. Assn. Clin. Radiology, Am. Soc. Hematology, Am. Soc. Blood and Marrow Transplantation (sec. 1993-95). Democrat. Roman Catholic. Office: Meml Sloan-Kettering Cancer Ctr 1275 York Ave New York NY 10021-6007

OREM, CASSANDRA ELIZABETH, health systems administrator; b. Balt., Sept. 26, 1940; d. Ira Julius and Mabel Ruth (Peeples) O. Diploma, Ch. Home and Hosp. Sch. Nursing, 1962; BS with honors, The Johns Hopkins U., 1968; MS, U. Md., 1972; cert., Balt. Sch. Massage, 1988; MA in Applied Psychology, U. Santa Monica, 1991, cert. in advanced applied psychology, 1992; cert., Waitley Masters Coaching Prog., 1996. Staff, charge nurse Ch. Home and Hosp., Balt., 1962-63; asst. instr. Ch. Home and Hosp. Sch. Nursing, Balt., 1963-64, instr., 1964-70, rsch., clin.-primary investigator, 1971-72; clin. nurse specialist Johns Hopkins Hosp., Balt., 1972-77, rsch., clin. co-investigator, 1975, asst. dir. nursing, 1977-79, asst. adminstr., dir. nursing, 1979-87; clin. assoc. faculty The Johns Hopkins U. Sch. of Nursing, 1984-87; program dir., instr. intermediate massage course Balt. Sch. Massage, 1988—, instr. advanced massage course, 1991—, program dir. advanced massage course, 1996, curriculum devel. coord., 1996—; network mktg. cons. UBP Assocs., 1991—, ptnr., educator, 1990-91; pres. Nursing Edn. and Cons. Svc., Inc., Balt., 1976-78, Oasis Health Systems, Inc., Balt., 1987—; spkr. workshop facilitator, cons. profl. topics, Health and Wellness, Personal Growth, Time Mgmt., 1973—. Author profl. booklet & audio publs., Patient Education Book and Related Materials, 1977, Time Management/Organizing System, 1995; contbr. chpts. and articles to profl. publs. Vol. Office on Aging, Balt., 1982-83, Boy Scouts Am., Balt., 1984-85. Mem. NOW, Am. Holistic Nurses Assn., Am. Assn. Nurse Massage Therapists, Balt.-Am. Massage Therapy Assn., Md. Assn. Massage Practitioners (advisor to nurse's coalition 1992), Ch. Home and Hosp. Sch. Nursing Alumni Assn. (treas. 1970-72, pres.-elect 1975-76), Johns Hopkins U. Alumnae Assn., Sigma Theta Tau. Democrat. Episcopalian.

OREN, DAN AHIASSAF, psychiatrist; b. Milw., Nov. 6, 1958; s. Gideon Ahiassaf and Rebeka Ahiassaf (Mayzels) O.; m. Jeanette Kuvin, Dec. 30, 1984; children: Sarah, Amalyah. BS, Yale Coll., 1979; MD, Yale U., 1984. Diplomate Am. Bd. Psychiatry and Neurology, Nat. Bd. Med. Examiners. Postdoctoral fellow and resident in psychiatry Yale U., New Haven, 1984-88; med. staff fellow NIMH, Bethesda, Md., 1988-89; sr. staff fellow NIMH, Bethesda, Md., 1989-90; lt. USPHS/NIMH, Bethesda, Md., 1990-91, lt. comdr., 1991-93, comdr., 1993-96; program chief NIMH, Bethesda, 1995-96; mem. faculty dept. psychiatry Yale U., 1996—. Author: Joining the Club: A History of Jews and Yale, 1985 (Yale U. Press Gov.'s award 1986), co-author: How to Beat Jet Lag, 1993. Mem. Am. Psychiat. Assn., Soc. Light Treatment and Biol. Rhythms (pres.-elect). Office: 25 Park St New Haven CT 06519

ORENSTEIN, DAVID STUART, optometrist; b. Bronx, N.Y., Mar. 23, 1954; s. Max and Muriel (Klein) O. BA, CUNY, Bronx, 1976; OD, CUNY, N.Y.C., 1979. Pvt. practice optometrist N.Y.C., 1980-87, Flushing, N.Y., 1987—; cons. optometrist Kateri Residence, N.Y.C., 1980—, Kings Harbor Nursing Home, Bronx, 1981—, Cardinal Cooke Nursing Home, N.Y.C., 1988—, Amsterdam Home, N.Y.C., 1992—. Bd. mem. Rotary Club, Flushing, 1990-94. Fellow Am. Acad. Optometry. Office: 36-03 162 St Flushing NY 11358

ORENSTEIN, ROBERT, internist; b. Hartford, Conn., Nov. 21, 1959; s. Milton David and Jacqueline Lillian (Freedman) O.; m. Amy Elisabeth Foxx, May 30, 1989. BS, Trinity Coll., Hartford, 1981; DO, U. Osto. Medicine/Health Scis., Des Moines, 1987. Diplomate Am. Bd. Internal Medicine with subspecialty in infectious diseases. Intern Botsford Gen. Hosp., Farmington Hills, Mich., 1987-88; resident in internal medicine Geisinger Med. Ctr., Danville, Pa., 1988-91; fellow in infectious diseases Med. Coll. Va., Richmond, 1991-93; asst. prof. dept. medicine Va. Commonwealth U., Richmond, 1993—; staff physician VA Med. Ctr., Richmond, 1993—, dir. HIV/AIDS program, 1993—; cons. HIV/AIDS Ctr., Va. Commonwealth U., 1993-95; clin. investigator McGuire VA Med. Ctr., Richmon, 1993—; assoc. Richmond AIDS Consortium, 1993—. Contbr. articles to profl. jours. Mem. ACP, Am. Osteo. Assn., Am. Soc. Microbiology, Infectious Diseases Soc. Am., Va. Infectious Diseases Soc. Home: 2530 Cedar Cone Dr Richmond VA 23233-2824 Office: Hunter-Homes McGuire VA Ctr 1201 Broad Rock Blvd (111C) Richmond VA 23249

ORENSTEIN, WALTER A., health facility administrator; b. N.Y.C., Mar. 5, 1948; m. Diane Rauzin; children: Eleza Tema, Evan William. BS, CCNY, 1968; MD, Albert Einstein Coll. Medicine, 1972. Intern U. Calif., San Francisco, 1972-73, resident in pediat., 1973-74; EIS officer divsn. immunization Ctr. for Disease Control, Atlanta, 1974-76, med. epidemiologist divsn. immunization, 1976-77, 80-82; resident pediat. Childrens Hosp. L.A., 1977-78; fellow infectious diseases U. So. Calif. Med. Sch., 1978-80; resident preventive medicine Ctrs. Disease Control, Atlanta, 1980-82, chief surveillance and investigations sect., 1982-88, dir. divsn. immunization, 1988-93; dir. nat. immunization program Ctrs. for Disease Control and Prevention, Atlanta, 1993—; cons. smallpox eradication program WHO, Uttar Pradesh, India, 1974-75; med. adv. bd. Ctrs. Disease Control, Atlanta, 1981-84, nat. vaccine adv. com., 1988—, adv. commn. on childhood vaccines, 1989—; clin. assoc. prof. dept. cmty. health Emory U. Sch. Medicine, 1985; adj. prof. The Rollins Sch. Pub. Health, 1992—; cons. and presenter in field. Editor Pediat. Infectious Disease Jour., 1987; contbr. articles to profl. jours. Asst.

surgeon gen. USPHS, 1995. Fellow Am. Acad. Pediat. (liaison mem., com. on infectious diseases 1989—, nat. vaccine adv. com.), Infectious Diseases Soc. Am., Pediat. Infectious Diseases Soc. (chmn. publs. com., mem. coun.); mem. APHA, Am. Epidemiological Soc., Soc. for Epidemiologic Rsch., Coun. the Pediat. Infectious Diseases Soc. Home: 50 Battle Ridge Dr Atlanta GA 30342-2451 Office: Nat Immunization Program Mailstop EO5 Atlanta GA 30333

ORENTREICH, NORMAN, physician, researcher; b. N.Y.C., Dec. 26, 1922; m. Roslyn Orentreich, June 22, 1946; children: Catherine Orentreich, David S. Orentreich, Sari Mass. BS, CUNY, 1943; MD, NYU Coll. Medicine, 1948. Diplomate Am. Bd. Dermatology. Asst. chief med. examiner USN, 1950-54; med. dir. Orentreich Med. Group, N.Y.C., 1953—; dir. Orentreich Found. for the Advancement of Science, N.Y., 1961—; head of hair clinic, skin & cancer unit NYU Med. Ctr., 1953-68; mem. bd. dirs. Animal Med. Ctr., N.Y.C., 1994, clin. prof. dermatology NYU Sch. Medicine, 1996. Mem. Am. Soc. for Dermatologic Surgery (pres. 1970-72), Am. Fedn. for Aging Rsch., Am. Acad. Cosmetic Surgery, Am. Contact Dermatology Soc., Endocrine Soc., Skin Pharmacology Soc., Skin Pharmacology Soc. Office: Orentreich Med Group 9095th Ave New York NY 10021

ORFORD, ROBERT RAYMOND, consulting physician; b. Winnipeg, Manitoba, Can., Apr. 18, 1948; came to U.S., 1988; s. Robert Raymond and Sarah Gloria L. (Gullden) O.; m. Dale Laura Stuart, June 2, 1972; children: Carolyn Tiffany, Andrew Craig, Loren Brent. BS, McGill U., 1969, MD, 1971; MS, U. Minn., 1975; MPH, U. Wash., 1976. Assoc. prof. cmty. medicine U. Alberta, Edmonton, Can., 1978-88; dir. med. svcs. Govt. of Alberta, Edmonton, Can., 1979-81, exec. dir. occupational health svcs., 1981-85, deputy min. cmty. occupational health, 1985-88; med. dir. employee health U. Alberta Hosp., Edmonton, Can., 1988; sr. assoc. cons. Mayo Clinic, Rochester, Minn., 1988-91, cons. preventive medicine, 1991—; asst. prof. Mayo Med. Sch., Rochester, 1988—; mem. Alberta Energy Resource Conservation Bd., 1988-89. Contbr. articles to profl. jours. Mem. Olmsted County Environ. Commn., Rochester, 1991-96, chair, 1994. Govt. of Can. Nat. Health fellow, 1975-76. Fellow Royal Coll. Physicians & Surgeons Can., Am. Coll. Occupational and Environ. Medicine, Am. Coll. Preventive Medicine, Aerospace Med. Assn.; mem. North Ctrl. Occupational and Environ. Medicine Assn. (pres. 1995), Internat. Commn. Occupational Health Medicine. Presbyterian. Home: 1136 Foxcroft Ln SW Rochester MN 55902 Office: Mayo Clinic Divsn Preventive Medicine 200 1st St SW Rochester MN 55905

ORHON, NECDET KADRI, retired physician; b. Manisa, Turkey, Aug. 13, 1928. MD, U. Istanbul, Turkey, 1951. Lic. to practice medicine in Ill., Iowa, Minn., Ohio, Va., Fla. Intern. U. Istanbul, Turkey, 1952-53; asst. residency in internal medicine Erlanger Hosp., Chattanooga, Tenn., 1953-54; resident in internal medicine Lloyd Noland Hosp., Birmingham-Fairfield, Ala., 1954-55; chief med. resident Good Samaritan Hosp., Lexington, Ky., 1955-56; internist Army Hosp., Turkey, 1956-58; chief resident in internal medicine, chief house doctor Glenwood Hills Hosps., Mpls., 1958-65, internist, chief house officer, 1968-69; fellow oncology Tuft U., Boston, 1965-66; internist Hillcrest Hosp., Birmingham, Ala., 1967-69; dir. emergency room. Mercy Med. Ctr., Springfield, Ohio, 1969-82; practice medicine specializing in internal medicine Springfield, Ohio, 1969-94; retired, 1994—. Mem. Clark County Med. Soc., Ohio Med. Assn. Home: 1157 Morningside Pl Sarasota FL 34236-1116

ORIHEL, THOMAS CHARLES, parasitology educator, research scientist; b. Akron, Ohio, Feb. 10, 1929; s. Joseph Andrew and Mary Susannah (Barno) O.; m. Dorothy Lila Williams, Dec. 27, 1952; children—Timothy Stewart, Charles Theodore, Susan Ethra, Adrianne Louise. B.S., U. Akron, 1950; M.S., U. Wash., 1952; Ph.D., Tulane U., 1959. Sr. scientist Tulane Delta Primate Ctr., Covington, La., 1963-85; prof. parasitology Tulane Med. Ctr., New Orleans, 1972—; William Vincent prof. tropical diseases Tulane Med. Ctr., 1982—; dir. Tulane U. Internat. Collaboration Infectious Diseases Rsch. Program, New Orleans, 1976-89; cons. NIH, Bethesda, Md., 1973-77; mem. expert panel WHO, Geneva, 1973-83; mem. U.S.-Japan Cooperative Med. Sci. Program, Bethesda, 1974-78; external examiner U. Queensland, Australia, U. Guelph, Ont., Can., U. Claude Bernard, Lyon, France, U. Malaya, Kuala Lumpur, Malaysia. Author books on subject of medical parasitology, 1976, 81, 84, 90, 94, 95; contbr. articles to Am. and internat. jours. Served to 1st lt. Med. Service Corps, U.S. Army, 1953-56, Korea. Mem. Am. Soc. Tropical Medicine and Hygiene (councilor 1975-78), Royal Soc. Tropical Medicine and Hygiene, Am. Soc. Microbiology, Southwestern Assn. Parasitologists (v.p. 1972-73), Am. Soc. Parasitologists, Sigma Xi. Home: 115 Bertel Dr Covington LA 70433-4815 Office: Tulane Med Ctr Dept Tropical Medicine 1430 Tulane Ave New Orleans LA 70112-2699

ORINGER, MAURICE JULES, oral surgeon; b. N.Y.C., June 18, 1905; s. Louis and Gerturde Cynthia (Trommer) O.; m. Helen Jane Ornstein, Apr. 11, 1953. DDS, NYU Coll. Dentistry, 1928. Diplomate Am. Bd. Oral Electrosurgery. Guest instr. Dept. Continuing Edn. 31 U.S. and Fgn. Dental Schs., 1951-89; profl. lectr. St. Louis U. Dental Sch., 1953-58; pres. Midtown Dental Soc., N.Y.C., 1953; prof. honoraire Ctr. de Perfectionnement en Odonto Stomatologie Cote d'Azur, France, 1966; founder Am. Acad. Dental Electrosurgery, N.Y.C., 1962, pres., 1963-67, exec. sec., 1968—; cons. ADA Coun. Dental Materials and Devices, Chgo., 1970—; chmn. ADA/ANSI Stds. Subcom. for Electrosurgery Device, Chgo., 1976—; adj. prof. Dept. Biomedical Engring. U. Miami, 1976-88; cons. Coles Electronic Corp., Phila., 1958-70, Ritter Co., Rochester, N.Y., 1973-75, Cavitron Corp., N.Y.C., 1970-72, Siemens, Bensheim, Germany, 1979-81. Author: Electrosurgery In Dentistry, 1962, 2d edit., 1975, Color Atlas of Oral Electrosurgery, 1984; co-editor: Dental Clinics North America, 1969; contbr. articles to profl. jours. Capt. AUS Dental Corps, CBI, 1942-46. Oringer award named in his honor Acad. Dental Electrosurgery. Mem. Am. Dental Assn., Am. Coll. Dentists, Am. Acad. Dental Electrosurgery, Royal Soc. Health. Jewish. Home: 15 W 81st St New York NY 10024-6022

ORLAND, FRANK, oral microbiologist, educator; b. Little Falls, N.Y., Jan. 23, 1917; s. Michael and Rose (Dorner) O.; m. Phyllis Therese Mrazek, May 8, 1943; children: Frank R., Carl P., June Rose, Ralph M. AA, U. Chgo., 1937, SM, 1945, PhD, 1949; BS, U. Ill., 1939, DDS, 1941. Diplomate Am. Bd. Med. Microbiology. With U. Chgo., 1941—; intern Zoller Meml. Dental Clinic, U. Chgo., 1941-42; Zoller fellow, asst. in dental surgery U. Chgo., 1942-49, instr., asst. prof., assoc. prof., prof. dental sci., 1949-88, prof. emeritus, 1988—, from instr. to assoc. prof. microbiology, 1950-58, rsch. assoc. prof., 1958-64; dir. Zoller Meml. Dental Clinic, 1954-66; prof. Fishbein Ctr. for Study History Sci. and Medicine, 1980-88, prof. emeritus, 1988—; attending dentist Country Home for Convalescent Children; past cons. Nat. Inst. Dental Rsch., NIH, Bethesda, Md.; mem. panel on dental drugs The Nat. Formulary; past chmn. dental adv. bd. Med. Heritage Soc. Author: The First Fifty-Year History of the International Association for Dental Research, 1973, Microbiology in Clinical Dentistry, 1982, William John Gies-His Contributions to the Advancement of Dentistry, 1992; editor: Jour. Dental Rsch., 1958-69, (Centennial brochure) Loyola U. Sch. Dentistry, 1983; editor, contbr. Microbiology in Clinical Dentistry, 1982; writer, prodr. 50th anniversary booklet Zoller Meml. Dental Clinic U. Chgo., 1987; contbr. articles to profl. jours. Past chmn. adv. coun. Forest Park (Ill.) Bd. Edn.; mem. Forest Park Citizens Com. for Better Schs.; past pres. Garfield Sch. PTA, 1953-55; chairperson heritage com. Bicentennial Commn. on Forest Park, 1983-85; editor Chronicles of Forest Park, 1976—. Recipient Rsch. Essay award Chgo. Dental Soc., 1955, Cook County Sheriff Medal of Honor award, 1993; named Citizen of Yr., Forest Park, 1989. Fellow AAAS, Inst. Medicine Chgo. (chmn. com. publ. comm.), Am. Acad. Microbiology (William J. Gies award 1994), Am. Coll. Dentists; mem. ADA (past chmn. coun. dental therapeutics), Internat. Assn. Dental Rsch. (pres. 1971-72, past councilor Chgo. sect., past chmn. program com., past chmn. com. on history), Am. Assn. Dental Schs. (past chmn. conf. oral microbiology past chmn. com. on advanced edn.), Am. Assn. Dental Editors (William Gies Editl. award 1968), Ill. State Dental Soc. (chmn. com on history), Fedn. dentaire Internat. (Commn. on History Rsch.), Am. Acad. History Dentistry (pres. 1976-77, Hayden-Harris award 1980), Hist. Soc. Forest Park (pres.), Soc. Med. History Chgo. (past pres.), Chgo. Lit. Club, Sigma Xi. Home: 519 Jackson Blvd Forest Park IL 60130-1807 Office: 521 Jackson Blvd Forest Park IL 60130-1807

ORLANDO, CARL, medical research and development executive; b. Palermo, Italy, Sept. 26, 1915; came to U.S., 1928; s. Peter and Maria (Bongiorno) O.; m. Ann Bovè, May 29, 1943; children: Ann Marie, Francine, Patricia, Charleen, Joan. BS, Columbia U., 1941; postgrad., Rochester U., 1943. Chief photo optics U.S. Army Elec. Commd., Ft. Monmouth, N.J., 1945-75; cons. pvt. practice, New Shrewsbury, N.J., 1975-79; v.p. rsch. & devel. Analytical R&D Inc., Eatontown, N.J., 1979-88; cons. rsch. & devel. Engring. Devel. Co., Tinton Falls, N.J., 1986-88; pres., rsch. & devel. dir. Sens-O-Tech Indsutries Inc., Eatontown, N.J., 1988—; chmn. bd. dirs. Sens-O-Tech Industries, 1988-92. Contbr. articles to profl. jours. Bd. dirs. Monmouth Regional High Sch., Tinton Falls, 1974; com. mem. Tinton Falls Environ. Unit, 1984; chmn. Entertainment Activities St. Dorothaas Ch., Eatontown, 1983. With USN, 1945. Recipient Monetary Suggestion award Signal Corp. Engring. Lab., 1948. Mem. Soc. Photographic Scientist & Engrs. (sr. mem.), Soc. Imaging Sci. & Tech., Elks, Battle Ground Country Club. Republican. Roman Catholic. Home and Office: 47 Willow Rd Tinton Falls NY 07724-3135

ORLANSKY, JESSE, psychologist; b. N.Y.C., Oct. 26, 1914; m. Grace Suydam; children: Michael, Susan, Karen. BSS, CCNY, 1935; MA, Columbia U., 1937, PhD, 1940. Diplomate Am. Bd. Profl. Psychology. Asst. psychology Columbia U., N.Y.C., 1939-40; instr. psychology CCNY, 1938-43; staff mem. The Psychol. Corp., N.Y.C., 1946-48; v.p. Dunlap and Assocs., Inc., Stamford, Conn., 1948-60; rsch. staff mem. Inst. for Def. Analyses, Alexandria, Va., 1960—. Editor, author: Military Value and Cost-Effectiveness of Training, 1989, The Value of Simulation for Training, 1994; editor and author procs. of various symposia. Recipient Exceptional Civilian Svc. medal, US Air Force, 1965, Commendation medal U.S. Marine Corps. 1978, Outstanding Scientific and profl. contributions to Military Psychology award, Am. Psychol. Assn., 1978. Mem. Am. Psychol. Assn. (Franklin V. Taylor award Div. Applied Exptl. and Engring. Psychologists 1983, pres. 1970), Inst. Def. Analyses (Andrew J. Goodpaster award 1988). Home: 7727 Rocton Ave Chevy Chase MD 20815-3915 Office: Inst for Def Analyses 1801 N Beauregard St Alexandria VA 22311-1733

ORLOFF, JOHN J., physician; b. Waterville, Maine, May 22, 1957; s. Paul J. and Germaine A. (Michaud) O.; m. Gwen M. Bogacki, Dec. 4, 1983; children: Jaclyn A., Kirsten E., Mark P. AB, Dartmouth Coll., 1979; MD, U. Vt., 1983. Diplomate Am. Bd. Internal Medicine, Am. Bd. Endocrinology. Intern, resident internal medicine U. Pitts., 1983-86, chief resident in medicine, 1986-87; endocrinology fellow Yale U. Sch. Medicine, New Haven, Conn., 1987-90, instr. in medicine, 1990-91, asst. prof. of medicine, 1991-96, assoc. prof. medicine, 1996—. Mem. ACP, AFCR, Endocrine Soc., Am. Soc. Bone and Mineral Rsch., Am. Soc. Cell Biology, AAAS. Office: Yale U Sch Med FMP 1 Endocrinology 333 Cedar St New Haven CT 06250

ORLUK, WILLIAM F., physician assistant, coroner; b. Lackawanna, N.Y., Feb. 17, 1942; s. Margaret Mary Krathaus; m. Patricia R. Nye, Sept. 10, 1970 (dec. Jan. 1984); 1 child, Tom; m. Patti Cooper, Aug. 20, 1990; children: Mark, Drew, Todd. Physician asst. diploma, Albany-Hudson Valley Coll., 1975. RPA-C. Attendant, venipuncturist Buffalo Gen. Hosp., 1961-66, acute care technician, clk. bus. office, 1968-73; physician asst. Hudson Headwaters Health Network, Chestertown, N.Y., 1975; coroner Warren County, Lake George, N.Y., 1982—. Mem. med. adv. bd. Head Start, Glens Falls, N.Y., 1990—; pres. sch. bd. North Warren Ctrl. Schs., Chestertown, 1994—; med. dir., bd. dirs. North Warren Emergency Medicine Squad, Chestertown, 1995—. With USN, 1962-70, Vietnam. Named VIP, North Warren C. of C., 1988; recipient cert. of achievement N.Y. State Sch. Bds. Assn., 1995. Mem. Am. Assn. Physician Assts., N.Y. State Soc. Physician Assts., NYSSCCME, NYSSBA. Republican. Roman Catholic. Home: PO Box 673 Chestertown NY 12817-0673

ORNE, MARTIN THEODORE, research psychiatrist, psychologist; b. Vienna, Austria, Oct. 16, 1927; s. Frank Edward and Martha (Brunner) O.; m. Emily Farrell Carota, Feb. 3, 1962; children—Franklin Theodore, Tracy Meredith. A.B., Harvard U., 1948, A.M., 1951, Ph.D., 1958; M.D., Tufts U., 1955; D.Sc. (hon.), John F. Kennedy U., 1980. Pvt. practice psychiatry Boston, 1959-64; pvt. practice psychiatry Phila., 1964—; lectr. Grad. Sch. Arts and Scis., Harvard U., 1958-59; instr. Harvard U. Med. Sch., 1959-62, assoc. in psychiatry, 1962-64; assoc. prof. psychiatry U. Pa. Med. Sch., 1964-67, prof., 1967—; dir. studies in hypnosis project Mass. Mental Health Center, Boston, 1960-64; dir. unit for exptl. psychiatry Inst. of Pa. Hosp., Phila., 1964-95, sr. attending psychiatrist, 1974-95; cons. VA Hosp., Phila., 1971-80; Mem. NIMH study sect., Washington, 1966-74, 80-84; exec. dir. Inst. Exptl. Psychiatry, Boston, 1961—. Editor: Internat. Jour. of Clinical and Exptl. Hypnosis, 1962-92, assoc. editor, editor emeritus, 1993—; editor (with R.E. Shor) The Nature of Hypnosis: Selected Basic Readings, 1965; contbr. numerous articles, also chpts. to sci. books, publs. Served with AUS, 1945-47. Rantoul scholar, 1949-50; Fulbright scholar, 1960; recipient Disting. Sci. Contbn. award for applications of psychology Am. Psychol. Assn., 1986. Fellow AAAS, AMA, Am. Psychiat. Assn., Am. Psychol. Assn. (bd. sci. affairs 1990-92), Am. Soc. Clin. Hypnosis, N.Y. Acad. Sci., Soc. CLin. and Exptl. Hypnosis (pres. 1971-73); mem. Assn. Psychophysiol. Study Sleep, Biofeedback Rsch. Soc., Am. Psychosomatic Soc., Internat. Soc. Hypnosis (pres. 1976-79), Psychiat. Rsch. Soc., Soc. Psychophysiol. Rsch. Soc. Psychotherapy Rsch., Royal Soc. Medicine (hon.). Home: 290 Sycamore Ave Merion Station PA 19066-1547 Office: 1955 Locust St Philadelphia PA 19103

OROSZ, CHARLES GEORGE, biomedical researcher, medical educator; b. Cleve., Jan. 9, 1949; s. George John and Mary Helen (Palmer) O.; m. Nancy Marie O'Linn, Aug. 23, 1974; children: Matthew Michael and Kathleen Elizabeth (twins), Molly Nielan. BS, Cleve. State U., 1971, MS, 1975, PhD, 1978. Postdoctoral fellow U. Wis., Madison, 1978-80; vis. rsch. fellow U. Minn., Mpls., 1980-81, asst. prof. lab. medicine and pathology, 1981-83; asst. prof. surgery Ohio State U., Columbus, 1983-87, dir. theraputic immunology rsch labs., 1981—, dir. Clin. Histocampatibility testing lab., 1981—, prof. dept surgery, pathology and med microbiology/immunology, 1995—; mem. study sect., site vis. teams Nat. Cancer Inst.-NIH. mem. editorial bds. for jour.Transplantation, jour of Heart Lung Transplantation, Immunopharmacology, Internat. jour. of Exptl. and Clin. Chemotherapy; contbr. over 100 articles to sci. jours. served with USNR, 1967-73. Recipient Reseach Award Nat. Kidney Found., 1984. Recipient Investigator award 1982, rsch. award NIH, 1984, 88, 90, Rsch awards NIH, 1993. Mem. Am. Soc. Histocompatability and Immunology Comprehensive Cancer Care Ctr., Transplantation Soc., Am. Assn., Am Soc Transplant Physicians, Immunologists, Inter-Am. Soc. for Chemotherapy, Leukemia Soc. Am. (bd. dirs. cen. Ohio chpt. 1984-86. spl fellow 1982). Roman Catholic. Avocations: woodworking, jogging. Office: Ohio State U Dept SurgeryMeans Hall Rm 355 1654 Upham Dr Columbus OH 43210

OROSZ, JUDY INEZ, pediatrician; b. Woodbury, Ga., July 16, 1945; d. Joseph Michael and Ruby Inez (Brown) O. Student U. Ga., 1963-64; B.S. in Biology, Ga. State U., 1967; M.D., Med. Coll. Ga., 1971; postgrad., So. Bapt. Theol. Sem., 1989—. Intern, Baroness Erlanger Hosp., Chattanooga, Tenn., 1971-72; resident T.C. Thompson Children's Hosp., Chattanooga, 1972-74, chief resident, 1973-74; pvt. practice medicine specializing in pediatrics, Cartersville, Ga., 1974-79; mem. staff Gracewood (Ga.) State Sch. and Hosp., 1979-81; asst. prof. pediatrics Med. Coll. Ga., Augusta, 1980-86, dir. ambulatory pediatrics, 1980-86; pres. med. staff Sam Howell Meml. Hosp., 1977, 78; with med. staff Eku (Nigeria) Bapt. Hosp., 1987-88, Immediate Care Ctrs., Louisville, 1989-91; pvt. practice pediatrics and family practice, Augusta, 1988-89; apptd. med. missionary Sudan Interior Mission, Egbe, Nigeria, 1991—. Mem. adv. bd. Bartow County Tng. Ctr., 1974-76; active Nat. Found. March of Dimes, 1976-77; v.p. bd. dirs. Augusta Child Advocacy Ctr., 1986. Named Dept. Pediatrics Tchr. of Yr. Med. Coll. Ga., 1981; recipient Ann. Social Work award Univ. Hosp., 1985. Mem. Richmond County Med. Soc., Med. Assn. Ga., AMA, Am. Acad. Pediatrics, Bapt. Med.-Dental Fellowship (fin. chmn. 1983-85, v.p. Ga. chpt. 1985-86, pres. 1986-87), Nat. Perinatal Assn., Med. Coll. Ga. Alumni Assn. (treas. women physician's council 1983-84). Baptist. Contbr. articles to profl. jours. Home: 4451 Forrest Dr Augusta GA 30907-1584 Office: ECWA SIM, PBM 2009, Jos Plateau State, Nigeria

O'ROURKE, INNIS, pediatrician; b. N.Y.C., 1951; s. Innis and Louise (Fraser) O'R.; m. Allison Gilchrist, July 20, 1985; children: Innis, Shea, Connor. BA, Yale U., 1973; MD, U. Central Del Este, San Pedro de Macoris, Dominican Republic, 1980. Diplomate Am. Bd. Pediatrics. Intern McKeesport (Pa.) Hosp., 1979-80; resident in pediatrics Winthrop-Univ. Hosp., Mineola, N.Y., 1980-83; pvt. practice Glen Cove, N.Y., 1983—. Fellow Am. Acad. Pediatrics; mem. Med. Soc. State N.Y., Nassau County Med. Soc. Office: 3 School St #203 Glen Cove NY 11542

ORR, EMMA JANE, pharmacist, educator; b. Pennington, Va., Sept. 30, 1956; d. Clyde Wilson and Monnie Lee (Daugherty) O.; m. Allen Emerson Clark, Oct. 24, 1981; 1 child, Katherine Wilson. BS in Pharmacy, Med. Coll. Va., 1979; D of Pharmacy with highest hons., U. Ky., 1981. Registered pharmacist, Va., Ky., Tenn. Asst. dir. pharmacy St. Mary's Hosp., Norton, Va., 1980-84, Norton Community Hosp., 1984-90; clin. coord. Hoston Valley Hosp., Kingsport, Tenn., 1990—; adj. faculty Mountain Empire C.C., Big Stone Gap, Va., 1981—; asst. clin. prof. dept. pharmacy and pharmaceutics Med. Coll. Va., Richmond, 1982—. Tchr., children's spkr. Ch. United Meth. Ch., Duffield, Va., Mountain Empire Older Citizens, Wise, Va., 1983-85. Named Young Career Woman of Yr. Bus. and Profl. Women's Club, 1983. Mem. Am. Soc. Hosp. Pharmacists, Am. Pharm. Assn., Va. Soc. Hosp. Pharmacists. Methodist. Home: 100 Quillen Dr Duffield VA 24244

ORR, RICHARD ANDREW, pediatrician, educator; b. St Mary's, Pa., Nov. 20, 1951; s. Clyde Richard And Ruth Virginia (Peters) O.; m. Margaret Elizabeth Engel, Aug. 8, 1982; children: Jessica, Nathaniel, Rebekah, Hannah, Joshua, Andrew. BA in Biology, W.Va. U., 1973, MD, 1977. Diplomate Am. Bd. Pediat., Am. Bd. Critical Care Medicine. Resident in pediat. W.Va. U. Hosp., Morgantown, 1977-80; fellow in critical care U. Pitts., 1980-81; assoc. dir. pediat. ICU Children's Hosp, Pitts., 1981—, med. dir. pediatric transport, 1983—; assoc. prof. anesthesiology, critical care medicine and pediat. U. Pitts. Sch. Med., assoc. prof. pediat.; bd. dirs., Am. Acad. Pediat. rep Commn. on Accreditation Air Med. Svcs., 1991—. Editor: Pediatric Transport Medicine, 1995; contbr. over 50 articles to med. jours. Instr. pediatric advanced life support Am. Heart Assn., Pitts., 1987—. Rsch. grantee Laerdal Found. Acute Medicine, 1991, 95. Fellow Am. Acad. Pediat. (critical care exec. com. 1990-93, transport med. exec. com. 1991—; mem. Soc. Critical Care Medicine, Nat. Assn. Emergency Med. Svc. Physicians, Air Medal Physician Assn. Republican. Mem. Christian and Missionary Alliance Ch. Office: Children's Hosp Pittsburgh 3705 5th Ave Pittsburgh PA 15213

ORR, ROY JOSEPH, hospital administrator; b. Bethany, Mo., Sept. 15, 1952; s. Jay Cedric and Carolyn Mae (Ellis) O.; m. Patrice Marie Kuta, Aug. 11, 1973; children: Sarah, Michaela, Kaitlyn, Hallie, Quentin. AA, Platte Coll., 1972; BS, U. Mo., 1974; MA, U. San Francisco, 1981. Occupational therapist Immanuel Med. Ctr., Omaha, 1974-79; administrative dir. Immanuel Rehab. Ctr., Omaha, 1979-80; dir. rehab. svcs. Bergan Mercy Hosp., Omaha, 1980-85, div. v.p., 1985-90; chief operating officer St. Elizabeth Hosp., Beaumont, Tex., 1990-92; pres., CEO McKenzie-Willamette Med. Svcs., Springfield, Oreg., 1992—. Bd. dirs. N.E. chpt. Arthritis Found., Omaha, 1978-86, pres. bd., 1980-81, chmn. bd., 1982, Nat. Svc. award 1986; mem. Leadership Beaumont, 1991-92; bd. dirs. So. Willamette Pvt. Industry Coun., Eugene, Oreg.; bd. dirs. Springfield C. of C., 1994—, United Way of Lane County, 1993—. Mem. Am. Coll. Healthcare Execs., Cardinal Club (v.p. 1991). Roman Catholic. Office: 1460 G St Springfield OR 97477-4112

ORR, STEVEN DEREK, health agency executive; b. Joplin, Mo., Feb. 11, 1940; s. Charles Thomas and Janice Laura (MacKinnon) O.; m. Maureen Jane Dumm, May 25, 1968; children—Sean Christopher, Brendan Huan. B.A., U. Ariz., 1972. Vol. Peace Corps, Panama, 1964-66; fgn. service officer Dept. State, Vietnam, 1966-68; mgr. Am. Express, N.Y.C., 1969-70; dir. edn. Planned Parenthood, Tucson, 1972-76; adminstr. Ariz. Med. Assn., Ft. Apache Indian Reservation, 1976-78; regional adminstr. Family Planning Internat. Assistance, Bogotá, Colombia and Miami, Fla., 1978-84; pres. SDO Consulting, Inc., TDY with USAID El Salvador for MIS/Logistics/Maintenance; lic. agt., fin. assets mgr. A.L. Williams Corp.; cons. Mgmt. Scis. for Health, Inc., The Futures Group, Inc., MD Resources, Inc., Juarez & Assocs., Inc., Devel. Assocs., Inc., Acad. for Ednl. Devel., Inc., U.S. Ctrs. for Disease Control, USAID; with Orange State Cons., 1985—; cons. Ariz. Dept. Pub. Health, 1975-78. Pres. Ariz. Pub. Health Assn., Phoenix, 1978, Miami-Killian High Sch. Band Patrons Assn. 1988-89. Served with USAF, 1957-60. Mem. Nat. Council Internat. Health, Med. Group Mgmt. Assn., Fla. Speakers Assn., Am. Mgmt. Assn., Nat. Coun. Returned Peace Corps Vols., Returned Peace Corp Vols. S. Fla (co-founder, v.p., treas. 1987-88, dir. 1995—). Club: Toastmasters.

ORRINGER, MARK BURTON, surgeon, educator; b. Pitts., Apr. 1943; s. Harry B. and Alta (Moses) O.; m. Susan Michaels, June 20, 1964; children: Jeffrey Scott, Lisa Jill. BA, U. Pitts., 1963, MD, 1967. Diplomate Am. Bd. Surgery, Am. Bd. Thoracic Surgery. Resident Johns Hopkins Hosp., Balt., 1967-73; from asst. prof. to prof. surgery U. Mich. Med. Sch., Ann Arbor, 1973-80, prof. surgery, 1980—; head sect. thoracic surgery U. Mich. Med. Sch., Ann Arbor, 1985—; dir. Am. Bd. Thoracic Surgery, 1988-95. Co-editor: (with Waldhausen) Complications in Cardiothoracic Surgery, Mosby Year Book, 1991, (with Zuidema) Shackelford's Surgery of the Alimentary Tract, vol. 1 - The Esophagus, 3d edit., 1991, 4th edit. 1995; contbr. over 150 articles to profl. jours., over 75 chpts. to books. Capt. USAR, 1974-76. Named among the best med. specialists in the U.S., Town and Country mag., 1984, 89, among the 400 best drs. in Am., Good Housekeeping mag., 1991; recipient Bicentennial Medal of Distinction, U. Pitts., 1987. Fellow ACP; mem. Thoracic Surgery Dirs. Assn. (sec., treas. 1991-95, pres. elect 1996), Soc. Thoracic Surgeons, Am. Coll. Chest Physicians, Am. Assn. Thoracic Surgery, Soc. Univ. Surgeons, Internat. Soc. Surgery, Am. Surg. Assn., Internat. Soc. Diseases Esophagus, Halsted Soc., Phi Beta Kappa, Alpha Omega Alpha. Office: U Mich Med Ctr 1500 E Med Ctr Dr Ann Arbor MI 48109

ORRIS, PETER, medical researcher, educator, consultant; b. L.A., Oct. 7, 1945; s. Leo and Gertrude (Weissman) O.; m. Sita Rao, May 23, 1978; children: Tara, Benjamin. BA, Harvard Coll., 1967; MPH, Yale U., 1970; MD, Chgo. Med. Sch., 1975. Diplomate Am. Bd. Preventive Medicine. Resident in internal medicine Cook County Hosp., Chgo., 1975-78, resident in occupl. medicine, 1977-79, attending physician, 1979—; attending physician U. Ill. Hosp. and Med. Ctr., 1990—; med. dir. Corp. Health Svcs. Northwest Cmty. Hosp., 1993—; assoc. prof. medicine I. Ill., Chgo.; dir. rsch. Great Lakes Ctr. Occupl. and Environ. Health, Arlington Heights, 1990—; dir. health hazard evaluation program U. Ill. Sch. Public Health, 1992—, clin. assoc. prof. environ. and occupl. health; co-chair Med. Profls. Task Force, Internat. Joint Commn. of the U.S. and Can., 1995—; med. adv. com. Internat. Brotherhood of Teamsters, AFL-CIO; med. adv. bd. John Redmond Found, IAFF, AFL-CIO; adj. assoc. prof. preventive medicine Nortwestern U. Med. Sch. Co-author chpts. to books: FIrefighters' Safety and Health, 1995, Preventive Medicine and Public Health, Occupational Health Services: A Guide to Program Plannig and Management, 1989, Modern and Traditional Healthcare in Developing Societies, 1988, Preventive Medicine and Public Health, 1987; reviewer Am. Jour. Public Health, Environ. Rsch., Jour. AMA, Jour. Occupl. Medicine, Jour. Health Svcs. Rsch.; mem. editl. bd. New Solutions, Physicians Forum Bul.; contbr. numerous articles to profl. jours. including Am. Jour. Indusl. Medicine, Ill. Morbidity and Mortality Rev., Am. Jour. Public Health, others. Fellow ACP, Am. Coll. Occupl. and Environ. Medicine (sele assessment com. 1983—); mem. Assn. Occupl. and Environ. Clinics (pres. 1994-95), Am. Med. Student Assn. (chair occupl. health and safety task force adv. com. 1992—), Chgo. Med. Soc. (councilor 1992—). Office: Cook County Hosp Occupl Med 720 S Wolcott Chicago IL 60615

ORSAY, CHARLES P., surgeon; b. Elgin, Ill., Sept. 30, 1949; s. E. Paul and Harriet S. (Preston) O.; m. Elizabeth J. Mueller, Oct. 20, 1984; children: Michael Preston, Stephen Charles. BS, U. Ill., 1971, MS, 1972; MD, U. Ill. Med. Sch., 1976. Diplomate Am. Bd. Surgery, Am. Bd. Colon & Rectal Surgery. Resident in gen. surgery Cook County Hosp., Chgo., 1976-81, resident in colon and rectal surgery, 1981-82, chmn. divsn. colon & rectal surgery, 1993—. Home: Cook County Hosp 1835 W Harrison Chicago IL 60612

ORSHAN, SUSAN AILEEN, women's health care specialist; b. Somerville, N.J., May 16, 1959; d. Martin Louis and Miriam (Ratner) O. BSN, U. Pa., 1981; MA, NYU, 1985, PhD, 1993. Cert. perinatal nurse ANA, cert. Lamaze childbirth educator Am. Soc. Psychoprophylaxis in Pregnancy/Lamaze. Teaching fellow, adj. instr. divsn. of nursing NYU, N.Y.C., 1985-89; adolescent pregnancy counselor St. Mary's Hosp., Hoboken, N.J., 1987-88; childbirth educator St. Vincent's Hosp. and Med. Ctr., N.Y.C., 1987-94, Robert Wood Johnson Univ. Hosp., New Brunswick, 1987-91; pvt. practice childbirth edn. Jersey City, 1987—; test cons. Nat. League for Nursing, N.Y.C., 1990-93; asst. prof. Rutgers Coll. Nursing, Newark, 1993—; mem. planning com. Rogerian Conf., N.Y.C., 1991-96. Health profl. adv. coun. No. N.J. chpt. March of Dimes, chair babies and you subcom. Fellow Am. Coll. Childbirth Educators; mem. ANA, N.J. State Nurses Assn., Assn. of Women's Health, Obstet. and Neonatal Nursing (corr. mem. nat. rsch. com., dist. III legis. com.), Am. Soc. for Psychoprophylaxis in Pregnancy/Lamaze, Sigma Theta Tau (pres. Upsilon chpt. 1992-94, region 5 mentor). Jewish. Home: 419 Sayre Dr Princeton NJ 08540 Office: Rutgers Coll Nursing University Heights Newark NJ 07102

ORT, PAUL JOSEPH, orthopedic surgeon, educator; b. Prague, Czechoslovakia, Apr. 15, 1936; s. Miloslav Ort; m. Vicky Harnik, Oct. 23, 1982. MD, Charles U., 1961. Diplomate Am. Bd. Orthopaedic Surgery. Rotating intern Bronx-Lebanon Hosp., N.Y.C., 1964-65; resident in gen. surgery Bellevue Hosp.-Cornell U., N.Y.C., 1965-67; resident in orthopaedic surgery Bellevue Hosp.-NYU, 1967-70; attending physician Cabrini Med. Ctr., N.Y.C., 1971-88; instr. in orthopedic surgery NYU Med. Ctr., N.Y.C., 1975-80, asst. prof. orthopedic surgery, 1980-87, assoc. prof. orthopedic surgery, 1987—; pvt. practice N.Y.C., 1971—. Fellow ACS, Am. Acad. Orthopaedic Surgery; mem. AMA, NYU Alumni Assn. (pres. 1989-91)m Bellevue Soc. (pres. 1994). Office: 530 1st Ave New York NY 10016

ORTEGA, E. ASTRID, nurse, educator; b. Merida, Yucatan, Mex., Mar. 3, 1945; d. Zanoni and Estela (Murillo) O. Diploma, R.I. Hosp. Sch. Nursing, 1966; BSN, Sacramento State U., 1977; MSN, U. Calif., San Francisco, 1980; cert. nurse practitioner, UCLA-Harbor Hosp., 1972. Ob.-gyn. nurse practitioner Santa Clara Valley Med. Ctr., San Jose, Calif.; perinatal outreach coord. Alta Bates Hosp., Berkeley, Calif.; primary health care nurse practitioner Santa Clara County Correctional Facilities, Milpitas, Calif.; asst. prof. Humboldt State U., Arcata, Calif.; family nurse practitioner Kaiser Permanente, Santa Rosa, Calif. Contbr. articles to prof. publs. Pres. Am. Heart Assn. (Humboldt, North Branch chpt.), 1st lt. Nurse Corps, U.S. Army, 1966-68, Vietnam. Named Nurse of Yr. Calif. March of Dimes, 1982. Mem. Nat. Assn. Hispanic Nurses (v.p. Alta, Calif. chpt. 1993), Assn. Chicana-Latina Nurses Santa Clara County (pres. 1988).

ORTENZIO, ROBERT A., health, medical products executive. Pres., COO Continetal Med. Systems, Inc., Mechanicsburg, Pa., 17055. Office: Continental Med Systems Inc 600 Wilson Ln PO Box 715 Mechanicsburg PA 17055*

ORTH, DAVID NELSON, physician, educator; b. East Orange, N.J., Mar. 5, 1933; s. John Joseph and Marjorie Adelaide (Wauters) O.; m. Linda Diana D'Errico, June 9, 1979; children by previous marriage: John Randall (dec.), Jennifer Stewart, Julie Thomas. Sc.B. in Chemistry, Brown U., 1954; M.D., Vanderbilt U., 1962. Intern, Osler med. service Johns Hopkins Hosp., Balt., 1962-63; fellow in medicine Johns Hopkins Hosp., 1962-65; asst. resident John Hopkins Hosp., 1963-65; mem. faculty dept. medicine Vanderbilt U. Sch. Medicine, Nashville, 1965—; prof. Vanderbilt U. Sch. Medicine, 1975—, joint dir. endocrinology div. dept. medicine, 1968-81, dir. cancer research and treatment ctr., 1972-77, dir. div. endocrinology, 1984—; scholar-in-residence Rockefeller Found. Bellagio (Italy) Study and Conf. Ctr., 1989; vis. scientist Vollum Inst. for Advanced Biomed. Rsch., Oreg. Health Scis. U., Portland, 1993-94. Contbr. numerous articles in field of endocrinology to med. jours. Served with U.S. Navy, 1954-57. John and Mary R. Markle scholar, 1968-73; Howard Hughes Med. Inst. investigator, 1969-75. Mem. AAUP, AAAS, ACP, Assn. Am. Physicians, Am. Soc. Clin. Investigation, Endocrine Soc. (sec.-treas. 1989-94), N.Y. Acad. Scis., Am. Fedn. Clin. Rsch., So. Soc. Clin. Investigation. Office: Vanderbilt U Med Ctr North 715 A MRB II Nashville TN 37232-6303

ORTIZ, JULIO ENRIQUE, plastic surgeon; b. San Juan, June 8, 1947; s. Epifanio and Mary Ortiz; m. Ana Silva, June 6, 1969; children: Ana A., Julio E., Annette. BS magna cum laude, U. P.R., 1969, MD, 1973. Diplomate Am. Bd. Surgery, Am. Bd. Plastic Surgery, Nat. Bd. Med. Examiners. Intern Brooke Army Med. Ctr., Ft. Sam Houston, Tex., 1973-74, resident in gen. surgery, 1974-77, chief resident gen. surgery svc., 1977-78; resident in plastic surgery Walter Reed Army Med. Ctr., Washington, 1979-80, chief resident, 1980-81; chief plastic surgery Tripler Army Med. Ctr., Moanalua, Hawaii, 1982-84, Brooke Army Med. Ctr., 1984-89; program dir. plastic surgery William Beaumont Army Med. Ctr., El Paso, 1989-91; pvt. practice Alamo Plastic Surgery, San Antonio, 1991—; asst. clin. prof. surgery U. Hawaii, 1982-84; clin. assoc. prof. surgery Uniformed Svcs. U. Health Scis., 1980—; cons. plastic surgeon; presenter in field. Contbr. articles to profl. jours. Decorated Legion of Merit, Army Commendation medal with oak leaf cluster. Fellow ACS; mem. Assn. Mil. Surgeons, Assn. Mil. Plastic Surgeons (sec.-treas. 1990-91), Am. Soc. Plastic and Reconstructive Surgery, Plastic Surgery Edn. Found., San Antonio Surg. Soc., San Antonio Plastic Surg. Soc., Tex. Med. Assn., Bexar County Med. Soc., Alpha Omega Alpha. Office: Alamo Plastic Surgery 1303 McCullough # 441 San Antonio TX 78212

ORTIZ, MARY THERESA, biomedical engineer, educator; b. N.Y.C., Mar. 25, 1957; d. Henry and Viola (Rega) O. BS, Wagner Coll., 1979; MS, Rutgers U., 1981, PhD, 1987. Emergency med. technician, N.Y. Adj. lectr. N.Y.C. Tech. Coll., Bklyn., 1981-89; teaching/rsch. asst. Rutgers U., New Brunswick, N.J., 1982-86; rsch. scientist N.Y. State Inst. for Basic Rsch., S.I., 1988-93; asst. prof. Kingsborough C. C., Bklyn., 1993—; adj. asst. prof. Coll. S.I., 1989-94. Contbr. articles to sci. jours. Mem. youth adv. coun. N.Y.C. Youth Bd. Beame Adminstrn., 1970's; participant N.Y.C. Tech. Coll. Access for Women, Bklyn., 1980's, Rutgers U. Coll. Engrs. Open House, Piscataway, 1985-86. Grad. Prof. Opportunities Program fellow Rutgers U., 1979-82, Grad. Student Dissertation and Research Support grantee, 1986; Women's Rsch. and Devel. Fund grantee CUNY, 1988. Mem. IEEE, N.Y. Acad. Scis. (judge city and boro sci. fairs), Nat. Engrs. Honor Soc., Kappa Mu Epsilon, Beta Beta Beta. Democrat. Roman Catholic. Home: 31 Ruth Pl Staten Island NY 10305-2430 Office: Kingsborough C C 2001 Oriental Blvd Brooklyn NY 11235-2336

ORTIZ-BUTCHER, CARMEN JULIE, medical educator; b. Johnson City, N.Y., July 26, 1954; d. Juan M. and Carmen M. (Garcia Vera) Ortiz de Valderrama;m. Albert Interian, July 27, 1979 (div. 1994); m. Jeffrey W. Butcher, June 15, 1992; children: Albert, Allan, Webb. BS magna cum laude, U. Miami, Coral Gables, Fla., 1978, MD, 1985. Diplomate Am. Bd. Internal Medicine and Nephrology. Intern, resident nephrology U. Miami, Coral Gables, 1986-89, asst. prof., 1989-94, assoc. prof., 1994—; dir. Renal Clinic, U. Miami, 1994-96. Mem. Woman's Emergency Network, Miami, 1995; bd. mem. Kidney Found. South Fla., Miami, 1994-96; chair med. adv. bd. Nat. Kidney Found. Fla., Orlando, 1995-96. Fellow ACP; mem. Alpha Omega Alpha. Office: 1600 NW 12th Ave RMSB 7168 Miami FL 33101

ORTIZ-BUTTON, OLGA, social worker; b. Chgo., July 12, 1953; d. Luis Antonio and Pura (Acevedo) Ortiz; m. Dennis Vesley, Aug. 11, 1973 (div. 1976); m. Randall Russell Button, Nov. 3, 1984 (div. Oct. 1993); children: Joshua, Jordan, Elijah. BA, U. Ill., 1975; MSW, Western Mich. U., 1981. Cert. social worker, sch. social worker. Social svcs. dir. Champaign County Nursing Home, Urbana, Ill., 1976; social svcs. and activity dir. Lawton (Mich.) Nursing Home, 1977; job developer Southwestern Mich. Indian Ctr., Watervliet, 1977-78; staff asst. New Directions Alcohol Treatment Ctr., Kalamazoo, 1978; counselor, instr. Alcohol Hwy. Safety, Kalamazoo, 1978-79; clin. social worker Mecosta County Community Mental Health, Big Rapids, Mich., 1981-84; program dir. substance abuse Sr. Svcs., Inc., Kalamazoo, 1984-85; sch. social worker Martin (Mich.) Pub. Schs., 1985-96; owner, therapist Plainwell (Mich.) Counseling Ctr., 1989—; S.W. cons. Med. Pers. Pool, 1993-94, G.L. Network Mktg., 1993—. Vol. social worker Hospice-Wings of Hope, Plainwell, 1984-85, mem. CQI bd., 1993—; supporter Students Against Aparteid South Africa, Kalamazoo, 1979-81; mem. World Vision and Countertop Ptnr., 1984—; sponsor, vol. People for Ethical Treatment of Animals, 1986-91; vol. helper Sparkies for Awana Club Ch., 1989-95; consortium mem. Mich. Post Adoption Svc. System, 1994—. NIMH Rural Mental Health grantee, 1979-81. Mem. NASW, Mich. Assn. Sch. Social Workers, Am. Assn. Christian Counselors. Office: Plainwell Counseling Ctr 211 E Bannister St Ste K Plainwell MI 49080-1372

ORTMAN, HAROLD R., prosthodontist; b. Buffalo, Dec. 19, 1917; s. Harold Taylor and Marguerite (Rodebaugh) O.; m. Betty Hellriegel (div.); children: Jeffrey, Lance, Jay, Paul; m. Virginia Love Ortman, June 30, 1960; step-children: William, Bruce Barton. DDS, U. Buffalo, 1941. Diplomate Am. Bd. Prosthodontists. (fellow). Instr. in removable prosthodontics U. Buffalo Dental Sch., 1942-46, asst. prof., 1947-51, assoc. prof., 1952-62, prof., 1962-88, chmn., head. dept. prosthodontics, 1962-88, prof. emeritus, 1988—; mem. exec. com. Sch. Dental Medicine U. Buffalo, 1970-88. Author: (with others) Complete Denture Prothodontics, 1979, 2d rev. edit., 1988; lectr: over 45 lectrs. on complete dentures in U.S. and 7 fgn. countries.; contbr. articles to profl. jours. Fellow Am. Coll. Dentists; mem. Am. Prosth. Soc. (all offices including v.p. and pres., exec. com.), Am. Dental Assn., Rocky Mt. Dental Club, Erie County Dental Assn. Home and Office: 3800 Main St Buffalo NY 14226

ORTMEYER, DALE HERBERT, psychologist; b. Charles City, Iowa, Mar. 1, 1926; s. Arthur Herman and Sarah Amelia (Stoeber) O.; m. Inge Salomon, Apr. 2, 1960; children: Daniel, Jason. BS, Iowa State U., 1949, MS, 1951; PhD, Columbia U., 1955. Lic. psychologist, N.Y., Conn. Psychoanalyst W. A. White Psychoanalytic Inst., N.Y.C., 1957-63; supervising psychologist Mental Hygiene Clinic, VA Hosp., N.Y.C., 1955-59; sr. psychologist Psychol. Clinic, Adelphi U., Garden City, N.Y., 1959-72; assoc. clin. prof. Psychol. Clinic, Adelphi U., 1967-72, cons. psychologist social svc. dept., 1968-75; pvt. practice psychology N.Y.C., 1955—; pvt. practice psychoanalysis Westport, Conn., 1973—; dir. continuing prof. edn. divsn. W.A. White Psychoanalytic Inst., N.Y.C., 1973-89, fellow tng. and supervision psychoanalyst; clin. prof. Adelphi U., 1968—: faculty Westchester Ctr. for Study of Psychoanalysis and Psychotherapy, White Plains, N.Y., 1976—; instr. psychiatry Columbia U., 1985—; sr. cons. Conn. Psychoanalytic Psychotherapy Ctr., 1990—. Contbr. articles to profl. jours. and books. Active Coun. for Nat. Register Health Svc. Providers in Psychology, 1975—. With U.S. Army, 1943-46. Mem. Conn. Soc. Psychoanalytic Psychologists (pres. 1988-90), AAAS, Am. Psychol. Assn., N.Y. State Psychol. Assn., Ea. Psychol. Assn., Am. Group Psychotherapy Assn., W.A. White Psychoanalytic Soc. (pres. 1995-96), Adelphi Soc. Psychoanalysis, Westchester Soc. Psychoanalysts, Nat. Accreditation Assn., Psychoanalytic Coun. for Advancement of Psychology Professions and Sci., Coun. Psychoanalytic Psychologists. Democrat. Home: 4 W Branch Rd Westport CT 06880-1248 Office: 1327 Lexington Ave New York NY 10128-1109

ORTOSKI, RICHARD A., osteopath; b. New Kensington, Pa., Mar. 30, 1958; s. Theodore Jerome and Laura Jean (Tadrzak) O. Student, Mercyhurst Coll., Erie, Pa., 1976-78; BS in Math., Allegheny Coll., 1980; DO, Phila. Coll. Osteo. Medicine, 1984. Diplomate Am. Osteo. Bd. Family Physicians with subspecialty in adolescent and young adult medicine, Nat. Bd. Med. Examiners; lic. physician, Mich., Pa. Intern Flint (Mich.) Osteo. Hosp., 1984-85, emergency/trauma unit staff physician, 1985-86; pvt. practice family and adolescent medicine Girard (Pa.) Family Health Care Ctr., 1986—; staff physician Health Care Ctr., 1986—; staff physician Eastside Med. Ctr., Erie, Pa., 1986-93; sch. dist. physician Girard Sch. Dist., 1986—; pre-match physician Wide World of Wrestling, Erie, 1987; emergency dept. physician Eastway Emergi-Ctr., Millcreek Cmty. Hosp., Erie, 1989-92; family medicine and manipulative therapy physician Lakecrest Med. Ctr., Edinboro, Pa., 1990-91; asst. med. advisor Erie County Dept. Health, pub. health officer, STD Clinic, Hispanic Coun., 1995—; staff physician State Correctional Instns. of Pa., 1993—, clin. dir. infectious diseases HIV/AIDS, 1995—; med. lab. dir. Sera-Tek Biologicals, 1995—; med. staff Great Lake Rehab. Hosp., Erie, Millcreek Cmty. Hosp., sec.-treas., 1994-96, resident/intern trainer; active med. cons. Vets. Affairs Med. Ctr., Erie; clin. prof. dept. gen. practice Phila. Coll. Osteo. Medicine; clin. asst. prof. dept. family medicine Lake Erie Coll. Osteo. Medicine, course dir. Physical Diagnosis Course HIV/AIDS, human sexuality, pub. health, clin. edn. coord. family medicine; med. examiner Nationwise Life Ins.; lectr. in field; condr. seminars in field. Med. advisor HIV/AIDS Task Force, Greater Erie chpt. ARC, 1993-95; adv. coun. for teen risk reduction Erie County, Pa., 1994—; med. dir. patient Seragate program County Wide Com., 1995—; clin. med. dir. Pa. Gov.'s Summer Sch. Excellence, 1995, 96. Reco'emt Cert. of Recognition Hurley Med. Ctr., Flint; Great Lakes scholar, Assn. Occpl. and Environ. Clinics, 1995-96. Roman Catholic. Office: Girard Family Health Care 649 Rice Ave Girard PA 16417

ORVIN, GEORGE HENRY, psychiatrist; b. Columbia, S.C., Aug. 6, 1922; s. Jesse Wright and Ruth Veril (Walton) O.; m. Rosalie Greer Salvo, Sept. 16, 1944; children: Candace, Jay Scott, Debra Anne, Nancy Lee. BS, The Citadel, 1943; MD, Med. U. S.C., Charleston, 1946; MD (hon.), The Citadel, 1996. Diplomate Am. Bd. Psychiatry. Pvt. practice Charleston, S.C., 1948-57; resident psychiatry Med. U. S.C., 1957-60; clin. asst. U. London, 1960-61; instr. Med. U.S.C., 1961; chief adolescent psychiatry Med. U. S.C., 1967-89, pres. faculty senate, 1977-79, prof. psychiatry, 1977-89, emeritus prof. psychiatry, 1993; founder, chmn. New Hope Treatment Ctrs., Inc., Charleston, 1984—. Author: Understanding the Adolescent, 1995; sr. editor Annals Adolescent Psychiatry, 1985; contbr. chpts. to books, articles to profl. jours. Vice-chmn. S.C. Com. Alcohol/Drug Abuse, 1973-89; mem. Gov.'s Cabinet for Children, 1984, Gov.'s Task Force Adolescent Pregnancies, 1985. Fellow Am. Psychiat. Assn. (life), Am. Soc. Adolescent Psychiatry (life), Royal Soc. Medicine, St. Andrews Soc., Citadel Brigadier Club (founder, pres. 1948-53). Episcopalian. Home: 126 Rutledge Ave Charleston SC 29401-1333 Office: New Hope Inc 225 Midland Pky Summerville SC 29485-8104

ORVIS, HAROLD HEACOCK, physician; b. Phila., Jan. 13, 1924; s. Harold Heacock and Leora Alice (Chappell) O.; m. Anna Ruth Schlaanstine, June 4, 1955; children: Stephen, Lynda, John. BS in Biology, Guilford Coll., 1948; MD, Columbia U., 1952. Diplomate Am. Bd. Internal Medicine. Intern D.C. Gen. Hosp., 1952-53; fellow in cardiology Washington Heart Assn., 1955-56; rsch. fellow NIH, Washington, 1956-57; resident George Washington Univ., Washington, 1958, asst. prof. medicine, 1958-63; assoc. prof. preventive medicine Univ. Ill., Chgo., 1963-66; assoc. clin. prof. medicine Hahnemann Univ., Phila., 1972-80; chief internal medicine The Chester County Hosp., West Chester, Pa., 1984-94; pvt. practice in internal medicine West Chester, 1971—; cons. cardiology VA Ctr., Martinsburg, W.Va., 1963-65; dir. rehab. ctr. Univ. Ill. Rsch. and Edn. Hosp., Chgo., 1963-66; med. bd. Easter Seal Soc., Chgo., 1965-66; dir. clin. investigations Atlas Chem. Industry, Wilmington, Del., 1966-71. Author Diet Manual Univ. Ill., 1966. Pres. Civitan Club, Chgo., 1965-66; scoutmaster Boy Scouts Am., Chester County, Pa., 1967-79. 1st lt. USAF, 1942-46. Fellow Am. Coll. Cardiology, Am. Coll. Chest Physicians, Coun. Geriatric Cardiology; mem. Am. Soc. Internal Medicine, Inst. Medicine Chgo., Am. Soc. Nephrology, Am. Soc. Clin. Pharmacists and Therapeutics, Sigma Xi, West Goshen (Pa.) Lions Club. Home and Office: 401 W Pleasant Grove Rd West Chester PA 19382-7117

ORWOLL, REBECCA LYNN, internist, hematologist, educator; b. Camden, N.J., May 10, 1949; d. Walter and Patricia Anne (Page) Schroth; m. Eric S. Orwoll, 1970 (div. 1988); children: Benjamin, Katherine, Elizabeth. AB cum laude, U. Mich., 1970; MA, U. Md., 1973; BS, Portland State U., 1975; MD magna cum laude, U. Oreg., Portland, 1979. Diplomate Am. Bd. Internal Medicine, Am. Bd. Hematology. Intern, resident in internal residence Oreg. Health Scis. U., Portland, 1979-82, fellow in hematology and med. oncology, 1982-84, clin. asst. prof., 1985—; pvt. practice Portland, 1984—. Mem. AMA, Am. Soc. Hematology, Am. Soc. Clin. Oncology, Am. Heart Assn. (mem. council), Oreg. Med. Soc., Multnomah County Med. Soc., Alpha Omega Alpha. Democrat. Unitarian. Office: Hematology Clin 5050 NE Hoyt St Ste 256 Portland OR 97213-2956

ORY, MARCIA GAIL, social science researcher; b. Dallas, Feb. 8, 1950; d. Marvin Gilbert and Esther (Levine) O.; m. Raymond James Carroll, Aug. 13, 1972. BA magna cum laude, U. Tex., 1971; MA, Ind. U., 1972; PhD, Purdue U., 1976; MPH, Johns Hopkins U., 1981. Rsch. asst. prof. U. N.C., Chapel Hill, 1976-77; from adj. asst. prof. to assoc. prof. sch. pub. health U. N.C., 1978-88; rsch. fellow U. Minn., Mpls., 1977-78; asst. prof. Sch. Pub. Health U. Ala., Bham, 1978-80; program dir. biosocial aging and health Nat. Inst. on Aging, Bethesda, Md., 1981-86; chief social sci. rsch. on aging Nat. Inst. on Aging, Bethesda, 1987—. Contbr. articles, editor vols. profl. jours. Mem. several nat. task forces on aging and health issues. Recipient Dept. of Health and Human Svcs. award, 1984, 85, 88, Am. Men and Women of Sci., 1989-90, Nat. Inst. of Health Dir.'s award, 1995; named Disting. Alumna by Purdue U. Fellow Gerontol. Soc. Am.; mem. APHA (gov. coun. 1986-88, program chmn. 1986, chmn.-elect 1989-91, chmn. 1992-93), Am. Sociol. Assn. (regional reporter 1984—, program com. 1986, nominations com. 1987, councilor-at-large 1992-93), Soc. Behavioral Medicine (program chmn. pub. health track 1988-89, program com. 1991-92), Phi Kappa Phi, Omicron Nu. Office: Nat Inst Aging Gateway Bldg Ste 533 7201 Wisconsin Ave # 9205 Bethesda MD 20892-9205

ORYSHKEVICH, ROMAN SVIATOSLAV, physician, physiatrist, dentist, educator; b. Olesko, Ukraine, Aug. 5, 1928; came to U.S., 1955, naturalized, 1960; s. Simeon and Caroline (Deneszczuk) O.; m. Oksana Lishchynsky, June 16, 1962; children: Marta, Mark, Alexandra. DDS, Ruperto-Carola U., Heidelberg, Ger., 1952, MD, 1953, PhD cum laude, 1955. Cert. Am. Assn. Electromyography and Electrodiagnosis, 1964; diplomate Am. Bd. Phys. Medicine and Rehab., 1966, Am. Bd. Electrodiagnostic Medicine, 1989. Research fellow in cancer Esptl. Cancer Inst., Rupert-Charles U., 1953-55; rotating intern Coney Island Hosp., Bklyn., 1955-56; resident in diagnostic radiology NYU Bellevue Med. Ctr.-Univ. Hosp., 1956-57; resident, fellow in phys. medicine and rehab. Western Res. U. Highland View Hosp., Cleve., 1958-60; orthopedic surgery Met. Gen. Hosp., Cleve., 1959; asst. chief rehab. medicine service VA West Side Med. Ctr., Chgo., 1961-74, acting chief, 1974-75, chief, 1975—; dir., coord. edn. U. Ill. Integrated Residency Program, Phys. Medicine & Rehab, 1974-89; clin. instr. U. Ill., 1962-65, asst. clin. prof., 1965-70, asst. prof., 1970-75, assoc. clin. prof., 1975-94, clin. prof., 1994—. Author, editor: Who and What in U.W.M.M., 1978; contbr. articles to profl. jours.; splty. cons. in phys. medicine and rehab. to editorial bd. Chgo. Med. Jours., 1978-89. Founder, pres. Ukrainian World Med. Mus., Chgo., 1977; founder, 1st pres. Am. Mus. Phys. Medicine and Rehab., 1980-91. Fellow AAUP, Am. Acad. Phys. Medicine and Rehab.; mem. Assn. Acad. Physiatrists, Am. Assn. Electromyography and Electrodiagnosis, Ill. Soc. Phys. Medicine and Rehab. (pres., dir. 1979-80), Ukrainian Med. Assn. N.Am. (dir., pres. chpt. 1977-79, fin. mgr. 17th med. conv. and congress Chgo. 1977, adminstr. and conv. chmn. 1979), World Fedn. Ukrainian Med. Assns. (co-founder and 1st exec. sec. research and sci. 1977-79), Internat. Rehab. Medicine Assn., Rehab. Internat. U.S.A., Nat. Assn. VA Physicians, AAAS, Assn. Med. Rehab. Dirs. and Coordinators, Nat. Rehab. Assn., Nat. Assn. Disability Examiners, Am. Med. Writers Assn., Biofeedback Research Soc. Am., Chgo. Soc. Phys. Medicine and Rehab. (pres., founder 1978-79), Ill. Rehab. Assn., Ukrainian Acad. Med. Scis. (founder, pres. 1979-80), Gerontol. Soc., Internat. Soc. Electrophysiol. Kinesiology, Internat. Soc. Prosthetics and Orthotics, Fedn. Am. Scientists. Ukrainian Catholic. Home: 1819 N 78th Ct Chicago IL 60635-3502 Office: 820 S Damen Ave Chicago IL 60612-3728

ORZAC, EDWARD SEYMOUR, otolaryngologist; b. N.Y.C., Jan. 11, 1917; s. Philip Edward Orzac and Gertrude (Wachtler) Orzac Cohen; m. Beatrice Fleiss, July 18, 1948; children: Carolyn, Virginia, Elizabeth. B., U. N.C., 1936, M., U. Va., 1937, MD, 1941; BA in History, Adelphi U., 1974; MA in Asian Studies, St. John's U., 1978. Diplomate Am. Bd. Otolaryngology. Intern Wilkes Barre Gen. Hosp., Pa., 1941-42; resident Morisania City Hosp., N.Y., 1945-46, 47-48, NYU-Bellevue Grad. Sch. Medicine, 1946-47; practice medicine specializing in otolaryngology, Valley Stream, N.Y., 1948-81; med. dir. Franklin Gen. Hosp., Valley Stream, 1973—; cons. otolaryngologist Nassau County Med. Ctr., 1983—; founder, dir. Gertrude Wachtler Cohen Hearing, Vertigo and Speech Ctr., Valley Stream, 1974—; asst. prof. clin. surgery SUNY-Stony Brook Med. Sch., 1971—; ann. vis. prof. Kasturba Med. Coll., Manipal Karnataka, India, 1975-82; adj. prof. speech and hearing Adelphi U., 1979—; assoc. adj. prof. hearing and speech, St. John's U. Contbr. articles to profl. jours. Chmn. United Jewish Appeal, Franklin Gen. Hosp. and South Nassau Communites Hosp., 1974; chmn. Israel Bond Drive, Franklin Gen. Hosp., 1965-72, co-chmn., Nassau County, 1976; chmn. Nassau Physicians and Dentists div. United Jewish Appeal, 1978-79; trustee North Shore Health Sys., 1996—. Served to maj. U.S. Army, 1942-45. Hon. fellow Acad. Gen. Edn., Kasturba Med. Coll., Manipal, Karnataka, 1979. Fellow Nassau Surg. Soc., Am. Acad. Ophthalmology and Otolaryngology, Am. Plastic Surgeons, Nassau Acad. Medicine, Am. Acad. Med. Dirs.; mem. Am. Coll. Emergency Physicians, Am. Coll. Physician Execs., Nassau County Soc. Otolaryngology (pres. 1959-60), Phi Alpha Theta. Home: 221 Albon Rd Hewlett NY 11557-2636 Office: Franklin Gen Hosp 900 Franklin Ave Valley Stream NY 11580-2145

OSBORN, GARY LEE, emergency physician; b. Columbus, Ohio, Jan. 21, 1959; s. Vernon Emery Osborn and Ruth Marie (Krieger) McQuay; m. Merri Lynn Dreier, Dec. 27, 1986; children: Malinda, Meredith, Marissa. BA in Chemistry, Miami U., Oxford, Ohio, 1981; DO, Ohio U. Coll. Osteo. Medicine, 1985. Diplomate Nat. Examiners for Osteo. Physicians and Surgeons, Am. Osteo. Bd. Family Practitioners. Intern Drs. Hosp., Columbus, Ohio, 1985-86; resident in family medicine Drs. Hosp., Columbus, 1987-88, staff physician emergency dept., 1991—; resident Ohio State U. Hosps., Columbus, 1986-87; physician emergency dept. Springs Meml. Hosp., Lancaster, S.C., 1988-91, med. dir., 1989-91; mem. regional devel. task force Charlotte Area Trauma Network, 1990-91; clin. asst. prof. Ohio U. Coll. Osteo. Medicine, 1991—; instr. osteo. grad. med. edn. dept. emergency medicine Drs. Hosp., 1991—, vice chmn. dept. emergency medicine, 1993—; program coord. Ohio Osteo. Emergency Medicine Edn. Coalition, 1991—; med. dir. Jerome Twp. Fire Dept., 1992—; corp. v.p. Drs. Emergency Group, Inc., 1995—; instr. ACLS, ATLS, PALS. Contbr. articles to profl. jours. Mem. Am. Osteo. Assn., AMA, Am. Coll. Osteo. Emergency Physicians, Am. Coll. Emergency Physicians, Am. Coll. Family Practice, Am. Coll. Physician Execs. Office: Drs Emergency Group PO Box 1089 Westerville OH 43081

OSBORN, JOEL C., cardiologist; b. Friona, Tex., June 11, 1951; s. Ernest F. and Valoris (Shafter) O.; m. Carlene K. Greeson, Aug. 10, 1973; children: Erin F., Loresn C., Lindsey J. BA in Biology, U. North Tex., Denton, 1972; MD, U. Tex., Galveston, 1976. Diplomate in internal medicine and cardiovascular diseases Am. Bd. Internal Medicine. Intern Univ. Med. Ctr., Jackson, Miss., 1976-77, resident in internal medicine, 1977-79, fellow in cardiology, 1979-81; pvt. practice physician Amarillo, Tex., 1981—; pres. med. staff High Plains Bapt. Hosp., Amarillo, 1990-91, chief cardiology divsn., 1994—, dir. cardiac catheterization lab., 1993—; sec. med. staff N.W. Tex. Hosp., Amarillo, 1992-93. Fellow Am. Coll. Cardiology. Office: Amarillo Diagnostic Clinic 6700 W 9th St Amarillo TX 79106

OSBORN, JUNE ELAINE, pediatrician, microbiologist, educator; b. Endicott, N.Y., May 28, 1937; d. Leslie A. and Dora W. (Wright) O.; divorced; children: Philip I. Levy, Ellen D. and Laura A. Levy (twins). BA, Oberlin (Ohio) Coll., 1957; MD, Western Res. U., 1961; DSc (hon.), U. Med. Dental Sch. N.J., 1990; DMS (hon.), Yale U., 1992; DSc (hon.), Emory U., 1993, Oberlin Coll., 1993; LHD (hon.), Med. Coll. Pa., 1994; DSc (hon.), Rutgers

U., 1994. Intern, then resident in pediatrics Harvard U. Hosp., 1961-64; postdoctoral fellow Johns Hopkins, 1964-65, U. Pitts., 1965-66; mem. faculty, prof. med. microbiology and pediat. U. Wis. Med. Sch., Madison, Wis., 1966-84; prof. pediat. and microbiology U. Wis. Med. Sch., 1975-84, assoc. dean Grad. Sch., 1975-84; dean Sch. Pub. Health U. Mich., 1984-93; prof. epidemiology, pediat. and communicable diseases U. Mich., Sch. Pub. Health and Med. Sch., 1984—; mem. rev. panel viral vaccine efficacy FDA, 1973-79, mem. vaccines and related biol. products adv. com., 1981-85; mem. exptl. virology study sect. Divsn. Rsch. Grants, NIH, 1975-79; mem. med. affairs com. Yale U. Coun., 1981-86; chmn. life scis. associateships rev. panel NRC, 1981-84; mem. U.S. Army Med. R&D Adv. Com., 1983-85; chmn. working group on AIDS and the Nation's Blood Supply, NHLBI, 1984-89; chmn. WHO Planning Group on AIDS and the Internat. Blood Supply, 1985-86. Contbr. articles to med. jours. Mem. task force on AIDS, Inst. of Medicine, 1986; mem. adv. com. Robert Wood Johnson Found. Health Svcs. Program, 1986-91; mem. nat. adv. com. on health of pub. program Pew and Rockefeller Founds.; mem. health promotion and disease prevention bd. IOM, 1987-90, Global Commn. on AIDS, WHO, 1988-92; chmn. Nat. Commn. on AIDS, 1989-93; trustee Kaiser Found., 1990—; trustee Case Western Res. U., Cleve., 1993—; mem. coun. Inst. Medicine, 1995—; mem. Nat. Vaccine Adv. Cte., HHS, 1995—. Grantee NIH, 1969, 72, 74-75, Nat. Multiple Sclerosis Soc., 1971; Scientific Freedom and Responsibility Award AAAS, 1994. Fellow Am. Acad. Arts and Scis., Am. Acad. Pediat., Am. Acad. Microbiology, Infectious Diseases Soc. Am.; mem. Am. Assn. Immunologists, Soc. Pediat. Rsch., Inst. Medicine. Office: U Mich Dept Epidemiology Sch Pub Health Ann Arbor MI 48109

OSBORN, LESLIE ANDREWARTHA, psychiatrist; b. Warrnambool, Victoria, Australia, Aug. 10, 1906; came to U.S., 1931, naturalized, 1938; s. Andrew Rule and Annie (Delbridge) O.; m. Dora Wright, June 12, 1931 (dec.); children: Anne L. Osborn Krueger Henderson, June E.; m. Gwen F. Arnold, Aug. 13, 1960 (dec. Mar. 12, 1976); m. Corinne H. Kirchmaier, June 7, 1985. Student, Wesley Coll., Melbourne, 1920-23; M.B., B.S., Melbourne Med. Sch., 1929; M.D., U. Buffalo, 1945. Diplomate: Am. Bd. Psychiatry and Neurology, 1944. Intern Melbourne Gen. Hosp., 1930-31; postgrad. Post Grad. Hosp., N.Y.C., 1934; in chest diseases Trudeau Sch. Tb, Saranac Lake, 1937; in neurology and psychiatry Columbia U., 1940; gen. practice medicine, physician Endicott-Johnson Med. Dept., Binghamton, N.Y., 1932-38; asst. physician Willard (N.Y.) State Hosp., 1938-41; psychiatrist Meyer Meml. Hosp.; assoc. psychiatry U. Buffalo, 1941-45; attending psychiatrist, dir. psychiatry Edward J. Meyer Meml. Hosp., psychiat. service, 1946-49; prof. psychiatry U. Buffalo Sch. Medicine, 1946, acting dir. dept. psychiatry, 1946-49, head dept., 1949-50; dir. Wis. Psychiat. Inst.; prof. psychiatry U. Wis. Med. Sch., 1950-60; dir. div. mental hygiene Wis. Dept. Pub. Welfare, 1950-60; dir. Walworth County Family Counseling Center, 1960; prof. psychiatry dept. neurology and psychiatry U. Nebr., 1960-66; dir. Swanson Clinic for Multiply Handicapped Children, Nebr. Psychiat. Inst., Omaha, 1960-64; med. dir. Winnebago County Mental Health Clinic, Rockford, Ill., 1966; dir. Mental Health Services, Tompkins County, 1967-68; pvt. practice psychiatry Seneca Falls, N.Y., 1968-74, Scottsdale, Ariz., 1974—. Author: Psychiatry and Medicine, 1952, Prognosis, A Guide to the Study and Practice of Clinical Medicine, 1966, Foundation Learning and Innumeracy, 1977, King of the Hill: Chess for Children: 1981, Preventing War: A Doctor's Trilogy: Vol. 1 Living in a Changed World, 1994. Fellow Am. Psychiat. Assn. (life). Presbyterian. Address: 4800 N 68th St Unit 110 Scottsdale AZ 85251-1142

OSBORN, MARK ELIOT, dentist; b. Buffalo, Apr. 22, 1950; s. Thomas Earl and Ruth Frances (Martin) O. BA, U. Mo., Columbia, 1972; DDS, U. Mo., Kansas City, 1977. Dir. Westport Free Health Clinic, Kansas City, Mo., 1974-76; clinician St. Louis Dept. Health, 1977- ; gen. practice dentistry Troy, Mo., 1978-92; pvt. practice St. Louis, 1993-94; mem. gen. practice staff Gravois-Gustine Dental Group, St. Louis, 1994—. Mem. ADA, Greater St. Louis Dental Soc., Am. Soc. Dentistry for Children, St. Louis Dental Rsch. Group, Delta Sigma Delta, Troy C. of C., Rotary (Troy chpt., dir. dental program 1985—, sec. 1988, pres. 1989, bd. dirs. 1989-91). Home: 360 W Point Ct Saint Louis MO 63130-4028 Office: 3921 Gravois Ave Saint Louis MO 63116

OSBORNE, MICHAEL PIERS, surgeon, researcher, health facility administrator; b. Sutton, Surrey, Eng., Jan. 6, 1946; came to U.S., 1980; s. Arthur Frederick and Leonora Kate Hope (Miller) O.; m. Carolyn Patricia Malkinson, June 22, 1974; children: James, Simon, Andrew, Emma. MB, BS, London U., 1970, MS in Surgery, 1980. Diplomate Royal Coll. Surgeons of Eng., Am. Coll. Surgeons. Intern Charing Cross Group of Hosp., England, 1970-71; resident Brompton Hosp., London, St. James Hosp., London, West Herts Hosp., Eng.; hon. lectr. surgery Royal Marsden Hosp., London, 1977-81; fellow in surg. oncology Meml. Sloan-Kettering Cancer Ctr., N.Y.C., 1980-81, attending surgeon, 1981-91, head breast cancer rsch. lab., 1984-91; chief breast surgery N.Y. Hosp.-Cornell Med. Ctr., N.Y.C., 1991—; prof. surgery Cornell U. Med. Coll., N.Y.C., 1991—; dir., CEO Strang Cancer Prevention Ctr., N.Y.C., 1991-95, pres., CEO, 1995—; dir. Strang- Cornell Breast Ctr., N.Y.C., 1991—; mem. adj. faculty Rockefeller U. Hosp., N.Y.C., 1981-89, vis. physician, 1983—; mem. sci. adv. com. Am.-Italian Found., N.Y.C., 1991—; bd. trustees Nat. Consortium Breast Ctrs., 1992-95; cons. Meml. Sloan-Kettering Cancer Ctr., N.Y.C., 1991—; pres. N.Y. Met. Breast Group, 1995—. Contbr. 12 chpts. to textbooks; contbr. over 100 articles to profl. jours. Recipient Gov.'s Clin. Gold medal Charing Cross Hosp. Med. Sch., 1970, Prize in Surgery, Charing Cross Hosp. Med. Sch., 1970, Raven prize British Assn. Surg. Oncology, 1978; Wellcome Trust fellow, 1975. Mem. N.Y. Acad. Scis., N.Y. Surg. Soc., Brit. Assn. Surg. Oncology, Soc. Surg. Oncology, Royal Soc. Medicine, Am. Soc. Breast Disease (trustee 1993-95), Am. Assn. Cancer Rsch., Am. Soc. Clin. Oncology, Internat. Soc. for Chemoprevention (sec.-gen.). Office: Strang Cancer Prevention Ctr 428 E 72d St Ste 600 New York NY 10021-4601

OSBORNE, PAUL DOUGLAS, hospital administrator; b. Blackwater, Va., Apr. 29, 1943; s. Paul James and Addie Mae (Bledsoe) O.; m. Susan Henry, Apr. 23, 1966; children: Karen D. Bennett, Amy Lynn. BA, Lynchburg Coll., 1965; MHA, Ga. State U., 1971. Health planner Ctrl. Va. Health Planning Coun., Lynchburg, Va., 1971-72; assoc. adminstr. N.E. Ga. Reg. Med. Ctr., Gainesville, Ga., 1972-76; adminstr. Mary Black Meml. Hosp., Spartanburg, S.C., 1976-80; v.p. Spartanburg (S.C.) Regional Med. Ctr., 1980-90; dep. supt. Ctrl. State Hosp., Milledgeville, Ga., 1990—. Bd. dirs. United Way Ctrl. Ga., 1993—, Regional Girl Scout Coun., 1987-90, Salvation Army, 1986-88; sr. warden St. Christopher's Episc. Ch., Spartanburg, 1983. Capt. U.S. Army, 1966-69, Vietnam. Fellow Am. Coll. Healthcare Execs., Milledgeville Country Club, Rotary. Home: 218 Pine Knoll Ln SE Eatonton GA 31024 Office: Ctrl St Hosp Dept Supt Milledgeville GA 31062

OSBORNE, RAYMOND LESTER, JR., radiologist; b. N.Y.C., Nov. 23, 1939; s. Raymond Lester and Margaret Forbes (Unangst) O.; m. Elizabeth Ann Parise, May 13, 1972 (div.); children: Alexandra Forbes, Raymond Lester III. AB with hons. in English, U. Pa., 1961; postgrad., U. Edinburgh, Scotland, 1959-60, U. Glasgow, Scotland, 1961-62; MD, CM, McGill U., Montreal, 1966. Diplomate Am. Bd. Radiology. Intern in surgery Royal Victoria Hosp., Montreal, 1966-67; resident in surgery Duke U. Med. Ctr., Durham, N.C., 1967-68; resident in diagnostic radiology Yale-New Haven Hosp., 1970-73; assoc. in radiology Duke U. Med. Ctr., Durham, 1973-74; asst. prof. Duke U. Med. Ctr., 1974-75; asst. roentenologist Meml. Sloan Kettering Cancer Ctr., N.Y.C., 1975-78; asst. prof. N.Y. Hosp./Cornell U. Med. Ctr., N.Y.C., 1975-78; clin. asst. prof. Yale U., New Haven, 1979—; sr. attending radiologist Middlesex Meml. Hosp., Middletown, Conn., 1978—. Author: The Radiology of Vertebral Trauma, 1980. Mem. Rep. Town Com., Durham, 1984—; mem. physicians' coun. Heritage Found. Lt. comdr. USNR, 1969-70. Decorated Navy Commendation medal, Vietnamese Medal of Honor, 1st class. Mem. AMA, Radiologic Soc. N.Am., Am. Coll. Radiology, Soc. Thoracic Radiology, Am. Roentgen Ray Soc., Conn. Radiologic Soc. (exec. bd.), Conn. Med. Soc., Soc. Med. Radiology, Interam. Coll. Radiology (designated B-reader for respiratory diseases), Nat. Inst. Occupl. Safety and Health, Assn. Am. Physicians and Surgeons, Alpha Omega Alpha. Repubican. Home: 9131 Town Walk Dr Hamden CT 06518-3727 Office: Radiologic Assocs PO Box 290 Middletown CT 06457-0290

OSBORNE, STEPHEN JEFFREY, laboratory administrator; b. Binghamton, N.Y., July 2, 1944; s. Orris Harder and Edith Autusta (Parmalee) O.; m. Judith Ann Hanicker, Sept. 17, 1966 (div. July 1993); children: David Michael, Deborah Ann Osborne Garvayo; m. Marsha christine Beach, July 30, 1994. BS in Med. Tech., Hartwick Coll., 1972. Cert. med. technologist. Med. technologist Binghamton Gen. Hosp., 1966-73, Southern Tier Med. Lab., Johnson City, N.Y., 1973-75; lab. supr. MDS Labs., Binghamton, 1975-84; chemistry instrument specialist Am. Monitor Corp., Indpls., 1984-87; lab. mgr. CMX Labs., Binghamton, 1987-89, Chenango Meml. Hosp., Norwich, N.Y., 1989-91, Bullhead Cmty. Hosp., Bullhead City, Ariz., 1992-94, Pershing Gen. Hosp., Love Lock, Nev., 1994-95. Deacon Presbyn. Ch., Binghamton, 1982—. With USNR, 1966-72, 83—, Desert Storm. Mem. Am. Med. Technologists, Nat. Cert. Agy. for Med. Lab. Pers., Clin. Lab. Mgmt. Assn. Republican. Home: 2832 W Emmaus Ave 8-308 Allentown PA 18103

OSBORNE-POPP, GLENNA JEAN, health services administrator; b. East Rainelle, W.Va., Jan. 5, 1945; d. B.J. and Jean Ann (Haranac) Osborne; m. Thomas Joseph Ferrante Jr., June 11, 1966 (div. Nov. 1987); 1 child, Thomas Joseph Osborne; m. Brian Mark Popp, Aug. 13, 1988. BA cum laude, U. Tampa, 1966; MA, Fairleigh Dickinson U., 1982; cert., Kean Coll., 1983. Cert. English, speech, dramatic arts tchr., prin./supr.; cert. nursing child assessment feeding scale and nursing child assessment tchg. scale, 1996. Tchr. Raritan High Sch., Hazlet, N.J., 1966; tchr. Keyport (N.J.) Pub. Schs., 1968-86, coord. elem. reading and lang. arts, 1980-84, supr. curriculum and instrn., 1984-86; prin. Weston Sch., Manville, N.J., 1986-88, The Bartle Sch., Highland Park, N.J., 1988-91, Orange Ave. Sch., Cranford, N.J., 1991-92; dir. The Open Door Youth Shelter, Binghamton, N.Y., 1992-94; child protective investigator supr. Dept. Health and Rehab. Svcs., Orlando, Fla., 1994-95; program supr. Children's Home Soc., Sanford, Fla., 1995; clin. supr. Healthy Families-Orange, Orlando, Fla., 1995—; regional trainer Individualized Lang. Arts, Weehawken, N.J., 1976-86; cons. McDougal/Little Pubs., Evanston, Ill., 1982-83; chair adv. bd. women's residential program Ctr. for Drug Free Living, Orlando, 1996. Contbr. chpt.: A Resource Guide of Differentiated Learning Experiences for Gifted Elementary Students, 1981. Sunday sch. tchr. Reformed Ch., Keyport, 1975-80, supt. Sunday sch., 1982-84. Mem. Order Ea. Star (Tampa, Fla.), Phi Delta Kappa. Republican. Methodist. Office: Healthy Families 623 S Texas Ave Orlando FL 32805

OSEVALA, MARK ALLAN, osteopath; b. Lancaster, Pa., Dec. 25, 1954; m. Deborah Osevala; children: Alexander, Nicholas, Katherine. BS, Pa. State U., 1977; postgrad., Lebanon Valley Coll., 1979; DO, Phila. Coll. Osteo. Medicine, 1985. Rotating intern Suburban Gen. Hosp., Norristown, Pa., 1985-86, resident in gen. surgery, 1986-90, chief surg. resident, 1987-88, 89-90; fellow in cardiothoracic and vascular surgery Jersey Shore Med. Ctr., Neptune, N.J., 1986-90, chief resident cardiothoracic surgery, 1991-92, mem. staff; Am. Cancer Soc. clin. fellow in oncology Pa. Hosp., Albert Einstein Med. Ctr., Phila., 1982, Am. Oncol. Hosp., Phila., 1983; presenter in field. Contbr. articles to profl. publs. Mem. Am. Osteo. Assn., Am. Coll. Osteo. Surgeons, Pa. Osteo. Med. Assn. (Golden Quill award 1987), Phi Lambda Upsilon. Home: 53 Jonathan Dr Tinton Falls NJ 07753

OSGOOD, DAVID ALDRICH, psychologist; b. Burlington, Vt., June 30, 1944; s. Edward F. Osgood and Muriel (Aldrich) Lane; m. Carla Newman, June 15, 1968; 1 child, Adam. BA, U. Vt., 1966; MPH, Yale U., 1972; EdD, U. Mass., 1991. Lic. psychologist, Vt. Sci. tchr. U.S. Peace Corps, Guyana, 1966-69; trainer U.S. Peace Corps, Trinidad, W.I., 1968; rsch. asst. U. W.I., Mona, Jamaica, 1970-71; dep. dir. Vt. State Office Child Devel., Montpelier, 1971-72; asst. dir. Ctr. for Svc.-Learning U. Vt., Burlington, 1972-85, psychologist Counseling Ctr., 1985—; psychologist The Growth Ctr, Essex Junction, Vt., 1980—. Editor: The Home Health Handbook, 1971. Mem. APA, Vt. Psychol. Assn., Assn. for Humanistic Psychology. Home: PO Box 81 Underhill Center VT 05490-0081 Office: U Vt Counseling Ctr 146 S Williams St Burlington VT 05401-3406

O'SHEA, ARTHUR JOSEPH, psychologist, educator; b. Boston, Sept. 23, 1928; s. Arthur and Delia Marie (Kelly) O'S.; m. Janet Margaret Scully, May 21, 1967; children: Jennifer Marie, Daniel Arthur, Elizabeth Marie. AB, Weston Coll., 1952; MA, Weston (Mass.) Coll., 1953; MEd, Boston Coll., 1963, PhD, 1967. Lic. psychologist, Mass.; diplomate Am. Bd. Vocat. Experts. Counselor, asst. prof. Northeastern U., Boston, 1966-68; assoc. dean Boston State Coll., 1968-73, prof., chair dept. psychology, 1973-82; pvt. practice Needham, Mass., 1974—; prof., dir. grad. counseling psychology program U. Mass., Boston, 1982-91, prof., 1991-92; chmn. bd. Career Planning Assocs., Inc., Needham. Editor: Guide for Occupational Exploration, 1984; author: (test) Career Decision-Making System, 1976; contbr. articles to profl. jours. Mem. APA, ACA (senator 1973-75), Mass. Assn. for Counseling and Devel. (pres. 1972-73), Am. Career Devel. Assn. Democrat. Roman Catholic. Home and Office: 289 Hillcrest Rd Needham MA 02192-4026

OSHER, HAROLD LOUIS, cardiologist, educator; b. Portland, Maine, Jan. 11, 1924; s. Samuel and Leah (Lazarovich) O.; m. Peggy Ann Liberman, June 18, 1950; children: Susan, Nancy, Judith, Samuel. BS summa cum laude, Bowdoin Coll., 1943; MD magna cum laude, Boston U., 1947; LHD (hon.), U. So. Maine, 1994. Diplomate Am. Bd. Internal Medicine, Am. Bd. Cardiovascular Disease. Internship internal medicine Boston City Hosp., 1947-48, residency, 1948-50; fellowship Beth Israel Hosp., 1950; staff mem. heart disease epidemiology study Nat. Heart Inst., Framingham, Mass., 1950-53; pvt. practice cardiology Portland, Maine, 1953—; dir. Cardiac Catheterization Lab. Maine Med. Ctr., Portland, 1955-74, asst. chief medicine, 1979-84, dir. div. cardiology, 1972-88, dir. emeritus, 1989—; asst. clin. prof. medicine Tufts U. Sch. Medicine, Portland, 1970-74, assoc. clin. prof., 1974-80; assoc. prof. medicine U. Vt., Portland, 1981—; heart disease cons. Maine's Regional Med. Program, Augusta, 1967-75, dir. coronary care project, 1968-72; dir. Med. Care Devel., Inc., Augusta, 1967-77, pres., 1971-75. Contbr. articles on cardiology to profl. jours. Recipient Brotherhood award Temple Beth El, Portland, 1968, Outstanding Svc. award New Eng. Regional Heart Com., Boston, 1976; rsch. fellow in hist. geography U. South Maine, 1990—. Fellow ACP, Am. Coll. Cardiology (gov. 1971-74); mem. Am. Heart Assn. (v.p. 1970-71, pres. Maine affiliate 1966-68, outstanding svc. award 1974), Maine Med. Assn., Cumberland County Med. Soc., Phi Beta Kappa. Jewish. Home: 66 Chadwick St Portland ME 04102-3511 Office: Maine Med Ctr 22 Bramhall St Portland ME 04102-3134

OSHER, ROBERT HENRY, ophthalmologist. MD, U. Rochester. Diplomate Am. Bd. Ophthalmology. Resident Bascom Palmer Eye Inst., Miami, Fla.; fellow Wills Eye Hosp., Phila., Bascom Palmer Eye Inst.; ophthalmic cons. Cin. Reds, 1990—; mem. faculty Am. and European Implant Socs., Cataract Congress; internat. lectr. in field. Co-author 5 books; editor Video Jour. Cataract & Refractive Surgery, Video Textbook of Viscosurgery, Internat. Advances in Phacoemulsification; reviewer Jour. Cataract and Refractive Surgery, Am. Jour. Ophthalmology, Archives of Ophthalmology; mem. editl. bd. European Implant Jour., Ophthalmology Times, Can. Cataract Jour.; contbr. articles to profl. jours.; developer intraocular lenses for cataract surgery; creator surg. videos (1st prize Am. and European Cataract Socs.). Coach Cin. Eye Inst. youth baseball and basketball. Recipient Heed Ophthalmic Fellowship award, Acad. Honor award, Maumenee award, Rayner award, Canon award. Mem. Outpatient Ophthalmic Surgery Soc. (exec. com.), Phi Beta Kappa, Alpha Omega Alpha. Office: Cin Eye Inst 10494 Montgomery Rd Cincinnati OH 45242

OSHIYOYE, ADEKUNLE EMMANUEL, physician, realtor; b. Lagos, Nigeria, Jan. 5, 1951; s. Alfred and Grace (Apena) O.; m. Olwwatoyin, Dec. 28, 1991; children: Adekunle Jr., Adedaye Justice. BS, N.Y.S.U., 1974; MD, American U., Monsterrat, Wis., 1979. Real Estate, Physician lic. Staff physician South Chgo. Hosp., Chgo., 1980-81, Cook County Hosp., Chgo., 1981-85, Mercy Hosp., Chgo., 1985-89; health physician City of Chgo. Dept. of Health, 1989—; cons. physician Dept. of Health, Chgo., 1989—. Med. Editor: African Connections, 1990—, Newsbreed Mag., 1990—. Organizer Harold Washington Coalition, Chgo., 1983—, operation push, Chgo. Mem. Am. Med. Assn., Cook County Physician Assn., Knights of Rose Croix #28, Eureka Lodge #64, Ancient Arabic Order of Mystic Shrine, Alpha Phi Alpha, Nigerian American Forum. Democrat. Apostolic. Home: PO Box 15187 Lansing MI 48901-5187

OSINSKI, MARGARET JEAN, occupational health nurse; b. Buffalo, June 20, 1939; d. Stanley Joseph and Rita (Milbrand) Sowa; m. Joseph George Osinski, Oct. 3, 1964; children: Joseph A. II, Susan M., Matthew S. Student, Canisius Coll., 1957-58; nursing diploma, Mercy Hosp. Sch. Nursing, Buffalo, 1960. RN; cert. occupational health nurse specialist. Staff nurse med. Kenmore Mercy Hosp., Kenmore, N.Y., 1960-61; staff nurse ob-gyn. Yonkers Gen. Hosp., Yonkers, N.Y., 1961; occupational health nurse Chevrolet div. Gen. Motors, Buffalo, 1961-66; staff nurse emergency Kenmore Mercy Hosp., 1974-80; occupational health nurse, safety coord. Nabisco Brands, Inc., Buffalo, 1980-87; occupational health nurse, employee assistance program coord Bell Aerospace Textron, Buffalo, 1987-91, safety rep., 1991—. Mem. Western N.Y. Assn. Occupational Health Nurses (pres. 1987-89), Am. & N.Y. State Assns. Occupational Health Nurses, Am. Bd. Occupational Health Nurses, Am. Soc. Safety Engrs., Employee Assistance Profls. Assn., Grand Island (N.Y.) Jr. Football. Republican. Roman Catholic. Home: 3098 Baseline Rd Grand Island NY 14072-1313

OSIYOYE, ADEKUNLE, obstetrician, gynecologist, educator; b. Lagos, Nigeria, Jan. 5, 1951; came to U.S., 1972; s. Alfred and Grace (Apena) Oshiyoye; m. Toyin Osinowo Oshiyoye, Dec. 28, 1991; children: Adekunle Jr., Adedayo Justice. Student, Howard U., 1972-73; BS, U. State of N.Y., 1974; postgrad., Columbia U., 1974-78; MD, Am. U., Montserrat, West Indies, 1979. Intern South Chgo. Community Hosp., 1980-81; intern dept. obstetrics-gynecology Cook County Hosp., Chgo., 1981-82, resident physician, 1982-84, chief resident physician dept. obstetrics-gynecology, 1984-85; assoc. prof. dept. obstetrics-gynecology Chgo. Osteo. Coll. Medicine, 1986—; health physician, cons. physician City of Chgo. Dept. Health, 1989—; attending physician St. Bernard Hosp., Chgo., 1985—, Hyde Park Hosp., Chgo., 1986—, Mercy Hosp., Chgo., 1987—, Roseland Hosp., Chgo., 1985—, Columbus Hosp., Chgo., 1985—, Jackson Park Hosp., Chgo., 1985—; coord. emergency rm. Cook County Hosp., 1983-85. Med. editor African Connections, 1990—; med. columnist Newsbreed Mag., 1990—; founding mem. Ob-Gyn Video Jour. Am. Organizer Harold Washington Coalition, Chgo., 1983-87; operation mem. Operation P.U.S.H., Chgo., 1987—; active Chgo. Urban League, 1989—, Cook County Dem. Party, 1988—; mem. Mayor's Commn. on Human Rels., Chgo., 1990—, State of Ill. Inaugural Com., 1991. Shell scholar, 1965-69; recipient Fed. Govt. scholarship award, 1972, Howard Univ. scholarship award, 1973, Fed. Govt. Nigeria grad. med. scholarship award, 1975-79, Cerebral Palsy rsch. award, 1977, Ob-gyn. Video Jour. award, 1989, Role Model award Chgo. Police Dept., 1991, 92, Chgo. Bd. Edn., 1991, Chgo. 100 Black Men, 1991, Gov.'s Recognition award, 1992; named one of Best Dressed Men in Chgo., Chgo. Defender, 1990, 91. Fellow Am. Coll. Internat. Physicians, Am. Coll. Obstetricians & Gynecologists; mem. AMA (physician recognition award 1986), Am. Coll. Glegal Medicine (edn. com.), Am. Soc. Law Medicine, Am. Pub. Heart Assn., Nat. Med. Assn., Ill. Med. Soc., Chgo. Med. Assn., Chgo. Gynecol. Soc., Cook County Physician Assn., Nigerian Am. Forum (chmn. health com., chmn. election com.), Cook County Hosp. Surg. Alumni Assn., Howard U. Alumni Assn. (regent, chmn. scholarship com. Chgo. chpt.), Eureka Lodge (investigating com.), Masons, Shriners, Order of Eastern Star, Alpha Phi Alpha (life mem., mem. Labor Day com., dir. ednl. programs Xi Lambda chpt. 1990—, co-chmn. courtesy Black & Gold com. 1989, 90, Recognition award 1991), Pan Hellenic Action Coun. (chmn. pub. rels. com.), Ill. Maternal and Child Health Coalition, Beta Kappa Chi. Apostolic. Home: PO Box 15187 Lansing MI 48901-5187 Office: Dept Health 37 W 47th St Chicago IL 60609-4657

OSKARSSON, HELGI J., medical educator, researcher. BA, Hamrahlid Coll., Reykjavik, Iceland, 1976; MD, U. Iceland, Reykjavik, 1983. Intern Regional Hosp., Akureyri, Iceland, 1983-84; sr. resident dept. internal medicine Landspitalinn U. Hosp. Iceland, 1984-85, sr. resident dept. pediats., 1985-86; resident internal medicine Med. Ctr. Loyola U., Maywood, Ill., 1986-89; fellow cardiology divsn. cardiovascular diseases U. Iowa Hosps. & Clinics, Iowa City, 1992-93; fellow assoc. Coll. Medicine U. Iowa, Iowa City, 1992-93; asst. prof. dept. internal medicine sect. cardiology U. Nebr. Med. Ctr., Omaha, 1993-95; asst. prof. divsn. cardiovascular diseases dept. internal medicine Coll. Medicine U. Iowa, 1995—. Contbr. articles to profl. jours. Grantee Am. Diabetes Found., 1996—, Max Baer Heart Rsch. grantee, 1995-96, Am. Heart Assn., 1995—. Office: U Iowa Hosps & Clinics Dept Internal Medicine 200 Hawkins Dr Iowa City IA 52242-7806

OSLAND, JACQUELINE S., surgeon; b. Fargo, N.D., Jan. 11, 1965; d. Glenn Harley and Joyce Ann (Gustafson) Rude; m. John Donald Osland, May 25, 1991. BA, N.D. State U., 1987; MD, U. N.D., 1991. Resident in gen. surgery U. Kans., Wichita, 1991—. Mem. Alpha Omega Alpha, Phi Kappa Phi. Home: 3821 Cranberry Wichita KS 67226

OSOFSKY, JOY DONIGER, psychology educator, researcher; b. N.Y.C., Sept. 9, 1944; d. Howard Eliot Doniger and Marion (Sterngold) Davidson; m. Howard Joseph Osofsky, Sept. 1, 1963; children: Hari, Justin, Michael. BA, Syracuse U., 1966, MA, 1967, PhD, 1969. Lic. psychologist, La., Kans. Asst. prof. Cornell U., Ithaca, N.Y., 1969-71; asst. prof. Temple U., Phila., 1972-73, assoc. prof., 1973-76; postdoctoral fellow Judge Baker Guidance Ctr., Boston, 1975-76; postdoctoral fellow Menninger Found., Topeka, 1976-79, staff psychologist, 1979-86; prof. psychology La. State U. Med. Ctr., New Orleans, 1986—. Editor: Handbook of Infant Development, 1978, 2d edit., 1987, Infant Mental Health Jour., 1987—. Recipient Harris award Chgo. Psychoanalytic Soc., 1990. Mem. Soc. for Rsch. in Child Devel. (sec. 1985-91), World Assn. for Infant Mental Health (pres.-elect 1989-92, pres. 1992—). Office: La State U Med Ctr 1542 Tulane Ave New Orleans LA 70112-2825

OSOWIEC, DARLENE ANN, clinical psychologist, educator, consultant; b. Chgo., Feb. 16, 1951; d. Stephen Raymond and Estelle Marie Osowiec; m. Barry A. Leska. BS, Loyola U., Chgo., 1973; MA with honors, Roosevelt U., 1980; postgrad. in psychology, Saybrook Inst., San Francisco, 1985-88; PhD in Clin. Psychology, Calif. Inst. Integral Studies, 1992. Lic. clin. psychologist, Mo., Ill. Mental health therapist Ridgeway Hosp., Chgo., 1978; mem. faculty psychology dept. Coll. Lake County, Grayslake, Ill., 1981; counselor, supr. MA-level interns, chmn. pub. rels. com. Integral Counseling Ctr., San Francisco, 1983-84; clin. psychology intern Chgo.-Read Mental Health Ctr. Ill. Dept. Mental Health, 1985-86; mem. faculty dept. psychology Moraine Valley C.C., Palos Hills, Ill., 1988-89; lectr. psychology Daley Coll., Chgo., 1988-90; cons. Gordon & Assocs., Oak Lawn, Ill., 1989—; adolescent, child and family therapist Orland Twp. Youth Svcs., Orland Park, Ill., 1993; psychology fellow Sch. Medicine, St. Louis U., 1994-95; clin. psychologist in pvt. practice Chgo., 1996—. Ill. State scholar, 1969-73; Calif. Inst. Integral Studies scholar, 1983. Mem. APA, Am. Psychol. Soc., Am. Women in Psychology, Am. Statis. Assn., Ill. Psychol. Assn., Calif. Psychol. Assn., Mo. Psychol. Assn., Gerontol. Soc. Am., Am. Soc. Clin. Hypnosis, Internat. Platform Assn., Chgo. Soc. Clin. Hypnosis, NOW (chair legal adv. corps, Chgo. 1974-76). Home: 6608 S Whipple St Chicago IL 60629-2916

OSS, GERTJAN VAN, anesthesiologist; b. Rosmalen, The Netherlands, July 31, 1952; s. Chris Van Oss and Maria (Van Uden) Schell; m. Annemie Van Aggelen, Nov. 20, 1977; children: Sander C.F., Ralph N.T. MD, Katholieke U., Njimegen, The Netherlands, 1977, cert. in anesthesiology, 1981. Head dept. pain treatment Hosp. Rijnstate, Arnhem, The Netherlands, 1989—. Chmn. Ronald McDonald Home, Arnhem, The Netherlands. Lt. col. Dutch Army Res., 1982—. Mem. Rotary. Roman Catholic. Home: Utrechtseweg 447, 6865 CL Doorwerth The Netherlands

OSSENBERG, HELLA SVETLANA, psychoanalyst; b. Kiev, Russia, June 10, 1930; came to U.S., 1957, naturalized, 1964; d. Anatole E. and Tatiana N. (Dombrovski) Donath; diploma langs. and psychology, U. Heidelberg, Germany, 1953; MS, Columbia U., 1968; cert. Nat. Psychol. Assn. Psychoanalysis, 1977, diplomate Am. Bd. Examiners; m. Carl H. Ossenberg, June 7, 1958. Sr. psychiat. social worker VA Mental Hygiene Clinic, N.Y.C., 1968-80, pvt. practice psychoanalysis, N.Y.C., 1975—; mem. Theodor Reik Cons. Center, 1978—; field instr. Columbia U., Fordham U. schs. social work. Mem. NASW, Acad. Cert. Social Workers, Nat. Psychol. Assn. Psychoanalysis, Nat. Assn. Advancement Phychoanalysis (Am. Bds. Accreditation and Certification), Am. Group Psychotheraphy Assn. (founder), Coun. Psychoanalytic Psychotherapists. Home: 820 W End Ave New York NY 10025-5371 Office: 345 W 58th St New York NY 10019-1145

OSSER, DAVID NEAL, psychiatrist; b. N.Y.C., Aug. 30, 1946; d. Abe A. and Edna (Meisel) O.; m. Stephanie D. Fleischer; children: Roselin Emily, Daniel Alexander. BA, Amherst Coll., 1968; MD, SUNY, Syracuse, 1972. Intern in psychiatry U. So. Calif., L.A., 1972-73; resident in psychiatry Mass. Mental Health Ctr., Harvard U., Boston, 1973-76; pvt. practice Needham, Mass., 1976—; asst. prof. psychiatry Harvard U. Med. Sch., 1976—, Tufts U. Med. Sch., 1978—, Taunton Med. Sch., 1976—, Faulkner Hosp., 1976—, Beth Israel Hosp., 1984—, Brockton VA Med. Ctr., 1995—. Author decision support software for psychopharmacology; contbr. articles to profl. jours. Mem. Am. Psychiat. Assn., Am. Soc. Clin. Psychopharmacology. Democrat. Jewish. Office: 150 Winding River Rd Needham MA 02192-1025

OSSIAS, ARTHUR LAWRENCE, physician, educator; b. N.Y.C., Mar. 24, 1940; s. David and Dora Ossias; m. Linda Machaelson; children: Geoffrey, Brian. BA, U. Rochester, 1961; MD, Yale U., 1965. Diplomate Am. Bd. Internal Medicine, Am. Bd. Hematology, Am. Bd. Med. Oncology. Asst. clin. prof. medicine Mt. Sinai Sch. Medicine, N.Y.C., 1974—; intern Univ. Rochester, 1965-66; residency Bronx Mcpl. Hosp. Ctr, 1968-70; fellowship Mt. Sinai Hosp, N.Y.C., 1970-72; asst. attending physician Mt. Sinai Med. Ctr., N.Y.C., 1974—. Surgeon USPHS, 1966-68. Fellow ACP; mem. Am. Soc. Hematology, Am. Soc. Clin. Oncology, Phi Beta Kappa. Office: 1112 Park Ave New York NY 10128-1235

OSSO, DONNA J., managed care administrator; b. Kew Gardens, N.Y., June 11, 1954. BA, Queens Coll., 1983; MPA, John Jay Coll., N.Y.C., 1990. Assoc. dir. N.Y.C. Health and Hosps., 1984-89; project coord. Mt. Sinai Med. Ctr., N.Y.C., 1990-92; provider svcs. rep. Sanus Health Plan, N.Y.C., 1992; provider rels. rep. MetraHealth, N.Y.C., 1992-93, contractor, 1993-95; cons. health svcs. Aetna Helath Plans, Hartford, Conn., 1995-96; mgr. provider rels. Aetna Helath Plans, N.Y.C., 1996—; cons. Med. Billing Techs., Whitestone, N.Y., 1988-92. Mayors Grad. scholar, N.Y.C., 1984. Mem. APHA, Am. Coll. Health Care Execs. (assoc.), Health Care Fin. Mgmt. Assn. Office: Aenta Helath Plans 2700 Westchester Ave Purchase NY 10577

OSSOFSKY, HELEN JOHNS (MRS. ELI OSSOFSKY), psychiatrist; b. Phila., Dec. 7, 1921; d. William Calloway and Gertrude (Schindele) Johns; A.B., Mt. Holyoke Coll., 1943; student Women's Med. Coll. Pa., 1950-52; M.D., Johns Hopkins U., 1954; m. Eli Ossofsky, Aug. 8, 1950, (dec. Oct. 1950); m. Charles E. Iliff, 1987. Intern Osler Med. Service, Johns Hopkins, 1954-55, resident Pediatrics Cornell U., N.Y. Hosp., 1955-56, Pediatrics Johns Hopkins, 1956-57; research assoc. Johns Hopkins Sch. Hygiene and Pub. Health, 1957-59; asst. prof. Georgetown U. Sch. Medicine, 1959-66, assoc. prof. pediatrics, 1966-79; supervisory med. officer D.C. Dept. Pub. Health, 1959-62, med. cons. div. mental retardation, 1967-69; child psychiatry consultation practice, McLean, Va., 1966—. Cons., Inst. Child Health and Human Devel., NIH, Bethesda, Md., 1962-63; cons. in med. tng. div. chronic diseases USPHS, 1964-65; cons. Va. Assn. Children with Learning Disabilities, Psychiatric Inst. Washington, 1972-88; cons. treatment of psychiat. disorders task force Am. Psychiat. Assn., 1986-89; fellow Am. Acad. Pediatrics, 1975; lectr. Cath. U. Sch. Cardiovascular Nursing, 1959-79; mem. advisory council Cybernetic Research Inst. Mem. AMA, Washington Psychiat. Soc., Am. Psychiat. Assn., Johns Hopkins Med. and Surg. Assn., Phi Beta Kappa. Author: Tumors of the Eye and Adnexa in Infancy and Childhood, 1962; also articles in profl. jours. Address: 1333 Merrie Ridge Rd Mc Lean VA 22101-1826

O'STEEN, RANDY A., nursing administrator; b. Oklahoma City, Sept. 14, 1954; s. Jim D. and June A. (Davis) O'S. AS, Oklahoma City Community Coll., 1981; BA in Mgmt., So. Nazarene U., Bethany, Okla., 1990. Charge nurse, post anesthesia care unit Bapt. Med. Ctr. of Okla., Oklahoma City, 1983-88, head nurse, post critical care unit, 1988-89, head nurse, nursing resource unit, 1989-91; dir. Nursing Systems, 1991-93; dir. systems and devel. Integris Health, Oklahoma City, 1993—. Editor newsletter Vital Signs, 1984-87. Mem. ANA, Am. Soc. Post Anesthesia Nurses, Okla. Nurses Assn., Okla. Soc. Post Anesthesia Nurses (pres. Oklahoma City chpt. 1983-86, chmn. publs. com. 1985-86), Am. Orgn. Nurse Execs., Okla. Orgn. Nurse Execs., Am. Med. Informatics Assn., Health Level Seven, Health Info. Mgmt. Sys. Soc. Home: 229 NW 33rd St Oklahoma City OK 73118-8613 Office: Integris Health Ste 200 5400 N Independence Ave Oklahoma City OK 73112-5300

O'STEEN, WENDALL KEITH, neurobiology and anatomy educator; b. Meigs, Ga., July 3, 1928; s. Wellna Hubert and Lillian (Powell) O'S.; m. Sandra Lynn Kraeer, July 30, 1983; children: Lisa Diane, Kerry Keith, Buckley Powell. BA, Emory U., 1948, MS, 1950; PhD, Duke U., 1958. Asst. prof. Jr. Coll. Emory U., Valdosta, Ga., 1948-49; instr. Emory U., Atlanta, 1950-51, prof. Sch. Medicine, 1968-77; from asst. prof. to prof. med. br. U. Tex., 1958-67; asst. prof. Wofford Coll., Spartanburg, S.C., 1951-53; prof., chmn. dept. neurobiology and anatomy, Bowman Gray Sch. Med. Wake Forest U., Winston-Salem, N.C., 1977-93, prof. emeritus, 1993—; mem. anatomy com. Nat. Bd. Med. Examiners, Phila., 1982-87. Contbr. over 150 articles to books, nat. and internat. jours. Served to lt. col. USAR. Recipient Golden Apple teaching award Med. Br. U. Tex., Galveston, 1967, Outstanding Tchr. award Emory U., 1973, Williams Disting. Teaching award Emory U., 1974, award for teaching excellence Bowman Gray Sch. Medicine, Wake Forest U. Mem. Am. Assn. Anatomists (exec. com. 1980-84, v.p. 1990-92), Assn. Anatomy Chairmen (exec. com. 1982-84, pres. 1990-91), So. Soc. Anatomists (pres. 1975-76), Soc. for Neurosci., N.C. Soc. Neurosci. (pres. 1980-81), Western N.C. Soc. Neurosci. (pres. 1987-88), Assn. Rsch. in Vision and Ophthalmology, Alpha Omega Alpha. Republican. Methodist. Office: Bowman Gray Sch of Medicine Wake Forest Univ Dept of Neurobiology & Anatomy Winston Salem NC 27157-1010

OSTER, MARTIN WILLIAM, oncologist; b. N.Y.C., Apr. 9, 1947; s. Joseph A. and Bella O.; B.A. summa cum laude, Columbia U., 1967, M.D., 1971; m. Karen A. Strauss, May 18, 1975; children—Bonnie Felice, Michelle Rae, Nancy Meredith. Intern, resident in medicine Mass. Gen. Hosp., Boston, 1971-73; clin. assoc. div. of cancer treatment Nat. Cancer Inst., Bethesda, Md., 1973-76; asst. prof. medicine Columbia Coll. Physicians and Surgeons, 1976-86, assoc. prof. clin. medicine, 1986—, asst. prof. medicine Cancer Rsch. Ctr., Columbia U., 1976-86, assoc. prof. medicine, 1986—; asst. attending physician Columbia-Presbyn. Med. Center, N.Y.C., 1976-86, assoc. attending physician, 1986—. Served with USPHS, 1973-76. Am. Cancer Soc. jr. faculty clin. fellow, 1976-79; diplomate Am. Bd. Internal Medicine and subsplty. med. oncology. Fellow ACP; mem. AMA (Physician Recognition awards 1976-78, 79-81, 82-84), Am. Assn. Cancer Rsch., N.Y. Cancer Soc., Am. Soc. Clin. Oncology, N.Y. Met. Breast Cancer Group, Phi Beta Kappa, Alpha Omega Alpha. Home: 6 Arrowhead Ln Armonk NY 10504-1301 Office: 161 Fort Washington Ave New York NY 10032-3713

OSTERKAMP, DALENE MAY, psychology educator, artist; b. Davenport, Iowa, Dec. 1, 1932; d. James Hiram and Bernice Grace (La Grange) Simmons; m. Donald Edwin Osterkamp, Feb. 11, 1951 (dec. Sept. 1951). BA, San Jose State U., 1959, MA, 1962; PhD, Saybrook Inst., 1989. Lectr. San Jose (Calif.) State U., 1960-61, U. Santa Barbara (Calif.) Ext., 1970-76; prof. Bakersfield (Calif.) Coll., 1961-87, emeritus, 1987—; adj. faculty, counselor Calif. State U., Bakersfield, 1990—; gallery dir. Bakersfield Coll., 1964-72. Exhibited in group shows at Berkeley (Calif.) Art, Ctr., 1975, Libr. of Congress, 1961, Seattle Art Mus., 1962. Founder Kern Art Edn. Assn., Bakersfield, 1962, Bakersfield Printmakers, 1976. Staff sgt. USAF, 1952-55. Recipient 1st Ann. Svc. to Women award Am. Assn. Women in C.C., 1989. Mem. APA, Assn. for Women in Psychology, Assn. for Humanistic Psychology, Calif. Soc. Printmakers. Home: PO Box 387 Glennville CA 93226-0387 Office: Calif State Univ Stockdale Ave Bakersfield CA 93309

OSTI, MATTIA FALCHETTO, medical educator; b. Genoa, Liguria, Italy, Feb. 18, 1962; s. Gianlupo and Maria Grazia (Zanelli Quarantini) O.; m. Domitilla Calamai, Sept. 24, 1995; 1 child, Gianlupo Marco. MD, U. Rome, 1986; specialist in radiology, U. La Sapienza, Rome, 1990, specialist in radiotherapy, 1994. Resident in cardiology U. Rome, 1986-90, resident in radiation oncology, 1990-94; asst. prof. U. La Sapienza, Rome, 1990—; asst. Inst. G. Roussy, Paris, 1996. Recipient awards Italian Inst. Health, Phila., 1992, Inst. Gustave Roussy, Paris, 1996. Fellow AIRO, SIRM, ESTRO. Home: V M Hergati 17/A, 00197 Rome Italy Office: Istituto Radiologia, Vie Regina Elena 326, 00161 Rome Italy

OSTLIND, DAN A., parasitologist; b. McPherson, Kans., June 19, 1936; s. Harry Dewey and Laura (Bartles) O.; m. Eleanor Ruth Ahlstedt, Oct. 5, 1958; 1 child, Dyanne Dee. MS, Kans. State U., 1962, PhD, 1966. Parasitologist Moorman Mfg. Co., Quincy, Ill., 1966-67; sr. rsch. parasitologist Merck & Co., Rahway, N.J., 1967-69, rsch. fellow, 1969-77, sr. rsch. fellow, 1977-86, sr. investigator, 1986—. Republican. Office: Merck & Co Research Dept Rahway NJ 07065

OSTROV, MELVYN R., physician; b. Bklyn., June 12, 1937; s. Alexander and Betty (Newman) O.; m. Irene Fishman, Dec. 24, 1959; children: Robert, David. BS, CUNY, 1959; MD, Chgo. Med. Sch., 1963. Diplomate Am. Bd. Internal Medicine, Am. Bd. Allergy and Immunology. Intern medicine and surgery Kings County Hosp., Bklyn., Calif., 1963-64; resident in internal medicine Kings County Hosp., Bklyn., Conn., 1964-66; resident in allergy Jewish Hosp. of Bklyn., 1966-67; chief of allergy U.S. Army Hosp., Ft. Ord, Calif., 1967-69; ptrn. Allergy Assocs. of Waterbury, Conn., 1969—; chief allergy clinic St. Mary's Hosp., Waterbury, 1969—, attending physician, 1969—; attending physician Waterbury Hosp., 1969—. Contbr. articles to profl. jours. With. Travel grantee Am. Coll. Allergists, 1967. Fellow Am. Acad. Allergy (travel grantee 1967); mem. Conn. Soc. Allergy, New Haven County Med. Soc., Conn. State Med. Soc. Office: Allergy Assocs Waterbury 475 Chase Pky Waterbury CT 06408

OSTROW, JAY DONALD, gastroenterology educator, researcher; b. N.Y.C., Jan. 1, 1930; s. Herman and Anne Sylvia (Epstein) O.; m. Judith Fargo, Sept. 9, 1956; children: George Herman, Bruce Donald, Margaret Anne. B.S. in Chemistry, Yale U., 1950; M.D., Harvard U., 1954; M.Sc. in Biochemistry, Univ. Coll., London, 1970. Diplomate Am. Bd. Internal Medicine. Am. Bd. Gastroenterology. Intern Johns Hopkins Hosp., Balt., 1954-55; resident Peter Bent Brigham Hosp., Boston, 1957-58; NIH trainee in gastroenterology, 1958-59; NIH trainee in liver disease Thorndike Mem. Lab. Boston City Hosp., 1959-62; instr. in medicine Harvard U., Boston, 1959-62; asst. prof. medicine Case-Western Res. U., Cleve., 1962-70; assoc. prof. U. Pa., Phila., 1970-76, prof., 1977-78; Sprague prof. medicine Northwestern U., Chgo., 1978-89, prof. medicine, 1989-95, prof. emeritus, 1995—, chief gastroenterology sect., 1978-87; vis. prof. gastrointestinal and hepatology dept. Acad. Med. Ctr., U. Amsterdam, The Netherlands, 1995—; med. investigator VA Hosp., Phila., 1973-78, VA Med. Ctr. Lakeside, Chgo., 1990-95. Editor, contbg. author: Bile Pigments and Jaundice, 1986. Asst. scoutmaster Valley Forge council Boy Scouts Am., Merion, Pa., 1972-78; asst. scoutmaster Northeast Ill. council Boy Scouts Am., 1978-81; vestryman St. Matthew's Episcopal Ch., Evanston, Ill., 1979-82; treas. Classical Children's Chorale, Evanston, 1982. Served to lt. comdr. M.C. USN, 1955-57. Recipient Gastroenterology Rsch. award Beaumont Soc., El Paso, 1979, Sr. Disting. Scientist award Alexander von Humboldt Found., Germany, 1989-90; NIH fellow, 1958-62, grantee, 1962-92; VA grantee, 1970-95. Mem. Am. Assn. Study Liver Diseases (councillor 1983-85, v.p. 1985-86, pres. 1987), Am. Gastroent. Assn. (chmn. exhibit com. 1969-72, mem. undergrad. tchg. project 1972-88), Am. Soc. Clin. Investigation, Am. Physiol. Soc. (asst. editor 1979-84), Internat. Assn. Study Liver, Peripatetic Club. Office: U Amsterdam Acad Med Ctr, Meibergdreef 9 Rm C2-111, 1105 AZ Amsterdam The Netherlands

OSTROWER, VICTORS, physician, educator; b. N.Y.C., Oct. 11, 1939; 4 children. BS, Marietta (Ohio) Coll., 1961; MD, N.Y. Med. Coll., N.Y.C., 1965. Intern U. Chgo., 1965-66; resident N.Y. Med. Coll., 1966-68, fellow in hematology, 1968-69; fellow in gastroenterology U. Colo., Denver. 1971-74; pvt. practice San Antonio; asst. prof. medicine and gastroenterology U. Tex. Health Sci. Ctr., San Antonio, 1974-80, clin. prof. medicine, 1980—. Office: Gastroenterology Clinic of San Antoino 7940 Floyd Curl Dr Ste 1050 San Antonio TX 78229

OSUCH, JANET ROSE, surgeon; b. Chgo., Mar. 12, 1948; d. Theodore and Shirley May (Gauthier) O. BS in Med. Tech., No. Ill. U., 1970; MD, Mich. State U., 1979. Diplomate Am. Bd. Surgery. Resident in surgery Northwestern McGaw Med. Ctr., Chgo., 1979-85; fellow surg. oncology Evanston (Ill.) Hosp., 1983-84; asst. prof. surgery Mich. State U., East Lansing, 1986-90, dir. surg. edn., 1987-93, assoc. prof., 1990-96, full prof., 1996—, med. dir. Comprehensive Breast Clinic, 1992—; advisor Mich. Dept. Pub. Health, Lansing, 1992—; panelist Quality Determinants of Mammography Clin. Practical Guidelines, Washington, 1993-94; nat. spokesperson Am. Cancer Soc., Atlanta, 1991—, U.S. Senate witness, 1993, 94; project leader, author Standardized Curriculum Breast and Cervical Project Ctr. Disease Control, 1994. Contbr. articles to profl. jours., chpts. to books. Fellow Am. Coll. Surgeons, Soc. Surg. Oncology; mem. AMA, Am. Soc. Breast Diseases, Nat. Surg. Adjuvant Breast Project, Am. Med. Women's Assn. (Bertha Van Hoosen award 1995), Assn. Women Surgeons, Alpha Omega Alpha. Office: Mich State U Dept Surgery B435 Clinical Ctr East Lansing MI 48824

OSWALT, ROBERT MCNEILL, psychology educator; b. Danville, Ill., Sept. 3, 1938; s. Robert Jhn and Katherine (McNeill) O.; m. Dorothy Jane Stein, July 11, 1970; children: Sarah, Michael, Mark. BA, DePauw U., 1960; MA, La. State U., Baton Rouge, 1962; PhD, La. State U., 1965. Lic. psychologist, N.Y. Staff psychologist The McMurray Co., Chgo., 1964-65; cons. Booz Allen & Hamilton, Chgo., 1965-67; prof. psychology Skidmore Coll., Saratoga, N.Y., 1967—. Contbr. articles to profl. jurs. Home: 8 Bryan St Saratoga Springs NY 12866-1706 Office: Skidmore Coll Dept Psychology Saratoga Springs NY 12866

OTA, DAVID M., physician, educator, health facility administrator; b. Santa Barbara, Calif., Feb. 16, 1948; m. Bette Brockway; children: Elizabeth, Britten. BS, U. Calif., Los Angeles, 1969; MD, U. Chgo., 1973. Diplomate Am. Bd. Surgery, Nat. Bd. Med. Examiners. Intern, asst. resident gen. surgery Johns Hopkins Hosp., 1973-75; surgical rsch. fellow dept. surgery U. Tex. Med. Sch., Houston, 1975-76; asst. and chief resident gen. surgery Hermann (U.) Hosp., Houston, 1976-79; sr. fellow surgical oncology U. Tex. M.D. Anderson Hosp. and Tumor Inst., Houston, 1979-80; asst. prof. surgery U. Tex. M.D. Anderson Cancer Ctr., Houston, 1980-85, assoc. prof., 1985-91, prof. surgery, 1991-93; asst. prof. U. Tex. Med. Sch., Houston 1980-85, assoc. prof., 1986-93, prof. surgery, 1991-93; prof. surgery U. Mo. Sch. Med., Columbia, 1993—; also chief divsn. surgical oncology, med. dir. U. Mo. Ellis Fischel Cancer Ctr., Columbia, 1993—; surgical oncology cons. Harry S. Truman Meml. Vets. Hosp., Columbia, 1994—, cons. Cooper County Meml. Hosp., Boonville, Mo., 1993—, Lake of Ozarks Gen. Hosp., Osage Beach, Mo., 1995—, Kelsey-Sebold Clinic, 1984—; vis. prof. U. Ky. Med. Ctr., Lexington, 1986; postgrad. adv. in field; physician adv. GenCare Health Sys. Inc., Columbia, 1995; surgeon adv. bd. Ethicon Endosurgery, 1992; assoc. examiner Am. Bd. Surgery, 1989; bd. dirs. Duchesne Acad. of Sacred Heart, 1991-93; mem. com. Cost-Effective Issues in Cancer Mgmt., Dept. Health, 1993—; spkr., presenter to over 25 confs., profl. assns., colls. and orgns. in field. Co-Author (with others) over 20 book chapters, 36 pub. abstracts;contbr. over 90 articles to profl. jours.; creator, Home IVH video tchg. film, 1982, OutpatientIVH tchg. manual, 1983, Laparascopic right hemocolectomy, 1993, Minimally Invasive Tissue Harvest for Microvascular Reconstruction (videotape), 1993 (certificate of Merit 1993), Laparascopic feeding jejunostomy, 1993; patentee for parenteral amino acid solution for difluoromethylornithine and other polyamine inhibitors, parenteral amino acid solutions for feeding cancer patients; mem. editl. bd. Jour. Nat. Cancer Inst. 1990—, Annals Surgical Oncology (assoc. sect. editor), ad-hoc reviewer Jour. Surgical Rsch., Surgery, Internat. Jour Cancer, Internat. Jour. Nutrition. Grantee Kelsey-Seybold Found., 1984-86, Travenol Labs. Inc., 1985-87, 1987-89, Caremark Inc. 1990-92, Ethicon EndoSurgery Inc., 1991, 1992, Cutter Labs., 1982-83, Hoffman LaRoche Labs., 1983, Abbott Labs., 1983, Physician's Review Svc, 1993, Nat. Cancer Inst., 1983-86, 85-88, 87-90, 1988-91, 93-96, Am. Inst. Cancer Rsch., 1987-89, Tex. Advanced Tech. Program, 1989-92; fellow Am. Cancer Soc., 1977. Mem. Am. Assn. Cancer Rsch., Am. Coll. Surgeons (Nat. and Mo. Chpts.), AMA, Am. Soc. Colorectal Surgeons, Am. Soc. Clinical Oncology, Am. Soc. Parenteral and Enteral Nutrition, Assn. Acad. Surgery (resident rsch. award 1976), Boone County Med. Soc., Internat. Assn. Vitamin and Nutritional Oncology, Soc. Surgery of Alimentary Tract, Soc. Surgical Oncology (mem. program com. 1988-91, stds. of care com., 1991—, tng. com. 1991, tng. exam com. 1991, chmn. corp. rels. com. 1991-95, Armand Hammer award, 1988-89), Soc. U. Surgeons, Tex. Med. Assn., Tex. Surgical Soc., Am. Inst. Cancer Rsch. (mem. grant review panel no. 2, 1987—). Office: Ellis Fischel Cancer Center 115 Business Loop 70 W Columbia MO 65203

OTENASEK, RICHARD JOSEPH, neurological surgeon; b. Balt., July 24, 1932; s. Richard Joseph and Mary Catherine (Hellman) O.; m. Margaret Dixon Bagli, Jan. 4, 1958; children: Catherine D., Elizabeth Page, Richard III, Frank H., John H. AB, Loyola Coll., 1954; MD, Johns Hopkins U., 1958. Diplomate Am. Bd. Neurol. Surgery. Surg. intern Johns Hopkins Hosp., Balt., 1958-59, asst. resident in neurosurgery, 1960-63, resident in neurosurgery, 1964, instr. neurosurgery, 1965-74, asst. prof. neurosurgery, 1974-93, assoc. prof. neurosurgery, 1993—; chief divsn. neurosurgery Greater Balt. Med. Ctr., Towson, Md., 1970-86; chief divsn. neurosurgery St. Joseph Med. Ctr., Towson, Md., 1991—, trustee, 1992—. Sr. asst. surgeon USPHS, 1959-61. Named Knight Sovereign Mil. Order of Malta. Fellow ACS (chmn. com. on applicants Md. chpt. 1987-92); mem. Am. Assn. Neurol. Surgeons, Congress Neurol. Surgeons, So. Neurosurg. Soc., Md. Neurosurg. Soc. (pres. 1985-88). Office: 120 Sister Pierre Dr Towson MD 21204

OTIS, RICHARD DICKINSON, pathologist; b. Meriden, Conn., Dec. 26, 1924; s. Fessendon Newport and Anna (Gerstenmaier) O.; m. Mary Tourtellot Hamlen, June 10, 1949; children: James H., Richard D. Jr., Christopher N., John B. Student premed. tng. program, Trinity Coll., 1945; MD, Yale U., 1949. Diplomate Am. Bd. Pathology, Internat. Bd. Cytopathology. Pathologist Sch. Medicine Yale U., New Haven, Conn., 1952-55; sr. pathologist, dir. anatomic pathology Hartford (Conn.) Hosp., Md., 1955-86; cons. pathologist Hartford (Conn.) Hosp., 1986—. Contbr. articles to profl. jours. Lt. USN, 1950-52. T. Stewart Hamilton grantee TSH Found.; Harvard U. fellow, 1979. Mem. AMA, Internat. Acad. pathologists, Internat. Acad. Cytology, New Eng. Cancer Soc., Coll. Am. Pathologists. Republican. Home and Office: 181 Meadow Neck Rd East Falmouth MA 02536-7712

OTNESS, SHIRLEY, retired nurse; b. Hedgesville, Mont., Nov. 3, 1931; d. Peter Loren Manaige and Marie (Harding) Manaige Steele; m. Les Otenss, Oct. 3, 1953; children: Janet R., Michael J., Sue A. Otness Pattyn. Diploma, St. Joseph's Sch. Nursing, 1952. RN, Mont. Charge nurse Teton Meml. Hosp., Choteau, Mont., 1952-53, 68-76; spl. duty nurse Teton Meml. Hosp., Choteau, 1957-64, staff nurse, 1965; nurse Dr. McAuley, Choteau, 1953-54; head nurse Teton County Nursing Home, Choteau, 1966-67, charge nuse, 1985-89, asst. dir. nursing, 1990-95; dental asst. Dr. Wibbeler, Choteau, 1977-85. Mem. Hosp. Bd, Choteau, 1980's, Luth. Ch. Bd., 1980's; v.p. Trinity Luth. Ch. Women, 1990's. Mem. Soroptimist (life, treas. 1970's), Home Demonstration Club (pres. 1960), Multiple Sclerosis Soc., Multiple Sclerosis Assn. (support group Conrad chpt.), Good Sam Club. Home: 1641 8th Ln NW Choteau MT 59422-9205

OTOLORIN, MICHAEL PRICE, physician; b. Abeokuta, Ogun, Nigeria, Nov. 4, 1914; s. E.A. and E.S. (Ogungbe) O.; m. I. F. Martins, Jan. 31, 1946; 6 children. Cert., King's Coll., Lagos, 1929-32; degree, Sch. Medicine, Lagos, 1938, Queen Mary's Hosp., London, 1949-50, Royal Inst. Pub. Health and Hygiene, London, 1959-50. Lic. Royal Coll. Physicians, London. House physician, surgeon Native Adminstrn. Hosp. Adeoyo, Ibadan, 1938-39; asst. med. officer Gen. Hosp. Lagos, 1940-44, Gen. Hosp. Maiduguri, P/Harcourt, 1944-45; med. officer G.H. Llorin, G.H. Offa, Nigeria, 1946-48, City Hosp. Kano, Gen Hosp. Wukari, Gen. Hosp. Ilorin, 1951-54; sr. med. officer Ibadan, 1955-57; chief health officer Western Region Nigeria, 1960-65; chief med. adviser to fed. govt. Lagos H.Q., 1965-69; ret.; v.p. World Health Assembly, Geneva, 1968, chmn. adminstrn., 1969, rep., Liberia, Monrovia, Sierralone, Freetown, 1969-75; chmn. Nursing and Midwifery Coun. Nigeria, 1965-69, Med. Coun. Nigeria, 1965-69; lectr. in field. Pres. Christian Social Union St. Peter's Cathedral; v.p. church Missionary Soc., Lagos. World Health Assembly fellow, 1960-61, 70; Order of St. John, 1969, DFMC Disting. fell, Med. Coll. Nigeria, 1994; recipient Merit award Christ Ch. Cathedral, Lagos, 1996, Archbishop of Nigeria & Diocesan Synod of Lagos, 1996. Fellow Med. Coll. Pub. Health, West African Coll. Physicians; mem. Med. and Dental Coun. Nigeria, (chmn. 1988—), Assn. Community Physicians Nigeria (pres. 1988—). Home: 5 Afolabi Lesi St, Ilupeju, Lagos Nigeria Office: 25 Ahmed Onibudo St, Victoria Island, Lagos Nigeria

O'TOOLE, EDWARD THOMAS, JR., microbiologist, educator; b. Frederick, Md., July 7, 1933; s. Edward Thomas and Margaret Russelle (Dorsey) O'T.; B.S., U. Md., 1958; postgrad. Balt. Med. Campus, 1959-66, Loyola Coll., 1960; Sc.M., Johns Hopkins Sch. Hygiene and Public Health, 1971; Ph.D., Union Grad. Inst., 1977; m. Edith Helen Stimson, Apr. 19, 1958; children: Shirley Hope, Edward Thomas III, Eugene Stanley. Tchr., dept. chmn., audio-visual coordinator Baltimore County Bd. Edn., Towson, Md., 1958-60; chief microbiologist St. Joseph Hosp., Balt., 1960-64; cons. microbiology and cytopathology Greater Balt. Med. Ctr. (formerly Hosp. for Women Md., Balt.), 1964-65; microbiologist Becton, Dickinson & Co., Hunt Valley, Md., 1964-65, chief microbiologist Biol. Safety and Control Labs., 1965-68; dir. sterility svcs. and clin. lab. Huntingdon Rsch. Ctr.,Inc., Balt., 1968-72; tchr. biology, health and social scis. Balt. City Bd. Edn., 1972-94, Community Coll. Balt., 1985-94, Dundalk Community Coll., Balt., 1988-93, Catonsville Community Coll., 1990-93, Essex Community Coll., 1990-93; microbiologist FDA, 1978-86; sr. partner firm E squared plus 3, Glyndon, Md., 1969—; cons. sterility svcs. and clin. lab., also microbial limits. Vol. instr. cardio-pulmonary resuscition and firearms safety; testing counselor Boy Scouts Am. Served with AUS, 1956-58. Registered specialist pathogenic microbiologist, and pub. health microbiologist specialist Nat. Registry. Mem. Am., Md. socs. med. technologists, Am. Soc. Clin. Pathologists, Am. Soc. Cytology, AAAS, Am. Inst. Biol. Scis., Am. Soc. Microbiology (sec.-treas. Md. br. 1969-74, spl. chmn. clin. meeting 1970, mem. archives com. 1974-80), Inst. Food Tech. Roman Catholic. Home: Geist Rd Glyndon MD 21071-5001 Office: PO Box 303 Riderwood MD 21139-0303

O'TOOLE, MICHAEL DORAN, psychologist; b. N.Y.C., Dec. 22, 1947; s. Lawrence Aloysius and Edith Cordella (Fralick) O'T.; m. Regina Holliday, Sept. 12, 1987; 1 child, Meredith Doran. BA, Am. U., 1970, MA, 1974; tng. group therapy, U. N.C., 1978. Cert. adult correctional officer, N.C., 1975, police info. network ltd., N.C., 1980, youth correctional officer, Dept. Human Resources, 1981, advanced youth correctional, N.C., 1983, profl. lectr., N.C., 1984, criminal justice instr., N.C., 1987, sheriff's edn. ltd. lectr., N.C., 1989, health svc. provider-psychology assoc., N.C., 1994. From recreation staff to asst. dir. Program for Mentally Retarded and Physically Handicapped Ctr, Washington, 1970-74; staff psychologist N.C. Dept. Corrections, McLeansville, 1975-81; chief psychologist Stonewall Jackson Sch., Concord, 1981—; instr. Ctrl. Piedmont C.C., Charlotte, N.C., 1984-88, N.C. Justice Acad., Salemberg, 1989-91. Photojournalist in field. Singer Christ Ch., Charlotte, 1981—. Mem. Psi Chi. Home: 2432 Oak Leigh Dr Charlotte NC 28262 Office: Stonewall Jackson Sch Dept Human Resources 1484 Old Charlotte Rd Concord NC 28027

OTT, CLARICE JEAN, social worker; b. Delhi, N.Y., June 18, 1944; d. Luther Ernest and Clara Grace (Helman) O. BA in English, Elizabethtown Coll., 1966; MSW, U. Pitts., 1973. Cert. social worker; lic. social worker, Pa. Tchr. secondary English World Ministries, Ch. of the Brethren, Nigeria, West Africa, 1966-69; caseworker Westmoreland County Bd. Assistance, Greensburg, Pa., 1970-73, social worker, 1973-75; social worker, counselor Dundalk Youth Svc. Ctr., Balt., 1975-83, supr. counseling svcs., 1976-83; family counselor New Day, Inc., Johnstown, Pa., 1983-84; social worker Conemaugh Valley Meml. Hosp., Johnstown, Pa., 1984—. Mem. NASW. Mem. Ch. of the Brethren. Home: 1100 Grove Ave Windber PA 15963-1562

OTT, ELINOR WHITFIELD, health services administrator; b. Fulton, Ala., Oct. 24, 1943; d. Oscar F. and Rubynell (Wade) Whitfield; m. Clayburn Ott, July 23, 1960; children: Kevin, Darnelle Ott Lewis, Ryan. Student, Am. Med. Records Assn., Chgo., 1975. Accredited in medical records tech., Ala. Health info. svcs. dir. II dept. mental health/retardatoin Thomasville (Ala.) Mental Health Rehab. Ctr., 1965—. Bd. dirs. 310 dual Disability Mental Retardation, Grove Hill, Ala., 1995—; sec. Health Information Task Force Subcom., Montgomery, Ala., 1995-96, mem., 1990—. Mem. Ala. Health Information Mgmt. Assn., Sandflat Home Ext. Club (pres. 1994—). Methodist. Home: Rt 2 Box 440 Grove Hill AL 36451 Office: DMH/MR Thomasville MH Rehab Ctr PO Box 309 Thomasville AL 36784

OTT, PAULA NISBET, nursing and emergency medical technician educator; b. Peoria, Ill., Nov. 21, 1944; d. Paul McCracken and Melcena Ellen (Arvin) Nisbet; m. Franklin Leo Ott, Nov. 8, 1966; children: Penelope, Jason, Cynthia. BSN, Ill. Wesleyan Coll., 1966; MEd, Northeast La. U., 1977. Cert. Indsl. Audiometric Tech., ARC Instr. First Aid and CPR, Basic and Advanced EMT Instr. Operating room supr. Glenwood Regional Med. Ctr., West Monroe, La., 1966; staff RN Rockford (Ill.) Meml. Hosp., 1966; mental health community nurse H. Douglas Singer Zone Ctr., Rockford, 1966-69; La.; instr. Delta Ouachita Regional Tech. Inst., West Monroe, 1969-88, dept. head health occupations, 1988—; nursing cons. GM Fisher Guide, Monroe, 1989—. Author: (with others) Cole's Basic Nursing Skills, 1991, Instructor's Guide and Concepts, 1991. La. Lung Assn. scholar, New Orleans, 1980; named Educator of Yr., La. Votech. Tchr. of Yr. State Dept. Edn., Baton Rouge, 1986. Mem. Am. Vocat. Assn. (policy com., region IV educator of yr., 1982), Nat. Assn. Health Occupation Tchrs. (treas., 1980-82, outstanding svc. award; 1983), La. Vocat. Assn. (parlimentary historian exec. coun., outstanding svc. award, 1982), La. Assn. Health Occupations Edn. (pres., past pres., exec. coun., tchr. of year, 1982), La. Soc. EMT Instr. Coords. (edn. com. chair, 1986—), Sigma Theta Tau Internat. Democrat. Mem. Assembly of God Ch. Home: RR 2 Box 198 Farmerville LA 71241-9582 Office: Delta-Ouachita Campus La Tech Coll 609 Vocational Pky West Monroe LA 71292-0127

OTTAVIANI, REGINA, psychologist; b. Towanda, Pa., Oct. 1, 1957; d. Julius James and Helen (Shanowski) O. BA, Bloomsburg State Coll., Pa., 1979; MA, The Am. U., Washington, 1983, PhD, 1985. Lic. psychologist, Md. Intern Crownsville Md. Hosp. Ctr., 1984-85; post-doctoral fellow U. Pa. Ctr. Cognitive Therapy, Phila., 1985-86; clin. practice in cognitive therapy Chevy Chase, Md., 1986—. Office: 4701 Willard Ave # 230 Bethesda MD 20815-4637

OTTE, LYNDA ELLEN, neonatal nurse; b. Washington, Apr. 14, 1946; d. Robert Grover and Esther Ellen (Watson) O. BSN, U. Md., 1968. RNC; cert. Nat. Cert. Corp. for the Ob-Gyn. and Neonatal Nursing Specialties. Staff nurse Children's Hosp., Washington, 1968-73, 76-78, nursery instr., 1973-74, primary nurse II, 1978-85, clin. mgr. I, 1985-88, 91-93, clin. nurse III, 1988-91; clin. nurse II, 1993-94; staff nurse George Washington U. Hosp., Washington, 1975-76, Anne Arundel Med. Ctr., Annapolis, Md., 1994—. Treas. bd. dirs. Prince George's Oak Pond Homeowners Assn., Bowie, Md., 1987—; vol. for ann. fund drive Am. Cancer Soc. Residential Campaign, Bowie, 1989, 91-93, 96; vol. Mothers March of Dimes, 1993-96, Am. Diabetes Assn. fund drive, 1994—, Nat. Kidney Found. Ask Your Neighbor campaign, 1996, Am. Lung Assn. of Md., 1996. Mem. Nat. Assn. Neonatal Nurses (charter), Washington Met. Assn. Neonatal Nurses (charter, co-chair strategic planning com. 1990-92, pres.-elect 1992-94, pres. 1994-96, co-chmn. mem. com. 1996—). Baptist. Home: 3060 New Oak Ln Bowie MD 20716-1350 Office: Anne Arundel Med Ctr Rebecca Clatanoff Pavilion 2001 Medical Pky Annapolis MD 21401

OTTEN, JOHN JOSEPH, oral-maxillofacial surgeon; b. Peoria, Ill., Oct. 22, 1963; s. Gerald Thomas and Delores (Mathews) O.; m. Molly Crawford, Aug. 12, 1963; children: Kathleen Kelly, Margaret Patricia, Steven Crawford. BS, Creighton U., 1985; DDS, U. Nebr., 1989; MD, La. State U., 1992. Resident in maxillofacial surgery La. State U. Med. Ctr., New Orleans, 1989—. With U.S. Army, 1982-96. Mem. AMA, ADA, Am. Assn. Oral and Maxillofacial Surgeons, So. Med. Assn. Republican. Roman Catholic. Home: 2807 N Knoxville Ave Peoria IL 61604-2869

OTTENSTEIN, DONALD, psychiatrist; b. N.Y.C., Feb. 2, 1922; s. Morris Zachary and Sadelle (Fertig) O.; m. Leah May Helpern, Dec. 24, 1944; children: Paul, John, Beth, Daniel. BS, Harvard U., 1942; MD, Columbia U. Intern Boston City Hosp., 1948-49; resident Mass. Mental Health Ctr., Roston, Mass., 1950-53; fellow D.O. Thom Clinic, Boston, 1955-56; cons. Met. State Hosp., Waltham, Mass., 1955-58; dir. South Shore Mental Health Ctr., Quincy, Mass., 1959-67; asst. psychiatrist Beth Israel Hosp., Boston, 1959—; attending psychiatrist McLean Hosp., Belmont, Mass., 1970-85, Newton Wellesley Hosp., 1979-85; asst. clin. prof. Harvard U. Med. Sch., Boston, 1974-89. Contbr. articles to profl. jours. Served to capt. U.S. Army, 1953-55. Fellow Mass. Med. Soc., Am. Psychiat. Assn., Am. Orthopsychiat. Assn., Am. Acad. Child Psychiatry. Home and Office: 65 Gale Rd Belmont MA 02178-3945

OTTINGER, MARY LOUISE, podiatrist; b. Valley City, N.D., July 8, 1956; d. Roy A. and Harriet A. Ottinger. BS, N.D. State U., 1978; D of Podiatric Medicine, Scholl. Coll. Podiatric Med., Chgo., 1983. Diplomate Am. Bd. Podiatric Surgery. Resident in podiatric medicine J.A. Haley VA Hosp., Tampa, Fla., 1983-84; podiatrist Med. Ctr. Podiatry Group, Augusta, Ga., 1984—. Author: (with others) Podiatric Dermatology, 1986. Fellow Am. Coll. Foot Surgeons; mem. Am. Podiatric Med. Assn., Ga. Podiatric Med. Assn., Am. Diabetes Assn. Methodist. Office: Med Ctr Podiatry Group 1515 Laney Walker Blvd Augusta GA 30904-5827

OTTO, CHARLES EDWARD, health care administrator; b. Somerville, N.J., Nov. 12, 1946; s. Hans and Virginia (Hegeman) O.; m. Wendy Ann Halsey; June 26, 1971; children: Eric, C. Halsey, Robert. BA, Hobart Coll., Geneva, N.Y., 1968; MBA, U. Pa., 1973. Adminstrv. asst. Mass. Gen. Hosp., Boston, 1970-71; adminstrv. resident Hosp. of U. of Pa., Phila., 1973; adminstrv. asst. Norwalk (Conn.) Hosp., 1974-76; exec. dir. Waveny Care Ctr., New Canaan, Conn., 1977-93; adminstr. Avery Heights Retirement Village, Hartford, Conn., 1994—; bd. chmn. Conn. Assn. of Non-Profit Facilities for the Aged, Wallingford, 1984-86; chmn. regional adv. group Conn. Community Care, Inc., Norwalk, 1983-85. Bd. chmn. S.W. Fairfield Am. Cancer Soc., Norwalk, 1985-87. Served to lt. (j.g.) USNR, 1968-70. Mem. Wharton Healthcare Alumni Assn. (bd. dirs. 1993-94), Rocky Point Club. Episcopalian. Home: 12 Lake Dr S Riverside CT 06878-2016

OTTONELLO, CARLO MAURIZIO, radiologist; b. Savona, Liguria, Italy, July 7, 1965; s. Ciacomo and Rosa (Arecco) O. MD cum laude, Genova (Italy) U., 1991. Resident rschr. radiology dept. Genova U., 1992—. Contbr. articles to profl. jours. 2d lt. M.C., Italian Army, 1994-95. Mem. Italian Soc. Sport Podology (mem. steeering com. 1995), Italian Assn. Radiology, Italian Mil. Med. Assn., Italian Assn. Res. Officers. Office: Genoa U Radiology Dept, Largo Rosanna Benzi 10, 16132 Genoa Italy

OU, LO-CHANG, physiology educator; b. Shanghai, China, Oct. 16, 1930; came to U.S., 1964; m. Cynthia Ou, June 10, 1960; children; Winnie, Edward, Emily, Joseph. BS, Peking U., Beijing, 1954; PhD, Dartmouth Coll., 1971. Teaching asst., dept. biochemistry Peking U., Beijing, 1954-60, lectr., dept. biochemistry, 1960-62; demonstrator, dept. physiology Hong Kong U., 1962-64; asst. prof., dept. physiology Dartmouth Med. Sch., Hanover, N.H., 1977-80, assoc. prof., dept. physiology, 1980-85, rsch. prof., dept. physiology, 1985—. NIH rsch. grantee, 1977—. Mem. Am. Physiol. Soc. Office: Dartmouth Med Sch Dept Physiology Lebanon NH 03756

OUALLINE, VIOLA JACKSON, psychologist; b. Edna, Tex., Oct. 17, 1927; d. S.R. Jackson and Myrtle Mae Wood; m. Charles M. Oualline Jr., Sept. 3, 1949; children: Stephen, Susan, Shari. BS, U. Houston, 1949; MS, North Tex. State U., 1962, PhD, 1975. Phys. therapist Hermann Hosp., Houston, 1948-49, pvt. practice, Austin, Tex., 1949-54, Miller Orthopedic Clinic, Charlotte, N.C., 1956-57; psychologist Dallas Easter Seal Soc., 1963-81, dir. psychology dept., 1981-93; pvt. practice, 1993—; psychol. cons. Mesquite Ind. Sch. Dist., Tex., 1974—, Duncanville Sch. Dist., Tex., 1974-76, Grand Prarie Ind. Sch. Dist., Tex., 1976-79. Mem. Am. Psychol. Assn., Tex. Psychol. Assn., Dallas Psychol. Assn., Am. Assn. Counseling Devel., Council for Exceptional Children, Chi Omega Mother's Club. Baptist. Avocations: reading; bicycle riding. Office: 11311 N Central Expy Ste 208 Dallas TX 75243

OUDHOF, HERMAN A. J., dentist; b. Utrecht, The Netherlands, Jan. 30, 1943; s. Abraham Oudhof and Jannelje Barneveldtvan; m. Johanne W. Volbrecht. Mem. ISLD, WALT. Office: Acta, Louwesweg 1, 1066 FA Amsterdam The Netherlands

OUELLETTE, DANIEL RONALD, pulmonary and critical care medicine specialist; b. Detroit, Sept. 9, 1956; s. Lois Emma Schramm Ouellette; m. Julie G. Michaelson, Nov. 27, 1978. BS, Pa. State U., 1977; MS, U. Pitts., 1980, MD, 1984. Diplomate Am. Bd. Internal Medicine, Am. Bd. Pulmonary Medicine, Am. Bd. Critical Care Medicine. Commd. U.S. Army, 1984—, advanced through grades to lt. col.; intern William Beaumont Army Med. Ctr., El Paso, Tex., 1984-85, resident in medicine, 1985-87, chief med. resident, 1987-88; pulmonary fellow Brooke Army Med. Ctr., San Antonio, 1988-90, critical care fellow, 1990-91, staff physician, 1994—; staff physician Fitzsimons Army Med. Ctr., Denver, 1991-94. Contbr. articles to profl. jours. Decorated Army Commendation medal, commissioned at 2nd lt., attained lt. col. 1994. Fellow Am. Coll. Chest Physicians; mem. Am. Thoracic Soc. Office: Brooke Army Med Ctr Pulmonary Clinic Fort Sam Houston TX 78234

OUELLETTE, JANE LEE YOUNG, biology educator; b. Charlotte, N.C., Dec. 29, 1929; d. James Thomas and Nancy Isabel (Yarbrough) Young; m. Armand Roland Ouellette, Aug. 3, 1951 (dec. Oct. 1984); children—Elizabeth Anne, James Young, Emily Jane, Frances Lee. B.A., Winthrop Coll., 1950; M.A., Oberlin Coll., 1952; postgrad. Coll. Medicine, Baylor U., 1974, U. Tex.-Houston, 1976-83, Tex. Woman's U., 1980-82. Lic. tchr., Tex. Tchr. Maria Regina High Sch., Hartsdale, N.Y., 1969-70, Spring Ind. Sch. System, Tex., 1972-78; coordinator biology program, prof., North Harris County Coll., Houston, 1979—. Meadow's fellow Baylor Coll. Medicine, 1989. Mem. Internat. Assn. for Study of Pain, Internat. Pain Found., N.Y. Acad. Sci., AAAS, Internat. Chronobiol. Soc., People to People Internat. Democrat. Home: 1619 Big Horn Dr Houston TX 77090-1862 Office: North Harris County Coll 2700 W Thorne Dr Houston TX 77073-3426

OUELLETTE, PAUL L., orthodontist; b. Oakland, Calif., July 23, 1944; s. Francis Patrick and Lanette (Heiser) O.; m. Patricia Bennett, June 12, 1975; children: Cindy, Jonathan, Jason, Danielle. BS, Tex. A&M U., 1966; DDS with honors, Loyola Sch. Dentistry, 1970, MS, cert. orthodontics, 1972. Asst. prof. orthodontics Emory U., Atlanta, 1972-74; pvt. practice Atlanta Orthodontic Care Ctrs., 1972-82, Family Dental Svcs., Melbourne, Fla., 1982-87, Dental Specialists, Winter Park, Fla., 1987—, Pickron Orthodontic Care, Atlanta, 1993—; v.p. Century 2001 Inc., Indian Harbour Beach, Fla., 1975—. Contbg. editor: Jour. Clin. Orthodontics, 1972-82; contbr. articles and revs. to profl. jours. Rsch. grantee U.S. Dept. Health, 1974. Mem. ADA, Am. Assn. Orthodontists, N.W. Dist. Dental Soc., Am. Track Assn., Atlanta Track Assn., Spacecoast Runners. Episcopalian. Home: 810 Mount Vernon Hwy NW Atlanta GA 30327 Office: Dental Specialists Winter Park Mall 500 N Orlando Ave Winter Park FL 32789

OVEREYNDER, JENNY COMPANJEN, human services administrator, social worker; b. The Hague, The Netherlands, July 30, 1938; d. Henry N. Companjen and Martina (Houtman) Udinktencate; m. Bernard W. Overeynder, Sept. 8, 1961 (dec. Nov. 1989); children: Ann, Julie, Helen. BS, U. Leiden, The Netherlands, 1960; MSW, Syracuse U., 1979. Cert. social worker; clin. social worker, N.Y. Social worker Hillside Children's Ctr., Rochester, N.Y., 1979-81; social worker birth defects clinic U. Rochester Med. Ctr., 1981-85, sr. social worker univ. program for devel. disabilities, 1985-94, project dir. tng. program in aging and devel. disabilities, 1987-94, assoc. in health svcs., 1994—; pres. Companion Assocs., Niskayuma, N.Y., 1994—; mem. aging com. N.Y. State Devel. Disabilities Planning Coun., Albany, 1987—. Mem. NASW, Am. Assn. Mental Retardation, Gerontol. Soc. Am. Office: U Rochester Med Ctr SCDD Box 671 601 Elmwood Ave Rochester NY 14642

OVERHOLSER, DONALD LEE, microbiology educator; b. Independence, Oreg., June 3, 1934; s. Ralph Donald Overholser and Murl (Little) Apperson; m. Barbara E. Gamberg, June 9, 1956; 1 child, Kristin E. Overholser Stewart. BS, Oreg. State U., 1961, MS, 1968; postgrad., U. Mont., 1961-63. Grad. teaching asst. of microbiology U. Mont., Missoula, 1961-63; sr. aquatic biologist Fish Com. of Oreg., Clackamas and Corvallis, 1963-66; microbiologist Oreg. State U., Corvallis, 1966-78, supervising microbiologist, 1978-88, asst. prof., 1981-88, sr. instr. microbiology, chief advisor undergrad. students, 1988-92; mem. emeritus faculty, 1992—. Author: Pathogenic Microbiology Laboratory Manual, 1990. With USCG, 1953-57. Recipient Gov.'s Mgmt. Svc. award State of Oreg., 1983, Oreg. State U. Dar Reese Excellence in Advising award, 1989. Mem. Am. Soc. for Microbiology, Masons, Elks, Sigma Xi, Phi Sigma. Office: Oreg State U Dept Microbiology Nash Hall # 220 Corvallis OR 97331-3804

OVERMAN, DENNIS ORTON, anatomist, educator; b. Union City, Ind., Oct. 16, 1943; s. E. Orton and Marjorie J. (Mills) O.; m. Sue A. Sappenfield, June 4, 1966; children: Andrew D., Michael M., Amy S. BA, Bowling Green State U., 1965; MS, U. Mich., 1967, PhD, 1970. Tchr. Community Sch., Tehran, Iran, 1967-68; rsch. assoc. U. Colo., Boulder, 1970-71; from instr. to asst. prof. dept. anatomy W.Va. U., Morgantown, 1971-76; assoc. prof. U. W. Va., Morgantown, 1976—; vis. lectr. U. B.C., Vancouver, Can., 1979; vis. rschr. U. Turku, Finland, 1993; clin. assoc. prof. dept. orthodontics, W.Va. U., Morgantown, 1985—. Author: (book chpt.) Bioethics and the Beginning of Life, 1990; editor: English transl. of Japanese textbook; mem. abstract com. Cleft Palate Jour., 1976—; contbr. articles to profl. jours. Bd. dirs. Christian Help, Inc., Morgantown, 1989—. Mem. Soc. for Devel. Biology, Teratology Soc. Democrat. Mem. Mennonite Ch. Home: 461 Overhill St Morgantown WV 26505-4824 Office: U W Va Dept Anatomy Morgantown WV 26506

OVERSTREET, JOHN TYLER, psychological examiner, therapist; b. Rockwood, Tenn., Dec. 5, 1958; s. E.M. and Jewell Lee (Crabtree) O.; m. Laura Jean Kiriluk, July 6, 1985; children: Abigail Mariah, Olivia Shiloh. BS, Tenn. Technol. U., 1983, MA, 1984. Lic. profl. counselor, Tenn., psychol. examiner, real estate affiliate broker, Tenn. Therapist Plateau Mental Health System, Cookeville, Tenn., 1986-88; psychol. examiner Plateau Mental Health System, Cookevillle, Tenn., 1988-89, sex abuse specialist, 1989, program mgr., 1989-92; social svc. worker Camelot Care Ctr., Inc., Kingston, Tenn., 1992-93; psychologist Health Mgmt. Sys. of Am., Harriman, Tenn., 1993—. Mem. APA (assoc.), Soc. for Personality and Social Psychology, Assn. for Treatment Sexual Abusers, Tenn. Assn. Psychol. Examiners (clin.), Tenn. Hist. Soc., Tenn. Assn. Child Care. Home: PO Box 966 Kingston TN 37763-0966 Office: Health Mgmt Sys Am 504 Dogwood Dr Harriman TN 37763

OVERSTREET, ROBIN MILES, parasitologist, researcher, educator; b. Eugene, Oreg., June 1, 1939; s. Robin M. and Laura (McGinty) O.; m. Kim Bunton, Mar. 31, 1964; children—Brian, Eric. B.A. in Gen. Biology, U. Oreg., 1963; M.S. in Marine Biology, U. Miami, 1966, Ph.D., in Marine Biology, 1968. NIH postdoctoral fellow in parasitology Tulane U. Med. Sch., New Orleans, 1968-69; head sect. parasitology Gulf Coast Rsch. Lab., Ocean Springs, Miss., 1969-92, sr. rsch. scientist, 1992—; adj. prof. U. So. Miss., U. Miss., La. State U., others; vis. prof. U. Queensland, 1984, 92, 95. Served with USN, 1956-62. Nat. Marine Fisheries Svc. grantee, 1969—, Miss.-Ala. Sea 1973-78, U.S.-Israel Binat. Sci. Found. 1974-75, Nat. Cancer Inst. 1982-88, USDA, 1985—, EPA 1990—, NSF, 1994—, others. Mem. Am. Soc. Parasitologists (editl. bd., assoc. editor 1979-95, v.p. 1991), Helminthological Soc. Washington (editl. bd. 1974—), Am. Micros. Soc. (bd. reviewers 1981-94), Am. Fish. Soc. (assoc. editor 1993—), Southeastern Soc. Parasitologists (v.p. 1991, pres. 1996), others. Author: Marine Maladies: Worms, Germs and Other Symbionts from the Northern Gulf of Mexico, 1978; contbr. numerous articles to profl. jours. Home: 13821 Paraiso Rd Ocean Springs MS 39564-2584 Office: Gulf Coast Rsch Lab Ocean Springs MS 39566-7000

OVERTON, SARITA ROSA, psychologist; b. South Haven, Mich., June 7, 1954; d. Samuel Edward and Rosa Jane (McGuire) O. BA in Psychology with honors, Mich. State U., 1976, MA in Rehab. Counseling, 1978, MA in Counseling Psychology, 1987, PhD in Counseling Psychology, 1988. Lic. psychologist, Mich. Dir. Job Club, Capital Area Community Svcs., Lansing, Mich., 1978-84; instr. rehab. counseling master's program Mich. State U., East Lansing, 1981-82, program teaching asst., 1985-87, coord. career assistance project, 1984, 84-85, clin. trainee Counseling Ctr., 1986, rsch. asst. disability mgmt. project, 1985-87; clin. trainee St. Lawrence Hosp., Lansing, 1986-87, psychologist Psychol. Svcs. and Addictions Clinic, 1987-91; psychologist Comprehensive Psychol. Svcs., P.C., East Lansing, 1990-95; pvt. practice psychologist Meridian Health and Wellness Ctr., East Lansing, 1995—; conf. and clin. presenter in field. Contbr. articles to profl. publs. Recipient Presdl. recognition award Mich. Rehab. Assn., 1986; grantee Nat. Inst. Handicapped Rsch., 1985; dissertation rsch. fellow Mich. State U., 1985. Mem. APA. Democrat. Office: Meridian Health and Wellness 139 Lake Lansing Rd Ste 200 East Lansing MI 48823

OVERWEG, NORBERT IDO ALBERT, physician; b. Enschede, The Netherlands; s. Ido and Bella Theresa (Lievenboom) O.; MD, U. Amsterdam, 1957; m. Angelique de Gorter; children: Eleonore, Elizabeth, Harold. Intern, Univ. Amsterdam Hosp., 1958-60; resident Rochester (N.Y.) Gen. Hosp., 1961-62; postdoctoral fellow dept. pharmacology Columbia U. Coll. Physicians and Surgeons, 1962-65; instr. dept. public health Columbia U., 1965-66; rsch. assoc. dept. surgery Columbia U., 1967-71; rsch. collaborator, asst. attending physician Brookhaven Nat. Lab., 1966-67; asst. prof. dept. physiology and pharmacology N.Y. U., 1971-78; cons. Lung Rsch. Ctr., Yale U. Sch. Medicine, 1972-73; pvt. practice medicine specializing in internal medicine, N.Y.C., 1967—; attending staff St. Clare's Hosp. and Health Center, Cabrini Med. Ctr.; clin. investigator antihypertension, anti-depressant, anti-anxiety, Alzheimer's Disease, migraine headache, panick attack, and gastro-intestinal drugs. NIH fellow, 1964-65. Mem. Am. Soc. Pharmcology and Exptl. Therapeutics, Am. Physiol. Soc., Am. Soc. Hypertension, Am. Coll. Clin. Pharmacology, N.Y. Acad. Scis., AAAS, AAUP, Royal Dutch Soc. Advancement of Medicine, Harvey Soc., Netherlands Am. Med. Soc., Eastern Hypertension Soc., N.Y. County Med. Soc., Med. Soc. of N.Y., Sigma Xi. Club: Netherlands of N.Y., Inc. Contbr. articles to profl. jour. Office: 133 E 73rd St New York NY 10021-3556

OWEIDA, STEVEN WASSEL, vascular surgeon; b. Fairburn, Ohio, Apr. 1, 1957; s. Nizer Nour and Margaret Louise (Antoua) O.; m. Patricia Jo. Minarchek, Sept. 7, 1985; children: Lindsey, Ryan, Erin, Jenne, Brenden. BS, U. Pitts., 1979; MD, Emory U., 1983. Diplomate Am. Bd. Surgeons; cert. added qualification in gen. vascular surgery. Resident in surgery Emory U. Hosp., Atlanta, 1983-88, fellow in vascular surgery, 1988-90; ptnr. Vascular Surgical Assocs., Marrietta, Ga., 1990—; staff surgeon Promina Kenneston Hosp., Marietta, 1990—, Promina Cross Hosp., Anstell, Ga., 1990—; mem. exec. com. Promina Kennston Hosp., Marietta, 1993; chmn. Los Svc. Com., Promina Kenneston Hosp., Marietta, 1993-95, mem. med. care evaluation com., 1994—; bd. dirs. Promina N.W. Health Systems, Marietta, Promina N.W. Health Network, 1995—. Contbr. articles to Jour. of Vascular Surgery, Surgical Forum, The Am. Surgeon; inventor and patentee (exptl. drugs) 1990. Pres. Herdoya Farm Homeowners Assn., Marietta, 1994-95. Fellow Am. Coll. of Surgeons; mem. So. Assn. of Vascular Sugreons, Med. Assn. Ga. (del. 1993—), Southeastern Surgical Congress, Cobb County Med. Soc. (mem. exec. com. 1992-94), Atlanta Vascular Soc. Office: Vascular Surgical Assocs. 140 Vann St Ste 340 Marietta GA 30060-7297

OWEN, BERNARD LAWTON, retired biology educator; b. Presidio, Tex., Nov. 10, 1929; s. Willis Lawton and Clara Esther (McEachern) O.; m. Colleen Young, Feb. 26, 1952; children: Cameron Lawton, Quentin Alan, Vincent Kyle. BS, Tex. A&M Coll., 1951, MS, 1954; PhD, Ala. Polytech. Inst., 1959. Entomologist USDA, Florence, S.C., 1958-59; asst. prof. Kans. Wesleyan U., Salina, 1959-65, prof. biology, 1966-95, ret., 1995; prof. emeritus Kans. Wesleyan U., 1996. 1st lt. inf. and M.S.C., U.S. Army, 1951-53. Mem. AAAS, Nat. Sci. Tchrs. Assn., Nat. Assn. Biology Tchrs., Soc. Coll. Tchrs. Sci., Nat. Assn. Advisors Health Professions, Human Anatomy and Physiology Soc., Kans. Acad. Sci. Office: Kans Wesleyan Univ 100 E Claflin Ave Salina KS 67401-6146

OWEN, DAVID BRUCE, pediatrician, educator; b. Albuquerque, Nov. 16, 1955; s. Donald Bruce and Ellen (Knox) O.; m. Karla Jo Kazilas, Jan. 1, 1981; children: Nicole, Jeffrey. BS, So. Meth. U., 1977; MD, U. Tex. Health Sci. Ctr., San Antonio, 1981. Diplomate Am. Bd. Psychiatry and Neurology, Am. Bd. Pediatrics. Pediatric intern Bexar County Hosp., 1981-82; resident in pediatrics, fellow in neurology U. Tex. Health Sci. Ctr., San Antonio, 1982-87; physician Dallas Pediatric Neurology Brain Tumor Clinic, 1987—; asst. clin. prof. Southwestern Med. Ctr., Dallas, 1987—; mem. staff Med. City Dallas, Children's Med. Ctr., Med. Ctr. Plano. Fellow Am. Acad. Pediatrics, Tex. Med. Assn., Am. Assn. Study Headache. Office: Dallas Pediatric Neurology 12801 N Central # 580 Dallas TX 75243

OWEN, DAVID MCINTOSH, physician; b. Gulfport, Miss., Oct. 6, 1935; s. Nat Jr. and Evelyn (McIntosh) O.; m. Sara Ann Cleveland, June 7, 1963; children: Susan, David Jr., Robert. BS, U. Miss., Oxford, 1956; MD, U. Miss., Jackson, 1960. Intern U. Tenn., Memphis, 1960-61; resident in internal medicine U. Miss., 1961-64, fellow in hematology and oncology, 1964-66; physician Hattiesburg (Miss.) Clinic, 1966—. Maj. USNG, 1961-71. Fellow ACP; mem. Am. Soc. Internal Medicine, Am. Soc. Clin. Oncology, Miss. State Med. Assn. (chmn. bd. trustees), Miss. State Med. Assn. (bd. trustees), Rotary Club (pres.). Office: Hattiesburg Clinic 415 S 28th Ave Hattiesburg MS 39401

OWEN, DUNCAN SHAW, JR., physician, medical educator; b. Fayetteville, N.C., Oct. 24, 1935; s. Duncan S. and Mary Gwyn (Hickerson) O.; m. Irene Lacy Rose, Oct. 22, 1966; children: Duncan Shaw III, Robert Burwell, Frances Gwyn. BS, U. N.C., 1957, MD, 1960. Diplomate Am. Bd. Internal Medicine (proctor 1977—). Intern Med. Coll. Va., Richmond, 1960-61; jr. asst. resident in medicine N.C. Meml. Hosp., Chapel Hill, 1961-62; asst. resident in medicine Med. Coll. Va., Richmond, 1964-65, fellow in rheumatic diseases, 1965-66; practice medicine specializing in internal medicine and rheumatology Richmond, Va., 1966—; instr. in medicine Med. Coll. Va., Richmond, 1966-67, asst. prof., 1967-71, assoc. prof., 1971-78, prof. dept. internal medicine, 1978—; Taliaferro/Scott Disting. prof. internal medicine Med. Coll. Va., Va. Commonwealth U., 1989—; dir. residency tng. Med. Coll. Va. Hosp.; dir. Rheumatology Clinics; mem. staff McGuire VA; dir. clin. tng. divsn. rheumatology, allergy, immunology, chmn. clin. activities comm., dept. internal mediine; chmn. med. adv. com. Richmond br. Arthritis Found., 1966-75, bd. dirs. 1966—, mem. nat. patient edn. com., 1979-80; med. advisor Social Security Adminstrn., HHS, 1967—; bd. dirs. Blue Shield Va., 1975-77, co-chmn. arthritis project Va. Regional Med. Program, 1975-76; bd. dirs. Univ. Internal Medicine Found., 1979—; prodr. Your Health TV series Va. Ednl. TV, 1978-79; prodr. Update in Medicine, Good Morning Virginia TV show, 1980; mem. various coms. in field. Contbr. numerous papers, chpts. in books, articles to profl. jours.; assoc. editor: Va. Med., 1978—; editorial reviewer Jour. AMA, 1979—, Arthritis Rheumatism, 1981—, Jour. Rheumatology, 1984—. Mem. usher's guild First Presbyn. Ch., Richmond, Va., 1966-70, deacon, 1974-77, chmn. of diaconate, 1976-77, elder, 1978—, chmn. witness com., 1978-80; co-chmn. physicians statewide capital funds campaign Va. Commn. U., 1986-87; bd. dirs. Mooreland Farms Assn., 1971-73, 77-81, Va. chpt. Arthritis Found., 1970-85; mem. Va. Mus., Richmond Symphony; bd. dirs. Richmond Area Health Care Coalition, 1980-84. Served to capt. MC, 1962-64. Recipient Army Commendation medal, 1964. Nat. Inst. Arthritis and Metabolic Diseases fellow, 1965-66; recipient Gerard B. Lambert award, 1974-75, Disting. Service award Arthritis Found., 1971. Fellow ACP, Am. Coll. Rheumatology; mem. AMA (expert on diagnostic and therapeutic tech. assessment program), Am. Rheumatism Assn. (exec. com. 1979-80), Richmond Acad. Medicine (pres. 1982, chmn. bd. 1983, parliamentarian 1988—), Med. Soc. Va. (com. on aging 1980-89, v.p. 1973, 75, del. 1972—, scholarship com. 1980-89), Richmond Soc. Internal Medicine (bd. dirs. 1971-73), Met. Richmond C. of C. (bd. dirs. 1981-94), Jr. Clin. Club (emeritus), Country Club Va., Custis Hunting and Fishing Club, Alpha Omega Alpha. Home: 8910 Brieryle Rd Richmond VA 23229-7704 Office: Med Coll Va Ambulatory Care Ctr PO Box 980647 Richmond VA 23298-0647

OWEN, HUGH THOMAS, dermatologist; b. Buffalo, July 6, 1947; s. Virgil Hugh and Jane (McKeown) O.; m. Barbara Jo Willette, June 7, 1969; children: Michelle Lynn, Barbara Ann, Hugh Thomas Jr. BS, Butler U., 1969; MD, Ind. U., Indpls., 1973. Intern St. Mary's Hosp., Evansville, Ind., 1973-74; fellow Marshfield (Wis.) Clinic, 1974-75; resident in dermatology Henry Ford Hosp., Detroit, 1975-77; pvt. practice Jeffersonville, Ind., 1977—. Mem. Am. Acad. Dermatology, So. Med. Assn., Ind. Med. Assn., Ky. Med. Assn., Ga. Med. Soc. Office: 320 W 13th St Jeffersonville IN 47130

OWEN, MINDY S., health facility administrator; b. Milw., June 13, 1951; d. Harold Lawrence and Lucille R. (Rute) Bender; m. William David Owen, Aug. 7, 1971; 1 child, Russell Timothy Cannon. BSN, Iowa Meth. Sch. Nursing, 1974. RN. Nurse ICU Milw. County Med. Complex, 1974-77; dir.

rehab. program Wesley Med. Ctr., Milw., 1977-84; regional dir. care mgmt. Intracorp, Chgo., 1984-91; gen. mgr. care mgmt. Neuro Care, Chgo., 1992-94; nat. dir. care mgmt. Quantum Health Resources, Indpls., 1994—; commr. Cert. of Case Mgrs., 1994—. Mem. Case Mgmt. Soc. Am. (pres.-elect 1989-91, pres. 1991-92, founder, bd. dirs., chair-elect 1996).

OWEN, RAY DAVID, biology educator; b. Genesee, Wis., Oct. 30, 1915; s. Dave and Ida (Hoeft) O.; m. June J. Weissenberg, June 24, 1939; 1 son, David G. BS, Carroll Coll., Wis., 1937, ScD, 1962; PhD, U. Wis., 1941, ScD, 1979; ScD, U. of Pacific, 1965. Asst. prof. genetics, zoology U. Wis., 1944-47; Gosney fellow Calif. Inst. Tech., Pasadena, 1946-47; assoc. prof. div. biology Calif. Inst. Tech., 1947-53, prof. biology, 1953-83, also chmn., v.p. for student affairs, dean of students, prof. emeritus, 1983—; research participant Oak Ridge Nat. Lab., 1957-58; Cons. Oak Ridge Inst. Nuclear Studies; mem. Pres.'s Cancer Panel. Author: (with A.M. Srb) General Genetics, 1952, 2d edit. (with A.M. Srb, R. Edgar), 1965; Contbr. articles to sci. jours. Recipient Gregor Mendel medal Czech Acad. Scis., 1965. Fellow AAAS; mem. Genetics Soc. Am. (pres., Thomas Hunt Morgan medal 1993), Am. Assn. Immunologists, Am. Soc. Human Genetics, Western Soc. Naturalists, Am. Soc. Zoologists, Am. Genetics Assn., Nat. Acad. Scis., Am. Acad. Arts and Scis., Am. Philos. Soc., Am. Acad. Allergy and Immunology (hon.), Internat. Soc. Animal Genetics (hon.), Sigma Xi. Home: 1583 Rose Villa St Pasadena CA 91106-3524 Office: Calif Inst Tech 156-29 156-29 Pasadena CA 91125

OWENS, ALBERT HENRY, JR., oncologist, educator; b. Staten Island, N.Y., Aug. 27, 1926; married, 1949; 4 children. BA, MD, Johns Hopkins U., 1949. Diplomate Am. Bd. Internal Medicine. Staff internal medicine Johns Hopkins U. Hosp., 1949-50, 52-53, 55-56; from instr. to assoc. prof. medicine Johns Hopkins U. Sch. Medicine, 1956-68, instr. pathobiology sch. hygiene and pub. health, 1957-76, prof. oncology and medicine, 1968—, dir. oncology ctr., 1973-92; dir. emeritus oncology ctr. Johns Hopkins U. Sch. Medicine, Balt., 1992—, disting. svc. prof., 1992—; fellow pharmacology and exptl. therapeutics, sch. medicine Johns Hopkins U., 1953-55; vis. physician Balt. City Hosp., 1957—. Fellow ACP, AAAS, Assn. Am. Physicians; mem. Am. Soc. Pharmacology and Exptl. Therapeutics, Am. Assn. for Cancer Rsch., Am. Assn. for Cancer Edn., Am. Soc. Clin. Oncology, Assn. Am. Cancer Insts., Internat. Soc. Exptl. Hematology, Nat. Coalition for Cancer Rsch., N.Y. Acad. Scis. Office: Johns Hopkins Oncology Ctr Ross Rsch Bldg Rm 361 720 Rutland Ave Baltimore MD 21205-2196

OWENS, CYNTHIA DENISE, physician; b. Detroit, Mar. 14, 1952; d. Jimmie Edwards Jr. and Anne Elizabeth (King) O.; divorced; 1 child, Luke. AD, Highland Park Jr. Coll., 1973; BA, Wayne State U., 1975; DO, Mich. State U., 1979. Internist pvt. practice, Quincy, Fla., 1984-86, Gastroenterology Clinic, Pascataway, Miss., 1986-94, Prevention Health Physicians, Biloxi, Miss., 1994—. Mem. NAACP, Am. Coll. Osteo. Internists, Am. Osteo. Assn., Am. Cancer Soc. (bd. dirs. 1996), Miss. State MEd. Assn., Singing River Med. Soc., So. Med. Soc. Office: Biloxi Vets Med Ctr 400 Vets Ave Biloxi MS 39531

OWENS, FLORA CONCEPCION, critical care nurse; b. Manila, Nov. 23, 1949; d. Felix and Marieta (Obsuna) Concepcion; m. George Owens, Feb. 13, 1976. Grad., San Juan de Dios Sch. Nursing, Pasay City, The Philippines, 1970; BSN, Concordia Coll., Manila, 1971. RN, Ill., Ark.; cert. in ACLS; CCRN. Staff nurse San Juan de Dios Hosp., 1970-71, Jefferson Meml. Hosp., Mt. Vernon, Ill., 1972, Russellville (Ark.) Nursing Home Ctr., 1973-76; staff nurse, relief supr. St. Mary's Regional Med. Ctr., Russellville, 1972-74, head nurse med. fl., 1975-76, insvc. coord. and unit mgr. med.-surg. ICU, 1976-90, staff nurse, charge nurse med.-surg. ICU, 1990—; instr. basic coronary care class, 1979-90, basic arrythmia class, 1979-91. Mem. AACN, CCRN, Ark. Tech. U. Nursing Honor Soc.

OWENS, GARY MITCHELL, family physician; b. Salisbury, Md., July 31, 1949; s. Avery Donovan and Elizabeth (Mitchell) O.; BA, U. Pa., 1971; MD, Thomas Jefferson U., 1975; m. Loretta Andrews; children: Aaron David, Scott Christopher, Stefanie Erin, Avery Tyler. Resident in family medicine Wilmington (Del.) Med. Center, 1975-78, chief resident, 1978, teaching assoc. dept. family medicine, 1978-91; practice medicine specializing in family practice, Wilmington, 1978-91; teaching assoc. dept. family medicine St. Francis Hosp., Wilmington, 1978-91; med. dir. Phoenix Steel Co., 1980-87; med. dir. Delaware Valley HMO, Delaware Plan, 1985-91, assoc. med. dir. quality assurance Del. Valley HMO, 1987-91, also chmn. credentials com.; med. dir. Keystone Health Plan East, Phila., 1991-94, sr. med. dir., 1994-95, sr. med. dir. Independence Blue Cross, 1995-96, v.p. patient care mgmt., 1996—; staff, coun. mem., chmn. reappointment com. Med. Ctr. Del., vice chmn. dept. family practice, 1990-91; cons. NorAm. Chem. Co., 1984-91. Diplomate Am. Bd. Family Practice. Fellow Am. Acad. Family Physicians; mem. Pa. Acad. Family Physicians, Alpha Omega Alpha. Roman Catholic. Home: S Palmer Dr Glen Mills PA 19342 Office: PO Box 7516 1901 Market St Philadelphia PA 19101-7516

OWENS, GREGORY RANDOLPH, physician, medical educator; b. Glendale, W. Va., Oct. 3, 1948; s. Elmer Herman and Anne Elizabeth (Kroggel) O.; m. Jane Marie Fleming, June 1, 1974; children: Gregory R. Jr., Allison Fleming. AB cum laude, Princeton U., 1970; MD, U. Pa., 1974. Diplomate Am. Bd. Internal Medicine, Am. Bd. Pulmonary Medicine, Am. Bd. Critical Care Medicine. Intern in internal medicine Hosp. U. Pa., Phila., 1974-75, residency in internal medicine, 1975-77, fellowship pulmonary disease, 1977-78, chief med. resident, 1978-79, fellowship pulmonary disease, 1979-80; asst. prof. medicine U. Pitts., 1980-86, assoc. prof. medicine, 1986-93, prof. medicine, 1993—, assoc. chief div. pulmonary medicine, 1984—; chief Montefiore U. Hosp., Pitts, 1991—; dir. Pulmonary Exercise Physiology Lab., Presbyn.-Univ. Hosp., Pitts., 1980-92, co-dir. Pulmonary Function Lab., 1980-92; co-dir. Occupl. Lung Clinic, Falk Clinic, Pitts., 1983-88. Contbr. articles to New Eng. Jour. Medicine, Am. Jour. Medicine, Jour. Lab. Clin. Medicine and others, presenter at profl. confs. Coach Oakmont (Pa.) Athletic Assn., 1988—, bd. dirs. Am. Lung Assn. Recipient Future Leaders Pulmonary Medicine award, Chgo., 1984, Preventive Pulmonary Acad. award NIH, 1988-93; grantee Health Rsch. and Svc. Found., 1980-85, NIH Lung Health Study, 1984-94, Lung Health Study II, 1994—. Mem. ACP, Am. Coll. Chest Physicians (Pa. gov. 1993—), Am. Thoracic Soc., Am. Fedn. for Clin. Rsch., Pa. Thoracic Soc. (pres. 1993-96). Office: U Pitts Sch Medicine 440 Scaife Hall 3550 Terrace St Pittsburgh PA 15261

OWENS, JOHN FRANKLIN, health care administrator, consultant, nurse; b. Slatington, Pa., May 19, 1935; s. William and Goldie Irene (Zerfass) O.; m. Shirley Ann Spade, June 15, 1957; children: Terri Ann Owens Albright, Rick Todd. Student, Orange County Community Coll., 1954-55; attended Sch. of Nursing, SUNY, 1954-57, student, 1954-57; student, Pa. State U., 1964, U. Pa., 1967. Pvt. practice, 1960-72, pvt. cons., 1961-72; nursing supr., instr. Easton (Pa.) Hosp., 1961-65, dir. in-svc. edn., 1963-65; dir. svcs. Northampton County Homemaker Svc., Bethlehem, Pa., 1965-67; exec. dir. Bucks County Homemaker-Home Health Aide Svc., Doylestown, Pa., 1967-72; zone mgr. UpJohn Healthcare Svcs., N.J., 1972-73; govt. adminstr. UpJohn Healthcare Svcs., 1973-79; zone mgr. UpJohn Healthcare Svcs., Fla., 1979-82; bus. mgr. UpJohn Healthcare Svcs., 1982-84, asst. to pres., 1984-85, regional mgr., 1985-88, govt. contracts nat. program mgr., 1989-90, dir. Nat. Govt. Affairs, 1990-91; pvt. cons. New Port Richey, Fla., 1991—; long term territory mgr. Kinetic Concepts, Inc., New Port richey, Fla., 1992-96; acct. exec. Kinetic Concepts, Inc., Hudson, Fla., 1994-96; ret., 1996. Author: PA Training Guide for Homemaker Home Health Aides, 1972, Government Contracting, 1990. Chmn. Bucks County Reps., Doylestown, 1972. With U.S. Army, 1953-54. Mem. Am. Pub. Health Assn., Am. Mgmt. Assn., Jr. Chamber Internat., Nat. Conf. on Aging, Jaycees (1st v.p. 1969-70, pres. 1970-71, chmn. bd. 1971-72). Republican.

OWENS, LINDSAY MEGGS, dentist; b. Tyler, TX, Feb. 9, 1952; s. W.B. and Sara Eden (Meggs) O.; m. Mersedeh Djafarihiri, Oct. 8, 1988. BS, Abilene Christian U., 1974; DDS, Baylor Coll. Dentistry-Dallas, 1983. Pvt. practice Dallas, 1983—. Active Heritage Found., Washington, 1987—; mem. health facilities bd. City of Dallas, 1993-95; two star donator Head Start Programs of Tex. Recipient Spl. Vol. of Yr. Dental Health Programs, Inc., 1992. Mem. ADA, Tex. Dental Assn. (jud. and ethics coun. 1994—), Dallas County Dental Soc. (jud. com. 1989-94, chmn. 1991-94). Mem. Ch. of Christ. Office: 6801 Snider Plz Ste 200 Dallas TX 75205-1374

OWENS, TOMAS PATRICIO, JR., family practice physician; b. Panama, Panama, Mar. 5, 1963; came to U.S., 1988; s. Thomas Patrick and Criseida Emilia (Saad) O.; m. Tammy Lea Jaqua, June 5, 1991; children: Thomas Patrick III, Emily Arlene. B.Sci., Letters and Philosophy, Colegio Javier, Panama, 1980; MD, U. Panama, 1986. Diplomate Am. Bd. Family Practice. Intern Complejo Hospitalario Metropolitano C.S.S., Panama, 1986-87, Sistema de Salud de Veraguas, Santiago, Panama, 1987-88; intern U. Okla. Health Sci. Ctr., Oklahoma City, 1988-89, resident, chief resident in family medicine, 1989-91, asst. prof. family medicine, 1993-95, clin. asst. prof. family medicine, 1995—, clin. asst. prof. internal medicine, 1995—; clin. rsch. fellow geriatric medicine Mayo Grad. Sch. Medicine, Rochester, Minn., 1991-93; asst. dir. residency program Great Plains Family Practice, Oklahoma City, 1995—; lectr. in field. Contbr. articles to profl. jours., chpts. to books; editor Revista Medica Cientifica AEMP, 1984-86. Vol. April 19 Bombing Heartland Found., Oklahoma City, 1995; vol. Okla. Hispanic Assn., 1993—; profl. adv. com. Fountains of Canterbury/Quality Lifestyles, Inc., Oklahoma City, 1993—. Okla. U. Health Sci. Ctr. Faculty Geriatric Medicine fellow, 1993—. Mem. ACP, AMA (Leadership Award for Resident Physicians 1990), Soc. Tchrs. Family Medicine (Excellence in Teaching award 1991), Am. Geriatric Soc., Am. Acad. Family Physicians, Internat. Ctr. for Family Medicine, Okla. Acad. Family Physicians (chmn. com. on aging 1995—), Okla. County Med. Soc. (editl. bd. 1995-96), Alpha Omega Alpha. Roman Catholic. Office: Gt Plains Family Practice 3300 NW 56 St #300 Oklahoma City OK 73112-4401

OWENS, WARNER BARRY, physical therapist; b. Detroit, Apr. 29, 1939; s. Wendell Lee and Flora Lucille (Maddox) O.; m. Frances Hutton, June 11, 1960 (div. May 1973); children—Jeffrey, Karen; m. Sandra Irene Olstyn, Nov. 16, 1974. B.S., UCLA, 1962. Staff phys. therapist Valley Phys. Therapy Ctr., Van Nuys, Calif., 1962-63; chief phys. therapist St. Joseph Med. Ctr., Burbank, Calif., 1963-70, dir. rehab., 1970—, bd. dirs. Credit Union, 1974-76, 83-91, pres., 1986-91; pres. Therapeutic Assocs. Inc., Sherman Oaks, 1992—; dir. Tetrad and Assocs., Sherman Oaks, 1972—; chmn. bd. dirs. Nat. Physical Rehab. Network, Inc.; mem. admissions com. phys. therapy option Calif. State U.-Northridge, 1976—. Childrens Hosp. Sch. Phys. Therapy Kate Crutcher scholar, 1961; recipient Outstanding Contbn. to Profession award Calif. State U.-Northridge, 1983. Mem. Am. Phys. Therapy Assn. (chmn. jud. com. 1981-82), Am. Coll. Sports Medicine, Phys. Therapy Dirs. Forum, Internat. Wine and Food Soc. (bd. dirs. San Fernando Valley 1979—, pres. 1980). Republican. Home: 4428 Gloria Ave Encino CA 91436-3451 also: 780 Rockbridge Rd Montecito CA 93108 Office: Therapeutic Assocs Inc 15060 Ventura Blvd Van Nuys CA 91403

OWENS, WILLIAM DON, anesthesiology educator; b. St. Louis, Dec. 12, 1939; s. Don and Caroline Wilhemena (Raaf) O.; m. Patricia Gail Brown, Dec. 12, 1964; children: Pamela, David, Susan. AB, Westminster Coll., 1961; MD, U. Mich., 1965. Diplomate Am. Bd. Anesthesiology. Resident and fellow Mass. Gen. Hosp. and Harvard Med. Sch., Boston, 1969-72; instr. Harvard Med. Sch., Boston, 1972-73; asst. prof. anesthesiology Washington U. Sch. Medicine, St. Louis, 1973-76, assoc. prof., 1976-82, prof., 1982—, chmn. dept., 1982-92; trustee Barnes Hosp., St. Louis, 1987-89; bd. dirs. Found. for Anesthesia Edn. and Rsch., 1990-95, Anesthesia Found.; bd. dirs. Am. Bd. Anesthesiology, 1984-86, sec.-treas., 1991-94, pres., 1995-96. Assoc. editor Survey of Anesthesiology, 1977-92; contbr. 50 articles to profl. jours., 7 chpts. to books. Served to lt. comdr. USN, 1966-69. Fellow Am. Coll. Anesthesiology; mem. Am. Soc. Anesthesiologists (bd. dirs. 1989-95, 1st v.p. 1995-96, pres.-elect 1996—), Internat. Anesthesia Rsch. Soc., Acad. Anesthesiology, Assn. Univ. Anesthesiologists. Office: Washington U Sch Med Dept Anesthesiology 660 S Euclid Ave Saint Louis MO 63110-1010 also: Am Bd Anesthesiology The Summit Ste 510 4101 Lake Boone Trail Raleigh NC 27607-7506

OWHOR, CLIFFORD NSIRIMOVU, physician; b. Portharcourt, Nigeria, Jan. 21, 1955; came to U.S., 1977; s. Ebenezar Wutchenne and Evelyn Oyinda (Wobeh) O.; m. Pattie Felicia Elliott, Aug. 20, 1983 (div. Oct. 1989); m. Mercy Bryson Pepple, May 29, 1992; children: Azubulke, Ahukwobi, Evelyn Nma. BS in Pre-Medicine, No. Ky. U., 1981; MD, U. Autonoma de Chihuahua, Mexico, 1987; MS in Biology, U. Detroit, 1992; BS in Medicine, Western Mich. U., 1994. Cert. physician asst. Lab. tech. Portharcourt Gen. Hosp., Nigeria, 1975-77; sub. sci. tchr. Cin. Pub. Sch., 1989-90; psychiat. asst. Ohio Dept. of Mental Health, Cin., 1988-90; lab. asst. molecular biology dept. U. Detroit Mercy, 1991-92; profl. in anatomy and physiology I-II Wayne County C.C., Detroit, 1991—; physician asst. NCCPA. Atlanta, 1995. Mem. Am. Med. Student Assn. Home: 13821 E 7 Mile Rd # 102 Detroit MI 48205

OWINGS, FRANCIS BARRE, surgeon; b. McColl, S.C., Mar. 9, 1941; s. Ralph Seer and Antoinette (Moore) O.; B.S., U. Miss., 1963, M.D., 1966; m. Judith Myers, Feb. 14, 1976; children—F. Patterson, Caroline C. Intern, San Francisco Gen. Hosp., 1966-67; resident in surgery U. Calif., San Francisco, 1969-74; surg. registrar Norfolk and Norwich Hosp., Norwich, Eng., 1971-72; practice medicine specializing in surgery, Atlanta, 1974—; mem. staff Crawford Long Hosp., pres. med. staff, 1981-82; mem. staff Piedmont Hosp.; clin. instr. surgery Emory U. Served to capt. USAF, 1967-69. Diplomate Am. Bd. Surgery. Fellow ACS, Southeastern Surg. Congress; mem. Med. Assn. Atlanta, Med. Assn. Ga., Naffziger Surg. Soc., Alpha Epsilon Delta, Sigma Chi, Phi Chi. Republican. Methodist. Home: 3400 Wood Valley Rd NW Atlanta GA 30327-1518 Office: 478 Peachtree NE Atlanta GA 30308

OWNBY, CHARLOTTE LEDBETTER, anatomy educator; b. Amory, Miss., July 27, 1947; d. William Moss and Anna Faye (Long) Ledbetter; m. James Donald Ownby, Sept. 6, 1969; children: Holly Ruth, Mary Faye. BS in Zoology, U. Tenn., 1969, MS in Zoology, 1971; PhD in Anatomy, Colo. State U., 1975. Instr. Okla. State U., Stillwater, 1974-75, asst. prof., 1975-80, assoc. prof., 1980-84, prof., 1984—; dir. electron microscope lab. Okla. State U., Stillwater, 1977—, head dept., 1990-95. Editor Proc. 9th World Congress Internat. Soc. Toxicology, 1989; editorial bd. Toxion, 1984—. Recipient SmithKline-Beecham award for rsch. excellence, 1992; NIH, USPHS grantee, 1979-92. Mem. Okla. Soc. Electron Microscopy (pres. 1977-78), Pan Am. Soc. Toxinology (pres. 1994—), Internat. Soc. of Toxinology (pres. 1994-97), Phi Beta Kappa, Sigma Xi, Phi Kappa Phi. Office: Okla State U Anatomy Pathology and Pharmacology Dept Physiol Scis 264 Vet Medicine Stillwater OK 74078

OWNBY, DENNIS RANDALL, pediatrician, allergist, educator, researcher; b. Athens, Ohio, July 14, 1948; s. Dillard Ralph and Miriam (Lee) O.; m. Helen Louise Engelbrecht, May 24, 1970; children: David Randall, Kathryn Louise. BS, Ohio U., 1969; MD, Med. Coll. Ohio, 1972. Diplomate Am. Bd. Allergy and Immunology, Am. Bd. Pediatrics, Nat. Bd. Med. Examiners. Intern and resident Duke U. Sch. Medicine, Durham, N.C., 1972-74, asst. prof., 1977-80; staff physician Henry Ford Hosp., Detroit, 1980—, dir. Allergy Rsch. Lab., 1986—; clin. asst. prof. pediat. U. Mich., Ann Arbor, 1980-86, clin. assoc. prof., 1986-95. Contbr. articles to med. jours., chpts. to books. Recipient Young Investigator award Nat. Inst. Allergy and Infectious Disease, 1978. Fellow Am. Acad. Pediatrics, Am. Acad. Allergy. Office: Henry Ford Hosp Dept Allergy & Clin Immunology 2799 W Grand Blvd Detroit MI 48202-2608

OWRE, DEANNE WELLMAN, speech language pathologist; b. Tulsa; d. Dean C. and Louise (Loomis) Wellman; m. Stein Owre, Aug. 28, 1965; children: Kristin, Nina. BA, U. Wyo., 1965; MS, Worcester State Coll., 1985. Speech, lang. pathologist Wyo. Easter Seal Soc., Cheyenne, N. Smithfield (R.I.) Pub. Schs., R.I. Hosp., Providence, Burrillville (R.I.) Pub. Sch. System; pvt. practice Burrillville; clin. supr. for speech-lang.-pathology Chiron Profl. Svcs., Providence, 1991-95. Mem. ASHA (recipient Outstanding Clin. Achievement award, mem. task force on support pers. 1993-95), R.I. Speech, Lang., Hearing Assn. (pres.), R.I. Bd. Examiners (chmn. Speech Pathology and Audiology Dept. of Health). Home: 4 Taber Hill Rd North Smithfield RI 02896

OWSLEY, WILLIAM CLINTON, JR., radiologist; b. Austin, Tex., Oct. 6, 1923; s. William Clinton and Lois (Lamar) O.; B.A., U. Tex., 1944; M.D., U. Pa., 1946; m. Betty Pinckard, 1949; 2 children. Intern, Hermann Hosp., Houston, 1946-47; resident Hosp. of U. Pa., Phila., 1949-52; instr. radiology U. Pa., 1950-52; practice medicine specializing in radiology, Houston, 1952—; mem. staff Hermann Hosp., Twelve Oaks Hosp., Bellville Hosp., St. Elizabeth Hosp., Brazos Valley Hosp.; assoc. clin. prof. radiology U. Tex. Served with USNR, 1947-48. Diplomate Am. Bd. Radiology. Fellow Royal Soc. Medicine (U.K.), Am. Coll. Radiology; mem. Am. Roentgen Ray Soc., Radiol. Soc. N.Am., Interam. Coll. Radiology, AMA. Republican. Baptist. Office: 4710 Greeley St Ste 230 Houston TX 77006-6254

OWYANG, CHUNG, gastroenterologist, researcher; b. Chung King, China, Nov. 20, 1945; arrived in Can., 1965; s. Chi and Ching-Ying (Fung) O.; m. Jeannette Lim; children: Stephanie, Christopher. BS with honors, McGill U., Montreal, Can., 1968, MD, 1972. Diplomate Am. Bd. Internal Medicine, Gastroenterology; lic. Gen. Med. Coun., U.K., Que., Can., Min. Med. lic., Mich. med. lic. Intern in internal medicine Montreal Gen. Hosp./McGill U., 1972-73, resident in internal medicine, 1973-75; clin. teaching fellow in internal medicine McGill U., 1974-75; fellow in gastroenterology Mayo Clinic and Found., Rochester, Minn., 1975-78; instr. internal medicine Mayo Med. Sch., Rochester, 1977-78; asst. prof. U. Mich., 1978-84, assoc. prof., 1984-88, assoc. chief divsn. gastroenterology, 1984-90, prof., 1988—, chief divsn. gastroenterology, 1991—, dir. med. procedures unit, 1992—, dir. Digestive Health Inst., 1992—; assoc. dir. Gastrointestinal Peptide Rsch. Ctr., U. Mich., 1984-95, dir. 1996—; cons. Rsch. Coun. Janssen Pharmaceutica Inc., 1985—, Ann Arbor VA Med. Ctr., 1978—, NIH, Bethesda, Md., 1989-94, FDA, Bethesda, 1995—; H. Marvin Pollard chair in gastroenterology, U. Mich., 1996—; speaker, presenter in field. Co-author: Textbook of Gastroenterology, 1991, 2d edit. 1995, Atlas of Gastroenterology, 1992; mem. edit. bd. Pancreas, 1986—, Am. Jour. Physiology, 1988—, Regulatory Peptide Letter, 1988—, Gastroenterology, 1990—, guest editor, 1991—, Digestive Diseases, 1993—; contbr. numerous chpts. to books, articles to profl. jours., jours. refereed. Grantee in field. Fellow ACP; mem. Am. Assn. Physicians, Am. Soc. Clin. Investigation, Am. Gastroenterological Assn., Am. Pancreatic Assn., Am. Diabetes Assn., Am. Fedn. Clin. Rsch., Am. Motility Soc., Ctrl. Soc. Clin. Rsch., Internat. Assn. Pancreatology, Midwest Gut Club. Office: U Mich Med Ctr 3912 Taubman Ctr Ann Arbor MI 48109

OXENHORN, SANFORD, psychiatrist; b. N.Y.C., June 29, 1926; s. Herman and Claire (Weinstein) O.; m. Miriam M. Hutter. BA, NYU, 1947; MD, SUNY, Bklyn., 1951; postgrad., N.Y. Psychoanalytic Inst., 1967. Diplomate Am. Bd. Psychiatry and Neurology, 1967. Rotating intern Jewish Hosp. of Bklyn., 1951-52; asst. resident in medicine Montefiore Hosp., Bronx, N.Y., 1952-53; fellow in hematology Kings County Hosp., Bklyn., 1953-54, Mt. Sinai Hosp., N.Y.C., 1955-56; asst. resident in medicine Maimonides Hosp., Blkyn., 1954-55; dir. hematology Maimonides Hosp., Bklyn., 1956-57; resident in psychiatry Bklyn. State Hosp., 1957-58; resident in psychiatry Albert Einstein Med. Ctr., Bronx, 1958-60, USPHS fellow in psychiatry, 1960-62; asst. prof. psychiatry Albert Einstein Coll. of Medicine, Bronx, 1962-74; assoc. clin. prof. psychiatry Coll. Medicine SUNY, Stony Brook, 1974—. With USNR, 1945-46. Mem. Am. Psychiat. Assn., N.Y. Psychoanalytic Assn. Office: PO Box 1550 Southampton NY 11969-1550

OXLEY, DWIGHT K(AHALA), pathologist; b. Wichita, Kans., Dec. 2, 1936; s. Dwight K. Jr. and Ruth Erdene (Warner) O.; m. Patricia Warren, June 18, 1961; children: Alice DeBloois, Thomas Oxley. AB, Harvard U., 1958; MD, U. Kans., 1962. Diplomate Am. Bd. Pathology (trustee 1992—), Am. Bd. Nuclear Medicine. Pathologist Wesley Med. Ctr., Wichita, 1969-74, Eisenhower Med. Ctr., Rancho Mirage, Calif., 1974-78, St. Joseph Health Ctr., Kansas City, Mo., 1978-88; chmn. dept. pathology Wesley Med. Ctr., 1988—. Bd. editors Archives of Pathology and Lab. MEdicine, Chgo., 1984-95, Clinica Chimica Acta, Amsterdam, 1980-86, Am. Jour. Clin. Pathology, Chgo., 1974-80. Sr. warden St. Stephens Episcopal Ch., Wichita, 1994. Lt. commdr. USN, 1964-69. Fellow Am. Soc. Clin. Pathologists (various offices), Coll. Am. Pathologists (various offices); mem. Am. Pathology Found. (bd. dirs. 1979-89), Kans. Soc. Pathologists (pres. 1993-96). Republican. Office: Wesley Med Ctr 550 N Hillside St Wichita KS 67214-4910

OXMAN, THOMAS ELLIOT, psychiatrist; b. Denver, May 15, 1949; s. Albert Charles and Leah (Hurwitz) O.; m. Judy Ann Heldman, May 27, 1971; children: Elliot Warren, Robert Charles, Annaleah H. AB in Philosophy, Dartmouth Coll., 1971; MD, U. Colo., 1975. Diplomate in psychiatry and geriatric psychiatry Am. Bd. Psychiatry and Neurology (mem. test com. 1987-95). Intern Mt. Zion Med. Ctr., San Francisco, 1976; resident in psychiatry Dartmouth Med. Sch., Hanover, N.H., 1979; fellow in consultation/liaison and cancer psychiatry Dartmouth Med. Sch., 1979-80; asst. prof. psychiatry and family medicine U. Cin. Med. Ctr., 1980-83; asst. prof. Dartmouth Med. Ctr., Hanover, 1983-87, assoc. prof. psychiatry and cmty. medicine, attending, 1987-95, prof., 1995—; assoc. dir. consultation liaison psychiatry svc. Dartmouth Hitchcock Med. Ctr., Hanover, 1983-90, dir. geriatric psychiatry, 1988—, mem. sci. rev. com. Hitchcock Found., 1988-95; mem. Mental Disorders of Aging rev. group NIMH, 1995—. Editor Internat. Jour. Psychiatry in Medicine, 1996—; contbr. articles to profl. jours. Recipient Merrell Resident Rsch. award Dartmouth Med. Sch., 1978; Rufus Choate scholar Dartmouth Coll., 1971; Mental Health Acad. awardee NIMH, 1987-90, Aging, Social Support and Phys. and Emotional Disability grantee, 1990-95; MacArthur Found. and Hartford Found. Depression in Primary Care grantee, 1995—. Fellow Am. Psychiat. Assn. (liaison com. on consultation/liaison psyhciatry 1982-88); mem. Phi Beta Kappa. Office: Dartmouth Med Sch Dept Psychiatry Lebanon NH 03756

OYAMADA, PAUL HERBERT, dentist, consultant, retired; b. Portland, Oreg., Oct. 19, 1921; m. Alice Yasuko Sono, Nov. 7, 1953; 1 child, Debra Kay. DMD, U. Oreg., 1950. Pvt. practice Portland, 1952-95; ret., 1995; dental cons. John Hancock Group, 1974-95, Blue Cross-Blue Shield, 1977-95, Washington Nat. Ins., 1985-95, Prin. Mut. Des Moines, 1985-95. Capt. U.S. Army, 1950-52, Korea. Fellow Am. Coll. Dentists (sect. chmn.), Internat. Coll. Dentists; mem. Oreg. Dental Assn. (pres. 1973-74, del. to ADA 1978-83), Multnomah Dental Soc. (pres. 1969-70), Lions (Roseway pres. 1951), Delta Sigma Delta. Avocation: fishing. Home: 13544 NE Klickitat Ct Portland OR 97230-2927

OZAKI, OSAMU, surgeon; b. Tokyo, Japan, Sept. 10, 1942; s. Seitaro and Shigeno (Nakagawa) O.; m. Momoko Makita, Apr. 24, 1973; children: Toru, Junko. MD, Tottori U., 1968, PhD, 1974. Asst. Tottori U. Hosp., Yonago, Japan, 1969-75, instr., 1975-83; chief surgeon Ito Hosp., Tokyo, 1983—; vis. prof. U. N.C., Chapel Hill, 1975, Tottori U., 1983—, Tokyo Women's Med. Coll., 1992—. Co-author: Surgical Mook 45, 1986, Clinical Visual Mook, 1986, Atlas of Endocrine Surgery, 1992; editor Atlas of Tumors of the Thyroid Gland, 1995; contbr. articles to profl. jours. Mem. AAAS, N.Y. Acad. Sci., Japanese Assn. Endocrine Surgery, Internat. Assn. Endocrine Surgery, Internat. Surg. Soc. Home: 3-37-1 Sendagaya, Shibuya, Tokyo 151, Japan Office: Ito Hosp, 4-3-6 Jingumae Shibuya, Tokyo 150, Japan

OZAWA, KEIYA, hematologist, researcher; b. Tatsuno-machi, Nagano-Ken, Japan, Feb. 23, 1953; s. Iwao and Taka (Ono) O.; m. Masami Inokuchi, Oct. 16, 1983; children: Sayaka, Tomo-o. MD, U. Tokyo, 1977, PhD, 1984. Resident in medicine Tokyo U. Hosp., 1977-79; with U. Tokyo, 1977-94; rsch. assoc. Jichi Med. Sch., Tochigi, 1980-82; staff fellow faculty medicine U. Tokyo, 1984-87; Fogarty fellow, clin. hematology br. Nat. Heart Lung and Blood Inst., NIH, Bethesda, Md., 1985-87; asst. prof. dept. hematology-oncology Inst. Med. Sci., 1987-90, assoc. prof., 1990-94; prof. dept. molecular biology Jichi Med. Sch., Tochigi, Japan, 1994—. Mem. editl. bd. Internat. Jour. Hematology, Kyoto, 1990-92, Japanese Jour. Clin. Oncology, 1993—, Japanese Jour. of Cancer Rsch., 1996—. Mem. AAAS, Am. Soc. Hematology, Am. Fedn. for Cin. Rsch., Internat. Soc. Hematology (Asian-Pacific divsn.), Internat. Soc. Exptl. Hematology, Japanese Soc. Immunology, Soc. Japanese Virologists, N.Y. Acad. Scis., Japanese Cancer Assn., Japanese Soc. Hematology (councilor 1990—), Japanese Soc. Internal Medicine, Japan Soc. Clin. Hematology (councilor 1991—), Japanese Soc. Gene Therapy (councilor 1995—), Am. Soc. for Microbiology, Japanese Soc. for Bone Marrow Transplantation, Japanese Soc. Transfusion Medicine, Japanest Soc. Host Def. Home: 3-1-3-C201 Gion, Minamikawachi-machi Kawachi Tochigi, Japan 329-04 Office: Jichi Med Sch Inst Hematol Dept Molec Biology, 3311-1 Yakushiji, Minamikawachi-machi Tochigi 329-04, Japan 329-04

ÖZBEK, SÜHA SÜREYYA, radiologist; b. Mugla, Turkey, July 29, 1961; s. Muhammet Sevket and Günten Özbek; m. Güliz Yakin, Sept. 28, 1990. MD, Ege U., Izmir, Turkey, 1985. Intern in radiology Ankara

(Turkey) U. Sch. Medicine, 1991; radiologist Ege U. Sch. Medicine, Izmir; cons. Tübitak, Ankara, 1995—. Contbr. articles to profl. publs. With Turkish Air Force, 1992-93. Mem. Soc. Med. Ultrasonography, Soc. Med. Imaging, N.Y. Acad. Scis. Home: 1740 sok No 4/2, Orkide Apt Daire 3, TR-35530 Karsiyaka-Izmir Turkey Office: Ege U Sch Medicine, Dept Diagnostic Radiology, TR-35100 Bornova Izmir Turkey

OZENBAUGH, BILLIE J., health facility administrator; b. Scottsbluff, Nebr., Nov. 17, 1941; d. Alva Emitt and Anna Grace (Brady) O. Student, Dushesne Cath. Women's Coll., Omaha, Nebr., 1960; diploma, St. Francis Sch. Nursing, Grand Island, Nebr., 1963; BSN-HCM, Metro State Coll., Denver, 1986. Staff nurse St. Mary Hosp., Scottsbluff, Nebr., 1963-67, head nurse surgery-OB, 1967-69; staff-charge nurse, ortho neuro St. Anthony Hosp. System, Denver, 1969-78, head nurse neuro trauma, 1978-80; nursing supr. Luth. Med. Ctr., Wheatridge, Colo., 1981-90; head nurse Spalding Rehab. Hosp., Wheatridge, 1990-93; program mgr. Spalding Rehab. Unit, 1993—. Home: 6245 W 61st Ave Arvada CO 80003-5609

OZER, MARK NORMAN, neurologist, hospital administrator; b. Cambridge, Mass., Jan. 17, 1932; s. Samuel Louis and Naomi (Smith) O.; m. Ann Teitler, Sept. 29, 1957 (div. Dec. 1978); children: Katherine, Elizabeth, Mark, Emily, Nicole; m. Martha Ross, Aug. 13, 1979. AB, Harvard U., 1953; MD, Boston U., 1957. Diplomate Am. Bd. Neurology. Intern Stanford Hosp., 1957-58; med. resident Stanford U. Svc., San Francisco Gen. Hosp., 1958-59; neurology resident Mt. Sinai Hosp., N.Y.C., 1959-60, 62-64; attending neurologist Children's Hosp. Nat. Med. Ctr., Washington, 1965-75; pres. Ozer Assocs., Washington, 1975-82; asst. chief SCI McGuire VA Med. Ctr., Richmond, Va., 1982-89; dir. stroke program Nat. Rehab. Hosp., Washington, 1989—, asst. med. dir., 1994—; asst. prof. neurology George Washington U., 1967-72, assoc. prof. child health and devel., 1973-84, prof., 1990—; assoc. prof. neurology Med. Coll. Va., 1984-90. Contbr. articles to profl. jours., chpts. to books. Capt. USAF, 1990-92. Home: 3420 38th St NW Washington DC 20016 Office: National Rehab Hosp 102 Irving St NW Washington DC 20016

ÖZTÜRK, YUSUF, pharmacologist, pharmacist; b. Ankara, Turkey, July 14, 1958; s. Erdoğan Ziya and Evin Fatma (Öke) Ö; m. Nilgün Kurtar, Oct. 28, 1989. BSc in Pharmacy, Ankara (Turkey) U., 1980, PhD in Pharmacology, 1985. Rsch. fellow Ankara (Turkey) U., 1980-85; postdoctoral rsch. fellow Anadolu U., Eskisehir, Turkey, 1985-86, asst. prof., 1986-87, head dept. pharmacology, 1987—, assoc. prof., 1987-92, prof., 1992—; mem. Faculty Bd., Anadolu U., Eskisehir, 1986—, mem. exec. com. of Faculty of Pharmacy, 1987-92. Contbr. numerous articles to profl. jours. Recruitment Field Army, 1983, Tokat, Turkey. Recipient fellowship of Turkish Sci. Tech. Rsch. Coun., 1981-83, Bursary for Congress Attendance, Brit. Coun., 1983, Fellowship UNIDO/UNDP, 1989. Mem. N.Y. Acad. Scis., Turkish Pharmacological Soc., IUPHAR. Home: Seyit Gazi Cad 24/13, Eskisehir Turkey Office: Anadolu U, Faculty Pharmacy, Tepebasi, 26470 Eskisehir Turkey

OZVATH, ROSE MARY HORNIK, independent home care nurse; b. Arlington, Va., July 29, 1951; d. Albert John and Charlotte (Mlynek) Hornik; m. Douglas Ozvath, Mar. 23, 1974; 1 child, Jared Matthew. Student, Alexandria Hosp. Sch. Nursing, Alexandria, Va., 1972. RN. Intravenous therapist, RN intensive care unit Pitts. Nursing Specialist, 1982-84; home health nurse, inservice coord. Family Home Health Svcs. Inc., McKeesport, Pa., 1984-88; utilization reviewer Olsten Health Care Svcs., Pitts., 1988; pvt. practice home health nurse Clairton, Pa., 1989—. Author: Home Health Care Infection Control Manual, Home Care IV Therapy Manual. Mem. steering com. Clairton Task Force Steel Valley Provider Coun., 1989-94; mem. adminstrv. bd. Coun. on Ministries, 1987-94; mem., sec. Clairton Ctrl. Cath. Sch. Bd., 1989-91; pres. United Meth. Women, Pine Run, Pa., 1989-91; bd. dirs. Christ for Clairton, 1989-94; tutor Christian Literacy Advs.; mem. Clairton Cmty. Planning Team, 1995; sec. adminstrv. bd. Pine Run United Meth. Ch. 1995—, coord. parish nurse, health ministry program, 1994—. Mem. League of Intravenous Therapy Edn. Home and Office: 231 Pennsylvania Ave Clairton PA 15025-2235

OZYAMAN, ISMAIL YAMAN, psychiatrist; b. Izmir, Turkey, May 22, 1929; came to U.S., 1962, naturalized, 1973; s. Halit and Feride O.; m. Guler Basaran, Apr. 1, 1955; children: Emre Ak, Ege Ozyaman-Cordell, Kenan Ozyaman. MD, U. Ankara, 1955. Diplomate Turkish Bd. Urology, Am. Bd. Psychiatry and Neurology; cert. mental health adminstr. Resident, U. Ankara Faculty of Medicine Urology Clinic, 1955-59; intern, Regina (Sask., Can.) Gen. Hosp., 1960-61, Grey Nuns' Hosp., Regina, 1961-62; resident St. Lawrence Psychiat. Center, Ogdensburg, N.Y., 1962-63; resident Harlem Valley Psychiat. Center, Wingdale, N.Y., 1963-64; resident Hudson River Psychiat. Center, Poughkeepsie, N.Y., 1967-68, chief service, 1970-84, also chmn. forensic and pharmacy and Mortality and Tissue coms.; urologist U. Ankara Faculty of Medicine, 1958; chief urology dept. Corlu Mil. Hosp., Turkey, 1959-60; chief urology service S.S. Yenisehir Hosp., Turkey, 1965-66; cons. Castlepoint (N.Y.) VA Hosp., 1977—; physicians' advisor Adirondack-Hudson-Mohawk Med. Peer Rev. Orgn.; cons. Greenhaven Correctional Facility, Stormville, N.Y., 1980-89; med. dir. Harlem Valley Psychiatric Ctr., Wingdale, 1984-89; cons. psychiatrist supreme and county cts., Dutchess County, N.Y., 1969-89, Dept. Mental Hygiene, 1989-93, Locum Tenens, 1993—. With Turkish Army, 1959-60. Home and Office: 3 Walnut Hill Rd Poughkeepsie NY 12603-4715

OZZELLO, LUCIANO, pathologist; b. Rivoli, Turin, Italy, July 18, 1926; s. John and Fina (Vallero) O.; m. Mary K. Vernier, Oct. 23, 1955; 1 child, Paul. MD, U. Turin, 1951. Asst. prof. pathology N.Y. Med. Coll., N.Y.C., 1958-60; asst. prof. surg. pathology Columbia U., N.Y.C., 1960-64, prof. surg. pathology, 1980-92, prof. emeritus surg. pathology, 1993—; attending pathologist Swedish Hosp., Seattle, 1964-68; dir. surg. pathology Michael Reese Hosp., Chgo., 1968-72; prof. and chmn. dept. pathology U. Lausanne, Switzerland, 1972-80; attending surg. pathologist Presbyn. Hosp., N.Y.C., 1980-92. Contbr. over 85 articles to profl. jours.; co-editor, author: The Breast, 1983. Mem. Am. Assn. Cancer Rsch., A.P. Stout Soc. Surg. Pathologists. Office: Columbia Univ Coll Physicians/Surgeons 630 W 168th St New York NY 10032

PAALMAN, MARIA ELISABETH MONICA, public health executive; b. Zwolle, Overyssel, The Netherlands, Dec. 7, 1951; d. Herman J. and Wieb (Lievestro) P. MS in Clin. Psychology, U. Groningen, 1977; postgrad. in psychotherapy, Pesso Psychomotor, Boston, 1982; MSc in Health Policy, Planning & Financing, London, 1996. Staff mem. Hoog Hullen-Ther. Comm., Eelde, Netherlands, 1977-79; asst. dir. Krauweelhuis-Ther.Comm., Amsterdam, 1979-82; dir. STD Found., Utrecht, 1983-93; cons. WHO, Geneva, 1990; mem. Nat. Com. AIDS Control, The Netherlands, 1983-93; nat. coord. campaigns on STDs, AIDS, safer sex, 1985-93; tech. asst. STD/AIDS EC, Tanzania, 1993-95. Editor: Dutch Std. Bull., 1983-93; editor Promoting Safer Sex, 1990; mem. bd. editors Internat. Jour. on STD and AIDS, 1989-93, AIDS Health Promotion Exch., 1991—, AIDS Edn. and Prevention, 1992—; contbr. articles to profl. jours. Mem. Internat. Soc. for STD Rsch. (bd. dirs. 1989-95). Home: PR Beatrixlaan 24, 4001 AH Tiel The Netherlands

PACE, LYNNE HOCHBERG, ophthalmologist; b. N.Y.C., May 13, 1951; d. Milton and Gloria (Friedman) Hochberg; m. Lawrence Frank Pace, Dec. 17, 1977; children: Lawrence, David, Daniel. BA, CUNY, 1971; MD, SUNY, Buffalo, 1975. Diplomate Am. Bd. Ophthalmology, Nat. Bd. Med. Examiners. Intern in internal medicine SUNY Buffalo Affiliated Hosps., 1975-76, resident in ophthalmology, 1976-79; staff ophthalmologist Buffalo VA Med. Ctr., 1979-84, sect. chief ophthalmology, 1984—; asst. clin. instr. SUNY-Buffalo Health Sci. Ctr., 1975-77, clin. instr., 1979-87, clin. asst. prof., 1987—. Mem. Buffalo Ophthalmologic Club. Office: Buffalo VA Med Ctr 3495 Bailey Ave Buffalo NY 14215

PACE, ROBERT SCOTT, internist, allergist, immunologist; b. Charlottesville, Va., July 19, 1951; s. Wesley Emory and Ruby Francis (Motley) P.; m. Kimberly Jane Huebert, Sept. 29, 1979; children: Kristin, Ryan, Jason. BS in Biology, Va. Tech., 1973; MD, Ea. Va. Med. Sch., 1976; internal medicine, U. Kans., 1979; allergy-immunology, U. Colo., 1989. Diplomate Am. Bd. Internal Medicine, Am. Bd. Allergy and Immunology, Nat. Bd. Med. Examiners. Pvt. practice internal medicine Greeley, Colo., 1979—; pvt. practice allergy-immunology Greeley, 1989—; asst. clin. prof. medicine U. Colo., Denver, 1981-89, assoc. clin. prof. medicine, 1989—. Pres. Weld County Heart Assn., Greeley, 1981-82; chmn. dept. medicine North Colo. Med. Ctr., Greeley, 1984-85. Recipient Physicians Recognition award AMA, Chgo., 1981-97. Fellow ACP, Am. Acad. Allergy, Asthma, Immunology, Am. Coll. Allergy, Asthma, Immunology. Office: 2000 16th St Greeley CO 80631

PACE, THOMAS MALCOLM, nursing manager; b. Demopolis, Ala., July 15, 1958; s. Malcolm P. and Doris Ann (Pyle) P.; m. Barbara W. Welborn, Jan. 17, 1983; 1 child, Heather Marie. Staff nurse trauma unit Our Lady of the Lake, Baton Rouge, 1985-89, adminstrv. coord., 1989—. Home: 7608 Debit Dr Baton Rouge LA 70817-5409

PACELLA, BERNARD LEONARDO, psychiatrist; b. Toronto, Ont., Can., July 25, 1912; m. Theresa Rita Domalakes; children: Karen Pacella Oldham, Richard B., Madelyn Joyce Nichols, Bernard Leonard Jr. BS, U. Colo., 1931, MD, 1935; post doctoral, N.Y. Psychoanalytic Inst., 1946-51. Cert. child, adolescent, and adult psychoanalyst; Diplomate Am. Bd. Psychiatry and Neurology. Intern Kings County Hosp., Bklyn., 1935-37, resident in pediatrics, 1937-38; resident in psychiatry Dept. Psychiatry Columbia U. and N.Y. State Psychiat. Inst., N.Y.C., 1938-40; rsch. fellow in psychiatry Columbia Presbyn. Med. Ctr., N.Y.C., 1940-41, instr. mil. psychiatry, 1943-46; lectr. clin. psychiatry Coll. Physicians and Surgeons Columbia U., 1942-44, assoc. clin. psychiatry, 1944-45, instr., 1945-47, asst. clin. prof., 1947-55, assoc. clin. prof., 1955-72, clin. prof., 1972-84, spl. lectr., mem. faculty Ctr. Psychoanalytic Tng. and Rsch., 1984—, clin. prof. emeritus, 1990—. Contbr. articles to profl. jours.; reviewer Psychoanalytic Quar. Pres. Margaret S. Mahler Psychiat. Rsch. Found., 1970-88, bd. dirs.; sec.-treas., bd. dirs. Sigmund Freud Archives; pres. Psychoanalytic Assistance Fund, 1974-89, bd. dirs.; bd. dirs. Freud London Mus.; co-trustee Mary S. Sigourney award, 1990. With Colo. N.G., 1930-35, M.C. USAR, 1935-40. Decorated Cavaliere Officiale dell Ordine al Merito (Italy), 1958. Fellow Am. Coll. Psychoanalysis, Am. Acad. Child and Adolescent Psychiatry, N.Y. Acad. Medicine, Am. Psychiat. Assn.; mem. AMA, Am. Orthopsychiat. Assn., Am. Soc. Adolescent Psychiatry, Am. Psychoanalytic Assn. (reviewer jour., pres.-elect 1990, pres. 1992—, treas. 1983—), Assn. Child Psychoanalysis, Group Advancement Psychiatry, Assn. Psychoanalytic Medicine, N.Y. Psychoanalytic Soc. and Inst. (bd. dirs.), Internat. Psychoanalytic Assn., N.Y. Coun. Child and Adolescent Psychiatry, Alpha Omega Alpha. Home and Office: 115 E 61st St New York NY 10021-8172

PACHECO, LUIS NOVOA, family practice physician; b. N.Y.C., May 26, 1956; s. Luis Felipe and Carmela (Novoa) P.; m. Donna Masters, July 14, 1984; children: Alana, Nigel. BA, Columbia U., 1979; MD, Ctrl. U., 1985. Diplomate Am. Bd. Family Practice. Intern and family practice resident U. So. Calif./CMC, 1986-89; med. dir. CMCLA Urgent Care Svcs., L.A., 1990-95, U. So. Calif. Family Practice Residency Program, L.A., 1990-96, U. So. Calif. Acute Care Ctr., L.A., 1994-95; asst. prof. family medicine U. So. Calif. Sch. Medicine, L.A., 1990—; dir. predoctoral edn. dept. family medicine U. So. Calif. Sch. Medicine, 1996—. Mentor Nat. Hispanic Student Mentor Assn., 1994—; spokesman Latino affairs Calif. Hosp. Med. Ctr., 1990—. Mem. Am. Coll. Legal medicine, Am. Coll. Occupational and Environ. Medicine, Calif. Acad. Family Physicians, Am. Coll. Sports Medicine. Office: U So Calif Sch Medicine Dept Family Medicine PMB-B205 Los Angeles CA 90033

PACIFICO, ALBERT DOMINICK, cardiovascular surgeon; b. Bklyn., Sept. 24, 1940; s. Dominick Vincent and Amelia Catherine (Jannelli) P.; m. Vicki Lynne Overton, May 16, 1980; children: Albert D., Nicole M., Paul V. B.S., St. Johns U., 1960; M.D., N.J. Coll. Medicine, 1964. Diplomate Am. Bd. Surgery, Am. Bd. Thoracic Surgery. Med. intern Jersey City Med. Ctr., Seton Gall Coll. Medicine, 1964-65; asst. resident in surgery Mayo Clinic, Rochester, Minn., 1965-67; research fellow in surgery U. Ala., Birmingham, 1967-69, sr. resident, then chief resident surgery, resident in thoracic and cardiovascular surgery, 1968-72, mem. faculty dept. surgery, 1970—, prof. surgery, 1978-83, John W. Kirklin prof. cardiovascular surgery, 1983—, vice chmn. dept. surgery, 1990, dir. div. cardiothoracic surgery, 1984—, dir. Congenital Heart Disease Diagnosis and Treatment Ctr., 1985—; mem. staff gen., thoracic and cardiovascular surgery Univ. Hosp., Birmingham, 1972—, VA Hosp., Birmingham, 1972—; mem. staff Children's Hosp., Birmingham, 1971—, chief gen., thoracic and cardiovascular surgery, 1984—. Author: (with others) Pediatric Cardiac Surgery, 1985, Cardiology, 1985, Textbook of Surgery, 13th edit., 1986, The Treatment of Congenital Cardiac Anomalies, 1986, Perspectives in Pediatric Cardiology, 1988, Current Therapy in Cardiothoracic Surgery, 1989, Decision Making in Surgery of the Chest, 1989, Cardiac Surgery: Cyanotic Congential Heart Disease, 1989, Reoperation in Cardiac Surgery, 1989, others; mem. editorial bd. Am. Jour. Cardiology, 1983—, Heart and Vessel, 1985—, Jour. Cardiac Surgery, 1985—; cons. editoral referee Ala. Jour. Med. Scis., 1974-75; contbr. articles to med. jours. Fellow ACS, Am. Coll. Cardiology, Am. Surg. Assn.; mem. AMA, Ala. State Med. Soc., Jefferson County Med. Soc., Am. Heart Assn. (Paul Dudley White Internat. Svc. Citation 1977), Am. Assn. Thoracic Surgery, Soc. Thoracic Surgeons, Am. Surg. Soc., Internat. Coll. Pediatrics, John Kirklin Soc., Congential Heart Surgeons Soc., Assn. Acad. Surgery, Ala. chpt. Mayo Clinic Alumni Assn., Panamanian Soc. Cardiology (hon.), Peruvian Soc. Thoracic and Cardiovascular Surgery (hon.), Soc. Nat. Inst. Cardiology Mex. (hon.), Cardiac Soc. Australia and New Zealand (corr.), Peruvian Soc. Cardiology (corr.), Alpha Omega Alpha. Republican. Roman Catholic. Office: Univ Ala UAB Station Dept Surgery Birmingham AL 35294

PACITTI, REGINA MARIE, school counselor; b. Waltham, Mass., Nov. 25, 1953; d. Domenic Anthony and Eleanor Catherine (Bonica) P. BA, Tufts U., 1975, MA, 1976; MEd, Boston Coll., 1980. Lic. social worker, Mass. Tchr. English Waltham Pub. Schs., 1975-84, sch. adjustment counselor, 1984-95, peer leadership coord., 1988-89, peer contact info., 1990—. Mem. Mass. Sch. Psychologists Assn., Fiore d'Italia Lodge Newton Sons of Italy, Dante Alighieri Soc., Newton Ctr. Italian Culture, Circolo Lettarario Italiano, Waltham Coll. Club. Roman Catholic. Home: 168 Longfellow Rd Waltham MA 02514 Office: Waltham High Sch 617 Lexington St Waltham MA 02154-3003

PACKARD, JOHN MALLORY, physician; b. Saranac Lake, N.Y., Sept. 25, 1920; s. Edward Newman and Mary Bissell (Betts) P.; m. Ann Maurine Schoonover, June 15, 1944; children: Michael David, John Mallory, Ann Maurine, Mary Betts, Charles Edward, Kris Asvananda, Frank Schoonover, Charlotte Mellen. B.A., Yale U., 1942; M.D., Harvard U., 1945. Diplomate Am. Bd. Internal Medicine. Intern Presbyn. Hosp., N.Y.C., 1945-46; resident in internal medicine Peter Bent Brigham Hosp., Boston, 1948-49; practice medicine specializing in internal medicine and cardiology Pensacola, Fla., 1954-68; prof. medicine, asso. dean Med. Sch. U. Ala., Birmingham, 1968-76; exec. dir. Ala. Regional Med. Program, Birmingham, 1968-73; corp. v.p. med. edn. Bapt. Med. Centers, Birmingham, 1976-92; ret. Contbr. articles to med. jours. Served with USN, 1946-54. Fellow ACP, Am. Coll. Cardiology, Council Clin. Cardiology; mem. Jefferson County Med. Soc., Med. Assn. Ala., AMA, Am. Soc. Internal Medicine, Ala. Soc. Internal Medicine (pres. 1981-82), Alpha Omega Alpha. Republican. Episcopalian.

PACKER, ROGER JOSEPH, neurologist, neuro-oncologist; b. Chgo., May 14, 1951; s. Harry and Mania (Kelmanowski) P.; m. Bernice Ruth Cizek, Mar. 28, 1976; children: Michael Joseph, Zehava Sarah. MB, Northwestern U., 1973, MD, 1976. Resident pediatrics Cin. (Ohio) Childrens Hosp., 1976-78; fellow child neurology Children's Hosp. Phila., Pa., 1978-81; attending neurologist Children's Hosp. Phila., 1981-89; prof. neurology and pediatrics U. Pa., Phila., 1981-89; chmn. neurology Childrens Nat. Med. Ctr., Washington, 1989—; prof. neurology and pediatrics George Washington U., Washington, 1989—; clin. prof. neurology Georgetown U., Washington, 1992—; clin. prof. neurosurgery U. Va., Charlottesville, Va., 1993—; chmn. brain tumor strategy group Childrens Cancer Group, Arcadia, Calif., 1989—. Author: New Trends in Neuro-Oncology, 1991; contbr. chpts. to books and articles to profl. jours. Grantee NIH, Am. Cancer Inst., others. Fellow Am. Acad. Pediatrics, Am. Acad. Neurology (chair sci. selection 1992—, chair neuro-oncology 1981), Child Neurology Soc. (chief liaison health plan reform 1991—). Office: Childrens Nat Med Ctr 111 Michigan Ave NW Washington DC 20010-2970

PADDISON, RICHARD MILTON, neurologist, educator; b. Rochester, N.Y., Aug. 20, 1919; s. Osborn Howard and Ruby (Rapp) P.; m. Josephine Butler Bowles, Dec. 18, 1943 (div. Nov. 1966); children: Richard Jr., Alice Jeannette, David Robert, Patricia Louise, Eileen Ruth, Wendy Ann; m. Vera Gay Davis, Nov. 20, 1966; children: Diane Bell, Stephen Matthew. AB, Duke U., 1943, MD, 1945. Diplomate Am. Bd. Psychiatry and Neurology. Intern Duke U. Hosp., Durham, N.C., 1945-46; instr. neurology and neuroanatomy U. Ga. Sch. Med., Augusta, 1948-49; resident in neurology Jefferson Med. Coll., Phila., 1949-51, instr. in neurology, 1952-53; resident in psychiatry Pa. Hosp., Phila., 1951-53; from asst. prof. to prof. La. State U. Med. Sch., New Orleans, 1964-84, head dept. neurology, 1965-79, med. dir. pvt. diagnostic clinics, 1979-82, dir. continuing med. edn. and alumni, 1982-84, prof. emeritus of neurology, 1984—; cons. Bur. Hearings and Appeals Soc. Security Adminstrn., New Orleans, 1972-95; med. dir. State of La. Office Preventive Medicine and Pub. Health, 1985-86; dir. Security Homestead, New Orleans, 1973-89. Contbr. to profl. books and jours., 1951-84; presenter lectures to profl. socs., 1952—. Regional rep. Duke Med. Sch., Durham, 1958-83; mem. Med. Adv. Bd. La. State Dept. Transp., Baton Rouge, 1976—; vol. tchr. La. State U. Med. Sch., 1984—. Served to capt. U.S. Army, 1946-48. Gitt Meml. vis. lectr., Washington U. Sch. Med., St. Louis, 1978; La. State U. Med. Sch. endowed lectureship named in his honor, 1979; endowed chair of neurology, La. State U. Sch. Med., 1989. Fellow Am. Acad. Neurology (com. chmn. 1958-70, disting. mem. 1987), ACP, Am. Electroencephalographic Soc., So. Electroencephalographic Soc. (past pres.);l mem. Soc. Clin. Neurologists (founder, past pres.), So. Yacht, Commanderie of Bordeaux (New Orleans). Methodist. Home: 1 Spinnaker Ln New Orleans LA 70124-1655

PADDOCK, PAULA J., geriatrics nurse; b. Rochester, N.Y., Oct. 26, 1956; d. Eugene J. and Marguerite R. (Bailey) O'Brien; m. Wayne W. Paddock, Jan. 3, 1981; children: Keith Allen, Eric William. AAS in Nursing, Community Coll. Finger Lakes, 1977. RN, N.Mex., N.Y. Float nurse, charge nurse emergency Lovelace Bataan Med. Ctr., Albuquerque, 1978-79; asst. head nurse pediatrics, charge surg. specialist St. Joseph Hosp., Albuquerque, 1979-83; head nurse Ontario County Health Facility, Canadaigua, N.Y., 1983-86; head nurse, relief supr. Hurlbut Nursing Home, Rochester, N.Y., 1986-88; nurse mgr. Episcopal Ch. Home, Rochester, 1988-90; asst. v.p. nursing, nurse mgr. Thompson Nursing Home, Canandaigua, 1990—; nurse trainer pediatrics in field. Mem. CNA (program coord., program instr., clin. evaulator), Nat. Nurses Assn. Home: 2115 Elton Rd Ionia NY 14475-9701

PADEN, CAROLYN EILEEN BELKNAP, dietitian; b. Takoma Park, Md., Dec. 10, 1953; d. Donald Julius and Lydian Allyne (Plyer) Belknap; m. Raymond Louis Paden, Dec. 29, 1985; children: Matthew Louis, Luke Andrew, Mark Anthony. BS in Home Econs. cum laude, Southern Coll., 1977; MS in Nutrition, Loma Linda (Calif.) U., 1983. Registered dietitian. Dietitic tech. Loma Linda U. Med. Ctr., 1978-82, nutritional support dietitian, 1982-84; clin. dietitian Mercy Meml. Med. Ctr., St. Joseph, Mich., 1984-86, mgr. clin. nutrition svcs., 1986-94; mem. adj. faculty Andrews U., Berrien Springs, Mich., 1994—; rschr. nutritional status of hospitalized patients Mercy Meml. Med. Ctr., St. Joseph, 1986, 87; cons. nutritional support various Berrien County hosps., 1984—; adj. prof. Andrews U., Berrien Springs, Mich., 1982—. Mem. Am. Dietetic Assn. Adventist. Home: 195 Knott Rd Niles MI 49120-9025 Office: Mercy Meml Med Ctr 1234 Napier Ave Saint Joseph MI 49085-2112

PADFIELD, STANLEY CHARLES, hospital administrator; b. Scranton, Pa., June 28, 1956; s. Stanley R. and Irene M. (Wietzel) P.; m. Gail D. Damon, Apr. 4, 1993; children: Stanley R.C., Zachary J.W. BS in Health Records Adminstrn., Temple U., 1978. Asst. dir., dir. med. records St. Agnes Med. Ctr. and Burn Ctr., Phila., 1978-80; dir. med. records NPW Med. Ctr., Wilkes-Barre, Pa., 1980-81, Med. Ctr. Ocean County, Point Pleasant, N.J., 1983-93; dir. Transcription, Ltd., Chgo., 1981-83; dir. health info. svcs. St. Elizabeth Hosp., Elizabeth, N.J., 1993—; mem. optical imaging task force N.J. Hosp. Assn., Princeton, 1995-96. Mem. Am. Health Info. Mgmt. Assn. (registered record adminstr., sgt.-at-arms 1979), N.J. Health Info. Mgmt. Assn. (chmn. legal com. 1984-85). Office: St Elizabeth Hosp 225 Williamson St Elizabeth NJ 07207

PADILLA, JOSÉ S., JR., surgeon; b. Mayagüez, P.R., Dec. 23, 1958; s. José S. and Lavinia (Feliciano) P.; m. Ingrid Oppenheimer, Dec. 24, 1978; children: José S. III, Valerie C., Francis J., Ingrid C. BA, St. Louis U., 1979, BS, 1980; MD, U. P.R., San Juan, 1984. Bd. cert. diplomate Am. Bd. Surgery. Staff surgeon, chief dept. surgery Aguadilla (P.R.) Regional Hosp., 1989-91; staff surgeon North Ark. Med. Ctr., Harrison, 1991—; assoc. prof. U. Autonoma de Guadalajara (Mexico) Sch. Medicine, 1990-91. Contbr. articles to profl. jours. Maj. U.S. Army, 1991. Fellow ACS; mem. AMA, Am. Soc. Gynecologic Endoscopists, Soc. Laparoendoscopic Surgeons, Ark. Med. Soc. Roman Catholic. Office: 715 W Sherman Ave Harrison AR 72602-1293

PADRÓN, MANUEL RICARDO, urologist; b. Havana, Cuba, Mar. 20, 1962; came to U.S., 1971; s. Manuel Antonio and America Cristina (Diaz-Mendez) P.; m. Christine Noel Berndt; children: Alejandro M., Noelle P. BS, U. Fla., 1984, MD, 1987. Diplomate Am. Bd. Urology. Intern, resident U. Fla., 1987-92; pvt. practice urology Echenique & Padrón, MD, P.A., Miami, Fla., 1992—; chmn. operative/invasive procedures quality team Mercy Hosp., Miami, 1994—. Fellow ACS; mem. Am. Urol. Assn., Elks, Phi Beta Kappa. Roman Catholic. Office: Echenque & Padrón 2931 Coral Way Miami FL 33145

PADULA, RICHARD THOMAS, retired cardiothoracic and vascular surgeon; b. Phila., Apr. 10, 1935; s. William V. and Marie T. (Musi) P.; m. Marta M. Meo, Dec. 26, 1959; children: Marta Anne Padula Jardon, Richard W., Thomas J., Robert J., William V III. BS in Biology, Ursinus Coll., 1957; MD, Jefferson Med. Coll., 1961. Bd. cert. Am. Bd. Surgery, Am. Bd. Thoracic Surgery, Gen. Vascular Surgery. Intern Phila. Gen. Hosp., 1961-62; resident in gen. and thoracic surgery Jefferson Med. Coll. Hosp., Phila., 1962-66; from instr. to assoc. prof. surgery Jefferson Med. Coll., Phila., 1966-71; prof. surgery, chief thoracic and cardiovascular surgery U. Tex. Med. Br., Galveston, 1971-86; pvt. practice cardiothoracic and vascular surgery Kansas City, Mo., 1976-95; ret., 1995; cons. thoracic and cardiovascular surgery USPHS, Galveston, 1972-76; chief thoracic and cardiovascular surgery Rsch. Med. Ctr., Kansas City, 1980-94. Contbr. chpts. to textbook and articles to profl. jours. 1st lt. USAR, 1962-64. Fellow ACS, Am. Coll. Cardiology; mem. Am. Assn. Thoracic Surgeons, Soc. for Thoracic Surgeons, Soc. for Vascular Surgery, Internat. Cardiovascular Soc., Soc. Univ. Surgeons, Kansas City Surg. Soc. (pres. 1994). Home and Office: 6600 Wenonga Terr Mission Hills KS 66208

PAFFENBARGER, RALPH SEAL, JR., epidemiologist, educator; b. Columbus, Ohio, Oct. 21, 1922; s. Ralph Seal and Viola Elizabeth (Link) P.; m. Mary Dale Higdon, Sept. 19, 1943 (dec.); children: Ralph, James (dec.), Ann, Charles, John (dec.), Timothy; m. Jo Ann Schroeder, July 20, 1991. A.B., Ohio State U., 1944; M.B., Northwestern U., 1946, M.D., 1947; M.P.H., Johns Hopkins U., 1952, Dr.P.H., 1954. Intern Evanston (Ill.) Hosp., 1946-47; research asst. pediatrics La. State U. and Charity Hosp., New Orleans, 1949-50; practice medicine, specializing in geriatrics Framingham, Mass., 1960-68; clin. asst. prof. preventive medicine U. Cin., 1955-60; lectr. biostatistics Sch. Pub. Health, Harvard U., 1961-62, clin. assoc. preventive medicine Med. Sch., 1963-65, lectr. epidemiology Sch. Pub. Health, 1965-68, vis. lectr., 1968-83, vis. prof. epidemiology, 1983-85, vis. lectr., 1986-88, adj. prof. epidemiology, 1988—; prof. epidemiology in-residence U. Calif. Sch. Pub. Health, Berkeley, 1968-69, adj. prof., 1969-80; prof. epidemiology Stanford U., 1977-93, prof. emeritus, 1993—; rsch. epidemiologist U. Calif., Berkeley, 1993—; commd. officer USPHS, 1947, med. dir., Atlanta, Ga., 1947-53, Bethesda, Md., 1953-55, Cin., 1955-60, Framingham, 1960-68, ret., 1968; mem. epidemiology and disease control study sect. NIH, 1972-76. Assoc. editor: Am. Jour. Epidemiology, 1972-75, 80—, editor, 1975-79; contbr. articles to profl. publs. Served with AUS, 1943-47. Recipient prize for Sports Scis. Internat. Olympic Com., 1996. Mem. AAAS, AMA, APHA, Am. Epidemiol. Soc., Am. Heart Assn., Internat. Epidemiol. Assn., Soc. Epidemiol. Rsch., Rsch. Soc. Am., Internat. Soc. Cardiology, Am. Assn. Suicidology, Marcé Soc., Am. Coll. Sports Medicine, Am. Acad. Sports Physicians, Nat. Fitness Leaders Assn., Royal Soc. Medicine, Phi Eta Sigma, Pi Kappa Epsilon, Delta Omega. Home: 892

Arlington Ave Berkeley CA 94707-1938 Office: Stanford U Sch Medicine Stanford CA 94305

PAGÁN, GILBERTO, JR., clinical psychologist; b. San Juan, P.R., Dec. 30, 1950; s. Gilberto Sr. and Juanita (Quiñones) P.; m. Grissele Camacho, Aug. 6, 1972; children: Mariel, Lauren. Exch. student, SUNY, Albany, 1969-70; BA in Psychology magna cum laude, U. P.R., 1972; MS in Devel. Psychology, Rutgers U., 1974, PhD in Clin. Psychology, 1984. Lic. psychologist, N.J.; cert. sch. psychology. Psychometrician Well Baby Clinic of New Brunswick, N.J., 1972-73; staff psychologist Community Orgn. for Mental Health and Retardation, Inc., Phila., 1976-77; intern in clin. psychology Multimodal Therapy Inst., Kingston, N.J., 1979-80; sch. psychologist New Brunswick Pub. Sch. System, 1980-83; mental health clinician Community Mental Health Ctr. U. Medicine and Dentistry N.J., Piscataway, 1983-93; sch. psychologist Perth Amboy Pub. Sch. Sys., 1993-95; pvt. practice clin. psychology Newark, 1988—; sch. psychologist Jersey City Pub. Sch. Sys., 1995—; assoc. in psychiatry Univ. of Medicine and Dentistry of N.J., Piscataway, 1988—; field supr. Rutgers U., New Brunswick, N.J., 1988—; cons. in field to clients including Bloomfield Pub. Sch. System, Div. of Youth and Family Svcs. of State of N.J., Project Head Start, Plainfield, N.J. Columnist San Juan Star, 1990-93, El Hispano, Phila., 1977-78; contbr. profl. publs.; presenter in field. Pres. N.J. chpt. Nat. Com. for Puerto Rican Statehood, 1990-95. NIMH fellow, 1978-79; predoctoral rsch. fellow Inst. for Rsch. in Human Devel., Divsn. Psychol. Studies of Ednl. Testing Svc., Princeton, N.J., 1974-75; recipient P.R. Psychol. Assn. award, 1972, Puerto Rican Action Bds. Parents Assn. award 1985; inducted into Nat. Honor Soc. in Psychology, 1973. Mem. APA, Am. Fedn. Tchrs., N.J. Psychol. Assn., Psi Chi. Democrat. Roman Catholic. Home: 422 Johnstone St Perth Amboy NJ 08861 Office: 467 Mount Prospect Ave Newark NJ 07104-2907

PAGANELLI, CHARLES VICTOR, physiologist; b. N.Y.C., Feb. 13, 1929; s. Charles Victor and Mary Barone (Spalla) P.; m. Barbara Harriet Slauson, Sept. 18, 1954; children: William, Kathryn, Peter, Robert, John. AB, Hamilton Coll., Clinton, N.Y., 1950; MA, Harvard U., 1953, PhD, 1957. Instr. physiology U. Buffalo, 1958-60, asst. prof., 1960-63; assoc. prof. SUNY, Buffalo, 1963-71, prof. physiology, 1971—. Editor: Physiological Function in Special Environments, 1990; contbr. articles to profl. jours. Recipient Elliott Coues award Am. Ornithologists Union, 1981. Mem. Sigma Xi, Phi Beta Kappa.

PAGANO, ALPHONSE FREDERICK, retired obstetrician, gynecologist; b. Bklyn., Nov. 23, 1909; s. Domenico Antonio Pagano and Amalia Rose (Foresta) Cundari; m. Adele Marie Savarese, May 20, 1939; children: Althea, Amelia, Alphonse Frederick. Ph Ch, Columbia U., 1930, BS, 1934; MD, SUNY, Bklyn., 1935. Diplomate Am. Bd. Ob.-Gyn. Asst. attending ob-gyn. Luth. Med. Ctr., Bklyn., 1938-48, assoc. attending ob-gyn., 1948-52, attending ob-gyn., 1952-88; mem. Malpractice Panel Supreme Ct. N.Y., 1965-85. Cons. Selective Svc. U.S.A., 1948-57; pres. Bay Ridge Med. Sco., 1952; chmn. membership com., 1952—; maternity mortality com. Kings County Med. Soc., 1955-85, chmn. adv. com. ob-gyn., 1965-88. 1st lt. USAR Med. Corps., 1935-42. Recipient Selective Svc. medal, Pres. Truman, Washington, 1948, Cert. Appreciation, Supreme Ct. Appellate Div., Kings County Med. Soc.; named Physician of Yr., 1966, Bay Ridge Med. Soc., Bklyn. Fellow ACS, Am. Coll. Ob.-Gyn. (founding). Republican. Roman Catholic. Home: 2 Westgate Dr Sayville NY 11782-3054

PAGANO, CHARLES DOMINIC, orthodontist; b. Pitts., July 9, 1946; s. Charles Samuel and Amelia Mary (Zaccari) P.; m. Katherine Quartuccio, July 5, 1969; children: Gino Michael, Leesa Marie. BA, St Vincent Coll., Latrobe, Pa., 1968; DMD, U. Pitts., 1971; Cert. in Orthodontics, U. Ill., 1974. Pvt. practice as orthodontist Monroeville, Pa., 1974—. Mem. ADA, Am. Assn. Orthodontists, Pa. Soc. Orthodontists, Pa. Denta Soc., Dental Soc. Western Pa. (bd. dirs. 1985-90). Roman Catholic. Office: 2735 Mosside Blvd Monroeville PA 15146-2736

PAGE, DONNA MARIE, health information manager; b. Oakland, Calif., Feb. 16, 1961; d. Robert Gary and Ada (Pagano) O'D.; m. Stephen Wade Page, Apr. 26, 1987. BA in Mass Comm., Calif. State U., Hayward, 1984. Dir. 401 Diagnostic Ctr., San Francisco, 1984-87; mktg. coord. AccuTax, Walnut Creek, Calif., 1987-89; health info. mgr. Rheem Valley Conv., Moraga, Calif., 1989—; health info. mgr. continuous quality improvement Regency Hills Conv., 1992—; cons. health info., quality assurance, Antioch, Calif., 1995—. Mem. Am. Health Info. Mgmt. Assn. (accredited record tech.), Contra Costa Continuity Care. Home: 1908 Powell Ct Antioch CA 94509

PAGE, EVA VERONICA, dermatologist; b. Arad, Rumania, Aug. 17, 1935; came to U.S., 1966; d. Alexander and Violet (Bernat) Gross; m. Tiberiu Gruber, 1958 (div. Nov. 1964); m. Ernest Page, June 5, 1967; 1 child, Thomas Julian. MD, U. Cluj, Rumania, 1959. Gen. practice medicine County of Oradea, Rumania, 1959-63, dist. physician, 1963-65; pediatric intern Michael Reese Hosp., Chgo., 1967-68; rsch. assoc. dept. medicine (cardiology) U. Chgo., 1966-67, resident in dermatology, 1968-70, instr. dermatology, 1970-71; dermatologist Dixie-Ashland Dermatology Assocs., Chicago Heights, Ill., 1972-75; dermatologist in pvt. practice Olympia Fields, Ill., 1975—. Contbr. articles to profl. jours. Fellow Am. Acad. Dermatology; mem. AMA, Ill. Med. Soc., Chgo. Med. Soc., Chgo. Dermatol. Soc. (v.p. 1990-91). Office: 2605 W Lincoln Hwy Olympia Fields IL 60461

PAGE, JOHN GARDNER, research administrator, scientist; b. Milw., Sept. 14, 1940; s. Raymond G. and Leone B. (Churchill) P.; m. Joyce Ann Krueger, July 7, 1962; children: Teresa Ann, Kimberly Christine. B.S., U. Wis.-Madison, 1963, M.S., 1966, Ph.D., 1967. Diplomate Am. Bd. Toxicology. Sr. Scientist NIH, Bethesda, Md., 1967-69, Eli Lilly Co., Indpls., 1969-77; dir. toxicology and pathology Rhone Poulenc, Inc., Ashland, Ohio, 1977-79; dir. toxicology, Toxigenics, Inc., Decatur, Ill., 1979-83; sr. rsch. advisor Battelle Meml. Inst., Columbus, Ohio, 1983-87; head preclin. toxicology div. So. Rsch. Inst., Birmingham, Ala., 1987—; adj. prof. U. Ill., 1981-83, U. Ala., Birmingham, 1988—. Contbr. articles to profl. jours. Bd. dirs. Am. Cancer Soc., Greenfield, Ind., 1973-77. Recipient Rennebohm Outstanding Tchr's award U. Wis., 1964. Mem. AAAS, Fedn. Am. Socs. Exptl. Biology, Am. Soc. Pharm. Exptl. Therapeutics, Soc. Toxicology, Am. Coll. Toxicology, Internat. Soc. for Study Xenobiotics, Sigma Xi, Rho Chi. Avocations: photography; hiking, fishing. Home: 3601 Crosshill Rd Birmingham AL 35223-1546 Office: So Research Inst 2000 9th Ave S Birmingham AL 35205-2708

PAGE, LESLIE ANDREW, disinfectant manufacturing company executive; b. Mpls., June 5, 1924; s. Henry R. and Amelia Kathryn (Steinmetz) P.; m. DeEtte Abernethy Griswold, July 6, 1952 (div. Sept. 1975); children: Randolph, Michael, Kathryn, Caroline; m. Mary Ellen Decker, Nov. 26, 1976. BA, U. Minn., 1949; MA, U. Calif., Berkeley, 1953; PhD, U. Calif., 1956. Asst. microbiologist, lectr. U. Calif., Davis, 1956-61; cons. San Diego Zoological Soc. Zoo Hosp., 1957-60; microbiologist, research leader Nat. Animal Disease Ctr., USDA, Ames, Iowa, 1961-79; ret., 1979, specialist in Chlamydial nomenclature and disease; med. text cons. Bay St. Louis, Miss., 1979-85; founder, pres., chmn. bd. Steri-Derm Corp., San Mateo, Calif., 1987—; cons. McCormick Distilling Co., Weston, Mo., 1994-95. Editor: Jour. Wildlife Diseases, 1965-68, Wildlife Diseases, 1976; contbr. chpts. to med. texts, over 70 articles to profl. jours.; patentee Liquid Antiseptic Composition. Pres. Garden Island Comty. Assn., Bay St. Louis, Miss., 1980-81; chief commr. East Hancock fire Protection Dist., Bay St. Louis, 1982-83; treas. Woodridge Escondido Property Owners Assn., 1986-88. Fellow Am. Acad. Microbiology (emeritus); mem. Wildlife Disease Assn. (pres. 1972-73, Disting. Svc. award 1980), Am. Soc. for Microbiology, Zool. Soc. San Diego, Sigma Xi, Phi Zeta (hon.). Home and Office: 1784 Deavers Dr San Marcos CA 92069

PAGE, LINDA JEWEL, mental health care educator; b. Quanah, Tex., Mar. 18, 1941; d. Wesley Lee and Eddie Lea (Fiero) P.; m. Roger Hollander, June 10, 1963 (div. Sept. 1973); children: Malika Jewel, Chantal Louise. BA, Mills Coll., 1963; MA, Princeton U., 1967, PhD in Sociology, 1973; MA in Counseling Psychology, Alfred Adler Inst., 1989. Assoc. prof. Northridge (Calif.) State U. (formerly San Fernando Valley State Coll.), 1964-68; lectr., assoc. prof. Concordia U. (formerly Sir George Williams), Montreal, Quebec, Can., 1970-73; teaching master Sir Sandford Fleming Coll., Lindsay, Ont., 1977-79; intern Rudolf Dreikurs Centre, Toronto, Ont., 1979-81; pvt. practice Toronto, 1981-87; dir., founder Psychotherapy Inst. Toronto, 1987-92; founder Med. Psychotherapy Inst., Chgo., 1992—; dean faculty counselling and psychotherapy Alfred Adler Inst. Ont., 1990-92, pres. Adler Grad. Sch. of Ont., 1992, core faculty, Adler Sch. Profl. Psychology, 1992; founder L.J. Page Pubs. and Prodns., Tools for Therapy, 1995. Co-editor: For What Time I Am In This World, 1978; writer poems: (children's album (Musical Chairs, 1980; scriptwriter (children's albums Big Bird and Oscar Go Camping in Canada, 1979, Kids on the Block, C'mon Along, We All Belong, 1986; asst. mng. editor New Century, 1989—; editor, writer, broadcaster Can. Broadcasting Corp., Kids Records, 1974-77; columnist G.P. Psychotherapist Newsletter, 1989-93. Chpt. chief Nichiren Shoshu Sokagakkai of Can., Toronto, 1990. Woodrow Wilson Found. fellow, 1963, NSF fellow, 1963-66. Mem. GP Psychotherapy Assn. (bd. dirs., chair rsch. com. 1991-93), Ont. Assn. Psychotherapsits (steering com., chair tng. liaison com. 1991-93), Internat. Assn. Neurolinguistics Programming (practitioner's cert. 1990, master track 1991), N.Am. Soc. Adlerian Psychology (rsch. com. 1989-93, del. assembly 1991), Soc. for Exploration of Psychotherapy Integration, Soc. for Psychotherapy Rsch., Ont. Assn. Cons., Counselors, Psychotherapists and Psychometrists, Phi Beta Kappa. Buddhist. Home: 5343 N Winthrop #2 Chicago IL Office: Adler Sch Professional Psychology 120 Carlton St Ste 312 Chicago IL

PAGE, NANCY E., pediatrics nurse, nursing consultant; b. Queens, N.Y., June 19, 1959; d. Gerard and Irene (Thomas) Lane; m. David Page, May 29, 1982; children: Meghan, Rebecca, Samantha. BS, SUNY, Brooklyn, 1981; MS, U. Rochester, 1986; postgrad., Syracuse U. RN, N.Y.; cert. in gen. pediatrics ANCC. Pediatric clin. nurse specialist SUNY Health Sci. Ctr., Syracuse, N.Y., 1986—; cons. in field to other hosps. Author: (with Arena) Implementing the Clinical Nurse Specialist Role in the Acute Care Setting, 1989, Application of the Impostor Phenomenon to the Clinical Nurse Specialist Role, 1992, Rethinking the Merger of the CNS and NP, 1994, (with Boeing) Visitation in the PICU: Controversy and Compromise, 1994. Mem. AACN (cert. pediatric RN), ANA, Assn. Care Children's Health, N.Y. State Nurses Assn.

PAGE, NANCY JEANETTE, nursing educator; b. Palo Alto, Calif., Jan. 30, 1954; d. Theodore Moreno and Lillian Margaret Ann Hogg; m. Bradley Page, Dec. 1984; children: Michael, Corey. Diploma, St. Luke's Hosp. Sch. Nursing, San Francisco, 1978; BSN, Calif. State U. Consortium, Long Beach, 1982; MSN, San Jose State U., 1989. CEN, CCRN, TNCC, ACLS instr. Staff nurse ICU Mills Hosp., San Mateo, Calif., 1978-85; staff nurse emergency rm. Alexian Bros. Hosp., San Jose, Calif., 1985-89; flight nurse Air Ambulance Inc., San Carlos, Calif., 1985-89; nursing educator Florence (S.C.) Gen. Hosp., 1985; nursing educator, emergency room, ICU North Bay Med. Ctr., Fairfield, Calif., 1985-87; asst. mgr. emergency dept. Kaiser Permanente Med. Ctr., South San Francisco, Calif., 1987-89; nursing instr. Yavapai Coll., Prescott, Ariz., 1989-96; staff nurse emergency dept. Yavapai Regional Med. Ctr., Prescott, Ariz., 1991—. Recipient Kellogg grant. Mem. AACN, ENA.

PAGE, ROY CHRISTOPHER, periodontist, educator; b. Campobello, S.C., Feb. 7, 1932; s. Milton and Anny Mae (Eubanks) P. BA, Berea Coll., 1953; DDS, U. Md., 1957; PhD, U. Wash., 1967; ScD (hon.), Loyola U., Chgo., 1983. Cert. in periodontics. Pvt. practice periodontics Seattle, 1963—; asst. prof. U. Wash. Schs. Medicine and Dentistry, Seattle, 1967-70, prof., 1974—, dir. Ctr. Research in Oral Biology, 1976-96; dir. grad. edn. U. Wash. Sch. Dentistry, 1976-80; dir. rsch. U. Wash. Sch. Dentistry, Seattle, 1976-94, assoc. dean rsch., 1994—; vis. scientist MRC Labs., London, 1971-72; cons., lectr. in field. Author: Periodontal Disease, 1977, 2d edit., 1990, Periodontitis in Man and Other Animals, 1982. Recipient Gold Medal award U. Md., 1957; recipient Career Devel. award NIH, 1967-72. Fellow Internat. Coll. Dentists, Am. Coll. Dentists, Am. Acad. Periodontology (Gies award 1982, fellowship award 1989); mem. ADA, Am. Assn. Dental Rsch. (pres. 1982-83), Am. Soc. Exptl. Pathology, Internat. Assn. Dental Rsch. (pres. 1987, basic periodontal rsch. award 1977). Home: 8631 Inverness Dr NE Seattle WA 98115-3935

PAGE, SEAN EDWARD, emergency medical care provider, educator; b. York, Pa., May 27, 1966; s. William C. and Patricia (Huber) P. BS in Biochemistry, Elizabethtown Coll., 1988; BSN, York Coll. Pa., 1991. Cert. EMS instr. ARC; cert. BCLS, BTLS, EMT. Health and EMS dep. Manchester Twp. Emergency mgmt. Agy., 1983-90, officer, 1990—; mem. continuing edn. staff York Hosp., 1990-91, clin. nurse I, team leader transitional care unit, 1991-93, charge nurse, 1993; med. officer York County Hazardous Materials Emergency Response Team, 1992-95; instr. nursing Harrisburg Area C.C., 1994—; dep. coroner York County, 1991-93; key resource person hazardous materials med. response Internat. Assn. Fire Chiefs and Nat. Fire Protection Agy., 1994—. Mem. com. health and safety Boy Scouts Am., 1990—; disaster human resource system ARC, 1993—, disaster svcs. instr., 1994—. Pam Abel Nursing scholarship; recipient Outstanding Emergency Med. Svcs. Vol. York County, 1990. Mem. Emergency Health Svcs. Fedn. (edn. and cert. com. 1990-95), Pa. Nurses Assn. (Dist. 20 bd. dirs. 1992-94), Phi Sigma Pi, Sigma Theta Tau. Home: 207 E Locust Ln York PA 17402-1033

PAGE, WINTHROP RANDOLPH, neurosurgeon; b. Rocky Ford, Colo., Aug. 23, 1917; s. Winthrop and Gladys P.; m. Nina Mary; children: John R., William H., Jennifer C. Boyd. Student, U. Va., 1935-38; MD, Yale U., 1942. Diplomate Am. Bd. Neurol. Surgery. Pvt. practice neurosurgery New Orleans, 1952-80; med. researcher W.R. Page Assocs., Inc., New Orleans, 1980—. Bd. dirs. Am. Cancer Soc., New Orleans, 1950-60, Multiple Sclerosis Soc., 1940-65; mem. La. Hwy. Safety Commn., 1967. Served with AUS, 1941-46, to capt. M.C., 1943-46, ETO. Decorated Bronze Star. Fellow ACS, Royal Soc. Health London; mem. Harvey Cushing Soc., Round Table Club N.C. (pres. 1968). Republican. Episcopal. Home: 1215 Pine St New Orleans LA 70118

PAGELS, CARRIE FANCETT, school psychologist, consultant; b. Newberry, Mich., Jan. 5, 1958; d. William Henry and Ruby Evelyn (Skidmore) F.; m. Jeffrey D. Pagels; 1 child, Cassandra Rose. B.A. in Psychology, Lake Superior State U., 1978; student Whittier Coll., 1976-77; M.A. in Sch. Psychology, U. S.C., 1981; Ph.D. in Sch. Psychology, 1984. Lic. psychologist; cert. sch. psychologist. Research asst. U. S.C., Columbia, 1979-80, 81-83; instr., 1983; instr. Lake Superior State U., Sault Ste. Marie, Mich., summer 1981; mental health cons. Head Start Program, Columbia, 1983-86, Charleston, 1987-95; child psychotherapist Counseling and Readjustment Services, Columbia, 1985-86; psychologist Children's Hosp., Columbia, 1983-86; clin. asst. prof. U. S.C. Sch. Medicine, Columbia, 1984-87; sch. psychologist Berkeley County Schs., 1986-87; pvt. sch. psychologist, North Charleston, 1987-94; sch. psychologist Erie 1 Boces presch., Depew, N.Y., 1995-96; cons. Richland Meml. Hosp., Columbia, 1983, Divorce Mediation Project, Columbia, 1982, Life Satisfaction Grant, Columbia, 1979-81. Contbr. chpt. to book. Campaign aide Dem. party, U.S. Senate race, Sault Ste. Marie, Mich., 1978. Stephenson scholar, 1978; NIMH fellow, 1980-81. Mem. Am. Psychol. Assn., Nat. Assn. of Sch. Psychologists, S.C. Assn. Sch. Psychologists, S.C. Psychol. Assn., Children with Attention Deficit Disorder, S.C. Acad. Profl. Psychologists, Low Country Assn. Sch. Psychologists (chmn. 1993-94), N.Y. Assoc. of Sch. Psycholgists. Democrat. Methodist. Avocations: writing fiction, computers, reading, crafts, walking. Home: 34 Short Rd West Falls NY 14170-9733

PAGLIARULO, MICHAEL ANTHONY, physical therapy educator; b. Amityville, N.Y., May 15, 1947; s. Anthony and Louise (Cipriani) P.; m. Patricia Marilyn Salm, Mar. 22, 1975; children: Michael, David, Elisa. BA in Biology, SUNY, Buffalo, 1969, BS in Phys. Therapy, 1970; MA in Phys. Therapy, U. So. Calif., 1974; EdD in Postsecondary Edn. Adminstrn., Syracuse U., 1988. Cert. phys. therapist, N.Y., Calif. Staff phys. therapist Brunswick Hosp. Ctr., Amityville, 1970; lectr. U. So. Calif., L.A., 1974-75, U. Calif., San Francisco, 1975-80; curriculum coord. Ithaca (N.Y.) Coll., 1980-82, asst. prof., 1982-84, acting dir., 1986-89, assoc. prof., dir., 1989-94, assoc. prof. phys. therapy, 1994—. Author: Introduction to Physical Therapy, 1996. Bd. dirs. Marin/Roundtree Homeowners Assn., San Rafael, Calif., 1978-80; cubmaster Boy Scouts Am., Ithaca, 1989-91. Capt. U.S. Army, 1970-72. Mem. Am. Phys. Therapy Assn. (bd. dirs. Calif. chpt. 1979-80, N.Y. chpt. 1989-91, Merit award 1988, 95, Norma Chadwick award 1993). Congregationalist. Office: Ithaca Coll Dept Phys Therapy Danby Rd Ithaca NY 14850

PAINE, ROBERT EDWARD, JR., internist; b. Roancke, Va., Apr. 27, 1925; s. Robert Edward and Edith Emily (Davis) P.; m. Alice Frances Parson, May 1, 1946; children: Emily Anne, Robert Parson. Student, U. Richmond, 1942-43; MD, Med. Coll. Va., 1947. Lic. Va. Intern, asst. resident Norfolk (Va.) Gen. Hosp., 1947-49; resident Lewis Gale Hosp., Roanoke, 1949-51, 53; pvt. practice Salem, Va., 1953-68; med. officer, alcohol rehab. staff Vets. Care Ctr., Salem, 1968-80. Lt. USN, 1943-45, WWII, 1951-53, Korea. Decorated Mil. Order World Wars; named Father of Yr. Roanoke Valley, 1982; recipient Red Cross Svc. award Roanoke Red Cross chpt., 1992, Outstanding Svc. award Boy Scouts Am. Troop 54, 1967. Mem. Island Ford Hunt Club, Lakeland Masonic Lodge, Roanoke Scottish Rite Bodies, Kazim Temple Shrine, Mayflower Soc. (Va. state surgeon), Kappa Sigma (50 year plaque). Presbyterian.

PAINTER, FRANK MCCORMICK, chiropractic physician; b. Newark, N.J., Aug. 28, 1948; s. Frank M. Jr. and Constance V. P.; 1 child, Justin. D of Chiropractic, Palmer Coll. of Chiropractic, 1993. bd. applicant to rehab. diplomate program L.A. Coll. of Chiropractic, 1995—. Series columnist (newspaper) Beacon, 1991-93. Sponsor Gompers Park Athletic Assn., 1995, Oak Park Village Players, Oak Park, Ill., 1995-96. Cert. of Merit Dept. of Diagnosis, 1993. Mem. Am. Chiropractic Assn., Internat. Chriopractic Assn., Found. for Chiropractic Edn. Rsch., Ill. Chiropractic Soc., Palmer Alumni Assn., Videofluorscopy Analysis Club (pres. 1992-93), Palmer Package Technique Club (v.p. 1992-93), Chi Rho Theta.

PAINTER, RUTH ROBBINS, retired environmental biochemist; b. Bethel, Conn., July 21, 1910; d. Bradford Hilton and Clara Mae (Davis) Robbins; m. Edgar Page Painter, July 4, 1940; children: Jane Painter Clapp, Page Robbins Painter. BS, U. Hawaii, 1931, MS, 1934. Cert. nutrition specialist. Nutrition investigator U. Hawaii, Honolulu, 1931-36; assoc. chemist USDA Bur. Home Econs., Washington, 1937; nutrition chemist Wash. State U., Pullman, 1937-40; asst. chemist agrl. toxicology pesticide residue rsch. U. Calif., Davis, 1960-66; assoc. specialist Environ. Toxicology, U. Calif., Davis, 1967-73, specialist, 1973-76; cons. Nutrition and Food Toxicology, Davis, 1940-60. Contbr. articles to profl. jours. and books. Pres. PTA Coun., Davis, 1959-60; chmn. UN Assn. Davis, 1963-65, chmn. Yolo County, Calif. chpt. ARC, 1988. Recipient Clara Barton medal Yolo County, Calif. ARC, U. Hawaii Gold medal, 1931. Mem. Am. Chem. Soc. (ret.), Inst. Food Technologists (profl.), Entomological Soc. Am. (emeritus, chmn. Yr. publs. 1973-75), Sigma Xi, Phi Kappa Phi. Home: 815 Miller Dr Davis CA 95616-3622

PAIROLERO, PETER CHARLES, surgeon; b. Bessemer, Mich., 1938. MD, U. Mich., 1963. Diplomate Am. Bd. Surgeons, Am. Bd. Thoracic Surgeons, Am. Bd. Gen. Vascular Surgeons. Intern St. Mary's Hosp., Duluth, Minn., 1963-64; resident gen. surgery Mayo Grad. Sch. Medicine, Rochester, Minn., 1966-71; fellow cerebral vascular resch. Mayo Grad. Sch. Medicine, Rochester, 1968-69, resident thoracic-cardio surgery, 1971-73. Mem. AMA. Office: 200 1st St SW Rochester MN 55905-0001*

PAK, WILLIAM LOUIS, biologist, researcher, educator; b. Suwon, Korea, Sept. 27, 1932; came to U.S., 1948; m. Marion Whitehouse, June 21, 1958; children: William L. Jr., Dorothy K. AB summa cum laude, Boston U., 1955; PhD, Cornell U., 1960. Inst. physics Stevens Inst. Tech., Hoboken, N.J., 1960-61, asst. prof. physics, 1961-65; asst. prof. biology Purdue U., West Lafayette, Ind., 1965-67, assoc. prof. biology, 1967-72, prof. biology, 1972-87, Oreffice disting. prof. biol. sci., 1987—; panel mem. Visual Scis. B Study Sect. NIH, 1972-75; mem. Vision Rsch. Rev. Com. Nat. Eye Inst., 1986-90; Roche Rsch. Found. vis. prof., Basel, Switzerland, 1984. Author: (with others) The Molecular Biology of the Retina, 1991, Molecular Genetics of Inherited Eye Disorders, 1994, Degenerative Diseases of the Retina, 1995; mem. editl. bd. Jour. Neurogenetics, 1982-88, mem. adv. bd., 1988—; contbr. articles to Cell, Procs. NAS U.S.A., Jour. Biol. Chemistry, Jour. Gen. Physiology, European Molecular Biology Orgn. Jour. Recipient rsch. career devel. award USPHS, McCoy award for rsch. Purdue U., 1982, merit award NIH, 1989, Friedenwald award Assn. for Rsch. in Vision and Ophthalmology, 1995. Mem. AAAS, Am. Physiol. Soc., Assn. Rsch. in Vision and Ophthalmology (Friedenwald award 1995), Biophys. Soc., Collegium of Disting. Alumni Boston U., Nat. Alumni Coun. Boston U., Phi Beta Kappa. Office: Purdue U Biol Sci Lilly Hall West Lafayette IN 47907-1392

PAKE, GEORGE EDWARD, research executive, physicist; b. Jeffersonville, Ohio, Apr. 1, 1924; s. Edward Howe and Mary Mabel (Fry) P.; m. Marjorie Elizabeth Semon, May 31, 1947; children—Warren E., Catherine E., Stephen G., Bruce E. B.S., M.S., Carnegie Inst. Tech., 1945; Ph.D., Harvard U., 1948. Physicist Westinghouse Research Labs., 1945-46; mem. faculty Washington U., St. Louis, 1948-56, 62-70; prof. physics, provost Washington U., 1962-69, exec. vice chancellor, 1965-69, Edward Mallinckrodt prof. physics, 1969-70; v.p. Xerox Corp.; mgr. Xerox Palo Alto (Calif.) Research Center, 1970-78, v.p. corp. research, 1978-83, group v.p., 1983-86; dir. Inst. for Research on Learning, Palo Alto, Calif., 1987-91, dir. emeritus, 1991—; prof. physics Stanford U., 1956-62. Author: (with E. Feenberg) Quantum Theory of Angular Momentum, 1953, Paramagnetic Resonance, 1962, (with T. Estle) The Physical Principles of Electron Paramagnetic Resonance, 1973. Mem. gov. bd. Am. Inst. Physics, 1957-59; bd. dirs. St. Louis Research Council, 1964-70; mem. physics adv. panel NSF, 1958-60, 63- 65; chmn. physics survey com. Nat. Acad. Sci.-NRC, 1964-66; Mem. St. Louis County Bus. and Indl. Devel. Commn., 1963-66; chmn. bd. Regional Indsl. Devel. Corp., St. Louis, 1966-67, St. Louis Research Council, 1967-70; mem. President's Sci. Adv. Com., 1965-69; Bd. dirs. St. Louis Country Day Sch., 1964-70, Central Inst. for Deaf, 1965-70; trustee Washington U., 1970—, Danforth Found., 1971—, U. Rochester, 1982—; trustee Ctr. for Advanced Study in Behavioral Scis., Palo Alto, 1986-92, The Exploratorium, San Francisco, 1987—; bd. overseers Superconducting Super Collider, Univs. Rsch. Assn., 1984-89. Fellow Am. Phys. Soc. (pres. 1977); mem. Am. Assn. Physics Tchrs., AAUP, AAAS, Am. Acad. Arts and Scis., Nat. Acad. Sci., Sigma Xi, Tau Beta Pi. Home: 2 Yerba Buena Ave Los Altos CA 94022-2208 Office: Inst for Rsch on Learning 66 Willow Pl Menlo Park CA 94025

PAKTER, JEAN, medical consultant; b. N.Y.C.; d. David and Lillian (Kunitz) P.; m. Arnold L. Bachman, Sept. 17, 1939 (dec. Dec. 1992); children: Ellen Bachman Mendelson, Donald M. BS, NYU, 1931, MD, 1934; MPH, Coll. U. Sch. Pub. Health, 1955. Bd. cert. pediatrics. Intern Mt. Sinai Hosp., N.Y.C., 1934-36, resident, 1937-39; pediatrician pvt. practice, N.Y.C., 1939-43; dir. Bur. Dept. Health, Marernity, Newborn & Family Planning, N.Y.C., 1950-82; cons., lectr. maternity, child health Coll. U. Sch. Pub. Health, N.Y.C., 1984—. Contbr. articles to profl. jours. Advisor March of Dimes, N.Y.C., 1975—. Recipient Fund for City of N.Y. Pub. Svc. award, 1974, Martha May Eliot award, 1990. Fellow Am. Acad. Pediatrics, Am. Pub. Health Assn., N.Y. Acad. Medicine (trustee 1979-83), N.Y. Obs. Soc. (assoc.); mem. Pub. Health Assn. N.Y.C. (bd. dirs. 1992-96), Women's City Club, Alpha Omega Alpha. Home: 1175 Park Ave New York NY 10128 Office: Coll U Sch Pub Health Ctr Population & Family 60 Haven Ave New York NY 10032

PAKULA, ANITA SUSAN, dermatologist; b. L.A., Nov. 20, 1961. BA, Pomona Coll., 1983; BS, Calif. Luth. Coll., 1985; MD, U. Calif., Irvine, 1988. Diplomat Am. Bd. Dermatology, NAt. Bd. Med. Examiners. Intern Evanston (Ill.) Hosp., 1988-89; resident Northwestern U. Med. Sch., Chgo., 1989-92; clin. instr. dermatology UCLA MEd. Ctr., 1993—; presenter in field. Contbr. articles to profl. jours. Fellow Am. Acad. Dermatology, Am. Soc. Laser Medicine and Surgery; mem. Soc. Pediatric Dermatology. Office: 3180 Willow Ln Ste 200 Westlake Village CA 91361

PALAD, ROSALINDA T., nurse practitioner; b. Masaya Bay, Laguna, The Philippines, Aug. 30, 1950; came to U.S., 1981; d. Graciano C. Taguiam and Zenaida E. Mendoza; m. Manuel T. Palad, June 21, 1975 (div. March 1995); children: Emmanuel Joseph, Thea Lynda. BSN, U. Manila, 1972; MSN, U. Philippines, 1975. RN, N.Y., N.J. Instr. U. Manila, 1972-75; Dean Coll. of Nursing Assumption Coll., San Fernando, Pomponga, The Philippines, 1975-

77; nurse practitioner St. Luke's Roosevelt Hosp. Ctr., N.Y.C., 1981—; rsch. assoc. Health Care Delivery Sys. in The Philippines, 1973, Job Satisfaction of Nurses in The Philippines, 1975. Mem. ANA, N.Y. State Nurses Assn., Philippine Nurses Assn. Republican. Roman Catholic. Home: 52 Mackay Ave Paramus NJ 07652 Office: St Lukes Roosevelt Hosp 1000 10th Ave New York NY 10019

PALADE, GEORGE EMIL, biologist, educator; b. Jassy, Romania, Nov. 19, 1912; came to U.S., 1946, naturalized, 1952; s. Emil and Constanta (Cantemir) P.; m. Irina Malaxa, June 12, 1941 (dec. 1969); children—Georgia Teodora, Philip Theodore; m. Marilyn G. Farquhar, 1970. Bachelor, Hasdeu Lyceum, Buzau, Romania; M.D., U. Bucharest, Romania. Instr., asst. prof., then assoc. prof. anatomy Sch. Medicine, U. Bucharest, 1935-45; vis. investigator, asst. assoc., prof. cell biology Rockefeller U., 1946-73; prof. cell biology Yale U., New Haven, 1973-83; sr. research scientist Yale U., 1983-89; prof.-in-residence, dean sci. affairs Med. Sch., U. Calif., San Diego, 1990—. Author sci. papers. Recipient Albert Lasker Basic Research award, 1966, Gairdner Spl. award, 1967, Horwitz prize, 1970, Nobel prize in Physiology or Medicine, 1974, Nat. Medal Sci., 1986. Fellow Am. Acad. Arts and Scis.; mem. Nat. Acad. Sci., Pontifical Acad. Sci., Royal Soc. (London), Leopoldina Acad. (Halle), Romanian Acad., Royal Belgian Acad. Medicine.

PALADINO, JOSEPH ANTHONY, clinical pharmacist; b. Utica, N.Y., May 5, 1953; s. Paul Francis and Jacqueline Ann (Monaco) P.; m. Carol Ann Jenny, June 5, 1976; children: Nicholas Joseph, Matthew Jerome, Kathryn Elizabeth. BS in Biology, Siena Coll., Loudonville, N.Y., 1975; BS in Pharmacy, Mass. Coll. Pharmacy, 1977; D Pharmacy, Med. U. S.C., 1982. Acting dir. pharmacy Utica (N.Y.) Psychiat. Ctr., 1978-80; decentralized pharmacist Med. U. Hosp., Charleston, S.C., 1980-82; asst. dir. pharmacy Rochester (N.Y.) Gen. Hosp., 1982-87, adj. med. staff, 1986-87; clin. instr. pediatrics U. Rochester Sch. Medicine, 1985-87; clin. asst. prof. pharmacy SUNY, Buffalo, 1989-93, clin. assoc. prof., 1994—; dir. pharmacokinetics Millard Fillmore Suburban Hosp., Williamsville, N.Y., 1987—; dir. clin. outcomes and econs. rsch. Millard Fillmore Health System, Buffalo; editorial adv. bd. Jour. of Infectious Disease Pharmacotherapy, 1993—; mem. adv. bd. several major pharm. cos.; 1st vis. prof. pharmacy Tayside Health Bd., Dundee, Scotland, 1992. Author book chpts.; contbr. numerous articles to med., pharmacy, pharmacology, pharmacoecon. and infectious disease jours. Big Bro., Big Bros. and Big Sisters, Albany, N.Y., 1972-80; bd. mem., den leader Cub Scouts, Clarence, N.Y., 1989-91; founding bd., coach Clarence Little League Football, 1992-94. Fellow Am. Coll. Clin. Pharmacy (founder, 1st chmn. Outcomes and Econs. Practice and Rsch. Network); mem. Am. Soc. Microbiology, Soc. Infectious Diseases Pharmacists, N.Y. Acad. Scis. Office: Millard Fillmore Suburban Hosp 1540 Maple Rd Williamsville NY 14221-3647

PALAHNIUK, RICHARD JOHN, anesthesiology educator, researcher; b. Winnipeg, Man., Can., Dec. 5, 1944; s. George and Teenie (Lukinchuk) P.; m. Patricia June Smando, July 15, 1967; children: Christopher, Daniel, Andrew. BS in Medicine, U. Man., 1968, MD, 1968. Head obstetric anaesthesia Health Scis. Ctr., Winnipeg, 1973-79; prof. and chmn. of anaesthesia U. Man., Winnipeg, 1979-89; prof. anesthesiology, head dept. U. Minn., Mpls., 1989—. Contbr. papers and book chpts. to profl. publs.; mem. editorial bd. Can. Jour. Anaesthesia, Toronto, 1985-89. Fellow Med. Rsch. Coun. Can., 1972, rsch. grantee, 1974-79. Fellow Royal Coll. Physicians of Can.; mem. Can. Anaesthetists' Soc., Am. Soc. Anesthesiology, Internat. Anesthesia Rsch. Soc. (editorial bd. Cleve. chpt. 1987—). Roman Catholic. Office: U Minn Med Sch 420 Delaware St SE Minneapolis MN 55455-0374

PALEK, JIRI, medical educator, researcher, academic administrator; b. Prague, Czechoslovakia, Aug. 6, 1934; came to U.S., 1968; s. Frant and Marie Palek; m. Marie Palek, Oct. 9, 1967; children: Michael, Nicole. MD, Charles U. Sch. Medicine, Prague, 1958. Clin. asst. prof. Med. Sch. Harvard U., Boston, 1973-74; assoc. prof. Med. Sch. U. Mass., Worcester, 1974-78; assoc. dir. div. hematology/oncology St. Vincent Hosp., Worcester, 1974-78; prof. Sch. of Medicine Tufts U., Boston, 1978—; chmn. dept. biomed. rsch., chief div. hematology/oncology St. Elizabeth's Med. Ctr., Boston, 1978—; cons. physician N.E. Deaconess Hosp., Boston, 1976-78; physician U. Mass. Med. Ctr., Worcester, 1976-78; mem. sci. adv. bd. Boston Sickle Cell Ctr., 1988—; reviewer hematology subsplty. panel residency rev. com. Accreditation Coun. for Grad. Med. Edn., 1989—; mem. hematology study sect. NIH, 1978-84; mem. editorial bd., guest editor various hematology jours. Contbr. numerous articles to profl. jours. NIH grantee, 1974—. Fellow ACP; mem. Assn. Am. Physicians, Am. Fedn. Clin. Rsch., Am. Physiol. Soc., Am. Soc. Cell Biology, Internat. Soc. Hematology (councillor 1989-90, v.p. 1990—), N.Y. Acad. Scis., Mass. Soc. Med. Rsch. (bd. dirs. 1987—), Leukemia Soc. Am., Red Cell Club, Boston Blood Club. Office: St Elizabeths Med Ctr 736 Cambridge St Brighton MA 02135-2997

PALENA, PETER V., ophthalmologist, retina specialist, educator; b. Phila., Apr. 15, 1938; s. Vincent and Susan Palena; m. Rosemary Catroppa, June 30, 1962; children: Peter V. Jr., Susan, David, Scott. AB in Biology, LaSalle Coll., Phila., 1959; MD, Jefferson Med. Coll., 1963. Diplomate Nat. Bd. Med. Examiners. Straight med. intern Jefferson Med. Coll. Hosp., Phila., 1963-64, resident in ophthalmology, 1966-69; Lancaster course in ophthalmology Colby Coll., Waterville, Maine, 1967; retinal fellow Wills Eye Hosp., Phila., 1969-70, mem. staff retina svc., 1981—; pvt. practice, Media, Pa., 1981—; mem. staff retina svc. Thomas Jefferson U. Hosp., Phila., 1970-81; clin. prof. ophthalmology Thomas Jefferson U., 1970—, Hahnemann Med. Coll., Phila., 1983-86; mem. staff Riddle Meml. Hosp., Media, 1970—, chief div. ophthalmology, 1984—, dir. Eye Care Ctr., 1994—; cons. Fair Acres Farms-Delaware County Hosp., Lima, Pa., 1970—; mem. Pa. Medicare Adv. Com., 1992—; mem. physicians adv. com. Blue Shield, 1988—. Contbr. articles to med. jours. Lt. comdr. M.C., USN, 1964-66; mem. USNR, 1966-69. Rsch. grantee NIH, 196-69, Lions Club Pa., 1971; retinal fellow Heed Fellowship, 1969-70, Nat. Inst. Neurol. Diseases and Blindness, 1969-70. Mem. ACS, AMA, Am. Acad. Ophthalmology (3d party reimbursement com.), Assn. for Rsch. in Vistion and Ophthalmology, Vitreous Soc., Pa. Med. Soc., Pa. Acad. Ophthalmology (exec. bd. 1988—, v.p., 3d party ins. policies and reimbursements com. 1989—), Delaware County Med. Soc., Phila. Med. Soc., Ophthalmic Club Phila. (life), Coll. Physicians Phila., Intercounty Med. Soc., Hare Honor Med. Soc., Alpha Epsilon, Alpha Epsilon Delta. Office: Riddle Eye Assocs Ste 3302 1098 W Baltimore Pike Media PA 19063 also: Wills Eye Hosp Retina Svc 9th and Walnut Sts Philadelphia PA 19107

PALERMO, DAVID STUART, retired psychology educator and administrator. BS in Psychology and Edn., Lynchburg Coll., 1951; MS in Psychology, U. Mass., 1953; PhD, U. Iowa, 1955. Rsch. assoc. Iowa Child Welfare Rsch. Sta. U. Iowa, 1955; asst. prof. psychology So. Ill. U., Carbondale, 1955-58; asst. prof. Inst. Child Devel. U. Minn., Mpls., 1958-63; vis. prof. dept. psychology U. Edinburgh, Scotland, 1969-70; sr. Fulbright scholar dept. psychology U. Sydney, Australia, 1975; prof. Inst. Advanced Psychol. Studies Adelphi U., Garden City, L.I., N.Y., 1978-79; assoc. prof. Pa. State U., University Park, 1963-66, prof., 1966—, assoc. dir. Ctr. for the Study of Child, Adolescent Devel., 1984-88, assoc. dean for rsch. and grad. studies, Coll. Liberal Arts, 1988-92; prof. emeritus, 1992—; assoc. The Behavioral and Brain Scis., 1982—. Editor Child Development Abstracts and Bibliography, 1971-74; editor Jour. Exptl. Child Psychology, 1973-83, mem. editorial bd., 1966—; mem. editorial bd. Jour. Verbal Learning and Verbal Behavior, 1964-77, Metaphor and Symbolic Activity, 1983—, Cognitive Devel., 1990-93; contbr. numerous articles to profl. jours. Recipient Career Devel. award Nat. Inst. of Child Health and Human Devel. award, 1965-70. Fellow APA; mem. Soc. for Rsch. in Child Devel., Ea. Psychol. Assn., Jean Piaget Soc., Sigma Xi.

PALERMO, NICHOLAS JOSEPH, osteopathic physician; b. Geneva, N.Y., Nov. 7, 1946; s. Nicholas Dominic and Theresa Marie (Bruno) P.; m. Wendy Jean Billings, Aug. 10, 1968 (div. Sept. 1988); children: Tina Anne, Nicholas Joseph Jr. BS in Biology, Norwich U., 1968; MS in Biology, Georgetown U., 1970; DO, Coll. Osteo. Medicine-Surgery, Des Moines, 1976. Cert. lab. dir. Intern Youngstown (Ohio) Osteo. Hosp., 1976-77; pvt. practice Youngstown, 1977-78, Manchester, Conn., 1978—; lab. dir. Manchester Profl. Lab. Inc., 1980—, Metpath Clin. Lab., Manchester, 1990-94; chmn. Conn. Bd. Osteo. Med. Examiners, Hartford, 1984—. Umpire Manchester Little League, 1981—; bd. dirs. March of Dimes, 1985; treas. Manchester Health Svcs., 1987-89. Capt. Med. Svc. Corps, U.S. Army, 1971-73. Recipient Men of Achievement award. Mem. Am. Coll. Family Practice (cert.), New Eng. Osteo. Assn. (bd. dirs.), Am. Osteo. Assn., New Eng. Coll. Osteo. Medicine (clin.), N.Y. Coll. Osteo. Medicine (clin.), Conn. Osteo. Med. Soc. (v.p. 1980-85, pres. 1986-95), Nat. Osteo. Found., AOA House of Dels., Mass. Soc. Bioenergetic Analyses, Hartford County Med. Assn., Manchester Med. Soc., Am. Legion, Student Osteo. Med. Assn. (life), UNICO, Sigma Sigma Phi (life), Epsilon Tau Sigma (life). Office: 225 Main St Manchester CT 06040-3539

PALESTINE, ALAN GARY, ophthalmologist; b. Middletown, N.Y., Apr. 30, 1952; s. Sol and Irene P.; m. Roberta, June 2, 1974 (div. Oct. 31, 1994); children: Sandra, Mark; m. Gail Ann, Sept. 3, 1995. BA, Cornell U., 1974; MD, U. Rochester, 1978. Diplomate Am. Bd. Ophthalmology. Chief clin. immunology nat. eye inst. NIH, Bethesda, Md., 1982-89. Office: 1145 19th St NW Washington DC 20036

PALEY, SHARON GREENBERG, clinical psychologist; b. Bklyn., Dec. 28, 1948; d. Milton J. and Henrietta (Weinrib) Greenberg; m. James A. Paley, Feb. 20, 1972; children: Jeremy Alexander, Erica Rachel. BS, Cornell U., 1970; MA, NYU, 1973; PhD, Syracuse U., 1981. Lic. psychologist, Conn., N.Y. Sch. psychologist Ithaca (N.Y.) City Sch. System, 1979-80; clin. psychologist Guilford, New Haven, Madison, Woodbridge, Conn., 1981—. Mem. Conn. Psychol. Assn. Democrat. Jewish. Home and Office: 75 Country Club Dr Woodbridge CT 06525-2509

PALINSKY, CONSTANCE GENEVIEVE, hypnotherapist, educator; b. Flint, Mich., May 31, 1927; d. George and Genevieve Treasa (Pisarski) Ignace; m. Joseph Palinsky, July 3, 1947; children: Joseph II, Mark Robert. Art student, Flint Inst. Arts, Oriental Artists Sch., others; numerous hypnosis studies including, Ethical Tng. Hypnosis Ctr., N.J. and Fla., Mid-West Inst., Hypnodye Found, Ill. and Fla.; tng., Nat. Guild Hypnotherapists. Cert NLP practitioner, neuro linguistics programmer. Owner, operator Palinsky Gallery of Art and Antiques, Flint, 1970-80; art lectr. Genesee County Grade Sch. System Flint Inst. Arts, 1972-74; owner, hypnosis cons. Hypno-Tech. Ctr., Flint, 1975-80; asst. mgr. Wethered-Rice Fine Jewelry, Flint, 1982-83; hypnotherapist, sr. cons. Dailey Life Ctr., Flint, 1985-95; mem. Am. Bd. Hypnotherapy, Calif.; numerous radio and TV shows and guest appearances, Flint, 1957—, ABC Nat. Network, 1959, Flint Calbe TV, 1972, others. Author: Constructive Personality Development, 1987, Secrets Revealed for Hypnosys Scripting, 1989, Designing Hypnosis Scripts for Relief of Multiple Sclerosis, 1994, Substance Abuse Issues Revealed of Effective Hypnosis Interventions, 1994, Light Tough Therapy for Stress-Headache and Back Pain Relief--A Form of Hypno-Acupressure, 1995; one-woman show Dell's Aircraft Gallery, 1958; group shows at Flint Inst. Arts, U. Mich., Purdue U., Lafayette, Inc., Flint Artist Market, Saginaw, Detrout and Grand Rapids, Mich., Japan, others; contbr. articles to profl. jours.; author scripts and software in hypnosis field. Bd. dirs. The Chapel of The Angles Bldg. Fund for Lapeer County, 1974-75; pub. speaker various civic orgns. Named Oil Colorist of Yr. Profl. Photographers of Mich., 1959; recipient Pub. Svc. award Genesee County Sheriff's Dept., 1974. Mem. Internat. Soc. Profl. Hypnosis (regional v.p. 1977-79), Internat. Soc. Profl. Hypnotists and Counselors, Internat. Med. and Dental Hypnotherapist Assn., Nat. Guild Hypnotherapists, Nat. Guild Hypnotists (rsch. award for hypnosis for relief of multiple sclerosis 1991), Questers Antique Study Group (various offices including pres. 1972-90), Internat. Psychic Arts Rsch. (founder, pres. 1974-75), Flint Artist Market Group (program dir., treas.), Flint Soc. Arts and Crafts (v.p., pres. 1958-59), Quota Club, others. Republican. Roman Catholic. Home: 2362 Nolen Dr Flint MI 48504-5201

PALISI, ANTHONY THOMAS, psychologist, educator; b. Rahway, N.J., Mar. 8, 1930; s. Anthony Francis and Marianne Catherine (Picone) P.; m. Dyane Cassidy, Apr. 19, 1954; children: Jane, Anthony Francis II, Phyllis, Damian-Marie. BS, Seton Hall U., 1951, MA, 1958; EdD, Temple U., 1973. Cert. secondary tchr., elem. prin., psychologist, rehab. counselor, N.J.; mem. Nat. Register Health Care Profls. in Psychology. Tchr., coach pub. schs. Rahway, 1953-60; sports editor Rahway News-Record, 1950-60; prin. elem. pub. sch. Franklin Twp., N.J., 1960-65; asst. prof. edn. Seton Hall U., 1965-73, assoc. prof., 1974-77, prof., 1977-82, acting grad. dean, 1976-77, dir., 1969-80, indsl. cons. group dynamics, 1967—. Contbr. articles and short stories to profl. jours. and popular periodicals. Mem. Rahway Bd. Edn. 1961-62; trustee Rahway Libr., 1961-68, pres. 1967-68. Recipient award N.J. Sportswriters' Assn., 1953. Mem. APA, ACA, Am. Mgmt. Assn. (coauthor video tng. program), N.J. Psychol. Assn., Assn. for Specialists in Group Work (mem. rsch. com. 1980-82), N.Y. Acad. Scis., Nat. Acad. Counselors and Family Therapists (chmn., exec. dir. 1988-93), Nat. Register of Health Svc. Providers in Psychology. Roman Catholic.

PALLARDY, THOMAS JOSEPH, counselor, psychology educator; b. Evergreen Park, Ill., Apr. 2, 1955; s. William Eugene and Mary Virginia (Kavanagh) P. AA, Morraine Valley Community Coll., 1985; B in Psychology, Governors State U., 1988. Cert. delinquency prevention specialist U. So. Calif. Delinquency Inst.; registered hypnotherapist Nat. Guild Hypnotists. Police officer Palos Hills (Ill.) Police Dept., 1976-83, div. comdr., 1979-83; football, basketball and baseball coach, tchr./counselor St. Laurence High Sch., Burbank, Ill., 1983—; cons. psychotherapy Oak Lawn and Chgo., Ill., 1986-94; pvt. practice counseling Oak Lawn, 1994—. With USN, 1973-76. Recipient Svc. to Mankind award Sertoma Club, 1981. Mem. Ill. High Sch. Assn. (ofcl. 1976—), Chgo. Cath. League Coaches Assn. (coach 1983—). Roman Catholic. Office: St Laurence High Sch 5556 W 77th St Oak Lawn IL 60459-1300

PALLAS, CHRISTOPHER WILLIAM, cardiologist; b. Chattanooga, Mar. 27, 1956; s. William Charles and Katherine (Rigas) P. Student, Vanderbilt U., 1974-75; BA in Biology, U. Tenn., 1978; MD, Wake Forest U., 1982. Diplomate Am. Bd. Internal Medicine, Am. Bd. Cardiology. Intern Med. Coll. Ga., Augusta, 1982-83, resident, 1983-85, chief med. resident, 1985-86, clin. fellow cardiology, 1986-88, instr. in cardiology, 1988-89, attending physician, 1988—, asst. prof. cardiology, 1989—, researcher clin. and basic cardiology, 1989—; cons. cardiovascular diseases VA Med. Ctr., Dublin, Ga., 1988-89, dir. coronary care unit, Augusta, 1988—. Contbr. articles to profl. jours. Fellow Am. Coll. Chest Physicians, Am. Coll. Cardiology; mem. AMA, Med. Assn. Ga., Richmond County Med. Soc. Greek Orthodox. Home: Ste 1601 # 1 Seventh St Augusta GA 30901 Office: Med Coll Ga Cardiology BA-A535 1120 15th St Augusta GA 30901-3157

PALMA, ROBERT ANTHONY, orthodontist; b. N.Y.C., Jan. 27, 1949; s. Anthony Ragusa and Ruth P.; m. Ann Marie, Dec. 23, 1978; children: Christopher, Jacqueline. BA, Gettysburg Coll., 1971; MS in Dentistry, MS in Orthodontics; DMD, Fairleigh Dickinson U., 1975. Gen. practice resident Cath. Med. Ctr. of Bklyn. and Queens, 1975-76. Mem. ADA, Am. Assn. Orthodontics, N.Y. Soc. Orthodontics, NE Soc. Orthodontists, Suffolk Dental Soc. Republican. Roman Catholic. Home: 1 Allenby Dr Fort Salonga NY 11768

PALMER, BEVERLY BLAZEY, psychologist, educator; b. Cleve., Nov. 22, 1945; d. Lawrence E. and Mildred M. Blazey; m. Richard C. Palmer, June 24, 1967; 1 child, Ryan Richard. PhD in Counseling Psychology, Ohio State U., 1972. Lic. clinical psychologist, Calif. Adminstrv. assoc. Ohio State U., Columbus, 1969-70; rsch. psychologist Health Svcs. Rsch. Ctr. UCLA, 1971-77; commr. pub. health L.A. County, 1978-81; pvt. practice clin. psychology Torrance, Calif., 1985—; prof. psychology Calif. State U., Dominguez Hills, 1973—. Reviewer manuscripts for numerous textbook pubs; contbr. numerous articles to profl. jours. Recipient Proclamation County of L.A., 1972, Proclamation County of L.A., 1981. Mem. Am. Psychol. Assn. Office: Calif State U Dominguez Hills Dept Psychology Carson CA 90747

PALMER, BRENT DAVID, microanatomy educator, reproductive biologist; b. Burbank, Calif., May 13, 1959; s. Warren Thayer and Yvonne Lita (McKelvey) P.; m. Sylvia Irena Karalius, June 26, 1982. BA, Calif. State U., Northridge, 1985; MS, U. Fla., 1987, PhD, 1990. Grad. asst. U. Fla., Gainesville, 1985-90; asst. prof. Wichita (Kans.) State U., 1990-91, Ohio U., Athens, 1991—; cons. U.S. EPA, 1992—, Environment Can., 1995—. Contbr. chpts. to books, articles on vertebrate reproductive biology and toxicology to profl. jours.; reviewer Biology of Reproduction, Champaign, Ill., 1988—, Harper Collins pubs., N.Y.C., 1991-93, Reproduction, Fertility and Devel., Australia, 1995—, Comments on Toxicology, Ind., Press, 1995—, Jour. Morphology, N.Y.C., 1995—, Environ. Health Perspectives, Biology of Reproduction, Gen. and Comprative Endocrinology, Am. Jour. Anatomy. Coord. Sci. Olympiad, Wichita, 1991, So. Ohio Dist. Sci. Day, 1992-94, Sci. and Engring. Fair, 1992-94. Rsch. grantee NIH, 1995—; recipient Best Student Paper award Herpetologists League, 1988, Stoye award Am. Soc. of Ichthyologists & Herpetologists, 1988, Student Rsch. award Soc. Study of Amphibian & Reptiles, 1989, Grants-in-aid of Rsch., Sigma Xi, 1989. Mem. AAAS, Am. Soc. Zoologists, Soc. Study Reproduction, Phi Beta Kappa. Office: Ohio U Dept Biol Scis Athens OH 45701-2979

PALMER, CAROL ANN, psychotherapist, editor, writer, artist, lawyer; b. Stamford, Conn., Sept. 20, 1949; d. Theodore Barclay and Mary Joan (Rekos) P. BA in English, Skidmore Coll., 1981; JD, Benjamin N. Cardozo Sch. Law, 1994. Lic. NASD-Series 7, 1985; cert. in hypnosis The Hypnosis Inst., N.Y.C. Editorial asst. Jour. of Quantum Electronics Internat. Brotherhood Elec. and Electronics Engrs., N.Y.C., 1970-71; mgr. color slide sect. The Bettmann Archive, N.Y.C., 1973-74; welfare advocate MFY Legal Services, Inc., N.Y.C., 1976-77; dir. rsch. capital punishment project NAACP Legal Def. and Ednl. Fund, Inc., N.Y.C., 1977-84; SEC/NASD compliance officer First Realty Res. Inc., N.Y.C., 1984-85; stockbroker N.Y.C., 1985; proofreader, editor mergers and acquisitions dept. Morgan Stanley & Co., N.Y.C., 1986-89; pvt. practice psychotherapy Bklyn., 1986—; assoc. Law Firm of Eileen Nadelson, 1995—; co-producer, co-host TV program Cable Investors Digest, N.Y.C., 1984-86. Founding editor (newsletter) Death Row, U.S.A. Mem. St. Ann and the Holy Trinity Episc. Ch., Bklyn. Pitney Bowes scholar 1967; recipient Laurel Girls' award State of Conn., 1967. Mem. Internat. Assn. of Counselors and Therapists, 62 Montague Street Housing Corp. (v.p. 1995—). Democrat. Roman Catholic. Home and Office: 62 Montague St Brooklyn NY 11201-3375

PALMER, EARL A., ophthalmologist, educator; b. Winchester, Ohio, July 2, 1940; m. Carolyn Mary Clark, June 13, 1963; children: Andrea, Aaron, Genevieve. BA, Ohio State U., 1962; MD, Duke U., 1966. Diplomate Am. Bd. Pediatrics, Am. Bd. Ophthalmology. Resident in pediatrics U. Colo. Med. Ctr., Denver, 1966-68; resident in ophthalmology Oreg. Health Scis. U., Portland, 1971-74; fellow Baylor Coll. Medicine, Houston, 1974-75; asst. prof. Pa. State U., Hershey, 1975-79; prof. Oreg. Health Scis. U., 1979—. Contbr. articles to profl. jours. Fellow Am. Acad. Pediatrics, Am. Acad. Ophthalmology (Honor award); mem. Am. Assn. Pediatric Ophthalmology and Strabismus (pres. 1996—). Office: Casey Eye Inst 3375 SW Terwilliger Blvd Portland OR 97201

PALMER, EDWARD L., social psychology educator, television researcher, writer; b. Hagerstown, Md., Aug. 11, 1938; s. Ralph Leon and Eva Irene (Brandenburg) P.; children: Edward Lee, Jennifer Lynn. BA, Gettysburg Coll., 1960; BD, Luth. Theol. Sem., Gettysburg, 1964; MS, Ohio U., 1967, PhD, 1970. Asst. prof. Western Md. Coll., Westminster, 1968-70; asst. prof. Davidson Coll., N.C., 1970-77, assoc. prof., 1977-86, chair, 1985—, prof., 1986—, Watson prof., 1991—; guest rschr. Harvard U., Cambridge, Mass., 1977; vis. scholar UCLA, 1984; cons. Council on Children, Media, Merchandising, 1978-79, 1st Union Bank Corp., Charlotte, N.C., 1975-79; NSF proposal reviewer, 1978—. Editl. reviewer Jour. Broadcasting and Electronic Media, 1978—; editor: Children and the Faces of TV, 1980; author: (book) Children in the Cradle of TV, 1987; contbr. to Wiley Ency. of Psychology, 1984, Lawrence Erlbaum Assocs., 1991, Sage Pub., 1993, 96; author jour. articles. Sec. A. Mecklenburg Child Devel. Assn., Davidson and Cornelius, N.C., 1974-78; bd. mem. pub. radio sta. WDAV, 1970-90. Telecommunications task force Rutgers U., 1981. Recipient Thomas Jefferson Teaching award Robert Earl McConnell Found., 1993. Mem. APA, Soc. Rsch. in Child Devel., Am. Psychol. Soc., Assn. Heads Depts. Psychology (chair 1994-96), Southeastern Psychol. Assn., Southeastern Soc. Social Psychologists, So. Assn. Pub. Opinion Rsch., Phi Beta Kappa (pres. Davidson chpt. 1985-86). Avocations: sunrise and sunset walks, writing poetry, bird watching, music composition and performance. Office: Davidson Coll PO Box 1719 Davidson NC 28036-1719

PALMER, HUBERT BERNARD, dentist, retired military officer; b. San Antonio, Sept. 6, 1912; s. Hubert Victor and Rosemary (Garvey) P.; student St. Mary's U., 1931-34; D.D.S., Baylor U., 1938; postgrad. George Washington U., 1946-47, U. Md., 1950-53; m. Elizabeth Harriet McAlary, Aug. 16, 1945; children—Hubert Bernard II, Robert Leldon. Commd. 1st lt. USAAF, 1938, advanced through grades to col. USAF, 1971; chief dept. dental research U.S. Army, 1946-50; chief dept. exptl. dentistry, USAF, 1953-54, chief research dentistry div. 1954-56; command dental surgeon, 1958-59, 63-65, 65-68; dental staff officer, 1959-62, dir. dental services, 1968-71; dir. Eastside Dental Clinic San Antonio Met. Health Dist., 1972-81; dir. Mirasol Dental Clinic, 1982-83; clin. asst. prof. U. Tex. Dental Sch., San Antonio, 1973-76. Decorated Legion of Merit, Commendation medal First Oak Leaf Cluster, Meritorious Service medal. Fellow AAAS; mem. Am. Dental Assn., Internat. Assn. Dental Research, Soc. Gen. Microbiology, Am. Soc. Microbiology, Omicron Kappa Upsilon. Contbr. articles to profl. jours. Research reduction decalcification tooth enamel. Home: 6115 Forest Timber St San Antonio TX 78240

PALMER, JEFFRESS GARY, hematologist, educator; b. Bklyn., Oct. 7, 1921; s. William Ware and Margaret Lee (Boswell) P.; m. Jane Ann Cartwright, Feb. 2, 1951; children: Kristin Cartwright, Julie Mitchell. BS, Emory U., 1942, MD, 1944. Intern N.C. Bapt. Hosp., 1944-45; resident in medicine Emory U., Atlanta, 1947-49; fellow hematology U. Utah, Salt Lake City, 1949-52; from asst. prof. to prof. medicine U. N.C., Chapel Hill, 1952—. Capt. M.C. AUS, 1945-47. Mem. AAAS, AAUP, AMA, Am. Fedn. for Clin. Rsch., So. Soc. for Clin. Investigation, N.Y. Acad. Scis., Am. Soc. Hematology. Home: Morgan Creek Rd Chapel Hill NC 27514

PALMER, JERRY P., medical educator, researcher, internist; b. N.Y.C., Apr. 5, 1944. BA in Biology, SUNY, 1966; MD cum laude, Upstate Med. Ctr., Syracuse, N.Y., 1970. Diplomate Am. Bd. Internal Medicine, Am. Bd. Endocrinology, Am. Bd. Metabolism. Intern Dartmouth Affiliated Hosps., Hanover, N.H., 1970-71, resident, 1971-72; sr. rsch. fellow divsn. endocrinology dept. medicine U. Wash., Seattle, 1972-74, acting instr. dept. medicine, 1974-75, dir. adminstrn. core diabetes endocrinology ctr., 1975—, dir. clin. rsch. core diabetes endocrinology rsch. ctr., 1975-88, 91—, acting asst. prof. dept. medicine, 1975-77, rsch. affiliate regional primate rsch. ctr., 1976—, asst. prof. dept. medicine, 1977-80, dep. dir. diabetes endocrinology rsch. ctr., 1977—, assoc. prof. dept. medicine, 1980-86, prof. dept. medicine, 1986—; assoc. med. staff Univ. Hosp., Seattle, 1975—; attending physician Seattle Pub. Health Hosp., 1975-82, Pacific Med. Ctr., Seattle, 1982-89; mem. med. staff Providence Med. Ctr., Seattle, 1988-89, VA Med. Ctr., Seattle, 1989—; chief divsn. endocrinology, metabolism and nutrition Seattle VA Med. Ctr., 1989—; dir. diabetes care ctr. U. Wash. Med. Ctr., 1991—; Pfizer vis. prof. U. Tex., Houston, 1996. Assoc. editor: Diabetes, 1984, 85, 86. Mem. Am. Diabetes Assn. (Wash. affiliate bd. dirs. 1975-83, Wash. affiliate v.p. 1976, 77, Wash. affiliate chmn. peer rev. com. 1984, 85, 86, mem. rsch. com. 1985, 86, 87, 88, ad hoc expert com. on immunotherapy of IDDM 1990, chmn. task force on profl. membership 1991-92, mem. publs. policy com. 1993-95, bd. dirs. 1994—, mem. scientific and med. meetings oversight com. 1995—, clin. rsch. grant 1996), Am. Fedn. for Clin. Rsch., Am. Soc. for Clin. Investigation, Endocrine Soc., King County Med., Western Assn. Physicians, Western Soc. for Clin. Rsch., Immunology Diabetes Soc. (pres. 1994-95), Alpha Omega Alpha. Office: VA Puget Sound Healthcare Sys 1660 S Columbian Way Seattle WA 98108-1597*

PALMER, JOHN ALBERT, JR., parapsychologist; b. Phila., Oct. 30, 1944; s. John Albert and Katharine (Royer) P. BA, Duke U., 1966; PhD, U. Tex., 1969. Asst. prof. McGill U., Montreal, Que., Can., 1969-71; rsch. assoc. U. Va. Med. Sch., 1971-75, U. Calif.-Davis, 1975-77, U. Utrecht, Netherlands, 1981-84; assoc. prof. John F. Kennedy U., Orinda, Calif., 1977-81; sr. rsch. assoc. Rhine Rsch. Ctr., Durham, N.C., 1984—. Co-author: Foundations of Parapsychology, 1986; editl. cons. Jour. Parapsychology, 1984-95, editor, 1995—; contbr. articles to profl. jours., chpts. to books. Recipient Weiss award Am. Soc. Psychical Rsch., 1977. Mem. Parapsychol. Assn. (pres. 1979, 92). Home: 501 Dupont Cir Apt 10 Durham NC 27705-2963 Office: Rhine Rsch Ctr 402 N Buchanan Blvd Durham NC 27701

PALMER, LEONARD ROBERT, optometrist; b. Bklyn., Oct. 29, 1930; s. Hyman and Sylvia (Weisenfeld) Perlmutter; m. Gloria Doris Feinman Palmer, Jan. 9, 1960; children: Mark, Denis. BS, Chgo. Coll. Optometry, 1952, OD, 1953; MS, Columbia U., 1954. Asst. med. dir. Nat. Coun. to Combat Blindness, Inc., N.Y.C., 1954-60; pvt. practice Bklyn., 1960—. 1st lt. Med. Svc. Corps, 1956-58. Mem. Bklyn. Optometric Soc. (v.p. 1965-67), Am. Optometric Assn. Jewish. Home: 163 Dover St Brooklyn NY 11235

PALMER, MARCIA ANN, healthcare management consultant, pharmacist; b. Hammond, Ind., Aug. 26, 1951; d. John J. and Millee (Ivan) P. BS in Pharmacy, Purdue U., 1974; MBA, Loyola U., 1984. Lic. pharmacist, Ind., Ill., Ariz., Fla. Staff pharmacist St. Margaret Hosp., Hammond, Ind., 1974-75; drug info. pharmacist to clin. coord. Ingalls Meml. Hosp., Harvey, Ill., 1975-77; dir. pharmacy Ingalls Meml. Hosp., Harvey, 1977-89; pres. Palmer Assocs., Healthcare Mgmt. Cons., Munster, Ind., 1989—; asst. prof. Purdue U., West Lafayette, Ind., 1972-89; tchg. assoc. U. Ill., Chgo., 1979-89; mem. adj. faculty pharmacy technician program South Suburban Coll., South Holland, Ill.; pres. Ill. Pharmacy Found., 1996—. Named Pharmacist Yr., Ill. Coun. Health-System Pharmacists, 1988. Mem. Am. Soc. Health-System Pharmacists, Am. Pharm. Assn., Am. Soc. Cons. Pharmacists, Acad. Managed Care Pharmacy, Am. Soc. Parenteral and Enteral Nutrition. Home: 1514 Cardinal Ct Munster IN 46321-3801 Office: Palmer Assocs 9245 Calumet Ave Ste 202 Munster IN 46321-2807

PALMER, ORRIN WILLIAM, psychiatrist; b. Mineola, N.Y., Mar. 23, 1957; s. Walter and Barbara Norma (Doctor) P.; m. Jill Renee Campbell, May 19, 1985; children: Devon Matthew, Danielle Nichole. BA, NYU, 1980; MD, NY Med. Coll., 1985. Diplomate Am. Bd. Psychiatry & Neurology. Intern Yale New Haven Hosp., 1985-86; resident, fellow Mt. Sinai Sch. Medicine, N.Y.C., 1986-90; med. dir. Evergreen Psychiatry & Psychology Assocs., Frederick, Md., 1991—; med. dir. psychiatry Frederick Meml. Hosp., 1990-93; med. dir. Allied Counseling Svcs., Frederick, 1996—. Mem. Am. Psychiat. Assn., Tourette Syndrome Assn. (med. adv. bd. 1990—), Md. Psychiat. Soc. Office: Evergreen Psychiatry 129-14 W Patrick St Frederick MD 21701

PALMER, PATTI LU, optometrist, medical officer; b. Paterson, N.J., Apr. 3, 1959; d. Albert and Frances C. (Ruit) Steenwyk; m. Mark R. Palmer, May 25, 1981; children: Benjamin, Joel. BS, Wheaton Coll., 1981, Pa. Coll. Optometry, 1985; OD, Pa. Coll. Optometry, 1985. Commd. 2d lt. U.S. Army, 1981, advanced through grades to maj., 1993; staff optometrist Walter Reed Army Med. Ctr., Washington, 1986-89; chief optometry First Armor Divsn., Mannheim, Germany, 1990-94, Third Armor Divsn., 1990-91, Raymond W. Bliss Army Cmty. Hosp., Sierra Vista, Ariz., 1994—; chief optometry R.W. Bliss Army Cmty. Hosp., Ft. Huachuca, Ariz., 1994—. Mem. Armed Forces Optometric Soc., Am. Optometric Assn. Office: MEDDAC ATTN: MCXJ-DS-OPT Fort Huachuca AZ 85613

PALMER, ROBERT FIELDS, neurosurgeon, educator; b. Portland, Oreg., Mar. 5, 1922; cons. Bur. of Hearings and Appeals, Social Security Adminstrn., Disability Evaluation, Oakland, Calif., 1967—; mem. neurosurgery adv. bd. Kentfield (Calif.) Rehab. Hosp., 1990—.; s. Arvis Richard and Capitola Georgia (Fields) P.; m. Mary Bernice Johnson, Oct. 5, 1944 (div. 1971); children: Elizabeth Ann, Ellen, Scott, Eileen, Eric, Edward; m. Melanie Marie Soares, Aug. 11, 1971; children: Anne Marie, Robert F. III, Georgia L., Margaret, James W. BA in Med. Scis., U. Calif., Berkeley, 1943; MD, U. Calif., San Francisco, 1946. Diplomate Am. Bd. Neurol. Surgery. Intern U. Calif. Hosp., San Francisco, 1946; post-doctoral rsch. fellow Atomic Energy Commn., The Rice Inst., Houston, 1949; asst. resident in gen. surgery U. Calif. Hosp., San Francsico, 1949-52, asst. resident in neurol. surgery, 1953-56, sr. resident in neurol. surgery, 1955-56; pvt. practice neurol. surgeon San Francisco, 1956—; clin. instr. dept. neurosurgery U. Calif., San Francisco, 1956-64, asst. clin. prof. dept. neurosurgery, 1964—; chief neurol. surgery Childrens Hosp., San Francisco, 1969-92. Contbr. articles to profl. jours. Physician San Francisco Giants, 1960-70; candidate for city coun., Mill Valley, 1963; participating subject Buck Ctr. for Rsch. on Aging, Mill Valley, 1991; vol. St. Anthony's Kitchen, San Francisco, 1991. Col. U.S. Army, 1938—. Recipient Commendation medal, cert. of appreciation U.S. Army, Operation Desert Storm, 1991; named one of Best Doctors, San Francisco Focus Mag., 1992. Office: 3600 California St San Francisco CA 94118

PALMER, ROGER FARLEY, pharmacology educator; b. Albany, N.Y., Sept. 23, 1931; m. Nelida Santiago, Apr. 1994. B.S. in Chemistry, St. Louis U., 1953; postgrad., Fla. State U., 1955-56, Woods Hole Marine Biology Lab., 1956; M.D., U. Fla., 1960. Intern Johns Hopkins Hosp., 1960-61, resident in medicine, 1961-62; asst. dept. biochemistry U. Fla., Gainesville, 1957; asst. medicine Osler Med. Service, 1960-62; instr. pharmacology and therapeutics U. Fla., 1962, asst. prof. pharmacology, therapeutics and medicine, 1964-67, assoc. prof. pharmacology and medicine, 1967-69, prof. medicine, chief div. clin. pharmacology, 1969-70, 81-82; prof., chmn. dept. pharmacology, prof. medicine U. Miami, Fla., 1970-81; clin. prof. medicine U. Miami, 1982—; chmn. pharmacology sect. Nat. Bd. Med Examiners, 1977-81; cons. Nat. Acad. Scis.; chmn. pharmacology sect. Nat. Bd. Med. Examiners, 1977-81. Editorial bd. Pharmacol. Revs.; assoc. editor Advances in Molecular Pharmacology; ad hoc editor Am. Heart Jour.; editor Horizons in Clinical Pharmacology, 1976; author abstracts; contbr. articles to profl. jours. Served with USAR. Mosby scholar, 1957-60; Markle scholar in acad. medicine, 1965-70; recipient Basic Sci. Teaching award U. Miami, 1975-76; Meritorious Service medal Am. Heart Assn., 1972; citation for meritorious Service So. Region Am. Heart Assn., 1979; Visitante Distinguido award, Costa Rica, 1979; Outstanding Tchr. award U. Miami, 1982. Mem. Am. Coll. Clin. Pharmacology, Am. Fedn. Clin. Rsch., Am. Therapeutic Soc. (prize essay award 1970), Am. Soc. Pharmacology and Exptl. Therapeutics, N.Y. Acad. Sci., So. Soc. Clin. Investigation, U.S. Pharmacopeia Revision Com., Internat. Study Group Rsch. Cardiac Metabolism, Royal Soc. Health, Am. Soc. for Internal Medicine, Key Biscayne Yacht Club (bd. govs. 1994—), Sigma Xi. Office: 24 W Enid Dr Key Biscayne FL 33149-2009

PALMER, SCOTT CRAIG, optometrist; b. Oceanside, N.Y., Dec. 11, 1966; m. Dana C. Palmer, May 15, 1993. BS cum laude, Briar Cliff Coll., 1989; OD, Ind. U., 1993. Intern pediat. clinic and contact lens clinic Ind. U., Bloomington; resident Hawley Army Comty. Hosp., Ft. Benjamin, Harrison, Indianapolis, Ind.; resident in eye disease Faust Eye Ctr., Marion, Ind.; with Family Eye Care Ctr., Garner, Iowa, 1993-94; optometrist Eyecare Ctr., Spencer, Iowa, 1994—. Mem. Am. Optometric Assn., Iowa Optometric Assn., Spencer Jaycees (sec. 1995-96), Spencer Rotary (bd. dirs, 1995-96), Beta Sigma Kappa. Lutheran. Home: 1407 Fairview Spencer IA 51301 Office: Eyecare Ctr 3 E 18th Box 707 Spencer IA 51301

PALMER, THOMAS HOWARD, JR., retired surgeon; b. Cambridge, Mass., Apr. 19, 1924; s. Thomas Howard and Elizabeth Agnes (Higgins) P.; m. Mary Ellen Herlihy, Feb. 20, 1954; children: Thomas H. III, Edward H., Anne M., David A., James L. Student, Harvard U., 1942-44; MD, Tufts U., 1948. Cert. Am. Bd. Surgery. Intern City Hosp., Boston, 1948-49; resident surgery New Eng. Med. Ctr., Boston, 1949-50, 52-55; staff surgeon Ea. Maine Med. Ctr., Bangor, 1955-89; staff surgeon St. Joseph Hosp., Bangor, 1955-89, chief of surgery, 1967-74, 80-85; med. staff pres. Ea. Maine Med. Ctr., Bangor, 1973-75; dir. Ea. Maine Healthcare, Bangor, 1982—; bd. dirs. Maine Peer Rev. Bd. (Med.) Bangor, 1988-89. Contbr. articles to med. jours. Trustee Ea. Maine Med. Ctr., Bangor, 1982-89. Lt. USN, 1943-45, 50-52, Korea. Henry B. Humphrey scholar Harvard U., 1942; Charlton Rsch. fellow Tufts U. Med. Sch., 1950; recipient Disting. Svc. award Ea. Maine Healthcare, 1957. Fellow ACS (pres. Maine chpt. 1969-70); mem. New Eng. Surg. Soc., Maine Med. Assn., Penobscot Med. Soc. Roman Catholic. Home: 332 Garland St Bangor ME 04401-5543

PALMER, TIMOTHY TROW, safety and health consultant; b. Evanston, Ill., Mar. 22, 1938; s. Clinton Foster and Josephine Margaret (Squires) P.; m. Eloise Ann Ellson, Jun 16, 1962; children: Timothy Foster, Jennifer Ann, Jonathan Blair. BA in Chemistry, Zoology, Carleton Coll., Northfield, Minn., 1960; MS in Zoology, U. Minn., 1964, PhD in Zoology, 1974; MS in Safety, U. So. Calif., L.A., 1981. Cert. safety profl.; registered profl. engr., Mass. Commd. U.S. Navy, 1964, advanced through grades to lt. comdr., ret. 1984; asst. to dir. Gorgas Meml. Lab., Panama, 1976-79; safety prog. mgr. NMRI, Bethesda, Md., 1979-84; pres. Tepee Ltd., Annapolis, Md., 1984-90; dir. environ. assessments and tng. Profl. Safety Cons. Co., Seabrook, Md., 1986—. Contbr. articles to profl. jours. Merit badge counselor Boy Scouts Am., Bloomington, Minn., 1967-76; risk mgmt. cons. Episcopal Diocese of Washington, 1981-88. Mem. Am. Soc. Safety Engrs., Nat. Safety Mgmt. Soc. (bd. dirs. 1985-87, 89-91, pres. 1987-89), Am. Nat. Standards Inst., Am. Soc. Tropical Medicine and Hygiene, Am. Legion, Masons. Republican. Episcopalian. Home: 3232 Chrisland Dr Annapolis MD 21403-4367 Office: Profl Safety Cons PO Box 891 Lanham Seabrook MD 20703-0891

PALMER-BEARD, DONNA, health facility administrator; b. Rockford, Ill., Apr. 15, 1948; d. Daniel J. and Lucille Lillian (Meilahn) Palmer; m. Edward W. Beard, Dec. 30, 1940. BS in Math. with honors, U. Ill., 1969. CPA, Ill. Auditor, supr. Coopers & Lybrand, Rockford, 1969-75; controller Ill. Hosp. and Health Svcs., Rockford, 1975-76; acctg. mgr. Swedish Am. Hosp., Rockford, 1976-88; adminstr., chief exec. officer St. Joseph Hosp., Belvidere, Ill., 1988-92; CFO DeKalb (Ill.) Clinic Chartered, 1992—.

PALOMBI, BARBARA JEAN, psychologist; b. Rockford, Ill, May 28, 1949; d. Frank and Vira Lavina (Gornet) P. BA, Luther Coll., Decorah, Iowa, 1971; MA, Pacific Lutheran U., Tacoma, Wash., 1974; PhD, Mich. State U., 1987. Career counselor Wright State U., Dayton, Ohio, 1974-77; asst. dean, dir. U. Calif., Irvine, 1977-80; grad. asst. Mich. State U., East Lansing, 1980-83, clin. intern, 1983-84; clin. intern Colo. State U., Ft. Collins, 1984-85; psychologist Ariz. State U., Tempe, 1985—, sr. psychologist, 1991—; tng. dir., psychologist Grand Valley State U., Allendale, Mich.; cons. in field. Contbr. articles and papers to profl. jours. Mem. U.S. Wheelchair Olympic Team, 1976, U.S. Wheelchair Team to the Internat. Stoke-Mandelville Games, 1979; alternative mem. U.S. Wheelchair Olympic Team, 1980; U.S. rep. Internat. Symposium on Sports, Physical Edn. and Recreation for the Handicapped, UNESCO, 1982. Grantee Nat. Sci. Found., U. Calif., 1977, 79; named Outstanding Handicapped Citizen Rock County 1982, Handicapped Profl. Woman of the Yr. Western Region, 1987. Mem. Am. Assn. Counseling and Devel. (Glen E. Hubele Nat. Grad. Student Research award 1988), Am. Coll. Personnel Assn. (bd. dirs. Div. VII-Counseling, mem. Div. VIII-Wellness, Burns B. Crookston Research award 1988, Commn. VII Grad. Student Research award 1988), Am. Psychology Assn. (rep. div. 17 handicapped task force). Democrat. Home: 11333 Brown St Allendale MI 49401 Office: Grand Valley State U Dept Psychology Allendale MI 49401

PALOMBO, JOSEPH, clinical social worker; b. Cairo, July 18, 1928; came to U.S., 1949; s. Albert H. and Regina (Costi) P.; m. Dorothy D. Denton, Aug. 4, 1957. PhB, New Sch. Social Rsch., N.Y.C., 1954; MA in Philosophy, Yale U., 1958; MSW, U. Chgo., 1959; cert. in child therapy, Inst. Psychoanalysis, Chgo., 1964. Cert. social worker, Ill. Pvt. practice Chgo., 1970—; dean Inst. Clin. Social Work, Chgo., 1981-92, founding dean, 1992—; assoc. dir. Rush Neurobehavioral Ctr. dept. pediats. Rush-Presbyn.-St. Luke's Med. Ctr., 1995—, assoc. dir. neurobehavioral ctr., 1995—; adminstrv. dir. child therapy program Inst. Psychoanalysis, 1970-78, mem. faculty, 1970—; adminstrv. dir. Barr-Harris Ctr. Inst. Psychoanalysis, Chgo., 1976-78; mem. faculty advanced cert. program Smith Coll. Sch. Social Work, 1985-87. Contbr. articles to profl. jours. Mem. NASW, Acad. Cert. Social Workers, Assn. Child Psychotherapists (pres. 1976), Nat. Acads. Practice in Social Work (founding), Ill. Soc. Clin. Social Workers, Chgo. Psycoanalytic Soc. (affiliate). Democrat.

PALOVCIK, REINHARD ANTON, research neurophysiologist; b. Dornheim, Hessen, Germany, June 30, 1950; came to U.S. 1956; s. Anton and Elfriede (Lankus) P. BS, U. Mich., 1973; MA, Wayne State U., Detroit, 1979, PhD, 1982. Rsch. asst. E.B. Ford Inst. Med. Rsch., Detroit, 1973-78; teaching asst. Dept. Psychology, Wayne State U., Detroit, 1978-79, grad. trainee, 1979-81, grad. asst., 1981-82; postdoctoral assoc. dept. physiology U. Fla., Gainesville, 1982-86, postdoctoral assoc. dept. neurosci., 1986-89, postdoctoral assoc. dept. neurosurgery, 1989-90, postdoctoral assoc. neurology dept., 1991, rsch. cons.; rsch. health scientist rsch. svc. VA Med. Ctr., Gainesville, 1990-95, clin. rsch. cons., 1995—. U. Mich. Regents Alumni scholar, 1969; NIMH predoctoral tng. grantee, 1979; NIH Nat. Rsch. Svc. awardee, 1983; Epilepsy Rsch. Found. Fla. postdoctoral grantee, 1990. Mem. AAAS, IEEE, APA, Soc. for Neurosci., Am. Statis. Assn., Internat. Neural Network Soc. Home: 2209 NE 15th Ter Gainesville FL 32609-8918

PALUMBO, FRANCIS XAVIER BERNARD, pharmacy educator; b. Scranton, Pa., June 19, 1945; s. Frank Bernard and Marcia Desales (Fidati) P.; m. Karen Ann Setterlund, June 26, 1971; 1 child, Janice Lynn. BS in Pharmacy, Med. U. S.C., 1968; MS, U. Miss., 1973, PhD in Health Care Adminstrn., 1974; JD, U. Balt., 1982. Bar: Md. 1983, D.C. 1990; lic. pharmacist S.C., Md. Asst. prof. pharmacy U. Md., Balt., 1974-79, assoc. prof., 1979-91, assoc. dir. Ctr. on Drugs and Pub. Policy, 1988—, prof., 1991—, chmn. dept. pharmacy practice and adminstrv. sci., 1991-93; atty. Hyman, Phelps & McNamara, P.C., Washington, 1988-89; mem. study sect. NIH, Bethesda, Md., 1984-88; cons. in field. Co-author: Containing Costs in Third Party Drug Programs, 1979. Bd. govs. Rodgers Forge Cmty. Assn., Balt., 1987-95; bd. dirs. Luth. Health Care Corp., Balt., 1988-93, Edenwald Continuing Care Retirement Cmty., 1996—. With U.S. Army, 1969-71. Mem. Am. Pharm. Assn. (chair econ., social and adminstrn. sci. 1992-93), Acad. Pharm. Rsch. and Sci. (pres. 1994-95), Am. Assn. Coll. Pharmacy, Md. State Bar Assn., Am. Assn. Pharm. Scientists, Am. Soc. Pharmacy Law. Home: 318 Overbrook Rd Baltimore MD 21212-1801 Office: U Md Sch Pharmacy 100 Penn St Baltimore MD 21201-1083

PALUMBO, STEVEN KEITH, physician; b. Bklyn., July 12, 1952; s. Frank Anthony and Lucy Marie (Pittaro) P.; divorced; 1 child, Robert. BA in Chemistry, CUNY, 1973; MD, SUNY, Bklyn., 1977. Diplomate Am. Bd. Plastic Surgery. Chief, plastic surgery Little Neck (N.Y.) Community Hosp., 1984-92; attending plastic surgeon Beth Israel North, N.Y.C., 1986—, Southampton (N.Y.) Hosp., 1995—; asst. prof. plastic surgery Albert Einstein Coll. of Medicine, Bronx, N.Y., 1984—. Author: (short story) The New Physician, 1982. Recipient Arthur Aufses Sr. prize in surgery, Mt. Sinai Hosp., N.Y.C., 1982, 1st prize in drawing Annenburg Art Festival, N.Y.C. Fellow ACS, Internat. Coll. Surgeons; mem. Songwriter's Guild. Office: 25 Montauk Hwy Quogue NY 11959-1609

PAN, MANUEL, cardiologist; b. Jerez, Spain, June 26, 1956; s. Manuel and Vicenta Ossorio (Alvarez) P.; m. Teresa Bajo, July 5, 1980; children: Manuel, Teresa. Staff cardiologist Reina Sofia Hosp., Cordoba, Spain, 1990-91; assoc. prof. Cordoba U., 1992—. Fellow European Soc. Cardiology. Home: Ave de Cervantes 16-5, 14008 Cordoba Spain Office: Reina Sofia Hosp, Ave Melindez Pidal 1, 14004 Cordoba Spain

PAN, TZU-MING, biotechnologist; b. Ching-Shui, Taiwan, Republic of China, Jan. 9, 1947; s. Wan-Chih and Teng (Yang) P.; m. Mei-Lan Chang, Dec. 25, 1973; children: Chia-Ying, Chia-Yu, Chia-Yueh. BS, Nat. Taiwan U., 1969, MS, 1972, PhD, 1978. Assoc. prof. Chinese Culture U., Taipei, 1978-82, prof., 1982-93, chmn., dir., 1988-92; prof. Yang-Ming Med. Coll., 1980—, Nat. Taiwan U., 1995—; chief divsn. bacteriology Nat. Inst. Preventive Medicine, Taipei, 1993—; com. of patent screening Ministry of Econ. Affairs, Taipei, Taiwan, 1987—, com. of waste reduction task force, 1991—; com. of standard method EPA, Republic of China, 1990—. Author: Organic Chemistry, 1984, Experiment in cHemistry, 1984, 86, 94, Experiment in Organic Chemistry, 1990, Preventive Medicine, 1995. Recipient Award of Rsch. and Writings Ministry of Edn., 1977, 79, Outstanding Tchrs. award, 1989, Youth Medal award Ministry of Youth, 1978, Outstanding Teaching Material award Ministry of Edn., 1992. Mem. Chinese Biochem. Soc., Chinese Tchrs. Assn. (exec. dir.), Biotech. Indsl. Assn. (exec. dir.), Chinese Agrl. Chem. Assn. (exec. dir.), Am. Chem. Soc., Am. Soc. Microbiology. Office: Nat Inst Preventive Med, 161 Kun Yang St Nan Kang, Taipei 11513, Taiwan

PANAGIDES, JOHN, pharmacologist; b. N.Y.C., Aug. 15, 1944; s. Chris and Sophie (Marmar) P.; m. Kathleen Ann Heimann, July 9, 1967; children: Christopher, Melissa, Adrienne. BS, CCNY, N.Y.C., 1966; MS, U. N.C., 1968; PhD, SUNY, Buffalo, 1972. Rsch. assoc. Rockefeller U., N.Y.C., 1972-73; sr. scientist Lederle Labs., Pearle River, N.Y., 1973-83; sr. clin. monitor Ayerst Labs., N.Y.C., 1983-87; dir. clin. projects, CNS Organon Inc., West Orange, N.J., 1987—. Contbr. articles to profl. jours. NDEA Title IV fellow, Chapel Hill, 1966-68. Mem. AAAS, Am. Soc. Pharmacology and Exptl. Therapeutics. Home: 7 Catawba Dr West Nyack NY 10994-2304 Office: Organon Inc 375 Mount Pleasant Ave West Orange NJ 07052-2724

PANAS, SONYA LEE SAWAYA, retired gerontology and pediatrics nurse; b. Douglas, Ariz., July 15, 1934; d. Edward G. and Ramona (Salem) Sawaya; m. Arnold M. Panas, May 12, 1956; children: Arnold Marc, Ramona Maria. Diploma, St. Mary's Hosp. Sch. Nursing, Tucson, 1956; student, U. Ariz. RN, Ariz. Psychiat. nurse VA Hosp., Miss., 1956; ob-gyn shift supr. St. Josephs, Tucson, 1960; night supr. Handmaker Nursing Home, Tucson, 1975; night charge nurse pediatrics unit St. Mary's Hosp. and Health Ctr., Tucson, 1975-83; asst. dir. nursing svc. Valley House Convalescent Ctr., Tucson, 1985; charge nurse, dir. nursing svc. Ariz. Elks Long Term Care Unit, Tucson, 1986-90; asst. dir. nursing, staff devel. coord. Santa Rosa Convalescent Ctr., Tucson, 1990-93; ret., 1993. Grey lady; former family svc. vol. USAF, Rhein Main AFB, Fed. Republic Germany, 1969-73.

PANAYI, GABRIEL STAVROS, medical educator; b. Nov. 9, 1940. BA with honors, U. Cambridge, Eng., 1962, MB, 1965, MD, 1972. House physician Queen Elizabeth II Hosp., Welwyn Garden City, Eng., 1965-66; med. rsch. coun. jr. fellow Kennedy Inst. Rheumatology Cen. Middlesex Hosp., London, 1967-69; house surgeon St. Mary's Hosp., London, 1966; sr. house officer in pathology Cen. Hosp., Nottingham, Eng., 1966, Cen. Middlesex Hosp., London, 1967; clin. rsch. fellow arthritis and rheumatism coun. diseases Northern Gen. Hosp., Edinburgh, Eng., 1970-73; lectr. in rheumatology dept. of medicine Guy's Hosp., London, 1973-76, sr. lectr., cons. arthritis and rheumatism coun. dept., 1976-80, prof. arthritis and rheumatism coun., chair rheumatology, 1980—; lectr. in field. Mem. editorial bd. Brit. Jour. Rheumatology, Clin. and Exptl. Immunology, Scandinavian Jour. Rheumatology, Scandinavian Jour. Immunology, Clin. Rheumatology, Jour. of Rheumatology, Clin. and Exptl. Rheumatology.; referee The Lancet, The New Eng., Jour. of Medicine, Arthritis and Rheumatism, Annals of Rheumatic Diseases; contbr. numerous articles to profl. jours. Recipient Margaret Holroyde prize Heberden Soc., 1975, Allesandro Robecci prize European League Against Rheumatism, 1979, Ballabio prize Italian Soc. Rheumatology. Mem. Am. Coll. Rheumatology, Brit. Soc. Immunology, Biochem. Soc., Brit. Soc. Rheumatology (past mem. exec. com., Heberden Orator 1992), Royal Soc. Medicine (past hon. sec. sect. of medicine, exptl. medicine and therapeutics 1977-79, libr. rep. sect. allergy and clin. immunology 1988-90, pres. sect. allergy and clin. immunology 1993-95), Greek Rheumatology Soc. (hon.), Italian Rheumatology Soc. (hon.). Office: Guys Hosp, Hunts House 4th Floor, London SE1 9RT, England

PANAYIOTOU, BARNABAS NICOS, consultant physician; b. Nicosia, Cyprus, June 17, 1959; arrived in Eng., 1974; s. Nicos and Machi (Constantinou) P.; m. Sandra Panayiotou. B Med. Sci. with honors, Nottingham (Eng.) U., 1981, BMBS, 1983. Registrar Gen. Hosp., Bolton, Eng., 1988-90; sr. registrar Gen. Hosp., Barnet, Eng., 1990-91; rsch. registrar Gen. Hosp., Leicester, Eng., 1991-93; sr. registrar Manor Hosp., Walsall, Eng., 1993-94, City Gen. Hosp., Stoke-on-Trent, Eng., 1994-96; cons. Manor Hosp., Walsall, 1996—. Contbr. articles to profl. jours., chpt. to book. Mem. Brit. Med. Assn., Med. Rsch. Soc., Brit. Geriatrics Soc., Royal Coll. Physicians Eng. Greek Orthodox. Office: Manor Hosp, Elderly Care Dept, South Wing, Walsall WS2 9PS, England

PANCHAL, PRAVIN D., physician; b. Ahmedabad, India, Sept. 16, 1941; s. D.A. and Kamalaben D. Panchal; came to U.S., 1968, naturalized, 1973; M.D., B.J. Med. Coll., 1964; m. Joan Dauginikas, June 20, 1970; children: Nita, Sheila, Lisa. Intern, South Side Hosp., Pitts., 1968-69; VA Hosp., Bronx, N.Y., 1969-71; chief rehab. med. services VA Hosp., Pitts., 1971-89; dir. rehab. svcs. Negley House Inc., Pitts., 1974-79; clin. dir. rehab. svcs. Cen. Med. Pavallion, Pitts., 1974-82; physiatrist South Side Hosp., Pitts., 1977—, chmn. phys. medicine and rehab., 1984—, dept. of medicine, 1989-91; med. dir. rehab. medicine Mercy Providence Hosp., 1992—; physiatrist, staff mem. Mercy Hosp., Pitts., 1994—; clin. asst. prof. orthopedic surgery U. Pitts. Sch. Medicine. Diplomate Am. Bd. Phys. Medicine and Rehab., Am. Bd. Quality Assurance and Utilization Rev. Physicians. Mem. Am. Acad. Rehab. Medicine, Internat. Med. Soc. Parapelegia, Am. Coll. Utilization Rev. Physicians, Pa. State Med. Soc. Contbr. rsch. papers in field. Home: 200 Highland Rd Pittsburgh PA 15238-2112 Office: 2000 Mary St Pittsburgh PA 15203-2054

PANES, PAUL BENJAMIN, educational psychologist; b. N.Y.C., June 18, 1928; s. Max and Sophie (Levine) P.; m. Hannah Gross, Oct. 29, 1955; children: Jonathan, Susan. BA, Bklyn. Coll., 1950, MA, 1951; EdD, NYU, 1968. Instr. Reading Inst., NYU, N.Y.C., 1957-61, dir., 1961-68; chmn. dept. basic skills Queensborough Community Coll., N.Y.C., 1968—. Author: Reading the Textbook, 1972, Reading Well in College, 1986; contbr. articles to ednl. jours. With M.I., U.S. Army, 1951-54, Korea. Office: Dept Basic Skills Queensborough Community Coll Bayside NY 11364

PANG, HERBERT GEORGE, ophthalmologist; b. Honolulu, Dec. 23, 1922; s. See Hung and Hong Jim (Chuu) P.; student St. Louis Coll., 1941; BS, Northwestern U., 1944, MD, 1947; m. Dorothea Lopez, Dec. 27, 1953. Intern Queen's Hosp., Honolulu, 1947-48; postgraduate course ophthalmology N.Y.U., Med. Sch., 1948-49; resident ophthalmology Jersey City Med. Ctr., 1949-50, Manhattan Eye, Ear, & Throat Hosp., N.Y.C., 1950-52; practice medicine specializing in ophthalmology, Honolulu, 1952-54, 56—; mem. staffs Kuakini Hosp., Children's Hosp., Castle Meml. Hosp., Queen's Hosp., St. Francis Hosp.; asst. clin. prof. ophthalmology U. Hawaii Sch. Medicine, 1966-73, now asso. clin. prof. Cons. Bur. Crippled Children, 1952-73, Kapiolani Maternity Hosp., 1952-73, Leahi Tb. Hosp., 1952-62. Capt. M.C., AUS, 1954-56, Diplomate Am. Bd. Ophthalmology. Mem. AMA, Am. Acad. Ophthalmology and Otolaryngology, Assn. for Rsch. Ophthalmology, ACS, Hawaii Med. Soc. (gov. med. practice com. 1958-62, chmn. med. speakers com. 1957-58), Hawaii Eye, Ear, Nose and Throat Soc. (pres. 1960), Pacific Coast Oto-Ophthalmological Soc., Pan Am. Assn. Ophthalmology, Mason, Shriner, Eye Study Club (pres. 1972—). Home: 346 Lewers St Honolulu HI 96815-2345

PANG, SHING-CHUN, chest physician; b. Hong Kong, Jan. 2, 1939; arrived in Australia, 1978; s. Siu-Wan and Mui (Chow) P.; m. Vivian Ying-Choi Wong, July 4, 1969; children: Ronald Tze-Ching, Donald Tze-Kei. MB BS, U. Hong Kong, 1964. Intern Queen Mary Hosp., Hong Kong, 1964-65; med. officer Med. and Health Dept., Hong Kong, 1965-72; cons. chest physician Kowloon Hosp., Hong Kong, 1972-78; chest physician Townsville Gen. Hosp., Queensland, Australia, 1978-79; chest physician Chest and TB Svcs., Perth, Australia, 1979-95, chest physician-in-charge disease control, 1995—; bd. dirs. Westcare Inc., Perth; mem. Indsl. Diseases Med. Panel, Perth, 1984—. Contbr. articles to profl. publs. Fellow Royal Coll. Physicians (Edinburgh), Am. Coll. Chest Physicians (v.p. 1974-75, pres. 1975-76); mem. Brit. Thoracic Soc., Thoracic Soc. Australia and New Zealand. Office: Perth Chest Clinic, 17 Murray St, Perth WA 6000, Australia

PANICO, ELAINE HARTMAN, nurse; b. Phila., July 13, 1924; d. Edward Earl and Eleanor Mayo (Adams) Hartman; children: Frederick, Robert, Eleanor, Lorne, Earl, John, William, Richard, Louise. BSN, State Coll. and Med. Ctr., 1946; BS in Edn., State Tchrs. Coll., 1946; postgrad., U. Pa., 1946-49. RN Summer Boys Camp, Winaukee, N.H., 1948; instr. Glassboro (N.J.) State Coll., 1948; coll. nurse, asst. Dean State Coll., Glassboro, 1946-48; asst. dir. nurses Osteo. Hosp., Phila., 1948-49, instr. pharm. math., 1948-49; eye surg. nurse Cornell-N.Y. Hosp., N.Y.C., 1949-50; surg. supr. Balt. City Hosps., 1950-52; nurse in charge Taj Mahal Med. Office, Atlantic City, N.J., 1990; surg. office nurse Ventnor, N.J., 1960—; pub. health spkr. elem. schs., Boston, 1950; RN internat. confs., Stony Brook, N.Y., 1980-85, A.C. Med. Ctr. Eye Clinic, Atlantic City, 1987-90; creator earliest postoperative surg. ICU, Balt. City Hosps., 1950-52. Cert. classic ballet, 1932-42. Bd. dirs. PTA, Ventnor, 1960-83, Atlantic Performing Arts Ctr., Atlantic City, 1970-90; mem. Holy Spirit Mothers Assn., Absecon, N.J., 1966-83; sponsor South Jersey Regional Theatre, Atlantic Community Concerts, Stockton Coll. Performing Arts; fin. sec. Atlantic City Med. Ctr. Aux., 1963; chmn. spl. projects Miss. Am. Pageant Scholarship Found., Very Important Hostess (V.I.H.), 1967—. Recipient Lifetime Recognition award Great Books Found., 1966-67, 15-yr. Gold award Miss Am. Pageant, 1982. Mem. AAUW, Atlantic County Med. Aux. (pres. 1984-90), U.S. Golf Assn., Internat. Platform Assn., RNs Cancer Heart Meml. Fund. (bd. dirs.), Hydrangea Club (chmn. 1964, Silver 15 Yr. award). Home: 102 S Dudley Ave Ventnor City NJ 08406-2837 Office: 10 S Somerset Ave Ventnor City NJ 08406-2846

PANITZ, LAWRENCE, physician; b. Bklyn., Apr. 30, 1928; s. Max and Gussie (Gorenstein) P.; B.A., NYU, 1962, M.D., 1966; m. Adrienne Ruth Luke, June 20, 1965; children: Jennifer, Michael. Intern, St. Joseph's Hosp., Syracuse, N.Y., 1966-67; practice gen. medicine, Elmsford, N.Y., 1967-90, Hawthorne, N.Y., 1968—; affiliated with Docs Physicians Beth Israel Med. Ctr., Shrub Oak, N.Y., Hartsdale, N.Y., Larchmont, N.Y., Yonkers, N.Y., Thornwood, N.Y., Crestwood, N.Y., New City, N.Y., West Haverstraw, N.Y., and numerous other cities, 1992—. mem. staff New Rochelle (N.Y.) Hosp., St. Agnes Hosp., White Plains, N.Y., Phelps Meml. Hosp., North Tarrytown, N.Y., Westchester County Med. Ctr., Valhalla, N.Y., Dobbs Ferry Hosp., Beth Israel Hosp. Med. Ctr., N.Y.C., New Rochelle (N.Y.) Hosp. Med. Ctr.; dep. dir. dept. family practice Phelps Meml. Hosp.; dir. Elmsford Med. Ctr.; police surgeon Tarrytown and North Tarrytown, Elmsford, Town of Greenburgh; med. dir. Margaret Chapman Sch. for Exceptional Child, Hawthorne; med. dir., prin. rschr. Clin. Tech. Assoc., Elmsford, N.Y., CNS Biosvcs., Pleasantville, N.Y.; physician Westchester County Correctional Health Dept., Valhalla; sch. physician Elmsford, N.Y. Served with U.S. Army, 1946-48; lt. col. M.C. USAR (ret.). Diplomate Am. Bd. Family Practice. Fellow Am. Acad. of Family Physicians, AMA, Med. Soc. of the State of N.Y., Westchester County Med. Soc., Westchester Acad. of Medicine. Jewish. Clubs: Shriners, Masons. Home and Office: 49 RoundABend Rd Tarrytown NY 10591-6518 Office: 5 Bradhurst Ave Hawthorne NY 10532-2154

PANNER, BERNARD J., pathologist, educator; b. Youngstown, Ohio, Oct. 9, 1928; s. Morris W. and Matilda (Giber) P.; m. Molly R. Seidenberg, Feb. 11, 1962; children—Morris J., Aaron M., Daniel Z. A.B. Western Res. U., 1949, M.D., 1953. Diplomate Am. Bd. Pathology. Intern in internal medicine Kings County Hosp., Bklyn., 1953-54; resident in pathology Boston City Hosp., 1954-55, Strong Meml. Hosp., Rochester, N.Y., 1958-60; asst. prof. pathology Sch. Medicine, U. Rochester, 1960-67, assoc. prof., 1967-72, prof., 1972-96, emeritus prof., 1996—; pathologist Strong Meml. Hosp., Rochester, 1972—; cons. Genesee Hosp., Rochester, 1974—. Contbr. articles to profl. jours. Served with USNR, 1955-57. Recipient Mapstone Teaching prize Sch. Medicine, U. Rochester, 1981. Mem. Internat. Acad. Pathology, Am. Assn. Pathologists, Internat. Soc. Nephrology, Am. Soc. Nephrology, Sigma Xi. Democrat. Jewish. Home: 330 Wilmot Rd Rochester NY 14618-2947 Office: U Rochester Sch Medicine Dept Pathology 601 Elmwood Ave Rochester NY 14642-0001

PANNO, FRANCIS VINCENT, prosthodontics, educator; b. N.Y.C., June 15, 1930; s. Francis and Viny (Macaluso) P.; m. Joan M. Donohue, Apr. 9, 1955; children: David F., Gregory J., Corey V., Susan A. Shephard. BS, Marquette U., 1952, DDS, 1956; cert. in prosthodontics, NYU, 1972. Diplomate Am. Bd. Prosthodontics. Grad. asst. dept. removable prosthodontics NYU-Coll. Dentistry, 1971-72, clin. asst. prof. removable prosthodontics, 1972-76, clin. assoc. prof. removable prosthodontics, 1976-79, dir. fixed prosthodontics of grad. prosthodontic program, 1976-79, assoc. prof. and chmn. dept. fixed prosthodontics, 1979-82, prof. and chmn. dept. fixed prosthodontics and occlusion, 1982-86, prof. prosthodontics, occlusion, implant dentistry, 1986—, chmn. dept. prosthodontics and occlusion, 1986-91, dir. implant dentistry, 1986-91, prof., head divsn. restorative and prosthodontic scis., 1991—; pvt. practice prosthodontics, Mamaroneck, N.Y., 1959—; dir. Elmsford Dental Clinic, 1960; cons. Conn. Gen. Inst. Co., 1974-82, Liberty Mutual Ins. Co., 1978-82, D.R. French Co., 1978-82, N.Y. State Dept. Edn.-Office Profl. Conduct, 1979—, N.Y. State Atty. Gen.'s Office, 1978—; lectr. in field. Contbr. articles to profl. jours. Lt. comdr. USN, 1956-59. Fellow Am. Coll. Prosthodontists, Am. Coll. Dentists (Meritorious Svc. to the Profession of Dentistry award 1992), Internat. Coll. Dentists, Am. Prosthodontic Soc. (Internat. Cir. Courses Lectr. award), Am. Acad. Operative Dentistry, Am. Acad. Fixed Prosthodontics, Fedn. Prosthodontic Orgns., Am. Acad. Fixed Prosthodontics, Acad. Denture Prosthetics (various coms.), Greater N.Y. Acad. Prosthodontics (pres. 1992), N.Y. Acad. Dentists, Westchester Shore Dental Soc. (past pres), Pierre Fauchard Internat. Honor Soc., Omicron Kappa Upsilon (past pres. Omega chpt., Disting. Prof. award); mem. Am. Bd. Prosthodontics, Dental Soc. State N.Y. (pub. and profl. rels. coun. 1974-79, state soc. spkrs. bur. 1977—, com. authoring consumers guide to dentistry, chmn. consumer affairs coun. 1978-81), Ninth Dist. Dental Soc. (chmn. mediation com. 1974-79, chmn. planning com. 1977-84, bd. govs. 1979-86, program chmn. 1992-93, pres. 1995, others), N.E. Gnathological Soc., Larchmont Yacht Club. Home: PO Box 479 69 Mead St Waccabuc NY 10597 Office: NYU 345 E 24 St New York NY 10010

PANOS, ANTHONY LAZARUS, surgery educator, researcher; b. Toronto, Ont., Can., Dec. 30, 1956; came to U.S., 1993; s. Lazarus and Patricia (Andreakos) P. MD, U. Toronto, 1980, MSc, 1989. Diplomate Am. Bd. Surgery, Am. Bd. Thoracic Surgery. Clin. fellow U. Toronto, 1993; chief cardiothoracic surgery Seattle VA Med. Ctr., 1993-95; asst. prof. surgery U. Wash., Seattle, 1993—. Contbr. articles to sci. jours., chpts. to books. Fellow Can. Lung Assn., 1984, Med. Rsch. Coun. Can., 1989. Fellow Royal Coll. Physicians and Surgeons Can.; mem. ACS (initiate), Am. Coll. Chest Physicians (assoc.), Assn. for Computing Machinery. Greek Orthodox. Office: U Wash Box 356310 1959 NE Pacific St Seattle WA 98195-6310

PANTALEO, THEODORE THOMAS, III, medical care development officer. BS, Regis Coll., 1979; M Healthcare Adminstrn., Golden Gate U., 1987. Commd. 2d lt. USAF, 1980, advanced through grades to maj.; dir. respiratory svcs. USAF Hosp., Grand Forks AFB, N.D., 1980-81; chief med. recruiting 3550th USAF Recruiting Squadron, Indpls., 1980-83; dir. pers. svcs. USAF Hosp., Mather AFB, Calif., 1986, dir. pat. svcs., 1986-89; pres. Pantaleo Cons., Enid, Okla., 1989; adminstr. USAF Clinic Vance, Vance AFB, Okla., 1989-92; managed care devel. officer HQ USAF/SGHA, Bolling AFB, D.C., 92—. Contbr. articles to profl. jours. Active various cmty. orgns. Fellow Am. Coll. Health Care Execs. Home: HQ USAF/SGHA 400 Luke Ave Washington DC 20332 Office: HQ USAF/SGHA Bolling AFB 170 Luke Ave Ste 400 Washington DC 20332-5113*

PANZARINO, SAVERIO JOSEPH, physician; b. East Orange, N.J., Nov. 29, 1930; s. Joseph Saverio and Pasqua (Binetti) P.; m. Suzanne Laico, Apr. 24, 1934; children: Laura, Kathleen. BA, Columbia Coll., 1952; MD, U. Rome, 1957. Diplomate Am. Bd. Surgery, Am. Bd. Pediat. Surgery. Intern St. Vincent's Hosp., N.Y.C., 1957-58; resident in gen. surgery Manhattan VA Hosp., N.Y.C., 1958-62; fellow in pediat. surgery Hosp. for Sick Children, London, 1962-63; pvt. practice, 1963-90; ret.; clin. assoc. surgery Columbia Coll. Physicians and Surgeons, N.Y.C., 1980-90; part-time med. legal cons., 1990—. Recipient Bowen Brooks scholarship N.Y. Acad. Medicine, 1962. Fellow ACS; mem. AMA, Am. Acad. Pediats. Home and Office: 10 Kenneth Ct Summit NJ 07901

PAOLI, DEE ANN, charge nurse, supervisor; b. Laurium, Mich., Sept. 5, 1953; d. Edward James and Elizabeth Jean (Beauchamp) Yotti; m. Mark Joseph Paoli, Jan. 27, 1979; children: James C., Marcus A. AAS cum laude, Monroe County Cmty. Coll., Monroe, Mich., 1993. RN, Mich. Charge nurse Lutheran Home, Monroe, Mich., 1993-94, charge nurse, supr., 1994—; commd. 2nd. lt. U.S. Army, 1994. Phi Theta Kappa. Home: 2500 E Sterns Erie MI 48133

PAOLINO, THOMAS J., JR., psychiatrist; b. Providence, May 10, 1940; s. Thomas Joseph and Florence (Dobie) P.; m. Barbara Paolino, Feb. 28, 1986; children: Pia, Thomas Joseph III, Adam. BA, Brown U., 1963; JD, George Washington U., 1967. Diplomate Am. Bd. Psychiatry and Neurology, Nat. Bd. Med. Examiners. Intern Tufts Med. Svc., Boston City Hosp., 1967-68; psychiat. resident Mass. Mental Health Ctr., Harvard Med. Sch., Boston, 1968-71; chief resident dept. psychiatry Cambridge Hosp., Harvard Med. Sch., Boston, 1970-71; clin. instr. in psychiatry Brown U. Med. Sch., Providence, 1973-74, asst. prof. in psychiatry, 1974-78; asst. prof. psychiatry Harvard Med. Sch., 1978-82; mem. psychiat. staff Miriam Hosp., Providence, 1983-85, Butler Hosp., Providence, 1983—; clin. asst. prof. Smith Coll. for Social Work, 1979-82; assoc. staff mem. Miriam Hosp., Providence; cons. VA Hosp., Providence, 1973-78; cons., lectr., presenter workshops in field. Co-author: The Alcoholic Marriage: Alternative Perspectives, 1977, Marriage and Marital Therapy: Psychoanalytic, Behavioral and Systems Theory Perspectives, 1978, Psychoanalytic Psychotherapy: Theory, Technique, Therapeutic Relationship and Treatability, 1981, The Basic Techniques of Psychodynamic Psychotherapy, 1986; contbr. articles, revs. to profl. publs. Chief psychiatrist employee assistance com. Providence Fire Dept., 1988—. Mem. Am. Psychiat. Assn., Am. Med. Soc. in Alcoholism, Inc., Am. Med. Writers Assn., Am. Advancement Psychotherapy, R.I. Med. Soc., Providence Med. Assn., Butler Hosp. Med. Staff Assn. (quality assurance com.). Home: 1055 N Main St Providence RI 02904-5718

PAONESSA, KENNETH JOSEPH, orthopaedic surgeon; b. Paterson, N.J., May 8, 1957; s. Joseph and Helen (Foytlin) P.; m. Mary Elizabeth Juillet, Dec. 18, 1982; children: James, Elizabeth, Robert. BS in Biology, Upsala Coll., 1979; MD, N.J. Med. Sch., 1984. Resident Seton Hall U., Paterson, N.J., 1984-89; orthopaedic surgeon Norwich (Conn.) Orthopaedic Group, 1990—; mem. trauma com. William Backus Hosp., Norwich, 1994—. Contbr. articles to profl. jours., chpts. to books. Sponsorship chmn. Southeastern Conn. Youth Hockey League, Norwich, 1995-96. Spine Surgery fellow NYU Med. Ctr., N.Y.C., 1989-90. Fellow Am. Acad. Orthopaedic Surgeons; mem. N.Am. Spine Soc., New England Spine Study Group (sec. 1994—), Scoliosis Rsch. Soc. Office: Norwich Orthopaedic Group 2 Clinic Dr Norwich CT 06360

PAPADAKOS, PETER JOHN, critical care physician; b. Bklyn., Feb. 4, 1957; s. John and Irene (Vahaviolos) P. BA, NYU, 1979; MD, CUNY, 1983. Intern, then resident in surgery The Roosevelt Hosp., N.Y.C., 1983-85; resident in anesthesiology Mt. Sinai Hosp., N.Y.C., 1985-87, fellow in critical care medicine, 1987-88; clin. dir. surg. ICU U. Rochester, N.Y., 1988—; asst. prof. anesthesiology Sch. Medicine U. Rochester, 1988—; adj. prof. respiratory care SUNY. Editor-in-chief Controversies in Critical Care; contbr. articles to profl. jours. Trustee Incurable Illness Found., N.Y.C., 1986-88. Recipient USN Rsch. award, 1975. Fellow Am. Coll. Chest Physicians; mem. Shock Soc., Soc. Critical Care, Thoracic Soc. Office: U Rochester 601 Elmwood Ave Rochester NY 14642-0001

PAPADATOS, GERALD, urologist; b. Athens, Greece; m. Elizabeth; children: Elizabeth, David. MD, Andrews U., 1971. Diplomate Am. Bd. Urology. Attending physician Cabrini Med. Ctr., N.Y.C., 1984—; attending physician Western Queens Cmty. Hosp., Astoria, N.Y., 1985—. Mem. Hellenic Med. Soc. Greek Orthodox. Home: 201 E 19th St New York NY 10003 Office: 28-25 33d St New York NY 11102

PAPAGEORGIOU, PANAGIOTIS, medical educator; b. Thessaloniki, Greece, Dec. 23, 1959. MD, Aristotelian U., Thessaloniki, 1984; PhD in Physiology, Harvard U., 1990. Cert. Ednl. Com. for Fgn. Med. Grads., FLEX; diplomate Am. Bd. Internal Medicine, subspecialty in cardiovasc. disease; lic. physician, Mass. Rsch. fellow Am. Heart Assn., Mass. affiliate, 1989-90; intern in medicine Beth Israel Hosp., Harvard Med. Sch., Boston, 1990-91, jr. asst. resident internal medicine, 1991-92, clin. cardiology fellow cardiovascular divsn., 1992-94, clin. electrophysiology fellow cardiovascular divsn., 1994-96, staff electrophysiologist, 1996—; tchg. fellow dept. cellular and molecular physiology Harvard U., 1985-90, clin. fellow medicine, 1990-95, instr., 1995—. Contbr. articles to profl. jours., chpts. to books. Greek Nat. scholar, 1977-84, Albert J. Ryan scholar Harvard Med. Sch., 1987-90; recipient clinician-investigator devel. award NIH, 1995, Clinician Scientist awrd AHA, Nat. Ctr., 1995. Mem. ACP, AMA, Tessaloniki Med. Soc., Am. Heart Assn., Mass. Med. Soc., Biophys. Soc., Am. Heart Assn. Basic Rsch. Coun., Am. Coll. Cardiology. Office: Beth Israel Hosp 330 Brookline Ave Boston MA 02215

PAPAIOANNOU, EVANGELIA-LILLY, psychologist, researcher; b. Thessaloniki, Greece, Mar. 22, 1963; came to U.S. 1984; d. Nicholas and Ekaterini (Goulias) P. Bus. studies certificate with high honors, Anatolia Coll., Thessaloniki, Greece, 1983; BA in Psychology magna cum laude, Smith Coll., 1986; postgrad., Am. U., 1989, Georgetown U., 1993—. Guest researcher NIH, Bethesda, Md., 1986—. Author articles in press and profl. jours. Active in Hellenic Soc. for the Health Scis., Bethesda, 1987—. Recipient: scholarships Smith Coll. and Anatolia Coll. Mem. APA, Jean Piaget Soc., Internat. Platform Assn., Washington Soc. for Jungian Psychology, Alliance Francaise, Smith Coll. Alumnae Assn., Anatolia Coll. Alumni Assn., Nat. Mus. Women in the Arts, Brazilian-Am. Cultural Inst., Smith Coll.First Group Scholars, Phi Beta Kappa, Psi Chi. Greek Orthodox. Home: Promenade Towers 5225 Pooks Hill Rd Apt 1711N Bethesda MD 20814-2051

PAPALIA, DIANE ELLEN, human development educator; b. Englewood, N.J., Apr. 26, 1947; d. Edward Peter and Madeline (Borrin) P.; m. Jonathan Finlay, June 19, 1976; 1 child, Anna Victoria Finlay. A.B., Vassar Coll., 1968; M.S., W.Va. U., 1970, Ph.D. (NSF fellow), 1971. Asst. prof. child and family studies U. Wis., Madison, 1971-75; assoc. prof. U. Wis., 1975-78, prof., 1978-87, coordinator child and family studies, 1977-79; adj. prof. psychology in pediatrics U. Pa. Sch. Medicine, 1987-89. Co-author: (with Sally W. Olds) A Child's World: Infancy Through Adolescence, 1975, 7th edit., 1996, Human Development, 1978, 6th edit., 1995, Psychology, 1985, 2d edit., 1988, (with Cameron J. Camp and Ruth Duskin Feldman) Adult Development and Aging, 1996; contbr. articles to profl. jours. Am. Council on Edn. fellow, 1979-80; U. Wis. grantee. Fellow Gerontol. Soc.; mem. Am. Psychol. Assn., Soc. Research in Child Devel., Nat. Council Family Relations, Psi Chi. Home: 316 E 18th St New York NY 10003

PAPANICOLAOU, GEORGE, vascular surgeon, educator; b. Greece, June 25, 1952. MD, Nat. U. Athens, 1977. Diplomate Am. Bd. Surgery. Surg. resident Univ. Hosp., Athens, Greece, 1980-82; intern in surgery Meth. Hosp., Bklyn., 1982-83; resident in surgery St. Mary's Hosp., Waterbury, Conn., 1983-87, chief resident, 1987-88; clin. fellow divsn. vascular surgery St. Vincent Med. Ctr./Med. Coll. Ohio, Toledo, 1988-89; sr. rsch. fellow divsn. vascular surgery U. Wash. Sch. Medicine, Seattle, 1993-94; clin. asst. prof. U. Nebr., 1991-92; clin. instr. in surgery U. So. Calif., 1994-96; clin fellow divsn. vascular surgery McGill U., Montreal, Que., Can., 1996-97; attending surgeon Bryan Meml. Hosp., Lincoln, Nebr., 1989-92, Lincoln Gen. Hosp., 1989-92, St. Elizabeth Health Ctr., Lincoln, 1989-92. Contbr. articles, abstracts to profl. jours. Fellow Royal Coll. Physicians and Surgeons Can.; mem. Can. Assn. Gen. Surgeons, King County Med. Soc. Office: LAC & USC Dept Surgery 1200 N State R 9900 Los Angeles CA 90033

PAPAPIETRO, SILVIO EMILIO, cardiologist; b. Santiago, Chile, Jan. 1, 1948; came to U.S., 1973; m. Patricia Sleman; children: Carolina, Claudio, Mauricio. BA, El Patrocinio de San Jose, Santiago, 1964; MD, U. Chile, Santiago, 1972. Diplomate Am. Bd. Internal Medicine. Fellow pharmacology U. Chile Med. Sch., Santiago, 1972-73; intern internal medicine Meml. Hosp., Worcester, Mass., 1973-74; resident internal medicine U. Ala., Montgomery, 1974-75, U. Okla. Health Sci. Ctr., Oklahoma City, 1975-76; fellow cardiovascular diseases U. Ala., Birmingham, 1976-78, cardiologist, 1978-81; cardiologist Carraway Meth. Med. Ctr., Birmingham, 1981—, dir. Cardiac Cath Lab., 1983-91, 95—; instr. medicine U. Ala., Birmingham, 1978-80, asst. prof., 1980-81, clin. asst. prof., 1981-85, clin. assoc. prof., 1985—. Bd. dirs., mem. Ala. affiliate, Jefferson-Shelby divsn. Am. Heart Assn., 1995—. Fellow ACP, Am. Coll. Cardiology (councillor Ala. chpt. 1994—), Am. Coll. Chest Physicians, Am. Heart Assn. (bd. dirs. Jeff-Shelby divsn. 1986-88); mem. AMA. Roman Catholic. Office: 1528 Carraway Blvd Birmingham AL 35234

PAPARELLA, MICHAEL M., otolaryngologist; b. Detroit, Feb. 13, 1933; s. Vincent Paparella and Angela Creat; m. Treva Buzard, Oct. 2, 1992; children: Mark, Steven, Lisa. BS, U. Mich., 1953, MD, 1957. Diplomate Am. Bd. Otolaryngology (guest examiner 1967-75, bd. dirs. 1976, mem. standards and residencies com. 1976, fgn. med. grads. com. 1978, credentials com. 1984-85, examiner 1976—); lic. physician, Mich., Mass., Ohio, Minn. Rotating intern Emanuel Hosp., Portland, Oreg., 1957-58; resident in otolaryngology Henry Ford Hosp., Detroit, 1958-61, jr. mem. staff, 1960-61; mem. geographic staff, asst. Mass. Eye and Ear Infirmary, Boston, 1963-64; instr. Harvard U. Med. Sch., Boston, 1963-64; asst. prof. otolaryngology, dir. otological research lab. Ohio State U., Columbus, 1964-67; mem. staff dept. otolaryngology Ohio State U. Hosps., 1964-67; prof., chmn. dept. otolaryngology U. Minn., Mpls., 1967-84, dir. otopathology lab., 1967—, clin. prof., 1984—; mem. staff U. Minn. Hosps., 1967-84; pres. Minn. Ear, Head and Neck Clinic, Mpls., 1984—; dir. Nat. Temporal Bone Bank Program Midwestern Ctr., Mpls., 1979—; cons. VA Hosp., Dayton, Ohio, 1964-67. Mem. editl. bd. Minn. Med. Assn. Medicine, The Laryngoscope, Modern Medicine, Am. Jour. Clin. Rsch, Am. Jour. Otolaryngology, Annals Otology, Rhinology & Larynology, Acta Oto-Laryngologica; editor: (films) Surgical Techniques and Auditory Rsch., Surgical Treatment for Intractable External Otitis, Tympanoplasty, parts 1 and 2, Endolymphatic Sac, Canalplasty; (books) Atlas of Ear Surgery, 1968, 2d ed., 1971, 3d ed., 1980, Biochemical Mechanisms in Hearing and Deafness, 1970, Clinical Otology: An International Symposium, 1971, Year Book of the Ear, Nose and Throat, 1972-75, Otolarynology: Basic Sciences and Related Disciplines, 1973, 2d ed. vol I, 1980, Otolarynology: Ear, vol. II, 1973, 2d ed., 1980, Otolaynrology: Head and Neck, vol. III, 1973, 2d ed., 1980, Year Book of Otolarynology, 1976—, Boies's Fundamentals of Otolaryngology: A Textbook of Ear, Nose and Throat Diseases, 5th ed., 1978, Ear Clinics International, vols. I-III. 1982, Medicassette Otolarynolgy, 1986; also contbr. numerous article to profl. pubs. Founder, sec., bd. dirs. Internat. Hearing Found., 1984—; mem. Presch. Med. Survey Vision and Hearing. Grantee NIH, Am. Otological Soc., Deafness Research Found., Hartford Found., Guggenheim Found., Bodman Found.; recipient Kobrak Research award, 1960, Amicitiae Sacrum honor Collegium Oto-Rhino-Laryngologicum, 1976; named Brinkman lectr. U. Nijmegen, Holland, 1986, Guest of Honor 5th Asia-Oceanic Meeting, Korea, 1983. Fellow ACS, Am. Acad. Ophthalmology and Otolaryngology (assoc. sec. continuing edn., assoc. sec., chmn. undergrad. edn. subcom., chmn. otorhinolaryngology self-improvement com., chmn. subcom. on evaluation new info. and edn. of hearing and equilibrium com., head and neck surgery equilibrium subcom. 1984-86, Merit award 1975); mem. Acad. Medicine Columbus County, Acad. Medicine Franklin County, Am. Assn. for Lab. Animal Scis., AMA, Am. Neurotology Soc. (audiology study com. 1976), Am. Otological Soc. (trustee research fund, pres.), Assn. Acad. Depts. Otolaryngology (pres. pro tem, organizer 1971-72, sec.-treas. 1972-74, pres. elect 1974-76, pres. 1976-78), Barany Soc., Better Hearing Inst. (adv. bd.), Deafness Research Found. (trustee, Centurion Club), Collegium Oto-Rhino-Laryngologicum Amicitiae Sacrum, Columbus Ophthalmology and Otolaryngological Soc., Hennepin County Med. Soc., Mpls. Hearing Soc. (bd. dirs.), Minn. Acad. Medicine, Minn. Acad. Ophthalmology and Otolaryngology (council), Minn. Coll. Surgeons, New England Otolaryngological Soc., Ohio State Med. Soc., Pan Am. Med. Assn., Soc. Univ. Otolaryngologists (exec. council 1969-71), Triological Soc. (v.p. middle sect. 1976, council mem. 1976, asst. editor), Alpha Kappa Kappa, Sigma Xi. Lodge: Lions (dir. hearing ctr., adv. council hearing ctr.). Office: 701 25th Ave S # 200 Minneapolis MN 55454-1443

PAPARONE, PAMELA ANN, nurse practitioner, medical surgical nurse; b. Jersey City, N.J., Apr. 16, 1953; d. Thomas Richard and Betty Ann (Richter) Devine; m. Philip William Paparone, Oct 2, 1976; children: Philip, Paige. BSN, Rutgers U., 1974; MSN, Seton Hall U., 1977. RN, N.J.; cert. nurse practitioner; med.-surg. clin. nurse specialist. RN Atlantic City Med. Ctr., 1974-75; surgical inservice nurse Atlantic City Med. Ctr., Pamona, N.J., 1975-76, clin. nurse specialist, 1978-80; instr. Russell Sage Coll., Troy, N.Y., 1977-78; nurse practitioner, clin. nurse specialist Philip Paparone, D.O., Absecon, 1978—; lectr. Stockton State Coll., Pomona, 1978-80. Author: The Lyme Disease Coloring Book, 1989; editl. review bd. Jour. Spirochetal and Tick Borne Diseases, 1994—; contbr. articles to profl. jours. Recipient Nurse Educator of the Year award Am. Assn. Office Nurses, 1989. Mem. Am. Acad. Nurse Practitioners, Sigma Theta Tau. Home: 714 N Harvard Ave Ventnor NJ 08406 Office: 72 W Jin Leeds Rd Absecon NJ 08201

PAPASTRAT, HELEN P(ANAYOTA), psychiatrist; b. Binghamton, N.Y., June 13, 1958; d. Peter H. and Mary A. (Angelopoulos) P. AB, Cornell U., 1980; MD, N.Y. Med. Coll., 1985. Intern Greenwich Hosp., 1985-86; resident Yale-New Haven Hosp., 1986-89; postdoctoral fellow dept. psychiatry Sch. Medicine Yale U., New Haven, 1985-89. Mem. Am. Psychiat. Assn., Alpha Omega Alpha. Greek Orthodox. Office: 133 Main St Binghamton NY 13905-2742

PAPAVASILIOU, STATHIS SPYRO, molecular endocrinologist; b. Athens, Attica, Greece, May 1, 1950; arrived in U.S., 1974, s. Spyro and Maria Papavasiliou; m. Antigone Antonios Syrigou, Aug. 7, 1974; children: Spyro, Anthony. M.D., U. Athens, Greece, 1974, Didactoricon, 1977. Diplomate Am. Bd. Internal Medicine. Fellow U. Calif.-San Francisco, 1974-77; intern Henry Ford Hosp., Mich., 1977-78, resident in medicine, 1980-82; fellow in endocrinology U. Mich., Ann Arbor, 1982-85, asst. rsch. scientist, 1985; physician internal medicine Sismanoglion Gen. Hosp., Athens, 1986-87; asst. prof. endocrinology U. Crete, Greece, 1987-93, assoc. prof. endocrinology, 1993—. Contbr. articles to med. books, jours. Mem. Am. Diabetes Assn. Bay Area Heart Research Com. fellow, 1976-77; recipient AMA Physicians Recognition award, 1982, Young Scientist award Mellon Found., 1984. Fellow ACP; mem. AAAS, N.Y. Acad. Scis., Hellenic Endocrine Soc. (exec. bd.). Avocations: music, chess, athletics. Office: U Crete, Med Sch, Heraklion Crete, Greece

PAPAZOGLOU, NICHOLAS, cardiologist; b. Iraklion, Crete, Greece, July 27, 1933; s. Michael and Aristea (Kokkinidis) P.; m. Calliope Apostolakis, Feb. 6, 1965; 1 son, Spyridon-Michael. M.D., U. Athens, 1957, Doctorate, 1963; Doctorate, U. Paris, 1961. Tng., U. Paris, 1960-63, Cardiothoracic Inst. of London, 1963; fellow Univ. Clinic Athens, 1964; sr. registrar cardiology clinic Nat. Ins. Hosp. of Athens, 1965-70, chief div. of cardiology, 1970—; vis. prof. in cardiology U. Athens, 1974; vis. lectr. Univ. Hosps. U.S., 1972, 74; mem. bd. examiners Ministry of Health. Served with Greek Health Service, 1957-60. Ednl. fellow French Ministry Fgn. Affairs, 1961-63. Mem. 5 nat. med. socs., Am. Coll. Chest Physicians, N.Y. Acad. Scis.; affiliate mem. French Cardiology Soc. (Paris), Royal Soc. Medicine (London). Author books in Greek: Myocardial Infarction, 1970; Modern Applied Clinical Cardiology, 1974; Cardiac Arrythmias, 1978, Ischemic Heart Disease, 1981; Clinical Cardiology, 1984; contbr. 200 research papers to Greek and fgn. med. jours. Home and Office: 64 Sina, 10672 Athens Greece

PAPE, BRIAN E., toxicologist, consultant; b. St. Louis, Oct. 13, 1943; s. Martin A. and Mary K. (Ratchford) P.; children: Jason, Kimberly, Katherine, Patricia. BA, Wash. U., St. Louis, 1966; MS, Mich. State U., E. Lansing, 1969, PhD, 1974; MBA, U. Mo., Columbia, 1982. Dir. toxicology U. Mo. Med. Ctr., Columbia, 1972-82, Mayo Clinic/NETS, Boston, 1986; assoc. prof. U. Mass. Med. Sch., Worcester, 1986—; cons. Pape & Assocs., 1986—. Home: 20 Tiger Rd Hudson NH 03051

PAPERNIK, DANIEL S., psychiatrist; b. N.Y.C., Apr. 29, 1937. AB, Union Coll., 1958; MD, SUNY, Bklyn., 1962, cert. psychoanalysis, 1974. Diplomate Am. Bd. Psychiatry and Neurology, Am. Bd. Med. Examiners. Intern Kaiser Foun. Hosp., San. Francisco; resident in psychiatry SUNY, Bklyn., 1965-68, from instr. psychiatry to clin. assoc. prof., 1968-80; clin. assoc. prof. psychiatry NYU Med. Ctr., N.Y.C., 1979-93, clin. prof., 1993—. mem. faculty psychoanalytic inst., 1979—, tng. and supervising analyst psychoanalytic inst., 1986—; psychoanalyst pvt. practice, N.Y.C.; candidate in psychoanalysis SUNY, Bklyn., 1967-74. Office: Daniel S Papernik MD PC 32 Gramercy Park S New York NY 10003-1709

PAPPA, KARL STEVEN, ophthalmologist; b. Cleve., Feb. 2, 1956; s. Steven Karl and Shirley Ann (Traxler) P.; m. Michelle Ann Urwin, Sept. 29, 1979; children: Christopher Steven, Rachael Therese. BS in Pharmacy summa cum laude, Ohio State U., 1979, PharmD, 1983, MD cum laude, 1987. Diplomate Am. Bd. Ophthalmology, Nat. Bd. Med. Examiners. Med./surg. intern Riverside Meth. Hosp., Columbus, 1988; ophthalmology resident Ohio State U., Columbus, 1988-91, glaucoma fellow, 1991-92; glaucoma and gen. ophthalmologist Grady Meml. Hosp., Delaware, Ohio, Grant Med. Ctr., Columbus; ophthalmologist Eye Surgery Ctr. of Ohio, Inc., Columbus, 1992—; clin. asst. prof. Ohio State U., Columbus; presenter in field. Contbr. articles to profl. jours. Mem. AMA, Am. Bd. Ophthalmology, Ohio Ophthalmol. Soc., Ohio State Med. Assn., Ohio State Pharm. Assn., Phi Delta Chi, Alpha Omega Alpha. Roman Catholic. Home: 4847 Pleasant Valley Dr Columbus OH 43220 Office: Eye Surgery Ctr Ohio Inc 303 East Town St #270 Columbus OH 43215

PAPPAS, CHARLES ENGELOS, plastic surgeon; b. Phila., May 20, 1946; s.Engelos George and Angelina (Biniaris) P.; m. Marilyn Ann Pappas; children: Evan, Angela, Chrysten. BA, BS, U. Pa., 1968; MD, Temple U., 1972. Intern, then resident in gen. surgery Johns Hopkins Hosp., Balt., 1972-75; resident in gen. surgery Temple U. Hosp., Phila., 1975-76, resident in plastic surgery, 1976-78, chmn. dept. plastic surgery, 1978-81, clin. assoc. prof. surgery, 1981—; chief dept. plastic surgery Meml. Hosp., Phila., 1986—; clin. assoc. plastic surgery Chestnut Hill Hosp., Phila., 1979—, chief/dir. dept. plastic surgery, 1994—; dir. Inst. for Aesthetic Plastic Surgery, Ft. Washington, Pa., 1985—; chmn. bd. Am. Gaming Industries, 1984—; dir., ptnr. Tristate Quicklube Co., 1982-91, Medars; pres., dir. two carwash cos., Phila., 1989—; med. dir. Fort Washington Surgery Ctr. Contbr. articles to profl. jours. Trustee Germantown Acad., Ft. Washington, 1986—, Commonwealth Nat. Country Club, Horsham, 1988—, Patrons' Charity Found. Fellow ACS, Royal Coll. Surgeons; mem. Am. Soc. Plastic Reconstructive Surgeons (diplomate), Am. Soc. Aesthetic Plastic Surgeons (diplomate), Phila. Soc. Plastic Surgeons (pres. 1990-92). Greek Orthodox. Office: Inst Aesthetic Plastic Surgery 467 Pennsylvania Ave Ste 202 Fort Washington PA 19034-3420

PAPPAS, GEORGE DEMETRIOS, anatomy and cell biology educator, scientist; b. Portland, Maine, Nov. 26, 1926; James and Anna (Dracopoulos) Pappatheodoros; m. Bernice Levine, Jan. 14, 1952; children: Zoe Alexandra, Clio Nicollette. BA, Bowdoin Coll., 1947; MS, Ohio State U., 1948, PhD, 1952; DSc (hon.), U. Athens, Greece, 1988. Vis. investigator Rockefeller Inst., N.Y.C., 1952-54; assoc. in anatomy Coll. Physicians and Surgeons, Columbia U., N.Y.C., 1956-57, asst. prof. anatomy, 1957-63, assoc. prof., 1963-66; prof. anatomy Albert Einstein Coll. Medicine, Yeshiva U., N.Y.C., 1967-77, prof. neurosci., 1974-77, vis. prof. neurosci., 1977—; prof., head dept. anatomy and cell biology U. Ill. Coll. Medicine, Chgo., 1977—; trustee Marine Biol. Lab., Woods Hole, Mass., 1975-81. Author: (with others) The Structure of the Eye, 1961, Growth and Maturation of the Brain, vol. IV, 1964, Nerve as a Tissue, 1966, The Thalmus, 1966, Pathology of the Nervous System, vol. 1, 1968, Structure and Function of Synapses, 1972, Methodological Approaches to the Study of Brain Maturation and Its Abnormalities, 1974, Advances in Neurology, vol.12, 1975, The Nervous System, vol. 1 The Basic Neurosciences, 1975, Cellular and Molecular Basis of Synaptic Transmission, 1988, also author many conf. procs.; contbr. over 200 articles to profl. jours.; former mem. editorial bd. Anatomical Record, Biol. Bull., Brain Rsch., Jour. Neurocytology, Microstructure; patentee method inducing analgesia by implantation of cells releasing neuroactive substances. Arthritis and Rheumatism Found. fellow, 1954-56; recipient career devel. award Columbia U., 1964-66; rsch. grantee NIH. Fellow AAAS, N.Y. Acad. Scis., Inst. Medicine Chgo.; mem. Am. Soc. Cell Biology (pres. 1974-75), Am. Assn. Anatomists (chmn. pub. policy com. 1981-82), Assn. Anatomy Chmn. (exec. com. 1978-80, pres. 1981-82), Electron Microscopy Soc. Am. (program chmn. 1984-85), N.Y. Soc. Electron Microscopy (pres. 1967-68), Soc. for Neurosci. (pres. Chgo. chpt. 1985-86), Harvey Soc., Internat. Brain Rsch. Orgn., Cajal Club, Sigma Xi. Home: 506 W Roscoe St Chicago IL 60657-3535 Office: U Ill Coll Medicine Dept Anatomy & Cell Biology 808 S Wood St Chicago IL 60612-7300

PAPPAS, JOHN, clinical psychologist; b. N.Y.C., Aug. 24, 1957; s. Dimitrios and Agnes (Tunis) P.; m. Lois M. McNally, Aug. 17, 1986. BS summa cum laude, U. Bridgeport, 1980; MA, New Sch. for Social Rsch., PhD, 1991. Lic. psychologist, N.Y. State. Psychology intern Hall-Brooke Found., Westport, Conn., 1986-87; clin. psychologist N.Y.C. Health Dept., 1987-88; clin. psychotherapist Washington Sq. Inst., N.Y.C., 1988-91; cons. Assessment Systems, Inc., N.Y.C., 1988-92; staff psychologist N.Y.C. Police Dept., 1987-92; dir. Downtown Profl. Cons., N.Y.C., 1990—; grad. teaching asst. New Sch., N.Y.C., 1985-86; rsch. asst. Yale U., New Haven, 1983-84. Author: Social Network Orientation and Psychotherapy, 1991; adv. bd. Healthway Mag. Recipient Herbert award in psychology U. Bridgeport, 1980. Mem. APA, AAAS, N.Y. Acad. Sci., N.Y. State Psychol. Assn., Mus. Modern Art. Office: Downtown Profl Cons 150 Broadway Ste 1005 New York NY 10038-4401

PAPPAS, MARIA ELENI, nurse; b. Encino, Calif., Oct. 1, 1960; d. Nicholas Constantine and Helen Cleo (Tannors) P. BSN, U. San Francisco, 1985; M in Nursing, UCLA, 1991. Cert. critical care nurse, pub. health nurse. Staff med./surg. nurse VA Med. Ctr., West L.A., 1985-87; staff nurse ICU VA Med. Ctr., San Francisco, 1987-88; staff nurse SICU St. Mary's Hosp., San Francisco, 1988-89; staff nurse ICU St. Joseph's Hosp., Burbank, Calif., 1989-91; clin. nurse specialist Northridge (Calif.) Hosp. Med. Ctr., 1991-95; asst. clin. prof. Sch. Nursing, UCLA, 1993—. Co-author: (manual) Brain Death Policy Manual, 1993. VA scholar U. San Francisco, 1984, Reynolds Estate scholar UCLA, 1991. Mem. Sigma Theta Tau (Outstanding Contbn. award 1989). Greek Orthodox. Home: 8012 Comanche Ave Winnetka CA 91306-1832 Office: Raytel Heart Ctr 10445 Balboa Blvd Granada Hills CA 91394-9400

PAQUETTE, MARY ELLEN, ophthalmologist; b. Tucson, Oct. 1, 1938; d. Garnet Douglas and Mascha V. (Dyck) Percy; m. Robert Emmett Paquette, Nov. 1, 1975; children: Connie Marie, Mary Kathryn. BSc in Biology magna cum laude, U. Ariz., 1960; MD, Stanford U., 1965. Diplomate Am. Bd. Ophthalmology. Intern U. Iowa, Iowa City, 1965-66; resident in ophthalmology Stanford (Calif.) U., 1966-69; pvt. practice Mountain View, Calif., 1969—. U. Ariz. scholar, 1957. Fellow Am. Acad. Ophthalmology; mem. AMA, Calif. Med. Assn., Santa Clara County Med. Soc., Kappa Alpha Theta (editor and scholarship chmn.), Phi Kappa Phi, Phi Beta Kappa. Office: 2500 Hospital Dr Bldg 4 Mountain View CA 94040

PÂQUIN, TRUDY, gerontological nurse; b. Wantagh, N.Y., May 23, 1954; d. William Carl and Gertrude Mary (Kryl) Bauer; m. Alfred Joseph Pâquin III, July 30, 1977. RN, AAS, John Tyler C.C., Chester, Va., 1982; BA magna cum laude, So. Conn. State U., 1993; gerontol. nurse cert., U. Conn., 1994, nurse mgmt. cert., 1995. Animal trainer, 1972—, pet therapist, 1974—; RN, educator Elm City Health Ctr., New Haven, 1983—; Alzheimer's rschr., 1995. Author: Pet Therapy Handbook, 1996, One Man's Journey to America, 1996; composer numerous musical works. Office: Elm City Health Ctr 50 Mead St New Haven CT 06511

PARA, MICHAEL FRANCIS, infectious disease physician, researcher; b. Akron, Ohio, Oct. 9, 1948; s. Adolph and Dorothy K. (Serfillipi) P.; m. Caroline Clement Whitacre, June 28, 1975; 1 child, Alexander Whitacre Para. BS, Mich. State U., 1970; MD, Ohio State U., 1974. Intern U. Chgo., 1974-75, resident, 1975-77, infectious diseases fellow, 1977-81; asst. prof. internal medicine Ohio State U., 1981-86, asst. prof. med. microbiology and immunology, 1981-86, assoc. prof., 1986-92, prof., 1992—; co-dir. East Ctrl. AIDS Edn. Ctr., Columbus, 1987-95; HIV adv. bd. Sandoz Pharms., 1994-96; HIV disease rsch. com. AIDS Clin. Trials Group NIH, 1993-96. AIDS and Hemophilia adv. Ohio Dept. Health, 1996. Firestone scholar Mich. State U., 1966; Damon Runyon-Walter Winchell rsch. fellow U. Chgo., 1978. Fellow ACP, Infectious Disease Soc. Am.; mem. AMA, Am. Fedn. Clin. Rsch., Ctrl. Soc. Clin. Rsch., Ohio State Med. Assn., Columbus Soc. Internal Medicine (pres. 1988), Sigma Xi. Office: 4725 U Hosp Clinic 456 W 10th Ave Columbus OH 43210

PARADIS, CAROL JEANNE, advanced practice nurse, counselor, mediator; b. Providence, Dec. 15, 1944; d. Ralph Joseph and Jeannette Clarice (Langelier) Petrucci; m. Daniel Kirby Paradis, Sept. 5, 1970 (div. 1993); children: Trent August, Scott LeMay. BSN, Boston U., 1966; M Nursing, UCLA, 1971; MA in Psychology, Regis U., 1995. RN, Colo.; cert. addictions counselor, Colo.; nat. cert. employee assistance profl. Nurse Univ. Hosp., Boston, 1966-67, Peter Bent Brigham Hosp., Boston, 1967-68; sr. clin. nurse surg. intensive care and Children's Hosp. Long Beach (Calif.) Meml. Hosp. Med. Ctr., 1968-71; faculty chmn. and adminstrv. asst. Presbyn. Sch. Nursing, Denver, 1972-80; mem. faculty Delta (Colo.) Montrose Vocat.-Tech. Sch., 1982-84; staff nurse Montrose (Colo.) Meml. Hosp., 1984-86; inpatient dir. Care Ctr. Montrose (Colo.) Hosp., 1986-91, outpatient dir. Care Ctr., 1987-95, employee assistance programs dir., 1989-95, dir. nurses, 1987, outpatient program dir., dir. employee assistance program, 1987-95; pvt. practice, 1995—; cons. Western Slope Employee Assistance Program, Home Psychiat. Health, U. Denver Sch. Nursing, 1981-82; instr. Mesa Coll. Outreach, 1984; mediator for bus. orgns., employee disputes and family/child disputes, 1992—. Speaker regional conf. Assn. Operating Rm. Nurses, 1974. Bd. dirs. Women's Resource Ctr., 1983-84; presenter Montrose Children's Mus., 1989; team mem. Montrose Community for Drug Free Colo., 1987—; leader local cub troop Boy Scouts Am.; active in various sch., ch. and communities activites. Recipient Bonnie Forquer award Nat. Coun. on Alcoholism and Drug Abuse, Mesa chpt., 1990. Mem. ANA, Colo. Nurses Assn., Employee Assistance Profls. Assn., Rocky Mountain Nurses Assn. (Colo. lobbyist Nurse Practice Act 1978), Colo. Psychiat. Nurses Assn., Friends of Nursing (scholarship coms. 1987-89), Alpha Phi. Roman Catholic. Home: 64669 W Ranger Rd Montrose CO 81401-7836 Office: 438 S Townsend Ave Montrose CO 81401

PARADISE, LOUIS VINCENT, educational psychology educator, university official; b. Scranton, Pa., Apr. 19, 1946; s. Louis Benjamin and Lucille (Bochicchio) P.; children: Christopher, Gabrielle,Victoria. BS, Pa. State U., 1968; MS, Bucknell U., 1974; PhD, U. Va., 1976. Lic. psychologist, profl. counselor; cert. sch. psychologist. Assoc. prof. Cath. U. Am., Washington, 1976-83; prof. edn., chmn. edn. leadership U. New Orleans, 1983-90, dean Coll. Edn., 1990-92, univ. exec. vice chancellor and provost, 1992-94, exec. vice chancellor for acad. affairs, 1994—. Author: Ethics in Counseling and Psychotherapy, 1979, Questioning: Skills for the Helping Process, 1979, Counseling in Community College, 1982. 1st lt. U.S. Army, 1968-72. DuPont scholar U. Va., 1974. Mem. APA, ACA (ethics com. 1986-89), Am. Edn. Rsch. Assn., So. Assn. Counselor Edn. (chmn. ethics com. 1988-89), Chi Sigma Iota (founding chpt. pres. 1985-87). Roman Catholic. Office: U New Orleans Office Acad Affairs New Orleans LA 70148

PARAGAS, ROLANDO G., physician; b. Philippines, Apr. 15, 1935; came to U.S., 1959; s. Epifanio Y. and Ester (Guiang) P.; m. Liwayway Galvey, May 5, 1963; children: Suzanne, Richard, Esther, Dawn. AA, U. Philippines, 1953; MD, Far Eastern U., 1958. Physician pvt. practice, Burlington, Iowa, 1968—. Fellow Am. Acad. Pediatrics; mem. AMA, Am. Assn. Filipino Physicians, Iowa Med. Soc., Philippine Physicians in Am. (assoc.). Office: 828 N 7th PO Box 249 Burlington IA 52601

PARAS, SOFIA DIMITRIA, counselor, writer, editor; b. Delaware, Ohio, Dec. 31, 1943; d. James Peter and Fotini Dimitria (Dellios) Stoycheff; m. Nicholas Andrew Paras, Dec. 8, 1968; 1 child, Alexandra Nicholas. BA, Ohio Wesleyan U., 1965; cert., Adelphi U., 1987. Tchr. Upper Arlington Schs., Columbus, Ohio, 1966-68; asst. tng. coord. personnel dept. Ohio State U. Hosps., Columbus, 1968-69, art fair coord., 1969; asst. tng. coord. personnel dept. New Eng. Deaconess Hosp., Boston, 1969-70; tng. coord. nursing dept. Meml. Hosp. of Sloan Kettering, N.Y.C., 1970-71; real estate salesperson Gen. Devel. Corp., 1971-72; adminstrv. asst. Ippocampos Maritime and Internship Fin. and Investments, Piraeus, Greece, 1976-81; office mgr. Internapa Fin. Svcs., Athens, Greece, 1981-86; adminstrv. dir. lawyer's asst. program Adelphi U., West Hempstead, N.Y., 1987-88, admissions counselor lawyer's asst. program, 1988—; cons. interior decorator hotel complex Paramount Tourist and Devel. Ltd., Paralimni, Cyprus, 1981-84; nat. nursing conf. coord. Meml. Hosp. Sloan Kettering, St. Louis, 1971. Editor Women's Internat. Club, Athens, 1978-84; author: (poetry) Observations, 1990, (screenplays) Contract I, 1990, Contract II, 1991, Mindlock, 1995, Reasonable in Richmond, 1996, Shipping Wars, 1996; editor: Traditional Hellenic Tastes (in Greek and English langs.), 1994. Theatre dir. Am. Farm Sch., Salonica, Greece, 1974; program coord. choir recitals St. Nicholas Greek Orthodox, Babylon, N.Y., 1989—; v.p. Internat. Women's Orgn. of Greece, Salonica, 1973-74; sec. Christian Orthodox Fellowship, Inc. Mem. Kappa Kappa Gamma, Theta Alpha Phi.

PARBHOO, SANTILAL PARAG, surgeon, consultant; b. Cape Town, South Africa, Jan. 16, 1937; came to Eng., 1962; s. Parag and Jasoda Pemi (Ramjee) P.; m. Constance Ann Craig, Jan. 8, 1969; children: Mark Santilal, Kathryn Elizabeth, Alan Vijay. MB BChir, Med. Sch. U., Cape Town, 1960; PhD, Queens U., Belfast, No. Ireland, 1967. House surgeon New Somerset Hosp., Cape Town, 1961; sr. house surgeon Edendale Hosp., Pietermaritzburg, 1961-62; clin. asst. Royal Victoria Hosp., Belfast, 1962-64, tutor, registrar, 1964-65; surgical registrar No. Ireland Hosps., 1965-68; rsch. fellow, lectr. Royal Free Hosp. and Sch. Medicine, London, 1968-72, sr. lectr., cons. surgeon, 1974-91, 1974-91, chmn. surg. bd. studies, 1984-91; surg. registrar Frenchay Hosp., Bristol, Eng., 1973-74; cons. surgeon Royal Free Hosp. (NHS Trust), London, 1991—, chmn. div. surgery, 1987-89; mem. med. adv. group Womens Nationwide Cancer Control Campaign, 1995—; advisor Marie Curie Found. Cancer Care Edn. Dept., 1993—; mem. coms. nat. U.K. Breast Screening program. Editor: Bone Metastasis: Monitoring & Treatment, 1983; contbr. articles to profl. jours. Dir. Breast Cancer Appeal, Royal Air Force Hosp., 1984—, Cancerkin; lectr. Reach to Recovery Internat. Program, Luxemburg, 1988, Trieste, Spain, 1992, Barcelona, Spain, 1994. Rsch. fellow Brit. Coun., Queens U., 1962-64, Interchange fellow Brit. Coun., U. Louvain, 1971, Rsch. Travelling fellow NATO, 1991-92; U. London and U. Tex. Southwest; Winnifrid Ladd scholar Royal Free Hosp. Sch. of Medicine, 1971. Fellow Royal Coll. Surgeons (Eng.), Surg. Rsch. Soc., Brit. Assn. Surg. Oncology, Egyptian Soc. Hepatology (medal 1989); mem. European Group on Lymphology, Gujerati Arya Assn., Hong Kong Soc. Surgeons (hon.). Office: Royal Free Hosp, Pond St, London NW3 2QG, England

PARDES, HERBERT, psychiatrist, educator; b. Bronx, N.Y., July 7, 1934; s. Louis and Frances (Bergman) P.; m. Judith Ellen Silber, June 9, 1957; children: Stephen, Lawrence, James. BS, Rutgers U., 1956, MD, SUNY, Bklyn., 1960; DSc (hon.) SUNY, 1990. Straight med. intern Kings County Hosp., 1960-61, resident in psychiatry, 1961-62, 64-66; asst. prof. psychiatry Downstate Med. Ctr., Bklyn., 1968-72, prof., chmn. dept., 1972-75; dir. psychiat. services Kings County Hosp., Bklyn., 1972-75; prof., chmn. dept. psychiatry U. Colo. Med. Sch., 1975-78; dir. psychiat. services Colo. Psychiat. Hosp., Denver, 1975-78; dir. NIMH, Rockville, Md., 1978-84; asst. surgeon gen. USPHS, 1978-84; prof. psychiatry Columbia U., N.Y.C., 1984—, chmn. dept., 1984—, dir. Psychiat. Inst., 1984-89, v.p. for health scis. and dean faculty of medicine, 1989—. Committeeman, Kings County Dem. Com., 1972-75; pres. sci. bd. Nat. Alliance for Research on Schizophrenia and Depression. Capt. M.C., AUS, 1962-64. Decorated Army Commendation medal; ann. hon. lectr. Downstate Med. Ctr. Alumni Assn., 1972, recipient Alumni Achievement medal, 1980, William Menninger award ACP, 1992, Dorothy Dix award Mental Illness Fedn., 1992, Vester Mark award, 1993. Mem. Assn. Am. Med. Colls. (chair-elect 1994-95, chair 1995-96), Am. Psychiat. Assn. (v.p. 1986-88, pres. 1989-90, Disting. Svc. award 1993), Inst. Medicine, Am. Psychoanalytic Assn., Coun. of Deans (adminstrv. bd., chair-elect 1993-94, chair 1994-95), Assoc. Med. Schs. N.Y. (pres. 1995—), Phi Beta Kappa, Alpha Omega Alpha. Contbr. articles to med. jours. Home: 15 Claremont Ave Apt 93 New York NY 10027-6814 Office: Columbia U Coll Phys & Surgeons Dept Psychiatry 630 W 168th St New York NY 10032-3702 also: NY State Psychiat Inst 722 W 168th St New York NY 10032-2603

PARDOLL, PETER MICHAEL, gastroenterologist; b. Bklyn., Oct. 24, 1946; s. Abraham Jacob and Lee (Nyfield) P.; m. Lois, June 29, 1969; children: Todd, Missy, Mindy. MD, Med. Coll. Va., 1971. Intern U. Miami Affiliated Hosps., 1971-72, resident, 1972-74; fellow gastroenterology U. South Fla., 1974-76; gastroenterologist pvt. practice, St. Petersburg, Fla., 1978-92; pres. Ctr. Digestive Diseases, St. Petersburg, Fla., 1992—; bd. dors. Palms of Pasadena Hosp., v.p. Founder, bd. dirs. Menorah Manor Home for Living, St. Petersburg. Maj. USAF, 1976-78. Gastroenterology fellow U. Sough Fla., 1974-76. Fellow Coll. Gastroenterology (chmn. com. practice affairs); mem. HCRA (gastroenterology rep., carrier adv. com.), Fla. Gastroenterology Soc. (sec., pres.-elect), Fla. Ind. Physicians Assn. (bd. dirs. region 5), Doctors Health Plan (bd. dirs.). Office: Ctr Digestive Diseases 1609 Pasadena Ave S Ste 3-M Saint Petersburg FL 33707

PARÉ DO, JOHN L., family practice physician; b. Sanford, Maine, Sept. 18, 1962; s. Laval P. and Theresa B. (Davis) Paré. BS in Medicine and Biology, U. New Eng., Biddeford, Maine, 1988, DO, 1992. Diplomate Am. Bd. Family Practice. Intern St. Elizabeth's Hosp., Utica, N.Y., 1992-93, resident in family practice, 1992-95, chief resident family practice medicine, 1994-95; family practice physician Prince William Hosp., Manassas, Va., 1995—. Recipient Family Practice Clin. Achievement award, 1993, Frank H. Boehm Sr. award Clin. Neurosci., 1994. Mem. AMA, Am. Osteo. Assn. Home: 11009 Kinship Ct #202 Manassas VA 22110-7759 Office: Gainesville Family Practice 7524 Linton Hall Rd Gainesville VA 22065

PAREJKO, RONALD ANTHONY, microbiology educator; b. Chgo., Oct. 21, 1940; s. Stanley and Victoria (Piotrowski) P.; m. Shirley Ann Smith, June 15, 1963; children: Catherine, Michael, Krystyna, Elizabeth. BS, U. Wis., Eau Claire, 1963; MS, U. Wis., Madison, 1964; PhD, U. Wis., 1969. Med. technologist St. Joseph's Hosp., Marshfield, Wis., 1963-64; rsch. asst. U. Wis., Madison, 1964-69; prof. of microbiology No. Mich. U., Marquette, 1969—; mem. Pre-Med. Adv. Bd., Marquette, 1972—; cons. med. edn. program Mich. State U., Escanaba, 1980-81. Contbr. articles to Sci., Jour. Bacteriology, Can. Jour. Microbiology, Proceedings NAS, Bull. Environ. Contam. Toxicology. Chmn. Marquette Twp. Planning Commn., 1987—. Mem. AAUP, Am. Soc. Microbiology (Pres.' fellow 1967), Sigma Xi, Alpha Epsilon Delta, Beta Beta Beta. Home: 1982 W Fair Ave Marquette MI 49855-2339 Office: No Mich U Biology Dept Marquette MI 49855

PARENT, J. REX, ophthalmologist; b. Ft. Wayne, Ind., Aug. 13, 1945; s. Harry Allen and Isabelle Eilene (Hopkins) P.; m. Connie Jo Parent, Feb. 23, 1968; children: J.R. Jr., Marcus Jason. BA, Hanover (Ind.) Coll.; MD, Ind. U. Med. Sch., Indpls. Diplomate Am. Bd. Ophthalmology. Intern Ind. U., Ft. Wayne, 1971-72; emergency rm. physician St. Joseph's Hosp., Ft. Wayne, 1972-73; retinal rsch. U. Louisville, 1973, resident, 1973-77, chief resident, asst. prof., 1977; pvt. practice, pres., CEO Ft. Wayne Ophthalmology, Inc., 1977—; clin. instr. Ind. U., Ft. Wayne, 1977—; pres., CEO Ft. Wayne Ophthalmic Surg. Ctr., 1986—. Lectr. in field. Humanitarian missions VOSH and Lions clubs, Honduras and other Ctrl. Am. countries, 1980s-94. Mem. AMA, Ind. State Med. Assn., Ft. Wayne Med. Soc., Am. Soc. Cataract and Refractive Surgery, Intraocular Lens Implant Soc., Outpatient Ophthalmic Surg. Soc., Am. Acad. Ophthalmology, Ind. Acad. Ophthalmology, Ft. Wayne Acad. Ophthalmology, Soc. for Excellence in Eyecare. Office: Ft Wayne Ophthalmology Inc 321 E Wayne St Fort Wayne IN 46802-2713

PARENTE, LOUISE, social worker; b. Bklyn., Apr. 11, 1945; d. Frank and Lucy (Coppola) Russo; m. John Parente Sr., Dec. 23, 1967; children: John Jr., Donald, Steven. B in Social Work summa cum laude, Kean Coll., N.J., 1984; MSW, NYU, 1985, PhD ABD, 1995. Cert. social worker, N.Y.; cert. eating disorder specialist. Pvt. practice S.I., N.Y., 1989—; staff social worker A Very Spl. Place, Inc., S.I., 1985-86; staff social worker, psychotherapist Children's Community Ctr., S.I. Mental Health Svc., 1986-88; clin. social worker, psychotherapist S.I. Hosp. Outpatient Psychiat. Clinic, 1988-95; part-time lectr. NYU, 1995-96. Chmn. Boy Scouts Am. Mem. NASW, Soc. Clin. Social Work Psychotherapists (corr. sec.), Acad. Cert. Social Workers, Acad. Eating Disorders, Am. Anorexia/Bulimia Assn., Internat. Assn. for Eating Disorder Profls., Alpha Delta Mu, Phi Kappa Phi, Kappa Delta Phi. Home: 103 Augusta Ave Staten Island NY 10312-3232

PARHAM, IRIS ANN, gerontology educator; b. Orange, Tex., Nov. 14, 1948; d. George Kevlin and Nina Mabel Parham; m. Edward Swarbrick, Aug. 9, 1975; 1 child, Erin Elsbeth. BA, U. Tex., 1970; MS, W. Va. U., 1973; PhD, U. So. Calif., 1976. Asst. prof. gerontology Va. Commonwealth U., Richmond, 1976-81, assoc., 1981-91, prof., 1991—; exec. dir. Va. Geriatric Edn. Ctr. Co-editor: Modular Gerontology Curriculum, 1982, vol. II, 1984, Access, 1990, Resource Guides-Geriatrics, 1990, Gerontological Social Work, 1992, Alcoholism & Aging, 1995; Jour. Social Issues, 1980; spl. editor: Jour. Minority Aging, 1984. Grantee Adminstrn. on Aging, 1978-79, 79-82, 85-87—, Adjusting to Widowhood Va., 1978-79, Temple U., 1983-84, Health Resources and Svcs. Adminstrn., 1985-90, 91-94. Mem. APA, So. Gerontol. Soc. (treas. 1984-87), Assn. Gerontology in Higher Edn., Sigma Xi. Avocation: photography. Office: Va Commonwealth U Gerontology Dept Med Coll Va MCV Box 980228 Richmond VA 23298

PARHAM, WILLIAM W., physician; b. Waycross, Ga., Dec. 28, 1962; s. Robert L. and Jo Ann (Barber) P.; m. Tamela T. Coppedge (div. Oct. 1989); m. Teri Alayne Herrald, June 3, 1995. AAS, Valdosta State Coll., 1987; ADN, South Ga. Coll., 1984; BS magna cum laude, Med. Coll. Ga., 1989; DO, U. Osteopathic Medicine & Health Scis., 1995. Paramedic Ware Emergency Svc., Waycross, 1982-85; nurse Satilla Regional Med. Ctr., Waycross, 1985-87, South Ga. Med. Ctr., Valdosta, 1987-89; physicians asst. instr. Med. Coll. Ga., Augusta, 1989-92; physicians asst. Broad Lawns Med. Ctr., Des Moines, 1993-95; resident in ob-gyn. Detroit Riverview Hosp., Detroit, 1995—; clin. instr. osteo. Mich. State U., Lansing, 1995. Health Edn. scholar Mercy Hosp., Des Moines, 1995, Ga. State Rural Physician scholar Ga. State Med. Bd., 1991. Mem. Am. Osteo. Assn., Sigma Sigma Phi. Office: Detroit Riverview Hosp 2151 E Jefferson Ave Detroit MI 48207

PARIENTE, RENÉ GUILLAUME, physician, educator; b. La Marsa, Tunisia, Sept. 1, 1929; s. Jules and Vera (Guttieres) P.; m. Dominique Savary, Dec. 26, 1971; children: Pierre, David, Benjamin. MD, U. Paris, 1962. Prof. medicine U. Paris, 1966—, head dept. intensive care and chest disease; bd. dirs. Inst. Nat. du Recherche Med. Mem. Soc. Française de Cardiologie, Soc. de Pathologie Respiratoire, Soc. de la Tuberculose, Soc. Française de Microscopie Electronique, Am. Soc. Chest Physicians, N.Y. Acad. Sci., Am. Thoracic Soc. Home: 12 rue de la Neva, 75008 Paris France Office: 100 G LeClerc, Beaujon Hosp, 92118 Clichy France

PARIS, DAVID ANDREW, dentist; b. Milw., Jan. 16, 1962; s. John Baptistia and Geraldine Louella (Grosso) P. BA, UCLA, 1985, DDS, 1989. Oral surgery extern VA, Phoenix, 1989; primary practitioner Aids Project L.A. Dental Clinic, 1990-94; assoc. M. Marchese D.D.S., Sun Valley, Calif., 1990-92, D. Pickrell DMD, West Hollywood, Calif., 1992-94, Dental Arts Assocs., Milw., 1994—, Family Dental Ctr., Milw., 1994—. Mem. ADA, Wis. Dental Assn., Calif. Dental Assn., Acad. Gen. Dentistry, Delta Sigma Delta.

PARIS, GEORGE L., plastic surgeon; b. Ridgway, Pa., Mar. 26, 1938; s. Arthur Mario and Ambrosine Grace (Furadori) P.; m. Mary Anne, Sept. 2, 1961; children: Jeanne, George. BS, Carnegie Mellon U., 1959; MD, Columbia U., 1963. Diplomate Am. Coll. Surgeons, Am. Bd. Ophthalmology. Intern, resident Stanford U., Palo Alto, Calif., 1963-70; fellow U. Calif., San Francisco, 1970-71, Oxford U., Eng., 1981; chmn. dept. ophthalmology Menlo Med. Clinic, Menlo Park, Calif., 1970—; mem. athletic bd. Stanford U., 1993-96; trustee Peninsula Ctr. for the Blind, Palo Alto, 1974-80, Sr. Coord. Commn., Palo Alto, 1976-82. Contbg. editor to books, 1978, 90, 95; editl. bd. Jour. of Ophthal. Plastic and Reconstructive Surgery, 1993-96, Brit. Jour. of Ophthalmology, 1995-96. Capt. U.S. Army, 1965-67, Japan. Fellow Am. Coll. Surgeons; mem. Am. Soc. Ophthal. Surgery (pres. 1994), Menlo Country Club (tournament chmn. 1990-96). Roman Catholic. Office: Menlo Med Clinic 1300 Crane St Menlo Park CA 94025

PARIS, MARK FRAZER, surgeon; b. Milw., Oct. 24, 1942; s. Milton and May (Frazer) P.; m. Diana Lea Smith, Aug. 5, 1972; 1 child, Stacy Anne. Student Vanderbilt U., 1960-62, Memphis State U., 1962-63; MD, U. Tenn., 1966; postgrad. La. State U., 1967-72. Diplomate Am. Bd. Surgery. Resident in surgery La. State U., 1967-72, clin. instr. surgery, 1970-72; fellow Lahey Clinic, Boston, 1970; chief surg. svcs. George AFB, Victorville, Calif., 1972-74; pres. Cove Surg. Assocs. Ltd., Roaring Spring, Pa., 1974-86; chief of surgery Nason Hosp., Roaring Spring, 1978-86, chief of staff, 1982-84; chief of surgery Hilton Head Hosp., 1988-90, bd. dirs., 1995—; ptnr. D&M Properties, Tampa, Fla., 1984—, Hilton Head Surg. Assoc., 1986—; med. dir. Bud Lite Triathalon, 1988, 89. Contbr. articles to profl. jours. Bd. dirs. Island Sch. Coun., 1988-89, pres., 1989. Served to maj. USAF, 1972-74. Decorated Air Force Commendation medal, 1973. Fellow ACS; mem. AMA, James Rives Surg. Soc., S.C. Med. Assn., Blair County Med. Soc. (pres. 1981), Beaufort County Med. Soc., S.C. Med. Soc. Republican. Jewish. Club: Balloon Fedn. Am. Avocations: hot air ballooning, boating, commercial pilot. Office: PO Box 21477 Hilton Head Island SC 29925-1477

PARISH, MARION ROBBINS, speech and language pathologist; b. Houston, Feb. 2, 1944; d. Walter Alvis and Maude Marion (Robbins) P.; BA, U. Tex., Austin, 1966; MA, Our Lady of Lake Coll., 1967. Speech pathologist Corpus Christi (Tex.) Speech and Hearing Center, 1966; instr., supr. undergrads. Our Lady of Lake Coll., San Antonio, 1967-72; dir./owner Speech Pathology Assocs., Houston, 1972—; founder, sch. head Parish Children's Sch., 1982—; cons. in field. Contbr. chpt. to Prospering In Private Practice. Active, Jr. League Houston. Named Outstanding Woman in Edn., YWCA, 1996, Liberty Bell award Young Lawyers Assn., 1996. Mem.

Houston Area Assn. Communication Disorders (past pres.), Am. Speech-Lang.-Hearing Assn., Tex. Speech-Lang.-Hearing Assn. (past pres.), Orton Soc., Houston Assn. for Communication Disorders (past pres.). Office: 11059 Timberline Rd Houston TX 77043-3829

PARK, CHAN HYUNG, cell biologist, physician; b. Seoul, Korea, Aug. 16, 1936; s. Chung Suh and Yoon Sook Yuh; m. Mary Hyungrok Kim, Apr. 16, 1966; 1 child, Christopher Myungwoo. MD, Seoul Nat. U., 1962, MS, 1964; PhD, U. Toronto, 1972. Diplomate: Am. Bd. Internal Medicine with subplty. of med. oncology. Asst. prof. U. Kans. Med. Ctr., 1974-80, assoc. prof., 1980-86, prof., 1986-89; prof., chief div. oncology/hematology dept. internal medicine Tex. Tech U. Health Scis. Ctr., 1989; dir. Cancer Ctr., head divsn. hematology/oncology dept. medicine Samsung Med. Ctr., Seoul, Korea, 1994—. Transl. novel from German to Korean; mem. editl. bd. Jour. Nutrition, Growth and Cancer, 1986-87; contbr. articles to biomed. and sci. jours. Recipient Rsch. Career Devel. award USPHS, NIH, 1979-84. Fellow ACP; mem. Am. Assn. Cancer Rsch., Am. Soc. Clin. Oncology, Am. Soc. for Blood and Marrow Transplantation, Am. Soc. Hematology, Internat. Soc. Hematotherapy and Graft Engring., Internat. Soc. Exptl. Hematology, World Marrow Donor Assn. Home: 50 Ilwondong Kangnamku, Seoul Republic of Korea

PARK, DAN DAE, podiatrist; b. Seoul, Korea, Feb. 15, 1961; came to U.S., 1974; s. Henry S. and Yun Hi (Back) P.; m. Hunni Pak, Apr. 22, 1989; children: Jocelyn, Justin, Richard. BA in Microbiology, U. Calif., Berkeley, 1984; DPM, U. Osteo. Medicine & Health, Des Moines, 1989. Diplomate Am. Bd. Pediatric Orthopaedics. Assoc. Met. Podiatry Assn., Phila., 1990-91; ptnr. Iawa Foot Care Ctr. P.C., Des Moines, 1992—. Fellow Am. Coll. Foot and Ankle Orthopedics and Medicine; mem. Am. Podiatric Med. Assn., Am. Diabetes Assn., Iowa Podiatric Med. Soc., Mid-Iowa Podiatric Med. Assn. (sec.-treas. 1993—), Pi Delta. Office: The Foot Ctr 2700 University Ave Ste 212 West Des Moines IA 50266

PARK, GLADYS JAYNAR, retired nurse; b. Waialua, Hawaii, Apr. 17, 1931; d. Joseph Ponciano and Alice (Sales) Jaynar; m. David Tai Young Park, Dec. 12, 1953; children: Sandra Eai Lan, Lawrence Jaynar. RN, Queen's Hosp. Sch. Nursing, Honolulu, 1953; BSN, U. Hawaii, 1960, MPH, 1973. Staff nurse Queen's Hosp., Honolulu, 1953-54; pvt. duty nurse, Honolulu, 1954-55; staff pub. health nurse Hawaii Dept. Health, Honolulu, 1955-64, supr. chest clinic, 1964-66, project supr., 1966-68, pub. health nursing supr., 1968-73, comprehensive health planning coordinator, 1974-77; comprehensive health planning officer, 1977-88; interim project dir., Maluhia Home Health Project, 1989, acting perinatal health svcs. sect. supr., 1991-92, perinatal quality assurance nurse cons., 1992-95; ret., 1995; mem. Honolulu Home Care Adv. Com., Honolulu, 1973-77; mem. Western Ctr. Health Planning Interim Adv. Bd., San Francisco, 1975-76; mem. Hawaii Bd. Audiology and Speech Pathology, Honolulu, 1979-82; mem. Govs. Adv. Com. Long Term Care, Honolulu, 1982-85; mem. Hawaii Sr. Ctr. Med. Adv. Com., 1975-77; mem. nursing adv. com. Dept. Commerce & Consumer Affairs Regulated Industries Office, 1995—. Trustee Palama Settlement, Honolulu, 1974-82; sec. Palolo Community Council, Honolulu, 1966-68; chmn. Palolo Community Action Program, 1966-68. Mem. Queen's Sch. Nursing Alumni Assn. (sec. 1954-55, 88-92, pres.-elect 1992-94, pres. 1994-96), Hawaii Nurses Assn. (membership chmn. 1966-68), APHA, Hawaii Pub. Health Assn. (pres. 1981), Am. Sewing Guild (sec. Honolulu chpt. 1988-89), Phi Kappa Phi. Clubs: Waialua '49 (sec. 1979—); Gen. Fedn. Women's (corr. sec. 1979) (Honolulu).

PARK, JON KEITH, dentist, educator; b. Wichita, Kans., May 26, 1938; s. William Ray and Eleanor Jeanette (Cunningham) P.; DDS, U. Mo., 1964; BA, Wichita State U., 1969; MS in Dental Hygiene Edn., U. Mo., 1971; MS in Oral Pathology, U. Md., 1982; cert. in dental radiology U. Pa. Sch. Dental Medicine, 1982. Diplomate Am. Bd. Oral and Maxillo-facial Radiology. Pvt. practice dentistry, Wichita, 1964-67; chmn. dept. dental hygiene Wichita State U., 1967-72; assoc. prof. oral diagnosis, dir. oral radiology Balt. Coll. Dental Surgery, U. Md., 1972—; program dir. U. Md. dental externship, 1974-77; lectr. Essex C.C., Harford County C.C.; cons. in radiology VA Hosp.; mem. Md. State Radiation Control Adv. Bd., 1981—; mem. Ute Pass Hist. Soc.; chmn. devel. com. Introduction to Basic Concepts in Dental Radiography, Dental Assisting Nat. Bd., Inc., Am. Dental Assts. Assn., 1991; editor Am. Acad. Oral and Maxillofacial Radiology Newsletter. Recipient U. Md. Media Achievement award, 1977, 78. Fellow Am. Acad. Dental Radiology; mem. ADA, Md. State Dental Assn., Balt. City Dental Soc. (ad hoc com. radiation safety), Am. Acad. Oral Pathology, Am. Acad. Oral and Maxillofacial Radiology (editor newsletter), Orgn. Tchrs. Oral Diagnosis, Am. Theater Organ Soc., Kans. Dental Hygienists Assn. (hon.), Balt. Music Club, Am. Acad. Oral and Maxillofacial Radiology (ednl. standards com.), Am. Assn. Dental Schs., Internat. Assn. Dental and Maxillofacial Radiology, Balt. Opera Guild, Engring. Soc. Balt., Met. Opera Guild, Balt. Symphony Orch. Assn., Ute Pass Community Assn., Univ. Club, Omicron Kappa Upsilon, Psi Omega. Episcopalian. Patentee pivotal design dental chair.

PARK, LEE CRANDALL, psychiatrist; b. Washington, July 15, 1926; s. Lee I. and Alice (Crandall) P.; m. Barbara Anne Merrick, July 1, 1953; children: Thomas Joseph, Jeffrey Rawson; m. Mary Woodfill Banerjee, Apr. 27, 1985; stepchildren: Stephen Kumar, Scott Kumar. Grad., Putney Prep. Sch., Vt.; B.S. in Zoology, Yale, 1948; M.D., Johns Hopkins, 1952. Diplomate Nat. Bd. Med. Examiners, Am. Bd. Psychiatry and Neurology. Intern medicine Johns Hopkins Hosp., Osler Clinic, Balt., 1952-53; resident psychiatry USN Hosp., Oakland, Calif., 1954, Henry Phipps Psychiat. Clinic, Johns Hopkins Hosp., Balt., 1955-59; asst. psychiatrist Henry Phipps Psychiat. Clinic, Johns Hopkins Hosp., 1955-59, staff psychiatrist, 1959—, staff dept. medicine, 1970—, dir. psychiat. outpatient svcs. and community psychiatry program, 1972-74, asst. dir. clin. svcs. dept. psychiatry, 1973-74, mem. departmental coun., 1974-76; fellow psychiatry Johns Hopkins U., 1955-59, faculty in psychiatry, 1959—, assoc. prof., 1971—, physician charge psychiat. svcs. student health svc., 1961-73; vis. psychiatrist Balt. City Hosp., 1960-61; co-prin., prin. investigator NIMH Psychopharmacology Rsch. Br. Outpatient Study of Drug-Set Interaction, 1960-68, co-dir. (with Eugene Meyer) Time-Limited Psychotherapy Rsch. Grant, 1969-73; pvt. practice psychiatry, 1964—; cons. Met. Balt. Assn. Mental Health, 1961-63, Bur. Disability Ins., Social Security Adminstrn., 1964-81; attending staff Seton Psychiat. Inst., 1966-73, exec. bd., 1970-73; staff Sheppard and Enoch Pratt Hosp., 1974—; rsch. includes borderline and narcissistic conditions, long-term effects of childhood emotional abuse, interrelationships of psychotherapy and pharmacotherapy, time ltd. psychotherapy, ethical considerations in clin. rsch. Contbr. articles and chpts. to profl. jours. and books. Served to lt. M.C., USNR, 1953-55, div. psychiatrist 1st Marine Div., Korea, staff psychiatrist USN Hosp., Camp Pendelton, Calif., 1954-55. Fellow AAAS, Am. Psychiat. Assn. (life mem. assembly 1983-93); mem. AMA, AAUP, Am. Psychosomatic Soc., Internat. Soc. Study of Personality Disorders, Am. Soc. Adolescent Psychiatry, Am. Coll. Neuropsychopharmacology, Am. Assn. Pvt. Practicing Psychiatrists, Md. Psychiat. Soc. (pres. 1978-79), Soc. Psychotherapy Rsch., N.Y. Acad. Scis., Group Therapy Network, Md. Interdisciplinary Coun. Children and Adolescents (treas. 1980-87), Med. and Chirurg. Faculty Md., Baltimore City Med. Soc., Baltimore County Med. Soc., Johns Hopkins Med. and Surg. Assn., Am. Assn. Pvt. Practicing Psychiatrists, Md. Assn. Pvt. Practicing Psychiatrists, SAR, Crandall Soc., Van Kouwenhoven-Conover Soc., Van Vorrhees Soc., Parke Soc., Nat. Soc. of the Sons and Daus. of the Pilgrims, Johns Hopkins Club (Balt.), Met. Club (Washington), Farmington Country Club (Charlottesville, Va.), Chevy Chase (Md.) Country Club, Phi Beta Pi. Home: 308 Tunbridge Rd Baltimore MD 21212-3803 Office: 1205 York Rd Ste 35 Lutherville Timonium MD 21093-6268

PARK, PAULINE KYONSOOK, surgeon; b. Phila.. BS, Pa. State U., 1980; MD, Jefferson Med. Coll., 1982. Diplomate Am. Bd. Surgeons; cert. added qualification critical care surgery. Instr. surgery Jefferson Med. Coll., Phila., 1987-90, asst. prof. surgery, 1990—; cons. Nat. Bd. Med. Examiners, Phila., 1987—; advisor Am. Women's Med. Assn. TMC chpt., Phila., 1993; mem. sci. adv. bd. Targeted Diagnostics and Therapeutics, Inc., Phila. 1994—. Fellow ACS; mem. Am. Assn. Acad. Surgery, Ea. Assn. For Surgery of Trauma. Office: Jefferson Med Coll Dept Surgery 1025 Walnut St Ste 607 Philadelphia PA 19107

PARK, RO JONG, physician; b. Seoul, Korea, Aug. 15, 1939; s. Woo Dong and Cha Nam (Han) P.; married, Jan. 15, 1966; 1 child, Charles. BS, Premed. Kyong Book U., Korea, 1969; MD, Kyung Book Med. Sch., Korea, 1963. Pvt. practice Three Rivers, Mich. Capt. Med. Corps Korean armed forces, 1963-67. Mem. AMA, Mich. Med. Soc., St. Joseph Med. Soc., Mich. Gen. Surgeons. Office: 172 E Michigan Three Rivers MI 49094

PARKER, CATHERINE SUSANNE, psychotherapist; b. Norwood, Mass., Nov. 4, 1934; d. George Leonard and Hazel Olga (Remmer) P. BA, Bates Coll., 1956; MSW, U. Denver, 1961. Diplomate Acad. Cert. Social Workers; cert. social worker, Colo. Social worker Taunton (Mass.) State Hosp., 1956-59; social worker Ft. Logan Mental Health Ctr., Denver, 1961-66, clin. team leader, 1966-72; dir. adult services Western Inst. Human Resources, Denver, 1973-74; pvt. practice psychotherapy Denver, 1974—; workshop facilitator Arapahoe C.C., 1986-90. Mem. NASW. Home: 6453 S Downing St Littleton CO 80121-2517 Office: Denver Mental Health 165 Cook St Ste 100 Denver CO 80206-5308

PARKER, CURTIS LLOYD, academic administrator, researcher, educator; b. Roanoke, Va., Mar. 28, 1942; s. James Owen Sr. and Verna Evelyn (Williams) P.; m. Dorothea Louise Valentine, June 2, 1964; children: Curtis Anthony, Lisa Ann. BS, Knoxville (Tenn.) Coll., 1965; PhD, U. Tenn., 1973. Postdoctoral investigator Oak Ridge (Tenn.) Nat. Lab., 1973-75; asst. prof. Bowman Gray Sch. of Medicine, Winston-Salem, N.C., 1975-80; assoc. prof. Atlanta U., 1981-83; assoc. prof. Morehouse Sch. of Medicine, Atlanta, 1983-85, prof., 1985-89, chmn. anatomy dept., prof., 1989—; adj. prof. Clark Atlanta U., 1983—, Ga. State U., Atlanta, 1989—; mem. faculty exch. program U. Fla., Gainesville, 1984—; dir. aids grant Morehouse Sch. of Medicine, Atlanta. Mem. jour. rev. com. Nat. Libr. of Medicine, Bethesda, Md., 1990—; bd. dirs. Nat. Coalition of Black Women, 1989—. NIH grantee, 1988—. Mem. Am. Soc. for Cell Biology, Am. Assn. Anatomists, Tissue Culture Assn., Alpha Phi Alpha. Democrat. Presbyterian. Home: 2941 Blue Grass Ln Decatur GA 30034-3312 Office: Morehouse Sch of Medicine 720 Westview Dr SW Atlanta GA 30310-1458*

PARKER, DEBORAH L. ROBERTS, counselor; b. Meridian, Miss., Mar. 15, 1952; d. Bernice (Roberts) Pringle; m. Curtis Edward Parker, Nov. 25, 1972; 1 child, Shana. BS, U. So. Miss., 1978; MEd, Miss. State U., 1980, EdSp, 1996. Lic. profl. counselor; nat. cert. counselor. Asst. PBX op., with client admissions dept. Weems Mental Health Ctr., Meridian, 1972-75, counselor children's svcs., 1981-86; career facilitator Meridian Pub. Schs., 1978-80; dir. gov.s youth grant Lauderdale County Juvenile Ctr., Meridian, 1980-81; adolescent counselor, case mgr. Laurel Wood Pscychiat. and Recovery Ctr., Meridian, 1986-89, adolescent program dir., 1989-93; counselor single parent/displaced homemaker Meridian C.C., 1993-94, acad. counselor, 1994—. Named one of Outstanding Young Women of Am., 1983. Mem. Alpha Lambda Delta, Delta Sigma Theta, Phi Delta Kappa. Roman Catholic. Home: 411 45th Ct Meridian MS 39301-1126 Office: Meridian Cmty Coll Hwy 19 N Meridian MS 39307

PARKER, GERALD M., physician, researcher; b. Olean, N.Y., Nov. 20, 1943; s. Richard and Kathleen (Manwaring) P.; m. Linda Kay Stuart, Dec. 28, 1968; children: Kimberly, Gerald, Cassandra, Kevin. B.A., Western Wash. U., 1965; D.O., Kirksville Coll. Osteopathy & Surgery, 1969. Intern, Art Centre Hosp., Detroit, 1969-70; ptnr. Doctor's Clinic, Amarillo, Tex., 1969—; dir. Southwest Inst. Preventive Medicine, Amarillo, 1978—, Hyperbaric Oxygen Ctr., Amarillo, 1979—. Contbr. articles to profl. jours. Appeared on That's Incredible TV show, 1982. Pres., Southwest Amarillo Little Dribblers Assn., 1979—; coach Girls Nat. Champion Basketball Teams, 1981, 83, 84, 85, 86, 87, 89. Fellow Am. Acad. Med. Preventics; mem. Southwest Acad. Preventive Medicine (pres. 1980—), Am. Osteopathic Assn. Methodist. Avocation: athletics. Office: Doctors Clinic 4714 S Western St Amarillo TX 79109-5950 also: 9577 Osuna Rd NE Albuquerque NM 87111-2271

PARKER, GLORIA ELIZABETH, medical technologist; b. Silver Spring, Md., Oct. 17, 1945; d. Oliver Albert Stehle and Rebecca Emily (Smalling) King; m. Daniel Franklin Giddens, Oct. 10, 1963 (div. May 1984); children: Daniel Franklin Jr., Danielle Francis Giddens Long; m. Leland Wesley Parker, July 20, 1986; 1 stepson, David Wesley Parker. Student, Macon (Ga.) Hosp., 1963-64, Santa Fe C.C., Gainesville, Fla., 1995—. Cert. med. technologist, N.J.; registered med. technologist. Med. technologist Raleigh (N.C.) Family Physicians, 1970-87; med. asst. Gainesville Med. Group, 1987-94, Gainesville Hematology-Oncology, 1994—. Vol. Ronald McDonald House, Gainesville, 1987—, Am. Cancer Soc., Gainesville, 1988-95, hospice, Gainesville, 1995—; Stephen min. Trinity United Meth. Ch., Gainesville, 1987—, mem. adminstrv. bd., 1994-95. Home: 7622 SW 11th Ave Gainesville FL 32607

PARKER, JOHN R., physician, pathologist; b. Rochester, Minn., Apr. 29, 1967; s. Joseph Corbin and Patricia (Singleton) P. BA, MD, U. Mo., Kansas City. Rsch. asst. U. Tenn. Meml. Hosp., Knoxville, 1985; autopsy technician Truman Med. Ctr., Kansas City, 1990-93. Contbr. articles to Annals of Clin. and Lab. Sci., Archives of Pathology, Jour. Okla. State Med. Assn. Organizer 4-H Summer Scholars Med. Terminology, Lakewood Hosp., 1989-91; co-chmn. Impaired Med. Student Coun., 1990-91. Recipient Richardson K. Noback Clin. Excellence award, 1993, Gov.'s commendation State of Okla., 1995, cert. of appreciation Office of Chief Med. Examiner, State of Okla., 1995, U. Okla. Lloyd and Ruth Rader Trust Scholarship award, 1995-96; Pathology Student fellow Truman Med. Ctr., 1989-90. Mem. AMA, Okla. State Med. Assn., Coll. Am. Pathologists, Am. Soc. Clin. Pathologists, U.S. and Can. Acad. Pathology, Mortar Board, Golden Key, Alpha Omega Alpha, Omicron Delta Kappa. Democrat. Office: Office of Chief Med. Examiner Ctrl Office 901 N Stonewall Oklahoma City OK 73117

PARKER, JOHN WILLIAM, pathology educator, investigator; b. Clifton, Ariz., Jan. 5, 1931; s. Vilas William and Helen E. Parker; m. Barbara A. Atkinson, June 8, 1957; children: Ann Elizabeth, Joy Noelle, John David, Heidi Susan. BS, U. Ariz., 1953; MD, Harvard U., 1957. Diplomate Am. Bd. Pathology. Clin. instr. pathology U. Calif. Sch. Medicine, San Francisco, 1962-64; asst. prof. U. So. Calif. Sch. Medicine, L.A., 1964-68, assoc. prof., 1968-75, prof., 1975—, dir. clin. labs., 1974-94, vice chmn. dept. pathology, 1985—, dir. pathology reference labs., 1991-94; assoc. dean sci. affairs U. So. Calif., 1987-89; co-chmn. 15th Internat. Leucocyte Culture Conf., Asilomar, Calif., 1982; chmn. 2d Internat. Lymphoma Conf., Athens, Greece, 1981; v.p. faculty senate U. So. Calif., 1991-92; bd. dirs. ann. meeting Clin. Applications of Cytometry, Charleston, S.C., 1988—. Founding editor (jour.) Hematological Oncology, 1982-93; assoc. editor Jour. Clin. Lab. Analysis, 1985—; co-editor: Intercellular Communication in Leucocyte Function, 1983; founding co-editor (jour.) Communications in Clin. Cytometry, 1994—; contbr. over 150 articles to profl. jours., chpts. to books. Named sr. oncology fellow Am. Cancer Soc., U. So. Calif. Sch. Medicine, 1964-69, Nat. Cancer Inst. vis. fellow Walter and Eliza Hall Inst. for Med. Research, Melbourne, Australia, 1972-73. Fellow Coll. Am. Pathologists, Am. Soc. Clin. Pathologists; mem. Am. Assn. Pathologists, Am. Soc. Hematology, Internat. Acad. Pathology, Clin. Cytometry Soc. (v.p. 1993, pres.-elect 1994-95, pres. 1995-97), Phi Beta Kappa, Phi Kappa Phi. Office: U So Calif Sch Medicine CSC 108 2250 Alcazar St Los Angeles CA 90033-4523

PARKER, JOSEPH CORBIN, JR., pathologist; b. Richmond, Va., Aug. 1, 1937; s. Joseph Corbin and Alice Cabell (Horsley) P.; m. Patricia Singleton, June 24, 1961; children: John Randolph, Nancy Jordan. BA, Va. Mil. Inst., 1958; MD, Med. Coll. Va., 1962; MS in Pathology, U. Minn., 1968. Fellow Mayo Clinic, Rochester, Minn., 1963-68; asst. prof. Duke U., Durham, N.C., 1969-70, Harvard U., Boston, 1970-71; assoc. prof. U. Ky., Lexington, 1971-75; prof. U. Miami, Fla., 1975-81; assoc. dean, prof. U. Tenn., Knoxville, 1981-86; prof. pathology, chmn. U. Mo., Kansas City, 1986-92; prof., chair dept. pathology U. Louisville Sch. Medicine, 1992-96, A.J. Miller prof., chair dept. pathology, 1996—; bd. dirs. Truman Med. Ctr., Kansas City, Mo., Hosp. Hill Health Svc., Kansas City. Author 4 chpts. in books; contbr. 100 articles to profl. jours. Bd. dirs. Multiple Sclerosis Soc., Knoxville, Tenn., 1985, Alzheimers Assn., Kansas City, 1988-91, U. Louisville Med. Sch. Fund. 1st lt. USAR, 1958-67. Recipient 1st Jackson -Hope medal Va. Mil. Inst., 1958; Caldwell award Alzheimers Assn., 1986. Fellow Am. Assn. Neuropathology, Am. Soc. Clin. Pathology, Coll. Am. Pathology, Assn. Clin. Scientists; mem. So. Med. Assn., Am. Acad. Neurology, Am. Soc. Neurol. Surgeons, Univ. Pathologists (pres.). Democrat. Unitarian. Home: 4606 Wolf Creek Pky Louisville KY 40241-5502 Office: U Louisville Sch Medicine Dept Pathology Louisville KY 40292

PARKER, LEANNE, nursing educator, nurse practitioner; b. Ogden, Utah, Jan. 6, 1961; d. Samuel LeGrande and Edith JoAnne (Dewey) P.; 1 child, Clinton D. Willard. AS, Weber State U., 1985; BS, U. Utah, 1987, MSc, 1994. Cert. women's health care nurse practitioner, ob-gyn. nurse practitioner, Nat. Certification Corp. for Obstetric and Neonatal Nursing. RN St. Benedict's Hosp., Ogden, 1986-87; nurse practitioner Planned Parenthood of Utah, Salt Lake City, 1989-96; asst. prof. Weber State U., Ogden, 1993—. Author (videotape) Clinical Teaching of Nurse-Midwifery and Nurse Practitioner Students: Teaching Strategies for Preceptors, 1993. Chair breast/cervical cancer task force Am. Cancer Soc., Ogden, 1994—. Recipient Faculty Vitality award Hemingway Found., 1995, Internat. Activities grant Weber State U., 1996. Mem. ANA, Utah Nurses Assn., Sigma Theta Tau. Office: Weber State Univ 3903 University Cir Ogden UT 84408

PARKER, LEROY ALBERT, JR., dental surgery educator; b. Newark, Feb. 12, 1930; s. Leroy Alston and Julia Elizabeth (Klena) P.; m. Ruth Elaine Wecht, June 19, 1954; children: Robert L., William L. DDS, Georgetown U., 1954; BA, Seton Hall U., 1962. Pvt. practice dentistry Union, N.J., 1956-61; dental educator U. Medicine and Dentistry, Newark, 1957-96; prof. emeritus, 1995—; interim dean U. Medicine and Dentistry of N.J., Newark, 1986-87; assoc. dir. clin. dental rsch. Johnson and Johnson, New Brunswick, N.J., 1965-66. Author: (handbook) Handbook of Dental Asepis, 1965, (chpt.) Clinical Oral Diagnosis, 1965, Peridontal Prosthesis, 1968. Lt. USN, 1954-56. Fellow Am. Coll. Dentists, Internat. Coll. Dentists; mem. ADA, Am. Assn. Dental Schs., Internat. Assn. Dental Rsch., N.J. Dental Assn., Essex County Dental Soc. Roman Catholic. Office: U Medicine & Dentistry NJ 110 Bergen St Newark NJ 07103-2400

PARKER, LYNDA MICHELE, psychiatrist; b. Phila., Sept. 28, 1947; d. Albert Francis and Dorothy Thomasinia (Herriott) P.; B.A., C. W. Post Coll., 1968; M.A. (Martin Luther King Jr. scholar 1968-70), N.Y.U., 1970; M.D., Cornell U., 1974; postgrad. N.Y. Psychoanalytic Inst., 1977-82. Intern, N.Y. Hosp., N.Y.C., 1975; resident in psychiatry Payne Whitney Clinic, N.Y.C., 1975-78; psychiatrist in charge day program Cabrini Med. Center, N.Y.C., 1978-79, attending psychiatrist, 1978—; admitting psychiatrist inpatient psychiat. treatment Payne Whitney Clinic, N.Y.C., 1978—, supr. psychiatry residents, 1978—, supr. long-term psychotherapy, 1980-82; attending psychiatrist N.Y. Hosp., Cornell Med. Center, 1979—; practice medicine specializing in psychiatry, N.Y.C., 1979—; instr. psychiatry Cornell U. Med. Coll., 1979-86, asst. prof., 1986—; instr. psychiatry, N.Y. Med. Coll., 1978—; psychiat. cons. Bldg. Service 32BJ Health Fund, 1983-89, Inwood House, N.Y.C., 1983-86, Time-Life Inc., 1986—, Ind. Med. Examiners, 1986—, Epilepsy Inst., 1986-87, asst. med. dir., 1987-88, med. dir., 1988; ind. med. examiner Rep. Health Care Rev. Sys. Mem. adv. bd. St. Bartholomew Community Presch., N.Y.C., 1990—. Mem. Am. Psychiat. Assn., Am. Womens Med. Assn. Episcopalian. Office: 219 E 69th St Apt 1J New York NY 10021-5453

PARKER, MICHAEL G(EORGE), management consultant; b. N.Y.C., Jan. 26, 1950; s. Al and Florence (Samuels) P.; m. Linda M. Prager, June 2, 1985; 1 child, Stephanie Danielle. BA, SUNY, Buffalo, 1970; postgrad., U. N.C., Chapel Hill, 1970-74; cert. in health svcs. adminstrn., NYU, 1977; MBA, Baruch Coll., CUNY, 1981. Prodn. editor Acad. Press, Inc., N.Y.C., 1974-75; grants adminstr. Meml. Sloan-Kettering Cancer Ctr., N.Y.C., 1975-78, pers. adminstr., 1978-79; planning analyst Mt. Sinai Med. Ctr., N.Y.C., 1979-82; founder, project mgr. The Cybertec Cons. Group, Inc., N.Y.C., 1982-90, v.p., 1991-93; mgr. KPMG Peat Marwick, N.Y.C., 1993-94, sr. mgr., 1994-96, prin., 1996—; pres. 101 W 23 Apt Inc., 1985-86; v.p. 244-246 Owners Corp., 1986-90, pres., 1990—. Mem. evaluation com. programs ARC, N.Y.C., 1980-82. Walter E. Heller fellow, 1981. Mem. Am. Soc. for Quality Control, N.Y. Soc. for Health Planning (treas. 1996—), N.Y. Acad. Sci., SUNY Buffalo Scis. Alumni Assn. (bd. dirs.), Beta Gamma Sigma. Home: 244 W 23rd St New York NY 10011-2324 Office: KPMG Peat Marwick LLP 11 Martine Ave White Plains NY 10606

PARKER, ROBERT ANDREW, psychologist, computer consultant; b. Jacksonville, Fla., Mar. 21, 1946; s. Farrand Drake and Laurel (Cook) P. BA with distinction in Psychology, Ohio State U., 1969; MA, U. Regina, Sask., Can., 1976, PhD, 1983. Lic. psychologist, N.Y. Psychologist Weyburn (Can.) Psychiat. Ctr., 1981-85; psychologist No. Westchester Guidance Clinic, Mt. Kisco, N.Y., 1985-87, cons., 1988—; sr. psychologist Abbott House, Irvington, N.Y., 1988-89, cons., 1989—; pvt. practice, White Plains, N.Y., 1988—; assoc. psychologist Rockland Children's Psychiat. Ctr., Orangeburg, N.Y., 1989—; cons. Westchester Mental Health Assn., White Plains, 1990—. Author: Waiting for Cargo, 1993; also articles; author computer programs Klopfer I, 1983, Exner I, 1986. Mem. APA, Soc. for Personality Assessment, Internat. Rsch. Soc., Internat. Soc. for Traumatic Stress Studies, Internat. Soc. for Prevention of Child Abuse and Neglect. Home: 16 Newcomb Pl White Plains NY 10606-2004

PARKER, ROBERT GEORGE, radiation oncology educator, academic administrator; b. Detroit, Mich., Jan. 29, 1925; s. Clifford Robert and Velma (Ashman) P.; m. Diana Davis, June 30, 1977; children by previous marriage: Thomas Clifford, James Richardson. BS, U. Wis., 1946, MD, 1948. Diplomate Am. Bd. Radiology (trustee 1978—, pres. 1988-90). Intern U. Nebr. Hosp., Omaha, 1948-49; resident in pathology Western Res. U., Cleve., 1949-50; resident in radiology U. Mich., Ann Arbor, 1950, 52-54, instr. in radiology, 1954-55; staff radiotherapist Swedish Hosp. Tumor Inst., Seattle, 1955-58; prof. radiology U. Wash., Seattle, 1958-77; prof. radiation oncology UCLA, 1977—. Lt. USN, 1950-52. Fellow Am. Coll. Radiology; mem. AMA (radiology residence rev. com.), Am. Soc. Therapeutic Radiologists (pres. 1975-76), Radiol. Soc. N.Am. (bd. dirs. 1984-90, pres. 1991-92), Am. Radium Soc. (bd. dirs. 1988-92, pres. 1992). Office: UCLA Ste B265 200 UCLA Medicine Plz Los Angeles CA 90095-6951

PARKER, ROBERT MICHAEL, toxicologist, anatomy educator; b. San Diego, Aug. 31, 1946; s. Thomas Jackson Parker and Sue Ellen (Randall) Muka; stepson Joseph Abbott Muka, Jr.; m. Karen May Green, Jan. 29, 1972; children: Jenifer May, Alexis Diane. BS, San Diego State Coll., 1970; MS, U. Calif.-Davis, 1975, PhD, 1980. Staff rsch. assoc. Calif. Primate Rsch. Ctr., Davis, 1976-80, postgrad. researcher, 1980-81; lectr. in biol. sci., Calif. State U., Sacramento, 1978; guest lectr. in embryology, Sch. Medicine U. Calif., Davis, 1980; lectr. in biology, Calif. State Coll., San Bernardino, 1982-84; asst. prof. anatomy Coll. Osteo. Medicine of the Pacific, Pomona, Calif., 1981-85; study dir., head reproductive and devel. toxicology Pathology Assocs., Inc., Nat. Ctr. for Toxicol. Rsch., Jefferson, Ark., 1985-91; mgr. toxicology TSI Redfield (Ark.) Labs., 1991-94; sr. scientist Argus Rsch. Labs., 1994—. Contbr. articles to profl. jours. Mem. Republican Presdl. Task Force, Washington, 1983-89, U.S. Senatorial Club, 1983-86, Jefferson County Rep. Cen. Com., 1985-86, coach Girls softball, 1985—; mem. sci. com. Southeast Ark. Arts and Sci. Ctr., 1985-86; vol. pub. schs., 1985—. Mem. AAAS, Teratology Soc., Soc. Toxicology, Sigma Phi Epsilon (alumni bd. 1975-78), Sigma Xi. Roman Catholic. Office: Argus Rsch Lab 905 Sheehy Dr Ste A Horsham PA 19044-1241

PARKER, ROY DENVER, JR., entomologist; b. San Diego, Jan. 18, 1843; s. Roy Denver and Helen Crowder (Connor) P.; m. E. Yvonne Wright, Sept. 2, 1967; children: John Michael, Preston Scott, Christopher Todd. AS, Kilgore Coll., 1963; BS, Tex. A&M U., 1966, MS with honors, 1968, PhD, 1979. Cotton field scout Tex. Agrl. Extension Svc., Knox City, 1965; leader cotton field scouts Tex. Agrl. Extension Svc., Lubbock, 1966; svc. mgr. Hunter Extermination Corp., San Antonio, 1971-72; county extension entomologist Tex. Agrl. Extension Svc., Weslaco, 1972-75; extension entomologist Tex. Agrl. Extension Svc., Corpus Christi, 1978—. Editor: (handbook) Cotton Demonstration Results in the Coastal Bend of Texas, 1983; editor procs. in field. Capt. Med. Svc. Corps, U.S. Army, 1968-71, Vietnam. Decorated Army Commendation medal, Bronze Star medal. Mem. Tex. Agrl. Extension Svc. Specialist Assn., Entomol. Soc. Am., Southwestern Entomol. Soc., Am. Registry of Profl. Entomologists, Alpha Zeta. Mem. Ch. of Christ. Home: 10713 Rockwood St Corpus Christi TX

78410-2715 Office: Tex Agrl Extension Svc RR 2 Box 589 Corpus Christi TX 78406-9704

PARKEY, ROBERT WAYNE, radiology and nuclear medicine educator, research radiologist; b. Dallas, July 17, 1938; s. Jack and Gloria Alfreda (Perry) P.; m. Nancy June Knox, Aug. 9, 1958; children: Wendell Wade, Robert Todd, Amy Elizabeth. BS in Physics, U. Tex., 1960; MD, S.W. Med. Sch., U. Tex., Dallas, 1965. Diplomate Am. Bd. Radiology, Am. Bd. Nuclear Medicine. Intern St. Paul Hosp., Dallas, 1965-66; resident in radiology U. Tex. Health Sci. Ctr., Dallas, 1966-69, asst. prof. radiology, 1970-74, assoc. prof., 1974-77, prof., 1977—, chmn. dept. radiology, 1977—, Effie and Wofford Cain Disting. chair in diagnostic imaging, 1994—; chief nuc. medicine Parkland Meml. Hosp., Dallas, 1974-79, chief dept. radiology, 1977—. Contbr. numerous chpts., articles and abstracts to profl. publs. Served as capt. M.C., Army N.G., 1965-72. NIH fellow Nat. Inst. Gen. Med. Sci., U. Mo., Columbia, 1969-70; Nat. Acad. Scis.-NRC scholar in radiol. research James Picker Found., 1971-74. Fellow Am. Coll. Cardiology, Am. Coll. Radiology; mem. Am. Coll. Nuclear Physicians (charter, ho. of dels. 1974—), Council on Cardiovascular Radiology of Am. Heart Assn., AMA, Assn. Univ. Radiologists, Dallas County Med. Assn., Dallas Ft. Worth Radiol. Soc., Radiol. Soc. N.Am., Soc. Chairmen of Acad. Radiology Depts., Soc. Nuclear Medicine (acad. council), Tex. Med. Assn., Tex. Radiol. Soc., Sigma Xi, Alpha Omega Alpha. Avocations: gardening, golf, tennis. Academic research interests: nuclear cardiology, development of new imaging technologies, medical education. Office: U Tex Southwestern Med Ctr Dallas Dept Radiology 5323 Harry Hines Blvd Dallas TX 75235-8896

PARKIN, JAMES LAMAR, otolaryngologist, educator; b. Salt Lake City, June 2, 1939; s. Elmer Lamar and Mary Ilene (Soffe) P.; m. Bonnie Dansie, July 1, 1963; children—Jeffrey, Brett, Matthew, David. B.S., U. Utah, 1963, M.D., 1966; M.S., U. Wash., 1970. Diplomate Am. Bd. Otolaryngology. Resident in otolaryngology U. Wash., Seattle, 1968-72; practice medicine specializing in otolaryngology, Salt Lake City, 1972—; chmn. div. otolaryngology U. Utah Sch. Medicine, Salt Lake City, 1974-93 , prof. surgery, 1981—, acting chmn. dept. surgery, 1982-84, 93-94, chmn. 1994—; pres. med. bd. Univ. Med. Ctr., Salt Lake City, 1983-85, chmn. exec. com. faculty practice orgn., 1994—; bd. govs. Utah Med. Ins. Assn., Salt Lake City, 1979-81. Guest editor Ear, Nose and Throat Jour., 1982; assoc. editor Archives of Otolaryngology. Bishop Ch. of Jesus Christ of Latter-day Saints, Salt Lake City, 1983-86, stake pres. 1986-96; leader Boy Scouts Am. Recipient Honor award Am. Acad. Otolaryngology, 1980. Fellow ACS, Am. Plastic and Reconstructive Surgery, Am. Laryngol., Rhinol. and Otological Soc., Am. Otological Soc., Am. Soc. Laser Medicine and Surgery, Am. Neurotology Soc.; mem. Assn. Acad. Depts. Otolaryngology (chmn. nat. faculty survey com. 1980-90, sec.-treas. 1982-84, pres. 1986-88), Soc. Univ. Otolaryngologists (pres. 1984-85), Am. Cancer Soc. (pres. Utah chpt. 1984-86), Soc. Otolaryngology-Maxillofacial Surgery (pres. Utah chpt. 1979). Home: 2390 Bernadine Dr Salt Lake City UT 84109-1206 Office: U Utah Health Scis Ctr 50 N Medical Dr Salt Lake City UT 84132

PARKINS, FREDERICK MILTON, dental educator, university dean; b. Princeton, N.J., Sept. 8, 1935; s. William Milton and Phyllis Virginia (Plyler) P.; m. Carolyn V. Rude; children: Bradford, Christopher, Eric. Student, Carleton Coll., 1953-56; D.D.S., U. Pa., 1960; M.S.D. in Pedodontics, U. N.C., Chapel Hill, 1965; Ph.D. in Physiology, 1969. Instr. pedodontics U. N.C., 1965-67; asst. prof. pedodontics U. Pa., 1967-68, dir. Dental Aux. Utilization program, chmn. pedodontics, 1968-69; assoc. prof., head pedodontics U. Iowa, Iowa City, 1969-72; prof., head pedodontics U. Iowa, 1972-75; asst. dean acad. affairs U. Iowa (Coll. Dentistry), 1974-75, asso. dean acad. affairs, 1975-79, dir. continuing edn., 1975-77; prof. pedodontics, dean Sch. Dentistry, U. Louisville, 1979-85, prof. pediatric dentistry, 1985—; mem. Hillenbrand Fellowship adv. com. Am. Fund Dental Health, 1980-85; cons. Div. Dental Health USPHS, 1969-72; dental cons., med. staff Children's Hosp. Phila., 1968-71; med. staff Kosair Children's Hosp. Louisville, 1983—; cons., mem. pedodontic adv. com. Council Dental Edn., 1974-80, chmn. pedodontic adv. com., 1978-80, cons. council on legislation, 1978-79; dental cons. Aux. Utilization VA, 1968-69; cons. Bur. Health Resources Devel., 1974-76, Dept. Army, 1980—, numerous others. Assoc. editor: Jour. Preventive Dentistry, 1973-79; editorial bd., 1980-83; editorial reviewer: Jour. Pediatrics, 1969—, Jour. Dental Edn, 1978—, Jour. AMA, 1979—; asso. editor: Jour. Clin. Preventive Dentistry, 1979-84; Contbr. chpts. to textbooks, articles to profl. publs. Bd. govs. Youth Performing Arts Coun., Louisville-Jefferson County Sch. Dist., 1980-89, pres., 1986-88; bd. govs. Regional Cancer Ctr., U. Louisville, 1979-84, Univ. Hosp., 1979-84; mem. human studies com. U. Louisville, 1988-90. Robert Wood Johnson Congl. fellow Inst. of Medicine, 1977-78; USPHS postdoctoral fellow, 1963-67; NIH grantee, 1971-75; Recipient Earle Banks Hoyt Teaching award, 1969. Fellow AAAS, Am. Acad. Pediat. Dentistry (chmn. rsch. com. 1972-73, Ann. Rsch. award 1968, chmn. advanced edn. com. 1974-75, chmn. dental care programs com. 1978-80); mem. ADA, Am. Coll. Dentistry, Am. Soc. Dentistry for Children (exec. bd. Iowa unit 1969-75, award com. 1973-76, edn. com. 1974-77, chmn. rsch. adv. com. 1973-76), Biophys. Soc., Internat. Assn. Dental Rsch., N.Y. Acad. Dentistry, Ky. Dental Assn. (exec. bd. 1979-84), Am. Assn. Dental Schs. (coun. deans 1979-85, chmn. pedodontics sect. 1976, chmn. continuing edn. sect. 1979, legis. com. 1978-83), Louisville Dental Alumni Assn. (bd. govs. 1979-84), Am. Assn. Dental Rsch. (nat. affairs com. 1978-85), Acad. Laser Dentistry (vice-chmn. rsch. and edn. 1996, cert. com.), Southeastern Soc. Pediat. Dentistry, U.S. Power Squadron (bd. govs. 1987-93, sec. 1989, adminstrv. officer 1990, exec. officer 1991, comdr. 1992), Omicron Kappa Upsilon (pres. Wa. chpt. 1991-92), Louisville Boat Club, Rotary. Unitarian. Home: 6424 Marina Dr Prospect KY 40059-8846 Office: U Louisville Sch Dentistry Dept Orth Pediatric &Geriatric Dent Rm 306 Louisville KY 40292

PARKS, DONALD HARRY, plastic surgeon; b. Newmarket, Ont., Can., May 6, 1943; s. Stuart Henry and Mary (Watson) P.; m. Janice Coe, Nov. 19, 1975; 1 child, Brianna. BA, U. Western Ont., 1966, MD, 1970. Assoc. prof., interim chief Shriner's Burns Inst., U. Tex. Med. Br., Galveston, 1976-82; prof., chief plastic surgery U. Tex. Med. Sch., Houston, 1982—. Editor: Burns in Children, 1988. Mem. Masons, Shriners. Office: U Tex Med Sch 6431 Fannin Ste 4156 Houston TX 77030

PARKS, JANET ELAINE, pharmacist; b. Watertown, S.D., Oct. 20, 1946; d. Dale O. and Della E. (Horn) P. BS, S.D. State U., 1970; MBA, U. Minn., 1981. Registered pharmacist, Minn., Wis. Staff pharmacist St. Luke's Hosp., Duluth, Minn., 1970-81; fin. cons. Parks & Parks, Marshall, Minn., 1981-82; pharmacy cons. J. Parks, Mason City, Iowa, 1982-85; night pharmacist St. Joseph Mercy Hosp., Mason City, 1982-85; dir. pharmacy Tomah Meml. Hosp., Wis., 1985-86; pharmacy cons. Tomah Care Ctr., 1985-86; mgr. pharmacy computer ops. St. Nicholas Hosp., Sheboygan, Wis., 1986-89; pharmacist Walgreen's Pharmacy, 1989—; cons. Meadow View Manor Nursing Home, Sheboygan, 1987-91. Fin. cons. Methodist Chs. Mem. AAUW, NAFE, Am. Soc. Hosp. Pharmacists (region sec. 1975), Nat. Assn. Future Women (photographer 1984), Phi Kappa Phi, Rho Chi. Methodist. Avocations: nature photography; needlecraft; cross-country skiing; bicycling; personal computers. Home: 9769 Dorset Ln Eden Prairie MN 55347-3137 Office: Walgreen's Pharmacy Mpls Dist 3566 Winnetka Ave N Minneapolis MN 55427-2022

PARKS, LAURENCE HALL, microbiologist, researcher; b. Glen Ridge, N.J., Oct. 18, 1946; s. Alan Hall Jr. and Jean Margaret (Collier) P.; m. Nancy Elaine Hurley, Dec. 31, 1976 (div. Oct. 1979); m. Deborah Lynn Smock, Aug. 23, 1980; children: Samuel Hall, Brieanna Noel. BS in Psychology with honors, U. Tenn., 1969; MS in Biology, U. Mo., Kansas City, 1977. Grad. teaching asst. dept. biology U. Mo., 1976-77; hepatitis technologist Cmty. Blood Ctr. Greater Kansas City, 1978, rsch. assoc., 1978-81, supr. hepatitis and epidemiology, 1981-86, supr. hepatitis and HIV reference, 1986-89, supr. Hepatitis Reference Lab., 1989-95, quality assurance specialist, 1995—. Contbr. abstracts to Transfusion, Comparative Biochemistry and Physiology, Viral Hepatitis and Liver Disease. Mem. sch. bd., treas. Global Montessori Acad., Kansas City, 1990-92. Mem. Am. Assn. Blood Banks, Am. Soc. for Microbiology. Democrat. Presbyterian. Home: 3816 Bell St Kansas City MO 64111-3916 Office: Community Blood Ctr Greater Kansas City 4040 Main St Kansas City MO 64111-2308

PARKS, ROWAN WESLEY, surgeon, research registrar; b. Belfast, No. Ireland, Mar. 5, 1966; s. Thomas George and Elizabeth (Mahood) P.; m. Janet Margaret McLuckie, Sept. 8, 1990; children: Matthew, Amy. MB, BCh, BAO, Queen's U., Belfast, 1989. Jr. house officer Royal Victoria Hosp., Belfast, 1989-90, Georgina Hadden rsch. fellow, 1994; sr. house officer Belfast Surg. Rotation, 1990-93, regional sr. house officer, 1993-95, registrar, 1995—. Recipient Fannin prize Intensive Care Soc. Ireland, 1995, Moyihan prize Assn. Surgeons of Gt. Britain and Ireland, 1996. Fellow Royal Coll. Surgeons Ireland; mem. Brit. Med. Assn. (Insole award 1995), Ulster Med. Soc. Office: Dept Surgery, Grosvenor Rd, BT12 6BJ Belfast Northern Ireland

PARMELEE, WALKER MICHAEL, psychologist; b. Grand Haven, Mich., Apr. 26, 1952; s. Walker Michael and Evelyn Mae (Essengerg) P.; m. Gayle Ann Klempel, Jan. 11, 1975; children: Morgan Christine, Kathryn Ann, Elizabeth Mae. BS, Ctrl. Mich. U., 1974, MA, cert. specialist in psychology, 1977; D in Counseling Psychology, Western Mich. U., 1986. Lic. psychologist, Mich. Sch. psychologist Oakridge Pub. Schs., Muskegon, Mich., 1977-82, Ravenna (Mich.) Schs., Muskegon Heights (Mich.) Schs., 1982-84; sr. staff therapist Steelcase Counseling Svcs., Grand Rapids, Mich., 1984-90; prin., psychologist Parmelee Psychology Ctr., Grand Haven, 1989—; consulting psychologist Chem. Dependency Clinic, Grand Haven, 1989—. Contbr. articles to profl. jours. Bd. dirs. Planned Parenthood, Muskegon, 1979-82, Harbinger Inc., Grand Rapids, 1986-90; elder 2d Ref. Ch., Grand Haven, 1989-92; mem. women and families adv. group Allegan, Muskegon, Ottawa Substance Abuse Agy., 1992—. Mem. Am. Psychol. Assn., Am. Group Psychotherapy Assn., Nat. Assn. Child Alcoholics, Mich. Psychol. Assn., Mich. Sch. Psychologists. Home: 215 Howard St Grand Haven MI 49417-1806 Office: Parmelee Psychology Ctr 321 Fulton Ave Grand Haven MI 49417-1231

PARMLEY, WILLIAM WATTS, cardiologist; b. Salt Lake City, Jan. 22, 1936; s. Thomas Jennison and Martha Lavern (Watts) P.; m. Shanna Lee Nielsen, Aug. 17, 1961; children: Michael William, John Nielsen, Todd Jennison, Ann. AB, Harvard U., 1957; MD, Johns Hopkins U., 1963. Intern Johns Hopkins Hosp., 1963-64, resident in medicine, 1964-65; clin. assoc. Nat. Heart Inst. NIH, Bethesda, Md., 1965-67; fellow in cardiology Peter Bent Brigham Hosp., Boston, 1967-69; asso. dir. cardiology Cedars-Sinai Med. Center, Los Angeles, 1969-73; mem. faculty dept. medicine U. Calif., San Francisco, 1974—; chief cardiology Moffitt Hosp., San Francisco, 1974—; established investigator Am. Heart Assn., 1971-74; chmn. Cardiovascular Bds., 1985-87. Editor Jour. the Am. Coll. Cardiology, 1992—; contbr. articles to profl. jours. Bishop Mormon Ch., 1977-82, stake pres., 1986-92, regional rep. 1992-95, area authority, 1995—. Served with USPHS, 1967-69. Fellow Am. Coll. Cardiology (pres. 1985-86), ACP; mem. Am. Soc. Clin. Investigation, Western Assn. Physicians, Assn. Am. Physicians, Phi Beta Kappa, Alpha Omega Alpha. Republican. Home: 2574 Roundhill Dr Alamo CA 94507-2236 Office: 1186 Moffitt Hosp 3D Parnassus Ave San Francisco CA 94143

PARNELL, DIANA DEANGELIS, dermatologist; b. Tacoma, Wash., May 18, 1940; d. Fulvio Garibaldi and Ruth Margaret (Nordlund) DeAngelis; m. Francis W. Parnell, Feb. 27, 1965; children—Cheryl Lynn, John Francis, Kathleen Diana, Alison Anne, Thomas William. B.S., Pa. State U., 1961; M.D., Georgetown U., 1965. Diplomate Nat. Bd. Examiners, Am. Bd. Dermatology. Intern, Univ. Hosps., U. Wis., Madison, 1965-66, resident in dermatology, 1966-69; dermatologist Univ. Health Service, U. Wis., Madison, 1969-70; practice medicine specializing in dermatology, Greenbrae, Calif., 1970-76, 78—, Ridgewood, N.J., 1976-78; corp. med. cons. indsl. dermatology, 1976-79; pres. Parnell Med. Corp., Greenbrae, 1980—; sec., bd. dirs. Parnell Pharms., San Rafael, Calif.; clin. instr. medicine U. Wis. Sch. Medicine, Madison, 1969-70; clin. instr. dermatology U. Calif. Sch. Medicine, San Francisco, 1970-76, 87-94, asst. clin. prof., 1994—; mem. staff Marin Gen. Hosp., Greenbrae, 1970—, Ross Gen. Hosp. (Calif.), 1970-75, 78-84, Valley Hosp. Ridgewood, N.J., 1976-78. Trustee dist. bd. Marin Hosp., 1992—, chair 1996—. Fellow Am. Acad. Dermatology; mem. Pacific Dermatol. Assn., San Francisco Dermatol. Soc., Am. Soc. Dermatol. Surgery, Delta Delta Delta. Home: PO Box 998 Ross CA 94957-0998 Office: 1100 S Eliseo Dr Ste 2 Greenbrae CA 94904

PARNELL, FRANCIS WILLIAM, JR., physician; b. Woonsocket, R.I., May 22, 1940; s. Francis W. and Dorothy V. (Lalor) P.; m. Diana DeAngelis, Feb. 27, 1965; children: Cheryl Lynn, John Francis, Kathleen Diana, Alison Anne, Thomas William. Student, Coll. Holy Cross, 1957-58; AB, Clark U., 1961; MD, Georgetown U., 1965. Diplomate: Nat. Bd. Med. Examiners, Am. Bd. Otolaryngology. Intern Univ. Hosps., Madison, Wis., 1965-66; resident in gen. surgery Univ. Hosps., Madison, 1966-67, otolaryngology, 1967-70; pvt. practice medicine specializing in otolaryngology San Rafael, Calif., 1972-75, Greenbrae, Calif., 1972-75, 78—; chmn., pres., CEO Parnell Pharms., Larkspur, Calif., 1982—; cons. corp. med. affairs, 1978-82; corp. med. dir. Becton, Dickinson & Co., Rutherford, N.J., 1976-78; clin. instr. U. Calif. at San Francisco, 1972-75, asst. clin. prof., 1975-76; Alt. del., U.S. Del. 27th World Health Assembly WHO, Geneva, 1974. Contbr. articles to profl. jours. Candidate Calif. State Assembly, 1988; bd. dirs. Marin Coalition, 1980-96, chmn., 1986-87; trustee Ross (Calif.) Sch. Dist., 1981-89; mem. governing bd. Marin Cmty. Coll. Dist., 1995—. Maj. M.C. AUS, 1970-72, lt. col. M.C., USAR, 1985-94. Fellow ACS (gov. 1988-94), Am. Acad. Otolaryngology. Home: PO Box 998 Ross CA 94957-0998 Office: 1100 S Eliseo Dr Greenbrae CA 94904-2004

PARNES, EDMUND IRA, oral and maxillofacial surgeon; b. Pitts., Apr. 16, 1936; s. David E. and Sara (Engelberg) P.; m. Elizabeth Cameron, Nov. 27, 1977; children: Dana, Mara, Lauren. Student Vanderbilt U., 1954-55, U. Miami, 1955-56; DMD, U. Pitts., 1960, Diplomate Am. Bd. Oral and Maxillofacial Surgery. Oral surgery intern Jackson Meml. Hosp., 1960-61; resident, teaching fellow anesthesiology Presbyn. Univ. Hosp., Pitts., 1963-64; sr. resident oral surgery Ben Taub Gen. Hosp., Houston, 1964-65; pvt. practice oral and maxillofacial surgery, Miami, Fla., 1965—; interim assoc. chief oral surgery Jackson Meml. Hosp., Miami, 1970-72; clin. assoc. prof. U. Miami, 1975—; lectr. in field. Capt. U.S. Army, 1961-63. Fellow Am. Assn. Oral and Maxillofacial Surgeons (mem. com. legislation 1972-73, com. sci. sessions 1979-86, trustee 1991-94, pres.-elect 1994-95, pres. 1995-96); mem. ADA, Fla. Soc. Oral and Maxillofacial Surgeons (pres. 1974-75), Fla. Dental Assn. (ho. of dels., trustee 1982-95, v.p. 1996—), S.E. Soc. Oral Surgeons, East Coast Dist. Dental Soc. (chmn. coms. 1980-84, pres. 1981-82), North Dade Dental Soc. (pres. 1971-72), Am. Soc. Dental Anesthesiology (pres. Fla. chpt. 1970), Alpha Omega (pres. 1977-78, regent 1983). Jewish. Office: 8700 N Kendall Dr Ste 221 Miami FL 33176-2206

PARNESS, HOWARD ARTHUR, internist; b. Bklyn., Mar. 28, 1942; s. Abraham and Frances (Bell) P.; m. Judith Kutler, Nov. 28, 1980 (div. Jan. 1988); 1 child, Amy; m. Ethel Siegal, Dec. 24, 1995. BS, CCNY, 1962; MD, SUNY, 1966. Diplomate Am. Bd. Internal Medicine, Am. Bd. Utilization and Quality Rev. Intern, then resident in internal medicine Kings County Hosp., Bklyn., 1966-68; resident L.A. County-U. So. Calif. Med. Ctr., 1970-72; pvt. practice L.A., 1972-75, Dallas, 1975—; bd. dirs. Wood Hill Imaging Ctr., Dallas. Vol. Jewish Fedn., Dallas, 1975—. Lt. comdr. USNR, 1968-70. Mem. AMA, Tex. Med. Assn., Dallas County Med. Soc., Tex. Soc. Internal Medicine. Democrat. Jewish. Office: 8210 Walnut Hill Ln Ste 810 Dallas TX 75231-4421

PARR, EUGENE QUINCY, retired orthopaedic surgeon; b. Erlanger, Ky., Aug. 4, 1925; s. Benjamin Franklin and Sallie Frances (Wright) P.; m. Joan Lykins, June 9, 1951; children—Eugene Quincy Jr., Jeffrey Wright, Valerie. Student Berea Coll., Ky., 1944-45, 46-48; M.D., U. Louisville, 1952; fellow Mayo Grad. Sch. Medicine, 1956-60. Diplomate Am. Bd. Orthopaedic Surgery. Intern Baroness Erlanger Hosp., Chattanooga, 1952-53; resident in orthopaedic surgery Mayo Clinic, Rochester, Minn., 1956-60; practice medicine specializing in orthopaedic surgery, Lexington, Ky., 1960-96, ret.; adminstrv. trustee Central Baptist Hosp., Lexington, 1975-84. Trustee Berea Coll., 1966-72. Fellow Am. Acad. Orthopaedic Surgeons; mem. Am. Assn. Hip & Knee Surgeons, Am. Acad. Disability Evaluating Physicians, Christian Med. Soc., Doctors Mayo Soc. (founding), Mid-Am. Orthopaedic Assn., Lexington Orthopaedic Soc. (pres. 1964-66), Ky. Orthopaedic Soc. (pres. 1986), Clin. Orthopaedic Soc., Phi Kappa Phi. Home: Foxtale Farm 1825 Keene Rd Nicholasville KY 40356-9433

PARRA, PAMELA ANN, physician, educator; b. New Orleans, La., Nov. 24, 1949; d. Morris Louis and Mary Elizabeth (Monaghan) P.; m. Garrett John Beadle, May 7, 1983; children: Erin Elizabeth, Ryan Garrett. BS, Loyola U., 1971; MD, Tulane U., 1975. Diplomate Am. Bd. Emergency Medicine. Emergency physician Lakewood Hosp., Morgan City, La., 1975-76, 81-86; resident Charity Hosp., New Orleans, 1976-79, staff physician, 1979-81; staff physician Baton Rouge (La.) Gen. Med. Ctr., 1986—; asst. prof. medicine La. State U., Med. Sch., New Orleans, 1989—. Fellow Am. Coll. Emergency Physicians (sec.-treas. La. chpt. 1993—); mem. La. State Med. Soc. Republican. Roman Catholic. Home: 1020 Pastureview Dr Baton Rouge LA 70810-4725 Office: Baton Rouge Gen Med Ctr 3600 Florida Blvd Baton Rouge LA 70806-3842

PARRIS, THOMAS GODFREY, JR., medical facility administrator; b. Phila., Jan. 30, 1937; married. BS, Pa. State U., 1958; M Health Care Adminstrn., U. Pitts., 1965. Adminstrv. resident Homestead (Pa.) Hosp., 1964-65; exec. assoc. to v.p. Assocs. Hosp. Svcs. of N.Y., N.Y.C., 1965-67; asst. adminstr. Hackensack (N.J.) Med. Ctr., 1967-68; assoc. exec. dir. Met. Hosp. Ctr., N.Y.C., 1968-73; adminstr., CEO Women and Infants Hosp. of R.I., Providence, 1973-76, exec. v.p., CEO, 1976-79, pres., CEO, 1979—. Contbr. articles to profl. publs. Active various cmty. orgns. Fellow Am. Coll. Health Care Execs. (regent R.I. 1984-90); mem. Am. Hosp. Assn. (mem. com., del., trustee 1985-88), R.I. Hosp. Assn. (bd. dirs. 1973—, exec. com. 1974-79, chair 1978-79, del. 1979-80). Office: Women & Infants Hosp RI 101 Dudley St Providence RI 02905*

PARRISH, MATTHEW DENWOOD, psychiatrist; b. Washington, Apr. 1, 1918; s. Forrest Denwood and Alice Lorena (Flynn) P.; m. Virginia John Bennet, Sept. 24, 1944 (div.); m. Marilyn Kay Arney, May 30, 1978; children: Megan, Maxwell. BA, U. Va., 1939; MD, George Washington U., 1950. Diplomate Am. Bd. Psychiatry. Intern Letterman Hosp., San Francisco, 1950-51; resident in psychiatry Walter Reed Hosp., Washingotn, 1951-54; commd. 2d lt. U.S. Army, 1941, advanced through grades to col., 1967, ret., 1971; chief tng. Ill. Dept. Mental Health, Chgo., 1972-74; supt. Singer Mental Health Ctr., Rockford, Ill., 1974-85, med. dir., 1985-93; child and adolescent psychiatrist, 1986-95, ret., 1996; clin. prof. psychiatry U. Ill., Chgo., 1972-76; clin. asst. prof. psychiatry Coll. Med., Rockford, 1976—. Editor in chief: U.S. Army Vietnam Medical Journal, 1967-68. Singer Mental Health Ctr., Rockford. Decorated Legion of Merit (2). Fellow Am. Psychiat. Assn. (life); mem. Soc. Med. Cons. in Armed Forces, Assn. Mil. Surgeons U.S.

PARRISH, OVERTON BURGIN, JR., pharmaceutical corporation executive; b. Cin., May 26, 1933; s. Overton Burgin and Geneva Opal (Shinn) P. B.S., Lawrence U., 1955; M.B.A., U. Chgo., 1959. With Pfizer Inc., 1959-74; salesman Pfizer Labs., Chgo., 1959-62; asst. mktg. product mgr. Pfizer Labs., N.Y.C., 1962-63; product mgr. Pfizer Labs., 1964-66; group product mgr. Pfizer Inc., 1966-67, mktg. mgr., 1967-68, v.p. mktg., 1969-70; v.p., dir. ops. Pfizer Labs., 1970-71; exec. v.p. domestic pharm. div. Prizer Labs., 1971-72; exec. v.p., dir. Pfizer Internat. Divsn., 1972-74; pres., chief operating officer G.D. Searle Internat., Skokie, Ill., 1974-75, pres., chief exec. officer, 1975-77; pres. Worldwide Pharm./Consumer Products Group, 1977-86; pres., chief exec. officer Phoenix Health Care, Chgo., 1987—; chmn., CEO, bd. dirs. Wis. Pharmiacal Co., Inc., 1990-96; co-chmn. Inhalon Pharms., 1991-95, also bd. dirs.; chmn. ViatiCare Ltd., 1993—, also bd. dirs.; chmn., CEO, bd. dirs. The Female Health Co., 1996—. Author: The Future Pharmaceutical Marketing; International Drug Pricing, 1971. Trustee Mktg. Sci. Inst.; trustee Food and Drug Law Inst., 1979—, Lawrence U., 1983—. Served to 1st lt. USAF, 1955-57. Mem. Am. Mktg. Assn., Am. Mgmt. Assn., Beta Gamma Sigma, Phi Kappa Tau. Home: 505 N Lake Shore Dr Chicago IL 60611-3427 Office: Phoenix Health Care 919 N Michigan Ave Chicago IL 60611-1601

PARROTTA, LYNDA A., counselor, foster care provider; b. Trenton, N.J., Nov. 13, 1952; d. Richard and Joan (Hoff) Jarvie; m. Michael A. Parrotta, Sept. 25, 1976; children: Michael, Carmen, Laura-Lynn, Scott, Carmeli, Lisa-Dawn. Student, Rutgers U., 1984, Phila. Coll., 1986. Tchg. family home provider DYFS, Trenton, 1984-85; mem. child placement rev. bd. N.J. Ct. Sys., Trenton, 1985-86; foster home profl. Concern, Doylestown, Pa., 1986-89, Bethanna Medically Needy Foster Home, 1989—; profl. in Biblically based therapeutic home placement for sexually abused and behavior problemed children. Mem. Nat. Foster Parent Assn. (region II), Assn. Children N.J., Spl. Needs Adoptive Parents N.J. (v.p.), County Foster Parent Assn. (Bucks County policy coun. head start rep.). Home: 3 Jennifer Ln Southampton PA 18966-1155

PARRY, RANDINE ELIZABETH, psychologist; b. Hartford, Conn., Sept. 6, 1947; d. William Brown and Mary Elizabeth (Caton) P.; children: Robert W. Parry-Cruwys, Brendon C. Parry-Cruwys. AB, Mt. Holyoke Coll., 1968; PhD (USPHS fellow, 1968-72), U. Chgo., 1977. Staff psychologist behavior analysis rsch. lab., dept. psychiatry, U. Chgo., 1971-74, dir. fluency clinic, 1974-77; dir. psychology Walter Fernald State Sch., Waltham, Mass., 1977-80, chief psychologist, 1980—; lic. psychologist SE Counseling Assocs., Norwood, Mass., 1980-82; vis. asst. prof. Northeastern U., Boston, 1977-80; cons. Human Resource Inst. of Franklin, Mass., 1979-81. Contbr. papers to profl. confs. chmn. ERA com., Chgo. chpt., 1974-77; mem. Belmont Day Sch. Parents Assn., 1984-94, Friends of Sturbridge Village, 1981-90, NE Aquarium, Mus. Fine Arts, Mus. Sci., Boston, 1979—, Framingham Civic League, 1987-92, bd. dirs., 1989-92, exec. bd., 1990-92; bd. dirs. Waverley Oaks Child Devel. Ctr., 1984-86. Mem. Am. Psychol. Assn., Eastern Psychol. Assn., New Eng. Psychol. Assn., Mass. Psychol. Assn., Assn. for Applied Behavior Analysis, Assn. for Advancement of Behavior Therapy, Assn. for Advancement of Psychology, Assn. for Women in Psychology, Boston Behavior Therapy Interest Group. Home: 15 Cherry Oca Ln Framingham MA 01702-5663 Office: Walter Fernald State Sch Dept Psychology 200 Trapelo Rd Waltham MA 02154-6332

PARSA, BRIAN B., surgeon, military officer; b. Kansas City, Mo., Mar. 24, 1959; s. Jalil and Marly (Johnson) P.; m. Irene Ella Burks Chapman Harrison Galzerau, Jan. 29, 1995 (sep.); 1 child, Jordan David. BA in Biology, U. Kans., 1981; DO, U. Health Sci., 1985. Faculty mem. U. Health Scis., Kansas City, Mo., 1986-88; commd. officer USAF, 1989, advanced through grades to lt. col.; flight surgeon USAF, various locations, 1989—. Named Jolly Green Assn. Rescue Mission of Yr., 1992, 93; recipient Sikorsky Helicopter Rescue award United Techs.-Sikorsky Aircraft Co., various 1992, 93; decorated Air Medal USAF, 1991, Air Force Commendation medal with 5 oak leaf clusters, 1993, S.W. Asia Svc. medal, 1994. Mem. Am. Osteo. Assn., Aerospace Med. Assn., Soc. USAF Flight Surgeons (Air Tng. Command Flight Surgeon of Yr. 1990, Air Combat Command Flight Surgeon of Yr. 1992).

PARSON, RHONDA S., emergency room nurse; b. Lawrenceburg, Tenn., Feb. 23, 1972; d. George E. and Dannie Sue (Owens) P. AAS, Columbia (Tenn.) State C.C., 1993. RN, Tenn., N.C.; cert. TNCC, ENPC, ACLS, PALS, CEN, MICN. Mem. nursing staff Maury Regional Hosp., Columbia, Tenn., 1993-94; emergency room nurse Hosp. Resource Mgmt., Lincolnton, N.C., 1994, Key Nursing Corp., Matthews, N.C., 1995, Cabarrus Meml. Hosp., Concord, N.C., 1995, Lexington (N.C.) Meml. Hosp., 1995—. Mem. Emergency Nurses Assn. Home: 355 Holloway Church Rd Lexington NC 27292

PARSONAGE, WILLIAM HERBERT, criminal justice educator; b. Mpls., Jan. 21, 1936; s. Charles William and Blanche Marion (Rue) P.; m. K. Susan Hoerschgen, May 6, 1961; children: David William, Mark Robert, Kara Lynn. BA, Hamline U., St. Paul, 1961; MA, U. S.D., Vermillion, 1963; D in Applied Sociology (hon.), Glen Mills Sch. Applied Sociology, Pa., 1981. Police officer Shorewood, Minn., 1957-61, Vermillion Police Dept., 1961-62; probation/parole agt. Minn. Dept. of Corrections, St. Paul, 1962-64, staff cons., 1964-67; asst. prof. law enforcement and corrections Pa. State U., University Park, 1967-73, assoc. prof. adminstrn. justice, 1973-96, prof. emeritus, 1996—, asst. dean Coll. Human Devel., 1984-87, assoc. dean Coll. Health and Human Devel., 1987-88; cons. Nat. Inst. of Corrections, Washington, 1988—. Author: Services to Delinquents and Families, 1970, Professional Experiences and Opportunities, 1971, Worker Safety In Probation and Parole, 1989; author and editor: Alcohol Use: A Look At Basic Issues, 1969, Perspectives on Victimology, 1979; contbr. articles to profl.

jours. Mem. citizens com. Pres.'s Com. on Juvenile Deliquency and Youth Crime, 1966-68; mem. Pa. Gov.'s Com. Juvenile Deliquency, 1972; mem. Gov.'s Adv. Com. on Probation, Pa., 1986—. Staff sgt. AUS, 1953-56. Mem. World Soc. Victimology, Acad. Criminal Justice Scis., Am. Soc. Criminology (bd. dirs. 1975-76), Chief Adult Probation Officers Assn., Pa. Prison Warden's Assn. Democrat. Mem. Ch. of Christ. Home: 1137 Dorum Ave State College PA 16801-4102 Office: Pa State U 918 Oswald Tower University Park PA 16802-6215

PARSONS, DANIEL LANKESTER, pharmaceutics educator; b. Biscoe, N.C., Sept. 10, 1953; s. Solomon Lankester and Doris Eva (Bost) P. BS in Pharmacy, U. Ga., 1975, PhD, 1979. Asst. prof. pharmaceutics U. Ariz., Tucson, 1979-82; asst. prof. Auburn (Ala.) U., 1982-86, assoc. prof., 1986-91, prof., 1991—, chmn. divsn., 1990—; cons. Wyeth-Ayerst, Phila., 1989-93, Technomics, Ardsley, N.Y., 1990-93; presenter in field. Author: (with G.V. Betageri and S.A. Jenkins) Liposome Drug Delivery Systems, 1993. Named Disting. Alumni Sandhills Coll., 1990, Tchr. of Yr., Pharmacy Student Coun., 1987, Grad. Faculty Mem. of Yr., Grad. Student Orgn., 1994. Mem. Am. Pharm. Assn., Am. Assn. Pharm. Scientists, Am. Coll. Clin. Pharmacology (mem. coun. 1990-93), Phi Kappa Phi, Kappa Psi (advisor 1990-95, Svc. award 1990, 95, Advisor award 1992, nat. scholarship com. 1995). Office: Auburn U Sch Pharmacy Auburn AL 36849

PARSONS, JAMES THOMAS, physician; b. Oak Ridge, Tenn., Apr. 12, 1951; s. James Alvin and Harriett Bate (Suddarth) P.; m. Patsy Marshall, May 11, 1953; twins: Amelia and Dianne. BS, Duke U., 1972, MD, 1976. Diplomate Am. Bd. Radiology. Prof. dept. radiation oncology U. Fla., Gainesville, 1980—, Rodney R. Million prof., 1989—, John P. Cofrin prof., 1996—. Mem. Am. Radium Soc., Am. Soc. Therapeutic Radiology and Oncology, Am. Coll. Radiology. Office: Univ Fla Box 100385 JHMHC Gainesville FL 32610

PARSONT, LAWRENCE M., ophthalmologist; b. N.Y.C., July 1, 1949; s. William and Charlotte P.; m. Ilene Parsont; children: Jason, Blair. BA, Columbia Coll., 1971, MD, 1975. Diplomate Am. Bd. Ophthalmology. Med. intern George Washington U., 1975-76; resident in ophthalmology Manhattan Eye and Ear, 1976-79; attending ophthalmologist/Cataract Clinic Manhattan Eye & Ear, 1979—; pvt. practice N.Y.C., 1979—. Mem. AMA, N.Y. County Med. Soc. Office: 799 Park Ave New York NY 10021

PARTAIN, CLARENCE LEON, radiologist, nuclear medicine physician, educator, administrator; b. Memphis, July 12, 1940; s. Archie Leon and Vergie (Young) P.; m. Judith Stafford, Jan., 1964; children: David Blane, Teri Ellyn, Amy Leigh. B.S.N.E., U. Tenn., 1963; M.S.N.E., Purdue U., 1965, Ph.D. in Nuclear Engring., 1967; M.D., Washington U., St. Louis, 1975. Diplomate: Am. Bd. Nuclear Medicine, Am. Bd. Radiology; registered profl. engr., Mo. Asst. prof. nuclear engring. U. Mo.-Columbia, 1968-71, assoc. prof., 1971-75; resident N.C. Meml. Hosp., Chapel Hill, 1975-79; assoc. prof. radiology U. N.C.-Chapel Hill, 1978-79; assoc. prof. Vanderbilt U., Nashville, 1980-85; prof. radiology and biomed. engring. Vanderbilt U., 1985—, vice chmn. radiology, 1989-92, dir. nuclear medicine, 1981-85, dir. magnetic resonance imaging, 1983-92, chmn. radiology, radiologist in chief, 1992—; cons. NIH, Bethesda, Md., 1980—. Author: Nuclear Magnetic Resonance (NMR) Imaging, 1983, NMR Imaging: Clinical Utility and Correlation, 1984, Thyroid and Parathyroid Imaging, 1986, Magnetic Resonance Imaging, 2d edit., 1988, Correlative Image: Nuclear Medicine, Magnetic Resonance, Computer Tomography, Ultrasound, 1988; editl. bd. Acad. Radiology, Magnetic Resonance Imaging, Jour. Magnetic Resonance Imaging, Jour. Nuclear Medicine. AEC Spl. fellow, 1964-66; grantee Nat. Inst. Neurosci., Communicative Diseases and Stroke, 1977-78. Fellow Am. Coll. Nuclear Physicians, Am. Coll. Radiology, Soc. Magnetic Resonance Imaging (bd. dirs.); mem. AMA, IEEE, Radiol. Soc. N.Am., Assn. Univ. Radiologists (exec. com.), Soc. Nuclear Medicine (trustee, Benedict Casson lectr. 1981), Am. Roentgen Ray Soc. (exec. coun.), Soc. Magnetic Resonance in Medicine (trustee), Internat. Soc. of Magnetic Resonance in Medicine (governance coun.), Sigma Phi Epsilon. Baptist. Home: 5471 Pinewood Rd Franklin TN 37064 Office: Vanderbilt U Med Ctr 1611 21st Ave S Nashville TN 37212-3103

PARTAIN, PATRICIA, hospital administrator; b. Ogdensburg, N.Y., Apr. 21, 1938; d. Walter Bernard and Vivian Agnes (Redmond) Fitzgerald; 1 child Felicia Anne Lewis Wilson. BS, Hartwick Coll., 1960. RN, N.Y.; cert. profl. in healthcare quality. Psychiatric unit supr. St. Joseph's Hosp., Hot Springs, Ark., 1981-83; home health team leader Ark. Healthcare, Hot Springs, 1984-85, Upjohn Healthcare Svc., Hot Springs, Ark., 1985-88; home health specialist Ark. Dept. Health, Hot Springs, 1988-91; healthcare cons. MQRS, Inc., Little Rock, 1991-92; quality mgr. John L. McClellan Meml. Vet.'s Hosp., Little Rock, 1992—. Mem. Ladies Guild, Little Rock, 1994-96; v.p. Questors Internat., Little Rock, 1996. Mem. Nat. Assn. Healthcare Quality, Ark. Assn. Healthcare Quality (bd. dirs. 1994-96), Pub. Health Nurses Assn. (chmn. legis. com. 1989), Sigma Theta Tau (mem. Kappa Rho chpt.). Roman Catholic. Home: 13120 Morrison Rd Little Rock AR 72212-3737

PARTHEMORE, JACQUELINE G., physician, educator; b. Harrisburg, Pa., Dec. 21, 1940; d. Philip Mark and Emily (Buvit) Parthemore; m. Alan Morton Blank, Jan. 8, 1967; children: Stephen Eliot, Laura Elise. BA, Wellesley Coll., 1962; MD, Cornell U., 1966. Rsch. edn. assoc. VA Hosp., San Diego, 1974-78; staff physician VA Med. Ctr., San Diego, 1978-79, asst. chief, med. svc., 1979-80, acting chief, med. svc., 1980-81, chief of staff, 1984—; rsch. edn. assoc. VA Hosp., San Diego, 1974-78; asst. prof. U. So. Calif. Sch. Medicine, San Diego, 1974-80; prof., assoc. dean U. Calif. Sch. Medicine, $D, 1985—; prof. medicine, assoc. dean U. Calif. Sch. Medicine, San Diego, 1985—; assoc. prof. U. So. Calif. Sch. Medicine, San Diego, 1980-85; staff physician VA Med. Ctr., San Diego, 1978-79, asst. chief med. svc., 1979-80, acting chief, 1980-81; $D $D, $D; mem. nat. rsch. resources coun. NIH, Bethesda, Md., 1990-94. Contbr. articles to profl. jours., chpts. to books. Bd. dirs. San Diego Vets. Med. Rsch. Found.; mem. adv. bd. San Diego Opera. Recipient Bullock's 1st Annual Portfolio award, 1985, San Diego Pres.'s Coun. Woman of Yr. award, 1985, YWCA Tribute to Women in Industry award, 1987. Fellow ACP; mem. Endocrine Soc., Am. Fedn. Clin. Rsch., Am. Bone and Mineral Soc., Nat. Assn. VA Chiefs Staff (pres. 1989-91), Am. Assn. Clin. Endocrinologists, Wellesley Coll. Alumnae Assn. (1st v.p. 1992-95). Office: VA Med Ctr 3350 La Jolla Village Dr San Diego CA 92161-0002

PARTINEN, MARKKU MIKAEL, neurologist; b. Helsinki, Finland, Dec. 4, 1948; s. Väinö and Kerttu Elisabeth (Havunen) P.; m. Helena Majanen; children: Eemil Väinö E., Evert Edvard J. MD, Faculty Medicine, Montpellier, France, 1975; DSc in Medicine, Epidemiology, Faculty Medicine, Helsinki, 1982; Docent Neurology, U. Helsinki, Leppävirta, Finland. Gen. practitioner Health Care Ctr., Leppavirta, Finland, 1975-76; asst. physician Clinic Neurophysiology and Medicine, Helsinki, 1975-78; resident in neurology U. Helsinki, 1978-82, asst. dept. pub. health sci., 1980-81, asst. prof. neurology, 1981-83, dir. sleep disorders unit, dept. neurology, 1983-84, staff neurologist, 1987—; dir. Ullanlinna Sleep Disorders Clinic and Research Ctr., Helsinki, 1984—, Vaajasalo Hosp., Kuopio, Finland, 1990-91; chief neurologist Kivelä Hosp., 1991-95; head R&D specialized health care Nat. Rsch. and Devel. Ctr. Welfare and Health, 1993-94; dir. Haaga Epilepsy & Sleep Rsch. Ctr., 1996—; sr. researcher epidemiology, Inst. Occupational Health, Helsinki, 1983-85; research fellow Sleep Disorders Ctr., Stanford, Calif., 1985-86; vis. lectr. Coll. Nurses, Helsinki, 1979-83; docent U. Helsinki, 1987. Spl. editor Annales Clin. Research (Sleep), 1985; editorial adv. bd. Jour. Sleep, 1986—; assoc. editor Jour. Sleep Rsch.; contbr. articles to profl. jours. Served to sub lt. medicine, Finnish Armed Forces, 1976-77. Sleep and Heart Found. fellow Cardiovascular Research Finland, 1980, internat. research fellow Fogarty Internat. Pub. Health Service-NIH, Stanford, Calif., 1985-86; grantee Paavo Nurmi Found., 1983-84, Miina Sillanpaa Found., 1983-87. Mem. Finnish Neurol. Soc., Finnish Brain Rsch. Soc., Scandinavian Sleep Rsch. Soc. (exec. bd. 1982—, pres. 1988—), European Sleep Rsch. Soc. (sci. com. 1986-90, v.p. 1992-94), Sleep Rsch. Soc. U.S., Finnish Sleep Rsch. Soc. (pres. 1988—), World Fedn. Sleep Rsch. Socs. (coordinating sec. 1996—). Evangelist Lutheran. Office: Haaga Ctr Neurol Rsch & Rehab, Makipellontie 15, 00320 Helsinki Finland

PARTINGTON, JOHN EDWIN, retired psychologist; b. Union Springs, N.Y., Nov. 13, 1907; s. Eliezer and Flora (Hobson) P.; m. Gwen L. Gray, Aug. 18, 1938. AB, Earlham Coll., 1929; MA in Psychology, U. Ky., 1938; postgrad., U. Chgo., 1946, Purdue U., 1959-62. Diplomate in counseling Am. Bd. Profl. Psychology; cert. psychologist, Ind. Tchr. Ky. Houses of Reform, Lexington, 1930-35; asst. to rsch. psychologist USPHS Hosp., Lexington, 1935-40; psychologist USES, Washington, 1940-42; counsellor VA, Roanoke, Va., 1946-50; psychologist US. Naval Exam. Ctr., Great Lakes, Ill., 1950-58; chief test devel. U.S. Army Enlisted Evaluation Ctr., Ft. Harrison, Ind., 1958-70; chief of rsch. U.S. Army Enlisted Evaluation Ctr., Ft. Harrison, 1970-72. Author: Leiter-Partington Adult Performance Scale, 1950, Helpful Hints for Better Living, 1990; contbr. articles to profl. jours. Chmn. adv. com. Ret. Sr. Vol. Program, 1973-88; chmn. ofcl. bd. Downtown Bapt. Ch., Lexington, Ky., 1989-91. Maj. AUS, 1942-46. Recipient Lt. Govs. Outstanding Kentuckian award, 1983. Mem. APA, Ind. Psychol. Assn. Address: 3458 Flintridge Dr Lexington KY 40517-1119

PARYANI, SHYAM BHOJRAJ, radiologist; b. Bhavnagar, Gujarat, India, July 18, 1956; came to U.S., 1966; s. Bhojraj Thakurdas and Sarswati (Shewarkanani) P.; m. Sharon Dale Goldman, May 12, 1979; children: Lisa Ann, Jason Bhojraj, Gregory Shyam. BSEE, U. Fla., 1975, MSEE, 1979, MD, 1979. Diplomate Am. Bd. of Radiology. Intern U. Tex., M.D. Anderson Hosp., Houston, 1979-80; resident Stanford (Calif.) U. Hosp., 1980-83, chief resident, 1983; dir. Williams Cancer Ctr., Bapt. Med. Ctr., Jacksonville, Fla., 1983—, Fla. Cancer Ctr., Jacksonville, Fla., 1985—; bd. dirs. Bapt. Med. Ctr., Jacksonville, 1986—, Meml. Med. Ctr., Jacksonville, 1987—, Meth. Hosp., Jacksonville, 1988—. Contbr. articles to profl. jours. Pres. Am. Cancer Soc., Jacksonville, 1992; bd. dirs. Jacksonville C. of C., 1991; adv. bd. Boy Scouts, 1990—. Mem. Am. Cancer Soc. (pres. 1992), Rotary Club. Republican. Hindu. Office: Fla Cancer Ctr 3599 University Blvd S Ste 1500 Jacksonville FL 32216-7400

PARZIALE, DEBORAH SHAYER, nursing educator; m. Alfred A. Parziale; 1 child, Michael. BSN, Northeastern U., 1973; MS in Nursing Edn., Russell Sage Coll., 1976. Prof. nursing program Ohlone Coll., Fremont, Calif.; instr. U. San Francisco. Contbg. author (book) Diagnostics. Mem. Phi Kappa Phi, Sigma Theta Tau.

PASCALI, ENZO, clinical immunology researcher, educator; b. Trieste, Italy, June 22, 1949; s. Vincenzo Pascali and Bice Pascali-Verderi. Degree in medicine, U. Trieste, Italy, 1974; specialist in allergy and clin. immunol., U. Firenze, 1978; specialist in hematology, U. Trieste, 1981. Med. diplomate. Intern med. clinic U. Trieste, 1974-75, asst. prof. med. clinic, 1975-81, researcher med. clinic, 1981—, prof. in charge clin. immunology Postgrad. Sch. Internal Med., 1991—, prof. in charge rheumatology faculty of medicine, 1992—, dir. lab. protidology and clin. immunology med. clinic, 1988—; invited lectr. Indian Coll. Allergy and Applied Immunology, Banaras Hindu U., Varanasi, 1992. Contbr. sci. articles to med. jours. Mem. Am. Assn. for Clin. Chemistry, N.Y. Acad. Sci., Italian Soc. Allergy and Clin. Immunology, Italian Soc. Immunology and Immunopathology. Office: U Trieste Inst Clin Med, Cattinara Hosp, 34149 Trieste Italy

PASCUCCI, RICHARD ANTHONY, osteopath, physician, rheumatologist, educator; b. Phila., Aug. 18, 1948; s. Robert Philip and Carmela Mary (Casale) P.; m. Patricia Comly, June 29, 1973; children: Richard Anthony Jr., Daniel, Amy Patricia, Matthew. BS in Biology, St. Joseph's U., Phila., 1970; DO, Phila. Coll. Osteopathic Medicine, 1975. Diplomate Am. Osteopathic Bd. Internal Medicine. Internship Suburban Gen. Hosp., Norristown, Pa., 1975-76, resident internal medicine, 1976-78; rheumatology fellow U. Louisville, 1978-80; attending physician Internal Medicine Assn., Norristown, 1980-84; assoc. prof. Coll. Osteo. Medicine Mich. State U., East Lansing, Mich., 1984-93; assoc. dean grad. med. edn. Phila. Coll. Osteo. Medicine, 1993—. Contbr. articles to profl. jours. Mem. athletic assn. St. Thomas Aquinas Sch., East Lansing, 1985-93; bd. dirs. Arthritis Found., Lansing, 1985-92. Fellow Am. Rheumatism Assn., Am. Coll. Osteo. Internists; mem. Am. Osteo Assn., Pa. Osteo. Med. Assn., Phila. Coll. Osteo. Medicine Alumni Assn., Phila. Rheumatism Soc., Mich. Assn. Osteo. Physicians and Surgeons, Nat. Bd. Osteo. Examiners (cert.), Am. Osteo. Bd. Internal Medicine and Rheumatology (cert., bd. dirs. 1992—). Republican. Roman Catholic.

PASCUZZI, ROBERT MARK, neurologist; b. Council Bluffs, Iowa, Oct. 1, 1953; s. Chris A. and Janice (Mayne) P.; m. Karen L. Roos; children: Anna, Janice. AB, Ind. U., Bloomington, 1976; MD, Ind. U., Indpls., 1979. Diplomate Am. Bd. Psychiatry and Neurology, Am. Bd. Electrodiagnostic Medicine. Intern Ind. U. Med. Ctr., Indpls., 1979-80; resident in neurology U. Va. Med. Ctr., Charlottesville, 1980-83, fellow in neuromuscular disease, 1983-85; prof. in neurology Ind. U. Sch. Medicine, 1995—; mem. med. staff Ind. U. Hosps., 1985—; chief neurol. svc. Wishard Meml. Hosp., stroke cons., mem. stroke site task force met. region. cen. Ind. unit Am. Heart Assn., 1988—; med. adv. bd. Nat. Myasthenia Gravis Found., 1988—; lectr. in field; presenter at profl. confs. Contbr. papers to profl. publs. Mem. Am. Acad. Neurology, Am. Soc. Neurol. Investigation (sec.-treas. 1987-88, pres. 1988-89), Am. Assn. Electrodiagnostic Medicine, Ind. Neurol. Soc., Am. Acad. Clin. Neurophysiology, Marion County Med. Soc., Cen. Soc. Neurol. Rsch. Office: Ind Univ Sch Medicine Regenstrief Health Ctr 1050 W Walnut St Indianapolis IN 46202-5254

PASETTI, LOUIS OSCAR, dentist; b. Tampa, Fla., Dec. 27, 1916; s. Joseph G. and Carmen (Gonzalez) P.; m. Mary Mendez, Jan. 11, 1942; children: Louis M., Arleen Pasetti Shearer. BS, U. Fla., 1937; DDS, Emory U., 1941; postgrad., U. Pa., 1978. Capt. U.S. Army, 1942-46; dentist pvt. practice Tampa, Fla., 1947—. Past. pres. Tampa Civitan Club, 1953; past lt. gov. Civitan Clubs of Tampa, 1962; past dep. gov. Civitan Internat., Tampa, 1964; fin. officer Am. Legion Post 248. Named Fla. Dentist of the Yr., Fla. Acad. Gen. Dentistry, 1983; recipient meritorious Svc. award Fla. Acad. Gen. Dentistry, 1989, Disting. Svc. award, 1985. Fellow Acad. Gen. Dentistry, Am. Coll. Dentists, Internat. Coll. Dentists, Acad. Dentistry Internat.; mem. ADA, Fla. Dental Assn., Fla. Acad. Gen. Dentistry (pres. 1981, Lifetime Achievement award 1996), Tampa Bay Acad. Gen. Dentistry (pres. 1977-78), Elks, Round Table of Civic Clubs of Tampa (sec. 1953), Palma Ceia Golf and Country Club. Democrat. Roman Catholic. Home: 10023 Hampton Pl Tampa FL 33618-4227 Office: 220 E Madison St Ste 250 Tampa FL 33602-4826

PASKAWICZ, JEANNE FRANCES, anesthesiologist; b. Phila., Mar. 3, 1954; d. Alex and Lillian (Pyluck) P. BSc, Phila. Coll. Pharmacy; MA, Villanova U., 1973; postgrad., St. Joseph U., 1979; PhD, Kensington U., 1984. Mem. anesthesiology staff Einstein Med. Ctr., Phila., 1990-94, Temple U. Hosp., 1994—; mem. detox./rehab. staff Presbyn. Med. Ctr., Phila., 1984—; house officer MCD-Elkins Park (Pa.) Campus, 1990—; mem. psychiatry staff Hahnemann U. Hosp., Phila., 1984-90; hostage negotiator Office of Mental Health, Phila., 1984-90; mem. surgery/anesthesiology staff Mt. Sinai Hosp., Phila., 1989-91. Bd. dirs. Phila. Coll. Pharmacy, St. Joseph U. Mem. NAFE, Am. Pain Soc., Nat. Parks Conservation Assn., North Shore Animal League, Amvets, DAV Comdrs. Club, Lambda Kappa Sigma.

PASKEY, MONICA ANNE, dietitian; b. Pasadena, Calif., Aug. 18, 1960; d. Harold Lloyd and Gloria Dolores (Swanson) Macomber; m. Dennis J. Paskey, Nov. 11, 1995; 1 child, Brittany Anne. Student, Mills Coll., 1978-80; BS cum laude, U. Conn., 1983. Registered dietitian. Clin. dietitian Marriott Corp., Washington, 1983-84; food svc. mgr. Marriott Corp., Virginia Beach, 1984-86; food svc. dir. Marriott Corp., Balt., 1987-88; oncology nutrition supr. Johns Hopkins U., Balt., 1988-89; cons. dietitian Beverly Enterprises, Balt., 1989-91; corp. menu mgr. Beverly Enterprises, Ft. Smith, Ark., 1991—; cons. dietitian, Virginia Beach, 1985-86. Author: (pamphlet) Campus Weekend Cooking Simplified, 1983; contbr. Beverly Enterprises Diet Manual, 1993, Thickened Liquids Manual, 1994. Recipient Spkr.'s award Eli Lilly, Inc., 1985. Mem. Am. Dietetic Assn., Va. Dietetic Assn., Tidewater Dist. Dietetic Assn. (treas. 1985-86), Md. Dietetic Assn. (job referral coord. 1987-89), Ark. Dietetic Assn. (media rep. 1996), Ark. Cons. Dietitians (health care facilities liaison 1992—, chair 1995-96). Roman Catholic. Office: Beverly Enterprises 5111 Rogers Ave Fort Smith AR 72919-3700

PASKINS-HURLBURT, ANDREA JEANNE, medical researcher; b. Eng., Apr. 26, 1943; d. Stanley and Josie Marie Betty Paskins; m. Douglas Herendeen Hurlburt, Sept. 7, 1968. BSc, McGill U., Montreal, Que., Can., 1965, MSc, 1970, PhD, 1974. Rsch. assoc. McGill, Montreal, 1974-77, Harvard Med. Sch., Boston, 1977-91. Home: 9809 Carmelita Dr Potomac MD 20854-4268

PASSAMANECK, RANDI LEA, medical technologist; b. Richmond, Va., May 18, 1942; d. Yale and Ann (Berman) P.; BS in Med. Tech., U. N.C., 1964; postgrad. Johns Hopkins Hosp., 1972-73. Research technologist USPHS Hosp., Balt., 1964-65; lab. scientist U. Md. Hosp., Balt., 1965-72, tech. and adminstrv. specialist, 1973-74; lab. assoc. Johns Hopkins Hosp., Balt., 1972-73; dir. tech. services ARC Blood Services, Chesapeake region, Balt., 1974-85; regulatory affairs specialist ARC, Washington, 1985-92; tech. support assoc. ARC, Washington, 1992-94, mfg. ops. assoc., 1995—. Bd. dirs. Mid-Atlantic Assn. Blood Banks, 1976-81, pres., 1979-80; mem. tech. workshop com. Am. Assn. Blood Banks, 1976-78; v.p. Washington-Balt. Blood Study Group, 1975-76; mem. tech. adv. com. ARC, 1982-84. Mem. Am. Soc. Clin. Pathologists, Am. Soc. Med. Tech., Internat. Soc. Blood Transfusion, Md. Soc. Med. Tech., Pa. Assn. Blood Banks, Regulatory Affairs Profls. Soc. Democrat. Jewish. Office: ARC 1616 N Fort Myer Dr Rosslyn VA 22209

PASSERO, MICHAEL ANTHONY, internal medicine physician, educator; b. Newark, Mar. 28, 1945; s. Anthony John and Connie (Blasi) P.; m. Mary Ann Cecere, June 14, 1969; children: Michael A. Jr., Christopher John. BA, Dartmouth Coll., 1966, MB, 1967; MD, Harvard U., 1969. Diplomate Am. Bd. Internal Medicine, Am. Bd. Pulmonary Diseases. Med. resident Duke U., Durham, N.C., 1969-72, pulmonary fellow, 1972-74; asst. prof. medicine Brown U., Providence, 1976-83, assoc. prof. medicine, 1984—; dir. pulmonary and critical care medicine Roger Williams Gen. Hosp., Providence, 1976—, assoc. chief medicine, 1984—; chmn. tchg. scholars com., Brown U. Sch. Medicine, dir. Biomed 281 Patho Physiology. Maj. M.C. U.S. Army, 1974-76. Named to Honorable Order of Ky. Cols. Fellow ACP, Am. Coll. Chest Physicians (gov. R.I. 1985-91); mem. Am. Thoracic Soc. (sec. eastern sect. 1984—). Office: Roger Williams Med Ctr 825 Chalkstone Ave Providence RI 02908-4728

PASSONS, GARY ALLEN, ophthalmologist; b. Chattanooga, Apr. 5, 1954; s. William E. and Betty Jean (Rogers) P.; m. Susan S., June 20, 1980; children: Travis, Taylor, Melanie. BA, Vanderbilt U., 1976; MD, U. Tenn., 1980. Intern Baptist Meml. Hosp., Memphis, 1980-81; resident U. Tenn., 1981-84. Fellow Am. Acad. Ophthalmology; mem. Memphis Eye Soc. Ophthalmology (pres. 1992-93), Tenn. Acad. Ophthalmology (bd. 1992). Home: 3622 Beaver Rim Dr Collierville TN 38017 Office: 6258 Poplar Memphis TN 38119

PASTERNAC, ANDRÉ, cardiologist; b. Toulouse, France, July 22, 1937; s. Jacques and Règine P.; came to Can., 1971, naturalized, 1978; adv. math. Lycée Henri IV, Paris, 1956; B.A. in Polit. Sci., Toulouse U., 1963, M.D., Med. Sch., 1968. Intern, Toulouse Univ. Hosp., 1962-63, resident, 1963-64, 66-68; resident Edouard-Herriot Hosp., Lyon, France, 1965-66; Fulbright scholar in cardiology Harvard U., 1968-71; research fellow Peter Bent Brigham Hosp., Boston, 1968-69; Milton fellow Children's Hosp., Boston, 1969-71; fellow in cardiology Toronto (Ont., Can.) U., 1971-72; staff cardiologist Montreal (Que., Can.) Heart Inst., 1972—; asst. prof. medicine U. Montreal, 1972-78, clin. assoc. prof., 1978—, clin. prof. medicine, 1994—; vis. assoc. prof. McGill U., Montreal, 1975-76; vis. lectr. U. Liège (Belgium), 1977, U. Madrid, 1977, U. Warsaw, 1979, 83; cons. Harley St. Clinic at Cromwell Hosp., London. Bd. dirs. Heart-Brain Rsch. Found. Inc., N.Y.C. Am. Field Svc. grantee, Oreg., 1954-55; specialist in cardiology, Paris, Montreal. Mem. French Cardiac Soc., European Soc. Cardiology, Canadian Cardiovasc. Soc., Am. Coll. Cardiology, Am. Heart Assn., Internat. Soc. Heart Rsch., Am. Fedn. Clin. Rsch., N.Y. Acad. Scis. Contbr. articles to profl. jours. Research in stress-related myocardial ischemia and dysfunction, mitral valve prolapse, cardiovascular drugs, cardiomyopathies, catecholamines, neuroendocrine control of the heart, stress and the heart. Home: 4175 Ste Catherine St W Apt 304, Westmount, PQ Canada H3Z 3C9 Office: Montreal Heart Inst, 5000 Belanger E, Montreal, PQ Canada H1T 1C8

PASTERNACK, ROBERT HARRY, school psychologist; b. Bklyn., Nov. 30, 1949; s. William and Lillian Ruth (Levine) P.; m. Jeanelle Livingston, Apr. 10, 1980; children: Shayla, Rachel. BA, U. South Fla., 1970; MA, N.Mex. Highlands U., 1972; PhD, U. N.Mex., 1980. Dir. Eddy County Drug Abuse Program, Carlsbad, N.Mex., 1972-73; adminstrv. intern U.S. Office Edn., Washington, 1975-76; exec. dir. Villa Santa maria, Cedar Crest, N.Mex., 1976-78; clin. dir. Ranchos Treatment Ctr., Taos, N.Mex., 1978-79; sch. psychologist N.Mex. Boys Sch., Springer, 1980—, supt., 1991; pres. Ensenar Health svcs., Inc., Taos, 1980—; exec. dir. Casa de Corazon, Taos, N.Mex., 1994—; instr. N.Mex. Highlands U., Las Vegas, 1980—, U. N.Mex., Albuquerque, 1980—; cons. N.Mex. Youth Authority, Santa Fe, 1988—, N.Mex. Devel. Disabilities Bur., Santa Fe, 1986—, various sch. dists. Author: Growing Up: The First Five Years, 1986; contbr. articles to profl. publs. Pres., bd. dirs. Children's Lobby, N.Mex., 1978, N.Mex. Spl. Olympics, 1986-88, Child-Rite, Inc., Taos, 1990; mem. Gov.'s Mental Health Task Force, Albuquerque, 1988—. Mem. Nat. Assn. Sch. Psychologists, Correctional Edn. Assn., Nat. Alliance Mentally Ill, N.Mex. Coun. on Crime and Delinquency. Home and Office: Enseñar Inc PO Box 3126 Taos NM 87571-3126 Office: Casa de Corazon PO Box 73 Taos NM 87571-0073

PASTERNACKI, LINDA LEA, critical care nurse; b. Green Bay, Wis., May 26, 1947; d. Paul John and Marion M. (Zagzebski) P.; (div.); children: Sam, Dan, Rachel Marie. Nursing diploma, St. Francis Sch. Nursing, Wichita, Kans., 1968; BS, Coll. St. Francis, Joliet, Ill., 1981, MS in Health Adminstrn., 1986. RN med.-surg., geriatrics, psychiatry St. Francis Hosp., Wichita, 1968-70; RN ICU-critical care unit Sunrise Hosp., Las Vegas, Nev., 1970-72; RN critical care unit Presbyn. Hosp., Albuquerque, 1972-75; RN med. ICU, surg. ICU VA Hosp., Albuquerque, 1976-81; RN emergency rm. Univ. Heights Hosp., Albuquerque, 1981-82; RN ICU, critical care unit Lovelace Med. Ctr., Albuquerque, 1982-86; RN ICU, emergency rm., surg. cornary care, intensive recovery room Presbyn. Hosp., Albuquerque, 1986-94; RN emergency rm., ICU, critical care unit St. Joseph Med. Ctr., Albuquerque, 1992-94; RN ICU, med.-surg. unit Transitional Hosp. Corp., Albuquerque, 1994—, admissions coord., 1995; hyperbaric therapy instr. Presbyn. Hosp., Albuquerque, 1975; clin. instr. U. N.Mex. EMT Sch., Albuquerque, 1980. Mem. AACN. Home: 10605 Central Park Dr NE Albuquerque NM 87123-4844 Office: Transitional Hosp Corp 700 High NE Albuquerque NM 87102

PASTORE, JOHN JAMES, family physician; b. N.Y.C., June 20, 1927; s. John and Maria (Chiariello) P.; m. Elisabeth M. Deltiel; children: John, Mark, Alexandra. BA, Hunter Coll.; MD, U. Paris, 1957. Med. dir. Cumberland County Med. Ctr., 1994; mem. S.J. Hosp. Systems, Bridgeton Divsn., 1993. Mem. N.J. Acad. Family Physicians (Family Physician of Yr. 1994, trustee 1969—, pres. 1978-79), Am. Acad. Family Physicians (publs. com. 1979-82), Nat. Acad. Family Physicians (alt. del. 1980-86), Cumberland County Med. Soc. (pres. 1982-83), N.J. Med. Soc. (trustee 1982-91), Am. Assn. Family Physicians (del. ho. of dels. 1987—, ins. and fin. svc. com. 1989-91). Home: 10 Silverbrook Dr Bridgeton NJ 08302

PASTOREK, NORMAN JOSEPH, facial plastic surgeon; b. Moline, Ill., Feb. 8, 1939; s. Joseph Andrew and Rose (Faurone) P.; m. Janice Marie Gloss, Apr. 27, 1986; children: Kate Haviland, Kelly Taylor. AB, Augustana Coll., 1960; MD, U. Ill., Chgo., 1964. Diplomate Am. Bd. Otolaryngology. Intern San Francisco Gen. Hosp., 1964-65; resident U. Ill. Hosps., Chgo., 1965-69; pvt. practice medicine specializing in facial plastic surgery N.Y.C; clin. asst. prof. N.Y. Hosp. Cornell Med. Coll., 1971-83, dir. div. facial plastic surgery dept. otolaryngology, 1977—, clin. assoc. prof., 1983-91, clin. prof., 1991—; examiner Am. Bd. Otolaryngology, 1971, 91-93. Author: Blepharoplasty, 1983, 3d edit., 1994; editor: Aesthetic Facial Surgery, 1990. Lt. comdr. USN, 1969-71. Fellow Am. Acad. Otolaryngology, Am. Bd. Otolaryngology (examiner 1991—), Am. Acad. Facial Plastic and Reconstructive Surgery (v.p. eastern region 1982-86, pres.-elect 1989-90, pres. 1990-91), ACS; mem. Alpha Omega Alpha. Republican. Episcopalian.

PASTORES, GREGORY MCCARTHY, physician, researcher; b. Bklyn., Sept. 4, 1959; s. Jovito Camara and Annie Harrington (McCarthy) P. MD, U. St. Thomas, 1983. Diplomate Am. Bd. Pediatrics, Am. Bd. Med. Genetics in Clin. Genetics and Clin. Molecular Genetics. Pediatric resident Mt. Sinai Med. Ctr., N.Y., 1986-89; fellow med. genetics Mayo Clinic Found., Rochester, Minn., 1989-91; med. and molecular genetics Mt. Sinai Sch. Medicine, N.Y., 1991-92, instr., pediatrics, genetics, 1992—, asst. prof. pediatrics, human genetics, 1993—. Roman Catholic. Home: 345 E 93rd St Apt 9H New York NY 10128-5518 Office: Mt Sinai Med Ctr Fifth Ave # 100th St New York NY 10029

PATAKY, PAUL ERIC, ophthalmologist; b. Phila., May 19, 1945; s. Andrew and Helen (Koffler) P.; m. Aimee Janet Margoles, June 13, 1971; Meryl Corinne, Lisa Ann. BS, Trinity Coll., 1966; MD, Pa. State Univ., 1971. Diplomate Am. Bd. Ophthalmology. Resident ophthalmology Mass. Eye & Ear Infirm, Boston, 1972-76; asst. in ophthalmology Harvard Medical Sch., Boston, 1976-79; ophthalmologist Dedham (Mass.) Medical Assocs., 1976-79, Paul E. Pataky M.D. P.A., Boynton Beach, Fla., 1979—; chmn. dept. of surgery Bethesda Meml. Hosp., Boynton Beach, 1988-89; pres. medical staff, 1990-91, chmn. credentials chmn., 1992-93, chmn. surgical care com., 1993—. Fellow Am. Acad. Ophthalmology; mem. Fla. Soc. Ophthalmology, AMA, Pan-Am. Assn. Ophthalmology, Palm Beach County Medical Soc., Fla. Medical Assn. Office: 2623 S Seacrest Blvd # 102 Boynton Beach FL 33435

PATARCA, ROBERTO, immunologist, molecular biologist, physician; b. Caracas, Venezuela, Feb. 12, 1958; came to U.S., 1981; s. Umberto Jose and Ivonne Noemi (Montero) P. MS, Ctrl. U. Venezuela, Caracas, 1981; PhD, Harvard U., 1987; MD, U. Miami, 1994. HCLD, Am. Bd. Bioanalysis. Computer programmer, systems analyst Centro Medico Docente La Trinidad, Caracas, 1978-81; rsch. fellow Mt. Sinai Sch. Medicine and Columbia U., N.Y.C., 1981-82, MIT-NASA Program, Boston, 1982; from rsch. fellow to asst. prof. pathology Harvard Med. Sch., Boston, 1982-90; asst. prof. medicine/immunology/microbiology U. Miami, Fla., Fla., 1994—; sci. dir. E.M. Papper lab. clin. immunology U. Miami, Fla., 1994—; teaching asst. Ctr. and Met. U., Caracas, 1977-80; lectr. and presenter in field. Co-editor Jour. Chronic Fatigue Syndrome and Critical Reviews in Oncogenesis/Clin. Mgmt. Chronic Fatigue Syndrome, 1994—; contbr. articles to profl. jours. Sub-guide Boy Scouts Am., Caracas, 1971-73; stake missionary Ch. of Jesus Christ of Latter Day Sts., Boston, 1985. Decorated Order of Merit (Venezuela); recipient Licha Lopez award Harvard Med. Sch., 1984, Richard A. Smith Rsch. award Dana-Farber Cancer Inst., 1989, Rsch. Distinction in Immunology U. Miami, 1994; Conicit and Gran Mariscal de Ayacucho Found. scholar, 1976-87, Am. Found. AIDS Rsch. scholar, 1990-93. Mem. AAAS, ACP, AMA, Fla. and Dade County Med. Assn., Clin. Immunology Soc., N.Y. Acad. Scis., Peruvian Soc. Immunology and Allergy, Alpha Omega Alpha. Home: 16445 Collins Ave Apt 328 Miami FL 33160-4562 Office: U Miami Sch Medicine PO Box 016960 Miami FL 33138

PATARLAGEANU, RADU CONSTANTIN, surgeon, consultant; b. Bucharest, Romania, Aug. 3, 1925; came to Germany, 1973; m. Constantin and Elena (Nestorescu) P.; m. Nora-Gerta Heidel, Aug. 16, 1952; children—Edda Antonia, Nora Joan. M.D., Faculty Medicine, Bucharest, Romania, 1949, D.Medicine, 1951, Traumatology, 1968, Resident surgeon State Hosp. 1, Brasov, Romania, 1949-55, cons. surgeon, 1955-57; cons. surgeon State Hosp., Budesti, Romania, 1962-64; chief surgeon State Hosp., Fierbinti, Urziceni, 1964-73; sr. surgeon Country Hosp., Sigmaringen, W.Ger., 1973-74; practice medicine specializing in surgery, Muhleim, W.Ger., 1974-89, ret., 1989; cons. medicine Shacko, Wieser, Lawton, Oswald Leibinger, Fridingen, Muhleim, Tuttlingen, Kolbingen, W.Ger., 1976-89. Columnist, reporter, contbr. articles to profl. jours. Chmn. Christian Democratic Union, 1983-85. Served as sgt. Med. Service, 1944. Polit. prisoner Law Ct. Bucharest, State Security Prison Malmaison, 1957-58. Mem. Medecins Union, U.S. Strategic Inst., Inst. Francais des Relations Internationales. Orthodox. Avocations: political economy studies, U.S. history, sovietology. Home: Berchenstrasse 2, D-78532 Tuttlingen 16, Germany

PATCHETT, STEPHEN EDMUND, physician, consultant; b. Cork, Ireland, Sept. 27, 1960; Arrived in England, 1990; s. Denis Maude and Iside (Pagarin) P.; m. Una Margaret O'Flanagan, May 21, 1988; children: Caoimhe, Elle. MB, BCH, BAO, U. Coll. Dublin, 1984; MRCPI, Royal Coll. Physicians, Dublin, 1987; MD, U.C.D., Dublin, 1992. Houseman St. Vincent's Hosp., Dublin, Ireland, 1984-88, sr. house officer, 1985-87, registrar, 1987-89; lectr. Meath Hosp., Dublin, 1989-90; rsch. fellow St. Bartholomew's Hosp., London, 1990-93, sr. registrar, 1993-95, sr. lectr., 1995—. Author: (book) Pocket Essentials of Clinical Medicine, 1995; contbr. articles to profl. jours. Mem. Am. Gastroenterological Assn., British Soc. Gastroenterology, British Medical Assn. Home: 216 Windsor Rd, SL6 2DW Maidenhead Berkshire England Office: Dept Gastroenterology, St Bartholomews Hosp, EC1A 7BE London England

PATEL, ANIL S., biomedical engineer, researcher, medical products executive; b. Baroda, India, June 28, 1939; came to U.S. 1961; s. Shankerbhai S. and Gangaben T. P.; children: Ravi, Sunil; m. Asha Rairkar, Aug. 22, 1992. BS, U. Baroda, India, 1960; MS, Purdue U., 1963; PhD, Northwestern U., 1966; postgrad., Stanford U., 1993. Sr. research scientist Baxter Travenol Labs. Inc., Morton Grove, Ill., 1968-74; chief scientist Cavitron Corp., N.Y.C., 1974-79; chief scientist and mgr. advanced products research Cooper Vision Systems div. Cooper Vision Inc. (formerly Cavitron Corp.), Irvine, Calif., 1979-83, Cooper Vision Inc. div., Bellevue, Wash., 1983-86, dir. advanced product research, chief scientist, Cooper Vision CILCO div. The Cooper Cos., Inc., Bellevue, 1986-89; dir. rsch. intra ocular lens Alcon Labs., Inc., Ft. Worth, 1989-92, sr. dir. rsch. surg. products, 1993—. Contbr. articles to profl. jours.; patentee in field. Organizer Highland Park (Ill.) Chess Club, 1970-74, White Plains Chess Club, N.Y., 1974-77. NIH postdoctoral fellow Northwestern U., 1966-67; recipient free passage from India to U.S., Ministry Sci. and Cultural Affairs of Govt. India, 1961. Fellow Am. Soc. Laser Medicine and Surgery (founder); mem. Assn. Advancement Med. Instrumentation (chmn. infrared warmers and incubators standards com. 1978-80, pulmonary function devices-spirometer standards subcom. 1978-80), Am. Nat. Standards Inst. (com. intraocular lenses standard 1988-94, viscoelastic ophthalmic devices 1992—, apptd. tech. expert del. U.S.A. tech. adv. group Internat. Standards Orgn. tech. com.), Am. Soc. Cataract and Refractive Surgery, Assn. Research in Vision and Ophthalmology, Inc., Internat. Soc. Refractive Keratoplasty, AAAS, IEEE, Soc. Biomaterials, Sigma Xi. Home: 4202 Brownwood Ln Arlington TX 76017-4126

PATEL, MULCHAND SHAMBHUBHAI, biochemist, researcher; b. Sipor, India, Sept. 9, 1939; came to U.S., 1965; s. Shambhubhai J. and Puriben (Patel) P.; m. Kankuben M. Patel; children: Sumitra, Yashomati, Mayank. BS, Gujarat U., 1961; MS, U. Baroda, 1964; PhD, U. Ill., 1968. Asst. prof. pediatric rsch. Sch. Medicine Temple U., Phila., 1970-72, rsch. asst. prof. medicine, 1972-75, rsch. asst. prof. biochemistry, 1970-75, rsch. assoc. prof. biochem. medicine, 1975-78; assoc. prof. biochemistry Case Western Res. U. Sch. Medicine, Cleve., 1978-86, prof., 1986-93; prof., chmn. biochemistry SUNY, Buffalo, 1993—; mem. NIH biochem. study sect. 2, 1984-88; mem. editl. bd. Jour. Biol. Chem., 1991—. Author, co-author research articles. Recipient Gold Medal in Biochemistry, U. Baroda, 1973, Fulbright Research Scholar award to India, 1987; prin. investigator, research grantee NIH. Mem. Am. Soc. for Biochemistry and Molecular Biology, Am. Inst. Nutrition, Biochem. Soc. London, Am. Soc. Neurochemists, Internat. Soc. Neurochemistry. Office: SUNY-Dept Biochemistry Sch Medicine 140 Farber Hall 3435 Main St Buffalo NY 14214

PATEL, PRAVIN CHATURBHAI, physician, consulting surgeon; b. Pij, Gujarat, India, Oct. 3, 1949; s. Chaturbhai Somabhai and Chanchalben Chaturbhai (Patel) P.; m. Nayana Pravinbhai, July 22, 1973; children: Nirav, Sonal. MBBS, U. Gujarat (India), 1965. Intern surgery, ob-gyn., medicine, 1971-72; sr. house officer SHO, gen. surgery New Civil Hosp., Ahmedabad, India, 1973-74, registrar gen. surgery, 1974; clin. attachment in gen. surgery St. Mary's Hosp., Eastbourne, Sussex, Eng., 1974; sr. house officer SHO, A&E, orthopedic surgery Leicester (Eng.) Royal Infirmary, 1975-76, sr. house officer SHO ENT, 1976, sr. house officer SHO gen. surgery, 1976-77; sr. house officer rotating SHO, A&E dept. with hand surgery, orthop. surgery with pediat. orthop. and gen. surgery with peripheral vascular surgery West Hill Hosp., Joyce Green Hosp., Dartford, Kent, Eng., 1977-78; registrar gen. surgery Kent Hosp., W. Hill Hosp., Dartford, Eng., 1978-79; registraar gen. surgery N. Oxfordshire sector Horton Gen. Hosp., Banbury, Oxon, Eng., 1980-82; registrar gen. surgery Victoria Hosp., Blackpool, Eng., 1982-84; specialist grade 1 gen. surgery King Faisal Hosp., Taif, Saudi Arabia, 1984-87; cons. surgeon, sr. registrar, registrar in gen. Medi-Call Locum Agy., Eng., 1987-88; dep. dir. surg. directorate depts. surgery, anesthesia & renal unit, cons. surgeon Armed Forces Hosp. so. region, Khamis Mushayt, Saudi Arabia, 1988-96; pvt. practice Middlesex, Eng. 1996—; mem. day surgery user's com., theatre user's com., med. exec. com., OR com., disaster planning com.; presenter in field. Contbr. numerous articles to profl. jours. Fellow Royal Coll. Surgeons. Home: 507 Kenton Rd Kenton-Harrow Middlesex, England HA3 O4L Office: Armed Forces Hosps. Program, PO Box 101, Khamis Mushayt Saudi Arabia

PATEL, RAFIQ KASSAMALI, surgeon; b. Bombay, Feb. 20, 1938; came to U.S., 1974; s. Kassamali and Rahembanc Patel; m. Yasmina Patel, July 7, 1967; children: Maheen, Samia, Riaz. BS, Xavier Coll., Bombay, 1955; MD, Dow Med. Coll., Karachi, Pakistan, 1960. Cert. diplomate of Brit. Bd. of Surgeons. Assoc. prof. surgery Dow Med. Coll. and Civil Hosp., Karachi, 1965-69; sr. surgeon S.I.T.E. Hosp., Mangcpir, Karachi, 1970-72; med. staff pres., chief of staff Fallston Gen. Hosp., Md., 1979; med. dir. Fallston Gen. Hosp., 1980-88, attending surgeon, 1975-92; attending surgeon Hartford Meml. Hosp., Havre de Grace, 1975-92; mem. Aga Khan Found., 1966-73; bd. dirs. Aga Khan Univ. Hosp., Karachi, 1985-92. Fellow Royal Coll. Surgeons, Am. Coll. Surgeons; mem. MED-CHI, Harford Med. Counties Soc. Republic. Republic. Muslim. Office: Walk-In Medical Ctr 1952 Pulaski Hwy Edgewood MD 21040-1617

PATEL, SHIRIS RANCHHODBHAI, anesthesiologist; b. Nikora, Gujarat, India, Nov. 1, 1957; came to U.S., 1987; s. Ranchhodbhai Lallubhai and Sushilaben-Ranchhodbhai Patel; m. Shila Shiris, Apr. 8, 1985; children: Amish, Alpesh. M.B.B.S., U. Ibadan (Nigeria), 1979, diploma in anesthesia, 1981. Cert. Am. Bd. Anesthesiologists. H.O. registrar, SNR registrar Univ. Coll. Hosp., Ibadan, 1979-85; registrar Royal Surrey County Hosp., Guildford, Eng., 1985-87, Lister Hosp., Stevenage, Eng., 1987; resident, fellow Montefiore Med. Ctr., Bronx, N.Y., 1988-89; attending, asst. prof. Albert Einstein Coll. of Medicine, Bronx, 1989-90; pvt. practice anesthesiology Carson, Newsome & Patel, MD, PA, Laurel, Md., 1990—; chmn. quality assurance anesthesiology dept. Carson, Newsome & Patel, MD, PA, Laurel, 1991—. Fellow Royal Coll. Surgeons Eng., Am. Soc. Anesthesiology. Hindu. Home: 8201 Darting Minnow Laurel MD 20723-1078

PATEL, TARUN R., pharmaceutical scientist; b. Borsad, Gujarat, India, Feb. 18, 1952; s. Ramesh C. and Savitaben R.; m. Nilima T. Patel, Feb. 17, 1981; children: Vishal, Shalini, Neha. BS in Pharmacy, Tex. So. U., 1975; PhD in Pharmaceutics, U. Iowa, 1980. Registered pharmacist Tex., Ill., Ind. Scientist Ortho Pharm. Corp., Raritan, N.J., 1980-82; sr. scientist Ortho Pharm. Corp., Raritan, 1982; group leader, mfg. engr. Bristol Labs., Syracuse, N.Y., 1982-83; mgr. process engring. Bristol Labs., Syracuse, 1983-84, dir. process engring., 1984-86; assoc. dir. process engring. Bristol Myers-USPNG, Evansville, Ind., 1986-90; dir. pharm. devel. Schering-Plough Corp., Memphis, 1990-94, sr. dir. pharm. devel., 1994—; adj. prof. U. Tenn., Memphis, 1991—. Contbr. articles to profl. jours. Recipient Remington award Tex. So. Univ., 1975. Mem. Am. Assn. Pharm. Scientists, Am. Pharm. Assn. Office: Schering-Plough Corp 3030 Jackson Ave Memphis TN 38112-2020

PATELL, MAHESH, pharmacist, researcher; b. Ahmedabad, Gujarat, India, June 14, 1937; came to U.S., 1962.; s. Kantilal K. and Maniben K. Patell; m. Rajeshvari S. Amin, Sept. 6, 1967; children: Milan, Rupel. BS in Pharmacy, L.M. Coll. of Pharmacy, Ahmedabad, 1960; MS in Pharmacy, St Louis Coll., 1964. Rsch. pharmacist Rexall Drug Co., St. Louis, 1968-74; mgr. tech. info. svcs. Cord Labs., Bloomfield, Colo., 1974-77; rsch. investigator K.V. Pharms., St. Louis, 1977-79; section head-health care product devel. Bristol Myers-Squibb, Hillside, N.J., 1979—. Mem. Am. Assn. Pharmaceutical Scientists, Controlled Release Soc., Pa. Mfg. Confectioners Assn. Hindu. Home: 4 Farrington St Edison NJ 08820-1921 Office: Bristol Myers Squibb 1350 Liberty Ave Hillside NJ 07205-1805

PATERSON, EILEEN, radiation oncologist, educator; b. Bklyn., Oct. 16, 1939; d. John Alexander and Frances (Rabito) P.; m. Bruce Leroy Benedict, Jan. 2, 1981. BA, Wilson Coll., Chambersburg, Pa., 1961; MD, Woman's Med. Coll. Pa., 1965. Diplomate Am. Bd. Radiation Oncology, Am. Bd. Nuclear Medicine. Intern Highland Hosp., Rochester, N.Y., 1965-66; resident radiology (radiation therapy) U. Rochester, 1966-69; asst. prof. radiation oncology U. Rochester, N.Y., 1970-83, assoc. prof., 1983—; chief dept. radiation oncology Rochester Gen. Hosp., 1983—; cons. Arnot Ogden Hosp., Elmira, N.Y., 1970-74, Genesee Hosp., Rochester, 1983—. Contbr. articles to med. jours. Mem. Am. Coll. Radiology, Am. Soc. Therapeutic Radiology and Oncology. Office: Rochester Gen Hosp 1425 Portland Ave Rochester NY 14621-3001

PATINKIN, TERRY ALLAN, physician; b. Oak Park, Ill., Feb. 1, 1950; s. Lester D. and Marcella Jaqueline (Steinburg) P.; m. Sandra Lee Friedman, Apr. 21, 1985; children: Jonathan, Zachary. BS, U. Ill., 1971; MD, U. Calif., San Francisco, 1975; MPH in health care mgmt., Harvard U., 1996. Diplomate Am. Bd. Emergency Medicine, Am. Bd. Family Medicine. Intern, resident in family practice U. Calif. San Francisco/Natividad Med. Ctr., Salinas, Calif., 1975-78; assoc. dir. family medicine residency program U. Calif. San Francisco/Natividad Med. Ctr., Salinas, 1978-90; dir. emergency dept. Natividad Med. Ctr., Salinas, 1985-91, dir. continuing med. edn., 1978-91, dir. undergrad. edn., 1978-90, emergency physician, 1979-91; emergency physician Sturdy Meml. Hosp., Attleboro, Mass., 1991-94; dir. emergency dept. Roger Williams Hosp., Providence, 1994—; asst. clin. prof. U. Calif., San Francisco, 1981-88, assoc. clin. prof., 1988-91; clin. asst. prof. Stanford U., 1990-93; asst. clin. prof. Brown U., Providence, 1995—. Fellow Am. Coll. Emergency Physicians; mem. U. Ill. Alumni Assn. (life), U. Calif. San Francisoco Alumni Faculty Assn. Office: Roger Williams Med Ctr 825 Chalkstone Ave Providence RI 02908

PATIPA, MICHAEL, ophthalmic plastic surgeon; b. Nathanya, Israel, July 12, 1949; came to the U.S., 1955; s. Eugene and Marie (Kirschenbaum) P.; m. Bonnie Black, Aug. 25, 1979; children: Leah, Elizabeth. BS, Emory U., 1971; MD, U. Miami, 1976. Intern Jackson Meml. Hosp., Miami, Fla., 1976-77; resident ophthalmology Med. Coll. Ga., Augusta, 1977-80; ophthalmic plastic and reconstructive fellow SX U. Tex., Houston, 1980-81; physician Oculoplastic and Orbital Cons., P.A., West Palm Beach, Fla.; Diplomate Am. Bd. Ophthalmology. Author: Plastic and Reconstructive Surgery of Eyelids, 1996; editor Cosmetic Surgery Jour. Survey of Ophthalmology, 1996; inventor in field. Fellow Am. Acad. Ophthalmology; mem. Fla. Soc. Ophthalmology (v.p. 1992—). Office: Oculplastic & Orbital Cons 2501 N Flagler Dr West Palm Beach FL 33407

PATRICELLI, ROBERT E., health care company executive; b. Hartford, Conn., Dec. 9, 1939; s. Leonard J. and Lydia E. Patricelli; m. Margaret Patricelli; children—Thomas, Alison. A.B. with high honors, Wesleyan U., Middletown, Conn., 1961; LL.B. cum laude, Harvard U., 1965. Bar: N.Y. 1967. White House fellow U.S. Dept. State, Washington, 1965-66; minority counsel U.S. Senate Subcom. Employment, Manpower and Poverty, Washington, 1966-69; dep. asst. sec., dep. undersec. HEW, Washington, 1969-71; v.p. Greater Hartford Process, Devco, Conn., 1971-75; adminstr. Urban Mass Transp. Adminstrn., U.S. Dept. Transp., Washington, 1975-77; v.p. govt. relations CIGNA Corp., Hartford, Conn., 1977-79, v.p., sr. v.p., exec. v.p. corp. services, 1979-83, pres. affiliated bus. group, 1983-86; chmn., chief exec. officer Value Health Inc., Avon, Conn., 1987—. Bd. dirs. Hartford Hosp., 1994—, Health Spring, Inc., 1994-95; bd. dirs. U.S. C. of C., 1990—, chmn. health and employee benefits com., 1990-94; trustee N.E. Utilities Corp., 1993—, Wesleyan U., 1993—. Recipient Disting. Alumnus award Wesleyan U., 1986; Fulbright scholar U. Paris, 1962. Mem. Inst. of Medicine. Office: Value Health Inc 22 Waterville Rd Avon CT 06001-2066

PATRICK, BERNARD SUTHERLAND, neurosurgeon; b. Booneville, Miss., Feb. 16, 1927; s. Bernard and Hortense P.; m. Jo Kurns, June 17, 1950; children: Karen Patrick Orsini, Kimberly Patrick Farrow, Kristen Patrick Mink, Kathleen Patrick Morgan. Student, Tulane U., 1944-45; BS, U. Miss., 1948; MD, U. Ill., Chgo., 1950. Diplomate Am. Bd. Neurol. Surgeons. Intern Augustana Hosp., Chgo., 1946-48; resident in gen. surgery St. Luke's Hosp., Chgo., 1953-54; resident in neuropathology U. Ill., Chgo., 1954; resident in neurology, neurosurgery U. Ill. Rsch. and Ednl. Hosps./St. Luke's Hosp., 1954-57; pvt. practice Memphis, 1957-68, Jackson, Miss., 1968—; instr. U. Tenn. Sch. Medicine, Memphis, 1957-68; assoc. prof. U. Miss. Sch. Medicine, Jackson, 1968-78, clin. assoc. prof., 1979-89, clin. prof., 1989—; presenter papers at med. confs.. Contbr. papers to med. jours. Capt., flight surgeon, USAF, 1951-53. Mem. Am. Assn. Neurol. Surgeons, Congress Neurol. Surgeons (pres. 1973), So. Neurosurg. Soc., AMA, ACS, Soc. Neurol. Surgeons, Assn. Am. Physicians and Surgeons, Memphis Neurol. Soc., Found. for Internat. Edn. in Neurosurgery (treas. 1974-80), Phi Kappa Epsilon. Office: B Patrick Neurol Surgery 971 Lakeland Dr Ste 620 Jackson MS 39216-4608

PATRICK, GEORGE MILTON, dentist; b. Accoville, W.Va., Sept. 27, 1920; s. Milton Michael and Martha Mary (Mullins) P.; m. Shirley Ann Rutherford, Mar. 22, 1952 (div. June 1966); 1 child, Geoffrey Milton (dec.); m. Jane Lee Austin, Oct. 1, 1971; stepchildren: Duke Anthony-Spencer Austin, T.L.C. Hughes. BS, Capital U., 1950; DDS, Ohio State U., 1955; postgrad., U. N.C., 1972. Gen. practice dentistry Columbus, Ohio, 1956-67; dir. mktg. and rsch. Kirkman Labs., Portland, Oreg., 1968; gen. practice dentistry specializing in orthodontics Columbus, 1968; pub. health dentist Ohio Dept. Health, Bowling Green, Ohio, 1968-80; practice dentistry specializing in pedodontics, 1980-82; pvt. practice computer cons. Columbus, 1982-87, mgmt. cons., 1987—; pres. Shamrock Patrick Cons., 1991—. Prodn. mgr. Vaud-Vilities, Columbus, 1979-86; singer First Community Ch., Columbus, 1972-90, Opera/Columbus Chorus, 1984-86. 2d lt. U.S. Army, 1942-46, ETO. Decorated Soldier's Medal Bronze Star, Purple Heart with Oak Leaf Cluster. Mem. ADA, Ohio Dental Assn., Columbus Dental Soc. (chmn. children's dental health week), Columbus Coun. World Affairs, Pub. Rels. Soc. (membership com. 1986), Career Execs. of Columbus (pres. 1987-91). Home and Office: 2610 Love Dr Columbus OH 43221-2645

PATRICK, JANET CLINE, personnel company executive; b. San Francisco, June 30, 1934; d. John Wesley and Edith Bertha (Corde) Cline; m. Robert John Patrick Jr., June 13, 1959 (div. 1988); children: John McKinnon, Stewart McLellan, William Robert. BA with distinction, Stanford U., 1955; postgrad. U. Calif.-Berkeley, 1957, George Washington U., 1978-82. English tchr. George Washington H.S., San Francisco, 1957, K.D. Burke Sch., San Francisco, 1957-59, Berkeley Inst., Bklyn., 1959-63; placement counselor Washington Sch. Secs., Washington, 1976-78, asst. dir. placement, 1978-81; mgr. med. personnel service Med. Soc. D.C., 1981-89, pres. Med. Pers. Svcs. Inc., 1989—. Chmn. area 2 planning com. Montgomery County Pub. Schs. (Md.), 1974-75; mem. vestry, corr. sec., Christ Ch., Kensington, Md., 1982-84, vestry, sr. warden, 1984-85, vestry, chmn. ann. giving com., 1986-89; chmn. long-range planning com., 1989-92, sec., 1992-93, jr. warden, 1994, co-chair capital campaign, 1996; fin. com. Montgomery County Pvt. Industry Coun., 1994. Mem. Met. D.C. Med. Group Mgmt. Assn., Phi Beta Kappa. Republican. Episcopalian. Club: Jr. League (Washington). Home: 5206 Carlton St Bethesda MD 20816-2306 Office: Med Personnel Svcs Inc 1707 L St NW Ste 250 Washington DC 20036-4201

PATRIZIO, PASQUALE, reproductive endocrinologist, andrologist, and infertility specialist; b. Torre Annunziata, Napoli, Italy, Jan. 31, 1959; came to U.S., 1988; s. Vincent and Assunta Patrizio; m. Teri Susan Ord, Aug. 27, 1993. MD summa cum laude, U. Naples, Italy, 1983. Diplomate of residency in ob-gyn., Italy; lic. physician, Calif., U.K., Italy; cert. Edn. Coun. for Fgn. Med. Grads. Intern in medicine and surgery U. Naples, 1983-84, resident in ob-gyn., 1983-87; postgrad. fellow in andrology U. Pisa, Italy, 1987-90; rsch. fellow in reproductive endocrinology and infertility U. Calif.-Irvine, Orange, 1988-90, resident in ob-gyn., 1989-93, clin. instr. in reproductive endocrinology and infertility dept. ob-gyn., 1993-94, asst. prof., 1994-95; dir. male infertility svc. Reproductive Endocrinology Fertility Ctr., San Antonio, 1995—; sr. house officer ob-gyn. Victoria Hosp. and Forth Park Hosp., Kirkcaldy, Fife, Scotland, 1986; sr. house officer ob-gyn. Royal Gwent Hosp., Newport, South Wales, 1987; clin. asst. in vitro fertilization and gametes intrafallopian transfer unit Dept. Reproductive Health, Bologna, Italy, 1987; pressenter in field. Contbr. chpts. to books, articles to med. jours. Recipient 1st prize for best rsch. paper Wyeth-Ayerst Labs., 1992; co-recipient Practicing Physician award Pacific Coast Fertility Soc., 1989, 92, 94, TAP Poster award Am. Fertility Soc., 1992; ACOG/Mead Johnson clin. fellow, 1992-93; Meml. Health Svcs. grantee, 1994-95. Fellow ACOG (jr.); mem. AMA, Am. Fertility Soc. (co-winner poster presentation 45th ann. meeting 1989), Am. Soc. Andrology, European Soc. Human Reprodn., Italian Soc. Fertility and Sterility (hon.), Italian Soc. Obstetricians & Gynecologists, Italian Soc. Andrology, Royal Coll. Obstetricians & Gynecologists (Eng.), Soc. for Study of Reprodn.

PATTEN, MAURINE DIANE, psychologist; b. Peoria, Ill., Aug. 30, 1940; d. Maurice H. and Esther Ann (Wilkenson) Foote; m. C. Alfred Patten, Aug. 26, 1961; children: Paul A., Bethany M. BS, Bradley U., 1961; MS, Chgo. State U., 1971; EdD, No. Ill. U., 1977. Lic. psychologist, Ill. Tchr. Elementary Schs., Skokie and Manhattan, Ill., 1961-63; dir. Southwest Coop Presch., Chgo., 1970-74; tchr. spl. edn. Dekalb County (Ill.) Spl. Edn. Assn., 1974-76, asst. dir., 1978-80; resource tchr. Sycamore (Ill.) Sch. Dist., 1976-78; asst. prof. Chgo. State U., 1980-81; pvt. practice as clin. psychologist Sycamore, 1981—; cons. Arthur Andersen & Co., St. Charles, Ill., 1981—; pvt. practice, 1981—. Fellow APA, Ill. Psychol. Assn. Methodist. Office: 964 W State St Sycamore IL 60178-1335

PATTERSON, DANIEL WILLIAM, dentist; b. Minot, N.D., Aug. 12, 1948; s. Girdell William and Fern Lemay (Sullivan) P. DDS, Northwestern U., 1974; Alumnus degree (hon.), U. Colo., 1977; BS in Biology, U.N.Y., 1993; M in Healthcare, U. Denver, 1994. Cert. health industry orgn., ops. U.Denver, 1993, cert. gerontology, 1996. Dentist Dan L. Hansen, DDS, P.C., Lakewood, Colo., 1974-75; pvt. practice dentistry Littleton, Colo., 1975-88; clin. instr. dept. applied dentistry U. Colo., Denver, 1981-83, lectr., 1983, clin. asst. prof. depts. restorative and applied dentistry, 1989-91, dir. advanced dentistry program, 1989-90, asst. prof. clin. track dept. restorative dentistry, 1991—. Mem. editorial adv. panel Dental Econs. Jour., 1981; also articles. Active Chatfield Jaycees, Littleton, 1976-81; vocal soloist, mem. Denver Concert Chorale, 1978-82. Lt. USN, 1968-74. Fellow Acad. Gen. Dentistry (bd. eligible certifying bd. gen. dentistry 1991); mem. ADA, Met. Denver Dental Soc., Colo. Dental Assn. (Pres.'s Honor Roll 1982-84), Mensa, Sedalia Wild Game Club. Lutheran. Home: 6984 N Fargo Trl Littleton CO 80125-9270 Office: U Colo Health Scis Ctr Sch Dentistry Box C-284 4200 E 9th Ave Denver CO 80262-0284

PATTERSON, D(OUGLAS) REID, pharmaceutical scientist; b. Port Arthur, Tex., July 30, 1945; s. Howard Hilliard and Rosa Nell (McPhail) P.; m. Mary Emilee Martin, Aug. 16, 1969; children: Keli Anne, Christopher Reid. BS, Tex. A&M U., 1968, DVM, 1969; PHD, U. Mo., 1976. Diplomate Am. Coll. of Lab. Animal Medicine, Am. Coll. Vet. Pathology, Am. Bd. Toxicology. Sr. staff pathologist Hazleton Labs. Am., Vienna, Va., 1975-78; head pathology Hazleton Labs. Europe, Harrogate, Eng., 1978-80; dir. medicine Hazleton Labs. Am., Vienna, 1980-81; supr. pathology/reproductive toxicology Shell Devel. Co., Houston, 1981-84; dir. pathology/toxicology Abbott Labs., Abbott Park, Ill., 1984-87, dir. drug safety, 1987-90; v.p. drug safety Abbott Labs, Abbott Park, Ill., 1990—; interim head neurosci. venture Abbott Labs., Abbott Park, Ill., 1992-93; adj. asst. prof. U. Tex. Med. Sch., Houston, 1983-84; asst. nat. program dir. Charles L. Davis, DVM Found., Sayre, N.Y., 1981-86. Contbr. articles to profl. jours. Mem. Lions Internat., Columbia, Mo., Houston, 1970-75; mem., v.p. Jaycees, Reston, Va., 1976-78; ruling elder Presbyn. Ch., Reston, Houston, 1976-78, 80-81. Named one of Outstanding Young Men of Am., Jaycees, 1977. Mem. Pharm. Mfg. Assn. (chmn. drug safety subsect. 1992-93), Soc. Toxicologic Pathologists (program chmn. 1988-91), Am. Coll. Vet. Pathologists (fin. com. 1985-91, councilor 1992-96), Gamma sigma Delta, Phi Kappa Phi, Phi Zeta, Sigma Xi. Republican. Office: Abbott Labs D-46G AP13A 100 Abbott Park Rd North Chicago IL 60064-3500

PATTERSON, HELEN CROSBY, clinical psychologist; b. Jackson, Miss., Nov. 12, 1947; d. Thomas Atkinson and Helen Elizabeth (Crosby) Patterson; m. Fred C. Craig, July 7, 1967 (div. July 1970); 1 child, Erin Crosby. BA in Psychology, Millsaps Coll., 1972; MS in Clin. Psychology, U. Wyo., 1976,

PhD in Clin. Psychology, 1978. Lic. clin. psychologist, Miss., N.Mex., Del. Coord., supervision and internships Antioch N.E. Grad. Sch., Keene, N.H., 1979-80; sr. clinician Jackson (Miss.) Mental Health Ctr., 1980-82; pvt. practice in Miss. and N.Mex., 1981—; clin. dir. Pain Mgmt. Ctr. St. Vincent Hosp., Santa Fe, N.Mex., 1990-91; psychol. cons. Disability Determination Svcs., Jackson, 1983—, Albuquerque, 1988-90, 91-93, Wilmington, Del., 1993-95; EAP cons., So. Beverage Co., Jackson, 1986-91, clin. dir. Pain Mgmt. Ctr., St. Vincent Hosp., Santa Fe, 1990-91. Mem. Hinds County Assn. for Children with Learning Disabilities, Jackson, 1985-88, Hinds County Mental Health Assn., Jackson, 1980-83. Mem. APA. Office: 11 Northtown Dr Ste 205 Jackson MS 39211 also: 3817 Don Juan Ct NW Albuquerque NM 87107-2812

PATTERSON, JAMES WILLIS, pathology and dermatology educator; b. Takoma Park, Md., Dec. 29, 1946; s. James Clark and Helen (Hendricks) P.; m. Julie Wyatt, Dec. 30, 1989; 1 child, James Wyatt. BA, Johns Hopkins U., 1968; MD, Med. Coll. Va., 1972. Diplomate Am. Bd. Dermatology, Am. Bd. Dermatopathology, Nat. Bd. Med. Examiners. Fellow dermatopathology Armed Forces Inst. Pathology, Washington, 1979-80; rotating intern in medicine Med. Coll. Va., Richmond, 1972-73, resident in dermatology, 1973-76, assoc. prof. pathology and dermatology, 1982-89, prof., 1989-92, dir. dermatopathology, 1982-92; clin. prof. dermatology and pathology Med. Coll. of Va., 1992-96; with Dermatology Assocs. of Va., 1992-96, Va. Dermatopathology Svcs., Richmond, 1992-96; prof. pathology and dermatology U. Va., 1996—; clin. instr. dermatology U. Colo. Med. Ctr., Denver, 1980-82; cons. in pathology McGuire VA Hosp., Richmond, 1982-92; cons. in pathology and dermatology Kenner Army Hosp., Ft. Lee, Va., 1982-95. Author: Dermatology: A Concise Textbook, 1987; contbr. over 100 articles on dermatology and pathology to med. jours.; asst. editor Jour. Cutaneous Pathology, 1989-94. Mem. nat. alumni schs. com. Johns Hopkins U., 1986—. With M.C., U.S. Army, 1976-82, col. Res. Recipient Stuart McEwen award Assn. Mil. Dermatologists, 1980, 82. Fellow ACP, Am. Acad. Dermatology, Am. Soc. Dermatopathology; mem. Va. Dermatol. Soc. (sec.-treas. 1984-88, v.p. 1988-89, pres. 1989-90), Johns Hopkins U. Alumni Assn. (pres. cen. Va. chpt. 1989), Tau Epsilon Phi (life). Republican. Presbyterian.

PATTERSON, JOHN C., clinical psychology researcher; b. Asheville, N.C.. BS in Psychology, Stephen F. Austin State U., MS in Psychology; PhD in Psychology, Tex. A&M U., 1981. Resident in psychology Wilford Hall USAF Med. Ctr., San Antonio, 1981; staff psychologist, maximum security unit Rusk State Psychiatric Hosp., Tex.; unit dir. USAF Sch. Aerospace Medicine; chief, aerospace clin. psychology function USAF Aeromed. Consultation Svc., 1985—; faculty mem. USAF Sch. Aerospace Medicine and U. Tex. Health Sci. Ctr., San Antonio (Psychiatry); internat. vis. lectr. in aeromed. neuropsychiatry; cons. in aerospace clin. psychology and neuropsychology evaluation; mem. NASA In-House Working Group on Astronaut Selection; cons. NASA. Contbr. over 30 articles to profl. jours.; rschr. in psychological factors associated with heart disease, aircrew and astronaut selection, spatial disorientation, aviator cognitive functioning, and airsickness; presenter in field. Recipient Armstrong Lab. Dirs. award for Rsch. 1993. Mem. APA, Aerospace Med. Assn. (Raymond F. Longacre award 1995), Am. Soc. Clin. Hypnosis, Internat. Neuropsychology Soc., AF Soc. for Clin. Psychologists, Bexar County Psychol. Assn. Office: USAF Aeromed Consultation Armstrong Lab Brooks AFB TX 78235

PATTERSON, JOHN RICHARD, obstetrician, gynecologist; b. Pekin, Ill., Aug. 7, 1932; s. John Sutton and Alma (Grove) P.; m. Anne Wayne Fuller, Dec. 27, 1958; children: John Richard Jr., Meredith Anne. AB in Chemistry, U. N.C., 1954, MD, 1958. Intern Med. Coll. Va., Richmond, 1958-59; resident in ob-gyn. U. Fla. Sch. Medicine, Gainesville, 1959-63; pvt. practice Danville (Va.) Ob-Gyn. Assocs., 1965—; mem. staff, bd. dirs. Danville Regional Med. Ctr. Capt. M.C., U.S. Army, 1963-65. Fellow Am. Coll. Ob-Gyn., Am. Fertility Soc., Danville-Pittsylvania Acad. Medicine. Office: Danville Ob-Gyn Assocs 101 Holbrook St Danville VA 24541-1732

PATTERSON, LLOYD CLIFFORD, psychiatrist; b. Toronto, Ont., Can., Jan. 16, 1917; came to U.S., 1942; s. William Henry and Florence May (Sonley) P.; m. Gloria May Patterson, Nov. 12, 1943; children: Diane Meisenheimer, Pamela DeBarr. MD, U. Western Ont., London, 1942. Diplomate Am. Bd. Psychiatry; cert. Am. Psychoanalytic Assn. Intern Hollywood Presybn. Hosp., L.A., 1942-43; fellow in intern medicine U. Calif. Hosp., San Francisco, 1943-44; resident in psychiatry Langley Porter Neuropsychiat. Inst., San Francisco, 1944-48; cons. psychiatrist student health U. Calif., Berkeley, 1960-70; assoc. clin. prof. U. Calif. Med. Sch., San Francisco, 1972—; dir. med. edn. Alta Bates Med. Ctr., Berkeley, 1988—; program chair Western Divisional Psychoanalytic meetings, San Francisco, 1966. Mem. East Bay Psychiat. Assn. (pres. 1962), No. Calif. Psychiat. Assn. (pres. 1968-69), San Francisco Psychoanalytic Soc. (pres. 1972-73), Am. Psychiat. Soc., Am. Psychoanalytic Soc., Calif. Med. Assn. (hosp. surveyor, mem. continuing med. edn. com. 1985-91, cons. CME com. 1992), Alameda Contra Costa Med. Assn. Home: 409 Cola Ballena Alameda CA 94501-3608 Office: 3021 Telegraph Ave Berkeley CA 94705-2013

PATTERSON, NANCY HORD, psychologist, registered nurse; b. Gainesville, Fla., Jan. 19, 1943; d. James Harvey and Crystal (Littlejohn) H.; children: Kathryn Gillis Jones, Crystal L. Gillis, Caren L. Gillis. AA, AS, Fla. Jr. Coll., 1971, 74; BA, U. North Fla., 1976, MA, 1978; PhD, U. Fla., 1984. Pres. Counseling Svcs., Inc., Jacksonville, 1978—; prof. Jacksonville U., U. North Fla., 1978—; adv. bd. Mental Health Assn., Jacksonville. Founder Nat. Graves' Disease Found., 1990. Mem. ANA, Assn. Ind. Psychotherapists (co-founder), Nat. Bd. Cert. Counselors. Office: 2 Tsitsi Ct Brevard NC 28712

PATTERSON, NANCY SYBLE, medical technologist; b. Tuskahoma, Okla., May 24, 1937; d. Paul Eugene and Lena Irene (Henderson) Moon; m. Truman Everett Patterson; children: Rex Everett, Teresa Annette Stuever, Diana J. Lohman, Jonathan Andrew. Grad. h.s., 1955. Cert. med. technician. Lab asst., tissue lab. St. Joseph Hosp., Wichita, Kans., 1955-56; histology technician St. Francis Hosp., Wichita, 1957-63; lab. technician Latimer County Gen. Hosp., Wilburton, Okla., 1979-85; med. technologist Choctaw Nation Indian Hosp., Talihina, Okla., 1985-87, Family Physicians, Wichita, 1988-91, Carriage Park br. Wichita Clinic, 1991—. Mem. Am. Soc. Med. Technologists, Am. Soc. Clin. Pathologists. Mem. Ch. of God. Office: Wichita Clinic Carriage Park Br 818 Carriage Pkwy Wichita KS 67209

PATTERSON, ROGER LEWIS, psychologist; b. Opelika, Ala., Oct. 30, 1939; s. Homer Lee and Ruby (White) P.; BA, Auburn U., 1963, MS, 1965; PhD, Fla. State U., 1971; m. Maritza Nunez de Gracia, Dec. 21, 1967; children: Anne Marie, Richard Allen. Clin. rsch. unit Camarillo (Calif.) State Hosp., 1969-72; psychologist and dir. day treatment Mental Health Ctr. of Escambia County, Pensacola, Fla., 1972-73; psychologist U. Ala. and Montgomery Police Dept., 1974-75; mem. faculty Fla. Mental Health Inst., Tampa, 1975-84, dir. gerontology program, 1977-84; adj. assoc. prof. dept. psychology U. So. Fla., 1977-84, clin. assoc. prof. dept. psychiatry Coll. Medicine 1984-85; assoc. project dir. Suncoast Gerontology Ctr., 1984; dir. geriatric psychosocial rehab. program VA Med. Ctr., Tuskegee, Ala., 1984-86; clin. coord. combined adult day health care and day treatment program VA Outpatient Clinic, Daytona Beach, Fla., 1986—; internat. speaker in field. Served with U.S. Army, 1961-62. Mem. APA, Am. Bd. Med. Psychotherapists (profl. adv. coun.), Behavior Therapy and Rsch. Soc. (clin. fellow). Author, editor books; contbr. chpts. to books, articles to profl. jours. Office: VA Outpatient Clinic 1900 Mason Ave Daytona Beach FL 32117-5103

PATTERSON, RONALD R(OY), health care systems executive; b. Baton Rouge, Mar. 4, 1942. BS, U. Houston, 1965; MS, Trinity U., San Antonio, 1973. Asst. adminstr. Med. Br. Tex. U., Galveston, 1972-75; asst. v.p. Hosp. Affiliates Internat., Nashville, 1975-81; chief oper. officer Affiliated Hosp. Systems, Houston, 1981-82; sr. v.p. Republic Health Corp., Dallas, 1982-88; pres. Miller Patterson Inc., Plano, Tex., 1988-89; ind. healthcare mgmt. cons. Plano, 1989-90; sr. v.p. Harris Meth. Health System, Ft. Worth, Tex., 1990-91; exec. v.p., COO Champion Healthcare Corp., Houston, Tex., 1991-96; exec. v.p., pres. healthcare ops. Paracelsus Healthcare Corp., Houston, 1996—; bd. govs. Fedn. Am. Health Systems, 1996—. Fellow Am. Coll. Healthcare Execs.; mem. Tex. Hosp. Assn. (vice chmn. multi-hosp. constituency 1987), Fedn. Am. Health Sys. (bd. govs. 1996—). Office: Champion Healthcare Corp 515 W Greens Rd Ste 800 Houston TX 77067

PATTERSON, ROY, physician, educator; b. Ironwood, Mich., Apr. 26, 1926; s. Donald I. and Helmi (Lantta) P. M.D., U. Mich., 1953. Diplomate: Am. Bd. Internal Medicine, Am. Bd. Allergy and Immunology. Intern U. Mich. Hosp., Ann Arbor, 1953-54; med. asst. research U. Mich. Hosp., 1954-55, med. resident, 1955-57, instr. dept. medicine, 1957-59; attending physician VA Research Hosp., Chgo., Northwestern Meml. Hosp.; mem. faculty Northwestern U. Med. Sch., Chgo., 1959—; prof. medicine Northwestern U. Med. Sch., 1964—, Ernest S. Bazley prof. medicine, chief sect. allergy-immunology dept. medicine. Editor: Jour. Allergy and Clin. Immunology, 1973-78. Served with USNR, 1944-46. Fellow Am. Acad. Allergy (pres. 1976), A.C.P.; mem. Central Soc. for Clin. Research (pres. 1978-79). Office: Northwestern U Med Sch Dept Medicine 303 E Chicago Ave Chicago IL 60611-3008

PATTERSON, RUSSEL HUGO, JR., neurosurgeon, educator; b. Apr. 1, 1929; s. Russel Hugo and Virginia (Fox) P.; m. Juliet Boyd, Nov. 25, 1955; children: Juliet Richie, Russel Hugo III, Alexander Canning. BA, Stanford U., 1948; MD, Cornell U., N.Y.C., 1952. Diplomate Am. Bd. Neurol. Surgery (vice chmn. 1981-82). Intern in surgery N.Y. Hosp., N.Y.C., 1952-53, asst. resident surgeon, 1955-57, asst. resident neurosurgeon, 1957-59, resident neurosurgeon, 1959-60, successively provisional asst., asst. attending, assoc. attending neurosurgeon, 1960-71, attending surgeon-in-charge, 1971—; rotating resident in neurosurgery Meml. Hosp., N.Y.C., 1957-60, cons. assoc. neurosurgeon, 1966—, assoc. attending surgeon, 1971—; asst. in surgery Cornell U. Med. Coll., N.Y.C., 1955-59, from instr. to clin. instr., 1959-63, asst. prof. surgery, 1963-68, assoc. prof., 1968-71, prof., 1971—; pvt. practice N.Y.C., 1962—. Contbr. numerous articles to profl jours. With M.C. U.S. Army, 1953-55. Mem. AMA, ACS, AAAS, Med. Soc. State N.Y., N.Y. County Med. Assn., N.Y. Soc. Neurosurgery (pres. 1976-78), Am. Assn. Neurol. Surgeons (pres. 1985-86), N.Y. Neurol. Soc., N.Y. State Neurosurg. Soc. (pres. 1972-73), Pan Am. Med. Assn., N.Y. Acad. Medicine, N.Y. Med. and Surg. Soc. (sec. 1973-75, pres. 1981), Internat. Soc. Surgery, Am. Surg. Assn., Soc. Neurol. Surgeons (pres. 1989-90), Am. Acad. Neurol. Surgeons (sec. 1972-76, pres.-elect 1982, pres. 1984), Soc. Stereotaxic and Functional Surgery, Internat. Soc. Pediatric Neurosurgery, Soc. Brit. Neurol. Surgeons (corr.), Nat. Med. Vets. Soc., German Neurosurgical Soc. Office: 525 E 68th St New York NY 10021-4873

PATTERSON, SAMUEL S., endodontist, educator; b. Indpls., Mar. 8, 1917; s. Abraham and Rose (Foreman) P.; m. Eunice Brenner, June 29, 1952; children: Alan B., Steven M. DDS, Ind. U., 1940, MSD, 1960. Diplomate Am. Bd. Endodontists. Instr. Ind. U., Indpls., 1949-52, asst. prof., 1952-55, assoc. prof., 1955-60, prof., dir. grad. endodontis, 1960-73; chmn. dept. endodontics Ind. U., Bloomington, 1973-86, prof. emeritis, 1986—; cons. VA, Indpls., 1977; dentist-in-residence Nat. VA, Washington, 1979-83; mem. active staff St. Vincent Health and Hosp. Ctr. Co-author: Endodontics, 1960, Surgical Endodontics, 1980, Methods of Endodontics, 1952. Maj. AUS, 1941-46. Recipient Maynard K. Hine award Ind. Dental Assn., 1990. Fellow Am. Coll. Dentists, Internat. Coll. Dentists; mem. Am. Assn. Endodontists (nat. pres. 1968-69, Edgar Coolidge award 1989), Ind. Dental Assn. (Maynard K. Hine award 1990), Indpls. Dental Assn. (pres. 1964-65, Honor Dentist of Yr. award 1988), Indpls. Athletic Club, Rotary. Home: 4536 N Meridian St Indianapolis IN 46208-3536 Office: 8402 Harcourt Rd Indianapolis IN 46260-2006 *Died Oct.15, 1993.*

PATTERSON, TINA MARIE, medical technologist; b. Sault Ste. Marie, Mich., Aug. 13, 1969; d. Donald Dean and Mary Anne (Carpenter) P. AAS, Jefferson C.C., Watertown, N.Y., 1989. Cert. med. lab. technician, med. technician. Med. lab. technician House of Good Samaritan Hosp., Watertown, N.Y., 1989-92, F.F. Thompson Hosp., Canandaigua, N.Y., 1992; med. lab. technologist Guthrie Meml. Clinic, Ft. Drum, N.Y., 1992—. Recipient Performance Commendation, Dept. Army, 1993, 95. Home: 234 Coffeen St Apt 3A Watertown NY 13601

PATTERSON, WALTER, cytotechnologist, osteopath; b. Stephenson, W.Va., Mar. 14, 1946; married Oct. 26, 1986; children: Kylie, Kawana. BS, Marshall U., 1973, MS, 1975; DO, W.Va. Sch. Osteo. Medicine, 1979. Med. dir. Family Health Group, National City, Calif., 1984-92; med. cons. Naval Hosp., Oceanside, Calif., 1992-94. With USN, 1980-84. Mem. Osteo. Family Physicians, Am. Soc. Clin. Pathologists. Home: 16 Frelinghuysen Ave Newark NJ 07114

PATTERSON, WILLIAM B., occupational and environmental medicine physician; b. Boston, Dec. 24, 1948; s. W. Bradford and Helen (Ross) P. BS, Harvard U., Boston, 1971; MD, U. Vt., 1976. Diplomate Am. Bd. Internal Medicine, Am. Bd. Preventive Medicine with subspecialty in occupl. and environ. medicine; lic. physician, Mass. Asst. vis. physician Boston City Hosp., 1979-83, intern and resident, 1976-79; dir. employee and occupl. health dept. health and hosps. City of Boston, 1982-83; occupl. physician Med. Products Group, Hewlett Packard Corp., 1983—; med. dir. occupl. health svcs. Choate-Symmes Health Svcs., Inc., 1983-86, dir. occupl. health svcs., 1986-90; v.p. occupl. health svcs. Wellesley Med. Mgmt. Inc. d/b/a Health Stop, 1990-92; pres. New Eng. Occupl. Health Svcs. d/b/a New Eng. Health Ctr., Wilmington, Mass., 1992—; med. dir. M/A-COM, Inc., 1994—; asst. prof. pub. health Boston U., 1985—, adj. asst. prof. pub. health, 1982-85, asst. prof. medicine, 1981—, instr. medicine, 1979-81, instr. socio-med. scis., 1979-82; cons. physician Mass. Registry Motor Vehicles, Boston, 1994-96; med. dir. Hale Hosp. Occupl. Health Program, Haverhill, Mass., 1992-96; cons. physician Army C.E., Waltham, Mass., 1992—; cons. in field; resident adv. com. occupl. medicine tng. program Boston U. Med. Ctr., 1988—, U. Mass. Med. Ctr., 1991—. Contbr. articles to profl. jours. Mem. worksite task force Mass. affiliate Am. Heart Assn., 1987-95, chmn. 1990-92, co-chmn. 1993-95. W.K. Kellogg Found. Nat. fellow, 1982-85. Mem. ACP, APHA, Mass. Coalition for Occupl. Health and Safety, Am. Coll. Occupl. and Environ. Medicine, Assn. of Occupl. and Environ. Clinics, New Eng. Coll. Occupl. and Environ. Medicine (bd. dirs. 1991—, program dir. 1992-93, v.p. 1993-94, pres. 1994-96), Roxbury Clin. Record Club. Office: New England Health Ctr 66B Concord St Wilmington MA 01887

PATTERSON-WENGER, PAMELA ANN, physical therapist; b. Clay Center, Kans., Oct. 10, 1954; d. Nolan John and Rachel Ann (Dinsmore) Patterson; m. James Donald Wenger, Dec. 8, 1979; 1 child, Patrick Nolan. Student, U. Kans., Lawrence, 1972-75; BS in Physical Therapy, U. Kans., Kansas City, 1976. Lic. physical therapist, Iowa, Kans., Nebr., Mo. Physical therapist dir. Profl. Physical Therapy Svcs., Hamburg, Iowa, 1977-81; physical therapist Physical Therapy Svcs., Hamburg, 1981-83; dir. physical therapy Restorative Health Svcs., Hamburg, 1983-86, Red Oak, Iowa, 1986-87; dir. physical therapy Community Hosp., Fairfax, Mo., 1987-93; phys. therapist Grape Cmty. Hosp., 1993—; dir. physical therapy Community Hosp. Assn. Home Health Agency, 1992-93; cons. Stanton (Iowa) Care Ctr., 1984-87, Malvern (Iowa) Care Ctr., 1984-85, Vista Garden Care Ctr., Red Oak, 1984-87, Good Samaritan Care Ctr., Red Oak, 1984-87, Red Oak Rehab. Agy., 1985-87, Bethesda Care Ctr., Tarkio, Mo., 1988-93. Active First Presby. Ch., Clay Center, 1976-83, United Trinty Ch., Hamburg, 1977—, Omaha Ballet, 1978—, Opera Omaha, 1978—, Hamburg Community Arts Council, 1985—. Mem. Am. Physical Therapy Assn., Orthopedic and Geriatric sections Am. Physical Therapy Assn., Iowa Physical Therapy Assn., Mo. Physical Therapy Assn. Republican. Home: 1510 Argyle St Hamburg IA 51640-1402

PATTON, JACK THOMAS, family practice physician; b. Rogers, Ark., Feb. 18, 1941; s. Jack Marcus and Jewell Selah (Pense) P.; m. Lynette Anne Carr, Sept. 2, 1960; children: Robert, John, Mark, Christopher. BA in History, Calif. State U., 1963; MD in Medicine, U. So. Calif., L.A., 1967; MA in Bib. Studies, Mennonite Brethren Bib. Sem., Fresno, Calif., 1980; MA in History, Calif. State U., Fresno, 1993. Cert. Bd. Med. Examiners, Calif., Hawaii. Intern Tripler Army Med. Ctr., Honolulu, 1967-68; resident in gen. practice Walson Army Hosp., Ft. Dix, N.J., 1968-70; med. supt. Nazarene Hosp., Papua New Guinea, 1973-80; chmn. family practice dept. Sharp Rees-Stealy, San Diego, 1981-86; chmn. occupational medicine Kaiser Permanente, Fresno, 1986-87; assoc. med. dir. Sharp Rees-Stealy, San Diego, 1987-92; med. dir. Summer Inst. Linguistics, Papua New Guinea, 1993-94; with family practice dept. Sharp Rees-Stealy Med. Group, San Diego, 1994—; family practice residency liaison Tripler Army Med. Ctr., Honolulu, 1972-73; chief medicine, dep. commr. Schofield Army Med. Clinics, Waihiwa, Hawaii, 1970-72. Mem. med. sch. support Salerni Collegium, U. So. Calif. Sch. Medicine, 1967-85; lectr. Ch.-Mission Inst., Mennonite Brethren Bib. Sem., 1984-92; sec. S.E. Asian task force Mennonite Brethren Ch. Fresno, 1990-93. Maj. U.S. Army, 1966-73. Mackenzie scholar U. So. Calif. Sch. Medicine, 1966-67. Fellow Am. Acad. Family Physicians; mem. Am. Bd. Family Practice (diplomate), Calif. Acad. Family Physicians, Royal Soc. Medicine (assoc., London). Home: 1461 S Willow Ave Fresno CA 93727 Office: Sharp Rees-Stealy Med Group 4510 Viewridge Ave San Diego CA 92123

PATTON, SUSAN OERTEL, clinical social worker, educator; b. Syracuse, N.Y., May 18, 1946; d. Robert William and Jane (VanWormer) Oertel; m. Joseph D. Patton, Jr., June 3, 1967; children: Jennifer, Joseph D. III. BA, SUNY, Geneseo, 1984; MSW, SUNY, Buffalo, 1987. Cert. social worker, N.Y.; lic. ind. social worker, S.C.; cert. employee assistance profl.; qualified clin. social worker; bd. cert. fellow in managed mental health care; diplomate in clin. social work. Counselor Profl. Counseling Svc., Gowanda, N.Y., 1987-88, Mental Health Mgmt., Rochester, N.Y., 1988-93; counselor The Health Assn., Rochester, 1988-89, sr. counselor, 1989-90, asst. dir. mktg. and tng., 1990-92; pvt. practice Rochester, 1988-93; employee assistance program dir. Recovery Ctr. EAP, Hilton Head, S.C., 1993-95; pres., dir. Employee Assistance Program, Inc., Hilton Head Island, S.C., 1995—; instr. Medaille Coll., Buffalo, 1990-93. Co-author: Treating Perpetrators of Sexual Abuse, 1990. Mem. NASW, Acad. Cert. Social Workers, Am. Bd. Cert. Managed Care Providers, S.C. Counselors Assn., Employee Assistance Profls. Assn. Office: Employee Assistance Program Carolina Bldg Ste 110 10 Office Park Rd Hilton Head Island SC 29928-7541

PATTON, THOMAS JAMES, sales and marketing executive; b. Cleve., Nov. 2, 1948; s. Michael Anthony and Delores (Bammerlin) P.; m. Thomasina Bernadette Cavallaro, Aug. 9, 1969; children: Thomasina, Thera V. A in Transp., Cleve. State U., 1971, BA in Mktg., 1973; BA, SUNY, Empire State, 1994. CLU; ChFC. Ins. salesman Manulife, Cleve., 1972-75, Mass. Mut., Cleve., 1976-80, Patton Ins. Assn., Inc., Avon Lake, Ohio, 1976—; ins. cons. Diversified Benefit Plans, Inc., Avon Lake, 1978-93, dir. sales and mktg., 1993—; pres. commerce Benefits Group, Inc. and Ins. Mktg. Group, Inc., 1995; prin. Cmty. Health Ptnrs., Ltd., Ill., 1994; pres. Commerce Benefits Group, Inc.; cons. Regional Sch. Consortium, Lorain County, Ohio, 1986—, County of Lorain, 1984—, City of Lorain, 1986—, County of Lorain, 1984—, City of Lorain, 1985—; prin. Comty. Health Ptnrs. Ltd.; bd. Italian Cultural Found. Pres. Lake Erie Rate Coun., Cleve., 1970-71; mem. Lorain County Dem. Ctrl. Com., Avon Lake, Ohio, 1986—; mem. com. Cleve. Leukemia Soc., 1985; bd. dirs. Villa Serena Sr. Housing, St. Francis Soc., Italian Cultural Found. Mem. Nat. Assn. Life Underwriters, Profl. Ins. Agts. Assn., Cert. Profl. Ins. Agts. Soc., Soc. Benefit Plan Adminstrn., Lorain County Life Underwriters, Irish Heritage, Order Italian Sons and Daus., Profl. Assn. Dive Instrs./Nat. Assn. Underwater Instrs. (SCUBA diving instr.). Roman Catholic. Office: Diversified Benefit Plan Inc PO Box 900 Elyria OH 44036-0900

PATTON, VALERIE BIERING, microbiologist; b. San Antonio, Aug. 12, 1949; d. Richard and Lillian G. (Gullett) Corner; m. Christopher Andrew Davis, June 6, 1969 (div. Nov. 1982); 1 child, Catherine Rice Davis; m. Paul Andrew Burk, Oct. 31, 1991; children: LaVerne F. Burk, Samantha A. Burk. AAS, NYU, 1980; BS, Southwest U., 1981; MS, Southwest U., 1986. Microbiologist U.S. Navy, Great Lakes, Ill., 1984-86; weekend evening shift supervisor Craven Regional Med. Ctr., New Bern, N.C., 1986—; instr. microbiology Craven Cmty. Coll., New Bern, 1987—; pres. V.P. Valuables, 1992—. Mem. Am. Soc. Clin. Pathologists, Am. Soc. Med. Techs., Am. Soc. Microbiologists. Republican. Home: 1736 Elmwood St New Bern NC 28560-8859

PAUL, DAVID FRANCIS, orthopedic surgeon; b. Worcester, Mass., July 3, 1946; s. Alexander and Margaret M. (Connelly) P.; m. Virginia Theresa Carr, June 15, 1969; children: Bridget J., Christina M., Alex M., Stephanie E., John R. BA, U. Notre Dame, 1968; MD, Tufts U., 1972. Diplomate Am. Bd. Orthopaedic Surgery. Intern Maine Med. Ctr., Portland, 1972-73; commd. 2nd lt. USAF, 1970, advanced through grades to lt. col., 1981; flight surgeon USAF Hosp., Clark AFB, Philippines, 1973-75, USAF Clinic, RAF Bentwaters, Eng., 1975-77; orthopedic surgery resident Wilford hall USAF Med. Ctr., Lackland AFB, Tex., 1977-81; active staff USAF Med. Ctr., Scott AFB, Ill., 1981-82, So. Maine Med. Ctr., Biddeford, 1982—; bd. dirs. Pharmx, Inc., Portland, Maine; pres. Orthopedic Surgery Assocs., Biddeford, 1985—. Fellow Am. Acad. Ortho. Surgeons; mem. maine Soc. Ortho. Surgeons, Maine Med. Assn. Roman Catholic. Office: Orthopedic Surgery Assocs 10 Wellspring Rd Biddeford ME 04005

PAUL, FRANK ALLEN, physician; b. Joshua Tree, Calif., Oct. 30, 1958; s. Louis Marion and Vivian Ann Paul. AA in Pharmacy and Marine Biology, Fullerton Coll., Calif., 1979; BA in Biochemistry and Biology, Calif. State U., Fullerton, 1982; DO, U. New Eng., 1990. Bd. cert. physician emergency medicine. Store mgr. Alpha Beta Markets, La Habra and Industry, Calif., 1977-81; constrn. supr. Louis M. Paul Constrn. Co., La Habra, 1977-82; co-owner Finecraft of Calif., Mfr./Jeweler, Claremont, Calif., 1978—; teaching fellow U. New Eng., Biddeford, Maine, 1988-89; intern Mt. Clemens (Mich.) Gen. Hosp., 1990-91, resident in emergency medicine, cons. staff, 1991-94; mem. staff Riverside Osteopathic Hosp., Trenton, Mich., 1995—; rsch. dir. Herpetol. and Ichthyol. Infectious Disease Rsch. Assocs.; clin. faculty mem. U. New England Coll. Osteopathic Medicine, 1994—. Contbr. publs. to Jour. Am. Osteo. Assn., Procs. of 3d Internat. Aquarium Congress, Handbook of Antimicrobial Therapy for Reptiles and Amphibians. Mem. AMA, Am. Osteo. Assn., Am. Acad. Osteopathy, Am. Coll. Emergency Physicians, Am. Coll. Osteopathic Emergency Physicians. Republican. Roman Catholic.

PAUL, LEONARD GEORGE, medical educator; b. Cleve., Oct. 16, 1924; s. Michael Joseph and Mary Elizabeth (Mandula) P.; m. Gertraud Erivd Johannes, May 2, 1947 (div. 1978); m. Nancy Kay Daubenspeck; children: Michael, Kathy, Stephen. BS, Cleve. State U., 1947; MD, Ohio State U., 1951. Intern Phila. Gen. Hosp., 1951-52; ptnr. Med. Group of Michigan City, Ind., 1952-75; assoc. prof. Ohio State U.-Med. Sch., Columbus, 1975-78; assoc. prof., dep. chmn. U. Calif., Irvine, 1978-82; prof., chmn. U. Tex. Health Sci. Ctr., San Antonio, 1982-95, prof. emeritus, chmn., 1995—; predoctoral chmn. Ohio State U., Columbus, 1976-78; residency dir. U. Calif. Irvine, 1978-82; chmn. U. Tex. Health Sci. Ctr., San Antonio. With U.S. Army, 1943-46. Mem. TAFP (dir. Alamo chpt.), AAFP, TMA (del.), AMA, RCMS (del. edn.), Alpha Omega Alpha. Home: 30019 Cantor Circle Fair Oaks Ranch TX 78015 Office: U Tex Health Sci Ctr 7703 Floyd Curl San Antonio TX 78284

PAUL, NORMAN LEO, psychiatrist, educator; b. Buffalo, N.Y., July 5, 1926; s. Samuel Joseph and Tannie (Goncharsky) P.; m. Betty Ann Byfield, June 6, 1951 (dec. May 1994); children: Marilyn, David Alexander. MD, U. Buffalo, 1948. Fellow pharmacology Coll. Medicine, U. Cin., Ohio, 1949-50; resident psychiatry Mass. Mental Health Ctr., Boston, 1952-55; fellow child psychiatry James Jackson Putnam Children's Ctr., Boston, 1957-58, 59, Mass. Gen. Hosp., Boston, 1958-59; chief psychiatrist Day Hosp. Mass. Mental Health Ctr., Boston, 1960-64; dir. conjoint family therapy Boston (Mass.) State Hosp., 1964-65, cons. in family psychiatry, 1965-70; assoc. clin. prof. dept. neurology Boston (Mass.) U. Sch. Medicine, 1977—; cons. Mental Health Ctr., Alaska Native Hosp., Anchorage, 1967, 68; cons. in family psychiatry Boston (Mass.) VA Hosp., 1967-71, Mass. Soc. for the Prevention of Cruelty to Children, Boston, 1993—; lectr. in psychiatry Harvard Med. Sch., Boston, 1976—; faculty assoc. Mgmt. Analysis Corp., Cambridge, Mass., 1979-82. Family therapist: (tv documentary) PBS-Trouble in the Family, 1965 (George Foster Peabody award 1965); co-author A Marital Puzzle, 1977, 86, German edit., 1987, French edit., 1995. Sponsor Mass. Orgn. to Repeal Abortion Laws, Boston, 1965-70; chair Audio Unit of Child Devel. and Mass Media, White House Conf. on Children and Youth, Washington, 1970; bd. trustees Cambridge (Mass.) Coll., 1977-89. Capt. USAF, 1950-52. Recipient Edward A. Strecker, M.D. award for young psychiatrist of yr., 1966, Cert. of Merit, Mass. Coun. on Family Life, Boston, 1967, Cert. of Commendation, Mass. Assn. for Mental Health, Boston, 1967, Disting. Achievement award Soc. for Family Therapy and Rsch., Boston, 1973. Fellow Royal Soc. Medicine, Am. Psychiat. Assn. (life); mem. Am. Assn.

Marriage and Family Therapy (bd. dirs. 1983-86), Am. Family Therapy Assn. (v.p. 1982-83, Disting. Contbn. award 1984), Assn. for Rsch. in Nervous and Mental Disorders, Group for the Advancement Psychiatry (chair com. on the family 1982-84). Office: 394 Lowell St Ste 6 Lexington MA 02173-2575

PAUL, OGLESBY, physician; b. Villanova, Pa., May 3, 1916; s. Oglesby and Laura Little (Wilson) P.; m. Marguerite Black, May 29, 1943 (dec. Sept. 1979); children: Marguerite, Rodman; m. Jean Lithgow, Jan. 17, 1981. A.B. cum laude, Harvard U., 1938, M.D. cum laude, 1942. Diplomate: in cardiovascular disease Am. Bd. Internal Medicine. Intern. Mass. Gen. Hosp., Boston, 1942-43; asst. medicine Harvard Med. Sch., 1946-49; clin. asso. prof. medicine U. Ill., 1952-62, clin. prof. medicine, 1962; asst. attending physician Presbyn.-St. Luke's Hosp., 1951-54, asso. attending physician, 1954-59, attending physician, 1959-62; chief div. medicine Passavant Meml. Hosp., Chgo., 1963-72; prof. medicine Northwestern U., 1963-77; med. dir. Univ. Med. Assos., 1973-75, v.p. health scis., 1973-75; prof. medicine Harvard U. Sch. Medicine, Boston, 1977-82, prof. medicine emeritus, 1982—; dir. admissions Harvard U. Sch. Medicine, 1977-82; sr. physician Brigham and Women's Hosp., Boston, 1977-82, sr. physician emeritus, 1982—; cons. U.S. Naval Hosp., Great Lakes, Ill., 1959-74; Mem. joint U.S.-U.K. Com. for Study Coronary and Pulmonary Disease, 1959—. Chmn. gov.'s adv. com. Ill. Regional Med. Program on Heart Disease, Cancer and Stroke, 1967-70; dirs. Internat. Soc. Cardiology Found. Served from lt. (j.g.) to lt. M.C. USNR, 1943-46. Fellow ACP, Am. Coll. Cardiology, Royal Soc. Medicine (Eng.); mem. Assn. U. Cardiologists, Am. Heart Assn. (pres. 1960-61), Chgo. Heart Assn. (pres. 1966-67), Am. Epidemiol. Soc., Am. Clin. and Climatol. Assn. Home: 10 Longwood Dr # 322 Westwood MA 02090 Office: Harvard U Med Sch Countway Libr 10 Shattuck St Boston MA 02115-6011

PAUL, RHONDA ELIZABETH, university program director, career development counselor; d. John and Vivian (Griffin) P. BA, Mich. State U., 1977; MA, Atlanta U., 1979; postgrad., Wayne State U., 1982—. Cert. counselor, Mich.; nat. cert. career counelor; lic. profl. counselor. Counselor, student affairs dept. Spelman Coll., Atlanta, 1978-79; life/career devel. specialist Wayne State U., Detroit, 1979-81, minority devel. counselor, 1981-83; prog. dir. recruitment dept. Wayne State Sch. of Medicine, Detroit, 1983—; cons./proprietor RP Career Assocs., Detroit, 1990—. Recipient Award of Pride, Mich. State U., Lansing, 1977, Spl. Recognition award Nat. Bd. for Cert. Counselors, 1993. Mem. NAACP, Am. Counseling Assn., Mich. Counseling Assn., Assn. Multicultural Counseling and Devel. (nat. stds. and cert. com.), Nat. Career Devel. Assn., Nat. Coalition of 100 Black Women (bd. dirs.), Alpha Kappa Alpha. Home: 4068 Cortland St Detroit MI 48204-1506 Office: Wayne State U Dept Recruitment Detroit MI 48202

PAUL, SANDRA JEFFREY, physician; b. Detroit, Aug. 23, 1957; s. Lloyd Julius and Doris (Siegel) P. BA, Brandies U., 1979; MD, U. Mich., 1983. Physician Mich. Endocrine Cons., Berkley, Mich., 1990—. Mem. AMA, Mich. State Med. Soc., Oakland County Med. Soc., Endocrine Soc., Soc. Obs. Medicine. Office: Mich Endocrine Soc 1695 W 12 Mile Rd #220 Berkeley CA 48072

PAUL, SHASHI DAMAN, surgeon, pediatrician; b. New Delhi, India, July 13, 1943; s. Jaswant Singh and Shakuntla Paul; children: Paresh, Sanjay, Arvin. Biomedical degree, U. Delhi Hindu Coll., New Delhi, 1961; MBBS, All India Inst. Med. Scis., New Delhi, 1965; cert., Edl. Commn. Fgn. Commn. Grads., Phila., 1965. Diplomate Am. Bd. Pedicatrics, Can. Bd. Pediatrics, Am. Bd. Family Practice, Am. Bd. Quality Assurance and Utilization Rev. Intern All India Inst. Med. Sci., New Delhi, 1966, Mt. Carmel Mercy Hosp., Detroit, 1967; resident in pediatrics Henry Ford Hosp., Detroit, 1968, Children's Hosp. of Mich., Detroit, 1968-71; practice medicine specializing in pediatrics Munster, Ind., 1971—; pediatrics registrar Hellington Hosp., Uxbridge, Middlesex, Eng., 1971; asst. prof. pediatrics Rush Med. Coll., Chgo., 1971—; mem. Am. Bd. Quality Assurance and Utilization Rev. Editor Jour. All India Inst. Med. Scis., 1964. Fellow Am. Acad. Pediatrics, Royal Coll. Physicians of Can., Am. Acad. Family Practice, Royal Coll. of Physicians and Surgeons of Ireland, Am. Bd. Quality Assurance and Utilization Rev.; mem. AMA (Physician Recognition award 1970, 73, 76, 79, 82, 85, 88, 91, 94), ACP. Home: 9524 Greenwood Ave Munster IN 46321 Office: 8224 Calumet Ave Munster IN 46321

PAUL, STEPHEN EDWARD, family practice; b. Atlantic City, Aug. 6, 1944; s. Joseph and Naomi B. (Brown) P.; m. Arlene Sheryl Lerman, Dec. 21, 1968 (div. May 1982); children: Ryan, Melissa; m. Lynn Susan Goldman, Dec. 14, 1985. BS, Alleghany Coll., 1966; DO, Phila. Coll. Osteo. Medicine, 1970. Diplomate Am. Bd. Family Practice. Intern Parkview Hosp., Phila., 1970-71; pvt. practice Maple Shade, N.J., 1972—; peer rev. com. PrimeCare/FPA Med., Newtown Square, Pa., 1995—; adv. bd. W.A.R., Collingswood, N.J., 1982-95. Mem. Am. Osteo. Assn., N.J. Assn. of Osteo. Physicians and Surgeons, Camden County Soc. of Osteo. Physicians and Surgeons, Am. Coll. Osteo. Family Physicians. Jewish. Office: 111 E Main St Maple Shade NJ 08052

PAUL, THOMAS WAYNE, psychotherapist; b. Vallejo, Calif., Mar. 25, 1950; s. Thomas Birdsall and Shirley Mae (Osterheld) P. BA, Goddard Coll., 1980, Ma, 1989. Cert. alcohol, drugs counselor, employee assistance profl.; nationally cert. addictions counselor. Civilian program coord., dir. community counseling ctr. Seneca Army Depot, Romulus, N.Y., 1981-85; svcs. mgr. Finger Lakes Alcoholism Counseling and Referral Agy., Seneca Falls, N.Y., 1985-86; dir. outpatient svc. dept., FLACRA, Clifton Springs, N.Y., 1985; dir. employee assistance program Maxwell Hall, Clifton Springs, 1985-86; regional svcs. coord. MEDIPLEX Group, Rochester, N.Y., 1986-87; co-owner Human Progress Enterprises, Newark, N.Y., 1986—; chem. dependency program coord. Hobart & William Smith Colls., Newark, 1985-88; pvt. practice in psychotherapy Geneva and Rochester, N.Y., 1985-88; dir., founder Adult Child & Co-dependency Ctr., Rochester, 1988—; pres. Finger Lakes Alcoholism Counseling & Referral Agy., Clifton Springs, 1983-84, Coun. on Alcoholism of Finger Lakes, Geneva, 1986—; treas. N.Y. State Coalition for Children of Addictions, 1987—, chmn. Rochester chpt., 1986—. Chmn. Combined Fed. Campaign United Way, Romulus, N.Y., 1983-84. Mem. Nat. Assn. Alcohol & Drugs Counselor, Nat. Assn. Children of Alcoholics, N.Y. Fedn. Alcoholism Counselors, Am. Counseling & Devel., N.Y. State Coalition for Children of Addictions. Home: 246 Grace Ave Newark NY 14513-2151 Office: 11 Goodman St N Rochester NY 14607-1501

PAUL, WILLIAM ERWIN, immunologist, researcher; b. Bklyn., June 12, 1936; s. Jack and Sylvia (Gleicher) P.; m. Marilyn Heller, Dec. 25, 1958; children: Jonathan M., Matthew E. AB summa cum laude, Bklyn. Coll., 1956; MD cum laude, SUNY-Downstate Med. Ctr., 1960, DSc (hon.), 1991. Intern, then asst. resident Mass. Meml. Hosp., Boston, 1960-62; clin. assoc. Nat. Cancer Inst. NIH, Bethesda, Md., 1962-64; postdoctoral fellow, instr. NYU Sch. Medicine, N.Y.C., 1964-68; sr. investigator Lab. Immunology Nat. Inst. Allergy and Infectious Diseases, NIH, Bethesda, 1968-70, chief Lab. Immunology, 1970—; dir. Office of AIDS Rsch. NIH, Bethesda, assoc. dir. AIDS rsch., 1994—; mem. bd. sci. advisors Jane Coffin Childs Meml. Fund for Med. Research, 1982-90; G. Burroughs Mider lectr. NIH, 1982; mem. sci. rev. bd. Howard Hughes Med. Inst., 1979-85, 87-91, mem. med. adv. bd., 1992-96; mem. bd. sci. cons. Meml. Sloan-Kettering Cancer Ctr., N.Y.C., 1984-92; chmn. adv. com. Harold C. Simmons Arthritis Rsch. Ctr., 1984-90; bd. dirs. Fed. Am. Soc. Experimental Biology, 1985-88; mem. bd. basic biology NRC, 1986-89; mem. select com. Alfred P. Sloan Jr. Prize, Gen. Motors Cancer Res. Fedn., 1986-87; sci. adv. coun. Cancer Rsch. Inst., 1985-94; mem. com. to visit div. med. sci., bd. overseers Harvard Coll., 1987-93; Carl Moore lectr. Sch. Medicine, Washington U., St. Louis, 1986; mem. adv. com. Pew Scholars Program in Biomed. Scis., 1988-91; Richard Gershon lectr. Yale U. Sch. Medicine, 1986; Nelson Med. lectr., U. Calif., Davis, 1988; Disting. Alumnus lectr., Univ. Hosp., Boston, 1989; Anderson med. lectr. U. Va., 1990, La Jolla sci. lectr., 1991, Wellcome vis. prof. Wayne State U., 1991, mem. Adv. Com. dept. of Molecular Bio., Princeton U., 1993-94, ann. lectr., Dutch Soc. for Immunology, 1992, Yamamura Meml. lectr. Osaka U., 1992, Kunkel lectr., Johns Hopkins U. Sch. of Medicine, 1993; Welcome vis. prof. SUNY Stony Brook, 1993; Benacerraf lectr. Harvard Med. Sch., 1993; Sulkin lectr. U. Tex. Southwestern Med. Ctr., 1995. Editor: Fundamental Immunology, 1984, 3rd edit., 1993, Ann. Rev. Immunology, Vols. 1-15, 1983—; adv. editor Jour. Exptl. Medicine, 1974—; assoc. editor Cell, 1985—; transmitting editor Internat. Immunology, 1989—; corr. editor Procs. Royal Soc. Series B, 1989-93; mem. editl. bd. Molecular Biology of Cell, 1990-92; contbg. editor Procs. NAS U.S.A., 1992-94; contbr. numerous articles to sci. jours. With USPHS, 1962-64, 75-96. Recipient Founders' prize Tex. Instruments Found., 1979, Alumni medal SUNY Downstate Med. Ctr., 1981, Disting. Svc. medal USPHS, 1985, 3M Life Scis. award, 1988, Tovi Comet-Wallerstein prize CAIR Inst., Bar-Ilan U., 1992, 6th ann. award for excellence in immunologic rsch. Duke U., 1993, Alumni honors Bklyn. Coll., 1994. Fellow Am. Acad. Arts and Scis.; mem. NAS, Inst. Medicine NAS, Am. Soc. Clin. Investigation (pres. 1980-81), Am. Assn. Immunologists (pres. 1986-87), Assn. Am. Physicians, Scandinavian Soc. Immunology (hon.). Office: NIH Bldg 31 Rm 4C02 31 Center Dr MSC 2340 Bethesda MD 20892-2340

PAULANKA, BETTY JANE, dean, nurse educator; b. Williamsport, Pa., Apr. 18, 1944; d. Stanley Paul Cahn and Frances Mae Leeser; m. Leonard William Paulanka, Oct. 22, 1965; children: Christie Ann, Eaine Frances. Diploma in nursing, U. Pa., 1965, MSN, 1977; BSN, Neuman Coll., 1976; EdD, Temple U., 1984. Staff nurse Med. Ctr. Del., Wilmington, 1974, Crozer-Chester (Pa.) Med. Ctr., 1976; from asst. to assoc. chair U. Del. Coll. Nursing, Newark, 1977-91, chair dept. nursing sci., 1987-92, course mgr., 1984-87, dean, 1992—; course mgr. dept. nursing sci. U. Del. Coll. Nursing, Newark, 1984-87, chair dept. nursing sci., 1987-91; adv. bd. De Valley Nurses Computer Network. HBO & Co. scholar, Alberta, Ga., 1991; grantee A. Fuld Found., 1990, rsch. grantee, 1991. Mem. Nat. Nurses Assn., Del. Nurses Assn., Pa. Assn. Adult Continuing Edn., Sigma Theta Tau, Sigma Xi. Home: 328 Staghorn Way West Chester PA 19380-5114 Office: Univ Delaware College Nursing Newark DE 19716*

PAULI, PAMELA ELLEN, health resource center coordinator; b. Portland, Oreg., May 7, 1955; d. Henry and Velma Lovene (Tedrick) P. BSN, Oreg. Health Scis. U., Portland, 1977; MN, U. Wash., Seattle, 1985. RN, Oreg.; cert. inpatient obstet. nursing. Staff/relief charge nurse Oreg. Health Scis. U., Portland, 1977-78, charge nurse, 1978-80, charge nurse obstetrics, 1980-83; relief charge nurse, staff nurse U. Wash. Hosps., Seattle, 1983-86; charge nurse/maternity St. Vincent Hosp. and Med. Ctr., Portland, 1986-93; clin. coord. health resource ctr. Providence Health Sys., Portland, 1993—; cmty. cons. Providence Health System, Portland, 1994. Contbr. articles to profl. jours. and newsletters. Vol. nurse Innovative Solutions Group, Portland, 1992—. Mem. ANA, Oreg. Nurses Assn., Oreg. Clin. Nurse Specialists, Sigma Theta Tau, Exec. Women's Golf. Office: Providence St Vincent Health Resource Ctr 9205 SW Barnes Rd Portland OR 97225

PAULISSEN, JAMES PETER, physician, county official; b. Chgo., Aug. 14, 1928; s. Joseph Edward and Louise Catherine (Muno) P.; m. Lorraine Antoinette Polly, Sept. 11, 1954; children—Linda, Steven, Mark, Daniel. Student Loyola U., 1946-49, M.D. cum laude, 1953; M.P.H., Johns Hopkins U., 1966. Diplomate Am. Bd. Pediatrics. Intern Milw. County Hosp., 1953-54; resident Milw. Children's Hosp., 1957-59; practice medicine specializing in pediatrics Wauwatosa Children's Clinic, Wis., 1959-65; chief Bur. Maternal and Child Health, Ill. Dept. Pub. Health, Springfield, 1966-70, chief Div. Family Health, 1970-76; exec. dir. DuPage County Health Dept., Wheaton, Ill., 1976-93; bd. dirs., mem. exec. com. Suburban Cook-DuPage Health Systems Agy., Oak Park, Ill., 1976-82; bd. dirs., past pres. Comprehensive Health Council Met. Chgo., 1977-87; dir. Sr. Home Sharing, Inc., Wheaton, 1981-83. Mem. Ill. Commn. on Children, 1971-85, vice chmn., 1983-85, chmn. Ill. Perinatal Adv. Com., 1981-84, mem. 1981-92; mem. Ill. Sch. Health Adv. Com., 1982-93, Gov.'s Adv. Council on Devel. Disabilities, 1973-76, Ill. Med. Determinations Bd., 1985; vice-chmn. Ill. Bd. Pub. Health Advisors, 1988-91; mem. adv. bd. div. Svcs. Crippled Children U. Ill., 1986-94; trustee DuPage County Med. Found., 1976-82, 86—; bd. dirs. DuPage Cmty. Clinic, 1993—, Cmty. Nursing Svc. of DuPage, 1993—; mem. cmty. benefit com. Ctrl. DuPage Health Sys., 1993—; del. White House Conf. for Children, 1970. Served to capt. USAF, 1954-56. Recipient Dir.'s award for Sustained Excellence Ill. Dept. Pub. Health, 1988, Ill. Pediatrician of Yr. award, 1992. Fellow Am. Acad. Pediatrics, Am. Pub. Health Assn., Am. Coll. Preventive Medicine; mem. Am. Acad. Pediatrics (mem. exec. com. Ill. chpt. 1978-81), Ill. Pub. Health Assn. (pres. 1977-78; Disting. Service award 1983, sec. 1988-92), Ill. Assn. Maternal and Child Health (pres. 1975-76). Avocation: model railroading. Home: 28w660 Hawthorne Ln West Chicago IL 60185-2472

PAULL, DOUGLAS EDWARD, thoracic surgeon; b. Dayton, Ohio, Apr. 4, 1956; s. William John and Alice Marie (Brownfield) P.; m. Lisa Dianne Kropp, Oct. 20, 1979; 1 child, Sara Melissa. BS in Zoology, Duke U. 1978, MD, 1982. Diplomate Am. Bd. Thoracic Surgery, Am. Bd. Surgery. Surg. resident N.Y. Hosp.-Cornell, N.Y.C., 1982-87; thoracic surgery fellow U. N.C., Chapel Hill, 1987-90; thoracic surgeon Wyo. Valley Health Care System, Wilkes-Barre, Pa., 1995—. Author: (with others) Yearbook of Critical Care, 1990; contbr. articles to profl. jours. Cancer Epidemology Fellowship NIH, 1981. Fellow ACS, Soc. of Thoracic Surgeons, Am. Coll. Chest Physicians (Boehringer Ingel Henn Rsch. award 1988), Southeastern Surg. Congress, Soc. of Air Force Surg. Surgeons, Chirurgio Soc., Alpha Omega Alpha. Roman Catholic. Home: 6 Farmhouse Rd Mountain Top PA 18707 Office: Surg Specialities Wyoming Valley 200 S River St Plains PA 18705

PAULSEN, DOUGLAS FRANK, biologist; b. Balt., Oct. 7, 1952; s. Douglas Frank and Janice Meriam (Benson) P.; m. Annamarie Angela Spillane, June 15, 1984; 1 child, Tai Josef. BA, Western Md. Coll., 1974; PhD, Wake Forest U., 1979. NIH postdoctoral fellow Calif. State U., Northridge, 1979-80; asst. prof. anatomy Sch. Medicine Morehouse Coll., Atlanta, 1980-88, assoc. prof. anatomy, 1988-95, prof. anatomy, 1995—; course dir. med. histology Morehouse Sch. Medicine, 1982-86, 1988—, prin. investigator, 1982—; vis. rschr. U. Iowa, Iowa City, 1986-87; mem. NIH, HED-2, IRG, 1990-94; mem. life sci. peer rev. panel NASA, 1993, 94, 96; mem. nutrition peer rev. panel USDA, 1996. Author: (textbook) Basic Histology: Examination and Board Review, 1990, 2d edit., 1993, 3d edit., 1996. Mem. Am. Assn. Anatomists, Soc. for Developmental Biology, Soc. for In Vitro Biology, Am. Soc. Cell Biology. Presbyterian. Home: 2477 Lost Valley Trl SE Conyers GA 30208-2440 Office: Morehouse Sch Medicine Dept Anatomy Atlanta GA 30310-1495

PAULSEN, J. KEVIN, physician, surgeon; b. Harvard, Ill., June 1, 1947; s. Lyle F. and M. Mercedes (Shields) P.; m. Pam Gielincki, June 22, 1974; children: Amy, Amanda. BS, U. Notre Dame, 1969; MD, U. Ill., 1973. Intern Henry Ford Hosp., Detroit, 1973-74; resident in surgery St. Francis Hosp., Peoria, Ill., 1974-78; active staff St. Francis Hosp., Peoria, 1978—, Meth. Hosp., Peoria, 1978—, Proctor Hosp., Peoria, 1978—. Fellow ACS; mem. Midwest Surg. Soc., Ill. State Surg. Soc. Address: 420 NE Glen Oak Ave Ste 301 Peoria IL 61603-3105

PAULSON, JEROME AVROM, pediatrician; b. Balt., July 31, 1949; s. Robert R. and Edna (Brenner) P.; m. Susan Miller, 1973 (div. 1980); m. Gwen Victor Gampel, July 2, 1989. BS in Biochemistry, U. Md., 1971; MD, Duke U., 1974. Diplomate Am. Bd. Pediatrics, Nat. Bd. Med. Examiners. Resident in pediatrics Johns Hopkins Hosp., Balt., 1974-76; resident in pediatrics Sinai Hosp., Balt., 1976-77, fellow in ambulatory pediatrics, 1977-78; asst. prof. pediatrics Case Western Res. U., Cleve., 1978-86; dir. sci. rsch. and pub. policy devel. Joseph P. Kennedy Jr. Found., Washington, 1986-87; dir. pediatrics Regional Inst. for Children and Adolescents, Rockville, Md., 1987-89; clin. assoc. prof. pediatrics Georgetown U., Washington, 1987—; exec. dir. Research!America, Alexandria, Va., 1989-90; assoc. prof. health care scis. and pediatrics George Washington U., Washington, 1990—, fellow Ctr. Health Policy Rsch., 1991—; mem. conf. on methodology/std. definitions for childhood injury rsch. Nat. Inst. Children and Human Devel., 1989; mem. health adv. com. Congressman James Moran, 8th Congl. Dist., Va., 1992-94; advisor Health Pages, 1994—. Contbr. articles to profl. jours., chpts. to books. Profl. adv. bd. Nat. Safety Town Ctr., Cleve., 1981-85; bd. dirs., pres. James Renwick Alliance, Washington, 1986-93, 95—. Recipient Cert. for Ednl. and Pub. Policy Activity, Ohio State Senate/Ho. of Reps., 1985; Robert Wood Johnson Health Policy fellow, 1985-86. Fellow Am. Acad. Pediatrics; mem. Ambulatory Pediatric Assn. Jewish. Office: George Washington Univ 2150 Pennsylvania Ave NW Washington DC 20037-2396

PAULSON, LORETTA NANCY, psychoanalyst; b. L.A., Nov. 5, 1943; d. Frank Morris and Rose (Kaufman) Fargo; m. Maurice Krasnow. BA, U. So. Calif., 1966; MS in Social Work, Columbia U., 1969; cert. psychoanalyst, C.G. Jung Inst., N.Y.C. Cert. clin. social worker, N.Y., Conn., N.J. Pvt. practice psychoanalysis N.Y.C. and Wilton, Conn., 1976—; faculty, supr., past vice chmn. Inst. Tng. Bd. Mem. NASW (diplomate in clin. social work), Internat. Assn. for Analytical Psychology (del., bd. dirs.), N.Y. Assn. for Analytic Psychology (pres., program com.), Conn. Soc. Clin. Social Work (com. on psychoanalysis). Democrat. Office: 6 Turtleback Rd Wilton CT 06897-1223 Office: 334 W 86th St Apt 1A New York NY 10024-3130

PAULSON-LEE, FRANKIE MAE, psychologist, administrator; b. LaCrosse, Wis.; d. Morgan Oliver and Grace Lorine (Bruhn) Nicholson; m. Clifton Arnold Paulson, Sept. 12, 1942 (dec. Aug. 8, 1975); children: I. Karon Paulson-Sherarts, Vicki Paulson-West, Craig T.; m. Merlin E. Lee, Apr. 28, 1984. BA summa cum laude, U. Minn., 1968, PhD, 1979. Lic. clin. psychologist, Minn., Tex., Ill.; Diplomate Am. Bd. Med. Psychotherapy. Staff psychologist Mpls. Children's Med. Ctr., 1973-84, Cigna Health Plan of Tex., Dallas, 1984-90; clin. dir. MCC Behavioral Care-Tex., Dallas, 1990-91; dir. clin. svcs. MCC Behavioral Care, Mpls., 1991-92, exec. dir., 1992-93; exec. dir. United Behavioral Sys., Rockford, Ill., 1993—. Mem. Aitkin County (Minn.) Human Resources Adv. Adminstrv. Bd., 1965-68; mem. examining panel for psychologists Tex. Bd. of Psychologists, Austin, 1989. Recipient NIMH fellowship, 1970-73. Mem. APA. Democrat. Lutheran. Home: 5501 Roanoke Rd Rockford IL 61107 Office: United Behavioral Systems 415 S Mulford Rd Rockford IL 61108

PAULSRUD, STEVEN GERHARDT, osteopathic physician; b. Iowa City, Iowa, Oct. 20, 1958; s. David Gerhardt and Joan Elizabeth (Swanson) P.; m. Kay Ellen Wadsworth, Aug. 21, 1982. BS in Sociology, Iowa State U., 1980; MSW, U. Iowa, 1984; DO, U. Osteo. Med. and Health Sci., Des Moines, 1994. Lic. in osteo. medicine, Iowa. Hosp. social worker St. Lukes Med. Ctr., Sioux City, Iowa, 1984-87, mgr. partial hosp. program, 1987-90; resident in family practice Cedar Rapids (Iowa) Med. Edn., 1994—. Iowa Dept. Human Svs. grantee, 1987. Mem. AMA, Am. Assn. Family Physicians. Lutheran. Home: 2001 Park Ave SE Cedar Rapids IA 52403 Office: St Lukes Med Edn Program 1026 A Avenue NW Cedar Rapids IA 52402

PAULUS, LYNN ANN, psychotherapist; b. Manitowoc, Wis., Aug. 26, 1957; d. Norman H. and M. Anita (Sheahan) P.; m. James R. Antisdel, July 11, 1981; children: Taylor P., Caitlin P. BA in Psychology, U. Wis., 1979, MSW, 1981; PsyD, Antioch Coll., 1997. Oncology social worker Columbia Hosp., Milw., 1981-82; co-coord. adult milieu program Michael Reese Psychosomatic & Psychiat. Inst., Chgo., 1982-84; asst. dir. day treatment program Evanston (Ill.) Hosp., 1984-85; dir. Riverside (Ill.) Day Hosp. (now MacNeal Day Hosp.), 1985-86; family therapist West Cen. Scvs., Lebanon, N.H., 1986-87, Dartmouth-Hitchcock Mental Health, Hanover, N.H., 1987-89; pvt. practice Manchester, N.H., 1990—. Mem. Alpha Delta Mu. Home: 78 Winter Hill Rd Goffstown NH 03045-1917 Office: 753 Chestnut St Manchester NH 03104

PAULUS, RONALD ALAN, health executive, physician; b. Carlisle, Pa., July 19, 1962; s. John E. Jr. and Margaret M. (Messinger) P.; m. Lori Nadine Griffie, Dec. 27, 1986. BS summa cum laude, U. Pa., 1984, MBA with distinction, 1988, MD, 1988. Health econs. rsch. specialist N.J. Hosp. Rate Setting Commn., Trenton, N.J., 1984-85; cons. Economed Svcs. Corp., Phila., Pa., 1987-88; med. resident dept. internal medicine UCLA Med. Ctr., 1988-89; v.p. opers, mng. dir. Salick Health Care, Inc., L.A., 1989-93; co-founder, COO Care Mgmt. Sci. Corp., Phila., Pa., 1993—; lectr. and presenter in field. Contbr. numerous articles to profl. jours. Mem. Am. Coll. Physician Execs. Republican. Methodist. Office: Care Mgmt Sci Corp 3600 Market St 6th Fl Philadelphia PA 19104

PAULY, JOHN EDWARD, anatomist; b. Elgin, Ill., Sept. 17, 1927; s. Edward John and Gladys (Myhre) P.; m. Margaret Mary Oberle, Sept. 3, 1949; children: Stephen John, Susan Elizabeth, Kathleen Ann, Mary Edward. B.S., Northwestern U., 1950; M.S., Loyola U., Chgo., 1952, Ph.D., 1955. Grad. asst. gross anatomy Stritch Sch. Medicine, Loyola U., Chgo., 1953-54; rsch. asst. anatomy Chgo. Med. Sch., 1952-54, research instr., 1954-55, instr. in gross anatomy, 1955-57, assoc. in gross anatomy, 1957-59, asst. prof. anatomy, 1959-63, asst. to pres., 1960-62; assoc. prof. anatomy Tulane U. Sch. Medicine, 1963-67; prof., head dept. anatomy U. Ark. for Med. Scis., Little Rock, 1967-83; prof., head dept. physiology and biophysics U. Ark. for Med. Scis., 1978-80, vice chancellor for acad. affairs and sponsored rsch., 1983-92, assoc. dean Grad. Sch., 1983-92, prof. anatomy, 1992-95, prof. emeritus, 1995—; tech. adviser Ency. Brit. Films, 1956; mem. safety and occupational health study sect. Nat. Inst. Occupational Safety and Health, Ctr. for Disease Control, 1975-79; vis. prof. faculty medicine Kuwait U., 1993, 94. Author: (with Hans Elias) Human Microanatomy, 1960, 3d edit. 1966, (with Elias and E. Robert Burns) Histology and Human Microanatomy, 1978; editor: (with Lawrence E. Scheving and Franz Halberg) Chronobiology, 1974, (with Heinz von Mayersbach and Lawrence E. Scheving) Biological Rhythms in Structure and Function, 1981, The American Association of Anatomists, 1888-1987. Essays on the History of Anatomy in America and a Report on the Membership-Past and Present, 1987, (with Lawrence E. Scheving) Advances in Chronobiology, 1987, (with Dora K. Hayes and Russel J. Reiter) Chronobiology: Its Role in Clinical Medicine, General Biology and Agriculture, 1990; editor Am. Jour. Anatomy, 1980-92; co-mng. editor Advances in Anatomy, Embryology and Cell Biology, 1980-95; mem. adv. editorial bd. Internat. Jour. Chronobiology, 1973-83; contbr. articles to profl. jours. Served with USNR, 1945-47. Recipient merit certificates AMA, 1953, 59; Bronze award Ill. Med. Soc., 1959; Lederle Med. Faculty award, 1966. Fellow AAAS; mem. Am. Assn. Anatomists (sec.-treas. 1972-80, pres. 1982-83, Centennial award 1987, Henry Gray award 1995), So. Soc. Anatomists (pres. 1971-72), Assn. Anatomy Chmn. (sec.-treas. 1969-71), Am. Physiol. Soc., Internat. Soc. Chronobiology, Pan-Am. Assn. Anatomy, Internat. Soc. Electrophysiol. Kinesiology, Internat. Soc. Steriology, Consejo Nacional de Profesores de Ciencias Morfologicas (hon.), Sigma Xi, Sigma Alpha Epsilon. Roman Catholic.

PAUMGARTNER, GUSTAV, hepatologist, educator; b. Neumarkt, Styria, Austria, Nov. 23, 1933; s. Gustav and Grete (Egghart) P.; grad. Bundesrealgymnasium, Graz, Austria; student Princeton U.; MD, U. Vienna, 1960; m. Dagmar List, June 24, 1963 (dec. 1988); m. Christel Köchert, June 26, 1993. Fellow pharmacology U. Vienna, 1961-63; resident internal medicine U. Vienna Hosp., 1963-65, 66-71; fellow medicine N.J. Coll. Medicine, 1965-66; assoc. dir. dept. clin. pharmacology U. Berne (Switzerland), 1974-79; prof. medicine, chmn. dept. Medicine II, U. Munich (Germany), 1979—; sec. European Assn. Study of Liver, 1971-73; pres. European Assn. Study of Liver, 1989, German Soc. Gastroenterology, 1992, German Assn. Study of Liver, 1995. Author: The Liver, Quantitative Aspects of Structure and Function, 1973; editor Jour. Hepatology; contbr. articles to profl. jours. Fellow Royal Coll. Physicians. Home: 13 Tassilostrasse, D-82166 Graefelfing Germany Office: Med Klinik II, Klinikum Grosshadern, D-81377 Munich Germany

PAUS, POVEL NICOLAY, internal medicine consultant; b. Oslo, Norway, June 23, 1939; s. Povel Nicolay and Bodil Hagerup (Holm) P.; m. Elisabeth Kielland, June 8, 1968; children: Povel Nicolai, Didrik, Henriette. B, Drammen (Norway) Latinskole, 1957; MD, U. Oslo, 1963, MSc, 1969, PhD, 1973. Intern Vestfold Sentralsykehus, Tønsberg, Norway, 1964; fellow Faculty of Medicine U. Oslo, 1966-71, asst. prof., 1971-73; fellow John Fogarty NIH U. Calif., La Jolla, 1973-74; resident Ullevål Hosp., Oslo, 1975-79, Nat. Hosp., Oslo, 1979-86; chief nephrology svc. Cen. Hosp. Akershus, Norway, 1986-92, med. dir., 1992-94; physician-in-chief Med. Clinic Ullevål U. Hosp., Oslo, Norway, 1995—. Author: Therapy in Dermatology, 1961; contbr. articles to profl. jours., chpts. to books. Lt. Norwegian Army, 1965-66. Mem. Norwegian Soc. Internal Medicine, Scandinavian Soc. for Study of Diabetes, Norwegian Med. Assn. (del. 1990-91), European Soc. for Study of Diabetes, Internat. Soc. Nephrology. Office: Ullevål U Hosp, N-0407 Oslo Norway

PAUSTENBACH, DENNIS JAMES, environmental toxicologist; b. Pitts., Oct. 29, 1952; s. Albert Paustenbach and Patricia Jean Iseman; m. Louise

Dunning, Feb. 23, 1985; children: Mark Douglas, Anna Louise. BSChemE, Rose-Hulman Inst. Tech., 1974; MS in Indsl. Hygiene, U. Mich., 1977; MS in Indsl. Psychology, Ind. State U., 1978; PhD in Environ. Toxicology, Purdue U., 1982. Diplomate Am. Bd. Toxicology, Am. Bd. Indsl. Hygiene, Bd. Cert. Safety Profls.; cert. indsl. hygienist, safety profl., environ. assessor. Chem. process engr. Eli Lilly & Co., Clinton, Ind., 1974-76; indsl. hygiene engr. Eli Lilly & Co., Lafayette, Ind., 1977-80; prof. toxicology and indsl. hygiene Purdue U., West Lafayette, Ind., 1979-82; risk assessment scientist Stauffer Chem. Co., Westport, Conn., 1982-84; mgr. indsl. and environ. toxicology Syntex Corp., Palo Alto, Calif., 1984-87; v.p. McLaren/Hart Environ. Engrng., Alameda, Calif., 1987-91, chief tech. officer, 1991—; cons. IBM, Kodak, Hercules, Exxon, GE, Ft. Wayne, Ind., 1980-82, Weyerhauser, 1980-82, 95, Maxus Energy Corp., 1980-82, 87-95, Hewlett-Packard, San Diego, 1984-86, Semicondr. Indsl. Assn., San Jose, Calif., 1984-86, Hughes Aircraft, L.A., 1987-92; com. mem. nat. coun. on radiol. protection and sci. adv. bd. U.S. EPA. Contbr. over 130 articles to profl. jours., 10 chpts. to books; author coll. textbook on environ. risk assessment. Recipient Kusnetz award in Indsl. Hygiene. Fellow Am. Acad. Toxicological Scis.; mem. AICE, Am. Indsl. Hygiene Assn., Soc. Toxicology, Soc. Risk Analysis, Soc. Environ. Toxicology and Chemistry, Soc. Exposure Assessment, Am. Conf. Govtl. Indsl. Hygienists, N.Y. Acad. Scis., Sigma Xi. Roman Catholic. Home: 65 Roan Pl Woodside CA 94062-4229 Office: McLaren/Hart Environ Engrng 1135 Atlantic Ave Alameda CA 94501-1145

PAVAN, MARY HINRICHSEN, pediatrician; b. Ames, Iowa, Jan. 25, 1946; d. J.J.L. and Margaret G. (Looft) Hinrichsen; m. Peter Reed Pavan, June 22, 1970; children: John Reed, Mary Margaret. AB, Radcliffe Coll., 1968; MD, Harvard U., 1972. Diplomate Am. Bd. Pediatrics. Pediat. intern U. Hosps., Cleve., 1972-73, pediat. resident, 1973-74; pediat. resident Children's Hosp. Nat. Med. Ctr., Washington, 1974-75; pediatric cons. Montgomery County Health Dept., Rockville, Md., 1975-76; pvt. practice Medford (Mass.) Pediatric Assocs., 1977-79; assoc. physician Divsn. Devel. Disabilities, U. Iowa, 1980-81; asst. prof. dept. pediatrics divsn. child devel. U. South Fla., Tampa, 1981—, multiple handicap specialsit, 1981—; dir. Early Intervention Program Dist. 5; pediatric dir. Tampa-St. Petersburg Craniofacial Ctr., also Dsit. 5 Spina Bifida Clinic. State of Fla. grantee, 1990—. Mem. Fla. Cleft Palate Craniofacial Assn. (v.p.), Am. Acad. Pediatrics, Am. Cleft Palate Craniofacial Assn., Phi Beta Kappa. Office: All Children's Hosp 801 6th St S Saint Petersburg FL 33701

PÄVLE, HEIKKI KALERVO, anesthesiologist; b. Jyväskylä Mlk, Finland, Sept. 14, 1954; s. Kauko K. and Irma T. (Karimo) P.; m. Anneli Marketta Himberg, July 26, 1980; children: Juhani, Matias. MD, Turku (Finland) U., 1980, cert. in anesthesiology, 1987, PhD, 1991. Jr. anesthesiologist Turku U. Hosp., 1983-87, sr. anesthesiologist, 1987, sr. lectr., asst. prof., 1988—, cons. anesthesiologist, 1988—, bd. dirs., 1993—. Mem. UEMS/EBA (bd. dirs. 1993—, Finnish rep.), Anesthesiologists in Finland (bd. dirs. 1984—), Finniah Assn. Drs. (bd. dirs. 1986-91, 95—). Office: Turku U Hosp, Dept Anesthesiology, 20520 Turku Finland

PAVLICK, PAMELA KAY, nurse, consultant; b. Topeka, Aug. 16, 1944; d. Cy Pavlick and June Lucille (Arnold) (dec.) Dull. Diploma nursing, St. Luke's Hosp., Kansas City, Mo., 1966; BA in Psychology magna cum laude, U. North Fla., 1982, MS in Health Adminstrn. summa cum laude, 1987. RN, Mo., Ill., Fla.; cert. ins. rehab. specialist; lic. rehab. provider, Fla. Clin. instr. St. Luke's Hosp., Kansas City, 1966-70; instr. lic. practical nursing Springfield (Ill.) Sch. Bd., 1970-72; nursing supr. Jacksonville Beach (Fla.) Hosp., 1972-74; pub. health nurse State of Fla., Ocala, 1974-76; dir. nursing Upjohn Health Care, Jacksonville, Fla., 1976-77, mem. adv. com.; med. rep. Travelers Ins. Co., Jacksonville, 1977-84; rehab. cons. Aetna Life & Casualty, Jacksonville, 1985—, rep. nurse cons. adv. coun., 1988-90. Mem. Am. Nurses Assn., Am. Assn. Rehab. Nurses, Nat. Assn. Rehab. Providers, Phi Kappa Phi. Republican. Episcopalian. Home: 14023 Tontine Rd Jacksonville FL 32225-2025 Office: Aetna Life & Casualty PO Box 2200 Jacksonville FL 32203-2200

PAVLOS, ANDREW JOHN, psychologist, educator; b. Toledo, Ohio, Jan. 7, 1937; s. John Andrew and Blanche M. (Waldeck) P.; m. Charlotte Y. Altizer, Aug. 3, 1960; children: Thomas V., Anthony T. BA cum laude, U. Toledo, 1957, MA, 1958; PhD, U. Nev., 1967; postdoctoral, Harvard U., 1992-93, 94-95. Asst. prof. psychology Jacksonville U., Fla., 1967-70; assoc. prof. psychology W.Va. State Coll., Institute, 1970-74; prof. psychology George Williams Coll., Downers Grove, Ill., 1974-86, Eureka (Ill.) Coll., 1986-90, Spring Hill Coll., Mobile, Ala., 1990-92; prof. Worcester (Mass.) State Coll., 1993-95. Author: Social Psychology and the Study of Deviant Behavior, 1978, The Cult Experience, 1982; contbr. articles to publs. Mem. Am. Psychol. Assn., Midwestern Psychol. Assn., Southeastern Psychol. Assn., Soc. for Philosophy and Psychology, So. Soc. for Philosophy and Psychology. Home: Apt 201 3915 Saint Charles Ave New Orleans LA 70115

PAWEL, RUTH, social worker, consultant; b. Prague, Czechoslovakia, Nov. 23, 1920; came to U.S., 1939; d. Hynek and Augusta (Axelrad) Littmann; m. Ernest Pawel, Mar. 23, 1943; children: Michael, Miriam. AB, Pa. State Coll., 1942; MA, Bryn Mawr Coll., 1944. Cert. social worker, N.Y. Caseworker Family Soc., Phila., 1942-45, Traveller's Aid Soc., N.Y.C., 1948-50, Jewish Family Svc., N.Y.C., 1950-54, West Queens (N.Y.) Guidance Ctr., 1954-56, North Shore Child Guidance, Great Neck, N.Y., 1956-58; pvt. practice Great Neck, 1958—; cons. Nassau County Bd. Coop. Ednl. Svcs., Great Neck. Mem. NASW (diplomate in clin. social work).

PAWELEC, GRAHAM PETER, immunologist; b. Cambridge, Eng., Nov. 23, 1951; s. Frank Robert and Hilary Irene (Lander) P.; m. Monika Rita Schneider, July 16, 1983; children: Michael Robert, Maria Elisabeth Sophie. MA, Cambridge (Eng.) U., 1973, PhD, 1982, Dozent, Tübingen U., 1987. Rsch. asst. dept. surgery U. Cambridge, 1974-78; established scientist 2nd dept. internal medicine U. Tübingen, Germany, 1978—; coord. European Union Concerted Action on Molecular Biology Immunosenescence. Translator sci. texts; contbr. over 150 articles to profl. jours. Deutsche Forschungsgeme grantee, 1983—, Deutsche Krebs grantee, 1991—; recipient Gerontology Rsch. award Sandoz Found., 1993. Mem. AAAS, Brit. Soc. Immunology, Brit. Transplantation Soc., Am. Soc. for Histocompatibility and Immunogenetics, German Soc. Immunology, European Found. for Immunogenetics. Office: Medizinische Klinik, Abt Innere Medizin II, D-72076 Tübingen Germany

PAWL, RONALD PHILLIP, neurosurgery educator; b. Chgo., July 26, 1935; s. Phillip Joseph and Ruby Helen (Graham) P.; m. Mary M. Rohner, July 11, 1959; children: Mary, Linda, Diane, Julie, Matthew, Michael. BS in Neurosurgery, Loyola U., Chgo., 1957, MD, 1961. Diplomate Am. Bd. Neurol. Surgery, Am. Bd. Pain Medicine (pres. 1995). Intern Resurrection Hosp., 1961-62; resident in gen. surgery and orthopedics Hines VA Hosp., 1962-63; resident in neurology and neurosurgery U. Ill., Chgo., 1963-66, asst. prof. neurosurgery, 1968-73; asst. chief neurosurgery Tripler Army Med. Ctr., Honolulu, 1966-68; assoc. prof. neurosurgery U. Ill., Chgo., 1973—; dir. pain treatment ctr. Lake Forest (Ill.) Hosp., 1978—. Author: Chronic Pain Primer, 1979; editor Seminars in Neurology, 1989; contbr. articles to Pain Diagnosis and Treatment, 1970-90. Capt. U.S. Army, 1966-68. Named Physician of Yr., Ill. Masonic Med. Ctr., Chgo., 1973. Mem. Ctrl. Neurosurg. Soc. (pres. 1979), Midwest Pain Soc. (pres. 1986), Am. Acad. Pain Medicine (treas. 1990), Chgo. Neurosurg. Soc. (pres. 1982). Roman Catholic. Office: 900 N Westmoreland Rd Lake Forest IL 60045-1674

PAWLOWSKI, DAVID ERIC, family practice physician; b. Highland Pk., Mich., Mar. 6, 1960; s. Paul Eugene and Lorraine Maxine (Nadolny) P.; m. Mary Therese-Pio Sulak, May 26, 1990; 1 child, Benjamin. BS in Chemistry, Wayne State U., Detroit, 1983; DO, Kirksville (Mo.) Coll. Osteo., 1987. Diplomate Am. Bd. Family Practice. Intern Farmington Hills, Mich., 1987-88; resident in family practice Garden City, Mich., 1988-89; sec. dept. family practice Garden City Hosp., 1991—.

PAWLSON, LEONARD GREGORY, physician; b. Victoria, Tex., 1943. MD, U. Pitts., 1969; MPH, U. Wash., 1976. Diplomate Am. Bd. Internal Medicine. Intern, affiliate hosps. Stanford U., 1969-70, resident in medicine, 1970-71; fellow in endocrinology U. Wash., 1973-75, Robert Wood Johnson clin. scholar, 1975-76; asst. prof. medicine and health care scis. George Washington U., Washington, 1976-80, assoc. prof. med. and health care scis., 1980-85, prof. health care scis., medicine, and health svcs. mgmt. and policy, 1985—, assoc. chmn. dept. health care scis., 1978-90, Mudoch head prof. preventive medicine, 1995—, acting chmn., 1987-90, chmn., 1990—; attending physician George Washington Hosp., 1976—. Robert Wood Johnson health policy fellow, 1986-87; bd. dirs. Bon Secours Hosp. System, 1993—, U.S. Soliders and Airmans Home, 1992—, Med. Faculty Assocs., 1990—. Mem. ACP, Am. Geriatrics Soc. (past pres. and chmn. bd., editor law and pub. policy sect. Jour. Am. Geriatrics Soc.); mem. Soc. Gen. Internal Medicine (past bd. dirs.), Assn. Tchrs. Preventive Medicine (chair pub. policy com.). Office: George Washington U Med Ctr Dept Health Care Scis 2150 Pennsylvania Ave NW Washington DC 20037-2396*

PAYN, STEPHEN BERT, psychiatrist, psychoanalyst; b. Swir, Vilna, Lithouania, Dec. 8, 1909; came to U.S., 1937; s. Nathan and Sophie (Swirski) P.; m. Rosalie Fox, Apr. 22, 1950. MD, Friedrich Wilhelms U., 1935; postgrad. psychoanalytic divsn., N.Y. Med. Coll., 1956-60. Diplomate Am. Bd. Psychiatry and Neurology. Intern Surg. U. Clinic, Berlin, 1935-36; intern Lebanon Hosp., N.Y.C., 1940-43, chief med. clinic, 1946-53; resident in psychiatry Grasslands Hosp., Valhalla, N.Y., 1953-56; attending psychiatrist Met. Hosp., N.Y.C., 1957—; mem. faculty psychiatry dept. N.Y. Med. Coll., Valhalla,, 1957—, clin. assoc. prof. Psychiatry, 1977—. Contbr. articles to profl. jours; assoc. editor: Jour. Psychoanalysis in Groups, 1965-75. Capt. M.C. A.U.S., 1943-46. Fellow AMA (life), Am. Psychiat. Assn. (life), Am. Acad. Psychoanalysis (life), Med. Soc. N.Y. State (life); mem. Am. Group Psychotherapy Assn., Soc. Med. Psychoanalysts (cert. group psychotherapist). Office: 137 E 36th St New York NY 10016-3528

PAYNE, DEBORAH ANNE, medical company officer; b. Norristown, Pa., Sept. 22, 1952; d. Kenneth Nathan Moser and Joan (Reese) Dewhurst; m. Randall Barry Payne, Mar. 8, 1975. AA, Northeastern Christian Jr. Coll., 1972; B in Music Edn., Va. Commonwealth U., 1979. Driver, social asst. Children's Aid Soc., Norristown, Pa., 1972-73; mgr. Boddie-Noell Enterprises, Richmond, Va., 1974-79; retail food saleswoman Hardee's Food Systems, Inc., Phila., 1979-81; supr., with tech. tng. and testing depts. Cardiac Datacorp., Phila., 1981-95; tng. supr. Raytel Cardiac Svcs., Forest Hills, N.Y., 1995—. Mem. bd. advisers Am. Biog. Inst., 1989. Mem. NAFE, Delta Omicron (pres. Alpha Xi chpt. 1978-79, pres. Epsilon province 1980-85, chmn. Eastern Pa. alumni 1986-88, Star award 1979), Am. Soc. Profl. and Exec. Women. Republican. Home: 4301 Chippendale St Philadelphia PA 19136-3628 Office: Raytel Cardiac Svcs 118-35 Queens Blvd Forest Hills NY 11375

PAYNE, DOUGLAS DEFREES, cardiothoracic surgeon, educator; b. Dayton, Ohio, Feb. 13, 1940; s. William Gebhart and Elizabeth (Defrees) P.; m. Geraldine Rupp, June 10, 1966. BA, Harvard U., 1962, MD, 1966. Diplomate Am. Bd. Surgery, Am. Bd. Thoracic Surgery. Cardiothoracic surgeon New England Med. Ctr., Boston, 1975—, vice chmn. dept. cardiothoracic surgery, 1985-93, acting chmn. dept. cardiothoracic surgery, 1993-94, chief Divsn. Cariothoracic Surgery, 1994—; assoc. prof. surgery Tufts U., Boston, 1982-90, prof. surgery, 1990—. Lt. col. U.S. Army, 1973-75, Korea. Fellow ACS; mem. Am. Heart Assn., Am. Coll. Chest Physicians. Soc. Thoracic Surgeons, Internat. Soc. for Heart Transplantation, Internat. Cardiovascular Soc. Office: New Eng Med Ctr 750 Washington St Boston MA 02111-1533

PAYNE, FRED J., physician; b. Grand Forks, N.D., Oct. 14, 1922; s. Fred J. and Olive (Johnson) P.; m. Dorothy J. Peck, Dec. 20, 1948; children: Chris Ann Payne Graebner, Roy S., William F., Thomas A. Student U. N.D., 1940-42; BS, U. Pitts., 1948, MD, 1949; MPH, U. Calif., Berkeley, 1958. Diplomate Am. Bd. Preventive Medicine. Intern, St. Joseph's Hosp., Pitts., 1949-50; resident Charity Hosp., New Orleans, 1952-53; med. epidemiologist Ctr. Disease Control, Atlanta, 1953-60; prof. tropical medicine La. State U. Med. Ctr., New Orleans, 1961-66; dir. La. State U. Internat. Ctr. for Med. Rsch. and Tng., San Jose, Costa Rica, 1963-66; exec. sec. 3d Nat. Conf. on Pub. Health Tng., Washington, 1966-67; epidemiologist Nat. Nutrition Survey, Bethesda, Md., 1967-68; chief pub. health professions br. NIH, Bethesda, 1971-74, med. officer, sr. rsch. epidemiologist Nat. Inst. Allergy and Infectious Diseases, 1974-78; asst. health dir. Fairfax County (Va.) Health Dept., 1978-94, dir. HIV/AIDS case mgmt. program, 1988-94, cons. epidemiologist 1994—; med. advisor Ams. for Sound AIDS Policy, 1996—; clin. prof. La. State U., 1966-79; cons. NIH, 1979-81; leader WHO diarrheal disease adv. team, 1960. Contbr. articles to profl. jours. Served with AUS, 1942-46, 49-52. Decorated Combat Medic Badge. Fellow Am. Coll. Preventive Medicine, Am. Coll. Epidemiology; mem. AAAS, AMA, Am. Soc. Microbiology, Internat. Epidemiology Assn., Soc. Epidemiologic Rsch., USPHS Commd. Officers Assn., Sigma Xi. Home: 2945 Ft Lee St Herndon VA 22071-1813 Office: 102 Eldon St Herndon VA 22071

PAYNE, MAXWELL CARR, JR., retired psychology educator; b. Nashville, Feb. 9, 1927; s. Carr and Mary Evans (Tarpley) P.; m. Juanita Campbell, Oct. 17, 1958; children: Maxwell Carr III, Elizabeth Campbell, Mary Allison. AB, Vanderbilt U., 1949; AM, Princeton U., 1950, PhD, 1951. Rsch. assoc. U. Ill., Urbana, 1951-54; asst. prof. psychology Ga. Inst. Tech., Atlanta, 1954-60, assoc. prof., 1961-65, prof., 1965-90, ret., 1991; cons. Lockheed-Ga. Co., Marietta, 1963; testing dir. Aircrew Ctr., Am. Insts. Rsch., Atlanta, 1960-75; faculty Atlanta Sch. Art, 1970; mem. Ga. State Bd. Examiners of Psychologists, 1970-74. Contbr. articles to profl. jours. Sunday Sch. tchr. Northside United Meth. Ch., Atlanta, 1989—. With USNR, 1944-46. Recipient Disting. Tchr. award Ga. Inst. Tech., 1970. Fellow AAAS; mem. Am. Psychol. Assn., Ga. Psychol. Assn. (Cert. of Merit), Southeastern Psychol. Assn., So. Soc. Philosophy and Psychology (treas. 1971-74, pres. 1985-86), Ga. Inst. Tech. Faculty Club (pres. 1970), Phi Beta Kappa, Sigma Xi, Phi Kappa Phi, Omicron Delta Kappa, Beta Theta Pi. Home: 3035 Farmington Dr NW Atlanta GA 30339-4704

PAYNE, MICHAEL CLARENCE, gastroenterologist; b. Chgo., June 30, 1955; s. Clarence H. and Mary P.; m. Cynthia Dillon, June 25, 1983; children: Morgan, Tyler, Dillon. AB in Biochem. cum laude, Harvard U., 1977, MD, 1982, MPH, 1982. Diplomate Am. Bd. Internal Medicine, Gastroenterology. Intern Beth Israel Hosp., Boston, 1988—, resident; fellowship New England Med. Ctr.; pvt. practice in gastroenterology Williamstown (Mass.) Med. Assocs., 1988—. Fellow Am. Coll. Gastroenterology; mem. ACP, AGA, ASGE, AMA. Office: Williamstown Med Assocs 197 Adams Rd Williamstown MA 01267

PAYNE, ROBERT WALTER, psychologist, educator; b. Calgary, Alta., Can., Nov. 5, 1925; s. Reginald William and Nora (Cowdery) P.; m. Helen June Mayer, Dec. 1948 (div. 1972); children: Raymond William, Barbara Joan, Margaret June; m. Josephine Mary Riley Adams, Mar. 1977 (div. 1982); children: George Reginald Alexander, Robin Charles; m. Jean Isobel Dawson, Aug., 1983. B.A., U. Alta., 1949; Ph.D., U. London, Eng., 1954. Lectr. psychology Inst. Psychiatry U. London, 1952-59; prof. psychology Queens U., Kingston, Ont., 1959-65; prof. psychology, chmn. dept. behavioral sci. Temple U. Med. Sch., Phila., 1965-73; prof. dept. psychiatry Temple U. Med. Sch., 1973-78; med. research scientist III Eastern Pa. Psychiat. Inst., Phila., 1965-78; prof. psychology U. Victoria, B.C., Can., 1978-91, prof. emeritus, 1991—, dean Faculty Human and Social Devel., 1978-83. Contbr. articles to profl. jours. Recipient Stratton Research award, 1964. Fellow Am. Psychol. Assn., Brit. Psychol. Soc., Canadian Psychol. Assn., Am. Psychopath. Assn. Home: 2513 Sinclair Rd, Victoria, BC Canada V8N 1B5

PAYNE, THOMAS WILLIAM, III, physicians assistants; b. Coatesville, Pa., Feb. 6, 1952; s. Thomas William II and Betty Sue (Hogg) P.; m. Dana Leigh Yost, Jan. 2, 1985; 1 child, Jennifer. BS in Med. Sci., Alderson-Broaddus Coll., Philippi, W.Va., 1975; MS in Human Resource Mgmt., U. Charleston, W.Va., 1994. Cert. physician asst., Pa., W.Va. Physician's asst. W.Va. Rehab. Ctr., Institute, 1976-77, Neurol. Assocs., Charleston, 1977-78; physician's asst. David A. Santrock, M.D., Inc., Charleston, 1978—, asst. office mgr., 1992—; career guidance presenter Coll. W.Va., Bekcley, 1994, clin. instr. physician asst. program, 1995—. Life mem. Martins Corner Fire Co., Coatesville, Pa., 1964—; eagle scout Boy Scouts Am., Chester County coun., 1962—. Fellow Nat. Assn. Physicians Assts., Am. Acad. Physicians Assts., W.Va. Assn. Physicians Assts. (legis. com. 1992-95, dir.-at-large, 1991, 93, 94, program dir. CME conf. 1992); mem. Seibukan Karate Club of Kanawha Valley (bd. dirs. 1990—). Republican. Home: 5138-A Lone Pine Ln Cross Lanes WV 25313 Office: 500 Donnally St Ste 100 Charleston WV 25301-1611

PAYNE PALACIO, JUNE ROSE, dietetics educator; b. Hove, Sussex, Eng., June 14, 1940; d. Alfred and Doris Winifred (Blanch) Payne; m. Moki Moses Palacio, Nov. 30, 1968; children: Carmen, Dora Jean, Lurene, Michael. AA, Orange Coast Coll., Costa Mesa, 1958-60; BS, U. Calif., Berkeley, 1960-63; postgrad., Dietetic Registration Mills Co, Oakland, 1963-64; PhD, Kans. State U., Manhattan, 1980-83. Registered dietitian. Asst. dir. foodservice, residence hall Mills Coll., Oakland, Calif., 1964-66; staff dietitian Servomation-Bay Cities, Inc., Oakland, 1966-67; food svc. dir. Host Internat., Inc., Honolulu, 1967-73; instr. Kapiolani Community Coll., Honolulu, 1984—, U. Hawaii, Honolulu, 1973-80; dir. dietetics Straub Clinic & Hosp., 1973-80; instr. Kans. State U., Manhattan, 1980-83, El Camino and Santa Monica (Calif.) Colls., 1984—; design cons. Clevenger Nutritional Svc., Santa Monica, 1984—; prof. dietetics Pepperdine U., Malibu, Calif., 1984—; instr. Ctr. for Dietetic Edn., Woodland Hills, Calif., 1986—. Contbr. articles to profl. jours. Mem. Am. Dietetic Assn. (ho. of dels., ethics com. AP4 rev. panel), Calif. Dietetic Assn. (pres. 1992-93). Republican. Episcopalian. Home: 24319 Baxter Dr Malibu CA 90265-4728 Office: Pepperdine U Dept Natural Scis 24255 Pacific Coast Hwy Malibu CA 90263-0001

PAYNTER, VESTA LUCAS, pharmacist; b. Aiken County, S.C., May 29, 1922; d. James Redmond and Annie Lurline (Stroman) Lucas; m. Maurice Alden Paynter, Dec. 23, 1945 (dec. 1971); children: Sharon Lucinda, Maurice A. Jr., Doyle Gregg. BS in Pharmacy, U. S.C., 1943. Lic. pharmacist. Owner, pharmacist Cayce Drug Store, S.C., 1944-52, Dutch Fork Drug Store, Columbia, S.C., 1955-60, The Drug Ctr., Cayce, 1963-81; pharmacist Lane-Rexall, Columbia, 1952-55; dist. pharmacist S.C. Dept. Health and Environ. Control, Columbia, 1983-90, ret., 1990. Named Preceptor of Yr., Syntex Co., student body U. S.C., 1981. Fellow, 5th Dist. Pharm. Assn., S.C. Pharm. Assn., S.C. Pub. Health Assn., Alpha Epsilon Delta; mem. China, India, Burma VA Assn. (assoc.), 14th Air Force Assn. (assoc.). Baptist. Lodges: Order of Eastern Star, Order of Amaranth, Sinclair Lodge, White Shrine of Jerusalem, Columbia Shrine #6. Avocations: travel, tennis, golf, art. Home: 2351 Vine St Cayce SC 29033-3000

PAZ, HAROLD LOUIS, internist and educator; b. N.Y.C., Jan. 3, 1955. BA in Biology and Psychology, U. Rochester, 1977, MD, 1982; MS in Life Sci. Engring., Tufts U., 1979. Diplomate Am. Bd. Internal Medicine, subspecialty in Pulmonary Medicine, Critical Care Medicine. Intern internal medicine Northwestern U. Med. Ctr., Chgo., 1982-83, resident internal medicine, 1983-85, chief medical resident, 1985-86; instr. clin. medicine Northwestern U., Chgo., 1985-86; fellow pulmonary and critical care John Hopkins U., Balt., 1986-88, fellow environ. health scis., 1986-88; asst. prof. medicine Hahnemann U., Phila., 1988-94, asst. prof. anesthesia, 1989-94, assoc. dean grad. med. edn., 1992—; assoc. prof. medicine Hahnemann U., 1992-94, dir. med. intensive care unit, 1988-94; assoc. hosp. med. dir. Ctr. for Clin. Outcomes, Hahnemann U., Phila., 1983-94; med. dir., assoc. dean for clin. affairs, assoc. prof. of clin. medicine UMDNJ, Robert Wood Johnson Med. Sch., New Brunswick, N.J., 1994-95; dean, CEO, assoc. prof. medicine U. Med. Group, 1995—. Editor Jour. Undergrad. Rsch., 1976, Med. Staff News newsletter, 1992—; cons. Annals Internal Medicine, Clin. Immunology and Immunopathology. Endowood fellow Johns Hopkins U., 1987-88; U. Rochester scholar, 1979. Fellow ACP, Am. Coll. Chest Physicians; mem. AMA, Am. Coll. Physician Execs., Am. Fedn. Clin. Rsch., Am. Thoracic Soc., Philip Drinker Soc. for Critical Care (pres. 1992-94). Office: UMDNJ Robert Wood Johnson Med Sch 125 Paterson St New Brunswick NJ 08901

PAZDERNIK, THOMAS LOWELL, pharmacology educator; b. Detroit Lakes, Minn., Jan. 3, 1943; s. Alvin Joseph and Irene Helen (Kersting) P.; m. Betty Catherine Platt, June 20, 1967; children: Lisa Ann, Nancy Lea. BS in Pharmacy, U. Minn., 1967; PhD in Medicinal Chemistry, U. Kans., 1971. NIH postdoctoral fellow U. Kans. Med. Ctr., Kansas City, 1971-73, asst. prof., 1973-77, assoc. prof., 1977-84, assoc. dean, 1986-89, prof. pharmacology, toxicology and therapeutics, 1984—; vis. rsch. scientist U. Helsinki, 1976. Contbr. articles to sci. publs. NIH career devel. awardee. Mem. Am. Soc. Pharmacology and Exptl. Therapeutics, Internat. Soc. Immunopharmacology, Soc. Toxicology (officer, com. mem. Cen. States chpt. 1986—), Soc. Neurosci. Roman Catholic. Home: 7807 Windsor St Shawnee Mission KS 66208-4027 Office: U Kans Med Ctr 39th and Rainbow St Kansas City KS 66103

PAZIRANDEH, MAHMOOD, rheumatologist, consultant; b. Hamadan, Iran, Jan. 1, 1932; came to U.S., 1966; naturalized U.S. Citizen, 1977; s. Rahim and Zahra (Shoushtar) P.; m. Parvin Danesh, Apr. 19, 1961; children: Bruce, Justin, Navid. MD, U. Tehran, 1958; postgrad., Eng., 1959-64, Pitts. U., 1967-68. Diplomate Am. Bd. Internal Medicine and Rheumatology. Asst. prof. Tehran U., Iran, 1964-67; clin. assoc. Cleve. Clinic Found., 1969-70; clin. instr. Case Western Res. U., Cleve., 1970-72, sr. clin. instr., 1972-78, clin. asst. prof., 1979-93, clin. assoc. prof., 1993—; dir. med. edn. Lake Hosp., Cleve., 1984-96, pres. med. staff, 1990-93; mem. CME com. Case Western Res. U. Sch. Medicine, 1994-96; dir. med. edn. Euclid Hosp., Cleve., 1971-73, dir. quality assurance, 1989-93. Contbr. articles to profl. jours. Speaker pub. edn. radio, TV and seminars, Cleve., 1984—; chmn. pub. forums Arthritis Found., Cleve., 1985—, trustee, 1986-96, chmn. pub. edn. com., 1987—. Recipient recognition svc. award Arthritis Found., 1976, Robert Stecher Vol. award, 1988, Nat. Vols. Svc. citation, 1989; Eng. and Iranian Govt. scholar, 1959-63. Fellow ACP, Am. Coll. Rheumatology; mem. Am. Soc. Internal Medicine, Ohio State Med. Assn. (del. 1989-96), Lake County Med. Soc. (pres. 1988—), Cleve. Rheumatism Soc. (pres. 1974), N.Y. Acad. Scis. Republican. Home: 124 Pheasant Ln Hunting Valley OH 44022-4043 Office: Case Western Res U 36100 Euclid Ave Willoughby OH 44094-4456

PAZZAGLINI, MARIO PETER, JR., psychologist; b. Endicott, N.Y., Mar. 9, 1940; s. Mario and Dina Julia (Albertini) P.; BA, SUNY, Binghamton, 1961; MA, George Washington U., 1965; PhD, U. Del., 1969. Staff psychologist Del. State Hosp., 1968-72, co-dir. adolescent program, 1972-77; with Bur. of Alcoholism and Drug Abuse State of Del., 1970-83; pvt. practice psychotherapy, Newark, Del., 1973—; mem. staff St. Francis Hosp., Wilmington, Del., 1977—; adj. asst. prof. psychology U. Del., 1972—; clin. instr. Jefferson Med. Sch.; cons. street drug rsch. HEW grantee, 1971, 1972. Author: The Book of Numbers, 1990, Symbolic Messages, 1992, (workbook) Street Drugs, 1995; contbr. articles to profl. jours. Mem. AAAS, Am. Psychol. Assn., N.Y. Inst. Gestalt Therapy, N.Y. Acad Scis, Sigma Xi. Democrat. Roman Catholic. Research in imagery and ancient use of symbols; also pioneer in-residence adolescent psychiat. treatment, drug treatment for State of Del. (11), street drug use patterns rsch. (11). Office: 523 Capitol Trl Newark DE 19711-3859

PEACH, PAUL E., physician, medical facility administrator; b. Owensboro, Ky., June 2, 1943; s. Elbert B. and Ermal M. (Bennett) P. Student, So. Meth. U., 1961-63; BS, Ind. U., 1965, JD, 1969; student, U. New Orleans, 1977-79; MD, La. State U., 1983. Bar: Ind., 1970; diplomate Am. Bd. Phys. Medicine and Rehab. Atty. pvt. practice Indpls., 1970-72; staff atty La. Dept. Health & Human Svcs., New Orleans, 1972-77; resident La. State U. Charity Hosp., New Orleans, 1983-84, Wadsworth VA Hosp., Cedars-Sinai Hosp., L.A., 1984-86; med. dir. Roosvelt Warm Springs (Ga.) Inst. for Rehab., 1986—; pvt. practice atty., New Orleans, 1972-77; clin. assoc. prof. Ctr. for Rehab. Medicine Emory U., Atlanta, 1987—. Author: (with others) Late Effects of Poliomyelitis, 1991, Effect of Compliance in Treatment Outcomes in Patients with Post-Polio Syndrome, 1991. Fellow Am. Acad. Phys. Medicine and Rehab.; mem. Med. Assn. Ga., Tri-County Med. Assn. Ga. (pres. 1990-91, 93-96), Ga. Soc. Phys. Medicine and Rehab. (pres. 1989-90, 95-96), Am. Acad. Electrodiagnostic Medicine (assoc.), Am. Hosp. Assn. (governing bd. 1988-91, del. rehab. sect. 1990). Home: Roosvelt Inst Box 336 Warm Springs GA 31830 Office: Roosvelt Inst for Rehab Box 1000 Warm Springs GA 31830-0268

PEACOCK, JAMES LOWREY, surgeon, educator; b. Atlanta, July 1, 1956; s. Erle Ewart and Mary Louise (Lowrey) P.; m. Lisabeth Bowen Todd, Oct. 3, 1982; children: Jennifer Sarah, Michael Todd. BA, Colo. Coll., 1978; MD, Tulane U., 1982. Surgery resident Vanderbilt U., Nashville, 1982-84, surgery chief resident, 1988-89; med. staff fellow Nat. Cancer Inst., Bethesda,

Md., 1984-86; asst. prof. surgery and oncology U. Rochester, N.Y., 1989-94; assoc. prof. surgery and oncology U. Rochester, 1995—; co-chmn. surgery com. Ea. Coop. Oncology Group, Denver, 1992—. Recipient Clin. Oncology Career Devel. award Am. Cancer Soc., Atlanta, 1992—. Fellow ACS; mem. AMA, Soc. Surg. Oncology, Assn. Acad. Surgery, Soc. Surg. Alimentary Tract. Office: U Rochester Med Ctr Surg 601 Elmwood Ave Rochester NY 14642

PEACOCK, JILLIAN MARY, university administrator; b. Glasgow, Scotland, Nov. 16, 1965; d. David Babes and Helen June (Walker) P. BSc in Cell Biology, U. Glasgow, 1987, PhD, 1991. Rsch. asst. U. Glasgow, 1987-90, postdoctoral rsch. assoc., 1990-94, rsch. adminstr., 1994—. Contbr. articles to profl. jours.; patentee in field. Mem. Internat. Assn. Dental Rsch., Phys. Soc. Office: U Glasgow, CRI, Glasgow G12 8QQ, Scotland

PEACOCK, WILLIAM FRANKLIN, IV, emergency medicine physician; b. Atlanta, Aug. 5, 1959; s. William Franklin Peacock and Gretchen Lenore (Elliott) Cochran; m. Judith Marie Baginski, Sept. 3, 1988; children: Ayla, Dakota. BS, Alma Coll., 1981; MD, Wayne State U., 1985. Assoc. residency dir. William Beaumont Hosp., Royal Oak, Mich., 1989-94; emergency ops. dir. Cleve. Clinic, 1994—. Office: Cleve Clinic Dept Emergency 9500 Euclid Cleveland OH 44195

PEARCE, DOUGLAS JAMES, physician; b. Terre Haute, Ind., Sept. 4, 1953; s. Robert Warren and Mary Jane (Powers) P.; m. Michelle Catherine Foote, Oct. 6, 1990; children: Brandon James, Lauren Michelle. BS, Ga. State U., 1979; MD, Med. Coll. of Ga., 1985. Diplomate Am. Bd. Internal Medicine, Am. Bd. Cardiology. Intern in internal medicine U. Rochester, N.Y., 1985-86; resident in internal medicine Wake Forest U., Winston-Salem, N.C., 1986-88; fellow in cardiology U. Ala., Birmingham, 1988-91; rsch. fellow Am. Heart Assn., Birmingham, 1990; chief fellow, cardiology U. Ala., Birmingham, 1991, asst. prof. medicine, 1991—, dir. coronary care unit, 1991—, co-dir. chest pain evaluation unit, 1995—; attending physician Birmingham VA Med. Ctr., Birmingham, 1991—; chmn. Ala. Commn. for Pre-Hosp. Cardiac Care, State of Ala., Montgomery, 1995—. Author: (book) Understanding Chest Radiographs, 1984; contbg. author texts in field. Mem. Ala. Conservancy, Birmingham, 1988—, Nature Conservancy, Am. Heart Assn., Birmingham, 1993—. Fellow Am. Coll. Cardiology, Am. Coll. Physicians; mem. Am. Coll. Cardiology (councilor 1994—), Alpha Omega Alpha.

PEARCE, JOHN KENNETH, psychiatrist, educator; b. Seattle, Mar. 15, 1935; s. J. Kenneth and Gladys (Gose) P.; m. Suzanne Elizabeth Schell, June 11, 1966; children: Sarah Elizabeth, Miranda Margaret. Student, U. Wash., 1953-57; MD, Yale U., 1961. Cert. in psychiatry. Intern U. Chgo. Clinics, 1961-62; resident Yale U., New Haven, 1962-64; fellow Austen Riggs Ctr., Stockbridge, Mass., 1964-66; fellow in child psychiatry Beth Israel Hosp., Boston, 1966-68; clin. instr. psychiatry Harvard U., 1968-73; faculty Ackerman Family Inst., N.Y.C., 1967-71, Cambridge Family Inst., Cambridge, Mass., 1975—, Kantor Family Inst., Cambridge, 1980—; med. dir. Island Counseling, Martha Vineyard Island, 1984—. Author: Exiles from Eden: Psychotherapy from an Evolutionary Perspective, 1989; editor: Ethnicity and Family Therapy, 1982, 86, Family Therapy: Combining Psychodynamic and Family Systems Approach, 1980. Mem. Human Behavior and Evolution Soc., Am. Family Therapy Assn. (bd. dirs. 1977-81, 82-85, sec. 1980-82, cert. recognition 1982, 85), Soc. for Family Therapy & Research (cert. recognition 1975, 83). Democrat. Congregationalist. Home and Office: 247 Lakeview Ave Cambridge MA 02138-2133

PEARL, RICHARD ALAN, neurologist, educator; b. N.Y.C., Feb. 2, 1943; s. Sam and Edith (Friedman) P.; m. Barbara Goldstein, Mar. 28, 1971; children: Laurie, Caroline, Jennifer. BA, U. Pa., 1964; MD, Georgetown U., 1968. Diplomate Am. Bd. Psychiatry and Neurology. Intern Mt. Sinai Hosp., N.Y.C., 1968-69, resident in neurology, 1969-70, 72-74; pvt. practice Smithtown, N.Y., 1974—; chief neurology St. John's Hosp., Smithtown, 1980—, Community Hosp. West Suffolk, Smithtown, 1980-90; asst. clin. prof. neurology Stony Brook (N.Y.) U. Hosp., 1980—. Lt. comdr. M.C., USN, 1972-74. Fellow Am. Acad. Neurology; mem. Assn. for Rsch. in Nervous and Mental Diseases, Alpha Omega Alpha. Office: 307 Middle Country Rd Smithtown NY 11787-2829

PEARL, WILLIAM RICHARD EMDEN, pediatric cardiologist; b. N.Y.C., Nov. 1, 1944; s. William Emden and Sara (Gilston) P.; m. Karlyn Katsumoto, July 9, 1978; children: Jeffrey, Kristine. BA, Queens Coll., 1966; MD, SUNY, Bklyn., 1970. Diplomate Am. Bd. Pediatrics, Am. Bd. Pediatric Cardiology. Intern Roosevelt Hosp., N.Y.C., 1970-71; resident N.Y. Hosp.-Cornell Med. Ctr., N.Y.C., 1971-72; fellow Albert Einstein Coll. Medicine, N.Y.C., 1972-74; asst. prof. U. Hawaii, Honolulu, 1974-76; asst. prof. Tex. Tech. Med. Sch., El Paso, 1976-82, assoc. prof., 1982-92; chief pediatric cardiology William Beaumont Army Med. Ctr., El Paso, 1976-94; assoc. prof. med. branch U. Tex. Med. Br., Galveston, 1994—; cons. Miami (Fla.) Children's Hosp., 1988, Driscol Children's Hosp., Corpus Christi, Tex., 1992, Thomason Hosp., El Paso, 1976-92. Contbr. articles to profl. jours. Col. USAR, 1974-92. N.Y. State Bd. Regents scholar, 1962-66, Fed. Health Careers scholar, 1967-70; NIH fellow, 1972-73; recipient Dept. of Army Commendation for outstanding sci. achievement, 1984. Fellow Am. Acad. Pediatrics, Am. Coll. Cardiology; mem. Am. Heart Assn. (coun. on cardiovascular disease in the young 1982). Office: U Tex Med Br Children's Hosp 301 University Blvd Galveston TX 77550-2708

PEARLMAN, MARTIN N., psychologist, educator; b. Bklyn., Apr. 28, 1938; s. Nathan and Mollie (Goldstein) P.; 1 child, Daniel. BA, Bklyn. Coll., 1958; MA, U. Mich., 1960; PhD, Rutgers U., 1975. Lic. psychologist, N.J. Sr. clin. psychologist Cen. Islip State Hosp., N.Y. Dept. Mental Health, 1963-67; clin. sch. psychologist Granite Sch. Dist., Salt Lake City, 1967-69; from instr. to full prof. Middlesex County Coll., Edison, N.J., 1969—, dir. mental health program, 1972-78; pvt. practice East Brunswick, N.J., 1978—; mem. Nat. Com. for Community Coll. Mental Health Programs, 1972-74. U.S. Pub. Health fellow, 1969-72. Mem. Am. Psychol. Assn. Office: Middlesex Coll Dept of Psychology Mill Rd Edison NJ 02819

PEARLMAN, RICHARD LEE, psychiatrist; b. N.Y.C., Jan. 8, 1943; s. Joseph and Eleanor (Levy) P.; m. Madlyne Diane, Jan. 31, 1965; children: Lisa, Bethany Lynn. AB, Clark U., 1963; MD, Tufts U., 1967. Diplomate Am. Bd. Psychiatry. Resident child psychiatry Albert Einstein Med. Ctr., Phila., 1967-69; resident adult psychiatry St. Vincent's Med. Ctr., S.I., N.Y., 1969-72; dir. out patient svc. North Richmond Community Mental Health Ctr., Staten Island, 1972-89; assoc. dir. North Richmond Community Mental Health Ctr., 1982—; dir. psychiatric residency program St. Vincents Med. Ctr., Staten Island, 1975—; clin. assoc. prof. N.Y. Med. Coll., 1985—. Contbr. articles to profl. jours. Lt. col. AUS, 1973-75. Mem. Am. Psychiat. Assn., N.Y. Med. Soc., Richmond County Med. Soc. (past pres.), Acad. Medicine (pres.). Office: 1260 Richmond Rd Staten Island NY 10304-2304

PEARLMUTTER, FLORENCE NICHOLS, psychologist, therapist; b. Bklyn., Mar. 17, 1914; d. William and Marie Elizabeth (Rugamer) Griebe; m. Wilbur Francis Nichols, Aug. 17, 1940 (dec. 1967); 1 child, Roger F.; m. F. Bernard Pearlmutter, June 27, 1969. BS, NYU, 1934, postgrad., 1965-75; MS, Yeshiva U., 1960. Psychologist P.P.P. Counseling Ctr., Northport, N.Y., 1967-69; hypno-therapist Robert E. Peck, M.D., Syosset, N.Y., 1969-75; therapist Arthur J. Gross, M.D., Hicksville, N.Y., 1975—; rsch. asst. and prof. rsch. in field. Mem. NEA, AAUW, Nassau County Psychol. Assn., N.Y. State Psychol. Assn. (assoc.), Nat. Women's Hall of Fame, Kappa Delta Pi.

PEARLSON, GODFREY DAVID, psychiatrist, educator; b. Sunderland, England, Jan. 30, 1950; came to U.S., 1975; s. Elias and Blanche (Book) P.; m. Judith G. Sirote. MA, Columbia U., 1975; MD, Newcastle on Tyne, England, 1974. Intern Newcastle-on-Tyne RVI, Newcastle, Eng., 1974; resident in psychiatry Johns Hopkins U., Balt., 1976-79, dir. psychiatry neuroimaging, 1989—, prof. mental hygiene, psychiatry, 1987—. Fellow Am. Psychopathological Assn., 1987. Fellow Am. Psychiat. Assn. Office: Johns Hopkins Hosp Meyer 3 166 600 N Wolfe St Baltimore MD 21287-7362

PEARN, JOHN HEMSLEY, pediatrician; b. Brisbane, Australia, Mar. 18, 1940; s. James Owen and Elizabeth Helen (Shaw) P.; m. Vena Beatrice White, Dec. 2, 1966; children: Owen Edward, Nigel John, Susan Cicely. BSc, U. Queensland, Australia, 1962, MB, BChir, 1964, MD, 1969. Registered med. practitioner, Queensland; cert. clin. geneticist; specialist cons. pediatrician and physician. Resident med. officer Royal Brisbane Hosp., 1965; clin. lectr., sr. lectr. and reader Royal Children's Hosp., Brisbane, 1968-85; sr. rsch. fellow U. London, Hosp. for Sick Children, 1971-72, Regional Neurol. Ctr., Westgate Hosp., Newcastle, Eng., 1973-74; clin. lectr. U. Queensland, 1966-67, prof., chmn. dept. child health, 1986—; vis. scholar Green Coll. U. Oxford, Eng., 1995; mem. med. ethics com. Australian Def. Force, 1991—. Author 20 books in field, including In the Capacity of A Surgeon, 1988, Venoms and Victims, 1988, Preventive First Aid, 1989, Fevers and Frontiers, 1990, New Horizons, 1992, Milestones of Australian Medicine, 1994; co-author: The Science of First Aid, 1996; contbr. articles to profl. jours. Nat. dir. tng. St. John Ambulance Australia, Brisbane, 1990—; councillor Australian Resuscitation Coun., 1987-93; exec. Child Accident Prevention Found., Melbourne, 1979-90, Pediat. Rsch. Soc., Australia, Melbourne, 1976. Col. M.C. Royal Australian Army, 1965—. Decorated Order of Australia, Res. Forces; decorated knight Order of St. John, 1996; Florey fellow Royal Soc. London, 1971-74; recipient Bancroft Oration award, 1991, Herbert Moran Oration award, 1991, Ashdown Oration medal Australasian Coll. of Tropical Medicine, 1995, citation Australia Med. Assn., 1995; Kenneth Russell orator Royal Australasian Coll. Surgeons, 1996. Fellow Royal Australian Coll. Physicians, Royal Coll. Physicians, Royal Coll. Physicians Edinburgh, Am. Coll. Tropical Medicine, Royal Hist. Soc. Queensland (v.p. 1989—), Royal Life Saving Soc. Australia; mem. Human Genetics Soc. (nat. pres. 1981-83), Parachute Regtl. Assn., United Svc. Inst., Australia Coll. Pediat. (chair Queensland 1993-96). Home: 121 Banks St, Brisbane Queensland 4051, Australia Office: Royal Childrens Hosp, Herston, Brisbane Queensland 4029, Australia

PEARSALL, HARRY JAMES, dentist; b. Bay City, Mich., Apr. 12, 1916; s. Roy August and Gladys Agnes (Tierney) P.; m. Betty Almina Dahlke, Oct. 5, 1946 (dec. Nov. 1982); 1 child, Paul Roy. BS, Marquette U., 1937, DDS, 1939. Gen. practice dentistry Bay City, 1939—; cons. Delta Dental Ins., Lansing, Mich., 1975-86. Mem. Bay City chpt. Revision Com., 1965-66; bd. dirs. Downtown Bay City, 1962-73. Served to maj. U.S. Army, MC, 1940-46. Mem. ADA, Am. Coll. Dentists, Internat. Coll. Dentists, Mich. Dental Assn. (pres. 1972-73, spl. com. on life mems.), Saginaw Valley Dental Soc. (pres. 1955-56), Bay County Dental Soc. (pres. 1950-51), Am. Legion. Lodge: Elks. Home: 1820 E Worfolk Dr Apt 1 Essexville MI 48732 Office: 404 Shearer Bldg Bay City MI 48708

PEARSE, WARREN HARLAND, association executive, obstetrician and gynecologist; b. Detroit, Sept. 28, 1927; s. Harry Albridge and Frances (Wressell) P.; m. Jacqueline Anne Langan, June 15, 1950; children: Kathryn, Susan, Laurie, Martha. B.S., Mich. State U., 1948; M.B., M.D., Northwestern U., 1950. Intern. Univ. Hosp., Ann Arbor, Mich., 1950-51; resident obstetrics and gynecology, 1951-53, 55-56; practice medicine specializing obstetrics and gynecology Detroit, 1956-58; mem. faculty U. Nebr. Med. Center Omaha, 1959-71, Found. prof., chmn. dept. obstetrics and gynecology, 1962-71; asst. dean U. Nebr. Med. Center Omaha (Med. Coll.), 1963-71, mem. residency rev. com. obstetrics and gynecology, 1968-71; dean Med. Coll. Va., Richmond, 1971-75; exec. dir. Am. Coll. Obstetrics and Gynecology, 1975-93; cons., 1993—; editor Women's Health Issues, 1993—; chmn. rsch. adv. group Maternal Child Health Svc., Health Scis. Mental Health Adminstrn., HEW, 1967—; cons. family planning Office Econ. Opportunity, 1970—. Author: (with R.W. Stander) Obstetrics and Gynecology at the University of Michigan, 1969; Contbr. chpts., articles tech. lit. Served from 1st lt. to capt. AUS, 1953-55. Mem. Am. Coll. Obstetrics and Gynecology (dist. sec., treas. 1964-68, vice chmn. 1968-71), Am. Gynecology Soc., Soc. Gynecology Investigation, Assn. Profs. Gynecology and Obstetrics (sec., treas. 1969—), Alpha Omega Alpha. Home: 350 S River Landing Rd Edgewater MD 21037-1549 Office: American College of Obs & Gyns 409 12th St SW Washington DC 20024

PEARSON, DENNIS LEE, optometrist; b. Portland, Oreg., June 21, 1951; s. Alvin Wesley and Pharaby Iva (Barnett) P.; m. Corinne Elaine Boggs, Aug. 27, 1972; children: Kathleen Erin, Erik Edward. BS in Chemistry, Portland State U., 1974; OD, Pacific U., Forest Grove, Oreg., 1978. Optometrist Drs. Diederich & Pearson, St. Helens, Oreg., 1979-83; pvt. practice Lebanon, Oreg., 1983—; adv. panel mem. managed care Vision Svc. Plan, Rancho Cucamunga, Calif., 1995—; adv. panel mem. laser refraction Laser Vision Ctr. at Pacific U., Portland, 1995—. Sch. bd. mem. Sodaville Sch. Dist., Oreg., 1989-93; bd. dirs. Lebanon Boys & Girls Club, 1989-91, 93-94; elder Lebanon Presbyn. Ch., 1992—. Mem. Am. Optometric Assn., Oreg. Optometric Assn. (bd. dirs. 1988—, pres.), Kiwanis Club of Lebanon, Lebanon C. of C. Office: 90 Market St Ste 20 Lebanon OR 97355

PEARSON, JACK WILLIAM, pharmaceutical executive; b. Orleans, France, Oct. 28, 1960; Came to U.S., 1961; BA in Psychology, Chemistry, Biology, Ind. U., 1983; MBA, Nat. U., Las Vegas, Nev., 1987. Sales rep. Glaxo, Inc., Las Vegas, 1985-88; dist. mgr. Glaxo, Inc., Sacramento, Calif., 1988-92; product mgr., mktg. adminstr. Glaxo, Inc., Durham, N.C., 1992-94; sr. mgr. health systems mktg. Glaxo Wellcome, Inc., Durham, 1994—; nat. adv. coun. Nat. Bus. Coalition Health, 1996—; mem. Midwest Bus. Group on Health, 1994—, users com. Nat. Commn. on Quality Assurance, 1994—; com. mem. Employer Purchasing Alliance, Tampa, 1995—. Mem. Am. Mgmt. Assn., Am. Coll. Healthcare Execs., Internat. Soc. for Econ. Evaluation of Medicines, Internat. Found. for Employer Benefit Plans, Soc. for Human Resource Mgmt. Office: Glaxo Wellcome Inc 5 Moore Dr Research Triangle Park NC 27709

PEARSON, LLOYD ERICK, orthodontist; b. Mpls., Feb. 20, 1933; s. Erik Olaf and Emma Fredda (Johnson) P.; m. June Marie Olson, Sept. 14, 1957; children: Cynthia Pearson Conner, Leslie M., Bradley L. DDS, U. Minn., 1957, MS in Orthodontics, 1959. Diplomate Am. Bd. Orthodontics (bd. dirs. 1984—, pres. 1990-91). Practice dentistry specializing in orthodontics Edina, Minn., 1959—. Contbr. articles to profl. jours. Mem. Am. Dental Assn., Minn. Dental Assn. (dental edn. com., del.), Am. Bd. Orthodontics (past pres.), Mpls. Dist. Dental Soc., Am. Assn. Orthodontists, Minn. Soc. Orthodontists (past pres., chmn. edn. com.), Midwestern Orthodontic Soc. (past pres.), Tweed Found. for Orthodontic Rsch., Omicron Kappa Upsilon. Office: 263 Southdale Med Bldg France Ave S Edina MN 55435

PEARSON, MARK LANDELL, molecular biologist; b. Toronto, Ont., Can., June 2, 1940; s. William Holmes and Marguerite Rachel (Landell) P.; m. Katharine Anne Brown, Aug. 2, 1962; children: Scott Wallace, Jennifer Anne. BASc, U. Toronto, 1962, MA, 1964, PhD, 1966. Asst. to assoc. prof. U. Toronto, 1969-79; sect. head devel. genetics NCI-FCRF, Frederick, Md., 1979-83, dir. lab. molecular biology, 1982-83; asst. dir. life scis. E.I. DuPont de Nemours & Co., Wilmington, Del., 1983-84, dir. molecular biology, 1985-90; exec. dir. cancer and inflamatory diseases rsch. The DuPont Merck Pharm. Co., Wilmington, 1991-92; CEO Darwin Molecular Corp., Kirkland, Wash., 1992-94; pres. Molecumetics, Ltd., Belleuve, Wash., 1994—; adj. prof. U. Toronto, 1969-79, U. Md., 1982-83, 86; sci. adv. bd. Genex Corp., Rockville, Md., 1978-83; bd. mem. Keystone Sympcsia on Molecular and Cellular Biology, 1986-93, exec. com., 1990-93; com. on sci. and the arts Franklin Inst., 1991-93. Trustee Life Sci. Rsch. Found., 1988, U. Del. Rsch. Found., 1990-92; mem. program adv. com. human genome NIH, 1988-92, Human Genome Orgn., 1989—; bd. dirs. Alliance Aging Rsch., 1989-92, joint informatics task force NIH/DOE, 1990-92, Wash. Biotech. Found., 1994—. Josiah Macy Jr. fellow, 1977-78; Helen Hay Whitney postdoctoral fellow, 1966-69. Mem. AAAS, Am. Chem. Soc., Am. Soc. Microbiology, Am. Soc. Virology, Biophys. Soc., Am. Soc. Cell Biology, Am. Soc. Biochem. and Molecular Biology, Am. Soc. Human Genetics, Am. Assn. for Cancer Rsch., Can. Biochem. Soc., Can. Soc. Cell Biology, N.Y. Acad. Sci. Home: 2405 91st Pl NE Bellevue WA 98004 Office: Molecumetics Ltd 2023 120th Ave NE # 400 Bellevue WA 98005

PEARSON, PATRICIA KELLEY, marketing representative; b. Carrollton, Ga., Jan. 21, 1953; d. Ben and Edith (Kelley) Rhudy; m. Ray S. Pearson, June 4, 1976; children: Chad, Jonathan, Kelly. BA in Journalism, Ga. State U., 1974; BSN, West Ga. Coll., 1990. RN Fla. Pub. rels. asst. Grady Meml. Hosp., Atlanta, 1974-77; editorial asst. Childers & Sullivan, Huntsville, Ala., 1977-78; sales rep. AAA Employment Agy., Huntsville, 1978-80; editor Wright Pub. Co., Atlanta, 1980-82; elect./electronic drafter PRC Cons., Atlanta, 1980-87; researcher Dept. Nursing at West Ga. Coll., Carrollton, 1989-90; med./surg. nurse Tanner Med. Ctr., Carrollton, Ga., 1989-90, Delray Community Hosp., Delray Beach, Fla., 1990-91; sales rep. Innovative Med. Svcs., 1991-94; with staff devel., employee rels. Beverly Oaks Rehab. and Nursing Ctr., 1994-95; sales rep./ pub. rels. rep. Columbia HCA, 1996—. Vol. Project Response. All-Am. scholar U.S. Achievement Acad., 1990, recipient Nat. Coll. Nursing award, 1989. Mem. NOW, Space Coast Bus. Writer's Guild, Omicron Delta Kappa. Democrat. Home: 139 Jamaica Dr Cocoa Beach FL 32931-2825

PEARSON, ROBERT EDWIN, psychiatrist; b. Toledo, Apr. 29, 1923; s. Albin L. and Elizabeth (Christ) Pearson; m. Karen S. Kamerschen, June 18, 1983; m. Katherine L. Gerrie, Oct. 15, 1955 (dec. 1981); children—Robert A., Michael A., Barbara A., Eric J., Brian S., Katherine E. B.S., Wayne U., 1949, M.D., 1952. Diplomate Am. Bd. Psychiatry and Neurology. Intern Highland Park (Mich.) Gen. Hosp., 1952-53; gen. practice medicine Boyne City, Mich., 1953-66; resident in psychiatry Traverse City State Hosp., Mich., 1966-69, dir. adult services, 1969-83; practice psychiatry, Houston, 1983—. Contbr. articles to profl. jours. Served to capt. AUS, 1941-46; ETO. Fellow Am. Soc. Clin. Hypnosis (pres. 1969-70, chmn. Edn. and Research Found. 1972-73), Soc. Clin. and Exptl. Hypnosis, AAAS. Roman Catholic. Home and Office: 10044 Lynbrook Dr Houston TX 77042-1558

PEARSON, THOMAS ARTHUR, epidemiologist, educator; b. Berlin, Wis., Oct. 21, 1950; married; 2 children. BA, Johns Hopkins U., 1973, MD, 1976, MPH, 1976, PhD in Epidemiology, 1983. Fellow cardiology Johns Hopkins Sch. Medicine, 1981-83, from asst. prof. to assoc. prof. medicine, epidemiology, 1983-88; prof. epidemiology Columbia U., 1988—, prof. meeidcine, 1995—; dir. Mary Imogene Bassett Rsch. Inst., 1988—; prof. medicine, Jane Forbes Clark chair in health rsch. Columbia U., N.Y.C., 1995—; chmn. monitoring bd. CARDIA project Nat. Heart, Lung and Blood Inst., 1987—; mem. rsch. com. Md. Heart Assn., 1986-88; chmn. data safety monitoring bd. HIT trial VA, 1994—; commr. Md. Coun. Phys. Fitness, 1985-88; mem. clin. applications and prevention commn. NIH, 1987-91, chmn., 1990-91. Mem. ACP, Am. Heart Assn. (nat. rsch. com. 1987-92, coun. epidemiology 1987—, vice chmn. 1994-95, chmn. 1996-98), Am. Fedn. Clin. Rsch., Am. Coll. Epidemiology, Am. Coll. Preventive Medicine, Am. Coll. Cardiology (prevention com.), Soc. Epidemiol. Rsch. (rsch. prize 1978). Office: Mary Imogene Bassett Med Rsch Inst 1 Atwell Rd Cooperstown NY 13326-1301

PEART, BRENDA C., cardiologist; b. Huntington, W.Va., Aug. 24, 1958. BS, Marshall U., 1980, MD, 1984. Diplomate Am. Bd. Internal Medicine. Pvt. practice Tucson, 1989-92; cardiologist Desert Cardiology of Tucson, 1992—; Bd. Dirs. HPPN, Tucson, 1995—. Mem. AMA, ACP, Am. Heart Assn., Am. Coll. Cardiology, Pima County Med. Soc. Office: North Tucson Heart Ctr c/o Desert Cardiology 1925 W Orange Grove Rd #201 Tucson AZ 85704

PECHÁŇ, JOZEF, internist; b. Trnava, Czechoslovakia, Nov. 6, 1935; s. Jozef and Anna (Marceková) P.; m. Viera Králiková, Nov. 20, 1965 (dec. 1987); children: Olga, Roman. MD, Comenius U., 1959; internist, Inst. Postgrad. Edn. Physician, 1962. House physician Faculty Hosp., Bratislava, Slovak Republic, 1959-61, head divsn. nuclear medicine, 1981—, prof. internal medicine, 1992—; reader internal medicine Comenius U., Bratislava, 1961-84, assoc. prof., 1984-92; pres. Faculty Hosp. Coun., 1996. Co-author: Internal Medicine, 1990 (Rector's prize 1990); contbr. articles to profl. jours.; editor: Slovak Med. Dr., 1991—. Mem. European Assn. Nuclear Medicine, Humboldt Club in Slovakia, Soc. Nuclear Medicine Slovak Med. Soc. (bd. dirs. 1964—, Gold medal 1995), Slovak Med. Chamber (pres. 1992-94, hon. pres. 1994—). Home: Sumracna 17, 821 02 Bratislava Slovak Republic Office: Faculty Hosp, 1st Dept Internal Medicine, Mickiewiczova 13, 813 69 Bratislava Slovak Republic

PECILE, ANTONIO MARIA, pharmacology educator; b. Padova, Italy, Oct. 3, 1929; s. Mario and Elisabetta (Pellizzari) P.; m. Marialuisa Pogliani, Sep. 26, 1964; children: Alessandro, Maurizio. MD, U. Padova, 1954. Rsch. assoc. U. Milan Med. Sch., 1955-61, asst. prof. pharmacology, 1962-69, assoc. prof., 1969-73, prof., 1973—, head Lab. of Experimental Endocrinology, 1969—, dir. postdoctoral pharmacology, 1982—, chmn. dept. pharmacology, 1982-88; referee European Bioscis. projects, 1988—; mem. advisory panel NATO, 1990—. Editor sci. books; contbr. over 200 articles to profl. jours.; organizer internat. meetings. NATO fellow, 1961. Mem. Rotary (pres. 1980-82, Paul Harris award 1982). Roman Catholic. Home: 62 Via Plinio, 20129 Milano Italy Office: Univ Dept Pharmacology, 32 Via Vanvitelli, 20129 Milan Italy

PECK, DONALD HARVEY, chiropractor; b. Oak Park, Ill., July 18, 1945; s. Donald Ray and Dorothy Sylvia (LaFlamme) P.; m. Mary Evelyn Lamb, June 15, 1964 (div. 1971); children: Donald Lee, Nancy Ellen; m. Cheryl Jean Cox, July 7, 1973; children: Richard Krom Watkins Jr., Bradley Alan, Steven Edward. AA, Mt. San Antonio Coll., 1966; DC, Palmer Coll. of Chiropractic, 1970. Diplomate Nat. Bd. Chiropractic Examiners. Engring. technician Besteel Corp., Industry, Calif., 1965-66, City of Ontario, Calif., 1966-67; supr. Mercy Hosp., Davenport, Iowa, 1967-70; pvt. practice chiropractor San Bernardino and Redlands, Calif., 1971-81; pvt. practice Cottonwood, Ariz., 1981—; instr. Yavapai Coll. Clarkdale, Ariz., 1982-88. Scoutmaster Calif. Inland Empire coun. Boy Scouts Am., 1974-81, Grand Canyon coun. Boy Scouts Am., 1981—; active Am. Youth Soccer Orgn., Cottonwood, 1977-92, regional commr., 1984-88; asst. varsity soccer coach Mingus Union High Sch., 1989-93; instr. trainer, chief instr. Ariz. Game and Fish Dept., Cottonwood, 1983—. Recipient Award of Merit Boy Scouts Am., 1980, Silver Beaver award, 1988; named Vol. of Yr. Verde Valley C. of C., 1987. Mem. Kiwanis (bd. dirs. 1985-87), Order of Arrow (vigil honor mem., Cert. Merit Boy Scout Am. Nat. Ct. of Honor 1990). Republican. Office: 703 S Main St Cottonwood AZ 86326-4615

PECK, ROGER GEORGE, internist; b. Russell, Kans., June 7, 1954; s. Ralph G. and Hester L. (Milberger) P.; m. Norma Linda Gutierrez, Dec. 28, 1975; children: David, Nathaniel, Alisia. BS, Ft. Hays State U., 1977; MD, U. Kans., 1981. Diplomate Am. Bd. Internal Medicine. Resident U. Kans. Med. Ctr., Wichita, 1981-84; mem. staff Ctrl. Kans. Med. Ctr., Great Bend, 1984—, chief of staff, 1991-93; ptnr. Great Bend Internists, Great Bend, 1984—; mem. Kans. Trauma Policy Group., Topeka, 1994—. Med. dir. Great Bend Emergency Med. Svcs., Kans. 1986—; Pres. Kans. Affiliate Am. Heart Assn., 1989-90. Mem. Am. Soc. Internal Medicine, Am. Soc. Electrocardiography, Am. Med. Assn. Republican. Roman Catholic. Office: Great Bend Internists Suite 2D 3623 Broadway Great Bend KS 67530

PECK, WILLIAM ARNO, physician, educator; b. New Britain, Conn., Sept. 28, 1933; s. Bernard Carl and Molla (Nair) P.; m. Patricia Hearn, July 10, 1982; children by previous marriage: Catherine, Edward Pershall, David Nathaniel; stepchildren: Andrea, Elizabeth, Katherine. A.B., Harvard U., 1955; M.D., U. Rochester, N.Y., 1960. Intern, then resident in internal medicine Barnes Hosp., St. Louis, 1960-62; fellow in metabolism Washington U. Sch. Medicine, St. Louis, 1963; mem. faculty U. Rochester Med. Sch., 1965-76, prof. medicine and biochemistry, 1973-76, head div. endocrinology and metabolism, 1969-76; John E. and Adaline Simon prof. medicine, co-chmn. dept. medicine Washington U. Sch. Medicine, St. Louis, 1976-89; physician in chief Jewish Hosp., St. Louis, 1976-89; prof. medicine and exec. vice chancellor med. affairs, dean sch. medicine, pres. univ. med. ctr. Washington U., St. Louis, 1989—; chmn. endocrinology and metabolism adv. com. FDA, 1976-78; chmn. gen. medicine study sect. NIH, 1979-81; chmn. Gordon Conf. Chemistry, PHysiology and Structure of Bones and Teeth, 1977; chmn. Consensus Devel. Conf. on Osteoporosis, NIH, 1984; co-chmn. Workshop on Future Directions in Osteoporosis, 1987; chmn. Spl. Topic Conf. on Osteoporosis, U.S. FDA, 1987; dir. Angelica Corp., Boatman's Trust Co., Allied Healthcare Products, Hologic, Reinsurance Group of Am. Editor Bone and Mineral Rsch. Annss., 1982-88; mem. editorial adv. bd. Osteoporosis Internat., other jours.; contbr. to med. jours. Pres. Nat. Osteoporosis Found., 1985-90. Served as med. officer USPHS, 1963-65. Recipient Mosby Book award Alpha Omega Alpha, 1960, Doran J. Stephens award U. Rochester Sch. Medicine, 1960, Lederle Med. Faculty award, 1967, NIH Career Program award, 1970-75, Commr.'s Spl. citation FDA, 1988, Humanitarian award Arthritis Found. Ea. Mo., 1995. Fellow ACP, AAAS;

mem. Am. Assn. Clin. Endocrinologists, Am. Geriatric Soc., Am. Soc. for Biochemistry and Molecular Biology, Am. Soc. Clin. Investigation, Am. Fedn. Clin. Rsch., Am. Diabetes Assn., Internat. Bone and Mineral Soc., Assn. Am. Physicians, Am. Soc. Bone and Mineral Rsch. (pres. 1983-84), Endocrine Soc., Orthopedic Rsch. Soc., Nat. Inst. Arthritis, Musculoskeletal and Skin Diseases (adv. coun. 1986-89), Assn. Am. Med. Colls. (adminstrv. bd. Coun. of Deans 1993—, chmn. elect 1996-97, group on bus. affairs rsch. task force), Sigma Xi, Alpha Omega Alpha (bd. dirs. 1992-95). Home: 2 Apple Tree Ln Saint Louis MO 63124-1601 Office: Washington U Sch Medicine 600 S Euclid Ave Saint Louis MO 63110-1093

PECORA, ANDREW A., physician, educator; b. Phila., Sept. 6, 1934; s. Arthur and Mary Louise (Giordano) P.; m. Rita R. Trombetti, June 17, 1961; children: Andrew Paul, Arthur Stevan, Paul Christian. BS, St. Joseph's Coll., Phila., 1957; DO, Phila. Coll. Osteo. Med., 1961. Diplomat Internal Medicine and Gastroenterology, Am. Bd. Internal Medicine. Asst. prof. medicine U. Medicine and Dentistry, U. N.J., Stratford, 1977-78, prof. medicine, 1978—, chmn. dept. medicine, 1978-93. Recipient Disting. Svc. award Am. Coll. Osteopathic Internists, 1989-90, Am. Osteopathic Bd. of Internal Medicine, 1984-94. Fellow Am. Coll. Osteopathic Internists (pres. sect. gastroenterology 1980-82, pres. 1988-89), Am. Coll. of Gastroenterology; mem. AOA, Am. Gastroenterology Assocs. Roman Catholic.

PEDDECORD, K(ENNETH) MICHAEL, medical educator; b. Hayden, Colo., Apr. 20, 1948; s. Paul Leo and Helen Mary (Murphy) P.; m. Mary Ann Bartle, Aug. 7, 1971; 1 child, Brenton. BS in Microbiology, Ariz. State U., 1970, MS in Microbiology, 1972; DrPH, U. Tex. Sch. Pub. Health, 1978. Health planner Ariz. Dept. Human Svcs., Phoenix, 1972; coord. quality control Hermann Hosp., Houston, 1975; asst. prof. Chgo. Med. Sch., 1978-81; asst. prof., assoc. prof. San Diego State U., 1981-90, prof., 1990—; cons. quality improvement, Calif. and Utah, 1981—; health outcomes cons., San Diego, 1994—. Contbr. articles to profl. jours. 1st lt. U.S. Army, 1972-74. Recipient Marriott Jour. award Med. Mgmt. Assn., 1992. Mem. APHA, Am. Coll. Healthcare Execs. (local program com., faculty assoc.), Pub. Health Leadership Soc. Roman Catholic. Office: Grad Sch Pub Health San Diego State Univ San Diego CA 92182

PEDDICORD, TOM E., pharmacist. DPharm, U. Nebr., 1994. Pharmacy resident Univ. Hosp./ U. Nebr. Med. Ctr., 1994-95; mem. U.S. Olympic com. doping control staff. Am. Soc. Hosp. Pharmacists fellow, 1996. Home: 5418 Grover St #105 Omaha NE 68106*

PEDERSEN, BENT CARL CHRISTIAN, cytogeneticist; b. Jutland, Denmark, Sept. 14, 1933; s. Jonathan and Lydia (Hansen) P.; m. Lene Reymann, July 3, 1965; children: Susanne, Kare. MB/BS, U. Copenhagen, 1960, MD, 1969; PhD, U. Cambridge, Eng., 1970. Assoc. researcher Inst. Human Genetics U. Copenhagen, 1961-67; sr. researcher Postgrad. Sch. of Medicine U. Cambridge, 1967-69; sr. researcher Cancer Rsch. Inst. Danish Cancer Soc., Aarhus, Denmark, 1970-78, assoc. rsch. dir., 1978-87, head dept. cytogenetics, 1987—. Author: Cytogenetic Evolution of Chronic Myelogenous Leukaemia, 1969, The Cytological Basis of Progression in Chronic Myeloid Leukaemia, 1970; contbr. articles to profl. jours. Recipient awards William Nielsens Found., 1971, 87, Generalkonsul Ernst Carlsens og Hustru Adolphine Carlsens Legat, 1989. Home: 94 Tingstedet, DK-8220 Brabrand Denmark Office: Danish Cancer Soc, Aarhus Amtssygehus, DK-8000 Aarhus C, Denmark

PEDERSEN, DARHL MAX, psychology educator; b. Orem, Utah, Oct. 12, 1935; s. Max Barlow and Edith (Aiken) P.; 1 child, Clark. BS, Brigham Young U., 1957, MS, 1958; PhD, U. Ill., 1962. Asst. prof. psychology Brigham Young U., Provo, Utah, 1962-65, assoc. prof., 1966-70, prof., 1971—; postdoctoral assoc. Ames Research Ctr., NASA, Moffett Field, Calif., 1969-70. Author: Psychological Tests and Measurements, 1965, Essentials for Understanding Statistics, 1978, Environmental Psychology, 1978, Learning Statistics, 1988. Commr. Provo council Boy Scouts Am., 1978—. NSF fellow, 1962. Mem. Sigma Xi (ann. lecture 1973), Phi Kappa Phi, Psi Chi. Republican. Mormon. Home: 1815 N 1550 E Provo UT 84604-5709 Office: Psychology Dept Brigham Young U Provo UT 84602

PEDICH, WOJCIECH KRYSTYN, cardiologist, gerontology educator; b. Warsaw, Poland, Feb. 5, 1926; s. Jan and Adela (Pocztarska) P.; m. Lucyna Aleksandrowicz; children: Marek, Ewa, Rafal, Magda, Marcin. Student, Med. Acad., Warsaw, 1951, MD, 1952; prof. medicine degree, Med. Acad., Bialystok, Poland, 1985. Med. diplomate; cert. cardiologist. Asst. Med. Acad., Warsaw, 1949-51; asst. County Hosp., Opole, Poland, 1951-56, ward head, 1956-64; ward head County Hosp. Bialystok, Bialystok, 1964-94; prof. gerontology Med. Acad., Bialystok, 1964—. Author: (handbook) Geriatrics, 1988, 2d edit., 1995; editor: Gerontopharmacology, 1987, 2d edit., 1991. Mem. Polish Cardiological Assn., Polish Gerontol. Soc. (pres. 1989—). Roman Catholic. Home: Wolodyjowski Str 8-30, 15-309 Bialystok Poland Office: Med Acad, Mickiewicza 1, Michiewicza 1, 15-230 Bialystok Poland

PEDINI, KENNETH, radiologist; b. Hartford, Conn., Mar. 19, 1940; s. Daniel Victor and Elizabeth Catherine Pedini; m. Egle Damijonaitis; children: David D., Julian A. AB in Philosophy, Trinity Coll., 1962; MD, Boston U., 1966. Diplomate Nat. Bd. Med. Examiners, Am. Bd. Radiology. Resident radiology Boston City Hosp., 1967-70, chief resident radiology, 1969-71, jr. staff radiologist, 1970-71; jr. staff radiologist U. Hosp., Boston, 1970-71; ptnr. Shawsheen Radiology, Andover, Mass., 1971—; sr. radiologist Lawrence (Mass.) Gen. Hosp., 1971-75, dir. radiology, 1976-87; sr. radiologist Melrose (Mass.)-Wakefield Hosp., 1971-93, chief radiologist, 1993—; pres. L & M Radiology Inc, Andover, Mass., 1994—; bd. trustees Lawrence Gen. Hosp., 1984-89; pres. L&M Radiology Inc., Andover, Mass., 1994—. Trustee Lawrence Gen. Hosp. Health Enterprises, Inc., 1990-93; mem. fin. com. Lawrence Gen. Hosp., 1986—; co-founder Andover Sch. of Montessori, 1975—; mem. alumni adv. com. Trinity Coll., 1995. Fellow Am. Coll. Radiology (councilor 1979-81); mem. Mass. Radiol. Soc. (pres. 1985-86, pres.-elect 1984-85, v.p. 1983-84, exec. com. 1977-87), Mass. Med. Soc., Stonehorse Yatch Club.

PEDLEY, TIMOTHY ASBURY, IV, neurologist, educator, researcher; b. Phoenix, Aug. 31, 1943; s. Timothy Asbury Pedley III and Mary Adele (Newcomer) Melis; m. Barbara S. Koppel, Mar. 17, 1984. BA, Pomona Coll., 1965; MD, Yale U., 1969. Cert. neurology, 1975, electroencephalography, 1975, clin. neurophysiology, 1993. Intern Stanford U. Hosp., 1967-70, resident in neurology, 1970-73, post-doctoral fellow in neurophysiology, 1973-75, asst. prof. neurology, 1975-79; assoc. prof. neurology Columbia U., 1979-83, prof., vice chmn. dept. neurology, 1983—; dir. comprehensive epilepsy ctr. Columbia-Presbyterian Med. Ctr., N.Y.C., 1983—. Contbr. articles to profl. jours. Bd. dirs. Epilepsy Found Am., 1984—, chmn. profl. adv. bd., 1985-87, pres., 1991-93, chmn. 1993-95. mem. rev. com. NIH Nat. Inst. Neurol. and Chronic Diseases and Strokes, 1985-89; vis. fellow in exptl. neurology Inst. Psychiatry, London, 1978; mem. merit review bd. neurobiology rsch., VA, 1992-96. Editor-in-chief Epilepsia, 1994—. Fellow Am. Acad. Neurology, Am. Electroencephalographic Soc. (pres. 1989-90, bd. dirs. 1981, 85); mem. Am. Neurol. Assn. (coun. 1992-94, treas. 1995—), Am. Epilepsy Soc. (treas. 1980-83, pres. 1991-92), Soc. for Neurosci., Internat. League Against Epilepsy (mem. exec. com. 1994—), Alpha Omega Alpha. Clubs: Yale (N.Y.C.), Met. Opera (N.Y.C.), Shenorock Shore (Rye, N.Y.). Office: The Neurological Inst 710 W 168th St New York NY 10032-2603

PEDRAZ, JOSE LUIS, pharmacist, educator; b. Salamanca, Spain, June 22, 1959; s. Jose Juan and Luisa (Muñoz) P.; m. Begoña Calvo, Nov. 15, 1986; children: Diana, Charles. Pharmacy Grad., U. Salamanca, Spain, 1981, PhD in Pharmacy, 1984; Hosp. Pharmacy Specialist, Ministry of Edn., Spain, 1989. Assoc. prof. U. Salamanca, Spain, 1986-92; prof. pharmacy and pharmaceutics U. of the Basque Country, Vitoria, Spain, 1992—, chmn. dept. pharmacy and pharmaceutics, 1992—; cons. Pharm. Industry, Spain, 1992—; sci. com. mem. Pharm. Tech. Teaching Assn., Spain, 1993. Author: (book chpt.) Interspecies PharmacoKinetics, 1990; contbr. articles to profl. jours. Grantee Ministry of Health, Spain, 1982-84, 87, Ministry of Edn., Spain, 1984-86; recipient award Spanish Royal Acad. Pharmacy, 1985. Fellow Mario Negri Inst.; mem. Spanish Soc. of Pharmacology, Am. Assn. Pharm. Scis., Spanish Pharm. Tech. Teaching Assn., Controlled Release Soc. Roman Catholic. Home: Bustinzuri 3-4 D, 01008 Vitoria Spain Office: U Basque Country Faculty Pharmacy, Marques de Urquijo S/n, 01006 Vitoria Spain

PEDRETTI, LORRAINE WILLIAMS, occupational therapy educator; b. Hackensack, N.J., Dec. 23, 1936; d. Julius Sr. and Angelina (LaValle) Williams; m. Robert Leland Pedretti, Dec. 18, 1971; 1 child, Mark Samuel. BS in Occupational Therapy, N.Y.U., 1959; MS in Occupational Therapy, San Jose State Coll., 1964. Staff occupational therapist Hartford (Conn.) Rehab. Ctr., 1964-67, Supr. occupational therapy dept., 1967-68; instr. Hartford Hosp., 1968; sr. occupational therapist, cons. Santa Clara (Calif.) Valley Med. Ctr., 1971; asst. prof. San Jose State U., 1968-78, assoc. prof., 1978-90, prof. occupational therapy, 1990-94. Author: audio-visual prodn. Occupational Therapy: Practice Skills for Physical Dysfunction, 1st edit., 1981, 2d edit., 1985, 3d edit., 1990, 4th edit., 1996. Recipient Meritorious Performance and Profl. Promise award, Affirmative Action Faculty Devel. award, San Jose State U., Eastern Seal Soc. scholarship, various grants. Mem. Am. Med. Writers Assn., Am. Occupl. Therapy Assn., Calif. Occupl. Therapy Assn., World Fedn. Occupl. Therapists, Text and Acad. Authors Assn. Home: 1482 Iris Ct San Jose CA 95125-3354

PEEBLES, CAROL LYNN, immunology researcher; b. Wellington, Kans., Jan. 20, 1941; d. Harry Alexander and Phyllis Dorothy (Pyle) P. BA, Kans. State Coll. of Pittsburg, 1962, MS, 1964; cert. med. technology, St. Francis Hosp., Wichita, Kans., 1965. Med. technologist St. Francis Hosp., Wichita, 1965-74; lab. supr. allergy and immunology Scripps Clinic and Rsch. Found., La Jolla, Calif., 1974-77; sr. rsch. asst. autoimmune disease ctr. Scripps Clinic and Rsch. Found., La Jolla, 1982—; lab. supr. rheumatology lab. U. Colo. Health Scis. Ctr., Denver, 1977-82. Author workshop manual; contbr. articles to sci. publs. Mem. Am. Coll. Rheumatology, AAAS, Am. Soc. Microbiology, Am. Soc. Med. Tech., Am. Soc. Clin. Pathology. Office: Scripps Rsch Inst Rm SBR6 10666 N Torrey Pines Rd La Jolla CA 92037-1027

PEEBLES-KLEIGER, MARY JOSEPHINE, psychologist; b. La Jolla, Calif., Dec. 21, 1950; d. David Coleman and Violet (Pankey) P. BA, Wellesley (Mass.) Coll., 1972; PhD, Case Western Res. U., 1977; postgrad., Topeka Inst. Psychoanalysis, 1980-89, 1992—, Wash. Inst. for Psychoanalysis, 1989-92. Lic. psychologist, Kans., Md.; Diplomate Am. Bd. Profl. Psychology. Intern clin. psychology Case Western Res. U. Med. Sch., Cleve., 1975-76; staff psychologist Gulf Coast Regional Health Mental Retardation Cmty. Svc. Ctr., Galveston, Tex., 1976-77; postdoct. fellow in child psychology Child and Adolescent Psychiatry div. U. Tex., Galveston, 1977-78; postdoct. fellow in clin. adult psychology The Menninger Found., Topeka, 1978-80, staff psychologist, faculty, supr., 1980-89, 1992—; psychologist Chestnut Lodge Hosp., Rockville, Md., 1989-92; pvt. practice Wheaton, Md., 1990-92. Contbr. articles to profl. jours.; also ednl. videotapes. Mem. adv. bd. Citizens for a Drug Free Community, Topeka, 1986-87. NIMH traineeship, 1972-75. Mem. Am. Psychol. Assn. (divs. psychoanalysis, psychotherapy, hypnosis, neuropsychology), Kans. Psychol. Assn. (bd. govs. 1986-89), Soc. Clin. and Exptl. Hypnosis, Soc. for Traumatic Stress Studies, Phi Beta Kappa. Office: Menninger PO Box 829 Topeka KS 66601-0829

PEELE, KIMBERLY A., ophthalmologist; b. Bellevue, Wash., Apr. 10, 1961; d. Fred Arthur and Dorothy Anne (Cooper) Piontkowski. BA in Biology, U. Calif., San Diego, 1983; MD, George Washington U., 1987. Commd. 2d lt. U.S. Army, 1983, advanced through grades to maj.; surg. intern Letterman Army Ctr., San Francisco, 1987-88; chief emergency svcs. McDonald Army Hosp., Newport News, Va., 1988-89; resident in ophthalmology Walter Reed Army Med. Ctr., Washington, 1989-92, neuro-ophthalmology fellow, 1992-93, mem. neuro-ophthlamology staff, 1993-94, 95—; orbital disease fellow Allegheny Gen. Hosp., Pitts., 1994-95; dir. orbital disease and oculoplastics Walter Reed Army Med. Ctr., Washington, 1995—; neuro-ophthalmology cons. Fitzsimons Army Med. Ctr., Denver, 1993-94. Contbr. articles to profl. jours., chpts. to books. Eye camp doctor Charitable Trust, New Delhi, India, 1996. Fellow Am. Acad. Ophthalmology; mem. N.Am. Soc. Neuro-Ophthalmology, Assn. Rsch. in Vision and Ophthalmology, Alpha Omega Alpha. Office: Walter Reed Army Med Ctr Ophthalmology Svc Georgia Ave NW Washington DC 20307-5001

PEELE, ROGER, hospital administrator; b. Elizabeth City, N.C., Dec. 24, 1930; s. Joseph Emmett and Catherine (Groves) P.; m. Diana Egan, June 15, 1963 (dec.); children: Amy, Rodney, Holly; m. Gail Nelson Oct. 15, 1992. A.B., U. N.C., 1955; M.D., U. Tenn., 1960. Cert. adminstrv. psychiatry, 1970 cert. forensic psychiatry, 1982. Intern St. Elizabeths Hosp., Washington, 1960-61; resident in psychiatry St. Elizabeths Hosp., 1961-64, tng. officer, 1964-67, chief of service William A. White div., 1967-69; dir. Area D Community Mental Health Center, 1969-73, asst. supt., 1974-75, 77-79, acting supt., 1975-77, chmn. dept. psychiatry, 1979—; clin. instr. psychiatry George Washington U., 1965-67, asst. clin. prof., 1967-71, assoc. clin. prof., 1971-79, clin. prof., 1979—; asst. dir. NIMH, 1978-79; chief clin. officer D.C. Commn. on Mental Health, 1987-91. Contbr. articles on clin., forensic and adminstrv. issues in Am. psychiatry to profl. jours. Served with USAF, 1950-53. Superior Service award HEW, 1967. Fellow Am. Coll. Psychiatry, Am. Psychiat. Assn. (speaker 1986-87, Adminstr. of Yr. 1989); mem. AMA, D.C. Med. Soc., Am. Assn. Psychiat. Adminstrs. (past pres.), Group for Advancement Psychiatry, Med. Soc. St. Elizabeth's Hosp. (past pres.), Fed. Physicians Assn. (past pres.). Episcopalian. Home: 5302 41st St NW Washington DC 20015-1904 Office: PO Box 39249 Washington DC 20016

PEELER, RICHARD NEVIN, internist, educator; b. Salisbury, N.C., Sept. 9, 1926; s. Banks Joseph and Agnes Goldie (Andrew) P.; m. Frances Anne Signorelli, Dec. 27, 1951; children: Lauren Marie, Anne Sullivan, Karen Andrew, Matthew George, Mark O'Brien. AB, Catawba Coll., 1947; MD, Johns Hopkins U., 1951. Intern, Johns Hopkins Hosp., Balt., 1951-52, resident, 1952-53, 55-56; fellow in medicine Johns Hopkins U., Balt., 1956-57, instr. medicine, 1952-57, asst. prof., 1977—; pvt. practice medicine specializing in internal medicine and infections disease, Annapolis, Md., 1957—; mem. staff Anne Arundel Med. Ctr., 1957—, pres. med. staff, 1969-71, dir. outpatient intravenous svcs., 1988—, sr. epidemiologist, 1993—; sr. ptnr. Annapolis (Md.) Med. Specialists, LLP. Contbr. articles to med. jours. Bd. dirs. Annapolis Life Care Ctr., 1981-84. With U.S. Army, 1954-56. Fellow ACP; mem. Am. Fedn. for Clin. Rsch., Am. Soc. for Microbiology, So. Med. Assn., Md. Med. and Chirurgical Faculty, Johns Hopkins Med.-Surg. Soc., Anne Arundel County Med. Soc., Annapolis Yacht Club, Johns Hopkins Club. Office: 900 Bestgate Rd # 300 Annapolis MD 21401-3066

PEELING, WILLIAM BRIAN, urologist, surgeon; b. Asansol, Bengal, India, Nov. 12, 1930; s. Harry Vivian and Dorothy (Maddocks) P.; m. Audrey Margaret Bloom, Aug. 6, 1957; children: Robert Halliday, Gillian Margaret. BA, St. John's Coll., Cambridge, Eng., 1954; MB BChir, London Hosp. Med. Coll., 1957; MA, St. John's Coll., Cambridge, 1958. Resident in tng. London Hosp.; Hugh Robertson fellow Presbyn. St. Luke's Hosp., Chgo., 1961-62; sr. registrar Cardiff Royal Infirmary, 1966-68; cons. surgeon Royal Gwent (Eng.) Hosp., 1968-74; cons. urologist Royal Gwent Hosp., Newport, Gwent, Eng., 1974—; prof. urol. surgery U. Wales, 1991; Chmn. British Prostate Group, Eng., 1979-82; hon. sec., vice chmn. Royal Soc. of Medicine (Urology sect.), London, 1979-83; hon. prof. urological surgery U. Wales, 1991. Contbr. articles and chpts. of books. Mem. Gwent (Eng.) Health Authority. Recipient Joseph Larmor award St. John's Coll., Cambridge, 1954, St Peter's medal, 1996, Assn. Urology Surgeons. Fellow Royal Coll. Surgeons; mem. British Assn. Urol. Surgeons Coun. (St. Peter's medal 1996). Anglican.

PEEPLES, MARK EDWARD, virology researcher, educator; b. Lancaster, Pa., Sept. 26, 1952; s. Robert Fred and Ruth Jane (Walters) P.; m. Rebecca Ann Brumberg, Nov. 5, 1977. BS, Heidelberg Coll., 1974; PhD, Wayne State U., 1978. Postdoctoral fellow Univ. Mass. Med. Sch., Worcester, 1978-80, instr., 1980-83; asst. prof. Rush Med. Coll., Chgo., 1983-88, assoc. prof., 1988-92, prof., 1992—, assoc. chmn., 1990—, head, sect. of virology, dept. immunology/microbiology, 1989—; cons. Cytel Corp., San Diego, 1990—; mem. grant rev. com. Am. Cancer Soc., Ill. divsn., Chgo., 1988-93; ad hoc mem. Reviewer's Res., Exptl. Viology Study Sect., NIH, 1993—; mem. microbiology test com. Nat. Bd. Med. Examiners, 1995—; sabbatical at NIH, 1995-96. Assoc. editor Virology, 1987—; contbr. chpt. to The Paramyxoviruses; contbr. articles to Virology, Jour. Virology, Jour. Exptl. Medicine, Cancer Rsch., Jour. Nat. Cancer Inst., Jour. Gen. Physiology, Gene, Neurology, Jour. Infectious Diseases, Jour. Clin. Microbiology, Proc. NAS. NIH Postdoctoral fellow, 1978-81, Rsch. Career Devel. awardee, 1988-93, grantee, 1985-88, 88-93, 90-95, 96; NSF U.S.-Australia Coop. Rsch. grantee, 1993-95. Mem. AAAS, Am. Soc. Virology, Am. Soc. for Microbiology, Soc. for gen. Microbiology, Sigma Xi (pres. Rush U. chpt. 1988-90). Office: Rush-Pres-St Luke Med Ctr Dept Immunology/Microbiol 1653 W Congress Pky Chicago IL 60612-3833

PEETERS, THEO LOUIS, biochemical engineering educator; b. Tienen, Belgium, Feb. 6, 1943; s. Henri and Josephine (Hendrickx) P.; m. Nadine Angèle Bonte, July 18, 1967; children: Bruno, Karen. Degree in biochem. engring., U. Leuven, 1965, PhD, 1968. Rsch. asst. Belgian Sci. Found., Leuven, Belgium, 1966-67, U. Ky., Lexington, 1968-69; rsch. asst. U. Leuven, 1970-79, lectr., 1983-93, chair dept. med. rsch., 1987-93; prof., 1993—; vis. prof. No. Ky. U., Highland Heights, 1980; coord. Belgian Rsch. Cmty., 1994-99. Contbr. 100 articles to profl. jours., chpts. to books. Lt. Belgian Air Force, 1966. Recipient Bio-therabel prize for gastroenterology, 1994. Office: Gut Hormone Lab, Gasthuisberg ON, B-3000 Leuven Belgium

PEETS, ROBERT L., osteopathic physician; b. Trenton, Mich., May 20, 1963; s. Richard Junior and Lois Elise (Walker) P.; m. Patricia Mary Haggerty, Aug. 29, 1986; 1 child, Rebecca Mary. BA, U. Mich., Dearborn, 1986; DO, Mich. State U., 1990. Diplomate Nat. Bd. Osteo. Med. Examiners. Intern Ingham Med. Ctr., Lansing, Mich., 1991; resident Grandview Hosp., Dayton, Ohio, 1992-95; ophthalmologist N.W. Dayton Eye Care, 1995—; clin. instr. Ohio U., 1992-95; instr. Mich. State U. Coll. Osteo. Medicine, East Lansing, 1990-91. Mem. Am. Acad. Ophthalmology, Am. Osteo. Assn., Ohio Ophthalmol. Soc., Am. Soc. Cataract and Refractive Surgery, Ohio Assn. Osteo. Physicians and Surgeons, Dayton Area Soc. Ophthalmology. Home: 149 Candle Ct Englewood OH 45322 Office: Northwest Dayton Eye Care 7643 N Main St Dayton OH 45415

PEIFFER, ARTHUR LEROY, health services executive; b. Borger, Tex., July 30, 1942; s. Clifton Lee and Eloise Mae (Brown) P.; m. Susan Jean Munn, Apr. 7, 1969 (div. 1973); children: Gregory Lloyd, Rochelle Jean. BS in Psychology and Sociology, Eastern N.Mex. U., 1965; MA in Counseling Psychology, U. N.Mex., 1968, postgrad., 1969-77; PhD in Behavioral Sci., Clayton U., 1978; grad. Sarus Inst. Biofeedback Tech. Lic. chem. dependency counselor, clin. social worker, marriage and family therapist, Tex.; cert. chem. dependency specialist, stress mgmt. educator, Tex. Psychol. counselor, div. vocat. rehab. N.Mex. Dept. Edn., Albuquerque, 1965-66; dir. counseling and testing Home Edn. Livelihood Program, OEO Project, N.Mex. Council of Chs., Albuquerque, 1966-67; instr. Western State Coll., Gunnison, Colo., summer 1968; doctoral intern, Nazareth Psychiat. Hosp., Albuquerque and U. N.Mex., 1968-69; psychometrist, U. N.Mex., Albuquerque, 1967-69; cons. psychologist, div. vocat. rehab., Inmate Program, N.Mex. State Penitentiary, Santa Fe, 1969-70, dir. placement, instr. psychology, Coll. of Santa Fe, 1969-70; cons. psychologist, div. vocat. rehab. Patient Program, Alcoholism Treatment Program, Albuquerque, 1970-71, chief clin. psychologist, 1971-72; program psychologist, adminstr. Alcohol Safety Action Program, Albuquerque, 1970-71; adj. prof. for internship programs, Eastern N.Mex. U., Portales, 1971-72; dir. clin. services La Hacienda Alcoholism Rehab. Facility (br. Nat. Living Ctrs., Inc.), Hunt, Tex., 1972-74, exec. dir. La Hacienda Alcoholism Treatment Ctr., Inc., Hunt, 1974-75; instr. psychology Schreiner Coll., Kerrville, Tex., 1972-75; founder-clin. dir. Stress, Tension, & Anxiety Tng. Clinic, Inc., Houston, 1975-77; dir. clin. services program for alcoholisms, addictions, stress and anxiety Houston Internat. Hosp. and Med. Ctr. Del Oro Hosp., East Dallas Hosp., Shoal Creek Hosp., Austin, 1975-77; v.p. Positive Alternatives to Anxiety, Stress, and Addictions, Inc., Houston, 1977-78; corp. staff specialist Hosp. Affiliates Internat., Inc., Gulf Coast Region, Houston, 1977-78; exec. v.p., full ptnr. Contemporary Health, Inc., nat. hdqrs., Houston, 1978-82; founder, exec. dir. Stress Mgmt. Research Assocs., Inc., Houston, 1978—; pres. Vista Health, Inc. of Calif., San Diego, 1981—; pres. Med. Programs, Inc., nat. hdqs., Houston, 1982—; pres. Vista Health Programs, Inc., nat. hdqrs., Houston, 1982—, Internat. HealthNet, Inc., Houston, 1986—; prin. Dr. Arthur L. Peiffer and Assocs., Inc., Houston. Charter mem. Republican presdl. task force; mem. Nat. Rep. Congl. Com.; campaign mem. Rep. Nat. Com., 1982. Mem. Tex. Assn. Alcoholism Counselors, Nat. Assn. Alcoholism Counselors and Trainers, Biofeedback Soc. Am., Am. Assn. Biofeedback Clinicians, Biofeedback Soc. Tex., Nat. Rehab. Counselors Assn., Council for Exceptional Children, Am. Personnel and Guidance Assn., Am. Group Psychotherapy Assn., World Congress Profl. Hypnotists, Am. Assn. Marriage and Family Therapy, Sigma Alpha Epsilon (founder mem. N.Mex.). Author: Alcohol, The Individual and the Automobile, 1972, cassette tape series: Stress Management Tng. Program, 1980; contbr. papers to profl. publs. and confs. Home: 3134 Robinson Rd Missouri City TX 77459-3232 Office: 17024 Butte Creek Rd Ste 201 Houston TX 77090-2329

PEINADO, BERNARDO, school psychologist, counselor; b. L.A., Feb. 5, 1961; s. Juan Cazares and Beatriz (Basurto) P. BA, U. Calif., San Diego, 1983; MS in Counseling, Calif. State U., L.A., 1986. Lic. ednl. psychologist; cert. sch. psychologist; marriage, family and child counselor intern; basic pupil pers. svcs. credential, C.C. counselor credential, C.C. student pers. worker credential; cert. applied behavioral analysis ednl. settings. Counselor's asst. early outreach program U. Calif., San Diego, 1981-83; counselor asst. compensatory edn. program L.A. Unified Sch. Dist., 1983-86; children's svcs. worker II L.A. County Dept. Children's Svcs., 1986-87; program coord. L.A. County Child Sexual Abuse Program, 1987-89; migrant counselor L.A. County Office of Edn., 1989-90; sch. psychologist intern Rosemead Unified Sch. Dist., 1990-91; sch. psychologists Bassett Unified Sch. Dist., La Puente, Calif., 1991—. Mem. Spanish Speaking Child Abuse Coun. of L.A., Calif. Tchrs. Assn.

PEIRO, JOSE MARIA, psychologist, educator; b. Torrent, Valencia, Spain, Mar. 5, 1950; s. Jose Maria and Amparo (Silla) P.; m. Otilia Alicia Salvador, Oct. 25, 1980; children: Teresa, Begoña. Lic. in philosophy, U. Valencia, Spain, 1975; lic. in psychology, U. Complutense, Madrid, 1976; PhD, U. Valencia, 1977. Asst. dept. psychology, assoc. prof. U. Valencia, 1976-81; prof. psychology U. Complutense, Madrid, 1981-82; prof. psychology U. Valencia, 1982-84, prof. social and orgnl. psychology, 1985—, dean psychology faculty; vis. prof. U. Sheffield, 1985, Argentina, 1989, U. Tillburg, 1992; mem. adv. bd. of the Work and Orgn. Rsch. Ctr. Univ. Tilburg. Author: Psicologia de la Organizacón, 1983, 91, Organizaciones Nuevas Perspectivas Psicosociológicas, 1990, Desencadenantes del estres laboral, 1993; co-author: Psicologia Contemporanea, 1981, Madurez Vocacional, 1986, Circulos de Calidad, 1993, Control del estres laboral, 1993; editor: Revista de Historia de la Psicologia, Revista de Psicologia Social Aplicada: co-editor: La socializacion laboral, 1987, Work and Organizational Psychology: European Contributions of the Nineties, 1995. Pres. Instituto Pro-Desarrollo Found., Torrent, 1982-87; v.p. Caja de Ahorros de Torrent, 1985-88. Mem. APA, European Network of Work and Orgnl. Psychologists, European Assn. Work and Orgnl. Psychology (pres.), Spanish Soc. Psychology (pres. Valencia br.), Colegio Ofcl. de Psicologos of Spain (exec. com. mem.). Office: U Valencia Psychology Fac, Avda Blasco Ibanez 21, 46010 Valencia Spain

PEISON, BERNARD, pathologist; b. Poland, Dec. 25, 1929; s. Max and Bascha P.; m. Karen Freda Perlmutter; children: David, Brenda. MD, Havana Med. Sch., 1955. Diplomate in anat. and clin. pathology and neuropathology Am. Bd. Pathology. Resident NYU Bellevue Med. Ctr., N.Y.C.; dir. labs. Rahway (N.J.) Hosp., 1969—; clin. assoc. prof. NYU Med. Ctr. Jewish. Home: 139 Deer Run Watchung NJ 07060 Office: Rahway Hosp 865 Stone St Rahway NJ 07065

PELCYGER, GWYNNE ELLICE, school psychologist; b. Bklyn., May 18, 1959; d. Iran and Elaine (Morley) P.; m. Aaron Blum, Dec. 21, 1991. BA, Hofstra U., 1981; MS, St. John's U., 1987. Cert. sch. psychologist, N.Y. Case mgr. Cath. Charities, N.Y.C., 1986-87; program mgr. Profl. Svc. Ctr. for Handicapped, N.Y.C.; consulting psychologist Graham Windom, N.Y.C., 1987-89; edn. specialist Assn. for Neurologically Impaired Brain Injured Children, N.Y.C., 1987-88; sch. psychologist N.Y.C. Bd. of Edn., 1988-92, Okeechobee (Fla.) County Sch. Bd., 1994—. Mem. APA, AACD, Nat.

Assn. Sch. Psychologists, N.Y. ACD, Fla. Assn. for Sch. Psychologists, Treasure Coast Counselors Assn., PhysChi Nat. Honor Soc. Office: 100 SW 5th Ave Okeechobee FL 34974-4221

PELL, SIDNEY, epidemiologist; b. N.Y.C., Dec. 13, 1922; m. Lola May, July 2, 1950. MBA, CCNY, 1952; PhD, U. Pitts., 1956. Biostatistician E.I. Du Pont de Nemours and Co., Wilmington, Del., 1955-76, mgr. epidemiology sect., 1976-82, sr. cons., 1982-85; epidemiology cons. Wilmington, 1985—; epidemiology cons. Del. Divsn. Pub. Health, Dover, 1986-95. Contbr. articles to New Eng. Jour. Medicine, Jour. Occupational Medicine, Jour. AMA. With U.S. Army, 1943-45, ETO. Recipient Merit in Authorship Hon. Mention, Inds. Med. Assn., 1959. Fellow Am. Coll. Epidemiology, Am. Heart Assn., Am. Pub. Health Assn. Home: 1416 Emory Rd Wilmington DE 19803-5120

PELLATT, JUDITH CAROLINE, clinical trials assistant; b. Newport, Eng., Nov. 22, 1955. Student, LSU Coll. Higher Edn., Southampton, Eng., 1990-93; BSc (hons.) in Podiatry; MSc, Columbia Pacific U. Cert. S.R.N., S.C.M. Staff nurse Queen Alexandra Hosp., Portsmouth, Eng., 1980-86; nat. sec. for U.K. Aid to the Ch. in Need (charity), Chichester, Eng., 1986-87; asst. to dir. Cega Air Ambulance, Chichester, 1986-87; surveillante Inst. Mont Olivet, Lausanne, Switzerland, 1989; rsch. asst. hematology lab. St. Marys Hosp., Portsmouth, 1989-90; part-time lectr. in psychology U. Portsmouth, 1994-95; full time clin. trials asst. Wessex Med. Oncology Unit, Southampton, Eng. Contbr. haematology articles to profl. jours. Mem. Soc. Chiropodists (student mem.). Roman Catholic.

PELLEGRINO, EDMUND DANIEL, physician, educator, former university president; b. Newark, June 22, 1920; s. Michael J. and Marie (Catone) P.; m. Clementine Coakley, Nov. 17, 1944; children: Thomas, Virginia, Michael, Andrea, Alice, Leah. BS, St. John's U., 1941, DSc (hon.), 1971; MD, NYU, 1944; 39 hon. degrees. Diplomate Am. Bd. Internal Medicine. Intern Bellevue Hosp., N.Y.C., 1944-45; asst. resident medicine Bellevue Hosp., 1948-49; resident medicine Goldwater Meml. Hosp., N.Y.C., 1945-46; fellow medicine NYU, 1949-50; supervising Tb physician Homer Folks Hosp., Oneonta, N.Y., 1950-53; dir. internal medicine Hunterdon Med. Center, Flemington, N.J., 1953-59; med. dir. Hunterdon Med. Center, 1955-59; prof., chmn. dept. medicine U. Ky. Med. Center, 1959-66; prof. medicine SUNY, Stony Brook, 1966-72; v.p. for health scis., dir. Health Scis. Center SUNY, 1968-73, dean Sch. Medicine, 1968-72; v.p. health affairs U. Tenn. System; chancellor U. Tenn. Med. Units, Memphis, 1973-75; prof. med. Yale U., New Haven, 1975-78; pres. Yale-New Haven Med. Center, 1975-78, Cath. U. Am., Washington, 1978-82; prof. philosophy and biology Cath. U. Am., 1978-82; John Carroll prof. medicine and med. ethics Georgetown U., Washington, 1982—; dir. Kennedy Inst. Ethics, Washington, 1983-88; dir. Ctr. for Advanced Study Ethics Georgetown U., Washington, 1988-94, dir. Ctr. for Clin. Bioethics, 1991—, acting chief Divsn. Gen. Internal Medicine, 1993-94. Founding editor Jour. Medicine and Philosophy, 1983—. Served with USAAF, 1946-48. Master ACP; fellow N.Y. Acad. Medicine; mem. Inst. Medicine of NAS, AMA, Assn. Am. Physicians, Medieval Acad. Am., Metaphys. Soc. Am., N.Y. Acad. Sci., Am. Clin. and Climatol. Assn. Office: Georgetown U Ctr for Clin Bioethics Washington DC 20007

PELLEGRINO, JAMES MARTIN, dentist; b. Massena, N.Y., Apr. 26, 1939; s. Frank A. and Mary E. (Martin) P.; m. Patricia Ann Viskovich, June 27, 1964; children: James, Lynn, Joanne, Andrea, Micheal. BS, Coll. of Holy Cross, 1961; DDS, SUNY, Buffalo, 1965. Pvt. practice Massena, 1965—. Bd. dirs. Massena Meml. Hosp., 1990, St. Law County Red Cross, Potsdam, N.Y., 1990. Mem. Am. Dental Assn., Dental Soc. (5th dist. pres.-elect 1994, pres. 1995), St. Law County Dental Soc. (pres. 1976), Massena Rotary (pres. 1975, Paul Harris fellow 1992), Monday Luncheon Club (pres. 1993), Elks, Knights of Columbus. Republican. Roman Catholic. Home: 24 Windsor Rd Massena NY 13662-1606 Office: 55 E Orvis St Massena NY 13662-2051

PELLEGRINO, PETER, surgeon; b. Camden, N.J., July 7, 1934; s. Peter and Alice (Alchin) P.; m. Barbara Ann Holdon, June 18, 1960; children: Peter Scott, Kathleen Ann, Lisa Marie. AB in Psychology, Franklin-Marshall Sch., 1956; MD, Hahnemann Med. Coll., 1960. Diplomate Am. Bd. Surgery. Intern, Hahnemann Hosp., Phila., 1960-61, surg. resident, 1961-62, surg. resident, 1965-67, 68, attending surgeon, 1969—; chief dept. surgery Kessler Hosp., Hammonton, N.J., 1969—. Served to capt., U.S. Army, 1962-65. Fellow ACS; mem. Am. Acad. Proctology, Soc. Abdominal Surgeons, AMA, N.J. Med. Soc., Hahnemann Alumni Assn. (1st v.p. 1984). Republican. Home: 3 Stafford Ct Berlin NJ 08009-2209 Office: 777 Profl Ctr Hammonton NJ 08037

PELLER, CHARLES HENRY, thoracic surgeon, educator; b. Albany, N.Y., May 8, 1930; s. Pincus and Tillie (Rockwitz) P.; m. Sherri Getz, Aug. 11, 1955; children: Howard D., Paul Ahron. BA in Chemistry, NYU, 1956, MD, 1960. Diplomate Am. Bd. Surgery, Am. Bd. Thoracic Surgery; lic. physician, N.Y., Ohio. Resident in gen. surgery U. Mich. Med. Ctr., Ann Arbor, 1960-65, resident in thoracic surgery, 1965-67, instr. surgery, 1963-67, asst. coord. for med. edn., 1964-65; pvt. practice thoracic surgery Aultman Hosp., Canton, Ohio, 1967-93; clin. assoc. prof. surgery Northeastern Ohio Univs. Coll. Medicine, Rootstown, 1976—; cons. Peer Rev. of Ohio, Columbus, 1993—. Author articles. Served with M.C., USN, 1950-54, Korea. Fellow ACS, Am. Coll. Chest Physicians; mem. AMA, Ohio State Med. Soc., John Alexander Thoracic Surg. Soc., Soc. Thoracic Surgery, Sierra Club (life). Home: 2665 Aspen Rd Ann Arbor MI 48108

PELLETIER, CLAUDE HENRI, biomedical engineer; b. Riviere-Ouelle, Can., Que., Dec. 15, 1941; s. Lucien Pelletier and Ernestine Michaud. Immatriculation sr., Coll. Universitaire U. Sherbrooke, 1961; B.Sc.A., U. Sherbrooke, 1966; M.Sc.A., Ecole Polytechnique, U. Montreal, 1972. Project engr. Alcan, Alma, Can., 1966-69; mgr. computer ctr. in physiology dept. faculty medicine U. Montreal, 1972-73; biomed. engr. Sacre-Coeur Hosp., Montreal, 1973-75; chief engr. biomed. engrng. dept. Montreal Heart Inst., 1975—; lectr. faculty of medicine U. Montreal, 1972-74, research asst. faculty of medicine, 1973-75; cons. Montreal Heart Inst., 1975—. Contbr. articles to profl. jours. Mem. Order of Engrs. Que., IEEE, Assn. Advancement Med. Instrumentation, Assn. Des Physiciens Et Ingenieurs Biomedicaux Du Que. Roman Catholic. Avocations: swimming; tennis. Home: 5732 Plantagenet, Montreal, PQ Canada H3S 2K3

PELLETIER, LAWRENCE LEE, JR., internist, infectious disease subspecialist; b. Bangor, Maine, Dec. 26, 1942; s. Lawrence Lee and Louise Elizabeth (Collins) P.; m. Mary Beacom Rowland, June 6, 1968; children: Christina Louise, Anne Elizabeth, Caron Elise. BA, Bowdoin Coll., 1964; MD, Columbia U., 1968. Diplomate Am. Bd. Internal Medicine, Am. Bd. Infectious Diseases. Internal medicine residency U. Kans. Sch. Medicine, Wichita, 1968-71, 73; fellow infectious diseases U. Washington, Seattle, 1973-75; asst. prof. internal medicine U. N.D. Sch. Medicine, Fargo, 1975-79; chief infectious disease ctr. Fargo VA Med. Ctr., 1975-79; assoc. prof. medicine U. Washington, Seattle, 1979-82; chief med. svc. Am. Lake VA Med. Ctr., Tacoma, Wash., 1979-82; prof. internal medicine U. Kans. Sch. Medicine, Wichita, 1982—; chief med. svc. Wichita VA Med. Ctr., 1982-96; program dir. in-residency U. N.D. Sch. Medicine, 1976-79; vice chmn. dept. internal medicine U. Kans. Sch. Medicine, Wichita, 1988—. Contbr. articles to profl. jours. Maj. U.S. Army, 1971-73. Recipient Disting. Physician award Am. Ex-Prisoners of War Assn., 1985. Fellow ACP, Infectious Diseases Soc. Am.; mem. Cen. Soc. for Clin. Rsch., Phi Beta Kappa, Sigma Xi. Office: Med Svc Wichita Kans Wichita KS 67218

PELLETIER, MURIEL T., health facility administrator, nurse; b. Manchester, N.H., June 19, 1950; d. Armand W. and Germaine (Demers) Tessier; m. Richard A. Pelletier, June 10, 1972; children: Lisa Marie, Amy Lyn. Diploma, Sacred Heart Sch. Nursing, Manchester, 1971; BS, Springfield Coll. RN, N.H. From staff nurse to infection control coord. Catholic Med. Ctr., Manchester, 1971—. Religious edn. tchr. St. Catherine of Siena, Manchester; chmn. child care adv. bd. Immaculate Heart of Mary, Concord, N.H. Mem. Nat. Assn. Health Care Quality, N.H. Asn. Infection Control & Epidemiology Profls., N.H. Assn. Health Care Quality. Office: Catholic Med Ctr 100 McGregor St Manchester NH 03102

PELLETIER, NANCY ANNE, obstetrical and gynecological nurse, educator; b. St. Louis, June 16, 1951; d. David Cooper Hill and Cenith Lorraine Gore; m. Russell Dean Pelletier, June 16, 1972; children: Kyle, Lindsay, Bradley. Cert. in practical nursing, Alexandria Hosp. Sch. of Practical Nursing, 1971; cert. in health edn., U. Md., 1973; AAS magna cum laude, No. Va. C.C., 1984. LPN, Va.; RN, Va. LPN in pediatrics Alexandria (Va.) Hosp., 1971-72, LPN in medications, 1972-73, LPN in post partum and intensive care nursery, 1977-84, nurse post partum and float pool, 1984-85, childbirth educator, 1978—; sch. nurse, tchr. health edn. Alexandria City Pub. Schs., 1973-76; lead nurse Ob-Gyn Assocs. No. Va., Alexandria, 1984-91; lead ob-gyn nurse Kaiser Permanente of Mid-Atlantic Region, Woodbridge, Va., 1991—; advisor Vocat. Edn. Clubs Am., Washington, 1974. Author: (pamphlet) A Nurse Discusses Your Cesarean Delivery, (teaching tool) Test Your Pregnancy Knowledge. Mem. NAACOG, Am. Soc. for Psychoprophylaxis in Obstetrics (cert. ACCE), Phi Theta Kappa.

PELLETIERE, VINCENT JAMES, plastic surgeon, cosmetic surgeon; b. Chgo., Oct. 23, 1943; s. John Patrick and Theresa (Tetti) P.; m. Joanne Elizabeth Pelletiere, May 2, 1970; children: Nicole, Christopher, Justin, Kelly. AB in Biology, U. Chgo., 1965; MD, U. Ill., 1969. Diplomate Am. Bd. Plastic and Reconstructive Surgery. Pvt. practice Barrington Plastic Surgery, Ltd., Inverness, Ill., 1978—; chief plastic surgery Northwest Cmty. Med. Ctr., Arlington Heights, Ill., 1992-95. To lt. comdr. USN, 1970-73. Mem. AMA, Am. Soc. Plastic and Reconstructive Surgery, Am. Soc. Aesthetic Surgery, Ill. Med. Soc., Chgo. Plastic Surgery Soc. Protestant. Home: 81 Hawley Woods Rd Barrington Hills IL 60010

PELLOW, RITA BOLL, psychologist; b. Pitts., Nov. 15, 1925; d. Raymond A. and Stella (Henson) B.; m. James A. Pellow, Jan. 30, 1948; children—James A., Michael R., David G., Lisa M. B.S., U. Pitts., 1964, M.S., 1966, Ph.D., 1970. Lic. clin. psychologist, cert. sch. psychologist. Pa. Staff psychologist Pitts. Child Guidance, 1968-69, Allegheny Intermediate Unit, 1970-80; pvt. practice clin. and sch. psychology, Pitts., 1977—. Mem. Am. Psychol. Assn., Pa. Psychol. Assn., Greater Pitts. Psychol. Assn., Am. Soc. Clin. Hypnosis, Western Pa. Soc. Clin. Hypnosis, Phi Beta Kappa, Sigma Xi, Mensa. Lodge: Zonta Internat. Home: The Brackenridge 1160 Bower Hill Rd Ph 4B Pittsburgh PA 15243-1358 Office: St Clair Bldg 1725 Washington Rd Ste 404C Pittsburgh PA 15241-1207

PELOQUIN, LORI JEANNE, clinical psychologist; b. Milw., Sept. 21, 1957; d. Wayne Joseph Peloquin and Jeanne Audrey (Ehlers) Driessen; m. Allen Theodore Retzlaff Jr., May 5, 1990; children: Austin Miles, Landry Quinn. Student, U. Wis., Eau Claire, 1975-76; BA summa cum laude, U. Minn., 1978; MA, U. Rochester, 1982, PhD, 1985. Lic. psychologist, N.Y. Teaching asst. U. Rochester, N.Y., 1981-83, instr. psychology, 1984; co-dir. Early Intervention Specialist Tng. Program Strong Ctr. for Devel Disabilities Rochester Sch. Medicine, 1992-94; instr. depts. pediatrics and psychiatry (psychology) U. Rochester Sch. Medicine and Dentistry, N.Y., 1984-93; sr. instr. dept. pediatrics and psychiatry U. Rochester Sch. Medicine and Dentistry, 1993—; pvt. practice Rochester, 1985—; cons. Rochester Children's Nursery and Bd. Coop. Ednl. Svcs., 1986-90, Hillside Children's Ctr., Rochester, 1985-87; planning coord. Crisis Intervention Program, Rochester, 1985-86; mem. steering com. Early Childhood Intervention Coun. Monroe County, 1989-90; mem. profl. adv. bd. Greater Rochester Attention Deficit Disorder Assn. Contbr. chpts. to books, articles to profl. publs. Mem. APA, Psychologists for Social Responsibility, Rochester Area Assn. Clin. Psychologists (v.p. 1987-89, pres. 1989-90, exec. com. 1990-91, ann. banquet com. chair 1991), Genesee Valley Psychol. Assn. (program com. 1991-93), Coalition for Svcs. to Parents with Devel. Disabilities (com. chmn. 1985-90, coord. 1988-90), N.Y. State Psychol. Assn., Assn. for Advancement of Psychology, Mental Health Assn., Phi Beta Kappa. Presbyterian. Office: 247 Park Ave Rochester NY 14607-2723

PELOQUIN, WILLIAM HENRY, ophthalmology; b. Genoa, Ohio, June 21, 1938; m. Joyce, 1961; children: Laura, Linda. BS, Capital U., 1960; MS, U. Cin., 1962; MD, Hahnemann Med. Sch., 1966. Diplomate Nat. Bd. Med. Examiners, Am. Bd. Ophthalmology. Intern Naval Hosp., Oakland, Calif., 1967, Aerospace Med. Inst., Pensacola, Fla., 1968; resident ophthalmology Naval Regional Med. Ctr., San Diego, 1973; from dir. pediat. ophthalmology to chmn. dept. ophthalmology Naval Hosp., Oakland, 1974-86; pvt practice ophthalmology Fullerton, Calif., 1986—; from asst. chmn. dept. ophthalmology to dir. pediat. ophthalmology Naval Regional Med. Ctr., San Diego, 1973-74. Mem. Am. Acad. Ophthalmology, Am. Soc. Cataract and Refractive Surgery, Calif. Assn. Ophthalmology, Calif. Med. Assn., Orange County Med. Assn., Orange County Soc. Ophthalmology, Soc. Mil. Ophthalmologists, Alpha Omega Alpha. Office: Ste 115 301 W Bastanchury Rd Fullerton CA 92635-3423

PELTON, LEROY HOWARD, social work educator; b. N.Y.C., Apr. 30, 1940; s. Myer and Rose (Stein) P. BS in Math. and Psychology, CUNY, 1961; MA in Psychology, New Sch. for Social Rsch., 1963; MSW, Rutgers U., 1985; PhD in Psychology, Wayne State U., 1966. Asst. prof. SUNY, Albany, 1966-73, Susquehanna U., Selinsgrove, Pa., 1973-75; program devel. specialist N.J. Div. Youth and Family Svcs., Trenton, 1975-79, spl. asst. to dir., 1979-81; rsch. assoc. Assn. for Children N.J., Newark, 1981-82; dir. child welfare Vera Inst. Justice, N.Y.C., 1982-83; policy and planning specialist N.J. Commn. for Blind and Visually Impaired, Newark, 1984-86; vis. lectr. Rutgers U., New Brunswick, N.J., 1985-86; vis. assoc. prof. U. Tenn., Knoxville, 1986-87; prof. social work Salem (Mass.) State Coll., 1987—. Author: The Psychology of Nonviolence, 1974, For Reasons of Poverty, 1989; editor: The Social Context of Child Abuse and Neglect, 1981; cons. editor Arete, 1989—; assoc. editor Children and Youth Svcs. Rev., 1990—; contbr. articles to profl. jours. Office: Salem State Coll Sch Social Work Salem MA 01970

PELTON, SHARON JANICE, emergency physician; b. Cohoes, N.Y., Oct. 21, 1944; d. William Joseph and Lily Marie (Carey) P.; m. John A. Martinec, Sept. 21, 1974 (div. Sept. 1977). BS, Rensselaer Poly. Inst., Troy, N.Y., 1966; MD cum laude, Albany Med. Coll., 1970. Diplomate Am. Bd. Emergency Medicine. Intern and resident Dartmouth Affiliated Hosps., Hanover, N.H., 1970-71; emergency physician Ill. Trauma Ctr. Sys., Ill. Emergency Depts., Neenah, Wis., 1971-73; co-initiator emergency physician coverage Theda Clark Hosp., Neenah, Wis., 1973-74; dir. emergency svcs. Oconto Falls (Wis.) Hosp., Naperville, Ill., 1974-76; asst. dir. emergency dept. Edward Hosp., Naperville, Ill., 1976-78; pvt. practice Meml. Hosp., Naperville, Ill., 1978-92; attending physician emergency dept. Meml. Hosp., Carbondale, Ill., 1992—; clin. asst. prof. So. Ill. U., Carbondale, 1994—; lectr. trauma nurse specialist program, Carbondale, 1994—. Advisor N.Am. Riding for Handicapped Assn., Harrisburg, 1995-96. Recipient award for doctor-patient relationship Lamb Found., 1970, Frederich H. Hesser award for excellence in neurology, 1970. Fellow Am. Coll. Emergency Physicians, Am. Acad. Family Physicians; mem. Am. Coll. Sports Medicine, Am. Med. Soc., Ill. State Med. Soc., Alpha Omega Alpha, Pi Delta Epsilon. Office: Meml Hosp Carbondale Carbondale IL 62901

PELZ, HERMAN H., physician; b. N.Y.C., May 28, 1931; s. Elias and Sima (Mansterman) P.; m. Janice G. nee Gersten, Mar. 1, 1958; children: Ellen, Daniel. BS, L.I. U., 1952; MD, SUNY, Bklyn., 1956. Diplomate Am. Bd. Allergy and Immunology. Pvt. practice specializing in internal medicine/allergies Elmhurst, N.Y., 1961—; chief allergy VA Hosp., Bklyn., 1962—, Wyckoff Hts. Hosp., Bklyn., 1963—; intern Mt. Sinai Hosp. of N.J., 1956-57; medicine residency VA Hosp., Bronx, 1957-58; fellowship in allergy Bklyn. Jewish Hosp., 1960-61, chief resident in medicine, 1961-62. Author: Primer in Allergy, 1978. Lt. USN 1958-60. Fellow Am. Acad. Allergy, Internat. Acad. Allergology, Am. Genetics Soc. Republican. Jewish. Office: 92-31 57th Ave Elmhurst NY 11373-5075

PEMBER, JOHN BARTLETT, social worker, educator; b. White Plains, N.Y., June 24, 1951; s. John Raymond and Allyn Marie (Case) P.; m. Deborah Ann Dudley, June 9, 1973; children: John Scott, Matthew Bartlett, Jenna Lynne. BA, Houghton (N.Y.) Coll., 1973; MSW, SUNY, Buffalo, 1978. Cert. social worker, N.Y. Social work asst. Cuba (N.Y.) Meml. Hosp. and Skilled Nursing Facility, 1973-76; staff social worker Wyoming County Mental Health, Warsaw, N.Y., 1978-80, supervising social worker, 1980-85; parole officer N.Y. State Div. Parole, Rochester, 1985-87; team supr., social worker II, Capital Dist. Psychiat. Ctr., Albany, N.Y., 1987—; pvt. practice Capital Area Christian Counseling Svc., Delmar, N.Y., 1988—; social work cons., Warsaw, 1978-87; instr. field work SUNY, Buffalo, 1982-85, SUNY, Albany, 1987—; clin. instr. dept. psychiatry Albany Med. Coll., 1991—. Mem. NASW. Office: Capital Area Christian Cons PO Box 313 Delmar NY 12054-0313

PEMBER-DOERR, JANICE JOY, recreational therapist; b. New Orleans, July 9, 1957; d. Robert Wayne and Marie Delcina (Bissonnette) Pember; m. Thomas Austin Doerr, May 20, 1983; children: Erich Thomas, Nathaniel Robert, Michael Patrick. BS in Psychology, Ctrl. Mich U., 1978, BS in Therapeutic Recreation, 1978, MA in Recreation and Park Adminstrn., 1979. Cert. therapeutic recreation specialist; cert. activity cons. Activity coord. Mt. Pleasant (Mich.) Housing Commn., 1977-80; recreational therapist Bay Med. Ctr., Bay City, Mich., 1980-83; mental health therapist Saginaw (Mich.) County Cmty. Mental Health, 1984; recreational therapy dir. Standish (Mich.) Cmty. Hosp., 1984—; adj. faculty Saginaw Valley State U., 1995—; geriatric cons. Health Care Cons., Bay City, 1984—; spkr. in field. Advisor Boy Scouts of Am., Standish, 1994—; leader, challenge 4-H, Bay City, 1981-83; leader brownies Girl Scouts Am., Hale, 1971-73. Mem. Mich. Assn. of Activity Profl. (bd. dirs. 1984—), Nat. Assn. of Activity Profls., Mich. Recreation and Park Assn., Nat. Recreation and Park Assn. (therapeutic br.). Roman Catholic. Home: 4317 Kuerbitz Dr Bay City MI 48706 Office: Standish Cmty Hosp 805 W Cedar Standish MI 48658

PEMBERTON, BOBETTE MARIE (HARMAN), nursing administrator; b. San Mateo, Calif., Oct. 20, 1952; d. William Adolph and Agnes Marie (Costa) Harman; m. William Charles Pemberton (div. Sept. 1993). BSN, U. San Francisco, 1975, PHN. RN, Calif., Hawaii, Fla.; cert. pub. health nurse, flight nurse, OR nurse. Recreation supr. Burlingame (Calif.) Recreation Ctr., 1968-74; nursing asst. III Stanford U. Med. Ctr., Palo Alto, Calif., 1974-75, staff nurse, 1976-78; clin. edn. supr., mobile ops. supr. Irwin Meml. Blood Bank, San Francisco Med Soc., 1978-87; OR staff nurse U. Calif., Davis, 1987-88; asst. dir. blood svcs. ARC, Farmington, Conn., 1988-89; coord. blood bank St. Anthony's Med. Ctr., St. Petersburg, Fla., 1989-90; dir. donor svcs. Hunter Blood Ctr., Clearwater, Fla., 1990-93; dir. nursing svcs. Blood Bank of Hawaii, Honolulu, 1993-95; dir. nursing Peninsula Blood Bank, 1995—; chairperson nursing edn. com. Calif. Blood Bank System, No. Calif. region seminar Irwin Meml. Blood Bank; mem. sci. com. Blood Bank Nurses Calif., Calif. Blood Bank System; nursing rep. Local 535; lectr. in field. With USAFR, 1983—. Mem. NAFE, Am. Bus. Women's Assn. (rec. sec., chairperson spring conf. Burlingame charter chpt., del. Kansas City conv.), Am. Assn. Blood Banks, Calif. Blood Bank Soc. (nursing and donor svcs. com., continuing edn. com.), Air Force Assn., Air Force Res. Officers Assn. Republican. Roman Catholic. Home: 512 Marin Dr Burlingame CA 94010

PEMBERTON, DIANE MARIE DUMAINE, nurse; b. New Orleans, Dec. 17, 1949; d. Randsdel Joseph and Doris (Gonzales) Dumaine; m. Richard N. Kenney, Feb. 3, 1968 (div. 1974); m. Anthony Martinez Jr., July 7, 1977 (div. Nov. 1988); children: Nicole F., Laura A.; m. Craig Pemberton, May 14, 1989; stepchildren: Stephen, Angela Ray. Lic. Vocat. Nurse, LPN, Jefferson Parish Vocat. Sch., La., 1969; cert. computer ops., Fed. Govt. Sch., Hammond, La., 1982; cert. in Reiki, Reiki of Tex., Houston, 1996. Critical care nurse ICU, CCU, recovery East Jefferson Gen. Hosp., Metairie, La., 1970-72; med.-surg. staff nurse Hotel Dieu Hosp., New Orleans, 1974-76; staff nurse, weekend charge nurse Eye Ear nose and Throat Hosp., New Orleans, 1976-77; city-wide staff relief nurse Med. Pers. Pool, New Orleans, 1978-80; pvt. duty nurse hosps. and pvt. homes Hammond & Ponchatoula, La., 1980-85; owner, dir., instr. The Computer Classroom, La. & Tex., 1982-87; computer literacy tchr. St. Augustine Cath. Elem. Sch., Houston, 1987-88, 89-90; clinic dir. sch. nurse St. Augustine Elem. Sch., Houston, 1988-90; sch. nurse dist. sub Pasadena (Tex.) Ind. Sch. Dist., Houston & Pasadena, 1990—; acting dir. Blood Ctr., Hammond, 1981. Author, poet: (poetry book) Whisperings of the Child First Born, 1982; poet Internat. Calendar LaLeche League, 1982; poet, photo-journalist, columnist The Poncatoula Times newspaper, 1981-85. Mem. Polit. and Moral Action Impact Grup, Sagemont Ch., Houston, 1995, 96; facilitator, founding-mother Concerned Christian Am. Citizens for True Justice, Houston, 1996; vol. Armory Army Nat. Guard Exam Rm., Ellington AFB, Houston, 1995-96; mem. Unity Ch. for Love and Light, Friendswood, Tex., vol. first healthcare team and Sunday sch. Recipient award of merit cert. Hollywood's (Calif.) Famous Poets Soc., 1995, 96. Mem. Am. Holistic Nurses Assn. (holistic nurse practitioner Houston 1995-96), Lic. Vocat. Nurses Assn. Tex., Rostcrucian Order Ancient Mystical Order Rosicrucis Order (matré 1992-94, Svc. award 1994). Republican. Home: PO Box 753191 Houston TX 77275-3191

PENA, ANTONIA MURILLO, physician, radiologist; b. San Diego, July 18, 1946; d. Blas and Elvira (Murillo) Pena. B.A., Loma Linda U., Riverside, Calif., 1968; M.D., 1973. Diplomate Nat. Bd. Radiology. Intern, White Meml. Med. Ctr., Los Angeles, 1973-74, resident, 1974-77; radiologist Paradise Valley Hosp., National City, Calif., 1978-79; neuroradiology fellow Los Angeles County-U.So. Calif. Med. Ctr., 1977-78, 79-80; radiologist Arlington Radiology Med. Group, Riverside, Calif., 1980—; attending staff Riverside Gen. Hosp. U. Med. Ctr., 1980—; assoc. staff Parkview Community Hosp., 1980—; med. dir. Magnetic Resonance Imaging Ctr., Parkview Community Hosp., 1985—; cons. radiologist Computerized Diagnostic Med. Group of Riverside, 1980—; cons. Veitch Student Health Ctr., Riverside, 1980—. Mem. Radiol. Soc. N.Am., Am. Coll. Radiology, Calif. Radiol. Soc., AMA, Calif. Med. Assn., Am. Assn. Women Radiologists, Inland Radiology Soc., Am. Soc. Neuroradiology (sr.), Riverside County Med. Soc. Republican. Seventh-Day Adventist. Office: 9851 Magnolia Ave Riverside CA 92503-3528

PENA, MARIA CARMEN, plastic surgeon; b. Sarria, Spain, July 13, 1949; d. Antonio and Carmen Amelia (Fernandez) P. BA, Medicine Sch., Santiago de Compostela, Spain, 1972; MD cum laude, U. Oviedo, 1985. Emergency physician R.S. Almurante Vierna, Vigo, Spain, 1972-73; staff asst. C.S. Enrique Sotomayor, Bilbao, Spain, 1973-74, C.N. Especialidades Quirurgigas, Madrid, Spain, 1974-77; registrar H. Ntra.Sra. Covadonga, Oviedo, 1977-88; pvt. practice Oviedo, 1986—; tchr. Medicine Sch., Oviedo, 1991. Contbr. articles to profl. jours. Mem. Compsion Nacional Cir. Plastica, Soc. Espanola Microciruga, Soc. Espanola de Cirucia Plastica. Office: Unidad Cirugia Plastica, Avenida de Galicia 9-4 D, 33005 Oviedo Spain

PENACHIO, ANTHONY JOSEPH, JR., psychotherapist. b. Stamford, Conn., Apr. 3, 1943; 1 child, Ariana. Cert. in psychotherapy, Am. Sch. Hynotherapy, 1978; DD, Aquarian Ch. of Jesus, 1978; PSD, Neotharian Sch. Philosophy, 1980. Cert. clin. registered hypnotherapist, psychotherapist, behavioral therapist. Counseling min., exec. dir. Inst. Clin. Tricotomy, Stamford; lectr. Contbr. articles profl. jours. Mem. Am. Coun. Hypnotherapist-Psychotherapist (bd. examiners), N.Y. Acad. Sci. Home and Office: 965 Hope St Stamford CT 06907-2227

PENCE, JOHN THOMAS, dietitian; b. Lafayette, Ind., June 21, 1941; s. M.O. and Florence (Lindley) P.; m. Karen Sue Turner, June 19, 1976. BS, Purdue U., 1963; MS, Kans. State U., 1970. Registered dietitian. Asst. dir. residence hall food service Kans. State U., Manhattan, 1973-82, head residence hall food service, 1982-87, assoc. dir., housing head residence hall food service, 1987—, instr. hotel, restaurant, instn. mgmt. dietetics, 1987—. Author: (with others) Recipes From the Heartland '80, 1980, Recipes From the Land of Ah's, 1982. Mem. Kans. Travel and Tourism Commn., 1987—; chmn. bd. dirs. Manhattan Community Sr. Svc. Ctr., 1990—. Recipient Silver Plate award Internat. Food Service Mfrs. Assn., 1987; named Kans. Employer Yr. Kans. Rehab. Assn., 1980. Mem. Am. Dietetic Assn., Am. Sch. Food Service Assn., Soc. For Advancement of Food Service Research, Nat. Assn. Coll. and Univ. Food Service (nat. treas. 1979-85, nat. pres. 1986-87, Meritorious Service award 1981, 83, 85). Republican. Methodist. Lodge: Kiwanis. Home: 2361 Grandview Ter Manhattan KS 66502-3729 Office: Kans State U Pittman Bldg Manhattan KS 66506

PENDERGRASS, HENRY PANCOAST, physician, radiology educator; b. Bryn Mawr, Pa., Jan. 29, 1925; s. Eugene Percival and Rebecca (Barker) P.; m. Carol Lowe Dodson, Aug. 27, 1960 (dec. Aug. 1993); children: Sharon (dec.), Lisa (dec.), Deborah, Margaret; m. Carol Minster Roberts, Oct. 2, 1994. Student, U.S. Naval Acad., 1944-46; A.B., Princeton U., 1948; M.D., U. Pa., 1952; M.P.H., Harvard U., 1969. Diplomate: Am. Bd. Radiology,

Am. Bd. Nuclear Medicine. Intern Pa. Hosp., 1953-54; mem. staff and faculty U. Pa. Med. Sch. and Univ. Hosp., Phila., 1953-58, 60-61; clin. asst. in neuroradiology Inst. Neurology Queen Sq., London, 1959-60; mem. staff and faculty Harvard U. Med. Sch. and Mass. Gen. Hosp., Boston, 1958-59, 61-76; prof. radiology Vanderbilt U. Sch. Medicine, Nashville, 1976-95, prof. emeritus, 1995—, vice chmn., 1976-89; adj. prof. radiology U. Pa. Med. Sch., 1996—. Mem. editorial bd. Am. Family Physician, 1980-94, Jour. Digital Imaging, 1987-96; contbr. chpts. to books, articles to med. jours. Mem. cancer control rev. com. Nat. Cancer Inst., 1975-79; Bd. dirs. state and local div. Am. Cancer Soc., 1976-85; mem. Project Hope Med. Mission, Peru, 1962; trustee Harpeth Hall Sch., Nashville, 1983-88. With U.S. Army, USN, 1943-46. Am. Cancer Soc. grantee, 1956-57; Nat. Cancer Inst. grantee, 1957-58; Nat. Inst. Neurol. Disease and Blindness grantee, 1959-60; Nat. Inst. Gen. Med. Scis. grantee, 1968-69; Distinguished Service award Am. Medical Assn., 1994. Fellow Am. Coll. Radiology (life mem., benefactor, counselor, steering com. 1968-73, bd. chancellors 1977-81), AMA (mem. Ho. of Dels. 1986—, sect. coun. on radiology 1978—, sec. 1987—, sect. on med. schs. 1979—, Disting. Svc. Gold medal 1994, grad. med. edn. adv. com. 1994—, chair 1996), Coun. Med. Splty. Socs., Am. Roentgen Ray Soc., Brit. Inst. Radiology, Ea. Radiol. Soc. (pres., trustee 1968-72, sci. program chmn. 1964, 72, 79), Assn. Univ. Radiologists, Mass. Radiol. Soc. (v.p. 1967-68, 75-76), Mass. Med. Soc. (counselor 1968-76), Nashville Acad. Medicine (chmn. com. on ethics 1981-82, Nat. Bd. Med. Examiners 1995—), Radiol. Soc. N.Am. (bd. dirs. 1972-77, chmn. 1975-76, pres.-elect and pres. 1977-78, Gold medal 1984, trustee RSNA Rsch. and Edn. Fund 1984-90, fund sec.-treas 1988-90), Am. Soc. Emergency Radiology, Tenn. Med. Assn., Tenn. Radiol. Soc. (pres.-elect, then pres. 1985-86, exec. com. 1984-88), Mid. Tenn. Radiol. Soc. (pres. 1984-85, sec., treas. 1985-94), Soc. Thoracic Imaging, Soc. Magnetic Resonance in Medicine, Sigma Xi, Delta Psi. Clubs: Belle Meade Country, Merion golf, Merion Cricket, Amateur Ski (N.Y.), Cap and Gown (Princeton, N.J.). Office: Vanderbilt U Sch Medicine 1121 21st Ave S Nashville TN 37232-2675

PENDLETON, ROBERT GRUBB, pharmacologist; b. Kansas City, Mo., Apr. 24, 1939. AA, Kansas City Jr. Coll., 1959; AB in Chemistry, U. Mo., 1961; PhD in Pharmacology, U. Kans., 1966. Sr. scientist SmithKline and French, Phila., 1966-67, assoc. sr. investigator, 1967-69, sr. investigator, 1969-74, asst. dir., 1974-79, assoc. dir., 1977-80, dir. pharmacology, 1980-81; dir. gastroenterology Merck, West Point, Pa., 1981-86; sr. dir. biology Rper Ctrl. Rsch., King of Prussia, Pa., 1986-90; sr. rsch. scholar Temple U., Phila., 1993—; cons. dir. pharmacology Sepracor, Inc., Marlborough, Mass., 1991—; adj. instr. life sci. C.C. of Phila., 1991—; lab. sci cons. Office of the Surgeon Gen., U.S. Army, Washington, 1989— Col U.S. Army Res., 1969—. Mem. Am. Soc. Pharmacology Exptl. Therapy, Am. Chem. Soc. (divsn. med. chem.), Soc. of Armed Forces Med. Lab. Scientist. Home: 1312 Sumneytown Pike Lower Gwynedd PA 19002 Office: Temple U Dept Biology Philadelphia PA 19122

PENDLEY, DONALD LEE, association executive; b. Jersey City, Nov. 5, 1950; s. Donald L. and Loretta M. (Purcell) P.; m. Donna Lynn Meade, Oct. 14, 1984; 1 child, Katelyn. BA, Montclair State Coll., 1972; MA, Syracuse U., 1974. Reporter/rewriter The Herald-News, Passaic, N.J., 1969-72; reporter The Dispatch, Union City, N.J., 1973; writer Keep America Beautiful, Inc., N.Y.C., 1974-75, communications dir., 1976-78, v.p. communications program devel., 1979-84; sr. v.p. communications Greater Newark C. of C., 1985-86; dir. pub. rels. Internat. Coun. Shopping Ctrs., N.Y.C., 1987-92; exec. dir. N.J. Hospice Orgn., Scotch Plains, N.J., 1993—. Creator, dir. theatre composer series William Carlos Williams Ctr., 1987-91; creator, dir. SRO Cabaret Series, 1991—. Pres. State Repertory Opera, South Orange, N.J., 1981-85, 92—, Ars Musica Chorale, Englewood, N.J., 1979-81. Recipient Award of Excellence Am. C. of C. Execs. 1986, Gold Key awards, Pub. Rels. News, 1982, 86. Mem. PRSA (accredited, sec.-treas. assn. sec. 1989-90, vice chmn. assn. sect. 1990-91, chmn. 1991-92), Am. Soc. Assn. Execs. (Gold Circle award 1988, comm. sect. coun. 1994-96), Am. Mensa, Ltd. (nat. devel. officer 1985-89, 96—, regional tng. officer 1989-93), Intertel. Home: 32 Hamilton Rd Glen Ridge NJ 07028-1109

PENDRAK, ROBERT FRANCIS, internist, insurance company medical director; b. Phila., June 26, 1946; s. Frank Joseph and Julia Ann (Kozlecki) P.; m. Jacqueline Celeste Kulpinski, June 15, 1968; children: Brian Todd, Erica Lynn. BS in Biology, St. Joseph U., Phila., 1968; MD, Hahnemann U., 1972; Assoc. in Risk Mgmt., Ins. Inst. Am., Malvern, Pa., 1995. Diplomate Am. Bd. Quality Assurance and Utilization Review Physicians; lic. physician. Pa. Intern in internal medicine Hahnemann Med. Coll. and Hosp., Phila., 1972-73, resident in internal medicine, 1973-74; resident in internal medicine Polyclinic Med. Ctr., Harrisburg, Pa., 1974-75; pvt. practice in internal medicine Pendrak, Kandra, Fierer, Kuskin Assocs., Ltd., Harrisburg, 1975-87; acting med. dir. Silver Spring health plan Phico Ins. Co., Mechanicsburg, Pa., 1987; assoc. med. dir. Phico Ins. Co., Mechanicsburg, 1987-88, med. advisor risk mgmt., 1988-94, med. dir. risk mgmt., 1994-95; v.p., med. dir., employee health physician Phico Group, Inc., Mechanicsburg, 1996—; med. dir. Commonwealth Pa. Bur. Vocat. Rehab. (Visual), Harrisburg, 1974-87; clin. asst. prof. medicine, Pa. State Coll. Medicine Med. Ctr., Hershey, Pa., 1978-89, clin. assoc. prof., 1989—; plant physician Harrisburg Steel Corp., divsn. of Harsco, 1982-86; vice chmn. Polyclinic Med. Ctr. Quality Assurance Utilization Rev. Com., 1978, 79, chmn., 1980-97; cons. to Dept. Defense, Armed Forces Medical-Legal Chest Pain Spcl. Rsch. Project. Contbr. articles to ins. and med. jours.; made presentations to over 500 groups including CEOs, Bds. of Trustees, med. staff, residents, nurses. Mem. five yr. planning com. Ctrl. Dauphin Sch. Dist., Pa., 1983-84; bd. dirs. Assn. for Retarded Citizens of Dauphin County (Pa.), 1993—, Lakevue Athletic Assn., 1987-95. Fellow Am. Soc. Healthcare Risk Mgmt., Am. Coll. Med. Quality; mem. Soc. Ins. Trainers and Educators, Am. Coll. Physician Execs. Home: 4787 Sweetbrier Terr Harrisburg PA 17111-3616 Office: Phico Group Inc 1 Phico Dr PO Box 85 Mechanicsburg PA 17055-0080

PENETAR, MARTIN CHRISTOPHER, osteopathic physician; b. Scranton, Pa., Nov. 19, 1962; s. Daniel L. and Anne Penetar; m. Barbara Catherine Penetar, June 2, 1993. BS in Biology, U. Scranton, 1984; DO, Phila. Coll. Osteo. Medicine, 1988. Emergency room physician Nesbitt Hosp., Kingston, Pa., 1990-92; pvt. practice family medicine, Clarks Summit, Pa., 1992—. Mem. AMA, Am. Osteo. Assn., Am. Coll. Gen. Practitioners, Am. Acad. Family Practice, Am. Coll. Emergency Physicians, Pa. Med. Soc. Home: 731 Beechwood Dr Dickson City PA 18519 Office: 203 Oakford Rd Clarks Summit PA 18411

PENICK, GEORGE DIAL, pathologistst; b. Columbia, S.C., Sept. 4, 1922; s. Edwin Anderson and Caroline Inglesby (Dial) P.; m. Marguerite Murchison Worth, Feb. 7, 1947; children: George Dial, Hal Worth, David Williams, Anderson Holladay, Marguerite Worth. Student, U. N.C, 1939-42, BS, 1944; MD, Harvard U., 1946. Intern in pathology Presbyn. Hosp. City Hosp., 1946-47; instr. pathology U. N.C., Chapel Hill, 1949-53, asst prof. pathology, 1953-56, assoc. prof. pathology, 1956-63, prof. pathology, 1963-70; prof., head dept. pathology U. Iowa, Iowa City, 1970-81, prof. pathology and dermatology, 1981-93; cons. Watts Hosp., Durham, N.C., 1949-70; attending pathologist N.C. Meml. Hosp., Chapel Hill, 1953-70; bd. dir. Nat. Heart Inst. Program, Project U. N.C.,1962-70; cons., bd. dirs. lab. svc. VA Med. Ctr., Iowa City, 1972-75. Contbr. articles to profl. jours. Capt. U.S. Army, 1947-49. Med. Sci. scholar John and Mary Markle Found., N.Y.C., 1953-58; recipient Disting. Svc. award Sch. of Med. U. N.C., 1979. Fellow Coll. Am Pathologists; mem. AMA, Am. Soc. Clin. Pathologists, Am. Assoc. Pathologists, Internat. Acad. Pathology, Phi Beta Kappa. Democrat. Episcopalian. Home: 3712C Reston Ct Wilmington NC 28403-6123

PENLAND, JAMES GRANVILLE, psychologist; b. Dallas, Mar. 1, 1951; s. James Marr and Katherine (Lindsley) P.; m. Michelle Elizabeth Stahl, Aug. 13, 1977; children: Abraham Christopher, Simon Peter, Zachary James. BA summa cum laude, Met. State Coll., 1977; MA, U. N.D., 1979, PhD, 1984. Instr. U. N.D., Grand Forks, 1978-83, statistician, 1981-84, psychologist, 1984-85; rsch. psychologist USDA, Agrl. Rsch. Svc., Grand Forks, 1985—; adj. prof. U. N.D., 1984—; cons. in field. Contbr. articles to profl. jours. Met. State Coll. scholar, 1977. Mem. APA, Am. Inst. Nutrition, Midwestern Psychol. Assn., N.D. Acad. Scis., Am. Statis. Assn., Nat. Acad. Sci., Sigma Xi. Home: 1804 S 36th St Grand Forks ND 58201 Office: USDA ARS 2420 2d Ave N Grand Forks ND 58202

PENLEY, DEBORAH WILLIAMSON, healthcare executive; b. Akron, Ohio, Oct. 4, 1949; d. Earl Eugene and Jacqueline Joan (Dugger) Williamson; m. Lloyd M. Penley, Dec. 20, 1968 (div. May 1984); children: Lisa C., Kristin M. BA in Mgmt., Malone Coll., 1990. Placements officer Inerlocal Community Action Program, New Castle, Ind., 1980-81; supr. Summit County Health Dept., Cuyahoga Falls, Ohio, 1982-84; profl. rels. coord. Health Am., Inc., Akron, Ohio, 1984-87; health svcs. mgr. Managed Health Care Svcs., Inc., Cleve., 1987-89; project mgr. United Am. Health Care Corp., Cleve., 1989-91, dir. provider svcs., 1991-94; assoc. Medimetrix Group, Cleve., 1994—; sr. assoc. Medimetrix Group, 1995—. Contbr. articles to local newspaper. Foster parent County Human Svcs., New Castle, 1979-80, World Vision Internat., Pasadena, Calif., 1988—. Mem. Am. Coll. Healthcare Execs., Women's Network, Evangelicals for Social Action, Christian Cmty. Health Fellowship, Christians for Bibl. Equality, Health Care Execs. Assn. N.E. Ohio. Office: Medimetrix Group 1500 North Point Tower 1001 Lakeside Ave E Cleveland OH 44114-1151

PENMASTA, RAJU A., research scientist; b. Bhimavaram, India, Sept. 22, 1952; came to U.S., 1982; s. Vijaya Rama Raju and Laksmikantamma (Sagi) P.; m. Aruna Penmasta, June 13, 1979; children: Naveen, Swetha. BS, New Sci. Coll., Hyderabad, India, 1974; MS, U. Ill., Chgo., 1986, PhD, 1988. Lectr. Osmania U., Hyderabad, 1978-82; rsch. asst. N.C. A & T U., Greensboro, 1982-84; rsch. asst. U. Ill., Chgo., 1984-88, rsch. assoc., 1988-90; sr. mgr. Steroids, Ltd., Chgo., 1990—. Contbr. articles to profl. jours. Am. Chem. Soc. Step grantee, 1986; NIH S.B.I.R. Phase I, 1992. Home: 711 Dunham Ln Bolingbrook IL 60440

PENN, ROBERT LAWRENCE, physician, educator; b. Buffalo, N.Y., Dec. 13, 1947; s. Haskell M. and Ida (Chirlin) P.; m. Rachel Tuttle, June 14, 1970. BA, SUNY, Buffalo, 1969, MD, 1973. Diplomate Am. Bd. Internal Medicine, Subspecialty in Infectious Diseases. Intern in internal medicine U. N.C./N.C. Meml. Hosp., Chapel Hill, N.C., 1973-74; resident in internal medicine U. N.C./N.C. Meml. Hosp., 1974-76; fellow infectious diseases U. Rochester (N.Y.) Sch. Medicine, 1976-79; asst. prof. medicine La. State U. Sch. Medicine, Shreveport, 1979-84, assoc. prof. medicine, 1984-91, prof. medicine, 1991—, chief infectious diseases sect., 1992—. Contbr. chpts. to books. Fellow ACP, Infectious Diseases Soc. Am.; mem. So. Soc. Clin. Investigation. Office: La State Univ Med Ctr Dept Medicine PO Box 33932 Shreveport LA 71130-3932

PENN, WILLIAM ROBERT, critical care nurse; b. Grundy, Va., June 30, 1961; s. Thomas J. and Kathleen (Little) P.; m. Mona Lisa Penn, Apr. 21, 1984; children: Andrew Robert, Emily Louise, William Samuel. ADN, Va. Appalachian Tricoll., Abingdon, 1986; BSN, Ea. Ky. U., 1991. RN, Ky.; cert. emergency nurse, ACLS, trauma nursing care course, BLS instr., PALS. Staff nurse med.-surg. unit Grundy Hosp. Inc., 1986-87; staff nurse telemetry unit Cen. Bapt. Hosp., Lexington, Ky., 1987; staff nurse ICU preceptor Good Samaritan Hosp., Lexington, 1988-90, staff nurse preceptor emergency room, 1990—; part-time LPN instr. Cen. Ky. Vocat. Tech. Inst., 1991-94. Mem. Emergency Nurses Assn. (sec. Bluegrass chpt. 1992-93).

PENNELL, DUDLEY JOHN, cardiologist; b. London, Sept. 8, 1958; s. Terence John and Irene Joan (Smith) P.; m. Elisabeth Ann Teo, Mar. 21, 1992. BA, Cambridge (Eng.) U., 1980, MB BChir, 1983, MA, 1984, MD, 1992; MRCP, 1986. Cardiology sr. house officer London Chest Hosp., 1985; renal sr. house officer St. Thomas' Hosp., London, 1986, cardiology registrar, 1988; cardiology registrar St. Peter's Hosp., Chertsey, Eng., 1987; lectr. Royal Brompton Hosp., London, 1988-92, cons., 1992—. Author: Thallium Myocardial, 1992, Nuclear Cardiology: Clinician's Guide, 1995; contbr. articles to profl. jours. Mem. Brit. Nuclear Cardiology Group (pres. 1994-96), Soc. for Cardiovascular Magnetic Resonance (vice chmn. 1995—), Am. Soc. Nuclear Cardiology (UK rep. internat. coun. 1995—), Royal Coll. Physicians. Office: Royal Brompton Hosp, Sydney St, London SW3 6NP, England

PENNELL, RICHARD CARLTON, surgeon; b. Newton, Iowa, Dec. 28, 1953; s. Robert E. and Phyllis Barbara (Cozad) P.; m. Christine Lisitano, June 25, 1977; children: Ryan C., Christopher P. BA in Chemistry, U. Mo., 1975; MD, St. Louis U., 1979. Diplomate Am. Bd. Surgery, Cert. gen. vascular surgery. Resident in surgery St. Louis U., 1979-84; fellow vascular surgery Mayo Clinic, Rochester, Minn., 1984-86; surgeon Meiners Surgery Group, St. Louis, 1986-95, West County Surgical Specialists, St. Louis, 1995—; councillor State of Mo. Southwestern Surgical Cong., 1995-98. Recipient Kinsella award Outstanding Resident, St. Louis U., 1984, Faculty Teaching award, 1994. Mem. Alpha Omega Alpha, Phi Beta Kappa. Methodist. Office: West County Surgical Specia Ste 7011B 621 S New Ballas Rd Saint Louis MO 63141

PENNEY, JOHN BRADBURY, JR., neurologist, educator; b. Winthrop, Mass., Dec. 10, 1947; s. John Bradbury Sr. and Margaret Spence (Pero) P.; m. Anne B. Young, Aug. 7, 1971; children: Jessica P., Ellen B. AB, Dartmouth Coll., 1969; MD, Johns Hopkins U., 1973; MS (hon.), Harvard U., 1991. Intern Baltimore City Hosp., 1973-74; resident neurology U. Calif., San Francisco, 1974-77; postdoctoral fellow VA, San Francisco, 1977-78; postdoctoral fellow, asst. prof., assoc. prof., prof. U. Mich., Ann Arbor, 1978-91; prof. neurology Harvard U., Cambridge, Mass., 1991—; neurologist Mass. Gen. Hosp., Boston, 1991—; sci. adv. bd. mem. Huntington's Disease Soc. Am., N.Y.C., 1983-90; cons. U.S. Venezuela Huntington's Project, Maracaibo, 1983—; med. adv. bd. mem. United Parkinson Found., Chgo., 1983—; exec. com. Parkinson Study Group, Rochester, N.Y., 1995—, Huntington Study Group, Rochester, 1993—. Contbr. articles to profl. jours. Treas. Venezuela Huntington's Disease Family Fund, Ann Arbor, 1988—. Recipient Weil award Am. Assn. Neuropathologists, 1972, Tchr. Investigation award NIH, 1980, grantee, 1994. Mem. AAAS, Am. Acad. Neurology, Am. Neurol. Assn., Soc. for Neurosci., Movement Disorder Soc. Office: Mass Gen Hosp Fruit St Boston MA 02114

PENNEY, RICHARD PATRICK, nurse; b. Melrose, Mass., Mar. 18, 1950; s. Francis Joseph and Rosemary (Joslin) P.; m. Nichole Penney, Dec. 24, 1977 (div. 1989); 1 child, Jason Scott. BA in Sociology and English, U. Mass., 1977; ADN, Durham Tech. C.C., 1994. CPR, ACLS. LPN Shattuck Hosp., Jamaica Plain, Mass.; SWIII, SWIII investigator Dept. of Social Security Child Protection, Boston, 1984-87. 2d lt. U.S. ANG, 1974-76. Republican. Home: 449 Fourth Ave S # 6 Naples FL 33940

PENNINGTON, DONALD HARRIS, physician; b. Clarksville, Ark., Sept. 13, 1945; s. John Powers and Verna Olive (Harris) P.; m. Susan Myree Snyder, Aug. 27, 1966 (div. Aug. 1982); children: Thomas Walter, Aimee Myree, John Herrick. BA, U. of the Ozarks, 1968; MD, U. Ark., 1972; wine diploma, Calif. Dept. Agr., 1973. Intern St. Vincent Infirmary, Little Rock, 1973; physician, founding ptnr. Clarksville Med. Group, P.A., 1972-93; physician Mercy Med. Svcs., Inc., Ft. Smith, Ark., 1993—; cons. family planning svcs. Ark. State Bd. of Health, 1973-93. Founding mem., musician Ft. Douglas (Ark.) Backporch Bluegrass Symphony, 1976-91; acoustic double bassist River Valley Jazz Union, Russellville, Ark., 1991—. Bd. dirs. Johnson County Regional Hosp., Clarksville, 1973-82; asst. ch. organist 1st United Meth. Ch., Clarkville, 1968—, full time organist 1st Presbyn. Ch., 1994—; active ACLU, Planned Parenthood Fedn., The League to Make a Difference, Sierra Club Legal Defense Fund, The Nature Conservancy; mem. Nat. Trust for Hist. Preservation, 1982—. Mem. AMA, Assn. Am. Physicians for Human Rights, Nat. Trust for Historic Preservation, Ark. Med. Soc. (county del. 1972—), Ark. Acad. Family Practice, Sierra Club, Legal Def. Fund, Drug Policy Found., Am. Guild Organists. Democrat. Home: 317 N Johnson St Clarksville AR 72830-2931

PENNY, RONALD, immunologist, educator; b. Warsaw, Poland, Dec. 28, 1936; arrived in Australia, 1940; s. Benjamin David and Cynthia (Berkman) P.; m. Naomi De Berg, Apr. 16, 1962; children: Mark, Sheira. MB, BS with honours, U. Sydney, Australia, 1959, MD, 1970; DSc, U. NSW, Australia, 1979. Diplomate Am. Bd. Med. Lab. Immunology. Jr. and sr. resident med. officer Royal Prince Alfred Hosp., Sydney, 1960-61, fellow in pathology, 1962, med. registrar, 1963, hon. asst. physician, 1967-69; lectr., demonstrator in histology U. Sydney, 1962, rsch. fellow, sr. rsch. fellow dept. medicine, 1964, 67-69; rsch. fellow dept. hematology Hammersmith Hosp., London, 1965; assoc. dept. medicine and Inst. Cancer Rsch., Columbia U. Coll. Physicians and Surgeons, N.Y.C., 1966; dir. Ctr. for Immunology St. Vincent's Hosp., Sydney; sr. lectr. medicine U. NSW, Sydney, 1970-72, prof. clin. immunology, mem. coun., 1981-85; chief commonwealth edn. and svcs. adviser Australian Nat. Coun. AIDS, Canberra, 1988-90; vis. prof. medicine Liverpool (Australia) U.; cons. Sydney AIDS Clinic; bd. examiners Royal Australian Coll. Ob-Gyn; rsch. adv. com. Asthma Found.; mem. Com. for Control HIV Infection in Intravenous Drug Users; numerous others. Mem. editorial bd. Jour. Clin. Lab. Immunology, AIDS, Jour. Immunology, Immunology and Medicine, Jour. Clin. Immunology and Immunopathology. Chmn. com. on AIDS strategy NSW Dept. of Health, Corrections Health Svcs. Bd., NSW State Govt. Decorated officer Order of Australia; Churchill fellow, 1972. Fellow R.C.P.A., Royal Australian Coll. Physicians; mem. R.A.C.D. (assoc.), Australian Soc. Immunology, Clin. Immunology Group, Am. Assn. Immunologists, Australian Rheumatism Assn., Transplantation Soc. Australia and New Zealand, Haematology Soc. Australia, Internat. Hematology Soc., Clin. Oncological Soc. Australia, Med. Oncology Group, Australia Soc. Med. Rsch., Am. Acad. Allergy and Immunology, Internat. Soc. for Interferon Rsch., Royal Australian Coll. Oncology (assoc.). Office: St Vincents Hosp Ctr for, Immunology, Victoria St, Sydney NSW 2010, Australia

PENROSE, CYNTHIA C., health plan administrator, consultant; b. Manila, Nov. 24, 1939; came to U.S., 1940; d. Douglas Lee Lipscomb Cordiner and Jane (Sturgeon) Edises; m. Douglas Francis Penrose, July 11, 1959 (div. 1981); children: Vicki Lynn, Lee Douglas; m. Alan Harrison Magazine, Aug. 30, 1984. BA, U. Calif.-Berkeley, 1963; MBA, U. Santa Clara, 1977. Cert. social svcs. V.p., dir. employment Resource Ctr. for Women, Palo Alto, Calif., 1973-78; bus. planner Raychem Corp., Menlo Park, Calif., 1979; adminstrv. mgr. Electric Power Research Inst., Palo Alto, 1979-83; sr. ptnr. MB Assocs., Washington, 1983-88; dir. ops. Utility Data Inst., Washington, 1984-85; dir. ops. Randmark, Inc., 1986-87; coordinator mkt. devel. for Mid-Atlantic States Kaiser Foundation Health Plan, Washington, 1987-88, asst. to assoc. regional mgr., 1988-94; market planner MetraHealth, Vienna, Va., 1995; exec. staff asst. United HealthCare, Vienna, 1995, dir. strategic planning, 1996—; bd. dirs. and treas. Unique Enterprises, Washington, 1985-87; sec. Wesley Property Mgmt. Co., 1987-89; bd. dirs. Wesley Housing Devel. Corp., 1988-89. Bd. dirs., v.p. LWV, Berkeley and Palo Alto, 1966-73; bd. dirs., sec. Am. Hospice Found., 1995—; chmn. program adv. council Resource Ctr. for Women, Palo Alto, 1980-83; mem. Affirmative Action Adv. Com. Palo Alto, 1975-76. Mem. Peninsula Profl. Women's Network (v.p. 1981-82), U. Calif. Alumni Assn., AAUW (Bicentennial br. sec. 1986-88), Capitol Area Soc. Healthcare Planning and Mktg., LWV. Democrat. Episcopalian. Avocations: swimming; nutrition and health; reading. Home: 1302 Chancel Pl Alexandria VA 22314-4707 Office: United Health Care 8330 Boone Blvd Ste 300 Vienna VA 22182

PENSLER, JAY MICHAEL, plastic surgeon, educator; b. Detroit, Apr. 29, 1954; s. Paul and Joyce (Keywell) P.; m. Laurie Ellen Olson, May 1985; children: Arielle, Alexander. BS Microbiology, U. Mich., 1976; MD, U. Chgo., 1980. Diplomate Am. Bd. Plastic Surgeons, Nat. Bd. Med. Examiners; lic. N.Y., Calif., Mass., Ill. Resident gen. surgery NYU Med. Ctr., 1980-83; resident plastic surgery U. Tex. Med. Br., Galveston, 1983-86; fellow craniofacial surgery Harvard U., Boston, 1986-87; plastic surgeon Northwestern Meml. Hosp., Chgo., 1987—; assoc. prof. surgery Northwestern U., Chgo., 1987-93; plastic surgeon Children's Meml. Hosp., Chgo., 1987—; surf. staff Columbus-Cabrini Med. Ctr., Chgo., 1990—, Evanston (Ill.)-Glenbrook Hosps., 1992—. Contbr. articles to profl. jours. Fellow Am. Coll. Surgeons (Met. Chgo. chpt.), Internat. Coll. Surgeons (Plastic Surgery); mem. AMA, Am. Acad. Pediatrics, Am. Assn. Pediatric Plastic Surgeons, Am. Burn Assn., Am. Cleft Palate-Craniofacial Assn., Am. Fedn. Clin. Rsch., Am. Soc. Bone and Mineral Rsch., Am. Soc. Maxillofacial Surgeons, Am. Soc. Plastic and Reconstructive Surgeons, Bioelec. Repair and Growth Soc., Blocker-Lewis Plastic Surgery Soc., Midwestern Assn. Plastic Surgeons, Chgo. Med. Soc., Chgo. Soc. Plastic Surgery. Office: Children's Surg Found Inc 2300 N Childrens Plz Chicago IL 60614-3318

PENTELLA, KAREN JO, neurology educator; b. Canton, Ohio, Aug. 19, 1954; d. Vincent Joseph and Rose Ruth (Norcia) P.; m. Wayne Andrew Stillings, Nov. 5, 1983; children: Nicole, Stephanie. BS, Ohio State U., 1976, MD, 1979. Bd. cert. Am. Bd. Neurology and Psychiatry. Med. intern Ohio State U. Hosp., Columbus, 1979-80; neurology resident Washington U. Med. Sch., St. Louis, 1980-83; clin. instr. neurology Washington U., St. Louis, 1983-95; chmn. biomed. ethic com. Christian Hosps., St. Louis, 1991-96. Mem. AMA, Mo. State Med. Assn., St. Louis Met. Med. Soc., Am. Acad. Neurology. Office: St Louis Neurol Inst Ste 202-10 11155 Dann Rd Saint Louis MO 63136

PENTNEY, ROBERTA JEAN, neuroanatomist, educator; b. Van Nuys, Calif., Jan. 11, 1936; d. Bernard Andrew and Helen Amelia (Sahm) Pierson; m. William M. Pentney, July 5, 1975; 1 child, William Robert. BA, Coll. Notre Dame, Belmont, Calif., 1960; PhD, U. Notre Dame, 1965. Asst. then assoc. prof. Coll. Notre Dame, Belmont, 1965-71; spl. fellow Coll. Phys. Sci. and Surgery, Columbia U., N.Y.C., 1971-74; from asst. prof. to prof. Sch. Medicine and Biomed. Sci. SUNY, Buffalo, 1974—; interim chmn. dept. anat. cell biology Sch. Medicine and Biomed. Sci. SUNY, Buffalo, 1992—. Contbr. articles to profl. jours. Mem. Am. Assn. Anatomists, Soc. for Neuroscis., Rsch. Soc. on Alcoholism, Gerontol. Soc., Sigma Xi. Office: SUNY Dept Anatomy Cell Bio 317 Farber Hall Buffalo NY 14214

PENTO, JOSEPH THOMAS, pharmacologist, educator; b. Masontown, Pa., Sept. 1, 1943; s. Joseph E. and Pearl (Marchando) P.; m. Maureen M. Daley, Jan. 25, 1969; children: Kelly Lynn, Christopher Thomas. BS, W.Va. U., 1965, MS, 1967; PhD, U. Mo., 1970. Postdoctoral fellow Miamonides Med. Ctr., N.Y.C., 1969-71; asst. prof. U. Okla., Oklahoma City, 1971-76, assoc. prof., 1976-79, prof. sect. head Coll. Pharmacy, 1979—. Contbg. editor Prous Pub., Barcelona, Spain, 1980—; contbr. articles, abstracts to profl. publs. NDEA fellow, 1967; grantee NSF, 1973-78, NIH, 1987—. Mem. Endocrine Soc., Soc. Exptl. Biol. Medicine, Am. Soc. Pharmacology and Exptl. Therapy, Metastasis Rsch. Soc., Sigma Xi. Office: U Okla Coll Pharmacy Health Scis Ctr 1110 N Stonewall Blvd Oklahoma City OK 73117

PENTON, DAVID NOEL, clinical psychologist; b. Baton Rouge, Dec. 24, 1941; s. Jules Denver and Lorena (Westbrook) P.; m. Carolyn Jean Yandle, Jan. 26, 1963 (div. Dec. 1980); children: John David, Steven Victor; m. Karen Maria Bishop, Dec. 26, 1981 (div. Feb. 1983). BS in Psychology, U. Southwestern La., 1964, MS in Psychology, 1974; PhD in Clin. Psychology, U. So. Miss., 1977. Lic. clin. psychologist, Miss.; cert. to do pre-commitments for state mental health hosps., Miss. Clin. psychologist, Gulfport, Miss., 1976-79; psychologist, outpatient dir., coord. staff devel. Singing River Mental Health Svcs., Pascagoula, Miss., 1976-79, also supr. all satellite ctrs., 1976-79; clin. psychologist The Personal Growth Ctr., Gautier, Miss., 1979—. Media rep. Taxpayers Against Govt. Waste. at. Mem. APA, Am. Assn. Orthomolecular Medicine, Miss. Psychol. Assn. (past chmn. edn. and tng. coms., past mem. nominating com., speaker 1980-82), Am. Soc. Clin. and Exptl. Hypnosis (nat. cert., nat. approved clin. hypnosis cons., proposed workshop faculty mem. 1985—), Am. Soc. Clin. Hypnosis (legis. com. 1992—), Kiwanis (bd. dirs., dir. Spl. Olympics program 1981), Psi Chi (past chmn. Gulfport chpt., mem. nat. suscriber's adv. bd. Howard Ruff's Fin. Success Report, Nat. Chmn. of Month award). Home and Office: 4113 Gautier-Vancleave Rd Gautier MS 39553-5151

PENUELAS, JOSEP, ecophysiologist; b. Vic, Catalonia, Spain, Jan. 30; s. Josep and Concepcio (Reixach) P.; m. Teresa Penarroya, July 13, 1985; children: Anna, Niria. BSc and MSc in Biology, U. Barcelona, Spain, 1980, BSc in Pharmacy, 1981, PhD in Biology, 1985. Pre-doctoral fellow Consejo Superior de Investigaciones Cientificas, Barcelona, 1981-82; pre-doctoral fellow U. Barcelona, 1982-85, asst. prof., 1986-87, assoc. prof., 1987-88, titular prof., 1988-90; staff scientist Inst. de Recerca Tech. Agroalimentaries, Barcelona, 1991-94, Ctr. Ecological Rsch. and Forestry Applications, Barcelona. Author: De la Biosfera a la Antroposfera, 1988, Brains, Sex, Biosphere and Evolution, 1992, El aire de la vida, 1992, Introducción a La Ecologia, 1993. Recipient several grants.

PENUGODA, HARAGOPAL KUSUMA, surgeon, urologist; b. Rajahmundry, Andhra Pradesh, India, Feb. 15, 1940; came to U.S., 1967; s. Veeranna and Veera Raju (Ambati) P.; m. Dwaraki Bai Yadama, May 1, 1966; children: Sarita, Namita. AS, Govt. Arts Coll., Rajahmundry, 1957; MD, Andhra Med. Coll., India, 1961, MS in Gen. Surgery, 1970. Resident in gen. surgery Guntur Med. Coll., India, 1963-65, asst. prof. anatomy, 1965-67; postdoctoral fellow St. Luke's, Nazareth, Temple U., St. Christopher's, Phila., 1967-73; resident in urology Temple U., Phila., 1968-72; pvt. practice urology, 1973—; pres. Urologic Assocs. Wilkes Barre, 1980—; chief dept. urology Wilkes Barre Gen. Hosp., 1991—. Contbr. Jour. Investigative Urology. Fellow ACS; mem. AMA, Am. Urologists Assn., Pa. Med. Soc., N.E. Pa. Urol. Soc., Luzerne County Med. Soc. Democrat. Hindu. Office: 35 W Linden St Wilkes Barre PA 18702-2619

PENZELL, DENNIS HOWARD, osteopathic physician; b. Bklyn., Apr. 12, 1952; s. Murray and Ruth Helen (Feinglass) P.; m. Joan Carol Rolland, Nov. 7, 1982; 1 child, Staci Janine. BS in Psychology, U. Md., 1974; MS in Physiology, George Washington U., 1976; DO, N.Y. Coll. Osteo. Medicine, 1981. Diplomate Nat. Bd. Osteo. Examiners, Am. Bd. Internal Medicine. Intern Meml. Gen. Hosp., Union, N.J., 1981-82; resident in internal medicine St. Barnabas Med. Ctr., Livingston, N.J., 1982-84; chief resident in internal medicine St. Barnabas Med. Ctr., 1984-85; staff internist Sun Coast Cmty. Health, Ruskin, Fla., 1985-88; med. dir. Sun Coast Cmty. Health, 1988—; bd. dirs. Nat. Assn. Cmty. Health Ctrs., Washington, 1992-93, Fla. Assn. Cmty. Health Ctrs., Tallahassee, 1992-94. Contbr. articles to profl. jours. Recipient Outstanding Clinician award Nat. Health Svc. Corps., 1989, 92, Nat. Health Svc. Corps. scholar, 1977-81; Am. Coll. Physician Execs. Mgmt. scholar, 1990. Fellow Am. Coll. Physicians; mem. AMA, Fla. Med. Assn., Hillsborough County Med. Assn. Office: Sun Coast Cmty Health Ctrs PO Box 1347 Ruskin FL 33570

PÉNZES, LÁSZLÓ GÉZA, biologist, educator; b. Budapest, Hungary, July 14, 1930; s. Antal József and Gizella Mária (Stefanovits) P.; m. Ilona Csáky, Nov. 15, 1951; 1 child, Tamás. Degree in agrl. engring., Univ. Agrl. Scis., Gödöllö, Hungary, 1955, Doctorate, 1960; PhD, Hungarian Acad. Scis., Budapest, 1960, DSc in Biol. Sci., 1982. Trainee Ministry for Food Industry, Budapest, 1955-56; postgrad. Inst. for Animal Husbandry, Budapest, 1956-59; sci. rschr. Ministry for Food Industry, Budapest, 1959-66; chief scientist, sci. adviser Semmelweis U. Medicine, Budapest, 1966—; nat. rep. Hungarian Assn. Gerontology, Budapest, 1966-84; guest prof. Bologna (Italy) U., 1993; TEMPUS coord. Joint European Project, 1991-94; habilitation Budapest U., 1996. Co-author: The Ageing, 1984, Centenarians in Hungary, 1990, Gerontopsychiatry, 1992; contbr. more than 130 articles in field to scientific jours.; mem. editorial bd. various scientific jours. Recipient Humboldt Univ. medallion U. Berlin, 1985, Ferdinand medal U. L'Aquila, Italy, 1995, Diploma of Merit, Semmelweis U. Medicine, 1993; UN scholar Internat. Atomic Energy Agy., Vienna, Austria, 1961-62. Mem. Hungarian Assn. Gerontology (pres. 1985-89). Home: Madách Imre ńt 2-6, 1075 Budapest Hungary Office: Semmelweis U Medicine, Rökk Szilárd utca 13, 1085 Budapest Hungary

PENZIEN, DONALD BAIRD, psychology educator; b. Bay City, Mich., July 22, 1957; s. C. Baird Penzien and Helene B. (Moore) Saylor; m. Suzanne Watterson, Aug. 11, 1979; 1 child, Caitlin Baird. AB in Psychology and Biology, Hope Coll., 1979; MS, Ohio U., 1982, PhD, 1986. Lic. psychologist, Miss. Rsch. design and statis. cons. dept. psychology Ohio U., Athens, 1980-85; rsch. cons. heart and health program Meml. Hosp., Pawtucket, R.I., 1985-86; rsch. cons. behavioral cardiology svc. Jackson VA Med. Ctr., 1986—; rsch. cons. chronic pain svc. San Diego VA Med. Ctr., 1990—; asst. prof. U. Miss. Med. Ctr., Jackson, 1986-91, dir. headache clinic, assoc. prof., 1991—. Author 3 books; sci. editor The Mississippi Psychologist, 1987-90; cons. editor: Annals of Behavioral Medicine; ad hoc reviewer Biofeedback and Self Regulation, 1986-96, Headache, 1991-94, Pain Digest, 1991-96, Health Psychology, 1986-94, Jour. Applied Behavioral Analysis, 1986-91, Jour. Cons. and Clin. Psychology, 1986-94, Pain Mgmt., 1986-91; contbr. articles to profl. jours. Ohio U. fellow, 1982; Muskegon Community scholar, 1975-77, Hope scholar, 1975-79, Mich. Competitive scholar, 1975-79, Biofeedback Soc. Am. scholar, 1981, 83; recipient numerous grants. Fellow Am. Assn. for Study of Headache; mem. APA (health psychology divsn., clin. psychology divsn.), Am. Acad. Pain Mgmt. (diplomate), Am. Pain Soc., Internat. Assn. Study of Pain, Internat. Headache Soc., Nat. Headache Found., Soc. Behavioral Medicine. Office: U Miss Med Ctr Dept Psychiatry/Human Behavior 2500 N State St Jackson MS 39216-4500

PENZINER, ALAN STUART, hematologist, oncologist; b. Jersey City, N.J., Oct. 16, 1951; s. Frederic and Gertrude (Kliman) P.; m. Paula Marantz Cohen, Aug. 22, 1982; children: Samuel, Katherine. BA, Yale U., 1973, MD, 1977. Resident in internal medicine U. Pitts. Hosps., 1977-80; instr. in medicine U. Pitts. Sch. Medicine, 1980-81; fellow in hematology-oncology NYU Med. Ctr., N.Y.C., 1981-84; pvt. practice Willingboro, N.J., 1984—; chmn. cancer com. grad. health system Rancocas Hosp., Willingboro, 1984—. Contbr. articles to profl. jours. Bd. mgrs. Burlington County chpt. Am. Cancer Soc., Mt. Laurel, N.J., 1984—. Fellow Acad. Medicine N.J.; mem. ACP, Am. Soc. Hematology, Am. Soc. Clin. Oncology, AMA, South Jersey Oncology Network (v.p. 1994—). Office: 1113 Hospital Dr Willingboro NJ 08046

PEPE, ELIZABETH MARIE, surgeon; b. Corona, Calif., Jan. 27, 1954; d. Matteo Larence and Helen Elizabeth (Brezina) P.; m. John Andrew Katalinas Jr., Aug. 9, 1975 (div. 1982); 1 child, Stephanie Alise Pepe-Katalinas. BS in Microbiology, U. Md., 1976; DO, Nova/Southeastern U., 1986. Diplomate Am. Bd. Osteo. Med. Examiners. Pres. Eastcoast Health Care Inc., DeLeon Springs, Fla., 1989—; owner, personal trainer De Leon Springs Fitness, 1993—; owner Eastcoast Med. Supply, De Leon Springs, 1991—; mem. adv. bd. Daytona Beach (Fla.) C.C., 1994-95. Asst. troop leader Girl Scouts U.S.A., De Leon Springs, 1991-93. Capt. U.S. Army, 1986-89. Mem. Am. Osteo. Assn., So. Med. Assn., Am. Coll. Osteo. Family Physicians, Fla. Soc. Am. Coll. Osteo. Family Physicians (trustee 1994-96, sec. bd. trustees 1995—), Lions (mem. scholarship adv. bd. 1992-93). Republican. Roman Catholic. Office: De Leon Springs Family Heal 4820 N Hwy 17 De Leon Springs FL 32130

PEPE, RICHARD KANE, nurse anesthetist; b. Meriden, Conn., May 4, 1953; s. Vincent and June (Segnella) P.; m. Patricia E. Pepe, Aug. 28, 1985. BS in Chemistry, U. Miami, Coral Gables, Fla., 1975, BSN, 1978; diploma in anesthesia, St. Raphael's, New Haven, 1981. Cert. RN anesthetist, addictions, BLS, ACLS, APRN advanced. Clin. nurse neonatal ICU St. Francis Hosp., Hartford, Conn., 1978-79; nurse anesthetist Jackson Meml. Hosp., Miami, Fla., 1981-83, Waterbury (Conn.) Hosp., 1983-84, Newington (Conn.) Children's Hosp., 1984-85, Bristol (Conn.) Hosp., 1985-91, Vet.'s Meml. Med. Ctr., Meriden, 1991—; co-chairperson Conn. Nurse Intervention Program, Meriden, 1991-92; founder Conn. Nurse Intervention Project. Author: Malignant Hyperthermia Protocol for the University of Miami Hospitals, 1981, (with Paul E. Pepe) Course Outline for Paramedic Training in Endotracheal Intubation, 1983; video prodr.: A Conspiracy of Silence, 1992, The World of Surgery, Pediatric Outpatient Surgery, Total Joint Replacement, Patient Satisfaction; contbr. articles to profl. jours.; founder POSIMED LLC software devel. for medicine. Mem. ANA, Am. Assn. Nurse Anesthetists, Conn. Assn. Nurse Anesthetists (bd. trustees 1987-89, chair well being com. 1988-92), Conn. Nurses Assn. (task force), Nat. Nurses Soc. on Addictions (task force), Malignant Hyperthermias Assn. of U.S., Internat. Anesthesia Rsch. Soc. (assoc.), Legislation for Impaired Nurses, Orange Key, Alpha Epsilon Delta, Omega Honorary Soc. Roman Catholic. Home: 210 Bradley Ave Meriden CT 06451-3964

PEPER, ERIK, psychophysiology educator, researcher; b. The Hague, May 28, 1944; came to U.S., 1957; m. Karen B. Williamson, Nov. 23, 1984; children: Eliot, Laura. BA, Harvard U., 1968; PhD, Union Grad. Sch., 1975. Co-dir. Biofeedback Family Therapy Inst., Berkeley, Calif., 1973—; mem. faculty San Francisco State U., 1976—, dir., 1995—; sports psychologist U.S. Rhythmic Gymnastics Team, 1981-85. Author: (book and tape) Breathing for Health, 1990; co-author: From the Inside Out, 1981, (computer program) Easy Breathing, 1990, Healthy Computing, 1996, Vreating Wellness: A Workbook Using Dynamic Relaxation, Imagery and Thought, 1992; co-editor: Mind/Body Integrated, 1979; mem. editl. bd. Biofeedback and Self Regulation Jour., 1990—. Mem. Assn. for Applied Psychophysiology and Biofeedback (pres. 1976-77), Biofeedback Soc. Calif. (pres. 1977-78), Soc. for Psychophysiol. Rsch., Soc. for Behavioral Medicine. Office: San Francisco State U 1600 Holloway Ave San Francisco CA 94132-1722

PEPITONE ARREOLA ROCKWELL, FRANCES MARIE, psychologist; b. San Mateo, Calif., June 3, 1941; d. Joseph Pepitone and Hope Norma (Arreola) Gunn; m. Don Arthur Rockwell, Dec. 23, 1965; children: Grant Arthur, Chad Arthur. RN, Highland Sch. Nursing, 1961; BA, Calif. State U., San Francisco, 1966; MA, Calif. State U., Sacramento, 1971; PhD, Calif. Sch. Profl. Psychology, 1974; postgrad., Harvard U., 1988. Asst. prof. psychology U. Calif., Davis, 1974-82, dir. women's resources and rsch. ctr., 1978-82, assoc. prof., 1982-84, asst. dean acad. affairs, 1982-84; assoc. prof. Drew Med. Sch., L.A., 1985-87; asst. dir. devel. programs Undergrad. Admissions and Rels. with Schs., UCLA, L.A., 1987-91; dir. psycho-social svcs., chief psychologist Rhonda Fleming Women's Clinic at UCLA, 1991-93; assoc. dean, faculty The Fielding Inst., Santa Barbara, Calif., 1993—; oral examiner Bd. Psychology State Calif. Editor: Dual Career Couples, 1980; style editor (jour.) Psychotherapy, 1980-84; contbr. articles to profl. jours. Founding mem. Yolo County (Calif.) Sex Assault Ctr., 1976-78; mem. sexual assault adv. com. State of Calif., 1982-83; com. mem. rape adv. panel Office of Criminal Justice, Sacramento, 1977; com. mem. Yolo County Health Assn., Davis, 1971-72; mem. site visitor team Coun. Pvt. Postsecondary & Vocat. Edn., 1995. Fellow APA (program reviewer 1985-86); mem. AAAS, Assn. Med. Colls. (women's liaison officer 1981-84), Coun. Nat. Register of Health Svc. Providers, Sigma Xi. Office: The Fielding Inst 2112 Santa Barbara St Santa Barbara CA 93105-3544

PEPLAU, HILDEGARD ELIZABETH, nursing educator; b. Reading, Pa., Sept. 1, 1909; d. Gustav and Ottylie (Elgert) P. Diploma, Pottstown Hosp. Sch. Nursing, 1931; BA, Bennington Coll., 1943; MA, Columbia U., 1947, EdD, 1953, DSc (hon.), 1983; cert., William Alanson White Inst., 1953; DSc (hon.), Alfred U., 1970, Duke U., 1974, Rutgers U., 1985, Ind. U., 1994, U. Ulster, No. Ireland, 1994; D of Nursing Sci. (hon.), Boston Coll., 1972; LHD (hon.), U. Indpls., 1987, Ohio State U., 1990. RN, N.J., Calif. Exec. officer Coll. Health Svc., Bennington (Vt.) Coll., 1938-43; dir. grad. program psychiatric nursing Tchrs. Coll., Columbia U., N.Y.C., 1948-53; exec. dir. ANA, Washington, 1969-70; dir. grad. program psychiatric nursing Rutgers U., New Brunswick, N.J., 1955-74, prof. emerita, 1974—. Author: Interpersonal Relations in Nursing, 1952; contbr. numerous articles to profl. publs. and jours., 1942—. 1st lt. Nurse Corps, U.S. Army, 1943-45. Mem. ANA, Am. Acad. Nursing (designated Living Legend 1994), Internat. Coun. Nurses (3d v.p. 1977-81, bd. dirs. 1973-77), Nat. League Nursing. Democrat. Lutheran. Home: 14024 Otsego St Sherman Oaks CA 91423-1225

PEPPER, DONALD ALLEN, dentist; b. Oakland, Calif., July 7, 1951; s. Alfred Moses and Rosaline (Frantz) P.; m. Giulie Lidan Chioini, Nov. 2, 1985; children: Giulene, Andrea. BS in Biology with honors, Stanford U., 1973; DDS, U. So. Calif., 1978. Dentist P.E. Tully, DDS & Assocs., Fremont, Calif., 1978-79; pvt. practice San Jose, Calif., 1979—. Chief Indian Princess YMCA, San Jose, 1989-90. Mem. ADA, Acad. Gen. Dentistry, Calif. Dental Assn. (treas.), No. Calif. Acad. Gen. Dentistry, Santa Clara County Dental Soc. Democrat. Jewish. Office: 6501 Crown Blvd Ste 104 San Jose CA 95120-2903

PEPPER, DOROTHY MAE, nurse; b. Merill, Maine, Oct. 16, 1932; d. Walter Edwin and Alva Lois (Leavitt) Stanley; m. Thomas Edward Pepper, July 1, 1960; children: Walter Frank, James Thomas. RN, Maine Med. Ctr. Sch. Nursing, Portland, 1954. RN, Calif. Pvt. duty nurse Lafayette, Calif.; staff nurse Maine Med. Ctr., Portland, 1954-56, Oakland (Calif.) VA Hosp., 1956-58; pvt. duty nurse, dir. RN's Alameda County, Oakland. Mem. Profl. Nurses Bur. Registry, Maine Writers and Pubs. Alliance.

PEPPER, NORMA JEAN, mental health nurse; b. Ellington, Iowa, Nov. 7, 1931; d. Victor F. and Grace Mae (Tate) Shadle; m. Bob Joseph Pepper, Dec. 28, 1956 (dec. Oct. 4, 1985); children: Joseph Victor, Barbara Jean, Susan Claire (dec.). Diploma in Nursing, Broadlawns Polk County Hosp., 1950-53; BSN, U. Iowa, 1953-55; MSN, U. Colo., 1955-60. Cert. mental health nurse. Head nurse Colo. Psychiatric Hosp., Denver, 1956; head nurse, Psychiatry Denver General Hosp., 1958-60; with Nurses Official Registry, Denver, 1960-73; staff nurse VA Med. Ctr., Denver, 1974-94; counselor VA Hosp. Employee Assistance Com., Denver, 1987-94. Mem. Colo. Nurses Assn. Home: 4836 W Tennessee Ave Denver CO 80219-3130

PEPPER, ROLLIN ELMER, microbiology educator, consultant; b. Glens Falls, N.Y., June 8, 1924; s. Henry Orville and Ruby Mae (Tucker) P.; m. Lucille Blackman, May 30, 1953 (dec.); children: Roger R., Barbara Pepper Moquin, Susan B.; m. Martha Charles, Mar. 3, 1990. B.A., Earlham Coll., 1950; M.S., Syracuse U., 1953; Ph.D., Mich. State U., 1963. Assoc. scientist Ethicon, Inc., Somerville, N.J., 1951-60; research assoc. Mich. State U., East Lansing, 1963-64; prof. biology Elizabethtown Coll., Pa., 1964-90, chmn. dept. 1967-77, prof. emeritus, 1990—; vis prof. biology U. Zambia, Lusaka, 1972-73; microbiology cons. Sporicidin Co., Rockville, Md., 1971-94, Baums Bologna, Elizabethtown, 1976-83; health officer Borough of Elizabethtown, 1981—. Contbr. articles to profl. jours., chpt. to book. Patentee in field. Pres. Elizabethtown Bd. Health, 1976-77. Mem. Ctrl. Atlantic State Assn. of Food and Drug Ofcls., Sigma Xi. Mem. Brethren in Christ Ch. Club: Elizabethtown. Lodge: Rotary (pres. 1983-84, youth exchange chmn. dist. 7390, 1978-81, Presdl. citation 1984, pres. Lancaster chpt. Friendship Force 1991-92). Avocations: travel, camping, photography. Home: 420 N Mount Joy St Elizabethtown PA 17022-1634 Office: Elizabethtown Coll Dept Biology Elizabethtown PA 17022

PEPPERBERG, IRENE MAXINE, biology educator; b. N.Y.C., Apr. 1, 1949; d. Robert and Yetta (Leibowitz) Platzblatt. SB, MIT, 1969; MA, Harvard U., 1971, PhD, 1976. Rsch. assoc. Purdue U., West Lafayette, Ind., 1977-84; vis. asst. prof. Northwestern U., Evanston, Ill., 1984-90; assoc. prof. ecology and evolutionary biology U. Ariz., Tucson, 1991—; scientific rev. bd. Marine World/USA, Vallejo, Calif., 1986—. Contbr. articles to Advances in the Study of Behavior, Perspectives in Ethology, 1991; contbr. articles to Jour. Comparative Psychology, Ethology, Animal Learning and Behavior, Semiotik, Netherland Jour Zoology. Rsch. grantee NSF, 1979-80, 84—, Harry Frank Guggenheim Found., 1982-84; NSF pre-doctoral fellow, 1969-71, John Simon Guggenheim fellow, 1996. Fellow Am. Behavior Soc.; mem. AAAS, Am. Ornithologists Union, Psychonomic Soc., Wilson Ornithol. Soc., Cooper Ornithol. Soc., N.Y. Acad. Scis., Assn. Field Ornithologists, Brit. Psychol. Soc., Ea. Psychol. Soc., Midwest Psychol. Soc., Am. Psychol. Assn. Office: U Ariz Bio Science West Tucson AZ 85721

PERACHA, MOHAMMAD HANIF, ophthalmologist; b. Sargodha, Punjab, Pakistan, Dec. 18, 1943; came to U.S., 1969; s. Maohammed Latif and Fatima Peracha; m. Khadija Khalid Kazak, May 29, 1977; children: Mohammed O., Latif H., Nabeel H., Zuhair H., Manal H. MBBS, Dow Med. Coll., Karachi, Pakistan, 1967; MD, Wayne State U., 1974. Diplomate Am. Bd. Ophthalmology. Pvt. practice Monroe, Mich., 1975—; clin. instr. Kresge Eye Inst., Detroit, 1975-80; pres. M. Hanif Peracha, MD, PC, Monroe, 1975-80. Pres. Pakistan Assn. of Detroit, 1984, 86, 88, Pak-Am. Friendship, Bloomfield, Mich., 1988, 90, 91; pres. Islamic Assn. Mich., Brownstown, 1990—. Mem. AMA, Am. Acad. Ophthalmology, Am. Soc. Cataract and Refractive Surgery, Mich. State Med. Assn., Assn. Pakistani Physicians N.Am. (treas. 1984-86, Lifetime Achievement award 1989), Monroe County Med. Soc., Grosse Ile Golf and Country Club. Office: Eye Surgeons Assocs PC 725 N Monroe St Monroe MI 48162

PERCIVAL, DARRYL L., pharmacy benefit executive; b. Phila., Nov. 15, 1951; s. Robert I. and Betty-Jane (Allen) P.; m. Kathleen Reynolds; children: Alexis, Dean. BS in Pharmacy, Phila. Coll. Pharm. & Sci., 1975. Registered pharmacist Pa., R.I. Pres. Percival Co., Warwick, R.I., 1980-86; gen. mgr. Flare Enterprises, Warwick, 1986-88; pharmacy supervisor Brooks Drug, Pawtucket, R.I., 1988-89; mgr. bus. devel. Hook-SuperX-Brooks Drug, Pawtucket, 1989-91; sr. v.p. Pequot Pharm Networkd divsn. of Mashautucket Pequot Tribal Nation, Ledyard, Conn., 1991—; adv. bd. CIBA-Geneva Labs., 1993—, Sandoz Labs., 1993—; regional bd. dirs. Am. Assn. Preferred Providers Orgns., 1992—. Asst. coach Little League, West Greenwich, R.I., 1995. Grantee USPHS, 1994. Fellow Am. Soc. Cons. Pharmacists, Am. Health Info. Mgrs. Assn. Home: 329 Fry Pond Rd West Greenwich RI 02817 Office: Pequot Pharm Network 1 Annie George Dr Ledyard CT 06339

PERCY, THOMAS, plastic and reconstructive surgeon; b. Pallithode, Thuravoor, India, July 1, 1945; came to U.S., 1970; s. Thomas Dennis and Kunjamma Thomas Louis; m. Celine James, Apr. 15, 1970; children: Dennis, Daphne, Alex, David. BSc, Sacred Heart Coll., Cochin, Kerala, India, 1964; M.B.B.S., Med. Coll., Trivandrum, Kerala, 1970. Diplomate Am. Bd. Surgery, Am. Bd. Plastic Surgery. Chief of surgery Kettering (Ohio) Med. Ctr., pres. med. staff; pvt. practice Miamisburg, OHio. Fellow ACS, Internat. Coll. Surgeons; mem. AMA, Am. Soc. Plastic and Reconstructive Surgeons, Ohio State Med. Assn., Montgomery County Med. Soc. (dir.-at-large, currently dir.), Miami Valley Assn. Indian Physicians (pres.), Ohio Valley Soc. Plastic and Reconstructive Surgeons. Home: 5049 James Hill Rd Kettering OH 45429 Office: 2130 Leiter Rd Ste 207 Miamisburg OH 45342-3674

PERDUE, WILLIAM LANG, II, general surgeon; b. Topeka, Oct. 29, 1949; s. William Lang and Margaret O'Neil (Archer) P.; children: Christopher Todd, Benjamin Blair; m. Sheri Cree Robert, Sept. 23, 1989. BA, Kans. U., 1971; MD, U. Kans., 1974. Resident in surgery U. Utah Affiliated Hosps., Salt Lake City, 1975-80; active med. staff Mercy Hosp., Council Bluff, Iowa, 1980-81, St. Francis Hosp., Topeka, Kans., 1981—, Stormont-Vail Hosp., Topeka, 1981—; assoc. clin. prof. surgery U. Kans., Topeka, 1984—; active med. staff Stormont-Vail Hosp., Topeka, 1981—; surgical cons. Blue Cross, Blue Shield, Topeka, 1984—; chmn. cancer com., St. Francis Hosp., Topeka, 1990-94. Mem. AMA, Kans. Med. Soc., Shawnee County Med. Soc., Soc. Civil War Surgeons, Am. Civil War Med. Assn. Home: 3727 Cobblestone Pl Topeka KS 66610 Office: W Lang Perdue II MD 631 Horne Ste 410 Topeka KS 66606

PEREIRA PINTO, JOSE HENRIQUE, immunologist, medical educator; b. Itajuba, MG, Brazil, June 1, 1947; s. Ailton Renno and Eny (Pereira) P.; 1 child, Henrique Motta. Degree, Colegio de Itajuba, 1965, MD, 1973. Head dept. med. clinic, internal medicine Faculdade Medicina, Itajuba, 1982-84, prof. dermatology, 1984-90, head dept. med. clinic, 1991-94, prof. immunology, 1991—. Office: Climed, RUA Americo De Oliveira No 3, 37500-000 Itajuba MG, Brazil

PEREL, JAMES MAURICE, pharmacology and psychiatry educator, researcher; b. Buenos Aires, Mar. 30, 1933; came to U.S., 1947, naturalized, 1954; s. Aria and Bella (Silverberg) P.; m. Noami Hookman, July 18, 1959 (div. 1971); 1 child, Allan B.; m. Audrey Feldman, Apr. 9, 1972; children: Alissa A., Stephen M. BS, CUNY, 1956; MS, NYU, 1961, PhD, 1964. Nuclear chemist N.Y. Naval Shipyard Lab., Bklyn., 1956-58; assoc. rsch. scientist NYU, Goldwater Meml. Hosp., N.Y.C., 1964-67; asst. prof. medicine and chemistry Emory U., Atlanta, 1967-70; asst. prof. psychiatry Columbia U. Coll. Physicians and Surgeons, N.Y.C., 1970-76; assoc. prof. clin. pharmacology, chief psychiat. rsch. N.Y. State Psychiat. Inst., N.Y.C., 1976-80; chief clin. pharmacology VA Med. Ctr. Highland Drive, Pitts., 1979-83; prof. psychiatry and pharmacology U. Pitts. Sch. Medicine, 1980—, acting chmn. dept. pharmacology, 1985-88; dir. clin. pharmacology Western Psychiat. Inst. and Clinic, Pitts., 1980—; prof. grad. neurosci., 1988—; postdoctoral fellow in clin. pharmacology NIH and NYU, 1964-67; lectr. chemistry CUNY, 1963-67; assoc. rsch. scientist N.Y. State Psychiat. Inst., 1970-76; cons., mem. grant-awarding study sects. NIH, NIMH. Mem. editorial bd. Psychopharmacology, Neuropsychobiology, Therapeutic Drug Monitoring; contbr. over 300 articles to sci. jours., chpts. to books. Recipient Founders Day award NYU, 1974, Julius Koch Meml. award Rho Chi, 1983; named Psychopharmacologist of Yr., U. Toronto, 1993; numerous rsch. grants, including NIH, NIMH, Founds. Fund for Rsch. in Psychiatry, pharm. cos., pvt. founds. Fellow Am. Inst. Chemists; mem. Am. Soc. Clin. Pharmacology and Therapeutics, Am. Soc. Pharmacology and Exptl. Therapeutics, Soc. for Biol. Psychiatry, Sigma Xi. Jewish. Office: U Pitts Sch Medicine 3811 Ohara St Pittsburgh PA 15213-2593

PERERA, THOMAS B., psychologist, educator; b. N.Y.C., Nov. 20, 1938; s. Lionel C. and Dorothy B. Perera; m. Gretchen G. Perera, Aug. 28, 1960; children: Daniel G., Thomas B. Jr. AB, Columbia Coll., 1961, MA, 1963, PhD, 1968. Cert. psychologist, N.Y., Vt. Asst. prof. psychology Barnard Coll., N.Y.C., 1966-74, vis. prof., 1975—; assoc. prof. Montclair State Coll., Upper Montclair, N.J., 1974-80, prof., 1980—; vis. prof.; cons. Columbia U., 1960—, Omni Systems Assn., 1978—, sr. rsch. scientist N.Y. State Psychiat. Inst., 1964-71. Contbr. computer programs, articles to profl. jours. Mem. AAAS, Am. Psychol. Assn., Eastern Psychol. Assn., Biofeedback Soc., Southeastern Psychol. Assn. Office: Montclair State Coll Valley and Normal Ave Montclair NJ 07043

PERETTI, MARILYN GAY WOERNER, human services professional; b. Indpls., July 30, 1935; d. Philip E. and Harriet E. (Meyer) Woerner; children: Thomas A., Christopher P. BS, Purdue U., 1957; postgrad., Coll. DuPage, 1980—, U. Wis., 1981—. Nursery sch. lab. asst. Mary Baldwin Coll., Staunton, Va., 1957-58; tchr. 1st grade, nursery sch. No. Ill. area schs., 1958-61; asst. tchr. of blind Glenbard E. H.S., Lombard, Ill., 1978-80; adminstrv. asst. Elmhurst Coll., 1980-81; dir. vol. svcs. DuPage Convalescent Ctr., Wheaton, 1981-95; dir. cmty. outreach Sr. Home Sharing, Inc., Lombard, Ill., 1996—; developer new vol. pos. for vis. the non-verbal handicapped, 1994; prodr. 4 ednl. slide programs on devel. countries, 1988-91; initiator used book collection for library project U. Zululand, S. Africa, 1993-94. Editor, designer newsletter Our Developing World's Voices, 1994—. Bd. dirs. Lombard YMCA, 1977-83, pres., 1980; vol. Chgo. Uptown Ministry, 1979; participant fact finding trips El Salvador, 1988, Honduras, 1989, Nicaragua, 1989, Republic of South Africa, 1991; mem. Nature Artists Guild of Morton Arboretum; vol. PADS, 1994—. Mem. Nature Artists Guild of Morton Arboretum. Office: Sr Home Sharing Inc 837 Westmore-Meyers Rd Lombard IL 60148

PEREZ, CARLOS A., radiation oncologist, educator; b. Colombia, Nov. 10, 1934; came to U.S., 1960, naturalized, 1969; children: Carlos S., Bernardo, Edward P. B.S., U. de Antioquia, Medellin, 1952, M.D., 1960. Diplomate: Am. Bd. Radiology (trustee 1985—). Rotating intern Hosp. U. St. Vincente de Paul, Medellin and Caldas, 1958-59; resident Mallinckrodt Inst. Radiology, Washington U. Sch. Medicine, St. Louis, 1960-63; mem. faculty Mallinckrodt Inst. Radiology, Washington U. Sch. Medicine, 1964—, prof. radiology, 1972—, dir. radiation oncology ctr., 1976—; fellow radiotherapy M.D. Anderson Hosp. and Tumor Inst., U. Tex., Houston, 1963-64. Co-editor: Principles and Clinical Practice of radiation Oncology, Principles and Practice of Gynecologic Oncology; editl. bd. Internat. Jour. Radiation and Physics, 1975—, Cancer, 1993—; contbr. articles to med. jours. Fellow Am. Coll. Radiology; mem. AAAS, AMA, Internat. Assn. Study Lung Cancer, Am. Soc. Clin. Oncology, Am. Soc. Therapeutic Radiologists (pres. 1981-82, Gold medal 1992), Am. Radium Soc., Am. Assn. Cancer Rsch., Am. Assn. Cancer Edn., Radiol. Soc. N.Am., Brit. Inst. Radiology, Mo. Radiol. Soc., Mo. Acad. Sci., Mo. Med. Soc., St. Louis Med. Soc., Greater St. Louis Soc. Radiologists, Radiation Rsch. Soc. Home: 78 Lake Frst Saint Louis MO 63117-1359 Office: Washington U Radiation Oncology Ctr 4511 Forest Park Ave Saint Louis MO 63108-2138

PEREZ, DIANNE M., medical researcher; b. Cleve., Dec. 13, 1959. BA in Chemistry and Biology with honors, Coll. of Wooster, 1982; PhD in Chemistry, Calif. Inst. Tech., 1988. Grad. rsch. asst. dept. chemistry Calif. Inst. Tech., Pasadena, 1982-87, grad. teaching asst. introductory chemistry and biochemistry, 1982-87; sr. rsch. scientist Specialty Labs., Inc., Santa Monica, Calif., 1987-88; fellow dept. eye rsch. Doheny Eye Inst., L.A., 1988-89; fellow dept. heart and hypertension rsch. Cleve. Clinic Found., 1989-91, rsch. assoc. dept. cardiovascular biology, 1992-93, project scientist dept. molecular cardiology, 1993-95, mem. asst. staff dept. molecular cardiology, 1996—; coord. Molecular Cardiology's Protein Group Seminar Series, Cleve. Clinic Found., 1994-95, supr. DNA Synthesis Core Facility Rsch. Inst., fellow's rep. Dept. Heart and Hypertension Rsch. to Divsn. Edn. Com.; adj. asst. prof. dept. pharmacology U. Ky., Lexington, 1994—; manuscript referee Molecular Pharmacology, Circulation Rsch., Cardiovascular Rsch., Jour. Pharmacology and Exptl. Therapeutics, Gene, Biochemistry; lectr. in field. Contbr. articles to profl. jours.; patentee in field. Lubrizol scholar Coll. of Wooster, 1980; recipient Nat. Rsch. Svc. award NIH, 1991; Glaxo grantee, 1994—. Mem. AAAS, Am. Soc. Pharmacology and Exptl. Therapeutics, Am. Heart Assn. (Established Investigator award 1996), Am. Chem. Soc. (cert.), Am. Soc. Biochemistry and Molecular Biology, Phi Beta Kappa, Iota Sigma Pi, Sigma Xi. Office: Cleve Clinic Found Rsch Inst 9500 Euclid Ave Cleveland OH 44195

PEREZ, FRANK J., healthcare administrator; b. Havanna, Cuba, Oct. 4, 1943; s. Julian N. and Silvia N. (Hernandez) P.; m. Carmen Rosario Perez, Apr. 10, 1966; children: Shelley, Vanessa, Karen. BS, Columbia Union Coll., 1970; M in Health Care Adminstrn., George Washington U., 1974. Exec. v.p. Christ Hosp., Jersey City, N.J., 1974-79; exec. dir. Bella Vista Hosp., Mayaquez, P.R., 1979-85, Caribe Hosp. Affiliates, Bayamon, P.R., 1985-88; pres. Atlantic Adventist Healthcare, Stoneham, Mass., 1988-94, Cmty. Hosps. of Ea. Middlesex, Stoneham, 1992-94, New England Meml. Hosp., Stoneham, 1988-94; pres., CEO Kettering (Ohio) Med. Ctr., 1994—; pres. State Health Facilities Com., Mayaquez, 1985-90. Co-author: The Conference Board, 1995; contbr. articles to profl. jours. Trustee Hospice of Dayton, Ohio, 1995-96, Dayton Ballet, 1995-96; bd. dirs. Ohio Quality Cardiac Care Found., Columbus, 1996. Recipient Presdl. Citation for Sustained Bus. Leadership Atlantic Union Coll., 1993. Fellow Am. Coll. of Healthcare Execs., Am. Hosp. Assn., Kettering Coll. of Med. Arts (bd. dirs. 1994-96), Greater Dayton Area Hosp. Assn. (bd. dirs. 1994-96), Dayton Area C. of C. (trustee 1996), PPS State Hosp. Assn. (bd. dirs., v.p., chmn. 1985-88). Office: Kettering Med Ctr 3535 Southern Blvd Kettering OH 45429

PEREZ, JEFFREY JOSEPH, optometrist; b. Aberdeen, Md., July 26, 1952; s. Jack Joseph and June C. (Champlin) P.; m. Sharon S. Cooper, June 10, 1979; children: Justin Joseph, Ashley Mary Louise. BA, U. Miss., 1974; BS, So. Coll. Optometry, 1977, OD, 1979. Assoc. with Dr. W.H. Starr, Gulfport, Miss., 1979-80; pvt. practice optometry, Gulfport, 1980—. U. Miss. scholar, 1974. Mem. Am. Optometric Assn., Men's Sr. Baseball League, Miss. Optometric Assn. (bd. dir., chmn. pub. rels. com. 1989), South Miss. Optometric Soc., Jaycees, Omega Delta. Roman Catholic. Club: Biloxi Alumni Band. Lodge: Elks. Home: 2473 Greenview Dr Gulfport MS 39507-2213 Office: 12296 Ashley Dr Gulfport MS 39503

PEREZ, JOSEPHINE, psychiatrist, educator; b. Tijuana, Mex., Feb. 10, 1941; came to U.S., 1960, naturalized, 1968. BS in Biology, U. Santiago de Compostela, Spain, 1971; MD, 1975. Clerkships in internal medicine, gen. surgery, otorhinolaryngology, dermatology and venereology Gen. Hosp. of Galicia (Spain), 1972-75; resident in gen. psychiatry U. Miami (Fla.), Jackson Meml. Hosp. and VA Hosp., Miami, 1976-78; practice medicine specializing in psychiatry, marital and family therapy, individual psychotherapy, Miami, Fla., 1979—; nuclear medicine technician, EEG technician, supr. Electrographic Labs., Encino, Calif., 1963-71; emergency room physician Miami Dade Hosp., 1975; attending psychiatrist Jackson Meml. Hosp., 1979—, asst. dir. adolescent psychiat. unit, 1979-83; mem. clin. faculty U. Miami Sch. Medicine, 1979—, clin. instr. psychiatry, 1979—. Mem. AMA (Physicians' Recognition award 1980, 83, 86, 89), Am. Assn. for Marital and Family Therapy (cert. clin. mem., treas. 1982-84, pres.-elect 1985-87, pres. 1987-89), Am. Psychiat. Assn., Am. Med. Women's Assn., Assn. Women Psychiatrists, South Fla. Psychiat. Soc. Office: 420 S Dixie Hwy Ste 4A Coral Gables FL 33146

PEREZ, KENNETH ALLEN, physician; b. Chgo., Aug. 22, 1963; s. Jesus Endriguez and Adela (Miranda) P. BS in biology, St. Joseph Coll., 1988; DO, Chgo. Osteopathic, 1992; BCFD in family medicine, Chgo. Osteo., 1995. Lab. technician Dyer Med. Clinic, Dyer, Ill., 1984-88; intern in medicine Chgo. Osteo., 1992-93, resident in family medicine, 1993-95. Contbr. articles to profl. jours. Mem. AMA, Am. Osteo. Assn., Ill. Physician and Surgeons. Roman Catholic. Home: 2156 Hart St Dyer IN 46311 Office: Olympia Fields Osteo 20201 S Crawford Ave Olympia Fields IL 60461

PEREZ, LOUIS ANTHONY, radiologist; b. N.Y.C., June 11, 1939; s. Salvatore Lawrence and Valvadina Rose (Ruscillo) P.; divorced, 1988; children: Lisa, Gregg, Nicole; m. Patricia Ann McVey, May 19, 1990; 1 child, Kelsey. BEE, Manhattan Coll., 1962; MD, SUNY, Bklyn., 1966. Diplomate Am. Bd. Radiology, Am. Bd. Nuclear Medicine. Chief nuclear medicine Misericordia Hosp., Bronx, 1973-75; cons. Manhattan Coll., Radiology Inst., Riverdale, N.Y., 1974-81; chief nuclear medicine Norwalk (Conn.) Hosp., 1975-82; dir. radiology Lawrence Hosp., Bronxville, N.Y., 1982—; asst. clin. prof. radiology Columbia U. Coll. Physicians and Surgeons, N.Y.C., 1995—. Contbr. articles to profl. jours., chpts. to books. Lt. comdr. USN, 1963-77. Grantee, Am. Cancer Soc., 1968-70, USPHS, 1974-75. Fellow Am. Coll. Radiology; mem. Soc. Nuclear Medicine (trustee 1985-89, 92—, chmn. sci. subcom. 1988—, chpt. pres. 1982), Am. Coll. Physician Execs., N.Y. State Med. Soc., Explorers Club, Alpine Club. Republican. Roman Catholic. Office: Diagnostic Imaging Svcs of Bronxville 45 Parkview Ave Bronxville NY 10708-2901 also: Lawrence Hosp Dept Radiology 55 Palmer Rd Yonkers NY 10708-5826

PEREZ, MARIO, psychiatrist; b. Santa Rosa, Antioquia, Colombia, Dec. 17, 1940; came to U.S., 1970; s. Rafael and Lucila (Roldan) P.; m. Himelda Velez, July 22, 1967; children: Carlos M., Eliana. BA, Colegio San Jose, Medellin, Colombia, 1958; MD, Antioquia U., 1965. Diplomate Am. Bd. Psychiatry and Neurology. Rsch. psychiatrist Fairfield Hills Hosp., Newtown, Conn., 1970-73; mem. attending staff Waterbury (Conn.) Hosp., 1996—; cons. staff mem. St. Mary's Hosp., Waterbury, Conn., 1991. Mem. MPA. Office: PO Box 3187 Newtown CT 06470-3187

PEREZ-BORJA, CARLOS M., neurologist, hospital executive; b. Quito, Ecuador, Oct. 24, 1927; came to U.S., 1959; s. Manuel V. Perez and Margot Borja; m. Rosa Enriquez, Sept. 6, 1954; children: Carmen, Patricia, Maria, Helena, Carlos. MD, U. Quito, 1952. Diplomate Am. Bd. Psychiatry and Neurology, Am. Bd. Electroencephalography. Asst. prof. neurology Wash. Med. Sch., Seattle, 1965-66; chief of medicine Macomb Hosp. Ctr., Warren, Mich., 1982-84, chief of neurology, 1969-96, vice chief of staff, 1995-96. Contbr. numerous rsch. papers to profl. jours. Fellow ACP, Am. Acad. Neurology, Am. EEG Soc., Pan Am. Coll. Physicians. Roman Catholic. Office: Ste 101 11900 E 12 Mile Rd Warren MI 48093

PEREZ-CASTRO, ANA VERONICA, developmental biology researcher; b. Lima, Peru, Jan. 27, 1962; came to U.S., 1986; d. Cesar Antonio and Ines Gladys (Marquina) P.; m. Alonso Castro, June 11, 1988. BS, Cayetano Heredia U., Lima, 1984, licentiate in chemistry and biology, 1985; MA, Columbia U., 1988, MPhil, 1990, PhD in Microbiology, 1992. Jr. prof. dept. chemistry Cayetano Heredia U., 1985-86; teaching asst. dept. microbiology U. Ga., Athens, 1987, Columbia U., N.Y.C., 1989; postdoctoral fellow life scis. div. Los Alamos (N.Mex.) Nat. Lab., 1992-95; prof. dept. biology U. N.Mex., Albuquerque, 1996—; speaker Fedn. Am. Socs. for Exptl. Biology, 1992, Baylor Coll. Medicine, Houston, 1992, Mexican Soc. Genetics, Guanajuato, 1993, Mexico City 1994. Contbr. articles to sci. jours. Recipient young scientist award Fedn. Am Socs. for Exptl. Biology, 1992; Nat. Coun. Sci. and Tech. grad. fellow Cayetano Heredia U., 1985-86; Fieger predoctoral scholar Norris Comprehensive Cancer Ctr., U. So. Calif., 1991-92. Mem. AAAS, Am. Soc. Microbiology, Am. Soc. Human Genetics. Home: 2546 Camino San Patricio Santa Fe NM 87505 Office: Univ NMex Dept Biology Castetter Hall Albuquerque NM 87131

PEREZ-CRUET, JORGE, psychiatrist, psychopharmacologist, psychophysiologist; b. Santurce, P.R., Oct. 15, 1931; s. Jose Maria Perez-Vicente and Emilia Cruet-Burgos; m. Anyes Heimendinger, Oct. 4, 1958; children: Antonio, Mick, Graciela, Isabelle. BS magna cum laude, U. P.R., 1953, MD, 1957; diploma psychiatry McGill U., Montreal, Que., Can., 1976. Diplomate Am. Bd. Psychiatry and Neurology, Nat. Bd. Med. Examiners, Am. Bd. Geriatric Psychiatry; lic. Can. Coun. Med. Examiners; cert. in quality assurance. Rotating intern Michael Reese Hosp., Chgo., 1957-58; fellow in psychiatry Johns Hopkins U. Med. Sch., 1958-60, instr., then asst. prof. psychiatry, 1962-73; lab. neurophysiologist and psychomatic lab. Walter Reed Army Inst. Rsch., Washington, 1960-62, cons., 1963-65; rsch. assoc. lab. chem. pharmacology NIH, Bethesda, Md., also rsch. assoc. adult psychiatry br. and lab. clin. sci. NIMH, Bethesda, 1969-73; psychiatry resident diploma course in psychiatry McGill U. Sch. Medicine, Montreal Gen. Hosp., 1973-76, Montreal Children's Hosp., 1975; prof. psychiatry U. Mo.-Mo. Inst. Psychiatry, St. Louis, 1976-78; chief psychiatry svc. San Juan (P.R.) VA Hosp., pharmacy and therapeutic com. 1978-92; also prof. psychiatry U. P.R. Med. Sch., 1978-92; prof. psychiatry U. Okla. Health Scis. Ctr., Okla. City VA Med. Ctr., 1992—; spl. adviser on mental health P.R. Senate, P.R. sec. health, 1989; spl. cons. NASA, 1965-69; cons. divsn. narcotic addiction and drug abuse NIDA, 1972-73. Capt. M.C., USAR, 1960-62; sr. surgeon USPHS, 1969-71, med. dir., 1971-73. Recipient Coronas award, 1957, Ruiz-Arnau award, 1957, Diaz-Garcia award, 1957, Geigy award, 1975, 76, AMA Recognition award, 1971, 76, 81, Horner's award, 1975, 76, Pavlovian award, 1978, Recognition cert. Senate of P.R., 1986, cert. of merit Gov. of P.R., 1986. Fellow Interam. Coll. Physicians and Surgeons, Royal Coll. Physicians and Surgeons Can. (sr., cert.); mem. Am. Psychiat. Assn., Am. Physiol. Soc., Pavlovian Soc., Am. Fedn. Clin. Rsch., Am. Assn. Geriatric Psychiatry, Am. Soc. Clin. Pharmacology and Therapeutics, Am. Soc. Pharmacology and Experimental Therapeutics, Soc. Neurosci., Nat. Assn. Healthcare Quality, Internat. Soc. Rsch. Aggression, Okla. Psychiat. Assn., Am. Soc. Clin. Psychopharmacology, Menninger Found., Okla. Assn. Health Care Quality. Roman Catholic. Home: 3304 Rosewood Ln Oklahoma City OK 73120-5604 Office: Oklahoma City VA Med Ctr 921 NE 13th St Oklahoma City OK 73104-5007

PEREZ-GUTIERREZ, ROBERTO, cardiologist; b. Santurce, P.R., Feb. 14, 1959; s. Roberto and Aurea E. (Gutierrez) P.; m. Mary Sol Cabrera, Jan. 17, 1987; children: Alexandra Marie, Roberto Gabriel. BS in Chemistry, U. P.R., 1979, MD, 1983. Cert. internal medicine and cardiology. Cardiology cons. San Francisco Hosp., Rio Piedras, P.R., 1988—; aux. prof. of medicine U. P.R. Sch. of Medicine, San Juan, 1988—; chief intensive care unit Carolina (P.R.) Regional Hosp., 1992—. Mem. ACP, Am. Coll. of Cardiology, Alpha Omega Alpha. Office: Torre San Francisco Ste 408 Ave de Diego 369 Rio Piedras PR 00923

PEREZ-REYES, EDWARD, molecular physiologist; b. Cheverly, Md., Feb. 18, 1957; s. Mario Perez-Reyes and Maria Gispert; m. Emilia Aranda Ripoll, June 15, 1984 (div. June 1989); m. Deborah Lynn Benuska, Apr. 13, 1991. PhD, U. Colo., 1986. Technician Nat. Inst. Environ. Health Scis., Research Triangle Park, N.C., 1978-80; postdoctoral fellow Baylor Coll. Medicine, Houston, 1986-91, asst. prof., 1991-92; asst. prof. Loyola U. Med. Ctr., Maywood, Ill., 1993—. Contbr. articles to profl. jours. Recipient Nat. Rsch. Svc. award NIH, 1988, Established Investigatorship award Am. Heart Assn., 1996; fellow NSF, 1980. Mem. Biophys. Soc. Home: 320 S Birchwood Dr Naperville IL 60540-5033*

PEREZ-VALDES, YVONNE ANN, nurse, educator; b. Tampa, Fla., May 18, 1946; d. Raimundo Abal and Encarnita (Perez) P. ASN, St. Petersburg Jr. Coll., 1978. Cert. ob-gyn., pediatric ICU nurse, RN, Fla. Nurse St. Joseph Hosp., Tampa, Fla., 1966-71, cardiologist office nurse mgr., 1976-78; ICCU nurse U. Community Hosp., Tampa, Fla., 1979-80; emergency rm. charge nurse, Intensive Coronary Care Unit asst. head nurse Centro Asturiano Hosp., Tampa, Fla., 1980-85; mem. faculty, head dept. nursing Tampa Coll., 1985-88; supr., dir. edn. Oakwood Nursing Home, Tampa, 1988-89; instr. health Hillsborough County Schs., Tampa, 1989-95; developer staff, mgr. risk, dir. edn. safety and pers. Meadowbrook Manor Tampa, 1994-95; faculty mem. Health Industry & Adv. Bd., Tampa, 1992-95; bilingual instr. for refugee asst. program Ideal Sch., Miami, Fla., 1980—; pvt. duty home health nurse, 1972-75; office nurse mgr. for cardiologist/internist, 1975-76. Author: Cry Out, I'm Listening. Mem.-at-large Nat. Rep. Com., Washington, 1991-92; mem. Presdl. Com., Washington, 1991-95, Senatorial Com., Washington, 1991-95. Name included Benefactor's Wall Am. Nursing Found. Bldg., Washington. Mem. ANA, ARC, Am. Cancer Assn., Am. Hispanic Nurses (chmn. 1992), Fla. Nurses Assn., Tampa Nurses Assn., St. Joseph's Hosp. Devel. Coun., Nat. Audubon Soc., Am. Diabetes Assn. Democrat. Roman Catholic. Office: Hillsborough County Schs Ctr for Tng 5410 N 20th St Tampa FL 33610-8213 also: Meadowbrook Manor Tampa 8720 Jackson Springs Rd Tampa FL 33615-3210

PERHACH, JAMES LAWRENCE, pharmaceutical company executive; b. Pitts., Oct. 26, 1943; s. James Lawrence and Elizabeth Louise (Hoffman) P.; m. Judith Irene Selter, Apr. 15, 1967; children: Laura Anne, Amy Elizabeth. BS, U. Dayton, 1966; MS, U. Pitts., 1969, PhD, 1971. Sr. scientist dept. pharmacology Mead Johnson Rsch. Ctr., 1971-74, sr. investigator dept. biol. rsch., 1974-76, sr. rsch. assoc. dept. biol. rsch., 1976-77, sr. rsch. assoc. dept. pathology and toxicology, 1977-78, prin. rsch. assoc. dept. pathology and toxicology, 1978-80; dir. pharmacology Wallace Biol. Rsch., Wallace Labs. div. Carter-Wallace Inc., Cranbury, N.J., 1980, exec. dir. biol. rsch., 1980-84, assoc. dir. clin. rsch., 1984-85, dir. clin. investigation, 1985-87, v.p. clin. pharmacology and pharmacokinetics, 1987—; vis. asst. prof. dept. pharmacy practice and adminstrn. Coll. Pharmacy Rutgers U., 1993—; adj. prof. toxicology Phila. Coll. Pharmacy and Sci., 1981—; assoc. faculty Evansville Ctr. Med. Edn., Ind. U., 1973-80; lectr. grad. physiology U. Evansville, 1973-79; scientific adv. bd. Clin. Rsch. Ctr., U. Med. Dentistry, N.J., 1995— apptd. med. pharmacologist, 1993, sec., 1994, chmn., 1985-865; mem. drug utilization rev. coun. State of N.J., 1983—; mem. substance abuse com. Tri-State Area Health Planning Coun., Evansville, 1972-75; mem. addictions mem. edn. program Evansville Ctr. for Med. Edn., 1972-78. Fellow Am. Coll. Clin. Pharmacology; mem. AAAS, Am. Soc. Clin. Pharmacology and Therapeutics, Am. Soc. Pharmacology and Exptl. Therapeutics, Am. Coll. Toxicology, European Soc. Toxicology, Soc. Exptl. Biology and Medicine, Soc. Neurosci., N.Y. Acad. Sci., Physiol. Soc. Phila., Drug Info. Assn., Sigma Xi. Home: 6 Highfield Ct Lawrenceville NJ 08648-1077 Office: Wallace Labs Half Acre Rd PO Box 1001 Half Acre Rd Cranbury NJ 08512

PERHEENTUPA, JAAKKO PENTTI, pediatrician; b. Eurajoki, Finland, Mar. 7, 1934; s. Antti and Suoma (Wikström) P.; m. Tuula Bäckman, June 19, 1964; children: Antti, Aaro, Laura, Ilkka, Inna. MD, U. Helsinki, Finland, 1959, D Med. Sci., 1967, Pediatrician, 1967, Pediatric Endocrinologist, 1979. Resident Children's Hosp./Univ. Helsinki, 1963-66, dir., 1984—; assoc. prof. Univ. Helsinki, 1973-84, prof., 1984—, chmn. pediatrics, 1984-93; fellow in pediatrics The Johns Hopkins U. and Hosp., Balt., 1966-68; vis. assoc., prof. pediatrics Univ. Calif. Med. Sch., L.A., 1982-83. Contbr. articles to profl. jours. Decorated comdr. Order of Finnish Lion; recipient Rosén von Rosenstein medal and lecture U. Uppsala, 1994. Mem. Endocrinol. Soc. Finland (hon.), Estonian Pediatric Assn. (hon.), European Soc. Pediatric Endocrinology (pres. 1981-82), Finnish Pediatric Assn. (pres. 1989-92), Finnish Acad. Sci. and Letters, Finnish Dental Soc. (corr.), Deutsche Gesellschaft Kinderheilkunde (corres. mem.). Office: Childrens Hosp, Stenbackinkatu 11, 00290 Helsinki Finland

PERIGYI, JO-ANN KATHERINE, nursing administrator; b. New Haven, Mar. 2, 1953; d. Arthur John Kelleher and Helen Katherine (Grady) Rohne; m. Carl Alexander Perigyi, July 14, 1984. AA, Norwalk Community Coll., 1977; BS in Nursing, U. Bridgeport, 1986; MA in Nursing Orgn. Exec. Role, Columbia U., 1988. Lic. practical nurse Jersey Shore Med. Ctr., Neptune, N.J., 1972-75; nursing asst., RN BentleyGardens, West Haven, Conn., 1975-78; staff nurse., mgr. patient care Park City Hosp., Bridgeport, Conn., 1978-85; intake facilitator Hosp. Home Health Care Conn., New Haven, 1986; from asst. dir. nurses to dir. nurses Regis Multi Health Ctr. Inc., New Haven, 1986-89; DON Homestead Health Ctr., Stamford, Conn., 1989-93, Mediplex of Stamford, Conn., 1993-94, Lord Chamberlain, Stratford, Conn., 1995—. Mem. Am. Mgmt. Assn. Roman Catholic. Home: 74 Cutiers Farm Rd Monroe CT 06468

PERIS, ANTONIO GARCIA, radiologist; b. Madrid, Feb. 5, 1961; s. Antonio Garcia Perez and Maria Peris Hernando; m. Rosa Maria Castro Esteban, Oct. 4, 1991; 1 child, Rodrigo Garcia Castro. RN, Puerta de Hierro Clinic, 1982; MD, Autonoma U., Madrid, 1988; specialist in radiodiagnostic, INSALVD, 1994. RN, Spain. Sr. radiologist mammography Hosp. Provincial, Toledo, Spain, 1995-96; sr. radiologist MRI Rosario Clinic, Toledo, 1995-96. Recipient Internat. award BRACCO, 1995. Mem. Toledo Med. Coll., SERAM. Office: Clinica del Rosario, Carretera de la Peraleda 3, 45004 Toledo Spain

PERKIN, GORDON WESLEY, international health agency executive; b. Toronto, Ont., Can., Apr. 25, 1935; came to U.S., 1962; s. Irvine Boyer and Jean (Laing) P.; m. Elizabeth Scott, Dec. 21, 1957; children: Scott, Stuart. MD, U. Toronto, 1959. Asst. dir. clin. research Ortho Research Found., Raritan, N.J., 1962-64; assoc. med. dir. Planned Parenthood Fedn. Am., N.Y.C., 1964-66; program advisor Ford Found., N.Y.C., 1966-67; regional program advisor Ford Found., Bangkok, 1967-69, Rio de Janeiro, 1973-76; program officer Ford Found., Mexico City, 1976-80; project specialist Ministry Fin. and Econ. Planning, Accra, Ghana, 1969-70; cons. World Health Orgn., Geneva, 1971-73; pres. Program for Appropriate Tech. in Health, Seattle, 1980—; affiliate prof. pub. health, U. Wash., Seattle. Contbr. numerous articles to profl. jours. Am. Pub. Health Assn. fellow, 1970. Mem. Planned Parenthood Fedn. Am. (bd. dirs. 1983-89), Planned Parenthood Seattle-King County (bd. dirs. 1982—, mem. exec. com. 1983-86), Nat. Coun. for Internat. Health (bd. govs. 1984-95), Nat. Acad. Scis. (com. mem. 1987-90), Alan Guttmacher Inst. (bd. dirs. 1985-90), Assn. Reproductive Health Profls., Alpha Omega Alpha. Office: PATH 4 Nickerson St Seattle WA 98109-1651

PERKIN, JAMES M., psychologist; b. Allentown, Pa., Nov. 9, 1952; s. David and Gloria (Green) P.; m. Andrea Howe, June 22, 1986. MS in Psychology, Duquesne U., 1977. Psychologist in pvt. practice Allentown, Bethlehem, Pa., 1980—; psychologist Lehigh County Juvenile Probation Office, Allentown, 1982—, Northampton County Juvenile Probation Office, Easton, Pa., 1983—, Pottsville (Pa.) Hosp., 1984—, Endeavor Inc., Bethlehem, 1985-92. Mem. Pa. Psychol. Assn. Office: 4825 Tilghman St Allentown PA 18104

PERKINS, DEBORAH J., hospital executive; b. East St. Louis, Ill., Aug. 25, 1950; d. Janet Francis Roberts; div. BS, So. Ill. U., 1972; BA, Hillcrest Med. Ctr., 1973; MBA, Pepperdine U., 1987. Registered record adminstr.; cert. quality assurance profl. Adminstrv. dir. clin. data St. Mary's Hosp., Reno, Nev., 1979-88; v.p. Md. Gen. Hosp., Balt., 1988—; cons., Reno and Balt., 1986—; pres. Nev. Health Info. Mgmt. Assn., Reno, 1981-85. Contbr. articles to profl. jours. Pres. Homeowners Assn.-Chase Lions Way, Columbia, Md., 1993—; mem. Jr. League of Reno and Balt., 1984—. Mem. Am. Coll. Healthcare Execs. (assoc.). Office: Md Gen Hosp 827 Linden Ave Baltimore MD 21201

PERKINS, DOUGLAS KENNEDY, emergency physician; b. Douglas, Ariz., Jan. 25, 1952; s. Ernest W. and Iris Virginia (Kennedy) P. BS in Biol. Scis., U. Ariz., 1974, BA in Psychology, 1975, MD, 1977. Fellow Am. Coll. Emergency Physicians (bd. cert. 1981).

PERKINS, HERBERT ASA, physician; b. Boston, Oct. 5, 1918; s. Louis and Anna (Robinson) P.; m. Frances Snyder, Sept. 2, 1942; children: Susan, Deborah, Dale, Karen, Erin. A.B. cum laude, Harvard U., 1940; M.D. summa cum laude, Tufts U., 1943. Intern Boston City Hosp., 1944, resident, 1947-48; practice medicine specializing in transfusion medicine, 1953—; clin. instr. Stanford Med. Sch., 1953-57, asst. clin. prof., 1957-58; hematologist Open Heart Surgery Team, Stanford Hosp., San Francisco, 1955-58, Jewish Hosp., St. Louis, 1958-59; dir. rsch. Irwin Meml. Blood Ctrs., San Francisco, 1959-78, med. and sci. dir., 1978-90, exec. dir., 1987-91, pres., 1991-93, sr. med. scientist, 1993—; asst. prof. medicine Washington U., St. Louis, 1958-59, U. Calif., San Francisco, 1959-66, assoc. prof., 1966-71, clin. prof., 1971—; v.p. Blood Rsch. & Devel. Found., 1995—. Co-editor: Hepatitis and Blood Transfusion, 1972; assoc. editor: Transfusion. Served to maj. M.C., U.S. Army, 1944-47. Mem. AAAS, Am. Assn. Blood Banks (chmn. sci. adv. com. 1972-73, chmn. standards com. 1968-71, chmn. com. on organ transplantation and tissue typing 1970-80, bd. dirs. 1982-86), Am. Soc. Hematology, Internat. Transfusion Soc., Am. Soc. Histocompatibility and Immunogenetics (pres. 1985-86), Nat. Marrow Donor Program (chair bd. dirs., chmn. com. on stds. 1987-94, chmn. fin. com. 1987-94). Home: 520 Berkeley Ave Menlo Park CA 94025-2323 Office: Irwin Meml Blood Ctrs 270 Masonic Ave San Francisco CA 94118-4417

PERKINS, MARVIN EARL, psychiatrist, educator; b. Moberly, Mo., June 1, 1920; s. Marvin Earl and Nannie Mae (Walden) P.; A.B., Albion Coll., 1942; M.D., Harvard U., 1946; M.P.H. (USPHS fellow), Johns Hopkins U., 1956; L.H.D., Albion Coll., 1968; grad. U.S. Army Command and Gen. Staff Coll., 1966, U.S. Army War Coll., 1972; m. Mary MacDonald, May 24, 1943 (div.); children: Keith, Sandra, Cynthia, Marvin, Mary, Irene; m. 2d, Sharon Johnstone, May 20, 1978; 1 dau., Sharon. Intern, Henry Ford Hosp., Detroit, 1946-47; post surgeon, hosp. comdg. officer Fort Eustis, Va., 1948; resident physician psychiatry Walter Reed Army Hosp., Washington, 1949-52; chief psychiatry br., psychiatry and neurology cons. div. Office U.S. Army Surgeon Gen., Washington, 1952-53, chief records rev. br., 1953-55; chief psychiat. svcs. div. D.C. Dept. Pub. Health, 1955-58, chief bur. mental health, 1959-60; lectr. Johns Hopkins U. Balt., 1960-65; adj. prof. Columbia U., 1961-67; prof. psychiatry Mt. Sinai Sch. Medicine of CUNY, 1967-72; clin. prof. psychiatry Coll. Physicians and Surgeons, Columbia U., 1972-77; prof. psychiatry N.Y. Coll. Medicine, 1977-78; prof. behavioral medicine and psychiatry U. Va. Sch. Medicine, 1978—; dir. N.Y.C. Community Mental Health Bd., 1960-68, commr. mental health svcs., 1961-68; dir. psychiatry Beth Israel Medical Center, N.Y.C., 1967-72, dir. Morris J. Bernstein Inst., 1968-72; dir. Community Mental Health Svcs. Westchester County, 1972-77; dir. psychiatry Westchester County Med. Center, 1977-78; med. dir. Mental Health Svcs. of Roanoke Valley, 1978-82; med. dir. Roanoke Valley Psychiat. Ctr., 1980-82, pres. med. staff, 1985-86; med. dir., pres. med. staff Catawba Hosp., 1988-91; psychiat., mental hygiene clinic VA Med. Ctr., Salem, Va., 1992-95; cons. psychiatrist Blue Ridge Cmty. Svcs., 1992—; med. dir. partial hospitalization program Alleghany Regional Hosp., Low Moor, Va., 1995—. With AUS, 1943-46; col. M.C. Res. ret. Diplomate in psychiatry Am. Bd. Psychiatry and Neurology; certified mental hosp. adminstr. Am. Psychiat. Assn. Fellow Am. Psychiat. Assn. (life), N.Y. Acad. Medicine (life); mem. AMA, Group Advancement Psychiatry, Roanoke Acad. Medicine, N.Y. Psychiat. Soc., Neuropsychiat. Soc. Va., Med. Soc. Va., State Hist. Soc. Mo. (life), Res. Officers Assn. (life) Mil. Order of World Wars (perpetual). Home: 3728 Forest Rd SW Roanoke VA 24015-4510 also: PO Box 20437 Roanoke VA 24018 Office: 1604 Boulevard Salem VA 24153 also: 865 Roanoke Rd Daleville VA 24083

PERKINS, NINA ROSALIE, social worker; b. Huntington, W.Va., July 17, 1953; d. Lloyd William and Violet Macil (Elkins) Fowler; m. Homer Chester Bartoe, Jan. 30, 1972 (div. Dec. 1979); m. Gary Michael Lovejoy, Aug. 9, 1982 (div. Mar. 1989); m. Raymond Wesley Perkins, Apr. 14, 1989 (div. Nov. 1989); 1 child, Homer David. BSW, Marshall U., 1982; postgrad., W.Va. U., 1989-95. Lic. social worker, W.Va.; cert. personal care provider. Child care worker Charles W. Cammack Children's Ctr., Huntington, 1983-84; ins. underwriter Mut. of Omaha, Shreveport, La., 1984-86; banquet mgr. Ramada Inn, Shreveport, 1986-87; ctr. coord. Cabell County Community Svcs. Orgn., Inc., Huntington, 1987-90, case mgr. sr. svcs., 1990-92; minority AIDS program coord. W.Va. Dept. Health, Charleston, 1988-90, cons. instr., 1990-92; social worker Marshall U. Sch. Medicine, Frank E. Hanshaw Geriatric Ctr., Huntington, 1990—; owner, adminstr. Sr. Care Mgmt. Svcs., Huntington, W.Va., 1991-92; dir. social svcs. Wayne Continuous Care Ctr., 1992—; charter mem. Cabell County Com. for Drug Info., Huntington, 1990—; mem. Huntington Area AIDS Task Force, 1988—; social work cons. for Region 2, Area Agy. on Aging Adv. Com.; cons. and guest lectr., 1991-96; mem. ethics com. W.Va. Dept. HHS Office Social Svcs., 1995—; mem. partial hospitilization adv. com. Prestera Ctr. Mental Health. Mem. Dem. Women's Club, Cabell County. Recipient Cert. for Concerned Citizenship, State of W.Va., 1982. Mem. W.Va. Assn. Dirs. Sr. Programs, NAFE, Internat. Plaform Assn., Inst. Noetic Scis. Democrat. Baptist. Office: Frank Hanshaw Geriatric Ctr 2900 1st Ave Huntington WV 25702-1271

PERKINS, WILLIAM HUGHES, speech pathologist, educator; b. Kansas City, Mo., Feb. 21, 1923; s. William C. and Edna (Hughes) P.; m. Jill Thompson, June 16, 1952; children: Christopher, Scott, Alizon, Kyle. BS, Southwest Mo. State U., 1943; MA, U. Mo.-Columbia, 1949, PhD, 1952. Lic. speech pathologist, Calif. Asst. prof. communications arts and scis., dept. speech sci. and tech. U. So. Calif., L.A., 1952-56, assoc. prof., 1956-60, prof., 1960-88, dir. Stuttering Ctr., 1957-88, disting. prof. emeritus, 1988—; adv. editor Coll.-Hill Press, San Diego, 1980-87. Author: Speech Pathology, 1967, Human Perspectives in Speech and Language Disorders, 1977; editor Jour. Speech and Hearing Disorders, 1977-81, Current Therapy of Communications Disorders, 1983-84, Functional Anatomy of Speech, Language and Hearing, 1986; editor-in-chief Seminars in Speech and Language, 1983-90, Recent Advances in Communications Disorders, 1984, Stuttering Prevented: A Guide for Parens, 1991, Stuttering and Science, 1996. Served to lt. comdr. USN, 1943-46. Fellow Am. Speech and Hearing Assn. (Honors of Assn. award 1983). Home: 5425 Weatherford Dr Los Angeles CA 90008-1048

PERKINSON, ROBERT RONALD, psychologist; b. Richmond, Va., Aug. 8, 1945; s. Gordon Archibald and Sarah (Haskins) P.; m. Elizabeth Godfrey Fly, July 27, 1968 (div. 1984); children: Robert Reps, Nyshie Page, Shane William; m. Angela Kaufman, Sept. 20, 1991. BS, Colo. State U., 1968; MS, Eastern Wash. State U., 1970; PhD, Utah State U., 1974. Lic. psychologist, Wyo., S.D. Juvenile ct. psychologist, Cedar City, Utah, 1971-72; cert. chem. dependency counselor level III, S.D.; nat. cert. gambling counselor; nat. cert. alcohol and drug counselor; psychologist in pvt. practice, Jackson, Wyo., 1974-83; dir. psychol. services Western Wyo. Mental Health Assn., Jackson, 1977-78, psychologist, 1983—; psychologist, clin. dir. Keystone Treatment Ctr., 1988—; cons. in field; chief psychologist Grand Teton Nat. Pk., Teton County Sheriff's Office and Police Dept. Copyrights: The Yellowstone Park Game, The Good Health Game, The Grizzly Control Team, Communication from God, Chemical Dependency Counseling, The Mystics. Contbr. articles to profl. jours. Mem. Am. Psychol. Assn., Wyo. Psychol. Assn., S.D. Psychol. Assn., S.D. Chem. Dependency Assn., Biofeedback Soc. Am. (bd. dirs. Wyo. br.), Wyo. Bd. Psychologist Examiners (sec.-treas., bd. dirs. S.D. coun. problem gambling), Nat. Register of Health Service Providers in Psychology. Address: PO Box 159 Canton SD 57013-0159

PERKOFF, GERALD THOMAS, physician, educator; b. St. Louis, Sept. 22, 1926; s. Nat and Ann (Schwartz) P.; m. Marion Helen Maizner, June 7, 1947; children: David Alan, Judith Ilene, Susan Gail. M.D. cum laude, Washington U., 1948. Intern Salt Lake City Gen. Hosp., 1948-49, resident, 1950-52; from instr. to asso. prof. medicine U. Utah, 1954-63; chief med. service Salt Lake VA Hosp., 1961-63; asso. prof., then prof. medicine Washington U. Sch. Medicine, St. Louis, 1963-79; chief Med. Service, St. Louis City Hosp., 1963-68, prof. preventive medicine and pub. health, dir. div. health care research, 1968-79; Curators prof. and assoc. chmn. dept. family and community medicine and prof. medicine U. Mo., Columbia, 1979-91, Curators prof. emeritus, 1991—; co-dir. program health care and human values U. Mo., 1984-85; chmn. nat. adv. com. Robert Wood Johnson Clin. Scholars Program, 1989-96; dep. dir. Robert Wood Johnson Found. Generalist Physician Initiative, 1991—; career rsch. prof. neuromuscular diseases Nat. Found. Neuromuscular Diseases, 1961; founder, dir. Med. Care Group of Washington U., 1968-78. Contbr. articles profl jours. Served as jr. asst. surgeon USPHS, 1953-54. John and Mary R. Markle scholar med. sci., 1955-60; Henry J. Kaiser Sr. fellow Ctr. Advanced Studies in Behavioral Sci., Stanford, 1976-77, 85-86. Mem. Am. Soc. Clin. Investigation, Soc. Tchrs. Family Medicine, Assn. Am. Physicians, Inst. Medicine (Nat. Acad. Scis.). Home: 1300 Torrey Pines Dr Columbia MO 65203-4826 Office: U Mo Sch Medicine Dept Family & Community Medicine M228 Med Scis Columbia MO 65212

PERL, ANDRAS, immunologist, educator; b. Budapest, Hungary, Sept. 20, 1955; came to U.S., 1985; s. Miklos and Ibolya (Molnar) P.; m. Katalin Banki, July 23, 1983; children: Annamaria, Marcel Adam, Daniel Peter. MD, Semmelweis Med. Sch., Budapest, 1979, PhD, 1984. Resident, fellow Semmelweis U. Med. Sch., 1979-84, asst. prof., 1984-85; cancer rsch. fellow U. Rochester, N.Y., 1985-88; sr. instr. dept. medicine U. Rochester, 1988-89; asst. prof. dept. microbiology and immunology SUNY, Buffalo, 1989-92; cancer rsch. scientist Roswell Park Cancer Inst., Buffalo, 1989-92; assoc. prof. medicine, microbiology & immunology SUNY, Syracuse, 1992—; presenter, lectr. in field. Contbr. articles to profl. publs. Grantee Am. Lupus Soc., 1994. Wilmot Cancer Rsch. fellow, 1985-88; recipient Arthritis Investigator award Arthritis Found., 1989—, Am. Lupus Soc. award, 1995, grant NIH, 1996—, grant Pardee Found. Cancer Rsch., 1991—. Mem. Am. Assn. Immunologists, N.Y. Acad. Scis., Clin. Immunology Soc. Office: SUNY Health Sci Ctr Coll of Medicine 750 E Adams St Syracuse NY 13210-2306

PERL, HAROLD, pediatrician; b. July 24, 1950; m. Esther Jayde Strauss, June 18, 1972; children: Ari, Sharona, Gil, Daniel. BA, Yeshiva Coll., 1972; MD, Albert Einstein Coll Medicine, 1975. Diplomate Am. Bd. Pediatrics, cert. neo-natal-peri-natal medicine. Dir. neonatology Hackensack (N.J.) U. Med. Ctr., 1991—; mem. biomed. ethics com. Hackensack U. Med. Ctr., 1985—. mem. health profls. adv. com. March of Dimes, No. N.J., 1982—. Office: Hackensack U Med Ctr 30 Prospect Ave Hackensack NJ 07601

PERLIN, SEYMOUR, psychiatrist, educator; b. Passaic, N.J., Sept. 27, 1925; s. Samuel and Fanny (Horowitz) P.; m. Ruth Joan Rudolph, Aug. 21, 1958; children: Jonathan Brian, Steven Michael, Jeremy Francis. Student, Johns Hopkins U., 1943-44; B.A. summa cum laude, Princeton U., 1946; M.D., Columbia U., 1950; grad., Washington Psychoanalytic Inst. Diplomate Am. Bd. Psychiatry and Neurology. Intern Univ. Hosp., Ann Arbor, Mich., 1951-52; resident N.Y. State Psychiat. Inst., 1950-51, 53-54, Manhattan State Hosp., 1952; practice medicine specializing in psychiatry and psychoanalysis Bethesda, Md., 1954-59, Stanford, Calif., 1959-60, N.Y.C., 1960-63, Balt., 1964-72, Bethesda, 1974—; chief div. psychiatry Montefiore Hosp., 1960-63; dir. clin. care and tng. Henry Phipps Psychiat. Clinic, Johns Hopkins Hosp., 1964-72; sr. research scholar Ctr. for Bioethics, Kennedy Inst., Georgetown U., Washington, 1974-78; clin. prof. psychiatry UCLA Sch. Medicine, 1973-74; clin. prof. psychiatry George Washington U. Sch. Medicine, 1974-76, prof., 1977—, also dir. residency tng., 1977-93; lectr. psychiatry Columbia U., 1963-64; assoc. prof. psychiatry Johns Hopkins Sch. Medicine, 1964-65, prof., 1966-72, dep. chmn. dept. psychiatry and behavioral scis., 1969-72; program dir. Fellowship Program in Suicidology, 1967-72; adv. council Univ. health services Princeton, 1970-82; vis. fellow Princeton U., 1973, Oxford U., 1974; Joseph P. Kennedy fellow medicine, law and ethics, 1974-75; chief sect. psychiatry Lab. Clin. Sci., NIMH, 1955-59, mem. clin. program-project com., 1967-70; fellow Ctr. Advanced Study in Behavioral Scis., 1959-60; chmn. mental health study sect. B, div. research grants NIH, 1964-66; cons. Community Mental Health Services, Md. Dept. Mental Hygiene, 1964-72; chmn. bd. dirs. Youth Suicide Nat. Ctr., 1985-87. Cons. editor: Jour. Suicide and Life Threatening Behavior, 1970-89; editorial bd.: Johns Hopkins Med. Jour, 1970-72; editor: Handbook for the Study of Suicide; co-editor: Ethical Issues in Death and Dying; contbr. numerous articles to med. jours. Served with USNR, 1944-46, with USPHS, 1954-58. Recipient Meirhoff award in pathology, 1950, Bicentennial Silver medal for achievement in psychiatry, 1967, both Coll. Phys. and Surg. Columbia. Fellow Am. Psychiat. Assn.; mem. Am. Coll. Psychiatry, Washington Psychoanalytic Soc., Med. Soc. D.C., Washington Psychiat. Soc., Am. Assn. Suicidology (pres. 1969-70, Dublin award 1978, ann. lectureship in suicidology in his name George Washington U. 1995). Home: 5125 Westbard Ave Bethesda MD 20816-1413 Office: Dept Psychiatry George Washington U Sch Medicine 2150 Pennsylvania Ave NW Washington DC 20037

PERLMAN, LEONARD G., psychologist, rehabilitation specialist, author, educator; b. Phila., Sept. 10, 1932; s. Aaron and Sophie P.; BS, Pa. State U., 1959, MS, 1961, EdD (HEW fellow), 1968; m. Gerry R. Wasserman, Oct. 13, 1963; children: Karyn Lisa, Diane Beth. Supervising psychologist Work Adjustment Center, Phila., 1961-66; chief Washington Field Office, NIMH, Bethesda, Md., 1968-73; assoc. exec. dir. Epilepsy Found. Am., Washington, 1973-76; pvt. practice psychology, Washington and Rockville (Md.), 1976—; coordinator Switzer Meml. Seminars in Vocat. Rehab., 1976—; professorial lectr. U. Md.; lectr. in field; lobbyist profl. orgns.; bd. dirs. Md. Gov.'s Com. on Employment of Handicapped, Montgomery County. Served with U.S. Army, 1953-55. Mem. Am. Psychol. Assn. (Washington liaison for nat. orgns. 1976—, pres. rehab. psychol. div. 1981-82), Am. Assn. Counseling and Devel., Am. Rehab. Counselors Assn., Nat. Rehab. Assn., Nat. Register Health Providers in Psychology. Author books, the most recent being: High Technology and Rehabilitation in the Information Age, 1984, Transitions to Work for Disabled Youth, 1986, The Aging Workforce: Implications for Rehabilitation, 1987, Making It on Your Own, 1987, 2d edit., 1991, 3d edit., 1991, Support Systems for Long-term Mentally Ill: Preparing for the Next Decade, 1988, The Worker with a Disability: Emerging Trends in the 1990's, 1990, Aging, Disability and the Nation's Productivity, 1991, Rehabilitation in the Private Sector: Insurance, Trends and Issues For the 21st Century, 1993, The Entrepreneur with a Disability, 1996; contbr. articles to profl. jours.

PERLMAN, STANLEY, physician, educator; b. N.Y.C., June 22, 1948; s. Herbert Charles and Ada Judith Perlman; m. Anne Broderick; children: Zachary, Laura, Neil, Claire, David. AB, U. Rochester, 1968; PhD, MIT, 1972; MD, U. Miami, 1979. Intern, then resident Children's Hosp., Boston, 1979-82, clin./rsch. fellow, 1982-83; asst. prof. Sch. Medicine U. Iowa, Iowa City, 1983-88, assoc. prof. Sch. Medicine, 1988-93, prof. Sch. Medicine, 1993—; clin. tchr. in ward, clinic, oper. rm. U. Iowa Hosp., Iowa City, 1983—; mem. site visit team NIH, Washington, 1993, Syracuse, N.Y., 1993; mem. merit rev. bd. VA, 1991-94; mem. rsch./fellowship com. pediatrics dept. U. Iowa, 1987-94. Mem. editl. bd. Virology, 1992—; contbr. 65 articles to profl. publs. Fellow Jane Coffin Child Meml. Fund, 1972-73, Helen Hay Whitney Found., 1973-77, Med. Found., Inc., 1982-83; recipient rsch. career devel. award NIH, 1989-94. Mem. Am. Acad. Pediatrics (chmn. com. on inf. disease 1989—). Office: U Iowa Hosp & Clinics Dept Pediatrics 207 Medical Labs Iowa City IA 52242

PERLMUTTER, LYNN SUSAN, neuroscientist; b. N.Y.C., Oct. 12, 1954; d. David Louis and Audrey Marilyn (Cherkoss) P.; m. Howard Jay Deiner, May 30, 1976; 1 child, Jocelyn Rae Perldeiner. BA with highest honors, SUNY, Stony Brook, 1976; MA, Mich. State U., 1980, PhD, 1984. Postdoctoral fellow U. Calif., Irvine, 1984-87; asst. prof. neurology and pathology U. So. Calif., L.A., 1987-94, sec. med. faculty assembly, 1990-92, assoc. prof. neurology and pathology, 1994; sci. coord. U. So. Calif. Bravo Med. Magnet H.S. Partnership, 1993-94; staff scientist pharm. divsn. Inst. Dementia Rsch., Bayer Corp., West Haven, Conn., 1994—; ad hoc reviewer John Douglas French Found., L.A., 1988, 91, Calif. Dept. Alzheimer's Disease Program, Sacramento, 1990, 92; mem. neurology rev. panel NIH, 1993, 94; chmn. blood-brain barrier session Internat. Conf. Alzheimer's Disease, Italy, 1992; organizer internat. symposium at Soc. Neuroscientists Africa, 1995. Contbr. articles to sci. jours. Coach Conn. state champions problem I, divsn. I, Odyssey of the Mind program, 1996. Travel fellow Internat. Conf. on Alzheimer's Disease, 1990, 92. Mem. AAAS, Soc. Neurosci., Electron Microscopy Soc. Am., Internat. Platform Assn., N.Y. Acad. Scis., Med. Faculty Women's Assn. (chmn. membership 1989-91), Phi Kappa Phi. Democrat. Jewish. Office: Bayer Corp Pharm Divsn Inst Dementia Rsch 400 Morgan Ln West Haven CT 06516-4140

PERLOFF, ROBERT, psychologist, educator; b. Phila., Feb. 3, 1921; s. Myer and Elizabeth (Sherman) P.; m. Evelyn Potechin, Sept. 22, 1946; children: Richard Mark, Linda Sue, Judith Kay. A.B., Temple U., 1949; M.A., Ohio State U., 1949, Ph.D., 1951; D.Sc. (hon.), Oreg. Grad. Sch. Profl. Psychology, 1984; D.Litt. (hon.), Calif. Sch. Profl. Psychology, 1985. Diplomate: Am. Bd. Profl. Psychology. Instr. edn. Antioch Coll., 1950-51; with personnel research br. Dept. Army, 1951-55, chief statis. research and cons. unit., 1953-55; dir. research and devel. Sci. Research Assos., Inc., Chgo., 1955-59; vis. lectr. Chgo. Tchrs. Coll., 1955-56; mem. faculty Purdue U., 1959-69, prof. psychology, 1964-69; field assessment officer univ. Peace Corps Chile III project, 1962; Disting. Svc. prof. bus. adminstrn. and psychology U. Pitts. Joseph M. Katz Grad. Sch. Bus., 1969-90, Disting. Svc. prof. emeritus, 1991—; dir. rsch. programs U. Pitts. Grad. Sch. Bus., 1969-77; dir. Consumer Panel, 1980-83; bd. dirs. Book Center; cons. in field, 1959—; adv. com. assessment exptl. manpower R & D labs. Nat. Acad. Scis., 1972-74; mem. rsch. rev. com. NIMH, 1976-80, Stress and Families rsch. project, 1976-79. Contbr. articles to profl. jours.; editor Indsl. Psychologist, 1963-65, Evaluator Intervention: Pros and Cons; book rev. editor Personnel Psychology, 1952-55; co-editor: Values, Ethics and Standards Sourcebook, 1979, Improving Evaluations; bd. cons. editors Jour. Applied Psychology; bd. advs. Archives History Am. Psychology, Psychol. Svc. Pitts., Recorded Psychol. Jours.; guest editor Am. Psychologist, 1972, Edn. and Urban Soc., 1977, Profl. Psychology, 1977; adv. editor Contemporary Psychology, 1994—. Bd. dirs., v.p. Sr. Citizens Svc. Corp., Calif. Sch. Profl. Psychology, Greater Pitts. chpt. ACLU; chmn. Nat. adv. com. Inst. Govt. and Pub. Affairs, U. Ill., 1986-89. Decorated Bronze Star; Robert Perloff Grad. Rsch. Assistantship in Inst. Govt. and Pub. Affairs, U. Ill., named in his honor, 1990; Robert Perloff Career Achievement award Knowledge Utilization Soc., named in his honor, 1991. Fellow AAAS, APA (mem.-at-large exec. com. div. consumer psychology 1964-67, 70-71, pres. div. 1967-68, mem. coun. reps. 1965-68, 72-74, chmn. sci. affairs com., div. consumer psychology 1968-69, edn. and tng. bd. 1969-72, chmn. finance com., treas. 1975-84, dir. 1974-82, chmn. investment com. 1977-82, pres. 1985, mem. adv. bd., memb. bd. sci. affairs 1994—, mem task force intelligence and Intelligence Tests, author column Standard Deviations in jour.), Ea. Psychol. Assn. (pres. 1980-81, dir. 1977-80); mem. Am. Psychol. Soc., Internat. Assn. Applied Psychology, Pa. Psychol. Assn. (Disting. Svc. award 1985), Assn. for Consumer Rsch. (chmn. 1970-71), Am. Psychol. Found. (v.p. 1988-89, pres. 1990-92), Am. Evaluation Assn. (pres. 1977-78, trustee 1995—), Soc. Psychologists in Mgmt. (Disting. Contbn. to Psychology Mgmt. award 1989, pres. 1993-94), Knowledge Utilization Soc. (pres. 1993-95), Sigma Xi (pres. U. Pitts. chpt. 1989-91), Beta Gamma Sigma, Psi Chi. Home: 815 Saint James St Pittsburgh PA 15232-2112

PERLOW, MARK JACOB, neurologist. BS, U. Mich., 1963; MD, Northwestern U., 1967. Diplomate Am. Bd. Neurology. Intern Cook County Hosp., Chgo., 1967-68; neurology resident and fellow Albert Einstein Coll. Medicine, Bronx, N.Y., 1968-72; staff scientist NIH, Bethesda, Md., and Washington, 1984-80; assoc. prof. neurology CUNY, Mt. Sinai Sch. Medicine, 1980-81; pvt. practice, neurology and neuro-rehab. Chgo. and Ind., 1981-87; assoc. prof. neurology U. Ill. Sch. Medicine, Chgo., 1983-87; pvt. practice, neurology Phoenix, 1987—. Contbr. over 125 articles to profl. jours. Major AUS, 1972-74. Fellow Am. Acad. Neurology; mem. Soc. for Neurosci., Endocrine Soc., Am. Neurol. Assn., Internat. Brain Rsch. Orgn. Office: 2632 N 20th St Phoenix AZ 85006

PERLSTEIN, ABRAHAM PHILLIP, psychiatrist; b. N.Y.C., Apr. 15, 1926; s. Benjamin William and Pauline (Gittler) P.; m. Shirley Anne Rubenstein, July 10, 1949; children: Judith Paula, Susan Carol, Bernard William. BS, U. Oreg., 1949; MD, NYU, 1953. Diplomate Am. Bd. Psychiatry and Neurology with added qualifications in Geriat. Psychiatry. Cons. alcoholism dir. SUNY, Bklyn., 1958—, clin. asst. prof. psychiatry, 1957—; med. dir. Peninsula Counseling Ctr., Woodmere, N.Y., 1973-78, psychiat. cons. geriatrics, 1978-90; pvt. practice Elmont, N.Y., 1957-90; assoc. psychiat. dir. Frankling Gen. Hosp., Valley Stream, N.Y., 1980-82; attending psychiatrist Kings County Hosp. Ctr., Bklyn., 1957-90, SUNY, U. Hosp. Bklyn., 1963-90, Franklin Gen. Hosp., Valley Stream, 1969-90; adj. clin. asst. prof. psychiatry Cornell U. Med. Coll., N.Y.C., 1978-90; assoc. attending psychiatrist North Shore U. Hosp., Manhasset, N.Y., 1978-90. Sgt. U.S. Army, 1944-46. Fellow Am. Psychiat. Assn. (life). Office: Columbia River Mental Health Svcs PO Box 1337 1950 Fort Vancouver Way Ste A Vancouver WA 98666

PERNEY, VIOLET HELEN, psychologist; b. Cleve., Jan. 24, 1938; d. Kazimir and Balbina (Brejnak) K.; m. Lawrence Perney, July 25, 1959 (dec. 1977); children: Teresa, Christine, Lawrence, Katherine, David. BA, Case Western Reserve, 1971, MA, 1973, PhD, 1975. Lic. psychologist. Psychologist Woman's Gen. Hosp., Cleve., 1975-76; asst. prof. S.W. Mo. State U., Springfield, Mo., 1976-86; pvt. practice psychology Springfield, 1978-87; dir. psychology Bryce Hosp., Tuscaloosa, Ala., 1987—; dir. behavioral medicine Mo. Rehab. Ctr., Mt. Vernon, 1985-87, dir. psychology Bryce Hosp., Tuscaloosa, Ala., 1987—. Mem. Am. Psychol. Assn., Ozark Area Psychol. Assn. (pres. 1984-85), Phi Beta Kappa. Office: Mo Rehab Ctr Mount Vernon MO 65712

PEROTTI, BEATRICE YEE-WA TAM, pharmacokineticist, research scientist; b. Hong Kong, Nov. 16, 1964; came to U.S., 1984; d. Kin-Fan Tam and Kam-Sheung So; m. Ronald Anthony Perotti, Jan. 29, 1988. Internat. baccalaureate, Lester Pearson Coll. Pacific, Victoria, B.C., 1984; BA, Mills Coll., 1988; PhD, U. Calif., San Francisco, 1994. Rsch. scientist Pfizer Ctrl. Rsch., Groton, Conn., 1994—; guest lectr. U. Calif., San Francisco, 1993. Author: Burger's Medicinal Chemistry and Drug Discovery, 1995; producer, performer (soprano recital) 300 Years of Classical Songs, 1986, Love Songs From the East and West, 1987; contbr. articles to profl. jours. Tutor Upward Bound, Oakland, Calif., 1985-87; soloist Brookside Cmty. Ch., Oakland, 1988-94, youth counselor, charity coord., 1989-94; vol. Project Open Hands, Oakland, 1993-94. U. Calif. rsch. fellow, 1986, AFPE Assn. fellow, 1992-94; Sir. Jack Cater trust scholar Hong Kong Edn. Dept., 1982-84; recipient Hong Kong Mills Club scholarship, 1984-87, Hellman music award Mills Coll., 1986-87, Gordon Rsch. Conf. Student Travel award, 1993, Greater Victoria Music award Greater Victoria Music Festival Assn., 1993. Mem. AAAS, ISSX, Am. Assn. Pharm. Scientists (AAPS Travel award 1992). Home: 268 Shore Rd Waterford CT 06385 Office: Pfizer Ctrl Rsch Eastern Point Rd Groton CT 06340

PERRET, GERARD ANTHONY, JR., orthodontist; b. New Orleans, Feb. 13, 1959; s. Gerard A. and Marie M. (Gamino) P.; m. Catherine J. McMahon, 1996. BS in Chemistry, U. N.C., 1981; DDS, La. State U., 1986, cert. orthodontics, 1989. Clin. asst. prof. La. State U. Sch. Dentistry, New Orleans, 1986-87; pvt. practice dentistry Lakeside Dental Group, Metairie, La., 1986-87; pvt. practice orthodontics Jacksonville, Fla., 1989-91, Tampa, Fla., 1991—; founder, pres. Orthogap, Inc., Tampa, 1993—. Patentee in field. Active New Tampa Cmty. Coun. Mem. ADA, Am. Assn. Orthodontists, Fla. Assn. Orthodontists, Hillsborough County Dental Soc., Hillsborough County Dental Rsch. Clinic, So. Assn. Orthodontists, Rotary (pres.-elect New Tampa), Omicron Kappa Upsilon. Office: 14201 Bruce B Downs Blvd Ste 2 Tampa FL 33613-3913

PERRICCI, ELLEN SMITH, physician, writer; b. Bethesda, MD, Apr. 26, 1955; d. John McCoach and Elizabeth Sherman (Sewell) Smith; m. Michael Anthony Perricci, Dec. 17, 1977; children: Anna Lucile, Joseph. BA magna cum laude, U. Utah, 1974, MD, 1978. Diplomate Am. Bd. Psychiatry & Neurology. Emergency staff physician Good Samaritan Hosp., Pottsville, Pa., 1980-83, Reading (Pa.) Hosp. and Med. Ctr., 1983-85; gen. physician Eastern Lebanon County Family Health Ctr., Myerstown, Pa., 1985-86; gen. physician, chmn. infection control com. Philhaven Psychiat. Hosp., Mt. Gretna, Pa., 1986-89; psychiatry resident Pa. State U., Hershey, 1989-94; chief of svc. Divsn. Med. Rev., Psychiatry Office of Med. Assistance Programs, Harrisburg, Pa., 1995; staff physician VA Hosp., Lebanon, Pa., 1995-96; med. dir. substance abuse treatment programs Lebanon VA Med. Ctr., 1996—; cons. physician Birthright, Reading, Pa., 1983-85; chief of svc. divsn. Psychiatry Med. Rev., Office of Med. Assistance Programs, Harrisburg, Pa., Jan.-June, 1995. Recipient scholarship Med. Assistance Program, Swaziland, Southern Africa, 1978; rsch. asst. grantee NIH, 1974. Mem. Christian Med. and Dental Soc. (nat. del. 1987-88), Christian Community Health Fellowship, Quentin Riding Club, Phi Beta Kappa.

PERRIN, EDWARD BURTON, health services researcher, biostatistician, public health educator; b. Greensboro, Vt., Sept. 19, 1931; s. J. Newton and Dorothy E. (Willey) P.; m. Carol Anne Hendricks, Aug. 18, 1956; children: Jenifer, Scott. BA, Middlebury Coll., 1953; postgrad. (Fulbright scholar) in stats, Edinburgh (Scotland) U., 1953-54; MA in Math. Stats., Columbia U., 1956; PhD, Stanford U., 1960. Asst. prof. dept. biostats. U. Pitts., 1959-62; asst. prof. dept. preventive medicine U. Wash., Seattle, 1962-65; assoc. prof. U. Wash., 1965-69, prof., 1969-70, prof., chmn. dept. biostats., 1970-72, prof. dept. health svcs., adj. prof. dept. biostats., 1975—, chmn. dept., 1983-94; prof. (hon.) West China U. of Med. Scis., Szechwan, Peoples Republic of China, 1988—; overseas fellow Churchill Coll., Cambridge U., 1991-92; sr. scientist Seattle Vets. Affairs Med. Ctr., 1994—; clin. prof. dept. cmty. medicine and internat. health Sch. Medicine, Georgetown U., Washington, 1972-75; dep. dir. Nat. Ctr. for Health Stats., HEW, 1972-73, dir., 1973-75; rsch. scientist Health Care Study Ctr., Battelle Human Affairs Rsch. Ctrs., Seattle, 1975-76, dir., 1976-78; dir. Health and Population Study Ctr. Batelle Human Affairs Rsch. Ctrs., Seattle, 1978-83; sr. cons. biostats. Wash./Alaska regional med. programs, 1967-72; biometrician VA Co-op Study on Treatment of Esopageal Varices, 1961-73; mem. Epidemiology and Disease Control Study Sect., NIH, 1969-73; chmn. health svcs. rsch. study sect., HEW, 1976-79; chmn. health svcs. R&D field program rev. panel, VA, 1988-91; chmn. health svcs. info. steering com. State of Washington, 1993-94; mem. nat. adv. coun. Agy. for Health Care Policy and Rsch. Dept. Health and Human Svcs., U.S. Govt., 1994—; mem. com. on nat. stats. NRC, NAS, 1994—; chmn. scientific adv. com. Med. Outcomes Trust, 1994—. Contbr. articles on biostats., health services and population studies to profl. pubs.; mem. editorial bd.: Jour. Family Practice, 1978-90, Public Health Nursing, 1992—. Mem. tech. bd. Milbank Meml. Fund, 1974-76. Recipient Outstanding Service citation HEW, 1975. Fellow AAAS, Am. Pub. Health Assn. (Spiegelman Health Stats. award 1970, program devel. bd. 1971, chmn. stats. sect. 1978-80, governing coun. 1983-85, stats. sect. recognition award 1989), Am. Statis. Assn. (mem. adv. com. to divsn. statis. policy 1975-77); mem. Assn. Health Svcs. Rsch. (pres. 1994-95), Inst. Medicine of Nat. Acad. Sci. (chmn. membership com. 1984-86, memb. bd. on health care svcs. 1987-96, forum health stats. 1994-95, chmn. com. on clin. evaluation 1990-93), Biometrics Soc. (pres. Western N.Am. Region 1971), Inst. Math. Stats., Internat. Epidemiologic Assn., Sigma Xi, Phi Beta Kappa. Home: 4900 NE 39th St Seattle WA 98105-5209 Office: U Wash Dept Health Svcs PO Box 357660 Seattle WA 98195-7660

PERRY, ARTHUR WILLIAM, plastic surgeon; b. Cornwall, N.Y., Jan. 2, 1957; s. Michael Martin and Harriet (Estrin) P. AB magna cum laude, Rutgers Coll., 1977; MD with distinction, Albany Med. Coll., 1981. Diplomate Am. Bd. Plastic Surgery. Clin. fellow in surgery Harvard Med. Sch., Boston, 1981-84; fellow in burn surgery Cornell U. Med. Coll., N.Y.C., 1984-85; resident in plastic surgery U. Chgo., 1985-87; clin. asst. prof. surgery UMDNJ-Robert Wood Johnson Med. Sch., New Brunswick, 1987—; clin. assoc. in surgery U. Pa., Phila., 1993—; mem. N.J. State Bd. Med. Examiners, Trenton, 1995—; mem. bus. devel. com. Carnegie Bank, Princeton, N.J., 1990—. Contbr. chpt. to book, articles to profl. jours. Recipient Gingrass award Plastic Surgery Rsch. Coun., 1981. Fellow ACS; mem. Am. Soc. Plastic and Reconstructive Surgeons, Am. Soc. Aesthetic Plastic Surgery, Alpha Omega Alpha. Office: 3055 Rte 27 Franklin Park NJ 08823

PERRY, BURTON LARS, pediatrician; b. Midland, Mich., Dec. 8, 1931; s. Willard Russell and Myrl Alice (Jacobsen) P.; m. Nancy Fawn Towsley, Aug. 24, 1956; children: Ellen, Willard. BS, U. Mich., 1953, MD, 1960. Diplomate Am. Bd. Pediats.; sub-bd. pediat. cardiology. Physician U. Mich., Ann Arbor, 1960-78, Childrens Hosp. Mich., Detroit, 1978—. 1st lt. infantry, U.S. Army, 1954-56. Home: 1416 Dicken Dr Ann Arbor MI 48103 Office: Childrens Hosp Mich 3901 Beaubien Detroit MI 48201

PERRY, CINDY ANN, health facility administrator; b. Oklahoma City, Mar. 12, 1958; d. Donald Paul Perry and Marilyn (Brittenham) Whitlock; m. Heath Lee Howitt, Mar. 27, 1978. AA cum laude, El Reno (Okla.) Jr. Coll., 1990; AAS cum laude, Rose State Coll., Midwest City, Okla., 1993. Accredited record technician. Coder Midwest City Regional Hosp., 1991-94; dir. medical records Beaver County Meml. Hosp., Beaver, Okla., 1994-95, Elmore Med. Ctr., Mountain Home, Idaho, 1995—. Mem. Am. Health Info. Mgmt. Assn., Okla. Health Info. Mgmt. Assn., Idaho Health Info. Mgmt. Assn., Treasure Valley Health Info. Mgmt. Assn. (nominating chmn. 1995-96), Beta Sigma Phi. Home: 1175 E 8th S Mountain Home ID 83647 Office: Elmore Med Ctr PO Box 1270 Mountain Home ID 83647

PERRY, E. ELIZABETH, social worker, real estate manager; b. Balt., Oct. 2, 1954; d. James Glenn and Pearl Elizabeth (Christopher) P.; 1 child, Linden Andrew. AA, C.C. of Balt., 1973; B in Art, Psychology, Social Work, U. Md., Balt., 1975, MSW, 1978. Asst. grant coord. Md. Conf. Social Concern, Balt., 1975; dir. social svcs. West Balt. Cmty. Health Care Corp., 1978-80; tng. counselor NutriSystem Inc. of Md., Balt., 1983-86; counselor/psychotherapist Switlik Elem. Sch., Marathon, Fla., 1988-89; program dir. emergency shelter Children's Home Soc., Miami, 1990-91; health educator, spokesperson Rape Treatment Ctr., Miami, 1991-94; CEO, pres. bd. Child Assault Prevention Project, Miami, 1993—; self-employed in real estate rehab. and mgmt., 1980—; pub. spkr. on women's and children's issues/sexual assault issues, 1990—. Bd. dirs. Partnership Way, 1993-95, ACHIEVE, 1995—; pub. citizen Dem. Nat. Com. Mem. AAUW, NOW (bd. dirs. Dade County 1994-95), Nat. Abortion Rights Action League, Amnesty Internat., People for the Am. Way, Psi Chi, Phi Theta Kappa. Democrat. Home: 5161 Alton Rd Miami Beach FL 33140 Office: Child Assault Prev Project Omni Mall Ste 1195 1601 Biscayne Blvd Miami FL 33132

PERRY, ELISABETH SCHERF, psychologist; b. Kasel-Trier, Germany, Aug. 24, 1952; came to U.S., 1976; d. Willibald and Brigitta (Jakobs) Scherf; m. R. T. Perry. AA in Maths., Columbia Basin Coll., Pasco, Wash., 1978; BS in Psychology with honors, U. Wis., 1982; MA in Psychology, Calif. Sch. Prof. Psychology, L.A., 1985, PhD in Clin. Psychology, 1988. Lic. psychologist, N.Mex.; cert. Am. Bd. Forensic Examiners. Psychologist

Psychol. Health Inc., Albuquerque, 1988-91, Los Lunas (N.Mex.) Sch. Dist., 1990-91; psychologist, dir. S.W. Psychol. Svcs., Santa Fe, 1991—; police psychologist Gallup (N.Mex.) Police Dept., 1992—, McKinley County Sheriff's Dept., Gallup, 1992—; psychologist, supr. Mesilla Valley, Gallup, 1995; sch. psychologist Los Alamos Schs., 1995. V.p. Santa Fe Child abuse Coun., 1991. Mem. APA, N.Mex. Psychol. Assn., Phi Kappa Phi. Office: SW Psychol Svcs 125 E Palace Ave Ste 62 Santa Fe NM 87544 also: 800 Trinity Dr Ste I Los Alamos NM 87544

PERRY, ERIC SCOTT, anesthesiologist; b. L.A., Nov. 9, 1962; s. Alvin Ralph and Rauna Grace (Miller) P.; m. Christine Lilian Rivers, Aug. 6, 1994. BS, U. Oreg., 1986; DO, U. Osteo. Med. & Health Scis., Des Moines, 1990. Diplomate Am. Bd. Anesthesiology. Intern Oakland Gen. Hosp., Madison Heights, Mich., 1990-91; resident anesthesiology U. Chgo. Hosps., 1991-94; fellow in anesthesia for cardiothoracic surgery Tex. Heart Inst., Houston, 1994; pvt. practice anesthesiologist Boswell Meml. Hosp., Sun City, Ariz., 1994—. Mem. AMA, Am. Osteo. Assn., Ariz. Osteo. Assn., Osteopathic Physicians and Surgeons of Calif., Maricopa County Med. Soc., Am. Soc. of Anesthesiologists, Internat. Anesthesia Rsch. Soc.

PERRY, HENRY DANIEL, ophthalmologist; b. Long Beach, N.Y., May 5, 1946; s. Benjamin and Frida Nine (Soria) P.; m. Mary Ann Nejman, June 2, 1974; children: David, Athena, Marc, Alicia. BA cum laude, Hofstra U., 1967; MD, U. Cin., 1971. Bd. cert. Am. Assn. Ophthalmology. Chief ophthalmology Walson Army Hosp., Fort Dix, N.J., 1977-79; chief cornea svc. U. Pa., Phila., 1977-78, L.I. Jewish Hosp., New Hyde Park, N.Y., 1979-83, North Shore U. Hosp., Manhasset, N.Y., 1984—, Nassau County Med. Ctr., East Meadow, N.Y., 1986—; med. dir. Lions Eye Bank for L.I., Manhasset, 1986—. Editor: Clinical Ophthlamology, 1992; contbr. chpts. to books. Vice chmn. Lions Eye Bank, Manhasset, 1995-96; capital campaign Portledge Sch., Locust Valley, 1996. Maj. U.S. Army, 1977-79. Recipient Rsch. award Fight for Signt, 1980, Rsch. award Eye Bank Assn. Am., 1994; rsch. grantee Lions Club Internat., 1989. Fellow ACS, Am. Acad. Ophthalmology (Honors award 1987); mem. Ea. Ophthalmic Pathology Soc., Nassau Acad. Medicine (chmn. 1995-96), Alumni Assn. Armed Forces Inst. (pres. 1995-96). Republican. Office: 2000 N Village Ave Rockville Centre NY 11570

PERRY, J. WARREN, health sciences educator, administrator; b. Richmond, Ind., Oct. 25, 1921; s. Charles Thomas and Zona M. (Ohler) P. BA, DePauw U., 1944; postgrad., Harvard U., 1948-49; MA, Northwestern U., 1952, PhD, 1955; DSc (hon.), D'Youville Coll., 1990, Med. Coll. of Ohio, 1996. Instr. St. John's Mil. Acad., Delafield, Wis., 1944-47; counselor, asst. prof. psychology U. Ill.-Chgo., 1953-56; dir. prosthetic-orthotic edn., asst. prof. orthopaedic surgery Northwestern U. Med. Sch., 1957-61; lectr. psychology U. Chgo., 1957-61; asst. chief div. tng. Vocat. Rehab. Adminstrn., HEW, 1961-64, dep. asst. commr. research and tng., 1964-66; prof. health scis. adminstrn. SUNY-Buffalo, 1966-85, founding dean Sch. Health Related Professions, 1966-77, dean and prof. emeritus, 1985—; Mary E. Switzer Meml. lectr. Dallas, 1977, Lexington, 1991; mem. task force for Legislation for Allied Health Professions, 1966-67; com. edn. allied health professions and svcs., coun. med. edn. AMA, 1968-73; nat. adv. com. Am. Dietetic Assn., 1970-75, chmn., 1972-75; nat. rev. com., regional med. programs HEW, 1969-72; mem. Inst. Medicine, NAS, 1973—, steering com. on manppower policy for primary care, bd. health promotion and disease prevention, 1981-83, sr. advisor, com. to study the role allied health, com. to study med. manpower in VA, 1988-91; spl. med. adv. com. VA, 1974-77; task force on manpower for prevention Fogarty Internat. Inst., NIH, 1975-76; acad. planning com. Mass. Gen. Hosp. Founding editor: Jour. Allied Health, 1972-78, editor emeritus, 1985—; contbr. articles to profl. jours. Bd. dirs., dir. com. opera edn. Lyric Opera Guild, Chgo., 1957-61; chmn. acad. divsn. dr., coun. trustees Buffalo Philharm. Orch., 1987-93; bd. dirs. Goodwill Industries Buffalo, 1969-76; trustee Cmty. Music Sch. Buffalo, 1977-80; adv. bd., v.p. Sisters of Charity Hosp., Buffalo, 1969-87, pres., 1986-88; bd. visitors U. Pitts., 1977-80; coun. trustees D'Youville Coll., Buffalo, 1978-88, trustee emeritus, 1989-95; bd. dirs. Am. Lung Assn. Western N.Y., 1975-92, pres., 1983; bd. dirs. ARC, Buffalo, Artpark State Performing Arts Ctr., Lewiston, N.Y., 1986—; Am. Lung Assn. N.Y. State, 1981-85, exec. com., 1989-92; chmn. N.Y. State Coalition Smoking or Health, Albany, N.Y., 1987-91; trustee Theodore Roosevelt Inaugural Site Found., 1987, pres., 1991-94; bd. advisors Buffalo Coun. on World Affairs, 1987-88; trustee Buffalo Opera Co., 1989-94, chmn. opera adv. coun., 1995—. Recipient Sustained Superior Svc. award HEW, 1965, Disting. Svc. award Am. Orthotics-Prosthetics Assn., 1966, Buffalo Opera Co., 1995, Chancellors award for adminstrv. svc. SUNY, 1977, 1st Allied Health Leadership award, 1988, Disting. Author award Jour. Allied Health, 1978, Cert. of Merit, AMA, 1979, Pres. Cir. PIN, Buffalo State Coll., 1993, 50th Anniversary Alumni citation De Pauw U., 1994, Outstanding Svc. award Theodore Roosevelt Inaugural Site Found., 1994, Brotherhood/Sisterhood award in health NCCJ Western N.Y., 1995, Christmas Seal Hall of Fame award ALA N.Y. State, 1995, Disting. Citizenship award Mayor of Buffalo, 1995; named Outstanding Individual Philanthropist, Nat. Soc. Fundraising Execs. Western N.Y., 1992, Ky. Col., 1969, Nebr. admn., 1964; J. Warren Perry Disting. Author award named in his honor Jour. Allied Health, 1984—, J. Warren Perry Meml. lectr. named in his honor SUNY, Buffalo, 1990—, J. Warren Perry Outstanding Vol. Leadership award named in his honor Western N.Y. chpt. ALA, 1994—; Perry Scholarships presented in his honor U. Buffalo Found., 1991—. Fellow Assn. Schs. of Allied Health Professions (pres. 1969-70, cert. of merit 1977, Pres.'s award 1978, Honors of Society 1984); mem. APA, Am. Dietetics Assn. (hon.), Am. Personnel and Guidance Assn., Nat. Rehab. Assn., Phi Beta Kappa, Phi Delta Kappa (pres. 1955), Delta Tau Delta. Home: 83 Bryant St Buffalo NY 14209-1836

PERRY, MICHAEL CLINTON, physician, medical educator, academic administrator; b. Wyandotte, Mich., Jan. 27, 1945; s. Clarence Clinton and Hilda Grace (Wigginton) P.; m. Nancy Ann Kaluzny, June 22, 1968; children: Rebecca Carolyn, Katherine Grace. BA, Wayne State U., 1966, MD, 1970; MS in Medicine, U. Minn., 1975. Diplomate Am. Bd. Internal Medicine, Am. Bd. Hematology, Am. Bd. Oncology. Intern in internal medicine Mayo Grad. Sch. Medicine, Rochester, Minn., 1970-71, resident, 1971-72, fellow, 1972-75; instr. Mayo Med. Sch., Rochester, 1974-75; asst. prof. U. Mo., Columbia, 1975-80, assoc. prof., 1980-85, prof., 1985—, chmn. dept. medicine, 1983-91, sr. assoc. dean, 1991-94, Nellie A Smith chair oncology, dir. div. hematology/oncology, 1994—; prin. investigator Cancer and Leukemia Group B, Nat. Cancer Inst., Hanover, N.H., 1982—, exec. com., 1982-84, 1987-90. Author, co-author 30 book chpts.; editor: Toxicity of Chemotherapy, 1984, The Chemotherapy Source Book, 1992, 96, Comprehensive Textbook of Thoracic Oncology, 1996; contbr. articles to profl. jours. Recipient Faculty Alumni award U. Mo., Columbia, 1985, Disting. Alumnus award Wayne State U., 1995. Fellow ACP; mem. Am. Soc. Hematology, Am. Soc. Clin. Oncology, Cen. Soc. Clin. Research, Am. Soc. Internal Medicine (Young Internist of Yr. 1981), Sigma Xi, Alpha Omega Alpha. Home: 1112 Pheasant Run Columbia MO 65201-6254 Office: U Mo-Columbia 516 Ellis Fischel Cancer Ctr 115 Business Loop 70 W Columbia MO 65203-3244

PERRY, NANCY ESTELLE, psychologist; b. Pitts., Oct. 30, 1934; d. Simon Warren and Estelle Cecelia (Zaluski) Reichard; children: Scott, Karen, Elaine. BS, Ohio State U., 1956, MA in Psychology, 1969, PhD in Psychology (EPDA fellow), 1973. Nurse, various locations, 1956-63; sch. psychologist Public Schs. Columbus (Ohio), 1970-72; human devel. specialist Madison County (Ohio) Schs., 1972-75; pvt. practice clin. psychology, cons. psychology, Worthington, Ohio, 1975-80; tchr. U. Wis. Sch. Nursing, Milw., 1980-88, Milw. Devel. Center, 1980-83; pvt. practice Assoc. Mental Health Services, 1983-87; pvt. practice Glendale Clinic for Stress Mgmt. and Mental Health Clinics, 1987—; faculty Wis. Profl. Schs.; adj. faculty U. Wis., Milw. Ohio Dept. Edn. grantee, 1973-76. Mem. APA, Wis. Psychol. Assn., Am. Soc. Clin. Hypnosis, Internat. Soc. Study of Dissociation, Am. Assn. Marriage and Family Therapists. Home: 2210 W Charter Mall Thiensville WI 53092-5451 Office: 5225 N Ironwood Ln Milwaukee WI 53217-4909

PERRY, RICHARD IRWIN, psychiatrist; b. Glen Cove, N.Y., June 1, 1942; s. Charles Daniel and Ann Alice (Antell) P.; m. Denise Murphy, Mar. 23, 1974; children: Allison, Jennifer. BS, Tufts U., 1964; MD, Cath. U. Louvain (Belgium), 1970. Diplomate Am. Bd. Psychiatry and Neurology, Am. Bd. Child Psychiatry. Intern Victoria Gen. Hosp., Halifax, N.S., Can., 1969-70; resident in psychiatry Bellevue Hosp., N.Y.C., 1970-72, fellow in child psychiatry, 1973-74, asst. attending psychiatrist, 1979—, chief child psychiatry inpatient unit, 1986—; staff psychiatrist Jewish Bd. Guardians, N.Y.C., 1972-74, Spence-Chapin Agy., N.Y.C., 1975-85, St. Vincent's Hosp., N.Y.C., 1978-79; asst. attending psychiatrist Univ. Hosp. NYU, 1979—; clin. prof. psychiatry Sch. Medicine NYU, N.Y.C., 1993; panel psychiatrist Children's Aid Soc., N.Y.C., 1975-79. Contbr. over 40 articles on child psychiatry to profl. jours. Fellow Am. Acad. Child and Adolescent Psychiatry; mem. Am. Psychiat. Assn. Office: 55 W 74th St New York NY 10023-2429

PERRY, RICHARD JAY, physician; b. Ft. Worth, Tex., Jan. 21, 1961; s. Billy Jay and Carol Joann (Evans) R.; m. Norma Jean Silva, June 9, 1990; children: Miles Jordan, Bryce Nicole. BS, Tex. A&M Univ., 1983, MS, 1985; DO, Tex. Coll. Osteopathic Med, 1990. Diplomate Am. Bd. Osteopathic. Internship Mt. Clemens (Mich.) Hosp., 1990-91; solo practice Sanger, Tex., 1991—; medical dir. Valley View (Tex.) Rural Clinic, 1996—, Cottonwood Manor, Denton, Tex., 1996—; utilization review com., Care Inn, Sanger, 1994—; clinical assoc. prof. UNT Health Sci., Ft. Worth, 1995—. Contbr. articles to profl. jours. Mem. Am. Osteopathic Assn., Tex. Osteopathic Medical Assn., Am. Osteopathic Acad. Sports Medicine, Am. Medical Soc. Sports Medicine (charter), Am. Osteopathic Coll. Family Practitioners, Tex. Soc. Osteopathic Family Practitioners, Tex. Medical Assn., Denton County Medical Soc., Sigma Sigma Phi, Lions Club. Office: Richard J. Perry DO P O Box 228 Sanger TX 76266

PERRY, SAMUEL RAY, physician assistant; b. Granville County, N.C., Sept. 6, 1947; s. George Thomas and Adelle (Wheelous) P.; m. Marcia Gaye Pegram, Apr. 5, 1968; children: Marcus Kyle (dec.), Jeremy Gray. AA in Livestock mgmt., N.C. State U., 1967; grad. surgeon asst., U.N.C., 1973. Cert. EMT-1, N.C. Surgeon asst. R.D. Noel/P.A. Reeder, MD, Oxford, N.C., 1973-93; orthopaedic physician asst. Durham (N.C.)-Chapel Hill Orthopaedics, 1993-94, Triangle Orthopaedics, Durham, 1994—; instr. emergency med. svcs. Vance-Granville Cmty. Coll., Henderson, N.C., 1976—; instr. CPR, Am. Heart Assn., Chapel Hill, 1978—; instr., coord. basic trauma life support, 1986—. EMT-1 Granville County Emergency Med. Svcs.; vol. Brassfield Vol. Fire Dept., 1985—; trustee Granville Med. Ctr., Oxford, 1995—. With U.S. Army, 1970-71. Democrat. Home: 1545 Hwy 96 Franklinton NC 27525 Office: Triangle Orthopaedics 2609 N Duke St Durham NC 27707

PERRY, SARAH TERESA ANDERSON (TERI PERRY), nurse manager, critical care nurse; b. Flushing, N.Y., Jan. 14, 1957; d. John Thomas and Dorothy Reu (James) Anderson; m. Dennis Michael Perry Sr., Oct. 17, 1981; children: John Thomas, Clayton Foster. ADN, Augusta (Ga.) Coll. Sch. Nursing, 1979; BSN, Med. U. of S.C., 1985, MSN, 1987. Shift supr. ICU U. Hosp., Augusta, Ga.; staff nurse III Roper Hosp., Charleston, S.C.; nurse mgr. Med. U. of S.C. Med. Ctr., Charleston, mem. biomed. ethics com., 1988-94; nurse mgr. CCU Med. Coll. of Ga., Augusta, 1994—, Med. Coll. Ga., Augusta, 1995—; registry coord. Nat. Registry of Myocardial Infarction 2, 1994—. Mem. AACN (pres. Charleston chpt. 1989-90, officer CSRA chpt.), S.C. Nurses Assn., Sigma Theta Tau. Home: 4826 Rocky Shoals Cir Evans GA 30809

PERRY, SEYMOUR MONROE, physician; b. N.Y.C., May 26, 1921; s. Max and Manya (Rosenthal) P.; m. Judith Kaplan, Mar. 18, 1951; children: Grant Matthew, Anne Lisa, David Bennett. BA with honors, UCLA, 1943; MD with honors, U. So. Calif., 1947. Diplomate: Am. Bd. Internal Medicine. Intern L.A. County Hosp., 1946-48, resident, 1948-51, mem. staff outpatient dept., 1951; examining physician L.A. Pub. Schs., 1951-52; sr. asst. surgeon Phoenix Indian Gen. Hosp., USPHS, 1952; charge internal medicine USPHS Outpatient Clinic, Washington, 1952-54; fellow hematology UCLA, 1954-55, asst. rsch. physician atomic energy project, 1955-57; asst. prof. medicine, head Hematology Tng. Program, Med. Ctr., 1957-60; instr. medicine Coll. Med. Evangelists, 1951-57; attending specialist internal medicine Wadsworth VA Hosp., Los Angeles, 1958-61; sr. investigator, medicine br. Nat. Cancer Inst., 1961-65, chief medicine br., 1965-68, mem. clin. cancer tng. com., 1966-69, chief human tumor cell biology br., 1968-71, assoc. sci. director clin. trials, 1966-71, assoc. sci. dir. program planning, divsn. cancer treatment, 1971-73, dep. dir., 1973-74, acting dir., 1974; spl. asst. to dir. NIH, 1974-78, assoc. dir., 1978-80, acting dep. asst. sec. health (tech.), 1978-79; acting dir. Nat. Ctr. Health Care Tech., OASH, 1978-80, dir., 1980-82; dep. dir. Inst. for Health Policy Analysis Georgetown U. Med. Ctr., Washington, 1983-89, prof. medicine, prof. cmty. and family medicine, 1983-93, adj. prof., 1993—, interim chmn. dept., 1989-90, chmn., 1990-93, dir. Inst. for Health Care Rsch. and Policy; sr. scholar Med. Tech. and Practice Patterns Inst., Washington, 1993—; dir. WHO Collaborating Ctr. on Health Tech., 1995—; mem. adv. com. on rsch. and on the therapy of cancer Am. Cancer Soc., 1966-70, adv. com. chemotherapy and hematology, 1975-77, chmn. epidemiology, diagnosis and therapy com., 1971, grantee, 1959-60; med. dir. USPHS, 1961-80; asst. surg. gen., 1980-82; mem. radiation com. NIH, 1963-70, co-chmn., 1971-73; pres. Nat. Blood Club, 1971; chmn. Interagy. Com. on New Therapies for Pain and Discomfort, 1978-80; mem. adv. panel on med. tech. and costs of medicare program Congress of U.S., 1982-84; chmn. criteria working group (bioseparation) NASA, 1984; cons. Nat. Ctr. Health Svcs. Rsch. and Health Care Tech., DHHS, 1985-90, Nat. Libr. of Medicine, 1985-89, Agy. for Health Care Policy and Rsch, DHHS, 1990—, Hosp. Assn. N.Y. State, 1990-91; mem. procedures rev. com. and profl. adv. panel Blue Cross/Blue Shield Nat. Capitol Area, 1987-93; advisor WHO Programme on Tech. Devel., Assessment and Transfer; mem. sci. com. Catalan office of Tech. Assessment, Barcelona, Spain, 1994—. Assoc. editor Internat. Jour. Tech. Assessment in Health Care, 1984—; mem. editl. bd. Jour. Health Care Tech., 1984-87, Health Tech.: Critical Issues for Decision Makers, 1987-90, Cts., Health and the Law, 1990-91. Bd. dirs. NIH Alumni Assn. Decorated comendador Order of Merit, Peru; comendador Orden Hipólito Unanue, Peru; Pub. Health Service commendation, 1967; Meritorious Service medal USPHS, 1980. Master ACP (adv. com. to gov. Md. on coll. affairs 1969-76, gov. for USPHS and HHS 1980-82, subcom. on clin. efficacy assessment 1982-85, chmn. health and pub. policy com. D.C. met. area 1987—, mem. gov.'s coun., D.C., 1992—); mem. APHA, Inst. Medicine of NAS (mem. evaluation panel coun. health care tech. 1987-90, com. on evaluation med. techs. in clin. use 1981-84, chmn. rev. com. on Inst. Medicine Report on Hip Fracture 1990, mem. rev. com. on renal disease 1990, rev. com. on artificial heart 1991), Patient Outcome Rsch. Team (chmn. adv. com. analysis of practice, hip fracture repair and hip replacement for osteoarthritis U. Md. 1990-94), Assn. Health Svcs. Rsch. (health svcs. rsch. adv. com. 1990-93), Assn. Acad. Health Ctrs., Internat. Soc. Tech. Assessment in Health Care (pres. 1985-87, bd. dirs. 1989-95, coord. spl. interest group on developing countries 1996—), NIH Alumni Assn. (bd. dirs. 1993—os Club. Office: Med Tech and Practice 2121 Wisconsin Ave NW Ste 220 Washington DC 20007-2258

PERRY, SHANNON ELIZABETH, nursing educator; b. Bloomington, Ill., Mar. 1, 1938; d. Joseph G. and Ruby M. (Aspel) Vogel; m. William J. Perry, Oct. 3, 1970; 1 child, Julie. Grad., St. Joseph Hosp. Sch. Nursing, Bloomington, 1959; BSN, Marquette U., 1969; MS, U. Colo., Denver, 1971; PhD, Ariz. State U., 1980. Instr. Ariz. State U., Tempe, 1973-76; nurse researcher Stanford (Calif.) U. Med. Ctr., 1985-86; dir. parent-infant nursing program Vanderbilt U., Nashville, 1979-85; prof. San Francisco State U., 1986—, dir. Sch. Nursing, 1994—. Contbr. articles to profl. jours. Robert Wood Johnson Clin. Nurse scholar, 1983-85. Fellow Am. Acad. Nursing; mem. ANA, ANA/Calif., Assn. Women's Health Obstet. and Neonatal Nurses, Sigma Theta Tau. Home: 1055 Rollins Rd Apt 201 Burlingame CA 94010-2526 Office: San Francisco State U Sch of Nursing 1600 Holloway Ave San Francisco CA 94132-1722

PERSING, JOHN ARTHUR, surgeon; b. Burlington, Vt., Apr. 16, 1948; s. Raymond Maurice and Natalie (Vespucci) P.; m. Susan Powers Light, June 22, 1971; children: Sarah Merriman, John Scott. BA cum laude, U. Vt., 1970, MD, 1974; MA (hon.), Yale U., 1992. Diplomate Am. Bd. Plastic and Reconstructive Surgery, Am. Bd. Neurological Surgeons. Resident gen. surgery Hosp. of the Univ. of Ariz., Tuscon, 1974-76; resident neurol. surgery Hosp. of the Univ. of Va., Charlottesville, 1976-82, resident plastic surgery, 1982-84, dir. cranial base surgery, 1988-92, vice chmn. dept. of plastic surgery, 1988-92, chief divsn. of craniofacial surgery, 1988-92; asst. prof. plastic and neurosurgery U. Va., Charlottesville, 1984-87, assoc. prof. of plastic and neurosurgery, 1987-89, prof. plastic and neurosurgery, 1989-92; prof. plastic surgery and neurosurgery Yale U. Sch. of Medicine, New Haven, Conn., 1992—, chief sect. of plastic surgery, 1992—; fellow Trumbull Coll. Yale U., New Haven, 1994—. Editor: Clinics in Plastic Surgery, July, 1995; co-editor Jour. of Craniofacial Surgery, 1992—, Scientific Foundations and Surgical Treatment for Craniosynostosis, 1989, Neurosurgery Clinics of North America, July, 1991; mem. editl. bd. Skull Base Surgery, 1994—; assoc. editor Annals of Plastic Surgery, 1994—; ad hoc reviewer Cancer, Head and Neck Surgery, Jour. of Neurosurgery, Neurosurgery, Plastic and Reconstructive Surgery, Pediatrics, Jour. of Dental Rsch. Recipient Donald D. Matson award Am. Assn. of Neurol. Surgeons, 1981. Mem. Am. Assn. Pediatric Plastic Surgeons (pres.-elect 1993-95, pres. 1995—), Am. Assn. Plastic Surgeons (membership com. 1994-95), Am. Soc. Plastic and Reconstructive Surgeons (coms.), Am. Cleft Palate-Craniofacial Assn. (coms.), Am. Soc. Maxillofacial Surgeons (coms., Bernd Speissl award 1991, Maxillofacial Surgeons Found. Rsch. award 1992), Assn. of Acad. Chmn. of Plastic Surgery (plastic surgery residency tng. evaluation com. 1993, chair issues com. 1994), Northeastern Soc. Plastic Surgeons (program com. 1995), Plastic Surgery Rsch. Coun. (program com. 1991-94). Office: Yale Plastic Surgery 333 Cedar St YPB 2 New Haven CT 06520-8041

PERSONS, MARJIE L., physician, surgeon, educator; b. Toronto, Mar. 9, 1954. BS, Houghton (N.Y.) Coll., 1976; MD, SUNY, Syracuse, 1980. Diplomate Am. Bd. Surgery. Resident in surgery Case Western Res. U. Integrated Residency, Cleve., 1980-85;, 1985—; asst. prof. surgery Case Western Res. U. Sch. Medicine, Cleve., 1980—. Office: Dept Surgery 11100 Euclid Ave Cleveland OH 44106

PERTSCHUK, LOUIS PHILIP, pathologist; b. London, July 4, 1925; s. Isaac M. and Rose P.; m. Andrea Roberts, June 28, 1985; children: Eric, Shawn, Brandy. AB, NYU, 1946; D.O., Phila. Coll. Osteo. Medicine, 1950. Diplomate: Am. Bd. Pathology. Instr. Downstate Med. Ctr., SUNY-Bklyn., 1974-75, asst. prof., 1975-79, assoc. prof., 1979-86, prof., 1986—; cons. Corning (N.Y.) Glass Works, 1982—, Zeus Sci. Co., 1982—, Abbott Labs., 1982—, Lifecodes Corp., 1989—, Oncor, Inc., Gaithersburg, Md., 1994—, Internat. Bioimmune Sys., Great Neck, N.Y., 1996—. Author: Immunocytochemistry for Steroid Receptors, 1990; editor: Localization of Putative Steroid Receptors, 1985. Served with U.S. Army, 1943-46. NCI/NIH grantee, 1979, 82, 85, 92. Fellow Coll. Am. Pathologists, Am. Soc. Clin. Pathologists; mem. Am. Assn. Pathologists, AAAS, Internat. Acad. Pathology, N.Y. Acad. Sci., Histochemical Soc. Current Work: Identification of steroid hormone binding sites in human neoplasms by histochemical and immunohistological techniques. Subspecialty: Pathology (medicine). Office: SUNY Health Sci Ctr at Bklyn 450 Clarkson Ave # 25 Brooklyn NY 11203-2012

PERVIN, LAWRENCE AARON, psychologist, educator, psychotherapist; b. Bklyn., Aug. 3, 1936; s. Murray and Mary (Ruthen) P.; m. Barbara Susan Zucker, June 21, 1958; children: David Joshua, Levi Jonathan. BA, CUNY, 1957; PhD, Harvard U., 1962. Asst. prof., clin. psychologist Princeton (N.J.) U., 1962-68; assoc. dean, assoc. prof. Rutgers U., New Brunswick, N.J., 1968-70; prof. Rutgers U., New Brunswick, 1970—. Author: Personality Theory Research, 6th edit., 1993; editor Psychol. Inquiry, 1990—. Fellow Am. Psychol. Assn., Am. Psychol. Soc. Office: Rutgers U Psychology Dept New Brunswick NJ 08903

PESCATORE, EARLE MILTON, JR., obstetrician/gynecologist; b. Ft. Lauderdale, Fla., Nov. 19, 1963; s. Earle Milton Sr. and Faith Lucille (Ouimette) P.; m. Keli Denise Raymond, Jan. 4, 1991. BA, William Penn Coll., 1985; DO, Southeastern U., North Miami Beach, Fla., 1989. Asst. dept. head Naval Hosp., Agana, Guam, 1994-96; gynecologist Pacificare Med. Ctr., Tamuning, Guam, 1995-96; staff ob.-gyn. Ohio Permanente Med. Group, Parma, Ohio, 1996—; med. cons. Social Security Adminstrn., Sinajana, Guam, 1995-96; gynecology cons. Healing Hearts Rape Crisis Ctr., Tamuning, Guam, 1995-96; author, presenter med. abstracts to profl. orgns. Lt. comdr. USN, 1987-96. Recipient award for osteo. principles, Merck, Sharpe, Dome, Miami, Fla., 1989. Fellow ACOG (jr.); mem. ACS (assoc.), Am. Coll. Physician Execs., Am. Assn. Gynecol. Laparoscopists. Office: 12305 Snow Rd Parma OH 44130

PESS, GARY MARTIN, hand and microsurgeon; b. Bklyn., June 13, 1956; s. Arthur H. and Thelma P.; m. Lois Nyberg, May 31, 1981; children: Matthew, Rachel, Rebecca. BS with honors, SUNY, Stony Brook, 1977; MD cum laude, Downstate Med. Ctr., 1981. Diplomate Am. Bd. Orthopedic Surgery, added qualification in hand surgery. Gen. surgery intern Beth Israel Hosp., N.Y.C., 1981-82; orthopedic surgery resident NYU Med. Ctr. Bellevue Hosp., N.Y.C., 1982-86; hand and microsurgery fellow Mass. Gen. Hosp. and Harvard U., Boston, 1986-87; partner Cen. Jersey Hand Surgery, Eatontown, N.J., 1987—; instr. gross anatomy NYU Med. Sch., N.Y.C., 1984-85, teaching asst., 1985-86; clin. instr. Harvard U. Med. Sch., Boston, 1986-87; clin. sr. instr. Hahnemann U., Phila., 1988—. Contbr. articles to profl. jours. Baseball, basketball and soccer coach Ocean (N.J.) Twp. Recreation, 1991—. Recipient Golden Apple Teaching award Mommouth Med. Ctr., Long Beach, N.J., 1990; Rsch. Pub. award Jersey Shore Med. Ctr., Neptune, 1989, 91. Fellow ACS, Am. Acad. Orthopedic Surgeons, Am. Soc. for Surgery of Hand; mem. Ea. Orthopedic Assn., N.Y. Hand Soc. (2d place presentation award 1984), Phila. Hand Soc., N.J. Orthopedic Soc., Mass. Gen. Hosp. Hand Club. Jewish. Home: 24 Pal Dr Asbury Park NJ 07712-2552 Office: Cen Jersey Hand Surgery 2 Industrial Way W Ste 1 Eatontown NJ 07724-2266

PESSIN, JEFFREY E., physiology educator; b. N.Y.C., Jan. 2, 1953; s. Al Pessin; m. Rene Debra Bronner, June 23, 1975; children: Jacob, Lauren, Melanie. BA in Chemistry, CUNY, 1975, MA in Chemistry, 1975; PhD in Biochemistry, U. Ill., 1980; postgrad., U. Mass., 1980. Grad. rsch. asst. U. Ill., Urbana, 1975-80; asst. prof. physiology U. Iowa, Iowa City, 1983-88, assoc. prof., 1988-91, prof., 1991—, assoc. dir. Diabetes and Endocrinology Rsch. Ctr., 1991—. Contbr. articles to Molecular and Cellular Biology, Endocrinology. Basil O'Connor rsch. scholar March of Dimes Birth Defects Found., 1987-90; grantee NIH, 1988-93. Mem. AAAS, NIH (mem. metabolism study sect. 1989-93), Am. Chem. Soc., Am. Diabetes Assn. (R & D award 1985-87, rsch. award 1995), Sigma Xi. Home: 924 Duck Creek Dr Iowa City IA 52246-8674 Office: U Iowa Dept Physiology and Biophysics 51 Newton Rd Iowa City IA 52242*

PESTANA, CARLOS, physician, educator; b. Tacoronte, Tenerife, Canary Islands, Spain, June 10, 1936; came to U.S., 1968, naturalized, 1973; s. Francisco and and Blanca (Suarez) P.; m. Myrna Lorena Serrato, Aug. 25, 1966; children—Becky Elizabeth, George Byron. B.S., Nat. U. Mex., 1952, M.D., 1959; Ph.D. in Surgery, U. Minn., 1965. Intern St. Mary of Nazareth Hosp., Chgo., 1959-60; resident Mayo Clinic, Rochester, Minn., 1961-65; surgeon Hosp. 20 de Noviembre Mexico City; asst. prof. surgery Nat. U. Mex., 1966-67; asst. prof. surgery U. Tex. Med. Sch. at San Antonio, 1968-70, asso. prof., 1970-74, prof., 1974—, asso. dean for acad. devel., 1971-73, asso. dean for student affairs, 1973-86, assoc. dean acad. affairs, 1986—. Recipient Edward John Noble Found. award, 1965, Piper Prof. award Minnie Stevens Piper Founds., 1972. Mem. ACS, AMA, Assn. Acad. Surgery, Nat. Bd. Med. Examiners, Tex. Med. Soc., Bexar County Med. Soc., San Antonio Surg. Soc., Soc. for Surgery Alimentary Tract, Assn. Am. Med. Colls., Priestley Soc., Sigma Xi, Alpha Omega Alpha. Home: 10123 N Manton Ln San Antonio TX 78213-1932 Office: 7703 Floyd Curl Dr San Antonio TX 78284-6200

PESTKA, SIDNEY, molecular biologist, microbiologist, educator; b. Drobin, Poland, May 29, 1936; s. Harry and Bernice P.; m. Joan Sparacin, June 19, 1960; children: Robert, Sharon, Steven. BA summa cum laude, Princeton U., 1957; MD, U. Pa., 1961; DSc (hon.), Rider Coll., 1987. Intern in pediatrics and medicine Balt. City Hosps., 1961-62; researcher in biochem. genetics lab. of Dr. Marshall W. Nirenberg NIH, 1962-66, researcher in protein synthesis Nat. Cancer Inst., 1966-69; sect. chief, assoc. mem. dept. biochemistry Roche Inst. Molecular Biology, 1969-74, sect. chief, full mem. dept. biochemistry, 1975-79, full mem., head lab. molecular genetics, 1980-86; prof., chmn. dept. molecular genetics & microbiology Robert Wood Johnson Med. Sch. U. Medicine & Dentistry of N.J., 1986—, prof. medicine, 1990—; adj. prof. pathology Columbia U., 1972—; Mayer lectr. life scis. MIT, 1986; Found. for Microbiology lectr., 1986-87; mem. editorial bd.

Pharmacology and Therapeutics, 1975—, Jour. Interferon and Cytokine Rsch., 1981—, Anticancer Rsch., 1981—, Cancer Communications, 1988-92, Jour. Nat. Cancer Inst., 1988-92, numerous others; assoc. editor Cancer Rsch., 1986-92, Jour. Biol. Regulators and Homeostatic Agts., 1986—, Virology, 1989—, Oncology Rsch., 1992—, numerous others; mem. editl. acad. Internat. jour. Oncology, 1993; column editor Pharm. Tech., 1988—; mem. scientific adv. com. Chimica oggi, 1986—; invited speaker, lectr., chmn., organizer numerous confs., symposiums and workshops. Author: Molecular Mechanisms and Protein Biosynthesis, 1977, Interferons Methods in Enzymology, vol. 78, 1981, vol. 79, 1981, vol. 119, 1986; author, co-author over 477 scientific papers. Apppointed to North Caldwell Bd. Health, 1973—, v.p, 1975-77, pres., 1977-79, 85-90; appointed to Breast Cancer Task Force Com. Nat. Cancer Inst., 1983-84, Breast Cancer Working Group Nat. Cancer Inst., 1984-87, Columbia U. Comprehensive Cancer Ctr., 1985—, N.J. Cancer Inst., 1995—, NAS Com. on Scholarly Communication with the People's Republic of China, 1986-89, Basic Pharmacology Adv. Com. Pharms. Mfrs. Assn. Found., Inc., 1986—, N.J. Cancer Com., Cancer Ctr. Task Force, UMDNJ-Robert Wood Johnson Med. Sch./Johnson & Johnson Task Force, 1988-89, Com. to Rev. Chairmanship of Dept. Environ. and Community Medicine, 1990-91, Basic Rsch. Rev. Com. Am. Found. AIDS Rsch., 1990-92; mem. search com. for dean of Robert Wood Johnson Med. Sch., 1988, for chair of dept. medicine, 1988-89, chmn. search com. for chair physiology/biophysics, 1988-89, mem. appointments & promotions com., 1990—, mem. search com. for dir. Cancer Ctr.; mem. exec. com. Oncology Task Force New Brunswick Affiliated Hosps., 1988-89; mem. sci. adv. bd. Rider Coll., 1990—; dir. grad. program Dept. Molecular Genetics & Microbiology, 1986—; chmn. Univ.-wide Cancer Com., 1986-92. Recipient Selman A. Waksman Award in Microbiology, 1977. Mem. AAAS, Am. Soc. for Biochemistry and Molecular Biology, Am. Soc. for Microbiology, N.Y. Acad. Scis., Internat. Soc. for Interferon Rsch. (councillor 1986-88, sec. 1989—, pres.-elect 1992-93, pres. 1994-95), Am. Soc. for Cancer Rsch., Inc., Assn. Med. Sch. Microbiology Chmn., Harvey Soc., Phi Beta Kappa, Sigma Xi. Office: Univ of Med & Dentistry of NJ Dept Molecular Genetics and Microbiology 675 Hoes Ln Piscataway NJ 08854-5635

PETERMAN, ANGELA RUTH, dermatologist; b. Balt., Dec. 6, 1952; d. John Francis and Ruth Audrey (Valentine) P.; m. Edward Ralph Ponatosh, May 20, 1989; children: Joshua, Caroline; stepchildren: Jeff, Ryan. BA cum laude, Wake Forest U., 1975; MD, Bowman Gray Sch. Medicine, 1980. Intern U. Mass. Med. Ctr., Worcester, 1980-83; resident Johns Hopkins Hosp., Balt., 1983-86, faculty mem., 1986-94; dermatologist pvt. practice, Annapolis, Md., 1986—; house staff coun. rep. Johns Hopkins Med. Instns., 1984-86; chmn. med. morbidity and mortality conf. U. Mass. Med. Ctr., Worcester, 1982-83; rsch. asst. oncology rsch. ctr. Bowman Gray Sch. Medicine, 1975-76; presenter in field. Contbr. articles to profl. jours. Organizer free med. clinic for homeless Lighthouse Shelter, Annapolis, 1995. Clin. fellow Johns Hopkins Med. Instns., 1985-86; recipient Janet M. Glasgow award, 1980, Annie J. Covington award, 1980. Fellow Am. Acad. Dermatology; mem. AMA, Am. Coll. Physicians, Am. Med. Women's Assn., Am. Cancer Soc., Am. Soc. Biologists, Southeastern Assn. Parasitologists, Md. Dermatology Soc., Med. Chiurgical Soc. Md., Collegiate Acad. Sci., Alpha Ometa Alpha, Beta Beta Beta, Alpha Epsilon Delta. Republican. Methodist. Home: 520 Horn Point Dr Annapolis MD 21403 Office: Ste 10 101 Ridgely Ave Annapolis MD 21401

PETERS, ALAN, anatomy educator; b. Nottingham, Eng., Dec. 6, 1929; came to U.S., 1966; s. Robert and Mabel (Woplington) P.; m. Verona Muriel Shipman, Sept. 30, 1955; children: Ann Verona, Sally Elizabeth, Susan Clare. BSc, Bristol (Eng.) U., 1951, PhD, 1954. Lectr. anatomy Edinburgh (Scotland) U., 1958-66; vis. lectr. Harvard, 1963-64; prof., chmn. dept. anatomy and neurobiology Boston U., 1966—; anatomy com. Nat. Bd. Med. Examiners, 1971-75; mem. neurology B study sect. NIH, 1975-79, chmn., 1978-79; affiliate scientist Yerkes Regional Primate Rsch. Ctr., 1984—. Author: (with S.L. Palay and H. deF Webster) The Fine Structure of the Nervous System, 1970, 3rd edit., 1991, Myelination, 1970; contbr. (with A.N. Davison) articles profl. jours.; mem. editorial bd. Anat. Record, 1972-81, Jour. Comparative Neurology, Neurocytology, 1972-89, 93—, Cerebral Cortex, 1990—, Studies of Brain Function, Anat. and Embryology, 1989-92; editor book series: (with E.G. Jones) Cerebral Cortex, 1984—. Served to 2d lt. Royal Army Med. Corps, 1955-57. Recipient Javits neurosci. investigator award NIH, 1986. Mem. Anat. Soc. Gt. Britain and Ireland (Symington prize anatomy 1962, overseas mem. coun. 1969), Assn. Anatomy Chmn. (pres. 1976-77), Am. Anat. Assn. (exec. com. 1986-90, pres. 1992-93), Am. Soc. Cell Biology, Soc. Neuroscis., Internat. Primatological Soc., Cajal Club (Harman lectr. 1990, Cortical Discoverer award 1991). Home: 16 High Rock Cir Waltham MA 02154-2207 Office: Boston U Sch Medicine Dept Anatomy and Neurobiology 80 E Concord St Roxbury MA 02118-2307

PETERS, CALVIN RONALD, plastic and reconstructive surgeon; b. New Orleans, Jan. 27, 1940; s. Arthur Henry and Christine Cecile (Moldaner) P.; m. Pamela Alice Orth, Sept. 4, 1965; children: Brandon Scott, Kendall Kyle. BS, La. State U., 1961, MD, 1964. Diplomate Am. Bd. Surgery, Am. Bd. Plastic Surgery. Intern USN Hosp., Portsmouth, Va., 1964-65; gen. surg. resident Ochsner Clinic, 1968-72; plastic surgery resident Duke U. Med. Ctr., Durham, 1972-75; asst. prof. plastic surgery Duke U. Med. Ctr., Durham, N.C., 1975-78; program dir., plastic surgery Cleve. Clinic, 1978-79; pres., founder Ctr. for Plastic and Reconstructive Surgery, Orlando, Fla., 1979—; chmn. dept. plastic surgery, Orlando Regional Med. Ctr., Orlando, 1981-86, Fla. Hosp. Med. Ctr., Orlando, 1981-86. Contbr. numerous articles, chpts. to profl. jours. and textbooks. With USN, 1965-68. Recipient Sr. Resident award Plastic Surgery Ednl. Found., Chgo., 1975. Fellow Am. Coll. Surgeons (bd. govs. 1980-86); mem. Am. Soc. Plastic and Reconstructive Surgeons, Am. Assn. Plastic Surgeons, Am. Soc. Maxillofacial Surgeons, Am. Soc. Aesthetic Plastic Surgeons, Orange County Med. Soc. (pres. 1989—), Fla. Soc. Plastic and Reconstructive Surgeons (pres. 1989—), Fla. Cleft Palate Soc. (pres. 1987-88), Interlachen Country Club, Winter Park Racquet Club. Republican. Episcopalian. Home: 467 Lakewood Dr Winter Park FL 32789-3939 Office: Ctr Plastic/Recon Surgery 2501 N Orange Ave Ste 310 Orlando FL 32804-4642

PETERS, CHARLES EUGENE, health care executive; b. DeWitt, N.Y., June 10, 1942; s. Albert C. Peters and Frances (Peters) Ruzekowicz; m. Marilyn Carpenter, Nov. 14, 1965; 1 child, Charles. BA, Bob Jones U., 1968; postgrad., SUNY, Binghampton, 1970-76, Broome C.C., Binghampton, 1970-73, No. Tex. State U., 1977, Northampton County Coll., 1978. Child welfare caseworker Greenville (S.C.) County Welfare Dept., 1968-69; assoc. adminstr. Montrose (Pa.) Gen. Hosp., 1969-77; adminstr. Presbyn. Homes/Lehigh Manor, Allentown, Pa., 1977-78; exec. dir. Heath Village, Hackettstown, N.J., 1978-87; pres. The Navesink House, Red Bank, N.J., 1987—; sec. N.J. Assn. of Non-profit Homes for the Aging. Former dir. Greater Red Bank (N.J.) C. of C., 1990. With USAF, 1960-63. Mem. Am. Coll. Health Care Adminstrs., Ea. Monmouth C. of C., Middletown C. of C. Baptist. Office: The Navesink House 40 Riverside Ave Red Bank NJ 07701

PETERS, ELEANOR WHITE, retired mental health nurse; b. Highland Park, Mich., Aug. 11, 1920; d. Alfred Mortimer and Jane Ann (Evans) White; m. William J. Peters, 1947 (div. 1953); children: Susannah J., William J. (dec.). RN, Christ Hosp. Sch. Nursing, Jersey City, 1941; BA, Jersey City State Coll., 1968; postgrad., U. Del., 1969-70; MS, SUNY, New Paltz, 1983. RN, N.J., N.Y. Mem. staff various area hosps. N.J., 1941-58; indsl. nurse Abex, Mahwah, N.J., 1958-68; sch. nurse Liberty (N.Y.) Ctrl. Sch., 1971-76; coord. practical nurse program Hudson County C.C., Jersey City, 1979-80; community mental health nurse Letchworth Village, Thiells, N.Y., 1981-96. Historian, Bishop House Found., Saddle River, N.J. Mem. AAUW (pres. Liberty-Monticello br. 1988-92), Am. Sch. Health Assn., Alpha Delta Kappa (sec. Mu chpt. 1973-75), Sigma Theta Tau (Kappa Eta chpt.). Republican. Lutheran. Home: PO Box 224 Saddle River NJ 07458-0224

PETERS, ELIZABETH ANN HAMPTON, nursing educator; b. Detroit, Sept. 27, 1934; d. Grinsfield Taylor and Ida Victoria (Jones) Hampton; m. James Marvin Peters, Dec. 1, 1956; children: Douglas Taylor, Sara Elizabeth. Diploma, Berea Coll. Hosp. Sch. Nursing, 1956; BS in Nursing, Wright State U., Dayton, Ohio, 1975; MS in Nursing, Ohio State U., Columbus, 1978. Therapist-RN Eastway, Inc., Dayton, Ohio, 1979-81; therapist family counseling svc. Good Samaritan-Community Mental Health Ctr., Dayton, Ohio, 1981-83; instr. Wright State U. Sch. Nursing, Dayton, 1983-84; clin. nurse specialist, pain mgmt. svcs., pain mgmt. program UPSA, Inc., Dayton, 1983-86; staff nurse Hospice of Dayton, Inc., 1985-86, dir. vol. svcs., 1986-89, dir. bereavement svcs., 1986-87; asst. prof. Community Hosp. Sch. Nursing, Springfield, Ohio, 1990-93, prof., 1993—. Author: (with others) Oncologic Pain, 1987. Mem. Clark County Mental Health Bd., Springfield, 1986-95; mem. New Carlisle (Ohio) Bd. Health, 1990—. Mem. ANA, Ohio Nurses Assn., Sigma Theta Tau. Home: 402 Flora Ave New Carlisle OH 45344-1329

PETERS, GEORGE NICHOLAS, surgical oncologist; b. Clarksdale, Miss., Apr. 8, 1947; s. Nicholas Emanuel and Lillie (Lemonis) P.; m. Janet Lee Straub, July 28, 1973; children: Nicholas George, Barton Frederick. BA, U. Miss.-Oxford, 1970; MD, U. Miss.-Jackson, 1974. Diplomate Am. Bd. Surgery. Surg. resident Baylor U. Med. Ctr., Dallas, 1974-79; vis. fellow in surgery Columbia Presbyn. Hosp., N.Y.C., 1979-80; surg., oncology fellow Roswell Park Meml. Inst., Buffalo, 1980; assoc. attending in surgery Baylor U. Med. Ctr., 1980—; attending staff Gaston Episcopal Hosp., Dallas, 1980-88. Contbr. articles to profl. jours. Mem. parish bd. Holy Trinity Greek Orthodox Ch., 1984-85, bd. v.p., 1985. Recipient award for achievement in pub. edn. Am. Cancer Soc., Tex. div., 1984, Sword of Hope award Am. Cancer Soc., 1987, Man of Yr. award Susan G. Komen Found., 1988, Leadership award Zeta Tau Alpha, Honorary award Holy Trinity Greek Orthodox Ch., 1995. Fellow ASC; mem. Soc. Surg. Oncology, Am. Soc. Clin. Oncology, Tex. Med. Assn., AMA, Dallas Soc. Gen. Surgeons, Dallas Am. Cancer Soc. (bd. dirs., med. v.p. 1985-87, pres. 1987-89), Am. Cancer Soc. (pres. elect 1989-91, pres. 1991-93 Tex. divsn., mem. detection and treatment com.), Am. Soc. Breast Disease (sec./treas. 1989-93, pres. 1993-95), So. Assn. Oncology, Southwest Surg. Congress., So. Med. Assn., Titanic Hist. Soc., Tex. Surg. Soc., Roswell Park Surg. Soc. Republican. Greek Orthodox. Lodge: Am. Hellenic Edn. Progressive Assn. Avocations: chess; painting; bicycling. Office: Baylor U Med Ctr 3409 Worth St Ste 300 Dallas TX 75246-2039

PETERS, JEFFREY LEE, psychiatrist; b. Akron, Ohio, Dec. 5, 1953; s. Ramon Lee and Phyllis Joy (Collier) P.; m. Patricia Marie Schaefer, Apr. 24, 1982. BA, Coll. of Wooster, 1976; MD, Case Western Reserve U., 1980. Diplomate Am. Bd. Psychiatry and Neurology (with added qualifications in geriatric psychiatry and addiction psychiatry). Staff psychiatrist V.A. Med. Ctr., Pitts., 1986-87, chief psychiatry, 1987—; asst. prof. U. Pitts. Sch. of Medicine, 1986-95; assoc. prof. U. Pitts. Sch. Medicine, 1995—; assoc. dir. Schizophrenia Research Unit, Pitts., 1986—. Contbr. numerous articles to profl. jours. Recipient Nat. Research Svc. award NIMH, 1984, Laughlin award Nat. Psychiat. Endowment, 1983, Phi Beta Kappa award, 1976, Dirs. award VA Mental Health and Behav. Scis. Svc., 1993, Comdrs. award Nat. Assn. Am. Ex-Prisoners of War, 1992. Fellow Assn. Acad. Psychiatry; mem. Am. Psychiat. Assn., Nat. Assn. V.A. Chiefs of Psychiatry. Republican. Presbyterian. Home: 134 Gordon St Pittsburgh PA 15218-1606 Office: VA Med Ctr Highland Dr Pittsburgh PA 15206

PETERS, JON D., physician; b. Washington, July 25, 1953. BS in Psychology with honors, U. Md., 1974; MD, Georgetown U., 1980. Diplomate Am. Bd. Psychiatry and Neurology. Intern in internal medicine Brown U. Sch. Medicine/Roger Williams Gen. Hosp., Providence, R.I., 1980-81; resident in neurology Georgetown U. Sch. Medicine/Washington Vets. Med. Ctr., Washington, 1983-86; gen. med. officer USPHS, Gallup, N.Mex., 1981-82; staff physician USPHS, Ranson, W.Va., 1982-83; attending neurologist Va. Neurologic Ctr., Ltd., Reston, Va., 1986—; physician advisor MedPartners, Inc., Birmingham, 1995—; clin. asst. prof. neurology Georgetown U. Sch. of Medicine, preceptor in neurology, others.; active staff Fairfax Hosp., Alexandria Hosp., Reston Hosp., Fair Oaks Hosp.; courtesy staff Nat. Hosp. for Orthopedics and Rehab., Mt. Vernon Hosp., others. Contbr. articles to profl. jours. lectr. in field. Mem. Phi Beta Kappa, Phi Kappa Phi. Home: 540 Springvale Rd Great Falls VA 22066 Office: Virginia Neurol Ctr Ltd Ste 419 1800 Town Center Dr Reston VA 22090

PETERS, JUDITH ROCHELLE, educator, administrator; b. Phila., July 16, 1951; d. John Bernard and Priscilla Jo (Johnson) P.; B.S (Senatorial scholar), Pa. State U., 1973; M.B.A., H.H.S.A., Cornell U. 1977. Sci. specialist Phila. Bd. Edn.; bd. mgrs. YMCA of West Phila., 1985-88; contractor adminstr., dir. edn. BEBASHI, Phila., 1988-91; health educator, dir. adolescent peer edn. program, founder and convener House of Chop Adolescent Support Group, The Children's Hosp. Phila., 1991—. Vol. Big Sisters Phila., ARC, Phila.; elder, gospel choir, fin. sec. Lombard Cen. Presbyn. Ch. USA, Phila.; sec., mem. bd. mgrs. YMCA West Phila.; bd. mgrs. Calvary United Meth. Ch., also vol. peer project. Mem. Presbyn. AIDS Network, Pa. Assn. Notaries, United Presbyn. Women, Am. Soc. Profl. and Exec. Women, Nat. Assn. Profl. and Exec. Women.

PETERS, MERCEDES, psychoanalyst; b. N.Y.C. Student Columbia U., 1944-45; BS, L.I. U., 1945; MS, U. Conn., 1953; tng. in psychotherapy Am. Inst. Psychotherapy and Psychoanalysis, 1960-70; cert. in Psychoanalysis Postgrad. Ctr. For Mental Health, 1976; PhD in Psychoanalysis, Union Inst., 1989. Cert. psychoanalyst Am. Examining Bd. Psychoanalysis; cert. mental health cons. Sr. psychotherapist Cmty. Guidance Svc., 1960-75; staff affiliate Postgrad. Ctr. for Mental Health, 1974-76; pvt. practice psychoanalysis and psychotherapy, Bklyn., 1961—. Contbr. articles to profl. jours. Bd. dirs. Brookwood Child Care Assn.; mem. vestry Grace Ch., Brooklyn Heights. Fellow Am. Orthopsychiat. Assn.; mem. LWV, NAACP, NASW, Postgrad. Psychoanalytic Soc., Wednesday Club. Office: 142 Joralemon St Brooklyn NY 11201-4709

PETERS, PHILLIP JOSEPH, endocrinologist, educator; b. Columbus, Ohio, Feb. 19, 1945; s. Phillip John and Elisabeth (Baas) P.; m. Janice Kassalow, Mar. 7, 1968; children: Julie Elaine, Jason Todd. BA, Harvard U., 1967; MD, W.Va. U., 1971. Diplomate Am. Bd. Internal Medicine, Am. Bd. Endocrinology and Metabolism. Intern in internal medicine W.Va. U. Med. Ctr., 1971-72, from resident to chief resident in internal medicine, 1974-76; fellow in endocrinology W.Va. U. Sch. Medicine, Morgantown, 1976-78, instr. in endocrinology and internal medicine, 1977-78, asst. prof. endocrinology and internal medicine, 1978-79; clin. asst. prof. endocrinology U. Ark. for Med. Scis., Little Rock, 1979-84, 91—; endocrinologist Little Rock Diagnostic Clinic, 1979—; med. dir. Diabetic Treatment Ctr. of Am., Little Rock, 1992-95. Pres., bd. dirs. Unitarian Universalist Ch. Little Rock, 1981-84; sec., bd. dirs. Chamber Music Soc. Little Rock, 1984-86. Capt. USAF, 1972-74. Named Outstanding Endocrinologist, Ark. Times, 1994-95. Fellow ACP, Am. Coll. Endocrinology; mem. Am. Assn. Clin. Endocrinologists, Am. Soc. Internal Medicine, Endocrine Soc., Harvard Club of Ark. (mem. exec. com. 1985—), Harvard U. Alumni Assn. (mid south regional dir. 1992-95). Home: 11 Shawbridge Ln Little Rock AR 72212 Office: Little Rock Diagnostic Ctr 10001 Lile Dr Little Rock AR 72205

PETERS, ROXANNE LEIGH, nurse practitioner, consultant; b. Gillette, Wyo., Sept. 11, 1954; d. Leonard Andrew and Margaret Rose (DeGering) McCullough; m. Michael James Thiry, Dec. 27, 1975 (div. Aug. 1978); m. John Peters, Oct. 28, 1978; 1 child, Mandi. BA in Nursing, Augustana Coll., Sioux Falls, S.D., 1976; BS in Bus. Adminstrn., Black Hills State U., 1995. RN, Wyo.; cert. nurse practitioner, physicians asst. Nurse Crook County Meml. Hosp., Sundance, Wyo., 1976-77; nurse practitioner So. Nev. Meml. Hosp., Las Vegas, 1978, Advanced Health Systems, Sundance, 1978-82; v.p. Med. Emergency Rescue Cons., Sundance, 1981—; bus. mgr., patient edn. coordinator N.W. Wyo. Med. Ctr., Sundance, 1986-88; assoc. prof. Eastern Wyo. Coll. Outreach Program, 1994—; cons. Parachute Med. Ruscue Service, Kalamazoo, Mich., 1981, Refugee Relief Internat., Boulder, Colo., 1983—. Treas., trustee Crook County Sch. Dist., Sundance, 1982-85; chmn. Crook County unit Am. Cancer Soc., Cheyenne, Wyo., 1983-88; trustee Bd. Coop. Ednl. Services, Gillette, 1982-85, vice chmn., 1984-85; bd. dirs. Crook County Family Violence and Sexual Assault Services, 1985-92, also vice chmn., vol. trainer; commr. Wyo. Commn. for Women, 1983-89; speaker Adolescent Drug/Alcohol Community Group, 1987-94; co-presenter Bush Faculty Devel. Conf.; presenter Midcontinent Inst. Undergrad. Rsch. Conf.; rechr., author Local Bank Rsch. project. Kellogg Found. grantee, 1977; S.D. Small Bus. Inst. Project winner, 1992. Fellow Wyo. Assn. Physician Assts. (bd. dirs. 1978); mem. Am. Acad. Physicians Assts. Republican. Home: PO Box 1070 Sundance WY 82729-1070 Office: 18 Valley Rd Sundance WY 82729

PETERS, THEODORE, JR., research biochemist, consultant; b. Chambersburg, Pa., May 12, 1922; s. Theodore and Miriam (Lenhardt) P.; m. Margaret Campbell, June 9, 1945; children: Theodore D., James C., Melissa Peters Barry, William L. BS in Chem. Engring., Lehigh U., 1943; PhD in Biol. Chemistry, Harvard U., 1950. Diplomate Am. Bd. Clin. Chemistry. Grad. asst. MIT, Cambridge, 1943-44; rsch. fellow Harvard Med. Sch., Boston, 1948-50; instr. U. Pa. Sch. Medicine, Phila., 1950-51; biochemist U.S. VA Hosp., Boston, 1953-55; rsch. biochemist Mary Imogene Bassett Hosp., Cooperstown, N.Y., 1955-88, rsch. scientist emeritus, 1988—; vis. scientist Carlsberg Laboratorium, Copenhagen, Denmark, 1958-59; guest worker NIH, Bethesda, Md., 1971-72; vis. rsch. prof. U. Western Australia, Perth, 1982; chmn. classification panel FDA, Washington, 1976-79; bd. dirs. Nat. Com. for Clin. Lab. Standards, Villanova, Pa., 1986-87. Author: All About Albumin, Biochemistry, Genetics, and Medical Applications, 1996; chmn. bd. editors Clin. Chemistry, 1979-84; contbr. articles to profl. jours. Chmn. Sewer Bd., Cooperstown, 1975—; mem. Water Bd., Cooperstown, 1973—; chmn. lake com. Otsego County Conservation Assn., Cooperstown, 1972-78. Comdr. USNR, 1944-47, 51-53. Recipient Gold medal Biol. div. Electron Microscope Soc. Am., 1966. Fellow Am. Assn. Clin. Chemistry (pres. 1988, awards 1976, 77, 91); mem. Am. Chem. Soc., Am. Soc. Biol. Chem. Molecular Biology (emeritus), Am. Soc. for Cell Biology (emeritus), Protein Soc., Nat. Acad. for Clin. Biochemistry (diplomate), Acad. Clin. Lab. Physicians and Scientists, Phi Beta Kappa. Home: 30 River St Cooperstown NY 13326-1317 Office: Mary Imogene Bassett Hosp Atwell Rd Cooperstown NY 13326

PETERS, THOMAS GUY, surgeon, educator; b. Cin., Oct. 3, 1945; s. Robert Lewis and Martha (Renter) P.; m. Dorothy Jean (Ruby) Geers; children: Elizabeth Jan, Andrew Thomas, Joseph Geers, Sarah Jane. BA, Miami U., Oxford, Ohio, 1966; MD, U. Cin., 1970. Diplomate, Am. Bd. of Surgery. Surgical intern Milwaukee County Gen. Hosp., 1970-71; surgical resident Medical Coll. Wis., Milwaukee, 1971-72, 74-77; fellow in transplantation U. Col., Denver, 1977-78; asst. prof. surgery U. Tenn., Memphis, 1978-84, assoc. prof. surgery, 1984-87, prof. surgery, 1987-88; dir. Jacksonville Transplant Ctr., Methodist Med. Ctr., Fla., 1988—; clin. prof. surgery U. Fla., 1989—, Uniformed Svcs. U. of the Health Scis., 1995—; clin. fellow Am. Cancer Soc., N.Y.C., 1975-76; assoc. examiner Am. Bd. Surgery, Phila., 1983—. Editor: National Transplantation Resource Directory, 1987, Organ and Tissue Donation: A Reference Guide for Clergy, 1989; contbr. articles to profl. jours., chpts. to books. Col. M.C. USAR. Recipient Resident Rsch. award Wis. Surg. Soc., 1976, 77, Outstanding Tchr. award U. Tenn. Alumni Assn., The Disting. Svc. awrad U. Tenn. Med. Ctr., 1984, The Trustees award Nat. Kidney Found., N.Y.C., 1987. Fellow Am. Coll. Surgeons; mem. Am. Soc. Transplant Surgeons, Soc. Med. Cons. to Armed Forces, Transplantation Soc., United Network for Organ Sharing. Home: 3601 River Hall Dr Jacksonville FL 32217-4277 Office: Jacksonville Transplant Ctr 580 W 8th St Ste 8000 Jacksonville FL 32209-6533

PETERS, UWE HENRIK, psychiatrist, neurologist, educator; b. Kiel, Germany, June 21, 1930; s. Maximilian Ferdinand and Erna Friederike (Sasz) P.; m. Anna Martini, 1989; children: Thomas, Eva Milena, Caroline Aksinja, Amadeus Christian, Florestan Eusebius. Student, U. Freiburg, Germany, U. Heidelberg, Germany; MD, U. Kiel, Germany, 1957. Physician, chief physiciaan Psychiat. and Nerve Clinic, Christian Albrecht U., Kiel, Germany, 1959-69; prof., chmn. neuropsychiatry Gutenberg U., Mainz, Germany, 1969-79; prof., chmn. dept. neurology and psychiatry U. Cologne, Germany, 1979—. Author: Dictionary of Psychiatry, 1971, 5th edit., 1996; author, editor 34 books; also over 300 articles. Fellow Am. Psychiat. Assn. (hon.); mem. German Soc. for Psychiatry and Nervous Diseases (pres. 1991-92), Com. World Psychiat. Assn., Internat. Assn. Germanophon Psychiatrists (pres. 1996—) and 15 other sci. socs. Office: Joseph-Stelzmann-Strasse 9, D-50931 Cologne Germany

PETERS, VICKIE JANN, health care educator; b. Los Angeles, May 1, 1951; d. Edward and Elsie (Galyardt) Neuvert; m. Milan James Peters, June 24, 1972; 1 child, Milan Anthony. BS, Mount St. Mary's Coll., 1973; MS, Calif. State U., 1977, MA, 1978. RN, Calif.; CPHQ. Adminstrv. dir. So. Calif. Orthopedic Rsch. and Edn. ctr., Van Nuys, 1988-92; nursing faculty Calif. State U., Dominguez Hills, 1988-92; nursing educator Valley Presbyn. Hosp., Van Nuys, 1973-87; quality assurance mgr. So. Calif. Renal Disease Coun., L.A., 1991-95; quality mgmt. dir. Hemodialysis, Inc., Glendale, Calif., 1995-96, prin., CEO VJP Quality Mgmt. Consultations, 1996—; cons. in field. Contbr. articles to profl. jours. Mem. The Cousteau Soc., Norfolk, Va., 1988. Mem. The Diabetes Educator Jour., AM. Assn. Diabetes Educators, Sigma Theta Tau, Phi Kappa Phi. Republican. Presbyterian. Home: 4228 Laurelgrove Ave Studio City CA 91604-1623

PETERS, WALTER R., surgeon, educator; b. Macomb, Ill., May 4, 1957; m. Gwenna G. Peters; children: Kathryn Elise, Pamela Lynn. BS in Chemistry with highest honors, Western Ill. U., 1978; MD, Washington U., 1982. Intern in surgery The Jewish Hosp. of St. Louis, 1982-83, asst. resident in surgery, 1983-86, chief resident in surgery, 1986-87, clin. fellow in colon and rectal surgery, 1987-88; clin. asst. in surgery Washington U. Sch. Medicine, 1982-88; active staff Boone Hosp. Ctr., Columbia, Mo., 1988; active staff Columbia (Mo.) Regional Hosp., 1988, chmn. dept. surgery, 1991-92; clin. asst. prof. surgery U. Mo., Columbia, 1991—; presenter in field. Contbr. articles to profl. jours. Recipient James L. O'Leary Neurosci. prize, 1979, Leon J. Fox Excellence in Orthopedics award, 1983-84. Mem. Phi Kappa Phi, Alpha Omega Alpha. Office: Ste 104 3401 Berrywood Dr Columbia MO 65201

PETERSDORF, ROBERT GEORGE, physician, medical educator; b. Berlin, Feb. 14, 1926; s. Hans H. and Sonja P.; m. Patricia Horton Qua, June 2, 1951; children: Stephen Hans, John Eric. BA, Brown U., 1948, DMS (hon.), 1983; MD cum laude, Yale U., 1952; ScD (hon.), Albany Med. Coll., 1979; MA (hon.), Harvard U., 1980; DMS (hon.), Med. Coll. Pa., 1982, Brown U., 1983; DMS, Bowman-Gray Sch. Medicine, 1986; LHD (hon.), N.Y. Med. Coll., 1986; DSc (hon.), SUNY, Bklyn., 1987, Med. Coll. Ohio, 1987, Univ. Health Scis., The Chgo. Med. Sch., 1987, St. Louis U., 1988; LHD (hon.), Ea. Va. Med. Sch., 1988; DSc (hon.), Sch. Medicine, Georgetown U., 1991, Emory U., 1992, Tufts U., 1993, Mt. Sinai Sch. Medicine, 1993, George Washington U., 1994; other hon. degrees. Diplomate Am. Bd. Internal Medicine. Intern, asst. resident Yale U., New Haven, 1952-54; sr. asst. resident Peter Bent Brigham Hosp., Boston, 1954-55; fellow Johns Hopkins Hosp., Balt., 1955-59; chief resident, instr. medicine Yale U., 1957-58; asst. prof. medicine Johns Hopkins U., 1957-60, physician, 1958-60; assoc. prof. medicine U. Wash., Seattle, 1960-62, prof., 1962-79, chmn. dept. medicine, 1964-79; physician-in-chief U. Wash. Hosp., 1964-79; pres. Brigham and Women's Hosp., Boston, 1979-81; prof. medicine Harvard U. Med. Sch., Boston, 1979-81; dean, vice chancellor health scis. U. Calif.-San Diego Sch. Medicine, 1981-86; clin. prof. infectious diseases Sch. Medicine Georgetown U., 1986-94; pres. Assn. Am. Med. Colls., Washington, 1986-94, pres. emeritus, 1994—; prof. medicine U. Wash., 1994—, disting. prof., 1995; disting. physician Vets. Health Adminstrn., Seattle, 1994—; cons. to surgeon gen. USPHS, 1960-75; cons. USPHS Hosp., Seattle, 1962-79; mem. spl. med. adv. group VA, 1987-94. Editor: Harrison's Priciples of Internal Medicine, 1968-90; contbr. numerous articles to profl. jours. Served with USAAF, 1944-46. Recipient Lilly medal Royal Coll. Physicians, London, 1978, Wiggers award Albany Med. Coll., 1979, Robert H. Williams award Assn. Profs. Medicine, 1983, Keen award Brown U., 1980, Disting. Svc. award Baylor Coll. Medicine, 1989, Scroll of Merit Nat. Med. Assn., 1990, 2d Ann. Founder's award Assn. Program Dirs. in Internal Medicine, 1991, Flexner award Assn. Amer. Med. Coll., 1994; named Disting. Internist of 1987, Am. Soc. Internal Medicine; Disting. Teacher award 1993, Amer. Coll. of Physicians. Felow AAAS, ACP (prs. 1975-76, Stengel award 1980, Disting. Tchr. award 1993), Am. Coll. Physician Execs. (hon.); mem. Inst. Medicine of NAS (councillor 1977-80), Assn. Am. Physicians (pres. 1976-77), Cosmos Club, Rainier Club. Home and Office: 1219 Parkside Dr E Seattle WA 98112-3717

PETERSEN, CHERYL ANN, hospital official; b. Boston, Sept. 23, 1964; d. Jack Leroy and Claudette (Lemire) P. BS, Tex. Woman's U., 1989. Coord. DRG Profl. Found. for Health Care, Jacksonville, Fla., 1990-91; dir. med. records Ed Fraser Meml. Hosp., Macclenny, Fla., 1991—. Vol. City Rescue Mission, Mus. Sci. and History, Jacksonville Zoo. Recipient Presdl. Sports award President's Coun. on Phys. Fitness and Sports, 1994. Mem. AHIMA (cert. RRA and CCS), Fla. HIMA, Nat. Zool. Soc., U.S. Taekwondo Union, World Taekwondo Fedn. Libertarian. Office: Ed Fraser Meml Hosp 159 N 3d St Macclenny FL 32063

PETERSEN, FINN BO, oncologist, educator; b. Copenhagen, Mar. 26, 1951; came to U.S., 1983; s. Jorgen and Ebba Gjeding (Jorgensen) P.; m. Merete Secher Lund, Mar. 7, 1979; children: Lars Secher, Thomas Secher, Andreas Secher. BA, Niels Steensen, Copenhagen, 1971; MD, U. Copenhagen, 1978. Intern in internal medicine Copenhagen, 1978-79, resident in hematology, 1980-83; fellow oncology Fred Hutchinson Cancer Rsch. Ctr. U. Wash., Seattle, 1983-85, assoc. researcher oncology, 1985-87, asst. mem. in clin. rsch., 1987-91, asst. prof., 1988-91, prof. medicine, 1992—; clin. dir. bone marrow transplant program U. Utah Sch. Medicine, 1992—. Author: Hematology, 1977; contbr. articles to profl. jours. Mem. AMA, AAAS, Internat. Soc. Exptl. Hematology, Am. Soc. Clin. Oncology, Am. Soc. Hematology, Assn. Gnotobiology. Office: U Uath Bone Marrow Transplant Program Div of Hematology and Oncology Salt Lake City UT 84132

PETERSEN, GAYLE ANNA, director clinical education; b. Moline, Ill., Aug. 11, 1961; d. LeRoy Francis and Barbara Jean (Korb) P. AS, Black Hawk Coll., 1981; BS, Coll. St. Francis, Joliet, Ill., 1987, MS, 1992. Cert. respiratory therapy technician, pulmonary function technologist; registered respiratory therapist. Respiratory therapist Luth. Hosp., Moline, Ill., 1981-84; dir. clin. edn. respiratory care programs Ill. Cen. Coll., East Peoria, 1984—; item writer Nat. Bd. for Respiratory Care, Shawnee Mission, Kans., 1985—; instr. CPR, Am. Heart Assn., 1985—, advanced cardiac life support provider, 1985-86. Mem. Am. Assn. Respiratory Care, Ill. Soc. for Respiratory Care (chmn. local chpt. 1984-86, 95—, v.p. 1989-90, chmn. pub. rels. 1989-91, chmn. recruitment 1991-92, chpt. rep. 1994-95, respiratory care accreditation bd. 1995-96). Home: 518 W Lawndale Ave Peoria IL 61604-1532 Office: Ill Ctrl Coll Dept Health and Pub Svcs 201 SW Adams Peoria IL 61635-0001

PETERSEN, KYLE, osteopath; b. Smithtown, N.Y., Apr. 10, 1968; s. Robert Ellis and Christina Mary (Dingwall) P. BS in Biotech. with distinction, Worcester Poly. Inst., 1990; DO with honors, U. Osteo. Medicine/Health Scis, 1994; cert. undersea med. officer, Naval Undersea Medicine Inst., 1995. Diplomate Am. Bd. Osteopathic Med. Examiners. Commd. ensign USN, 1990, advanced through grades to lt., 1994; intern dept. internal medicine US Naval Hosp., Portsmouth, Va., 1994-95; diving, emergency rm. physician US Naval Hosp., Roosevelt Roads, P.R., 1996—. Mem. ACP, Am. Osteo. Assn., Assn. of Mil. Osteo. Physicians and Surgeons. Presbyterian. Office: US Naval Hosp Roosevelt Rds PSC 1008 Box 3007 FPO AA 34051

PETERSEN, ROBERT ALLEN, pediatric ophthalmologist; b. N.Y.C., Dec. 30, 1933; s. Harold Marinus and Elinor Louise (Buckley) P.; m. Veronica Margiana Stinnes, Dec. 22, 1956; children: Anne, Catherine, John. BS, CUNY, 1955; MD, Columbia U., 1959, DrMedSc, 1964. Diplomate Am. Bd. Ophthalmology. Med. resident Presbyn. Hosp., N.Y.C., 1959-61; USPHS postdoctoral fellow Columbia U. Coll. Physicians and Surgeons, N.Y.C., 1961-62; USPHS preclin. trainee Howe Lab. of Ophthalmology, MEEI, Boston, 1962-63; resident in ophthalmology Mass. Eye and Ear Infirmary, Boston, 1963-66; instr. in ophthalmology to asst. prof. Harvard Med. Sch., Boston, 1970—; assoc. in Ophthalmology to sr. assoc. Children's Hosp., Boston, 1966—. Contbr. over 40 articles to profl. jours. Cons., vision task force Mass. Dept. Pub. Health, 1981-85. Major U.S. Army, 1967-69, South Vietnam. Various rsch. grants NIH, 1961-63, 94—. Fellow Am. Acd. Ophthalmology, Am. Acad. Pediatrics; mem. Am. Assn. for Pediatric Ophthalmology and Strabismus (bd. dirs. 1974-76, edn. com. 1987—, chair Costenbader Lectureship com. 1993—, chair site selection com. 1995—), New Eng. Ophthal. Soc. Mem. Soc. of Friends. Office: Children's Hosp 300 Longwood Ave Boston MA 02115-5724

PETERSEN, SCOTT RICHARD, surgeon, health facility administrator; b. Salt Lake City, Jan. 31, 1949; s. Thad Landeen and Bette Jane (Peck) P.; m. Cecile Norma Christensen, Sept. 10, 1971 (div. Oct. 1981); children: Lisa Ashley Nielsen, Scott Benjamin; m. Elizabeth Umphred, Dec. 5, 1981; children: Breck, Lee. BS in Med. Biology, U. Utah, 1972, MD, 1974. Diplomate Am. Bd. Surgery. Intern U. Calif., San Francisco, 1974-75; resident in surgery U. Utah Affiliated Hosp., Salt Lake City, 1975-79; NIH fellow San Francisco Gen. Hosp., 1977-78; asst. prof. dept. surgery U. Utah Sch. Med., Salt Lake City, 1980-82; asst. chief surgery Kaiser Found. Hosp., Honolulu, 1982-83; dir. trauma John C. Lincoln Hosp., Phoenix, 1983-91; dir. trauma ctr. St. Joseph's Hosp. and Med. Ctr., Phoenix, 1991—; assoc. clin. prof. surgery U. Nebr. Med. Ctr., Omaha, 1986—; chmn., bd. dirs. Ariz. Emergency Med. Sys., Phoenix, 1992—; vice chmn. state trauma adv. bd. Dept. Health Svcs. Ariz., Phoenix, 1994—. Contbr. over 50 articles to profl. pubs. Treas., founding mem. U.S. Marshals Posse Dist. Ariz., Phoenix, 1989—; bd. dirs. White Mt. Range Riders, Springerville, Ariz., 1985—. Recipient Roch award U. Utah Coll. Med., 1974; grantee NIH, 1994. Fellow ACP (Ariz. state chmn. 1995—, Resident's award 1978); mem. Am. Assn. Surgery of Trauma, Phoenix Surg. Soc. (pres. 1995—), Western Trauma Assn., S.W. Surg. Assn. Republican. Office: Trauma Ctr St Josephs Hosp 350 W Thomas Rd Phoenix AZ 85013

PETERSON, ALAN LEE, psychologist; b. Riverside, Calif., Jan. 16, 1958; s. Charles William and Jean Edith Peterson; m. Sandra Karen Hicks, Apr. 8, 1980; children: Dane Alan, Stefan Alan. BA, U. Cen. Fla., 1980; MS, Nova U., 1986, PhD, 1990. Lic. psychologist. Commd. 2d lt. USAF, 1980, advanced through grades to capt., 1986; adjutant Holloman AFB, Alamogordo, N.Mex., 1980-84; chief resident clin. psychology Wilford Hall USAF Med. Ctr., San Antonio, 1988-89, postdoctoral fellow behavioral health psychology, 1989-90; chief health psychology svcs. Keesler USAF Med. Ctr., Biloxi, Miss., 1990-93; chief behavioral health psychology RAF Lakenheath Hosp., 1993—; adj. prof. U. So. Miss., Long Beach, 1990-93; internat. authority on behavioral treatment of Tourette syndrome; presenter in field. Contbr. articles to sci. jours. Rsch. grantee Tourette Syndrome Assn., Bayside, N.Y., 1986. Mem. APA, Assn. for Advancement of Behavior Therapy, Soc. Behavioral Medicine, Soc. Air Force Clin. Psychologists, Assn. Applied and Preventive Psychology, Miss. Psychol. Assn. Office: RAF Lakenheath Hosp PO Box 2967 APO AE 09464

PETERSON, ANNAMARIE JANE, medical record administrator; b. Eveleth, Minn., Aug. 9, 1936; d. Martin Henry and Agnes Elizabeth (Nyfors) Brown; m. Carl Dewane Peterson, Oct. 7, 1956 (div. Jan. 1968); children: Martine C. Peterson Trihey, Karin R. Peterson Harris, Carl Frederick (dec.). Student, Va. Jr. Coll., 1955, U. Minn., 1956; BA, Coll. of St. Scholastica, 1973. Pvt. practice interior design and drapery cons. Duluth and Two Harbors, Minn., 1966-72; dir. med. records Holy Family Hosp., Superior, Wis., 1973-75; dir. health info. svcs. Miller-Dwan Med. Ctr., Duluth, 1975—; clin. supr. Coll. of St. Scholastica, Duluth, 1973—; mem. supervisory com. med. secretarial program Duluth Tech. Coll., 1979—; cons. St. Francis Nursing Home, Superior, 1975-78, Pk. Point Manor, Duluth, 1982-84; cons., com. mem. to develop med. transcription telecomms. project NorthSpan, Duluth, 1987-89. Dem. Farmer Labor del., 1988; chmn. Lake County Devel. Commn., 1984-92; mem. Lake County Housing and Redevel. Authority, 1984—, chmn., 1992—; mem. Knife River Community Coun., 1989, Lake County Steering Com. for Blanding Community Leadership Program, 1989, Two Harbors Vision & Heritage Commn., 1994—; mem. fund. distbn. panel Duluth United Way, 1990-94; active Duluth Clinic Inst. Rev. Bd., 1978-94, Duluth Vis. and Conv. Bur.; del. People to People Health Info. Del., China, 1995. Mem. Am. Health Info. Mgmt. Assn., Minn. Health Info. Mgmt. Assn. (nominating com. 1980, bylaws com. 1981, del. dir. 1989, pres.-elect 1990, pres. 1991-92), N.E. Minn. Med. Records Assn. (program chmn. 1977-79, pres. 1987-89), Two Harbors Area C. of C., North Shore Assn., Altrusa Club Duluth. Presbyterian. Home: Depot Campground Scenic Hwy 61 Knife River MN 55609 Office: Miller Dwan Med Ctr 502 E 2nd St Duluth MN 55805-1913

PETERSON, BRUCE DWIGHT, hospital administrator; b. Joliet, Ill., Aug. 30, 1948; s. Sidney Bernard and Doris (Goodwick) P.; m. Susan Marie Hazelo, June 23, 1973; children: Kristin, Jessica, Jonathan. BSME, GM Inst., 1971; MBA, U. Wis., Whitewater, 1982; MHA, U. Minn., Mpls., 1991. Registered profl. engr., nursing home adminstr. Coop. student GM, Janesville, Wis., 1966-79, indsl. engr., 1970-75, plant engr., 1975-82; v.p. Jane Lamb Health Ctr., Clinton, Iowa, 1982-89; adminstr. Mercer County Hosp., Aledo, Ill., 1989—; Mercer County Health Dept., 1989—. Bd. dirs. Skyline Ctr., Clinton, 1983-88, Skyline Residential Svcs., Clinton, 1984-88, New Life Crisis Pregnancy Ctr., Clinton, 1987-89, Mercer Found. for Health, Aledo, 1990—; chmn. Greater Quad City Hosp. Coun., 1992-93. Mem. Am. Coll. Healthcare Execs., Healthcare Fin. Mgmt. Assn., Nat. Rural Health Assn., Ill. Hosp. Assn., Ill. Rural Health Assn., Ill. Pub. Health Assn., Aledo C. of C., Aledo Kiwanis (v.p. 1990-91, pres. 1992-93). Office: Mercer County Hosp 409 NW 9th Ave Aledo IL 61231-1258

PETERSON, CARL MARVIN HARLAN, surgeon; b. Barksdale Field, La., Oct. 24, 1943; s. Carol Monroe and Mary Ellen (Peterson) P.; m. Datha Darlene Guest, Apr. 9, 1966; children: Shelley, David, Sue Lynn, Jared, Joseph. BS in Edn., N.W. Mo. State Coll., Maryville, 1965, BA in Biology, 1968; MD, U. Mo., 1974. Diplomate in surgery Am. Bd. Surgery. Intern Mercy Hosp., Des Moines, 1974-75; resident surgery VA Hosp., Des Moines, 1975-79, staff gen. surgeon, 1979—. Contbr. articles to profl. jours. Bd. dirs. Beaverdale Little League, Des Moines, 1988-90. With U.S. Army, 1963. Fellow ACS; mem. Am. Soc. Gastrointestinal Endoscopy. Home: 3330 Douglas Ave Des Moines IA 50310

PETERSON, CAROL ANN, health care consultant; b. Atlanta, July 29, 1947; d. Francis Andrew and Margie Nell (Hollehan) Ferko; m. Franz Richard Peterson, Sept. 22, 1972; 1 child, Jamie Elizabeth. BSN, U. Ariz., 1969; M in Nursing, U. S.C., 1981. RN, Fla. Staff nurse U.S. Naval Hosp., San Diego, 1969-71, U.S. Naval Dispensary, Adak, Ala., 1971-72; charge nurse Naval Hosp. Boston, Chelsea, Mass., 1972-74; charge nurse, patient care coordinator for staffing Naval Regional Med. Ctr., Charleston, S.C., 1977-80; charge nurse, patient care coordinator Naval Regional Med. Ctr., Jacksonville, Fla., 1981-84; instr. Naval Sch. Health Scis., Bethesda, 1984-88; asst. dir. nursing svcs. Operation Desert Shield, 1990-91; clin. instr. Nat. Naval Med. Ctr., Bethesda, 1974-77, assoc. dir. nursing, 1988-92; dir. nursing svc. Orlando Naval Hosp., 1992-95; ret. U.S. Navy, 1995.; cons. and trainer CP Consults, Orlando, Fla., 1995-96; asst. prof. nursing Fla. Hosp. Coll. Health Scis., Orlando, 1996—. Mem. Assn. for Psychol. Types, Sigma Theta Tau. Roman Catholic. Home: 3868 Golden Meadow Ct Oviedo FL 32765-9207

PETERSON, DONALD DUANE, physician; b. Bozeman, Mont., Dec. 16, 1949; s. Robert Duane and Gretchen Anne (Lehman) P.; m. Rosemary de Lourdes Casey; children: Donald, James, Timothy, Rosemary. BS, U. Notre Dame, 1971; MD, Harvard Med. Sch., 1975. Diplomate Am. Bd. Internal Medicine, Bd. Pulmonary Diseases, Bd. Critical Care Medicine, Bd. Sleep Disorders Medicine. Asst. prof. medicine Jefferson Med. Coll., Phila., 1982-91, assoc. prof., 1991—; dir. Sleep Disorders Ctr., chief divsn. pulmonary and critical care medicine Lankenau Hosp., Wynnewood, Pa., 1989—; sec. crit. care exam. com. Am. Bd. Internal Medicine, 1989-95. Contbr. articles to profl. jours. and publs. Fellow Am. Coll. Physician, Am. Coll. Chest Physicians, Am. Thoracic Soc., Am. Sleep Disorders Assn., Laennec Soc. (pres. 1985). Roman Catholic. Home: 910 Stony Ln Gladwyne PA 19035 Office: 230 Lankenau Med Bldg Wynnewood PA 19096

PETERSON, DONALD FRED, physiologist, educator; b. Great Bend, Kans., Aug. 4, 1941; s. Donald F. and Mary K. (Doerr) P.; m. Bonnie Jean Campbell, July 30, 1967; children: Cori, Bailey, Ronald. Student, U. Sorbonne, Paris, 1962-63; BS in Zoology, Kans. State U., 1965, PhD in Physiology, 1970. Postdoctoral fellow U. Utah Med. Ctr., Salt Lake City, 1969-71; instr. U. Tex. Health Sci. Ctr., San Antonio, 1971-73, asst. prof., 1973-77, assoc. prof., 1977-78; assoc. prof. Oral Roberts U. Med. Ctr., Tulsa, 1978-88, prof., chmn. physiology, 1988-90; prof., chmn. physiology Kirksville (Mo.) Coll. Osteo. Medicine, 1990—. Mem. extra-curricular task force Kirksville (Mo.) Sch. Dist., 1995, pres. Kirksville Boosters, 1994-95. Recipient Rsch. Career Devel. award NIH, 1976. Fellow Am. Physiol. Soc.; mem. Am. Heart Assn. (chmn. Mo. peer rev. com. 1995-96, bd. dirs. and exec. com. Mo. affiliate 1996—), Sigma Xi. Mem. Ch. of Christ. Home: 2201 Crestline Dr Kirksville MO 63501-5709 Office: Kirksville Coll. Osteo Med Dept Physiology 800 W Jefferson Kirksville MO 63501-1443

PETERSON, DONALD ROBERT, psychologist, educator, university administrator; b. Pillager, Minn., Sept. 10, 1923; s. Frank Gordon and Ruth (Friedland) P.; m. Jean Hole, Feb. 10, 1952 (div.); children: Wendy, Jeffrey, Roger, Lisa; m. Jane Snyder Salmon., Dec. 21, 1974. BA, U. Minn., 1948, MA, 1950, PhD, 1952. Mem. faculty U. Ill., Urbana, 1952-75, prof. clin. psychology, 1963-75, head div. clin. psychology, 1963-70, dir. Psychol. Clinic, 1961-70, dir. D. Psychology program, 1970-75; dean Grad. Sch. Applied and Profl. Psychology Rutgers U., New Brunswick, 1975-89; pres. Nat. Coun. Schs. of Profl. Psychology, 1981-83. Author: The Clinical Study of Social Behavior, 1968; co-author: Close Relationships, 1983; also articles; editor Jour. Abnormal Psychology, 1970-72. With AUS, 1943-46. Mem. N.J. Psychol. Assn., Am. Psychol. Assn. (awards for disting. contbns. to practice of psychology 1983, disting. contbns. to edn. and tng. 1989). Office: Rutgers U Grad Sch Applied & Profl Psychology New Brunswick NJ 08903

PETERSON, DOUGLAS ARTHUR, physician; b. Princeton, N.Y., Sept. 13, 1945; s. Arthur Roy William and Marie Hilma (Anderson) P.; m. Virginia Kay Eng., June 24, 1967; children: Rachel, Daniel, Rebecca. BA, St. Olaf, 1966; PhD, U. Minn., 1971, MD, 1975. Postdoctoral fellow U. Pitts., 1971-72; intern Hennepin County Med. Ctr., Mpls., 1975-76, resident in medicine, 1976-78; physician Bloomington Lake Clinic, Mpls., 1978-82; staff physician Mpls. VA Med. Ctr., Mpls., 1992—, chief compensation and pension, 1992—; asst. prof. U. Minn., 1985—. Bd. dirs. Rolling Acres Home, Victoria, Minn., 1985—. Lt. Col. M.C., USAR. Mem. AAAS, Am. Assn. Pathologists, N.Y. Acad. Scis. Home: 5008 Queen Ave S Minneapolis MN 55410 Office: VA Med Ctr One Veterans Dr Minneapolis MN 55417

PETERSON, JACK EDWIN, industrial hygiene consultant, chemical engineer; b. Bremerton, Wash., Feb. 7, 1928; s. Clarence Edwin and Hulda Doris (Lund) P.; m. Cecelia Frances Miller, Sept. 7, 1952; children: Brian Lee, Eric Wayne. BSChemE, Wash. State U., 1951; MSChemE, U. Mich., 1952, PhD in Indsl. HEalth, 1968. Registered profl. engr., Wis.; cert. indsl. hygienist. Environ. health engr. Dow Chem. Co., Midland, Mich., 1952-65; from asst. to assoc. prof. Marquette U., Milw., 1968-80, Med. Coll. Wis., Milw., 1968-75; prcf. U. Ill., Chgo., 1977-80; prof. allied health U. Wis.-Parkside, Kenosha, 1984-86; indsl. hygienist cons. Peterson Assocs., Brookfield, Wis., 1975-91; indsl. hygiene cons. Alpine, Calif., 1991—. Author: Industrial Health, 1977, 2nd rev. edit., 1991; contbr. articles to Jour. Applied Physiology, Am. Indsl. Hygiene Assn. Jour., Sci. Cpl. U.S. Army, 1945-46, PTO. Mem. Am. Indsl. Hygiene Assn. (Outstanding Papers awards 1962, 70, Wis. chpt. Byron A. Berg award 1989), Am. Acad. Indsl. Hygiene (councilor 1975-78, v.p. 1995, Henry F. Smyth award 1987). Office: 2830 Via Viejas Oeste Alpine CA 91901-3152

PETERSON, JAMES HILL, otolaryngology surgeon; b. Ovid, Colo., June 17, 1937; s. Arthur E. and Tressa (Hill) P.; m. Sylvia Ann Rigg, June 3, 1961; children: Anne-Marie, James Jr., Amanda. MD, U. Nebr., 1966. Diplomate Am. Bd. Otolaryngology. Intern Good Samaritan Hosp., Phoenix, 1966-67; resident in ear, eye, nose and throat U. Kans. Med. Ctr., Kansas City, 1969-73; surgeon No. Colo. Ear, Nose and Thraot Hosp., Greeley, Colo., 1973—; surgeon Ft. Morgan Cmty. Hosp., Greeley, Colo., 1973—; staff ear, nose and throat physician No. Colo. Med. Ctr., Sterling Regional Med. Ctr., McKee Med. Ctr., Loveland, Colo., East Morgan County Hosp., Brush, Colo., Wray Cmty. Hosp.; tchg. cons. U. Colo. Served to capt. U.S. Army, 1967-69. Fellow Am. Acad. Otolaryngology-Head and Neck Surgery; mem. Rotary. Republican. Office: 2528 16th St Greeley CO 80631-4902

PETERSON, JAMES ROBERT, retired engineering psychologist; b. St. Paul, Apr. 16, 1932; s. Palmer Elliot and Helen Evelyn (Carlson) P.; BA in Psychology cum laude, U. Minn., 1954; MA in Exptl. Psychology, 1958; PhD in Engring. Psychology, U. Mich., 1965; m. Marianna J. Stockvig, June 26, 1954; 1 child, Anne Christine. Devel. engr. Honeywell Inc., 1961-65, sr. devel. engr., 1965-67, staff engr., 1967-90, sr. project staff engr., 1990-93, ret., 1993; Honeywell sponsor rep. Shuttle Student Involvement Program, 1982, 84. Served with USMC, 1954-57, with Res., 1957-62. Assoc. fellow AIAA; mem. Human Factors and Ergonomics Soc. (life), Air & Space Mus. (charter), Smithsonian Inst. Club: Mason. Contbr. articles to profl. jours. Achievements include invention of Apollo translation hand controller; participation in development work on all U.S. Manned Space Programs (Mercury, Gemini, Apollo, Lunar Excursion Module, Manned Orbiting Laboratory, Space Shuttle and Space Station) as member/manager of associated human factors groups. Home: 3303 San Gabriel St Clearwater FL 34619-3341

PETERSON, JANET ANNE, pharmaceutical executive; b. Jersy City, June 15, 1961; d. Arthur Conrad and Gail Lois (Flury) P.; m. Mark Edward Bell, May 26, 1984; children: Matthew, Thomas, Andrew. BS cum laude, U. Mass., 1983; MS, Rutgers U., 1988, PhD, 1992. Lab. technician N.Y. Blood Ctr., N.Y.C., 1984-85; adj. prof. Kean Coll., Union, N.J., 1990-91; assoc. med. dir. Roberts Pharmaceutical, Eatontown, NJ, 1992-93; assoc. dir. med. affairs Enzon, Inc., Piscataway, N.J., 1993-94; assoc. dir. safety evaluation and epidemiology Pfizer Inc., N.Y.C., 1994-96; assoc. dir. sci. affairs Pfizer Internat. Inc., N.Y.C., 1996—; freelance med. writer, Highlands, N.J., 1990-92. Recipient Nat. Rsch. Svc. award, NIH, 1986-91. Mem. AAAS, Drug Info. Assn., N.Y. Acad. Scis. Roman Catholic. Home: 33 Shrewsbury Ave Highlands NJ 07732-1740 Office: Pfizer Inc Regulatory Affairs Divsn 235 E 42nd St New York NY 10017-5703

PETERSON, KENT WRIGHT, physician; b. Portsmouth, Va., Apr. 16, 1943; s. Gerald Milton and Julia Elizabeth (Hoover) P.; m. Virginia Mae Sonne, Dec. 26, 1979; children: Liesl Lynn, Owen Sonne. B.A., U. N.C., Chapel Hill, 1964; M.D., U. Pa., 1968. Diplomate Am. Bd. Gen. Preventive Medicine and Occupational Medicine. Intern U. Wis., 1968-69, resident, 1970-71; Robert Wood Johnson clin. scholar George Washington U., 1975-77; family physician E. Madison Clinic, Madison, Wis., 1969; chief med. officer policy devel. U.S. Cost of Living Council, Washington, 1973-74; assoc. dir. Assn. Univ. Programs in Health Adminstrn., Washington, 1974-77; exec. v.p. Am. Coll. Preventive Medicine, Washington, 1977-81; corp. mgr. preventive and environ. medicine IBM Corp., White Plains, N.Y., 1981-84; corp. med. dir. Am. Standard, N.Y.C., 1984-86; pres. Occupational Health Strategies, Charlottesville, Va., 1984—; clin. asst. prof. Georgetown U. Sch. Medicine, 1979-85; clin. assoc. prof. NYU dept. environ. medicine, 1985—; rep. to Coun. Med. Specialty Socs., 1980-86; mem. Accreditation Coun. for Continuing Med. Edn., 1981-86; treas. Med. Rev. Officer Cert. Coun., 1992—; v.p. Am. Bd. of Ind. Med. Examiners, 1995—. Author books including Directory of Occupational Health and Safety Software, 9th edit., 1996, Handbook of Health Risk Appraisals, 3d edit., 1996; contbr. nuermous articles to profl. jours. and chpts. to books. Pres. Children of the Americas Found., 1979-84. Served to maj. M.C. U.S. Army, 1971-73. Fellow Am. Coll. Preventative Medicine, Am. Coll. Occupl. and Environ. medicine (chmn. computers in occupl. medicine com. 1986-90); mem. AMA, APHA, Assn. Tchrs. Preventive Medicine, N.Y. Acad. Medicine, Ramazzini Soc., Soc. Prospective Medicine (officer) World Future Soc., Coun. for Liveable World, Va. Occupl. Medicine Assn. (pres. 1988-90). Home: 7767 Faber Rd Faber VA 22938-9715 Office: Occupational Health Strategies Inc 901 Preston Ave Ste 400 Charlottesville VA 22903-4491

PETERSON, LARRY JAMES, medical educator, oral surgeon; b. Winfield, Kans., Apr. 23, 1942; m. Susan Bartlett; children: Brie, Tucker. BS, U. Kans., 1964; DDS cum laude, U. Mo., Kans. City, 1968; MS, Georgetown U., 1971. Diplomate Am. Bd. Oral and Maxillofacial Surgery. Oral surgery resident Georgetown U. Sch. Dentistry, Washington, 1968-71; active staff Eugene Talmadge Meml. Hosp., Augusta, Ga., 1971-75, John N. Dempsey Hosp., Farmington, Conn., 1975-82, Ohio State U. Hosp., Columbus, 1982—, Children's Hosp., Columbus, 1982—; asst. prof. oral surgery Med. Coll. Ga. Sch. Dentistry, Augusta, 1971-74, assoc. prof. oral surgery, 1974-75; assoc. prof. oral and maxillofacial surgery U. Conn. Sch. Dental Medicine, Farmington, 1975-81; program dir. oral and maxillofacial surgery residency U. Conn. Affiliated Program, Farmington, 1980-82; prof. oral and maxillofacial surgery U. Conn. Sch. Dental Medicine, Farmington, 1981-82; prof., chmn. oral and maxillofacial surgery and pathology Ohio State U. Coll. Dentistry, Columbus, 1982—; adv. com. Am. Bd. Oral and Maxillofacial Surgeons 1980-86, assoc. subject leader 1982-84, subject leader 1984-86. Editor: (textbook) Contemporary Oral and Maxillofacial Surgery, (multi-vol. ref. book) Principles of Oral and Maxillofacial Surgery; contbr. over 40 articles to profl. jours., 25 chpts. to books; editor oral surgery sect. Clinical Dentistry, 1981-87, oral and maxillofacial surgery sect. Oral Surgery, Oral Medicine, Oral Pathology, 1992—, editor-in-chief 1993—; editl. bd. Jour. Oral and Maxillofacial Surgery 1991-92; presenter in field. Recipient awards Am. Coll. Dentists, 1984, Internat. Coll. Dentists, 1992; Mosby scholar 1968. Fellow Am. Dental Soc. of Anesthesiology; mem. ADA (cons., oral and maxillofacial surgery site visitor, commn. on dental accreditation 1985-91, nat. dental bd. test constrn. com. oral and maxillofacial surgery 1985-90, nat. dental bd. part II restructuring com. 1987-92, cons. coun. on dental therapeutics 1980-92), Am. Assn. of Oral and Maxillofacial Surgeons (rsch. adv. com. 1976-79, test constrn. com. 1978-91, com. on scientific sessions 1991-94, com. on residency edn. and tng. 1992—, del. Ho. Dels. 1991-94), Internat. Assn. for Dental Rsch., Am. Assn. Dental Schs., Acad. of Osteointegration, Assn. for Acad. Surgery, Surg. Infection Soc., Alliance for Prudent Use of Antibiotics, Ohio Dental Assn., Ohio Soc. Oral and Maxillofacial Surgeons, Great Lakes Soc. Oral and Maxillofacial Surgeons, Columbus Dental Soc., Sigma Xi, Omicron Kappa Upsilon. Office: Ohio State U Coll Dentistry Dept Oral and Max Surgery 305 West 12th Ave Columbus OH 43210-1241*

PETERSON, PAUL QUAYLE, retired university dean, physician; b. Marissa, Ill., June 30, 1912; s. Charles Logan and Phoebe (Lewis) P.; m. Kathryn Lentz, Aug. 1936; children—Philip Lewis, Frances Anne; m. Mildred Cook Allison, Dec. 7, 1957; foster children—Patricia Elaine Allison, Susan Claire Allison. B.S., U. Ill., 1933, M.D., 1937; M.P.H., U. Mich., 1946. Diplomte Am. Bd. Preventive Medicine (service mem., vice chmn. 1976—). Intern Bethesda Hosp., Cin., 1936-37; gen. resident Meml. Hosp., Lima, Ohio, 1937-38; gen. practice medicine McLeansboro, Ill., 1939-40; practice medicine specializing in preventive medicine, 1940-46; health officer Breckenridge, Meade and Hancock counties, Ky., 1940-41, Warren, Simpson and Allen counties, 1942-45; regional cons., div. local health Ky. Health Dept., 1946-47; chief bur. direct services, asst. to dir. Ohio Dept. Health, 1948-51; asst. prof. preventive medicine Ohio State U., 1948-51; chief health div. Mut. Security Mission to China, Taipei, Taiwan, 1952-53; chief health and sanitation div. USOM (asso. states Cambodia, Laos and Vietnam), 1954; chief program services, div. internat. health USPHS, Washington, 1955; chronic disease program USPHS, 1957; asst. dir. Nat. Inst. Allergy and Infectious Diseases, NIH, 1958-61; dep. chief div. pub. health methods Office Surgeon Gen., 1961-62, chief div., 1962-64; asst. surgeon gen. USPHS, 1964, asso. chief bur. state services (community health), 1964-67; dep. dir. Bur. Health Services, 1967-68; asso. adminstr. Health Services and Mental Health Adminstrn., 1968-70; dep. surgeon gen., 1970; dean Grad. Sch. Pub. Health, U. Ill., Chgo., 1971-82, dean emeritus, 1982—; dir. office rsch. Ctr. Study Patient Care, U. Ill. Med. Ctr., 1979-86; dir. Ill. Dept. Pub. Health, 1977-79, Am. Bur. Med. Aid to China; mem. residency rev. com. Liaison Com. Grad. Med. Edn., 1976—; cons. Ctr. for Health Services Research, 1982—. mem. editorial bd. Pub. Health Service World, Mil. Medicine. Commr. USPHS, 1941. Recipient Disting. Service award U. Ill. Alumni Assn., 1984. Fellow Am. Pub. Health Assn. (chmn. program area com. pub. health adminstrn.); mem. Am. Assn. Pub. Health Physicians (pres. 1975-76), AMA (intersplty. adv. bd. 1975-77), Assn. Schs. Pub. Health (exec. com. 1975—), Pub. Health Service Commd. Officers Assn. (sec. D.C. 1959), AAAS, Assn. Mil Surgeons, Am. Coll. Preventive Medicine (regent 1975—), Ill. Hosp. Assn. (exec. bd. 1974-77, cert. correctional health com. of profl. cert. bd. 1990), Nat. Inst. of Health Alumni Assn. bd. dirs., 1993—, Phi Beta Pi (pres. 1935), Delta Omega. Methodist. Home: 1600 N Oak St Arlington VA 22209-2751

PETERSON, SHARON L., community health nurse; b. New Castle, Pa., June 26, 1950; d. Paul Lewis and Beatrice Marie (Payne) Zook; m. Mark J. Peterson, Aug. 5, 1972; children: Eric James, Daniel Mark, Krista Marie. BSN, Roberts Wesleyan Coll., 1972. RN, Pa., cert. comm. health. Comm. health nurse II Pa. Dept. of Health, Seneca, Pa. Facilitator Venango-Forest Prenatal Task Force, Venango-Forest Cmty. Health Action Team. Mem. ANA, Pa. Nurses Assn., Sigma Theta Tau, Clarion U. Pa. Nursing Honor Soc.

PETERSON, W(ALTER) SCOTT, ophthalmic surgeon; b. Newton, Kans., Sept. 5, 1944; s. Walter F. and Elizabeth (Wiebe) P.; m. Jean Louise Murray, Dec. 16, 1967; children: James Scott, Hilary Jean. BA summa cum laude, Yale U., 1966, MD, 1971. Diplomate Am. Bd. Ophthalmology. Ophthalmic surgeon OptiCare Eye Health Ctr., 1974—; mem. tchg. faculty Med. Sch. Yale U., New Haven, 1975—. Author: An Approach to Paterson, 1967. Bd. dirs. Waterbury Found., 1985—, v.p., 1996—; trustee Dickinson Coll., 1993—. Recipient Med. Sci. award Am. Diabetes Assn., 1980. Fellow ACS, Am. Acad. Ophthalmology; mem. MLA, New England Ophthal. Soc., William Carlos Williams Soc; Phi Beta Kappa Assocs. Office: Opti Care Eye Health Ctr 87 Grandview Ave Waterbury CT 06708-2514

PETERSON, WILLIAM FRANK, physician, administrator; b. Newark, Sept. 28, 1922; s. Edgar Charles and Margaret Benedict (Heyn) P.; m. Margaret Henderson Lee, June 28, 1946 (div. 1978); children: Margaret Lee, Edward Charles; m. 2d, Mary Ann Estelle McGrath, Nov. 29, 1980. Student, Cornell U., 1940-43; MD, N.Y. Med. Coll., 1946. Commd. lt. U.S. Air Force, 1946, advanced through grades to col., 1963; med. officer U.S. Air Force, 1946-70; chmn. dept. ob-gyn Washington Hosp. Ctr. 1970-92; dir. Women's Clinic. Washington, 1971-96, Ob-Gyn Ultrasound Lab., Washington, 1974-92; ret. 1996. Contbr. articles to profl. jours. Chmn., Maternal Mortality Com., 1981-96. Decorated Legion of Merit, 1960, 70; Cert. Achievement, Office Surgeon Gen., USAF, 1967. Fellow Am. Coll. Ob-Gyn, ACS, Nat. Bd. Med. Examiners (diplomate), Washington Gynecol. Soc. (exec. council 1980-85). Republican. Episcopalian. Home: 50 Stonegate Dr Silver Spring MD 20905-5701

PETITE, MICHAEL JAMES, psychiatrist; b. Youngstown, Ohio, Feb. 17, 1937; s. James Richard and Mary (Martin) P.; m. Jeannette Alessio, Apr. 27, 1963; children: Christopher More, Jennifer Kristen. AB in Biology, Georgetown U., 1959; M.D., Ohio State U., 1963. Diplomate Am. Bd. Psychiatry. Intern Georgetown Hosp., Washington, 1963-64, resident, 1964-67; practice medicine specializing in psychiatry Washington, 1969—; clin. assoc. prof. Georgetown Med. Sch., Washington, 1981—; cons. Georgetown U. Student Health Service, Washington, 1969—; mem. staff Sibley Meml. Hosp., Washington. Fellow Am. Psychiatr. Assn.; mem. AMA. Roman Catholic.

PETKUS, ALAN FRANCIS, microbiologist; b. Chgo., Feb. 4, 1956; s. Frank Anthony and Valeria (Shimkus) P.; m. Karan Elaine Blakely, Apr. 21, 1990; children: Sabrina Marie, Alexandra Louise. BS, Ill. Benedictine Coll., Lisle, 1979; PhD, Chgo. Med. Sch., North Chicago, 1986. Technologist Palos Community Hosp., Palos Heights, Ill., 1973-79, med. technologist, 1979-86; microbiologist South Bend (Ind.) Med. Found., 1986-91; microbiology dir. Met. Hosp., Grand Rapids, Mich., 1991—. Mem. AAAS, Am. Soc. Clin. Pathologists, Am. Soc. Microbiology, N.Y. Acad. Sci., Ill. Soc. Microbiology, South Ctrl. Assn. Microbiology. Roman Catholic. Office: Met Hosp 1919 Boston St SE Grand Rapids MI 49506-4160

PETRACEK, MICHAEL RAY, surgeon; b. Covina, Calif., Jan. 10, 1946; s. Raymond Frank and Hazel Maude (Morrison) P.; m. Constance E. Ryder, Sept. 22, 1971; children: Kristen L., Kara M., Katherine M. BS, Baylor U., 1967; MD, Johns Hopkins U., 1971. Surg. internship Johns Hopkins Hosp., Balt., 1971-72, asst. resident surgery, 1972-73; asst. resident surgery Vanderbilt U. Hosp., Nashville, 1975-78, chief surg. resident, 1978-79, resident in cardiothoracic surgery, 1979-81; cardiac and thoracic surgeon St. Thomas Hosp., Nashville, 1981—, Cardiovascular Surgery Assocs., P.C., Nashville, 1981—; asst. clin. prof. cardio-thoracic surgery Vanderbilt U. Sch. Medicine, 1982—. Contbr. 23 articles to med. jours. Bd. dirs. Nashville br. Nat. Kidney Found. Served to capt. Med. Svc. Corps, U.S. Army, 1973-75. Fellow ACS; mem. AMA, Internat. Coll. Surgeons, Inter. Soc. for Heart Transplantation, Soc. Toracic Surgeons, Johns Hopkins Med. and Surg. Soc., So. Thoracic Surg. Assn., Nashville Cardiovascular Soc., Nashville Acad. Medicine, Tenn. Med. Assn., Nashville Surg. Soc., N.Am. Soc. Pacing and Electrophysiology, United Network of Organ Sharing, H. William Scott Soc. Republican. Baptist. Office: Cardiovascular Surgery Assocs 4230 Harding Rd Ste 501 Nashville TN 37205-2013

PETRALI, JOHN PATRICK, anatomist, researcher, pathologist; b. Fairview, N.J., July 30, 1933; s. John and Yolanda (Stigliano) P.; m. Sadie Belle Hose, Dec. 7, 1963 (div. 1980). Student, Boston U., 1956-58; BS cum laude, Davis and Elkins, 1955; PhD, U. Md., Balt., 1969. Cert. electron microscopy technologist, Md. Rsch. anatomist, team leader U.S. Army Med. Rsch. Inst., Aberdeen Proving Ground, 1962—; asst. prof. dept. anatomy U. Md., 1969-72, assoc. prof., 1975-80, adj. assoc. prof., 1990—; advisor/ cons. Md. Optical Assn., Balt., 1985. Editl. bd. Jour. Ophthamology, 1987; contbr. chpt. to book and articles to profl. jours. Bd. dirs. Forward Step, Edgewood, Md., 1978-81; treas., pres., coun. mem. coun. Civic Improvement Assn., Edgewood, 1970-75; treas., mem. coun. Civic Assn., Priestford Hills, Md., 1988-90. With U.S. Army, 1958-60. Recipient Achievement awards U.S. Med. Rsch. Labs., 1990-95, Comdr.'s medal, 1992, Exhibit awards Microscopy Soc. Am., 1994-95. Mem. Chesapeake Soc. Microscopy (pres., v.p., coun.). Home: 204 Goucher Way Churchville MD 21028 Office: US Army Med Rsch Inst Ricketts Point Rd Aberdeen Proving Ground MD 21010-5425

PETRENKO, VALERY ALEXANDROVICH, molecular biologist; b. Kalinin, Russia, Apr. 9, 1949; s. Alexander M. and Valentina M. (Vasilenko) P.; m. Natalia I. Popolova, Apr. 12, 1969; children: Anton, Polina. BS/MS in Chemistry, Moscow State U., 1972, D Chemistry, 1988; PhD in Bioorganic Chemistry, Inst. Organic Chemistry, Moscow, 1976; Prof., Supreme Attestation Com., Moscow, 1992. Jr. rsch. worker Inst. Organic Chemistry, Moscow, 1975-77; sr. rsch. worker Int. Molecular Biology, Novosibirsk, Russia, 1977-82, head lab. nuclear acids, 1982-85; asst. sci. dir. Inst. Biol. Active Substances, Berdsk, Russia, 1985-89, dir., 1989-95; asst. sci. gen. dir. NPO Vector, Novosibirsk, 1989-95; vis. prof. U. Mo., Columbia, 1993-95, rsch. prof., 1995—; sci. cons. State Rsch. Ctr. for Virology and Biotech., Novosibirsk, 1995—; mem. spl. bd. dissertation def. Novosibirsk Inst. Bioorganic Chemistry, 1990-93. Contbr. articles to internat. and Russian jours.; 13 inventions in field. Grantee State Sci. and Tech. Program, Moscow, 1991-92, Russian Found. for Fundamental Studies, Moscow, 1993. Office: U Mo-Columbia Dept Biol Scis 406 Tucker Hall Columbia MO 65211

PETRETICH, CATHERINE ANN, biomedical researcher; b. Youngstown, Ohio, Aug. 8, 1970; d. Stephen John and Catherine Marie (Bestic) P. BA in Psychology, U. Toledo, 1993. Lab. asst. dept. pharmacy U. Toledo, 1988, teaching asst.'s asst. dept. chemistry, 1990; technologist dept. toxicology N.Am. Sci. Assocs., Northwood, Ohio, 1989-93, rsch. assoc., 1993-94; biomed. rsch. tech. dept. physiology and molecular medicine Med. Coll. Ohio, Toledo, 1994—; team leader NAmSA Continuing Edn. Team, Northwood, 1993-94. Mem. Ohio Acad. Sci. (judge 1993-95), Am. Assn. for Lab. Animal Sci. Home: 1840 Garden Ridge Dr Apt 6 Toledo OH 43614 Office: Med Coll Ohio 3000 Arlington Ave Toledo OH 43613

PETRICK, DALE LEE, dentist; b. Bentleyville, Pa., Feb. 26, 1942; s. Stanley and Rose Ann Petrick. BS in Mech. Engring., Pa. State U., 1963; MS in Mgmt., Rensselaer Poly. Inst., 1970; DDS, UCLA, 1987. Assoc. scientist missiles and space divsn. Lockheed, Sunnyvale, Calif., 1963-64; plant engr. Monsanto Co., Santa Clara, Calif. and Springfield, Mass., 1964-68; gas turbine engr. United Techs. Corp., Hartford, Conn., 1968-76; group leader long-distance bicycle tours Bike Centennial, Missoula, Mont., 1976-81; ski instr., program dir. Trapp Family Lodge Ski Touring Ctr., Stowe, Vt., 1977-81; assoc. dentist, Dr. Larry Cohen, Oxnard, Calif., 1987-88; gen. practice dentistry Cathedral City, Calif., 1988—. Mem. ADA, Calif. Dental Assn. Democrat. Home: 67405 Rango Rd Cathedral City CA 92234-3492 Office: 31855 Date Palm Dr Cathedral City CA 92234-3100

PETRIE, JACK B., medical educator; b. Pitts., Apr. 17, 1952; s. Jack B. and Lorraine Elnor (Shilling) P.; m. Beverly Sue Geber, Jan. 14, 1987; children: Ian, Benjamin. BS, Mich. State U., 1974; MD, Rush Coll., Chgo., 1981. Diplomate Am. Bd. Internal Medicine. Intern, resident Mayo Clinic, Rochester, Minn.; resident Midway Hosp., St. Paul, Minn.; mem. staff Aspen Med., St. Paul, 1984-96; asst. clin. prof. U. Minn., Mpls., 1995—. Med. dir. Minn. Dept. of Corrections, St. Paul, 1989-95. Fellow ACP. Home: 15100 N Square Lake Tr Stillwater MN 55082 Office: Aspen Med Group 1020 Bandana Blvd Saint Paul MN 55108

PETRIE, LUCINDA ALICIA, medical technician; b. Marshalltown, Iowa, May 17, 1951; d. Bernard Chesley and Alice May (Ogan) Malloy; m. David Michael Petrie, Nov. 19, 1976; children: Andrea Joan, Philip Randolph. AA, Marshalltown Coll., 1971; BA, U. Iowa, 1974. From diagnostic med. sonographer to chief sonographer Marshalltown Med. and Surg. Ctr., 1976-79; asst. diagnostic med. sonographer Wolfe Eye Clinic, Marshalltown, 1979-81, chief sonographer, 1981—; guest faculty mem. intensive workshop in ophthalmic U. Iowa, 1981; dir./presenter gen. ultrasound Iowa Registry Rev., 1978. Contbr. rsch. articles to profl. publs. Mem. exec. bd. Iowa chpt. Heal the Children, 1989-91; mem. Nat. Trust for Hist. Preservation, 1992-93. Mem. AAUW, PTA, Am. Soc. Ultrasound Tech. Specialists (Iowa rep. 1978-80, bd. dirs. 1978-80), Assn. Registered Diagnostic Med. Sonographers, Am. Inst. Ultrasound in Medicine, Soc. Diagnostic Med. Sonographers, Am. Assn. Ophthalmic Standardized Echography, Soc. Internat. Diagnostic Ultrasound in Ophthalmology, U. Iowa Alumni Assn. (life). Roman Catholic. Office: Wolfe Eye Clinic PC 309 E Church St Marshalltown IA 50158-2946

PETRIE, WILLIAM MARSHALL, psychiatrist; b. Louisville, Oct. 19, 1946; s. Garner McReynolds and Claire (Samuels) P.; m. Patricia L. Roberts, Aug. 3, 1968; children: Christopher W., Ellen M., Shelley M.; m. Lori L. Molchin, Oct. 1, 1994. BA, Vanderbilt U., 1968, MD, 1972. Research psychiatrist NIMH, Rockville, Md., 1975-77; asst. prof. dept. psychiatry Vanderbilt Med. Ctr., Nashville, 1977-81, assoc. prof., 1981-82, assoc. clin. prof., 1982-87, clin. prof., 1992—; pvt. practice psychiatry Psychiat. Cons., P.C., Nashville, 1982—; clin. instr. Georgetown U. Med. Ctr., 1975-77; cons. psychopharmacology rsch. br. NIMH, 1977-80; rschr. in geriatric psychopharmacology; med. dir. memory Study Ctr., 1987—. Mem. editorial bd. Gen. Hosp. Psychiatry, 1995—, Audic Digest Psychiatry, 1996—; author numerous articles and book chpts. on psychopharmacology and geriatric psychiatry. Fellow Am. Psychiat. Assn. (pres. mid. Tenn. dist. br. 1986-87); mem. AMA, Tenn. Med. Assn., Am. Assn. Geriatric Psychiatrists. Am. Coll. Psychiatrists. Democrat. Methodist. Office: Psychiat Cons PC 310 25th Ave N Nashville TN 37203-1515

PETRO, JANE A., plastic and reconstructive surgeon; b. Erie, Pa., Dec. 17, 1946; d. William Irwin and Virginia (Douglas) Arbuckle; m. Denis J Petro, Mar. 28, 1969 (div. 1982); 1 child, Noah Edward. BS, Eckerd Coll., St. Petersburg, Fla., 1968; MD, Pa. State U., 1972. Diplomate Am. Bd. Surgery, Am. Bd. Plastic and Reconstrv. Surgery. 0; gen. surg. resident U. Louisville, 1972-74, Harrisburg Hosp., Pa., 1974-76; plastic surgery resident Pa. State U., Hershey, 1977-79; burn/microsurg. fellow Albert Einstein Coll. Medicine, Bronx, 1979-80; asst. prof. surgery N.Y. Med. Coll., Valhalla, 1981—; assoc. prof. surgery N.Y. Med. Coll., 1981—; assoc. dir. burns Westchester County Med. Ctr., Valhalla, 1981—, chief surg. HIV svcs., 1991—; courtesy affiliate dept. surg. divsn. plastic surgery Phelps Meml. Hosp., 1989—; chief pediatric plastic surgery St. Agnes Hosp., 1992—; mem. plastic and reconstructive surgery device adv. panel FDA, 1993—. Contbr. articles to profl. jours. Recipient Physicians Recognition award AMA, 1977, 90, 92, McArthur Alumni award for disting. achievement Eckerd Coll., 1980, My Sister's Place Ann. Leadership awrad, 1991. Mem. ACS, AAAS, APHA, Am. Soc. Plastic and Reconstructive Surgeons (AIDS task force com. 1991—), Am. Assn. Physicians for Human Rights (chmn. women's issues com. 1992—), Am. Trauma Soc., Assn. Women Surgeons, Am. Burn Assn., Am. Cleft Palate Assn., Am. Med. Women's Assn. (Cmty. Svc. award 1993), Am. Soc. Law, Medicine and Ethics, N.Y. Acad. Scis., N.Y. Acad. Medicine, Acad. Compensation Medicine, Am. Fedn. Clin. Rsch. N.Y. Soc. Plastic and Reconstructive Surgery, N.Y. Regional Head and Neck Soc., Soc. Office Based Surgery, N.E. Soc. Plastic and Reconstructive Surgeons, Undersea and Hyperbaric Med. Soc., Westchester County Med. Soc. (chmn. plastic surgery sect. 1990—, com. on women 1992—), Alpha Omega Alpha. Democrat. Presbyterian. Office: Westchester County Med Ctr Burn Unit Valhalla NY 10595

PETRONE, WILLIAM FRANCIS, physician, microbiologist, corporate executive; b. Bklyn., Sept. 12, 1949; s. Arthur Carmen and Helen (Kenny) P.; m. Kathleen Anne Baron, Aug. 25, 1979; children: William Gaetano, Katherine Bridget, Jason Daniel. BA, U. Conn., 1972; MS, U. Mass., 1974; PhD, U. R.I., 1978; MD, U. South Ala., 1984. Diplomate Am. Bd. Pediatrics, Pediatric Emergency Medicine. Rsch. assoc. Coll. Medicine U. South Ala., Mobile, 1978-80; resident in pediatrics Orlando (Fla.) Regional Med. Ctr., 1984-85, W.Va. Univ. Med. Ctr., 1985-87; emergency rm. physician, dir. pediatric emergency svcs. Mercy Hosp., Springfield, Mass., 1987—; pres. Med. Simulation Software. Contbr. articles on inflamation and white blood cell function to sci. jours. Fellow Am. Acad. Pediat., Am. Coll. Emergency Physicians; mem. AAAS, AMA, N.Y. Acad. Scis., Sigma Xi. Roman Catholic. Office: Mercy Hosp Emergency Unit PO Box 9012 Springfield MA 01012

PETROS, ANDRANICK JOSEPH, pediatrician, consultant; b. Bombay, Nov. 26, 1955; arrived in Eng., 1962; s. Sahak Azgaser and Gertrude Blanche (Michael) P.; m. Louise Olwen Neville; children: Gregory, Claire. MBBS, Middlesex Hosp., London U., 1979; MSc, Christ Ch., Oxford U., 1986. Sr. house officer Hammersmith Hosp., England, 1985-86; registrar anesthesia U. Coll. Hosp., England, 1986-89; sr. registrar intensive care St. George's Hosp., England, 1989-91; fellow in pediat. intensive care Toronto (Can.) Hosp. for Sick Children, 1991; cons. intensivist Royal Liverpool Children's Hosp., 1992-94; cons. pediat. intensivist Royal Brompton Hosp., London, 1994-96, Great Ormond St. Hosp. for Sick Children, London, 1996—. Med. Rsch. Coun. scholar, Oxford, 1981. Mem. Royal Coll. Physicians (U.K.). Office: Royal Brompton Hosp, Sydney St, London SW13 GNP, England

PETROVIC, ALEXANDRE GABRIEL, physician, physiology educator, medical research director; b. Belgrade, Yugoslavia, July 10, 1925; naturalized French citizen; s. Gabriel M. and Maria S. (Miskovic) P.; m. Suzanne Durry, Feb. 25, 1956; 1 child, Nicole Gasson. MD, Strasbourg Med. Sch., 1954; DSc, Strasbourg U., 1961; postgrad. McGill U. Med. Sch., 1961-52. Assoc. staff physician, asst. prof. Northwestern U. Med. Sch., Chgo., 1965-68; prof. U. Montreal Med. Sch., 1970-71; dir. rsch. Nat. Inst. Health and Med. Research, Strasbourg, 1968-94; prof. human physiology U. Louis Pasteur Med. Sch., Strasbourg, 1976-90, lectr. in biomed. rsch., methodology, 1989—, also mem. sci. coun.; vis. rsch. scientist Center for Human Growth and Devel., U. Mich., Ann Arbor, 1976-78; vis. prof. La. State U. Med. Ctr., New Orleans, 1979—; van der Klaauw prof. U. Leiden, Netherlands, 1985; prof. U. Cattolica del Sacro Cuore, Rome, Italy, 1992—; prof. honoris causa U. Camilo Castelo Branco, São Paulo, Brazil; charge of French med. missions to USSR, 1969, Yugoslavia, 1969, 74, 76, 78, 81, Argentina, Peru, Brazil and Chile, 1974, U.S., 1977, 78, 82, Cuba, 1986. Recipient prize Vlès, Strasbourg Med. Sch., 1954, prize Laborde, Biol. Soc., 1961, E. Sheldon Friel award European Orthodontic Soc., 1976, Calvin Case award for orthodontic rsch., 1984, Disting. Sci. Craniofacial Biology Rsch. award Internat. Assn. Dental Rsch., 1994. Mem. Soc. Cryobiology (charter), Acad. Medicine (Belgrade) (honor mem.), Academia Ibero-Latino-Am. de Disfuncion Craneomandibular, Club Internat. de Morphologie Faciale, Assn. des Physiologistes, European Tissue Culture Soc., etc. Contbg. author various books and sci. papers on a cybernetic theory of the mechanisms of craniofacial bone growth, on cytopathogenesis of craniostenosis and on philosophy of biomed. research; discovered feasibility of orthopedically stimulating the growth of the mandible; described new ways in orthodontic decision making; pioneer research studies on treatment of otospongiosis by sodium fluoride and disphosphonates, on theory of auto-immune origin of otospongiosis; new classification of bone tumors; discovered possibility of prefecondatory hereditary male contribution by penetration of spermatozoary DNA into intraovarian ovocytes. Home: 2 rue de Rome, 67000 Strasbourg France Office: Inst Nat la Sante et la Recherche Medicale, 2 Rue de Rome, 67000 Strasbourg France

PETRUCELLI, R(OCCO) JOSEPH, II, nephrologist; b. Meriden, Conn., Sept. 20, 1943; s. Rocco Joseph and Marguerite Robena (Colwell) P. BA, Yale U., 1965; MD, Harvard U., 1969. Diplomate Am. Bd. Internal Medicine, Am. Bd. Nephrology. Intern, then resident Mt. Sinai Hosp., N.Y.C., 1969-72; fellow in nephrology U. Calif. San Francisco Med. Ctr., San Francisco, 1972-74; asst. prof. Mt. Sinai Sch. Medicine, 1978-92; assoc. prof. N.Y. Med. Coll., 1992—; vis. rschr. Karolinska Inst., Stockholm, 1970-71; exec. com. End Stage Renal Disease, N.Y.C., 1980-90, pres. 1985. Author: Medicine: An Illustrated History, 1978, transl. into fgn. langs., 1978-96. Pres. Bklyn. Opera Soc.; mem. med. adv. bd. Nat. Kidney Found., 1987-94, v.p., 1994; treas. Friends of Rare Book Rm. of N.Y. Acad. Medicine, 1993, sec., 1994. Recipient Richard Cabot prize Harvard Med. Sch., 1969, Boylston prize Boylston Med. Soc., 1969, John P. McGovern prize Baylor Coll. Medicine, Houston, 1993. Fellow N.Y. Acad. Medicine (libr. com. 1975—), Am. Soc. Nephrology, Internat. Soc. Nephrology. Democrat. Episcopalian. Home: 19 Fulton Ave Rye NY 10580-2515 Office: Chief Nephrology New Rochelle Med Ctr 16 Guion Pl New Rochelle NY 10801-5503

PETRUS, JOHN J., oncologist; b. Cleve., Jan. 25, 1960; s. Nicholas Edward and Therese Joan (Sanko) P.; m. Sharon Lynn Dilauro, Apr. 28, 1984; children: Nicholas Jared, Alexandra Marie, Jeremiah John. BS, Youngstown State U., 1984; MD, Northeastern Ohio Univs., 1984. Dir. oncology Alliance (Ohio) Cmty. Hosp., 1990-91; chief hematology-oncology Akron (Ohio) Gen. Med. Ctr., 1991—, chmn. biomed. ethics, 1994—; asst. prof. internal medicine Northeastern Ohio Univs. Coll. Medicine, Rootstown, Ohio, 1990-95, assoc. prof. clin. internal medicine, 1995—; med. dir. Hospice Ctr. Vis. Nursing Svc., Akron, 1995—, mem. profl. adv. bd., 1993—, chaplain residency program Akron Gen. Med. Ctr., 1994—. Co-chair Decisions-A Community Directive on Examining Ethical Concerns, Akron, 1994—. Republican. Byzantine Catholic. Home: 2822 Valley Rd Cuyahoga Falls OH 44223 Office: Akron Gen Med Ctr 400 Wabash Ave Akron OH 44302

PETRUS, RICHARD JOHN, medical association adminstrator; b. N.Y.C., Aug. 15, 1952; m. Carol Anne Petrus, Sept. 15, 1979; children: Brian, Kevin. BA in Biology, Syracuse U., 1974; AAS in Respiratory Care, Westchester Cmty. Coll., Valhalla, N.Y., 1978; postgraduate in health sci., New Sch. for Social Rsch., 1996—. Lic. respiratory therapist, N.Y.; cert. profl. health care quality. Respiratory therapist St. Luke's Hosp., Newburgh, N.Y., 1974-75, Alcare Home Care, Nyack, N.Y., 1976-77, Phelps Meml. Hosp., North Tarrytown, N.Y., 1977-78; respiratory care coord. Lincare Homecare, Elmsford, N.Y., 1978-79; dir. respiratory care St. Anthony Cmty. Hosp., Warwick, N.Y., 1980—, v.p. quality mgmt., 1982%, risk mgr., 1988—; respiratory care cons. Orange County Dept. Residential Health Care, Goshen, N.Y., 1986—. Mem. Am. Assn. Respiratory Care, Nat. Assn. Healthcare Quality. Home: 29 Robert Dr Warwick NY 10990 Office: St Anthony Community Hosp 1519 Maple Ave Warwick NY 10990

PETTEE, DANIEL STARR, neurologist; b. N.Y.C., Feb. 15, 1925; s. Allen Danforth and Helen Marien (Starr) P.; m. Dimetra Marie Peters, June 24, 1961; children: William, Margaret, Allen. BA, Yale U., 1951; MD, Columbia U., 1955. Diplomate Am. Bd. Psychiatry and Neurology, 1965, Am. Bd. Clin. Neurophysiology, 1984. Rotating internship Strong Meml. Hosp. U. Rochester, N.Y., 1955-57, residency neurology, 1957-62; neurologist pvt. practice, Rochester, N.Y., 1962-96; clinic dir. Rochester (N.Y.) Area Multiple Sclerosis Chpt., Rochester, N.Y., 1962-76; assoc. prof. neurology U. Rochester (N.Y.) Sch. Medicine, 1978-96, emeritus assoc. prof., 1996—; clin. assoc. dept. neurology Strong Meml. Hosp., Rochester, 1978—; head neurology div. dept. medicine The Genesee Hosp., Rochester, 1972-96; pres. Genesee Neurol. Assocs., Rochester, 1974-96; mem. bd. dirs. Rochester (N.Y.) Area Multiple Sclerosis Chpt., 1970-76. Contbr. articles to profl. jours. Mem. bd. dirs., singer Rochester (N.Y.) Oratorio Soc., 1960-61, 1955-78. Recipient Purple Heart, Bronze Star U.S. Army, 1944, Bronze Hope Chest for Svc. award Rochester (N.Y.) Area Multiple Sclerosis Chpt., 1976. Mem. N.Y. Acad. Sci., Rochester Acad. Sci. (astronomy sect. 1989—, bd. dirs. astronomy sect. 1993-94). Home: 150 Summit Dr Rochester NY 14620-3130 Office: Genesee Neurol Assocs 222 Alexander St Rochester NY 14607-4005

PETTEGREW, JAY W., neurology and psychiatry educator; b. Peoria, Ill., May 19, 1944; s. James Elting and Elsie Lucille (Bowyer) P.; m. Nancy J. Minshew; children: Jonathan, Jared, Heather. Student, U. Ill., 1962-65; MD, U. Ill., Chgo., 1965-69. Cert. Am. Bd. Psychiatry and Neurology with spl. competence in child neurology. Asst. prof. neurology and pediatrics U. Tex. Health Sci. Ctr., Dallas, 1977-84, coord. pediatrics neurology tng. program, 1978-84; assoc. prof. psychiatry and neurology U. Pitts., Western Psychiat. Inst. and Clin., 1984-90, dir. div. neurophysics, 1984—; prof. psychiatry (with tenure) and neurology U. Pitts., Western Psychiat. Inst. and Clinic, 1990—; assoc. dir. Drug Design Inst. U. Pitts. Sch. of Medicine, 1985—; dir. Ctr. for Membrane Studies U. Pitts., 1989—, dir. Alzheimer's Disease Rsch. Ctr., 1989—; examiner AM. Bd. Psychiatry and Neurology, 1980—. Author: Nuclear Magnetic Resonance: The Principles and Applications of NMR Spectroscopy and Imaging to Biomedical Research, 1989; contbr. chpt. The Science and Practice of Clinical Medicine, 1980, Genetic Research Strategies in Psychobiology and Psychiatry, 1980, and many others; contbr. over 40 articles to Jour. Am. Chem. Soc., New Eng. Jour. Medicine, Jour. Neurochemistry, Neurochemistry Rsch., Trans. Am. Neurol. Assn., Life Scis., Jour. Affective Disorders, Muscle and Nerve, and many others. Lt. comdr. USNR, 1975-77. Fellow Am. Acad. Neurology, Am. Psychopathological Assn. Inc.; mem. AAAS, Child Neurology Soc., Internat. Child Neurology Assn., Internat. Soc. Magnetic Resonance, The N.Y. Acad. Scis., Soc. Biol. Psychiatry, Soc. for Magnetic Resonance Imaging, So. Child Neurology Soc., Soc. for Neuroscience, Phi Eta Sigma, Omega Beta Pi. Home: 630 S Linden Ave Pittsburgh PA 15208-2813 Office: U Pitts Sch Medicine Western Psychiat Inst Clin Pittsburgh PA 15213

PETTERSSON, ULF GÖSTA, geneticist, virologist, molecular biologist; b. Nyköping, Sweden, Sept. 24, 1942; s. Gösta Albert and Aina Maria (Lindberg) P.; m. Birgitta Karolina Strömstedt, Apr. 3, 1965; children: Magnus, Anna. MD, Uppsala (Sweden) U., 1970, D in Medical Sci., 1971. Rsch. asst. Uppsala U., 1965-71, asst. prof. microbiology, 1973-81, prof. med. genetics, 1981—; postdoctoral fellow Cold Spring Harbor (N.Y.) Lab., 1971-72, sr. staff scientist, 1972-73; dir. Beijer Lab., Uppsala, 1990—. Mem. editorial bd. Human Heredity, Archives of Virology. Recipient The Svedberg award Swedish Biochem. Assn., Sweden, 1980, Fernström award Fernström Found., Lund, Sweden, 1983, Lennander Lecture award, Swedish Soc. Medicine, Lund, 1989. Mem. Am. Soc. Microbiology, N.Y. Acad. Scis., Royal Acad. Scis., Academia Europea, Human Genome Orgn., European Molecular Biology Orgn. Home: Sveavägen 5, S-752 36 Uppsala Sweden Office: Dept Med Genetics, BMC Box 589, S-75123 Uppsala Sweden

PETTIJOHN, JOYCE LORRAINE, pharmacist, educator; b. Portland, Oreg., Jan. 7, 1955; d. E.I. and Verona M. (McKittrick) Pettijohn; B.S. with honors in Pharmacy, Oreg. State U., 1978; postgrad. in bus. adminstrn. U. Puget Sound, 1980-81. With St. Vincent's Hosp., Portland, 1977, Lakeshore Clinic Pharmacy, Kirkland, Wash., 1978, Evergreen Pharm. Services, Kirkland, 1979-93; pres. Performance Med., Inc., Seattle, 1994—; dir. Health Products, Inc., Kirkland, 1981-85; found. mem. Fred Hutchinson Cancer Rsch. Ctr., 1995—. Trustee Friends of Seattle Pub. Libr., 1996—. Lic. pharmacist, Wash., Calif., Oreg. Mem. adv. bd. long term care King County, 1991-94. Mem. Am. Pharm. Assn., Am. Soc. Cons. Pharmacists. Avocations: photography, sailing. Office: Performance Med Inc PO Box 758 Kirkland WA 98083

PETTINE, LINDA FAYE, physical therapist; b. New London, Conn., Nov. 11, 1958; d. Robert Anderson and Pauline Priscilla (Johnson) Erwin; m. H. Louis Pettine Jr., Mar. 6, 1982. BS, U. Conn., 1980; student, Quinnipiac Coll., Hamden, Conn., 1989-91. Registered phys. therapist, Conn. Staff phys. therapist Worcester (Mass.) Hahneman Hosp., 1980, Newport (R.I.) Hosp., 1980-82, Middlebury Orthopaedic Group, Waterbury, Conn., 1982; staff phys. therapist Easter Seal Rehab. Ctr. of Cen. Conn., Meriden, 1982-84, hosp. and rehab. ctr. coord., 1984-86; co-founder Pettine & McDiarmid Phys. Therapy, Cheshire and Wallingford, Conn., 1986-88; pres. Keystone Phys. Therapy & Sports Medicine P.C., Cheshire and Wallingford, Conn., 1988—; lectr. Diabetes Edn. Program, Meriden, 1985; cons. Waterbury (Conn.) Nursing Ctr., 1986-87. Mem. adv. bd. Waterbury Continuing Edn. program, 1985; guest speaker Conn. chpt. Am. Diabetes Assn., Meriden, 1986, Arthritis Support Group, Meriden, 1986, Meriden Indsl. Mgr. Assn., 1986. Katherine Wyckoff and Margaret Wyckoff Moore Endowed scholar, 1991. Mem. Am. Phys. Therapy Assn. (pvt. practice sect.), Conn. Phys. Therapy Assn. (program com. chair 1991-92, qualified peer reviewer 1995—). Office: Keystone Phys Therapy & Sports Medicine PC 675 S Main St Cheshire CT 06410-3153 also: 850 N Main Street Ext Wallingford CT 06492-2400

PETTINGA, FRANK L., health facility administrator, physician; b. Hudsonville, Mich., May 28, 1926; s. Rhine C. and Adrianna L. (Landaal) P.; m. E. Suzanne Leestma, June 24, 1952; children: Debora Pettinga Toering, Jan, Fredrick, Cynthia Pettinga Hiskes. BA, Calvin Coll., 1947; MA in Pharmacology, Boston U., 1948, MD, 1952; MPH, U. Mich., 1981. Diplomate Am. Bd. Family Practice. Resident Wayne County Gen. Hosp., Detroit, 1952-54; pvt. practice family medicine Muskegon, Mich., 1954-73; minister consular U.S. State Dept., 1973-86; v.p., med. dir. Hackley Hosp., Muskegon, 1986-94; med. dir. healthcare programs U.S. State Dept., Washington, 1980-82. Contbr. articles to profl. jours. Pres. Western Mich. Christian H.S. Bd., Muskegon, 1963-66; bd. trustees Calvin Coll., 1992-96. With USN, 1944-46. Mem. Muskegon County Soc. (pres. 1966), Calvin Coll. Alumni Assn. (pres. 1989-90). Mem. Reformed Ch. Am. Office: Hackley Hosp 1700 Clinton St Muskegon MI 49442-5502

PETTIT, JOHN W., administrator; b. Detroit, Mar. 6, 1942; s. John W. and Clara (Schartz) P.; m. Kathleen Endres, Aug. 8, 1970; children: Julie, Andrew, Michael. BBA, U. Notre Dame, 1964; MBA, Mich. State U., 1974. CPA, Mich. Acct. Ernst & Ernst, Detroit, 1964-67; chief acct. Detroit Inst. Tech., Detroit, 1967-69; controller, dir. adminstrn. & fin. Mich. Cancer Found., Detroit, 1969-80; chief adminstrv. officer Dana-Farber Cancer Inst., Boston, 1980-94; exec. v.p., chief oper. officer John Wayne Cancer Inst., Santa Monica, Calif., 1995—; grant reviewer Nat. Cancer Inst., Bethesda, Md., 1979—. Pres. advanced mgmt. program Mich. State U., 1978-79. Mem. Am. Inst. CPA's. Office: John Wayne Cancer Inst 2200 Santa Monica Blvd Santa Monica CA 90404-2301

PETTITT, BARBARA JEAN, pediatric surgeon; b. Niagara Falls, N.Y., Feb. 2, 1952; d. Robert Andrew and Joan Marilyn (Boore) P.; m. Richard Allen Schieber, May 24, 1981; children: Christine Pettitt Schieber, Lucy Pettitt Schieber, Brian Pettitt Schieber. BA in Chemistry magna cum laude, Cen. Coll., Pella, Iowa, 1972; D of Medicine, Northwestern U., Chgo., 1976. Diplomate Am. Bd. Surgery with certificates of spl. competence in pediatric surgery and surg. critical care; lic. pediatric surgeon, Calif., Pa., Ga. Student fellow in rehab. medicine Rehab. Inst. Chgo., spring 1974; intern in straight surgery Los Angeles County-U. So. Calif. Med. Ctr., 1976-77, resident in gen. surgery, 1977-81; resident in pediatric surgery Childrens' Hosp. Pitts., 1982-84; asst. prof. surgery and pediatrics dept. Sch. Medicine Emory U., Atlanta, 1985—; mem. staff Henrietta Egleston Hosp. for Children, Atlanta, 1985-86; mem. staff Grady Meml. Hosp., Atlanta, 1985—, chief pediatric surg. svc., 1990—; chief of surgery Hughes Spalding Children's Hosp., 1993—; instr. ATLS, PALS; active various coms. Henrietta Egleston Hosp. for Children, 1985-86, Grady Meml. Hosp., 1986—, Hughes Spalding Children's Hosp., 1992—; lectr., presenter many profl. and ednl. orgns., 1983—. Contbg. author: (with M. Rowe) Pediatric Surgery, 4th edit., 1986; contbr. articles to profl. publs. Bd. dirs., trustees DeKalb Choral Guild, Atlanta, 1988—; pres. Summit Cmty. Assn., 1992—; chairperson health and safety com. Arbor Montessori Sch. Rsch. grantee Rsch. Corp., summer 1971, NIH, 1983-84; Rollscreen full-tuition scholar, 1969-72, Ruth G. White scholar Calif. State P.E.O., 1974-75; recipient 1st prize Bernard Baruch Essay Contest, Am. Congress Rehab. Medicine, 1975; named Outstanding Young Woman of Yr., State pf Pa., 1984, State of Ga., 1986, Disting. Alumna Ctrl. Coll., 1990. Fellow ACS, Am. Acad. Pediatrics (surg. sect., critical care sect.); mem. AMA, Am. Med. Womens' Assn., Southeastern Surg. Congress, Am. Pediatric Surg. Assn., Assn. Women Surgeons, Am. Soc. Parenteral and Enteral Nutrition, La.A. County-U. So. Calif. Med. Ctr. Soc. Grad. Surgeons, Phi Delta Epsilon (pres. med. sch. chpt. 1974-75, undergrad. midwest regional coord. 1974-75, nat. exec. com. 1976-80, nat. intern-resident liaison com. 1980-85, nat. constn. and bylaws com. 1986—, Isadore Pilot award Chgo. chpt. 1975, nat. svc. award 1976), Soc. Critical Care Medicine, Ga. Surg. Soc., Assn. Surg. Edn. Democrat. Episcopalian. Office: Emory Univ Sch Medicine Dept of Surgery 69 Butler St SE Atlanta GA 30303-3033

PETTUS, SALLY LOCKHART, psychologist; b. N.Y.C., Aug. 17, 1937; d. Alfred Sherman and Jane Clay (Zevely) Foote; m. Charlton Messick Pettus, June 21, 1958 (div. 1974); children: Charlton, Cybele; m. William Frank Wyatt Jr., Sept. 10, 1989. Student, Vassar Coll., 1955-58; AB, Roger Williams Coll., 1972; EdD, Boston U., 1977. Lic. Psychologist. Psychol. cons. Ipswich (Mass.) Sch. System, 1975-77, Human Resource Inst., Brookline, Mass., 1975-77, New England Meml. Hosp., Stoneham, Mass., 1977-78; sr. psychologist Newton (Mass.) Guidance Clinic, 1978-82; clin. assoc. East Side Ctr., Providence, 1987-89; sr. psychologist Netrowest Youth Guidance, Framingham, Mass., 1982-91; clin. psychologist Providence, 1989—; clin. supr. Women's Protective Svcs., Framingham, 1987-90; reviewer in field. Mem. APA, Nat. Register Health Svc. Providers in Psychology, Mass. Psychol. Assn., R.I. Psychol. Assn., Am. Soc. Clin. Hypnosis.

PETTY, DAVID TALMAGE, surgeon; b. Istanbul, Turkey, Sept. 19, 1921; s. DeWitt Talmage and Beatrice Elizabeth (Worthington) P.; m. Mary Kathryn Toft, Dec. 19, 1943 (div. 1957); children: Miriam Elise Petty Dewhurst, David William; m. Yvonne Caroline DelMagro, July 11, 1959; children: Carol Jean, Mark Lawrence, Gail Marie, Guy Robert. BS in Physiology, U. Chgo., 1943; MD, Northwestern U., 1947, MS in Pathology, 1952; MS in Surgery, U. Ill., 1954. Diplomate Am. Bd. Surgery. Intern U.S. Naval Hosp., Bremerton, Wis., 1946-47; resident VA Hosp., Hines, Ill., 1950-53; instr. in surgery Chgo. Med. Sch., 1954-56; asst. chief surgery VA Hosp., Chgo., 1956-58; pvt. practice Chgo., 1958—; staff surgeon VA Med. Ctr., North Chicago, Ill., 1988—, U.S. Naval Hosp., Great Lakes NTS, 1988—; mem. bd. appeals McHenry County Dept. Health, Woodstock, Ill. Comdr. USNR, 1943-51. Fellow ACS; mem. Chgo. Surg. Soc., Am. Fedn. Clin. Rsch. (sr.), Chgo. Med. Soc. (past pres., mem. various coms., former br. pres.), Ill. State Med. Soc. (past chmn. med. legal coun.), Sigma Xi. Office: 151 N Michigan Ave Chicago IL 60601

PETTY, ELIZABETH MARIE, geneticist, pediatric; b. Chgo., July 13, 1959; d. Ralph David and Joyce Elizabeth (Carlson) Petty; m. Karen Milner, Dec. 15, 1985. BA, Clarke Coll., 1981; MD, U. Wis., 1986. Diplomate Nat. Bd. Med. Examiners, Am. Bd. Med. Genetics, Molecular Genetics and Clin. Genetics, Am. Bd. Pediatrics. Pediatric intern and resident U. Wis., Madison, 1986-89; postdoctoral genetics fellow Yale U., New Haven, 1989-92, postdoctoral assoc. in genetics, 1992-93; asst. prof. U. Mich., Ann Arbor, 1994—; DNA expert witness State of Ohio, 1995—; peer reviewer various jours., 1994—; mem. genome ethics com. U. Mich., 1994—, comprehensive cancer ctr. mem., 1995—. Contbr. articles to profl. jours., chpts. to books. Participant Gay and lesbian Health Group, Ann Arbor, 1994—. Recipient Clin. Investigator award NIH/Nat. Cancer Inst., 1995—. Mem. AAAS, AMA, Am. Soc. Human Genetics, European Soc. Human Genetics. Office: Yale U Sch Med Dept Human Gene/Peds 333 Cedar St # W305 New Haven CT 06510-3206*

PETZ, THOMAS JOSEPH, internist; b. Detroit, Feb. 10, 1930; s. Arthur J. and Marie (McCarthy) P.; m. Catherine Crowe, June 13, 1959; children: Thomas Jr., William, David, John, Catherine. BS, U. Detroit, 1951; MD, Wayne State U., 1955. Diplomate Am. Bd. Internal Medicine and Pulmonary Disease. Intern Harper Hosp., Detroit, 1955-56, resident, 1958-59, 60-62; resident U. Calif., San Francisco, 1959-60; clin. instr. Wayne State U., Detroit, 1962-72, assoc. prof., 1972-76, clin. assoc. prof., 1976-95, clin. prof., 1996—; pvt. practice pulmonary disease and internal medicine Detroit, 1962-72, St. Clair Shores, Mich., 1977—; chief pulmonary Wayne State U., Detroit, 1974-76, Harper Hosp., Detroit, 1972-79; dir. med. intensive care unit Harper Hosp., Detroit, 1977-83; chmn. dept. medicine Bon Secours Hosp., Grosse Pointe, Mich., 1984-86; chmn. Gen. Motors human rsch. com., 1995. Bd. govs. Wayne State Sch. of Medicine Alumni Assn., Detroit, 1981-85. Fellow Detroit Acad. Medicine (pres. 1982-83), Am. Coll. Chest Physicians; mem. Am. Coll. Physicians, Detroit Med. Club. Republican. Roman Catholic. Office: 23201 Jefferson Ave Saint Clair Shores MI 48080-1903

PETZOLD, ANITA MARIE, psychotherapist; b. Princeton, N.J., June 2, 1957; d. Charles Bernard and Kathleen Marie (McDonald) P. AS in Bus., Indian River C.C., Ft. Pierce, Fla., 1986; BS in Liberal Studies, Barry U., 1988; MS in Human Svcs. Adminstrn., Nova U., 1989, postgrad., 1989-91; PhD in Human Svcs. Adminstrn., LaSalle U., 1994. Lic. mental health counselor, Fla.; cert. addictions profl.; internat. cert. alcohol and drug abuse counselor; nat. cert. counselor; cert. employee assistance counselor; nat. cert. clin. mental health counselor; nat. cert. addictions counselor; cert. DUI instr. Admissions coord. The Palm Beach Inst., West Palm Beach, Fla., 1985-86; dir. admissions Heritage Health Corp., Jensen Beach, Fla., 1986-89; drug abuse strategy coord. Martin County Bd. of County Commrs., Stuart, Fla., 1989—; mem. Drug Resource Team for the 12th Congl. Dist., Fla., 1990—, Juvenile Justice Assn. of the 19th Jud. Ct., Fla., 1993—; grant writer in field. Vol. Hist. Soc. Martin County, Stuart, 1986—; mem. United Way Martin County, Stuart, 1993; mem. bd. dirs. Cmty. AIDS Adv. Project, Stuart, 1993; chmn. treatment com. Martin County Task Force on Substance Abused Children, Stuart, 1993—. Recipient Outstanding Cmty. Svc. award United Way Martin County, Stuart, 1993. Mem. NASW, Am. Mental Health Counselors Assn., Nat. Criminal Justice Assn., Nat. Assn. Alcoholism and Drug Abuse Counselors, Nat. Consortium Treatment Alternatives to St. Crime Programs, Am. Coll. Addiction Treatment Adminstrs., Am. Labor-Mgmt. Adminstrs., Fla. Alcohol and Drug Abuse Assn. Republican. Roman Catholic. Office: Martin County Bd County Commrs 400 SE Osceola St Stuart FL 34994-2577

PEVEHOUSE, BYRON CONE, neurosurgeon, company official; b. Lubbock, Tex., Apr. 5, 1927; s. William Monrow and Myrtle Elizabeth (Cone) P.; m. Maxine E. Smith, June 16, 1951 (dec. July 1978); children: Deann Pevehouse Freitag, Carol Pevehouse Palato, Lesa Pevehouse Howell; m. Lucille Seguin, Jan. 30, 1981. BS, Baylor U., 1948; MD, Baylor Coll. Med., 1952; MSc, McGill U., 1960. Diplomate Am. Bd. Neurosurgery. Intern Colo. Gen. Hosp., Denver, 1952-53; resident in gen. surgery U. Oreg. and V.A. Hosps., Portland, 1953-54; resident in neurol. surgery U. Calif. Med. Ctr., San Francisco, 1954-58; prof. neurosurgery U. Calif., San Francisco, 1960—; practice medicine specializing in neurosurgery San Francisco, 1960—; pres. Pevehouse Devel. Co., Lubbock, Tex., 1972—. Trustee Pacific Presbyn. Med. Ctr., San Francisco, 1983—. NSF fellow Montreal (P.Q., Can.) Neurol. Inst., 1958-59, Spl. Postdoctoral fellow in neurology and neurophysiology USPHS, Inst. Neurology, Queen Sq., London, 1959-60. Mem. Am. Assn. Neurol. Surgeons (pres. 1983-84), The Soc. Neurol. Surgeons (pres. 1987-88), Neurosurgical Assocs. Med. Group (pres.), Olympic Club. Office: Neurosurg Assocs 50 Museum Way San Francisco CA 94114-1428

PEYMAN, DOUGLAS ALASTAIR RALPH, clinical psychology educator, consultant; b. Vancouver, Can., Oct. 11, 1920; s. James Albert and Ruth McLean (McKenzie) P.; m. Lila Anne Wilcox, Oct. 5, 1946; children: Carol Anne, Kathleen Margaret, Pamela Eileen, Linda Diane. BA, U. B.C., 1943, MA, 1946; PhD, U. Wash., Seattle, 1951. Diplomate Am. Bd. Psychology. Assoc. psychology dept. U. Wash., 1947-50; asst. prof. psychology dept. U. Ala., Tuscaloosa, 1950-55, assoc. prof. psychology dept., 1955-64, prof. psychology dept., 1964-75; prof., head psychology dept. Miss. State U., Starkville, 1975-90, prof. emeritus, 1990—; dir. psychology dept. Ala. State Hosps., Tuscaloosa, 1956-71. Contbr. articles to profl. jours. Fellow Soc. for Personal Assessment; mem. Am. Psychol. Assn. (life), Southeastern Psychol. Assn. (life), Miss. Psychol. Assn. (life). Unitarian. Home: 996 Sandhurst Rd Starkville MS 39759-9301 Office: Miss State U PO Box 6161 Mississippi State MS 39762-6161

PEZZUTO, JOHN MICHAEL, pharmacology educator; b. Hammonton, N.J., Aug. 29, 1950; s. Michael L. and Elizabeth (Brown) P.; m. Mimi Faith Rotstein, Aug. 29, 1986; 1 child, John-Henry Albert; 1 child from previous marriage, Jennifer Anne. AB, Rutgers U., 1973; PhD, Coll. Medicine and Dentistry N.J., 1977. Postdoctoral assoc. MIT, Cambridge, 1977-79; instr. chemistry U. Va., Charlottesville, 1979-80; asst. prof. U. Ill.-Chgo., 1980-84, assoc. prof.,1984-91, prof., 1991—; assoc. dir. U. Ill. Cancer Ctr, 1991-95; editor-in-chief Internat. Jour. Pharmacognosy, 1991-95, editor-in-chiefCombinatory chemistry and high throughput screening, 1996—; interim head dept. med. chemistry and pharmacognosy, U. Ill., Chgo., 1992-95; dir. program for collaborative rsch. in the pharm. scis. U. Ill., Chgo., 1995—; pres., co-founder Internat. Therapeutics Inc., River Forest, Ill., 1996—. Editor: Biotechnology and Pharmacy; contbr. articles to sci. jours. and books. NIH fellow, 1977-80, Rsch. fellow Alexander von Humboldt Found., 1990-91; NIH Research Career Devel. awardee, 1984-89, grantee Nat. Cancer Inst., 1984-78, Nat. Inst. Dental Research, 1984-85. Mem. AAAS, Am. Chem. Soc., Am. Soc. Pharmacognosy, Am. Assn. Cancer Research, N.Y. Acad. Scis., Am. Soc. Biol. Chemists. Home: 846 Bonnie Brae Pl River Forest IL 60305-1510 Office: U Ill 833 S Wood St Chicago IL 60612-7229

PFAFF, WILLIAM WALLACE, medical educator; b. Rochester, N.Y., Aug. 14, 1930; s. Norman Joseph and Eleanor Blakesley (Wells) P.; m. Patricia Ann Clark; children: Nancy, Karen, Margaret, Mary Catherine. AB, Harvard U., 1952; MD, SUNY, 1956. Intern U. Chgo., 1956-58; sr. asst. surgeon NIH, Bethesda, Md., 1958-60; resident Stanford U. Med. Ctr., Palo Alto, Calif., 1960-65; asst. prof. U. Fla., Gainesville, 1965-68, assoc. prof., 1968-71, prof. surgery, 1971-95, prof. emeritus, adj. prof., 1995—, dir. organ transplant programs, 1971-95; bd. dirs. United Network for Organ Sharing, Richmond, Val; pres., com. chair Southeastern Organ Procurement Found., Richmond, 1973-95. Fellow Am. Coll. Surgeons; mem. Am. Surg. Assn., Am. Soc. Transplant Surgeons, So. Surg. Assn., Transplantation Soc., Alachua County Med. Soc. (pres. 1977-78). Home: 2445 NW 15 Pl Gainesville FL 32605 Office: U Fla Dept Surgery PO Box 100286 Gainesville FL 32610-0286

PFAFFLIN, SHEILA MURPHY, psychologist; b. Pasadena, Calif., July 31, 1934; d. Leonard Anthony and Honora (Shields) Murphy; m. James Reid Pfafflin, Sept. 7, 1957. BA, Pomona Coll., 1956; MA, Johns Hopkins U., 1958, PhD, 1959. Mem. tech. staff AT&T Bell Labs., Murray Hill, N.J., 1959-75; dist. mgr. AT&T, Morristown, N.J., 1975—; Chair sub com. on Women-Com. on Equal Opportunities in Sci. and Tech., NSF, Washington, 1981-85; mem. adv. coun. Math/Sci. Tchr. Supply and Demand, N.J. Dept. Higher Edn., 1982-83; mem. adv. bd. for Maths., Sci. and Computer Sci. Teaching Improvement Grants, N.J. Dept. Higher Edn., 1984-89. Co-editor: Expanding the Role of Women in the Sciences, 1978, Scientific-Technological Change & the Role of Women in Development, 1981, Psychology & Educational Policy, 1987; contbr. articles to profl. jours. Trustee Ramapo Coll. of N.J., Mahwah, N.J., 1984—; adv. bd. Project "SMART", Girls Clubs of Am., N.Y.C., 1984—, Consortium for Ednl. Equity, Rutgers U., New Brunswick, N.Y., 1983—; pres. Assn. for Women in Sci. Ednl. Found., Washington, 1982—. Fellow AAAS, N.Y. Acad. Scis., Am. Psychol. Assn.; mem. Assn. for Women in Sci. (pres. 1980-81, Women Scientist award, Met. Chpt., 1987), Phi Beta Kappa, Sigma Xi. Home: 173 Gates Ave Gillette NJ 07933-1719 Office: AT&T 100 Southgate Pkwy Rm 3F07 Morristown NJ 07960-6441

PFALZER, FRANK A., retired general surgeon and educator; b. Buffalo, July 3, 1923; s. Frank Anthony and Claire Marie (Zindel) P.; m. Patricia Joan Funnell, Feb. 10, 1953; children: Nancy J. Swartzman, Peter A., David F., Mary Jo Malik, William J., Marta E. Jackson. BS in Chemistry, Canisius Coll., Buffalo, 1944; MD, SUNY, Buffalo, 1949. Diplomate Am. Bd. Surgery. Attending surgeon U.S. VA Med. Ctr., Buffalo, 1957-70, cons. in surgery, 1970-89; clin. instr. surgery SUNY, Buffalo, 1957-89; staff surgeon Kenmore (N.Y.) Mercy Hosp., 1957-89, pres. med. staff, 1972, emeritus staff gen. surgery dept., 1989—. Contbr. articles to profl. jours. 1st lt. M.C., U.S. Army, 1953-55, Korea. Decorated Bronze Star. Fellow ACS, Buffalo Surg. Soc. Republican. Roman Catholic. Home: 2 Laurel Oak Rd Fernandina Beach FL 32034-6524

PFEFFER, CYNTHIA ROBERTA, psychiatrist, educator; b. Newark, May 22, 1943; d. Edward I. and Ann Pfeffer. BA, Douglas Coll., 1964; MD, NYU, 1968. Assoc. dir. child psychiatry inpatient unit Albert Einstein Coll. Medicine, Bronx, N.Y., 1973-79; chief child psychiatry inpatient unit N.Y. Hosp. Cornell Med. Ctr., White Plains, N.Y., 1979—; assoc. prof. clin. psychiatry Cornell U. Med. Coll., N.Y.C., 1984—; prof. psychiatry Cornell U. Med. Coll., 1989—; pres. N.Y. Coun. on Child and Adolescent Psychiatry, N.Y.C., 1989—. Author: The Suicidal Child, 1986, Difficult Moments in Child Psychotherapy, 1988; editor: Youth Suicide: Perspectives on Risk and Prevention, 1989. Recipient Erwin Stengel award Internat. Assn. Suicide Prevention, 1987, Wilford Hulse award N.Y. Coun. on Child & Adolescent Psychiatry, 1989, Sigmund Freud award Am. Soc. Psychoanalytic Physicians, 1994. Fellow Am. Psychiat. Assn., Am. Acad. Child and Adolescent Psychiatry (councillor-at-large 1989—, Norbert Rieger award 1988), Am. Psychopathological Assn.; mem. Am. Assn. Suicidology (pres. 1987, Young Contbrs. award 1981, 82). Office: NY Hosp Westchester Div 21 Bloomingdale Rd White Plains NY 10605-1504 also: 40 E 89th St New York NY 10128-1215

PFEFFER, WAYNE LOWELL, medical center administrator; b. N.Y.C., Mar. 21, 1952; s. Martin I. and Roslyn (Israel) P.; m. Elizabeth A. Pfeffer, Aug. 7, 1986; children: Michelle, Katie. BS in Bus. Orgn. and Mgmt. Acctg., SUNY, Buffalo, 1974; MHSA, St. Joseph Coll., Widham, Maine, 1996. Chief acct. trainee VA Med. Ctr., Bronx, N.Y., 1974-75; chief acct. VA Med. Ctr., Portland, Oreg., 1975-78; asst. chief fiscal svcs. VA Med. Ctr., Dayton, Ohio, 1978-79; CFO VA Med. Ctr., Newington, Conn., 1979-80, L.A., 1980-81, San Diego, 1981-87; assoc. dir. tng. VA Med. Ctr., Long Beach, Calif., 1987-88; assoc. dir. VA Med. Ctr., Boise, Idaho, 1988-92, Lexington, Ky., 1992—; pres. Fed. Exec. Assn., Lexington, 1994—; chief Network Assn. Dirs., 1993-95. Pre-litigation screning panel mem. City Boise, 1989-92. Mem. Am. Coll. Health Care Execs. Office: VA Med Ctr 2250 Leestown Rd Lexington KY 40511

PFEIFER, EUGENE, clinical pharmacist, nursing home consultant; b. Melrose Park, Ill., Apr. 16, 1945; s. Eugene Paul and Leota Agnus (Dreher) P.; 1 child, Jennifer Lynn; m. Virginia A. Perun. BS in Zoology, No. Ill. U., 1967; BS in Pharmacy, U. Ill., Chgo., 1970; MBA, Keller Grad. Sch. Mgmt., 1983; PharmD, Purdue U., 1995. Registered pharmacist, Ill., Va. Dir. pharmacy Westlake Cmty. Hosp., Melrose Park, 1970-71; staff pharmacist Northwestern Meml. Hosp., Chgo., 1975-77; pharmacist in charge Whitehall Convalescent and Nursing Home, Chgo., 1975-76; asst. dir. pharmacy/metabolic support svc. St. Mary of Nazareth Hosp. Ctr., Chgo., 1977-85; pharmacy mgr./cons. pharmacist Conva-Care, Inc., Glenview, Ill., 1985-87; cons., pharmacist-in-charge Healthcare Pharmacy, Chgo., 1987-88; pharmacist VA Med. Ctr., Danville, Ill., 1988-89, Covenant Med. Ctr., Urbana, Ill., 1989-93; staff clin. pharmacist USMC, Danville, Ill., 1990-96; staff clin. pharmacist Ball Meml. Hosp., Muncie, Inc., 1996—; off-site preceptor pharmacy residency program Rush Presbyn. St. Luke's Med. Ctr., Chgo., 1978-83. Mem. exec. coun. Boy Scouts Am. With USN, 1971-75. Mem. Am. Soc. Health Sys. Pharmacy, Am. Coll. Clin. Pharmacy, Kappa Psi. Roman Catholic. Contbr. articles to profl. jours. Home: 7812 O'Hare Cir Yorktown IN 47396 Office: Ball Meml Hosp Pharmacy Dept 2400 University Muncie IN 47396

PFEIFER, MARK EDWARD, podiatrist; b. Milw., Sept. 15, 1956; s. Edward George and Dorothy Lucille (Rosa) P. AS, U. Wis., 1976; BS, St. Norbert Coll., 1978; DPM/BS, Ill. Coll. Podiatric Medicine, 1983. Diplomate Am. Bd. Podiatric Orthopedics and Primary Medicine. Radiology fellow Ill. Coll. Podiatric Medicine, 1983-84, radiology faculty, 1983-84; med., surg. resident VA Med. Ctr., North Chicago, 1992-94; physician Northwoods Foot Specialist, Eagle River, Wis., 1986—, Lakeland Med. Ctr., Elkhorn, Wis., 1995—; Con. VA Med. Ctr., 1995—; adv. com. Gateway Tech. Coll., Elkhorn, 1995—. Sponsor, lectr. Am. Heart Assn. Fitnesswalk, Eagle River, Wis., 1986—; bd. dirs. Town of Lincoln Mining Impact and Devel. Com., Crandon, Wis., 1990-92. Recipient Cert. of Appreciation Ill. Podiatric Med. Students Assn., 1982, Cert. of Svc., 1982. Fellow Am. Coll. of Podiatric Radiologists, Am. Soc. of Podiatric Dermatology; mem. Wis. Soc. of Podiatric Medicine, Am. Podiatric Med. Assn., Am. Pub. Health Assn.,. Home: Rt 1 Box 311 Argonne WI 54511 Office: Northwoods Foot Specialists 201 Hospital Rd Eagle River WI 54521

PFEIFFER, STEVEN EUGENE, molecular cell biologist, educator; b. Watertown, Wis., Aug. 13, 1940; s. Roy Henry and Doris (Haugen) P.; m. Carol Lee Aldrich, June 24, 1965; children: Julie Kristen, Carin-anna, Shaili Margreta. BA, Carleton Coll., 1962; PhD, Washington U., 1967. Postdoctoral fellow Brandeis U., Waltham, Mass., 1967-69; from asst. prof. to prof. U. Conn. Med. Sch., Farmington, 1969—; vis. scientist Pasteur Inst., Paris, 1976-77, European Molecular Biology Lab., Heidelberg, Germany, 1984-85, 93; mem. adv. com. on rsch. Nat. Multiple Sclerosis Soc., N.Y.C., 1989-95; mem. com. on space biology and medicine Nat. Rsch. Coun., 1995—. Mem. editl. bd. Jour. Neurosci. Rsch., 1979—, Devel. Neurosci., 1982—, Internat. Jour. Devel. Neurosci., 1991—. Clarinetist Farmington Valley Symphony Orch., 1981—. Josiah Macy Jr. Faculty scholar, 1976-77; Fulbright fellow, 1983-84; Deutsche Academicer Austausch Dienst fellow, 1993; Jacob Javits Neurosci. Investigator award, 1995—. Mem. Am. Soc. Neurochemistry, Soc. for Neurosci., Am. Assn. for Cell Biology. Unitarian. Office: U Conn Med Sch Farmington Ave Farmington CT 06030-0001

PFEIFFER, STEVEN IRA, psychologist; b. N.Y.C., Nov. 10, 1950; s. Murray Robert and Phyllis Selma (Levine) P.; m. Jan Stephanie Leslie, Aug. 25, 1979; 1 child, Andrea Beth. BA, SUNY, Oneonta, 1972; MA, Fairleigh Dickinson U., 1974; PhD, U. N.C., 1977. Diplomate Am. Bd. Profl. Psychology; lic. psychologist. Prof. Fla. Internat. U., Miami, 1977-78, Fordham U., N.Y.C., 1978-80, No. Ariz. U., Flagstaff, 1980-82; staff psychologist dept. pediatrics Ochsner Clinic, New Orleans, 1982-87; exec. dir. Inst. Clin. Tng. and Rsch., Inc., Devon, Pa., 1987-95; vis. prof. clin. psychology Drexel U., Phila., 1995-96; prof. Kent (Ohio) State U., Kennett Square, Pa., 1996—; adj. prof. dept. psychiatry U. Pa. Sch. Medicine; clin. psychologist, Paoli, Pa., 1988—. Author: Inpatient Treatment of Children and Adolescents, 1992; editor-in-chief Clin. Child Psychology, 1985; editor Comprehensive Mental Care Jour.; also articles. Lt. USNR, 1986-95. U.S. Dept. Edn. grantee, 1979; NIMH fellow, 1974-75. Fellow Am. Psychol. Assn.; mem. Am. Assn. Mental Retardation, Am. Orthopsychiat. Assn., Coun. for Exceptional Children. Office: Kent State U Grad Sch Edn Kent OH 44242

PFENNINGER, KARL H., cell biology and neuroscience educator; b. Stafa, Switzerland, Dec. 17, 1944; came to U.S., 1971, naturalized, 1993; s. Hans Rudolf and Delie Maria (Zahn) P.; m. Marie-France Maylié, July 12, 1974; children—Jan Patrick, Alexandra Christina. M.D., U. Zurich, 1971. Research instr. dept. anatomy Washington U., St. Louis, 1971-73; research assoc. sect. cell biology Yale U., New Haven, 1973-76; assoc. prof. dept. anatomy and cell biology Columbia U., N.Y.C., 1976-81, prof., 1981-86; prof., chmn. dept. cellular and structural biology U. Colo. Sch. Medicine, Denver, 1986—; dir. interdeptmental program in cell and molecular biology Columbia U. Coll. Physicians and Surgeons, N.Y.C., 1980-85; chmn. Given Biomed. Inst., Aspen, Colo., 1992-93. Author: Essential Cell Biology, 1990; contbr. articles to profl. jours. Recipient C.J. Herrick award Am. Assn. Anatomists, 1977; I.T. Hirschl Career Scientist award, 1977; Javits neurosci. investigator awards NIH, 1984, 91. Mem. AAAS, Am. Soc. for Cell Biology, Am. Soc. for Biochemistry and Molecular Biology, Toxicology Forum (bd. dirs. 1995—), Harvey Soc., Soc. for Neurosci., Internat. Brain Rsch. Orgn., Internat. Soc. for Neurochemistry. Office: U Colo Health Scis Ctr Dept Cellular and Structural Biology B-111 4200 E 9th Ave Denver CO 80262

PFEUFFER, THOMAS HANS, biochemist, researcher; b. Schweinfurt, Germany, Feb. 11, 1938; s. Leo and Sophie (Pröschel) P.; m. Elke Pichler. Pharm. Chemist U., Würzburg, Germany, 1963; PhD, Univ. Würzburg, Germany, 1966. Capt. German Army, 1966-67; asst. prof. U. Würzburg, Germany, 1968-80, assoc. prof., 1980-91; full prof., dept. head U. Düsseldorf, Germany, 1991—. Mem. Brit. Bio-Chem. Soc., German Soc. Biol. Chemistry. Home: Espenstr 99, 41470 Neuss Germany Office: Heinrich-Heine Univ Inst, Physiologische Chemie II, Universitätsstr 1, 40225 Düsseldorf Germany

PFISTER, ALBERT JAMES, cardiac surgeon; b. Sayre, Pa., June 23, 1951. AB, Dartmouth Coll., 1973; MS, Rutgers U., 1976; MD, Med. U. of S.C., 1981. Diplomate Nat. Bd. Med. Examiners, Am. Bd. Surgery, Am. Bd. Thoracic Surgery. Intern in surgery N.Y. Hosp./Cornell Med. Ctr., N.Y.C., 1981-82, resident in surgery, 1982-86; fellow in cardiothoracic surgery George Washington U. Med. Ctr., Washington, 1986-88; attending cardiac surgeon Washington Hosp. Ctr., 1988—, co-dir. heart transplantation, 1990-94; clin. in surgery George Washington U. Sch. Medicine, Washington, 1991—. Fellow ACS; mem. AMA, Soc. Thoracic Surgeons, D.C. Med. Soc. Office: 11706 New Hampshire Ave NW Washington DC 20009

PFISTER, RICHARD CHARLES, physician, radiology educator; b. Ypsilanti, Mich., Nov. 27, 1933; s. Emil Robert and Francis Josephine (LeForge) P.; m. Sally DeAnn Haight, Dec. 31, 1956 (div. 1980); children: Kirk Alan, Gary Raymond, Karen Dawn, James Kevin, William Charles. BS, Ctrl. Mich. U., 1958; MD, Wayne State U., 1962. Assoc. prof. radiology Harvard

Med. Sch. and Mass. Gen. Hosp., Boston, 1966-89; med. officer FDA, Washington, 1989-90; prof. radiology U. South Ala., Mobile, 1990-92, La. State U., New Orleans, 1993—. Editor, author: Interventional Radiology, 1982. With U.S. Army Med. Corps, 1953-55. Recipient Investigator award NIH, Washington, 1972. Fellow Am. Coll. Radiology; mem. AMA, Soc. Uroradiology (pres. 1984-85), Radiologic Soc. N.Am., Am. Roentgen Ray Soc., Soc. Cardiovascular Interventional. Office: LSU Med Ctr 1542 Tulane Ave New Orleans LA 70112-2825

PFLUM, WILLIAM JOHN, physician; b. N.Y.C., July 30, 1924; s. Peter Arthur and Caroline (Schmidt) P.; BS, Georgetown U., 1947; MD, Loyola U., Chgo., 1951; m. Roseann Sarah Stubing, Oct. 13, 1956; children: Carol Jean, Jeannine, Suzanne, Denise, Peter. Intern, St. Vincent's Hosp., N.Y.C., 1951-52, resident in internal medicine, 1954-55; resident in internal medicine NYU div. Goldwater Meml. Hosp., N.Y.C., 1952-53; resident in allergy Inst. Allergy, Roosevelt Hosp., N.Y.C., 1956; attending internal medicine (allergy and immunology) Overlook Hosp., Summit, N.J., 1958—; assoc. attending Inst. Allergy, Immunology and Infectious Diseases, Roosevelt Hosp., N.Y.C., 1957-92; pvt. practice medicine, specializing in allergy and immunology, Summit, 1957-92; ret.; cons. in field. Participant Boston Marathon, 1971-95. Served with USAAF, 1943-45; ETO. Decorated Purple Heart, Air medal with two clusters, POW medal. Diplomate Am. Bd. Allergy and Immunology. Fellow Am. Acad. Allergy, Am. Coll. Allergists, Am. Assn. Clin. Immunology and Allergy; mem. Summit Med. Soc., Am. Assn. Clin. Immunology and Allergy (pres. Mid-Atlantic region 1975-76), Disabled Am. Vets., Mil. Order Purple Heart, Am. Ex-Prisoners of War, 8th Air Force Hist. Soc., World Marathon Runners Assn., Robert A. Cooke Allergy Alumni Assn. Roman Catholic. Home: 16 Packer Ave Rumson NJ 07760-2028

PFORR, MARY MARTHA, retired public health administrator, consultant; b. Balt., Apr. 26, 1948; d. Karl George and Mary Theresa (Krecz) Smith; m. William John Pforr Jr., Feb. 9, 1983; children by previous marriage: M. Melissa, Patrick W. AA, Anne Arundel Community Coll., 1972; BS in Nursing, U. Md., Balt., 1974; MPH, Johns Hopkins U., 1976. Diplomate in quality assurance; cert. nurse adminstr., master hypnotherapist, health edn. specialist, neuro-linguistics practioner, nutrition counselor, master time line therapy practitioner. Asst. prof. nursing Anne Arundel Community Coll., Arnold, Md., 1976-80; dir. tng. Neighborhood Devel. Collaborative, Washington, 1980-81; supr. pub. health nurse Vis. Nurses Assn., Balt., 1981-82; dir. quality assurance Consumer Health Svcs., Inc., Annapolis, Md., 1982-83; program dir. Balt. County Health Dept., Towson, Md., 1983-84; claims specialist Blue Cross Md., Towson, Md., 1984-85; asst. dir. Staff Builders Inc., Balt., Md., 1985-87; nursing instr. South Balt. Gen. Hosp, 1987-88; chief div. quality control State Md. Mental Hygiene Adminstrn., Balt., 1988-94; ret., 1994; cons. Earl Delarue, Esquire, Towson, 1987, Mark Shar, Esquire, Balt., 1979, nutrition counselor; chmn. editor Md. Nursing Assn., Balt., 1974; spkr., presenter Internat. Conf. Psychiat. Care. Co-author Geriatric Nursing Assistant, 1980; contbr. articles to profl. jours. Leader Girl Scouts U.S., Pasadena, Md., 1980; den mother Boy Scouts Am., Pasadena, Md., 1980; coord. ARC Anne Arundel County Health Fairs, Balt., 1981. Recipient Leadership award ARC, 1980; CETA grantee State Md., 1979. Mem. AAHPERD, Md. Quality Assurance Profls., Am. Coll. Med. Quality, Nat. Assn. Quality Assurance and Utilization Rev., Am. Coll. Utilization Rev. Physicians, Md. Pub. Health Assn. (v.p. 1987-89), Pub. Risk Mgmt. Assn., Am. Coll. Health Care Execs., Nat. Assn. Cert. Hypnotherapists, Nat. Bd. Cert. Clin. Hypnotherapists, Soc. Pub. Health Educators, Soroptimists (sec. 1982-84), Women of Moose, Sigma Theta, Sigma Zeta. Democrat. Roman Catholic. Home: 226 Bar Harbor Rd Pasadena MD 21122-3021

PHAM, SI MAI, cadiothoracic surgeon, medical educator; b. Ninh Hoa, Khanh Hoa, Vietnam, Oct. 6, 1955; came to U.S. 1975; s. Tro Pham and Nhung Thi Mai; m. Marie Christine Pham, Sept. 9, 1987; children: Benjamin Bartley, Anthony Ninh. Student, U. Saigon, Sch. Pharmacy, Vietnam, 1973-75; BS in Chem. magna cum laude, Lebanon Valley Coll., Annville, Pa., 1979; MD, U. Pitts., 1983. Diplomate Am. Bd. Surgery, Am. Bd. Thoracic Surgery. Intern, resident gen. surgery U. Pitts., Pitts., Pa., 1983-86, rsch. fellow, cardiothoracic surgery, 1986-87, sr. and chief resident, gen. surgery, 1987-89, resident cardiothoracic surgery, 1989-92, asst. prof. surgery, Sch. of Medicine, 1992—, dir. adult cardiac transplant program, Sch. of Medicine, 1993—; dir. extracorporeal membrane oxygenation svc. Presbyterian U. Hosp., Pitts., Pa., 1993—. Contbr. chpts. to books, articles to profl. jours. Recipient Am. Chem. award, 1979, Radiology award U. Pitts., 1983; ACS Faculty fellowship award, 1994—; grantee Children's Hosp. Pitts., 1987, Am. Heart Assn., 1987-88, 94—, Thoracic Surgery Found., 1996-97, Presbyn. U. Hosp., 1987-89. Fellow Am. Coll. Surgeons; mem. Am. Soc. Artificial Internal Organs, Internat. Soc. Heart and Lung Transplantation, Soc. Critical Care Medicine, Am. Assn. Advancement of Sci., Am. Soc. Transplant Surgeons, Soc. Thoracic Surgeons, Extracorporeal Life Support Organization, Phi Alpha Epsilon. Home: 305 Marberry Dr Pittsburgh PA 15215-1437 Office: U Pitts Med Ctr Divsn CTS 200 Lothrop St Rm C-700 Pittsburgh PA 15213-2546

PHARES, JAMES STEPHEN, physician assistant; b. Hamilton, Ohio, Apr. 6, 1947; s. Murray Allen and Mary Lou (Stephens) P.; m. Claudette Harrison Halstead, July 3, 1969 (div. Oct. 1978); 1 child, Amber Dawn; m. Dawn Ester Diener, Feb. 16, 1980; 1 child, Hannah Marie. AAN, Miami U. Middletown, 1974; BS, Duke U., 1978. Staff nurse Duke Med. Ctr., Durham, N.C., 1974-76; physician asst. Blackfeet Indian Health Svcs. Hosp., Browning, Mont., 1978-80, Cardiovas. & Thoracic Surgeons Greensboro, N.C., 1980-87, Heart-Lung & Vasc. Inst. Scripps Clinic, La Jolla, Calif., 1987-90, Dr. Thomas Mabee, Davenport, Iowa, 1990—. Fellow Am. Acad. Physician Assts., Nat. Rural Health Assn., Acad. Physician Assts. in Cardiovasc. Surgery, Iowa Physician Asst. Soc. Republican. Methodist. Home: 3205 Quail Ridge Rd Bettendorf IA 52722-5338 Office: Profession Possibilities 1228 E Rasholme Ste 100 Davenport IA 52803

PHARIS, MARY EVANS, psychology educator; b. Milw., July 3, 1938; d. Silas McAfee and Lorraine (McManamy) Evans; m. David Bunsen Pharis, Aug. 6, 1966; children: Christopher, Michael. Student, Stanford U., 1956-58; BS, U. Wis., 1960; AM, U. Chgo., 1962; PhD, U. Tex., 1978. Lic. psychologist, Tex.; diplomate Am. Bd. Psychology. Case worker Scholarship & Guidance Assn., Chgo., 1962-66; social work tng. Michael Reese Hosp. Psychiatry, Chgo., 1966-68; coord. spl. svc. Evanston Ind. Sch. Dist., Evanston, Ill., 1968-70; instr. Ill. Coll. and MacMurray Coll., Jacksonville, Ill., 1972-74; intern psychology Counseling Ctr. U. Tex., Austin, 1978-79; spl. asst. to chief Mental Health Study Ctr. NIMH, Adelphi, Md., 1980-81; asst. prof. U. Tex., Austin, 1981-84, assoc. prof. psychology, 1984—; pvt. practice Austin, 1984—; examiner Am. Bd. Profl. Psychology, 1990—; cons. in field. Author of book and contbr. chpts. to books; contbr. articles to profl. jours. Adv. com. family life Child and Family Svcs., Austin, 1982—; mem. com. capital area needs assessment project United Way, 1984; mem. Child and Adolescent Needs Task Force, Travis County, 1984; bd. dirs. Austin Teenage Parent coun., 1986-88. Fellow Lindsey Barbee, 1960-61, faculty U. Chgo., 1961-62, NIMH, 1976-78, Congrl. Sci., 1979-80, 82-84, Clara Pope Willoughby Centennial, 1985—. Mem. Ill. Soc. Clin. Social Work (founder), Am. Orthopsychiat. Assn., Am. Psychol. Assn. Tex. Psychol. Assn., Capital Area Psychol. Assn., Soc. Rsch. in Child Devel., Am. Bd. Profl. Psychology (life), Tex. Ex-Students Assn. (life), Stanford Alumni Assn. (life), Phi Kappa Phi (life). Home: 5400 Ridge Oak Dr Austin TX 78731-4816

PHELAN, JEFFREY PATRICK, obstetrician and gynecologist; b. Boston, Apr. 7, 1946; m. Marilyn Marcy, May 3, 1969; children: Kelly Elizabeth, Shane Patrick, Shannon Leigh. MD, U. Miami, 1973; JD, Loyola Law Sch., 1988. Diplomate Am. Bd. Ob-Gyn. Intern, resident Naval Regional Med. Ctr., Portsmouth, Va., 1973-77; obstet. cons. Pregnant Cardiac Clinic U. So. Calif.-L.A. County Med. Ctr., 1981-83, dir. Normal Birth Ctr., 1981-88, dir. External Cephalic Version Clinic, 1982-85, obstet. cons. Post Date Clinic, 1984-86, assoc. dir. Women's ICU, 1984-88, dir. antepartum fetal surveillance, 1984-88; dir. maternal-fetal medicine Queen of the Valley Hosp., West Covina, Calif., 1987-91; co-dir. maternal-fetal medicine Pomona (Calif.) Valley Hosp. Med. Ctr., 1987—; dir. maternal-fetal medicine San Antonio Hosp., Upland, Calif., 1991—; co-dir. maternal-fetal medicine Garfield Med. Ctr., 1995—. Editor: Critical Care Obstetrics, 1987, Cesarean Delivery, 1988, Prevention in Prematurity, 1992; editor jour. Ob-Gyn. and the Law, 1989; perinatal editor Jour Perinatology, 1993; editor in chief OBG Mgmt., 1994; co-editor: Critical Care Obstetrics, 2d edit., 1991, Handbook of Critical Care Obstetrics, 1994. Named Best Doctor in Am., 1994. Fellow Am. Coll. Ob-Gyn. (1st award for sci. presentation 1989), Am. Coll. Legal Medicine; mem. ABA, Calif. Bar Assn., Soc. Perinatal Obstetricians (Soc. award 1989). Office: 1030 S Arroyo Pky # 200 Pasadena CA 91105

PHELPS, CHARLES ELLIOTT, economics educator; b. N.Y.C., Apr. 20, 1943; s. McKinnie L. and Carolyn (McCleery) P.; m. Dale L. King, Sept. 2, 1967; children: Darin, Teresa. BA in Math., Pomona Coll., 1965; MBA, U. Chgo., 1968, PhD, 1973. Economist RAND Corp., Santa Monica, Calif., 1973-84; prof. econs. U. Rochester, N.Y., 1984—; provost U. Rochester, 1994—; cons. JUREcon, Inc., L.A., 1977-86; pvt. cons., Rochester, N.Y., 1986—. Author: Health Economics, 1996; also over 70 articles. Fellow Nat. Bur. for Econ. Rsch.; mem. Inst. Medicine, Am. Econ. Assn., Soc. for Med. Decision Making (trustee 1991-93), Assn. for Pub. Policy Analysis (sec. 1982-91). Office: Office of the Provost U Rochester 200 Administration Bldg. Rochester NY 14627-0001

PHELPS, KATHRYN ANNETTE, mental health counseling executive, consultant; b. Creswell, Oreg., Aug. 1, 1940; d. Henry Wilbur and Lake Ilene (Wall) M.; children: David Bryan (dec.), Derek Alan, Darla Ailene. BS in edn., Western Oreg. State Coll., 1962; MSW, Columbia State U., 1992, PhD, 1993. Tchr. Germany, Thailand, U.S., 1962-88; acct. exec. ins. industry; weight-loss counselor, alchohol/drug abuse prevention/intervention counselor teens, 1990-93; counselor Eugene, 1989-94; sr. exec. v.p., edn. dir. Light Streams, Inc., Eugene, 1993—; sr. exec. v.p., therapist Comprehensive Assessment Svcs./The Focus Inst., Inc., Eugene, 1994—; mental health counselor in pvt. practice; ednl. cons. specializing in learning testing Comprehensive Assessment Svcs., Eugene, 1996—; co-owner, co-founder Comprehensive Assessment Svcs., LLC, 1995—; cons. consumer edn. Author: Easy Does It, books 1 & 2; hosted weekly TV cooking segment, Portland and U.S. Guardian Jobs Daughters, 1980-82; bd. dirs., den mother Cub Scouts, Boy Scouts, Kansas, Oreg., 1974-82; coach girls volleyball, 1974-80; vol. in orphanages, elderly nursing homes, Thailand, Germany, U.S., 1954-95; sunday sch. tchr., 1956-90; sponsored exchange student, 1984-88. Mem. Am. Bd. Disability Analysts, Eastern Star, Nat. Assn. Social Workers, Am. Counseling Assn., Columbia State U. Alumni Assn., Women's Internat. Bowling Conf. Home: 3838 Kendra St Eugene OR 97404 Office: Comprehensive Assessment Sv The Focus Inst Inc 400 E 2d St Ste 103 Eugene OR 97401

PHELPS, MICHAEL EDWARD, biophysics educator; b. Cleve., Aug. 24, 1939; s. Earl E. and Regina Bridget (Hines) P.; m. Patricia Emroy, May 15, 1969; children: Patrick, Kaitlin. B.A., Western Wash. State U., 1965; Ph.D., Washington U., St. Louis, 1970. Asst. prof. Washington U. Sch. Medicine and Engring., 1970-73, assoc. prof., 1973-75; assoc. prof. dept. radiology U. Pa., Phila., 1975-76; prof. biomath. UCLA, 1976—, prof., chief div. nuclear medicine and biophysics, 1980—, dir. Crump Inst. for Biol. Imaging; mem. study sect. NIH, Bethesda, Md., 1974-78. Author: Reconstruction Tomography in Diagnostic Radiology and Nuclear Medicine, 1977, Physics in Nuclear Medicine, 1980, Principles of Tracer Kinetics, 1983; contbr. articles to profl. jours. Recipient Von Hersey Found. award, 1975, Von Hersey Found. award, 1982, Von Heresy prize Von Heresy Found., Zurich, 1978, 82, E.O. Lawrence award Dept. Energy, 1983, Rosenthal award Am. Coll. Physicians, 1987; holder Jennifer Jones Simon endowed chair, 1983; named Disting. Alumnus Western Wash. State U., 1980. Fellow Am. Heart Assn.; mem. Inst. Medicine NAS (elected), Soc. Nuclear Medicine (Aebersold award 1983), Internat. Soc. Cerebral Blood Flow and Metabolism (Excellence award 1979), N.Y. Acad. Scis. (Sarah L. Poiley award 1984), Soc. Neuroscis., Am. Coll. Physicians (Rosenthal award). Roman Catholic. Home: 16720 Huerta Rd Encino CA 91436-3544

PHIBBS, CLIFFORD MATTHEW, surgeon, educator; b. Bemidji, Minn., Feb. 20, 1930; s. Clifford Matthew and Dorothy Jean (Wright) P.; m. Patricia Jean Palmer, June 27, 1953; children—Wayne Robert, Marc Stuart, Nancy Louise. B.S., Wash. State U., 1952; M.D., U. Wash., 1955; M.S., U. Minn., 1960. Diplomate Am. Bd. Surgery. Intern Ancker Hosp., St. Paul, 1955-56; resident in surgery U. Minn. Hosps., 1956-60; practice medicine specializing in surgery Oxboro Clinic, Mpls., 1962—, pres., 1985—; cons. to health risk mgmt. corps., 1994—; mem. Children's Hosp. Ctr., Northwestern-Abbott Hosp., Fairview-Southdale Hosp., Fairview Ridges Hosp.; clin. asst. prof. U. Minn., Mpls., 1975-78, clin. assoc. prof. surgery, 1978—; med. dir. Minn. Protective Life Ins. Co. Contbr. articles to med. jours. Bd. dirs. Bloomington Bd. Edn., Minn., 1974—, treas., 1976, sec., 1977-78, chmn., 1981-83; mem. adv. com. jr. coll. study City of Bloomington, 1964-66, mem. community facilities com., 1966-67, advisor youth study commn., 1966-68; vice chmn. bd. Hillcrest Meth. Ch., 1970-71; mem. Bloomington Adv. and Rsch. Coun., 1969-71; bd. dirs. Bloomington Symphony Orch., 1976—, Wash. State U. Found., trustee, 1990—; dir. bd. mgmt. Minnesota Valley YMCA, 1970-75; bd. govs. Mpls. Met. YMCA, 1970—; bd. dirs. Bloomington Heart-Health Found., 1989—, Martin Luther Manor, 1989; pres. Oxboro Clinics, 1985—; bd. dirs. Bloomington History Clock Tower Assn., 1990—; bd. dirs. Fairview Hosp. Clinic, 1994—. Capt. M.C., U.S. Army, 1960-62. Mem. ACS, AMA (Physician Recognition awards 1969, 73, 76, 79, 82, 85, 88, 91, 94), Assn. Surg. Edn., Royal Soc. Medicine, Am. Coll. Sports Medicine, Minn. Med. Assn. (del. 1991-94), Minn. Surg. Soc., Mpls. Surg. Soc., Hennepin County Med. Soc., Pan-Pacific Surg. Assn., Jaycees, Bloomington C. of C. (chmn. bd. 1984, chmn. 1985-86). Home: 9613 Upton Rd Minneapolis MN 55431-2454 Office: 600 W 98th St Minneapolis MN 55420-4773

PHIBBS, GARNETT ERSIEL, engineer, educator, minister, religious organization administrator; b. Clinchfield, Va., Oct. 12, 1922; s. Willie McDonald and Alma Irene (Horton) P.; m. Aug. 18, 1945 (div. 1972); children: Gerald Edwin, David Miller, Robert Lee. BA, Bridgewater (Va.) Coll., 1943; MRE, Bethany Theol. Sem., 1945; MDiv, Yale U., 1952, STM, 1954; postgrad., Boston U., Princeton U., St. Louis U. Cert. tchr., Calif.; ordained min. Ch. of the Brethren, 1945. Pastor Ch. of the Brethren, Bassett, Va., 1945-50, Champaign, Ill., 1955-56, Wilmington, Del., 1956-57, Glendale, Calif., 1969-70; pastor Niantic (Conn.) Bapt. Ch., 1950-51, Congl. Ch. (now United Ch. of Christ), Killingworth, Conn., 1951-55; exec. dir. Coun. of Chs., Trenton, N.J., 1957-62, Toledo, 1962-69; exec. dir. Citizens Aiding Pub. Offenders, Toledo, 1974-76; engr. Beverly Hills (Calif.) Hotel, 1981-91; mem., cons., leader Parents Without Ptnrs., 1972-90, ; mem. Habitat for Humanity, 1989-91; cons. North Toledo Community Orgn., 1977; co-founder Rescue Crisis Svc.; founder Interfaith Housing Corp., Toledo. Author: Bethel Memory Makers, 1977; contbr. articles to profl. jours. Mem. Toledo Bd. of Cmty. Rels., 1962-69, Ohio State Civil Rights Commn. of N.W. Ohio, Toledo, 1966-68, U.S. Civil Rights Commn., Toledo, 1965-69, Planned Parenthood Bd., Sister City Com. Toledo, Spain; mem., past pres. Kiwanis Internat., 1945-69; founding bd. dirs. West Hollywood Homeless Orgn. founder Charlotte Interfaith Network for Gays and Lesbian Equality; charter mem. Common Cause, Ams. United for Separation Ch. and State. Recipient Community Svc. award NAACP, 1960, So. Calif. Regional award Parents Without Parents, 1980; named Man of the Yr., ACLU, 1969. Mem. Internat. Union Oper. Engrs., Am. Correctional Assn., Am. Assn. for Pub. Adminstrs., Calif. Assn. Marriage and Family Counselors, Halfway House Assn, Parents and Friends of Gays and Lesbians (bd. sec. Time-Out Youth). Democrat. United Church of Christ. Home: 5945 Reddman Rd Charlotte NC 28212

PHIFER, CYNTHIA ANN, health facility administrator; b. Allentown, Pa., Dec. 10, 1960; d. Frederick A. and Annette A. (Barnack) Mihalow; m. Craig Phifer, Oct. 6, 1985. BS, Bloomsburg State Coll., 1981, MS, 1982; cert. health care adminstrn., Widener U., Chester, Pa., 1989; postgrad., Pa. State U. Speech/lang. pathologist Main Line Speech Cons., Haverford, Pa., 1982-84, Montgomery County Intermediate Unit #23, Norristown, Pa., 1982-85; clin. dir. speech and lang. pathology Montgomery Hosp. Med. Ctr., Norristown, 1985-95; dir. Weehab Sta., dir. speech and lang. pathology Rehab. Sta., 1995—; vis. lectr. Cabrini Coll., Montgomery County C.C., 1992—; guest presenter Early Childhood Conf., 1992, 94; tech. cons. UltraVoice, Ltd., 1993—, Theraspoons, 1993—; mem. profl. adv. com. Montgomery Home Care. Mem. Am. Speech, Lang. and Hearing Assn., Pa. Speech, Lang. and Hearing Assn. (profl. standards and practices com. 1990—), NE Pa. Speech and Hearing Assn., SE Pa. Speech and Hearing Assn. Office: Montgomery Hosp Powell And Fornance St Norristown PA 19401

PHILIP, PHILIP H., psychiatrist; b. Poland, Nov. 16, 1920; arrived in Canada, 1921, came to U.S., 1950; s. Harry Starr and Jenny Amsterdam.; m. Susanne Miller, July 10, 1983 (div. May 10, 1990); children: Eric D., Craig F., Susan L. MD, U. Toronto Med. Sch., 1944. Diplomate Am. Bd. Psychiatry and Neurology, Am. Bd. Child Psychiatry, 1964,. Dir. Cmty. Child Guidance Clin. of Washington U., St. Louis, 1953-55; chief children's outpatient clinic Nebr. Psychiat. Inst., Omaha, 1955-69; staff psychiatrist Student Health Ariz. State U., Tempe, 1992—; psychiatric examiner Episcopal Diocese of Nebr., Omaha, 1968-84; psychiatric cons. SAC/Offut AFB, Omaha, Nebr., 1978-82, dept. oncology, Meth. Hosp., Omaha, 1981-83; psychiatrist Boys Town, 1981-84. Capt. Royal Canadian Army Med. Corps, 1942-45. Fellow AMA, Am. Psychiatric Assn. (life). Office: Ariz State U Student Health PO Box 872104 Tempe AZ 85287-2104

PHILIPPILLAI, MARY RAJAPUSHPAM, nurse; b. Trincomal, Sri Lanka, Jan. 27, 1947; d. Augustinpillai Rajah and Theresammah (Ponnampalam) P.; m. Alan Francis Javel, Apr. 24, 1976; 1 child, Avril Therese. BS, Upsala Coll., E. Orange, N.J., 1984; MA in Psychology, Antioch U., 1994. Grad. nurse Beth Israel Med. Ctr., Newark, N.J., 1972-74; clin. nurse II U. Calif., San Francisco, 1974-78; staff nurse Mills Meml. Hosp., San Mateo, Calif., 1978-79, Royal Infirmary, Edinburgh, Scotland, 1980; relief charge nurse Watsonville (Calif.) Community, 1980; staff nurse St. Barnabas Med. Ctr., Newark, 1981-82; charge nurse Panorama Convalescent Ctr., Olympia, Wash., 1982-87; staff nurse St. Peter Hosp., Olympia, Wash., 1987—; pvt. practice Olympia, Wash.; employee assistance counselor St. Peter Hosp., Olympia, Wash., 1995—. Mem. advocations com. St. Michael's Ch., Olympia,, 1985—, liaison social justice com., social action commn., bd. mem. for bread for the world in dist. 3, Olympia, 1985—. Home: 6426 Woodard Bay Rd NE Olympia WA 98506-1550

PHILIPSON, LENNART CARL, microbiologist, science administrator; b. Stockholm, July 16, 1929; s. Carl and Greta (Svanström) P.; m. Malin Jondal, 1954; children: Niklas, Andreas, Tomas. MD, Uppsala (Sweden) U., 1957, D in Med. Scis., 1958, PhD (hon.), 1982, Dr. Med. (hon.), 1987, 94. Rsch. asst. Inst. Bacteriology Uppsala U., 1953-57, rsch. asst. Inst. Biochemistry, 1957-58, asst. prof. Inst. Virology, 1958-59; Sophie Fricke fellow Swedish Royal Acad. Sci. Rockefeller Inst., N.Y.C., 1959-61; from asst. to assoc. prof. virology, Swedish Med. Rsch. Coun. Uppsala U., 1961-68, founder, dir., The Wallenberg Lab., 1967-76, prof. microbiology, dept. microbiology, 1968-82; dir. gen. European Molecular Biology Lab., 1982-93; dir. Skirball Inst. Biomolecular Medicine, NYU Med. Ctr., N.Y.C., 1993—; vis. prof. Columbia U., 1971, MIT, 1977. Mem. editl. bd. EMBO Jour., 1982-86, 93—, Molecular Biology and Medicine, 1983-86, Jour. Virology, 1972-90, Nucleic Acid Rsch., 1983-91, BBA Revs. on Cancer, 1980—, Cancer Letters, 1985—, Genomics, 1986—; contbr. articles to profl. jours. Recipient Axel Hirsch prize Karolinska Inst., 1976, hon. prof. sci. faculty, Heidelberg U., Fed. Rep. Germany, 1985; fgn. assoc. U.S. NAS, Washington, 1992. Fellow Am. Acad. Microbiology; mem. Swedish Royal Acad. Sci., Royal Swedish Acad. Engring. Scis., European Molecular Biology Orgn., Heidelberg Acad. Scis., Soc. for Gen. Microbiology, N.Y. Acad. Scis., Swedish Soc. for Microbiology, Fedn. of European Biochem. Socs., Harvey Soc. (N.Y.). Office: NYU Med Ctr Skirball Inst Biomolecular Medicine 550 1st Ave New York NY 10016-6481

PHILLIPS, ARTHUR WILLIAM, JR., biology educator; b. Claremont, N.H., Sept. 25, 1915; s. Arthur William and Jane Helen (Daley) P.; m. Mary Catherine Mich, Oct. 21, 1950; children: Marilynn, William (dec.). BS, U. Notre Dame, 1939, MS, 1941; DSc, MIT, 1947. Rsch. asst. Lobund lab. U. Notre Dame, Ind., 1937-41, rsch. scientist, 1943-45; rsch. assoc. MIT, 1947-49; rsch. assoc. prof., head div. bioengring. Lobund lab. U. Notre Dame, Ind., 1949-54; rsch. scientist dept. biology and bioengring. MIT, Cambridge, 1942-43, rsch. fellow dept. food tech., 1945-47, rsch. assoc. dept. food tech., 1947-49; rsch. assoc. prof. dept. bacteriology Syracuse (N.Y.) U., 1954-58, prof. microbiology, 1959-86, prof. emeritus, 1986—, founder, dir. biol. rsch. labs., 1955-65, head radiation and isotope lab., 1956-63, dir. germ-free life rsch. lab., 1956-84; mem. Internat. Congress on Nutrition, Washington, 1960, Internat. Congress for Microbiology, Montreal, Can., 1962, Moscow, 1966, Internat. Congress for Germ-Free Life Rsch., Nagoya, Japan, 1967; mem. com. on nutrition NAS-NRC, Washington, 1964-66; mem. Conf. on Germ-Free Life and Gnobiotics, Madison, Wis., 1986, Internat. Conf. on Gnotobiology, Versailles, France, 1987; cons. NSF, Washington, Cradle Soc. Inc., Evanston, Ill., GE, Syracuse, Am. Cyanamid, Pearl River, N.Y., Carnation Co., L.A., C.V. Mosby, St. Louis, Can. Dry Corp., Greenwich, Conn., Chocolate Mfrs. Assn., Washington, Continental Can Co., Syracuse. Contbr. articles to profl. jours., chpts. to books. Refrigeration Rsch. Found. fellow, 1945-47; NIH grantee, 1956-80. Mem. Am. Soc. for Microbiology (placement com. 1968-78), Gnotobiotics Assn., Soc. for Gen. Microbiology. Home: Clark Hollow Rd East Poultney VT 05741-0604 Office: Syracuse U Dept Biology 108 College Pl Syracuse NY 13244-1270

PHILLIPS, DAVID HUNTER, biochemist, genetic toxicologist, researcher; b. London, Feb. 26, 1953; s. Ronald Aubrey and Margaret (Hunter) P.; m. Janet Carter, Sept. 16, 1978; children: Thomas Hunter, Jonathan Leo Hunter. BA, Oxford (Eng.) U., 1975; PhD, U. London, 1978. Rsch. assoc. U. Wis., Madison, 1978-80; rsch. affiliate Stanford (Calif.) U., 1980-81; rsch. scientist Inst. Cancer Rsch., London, 1981—. Co-editor: Postlabelling Methods for Detection of DNA Adducts, 1993, Environmental Mutagenesis, 1995; contbr. over 130 articles to profl. pubs. Mem. Royal Coll. Pathologists, Am. Assn. Cancer Rsch., U.K. Environ. Mutagen Soc. Office: Inst Cancer Rsch Haddow Lab, Cotswold Rd, Sutton SM2 5NG, England

PHILLIPS, DENISE, critical care nurse; b. Orange, N.J., July 11, 1960; d. James Henry Phillips and Gracie Estelle (Reed) Brown. Diploma in nursing, Riverside Hosp. Sch. Nursing, Newport News, Va., 1985; cert. in paralegal studies, Hampton U., 1990. RN, Va., Fla., Md., N.Y.; cert. BLS instr., ACLS; instr. cert. nurse asst. and LPN programs. Nurse asst. Riverside Hosp., Newport News, 1981-86; Riverside Hosp. Riverside Regional Med. Ctr., Newport News, 1986-91; staff nurse Traveling Nurse Corp., Malden, Mass., 1991-93; dir. staff devel. Va. Health Svcs., Inc., Newport News, 1993-95; asst. dir. nursing svcs. James Pointe Care Ctr., Newport News, Va., 1995—; per diem nurse adminstr. Sentara Hampton (Va.) Gen. Hosp., 1994—; asst. dir. of nursing svcs. James Point Care Ctr., Newport News, Va., 1995—; LPN, cert. nurse asst. instr. Career Devel. Ctr., Newport News, 1989-91; lectr. on decreasing profl. liability for healthcare workers, 1990—. Contbr. article to Health Care Digest, 1995. Vol. Williamsburg (Va.) area Girl Scouts U.S., 1990-92. Mem. ACCN, Nat. League of Nursing. Home: 7402 Vernon Pl Newport News VA 23605 Office: 5015 Huntington Ave Newport News VA 23605

PHILLIPS, EDUARDO, surgeon, educator; b. Guadalajara, Mex., Oct. 25, 1943; m. Marion Paulette Khan; children: Mark, Anthony, Cynthia. MD with honors, Nat. U. Mexico City, 1967. Diplomate Am. Bd. Surgery. Rotating intern Hosp. Frances, Mexico City, 1966, resident in gen. surgery, 1967-69; rotating intern Sinai Hosp., Detroit, 1969, resident in gen. surgery, 1970-73, coord. surg. edn., 1974-76, chief surg. endoscopy, 1984—, acting chmn. dept. surgery, 1991, chmn. dept. surgery, 1992—; clin. asst. prof. Wayne State U., Detroit, 1992—. Contbr. articles to profl. jours. Fellow Internat. Coll. Surgeons (pres. Mich. divsn. 1995—, vice regent Mich 1993-95, regent Mich. 1995—, Vice Regent of Yr. 1993), Am. Coll. Surgeons; mem. AMA, Am. Soc. for Laser Medicine and Surgery, Am. Soc. Abdominal Surgeons, Am. Soc. Gastrointestinal Endoscopy, Am. Soc. Bariatric Surgery, Acad. Surgery Detroit (coun mem., chair membership com., chmn. membership com. 1995—), Detroit Gastroent. Soc. (pres. 1985-86), Detroit Surg. Assn., Mich. State Med. Soc., Crohn's and Colitis Found. Am., Inc., Soc. Laparoendoscopic Surgeons, Mich. Soc. Gen. Surgeons, Wayne County Med. Soc., Mich. Soc. Gastrointestinal Endoscopy, Frederick A. Coller Surg. Soc., Southeastern Mich. Surg. Soc. Jewish. Office: Sinai Hosp 6767 W Outer Dr Detroit MI 48235

PHILLIPS, ELAINE LEE, psychologist, educator; b. Atlanta, Nov. 13, 1950; d. Irving and Norma Young; m. Douglas Chambers. BA summa cum laude, Western Mich. U., 1973, MA, 1975, PhD, 1986. Lic. psychologist, Mich. Sch. psychologist Eastern Svc. Dist., Galesburg, Mich., 1975-77;

coord. Family and Children's Svcs. Barry County Mental Health, Hastings, Mich., 1977-82; psychologist Pheasant Ridge Ctr., Kalamazoo, 1982-83, Kalamazoo Regional Psychiat. Hosp., 1983-87; assoc. prof. Western Mich. U., Kalamazoo, 1987—; cons. in field; presenter on health beliefs and practices of Am. youth, physician psycho-social assessment adolescents. Contbr. articles to profl. jours. Bd. dirs. Hospice Greater Kalamazoo, 1987—, mem. clin. records evaluation and rev. com., 1987—, mem. program evaluation and adv. com., 1987—, chmn. bereavement evaluation com., 1989—; sec. Commn. on Status Women, 1989-90, pres., 1990-92. Kalamazoo Consortium Higher Edn. grantee, 1989. Mem. APA, Women in Psychology and Clin. Group Psychology. Office: Western Mich U Kalamazoo MI 49008

PHILLIPS, GRETCHEN, clinical social worker; b. Erie, Pa., July 14, 1941; life ptnr. Beverly Campbell, June 10, 1989. BA, Mercyhurst Coll., 1966; MSW, Yeshiva U., 1972; postgrad., Advanced Ctr. Psychotherapy, 1972-73, Washington Sq. Inst., 1973-77. Bd. cert. diplomate clin. social work; cert. social worker, N.Y. Psychiat. social worker, forensic social worker Creedmoor Psychiat. Ctr., Queens Village, N.Y., 1972-80; Med. social worker Bellevue Hosp. Ctr., N.Y.C., 1980-83; intake probation officer N.Y.C. Probation, Family Court, Bklyn., 1983—. Mem. NASW, Am. Group Psychotherapy Assn., Internat. Soc. for Traumatic Stress Studies (N.Y. chpt.). Home: 125 Radford St # 3C Yonkers NY 10705-3049 Office: Probation Intake Kings Family Ct 283 Adams St Brooklyn NY 11201-2898

PHILLIPS, HELEN ALVEY, medical technologist; b. Derby, Ind., Mar. 23, 1941; d. Richard Clifton and Sarah Helen Alvey; m. David G. Krider, Aug. 20, 1963 (div. Jan. 1980); children: Lynette Elizabeth Krider Safrit, Randall Phillip (dec.). Med. technologist, Elkhart U., 1963; Assoc. Degree in Med. Tech., Ind. U., 1970. Cert. clin. lab. scientist Nat. Cert. Agy. Chem. and instrument specialist Northern Ind. Med. Labs. of Robert McBride, Michigan City, Ind., 1974-83, N.T. DeHaven Lab., Charlotte, N.C., 1983-85; generalist med. technician Univ. Hosp. Carolinas Med. Ctr., Charlotte, N.C., 1985-87, Mercy Hosp., Charlotte, N.C., 1987-89; generalist, safety officer, med. technologist Frye Regional Med. Ctr., Hickory, N.C., 1989—. Master gardener N.C. Agrl. Ext., Newton, N.C., 1990—; v.p. Rags to Riches Investment Club, Hickory, 1995-96; pres.-elect Piedmont Lab. Edn. Soc., N.C., 1995-96, pres., 1996—; v.p. Catawba Valley Outing Club, Hickory, 1996; missions com. mem. First United Meth. Ch., 1994—. Mem. Am. Soc. Clin. Pathologists (cert. med. lab. technician), Am. Med. Technologists (cert. med. technologist). Home: 1204 Second St SE Conover NC 28613 Office: Frye Regional Med Ctr 420 North Center St Hickory NC 28601

PHILLIPS, JOHN P(AUL), retired neurosurgeon; b. Danville, Ark., Oct. 14, 1932; s. Brewer William Ashley and Wave Audrey (Page) P.; AB cum laude, Hendrix Coll., 1953; MD, U. Tenn., 1956; m. June Helen Dunbar, Dec. 14, 1963; children: Todd Eustace, Timothy John Colin, Tyler William Ashley. Intern, Charity Hosp. La., New Orleans, 1957; resident in surgery U. Tenn. Hosps., 1958; resident in neurol. surgery U. Tenn. Med. Units, 1958-62; practice medicine, specializing in neurol. surgery, Salinas, Calif., 1962-93; retired 1993; chief of staff, chief of surgery Salinas Valley Meml. Hosp.; mem. staffs Community Hosp. Monterey Peninsula, U. Calif. Hosp., San Francisco; asst. clin. prof. U. Calif., 1962—. Commd. Ky. col. Diplomate Am. Bd. Neurol. Surgeons. Mem. ACS, Internat. Coll. Surgery, Harvey Cushing Soc., Congress Neurol. Surgery, Western Neurosurg. Assn., AMA, San Francisco Neurol. Soc., Pan Pacific Surg. Assn., Alpha Omega Alpha, Phi Chi, Alpha Chi. Home: 6 Mesa Del Sol Salinas CA 93908-9324

PHILLIPS, KAREN KAY, physician, medical director; b. Ord, Nebr., May 1, 1958; m. Ronald Lee Phillips. BS, U. Nebr., 1980; MD, U. Nebr., Omaha, 1984; MPH, UCLA, 1988. Bd. cert. diplomate Am. Bd. Internal Medicine, Am. Bd. Preventive Medicine; cert. occupl. medicine. Assoc. med. dir. Barlow Occupl. Health Ctr., Whittier, Calif., 1989-92; med. cir. Co. Care, Lincoln, Nebr., 1994—; clin. instr. dept. preventive medicine USC Sch. Medicine, L.A., 1989-91, clin. asst. prof. dept. preventive medicine, 1991-92; invited participant adv. com. for malathion State of Calif. Dept. Health Svcs., L.A., 1990-92; physician advisor Blue Cross/Blue Shield of Nebr., Omaha, 1993—; ind. med. examiner Nebr. Workers' Comp Ct., Lincoln, 1994—; cert. med. rev. officer Company Care Drug Testing Program, Lincoln, 1994—. Contbr. chpt. to book and articles to profl. publs. Active PEO, Lincoln, 1994, Daug. of the Nile, Lincoln, 1995. Four Yr. Regents' scholar U. Nebr., Lincoln, 1976-80. Fellow Am. Coll. Occupl. and Environ. Medicine; mem. ACP, AMA, APHA, Great Plains Coll. Occupl. and Environ. Medicine. Office: Company Care 1000 W O St Ste A Lincoln NE 68528

PHILLIPS, LINDA DARNELL ELAINE FREDRICKS, psychiatric and geriatrics nurse; b. Calgary, Alta., Can., July 23, 1940; came to U.S., 1964; d. Richard and Adeline Ruth (Kuch) Fredricks; m. Marion Rolley Phillips, June 25, 1960 (div. 1962). Cert. in nursing with honors, Broward C.C., Ft. Lauderdale, Fla., 1983. Exec. sec. Grandeur Motor Cars, Pompano Beach, Fla., 1975-80; charge nurse Las Olas Hosp., Ft. Lauderdale, 1983-85; nurse Med. Pers. Pool, Ft. Lauderdale, 1984-85; pvt. duty nurse, Ft. Lauderdale, 1985—; pres., v.p. L.P.R.N. Inc., 1992-93; cons. nurse Waterford Point Condo, Pompano Beach, Fla., 1980-90. Mem. Fla. Nurses Assn., Internat. Platform Assn. Address: 2910 NE 55th St Fort Lauderdale FL 33308-3452

PHILLIPS, LINDA LOU, pharmacist; b. Mason City, Iowa, Sept. 3, 1952; d. Reece Webster and Bettye Frances (Martin) Phillips. BS in Polit. Sci., So. Meth. U., 1974; BS in Pharmacy, U. Ark., 1976; MS in Pharmacy, U. Houston, 1980. Registered pharmacist, Tex. Pharmacy intern Palace Drug Store, Forrest City, Ark., 1976-77; pharmacy resident Hermann Hosp., Houston, 1978-79; dir. pharmacy Alvin Cmty. Hosp., (Tex.), 1979-80; relief pharmacist Twelve Oaks Hosp., Houston, 1980; cons. pharmacist Health Facilities, Inc., Houston, 1980-81; pharmacy supr. Meth. Hosp., Houston, 1981—; sec. spl. interest group, IBAX Pharmacy, 1990-93; chmn. HBO and Co., Series 4000, materials mgmt. spl. interest group, 1994—. Mem. Am. Soc. Hosp. Pharmacists, So. Meth. U. Alumni Assn., Ark. Alumni Assn., Rho Chi, Pi Sigma Alpha. Republican. Methodist. Club: Girls' Cotillion (bd. dirs. 1983-85). Home: 7400 Bellerive Dr Apt 403 Houston TX 77036-3045 Office: Meth Hosp Pharmacy 6565 Fannin St Houston TX 77030-2704

PHILLIPS, MARGARET A., pharmacology educator. BS in Biochemistry, U. Calif., Davis, 1981; PhD in Pharm. Chemistry, U. Calif., San Francisco, 1988. Asst. prof. dept. pharmacology U. Tex. Southwestern Med. Ctr., Dallas, 1992—. Contbr. articles to profl. jours. Postdoctoral fellow U. Calif., 1988-92; recipient Lyndon Baines Johnson award Am. Heart Assn., 1993, Established Investigator award, 1996, Young Investigator award Burroughs Wellcome, 1995. Mem. AAAS, Am. Chem. Soc., Am. Soc. Biochemistry and Molecular Biology, Protein Soc. Office: U Tex Southwestern Med Ctr Dept Pharmacology 5323 Harry Hines Blvd Dallas TX 75235

PHILLIPS, MICHAEL GRAY, physician assistant, medical association administrator; b. Elnora, Ind., Dec. 30, 1945; s. Grover Gerald and Dora Leona (Gray) P.; m. Channing Lee Schular, June 17, 1987; children Michael Thad, Laurie Lynn, Justin Michael. B in Health Sci., Duke U., 1973, cert. physician assoc., 1988. Cert. Am. Bd. Transplant Coord., Nat. Commn. on Cert. of Physician Assts., Am. Registry Radiol. Technologists. Pvt. practice Boca Raton, Fla., 1973-74, Crescent City, Fla., 1974-75; chief of organ and tissue donation Duke U., Chapel Hill, N.C., 1975-81, U. N.C., Durham, N.C., 1975-81; dir. Alabama Organ Ctr., Birmingham, 1981—; instr. surgery Sch. Med. U. Ala., Birmingham, 1988—; adj. prof. Sch. Health Related Professions U. Ala., Birmingham, 1992-95, instr. Sch. Health Related Professions, 1995—. Author, editor (handbook): Organ Procurement Coordinator's Handbook, 1986 (citation 1986), 1987 (merit award 1987), author 3d. rev. edit., 1995; Editor (book): Organ Procurement, Preservation in Transplantation, 1992. Co-chmn. organ procurement and distbn. com. United Network for Organ Sharing, Richmond, Va., 1990-92, mem. liver a nd intestine com., 1994—, Upjohn/Southeastern Organ Procurement Found., Richmond, 1987-88, mem. preservation com., 1988. Recipient merit award Physician Assts. Alumni Assn., Duke U., 1983. Fellow Am. Acad. Physician Assts; mem. Internat. Soc. for Heart Transplantation, North Am. Transplant Coord. Orgn.(mem. faculty selection com. 1987-88), Masons. Office: Alabama Organ Center Ste 1001 201 S 20th St Birmingham AL 35233

PHILLIPS, RICHARD HART, psychiatrist; b. Atlanta, June 23, 1922; s. Wendell Brooks and Margaret (Hart) P.; married Mar. 10, 1945; children: Valerie, Richard Jr., Hugh, Nancy, Mark. BS, U. N.C., 1943; MD, NYU, 1945. Intern U.S. Naval Hosp., Camp Lejeune, N.C., 1945-46; resident med.-surg. Harrisburg Hosp., Harrisburg, Pa., 1948; resident, chief resident psychiatry Duke U. Hosp., Durham, N.C., 1949-51; instr. psychiatry U. Pa., Phila., 1952-53; sr. psychiat. cons. Consolidated Industries Greater Syracuse, Syracuse, N.Y., 1976-89; from asst. prof. to prof. health sci. ctr. SUNY, Syracuse, 1953-92, prof. emeritus, 1992—; dir. adult psychiat. clinic health sci. ctr. SUNY, 1981-92. Author: (poetry) Bindweed, 1988; contbr. sci. and popular articles on psychology to jours. Pres. bd. dirs. Marcellus (N.Y.) Free Libr., 1968-75. Lt. (j.g.) USNR, 1943-48. Fellow Am. Psychiat. Assn. (life); mem. Soc. Children's Book Writers, Thursday Night Club. Republican. Home: 4149 Bishop Hill Rd Marcellus NY 13108-9613 Office: SUNY Health Sci Ctr 750 E Adams St Syracuse NY 13210-2306

PHILLIPS, ROBERT HASKELL, physician; b. Stillwater, Okla., July 24, 1942; s. Elmer Dean Phillips and Alwina Erna (Friend) Arnold; m. Doris Irene Hutson, June 8, 1974; children: Christopher Dean, Brandon Tyler. BS in Pharmacy, Southwestern Okla. State U., 1965; MD, U. Okla., 1969. Cert. Am. Bd. Surgeons; diplomate Am. Bd. Surgery. Intern-resident VA Hosps., U. Okla., Oklahoma City, 1969-71; resident VA Hosps., U. Okla., 1973-76; staff physician Stillwater Med. Ctr., 1976—, chief staff, 1981-82. Bd. dirs. Hospice, Stillwater, 1979-89, Friends Music, Stillwater, 1988—. Lt. comdr. USN, 1971-73, Vietnam. Decorated Bronze Star. Fellow ACS (councilman Okla. chpt. 1990—, pres. 1995-96); mem. Okla. State Med. Assn. (trustee), Okla. Surg. Assn. (pres. 1992-93), Southwestern Surg. Assn., Kiwanis (bd. dirs. Stillwater chpt. 1986-88, 90-92). Methodist. Office: 801 S Walnut Stillwater OK 74074-4226

PHILLIPS, ROBIN KENNETH STEWART, colorectal surgeon; b. Eng., Nov. 18, 1952; s. John Fleetwood Stewart and Mary Gordon (Shaw) P.; m. Janina Fairley Nowak, June 14, 1975; children: Eva Elizabeth, Henry Elliot. MBBS, Royal Free U., London, 1975; MS, U. London, 1984. Cons. surgeon St. Mark's Hosp., Harrow, Eng., 1987—, chmn. dept. surgery, 1994—; sr. lectr. St. Bartholomew's Hosp., 1987-90; cons. surgeon Homerton Hosp., 1990-93; dir. polyposis registry Imperial Can. Rsch. Fund, 1993—; hon. adminstrv. dir. Leeds Castle Polyposis Group, 1994—. Editor: Modern Coloproctology, 1993, Familial Adonomations Polyposis, 19994, Anal Fistula, 1996. Fellow Royal Soc. Medicine (coun. mem.), Royal Coll. Surgeons Eng. Office: St Marks Hosp, Northwick Pk Watford Rd, Harrow HA1 3UJ, England

PHILLIPS, SHELLEY, psychologist, writer; b. Melbourne, Victoria, Australia, Mar. 18, 1934; children: Catherine, Odette. BA in Lit. and History with honors, U. Melbourne; PhD in Psychology, U. Sydney (Australia), 1973. Registered psychologist. Lectr. child devel. U. NSW, Sydney, 1972-77; guest lectr. Ga. State U., Atlanta, 1975; vis. fellow U. Birmingham (Eng.), 1975-76; vis. prof. U. Alta. (Can.), 1975-76; vis. scholar Inst. of Edn., London U., 1979, 82-83; sr. lectr. U. NSW, Sydney, 1977-85, dir. unit for child studies, 1979-85; dir. Found. for Child and Youth Studies, Sydney, 1985-90; pvt. practice psychol. cons. Sydney, 1985—; vis. scientist, program assoc. Tavistock Clinic, London, 1975, 78, 83; vis. scholar Inst. Early Childhood, Melbourne, 1982; chairperson children's programme com. Australian Broadcasting Tribunal, Sydney, 1984-87; lectr. Inst. of Psychiatry, Sydney, 1985-91; occasional lectr. staff tng. A.C.T. Schs.' Authority, Canberra, Australia, 1979-86. Author: Medieval Thinking, 1972, Young Australians, 1979, Self Concept and Sexism in Language, 1982, Relations with Children, 1986, Beyond the Myths, Mother Daughter Relations in Psychology, History, Literature and Everyday Life, 1991, Mothers and Daughters in Jane Austen, 1994. Mem. Australian Psychol. Soc., Australian Soc. Authors, Australian Soc. Women Writers, Bd. Ednl. and Devel. Psychologists, Nat. Trust Australia, Jane Austen Soc., Australian Book Coun., U. Sydney Alumni Assn. Office: 21/3 Plunkett St, Kirribilli NSW 2061, Australia

PHILLIPS, SPENCER KLECKNER, retired surgeon; b. Freeport, Ill., Nov. 6, 1914; s. Nelson Chancellor and Bertha Diana (Kleckner) P.; m. Marjorie Ann Figi, July 19, 1948; children: Julia Mae, Spencer Frederick. BA, Colgate U., 1935; MB, Northwestern U., 1939, MD, 1940; MS in Surgery, U. of Minn., 1947. Diplomate Am. Bd. Gen. Surgery. Surg. fellow Mayo Found., Rochester, Minn., 1941, 46-47; 1st asst. surgery Mayo Clinic, Rochester, 1947-48; practice medicine specializing in surgery Freeport, Ill., 1948-85; dir. of surgery Freeport Meml. Hosp., Freeport, 1983-85; asst. sec., bd. dirs. Scientific Safety Tech., Inc., Wood Dale, Ill., 1987-88; bd. dirs. Cartel, Inc., Woodstock, Ill. Contbr. articles to profl. jours. Commr. Freeport Drug and Alcohol Commn., 1988-95. Comdr. USNR, 1941-45, PTO. Decorated Legion of Merit. Fellow ACS; Phi Beta Kappa, Alpha Omega Alpha. Home: 1769 Highland Dr Freeport IL 61032-4605

PHILLIPS, TANIA JEANNE, dermatologist, researcher; b. Colombo, Sri Lanka, May 5, 1955; came to U.S., 1986; m. Jeffrey Dover, July 15, 1987; children: Sophie, Isabel. MB, BS, Guys Hosp. Med. Sch., London, 1979. Cert. dermatologist, Can. Intern New Cross Hosp., London; intern in surgery Royal Sussex County Hosp., Brighton, U.K., 1979-80; resident Whittington Hosp., London, 1980-82, Brompton Hosp., London, 1982-83, London Chest Hosp., 1982-83; chief resident in dermatology Royal London Hosp., 1983-86; dermatology fellow Boston U. Sch. Medicine, 1986-90, asst. prof. dermatology, 1990-93; vis. physician Univ. Hosp., Boston, 1990—, dir. wound healing clinic, 1990—; attending dermatologist Boston City Hosp., 1990—; dir. dermatology clin. rsch. ctr. Boston U. Med. Ctr., 1991—, assoc. prof. dermatology, 1993—; guest lectr. in field; adv. bd. Internat. Com. on Wound Mgmt., 1990—; selected participant NIH, Bethesda, 1988. Contbr. over 50 articles to profl. jours.; adv. bd. Wounds Jour., 1990—, Jour. Geriatric Dermatology, 1990—. Recipient Venous Rsch. award Am. Venous Forum, 1989, Young Investigator award Am. Soc. Dermatology and Surgery, 1989. Office: Boston Univ Medical Ctr 80 E Concord St Boston MA 02118

PHILLIPS, THEODORE LOCKE, radiation oncologist, educator; b. Phila., June 4, 1933; s. Harry Webster and Margaret Amy (Locke) P.; m. Joan Cappello, June 23, 1956; children: Margaret, John, Sally. BSc, Dickinson Coll., 1955; MD, U. Pa., 1959. Intern Western Res. U., Cleve., 1960; resident in therapeutic radiology U. Calif., San Francisco, 1963, clin. instr., 1963-65, asst. prof. radiation oncology, 1965-68, assoc. prof., 1968-70, prof., 1970—, chmn. dept. radiation oncology, 1973—; rsch. radiobiologist U.S. Naval Radiologic Def. Lab., San Francisco, 1963-65; rsch. physician Lawrence Berkeley Lab. Contbr. numerous articles to profl. publs. With USNR, 1963-65. Nat. Cancer Inst. grantee, 1970-96. Mem. Am. Soc. Therapeutic Radiologists (pres. 1984), Am. Soc. Clin. Oncology, Radiol. Soc. N.Am., Hyperthermia Soc. (pres. 1994), Am. Assn. Cancer Rsch., Calif. Med. Assn., Am. Coll. Radiology, Radium Soc., No. Calif. Radiation Oncology Assn., Inst. Medicine, Phi Beta Kappa, Alpha Omega Alpha. Democrat. Office: U Calif San Francisco Dept Radiation Oncology L-75 Box 0226 San Francisco CA 94143

PHILLIPS, WALTER MILLS, III, psychologist, educator; b. N.Y.C., Sept. 29, 1947; s. Walter Mills and Grace Mary (Mullen) P. BS, Fordham U., 1970; MA, U. S.D., 1973, PhD, 1975. Lic. clin. psychologist, Conn.; diplomate Am. Coll. Forensic Examiners; m. Anne Marie Boyle, July 3, 1971; children: Jonathan, Elizabeth. Adolescent resident counselor Hawthorne (N.Y.) Cedar Knolls Sch., 1970-71; NIMH tng. fellow, 1971-75; clin. psychology intern Inst. of Living, Hartford, Conn., 1974-75, clin. staff psychologist, 1975-79, sr. staff psychologist, 1979-82, asst. dir. dept. clin. psychology, 1980-82, dir. clin. psychology tng., 1980-82; co-dir. outpatient psychiatry U. Conn., Farmington, 1982-88; asst. prof. psychiatry, dir. psychiatry evaluation svc. U. Conn. Health Ctr., 1982-88 ; pvt. practice psychotherapy, Hartford, 1976—, dir. Anxiey Rsch. and Treatment Ctr., 1985-88; dir. adolescent/young adult svc. Grandview Psychiat. Resource Ctr., Waterbury, Conn., 1988-90; dir. psychology Waterbury Hosp., 1990—; asst. clin. prof. psychiatry Sch. Medicine Yale U., New Haven, Conn., 1988—; mem. psychology exec. com. Sch. Medicine Yale U., New Haven. Mem. Am. Psychol. Assn., Conn. Psychol. Assn., Soc. Psychotherapy Rsch., Soc. Personality Assessment, Conn. Hosp. Assn. (chmn., dir. psychology conf.), N.Y. Acad. Scis., Sigma Xi. Contbr. articles to profl. jours. Home: 70 Beverly Dr Avon CT 06001-3528 Office: 60 Westwood Ave Ste 115 Waterbury CT 06708-2460

PHILLIPS, WILLIAM AULT, pediatric dentist; b. Louisville, June 28, 1946; s. Clyde Custer, II, and Geraldine (Ault) P.; m. Karen Walters, June 28, 1969 (div.); children: Taylor Brett, Hayden Reign. DMD, U. Ky., 1971; MSD, Boston U., 1973; MS in Bus. Mktg. Webster U., 1993, MBA, 1994. Diplomate Am. Acad. Pediatric Dentistry; Am. Bd. Pediatric Dentistry (chmn. 1988). Pvt. practice pediatric dentistry, Louisville, 1973—; clin. instr. U. Louisville, 1973-78. Trustee Coun. Retarded Citizens, 1978-81; dir. Community Coordinated Child Care, 1980—. Fellow Am. Acad. Pediatric Dentistry, Am. Soc. Dentistry for Children, Acad. of Gen. Dentistry, Pierre Fauchard Acad. Republican. Presbyterian. Avocations: riding Harley Davidsons, sailing, water skiing, traveling, running. Home: 208 Totem Rd Louisville KY 40207-1533 Office: 1001 Dupont Sq N Louisville KY 40207-4612

PHILLIPS, WILLIAM ROBERT, physician; b. Wash., Apr. 26, 1950. BA, U. Wash., 1971, MD, 1975, MPH, 1975. Diplomate Nat. Bd. Med. Examiners, Am. Bd. Family Practice, Am. Bd. Preventive Medicine; lic. physician and surgeon, Wash. Resident family practice Providence Med. Ctr., Seattle, 1975-78; resident preventive medicine U. Wash. Sch. Pub. Health & Cmty. Medicine, Seattle, 1976-79; vis. prof. U. Auckland, New Zealand, 1979, U. Tasmania, Hobart, Australia, 1979, U. Zimbabwe, Harare, 1993; clin. prof. family medicine U. Wash., Seattle, 1994—; chief staff Ballard Cmty. Hosp., Seattle, 1985, chief family practice, 1984. Contbr. articles to profl. jours. Bd. trustees Ballard Cmty. Hosp., Seattle, 1985. Recipient USPHS primary care policy fellowship, 1995. Fellow Am. Acad. Family Physicians (Mead Johnson award 1976, Warner-Chilcottaward 1979), Am. Coll. Preventive Medicine; mem. N.Am. Primary Care Rsch. Group (pres., rsch. awards), Soc. Tchrs. of Family Medicine. Office: 1801 NW Market St Seattle WA 98107

PHILLIS, HUGH RICHARD, orthodontist, educator; b. Toledo, Ohio, Sept. 24, 1955; s. Richard Waring and Marilyn Anne (Hughey) P.; m. Mary Elizabeth Fecteau, Dec. 20, 1980; children: Nicole, Daniella, Andrea, Stephanie, Kendra, Hugh. Diplome Sovietologe, U. Fribourg, Switzerland, 1976; BS, Pa. State U., 1977; DMD, Tufts U., 1980, cert. in orthodontics, 1982. Diplomate Am. Bd. Orthodontics. Dentist Franklin (Mass.) Dental Assocs., 1980-81, Office of Drs. Cohen and Silvestri, Boston, 1981-82; orthodontist Office of Dr. Milton Meyers, Lawrence, Mass., 1982-83, Office of Dr. T. Arthur Babineau, Nashua, N.H., 1982-91; pvt. practice orthodontics Nashua, 1991—; asst. clin. prof. Sch. Dental Medicine Tufts U., Boston, 1982—. Founder, incorporator Spina Bifida Assn. of N.H., Nashua, 1989-93; trustee Nashua Ctr. for Arts, 1991-92; mem. adv. bd. Nashua Symphony Assn., 1993—. Fellow Am. Coll. Dentists, Internat. Coll. Dentists; mem. ADA, Am. Assn. Orthodontists (chair coun. on membership 1988-95), Tufts Assn. Orthodontists (pres. 1995-96), Greater Nashua Dental Soc. (pres. 1987-88), Coll. Diplomates of Am. Bd. Orthodontics, Edward H. Angle Soc. (affiliate eastern component), Northeastern Soc. Orthodontics (sec.-treas. 1995—), Am. Assn. Orthodontics Found. (chair N.H. campaign 1991—), Omicron Kappa Upsilon. Office: 505 W Hollis St # 201 Nashua NH 03062

PHILLIS, JOHN WHITFIELD, physiologist, educator; b. Port of Spain, Trinidad, Apr. 1, 1936; came to U.S., 1981; s. Ernest and Sarah Anne (Glover) P.; m. Pamela Julie Popple, 1958 (div. 1968); children: David, Simon, Susan; m. Shane Beverly Wright, Jan. 24, 1969. B in Vet. Sci., Sydney (Australia) U., 1958, D in Vet. Sci., 1976; PhD, Australian Nat. U., Canberra, 1961; DSc, Monash U., Melbourne, Australia, 1970. Lectr./sr. Monash U., 1963-69; vis. prof. Ind. U., Indpls., 1969; prof. physiology, assoc. dean rsch. U. Man., Winnipeg, Can., 1970-73; prof., chmn. dept. physiology U. Sask., Saskatoon, Can., 1973-81, asst. dean rsch., 1973-75; prof. physiology, chmn. dept. physiology Wayne State U., Detroit, 1981—; Wellcome vis. prof. Tulane U., 1986; mem. scholarship and grants com. Can. Med. Rsch. Coun., Ottawa, Ont., 1973-79; mem. sci. adv. bd. Dystonia Med. Rsch. Found., Beverly Hills, Calif., 1980-85; mem. sci. adv. panel World Soc. for Protection of Animals, 1982—. Author: Pharmacology of Synapses, 1970; editor: Veterinary Physiology, 1976, Physiology and Pharmacology of Adenosine Derivatives, 1983, Adenosine and Adenine Nucleotides as Regulators of Cellular Function, 1991, The Regulation of Cerebral Blood Flow, 1993, Novel Therapies for CNS Injuries: Rationales and Results, 1996; editor Can. Jour. Physiology and Pharmacology, 1978-81, Progress in Neurobiology, 1973—. Mem. grants com. Am. Heart Assn. of Mich., 1985-90, mem. rsch. coun., 1991-92, mem. rsch. forum com., 1991—, chair, 1992-93. Wellcome fellow London, 1961-62; Can. Med. Rsch. Found. grantee, 1970-81, rsch. prof., 1980; NIH grantee, 1983—. Mem. Brit. Pharmacol. Soc., Physiol. Soc., Can. Physiol. Soc. (pres. 1979-80), Am. Physiol. Soc., Soc. Neurosci., Internat. Brain Rsch. Orgn. Office: Wayne State U Dept Physiology 540 E Canfield St Detroit MI 48201-1928

PHILMON, MARTHA VIRGINIA, nursing administrator; b. Lake Charles, La., June 8, 1940; d. James Washington Sr. and Clara Virginia (McCurley) P. Diploma, Mather Sch. Nursing, New Orleans, 1961; student, Tex. Women's U., 1968-69. RN, La. Nursing supr. Calcasieu Cameron Hosp., Sulphur, La., 1962-65; supr. M.D. Anderson Hosp., Houston, 1965-70; head nurse Hartford (Conn.) Hosp., 1973-75; adminstr. Wasatch Med. Mgmt., Salt Lake City, 1978-79, DON in 3 nursing homes, 1976-82; DON in 3 nursing homes Gen. Health Systems, Baton Rouge, 1982-87, 89-90; DON Heritage Hosue Nursing Home, Baton Rouge, 1987-89; DON, acting br. mgr. Kimberly Quality Care, Baton Rouge, 1990-92; clin. dir. Golden Age Home Care Ctr., Baton Rouge, 1992—. Capt. USAF, 1970-72. Mem. La. State Nursing Home Assn. (officer), Nat. Assn. Home Care, Nurses in Action (treas.). Baptist.

PHINNEY, JEAN SWIFT, psychology educator; b. Princeton, N.J., Mar. 12, 1933; d. Emerson H. and Anne (Davis) Swift; m. Bernard O. Phinney, Dec. 11, 1965; children: Peter, David. BA, Mass. Wellesley Coll., 1955; MA, UCLA, 1969, PhD, 1973. Asst. prof. psychology Calif. State U., L.A., 1977-81, assoc. prof. psychology, 1981-86, prof. psychology, 1986—. Editor: Children's Ethnic Socialization, 1987; asst. editor Jour. Adolescence; contbr. articles to profl. jours. NIH grantee. Mem. APA, Soc. for Rsch. in Child Devel., Soc. for Rsch. in Adolescence, Internat. Soc. for Study of Behavior Devel. Office: Calif State U Dept Psychology 5151 State University Dr Los Angeles CA 90032

PHIPPS, CLAUDE RAYMOND, research scientist; b. Ponca City, Okla., Mar. 15, 1940; s. Claude Raymond Louis and Deva Pauline (DeWitt) P.; m. Lynn Malarney, Dec. 1, 1962 (div. Feb. 1989); 1 child, David Andrew; life ptnr. Shanti E. Bannwart. BS, MIT, 1961, MS, 1963; PhD, Stanford U., 1972. Rsch. staff Lawrence Livermore (Calif.) Nat. Lab., 1972-74; rsch. staff Los Alamos (N.Mex.) Nat. Lab., 1974-95, project leader engine support sys. tech. program, 1993; assoc. dir. Alliance for Photonic Tech., Albuquerque, 1992-95; CEO Photonic Assocs., Santa Fe, 1995—; co-instr. (with Shanti E. Bannwart) "Pairs" Relationship Tng., Santa Fe, N.Mex., 1990—; dir. Santa Fe Investment Conf., 1987; mem. program com. MIT Workshop on High Temperature Superconductors, Cambridge, 1988; mem. Instl. R & D Com., Los Alamos Nat. Lab., 1990-92, project leader laser effects, 1982-87, mem. internat. rsch. tour, Australia, Japan, Scotland, 1988-89; invited discussion leader Gordon Conf. on Laser Particle Interactions, N.H., 1992. Co-author: Laser Ionization Mass Analysis, 1993; author internat. lecture series on laser surface interactions, Berlin, Antwerp, Marseilles, Xiamen, Cape Town, Durban, 1987—; contbr. articles to profl. jours. Lt. USN, 1963-65. Grad. fellow W. Alton Jones Found., N.Y.C., 1962-63. Home and Office: Photonic Assocs 1621 Calle Torreon Santa Fe NM 87501

PIACITELLI, JOHN J., county official, educator, pediatrician; b. Providence, Sept. 1, 1936; s. Joseph A. and Elsie (Mignacca) P.; m. Carol Ann Keirn, Aug. 19, 1961; 1 child, James. BS, U. R.I., 1958; MA, SUNY, Buffalo, 1963; MD, Creighton U., 1964. Diplomate Am. Bd. Pediatrics. Intern Buffalo Gen. Hosp., 1964-65; pediatric resident Children's Hosp. of Buffalo, 1965-67; pediatrician U.S. Army Hosp., Ft. Polk, La., 1967-69, East Nassau Med. Group, North Babylon, N.Y., 1969-79; dir. Charlotte County Pub. Health Unit, Punta Gorda, Fla., 1980—; asst. clin. instr. SUNY, Buffalo, 1965-67, instr. in clin. pediatrics, L.I., 1972-79, asst. prof. pediatrics, 1979. Contbr. articles to profl. jours. Mem. health adv. com. Charlotte County Sch., 1981—; mem. local planning orgn. adv. com., Charlotte

County, Fla., 1986-87; mem. Indigent Health Care Adv. Bd., Charlotte County, 1988—; chmn. Charlotte County AIDS Task Force, 1988-91; chmn. adv. com. Head Start Health Svcs., 1991-94. Maj. U.S. Army, 1967-69. Fellow Am. Acad Pediatrics (cert.), Internat. Coll. Pediatrics; mem. Am. Coll. Physician Execs., Nat. Assn. County and City Health Officials, Fla. Pub. Health Assn., Fla. Assn. County Health Officers, Fla. Med. Assn., Fla. Pediatric Soc., Charlotte County Med. Soc. Office: Charlotte County Pub 514 E Grace St Punta Gorda FL 33950-6121

PIACSEK, BELA EMERY, biology educator, researcher; b. Budapest, Hungary, Apr. 17, 1937; came to U.S., 1952, naturalized, 1958; s. Stephen Elek and Adriene Anna (Vasarhelyi) P.; m. Eniko Mary DePottyondy, June 9, 1962; children: Kristina Marie, Steven Bela, Kathleen Elizabeth, Thomas Charles. B.S., Notre Dame U., 1959, M.S., 1961; Ph.D., Mich. State U., 1966. Research fellow Harvard Sch. Medicine, Boston, 1966-68; asst. prof. Marquette U., Milw., 1968-73, assoc. prof., 1973-79, prof., 1979—. Contbr. chpts. to books, articles to profl. jours. Active St. Luke Choir, Brookfield, Wis., 1974—. Mem. Am. Physiol. Soc., Endocrine Soc., Soc. Study Reprodn. Roman Catholic. Avocations: classical music, distance running, tennis, gardening. Office: Marquette U Dept Biology 530 N 15th St Milwaukee WI 53233-2214

PIATNEK-LEUNISSEN, DOROTHY ANN, internist; b. Lawrence, Pa., Feb. 8, 1928; d. Andrew Paul and Mary Theresa (Batrla) Piatnek; married, May 12, 1962. BA, Seton Hill Coll., 1949; MA, Mt. Holyoke Coll., 1951; PhD, U. Pitts., 1956; MD, Med. Coll. Pa., 1974. Intern, resident in medicine Bryn Mawr (Pa.) Hosp., 1974-76; rsch. asst. Jefferson Med. Coll., Phila., 1951-53; rsch. assoc. Grad. Sch. Pub. Health U. Pitts., 1956-62; asst. prof. physiology Hahnemann Med. Coll., Phila., 1962-69; pvt. practice internal medicine Med. Cardiology Assocs., Media, Pa., 1976—. Contbr. numerous articles to profl. jours. Mem. AMA, Pa. State Med. Soc., Delaware County Med. Soc., Am. PHysiol. Soc., N.Y. Acad. Scis., Sigma Xi, Alpha Lambda Delta. Republican. Roman Catholic. Home: 121 Bryn Mawr Ave Newtown Square PA 19073 Office: Med Cardiology Assoc 1078 W Baltimore Pike Media PA 19063

PIAZZA, DANIEL HALLER, urologist; b. Aurora, Ill., Feb. 25, 1946; s. Eugene and Sylvia Henrietta (Schildt) P.; m. Joyace Ann Zemrow, June 15, 1974; children: Elizabeth, Matthew. AB, Stanford U., 1968; MD, U. Ill., 1972. Intern Rush Presbyn. St. Lukes Med. Ctr., Chgo., 1972-73; resident Loyola U. Hosp., Maywood, Ill., 1973-74, U. Mich. Med. Ctr., ann Arbor, 1976-79; pvt. practice N.W. Urol. Assocs., Arlington Heights, Ill., 1979—. Maj. M.C., U.S. Army,. 1974-76. Decrated Nat. Def. ribbon, Army Commendation medal, Cert. of Achievement. Mem. AMA, Am. Urol. Assn., Ill. Urol. Soc., Ill. Med. Soc., Chgo. Urol. Soc., Chgo. Med. Soc., 38th Parallel Med. Soc. Roman Catholic. Office: NW Urol Assocs 2010 S Arlington Heights Rd Arlington Heights IL 60005

PIAZZA, DIANNA MARIE, orthopaedic physician assistant; b. N.Y.C., Nov. 5, 1947; d. Rosario Joseph and Nancy Theresa (Campayana) P. RN, N.Y.C. C.C., Bklyn., 1967; Physician Asst., USPHS PAT, S.I., N.Y., 1977; BS in Health Sci., Charter Oak Coll., Hartford, Conn., 1982; BS in Psychology, Sacred Heart U., Fairfield, Conn., 1985, MEd, 1985; DEd, Nova U., Ft. Lauderdale, Fla., 1992. Nursery sch. tchr. Immaculate Heart of Mary, Elizabeth, N.J., 1969-72, St. Margaret Mary, Shelton, Conn., 1979—; nurse Morristown (N.J.) Meml., 1969-75; orthpaedic physician asst. St. Vincent's Med. Ctr., Bridgeport, Conn., 1977-88, Dr. Garver, Bridgeport, 1988-93, Dr. Belkin, Dr. Redler & Dr. Boone, Trumbull, Conn., 1993-96, Waterbury (Conn.) Hosp., 1996—; adj. prof. edn. Sacred Heart U., Fairfield, 1985-89; adj. prof. medicine Quinnipiac Coll., Hamden, Conn., 1993—; mem. adv. bd. for physician asst. Quinnipiac Coll., Hamden. Author: Preop Teaching of Children 3-11 Years of Age, 1992. Fellow Am. Assn. Physicians Assts. Republican. Roman Catholic. Home: 67 Chamberlain Dr Huntington CT 06484

PIAZZA, DUANE EUGENE, biomedical researcher; b. San Jose, Calif., June 5, 1954; s. Salvador Richard and Mary Bernice (Mirassou) P.; m. Sandra Patrignani, Sept. 19, 1992. BS in Biology, U. San Francisco, 1976; MA in Biology, San Francisco State U., 1986. Staff rsch. assoc. I U. Calif., San Francisco, 1975-81; sr. rsch. technician XOMA Corp., San Francisco, 1981-82; biologist II Syntex USA Inc., Palo Alto, Calif., 1982-85; pres., cons. Ryte For You, Oakland, Calif., 1985—; rsch. assoc. I Cetus Corp., Emeryville, Calif., 1986-90; rsch. assoc. II John Muir Cancer and Aging Rsch. Inst., Walnut Creek, Calif., 1991-92; rsch. assoc. Pharmagenesis, Palo Alto, Calif., 1993—. CPR & first aid instr. ARC, 1980-92, vol. 1st aid sta. instr., Santa Cruz, 1985-86, vol. 1st aid sta. disaster action team, Oakland, 1986—, br. chmn. disaster action team, 1987-88; treas. Reganti Homeowner Assn., 1990-92. Mem. AAAS, Am. Soc. Microbiology, N.Y. Acad. Scis., Astron. Soc. Pacific, Planetary Soc., Mt. Diablo Astronomy Soc. Republican. Roman Catholic. Home: 1055 Rebecca Dr Boulder Creek CA 95006-9442

PIAZZA, GARY GERARD, orthopedist; b. N.Y.C., Mar. 28, 1952; s. Anthony F. and Camille Teresa (Gebbia) P.; m. Janis Mary Mascolino, June 9, 1974. BA, Ohio State U., 1975; DO, Coll. Osteopathic Medicine, Chgo., 1980. Diplomate Nat. Bd. Examiners of Osteopathic Physicians and Surgeons. Staff Avenel (N.J.)-Iselin Med. Group, 1981-82, Family Med. Ctr., Woodbridge, N.J., 1982-84; resident Meml. Gen. Hosp., Union, N.J., 1984; pvt. practice Colonia, N.J., 1985; staff Sunrise House, Lafayette, N.J., 1986-88, Mini-Mall Med. Ctr., Darlin, N.J., 1989-93, Orthopaedic Office, Clifton, N.J., 1993—. Mem. AAAS, Am. Osteo. Assn., Am. Coll. Family Practitioners, N.Y. Acad. Sci., Alpha Epsilon Delta, Helix, Sigma Sigma Phi. Republican. Home: 7 Carriage Pl Edison NJ 08820-4021

PIAZZA, RICHARD SAMUEL, health facility administrator; b. Beloit, Wis., Feb. 17, 1957; s. Samuel Henry Piazza and Evelyn Mae (Meyer) Piazza Cooper; m. Jo Ellen Buffington, Jan. 30, 1980; 1 child, Anthony Richard. Cert. in surg. tech., Portsmouth Naval Reg. Med. Ctr, Va., 1977; BS, Pitts. State U., 1983; DO, Kirksville (Mo.) Coll. Osteo., 1987. Diplomate Am. Coll. Osteo. Family Physicians. Intern Still Regional Med. Ctr., Jefferson City, Mo., 1987-88; resident Des Moines Gen. Hosp., 1988-90; assoc. dir. med. ctr. No. Calif. Group Physicians, Sacramento, 1990-92; staff physician, dir. family practice residency Riverside Health Sys. Maize Rd. Clinic, Wichita, Kans., 1992—; dir. Kans. Neurol. Testing Ctr., Wichita, 1995—. Contbr. articles to profl. jours. With USN, 1975-80. Mem. Am. Osteo. Assn., Kans. Osteo. Med. Assn., Iowa Osteo. Med. Soc., Osteo. Physicians and Surgeons Calif., Sedgwick County Osteo. Soc. Republican. Episcopalian. Home: 2355 N Tee Time Ct Wichita KS 67205 Office: Riverside Health Sys 501 N Maize Rd Wichita KS 67212

PICARD-AMI, LUIS ALBERTO, plastic surgeon; b. Waterbury, Conn., Mar. 1, 1958; s. Luis Alberto and Patricia (Vogan) P.; m. Adelita Alvarado, Feb. 21, 1981; children: Alexandra, Luis Demetrio, Alberto Arturo. MD, U. Panama, Republic of Panama, 1983; MSc, McGill U., 1991. Intern Nicolas Solano Gen. Hosp., La Chorrera, Panama, 1984-85; internship Social Security Met. Hosp., Panama City, Panama, 1983-84; microsurgical rsch. Royal Victoria Hosp., Montreal, 1987-88; residency plastic surgery McGill U., Montreal, Can., 1989-91, general surgery residency, 1985-89; fellowship cleft lip & palate surgery U. Miami, 1991; pvt. practice Miami, 1992—. Contbr. articles to profl. jours. With U.S. Army Res., 1989—. Fellow ACS (assoc.), Royal Coll. Physicians & Surgeons of Can.; mem. AMA (Physicians Recognition award 1991-94), Am. Soc. Plastic and Reconstructive Surgery, Can. Soc. Plastic Surgeons (assoc.), Fla. Soc. Plastic and Reconstructive Surgeons, Latin Am. Soc. Plastic Surgeons (sec.), Greater Miami Soc. Plastic and Reconstructive Surgeons, McGill U. Plastic Surgery Soc., Fla. Med. Assn., Dade County Med. Assn., Panamanian Med. Assn. Roman Catholic. Office: 351 NW 42nd Ave Ste 501 Miami FL 33126-5670

PICCO, JOSEPH ANTHONY, dental oncologist, dentist; b. Waverly, N.Y., Mar. 1, 1965; s. Gennaro R. and Bianca Aurora (Mercaldo) P. BA in Biology and Psychology, U. Rochester, 1987; DDS, SUNY, Buffalo, 1991. Tng. in dental oncology Roswell Park Cancer Inst., Buffalo, 1991-92; pvt. practice gen. and oncological dentistry, Waverly and Binghamton, N.Y., 1992; gen. dentist Sullivan Park Nursing Facility, Endicott, N.Y., 1992—; dentist, oncologist Andover (N.Y.) Dental Clinic, 1992—, Broome County, Binghamton, 1995—, Guthrie Health Care, Waverly 1995—; mem. adv. bd., cons. Am. Cancer Soc., Waverly, 1994—. Recipient William Sky award U. Rochester, 1996. Mem. Valley Dental Soc., Rotary (v.p. Waverly 1993—). Roman Catholic. Home: RR 3 Box 67A Gillett PA 16925 Ofice: 37 Chemung St Wavelry NY 14892

PICCOLO, JOSEPH ANTHONY, hospital administrator; b. Phila., Aug. 1, 1953; s. Rudolph and Mary C. (Mellela) P.; m. Elizabeth J. Mullarkey, Mar. 24, 1984; children: Mary E., Sarah C., Theresa N. BA, U. Pa., 1975; MBA, LaSalle U., 1992. Mgr. health sci. store U. Pa., Phila., 1973-76; mgr. univ. store Hahnemann U., Phila., 1976-86 adminstr., clin. sr. instr. dept. pathology/lab. medicine, 1986-94; assoc. adminstr. Fox Chase Cancer Ctr., Phila., 1994—; v.p. Hahnemann Found. Pathology, Phila., 1986-94. Author: (with others): Health Science Store Manual, 1985. Bd. dirs. Big Sisters of Phila., 1996—. Mem. Med. Group Mgmt. Assn., Am. Mgmt. Assn., Healthcare Fin. Mgmt. Assn., Hahnemann Pathology Assocs., Inc. (v.p., treas. 1986-94), Big Sisters of Phila. Inc. (bd. dirs., 1996—). Office: Fox Chase Cancer Ctr 7701 Burholme Ave Philadelphia PA 19111-2412

PICHAL, HENRI THOMAS, electronics engineer, physicist, consultant; b. London, Feb. 14, 1923; came to the U.S., 1957; s. Henri and Mary (Conway) P.; m. Vida Eloise Collum Jones, Mar. 7, 1966; children: Chris C., Henri T. III, Thomas William Billingsley. MSc in Engring., U. London, 1953, PhD in Physics, 1955. Registered profl. engr., Wash., Fla. Product engr. John Fluke Mfg. Corp., Everett, Wash., 1970-73; engring. specialist Harris Corp., Melbourne, Fla., 1973-75; pres., prin. Profl. Engring. Co., Inc., Kissimmee, Fla., 1975-91. Contbr. articles to Electronics, Microwaves, and others. Named one of Two Thousand Men Achievement, 1972. Mem. Inst. Physics, Am. Phys. Soc., Fla. Engring. Soc. (sr.), Inst. Environ. Scis. (sr.), IEEE (past chmn. microwave theory and techniques communications systems), Aerospace/Navigational Electronics, Space Electronics and Telemetry, Mil. Electronics. Republican. Home: PO Box 969 Kingston WA 98345-0969

PICK, ROBERT YEHUDA, orthopedic surgeon, consultant; b. Haifa, Israel, 1945; came to U.S., 1957; s. Andre B. and Hanna (Gross) P.; m. Roni L. Kestenbaum, Sept. 25, 1977; children: Benjamin A., Joseph E., Jennifer L., Abigail I. BA, B in Hebrew Lit., Yeshiva U., 1967; MD, Albert Einstein Coll. Med., 1971; MPH, Harvard U., 1979. Diplomate Nat. Bd. Med. Examiners, Am. Bd. Orthopaedic Surgery. Intern Brookdale Hosp., Bklyn., 1971-72; resident in orthopedic surgery Albert Einstein-Bronx (N.Y.) Mcpl. Hosp. Ctr., 1972-74; resident in orthopedic surgery USPHS Hosp., Staten Island, N.Y., 1974-75, asst. chief orthopedic surgery, 1975-77; asst. chief orthopedic surgery USPHS Hosp., Boston, 1977-78; fellow orthopedic trauma Boston City Hosp., 1979-80, assoc. dir. orthopedic surgery, 1980-84, dir. pediatric orthopedics, 1981-83; practice medicine specializing in orthopedic surgery Newton Ctr., Mass., 1984—; instr. orthopedic surgery Boston U., 1980-82, asst. prof., 1982—; adj. asst. prof. health scis. and orthopedics Touro Coll., N.Y.C., 1976-78; dir. spinal screening program Dept. Health and Hosps., Boston, 1979-82; dist. med. advisor U.S. Dept. Labor, Boston, 1984—; cons. Boston Retirement Bd., 1983-84, New Eng. Telephone, Boston, 1985—, Commonwealth of Mass. Pub. Employee Retirement Adminstrn., Boston, 1985-90. Contbr. articles on med. issues to profl. jours. Trustee Young Israel Jackson Heights, Queens, N.Y., 1969-76, pres., 1976-77; sec. Young Israel Brookline, Mass., 1978-79; trustee Maimonides Sch., Brookline, 1990—. Served to lt. comdr. USPHS, 1975-78. Fellow Am. Acad. Orthopedic Surgeons; mem. Am. Physicians Fellowship for Medicine in Israel (trustee 1975—, exec. com. 1976—, asst. treas. 1987-90, treas. 1990—, Man of Yr. award 1977), Nat. Inst. Occupational Safety and Health (traineeship 1978-79), Mensa.

PICKARD, JEFFREY, physician; b. N.Y.C., Apr. 18, 1952; s. Lawrence and Ruth Harriet (Hochberg) P.; m. Connie Gale St. Clair, Mar. 19, 1988; children: Kyle Michelle, Kasey Lawrence, Kevin James. BA, Johns Hopkins U., 1974; MD, George Washington U., 1978. Asst. prof. medicine Denver Gen. Hosp., 1985-92, clin. assoc. prof medicine, 1992—; physician pvt. practice, Estes Park, Colo., 1994—; mem. Colo. Diabetes Adv. Coun., Denver, 1985-94. Co-author: (chpts.) Cardiology Secrest, 1994, Primary Care Secrets, 1994. Mem. Am. Coll. Physicians, Soc. Obs. Medicine, Soc. Gen. Internal Medicine. Office: 555 Prospect Ave Ste D Estes Park CO 80517

PICKARD, MYRNA RAE, dean; b. Sulphur Springs, Tex., Oct. 10, 1935; d. George Wallace and Ellie (Williams) Swindell; m. Bobby Ray Pickard, May 17, 1957; 1 child, Bobby Dale. B.S. summa cum laude, Tex. Wesleyan Coll., 1957, M.Ed., 1964; M.S., Tex. Women's U., 1974; EdD, Nova U., 1976. Instr. John Peter Smith Hosp., Fort Worth, 1956-58; pub. health nurse Forest County Health Dept., Hattiesburg, Miss., 1958-60; asst. nurse adminstrn. John Peter Smith Hosp. Sch. Nursing, Fort Worth, 1960-70, nurse adminstr., 1970-73; assoc. dean, dean U. Tex. System Sch. Nursing, Fort Worth, 1971-76; dean U. Tex. Sch. Nursing, Arlington, 1976-95; prof. nursing, 1976—; cons. in field; adv. com. Rural Health Rsch. Ctr., U. N.D., 1990. Mem. editorial bd. Jour. Rural Health, 1985-92, 94; contbr. articles to profl. jours., chpt. in book. Pres. Tex. League for Nursing, 1986-89. Fellow Am. Acad. Nursing; mem. ANA, Nat. League Nursing, Nat. Rural Health Assn. (bd. dirs., treas. 1990-92), Sigma Theta Tau. Methodist. Home: 8301 Anglin Dr Fort Worth TX 76140-4213 Office: U Tex Box 19407 Arlington TX 76019

PICKENS, WILLIAM STEWART, cardiologist; b. Bentonville, Ark., Dec. 16, 1940; s. William Craig and Mary Elizabeth (McFarland) P.; BS, U. Ark., Fayetteville, 1962; MD, U. Ark., Little Rock, 1966; children from previous marriage: Holly, Heather, Brian; m. Wanda J. Godwin. Diplomate Am. Bd. Internal Medicine (subspecialty cardiovascular diseases). Rotating intern Tampa (Fla.) Gen. Hosp., 1966-67; resident in radiology U. Fla. Med. Ctr., Gainesville, 1970-72; resident in internal medicine, then fellow in cardiology U. South Fla. Med. Center, Tampa, 1972-75; fellow in cardiovascular radiology U. Fla. Med. Center, 1974; staff physician VA Hosp., Tampa, 1974-75; practice medicine specializing in cardiology, Pensacola, Fla., 1976—; mem. staff Baptist Hosp., Sacred Heart Hosp.; asst. prof. radiology and internal medicine U. Ark., Little Rock, 1975-76 clin. assoc. prof. medicine Tulane U., 1983—; v.p. ECG Systems Inc.; bd. dirs. Mobil Diagnostics, 1985—; trustee Peer Rev. Orgn. State Fla., 1986-91. Benefactor Pickens found. for Edn., 1990. Served as officer M.C., USAF, 1967-72; maj. Res. Rockefeller scholar, 1958-59; U. Ark. Alumni scholar, 1958-60; Edn. Found. scholar, 1958-62; Barton Found. scholar, 1965; C.V. Mosby scholar, 1966. Fellow Am. Coll. Cardiology, Am. Council on Clin. Cardiology; mem. Am. Soc. Nuclear Cardiology (founding), Sigma Xi (assoc.), Alpha Omega Alpha, Phi Eta Sigma, Alpha Epsilon Delta. Republican. Episcopalian. Office: 1717 N E St Ste 331 Pensacola FL 32501-6335

PICKERING, JACK EDWARD, cardiologist; b. Hutchinson, Kans., Aug. 26, 1932; s. Jesse Clayton and Alta Lucille (McKibben) P.; m. Linda Fay Auman, June 27, 1959; children: Aminda Halsey, Nandrea Courts, Creighton. BS, U. Kans., 1954, MD, 1958. Intern Jefferson Med. Coll., Phila., 1958-59; epidemiologist CDC, Atlanta, 1959-61; resident USPHS Hosp., S.I., N.Y., 1961-62; staff mem. Nat. Heart Inst., Bethesda, Md., 1962-63; fellow in cardiology U. Pa., Phila., 1963-65; rschr. Wyeth Labs., Radnor, Pa., 1965-69; cardiologist/rschr. Lancaster Hosp., Wynnewood, Pa., 1969—. With USPHS, 1959-65. Fellow ACP, Am. Coll. Cardiology. Home: 602 Winsford Rd Bryn Mawr PA 19111 Office: 100 Lancaster Ave Ste 316 Wynnewood PA 19096-3426

PICKETT, BETTY HORENSTEIN, psychologist; b. Providence, R.I., Feb. 15, 1926; d. Isadore Samuel and Etta Lillian (Morrison) Horenstein; m. James McPherson Pickett, Mar. 10, 1952. A.B. magna cum laude, Brown U., 1945, Sc.M., 1947, Ph.D., 1949. Asst. prof. psychology U. Minn., Duluth, 1949-51; asst. prof. U. Nebr., 1951; lectr. U. Conn., 1952; prof. assoc. psychol. scis. Bio-Scis. Info. Exchange, Smithsonian Instn., Washington, 1953-58; exec. sec. behavioral scis. study sect. exptl. psychology study sect. div. research grants NIH, Washington, 1958-61; research cons. to mental health unit HEW, Boston, 1962-63; exec. sec. research career program NIMH, 1963-66, chief cognition and learning sect. div. extramural research program, 1966-68, dep. dir., 1968-74, dir. div. spl. mental health programs, 1974-75, acting dir. div. extramural research program, 1975-77; assoc. dir. for extramural and collaborative research program Nat. Inst. Aging, 1977-79; dep. dir. Nat. Inst. Child Health and Human Devel., Bethesda, Md., 1979-81; acting dir. Nat. Inst. Child Health and Human Devel., 1981-82, dir. Div. Rsch. Resources, 1982-88; mem. health scientist adminstr. panel CSC Bd. Examiners, 1970-76, 81-88; mem. coun. on grad. edn. Brown U. Grad. Sch., 1989-91. Contbr. articles to profl. jours. Mem. APA, Am. Psychol Soc., Psychonomic Soc., Assn. Women in Sci., AAAS, Phi Beta Kappa, Sigma Xi. Home: Morgan Bay Rd PO Box 198 Surry ME 04684-0198

PICKETT, HAL GENE, prosthodontist; b. Oakley, Idaho, Apr. 14, 1926; s. Eugene and Emma Adelaide (Mabey) P.; m. Patty Ann Monson, Jan. 18, 1957 (div. June 1981); children: Rex, Eric, Clarke, Sharon, Lynda. BS in Zoology, U. Idaho, 1950, MS in Zoology, 1952; DMD, U. Oreg., 1956; MS in Prosthodontics, U. Iowa, 1967. Capt. U.S. Army, 1944-46. Mem. ADA, Internat. Coll. Dentists, Rotary. Republican. Mem. LDS Ch. Home: 3204 Kootenai Boise ID 83705 Office: 909 Warren Boise ID 83706

PICKETT, JACKIE LOUISE, computer operator; b. Nashville, Sept. 13, 1961; d. James Cleveland and Gladys Virginia (Hooper) P.; 1 child, Jeremy Daniel. Installment loan clerk Third Nat. Bank, Nashville, 1979-83; data entry tech. Matthew Walter Health Ctr., Nashville, 1984-88, computer operator, 1994—; liaison operator Vanderbilt Med. Ctr., Nashville, 1988-94. Address: 1501 Herman St Nashville TN 37208-3369

PICKETT, NANCY ELIZABETH, vocational rehabilitation consultant, case manager, government council executive; b. Barksdale AFB, La., Nov. 7, 1948; d. Richard Dewey and Evelyn (Weis) P.; m. Wendell Alfred Smith III, May 31, 1968 (div. 1976); children: Melinira Lynne, Wendell Alfred, IV. BA, Nicholls State U., 1970, MEd, 1972. Tchr. Cert. Vocat. expert; qualified mental retardation profl.; lic. profl. counselor, rehab. counselor. St. Charles Sch. Bd., Luling, La., 1970-71; counselor, coordinator River Parishes Council Govt., Convent, La., 1973-74, exec. dir., Boutte, La., 1974-86; exec. asst. Centec Corp., New Orleans, 1986-87; vocat. rehab. cons. Crawford Health and Rehab., Metairie, La., 1987-89; mgr., Alexandria, 1989-92, vocat. counselor/supr., Las Vegas, 1993-94; vocat. counselor, med. case mgr. MED/VOC, Inc., Las Vegas, 1994—; pres. pvt. industry council, LaPlace, La., 1981-83; pvt. practice trainer, cons., Boutte, La., 1979-87; mem. bd. examiners La. Licensed Vocat. Rehab. Counselors, 1992; mem. adv. bd. La. Family Planning Program, New Orleans, 1976-90. Editor: Directory Community Resources, 1977. Del. White House Conf. Families, Mpls., 1978, La. Gov.'s Conf. Libraries, Baton Rouge, 1978; founding bd. dirs. St. Charles Community Theatre, Luling, La., 1979-84; bd. dirs., v.p. S.E. La. Girl Scout Coun., New Orleans, 1978-83. Nat. Merit scholar, 1966. Mem. Am. Soc. for Tng. and Devel. (bd. dirs., treas. 1984, chmn. position referral 1983), Service Delivery Area Dirs. Assn., La. Assn. Rehab. Profls. Pvt. Sector (bd. dirs. 1992). Office: MED/VOC Inc 4550 W Oakey Blvd Ste 111 Las Vegas NV 98102

PICKETT, STEPHEN ALAN, hospital executive; b. Ft. Payne, Ala., Dec. 22, 1953; s. James Benjamin Pickett and Dorothy Jane (Howell) Pickett Fancher; m. Nell Annette Horsley, Mar. 5, 1977; children: Stefanie Leigh, Allison Marie. BBA, U. Montevallo, 1976; MPH, Tulane U., 1995. CPA, Ala. Sr. acct. Ernst & Whinney, Birmingham, Ala., 1976-78; contr. East End Meml. Hosp., Birmingham, 1978, v.p. fin., 1979-84; v.p. fin. W.Va. U. Hosps., Morgantown, 1985-87, exec. v.p., adminstr., 1987-91; adminstr., COO Tulane U. Hosp. and Clinic, New Orleans, 1991-95, CEO, 1995—; bd. dirs. Met. Hosp. Coun., 1991—, Associated Hosp. Svcs., 1991—. Active sustaining mem. campaign Birmingham coun. Boy Scouts Am., 1978; mem. Jefferson County Republican Exec. Com., Birmingham, 1982, First Baptist Ch. New Orleans (fin. com. 1993—). Fellow Healthcare Fin. Mgmt. Assn.; mem. Am. Inst. C.P.A.s, Ala. Soc. C.P.A.s, U. Montevallo Alumni Assn. (life), Alpha Tau Omega Alumni Assn. Baptist. Lodge: Rotary. Home: 185 Lakewood Estates Dr New Orleans LA 70131-8364 Office: Tulane U Hosp & Clinic 1415 Tulane Ave New Orleans LA 70112-2605

PICKLE, LINDA WILLIAMS, biostatistician; b. Hampton, Va., July 19, 1948; d. Howard Taft and Kathryn Lee (Riggin) Williams; 1 child from previous marriage, Diane Marie; m. James B. Pearson, Jr., Oct. 14, 1984. BA, Johns Hopkins U., 1974, PhD in Biostats., 1977; postgrad., George Washington U., 1986-87. Computer programmer Comml. Credit Computer Corp., Balt., 1966-69; systems analyst, computer programmer Greater Balt. Med. Ctr., Balt., 1969-72; grad. teaching asst. biostats. Johns Hopkins U., Balt., 1974-77; adj. asst. prof. div. biostats. and epidemiology Georgetown U. Med. Sch., Washington, 1983-88, assoc. prof. div. biostats and epidemiology, 1988-91, dir. biostats. unit, V.T. Lombardi Cancer Rsch. Ctr., 1988-91; biostatistician Nat. Cancer Inst. NIH, Bethesda, Md., 1977-88; math. statistician office rsch. methodology Nat. Ctr. for Health Stats., Hyattsville, Md., 1991—. Author: Atlas of U.S. Cancer Mortality Among Whites: 1950-80, 1987, Atlas of U.S. Cancer Mortality Among Nonwhites: 1950-1980, 1990, 96; contbr. articles to med. and statis. jours. Sr. troop leader Girl Scouts U.S., 1981-83; sci. fair judge, 1983—. Mem. The Biometric Soc., Am. Statis. Assn., Soc. Epidemiologic Research, Soc. Indsl. and Applied Math., Sigma Delta Epsilon (pres. Omicron chpt. 1984), Phi Beta Kappa.

PICKLEMANN, JACK R., surgeon. MD, McGill U., Montreal, Que., Can., 1964. Intern Royal Victoria Hosp., Montreal, Que., Can., 1964-65; resident in surgery U. Chgo. Med. Ctr., 1967-73; prof. surgery Loyola U. Chgo.; attending physician Loyola Med. Ctr., Maywood, Ill. Mem. ACS. Office: Loyola U Med Ctr 2160 S 1st Ave Maywood IL 60153*

PICKTON, THOMAS EMIL, psychologist; b. Akron, Ohio, Oct. 11, 1949; s. Robert James and Carolyn Jane (Schweitzer) P.; m. Kimberly Ann, Aug. 26, 1995; children: Elizabeth Jane, Patrick Thomas. BEd, Miami U., Oxford, Ohio, 1972; MEd, Xavier U., Cin., 1975; MS, U. Nebr., Kearney, 1981, EdS, 1982; PhD, U. Miss., 1986. Lic. psychologist, Ohio. Speech pathologist Hamilton Local Schs., Columbus, Ohio, 1972-74; cons. supr. Ednl. Svc. Unit #9, Hastings, Nebr., 1974-79; assoc. psychologist South Ctrl. Community Mental Health Ctr., Hastings, 1979-82; instr. U. Miss., Oxford, 1982-84; psychology intern Wichita (Kans.) Guidance Ctr., 1984-85; psychologist Child and Adolescent Svc. Ctr., Canton, Ohio, 1985-88, Kunstel, Grzegorek and Assocs., Stow, Ohio, 1988-94, Thomas Pickton & Assocs., Stow, Ohio, 1994—. Mem. Am. Psychol. Assn., Ohio Psychol. Assn., Phi Gamma Delta. Democrat. Presbyterian. Office: Thomas Pickton & Assocs 4301 Darrow Rd Ste 4400 Stow OH 44224

PICKUS, FRANCINE SHEILA, speech and language pathologist; b. N.Y.C., Jan. 5, 1957; d. Walter and Selma (Rubin) Grubert; m. Jay I. Pickus, July 8, 1979; children: Aaron Joshua, Heather Alyse. BA cum laude, Queens Coll., 1978; MS, Bklyn. Coll., 1981. Cert. clin. competence, tchr. speech and hearing handicapped; lic. speech-lang. pathologist, N.Y. Substitute speech tchr. BOCES III, Dix Hills, N.Y., 1981; asst. speech-lang. pathologist L.I. Developmental Ctr., Melville, N.Y., 1981-84; pvt. practice as speech-lang. pathologist North Babylon, N.Y., 1985—; speech-lang. pathologist L.I. Developmental Ctr., Melville, 1986-88. Author: The Importance of Communicating and Recognizing Speech-Language and Hearing Disorders. Recipient Knights of Pythias scholarship, Hebrew-AYIN award, Alexander Lamport Hebrew award. Mem. Am. Speech, Lang. and Hearing Assn. (cert.), L.I. Speech, Lang. and Hearing Assn., N.Y. State Speech-Language-Hearing Assn. Home and Office: 20 Barnum St North Babylon NY 11703

PICON, EDITH, speech pathologist; b. Newark, N.J.; d. Leo and Gloria (Berger) Jarecki; m. Scott Picon, Apr. 18, 1982; children: Jaclyn, Erica. BS, Ithaca Coll., 1980; MA, Montclair State Coll., 1981. Cert. clin. competence, lic. speech pathologist, N.Y., N.J. Speech-lang. pathologist Pouch Ctr. for Spl. People, Staten Island, N.Y., 1981-85; speech-lang. pathologist Ctr. for Communications Disorders, Livingston, N.J., 1987-88; pvt. practice Florham Park, N.J., 1985—. Recipient award for Continuing Edn. Mem. N.J. Speech and Hearing Assn., Early Intervention Coalition, Am. Speech and Hearing Assn., Morris County Speech and Hearing Assn., Neuro Devel. Treatment Assn. Home and Office: 2 Country Club Ln Florham Park NJ 07932

PICON, MARIA CRISTINA, plastic surgeon; b. San Juan, Argentina, Feb. 15, 1952; d. Francisco de Paula and Maria J. (Linares) Picon Ibañez. MD, U. Nat. Buenos Aires, 1975. Resident Alfaro Hosp., Buenos Aires, 1976-79, Brit. Hosp., Buenos Aires, 1979-83; chief resident Rivadavia Hosp., Buenos Aires, 1979-90, plastic surgeon, 1984-90. Author: Cirugia Plastica, 1993;

contbr. articles to nat. and internat. jours. Vocal AIME, Buenos Aires, 1994, treas., 1995-96. Mem. Assn. Medica Argentina, Assn. Argentina de Cirugia, A de CP de Buenos Aires: Assn. de Cirugfa Plastica de Buenos Aires (internat. corr. participant), Internat. Plastic Reconstructive Aesthetic Surgery, Assn. Ibero Am. de Mujeres Empresarias, Am. Soc. Aesthetic Plastic Surgery, Inc. Office: Vicente Lopez 2251, 1128 Buenos Aires Argentina

PICON-WAGONER, DORA AMALIA, neurologist; b. San Juan, P.R., Mar. 20, 1950; d. Guido F. Picon and Rosa L. Ramirez; children: Dora, Daphne, Dariush; m. Kent A. Wagoner, June 10, 1995. BA, U. P.R., 1970; MD, U. Central del Este, San Pedro, R.D., 1982; postgrad., Wayne State U., Detroit, 1986, Wayne State U., 1987. From neurology resident to EEG fellow Wayne State U., Detroit, 1982-87; neurologist pvt. practice, Richmond, Ky., 1995—; ethics com. Holy Cross Hosp., Detroit 1988—, South Macomb Hosp. Mem. AMA, American Acad. Neurology. Office: Med Arts Bldg 527 West Main St Richmond KY 40475

PIDOUX, JEAN MARIE, physician; b. Lausanne, Switzerland, Sept. 9, 1945; s. Georg and Beatrice (Mercier) P.; m. Elaine Gaudin (div. 1977); m. Marianne Vogt (div. 1991); 1 child, Romain. MD, Med. Sch. Lausanne, 1972, PhD in Forensic Medicine, 1977, Specialist, Ear/Nose and Throat, 1978. MD. Resident Chx-de-Fonds Hosp., La Chx-de Fonds, 1973-74, CHUV, Lausanne, 1974-77; chief resident U. Hosp., Geneva, 1977-78; pres. med. exams. Lausanne, 1986—; med. adviser Winterthur Ins., 1986—; bd. dirs. cos., chmn., pres. various cos. Author two books in field. Mem. City Coun., Lausanne, 1981-91; dep. of Lausanne, 1991-94, officer Med. Corp., 1973—. Mem. Golf Club (Lausanne and Gland), numerous med. assns. Conservative. Office: 8 Grand Chene, 1003 Lausanne Switzerland

PIECH, MARY LOU ROHLING, medical psychotherapist, consultant; b. Elgin, Ill., Jan. 20, 1927; d. Louis Bernard and Charlotte (Wylie) Rohling; m. Raymond C. Piech, Feb. 12, 1950 (dec. Feb. 1985); 1 child, Christine Piech. BA, U. Ill., 1948, MA, 1953; postgrad., Ill. Inst. Tech., 1966-68, Union Inst., 1991-96. Cert. clin. psychologist, Ill.; diplomate Am. Bd. Med. Psychotherapy. Instr. psychology Elmhurst (Ill.) Coll., 1555-61; asst. prof. psychology North Cen. Coll., Naperville, Ill., 1961-67, Elmhurst (Ill.) Coll., 1968-81; med. psychotherapist Shealy Pain & Health Rehab. Ctr., LaCrosse, Wis., 1977-82, Shealy Inst. Comprehensive Health Care, Springfield, Mo., 1982—. Author, editor: (video series) Mental Health, 1982, (audio tape series) Holistic Mental Health, 1983. Recipient award Lilly Found., Elmhurst Coll., Shealy Inst., 1977. Fellow Am. Bd. Med. Psychotherapy; mem. APA, N.Am. Soc. Adlerian Psychology, Assn. Psychol. Type (life), Phi Beta Kappa, Phi Kappa Phi, Mortar Bd. Office: Shealy Inst 1328 E Evergreen St Springfield MO 65803-4400

PIEKARSKI, IRENE MARY, physician; b. Cobleskill, N.Y., Dec. 20, 1942; d. Leon Thaddeus and Irene Hyacinth (Glogowski) P.; m. John Robert Dorr, Aug. 30, 1965 (div. Dec. 1985); children: Jessica R., Ellen J., Zachary R. AB, Vassar Coll., 1964; MD, U. Calif., 1968. Diplomate Am. Bd. Emergency Medicine. Emergency physician Lettermann Gen. Hosp., San Francisco, 1970; emergency physician Kaiser Permanente, Honolulu, 1971, Richmond, Calif., 1972-73; emergency physician Martin Army Hosp., Columbus, Ga., 1974-75, St. Vincent Hosp., Billings, Mont., 1975-88; primary care physician CarePlus Med. Ctr., Seattle, 1988—. Fellow Am. Coll. Emergency Physician. Roman Catholic. Office: CarePlus Med Ctr 14731 Aurora Ave N Seattle WA 98133

PIEL, CAROLYN FORMAN, pediatrician, educator; b. Birmingham, Ala., Oct. 18, 1918; d. James R. and Mary Elizabeth (Dortch) Forman; m. John Joseph Piel, Aug. 3, 1951; children: John Joseph, Mary Dortch, Elzabeth Forman, William Scott. BA, Agnes Scott Coll., 1940; MS, Emory U., 1943; MD, Washington U., St. Louis, 1946. Diplomate Am. Bd. Pediatrics (examiner 1973-88, pres. 1986-87); diplomate Am. Bd. Pediatric Nephrology. Intern Phila. Gen. Hosp., 1946-47; resident Phila. Children's Hosp., 1947-49; fellow Cornell U. Med. Sch., N.Y.C., 1949-51; from instr. to assoc. clin. prof. Stanford U. Sch. Medicine, San Francisco, 1951-59; from asst. prof. to prof. Sch. Medicine, U. Calif., San Francisco, 1959-89, emeritus prof., 1989—. Author, co-author research articles in field. Bd. mem. San Francisco Home Health Service, 1977-83. Emeritus mem. Soc. for Pediatric Research, Am. Pediatric Soc., Am. Soc. for Pediatric Nephrology, Am. Soc. Nephrology, Western Soc. for Pediatric Nephrology (pres. 1960). Democrat. Presbyterian. Home: 2164 Hyde St San Francisco CA 94109-1701 Office: U Calif PO Box 748 San Francisco CA 94143

PIEL, GERARD, medical science editor, publisher; b. Woodmere, L.I., N.Y., Mar. 1, 1915; s. William F.J. and Loretto (Scott) P.; m. Mary Tapp Bird, Feb. 4, 1938; children: Jonathan Bird, Samuel Bird (dec.); m. Eleanor Virden Jackson, June 24, 1955; child, Eleanor Jackson. A.B. magna cum laude, Harvard U., 1937; D.Sc., Lawrence Coll., 1956, Colby Coll., 1960; U. B.C., Brandeis U., 1965, Lebanon Valley Coll., 1977, L.I. U., 1978, Bard Coll., 1979, CUNY, 1979, U. Mo., 1985, Blackburn Coll., 1985; Litt.D., Rutgers U., 1961, Bates Coll., 1974; L.H.D., Columbia, 1962, Williams Coll., 1966, Rush U., 1979, Hahnemann Med. Coll., 1981, Mt. Sinai Med. Sch., 1985; LL.D., Tuskegee Inst., 1963, U. Bridgeport, 1964, Bklyn. Poly. Inst., 1965, Carnegie-Mellon U., 1968, Lowell U., 1986; Dr. (honoris causa), Moscow State (Lomonosov) U., 1985. Sci. editor Life mag., 1938-44; asst. to pres. Henry J. Kaiser Co. (and assoc. cos.), 1945-46; organizer (with Dennis Flanagan, Donald H. Miller, Jr.), pres. Sci. Am., Inc., 1946-84, chmn., 1984-87, chmn. emeritus, 1987-94; pub. mag. Sci. Am., 1947-84. Translated editions: Le Scienze, 1968, Saiensu, 1971, Investigacion y Ciencia, 1976, Pour la Science, 1977, Spektrum der Wissenschaft, 1978, KeXue, 1979, V Mire Nauki, 1983, Tudomany, 1985, Majallat Al Oloom, 1986, Erde im Gleichgewicht, 1994; author: Science in the Cause of Man, 1961, The Acceleration of History, 1972, Only One World, 1992. Chmn. Commn. Delivery Personal Health Services City N.Y., 1967-68; trustee Am. Mus. Nat. History, N.Y. Bot. Garden, René Dubos Ctr.; trustee emeritus Radcliffe Coll., Phillips Acad., Mayo Clinic, Henry J. Kaiser Family Found., Found. for Child Devel.; pub. mem. Am. Bd. Med. Specialities; bd. overseers Harvard U., 1966-68, 73-79. Recipient George Polk award, 1961, Kalinga prize, 1962, Bradford Washburn award, 1966, Arches of Sci. award, 1969; Rosenberger medal U. Chgo., 1973, A.I. Djavakhishvili medal U. Tbilisi, 1985; named Pub. of Yr. Mag. Pubs. Assn., 1980. Fellow Am. Acad. Arts and Scis., AAAS (pres. 1985, chmn. 1986); mem. Coun. Fgn. Rels., Am. Philos. Soc., Nat. Acad. Sci. Inst. Medicine, Harvard Club, Century Club, Met. Opera Club, Cosmos Club, Somerset Club, Phi Beta Kappa, Sigma Xi. Home: 1115 5th Ave New York NY 10128-0100

PIEMME, THOMAS E., medical educator. BS with high honors, U. Pitts., 1954, MD, 1958; postgrad., Ohio State U., 1964-65. Diplomate Nat. Bd. Med. Examiners; cert. Am. Bd. Family Practice. Intern Health Ctr. Hosps., Pitts., 1958-59, asst. resident in medicine, 1959-60; jr. asst. resident in medicine Peter Bent Brigham Hosp., Boston, 1960-61, fellow/AHA, asst. in medicine, 1961-63; rsch. cardiologist, chief bioanalysis br. Envrion. Med. Div. USAF, Wright-Patterson AFB, Ohio, 1964-66; asst. prof. medicine U. Pitts. Sch. of Medicine, 1966-69; asst. chief of medicine Presbyn. U. Hosp., Pitts., 1966-69; prof. medicine, dir. Divsn. Gen. Medicine George Washington U. Sch. of Medicine, 1969-74; various to prof. health care scis. and medicine, assoc. dean George Washington U. Sch. Medicine, 1977—, 1987—. Contbr. articles to profl. jours and publs. Maj. USAF. Scholar of John and Mary Markle Found., 1966-71; recipient Disting. Svc. award Nat. Bd. Med. Examiners, 1984, others. Mem. AAAS, AMA, AAUP, Am. Fedn. Clin. Rsch., Aerospace Med. Assn., Assn. Am. Med. Colls., Am. Soc. Internal Medicine, Am. Heart Assn., Soc. Tchrs. of Family Medicine, Assn. Phys. Asst. Programs, Am. Acad. Family Physicians, Alliance for Continuing Med. Edn., Soc. for Med. Decision Making (adminstrv. dir.), Phi Beta Kappa, Alpha Omega Alpha, others. Office: George Washington U Office Continuing Med Edn 2300 K St NW Washington DC 20037

PIEPER, JAY BROOKS, hospital executive; b. Atlantic, Iowa, Sept. 11, 1943; s. Elmer Paul and Leona Bertha (Knop) P.; m. Beverly Jeanne Schultz, Aug. 12, 1967; 1 child, Cynthia Marie. BA, Cornell Coll., 1965; MBA, Washington U., St. Louis, 1967; sr. v.p., CFO. Staff acct. Pabst Brewing Co., Milw., 1967-69, corp. fin. mgr., 1969-72, treas., 1972-81, asst. to pres., 1976-79, v.p. corp. devel., 1979-81; v.p., treas., sec. Midland Glass Co., Inc., Cliffwood, N.J., 1981-84; asst. prof. fin. Monmouth Coll., Long Branch, N.J., 1985-86; sr. v.p., CFO Brigham Med. Ctr., Inc., Boston, 1986-96, Brigham and Women's Hosp., Boston, 1986-96; ptnr. PRS Fin., Inc., Little Silver, N.J., 1985—; treas. Bioscis. Rsch. Found., Inc., 1986—; v.p. corp. devel. treasury affairs Ptnrs. Healthcare Sys., Inc., Boston, 1995; bd. dirs. AutoImmune Techs., Chartwell, Inc., WorldCare, IH Solutions. Mem. Fin. Execs. Inst. (chmn. com. on info. mgmt. sys. 1994—). Lutheran. Home: 48 Draper Rd Wayland MA 01778-2125 Office: Brigham Med Ctr Inc 75 Francis St Boston MA 02115-6110

PIEPHO, ROBERT WALTER, pharmacy educator, researcher; b. Chgo., July 31, 1942; s. Walter August and Irene Elizabeth (Huybrecht) Apfel; m. Mary Lee Wilson, Dec. 10, 1981. BS in Pharmacy, U. Ill.-Chgo., 1965; PhD in Pharmacology, Loyola U., Maywood, Ill., 1972. Registered pharmacist, Ill., Colo. Assoc. prof. U. Nebr. Med. Ctr., Omaha, 1970-78; prof. pharmacy, assoc. dean Sch. Pharmacy U. Colo., Denver, 1978-86; prof. pharmacol., dean U. Mo. Sch. Pharmacy, Kansas City, 1987—. Contbr. articles to profl. jours., chpts. to books. Pres. Club Monaco Homeowners Assn., Denver, 1980-82. Named Outstanding Tchr. U. Nebr. Coll. Pharmacy, 1975; recipient Arthur Hassan Colo. Pharmacal Assn., 1983, Excellence in Teaching U. Colo. Med. Sch., 1983. Fellow Am. Coll. Clin. Pharmacology (regent 1983-88, 91-96), Am. Coll. Apothecaries; mem. Am. Soc. Hosp. Pharmacists, Am. Soc. Pharmacology and Exptl. Therapeutics, Rho Chi. Roman Catholic. Office: U Mo Sch Pharmacy 5005 Rockhill Rd Kansas City MO 64110-2239

PIERCE, ALAN KRAFT, physician, educator; b. Houston, Sept. 3, 1931; s. Fred Allan and Esther Beth (Schmidt) P.; m. Dorothy Louise Manes, Dec. 23, 1958; children—Katherine Neal, Alan Kent. Student, Rice U., 1948-51; M.D., Baylor U., 1955. Intern Univ. Hosps. of Cleve., 1955-56; resident Parkland Meml. Hosp., Dallas, 1958-61; practice medicine, specializing in pulmonary diseases Dallas, 1962—; from instr. to prof. U. Tex. Southwestern Med. Sch., Dallas, 1963-84; med. dir. Aston Ambulatory Care Ctr., 1984-87, Parkland Meml. Hosp., 1987-96. Served to capt. USAF, 1956-58. Fellow A.C.P.; mem. Am. Thoracic Soc. (pres. 1972-73), Tex. Thoracic Soc. (pres. 1969-70), Am., Central, So. socs. for clin. research, Am. Assn. Physicians. Home: 3537 Villanova St Dallas TX 75225-5008 Office: U Tex Southwestern Med Sch 5323 Harry Hines Blvd Dallas TX 75235-9034

PIERCE, CHESTER MIDDLEBROOK, psychiatrist, educator; b. Glen Cove, N.Y., Mar. 4, 1927; s. Samuel Riley and Hettie Elenor (Armstrong) P.; m. Jocelyn Patricia Blanchet, June 15, 1949; children: Diane Blanchet, Deirdre Anona. AB, Harvard U., 1948, MD, 1952; ScD (hon.), Westfield Coll., 1977, Tufts U., 1984. Instr. psychiatry U. Cin., 1957-60; asst. prof. psychiatry U. Okla., 1960-62, prof., 1965-69; prof. edn. and psychiatry Harvard U., 1969—; pres. Am. Bd. Psychiatry and Neurology, 1977-78; mem. Polar Research Bd.; cons. USAF. Author publs. on sleep disturbances, media, polar medicine, sports medicine, racism; mem. editorial bds. Advisor Children's TV Workshop; chmn. Child Devel. Assn. Consortium; bd. dirs. Action Children's TV. With M.C. USNR, 1953-55. Fellow Royal Australian and N.Z. Coll. Psychiatrists (hon.), Gt. Britain Royal Coll. Psychiatrists (hon.); mem. Inst. Medicine, Black Psychiatrists Am. (chmn.), Am. Orthopsychiat. Assn. (pres. 1983-84). Democrat. Home: 17 Prince St Jamaica Plain MA 02130-2725

PIERCE, GEORGE EMORY, surgeon, researcher; b. Washington, Iowa, July 15, 1933; s. George Owens and Jessie (Culver) P.; m. Carolyn Bell, Oct. 6, 1962; children: Cathryn Lynn Pollinger, William Brooks. Student, U. Utah, 1951-52; BS, U. Wyo., 1955; postgrad., Johns Hopkins U., 1955-56, MD, 1960. Diplomate Am. Bd. Surgery, Am. Bd. Thoracic Surgery, Am. Sub-Bd. Vascular Surgery. Intern Johns Hopkins Hosp., Balt., 1960-61, resident in surgery, 1961-62, 64-65; resident in gen. and thoracic surgery U. Wash., Seattle, 1965-69, asst. prof. surgery, 197--71; asst. prof. surgery U. Colo., Denver, 1971-72; assoc. prof. surgery U. Kans., Kansas City, 1972-77, prof.surgery, 1978—; attending surgeon, chief surg. svc. VA Med. Ctr., Kansas City, Mo., 1979—; attending surgeon U. Kans. Med. Ctr.; mem. med. adv. bd. Nat. Kidney Found. Kans. and We. Mo., 1976—; bd. dirs. Midwest Organ Bank, Kansas City, Kans., 1974—, pres., 1980-81. Contbr. numerous articles to profl. jours. Lt. col. USPHS, 192-64. Mem. AMA, ACS, Am. Assn. Cancer Rsch., Am. Assn. Immunologists, Am. Coll. Cardiology, Am. Soc. Transplant Surgeons, Am. Surg. Assn., Assn. for Acad. Surgery, Assn. VA Surgeons, Ctrl. Surg. Assn., Halsted Soc., Internat. Surg. Soc., Midwestern Vascular Surg. Soc., Reticuloendothelial Soc., Soc. for Surg. Oncology, Soc. Univ. Surgeons, Soc. for Vascular Surgery, Southwestern Surg. Congress, Transplantation Soc., Western Surg. Assn., Western Trauma Assn., Wyandotte County Med. Soc., Phi Beta Kappa, Sigma Xi. Office: U Kans Med Ctr Dept Surgery 3901 Rainbow Blvd Kansas City KS 66160-0001

PIERCE, MARIANNE LOUISE, pharmaceutical and healthcare companies executive, consultant; b. Atchison, Kans., Apr. 22, 1949; d. James Arthur and Marian Louise (Patton) P.; m. Woodrow Theodore Lewis Jr., June 23, 1973 (div. June 1981). Student, Barnard Coll.; AB, Columbia U., 1970, MBA, 1975. Dep. dir. N.Y. Model Cities, N.Y.C., 1971-73; assoc. corp. fin. Citibank Mcht. Banking, N.Y.C., 1975-77; sr. assoc. N.Y.C., San Francisco, N.Y.C., 1977-82; dep. biotech. dir. Ciba Geigy A.G., Basel, Switzerland, 1982-86; pres., chmn. bd. dirs. Life Scis. Assocs., Ltd., N.Y.C., 1986—; mng. ptnr. Patton, Pierce, Brandon & Co., 1986—; pres., CEO, chmn. XXygen, Inc., New Haven, 1991—. Author: (pamphlet) Developing Biotechnology Strategies for Multinational Corporations, 1985, Managing Successful Strategic Alliances, 1990, New Realities in Drug Discovery, 1995, Drug Discovery Economics, 1996, The Pharmaceutical Industry: Challenges for the Future, 1996. Mem. Internat. Soc. Pharm. Engring., Brit. Biotech. Assn., Comml. Devel. Assn., Practicing Law Inst., Univ. Club (N.Y.C.).

PIERCE, NORMAN BRAYTON, psychologist; b. Acushnet, Mass., Sept. 11, 1940; s. Norman and Hazel May (Gifford) P.; A.B., Bowdoin Coll., 1962; S.T.B., Boston U., 1966, M.A., 1973, Ph.D., 1980; m. Patricia M. Jobe, June 26, 1965 (div.); children: Christine Ruth, Matthew Jobe. Ordained to ministry, Meth. Ch., 1967; registered marriage and family therapist, psychologist. Pastor Wareham and Marion United Meth. Chs., 1966-68, East Bridgewater United Meth. Ch., 1968-71; psychotherapist in pvt. practice, Hingham, Mass., 1971-82; assoc. dir. South Shore Pastoral Counseling Center, Hingham, 1982-85, staff psychologist South Shore Counseling Ctr., 1985—, Bellville Counseling Assocs., Boston, 1992-93; pvt. practice, Boston, 1993—; sex therapist human sexuality program McLean Hosp., 1994—; clin. supr. Boston Inst. Psychotherapies, 1981-88, 92—, assoc. dir. postgrad. ctr., 1986-91; treas., fin. mgr. Pierce Galleries, Inc., 1971-77. Recipient Goodwin French prize, 1959; James Bowdoin scholar, 1959-62; Nat. Meth. scholar, 1963; Albert Danielsen pastoral counseling fellow, 1975-77; Paul Johnson teaching fellow, 1977-78. Diplomate Am. Inst. Counseling and Psychotherapy. Mem. APA, Am. Assn. Marriage and Family Therapy, Mass. Assn. for Psychoanalytic Psychology, New Eng. Soc. Clin. Hypnosis, New England Assn. Lesbian, Gay, Bisexual Psychologists (steering com. 1992—), Phi Beta Kappa. Office: 738 Main St Hingham MA 02043-3327 also: 25 Huntington Ave Ste 406 Boston MA 02116-5713

PIERCE, SANDY FISHER, physician assistant; b. Milford, Del., May 7, 1951; d. Willard Hall and Elizabeth (Oliphant) F.; m. Glenn Thomas Pierce, June 2, 1974; children: Jennifer Marie, Ryan Thomas. BS in Biology cum laude, Wake Forest U., 1973; Physician Asst., Bowman Gray Sch. Medicine, Winston-Salem, N.C., 1976. Cert. physician asst., N.C.; BCLS; ACLS. Physician asst. Dr. Coffman, Norlina, N.C., 1976-77, Dr. Hal Stuart, Elkin, N.C., 1977-85, VA Med. Ctr., Asheville, N.C., 1985—. Deacon, Sunday sch. tchr., mem. choir First Bapt. Ch., Asheville, 1985—; mem. adv. bd. Mountain Area Health Edn., Asheville, 1994-95. Named Outstanding Younr Woman of Am., 1983. Mem. Am. Acad. Physician Assts. (del. 1983, 87, 89, 91, 92, 94, chief del. 1987, 89), N.C. Acad. Physician Assts. (bd. dirs. 1983-87, pres. 1986, chair various coms., Presdl. award 1987), VA Physician Asst. Assn., Jaycettes (exec. v.p., pres. 1979-80), PTA, PTO, Beta Beta Beta. Home: 17 Brushwood Rd Asheville NC 28804 Office: VA Med Ctr 1100 Tunnel Rd Asheville NC 28805

PIERCE, VERLON LANE, pharmacist, small business owner; b. Greensburg, Ky., July 13, 1949; s. Ogle Lee and Aleene (Hall) P.; m. Brenda Mildred Russell, May 20, 1973; children: Amanda Lee, Daniel Russell. BS in Math. and Chemistry, Western Ky. U., 1972; BS in Pharmacy, U. Ky., 1975. Relief pharmacist Shugart & Willis Drug Store, Franklin, Ky., 1975-78; staff pharmacist Franklin Simpson Meml. Hosp., Franklin, 1976-79; owner, pres. pharmacist Medicine Shoppe, Bowling Green, Ky., 1978—; pres. Westland Drug Inc., Bowling Green, 1984-89; pres. JP Solutions, Inc., DBA Option Care, 1988—; sec. 21st Investment Group, Bowling Green, 1984—. Recipient Franny award Internat. Franchise Assn., 1980; Hall of Fame bust Medicine Shoppe, St. Louis, 1983. Mem. 4th Dist. Pharmacy Group (pres. 1983-84), Ky. Pharmacy Assn., Masons, Shriners. Democrat. Baptist. Avocations: golf, swimming. Home: 1414 Mount Ayr Cir Bowling Green KY 42103-4709 Office: Medicine Shoppe 818 Us 31W Byp Bowling Green KY 42101-2314

PIERCE, WILLIAM SCHULER, cardiac surgeon, educator; b. Wilkes-Barre, Pa., Jan. 12, 1937; s. William Harold and Doris Louis (Schuler) P.; m. Peggy Jayne Stone, June 12, 1965; children: William Stone, Jonathan Drew. B.S., Lehigh U., 1958; M.D., U. Pa., 1962. Intern U. Pa., 1962-63; resident in surgery Hosp. U. Pa., 1963-70; asst. prof. M.S. Hershey Med. Ctr., Pa. State U. Coll. Medicine, Hershey, 1970-73, assoc. prof., 1973-77, prof. surgery, 1977—, chief divsn. cardiothoracic surgery, 1991-95; assoc. chmn. dept. surgery, dir. rsch., dept. surgery, 1995—. Contbr. over 300 articles to profl. jours.; inventor cardiac valve, blood pump. Served with USPHS, 1965-67. Fellow ACS; mem. AMA, AAAS, Internat. Cardiovascular Soc., Am. Soc. Artificial Internal Organs, Soc. Vascular Surgery, Am. Heart Assn., Assn. Acad. Surgery, Inst. Medicine, So. Pa. Assn. Thoracic Surgery, Soc. Univ. Surgeons, Am. Surg. Assn., Soc. Clin. Surgery. Office: Milton S Hershey Med Ctr PO Box 850 Hershey PA 17033-0850

PIERING, WALTER FREDERICK, clinical medicine educator; b. Wauwatosa, Wis., Jan. 2, 1936; m. Beatrice A. Nelson; children: Andrew, Peder, Karen, Paul. BS in Psychology, U. Wis., 1958, MD, 1962. Diplomate Nat. Bd. Med. Examiners, Am. Bd. Internal Medicine; cert. comml. pilot. Rotating intern Milw. County Gen. Hosp., 1963-66; clin. fellow in medicine Marquette Sch. Medicine (now Med. Coll. Wis.), Milw., 1966-68; instr. in medicine Med. Coll. Wis., Milw., 1966-69, asst. prof. medicine, 1969-75, assoc. prof. medicine, 1975-89, prof. medicine, 1989—; sr. attending physician dept. medicine Milw. County Med. Complex, 1966—, dir. hemodialysis ctr. dept. medicine, 1968-81; sr. staff Froedtert Meml. Luth. Hosp., Milw., 1981—; med. dir. dialysis unit Milw., 1981—, vice chief of staff, 1990-92, chief of staff, 1992-94; cons. nephrology Zablocki VA Med. Ctr., Wood, Wis., 1969—, Waukesha (Wis.) Meml. Hosp., 1973—, Good Samaritan Med. Ctr., Milw., 1974-88, Elmbrook Meml. Hosp., Brookfield, Wis., 1978—, West Allis (Wis.) Meml. Hosp., 1983—, St. Nicholas Hosp., Sheboygan, Wis., 1982—, Columbia Hosp., Milw., 1991—; mem. coun. on dialysis and transplantation Nat. Kidney Found., 1975—, program com., 1980, dialysis and transplantation forum, 1981, Med. Vol. of Yr. 1975-76); lectr. in field. Contbr. articles to profl. jours. Staff sgt. Wis. Air N.G., 1954-61. Recipient Rsch. grant Dialysis Rsch. Fund, 1975—, grant Nat. Kidney Found. Wis., 1980, 81, 84. Fellow Am. Coll. Physicians; mem. Am. Soc. Nephrology, Am. Soc. for Artificial Internal Organs, Internat. Soc. Nephrology, Am. Fedn. for Clin. Rsch., Milw. Acad. Medicine (membership com. 1988-89), Internat. Soc. for Peritoneal Dialysis, Renal Physicians Assn., Wis. Nephrology Assn. (dir., founder), U. Wis. Med. Alumni Assn. (life). Home: 16595 Shoreline Dr Brookfield WI 53005 Office: Med Coll Wis 9200 W Wisconsin Ave Milwaukee WI 53227

PIERINI, KENNETH WILLIAM, family physician; b. Chgo., May 2, 1940; s. William Lino and Margaret Florence (Jones) P.; m. Georgia Bealle Silver, Aug. 24, 1973; children: Margaret Elizabeth, William Michael. BS, Grinnell Coll., 1962; MS, Loyola U., 1964; MD, U. Seville, Cadiz, Spain, 1972. Resident physician Luth. Gen., Park Ridge, Ill., 1973-76, clin. assoc., 1976-78, attending physician, 1978—; clin. assoc. Fahey Med. Ctr., Des Plaines, Ill., 1977-78; clin. assoc. prof. U. Ill. Coll. of Medicine, Chgo., 1979-86, Chgo. Med. Sch., North Chicago, Ill., 1993—; pvt. practice Niles, Ill., 1978—. Fellow Am. Bd. Family Practice; mem. Ill. Acad. Family Physicians (mem.-at-large 1978—, del. Maine chpt. 1980-92, bd. dirs. 1987-90). Roman Catholic. Office: 8780 W Golf Rd Ste 100 Niles IL 60714

PIERONI, ROBERT EDWARD, internist, educator; b. Portland, Maine, June 20, 1937; s. Ansel Kirby and Agnes Mary (Dumais) P.; m. Dorothy Louise McDonnell, Oct. 3, 1970; children: Michelle Kirby, Robert Francis. BS, Boston Coll., 1959; MD, Pa. State U., 1971. Diplomate Am. Bd. Internal Medicine, Am. Bd. Family Practice, Am. Bd. Allergy and Immunology, Am. Bd. Geriatric Medicine, Am. Bd. Quality Assurance. Chemist Mass. Dept. Pub. Health, Boston, 1962-71; sr. bacteriologist Mass. Dept. Pub. Health, 1971-74; asst. prof. internal medicine U. Ala., Tuscaloosa, 1974-76, assoc. prof. dept. internal medicine and family practice, 1976-81, prof. internal medicine and family practice, 1981—; cons. VA Hosp., Bryce Hosp. and Partlow State Hosp., Tuscaloosa, 1974—. Contbr. more than 250 textbooks, articles and chpts.; mem. editorial bd. various jours. Col. U.S. Army, 1961—. Decorated Bronze Star, 1991, Commendation for Valor; recipient Golden Stethoscope award, 1982, Faculty Recognition award, 1986, Ala. Golden Eagle Humanitarian award Ala. Sr. Citizens Hall of Fame, 1988. Mem. AMA, ACP, Am. Coll. Allergy and Immunology, Am. Gerontol. Soc., Am. Acad. Family Physicians, Physicians for Human Rights, Undersea and Hyperbaric Med. Soc., C. of C., VFW, Am. Legion. Democrat. Roman Catholic. Home: 398 Riverdale Tuscaloosa AL 35406-1802 Office: U Ala Dept Internal Medicine PO Box 870326 Tuscaloosa AL 35487-0326

PIERRE, GLENN N., optometrist; b. Chgo., Aug. 4, 1951; s. Glenn L. and Elsabeth P. (Clark) P.; m. Debbie Ann Schwarz, May 28, 1983; children: Nicole, Danielle. BS, Ill. State U., 1974; OD, Ill. Coll. Osteopathy, 1977. Pvt. practice optometry Colorado Springs, 1977—. Mem. Am. Optometric Assn., Colo. Optometric Assn., Rotary. Republican. Roman Catholic. Home: 4215 Bromley Pl Colorado Springs CO 80906 Office: Archdale Eyecare 709 N Union Colorado Springs CO 80909

PIERSON, ELLERY MERWIN, psychometrist; b. Eugene, Oreg., Mar. 31, 1935; s. Russell Alford and Doris Amanda (Howard) P.; m. Barbara Suzannah Weber, Nov. 27, 1958; children: Suzanne Christine, Audrey Elaine. BS, Portland State Coll., 1957; MEd, Rutgers U., 1965; PhD, U. Pa., 1975. Rsch. asst. Columbia Coll. Physicians and Surgeons, N.Y.C., 1957-58; lab. asst. RCA, Somerville, N.J., 1958-60; welfare investigator Middlesex County Welfare Bd., New Brunswick, N.J., 1960-61; rsch. asst. Ednl. Testing Svc., Princeton, N.J., 1961-66; rsch. psychologist Franklin Inst. Rsch. Labs., Phila., 1966-67; rsch. assoc. Sch. Dist. Phila., 1967-75, mgr. in rsch., 1975-96, dir. assessment, 1996; cons. Livingford Assocs. Mem. Am. Ednl. Rsch. Assn., Nat. Coun. Measurement in Edn., Lions (club sec. 1984—).

PIERSON, RICHARD NORRIS, JR., medical educator; b. N.Y.C., Sept. 22, 1929; s. Richard Norris and Dorothy (Stewart) P.; m. Alice Roberts, Aug. 26, 1974; children by previous marriage: Richard N., Olivia Tiffany, Alexandra de Forest, Cordelia S.C.; stepchildren: Alice W. Dunn, Eric C.W. Dunn. BA, Princeton U., 1951; MD, Columbia U., 1955. Diplomate Am. Bd. Internal Medicine, Am. Bd. Nuclear Medicine. Resident St. Luke's Roosevelt Hosp., N.Y.C., 1955-61, assoc. dir., 1961-65, dir. div. nuclear medicine, 1965-89, dir. body composition unit, 1965—, attending physician, 1975—; prof. clin. medicine Columbia U., 1980—; dir. medicine Hackensack Hosp., 1973-74; staff assoc. Brookhaven Nat. Lab., 1970—; research scholar Lawrence Radiation Lab., Berkeley, Calif., 1970-71, bioengring. inst. Columbia U., 1976—, chmn., 1989-94. Editor: Quantitative Radiocardiography, 1975. Contbr. articles to profl. jours. Bd. dirs. Englewood Health Dept., N.J., 1966-74; warden St. Paul's Ch., 1980-82, bd. dirs. Empire Blue Cross/Blue Shield, N.Y., 1978-91, v.p., 1990-91. Lt. USNR, 1956-58. NIH grantee, 1973-76, 86—; John A. Hartford Found. grantee, 1967-70. Fellow N.Y. Acad. Medicine, ACP; mem. AAAS, APS, AIN, N.Y. County Med. Soc. (pres. 1978-79), N.Y. County Health Svc. Rev. Orgn. (chmn. 1980-82), Am. Bur. Med. Advancement in China (pres. 1979-87), Am. Med. Rev. Rsch. Ctr. (pres. 1985-89, N.Y. State del. to AMA 1978-90), Alliance for Continuing Med. Edn. (pres. 1985-89), Soc. Nuclear Medicine (greater N.Y. area pres. 1982-83, trustee 1991—, del. to AMA 1991—, Berson-Yalow award 1995), P&S Alumni Assn. (pres. 1989-91), Century Club, Englewood Field Club. Home: 60 Lincoln St Englewood NJ 07631-3117 Office: St Lukes Roosevelt Hosp Ctr 1111 Amsterdam Ave New York NY 10025-1716

PIERZ, JOSEPH J., orthopaedist, surgeon; b. Yonkers, N.Y., Nov. 14, 1946; s. Joseph John and Irene Y. Pierz; m. Ann K. Kaczor, May 20, 1972; children: Brian, Elizabeth, Christopher. BA in Biology, Boston U., 1968; MD, U. Conn., Farmington, 1972. Diplomate Am. Bd. Orthop. Surgery. Rotating intern St. Mary's Hosp. and Med. Ctr., San Francisco, 1972-73, resident in surgery, 1973-74, resident in orthopedics, 1974-77; orthop. surgeon Oneida (N.Y.) Orthop. Assoc., 1977—; clin. instr. Upstate Med. Ctr., Syracuse, N.Y., 1977-87; clin. asst. prof. SUNY Health Sci. Ctr., Syracuse, N.Y., 1987—. Fellow ACS, Am. Acad. Orthop. Surgeons; mem. N.Y. State Orthop. Soc. (bd. dirs., pres. 1995—). Office: Oneida Orthop Assoc PC 357 Genesee St Ste 2 Oneida NY 13421

PIES, RONALD WILLIAM, physician, writer; b. Rochester, N.Y., June 12, 1952. AB, Cornell U., 1974; MD, SUNY, Syracuse, 1978. Diplomate Am. Bd. Psychiatry and Neurology. Intern then resident SUNY Upstate Med. Ctr., 1978-82; assoc. clin. prof. psychiatry Sch. Medicine Tufts U., Boston, 1988—; dir. tng. edn. Bay Cove-Tufts Mental Health Ctr., Jamaica Plain, N.Y., 1987-88. Author: Inside Psychotherapy, 1983, Psychotherapy Today, 1991, also poetry. Laughlin fellow Am. Coll. Psychiatry, 1980. Mem. Am. Psychiat. Assn., AMA, Am. Acad. Psychiatry and the Law. Office: Tufts U Sch Medicine 750 Washington St Boston MA 02111-1533

PIETRELLI, LARRY ALAN, research scientist; b. San Francisco, May 4, 1952; s. Baptista David and Vega Elaine Pietrelli; m. Nancy Louise Saylor, July 20, 1985; 1 child, Sarah. AS, City Coll. San Francisco, 1973; BA, San Francisco State U., 1978, MA-C, 1980. Rschr. in toxicology Cutter Biol., Berkeley, Calif., 1980-83; clin. rsch. Cutter Biophys., Berkeley, Calif., 1983-87; sr. clin. rschr. Xoma Corp., Berkeley, Calif., 1987-89, sr. clin. rsch. asst., 1989-92; sr. clin. rsch. asst. Cetus, Emeryville, Calif., 1989; mgr. clin. rsch. Sequus Pharm. Inc., Menlo Park, Calif., 1992—. Deacon Hillcrest Ch., Pleasant Hill, Calif., 1992-93. Mem. Am. Soc. Microbiology, Drug Info. Assn. Home: 367 Blue Oak Ln Clayton CA 94517 Office: Sequus Pharm Inc 960 Hamilton Ct Menlo Park CA 94502

PIETROLETTI, RENATO, surgeon, researcher; b. Rome, Sept. 2, 1958; s. Giulio P. and Fernanda Tarquini; m. Patrizia Pedica, Mar. 17, 1988; children: Lorenzo, Damiano. MD, U. Rome, 1983, PhD, 1990. Intern dept. surgery U. Rome, 1980-83, resident, 1983-88; fellow dept. of histochem Hammersmith Hosp., London, 1984-85, U. Amsterdam, 1987-88; asst. staff surgeon U. L'Aquila (Italy), 1988—; cons. proctology clin. U. L'Aquila, Italy, 1989, stoma care clinic, 1989—; cons. endoscopist Found. Cancer Prevention, Rome, 1992-94,. Fellow Italian Soc. Surgery, Italian Soc. Coloproctology, Italian Soc. Endoscopy. Office: U Aquila Dept Surgery, Via Vetoio Blocco 11, Coppito L'Aquila AQ, Italy

PIETROPAOLO, MASSIMO, medical educator, researcher; b. Palmi, Italy, Feb. 24, 1957. MD, U. Perugia, 1983. From resident to sr. resident Inst. Internal Medicine and Endocrine and Metabolical Scis. U. Perugia Sch. Medicine, Italy, 1983-87, clin. fellow, 1988-89, investigator, physician on staff, 1991-95; rsch. fellow in medicine Joslin Diabetes Ctr. Harvard Med. Sch., Boston, 1989-92; rsch. fellow Barbara Davis Ctr. for Childhood Diabetes U. Colo. Health Scis. Ctr., Denver, 1992-95; rsch. asst. prof. pediats. and medicine divsn. immunogenetics dept. pediats. Rangos Rsch. Ctr. U. Pitts. Sch. Medicine, 1995—. Mem. editl. bd. Diabetes, 1996, Nutrition and Metabolism, 1996. Recipient Postdoctoral fellowship award Juvenile Diabetes Found., 1990-92, 93-95. Mem. AAAS, Am. Fedn. for Clin. Rsch., Am. Diabetes Assn. (career devel. award 1995), N.Y. Acad. Scis. Office: U Pittsburgh Sch Med Rangos Rsch Ctr Children Hosp 3460 5th Ave Pittsburgh PA 15213*

PIFFL, RONALD JAMES, optometrist; b. Madison, Wis., Mar. 23, 1967; s. Victor Joseph Jr. and Margaret Ann (Zieglar) P.; m. Kathryn Aileen Chapin, June 23, 1990. BS in Zoology, U. Wis., Madison, 1989; DO, Ill. Coll. Optometry, 1993. Lic. optometrist, Wis. Optometrist Kindy Optical, Wisconsin Rapids, Wis., 1993-96, Wausau, Wis., 1994-96; optometrist Shopko Optical, Marshfield, Wis., 1996—. Mem. Wis. Optometric Assn. Roman Catholic. Office: Shopko Optical 1306 N Central Ave Marshfield WI 54449

PIGG, MARGARET ANN, psychiatric services administrator, counselor; b. Cape Girardeau, Mo., Apr. 3, 1965; d. Alan H. and Ann M. (Virobik) Held; m. Timothy John Pigg, Oct. 22, 1988; children: Jesse Allen, Kellie Jo. BA, U. Mo., 1987; MEd, U. Mo., St. Louis, 1990. Lic. profl. counselor., Mo. Children's therapist Comtrea, Inc., Festus, Mo., 1987-88, therapist, program coord., 1988-90, cmty. support worker, 1990-91, dir. cmty. support, 1991—. Author psychoednl. program K.I.D.S (Kids In Divorce Supported), 1989.

PIGMAN, HARRY TSCHOPIK, pathologist, consulting computer scientist; b. New Orleans, Dec. 19, 1952; s. Hope (Tschopik) P.; m. Mignon Glass, Apr. 30, 1988; 1 child, Zosia. BA, Conn. Coll., 1974; MD, Tulane U., 1981. Asst. prof. pathology Med. Sch. Tulane U., New Orleans, 1985-87, clin. asst. prof. pathology Med. Sch., 1987—; asst. chief lab. svc. VA Hosp., Biloxi, Miss., 1987—. Developer (computer programs) Lab Manager, 1988, Max Efficiency, 1988, ROC Analyzer, 1989. Fellow Am. Soc. Clin. Pathologists; mem. Am Med. Infos. Assn., Soc. for Med. Decision Making, Group for Rsch. in Pathology Edn. Home: 831 Pine St New Orleans LA 70118-5120 Office: Dept of Vets Affairs Med Ctr 400 Veterans Ave Biloxi MS 39531-2420

PIGNO, MARK ANTHONY, prosthodontist, educator, researcher; b. Lake Charles, La., May 17, 1960; s. Frank Anthony and Geraldine (Carnahan) P.; m. Eileen Marie Failla, May 18, 1991; children: Alexandra Constance, Nathaniel Anthony. BS, McNeese State U., 1983; DDS, La. State U., 1989, cert. in prosthodontics, 1991; cert. in maxillofacial prosthetics, MD Anderson Cancer Ctr., Houston, 1992. Asst. prof. U. Mo., Kansas City, 1992-93, U. Tex. Health Sci. Ctr., San Antonio, 1993—; mem. Craniofacial Anomalies Bd. U. Tex. Health Sci. Ctr., San Antonio, 1995—. Contbr. articles to dental jours. Grantee U. Tex. Health Sci. Ctr., 1995. Fellow (assoc.) Am. Acad. Maxillofacial Prosthetics (Ann. Rsch. award 1992); mem. Am. Dental Assn., Am. Coll. Prosthodontists (com. mem. 1991—), Am. Assn. Dental Schs., Am. Assn. Dental Rsch. Roman Catholic. Office: U Tex Health Sci Ctr 7703 Floyd Curl Dr San Antonio TX 78284-7912

PIKE, DAVID M., physician assistant; b. Canandaguia, N.Y., May 28, 1952; s. Wesley G. and Margaret (Van De Montal) P.; m. Charlene Covers, Nov. 27, 1976; children: Kristin, Chad, Erik. BS, CCNY, 1983; postgrad., Sanford U., 1990. ACLS. Physician asst. Arnold Gregory Meml. Hosp., Albion, N.Y., 1983-89, U. Rochester, N.Y., 1989-93, Oak Orchard Cmty. Health Ctr., Albion, 1993—; physician asst. N.Y. State Dept. Corrs., Albion, 1994—, Sisters of Charity Hosp., Buffalo, 1989—; clin. instr. family medicine D'Youville Coll., Buffalo, 1993—; clin. instr. geriatric medicine Albany Physician Asst. Program, 1989-93. Active AIDS Task Force, Albion, 1996, Orleans County Hospice Com., Albion, 1993. With USN, 1985—. Fellow Am. Acad. Physician Assts., N.Y. State Soc. Physician Assts., Am. Mil. Surg. Assn. Office: Oak Orchard Cmty Health Ctr 301 W Ave Albion NY 14411

PILCHER, ELLEN LOUISE, rehabilitation counselor; b. Washington, Feb. 5, 1949; d. Donald Everett and Edna Lois (Walker) P.; m. Adam J. Buzon Jr., July 27, 1974 (div. Apr. 1991). BA in Psychology, So. Ill. U., 1971, MA in Rehab. Counseling, 1973. Social svcs. asst. Dept. Army, Ft. Huachuca, Ariz., 1973-74, New Ulm, Germany, 1974-75, Ft. Sill, Okla., 1977-87; counselor Goodwill Industries, Lawton, Okla., 1976-77; ind. living specialist Ariz. Bridge to Ind. Living, Phoenix, 1984-87; disability specialist Samaritan Rehab. Inst., Phoenix, 1987-89; disability cons. Peoria, Ariz., 1989—; founder Problems of Architecture and Transp. to Handicapped, Lawton, Okla., 1976-79; founder, past pres. Polio Echo Support Group, Phoenix, 1985—; co-founder, bd. mem. Disability Network of Ariz., Phoenix, 1986—; disability speaker Easter Seal Soc. and free lance, Phoenix, 1984—; producer, host Cable Community Svc. TV Show, Glendale, Ariz., 1987-91; mem. nat. adv. bd. Polio Support Groups, St. Louis, 1987. Named Ms. Wheelchair Ariz. Good Samaritan Med. Ctr., Phoenix, 1986, Second Runner-Up Ms. Wheelchair Am., Ms. Wheelchair Am. Assn., Richmond, Va., 1986, Outstanding Bus. Person Ariz. Parks/Recreation, 1987; recipient Celebration of Success award Impact for Enterprising Women, Phoenix, 1989, Extraordinary Personal Achievement award Lions Club Found., Phoenix, 1987. Mem. NOW (co-founder Lawton chpt. 1982, Glendale, Ariz. chpt. 1984), Nat. Rehab. Assn., Nat. Rehab. Counselors Assn., Ariz. Rehab. Assn., Ariz. Rehab. Counselors Assn. Democrat. Unitarian.

PILCZ, MALETA, psychotherapist; b. Poland, June 5, 1945; came to U.S., 1949; s. Victor and Hana (Oks) P. BA in Psychology, Bklyn. Coll., 1967; MA in Social Work, U. Chgo., 1969. Diplomate Am. Bd. Examiners Clin. Social Work; cert. social worker, N.Y. Psychotherapist Scholarship and Guidance Assn., Chgo., 1969-71; family therapist, supr. Northwestern Meml. Hosp., Chgo., 1972-75; pvt. practice, psychotherapist, cons. Chgo., 1974-80, N.Y.C., 1980—; field work instr. U. Chgo. Sch. of Social Svcs., 1974-75; instr. dept. psychiatry Northwestern U. Med. Sch., 1973-75; cons. faculty Ctr. for Family Studies, Family Inst. Chgo., 1978-80; assoc. staff Ackerman Inst. Family Therapy, N.Y.C., 1983-88; part-time instr. Hunter Coll. Sch. of Social Work, N.Y.C., 1985-88; cons. N.Y.C. Bd. Edn., 1988—. Author: Understanding the Survivor Family; thematic cons. documentary film The Legacy, 1979 (Cigne Gold Eagle, Red Ribbon Am. Film Festival, 1980). Fellow Am. Orthopsychiat. Assn.; mem. NASW (diplomate clin. social work), Am. Group Psychotherapy Assn., Acad. Cert. Social Workers. Office: 330 E 46th St Apt 12D New York NY 10017-3076

PILEWSKI, NORBERT ANTHONY, pharmacognosy educator, pharmacist; b. Oil City, Pa., Dec. 15, 1938; s. John Walter Pilewski and Martha Mary Walentowski; m. Charlotte Marie Kersavage, Sept. 5, 1964; children: Michael John, Kathleen Marie. BS in Pharmacy, U. Pitts., 1961, MS in Pharmacognosy, 1963; PhD in Pharmacognosy, Ohio State U., 1967. Registered pharmacist, Pa., Ohio. Part-time staff pharmacist Presbyn.-Univ. Hosp., Pitts., 1961-63, Magee-Womens Hosp., Pitts., 1961-63; part-time retail pharmacist Chain and Ind. Pharmacies, Pitts., 1961-63, 67-78, Columbus, Ohio, 1963-67; asst. prof. pharmacognosy Duquesne U., Pitts., 1967-71; assoc. prof. pharmacognosy Duquesne U., 1971—; part-time pediatric staff pharmacist Children's Hosp. of Pitts., 1978-91; faculty liaison Am. Soc. Health Systems Pharmacists, Pitts., 1992-96; adj. prof. med. microbiology Pitts. U. Mortuary Sci., 1972-77; faculty advisor Western pa. Soc. Hosp. Pharmacists, Pitts., 1992-96, Kappa Psi Profl. Pharmacy Frat., Pitts., 1967—. Cubmaster, scoutmaster, roundtable commr. Boy Scouts Am., Pitts., 1974—; mem. German-Am. Nat. Congress, Pitts., 1987—; nat. sec. Inst. for German-Am. Rels., Pitts., 1990—; music libr., 2d tenor Teutonia Maennerchor, Pitts., 1990—; mem. 1st aid com., CPR instr. ARC, 1988—. Inst. Intereuropean Studies Travel grantee Inst. for Fgn. Cultural Rels., Berlin, Hamburg, Lambrecht, 1989, Bundestag Adm./Freie U. Berlin Travel grantee Coun. on Internat. Edn. Exch., Bonn, Berlin, 1991; rsch. scholar Am. Found. Pharm. Edn., Columbus, Ohio, 1963-67; recipient Silver Beaver award Boy Scouts Am., 1990, Vigil Honor, 1992. Omicron Delta Kappa. Republican. Roman Catholic. Home: 118 Audbert Dr Pittsburgh PA 15236-1934 Office: Duquesne U Sch Pharmacy Rm 415 Mellon Hall Pittsburgh PA 15282-1504

PILGERAM, LAURENCE OSCAR, biochemist; b. Great Falls, Mont., June 23, 1924; s. John Rudolph and Bertha Roslyn (Phillips) P.; m. Cynthia Ann Moore, Apr. 16, 1971; children: Karl Erich, Kurt John. AA, U. Calif., Berkeley, 1948, BA, 1949, PhD, 1953. Instr. dept. physiology U. Ill. Profl. Coll., Chgo., 1954-55; asst. prof. dept. biochemistry Stanford (Calif.) U. Sch. Medicine, 1955-57; dir. arteriosclerosis research lab. U. Minn. Sch. Medicine, Mpls., 1957-65, Santa Barbara, Calif., 1965-71; dir. coagulation lab., assoc. dir. Cerebrovascular Research Ctr., Baylor Coll. Medicine, Tex. Med. Ctr., Houston, 1971-75; dir. Thrombosis Control Labs., Palo Alto, Calif., 1975-79, Santa Barbara, 1979—; cons. NIH, Bio-Sci. Labs., FDA; del. Council on Thrombosis and Council on Strokes, Am. Heart Assn. Assembly. Co-editor: Nutrition and Thrombosis for the Nat. Dairy Council, 1973; contbr. sci. articles to profl. jours. Recipient CIBA award, London, 1958, Karl Thomae award, Germany, 1973; NIH grantee, 1954-75; LIfe Ins. Med. Research Fund fellow, 1952-54. Mem. Am. Soc. for Biochemistry and Molecular Biology. Office: PO Box 1583 Goleta PO Santa Barbara CA 93116

PILGRIM, DEBORAH ANNICE, psychotherapist; b. Bklyn., Sept. 18, 1956; d. Charles Montague and Nellian Claire (Holloway) P. AB, Smith Coll., 1978; EdM, Harvard U., 1979; EdD, George Washington U., 1986. Rsch. analyst/supr. Crown Hts. Community Corp., Bklyn., summers 1974, 76; supr. Urban League Tutorial Program, Bklyn., summers 1975,77; substitute tchr. Smith Coll. Lab. Campus Sch., Northampton, Mass., 1978; dir. Crown Hts. North Multi-Svc. Ctr. Tutorial Program, Bklyn., summer 1978; psychology extern Cath. U. Am., Washington, 1980-81; psychiat. teaching fellow Boston U. Sch. Medicine, 1981-82; clin. psychology intern Boston City Hosp., 1981-82; psychology teaching fellow Harvard U., Cambridge, Mass., 1987, staff psychologist, 1985—; lectr. and cons. in field. Artist original sculpture in King's Plaza Ctr. in Bklyn., 1971. Prodn. mem. Brookline (Mass.) Community Theater; resident mem. Concerned Black Citizens of Brookline; recruiter/interviewer Smith Coll.; mem. admissions com. Harvard U. Grad. Sch. Edn., 1978-79. NIMH grantee, 1981-82. Mem. APA, Assn. Black Psychologists, Am. Assn. for Counseling and Devel., Assn. for Multi-Cultural Counseling and Devel. (co-chair nat. conv. 1988-89), The Coalition of 100 Black Women (Boston chpt.), Phi Delta Kappa. Democrat. Episcopalian. Office: Harvard U Bur Study Counsel 5 Linden St Cambridge MA 02138-5004

PILISUK, MARC, community psychology educator; b. N.Y.C., Jan. 19, 1934; s. Louis and Charlotte (Feferholtz) P.; m. Phyllis E. Kamen, June 16, 1956; children: Tammy, Jeff. BA, Queens Coll., 1955; MA, U. Mich., 1956, PhD, 1961. Asst. prof., assoc. rsch. psychologist U. Mich., Ann Arbor, 1961-65, founder teach-in, 1965; assoc. prof. Purdue U., West Lafayette, Ind., 1965-67; prof.-in-residence U. Calif., Berkeley, 1967-77; prof. community psychology U. Calif., Davis, 1977—; vis. prof. U. Calif., Wright Inst., 1991—; cons. Ctr. for Self Help Rsch., Berkeley, Calif., 1991-93; prof. psychology Saybrook Inst. and Grad. Ctr., San Francisco, 1993—. Author: International Conflict and Social Policy, 1972, The Healing Web: Social Networks and Human Survival, 1986; editor: The Triple Revolution, 1969; Poor Americans, 1970; Triple Revolution Emerging, 1972; How We Lost the War on Poverty, 1973. NIMH fellow, 1959-60; NSF grantee, 1962-66; Nat. Inst. Alcoholism and Drug Abuse tng. grantee, 1973-77. Fellow Soc. for Community Rsch. and Action, Soc. for Psychol. Study Social Issues (council), APA (pres.-elect divsn. peace psychology 1996), Am. Orthopsychiat. Assn.; mem. ACLU, Am. Soc. on Aging, Am. Pub. Health Assn., Psychologists for Social Responsibility, Faculty for Human Rights in C.Am.

PILL, CYNTHIA JOAN, social worker; b. N.Y.C., Mar. 30, 1939; d. Alfred and Edna (Strauss) Fruchtman; BS cum laude, Jackson Coll., Tufts U., 1961; MS, in Social Work, Simmons Coll. 1963; PhD in Social Work, 1988; m. Robert Pill, July 29, 1961; children: Laura, Daniel, Karen. Clin. social worker Concord (Mass.) Family Service, 1965-78; coordinator family life edn. Family Counseling Service, Newton, Mass., 1979-83; pvt. practice clin. social work, Newton, Mass., 1979—; co-founder, clin. social worker Remarriage Counseling Collaborative, Newton, Mass., 1981-87; cons. Hospice of the Good Shepherd Inc., 1979-84; rsch. advisor Smith Coll. Sch. for Social Work, Northampton, Mass., 1988—; adj. asst. prof. Simmons Coll. Sch. Social Work, Boston, 1989-93. Vol. coordinator Hospice at Home, Sudbury, Mass., 1986-88. Lic. ind. clin. social worker. Mem. Mass. Acad. Clin. Social Work, Inc., Nat. Assn. Social Workers, Register Clin. Social Workers (bd. cert. diplomate). Contbr. to profl. publs. Address: 14 Mason Rd Newton Center MA 02159-1506

PILLARD, RICHARD COLESTOCK, psychiatrist, educator; b. Yellow Springs, Ohio, Oct. 11, 1933; s. Basil H. and Lilian E. (Schueler) P.; m. Cornelia Cromwell, June 20, 1958 (div. 1967); children: Victoria L., Cornelia T.L., Elizabeth J. BA, Antioch Coll., 1955; MD, U. Rochester, 1959. Diplomate Nat. Bd. Med. Examiners. Intern medicine Boston City Hosp., 1959-60; resident in psychiatry Boston State Hosp., 1960-62; research fellow in psychiatry Boston U. Sch. Medicine, 1964-66, head basic studies unit Psychopharmacology Lab., 1968-77, dir. Family Studies Lab., 1977—, prof. psychiatry, 1984—; assoc. vis. physician Univ. Hosp., Boston, 1968—, Dr. Solomon C. Fuller Mental Health Ctr., 1985—, med. dir., 1985-93; expert cons. FDA, 1974-77; med. adviser Homophile Community Health Service, Boston, 1970-80. Co-author: Wild Boy of Burundi, 1978; contbr. articles to profl. jours. Mem. exec. com. Gay and Lesbian Physicians of New England, Boston, 1982-84. Spl. research fellow USPHS, 1966-67; Recipient Research scientist Devel. award USPHS, 1967-72. Fellow Am. Psychiat. Assn. (life); mem. Mass. Psychiat. Soc., Am. Coll. Neuropsychopharmacology, Soc. for Sci. Study of Sex, Internat. Acad. Sex Rsch. Home: 6 Bond St Boston MA 02118

PILLAY, VEERASAMY K.G., physician; b. Durban, Natal, South Africa, Jan. 3, 1931; came to U.S. 1966.; s. Kista and Muthamma (Govender) P.; m. Kamalamma R. Naidoo, July 13, 1972; children: Sankara, Shoba. MD, U. Natal, Durban, 1957. Diplomate in internal medicine and nephrology Am. Bd. Internal Medicine. Asst. prof. medicine Chgo. Med. Sch., 1969-72; staff nephrologist Cook County Hosp., Chgo., 1969-72; assoc. prof. U. Ill., Chgo., 1972-75, prof. medicine, 1975—; chief of nephrology VA Westside Med. Ctr., Chgo., 1972-76, assoc. chief of staff for edn., 1976—. Fellow Royal Coll. Physicians (London), Royal Coll. Medicine (South Africa). Home: 107 Thatcher Ave River Forest IL 60305 Office: V A Westside Med Ctr 820 S Damen Chicago IL 60612

PILLINGER, MICHAEL H., physician; b. Queens, N.Y., July 13, 1959; s. James J. and Evelyn S. P.; m. Judy Goldman. BA in Biochemistry cum laude, Harvard Coll., 1981; MD, NYU, 1987. Diplomate Nat. Bd. Med. Examiners, Am. Bd. Internal Medicine, Am. Bd. Rheumatology. Resident in internal medicine Albert Einstein Coll. Medicine, 1987-90; fellowship in rheumatology NYU Med. Ctr./Hosp. for Joint Diseases, 1990-93; tchg. asst. NYU Sch. Medicine, 1990-93, instr., 1993—, faculty Post-Grad. Med. Sch. Seminar, 1994—; guest lectr. in medicine SUNY Coll. of Optometry, 1990—; rschr. in field. Bd. dirs. Coyote Theatre Co., Chappaqua, N.Y., 1995—. Recipient Arthritis Investigator award (Hulda Irene Duggan award) 1995-98, award N.Y. Arthritis Found. (Ruth M. Hagedorn award) 1994-95, Skirball Clin. fellowship 1994; grantee Am. Cancer Soc. 1996, N.Y. Arthritis Found. 1994, others. Democrat. Jewish. Office: NYU Med Ctr Dept Medicine 550 First Ave Rm NB16NI New York NY 10016

PILLSBURY, HAROLD CROCKETT, otolaryngologist; b. Balt., 1947. MD, George Washington U., 1972. Intern U. N.C., Chapel Hill, 1972-73, resident in surgery, 1973, prof.; resident in otolaryngology N.C. Meml. Hosp., Chapel Hill, 1973-76, mem. staff, 1976—. Mem. ACS, AMA, AAFPRS, AAO-NHS, Alpha Omega Alpha. Office: U NC Womack Bldg CB7070 610 Burnett Chapel Hill NC 27599*

PILLSBURY, JULIA MARIE, former nurse, pediatrician; b. Phila., Feb. 28, 1952; d. James Joseph and Julia Marie (McMonigle) Reddy; m. James S. Pillsbury, Oct. 23, 1982; children: John Ryan, Michael Brendan. AS in Nursing, Gwynedd Mercy Coll., 1972, BS in Nursing, 1974; postgrad., Phila. Coll. Osteo. Medicine, 1981. Instr. nursing Episcopal Hosp., Phila., 1974-75, staff nurse, 1975-76, head nurse, 1976-77; intern pediatrics Fitzsimmons Army Med. Ctr., Aurora, 1981-82, resident pediatrics, 1982-84; gen. pediatrician, clin. instr. pediatrics USAF Hosp., Eglin AFB, Fla., 1984-85; pediatrician USAF Hosp., Whiteman AFB, Mo., 1985-86, chief dept. pediatrics, 1986-88; pediatrician USAF Hosp., Dover, Del., 1989-91; adolescent medicine specialist The Wellness Ctr. Dover (Del.) High Sch., 1990—; physician newborn svc. spl. care nursery Kent Gen. Hosp., Dover, 1990-91; pres. Sweet Delights, Inc., 1990—; cons. Johnson City Child Advocacy Com., Warrensburg, Mo., 1986-88, Child Advocacy Com., 1986-88, Child Devel. Ctr., 1986-88; lectr. Sacred Heart Ch., Warrensburg, 1985-89; instr. Whiteman AFB, Mo., 1985-88; adv. coun. Parent Early Edn. Ctr. Mem. Del. Task Force for Child Abuse Investigation and Child Death Protocols. Maj. USAF, 1984-88. Named One of Outstanding Young Women in Am., 1986. Fellow Am. Acad. Pediatrics, Am. Coll. Osteo. Pediaticians, Assn. Mil. Osteo. Physicians and Surgeons, Am. Osteo. Assn. Democrat. Roman Catholic. Home: 141 Shinnecock Rd Dover DE 19904-9446 Office: The Ctr Pediatric and Adolescent Medicine 942 Walker Rd Dover DE 19904-2729

PILOUS, BETTY SCHEIBEL, nurse; b. Cleve., July 30, 1948; d. Raymond W. and Dorothy E. (Groth) S.; m. Lee Alan Pilous, Sept. 11, 1970; 1 child. Diploma in nursing, Huron Rd. Hosp., Cleve., 1970; BSBA, St. Joseph's Coll., 1989, MHSA, 1995. RN, Ohio; cert. med.-surg. nurse, nursing adminstr. Nurse Huron Rd. Hosp., Cleve., 1970-71, Hillcrest Hosp., Cleve., 1974-77; head nurse, relief supr. Oak Park Hosp., Oakwood, Ohio, 1977-81; head nurse med.-surg. Bedford Hosp., Ohio, 1981-87; dir. inpatient svcs. Meridia Euclid Hosp., Euclid, Ohio, 1987-93, coord. hosp. info. system for nursing, chair nurse practice com., los com. nursing liason; DON, Manor Care, Willoughby, Ohio; team leader referral/assessment Hospice Western Res. Former instr. ARC; chair nurse practice com. Am. Heart Assn.; mem. nursing standards com. Cmty. Hosp. of Bedford; mem. health and safety com. Twinsburg Schs., Ohio, 1984, mem. curriculum com., 1981-83; chairperson standards com. Cmty. Hosp. of Bedford; former counselor jr. high youth 1st Congl. Ch., Twinsburg; past chair adv. bd. chairperson Brecksville Rainbow Assembly for Girls, 1992; mem. Twinsburg Libr. Levy Com., 1991. Recipient Paradiam award, 1991. Mem. Ohio Citizen League Nursing Nurse Execs. Network (former sec.), Ohio Hosp. Assn., Ohio Orgn. Nurse Execs., Ohio Directors of Nursing Assocs. Long Term Care, Nat. League Nursing, Southeast Cleve. Mid Mgrs. Ohio Orgn. Nurse Exec., Acad. Med.-Surg. Nursing (charter mem.), Networking Group Nurse Mgrs. (initiated), Order Eastern Star, Sigma Theta Tau, Iota Psi. Avocation: hiking.

PILSNER, JOYCE MARION, health services administrator; b. N.Y.C., Jan. 30, 1925; d. Sol and Estelle (Schaffle) Mayersohn; m. Harry Pilsner, Dec. 20, 1947; 1 child, Toby Jane. AB, Hunter Coll., 1944; MA, Columbia U., 1946, cert. Inst. for Not-for-Profit Mgmt., 1977. Tchr. N.Y.C., 1945-67; rsch. assoc. Inst. Community Studies Sarah Lawrence Coll., Bronxville, N.Y., 1968-69, asst. to dean, 1968-70; rsch. assoc., field coordinator Consortium on Community Crises Cornell U., Ithaca, N.Y., 1970-71; exec. dir. Riverdale Mental Health Ctr., Bronx, N.Y., 1971—; sec. Citywide Behavioral Network, 1986—. Membership chmn. corr. sec. Riverdale Cmty. Coun.; mem. dist. bd. Comprehensive Health Planning Agy.; mem., sec. sub-regional com. Bronx Fedn. Mental Health and Mental Retardation Agys.; bd. dirs. Riverdale Sr. Ctr., 1974-82; bd. dirs. Coalition of Vol. Mental Health Agys., 1975—, v.p., 1975-90, sec., 1995—; mem. Cmty. Bd. B, Bronx, 1975—, chmn. health com., ethics com., youth com., 2d v.p., 1989-96, 96—, 1st v.p., 1990-93, chmn., 1993-95; mem. cmty. adv. bd. North Ctrl. Bronx Hosp., 1983-89, chmn. health, membership and nominating coms.; mem. Users Group,. Info. Scis. Divsn. Nathan Kline Inst., 1984-87, exec. com., sec., 1985-86; borough outreach com. Greater N.Y. Fund/United Way, 1985-89. Named Riverdalian of Yr., 1979; recipient Cert. of Meritorious Svc. N.Y.C. Mayor Edward I. Koch, 1986, Cmty. Svc. award Benjamin Franklin Dem. Club, 1992, Cleveland E. Dodge award, 1995. Fellow Am. Orthopsychiat. Assn.; mem. Riverdale Mental Health Assn. (dir. 1965-71, chmn. pub. rels., editor newsletter), UN Assn. (dir. Riverdale chpt., chmn. publicity), East Hampton House Owners Ltd. (bd. dirs., v.p. 1986, pres. 1988—), Alumni Assn. Inst. for Not-for-Profit Mgmt. (exec. com. 1987-89), Bronx Mental Health Coun. (chmn. legis. com. 1980-94). Home: 4721 Delafield Ave Bronx NY 10471-3311 Office: Riverdale Mental Health Assn 5676 Riverdale Ave Bronx NY 10471-2138

PIMENTA, JOSE MANUEL ARAUJO GUERRA, surgeon; b. Barreiro, Setubal, Portugal, May 15, 1954; s. Manuel Guerra and Celeste da Conceição (Araujo) P.; m. Maria Helena Santos da Gama Lanca Guerra Langa, Oct. 11, 1975; children: Marta da Gama Lanca Guerra, Pedro da Gama Lanca Guerra. Complementar, Liceu Barreiro, Portugal, 1973; Superior, Faculty Medicine Lisboa, Portugal, 1981. Gen. physician H.D. Barreiro, 1982-85; complemental internal clin. pathology H.D. Chaves, 1985-86; complemental internal stomatology H. Civis Lisboa, Portugal, 1986-89; complemental internal gen. surgery H.D. Barreiro, 1989-95, gen. surgeon, 1995; stomatologist CIREST, Barreiro, 1989—. Mem. Ordem Dos Medicos Lisboa, Sociedade Portuguesa de Estomatologia. Home: R Jose Magro 6, 10o, 2830 Barreiro Portugal Office: CIREST, R Dr M Manuel Pachelo Nobre 105 3o dt, 2830 Barreiro Setubal, Portugal

PIMENTAL, LAURA, emergency physician; b. Prestwick, Scotland, Jan. 27, 1958; came to U.S., 1958; BS, Georgetown U., 1979, MD, 1983. Diplomate Am. Bd. Emergency Medicine, Nat. Bd. Med. Examiners. Intern Walter Reed Army Med. Ctr., Washington, 1983-84; resident in emergency medicine Madigan Army Med. Ctr., Tacoma, Wash., 1984-86; chief resident dept. emergency medicine Madigan Army Med. Ctr., Tacoma, 1986; staff physician Tripler Army Med. Ctr., Honolulu, 1986-87, asst. chief emergency med. scvs., 1987-88; attending emergency physician Brooke Army

Med. Ctr., San Antonio, Tex., 1989-90; dir. edn. dept. emergency medicine Mercy Med. Ctr., Balt., 1992-93; dir. emergency svcs. Bon Secours Hosp., Balt., 1993-94; attending physician dept. emergency medicine Univ. Hosp., Balt., 1990—; attending physician dept. emergency medicine Mercy Med. Ctr., Balt., 1990—, acting chmn. dept. emergency medicine, 1996—; mem. affiliate faculty ACLS, Mil. Tng. Network, San Antonio, Tex., 1988, emergency medicine tchg. faculty Brooke Army Med. Ctr., San Antonio, 1989-90; asst. prof. dept. surgery U. Md. Sch. of Medicine, Balt., 1990—. Contbr. articles to profl. jours.; presenter, lectr. at nat. and internat. sci. confs. Named Best Resident and Best Overall Presenter, So. Med. Assn.-Am. Coll. Emergency Physicians Case Presentation Competition, New Orleans, 1984. Mem. Am. Coll. Emergency Physicians, Am. Acad. Emergency Medicine, Christian Med. and Dental Soc. Home: 14 Old Dominion Ct Catonsville MD 21228

PIMENTAL, PATRICIA ANN, neuropsychologist, consulting company executive, author; b. Warwick, R.I., Feb. 2, 1956; d. Thomas Robert and Veronica Madeleine (Costa) P.; m. John V. O'Hara, Dec. 16, 1989; children: John Bernard, Padraic James. BS in Pre-Med, Speech Pathology, Northwestern U., 1978, MA in Speech Pathology with honors, 1980; PsyD in Clin. Psychology with honors, Chgo. Sch. Profl. Psychology, 1987. Lic. psychologist, speech pathologist, Ill.; diplomate Am. Bd. Vocat. Neuropsychology, Am. Acad. Pain Mgmt., Am. Bd. Prof. Disability Cons., Am. Bd. Profl. Neuropsychology. Clin. psychology extern child psychology clinic U. Ill., Chgo., 1984-85, dir. psychol. svcs. dept. phys. medicine and rehab., 1987-91, asst. prof. dept. phys. medicine and rehab., 1987-91; clin. psychology extern Filmore Mental Health Ctr., Berwyn-Cicero (Ill.) Sr. Svcs., 1985-86; clin. psychology intern St. Elizabeth's Hosp., Chgo., 1986-87; mem. faculty Chgo. Sch. Profl. Psychology, 1991—; pres. Neurobehavioral Medicine Cons., Ltd., Oak Brook, Ill., 1991—. Sr. author: Neuropsychological Aspects of Right Brain Injury, 1989, The Mini Inventory of Right Brain Injury, 1989; contbr. articles and revs. to profl. jours., chpts. to books; manuscript reviewer Archives Phys. Medicine and Rehab., 1990; book reviewer Contemporary Psychology, 1991. Vol. trainer ARC Disaster Stress Relief Program, 1991—; leader U. Ill. Stroke Club, 1988-91; bd. dirs. Older Adult Rehab. Svcs., Cicero, 1987-90; active Chgo. Anti-Cruelty Soc., Lincoln Park Zool. Soc. Named one of Outstanding Young Women Am., 1984, 92; Am. Cancer Soc. scholar, 1979; recipient Outstanding Manuscript of Yr. award Am. Jour. of Pain Mgmt., 1993. Fellow Am. Coll. Pain Neuropsychology; mem. APA, Am. Pain Soc., Ill. Psychol. Assn. (adv. bd. 1989-93, chair-elect, chair health and rehab. sect. 1991-92, 92-93, chair prescription privilege task force 1992-95, continuing edn. chair/clin. practice sect. 1993-95, pres.-elect 1995-96, pres. 1996—), Nat. Brain Injury Rsch. Found. (med. adv. coun. 1992—), Internat. Neuropsychol. Soc., Nat. Acad. Neuropsychology, Am. Congress Rehab. Medicine, Soc. Clin. and Exptl. Hypnosis, Midwest Neuropsychology Group, Am. Speech and Hearing Assn. Roman Catholic. Office: Glen Oaks Hosp Med Ctr Neurobehavioral Medicine 701 Winthrop Ave Glendale Heights IL 60139

PIMENTEL, EDGAR ANDREW, physician; b. Bayshore, N.Y., Feb. 16, 1963; s. Mariano Balbin and Sinen Sadiua (Pe) P. BA, U. Md., 1987; DO, U. New Eng., 1991. Diplomate Nat. Bd. Osteopathy. Chief resident in family practice St. Barnabas Hosp., Bronx, N.Y., 1995-96. Active Rep. nat. com.,1993-9. Mem. AMA, Am. Osteo. Assn. (intern-resident com. 1995—), Soc. of Tchrs. of Family Medicine, Mass. Med. Soc., Phi Beta Kappa. Roman Catholic.

PIMPINELLA, RONALD JOSEPH, surgeon; b. Utica, N.Y., Sept. 27, 1935; s. Joseph and Josephine (Payne) P.; B.A. magna cum laude, Syracuse U., 1956; M.D., U. Rochester, 1960; children: Andrea, Giancarlo. Intern, Albany (N.Y.) Med. Center, 1960-61; resident in ear-nose-throat Columbia Presbyn. Med. Ctr., 1962-65; chief ENT, Martin Army Hosp., Ft. Benning, Ga., 1965-67; practice medicine specializing in otolaryngology and facial plastic surgery, Torrington, Conn., 1967-88; ret.; chief otolaryngology Charlotte Hungerford Hosp. Capt. U.S. Army, 1965-67. Fellow Am. Assn. Ophthalmology and Otolaryngology, Am. Acad. Facial Plastic and Reconstructive Surgery, ACS; mem. AMA, Conn. Med. Soc. (pres. otolaryngology sect. 1978-83). Roman Catholic. Contbr. articles to med. jours. Home: 8900 SW 97 Lane Rd Unit D Ocala FL 34481

PINA-CABRAL, JOSÉ MANUEL GONCALVES, physiology educator; b. V.N. Gaia, Porto, Portugal, Dec. 9, 1929; s. Manuel Pereira and Maria Luisa (Gonçalves) Pina-C.; m. Maria Idalina Tavares, Aug. 14, 1959; children: Maria Paula, Helena Maria, Francisco Manuel, José Jorge, João Filipe. Diploma Faculty Medecine, Porto, 1952. Med. doctor Faculty Medecine of Porto, 1945-52, PhD, 1952-63, aggregate prof., 1963-72, full prof., 1972-95; mem. Scientific Coun. Faculty Medecine of Porto, dir. Lab. Physiology, dean Faculty of Medecine of Porto, 1974-76. Contbr. articles to profl. jours. Mem. Portuguese Soc. Physiology, Portuguese Soc. Electron Microscopy, Portuguese Soc. Haematology, Internat. Soc. Thrombosis and Haemostasis, Internat. Soc. Haematology, European Thrombosis Rsch. Orgn. Socialist. Mem. Lusitanian Ch. Home: Avenida da Boavista, 2066-H 65, 4100 Porto Portugal Office: Faculty of Medicine Porto, Al Prof Hernâni Monteiro, 4200 Porto Portugal

PINCHUCK, CURT PAUL, psychiatrist; b. Bklyn., Feb. 6, 1960. BA, Columbia Coll., N.Y.C., 1982; MD cum laude, SUNY, Buffalo, 1987. Intern, then resident in psychiatry NYU Med. Ctr., N.Y.C., 1987-91; teaching asst. in psychiatry Tisch Hosp., The Univ. Hosp. of NYU Med. Ctr., 1990-94; staff psychiatrist Hillside Hosp. of the L.I. Jewish Med. Ctr., 1991-93; asst. prof. psychiatry Albert Einstein Coll. Medicine, 1993-94; clin. asst. prof. psychiatry Mount Sinai Sch. Medicine, 1995-96; med. dir. Interborough Devel. & Consultation Ctr., Inc., Bklyn., 1996—; instr. in psychiatry Albert Einstein Coll. of Medicine, Yeshiva U., 1991-93; consulting psychiatrist New Hope Guild Tikvah Program, Bklyn., 1995—; asst. attending Maimonides Med. Ctr., 1996—. Editor: The First Annual 1991-92 New York City Psychiatric Fellowship and Research Guide, 1990. Recipient Gilbert M. Beck meml. prize in psychiatry for acad. excellence SUNY at Buffalo Sch. Medicine, 1987. Mem. APA (presenter ann. mtgs. 1985, 86), Mesorah Soc. for Traditional Judaism, Alpha Omega Alpha, Phi Lambda Kappa. Office: Interborough Devel & Consultation Ctr Inc 1670-78 E 17th St Brooklyn NY 11229

PINCUS, DEBBIE SUE, psychotherapist; b. Glencove, N.Y., June 30, 1953; d. William and Reva (Napers) P.; m. Richard J. Ward, Sept. 24, 1989. BS magna cum laude, U. Bridgeport, 1975, MS, 1976. Tchr. Lerox Sch., N.Y.C., 1976-78, Horace Mann Barnard Sch., Riverdale, N.Y., 1978-1984; pvt. practice N.Y.C., Larchmont (N.Y.), N.Y.C., 1983—; dir. counseling svcs. Coll. of Mt. St. Vincent, N.Y.C., 1984-91, Physician's Smokestopping Clinic, N.Y.C., 1984-90. Author: Sharing, 1983, Feeling Good About Yourself, 1989, Citizenship, 1990, Manners Matter, 1992, Getting Along With Others, 1993. Mem. ACA.

PINCUS, JONATHAN HENRY, neurologist, educator; b. Bklyn., May 4, 1935; s. Joseph Bernhard and Hannah Martha (Palestine) P.; m. Cynthia Sterling Deery, Jan., 1961 (div. 1983); children: Daniel, Jeremy, Adam; m. Fortuna Mizrahi Fries, Nov. 1983 (div. 1995). AB, Amherst Coll., Mass., 1956; MD, Columbia U., 1960; MA, Yale U., 1973. Asst. prof. neurology Yale U., New Haven, 1965-69, assoc. prof. neurology, 1969-73, prof. neurology, 1973-86; prof., chmn. neurology Sch. Medicine Georgetown U., Washington, 1987-95, prof. neurology, 1987—. Author: Behavioral Neurology, 1974, 3d edit., 1986. Fellow Am. Acad. Neurology (v.p. 1991-93); mem. Am. Neurol. Asns. (counselor 1984-86). Office: Georgetown Univ Hosp Dept Neurology 1st Fl Bles Bldg 3800 Reservoir Rd NW Washington DC 20007-2196

PINCUS, PATRICIA HOGAN, nurse; b. Lockport, N.Y., Dec. 4, 1945; d. George W. and Theresa J. (Harrington) Wendel; children: Jennifer, Molly, Peter. RN, Mercy Hosp. Sch. Nursing, Buffalo, 1966; MPH, U. Rochester, 1985; BS, Empire State Coll., Rochester, N.Y., 1977. RN, N.Y.; cert. infection control nurse. Instr. Empire Nine Emergency Med. Tech. Program, Rochester, 1976; infection control practitioner dept. medicine U. Rochester Med. Ctr., 1975-79, asst. nursing practice coord. dept. nursing, 1979-80; tech. assoc. IDU Univ. Rochester, 1980-92, nurse mgr. Clin. Rsch. Ctr., 1992—. Contbr. numerous articles to profl. jours. Mem. ANA, AONE, Nat. Assn. Gen. Clin. Rsch. Ctr. Nurse Mgrs., Genesee Valley Nurses Assn., Assn. for Practitioners in Infection Control (bd. dirs.), Western N.Y. State Infection Control Officers (bd. dirs.). Home: 14 W Jefferson Rd Pittsford NY 14534-1902 Office: Univ Rochester Med Ctr Box 619-13 609 Elmwood Ave Rochester NY 14620-2913

PINCUS, STEPHANIE HOYER, dermatologist, educator; b. Lakehurst, N.J., Feb. 28, 1944; d. Ernest Carl and Aviva (Silbert) Hoyer; m. David Frank Pincus, Aug. 22, 1965 (div. Dec. 1984); children: Matthew Jonah, Tamara Hope; m. Allan Roy Oseroff, Mar. 24, 1985; 1 child, Benjamin Henry Oseroff. BA, Reed Coll., 1964; MD cum laude, Harvard U., 1968. Diplomate Am. Bd. Dermatology, Am. Bd. Internal Medicine. Intern Boston City Hosp., 1968-69; rsch. fellow U. Wash., 1969-71; resident internal medicine U. WN, 1971-72, resident-fellow dermatology, 1972-74; fellow instr. dept. dermatology Harvard Med. Sch., 1974-75; asst. prof. medicine U. Wash., Seattle, 1975-77; lectr. Sch. Medicine Boston U., 1977-89; asst. prof. medicine Sch. Medicine Tufts U., Boston, 1977-82, mem. dept. immunology, 1977-89, asst. prof. dermatology, 1979-82, assoc. prof. dermatology and medicine, vice chairperson dermatology, 1982-89; prof. medicine and dermatology, chairperson dermatology SUNY, Buffalo, 1989—. Dermatology Found. fellow, Evanston, Ill., 1974-75, 77-78; Vets. Adminstrn. rsch. assoc., 1975-77; recipient Clin. Investigator award NIH, Bethesda, Md., 1979-81. Mem. Am. Contact Dermatitis Soc. (mem. liaison com. 1993—), Women's Dermatologic Soc. (bd. dirs. 1992—), Soc. Investigative Dermatology (chmn. com. on govt. and pub. rels. 1992-96), Profs. of Dermatology (mem. program com. 1993—), Internat. Soc. for Study of Vulvar Diseas (mem. exec. com. 1993-95), Harvard Med. Alumni (pres. 1995-96), Phi Beta Kappa, Alpha Omega Alpha. Office: SUNY 100 High St Ste C319 Buffalo NY 14203-1126

PINE, CHARLES JOSEPH, clinical psychologist; b. Excelsior Springs, Mo., July 13, 1951; s. Charles E. and LaVern (Upton) P.; m. Mary Day, Dec. 30, 1979; children: Charles Andrew, Joseph Scott, Carolyn Marie. BA in Psychology, U. Redlands, 1973; MA, Calif. State U.-L.A., 1975; PhD, U. Wash., 1979; postdoctoral UCLA, 1980-81. Diplomate in Clinical Psych. Am. Bd. Profl. Psych. Lic. psychologist, Calif., Fla. Psychology technician Seattle Indian Health Bd., USPHS Hosp., 1977-78; psychology intern VA Outpatient Clinic, L.A., 1978-79; instr. psychology Okla. State U., 1979-80, asst. prof., 1980; asst. prof. psychology and native Am. studies program Wash. State U., 1981-82; dir. behavioral health services Riverside-San Bernardino County Indian Health Inc., Banning, Calif., 1982-84; clin. psychologist, clin. co-dir. Inland Empire Behavioral Assocs., Colton, Calif., 1982-84; clin. psychologist VA Med. Ctr., Long Beach, Calif., 1984-85; clin. psychologist, psychology coordinator Psychiatry div. VA Med. Ctr., Sepulveda, Calif., 1985-93; clin. dir. Traumatic Stress Treatment Ctr., Thousand Oaks, Calif., 1985-93; assoc. clin. prof. UCLA Sch. Medicine, 1985—, Fuller Grad. Sch. Psychology, Pasadena, Calif., 1985-93, indep. practitioner Orlando, 1993-94; adj. assoc. prof. Calif. Sch. Profl. Psychology, L.A., 1989—; mem. adj. faculty, psychologist, administv. coord. alcohol and drug abuse U. Ctrl. Fla.; rsch. assoc. Nat. Ctr. for Am. Indian and Alaska Native Mental Health Rsch., U. Col. Health Sci. Ctr., Denver, 1989—; psychologist alcohol and drug abuse treatment program, Orlando VA Outpatient divsn. Tampa VA Med. Ctr., 1993—; cons. NIH, 1993—; mem. L.A. County Am. Indian Mental Health task force, 1987-92. Editorial cons. White Cloud Jour., 1982-85; cons. Dept. Health and Human Services, USPHS, NIMH, 1980. Vol. worker Variety Boys Clubs Am., 1973-75; coach Rialto Jr. All-Am. Football League, 1974, Conejo Youth Flag Football Assn., pres., 1990, coach, bd. dirs. Westlake Youth Football, 1991-92; coach. Conejo Valley Little League, Dr. Phillips Little League, 1993—; co-commr., coach Dr. Phillips Pop Warner Football, 1993—. U. Wash. Inst. Indian Studies grantee, 1975-76, UCLA Inst. Am. Cultures grantee, 1981-82. Fellow Am. Psychol. Assn. (chair task force on service delivery to ethnic minority populations bd. ethnic minority affairs 1988—, bd. ethnic minority affairs 1985-87), Acad. Clin. Psychology; mem. Soc. Indian Psychologists (pres. 1981-83), Nat. Register Health Svc. Providers in Psychology, Calif. Psychol. Assn. Found. (bd. dirs. 1990-92), N.Y. Acad. Sci., Soc. for Psychol. Study Ethnic Minority Issues (exec. com. 1987-88), Sigma Alpha Epsilon. Republican. Roman Catholic. Contbr. psychol. articles to profl. lit.

PINEDA, ANSELMO, neurosurgery educator; b. Lima, Peru, Apr. 3, 1923; s. Anselmo Vicente and Juana (Munayco)P.; m. Monique Yvonne Martin, Mar. 15, 1955; children: Patricia M., Richard A., Gilbert V., Katherine A. MD, San Marcos U., Lima, 1951; MS, Northwestern U., 1962. Diplomate Am. Bd. Neurol. Surgery. Rotating intern Loayza Hosp., Lima, 1950-51; head histology sect. Leprosy dept. Ministry Pub. Health, Lima, 1951; asst. pathologist Nat. Inst. Neoplastic Diseases, 1952; vol. asst. lab. normal and path. histology nervous system San Marcos U. Sch. Medicine, 1953; rotating intern Augustana Hosp., Chgo., 1954, resident in gen. surgery, 1955; jr. asst. resident in neurosurgery U. Chgo., 1955-56, sr. asst. resident in neurosurgery, 1956-57, chief resident in neurosurgery, 1957-58; assoc. instr. neurosurgery U. Tex., 1958-61; assoc. neurosurgeon John Sealy Hosp., Galveston, Tex., 1960-61, attending neurosurgeon, 1961; acting chief neurosurgery VA Hosp., Long Beach, Calif., 1962-63; assoc. clin. prof., mem. Brain Research Inst. UCLA, 1962—; cons. VA Hosp., Long Beach, 1966-67. NIH spl. fellow in Neuroanatomy Northwestern U., 1961-62. Fellow ACS, Am. Coll. Angiology, Royal Soc. Medicine; mem. AAUP, AAAS, AMA, Congress of Neurol. Surgeons, World Med. Assn., Am. Assn. Neurol. Surgeons, Calif. Med. Assn., Orange County Med. Assn., Am. Acad. Neurology, Am. Assn. Neuropathologists, Internat. Coll. Surgeons, Am. Assn. Anatomists, Am. Assn. Trauma, Am. Soc. Stereotaxic and Functional Neurosurgery, N.Y. Acad. Scis., Internat. Assn. Study Pain, Sigma Xi. Home: 16571 Carousel Ln Huntington Beach CA 92649-2115 Office: 2880 Atlantic Ave Ste 160 Long Beach CA 90806-1715

PINELESS, HAL STEVEN, neurologist; b. Chgo., Oct. 19, 1954; s. William and Sophie (Lubnicka) P.; m. Edy Dianne Rudnick, Mar. 10, 1985; children: Adam, Emily. BS in Zoology, U. Ill., 1976; DO, Chgo. Coll. Osteo. Medicine, 1981. Diplomate Am. Osteo. Bd. Neurology and Psychiatry. Intern Chgo. Osteo. Hosp., 1981-82; resident Loyola U. Med. Ctr./Hines (Ill.) VA Ctr., 1982-85; asst. prof. neurology Chgo. Coll. Osteo. Medicine, 1985-86; pvt. practice Winter Park, Fla., 1986—; pres. med. staff Fla. Hosp. East Orlando, 1990-93, bd. trustees, 1990-94. Contbr. articles to profl. jours and newspapers. Mem. AMA, Am. Osteo. Assn., Am. Acad. Neurology, Am. Coll. Neuropsychiatrists, Nat. Headache Found. Office: 1890 Semoran Blvd Ste 255 Winter Park FL 32792

PINERO, CARLOS, cardiologist; b. Seville, Spain, Dec. 2, 1937; s. Antonio Pinero and Carlota Galvez; m. Maria Luisa Gonzalez, May 12, 1968; children, Pilar, Carlos. MD, Med. Sch., Seville, Spain, 1964, PhD, 1985. Intern Englewood (N.J.) Hosp., 1968-69, medical resident, 1969-71; resident in cardiology Montefiore Hosp, Bronx, N.Y., 1971-73; chief CCU U. Hosp., Seville, 1974-86; chief svc. cardiology Hosp. Gen., Cadiz, Spain, 1987—; assoc. prof. Sch. Med., Cadiz, 1991—. Mem. Soc. Española Cardiology, Soc. Andaluza Cardiology (jour. editor 1991). Home: Parlamento 5, Cadiz 11008, Spain Office: Clinica La Salud, Feduchy 8, Cadiz 1001, Spain

PINES, BEVERLY IRENE, psychologist; b. Bklyn., Nov. 11, 1925; d. Solomon and Jeannette (Radin) Grobstein; B.A., Bklyn. Coll., 1944, M.A., 1948; Ph.D., N.Y. U., 1957; postgrad. Walden U.; m. Matthew Pines, Jan. 29, 1949; children—Elyse Pines Rosenstein, Elliot. Student psychologist Kings County (N.Y.) Hosp., 1945-47; med. asst. to physicians, 1942-49; instr., lectr. Bklyn. Coll., 1946-50, student guidance counselor, 1946-50, group therapist, 1948-50; pvt. practice psychol. and psychotherapist marriage and divorce counseling, family therapy, community health service-health fairs. Bklyn., 1948—; participating psychologist G.H.I. Nat. Register Health Service Providers in Psychology, Blue Cross Blue Shield Wrap Around plus Ins. Plans and Medicaid and Medicare. Lic. psychologist, N.Y. Mem. Am., N.Y. State, Bklyn. psychol. assns., Am. Soc. Clin. Hypnosis Edn. and Research Found., Bklyn. Coll. Alumni Assn. Jewish. Address: 637 E 8th St Brooklyn NY 11218-5905

PINES, JEFFREY M., psychiatrist; b. N.Y.C., Jan. 12, 1947. AB, Columbia Coll., 1969; MD, Columbia U., 1973. Diplomate Am. bd. Psychiatry and Neurology. Intern medicine Presbyn. Hosp., N.Y.C., 1973-74; resident medicine Presbyn. Hosp., 1974-76; rheumatology fellow Hosp. for Spl. Surgery, N.Y.C., 1976-77; resident psychiatry N.Y. State Psychiat. Inst., Presbyn. Hosp., 1977-80; fellow consultation-liaison psychiatry Presbyn. Hosp., N.Y.C., 1980-81, asst. attending, 1983-94, assoc. attending, 1994—; asst. prof. clin. psychiatry Columbia U., N.Y.C., 1983-94, assoc. prof. clin. psychiatry, 1994—. Mem. Am. Psychiatric Assn., Alpha Omega Alpha. Office: Presbyn Hosp 161 Ft Washington Ave New York NY 10032-3713

PINILLA, ANA RITA, neuropsychologist, researcher; b. N.Y.C., May 20, 1957; d. Louis and Luz Maria (Diaz) P.; m. Jorge Rosado Rosado, Dec. 01, 1979; children: Jorge Javier, Juan Carlos, Ana Mari. BS magna cum laude, U. P.R., Rio Piedras, 1978; MS, Caribbean Ctr., San Juan, P.R., 1980, PhD, 1988. Lic. psychologist, P.R. Prof. psychology Inter-Am. U., San Juan, 1980-91; neuropsychologist Neuropsychol. Svcs. to Developmental Deficiencies Children, Bayamon, P.R., 1987-88; asst. dir. Gov.'s Prevention Program, San Juan, 1988-90; exec. dir. Learning Disability Ctr., San Juan, 1990-94; external evaluator prevention program Roberto Clemente Sports City, Carolina, P.R., 1990-95; cons. in edn. programs Gov.'s Office; adviser, evaluator drug prevention programs, 1994—; clin. dir. options P.R.; cons. in field. Author: Analysis of Wisc-R, 1988; contbr. articles to profl. publs. Mem. Internat. Neuropsychol. Soc., Nat. Acad. Neuropsychology.

PINKE, JAMES RICHARD, ophthalmologist; b. Oceanside, N.Y., Oct. 25, 1952; s. E. Mitchell and Joyce F. (Schwartz) P.; m. Ellen Ruth Lewis, July 24, 1982; children: David, Russell, Chelsey. BS magna cum laude, Tufts U., 1974, MD, Tufts New Eng. Med. Ctr., 1978. Diplomate Am. Bd. Ophthalmology. Med. intern Faulkner Hosp., Jamaica Plain, Mass., 1978-79; resident in ophthalmology Tufts New Eng. Med. Ctr., 1979-82; pvt. practice ophthalmology Shelton, Conn., 1982—. Fellow Am. Acad. Ophthalmology; mem. AMA, Am. Soc. Cataract and Refractive Surgeons, Fairfield County Med. Assn., Naugatuck Valley Med. Soc. (pres. 1990). Office: 9 Cots St Shelton CT 06484-3855

PINKENBURG, RONALD JOSEPH, ophthalmologist; b. Houston, Nov. 25, 1940; s. William Joseph and Winnie Vale (Downs) P.; BA cum laude, U. St. Thomas, 1963; MD, Baylor U., 1967; m. Patricia Anne Regan, Oct. 21, 1967; children: Lisa, Anne Marie, Steven, Renée. Intern, U. Iowa, 1967-68; resident U. Okla., 1971-74, asst. clin. prof. ophthalmology, 1974-88; assoc. clin prof. opthalmology, U. Tex. Health Sci. Ctr., Tyler, 1988-93; gen. practitioner So. Calif. Permanente Med. Group-Kaiser Found. Hosp., Fontana, 1970-71; pvt. practice medicine specializing in ophthalmology, Tyler, Tex., 1974—; mem. staff Med. Center Hosp., Tyler, Mother Francis Hosp., Tyler. Bd. trustees, Tex. Med. Assn. Ins. Trust, 1988-89, chmn. bd. trustees, 1989—; served with USAF, 1968-70. Fellow ACS, Royal Soc. Medicine, Tex. Soc. Opthalmology and Otolaryngology; mem. AMA, Smith County Med. Soc. (pres. elect 1991-92, pres. 1992-93), Tex. Med. Assn. (chmn. com. assn. ins. programs 1981-88), Tex. Ophthalmology Assn. (pres. elect 1987-88, pres. 1988-89), Am. Acad. Ophthalmology, Am. Intraocular Implant Soc., Retina Found. SW (bd. med. advisors). Roman Catholic. Home: 311 Cumberland Rd Tyler TX 75703-5412 Office: 820 S Baxter Ave Tyler TX 75701-2225

PINKSTAFF, CARLIN ADAM, anatomist; b. Louisville, Ill., June 10, 1934; s. Lester D. and Helen Eva (Armstrong) P.; m. Delores Aileen McCallum, Jan. 1, 1958; 1 child, Cheryl Ann. Student, Vincennes U., 1956-58; BS with honors, Eastern Ill. U., 1960; PhD, Emory U., 1964. Instr. anatomy U. Oreg. Dental Sch., Portland, 1964-65, asst. prof., anatomy, 1965-67; asst. prof., anatomy W.Va. U., Sch. Medicine, Morgantown, 1967-70, assoc. prof., anatomy, 1970-81, prof. anatomy, 1981—; vis. prof. U. Ibadan, Nigeria, 1973, Yerkes Regional Primate Ctr., Atlanta, 1973, St. Georgia's U. Sch. Medicine, Grenada, W.I., 1979, 90, 91, Semmelweis U. Medicine, Budapest, Hungary, 1982; cons. in histochemistry, FDA, Div. Pathology, Washington, 1979-80. Editorial bd.: European Jour. of Histochemistry, 1984—, Jour. of Histochemistry and Cytochemistry, 1992—; contbr. articles to profl. jours., books. With USMC, 1954-56. Mem. Am. Assn. Anatomists, Histochem. Soc., Internat. Fedn. Socs. for Histochemistry and Cytochemistry, N.Y. Acad. Scis., Internat. Assn. Dental Rsch., Am. Assn. Dental Rsch., Am. Assn. Dental Schs., AAAS, Am. Soc. Mammalogists, Fedn. Am. Socs. for Exptl. Biology. Home: 1200 Philip St Morgantown WV 26505-7119 Office: WVa U Dept Anatomy Morgantown WV 26506

PINKUS, LAWRENCE MARK, biochemist; b. Bklyn., Mar. 10, 1945; s. Albert Sydney and Sereta Tessler. BS, Johns Hopkins U., 1966; PhD in Biochemistry, Cornell U. Med. Coll., 1973. Staff fellow Nat. Inst. Health, Bethesda, Md., 1973-77; asst. prof. Medicine and Biochemistry SUNY, Stony Brook, N.Y., 1977-83; Nassau County Med. Ctr., 1977-83; sr. research biochemist A. H. Robins Co., Richmond, Va., 1983-86, research assoc., 1986-90; scientific rev. adm. oral biology and medicine NIH Divsn. Res. Grants, 1991-94, with Pathology A Renal and Vascular Pathology, 1994—; advisor Pharm. Mfrs. Am. Rsch. Found., 1988—. Author 25 sci. papers and 4 chpts. in book. Grantee Nat. Inst. of Health, fellow, 1968-73. Mem. Am. Soc. of Pharmacology and Exptl. Therapeutics. Jewish. Clubs: NIH Fencing, U.S. Fencing Assn. (S.E. sect. chmn. 1989-91, nat. rank 3rd vets. sabre, 1995-96, Olympic Festival Sabre Team Gold medalist, 1987, Va. state champion 1986, 87, 89, 91). Office: Nat Inst of Health 6701 Rockledge Dr Rm 4140 Bethesda MD 20892-7802

PINNELL, SHELDON RICHARD, physician, medical educator; b. Dayton, Ohio, Feb. 3, 1937; s. Jacob and Nevella P.; m. Doren Madey, 1983; children: Kevin, Alden, Tyson. AB, Duke U., 1959; MD, Yale U., 1963. Intern in medicine U. Minn. Hosp., 1963-65; resident in dermatology Harvard U., 1968-71; prof. medicine Duke U. Med. Ctr., Durham, N.C., 1978—, chief div. dermatology, 1982—; asst. prof. of biochemistry, 1988—, J. Lamar Callaway prof. dermatology, 1989—; med. dir. Fibrogen, 1994—. Contbr. over 100 articles to profl. jours.; four patents in field. Office: Duke U Med Ctr PO Box 3135 Durham NC 27715-3135

PINO, CHRISTOPHER JOSEPH, clinical psychologist; b. Canastota, N.Y., Oct. 12, 1942; s. James and Josephine (Tianello) P.; m. Betsey Nelson, Sept. 2, 1967 (div. Apr. 1977); m. Lynn G. English, June 11, 1977; children: Lucienne, Christopher James, Marisa. BA in Psychology, Alfred U., 1965; MA in Psychology, Miami U., Oxford, Ohio, 1966; PhD, Ill. Inst. Tech., 1969. Lic. psychologist. Intern in psychology H.O. Singer Zone Ctr., Rockford, Ill., 1966-67; clin. psychologist J.J. Madden Zone Ctr., Chgo., 1967-68, H.U. Read Zone Ctr., Chgo., 1968-69; supr. clin. psychologist Orleans County Mental Health Clinic, Albion, N.Y., 1969-70; assoc. prof. psychology D'Youville Coll., Buffalo, 1970-80; exec. dir. Monsignor Carr Inst., Buffalo, 1980—; clin. psychologist Buffalo, 1970—; assoc. prof. counselor edn. Canisius Coll., 1983-86; adj. faculty counseling psychology SUNY, Buffalo, 1992—, assoc. prof. Sch. of Social Work, 1995—. Author: Divorce, Remarriage and Blended Family, 1984, Personalized Marriage Preparation and Enrichment, 1986, Training Consultants, 1985, Imagery in Family Diagnosis and Therapy: CVFES Sourcebook, 1991. Bd. dirs. Crisis Services, Buffalo, Step Family Assn. of W. N.Y. Mem. APA, Psychol. Assn. We. N.Y. (sec. 1975-76), Mental Health Assn. Erie County (bd. dirs. 1980-86), Step-Family Assn. Am. (bd. dirs.). Democrat. Roman Catholic. Home: 4070 Harris Hill Rd Williamsville NY 14221-7403 Office: Monsignor Carr Inst 76 W Humboldt Pky Buffalo NY 14214-2605

PINO, H. EDUARDO, clinical psychologist; b. Santiago, Chile, Sept. 25, 1949; came to U.S., 1968; s. Orozimbo and Sylvia (Garrido) P. BS, St. Joseph's U., Phila., 1973; MS, Hahnemann Med. Coll., 1977; D in Psychology, Hahnemann U. and Hosp. (now called Allegheny U. Health Scis.), 1985; cert. in mediation, Phila. Child Custody Mediation project and Temple U. Law Sch. Psychiat. asst. part-time Hahnemann Hosp. Emergency Rm., Phila., 1975-76; psychol. examiner Hahnemann Cmty. Mental Health Ctr., Phila., 1975-78; sr. clin. psychol. intern Montgomery County Emergency Svcs., Norristown, Pa., 1982-84, staff psychologist part-time, 1983-84; staff psychotherapist CAMCARE Health Corp., Camden and Pennsauken, N.J., 1984-85; forensic psychologist Lenape Valley Found., Bucks County, Pa., 1985-86; staff psychologist Eagleville (Pa) Hosp., 1985; cons. clin. psychologist Eugenia Hosp., Flourtown, Pa., 1984-86; ct. clin. psychologist Ct. of Common Pleas, Phila., 1986-91; pvt. practice Phila., 1991—; cons. in group treatment for sexual offenders and individual victims of sexual abuse Joseph J. Peters Inst., Phila., 1991—. Contbr. articles to profl. jours. Recipient award for Outstanding Achievement and Accomplishment in Scholarship Rotary Internat. Fellow Pa. Psychol. Assn. (mem. editl. com. 1989—, cons. editor 1989-90, 91-92, 92-93, 94—); mem. APA (internat. affairs com. chairperson psychology law divsn. 1990-91, 91-92, psychol. hypnosis divsn. 1993—), APHA, Am. Orthopsychiat. Assn., Am. Profl. Soc. on Abuse of Children, Internat. Soc. Family Law, Internat. Soc. Study Dissociation (Phila. study group for MPD and Dissociative States 1992—). Office: PO Box 2130 Philadelphia PA 19103-0130

PINO, HARRY, health center manager; b. Vega Baja, P.R., Oct. 17, 1959; s. Israel and Ada (Raimundi) P.; m. Elizabeth Ann Chesnut, Mar. 25, 1995; 1 child, Charles. BS, U. P.R., 1983; MS, Ind. U., 1985, postgrad. Profl. tennis pro Hyatt Dorado Beach, P.R., 1978-85; asst. prof. U. P.R., 1985-90; health and fitness coord. Meth. Hosp., Indpls., 1990—, Meth. Occupl. Health Ctrs., Indpls., 1990—; cons. Roche Pharm., Manati, P.R., 1989-90. Named to Hall of Fame in tennis, U. P.R., 1996. Mem. Am. Coll. Sports Medicine, U.S. Profl. Tennis Assn. Home: 11243 Boston Way Fishers IN 46308 Office: Meth Occupl Health Ctrs 1800 N Meridian St #305 Indianapolis IN 46202

PINO, ROBERT S., radiologist; b. Bklyn., May 20, 1939; s. Carmine M. and Olga (Aversa) P. BA, NYU, 1960; MD, SUNY, 1960. Diplomate Am. Bd. Pediatrics, Am. Bd. Radiology. Intern N.Y. Hosp., N.Y.C., 1964-65, resident pediatrics, 1965-67; pvt. practice pediatrics Ft. Lee, N.J., 1969-74; resident radiology N.Y. Hosp., N.Y.C., 1974-76, chief resident radiology, 1976-77; chmn. St. Mary's Hosp., Passaic, N.J., 1977—, dir. radiology, 1986—. Maj. U.S. Army, 1967-69. Home: 2055 Center Ave Fort Lee NJ 07024 Office: St Marys Hosp 211 Pennington Ave Passaic NJ 07055

PINSKER, WALTER, allergist, immunologist; b. Bay Shore, N.Y., Mar. 27, 1933; s. Albert and Irene (Kuchlick) P.; m. Tillene Giller, June 15, 1958; children: Neil, Andrew, Susann. BA, U. Rochester, 1954; MD, Chgo. Med. Sch. U. Health Sci., 1958. Diplomate Am. Bd. Allergy and Immunology. Intern L.I. Jewish Hosp., New Hyde Park, N.Y., 1958-59; resident internal medicine Bklyn. VA Hosp., 1959-60; resident internal medicine Long Beach (Calif.) VA Hosp., 1960-61, resident allergy and immunology, 1961-62; chief of allergy Letterman Army Hosp., San Francisco, 1962-64; pres. Bay Shore Allergy Group, 1964-94; attending physician Mather Hosp., Port Jefferson, N.Y., St. Charles Hosp., Port Jefferson, 1981, Southside Hosp., Bay Shore, 1964—, Good Samaritan Hosp., West Islip, N.Y., 1964—, asst. clin. prof. medicine SUNY, Stony Brook, 1968—. Contbr. articles to profl. jours. Bd. visitors Pilgrim State Hosp., Brentwood, N.Y., 1974-77; pres. Suffolk Assn. Children with Learning Difficulties, N.Y., 1972-74; trustee Leeway Sch., Stony Brook, 1974-75, Bay Shore Jewish Ctr., 1974-84; com. for handicapped West Islip Schs., 1971—. Capt. U.S. Army, 1962-64. Named Co-Humanitarian of Yr. L.I. Adults and Children with Learning and Developmental Disabilities, 1994; recipient Physician's Recognition award AMA, 1969—. Fellow Am. Acad. Allergy and Immunology, Am. Coll. Allergy and Immunology, Am. Assn. Certified Allergists, Am. Coll. Chest Physicians, Am. Assn.- Study of Headaches, N.Y. Acad. Scis., Suffolk Acad. Medicine, Nassau-Suffolk Allergy Soc. (officer, bd. dirs. 1970—, pres. 1980-82). Office: Bay Shore Allergy Group P C 649 W Montauk Hwy Bay Shore NY 11706-8222

PINSKI, GABRIEL, psychiatrist; b. N.Y.C., Sept. 9, 1937; s. Henry and Anna (Kopekin) P.; m. Avivah Rachelle Zuchman, June 14, 1960; children: Shira Beth, David Aaron, Ari Isaac. AB, Columbia Coll., N.Y.C., 1957; PhD in Physics, U. Rochester, 1964; MS in Stats., Temple U., Phila., 1981; MD, U. Aut de Cd Juarez, Mexico, 1982. Instr. physics Syracuse (N.Y.) U., 1963-65; asst. prof. physics Drexel U., Phila., 1965-70; corp. ops. rsch. analyst Sun Oil Co., Phila., 1970-73; rsch. advisor Computer Horizons, Inc., Cherry Hill, N.J., 1973-77; sr. rsch. scientist Inst. Sci. Info., Phila., 1977-80; intern medicine Mercy Cath. Med. Ctr., Darby, Pa., 1982-83; resident psychiatry Thomas Jefferson U. Hosp., Phila., 1983-86; staff psychiatrist Community Coun. Mental Health/Mental Retardation, Phila., 1986—; psychiatrist Univ. City Counseling Ctr., Phila., 1988-94, Fitzgerald Mercy Crisis Ctr., Darby, Pa., 1983—. Contbr. articles to profl. jours. Mem. Am. Psychiat. Assn., AMA, Am. Phys. Soc., Ops. Rsch. Soc. Am., Sigma Xi. Home: 411 Witley Rd Wynnewood PA 19096-2424 Office: Community Coun 4900 Wyalusing Ave Philadelphia PA 19131-5127

PINSKY, ABE, psychiatrist, educator; b. N.Y.C., Mar. 9, 1914; s. Benjamin and Yetta (Zaretsky) P.; m. Marcia Kerr; children: David, Ruth. BS, BYU, 1933, MD, 1937. Diplomate Am. Bd. Psychiatry and Neurology. Pvt. practice Bklyn., 1948—; clin. asst. prof. psychiatry SUNY Downstate Med. Ctr., Bklyn., 1948—. Mem. Assn. for Advancement Psychoanalysis, Am. Inst. for Psychoanalysis (assoc. dean 1979—), ACLU. Democrat. Jewish. Office: 1 Hanson Pl Brooklyn NY 11243

PINSKY, STANLEY THEODORE, radiologist; b. Ruleville, Miss., June 25, 1928; s. Hyman and Gertie Ethel (Oser) P.; m. Sonja Stahl, Aug. 11, 1957; children: H. Mark, David J., Susan L., Debra A. BA, Ohio State U., 1951, MD, 1955. Diplomate Am. Bd. Radiology, Am. Bd. Nuclear Medicine. Chief radiology St. Vincent Med. Ctr., Toledo, 1969-95; prof. radiology Med. Coll. Ohio, Toledo, 1995—; pres. Cons. Radiologist Corp., Toledo, 1960-94. Sgt. U.S. Army, 1946-48. Fellow Am. Coll. Radiology, Am. Coll. Nuclear Medicine; mem. Ohio State Radiology Soc. (silver medal 1985). Office: Med Coll Ohio 3000 Arlington Toledo OH 43623

PINSKY, STEVEN MICHAEL, radiologist, educator; b. Milw., Feb. 2, 1942; s. Leo Donald and Louise Miriam (Faldberg) P.; m. Sue Brona Rosenzweig, June 12, 1966; children—Mark Burton, Lisa Rachel. BS, U. Wis., 1964; MD, Loyola U., Chgo., 1967. Resident in radiology and nuclear medicine U. Chgo., 1968-70, chief resident in diagnostic radiology, 1970-71, asst. prof., 1973-77, then assoc. prof. radiology and medicine, 1977-84, prof., 1984-89; prof., chmn. dept. radiology U. Ill., 1989— ; dir. nuclear medicine Michael Reese Med. Ctr., Chgo., 1973-87, vice-chmn. radiology, 1984-87, chmn. radiology, 1987-93, v.p. med. staff, 1986-87, pres., 1988-89, trustee, 1984-86, 90-93; dir. nuclear medicine tech. program Triton Coll., River Grove, Ill., 1974-87. Contbr. chpts. to books, articles to med. jours. Rsch. fellow Am. Cancer Soc., 1969-70. Maj., M.C., U.S. Army, 1971-73. Fellow Am. Coll. Nuclear Physicians (Ill. del., treas. 1982-84), Am. Coll. Radiology (alt. councilor 1986-92, councilor 1993—); mem. Soc. Nuclear Medicine (trustee 1979-87, pres. central chpt. 1980-81), Radiologic Soc. N.Am. (councilor 1994—, chmn. tech. exhibits com. 1994—, edn. coun. 1994—), Ill. Radiologic Soc. (sec./treas. 1992-94, pres.-elect 1994-95, pres. 1995-96). Home: 1821 Lawrence Ln Highland Park IL 60035-4326 Office: U Ill Hosp 1740 W Taylor St Chicago IL 60612-7232

PINSON, CHARLES WRIGHT, medical educator; b. May 29, 1952. Student, Miami U., 1970-72; BA, U. Colo., 1974, MBA, 1976; MD, Vanderbilt U., 1980. Intern Oreg. Health Sci. U., 1980-81, resident, 1981-85, chief resident, 1985-86; staff surgeon Portland Vets Affairs Med. Ctr., 1988-90; asst. prof. physiology Oreg. Health Scis. U., 1988-90, asst. prof. surgery, 1988-90, assoc. prof. surgery, 1990; staff surgeon Nashville Vets. Affairs Med. Ctr., 1990—; prof. surgery, mem. divsn. surg. oncology Vanderbilt U., Nashville, 1990—; presenter in field. Contbr. articles to profl. jours., chpts. to books. Gastrointestinal Surgery fellow Lahey Clinic Med. Ctr., 1986-87, Harvard U., 1987-88, Oreg. Am. Heart Assn. Postdoctoral fellow, 1983-84; Good Samaritan Hosp. Martin A. Howard scholar, 1985, St. Vincent Hosp. and Med. Ctr. Resident scholar, 1986; recipient Culler Physics prize, 1972, John and Julia Sawyers Rsch. award, 1995. Fellow Am. Coll. Surgeons; mem. Am. Assn. Study Liver Disease, Am. Gastroenterological Assn., Am. HEart Assn., Am. Hepatopancreatobiliary Assn. (mem. com. 1994—), Am. Inst. Phusics, Am. Liver Found., Am. Physiologic Soc., Am. Soc. Transplant Surgeons, Assn. Acad. Surgery, Assn. Surg. Edn., Assn. Program Dirs. in Surgery, Internat. Fedn. Surg. Colls., Internat. Liver Transplantation Soc., Internat. HEpato Pancreato Biliary Assn., Mass. Med. Soc., Nashville Surg. Soc. (mem. com. 1993-94), North Pacific Surg. Assn. (scientific progra, 1990-92, chmn. 1991), Pacific Northwest Transplantation Soc., The Pancreas Club, Portland Surg. Soc., Royal Soc. Medicine, Soc. Surgery Alimentary Tract, Soc. Surg. Chmn., Soc. Surg. Oncology, So. Med. Assn., Southeastern Surg. Congress, Tenn. Transplant Soc., Western Assn. Transplant Surgeons, Western Surg. Assn., World Assn. Hepaticopancreaticobiliary Surgery (founder), Alpha Omega ALpha, Phi Beta Kappa, Sigma Pi Sigma. Office: Vanderbilt U Med Ctr Oxford House Ste 801 Nashville TN 37232*

PINSON, THOMAS MICHAEL, emergency room physician; b. Wyandotte, Mich., Apr. 2, 1951; s. Thomas Oliver and Irene Ann (Bencik) P.; m. Susan Marie Stroia, June 23, 1991; 1 child, Alexis. DO, Mich. State U., 1986. Dir. emergency rm. Madison Cmty. Hosp., Madison Heights, Mich., 1989—; dir. outpatient drug abuse Shar House, Detroit, 1989-94. Mem. Am. Coll. Emergency Physicians, Am. Osteo. Assn. Roman Catholic. Office: Madison Cmty Hosp 30671 Stephenson Hwy Madison Heights MI 48071

PINTER, GABRIEL GEORGE, physiology educator; b. Bekes, Hungary, June 23, 1925; came to U.S., 1958; s. Lajos and Regina (Szilagyi-Farkas) P.; m. Berit Helgesen, Dec. 19, 1958 (dec. May 1980); children: Renee Astrid, Eva Ingelill; m. Vera Lederer Dallos, May 23, 1984. M.D., U. Sch. of Medicine, Budapest, Hungary, 1951. Asst prof. U. Sch. Medicine, Budapest, 1951-56; rsch. assoc. U. Inst. Med. Rsch., Oslo, Norway, 1957-58; asst. prof. U. Tenn., Memphis, 1958-61; from asst. prof. to prof. U. Md., Balt., 1961-92, ret.; vis. prof. King's Coll., London, 1990-94. Contbr. articles to profl. jours. Recipient A.V. Humbolt prize Fed. Republic of Germany, 1980; Swedish Royal Med. Soc. fellow, Uppsala, Sweden, 1972. Mem. Am. Physiol. Soc., Physiol. Soc. Great Britain, Scandinavian Physiol. Soc., European Soc. Microcirculation.

PIOMBINO, NICHOLAS, psychotherapist; b. N.Y.C., Oct. 5, 1942; s. Nicholas Bruce and Ruth Mary (Rothbart) P. BA with honors, CCNY, 1964; MSW, Fordham U., 1971; cert. in adult psychoanalysis and psychotherapy, Postgrad. Ctr. Mental Health, N.Y.C., 1982. Diplomate in clin. social work; cert. psychotherapist, social worker, N.Y. Social worker Manhattan State Hosp., N.Y.C., 1971-73; pvt. practice psychotherapy N.Y.C., 1976—; sch. social worker N.Y.C. Bd. Edn., 1974—; staff psychotherapist Postgrad. Ctr. Mental Health, 1978-86; supr., mem. faculty Psychoanalytic Inst. N.Y. Counseling and Guidance Svc., N.Y.C., 1987—. Author: Poems, 1988, (essays) The boundary of Blur, 1993; contbr. articles and poems to numerous publs. Mem. Postgrad. Psychoanalytic Soc., Soc. Clin. Social Work Psychotherapists. Home: 119 W 95th St New York NY 10025-6636 Office: 680 W End Ave New York NY 10025-6815

PIORE, EMANUEL RUBEN, physicist; b. Wilno, Russia, July 19, 1908; came to U.S., 1917; s. Ruben and Olga (Gegusin) P.; m. E. Nora Kahn, Aug. 26, 1931; children—Michael Joseph, Margot Deborah, Jane Ann. A.B., U. Wis., 1930, Ph.D., 1935, D.Sc. (hon.), 1966; D Sc. (hon.), Union U., 1962. Asst. instr. U. Wis., 1930-35; research physicist RCA, 1935-38; engr.-in-charge TV lab. CBS, 1938-42; head spl. weapons group, bur. ships U.S. Navy, 1942-44; head electronics br. Office Naval Research, 1946-47, dir. phys. sci., 1947-48, dep. for natural sci., 1949-51, chief sci., 1951-55; v.p., dir. Avco Mfg. Corp., 1955-56; dir. research IBM Corp., 1956-61, v.p. research and engring., 1961-63, v.p., group exec., 1963-65 v.p., chief scientist, 1965—; also dir.; physicist research lab. electronics MIT, 1948-49; dir. Sci. Research Assocs., Inc., Health Advancement, Inc., Paul Revere Investors, Guardian Mut. Fund.; adj. prof. Rockefeller U., 1974—. Mem. Pres.'s Sci. Adv. Com., 1959-62; mem. Nat. Sci. Bd., 1961—; bd. dirs. N.Y. State Found. for Sci.; past bd. dirs. NSF; chmn. vis. com. Nat. Bur. Standards; chmn. bd. Hall of Science, N.Y.C.; mem. corp. Woods Hole Oceanographic Instn.; mem. exec. com. Resources for Future; bd. dirs. Stark Draper Lab., Nat. Info. Bur., Meml. Cancer Hosp.; mem. vis. com. to elec. engring. dept. Mass. Inst. Tech., 1956-57; vis. com. Harvard Coll., 1958-70; trustee Sloan-Kettering Inst. Cancer Research; mem. N.Y.C. Bd. Higher Edn., 1976—. Served to lt. comdr. USNR, 1944-46. Recipient Indsl. Research Inst. award, 1967; Distinguished Civilian medal Dept. Navy; Kaplun award Hebrew U., 1975. Fellow AAAS, Royal Soc. Arts (London, Eng.), Am. Phys. Soc., IEEE, Am. Acad. Arts Scis.; mem. Sci. Research Soc. Am., Sci. Research Assn. (dir.), Nat. Acad. Sci., Nat. Acad. Engring., Am. Inst. Physics (dir.), Am. Philos. Soc. (sec. 1985—), Sigma Xi. Clubs: University (N.Y.C.), Cosmos (Washington), Century (N.Y.C.). Home: 2 Fifth Ave New York NY 10011

PIORE, NORA KAHN, economist, health policy analyst; b. N.Y.C., N.Y., Nov. 28, 1912; d. Alexander and Sara (Rosenbaum) Kahn; m. Emanuel R. Piore, Aug. 26, 1931; children: Michael Joseph, Margot Deborah. Jane Anne. B.A., U. Wis., 1933, MA, 1934. Research economist health legislation subcom. U.S. Senate, Washington, 1950-53; spl. asst. to commr. N.Y.C. Dept. Health, 1957-68; adj. prof. urban affairs Hunter Coll., N.Y.C., 1962-72; dir. N.Y.C. Urban Med. Econs. Research Ctr., 1960-68; vis. scientist Assn. Aid of Crippled Children, N.Y.C., 1968-72, study dir. hosp. ambulatory care svcs. in U.S., 1968-72; prof. pub. health econs. Columbia U. Sch. Pub. Health, N.Y.C., 1972-82; assoc. dir. Columbia U. Ctr. Community Health Systems, N.Y.C., 1971-82, cons. Health Services Research, 1982—; sr. program cons. Commonwealth Fund, N.Y.C., 1982-88; sr. fellow United Hosp. Fund, N.Y.C., 1982-90; dir. Health Svcs. Improvement Fund (Blue Cross-Blue Shield), 1984—, Sun Valley Health Forum, Boise, Idaho, 1978-88; active numerous coms., founds., task forces, funds in field; cons. Carnegie Corp. N.Y., R.I. Health Svcs. Rsch. Corp., Robert Wood Johnson Found., Pew Meml. Trust; mem. N.Y. State Hosp. Rev. and Planning Coun., 1976-84. Contbr. chpts. to books, articles to profl. jours. Recipient Merit award N.Y. Pub. Health Assn., 1977 Career Scientist award N.Y. Health Rsch. Coun., 1961-65, 66-71; Belding scholar Assn. Aid Crippled Children, 1968; grantee USPHS, 1980. Fellow Am. Pub. Health Assn., N.Y. Acad. Medicine; mem. Am. Econs. Assn., AAAS, Health Services Research Assn., Assn. Social Scientists in Health, Inst. Medicine, Nat. Acad. Sci.. Phi Beta Kappa. Clubs: Cosmopolitan, Women's City (N.Y.C.).

PIOVANETTI, SIMON, pediatrician; b. Sabana Grande, P.R., Mar. 27, 1920; s. Antonio and Juanita (Bonelli) Prowik; m. Priv K.; 1 child, Yvette. MD, Jefferson Med. Coll., 1951. Dir. dept. pediatrics Ashfor & Presbyn. Cmty. Hosp., Hatorey, P.R., 1985—. 1st lt. U.S. Infantry, 1941-46. Mem. Am. Acad. Pediatrics. Home: 609 Cuevillas Apt 7B San Juan PR 00907 Office: 400 Domenech San Juan PR 00918

PIPER, JAMES HOWARD, JR., managed care administrator; b. Manchester, Tenn., Nov. 10, 1952; s. James Howard and Dorothy Nell (McCool) P.; m. Janet Hagan, Apr. 2, 1971; children: James Howard III, Daniel Frederick. BA, West Ga. Coll., 1977; MS in Health Sys., Ga. Inst. Tech., 1979. Grad. rsch. asst. Ga. Inst. Tech., Atlanta, 1977; mgmt. engr. Ga. Bapt. Med. Ctr., Atlanta, 1978-79; health sys. analyst Blue Cross Blue Shield Ga., Atlanta, 1979-81, mgr. instnl. affairs, 1982-84, 88-93, asst. v.p. instnl. affairs, 1984, asst. v.p. pvt. reimbursement, 1985-86, asst. v.p. provider affairs, 1986-87; sr. v.p. managed care programs Anchor Hosp., 1993-96; v.p. managed care Am. Sudden Infant Death Syndrome Inst., Atlanta, 1996—; mem. bd. and rev. com. North Ctrl. Ga. Health Sys. Agy., 1986,. Ordained deacon Eastside Bapt. Ch., Marietta, Ga., 1981; mem. men's ministry com. 1st Bapt. Ch., Woodstock, Ga., 1994-96. Mem. Healthcare Fin. Mgmt. Assn. (managed care forum 1995, judging com. outstanding achievement award for chpt. edn. 1995, for chpt. projects 1996; bd dirs. Ga. chpt. 1986-88, treas. 1989-90, sec. 1990-91, program chairperson 1991-92, pres.-elect 1992-93, pres. 1993-94, chmn. nominating com. 1994-95, mem. adv. com. 1994-96, past pres. 1994-95, Follmer bronze merit award 1987, Reeves silver merit award 1989, Muncie gold merit award 1994, GLD chpt. achievement award 1994, Charles H. Anderson President's award 1995, Robert M. Shelton award 1995), Healthcare Info. and Mgmt. Sys. Soc. (charter Ga.), Ga. Hosp. Assn. (uniform billing com. 1983-90, coun. on smaller hosps. 1985-87, coun. on fin. 1993-94), Ga. Soc. for Managed Care (sec. 1994-96), Kappa Mu Epsilon. Home: 1474 Rosebay Ct Marietta GA 30066 Office: Am Sudden Infant Death Syndrome Inst 6065 Roswell Rd Ste 876 Atlanta GA 30328

PIPITONE, PHYLLIS L., psychologist, educator, author; b. Chgo.; m. S. Joseph Pipitone, Aug. 28, 1948 (dec.); children: Guy, Daniel, Paul; m. Thomas A. Cox, Jan. 3, 1980. Student Chgo. Conservatory Music, 1941-44, Peabody Conservatory Music, 1945, Chgo. Tchrs. Coll., 1946-47, So. Meth. U., 1951-52; MA, U. Akron (Ohio), 1967; PhD, Kent (Ohio) State U., 1974. With B.S. & H. Advt. Agy., Chgo., 1941-43; instr. piano and theory Music Acad. Chgo.; psychologist, instr. U. Akron and Kent State U., 1970-79; pvt. practice psychology, Akron, 1967—; lectr. in field in U.S and abroad. Served with WAC, AUS, 1944-46. NIMH grantee, 1974, HEW Child Devel. fellow, 1974. Mem. Am. Psychol. Assn., Nat. Assn. Sch. Psychologists, Mensa, Council Exceptional Children, Am. Hypnosis Soc., Kent Psi Research Group, Assn. Study/Dreams, Am. Soc. Psychical Research, Phi Delta Kappa. Clubs: Tuesday Musical, Weathervane Theatre Women's Bd., Akron Women's City, Wadsworth Women's. Home: 224 Pheasant Run Wadsworth OH 44281-2344

PIPKIN, DAVID LAVON, medical facility administrator; b. Balt., Aug. 27, 1962; s. David Lavon and Mildred Lynn (Fleetwood) P.; children: Erika Monique Jones, David Lavon IV. BS, Coppin State Coll., 1989. Asst. adminstr. Villa St. Michael, Balt., 1992-93; adminstr. Ashburton Nursing Ctr., Balt., 1993-95, Northwest Nursing Ctr., Balt., 1995—. Home: 1451 Barrett Rd Baltimore MD 21207

PIPPIN, JAMES REX, health care company executive, educator; b. Clovis, N.Mex., Apr. 3, 1949; s. C.A. and J. (Davis) P.; m. Annette Jacqueline Charsha, Feb. 6, 1971; children: Ken, Matthew, Sabrina. BS, Ea. N.Mex. U., 1971; MPA, U. Ariz., 1973. Cert. health care adminstr., Ill. Adminstr. The Mayflower, Grinnell, Iowa, 1973-78; exec. dir. Mayflower Homes, Inc., Grinnell, 1978-80; pres., CEO, Lifelink Corp., Bensenville, Ill., 1980—; preceptor, adj. prof. George Washington U., Washington, 1985—. Contbr. articles to profl. jours. Mem. Am. Coll. Health Care Adminstrs., Am. Assn. Homes for Aging (treas. 1988-90, Profl. of Yr. award 1979), Coun. for Health and Human Svcs. (pres. 1990-92, Exec. of Yr. award 1985), Ill. Assn. Homes for Aging (pres. 1986-88), Ill. Child Care Assn. (bd. dirs.), Internat. Assn. Svcs. for the Aging (bd. dirs. 1995—). Republican. Mem. United Ch. of Christ. Office: Lifelink Corp 331 S York Rd Bensenville IL 60106-2673

PIPPIN, JOHN JOSEPH, cardiologist; b. Brookline, Mass., Jan. 7, 1950; s. John Charles and Shirley Ann (Marson) P. AB in History, Harvard U., 1971; MD, U. Mass., 1980. Diplomate Am. Bd. Internal Medicine. Police officer Harvard U., Cambridge, Mass., 1971-76, City of Cambridge, 1976; resident in medicine New Eng. Deaconess Hosp., Boston, 1980-83, chief resident, 1983-84, fellow in cardiology, 1984-86; fellow in nuclear cardiology U. Tex. Southwestern Med. Sch., Dallas, 1986-87; asst. prof. medicine Med. Coll. Va., Richmond, 1987-91; assoc. prof. medicine U. Okla. Health Sci. Ctr., Tulsa, 1992—; pvt. practice cardiology Okla. Heart, Inc., Tulsa, 1991—; dir. nuclear cardiology Hillcrest Med. Ctr., Tulsa, 1991—, Cardiovascular Assessment Ctr., 1991, dir. James D. Harvey Rsch. Ctr., 1995, chmn. Instl. Review Bd. Contbr. 35 abstracts, 14 articles to profl. jours; author 3 monographs. Recipient Clinician-Scientist award Am. Heart Assn., 1986-91. Fellow Am. Coll. Cardiology, Am. Soc. Nuclear Cardiology, Soc. Nuclear Medicine. Office: Okla Heart Inc 1265 S Utica Ave Tulsa OK 74104

PIRISI, MARIO, physician, researcher; b. Nuoro, Sardinia, Italy, June 13, 1956; s. Salvatore and Maria (Tanda) P.; m. Anna Rita Tuveri, Aug. 26, 1982; children: Matteo, Alessandro. MD cum laude, Med. Sch. Sassari, Italy, 1981, postgrad., 1982-86. Vis. fellow Hall Inst., Melbourne, Australia, 1987-88; registrar Gen. Hosp., Nuoro, Italy, 1989-90; rsch. fellow Med. Sch. Udine, Italy, 1990—. Contbr. articles to med. jours. Lt. Italian Army, 1983-84. Mem. European Assn. Study of the Liver, Italian Assn. Study of the Liver, Italian Soc. Gastroenterology. Home: 10 Via Dei Pini, I-33010 Pagnacco Italy Office: Univ Hosp, Cattedra Medicina Interna, 1 Ple S M Misericordia, I-33100 Udine Italy

PIRNIE, THOMAS DUNCAN, school adjustment counselor; b. Agawam, Mass., Sept. 19, 1945; s. Mavis (Cooper) P.; m. Leslie Hall, Feb. 23, 1967; children: Kristina, Jennifer, Jason. BS in Edn., Westfield State Coll., 1975; MEd, Am. Internat. Coll., 1978; CAS, Springfield Coll., 1990. Lic. social worker, Mass. Tchr. Southwick (Mass.) Pub. Schs., 1975-77, 78-80, sch. adjustment counselor, 1980-88; drop-out prevention counselor West Springfield (Mass.) Jr. H.S., 1988-89; sch. adjustment counselor Westfield (Mass.) H.S., 1990—. Sgt. USMC, 1965-69, Vietnam. Office: Westfield HS 177 Montgomery Rd Westfield MA 01085-1062

PIRODSKY, DONALD MAX, psychiatrist, educator; b. Freeport, N.Y., Feb. 2, 1945; s. Max and Doris Geilhard (Biedermann) P.; children: Laura Anne, Jason Donald. BA, Hofstra U., 1966; MD, SUNY, Syracuse, 1970. Diplomate Am. Bd. Psychiatry and Neurology, Nat. Bd. Med. Examiners. Med. intern Northwestern U. Med. Ctr., Chgo., 1970-71; resident in psychiatry Strong Meml. Hosp., Rochester, N.Y., 1973-74, U. Ariz. Med. Ctr., Tucson, 1974-76; instr. psychiatry SUNY Health Sci. Ctr., Syracuse, 1976-78, attending psychiatrist, 1976—, asst. prof. psychiatry, 1978-85, mem. exec. com. of med. coll. assembly, 1979-82, clin. assoc. prof., 1985—; pvt. practice Syracuse and Fayetteville, N.Y., 1976—; staff psychiatrist, dir. consultation/liaison svc. Syracuse VA Med. Ctr., 1976-87, chmn. pharmacy rev. and therapeutic agts. com., 1980-86; psychiat. cons. Ariz. Sch. for Deaf and Blind, Tucson, 1975-76, Syracuse Devel. Ctr., 1977—, Rochester Sch. for Deaf, 1978-81; ex-officio mem. Family Counseling Agy., Tucson, 1975-76. Author: Primer of Clinical Psychopharmacology: A Practical Guide, 1981, (with Jerry S. Cohn) Clinical Primer of Psychopharmacology: A Practical Guide, 2d edit., 1992; contbr. articles to profl. jours., chpts. to med. books. Lt. comdr. USPHS, 1971-73. Fellow Am. Psychiat. Assn.; mem. AMA, Am. Psychosomatic Soc., Am. Assn. Mental Retardation, Med. Soc. State of N.Y., Onondaga County Med. Soc. Episcopalian. Office: 7000 E Genesee St Fayetteville NY 13066-1131

PIRONTI, PASCAL ANTHONY, urologist; b. Newark, Feb. 2, 1934; s. Louis and Rose P.; B.A., Johns Hopkins U., 1955; M.D., Hahnemann Med. Coll., 1959; m. June 29, 1963; children—Louis, Carolyn. Intern, Hahnemann Hosp., Phila., 1959-60, resident in gen. surgery, 1960-61, resident in urology, 1961-64; individual practice medicine specializing in urology, Summit, N.J., 1964—; chmn. dept. urology, attending urologist Overlook Hosp., Summit, 1970—, chmn. dept. surgery, pres., 1986-87; urologist Children's Specialized Hosp., Mountainside, N.J., 1970—; cons. staff VA Hosp., Lyons, N.J.; asso. urology Columbia U., N.Y.C., 1975—. Sec.-treas., v.p. Overlook Hosp., 1977—. Served with M.C., U.S. Army, 1967-68; Vietnam. Decorated Army Commendation medal; diplomate Am. Bd. Urology. Fellow A.C.S., Acad. Medicine N.J.; mem. Union County (v.p. 1977-78, pres. 1980-81), N.J. (del. 1975—) med. socs., AMA, Soc. Surgeons N.J., Am. Urol. Assn., Am. Assn. Clin. Urologists, Am. Fertility Soc. Roman Catholic. Club: Plainfield Country. Office: 475 Springfield Ave Summit NJ 07901-2604

PIROTTE, PATRICK JOSEPH, optometrist; b. Wichita, Kans., Nov. 21, 1957; s. Thomas Aquinas and Doris Jean (Cohn) P.; m. Andrea Gonzales, Oct. 10, 1987; children: Maria, Benjamin. Student, U. Kans., 1978-81; BS in Visual Sci., So. Calif. Coll. Optometry, 1983, OD, 1985. Pvt. practice, Wichita, 1985—; dir. Kans. Low Vision Clinic, Wichita, 1986—; mem. staff, cons. HCA/Columbia Wesley Rehab. Hosp., Wichita, 1992—. Mem. Am. Optometric Assn., Kans. Optometric Assn., Coll. Optometrists in Vision Devel. Office: 746 N Maize Rd Ste 100 Wichita KS 67212

PIROZZI, PATRICK J., oral and maxillofacial surgeon; b. Bklyn., Nov. 29, 1955; s. Michael James and Patricia Ann (O'Donnell) P.; m. Rosemarie Sardo, Nov. 12, 1983; children: Kelly Marie, Patrick Sardo. BS, Notre Dame U., 1977; DMD, Fairleigh Dickinson U., 1981; specialty cert., Lincoln Med. Ctr., 1981-84. Diplomate Am. Bd. Oral and Maxillofacial Surgery. Assoc. pvt. practice Dr. Anthony Arthur, Bronx, 1984-87, Dr. Paul Gates, Paterson, N.J., 1984-86; assoc. prof. Fairleigh Dickinson Dental Sch., Hackensack, N.J., 1984-88; pvt. practice Montville (N.J.) Oral Surgery Assocs., 1987—; chmn. dental credentials St. Clares Hosp., Denville, N.J., 1996—; chmn. dept. dentistry N.W. Covenant Med. Ctr., Denville, 1996—. Active Serra Club, Somerset County, N.J., 1992-94; coach Watchung (N.J.) Little League, 1995—. Fellow Dental Soc. Anesthesiology, Am. Dental Soc. Anesthesiology, Am. Assn. Oral-Maxillofacial Surgeons, Coll. Oral-Maxillofacial Surgeons; mem. ADA, N.J. Soc. Oral-Maxillofacial Surgeons, Sons of Italy. Republican. Roman Catholic. Office: Montville Oral Surg Assocs Ste H-2 150 River Rd Montville NJ 07045

PISCIOTTA, VIVIAN VIRGINIA, psychotherapist; b. Chgo., Dec. 7; d. Vito and Mary Lamia; m. Vincent Diago Pisciotta, Apr. 1, 1951; children: E. Christopher, Vittorio, V. Charles, Mary A. Pisciotta Higley, Thomas Sansone. BA in Clin. Psychology, Antioch U., 1974; MSW, George Williams Coll., 1984; postgrad., Erickson Inst. of No. Ill., 1990. Lic. clin. social worker; diplomate in clin. social work. Short-term therapist Woman Line, Dayton, Ohio, 1976-79; psychotherapist Cicero (Ill.) Family Svcs., 1982-83, Maywood (Ill.) - Proviso Family Svcs., 1983-84, Maple Ave. Med. Ctr., Brookfield, Ill., 1985-88, Met. Med. Clinic, Naperville, Ill., 1986-88; allied staff Riveredge Psychiat. Hosp., Forest Park, Ill., 1986—, Linden Oaks Hosp., Naperville, Ill., 1990—; psychotherapist, pvt. practice Oakbrook, Ill., 1988—; psychotherapist, co-founder Archer Austin Counseling Ctr., Chgo., 1988-89; psychotherapist, founder Archer Counseling Ctr., Chgo., 1989—;

allied staff Linden Oaks Psychiat. Hosp., Naperville, 1990—; substitute tchr. Chgo. Pub. High Sch., 1981. Author treatment prog., workshops in field. Co-founder Co-op Nursery Sch., Rockford, Ill., 1956; leader Great Books of the Western World series, Piqua, Ohio, 1977, Rockford, 1960-65; leader Girl Scouts U.S., St. Bridget Sch., Rockford, 1968-71. Mem. Assn. Labor-Mgmt. and Cons. on Alcoholism, Soc. Clin. Exptl. Hypnosis, Nat. Assn. Social Workers, Acad. Cert. Social Workers, Nat. social Wk. Register, Antioch Univ. Alumnus Assn. Rockford Coll. Alumnae Orgn. (newsletter contbr. 1972-73), Soc. for Clin. and Exptl. Hypnosis (assoc. mem.), Internat. Soc. for Clin. and Exptl. Hypnosis (assoc. mem.). Republican. Roman Catholic. Office: Archer Counseling Ctr 7002 W Archer Ave Ste 2B Chicago IL 60638-2202

PISKACEK, VLADIMIR RICHARD, psychiatrist; b. Pilsen, Czechoslovakia, Apr. 13, 1929; came to U.S., 1958, naturalized, 1964; s. Frank and Ludmila (Drchovska) P. MD, Charles IV U., Prague, Czechoslovakia, 1956. Intern Coney Island Hosp., N.Y.C., 1958-59; resident Bellevue Hosp., N.Y.C., 1962-65; fellow Mt. Sinai Hosp., N.Y.C., 1965-66; resident Psychiat. Inst., Columbia U., N.Y.C., 1967-68; practice medicine specializing in psychiatry Manhasset, N.Y., 1971—; sr. attending psychiatrist North Shore Univ. Hosp.; instr. psychiatry Columbia U. Med. Sch., 1968-73; asst. dir. Madeline Borg Child Guidance Clinic, N.Y.C., 1969-71; med. dir. Nassau Ctr. for Developmentally Disabled, 1978—; clin. asst. prof. psychiatry Cornell U. Med. Coll., 1978—. Author: (with M. Golub) Psychiatric and Social Work Problems of Children of Interracial Marriages, 1973; Deja Vu in Tibet, 1982; book Bender Gestalt Performance in Children of Papua, New Guinea, 1983. Recipient award Congresso Panamericano de Hipnologia e Medicina Psicossomatica, Rio de Janeiro, Brazil, 1978. Mem. AMA (Physician's Recognition award), Am. Psychiat. Assn. Home: 10 Grace Ave 8D Great Neck NY 11021 Office: 225 Middle Neck Rd Great Neck NY 11021-1100

PISTOLE, THOMAS GORDON, microbiology educator, researcher; b. Detroit, Sept. 17, 1942; s. Leotis Merton Pistole and Lillian Nell (Bosley) Besser; m. Donna Dulcie Straw, Sept. 11, 1965; children: James Alexander, Jennifer Katharine. PhB, Wayne State U., 1964, MS, 1966; PhD, U. Utah, 1969. Postdoctoral fellow U.S. Army, Frederick, Md., 1969-70; research assoc. U. Minn., Mpls., 1970-71; asst. prof. U. N.H., Durham, 1971-77, assoc. prof., 1977-83, prof., 1983—, chmn., 1983-92; vis. scientist Weizmann Inst., Rehovot, Israel, 1979; vis. prof. U. Edinburgh, Scotland, 1986. Co-editor: Biomedical Application of the Horseshoe Crab, 1979; mem. editorial bd. Jour. Invertebrate Pathology, 1988-90. NRC fellow, 1969-70, NIH sr. internat. fellow, 1986; grantee NIH, 1975-77, 89-93, 96—, NSF, 1981-84. Mem. Am. Soc. for Microbiology, Am. Assn. Immunologists, Internat. Soc. Devel. and Comparative Immunology, Soc. for Leukocyte Biology. Office: U NH Dept Microbiology Durham NH 03824

PISTONE, LISA MARIAN MOLOY, clinical psychologist; b. Phila., Jan. 13, 1959; d. Carmen Dominic and Florence Pauline (Ciarrorchi) P. BA, U. Pa., 1980; MS, U. Fla., 1984, PhD, 1989. Lic. clin. psychologist. Postdoctoral fellow U. Rochester, N.Y., 1988-90; coord. psychol. svcs. Charleston (W.Va.) Area Med. Ctr., 1990—; clin. asst. prof. W.Va. U., Charleston, 1990—; vol. mem. Critical Incidents Stress Mgmt. Team, Charleston, 1991-95; trainee Nat. Inst. Dental Rsch., U. Fla., 1985-87, USPHS, 1982-83. Rsch. grantee Div. Sponsored Rsch., U. Fla., 1983. Mem. APA, Soc. Behavioral Medicine. Office: Assocs in Health Psychology 7C Trolley Square Newark DE 19711

PI-SUNYER, F. XAVIER, medical educator, medical investigator; b. Barcelona, Catalonia, Spain, Dec. 3, 1933; came to U.S., 1942; s. James and Mercedes (Diaz) Pi-S.; m. Penelope Wheeler; children: Andrea, Olivia, Joanna. BA, Oberlin (Ohio) Coll., 1955; MD, Columbia U., 1959; MPH, Harvard U., 1963. From instr. to asst. prof. Coll. of Physicians & Surgeons, Columbia U., N.Y.C., 1965-76, assoc. prof., 1976-85, prof. clin. medicine, 1985-91; prof. St. Luke's-Roosevelt Hosp. Ctr., N.Y.C., 1991—; from asst. to assoc. attending physician St. Luke's Hosp., N.Y.C., 1965-75; attending physician St. Luke's-Roosevelt Hosp. Ctr., N.Y.C., 1975—, chief div. endocrinology, diabetes and nutrition, 1988—, dir. Obesity Rsch. Ctr., 1988—; dir. Joslin Diabetes Ctr. at St. Luke's Hosp., 1994—, Van Itallie Ctr. for Nutrition and Weight Mgmt., 1994—; mem. adj. faculty Rockefeller U., 1984—; vis. physician Rockefeller U. Hosp., 1984—; attending physician Presbyn. Hosp., 1985—; sr. investigator N.Y. Heart Assn., 1968-73; Hsien Wu investigator St. Luke's-Roosevelt Hosp., 1982-90; Sigma Xi lectr. Pa. State U., 1989; Howard Heinz vis. prof. Med. Coll. Pa., 1987; pfizer vis. prof. in diabetes Boston U./Tufts U./Harvard U., 1995; mem. C study sect. NIDDKD, 1988-92, mem. task force on obesity, 1990—, mem. nutrition study sect., 1983-87; v.p. Am. Bd. Nutrition, 1987-88. Contbr. numerous articles to profl. jours. Fogarty Internat. fellow NIH, 1979-80. Mem. Am. Soc. for Clin. Nutrition (coun. 1987-90, pres. 1989-90), Am. Diabetes Assn. (exec. com. 1990-93, pres. 1992-93), N.Am. Assn. Study Obesity (v.p. 1992-93, pres. 1994-95), N.Y. State Health Rsch. Coun., N.Y. Acad. Medicine (com. on pub. health 1983—). Home: 305 Riverside Dr New York NY 10025-5286 Office: St Luke's-Roosevelt Hosp Ctr Dept Medicine 1111 Amsterdam Ave New York NY 10025-1716

PITAS, GRZEGORZ ADAM, anesthesiologist; b. Gorzów, Poland, May 9, 1965; s. Stefan Józef and Donata Maria (Mozol) P.; m. Barbara Katarzyna Marczyk, Aug. 31, 1991; children: Adam, Anna. MD, Med. Acad., Poznań, Poland, 1989. Intern Town Hosp., Gorzów, 1989-90, resident in anesthesiology, intensive therapy, and hemodialysis unit, 1990-93, physician, 1989-94, attending physician emergency medicine unit, 1990—; attending physician in anesthesiology and intensive care County Hosp., Gorzów, 1995—; cons., area mgr. Boehringer Mannheim, Warsaw, Poland, 1994-95. Author: Monitoring in Anaesthesia, 1992. Home: Popmiejska 33/2, 66-400 Gorzów Poland Office: County Hospital, Anesthesiology/Int Care, Dekerta 1, 66-400 Gorzów Poland

PITCHUMONI, CAPECOMORIN SANKAR, gastroenterologist, educator; b. Madura, India, Jan. 20, 1938; came to U.S., 1967; s. Sankara and Jaya (Lekshmi) Iyer; m. Prema Iyer, Nov. 11, 1964; children: Sheila, Shoba, Suresh. Student, St. Xavier Coll., India, 1953-55; M.B. B.S., Trivandrum Med. Coll., India, 1959, M.D., 1965. Intern Med. Coll., Trivandurm, India, 1961-63; resident in gastroenterology Yale U., 1967-69; N.Y. Med. Coll., 1969-72; practice medicine specializing in gastroenterology N.Y.C., 1972—; asst. prof. medicine Kottayam Med. Coll., India, 1967; asst. prof. medicine N.Y. Med. Coll., 1972-75, assoc. prof., 1975-80, prof. clin. medicine, 1980-85, prof. medicine, 1985—, assoc. prof. preventive and social medicine, 1975-86, prof. community and preventive medicine, 1986—; chief sect. gastroenterology Our Lady of Mercy Med. Ctr., N.Y., 1980—; assoc. dir. medicine Our Lady of Mercy Med. Ctr., N.Y.C., 1985—, program dir. internal medicine, 1987—; dir. medicine, 1992. Contbg. author med. textbooks; contbr. articles to profl. jours. Recipient Om Prakash award Indian Soc. Gastroenterology, 1976, Outstanding Scientist of Yr. award MV Spltys., Madras, 1994, Oration award Thangavelu Endowment, 1994. Fellow Royal Coll. Physicians and Surgeons Can., ACP, Am. Coll. Gastroenterology, Am. Coll. Nutrition; mem. Am. Soc. for Gastrointestinal Endoscopy, Assn. Physicians India, Am. Coll. Nuitrition, Am. Gastroent. Assn., India Soc. Gastroenterology (life), Am. Inst. Nutrition, N.Y. Gastroent. Assn., N.Y. Acad. Scis., N.Y. Soc. Gastrointestinal Endoscopy, Am. Soc. for Clin. Nutrition. Hindu. Home: 178 Fairmount Ave Glen Rock NJ 07452-3014 Office: 600 E 233rd St Bronx NY 10466-2697

PITKIN, ROY MACBETH, physician, educator; b. Anthon, Iowa, May 24, 1934; s. Roy and Pauline Allie (McBeath) P.; m. Marcia Alice Jenkins, Aug. 17, 1957; children: Barbara, Robert Macbeth, Kathryn, William Charles. B.A. with highest distinction, U. Iowa, 1956, M.D., 1959. Diplomate Am. Bd. Obstetrics & Gynecology, 1967. Intern King County Hosp., Seattle, 1959-60; resident in ob-gyn U. Iowa Hosps. and Clinics, Iowa City, 1960-63; asst. prof. ob-gyn U. Ill., 1965-68; assoc. prof. ob-gyn U. Iowa, Iowa City, 1968-72; prof. U. Iowa, 1972-87, head dept. ob-gyn, 1977-87; prof. UCLA, 1987—, head dept. ob-gyn., 1987-95; mem. residency rev. com. ob-gyn, 1981-87, chmn. 1985-87. Editor-in-chief: Year Book of Obstetrics and Gynecology, 1975-36; editor-in-chief: Clinical Obstetrics and Gynecology, 1979; editor: Obstetrics and Gynecology, 1985. Contbr. articles to med. jours. Served to lt. comdr. M.C. USNR, 1963-65. NIH career awardee, 1972-77. Fellow Royal Obstetricians and Gynecologists (ad eundem); mem. AMA (Goldberger award in clin. nutrition 1982), Am. Coll. Obstetricians and Gynecologists, Am. Gynecol. and Obstet. Soc. (pres. 1994-95), German Soc. Gynecology and Obstetrics (hon. 1992), Ctrl. Assn. Obstetricians and Gynecologists, Soc. Gynecologic Investigation (pres. 1985-86), Soc. Perinatal Obstetricians (pres. 1978-79), NAS, Inst. of Medicine. Presbyterian. Office: UCLA Sch Med Dept Ob-Gyn Los Angeles CA 90024-1740

PITT, BERTRAM, cardiologist, educator, consultant; b. Kew Gardens, N.Y., Apr. 27, 1932; s. David and Shirley (Blum) P., m. Elaine Liberstein, Aug. 10, 1962; children—Geoffrey, Jessica, Jillian. BA, Cornell U., 1953; MD, U. Basel, Switzerland, 1959. Diplomate Am. Bd. Internal Medicine, Am. Bd. Cardiology. Intern Beth Israel Hosp., N.Y.C., 1959-60; resident Beth Israel Hosp., Boston, 1960-63; fellow in cardiology Johns Hopkins U., Balt., 1966-67; from instr. to prof. Johns Hopkins U., 1967-77; prof. medicine, dir. div. cardiology U. Mich., Ann Arbor, 1977-91, assoc. chmn. dept. medicine, 1991—. Author: Atlas of Cardiovascular Nuclear Medicine, 1977; editor: Cardiovascular Nuclear Medicine, 1974. Served to capt. U.S. Army, 1963-65. Mem. ACP, Am. Coll. Cardiology, Am. Soc. Clin. Investigation, Assn. Am. Physicians, Am. Physiol. Soc., Am. Heart Assn., Assn. Univ. Cardiologists, Am. Coll. Chest Physicians, Royal Soc. Mich. Home: 24 Ridgeway St Ann Arbor MI 48104-1739 Office: U Mich Divsn Cardiology 1500 E Medical Center Dr Ann Arbor MI 48109-0999

PITT, WILLIAM ALEXANDER, cardiologist; b. Vancouver, B.C., Can., July 17, 1942; came to U.S., 1970; s. Reginald William and Una Sylvia (Alexander) P.; m. Judith Mae Wilson, May 21, 1965; children: William Matthew, Joanne Katharine. MD, U. B.C., Vancouver, 1967. Diplomate Royal Coll. Physicians Can. Intern, Mercy Hosp., San Diego, 1967-68, resident, 1970-71; resident Vancouver Gen. Hosp., 1968-70, U. Calif., San Diego, 1971-72; assoc. dir. cardiology Mercy Hosp., San Diego, 1972-92; with So. Calif. Cardiology Med. Group, San Diego, 1984—; pvt. practice Clin. Cons. Cardiology; bd. trustees San Diego Found. for Med. Care, 1983-89, 91—, pres., chmn. bd. trustees, 1986-88, med. dir., 1991—; bd. dirs. Mut. Assn. for Profl. Services, Phila., 1984-92; pres. Alternet Med. Svcs., Inc., 1992-95, San Diego IPA, 1996—. Fellow Royal Coll. Physicians Can., Am. Coll. Cardiology (assoc.); mem. AMA, Am. Heart Assn., Calif. Med. Assn., San Diego County Med. Soc., San Diego County Heart Assn. (bd. dirs. 1982-88). Episcopalian. Office: So Calif Cardiology Med Group 6386 Alvarado Ct Ste 101 San Diego CA 92120-4906

PITTA, PATRICIA JOYCE, psychologist; b. N.Y.C., July 3, 1947; d. John Joseph and Mildred (Gioiosa) P.; m. Eric Eugene Kirk; children: Eric Jon, Kevin. BA, Queens Coll., 1968; MS, Hunter Coll., 1972; PhD, Fordham U., 1975. Diplomate Am. Bd. Family Psychology. Recreational therapist Roosevelt Hosp., N.Y.C., 1968-73, psychology intern, 1973-74; staff psychologist NYU Med. Ctr., 1974-78, clin. instr., 1975—; pvt. practice psychology Manhasset, N.Y., 1977—; chief psychologist St. John's Episc. Hosp., Smithtown, N.Y., 1978-79; cons. North Shore U. Hosp., Manhasset, 1979-84; mem. faculty L.I. family therapy div. Inst. Psychoanalysis; supr. psychologist Clin. Psychology Doctoral Program St. John's U., N.Y.; media psychologist, relationship expert Nat. & Local T.V.; mem. bd. dirs., task force head divsn. pvt. practice APA, 1994—; lectr. in field. Contbr. articles to profl. jours., newspapers. Bd. dirs. Assn. for Retarded Children, 1988-92. Mem. APA (bd. dirs. ind. practice divsn.), Nassau County Psychol. Assn. (pvt. practice com. 1986-88, bd. dirs. 1987—, social issues com. 1988—), Working Woman Manhasset, L.I. Ctr. Bus. and Profl. Women, L.I. Assn. Marriage and Family Therapy (bd. dirs. 1992—, sec. 1993—, pres. 1995—). Office: 35 Bonnie Heights Rd Manhasset NY 11030-1636

PITTELKOW, MARK ROBERT, physician, dermatology educator, researcher; b. Milw., Dec. 16, 1952; s. Robert Bernard and Barbara Jean (Thomas) P.; m. Gail L. Gamble, Nov. 26, 1977; children: Thomas, Cameron, Robert. BA, Northwestern U., 1975; MD, Mayo Med. Sch., 1979. Intern then resident Mayo Grad. Sch., 1979-84, post-doctoral exptl. pathology, 1981-83; from asst. to assoc. prof. dermatology Mayo Med. Sch., Rochester, Minn., 1984-95, prof. dermatology, 1995—, assoc. prof. biochemistry and molecular biology, 1992—; cons. Mayo Clinic/Found., Rochester, 1984—. Fellow Am. Acad. Dermatology; mem. AAAS, Am. Dermatol. Assn., Soc. Investigative Dermatology, Am. Burn Assn., Am. Soc. Cell Biology, N.Y. Acad. Scis., Chi Psi. Home: 721 12th Ave SW Rochester MN 55902-2027 Office: Mayo Clinic 200 1st St SW Rochester MN 55905-0001

PITTELL, ROBERT S., pediatrician; b. Buffalo, Apr. 25, 1930; s. Bernard E. and Dorothy (Jacobson) P.; m. Elaine B. Davis, June 23, 1956; children: Scott, Jeffrey, Lynn. BA cum laude, U. Buffalo, 1954, MD, 1955. Diplomate Am. Bd. Pediatrics. Intern U.S. Naval Hosp., St. Albans, N.Y., 1955-56; resident in pediatrics U.S. Naval Hosp., Chelsea, Mass., 1956-58; staff pediatrician U.S. Naval Hosp., Jacksonville, Fla., 1958-60; fellow in pediatric neurology Children's Med. Ctr., Boston, 1960-61; pediatrician Pediatric Assocs., Hollywood, Fla., 1961—. Pres. Jewish Fedn. South Broward, Hollywood, Fla., 1980-82. Lt. USN, 1955-60. Mem. Fla. Pediatric Soc., Am. Acad. Pediatrics, Am. Birding Assn. Office: Pediatric Assocs 4500 Sheridan St Hollywood FL 33021

PITTILLO, JACK DANIEL, biology educator, researcher, consultant; b. Hendersonville, N.C., Oct. 25, 1938; s. Louia and Mattie Ruth (Hill) P.; m. Jean Henri Farr, Aug. 23, 1966; children: Heather Ann, Shane Keven. AB, Berea Coll. (Ky.), 1961; MS, U. Ky., 1963; PhD, U. Ga., 1966. Grad. and rsch. asst. U. Ky., 1961-63, U. Ga., 1963-66; asst. prof. biology Western Carolina U., 1966-71, assoc. prof., 1971-77, prof., 1977—; researcher Nat. Park Svc., Atlanta, 1975-77, Highlands Biol. Sta., 1990-94; prin. biologist N.C. Natural Heritage Program, 1990-94. Active Cullowhee United Meth. Ch., 1968—, mem. adminstrv. bd., 1968—. NSF grantee, 1982-85; Outstanding Individual Trails award N.C., 1985, Ester Cunningham Conservation award, 1989, Paul A. Reid Disting. Svc. award, 1991-92, Gov. award of Excellence, 1992. Mem. Ecol. Soc. Am., Assn. Southeastern Biologists (rsch. award 1985), N.C. Acad. Sci., So. Appalachian Bot. soc. (pres. 1977-78, newsletter editor 1993—), N.C. Bartram Trail Soc. (pres. 1979-85, editor newsletter 1979-93, bd. mem. 1993—), Sigma Xi. Democrat. Office: Dept Biology Western Carolina Univ Cullowhee NC 28723

PITTLE, LESTER B., physician, medical facility administrator; b. Newark, N.J., Apr. 7, 1947; s. Jack R. and Anne (Hart) P.; m. Maria Cecilia Amado, Mar. 26, 1978; children: Arie, Moshe. BS in Psychology, U. Mich., Ann Arbor, 1969; MD, U. Va., Charlottesville, 1972; MPH, U. Wash., Seattle, 1980. Diplomate Am. Bd. Internal Medicine. Clinic physician Pike Market Med. Clinic, Seattle, 1981-89, med. dir., 1989—; mem. exec. coun. breast and cervical health program State Dept. of Health, Olympia, Wash., 1994—; chair Cmty. Health Coun. King's County, Seattle, 1993-95; physician rep. Western Wash. Bd. Cmty. Health Plan, Seattle, 1992-94. Recipient Outstanding Clinician's Achievement award Northwest Regional Primary Care Assn., Seattle, 1993. Mem. King County Med. Soc. Office: Pike Market Med Clinic 1930 Post Alley Seattle WA 98101

PITTMAN, JACQUELYN, mental health nurse, nursing educator; b. Pensacola, Fla., Dec. 22, 1932; d. Edward Corry Sr. and Hettie Oean (Wilson) P. BS in Nursing Edn., Fla. State U., 1958; MA, Columbia U., 1959, EdD, 1974. Physician asst. Med. Ctr. Clinic, Pensacola, 1953-55; clin. instr., asst. dir. nursing svc. Sacred Heart Hosp., Pensacola, 1955-56; instr.psychiatric nurse Fla. State Hosp., Chattahoochee, 1958, Pensacola Community Coll., 1959-60, 62-63; chmn. div. nursing Gulf Coast Community Coll., Panama City, Fla., 1963-66; asst. prof. U. Tex., Austin, 1970-72, assoc. prof., 1972-80; prof. nursing, coord. curriculum and teaching Grad. Program La. State U. Med. Ctr. Sch. Nursing, New Orleans, 1980—; curriculum cons. Nicholls State U., Thibodaux, La., 1982, Our Lady of the Lake Sch. Nursing, Baton Rouge, 1983; rsch. liaison So. Bapt. Hosp., New Orleans, 1987-89, Med. Ctr. La., 1992—; mem. Sci. Misconduct Inquiry com. La. State U. Med. Ctr., 1992—; adv. bd. Sister Henrietta Guyot Professorship. Tchr. Christian edn. program for mentally retarded St. Ignatius Martyr Ch., 1979-80; tchr. initiation team Rite of Christian Initiation of Adults, Our Lady of the Lake Cath. Ch., Mandeville, La., 1983-86; ethics com., bd. trustees Hotel Dieu Hosp., New Orleans, 1987-91; v.p., bd. dirs. St. Tammany Guidance Ctr., Inc., Mandeville, 1987-91; mem. Dem. Nat. Comm., Presdl. Task Force, 1992, Ctr. for Study of Presidency; judge Internat. Sci. and Engring. Fair Assn., 1990, 92; del. La. State Nurses' Assn. State Conv., 1992, 94; assoc. Libr. of Congress, Smithsonian Instn. Mem. ANA, LWV, N.Y. Acad. Scis., Acad. Polit. Sci., Libr. of Congress Assocs., Nat. Trust for Hist. Preservation, La. Endowment for Humanities, La. Nurses Assn. (archivist 1987—, state task force com. to preserve hist. documents 1987—), So. Nursing Rsch. Soc., Nat. League Nursing, Boston U. Nursing Archives, Women's Inner Cir. Achievement N.Am. Cmtys., Internat. Order of Merit, World Found. Successful Women, Wilson Ctr. Assocs., Kappa Delta Pi, Sigma Theta Tau. Democrat. Roman Catholic. Address: 204 Woodridge Blvd Mandeville LA 70471-2604 Office: La State U Med Ctr 1900 Gravier St New Orleans LA 70112-2232

PITTMAN, JAMES ALLEN, JR., physician, educator; b. Orlando, Fla., Apr. 12, 1927; s. James Allen and Jean C. (Garretson) P.; m. Constance Ming-Chung Shen, Feb. 19, 1955; children—James Clinton, John Merrill. BS, Davidson Coll., 1948; MD, Harvard, 1952; DSc (hon.), Davidson Coll., 1980, U. Ala., Birmingham, 1984. Intern, asst. resident medicine Mass. Gen. Hosp., Boston, 1952-54; tchg. fellow medicine Harvard U., 1953-54; clin. assoc. NIH, Bethesda, Md., 1954-56; instr. medicine George Washington U., 1955-56; chief resident U. Ala. Med. Ctr., Birmingham, 1956-58, instr. medicine, 1956-59, asst. prof., 1959-62, assoc. prof., 1962-64, prof. medicine, 1964—, dir. endocrinology and metabolism div., 1962-71, co-chmn. dept. medicine, 1969-71, also prof., physiology and biophysics, 1967-92; dean U. Ala. Med. Ctr. (Sch. Medicine), 1973-92; asst. chief med. dir. rsch. and edn. in medicine U.S. VA, 1971-73; prof. medicine Georgetown U. Med. Sch., Washington, 1971-73; mem. endocrinology study sect. NIH, 1963-67; mem. pharmacology and endocrinology fellowships rev. coms., 1967-68; mem. grad. med. edn. nat. adv. com. HEW; mem. HHS coun. on Grad. Med. Edn., 1986-90; mem. nat. adv. rsch. resources coun. NIH, 1991-95; hon. prof. Chung Shan Med. and Dental Coll., Taiwan, 1995; sr. advisor Internat. Coun. on Control of Iodine Deficiency Diseases, 1994-95. Author: Diagnosis and Treatment of Thyroid Diseases, 1963; Contbr. articles in field to profl. jours. Master ACP; fellow Am. Coll. Endocrinology; mem. Assn. Am. Physicians, Endocrine Soc., Am. Assn. Clin. Endocrinologists, Am. Thyroid Assn., N.Y. Acad. Scis. (life), Soc. Nuclear Medicine, Am. Diabetes Assn., Am. Chem. Soc., Wilson Ornithol. Club (life), Am. Ornithologists Union (life), Am. Fedn. Clin. Rsch. (pres. So. sect., nat. coun. 1952-66), So. Soc. Clin. Investigation (Founder's medal 1993), Harvard U. Med. Alumni Assn. (pres. 1986-88), Phi Beta Kappa, Alpha Omega Alpha, Omicron Delta Kappa. Office: U Ala Sch of Med CAMS 75 SDB Birmingham AL 35294-0007

PITTS, FREDERICK WILLIAM, neurosurgeon; b. Detroit, Oct. 14, 1929; s. Frederick William and Edna Virginia (Green) P.; m. Dolores Barbara Scott, Aug. 17, 1957; children: Frederick, Linda, Victoria, John. BS, U. Pitts, 1950; MD, U. Pa., 1954. Diplomate Am. Bd. Neurol. Surgery. Intern U. Pa. Hosp., Phila., 1954-55, resident, 1957-62; fellow neuropathology Phila. Gen. Hosp., 1962-63; from asst. instr. to asst. prof. neurosurgery U. Pa., Phila., 1957-67; from assoc. prof. to prof. neurol. surgery U. So. Calif., L.A., 1967-73, clin. prof. surgery, 1973—; pvt. practice L.A.; neurosurgery sect. chmn. Hosp. Good Samaritan, L.A., 1974—; attending physician U. Pa. Hosp., Phila., 1962-67, Phila. Gen. Hosp., 1962-67, LAC-USC Med. Ctr., 1967-73, Santa Fe Meml. Hosp., L.A., 1972-73, Verdugo Hills Hosp., Glendale, Calif., 1976-86, Glendale Adventist Med. Ctr., 1976-81, Childrens Hosp. L.A., 1972-85, Calif. Hosp., L.A., 1978-87, St. Vincent Med. Ctr., L.A., 1981-92, Orthop. Hosp., L.A., 1982—, Northern Inyo Hosp., Bishop, Calif., Memmoth Hosp., Mammoth Lakes, Calif.; founding mem., vice chmn. bd. Preferred Health Network, 1983-85, chmn., 1986. Contbr. articles to profl. jours. Capt. U.S. Army, 1955-57. Mem. AMA, ACS (So. Calif. chpt.), Am. Assn. Neurol. Surgeons, Am. Assn. Stereotactic and Functional Neurosurgery, Internat. Assn. for Study of Pain, Calif. Med. Assn., Calif. Assn. Neurol. Surgeons, We. Neurosurg. Soc., L.A. Acad. Medicine,L.A. County Med. Assn., So. Calif. Neurosurg. Soc., Phi Rho Sigma, L.A. Yacht Club, Geter C. Shidle Masonic Lodge 650. Office: 1245 Wilshire Blvd #305 Los Angeles CA 90017

PITTS, MARK ALEXANDER, oral and maxillofacial surgeon; b. Cleveland, Tenn., Aug. 30, 1961; s. Doughton Alexander and Geraldine (Brown) P.; m. Shawn Elizabeth Myers, Dec. 31, 1995. BS, Lee Coll., 1982; DDS, U. Tenn., Memphis, 1988. Gen. practice resident Brigham & Women's Hosp., Boston, 1988-89; oral surgery resident U. Md. Hosp., Balt., 1989-93; pvt. practice Frederick, Md., 1993—. Recipient Jack E. Wells award U. Tenn., 1988; Omicron Kappa Upsilon scholar, 1988. Mem. ADA, Md. Dental Assn., Am. Assn. Oral and Maxillofacial Surgery, Frederick County Dental Soc. (mem.-at-large), Rotary (chpt. v.p., pres. elect 1993—). Office: 2100 Old Farm Dr Frederick MD 21702

PITTSCHIELER, KLAUS, pediatrician; b. Bozen, Italy, Jan. 6, 1949; s. Karl and Brunhilde (Langer) P.; m. Antoinette Marthe Schaack, Dec. 17, 1975; children: Thomas, Sabine. MD, U. Innsbruck, 1973; degree in pediatrics, U. Padova, 1977; degree in pediatric gastroenterology, SUNY, Buffalo, 1987. Intern, resident Verona, 1973-76, Padua, 1977; asst. Gen. Hosp., Bozen, 1974-81, assoc., 1981-95, dir. dept. pediatrics, 1996—; dir. rsch. lab., Bozen, 1988; prof. pediatrics U. Innsbruck, 1992, U. Rome, Italy, 1994, U. Verona, Italy, 1995. Author, editor: Alpha-1-Antitrypsin Deficiency, 1994; patentee Coeliac Disease Test; contbr. articles to profl. jours. Mem. ESPGAN. Roman Catholic. Office: Ospedale Regionale, Lorenz Boehler 5, 39100 Bozen Italy

PIVA, ENRICO ERNESTO, physician; b. Torino, Italy, Jan. 1, 1958; came to U.S., 1970; s. Terzo and Gemma Giacinta (Mazza) P. BA in Biology, East Carolina U., 1982; physician asst., Bowman Gray Sch. of Medicine, 1985; DO, W.Va. Sch. of Medicine, 1995. EMT Pitt County Meml. Hosp., Greenville, N.C., 1982; physician asst. in pvt. practice Advance, N.C., 1985-88, Winston-Salem, N.C., 1988-91; intern in osteopathy Greebrier Valley Hosp., Lewisburg, W.Va., 1995—. Pres.-elect Winston-Salem Adult Soccer League, 1988-90, head of referees, 1990-91. Rural Health grantee The Kellog Found., Rainelle, W.Va., 1994-95. Mem. Am. Osteopaathic Assn., Sigma Sigma Phi. Roman Catholic. Home: 409 E Washington St Lewisburg WV 24901

PIVIN, JEANETTE EVA, psychotherapist; b. Fall River, Mass., Feb. 24, 1932; d. Oscar and Ida Antoinette (Gauthier) P. B in Edn., Cath. Tchrs. Coll., 1956; MA in Theology, U. Notre Dame, 1967; cert. clin. pastoral edn., Worcester State Hosp., 1975; cert. interior design, Hall Inst. Tech., 1989; cert. divorce mediator, Roger Williams Univ, 1995. Tchr. St. Matthew Sch., Cranston, R.I., 1956-64; assoc. prof. religious studies Salve Regina U., Newport, R.I., 1967-74; staff counselor La Salette Counseling Svcs., Attleboro, Mass., 1975-80; pastoral counselor Interfaith Counseling Ctr., Providence, R.I., 1975—; pvt. practice Providence, 1980—. Home and Office: 139 Woodbine St Providence RI 02906-2543

PIZZO, SALVATORE VINCENT, pathologist; b. Phila., June 22, 1944; s. George J. P. and Aida (Alcaro) Lepore; m. Carol Ann Kurkowski, Dec. 28, 1968 (div. 1987); children: Steven, David, Susan. PhD, Duke U., 1972; BS, St. Joseph's Coll., 1966; MD, Duke U., 1973. Asst. prof. Duke U. Med. Ctr., Durham, N.C., 1976-80, assoc. prof., 1980-85, prof., 1985—, dir. med. scientist tng. program, 1987—, chmn., 1991—; mem., chmn. program rev. com. NIH, Bethesda, Md., 1986-90; vice chmn. Gordon Conf. Proteases, Holderness, N.H., 1990, chmn., 1992-96; cons. in field, 1980—; mem. Cellular and Molecular Basis of Disease Rev. Com., 1992—. Contbr. articles to profl. jours. Grantee NIH, 1976—, Am. Cancer Soc., 1976—. Mem. Am. Heart Assn. (exec. com. Thrombosis coun. 1990, 92), Am. Chem. Soc., Am. Assn. Pathologists (program com. 1985-88, long range planning com. 1990-92), Am. Soc. Biological Chemists, Alpha Sigma Nu, Phi Beta Kappa, Alpha Omega Alpha, Sigma Xi. Office: Duke U Med Ctr PO Box 3712 Durham NC 27710

PIZZOFERRATO, THOMAS ATTILIO, pharmacist; b. Hartford, Conn., July 23, 1951; s. Attilio and Myra (Ferreira) P.; m. Dana Lorraine Bragg, June 29, 1974; 1 child, Lauren. BS in Pharmacy, U. Conn., 1974; MBA in Health Care, Rensselaer Poly. Inst., 1985. Bd. cert. Nutritional Support Pharmacist. Staff pharmacist Dougherty Drug, Windsor, Conn., 1972-74, Sless Pharmacy, Hartford, Conn., 1974; staff pharmacist St. Francis Hosp., Hartford, Conn., 1974-80, supr., 1980-85, asst. dir., 1985—; cons. in field. Mem. Polit. Action Com., East Granby, Conn., 1995—. Mem. Am. Soc.

Parenteral and Enteral Nutrition, Conn. Soc. Hosp. Pharmacists. Independent. Office: St Francis Hosp Med Ctr 114 Woodland St Hartford CT 06105

PLAA, GABRIEL LEON, toxicologist, educator; b. San Francisco, May 15, 1930; arrived in Can., 1968; s. Jean and Lucienne (Chalopin) P.; m. Colleen Neva Brasefield, May 19, 1951; children: Ernest (dec.), Steven, Kenneth, Gregory, Andrew, John, Denise, David. BS, U. Calif., Berkeley, 1952; PhD, U. Calif., San Francisco, 1958. Diplomate Am. Bd. Toxicology. Asst. toxicologist City/County San Francisco, 1954-58; asst. prof. Sch. Medicine Tulane U., New Orleans, 1958-61; assoc. prof. U. Iowa, Iowa City, 1961-68; prof. U. Montreal, 1968-95, chmn. dept. pharmacology, 1968-80, vice-dean Faculty Medicine, 1982-89, dir. Interuniv. Ctr. Rsch. in Toxicology, 1991-95; ret., 1995, prof. emeritus, 1996; Dorothy Snider disting. lectr. U. Ark., 1995; chmn. Can. Coun. Animal Care, Ottawa, Ont., Can., 1985-86. Editor Toxicology and Applied Pharmacology, 1972-80; contbr. over 200 articles to profl. jours. 1st lt. U.S. Army, 1952-53, Korea. Recipient Thienes award Am. Acad. Clin. Toxicology, 1977. Mem. Am. Soc. Pharmacology, Soc. Toxicology Can. (pres. 1981-83, Henderson award 1969, award of distinction 1994), Pharm. Soc. Can. (pres. 1973-74), Soc. Toxicology (pres. 1983-84, Achievement award 1967, Lehman award 1977, Edn. award 1987, Amb. award 1987, Merit award 1996), Acad. Toxicological Scis. Roman Catholic. Home: 236 Meredith Ave, Dorval, PQ Canada H9S 2Y7 Office: U Montreal Dept Pharmacology, PO Box 6128 Sta A, Montreal, PQ Canada H3C 3J7

PLACE, DENISE LISETTE MARIE WESCOTT, quality management professional; b. Concord, N.H., June 13, 1961; d. Joseph Michael Wescott and Georgette Aline Marie (Dupont) Lavalliere. BSBA, U. N.H., 1983. Cert. profl. in health care quality. Vice pres. AIESEC U.S., Inc., N.Y.C., 1983-84; mktg. mgr. asst. CODAREC, Brussels, 1984; mgr. Francestown Village Store, 1985-88; adminstrv. asst. Dept. Quality Mgmt., Health N.E., Inc., Manchester, N.H.; quality mgmt. adminstr. Elliot Hosp., Manchester, N.H., 1988—; session leader, chmn. U.S. regional conf. AIESEC, Ohio, 1983, corp. fundraising session leader, Boston, 1986, chmn. nat. conf., Belgium, 1984; acct. rep. mktg. staff U. N.H., Durham, 1981, pres., 1982-83. Fundraiser N.H. Kidney Found., U. N.H., 1982; mem. fellowship rev. bd. Nat. Healthcare Quality Edn. Found, 1996. Mem. Nat. Assn. for Healthcare Quality, N.H. Assn. for Healthcare Quality (prs. 1993-95).

PLACEK, MARJORIE YOUNGBLOOD, healthcare management consultant; b. Cleve., Oct. 26, 1944; d. Melvin Anthony and Magdalene Anna (Suppan) Youngblood. BSN, Case Western Res. U., 1968; MSIA, Carnegie Mellon U., 1988; MN, U. Pitts., 1974, MNEd, 1980. RN, Pa. Staff devel. inst., clin. specialist Fairfax (Va.) Hosp., 1975-76; asst. dir. nursing, dir. staff devel.-patient edn. West Penn Hosp., Pitts., 1976-82, dir. quality assurance, 1982-87; v.p. quality improvement Lancaster (Pa.) Gen. Hosp., 1989-91; cons. Wolf Adv. Internat., 1991; cons. quality improvement.mgmt. devel. Placek Assocs., 1992—; speaker on quality improvement and quality assurance. Mem., chair allocations panel Lancaster County, United Way, 1989—, restructuring task force, 1990; chair strategic planning com. Lancaster-Lebanon Literacy Coun., 1989—, bd. dirs., planning com., 1990—, pres. bd. literacy coun., 1992. Cecilia A. Evans scholar. Mem. AAUW, ANA, NAFE, Am. Oper. Rm. Nurses, Assn. Quality and Participation, Am. Soc. for Quality Control, Am. Hosp. Assn., Am. Mgmt. Assn., Am. Coll. Healthcare Execs., Nat. League for Nursing, Rotary Club, Lancaster C. of C., Sigma Theta Tau. Home and Office: 3107 Dale Dr Lancaster PA 17601-1513

PLAIR, WENDELL SAMUEL, psychologist; b. Charlotte, N.C., Aug. 31, 1921; s. William Samuel and Alice Geneva (Oglesby) P.; BS, Johnson C. Smith U., 1942; MS, Howard U., 1967, PhD, 1994; m. Willa Mae Vaught, Mar. 6, 1950; 1 dau., Barbara Ann. With Airway Sales and Services, Inc., Washington, 1951-63; research asst. NIH, Bethesda, Md., 1963-66; staff psychologist DC Dept. Corrections, Lorton facility, 1967-69, research psychologist, rsch. and planning div., 1970-72; mental health coordinator, mental health svcs. D.C. Detention Center, 1973-87; group therapist Georgetown U. Clinic, 1970-71; mem. adv. bd. Parental Imprisonment and Child Socialization Project, Howard U., 1974-76. Served with USNR, 1945-46. Recipient Outstanding Performance awards D.C. Govt., 1976, 80, Quality Service award, 1982. Mem. D.C. Psychol. Assn., Am. Psychol. Assn., Assn. Black Psychologists, Am. Assn. Correctional Psychologists, Soc. Psychol. Study Social Issues, Omega Psi Phi. Clubs: Pigskin of Washington, Masons. Home: 1314 Nicholson St Hyattsville MD 20782-1512

PLAKANS, SHELLEY SWIFT, social worker, psychotherapist; b. Boston, Aug. 29, 1943; d. William Nye and Phyllis (Childs) Swift; m. John Joseph Guinan Jr. (div. 1975); children: Ashley, Lindsey Guinan, John Jeffrey, Daniel Plakans; m. John Plakans. AB, Wheaton Coll., 1965; MEd, Fitchburg (Mass.) State Coll., 1977; MSW, Simmons Sch. of Social Work, Boston, 1987. Lic. ind. clin. social worker, Mass.; bd. cert. diplomate. Staff psychologist Ayer (Mass.) Guidance Ctr., 1978-81; substance abuse specialist Family Counseling and Guidance Ctrs., Danvers, Mass., 1990-91; pvt. practice psychotherapy Boston North Shore Assocs., Salem, 1985-90, NEPA, Salem, 1990-94. Mediator Lynn (Mass.) Youth Resource Bur., 1986-87, Marblehead Cmty. Counseling Ctr., 1994-96. Mem. Nat. Assn. Social Workers, Mass. Acad. Clin. Social Work, Inc., Am. Soc. Clin. Hypnosis, Internat. Soc. Clin. Hypnosis. Office: 1 Pleasant Ln Marblehead MA 01945-2341

PLAKUN, ERIC MARTIN, psychiatrist, educator; b. N.Y.C., Aug. 1, 1947; s. Charles and Lucille (Stein) P.; m. Catherine Mary Furst, Oct. 18, 1980; children: Noah, Caleb, Samantha. BA, Hofstra U., 1968; MD, Columbia U., 1972. Diplomate Am. Bd. Psychiatry and Neurology (written test com. 1987—), Am. Bd. Forensic Examiners, Am. Bd. Forensic Medicine. Intern Dartmouth Hitchcock Affiliated Hosps., Hanover, N.H., 1972-73; family practitioner Black River Med. Group, Cavendish, Vt., 1973-75; resident in psychiatry Dartmouth Hitchcock Affiliated Hosps., Hanover, N.H., 1975-78; fellowship in psychoanalytic psychotherapy, asst. med. staff Austen Riggs Ctr., Stockbridge, Mass., 1978-82, assoc. med. staff, 1982-88, sr. med. staff, 1988—, dir. admissions, 1981—; acting dir. rsch. Austen Riggs Ctr., Stockbridge, 1992-93, dir. program devel. and rsch., 1995—; clin. instr. psychiatry Harvard U. Med. Sch., Cambridge, Mass., 1982—; mem. Cen. Collaborative Rsch. Group, Chgo., 1986-93; mem. New Eng. Study Group on Personality Disorders, Boston, 1990; mem. written test com. Am. Bd. Psychiatry and Neurology, 1987—, oral examiner, 1991—; numerous presentations of sci. data and chairing of sci. symposia. Editor: New Perspectives on Narcissism, 1990; contbr. articles to med. jours., chpts. to books. Mem. ad hoc adv. com. on growth Town of Stockbridge, 1986-87, mem. zoning bylaws revision com., 1987-89, mem. land trust study com., 1989-90, mem. planning bd., 1989—, mem. master plan com., 1995—. Recipient Excellence in Teaching award Yale Physicians Assoc. Program, 1975; named Outstanding Young Men of Am., 1984. Fellow Am. Psychiat. Assn.; mem. AAAS, Assn. for Rsch. in Personality Disorders, Mass. Psychiat. Assn., Mass. Med. Soc., Berkshire Dist. Med. Soc., Am. Acad. Psychoanalysis, Am. Coll. of Forensic Examiners, Sigma Xi. Office: Austen Riggs Ctr Box 962 25 Main St Stockbridge MA 01262-0962

PLATA-SALAMÁN, CARLOS RAMON, neuroscientist; b. Guadalajara, Jalisco, Mex., Feb. 7, 1959; came to U.S., 1988; s. Manuel Plata and Eva Maria Salamán; m. Kyoko Matsumoto, Mar. 12, 1987. MD, U. Guadalajara, 1984; D of Med. Sci., Kyushu U., Fukuoka, Japan, 1988. Lectr. in pathophysiology, coord. rsch. sect. Dept. Pathophysiology Faculty of Medicine U. Guadalajara, 1979-82; coord. sci. activities Soc. of Boarding Med. Students, Civil Hosp. of Guadalajara, 1981-82; collaborator exptl. physiology teaching program for med. students Kyushu U., 1984-88; postdoctoral fellow Inst. Neurosci. U. Del., Newark, 1988-90, lectr. neurobiology, neuroimmunology, neurosci., and physiology Sch. Life and Health Scis., 1990—, assoc. prof. Sch. Life and Health Scis., 1990—; referee Am. Jour. Physiology, Neurosci. Letters, Peptides, Life Scis., Nutrition, Pharmacology Biochemistry and Behavior, Obesity Rsch., Brain Behavior and Immunity, Brain Rsch. Bull., Neurosci., Physiology and Behavior. Contbr. articles to profl. jours. including Jour. Neurophysiology, Brain Rsch., Am. Jour. Physiology, Physiology and Behavior, Jour. Physiology (London), Pharmacology, Biochemistry and Behavior, Peptides, Life Scis., NeuroReport, Neurosci. Letters, Brain Rsch. Bull., Neurosci. Biobehavior Rev., Digestive Diseases, European Jour. Pharmacology, Brain, Behavior and Immunity, Neurosci. Rsch. Comm., Molecular Brain Rsch., Nutrition, Jour. Molecular Neuroscience, Obesity Rsch., Jour. Neurosci. Methods; mem. editl. bd. Am. Jour. Physiology, Nutrition, Physiology and Behavior. Mem. AAAS, Am. Physiological Soc., N.Y. Acad. Scis., Soc. for Neurosci., Internat. Neuropeptide Soc., N.Am. Soc. for Neuroimmunomodulation, Pavlovian Soc., Soc. for the Study of Ingestive Behavior, Internat. Soc. for Neuroimmunomodulation, Human Anatomy and Physiology Soc. Office: Sch Life and Health Scis U Del Newark DE 19716-2590

PLATSOUCAS, CHRIS DIMITRIOS, immunologist; b. Athens, Greece, Apr. 17, 1951; came to U.S., 1973; s. Dimitrios Evagelos and Maria (Tsonidis) P.; m. Emilia L. Oleszak, Oct. 18, 1985. BS, U. Patras (Greece), 1973; postgrad., Purdue U., 1974; PhD, MIT, 1978. Rsch. fellow/assoc. Meml. Sloan-Kettering Cancer Ctr., N.Y.C., 1978-80, asst. mem., 1980-85, asst. prof., 1981-85, head lab. biol. response modifiers, 1981-85; assoc. prof. dept. immunology M.D. Anderson Cancer Ctr., Houston, 1985-89, prof., dep. chmn., 1989-93, Ashbel Smith professorship, 1991-92, H.L. and O. Stringer professorship in cancer rsch., 1992-93; L.H. Carnell prof. and chmn. dept. microbiology, immunology Temple U. Sch. Medicine, Phila., 1993—; biotech. cons., sci. reviewer study sects. NIH, Bethesda, 1982—. Contbr. numerous articles to profl. jours. Nat. Rsch. Svc. award NIH, 1978-79; NIH grantee, 1982—, Am. Cancer Soc. grantee, 1980-91. Mem. Am. Assn. Immunologists, Am. Soc. Hematology, Am. Assn. Biochem & Molecular Biology, Am. Assn. Pathologists. Greek Orthodox. Office: Temple U Sch Medicine Dept Microbiology and Immunology 3400 N Broad St Philadelphia PA 19140-5196

PLATT, ALEXANDER BRADFORD, psychologist; b. N.Y.C., Mar. 2, 1935; s. Leonard Scranton and Rachel Mary (McClurg) P.; m. Patricia Ann Edwards, June 18, 1960; children—Alexander Bradford, Corinne Patricia. B.A., Washington and Lee U., 1957; M.A., Columbia, 1958, Ph.D., 1966. Vocational counselor YMCA Vocat. Service Center, N.Y.C., 1959-60; asst. to dean students Sch. Gen. Studies, Columbia U., 1960-62, dean students, 1962-66; prof. psychology Briarcliff Coll., Briarcliff Manor, N.Y., 1966-67; assoc. dean student affairs Columbia Coll., Columbia U., 1967-68; mgmt. cons. Rohrer, Hibler & Replogle, N.Y.C., 1968-69; v.p., dir. instructional systems div. Grolier Ednl. Corp., N.Y.C., 1969-77; gen. ptnr. Keyes, Platt & Dineen, Darien, Conn., 1977-80; pres. Platt and Assocs., Inc., 1981—. Mem. Am. Psychol. Assn. Home: 30 Willowmere Ave Riverside CT 06878-2517

PLATT, BRYCE ORION, critical care nurse; b. Bakersfield, Calif., Apr. 13, 1953; s. William Barry and Jewell Charlene (Edwards) Platt; m. Dolores Ramos, May 12, 1973 (div. 1986); children: Amber Nicole, Christopher Bryce; m. Mary Ann McGrath, Oct. 31, 1990. Calif. State Coll., 1975; postgrad., U. Ariz., 1990—. RN, Calif., Ariz. Staff nurse ICU U. Calif. Irvine Med. Ctr., Orange, 1975-76; free-lance ICU nurse Calif., 1976-83; staff nurse ICU St. Joseph Hosp., Orange, 1983-90; staff nurse St. Joseph Hosp., Tucson, Ariz., 1991—. Mem. Am. Assn. Critical Care Nursing, Am. Chem. Soc., Genetics Soc. Am., Am. Geophys. Soc., Math. Assn. Am., Internat. Union Pure and Applied Chemistry, U.S. Naval Inst., Soc. for Creative Assn., Am. Genetic Assn., Soc. for Study of Evolution, Soc. for Molecular Biology and Evolution, Mensa. Republican. Home: 2670 W Saddleranch Pl Tucson AZ 85745-3544 Office: Univ of Ariz Biol Scis W Tucson AZ 85745

PLATT, HOWARD A., neurosurgeon; b. Phila., Oct. 27, 1935; s. Harry and Florence (Needleman) P.; m. Vera Neuman, Mar. 15, 1970; children: Raphael, Karen, Michael. AB in English, Lafayette Coll., 1957; MD, Jefferson Med. Coll., 1961. Diplomate Am. Bd. Neurologic Surgery. Intern Albert Einstein Med. Ctr., Phila., 1961-62; resident Episcopal Hosp., Phila., 1962-64; resident/fellow Cleve. Clinic Hosp., 1964-67; staff neurosurgeon US Naval Hosp., Memphis, Tenn., 1967-69, Rambam Hosp., Haifa, Israel, 1969-70; neurosurgeon, pvt. practice Lebanon, Pa., 1970-73, Scranton, Pa., 1973—; cons. neurosurgeon, Riverfront Med. Svcs., Syracuse, N.Y., 1986-96. Lt. comdr. USN, 1967-69. Mem. AMA, Pa. Med. Soc., County Med. Soc., Congress of Neurol. Surgeons.

PLATT, JENNIE RONALDS, neurosensory and geriatrics nurse, researcher; b. Bronx, N.Y., June 5, 1953; d. John David Ronalds and Mary Dolores (Borowich) P. BSN, Thomas Jefferson U., 1993; postgrad., U. Pa., 1993—. RN, Pa. Staff nurse, neurosensory and acute stroke unit Thomas Jefferson U. Hosp., Phila., 1993—. Contbr. articles to acad. pubs. Mem. World Affairs Coun., Sigma Theta Tau. Home: 537 League St Philadelphia PA 19147 Office: Thos Jefferson U Hospital 9NE/Acute Stroke 111 S 11th St Philadelphia PA 19107

PLATT, JEROME JOSEPH, psychologist, educator; b. N.Y.C., May 3, 1941; s. Benjamin and Rose (Weissman) P.; m. Arleen Kay Adair, Jan. 20, 1964; 1 son, Gregory. A.B., U. Mo., 1961; M.S., U. Ga., 1965, PhD, 1967. NASA predoctoral trainee U.Ga., 1967; Clin. research psychologist, sr. instr. in psychiatry Hahnemann Med. Coll. and Hosp., 1968-71, asst. prof. mental health scis., 1971-73, assoc. prof., 1973-77, prof., 1977-86, assoc. dir. grad. edn. in psychology, 1977-82; dir. research Hahnemann mental health services at Phila. prisons, 1978-81; clin. fellow Temple U. Sch. Medicine, Phila., 1978-80; prof. dir. div. rsch. Hahnemann Univ. Dept. Mental Health Scis., 1981-86; prof. psychiatry/dir. Ctr. Excellence in Addiction Treatment Rsch. U. Medicine and Dentistry of N.J., Camden, N.J., 1986-91, asst. dean for clin. rsch., 1987-88, acting assoc. dean for rsch., 1988-90; assoc. dean for rsch. Rsch. U. Medicine and Dentistry of N.J. S.O.M. Camden, 1990-91; prof., dir. divsn. addiction rsch. and treatment Med. Coll. of Pa. and Hahnemann U., 1991—; adj. prof. psychiatry and human behavior Jefferson Med. Coll., 1984-89; rep. U.S. Dept. State/Fed. Republic Germany workshop on drug abuse treatment, 1985; cons. in field; chmn. organizing prog. coms. Duth/Am. Conf. on Effectiveness of Drug Abuse Treatement, 1987; mem., chmn. peer rev. com. Nat. Inst. Drug Abuse, 1984—; chmn. NIH, Nat. Inst. Druge Abuse Health Svcs. Rsch. Subcom., 1996—; chmn. organizing and prog. coms. German/Am. Conf. on Drug Abuse Sys., 1989; mem. various adv., blue ribbon, other coms., 1986—; vis. scientist, Inst. Therapieforschung, Munich, 1990. Author or editor several books, including Heroin Addiction: Theory, Research, and Treatment, 1977, 2d edit., 1986 (transl. into German 1982), The Psychological Consultant, 1979, The Effectiveness of Drug Abuse Treatment, 1990, Drug Addiction Treatment Research, 1992, Heroin Addiction, Vol. 2, The Addict, The Treatment Process, and Social Control, 1995, Heroin Addiction, Vol. 3, Treatment Advances and AIDS, 1995, Cocaine Addiction: Theory, Research, and Treatment, 1996; contbr. numerous articles to profl. jours. Bd. dirs. Burlington County chpt. Am. Cancer Soc., 1976-79; mem. Mayor's Commn. on Health in the 80s City of Phila., 1982. Grantee Nat. Inst. Drug Abuse, 1978—; clin. fellow Behavior Therapy and Rsch. Soc. Fellow Pa. Psychol. Assn., Am. Coll. Forensic Psychology, Am. Psychol. Assn.; mem. N.J. Psychol Assn., Eastern Psychol. Assn., AAAS, Sigma Xi. Office: Med Coll Pa Hahnemann U Sch Medicine MS982 Broad & Vine Sts Philadelphia PA 19102-1192

PLATT, LAWRENCE D., obstetrician and gynecologist; b. Detroit, Oct. 19, 1947; m. Wendy; children: Joshua, Adeena, Ari. BA, Wayne State U., 1968, MD, 1972. Diplomate Am. Bd. Obstetrics and Gynecology, Nat. Bd. Med. Examiners. Intern, resident, chief resident Sinai Hosp. Detroit, 1972-76; fellow in maternal-fetal medicine U. So. Calif. Sch. Medicine, L.A., 1976-78; from clin. instr. to prof. ob/gyn U. So. Calif. Med. Ctr., L.A., 1978-90; prof. dept. ob/gyn UCLA, 1990—; med. dir. perinatal svc., St. John's Hosp. and Health Ctr., Santa Monica, Calif., 1992-94; attending staff Children's Hosp., L.A., 1981-96, Cedars-Sinai Med. Ctr., L.A., 1985—, Valley Presbyn. Hosp., Van Nuys, Calif., 1994— ; acad. cons. staff St. John's Med. Ctr., Santa Monica, 1987—, Queen of Angeles-Hollywood Presbyn. Med. Ctr., L.A., 1988-96; vice chmn. dept. ob/gyn UCLA Med. Sch., 1992—. Editor Ultrasound in Ob/Gyn, 1990—; mem. editl. bd. Jour. Perinatology, 1985—, Jour. Ultrasound in Medicine, 1986—, Diagnostic Med. Soc., 1987-93, Ultrasound Quar., 1988—, Am. Jour. Cardiac Imaging, 1987-95, Jour. Maternal-Fetal Investigation, 1991—, Jour. Soc. Gynecol. Investigation, 1993—. Health profl. adv. com. March of Dimes, 1986-93; profl. adv. bd. pre-natal diagnosis com. Nat. Tuberous Sclerosis Assn.; mem. L.A. Assembly Exec. Com. Fellow Am. Coll. Obstetricians and Gynecologists; mem. Am. Coll. Physician Execs., Am. Soc. Human Genetics, Internat. Soc. Ob/Gyn Ultrasound, Soc. Obstetrical and Gynecol. Ultrasound (sec. treas. 1978-80, vice-chmn. 1980-82, chmn. 1982-84, exec. bd. 1984—), Pacific Coast Ob-Gyn Soc., L.A. Soc. Obstetrics and Gynecology (pres. 1996—), Daniel Morton Soc., Am. Inst. Ultrasound in Medicine (bd. govs. 1984-86, v.p. 1986-90), Soc. Obstetric Anesthesia & Perinatology, Alfred I. Sherman Soc., L.A. Radiology Soc. (ultrasound sect.), Soc. Gynecol. Investigation, Calif. Perinatal Assn., Soc. Perinatal Obstetricians. Office: Cedars Sinai Med Ctr 8700 Beverly Blvd Los Angeles CA 90048

PLATT, REGINALD, III, physician; b. Houston, Dec. 18, 1928; s. Reginald Jr. and Cecile Louise (Hoffman) P.; div.; children: Reginald IV, Cynthia Elizabeth Platt Wegman, Kathryn Nell Platt Meeks, Mark Jonathan, Jennifer Holly. BS, U. Houston, 1965; DO, Kirksville Coll. Osteopathy and Surgery, 1969. Diplomate Am. Bd. Examiners for Osteopathic Physicians and Surgeons of U.S.A. Intern Davenport (Iowa) Osteopathic Hosp.; commd. ensign USNR, 1953, advanced through grades to lt. comdr., naval aviator, 1953-70, ret., 1970; physician Platt Osteo. Clinic, Houston, 1970—. Mem. Am. Osteo Assn., Tex. Osteo. Med. Assn., Tex. Med. Assn., Harris County Osteo. Med. Soc. (dist. pres. 1981), Harris County Med. Soc. Office: # 108 4119 Montrose Blvd Houston TX 77006-4936

PLAUNTZ, ARTHUR CARL, urologist; b. Milw., June 6, 1934; s. Arthur Carl and Gertrude (Kohlhoff) P.; m. Alice Dorothy LaFrance, Dec. 27, 1966; children: Arthur, Julia, Laura, Joseph, Andrew. MD, Med. Coll. Wis., 1958. Intern St. Joseph's Hosp., Milw., 1959; residency Milw. County Hosp.; pvt. practice Riverview Clinic, Janesville, Wis., 1967-94, Health Net of Janesville, 1994—, Dean Med. Ctr., Janesville, 1995-96; mem. exec. bd. Riverview Clinic, Janesville; chief of surgery Mercy Hosp., Janesville. Contbr. articles to profl. jours. Capt. U.S. Army, Viet Nam, 1966-67. Mem. AMA, Am. Urol. Assn., Am. Fertility Soc., Urology Soc. (bd. dirs. 1986—), Rock County Med. Soc. (pres.). Office: Dean Med Ctr Riverview Clin 580 N Washington St Janesville WI 53545

PLAVSIC, BRANKO MILENKO, radiology educator; b. Zagreb, Yugoslavia, Croatia, Feb. 14, 1947; came to U.S., 1989; s. Milenko and Nevenka P.; m. Valerie H. Drnovsek, Aug. 26, 1991. MD, U. Zagreb, 1972, MS, 1974, PhD, 1975. Asst. prof. U. Zagreb, 1986, prof. radiology, chief abdominal radiology, 1988; prof. radiology, vice-chmn., dir. abdominal radiol./rsch. Tulane U., New Orleans, 1991—. Co-author: (with A.E. Robinson, R.B. Jeffrey) Gastrointestinal Radiology: A Concise Text, 1992; contbr. articles to profl. jours. Home: 4460 Lennox Blvd New Orleans LA 70131-8348 Office: Tulane U Med Ctr Dept Radiology 1430 Tulane Ave New Orleans LA 70112

PLAYFORD, RAYMOND JOHN, gastroenterologist; b. Manchester, Eng., Mar. 11, 1960; s. Gordon Jack and Marjorie (Jones) P.; m. Edith Diane Cooke; children: Richard Charles, Christopher John. BSc with honors, U. London, 1981; MB, BS, St. Bartholomews Hosp., London, 1984; PhD, U. London, 1992. Sr. house officer Royal Marsden Hosp., London, 1986-87; registrar Ealing Hosp., London, 1987-88; registrar Hammersmith Hosp., London, 1988-89, cons. physician, 1995-96; tng. fellow Med. Rsch. Coun., London, 1989-91; chief gastroenterology U. Leicester, Eng., 1996—; vis. lectr., Tokyo, 1995; vis. prof. Royal Postgrad. Med. Sch., London, 1996. Contbr. articles to profl. jours. Clinician scientist grantee Med. Rsch. Coun., London, 1992, sr. fellowship grantee Wellcome Trust, 1995; recipient Rsch. medal Brit. Soc. Gastroenterology, 1995. Mem. Brit. Soc. Gastroenterology, Athenaeum Club. Mem. Ch. of Eng. Office: Leicester Gen Hosp, Gwendolen Rd, Leicester LE54PW, England

PLAZZI, GIUSEPPE, neurologist, researcher; b. Ravenna, Italy, July 20, 1959; s. Luigi and Laura (Angelini) P.; m. Diamante Marzotto, Dec. 23, 1987; children: Matteo, Jacopo, Oliviero. Degree in Medicine, U. Bologna, Italy, 1989, postgrad. specialty in Neurology, 1993. Fellow Neurology Inst., U. Bologna, Italy, 1989-94, physician in charge sleep lab., 1994—; adv. Epilepsy Ctr. Neurology Inst., U. Bologna, 1994. Contbr. articles to profl. jours. Home: Via Carlo Cattaneo 34, 48100 Ravenna Italy Office: Neurology Inst U Bologna, Via Ugo Foscolo 7, 40123 Bologna Italy

PLENS, OLE EMIL, psychiatrist, administrator; b. Copenhagen, Denmark, Feb. 20, 1948; s. Erik Emil and Carla (Jeppesen) P. MD, U. Copenhagen, 1975. Rotating resident Danish and Swedish Hosps., 1975-78; trainee psychiat. open ward Helsingborg (Sweden) Hosp., 1980-82; cons. psychiatrist Helsingborg Hosp., 1982-83; head psychiatrist gero-psychiat. unit Herning (Denmark) Hosp., 1983-84, Helsingborg Hosp., 1986—; pvt. practice Angelholm, 1989—. Flight surgeon Royal Danish Air Force, 1978-79. Mem. European Psychogeriatric Assn., Swedish Med. Assn., Danish Gerontopsychiat. Club, Swedish Motor Club. Home: Kullabergsregen 11, 260 42 Molle Skane, Sweden Office: Storgatan 22, 262 32 Angelholm Skane, Sweden

PLEVRIS, JOHN (IOANNIS), gastroenterologist, educator; b. Athens, July 17, 1959; arrived in Scotland, 1987; s. Nicholas and Amalia (Petichaki) P.; m. Melpomeni Papaioannou, Mar. 6, 1986; children: Nicholas, Athanasios, Constantinos. Med. Degree, U. Athens, 1983, MD, 1994; PhD, U. Edinburgh, 1995. Resident Naval Mil. Hosp., Athens, 1985-86; asst. in gen. medicine Laikon Hosp., Athens, 1986-87; sr. house officer in medicine Royal Infirmary, Edinburgh, 1987-89; William Gibson fellow in gastroenterology U. Edinburgh/Royal Infirmary, 1989-92; registrar in gastroenterology, hepatology, liver transplant Royal Infirmary, Edinburgh, 1992-95; lectr. gastroenterology and hepatology U. Edinburgh, 1995—, supr. postgrad. students in medicine, 1992—. Contbr. over 35 articles to profl. jours. and books. U. Edinburgh scholar, 1989. Mem. Royal Coll. Physicians (U.K.), Royal Coll. Physicians (Edinburgh), Hellenic Soc. Gastroenterology, Brit. Soc. Gastroenterology, NY. Acad. Scis., European Assn. Study of the Liver. Christian Orthodox. Office: U Edinburgh Dept Medicine, 1 Lauriston Pl, Edinburgh EH3 9YW, Scotland

PLIMPTON, CALVIN HASTINGS, physician, university president; b. Boston, Oct. 7, 1918; s. George Arthur and Fanny (Hastings) P.; m. Ruth Talbot, Sept. 6, 1941; children: David, Thomas, George (dec.), Anne, Edward. B.A. cum laude, Amherst Coll., 1939; M.D. cum laude, Harvard, 1943, M.A., 1947; Med. Sci.D., Columbia, 1951; LL.D., Williams Coll., 1960, Wesleyan U., 1961, Doshisha U., Kyoto, Japan, 1962, St. Lawrence U., 1963, Amherst U., 1971; L.H.D., U. Mass., 1962; D.Sc., Rockford Coll., 1962, St. Mary's, 1963, Trinity Coll., 1966, Grinnell (Iowa) Coll., 1967; Litt.D., Am. Internat. Coll., 1965, Mich. State Coll., 1969; DSc, N.Y. Med. Coll., 1986. Diplomate: Nat. Bd. Med. Examiners, Am. Bd. Internal Medicine. Intern, asst. resident, resident medicine Presbyn. Hosp., N.Y.C., 1947-50; asst. attending physician Columbia-Presbyn. Med. Center, 1950-60; asso. medicine (Coll. Phys. and Surg.), 1950-59, asst. prof. clin. medicine, 1959-60; prof. medicine, chmn. dept. Am. U. Beirut, Am. U. Hosp., Beirut, Lebanon, 1957-59; pres. Amherst Coll., 1960-71; pres. Downstate Med. Center, SUNY, 1971-79, dean med. sch., 1971-74, 76-79, prof. medicine, 1971-82, prof. emeritus, 1982—; pres. Am. U., Beirut, 1984-87; vis. prof. Columbia Presbyn. Med. Center, 1976-77. Trustee Am. U., Beirut, 1960-90, trustee emeritus, 1990—, chmn. bd., 1965-82; trustee World Peace Found., 1962-77, Phillips Exeter Acad., 1963-76, Commonwealth Fund, 1962-83, Hampshire Coll., 1963-71, U. Mass., 1962-70, L.I. U., 1972-82, N.Y. Law Sch., 1976-84; mem. Harvard Bd. Overseers, 1969-75. Capt. U.S. Army, 1944-46, ETO. Decorated comdr. Order of Cedars Lebanon; recipient award Nat. Geog. Soc., award New Eng. Soc., John Phillips award Phillip Exeter Acad. Fellow ACP; mem. Am. Acad. Arts and Scis., Coun. Fgn. Rels., Soc. Mayflower Descs., Harvey Soc., Alpha Omega Alpha, Sigma Xi. Clubs: Century, Univ. (N.Y.C.), Charaka (N.Y.C.), Riverdale Yacht (N.Y.C.), Pilgrims (N.Y.C.); Tavern Boston. Home and office: 4600 Palisade Ave Bronx NY 10471-3508

PLOTKIN, GARY ROBERT, physician; b. Jersey City, June 2, 1944; s. Charles and Rose (Wexler) P. B.S., B.Ph., Rutgers U., 1967; M.D., N.J. Coll. Medicine, 1972. Diplomate Am. Bd. Internal Medicine; cert. subspecialty infectious diseases. Intern, Downstate Med. Ctr.-Kings County Hosp. Ctr., Bklyn. 1972-73, resident, 1973-75; fellow in infectious disease U. Fla., Shands Teaching Hosp., Gainesville, 1975-76, NYU-Bellevue Hosp., 1976-77; assoc. dept. infectious diseases Geisinger Med. Ctr., Danville, Pa., 1977-81; physician Trover Clinic, Madisonville, Ky., 1981-82, Danville Internal Medicine, Va., 1982-83; chief infectious diseases VA Med. Ctr., Wilkes-Barre, Pa., 1983-92 ; clin. asst. prof. dept. medicine Hahnemann U. Sch. Medicine, Phila., 1983-92; assoc. prof. dept. Emergency Medicine, St. Joseph Fatima Hosp., North Providence, R.I., 1992-95, East Naples Med. Ctr., Naples, Fla., 1996—. Contbr. articles to profl. jours., chpts. to books. Fellow ACP;

mem. Infectious Diseases Soc. Am., Am. Fedn. Clin. Research, Am. Thoracic Soc., Am. Soc. Microbiology, N.Y. Acad. Sci., Sigma Xi. Jewish. Home: 283 Edgewater Ct Marco Island FL 33937 Office: East Naples Med Ctr 5432 Rattlesnake Hammock Rd Naples FL 33962

PLOTKIN, STANLEY ALAN, medical virologist; b. N.Y.C., May 12, 1932; s. Joseph and Lee (Fishbein) P.; m. Susan Lannon, Nov. 24, 1979; children: Michael, Alec. BA, NYU, 1952; MD, SUNY, N.Y.C., 1956; MA (hon.), U. Pa., 1974. Diplomate Am. Bd. Pediatrics, Am. Acad. Pediatrics. Intern Cleve. Met. Gen. Hosp., 1956-57; resident pediatrics Phila. Children's Hosp., 1961-62, dir. div. infectious diseases, sr. physician, 1969-90; registrar Hosp. for Sick Children, London, 1962-63; assoc. mem. Wistar Inst., Phila., 1963-74, prof. virology, 1974—; asst. prof. pediatrics U. Pa., Phila., 1966-71, assoc. prof., 1971-74, prof., 1974-91; prof. emeritus, 1991—; assoc. chmn. dept. pediatrics U. Pa., Phila., 1986-88; med. and sci. dir. Pasteur-Mérieux-Connaught Labs., Marnes-la-Coquette, France, 1991—. Assoc. editor: Am. Jour. Epidemiology, 1967-87, Proc. Soc. Exptl. Biology and Medicine, 1968-85, Pediatric Infectious Disease jour., 1982-87, Vaccine jour., 1983—, Molecular and Cellular Probes jour., 1987—. Served as med. officer USPHS, 1957-60. Joseph P. Kennedy Found. grantee, 1964-66, Hartford Found. grantee, 1971-73, NIH grantee, 1973—; recipient Bruce medal ACP, 1987; named Disting. Physician Pediatric Infectious Diseases Soc., 1993. Mem. Soc. Pediatric Rsch., Am. Pediatric Soc., Infectious Diseases Soc. Am.,Am. Epidemiology Soc., Am. Soc. Microbiology, Am. Acad. Pediatrics (chmn. infectious diseases com. 1987-90). Home: 29 rue du, Général Delestraint, 75016 Paris France Office: Pasteur-Mérieux-, Connaught, 3 Av Pasteur, 92430 Marnes-la-Coquette France

PLOTNICK, GARY DAVID, cardiologist; b. Balt., Nov. 23, 1941; s. Alvin Bernard and Evelyn Ruth (Altschul) P.; m. Leslie Karcl Parker, Feb. 11, 1967; children: Michael, Daniel. BA, Johns Hopkins U., 1962; MD, U. Md., 1966. Resident U. Md. Hosp., Balt., 1966-72; gen. med. officer USN, Danang, Vietnam, 1968-69; rsch. fellow Johns Hopkins Hosp., Balt., 1972-74; from asst. prof. to prof. Sch. of Medicine U. Md., Balt., 1974—; assoc. prof. Johns Hopkins Sch. Medicine, 1988—; dir. echocardiography U. Md. Hosp., 1986—, dir. cardiology fellowship, 1987—; editorial bd. Jour. Am. Coll. Cardiology, 1987-93, Jour. Non-Invasive Cardiology, 1987—. Fellow Am. Coll. Cardiology, Coun. of Clinical Cardiology, Am. Coll. Physicians;mem. Am. Soc. Echocardiography (bd. dirs.). Democrat. Jewish. Home: 7918 Winterset Ave Baltimore MD 21208-3111 Office: Univ Hosp 22 S Greene St Baltimore MD 21201-1544

PLOTZ, PAUL HUNTER, research physician; b. Bklyn., Oct. 19, 1937; s. Milton B. and Helen (Ratnoff) P.; m. Judith Abrams, Sept. 1, 1963; children: John M.G., David A. AB, Harvard U., 1958, MD, 1963. Intern, resident Beth Israel Hosp., Boston, 1963-65; clin. assoc. NIH, Bethesda, Md., 1965-68; Helen Hay Whitney fellow Nat. Inst. for Med. Rsch., London, 1968-70; sr. investigator Arthritis and Rheumatism br. NIH, Bethesda, 1970-84, chief connective tissue diseases sect., 1984—; chief arthritis and rheumatism br. NIH, Bethesda, 1994—; clin. prof. Uniformed Svcs. U. Health Scis., Bethesda, 1983—. Contbr. chpts. to books, articles to profl. jours. Co-chmn. Com. of Concerned Scienetists, N.Y.C., 1985—. Capt. USPHS. Recipient prize Société Francaise de Rhumatologie, Paris, 1981, Philip Hench award Assn. Mil. Surgeons U.S., 1984, Outstanding Svc. medal USPHS, 1991. Fellow ACP (gov. for HHS 1990—); mem. Am. Soc. for Clin. Investigation, Am. Coll. Rheumatology, Am. Assn. Immunologists. Office: NIH Arthritis & Rheumatism Clin Ctr 9N244 Bethesda MD 20892-1820

PLOTZ, RICHARD DOUGLAS, pathologist; b. Bklyn., Aug. 15, 1948; s. Charles Mindell and Lucille (Weckstein) P.; m. Judith Anker, Mar. 28, 1971; children: Martha Anne, Michael David. AB cum laude, Harvard U., 1971; MD, U. Pitts., 1977; MPH, Boston U., 1992. Resident Brown U., Providence, 1977-81; staff pathologist Women & Infants Hosp., Providence, 1982-88; med. dir. Corning Metpath (formerly Damon Clin. Lab.), Westwood, Mass., 1988-95, CytoStat, Pawtucket, R.I., 1996—. Del. White Ho. Conf. on Libr. & Info. Svcs., Washington, 1979. Fellow Coll. Am. Pathologists (inspector lab. accreditation program); mem. New Eng. Soc. Pathologists, R.I. Med. Soc., R.I. Soc. Pathologists. Democrat. Jewish. Home: 104 11th St Providence RI 02906-2912 Office: CytoStat 129 School St Pawtucket RI 02860-5344

PLOURDE, SHARON K., nursing administrator; b. Washington, Apr. 13, 1961; d. William J. and Anita Faye (Pickett) Davis; m. Edward John Plourde, Jr., Oct. 26, 1984; children: Jennifer, Fawne, Megan. BSN, Alderson-Broaddus Coll., Philippi, W.Va., 1984. RN, Md. Staff nurse med.-surg. unit AMI Doctors' Hosp., Lanham, Md.; head nurse med-surg. pediatric units So. Md. Hosp., Clinton; supr. patient care St. Mary's Hosp., Leonardtown, Md.

PLUM, FRED, neurologist; b. Atlantic City, Jan. 10, 1924; s. Fred and Frances (Alexander) P.; children—Michael, Christopher. Carol; m. Susan Butler, Apr. 23, 1990. BA, Dartmouth Coll., 1944, postgrad., 1944-45; MD, Cornell U., 1947; MD (hon.), Karolinska Inst., Stockholm, 1982; DSc (hon.), L.I. U., 1990. Resident N.Y. Hosp., 1947-50, physician to outpatients, 1950-53, neurologist-in-chief, 1963—; instr. neurology Sch. Medicine Cornell U., 1950-53, Anne Parrish Titzell prof. neurology, 1963—, chmn. dept. neurology, 1963—; head neurology sect. U.S. Naval Hosp., St. Albans, N.Y., 1951-53; from asst. prof. to prof. neurology Sch. Medicine U. Wash., 1953-63; vis. scientist U. Lund, Sweden, 1970-71; vis. physician Rockefeller U. Hosp., 1975-85; assoc. neurosci. research program MIT and Rockefeller U., 1977-87; mem. neurology study sect., 1964-68, grad. tng. com., 1959-63, 71, nat. adv. council, 1977-81, Nat. Inst. Neurol., Communicative Disorders and Stroke, 84-86; past pres. McKnight Endowment Fund for Neurosci., 1986-90. Author: Diagnosis of Stupor and Coma, 1966, 3d edit., 1980, Clinical Management of Seizures, 1976, 2d edit., 1983, (with others) Cecil Essentials of Medicine, 1986, 3d edit., 1995; editor, contbg. author: Cecil's Textbook of Medicine, 1968, 2d edit., 1996; chief editor neurology sect. Contemporary Neurology series; editor: Recent Trends in Neurology, 1969, 2d edit., 1989, Brain Dysfunction in Metabolic Disorders, 1974; mem. editorial bd. Archives Neurology, 1958-68; chief editor, 1972-76; founding editor Annals of Neurology, 1977—; contbr. articles to scientific and profl. jours. Mem. Inst. of Medicine, Nat. Acad. Sci., Am. Neurol. Assn. (v.p. 1974-75, pres. 1976-77, Jacoby award 1984), Am. Acad. Neurology (past mem. council), Soc. Neurosci., Am. Soc. Clin. Investigation, Assn. Rsch. Nervous Mental Diseases (pres. 1973, 87), Assn. Am. Physicians, Alpha Omega Alpha; hon. mem. Can., Brit., French, Italian, Swiss neurol. socs. Office: Cornell U Medical Coll 1300 York Ave New York NY 10021-4805

PLUMB, VANCE JOHN, cardiologist, educator; b. Belleville, Ill., Sept. 13, 1948; s. Howard Earl and Elvira (Van Bockern) P.; m. Naonal Billie Newman, Jan. 31, 1970; children: Heather, Tara, John, Tyler. BS, Hampden-Sydney Coll., 1970; MD, Duke U., 1973. Diplomate Am. Bd. Internal Medicine, Am. Bd. Cardiovasc. Disease. Resident, then chief resident in internal medicine U. Ala., Birmingham, 1973-76, fellow in cardiology, 1977-79, instr. to assoc. prof. in medicine, 1976-89, prof., 1989—, assoc dir. divsn. cardiology, 1985—; chair clin. practice com. Kirkland Clinic, Birmingham, 1993-95. Contbr. numerous articles to profl. jours. Elder Presbyn. Ch., Birmingham, 1982—. Fellow Am. Heart Assn.(recipient tchg. award coun. clin. cardiology, 1990), Am. Coll. Cardiology; mem. ACP, N.Am. Soc. Pacing and Electrophysiology. Office: U Ala at Birmingham 321 K THT Birmingham AL 35294

PLUMMER, ALICE TOLBERT, psychiatrist; b. Washington, Aug. 21, 1953; d. Alvin Joseph and Cleora (Cato) Tolbert; m. Harold David Plummer, Dec. 24, 1977; children: David Joseph, Jessica Danielle. BA, Mt. Holyoke Coll., 1975; MD, George Washington U., 1979. Lic. physician, N.J., Pa. Intern Howard U. Hosp., Washington, 1979-80; resident St. Elizabeths Hosp., Washington, 1980-83; psychiatrist in charge vol. unit Nat. Health Svc. Corps Newark Beth Israel Med. Ctr., 1983-88; dir. psychiat. svcs. Morristown (N.J.) Meml. Hosp., 1988—; instr. clin. psychiatry U. Medicine and Dentistry N.J., Newark, 1986-88, Columbia U. Coll. Physicians and Surgeons, N.Y.C., 1990—; cons. Applied Skills Industries Lynch Programs, Huntington Valley, Pa., 1990-92, SPECTRUM for Living, Closter, N.J., 1995—; unit chief Pathways, 1992-94, clin. dir.; assoc. clin. dir. Outpatient Mental Health Svc. Ramapo Ridge Psychiat. Hosp., Christian Health Care Ctr., Wyckoff, N.J., 1994—.

PLUMMER, JACK MOORE, psychologist; b. Galveston, Tex., Apr. 19, 1940; s. Jack Moore and Sarah Carroll (Cochran) P.; m. Rose Marie Taylor, July 22, 1960; children: Cynthia Marie, Edward Moore, Elizabeth Anne, Sarah Lorraine, Jack Moore. BA, St. Mary's U., 1962; MS, Trinity U., 1968; PhD, Tex. Tech. U., 1969; AAS in Criminal Justice, Garland County Community Coll., 1978. Psychologist Okla. rehab. div. Okla. State Reformatory, Granite, 1968-69; dir. tng. Ark. Rehab. Rsch. and Tng. Ctr., Hot Springs, 1970-71; pvt. practice psychology, Hot Springs, 1971—; exec. dir. Plummer Assocs. for Consultation and Tng., 1982—; dir. Ark. Behavioral Svcs. Clinic, 1983—; exec. officer Tng. Inst. for Edn. in Security, 1983—; clin. dir. Transpersonal Psychology Inst., Pine Bluff, Ark., 1989-91; psychol. cons. to Rehab. Svcs., Dept. Correction, Probation and Parole Div., also to physicians, attys., cts., law enforcement agys.; instr. Garland County C.C., Hot Springs, 1973—; continuing edn. instr. nursing degree program Coll. St. Francis, Joliet, Ill., 1979—; cons. Parents Without Ptnrs. Mem. bd. L.P.N. nurse program Ouachita Vocat.-Tech. Sch., Hot Springs, 1979—. Fellow Ark. Psychol. Assn.; mem. Nat. Rehab. Assn., Nat. Rehab. Counseling Assn., Am. Psychol. Assn., Ark. Psychol. Assn. (chmn. fellow status rev. com. 1980, 81, chmn. profl. standards rev. com. 1982, 83), Hot Springs Psychol. Assn. (pres. 1979, 80), Internat. Soc. for Study Symbols, Elks, Lions. Democrat. Roman Catholic. Contbr. articles to profl. jours., chpt. in Handbook of Measurement and Evaluation in Rehabilitation. Address: 614 Ridgeview Dr Hot Springs National Park AR 71901-7901 Office: Health Support Svcs 500 Albert Pike Ste B Hot Springs National Park AR 71913

PLUNKETT, F.X., orthopedic surgeon; b. Pitts., Mar. 23, 1949; s. John F. and C. Inez (McCoy) P. BA, Yale U., 1971; MD, u. Pitts., 1975. Intern Ranchos Los Amigos Hosp., Downey, Calif., 1975-76, resident, 1976-77; resident in orthopedic surgery U. Pitts., 1977-80; pvt. practice Gateway Orthopedics, Inc., Pitts., 1980-86, Pitts., 1986-96; assoc. med. dir. MetraComp, Pitts., 1993-96, med. dir. nat. specialty rev. svcs., 1996—; bd. dirs. PMSLIC, Harrisburg, Pa.; clin. instr. U. Pitts. Sch. Medicine Dept. Orthopedic Surgery, 1980—. Mem. Am. Med. Soc., Allegheny County Med. Soc., Pa. Med. Soc., Am. Acad. Orthopedic Surgeons, Interstate Orthopedic Assn., Eastern Orthopedic Soc. Home: 12 Ellsworth Terr Pittsburgh PA 15213

PLUNKETT, MICHAEL C., psychotherapist; b. Nyack, N.Y., Feb. 23, 1953; s. Stephen J. Jr. and Naomi M. (Davies) P.; m. Barbara E. Plunkett, Sept. 2, 1983; 1 child, Joshua E. BSBA, St. Thomas Aquinas Coll., 1975; MA in Psychology, U. No. Colo., 1986. Lic. profl. counselor, Colo.; cert. addiction counselor, Colo., instr. in prevention of HIV disease among substance abusers, Nat. Inst. Drug Abuse, instr. in outreach and retention of methadone clients. Diagnostic coord. El Paso County Dept. Health and Environ./McMaster Ctr., Colorado Springs, 1987-95, prevention & outreach supr. Prevention HIV IHEPB among IDUs; instr. psychology Pikes Peak C.C., Colorado Springs, 1988—; mem. Colorado Springs HIV Edn. and Prevention Consortium. Bd. dirs. So. Colo. AIDS Project, HIV Edn. and Prevention Consortium, Colorado Springs, 1995; mem. ad hoc com. HIV Prevention Cmty. Planning Com., 1994; bd. dirs. Pikes Peak region Nat. Coun. Alcoholism and Drug Dependency, 1988-91, vice-chmn., 1990; mem. subcom. on needle exch. Gov.'s AIDS Coun.; active Coloradans Working Together, 1995—, Safety Network Project, 1996; mem. subcom. needle exch. Govs. Aid Coun. Office: El Paso County Health and Environ 301 S Union Blvd Colorado Springs CO 80910-3123

PO, JOANNA MALATA VILLAREÑA, nursing administrator; b. Iloilo, The Philippines, Sept. 11, 1943; came to U.S., 1969; d. Vivencio and Mercedes (Malata) V.; m. Antonio Ty Po, Jan. 31, 1970; children: Joanne, Jeanne. Student pre-nursing, U. Philippines, 1962-64; diploma in nursing, Abad Santos Ednl. Instn., Quezon City, The Philippines, 1967; BS in Nursing, Philippine Women's U., Manila, 1968; MS in Nursing, Tex. Woman's U., Houston, 1985. RN, Tex, advanced practice nurse, clin. nurse specializing in med.-surg. nursing, Tex.; cert. med.-surg. nurse ANCC, cardiovascular specialist Meth. Hosp. Asst. headnurse/ charge nurse Meth. Hosp. Cardiovascular Unit, Houston, 1969-74; head nurse Meth. Hosp. Cardiovascular Intermediate Care Unit, Houston, 1974-78; headnurse/ asst. nurse mgr. Meth. Hosp. Dept. Radiology, Houston, 1978-94; divsn. nurse mgr. U. Tex. M.D. Anderson Cancer Ctr., Diagnostic Imaging, Houston, 1995—. Author: (manual) Radiology Nursing Resource Manual, 1982, rev. 2d edit., 1987; inventor: Rolling pole that holds intravenous bottles and blood pressure measurer, 1980. Named Hartmann Centennial Lectr. Radiology Centennial Inc., Am. Coll. Radiology, Chgo., 1995. Mem. Am. Radiol. Nurses Assn. (mem. exec. bd. 1994—, lifetime, charter mem.), Tex. Gulf Coast Radiology Nurses Chpt. (bd. dirs. 1978—), Philippine Nurses Assn. Met. Houston (Leadership award 1984, Mgmt. Excellence award 1994). Republican. Roman Catholic. Office: U Tex M D Anderson Cancer Ctr Box 57 1515 Holcombe Blvd Houston TX 77030

PO, VICENTE H., surgeon; b. Manila, The Philippines, July 24, 1928; came to U.S., 1956; s. Sun Hang and Yu Chian Po; m. Lorraine Adler, Jan. 27, 1961; children: Michele, Jennifer. MD, U. Santos Tomas, 1956. Diplomate Am. Bd. Gen. Surgery, Thoracic Cardio Vascular Surgery. Intern Little Co. of Mary Hosp., Evergreen Park, Ill., 1956-57; resident Bronx (N.Y.)-Lebanon Hosp. Ctr., 1957-61, Latter Day Saints Hosp., Salt Lake City, 1961-63; staff surgeon McKnight T.B. Sanitorium, San Angelo, Tex., 1963-64, VA Hosp., Topeka, 1965-68, Ingals Meml. Hosp., Harvey, Ill., 1968—; surgeon South Suburban Hosp., Hazel Crest, Ill., 1970-91. Contbr. articles to profl. jours. Mem. AMA, ACS, Ill. State Med. Soc., Chgo. Med. Soc. Home: 230 Brenner Ct Crete IL 60417 Office: 3235 Vollmer Rd Flossmoor IL 60422

POBER, ZALMON, physiologist, educator; b. Phila., July 31, 1939; s. Benjamin and Sarah Ann (Marcus) P.; m. Cheryl Ann Goodman, June 4, 1969. BS, Drexel U., 1962; MBA, Western New Eng. Coll., 1984; MS, Thomas Jefferson U., 1965, PhD, 1968. Physiologist R&D Command U.S. Army, Natick, Mass., 1968-76; asst. prof. Mass. Coll. Pharmacy, Springfield, 1976-81, assoc. prof., 1981—; cons. Continuing Profl. Edn. Svcs., Springfield, 1984—. Contbr. articles to profl. jours.; patentee in field. Mem. Am. Physiol. Soc., N.Y. Acad. Sci., Sigma Xi. Home: 5 Applewood Cir Easthampton MA 01027-1309 Office: Mass Coll Pharmacy 24 Bellamy Rd Springfield MA 01119-2416

POBERESKIN, LOUIS HOWARD, neurosurgeon; b. Chgo., Aug. 16, 1948; s. Meyer and Sarah P.; m. Laurelle Baxter, Nov. 4, 1980; children: Sarah, Lisa. BS, Case Western Res. U., Cleve., 1970; MD, Case Western Res. U., 1974. Neurosurgeon U. Va., Charlottesville, 1974-80, Cambridge U., Eng., 1980-85, Derriford Hosp., Plymouth, Eng., 1985—. Mem. Alpha Omega Alpha, Phi Beta Kappa. Office: Dept Neurosurgery, Derriford Hospital, Plymouth England PL6 8DM

POBLETE, RITA MARIA BAUTISTA, physician, educator; b. Manila, May 19, 1954; came to U.S., 1980; d. Juan Gonzalez and Rizalina (Bautista) Poblete. BS, U. Philippines, 1974, MD, 1978. Diplomate Am. Bd. Internal Medicine and Infectious Disease. Intern, resident Wayne State U./Detroit Med. Ctr., 1982-85, fellow in infectious disease, 1986-87; fellow in infectious disease Chgo. Med. Sch./VA Hosp., North Chicago, Ill., 1985-86; fellow in spl. immunology U. Miami (Fla.)-Jackson Meml. Hosp., 1987-89; adj. clin. instr. dept. of medicine U. Miami, 1989-90, asst. prof. medicine, 1990-94; infectious disease cons. Cedars Med. Ctr. and Mercy Hosp., Miami, 1994—. Contbr. articles to med. jours. Mem. Am. Soc. for Microbiology, Am. Soc. Internal Medicine, World Found. Successful Women. Office: Cedars Med Ctr 1295 NW 14th St Ste E Miami FL 33125-1600

POCCHIARI, MAURIZIO, neuroscientist; b. Rome, June 25, 1953; s. Francesco and Giuliana (Tommasi) P.; m. Myriam Tinti, Mar. 4, 1978; children: Eleonora, Lorenza. MD, Cath. U., Rome, 1977, specialist in neurology, 1981. Postdoctoral fellow Nat. Rsch. Coun., Rome, 1978-80; asst. prof. neurology Cath. U., Rome, 1980-87; assoc. prof. microbiology U. Lecce, Italy, 1987-91; assoc. prof. gen. pathology U. Aquila, Italy, 1991; head rsch. lab. of virology Inst. Superiore di Sanitá, Rome, 1992—; vis. fellow NIH, Bethesda, Md., 1980-83; chief Nat. Registry Creutzfeldt-Jakob Disease, Rome, 1993—. Contbr. articles to profl. jours. Mem. Am. Soc. for Microbiology, Am. Soc. for Virology. Home: Via Val Brembana 13, 00141 Rome Italy Office: Inst Superiore di Sanitá, Viale Regina Elena 299, 00161 Rome Italy

POCCIA, DOMINIC LOUIS, biology educator; b. Utica, N.Y., Aug. 8, 1945; s. Louis Joseph and Frances Marie (Surace) P.; m. Alison Gordon, May 18, 1971 (div. 1979); 1 child, Joseph; m. Clara Pinto Correia, Aug. 20, 1994. BS, Union Coll., 1967; AM, Harvard U., 1968, PhD, 1971; AM (hon.), Amherst Coll., 1987. Asst. prof. Wellesley (Mass.) Coll., 1971-72, SUNY, Stony Brook, 1974-78; asst. prof. Amherst (Mass.) Coll., 1978-82, assoc. prof., 1982-87, chair, biology dept., 1983-85, prof., 1987—; vis. scholar U. Calif., Berkeley, 1986-87; vis. prof. Stanford U. Hopkins Marine Sta., Pacific Grove, Calif., 1988; adj. prof. U. Mass., Amherst, 1984—. Author: Molecular Aspects of Spermatogenesis, 1994; contbr. articles to profl. jours.; assoc. editor Jour. Exptl. Zool., Molecular Reprodn. Devel. Recipient grants NIH, 1975-86, 89, 91, 93-94, NSF, 1990—. Mem. Am. Soc. Cell Biology, Phi Beta Kappa, Sigma Xi.

POCKROS, PAUL JOSEPH, gastroenterologist; b. Cin., July 1, 1952; s. Marvin Ned Pockros and Sophia (Mansbach) Ralson; m. Ann Marie Whealen, July 6, 1980; children: Lara, Jacob, Alana. BA, U. Calif. San Diego, 1974; MD, U. So. Calif., 1978. Diplomate Am. Bd. Gastroenterology, Am. Bd. Internal Medicine. Intern in internal medicine U. So. Calif. Med. Ctr., L.A., 1978-79; resident in internal medicine USC Med. Ctr., L.A., 1979-81; from fellow in gastroenterology to gastroenterologist Scripps Clinic & Rsch. Found., La Jolla, Calif., 1981—; fellow hepatology USC/Rancho Los Amigos Hosp., 1984-85; head divsn. gastro/hepatology Scripps Clinic & Rsch. Ctr., 1996—; med. dir., liver transplantation co-dir. Liver Disease Ctr., Scripps Clinic & Rsch. Ctr. Founding mem. Am. Liver Found., 1989. Fellow Am. Coll. Physicians; mem. Am. Assn. Study of Liver Disease, Am. Gastroenterology Assn., Am. Soc. Transplant Physicians, Am. Liver Found. (bd. dirs. 1990—), S.D. Gastroenterol. Soc. (pres. 1992). Democrat. Jewish. Home: PO Box 9905 Rancho Santa Fe CA 92067 Office: Scripps Clinic 10666 N Torrey Pines Rd La Jolla CA 92037

POCOSKI, DAVID JOHN, cardiologist; b. Waterbury, Conn., July 15, 1945; s. Edward J. and Stella E. (Kolpa) P.; m. Madelyn M. Pocoski, Sept. 25, 1971; 1 child, Sarah C. BA, U. Conn., 1967; MD magna cum laude, Upstate Med. Ctr., Syracuse, N.Y., 1971. From intern to fellow in cardiology U. Rochester, N.Y.; pres. Osler Clinic of Medicine, Melbourne, Fla. Maj. USAF, 1974-76. Mem. AMA; Fellow Am. Coll. Cardiologists. Republican. Roman Catholic. Office: 930 S Harbor City Blvd Melbourne FL 32901-1963

PODA, GEORGE ALEX, retired occupational medicine physician; b. Jamestown, N.Y., Apr. 26, 1921; s. Alex Legor and Olympia (Nicole) P.; m. Anna Michele; children: George Jr. (dec.), Deborah Ann, Steven Michael. MD, U. Buffalo, 1945. Chief resident Women's Homeopathic Hosp., Phila., 1946-48; sr. physician DuPont, Buffalo, Newport, Ind., 1948-52; lt. USNR, Bremerton, Wash., 1952-55; from sr. physician to med. supt. DuPont Savannah River Plant, Aiken, S.C., 1955-86. Fellow Am. Occupl. Environ. Medicine. Home: 12 Longwood Dr Aiken SC 29803

PODGOR, MARVIN JAY, medical researcher; b. Oak Ridge, Tenn.; s. Samuel and Charlotte L. Podgor; m. Debbie A. Goldscheider; children: Melinda, David. BA, U. Rochester, 1973; MS, George Washington U., 1978, PhD, 1992. Statistician Nat. Eye Inst., Bethesda, Md., 1973-91, math. statistician, 1991-95; chief statis. methods and analysis sect. Nat. Eye Inst., Bethesda, 1995—. Assoc. editor Am. Jour. of Epidemiology; contbr. articles to profl. jours. Mem. Am. Statis. Assn., Internat. Biometric Soc. Office: Nat Inst of Health MSC 2510 31 Center Dr Bethesda MD 20892-2510

PODGORNY, GEORGE, emergency physician; b. Tehran, Iran, Mar. 17, 1934; s. Emanuel and Helen (Parsian) P.; came to U.S., 1954, naturalized, 1973. B.S., Maryville Coll., 1958; postgrad. Bowman Gray Sch. Medicine, 1958; M.D., Wake Forest U., 1962; m. Ernestine Koury, Oct. 20, 1962; children: Adele, Emanuel II, George, Gregory. Intern in surgery N.C. Bapt. Hosp., Winston-Salem, 1962-63, chief resident in gen. surgery, 1966-67, in cardiothoracic surgery, 1967-69; sr. med. examiner Forsyth County, N.C., 1972—; dir. dept. emergency medicine Forsyth Meml. Hosp., Winston-Salem, 1974-80; sec.-treas. Forsyth Emergency Services, Winston-Salem, 1970-80; clin. prof. emergency medicine East Carolina U. Sch. Medicine, Greenville, 1984—, chmn. residency rev. com. on emergency medicine, 1980-88; mem. Accreditation Coun. for Grad. Med. Edn. Dir. Emergency Med. Svcs. Project Region II of N.C., 1975—; chmn. bd. trustees Emergency Medicine Found.; chmn. residency rev. com. emergency medicine Accreditation Coun. Grad. Med. Edn.; founder Western Piedmont Emergency Med. Svcs. Coun., 1973; mem. N.C. Emergency Med. Svcs. Adv. Coun., 1976-81; assoc. prof. clin. surgery Bowman Gray Sch. Medicine, Wake Forest U., Winston-Salem, 1979—. Bd. dirs. Piedmont Health Systems Agy., 1975-84; trustee Forsyth County Hosp., Authority, 1974-75; bd. dirs. N.C. Health Coordinating Coun., 1975-82, Medic Alert Found. Internat. Fellow Internat. Coll. Surgeons, Internat. Coll. Angiology, Royal Soc. Health (Great Britain), Royal Soc. Medicine, Southeastern Surg. Congress; mem. Am. Coll. Emergency Physicians (charter, pres. 1978-79), AMA, (chmn. coun. of sect. emergency medicine 1978-90, alt. del. for Am. Coll. Emergency Physicians, 1990—), Am. Bd. Emergency Medicine (pres. 1976-81). Contbr. articles to profl. publs. on trauma, snake bite and history of medicine; editorial bd. Annals of Emergency Medicine, Med. Meetings. Home and Office: 2115 Georgia Ave Winston Salem NC 27104-1917

PODGORNY, RICHARD JOSEPH, biologist, science administrator; b. Chgo., Jan. 27, 1944; s. Leon and Mary Agatha (Gryzik) P.; m. Dorothy Mary Dorece, June 11, 1966; 1 child, Nicole Marie. BA, St. Mary's Coll., 1966; MS, Am. U., 1971; PhD, Georgetown U., 1975; postgrad., Fed. Exec. Inst., 1989. Quality control supr. Capital Aerosol Packaging Co., Melrose Park, Ill., 1965-66; Peace Corps vol., Adi Teclesan, Ethiopia, 1966-68; sci. dept. chmn. and tchr. Western Sr. High Sch., Washington, 1968-76; dir. marine scis. D.C. Pub. Sch. Systems, 1976-79; mgr. nat. sanctuaries programs U.S. Dept. Commerce, NOAA, Washington, 1979-82, chief user affairs/mktg. unit, external affairs staff, 1983-86, chief internat. affairs Nat. Ocean Service, 1986-94, sr. advisor, pres. Coun. Sustainable Devel., 1994—; U.S. del. to Intergovtl. Oceanographic Commn., 1986—, South Pacific Commn., 1989—; bd. dirs. Pacific Congress Internat., 1987—; lectr. in field; cons. in field. Author: Introduction to Marine Science, 1977; Ocean Ecology, 1978; contbr. articles to profl. jours. Vice pres., bd. dirs. Friends of Arlington County Parks, 1982-86; chmn. bd. dirs. planning com. Burgundy Farm Country Day Sch., Inc., 1980-86. NSF scholar, 1969-71; Georgetown U. fellow, 1972-75; recipient service commendation Emperor Haile Sallassie, 1967. Mem. AAAS, Oceanography Soc., Marine Tech. Soc., Sigma Xi. Roman Catholic. Clubs: Capital Yacht, Skyline Health and Racquet. Home: 4858 28th St S Arlington VA 22206-1370 Office: US Dept Commerce NOAA Office Sustainable Devel Rm 5222 14th St & Constitution Ave NW Washington DC 20011-6930

PODGORSAK, MATTHEW BORUT, clinical physicist, educator; b. Jesenice, Slovenia, May 22, 1966; came to U.S., 1969; s. Ervin B. and Ana (Ambrozic) P.; m. Kristine Ann Knudson, Dec. 23, 1992; children: Alexander Rudolf, Anthony Thomas. BSc, McGill U., Montreal, 1987, MSc, 1990; PhD, U. Wis., 1993. Clin. physicist Hotel-Dieu Hosp., Montreal, 1990; clin. physicst, asst. prof. Roswell Park Cancer Inst., Buffalo, 1993—. Recipient 3d prize Young Investigators' Symposium, Am. Assn. Physicists in Medicine, 1990. Home: 50 Spring Meadow Dr Williamsville NY 14221 Office: Roswell Park Cancer Inst Elm And Carlton St Buffalo NY 14263-0001

PODHORETZ, HARRIETTE, psychologist, psychoanalyst; b. N.Y.C., Nov. 28, 1932; d. John and Leah (Bressler) Miller; m. Jan. 22, 1958; children: Jane, James. BS in Edn., CCNY, 1953, MA in English Edn., 1966; profl. diploma in psychology, Fordham U., N.Y.C., 1973; PhD in Psychology, Fordham U., 1974. Lic. psychologist, N.Y.; grad. psychoanalyst. Tchr. N.Y.C. Pub. Schs., 1953-59; psychotherapist Jamaica Ctr. Psychotherapy, N.Y.C., 1968-72; psychotherapist in pvt. practice N.Y.C., 1972-75, pvt. practice psychology, 1975—; pvt. practice psychology Scarsdale, N.Y., 1979-96; tng. analyst Nat. Psychol. Assn. for Psychoanalysis, 1976—. Contbr. chpts. to books. Mem. APA, N.Y. Psychol. Assn., N.Y. State Psychol. Assn., Nat. Psychol. Assn. for Psychoanalysis. Home: 300 E 59th St # 1701 New York NY 10022 Office: 51 E 42nd St New York NY 10017-5404

PODIMATAS, YIANNIS, pharmacist; b. Karditsa, Greece, July 11, 1956; s. Aggelos and Photini (Velimezi) P. BPharm., Athens (Greece) U., 1978. Sci. collaborator Med. Sch. Athens U., 1978-81; clint svc. mgr. A.G. Nielsen Hellas Ltd., Athens, 1981-83; product mgr. BDF, Athens, 1983-88, SmithKline Beecham CISA, Athens, 1988—. Home: Hymetus 80A, 155 61 Cholargos Athens, Greece Office: Smithkline Beecham CISA, Xanthou 32 Athens, 154 51 N Psychico Greece

PODOJIL, RONALD EUGENE, physician assistant; b. Saulte Ste Marie, Mich., Sept. 14, 1950; s. Lawrence Robert and Evelyn Anesthasia (Lomand) P.; m. Susan Hortick, Mar. 30, 1972 (div. Jan. 1985); children: Ronald Arthur, Kelly Rene; m. Sharon Jean Baluha, Mar. 7, 1985; children: Edward Lawrence, Andrew Robert. BS in Med. Sci., U. Nebr., 1977; MS in Clin. Counseling, Our Lady of the Lake U., San Antonio, 1984. Commd. 2d lt. USAF, 1970, advanced through grades to capt.; physician asst. Primary Care, USAF Hosp., Dyess AFB, Tex., 1976-79, Kelly AFB, Tex., 1979-84; sr. physicians asst. Family Practice, USAF Clinic, Bolling AFB, 1984-86, Primary Care, Malcol Grow Med. Ctr., Andrews AFB, Md., 1986-90; physicians asst. Kaiser Permante, Landover, Md., 1989-90; physician asst., admission coord. Dutcher Treatment Ctr., Middletown, Conn., 1990-91; physician asst. Chatham Family Practice, East Hampton, Conn., 1991-96, Pequot Health Ctr, Groton, Conn., 1995—; clin. preceptor Quinniac Coll. Pa. Program, Hamden, Conn., 1995—. Cub master Boy Scouts Am., San Antonio, 1980-82, Troop 979, Clinton, Md., 1986-89; various ch. coms. St. Luke Luth. Ch., Gales Ferry, Conn., 1982—. Fellow Am. Acad. of Physician Asst., Conn. Acad. of Physician Assts., Soc. South Tex. Physician Asst. (pres. 1979-82). Democrat. Lutheran. Home: 44 Daisy Hill Dr Oakdale CT 06370

PODOLOFF, DONALD ALAN, physician; b. N.Y.C., Dec. 23, 1938; s. Samuel and Ruth (Satz) P.; m. Mary Ellen Sutton, Jan. 14, 1966; children: John, Andrew, Jennifer, Michael. BA with honors, NYU, 1959; MD, SUNY, N.Y.C., 1964. Diplomate Am. Bd. Internal Medicine, Am. Bd. Radiology, Am. Bd. Nuclear Medicine. Intern Beth Israel Med. Ctr., N.Y.C., 1964, resident internal medicine, 1965-68, chief resident, 1967-68; resident diagnostic radiology Lackland AFB, Wilford Hall USAF Hosp., San Antonio, 1970-73; dir., dept. nuclear medicine Diagnostic Clinic of Houston, 1975-86; dep. chmn., dept. nuclear medicine M.D. Anderson Cancer Ctr., Houston, 1993—, head sect. clin. nuclear medicine dept. nuclear medicine, 1989-93. Contbr. articles to profl. jours.; contbr.: (book) Critical Reviews in Diagnostic Imaging, 1989, Advances in Nuclear Medicine, 1988. Mem. Congregation Beth Israel, Friends of KUHF. Lt. col. USAF, 1968-75. Mem. AMA, Am. Coll. Nuclear Physicians, Soc. Nuclear Medicine, Radiol. Soc. N.Am., Am. Coll. Radiology, Tex. Assn. of Physicians in Nuclear Medicine. Jewish. Home: 921 W Main St Houston TX 77006 Office: MD Anderson Cancer Ctr 1515 Holcombe Blvd Houston TX 77030-4009

PODRUG, DINKO, psychiatrist, educator; b. Zagreb, Croatia, Feb. 1, 1952; came to U.S., 1977.; MD, U. Zagreb, 1975; Med ScD, SUNY, Bklyn., 1988. Diplomate Am. Bd. Psychiatry and Neurology. Resident in psychiatry NYU-Bellevue Med. Sch., N.Y.C., 1977-81; rsch. fellow SUNY Health Scis. Ctr., Bklyn., 1981-85, attending psychiatrist, 1981—, dir. psychiatry clerkship, 1985-88, clin. assoc. prof., 1991, dir. inpatient psychiatry, 1996—; pvt. practice, N.Y.C., 1981—. Co-author: Transference in Brief Psychotherapy, 1985. Office: 52 E End Ave New York NY 10028-7954

PODURI, KANAKADURGA RAO, physician; b. Attili, Andhra, India, Jan. 21, 1944; came to U.S., 1970; d. Sri Ramarao and Sita (Pusuluri) Ayyagari; m. S.R.S. Rao Poduri, Aug. 22, 1970; children—Annapurna, S. Ramgopal. Student Andhra U., Waltair, India, 1961; M.B.B.S., Karnatak U., Hubli, India, 1970; M.D., SUNY, 1984. Diplomate Am. Bd. Phys. Medicine and Rehab. Extern St. Mary's Hosp., Rochester, N.Y., 1971-72, intern, 1972-73, resident in phys. medicine and rehab. Strong Meml. Hosp., Rochester, 1976-80; clin. instr., asst. physician U. Rochester Med. Ctr., 1981—; med. dir. Rochester Rehabilitation Ctr., 1986—; clin. faculty Strong Meml. Hosp., Rochester, 1981—; clin. faculty rehab. unit area hosps., Rochester, 1981—, cons., 1981—, clin. asst. prof., 1987—. Mem. AMA (clin. instr. 1981—, physician's recognition award 1980, 83, asst. prof. 1980, 83, 86, 89, 92, 95), Med. Women's Assn. Rochester, Am. Acad. Phys. Medicine and Rehab. Hindu. Home: 66 Irving Rd Rochester NY 14618-2306 Office: Rochester Rehabilitation Ctr 1000 Elmwood Ave Rochester NY 14620-3004

POEPPEL, ERNST, medical psychologist; b. Schwessin, Pomerania, Germany, Apr. 29, 1940; s. Ernst and Elfriede (Bartelt) P.; children: David, Julie, Lili. PhD, Innsbruck (Austria) U., 1968; privatdozent, Med. Sch. Munich, 1974; univ.-dozent, Philos. Faculty, Innsbruck, 1976. Researcher Max-Planck-Soc., Andechs, Fed. Republic Germany, 1965-70; rsch. assoc. dept. psychology MIT, Cambridge, Mass., 1971-73; staff scientist Neurosci. Rsch. Program, Boston, 1972-73; scientist Max-Planck-Soc., Munich, 1974-76; prof. med. psychology Med. Faculty, Munich, 1976—; chmn. Inst. Med. Psychology, Munich, 1977—. Author: Lust & Schmerz, 1982/93, Grenzen d. Bewusstseins, 1985, English edit., Mediz. Psychol., 1990. With reserves German Navy, 1961-62. Recipient Levinson award Am. Poetry Assn., 1983, Purkinje medal Czechoslovak Medical Soc., 1988. Mem. German Soc. for Med. Psychology. (pres. 1991—). Office: Forschungszentrum Jülich, Postfach 1913, D-2425 Jülich Germany

POGÁTSA, GÁBOR, internist; b. Budapest, Feb. 25, 1932; s. Jozsef and Paula (Toth) P.; m. Gizella Pogátsa, July 31, 1957; children: Adrienn, Marta, Balazs. MD, Semmelweis U., 1956, internist, 1960; PhD, Hungarian Acad. Sci., 1968, DSc, 1980. Intern, resident 3rd Med. Clinic Semmelweis U., Budapest, 1956-59, asst. prof., 1959-67; prof. Semmelweis U., Budapest, 1992—; sr. mem. Nat. Inst. Cardiology, Budapest, 1967-80, head rsch. dept., 1980-92; dep. mgr. Hungarian Ctr. Clin. Pharmacy, Budapest, 1986-91; dep. chief mgr. Nat. Inst. Cardiology, 1993—; mem. adv. bd. Jour. Exptl. Clin. Cardiology, 1993-94. Contbr. chpts. to books. Mem. St. Luke's Soc. Hungarian Physicians (pres. 1990—), Conservative Com. Nat. Sci. Rsch. Fund (pres. 1989—), Diabetes Com. Nat. Inst. Internat. Med. Paed. (pres. 1989—), Hungarian Diabetes Assn. (v.p. 1987—), Hungarian Soc. Cardiology (mem. ethical sect. 1987). Roman Catholic. Home: 28 Maros, H 1122 Budapest Hungary Office: Nat Inst Cardiology, 29-31 Haller, H-1096 Budapest Hungary

POGO, GUSTAVE JAVIER, cardiothoracic surgeon; b. Buenos Aires, Feb. 7, 1957; came to U.S., 1964; s. Angel Oscar and Beatriz (Garcia-Tuñon) P.; m. Janis Teitler, Feb. 17, 1983; children: Michael Tyler, Katherine Elizabeth. BA, NYU, 1979, MD, 1983. Gen. surgery resident North Shore Univ. Hosp., Manhasset, N.Y., 1983-88; cardiothoracic surgery resident Mt. Sinai Sch. Medicine, N.Y.C., 1988-91; attending, cardiothoracic surgery North Shore Univ. Hosp., Manhasset, 1991—. Contbr. articles to profl. jours. Fellow ACS, Am. Coll. Chest Physicians, Am. Coll. Cardiology; mem. Soc. Thoracic Surgery. Office: North Shore Univ Hosp 300 Community Dr Manhasset NY 11030-3801

POGORELEC, EUGENE DOMINIC, physician; b. Passaic, N.J., Aug. 5, 1953; s. Albert Frank and Anna Emily (Paciga) P.; m. Irene Dobko, Dec. 27, 1975; children: Joshua M., Jordan M., Jeremy M., Lauren M., Evan J. Student, Marietta Coll., 1971-74; Do, Kirksville Coll. Osteo. Med., 1978. Intern Doctors Hosp. of Stark County, Massillon, Ohio, 1978-79; pres. Family Practice Assocs., Inc., Massillon, 1979—, Diversified Health Care, Inc., Massillon, 1980—. Fellow Am. Coll. Osteo. Family Physicians (cert., bd. govs. 1993—), Am. Osteo. Assn., Ohio Osteo. Assn. (pres. 1995—), Kirksville Coll. Osteo. Medicine Alumni Assn. (pres. 1994-95). Office: Family Practice Assocs Inc 2300 Wales Rd Massillon OH 44646

POHL, ROBERT BRYANT, psychiatrist, researcher; b. Windsor, Ont., Can., Sept. 6, 1948; s. John Bryant and Jeannette (Demers) P.; m. Linda Therese Ray; children: Steven, Kristin, Elisabeth. MD, Wayne State U., 1973. Diplomate Am. Bd. Psychiatry and Neurology. Resident in psychiatry Lafayette Clinic, Detroit, 1973-76; asst. prof. Wayne State U., Detroit, 1978-87, assoc. prof., 1987-91, prof., 1991—, dir. psychiat. residency programs, 1982-93; dir. outpatient dept. Lafayette Clinic, Detroit, 1979-92, interim assoc. chmn. dept. psychiatry, 1990-94; dir. Univ. Psychiatric Ctr., Detroit, 1993-95; Contbr. articles to profl. jours. Mem. Am. Psychiat. Assn., Soc. Biol. Psychiatry, Collegium Internat. Neuro-Psychopharmacologicum. Office: Univ Psychiatric Ctr 2751 E Jefferson Ave Ste 200 Detroit MI 48207-4100

POHL, SHARON RENEE, optometrist; b. Coldwater, Ohio, May 9, 1967; d. Carl Henry and MaryAnn Bernadine P.; m. David Allen Berchtold, July 17, 1993. BS in Physiol. Optics, Ohio State U., 1990; OD, The Ohio State U., 1992. Resident in rehabilitative optometry U. Calif., Berkeley, 1993; apprentic optician Pearle Vision Franchise, Columbus, Ohio, 1990-92; low vision residency VA, Palo Alto, Calif., 1992-93; primary eye care optometry Royal Optical, Waukegan, Ill., 1993-94; primary eye care cons. Dr. Walter Fried, Gurnee, Ill., 1994; contact lens cons. Dr. Walter Fried, Gurnee, 1995; low vision optometrist Chgo. Lighthouse for the Blind, 1994—; low vision and contect lens cons. Med. Eye Svcs., Ltd., Gurnee, Ill., 1995—; cons. VISX, San Jose, Calif., 1993; continuing edn. class spkr. VA Hosp., Menlo Park, Calif., 1993; continuing edn. lectr. Discovery 95 The Third Low Vision Conf., Chgo., 1995; cmty. svc. lectr. Insights: Learning About and Managing Low Vision, Chgo., 1995, lectr. in field. Mem. The Ohio State U. Alumni Assn., Columbus, 1990—; scholarship chmn. Great Lakes Officers and Spouses Assn., Great Lakes, Ill., 1994—; vol. I CARE Internat., 1993; student vol. Optometric Svcs. for Humanity, 1988-92. Recipient Davisson Hanley Alumni scholarship Ohio State U. Alumni Assn., 1985, 86, Ann Tweedale Alumni scholarship, 1987, 88, scholarship in optometry Ohio State U. Coll. of Optometry, 1991, 92. Mem. Am. Optometric Found. (William Feinbloom scholarship 1992), Ohio State U. Optometry Alumni Assn. (life), Ill. Vol. of Optometric Svcs. for Humanity, . Roman Catholic. Office: Chgo Lighthouse for People Who Are Blind 1850 W Roosevelt Rd Chicago IL 60608

POHLMAN, JANET ELIZABETH, healthcare executive, consultant; b. N.Y.C., Oct. 29, 1938. Diploma in nursing, NYU, 1959, MA, 1981; BA, Queens Coll., 1977; cert. ergonomics in occupl. health, Rutgers U.; cert. EPA hazardous waste mgmt., Harvard U.; cert. advanced safety, Nat. Safety Coun.; cert. radiol. safety tng., Ga. State U.; cert. CPR, emergency cardiac care, Am. Heart Assn.; cert. compliance course for safety officers, U.S. Dept. Labor; cert. asbestos safety tng., N.Y. Dept. Health. RN, N.J., N.Y., Mass.; cert. occupl. health nurse, safety profl., hazard control mgr., occupl. hearing conservationist. Staff nurse Elmhurst (N.Y.) Gen. Hosp., 1959-63; pvt. practice spl. nurse, 1963-74; occupl. health nurse Allied Stores Corp., Flushing, N.Y., 1974-77; staff nurse N.Y. Telephone, N.Y.C. 1977-79, paramedic svcs. asst. supr., 1979-81, paramed. svcs. supr., 1981-83; assoc. dir. corporate safety and health NYNEX, N.Y.C., 1983-90, dir. paramed. svcs., 1990-95. Mem. Am. Assn. Occupl. Health Nurses, Greater N.Y. Assn. Occupl. Health Nurses (past dir., sec., past editor newsletter), Am. Soc. Safety Engrs.

POHLODEK, KAMIL, gynecologist and obstetrician; b. Bratislava, Slovakia, May 2, 1959; s. Viliam and Dobroslava (Horká) P.; m. Janka Gráňáková, Febr. 4, 1994; 1 child, Daniel Pohlodek. MD, U. Bratislava, 1984, specialist Ob/Gyn 1st degree, 1987, specialist Ob/Gyn 2d degree, 1995. Cert. specialist for breast cancer detection. Jr. asst. 2d dept. ob/gyn U. Bratislava, 1984-87, sr. asst., 1987-91; rsch. asst. dept. ob/gyn U. Heidelberg, 1991-94; fellow dept. ob/gyn U. Bern, Switzerland, 1992; fellow Rush-Presbyn.-St. Luke's Med. Ctr., Chgo., 1993—. Contbr. chpts. to book in field. Mem. Slovak Soc. Physicians (award for best publication 1994), Slovak Soc. Ob/Gyn, German Soc. Senology, European Soc. Mastology. Office: U Hosp Bratislava 2d Dept ObGyn, Sulekova 20, 811 03 Bratislava Slovak Republic

POINT, WARREN, internist; b. Charleston, W.Va., Aug. 21, 1921; s. Walter Warren and Maude (Brown) P.; m. Virginia Anne Parry, 1945; 3 children. BA, W. Va. U., 1942; MD cum laude, Harvard U., 1945. Diplomate Am. Bd. Internal Medicine. Med. intern Harvard Svc./Boston City Hosp., 1945-46, asst. resident, 1946, 48-49; clin. and research fellow in gastroenterology Mass. Gen. Hosp., 1949-51; pvt. practice internal medicine and gastroenterology Mass. Gen. Hosp., Boston, 1951-77; group practice of internal medicine and gastroenterology Med. Dept., MIT, Cambridge, 1967-77; faculty group practice internal medicine/gastroenterology Charleston div. W.Va. U. Med. Ctr., 1977—; Warren Point Endowed Chair Sch. Medicine, 1989—; prof. W.Va. U. Sch. Medicine, 1977-91, assoc. chmn. dept. medicine, 1977-88, prof. emeritus, 1991—; cons. gastroenterology Mt. Auburn Hosp., Cambridge, Mass., 1955-77, Children's Hosp., Boston, 1955-85; bd. dirs. Charleston Nat. Bank. Contbr. articles to profl. jours. Trustee U. Charleston, 1982—, chmn. bd., 1990—, chmn. acad. affairs com., 1988—; bd. dirs. United Way of Kanawha Valley, 1988, CAMC Found., 1978—; trustee W.Va. Symphony Orch., 1985-90. Fellow ACP (master, gov. 1983-87, exec. com. 1986-87, Laureate award 1987); mem. AMA, Am. Gastroenterol. Assn., W.Va. Med. Assn. (coun. 1986-90), Kanawha Med. Soc. (coun. 1986-90), Assn. Program Dirs. Internal Medicine, Northeast Med. Assn., Boylston Med. Soc., Phi Beta Kappa, Alpha Omega Alpha. Home: 1623 Louden Heights Rd Charleston WV 25314-1545

POKKY, ERIC JON, pharmacist; b. Ft. Worth, Oct. 24, 1957; s. Arne Huntus and Helen Theodora (Tienvieri) P.; m. Catherine Ann Miller, June 13, 1987; 1 child, Allison Christine. Student, U. Tex., Arlington, 1976-80; BS in Pharmacy, U. Houston, 1983; postgrad., Midland (Tex.) Coll., 1984. Cert. anticoagulation therapist; cert. Parkinson's disease therapist. Rec. engr. Hallmark Prodns./Sundown Rec. Studios, Friendswood, Tex., 1980-83; salesman, cons. Future Sys., Midland, 1983-86; pharmacist Town and Country Drug, Odessa, Tex., 1983-92; outpatient pharmacy supr. Med. Ctr. Hosp., Odessa, 1992-95, clin. pharmacy coord., 1995—; pres. ECF Cons. Svcs., 1989—. Fellow Am. Soc. Cons. Pharmacists; mem. Am. Pharm. Assn., Am. Soc. Consulting Pharmacists, Permian Basin Pharm. Assn. (v.p. 1986-88, pres. 1988—), Permian Basin Immunization Coalition, Am. Soc. Hosp. Pharmacists, Am. Soc. Cons. Pharmacists, Tex. Soc. Hosp. Pharmacists, Tex. Pharm. Assn. (del. to house 1994—), West Tex. Pharm. Assn., Kappa Psi (sec. 1982-83). Republican. Lutheran. Home: 4420 Haner Dr Odessa TX 79762-4671 Office: Med Ctr Hosp PO Box 7239 Odessa TX 79760-7239

POKORNOWSKI, RONALD FELIX, internist; b. Chgo., July 8, 1933; s. Felix Florian and Isabella Helen (Mrazek) P.; m. Joan Barbara Krygier, Feb. 8, 1958; children: Barbara Karen, John Ronald. Grad. pre-med., Marquette U., 1953, MD, 1957; MD (hon.), Med. Coll. Wis., 1977. Resident internal medicine Northwestern U., Evanston and Chgo., Ill., 1961-64; gen. practice internal medicine Wheaton, Ill., 1964-72; pres. Ctrl. DuPage Internist Assocs., S.C., Carol Stream, Ill., 1972—, also bd. dirs.; v.p. Cen. DuPage Hosp. Med. Staff, 1968-69, pres., 1969-70, mem. bd. govs.; chief med. cons. DuPage Convalescent Ctr., 1980-83; bd. dirs. Allmed Inc., Libertyville, Ill., Fun 'N Travel, Wheaton. Mem. DuPage County Bd. Health, 1993—. Capt. U.S. Army, 1958-61. Mem. AMA, Am. Soc. Addiction Medicine, Ill. Med. Soc., DuPage County Med. Soc. (bd. dirs., alt. del. to Ill. State Med. Soc.), Nat. Assn. Children of Alcoholics. Republican. Roman Catholic. Home: 26w260 Blair St Winfield IL 60190-1104 Office: Cen DuPage Internist Assocs SC 381 S Main Pl Carol Stream IL 60188-2452

POKORNY, ALEX DANIEL, psychiatrist; b. Taylor, Tex., Oct. 18, 1918; s. John Robert and Olga Frances (Susen) P.; m. Jeanice Brooke Allen, Mar. 13, 1948; children: Martha, Ross, Ellen, Sally. BA, U. Tex., 1939; MD, U. Tex., Galveston, 1942. Diplomate Am. Bd. Psychiatry and Neurology. Psychiatrist VA Hosp., Houston, 1949-55, chief psychiatry and neurology svc., 1955-73; from instr. to prof. psychiatry Baylor Coll. Medicine, Houston, 1949-89, acting chmn. dept. psychiatry, 1968-72, vice chmn. dept. psychiatry, 1972-89, ret. Editor (with others) 7 books, including Phenomenology and Treatment of Anxiety, 1979, Phenomenology and Treatment of Alcoholism, 1980, Phenomenology and Treatment of Psychosexual Disorders, 1983, Phenomenology and Treatment of Psychiatric Emergencies, 1984; editor numerous publs.; contbr. 100 articles to profl. jours. Capt. U.S. Army, 1943-46. Recipient Amersa award for Excellence in Med. Edu. Assn. Med. Edn. & Rsch. Substance Abuse, 1989, Dublin award Am. Assn. Suicidology, 1992. Fellow AAAS, Am. Psychiat. Assn. (life), Am. Coll. Psychiatrists (life); mem. Soc. Psychophysiological Rsch. Home: 813 Atwell St Bellaire TX 77401-4718

POLAN, GARY DAVID, optometrist; b. Chgo., July 3, 1956; s. Seymour and Rena (Schneider) P. BA, U. So. Calif., 1978; BS, So. Calif. Coll. Optometry, 1982, OD, 1984. Pvt. practice Pacific Palisades, Calif., 1985—; mem. Pacific Palisades Health Profls., 1992-94; radio talk show guest during Vision Care Month, L.A., 1988. Contbr. articles to profl. jours.; patent pending for product in field. Mem. Pacific Palisades C. of C. Democrat. Home: 1550 Palisades Dr Pacific Palisades CA 90272 Office: 881 Alma Deal Dr Ste T4 Pacific Palisades CA 90272

POLAN, MARY LAKE, obstetrics and gynecology educator; b. July 17, 1943. Student, Smith Coll., Paris, 1963-64; BA cum laude, Conn. Coll., 1965; PhD in Biophysics and Biochemistry, Yale U., 1970, MD, 1975. Diplomate Am. Bd. Ob-Gyn., Am. Bd. Reproductive Endocrinology, Nat. Bd. Med. Examiners. Postdoctoral fellow dept. biology, NIH postdoctoral fellow Yale U., New Haven, 1970-72, resident dept. ob-gyn. Sch. Medicine, 1975-78, fellow in oncology, then fellow in endocrinology-infertility, 1978-80, asst. instr., then lectr. molecular biophysics-biochemistry, 1970-72, instr., then asst. prof. ob-gyn., 1978-79, 80-85, assoc. prof., 1985-90; clin. clk. in ob-gyn. and pediat. Radcliffe Infirmary, Oxford (Eng.) U. Med. Sch., 1974; instr. Pahlavi U., Shiraz, Iran, 1978; Katharine Dexter McCormick and Stanley McCormick Meml. prof. Stanford (Calif.) Sch. Medicine, 1990—, chmn. dept. gynecology and obstetrics, 1990—; vis. prof. Hunan Med. Coll., Changsha, China, 1986; mem. med. bd. Yale-China Assn., 1987-90; liaison com. on ethics in modern world Conn. Coll., New London, 1988-90; mem. med. adv. bd. Ova-Med Corp., Palo Alto, Calif., 1992—, Vivus, Menlo Park, Calif., 1993—; bd. dirs. Metra Biosys., Palo Alto, Quidel, San Diego, LipoMatrix, Palo Alto, Stanford Health Svcs., 1994—; mem. reproductive endocrinology study sect. NIH, 1989-90, co-chmn. task force on opportunities for rsch. on woman's health, 1991. Author: Second Seed, 1987; guest editor: Seminars in Reproductive Endocrinology, 1984, Infertility and Reproductive Medicine Clinics of North America: GnRH Analogues, Vol. 4, 1993; editor; (with A.H. DeCherney) Surgery in Reproductive Endocrinology, 1987, (with DeCherney, S. Boyers and R. Lee) Decision Making in Infertility; ad hoc reviewer Jour. Clin. Endocrinology and Metabolism, Fertility and Sterility, Ob-Gyn., also others; contbr. numerous articles to med. jours., chpts. to books. Fellow NRSA, 1981-82; grantee NIRA, 1082-85, HD, 1985-90, NRSA, 1987-88, Johnson & Johnson, 1993-96; scholar Assn. Acad. Health Ctrs., 1993—. Fellow ACOG (PROLOG task force for reproductive endocrinology and infertility 1988-89, rep. to CREOG coun. 1994-97); mem. Am. Fertility Soc., Soc. for Gynecologic Investigation, Soc. for Reproductive Endocrinologists, Am. Gynecologic and Obstetric Soc., Inst. Medicine (com. on rsch. capabilities of acad. depts. ob-gyn. 1990-91, bd. on health scis. policy 1992—), San Francisco Gynecologic Soc., Bay Area Reproductive Endocrine Soc., Phi Beta Kappa. Home: 4251 Manuela Ct Palo Alto CA 94306-3731 Office: Stanford U Sch Medicine 300 Pasteur Dr Rm Hh333 Stanford CA 94305-2203*

POLAN-CURTAIN, JODIE LEA, physiologist researcher; b. Galliano, La., Sept. 4, 1963; d. John Lee and Janice Eleanor (Ferris) Polan; m. James Barry Curtain, Sept. 3, 1988; 1 child, Johnna Lela. BS in Biology, U. Tex., San Antonio, 1984, MS in Biology, 1989. Teaching asst. U. Tex., San Antonio, 1989, rsch. assoc. I, 1989-90, teaching assoc., 1990-93, rsch. assoc. II, 1990-93; sr. rsch. asst. U. Tex. Health Sci. Ctr., San Antonio, 1994—. Contbr. articles to profl. jours. Mem. AAAS, Soc. Neurosci. Address: 4302 Spiral Creek San Antonio TX 78238

POLAND, ALAN PAUL, oncology educator. Prof. oncology McArdle Lab. for Cancer Rsch. U. Wis., Madison. Recipient Founders award Chem. Industry Inst. Toxicology Bristol-Myers Squibb Found., 1996. Office: U Wis McArdle Lab Cancer Rsch 450 N Randall Ave Madison WI 53706-1506*

POLANSKI, JERZY A., surgeon, medical educator; b. Karpacz, Poland, Nov. 30, 1945; s. Tadeusz P. and Irena (Taguszewska) Polanska; m. Krystyna Pyrgiel; children: Rafael, Margaret. Med. Dr., Warsaw Med. Sch., 1969; MD, Polish Acad. Sci., 1972. Specialist in gen. surgery, 1978. Asst. Polish Acad. Sci., Warsaw, 1969-72, sr. asst., 1973-74; sr. asst. Warsaw Med. Sch., 1974-78, asst. prof., 1978-81, prof. surgery, 1983—, head dept. surgery, 1988—; S.M.O. jr. tutor Royal Victoria Hosp., Belfast, 1972-73; rsch. assoc. Sinai Hosp., Detroit, 1982. Author: Oncologic Liver Tumors, 1993, Surgery of the Liver and Biliary, 1994. Mem. Warsaw Med. Chamber (v.p. 1990-96), Polish Surg. Assn. (pres. Warsaw chpt. 1995—). Office: 3rd Dept Surgery Warsaw Med Sch, Stepinska 19/25, 00739 Warsaw Poland

POLASKY, HILDEGARDE ELAINE, medical technologist; b. Carlisle, Pa., Jan. 27, 1943; d. Paul John and Emma (Holtz) Fisher; m. Raymond Joseph Polasky, June 15, 1968; children: Heather Ann Polasky Nance, Ethan Paul, Justin Raymond. Tech. cert., Franklin Sch. Sci. and Arts, 1961; student, Millersville State Coll. Med. technologist Mercy Hosp., Altoona, Pa., 1961-65, Lancaster (Pa.) Osteo. Hosp., 1965-67; med. technologist, supr. Anat. and Pathol. Lab., Flagstaff, Ariz., 1967-70; med. technologist generalist Santa Fe (N.Mex.) Med. Lab., 1973-84, Darlene Thonington, M.D., Santa Fe, 1985-87, Lovelace Health Systems, Santa Fe, 1987—. Mem. Am. Med. Technologists Assn., N.Mex. State Soc. Med. Technologists (treas. 1987—, editor profl. jour. 1994—). Home: 1612 Ben Hur Dr Santa Fe NM 87501

POLENZ, JOANNA MAGDA, psychiatrist; b. Cracow, Poland, Oct. 20, 1936; came to U.S., 1961; d. Mieczyslaw and Nusia (Goldberger) Uberall; m. Daryl Louis Polenz, July 8, 1962 (div. 1991); children: Teresa Ann, Daryl Philip, Elizabeth Sophia. MD, U. Sydney, Australia, 1960; MPH, Columbia U., 1992. Diplomate Am. Bd. Psychiatry and Neurology. Intern Bklyn. Hosp., 1961-62; resident Mt. Sinai Med. Ctr., N.Y.C., 1962-65; ednl. fellow Mt. Sinai Med. Ctr., 1965-66, rsch. assoc., 1966-67; med. dir. Tappan Zee clin. Phelps Meml. Hosp., Tarrytown, N.Y., 1968-71, dir. dept. psychiatry, 1972-77; sr. attending psychiatrist Meml. Hosp. Ctr., 1972-93; pvt. practice Briarcliff Manor, N.Y., 1971-91; physician Joint Commn. Accreditation of Healthcare Orgns., Oakbrook Terrace, Ill., 1993—; lectr. in field. Author: In Defense of marriage, 1981; (with other) Test Your Marriage IQ, 1984, Test Your Success IQ, 1985; contbr. articles to profl. jours.; numerous TV appearances including Phil Donahue, 1988, Oprah Winfrey 1984. Grant Found. grantee, 1970. Fellow Am. psychiatric Assn., Royal Soc. for Health; mem. AMA, N.Y. Acad. Scis., Pan Am. Med. Assn., Westchester Psychiatric Assn. (sec. 1982-85, chair person fellowship com. 1989). Home: 1755 York Ave Apt 31E New York NY 10128

POLESON, KATHRYN LANE, dentist; b. Moscow, Idaho, Dec. 2, 1947; m. Thomas S. Dowdy. BS, U. Idaho, Moscow, 1970; DMD, Oreg. Sch. Dentistry, 1975. Vol. dentist Dental Health Internat., Lesotho, South Africa, 1974, Agy. for Internat. Devel., Cameroon, Africa, 1975; dental clinic coordinator Multnomah County Health, Portland, 1978-81; gen. dentist Army Dental Clinic, Frankfurt, Germany, 1981-84; pvt. practice Portland, 1985—, Vancouver, Wash., 1991—; chmn. Internat. Rels. Am. Student Dental Assn., 1973-75; instr. Oreg. Health Scis. Ctr., Portland, 1978-81; dentist Dammasch State Hosp., 1978-79, Wilsonville, Oreg., 1986—. Mem. S.W. Wash. Leaders, 1991—; aux. work Oreg. Symphony Orch. Capt. U.S. Army, 1975-77; maj. USAR, 1983—. Master Acad. Gen. Dentistry; mem. ADA, Clark County Dental Soc., Wash. State Dental Assn., Am. Assn. Women Dentists (nat. del. 1989-90, dist. trustee 1991-93), Am. Dental Soc. Europe. Office: 916 SE 164th Ave Vancouver WA 98683-9642

POLI, KIM ANN, internist; b. Dayton, Ohio, Feb. 28, 1966; d. Corrado and Antoinette Dolores (Watkins) P. BS, U. Mass., 1988, MD, 1992; postgrad., U. Siena, Italy, 1985. Diplomate Am. Bd. Internal Medicine; lic. physician, Mass. Rsch. fellow U. Mass. Med. Ctr., Tocachi, Ecuador, 1989; internal medicine resident Deaconess Hosp., Boston, 1992-95, cardiology fellow/physician, 1996—; cardiovascular rsch. fellow Framingham Heart Study, Boston U., 1995-96. Home: 29 5th Ave Rd W Shrewsbury MA 01545 Office: Deaconess Hosp Dept Cardiology Deaconess Rd Boston MA 02215

POLICASTRO, ANTHONY MICHAEL, retired military officer, pediatrician; b. Bklyn., Nov. 27, 1946; s. Anthony Albert and Philomena (Pucci) P.; m. Joan Eleanor Lober, June 20, 1970; children: Lorraine Angela, Barbara Ann, Denise Marie. BS in Biology with honors, Manhattan Coll., 1968; MD summa cum laude, SUNY, Bklyn., 1972. Diplomate Am. Bd. Pediatrics. Resident in pediatrics Tufts New Eng. Med. Ctr., Boston, 1972-75; commd. capt. USAF, 1975, advanced through grades to col.; pediatrician USAF, Dover AFB, Del., 1975-76; pediatrician Malcolm Grow Med. Ctr. USAF, Andrews AFB, Md., 1976-80, asst. chairperson pediatrics, 1980-82, dir. med. edn., 1982-84; chief hosp. services USAF Hosp., Upper Heyford,

Eng., 1984-86; hosp. comdr. 363 med. group USAF, Shaw AFB, S.C., 1986-89; hosp. comdr. 1st Med. Group USAF, Langley AFB, Va., 1989-95; sr. v.p. med. affairs Nanticoke Meml. Hosp., Seaford, Del., 1995—; clin. assoc. prof. pediatrics Uniformed Services U. of Health Scis., 1977-93. Contbr. articles to profl. jours. Recipient Make it Click award Nat. Safety Council, 1982. Fellow Am. Acad. Pediatrics (Make it Click award 1982); mem. Assn. Mil. Surgeons U.S., Soc. Devel. and Behavioral Pediatrics. Roman Catholic. Home: Rt 5 Box 23 B Seaford DE 19973

POLIN, STANTON GORDON, physician, surgeon, medical educator; b. Chgo., Jan. 24, 1933; s. Abraham Noah and Dorothy (Blacher) P.; m. Leah Goldstein, July 1, 1962; children: Abby Joy, Bonnie Sue, Brian Alan, Jonathan Evan. BS, U. Ill., Chgo., 1955, MD, 1957; MHA, U. Colo., 1995. Diplomate Am. Bd. Surgery, Am. Bd. Thoracic-Cardiovascular Surgery. Intern Michael Reese Hosp., Chgo., 1957-58, resident in gen. surgery, 1958-62; resident in cardiovasc. surgery VA Hosp., Hines, Ill., 1962-63; resident in cardiovasc. thoracic surgery Baylor U., Houston, 1963; pvt. med. practice Chgo., 1963-67, 69—; assoc. prof. Chgo. Med. Sch., 1964—; rschr. Michael Reese Hosp., Chgo., 1975-90; pres. Thorek Hosp. Med. Staff; lectr. in field. Contbr. articles to profl. jours. Chmn. doctors divsn. Israel Bond Orgn., Chgo., 1990-95; chmn. fund raising Am. Heart Assn., Skokie, Ill., 1994. Comdr. USN, 1967-69, USNR, 1969-93. Fellow ACS. Office: 4801 Peterson Ave Chicago IL 60646

POLING, STEVEN N., podiatrist; b. Passaic, N.J., Sept. 6, 1954; s. Stephen Frank and Angela Poling; m. Gail Ziegler, May 30, 1987; children: Matthew Stephen, Michael Anthony. BS in Pharmacy, Bklyn. Coll., 1977; D in Podiatric Medicine, Ill. Coll. Podiatric Medicine, Chgo., 1985. Diplomate Am. Bd. Podiatric Orthopedics, Am. Coun. Cert. Podiatric Physicians and Surgeons. Resident Roseland (N.J.) Surg. Ctr., United Hosps.-Presbyn. Hosp., Newark, N.J., West Essex Gen. Hosp., Livingston, N.J.; pvt. practice Rutherford, N.J.; mem. staff St. Mary's Hosp., Passaic, Roseland Surg. Ctr., Passaic Gen. Hosp., Montclair (N.J.) Cmty., Passaic Beth Israel Hosp., Clifton (N.J.) Surg. Ctr., Meadowlands Hosp., Secaucus, N.J., Brookhaven Health Care Ctr., East Orange, N.J.; lectr. and cons. in field. Contbr. articles to profl. jours. Mem. Am. Assn. Podiatric Physicians and Surgeons, Am. Podiatric Arthroscopy Assn., Am. Heart Assn. (bd. dirs.), N.J. Spl. Olympics Med. Staff, N.J. March of Dimes (com.). Office: 240 Park Ave Rutherford NJ 07070

POLITOFF, ALBERTO LIFSCHITZ, neurologist, neurobiologist; b. Santiago, Chile, July 31, 1935; came to U.S., 1964; s. Leonidas and Emilia (Lifschitz) P.; m. Ida Marticorena, June 2, 1979; 1 child, Violeta. MD, U. Chile, 1960. Asst. prof. physiology Boston U. Med. Sch., 1973-78, assoc. prof., 1978-81; assoc. prof. neurology SUNY L.I. Hosp., New Hyde Park, 1985-89; assoc. prof. U. N.D. Med. Sch., Fargo, 1989—. Author: Introduccion a la Neurologia; contbr. articles to profl. jours. Recipient NIH grants, 1974, Muscular Dystrohpy grants, 1978. Office: U ND Med Sch 1919 Elm St Fargo ND 58102-2416

POLJAK, SILVIA, pharmacist; b. Belisce, Croatia, Jan. 19, 1966; d. Franjo and Milka (Kitin) P. BS in Pharmacy, Zagreb U., 1989. Prodn. engr. Pliva, Zagreb, 1990-93, pharm. devel. process engr., 1993—. Mem. Croatian Pharm. Soc., ISPE. Office: Pliva, Ulica Grada Vukovara 49, 10 000 Zagreb Croatia

POLK, HIRAM CAREY, JR., surgeon, educator; b. Jackson, Miss., Mar. 23, 1936; s. Hiram Carey and Dorris (Hemby) P.; m. Susan Galandiuk; children: Susan Elizabeth, Hiram Cary. BS, Millsaps Coll., 1956; MD, Harvard U., 1960. Intern Barnes Hosp., St. Louis, 1960-61; resident Barnes Hosp., 1961-65; instr. in surgery Washington U., St. Louis, 1964-65; asst. prof. surgery U. Miami, Fla., 1965-69; assoc. prof. U. Miami, 1969-71; prof. chmn. dept. surgery U. Louisville, 1971—; pres., chmn. bd. Univ. Surg. Assocs., P.S.C., 1971—; chmn. bd. Clin. Services Assn., Inc.; mem. merit rev. bd. for surgery VA, 1983-85. Author: (with H.H. Stone) Contemporary Burn Management, 1971, Hospital-Acquired Infections in Surgery, 1977; (with B. Gardner, H.H. Stone and W.L. Sugg) Basic Surgery, 1978, (with H.H. Stone and B. Gardner) 2d edit., 1983, 3d edit., 1987, 4th edit., 1992, 5th edit., 1995; (with D.C. Carter) Trauma, 1982; (with J.E. Conte Jr. and L.S. Jacob) Antibiotic Prophylaxis in Surgery: A Comprehensive Review, 1984; (with J.D. Richardson and L.M. Flint Jr.) Trauma: Clinical Care and Pathophysiology, 1987; contbr. numerous articles to profl. publs.; mem. editl. bd. So. Med. Jour., 1970-72, Jour. Surg. Rsch., 1970-72, 75-77, 78-80, Current Problems in Surgery, 1973—, Surgery, 1975-85, Current Surgery, 1977—, Current Surg. Techniques, 1977—, Emergency Surgery: A Weekly Update, 1977—, Collected Letters in Surgery, 1978—, Brit. Jour. Surgery, 1981-94; chief editor Am. Jour. Surgery, 1986—. Bd. govs. Trover Clinic Found., Madisonville, Ky. Mem. ACS (gov. 1972-80, commn. on cancer 1975-80), AMA, Allen O. Whipple Soc. (exec. coun. 1977-80), Am. Assn. Cancer Edn. (exec. coun. 1968-72), Am. Assn. Surgery of Trauma, Am. Burn Assn., Am. Cancer Soc. (pres. Ky. div. 1989-90, nat. del. dir. 1989-92, 93-95), Am. Surg. Assn. (sec. 1984-89), Acad. Surgery (pres. 1975-76), Cen. Surg. Assn., Assn. Am. Med. Colls. (chmn. ad hoc com. on Medicare and Medicaid 1978-79), Collegium Internationale Chirurgiae Digestivae (sec.-treas. 1981-86, pres. 1986-87), Council on Public Higher Edn. (task group on health scis.), Halsted Soc., Jefferson County Med. Soc., Ky. Med. Assn., Ky. Surg. Soc. (pres. 1982-83), Louisville Surg. Soc. (pres. 1989-90), Residency Rev. Com. for Surgery (vice chmn. 1981-83, chmn. 1983-85), Société Internationale de Chirurgie, Soc. Surgery Alimentary Tract (treas. 1975-78, pres. 1985-86), Soc. Clin. Surgery, Soc. Surg. Chairmen, Soc. Surg. Oncology (pres. 1984-85), Soc. Univ. Surgeons (treas. 1971-74, pres. 1979-80), Southeastern Surg. Congress (exec. coun. for Ky. 1985-86, pres. 1994-95), So. Med. Assn. (vice chmn. sect. on surgery 1969-70, chmn. sect. 1972-73, sec. 1970-72, exec. coun. for Ky. 1971-77, 89-90), So. Surg. Assn. (pres. 1988-89), Alpha Omega Alpha. Home: 5609 River Knolls Dr Louisville KY 40222 Office: U Louisville Dept Surgery Louisville KY 40292

POLLACK, EMANUEL DAVIS, neuroscience educator; b. Chgo., Mar. 29, 1942; s. Louis and Helen May (Freedman) P.; m. Christine Florence Kozlowski, Oct. 22, 1977; children: Jennifer Kristin, Brian Andrew. BS, Roosevelt U., Chgo., 1964; MS, U. Iowa, 1967, PhD, 1970. Rsch. fellow Yeshiva U. Albert Einstein Coll. Medicine, Bronx, N.Y., 1970-72; rsch. scientist Ill. Inst. for Devel. Disabilities, Chgo., 1972-79, adminstrv. rsch. scientist, 1979-90; assoc. prof. biol. scis. U. Ill., Chgo., 1976—, rsch. assoc. prof., 1978-94, assoc. prof. anatomy and cell biology, 1993—, dir. biomed. scis., 1979-91, dir. developmental and behavioral neurosci., 1991-94, chmn. neurosci. com., 1983-94, fellow Honors Coll., 1989—; asst. dean Coll. Liberal Arts and Scis. U. Ill., Chgo., 1994—; cons. Ill. EPA, Chgo., 1975-80, scientist vol. Mus. Sci. and Industry, Chgo, 1985—; mem. bd. edn. Evanston/Skokie Sch. Dist. 65, Ill, 1991-95, pres. 1993-95; mem. bd. control Low Incidence Coop. Agreement/ Regional Hearing Impaired Program, Ill. 1991-95; cons. to various sci. publs. Editor: Developmental Neurobiology of the Frog, 1988; contbr. articles and abstracts to sci. jours., chpts. to books. Trustee Roosevelt U., 1989-92. Mem. AAAS, Soc. for Neurosci., Internat. Brain Rsch. Orgn., Am. Soc. for Cell Biology, N.Y. Acad. Scis., Roosevelt U. Alumni Assn. (bd. govs. 1983, pres. 1988-91). Home: 8632 Lawndale Ave Skokie IL 60076-2334 Office: U Illinois M/C 066 845 W Taylor St Chicago IL 60607-7060

POLLACK, MARVIN, ophthalmologist; b. Bklyn., Mar. 11, 1944; s. Ben and Ida (Kassera) P.; m. Gloria Wiederkehr, Sept. 6, 1965; children: Aryeh, Shalom, Joshua, Bracha, Rebecca, Miriam. BA, Yeshiva U., 1963; MD, Albert Einstein Coll. Medicine, 1967. Intern Lincoln Hosp., Bronx, N.Y., 1967-68; resident in ophthalmology Albany (N.Y.) Med. Ctr., 1968-71; pvt. practice Bklyn., 1973—; asst. in ophthalmology Maimonides Hosp., Bklyn. Lt. comdr. USNR, 1971-73. Fellow Am. Acad. Ophthalmology; mem. Med. Soc. County of Kings, Med. Soc. State of N.Y. Jewish. Office: 4701 15 Ave Brooklyn NY 11219

POLLACK, ROBERT ELLIOT, biologist, educator; b. Bklyn., Sept. 2, 1940; s. Hyman Ephraim and Molly (Pollack) P.; m. Amy Louise Steinberg, Dec. 23, 1961; 1 child, Marya. BA in Physics, Columbia U., 1961; PhD in Biology, Brandeis U., 1966. Asst. prof. pathology Med. Sch. NYU, N.Y.C., 1969-70; sr. scientist Cold Spring Harbor Lab., N.Y., 1971-75; prof. microbiology Med. Sch., SUNY-Stony Brook, 1975-78; prof. biol. sci. Columbia U., N.Y.C., 1978—; dean Columbia Coll., N.Y.C., 1982-89; bd. dirs. Applied Microbiology, Inc.; instr. Pratt Archtl. Sch., Bklyn., 1970; vis. prof. pharmacology Albert Einstein Coll. Medicine, Bronx, N.Y., 1977-92; lectr. Rosenthal Colloquium, March of Dimes, 1989; McGregory lectr. Colgate U., 1979; du Vigneaud lectr. Med. Sch., Cornell U., 1983. Co-editor: Readings in Mammalian Cell Culture, 1973, 3d rev. edit., 1981, Signs of Life, 1984 (translations in 7 langs., Lionel Trilling award 1995); mng. editor BBA Revs. on Cancer, 1980-86; contbr. numerous rsch. articles on molecular cell biology to profl. jours. Trustee N.Y. Found., 1986—, Brandeis U., 1989-94, Solomon Schechter Sch. of N.Y.C., 1996—; mem. World Econ. Forum, 1995—. Recipient Rsch. Career Devel. award NIH, 1974, Alexander Hamilton medal, 1989, Lionel Trilling award Columbia U., 1995; NIH spl. fellow Weizmann Inst., Rehovot, Israel, 1970-71; grantee Nat. Cancer Inst., NIH, 1968-92, Am. Cancer Soc., 1985-94; John Simon Guggenheim fellow, 1993. Fellow AAAS; mem. N.Y. Acad. Scis., Am. Soc. Microbiology. Jewish. Office: Columbia U Dept Biol Scis 749 Fairchild Hall New York NY 10027

POLLACK, ROBERT WILLIAM, psychiatrist; b. N.Y.C., May 22, 1947; s. George and Esther P.; m. Pam Gregory, Sept. 15, 1984; 1 child, Jessie. BS in Biology, Yale U., 1969; MD, SUNY Downstate Med. Ctr., Bklyn., 1973. Diplomate Am. Bd. Psychiatry and Neurology. Tng. resident U. Fla., 1973-76, chief resident Dept. of Psychiatry, 1975-76; asst. prof. Dept. of Psychiatry U. Fla., Gainesville, 1976-77; clin. asst. prof. dept. psychiatry Shands Hosp., Gainesville, 1977—; chief dept. psychiatry Fla. Hosp., Orlando, 1983, 84; clin. dir. assessment and evaluation team West Lake Hosp., Longwood, Fla., 1984-87, clin. dir. intensive evaluation unit, 1987-89; med. dir. Fla. Psychiat. Assocs., Winter Park, 1989—, Fla. Psychiat. Mgmt., Winter Park, 1990—, FPM Behavioral Health, 1993—; med. dir. consultation, liaison svc., and spl. med. unit Winter Park Meml. Hosp., 1992. Contbr. 4 articles to profl. jours.; author sci. reports. Chmn. Retinitis Pigmentosa Casino Night, Orlando, 1988-92; vice-chmn. nat. championship com. U.S. Blind Golfers Assn., 1991-92, chair 48th ann. championship com., 1992-93; bd. dirs. Tennis with a Different Swing, Orlando, 1988-92. Mem. Alaqua Country Club (bd. dirs.). Office: FPM Behavioral Health 1276 Minnesota Ave Winter Park FL 32789-4833

POLLARD, HARVEY B., physician, neuroscientist; b. San Antonio, May 26, 1943. BA in Biology, Rice U., 1964; MS in Biochemistry, U. Chgo., 1969, MD, 1969, PhD, 1973. Rsch. assoc. NIH-Nat. Inst. Arthritis and Metabolic Diseases, Bethesda, Md., 1969-71, sr. investigator, 1972-74, 1977-79, sect. chief, 1979-81; lab. chief Nat. Inst. Diabetes, Digestive and Kidney Diseases, Bethesda, 1981—. Contbr. over 200 articles to profl. jours. With USPHS, 1969—. Recipient Commendation medal USPHS, 1982, Alumni award for Disting. Svc., U. Chigo. Alumni Assn., 1989, NIH Inventor's award, 1991. Mem. Biophys. Soc., Soc. for Neurosci., Am. Soc. for Pharmacology and Exptl. Therapeutics, Soc. for Cell Biology. Office: Nat Inst Diabetes Digestive & Kidney Disease 9000 Rockville Pike Blg 8 Rm 403 Bethesda MD 20892

POLLARD, JAMES ASHWELL, dentist; b. Lynchburg, Va., Feb. 1, 1946; s. Paul Alexander and Edna Charlotte (Ashwell) P.; m. Martha Bradley Handy; children: James Ashwell Pollard, Jr., Martha Elizabeth Pollard. BA, U. Va., 1968; DDS, Med. Coll. Va., 1972. Dentist USN, Rota, Spain, 1972-75; pvt. practice Onancock, Va., 1975-78, Lynchburg, Va., 1978—. Mem. ADA, Va. Dental Assn., Lynchburg Dental Soc. Home: 504 Elmwood Ave Lynchburg VA 24503-4412 Office: 7217 Timberlake Rd Lynchburg VA 24502-2336

POLLARD, LESLIE JUNE, surgical laser laparoscopic consultant; b. Dallas, Oct. 6, 1954; s. Jodie Moseley and Winifred Nadine (Robinson) P. BS in Med. Tech., U. Tex., Galveston, 1977; AAS, Tex. State Tech. Inst., Waco, 1984. Cert. proficiency Am. Assn.Clin. Pathologists. Hematology specialist U. Tex., Galveston, 1977-81, rsch. specialist, 1981-82; dir. laser/laparoscopic svc. Meml. Mission Hosp., Asheville, N.C., 1984-90; dir. laser/laparoscopic surgery St. Joseph's Hosp., Asheville, 1990—; instr. N.C. Biomed. Soc., Raleigh, N.C., 1990-94; advisor Med. Laser Safety Officer Soc., Denver, 1992-94; pres. Med. Laser Cons., Asheville, 1986—; instr., advisor Health Adventure, Asheville, 1995—. Author: Clinical Laser Specialist Handbook, 1991. Vol. Big Bros./Big Sisters, Asheville, 1986-91, Parks & Recreation Dept., Asheville, 1984-91, Buncombe County Schs., Asheville, 1990—. Mem. Am. Soc. for Lasers in Medicine and Surgery, Am. Soc. Clin. Pathologists, N.C. Biomed. Sco. Office: St Josephs Hosp 428 Biltmore Ave Asheville NC 28801

POLLARD, ROBERT Q., JR., psychologist; b. Rochester, N.Y., Sept. 22, 1958; s. Robert Q. and Jeanne Loretta (Clark) P.; m. Pamela Rose White, Oct. 14, 1989; 1 child, Matthew. BS in Biology and Psychology cum laude, Union Coll., Schenectady, 1980; MA in Clin. Psychology, SUNY, Buffalo, 1983, PhD in Clin. Psychology, 1984. Lic. psychologist, Calif., Ohio, N.Y. Psychologist, clinician specialist Community Ctr. for Deaf, Columbus, Ohio, 1984-86; psychologist Calif. Sch. for Deaf, Fremont, 1986; clin. and rsch. psychologist U. Calif. Ctr. on Deafness, San Francisco, 1986-90; asst. prof., psychologist U. Rochester Med. Ctr., 1990—; founder, mgr. Deaftek Psych, 1988-95. Founder program for deaf trainees. Mem. APA (founder, pres. spl. interest sect. on deafness divsn. 22 1990—, chmn. com. on disability issues in psychology 1991, bd. advancement psychology in pub. interest 1995—, Disting. Contribution to Psychology in Pub. Interest award 1994), Am. Deafness and Rehab. Assn. (mental health sect.). Office: U Rochester Med Ctr Dept Psychiatry 300 Crittenden Blvd Rochester NY 14642-0001

POLLARD, THOMAS DEAN, biologist, educator; b. Pasadena, Calif., July 7, 1942; s. Dean Randall and Florence Alma (Dierker) P.; m. Patricia Elizabeth Snowden, Feb. 7, 1964; children: Katherine, Daniel. BA, Pomona Coll., Claremont, Calif., 1964; MD, Harvard U., 1968. Intern Mass. Gen. Hosp., Boston, 1968-69; staff assoc. NIH, Bethesda, Md., 1969-72; from asst. prof. to assoc. prof. Harvard Med. Sch., Boston, 1972-78; prof., dir. dept. cell biology and anatomy Johns Hopkins Sch. Medicine, Balt., 1977-96; pres. Salk Inst. for Biological Studies, LaJolla, Calif., 1996—; mem. Commn. on Life Sci., NRC, 1990—, chair, 1993—; mem. coun. Nat. Inst. Gen. Med. Scis., NIH. Recipient Lewis S. Rosentiel Disting. Work in Basic Med. Rsch. award Brandeis U., 1996; Guggenheim fellow, 1984. Fellow AAAS, Am. Acad. Arts and Scis.; mem. NAS, Am. Soc. Cell Biology (pres. 1987-88, K. R. Porter lectr. 1989), Biophys. Soc. (pres. 1992-93), Marine Biol. Lab. (trustee 1991—). Office: Salk Inst Dept Cell Biology-Anatomy 10010 N Torrey Pines Rd LaJolla CA 92037-2105

POLLIACK, AARON, hematology educator; b. Capetown, South Africa, Jan. 12, 1939; came to Israel, 1962; s. Majrym and Ida (Kopelowitz) P.; m. Lily Polliack, Apr. 3, 1962; children: Meira, Vered, Ronen. MB ChB, Captetown U., 1961, MD, 1968. Resident dept. pathology Hadassah U. Hosp. and Hebrew U. Med. Sch., Jerusalem, 1965-68; Internat. Fogarty fellow Meml. Sloan-Kettering Cancer Ctr., N.Y.C., 1972-74; with dept. hematology Hadassah U. Hosp., Jerusalem, 1968—; head of lymphoma, leukemia unit dept. hematology Hadassah U. Hosp. and Hebrew U. Med. Sch., Jerusalem, 1978—, prof. hematology and medicine, 1978—; EMBO vis. prof. Karolinska Inst., Sweden, 1976; vis. prof. Harvard Med. Sch.-Dana Farber Cancer Ctr., Boston, 1982, Capetown U. Med. Sch., 1984, Royal Postgrad. Med. Sch.-Royal Marsden Hosp., London, 1989-90. Author: Essential Drugs and Regimens in Hematological Oncology, 1992, Scanning EM atlas of Leukocytes Springer Verlag, 1978, Human Leukemia, 1982, Chronic Lymphocytic Leukemia, 1988, Benign and Malignant Lymphadenopathies, Scanning EM Atlas of Normal and Malignant Leukocytes, 1993; editor-in-chief: Leukemia and Lymphoma, 1990—. Capt. Israel Def. Forces. Mem. Israel Soc. Hematology (pres. 1992-95). Jewish. Office: Hadassah U Hosp Hebrew U Med Sch, Lymphoma-Leukemia Unit Dept Hematology, Jerusalem Israel

POLLICK-GISONDI, SHARON, dentist; b. Phila., Dec. 20, 1960; d. John Louis and Rosemary (Madden) Pollick; married, Oct. 17, 1992. BS, Thomas Jefferson U., 1982; DMD, Temple U., 1988. Resident La. State U., New Orleans, 1988-90, Montefiore Med. Ctr., Bronx, 1990-94; pvt. practice as oral and maxillofacial surgeon Patchogue, N.Y., 1994—; staff mem. Stony Brook Univ. Hosp. and Sch. Dental Medicine, Montefiore Med. Ctr./Albert Einstein Coll. Medicine, Bronx, N.Y., Beth Israel Med. Ctr., N.Y.C., Brookhaven Meml. Hosp. Med. Ctr. Office: 250 Patchague Rd # 10 Patchogue NY 11772

POLLOCK, ALAN ALBERT, physician; b. Newark, N.J., July 10, 1946; s. David Albert and Margaret (Bergman) P.; m. Patricia Ann Provetto; children: Matthew, Zachary. AB magna cum laude in French Lit., Bowdoin Coll., 1968; MD, N.Y. Medical Coll., 1972. Diplomate Am. Bd. Internal Medicine, Am. Bd. Infectious Diseases. Clin. asst. prof. medicine NYU Sch. Medicine, N.Y.C.; attending physician Lenox Hill Hosp., N.Y.C.; pvt. practice infectious disease and internal medicine N.Y.C. Contbr. articles to profl. jours. Mem. Am. Coll. Physicians, Am. Soc. Microbiology, Infectious Diseases Soc. Am. Office: Alan A Pollock MD 184 E 70th St New York NY 10021

POLLOCK, BRUCE GODFREY, physician; b. Toronto, Aug. 18, 1952; s. Ira Justus and Sheila Joy (Godfrey) P.; m. Judith Arluk, May 18, 1982; children: Debra, Ariel. BS, U. Toronto, 1975, MD, 1979; PhD, U. Pitts., 1987. Chief resident Clarke Inst. of Psychiatry, Toronto, 1982-83; postdoctoral fellow U. Pitts., 1983-84, asst. prof. dept. psychiatry, 1984-90, assoc. dir. clin. pharmacology dept. psychiatry, 1987-95, assoc. prof. dept. psychiatry and pharmacology, 1990-96, dir. geriatric psychopharm. dept. psychiatry, 1995—, prof. dept. psychiatry, 1996—. Contbr. about 80 articls to profl. jours.; contbg. author books in field. Centennial fellow Med. Rsch. Coun. of Can., Ottawa, 1983, Merck fellow geriatric clin. pharmacology, Am. Fedn. for Aging Rsch., N.Y.C., 1988; recipient acad. award geriatric mental health NIMH, Bethesda, Md., 1992. Fellow Royal Coll. Physicians Can. Home: 7032 Meade Pl Pittsburgh PA 15208 Office: Western Psychiat Inst/Clin 3811 O Hara St Pittsburgh PA 15213

POLLOCK, CARYL JEAN, internist; b. Chgo., Sept. 24, 1950; d. Michael William and Bobbette J. Coglianese; m. William Gaither Murchison, May 5, 1993. BA in Psychology cum laude, No. Ill. U., 1972; MS in Physiology, Loyola U., 1976; DO, Coll. Osteopathic Medicine, 1978. Diplomate Am. Bd. Internal Medicine; lic. physician, Colo., Ill. Intern Chgo. Osteopathic Med. Ctr., 1978-79, resident, 1979-82; chmn. medicine dept. Eisenhower Hosp., Colorado Springs, 1986-90; quality assurance com. mem. Meml. Hosp., Colorado Springs, 1990-95; credentials com. mem. Colorado Springs Health Ptnrs., 1995—. Exhibited in group show at Poor Richard's Expresso Bar, 1993; contbr. articles to profl. jours. Mem. El Paso County Search and Rescue, Colorado Springs, 1995—. Mem. Am. Coll. Osteopathic Internists, Am. Osteopathic Assn., Colorado Med. Soc., El Paso County Med. Soc. (credentials com. 1989-93). Office: Colo Springs Health Ptnrs 209 S Nevada Colorado Springs CO 80903

POLLOCK, DIANA LYNN, neurologist; b. Berkeley, Calif., Dec. 2, 1957; d. Richard Edward and Marjorie Helen (Smith) P.; m. Paul Scott Denker, July 23, 1980. BA, Washington U., St. Louis, 1978; MD, St. Louis U., 1982. Diplomate Am. Bd. Internal Medicine, Am. Bd. Neurology. Specialist in internal medicine U. So. Fla., Tampa, 1982-85, specialist in neurology, 1991-94; primary care dir. Pinellas County Health Dept., St. Petersburg, Fla., 1985-88; dir. immediate care Suncoast Med. Clinic, St. Petersburg, 1988-91; pvt. practice Clin. Neurol. Specialties, Clearwater, Fla., 1994—. Mem. Am. Acad. Neurology, Phi Beta Kappa. Office: 1011 Jeffords St Bldg A Clearwater FL 34616

POLLOCK, GEORGE HOWARD, psychiatrist, psychoanalyst; b. Chgo., June 19, 1923; s. Harry J. and Belle (Lurie) P.; m. Beverly Yufit, July 3, 1946; children: Beth L. Pollock Ungar, Raphael E., Daniel A., Benjamin B., Naomi R. Pollock Sneider. B.S., U. Ill., 1944, M.D. cum laude, 1945, M.S., 1948, Ph.D., 1951. Diplomate Am. Bd. Psychiatry and Neurology. Intern Cook County Hosp., Chgo., 1945-46; resident Ill. Neuropsychiat. Inst., Chgo., 1948-51; practice medicine, specializing in psychiatry Chgo., 1948-91; clin. assoc. prof. dept. psychiatry Coll. Medicine, U. Ill., 1955-64, clin. prof., 1964-72; prof. psychiatry Northwestern U., 1972-93, Dunbar prof. psychiatry and behavioral scis. emeritus, 1993—, dir. rsch. dept. psychiatry/behavioral scis.m 1988-93, emeritus, 1993—; faculty Inst. for Psychoanalysis, Chgo., 1956-92, asst. dean edn., 1960-67, tng. analyst 1961-92, supervising analyst, 1962-92, dir. rsch., 1963-71, pres., 1971-89; exch. program participant Hampstead Child Therapy Clinic, 1962-63; pres. Ctr. Psychosocial Studies, 1972-90. Chmn. bd. editors Ann. of Psychoanalysis, 1971-89; mem. editorial bd. Jour. Am. Psychoanalytic Assn., 1971-74; mem. editorial bd. sect. psychoanalysis Psychiat. Jour. U. Ottawa Faculty Medicine, 1976—; corr. editor Jour. Geriatric Psychiatry, 1975—; Med. Problems of Performing Artists, Psychoanalytic Edn., Psychoanalytic Psychology, Internat. Forum for Psychoanalysis, Internat. Jour. Behavioral Scis. and the Law, Internat. Psychogeriatrics, Depression and Stress. Mem. med. adv. com. Planned Parenthood Assn., 1966-70; pres. governing bd. Parents Assn. Lab. Schs., U. Chgo., 1966-70; mem. med. adv. coun. Asthma and Allergy Found. for Greater Chgo. Capt. U.S. Army, 1946-48. Commonwealth fellow, 1951; research grantee Founds. Fund for Research in Psychiatry, 1960-65. Fellow Am. Coll. Psychiatrists, Am. Orthopsychiat. Assn., Am. Psychiat. Assn. (treas. 1980-86, pres. 1987-88), Am. Coll. Psychoanalysts (pres. 1985-86); mem. Internat. Psychogeriatrics (mem. editorial bds.), Am. Acad. Polit. and Social Sci., Am. Anthrop. Assn., Nat. Council on Family Relations, AAAS, AAUP, Profs., Am. Electroencephalographic Soc., Am. Heart Assn., Assn. for Research in Nervous and Mental Disease, Soc. for Exptl. Biology and Medicine, Ill., N.Y. acads. scis., Chgo. Psychoanalytic Soc. (pres. 1984-85), Soc. for Gen. Systems Research, AMA, World Med. Assn., Am. Name Soc., Am. Psychoanalytic Assn. (pres. 1974-75), Am. Psychol. Assn., Am. Psychosomatic Soc., Am. Pub. Health Assn., Am. Sociol. Assn., Assn. Am. Med. Colls., Ill. Psychiat. Soc. (pres. 1973-74), Sigma Xi, Alpha Omega Alpha, numerous others. Home: 5759 S Dorchester Ave Chicago IL 60637-1726 Office: 30 N Michigan Ave Chicago IL 60602-3400

POLLOCK, TONY JOE, nurse consultant; b. St. Mary's, Ohio, Apr. 10, 1961; s. Gary D. and Loretta J. (Lowe) P. BSN, U. Minn., 1983. CCRN, CEN. Staff nurse ICU VA Med. Ctr., Martinez, Calif., 1986-88; charge nurse emergency room Mad River Community Hosp., Arcata, Calif., 1988-90; staff emergency med. technician, paramedic Hupa Health Assn. EMS, Hoopa, Calif., 1989-91; charge nurse emergency svcs. Health One Unit Hosp., Fridley, Minn., 1991-93; mgr. NurseLine United Healthcare, Golden Valley, Minn., 1993-95; sr. ptnr. Midwest Legal Nurse Cons., Inc., Edina, Minn., 1995—; staff nurse Park Nicollet Clinic Phone Care, Wayzata, Minn., 1995—. Capt. Nurse Corps, U.S. Army, 1983-86. Home: 601 S 9th St Minneapolis MN 55404-1179 Office: PO Box 39155 Edina MN 55439

POLLY, STUART MCGRATH, health facility administrator; b. Washington, July 9, 1940; s. Stanley Robert and Sylvia Vannah (McGrath) P.; m. Judith Deanne Gillis, July 3, 1965 (div. July 1976); children: Matthew Stuart, Alison Rees; m. Dianne Elaine Kammerer, June 27, 1980; children: Alexandra Vanessa, Samantha Ashley. AB in Biology, Dartmouth Coll., Hanover, N.H., 1962; MS in Bacteriology, U. Fla., 1964, MD, 1968. Diplomate in infectious disease Am. Bd. Internal Medicine. Resident in internal medicine AB Chandler Tchg. Hosp. U. Ky., Lexington, 1968-70; fellow Shands Teaching Hosp., Gainesville, Fla., 1972-73; resident in internal medicine Shands Tchg. Hosp. U. Fla., Gainesville, 1973-74; asst. prof. microbiology and medicine Creighton U., 1974-80; dir. infectious disease St. Joseph Hosp., Omaha, 1974-80; assoc. prof. medicine Tex. Tech. U., El Paso, 1980-86; chief med. svc. Thomason Gen. Hosp., El Paso, Tex., 1980-90; prof. medicine and microbiology Tex. Tech. U., El Paso and Lubbock, Tex., 1986-90; med. dir. Regional Med. Ctr., Memphis, 1990-92; prof. medicine U. Tenn., Memphis, 1990—; chief med. officer, sr. v.p. clin. affairs Regional Med. Ctr., Memphis, 1992—; bd. dirs. Mid-South Family Health Care Ctr., BOD Memphis Managed Care Co., BOD Primary Care Svcs. Inc.; assoc. med. dir. TLC Family HealthCare, Memphis, 1995—. Lt. comdr. M.C., USN, 1970-72. Fellow ACP; mem. AMA (rep. 1982—), Am. Coll. Physician Execs., Tenn. Med. Assn., Memphis/Shelby County Med. Soc., Leadership Memphis. Office: Regional Med Ctr 842 Jefferson Ave Memphis TN 38103

POLOGEORGIS, GEORGE JOHN, oncologist, surgeon, researcher; b. Athens, Attika, Greece, Feb. 10, 1948; s. John George and Evangelia John (Micheletou) P. MD, Athens U., 1972; cert., E.C.F.M.G., U.S.A., 1972. Intern surg. dept. Halkis (Evia Island, Greece) State Hosp., 1974-75, Evreux (Normandy, France) State Hosp., 1976-78, Chartres State Hosp., Eure-Et-Loire, France, 1979-80, Germain-En-Laye Hosp., Paris, 1980-81; gen. practitioner Sfakia Country Infirmary, Crete Island, Greece, 1976-77; resident surg. dept. Centre Réné-Huguenin Cancer Hosp., Paris, 1981-82, Notre-Dame-Du-Perpétuel-Secours Hosp., Paris, 1982-83; asst. surg. dept. Inst. Gustave-Roussy Cancer Hosp., Villejuif, France, 1983-84, Children's Hosp.

P. & A. Kyriakou, Athens, 1984-85, Hellenic Anticancer Inst., Athens, 1985—; asst. Paris U. Affiliate Hosp., Inst. Gustave-Roussy, Faculty Kremlin-Bicêre. Contbr. articles to profl. jours. Mem. Alive As Before, 1989. Lt. Greek Army, 1973-74. Athens U. scholar, 1971, 72. Mem. Hellenic Surg. Soc./Coll. Surgeons, Hellenic Anticancer Soc., Hellenic Soc. Oncology, Hellenic/Internat. Soc. Mastology Athens, Athens Tennis Club, Tatoi Riding Club. Home: 59 Ypsilantou St, GR-11521 Athens Greece Office: St Savvas Hosp, 171 Alexandras Ave, GR-11522 Athens Greece

POLSKY, LOUIS SANFORD, obstetrician, gynecologist; b. Longview, Tex., July 20, 1932; s. Sam and Ruth (Glass) P.; m. Joyce Misthal, Jan. 22, 1961; children: Gary Steven, Jay Howard, Jeffrey Carl. BA, U. Tex., 1954; MD, U. Tex., Galveston, 1958. Intern Phila. Gen. Hosp., 1958-59, resident, 1961-64; pres. Prospect Women's Med. Ctr., P.A., Hackensack, N.J., 1980—. Contbr. articles to profl. jours. Lt. USN, 1959-61. Fellow ACS, Am. Coll. Ob-Gyn., Am. Fertility Soc., Gyn. Laser Soc., Am. Colposcopists, Am. Lararoscopists. Jewish. Office: Prospect Women's Med Ctr 120 Prospect Ave Hackensack NJ 07601-2256

POLSKY, MARK DAVID, emergency physician; b. St. Louis, Aug. 21, 1954; s. Selwyn Jean and Betty Ruth (Murnan) P.; m. Jonna Marie Avella, Jan. 1, 1996. AD in Respiratory Therapy, Kans. U. Med. Ctr., 1979; BA in Natural Sci., Avila Coll., 1984; DO, Kirksville Coll. Osteo., 1988. Diplomate Am. Bd. Emergency Medicine, Osteo. Emergency Medicine. Emergency physician Martin Meml. Med. Ctr., Stuart, Fla., 1992—; med. dir. Hobe Sound (Fla.) Ambulance, 1994—; instr. PALS, Am. Heart Assn. Mem. Am. Coll. Emergency Physicians, Am. Osteo. Assn., Fla. Assn. Emergency Med. Dirs. Home: 8169 SE Pilots Cove Terr Hobe Sound FL 33455 Office: Martin Meml Med Ctr 300 SE Hospital Dr Stuart FL 34994

POLSKY, MICHAEL, neurologist; b. Bklyn., July 26, 1938; s. Edward and Sarah (Rabinowitz) P.; m. Rita Klaitman, Aug. 17, 1968; children: Yarom, Ronen, Sarit, Avital. BA, Bklyn. Coll., 1960; MD, Faculté de Medecine Lariboisiere-St. Louis, Paris, 1969. Diplomate Am. Bd. Neurology. Intern Jeffrey Hale's Hosp., Quebec City, Can., 1969-70; resident in internal medicine Bronx VA Hosp., N.Y., 1970-71; commed. 2d lt. U.S. Army, 1971, advanced through grades to lt. col., resigned, 1980; neurologist Walter Reed Army Med. Ctr., Washington, 1971-74; from asst. chief to acting chief Neurology Service Brooke Army Med. Ctr., San Antonio, 1974-80; practice medicine specializing in neurology Las Cruces, N.Mex., 1980—. Lt. col. USAR, 1987—. Mem. AMA, Am. Acad. Neurology, N.Y. Acad. Scis., Wilderness Med. Soc. Jewish. Office: 2467 Telshor Blvd Las Cruces NM 88001

POLSON, DONALD ALLAN, surgeon; b. Gallup, N.Mex., May 12, 1911; s. Thomas Cress and Carrie Fern (Cantrall) P.; m. Cecily, Lady Avebury, Nov. 9, 1946; 1 child, Carolyn Kathleen. Student Stanford U.; MD, Northwestern U., 1936, MSc, 1947. Diplomate Am. Bd. Surgery. Intern, then resident in surgery St. Luke's Hosp., Chgo., 1936-38; practice medicine specializing in gen. surgery, Phoenix, 1947-83; formerly chmn. Drs. Polson, Berens & Petelin, Ltd.; chief staff Maricopa County Hosp., 1952-53, St. Joseph's Hosp., 1961; bd. dirs. Ariz. Blue Shield, 1950-55, pres., 1956. Served to col. M.C., AUS, World War II. Mem. AMA, ACS, Ariz. Med. Assn. (dir. 1955-60), Maricopa County Med. Soc. (pres. 1954), Phoenix Surg. Soc. (pres. 1959), White Mountain Country Club, Alpha Omega Alpha, Nu Sigma Nu. Republican. Episcopalian. Home: 7619 N Tatum Blvd Paradise Valley AZ 85253-3378

POLZIEN, PAUL ADALBERT, physician; b. Roessel, East Prussia, Fed. Republic of Germany, Oct. 18, 1918; s. Paul and Martha (Pusch) P.; m. Edith Helene Berndt, Aug. 18, 1978 (dec. Jan. 1991); children: Paul, Peter. Med. Degree, U. Erlangen, Fed. Republic of Germany, 1946, MD, 1946. Asst. internal medicine U. Erlangen, Heidelberg, Fed. Republic of Germany, 1946-48; asst. physiologist U. Erlangen, Fed. Republic of Germany, 1948-50; asst. psychotherapy U. Tuebingen, Fed. Republic of Germany, 1951; asst. internal medicine and psychotherapy U. Wuerzburg, Fed. Republic of Germany, 1951-53; specialist in internal medicine Medizinische Poliklinik U., Wuerzburg, Fed. Republic of Germany, 1953-64, dep. head, 1964-81, standing-in for dept. head, 1981-82; pvt. practice medicine specializing in internal medicine Wuerzburg, Fed. Republic of Germany, 1983—; professorship U. Wuerzburg, 1957. Author: Physiology of Hypnotic State as Somatic Base for Neurosis, 1958. Recipient Ernst-Von-Bergmann Placque Bundesärztekammer, 1977. Mem. Deutsche Gesellschaft Fuer Innere Medizin, Deutsche Ges. F. Herz-Kreislaufforschung, Internat. Com. for the Coordination of Clin. Application and Teaching in Autogenic Tng. (found.), Deutsche Gesellschaft Fuer Autogenes Tng. and Hypnosis, Psychotherapeutisches Kolleg U. of Wuerzburg (found.). Office: 23 Trautenauer Strasse, Wuerzburg D97074, Germany

POMAZAL, ANDREW MICHAEL, physician; b. Milw., Nov. 20, 1950; s. John and Elizabeth (Aitcheson) P.; m. Deborah Ann Dabney, May 3, 1975; children: Gregory, Jason, Tyra, Michael, Joshua. BS, Southern Oregon State Coll., 1981; D in chiropractic, Western States Chiro. Coll., 1983; DO, Univ. New Eng., 1996. Diplomate Am. Bd. Pain Mgmt. Clinician Pine Tree Chiropractic, Klamath Falls, Oreg.; instr. ODOC; instr. pharmacology Emergency Medicine Western States Chiropractic Coll., Portland, Oreg. Contbr. articles to profl. jours. Bd. govs. Oreg. Chiropractic Physicians Assn., 1990-91, Chiropractic Assn. Oreg., 1992-93; bd. dirs. Kiwanis Klamath Falls, 1992. With Navy, 1969-73, Coast Guard Res., 1974-78. Office: Pine Tree Chiropractic 832 Klamath Ave Klamath Falls OR 97601

POMERANCE, HERBERT HART, pediatrician; b. N.Y.C., Mar. 28, 1918; s. Nathaniel and Ida (Warfman) P.; m. Ruth Elizabeth Segal, Dec. 25, 1940; children: Glenn N., Roger M. BS, NYU, N.Y.C., 1937; MD, Columbia U., 1941. Licentiate Am. Bd. Pediatrics. Intern Meml. Hosp., Wilmington, Del., 1941-42; resident Gouverneur Hosp., N.Y.C., 1946-47, Willard Parker Hosp., N.Y.C., 1947; chief resident Lincoln Hosp., N.Y.C., 1948; pvt. practice pediatrics N.Y.C., 1949-70; chmn. pediatrics Charleston (W.Va.) Area Med. Ctr., 1970-73; prof., chmn. dept. pediatrics W.Va. U. Sch. Medicine, Charleston, 1973-84; prof. pediatrics U. South Fla., Tampa, 1984—, prof., chmn. pediatrics, 1990-91. Author: Growth Standards in Children, 1979; co-editor: Topics in Pediatrics, 1990. Maj., M.C., U.S. Army, 1942-46. Fellow Am. Acad. Pediatrics (chpt. chmn. W.Va. chpt. 1976-82, mem. com. on practice 1974-84, chmn. com. on comm. Fla. chpt. 1990—). Home: 4936 Bay Way Dr Tampa FL 33629 Office: U South Fla 1 Davis Blvd Ste 307 Tampa FL 33606

POMERANTZ, JACOB, retired physician; b. Phila., Aug. 9, 1907; s. Abraham and Rebecca (Winokur) P.; m. Mollie Esther Orloff, June 3, 1931 (dec. 1987); children: Marc A., Rachel Ann Pomerantz Schonberger; m. Charlotte Feldstein, May 29, 1988. BA, U. Pa., 1927; MD, Temple U., 1931. Intern Temple Univ. Hosp., Phila., 1931-33; pvt. practice Phila., 1933-72; regional med. dir. United Parcel Svc., Chgo., 1973-84; ret., 1984. Maj. USAF, 1942-46. Fellow Am. Occupational Med. Assn.; mem. AMA, Chgo. Med. Assn. (emeritus), Ill. Med. Assn. (emeritus). Home: 2460 Peachtree Rd NW Apt 412 Atlanta GA 30305-4154

POMERANTZ, JAY MARTIN, psychiatrist; b. Bklyn., Apr. 8, 1939; s. Eli and Rita (Migdal) P.; m. Farida Attia, July 2, 1967; children: Anne, Maurice. AB, Hamilton Coll., Clinton, N.Y., 1959; MD, Yale U., 1963. Staff physician Peace Corps, Panama, 1964-65; med. dir. for Latin Am. Peace Corps, Washington, 1965-66; resident in psychiatry Mass. Mental Health Ctr., 1966-69; asst. reg. mental health adminstrn. Mass. Dept. Mental Health, Springfield, 1966-70; reg. mental health adminstr. Mass. Dept. Mental Health, 1970-71; pvt. practice psychiatry Longmeadow, Mass., 1970—; clin. instr. Tufts Med. Sch., Boston, 1974—. Author: The Bethlehem Diaries: Student-Mental Patient Encounters, 1974; contbr. articles to profl. jours. Bd. dirs. Child & Family Svc. of Springfield, 1972. With USPHS, 1964-66. Fellow APA; mem. Mass. Psychiat. Soc. (pres. western Mass. chpt. 1979-80, counselor 1979-80). Office: 123 Dwight Rd East Longmeadow MA 01106-1748

POMERANTZ, MARVIN, thoracic surgeon; b. Suffern, N.Y., June 16, 1934; s. Julius and Sophie (Luksin) P.; m. Margaret Twigg, Feb. 26, 1966; children: Ben, Julie. AB, Colgate U., 1955; MD, U. Rochester, 1959. Diplomate Nat. Bd. Med. Examiners, Am. Bd. Surgery, Am. Bd. Thoracic Surgery (dir. 1989—). Intern Duke U. Med. Ctr., Durham, N.C., 1959-60, resident, 1960-61, 63-67, instr. surgery, 1966-67; asst. prof. surgery U. Colo. Med. Sch., Denver, 1967-71, assoc. prof. surgery, 1971-74, assoc. clin. prof. surgery, 1974-93, prof. surgery, chief gen. thoracic surgery, 1992—; chief thoracic and cardiovascular surgery Denver Gen. Hosp., 1967-73, asst. dir. surgery, 1967-70, assoc.dir. surgery, 1970-73; pvt. practice Arapahoe CV Assocs., Denver, 1974-92; clin. assoc. surgery br. Nat. Cancer Inst., 1961-63; mem.staff Univ. Hosp., Denver, Denver Gen. Hosp., Rose Med. Ctr., Denvr, St. Joseph's Hosp., Denver, Englewood, Colo., Porter Meml. Hosp., Denver, Swedish Med. Ctr., Englewood, Denver VA Med. Ctr., Children's Hosp., Denver, U. Coll. Health Sci. Ctr., 1992—, bd. dirs., 1995-97. chmn., 1997, Am. Bd. Thoracic Surgery. Guest editor Chest Surgery Clinics N.Am., 1993; contbr. numerous articles to profl. publs., chpts. to books. Fellow ACS, Am. Coll. Chest Surgeons; mem. AMA, Western Thoracic Surg. Assn. (v.p. 1992, pres. 1993-94, counselor-at-large 1988-90), Am. Assn. Thoracic Surgeons (program com. 1991), Am. Heart Assn. (bd. dirs. Colo. chpt. 1993), Arapahoe Med. Soc., Colo. Med. Soc., Denver Acad. Surgery (pres. 1980), Internat. Cardiovascular Soc., Rocky Mtn. Cardiac Surgery Soc., Rocky Mtn. Traumatologic Soc., Soc. Thoracic Surgeons (nomenclature/coding com. 1991-95, standards and ethics com., govt. rels. com., chmn. program com. 1994-95), Soc. Vascular Surgeons, Am. Bd. Thoracic Surgery (vice chmn. 1996—). Office: UCHSC Divsn CTS 4200 E 9th Ave # C310 Denver CO 80220-3706

POMERANZ, HARRY, physician assistant, clinician, educator; b. Haifa, Israel, June 5, 1952; s. Joseph Pomeranz and Irene Steinker; m. Carol Ann Schaeffler, May 20, 1973; 1 child, Joshua. BS, L.I. U., 1978; postgrad., Hunter Coll., 1990-92, L.I. U., 1995. Cert. physician asst., family practice and surgery. Physician asst. dept. emergency medicine Beth Israel Med. Ctr., N.Y.C., 1980-83; chief physician asst. dept. emergency medicine Meth. Hosp.-N.Y. Hosp., Bklyn., 1983-94, Bklyn. Hosp. Ctr./NYU, 1994—; instr. ACLS, Am. Heart Assn., N.Y.C., 1986—, Advanced Pediat. Life Support, 1989—; instr. physician asst. program Bklyn. Hosp./L.I. U., 1994—; lectr. in emergency medicine Bklyn. Hosp. Emergency Medicine Residency Program, 1994—. Mem. Soc. Emergency Medicine Physician Assts. (founding mem), Physician Assts. for Social Change (founding mem.), Am. Acad. Physician Assts., N.Y. State Soc. Physician Assts. Home: 687 East 24th St Brooklyn NY 11210 Office: Bklyn Hosp Ctr 121 Dekalb Ave Brooklyn NY 11201

POMERANZ, JEROME RAPHAEL, dermatologist; b. Newark, Dec. 29, 1930; s. Raphael and Zina (Rubinow) P.; m. Jacqueline R. Goldenberg, June 15, 1953 (div. 1973); m. Barbara P. Barna, May 5, 1978; children: Russell Carl, William Eric, Emily Suzanne. BS, George Washington U., 1952; MD, Boston U., 1956. Diplomate Am. Bd. Dermatology, Am. Bd. Pathology. Intern, then resident Johns Hopkins Hosp., Balt., 1957-58, resident in dermatology, 1960-63, fellow in allergy, 1963-65, mem. staff; assoc. prof. dermatology Case Western Res. U., Cleve., 1965—, assoc. prof. pathology, 1967—; dir. dermatology Metro Health Med. Ctr., 1965-92, mem. staff, 1992—. Contbr. articles to profl. jours. Served to capt. M.C., U.S. Army, 1958-60. Fellow ACP, Am. Am. Acad. Dermatology; mem. AAAS, NAS (drug efficacy studyjpanel 1967-69, com. to rev. use of ionizing radiation for treatment of benign diseases 1975-78), Am. Dermatol. Assn., FDA Bur. Drugs (dermatology adv. com. 1981-85, 92-94), Cleve. Dermatol. Soc. (pres. 1973-75), Am. Soc. Dermatopathology, Soc. Investigative Dermatology (membership com. 1975, 76, 77, chmn. 1977, audit com. 1993—), Assn. Profs. Dermatology, N.Y. Acad. Scis., Cleve. Acad. Medicine. Home: 490 Merrimak Dr Berea OH 44017-2241 Office: Cleve Skin Pathology Lab 2475 E 22d St Rm 611 Cleveland OH 44115

POMEROY, BRUCE MARCEL, critical care nurse, educator; b. East St. Louis, Ill., July 11, 1959; s. Martin Bruce and Loretta Emma (Klasing) P. ADN, Kaskaskia Jr. Coll., Centralia, Ill., 1979; BSN, McKendree Coll., Lebanon, Ill., 1981; MSN, St. Louis U., 1992. RN, Ill., Mo.; cert. ACLS provider, BLS instr. Staff and charge nurse Washington County Hosp., Nashville, Ill., 1979-81; staff nurse ICU-telemetry-orthopedic units St. Elizabeth Hosp., Belleville, Ill., 1981-83; staff nurse/ preceptor ICU, critical care nursing edn. instr. Meml. Hosp., Belleville, 1983—; house supr. Deaconess Hosp., St. Louis, 1995—; clinical nursing instr. Belleville Area Coll., 1992-93, Kaskaskia Coll, Centralia, Ill., 1993—; clinical nursing instr., Sch. Nursing. Luth. Med. Ctr., St. Louis. Mo., 1995—; clin. nursing instr. Sch. Nursing, Deaconess Coll. Nursing, St. Louis, 1996—. Mem. sr. choir St. Peter's United Ch. of Christ; v.p. ch. coun. St. Paul's United Ch. Christ, Okawville, Ill. Mem. AACN (co-founder Metro East chpt.), nat. League Nursing, N.Am. Nursing Diagnosis Assn., McKendree Coll. Nursing Hon. Soc. (charter), Sigma Theta Tau, Sigma Zeta, Phi Theta Kappa. Home: PO Box 66 316 W Elm St Okawville IL 62271-0066

POMEROY, KENT LYTLE, physical medicine and rehabilitation physician; b. Phoenix, Apr. 21, 1935; s. Benjamin Kent and LaVerne (Hamblin) P.; m. Karen Jodelle Thomas (dec. Dec. 1962); 1 child, Charlotte Ann; m. Margo Delilah Tuttle, Mar. 27, 1964 (div. Jan. 1990); children: Benjamin Kent II, Janel Elise, Jonathan Barrett, Kimberly Eve; m. Brenda Pauline North, Sept. 1, 1990. BS in Phys. Sci., Ariz. State U., 1960; MD, U. Utah, 1963. Diplomate Am. Bd. Phys. Medicine and Rehab., Am. Bd. Pain Medicine. Rotating intern Good Samaritan Hosp., Phoenix, 1963-64; resident in phys. medicine and rehab. Good Samaritan Hosp., 1966-69, asst. tng. dir. Inst. Rehab. Medicine, 1970-74, dir. residency tng., 1974-76, asst. med. dir., 1973-76; dir. Phoenix Phys. Medicine Ctr., 1980-85, Ariz. Found. on Study Pain, Phoenix, 1980-85; pvt. practice, Phoenix and Scottsdale, Ariz., 1985—; lectr. in field. Contbr. articles to med. jours. Leader Theodore Roosevelt coun. Boy Scouts Am.; mem. exec. posse Maricopa County Sheriff's Office, Phoenix, 1981—, posse comdr., 1992-94, qualified armed posseman; mem. med. adv. bd. Grand Canyon-Saguaro chpt. Nat. Found. March of Dimes, 1970-78. Recipient Scouter's Tng. award Theodore Roosevelt coun. Boy Scouts Am., 1984, Scouter's Woodbadge, 1985. Mem. AMA, Am. Acad. Phys. Medicine and Rehab., Internat. Rehab. Medicine Assn., Am. Assn. Orthopaedic Medicine (co-founder, sec.-treas. 1982-88, pres. 1988-90), Pan Am. Med. Assn. (diplomate), Prolotherapy Assn. (pres. 1981-83), Am. Pain Soc., Western Pain Soc., Am. Assn. for Study Headache, Am. Thermographic Soc. (charter), Am. Soc. Addiction Medicine (sec. Ariz. chpt.), Am. Acad. Pain Medicine, Nat. Eagle Scout Assn., Acad. Clin. Neurophysiology, Ariz. Soc. Phys. Medicine (pres. 1977-78), Ariz. Med. Assn., Maricopa County Med. Soc., others, Nat. Sheriff's Assn. Law Enforcement Alliance of Am. Mem. LDS Ch. Address: 2536 N 3rd St Ste 3 Phoenix AZ 85004-1308

POMEROY, LEON RALPH, psychologist; b. Westfield, Mass., Dec. 6, 1933; s. L. Ralph and Rachel (Harlow) P.; m. Wendy Anwar, Oct. 17, 1985. BA, U. Mass., 1959, MA, 1961; PhD, U. Tex. Austin, 1967. Lic. psychologist, N.Y., N.J.; cert. addictions specialist. Rsch. scientist Clayton Found. Biochem. Inst. U. Tex. Austin, 1962-65, rsch. biomed. engr., 1965-67; asst. prof., assoc. prof. L.I. U., N.Y.C., 1967-72; assoc. prof. Kean Coll., Union, N.J., 1972-73; clin. psychologist, dir. Behavioral Medicine VA Med. Ctr., Bklyn., 1973—; pres. Behavioral Axiology, Ltd., N.Y.C.; pvt. practice, Manhattan, 1972—; adj. assoc. prof. CUNY, 1968-72, 78, New Sch. for Social Rsch., 1977-78, NYU, 1974-76. Contbr. articles to profl. jours. Bd. dirs. Hartman Inst., 1982—. Inst. Advanced Study in Radional and Cognitive Psychotherapies fellow, 1970-73. Mem. Internat. Acad. Preventive Medicine (pres. 1974-75, bd. dirs. 1972-82, editor-in-chief publs. 1971-87). Home: 1619 3d Ave Apt 19 DE New York NY 10128

POMPOSELLI, FRANK BERNARD, JR., vascular surgeon; b. Rutherford, N.J., July 16, 1952; s. Frank B. Sr. and Constance Pomposelli. BS, Boston Coll., 1974; MD, Boston U., 1979. Intern, then resident New Eng. Deaconess Hosp., Boston; fellow NYU Med. Ctr., N.Y.C.; asst. prof. surgery Harvard Med. Sch., New Eng. Deaconess Hosp., Boston, 1987—. Office: 110 Francis St 5B Boston MA 02215

PONCE, SANTIAGO PEDRO, nephrologist; b. Lisbon, Portugal, Sept. 23, 1953; s. Santiago Jervis and Maria Avsenda (Magalhães) P.; m. Olga Murgado, July 30, 1975; 1 child, Pedro Miguel. MD, Lisbon U., 1976. Bd. cert. nephrologist, Portugal, bd. cert. intensivist, European comty. Resident in internal medicine SUNY, 1981-82; renal fellow Hospitais Civis Lisbon, 1982-86, Tufts U., 1983, Harvard U., 1984; staff nephrologist Hosp. S. Cruz, Portugal, 1987-92; chief nephrology svc. Hosp. Garcia de Urta, Portugal, 1993—; clin. dir. Hosp. CUF, Portugal, 1990-93; chief of intensive care unit CUF, Portugal, 1987—; clin. dir. Med. Care Dialysis Unit, Portugal, 1985—; nephrology cons. Brit. Hosp., Portugal. Contbr. med. rsch. articles to profl. jours. Mem. ethics and discipline com. Portuguese Med. Assn., 1990-93; head ethics com. Hosp. Garcia de Urta, 1993—. Mem. Portuguese Soc. Nephrology (sec. gen. 1986-91), Internat. Soc. Nephrology, Portuguese Soc. Intensive Care. Roman Catholic.

PONTE, CHARLES DENNIS, pharmacist, educator; b. Waterbury, Conn., Jan. 17, 1953; s. Americo Joseph and Irene (Poirier) P. BSc in Pharmacy, U. Conn., 1975; D Pharmacy, U. Utah, 1980. Diplomate Am. Acad. Pain Mgmt.; cert. diabetes edn.; bd. cert. pharmacotherapy specialist. Intern Woodbury (Conn.) Drug Co., 1975; hosp. pharmacy resident Yale-New Haven Hosp., 1975-76, ambulatory staff pharmacist, 1976-78; prof. clin. pharmacy, family medicine Robert C. Byrd Health Scis. Ctr. of W.Va. U., Morgantown, 1980—, also dir. PharmD program; mem. adv. bd. ambulatory care and family practice Annals Pharmacotherapy, Cin., 1985—; mem. adv. panel on family practice U.S. Pharmacopeial Conv., Inc., Rockville, Md., 1990—; mem. vis. faculty Upjohn Co., Kalamazoo, 1986; coord. Sch. Pharmacy, Spencer State Tng. Ctr., 1984-88; participant Practical Aspects of Diabetes Care: Conf. for Pharmacy Educators, 1989; chmn. Van Liere Rsch. Convocation for Med. Students, 1990; mem. splty. coun. on nutritional support pharmacy practice Bd. Pharm. Spltys., 1994—. Contbr. to profl. publs. Grantee Robert Wood Johnson Found., 1981. Fellow Am. Coll. Clin. Pharmacy, Am. Soc. Hosp. Pharmacists (practice interest adv. panel 1990-92); mem. Am. Coll. Clin. Pharmacy, Am. Coll. Clin. Pharmacology, Soc. Tchrs. Family Medicine, Am. Diabetes Assn. (pres. W.Va. affiliate 1985-86), Sigma Xi, Phi Kappa Phi, Phi Lambda Sigma, Rho Chi. Roman Catholic. Office: WVa U Robert C Byrd Health Sci Ctr Sch Pharmacy Morgantown WV 26506

PONTEROTTO, JOSEPH GERARD, psychology educator; b. Bronx, N.Y.. BA magna cum laude, Iona Coll., 1980; MA, U. Calif., Santa Barbara, 1981, PhD, 1985. Asst. prof., counseling psychology Univ. Nebr., Lincoln, 1985-87; asst. prof., counseling psychology Lincoln Ctr. Fordham U., 1987-90, assoc. prof., program coord., 1990-93, prof., 1994—. Mem. editl. bd. Jour. Multicultural Counseling and Devel., 1985-87, 87-90, Ednl. Psychology Rev., 1988-90, The Counseling Psychologist, 1989-91, Jour. Counseling Psychology, others; author: (with others) Affirmative Action on Campus, 1990, Handbook of Racial/Ethnic Minority Counseling Research, 1991, Preventing Prejudice, 1993, Handbook of Multicultural Counseling, 1995, Handbook of Multicultural Assessment, 1996; contbr. chpts. to books, articles to profl. jours. Fellow APA, Am. Assn. Applied and Preventive Psychology. Office: Fordham Univ Lincoln Ctr Div Psychol & Ednl Svcs New York NY 10023-7478

PONTES, JOSE EDSON, urologist; b. Fortaleza-Ceara, Brazil, Mar. 26, 1941; came to U.S., 1966; s. Edson M. and Teresita S. (Silva) P.; m. Susan Faye Kunert; children: Daniel, David. BS, Collegio S. Joao, Fortaleza-Ceara, 1958; MD, Fed. U. Ceara, 1964; PhD (hon.), U. Fortaleza-Ceara. Clin. instr. urology Wayne State U., Detroit, 1971-73, asst. prof., 1973-75, assoc. prof., 1976-80, prof. and chmn. dept. urology, 1990—; assoc. prof. urology SUNY, Buffalo, 1980-84; chief dept. urology/oncology Roswell Park Meml. Unit, Buffalo, 1980-84; head sect. urology/oncology Cleve. Clinic Found., 1984-90. Mem. Brazilian Acad. Medicine. Republican. Office: Harper Professional Bldg 4160 John R St #1017 Detroit MI 48201-2020

PONTIOUS, JAMES MICHAEL, medical educator; b. Ada, Okla., Nov. 16, 1952; s. James D. and Dorothy Mae (Postlewaite) P.; m. Myrna Louise Kirk, May 29, 1975; children: Jessica Michaela, James Benjamin, Jonathan Kirk. BS with honors, Okla. Bapt. U., 1975; MD, Okla. U., 1979. Resident U. Okla./ Shawnee Family Medicine; asst. prof. family medicine Okla. U., Oklahoma City, 1982-84; physician pvt. practice, Madill, Okla., 1984-89; asst. prof., program dir. Okla. U./Enid Family Medicine, 1989—; bd. dirs. Meadowlake Hosp., Enid, Ambulatory Sentinel PracticeNEtwork, Denver, Hospice Ctr. of Love, Enid. Mem. adv. coun. Enid Met. Health Planning, 1990—. Mem. AMA, Am. Acad. Family Practice, Okla. State Med. Assn., Okla. Acad. Family Practice, Soc. Tchrs. Family Medicine. Democrat. Baptist. Office: Okla U/Enid Family Medicine 620 S Madison Ste 304 Enid OK 73701

PONTIROLI, ANTONIO ETTORE, medical educator; b. Milan, Italy, July 25, 1947; s. Luigi and Andreina (Bardelli) P.; m. Paola Giuliana Rietti, Dec. 2, 1972; children: Andrew, Francesca. Sci. diploma, Leonardo Da Vinci, Milan, 1965; medical diploma, State U., Milan, 1971. Vol. physician State U., Milan, 1971-72; staff physician Inst. San Raffaele, Milan, 1973-75; rsch. assoc. Wayne State U., Sinai Hosp., Detroit, 1976; established investigator State U., Milan, 1977-88, assoc. prof., 1988-95, prof. internal medicine, 1995—; vice chmn. Inst. San Raffaele, Milan, 1981—, clin. investigations, 1988—; lectr. in field. Contbr. articles to profl. jours.; inventor in field. Recipient Lepetit prize, State U., Milano, 1972. Mem. Endocrine Soc. USA, European Soc. Clin. Investigation (councilor 1993-96, pres. 1996—), European Assn. Study Diabetes, Soc. Italian Diabetes (scientific coun. 1986—), Soc. Italian Endocrinology, Sport Club Milan. Home: Residenza Cerchi-Milano 2, 20090 Segrate Italy Office: Inst San Raffaele, Via Olgettina 60, 20132 Milan Italy

PONTIUS, ANNELIESE ALMA, psychiatrist; b. Chemnitz, Saxony, Germany, May 19, 1921; came to U.S., 1957; d. Karl Gottfried Mueller and Clara (Alma) Mueller Otto; m. Johann Jakob Pontius, July 7, 1951. MD, Johann Wolfgang Goethe U., Frankfurt, Germany, 1950; Grad., Munich Analytic Inst., Fed. Republic of Germany, 1953. Diplomate Am. Bd. Psychiatry and Neurology. Intern U. Hosps., Franfurt, 1950-51; resident McGill U., Montreal, Que., Can., 1955-57, Auspices Mass. Tng. Faculty, Worcester, 1957-59; rsch. assoc. child psychiatry Lenox Hill Hosp., N.Y.C., 1962-64; pvt. practice N.Y.C., 1966—; vis. neuro-psychiatrist NYU Med. Ctr., 1969-76; vis. scientist NIMH, Rockville, Md., 1971-72; clin. assoc. in psychiatry Mass. Gen. Hosp., Boston, 1984—; asst. clin. prof. NYU, 1972-76; asst. psychiatrist McLean Hosp., Belmont, Mass., 1977-84, asst. clin. prof., 1981-86; assoc. clin. prof. Harvard Med. Sch., 1986—. Assoc. editor internat. jour. Biosocial & Med. Rsch., Tacoma, Wash., 1983—; contbr. over 70 articles to profl. jours. Med. expert U.S. Dept. Health and Human Svcs., N.Y.C., 1968—. Fellow N.Y. Acad. Medicine, Explorers Club; mem. AAAS, Am. Psychiat. Assn., N.Y. Acad. Scis., Internat. Assn. Analytical Psychology, Am. Acad. Psychiatry and Law. Home and Office: 165 E 60th St New York NY 10022-1230

PONTOLILO, BRIAN A., physical therapist; b. Boston, Nov. 12, 1949. BS in Phys. Therapy, Marquette U., 1972; MPS in Healthcare Adminstrn., L.I. U., 1978. Lic. phys. therapist, Mass., R.I. V.p. bus. devel. Mediplex Group, Wellesley, Mass., until 1993; v.p. corp. svcs. St. Luke's Hosp., New Bedford, Mass., 1993-94; pres. Chiron Profl. Svcs., Warwick, R.I., 1994—. Office: Chiron Profl Svcs 100 Jefferson Blvd Warwick RI 02888

PONTORIERO, MICHAEL ANTHONY, cardiothoracic surgeon, educator; b. Newark, Sept. 22, 1959; s. Antonio Rocco and Maria Pontoriero; m. Mary Theresa Pugliese, Sept. 24, 1988; 1 child, Maria Isabella. BS in Chemistry summa cum laude, Fordham U., 1981; MD, UMDNJ/N.J. Med. Sch., Newark, 1985. Diplomate Am. Bd. Surgery, Am. Bd. Thoracic Surgery. Intern in gen. surgery U. Medicine and Dentistry N.J./N.J. Med. Sch., Newark, 1985-86, resident, 1986-90, clin. asst. prof. surgery, 1994—; fellow in cardiothoracic surg. rsch. Tufts U. Sch. Medicine and Dentistry-New Eng. Med. Ctr., Boston, 1990-91, resident in cardiothoracic surgery, 1991-93; pvt. practice, Belleville, N.J., 1993—. Contbr. articles to med. jours. Fellow ACS, Am. Coll. Chest Physicians, Am. Coll. Cardiology; mem. Soc. Thoracic Surgeons, N.J. Soc. Thoracic Surgeons, Phi Beta Kappa. Office: Thoracic Cardiovasc Surg Group 5 Franklin Ave Ste 302 Belleville NJ 07109

POOL, JOHN THOMAS, health services coordinator, consultant; b. Spokane, Wash., July 13, 1943; s. Dean Layton and Alice Gwendalyn (Rygg) P.; m. Elaine W. Wirkkunen, Mar. 25, 1972; children: Matthew, Erik. BA in Econs., U. Wash., 1966. Detective Univ. Police Dept., Seattle, 1970-74; spl. agt. Drug Enforcement Adminstrn., Seattle and El Paso, Tex., 1976-83; tng. coord. Drug Enforcement Adminstrn., Dallas, 1983-88; demand reduction coord. Drug Enforcement Adminstrn., Seattle, 1988-95; exec. dir. Wash.

Drug Free Bus., Bellevue, 1995—; bd. dirs. Alaskans for Drug Free Youth, Ketchikan, 1989—, Gov.'s Substance Abuse Coun., Olympia, Wash., 1991-93; mem. bd. advisors Wash. State Substance Abuse Coalition, Bellevue, 1989—; advisor bd. dirs. Oreg. Partnership, 1994—; mem. Internat. Drug Strategy Inst., 1994—, Nat. Demand Reduction Adv. Coun., 1991-95. Author: (book) Creating The Drug Free Business, 1990; editor newsletter Business Taking Action, 1993—. Intelligence officer USN, 1966-70. Mem. Alpha Sigma Phi. Office: Wash Drug Free Bus 12729 NE 20th Ste 17 Bellevue WA 98005

POOLE, ANDREW EDWARD, pediatric dentist, human geneticist, educator; b. Burton-on-Trent, Staffordshire, Eng., Aug. 4, 1935; came to U.S., 1962; s. Reginald Leslie and Eunice Winifred (Salt) P.; m. Deirdre-Anne Farnan, Dec., 1982; children: Nichola Ruth, Timothy Sean, Amelia Anne. BDS, London Hosp. Dental Sch., 1960; MS, U. Rochester, 1965, PhD, 1970. Instr. London Hosp., 1961-62, U. Rochester, N.Y., 1965-70; asst. prof. U. Conn. Health Ctr., Farmington, 1970-74, assoc. prof., 1974-85, prof. pediatric dentistry, 1985-96; dir. craniofacial disorders team Conn. Childrens Med. Ctr., 1996—; co-dir. U. Conn. Craniofacial Disorders Team, 1981-84, dir. 1985-96; mem. Craniofacial Disorders Team, Conn. Children's Med. Ctr., 1996—. Guest editor Dental Clinics N. Am., 1975. Contbr. articles to profl. publs., chpts. to books. Fellow Eastman Dental Dispensary, 1962-65, U. Rochester, 1965-70; NIH grantee, 1970—. Mem. Royal Coll. Surgeons, Internat. Assn. Dental Research, Am. Acad. Pedodontics, Am. Assn. Human Genetics, AAAS, Soc. Craniofacial Genetics (sec.-treas. 1984-92, pres. 1992-93), Am. Coll. Med. Genetics, Sigma Xi. Home: 820 Prospect Ave Hartford CT 06105-4232 Office: U Conn Health Ctr Farmington Ave Farmington CT 06032 also: Conn Childrens Med Ctr 282 Washington St Hartford CT 06106

POOLE, THOMAS A., ophthalmologist; b. Miflington, Pa., June 26, 1940. AB, U. Pa., 1962; MD, Harvard Med. Sch., 1966. Diplomate Am. Bd. Ophthalmologists. Surgeon, dir. Manhattan Eye & Ear & Throat Hosp., N.Y.C., 1973—. Capt. USAF, 1967-69. Office: 4 East 77th St New York NY 10021

POOLE, WILLIAM LANNON, JR., dermatologist; b. Birmingham, Ala., Mar. 28, 1939; s. Wiliam L. Sr. and Mildred (Yates) P.; m. Mary Dudley; children: Shannon, Kimberly, Bill III. MD, U. Ala., 1964. Diplomate Am. Bd. Dermatology. Pvt. practice East Central, Ala. With U.S. Army, Vietnam, 1966-68. Mem. Am. Acad. Dermatology, Am. Soc. Dermatological Surgery, Ala. Dermatology Soc. Office: Craddock Clinic 308 W Hickory Sylacauga AL 35150

POOLE-WILSON, PHILIP ALEXANDER, cardiology educator; b. London, Apr. 26, 1943; s. Denis Smith and Monique Michelle (Gosse) P.-W.; m. Mary Elizabeth Tattersall, Oct. 25, 1969; children: William, Michael, Oenone. BA, Cambridge (Eng.) U., 1964, MB BChir, 1967, MD, 1975, MA, 1991. Lectr. St. Thomas Hosp., London, 1972-76; sr. lectr., hon. cons. physician Cardiothoracic Inst. Nat. Heart Hosp., London, 1976-80; prof. cardiology U. London, 1980-88, sr. Marks Brit. Heart Found. prof. cardiology Nat. Heat and Lung Inst., 1988—. Contbr. articles to profl. jours. Mem. coun. Brit. Heart Found., 1985. Fellow Royal Coll. Physicians, European Soc. of Cardiology, Am. Coll. Cardiology; mem. European Soc. Cardiology (bd. dirs. 1988, pres. 1994-96), Internat. Soc. for Heart Disease (treas. 1989-95), Athenaeum (London). Office: Nat Heart Lund Inst, Dovehouse St, London SW3 6LY, England

POOR, CLARENCE ALEXANDER, physician; b. Ashland, Oreg., Oct. 29, 1911; s. Lester Clarence and Matilda Ellen (Doty) P.; AB, Willamette U., 1932; MD, U. Oreg., 1936. Diplomate Am. Bd. Internal Medicine. Intern U. Wis., Madison, 1936-37, resident in internal medicine, 1937-40, instr. dept. pathology Med. Sch., 1940-41, clin. instr., clin. asst. dept. internal medicine, 1942-44; pvt. practice medicine specializing in internal medicine, Oakland, Calif., 1944—; mem. emeritus staff Highland Alameda County Hosp., Oakland, 1949—; mem. staff Providence Hosp., Oakland, 1947—, pres. staff, 1968-69; staff mem. Samuel Meritt Hosp., Oakland, 1958—; staff mem. Summit Med. Ctr. (merger Providence Hosp. and Samuel Merritt Hosp.), 1991—. Mem. Nat. Coun. on Alcoholism, 1974—, bd. dirs. Bay Area, 1977—. Mem. Am., Calif., Alameda-Contra Costa med. assns., Alameda County Heart Assn. (trustee 1955-62, 72-82, pres. 1960-61), Calif. Heart Assn. (dir. 1962-72), Soc. for Clin. and Exptl. Hypnosis, Am. Soc. Clin. Hypnosis, San Francisco Acad. Hypnosis (dir. 1966—, pres. 1973). Home: 1241 Westview Dr Berkeley CA 94705-1650 Office: 400 29th St Ste 201 Oakland CA 94609-3547

POPACK, MIRIAM, social worker; b. N.Y.C.; d. Harry and Anna Spalter; m. Samuel Isaac Popack; children: Chana, Yisroel Meir, Yosef Yitzchok, Tobi, Rivkah, Zeesy. MS in Edn., L.I. U., 1982; MSW, YU Wurzweiler Sch. Social Work, 1986; CSW, SUNY, 1986. Cert. social worker, N.Y.; qualified clin. social worker. Sch. social worker Counterforce, N.Y.C., 1982—, family therapist, 1986—; coord. regional convs., 1966—. Mem. Presidium of Internat. Chabad Women's Orgn.

POPE, HARRISON GRAHAM, JR., psychiatrist, educator; b. Lynn, Mass., Dec. 26, 1947; s. H. Graham and Alice (Rider) P.; m. Mary M. Quinn, June 7, 1974; children: Kimberly, Hilary, Courtney. AB summa cum laude, Harvard U., 1969, MPH, 1972, MD, 1974. Diplomate Am. Bd. Psychiatry and Neurology. Resident in psychiatry McLean Hosp., Belmont, Mass., 1974-77, clin. rsch. fellow Mailman Rsch. Ctr., 1977-79, asst. psychiatrist, 1979-84, assoc. psychiatrist, 1984-92, psychiatrist, 1992—, chief biol. psychiatry lab., 1984—; Dupont-Warren rsch. fellow Harvard Med. Sch., Boston, 1976-77; instr. psychiatry Harvard Med. Sch., Boston, 1977-82, asst. prof., 1982-85, assoc. prof., 1985—; staff psychiatrist Hampstead (N.H.) Hosp., 1976-80; vis. fellow The Maudsley Hosp., London, 1977, Hôp. Ste. Anne, Paris, 1977; mem. Am. Psychiat. Assn., 1976-80, adv. com. on schizophrenic, paranoid and affective disorders, 1979, adv. com. on preparation of DSM-III-R, 1984, task force on nomenclature and stats., 1979, 84. Author: Voices from the Drug Culture, 1971, The Road East, 1974, (with J.I. Hudson) New Hope for Binge Eaters: Advances in the Understanding and Treatment of Bulimia, 1984; co-editor: The Psychobiology of Bulimia, 1987, Use of Anticonvulsants in Psychiatry: Recent Advances, 1988; contbr. over 250 papers on biol. psychiatry, with particulary emphasis on diagnosis of psychotic disorders, treatment of mood disorders and eating disorders, and substance abuse, particularly abuse of anabolic steroids by athletes; mem. editl. bd. European Psychiatry, Paris, 1984—, Internat. Jour. of Eating Disorders, 1984—, Jour. Clin. Psychiatry, 1993—. Named one of Outstanding Americans under 40 Esquire mag., 1984; fellow Scottish Rite Schizophrenia Program, No. Masonic Jurisdiction, 1977-81, Charles A. King Trust, Boston, 1977-79. Office: McLean Hosp 115 Mill St Belmont MA 02178-1041

POPE, PRESTON CARLETON, anesthetist, nurse; b. Hartford, Conn., Apr. 8, 1950; s. Preston Louis and Doris Lucinda (Stewart); m. Delair Moses, Aug. 28, 1971; children: Chad, Ryan. Diploma, New Britain Gen. Sch. Nursing, 1972, cert. in anesthesia, 1974. Cert. nurse anesthetist, advanced practice RN; notary pub., Conn., justice of the peace, Conn.; pvt. investigator, Conn.; hypnotherapist; NRA small arms instr.; lic. comml. sea capt., pilot, nuisance wildlife control operator. Staff anesthetist Bristol (Conn.) Hosp., 1974-78; staff anesthetist Harford Hosp., 1978-79, 81—, chief anesthetist, 1987—. Alumni pres. New Britain Sch. Nurse Anesthesia. Capt. USAF, 1979-81. Mem. NRA (life), Am. Assn. Nurse Anesthetists, Nat. Assn. Federally Lic. Firearms Dealers, Boat Owners Assn. Am., Aircraft Owners and Pilots Assn., Nat. Notary Assn. Republican. Home: 102 Simpkins Dr Bristol CT 06010-2688

POPE, RICHARD M., rheumatologist; b. Chgo., Jan. 10, 1946. Student, Procopius Coll., 1963-65, U. Ill., 1965-66; MD, Loyola U., 1970. Diplomate Am. Bd. Internal Medicine. Intern in medicine Med. Ctr. Michael Reese Hosp., Chgo., 1970-71, resident in internal medicine, 1971-72; fellow in rheumatology U. Wash., Seattle, 1972-74; asst. clin. prof. medicine U. Hawaii, 1974-77; asst. prof. medicine U. Tex. Health Sci. Ctr., San Antonio, 1976-81, assoc. prof. medicine, 1981-85; assoc. prof. medicine Northwestern U. Med. Sch., 1985-88, prof. medicine, 1988—; attending physician Northwestern Meml. Hosp., Chgo., 1985—, VA Lakeside Med. Ctr., Chgo., 1985—, Rehab. Inst. Chgo., 1985—; chief divsn. rheumatology VA Lakeside Med. Ctr., 1985-91, divsn. arthritis-connective tissue diseases Northwestern U. and Northwestern Meml. Hosp., 1989—, Northwestern Med. Faculty Found., 1989—; mem. program com. Ctrl. Soc. Clin. Rsch., 1987, ctrl. region Am. Rheumatism Assn., 1987; mem. sci. com. Ill. chpt. Arthritis Found., 1988-1992, bd. dirs., 1990—, mem. chpt. review grants subcom., 1983-88, chmn. chpt. rsch. grant subcom., 1986-88, mem. rsch. com., 1986-88; mem. site visit teams NIH, 1986, 87, 89; cons. reviewer VA Merit Review Bd., 1984, 87, 91; cons. reviewer Arthritis Soc. Can., 1986, 87; mem. editorial adv. bd. Arthritis and Rheumatism Jour. Lab. and Clin. Medicine, 1992—. Author: (with others) The Science and Practice of Clinical Medicine, 1979, Proceedings of the University of South Florida International Symposium in the Biomedical Sciences, 1984, Concepts in Immunopathology, 1985, Biology Based Immunomodulators in the Therapy of Rheumatic Diseases, 1986, Primer on the Rheumatic Diseases, 1988; contbr. numerous articles to profl. jours. With U.S. Army, 1974-76. Anglo-Am. Rheumatology fellow, 1983. Mem. Am. Coll. Physicians, Am. Coll. Rheumatology (councillor ctrl. region coun. 1990—, program com. 1983-86, 91), Am. Assn. Immunologists, Am. Fedn. Clin. Rsch., Am. Soc. Clin. Investigation, Lupus Found. Ill. (mem. adv. bd. 1990-93), Chgo. Rheumatism Assn. (pres. 1991-93), Ctrl. Soc. Clin. Investigation, Soc. Irish and Am. Rheumatologists (sec., treas. 1989-93), Univ. Rheumatology Coun. Chgo., Alpha Omega Alpha. Office: Northwestern U Multipurpose Arthritis Ctr 303 E Chicago Ave Chicago IL 60611-3008

POPEL, GEORGE, ophthalmologist; b. Lviw, Ukraine, Sept. 30, 1942. BS, Fordham U., 1965; MD, Cornell U., 1969. Diplomate Am. Bd. Ophtaholmology. Intern Temple U. Hosp., Phila., 1969-70; resident neurology Mt. Sinai Hosp., N.Y.C., 1970-71; resident ophthalmology N.Y. Eye & Ear Infirmary, N.Y.C., 1971-74; specialist cataract & glaucoma surgery, refractive surgery Eye Ctr. of Del., Wilmington, 1974—. Mem. Phi Beta Kappa. Office: Eye Ctr Del 213 Greenhill Ave Wilmington DE 19805-1844

POPESCU, VALERIAN, medical educator, physician; b. Negresti, Romania, Oct. 26, 1912; arrived in France, 1985; s. Constantin D. and Kira M. (Boboc) P.; m. Colette T. Elisievici, Dec. 5, 1943; children: Kira-Cristinel, Qana-Manuela. BS, Basarab, Bucharest, Romania, 1931; D in Medicine and Surgery, Faculty Medicine Bucharest, 1939; specialist in stomatology, Inst. STomatology, Bucharest, 1943; specialist in maxillo-facial surgery, Inst. Medicine, Bucharest, 1949, Dr.Docent (hon.), 1960. Intern Bucharest's Hosps., 1934-41; resident Maxillo-Facial Surgery Clinic, Bucharest, 1941-48, clin. asst. prof., 1942-49, prof., clinic head, 1949-85, dean faculty stomatology, 1962-76; hon. prof. Med. Inst., Bucharest, 1985; prof. oral-maxillofacial surgery Ecol. U., Bucharest, 1990; expert WHO, Geneva, 1968, Mission WHO in Tunisia, 1972; pres. various internat. congresses, 1970, 72, 81; pres. Romanian Soc. Stomatology, 1948-73, Union Med. Scis. Socs. Romania, 1969-73. Author: Maxillo-Facial Surgery, 1966 (award 1968), Emergencies in Stomatology, 1969, Anesthesia in Stomatology, 1971, Radiodiagnosis in Stomatology, 1973-85, numerous others; editor-in-chief Acta Stomatologica Internationalia, 1980—, Stomatologia, 1954-90; mem. editorial bd. Maxillo-Facial Surgery, 1972—; contbr. articles, papers in field; originator 12 surgical methods and techniques. Lt. M.C., Romanian Army, 1941-42. Recipient Magitot prize Acad. Medicine France, 1968, Nat. prize Minister of Edn. of Romania, 1968, medal d'Or Acad. Arts. Mem. Romanian Acad., Med. Scis. Acad. (pres. 1969), Internat Assn. Stomatology (pres. 1975-79, hon. pres. 1979), Internat. Assn. Maxillofacial Surgery (founding, v.p. 1970), European Assn. Maxillofacial Surgery (founding, counselor 1970), Acad. de Chirurgie Dentaire de France, N.Y. Acad. Scis., Royal Soc. Medicine (fgn.), Fedn. Dentaire Internat. (commn. dental edn and rsch.), European Acad. Implantology (founding, gen sec.). Mem. Orthodox Ch. Home: 81 Bis Ave Secrétar, 75019 Paris France

POPKIN, DAVID R., academic dean, obstetrician, gynocologist; m. Linda Popkin, 1964; 4 children. Dean U. Saskatchewan Coll. Medicine, Can. Office: Coll Medicine, Health Scis Bldg 107, Wiggins Rd Rm B103, Saskatoon, SK Canada S7N 5E5*

POPLAWSKI, PAUL EDWIN, psychologist; b. Phila., Aug. 22, 1949; s. Edwin Joseph and Ellen Catherine (Jones) P.; BA in Psychology, U. Del., 1972; M in Human Services, Lincoln U., 1978; PhD in Psychoednl. Processes, Temple U., 1989. Lic. psychologist. Clin. supr., psychotherapist Bur. Alcoholism and Drug Abuse, Newark, Del., 1971-75, dir. Newark Counseling Ctr., 1975-76, dir. tng. and edn., 1979—, coordinating state troubled employees program, 1983—, dir. outpatient care, Wilmington, Del., 1976-79; co-founder Nat. Tng. Network, 1982, Psychology of Music Rsch., 1984; pvt. practice psychotherapy, Newark, Del., 1976—. Composer electronic music. Nat. Inst. Alcohol Abuse and Alcoholism grantee, 1979-82, Nat. Inst. Drug Abuse grantee, 1979-83. Mem. Am. Soc. Tng. and Devel., N.Y. Inst. for Gesalt Therapy. Roman Catholic. Home: 200 Unami Trl Newark DE 19711-7509 Office: Divsn Alcoholism Drug Abuse and Mental Health 1901 N Dupont Hwy New Castle DE 19720-1100

POPLAWSKY, ALEX JAMES, experimental psychology educator; b. Scranton, Pa., July 12, 1948; s. Alex James and Archangel (Russo) P.; m. Deborah Ann Grembacki, June 10, 1972; children—Alexander John, Jonathan David. B.S., U. Scranton, 1970; M.S., Ohio U., 1972, Ph.D., 1974. Asst. prof. exptl. psychology Bloomsburg U. of Pa., 1974-79, assoc. prof., 1979-82, prof., 1982—; vis. assoc. prof. SUNY-Binghamton, 1981-82, rsch. assoc., 1988-89. Contbr. articles to profl. jours. Commonwealth teaching fellow, 1978-79. Mem. Am. Psychol. Soc., Eastern Psychol. Assn., Psychonomic Soc., Soc. Neurosci., Internat. Brain Rsch. Orgn., Internat. Behavioral Neurosci. Soc., Sigma Xi, Psi Chi, Phi Kappa Phi. Democrat. Roman Catholic. Home: 106 Charlene Dr Danville PA 17821-9157 Office: U of Bloomsburg Dept Psychology Bloomsburg PA 17815

POPMA, JEFFREY J., interventional cardiologist, laboratory director; b. Morristown, N.J., June 17, 1955; s. Eugene John and Maxine Mary (Guinon) P.; m. Theresa Anne Bucher; children: Jessica, Nicole, Christopher. BA in Economics, Stanford U., 1977; MD with highest distinction, Ind. U., 1981. Diplomate Am. Bd. Internal Medicine. Flexible intern U. Calif.-Valley Med. Ctr., San Fransisco, 1981-82; intern in internal medicine U. Tex. Southwestern Med. Ctr., Dallas, 1982-83, resident in internal medicine, 1983-85, chief resident, 1985-86, fellow in cardiology, 1986-89; fellow in interventional cardiology U. Mich. Med. Ctr., Ann Arbor, 1989-90, dir. angiographic core lab., 1990-91, asst. prof. dept. internal medicine, 1990-91; lectr. dept. internal medicine U. Mich., Ann Arbor, 1990; dir. angiographic core lab. Washington Hosp. Ctr., 1991—, assoc. dir. investigational angioplasty program, 1991—; mem. Instl. Rev. Bd. Medlantic Rsch. Found., 1992—; mem. steering com. New Approaches to Coronary Intervention Registry, 1992—, mem. ops. com., 1992—; pub. com. Angiopeptin Trials, 1992—, steering com., 1992—; co-chmn. data and quality assurance com. Nat. Cardiovascular Network, 1993—; angiographic com. TOTAL study, 1994—. Co-author (textbook) Atlas of Interventional Cardiology, 1994; contbr. chpts. to textbooks including Clinical Use of the Palmaz-Schatz Stent, 1993, Advances in Interventional Cardiology: New Technologies and Strategies for Diagnosis and Treatment, 1994, others; contbr. over 100 articles to sci. pubs. including Circulation, Am. Jour. Cardiology, Jour. Interventional Cardiology, others; editl. bd. Am. Jour. Cardiology, 1992—; reviewer Circulation, 1993—, Catheterization and Cardiovascular Diagnosis, 1993—, Cardiology in the Elderly, 1994—, Jour. of Am. Coll. Cardiology, 1994—. Mem. AAAS, Alpha Omega Alpha. Home: 5815 Bradley Blvd Bethesda MD 20814 Office: Washington Cardiology Ctr 110 Irvine St Ste 4B1 Washington DC 20010

POPOVSKY, MARK ALAN, physician; b. Boston, Aug. 1, 1950; s. Samuel and Sally Lillian (Taitz) P.; m. Andrea Leigh Lavender, June 7, 1981; 1 child, Erica Yael. BA magna cum laude, U. Mass., 1972; MD with honors, U. Vt., 1977. Diplomate Am. Bd. Pathology. Intern/resident anatomic/clin. pathology NIH, Bethesda, Md., 1977-81; fellow transfusion medicine Mayo Clinic, Rochester, Minn., 1981-82, staff cons., 1982-85; asst. prof. med. lab. Mayo Med. Sch., Rochester, Minn., 1982-85; med. dir. N.E. region ARC, Dedham, Mass., 1985—, chief med. officer New Eng. region, 1995-96, prin. officer New Eng. region, 1996—; asst. prof. pathology Harvard U., Boston, 1985—; staff physician Beth Israel Hosp., Boston, 1985—; clin. prof. pathology and lab. medicine Boston U., 1993—; del. Interam. Com. of Red Cross on Orgn. of Blood Transfusion Svcs., Geneva, Switzerland, 1986-90; mem. adv. bd. New Eng. region Aplastic Anemai Found., 1988-89; mem. expert panel on autogous transfusion Nat. Heart, Lung, Blood Inst., 1993-94, mem. nat. blood resource edn. program coord. commn., 1992-93; chmn. biomed. tech. curriculum com. Drew Inst., ARC, 1995—. Editor: Transfusion Reactions, 1996; mem. editl. bd. Nat. Intravenous Therapy Assn., 1984, Immunohematology, 1992—, Am. Jour. Clin. Pathology, 1993—; contbr. over 55 articles to profl. jours., over 25 chpts. and monographs to books. Lt. comdr. USPHS, 1977-81. Recipient Herbert Martin Sr. Excellence award U. Vt., 1977, Donor Svcs. Recognition award ARC, 1993, Morton Grove-Rasmussen award Mass. Assn. Blood Banks, 1996. Mem. Am. Assn. Blood Banks (chmn. biotech. work group, sci. sect. coord. com. 1990-92, chmn. Latin Am. affairs work group 1991-93, chmn. transfusion practices com. 1995—), Am. Soc. Hematology, Minn. Assn. Blood Banks (v.p. 1984-85), Phi Beta Kappa, Phi Kappa Phi. Office: ARC NE Region 180 Rustcraft Rd Dedham MA 02026-4554

POPP, CHARLOTTE LOUISE, health development center administrator, nurse; b. Vineland, N.J., July 26, 1946; d. William Henry and Elfriede Marie (Zickler) P. Diploma in Nursing, Luth. Hosp. of Md., Balt., 1967; BA in Health Edn., Glassboro (N.J.) State Coll., 1972; MA in Human Devel., Fairleigh-Dickinson U., 1981. Cert. Sch. Nurse, N.J., Health Educator, N.J. Charge nurse Newcomb Hosp., Vineland, N.J., 1967-71; supr. Vineland Rehab. Ctr., 1971-72; charge nurse Bridgeton (N.J.) Hosp., 1972-73; dir. insvc. edn. Millville (N.J.) Hosp., 1973-76; dir. hosp. insvc. edn. Vineland Devel. Ctr. State of N.J., 1976-78, program asst. Vineland Devel. Ctr., 1978-87; dir. habilitation planning services State of N.J., Vineland Devel. Ctr., 1987—, lead program coord. Vineland Devel. Ctr., 1981—; exam proctor State of N.J. Bd. Nursing, Newark, 1973-91. Editorial rev. bd. (jour.) Nursing Update, 1973-77. Instr. basic life support, Am. Heart Assn., bd. dirs. Tri-county chpt., 1979-83, South Jersey chpt., 1983-90. Mem. ANA, N.J. State Nurses Assn., Am. Assn. Mental Retardation, South Jersey Insvc. Exch. (life), Smithsonian Assn., Luth. Hosp. of Md. Alumni Assn., Glassboro State Coll. Alumni Assn., Fairleigh-Dickinson U. Alumni Assn. Lutheran. Office: Vineland Devel Ctr 1676 E Landis Ave Vineland NJ 08360-2901

POPP, JEFFREY COLLINS, ophthalmologist, educator, plastic surgeon; b. Lincoln, Nebr., Nov. 11, 1953; s. Kenneth Leroy and Bess Rhea (Bales) P.; m. Barbara Joann Watson, July 24, 1982; children: Collin, Christopher, Cameron. Student, U. Nebr., 1972-74, 75, Ariz. State U., 1974-75, U. Oregon, 1978, Wash. U., St. Louis, 1978; MD, U. Nebr., 1979. Diplomate Am. Bd. Ophthalmology. Resident in ophthalmology dept. ophthalmology U. Nebr., Lincoln, 1979-82; resident in ophthalmology U. Tex., Houston, 1980; fellow in ophthalmic plastic and reconstructive surgery U. Ariz. Med. Sch., Tucson, 1982-83; pvt. practice Omaha, 1983-85, Atlanta, 1985-86, Lincoln, 1986—; clin. instr. ophthalmic plastic and reconstructive surgery Dept. Ophthalmology U. Ariz. Health Scis. Ctr., Tucson, 1982-83, U. Nebr. Coll. Med., Omaha, 1983-85, Emory U. Sch. Med., Atlanta, 1985-86; clin. assoc. prof., dir. Oculoplastic, Orbital and Oncology Svc. Dept. Ophthalmology, U. Nebr. Coll. Med., Omaha, 1986—; cons. Phoenix VA Hosp., Tucson VA Hosp., Maricopa County Hosp.; lectr. in field. Contbr. chpts. to books, articles to profl. pubs. Bd. Dirs. Myasthenia Gravis Found. N.E. Chpt., 1989. U. Ariz. Med. Sch. fellow, 1982-83. Fellow ACS, Am. Acad. Ophthalmology (Honor award 1993), Am. Soc. Ophthalmic Plastic Reconstructive Surgery, Am. Acad. Facial Plastic Reconstructive Surgery, Am. Acad. Cosmetic Surgery, Am. Coll. Oral Maxillofacial Surgeons, Am. Acad. Aesthetic Restorative Surgery; mem. AMA, Nebr. Acad. Ophthalmology, Omaha Eye Soc., Am. Soc. Liposuction Surgery Inc., European Soc. Ophthalmic Plaxstic Reconstructive Surgery (assoc.). Office: Cosmetic and Oculoplastic Surgery 9140 W Dodge Rd # 408 Omaha NE 68114

POPPERS, PAUL JULES, anesthesiologist, educator; b. Enschede, Netherlands, June 30, 1929; came to U.S., 1958; naturalized, 1963; s. Meyer and Minca (Ginsburg) P.; m. Ann Feinberg, June 3, 1969; children: David Matthew, Jeremy Samuel. MD, U. Amsterdam, 1955. Diplomate Am. Bd. Anesthesiology. Instr. anesthesiology Columbia U., N.Y.C., 1962-63, assoc., 1963-65, asst. prof. anesthesiology, 1965-71, assoc. prof. anesthesiology, 1971-74; prof., vice chmn. dept. anesthesiology NYU, 1974-79; prof., chmn. dept. anesthesiology SUNY, Stony Brook, 1979—; cons. Brookdale Med. Ctr., Bklyn., 1975—, VA Med. Ctr., Northport, N.Y., 1979—, The N.Y. Hosp. Med. Ctr. of Queens (formerly Booth Meml. Hosp.), Flushing, N.Y., 1979—, L.I. Jewish Med. Ctr., New Hyde Pk., N.Y., 1980—, Ea. L.I. Hosp., Greenport, N.Y., 1995—, Am. Hosp. Paris, 1989-93; cons., lectr. Author: Regional Anesthesia, 1977; editor: Beta Blockade and Anaesthesia, 1979; sect. editor Jour. Clin. Anesthesia, 1990—; mem. editorial bd. Internat. Jour. Clin. Monitoring and Computing, 1990—, Gynecologic and Obstetric Investigation, 1996—; internat. bd. editors Anaesthesiology Digest, 1991-94; contbr. numerous articles to profl. jours. NIH postdoctoral rsch. fellow, 1961; recipient medal Polish Acad. Scis., Poland, 1987, Univ. medal Jagiellonian U., Krakow, Poland, 1987, 1st Sci. award Post-grad. Assembly in Anesthesiology; named Hon. Prof. Anesthesiology, U. Leiden, The Netherlands, 1977. Fellow Am. Coll. Anesthesiology, Am. Coll. Ob-gyns., Royal Soc. Medicine, Post-grad. Assembly in Anesthesiology (hon. chmn. 1989—); mem. Am. Soc. Anesthesiologists, Assn. Univ. Anesthesiologists, Soc. Acad. Anesthesia Chmn., Internat. Anesthesia Rsch. Soc., Soc. Obstetric Anesthesia and Perinatology, Am. Soc. Regional Anesthesia, Jerusalem Acad. Medicine, Am. Soc. Pharmacology and Exptl. Therapeutics, Fedn. Am. Soc. Exptl. Biology, Sigma Xi. Office: SUNY Sch Medicine Health Scis Ctr Stony Brook NY 11794-8480

POPSON, RICHARD DENNIS, social worker; b. Cleve., June 25, 1950; s. Thomas James and Ann (Baker) P.; m. Karen Brason, Aug. 4, 1973; children: Jennifer, Stephanie, Rachel. BA in Psychology, Elizabethtown (Pa.) Coll., 1974; MSW, SUNY, Buffalo, 1977. Cert. social worker. Social worker Children's Aid Soc. Pa., Phila., 1977-79, Delaware County Children and Youth Svcs., Upper Darby, Pa., 1979-80; crisis counselor Springville (N.Y.) Community Counseling Ctr., 1980-82, sr. clinician, 1982-83, program dir., 1983-86; pvt. practice Popson Counseling Assocs., Hamburg, N.Y., 1985—; dir. pub. rels. Willcare, Inc., Hamburg, 1986-89; mental health clinic coord. Orleans County Mental Health, Albion, N.Y., 1989-90. Mem. NASW. Office: Popson Counseling Assocs 40 Main St Hamburg NY 14075-4905

PORCERELLI, JOHN HOWARD, clinical psychology, educator; b. Detroit, June 25, 1957; s. Joseph Francis and Maria Celeste (Andreozzi) P.; m. Mary Anne Manzano, July 23, 1988; children: Daniel, Jonathan. BA with high distinction, U. Mich., Dearborn, 1984; MA, U. Detroit, 1987, PhD, 1990. Lic. psychologist, Mich. Postdoctoral fellow Wayne State U. Sch. Medicine, Detroit, 1990-92, psychotherapy supr., 1993—; rsch. and clin. cons. Detroit Psychiat. Inst., 1992—; pvt. practice, Birmingham, Mich., 1992—; adj. clin. prof. U. Detroit Mercy, 1994—; adj. asst. prof. Wayne State U. Sch. Medicine; mem. adv. bd. South Woodward Clinic, Birmingham, 1993—. Contbr. articles to profl. jours. Mem. APA, Mich. Psychol. Assn., Mich. Psychoanalytic Soc. (liaison to grad. programs, com. mem.), Mich. Psychoanalytic Inst. (pres.-elect candidate orgn. 1995-96), Soc. Personality Assessment. Home: 1165 S Eton St Birmingham MI 48009-7141 Office: 111 S Woodward Ste 240 Birmingham MI 48009

POREMBKA, DAVID THOMAS, anesthesia and surgery educator; b. Latrobe, Pa., Nov. 28, 1953; m. Diane Irene Siefert; children: Daniela, Nathanael, Anna, Sarah. BS in Biology/Chemistry cum laude, U. Pitts., 1975; DO, Mich. State U., 1981. Diplomate Nat. Bd. Examiners, Am. Bd. Anesthesiology, Am. Bd. Critical Care Medicine subspecialty; cert. advanced trauma life support; lic. Mich., Ohio. Intern Botsford Gen. Hosp., Detroit, 1981-82, anesthesiology resident, 1982-83; anesthesiology resident Cleve. Clinic Found., 1984-86, anesthesiology chief fellow, surgical intensive care medicine, 1986-87, clin. fellow A, SICU rsch. assoc., 1987-88; assoc. prof. clin. anesthesiology, critical care medicine Univ. Cin. Coll. of Medicine, 1988—; assoc. dir. trauma/surg. intensive care unit Dept. Anesthesiology, Univ. Cin. Coll. of Medicine, 1988—; dir. transesophageal echocardiography Univ. Cin. Coll. of Medicine, 1988—, acting dir. cardiac anesthesia, 1989-90, 90—, asst. prof. clin. surgery, 1990-93, assoc. prof. of anesthesia, 1993—, assoc. prof. of surgery, 1994—; anesthesiology rsch. assoc., dept. anesthesiology Univ. Pitts. (Pa.) Sch. of Medicine, 1977-78; cons. Baxter-Edwards, Advanced Tech. Labs.; vis. prof., presenter and lectr. in field. Contbr. articles to profl. jours.; patentee method for automatic contar extraction with echocardiography. Fellow Soc. Critical Care Medicine (chair anesthesia sect. 1995—, program com. 1993—, workforce com. 1994—, continuing edn. com.

1994—, multidisciplinary rev. bd. 1994—), Coll. Chest Physicians; mem. Am. Coll. Chest Physicians, Am. Heart Assn., Am. Soc. Anesthesiology, Am. Soc. Critical Care Anesthesiologists, Am. Soc. Echocardiography, Internat. Anesthesia Rsch. Soc., Mich. Soc. Critical Care Medicine, Ohio Soc. Anesthesiologists, Soc. Cardiovascular Anesthesiologists (edn. com. 1990—), Cin. Soc. Anesthesiology. Office: Univ Cin 231 Bethesda Ave Cincinnati OH 45229-2827

PORESKY, ROBERT HAROLD, psychology educator; b. Allentown, Pa., Sept. 10, 1941; s. Milton Nathan and Betty L. (Chernoff) P.; m. Barbara Keebaugh, Sept. 2, 1964; children: Pamela, Laura. BA, Cornell U., 1963, MA, 1967, PhD, 1969. Lic. psychologist, Kans. Assoc. prof. family studies and human svcs. Kans. State U., Manhattan, 1972-77, assoc. prof., 1977—, acting dept. chmn., 1979-80, dir. Computer Assited Telephone Interviewing Lab., 1996—. Author, editor: (book) Caring for Children Today, 1979; contbr. articles to profl. jours. Bd. dirs. various child care ctrs. Mem. APA, Nat. Assn. for Edn. of Young Children, Soc. Rsch. in Child Devel., Am. Assn. for Pub. Opinion Rsch., Nat. Network of State Polls, Midwest Assn. for Edn. Young Children (bd. dirs. 1986—), Kans. Assn. for Edn. Young Children (prs. 1978-80, treas. 1986). Home: 3905 Barbara Ln Manhattan KS 66502-7573 Office: Kans State U 312 Justin Hall Manhattan KS 66506-1403

PORIES, WALTER JULIUS, surgeon, educator; b. Munich, Germany, Jan. 18, 1930; came to U.S., 1940; s. Theodore Francis and Frances (Lowin) P.; m. Muriel Helen Aronson, Aug. 18, 1951; children: Susan E., Mary Jane, Carolyn A., Kathy G.; m. Mary Ann Rose McCarthy, June 4, 1977; children: Mary Lisa, Michael McCarthy. BA, Wesleyan U., Middletown, Conn., 1952; MD with honors, U. Rochester, 1955. Diplomate: Am. Bd. Surgery, Am. Bd. Thoracic Surgery. Intern Strong Meml. Hosp., Rochester, N.Y., 1955-56, resident, 1958-62; chmn. dept. surgery Wright-Patterson AFB, Ohio, 1952-67; asst. prof. surgery and oncology U. Rochester, 1967-69; prof. surgery and assoc. chmn. dept. surgery U. Cleve., 1969-77; prof. surgery East Carolina U., Greenville, N.C., 1977—, chmn. dept. surgery, 1977—; chief surgery Pitt County Meml. Hosp., 1977—; prof. surgery U. Health Scis. of Uniformed Svcs., 1982—; founder, assoc. dir. Rochester Cancer Ctr., 1967-69; founder, dir. Cleve. Cancer Ctr., 1972-77, Hospice of Cleve., 1975; founder, chmn. bd. Hospice of Greenville, 1981; med. dir. Home Health Care of Greenville, 1978-83; founder, chmn. bd. Ctr. for Creative Living, 1985-91. Author: Clinical Applications of Zinc Metabolism, 1974; editor: Operative Surgery series, vols. 1-4, 1979-83, Office Surgery for Family Physicians, 1985; editor in chief Current Surgery, 1990—; editor Nat. Curriculum for Residency in Surgery, 1988—, mem. residency rev. com., 1992—; contbr. articles to profl. jours. Bd. dirs. Boy Scouts Am., Cleve., 1974-77, Greenville Arts Mus., 1980-82; pres., CEO, chmn. bd. dirs. Ea. Carolina Health Orgn. Maj. USAF, 1955-67; col. USAR, 1979-91, comdr. USAF Hosp., Durham, N.C.; activated Desert Shield, 1990. Decorated Legion of Merit; Thorndyke scholar, 1948-51; recipient McLester award USAF, 1966, Miss. Magnolia Cross, 1989, Presdl. citation for Desert Shield, 1994; named to Hon. Order of Ky. Cols., 1965. Fellow ACS, Am. Coll. Cardiology, Am. Coll. Chest Physicians; mem. Soc. for Vascular Surgery, Soc. Surg. Oncology, Soc. Univ. Surgeons, Am. Surg. Assn., Soc. Environ. Geochemistry (past pres.), Residency Rev. Com. for Surgery, So. Surg. Assn., Soc. for Thoracic Surgery, Ea. Carolina Health Orgn. (pres., chmn. bd. 1994—), Assn. Programs Dirs. in Surgery (pres. 1995-96), N.C. Surg. Assn. (pres. 1995-96), Greenville Country Club, Phi Kappa Phi. Republican. Roman Catholic. Home: Deep Sun Farm 7464 NC 43 N Macclesfield NC 27852 Office: East Carolina U Dept Surgery Greenville NC 27858

PORT, FRIEDRICH KONRAD, nephrologist, epidemiologist; b. Heidelberg, Germany, Mar. 17, 1938; came to U.S., 1965; MD, U. Erlangen-Nüremberg, Germany, 1964; MS, U. Minn., 1975. Diplomate Am. Bd. Internal Medicine. Resident in internal medicine Mayo Clinic, Rochester, Minn., 1968-70; fellow nephrology Mayo Clinic, Rochester, 1970-72, assoc. cons., 1972-73; chief of dialysis unit U. Mainz, Germany, 1973-74, VA Med. Ctr., Ann Arbor, Mich., 1974-90; from asst. prof. to prof. internal medicine U. Mich., Ann Arbor, 1974—; prof epidemiology U. Mich. Sch. Pub. Health, Ann Arbor, 1989—; interim dir. Divsn. of Nephrology, U. Mich., Ann Arbor, 1977-78; dir. Mich. Kidney Register, Ann Arbor, 1984-94, dep. dir. U.S. Renal Data System-Coord. Ctr., Ann Arbor, 1988—; co-dir. Kidney Epidemiology and Cost Ctr., Ann Arbor. Contbr. 110 articles to peer rev. profl. jour., 35 chpts. to books or books. Fellow Am. Coll. Physicians; mem. Am. Soc. Nephrology (edtl. bd.), Am. Kidney Found. (edtl. bd.). Office: U Mich Kidney Epedemiol & Cost Ctr 315 W Huron Ste 240 Ann Arbor MI 48103

PORTELE, GERHARD LUDWIG, psychotherapist, educator; b. Prague, Czechoslovakia, Apr. 18, 1933; s. Otto and Hermine (Ludwig) P.; m. Marei Eiermann, June 27, 1952; children: Kristin, Regina. Cert. primary sch. tchr., U. Heidelberg, Germany, 1954; diploma in sociology, U. Mannheim, Germany, 1968, Dr.Phil, 1972. Rsch. asst. U. Mannheim, 1968-77; prof. U. Hamburg, Germany, 1977—. Author: (book) Motivation und Lernen, 1972, Entfremdung Bei Wissenschaftlern, 1981, Autonomie, Macht, Liebe, 1989, Der Mensch 1St Kein Waegelchen, 1992. Office: U Hamburg, Sedanstr 19, 2000 Hamburg 13, Germany

PORTER, CLARENCE A., academic dean; b. McAlester, Okla., Mar. 19, 1939; s. Lloyd C. and Myrtle E. (Johnson) P.m. Olga Marzart-porter; children—Richard Alan, Cory Steven. B.S. in Biology, Portland State Coll., 1962; M.S. in Zoology, Oreg. State U., 1964, Ph.D. in Zoology, 1966. Asst. prof. gen. sci. Portland State U., 1966-70, assoc. prof., 1970-72, exec. asst. to pres., 1970-72; asst. v.p. acad. affairs U. N.H., 1972-76; assoc. vice chancellor acad. affairs State Univ. System of Minn., 1977-78; exec. dir. Phyllis Wheatley Community Ctr., Mpls., 1978-82; ednl. cons., Hopkins, Minn., 1982-83; v.p. for acad. affairs Cheyney U. (Pa.), 1983-84; dean Inst. Natural Scis., Montgomery Coll., Takoma Park, Md., 1984—. Contbr. articles to sci. jours. Bd. dirs. Mpls. Aquatennial, 1980-82, Urban Concerns Workshop Inc., 1979-82, Nat. Coun. Black Am. Affairs, (NE. region, 1995—), Helminthological Soc. Wash., Sigma Xi. Office: Montgomery Coll Inst Natural Scis Takoma Park MD 20912

PORTER, GEORGE HOMER, III, physician, medical foundation executive; b. Charlotte, N.C., Sept. 7, 1933; s. George Homer Jr. and Sallie Mapp (Jacob) P.; m. Virginia Pillow, Apr. 5, 1958; 1 child, Virginia Mapp (dec.). AB, Duke U., 1954, MD, 1958. Diplomate Am. Bd. Internal Medicine, Am. Bd. Hematology, Am. Bd. Med. Oncology. Intern internal medicine Duke U. Med. Ctr., Durham, N.C., 1958-59; asst. resident medicine, instr. medicine Barnes Hosp., Washington U. Sch. Medicine, St. Louis, 1959-60; sr. resident physician The Peter Bent Brigham Hosp., Boston, 1960-61; clin. assoc. medicine, fellow hematology NIH, Bethesda, Md., 1961-64; staff hematologist-oncologist Ochsner Clinic, New Orleans, 1965—; trustee, mem. exec. com. Alton Ochsner Med. Found., New Orleans, 1973—, pres., chief exec. officer, 1980-91; pres., 1991—; prin. investigator Southeastern Cancer Study Group, 1973-78; bd. dirs. Eye, Ear, Nose and Throat Hosp., New Orleans, 1986—, Hibernia Corp., Hiberna Nat. Bank, New Orleans, 1980-92. Bd. dirs. Am. Cancer Soc., New Orleans, 1978-89, La. Cancer and Lung Trust Fund, 1980—, Leukemia Soc. Am., 1968-72, The Chamber, New Orleans, 1984-88, Bus. Task Force on Edn., New Orleans, 1985—, Bur. Govtl. Rsch., New Orleans, 1988—, Metrovision Partnership, New Orleans, 1990—. Named Tchr. of Yr., Alton Ochsner Med. Found., 1967. Fellow ACP (life), Internat. Soc. Hematology; mem. AMA, ABA (mem. sect. on med. schs.), AAAS, Internat. Assn. for Study Lung Cancer (founding), Am. Fedn. Clin. Rsch., Am. Hosp. Assn., Am. Assn. Clin. Oncology, Am. Assn. Hematology, Am. Soc. Internal Medicine, Internat. AIDS Soc., La. Med. Soc., Orleans Med. Soc. Soc. Surg. Oncology, Am. Coll. Legal Medicine (assoc.-in-medicine, bd. trustees NO/AIDS Task Force, bd. dirs. Acad. Med. Ctr. Consortium), Internat. Soc. for AIDS Edn., Assn. for Health Care Rsch., Mensa, SAR, Royal Soc. St. George, Milton Soc., Confrerie chevaliers du Tastevin, New Orleans Country Club, Boston Club, Century Assn. (N.Y.C.), Phi Beta Kappa. Office: Alton Ochsner Med Found 1516 Jefferson Hwy New Orleans LA 70121

PORTER, HOWARD LEONARD, III, health policy consultant; b. Denver, July 12, 1945; s. Howard Leonard and Margaret (Johnson) P.; m. Mary Ellen Biciste, June 22, 1968; 1 child, Andrew James. BA, Monmouth (Ill.) Coll., 1967; MS, U. Ill., Champaign, 1968; MBA U. Fla., 1995. Pres. The Porter Co., 1968—; sr. v.p., exec. dir. HCI Preferred Care, Inc., Auberndale, Fla., 1992—; COO Heritage Summit Health Care of Fla., Inc., 1996—; v.p. Roswell E. Johnson Inst. Comm. Rsch., 1992—. Served with Med. Service Corps, USAF, 1969-72. Mem. Phi Kappa Phi (hon.). Republican. Presbyterian. Contbr. articles to profl. publs. Home: 2068 Katie Ct Winter Haven FL 33884-3113 Office: PO Box 7533 Winter Haven FL 33883-7533

PORTER, IAN HERBERT, pediatric educator, medical center administrator; b. Copenhagen, Denmark, Nov. 14, 1929; s. Reginald and Ingeborg (Grandjean) P.; divorced; children: Julian, Robert. MB BS, St. Thomas's Hosp.-London U., 1956. Resident St. Thomas's Hosp., London, 1956-58, Royal Postgrad. Med. Sch., London, 1958-59; fellow The Johns Hopkins U. Sch. Medicine, Balt., 1960-62; rsch. fellow Royal Postgrad. Med. Sch., London, 1962-63; chief med. genetics Albany (N.Y.) Med. Coll., 1963-80, chair dept. pediatrics, 1968-79; dir. birth defects inst. N.Y. State Dept. Health, Albany, 1967-84; med. dir., v.p. med. affairs Albany Med. Ctr., 1986—; mem. N.Y. State Coun. Grad. Med. Edn., 1990-94. Mem. editorial bd. Am. Jour. Med. Genetics, 1980—. Bd. dirs. St. Gregory's Sch. for Boys, Albany, 1969-75; v.p. Albany Inst. History and Art, 1979-80, 87-89. Fellow Am. Acad. Pediatrics (trustee 1982-91, bioethics com. 1990—); mem. Am. Soc. Human Genetics (bd. dirs. 1972-75), Soc. Pediatric Rsch., Soc. Health and Human Values, Coll. Physician Execs., Am. Pediatric Soc., Alpha Omega Alpha. Home: 205 Jay St Albany NY 12210-1807 Office: Albany Med Ctr New Scotland Ave Albany NY 12208-3516

PORTER, JACK, clinical psychologist; b. Phila., Apr. 15; s. Harry and Rose (Solomon) P. BS in Edn., Temple U., 1951, MEd, 1952, DEd, 1959. Diplomate Am. Bd. Sexology; lic. psychologist, Pa., sch. psychologist, Pa. Pvt. practice psychotherapy and forensics pvt. practice, Suburban Phila., 1959—; prof. West Chester (Pa.) U., 1968—. Bd. dirs. Fedn. Day Care Svcs., Human Svcs. Ctr.; past pres. Bd. Jewish Edn. Fellow Am. Acad. Clin. Sexologists (life); mem. Am. Psychol. Assn., Pa. Psychol. Assn. (past pres.), Pa. Psychol. Found. (founding pres.), Eastern Psychol. Assn., Phila. Soc. Clin. Psychols. (Disting. Svc. award). Home and Office: 1205 Manoa Rd Wynnewood PA 19096-3325

PORTER, JEFFERY SCOTT, physician, pharmacist; b. Ft. Belvoir, Va., July 8, 1961; s. Warren Frank and Willodene (Phillips) P. BS in Pharmacy, Ohio No. U., 1986; DO with hons., Tex. Coll. Osteo. Medicine, 1994. Registered pharmacist, Tex. Pediat. resident William Beaumont Army Med. Ctr., El Paso, Tex. Capt. USAF, 1987-90, U.S. Army, 1994. Scholarship U.S. Army, 1990. Mem. Am. Coll. of Gen. Practitioners (pres. Zeta chpt. 1991-92), Rho Chi, Tau Kappa Epsilon, Kappa Psi, Phi Lambda Sigma, Psi Sigma Alpha, Phi Beta Fi. Home: 810 Mesita Dr El Paso TX 79902-1816

PORTER, LEAH LEEARLE, biological researcher; b. Remington, Va., Sept. 19, 1963; d. James Wallace and Earline Yvonne (Moore) P. BS, U. Md., 1985; MS, Cornell U., 1990, PhD, 1993. Biol. technician U.S. Dept. Agr., Beltsville, Md., 1981-85; agrl. cons. Md. Dept. Agr., College Park, 1985; cons., office mgr. Carpigraphics, Inc., Beltsville, 1985-86; grad. rsch. asst. Cornell U., Ithaca, N.Y., 1986-94; cons., mktg. asst. LeEarle Enterprises, Ithaca, 1988-94; mgr. internat. project Glahe Cons. Group, Washington, 1994-95; rsch. mgr. Chem. Mfrs. Assn., Washington, 1995—; cons., mktg. asst. Le Earle Enterprises, Ithaca, 1988-93. Md. State Senate scholar, 1984-85; faculty grad. fellow Cornell U., 1986-87. Fellow N.Y. Acad. Scis.; mem. Am. Phytopathological Soc., Assn. Women in Sci., Black Grad. and Profl. Students, Alpha Chi Sigma, Zeta Phi Beta. Democrat. Baptist. Office: 1300 Wilson Blvd Arlington VA 22209

PORTER, RODNEY WAYNE, physician; b. Stockton, Calif., May 4, 1946; s. Clarence M. and Zula S. (Plylar) P.; m. Leslie Joan Wilson, Aug. 11, 1978; 1 child, Adam. AA, San Joaquin Delta Coll., 1966; BS, Harding U., 1979; MD, U. Ark., 1984. Resident physician Area Health Edn. Ctr., Ft. Smith, Ark., 1984-85, Tex. Tech. Regional Health Ctr., Odessa, Tex., 1985-86; pvt. practice Russellville, Ark., Corning, Ark., 1986—. With U.S. Army, 1966-69. Recipient Physician's Recognition award AMA, 1989. Mem. Assn. Am. Physicians and Surgeons, NRA (life), Am. Legion. Republican. Mem. Ch. of Christ. Home and Office: 1601 Lockwood Dr Corning AR 72422-3003

PORTER, ROGER JOHN, medical research administrator, neurologist, pharmacologist; b. Pitts., Apr. 4, 1942; s. John Keaggy and Margaret (Parker) P.; m. Candace Marie Leland, Feb. 17, 1968; children: David, Stacey. BS, Eckerd Coll., 1964; MD, Duke U., 1968. Diplomate Nat. Bd. Med. Examiners, Am. Bd. Neurology, Am. Bd. Electroencephalography. Intern U. Calif. at San Diego, 1968-69; resident in neurology U. Calif. at San Francisco, 1971-74; fellow Rsch. Tng. Program Duke U., Durham, N.C., 1966-67; staff assoc. sect. epilepsy Nat. Inst. Neurol. Diseases and Stroke, NIH, Bethesda, Md., 1969-71; investigator U. Calif., San Francisco, 1972-73; sr. rsch. assoc. epilepsy br., Neurol. Disorders Program Nat. Inst. Neurol. and Communicative Disorders and Stroke, NIH, Bethesda, 1974-78, asst. chief epilepsy br., 1977-79, acting chief, 1979-80, acting chief clin. epilepsy sect., IRP, 1979-84, chief epilepsy br., Neurol. Disorders Program 1980-84, chief med. neurology br. and clin. epilepsy sect. IRP, 1984-87; dep. dir. Nat. Inst. Neurol. Disorders and Stroke, NIH, Bethesda, 1987-92; v.p., clin. pharmacology Wyeth-Ayerst Rsch., Radnor, Pa., 1992—; adj. prof. neurology U. Pa., 1993—; prof. neurology Uniformed Svcs. U. Health Scis., Bethesda, 1980-93, adj. prof. pharmacology, 1982—; cons.-lectr. neurology Nat. Naval Med. Ctr., Bethesda, 1978-93; chmn. White House Subcom. on Brain and Behavioral Scis., 1990-92; scholar-in-residence Assn. Am. Med. Colls., Washington, 1989-90; mem. NIMH/Nat. Inst. Neurol. Disorders and Stroke Coun. of Assembly of Scientists, 1983-86, pres., 1985-86; mem. pharmacy and therapeutics com. NIH, 1977-86, chmn., 1978; mem. instnl. rev. bd. human subjects Nat. Inst. Neurol. Disorders and Stroke, 1984-87, chmn., 1986-87. Author/editor 10 books; mem. editl. bd. Acta Neurologica Scandanavica, Annals of Neurology, Epilepsia; contbr. numerous papers, book chpts., abstracts to profl. publs.; writer, contbr. 5 motion pictures, 1 exhibit. Bd. trustees Eckerd Coll., 1994—. With USPHS, 1969-92. Recipient USPHS Commendation medal, 1977, MacArthur Outstanding Alumnus award Eckerd Coll., 1977, Fulbright Disting. Prof. award, 1985, USPHS Meritorious Svc. medal, 1986, Dept. Def. Meritorious Svc. medal, 1989, Disting. Alumnus award Duke Duke U. Med. Ctr., 1989, USN Commendation medal, 1991, USPHS Disting. Svc. medal, 1991; scholar in residence Assn. Am. Med. Colls., Washington, 1989-90. Fellow Am. Acad. Neurology, Am. Neurol. Assn.; mem. Am. Electroencephalographic Soc., Am. Epilepsy Soc. (pres. 1989-90), Soc. Neurosci., Am. Soc. Clin. Pharmacology and Therapeutics, Am. Soc. Neurologic Investigation (hon.), Internat. League Against Epilepsy (sec.-gen. 1989-93). Home: 461 Timber Ln Devon PA 19333-1232 Office: Wyeth-Ayerst Rsch PO Box 8299 Philadelphia PA 19101

PORTER, STEPHEN ROSS, dental and medical educator; b. Lanark, Scotland, Sept. 13, 1957; s. Richard and Catherine Mary Porter. BSc, Glasgow (Scotland) U., 1979, BDS, 1982; PhD, Bristol (Eng.) U., 1987, MB BChir, 1991, MD, 1993. House officer Bristol Dental Sch., 1982-83, MRC rsch. tng. fellow, 1983-86; registrar John Radcliffe Hosp., Oxford, Eng., 1986-87; hon. lectr. U. Bristol, 1987-91, lectr., 1992-93; sr. lectr. Eastman Dental Inst., London, 1993—. Co-author: Medicine and Surgery for Dentistry, 1993, Atlas of Oral Diseases, 1996, Innovations and Developments in Non-Surgical Care of Orofacial Diseases, 1996, Oral Health Care for Those With HIV Disease and Other Special Needs, 1995. Fellow Royal Coll. Surgeons Eng., Royal Coll. Surgeons Edinburgh. Office: Eastman Dental Inst, Dept Oral Medicine, 256 Grays Inn Rd, London WC1X 8LD, England

PORTER, WAYNE RANDOLPH, dermatologist; b. Washington, Jan. 10, 1948; s. James Randolph and Betty Rose (Burgess) P.; BS, MIT, 1970; MD, Duke U., 1973. Intern, U. Miami Affiliated Hosps., 1973-74, resident in internal medicine U. Miami Sch. Medicine (Fla.), 1973-76, resident in dermatology, 1976-78, clin. instr., then asst. prof. dermatology, 1978-85, assoc. prof., 1985—; practice medicine specializing in dermatology, North Miami Beach, 1978—; mem. staff U. Miami-Jackson Meml. Hosp., North Shore Med. Ctr., Parkway Regional Med. Ctr., Aventura Hosp. Diplomate Am. Bd. Internal Medicine, Am. Bd. Dermatology. Mem. med. adv. bd. Dade-Broward chpt. Lupus Found. Am. Fellow Internat. Soc. for Dermatologic Surgery, Am. Acad. Dermatology, Am. Soc. Dermatologic Surgeons; mem. AMA, Dade County Med. Assn., Fla. Med. Assn., Fla. Dermatology Soc., Miami Dermatol. Soc., So. Med. Assn., ACP, Internat. Soc. Pediatric Dermatology, Miami Dermatol. Soc. (pres.). Club: Bath Club (Miami beach). Home: 3550 Rockerman Rd Miami FL 33133 Office: 909 N Miami Beach Blvd Miami FL 33162-3712

PORTER, WILLIAM HUDSON, clinical chemist; b. Wilson, N.C., Mar. 12, 1940; s. Frank L. and Mildred McCollum P.; m. Faye Hardee, Mar. 23, 1963; children: Tracy M., Mark W. BS, The Citadel, 1962; MS, Med. U. S.C., 1967; PhD, Vanderbilt U., 1971. Diplomate Am. Bd. Clin. Chemistry (bd. dirs. 1985-91). Postdoctoral fellow Fla. State U., Tallahassee, 1970-72; asst. rsch. prof. U. Tenn. Meml. Rsch. Ctr., Knoxville, 1972-74; asst. prof. Med. U. S.C., Charleston, 1974-78; assoc. prof. clin. chemistry U. Ky. Med. Ctr., Lexington, 1978-86, prof., 1986—. Contbr. articles to profl. jours. Mem. Nat. Registry in Clin. Chemistry (bd. dirs. 1991-93), Am. Assn. for Clin. Chemistry, Assn. of Clin. Scientists, Am. Chem. Soc., Am. Soc. Biochemistry and Molecular Biology. Office: Univ of Ky Med Ctr HA616 Dept Pathology Lab Medicine Lexington KY 40536

PORTERFIELD, CRAIG ALLEN, psychologist, consultant; b. Geneva, N.Y., May 11, 1955; s. Paul Laverne and Elizabeth Louise (Mearns) P.; m. Alta Marie Herring, Aug. 1977; children: Aleine Michelle, Brian Matthew. Student, Sorbonne U., Paris, 1975-76; BA, St. John Fisher Coll., 1977; MA, U. Tex., Austin, 1982, PhD, 1985. Lic. psychologist, N.Y., Del.; cert. sch. psychologist, N.Y. Program evaluation intern Austin Ind. Sch. Dist., 1980, psychol. intern, 1982-83; program evaluator Austin Child Guidance Ctr., 1981-82; evaluation mgr. Child, Inc., Austin, 1981-82; staff therapist Psychotherapy Inst., Austin, 1984-85; consulting psychologist Albany (N.Y.) Psychol. Assocs., 1987-90; staff psychologist Berkshire Farm Ctr. and Svcs. for Youth, Canaan, N.Y., 1985-87, dir. rsch., 1987-90; psychologist Del. Psychiatric Svcs., Dover, 1990-94; sr. psychologist Del. Psychiatry Svcs., Del., 1994-95; pvt. practice psychology Dover and Milford, Del., 1995—; adj. asst. prof. SUNY, Albany, 1986-87, 89-91; psychologist privileges dept. psychiatry Kent Gen. Hosp., Dover, 1990—, Milford Meml. Hosp., 1995—; mem. adv. com. life skills curriculum Lake Forest Sch. Dist., Harrington, Del., 1991; co-founder, advisor Children with Attention Deficit Disorders Kent County, Del., 1991—; active Children with Attention Deficit Disorders State Coun. Del., 1993—. Grantee N.Y State Integrated Task Force on Substance Abuse Programs for Youth, 1988; recipient Presenter of Yr. Del. Coun. on Exceptional Children, 1996. Mem. APA, Assn. Advancement of Psychology, Nat. Register of Health Svcs. Providers in Psychology, Wild Quail Country Club, Preservation Delaware. Home: 109 N Main St Camden Wyoming DE 19934-1229

PORTER-O'GRADY, TIMOTHY, health science consulting executive; b. Edmonton, Alta., Can., Mar. 29, 1947; came to U.S., 1969; s. Thomas Joseph O'Grady and Margaret Porter; m. Josephine Nelson, May 13, 1969 (dec.). AA In SCi., Lower Columbia Coll., 1973; BS, Seattle U., 1975; MA, U. Wash., 1977; EdD, Nova Southeastern U., 1983; PhD, LaSalle U., 1995. Staff nurse Providence Med. Ctr., Seattle, 1973-75, clin. supr., 1975-77; patient care adminstr. Alleghany Regional Hosp., Covington, Va., 1977-79; v.p. patient care services Drs. Meml. Hosp., Richmond, Va., 1979-80; nurse adminstr. St. Joseph's Hosp., Atlanta, 1980-84; pres., bd. dirs. Affiliated Dynamics Inc., Atlanta, 1985-91; pres. Tim Porter-O'Grady Assocs., Inc., Atlanta, 1992—. Author: Shared Governance, 1984, Participatory Management, 1986, Nursing Finance, 1987, Reorganization of Nursing Practice, 1990, Implementing Shared Governance, 1992, The Nurse Managers Problem Solver, 1994, Leadership Revolution in Health Care, 1995; contbr. over 125 articles to profl. jours. Mem. governing bd. Atlanta Cmty. Health Program, 1987-89; trustee Ga. Nurses' Found., Atlanta, 1988-92; mem. adv. bd. Ga. State Dept. Human Resources, Atlanta, 1987—; chmn. bd. AID Atlanta, 1991-92, vice chair, 1992-94; chmn. Ga. Health Reform Project, 1994-95; bd. dirs. Nat. Franciscan Health Sys., 1996—. Homeless health care grantee U.S. Dept. HHS, 1987, 89. Fellow Am. Acad. Nursing, N.Y. Acad. Scis.; mem. ANA (nat. cert. advanced adminstrn. and gerontology), AIDS Rsch. Consortium of Atlanta, Am. Coll. Health Execs., Gerontology Soc. Am., Amnesty Internat. (health care profl. divsn.), Forum for Nurse Execs. (bd. dirs. 1991-94), Sigma Theta Tau. Democrat. Roman Catholic. Home and Office: 1710 Barnesdale Way NE Atlanta GA 30309-2602

PORTMAN, RONALD JAY, pediatric nephrologist, researcher; b. Portsmouth, N.H., June 8, 1950; s. Harry and Sylvia Rosa (Applebaum) P.; m. Joan Marie Welch, June 29, 1974; children: Wendi Alana, Shayna Matana, Solomon Zachary. BS, Northeastern U., 1973; MD, Dartmouth Coll., 1976. Diplomate Am. Bd. Pediat., Am. Bd. Pediatric Nephrology. Commd. officer U.S. Army, 1976, advanced through grades to maj.; pediatric house officer Fitzsimons Army Med. Ctr., Denver, 1976-79, pediatric nephrologist, 1983-86; chief dept. pediat. Würzburg (Germany) Army Hosp., 1979-81; fellow in pediatric nephrology Washington U., St. Louis, 1981-83; resigned, 1986; pediatric nepnrologist U. Tex. Med. sch., Houston, 1986-92, dir. divsn. pediatric nephrology and hypertension, 1992—; dir. pediat. spl. care unit and Hermann Chronobiology Ctr., Hermann Hosp., Houston, 1992—; mem. med. adv. bd. Nat. Kidney Found. S.E. Tex., Houston, 1986—; cons. M.D. Anderson Hosp., Houston, 1986—, Chronobiology Ctr. Tel Hashomer, Tel Aviv, 1995—; mem. med. rev. bd. End Stae for Disease Network 14, Dallas, 1992—. Contbr. numerous articles to med. jours., chpts. to books. Bd. dirs. Congregation Brith Saalom, Bellaire, Tex., 1990-94. Recipient svc. award Nat. Kidney Found., 1995; numerous rsch. grants. Mem. Am. Soc. Pediatric Nephrology, Am. Soc. Nephrology, Am. Soc. Hpertension, Internat. Soc. Chronobiology, N.Am. Pediatric Renal Transplant Study Group, S.W. Pediatric Nephrology Study Group. Jewish.

PORTNOW, STANLEY LEWIS, psychiatrist, educator; b. Newark, N.J., Apr. 24, 1929; s. Michael Philip and Anna (Schuman) P.; m. Faye Darlene Allen, Nov. 23, 1933; children: Elisabeth Rose, Jana Lynn, Kara Jyme. AB, N.Y.U., 1950; MD, U. Zurich, 1956; JD, Fordham U., 1986. Diplomat, Am. Bd. Psychiatry & Neurology, Am. Bd. of Forensic Psychiatry. Asst. clin. prof. of Psychiatry NYU Sch. Med., N.Y.C., 1969-74, clin. assoc. prof. of Psychiatry, 1974-83, clin. prof. psychiatry, 1983—; dir. of Psychiatry, Forensic Psychiatry, NYU Sch. of Med., 1969-72, N.Y.C. Com. Mental Health Bd., 1965-69. Author: several articles on insanity defense, personality disorders, and Law and Psychiatry, 1960-88. Lt. Med. Corps, U.S. Army, 1958-66. Fellow Am. Psychiatric Assn., N.Y. Acad. Medicine; mem. Am. Acad. of Psychiatry & Law (pres. 1982), Am. Bd. Forensic Psychiatry (bd. dirs. 1976-82), Am. Bd. Forensic Psychiatry (sec. 1979-81). Office: 823 Park Ave New York NY 10021-2849

POSER, ERNEST GEORGE, psychologist, educator; b. Vienna, Austria, Mar. 2, 1921; emigrated to Can., 1942, naturalized, 1946; s. Paul and Blanche (Furst) P.; m. Maria Jutta Cahn, July 3, 1953; children: Yvonne, Carol, Michael. B.A., Queen's U., Kingston, Ont., 1946, M.A., 1949; Ph.D., U. London, 1952. Diplomate: Am. Bd. Profl. Psychologists; registered psychologist, B.C. Asst. prof. U. N.B., 1946-48; chief psychologist N.B. Dept. Health, 1952-54; prof. psychology McGill U., Montreal, 1954-83; assoc. prof. psychiatry Faculty Medicine McGill U., 1963-83; adj. prof. dept. psychology U. B.C., 1984—; dir. behavior therapy unit Douglas Hosp. Center, Montreal, 1966-83. Author: Adaptive Learning: Behavior Modification with Children, 1973, Behavior Therapy in Clinical Practice, 1977. hon. fellow Middlesex Hosp., London, 1964. Fellow Canadian Psychol. Assn., Am. Psychol. Assn.

POSEY, DELMA POWELL, dermatologist; b. Mexia, Tex., Feb. 2, 1937; s. Delma Ross and Lois Lorene (Sikes) P.; m. Patsy Ruth Fitts, Aug. 13, 1960; children: Daniel, Patrick, Julie. BS, Tex. A&M U., 1959; MD, Baylor U., 1963. Commd. 2d lt. U.S. Army, 1963, advanced through grades to major, 1968, ret., 1971; intern William Beaumont Gen. Hosp., El Paso, Tex., 1963-64; resident Brooke Gen. Hosp., San Antonio, 1965-68; staff physician Scott and White Clinic, Temple, Tex., 1971—. Fellow Am. Acad. Dermatology. Mem. Christian Ch. Office: Scott and White Clinic 2401 S 31st St Temple TX 76508-0001

POSEY, JOHN ALTON, JR., internist; b. Houston, Apr. 11, 1942; s. John Alton and Maude Enna (Paxton) P.; m. Ruth Ann Shafran, Mar. 3, 1973; children: Jennifer Ellen, Kristen Lea, John Alton III. Student, Lamar State Coll. Tech., 1960-62; BS in Mech. Engring., U. Tex., 1965, MS in Mech. Engring., 1968; MD, U. Tex., Galveston, 1975; PhD, Baylor Coll. Medicine, 1972. Registered profl. engr.; diplomate Nat. Bd. Med. Examiners, Am. Bd. Internal Medicine. Intern St. Luke's Episcopal Hosp., Houston, 1975-76;

resident internal medicine Baylor Coll. of Medicine Affiliated Hosps., Houston, 1976-78; asst. clin. instr. dept. internal medicine Baylor Coll. Medicine, Houston, 1975-78, clin. instr. dept. internal medicine, 1981-87, clin. asst. prof. dept. internal medicine, 1987—; pvt. practice gen. internal medicine Houston, 1978—; asst. instr. dept. physiology Baylor Coll. Medicine, 1971-72, instr., 1972, adj. instr., 1972-75. Contbr. articles to profl. jours. Recipient Nat. Sci. Found. scholarship, 1964, Nat. Inst. Health fellowship, 1969-71. Mem. AMA, Tex. Med. Assn., Harris County Med. Assn., Am. Coll. Physicians, Tex. Soc. Internal Medicine, Houston Soc. Internal Medicine, U. Tex. Circle (charter mem.), Omicron Delta Kappa, Tau Beta Pi (pres. Tex. Alpha chpt. 1965-66, chmn. nat. conv. com. 1966), Pi Tau Sigma (pres. Tex. Kappa chpt. 1964-65). Methodist. Office: Cheng Posey & Assocs 6624 Fannin St Ste 2360 Houston TX 77030-2335

POSEY, LORAN MICHAEL, pharmacist, editor; b. Albany, Ga., Aug. 22, 1955; s. Loran Willis and Rubye Jane (Lumpkin) P.; m. Teresa Maria McCoy, June 27, 1975 (div. Mar. 1983); m. Cheryl Ann Emerling, Jan. 31, 1989; children: Evan Michael, Alan Michael, Loran Michael. BS in Pharmacy, BS in Microbiology, U. Ga., 1979, postgrad., 1996—. Registered pharmacist, Ga. Sr. editor Am. Soc. Hosp. Pharmacists, Bethesda, Md., 1980-85; pres. PAS Pharmacy/Assn. Svcs., Athens, Ga., 1985—, PNN Pharmacotherapy News Network, Athens, 1994—; dir. adminstrv. svcs. Ill. Soc. Hosp. Pharmacists, 1986-92, Va. Soc. Hosp. Pharmacists, 1990—; exec. dir. Phi Delta Chi Pharmacy Frat., 1983—, Ga. Soc. Hosp. Pharmacists, 1993-95. Author: Pharmacy Cadence, 1992; editor: Pharmacotherapy: A Pathophysiologic Approach, 1989, 2d edit., 1992; editor The Cons. Pharmacist, 1986, Jour. Managed Care Pharmacy, 1995. Mem. Am. Med. Writers Assn. (chpt. pres. 1988-89, Pres.'s award 1988), Profl. Frat. Assn. (com. chair 1986-90), Am. Soc. Assn. Execs., Ill. Coun. Hosp. Pharmacists (hon.), Phi Delta Chi. Office: PAS Pharmacy/Assn Svcs PO Box 6565 Athens GA 30604

POSNER, DAVID MARK, family physician; b. N.Y.C., June 27, 1945; s. Herbert and Anne (Seidman) P.; children: Nicole, Eric, Andrea Kate. Student, Bard Coll., 1958; BA, Hofstra U., 1962; DO, U. Health Scis., Kansas City, Mo., 1972; MBA, Loyola Coll., Balt., 1991. Diplomate Am. Bd. Family Practice. Pvt. practice Balt., 1981—; assoc. dir. dept. med. affairs Prudential Health Care Sys., 1994; chief exec. officer Triam Aviation Inc., Balt., 1990—; bd. dirs. Cygne Cons. Inc., Balt. Asst. surgeon gen. Pub. Health Svc., 1972-73. Mem. Am. Coll. Physician Execs. Home: 4348 Wild Filly Ct Ellicott City MD 21042-5931 Office: Capitol Hill Med Ctr 412 1st St SE Washington DC 20003

POSNER, JEROME BEEBE, neurologist, educator; b. Cin., Mar. 20, 1932; s. Philip and Rose (Goldberg) P.; m. Gerta Grunen, Aug. 29, 1954; children: Roslyn, Joel, P.J. BS, U. Wash., 1951, MD, 1955. Intern King County Hosp., Seattle, 1955-56; asst. resident in neurology U. Wash. Affiliated Hosps., Seattle, 1956-59; fellow in neurology U. Wash. Affiliated Hosps., 1958-59; spl. fellow NIH, U. Wash., 1961-63; instr. medicine U. Louisville Sch. Medicine, 1959-61; attending neurologist King County Hosp., 1962-63; asst. prof. neurology Cornell U. Med. Coll., N.Y.C., 1963-67; assoc. prof. Cornell U. Med. Coll., 1967-70, prof., 1970—, vice chmn. dept. neurology, 1978-87; asst. attending neurologist N.Y. Hosp., 1963-67, asso. attending neurologist, 1967-70, attending neurologist, 1970—; asso. Cotzias Lab. of Neuro-Oncology, Sloan Kettering Inst. Cancer Research, N.Y.C., 1967-76; mem. Cotzias Lab. of Neuro-Oncology, Sloan Kettering Inst. Cancer Research, 1976—; chief neuropsychiat. service, attending physician dept. medicine Meml. Hosp. for Cancer and Allied Diseases, 1967-75, attending physician, 1975—, chmn. dept. neurology, 1975-87, 89—, Cotzias chair neuro-oncology, 1986; clin. rsch. prof. Am. Cancer Soc., 1996—; mem. med. adv. bd. Burke Rehab. Ctr., White Plains, N.Y., 1973—; adj. prof., vis. physician Rockefeller U. and Hosp., N.Y.C., 1973-75; mem. neurology B study sect. NIH, 1972-76. Author: (with F. Plum) Diagnosis of Stupor and Coma, 3d edit., 1980, (with H. Gilbert and L. Weiss) Brain Metastasis, 1980, Neurologic Complications of Cancer, 1995; mem. editorial bd. Archives of Neurology, 1971-76, Annals of Neurology, 1976-80, Am. Jour. Medicine, 1978-93, Neurology, 1992—; contbr. articles to med. jours. Served with M.C. U.S. Army, 1959-61. Fellow AAAS; mem. AMA, Am. Acad. Neurology (Farber Brain Tumor award 1988), Am. Assn. Cancer Rsch., Am. Fedn. Clin. Rsch., Am. Neurol. Assn., Am. Physiol. Soc., Assn. Am. Physicians, Harvey Soc., N.Y. Acad. Sci. Inst. of Medicine, Soc. Neurosci., Can. Neurol. Soc. (hon.), Alpha Omega Alpha. Office: Meml Sloan-Kettering Cancer 1275 York Ave New York NY 10021-6007

POSNER, RONALD EDGAR, physician, ophthalmologist; b. Cleve., Oct. 31, 1936; s. Alan and Betty (Krasny) P.; m. Linda A. Maron, Aug. 21, 1960; children: David, Laura Posner Dim. BA, Western Res. U., 1959, MD, 1963. Diplomate Am. Bd. Ophthalmology. Intern Mt. Sinai Hosp., Cleve., 1963-64, resident in ophthalmology, 1964-67; pvt. practice Painesville and Mentor, Ohio., 1969—; chmn. bd., co-founder Western Res. Health Plan, Cleve., 1981-85. Contbr. articles to profl. jours. Lt. comdr. USPHS, 1967-69. Fellow ACS (credential com.), Am. Acad. Ophthalmology; mem. Am. Soc. Cataract and Refractive Surgery, Ohio Ophthal. Soc., Ohio and Lake County Med. Soc., Cleve. Ophthal. Soc. (treas.).

POSNICK, JEFFREY CRAIG, plastic surgeon; b. Mpls., Mar. 1, 1952; s. Irving H. and Nan (Fine) P.; m. Patricia Joan Grundlegar, Jan. 7, 1989; children: Joshua, David. BA, U. Minn., 1973; DMD, Harvard U., 1977; MD, Vanderbilt U., 1979. Diplomate Am. Bd. Oral/Maxillofacial Surgery, Am. Bd. Plastic Surgery. Resident oral/maxillofacial surgery Vanderbilt U. Hosp., Nashville, 1977-79, resident gen. surgery, 1979-80, resident oral/massillofacial surgery, 1980-81; resident gen. surgery Mass. Gen. Hosp., Boston, 1981-83; fellow pediatric craniofacial surgery U. Pa., Phila., 1983; resident plastic surgery Ea. Va. Sch. Medicine, Norfolk, 1984-86; dir. craniofacial surgery Hosp. for Sick Children, U. Toronto, Ont., Can., 1986-92; dir. Craniofacial Ctr. Georgetown Children's Med. Ctr., Georgetown U. Med. Ctr., Washington, 1992—. Contbr. articles to profl. jours. Rsch. grantee Med. Rsch. Coun. Can., 1990, Plastic Surg. Edn. Found., 1990, Saudi Arabia Edn. Found., 1992, Cleft Palate Found., 1995. Fellow ACS, Royal Coll. Surgeons (Can.); mem. Internat. Soc. Craniofacial Surgeons, Am. Cleft Palate/Craniofacial Assn. Home: 10100 Counselman Rd Potomac MD 20854 Office: Georgetown U Med Ctr Divsn Plastic Surgery 3800 Reservoir Rd Washington DC 20007

POST, DAVID L., clinical psychologist; b. N.Y.C., July 18, 1949; s. Joseph and Anne (Bretzfelder) P.; m. Belinda M., May 31, 1975; children: Christopher Thomas, Joel Matthew. BA, U. Chgo., 1971; MA, New Sch. Social Rsch., 1973; PhD, Brandeis U., 1978. Lic. psychologist, Mass.; Diplomate Am. Bd. Med. Psychotherapists. Prin. psychologist John T. Berry Rehab. Ctr., North Reading, Mass., 1978-80; staff psychologist Family Counseling & Guidance Ctr., Danvers, Mass., 1980-86; clin. psychologist pvt. practice, Chestnut Hill, Mass., 1986—; cons. in field. Contbr. articles to profl. jours. Named Suzanne Feld Meml. Fellow in Psychology Brandeis U., 1974-76. Mem. APA, Mass. Psychol. Assn., Mass. Soc. Clin. Psychologists (pres. 1987-89). Office: 31 Oakmont Rd Newton MA 02159-2530

POST, MARY ANN, nurse; b. La Porte, Ind.; d. Kenneth William and Lucille M. (Helm) P. BA, Chapman Coll., 1974; BSN, Sonoma Staet U., 1979; MS in Nursing, U. Tex. Health Sci. Ctr., 1983. RN, Ariz. Commd. 2d lt. USAF, 1969, advanced through grades to col., retired, 1995; dir. utilization mgmt. Humana Inc., Louisville, 1995; cons. in field. Mem. exec. bd. Bexar County Battered Women's Shelter, San Anton, Tex., 1982-83; mem. Ba. Peninsula Divsn. Am. Heart Assn., Hampton, 1985. Decorated Legion of Merit, Meritorious Svc. medal, Commendation medal. Mem. ANA, am. coll. Healthcare Execs., Sigma Theta Tau. Home: 1505 Crystal Dr #916 Arlington VA 22202

POST, ROBERT LICKELY, physiologist; b. Phila., Nov. 4, 1920; s. Levi Arnold and Grace Hutcheson (Lickely) P.; m. Grace Elizabeth Rawlings, Oct. 22, 1947. BS magna cum laude, Harvard U., 1942, MD, 1945. Intern Hartford (Conn.) Hosp., 1945-46; instr. Med. Sch. U. Pa., Phila., 1946-48, vis. scholar, 1991—; from instr. to prof. Med. Sch. Vanderbilt U., Nashville, 1948-91. Recipient Cole award Biophys. Soc., 1983. Home: 3300 Darby Rd Apt 6303 Haverford PA 19041-1074 Office: U Pa Sch of Medicine Dept Of Physiology Philadelphia PA 19104-6085

POSTER, DON STEVEN, internist, hematologist, oncologist; b. N.Y.C., Nov. 19, 1950. BA, Pace U., N.Y.C., 1970; DO, U. Osteopathic Health Sci., Des Moines, 1973. Diplomate Am. Bd. Internal Medicine, Am. Bd. Med. Oncology, Am. Bd. Hematology (fellow). Intern USPHS Hosp., S.I., 1973-74; resident in medicine SUNY and Northport VA Hosp., 1975-77; fellow hematology and oncology Roswell Park Meml. Inst., Buffalo, 1977-79; investigator NCI/NIH, Bethesda, Md., 1979-81; med. oncologist North Miami Beach, Fla., 1981—. Editor: Treatment of Nausea and Vomiting, 1981; contbr. articles to profl. jours. Bd. dirs. United Charities, Hollywood, Fla., 1989. With USPHS, 1978-81. Am. Cancer Soc. fellow, 1977-79. Fellow Am. Coll. Clin. Pharmacology, Am. Coll. Medicine.

POSTHUMA, ALBERT ELWOOD, surgeon; b. Grand Rapids, Mich., Apr. 25, 1919; s. Gerrit Pylman and Alice (Mandemaker) P.; A.B., Calvin Coll., 1940; M.D., U. Mich., 1943, M.S. 1949; m. Jean L. Swann, Aug. 17, 1974; children by previous marriage: Beth Alicia Posthuma Jenkins, Ann Maureen Posthuma Eizyk, Jane Marie Robertson, Susan Swann Gregory. Intern, St. Mary's Hosp., Grand Rapids, 1943-44, resident, 1944-46, 48-50; practice medicine specializing in surgery, 1950-86; cons. surgeon St. Mary's Hosp., 1972—, chief of staff, 1972-78; cons. surgeon Ferguson-Droste-Ferguson hosps. Pres., Kent County Med. Found., 1979. Served from 1st lt. to capt. AUS, 1946-48. Recipient citation U. Mich., 1949. Diplomate Am. Bd. Surgery. Fellow A.C.S.; mem. Pan-Pacific Surg. Assn., Kent County Med. Soc. (pres. 1978-79). Club: Blythefield Country. Home: 6025 Belinda Dr NE Rockford MI 49341-9444

POSTON, ANN GENEVIEVE, psychotherapist, nurse; b. Sioux City, Iowa, July 28, 1936; d. Frank Earl and Ella Marie (Stanton) Gales; m. Gerald Connell Poston, June 27, 1959; children: Gregory, Mary Ann, Susan. BSN, Briar Cliff Coll., 1958; MA, U. Mo., 1978; postgrad., Family Inst. of Kansas City, Inc., 1989-91. RN, Kans., Mo.; lic. counselor, Mo. Staff nurse, sr. team leader St. Joseph Mercy Hosp., Sioux City, 1958-59; head nurse St. Anthony's Hosp., Rock Island, Ill., 1960, charge nurse, 1966-69; charge nurse St. Mary's Hosp., Mpls., 1970-71, North Kansas City (Mo.) Hosp., 1972-73, Tri-County Mental Health Ctr., North Kansas City, 1973-79; psychotherapist VA Med. Ctr., Kansas City, 1979-84, Leavenworth, Kans., 1984-85; psychotherapist The Kans. Inst., Olathe, 1985-95; psychotherapist, marriage and family therapist Psychiatry Assocs., Chartered, Overland Park, Kans., 1994—; cons. Synergy House, Parkville, Mo., 1974-75, North Kansas City Hosp., 1978-79, VA Hosps., Kansas City and Leavenworth, 1979-85, Cath. Charities, Kansas City, 1983-87, Olathe Med. Ctr., 1985-95, Humana Med. Ctr. Overland Park, Kans., 1986-95, St. Joseph Med. Ctr., Kansas City, Mo., 1990-95; psychotherapist, marriage & famiy therapist Cath. Charities, Kansas City, Mo., 1996—, Shawnee Mission (Kans.) Med. Ctr., 1996—. Author, presenter (video) Depression & Suicide, 1980. Third officer King's Daus., Moline, Ill., 1960-69; campaign worker Rep. Party, Moline, 1963-68; community asst. New Mark Community Affairs, Kansas City, 1972-76; nursing rep. Combined Fed. Campaign, Kansas City, 1982; coord. mental health program com. Midwest Health Congress, Kansas City, 1981. Mem. ACA, ANA (cert.), Internat. Assn. for Marriage and Family Counselors, Am. Assn. Marriage and Family Therapy (clinical), Nat. Bd. Cert. Counselors, Mo. Assn. Marriage and Family Therapy, Sigma Theta Tau. Roman Catholic.

POSTON, WALKER S. O, medical educator. BA in Biol. Scis., U. Calif., Davis, 1983, PhD, 1990. Intern, resident USAF Med. Ctr., Wright-PAtterson AFB, Ohio, 1989-90; dir. psychology svcs., asst. chief mental health svcs. 9th Med. Group, Beale AFB, 1990-92; chief health and rehab. psychology svc. Malcolm Grow Med. Ctr., 1993-95, faculty, 1993-95; clin. asst. prof. dept. med. and clin. psychology F. Edward Herbert Sch. Medicine, Bethesda, Md., 1993-95; asst. prof. medicine Baylor Coll. Medicine, Houston, 1995—. Contbr. articles to profl. jours. Recipient Minority Scientist Devel. award Am. Heart Assn., 1995; U. Calif. Doctoral scholars fellow, 1984-85, 85-86, 86-87, 88-89, Clin. fellow Wilford Hall Med. Ctr., Lackland AFB, 1992-93; Nat. Merit scholar, 1979-80. Office: Baylor Coll Medicine Behavior Medicine Rsch Ctr 6535 Fannin MS F-700 Houston TX 77030*

POTASH, SETH DAVID, ophthalmologist, educator; b. N.Y.C., Nov. 19, 1962; s. Jacob I. and Rhoda L. (Isaacson) P.; m. Linda S. Jacobs, Sept. 7, 1991; 1 children: Emily K., Samuel I. BA, Johns Hopkins U., 1984; MD, SUNY, Stony Brook, 1988. Diplomate Am. Bd. Med. Examiners; bd. cert. diplomate Am. Bd. Ophthalmology. Intern internal medicine Winthrop Univ. Hosp., Mineola, N.Y., 1988-89; resident ophthalmology Lenox Hill Hosp., N.Y.C., 1989-92; fellow glaucoma N.Y. Eye and Ear Infirmary, N.Y.C., 1992-93; pvt. practice ophthalmology White Plains, N.Y., 1993—; clin. instr. N.Y. Med. Coll., Valhalla, 1993—, N.Y. Eye and Ear Infirmary, N.Y.C., 1993—. Contbr. chpt. to book and articles to profl. jours. Rsch. grantee A.R.V.O., 1993. Fellow Am. Acad. Ophthalmology; mem. N.Y. State Ophthalmol. Soc., N.Y. Glaucoma Soc., Med. Soc. State N.Y., Westchester County Med. Soc., Alpha Omega Alpha. Office: 170 Maple Ave White Plains NY 10601

POTLURI, VENKATESWARA RAO, medical facility administrator; b. Krishna Dist., India, Jan. 1, 1955; came to U.S., 1983; s. Venkata Krishnaiah and Bulli Ademma (Koduru) P.; m. Padma Sree Peddu, Dec. 4, 1986; children: Vani, Vamsee Krishna, Varun. BSc, ANR Coll., Gudivada, India, 1975; MSc, AU Coll. Sci. and Tech., Waltair, India, 1977; MPhil, Delhi (India) U., 1979, PhD, 1982. Diplomate Am. Bd. Med. Genetics. Postdoctoral fellow Mt. Sinai Med. Ctr., N.Y.C., 1983-85, vis. asst. prof., 1985-87; lab. dir., adj. mem. med. staff Norwalk (Conn.) Hosp., 1987—. Fellow Am. Coll. Med. Genetics (founding); mem. Am. Soc. Human Genetics, New Eng. Regional Genetics Group. Home: 33 Ledgewood Dr Norwalk CT 06850-1813 Office: Norwalk Hosp Cytogenetic Lab Dept Path Maple St Norwalk CT 06856

POTTASH, RUBEN ROBERT, psychiatrist; b. Phila., Aug. 9, 1914; s. Harry and Bessie (Krell) P.; m. Myra Elizabeth Cohn, Oct. 22, 1938; children: Steven J., A. Carter. BA, Pa. State U., 1935; MD, Thomas Jefferson U., 1939. Diplomate, Am. Bd. Psychiatry and Neurology. Pvt. practice Phila., 1940-55; resident Inst. Pa. Hosp., Phila., 1955-57, U. Pa., Phila., 1957-59; pvt. practice Wynnewood, Pa., 1990-95; ret., 1995; intern Sacred Heart Hosp., Allentown, Pa., 1939-40; cons. Phila. Child Guidance Clinic, 1976-85, U.S. Naval Hosp., Phila., 1976-85; cons. Inst. Pa. Hosp., 1979-86, hon. cons., 1990. Maj. M.C., USAF, 1943-46, PTO. Fellow Am. Psychiat. Assn. (life), Pa. Psychiat. Soc., Phila. Psychiat. Soc.; mem. Am. Psychoanalytic Assn.

POTTER, BENJAMIN FRANKLIN, JR., clinical psychologist; b. Durham, N.C., July 7, 1940; s. Benjamin F. and Mary Belle (McDade) P.; m. Nancy Northcott, Dec. 27, 1968; children: Elizabeth, Rebecca. BA, U. N.C., 1962; MDiv, U. Theol. Sem., 1966; MA, Appalachian State U., 1980; Psychology D, Wright State U., 1982. Ordained to ministry Meth. Ch. Pastor Wesley Meml. United Meth. Ch., Columbia, N.C., 1968-72, Princeton (N.C.) United Meth. Ch., 1972-75, Aldersgate United Meth. Ch., Durham, 1975-78; instr. dept. philosophy and religion Appalachian State U., Boone, N.C., 1979; psychology intern Broughton Hosp., Morganton, N.C., 1982-83; psychologist Gaston Mental Health Ctr., Gastonia, N.C., 1983-85; dir. psychol. svc. Gaston-Lincoln Mental Health Program, Gastonia, 1985-86; pvt. practice Gastonia, 1984—; coord. psychology Gaston Meml. Hosp., Gastonia, 1986—. Mem. APA, N.C. Psychol. Assn. Methodist. Office: Gaston Meml Hosp PO Box 1747 2525 Court Dr Gastonia NC 28054-2142

POTTER, JACK ARTHUR, optometrist; b. Peoria, Ill., Sept. 7, 1917; s. John Bernard Potter and Mary Bernadot Purcell; m. Charlotte Helen Brubaker, Apr. 5, 1941 (dec. Jan 1974); children: Jack Allen, Lynn Ann; m. Dorothy Grantz Styx, July 24, 1975. OD, Ill. Coll. Optometry, 1938; postgrad., Purdue U., 1946. Pvt. practice optometry East Peoria, Ill., 1938—; coordinator optometry St. Francis Hosp., Peoria, 1975-82; lectr. Bradley U., Peoria, 1949-72. Contbr. articles on reading and vision problems to profl. jours. Served with U.S. Army, 1941-45. Fellow Am. Acad. Optometry; mem. Am. Optometric Assn. (bd. trustees 1967-73, sec., treas. 1973-75), Ill. Optometric Assn. (pres. 1965-67, Optometrist of Yr. 1967, Disting. Svc. award 1975, del. for life), Ill. Valley Optometric Soc. (pres.). Republican. Mem. Christian Ch. Lodges: Masons, Shriners. Home: 609 Hilldale Ave Washington IL 61571-1607 Office: 2400 N Main St East Peoria IL 61611-1735

POTTER, JAMES DOUGLAS, pharmacology educator; b. Waterbury, Conn., Sept. 26, 1944; s. Herbert Eugene and Jean Gladys (Troske) P.; m. Priscilla F. Strang, Aug. 9, 1985; children: Liesse, Andrew, Ian Brown. BS, George Washington U., 1965; PhD, U. Conn., 1970; postgrad. (fellow) Boston Biomed. Rsch. Inst., 1970-74. Staff scientist Boston Biomed. Research Inst., 1974-75; assoc. in neurology Harvard U. Med. Sch., 1974-75; asst. prof. cell biophysics Baylor Coll. Medicine, 1975-77; assoc. prof. pharmacology U. Cin., 1977-81, prof., 1981-83; chmn., prof. dept. molecular and cellular pharmacology U. Miami, 1983—; grant reviewer in field. Grantee NIH, 1978-81, 83—, Nat. Heart Lung and Blood Inst., 1978— (Merit award 1989—), Muscular Dystrophy Assn., 1983-94. Fellow Muscular Dystrophy Assn.; mem. AAAS, Am. Chem. Soc., Am. Soc. Pharmacology and Exptl. Therapeutics, Assn. for Med. Sch. Pharmacology (chmn.), Internat. Soc. Heart Rsch., Am. Heart Assn. (established investigator 1974-79), Am. Soc. Biochem. and Molecular Biologists, Cardiac Muscle Soc. (sec.-treas. 1992-94, pres. 1994-96), Biophys. Soc., Sigma Xi. Contbr. articles to profl. jours. Home: 7240 SW 127th St Miami FL 33156-5336 Office: U Miami Sch Medicine Dept of Molecular & Cellular Pharm 1600 NW 10th Ave Miami FL 33136

POTTER, MICHAEL TERRY, dentist; b. San Francisco, Nov. 9, 1949; s. William Harry and Polly Potter Switt, m. Sue Ann Potter; children: William Michael, Jeffrey Matthew. BA, East Carolina Univ., 1971; DDS, Univ. N.C., 1975; cert., Wilford Hall Medical Ctr., 1988. Diplomate Am. Bd. Prosthodontics. Gen. dentist USAF, 1975-88, prosthodontist, 1988—; chief of dept. prosthodontics Sheppard Air Force Base, Wichita Falls, Tex., 1995—; instr. in prosthodontics Advanced Edn. in Gen. Dentistry Program Deesler AFB, 1988-91, Sheppard AFB, 1995—. Col. U.S. Air Force, 1975—. Fellow Am. Coll. Prosthodontist; mem. Am. Dental Assn. Republican. Roman Catholic. Office: 82nd Medical Group SGD 149 Hart St Ste 1 Sheppard AFB TX 76311

POTTER, PATRICIA ANN, psychiatrist; b. Portsmouth, Va., Sept. 22, 1951; d. Maxwell Gideon and Bernice Vivian (Padget) P. BA, Harvard U., 1973; MD, Tufts U., 1977. Diplomate Am. Bd. Psychiatry and Neurology, Am. Bd. Psychiatry, Am. Bd. Child Psychiatry. Intern in medicine Meml. Hosp., Worcester, Mass., 1977-78; resident in psychiatry Tufts Affiliated Hosps., Boston, 1978-82; fellow in child psychiatry McLean Hosp., Belmont, Mass., 1982-84, asst. child psychiatrist, 1984—; instr. in psychiatry Harvard U. Med. Sch., Boston, 1984—; cons. psychiatrist Thom Clinic, Boston, 1984-88, Brandeis U., Waltham, Mass., 1987—. Mem. Mass. Psychiatric Soc., Mass. Med. Soc., Am. Acad. Child and Adolescent Psychiatry, N.Eng. Coun. Child and Adolescent Psychiatry, Am. Psychiatric Assn., Am. Psychoanalytic Assn. Office: 1280 Massachusetts Ave Cambridge MA 02138-3840

POTTS, ANTHONY VINCENT, optometrist, orthokeratologist; b. Detroit, Aug. 10, 1945; m. Susan Claire, July 1, 1967; 1 child, Anthony Christian. Student, Henry Ford Community Coll., 1964-65, Eastern Mich. U., 1965-66; OD, So. Coll. Optometry, 1970; MS in Health Svcs. Mgmt., LaSalle U., 1995. Practice orthokeratology and contact lenses Troy, Mich., 1975—; adj. prof. optometry Ill. Coll. Optometry; lectr., author orthokeratology, contact lenses and astigmatism. Lt. USNR, 1971-73, lt. MSC USNR, 1992—. Fellow Internat. Orthokeratology Soc. (membership chmn. 1976-83, bd. dirs. local chpt. 1976-83, chmn. Internat. Eye Rsch. Found. sect. 1981-83, bd. dirs. nat. chpt. 1985—, adminstrv. dir. nat. chpt. 1985—, chmn. nat. chpt. 1987—), Am. Acad. Optometry; mem. Am. Optometric Assn., Armed Forces Optometric Soc., Nat. Eye Rsch. Found., Naval Order Am., Assn. of Mil. Surgeons of U.S., Naval Hosp. Great Lakes. Roman Catholic. Office: Med Sq Troy 1575 W Big Beaver Rd # 11C Troy MI 48084-3525

POTTS, JOHN THOMAS, JR., physician, educator; b. Phila., Jan. 19, 1932; married; 3 children. B.A., LaSalle Coll, Phila., 1953; M.D., U. Pa., Phila., 1957. From intern to asst. resident in medicine Mass. Gen. Hosp., Boston, 1957-59; resident Nat. Heart Inst., 1959-60, research fellow in medicine, 1960-63, sr. research staff, 1963-66, head sect. polypeptide hormones, 1966-68; chief endocrine unit Mass. Gen. Hosp., Boston, 1968-81, chief gen med. svc., 1981—; from asst. to assoc. prof. medicine Harvard U. Med. Sch., Boston, 1968-75, prof., 1975-81, Jackson prof. clin. medicine, 1981—; chief endocrine unit Mass. Gen. Hosp., Boston, 1968-81, chief gen. med., 1981—. Recipient Ernest Oppenheimer award, Andre Lichwitz prize Endocrine Soc., 1968, Fred Conrad Koch award Endocrine Soc., 1991, William F. Neumann award Am. Soc. Bone and Mineral Rsch. Fellow AAA; mem. Am. Soc. Biol. Chemistry, Endocrine Soc. (pres. 1987), Assn. Am. Physicians, Am. Fedn. Clin. Research, Am. Soc. Clin. Investigation, Inst. Medicine. Office: Mass Gen Hosp Med Svcs Fruit St Boston MA 02114-2620*

POTTS, NANCY DEE NEEDHAM, psychologist, b. Dec. 21, 1947; d. Sidney Boyd and Katie Sue (McDonald) N. BA, Baylor U., 1970; MEd, Sam Houston U., 1974; EdD, U. Houston, 1979. Lic. marriage and family therapist. Tchr. Spring Branch (Tex.) Ind. Sch. Dist., 1971-73; therapist, program cons. Ctr. for Counseling, Houston, 1973-75; psychologist, ptnr. Marriage, Family & Divorce Cons., Houston, 1975-81; pres. The Peace Inst. Universal Christianity, 1986—; speaker, workshop leader in field. Mem. Am. Psychol. Assn., Psychologists for Social Responsibility, Am. Assn. Marriage and Family Therapists, AAUW. Author: Beginning Again: Challenge of Formerly Married, 1976, Counseling Single Adults, 1978, Loneliness: Living Between the Times, 1978, Women of Vision, Women of Peace, 1994, As the Spirit Moves, 1994. Office: 303 Camp Craft Rd Ste 250 Austin TX 78746-6569

POULOS, JAMES THOMAS, endocrinologist, educator; b. Lynn, Mass., Apr. 11, 1938; s. Thomas Dimitrios and Christine Julia (Zorzy) P.; m. Mary Margaret White, June 22, 1963; 1 son, Christopher Kreag. BS, Tufts U., 1959, MD, 1963. Diplomate Am. Bd. Internal Medicine, Am. Bd. Endocrinology and Metabolism. Intern, New Eng. Med. Ctr., Boston, 1963-64, resident 1964-65; resident and fellow in endocrinology U. Chgo., 1967-70; practice medicine specializing in endocrinology Arnett Clinic, Lafayette, Ind., 1970—, v.p., bd. dirs., 1979-95; adj. prof. clin. pharmacology Purdue U., West Lafayette, Ind., 1976—; clin. faculty Ind. U. Sch. Medicine; bd. dirs. Lafayette Home Hosp., 1980-85, dir., pres. med. staff, 1978-79; pres. Arnett HMO, 1986—; dir. N. Cemn Health Svcs., 1985—. Active Nat. Rep. Senatorial Com., Natl. Rep. Congl. Com. Served with M.C., U.S. Army, 1965-67. Fellow ACP, Am. Assn. Clin. Endocrinologists; mem. AMA, ACP, Am. Diabetes Assn. (dir. Ind. chpt. 1980—, pres. 1986-88, bd. dirs. 1986—, com. profl. practice 1987-88, pres. 1994—), Internat. Diabetes Federation, Am. Lung Assn. (pres. West Cen. Ind. 1982-83), Lafayette C. of C. Co-author: The Metabolic Influence of Progestins Advances in Metabolic Disorders, 1971; contbr. articles to profl. publs. Home: 1000 Windwood Ln West Lafayette IN 47906-4737 Office: 2600 Greenbush St Lafayette IN 47904-2477

POULOS, PETER PETER, thoracic surgeon, lawyer; b. Orange, N.J., Feb. 18, 1922; s. Peter Spiro and Jennie (Polychronopoulos) P.; m. Helen Siganos, Aug. 22, 1948; children: Paul, John, Eoanna, Maria. BS in Aero. Engring., MIT, 1947; MD, Cornell U., 1952; JD, Rutgers U., Newark, 1989. Bar: N.J. 1990; diplomate Am. Bd. Gen. Surgery, Am. Bd. Thoracic Surgery. Surg. intern Bellevue Hosp., N.Y.C., 1952-53, resident in surgery, 1953-55; NIH rsch. fellow in physiology Cornell Med. Coll., N.Y.C., 1955-56; resident in surgery Manhattan VA Hosp., N.Y.C., 1956-58; resident in thoracic surgery Triboro Hosp., N.Y.C., 1958-60; founder, dir. Heart Inst., Newark, 1960-77; pvt. practice thoracic surgery various hosps. Newark,, Elizabeth and Livingston, N.J., 1977-86; dir. Med. Law Inst., Maplewood, N.J., 1990-95; cons. various law firms, N.J., 1990-95; clin. prof. surgery U. Med. N.J., Newark, 1962-95; lectr. medicine for lawyers Med. Law Inst., Maplewood, 1990-95. Contbr. articles to profl. jours. 1st lt. USAAF, 1943-45, Eng. Decorated Air medal with silver oak leaf cluster. NIH fellow, Cardiovascular Rsch. fellow, Cornell Med. Coll. fellow, 1955-58. Fellow ACS, Am. Soc. Law and Medicine; mem. AMA, N.J. Am. Med. Soc., N.J. Bar Assn., Rsch. Soc., Tau Beta Pi, Sigma Xi. Greek Orthodox. Home: Maplewood N.J. *Died Dec. 13, 1994.*

POULSEN, ERIK FANGEL, gynecologist; b. Copenhagen, May 29, 1934; s. Richard Fangel and Inger (Wiberg) P.; m. Estrid Hald, Oct. 17, 1962 (div. 1977); children: Anne Mette, Peter; m. Birte Andersen, June 27, 1981; 1 child, Mikkel. Student, Østersøgade, 1953; MD, U. Copenhagen, 1962. Staff doctor U. Hosp., Copenhagen, 1961-70, Odense, Denmark, 1976-80; staff doctor Urban Hosps., Copenhagen, 1970-76; pvt. practice Odense, 1980—. Author: Smil Med Doktoren, 1966, Kvindens Sygdomme, 1969, Børnesygdomme, 1977, Foer Du Elsker, 1979; columnist BT (daily newspaper) Doctors Column, 1967—. Bd. dirs. Christian Children's Fund, Richmond, Va., 1981-87, Boernefonden, Copenhagen, 1971—, pres., 1981-87, Health Call/Telephone, Denmark, 1991—, TV-Doctor, 1992—, Med. Libr. Diatel/Internet/Netscape, 1996—. Mem. Danish Soc. Ob-Gyn. (bd. dirs.). Home: Carl Baggersalle 45, 5250 Odense SV Denmark Office: Vestergade 39, 5000 Odense Denmark

POULSEN, LAWRENCE LEROY, research scientist; b. Salmon, Idaho, Nov. 27, 1933; s. William LeRoy and Eva (Martin) P.; m. Maclovia Torres, Feb. 1, 1957; children: William, Nancy, Judith, Doris, Kenneth, Tammy. AA, Riverside City Coll., 1953; BA, U. Calif., Riverside, 1965, DPhil, 1970. Phys. sci. tech. USDA, Riverside, Calif., 1957-65; rsch. assoc. dept. biology Tex. A&M U., College Station, 1969-70; assoc. rsch. scientist Clayton Found., Austin, Tex., 1971-80, rsch. assoc., 1980-89; rsch. assoc. dept. chemistry U. Tex., Austin, 1990—; lectr. and cons. in field. Inventor in field. Bishop LDS Ch., Austin, 1986-91, high counselor, 1991-95; scoutmaster, dist. com. Boy Scouts Am., Austin, 1970-86. Postdoctoral fellow U. Calif., 1965-69, Pub. Health Svc., 1968-69, 71-74, Welch Found., 1969-70. Mem. Am. Soc. Biochemistry and Molecular Biology. Mem. LDS Ch. Home: 6314 Libyan Dr Austin TX 78745 Office: U Tex Dept Chemistry Austin TX 78712

POULTON, ROBERTA DORIS, nurse, consultant; b. Balt., Oct. 19, 1943; d. Charles Robert and Mary Doris (Guercio) P. Nursing diploma Md. Gen. Hosp., 1964. Staff nurse Md. Gen. Hosp., Balt., 1964-67, Project Hope, Colombia, 1967, Tunisia, 1969-70; staff nurse St. Agnes Hosp., Balt., 1968-69, team leader, 1972-83, staff nurse-preceptor, 1983-88, nurse mgr. pediatric emergency room and ambulatory svcs., 1988-93, St. Agnes Hosp., Balt., 1970—; pediat. hemophilia coord., 1994—; pediat. ambulatory specialty clin. nurse; cons., Girl Scouts U.S.A., Balt., 1972—, Bapt. Conv. Md., 1963—. Vol. CPR instr. ARC, Balt., 1972—. Mem. AACN, Am. Nurses Assn., Md. Nurses Assn., Nurses, Appalachian Trial Conf. Democrat. Baptist.

POUNDER, DERRICK JOHN, forensic medicine educator; b. Rhondda, Wales, Feb. 25, 1949; s. Wilfred and Lilian (Jones) P.; m. Georgina Kelly, Nov. 28, 1975; children: Sibéal, Emlyn, Sinéad. MB, ChB, U. Birmingham, Eng., 1973. Cert. pathology. Intern Charitable Infirmary and Dr. Stevens' Hosp., Dublin, Ireland, 1973-74; resident St. Laurence's Hosp., Dublin, 1975-77; resident Inst. Med. and Vet. Sci., Adelaide, Australia, 1977-80, specialist pathologist, 1980-85; sr. lectr. forensic pathology U. Adelaide, 1984-85; dep. chief med. examiner Edmonton, Can., 1985-87; prof. forensic medicine U. Dundee, Scotland, 1987—. Chmn. Physicians for Human Rights, U.K., 1990-93; exec. mem. Australian Coun. Salaried Med. Officers' Assns., 1978-84. Named Freeman, Llantrisant, Wales. Fellow Royal Coll. Pathologists Australasia, Faculty Pathologists Royal Coll. Physicians Ireland, Hong Kong Coll. Pathologists; mem. Nat. Assn. Med. Examiners, Can. Soc. Forensic Sci., Am. Acad. Forensic Scis., Brit. Assn. Forensic Medicine, Forensic Sci. Soc. India (life), Romanian Legal Med. Soc. (hon.), Sci. Soc. Legal Med. Azerbaijan (hon.), Royal Nat. Lifeboat Inst. (life), Nat. Trust Scotland (life), Scotch Malt Whisky Soc., Woodland Trust (life). Mem. Scottish Nat. Party. Home: 12 Hill St Broughty Ferry, Dundee DD5 2JL, Scotland Office: The Royal Infirmary, Dundee DD1 9ND, Scotland

POUSSAINT, ALVIN FRANCIS, psychiatrist, educator; b. N.Y.C., May 15, 1934; s. Christopher Thomas V. and Harriet (Johnston) P. BA, Columbia U., 1956; MD, Cornell U., 1960; MS, UCLA, 1964. Intern UCLA Ctr. for Health Sci., 1960-61, resident in psychiatry Neuropsychiat. Inst., 1961-64, chief resident, 1964-65; So. field dir. Med. Com. Human Rights, Jackson, Miss., 1965-66; asst. prof. psychiatry Tufts U. Med. Sch., 1966-69; assoc. prof. psychiatry, assoc. dean students Harvard Med. Sch., 1969-75, 78—, prof. psychiatry, 1993—, dean students, 1975-78; cons. HEW, 1969-73; chmn. select com. on Edn. of Black Youth. Author numerous articles in field. Nat. treas. Black Acad. Arts and Letters, 1969-70, Med. Com. Human Rights, 1966—. Recipient Michael Schwerner award, 1968, Am. Black Achievement award in Bus. and the Professions Johnson Pub. Co., Inc., 1986, John Jay award for Disting. Profl. Achievement Columbia Coll., N.Y., 1987, Medgar Evers Medal of Honor Beverly Hills/Hollywood chpt. NAACP, Hollywood, Calif., 1988, and numerous hon. degrees. Fellow AAAS, Am. Orthopsychiatric Assn., Am. Psychiat. Assn. (mem. com. on Black Psychiatrists 1970-75); mem. Nat. Med. Assn., Am. Acad. of Child Psychiatry, Children's Longwood. Office: Judge Baker Ctr 295 Longwood Ave Boston MA 02115-5794

POUTASSE, EDMUND JOSEPH, health care consultant; b. Boston, June 16, 1931; s. Edmund Joseph and Mae Francis (Vahey) P. AA, Boston U., 1952, BS, 1954, MS, 1969. Sr. pub. health advisor USPHS, Atlanta, 1963-72; ptnr. Laffin, Dodge & Ptnrs., Waltham, Mass., 1972-74; v.p. Health Care Fin. Cons., Newport Beach, Calif., 1974-78; exec. dir. Hi-Desert Med. Found., Joshua Tree, Calif., 1978-81; cons. Hyannis, Mass., 1981—. Columnist op-ed page Cape Cod Times, 1983—. Served as sgt. USAF, 1954-58. Mem. VFW, DAV. Home: 226 Old Bass River Rd Apt 110 South Dennis MA 02660-3806

POWELL, BARBARA, clinical psychologist; b. Dexter, Mo., Apr. 25, 1929; d. Clarence Albert and Ethel (Mohrstadt) P.; m. Richard W. O'Neill, Jan. 3, 1953 (div. 1966); children: Richard W., Susan P., Jennifer A., Julia K.; m. Charles J. McCarthy, May 13, 1967 (div. 1978); m. David S. Burt, June 16, 1983 (div. 1990). BA, Wellesley Coll., 1950; MA, Columbia U., 1967; PhD, Fordham U., 1975. Copywriter, Parade mag., 1951-52, McCall's, 1952-53; publicity dir. Silvermine Guild Art, New Canaan, Conn., 1964-66; reporter Bridgeport (Conn.) Post, 1964-69; psychologist Dunlap & Assos., Darien, Conn., 1966-67; dir. Guidance Center for Women, U. Conn., 1968-69; intern N.Y. Hosp., Westchester, 1972-73; psychologist St. Mary's in-the-field, Valhalla, N.Y., 1973-77, Behavior Therapy Inst., White Plains, N.Y., 1975-78; pvt. practice clin. psychology, Rowayton, Conn., 1976—; lectr. U. Conn., 1976-77; co-founder, assertive tng. leader Woman's Place, Darien. USPH grantee, 1970-71. Mem. Am. Psychol. Assn., Am. Assn. Marriage and Family Therapists, Am. Assn. Advancement Behavior Therapy, Soc. Clin. and Exptl. Hypnosis, Phi Beta Kappa, Sigma Xi. Author: Careers for Women after Marriage and Children, 1965; How to Raise a Successful Daughter, 1979; Overcoming Shyness, 1979; The Complete Guide to Your Child's Emotional Health, 1984; Alone, Alive and Well, 1985; Good Relationships Are Good Medicine, 1987. Address: PO Box 1036 Block Island RI 02807-0997

POWELL, DEBORAH ELIZABETH, pathologist; b. Lynn, Mass., 1939. MD, Tufts U., 1965. Diplomate Am. Bd. Pathology. Intern Georgetown Med. Ctr., Washington, 1965-66; resident in pathology NIH, Bethesda, Md., 1966-69; with A.B. Chandler Med. Ctr., Lexington, Ky.; prof. U. Ky. Mem. Am. Assn. Pathologists, Internat. Assn. Pathologists, ASC. Office: Acad Faculty 800 Rose St Lexington KY 40536-0001*

POWELL, DON WATSON, medical educator, physician, physiology researcher; b. Gadsden, Ala., Aug. 29, 1938; s. Gordon C. and Ruth (Bennett) P.; m. Frances N. Rourke; children: Mary Paige, Drew Watson, Shawne Margaret. BS with honors, Auburn U., 1960; MD with highest honors, Med. Coll. Ala., Birmingham, 1963. Diplomate Am. Bd. Internal Medicine, Am. Bd. Gastroenterology. Intern, resident P.B. Brigham Hosp., Boston, 1963-65; resident Yale U. Sch. Med., New Haven, 1968-69, spl. NIH fellow in physiology, 1969-71; asst. prof. medicine U. N.C., Chapel Hill, 1971-74, assoc. prof., 1974-78, prof., 1978-91; chief divsn. digestive diseases U. N.C., 1977-91, dir. Ctr. Gastrointestinal Biol. Diseases, 1985-91, assoc. chmn. clin. affairs dept. medicine, 1989-91; Edward Randall and Edward Randall, Jr. Disting. Chmn., prof. dept. internal medicine, prof. dept. physiology and biophysics Med. br. U. Tex., Galveston, 1991—; cons. WHO, Geneva, 1980-82, Burroughs-Wellcome, Inc., Research Triangle Park, N.C., 1981-82, Hoffman-LaRoche, Inc., Nutley, N.J., 1982—; mem. merit rev. bd. VA, 1977-80; mem. gen. medicine A-2 study sect. NIH, 1985-89, mem. Nat. Inst. Diabetes Digestive and Kidney Diseases Adv. Coun., 1994—; coun., bd. rep. adv. com. to dir.NIH, 1996—. Assoc. editor: Textbook of Gastroenterology, Atlas of Gastroenterology; mem. editl. bd. Am. Jour. Physiology, Gastrointestinal and Liver Physiology, 1979—, Am. Jour. Med. Sci., 1984-92, Regulatory Peptide Letter, 1990—, Annals of Internal Medicine, 1993-96; contbr. over 100 articles to profl. jours. Capt. U.S. Army Med. Corps, 1965-68. Recipient Rsch. Career Devel. award NIH, 1973-78, Merit award, 1987, Outstanding Physician of Yr. award Gulf Coast chpt. Crohn's Colitis Found. Am., 1994. Fellow ACP (mem. med. knowledge self-assessment program VII gastroenterology com. 1983-85); mem. Am. Physiol. Soc., Am. Gastroenterol. Assn. (v.p. 1991-92, pres. 1993-94), Gastroenterology Rsch. Group (chmn. 1988-89), So. Soc. Clin. Investigation, Federated Socs. Gastroenterology and Hepatology (chmn. 1996—), Assn. Am. Physicians, Assn. Prof. Medicine, Am. Clin. and Climatol. Assn. Office: U Tex Med Br 4.108 John Sealy Annex 301 University Blvd Galveston TX 77555-0567

POWELL, GAYLE MARIE, pediatrics nurse; b. Santa Maria, Calif., Mar. 3, 1961; d. Galen Lee and Kathryn Clair (Murray) Oden; m. William Alford Powell, Nov. 8, 1980 (div. Oct. 1983); children: Kathryn Renee, Lesa Marie, Jessica Marie. A in Applied Sci. and Nursing, Penn Valley C.C., Kansas City, 1992; AA, Longview C.C., Kansas City, 1993. RN, Mo. Nursing asst. Hiber Nursing Home, Grandview, Mo., 1981-82; staff nurse St. Mary's Hosp., Blue Springs, Mo., 1993—. Named Alumnus of Yr. JTPA Svc. Delivery Area 12, Independence, Mo., 1993. Democrat. Lutheran. Office: St Mary's Hosp 201 NW R.D. Mize Rd Blue Springs MO 64014

POWELL, IRIS CUNDIFF, nurse; b. Pittsylvania County, Va., Nov. 22, 1935; d. Beverly Davis and Helen Josephine (Southall) Cundiff; m. James Frederick Powell, June 27, 1959; 1 son, James Frederick. Diploma, Roanoke Meml. Hosp. Sch. Nursing, 1957; B.S., U. Va., 1959; postgrad. Catholic U. Am., 1968-69; M.S., Radford Coll./Univ., 1971. Supr., U. Va. Hosp., Charlottesville, 1959-61; instr. nursing Va. Baptist. Hosp., Lynchburg, 1962-67; asst. prof. nursing Radford U. (formerly Radford Coll.), Va., 1970-72; pub. health nurse Montgomery County Health Dept., 1972-74; assoc. prof. nursing. Va. Western Community Coll., 1975-83, dir. nursing program, 1982-83; nursing instr., Technical Coll. of Alamanace (now Alamanace Community Coll.), 1984-86, maternity nursing instr., 1986-90; nurse health svcs Elon (N.C.) Coll., 1991-94, Ea. Guilford (N.C.) H.S., 1995. Active Mothers March of Dimes, Cancer Crusade, Red Cross Bloodmobile, United Way, Newcomers of Burlington, N.C., N.C. AD Council. Mem. Va. Coun. Assoc., Elon Coll. Health Svcs., N.C. Degree Nursing Edn., Va. Dist. II Nurses Assn., Am. Nurses Assn., Va. Nurses Assn. Baptist. Lodge: Order Eastern Star. Home: 645 Indian Valley Dr Burlington NC 27217-8955

POWELL, JAMES BOBBITT, biomedical laboratories executive, pathologist; b. Burlington, N.C., Aug. 28, 1938; s. Thomas Edward and Sophia (Sharpe) P.; m. Pamela Oughton, Sept. 12, 1969 (div. Sept. 1979); 1 child, Daphne Oughton; m. Anne Ellington, Oct. 20, 1984; children: James Bobbitt (dec.), John Banks, James Rosser, Helen Bobbitt. BA, Va. Mil. Inst., 1960; MD, Duke U., 1964. Diplomate Am. Bd. Pathology. Intern, Duke U. Med. Ctr., Durham, N.C., 1964-65; resident Cornell Med. Ctr., N.Y.C., 1965-67, Englewood Hosp., N.J., 1967-69; founder Biomed. Labs., Burlington, 1969—; pres. Roche Biomed. Labs., 1982-95, pres., CEO Lab. Corp. Am. Holdings, 1995—, Warren Land Co.; bd. dirs. FirstSouth Bank, Burlington, N.C. Trust Co. Contbr. articles to sci. publs. Trustee Elon Coll. (N.C.), 1981—, N.C. Sch. Sci. and Math.; mem. bd. visitors Duke U. Med. Ctr.; chmn. Alamance Found.; interim bd. edn. Alamance-Burlington, N.C. Served as maj. M.C., U.S. Army, 1969-72. Fellow Am. Soc. Clin. Pathologists, Coll. Am. Pathologists; mem. Alamance Country Club. Republican. Methodist. Avocations: tennis, U.S. military history. Home: 2307 York Rd Burlington NC 27215-3360 Office: LabCorp 358 S Main St Burlington NC 27215-5837

POWELL, JEFFREY HAIDON, optometrist; b. Butler, Mo., Apr. 9, 1948; s. Jack and Mona P.; m. Mary Jane Goodson, Sept. 7, 1968; children: Shawn, Ryan, Craig. Student, Ctrl. Mo. State U., 1968; D of Optometry, So. Coll. of Optometry, 1972. Lic. optometrist, Mo., Colo. Optometrist USAF, 1972-75, pvt. practice, Maryville, Rockport, Mo., 1975—. fficer USAF, 1972-75; ret. lt. col. Mo. Air Nat. Guard. Mem. Am. Optometric Assn., Mo. Optometric Assn. (trustee 1976-81), Air Nat. Guard Optometric Soc. Baptist. Office: Powell Optometry & Optical 2320 S Main Maryville MO 64468

POWELL, JOHN CLARK, cardiothoracic surgeon; b. Paintsville, Ky., Oct. 11, 1961; s. Glenn Richard and Elizabeth Lou (Vanhoose) P.; m. Donna Jo Roberts, Nov. 17, 1984; children: Luke Richard, Daniel Glenn, Philip John, Samuel Clark. Student, U. Ky., 1979-82; MD, Washington U., St. Louis, 1986. Diplomate Am. Bd. Surgery, Am. Bd. Thoracic Surgery. Resident in gen. surgery Ind. U. Sch. Medicine, 1986-91, fellow in cardiothoracic surgery, 1991-93; pvt. practice cardiothoracic surgery, 1993—; pvt. practice, Owensboro, Ky.; staff physician Owensboro-Mercy Health Sys., 1993—. Lt. comdr. USNR, 1989-96. Fellow Am. Coll. Chest Physicians. Baptist. Office: 815 E Parrish Ave Ste 440 Owensboro KY 42303-3222

POWELL, MICHAEL ROBERT, biophysicist, physiologist, chemist; b. Detroit, Nov. 23, 1941; s. Herschel Homer and Julia (Dickun) P.; m. Mary Grace Power, Aug. 8, 1964; children: Andrew, Christie, Kevin, Eric. B.S. in Chemistry, Mich. State U., 1963, M.S. in Biophysics, 1966, Ph.D., 1969. Research biophysicist Union Carbide, Tarrytown, N.Y., 1969-75; dir. biophysics dept. Inst. Applied Physiology and Medicine, Seattle, 1975-89, Space Biomedical Rsch. Inst., 1989—; head environ. physiology/biophisics sect. NASA/Johnson Space Ctr., Houston. Mem. Am. Chem. Soc., Biophys. Soc., Am. Physiol. Soc., Aerospace Med. Soc., Undersea Med. Soc. Republican. Roman Catholic. Office: NASA Johnson Space Ctr # SD-5 Houston TX 77058

POWELL, ROBERT CHARLES, marriage and family counselor; b. Champaign, Ill., Sept. 19, 1958; s. William York and Betty (Holt) P.; m. Trudy Suedell Graham, May 5, 1986; children: Emily, Amy. BS, We. Ill. U., 1981, MS, 1985. Pvt. practice LaSalle, Ill., 1990—; counselor Luth. Social Svcs., Dixon, Ill., 1994—; founder, leader support group for parents, Peru, Ill., 1990—; co-founder Human Resource Network. Chmn. steering com. Ill. Valley Christian Ch., Peru, 1989-90; bd. dirs. LaSalle County Habitat for Humanity. Mem. AACD, Internat. Assn. Marriage and Family Counselors. Office: 2513 5th St Peru IL 61354-2401

POWELL, THOMAS GAYLE, physician assistant; b. Houston, May 18, 1946; s. Allen Thomas and Nellie Beatrice (Taylor) P.; m. Connie Thomas, Sept. 7, 1968 (div. May 1978), Nancy Jean Hoffman, Oct. 19, 1979 (div. Oct. 1983); children: Kathryn Christine Powell Mitchell, Julia Marie Powell; m. Sally Ann Smyer Powell, Jan. 19, 1985; children: Christopher Vasil Barnick, Jennifer Marie Barnick, Patricia Ann Barnick. AA, Fla. Jr. Coll., Jacksonville, 1972; BS, U. Nebr., 1976. Cert. physician asst. Dept. head mil. medicine NAS Branch Clinic, Jacksonville, 1976-79, Kingsville, Tex., 1984-89; emergency response coord. USS Forrestac CV59, Mayport, Fla. 1979-80; coord. emergency rm. and chronic illness clinic Naval Hosp., Agana, Guam, 1980-84; asst. prof. emergency medicine Guam C.C., Migelo, Guam 1982-84; regional sr. Pa. Naval Regional Med. Ctr., Corpus Christi, Tex., 1984-89; emergency response coord. Med. Dept. USS Lincoln CVN 72, Alameda, Calif., 1989-91; sr. PA and clinic head Naval Hosp., Camp Lejeune, N.C., 1991-95; head Merkel (Tex.) Med. Clinic, 1995—; cons., founding mem., charter author Guam Task Force on Family Abuse and Sex and Assault, Agana, 1982-84; cons./advisor Svc. Source Selection Bd., Denver, 1994-95, Guam High Blood Pressure Coun., Agana, 1982-84, Abilene Regional Med. Ctr., 1995. Neighborhood commr. Boy Scouts Am., Jacksonville, N.C., 1970; asst. Spl. Olympics, multiple states, 1981-89; cons. emergency medicine Merkel Vol. Rescue, 1995—; coord. Toys for Tots, Merkel, 1995. Lcdr. USN, 1965-95. Named to Ancient Order of Chammori, Gov. of Guam, 1983; decorated Meritorious Svc. medal, Purple Heart (six medals). Fellow Am. Acad. Physician Assts., Naval Assn. and Physician Assts. (bd. dirs. 1978—); mem. Guam High Blood Pressure Coun. (pres., bd. dirs. 1981-95), Lions, Kiwanis (v.p., bd. dirs. Agana club 1981-83, pres., v.p. Kingsville, Tex. club 1984-89), Mil. Order of Purple Heart (life, charter, jr. vice comdr. 1994-95). Home: 124 FM 2035 Merkel TX 79536 Office: Merkel Med Clinic 1508 N First St Merkel TX 79536

POWELL, THOMAS ROGER, rheumatologist, educator; b. Detroit, Jan. 14, 1947; s. George Wayne and Margaret Ellen (Krull) P.; m. Deborah Neal Gerwig, May 27, 1972; children: Jessica Meagan, Britton Thomas. BA, Boston U., 1968; MD, George Washington U., 1972. Diplomate Am. Bd. Internal Medicine, Am. Bd. Rheumatology. Intern, resident U. Calif., Irvine, 1970-75, fellow in rheumatology, 1977-79; pvt. practice rheumatology, Orange, Calif., 1979—; asst. clin. prof. U. Calif. Med. Sch., Irvine, 1980—. Bd. dirs. Orange County br. Arthritis Found., Santa Ana, Calif., 1985-90. Maj. M.C., U.S. Army, 1975-77. Fellow Am. Coll. Rheumatology; mem. ACP, Am. Soc. Internal Medicine, Calif. Med. Assn., Orange County Acad. Internal Medicine (past pres.), Orange County Med. Assn., Alpha Omega Alpha. Office: 1000 W La Veta Ste 203 Orange CA 92668

POWELL, TIMOTHY JAMES, physician; b. Myrtle Creek, Oreg., Mar. 21, 1950; s. Dean Leroy and Josephine (Wright) P.; m. Katherine Lynn Moore, Aug. 30, 1975; children: Matthew David, Angela Jo, Esther Nicole. BS in Pharmacy, Oreg. State U., 1973, MD, 1977. Resident San Bernardino (Calif.) County Hosp., 1977-80; physician Dr. Zastrow, Roseburg, Oreg., 1980-86, pvt. practice, Roseburg, Oreg., 1986—; chief of staff, mem. adv. bd. Mercy Hosp., Roseburg, Douglas Cmty. Hosp. Named Douglas Counselor of Yr. Oreg. Lung Assn., 1982. Mem. Oreg. Med. Soc. (del. young physicians sect., nurse practitioner pharmacy adv. bd.). Republican. Office: 2510 NW Med Park Dr Roseburg OR 97470

POWERS, JAMES MATTHEW, neuropathologist; b. Cleve., Sept. 15, 1943; s. Alfred Patrick and Margaret Anne (Gunther) P.; m. Karen P. Smith, 1983; children: Kristin, Scott, Conor. BS in Biology, Manhattan Coll., 1965; MD, U. S.C., Charleston, 1969. Diplomate in anatomic pathology and neuropathology Am. Bd. Pathology. Asst. prof. pathology Med. U. S.C., Charleston, 1973-76; dir. electron micros. lab. VA Hosp., Charleston, 1973-76; assoc. prof. pathology Med. U. S.C., Charleston, 1976-80, prof. pathology, 1980-88; vice chmn. dept. pathology Columbia Coll. Physicians and Surgeons, N.Y.C., 1989-92; assoc. chair of edn., dir. residency tng. program U. Rochester, N.Y., 1994—; prof., dir. neuropathology U. Rochester, 1992—; sec. Biol. Stain Commn., 1994—. Author: (book chpt.) Andersen's Pathology, 10th edit., 1996, (practice guidelines) Archives Pathology and Laboratory Medicine, 1995; mem. editl. bd. Human Pathology, 1991—, Brain Pathology, 1995—, Acta Neuropathologica, 1995—, Biotech. and Histochemistry, 1994—, Modern Pathology, 1996—. Mem. Internat. Soc. Neuropathology (v.p. 1994—), Am. Assn. Neuropathologists (pres. 1993, Moore award 1975, 76, 77, 81), U.S.-Can. Acad. Pathology, Am. Assn. Pathologists, N.Y. Acad. Scis., Coll. Am. Pathologists. Office: U Rochester Box 626 601 Elmwood Ave Rochester NY 14642

POWERS, JOHN MICHAEL, neurologist; b. San Diego, Apr. 12, 1945; s. George Harold and Dorothy Elizabeth (Howe) P.; m. Linda Rose Bird, Aug. 24, 1968; children: Wendy Lynne, Megan Anne. BA in Biology, Grinnell Coll., 1967; MD, U. Iowa, 1971. Cert. Am. Bd. Psychiatry and Neurology. Intern Ohio State U. Hosp., 1971-72; resident in neurology U. Iowa Hosps. and Clinics, 1972-77; neurologist St. Luke's Med. Ctr., 1977—, St. Joseph's Hosp. and Med. Ctr., 1977—, Good Samaritan Med. Ctr., 1977—; neurologist Healthwest Regional Med. Ctr., 1977-94; dir. Clin. Neurophysiology Lab. St. Lukes Med. Ctr., Phoenix, 1977—, mem. instnl. rev. com., 1981—, mem. dept. medicine 1981-93, chmn. dept. medicine 1983-85, mem. exec. com. 1983-93, sec.-treas. med. staff, 1986-87, v.p. med. staff, 1988-89, pres. med. staff, 1990-91, mem. by-laws com., 1992—, mem. nominations com., 1992—; dir. sect. neuro-ophthalmology, Divsn. Neurology, Barrow Neurol. Inst., 1978-95; bd. trustees St. Lukes Health Sys., Phoenix, 1990-95, vice-chmn., 1993-95, chmn. quality mgmt. com. 1992-95; vice chair, trustee St. Lukes Charitable Trust, Phoenix, 1995—; trustee St. Luke's OriNDa Health sys., 1995—; presenter in field. Editor Neurology Sect., Ariz. Medicine, 1982-85; contbr. articles to profl. jours. Mem., pres. Madison Sch. Bd., Phoenix, 1982-85; mem. libr. bd. Maricopa County Med. Soc., 1984-86; mem. citizen's bond adv. com. Phoenix Union H.S. Dist., 1987, blue ribbon com. on sch. fin., 1989, chmn. instrnl. support subcom., 1989; mem.-at-large Barrow Neurol. Inst. Bd., 1987-90. Maj. U.S. Army, 1973-75. Decorated Army Commendation medal, 1975. Fellow Am. Acad. Neurology; mem. AMA (Physician Recognition award), Ariz. Med. Assn. (del. 1982—, mem. com. of reports and resolutions 1988, 89, chmn., 1990, sec. exec. com. 1994-96), Maricopa County Med. Soc. (bd. dirs. 1987-89, chmn. membership com. 1989), Nat. Multiple Sclerosis Soc. (profl. adv. com. Desert S.W. chpt. 1982-95, bd. trustees 1992-95, Hall of Fame award 1990, Ruth Demoplos award 1993, nat. bd. PAC chairs 1992-96), Alpha Omega Alpha. Office: Affiliated Neurologists Ltd 525 N 18th St #602 Phoenix AZ 85006

POWERS, JOHN MICHAEL, dental educator, researcher; b. Ft. Wayne, Ind., Apr. 16, 1946; s. Wesley R. and Mary A. (Leak) P.; m. Susan Mitchell, Dec. 21, 1968; children: Kenneth, Karen. BS, U. Mich., 1967, PhD, 1972. Asst. prof., assoc. prof., prof. U. Mich. Sch. Dentistry, Ann Arbor, 1972-88; prof. U. Tex. Dental Br., Houston, 1988—, chmn., 1988-93, dir. Biomaterials Rsch. Ctr., 1994—; sr. v.p. Dental Cons. Inc., Ann Arbor, 1983—. Author: Dental Materials-Properties and Manipulation, 1996; editor (newsletter) Dental Advisor, 1984; mem. editl. bd. Jour. Clin. Dentistry, Am. Jour. Dentistry, Dental Materials; contbr. articles to dental jours. Chmn. Sugar Land (Tex.) Recycling and Environ. Adv. Bd., 1995—. Fellow Acad. Dental Materials; mem. ADA (assoc.), Am. Assn. Dental Schs., Internat. Assn. for Dental Rsch. (pres. dental materials group 1983-84), Soc. for Biomaterials (charter), Sigma Xi, Phi Kappa Phi, Omicron Kappa Upsilon (hon.). Methodist. Office: U Tex Dental Br 6516 John Freeman Houston TX 77030-3402

POWERS, MARY MARGARET, physician assistant; b. S.I., N.Y., Nov. 5, 1963; d. John J. and Ellen K. (Powis) P. BS, St. John's U., Jamaica, N.Y., 1986. Cert. phys. asst. Resident Yale U./Norwalk (Conn.) Hosp., 1986-87; unit clk. Bayley Seton Hosp., S.I., 1981-86; orthopedic physician asst. Hampshire Orthopedics, Northampton, Mass., 1987—; sports medicine physician asst. to football and lacross teams U. Mass., Amherst, 1987—. Mem. Am. Acad. Physician Assts., Mass. Assn. Physician Assts. Roman Catholic. Home: 9 Kennedy Dr Hadley MA 01035 Office: Hampshire Orthopedics 6 Hatfield St Northampton MA 01060-1556

POWERS, MELINDA SUE, osteopath; b. Lubbock, Tex., Sept. 27, 1958; d. Russell Done and Alva Sue (Hailes) Williamson; m. Mack Arthur Powers, Jr., Dec. 27, 1980; children: Stephanie, Adam, Michael, Laura. BS, Lubbock Christian Coll., 1980; MS, Eastern N.Mex. State U., 1993; DO, Kirksville Coll. Osteo. Med., 1997. Intern/extern Kirksville (Mo.) Coll. Osteopathic Medicine, 1993—. Mem. Am. Assn. Osteopathic Family Practitioners, Am. Osteopathic Assn., Cranial Acad. Mem. Ch. Christ. Home: 1110 Sleepy Hollow Garland TX 75043

POWERS, PAUL CHARLES, cardiothoracic surgeon; b. Cleve., Aug. 17, 1941; s. Earl Francis and Lillian (White) P.; m. Julie Ann Hillier, Oct. 9, 1965; children: susan, Wendy, Christopher. BS, U. Notre Dame, 1963; MD, St. Louis U., 1967. Diplomate Am. Bd. Surgery, Am. Bd. Thoracic and Cardiovascular Surgery. Resident in gen. and thoracic surgery Ind. U. Med. Ctr., Indpls., 1967-73; thoracic surgeon U.S. Naval Hosp., Phila., 1973-75; staff cardiovascular surgeon Ball Meml. Hosp., Muncie, Ind., 1975—, chmn. dept. surgery. Lt. comdr. USN, 1973-75. Fellow ACS, Soc. Thoracic Surgery, Am. Coll. Chest Physicians, Rotary. Office: Cardio Thoracic Vascular Surg Assoccs PC 2525 University Ave Ste 502 Muncie IN 43704

POWERS, PAULINE SMITH, psychiatrist, educator, researcher; b. Sept. 23, 1941; m. Henry P. Powers; children: Jessica, Samantha. AB in Math., Washington U., 1963; MD, U. Iowa, 1971. Med. intern Emanuel Hosp., Portland, Oreg., 1971-72; psychiatry resident U. Iowa, Iowa City, 1972-74, U. Calif., Santa Barbara, 1974-75; from asst. prof. to assoc. prof. psychiatry Coll. Medicine U. So. Fla., Tampa, 1975-85, prof., 1985—, dir. eating disorder program, 1979—, dir. psychosomatic medicine divsn., 1979—. Author: Obesity: The Regulation of Weight, 1980; editor: The Current Treatment of Anorexia Nervosa and Bulimia, 1984. Fellow Am. Psychiat. Assn. (Dorfman Jour. Paper award 1987, Rush Gold Outstanding Exhibit medal 1976); mem. Acad. Eating Disorders. Office: U So Fla Coll Medicine Dept Psychiatry 3515 E Fletcher Ave Tampa FL 33613

POWERS, ROBERT DAVID, physician; b. Plainfield, N.J., Nov. 6, 1953; s. John B. and Marian E. (Kuhn) P.; m. Sally Ann Harmet, 1978; children: Alison, Elizabeth, Carolyn. BA, Amherst Coll., 1975; MD, U. Va., 1979. From asst. to assoc. prof. U. Va., Charlottesville, 1983-94; assoc. prof. U. Conn., Farmington, 1994—. Office: Hartford Hosp Dept Emergency Medicine Hartford CT 06115

POWERS, RUNAS, JR., rheumatologist; b. Jackson's Gap, Ala., Dec. 11, 1938; s. Runas and Geneva (Burton) P.; m. Mary Alice Shelton, Feb. 4, 1969; children: Tiffany, Trina, Runas Coley III. BS, Tenn. State U., 1961; MD, Meharry Med. Coll., Nashville, 1966. From intern to resident in internal medicine Hurley Hosp., Flint, Mich., 1966-67, 69-72; postdoctoral fellow Stanford (Calif.) Med. Ctr., 1972-76; pvt. practice Alexander City, Ala. Contbr. with others articles to Jour. of Rheumatology, Alcohol Myopathy and Myoglobinuric Nephrosis. Lt. comdr. MD, USN, 1967-69. Decorated Purple Heart, Bronze Star; named Man of Yr. Alexander City C. of C., 1991. Fellow Am. Coll. Rheumatology; mem. AMA, N.Y. Acad. Sci, Ala. State Med. Assn., Nat. Med. Assn., Am. Fedn. Clinical Rsch. Office: 3368 Highway 280 Ste 108 Alexander City AL 35010-4621

POWERS, WILLIAM JOHN, neurologist; b. Northampton, Mass., Apr. 28, 1949; s. John Bernard and Marian Erna (Kuhn) P.; m. Karen Diane McElvany, Mar. 9, 1983; children: Katherine Elizabeth, Brian Ward. AB, Dartmouth Coll., 1971; MD, Cornell U., 1975. Resident dept. internal medicine Duke U., Durham, N.C., 1975-77; resident dept. neurology U. Calif., San Francisco, 1977-80; instr. depts. neurology/radiology Washington U., St. Louis, 1980-82, asst. prof., 1982-87, assoc. prof., 1987—; neurologist-in-chief Jewish Hosp., St. Louis, 1986-92; chmn. Neurol. Disorders Program Project Rev. A com. NIH, 1994—. Office: Washington Univ Med Ctr East Bldg Imaging Ctr 4525 Scott Ave Box 8225 Saint Louis MO 63110

POWSNER, EDWARD RAPHAEL, physician; b. N.Y.C., Mar. 17, 1926; m. Rhoda Lee Moscovitz, June 8, 1950; children: Seth, Rachel, Ethan, David. SB in Elec. Engring., MIT, 1948, SM in Biology, 1949; MD, Yale U., 1953; MS in Internal Medicine, Wayne State U., 1957; MHSA, U. Mich. Diplomate Am. Bd. Nuclear Medicine, Am. Bd. Pathology in clin. pathology and anatomic pathology, Am. Bd. Internal Medicine; lic. physician, Mich., Calif., N.Y. Intern Wayne County Gen. Hosp., Eloise, Mich., 1953-54, resident internal medicine, 1954-55; resident internal medicine Detroit Receiving Hosp., 1955-56; fellow in hematology Wayne State U. and Detroit Receiving Hosp., 1957-58; clin. investigator VA Hosp., Allen Park, Mich., 1958-61, chief nuclear medicine svc., 1961-78; dir. clin. labs. Mich. State U., East Lansing, 1978-81; staff pathologist Ingham Med. Ctr., Lansing, Mich., 1978-81; dir. nuclear medicine St. John Hosp., Detroit, 1982-95; rsch. asst. biology MIT, 1948-49, 50; asst. instr. medicine Wayne State U. Coll. Medicine, 1954-56, instr., 1959-61; assoc. prof. pathology Wayne State U. Sch. Medicine, 1961-68, assoc. medicine, 1961, prof. pathology, 1968-78; prof. pathology Mich. State U., 1978-81, assoc. chairperson, 1980-81, clin. prof., 1981-82; chief clin. labs. Detroit Gen. Hosp., 1969-73; chief lab. svcs. Health Care Inst., Wayne State U., 1976-78; mem. adv. coun. Nuclear Medicine Tech. Cert. Bd., 1990-91. Bd. editors Am. Jour. Clin. Pathology, 1963-76, 83-88; author 1 textbook, 10 chpts., 48 peer reviewed papers, 19 abstracts and other publs. With U.S. Army, 1944-47. Mem. AMA (sect. coun. on pathology), Am. Soc. Clin. Pathologists (rep. 1987-89, 93—, govt. rels. com. 1993—, mem. coun. nuclear medicine 1978-82, chmn. 1982-84), Am. Coll. Nuclear Physicians, Am. Soc. Nuclear Cardiology, Coll. Am. Pathologists, Detroit Acad. Medicine, Mich. Soc. Pathologists, Mich. State Med. Soc., Soc. Nuclear Medicine, Washtenaw County Med. Soc., Sigma Xi, Tau Beta Pi. Office: Eastside Nuclear Medicine 18530 Mack Ave Ste 134 Grosse Pointe MI 48236 also: St John Hosp & Med Ctr 22101 Moross Rd Detroit MI 48236

POWSNER, SETH M., psychiatrist, educator; b. New Haven, May 29, 1953; s. Edward Raphael and Rhoda Lee (Moscovitz) P.; m. Elizabeth C. Yen, Aug. 18, 1985. BSEE, MIT, 1974; MD, Yale U., 1978. Practice medicine specializing in psychiatry Chgo., 1982-86; unit chief Charter Barclay Hosp., Chgo., 1983-84; asst. dir. psychiat. tng. Michael Reese Hosp., Chgo., 1983-84; psychiatrist Ill. State Psychiat. Inst., Chgo., 1984-85; research cons. U. Chgo. Med. Sch., Chgo., 1985-86; asst. professor Yale Med. Sch., New Haven, 1986-92, assoc. prof., 1992—; chief psychiat. consultation svc. Yale-New Haven Hosp., 1993—. Contbr. articles to profl. jours. Mem. AMA, IEEE, Am. Psyciat. Assn., Assn. for Computing Machinery. Office: Yale U Dept Psychiatry 20 York St Rm 2039 Cb New Haven CT 06504

POZNANSKI, ANDREW KAROL, pediatric radiologist; b. Czestochowa, Poland, Oct. 11, 1931; came to U.S., 1957, naturalized, 1964; s. Edmund Maurycy and Hanna Maria (Ceranka) P.; children: Diana Jean, Suzanne Christine. B.Sc., McGill U., 1952, M.D.C.M., 1956. Diplomate: Am. Bd. Radiology, Royal Coll. Physicians and Surgeons Can. Intern Montreal (Que., Can.) Hosp., 1956-57; resident Henry Ford Hosp., Detroit, 1957-60; staff radiologist Henry Ford Hosp., 1960-68, U. Mich. Med. Center, Ann Arbor, 1968-79; co.-dir. pediatric radiology C.S. Mott Children's Hosp., Ann Arbor, 1971-79; radiologist-in-chief Children's Meml. Hosp., Chgo., 1979—; prof. radiology U. Mich., 1971-79, Northwestern U. Med. Sch., 1979—; bd. dirs. Nat. Coun. on Radiation Protection, 1983-90; mem. Internat. Commn. on Radiologic Protection, 1981-89; mem. adv. panel on radiologic devices FDA, 1975-77, chmn., 1976-77; trustee Am. Bd. Radiology, 1993—. Author: The Hand in Radiologic Diagnosis, 1974, 2d edit., 1983, Practical Approaches to Pediatric Radiology, 1976; bd. editors: Skeletal Radiology, 1975-95, Radiographics, 1980-84, Pediatric Radiology, 1986-91. Fellow Am. Coll. Radiology; mem. AMA, Am. Roentgen Ray Soc. (pres. 1993-94), Soc. Pediatric Radiology (pres. 1980-81), Radiol. Soc. N.Am., Assn. Univ. Radiologists, John Caffey Soc., Am. Assn. Phys. Anthropologists, Internat. Skeletal Soc. (founder, pres. 1992-94), Can. Assn. Radiologists (hon.), Polish Radiol. Soc. (hon.), Teratology Soc., Alpha Omega Alpha. Home: 2400 N Lakeview Ave Chicago IL 60614-2747 Office: Childrens Meml Hosp 2300 N Childrens Plz Chicago IL 60614-3318

POZZILLI, PAOLO PARIDE, diabetologist; b. Rome, Jan. 8, 1951; s. Giuliano and Teodora (La Cava) P.; m. Raffaella Buzzetti. MD, U. Rome, 1986, D. in Endocrinology, 1989. Rsch. fellow to sr. rsch. fellow St. Bartholomew's Hosp., London, 1979-81, Juvenile Diabetes Found., N.Y.C., 1982-83; sr. chief investigator U. Rome Med. Sch., 1983-85; cons. physician U. London, 1985—; prof. Erasmus U., Brussels, Belgium, 1989—; prof. immunoendocrinology U. Rome "La Sapienza", 1992—. Author: Immunotherapy Type I Diabetes, 1989; editor: Diabetes, Prevention and Therapy, 1990—; contbr. articles to profl. jours. Recipient Morgagni award European Soc. for Metabolism, Padua, Italy, 1989. Fellow Internat. Diabetes Found., British Diabetic Assn. (A Cudworth award 1984), Internat. Diabetes Immunotherapy Group (sec. gen. 1989-92), Italian Soc. of Diabetes (chmn. genetics group 1995—, mem. Coun. of Immunology 1995—), Royal Soc. Medicine, Aniene Club. Office: II Clinica Medica, 00161 Rome Italy

PRACHT, DRENDA KAY, psychologist; b. Carrollton, Mo., Jan. 15, 1952; d. Ethan Lyle Pracht and Wilma Esteleen (Henderson) Lucas; 1 child, Matthew Kent. BA in Psychology, William Jewell Coll., 1974; MS in Clinical Psychology, Cen. Mo. State U., 1976; postgrad. in clin. psychology, Fielding Inst., Santa Barbara, Calif., 1987—. Lic. psychologist, marriage and family therapist, Minn., Kans.; lic. psychologist, Mo., Minn. Therapist Briscoe Carr Cons., Kansas City, Mo., 1978-79; psychologist Crittenton Ctr., Kansas City, 1979-81, Cen. Minn. Mental Health Ctr., St. Cloud, 1981-85, St. Cloud Hosp., 1985-87; gen. practice psychology St. Cloud, 1985-92, Kansas City, 1992—; cons. St. Benedicts Ctr., Country Manor, 1986-92. Mem. Cen. Minn. Child Abuse Team, St. Cloud, 1981-85; bd. dirs. Cen. Minn. Child Care Assn., St. Cloud, 1982-83. Mem. Am. Psychol. Assn., Cen. Minn. Psychol. Assn. (pres. 1984-85), Minn. Lic. Psychologists, Minn. Psychol. Assn., Alpha Delta Pi Aumni Assn. Presbyterian. Office: Ste 110 4500 College Blvd Overland Park KS 66211

PRADO, WILLIAM MANUEL, psychologist, educator, b. N.Y.C., Oct. 20, 1927; s. Manuel Fernando and Amor Maria (Bango) P.; m. Elizabeth Ann Avery, Aug. 16, 1953; children: Cheryl, Stuart, Mark. B.A., Johns Hopkins U., 1950; M.A., U. Ala., 1953; Ph.D., U. Okla., 1958. Staff psychologist VA Hosp., Little Rock, 1958-65, asst. chief psychology services, 1961-82; asst., assoc. and adj. prof. psychology Philander Smith Coll., Little Rock, 1967-85; instr. Little Rock U., 1959-69; clin. psychologist in pvt. practice, Little Rock, 1961—; cons. in field. Contbr. articles to profl. jours. Served with U.S. Army, 1946-47. Recipient Math and Sci. Gold medal Rensselaer Poly. Inst., 1944. Mem. Am. Psychol. Assn., Ark. Assn. Profl. Psychologists, Ark. Psychol. Assn. Democrat. Roman Catholic. Avocations: music; art; movies.

PRAEGER, MARK ALBERT, surgeon; b. Great Bend, Kans., Aug. 5, 1942; s. Walter Grizzell and Mary Edith (Kendall) P.; m. Sandra Lee Kaiser, June 6, 1965; children: Gretchen Lee, John David. BA, U. Kans., 1964; MD, U. Kans., Kansas City, 1968. Rotating intern Fitzsimmons Gen. Hosp., Denver, 1968-69, resident gen. surgery, 1969-73; asst. chief surgery Silaj B. Hayes Hosp., Fort Ord, Calif., 1973-75; tchg. staff surgery Madigan Army Med. Ctr., Tacoma, 1975-77; active staff Lawrence (Kans.) Meml. Hosp., 1977—; vice chair Health Care Stabilizatyion Fund Bd. Dirs., Topeka, 1995—. Lt. col. U.S. Army, 1967-77. Decorated Army Commendation medal U.S. Army, 1975, 77. Fellow ACS; mem. Kans. Chpt. ACS (coun. 1990-96, pres. 1995-96), AMA, Kans. Med. Soc., Douglas County Med. Soc. (treas. 1978-80), Lawrence C. of C. (bd. dirs. 1995-96). Republican. Presbyterian. Office: Lawrence Surgery Assocs PA 1112 W 6th Ste 204 Lawrence KS 66044

PRAESTHOLM, JOHANNES, radiologist; b. Lemvig, Denmark, May 26, 1928; s. Niels B.A. and Annemarie P. (Houlind) P.; m. Ingibjorgdl F.M. (Reynberg) July 24, 1954; children: Niels, Per, Annemarie, Birgitta. MD, U. Aarhus, Denmark, 1959; D Medicine, U. Copenhagen, 1979. Resident Viborg County Hosp., Denmark, 1959-62; asst. surgeon Nat. Hosp., Faeroe Islands, 1963-64, Gentofte Hosp., Denmark, 1964-67; sr. resident Nat. Hosp., Copenhagen, Denmark, 1967-70, Glostrup Hosp., Denmark, 1970-71, Nat. Hosp., Copenhagen, 1971-73; cons. radiologist Bispebjerg Hosp., Copenhagen, 1973-82, Hvidovre Hosp., Copenhagen, 1982-94; cons. Med. Hist. Mus., Copenhagen, 1995—; lectr. U. Copenhagen, 1981-91. Contbr. articles to profl. publs. Mem. Danish Radiol. Soc. (chmn. 1984-87), Scandinavian Neuroradiol. Soc. (chmn. 1986-87). Home: Skovbrinken 21, DK-3450 Allerod Denmark Office: Med Hist Mus, Bredgade 62, DK-1260 Copenhagen Denmark

PRAGER, ELLIOT DAVID, surgeon, educator; b. N.Y.C., Sept. 10, 1941; s. Benjamin and Sadye Zelda (Newman) P.; m. Phyllis Damon Warner, July 1, 1967; children: Rebecca, Sarah, Katherine. AB, Dartmouth Coll., 1962; MD, Harvard U., 1966. Diplomate Am. Bd. Surgery, Am. Bd. Colon and Rectal Surgery. Surg. resident Roosevelt Hosp., N.Y.C., 1966-71; colonrectal fellow Lahey Clinic, Boston, 1971-72; staff surgeon Sansum Clinic, Santa Barbara, Calif., 1974—; dir. colorectal fellowship Sansum Clinic, Santa Barbara, 1982—, chief of surgery, 1986-94; dir. surg. edn. Cottage Hosp., Santa Barbara, 1994—; mem., vice chair Residency Rev. Com., 1992—. Author: (with others) Operative Colorectal Surgery, 1994, Current Therapy in Colon and Rectal Surgery, 1990; contbr. articles to profl. jours. Lt. comdr. USN, 1972-74. Fellow Am. Coll. Surgeons (adv. coun. 1992—), Am. Soc. of Colon and Rectal Surgeons (v.p. 1992, sec. of program dirs., 1990—). Office: Sansum Clinic 317 W Pueblo Santa Barbara CA 93102

PRAHAN, AVINASH CHINTAMANI, nephrologist, consultant; b. Thana, India, June 13, 1948; s. Chintamani Gopal and Suhasini C. Pradhan; m. Medha A. Pradhan, Oct. 27, 1973; children—Pradnya, Vidya. Student, R. Ruia Coll., Bombay, India; M.B.B.S., G.S. Med. Coll., Bombay. Diplomate Am. Bd. Internal Medicine, Am. Bd. Nephrology, Am. Bd. Geriatrics. Intern, Highland Park Gen. Hosp. (Mich.), 1972-73, resident VA Med. Ctr., Bklyn., 1973-76; fellow in nephrology Albany Med. Ctr. (N.Y.), 1976-78; chief med. service Fort Lyon VA Med. Ctr. (Colo.), 1978-82, Dublin VA Med. Ctr. (Ga.), 1983—; cons. in medicine. Recipient commendations VA Med. Ctr., 1980, 82, 85-86. Mem. Am. Coll. Physicians, Assn. VA Chiefs Med. Service. Home: 1201 Shamrock Dr Dublin GA 31021-3024 Office: Dublin VA Med Ctr Dublin GA 31021

PRAINITO, SALVATORE, physician; b. Borgetto, Italy, Jan. 8, 1968; came to U.S., 1973; s. Nicolo and Lucrezia (Rappa) P.; m. Helene Iris Gross, June 14, 1992. BA in Biology, NYU, 1990; DO, N.Y. Coll. Osteo. Medicine, 1994. Diplomate Nat. Bd. Osteo. Med. Examiners. House staff Luth. Med. Ctr., Bklyn., 1994-97, resident in family practice dept. family practice; house staff rep. Luth. Med. Ctr., 1995—. Mem. AMA, Am. Acad. Family Physicians, Am. Osteo. Assn., Acad. Osteo. Family Physicians, N.Y. State Acad. Family Physicians. Roman Catholic. Office: Luth Med Ctr 150 55th St Brooklyn NY 11220

PRAKASH, RAVI, physician, educator; b. Meerut, U.P., India, Feb. 22, 1941; s. Daya Ram and Ramkali Devi Bansal; m. Odette Agustin, June 10, 1978; children: Gennifer Gita, John Paul Ravi, Jonathan Dayaram. BSc, Agra U., 1958; MD, All India Inst. Med. Scis., New Delhi, 1963. Diplomate: Diplomate Am. Bd. Internal Medicine. Fellow in cardiology Cedars-Sinai Med. Center, 1970-71; asst. prof. medicine U. Ill., 1971-73; asst. prof., then assoc. prof. medicine U. Calif., Irvine, 1973-79; prof. medicine UCLA Sch. Medicine, 1981-92, vice chmn. dept. medicine, 1989-90; chmn. dept. medicine Charles R. Drew U. Medicine and Sci., L.A., 1989-90; chief cardiology King-Drew Med. Ctr., L.A., 1979-90; pres. Am. Heart Inst., 1987—. Contbr. articles to profl. jours. Capt., M.C. Indian Army, 1963-66. Recipient Outstanding Tchr. award Long Beach VA Hosp., 1974, 76. Fellow ACP, Am. Coll. Cardiology; mem. Am. Heart Assn. Office: 4305 Torrance Blvd Ste 405 Torrance CA 90503-4404

PRASHER, DEEPAK KUMAR, research scientist; b. Jodhpur, India, May 21, 1951; arrived in Eng., 1963; s. Santosh Kumar and Prakash (Rishi) P.; m. Sumon Tah, July 18, 1976; children: Anchal, Neha, Varun. BSc with hons., U. Manchester, Eng., 1973; PhD, U. London, 1982. Computer engr. ICL, Kidsgrove, Eng., 1973-75; rschr. Coventry U., 1975-77; scientist Med. Rsch. Coun., London, 1977-93; reader Univ. Coll., London, 1993—; cons. CMC, India, 1985-88, St. George's Hosp., London, 1988-93. Contbr. articles to profl. jours., chpts. to books. Gov. sch., London, 1994—. Grantee UCL, London, 1994, LORS, London, 1994, European Union, Brussels, 1996. Mem. Am. Acad. Sci., Assn. Otolaryngology Rsch., IEE, EEG Soc. Office: Inst Laryngology & Otology, 330 Grays Inn Rd, London WC1X 8EE, England

PRATER, THOMAS GEORGE, ophthalmology; b. Springfield, Mo., May 3, 1957; s. B.G. and Marie (Haas) P.; m. Kimberley Alexander Prater, July 4, 1987; children: Alexandra Marie, Bronwyn Elizabeth. BA in Chemistry, So. Meth. U., 1979; MD, Washington U., St. Louia, 1983. Diplomate Am. Bd. Ophthalmology. Resident in ophthalmology Washington U. Med. Ctr., St. Louis, 1984-87; pvt. practice, Springfield, 1987—; sec. med. staff Lester E. Cox Med. Ctr., Springfield, 1994-95. Bd. dirs. Vis. Nurses Assn. S.W. Mo., Springfield, 1991-94; mem. adv. com. Hammons Hall for Performing Arts, Springfield, 1993-96. Fellow ACS, Am. Acad. Ophthalmology; mem. AMA, Mo. Med. Assn., Mo. Ophthal. Assn., Greene County Med. Soc. (chmn. pub. policy com. 1989, 95), Springfield Area C. of C. (pres. health care com. 1991-93, bd. dirs. 1995-98). Office: Eye Surgeons Springfield 3800 S National Ave Ste 500 Springfield MO 65807

PRATKANIS, ANTHONY RICHARD, social psychologist, educator; b. Portsmouth, Va., Apr. 2, 1957; s. Tony R. and Rosemarie (Gray) P. B.S. summa cum laude, Eastern Mennonite Coll., 1979; M.A., Ohio State U., 1981, Ph.D., 1984. Research assoc. Ohio State U., Columbus, 1981-83; postdoctoral fellow Carnegie-Mellon U., Pitts., 1983-84; asst. prof. indsl. adminstrn. and psychology, U. Calif., Santa Cruz, 1984-87, asst. to assoc. prof. psychology, 1987-95, prof. psychology, 1995—; expert legal witness; reviewer acad. jours. Author: (with E. Aronson) The Age of Propaganda, 1992; contbr. prof. papers, book chpts. J.B. Smith scholar Eastern Mennonite Coll., Harristonburg, Va., 1975-79; editor (with A. Greenwald and S. Breckler): Attitude Structure and Function. Fellow APA, Soc. for Personality and Social Psychology; mem. Midwestern Psychol. Assn., Soc. Exptl. Social Psychology. Democrat. Avocations: reading; personal computers. Research includes attitudes, persuasion, the self, consumer behavior. Home: 218 Dickens Way Santa Cruz CA 95064-1009 Office: U Calif Bd Psychology Santa Cruz CA 95064

PRATT, ANNE CAROLINE, forensic psychologist; b. Chgo., July 7, 1953; d. Richard Putnam and Alice Marie (Clancy) P. BA, Goddard Coll., 1975; MA, U. R.I., 1983, PhD, 1985. Lic. psychologist, Mass., Conn.; cert. designated forensic psychologist, Mass. Kindergarten tchr. Twinfield Elem. Sch., Marshfield, Vt., 1977-78; psychol. technician Lansdowne Mental Health Ctr., Ashland, Ky., 1978-80; psychologist Northampton (Mass.) State Hosp., 1985-86; forensic psychologist Forensic Svcs., Springfield, Mass., 1986-92; pvt. practice, Springfield, 1989-92; psychologist Traumatic Stress Inst., South Windsor, Conn., 1992—; pres. Forensic Psychology Assocs., Inc., 1989-91. Mem. APA, Am. Psychology and Law Soc., Internat. Soc. for Traumatic Stress Studies. Office: 22 Morgan Farms Dr South Windsor CT 06074-1369

PRATT, DONALD GEORGE, physician; b. Higgins, Tex., Oct. 19, 1946; s. George Horace and Esta Vici (Barker) P. BS in Biomed. Sci., West Tex. State U., 1970; MD, U. Tex., Galveston, 1974. Diplomate Am. Bd. Family Practice, Am. Bd. Radiology (Radiation Oncology). Intern Scott & White Meml. Hosp., Temple, Tex., 1974-75, resident in gen. surgery and pathology, 1975-77, physician, 1979-83; resident in family practice McLennan County Med. Edn. and Rsch. Found., Waco, Tex., 1977-79; physician Family Practice Assocs., El Paso, Tex., 1983; owner, pvt. contractor Minor Emergency Ctrs., Amarillo, Tex., 1983-85; resident in radiation therapy U. Tex., Galveston, 1985-88; ptnr. Cons. in Radiation Oncology, P.A., Amarillo, 1988—, pres., 1994—; dir. dept. radiation oncology Harrington Cancer Ctr., Amarillo, 1994—; pres. Cons. in Radiation Oncology, 1994—; pres. staff Harrington Cancer Ctr., 1995—; prin. investigator Radiation Oncology Group, 1988-95; pres. of staff Harrington Cancer Ctr., 1995—, also bd. dirs. Mem. AMA, Am. Soc. Therapeutic Radiology and Oncology, Am. Acad. Family Physicians, Tex. Med. Assn., Potter/Randall County Med. Soc., Tex. Radiol. Soc. Home: 3623 Tripp Ave Amarillo TX 79121-1809 Office: Cons Radiation Oncology PA 1600 Coulter Dr Ste 402 Amarillo TX 79106-1719

PRATT, GEORGE JANES, JR., psychologist, author; b. Mpls., May 3, 1948; s. George Janes and Sally Elvina (Hanson) P.; married; 1 child, Whitney Beth. BA cum laude, U. Minn., 1970, MA, 1973; PhD with spl. commendation for overall excellence, Calif. Sch. Profl. Psychology, San Diego, 1976. Diplomate Am. Bd. Med. Psychotherapists, Am. Acad. Pain Mgmt.; lic. psychologist, Calif. Psychology trainee Ctr. for Behavior Modification, Mpls., 1971-72, U. Minn. Student Counseling Bur., 1972-73; predoctoral clin. psychology intern San Bernardino County (Calif.) Mental Health Svcs., 1973-74, San Diego County Mental Health Services, 1974-76; mem. staff San Luis Rey Hosp., 1977-78; postdoctoral clin. psychology intern Mesa Vista Hosp., San Diego, Calif., 1976; clin. psychologist, dir. Psychology and Cons. Assocs. of San Diego, 1976—; chmn. Psychology and Cons. Assocs. Press, 1977—; bd. dirs. Optimax, Inc., 1985—; pres. George Pratt Ph.D., Psychol. Corp., 1979—; chmn. Pratt, Korn & Assocs., Inc., 1984—; mem. staff Scripps Meml. Hosp., La Jolla, Calif., 1986—, chmn. psychology, 1993—; founder La Jolla Profl. Workshops, 1977; clin. psychologist El Camino Psychology Ctr., San Clemente, Calif., 1977-78; grad. teaching asst. U. Minn. Psychology and Family Studies div., 1971; teaching assoc. U. Minn. Psychology and Family Studies div., Mpls., 1972-73; instr. U. Minn. Extension div., Mpls., 1971-73; faculty Calif. Sch. Profl. Psychology, 1974-83, San Diego Evening Coll., 1975-77, Nat. U., 1978-79, Chapman Coll., 1978, San Diego State U., 1979-80; vis. prof. Pepperdine U., L.A., 1976-80; cons. U. Calif. at San Diego Med. Sch., 1976—, also instr. univ., 1978—; psychology chmn. Workshops in Clin. Hypnosis, 1980-84; cons. Calif. Health Dept., 1974, Naval Regional Med. Ctr., 1978-82, ABC-TV; also speaker. With USAR, 1970-76. Fellow Am. Soc. Clin. Hypnosis (cert., approved cons.); mem. APA, Internat. Soc. Hypnosis, San Diego Psychology Law Soc. (exec. com.), Am. Assn. Sex Educators, Counselors and Therapists (cert.), San Diego Soc. Sex Therapy and Edn. (past pres.), San Diego Soc. Clin. Hypnosis (past pres.), San Diego Psychol. Assn., Soc. Clin. and Exptl. Hypnosis., U. Minn. Alumni Assn., Nat. Speakers Assn., Beta Theta Pi. Author: Rx for Stress, 1994, HyperPerformance, 1987, A Clinical Hypnosis Primer, 1984, 88, Release Your Business Potential, 1988, Sensory/Progressive Relaxation, 1979, Effective Stress Management, 1979, Clinical Hypnosis: Techniques and Applications, 1985; contbr. chpts. to various books. Office: Scripps Hosp Med Bldg 9834 Genesee Ave Ste 321 La Jolla CA 92037-1216

PRATT, GEORGE LORING, surgeon; b. Balt., Jan. 19, 1946; s. Loring Withee and Jeanette Irene (Burque) P.; m. Ann Carolyn Pratt, Sept. 22, 1973; children: Jennifer Ann, Emily Christine. BA, U. Maine, 1969; MS, Midwestern State U., 1978; DO, U. Health Scis., Kansas City, Mo., 1983. Lic. physician, Maine, N.Y., Nebr. Commd. 2d lt. USAF, 1972, advanced through grades to maj., 1995; flight surgeon USAF, Omaha, 1972-95. Author: "Charlie" A Novel About A Read Gentelman, 1995. Recipient USAF Commnedation medal. Fellow Air Force Soc. Flight Surgeons; mem. AMA, AOA, Aerospace Medicine. Home: 1332 Camp Gifford Rd Bellevue NE 68005 Office: 55 Med Group Offutt AFB NE 68113

PRATT, HARRY DAVIS, retired entomologist; b. North Adams, Mass., Apr. 13, 1915; s. Harry Edward and Ethel Mae (Davis) P.; m. Caroline Georgine Kreiss, Apr. 13, 1944 (dec. May 1951); children: Harry Davis Jr., Katherine Maria Pratt Garrison, George Kreiss; m. Dora Belle Ford, Nov. 29, 1952. BS, Mass. State Coll., 1936, MS, 1938; PhD, U. Minn., St. Paul, 1941. Registered profl. entomologist. Asst. entomologist USPHS Malaria Control War Areas, San Juan, P.R., 1942-46; chief med. entomol. lab. USPHS Communicable Disease Ctr., Atlanta, 1946-53, chief insect rodent tr., 1953-63, chief Aedes aegypti control tng., 1964-68; chief insect rodent control tng. Environ. Control Agy., Atlanta, 1968-72; cons., tchr., writer Atlanta, 1972—; spl. cons. Econ. Coop. Adminstrn., Saigon, Vietnam, 1950, WHO, Geneva, 1966, Kuala Lumpur, Malaysia, 1969. Fellow Entomol. Soc. Am. (life); mem. Am. Mosquito Control Assn. (pres. 1967), Entol. Soc. Washington, Ga. Entomol. Soc. Mem. Christian Ch. (Disciples of Christ). Home: 879 Glen Arden Way NE Atlanta GA 30306-3407

PRATT, HILLEL, neurophysiologist; b. Haifa, Israel, Aug. 5, 1948; s. Baruch and Mona (Levinson) P.; m. Toby Kirschenbaum, Oct. 20, 1979; children: Gad, Shi. BS, Hebrew U., Jerusalem, 1972, PhD, 1977. Instr. Hebrew U., Jerusalem, 1973-77; postdoctoral fellow U. Calif., Irvine, 1977-79; lectr. Israel Inst. Tech., Haifa, 1979-82, sr. lectr., 1982-88, assoc. prof., 1988-96, prof., 1996—. Cons. editor Jour. Electroencephalography and Clinical Neurophysiology; editl. bd. Audiology, Brit. Jour. Audiology. Mem. Israel Soc. for Clin. Neurophysiology (pres.), Israel Soc. for Auditory Rsch. (exec. bd.), Collegium Otorhinolaryngol. Amicitae Sacrum. Home: PO Box 186, Nofit 36001, Israel Office: Evoked Potentials Lab, Gutwirth Bldg, Haifa 32000, Israel

PRATT, LAWRENCE ARTHUR, thoracic surgeon, foreign service officer; b. Paris, Ill., Dec. 20, 1907; s. Luther F. and Katherine (Kaufman) P.; m. Mai Thi NgocSuong, May 7, 1974; children: Elizabeth, Lawrie Porter, D. Jane. B.S., Wayne State U., Detroit, 1930, M.B., M.A., M.D., 1934, M.Ed., 1960; LL.B., Woodrow Wilson Coll. Law, Atlanta, 1943. Diplomate: Am. Bd. Surgery, Am. Bd. Thoracic Surgeons. Intern Grace Hosp., 1934-35; practice thoracic surgery Detroit, 1935-41, 46-63; attending thoracic surgeon Grace, Detroit Meml. hosps.; courtesy staff St. John's Hosp.; cons. thoracic surgeon Holy Cross, Highland Park Gen. hosps., Detroit; U.S. fgn. svc. officer, 1963—; vis. prof. medicine U. Saigon, Vietnam, 1963-75; med. dir. Urban Health Clinic of Orange County, Calif., 1981—; exec. v.p. Am. Fedn. Med. Ctrs., Inc., 1953-54; chief med. dental edn. divsn. AID/PH, Vietnam; cons. Vietnam Min. Edn., 1974-75; assoc. dean Minh Duc. Med. Sch., Saigon, 1974-75; cons. HEW, 1975-77; spl. asst. HEW (Divsn. Medicine Bur. Health Manpower), 1976; cons., mem. White House Task Force Internat. Health Policy, 1977; mem. World Bank Task Force Internat. Health Policy and Manpower, 1977, U.S. Pub. Health Assn.; leader design team Health Care Program, Mauritania, West Africa, 1978; physician in charge Refugee Transit Camps, Malaysia, 1980; med. dir. Urban Health Clinic, Orange County, Calif., 1981-84, Spl. Disease Specialist 1981—; cons. physician overseas ops. World Cons., Irvine, Calif., 1984-85; cons. to min. health, Rabat, Morocco, 1986; sr. cons. World Care Inc., 1988—; mem. Nat. Coun. for Internat. Health, 1988—; chmn. bd. dirs. Boarne Seven Seas Devel. Corp., 1993—. Author: Total Development for Survival, 1986. bd. dirs. Sun Yet Middle Sch., Zhongshan, Quandong Province, People's Republic of China, 1986—; chmn. bd. 100 For 1 Systems Corp., 1986—. Lt. col., M.C. AUS, 1941-46. Active U.S-Mexican Border Health Assn., 1986—. Recipient Unit citation; medal of Culture and Edn.; medal of Merit Vietnam). Fellow ACS (life), Am. Coll. Chest Physicians; mem. AMA,

Mich. Med. Soc., Wayne County Med. Soc., Internat. Bronchoesophagol. Assn. (founder), Am. Bronchoesophagol. Assn., 4th Aux. Surg. Group Assn. (pres. 1955-56), Wayne State U. Med. Alumni Assn. (pres. 1956-57), Ga. Bar Assn., Am. Bd. of Surgery (diplomat), Am. Bd. of Thoracic Surgery (diplomat). Clubs: Essex Cricket (Eng.); Lambs (N.Y.C.); Scarab (Detroit), Detroit Skating (Detroit); Grosse Pointe Yacht, Grosse Pointe Hunt, Am. Radio Relay League, El Cajon (Calif.) Radio. Home: 2302 Lowell Ln Santa Ana CA 92706-1932

PRATT, MARTHA LEE, nurse; b. Chattanooga, Tenn., Mar. 25, 1957; d. Joseph Hilliard and Thelma (Lee) Anders; m. Frank Martin Pratt, Jr., Dec. 9, 1977; children: Jessica Kristin, Andrew Brett. BSN, U. Ala.-Birmingham, 1979. Nurse's aide Univ. Hosp., Birmingham, 1977-79, staff nurse, 1979-80, shift mgr. burn dressing team, 1980—, speaker Burn Ctr., 1980—; researcher Robert Wood Johnson Found., Birmingham, 1985-88. Tchr. Valley Creek Baptist Ch., Hueytown, Ala., 1984-85. Recipient Clin. Excellent in Nursing U. Ala. Hosp., 1988. Mem. Am. Burn Assn., Nat. Burn Prevention Com. Democrat. Avocations: horseback riding, boating, camping, reading. Home: 149 Greenridge Rd Bessemer AL 35023-3703 Office: University Hosp JT Rm 1010A 619 19th St S Birmingham AL 35233-1924

PRATT, PHILIP CHASE, pathologist, educator; b. Livermore Falls, Maine, Oct. 19, 1920; s. Harold Sewell and Cora Johnson (Chase) P.; m. Helen Clarke Deitz, Feb. 4, 1945; children: William Clarke (dec.), Charles Chase (dec.). A.B., Bowdoin Coll., 1941; M.D., Johns Hopkins U., 1944. Diplomate: Am. Bd. Pathology. Intern in pathology Johns Hopkins Hosp., 1944-45, asst. resident in pathology, 1945-46; pathologist Saranac Lab., Saranac Lake, N.Y., 1946-52; asst. dir. Saranac Lab., 1952-55; instr. Ohio State U., 1955-57, asst. prof. pathology, 1957-62, assoc. prof., 1962-66; assoc. prof. Duke U. Med. Ctr., 1966-71, prof., 1971-90, prof. emeritus, 1991—. Author: (with V.L. Roggli and S.D. Greenberg) Pathology of Asbestos Related Diseases, 1993; contbr. numerous articles to profl. publs. Fellow Am. Coll. Chest Physicians, Coll. Am. Pathologists; mem. AAAS, Am. Thoracic Soc., Am. Soc. Exptl. Pathology, Am. Assn. Pathologists and Bacteriologists, Internat. Acad. Pathology, Royal Soc. Health. Unitarian. Office: PO Box 3712 Davison Bldg Durham NC 27710

PRATT, SUZANNE GARRETT, gynecologist; b. La Grange, Ga., Mar. 9, 1948; d. Roswell and Susie Turner (Keller) Garrett; m. Frank Graham Pratt III, Sept. 18, 1971; children: Frank Graham, Edward Garrett. BS summa cum laude, U. Ga., 1970; MD, Med. Coll. Ga., 1973. Diplomate Am. Bd. Ob-Gyn. Resident Med. Coll. Ga., Augusta, 1973-77; physician D.D. Eisenhower Army Med. Ctr., Ft. Gordon, Ga., 1977-79; practice medicine specializing in gynecology, Rome, Ga., 1980-89, pvt. practice limited to gynecology, 1989—; coord. ob-gyn family practice residency program Floyd Med. Ctr., Rome, 1983-84. Nat. Merit scholar U. Ga. Found., 1966-70. Fellow Am. Coll. Ob-Gyn.; mem. Floyd-Polk-Chattooga Med. Soc. (sec. 1982-84), Ga. Soc. Ob-Gyn., Med. Assn. Ga., Endometriosis Assn. (bd. dirs., v.p. edn. and community rels. 1987-88), Zodiac, Phi Beta Kappa, Phi Kappa Phi. Avocation: reading. Home: 3 Hilldale Ln Rome GA 30165-4310 Office: Three Rivers Gynecology 909 N 5th Ave Rome GA 30165-2706

PRATTICHIZZO, FERNANDO ANTONIO, physician; b. Foggia, Italy, May 14, 1956; s. Michele and Maria Giuseppa P. MD, U. Padua, 1981. Asst. internal medicine Gen. Hosp., San Miniato, 1988-93; first level med. mgr., 1994—. Fellow Am. Coll. Angiology; mem. AAAS. Home: via 2 Giugno 6, 50057 Empoli Italy Office: General Hospital, Dept Internal Medicine, Piazza XX Settembre, 56027 San Miniato Italy

PREJEAN, CURTIS ANTHONY, cardiothoracic surgeon; b. Churchpoint, La., May 16, 1953; s. Curtis Anthony and Elsie (Cary) P.; m. Mary McGovern, June 14, 1981; 1 child, Phillip. BS, U. S.W. La., Lafayette, 1975; MD, La. State U., Shreveport, 1979. Resident in gen. surgery La. State U. Hosp., Shreveport, 1979-84; resident in cardiothoracic surgery Case Western Res. U., Cleve., 1984-86; assoc. staff Cleve. Clinic Found., 1986-87; staff surgeon Good Samaritan Hosp., L.A., 1987—. Contbr. articles to profl. jours. Fellow ACS, Am. Coll. Thoracic Surgery, Thoracic Surgery Soc., Internat. Coll. Surgeons; mem. AMA. Office: Kay Med Group 123 S Alvarado St Los Angeles CA 90057

PRELL, JOEL JAMES, medical group administrator; b. L.A., Aug. 16, 1944; s. Samuel and Mary Devorah (Schwartz) P.; children: Vanessa S., Matthew. BA, U. So. Calif., L.A., 1967; cert. fin. mgmt., Ohio State U., 1979; M. Pub. Health, UCLA, 1981. Various positions, 1967-72; chief adminstrv. office sr. adminstrv. analyst L.A. County, 1972-73; dep. regional dir. for planning and community rels. L.A. County Dept. Health Svcs. Region, 1973-75; adminstr. ambulatory care L.A. County Harbro Gen. Hosp., 1975-76; assoc. dir. hosp. and clinics ambulatory care svcs. U. Calif.-Irvine Med. Ctr., 1976-78; asst. to the dir. rsch. and analysis unit U. Calif., Davis, 1978-80; v.p. profl. svcs. San Pedro Peninsula Hosp., 1981-84; sr. v.p. South Coast Med. Ctr., 1984-87; pres., CEO Harbor Health Systems, Inc., 1987-90; CEO Santa Monica (Calif.) Plz. Med. Group, Inc., 1990-93; administrator Pathology Cons. Med. Group, Torrance, Calif., 1993—; spl. asst. to the contr. UCLA Hosp. and Clinics, 1980-81, adminstr. emergency medicine ctr., 1981. Mem. Hosp. Coun .So. Calif. (polit. action steering com., chmn. legis. affairs com.), Calif. Hosp. Polit. Action Com. (bd. dirs.), Health Care Execs. So. Calif., UCLA Health Svcs. Adminstrs. Alumni Assn. (pres.), Med. Group Mgmt. Assn., Am. Coll. Health Care Adminstrs., Friends of Westwood. Office: Pathology Cons Med Group 20221 Hamilton Ave Torrance CA 90502-1321

PREMACK, DAVID, psychologist; b. Aberdeen, S.D., Oct. 26, 1925; s. Leonard B. and Sonja (Liese) P.; m. Ann M. James, Oct. 26, 1951; children: Ben, Lisa, Timothy. BA, U. Minn., 1949, PhD, 1955. Rsch. assoc. Yerkes Labs. Primate Biology, Orange Park, Fla., 1955; rsch. assoc., asst. prof. psychology U. Mo., Columbia, 1956-58; assoc. prof. U. Mo., 1959-62, prof., 1963-64; prof. U. Calif., Santa Barbara, 1965-75; vis. prof. Harvard U., 1970-71; prof. U. Pa., 1975—; artist-in-residence Yaddo, Saratoga Springs, N.Y., 1955; fellow Van Leer Jerusalem Inst., 1980, Inst. for Advanced Study, Berlin, 1985-86; vis. scientist Japan Soc. for Promotion Sci., 1980; univ. rsch. lectr. U. Calif., Santa Barbara, 1973; mem. sci. gov. bd. Fyssen Found., Paris, 1989—; assoc. neurosci. rsch. program, La Jolla, Calif., 1991—. Author: Intelligence in Ape and Man, 1976, (with Ann James Premack) The Mind of an Ape, 1983, Gavagai! Or the Future History of the Animal Language Controversy, 1986 (with Dan Sperber and Ann James Premack) Causal Cognition: A Multidisciplinary Debate, 1995; mem. editorial bd. Jour. Exptl. Psychology: Animal Processes, 1976—, Cognition, 1977—, Brain and Behavior Sci., 1978—, Jour. Cognitive Neurosci. Served with U.S. Army, 1943-46. Ford Found. teaching intern, 1954; USPHS postdoctoral fellow, 1956-59; Social Sci. Research Council fellow, summer 1963; Center for Advanced Study in Behavioral Scis. fellow, 1972-73; Guggenheim fellow, 1979-80; grantee NSF, 1961—, USPHS, 1960-80; recipient Kenneth Craik Research award St. John's Coll.-Cambridge U., 1987, Internat. Sci. prize Fyssen Found., Paris, 1987. Fellow AAAS; mem. Soc. Exptl. Psychologists. Office: 3815 Walnut St Philadelphia PA 19104-3604 also: CREA, Ecole Polytechnique, 1 rue Descartes, 75005 Paris France

PRENDERGAST, ROBERT ANTHONY, pathologist educator; b. Bklyn., Nov. 6, 1931. BA, Columbia U., 1953; MD, Boston U., 1957. Intern Bellevue Hosp., 1957-58; resident Boston City Hosp., 1958-59, Meml. Sloan-Kettering Hosp., 1959-61; vis. physician Rockefeller U., 1963-65, asst. prof., 1965-70; Assoc. prof. opthamology and pathology, sch. medicine Johns Hopkins U., 1970—; prof. Rsch. Prevent Blindness, Inc., 1971—. Mem. Am. Assn. Immunology, Am. Soc. Exp. Pathology, Transplantation Soc., Reticuloendothelial Soc. Office: Johns Hopkins Univ Wilmer Inst Ophthalmic Immunology Lab Baltimore MD 21287-9142

PRENDERGAST, WILLIAM JOHN, ophthalmologist; b. Portland, Oreg., June 12, 1942; s. William John and Marjorie (Scott) P.; m. Carolyn Grace Perkins, Aug. 17, 1963 (div. 1990); children: William John, Scott; m. Sherryl Irene Guenther, Aug. 25, 1991. BS, U. Oreg., Eugene, 1964; MD, U. Oreg., Portland, 1967. Diplomate Am. Bd. Ophthalmology. Resident in ophthalmology U. Oreg., Portland, 1970-73; pvt. practice specializing in ophthalmology Portland, 1973-82; physician, founder, ptnr. Oreg. Med. Eye Clinic, Portland, 1983—; founder, pres. (Focus Group) Inc. Focus Group Inc., Ophthalmic Clinic Networking Venture, Portland, 1992—; clin. asst. prof. ophthalmology Oreg. Health Sci. U., 1985—; pres. Focus Group. Vol. surgeon N.W. Med. Teams, Oaxaca, Mexico, 1989, 90. With USPHS, 1968-70. Fellow Am. Acad. Ophthalmology; mem. Met. Bus. Assn., Multnomah Athletic Club, Mazamas Mountaineering Club, Portland Yacht Club, Phi Beta Kappa, Alpha Omega Alpha. Office: Oregon Med Eye Clinic 1955 NW Northrup St Portland OR 97209-1614

PRENSKY, ARTHUR LAWRENCE, pediatric neurologist, educator; b. N.Y.C., Aug. 31, 1930; s. Herman and Pearl (Newman) P.; m. Sheila Carr, Nov. 13, 1969. A.B., Cornell U., 1951; M.D., N.Y. U., 1955. Diplomate: Am. Bd. Psychiatry and Neurology. Intern Barnes Hosp., St. Louis, 1955-56; resident and research fellow in neurology Harvard U., Mass. Gen. Hosp., Boston, 1959-66; instr. neurology Harvard Med. Sch., 1966-67; mem. faculty Washington U. Sch. Medicine, St. Louis, 1967—; prof. pediatrics and neurology Washington U. Sch. Medicine, to 1975, Allen P. and Josephine B. Green prof. pediatric neurology, 1975—; pediatrician St. Louis Children's Hosp.; neurologist Barnes and Allied Hosps., Jewish Hosp., St. Louis. Author: (with others) Nutrition and the Developing Nervous System, 1975; editor: (with others) Neurological Pathophysiology, 2d edit, 1978, Advances in Neurology, 1976; mem. editorial bd. Pediatric Neurology, 1984-90, Jour. Child Neurology, 1985—. Served with USAF, 1957-59. Fellow Am. Acad. Neurology; mem. Am. Neurol. Assn., Am. Soc. Neurochemistry (mem. council 1973-77), Central Soc. Neurol. Research (pres. 1977-78), Child Neurology Soc. (pres. 1979-80), Am. Pediatric Soc., Internat. Child Neurology Assn., Japanese Soc. Child Neurology, Profs. Child Neurology (pres. 1984-86). Home: 15 Monarch Hill Ct Chesterfield MO 63005-4004 Office: 400 S Kingshighway Blvd Saint Louis MO 63110-1014

PRENTICE, ROBERT CRAIG, cardiologist; b. Chgo., Sept. 2, 1951; s. Robert Lee and Helen (Virginia) P.; m. Mary Ellen Toomey, Oct. 3, 1981; children: Ryan, Laura, Sarah. BA, Wabash Coll., Crawfordsville, Ind., 1973; MA, So. Ill. U., 1978; DO, Chgo. Coll. Osteo. Medicine, Chgo., 1982; PhD, U. Ill., 1982. Faculty asst. So. Ill. U., Carbondale, 1974-78; med. scientist Chgo. Osteo. Hosp., 1978-82; resident in medicine Hines (Ill.) VA Hosp., 1982-85; fellow in cardiology Loyola U., Maywood, Ill., 1985-87; staff asst. prof. medicine Loyola U., 1987-88; cardiologist Olympia Fields (Ill.) Med. Ctr., 1988-90; cardiologist, dir. cardiac lab. Michael Reese Hosp., Chgo., 1990-92; pvt. practice interventional cardiology Blue Island, Ill., 1992—; rsch. asst. U. Ill., 1980-82; dir. cardiac lab. Michael Reese Hosp., 1990-92. Grantee Chgo. Heart Assn., 1985. Fellow ACP, SCAI, Am. Coll. Cardiology; mem. AMA, Chgo. Med. Soc. Office: 3611 W 183rd St Hazel Crest IL 60429-2029

PRESCOTT, JANELLE, medical and surgical nurse; b. Uniontown, Pa., Jan. 5, 1965; d. Robert Lee and Pauline (Marcinek) Smith; m. Marvin Levi Prescott, Oct. 14, 1989; 1 child, Aaron Michael. Diploma, Uniontown Hosp. Sch. Nursing, 1988, Finesse Finishing Sch., Uniontown, 1986. RN, Pa. Nurse Uniontown Hosp., 1988—. Mem. U.S. Friendship Ambs., 1987—. Home: PO Box 1381 Uniontown PA 15401-1381

PRESCOTT, LAURIE FRANCIS, clinical pharmacology educator, physician; b. London, May 13, 1934; s. Frederick and Jessica (Raison) P.; m. Josephine Anne Carpentieri, Dec. 12, 1957; children: Nicholas, Katherine, Caroline, Christina; m. Jennifer Ann Gorvin, Sept. 6, 1980. MA, U. Cambridge, Eng., 1957, MB, BChir, 1960, MD, 1968. Resident medicine Boston City Hosp., 1962-63; rsch. fellow Johns Hopkins Hosp., Balt., 1963-65; lectr. dept. therapeutics U. Aberdeen, 1965-69; sr. lectr., reader dept. clin. pharmacology U. Edinburgh, Scotland, 1969-85, prof. clin. pharmacology, 1985—; cons. physician The Royal Infirmary, Edinburgh, 1969—. Author: Paracetamol (Acetaminophen): A Critical Bibliographic Review, 1996; editor: Drug Absorption, 1979, Handbook of Clinical Pharmacokinetics, 1983, Rate Control in Drug Therapy, 1985, Novel Drug Delivery, 1989. With RAF, 1954-56. Fellow Royal Coll. Physicians Edinburgh, Royal Soc. Edinburgh, Royal Coll. Physicians (London), Faculty Pharm. Physicians. Home: Redfern 24 Colinton Rd, Edinburgh EH10 5EQ, Scotland Office: Western Gen Hosp, Clin Pharmacology Unit Crewe Rd, Edinburgh EH4 2XU, Scotland

PRESCOTT, WILLIAM GLENN, psychiatrist; b. Portland, Oreg., Sept. 24, 1936; s. Glenn Leroy and Willmina (Long) P.; m. Katherine Lee Finnel, June 16, 1960 (div. 1975); children: Tracy K., Erin A., Shannon L., Bryn W., Duncan M.; m. Barbara Ann Carlson, Oct. 19, 1982; children: William G., Anna E., Andrew D. BS, Portland State U., 1959; MS, U. Oreg., 1963, MD, 1963; diploma in psychiatry, Harvard U., 1972. Diplomate Am. Bd. Psychiatry and Neurology, Am. Bd. Geriatric Psychiatry. Dir. USPHS Clinic, San Juan, P.R., 1972-75; chmn. dept. psychiatry USPHS Hosp., San Francisco, 1975-81; dir. Cuban-Haitian Unit NIMH, Washington, 1981-84; supt. St. Elizabeth's Hosp., Washington, 1984-87; asst. surg. gen. USPHS, 1984-87; med. dir. Brook Ln. Psychiat. Ctr., Hagerstown, Md., 1987—; consulting psychiatrist Nortcote Cmty. Mental Health Ctr., Falmerston North, New Zealand, 1992-93; cons. in field. Contbr. articles to profl. jours. Med. officer CAP, Oreg., Md., Mass., D.C., 1951—. Served to rear adm. (asst. surgeon gen.) USPHS, 1964-87. Decorated Bronze medal of Valor, D.S.M., Meritorious Svc. medal, Outstanding Svc. medal; Selling fellow U. Oreg., 1961-63. Mem. Am. Psychiat. Assn., Wash. Psychiat. Soc., Acad. Psychomatic Medicine, Am. Assn. Psychiat. Adminstrs., Am. Coll. Health Care Execs., Am. Acad. Psychiatry and the Law, Am. Coll. Mental Health Adminstrs., Am. Assn. Mental Health Adminstrs. Methodist. Home: 12909 Old Annapolis Rd Mount Airy MD 21771-7809 Office: Brooklane Psychiatric Ctr PO Box 1945 Hagerstown MD 21742

PRESMANES, WILLA SUMMEROUR, mental health systems evaluator; b. Baton Rouge, Jan. 12, 1948; d. William Henry and Mildred Katherine (Hazen) Summerour; m. Gregory T. Presmanes, Dec. 26, 1970; 1 child, Alison.; d. William Henry and Mildred Katherine (Hazen) Summerour; m. Gregory T. Presmanes, Dec. 20, 1970; 1 child, Alison. BA in Psychology, U. Ga., 1970; MEd in Counseling, Ga. State U., 1976, MA in Psychology, 1981. Psychiat. asst. Northside Hosp. Mental Health Ctr., Atlanta, 1971-74; program evaluator Ga. Mental Health Inst., Atlanta, 1976-79; staff rsch. psychologist DeKalb Bd. Health, Decatur, Ga., 1979-93; MIS stats. analyst DeKalb Cmty. Svc. Bd., Decatur, Ga., 1993—; counselor Community Friendship, Atlanta, 1977-78, Griffen Health Dept., Atlanta, 1976-77. Author: Comprehensive Service Plans, 1989, Balanced Service System Plans, 1978, Behaviorally Anchored Rating Scales, 1981, Quality Assurance Monitoring, 1977; co-author: (functional assessment) Daily Living Activities, Functional Assessment for Severely Mentally Ill, Mentally Retarded, Substance Abusers or Dually Diagnosed in DeKalb County. Pub. Dunwoody United Meth., Atlanta, 1990—; bd. dirs. Atlanta Figure Skating Club, 1990—; historian Mount Vernon Sch. Sandy Springs, Atlanta, 1988-89. Named Outstanding Young Women in Am., 1982. Mem. Nat. Coun. Community Mental Health.

PRESSMAN, SCOTT HUGHES, ophthalmologist; b. Eugene, Oreg., Aug. 6, 1950; s. E. Charles and Hope Hughes P.; m. Beverly Kay Glover, Mar. 29, 1975; children: Peter, Nicole, Andrew. BS, U. Oreg., 1974; MD, Oreg. Health Sci. U., 1976. Diplomate Am. Bd. Ophthalmology. Dir. emergency physicians St. Elizabeth Hosp., Baker, Oreg., 1977-80; ophthalmology resident Ea. Va. Med. Sch., Norfolk, Va., 1980-83; fellowship in pediatric ophthalmology U. iowa, Iowa City, 1983-84; fellow Am. Bd. Ophthalmology, 1984; asst. prof. ophthalmology U. Utah, Salt Lake City, 1986—. Author: (book) Common Ophthalmic Proceedures, 1986; contbr. articles to profl. jours. Fellow Am. Bd. Ophthalmology; mem. Idaho Ophthalmology Soc. (pres. 1993-95), Idaho Med. Soc., Am. Assn. Pediatric Ophthalmology, Am. Acad. Ophthalmology. Office: The Eye Assocs Ste 302 901 N Curtis Boise ID 83706

PRESTI, JOSEPH CHARLES, JR., urologist; b. San Francisco, June 15, 1958; s. Joseph C. and Angelina A. (Alioto) P.; m. Micaela Thompson, Dec. 7, 1985. AB, U. Calif., Berkeley, 1980; MD, U. Calif., Irvine, 1984. Diplomate Am. Bd. Urology. Resident gen. surgery U. Calif., San Francisco, 1984-86, resident urology, 1986-89; fellow urologic oncology Meml. Sloan Kettering Cancer Ctr., N.Y.C., 1989-92; asst. prof. dept. urology U. Calif., San Francisco, 1992—; prin. investigator merit rev. VA Rsch. Office, 1993-95. Recipient Clin. Oncology fellowship, Am. Cancer Soc., 1989-92, Clin. Oncology Career Devel. award, 1993-96. Fellow Am. Coll. Surgeons; mem. Am. Urol. Assn. (western sect.), Am. Assn. Cancer Rsch. Democrat. Roman Catholic. Office: U Calif San Francisco Mt Zion Cancer Ctr Urol Onc 2356 Sutter St San Francisco CA 94115

PRESTON, ANDREW JOSEPH, pharmacist, drug company executive; b. Bklyn., Apr. 19, 1922; s. Charles A. and Josephine (Rizzutto) Pumo; BSc, St. John U., 1943; m. Martha Jeanne Happ, Oct. 10, 1953; children: Andrew Joseph Jr., Charles Richard, Carolyn Louise, Frank Arthur, Joanne Marie, Barbara Jeanne. Cert. bus. intermediary. Mgr. Press Club, Bklyn. Nat. League Baseball Club, 1941-42; purchasing agt. Drug and Pharm. div. Intrassind, Inc., 1947; chief pharmacist Hendershot Pharmacy, Newton, N.J., 1949; agt. Bur. of Narcotics, U.S. Treasury Dept., 1948-49; owner Preston Drug & Surg. Co., Boonton, N.J., 1949-86; CEO Preston Pharmaceutics, Inc., Butler, N.J., 1970-80, Preston Bus. Cons., Inc., Kinnelon, N.J., 1987—; commr. N.J. State Bd. Pharmacy, 1970-72, pres., 1973; organizer State of N.J. Drug Abuse Speakers Program, 1970-76; chmn. Morris County Drug Abuse Coun., 1969-70; lectr. drug abuse and narcotic addiction various community orgns., 1968-78; mem. adv. bd. Nat. Community Bank, Boonton, N.J., 1973. Chmn. bldg. fund com. Riverside Hosp., Boonton, 1963; mem. Morris County (N.J.) Rep. Fin. Com., 1972; pres. Ronald Reagan N.J. Re-Election Adv. Bd., 1984; mem. exec. com. Gov. Tom Kean Annual Ball, 1985-86; chmn. Pharmacists of N.J. for election of Pres. Ford, 1976, Pharmacists for Gov. Tom Kean, 1981-84, N.J. Pharmacists for Reagan/Bush '84; mem. exec. com. Morris County Overall Econ. Devel. Com., 1976-82; chmn. Pharmacists for Fenwick, 1982; v.p. Kinnelon Rep. Club, 1980, Rep. Com., Kinnelon, 1990; adv. com. to Congressman Dean Gallo on Pres. Clinton's Health Security Plan, 1994. Served to lt. (j.g.), USNR, 1943-46. Recipient Bowl Hygeia award Robbins Co., 1969, E.R. Squibb President's award, 1968, N.J. Pharm. Square Club award, 1969. Mem. Am. Pharm. Assn., N.J. Pharm. Assn. (mem. econs. com. 1960-65, pres. 1967-68, Oscar Singer Meml. award 1987, William H. McNeil award 1994), Nat. Assn. of Retail Druggists, Internat. Narcotic Enforcement Officers Assn., N.J. Narcotic Enforcement Officers Assn., Nat. Assn. Realtors, N.J. Assn. Realtors, Morris County Bd. Realtors, Internat. Bus. Brokers Assn. (cert. bus. intermediary), Inst. Bus. Appraisers, Pharmacists Guild Am. (pres. N.Y. div. 1946-47), Pharmacists Guild of N.J., N.J. Public Health Assn., Morris County Pharm. Assn., Morris-Sussex Pharmacists Soc., Am. Legion, St. John's Alumni Assn. Roman Catholic. Clubs: Elks, K.C., Smoke Rise. Contbr. editorials to profl. jours. Home and Office: 568A Pepperidge Tree Ln Kinnelon NJ 07405-2213

PRESTON, CHARLES BRIAN, orthodontist, school administrator; b. Johannesburg, South Africa, Nov. 19, 1937; s. David Charles and Mary (Meerkotter) P.; m. Joy Pretorius, Jan. 1, 1966; 1 child, Bridgette. B.D.S., Witwatersrand Sch. Dentistry, 1961, diploma orthodontics, 1973, M.Dent., 1974, Ph.D., 1988 Lectr. dentistry Sch. Dentistry, Johannesburg, 1967-73, lectr. orthodontics, 1973-77, acting head dept. orthodontics, 1977-79, prof., head dept. orthodontics, 1979-84, dep. dean, 1983, 84, 85, 86; dean and mgr. Oral and Dental Teaching Hosp. U. of the Witwatersrand, 1987—. Cons., referee Am. Jour. Orthodontics. Internat. editor Seminars in Orthodontics; contbr. articles to profl. jours. Active South African Council Alcoholism; life mem. Operation Wild Flower. Recipient Middleton-Shaw award Dental Assn. of South Africa, 1987; grantee Research, Edn. and Devel. Fund, 1979-80, Med. Research Council, 1979-82; Elida Gibbs research fellow Dental Assn. South Africa, 1979-80. Mem. South African Soc. Orthodontists (exec. bd.), European Orthodontic Soc., Am. Assn. Orthodontists, Am. Assn. Dental Schs., South African Interim Med. Coun., Internat. Assn., Dental Research, South African Coll. Medicine (assoc.), Fed. Coun. of the Dental Assn. of South Africa, Med. and Dental Coun. of South Africa, Aircraft Owners and Pilots Assn., Univ. Flying Club (chmn. 1980-81), Emmarentia Sailing Club, Lions, Alpha Omega. Office: U Witwatersrand, 1 Jan Smuts Ave, Johannesburg 2001, South Africa

PRETLOW, THERESA PACE, biomedical educator, researcher; b. Rochester, N.Y., July 8, 1939; d. Peter and Mary (Stefano) Pace; m. Thomas Garrett Pretlow II, June 29, 1963; children: James Michael, Joseph Peter, David Mark. BS, Le Moyne Coll., 1961; PhD, U. Rochester, N.Y., 1966. Postdoctoral fellow in bacteriology U. Wis., Madison, 1965-67; rsch. assoc. dept. pathology U. Ala., Birmingham, 1974-77, from rsch. instr. to asst. prof. dept. pathology, 1978-83; asst. prof. Inst. Pathology Case Western Res. U., Cleve., 1983-89, assoc. prof. Inst. Pathology, 1989-96; prof. Inst. Pathology Case Western Res. U., Cleve., 1996—; mem. spl. study sects., ad hoc mem. study sect. on metabolic pathology NIH. Assoc. editor Cancer Rsch.; ad hoc reviewer Am. Gastroent. Assn., NAS, Carcinogenesis, VA Merit Rsch.; contbr. over 80 articles to profl. jours. Vol. leader Boy Scouts Am., Birmingham and Cleve., 1976-94. Grantee Nat. Cancer Inst., Am. Inst. Cancer Rsch., Am. Cancer Soc., Wendy Will Case Cancer Fund; recipient Silver Beaver and St. George awards Boy Scouts Am. Mem. Am. Assn. for Cancer Rschrs. (ad hoc reviewer, assoc. editor Cancer Rsch. 1996), Am. Soc. Investigative Pathology, Am. Soc. Cell Biologists, Histochem Soc. (councilor 1992-96, pres. elect 1995, pres. 1996-97, ad hoc reviewer), Women in Cancer Rsch. (sec.-elect 1995-96, sec., 1996-98). Roman Catholic. Office: Case Western Res U Inst Pathology 2085 Adelbert Rd Cleveland OH 44106-2622

PRETLOW, THOMAS GARRETT, physician, pathology educator, researcher; b. Warrenton, Va., Dec. 11, 1939; s. William Ribble and May (Tiffany) P.; m. Theresa Pace, June 29, 1963; children: James Michael, Joseph Peter, David Mark. A.B., Oberlin Coll., 1960; M.D., U. Rochester, 1965. Intern, Univ. Hosps., Madison, Wis., 1965-66, fellow McArdle Lab., 1966-67; research assoc. Nat. Cancer Inst., Bethesda, Md., 1967-69; asst. prof. pathology Rutgers Med. Sch., Piscataway, N.J., 1969-70; assoc. prof. pathology, U. Ala., Birmingham, 1971-73, prof. pathology, 1974-83, prof. biochemistry, 1982-83; vis. prof. pathology Harvard Med. Sch., Boston, 1983-84; prof. pathology Case Western Res. U., Cleve., 1983—, prof. oncology, 1987—, prof. environ. health scis., 1991—, prof. urology, 1994—; cons. NIH, Bethesda, 1976-95, Am. Inst. Cancer Rsch., 1995—; mem. editorial bd. Cell Biophysics, Cambridge, Mass., 1978-82. Editor: Cell Separation: Methods and Selected Applications, 5 vols., 1982, 83, 84, 87, Biochemical and Molecular Aspects of Selected Cancers, 2 vols., 1991, 94. Mem. exec. bd. Birmingham council Boy Scouts Am., 1979-83, Greater Cleve. council Boy Scouts Am., 1984-90. Served to lt. comdr. USPHS, 1967-69. Recipient Research Career Devel. award Nat. Cancer Inst., 1973-78; grantee for cancer research. Mem. Am. Assn. Pathologists, Am. Assn. Immunologists, Internat. Acad. Pathology, Am. Soc. Clin. Oncology, Am. Assn. Cancer Research. Club: Serra (pres. Birmingham chpt. 1982-83). Avocations: camping, fishing, Boy Scouts, classical music, biking. Home: 3061 Chadbourne Rd Cleveland OH 44120-2446 Office: Inst of Pathology Case Western Reserve U Cleveland OH 44106

PRETRE, LINDA TERRY, medical records administrator; b. Washington, Mar. 5, 1964; d. Harold and Rusty Kaye; m. John Edward Pretre, Sept. 20, 1986; children: Phillip, Jennifer. BS in Med. Records Adminstrn., St. Louis U., 1986. Cert. coding specialist; registered record adminstr. Med. records practitioner St. John's Mercy Med. Ctr., St. Louis, 1985-86; DRG coord. Normancy/Met. Hosp. West, St. Louis, 1986-90; dir. med. records Great Rivers Mental Health Svcs., St. Louis, 1990-91; med. records mgr. Doctors Hosp., Wentzville, Mo., 1991-96; sr. healthcare cons. Ernst & Young LLP, St. Louis, 1996—; med. records cons. Centrec Care, Inc., St. Louis, 1989—. Grad. Vision West, Western St. Charles County, Mo., 1985. Mem. Am. Health Info. Mgmt. Assn., Mo. Health Info. Mgmt. Assn. (bd. dirs. 1990-), Eastern Mo. Health Info. Assn. (bd. dirs. 1987-96, corr. and rec. sec. 1995). Home: 1055 Oakwood Farms Ln Ballwin MO 63021 Office: Ernst & Young LLP 701 Market St Ste 1400 Saint Louis MO 63101

PREVOR, RUTH CLAIRE, psychologist; b. N.Y.C., June 20, 1944; d. Gustav and Greta (Dreifuss) Strauss; m. Sydney Joseph P., July 4, 1963; children: Joy, Grant, Jed. BA, U. P.R., 1966; PhD, Caribbean Ctr. of Postgrad., Studies, San Juan, 1988. Cert. forensic psychologist, critical incident stress debriefing. Asst. dean Caribbean Ctr. of Postgrad. Studies, 1986-87; dir. prenatal edn. Ashford Meml. Hosp., San Juan, 1987; pvt. practice San Juan, 1984—; advisor, field faculty Vt. Coll., Norwich U., 1990-91; trustee Caribbean Ctr. for Advanced Studies, San Juan, Miami, Fla., 1990—. Bd. dirs. Jewish Community Ctr., Miramar, P.R., 1986—, bd. dirs. pre-sch., 1990—; pres. Home and Sch./St. John's Prep., San Juan, 1980-81, P.R. chpt. Hadassah Sch., 1972-74; presdl. adv. com., 1990-92. Mem. Am. Psychol. Assn., Assn. of Psychology of P.R. (hon. award 1984), Caribbean Counselors Assn., Caribe Hilton Club, Nat. Assn. Children with Learning

Disabilities, Nat. Register Health Svc. Providers in Psychology. Jewish. Office: Ashford Med Ctr San Juan PR 00907

PREWITT, TAYLOR ARCHIE, III, cardiologist; b. Little Rock, Jan. 11, 1938; s. Taylor Archie Jr. and Mary (Wheeler) P.; m. Mary Bowden, Aug. 14, 1960; children: Kendrick, Ellen, Sally. BA, U. Ark., 1959; MD, Washington U., St. Louis, 1963. Diplomate Am. Bd. Internal Medicine, Am. Bd. Cardiovascular Disease. Intern, then resident in cardiovascular desease and internal medicine, fellow in cardiology N.C. Meml. Hosp., Chapel Hill, 1963-67; sr. fellow in cardiology Cardiothoracic Inst. Brompton Hosp., London, 1974; cardiologist Cooper Clinic, P.A., Ft. Smith, Ark., 1969—; pres. Cooper Clinic, P.A., 1988-89; assoc. clin. prof. dept. medicine U. Ark. Coll. Medicine, Little Rock. Trustee St. Edward Mercy Med. Ctr., 1990-93. With USPHS, 1967-69. Fellow ACP (governor for Ark. 1995-99), Am. Coll. Cardiology (gov. Ark. chpt. 1983-86); mem. Am. Heart Assn. (pres. Ark. chpt. 1990-92), Sebastian County Med. Soc. (pres. 1990), Rotary (pres. Ft. Smith 1992-93). Methodist. Office: Cooper Clinic PA PO Box 3528 Fort Smith AR 72913-3528

PREZIO, JOSEPH ANTHONY, nuclear medicine physician; b. Troy, N.Y., Dec. 30, 1933. MD, Georgetown U., 1959. Intern Mercy Hosp., Buffalo, N.Y., 1959-60; resident D.C. Gen. Hosp., Washington, 1960-61, Georgetown Hosp., Washington, 1961-62; fellow endocrinology Georgetown Hosp., 1962-64; resident Mercy Hosp.; chmn. dept. nuclear medicine SUNY, Buffalo. Mem. AMA, Am. Coll. Nuclear Physicians, Endocrine Soc., Soc. Nuclear Medicine. Office: PO Box 273 Chautauqua NY 14722-0273 also: SUNY Sch Medicine Dept Nuclear Medicine 105 Parker Hall 3435 Main St Buffalo NY 14214-3001*

PRIBOR, HUGO CASIMER, physician; b. Detroit, June 12, 1928; s. Benjamin Harrison and Wanda Frances (Mioskowski) P.; m. Judith Elinor Smith, Dec. 22, 1955: children: Jeffrey D., Elizabeth F., Kathryn A. BS, St. Mary's Coll., 1949; M.S., St. Louis U., 1951, Ph.D., 1954, MD, 1955. Diplomate Am. Bd. Pathology. Intern Providence Hosp., Detroit, 1955-56; resident pathologic anatomy and clin. pathology NIH, Bethesda, Md., 1956-59; field investigator gastric cytology rsch. project Nat. Cancer Inst., Bowman-Gray Sch. Medicine, Winston-Salem, N.C., 1959-60; assoc. pathologist, dir. clin. lab. Bon Secours Hosp., Grosse Pointe, Mich., 1960-63; pathologist, dir. labs. Samaritan Hosp. Assn., East Side Gen. Hosp., Detroit, 1963-64, Anderson Meml. Hosp., Mt. Clemens, Mich., 1963-64; cons. pathologist Middlesex County Med. Examiners Office, New Brunswick, N.J., 1964-73; dir. dept. labs., chief pathologist, sr. attending physician Perth Amboy (N.J.) Gen. Hosp., 1964-73; chmn., chief exec. officer Ctr. Lab. Medicine, Inc., Metuchen, N.J., 1968-77; v.p. med. affairs Damon Corp., Med. Svcs. Group, 1977-78; exec. med. dir. MDS Health Group, Inc., Red Bank, N.J., 1978-80; med. dir. Internat. Clin. Labs., Inc., Nashville, 1981-88; med. dir. SmithKline Beechman Clin. Labs., Nashville, 1990—; physician, pathologist Assoc. Pathologists (P.C.), Nashville, 1981—; rsch. assoc. dept. pathology St. Louis U. Sch. Medicine, 1954-55; instr. pathology Bowman-Gray Sch. Medicine, Winston-Salem, N.C., 1959-60; asst. prof. chemistry U. Detroit, 1961-64; instr. pathology Wayne State U. Sch. Medicine, Detroit, 1961-64; clin. assoc. prof. dept. pathology Med. Sch. Rutgers U., The State U., New Brunswick, N.J., 1966-68; cons. Health Facilities Planning and Constrn. Svc., USPHS, HEW, Rockville, Md., 1970-71; prof. biomed. engring. Coll. Engring., Rutgers, The State U., New Brunswick, N.J., 1971-75, 80-82; chmn. bd. trustees St. Mary's Coll., Winona, Minn., 1972-74, chmn. fin. com., 1971-72; clin. prof. pathology Vanderbilt U. Sch. Medicine, Nashville, 1981—. Author: (with G. Morrell and G. H. Scherr) Drug Monitoring and Pharmacokinetic Data, 1980, The Laboratory Consultant, 1992; contbr. articles to profl. jours. Fellow Am. Soc. Clin. Pathologists (Silver award 1968); mem. AMA , Am. Assn. Exptl. Pathology, Coll. Am. Pathologists (chmn. subcom. 1974-78), Internat. Acad. Pathology, Pan Am. Med. Assn. (life), N.J. State Med. Soc., Acad. Medicine N.J. (chmn. clin. pathology sect. 1965-67), N.J. Soc. Pathologists (exec. com. 1965-67), Sigma Xi. Republican. Roman Catholic. Home: 6666 Brookmont Ter #1111 Nashville TN 37205

PRICE, ALEXANDER, retired osteopathic physician; b. Stepanitz, Russia, Mar. 7, 1913; came to U.S., 1921; s. Abraham and Mariam (Cohen) P.; m. Frances Ahrens, 1944 (dec. Sept. 1987); children: John O., Carl A. BA, U. Pa., 1936; DO, Phila. Coll. Osteo. Medicine, 1941; postgrad., Columbia U., 1947-57. Diplomate Am. Osteo. Bd. Internal Medicine, Am. Osteo. Bd. Cardiology. Intern Warren Hosp., Phillipsburg, N.J., 1941-43; postgrad. in cardiology and internal medicine; pvt. practice Camden and Cherry Hill, N.J., 1943-44, 46-80, 82-87, Ft. Lauderdale, Fla., 1980-82; mem. med. staff Met. Hosp., Phila., 1948-63, chief staff, 1961-63; mem. med. staff Cherry Hill (N.J.) Hosp., 1960-87, chmn. dept. medicine, 1960-72, chmn. div. cardiology, 1960-80; ret., 1987; assoc. clin. prof. medicine Phila. Coll. Osteo. Medicine, 1965-80; clin. prof. medicine N.J. Sch. Osteo. Medicine, Rutgers U., Camden, 1970—; physician, cons. in cardiology Primary Health Care Clinic, Broward County, Fla., 1991—. Contbr. numerous articles to osteo. medicine jours. Vol. Medivan (home health care for elderly poor, indigent, disabled), Broward County, Fla., 1988—. With M.C., AUS, 1944-45, MTO. Fellow Am. Coll. Osteo. Internists (pres. 1974-75, Meml. lectr. ea. div. 1970, Meml. lectr. nat. div. 76, Disting. Svc. award 1977), Coll. Physicians Phila.; mem. Am. Osteo. Assn., N.J. Osteo. Assn., Masons. Home: 1071 NW 85th Ave Fort Lauderdale FL 33322-4622

PRICE, ANN LAURIE, senior health program manager; b. Tuskegee Inst., Ala.; d. Edward James and Katie Beatrice (Griffin) Middleton; m. Frederick D. Price, Jr., Feb. 26, 1972; 1 child, Anne Monique. BS in Nursing Edn., Tuskegee Inst.; postgrad., Howard U.; MPA, Am. Univ., 1980; Diploma, Army Mgmt. Staff Coll., 1989. Diplomate Am. Coll. Healthcare Execs.; RN, Ala. Clin. mgr. child health multidisciplinary clinic Prince Georges County Health Dept., Cheverly, Md., 1976-78; occupl. health nurse, liaison Dept. of Health and Human Svcs., Rockville, Md., 1978-80, internat. health analyst spl. projects, tech. asst., 1980-81; program mgr., analyst comml. contracts Dept. of Army, Washington, 1981-86; health program mgr., policy analyst Dept. of the Army Office of the Surgeon Gen., Falls Church, Va., 1986-96; faculty mem. worldwide internal rev. confs. Dept. of the Army, Washington, D.C., Tex. and Colo., 1990, 91, 93; faculty nat. healthcare conf. Nat. Managed Healthcare Congress, Washington, 1993; career mentorship program sponsor Dept. of the Army, Washington, 1993-95; presenter, mem. South African Nat. Congress Africare, Washington, 1995; group facilitator Nat. Seminar Wesley Theolog. Sem., Md., 1995. Contbr. articles to profl. jours. Bd. dirs. Music Boosters Assn., Elizabeth Seton H.S., Bladensburg, Md., 1991, 92; chair African activities com. Alpha Kappa Alpha, Washington, 1993, 94; mem. adminstrv. bd. Asbury United Meth. Ch., Washington, 1995-96. Recipient Mayoral Recognition/Cert. for Immunization Campaign, Mayor, Washington, 1992, Adminstr.'s citation The Health Care Financing Adminstrn., 1993, recognition for evaluation of health care contracts Office of Sec. of Def., 1993. Mem. Assn. Healthcare Execs., Assn. Healthcare Adminstrs., Dept. of Def. Sr. Profl. Women, Am. Assn. Budget and Program Analysis, Order of Eastern Star, Alpha Kappa Alpha. Methodist.

PRICE, BRUCE H., neurologist, clinician, researcher; b. Seattle, July 24, 1949; s. Richard H. and Harriet (Kinloch) P.; m. Andrea K. Wolf, Mar. 15, 1975 (div. June 1989); m. Eileen Salmanson, Oct. 15, 1994; children: Douglas Brian, Shannon Michelle. BA, Harvard U., 1971; MD, U. Cin., 1975. Diplomate Am. Bd. Neurology and Psychiatry. Resident in internal medicine Christ Hosp., Cin., 1975-79; resident in neurology U. Colo. Health Scis. Ctr., 1979-82; fellow in behavior neurology Beth Isreal Hosp./Harvard Med. Sch., Mass., 1982-84; instr. in neurology Harvard Med. Sch., Boston, 1982—; chief dept. neurology McLean Hosp./Harvard Med. Sch., Belmont, Mass., 1994—; assoc. in neurology Mass. Gen. Hosp., Boston, 1994; spkr. in field. Author books in field; contbr. articles to profl. jours. Active Physicians for Human Rights, Boston, 1984—, Medicine Without Borders, N.Y.C., 1990—. Alzheimer's Assn. grantee, 1986. Mem. Am. Acad. Neurology, Am. Neuropsychiat. Soc., Boston Soc. of Psychiatry and Neurology (head com.). Office: McLean Hosp 115 Mill St Belmont MA 02178

PRICE, CHRISTOPHER PHILIP, clinical biochemistry educator; b. Cheltenham, Eng., Feb. 28, 1945; s. Philip Bright and Frances (Fox) P.; m. Elizabeth Ann Dix, July 13, 1968; children: Carolyn Sarah, Emma Jane. BS, U. London, 1967; PhD, U. Birmingham, 1972; MA (hon.), U. Cambridge, 1983. Prin. biochemist East Birmingham Hosp., Birmingham, 1972-76; cons. biochemist Gen. Hosp., Southampton, 1976-80, Addenbrookes Hosp., Cambridge, 1980-88; prof. clin. biochemistry St. Bartholomew's and Royal London Sch. Medicine, 1988—. Editor: Principals and Practice of Immunoassay, 1991, Centrifugal Analysis in Clinical Chemistry, 1980. Fellow Royal Soc. Chemistry, Royal Coll. Pathologists; mem. Assn. Clin. Biochemists (chmn. 1991-94), Am. Assn. Clin. Chemistry, Biochem. Soc. Office: St Bartholomews and, Royal London Sch Medicine, Turner St, London E1 2AD, England

PRICE, DOUGLAS ARMSTRONG, chiropractor; b. Pitts., Feb. 17, 1950; s. Walter Coachman and Janet (Armstrong) P.; m. Ann Georgette Martino, Jan. 31, 1989; 4 children. BA, Brown U., 1972; D Chiropractic, Life Chiropractic Coll., Atlanta, 1983. Diplomate Am. Bd. Chiropractic Examiners; cert. rehab. doctor; life extension physician; independent medical examiner, Fla. Owner, CEO Athletic Attic-Westshore, Tampa, Fla., 1976-80, Applied Biomech. and Musculoskeletal Rehab., Tampa, 1989—, All Am. Chiropractic Clinic; pvt. practice Tampa, 1984-94, Manalapan, Fla., 1994—; dir. Myofascial Therapy Found. Producer therapeutic exercise video for cervical and lumbar rehab.; contbr. articles to profl. jours. Magnetic Resonance Imaging fellow; named to Brown U. Athletic Hall of Fame; Southeastern Masters Champion Shotput, Discus, 1990-91. Fellow Am. Coll. Sports Medicine, Chiropractic Rehab. Assn., Am. Gerontology Assn.; mem. APHA, Am. Chiropractic Assn., Fla. Chiropractic Assn., Hillsborough County Chiropractic Soc. (bd. dirs. 1990-93, pres. 1992-93), Palm Beach Chiropractic Soc. Democrat. Roman Catholic. Home: 731 N Atlantic Dr Lantana FL 33462-1911 Office: 204 S Ocean Blvd Mawalapan FL 33462-3312

PRICE, ELY, dermatologist; b. N.Y.C., Aug. 9, 1932; s. Jacob and Mary (Flattau) P.; m. Ilona Brodie, Apr. 30, 1988; children from previous marriage: Jeremy, Andrew. BS cum laude, CCNY, 1953; AM, Ind. U., 1956; MD, U. Lausanne, Switzerland, 1964. Diplomate Am. Bd. Dermatology. Intern Brookdale Hosp. Med. Ctr., Bklyn., 1964-65, resident internal medicine, 1965-66; fellow Mt. Sinai Hosp., N.Y.C., 1965-66; practice dermatology Bay Ridge Skin and Cancer Dermatology, P.C., Bklyn., 1969—; attending dermatology Bklyn. Hosp., 1985-96; attending-in-charge, head dermatology Maimonides Med. Ctr., Bklyn., 1985—; clin. assoc. prof. dermatology SUNY Sci. Ctr., Bklyn., 1985—; cons. in medicine Luth. Med. Ctr., Bklyn., 1988—; cons. in dermatology Victory Med. Hosp., Bklyn., 1989—. Fellow ACP, Am. Acad. Dermatology, N.Y. Acad. Medicine. Home: 674 W Fingerboard Rd Staten Island NY 10305 Office: Bay Ridge Skin & Cancer Dermatology PC 9921 4th Ave Brooklyn NY 11209

PRICE, FRANCES KIE, hospital administrator; b. Franklin, Ky., Jan. 30, 1950; d. Atha and Dorothy Louise (Poole) Kie; m. James Lewis Price, Feb. 29, 1981; children: Shelley, Tina, Jeremy, James. Ctrl. svc. tech. Jesse Holman Jones Hosp., Springfield, Tenn., 1986-88, surg. technologist, 1988-90, ctrl. svc. supr., 1990—, recall and chem. inventory mgr., 1993—. Tng. Agy. mgr. Am. Heart Assn., 1993—. Recipient cert. Excellence ARC, 1993; named Parent of Yr. So. Ky. Head Start, 1987. Mem. NAFE, Internat. Assn. Healthcare Ctrl. Svc. Materials Mgmt., Am. Soc. Healthcare Ctrl. Svc. Personnel (Sterile Bowl 1992, advanced mem. award, 1995), Internat. Registry Environ. Engrs. and Profls. (environ. compliance mgr. 1994), Assn. Surg. Technologists, Tenn. Soc. Healthcare Ctrl. Svc. Personnel, Midstate Soc. Healthcare Ctrl. Svc. Personnel, Women's Writers Guild. Office: North Crest Med Ctr 1 N Crest Dr Springfield TN 37172-2941

PRICE, FREDRIC VICTOR, physician, educator, researcher; b. Wilmington, Del., Nov. 4, 1957; s. Martin Burton and Mollie (Saline) P.; m. Ellen S. Wilson, Nov. 30, 1985; children: George, Olivia. BA, Yale U., 1980; MD, U. Louisville, 1986. Diplomate Am. Bd. Ob-Gyn.; cert. gynecologic oncologist. Resident in ob-gyn. U. Pitts., 1986-90; fellow in gynecologic oncology Yale U., New Haven, Conn., 1990-92; asst. prof. U. Pitts., 1993—; attending physician Magee-Womens Hosp., Pitts., 1992—; peer reviewer Obstetrics and Gynecology, L.A., 1996, Gynecologic Oncology, San Diego, 1994—; grant reviewer FDA, Rockville, Md., 1995. Contbr. articles to profl. jours. Felix Rutledge fellow M.D. Am. Cancer Ctr., 1989; recipient Clin. Oncology award Am. Cancer Soc., 1991, Bristol-Myers Squibb Clin. Rsch. award Bristol-Myers Oncology, 1995. Fellow Am. Coll. Obstetric Gynecology, ACS. Office: U Pitts Magee-Womens Hosp 300 Halket St Pittsburgh PA 15213

PRICE, GAIL J. GOODMAN, marriage and family therapist, deaf and hearing impaired specialist; b. L.A., July 17, 1950; d. David S. and Ruth M. (Eholnikoff) Goodman; children: Gregory David, Jeffrey Ranen. BA, Calif. State U., Northridge, 1972; MEd, U. Ariz., 1973; postgrad, Chapman U., 1975-77. Lic. marriage, family and child counselor. Tchr. L.A. Unified Sch. Dist., 1973-74; dir. multi-handicapped programs Ennoble Group Homes, Inglewood, Calif., 1979; deaf-blind specialist San Francisco Lighthouse for the Blind, 1979-81; supr. social svcs. Foothill Health and Rehab. Ctr., Sylmer, Calif., 1981-83; dir. counseling ctr. Planned Parenthood of Orange County, Santa Ana, Calif., 1985-88; pvt. practice marriage, family and child counselor Orange, Calif., 1984—. U. Ariz. fellow, 1972-73. Mem. Nat. Assn. Deafness, Calif. Assn. Marriage & Family Therapists, Internat. Soc. for the Study Dissociation, Greater L.A. Coun. Deafness, Kappa Delta Pi. Home: 13642 Carroll Way Tustin CA 92780-1846 Office: 221 S Glassell Orange CA 92666

PRICE, HARVEY RAYMOND, safety, environmental health services administrator; b. Ochsenfurt, Germany, Apr. 27, 1947; s. Randall Dean and Annemarie (Biesecke) P.; m. Elizabeth Ann Panoske, May 29, 1974; 1 child, Joseph Raymond Dean. AAS, Cen. Tex. Coll., 1979; BS, U. Ctrl. Tex., 1981; MA, Webster U., 1991; MS, Regis U., 1995. Cert. protection officer; cert. fraud examiner, cert. healthcare protection adminstr., healthcare risk mgr. Enlisted USMC, 1966; transfered to U.S. Army, 1969; investigative supr., spl. agt. Criminal Investigative Divsn., 1979-82, spl. agt. supr., 1982-86, dir. exec. protection Europe, Mid. East, Africa, 1986-89; spl. agt. in charge Criminal Investigative Divsn., Denver, 1989-91; retired Criminal Investigative Divsn., 1991-94; dir. safety and risk mgmt. Regional West Med. Ctr., Scottsbluff, Nebr., 1991-94; environ. care cons. St. Joseph Hosp., Denver, 1994—; chmn. safety com., hazardous materials com., disaster com. Regional West Med. Ctr., 1991-94. Active Local Emergency Planning Commn., Scottsbluff, 1991, Hazardous Waste Planning Commn., Scottsbluff, 1991. Decorated Bronze Star with two bronze oak leaf clusters, Air medal with three bronze oak leaf clusters, 1970-72; Airborne badge (Germany); Cross of Gallantry (Vietnam). Mem. Internat. Assn. Healthcare Safety and Security, Assn. Cert. Fraud Examiners, Am. Soc. Indsl. Security, Am. Soc. Healthcare Risk Mgrs., Retired Officers Assn., Masons, Shriners, Alpha Phi Sigma. Episcopalian. Office: Hosp Shared Svcs 1395 S Platte River Dr Denver CO 80223-3467

PRICE, HOWARD CHARLES, chemist; b. South Gibson, Pa., Feb. 26, 1942; s. Howard Thomas and Rachael Emma (Michael) P.; m. Delores Ann Wilson, July 1, 1967; children: Susanne, Thomas. BS, Dickinson Coll., Carlisle, Pa., 1963; postgrad., Brown U., Providence, 1963-64; PhD, SUNY, Binghamton, 1971. NIH postdoctoral fellow Albert Einstein Coll. Medicine, Bronx, 1970-71; asst. prof. chemistry Marshall U., Huntington, W.Va., 1971-77, assoc. prof., 1978-80; sr. rsch. chemist Adv. Tech. Dept., Zimmer Inc., Warsaw, Ind., 1981-83, rsch. & devel. mgr., 1984-86, rsch. & devel. group mgr., 1987-88; R & D dir. Rsch. Labs., Warsaw, Ind., 1988-90; R & D devel. dir. Advanced Technology Dept., Zimmer Inc., Warsaw, Ind., 1991-92; dir. materials technology divsn. Family Health Internat., Research Triangle Park, N.C., 1992-95; vis. prof. Ohio U., Ironton, 1973-74. Contbr. articles to profl. jours.; author: Pennsylvania Game News, 1982; patentee in field. Band booster Warsaw Community High Sch., 1985-89. 1st lt. U.S. Army, 1964-66. Grantee, Spectroscopy Soc. of Pitts., 1980, Sigma Xi, 1975, NSF and Marshall U., 1973-80. Mem. ASTM, ASM, Am. chem. Soc. (sect. treas. 1975-76), Soc. for Biomaterials, Orthopaedic Rsch. Soc., Soc. Plastics Engrs., N.Y. Acad. Scis., Tissue Engring. Soc., Sigma Xi. Home: 1032 Lakeshore Dr Wendell NC 27591-8640 Office: Four M PO Box 549 Wendell NC 27591

PRICE, JAMES GORDON, physician; b. Brush, Colo., June 20, 1926; s. John Hoover and Rachel Laurette (Dodds) P.; m. Janet Alice McSween, June 19, 1949; children: James Gordon II, Richard Christian, Mary Laurette, Janet Lynn. B.A., U. Colo., 1948, M.D., 1951. Diplomate: Charter diplomate Am. Bd. Family Practice (dir., pres. 1979). Intern Denver Gen. Hosp., 1951-52; practice medicine specializing in family medicine Brush, 1952-78; prof. family practice U. Kans. Med. Ctr., 1978-93; chmn. dept. U. Kans. Med. Center, 1982-90, exec. dean, 1990-93, prof. emeritus in family practice, 1993—; mem. Inst. Medicine, Nat. Acad. Scis., 1973—; med. editor Gen. Learning Corp., 1973-92. Editorial bd.: Med. World News, 1969-79; editor: Am. Acad. Family Physician Home Study Self Assessment Program, 1978-83; contbr.: (column) Your Family Physician, 1973-90. Trustee Family Health Found. Am., 1970-82. Served with USNR, 1943-46. Charter fellow Am. Acad. Family Physicians (pres. 1973); mem. Phi Beta Kappa, Alpha Omega Alpha. Home: 12205 Mohawk Rd Shawnee Mission KS 66209-2137

PRICE, JAMES MELFORD, physician; b. Onalaska, Wis., Apr. 3, 1921; s. Carl Robert and Hazel (Halderson) P.; m. Ethelyn Doreen Lee, Oct. 23, 1943 (div.); children: Alta Lee, Jean Marie, Veda Michele; m. Charlotte E. Schwenk, Sept. 27, 1986; children: Shirley S. Bunn, Cindy S. Davis, Irene S. McCumber. BS in Agr., U. Wis., 1943, MS in Biochemistry, 1944, PhD in Physiology, 1949, MD, 1951. Diplomate Am. Bd. Clin. Nutrition. Intern Cin. Gen. Hosp., 1951-52; mem. faculty U. Wis. Med. Sch., 1952—, prof. clin. oncology, 1959—, Am. Cancer Soc.-Charles S. Hayden Found. prof. surgery in cancer research, 1957—; on leave as dir. exptl. therapy Abbott Labs., 1967—, v.p. exptl. therapy, 1968, v.p. corp. research and exptl. therapy, 1971—, v.p. corp. sci. devel., 1976-78; v.p. med. affairs Norwich-Eaton Pharms., 1978—, v.p. internat. R&D, 1980-82; pres. RADAC Group, Inc., 1982-90, Biogest Products, Inc., 1984-88; mem. metabolism study sect. NIH 1959-62, chairman B study sect., 1964-68; sci. adv. com. PMA Found.; chmn. research adv. com. Ill. Dept. Mental Health; sci. com. Nat. Bladder Cancer program; mem. Drug Research Bd. Nat. Acad. Scis./NRC. Bd. dirs. Grandview Coll., Des Moines, 1977-78. Served with USNR, 1944-45. Fellow Am. Coll. Nutrition, Royal Soc. Medicine London; mem. Am. Soc. Pharmacology and Exptl. Therapeutics, Am. Assn. Cancer Research, Am. Cancer Soc. (com. etiology 1957-61), Pharm. Mfrs. Assn. (chmn. research and devel. sect. 1974-75), Am. Soc. Biol. Chemists, Am. Inst. Nutrition, Am. Soc. Clin. Nutrition, Research Dirs. Assn. Chgo., Soc. Exptl. Biology and Medicine, Soc. Toxicology. Spl. research trytophan metabolism, metabolism vitamin B complex, chem. carcinogenesis; research and devel. pharm., diagnostic and consumer products; licensing and bus. devel. Avocation: pvt. pilot. Home: PO Box 211 Edmeston NY 13335-0211

PRICE, JANIS, medical center administrator; b. N.Y.C.; d. Marvin Howard and Helen (Saks) Davidson; m. H. Laurence Price, May 28, 1972; children: Sarah Lynn, David Matthew. BA, SUNY, Brockport, 1972. Cert. healthcare access mgr. Admissions clk. U. Mich. Med. Ctr., Ann Arbor, 1972-74, patient rep., 1974-76, admissions supr., 1976-82, asst. admitting mgr., 1982-85, admissions mgr.-psychiatry, 1985-89, asst. dir. psychiatry, 1989—; speaker in field. Contbr. articles to profl. jours. and chpts. to books. Tutor Washtenaw Literacy program, 1994—. Recipient JFK Good Citizenship award Reader's Digest, 1968. Mem. Nat. Assn. Healthcare Access Mgmt. (nomination chmn. 1989-92, strategic planning chairperson 1992-93, Doris Gleason Publ. award 1989), Hosp. Admitting Mgrs. S.E. Mich. (pres. 1985-89, editor newsletter 1989-93, Pres.'s award 1993), Med. Group Mgmt. Assn., Acad. Practice Assembly, Adminstrs. in Acad. Psychiatry (mem.-at-large 1993-94, assoc. editor newsletter 1989-94, editor newsletter 1994—). Jewish.

PRICE, JEANNINE ALLEENICA, clinical psychologist, computer consultant; b. Cleve., Oct. 29, 1949; d. Q. Q. and Lisa Denise (Wilson) Ewing; m. T. R. Price, Sept. 2, 1976. BS, Western Res. U., 1969; MS, Vanderbilt U., 1974; MBA, Stanford U., 1985. Cert. alcoholism counselor, Calif. Health Service coordinator Am. Profile, Nashville, 1970-72; exec. dir. Awareness Concept, San Jose, Calif., 1977-80, counselor, 1989—, exec. dir., 1989-90, v.p. Image Makers (formerly Awareness Concepts), 1994—; mgr. employee assistance program Nat. Semiconductor, Santa Clara, Calif., 1980-81; mgmt. cons. employee assistant programs. Mem. Gov.'s Adv. Council Child Devel. Programs. Mem. Am. Bus. Women's Assn., NAFE, AAUW, Coalition Labor Women, Calif. Assn. Alcohol counselors, Almaca. Author: Smile a Little, Cry a Lot, Gifts of Love, Reflection in the Mirror, The Light at the Top of the Mountain, The Dreamer, The Girl I Never Knew, An Act of Love, Walk Toward the Light.

PRICE, LARRY DEAN, cardiologist; b. Cleburne, Tex., Jan. 31, 1954; s. Truitt Evlyn and Pearlene (Sledge) P.; m. Ramona Ann Bradford, Feb. 4, 1984; children: Eric, Jason, Justin. BS, Baylor U., 1974, MA, 1975; DO, Tex. Coll. Osteo. Medicine, 1980. Cert. Am. Bd. Internal Medicine in Internal Medicine, Cardiology, Critical Care Medicine, Clinical Cardiac Electrophysiology. Intern Ft Worth Osteo. Med. Ctr., 1980-81; resident in internal medicine Scott and White Meml. Hosp., Temple, Tex., 1981-84, fellowship in cardiology, 1984-86; fellowship in critical care medicine Mayo Clinic, Rochester, Minn., 1986-87; cardiologist Scott and White Clinic, Temple, Tex., 1987—; asst. prof. internal medicine and surgery Tex. A&M U. Coll. of Medicine, Temple, 1987—. Fellow Am. Coll. Cardiology; mem. AMA, N.Am. Soc. Pacing and Electrophysiology. Office: Scott and White Clinic 2401 S 31st St Temple TX 76508-0001

PRICE, MARGARET PRYSE, nursing administrator; b. Port Clinton, Ohio, Oct. 9, 1945; d. Dudley N. and Mildred L. (Osborn) Sparks; m. Marvin P. Price, Jan. 19, 1968; children: David A., Evan A. Diploma, Henry Ford Hosp. Sch. Nursing, 1966; BSN, Madonna U., 1975; MS in Adminstrn., Cen. Mich. U., 1987. RN, Mich., N.C.; diplomate Am. Coll. Healthcare Execs.; cert. advanced nurse adminstr. Head nurse ICU Pontiac (Mich.) Gen. Hosp.; head nurse neurosurgery and neuro/med-surg. ICU Crittenton Hosp., Rochester, Mich.; dir. CCU Huron Valley Hosp., Commerce, Mich.; v.p. patient care svcs. Huron Valley Hosp., Milford, Mich.; chief nurse exec. Margarete R. Pardee Meml. Hosp., Hendersonville, N.C. Lay leader St. Paul's United Meth. Ch., Rochester. Mem. S.E. Mich. Neursci. Nurses (founder, pres., bd. dirs.), Mich. Orgn. Nurse Execs. (dir. Dist 1 S.E. Mich.), Am. Orgn. Nurse Execs., N.C. Orgn. Nurse Execs.

PRICE, RICHARD TAYLOR, family physician; b. Perkasie, Pa., Apr. 4, 1930; s. Harold Norwood and Florence Mae (Spoerl) P.; m. Kathleen Ann Schnerr, Aug. 9, 1958; children: Steven Taylor, Sally Ann. BA, Lehigh U., 1951, MS, 1952; MD, Jefferson Med. Coll., 1956. Intern/resident Meth. Hosp., Phila., 1956-57; family physician Perkasie, 1957-58; ptnr. Pennridge Med. Assocs., Perkasie, 1960-95, TriValley Primary Care, Perkasie, 1995—; med. dir. Pennridge Sch. Dist., Perkasie, 1960—; pres. med.-dental staff Grandview Hosp., 1969; clin. instr. dept. family medicine Thomas Jefferson U., Phila., 1976—. Bd. dirs. Grandview Found., Sellersville, 1990-92; trustee Grandview Hosp., 1990-91. Mem. AMA, Am. Acad. Family Practice, Pa. Med. Soc., Bucks County Med. Soc., Pennridge C. of C., St. Stephen's U. C. of C. Republican. Office: Pennridge Med Assocs 1301 N 5th St Perkasie PA 18944-2256

PRICE, RONALD LEWIS, ophthalmologist; b. Pitts., May 27, 1939; s. Christina Anita Bowers, June 11, 1962; children: Diana Price-Hanson, Cynthia, Kimberly. BA, Oberlin (Ohio) Coll., 1961; MD, Columbia U., 1965. Dipolmate Am. Bd. Ophthalmology. Intern Straight Med. Health Ctr. Hosps. U. Pitts., 1965-66; resident in ophthalmology U. Louisville, 1966-70; fellow in pediatric ophthalmology, strabismus Childrens Hosp., Washington, 1970-71; staff physician Cleve. Clinic Found., 1971-91; asst. clin. prof. Case Western Res. U., Cleve., 1991—; bd. trustees Cleve. Clinic Found., 1986-88, Quality Info. Mgmt. Corp., Cleve., 1991-94; bd. dirs. Cleve. Skilled Industries, 1986—; mem. adv. bd. Ohio Vision Network. Contbr. articles to profl. jours. Trustee Robert Page Singers, Cleve., 1984-89. Recipient Honor award Am. Acad. Ophthalmology, 1987, Hudson Disting. Svc. award Acad. Medicine Cleve., 1995. Mem. AMA (del.), Am. Assn. Pediatric Ophthalmology and Strab. (past dir., honor award 1990), Ohio State Med. Assn. (councilor 1990-94), Acad. Medicine Cleve. (pres. 1989-90). Home: 21450 Fairmount Blvd Shaker Heights OH 44118 Office: Univ Ophthalmology Assocs 1611 S Green Rd Ste 300 Cleveland OH 44121

PRICE, THEODORA HADZISTELIOU, individual and family therapist; b. Athens, Greece, Oct. 1, 1938; came to U.S. 1967; d. Ioannis and Evangelia (Emmanuel) Hadzisteliou; m. David C. Long Price, Dec. 26, 1966 (div. 1989); children: Morgan N., Alkes D.L. BA in History/Archaeology, U. Athens, 1961; DPhil, U. Oxford, Eng., 1966; MA in Clin. Social Work, U.

Chgo., 1988; Diploma in Piano Teaching, Nat. Conservatory, Athens, 1958. Lic. clin. social worker. Mus. asst. and resident tutor U. Sydney, Australia, 1966-67; instr. anthropology Adelphi U., N.Y.C., 1967-68; archaeologist Hebrew Union Coll., Gezer, Israel, 1968; asst. prof. classical archaeology/art U. Chgo., 1968-70; jr. rsch. fellow Harvard Ctr. Hellenic Studies, Washington, 1970-71; clin. social worker Harbor Light Ctr., Salvation Army, Chgo., 1988-89; therapist Inst. Motivational Devel., Lombard, Ill., 1989-90; caseworker Jewish Family & Community Svc., Chgo., 1989-90; staff therapist Family Svc. Ctrs. of South Cook County, Chicago Heights, 1990-91; pvt. practice child, adolescent, family therapy Bolingbrook, Ill., 1991—; dir. counseling svcs., clin. supr., psychotherapist The Family Link, Inc., Chgo., 1993; therapist children, adolescents and families dept. foster care Catholic Charities, Chgo., 1993-94; individual and family therapist South Ctrl. Cmty. Svcs. Individual-Family Counseling Svcs., Chgo., 1994—; staff therapist Cen. Bapt. Family Svcs., Chgo., 1991, Gracell Rehab., Chgo., 1991-92; casework supr., counselor Epilepsy Found. Greater Chgo., 1992-93; lectr. in field; bd. mem., counselor Naperville Sch. for Gifted and Talented, 1982-84. Author: (monograph) Kourotrophos, Cults and Representations of the Greek Nursing Deities, 1978; contbr. articles to profl. jours. Meyerstein Traveling awardee, Oxford, Eng., 1963, 64; Sophocles Venizelos scholar, 1962-65; nominated Internat. Woman of Yr. for 1995-96 Internat. Biog. Ctr., 20th Century Achievement award, 1996. Mem. NASW, Nat. Acad. Clin. Social Workers, Ill. Clin. Social Workers. Home and Office: 10 Pebble Ct Bolingbrook IL 60440-1557

PRICE, THOMAS FRANKLIN, health care administrator; b. Buffalo, May 15, 1947; s. Irving Llewellyn Price; m. Margaret Elaine Walker, June 21, 1978; children: Tommy, Megan. BSBA, Ithaca Coll., 1969; MS in Health Adminstrn., Columbia U., 1971. Staff assoc. Hosp. Survey Com., Phila., 1971-75; v.p. Pa. Hosp., Phila., 1975-86; sr. v.p., dir. instnl. svcs. Chestnut Hill Health Care, Phila., 1986—; chmn. The Forum-Delaware Valley Health Edn. and Rsch. Found., Phila., 1987. Bd. dirs. Citizens Coalition for Energy Efficiency, Phila., 1980-94; mem. exec. com., bd. dirs. Chestnut Hill Civic Assn., Phila., 1986-95. Recipient vol. recognition award United Way Southeastern Pa., 1982, cost containment award Hosp. Assn. Pa., 1982. Mem. Am. Coll. Healthcare Execs. (cert. health exec., co-chmn. regional adv. coun. 1993-95), World Affairs Coun. Phila. Home: 1201 Limberlost Ln Gladwyne PA 19035 Office: Chestnut Hill Health Care 8835 Germantown Ave Philadelphia PA 19118-2718

PRICE, TREVOR ROBERT PRYCE, psychiatrist, educator; b. Concord, N.H., Nov. 29, 1943; s. Trevor Alaric and Beatrice (Dinsmore) Pryce; m. Margaret Ann Bowring, June 8, 1991; children: Meghan Jennifer, Sara Brittany; children by previous marriage: Trevor Breton, Elizabeth Anne. BA, Yale U., 1965; MD, Columbia U., 1969. Diplomate Am. Bd. Psychiatry and Neurology (examiner 1985—), Am. Bd. Internal Medicine, Nat. Bd. Med. Examiners. Intern in medicine Med. Ctr. U. Calif., San Francisco, 1969-70; resident in internal medicine Med. Ctr. of U. Calif., San Francisco, 1972-74; resident in psychiatry Dartmouth Med. Sch., Hanover, N.H., 1974-77, asst. prof., assoc. prof. psychiatry and medicine, 1977-85; assoc. prof., prof. psychiatry U. Pa. Sch. Medicine, Phila., 1985-88; dir. psychiat. in-patient svcs. Hosp. of U. Pa., 1985-88; prof. psychiatry Med. Coll. Pa., Pitts., 1989-90, prof. psychiatry and medicine, 1991-95; tenured prof. psychiatry Med. Coll. Pa., 1993—; chmn. dept. psychiatry Med. Coll. Pa. and Hahnemann U., Allegheny Campus, Pitts., 1989-95, 1995—; sr. assoc. dean Med. Coll. Pa. and Hahnemann U., Pitts., 1993-95; pres. Allegheny Neuropsychiat. Inst. Med. Coll. Pa., Pitts., 1992-94; exec. dir. Allegheny Neuropsychiat. Inst., Pitts., 1994—; tenured prof. Psychiatry, chmn. dept. Psychiatry Med. Coll. of Pa. Hahnemann Sch. Medicine Allegheny U. Health Scis., 1995—; bd. dirs. Coll. Health Consortium, Inc., Phila., Highland Dr. Rsch. and Edn. Found., Yale Club Pitts., Pitts. Psychoanalytic Found.; mem. blue ribbon bd. Alzheimer's Disease Alliance, Western Pa., 1989—. Mem. editl. bd. Convulsive Therapy, 1984-94, Jour. Neuropsychiatry and Clin. Neurosci., 1992—, Alleghany Gen. Hosp. Jour. Neurosci., 1992—, Seminars in Neuropsychiatry, 1995—; editl. reviewer 12 psychiat. and med. jours., 1978—; contbr. chpts. to books and articles in profl. jours. Mem. N.H. Commn. on Laws Effecting Mental Health, 1974-75; bd. dirs. Advanced Studies Program, Friends of St. Paul's Sch., Concord, N.H., 1983-87. Recipient William C. Menninger award Ctrl. Neuropsychiat. Assn., 1977, Faculty Teaching award dept. psychiatry Dartmouth Med. Sch., 1984, Pres. award for Exceptional Achievement AHERF, 1994, numerous grants. Fellow Am. Psychiat. Assn.; mem. Pa. Psychiat. Assn., Am. Coll. Psychiatrists, Am. Assn. Chairmen of Depts. Psychiatry, Soc. Biol. Psychiatry, Am. Neuropsychiat. Assn. (bd. dirs., exec. dir. 1995), Assn. for Acad. Psychiatry, Am. Assn. Dirs. Psychiat. Residency Tng., Assn. Acad. Psychiatry, Assn. Convulsive Therapy, Assn. Medicine and Psychiatry, Yale Club Pitts., H-Y-P Club Pitts. Office: Med Coll Pa Hahnemann Sch of Medicine Dept Psychiatry 320 E North Ave Pittsburgh PA 15212-4772 also: Broad and Vine Sts M/S 403 Philadelphia PA 19102-1192 also: Eastern Pa Psychiat Inst Rm 166 3200 Henry Ave Philadelphia PA 19129

PRICE, WESTCOTT WILKIN, III, health care company executive; b. Glendale, Calif., May 6, 1939; s. Westcott Wilkin Jr. and Edna Johnson P.; m. Hillary Clark Haney, Apr. 12, 1941; children: Christopher, Gretchen, Wendy. BS in Bus., U. Colo., 1961; MBA, U. So. Calif., 1967. V.p., COO Calif. Med. Ctrs., L.A., 1970-73; pres., CEO Wm. Flaggs Inc., Commerce, Calif., 1973-80; pres., vice chmn. FHP Inc., Fountain Valley, Calif., 1981—. Bd. dirs. FHP Found., Long Beach, Calif., 1985—; bd. govs. U. So. Calif. Sch. Pub. Adminstrn., Los Angeles, 1987—. Served to lt. (j.g.) USN, 1961-63. Republican. Episcopalian. Club: Calif. (Los Angeles). Office: FHP Internat Corp 9900 Talbert Ave Fountain Valley CA 92708*

PRICE, WILLIAM HENRY, physician, educator, consultant, researcher; b. Swansea, Wales, June 11, 1932; s. David George and Nellie Gertrude (Thomas) P.; m. Mary Jackson, Mar. 2, 1957; children: David J., John S., Gillian M., Jacqueline F. BSc, U. Wales, Cardiff, 1952; MB, BCh, Welsh Nat. Sch. Medicine, Cardiff, 1955. Intern United Cardiff Hosps., 1955-56; resident, pathology Royal Devon and Exeter Hosp., 1956-58; resident, cardiology Nat. Heart Hosp., London, 1958-59; resident, internal medicine Ea. Gen. Hosp., Edinburgh, 1959-63; sr. registrar Newcastle Regional Hosp. Bd., Newcastle upon Tyne, Eng., 1963-65; staff Med. Rsch. Coun. clin. effects of radiation rsch. unit Western Gen. Hosp., Edinburgh, Scotland, 1965-67, clin. scientist, head clin. studies MRC Cytogenetics Unit, 1967-87, clin. scientist MRC human genetics unit, 1987-92; clin. dir. med. svcs. Western Gen. Hosps. Nat. Health Svc. Trust, Edinburgh, 1992-95; lectr. medicine U. Edinburgh, 1967-69, sr. lectr., 1969—; cons. physician Lothian Health Bd., Edinburgh, 1969—. Contbr. articles to med. jours. on peripheral circulation, dyspepsia, disorders of sexual devel., clin. cytogenetics, genetics of coronary heart disease, also chpts. to books. Fellow Royal Coll. Physicians, Royal Soc. Medicine; mem. Scottish Soc. Physicians (sr.), Brit. Med. Assn. Anglican. Home: 4 Strathalmond Rd, Edinburgh EH4 8AD, Scotland Office: Western Gen Hosp, Crewe Rd, Edinburgh EH4 2XU, Scotland

PRICKETT, DAVID CLINTON, physician; b. Fairmont, W.Va., Nov. 26, 1918; s. Clinton Evert and Mary Anna (Gottschalk) P.; m. Mary Ellen Holt, June 29, 1940; children: David C., Rebecca Ellen, William Radcliffe, Mary Anne, James Thomas, Sara Elizabeth; m. Pamela S. Blackstone, Nov. 17, 1991. AB, W.Va. U., 1944; MD, U. Louisville, 1946; MPH, U. Pitts., 1955. Lab. asst., instr. in chemistry, W.Va. U., 1943; intern, Louisville Gen. Hosp., 1947; surg. resident St. Joseph's Hosp., Parkersburg, W.Va., 1948-49; gen. practice, 1949-50, 55-61; physician USAF, N.Mex., 1961-62, U.S. Army, Calif., 1963-64, San Luis Obispo County Hosp., 1965-66, So. Calif. Edison Co., 1981-84; assoc. physician indsl. and gen. practice Los Angeles County, Calif., 1967—; med. dir. S. Gate plant GM, 1969-71; physician staff City of L.A., 1971-76; relief med. practice Applachia summer seasons, 1977, 1986, 1988-95. Med. Officer USPHS, Navajo Indian Reservation, Tohatchi (N.Mex.) Health Ctr., 1953-55, surgeon, res. officer, 1957-59; pres. W.Va. Pub. Health Assn., 1951-52, health officer, 1951-53, sec. indsl. and pub. health sect. W.Va. Med. Assn., 1956. Author: The Newer Epidemiology, 1962, rev., 1990, Public Health, A Science Resolvable by Mathematics, 1965. Served to 2d lt. AUS, 1943-46. Dr. Thomas Parran fellow U. Pitts. Sch. Pub. Health, 1955; named to Hon. Order Ky. Cols. Mem. Am. Occupational Med. Assn., Western Occupational Med. Assn., Am. Med. Assn., Calif. Med. Assn., L.A. County Med. Assn., Am. Acad. Family Physicians, Phi Chi. Address: PO Box 4032 Whittier CA 90607-4032

PRIDA, XAVIER E., cardiologist; b. Tampa, Fla., Nov. 23, 1953; s. Luciano Leopoldo and Alice Mercedes (Martinez) P.; m. Ember Josephine Cacciatore, May 8, 1976; children: Adam Xavier, Alexis Christina, Aaron Christopher. BS, . Fla., 1975; MD, U. Miami, Fla., 1980. Diplomate ACP. Resident in medicine N.Y. Hosp./Gen. Med. Ctr., N.Y.C., 1980-83; fellow in cardiology U. Fla./Shands Med. Ctr., Gainesville, Fla., 1983-86, chief resident in medicine, 1986-87; pvt. practice Tampa, 1987—. Fellow Am. Coll. Cardiology. Office: 2727 W Martin Luther King Tampa FL 33607-6382

PRIEBE, STEFAN, psychiatrist; b. Berlin, Oct. 24, 1953; s. Karl Heinz and Barbara (Schippert) P.; children: Roman, Marian Karl. Abitur, Canisius-Kolleg, Berlin, 1973; Dipl.-Psychologist, U. Hamburg, 1978, MD, 1980; DSc, Free U. Berlin, 1991. Rsch. fellow Middlesex Hosp., London, 1981, Neurol. Dept., U. Hamburg, 1981; asst. Albertinen Hosp., Hamburg, 1982-83; rsch. fellow dept clin. psychiatry Free U. Berlin, 1983-88, dep. head dept. social psychiatry, 1988-91, acting head dept. social psychiatry, 1991—; rschr. Med. Rsch. Inst., Palo Alto, Calif., 1983, Social Psychiat. U. Hosp., Berne, Switzerland, 1986, Med. Rsch. Coun., Social Psychiat. Unit, London, 1985. Editor and author several books; contbr. articles to profl. jours. Mem. Internat. Assn. for Psychotherapy Rsch., Deutsche Gesellschaft für Psychiat., Psychoth. und Nervenheilkunde, Deutscher Fachverband für Verhaltenstherapie, Platane 19 e.V (pres.), German Assn. for Social Psychiatry (chair rsch. com. 1995—), Dahlemer Tennis Club. Office: Free U, Platanenallee 19, 14050 Berlin Germany

PRIEBE, WALDEMAR ANTONI, bioorganic and medicinal chemistry educator; b. Wroclaw, Poland, Jan. 17, 1943; came to U.S., 1979; s. Janusz and Maria (Sosnowska) P.; m. Teresa Szwarocka, Feb. 23, 1974; children: Anna, Chris, Elizabeth. MS, U. Warsaw, Poland, 1971; PhD, Polish Acad. Scis., Warsaw, 1978. Postdoctoral fellow dept. chemistry Ohio State U., Columbus, 1979-81, rsch. assoc., 1982-85; assoc. prof. medicinal chemistry U. Tex. M.D. Anderson Cancer Ctr., Houston, 1986—; adj. prof. medicinal chemistry U. Houston, 1986—. Author and editor, organizer of nat. and internat. sci. symposiums; editl. bd. mem. Current Pharmaceutical Design; contbr. articles to profl. jours; patentee in field. Mem. AAAS, AACR (Am. Assn. for Cancer Rsch.), Am. Chem. Soc., Internat. Union Pure and Applied Chemistry, Polish Chem. Soc., N.Y. Acad. Scis. Roman Catholic. Office: U Tex MD Anderson Cancer Ctr 1515 Holcombe Blvd Houston TX 77030-4009

PRIESMAN, ELINOR LEE SOLL, family dynamics administrator, mediator, educator; b. Mpls., Jan. 19, 1938; d. Arthur and Harriet Lucille (Premack) Soll; m. Ira Morton Priesman, Mar. 30, 1958; children: Phillip Sherman, Artyce-Joy Erin. PhD, Union Inst., 1993. Cert. mediator, Va.; cert. family life educator. Nursery sch. tchr. Jewish Comty. Ctr., Santa Monica, Calif., 1958-59; head tchr. Altrusa Day Nursery, Battle Creek, Mich., 1959-60; prin. Arlington/Fairfax Jewish Ctr., Arlington, Va., 1966-67; tchr. grades 1-10 Congregation Olam Tikvah, Fairfax, Va., 1970-75; dir. Creative Play Nursery Sch., Fairfax, Va., 1970-71; tchr. high sch. Temple Sinai, Washington, Va., 1976-78; prin. Congregation Olam Tikvah, Fairfax, Va., 1975-76; asst. to pres.-emeritus Coun. for Advancement and Support of Edn., McLean, Va., 1987-90; cons. to univ. Union for Experimenting Colls. and Univs., McLean, Va., 1988-90; dir. family dynamics inst. Fairfax; mem. doctoral com. Union Inst., Cin., 1991-92, 92—; faculty mentor Ea. U., Albuquerque, 1993—. Author: The Empowered Parent, 1993, A New Perspective on Parenting, 1994 (Spanish, Korean translations 1996), A New Perspective on Parenting for Attorneys and Mediators, 1995; editor: Empowered Parenting newsletter, 1991-92. Pres. No. Va. Artistic Skating Club, Manassas, 1983-85; chair edn. com. Olam Tikvah Synagogue, Fairfax. Recipient Pres.'s award Olam Tikvah Synagogue, 1976. Mem. N.Am. Soc. Adlerian Psychology, Nat. Coun. on Family Rels., Children's Rights Coun., Acad. Family Mediators, No. Va. Mediation Svc. (mediator), Hadassah (life, Alexandria chpt. pres. 1966-67, Esther award 1965). Jewish. Office: Family Dynamics Inst 9302 Swinburne Ct Fairfax VA 22031-3027

PRIEST, MARSHALL FRANKLIN, III, cardiologist; b. Rio de Janeiro, Feb. 27, 1943; came to the U.S., 1945; s. Marshall Franklin Jr. and Eleanor Margaret (Harris) P.; m. Martha Prather, June 11, 1966; children: Paula Carol, Molly McCall, Marshall Franklin IV. BS, U. Tenn., 1965, MS, 1969, MD, 1973. Bd. cert. internal medicine and cardiovascular disease. Intern U. Tenn. Affiliated Hosp., Memphis, 1973-74; resident U. Tex. Affiliated Hosp., Memphis, 1974-76; cardiology fellow U. Ala. Hosps., Birmingham, 1976-78, instr. medicine and cardiology, 1978-79; cardiologist Boise (Idaho) Heart Clinic, 1979-94, Idaho Cardiology Assocs., Boise, 1994—; clin. asst. prof. medicine U. Washington. Fellow Am. Coll. Cardiology, Am. Heart Assn. (coun. on clin. cardiology); mem. Alpha Omega Alpha. Office: Idaho Cardiology Assocs 300 E Jefferson Ste 201 Boise ID 83712

PRIEST-MACKIE, NANCY RAY, nutrition consultant; b. Tampa, Fla., Dec. 1, 1934; d. Tommy Rex and Louise Virginia (Pierce) Priest; m. Harry Arendt Mackie, Aug. 6, 1983 (dec. 1991); children from previous marriage: Barbara Ellen, Allison Claire, Samuel Priest, Marjorie Lee. BS in Dietetics, Maryville Coll., 1956; postgrad., Nicholls State U., Thibodaux, La., 1979; MPH, Tulane U., 1981. Lic. dietitian, La.; lic. nutritionist. Clin. dietitian Baton Rouge (La.) Gen. Hosp., 1956-57; research dietitian East La. State Mental Hosp., Jackson, 1957-58; instr. Nicholls State U., Thibodaux, La., 1977-79; clin. dietitian East Jefferson Gen. Hosp., Metairie, La., 1980, Highland Park Hosp., Covington, La., 1981-83; renal cons. Washington Parish Dialysis Ctr., Bogalosa, La., 1985-86, St. Tammany Parish Dialysis Ctr., Covington, La., 1983-89; nutrition cons. Hope St. Nutrition Clinic Covington, 1983—; renal cons. Home Intensive Care, Hammond, La., 1988-96, Renal Treatment Ctrs., Inc., New Orleans, 1989-91; cons. quality care dialysis Dialysis Ctr., Hammond, La., 1988—, Bogalusa (La.) Cmty. Med. Ctr., 1990-96, St. Helena Parish Dialysis Ctr., 1994—, Renal Mgmt. Assn., New Orleans, 1996—; schizophrenia rschr. Tulane U. Med. Sch., Jackson, La., 1957-58; dir. Hope St. Exptl. Weight Loss Clinic, Covington, 1987, Hadden Hall adv. coun. St. Tammany Coun. on Aging, Inc., 1987—. Author: A First Novel; also other writings. Pres. Golden Meadow Homemakers, La., 1960-61; bd. pres. Council on Aging, Lafourche Parish, La., 1964-66. Mem. Am. Dietetic Assn. (registered), Renal Dietitians Assn., New Orleans Dietetic Assn., Bus. and Profl. Women, Cons. Nutritionists La., La. Cons. Dietitians in Pvt. Practice, A Practice Group of Am. Dietetic Assn. (chmn.). Home and Office: Hope St Nutrition Clinic Ltd 138 N New Hampshire St Covington LA 70433-3236

PRIEWE, RAYMON DEAN, osteopath; b. Oklahoma City, Okla., Feb. 9, 1954; s. Richard John and Gerda (Linke) P.; m. Sima Emine Günday, May 1, 1981. AA magna cum laude, Seminole Community Coll., Sanford, Fla., 1974; student, Baptist Coll. of Charleston, S.C., 1977-79; BA, U. So. Fla., 1981; D of Osteopathy, Southeastern Coll. Osteopaths, North Miami Beach, Fla., 1986. Advanced cardiac life support instr., advanced trauma life support provider. Medical officer Naval Aerospace Med. Inst., Pensacola, Fla., 1987-88; flight surgeon, head occupl. health Naval Med. Clinic, Key West, Fla., 1988-90; resident in anesthesiology U. Miami, Titusville, Fla., 1990-93; pvt. practice Titusville, Fla., 1993—. Lt. USNR, 1986-90, lt. comdr., 1990—. Mem. Am. Soc. Anesthesiologists, Internat. Anesthesia Rsch. Soc., Fla. Soc. Anesthesiologists, Am. Osteopathic Assn., Assn. Mil. Surgeons of the U.S., Aerospace Med. Assn., Soc. USN Flight Surgeons, Am. Assn. Mil. Osteopathic Physicans and Surgeons. Republican. Roman Catholic. Home: 3642 Thal Rd Titusville FL 32796-4017 Office: PO Box 1827 Titusville FL 32781-1827

PRIGMORE, CHARLES SAMUEL, social work educator; b. Lodge, Tenn., Mar. 21, 1919; s. Charles H. and Mary Lou (Raulston) P.; m. Shirley Melaine Buuck, June 7, 1947; 1 child, Philip Brand. A.B., U. Chattanooga, 1939; M.S., U. Wis., 1947, Ph.D., 1961; extension grad., Air War Coll., 1967, Indsl. Coll. Armed Forces, 1972. Social caseworker Children's Svc. Soc., Milw., 1947-48; social worker Wis. Sch. Boys, Waukesha, 1948-51; supt. tng. Wis. Bur. Probation and Parole, Madison, 1951-56; supt. Tenn. Vocat. Tng. Sch. for Boys, Nashville, 1956-59; assoc. prof. La. State U., 1959-64; ednl. cons. Coun. Social Work Edn., N.Y., 1962-64; exec. dir. Joint Commn. Correctional Manpower and Tng., Washington, 1964-67; prof. Sch. Social Work, U. Ala., 1967-84, prof. emeritus, 1984—, chmn. com. on Korean relationships; Fulbright lectr., Iran, 1972-73; vis. lectr. U. Sydney, 1976; cons. Iranian Ministry Health and Welfare, 1976-78; frequent lectr., workshop leader. Author: Textbook on Social Problems, 1971, Social Work in Iran Since the White Revolution, 1976, Social Welfare Policy Analysis and Formulation, 1979, 2d edit., 1986; editor 2 books; contbr. articles to profl. jours. Adv. Com. for Former Prisoners of War VA, 1981-83; chmn. Prisoner of War Bd., State of Ala., 1984-89; state comdr. Am. Ex-Prisoners of War, Ala., 1985-86, nat. legis. officer, 1985—, nat. dir., 1989-92, nat. sr. vice comdr., 1993—, nat comdr., 1994-95; gov.'s liaison U.S. Holocaust Meml. Coun., 1983-89; mem. Ala. Bd. Vets. Affairs, 1986-89, Ala. Bicentennial Commn. on Constn., 1987-90; bd. dirs. Community Svcs. Programs of W. Ala., 1985-89, others in past. Served to 2d lt. USAAF, 1940-45, prisoner of war, Germany, 1944-45; lt. col. Res., ret. Decorated Air medal with oak leaf cluster; recipient Conservation award Woodmen of the World, 1971; Fulbright rsch. fellow Norway, 1979-80. Fellow Am. Sociol. Assn., Royal Soc. Health; mem. Acad. Cert. Social Workers, Nat. Coun. Crime and Delinquency, Tuscaloosa Country Club, Capitol Hill Club, Alpha Kappa Delta, Beta Beta Beta. Home: 923 Overlook Rd N Tuscaloosa AL 35406-2122 Office: PO Box 870314 Tuscaloosa AL 35487-0314

PRIHODA, ALTON ROY, pediatrician, educator; b. Freeport, Tex., Sept. 1, 1955; s. Eddie L. and Henrietta S. (Vrazel) P.; m. Lee Ann Pate, June 16, 1979; children: Andrew, Nathan, Bryan. BS, Tex. A&M U., 1977; MD, U. Tex., Houston, 1981. Diplomate Am. Bd. Pediatrics. Resident in pediatrics U. Tex. Med. Br., Galveston, 1981-84; pvt. practice Wharton and El Campo, Tex., 1984-88, Baytown, Tex., 1988—; instr. family practice residency program U. Tex., Houston, 1989—; chief pediatrics South Tex. Med. Clinics, P.A., Wharton, 1985-88, Gulf Coast Med. Ctr., Wharton, 1986-88, San Jacinto Meth. Hosp., Baytown, 1991—. Contbr. articles to med. jours. Cons. Goose Creek Consol. Ind. Sch. Dist., Baytown, 1988—. Recipient Outstanding House Staff award U. Tex. Med. Br., 1984. Fellow Am. Acad. Pediatrics; mem. AMA, Tex. Med. Assn., Harris County Med. Soc., Wharton-Matagorda County Med. Soc. (sec. 1986, v.p. 1987, pres. 1988), Rotary, KC, Phi Eta Sigma, Phi Kappa Phi, Beta Beta Beta. Roman Catholic. Office: One Child Place Pediatrics 4201 Garth Rd Ste 318 Baytown TX 77521-3156

PRILLAMAN, WILLIAM NORMAN, orthodontist; b. Newport News, May 30, 1967; s. William Norman and Kaye (Catron) P.; m. Sonya Rachelle Wood, Mar. 6, 1993. BA in Biology, U. Va., 1989; DDS, N.C. Sch. Dentistry, 1993; Cert. in Orthodontics, Med. Coll. Va., 1995. Lic. dentist Va. Orthodontist in pvt. practice Martinsville, Va., 1995—. Bd. dirs. Habitat for Humanity, Martinsville, 1996—; asst. scoutmaster Boy Scouts Am., Martinsville, 1995—; youth counselor United Meth. Ch., Martinsville, 1995—; asst. basketball/soccer coach Recreation Dept., Martinsville, 1995—; resident selection com. mem. orthodontic dept. Med. Coll. Va., 1995—. Mem. Am. Assn. Orthodontists, Va. Assn. Orthodontists, Piedmont Dental Soc. (v.p. 1995—), Kiwanis. Home: 717 Beverly Way Martinsville VA 24112 Office: 25 Cleveland Ave Ste E Martinsville VA 24112

PRIMM, RICHARD KIRBY, physician; b. Thomasville, N.C., May 23, 1944; s. Richard Wesley and Gertrude (Berrier) P.; m. Sharon Kay Lucas, Dec. 28, 1968; children: Heather, Lucas. BA, Duke U., 1966; postgrad., Baylor U., 1966-67; MD, U. N.C., 1970. Intern internal medicine Vanderbilt U. Hosp., Nashville, 1970-71, resident in internal medicine, 1973-75, chief resident, 1975-76; fellow cardiovascular diseases U. Ala., Birmingham, 1976-78, chief fellow, instr. medicine, 1978-79; asst. prof. medicine Vanderbilt U. Sch. Medicine, Nashville, 1979-84; staff cardiologist Wenatchee (Wash.) Valley Clinic, 1984—; clin. asst. prof. medicine U. Wash., Seattle, 1985-91, clin. assoc. prof. medicine, 1991—; dir. dept. cardiology Wenatchee Valley Clinic, 1987-91. Contbr. articles to profl. jours. Med. dir. Wenatchee Cardiac Rehab. Program, 1985--. Capt. U.S. Army, 1971-73. Recipient Heusner Pupil award U. N.C., 1969, Hillman Teaching Excellence award Vanderbilt U., 1976. Fellow Am. Coll. Cardiology; mem. Am. Heart Assn., AMA, U. N.C. Alumni Coun., Wash. Heart Assn. (bd. trustees 1990—), Physicians for Social Responsibility, North Pacific Soc. of Internal Medicine, Alpha Omega Alpha. Democrat. Home: 141 Heather Ln Wenatchee WA 98801-9644 Office: Wenatchee Valley Clinic 820 N Chelan Ave Wenatchee WA 98801-2028

PRIMROSE, WILLIAM ROBERTSON, geriatrician, consultant; b. Glasgow, Scotland, June 2, 1952; s. David Anderson and Marjorie Black (Snodgrass) P.; m. Catherine Seonaid Wilson, June 6, 1978; children: John Robertson, Kenneth Wilson, Eilidh Catherine, Colin William. B in Med. Biology, MB, B in Chirurgery, Aberdeen (Scotland) U., 1976; diploma in Obstetrics, Otego U., Dunedin, New Zealand, 1980. Diplomate Joint Com. of Higher Med. Tng. in gen. medicine, geriatric medicine. Resident in gen. medicine Royal Alexandra Infirmary, Paisley, Scotland, 1976-77; resident in surgery Aberdeen Royal Infirmary, 1977; sho/registrar in gen. medicine So. Gen. Hosp., Glasgow, 1977-79; sr. house officer/registrar in gen. medicine, psychiatry Timaru Hosp., New Zealand, 1979-80; gen. practice trainee Govan Health Centre, Glasgow, 1980-81; registrar in respiratory medicine and infectious diseases King's Cross Hosp., Dundee, Scotland, 1981-83; sr. registrar in gen. medicine and geriatric medicine Longmore, Edinburgh, 1983-86, Royal Victoria, Edinburgh, 1983-86, City and Ea. Gen. Hosp., Edinburgh, 1983-86; cons. physician dept. medicine for elderly Woodend Hosp., Aberdeen, Scotland, 1986—; hon. sr. lectr. Aberdeen U., 1986—; chmn. med. adv. com. Priority U., Aberdeen, 1991-93; chmn. clin. audit com. Grampian Healthcare, 1995—. Contbr. articles to profl. jours. Mem. mgmt. com. Age Concern, Aberdeen, 1987—. Recipient Astra award, 1981, rsch. grant Lothian Health Bd., 1984, audit grants Grampian Health Bd., 1990, 91, rsch. grant, 1994. Fellow Royal Coll. Physicians and Surgeons (cert., mem. exam. com. 1990—); mem. Royal Coll. Gen. Practitioners (cert., referee jour. 1988—), Scottish Soc. Physicians, Brit. Geriat. Soc. Methodist.

PRINCE, ANGIE BENNETT, psychotherapist; b. Athens, Ga., Sept. 21, 1952; d. Charles Curtis and Margaret Adeline (Hanson) Bennett; m. Thomas Chafer Prince, III, Apr. 7, 1979; children: Rollin Thomas, Nathan Chafer, Merry Katherine. BA, U. Ga., 1975; MEd, Ga. State U., 1978; grad., Psychol. Studies Inst., 1978. Lic. psychol. examiner, counselor, Tenn.; reg. lobbyist, Tenn. V.p. Russell, Montgomery and Assocs., Knoxville and Nashville, Tenn.; counselor, pvt. practice Knoxville Counseling Ctr.; pres. Prince & Assocs., Knoxville. Mem. Knox County Rep. Exec. Com., precinct del.; mem. Jr. League Knoxville; com. mem. Leadership Knoxville, 1994; mem. Cedar Springs Presbyn. Ch., leader marriage preparation sem., group leader for survivors of sexual abuse; vol. Cedar Bluffs Schs. Mem. ACA, Am. Mental Health Counselor Assn., N.Am. Assn. Masters in Psychology (charter), Tenn. Assn. Psychol. Examiners (pres. 1994, 95), Knoxville Assn. Psychol. Examiners (past treas.), Christian Assn. Psychologists, Akima Club (assoc.).

PRINCE, GEORGE EDWARD, pediatrician; b. Erwin, N.C., Nov. 25, 1921; s. Hugh Williamson and Helen Herman (Hood) P.; m. Millie Elizabeth Mann, Nov. 26, 1944; children: Helen Elizabeth, Millie Mann, Susan Hood, Mary Lois. MD, Duke U., 1944. Diplomate Am. Bd. Pediatrics, Am. Bd. Med. Examiners. Intern Boston Children's Hosp. Harvard Svc., Boston, 1944-45; resident pediatrics Children's Hosp., Louisville, 1945-47; instr. pediatrics U. Louisville, 1947; founder Gastonia (N.C.) Children's Clinic, 1947, pediatrician, 1947-86; pub. health physician Gaston County Health Dept., Gastonia, N.C., 1986-95, med. dir., 1995-96; chmn. bd. dirs. Carolina State Bank; bd. dirs. So. Nat. Bank, Gastonia, 1979-95, Hospice, Gastonia, 1987-92; organizer, dir. AIDS Adv. Coun., Gaston County, N.C., 1988-94; coord. N.C. chpt. Pediatric Rsch. in Office Setting, 1986-92. Contbr. articles to profl. jours. Mem. Gaston County Human Rels. Com., Gastonia, 1966; mem. Sch. Health Adv. Coun., Gaston County, 1980-96. Maj. USAF, 1955-57. Recipient Balthis Heart Assn. award Gaston County, 1981, Good Ambassador award Health Dept., 1986. Fellow Am. Acad. Pediatrics (pres. N.C. chpt. 1984-86); mem. AMA, N.C. Pediatric Soc. (hon., pres. 1970), N.C. Med. Soc., Gaston County Med. Soc. (pres. 1966), Rotary (pres. 1984), County Club (bd. dirs. 1975-76). Democrat. Methodist. Home: 2208 Cross Creek Dr Gastonia NC 28056-8808 Office: Gaston County Health Dept 991 Hudson Blvd Gastonia NC 28052-6430

PRINCE, JACQUELYNNE BOLANDER, nurse, consultant; b. Norfolk, Va., July 4, 1955; d. Jack C. Bolander and Particia (Loud) Bolander Melvin; m. John Martine Prince, Jr., Oct. 1, 1977; children:Emily Alene, John Ryland, Christopher. B.S., Med. Coll. of Va., 1978; M.S., Tex. Woman's U., 1985. Cert. critical care registered nurse, med.-surg CNS. Staff nurse Med. Coll. of Va., Richmond, 1978-80; asst. nurse coord. Parkland Hosp., Dallas,

1980-82, supr., 1982-83; head nurse N.C. Meml. Hosp., Chapel Hill, 1983-85; coord. critical care edn. Wise Appalachian Regional Hosp., Wise, Va., 1985-86; coord. continuing edn. Norton (Va.) Community Hosp., 1986-91, mem. bd. dentistry State of Va., 1991-92; clin. nurse splist. Fort Sanders Parkwest Hosp., Knoxville, 1992—; cons. in field. Contbr. articles to profl. publs., chpt. in book. Instr. Advanced Cardiac Life Support, Am. Heart Assn., Dallas, Chapel Hill, N.C., 1980—; chmn. health adv. com. Norton City Schs.; chmn. Wise Sch. Dance, 1987-89, bd. dirs., 1987-91; v.p. PTA. Mem. ANA, Assn. Critical Care Nurses (bd. dirs.), N.C. Meml. Collaborator Practice Com., Wise County Med. Soc. Auxilliary (pres. 1988, chmn. health com. 1989-91, v.p. 1991), Parkland Woman's Club (project svc. chmn. 1980-83). Baptist. Avocations: skiing, quilting, reading, running. Home: 809 Bennett Pl Knoxville TN 37909-2348 Office: Ft Saunders Parkwest Hosp 9333 Parkwest Blvd Knoxville TN 37923

PRINCE, JULIUS S. (BUD), retired foreign service reserve officer; b. Yonkers, N.Y., July 21, 1911; s. Julius and Clara B. (Rich) P.; m. Eleanora Molloy, July 6, 1943; children: Thomas Marc, Tod Ainslee (dec.), Richard M. Johnson. B.A., Yale U., 1932; M.D., Columbia U., 1938, M.P.H., 1948; Dr.P.H., Harvard, 1957. Intern Sinai Hosp., Balt., 1939-40; asst. resident medicine N.Y. U. div. Goldwater Meml. Hosp., 1941-42; dist. state health officer N.Y. State Dept. Health, Jamestown, 1948-58; chief pub. health div. USAID, Ethiopia, 1958-67; prin. investigator demonstration and evaluation project AID, Ethiopia, 1959-67; chief Africa div. Population and Humanitarian Affairs, Population Office, AID, Washington, 1967-73; dir. Africa Regional Population Office, Accra, Ghana, 1973-74; chief health, population and nutrition projects AID, Ghana, 1974-76; cons. internat. health APHA, 1977-78, Pacific Cons., Inc., 1978-82, RONCO Inc., 1982; pub. health specialist/sr. health advisor One Am., Inc., 1982-87; sr. pub. health and nutrition specialist Internat. Sci. and Tech. Inst. Inc., 1985-94; cons. on internat. health, 1985—; report on sustainability of AID supported health, population and nutrition programs, Ghana, 1963-85, Ctr. Devel. Info. and Evaluation AID, 1988, Annotated History of AID-Supported Health and Nutrition Rsch.: From Outset to Present, Introduction and Background, AID Office Health, 1991, Compendium of Abstracts, 1985-92, rsch. by historically black colls. and univs. under AID Univ. Ctr./Rsch. and Univ. Devel. Linkages, 1985-92. Contbr. chpt. to book. Served from lt. to maj. M.C. Royal Canadian Army, 1942-46. Recipient Letter of Commendation, Adj. Gen. Can. Army, 1946, Superior honor award AID, 1968, Letter of Commendation, 1977. Fellow APHA, Soc. Applied Anthropology, Washington Acad. Scis., Royal Soc. Health; mem. AMA, N.Y. State Pub. Health Assn. (pres. 1957), Pan Am. Med. Assn., Am. Assn. World Health (emeritus mem. bd. dirs.), Internat. Soc. Hypertension in Blacks, Population Assn. Am., Soc. Internat. Devel., Nat. Coun. Internat. Health (award 1992), World Med. Assn., Soc. Prospective Medicine, Can. Soc. Internat. Health. Home and Office: 7103 Pinehurst Pky Chevy Chase MD 20815-3144

PRINCEVAC, SINISA MOMIR, physician, medical facility administrator; b. Croatia, May 12, 1941; came to U.S., 1971, naturalized, 1976; s. Momir Marko and Zlata Josip (Hopental) P.; m. Spasena D. Andelkovich, July 29, 1968; children—Boby, Otmar. M.D., Med. Facility Belgrade, Yugoslavia, 1966. Diplomate Am. Bd. Family Practice. Resident in internal medicine Columbus Hosp., Chgo., 1972-74; mgr. Health Care and Assoc. Med. Services Ltd., Chgo., 1977—. Mem. Rep. Party Task Force, 1983-82, Presdl. Task Force, 1983. Served to lt. Yugoslav Army, 1967-68. Mem. Chgo. Med. Soc., Ill. Med. Soc., AMA, Am. Mgmt. Assn., Internat. Assn. Physicians, Chinese Medicine Assn. Serbian Orthodox. Avocations: organized crime, econs. and bus. mgmt., real estate investments. Office: 2475 W Gunnison St Chicago IL 60625-2811

PRINEAS, JOHN WILLIAM, neurologist; b. Junee, NSW, Australia, May 30, 1935; came to U.S., 1974; s. Peter John and Nancy (McDonald) P.; m. Eileen Crisp, Jan. 9, 1960; children: Claire Beatrice Elizabeth Prineas McPhail, Sara Lianne, Peter John Edward. MB, BS with honors, Sydney U., 1958. House physician Royal Prince Alfred Hosp., Sydney, 1958; sr. resident cardiology Glasgow Royal Infirmary, 1960-61; sr. resident gastroenterology Royal Free Hosp, London, 1961; sr. resident, registrar, sr. registrar Nat. Hosps. for Nervous Diseases, Maida Vale, London, 1962-64; sr. registrar neurology The London Hosp., 1964; first asst. neurology U. Newcastle-Upon-Tyne, 1964-67; rsch. fellow neuropathology Albert Einstein Coll. Medicine, N.Y.C., 1967-69; sr. rsch. fellow neurology U. Sydney, 1971-72, sr. lectr. medicine, 1973; prof. dept. neurology and neuropathology U. Medicine and Dentistry N.J. Med. Sch., Newark, 1974—; vis. prof. pathology Albert Einstein Coll. Medicine, N.Y.C., 1976-84; attending neurologist VA Hosp., East Orange, N.J., 1976—. Contbr. articles to profl. jours. Fellow Nat. Multiple Sclerosis Soc., N.Y.C., 1967-69, Wellcome Found. sr. rsch. fellow dept. medicine Sydney U., 1970-72. Fellow Royal Coll. Physicians (London), Royal Coll. Physicians (Edinburgh), Australian Neurol. Assn. (hon.), Royal Microscopical Soc.; mem. Am. Assn. Neuropathologists (Weil awards 1969, 75, Moore award 1976), Am. Neurol. Assn. Office: VA Hosp Neurology 127 Tremont Ave East Orange NJ 07019

PRINEAS, RONALD JAMES, epidemiologist, educator; b. Junee, New South Wales, Australia, Sept. 19, 1937; came to U.S., 1973; s. Peter John and Nancy (MacDonald) P.; m. Julienne Swynny, Apr. 21, 1961; children: Matthew Leigh, Anna Mary, John Paul, Miranda Jane. MBBS, U. Sydney, Australia, 1960; PhD, U. London, 1969. Med. house officer Prince Henry Hosp., Sydney, 1961; sr. med. house officer Royal Perth Hosp., Australia, 1962; registrar in medicine Royal Glasgow Infirmary, Scotland, 1963-64; research fellow London Sch. Hygiene and Tropical Medicine, 1964-67, lectr., 1967-68; asst. in medicine U. Melbourne, Australia, 1968-72; prof. epidemiology U. Minn., Mpls., 1973-88, prof. medicine, 1974-88; prof., chair epidemiology and pub. health U Miami, Fla., 1988—; cons. WHO, Geneva, 1976—, Nat. Heart Lung and Blood Inst., 1976—; prin. investigator Nat. Health Lung and Blood Inst., 1973—. Author books, including; Blood Pressure Sounds; Their Measurement and Meaning, 1978; The Minnesota Code Manual of Electrocardiographic Findings, 1982; also numerous articles. Recipient numerous cardiovascular disease research grants and contracts. Mem. Fla. affiliate Am. Heart Assn., Mpls., 1973—, chmn. adv. groups, 1975—. Fellow Royal Coll. Physicians Edinburgh, Am. Coll. Cardiology, Am. Pub. Health Assn., Soc. Epidemiologic Research, Am. Heart Assn. Council on Epidemiology, Internat. Soc. Hypertension, Council on Human Biology, Internat. Soc. Cardiology, Soc. Controlled Clin. Trials, Am. Coll. Epidemiology, Am. Soc. Epidemiology, Internat. Soc. Human Biology; mem. Royal Coll. Physicians London. Avocations: reading; raising a family. Office: U Miami Sch Medicine Dept Epidemiology & Pub Health PO Box 669R Miami FL 33101-0116

PRINS, DAVID, speech pathologist, educator; b. Herkimer, N.Y., Oct. 4, 1930; s. Tunis W. and Harriet Z. (Baker) P.; m. Gloria B. Fleming, June 4, 1955; children: Leslie, Steven, Douglas, Michael. BA, Central Coll. Iowa, 1952; MA, U. Mich., 1957, PhD, 1961. Tchr. Denison (Iowa) H.S., 1954-55; instr. U. Mich., 1960-63, asst. prof., 1963-66, assoc. prof., 1966-69; asst. dir. U. Mich. Speech and Hearing Camp, 1960-64, dir., 1964-69; dir. program in speech and hearing scis. U. Wash., 1974-75, assoc. prof., 1969-72, prof., 1973-92, chmn. dept. speech and hearing scis., 1975-79, assoc. dean Coll. Arts & Scis., 1979-88, prof. emeritus, 1992—; vis. prof. U. Va. Contbr. articles in field of stuttering and articulation disorders to profl. jours. Served with U.S. Army, 1952-54. Mem. AAAS, Am. Speech and Hearing Assn., Wash. Speech and Hearing Assn., Mich. Speech and Hearing Assn. (past pres.), Phi Beta Kappa, Phi Kappa Phi. Office: U Wash Dept Speech And Scis Seattle WA 98105-6246

PRINZ, RICHARD ALLEN, surgeon. MD, Loyola U., Chgo., 1972. Diplomate Am. Bd. Surgery. Intern Barnes Hosp., St. Louis, 1972-73, resident in surgery, 1973-74; resident in surgery Loyola U., Chgo., 1974-77, attending surgeon, 1980-93; staff Rush Presbyn.-St. Luke's Med. Ctr., Chgo., 1993—; prof., chmn. Rush U., Chgo., 1993—. Mem. Alpha Omega Alpha. Office: Rush Presbyn/St Luke Med Ct 810 Professional Bldg 1725 W Harrison St Chicago IL 60612*

PRIOR, JOHN THOMPSON, pathology educator; b. St. Albans, Vt., July 24, 1948; s. Thomas William and Pauline Agnes Prior; m. Elizabeth Titus Troy, July 24, 1948; children: Anne, Polly, John Jr., Thomas, Jeffrey, Timothy. BS, U. Vt., 1939, MD, 1943. Diplomate Am. bd. Pathology. Resident in pathology Binghamton (N.Y.) City Hosp., 1946-47; fellow in pathology Syracuse (N.Y.) U. Med. Coll., 1947-49; asst. prof. pathology SUNY, Syracuse, 1949-54, assoc. prof., 1954-63, prof., 1963-72, clin. prof. pathology, 1972—; active ARC Blood Bank, Syracuse, 1966-70; pres. N.Y. State Assoc. Lab., Syracuse, 1959-60; med. dir. PSRO Ctrl. N.Y., Syracuse, 1983-84; mem. N.Y. Stat Hosp. Rev. & Planning Assn., Albany, 1980-82; bd. dirs. Am. Med. Peer Rev. Assn., 1985-90. Contbr. articles to profl. jours. Bd. dirs. Lung Assn. Ctrl. N.Y., Syracuse, 1994—. Col. M.C., U.S. Army, 1944-77. Recipient William Hammond Citation, N.Y. State Jour. Medicine, N.Y.C., 1984, Disting. Alumnus award U. Vt., Burlington, 1994. Mem. Onondaga County Med. Soc. (pres. 1974, disting. svc. award 1981). Home: 4615 Pewter Ln Manlius NY 13104

PRIOR, REED RICHARD, biotechnology executive; b. Saginaw, Mich., Oct. 3, 1951; s. Richard Walter and Carol Ruth (Fogt) P.; m. Mary Theresa Murphy, June 11, 1978; children: Adam G., Colleen A., Leigh K. BS in Biophysics, Mich. State U., 1973; MBA, Harvard U., 1980. Product mgr. Millipore Corp., Bedford, Mass., 1979-80; group mktg. mgr. Waters/Millipore, Milford, Mass., 1980-81, dir. internat. mktg., 1981-83; v.p. Promega Biotec, Madison, Wis., 1983-85, Marine Venture Capital, Inc., Milw., 1985-86; pres., CEO i-STAT Corp., Princeton, N.J., 1986-90, Genex Corp., Gaithersburg, Md., 1990-91; pres., CEO, bd. dirs. Receptor Labs., Inc., Chgo., 1992-95, ActiMed Labs., Inc., Burlington, N.J., 1995—; airline transport pilot. Office: ActiMed Labs Inc 5 Terri Ln Burlington NJ 08016

PRIOUR, DONALD JAMES, ophthalmologist; b. Kerrville, Tex., May 23, 1946; s. James W. and Bertha (Real) P.; m. Jane Wynett, July 27, 1968; children: Donald J. Jr., Amy Rebecca. AA, Schreiner Coll., Kerrville, 1966; BA, U. Tex., 1968; MD, U. Tex., Galveston, 1972. Diplomate Am. Bd. Ophthalmology, Am. Bd. Eye Surgery. Intern Baylor Coll. Medicine, 1972-73; resident U. Tex. Med. Br., Galveston, 1973-76; chief of staff Sid Peterson Meml. Hosp., Kerrville, Tex.; pvt. practice; pvt. practice Kerrville, 1976—. Contbr. articles to med. and archeology jours. Pres. Am. Cancer Soc., 1978. Fellow ACS, Am. Acad. Ophthalmology; mem. AMA (Physicians' Recognition award), Am. Coll. Eye Surgeons (cert.), Kerr, Kendal, Bandra Counties Med. Soc. (pres.), Phi Theta Kappa, Alpha Epsilon Delta. Office: 961 Water St Kerrville TX 78028-3550

PRISANT, L(OUIS) MICHAEL, cardiologist; b. Albany, Ga., Dec. 25, 1949; s. Bennie Martin and Mozelle (Cosper) P.; m. Rose Corinth Trincher, June 28, 1975; children: Michelle Elizabeth, Louis Michael. BA, Emory U., 1971; MD, Med. Coll. Ga., 1977. Diplomate Am. Bd. Internal Medicine, Am. Bd. Cardiovascular Diseases, Am. Bd. Geriatric Medicine, Am. Bd. Clin. Pharmacology, Nat. Bd. Med. Examiners. Intern Med. Coll. Ga., Augusta, 1977-78; resident Med. Coll. Ga., 1978-80; chief med. resident, 1979-80; cardiology fellow Med. Coll. Ga., 1980-82, instr., 1982-83, asst. prof. medicine, 1983-89, assoc. prof. medicine, 1989-94, prof., 1994—; cons. in field; lectr. in field. Contbr. 85 articles and 88 abstracts to profl. jours., 5 chpts. to books; author of 6 monographs; manuscript reviewer med. jours. FOE grantee, 1989, Rorer, 1989, Am. Cyanamid, 1988, Sandoz, 1989-93, Merck, 1990-92, Squibb, 1991, Lorex, 1991, NIH, 1991, Lederle, 1993, Ciba-Geigy, 1993. Fellow ACP, Am. Coll. Cardiology, Am. Coll. Clin. Pharmacology, Am. Coll. Chest Physicians; mem. AMA (Physician's Recognition award 1982-95), AAUP, Am. Fedn. Clin. Rsch., Am. Heart Assn., Am. Soc. Echocardiography, Am. Soc. Hypertension, Am. Soc. Internal Medicine, Internat. Soc. for Hypertension in Blacks, Ga. Heart Assn., Assn. for Advancement Med. Instrumentation, Ga. Med. Care Found., Med. Assn. Ga., Richmond County Med. Soc., Ahlquist Soc. (pres.), AMA Physician, Phi Delta Epsilon, Alpha Phi Omega, Tau Epsilon Phi. Jewish. Office: Med Coll Ga Sect Cardiology Rm CK-151 Augusta GA 30912-3150

PRISCO, DOUGLAS LOUIS, physician; b. N.Y.C., Nov. 30, 1945; s. Frank James and Isabel (Gaetano) P.; AB, Georgetown U., 1967; postgrad. N.Y. U., 1967-68; MD, U. Rome, 1974; m. Marianne Paula Mangano, Jan. 8, 1972; children: Jennifer Leigh, Douglas Louis, Dana Lauren, Andrew Michael. Intern, Mt. Sinai Svcs., Elmhurst, N.Y., 1974-75, resident in medicine, 1975-77, pulmonary medicine fellow, 1977-79; practice medicine specializing in pulmonary medicine, N.Y.C., New Hyde Park, N.Y., 1979-81; clin. asst. in medicine Bklyn. Hosp., 1979-81; pulmonary cons. and admitting physician Booth Meml. Hosp.; chief pulmonary medicine Deepdale Gen. Hosp.; clin. asst. Mt. Sinai Sch. Medicine N.Y.C., 1977-79; physician adviser St. Barnabas Hosp., 1981-82; pres. Met. Pulmonary Assocs., P.C., 1980—, Met. Pulmonary, P.C., 1985—; physician adv. to Queens County Profl. Standards Rev. Orgn., 1979-85; co-chmn. quality assurance com. downstate region Island Peer Rev. Orgn., 1990—, vice- chmn. pro-tem regional quality assurance com., N.Y., 1993—. Bd. dirs. Queens County Profl. Standards Rev. Orgn., 1984-85; med. dir., chief pulmonary diseases Little Neck Cmty. Hosp. (formerly Deepdale Gen. Hosp.), 1993—, adminstr. med. affairs, 1993—; pres. Med. Staff Soc. 1992—, v.p. med. bd. 1993—; mem., cons. Queens div. Island Peer Rev. Orgn., 1985—. Diplomate Am. Bd. Internal Medicine, sub-bd. Pulmonary Diseases. Mem. Rep. Senatorial Inner Cir., 1990. Fellow Am. Coll. Chest Physicians; mem. ACP, Am. Lung Assn. Queens (bd. dirs. 1988—), Queens County Med. Soc. Roman Catholic. Club: Port Washington Yacht (former chmn. jr. activities 1987-88, fleet surgeon 1991-93, 95—, bd. dirs. 1995—), Capitol Hill Club (Washington), Intergrated Delivery Systems of N.Y. (vice chmn., chmn., 1995—). Office: 1575 Hillside Ave New Hyde Park NY 11040-2501

PRISCO, FRANK J., psychotherapist; b. N.Y.C.; s. Frank J. and Isabel (Gatano) P.; m. August Frances; children: Frank, Christian, Meredith. BS in History, NYU, 1964, MA in History and Psychology, 1972, PsyD/Psychoanalysis, 1980. Cert. psychoanalyst, cert. med. hypnotherapist. Cons./staff therapist Creedmore Psychiat. Ctr.; faculty Psychanalytic Inst., L.I.; psychoanalyst, pvt. practice Ctr. for Modern Psychoanalytic Studies. Eucharistic min. Cath. Ch. Recipient Soc. of Emil award. Mem. AAAS, Am. Assn. Guidance and Counseling, N.Y. Acad. Scis., Nat. Assn. Advancement Psychoanalysis, Am. Poetry Assn. (Poet Merit award 1988, 89, 90).

PRISCO, NICHOLAS ALLEN, hospital administrator; b. Englewood, N.J., Aug. 4, 1943; s. Nicholas T. and Ruth Esther (Allen) P.; m. Sarah Jane Watson, Aug. 16, 1969; children: Kimberly Anne, Ginger Marie, Nicholas Edwin. BA, U. Calif., 1967; M in Hosp. & Health Svcs. Adminstrn., Cornell U., 1973. Diplomate Am. Coll. Healthcare Execs. Asst. adminstr. Tompkins County Hosp., Ithaca, N.Y., 1973-75; adminstr. Little Falls (N.Y.) Hosp., 1975-86; ceo Sunbury (Pa.) Cmty. Hosp., 1986—. Capt. USAMSC, 1967-71, Vietnam. Office: Sunbury Cmty Hosp 350 N 11th St PO Box 737 Sunbury PA 17801

PRITCHETT, ALLEN MONROE, healthcare administrator; b. St. Louis, June 29, 1949; s. Allen M. Jr. and Jane (Baird) P.; m. Linda Jasper (div. Apr. 1980); 1 child, Brett A. (dec.). AA, Meramec Coll., 1969; BS, U. Mo., 1971; MA, Webster U., 1978. Tchr. social studies Union (Mo.) High Sch., 1971-77; mgr. edn. and tng. Luth. Med. Ctr., St. Louis, 1977-78, asst. dir. human resources, 1978-81; dir. pers. Grandpa John's, Inc., Murphysboro, Ill., 1981-82; mgmt. instr. So. Ill. U., Carbondale, 1982-84; dir. human resources Meml. Hosp., Carbondale, 1984-93; v.p. So. Ill. Hosp. Svcs., Carbondale, 1993-95; pres. Pritchett/Baird Assocs., 1995—; mem. coun. on healthcare human resources Ill. Hosp. Assn., 1991-93; bd. dirs. So. Ill. Regional Social Svcs., Inc., 1994—, sec./treas., 1996—; So. Ill. U. Coll. Bus. Ctr. for Mgmt. and Exec. Devel., 1987-93. Mem. bus. adv. com. Carbondale Cmty. H.S., 1984-95; mem. So. Ill. Bus./Employer Advisors, Carbondale, 1984—; mem. Carbondale Postal Customer Adv. Coun., 1995-96; mem. human resources adv. bd. Commerce Clearing House, 1995-96. Mem. So. Ill. Healthcare Human Resources Assn. (pres. 1987-88, 90-91, exec. com. 1986—, sec. 1986-87), Am. Soc. Healthcare Human Resources Adminstrn. (pres. So. Ill. chpt. 1987-88, 90-91), Soc. for Human Resource Mgmt., Am. Coll. Healthcare Execs. (diplomate), Carbondale C. of C. (bd. dirs. 1995-96).

PRITHAM, HOWARD GEORGE, surgeon; b. Waltham, Mass., Oct. 13, 1940; s. Howard Charles and Dorothy Clark (Thayer) P.; m. Ellen Barbara Davis, Sept. 3, 1965; children: David, Ellen Jean, Gregory. BS, Tufts Coll., 1962; MD, Tufts Med. Coll., 1966. Diplomate Am. Bd. Surgery. Resident in surgery Mary Hitchcock Hosp., Lebanon, N.H., 1970-74; mem. staff in surgery Littleton (N.H.) Regional Hosp., 1974—. Lt. Comdr. USN, 1967-70. Fellow ACS; mem. Northeast Med. Assn., New Eng. Surg. Soc. Office: 105 Cottage St Littleton NH 03561-1821

PRITIKIN, ROLAND I., ophthalmologic surgeon, writer, lecturer; b. Chgo., Jan. 9, 1906; s. Edward and Bluma (Saval) P.; m. Jeanne DuPre Moore, May 25, 1940 (dec. May 1988); children: Gloria Anne, Karin (Mrs. Craig Howard Heiser). B.S., Loyola U., 1928, M.D., 1930; diploma, U.S. Army Command and Gen. Staff Coll., 1964. Diplomate: Am. Bd. Ophthalmology. Eye department Loyola U. School Medicine, 1933-35; resident Ill. Eye and Ear Infirmary, 1936-38, staff, 1939-48; vis. eye surgeon, Shikarpur, Sind, Pakistan, under Sir Henry Holland, 1939, 57, 60, 63, 66, 71, vis. eye surgeon Ethiopia, 1972; cons. Rockford industries, 1946—; pvt. practice ophthalmology Rockford, 1946—; pres. staff Winnebago County (Ill.) Hosp., 1950; lecture, research tour, Western Europe, Near and Middle East, 1951, vis. eye surgeon, Pakistan, 1960; cons. in ophthalmology HHS; hearing officer Social Security Adminstrn.; vis. eye clinics Vienna, Zurich, Paris, 1934. Author: Essentials of Ophthalmology, 1950, 3d edit., 1975, World War Three Is Inevitable, 1976; contbr. Ency. Americana supplements, 1946-80, reg. vols., 1955-72, articles on ophthalmology various med. jours., also sects. on spectacles and contact lenses to Acad. Am. Ency. Med. Res. Officers; chmn. meeting on computers in ophthalmology Internat. Symposium on Bio-Engring. in Ophthalmology, Haifa, Israel, 1975, Ctr. For Global Security, 1978—; life mem. Weizmann Inst., Sci. Served as col. M.C. AUS, 1941-45; brig. gen. Ill. N.G., ret. Recipient 1st award World Medical Assn., 1964; Quetta Mission Hosp. medal, 1964; Physician's Recognition award AMA, 1972, 75, 77, 83, 86, 89, 92, Cert. award VFW, 1986, Cert. award Chapel of the Four Chaplains, 1980, Super Sr. award Winnebago County Coun. on Aging, 1991, Cert. Appreciation for 25 yrs. vol. cons. ophthalmology U.S. Army Health Svcs. Command; named Commodore State of W.Va., 1980, Ky. Col., 1982; decorated Army Commendation medal, 1965, Order St. John of Jerusalem by Queen Elizabeth II, 1970; promoted to Comdr. by Queen Elizabeth II, 1993. Fellow Indsl. Med. Assn., Am. Med. Writers Assn., Soc. Mil. Ophthalmologists (bd. govs., 1st life), AMA, A.C.S., Internat. Coll. Surgeons, AAAS, Am. Geriatrics Soc., Royal Soc. Health, Am. Coll. Nuclear Medicine (distinguished mem., founding mem.), Instituto Barraquer, Barcelona; assoc. Royal Soc. Medicine London; mem. Internat. Assn. Secs. Ophthalmol. and Otolaryngol. Socs. (editor ophthalmology 1973-80), Ill., Winnebago County med. socs., Am. Nuclear Soc., Am. Acad. Ophthalmology and Otolaryngology, Chgo. Ophthal. Soc., Assn. Mil. Surgeons U.S., Rock River Valley Ophthalmology Assn. (sec. 1978—), World Med. Assn., Pan-Am. Assn. Ophthalmology, Am. Assn. History of Medicine, Assn. Am. Phys. and Surg., Internat. Assn. Prevention of Blindness, Joseph Waring Meml. Library Assn. History of Medicine, Soc. Med. Cons. to Armed Forces, N.Y. Acad. Scis., Contact Lens Soc. of Ophthalmologists, Nat. Soc. Prevention Blindness, Henry Holland Hosps. Alumni Assn. and Fund (pres.), Internat. Assn. Against Trachoma, Assn. Research Ophthalmology, Soc. Nuclear Medicine, Pan Am. Soc. Ophthalmic Microsurgery (charter), Ophthalmol. Soc. Canary Islands (hon.), Internat. Soc. History Medicine (hon.), Am. Coll. Eye Surgeons (life mem.), C. of C., 33d Div. War Vets. Assn. (surgeon 1975-85), Am. Legion, Res. Officers Assn. U.S., Internat. Agy. Prevention Blindness, Ophthalmol. Soc. Pakistan (life), others. Club: Univ. (Rockford). Home: Independence Village 3655 N Alpine Rd Apt B-302 Rockford IL 61114-7324 Office: Talcott Bldg Rockford IL 61101

PRITZ, MICHAEL BURTON, neurological surgeon; b. New Brunswick, N.J., Oct. 8, 1947; s. John Ernest and Helen Violet (Rockoff) P.; m. Edmay Marie Gregorcy, Feb. 18, 1973; children: Edmond Louis, Benjamin David. BS, U. Ill., 1969; PhD, Case Western Res. U., 1973, MD, 1975. Diplomate Am. Bd. Neurol. Surgery. Asst. prof. neurol. surgery U. Calif. Irvine Med. Ctr., Orange, 1981-85, assoc. prof., 1985-93; prof., 1993, U. Calif. Irvine Med. Ctr., Orange, 1993—; prof. sect. neurol. surgery Ind. U. Sch. Medicine, Indpls., 1993—, prof. neurol. surgery, 1993—. Contbr. articles to profl. jours. Recipient Herbert S. Steuer award Case Western Res. U., Cleve., 1975; NSF fellow, 1968; Edmund J. James scholar U. Ill., Champaign, 1968-69. Mem. Soc. Neurosci., Am. Assn. Anatomists, Am. Assn. Neurol. Surgeons, Congress Neurol. Surgeons, Soc. Neurol. Surgeons of Orange County (pres. 1985-86, sec.-treas. 1984-85).

PRO, JOHN PAUL, psychotherapist; b. Pitts., Apr. 7, 1925; s. John Battista and Mary (DiBartalo) P.; m. Katherine Mary Vazzano, June 2, 1945; children: Patricia, Paul, Carol, Anita, Robert. BEd, Duquesne U., Pitts., 1949; BD, Pitts.Xenia Sem., 1957; MDiv, ThM, Pitts. Sem., 1972, 69; DMin, Luther Rice Sem., Jacksonville, Fla., 1977; DD, Alderson-Broaddus Coll., 1978. Diplomate Am. Assn. Pastoral Counselors. Staff counselor Luth. Counseling Ctr., Pitts., 1965-68; dir. Luth. Counseling Ctr., 1968-70; staff counselor Pitts. Pastoral Inst., 1970-88, supr., 1980-88, instr., 1975-88; pvt. practice pastoral psychotherapy Jeannette, Pa., 1988—; cons. in field. Author: Evangelism in Pastoral Counseling, 1980. Bd. dirs. United Fund, Jeannette, Pa., 1967; nat. counselor Italian Sons & Daus. of Am., Pitts. Mem. Am. Assn. Marriage and Family Therapists (clin. mem.). Antiochian Orthodox Ch. Home and Office: 436 Sloan Ave Jeannette PA 15644-1658

PROAKIS, ANTHONY GEORGE, pharmacologist; b. Chios, Greece, May 26, 1940; came to the U.S., 1946; s. George John and Fotine (Parikakis) P.; m. Nancy Lee Pietranton, Feb. 23, 1963; children: Lisa Ann, Andrea Lynn, Steven Anthony. BS in Pharmacy, W.Va. U., 1962; PhD in Pharmacology, Purdue U., 1972. Pharmacist Medco Pharmacies Inc., L.A., 1962-63, mgr., 1963-66, v.p., 1966-67; gen. mgr. Guardian Pharmacies Inc., L.A., 1967-69; sr. rsch. biologist A.H. Robins Rsch. Labs., Richmond, Va., 1972-77, rsch. assoc., 1977-80, group mgr., 1980-90; pharmacologist U.S. FDA, Rockville, Md., 1990—; adj. asst. prof. Med. Coll. Va., Richmond, 1989—; grant reviewer Am. Heart Assn., Richmond, 1982-86. Contbr. articles to profl. jours.; patentee in field. NIH postdoctoral fellow, 1969-72. Fellow Am. Coll. Clin. Pharmacology; mem. Am. Soc. for Pharmacology and Experimental Therapeutics, Soc. for Experimental Biology and Medicine, Am. Heart Assn., Rho Chi, Phi Kappa Phi, Sigma Xi. Home: 2200 Normandstone Dr Midlothian VA 23113-9652 Office: US FDA HFD-110 5600 Fishers Ln Rockville MD 20852-1750

PROBSTFIELD, JEFFREY LYNN, internist; b. Fargo, N.D., June 27, 1941; s. George Berg and Alda Gail (Abbott) P.; m. Margaret Helen Belgum, Dec. 28, 1965; children: Erik, Kathryn, Cindy, Dawn, Shannon, Laura. BA, Pacific Luth. U., Tacoma, Wash., 1963; MD, U. Wash., 1967; postgrad., U. Minn., 1970-74. Diplomate Am. Bd. Internal Medicine. Rotating intern Hennepin County Gen. Hosp., Mpls., 1967-68; resident in internal medicine U. Minn., Mpls., 1968-71, fellow in clin. pharmacology, 1971-75, asst. prof. medicine, 1975-78; asst. prof. medicine Baylor Coll. Medicine, Houston, 1978-84; sci. project officer Clin. Trials Br., NHLBI, Bethesda, Md., 1984-93; prof. internal medicine Uniformed Svcs. Univ. Health Sci., Bethesda, Md., 1991-93; project dir., co-prin. investigator The Womens Health Initiative Coord. Ctr. Fred Hutchinson Cancer Rsch. Ctr., Seattle, 1993-95; prof. epidemiology Sch. Pub. Health, U. Wash., Seattle, 1993—. Contbr. over 90 articles to profl. jours., chpts. to books; editor, author: The Handbook of Health Behavior Change, 1990; editor/author monograph: The Systolic Hypertension in the Elderly Program, 1991. Bd. regents Pacific Luth. U., Tacoma, 1981-90; bd. dirs. Westbury Am. Little League, Houston, 1980-84; coach baseball Gaithersburg (Md.) Sports Assn., 1985-90; coach basketball Montgomery County Recreation Dept., Gaithersburg, 1985-90. Lt. comdr. USN, 1967-84. Fellow, Epidemiology Coun. Am., 1986, Am. heart Assn., Arteriosclerotic Coun., 1984. Fellow ACP, Am. Coll. Cardiology, Am. Coll. Geriatric Cardiology; mem. AAAS, Am. Soc. Clin. Pharmacology and Therapeutics, Soc. for Clin. Trials (bd. dirs. 1990-94). Republican. Lutheran. Office: Divsn Pub Health Scis FHCRC MP702 1124 Columbia St Seattle WA 98104-2015

PROCIDANO, MARY ELIZABETH, psychologist, educator; b. New Rochelle, N.Y., Apr. 1, 1954; d. John D'Arge and Dorothy Diane (Utter) P.; m. Stephen Anthony Buglione, Aug. 9, 1986; children: Daniel Stephen, Katherine Mary, Anne Elizabeth. BS summa cum laude with honors, Fordham U., 1976; PhD, Ind. U., 1981. Lic. psychologist. Assoc. instr. Ind. U., Bloomington, 1979-80; intern in clin. psychology Inst. of Living, Hartford, Conn., 1980-81; asst. prof. Fordham U., Bronx, N.Y., 1981-90, asst. chair psychology dept., 1984-87, chair Inst. Rev. Bd. for Protection of Human Subjects, 1986-94, assoc. prof., mem. faculty senate, 1992-96, also mem. coll. coun. and various coms., advisor; pvt. practice clin. psychology Scarsdale, N.Y., 1992—; assoc. dean Fordham U. Grad. Sch. of Art's and Scis., 1996—. Cons. editor Jour. of Personality and Social Psychology, 1989—; contbr. articles and chpts. to profl. and scholarly jours. and books. Faculty fellow Fordham U., 1990; rsch. and faculty devel. grantee Fordham

U. Mem. Am. Psychol. Assn., Ea. Psychol. Assn., Assn. for Advancement Behavior Therapy, Phi Beta Kappa, Sigma Xi, Psi Chi. Roman Catholic. Office: Fordham U Dept Psychology Bronx NY 10458

PROCKOP, DARWIN JOHNSON, biochemist, physician; b. Palmerton, Pa., Aug. 31, 1929; s. John and Sophie (Gurski) P.; m. Elinor Sacks, Apr. 15, 1961; children: Susan Elizabeth, David John. AB, Haverford Coll., 1951; MA, Oxford U., 1953; MD, U. Pa., 1956; PhD, George Washington U., 1962; DSc (hon.), U. Oulu, 1983, U. So. Fla., 1993. Investigator NIH, 1957-61; assoc., asst. prof., asso. prof., prof. medicine and biochemistry U. Pa., Phila., 1961-72; prof., chmn. dept. biochemistry U. Medicine and Dentistry of N.J. (Rutgers Med. Sch.), Piscataway, N.J., 1972-86; prof., chmn. dept. biochemistry and molecular biology Jefferson Med. Coll., Phila., 1986-96; prof., dir. Ctr. for Gene Therapy, Med. Coll. Pa./Hahnemann U., Phila., 1996—; dir. Jefferson Inst. Molecular Medicine, 1986-96. Contbr. articles to profl. jours.; research on collagen. Served with USPHS, 1958-61. Fulbright fellow Oxford U., 1951-53; NIH, grantee, 1961—; recipient Disting. Alumnus award George Wash. U., 1991, U. Pa., 1994. Mem. NAS, Inst. Medicine, Acad. Finland, Soc. Biol. Chemists, Am. Soc. Clin. Investigation, Am. Assn. Physicians, Phi Beta Kappa, Alpha Omega Alpha. Home: 291 Locust St Philadelphia PA 19106-3913

PROCTOR, BRIAN DONALD, ophthalmologist; b. Highland Park, Mich., Oct. 14, 1963; s. Howard Donald and Janet (Twork) P.; m. Linda Susan (Parrett), Qug. 25, 1990. BS, Kalamazoo Coll., 1986; DO, Mich. State U., 1990. Diplomate Am. Bd. Ophthalmology, Am. Bd. Otorhitolaryngology. Intern BiCounty Hosp., Highland Park, 1990-91; resident in ophthalmology Detroit Ophthalmology Consortium, 1991-94, chief resident in opthalmology, 1992-94; physician Gottlieb Meml. Hosp., Melrose Park, Ill., 1994—; adj. faculty resident tng. Chgo. Coll. Osteopathic Medicine, Hyde Park, Ill., 1996—; presenter in field. Contbr. articles to profl. pubs. Vol. Nat. Eye Care Project, Melrose Park, 1995-96. Recipient Osteopathic Concept award Mich. State U., 1990. Mem. Am. Osteo. Colls. Ophthalmology, Am. Acad. Ophthalmology, Am. Osteo. Assn., Ill. Assn. Osteo. Physicians and Surgeons, Chgo. Med. Soc. Office: Gottlieb Eye Ctr 675 W North Ave Melrose Park IL 60160

PROCTOR, JOHN HOWARD, industrial and organizational psychologist; b. Bronx, N.Y., June 3, 1931; s. John Carol and Carolyn Elizabeth (Slade) P.; m. Karen Jane Boyer Crye, Apr. 21, 1984; children: Donna Lynn, Susan Carol, John Christopher, John Crye, Christopher Lynn Crye, James Alexander. BS, Davidson Coll., 1953; MS, Purdue U., 1954, Ph.D., 1958. Diplomate Am. Bd. Profl. Psychology (sec. Mideast Regional Coun. 1989-93). Cons. Humble Oil & Refining Co., 1957-58; dir. tng. and personnel rsch. Bleached Bd. div. W.Va. Pulp and Paper Co., 1958-60; mem. tech. staff Mitre Corp., 1960-64; sr. project dir. Data Dynamics Inc., 1964-66; gen. mgr. Eastern ops. Mellonics div. Litton Systems Inc., Ft. Walton Beach, Fla., 1966-70; pres. Data Solutions Corp., Vienna, Va., 1970-85, also chmn. bd.; sr. v.p. B-K Dynamics, Inc., Rockville, Md., 1985-93; prin. John H. Proctor Assocs., 1993—. Mem. adv. com. on rights and responsibilities of women HEW, 1976; mem. Nat. Def. Exec. Res.; del. White House Conf. on Aging, 1982; sec. gen. elect World Acad. Art and Sci., 1987-96; deacon-elect Columbia Bapt. Ch., 1991—. With AUS, 1954-56. Fellow World Acad. Art and Sci., Washington Acad. Scis. (life, bd. mgrs. 1991, pres. elect 1992), Spanish Royal Acad. Pharmacy (corr.); mem. APA, Soc. for Indsl. and Orgnl. Psychology, Am. Bd. Indsl. and Orgnl. Psychology (bd. dirs. 1992—), Internat. Assn. Creative Intelligentsia (Russia, presdl. coun. 1995), River Bend Golf and Country Club (pres. 1986-88), Sigma Xi. Author: (with W.M. Thornton) Training: A Handbook for Line Managers, 1961; editor: (with Lorenz K.Y. Ng) Management of Pain and Stress, 1985; contbr. to Strategies for Public Health: Promoting Health and Preventing Disease, 1982; Just Who Do You Think You Are?, 1992; contbr. articles to profl. jours. Home and Office: 308 East St NE Vienna VA 22180-3618

PROCTOR, PAUL WAINWRIGHT, psychologist, educator; b. Kansas City, Mo., Sept. 14, 1915; s. Paul Bullard and Jessie Elizabeth (Wainwright) P.; m. Shizu Asahi, Nov. 23, 1945. BSBA, Washington U., 1936; MA, Columbia U., 1945; postgrad. Johns Hopkins U., 1947, Claremont Coll., 1948; PhD, NYU, 1948-52. Cert. psychologist, sch. psychologist, N.Y. Tchr. social studies and remedial reading Friends Sch., Balt., 1945-47; asst. psychologist U. Md. Hosp., Balt., 1947; tchr. remedial reading Slade Sch., Olney, Md., 1947-48; psychologist, tchr. NYU, Reading Inst., 1948-50; asst. dir., sr. psychologist N.Y. U. Testing and Advisement Ctr., 1950-70; instr. psychol. tests and measurements Bank St. Coll. of Edn., 1970; psychologist, dir. Internat. Sch. Psychol. Svc., 1964-65, 70-71; assoc. prof., counselor Kingsborough Community Coll., Bklyn., 1971—; cons. in field. Exec. bd. Metro. Coll. Mental Health Assn., 1980-82. Kansas City Honor scholar, 1932-33, 34-36. Mem. Am. Psychol. Assn., Am. Counseling Assn., Nat. Career Devel. Assn., N.Y. Psychol. Assn., Ea. Psychol. Assn., Soc. for Personality Assessment, Nat. Assn. Sch. Psychologists, Internat. Coun. Psychologists, Soc. Friends. Home: 44 W 10th St New York NY 10011-8762 Office: Kingsborough Community Coll Manhattan Beach Brooklyn NY 11235

PROFFIT, WILLIAM ROBERT, orthodontics educator; b. Harnett County, N.C., Apr. 19, 1936; s. Glenn Theodore and Edna Marie (Queener) P.; m. Sara Thomas, Sept. 20, 1953; children: Lola Ann, Edward Thomas, Glenn Theodore. BS, U. N.C., 1956, DDS, 1959; student, Campbell Coll., Buies Creek, N.C., 1952-53; PhD, Med. Coll. Va., 1962; MS, U. Wash., 1963; FDS, Royal Coll. Surgeons, 1990. Am. Bd. Orthodontics. Investigator Nat. Inst. Dental Research, Bethesda, Md., 1963-65; asst. prof. orthodontics U. Ky., Lexington, 1965-68, assoc. prof., 1968-71; prof. U.Ky., Lexington, 1971-73; prof. orthodontics U. Fla., Gainesville, 1973-75; prof., chmn. dept. orthodontics U. N.C., Chapel Hill, 1975—, Kenan prof., 1992; cons. NIH, Bethesda, 1974, 76—. Author: Contemporary Orthodontics, 1986, 2d edit., 1993; co-author: Surgical Correction of Dentofacial Deformity, 1980, Surgical-Orthodontic Treatment, 1990; contbr. articles to sci. jours. Served to lt. comdr. USPHS, 1963-65. Fulbright research scholar U. Adelaide, Australia, 1972. Mem. Am. Assn. Orthodontists (council on research 1970-76), ADA, Internat. Assn. Dental Research, Phi Beta Kappa. Democrat. Presbyterian. Home: 620 Rock Creek Rd Chapel Hill NC 27514-6716 Office: U NC Sch Dentistry Orthodontics Dept Chapel Hill NC 27599

PROKESCH, CLEMENS ELIAS, physician; b. Dorchester, Mass., Nov. 21, 1918; s. Solomon Zischa and Ray Lillian (Brooks) P.; m. Jeanne Harriet Chase, Apr. 29, 1945 (dec. May 1976); children: Richard Chase, Steven Edward, Linda Dale Prokesch Foster; m. Natalie Gourse, July 27, 1980. BS, Yale U., 1939; MS, MIT, 1945; MD, N.Y. Med. Coll., 1949; cert. in internal medicine, NYU Postgrad. Med. Sch., 1952. Intern Englewood (N.J.) Hosp., 1949-50, resident in internal medicine, 1950-51; pvt. practice, 1954—; sr. active attending physician Lawrence and Meml. Hosp., New London, Conn., 1954—. Capt. USAF, 1952-54. Fellow ACP; mem. German Soc. Ea. Conn. (v.p.), Thames Stamp Club (pres. 1959-84, pres. emeritus 1984—). Democrat. Jewish. Home: 30 Admiral Dr New London CT 06320-4202 Office: 435 Montauk Ave New London CT 06320-4629

PROKOP-ROBERTS, JOAN DIANE, nursing educator, folk dance educator; b. Berwyn, Ill., June 24, 1946; d. Otto James and Pauline Anne (Smith) Prokop; m. Ronald Roberts, Aug. 1972 (div. Aug. 1976). BS in Nursing, U. Md., 1968; M in Nursing, UCLA, 1976. RN, Calif.; cert. orthopedic nurse, nursing staff devel. Staff nurse surg. unit, relief nurse supr. Victor Valley Hosp., Victorville, Calif., 1971-72; nursing supr. Sherman Oaks (Calif.) Community Hosp., 1974; surg. asst. Dr. Richard Dauphine, Monterey, Calif., 1979-80; nursing supr. Eskaton Monterey Hosp., Monterey, Calif., 1976-83, Natividad Med. Ctr., Salinas, Calif., 1983-84; sr. instr. Natividad Med. Ctr., Salinas, 1984-90, dir. ednl. svcs., 1990-93; sr. instr., 1993—; coord., instr. Pro-Ed Svcs., Marina, Calif., 1977-82; instr. adult Israeli Folkdance classes, 1983—, children's classes, 1991—, coord. performing group 1985—. Contbr. articles to Orthopedic Nursing Assn. Jour. Maj. Nurse Corps, U.S. Army, 1964-71, USAR, 1971-86. Mem. Nat. Assn. Orthopedic Nurses, Nat. Nursing Staff Devel. Orgn., Tri-County Educator's Network (founder 1990), Sigma Theta Tau. Home: 119 Redondo Ct Marina CA 93933-2133 Office: Natividad Med Ctr 1330 Natividad Rd Salinas CA 93906-3101

PROLL, GEORGE SIMON, psychologist; b. Würzburg, Germany, June 30, 1931; s. Jack Ignatz and Irma (Kramer) P.; came to U.S., 1936, naturalized, 1943; B.A., Yale, 1953; M.A., Boston U., 1958, Ph.D., 1962; m. Rita Rosina Rado, Aug. 9, 1954; children—Lauren, Douglas. Intern clin. psychology VA, Brockton, also Bedford, Lowell (all Mass.), 1958-62; dir. dept. psychology, psychologist mental health clinic Trenton Psychiat. Hosp., 1962-67, East Hosp., 1973-75; prin. clin. psychologist Ancora Psychiat. Hosp., 1975—, dir. psychology tng. program, 1980-86; dir. profl. services Youth Reception, Correction Center, Yardville, N.J., 1967-73; pvt. practice clin. psychology, Willingboro, N.J., 1969—. Mem. exec. bd. Psychol. Services Center, Trenton, 1965-66; mem. Drug Study Commn., Willingboro, 1971-72; mem. steering com. Community Mental Health Center, Princeton, N.J., 1973. Served with USN, 1955-57. Winner several chess competitions, including State N.H., 1957, State Mass., 1962, So. N.J., 1971, 74, N.J. Amateur Class A, 1972, South Jersey, 1983, first place, 1984, Chess Trophy U.S. Amateur Championship, 1990, 94. Mem. Am., N.J. (Burlington County rep. to legis. com. 1968-72), psychol. assns. Club: Cherry Hill (N.J.) Chess. Home: 48 Trebing Ln Twin Hill Park Willingboro NJ 08046 Office: Ancora Psychiat Hosp Hammonton NJ 08037-9699

PROMISLOFF, ROBERT ALAN, medical educator, health facility administrator. BA, Temple U., 1969; DO, Phila. Coll. Osteopathic Medicine, 1973. Diplomate Am. Bd. Internal Medicine. Intern straight internal medicine Phila. Gen. Hosp., 1973-74; resident Hahnemann U. Hosp., Phila., 1974-76, apptd. chief resident and tchg. fellow sr. resident, 1975-76, fellow pulmonary diseases, 1976-78, dir. sch. respiratory therapy, 1985-87, acting dir. divsn. pulmonary diseases, 1985-87, med. dir. dept. respiratory therapy, 1985-90, med. dir. pulmonary function lab., 1985-90, clin. dir., dir. pulmonary fellowship program pulmonary divsn., 1987-89; dir. pulmonary divsn. Havertown (Pa.) Cmty. Hosp., 1981—; sec. med. staff Haverford (Pa.) Cmty. Hosp., 1983-84, pres. med. staff, 1985—; asst. prof. clin. medicine Sch. Medicine Hahnemann U., Phila., 1986-88, clin. assoc. prof. medicine Sch. Medicine, 1988—. Fellow Am. Coll. Physicians, Am. Coll. Chest Physicians (coun. critical care); mem. Pa. County Med. Soc., Pa. Soc. Pulmonary Disease. Home: 516 Hoffman Dr Bryn Mawr PA 19010 Office: Respiratory Assocs Ltd West Bldg 101 City Line Ave Wynnewood PA 19096

PRONG, LINDA LEE, counselor, educator; b. Detroit, Apr. 9, 1953; d. Franklin and Patricia Ann (Bishop) St. Louis; children: Clint Stephen, Nathan Carl, Paul David. BSW, Wayne State U., 1987, MSW, 1988; postgrad., UCLA, 1991. Dir. social svcs. Pathways Vol. Hospice, Long Beach, Calif.; missionary to Chile Delta (Ohio) Ch. of Christ; coord. AIDS program La Casa, Detroit; chmn. AIDS Conf., Wayne State U., Detroit, 1988; adj. prof. Calif. State U., Long Beach; asst. prof. Pacific Christian Coll., Fullerton, Calif. Recipient hon. mention Leadership award Wayne State U., Exceptional Svc. award Sch. Social Work, Wayne State U., 1990, Gold Fellowship, UCLA, 1990. Mem. NASW, Nat. Hospice Orgn., Calif. Hospice Orgn.

PRONOVE-IRREVERRE, PACITA, medical officer; b. Manila, Philippines, Oct. 12, 1919; d. Ricardo Avenido and Dolores (Laico) Pronove; m. Filadelfo Irreverre, Dec. 30, 1950. AA, U. Philippines, 1939, MD, 1944. Diplomate Am. Acad. Pediatrics. Physician Pasay City Health Dept., Philippines, 1946-52; pediatric resident Childrens Hosp., Washington, 1952-54; rsch. assoc. NIH, Bethesda, Md., 1959-61, scientist, adminstr., 1961-73. co-discoverer Bartter's Syndrome. Pres. Pasay City Jr. Women's Club, Manila, 1948, Philippine Jr. Women's Clubs, Manila, 1950. Outstanding Alumnae award U. Philippines Coll. Medicine, 1987. Home: 4470 N Camino De Carrillo Tucson AZ 85750-6307

PROPST, MICHAEL TRUMAN, pathologist; b. Lebanon, Oreg., July 3, 1940; s. Lynn Edward and Vera Ruth (Forbes) P.; m. Susan Jean Joesting, Dec. 26, 1974; children: Christopher M., Andrew J., Matthew A., Michael Jonathan, Edwin Cam. BS, Oreg. State U., 1962; MD, U. Oreg., 1966. Diplomate Am. Bd. Pathology. Pathologist Humana Hosp., Anchorage, 1974-84; med. examiner State of Alaska, Anchorage, 1975-94; med. dir. Physicians Med. Lab., Anchorage, 1984-94; chief med. examiner State of Alaska, Anchorage, 1994—. Served to maj. USAF, 1971-74. Fellow Coll. Am. Pathologists, Am. Soc. Clin. Pathologists, Am. Acad. Forensic Scientists, Royal Soc. Medicine (Gr. Britain), ; mem. Nat. Assn. Med. Examiners. Episcopalian. Office: State Med Examiner 5700 E Tudor Rd Anchorage AK 99507

PRÓSPERO, FLÁVIO CORRÊA, health care company executive; b. São Paulo, Brazil, Oct. 2, 1942; s. Dalmo and Maria (Corrêa) P.; m. Maria Ines Rimoli, Jan. 17, 1967 (div. Jan. 1981); children: Marcos R., Luciano R., Flávia Rimoli; m. Nereide Aparecida Bonato, Feb. 8, 1983; 1 child, Saulo José Bonato. B in Engring., Poly Sch. U. São Paulo, 1966; postgrad., Getulio Vargas Found., São Paulo, 1975. Cert. engineer. Engring. trainee Alcan, São Paulo, 1965-66; sys. analyst IBM, São Paulo, 1967-68; project devel. engr. Asplan S.A., São Paulo, 1968-70; project mgr. Simonsen Assocs., São Paulo, 1971; investment mgr. Denasa-Bank of Investment, São Paulo, 1972-74; pres. Denasa São Paulo, 1974-75; mgr. planning and control Villares Industria de Base, São Paulo, 1976-80; gen. mgr. Logos Engenharia S.A., São Paulo, 1980-94; pres. Logos Pró-Saúde S.A., São Paulo, 1987—; cons. Planasa S.A., São Paulo, 1967-69; prof. bus. Alvares Penteado Found., São Paulo, 1974-80; prof. mgmt. constrn. Getulio Vargas Found., São Paulo, 1983-92. Pres. Terrafoto S.A., São Paulo, 1983-87, G.E.G.E., São Paulo, 1989-90, Life Quality Group, São Paulo, 1991-92, Sorri Brazil, São Paulo, 1993-94. Mem. Brazilian Soc. of Quality Life (pres. 1995—). Brazilian Social Democrat. Roman Catholic. Home: Rua Vergueiro 3645 Apt 610, 04101-300 São Paulo Brazil Office: Logos Pró-Saúde SA, Rua Sampaio Viana 253, 04004000 São Paulo Brazil

PROUDFIT, CAROL MARIE, pharmacologist; b. Cin., Nov. 22, 1937; m. Herbert K. Proudfit, Sept. 12, 1970 (div. 1981); 1 child, Amanda. BS, U. Cin., 1959; PhD, U. Kans., 1971; MBA, Rosary Coll., 1986; MPH, U. Ill., 1995. Lectr. Triton Coll., River Grove, Ill., 1974, Northwestern U. Evanston, Ill., 1975, U. Ill. Med. Ctr., Chgo., 1975—; sr. scientist AMA, Chgo., 1976-88, asst. div. dir., project mgr. drug evaluations, 1988—; reviewer drug monographs U.S. Pharmacopeia, Washington, 1984—. Mem. editl. bd. Drug Evaluations Ann. and Subscription, 1990-95; contbr. articles to profl. jours. Pres. Sounds of Joy Choristers, Oak Park, Ill., 1980-83; print chmn. Oak Park Camera Club, 1977-1979. Mem. APHA, Drug Info. Assn., Am. Soc. for Reproductive Medicine, Am. Soc. Clin. Pharmacology and Therapeutics, Am. Diabetes Assn. Office: AMA Group on Sci Tech Health 515 N State St Chicago IL 60610-4320

PROUGH, RUSSELL ALLEN, biochemistry educator; b. Twin Falls, Idaho, Nov. 5, 1943; s. Elza Leroy and Beulah Elsie (Huddleston) P.; M. Betty Marie Ehlers, Dec. 26, 1965; children: Jennifer Sally, Kimberly Marie. BS in Chemistry, Coll. of Idaho, 1965; PhD in Biochemistry and Biophysics, Oreg. State U., 1969. Postdoctoral fellow VA Hosp., Kansas City, Mo., 1969-72; instr. biochemistry U. Tex. Southwestern Med. Sch., Dallas, 1972-73, asst. prof. biochemistry, 1973-77, assoc. prof. biochemistry, 1977-82, prof. biochemistry, 1982-86; prof., chmn. dept. biochemistry U. Louisville Sch. Med., 1986—; mem. NIH Toxicology Study Sect., 1984-88, State of Nebr. Smoking Disease and Cancer Rsch. Program, 1984-91. Assoc. editor Drug Metabolism and Disposition, 1994—. Recipient Rsch. Career Devel. award USPHS. Mem. Am. Soc. Biochemistry and Molecular Biology, Am. Assn. Cancer Rsch., Am. Soc. Pharmacology and Exptl. Therapeutics, Internat. Soc. for Study of Xenobiotics, Sigma Xi. Lutheran. Office: U of Louisville Dept of Biochemistry Louisville KY 40292

PROUT, CURTIS, physician; b. Swampscott, Mass., Oct. 13, 1915; s. Henry Byrd and Eloise (Willett) P.; m. Daphne Brooks, June 27, 1939 (div. 1985); children: Diana P. Cherot, Daphne P. Cook, Rosamond P. Warren, Phyllis P. Brosius; m. Diane Neal Emmons, Dec. 7, 1985. AB, Harvard U., 1937, MD, 1941. Diplomate Am. Bd. Internal Medicine. Intern Peter Bent Brigham Hosp., Boston, 1942; resident in internal medicine Johns Hopkins Hosp., Balt., 1943; research fellow Mass. Gen. Hosp., Boston, 1943-45; practice medicine specializing in internal medicine, 1945—; asst. dir. Univ. Health Services Harvard U., Cambridge, Mass., 1961-72; dir. prison health project Office of Econ. Opportunity, 1972-74; asst. dean Harvard Med. Sch., Boston, 1980-90, asst. clin. prof., 1975-82; trustee Humane Soc. of Mass., Boston, 1975-87; bd. dirs. Nat. Commn. on Correctional Health Care, 1980—, chmn., 1990; dir., treas. The Med. Found., Boston, 1980—. Chmn. Bd. Health, Dover, Mass., 1960-75. Fellow Am. Coll. Physicians, Mass. Med. Soc.; mem. AMA, Am. Clin. and Climatol. Assn. Clubs: Tavern (Boston) (pres. 1980-82); Manchester Yacht (Mass.). Home: 115 School St Manchester MA 01944-1232 Office: 319 Longwood Ave Boston MA 02115-5710

PROUT, GEORGE RUSSELL, JR., medical educator, urologist; b. Boston, July 23, 1924; s. George Russell and Marion (Snow) P.; m. Loa Katherine Wheatley, Oct. 17, 1950; children: George Russell III, Elizabeth Louise. Student, Union Coll., 1943, DSc (hon.), 1990; MD, Albany Med. Coll., 1947, DSc (hon.), 1988; MA (hon.), Harvard U., 1969. Intern Grasslands Hosp., Valhalla, N.Y., 1947-48; resident N.Y. Hosp., N.Y.C., 1952-56; asst. attending physician Meml. Ctr. for Cancer and Allied Disease, N.Y.C., 1956-57; asst. clinician in surgery James Ewing Hosp., N.Y.C., 1956-57; assoc. prof., chmn. div. urology U. Miami, 1957-60; prof., chmn. div. urology Med. Coll. Va., 1960-69; chief urol. svc. Mass. Gen. Hosp., Boston, 1969-89; prof. surgery Harvard Med. Sch., 1969-89; emeritus prof. surgery Harvard Med. Sch., Boston, 1989—; hon. urologist Mass. Gen. Hosp., Boston, 1993—; chmn. Adjuvants in Surg. Treatment of Bladder Cancer; mem. adv. task force to Nat. Cancer Inst., 1968—, expert cons. divsn. surveillance, 1991—, Finland coop. ATBC study, 1991—; chmn. Nat. Bladder Cancer Group, 1973-86. Editor-in-chief Urologic Oncology, 1994—. With USNR, 1950-52. Fellow ACS, Acad. Medicine Toronto (corr.); mem. AMA, AAUP, Am. Urol. Assn., Can. Urol. Assn., Am. Cancer Soc., Soc. Pelvic Surgeons, Soc. Surg. Oncology, Soc. Univ. Urologists, Dallas. So. Clin. Soc. (hon.), Am. Assn. Genitourinary Surgeons, Soc. Pediatric Urology, Soc. Urol. Oncology, Soc. Internat. Urologists, Soc. Basic Urol. Rsch., Alpha Omega Alpha. Home and Office: 27 W Prospect Bay Dr Grasonville MD 21638-9668 Winter address: 224 Corsair Rd Marathon FL 33050

PROVENZANO, JOSEPH J., emergency and family practice physician; b. Houston, Dec. 14, 1954; s. Joe Johnnie and Margaret Gladys (Toman) P.; m. Mimi Dygert, Dec. 27, 1979 (div. Dec. 1987); m. Lisa Michelle Masson, May 7, 1989; children: Destie Jo, Gina Gayl, Noelle Joy. BS, U. Houston, 1977; DO, Tex. Coll. Osteopathic Med., 1983. Diplomate Am. Bd. Family Practice. Pharmacist Eckerds Pharmacy, Houston, 1977-79; emergency physician Fishcer Mangold, Wichita Falls, Tex., 1980-90; physician Gould Med., Modesto, Calif., 1990—. Fellow Am. Acad. Family Practice; mem. Calif. Med. Assn., Tex. Med. Assn., Tex. Osteopathic Med. Assn. Office: Gould Med Found 600 Coffee Rd Modesto CA 95355

PROVINE, ROBERT RAYMOND, psychology educator; b. Tulsa, May 11, 1943; s. Robert William and Thelma Fern (Morgan) P.; children—Kimberly G., Robert W. B.S., Okla. State U., 1965; Ph.D., Washington U., St. Louis, 1971. Research assoc. Washington U., 1971-72, research asst. prof. 1971-74; asst. prof. to prof. psychology, researcher neural and behavioral devel., human ethology U. Md. Baltimore County, Balt., 1974—. Contbr. articles to profl. jours., chpts. in books. Mem. Soc. for Neurosci., Psychonomic Soc., Animal Behavior Soc., Am. Psychol. Soc., Internat. Soc. for Developmental Psychobiology, Sigma Xi, Psi Chi. Avocations: astronomy; photography, Tae Kwon Do. Office: Dept Psychology U Md Baltimore County Baltimore MD 21228

PROVOST, RHONDA MARIE, nurse anesthetist; b. Quincy, Mass., Sept. 13, 1948; d. John Stanley and Roberta Adelaide (Tangstrom) P. RN, Quincy City Hosp. Sch. Nursing, 1969, Nurse Anesthetist, 1971; BS, George Washington U., 1982. Cert. registered nurse anesthetist. Staff anesthetist, instr. Children's Hosp. Med. Ctr., Boston, 1971-77; staff anesthetist George Washington U. Med. Ctr., Washington, 1977-78; dir. Sch. of Anesthesia, New Eng. Med. Ctr. Hosp., Boston, 1978-79; staff anesthetist Kaiser-Permanente Med. Group, Redwood City, Calif., 1979-88, chief anesthetist, 1988-89, Santa Rosa, Calif., 1989-91, staff anesthetist, 1991—; freelance anesthetist Pregnancy Counseling Ctr., San Jose, Calif., 1983-84, Plastic Reconstructive Ambulatory Ctr., Los Altos, Calif., 1984-85; treas. Specific Publs., Inc., 1983—, v.p., sales dir., 1991—. Co-author: Indoor Exercise Book, 1981, Advanced Indoor Exercise Book, 1982, Feeling Fit in Your Forties, 1986; also articles; TV race commentator 2d Ann. Manila Internat. Marathon, 1983. Sec. bd. dirs. Grant Ave. Condominium Owners Assn., Palo Alto, Calif., 1984, v.p. bd. dirs., 1985. Mem. Am. Assn. Nurse Anesthetists, Calif. Assn. Nurse Anesthetists, Toastmasters. Roman Catholic. Avocations: triathletics, ultradistance running, piano, snow skiing. Home: 7050 Giusti Rd Forestville CA 95436-9637 Office: The Permanente Med Group 401 Bicentennial Way Santa Rosa CA 95403-2149

PROVOST, THOMAS TAYLOR, dermatology educator, researcher; b. Pitts., Mar. 21, 1938; s. Charles Thomas and Marcelle K. (Taylor) P.; m. Carol Sara Christie, July 2, 1960; children: Charles T., Christie Lynn, Thomas Wright. AB, U. Pitts., 1958, MD, 1962. Resident in dermatology Dartmouth Med. Ctr., Hanover, N.H., 1966-67, U. Oreg. Med. Ctr., Portland, 1967-68; fellow in immunology SUNY, Buffalo, 1969-72, asst. prof. dermatology, 1972-75, assoc. prof., 1975-78; assoc. prof. Johns Hopkins U. Med. Sch., Balt., 1978-82, prof., dept. chmn., 1982—. Lt. commdr. USPHS, 1962-64. Mem. Soc. Investigative Dermatology, Soc. Clin. Investigation. Office: Johns Hopkins U Sch of Medicine 720 Rutland Ave Baltimore MD 21205-2109

PRUCHNIEWSKI, JAMES, podiatrist; b. Buffalo, Dec. 27, 1947; s. Frank and Leona (Czechowski) P. BS, Niagara U., 1969; MS, Canisius Coll., 1972; DPM, Scholl Coll. Podiatric Med., 1986. Diplomate Am. Bd. Podiatric Orthopedics & Primary Podiatric Medicine, Am. Acad. Pain Mgmt., Am. Acad. Ambulatory Foot Surgery. Tchr. Lancaster (N.Y.) Ctrl. Schs., 1969-82; podiatrist North Lakeland (Fla.) Foot Clinic, 1988—. Dir. religious edn. St. Bernard Roman Catholic Ch., Buffalo, 1969. Fellow Am. Coll. Foot & Ankle Orthopedists. Democrat. Office: North Lakeland Foot Clinic 930 Marcum Rd Lakeland FL 33809

PRUETT, CLAYTON DUNKLIN, biotechnical company executive; b. Montgomery, Ala., June 16, 1935; s. William Rogers and Myra Eleanor (Ganey) P.; m. Barbara Clapp, Feb. 22, 1974; children: Christopher Blair, Tyler Michael. BSCE, Auburn U., 1956. Profl. engr., Ala. Civil engr. Ala. State Hwy Dept., Montgomery, 1956-57; lt. USAF, 1957; civil engr. USAF, Andrews AFB, 1959-64; staff assoc. Gen. Atomic div. Gen. Dynamics, La Jolla, Calif., 1964-68; exec. v.p. Enviro-Med Inc., La Jolla, 1968-73; chmn. bd. CDP Svcs., Inc., Atlanta, 1973—; pres., CEO Advanced Cancer Techs., Inc., Atlanta, 1988-95. Bd. dirs. Am. Cancer Soc., 1986-90, U. Calif., San Diego Cancer Ctr. Found, 1989—, Nat. Childhood Cancer Found., 1990—. Mem. San Diego Yacht Club. Home: PO Box 2304 Rancho Santa Fe CA 92067-2304 Office: CDP Svcs Inc 1050 Crown Pointe Pky Atlanta GA 30338-7707

PRUETT, KYLE DEAN, psychiatrist, writer, educator; b. Raton, N.Mex., Aug. 27, 1943; s. Ozie Douthitt Pruett and Velma Lorraine Smith; children: Elizabeth Storr, Emily Farrar. BA in History, Yale U., 1965; D of Medicine, Tufts U., 1969. Intern Mt. Auburn Hosp.-Harvard U., 1969-70; resident in psychiat. medicine Tufts-New England Med. Ctr., Boston, 1970-72; child psychiatry fellow Child Study Ctr., Yale U., New Haven, 1972-74, asst. clin. prof. psychiatry, 1975-79, assoc. clin. prof., 1979-87, clin. prof., 1987—; dir. child devel. unit Yale U., 1982—; attending physician dept. child psychiatry Yale-New Haven Hosp., 1972—; cons. psychiatrist Guilford (Conn.) Pub. Schs., 1977—; vis. scholar Sch. Medicine, U. Vt., 1987, Sch. Medicine, U. N.Mex., 1988; mem. editorial bd. Med. Problems of Performing Artists jour., 1983—, Good Housekeeping mag., 1987—; bd. dirs. Zero to Three: Nat. Ctr. for Clin. Infant Programs, Washington; cons. CBS News, Lifetime. Author: The Nurturing Father, 1988 (Am. Health Book award 1988); contbr. numerous articles to profl. jours.; host biweekly TV series Your Child 6 to 12 with Dr. Kule Pruett Lifetime TV, 1993-94. Mem. med. adv. bd. Scholastic, Inc., 1988—, Yale U. Program for Humanities in Medicine, 1989—, World Assn. for Infant Mental Health, 1979—, CBS-TV Family Time, 1989—, Wellesley Child Study Ctr.; prin. tenor Conn. Chancel Opera Co., New Haven, 1983—. Vis. fellow Anna Freud Clinic, London, 1975; recipient Mayoral Citation, City of Indpls., 1987. Mem. Am. Acad. Child and Adolescent Psychiatry, Am. Psychiat. Assn., Soc. for Rsch. in Family Therapy, Physicians for Social Responsibility, Nat. Assn. Physician Broadcasters (CBS news cons. 1989—), Zero to Three (Nat. Ctr. for Clin. Infant Programs pres.-elect 1995—), Yale U. Glee Club Alumni Assn. (pres.

1985-89). Home: 10 Fernwood Dr Guilford CT 06437-2349 Office: Yale Child Study Ctr 333 Cedar St New Haven CT 06510-3206

PRUITT, ALBERT W., dean; b. Anderson, S.C., Jan. 1, 1940; s. James Ernest and Jennie L. (Burdette) P.; m. Ellanor Frances Hanson, June 3, 1961; 1 child, Nora Taplin Pruitt Krist. BA, Emory U., 1961, MD, 1965. Mem. pediatrics faculty Emory U. Sch. Medicine, Altanta, 1972-82; chmn. pediatrics Med. Coll. Ga., Augusta, 1982-92; dean. coll. medicine, v.p. med. affairs USA Coll. Medicine, Mobile, Ala., 1992—. Contbr. articles to profl. jours., chpts. to books. Maj. U.S. Army, 1978-80. Fellow Am. Acad. Pediatrics (com. chair), Ga. Acad. Pediatrics (pres.); mem. Alpha Omega Alpha. Episcopalian. Office: U South Ala Coll Medicine CSAB170 307 University Blvd Mobile AL 36688

PRUITT, ALICIA COMPTON, clinical nurse, emergency room nurse; b. Houston, July 19, 1967; d. Escol Burvis and Janet Elaine (Dreusedow) Compton; m. William Steven Pruitt, Dec. 23, 1991; children: Nicholas, Thomas. Student, Tex. Tech U., 1987; BSN, Midwestern State U., Wichita Falls, Tex., 1993. RN, Tex.; cert. emergency nurse; cert. sexual assault nurse examiner; cert. BLS, ACLS, ACLS instr., PALS, BLS instr., TNCC. Cmty. svc. officer City of Wichita Falls, Tex., 1988-90; clin. asst. Wichita Gen. Hosp., Wichita Falls, 1992-93, nurse, 1993—. Mem. ANA, Emergency Nurses Asn., Sigma Theta Tau Internat. (Xi Iota chpt.). Republican. Presbyterian. Office: Wichita Gen Hosp Emergency Dept 1600 8th St Wichita Falls TX 76301

PRUITT, JEFFREY ALLYN, surgeon, educator; b. Dayton, Ohio, July 3, 1961; s. John Albert and Martha Sue (Burnsides) P.; m. Kristine S. Grenda, Jan. 27, 1990; 1 child, Lauren. BS in Engring., Wright State U., 1983; MD, Med. Coll. Ohio, 1987. Diplomate Am. Bd. Surgery. Surgeon Defiance (Ohio) Clinic, 1993—; clin. assoc. prof. surgery Med. Coll. Ohio, Toledo, 1993—; bd. mem. NWO Advs. for Women's Health. Fellow ACS (assoc.); mem. AMA, Ohio State Med. Assn., Defiance County Med. Soc., Soc. Laproendoscopic Surgeons. Office: Defiance Clinic 1400 E Second St Defiance OH 43512

PRUS, JOSEPH STANLEY, psychology educator, consultant; b. Glen Cove, N.Y., Mar. 9, 1952; s. Joseph Stanley and Constance Mary (Lamp) P.; m. Audrey Kaye Mink, Apr. 19, 1980; children: Erin Marie, Elizabeth Lauren Scudder. Student, St. John Fisher Coll., Rochester, N.Y., 1970-72; BA, U. Ky., 1974, MA, 1975, PhD, 1979. Lic. sch. psychologist, S.C., Ky.; nat. cert. sch. psychologist. Coord. psychology human devel. program U. Ky., Lexington, 1978-79, assoc. dir. human devel. program, 1979-80; from asst. to assoc. prof. Winthrop U., Rock Hill, S.C., 1980-89, prof., 1989—, dir. Office of Assessment, Sch. Psychology Program, 1988—; cons. Cardinal Hill Hosp., Lexington, 1977-80, U. Ariz., Tucson, 1984-85, Lancaster (S.C.) Mental Retardation Bd., 1987—; numerous presentations in field. Author: Handbook of Certification for School Psychologists, 1989; also numerous articles. Bd. dirs. Wesley Found., 1985-87; chmn. bd. dirs. Rock Hill Girls' Home, 1987-91. Recipient Disting. Prof. award Winthrop U., 1989; numerous grants from state and nat. agys. Mem. APA, NASP (presdl. citation 1993, 96), S.C. Assn. Sch. Psychologists (Outstanding Contbns. to Sch. Psychology award 1991), Phi Beta Kappa, Psi Chi. Home: 2430 Colebrook Dr Rock Hill SC 29732-9411 Office: Winthrop U Dept Psychology Rock Hill SC 29733

PRUSINER, STANLEY BEN, neurology and biochemistry educator, researcher; b. Des Moines, May 28, 1942; s. Lawrence Albert and Miriam (Spigel) P.; m. Sandra Lee Turk, Oct. 18, 1970; children: Helen Chloe, Leah Anne. AB cum laude, U. Pa., 1964, MD, 1968; PhD (hon.), Hebrew U., Jerusalem, 1995. Diplomate Am. Bd. Neurology. Intern in medicine U. Calif., San Francisco, 1968-69, resident in neurology, 1972-74, asst. prof. neurology, 1974-80, assoc. prof., 1980-84, prof., 1984—, prof. biochemistry, 1988—, acad. senate faculty rsch. lectr., 1989-90; prof. virology U. Calif., Berkeley, 1984—; mem. neurology rev. com. Nat. Inst. Neurol. Disease and Strokes, NIH, Bethesda, Md., 1982-86, 90-92; mem. sci. adv. bd. French Fedn., L.A., 1985—; mem. sci. rev. com. Alzheimer's Disease Diagnostic Ctr. & Rsch. Grant Program, State of Calif., 1985-89; chmn. sci. adv. bd. Am. Health Assistance Found., Rockville, Md., 1986—. Editor: The Enzymes of Glutamine Metabolism, 1973, Slow Transmissible Diseases of the Nervous System, 2 vols., 1979, Prions--Novel Infectious Pathogens Causing Scrapie and CJD, 1987, Prion Diseases of Humans and Animals, 1992, Molecular and Genetic Basis of Neurologic Disease, 1993, Prions Prions Prions, 1996—; contbr.more than 200 articles to profl. jours. Mem. adv. bd. Family Survival Project for Adults with Chronic Brain Disorders, San Francisco, 1982—, San Francisco chpt. Alzheimer's Disease and Related Disorder Assn., 1985—. Lt. comdr. USPHS, 1969-72. Recipient Leadership and Excellence for Alzheimer's Disease award NIH, 1990—, Potamkin prize for Alzheimer's Disease Rsch., 1991, Presl. award, 1993, Med. Rsch. award Met. Life Found., 1992, Christopher Columbus Discovery award NIH and Med. Soc. Genoa, Italy, 1992, Charles A. Dana award for pioneering achievements in health, 1992, Dickson prize for outstanding contbns. to medicine U. Pitts., 1992, Max Planck Rsch. award Alexander von Humboldt Found. and Max Planck Soc., 1992, Gairdner Found. Internat. award, 1993, Disting. Achievement in Neurosci. Rsch. award Bristol-Myers Squibb, 1994, Albert Lasker award for Basic Med. Rsch., 1994, Caledonian Rsch. Found. prize Royal Soc. Edinburgh, 1995, Paul Ehrlich and Ludwig Darmstaedter award Germany, 1995, Paul Hoch award Am. Psychopathol. Assn., 1995, Wolf prize in medicine, 1996, ICN Virology prize, 1996, Charles-Leopold prize French Acad. Scis., 1996, Keio Internat. award in medicine, 1996, Victor and Clara Soriano award World Fedn. Neurology, 1996; Alfred P. Sloan Rsch. fellow U. Calif., 1976-78; Med. Investigator grantee Howard Hughes Med. Inst., 1976-81; grantee for excellence in neurosci. Senator Jacob Javits Ctr., NIH, 1985-90. Mem. NAS (Inst. Medicine, Richard Lounsbery award for extraordinary achievements in biology and medicine 1993), Am. Acad. Arts and Scis., Am. Acad. Neurology (George Cotzias award for outstanding rsch. 1987, Presdl. award 1993), Am. Assn. Physicians, Am. Soc. Microbiology, Am. Soc. Neurochemistry, Internat. Soc. Neurochemistry, Am. Soc. Virology, Am. Neurol. Assn., Am. Soc. Clin. Investigation, Am. Soc. Cellular Biology, Am. Soc. Molecular Biol. Biochemistry, Protein Soc., Concordia Argonaut Club.

PRUSOFF, WILLIAM HERMAN, biochemical pharmacologist, educator; b. N.Y.C., June 25, 1920; s. Samuel and Mary (Metrick) P.; m. Brigitte Auerbach, June 19, 1948 (dec. Apr. 1991); children—Alvin Saul, Laura Ann. B.A., U. Miami, Fla., 1941; M.A., Columbia U., 1947, Ph.D., 1949. Research assoc., instr. pharmacology Western Res. U., 1949-53; mem. faculty Yale Med. Sch., 1953—, prof. pharmacology, 1966-90, prof. emeritus. sr. rsch. scientist, 1990—, acting chmn. dept., 1968; cons. in field, 1965—. Mem. Am. Assn. Cancer Rsch., Am. Chem. Soc., Am. Soc. Biol. Chemists, Am. Soc. Pharmacology and Exptl. Therapeutics, Soc. Chinese Bioscientists in Am., Sigma Xi, Internat. Soc. for Antiviral Rsch. Home: De Forest Dr Branford CT 06471 Office: Yale U Sch Medicine New Haven CT 06510

PRUSZENSKI, AMY DEE, optometrist; b. Bethesda, Md.. BS, MIT, 1989; D of Optometry, New England Coll. Optometry, 1989. Optometrist Rockingham Eye Assocs., Salem, N.H., 1993-95; instr., researcher New England Coll. Optometry, Boston, 1993—; optometrist pvt. practice, Newington, N.H., 1995—. Recipient Grederick Brock award, 1993. Mem. Am. Optometric Assn., New England Coun. Optometrists, N.H. Optometric Assn. Office: Sears Optical Fox Run Mall Newington NH 03801

PRUZANSKY, MARK ELIOT, orthopedic surgeon, hand surgeon, sports physician; b. N.Y.C., July 4, 1948; s. Leon and Pearl (Buchbinder) P.; m. Sheila Erlich, Sept. 8, 1979; children: Jason, Julie. BA cum laude, Columbia U., 1970; MD, Mt. Sinai Med. Sch., 1974. Diplomate Am. Bd. Orthopedic Surgery; bd. cert. in hand surgery. Cert. in endoscopic carpal tunnel release surgery, 1992. Fellow, hand surgery So. Bapt. Hosp., New Orleans, 1978-79, Presbyn. Hosp., San Francisco, 1979-80; surgeon-in charge,, orthopedic hand surgery L.I. Jewish-Hillside (N.Y.) Med. Ctr., 1980-81; fellow, sports medicine Valley Presbyn. Hosp., Van Nuys, Calif., 1983; asst. prof. clin. orthopedics Mt. Sinai Med. Sch., N.Y.C., 1983—; asst. attending staff Beth Israel North Med. Ctr., N.Y.C., 1987—; pvt. practice Pruzansky Hand, Athletic and Sports Trauma Inst., N.Y.C., 1979—; lectr. Genentech Corp., San Francisco, 1988; cons. N.Y. Road Runners Club, 1983—, Dalton Sch. Teams, 1990—. Designed laser disc monitor for patient edn. and injury prevention, touchscrean and video ednl. ctr., computerized, for latient learning about hand, athletic, knee, and shoulder problems, treatment, prevention, and surgery; invented operation for chronic tennis elbow; author: (3 books) Operative Orthopedics, 1995; Complications of Orthopaedic Surgery, 1986; Medical, Surgical, Gynecological Complications of Pregnancy, 1992; contbr. articles to profl. jours. Fellow Am. Acad. Orthopedic Surgery. Office: Pruzansky Hand Athletic & Sports Trauma Ins 975 Park Ave New York NY 10028

PRYOR, CAROL GRAHAM, obstetrician, gynecologist; b. Savannah, Ga.; m. Louis O.J. Manganiello, June 11, 1950; children: Carol Helen, Victoria Manganiello Mudano. AB, Ga. Coll., 1943; MD, Med. Coll. Ga., 1947. Rotating intern City Hosps., Balt., 1947-48; asst. resident pathology Baroness Erlanger Hosp., Chattanooga, 1948; intern. obstetrics City Colls., Balt., 1949; coll. physician Ga. State Coll. for Women, Milledgeville, Ga., 1949-50; resident obstetrics City Hosps., Balt., 1950-51; asst. resident gynecology Univ. Hosp., Balt., 1951-52; sr. resident ob-gyn. Univ. Hosp., Augusta, Ga., 1952; pvt. practice ob-gyn. Augusta, 1952—. Mem., former pres. Iris Garden Club, Augusta; mem. coun. on maternal and infant health State of Ga., Atlanta, 1981-90; mem. edn. found. AAUW, 1961-63, state v.p., br. pres., 1963-65. Recipient Cert. of Achievement-Community Leadersip, Ga. div. AAUW, 1982; named Med. Woman of Yr., Ga. br. 51 Am. Med. Women's Assn., 1961. Fellow am. Coll. Surgeons (1st woman mem. Ga. chpt. 1956), Am. Coll. Ob-Gyn.; mem. AMA, Richmond County Med. Soc., So. Med. Assn., So. Surg. Congress, Delta Kappa Gamma. Democrat. Methodist. Office: 2316 Wrightsboro Rd Augusta GA 30904-6220

PRYOR, JAMES CLIFTON, psychiatrist, psychotherapist; b. Greenville, S.C., June 1, 1959; s. William Watkins and Julia Ann (Smoot) P.; m. Rachel Flora Williams, Dec. 18, 1982; children: Zachary Ward, Rebecca Benn. BS in Chemistry magna cum laude, Furman U., 1981; MD, Med. U. S.C., 1985. Diplomate Nat. Bd. Med. Examiners. Resident in psychiatry Duke U. Med. Ctr., Durham, N.C., 1985-89; fellow in psychopharmacology Vanderbilt U. Med. Ctr., Nashville, Tenn., 1989-90, instr. psychiatry, 1990-91, med. dir., mental hygiene clinic, 1989-90, asst. prof. psychiatry, 1991-93, unit chief, psychiatry in-patient unit, 1992-93; pvt. practice Aiken, S.C., 1993-94; sr. psychiatrist Lexington County Cmty. Mental Health Ctr., West Columbia, S.C., 1994—. Contbr. chpts. to books. Laughlin fellow Am. Coll. Psychiatrists, 1989. Mem. Phi Beta Kappa. Office: Lexington County Cmty Mental Hlth Ctr 1910 Sunset Blvd West Columbia SC 29169

PRYOR, JON L., urologist; b. Hartford, Conn., Oct. 5, 1956; s. Richard and Elizabeth P.; m. Laurie E. Stevens, June 23, 1979; children: Emily, Thomas, Samuel. BA, Carleton Coll., 1979; MD, U. Minn., 1983; MS, U. Va., 1989. Diplomate Am. Bd. Urology. Resident in surgery Hennepin County Med. Ctr., Mpls., 1983-85; resident in urology U. Va., Charlottesville, 1985-89; fellow Am. Found. Urol. Disease, Mpls., 1989-91; asst. prof. U. Minn., Mpls., 1991-96, assoc. prof., 1996—; urol. clin. dir. U. Minn., 1993-95; pres. Minn. Urology, P.A., Mpls., 1995—. Co-editor: Handbook of Andrology. Grantee NIH, 1992—. Mem. Am. Urol. Assn., Am. Soc. Reproductive Medicine, Am. Soc. Andrology (exec. coun. 1994—). Office: Dept Urol Surgery 420 Delaware St SE Minneapolis MN 55455

PRYOR, KAREN WYLIE, biologist, writer; b. N.Y.C., May 14, 1932; d. Philip Gordon Wylie and Sally Ondeck; m. Taylor A. Pryor, June 25, 1954 (div. 1973); children: Tedmund, Michael, Gale; m. Jon M. Lindbergh, May 14, 1983. BA in English, Cornell U., 1954; postgrad., U. Hawaii, 1957-59, NYU, 1977-79, Rutgers U., 1979-82. Founder, curator Sea Life Park Oceanarium, Honolulu, 1960-71; copywriter Fawcett-McDermott, Honolulu, 1973-76; drama critic Honolulu Advertiser, 1971-75; free lance writer, 1963—, marine mammal cons., 1970—; sci. advisor U.S. Tuna Found., Washington, 1976-82; cons. NSF, NASA, Nat. Geographic Soc., 1976—; commr. Marine Mammal Commn., Washington, 1984-87; pres. Sunshine Books, Inc., 1992—; pub. and video prodr. Author: Nursing Your Baby, 1963, rev. edit., 1973, Lads Before the Wind: Adventures in Porpoise Training, 1975, Don't Shoot the Dog! The New Art of Teaching and Training, 1984 (Excellence in Media award APA 1984), How to Teach Your Dog to Play Frisbee, 1985, (with K.S. Norris) Dolphin Societies: Discoveries and Puzzles, 1991; editor: Crunch and Des: Classic Stories of Salt Water Fishing by Philip Wylie, 1991, (with Gale Pryor) Nursing Your Baby, 1991, Karen Pryor on Behavior, 1995; contbr. articles to profl. jours. Mem. Internat. Marine Animal Trainers Assn., Assn. for Behavior Analysis, Animal Behavior Soc., Assn. Zoos and Aquariums, Authors Guild, Marine Mammal Soc. (charter), Soc. Women Geographers, Cosmopolitan Club. Home: 44811 SE 166th St North Bend WA 98045-9007

PUCILLO, ANTHONY LOUIS, physician; b. Mt. Vernon, N.Y., Jan. 29, 1952; s. Louis and Dorothy (Merola) P.; m. Lauren Beth O'Connor, Nov. 10, 1984; 1 child, Andrew. BA, Johns Hopkins U., 1974; MD, Mt. Sinai Sch. Med., 1978. Diplomate Bd. in Internal Medicine and Cardiology. Intern Columbia-Presbyn. Med. Ctr., N.Y., 1978-79; resident in medicine Columbia-Presbyn. Med. Ctr., 1979-81, fellow in cardiology, 1981-84; asst. prof. medicine N.Y. Med. Coll., 1984-90, assoc. prof. medicine, 1990—. Contbr. articles to profl. jours. Fellow Am. Coll. Cardiology; mem. Phi Beta Kappa, Alpha Omega Alpha. Office: Divsn Cardiology Westchester County Med Ctr Valhalla NY 10595

PUCKETT, JAMES BUTLER, internist, educator; b. Charlotte, N.C., Oct. 20, 1947; s. William Olin and Virginia Lewis (House) P.; m. Margaret Ann Tucker, Aug. 18, 1973; 1 child, James William. BS, Davidson (N.C.) Coll., 1970; MD, U. N.C., 1974. Diplomate Am. Bd. Internal Medicine. Intern in medicine Med. Coll. Va., Richmond, 1974-75; resident in internal medicine Bowman Gray Sch. Medicine, Winston-Salem, N.C., 1977-79, fellow in med. oncology, 1979-81; asst. prof. Sch. Medicine U. S.C., Columbia, 1981-83; pvt. practice, H and M Med. Clinic, P.A., Concord, N.C., 1984-90, Asheville, N.C., 1990—; cons. asst. prof. medicine Duke U. Sch. Medicine, Durham, N.C., 1988-90. Contbr. numerous articles to profl. jours. Mem. First Bapt. Ch., Asheville, N.C.; asst. Boy Scouts Am., Concord, 1988-90; active Cabarras County Bd. Health, Concord, 1984-87; v.p. Am. Cancer Soc., Concord, 1988-89, bd. dirs., 1984-90. Capt. U.S. Army, 1975-77. Bullitt Fund scholar U. N.C., 1970-74. Fellow ACP; mem. AMA, N.C. Med. Soc., Buncombe County Med. Soc., Piedmont Oncology Assn., Am. Soc. Clin. Oncology. Democrat. Home: 8 Greenwood Rd Asheville NC 28803-3111 Office: Asheville Hematology Oncology Assocs One Doctor's Dr Asheville NC 28801

PUDER, DOUGLAS RICHARD, pediatrician; b. Newark, Dec. 29, 1953; s. Richard and Miriam (Schoenberger) P.; m. Kathleen Engle (div.); 1 child, Jennifer Engle; m. Kathleen, Oct. 9, 1994; 1 child, Janice. BA, Sarah Lawrence Coll., 1975; MD, NYU Sch. Medicine, 1982. Resident in pediatrics NYU Sch. Medicine, 1982-85, fellowship, 1985-87; pediatrician Clarkstown Pediatrics, Nanuet, N.Y., 1987—; dir. dept. pediatrics, Nyack (N.Y.) Hosp., 1991—; asst. clin. prof. N.Y. Med. Coll., Valhalla, 1987—. Editor Clarkstown Parentletter, 1990—. Fellow Am. Acad. Pediatricians (art dir. N.Y. state newsletter). Jewish. Office: Clarkstown Pediatrics 259 N Middletown Rd Nanuet NY 10960

PUENTE, ANTONIO ENRIQUE, psychology educator; b. Habana, Cuba, Feb. 14, 1952; came to U.S., 1960; s. Antonio A. and Silvia (Llanso) P.; m. Linda Newman, June 11, 1977; children: Krista, Antonio Nicolas, Lucas. AA, Fla. Jr. Coll., 1972; BA, U. Fla., 1973; MS, PhD, U. Ga., 1978. Lic. psychologist, N.C. Asst. prof. neuroanatomy Sch. Medicine, St. George's U., Grenada, W.I., 1978; clin. psychologist NE Fla. State Hosp., Macclenny, 1979-81; vis. prof. to prof. psychology U. N.C., Wilmington, 1981—. Author 6 books, numerous articles, editor neuropsychology series and jour. Fulbright scholar, Argentina, 1982. Fellow APA (divsn. 2, 40, continuing edn. com. chair, mem.-at-large and coun. rep. divsn. neuropsychology, chair conv. bd.); mem. Internat. Neuropsychol. Soc., Nat. Acad. Neuropsychologists (pres. 1990), Soc. Interamericana de Psicologia, N.C. Psychol. Assn. (pres. 1989-90), N.C. Psychol. Found. (founding pres.). Republican. Roman Catholic. Home: 1916 Lunar Ln Wilmington NC 28405-4211 Office: U NC Dept Psychology Wilmington NC 28403

PUESCHEL, SIEGFRIED M., pediatrician, educator; b. Waldenburg, Germany, July 28, 1931; came to U.S., 1961; naturalized, 1971; widowed. Student, Braunschweig Coll., Germany, 1953-55, Leibniz Coll., Tubingen, Germany, 1955-56, U. Tubingen, Germany, 1955-57, Free U., Berlin, 1957-58, U. Freiburg, Germany, 1958; MD summa cum laude, Med. Acad., Dusseldorf, Germany, 1960; MPH, Harvard U., 1967; PhD, U. R.I., 1985; JD, So. New Eng. Sch. Law, 1996. Diplomate Am. Bd. Pediatrics, Am. Bd. Med. Genetics. Intern Mercer Hosp., Trenton, N.J., 1961-62; jr. resident in pediatrics Children's Hosp., Honolulu, 1962-63; asst. resident in pediatrics Children's Hosp. Med. Ctr., Boston, 1963-64, asst. in mental retardation, 1967-68, assoc. in mental retardation, 1968-75, dir. Down Syndrome Program, 1970-75, dir. PKU Clinic, 1972-75; sr. resident in pediatrics Montreal Children's Hosp., 1964-65, fellow in biochemical genetics/metabolism, 1965-66; assoc. physician R.I. Hosp., Providence, 1975-79, dir. child devel. ctr., 1975-94, dir. PKU and Amino Acid Program, 1975—, dir. Down Syndrome Program, 1978—, physician, 1979—; instr. pediatrics Harvard U., Cambridge, Mass., 1968-74, asst. prof. in pediatrics, 1974-75, lectr. in pediatrics, 1975—; asst. prof. in pediatrics Brown U., Providence, 1975-77, assoc. prof. in pediatrics, 1977-85, prof. in pediatrics, 1985—; consulting pediatrician Waltham (Mass.) Hosp., 1968-75; cons. in genetics Lying in Hosp., Boston, 1969-75, Women and Infants Hosp., Providence, 1975—; cons. Devel. Evaluation Clinic Children's Hosp. Med. Ctr., Boston, 1975—; mem. prevention of mental retardation com. Internat. League of Socs. for Persons with Mental Handicaps; mem. rsch., prevention and program svc. com. Assn. for Retarded Citizens U.S.; mem. nat. conf. on rsch. perspectives in down syndrome Nat. Inst. Child Health and Rehab. Svcs.; mem. state-of-the-art conf. on down syndrome Office Spl. Edn. and Rehab. Svcs. U.S. Dept. Edn.; mem. nat. adv. child health and human devel. coun. NIH, Washington; mem. sub-com. on tng., edn. and quality assurance-tech. assistance Devel. Disabilities Coun., R.I.; mem. med. adv. com. Spl. Olympics. Author chpts. to books; mem. editl. bd. Down Syndrome Papers and Abstracts for Profls., Exceptional Parents, Down's Syndrome: Rsch. and Practice; reviewer numerous jours.; contbr. articles to profl. jours. Grantee Mass. Dept. Health, 1968, Vigneron Meml. Fund, 1984-85, Charlotte Taylor Fund, 1985-86, Dept. Health and Human Svcs., 1982-86, March of Dimes Nat. Found., 1987-89, Sigma-Tau Pharm., Inc., 1990-93; recipient Recognition award March of Dimes, 1976, Recognition award Blackstone Valley chpt. R.I. Assn. for Retarded Citizens, 1979, Fogarty Founders award, 1988, Edn. award Muscular Dystrophy Assn., 1985, 86, Muscular Dystrophy Tchg. award, 1988, Recognition award Devel. Ctr. for Handicapped Personsn-Utah State U., 1986, Down Syndrome Assn. of Greater Cin. award, 1986, Colegion John Langdown Down award Mexico City, 1987, Disting. Rsch. award Assn. for Retarded Citizens of U.S., 1990, Conn. Down Syndrome Assn. award, 1991, Sindrome de Down award Asociación Down de Monterrey (Mexico), 1994. Fellow Am. Acad. Pediatrics, Am. Coll. Med. Genetics (founder); mem. AAAS, Am. Assn. Mental Retardation (Profl. Contbn. award 1991), Am. Acad. Cerebral Palsy and Devel. Medicine, Am. Pediatric Soc., Am. Soc. Human Genetics, Nat. Down Syndrome Congress (past pres., Recognition for Disting. Svc. award 1980, Mid-Hudson Valley award 1983, Achievement in Rsch. award 1988, Outstanding Physician award 1991), N.Y. Acad. Sci., R.I. Med. Soc., New Eng. Regional Genetics Group, Soc. Inherited Metabolic Disorders, Down Syndrome Soc. R.I. (award 1985), Assn. for Children with Down Syndrome (bd. dirs.). Office: RI Hosp Child Devel Ctr 593 Eddy St Providence RI 02903-4923

PUGH, DAVID MILTON, physician, medical educator; b. Phila., July 13, 1929; s. Edward J. and Pauline S. (Stroedtman) P.; m. Virginia Wightman, June 25, 1955; children: Laurie, Catherine, Daniel. A.D., U. Rochester, 1951; M.D., Yale U., 1958. Intern, U.S. Naval Hosp., Bethesda, Md., 1958-59; resident in medicine U. Wash. Hosp., Seattle, 1959-61, fellow in cardiology, 1961-64; asst. prof. cardiology, U. Kans. Med. Ctr., Kansas City, 1965-70, assoc. prof., 1970-76, prof., 1976—. Served to lt. comdr. USNR, 1951-54, Korea, 1958-59. Fellow Am. Heart Assn. (council clin. cardiology 1970—), Am. Coll. Cardiology (pres. Kans. affiliate 1981-82), ACP, Am. Coll. Chest Physicians; mem. Wyandotte County Med. Soc. (pres. 1982). Office: U Kans Sch Medicine Cardiovascular Sect 39th & Rainbow Kansas City KS 66103 Office: 6445 Nall Ave Shawnee Mission KS 66202-4344

PUGH, DIANE LEIGH, physician; b. Memphis, Sept. 12, 1964; d. Danny Martin and Darlene (Mallory) P. BS, U. Fla., 1986; DO, Southeastern Coll. Osteo. Med., 1990. Family practice resident Fla. Hosp. East, Orlando, 1990-94; family physician Lakewood Pk. Family Practice, Ft. Pierce, Fla., 1995—; obstetric fellow Fla. Hosp. South, Orlando, 1994; alt. dir. Hospice of the Treasure Coast, Ft. Pierce, 1995—, Red Cross Bd. St. Lucie County, 1996—. Rsch. asst. March of Dimes, U. Fla., 1984-86. Mem. Am. Osteo. Assn., Am. Coll. Osteo. Family Physicians, Fla. Osteo. Med. Assn. Baptist. Office: Lakewood Pk Family Practice 5061 Sunshine State Pkwy Fort Pierce FL 34951

PUGH, JAMES EDWIN, JR., neurologist; b. Phila., Dec. 3, 1941; s. James Edwin and Loretta (Day) P.; m. Faye Cook, Feb. 6, 1971; children: Christopher Brent, William Evan. AB, Princeton U., 1963; MD, U. Pa., 1967; PhD, U. Mich., 1976. Diplomate Am. Bd. Psychiatry and Neurology, Am. Bd. Clin. Neurophysiology. Intern in surgery U. Calif. San Francisco, 1967-68; resident in neurology U. Mich., Ann Arbor, 1975-78, fellow in EEG, 1979-80, asst. prof., neurology, 1980-83; clin. asst. prof. medicine U. N.C., Charlotte, 1984-94; neurologist Mechlenburg Neurol. Assocs., Charlotte, 1983—; cons. 3M Corp., St. Paul, Minn., 1994-95. Contbg. author books in field. Med. dir. Ataxia Clin, Charlotte Inst. of Rehab., 1988—; mem. ethics com. Presbyn. Hosp., Charlotte, 1993—. Lt. USN, 1968-70. Rsch. tng. grantee NINDS/NIH, U. Mich., 1971-74. Fellow Am. Acad. Neurology, Am. Electroencephalographic Soc.; mem. Mecklenburg County Med. Soc., N.C. State Med. Soc., Physicians for Social Responsibility. Home: 2154 Norton Rd Charlotte NC 28207 Office: Mecklenburg Neurol Assocs 1900 Randolph Rd Charlotte NC 28207

PUGH, JAMES WHITWORTH, biomedical engineer; b. Jan. 4, 1946. BS in Metallurgy, MIT, 1968, PhD in Biomedical Engring., 1972. Registered profl. engr., N.Y.; USCG Operator's Lic.; lic. pvt. pilot. Postdoctoral fellow in bioengring. MIT, Cambridge, 1972; dir. biomechanics lab. Hosp. for Joint Diseases & Med. Ctr., 1972-79; dir. div. bioengring. Hosp. for Joint Diseases Orthopaedic Inst., 1979-84; rsch. prof. dept. orthpaedics, tech. dir. Gait Lab. SUNY, Stony Brook, 1985-86; dir. biomed. engring., metallurgy, materials sci. Inter-City Testing & Cons. Corp., Mineola, N.Y., 1986—; asst. prof. orthopaedics Mt. Sinai Sch. Medicine, SUNY, 1973-81, assoc. prof., 1981-84; adj. assoc. prof. dept. occupl. health and safety NYU, 1981-85; adj. assoc. prof. Cooper Union Sch. Engring., N.Y.C., 1982-85, vis. prof. bioengring., 1986-87, adj. prof. bioengring., 1995—; rsch. prof. dept. orthopaedics SUNY, 1985-86; affiliate prof. bioengring. U. Wash., Seattle, 1989—. Contbr. numerous articles to profl. jours. Mem. ASME, ASTM, AAAS, NSPE, Am. Soc. Metals, Soc. Automotive Engrs., Orthopaedic Rsch. Soc., N.Y. State Soc. Profl. Engrs., Soc. for Biomaterials, Joint Med. Study Group, Soc. Plastics Engrs., Nat. Assn. Profl. Accident Reconstructionists, Sigma Xi. Home: 620 Broadway # 2F New York NY 10012-2616 Office: 3550 Watt Ave Sacramento CA 95821

PUGH, KIMBERLY RENEE, mental health nurse; b. Portsmouth, Va., Aug. 2, 1971; d. Isaiah and Phyllis (Edwards) P. ADN, Norfolk State U., 1993, BS summa cum laude, 1994. RN, Va. Staff nurse Riverside Convalescent Ctr., Newport News, Va., 1993-94, Eastern State Mental Health Hosp., Williamsburg, Va., 1994—. Mem. NAACP, Nat. Black Nurses' Assn. Democrat. Baptist. Home: 603 Burton St Hampton VA 23666

PUI, CHING-HON, hematologist, oncologist, educator; b. Hong Kong, Aug. 20, 1951; came to U.S., 1976; s. Y.T. and Lan Kwan (Ho) Bay-P. MD, Nat. Taiwan U., 1976. Diplomate Am. Bd. Pediat., Am. Bd. Pediatric Hematology and Oncology. Intern St. Louis City Hosp., 1976-77; resident St. Jude Children's Rsch. Hosp., Memphis, Tenn., 1977-79, fellow in pediatric hematology/oncology, 1979-81, rsch. assoc., 1981-82, asst. mem., 1982-86, assoc. mem., 1986-90; assoc. prof. of pediatrics U. Tenn., Memphis, 1986-90, prof. pediatrics, 1990—; mem. depts hematology-oncology, pathology and lab. St. Jude Children's Rsch. Hosp., Memphis, 1990—, dir. lymphoid disease program, vice chmn. dept. hematology and oncology, 1994—; co. dir.dept. hematological malignancies program, 1995—; prin. investigator pediatric oncology group St. Jude, St. Louis, 1990—; reviewer spl. ad hoc rev. com. Nat. Cancer Inst., Bethesd, Md., 1990—. Contbr. articles to profl. jours. Recipient Book Coupon award Nat. Taiwan U., 1971, 74, 75. Fellow Am. Acad. Pediat., Am. Soc. Clin. Oncology, Am.

Assn. Cancer Rsch., Am. Soc. Hematology, Soc. Pediatric Rsch., Pediatric Oncology Group; mem. AAAS, Am. Soc. Clin. Investigation. Office: St Jude Childrens Rsch Hosp 332 N Lauderdale St Memphis TN 38105-2729

PUJADAS, WILLIAM GEORGE, general and reconstructive orthopaedic surgeon; b. Chgo., July 7, 1951; s. Guillermo Manuel and Yolanda Esperanza (Demoya) P.; m. Alice Joy Pujadas; children: William, Kaysee, Korrie. MD, U. Guadalajara, Mex., 1975. Diplomate Am. Bd. Orthopedic Surgery. Resident in gen. surgery, resident in orthopedics, chief resident, pvt. practice, 1982—; founding ptnr. Jacksonville (Fla.) Orthopedic Inst., 1993—. Mem. AMA, N.E. Fla. Orthopaedic Soc. (past pres.), So. Orthopaedic Soc., Am. Acad. Orthopaedic Surgery, Am. Foot and Ankle Soc. Roman Catholic. Office: Jacksonville Orthopaedic Inst 1325 San Marco Blvd Jacksonville FL 32217

PULIAFITO, CARMEN ANTHONY, ophthalmologist, laser researcher; b. Buffalo, Jan. 5, 1951; s. Dominic F. and Marie A. (Nigro) P.; m. Janet H. Pine, May 19, 1979. AB cum laude, Harvard Coll., 1973, MD magna cum laude, 1978; postgrad., U. Pa. Diplomate Am. Bd. Ophthalmology. Intern Faulkner Hosp., Tufts U. Sch. Medicine, 1978-79; resident Mass. Eye and Ear Infirmary, Boston, 1979-82, retina fellow, 1982-83; instr. Harvard Med. Sch., Boston, 1983-85, asst. prof., 1985-89, assoc. prof., 1989-91; dir. divsn. continuing edn. dept. ophthalmology Harvard Med. Sch., 1989-91; vis. scientist MIT Regional Laser Ctr., Cambridge, 1982—, asst. prof. health scis. and tech. program, 1987-89, assoc. prof., 1989-91; mem. staff Mass. Eye and Ear Infirmary, Boston, 1983; dir. Morse Laser Ctr., Mass. Eye and Ear Infirmary, 1986-91, dir. New Eng. Eye Ctr., 1991—; prof., chmn. dept. ophthalmology Tufts U. Sch. Medicine, 1991—; adj. prof. biomed. engring. Tufts U., 1991—; chmn. med. bd. New Eng. Med. Ctr. Hosps., 1994—, ophthalmologist in chief, 1991—; assoc. examiner Am. Bd. Ophthalmology, 1990—. Author: (with D. Albert) Foundations of Ophthalmic Pathology, 1979, (with R. Steinert) Principles and Practice of Ophthalmic YAG Laser Surgery, 1984, Lasers in Surgery and Medicine: Principles and Practice, 1996, (with M.R. Hee, J.S. Schuman and J.G. Fujimoto) Optical Coherence Tomography of Ocular Diseases, 1996, (with E. Reichel) Atlas of Indocyanine Green Angiography, 1996; editor-in-chief Lasers in Surgery and Medicine, 1987-95, Ophthalmic Surgery and Lasers, 1995—; contbr. about 100 articles to profl. jours. Pres. Am. Soc. for Laser Medicine and Surgery, 1994-95; v.p. Mass. Soc. Eye Physicians and Surgeons, 1994-96; assoc. examiner Am. Bd. Ophthalmology, 1990—; retina trustee Assn. Rsch. in Vision and Ophthalmology, 1995—. Recipient Richard and Hinda Rosenthal award in visual scis., 1994, Man of Vision award Boston Aid to the Blind, 1993, Leon Goldman award Biomed. Optics Soc., 1993, I Migliori award Pirandello Lyceum of Mass., 1994. Fellow Am. Acad. Ophthalmology, Am. Soc. for Laser Medicine and Surgery (pres. 1994-95); mem. Mass. Soc. Eye Physicians and Surgeons (v.p. 1994-96). Roman Catholic. Home: 69 Pigeon Hill Rd Weston MA 02193-1641 Office: New Eng Eye Ctr 750 Washington St Boston MA 02111-1533

PULIER, MYRON LEOPOLD, psychiatrist; b. Passaic, N.J., Feb. 28, 1941; s. Emanuel and Sonia (Serbin) P.; m. Anita Salzman, Feb. 6, 1965; children: Eric, Gregory. BA in Math., Harvard Coll., 1962; MD, Albert Einstein Coll. Medicine, 1965. Diplomate Am. Bd. Psychiatry and Neurology. Intern (rotating) Greenwich Hosp., Greenwich, Conn., 1965-66; resident psychiatry Hillside Hosp., Glen Oaks, N.Y., 1966-69; chief psychiatrist U.S. Army Health Clinic, Pentagon, Washington, 1969-71; research psychiatrist Hillside Hosp., Glen Oaks, 1971-72; attending psychiatrist L.I. Jewish Hosp., New Hyde Park, N.Y., 1971-72; research psychiatrist Rockland Research Inst., Orangeburg, N.Y., 1972-74; attending psychiatrist Bergen Pines County Hosp., Paramus, N.J., 1972—, Pascack Valley Hosp., Westwood, N.J., 1972-73, Hackensack Med. Ctr., Hackensack, N.J., 1973—, Holy Name Hosp., Teaneck, N.J., 1987—; asst. clin. prof. N.J. Med. Sch., U. Medicine and Dentistry, 1994—; dir. R&D MEGAsoft Assocs., Hackensack, 1983—; chair profl. adv. bd. Passaic Bergen chpt. Nat. Multiple Sclerosis Soc., Teaneck, 1984-92; cons. psychiatrist Gimbel Multiple Sclerosis Ctr., Teaneck, 1986—; med. psychiat. dir. PruCare No. N.J., Parsippany, 1987-93; chair instnl. rev. bd. Bergan Pines County Hosp., Paramus, N.J., 1986-95; co-dir. MPC Clinic, Hackensack, 1991-95; rsch. forum leader InterPsych, 1995—. Co-author: Preserving Psychiatric Confidentiality, 1972; contbr. articles to profl. jours.; author (computer lang.) Babel, 1984; calender editor Self Help & Psychology mag., 1995—; inventor Pulier Electronic Tachystoscope, 1987. Pres. bd. trustees The Children's Ctr., Tenafly, N.J., 1972-73. Major USAR, 1969-71. Mem. Am. Psychiat. Assn. (cons. com. on telemed. svcs. Coun. on Internal Org., 1996—), N.Y. Soc. for Adolescent Psychiatry, Am. Acad. Clin. Psychiatry. Office: 211 Essex St Ste 301 Hackensack NJ 07601-3246

PULITZER, ROSLYN K., social worker, psychotherapist; b. Bronx, N.Y., Apr. 25, 1930; d. George and Laura Eleanor (Holtz) P. BS in Human Devel. and Life Cycle, SUNY, N.Y.C., 1983; MSW, Fordham U., 1987; postgrad., Masterson Inst., N.Y.C., 1991. cert. in psychoanalytic psychotherapy of the personality disorders, Masterson Inst., N.Y.C.; lic. clin. social worker, N.Y. Clinic dir. Resources Counseling and Psychotherapy Ctr., N.Y.C., 1985-89; social worker, clin. supr. methadone maintenance treatment program Beth Israel Med. Ctr., N.Y.C., 1989—; cons. therapist, clin. supr. Identity House, N.Y.C., 1980—, exec. dir., 1985, clin. dir., 1993-94. Mem. regional adv. coun. N.Y. State Div. Human Rights, N.Y.C., 1975-76; mem. Community Bd. 6, N.Y.C., 1978-81; founder, legis. chmn. N.Y. State Women's Polit. Caucus, 1978-80. Mem. NASW, Acad. Cert. Social Workers, Soc. Masterson Inst., N.Y. Milton Erickson Soc. for Psychotherapy and Hypnosis (cert.). Home: 110 Bank St Apt 5F New York NY 10014-2171

PULSIFER, MARGARET BIGWOOD, psychologist; b. Boston, Nov. 16, 1959; d. Harold Smith and Brenda (MacHugh) Bigwood; m. Peter Emery Pulsifer, Aug. 2, 1987. BA, Boston Coll., 1981, MA, 1983; PhD, SUNY, Buffalo, 1989. Lic. psychologist, Md. Clin. psychology extern, St. Elizabeths Hosp., Washington, 1987-88, clin. psychology intern, 1988-89; postdoctoral fellow Johns Hopkins U. Sch. Med., Balt., 1989-90; pediatric psychologist Kennedy Krieger Inst./Johns Hopkins U., Balt., 1990-94; asst. prof. dept. psychiatry Johns Hopkins Sch. Medicine, Balt., 1994—. Mem. Jr. League of Washington, 1989—. Mem. Am. Psychol. Assn., Md. Psychol. Assn., Nat. Acad. Neuropsychology. Office: Johns Hopkins Sch Medicine Dept Psychiatry 600 N Wolfe St # 218 Baltimore MD 21205-2110

PUNG, ROSALYN ALYCE (ROSIE PUNG), nursing educator; b. Shelbyville, Ind., May 3, 1948; d. William O. and Dorothy Alice (Roupp) Hill; m. Ronald J. Pung, Aug. 25, 1984; 1 child, Bradley Scott Smith. ASN, Ind. U., 1969, BSN, 1983, MSN, 1985. Head nurse Winona Hosp., Indpls., 1976; hemodialysis staff nurse renal dept. Ind. U. Med. Ctr., Indpls., 1976-78, hemodialysis home nurse coordinator renal dept., 1978—79, adult dialysis units nursing dir. renal dept., 1979-85; clin. lectr. Ind. U. Sch. Nursing, Indpls., 1985, 88; nurse analyst Associated Group Blue Cross/Blue Shield of Ind., 1985-88; project SIHO office mgr. Southeastern Ind. Health Orgn., Columbus, 1987-88; relief mgr. Chgo. U. Heights Hosp. Community Hosp. South, Indpls., 1988-90; nurse med. cons. Holland and Holland Law Firm, Indpls., 1988-90; ASN clin. instr. Henry Ford Community Coll., Dearborn, Mich., 1990-91; relief supr. McPherson Hosp., Howell, Mich., 1990-91, dir. med./surg. svcs., 1991-92; clin. coord. Huron Valley Hosp., Milford, Mich., 1992-94; office mgr. Harper Physicians Group, Detroit, 1994—; rev. and med.-legal cons.; hemodialysis cons. HCFA project Sys. Sci., Inc., Washington, 1980-81, R&R Assocs. Personal Bus. Devel., 1996, Cobe Labs., Denver, 1984, Travenol Labs., Chgo., 1983. Contbg. author: Nursing Theorists and Their Work, 1986. Mem. Am. Nephrology Nurses Assn., Nat. Assn. Exec. Women, Ind. State Nurses Assn., Am. Nurses Assn., Sigma Theta Tau. Home: 3260 Ravinewood Commerce Township MI 48382-1475 Office: HPOB 4160 John R St Ste 729 Detroit MI 48201-2014

PURCELL, J. KENNETH, exercise physiologist, technology coordinator, educator; b. Brooksville, Fla., Aug. 15, 1947; s. Edwin M. and Madge (Davis) P.; m. Lynda Carter, Dec. 21, 1968; 1 child, David. AA, Cen. Fla. Community Coll., Ocala, 1967; BS in Edn., Ga. So. U., 1969, MST in Phys. Edn., 1972; PhD in Exercise Physiology, Fla. State U., 1975. Phys. edn. tchr., coach New Ellenton (S.C.) Jr. High Sch., 1969-70; chemistry, biology tchr. Evans County High Sch., Claxton, Ga., 1970-71; phys. edn. tchr. Cairo (Ga.) Pub. Schs., 1971-72; assoc. prof. dept. health, phys. edn., recreation Murray (Ky.) State U., 1974—, tech. coord. coll. edn., 1992—; fitness cons. Paducah (Ky.) Gaseous Diffusion Plant, 1983-85; rsch. cons. Office of Gov., Frankfort, Ky; cons. Govs. Coun. on Phys. Fitness, Sports, Franfurt, 1984-86. Contbr. articles to profl. jours. Mem. Cong. of Faculty Senate Leaders, Ky., 1979-81; pres. Murray State U. Faculty Senate, 1980-81; state coord. Jump Rope for Heart, Ky., 1980-84. Recipient Disting. Svc. award, Am. Heart Assn., Lousiville, 1981. Mem. AAHPERD (life), Ky. Assn. Health, Phys. Edn., Recreation and Dance (Merit award 1977, Disting. Svc. award 1992), Am. Coll. Sports Medicine, Phi Delta Kappa (pres. Murray chpt. 1996), Phi Kappa Phi, Phi Epsilon Kappa. Baptist. Office: SED Murray State U PO Box 9 Murray KY 42071-0009

PURCELL, ROBERT HARRY, virologist; b. Keokuk, Iowa, Dec. 19, 1935; s. Edward Harold and Elsie Thelma (Melzl) P.; m. Carol Joan Moody, June 11, 1961; children: David Edward, John Leslie. BA in Chemistry, Okla. State U., 1957; MS Biochemistry, Baylor U., 1960; MD, Duke U., 1962. Intern in pediatrics Duke U. Hosp., Durham, N.C., 1962-63; officer USPHS, 1963, advanced through grades to med. dir. (O-6), 1974; with Epidemic Intelligence Svc., Communicable Disease Ctr. Atlanta; assigned to vaccine br. Nat. Inst. Allergy and Infectious Diseases, Bethesda, Md., 1963-65; sr. surgeon Lab. Infectious Diseases, NIH, Bethesda, Md., 1965-69, med. officer, 1969-72, med. dir., 1972-74, head hepatitis viruses sect., 1974—; organizer, invited participant, speaker numerous nat. and internat. symposia, confs., workshops, meetings; temporary advisor WHO, 1967—; expert cons. in hepatitis U.S.—China, U.S.—Taiwan, U.S.—Japan, U.S.—Russia, U.S.—India, U.S.—Pakistan Bilateral Sci. Agreements; lectr. various virology classes. Mem. editl. bd. and/or reviewer Am. Jour. Epidemiology, Gastroenterology, Hepatology, Infection and Immunity, Jour. Clin. Microbiology, Jour. Infectious Diseases, Jour. Med. Virology, Jour. Nat. Cancer Inst., Nature, Sci.; contbr. over 500 articles to profl. jours., chpts. to books; numerous patents in field. Decorated D.S.M.; recipient Superior Svc. award USPHS, 1972, Meritorious Svc. medal USPHS, 1974, Gorgas medal, 1977, Disting. Alumni award Duke U. Sch. Medicine, 1978, Eppinger prize 5th Internat. FALK Symposium on Virus and Liver, Switzerland, 1979, Medal of City of Turin, Italy, 1983, Gold medal Can. Liver Found., 1984, Inventor's Incentive award U.S. Commerce Dept., 1984; fellowships Baylor U., 1959-60, Duke U., 1960-62. Fellow Washington Acad. Scis.; mem. Am. Epidemiology Soc., Am. Soc. Microbiology, Am. Soc. Virology, Am. Acad. Microbiology, AAAS, Soc. Epidemiol. Rsch., Infectious Diseases Soc. Am. (Squibb award 1980), N.Y. Acad. Scis., Am. Soc. Clin. Investigation, Assn. Am. Physicians, Am. Coll. Epidemiology, Am. Assn. Study of Liver Diseases, Internat. Assn. Study and Prevention Virus Associated Cancers, Internat. Assn. Biol. Standardization, Internat. Assn. Study Liver, Soc. Exptl. Biology and Medicine (Disting. Scientist award 1986), Nat. Acad. Scis. Office: NIH Lab Infectious Diseases NIH Bldg 7 Rm 202 7 Center Dr MSC 0740 Bethesda MD 20892-0740

PURPURA, DOMINICK P., neuroscientist, university dean; b. N.Y.C., Apr. 2, 1927; m. Florence Williams, 1948; children—Craig, Kent, Keith, Allyson. A.B., Columbia U., 1949; M.D., Harvard U., 1953. Intern Presbyn Hosp., N.Y.C., 1953-54; asst. resident in neurology Neurol. Inst., N.Y.C., 1954-55; Prof., chmn. dept. anatomy Albert Einstein Coll. Medicine, Yeshiva U., N.Y.C., 1967-74, sci. dir. Kennedy Ctr., 1969-72, dir. Kennedy Ctr., 1972-82, prof., chmn. dept. neurosci., 1974-82, dean, 1984—; dean Stanford U., Calif., 1982-84; mem. neurophysiol. panel Internat. Brain Rsch. Orgn., pres. 1987—; v.p. med. affairs UNESCO, 1961—; chmn. internat. congress com. Internat. Brain Rsch. Orgn./World Found. Neuroscientists, 1983—. Mem. editorial bd. Brain Rsch., 1965—, editor-in-chief, 1975—; editor-in-chief Brain Rsch. Revs., 1975—, Developmental Brain Rsch., 1981—, Molecular Brain Rsch., 1985—, Cognitive Brain Rsch., 1991—. Served with USAAF, 1945-47. Fellow N.Y. Acad. Scis.; mem. Inst. Medicine of Nat. Acad. Scis., Nat. Acad. Scis., Am. Acad. Neurology, Am. Assn. Anatomists, Am. Assn. Neurol. Surgeons, Am. Epilepsy Soc., Am. Physiol. Soc., Assn. Research in Nervous and Mental Disease, Soc. Neurosci., Sigma Xi. Office: Yeshiva U Albert Einstein Coll Medicine 1300 Morris Park Ave Bronx NY 10461-1926

PURSELL, PAUL DENNIS, rehabilitation director; b. Altadena, Calif., Jan. 26, 1950; s. Robert Ralph and Thelma (Winifred) P. BS, Calif. State U., 1972. Registered phys. therapist. Asst. athletic trainer Orange County Ramblers Football, Inc., Anaheim, Calif., 1968, Calif. State U., Long Beach, 1968-71; athletic trainer U.S. Olympic Track & Field Tng. Camp, San Diego, 1971; phys. therapy aide Fountain Valley (Calif.) Community Hosp., 1971-72; chief phys. therapy Tustin (Calif.) Community Hosp., 1972-78; disaster planning coord. St. Joseph Hosp., Orange, Calif., 1984-90, 94—, dir. human devel., 1987-91, dir. phys. rehab. svcs., 1978—; instr. Calif. State U., Long Beach, 1989—; pres. Calif. Phys. Therapy Fund, Inc., Sacramento, 1983-84; chmn. bd. Orange County/Long Beach Health Edn. Ctr., 1984-85, Health Assocs. Fed. Credit Union, 1985-86. Chmn. Calif. Allied Health Coalition, Sacramento, 1983-84; speaker of assembly Orange County (Calif.) Health Planning Coun., 1986-87; trustee Gail Pattison Youth Leadership Trust, Orange, 1990-91; mem. mgmt. audit com., City of Orange, 1991-95, ad hoc fin. com., 1993; chmn. bd. Leadership Orange, 1992-94; mem. Orange Citizen of Yr. Selection Com., 1988-89; pres. adv. coun. phys. therapy Calif. State U., Long Beach, chmn. 1987—; mem. Orange County Charter Commn., 1995. Recipient Commendation for Volutneerism, Carnation Found., 1984. Mem. Am. Phys. Therapy Asn. (pres. Calif. chpt. 1983-84, Outstanding Svc. award 1980, 84), Nat. Fire Protection Assn., Orange County/Long Beach Health Consortium (chmn. bd. 1984-85), Orange C. of C. (pres. 1990-91),. Democrat. Roman Catholic. Office: St Joseph Hosp 1310 W Stewart Dr Ste 203 Orange CA 92667 Address: 2700 Dunstan Dr Tustin CA 92680-1336

PUSCHETT, JULES B., medical educator, neprhrologist, researcher; b. Hazelton, Pa., Mar. 13, 1934; m. Diane Puschett; children: Mitchell, Lynne. BA magna cum laude, Lehigh U., 1955; MD, U. Pa., 1959. Intern Jackson Meml. Hosp., Miami, 1959-60; resident, fellow endrocrinology and metabolism Univ. Hosp., Balt., 1963-66; postdoctoral fellow in medicine NIH Inst. Arthritis and Metabolic Disease, Bethesda, Md., 1966-68; fellow, renal-electrolyte sect. U. Pa. Sch. Medicine, Phila., 1966-68; rsch. assoc. VA Hosp., Phila., 1968-70, staff to chief renal-electrolyte sect. dept. medicine, 1968-73, clin. investigator, 1970-73; head renal-electrolyte divsn. Allegheny Gen. Hosp., Pitts., 1973-78; dir. renal-electrolyte divsn. fellowship tng. program U. Pitts. Sch. Medicine, 1976-78; chief renal-electrolyte divsn. dept. medicine U. Ark. for Med. Scis., Little Rock, 1979-80, U. Pitts Sch. Medicine, 1980-90; interim chief sect. nephrology dept. medicine Tulane U. Sch. Medicine, New Orleans, 1990-92; chmn. dept. medicine Tulane U. Sch. Medicine, New Orleans, 1990—; instr. medicine U. Pa. Sch. Medicine 1967-79, assoc. in medicine 1969-70, asst. prof. medicine 1970-73; clin. assoc. prof. medicine U. Pitts. Med. Sch. 1973-78; prof. medicine U. Ark. Med. Scis. 1979-80; prof. medicine U. Pitts. Sch. Medicine 1980-90; prof. medicine Tulane U. Sch. Medicine 1990—. Editor: The Diuretic Manual, 1984, Diuretics: chemistry, Pharmacology and Clinical Applications, 1984, Disorders of Fluid and Electrolyte Balance: diagnosis and Management, 1985, Diuretics II: Chemistry, Pharmacology and Clinical Applications, 1986, Diuretics III, 1989, Diuretics IV, 1993; contbr. over 170 articles to profl. jours.; spkr. and presenter in field; editl. bd. Am. Jour. Med. Scis., Am. Jour. Nephrology (sect. editor Physiology for the Nephrologist), Cardiovasc. Risk Factors, Internat. Jour. Artificial Organs, Southern Med. Jour. Chmn. 1st Ann. Kidney Ball, Nat. Kidney Found. of Western Pa., 1988, chmn. 2d Ann. Kidney Ball, 1989. With USN 1960-63. Coxe Meml. schlar, Lehigh U., 1951; named Outstanding Tchr. Yr., Owl Club, Tulane U., 1991, 94. Fellow ACP; mem. AMA, AAAS, Am. Fedn. Clin. Rsch., Am. Soc. Artificial Internal Orgnas. Am. Soc. Nephrology (chmn. audit com. 1992), Nat. Kidney Found. (pub. policy com. 1989, vol. svc. award 1990), Internat. Soc. Nephrology, Am. Heart Assn. Coun. on the Kidney in Cardiovasc. Disease (chmn. subcom. on scientific confs. 1991-92, exec. com. 1991-95, long-range planning com. 1992—), Am. Heart Assn. Coun. for High Blood Pressure Rsch., Am. Physiol. Soc., Fedn. Am. Socs. for Exptl. Biology, Am. Geriat. Soc., Ctrl. Soc. for Clin. Rsch., Soc. for Exptl. Biology and Medicine, Am. Soc. Clin. Pharmacology and Therapeutics, Am. Coll. Clin. Pharmacology, Endocrine Soc., Am. Soc. Renal Biochemistry and Metabolism, Am. Soc. Hypertension (Outstanding Tchr. Yr. 1986), Internat. Soc. Nutrition and Metabolism in Renal Disease, Am. Soc. Bone and Mineral Rsch., European Dialysis and Transplant Assn., Nat. Kidney Found. of Western Pa. (med. adv. com. 1981, chmn. 1981-83, Gift of Life award 1991), Nat. Kidney Found. of La. (mem.-at-large, trustee 1991), So. Med. Assn., So. Soc. Clin. Investigation (councilor 1992-94, sec.-treas. 1994-95), La. State Med. Soc., Orleans Parish Med. Soc. (membership com. 1993, long-range planning com. 1993), La. Soc. Internal Medicine, S.E. Clin. Club, Midwestern Salt and Water Club, Phi Beta Kappa, Alpha Epsilon Delta. Office: Tulane Univ Sch Medicine Dept Medicine SL 12 1430 Tulane Ave New Orleans LA 70112-2699

PUSTKA, RICHARD ALFONS, physician assistant; b. Denver, Mar. 7, 1946; s. Alfons and Ann (Rizzolo) P.; m. Mary Ann Moore, Jan. 15, 1966; children: Angela, Sarah. Student, Kans. State Tchrs. Coll., 1964-66; grad. physician asst., USPHS Hosp., S.I., N.Y., 1973. Cert. physician asst., N.Y., Iowa, Mo. Physician asst., Boone, Iowa, 1973-91, Iowa Heart Ctr., Des Moines, 1992-93; physician asst., dir. Iowa Heart, Lung and Vascular Surgeons, Des Moines, 1993—; collaborator Rural Health Act, U.S. Senate, Washington, 1975. Contbr. articles to med. jours. Vol. tree planter Johnny Appleseed Found., Boone, 1985-95. With USN, 1967-69, Vietnam. Decorated Silver Star, Purple Heart, Vietnamese Cross of Gallantry; recipient Gov.'s Leadership award State of Iowa, 1978, 85. Fellow Am. Acad. Physician Assts. (jud. affairs com. 1980-81), Iowa Physician Assts. Soc. (founding pres. 1973), Am. Assn. Physician Assts. in Occupl. Medicine. Roman Catholic. Office: Iowa Heart Lung & Vascular Surg PC 411 Laurel St Ste 2350 Des Moines IA 50314

PUTHENVEETIL, JOS ANTHONY, laboratory executive; b. Cochin, Kerala, India, Apr. 2, 1947; came to U.S., 1972; s. Peter Joseph and Angela (Thengaparackal) P.; m. Tresa Joseph Maliekal, Apr. 14, 1973; children: Peter, Marietta, Joseph. BS, Kerala U., India, 1969; BBA, Northwestern Bus. Coll., 1973. Lab. technologist United Med. Lab., Chgo., 1973-74; lab. adminstr. Westlawn Med. Lab., Chgo., 1974-76; pres. Roseland Med. Lab., Chgo., 1976-77; v.p. Foster Western Med. Lab., Chgo., 1977—; pres., CEO Med. World Lab., River Forest, Ill., 1984—; chmn. Pro-Vet Labs., River Forest; bd. dris., exec. v.p. Superior Printed Circuits, Inc., Wheeling, Ill.; Oak Brook, Ill., 1981—, Promed Mgmt., Inc., River Forest; bd. dirs. Diapers India, Ltd., Bombay, Golden Shrimp Hatchery, Inc., Cochin, India. Founder, chmn. Care and Share, USA, River Forest, 1989; pres. Indo-Am. Friendship Soc., Westmont, 1981; chmn. Nat. South Asian AIDS Orgn., River Forest, 1992. Named Businessman of Yr. Indo-Am. Forum, 1989; recipient Son of India, Indian Christian Assn., 1992, Community Svc. award Fedn. of Christians, 1990, Svc. Excellence award Cen. Wis.-Indians, 1990; Paul Harris fellow Rotary Internat., 1990. Home: 209 Roslyn Rd Oak Brook IL 60521-2516 Office: Med World Lab Inc 7716 Madison St River Forest IL 60305-2102

PUTMAN, CHARLES E(D), medical educator, clinician, academic administrator, radiologist; b. Cleburne, Tex., July 22, 1941; s. Edna P.; m. Mary Clark, June 19, 1966; children: Camille Clark, Shannon Bandy, Charles Garrett. B.A., U. Tex.-Austin, 1963; M.D., U. Tex. Med. Br., Galveston, 1967. Diplomate: Am. Bd. Internal Medicine, Am. Bd. Radiology. Intern U. Iowa City, Iowa City, 1967-68; resident U. Tex. Med. Br., Galveston, 1968-71, U. Calif.-San Francisco, 1971-73; asst. prof. radiology Yale U., New Haven, 1973-75, assoc. prof. radiology and internal medicine, 1976-77, clin. dir. diagnostic radiation, 1976-77; prof. radiology, chmn. dept. radiology Duke U. Med. Ctr., Durham, N.C., 1977-85, James B. Duke prof., 1983—, chief of staff, 1982—, vice chancellor for health affairs, vice provost, 1985-86; vice provost Sch. Med., Research, Devel. Duke U. Med. Ctr., Durham, 1986-89. Author: Intensive Care Radiology Imaging of the Critically Ill, 1982, 3d edit. 1991Pulmonary Diagnosis Imaging and Other Techniques, 1982. Mem. Fleischner Soc., Assn. Univ. Radiologists (pres.-elect 1983), Soc. Chairmen Acad. Radiology Depts. (pres. 1983), Am. Coll. Radiology. Office: Duke U 212 Allen Bldg Box 90026 Durham NC 27708-0026*

PUTNAM, J. DAVID, optometrist; b. Waverly, N.Y., June 15, 1926; s. Israel and Ethel Lorena (Dibble) P.; m. Janine Ann Smith, Feb. 23, 1990; children: Meyanne, Deborah. BS in Optometry, Pa. Coll. Optometry, 1948. Pvt. practice, optometrist Sayre, Pa., 1952—. Patentee in field of thermal energy. Marine engr. USMCC, 1943-45. Mem. Elks, Moose, VFW, Am. Legion, Cath. War Vets. Republican.

PUTNAM, RICHARD WORCESTER, dentist; b. Gainesville, Fla., Dec. 20, 1945; s. Charles Worcester and Jean Madden (Hampson) P.; m. Joanne White, Dec. 23, 1967; children: Joseph Worcester, Charles Jason. BS in Biology, Emory U., 1967, DDS, 1971. Instr. Camp Cherokee for boys, Clarksville, Ga., 1966-67; bus driver Atlanta Transit System, Atlanta, 1968-69; gen. practice dentistry, Blairsville, Ga., 1973—; staff mem. Blairsville Gen. Hosp., 1973-76, Union Gen. Hosp., Blairsville, 1974—; lctr. Am. Cancer Soc., Union County Sch. System; pub. health dentist Union County, Ga., 1981-88. Chmn. awards, publicity Union County Bicentennial Com., 1976; mem. forensic identification team State of Ga., 1992—. Served as capt. U.S. Army Dental Corps, 1971-73. Featured Country Dentist, Dental Mgmt. Mag., 1979; Fla. Bd. Regents scholar, 1967-71. Mem. Mountain Area Dental Study Group (founder), ADA, Ga. Dental Assn., No. Dist. Dental Soc., N. Am. Norwegian Red Cattle Assn. (bd. dirs. 1983-88, first registered breeder Norwegian Red cattle in Ga., 1974), Jaycees, Phi Gamma Delta (charter, treas. 1964-65, historian 1965-66), Delta Sigma Delta (social chmn. 1969-70). Lodge: Kiwanas (bd. dirs. 1974—, chmn. various coms. 1979—). Avocations: kayaking; physical fitness. Home and Office: PO Box 2059 Blairsville GA 30514

PUTNAM, WILLIAM SHIELDS, gastroenterologist, educator; b. Roanoke, Va., Mar. 29, 1955; s. Robert Walbridge and Marilyn Marie (Mitchell) P.; m. Bonnie Carol Bean, Oct. 29, 1978; children: William Shields Jr., Alexandra Carol. BA summa cum laude, Duke U., 1977, MD, 1980. Diplomate Am. Bd. Internal Medicine. Resident Duke U. Med. Ctr., Durham, N.C., 1981-84; emergency room physician Alamance County Hosp., Burlington, N.C., 1984-85; fellow U. Calif., San Francisco, 1985-87; assoc. Duke U. Sch. Medicine, 1987-88, asst. prof., 1988-90; clin. asst. prof. U. Wash., Seattle, 1990—; pvt. practice Seattle. Contbr. articles to med. jours. Fellow ACP; mem. Am. Fedn. Clin. Rsch., Am. Gastroenterol. Assn., Am. Coll. Gastroenterology, Am. Soc. Gastrointestinal Endoscopy, Wilderness Soc., Amnesty Internat., Alpha Omega Alpha. Home: 5908 36th Ave NW Seattle WA 98107-3341 Office: 11027 Meridian Ave N # 100 Seattle WA 98133

PUYAU, FRANCIS ALBERT, physician, radiology educator; b. New Orleans, Dec. 1, 1928; s. Frank Albert and Rose Sue (Jones) P.; m. Geraldine Sally diBenedetto, June 6, 1951; children: Michael, Stephen, Jeanne Marie, Julie, Melissa. B.S., Notre Dame U., 1948; M.D., La. State U., 1952. Diplomate Am. Bd. Pediatrics, Am. Bd. Pediatric Cardiology, Am. Bd. Radiology. Intern Charity Hosp., New Orleans, 1952-53; resident in pediatrics Charity Hosp., 1955-57; instr. pediatrics La. State U. Sch. Medicine, New Orleans, 1957-59; asst. prof. La. State U. Sch. Medicine, 1959-61, clin. asso. prof., 1968-71, prof. radiology and pediatrics, 1971-74, acting head dept. radiology, 1971-72, head dept., 1972-74; asst. prof. pediatrics Vanderbilt U., 1961-68; fellow dept. diagnostic radiology Charity Hosp., New Orleans, 1968-70; prof. radiology and pediat. Tulane U. Sch. Medicine, New Orleans, 1974—, prof. medicine, 1974-95; acting chmn. dept. pediatrics Tulane U. Sch. Medicine, 1976-78; cons. St. Tammany Hosps., Covington, La., 1968-81; dir. cardiac catherization lab. dept. cardiology Charity Hosp., New Orleans, 1970-85; staff radiologist Our Lady of the Lake Regional Med. Ctr., Baton Rouge, 1986-93; mem. staff Hotel Dieu, New Orleans, 1973-80; head x-ray dept. Children's Hosp. of New Orleans, 1976-82. Contbr. articles to med. jours. Served with USPHS, 1953-55. Fellow Am. Coll. Cardiology, Am. Coll. Radiology; mem. East Baton Rouge Med. Soc., So. Soc. Pediatric Research, Am. Coll. Radiology, La. Radiology Soc., New Orleans Radiology Soc. (pres. 1985), New Orleans Pediatric Soc., Soc. Chmn. Acad. Radiology Depts., Radiol. Soc. N.Am., Am. Roentgen Ray Soc., Assn. Univ. Radiologists, Southern Yacht Club (New Orleans), Alpha Omega Alpha. Roman Catholic. Home: 458 Shady Lake Pky Baton Rouge LA 70810-4322 Office:

Tulane U Med Ctr Dept Radiology 1415 Tulane Ave New Orleans LA 70112-2605

PYERITZ, REED EDWIN, medical geneticist, educator, research director; b. Pitts., Nov. 2, 1947; s. Paul L. and Ida Mae (Meier) P.; m. Jane Ellen Tumpson, May 28, 1972; 2 children. SB in Chemistry, U. Del., 1968; AM, Harvard U., 1971, PhD in Biochemistry, 1972, MD, 1975. Diplomate Am. Bd. Internal Medicine, Am. Bd. Med. Genetics. Intern Peter Bent Brigham Hosp., Boston, 1975-76, resident, 1976-77; resident Johns Hopkins Hosp., Balt., 1977-78; from instr. to prof. medicine and pediatrics Sch. Medicine, Johns Hopkins U. Balt., 1978-93, chair dept. human genetics, prof. human genetics, medicine and pediatrics, 1994—; dir. Inst. Med. Genetics Allegheny U. Health Sci., 1993—; chmn. dept. human genetics Allegheny Singer Rsch. Inst., Pitts., 1993—; chief physician Md. Athletic Commn., Balt., 1978-93; chmn. med. adv. bd. Nat. Marfan Found., N.Y.C., 1982-93; med. dir. Alliance of Genetic Support Groups, 1994—; mem. rsch. adv. bd. Nat. Orgn. Rare Disorders, 1989—; mem. rsch. adv. com. Am. Heart Assn., 1996—. Co-editor Principles and Practice of Medical Genetics; mem. editorial bd. New Eng. Jour. Medicine; sect. editor Am. Jour. Med. Genetics; contbr. numerous articles to profl. publs. NIH Grantee. Fellow ACP, Am. Coll. Med. Genetics (dir. 1992-94, pres.-elect 1995-96); mem. Am. Soc. Human Genetics (chair program com. 1994-95), Am. Heart Assn., AAAS, Hastings Ctr. Office: Allegheny Singer Rsch Inst 320 E North Ave Pittsburgh PA 15212-4772

PYHEL, HELMUT JACK, cardiologist; b. Patterson, N.J., July 6, 1944; s. Helmut Joseph and Frieda (Alber) P.; m. Gail A. Kulbick, Aug. 24, 1969; children: Christopher, Allison. BA, Seton Hall U., 1966; MD, Hahnemann U., 1970. Diplomate Am. Bd. Internal Medicine, Am. Bd. Internal Medicine in Cardiovascular Disease. Intern in internal medicine Hahnemann Hosp., Phila., 1970-71, resident in internal medicine, 1973-75; fellow in cardiology Ind. U. Sch. Medicine, 1975-77; pvt. practice St. Petersburg, 1977—; dir. heartcare cardiac rehab., dir. coronary care unit St. Anthony's Hosp., St. Petersburg, pres. med. staff, 1992-93; clin. asst. prof. U. South Fla., St. Petersburg; med. staff St. Anthony's Hosp., Bayfront Med. Ctr., All Children's Hosp., Edward White Hosp. Contbr. articles to profl. jours. Capt. U.S. Army, 1971-73. Fellow Am. Coll. Cardiology; mem. AMA, Fla. Med. Assn., Pinellas County Med. Soc., Alpha Omega Alpha. Office: 1000 16th St N Saint Petersburg FL 33705

PYLE, HOYTE REMUS, JR., nephrologist; b. Ft. Smith, Ark., Apr. 25, 1937; s. Hoyte R. and Wanda N. (Chastain) P.; m. Dianna Wingfield, June 13, 1963; children: Hoyte R. III, Summer I. BA, U. Ark., 1959, MD, 1963. Diplomate Am. Bd. Internal Medicine. Intern, then resident U. Ark. for Med. Scis., Little Rock; dir. dialysis unit VA Hosp., Little Rock, 1969-70; pvt. practice Little Rock, 1970—. Lt. comdr. USN, 1967-69. Fellow ACP; mem. Am. Soc. Nephrology, Internat. Soc. Nephrology, Ark. Med. Soc. Republican. Baptist. Office: Little Rock Internal Med 5918 Lee Ave Little Rock AR 72205

PYLES, ROBERT LINDSAY, psychiatrist, educator; b. Winston-Salem, N.C., Mar. 22, 1936; s. Robert Kelso and Elizabeth (Waggoner) P.; m. Barbara Therese Cannon; children: Marybeth, Christopher, Kimberley, Robert, Michael. BA with honors, U. Va., 1958; MD, Harvard U., 1962. Chief resident in psychiatry Mass. Mental Health Ctr., Boston, 1965-66; pvt. practice Wellesley Hills., Mass.; instr. psychiatry Harvard U., Boston, 1969—; assoc. in psychiatry Beth Israel Hosp., Boston, 1973—; mem. faculty Psychoanlytic Inst. New Eng., Cambridge, Mass., 1975—, chmn. faculty, 1978-79, bd. dirs. 1977—, tng. analyst, 1988—; supr. Faulkner Hosp., Jamaica Plains, Mass., 1987—, Mt. Auburn Hosp., Cambridge, 1988—; cons. Polaroid Corp., Cambridge, 1969—, Sports Medicine Resource, Brookline, Mass., 1983—; med. dir. Mass. Coun. on Compulsive Gambling, Boston, 1985—; bd. dirs. Found. for Study Compulsive Gambling, Washington, 1982—. Contbr. articles to med. jours. Mem. steering com. Mass. Gambling Authority, 1988—; mem. Commn. on Non-Med. Clin. Tng., N.Y.C., 1987—; chmn. Adv. Com. on Problem Gambling, Cambridge, 1988—; bd. dirs. Internat. Found. on Problem Gambling, Boston, 1989—. Lt comdr. M.C., USN, 1963-66. Mem. Am. Psychiat. Assn., Internat. Psychoanalytic Assn., Am. Psychoanalytic Assn. (pres.-elect 1996), Mass. Med. Soc., Greater Boston Track Club, Phi Beta Kappa, Phi Eta Sigma. Home and Office: 367 Worcester St Wellesley MA 02181-5346

PYNES, LEONARD TERRY, physician, dermatologist; b. Dothan, Ala., June 28, 1952; s. Fair Daniel and Frances Idell (Hobbs) P.; m. Joanne Patricia Clark, June 3, 1972; children: Anna Elizabeth, Sarah Allison, Mary Kathryn. AS, Wallace C.C., 1972; BS, U. Ala., 1974; MD, U. South Ala., 1978. Diplomate Am. Bd. Internal Medicine, Am. Bd. Dermatology. Intern Carraway Meth. Med. Ctr., Birmingham, Ala., 1978-79, resident internal medicine, 1979-81; resident dermatology Med. Ctr. U. Ala., Birmingham, 1981-83. Fellow Am. Acad. Dermatology; mem. AMA (Physicians Recognition award 1984), ACP, Med. Assn. State Ala. (Physicians Recognitin award 1984), Houston County Med. Soc. Office: 279 W Main St Dothan AL 36301-1644

PYSH, JOSEPH JOHN, neurologist; b. Olyphant, Pa., Nov. 14, 1935; s. John Andrew and Anna Mary (Marusin) P.; m. Deborah Ann Prass, Dec. 15, 1991. BA in Biology, Wayne State U., 1958; DO, Chgo. Coll. Osteo. Medicine, 1962; PhD in Neuroanatomy, Northwestern U., Chgo., 1967. From instr. to assoc. prof. anatomy Northwestern U., Chgo., 1966-86, acting chmn. cell biology and anatomy, 1978-81, resident physician in neurology, 1983-86; assoc. prof. neurology Mich. State U., East Lansing, 1986-95, prof. neurology, 1995—; grant referee NSF, Washington, 1974—; frequent CME neurology speaker in field. Contbr. numerous articles to profl. jours; manuscript reviewer various orgns., Washington and N.Y.C. NIH grantee, 1969-82. Mem. AAAS (life), NIH (mem. rsch. grant neurology study sect. 1976-77), Am. Acad. Neurology, Am. Coll. Neuropsychiatrists, Am. Soc. Cell Biology, Am. Assn. Anatomists, Soc. Neurosci., Sigma Xi. Republican. Office: Mich State U Coll Osteo Medicine Dept Internal Medicine B305 W Fee East Lansing MI 48824

QADEER, SHEIKH ABDUL, psychiatrist; b. Delhi, India, Apr. 2, 1940; came to U.S., 1972; s. Sheikh Abdul and Akbari Begum Kareem; m. Moiney Aziz, June 1, 1951; children: Farzana, Omar, Rubina, Usman. M.B., BS, Dow Med. Coll., Karachi, Pakistan, 1964; D.P.M., R.C.P., R.C.S., Royal Colls. Physicians & Surgeons, England, 1969; M.R.C. in Psychiatry, Royal Coll. Psychiatrist-United Kingdom, England, 1972. Cert. psychiatrist, N.Y.; bd. cert. forensic examiner. Resident in psychiatry various locations in England, 1967-69; intern Jinnah Postgrad. Med. Ctr., Karachi, Pakistan, 1964-67; House officer Goodmayes Hosp., London, 1967-69; registrar Goodmayes Hosp., 1969-72; staff psychiatrist Elmira Psychiat. Ctr., Elmira, N.Y., 1972-75; cons. psychiatrist Elmira, Corning, N.Y., 1975; unit chief Elmira Psychiat. Ctr., 1975—; cons. psychiatrist area hosps., Elmira, 1975—; pres. Med. Staff Orgn., Elmira Psychiat. Ctr., 1982-84. Mem. Am. Psychiat. Assn., Med. Soc. State N.Y., Twin Tier Assn. Psychiatrists N.Y./Pa. (pres. 1986-89). Muslim. Home: 62 Orchard Dr Big Flats NY 14814-9753

QIAO, QING, pediatrician, researcher; b. Qingdao, Shandong, China, Feb. 6, 1959; Arrived in Finland, Nov. 1992; s. Tinglan Qiao and Yumin Li; m. Jinlong Zhang, Dec. 20, 1984; children: Zhang, Nan. MB, Qingdao Med. Coll., 1983. Resident, asst. Qingdao Med. Coll., 1983-87, chief resident, 1987-88, lectr., 1988-92; vis. scholar Children's Hosp. of U. Helsinki, Finland, 1992-93; rschr. dept. pub. health sci. and gen. practice U. Oulu, Finland, 1993—. Office: U Oulu Dept Pub Health Sci Gen Practice, Aapistie 1, 90220 Oulu Finland

QUAIFE, MARJORIE CLIFT, nursing educator; b. Syracuse, N.Y., Aug. 21. Diploma in Nursing with honors, Auburn Meml. Hosp; BS, Columbia U., 1962, MA, 1978. Cert. orthopaedic nurse; cert. in nursing continuing edn. and staff devel.; BLS instr. Staff instr. Columbia Presbyn. Hosp., N.Y.C.; content expert for computer assisted instrn. program-ctrl. venous catheters. Contbr. articles to numerous profl. publs. Mem. ANA, N.Y. State Nurses Assn., Nat. Assn. Orthopaedic Nurses, Nat. Assn. Nursing Staff Devel., Nat. Assn. Vascular Access Networks, Intravenous Nurses Soc., Sigma Theta Tau.

QUALEY, THOMAS LEO, JR., human services administrator; b. Kearny, N.J., Dec. 3, 1946; m. Jeanne P., Dec. 26, 1970; children: Kathlyn Jeanne, Theresa Marie. BA, Coll. Santa Fe, 1969; BSN, McNeese State U., 1986, MSN, 1995; MSHHA, U. Ala., Birmingham, 1975. Cert. gerontol. nurse, cert. nursing adminstr., advanced nursing facility adminstr. Health planner New Orleans Area Health Systems Agy.; adminstr. Oak Park Care Ctr., Lake Charles, La., Jefferson Davis Nursing Home, Jennings, La.; health care cons. Contbr. article to profl. jour. With U.S. Army, 1972-75. Fellow Royal Soc. Health; mem. Am. Coll. Health Care Adminstrs., Sigma Theta Tau (charter Kappa Psi chpt., v.p.). Home: 318 E Norwood Dr Jennings LA 70546-6028

QUAN, STUART FUN, internist, educator; b. San Francisco, May 16, 1949; s. Stuart Fun and Mabel (Wing) Q.; m. Diana Lee, Dec. 18, 1971; children: Jason Stuart, Jeremy Ryan-Stuart. AB, U. Calif., Berkeley, 1970; MD, U. Calif., San Francisco, 1974. Diplomate Am. Bd. Internal Medicine, Am. Bd. Pulmonary Diseases, Am. Bd. Critical Care Medicine, Am. Bd. Sleep Medicine. Intern in internal medicine U. Wis., Madison, 1974-75, resident, 1975-77; fellow in critical care and emergency medicine U. Calif., San Francisco, 1977-79; fellow in pulmonary medicine U. Ariz., Tucson, 1979-80, from instr. to asst. prof. medicine, 1980-86, assoc. prof. medicine, 1986-1992, prof. medicine & anesthesiology, 1992—, med. dir. respiratory care, 1980—; med. dir. ICU Univ. Med. Ctr., Tucson, 1980-87; med. dir. Vencor Hosp., Tucson, 1994—; dir. Sleep Disorders Ctr. U. Ariz., Tucson, 1984—, chief pulmonary and crit. care medicine sect., 1987—, assoc. head dept. medicine, 1995—; chmn. and cons. adv. panel on anesthesia and respiratory devices FDA, 1987-89; mem. Am. Bd. Sleep Medicine, 1991-96. Co-author: Respiratory Diseases--A Pathophysiological Approach, 1984; contbd. chpts. to various books; contbr. numerous articles to med. jours. Pres. Gymnastics Support Orgn., Tucson, 1985-87. Fellow Am. Coll. Chest Physicians, Am. Sleep Disorders Assn. (chmn. accreditation com. 1995—); mem. Am. Thoracic Soc., Am. Fedn. Clin. Rsch., Nat. Assn. Med. Dirs. Respiratory Care, Soc. for Critical Care Medicine, Phi Beta Kappa, Alpha Omega Alpha. Office: U Ariz Div Respiratory Scis 1501 N Campbell Ave Tucson AZ 85724-0001

QUANBECK, DEBORAH SHELDON, pediatric orthopaedic surgeon; b. Mpls., May 16, 1957; d. Harold Clark and Claire Gladys (Hairdahl) Sheldon; m. Thomas Henry Quanbeck, June 20, 1981; children: Amy Elizabeth, Zachary Andrew. BA, St. Olaf Coll., 1979; MD, U. Minn., 1985. Diplomate Am. Bd. Orthopaedic Surgery. Resident in orthopaedic surgery U. Minn., Mpls., 1985-90; pediatric orthopaedic surgery fellow Shriners Hosp., Mpls., 1990-91, staff pediatric orthopaedic surgeon, 1991—, med. dir. ambulatory care unit, 1993—; pediatric orthopaedic surgery fellow Gillette Hosp., St. Paul, 1990-91, staff pediatric orthopaedic surgeon, 1992-93; clin. assoc. prof. U. Minn., Mpls., 1995—. Rsch. grantee Shriners Hosp., 1995. Fellow Am. Acad. Orthopaedic Surgeons; mem. Twin Cities Orthopaedic Soc. (pres. 1991-92). Office: Shiners Hosp Twin Cities Unit 2025 E River Rd Minneapolis MN 55414

QUARLES, FRANKIE BRUNSON, obstetrician, gynecologist; b. Winston-Salem, N.C., Dec. 7, 1956; s. Larnzer and Cora Teal (Felder) Q.; divorced; children: Candyce Lynne, Kareem Brunson, Brandon, Jordan-Christopher Champen. BA, Queens Coll, CUNY, 1981; DO, N.Y. Coll. Osteo. Medicine, 1989. Diplomate Nat. Bd. Osteo. Med. Examiners. Resident in ob/gyn. Am. Med. Assn., Bedford-Stuyvesant, N.Y., 1990-94; mem. med. staff Riker's Island Correctional Facility, Elmhurst, N.Y., 1991-94; attending obstetrician/gynecologist Crouse Irving Meml. Hosp., Upstate U. Med. Ctr., St. Joseph's Hosp., Syracuse, N.Y., 1994—. Active Father's Rights Assn., Syracuse, 1994; mem. Nat. Health Svc. Corps., Dept. Health and Human Svcs., U.S. Pub. Health Svcs., 1994—. Fellow Am. Coll. Ob/Gyn. (jr.). Home: PO Box 385 Manlius NY 13104-0385

QUARLES, JOHN MONROE, microbiologist, educator; b. Chattanooga, May 24, 1942; s. John Monroe and Helen Marie (Taylor) Q.; 1 child, Bryan Stephen. BS, Fla. State U., 1963, MS, 1965; PhD, Mich. State U., 1973. Registered microbiologist. Rsch. scientist Ctrs. for Disease Control, Atlanta, 1965-66; postdoctoral fellow Oak Ridge (Tenn.) Nat. Labs, 1973-76; prof. Coll. of Medicine Tex. A&M U., College Station, Tex., 1976—; dir. grad. studies Tex. A&M U. Health Sci. Ctr., 1989-92, dir. Ctr. for Flow Cytometry & Image Analysis, 1994—. Lt. USN, 1966-69. Mem. Am. Soc. for Microbiology, Am. Soc. for Virology, Soc. for Analytical Cytology. Office: Tex A&M U Coll Medicine Dept Med Microbiology College Station TX 77843

QUATTRONE-CARROLL, DIANE ROSE, clinical social worker; b. N.Y.C., July 18, 1949; d. Mario Anthony and Filomena (Serpico) Quattrone; m. Rene Eugene Carroll Jr., June 7, 1980; children: Jenna Cristine, Jonathan Rene. BA cum laude, Bklyn. Coll., 1971; MSW, Rutgers U., 1974. Lic. marriage and family counselor, lic. clin. social worker, N.J.; bd. cert. diplomate in clin. social work. Clin. social worker, field instr. Essex County Guidance Ctr., East Orange, N.J., 1974-82; exec. dir. Psychotherapy Info. and Referral Svc., Madison, N.J., 1982-87; pvt. practice Sparta, N.J., 1982—. Nat. Assn. Social Workers.

QUEBBEMAN, EDWARD J., surgery educator; b. Ill., July 6, 1946; m. Pamela; children: Edward, Elizabeth, Jonathan. BS, No. Ill. U., 1968; MD, U. Ill., 1972; PhD, Med. Coll. Wis., 1978. Diplomate Am. Bd. Surgery. Resident in surgery Med. Coll. Wis., Milw., 1972-78, fellowship in physiology, 1974-75, asst. instr. surgery, 1974-78, asst. prof. surgery, 1978-85, assoc. prof. surgery, 1985-92, asst. prof. physiology, 1978—, prof. surgery, 1992—; dir. nutritional support Milw. County Med. Complex, 1978—; dir. surg. ICU Froedtert Meml. Hosp., Milw., 1980—; instr. Adv. Trauma Life Support, 1990—; chmn. ICU Com., 1980—. Contbr. articles to profl. jours. and chpt. to book. Mem. Am. Coll. Surgeons (mem. com. on trauma, bd. govs. sub. com. on AIDS, mem. com. on the environ. 1985-95), Quality Coun. Office: Med Coll Wis 9200 W Wisconsin Ave Milwaukee WI 53226

QUEEN, SANDY (SANDRA JEAN QUEEN), psychologist, trainer, small business owner; b. Washington, Jan. 25, 1946; d. Ralph Edward and Nettie Mae (Peeler) Bort; m. Roy Queen (div. 1973); children: David Brice, Lara Renee, Wendy Joy. BS in Psychology summa cum laude, Towson State U., 1975. Mem. staff social svc. dept. St. Joseph Hosp., Towson, Md., 1973-76; outreach dir. St. Joseph Hosp., Towson, 1980-82; legal rsch. aide, office mgr. Ellin and Assocs., Balt., 1976-77; mkt. mgr. east coast Nat. Med. Cons., Kansas City, Mo., 1977-80; owner, dir. Lifeworks, Columbia, Md., 1982—; wellness coord. St. Anthony Sch., Balt., 1975—, Goucher Coll., 1981-87, Nat. Wellness Conf., Stevens Point, Wis., 1982—, Nat. Humor Conf., 1996; adv. coun. Gov.'s Coun. on Physical Fitness, Balt. 1990—; cons.Ministry of Sport and Recreation, Australia, 1991—, Singpore Kidney Found. Author: Wellness for Children, 1982, Wellness for Youth, 1992, vol. II, 1993; (curriculi) Well and Wonderful, 1982, Child Abuse Resistance, 1985. Chmn. edn. com. Nat. Cancer Soc., Towson, 1981-83, pub. info. com. Am. Heart Assn., Balt., 1982-83; race dir. Am. Heart Assn., Balt., 1982-84; commr. Gov's Coun. on Physical Fitness, Balt., 1984-90; mem. Md. Wellness Com., Balt., 1991—; owner Lifeline Publs., 1993. Recipient Spl. Svc. award, Jaycees of Md., 1982, Am. Heart Assn., 1983. Democrat. Baptist. Office: Lifeworks PO Box 2668 Columbia MD 21045-1668

QUEENAN, JOHN THOMAS, obstetrician, gynecologist, educator; b. Aurora, Ill., June 4, 1933; s. John William and Alice Margaret (Thomas) Q.; m. Carrie Ethel Neher, June 15, 1957; children: John Thomas Jr., Carrie Lynne. BS cum laude, U. Notre Dame, 1954; MD, Cornell U., 1958. Diplomate Am. Bd. Ob-Gyn., Am. Bd. Maternal-Fetal Medicine. Intern, Bellevue Hosp., N.Y.C., 1958-59; resident N.Y. Hosp., 1959-62; instr. Cornell U., 1962-65, clin. asst. prof. ob-gyn, 1965-70, assoc. prof., 1970-72; prof. ob-gyn, chmn. dept. ob-gyn U. Louisville, 1972-80; chief ob-gyn. Norton-Children's Hosps., Louisville Gen. Hosp., 1972-82; prof., chmn. dept. ob-gyn Georgetown U., 1980—, obstetrician and gynecologist-in-chief Georgetown U. Hosp., 1980—; spl. adv. ob-gyn devices panel FDA, 1978—. Bd. dirs. ARC, Greenwich, Conn., 1970-72. Fellow Am. Gynecol. and Obstet. Soc.; mem. Am. Coll. Obstetricians and Gynecologists, ACS, Am. Fertility Soc., Nat. Perinatal Assn. (pres. 1976-78), So. Perinatal Assn. (pres. 1975), Royal Soc. Medicine, Round Hill Club (Greenwich), Cosmos Club (Washington), Chevy Chase Club (Md.), Edgartown Yacht Club (Mass.), Alpha Omega Alpha. Author: Modern Management of the Rh Problem, 1977; Management of High Risk Pregnancy, 1980, 2d edit., 1985, 3d edit., 94; (with Carrie N. Queenan) A New Life, 1980, 2d edit., 1986, (with Kimberly K. Leslie) Preconceptions: Preparation for Pregnancy, 1989; editor: (with John C. Hobbins) Protocols for High Risk Pregnancies, 1982, 3d edit., 1995; editor-in-chief Contemporary Ob-Gyn, 1973—. Home: 3257 N St NW Washington DC 20007-2845 Office: Georgetown U Hosp 3800 Reservoir Rd NW Washington DC 20007-2196

QUEN, JACQUES MARC, psychiatrist, educator; b. N.Y.C., Oct. 23, 1928; s. Mardochée J. and Sarina Q. BS, Bethany Coll., 1948; MS, Brown U., 1950; MD, Yale U., 1954. Diplomate Nat. Bd. Med. Examiners, Am. Bd. Forensic Psychiatry (bd. dirs. 1979-82), Am. Bd. Neurology and Psychiatry. Intern Kings County Hosp., Bklyn., 1954-55; jr. asst. resident West Haven (Conn.) VA Hosp., 1955-56, chief resident, 1957-58; sr. asst. resident Grace-New Haven Cmty. Hosp., 1956-57; sr. psychiatrist outpatient unit Montefiore Hosp., Bronx, N.Y., 1960-61; asst. dept. psychiatry Cornell U. Med. Coll., N.Y.C., 1961-63, clin. instr., 1963-66, clin. asst. prof., 1966-71, clin. assoc. prof., 1971-78, clin. prof., 1978—; cons. psychiatrist Beth Abraham Home for Chronic Disease, N.Y.C., 1961-63; psychiatrist-in-charge Welfare Med. Care Project, N.Y. Hosp., N.Y.C., 1961-63. Assoc. editor Yale U. Jour. Biology and Medicine, 1950-54, Bull. Am. Acad. Psychiatry and Law, 1974-83, Jour. History Medicine and Allied Scis., 1986-88; mem. editorial bd. Classics in Psychiatry, 1974-76, Mental Health, 1977-80. Served with U.S. Army, 1958-60. Fellow Am. Psychiat. Assn. (life); mem. AAAS, Am. Acad. Forensic Scis., Am. Acad. Psychiatry and Law (assoc. editor bull. 1974-83, Disting. Svc. award 1986, golden award 1992), Am. Acad. Psychoanalysis, Am. Assn. History Medicine, N.Y. Acad. Medicine, N.Y. County Med. Soc., N.Y. State Med. Soc., Sigma Xi.

QUENCER, ROBERT MOORE, neuroradiologist, researcher; b. Jersey City, Nov. 14, 1937; s. Arthur Bauer and Isabell (Moore) Q.; m. Christine F. Thomas, Sept. 16, 1972; children: Kevin, Keith. BS, Cornell U., 1959, MS, 1963; MD, SUNY, Syracuse, 1967. Diplomate Am. Bd. Radiology, Nat. Bd. Med. Examiners; cert. of added qualifications in neuroradiology. Intern Jackson Meml. Hosp., Miami, Fla., 1967-68; resident in radiology Columbia U., N.Y.C., 1968-71, fellow in neuroradiology, 1971-72; asst. prof. Downstate Med. Ctr., Bklyn., 1972-76; assoc. prof. U. Miami, 1976-79, prof., 1979-92, chmn., prof., 1992—, chief sect. neuroradiology, 1976-86, dir. divsn. magnetic resonance imaging, 1986-92; vis. prof. U. Tenn. Coll. Medicine, Memphis, 1982, Downstate Med. Ctr. Coll. Medicine, Bklyn., 1992, U. Vt. Coll. Medicine, Burlington, 1983, N.Y. Med. Coll., Valhalla, 1984, U. Va. Sch. Medicine, Charlottesville, 1984, U. Ky. Sch. Medicine, Lexington, 1985, Yale U. Sch. Medicine, New Haven, 1986, Columbia U. Sch. Medicine, N.Y.C., 1986, The Mayo Clinic & Found., Rochester, Minn., 1987, Med. Coll. Va., Richmond, 1988, U. Pa. Sch. Medicine, Phila., 1988, Harvard U. Sch. Medicine/Mass. Gen. Hosp., Boston, 1989, U. Conn., Farmington, 1990, Kumamoto, Japan, 1993, U. Man., Can., 1992; Phaler lectr. Phila. Roentgen Soc., 1995; dir. programs in dept. radiology U. Miami Sch. Medicine, 1984, 86, Med. Coll. Wis., Tucson, 1990, 92, Kauai, Hawaii, 1991, Whistler, B.C., 1990; guest lectr. at ASEAN Congress of Radiology, Malaysia, 1992, Royal Australia Radiology Soc., Brisbane, 1993; adv. cons. NIH, 1987, 90; sci. merit reviewer V.A., 1987; presenter, lectr. in field. Author: Neurosonography, 1988; dep. editor Am. Jour. Neuroradiology, 1984—; assoc. editor for neuroimaging Yearbook of Neurology and Neurosurgery, 1991—; book reviewer Am. Jour. Neuroradiology, 1984—, Paraplegia, 1989—, Radiographics, 1991—, Pediatrics, 1993—; mem. editorial bd. Jour. Clin. Neuro-Ophthalmology, 1980—; contbr. articles to profl. jours. Pres. Am. Soc. Neuroradiology, 1994-95; prin. investigator NIH Grant on imaging/pathology of spinal cord injury. Lt. (j.g.) USN, 1959-61. Fellow Am. Coll. Radiology, Am. Soc. Neuroradiology (pres. 1994-95, program com. 1985-89, 92, editl. com. 1984—, publs. com. 1984—); mem. AMA, Radiol. Soc. N.Am. (program subcom. on neuroradiology 1990-94), Southeastern Neuroradiol. Soc. (founder, pres. 1980-81, examiner for bd. certification in radiology and neuroradiology), Dade County Med. Assn., Soc. Chmn. Acad. Radiology Depts., Fla. Radiol. Soc. (magnetic resonance com. 1991-92), Alpha Omega Alpha. Office: U Miami 1150 NW 14th St Miami FL 33136-2106

QUERESHI, MOHAMMED YOUNUS, psychology educator, consultant; b. Haripur Hazara, Pakistan, Dec. 12, 1929; came to U.S., 1953; s. Mohammed Noor and Meryam Khatoon Q.; m. Nora Jane Knapp, May 27, 1958 (div. Nov. 1979); children—Ahmed, Amna, Shukria, Shawn; m. Farzana Kaukab, May 17, 1980; children—Ajmel, Sabeeha, Azem. Ph.D., U. Ill., 1958. Lic. psychologist, Wis. Asst. prof. psychology U. Minn., Duluth, 1960-62, U. N.D., Grand Forks, 1962-64; assoc. prof. psychology Marquette U., Milw., 1964-70, prof., 1970—, chmn. dept. psychology, 1971-77; cons. psychologist. Pres. 81st Street Sch. PTA, 1968-70; merit badge counselor Milw. County council Boy Scouts Am., 1973-88; pres. Islamic Assn. Greater Milw., 1978-83. NIH grantee, 1962-69; Office of Edn. grantee, 1970-71; TOPS Club grantee, 1969-76. Mem. Am. Psychol. Assn., Psychometric Soc., AAAS, Sigma Xi. Author: Statistics and Behavior: An Introduction, 1980, 2nd edit., 1991; contbr. articles to sci. and profl. jours. Home: 2759 N 68th St Milwaukee WI 53210-1204 Office: Marquette U Schroeder Health Complex PO Box 1881 Milwaukee WI 53201

QUEVEDO, ARTURO R., ophthalmologist, consultant; b. Guatemala, Guatemala, Dec. 14, 1937; s. Arturo Quevedo and Marian Campbell Laberée; m. Amelia Guadalupe Widmann, June 14, 1971 (div. 1975); 1 child, Arturo Robert Quevedo. AB in Biochemistry, Harvard U., 1959; MD, McGill U., Montreal, Que., 1963. Diplomate Nat. Bd. Med. Examiners, Am. Bd. Ophthalmology. Resident Mass. Eye and Ear Infirmary, Boston, 1965-68, postgrad. resident in retina, 1968; chief dept. ophthalmology Roosevelt Hosp., Guatemala, 1969-76, dir. ophthalmology postgrad. program, 1970—, cons. ophthalmologist, 1976—; prof. U. San Carlos, Guatemala, 1974—; dir. teaching Hosp. Rodolfo Robles, Guatemala, 1970-83; bd. dirs. Comité Pro Ciegos, Guatemala, 1970-80. Fellow Am. Acad. Ophthalmology; mem. Pan Am. Assn. Ophthalmology, Guatemalan Assn. Ophthalmology. Office: Zona 13, 11 Calle 15-62, Guatemala City Guatemala

QUICK, VALERIE ANNE, sonographer; b. Alta., Can., Feb. 14, 1952; came to U.S., 1953; d. Kenneth Conrad and Kathryn (Maller) Bjorge. Grad. high sch., Salinas, Calif. Registered adult and pediatric echocardiographer, abdomen, small parts and ob-gyn sonographer; registered cardiovasc. technician. Chief EKG technician Natividad Med. Ctr., Salinas, 1978-81, chief ultrasound dept., 1981-94, chief cardiac echo lab., 1995—. Mem. Am. Inst. Ultrasound in Medicine, Am. Soc. Echocardiography, Nat. Soc. for Cardiopulmonary Technicians, Soc. Pediat. ECHO, Soc. Diagnostic Med. Sonographers, Am. Heart Assn., Am. Registry Diagnostic Med. Sonographers. Office: PO Box 6694 Salinas CA 93912-6694

QUIE, PAUL GERHARDT, physician, educator; b. Dennison, Minn., Feb. 3, 1925; s. Albert Knute and Nettie Marie (Jacobson) Q.; m. Elizabeth Holmes, Aug. 10, 1951; children: Katie, Bill, Paul, David. B.A., St. Olaf Coll., 1949; M.D., Yale U., 1953; PhD (hon.), U. Lund, 1993. Diplomate Am. Bd. Pediatrics, Nat. Bd. Med. Examiners (mem.). Intern Hennepin County Hosp., 1953-54; pediatric resident U. Minn. Hosps., 1957-59; mem. faculty U. Minn. Med. Sch., 1959—, prof. pediatrics, 1968—, prof. microbiology, 1974—; assoc. dean of students, 1992—; Am. Legion meml. heart research prof. U. Minn. Med. Sch., 1974-91, Regents prof., 1991, interim dir. Ctr. for Biomed. Ethics, 1985-86; attending physician Hennepin County Hosp., 1959-91; cons. U. Minn. Nursery Sch., 1959-91; chief of staff U. Minn. Hosp., 1979-84; vis. physician Radcliffe Infirmary, Oxford, Eng., 1971-72; mem. Adv. Allergy and Infectious Disease Coun., 1976-80; mem. pediat. com. NRC, 1978; mem. bd. sci. counselors Gamble Inst., 1985-90; vis. prof. U. Bergen, 1991; hon. prof. U. Hong Kong Med. Sch., 1995; vis. prof. pediat. Chubu Hosp., Nagasaki, Japan, 1996. Mem. editorial bd. Pediatrics, 1970-76, Rev. Infectious Diseases, 1989-92. Served with USNR, 1954-57; med. officer. Recipient E. Mead-Johnson award Am. Acad. Pediatrics, 1971; Guggenheim fellow, 1971-72; John and Mary R. Markle scholar, 1960-65; Alexander Von Humbolt fellow, 1986. Mem. Inst. Medicine of NAS, N.W. Pediatrics Soc., Minn. Med. Found. (pres. 1986-88), Am. Fedn. Clin. Rsch., Am. Soc. Microbiology, Infectious Diseases Soc. Am. (coun. 1977-82, pres. 1985, Bristol award 1994), Soc. Pediatric Rsch., Am. Pediatric Soc. (coun. 1976-83, pres. 1987-88), Am. Soc. Clin. Investigation, Minn. Acad. Pediatrics, Am. Acad. Pediatrics, Assn. Am. Physicians, Minn. Acad.

Medicine (pres. 1993-94). Home: 2154 Commonwealth Ave Saint Paul MN 55108-1717 Office: U Minn Hosp PO Box 483 Minneapolis MN 55440-0483

QUIGLEY, GEORGE J., ophthalmologist; b. Indpls., July 9, 1940; s. Joseph B. and Denoe M. (Wolford) Q.; m. Kay A. Heidenreich, Feb. 4, 1967; children: Kimberly, Marc. AB, Ind. U., 1962; MD, Ind. U. Sch. Medicine, Indpls., 1965. Diplomate Am. Bd. Ophthalmology. Resident Ind. U. Sch. Medicine, Indpls., 1968-71; pvt. practice Indpls., 1971—. Lt. comdr. USN, 1966-68. Fellow Am. Acad. Ophthalmology; mem. Ind. State Med. Soc., Ind. Acad. Ophthalmology, Indpls. Med. Soc., Indpls. Ophthalmol. Soc. Home: 7810 Providence Cir Indianapolis IN 46250 Office: 1400 N Ritter Ave #271 Indianapolis IN 46219

QUIGLEY, HERBERT JOSEPH, JR., pathologist, educator; b. Phila., Mar. 6, 1937; s. Herbert Joseph and Mary Kathleen (Carney) Q.; m. Jacqueline Jean Stocksdale, Nov. 28, 1965 (div. 1974); 1 child, Amelia Anne. BS in Chemistry, Franklin and Marshall Coll., 1958; MD, U. Pa., 1962. Diplomate Am. Bd. Pathology. Chief pathology U.S. Naval Hosp., Key West, Fla., 1966-68, Monroe County Hosp., Key West, 1966-68; from asst. prof. to assoc. prof. pathology Creighton U., Omaha, 1968-72; chief pathology service VA Med. Ctr., Omaha, 1968-88; prof. pathology Creighton U., 1972—; dir. Triton-Chito Inc., Omaha. Contbr. articles to profl. jours. Patentee in field. Bd. dirs., for pres. chmn. Nebr. Assn. Earth Sci. Clubs, Omaha, 1972—. Served to lt. comdr. USNR, 1966-68. Recipient Career Devel. award NIH, 1962-66; Borden prize med. research Borden Co., Inc., 1962; fellow NIH, Nat. Cancer Inst., 1958-62. Fellow Coll Am. Pathologists, Am. Soc. Clin. Pathologists, Am. Inst. Chemists; mem. Nebr. Assn. Pathologists, N.Y. Acad. Scis. Republican. Roman Catholic. Avocations: paleontology, geology. Home: 9511 Mockingbird Dr Omaha NE 68127-2423 Office: VA Med Center 4101 Woolworth Ave Omaha NE 68105-1850

QUILES, DORIS ANN, health facility administrator; b. Valley Forge, Pa., June 23, 1955; d. William I. and Magdalena (Messinger) Q. BSN, Ind. U., Pa., 1977; MS in Psychiat.-Mental Health Nursing, U. Pa., 1981. RN, Pa. Staff nurse Inst. Pa. Hosp., Phila., 1977-81, Lankenau Hosp., Wynnewood, Pa., 1979-80; from clin. nurse to asst. acting dir. patient mgmt. Phila. State Hosp., 1981-86; staff devel. coord. Hampton Hosp., Rancocas, N.J., 1986-87; asst. hosp. dir. psychiat., med., emergency svcs. Temple U. Hosp., Phila., 1987—; presenter in field. Bd. dirs. Womans Christian Alliance, Phila., 1995—. Recipient Legion of Honor, Chapel of Four Chaplains, Phila., 1984. Mem. ANA, Southeastern Orgn. Nurse Leaders, Sigma Theta Tau. Home: 119 W College Ave Yardley PA 19067 Office: Temple Univ Hosp 3401 N Broad St Philadelphia PA 19140-5103

QUILLIAN, WARREN WILSON, II, pediatrician, educator; b. Miami, Fla., Jan. 21, 1936; s. Warren Wilson and Rosabel (Brown) Q.; m. Sallie Ruth Creel, July 26, 1958; children: Rutledge, Ruth, Warren C., Frances. MD, Emory U., 1961. Diplomate Am. Bd. Pediat. (examiner 1966—, bd. dirs. 1974-80, 1992—, treas. 1978, v.p. 1979, pres. 1980). Intern in pediatrics Vandertilt U., Nashville, 1961-62; resident Children's Hosp. Med. Ctr., Harvard U., Boston, 1962-63; chief resident Grady Meml. Hosp., Emory U., Atlanta, 1963-64; pvt. practice, Coral Gables, Fla., 1966; instr., asst. clin. prof., assoc. clin. prof., now clin. prof. pediat. U. Miami Med. Sch., 1966—; active staff, bd. dirs. Miami Children's Hosp.; active staff Jackson Meml. Hosp.; chief pediat. Doctors' Hosp.; mem. courtesy staff Mercy Hosp., Bapt. Hosp., South Miami Hosp., Cedars of Lebanon Hosp.; chmn. health adv. com. Dade County Schs.; bd. dirs., v.p. Am. Bd. Pediat. Found., 1991—; mem. adv. bd. McGlannon Sch.; cons. Fla. Div. Med. Svcs.; bd. dirs. Bank Coral Gables. Contbr. articles to med. jours. Hon. bd. dirs. Soc. for Abused Children of Children's Home Soc., Miami, 1980-84; mem. Coral Gables Code Enforcement Bd., 1986-88; team-sch. physician Coral Gables Sr. H.G., 1980-88; bd. dirs. Dade County March of Dimes, Miami, 1968-72; bd. advisors Dade County Assn. Retarded Children, 1986-76; trustee Emory U., 1991—; mem. coun. ministries, youth coord., mem. fin. com., Sunday sch. tchr. United Meth. Ch. Coral Gables, 1966—; mem. parrish rels. com.; mem. bd. advisors The Growing Place. Capt. M.C., U.S. Army, 1964-66. Recipient citation of merit Emory U., 1980, alumni commendation Miami Children's Hosp., 1983, Teaching award U. Miami Sch. Medicine, 1995. Fellow Am. Acad. Pediat.; mem. AMA, Fla. Med. Assn. (sch. health com.), Fla. Pediatric Soc. (past chmn. sch. health com.), So. Med. Assn., Dade County Med. Assn. (sch. health com., continuing edn. com.), Empirical Soc. (past pres.), So. Soc. for Pediatric Rsch., So. Perinatal Soc., Greater Miami Pediatric Soc. (past pres., chmn. legis. and sch. health com.), Miami Med. Forum (past pres., Maxwell Cup 1985), Alpha Omega Alpha, Omicron Delta Kappa, Alpha Epsilon Upsilon, Phi Delta Theta. Democrat. Office: 305 Granello Ave Coral Gables FL 33146-1806

QUINN, CHRISTINE AGNES, radiologist; b. Cleve., Sept. 23, 1946; d. Paul Leo and Estelle Christine Q.; m. Paul C. Janicki, July 11, 1970; children: Sarah Christine, Megan Alexandra. B.A., Marquette U., 1967; M.D., Med. Coll. Pa., 1971. Diplomate Am. Bd. Radiology. Intern, St. Luke's Hosp., Cleve., 1971-72; resident in diagnostic radiology Cleve. Clinic Found., 1972-75, radiologist, 1975-81; radiologist Marymount Hosp., Cleve., 1981-93, radiologist Clev. Clinic Found., 1993—; physician dir. Techniques in Mammography Conf., 1989—. Co-author: Positioning Techniques for Mammographers, 1991; contbr. to CRC Handbook Series, vol. II, 1977; contbr. articles to profl. jours. Trustee Am. Cancer Soc. Named Women's Health Champion of Northeast Ohio, Cleve. mag., St. Alexis Hosp., 1991. Mem. AMA, Radiol. Soc. N.Am., Am. Coll. Radiology, Soc. Nuclear Medicine, Ohio Med. Soc., Cuyahoga County Med. Soc. Home: 2781 Sherbrooke Rd Cleveland OH 44122-1829 Office: Cleve Clinic 9500 Euclid Ave Cleveland OH 44195

QUINN, CHRISTOPHER JOSEPH, optometrist; b. Orange, N.J., Dec. 11, 1956; s. Joseph John and Mary Jane Quinn; m. Susan C. Heidt, Aug. 27, 1983; children: Kelly Brooke, William Christopher. BA in Biology, Ind. U., 1978; OD, Pa. Coll. Optometry, 1985. Dir. Omni Eye Svcs., Iselin, N.J., 1986—; bd. dirs. N.J. Optometric Assn., Trenton, 1987-93, sec.-treas., 1995-96, Optometrist of Yr. 1993. Contbr. chpt. in book. Mem. APHA, Am. Acad. Optometry, Am. Optometric Assn. Office: Omni Eye Svcs 485 Rt #1 S Bldg A Iselin NJ 08830

QUINN, EDWARD FRANCIS, III, orthopedic surgeon; b. Washington, Apr. 28, 1944; s. Edward F. Jr. and Louise Q.; m. Audrey Dickinson; 1 child, Edward Francis IV. BS, U. Md., 1968, MD, 1969. Diplomate Am. Bd. Orthopedic Surgery, Am. Bd. Neurol. and Orthopedic Surgery. Intern Ohio State Univ. Hosp., Columbus, 1969-70; resident USN Hosp., Bethesda, Md., 1971-74; staff Milford (Del.) Meml. Hosp., 1975—, pres. med. staff, 1991-93, chief surgery, 1993—; cons. staff Beebe Hosp., Lewes, Del., 1975-92, Nanticoke Meml. Hosp., Seaford, Del., 1975-90, Kent Gen. Hosp., Dover, Del., 1981-90, attending staff, 1990-94. Bd. advisors So. Campus of Goldey Beacon Coll., 1987-91. Lt. comdr. USN, 1970-75. Fellow ACS, Am. Acad. Neurol./Orthopeadic Surgery, Internat. Coll. Surgeons; mem. AMA, Med. Soc. Del., Sussex County Med. Soc., Am. Fracture Assn., So. Med. Assn., Del. Soc. Orthopaedic Surgeons, Ea. Orthopaedic Assn., So. Orthopaedic Assn., Acad. Neuro-Muscular Thermography, Chemonucleolysis Adv. Bd., Milford Rotary Club, Rotary Internat. (Paul Harris fellow 1986), Am. Acad. Disability Evaluation Rsch. Physicians, Am. Legion, So. Del. C. of C. (bd. dirs. 1983-90). Republican. Office: Dickinson Med Group 800 N Dupont Blvd Milford DE 19963-1031

QUINN, GRAHAM EARL, ophthalmologist; b. Raleigh, N.C., May 28, 1947; s. Graham S. and Edna (Moore) Q.; m. Dianne McDonald; children: Graham, Elizabeth, Hunter. AB, Duke U., 1965-69, MD, 1973. Diplomate Am. Bd. Ophthalmology. From instr. to assoc. prof. ophthalmology Children's Hosp., Phila., 1979—; cons. Pa. Hosp., Phila., 1979—, U. Pa. Med. Ctr., Phila., 1980—, Med. Coll. Pa., Phila., 1984—, Albert Einstein Med. Ctr., Phila., 1984—. Mem. Am. Assn. Pediat. Ophthalmology, Am. Acad. Pediatrics, Am. Acad. Pediatric Ophthalmology, Am. Acad. Ophthalmology. Office: Childrens Hosp Phila 34th St/Civic Ctr Blvd Philadelphia PA 19104

QUINN, LOIS MARIE, health services administrator; b. Boston; d. Charles Edward and Grace Marie (Lowder) Seabrook; R.N., Boston City Hosp.; B.A., Glassboro State Coll., 1977; M.A., Central Mich. U., 1982; m. Richard Edward Quinn; children—Deborah Marie, Christopher Edward, Erin Elizabeth, Patrick Richard. Pediatric staff nurse Boston City Hosp.; staff nurse, coronary care nurse, supr., patient edn. coordinator, dir. nursing service Rancocas Valley Hosp., Willingboro, N.J., 1967-78; nursing mgmt. cons. Am. Medicorp., Bala Cynwyd, Pa., 1977-78; asst. adminstr. Washington Meml. Hosp., Turnersville, N.J., 1978-80; pres. Lois Quinn Assocs., Nursing Mgmt. Cons., Willingboro, N.J., 1980-83; mgr. nursing services Universal Health Services, Inc., King of Prussia, Pa., 1983-84, dir. mgmt. services, profl. standards, 1984-90, dir. profl. svcs. Am. Healthcare Mgmt., Inc. 1990-93; v.p. profl. affairs, Am. Healthcare Mgmt., Inc., 1993-94; sr. v.p. profl. affairs Primary Health Sys., L.P., 1994—. Cert. nursing adminstr. Mem. Amnesty Internat., Coop. Am., Bread for the World. Mem. Common Cause, Am. Nurses Assn., Pa. Nurses Assn., N.J. Nurses Assn. (coordinator So. N.J. nursing adminstrs. and educators 1975-77), Sigma Iota Epsilon. Roman Catholic. Developer of proprietary automated quality measurement and productivity systems; featured in newspaper articles and nat. publs Address: 360 Old Forge Crossing Devon PA 19333

QUINN, MARK T., medical educator; b. San Jose, Calif., June 11, 1958. BA in Biology and Chemistry, Point Loma Coll., 1982. PhD in Physiology and Pharmacology, U. Calif., San Diego, 1987. Postdoctoral rsch. assoc. Rsch. Inst. Scripps Clinic, La Jolla, Calif., 1988-89; sr. rsch. assoc. Mont. State U., Bozeman, 1989-90, asst., assoc. rsch. prof., 1991-95, asst. prof., 1995—. Contbr. articles to profl. jours. Recipient Investigator award Arthritis Found., 1991, Health FIRST award NIH, 1992—, Charles and Nora Wiley Meritorious Rsch. award, 1993; grantee Am. Cancer Soc., 1989, Am. Lung Assn., 1991-93, Arthritis Found., 1994—, USDA, 1995—; U. Calif. Regents fellow, 1981, Point Loma Coll. Rsch. Assocs. fellow, 1981, San Diego & Grad. Opportunity Rsch. fellow, 1986-87, Arthritis Found. Postdoctoral fellow, 1989-91. Mem. Am. Soc. Cell Biology, Am. Heart Assn. (coun. basic rsch., Established Investigator award 1996—), Soc. Leukocyte Biology. Office: Mont State U Dept Vet Molecular Biology Bozeman MT 59717

QUINN, PETER D., oral and maxillofacial surgeon; b. Scranton, Pa., June 12, 1948. BS, U. Scranton, 1970; DMD, U. Pa., 1974; MD, Med. Coll. Pa., 1981. Chmn. oral and maxillofacial surgery dept. U. Pa. Sch. Dental Medicine, Phila., 1986—; chmn. oral and maxillofacial surgery and hosp. dentistry U. Pa. Med. Ctr., Phila., 1992—. Fellow Am. Assn. Oral and Maxillofacial Surgeons. Office: U Penn Med Ctr 3400 Spruce St Philadelphia PA 19104

QUINN, PHILIP FRANCIS, psychologist, educator; b. Chgo., Feb. 8, 1932; s. William Martin and Helen Gertrude (Coffey) Q.; m. Jo Ann Farina, June 10, 1974; children—Allain, Megan, Colleen. Student Loyola U., Chgo., 1949-51, M.A. in Sociology, 1960, Ph.D. in Counseling, 1972; B.A., Xavier U., 1955; S.T.B., West Baden Coll., 1965; diploma div. Religion and Psychiatry, Menninger Sch. Psychiatry, 1966. Ordained priest Roman Catholic Ch., 1964; laicized, 1973. Instr. sociology Xavier U., Cin., 1967-69; teaching asst. dept. counseling and guidance Grad. Sch. Edn., Loyola U., Chgo., 1970-71; dir. pastoral counseling ctr. St. Joseph's Hosp. Mental Health Ctr., Tampa, Fla., 1971-73; clin. asst. prof. psychiatry U. South Fla. Coll. Medicine, Tampa, 1972-73; assoc. prof. dept. social sci. U. Tampa, 1973—, chair criminology and social work, 1991-93; pvt. practice psychology, Tampa, 1973—; cons. Tampa Community Correctional Ctr., 1975, Dixie Hollins High Sch., 1979. Bd. dirs. DWI Counter Attack, 1977-80, 84—, Cath. Social Services, Tampa, 1981-83; vol. psychol. services Tampa Police Dept., 1981-84. Voted One of the Top Psychotherapists in U.S. Town and Country mag., 1988. Mem. Am. Psychol. Assn., Am. Assn. Marriage and Family Therapy . Contbr. articles to profl. jours. Office: Univ Profl Ctr 3500 E Fletcher Ave Ste 522 Tampa FL 33613-4711

QUINNAN, GERALD VINCENT, JR., medical educator; b. Boston, Sept. 7, 1947; s. Gerald Vincent and Mary (Lally) Q.; children: Kevin, Kylie, Kathleen, John, Gerald; m. Leigh A. Sawyer. AB in Chemistry, Coll. Holy Cross, 1969; MD cum laude, St. Louis U., 1973. Diplomate Am. Bd. Internal Medicine. Intern, resident, fellow Boston U. Med. Ctr., 1973-77; med. officer Bur. Biologics, USPHS, Bethesda, Md., 1977; advanced through grades to asst. surgeon gen. USPHS, 1992; dir. herpes virus br., dep. dir. div. virology Bur. Biologics, Bethesda, 1980-81; dir. div. virology Ctr. for Drugs and Biologics, Bethesda, 1981-88; dep. dir. Ctr. Biologics Evaluation and Rsch., Bethesda, 1988-93, acting dir., 1990-92; prof. uniformed svcs. U. Health Scis., Bethesda, 1993—. Contbr. chpts. to books, numerous articles to profl. jours.; editl. bd./reviewer several jours. Fellow Infectious Diseases Soc. Am.; mem. AAAS, Am. Soc. for Microbiology, Am. Soc. for Clin. Investigation, Sigma Xi, Alpha Omega Alpha. Roman Catholic. Office: Uniformed Svcs U Hlth Scis Div Tropical PH 4301 Jones Bridge Rd Bethesda MD 20814

QUINONES-BALDRICH, WILLIAM J., surgeon, educator; b. San Juan, P.R., Jan. 2, 1953; s. William Quinones and Maria Cecilia Baldrich; m. Sherrylin H. Hernandez-Linares; children: William, Jose. BS magna cum laude, U. P.R., San Juan, 1973, MD, 1977. Intern, then resident Thomas Jefferson U. Hosp., Phila., 1977-82; fellow in vascular surgery UCLA Med. Ctr., 1982-84; adj. asst. prof. surgery Sch. Medicine UCLA, 1982-84, asst. prof. surgery, 1984-90, assoc. prof. surgery, 1990-96, prof. surgery, 1996—; pres. R&D, 1987—. Recipient Bristol award Puerto Rican Med. Assn., 1977. Fellow ACS; mem. Peripheral Vascular Surgery Soc. (sec. 1991-93, pres. 1994-95), Internat. Soc. Vascular Surgery, Soc. for Vascular Surgery, Western Vascular Soc., So. Calif. Vascular Surgery Soc., Bay Surgery Soc. (sec. 1994-95, pres. 1996—). Office: Westwood Plz 200 UCLA Med Plz # 530 Los Angeles CA 90095-6958

QUINTANILLA, ANTONIO PAULET, physician, educator; b. Peru, Feb. 8, 1927; came to U.S., 1963, naturalized, 1974; s. Leandro Marino and Edel Paulet Q.; m. Mary Parker Rodriguez, May 2, 1958; children: Antonio Paulet, Angela, Francis, Cecilia, John. PhD, San Marcos U., 1948, MD, 1957. Assoc. prof. physiology U. Arequipa, Peru, 1960-63; assoc. in physiology Cornell U., N.Y., 1963-64; prof. physiology U. Arequipa, 1964-68; assoc. prof. medicine Northwestern U., 1969-80, prof., 1980—; chief renal sect. VA Lakeside Hosp., 1976-90; cons. nephrologist Northwestern Meml. Hosp., Evanston Hosp., 1990—; lectr. nat. Ctr. Advanced Med. Edn., Chgo.; mem. adv. bd. Kidney Found. Ill., Am. Fedn. Clin. Rssch. Fellow ACP; mem. Chgo. Heart Assn. (hypertension council), Central Soc. Clin Rsch., Am. Soc. Clin. Pharmacology and Therapeutics, Am., Internat. socs. nephrology, Chgo. Soc. Internal Medicine, Am. Physiol. Soc. Contbr. articles on renal disease to med. jours.; author books, poetry, short stories. Home: 9352 Karlov Ave Skokie IL 60076-1415 Office: 2650 Ridge Ave Evanston IL 60201-1718

QUINTERO DEL RIO, GLORIA MARIA, medical record adminstrator; b. San Juan, P.R., Sept. 2, 1966; d. Hector Quintero and Iris Del Rio. BS in Biology, U. P.R., Rio Pedras, 1989, Assoc. Emergency Med. Tech., 1990; MS in Med. Record Adminstrn., U. Puerto Rico, Rio Pedras, 1992. Rschr. Coll. of Health Related Professions, Rio Piedras, P.R., 1991-92; med. record dir. Carolina (P.R.) Regional Hosp., 1992-93; asst. exec. dir. P.R. Dept Health, Santurce, 1993; regional med. record adminstr. P.R. Dept Health, Bayamón, 1993-94; med. records auditor P.R. Dept Health, Santurce, 1994-95; accreditation coord. P.R. Dept Health, Rio Pedras, 1995—. Recipient Nat. Collegiate award U.S. Achievement Acad., 1990. Mem. Am. Health Info. Mgmt. Assn. (registered record adminstr.), P.R. Health Info. Mgmt. Assn. Home: Ste 1 # 610 Tintillo Hills Guaynabo PR 00966 Office: Univ Hosp PR Med Ctr Bo Monacillos Rio Piedras PR 00935

QUINTIN, LUC, anesthesiologist; b. Paris, Oct. 4, 1950; s. Jean Quintin and Anne Flatres; children: Marc, Yann. MD, Brest, France, 1977; Fellow Anesthesiology, Paris-Creteil, 1977; PhD, Lyon, France, 1984. Sr. investigator Roussel-Hoechst Pharmaceuticals, Paris-Romainville, 1983-86; established investigator Ctr. Nat. de la Recherche Scientifique, 1988—; anesthetist Hosp. H. Mondor, Paris-Creteil, 1978-79, 1983-90; sr. resident Royal Victoria Hosp., Montreal, 1979-80; anesthetist Hosp. Cardiologique, Lyon, 1980-83, Hosp. E. Herriot, Lyon, 1990—; cons. Bohringer-Ingelheim, France, 1986-92, UCB S.A., Belgium, 1992-94. Jr. officer French Army, 1976. Mem. Am. Soc. Anesthesiology, Am. Soc. Neurosci. Office: Physiology Sch Medicine, 69 373 Lyon France

QUINTON, RONALD RAY, thoracic surgeon; b. Peru, Ind., Apr. 11, 1950; s. William Raymond and Katherine Nellie (Aspnwall) Q.; m. JoNell Smith, Apr. 29, 1979; children: Joseph Blake, Nicholas Solon, Leah Ashley. BS, USAF Acad., 1972; MD, Tulane U., 1976. Diplomate Am. Bd. Thoracic Surgery, Am. Bd. Surgery. Commd. 2d lt. USAF, 1972, advanced through grades to lt. col., separated, 1989; staff thoracic surgeon LDS Hosp., Salt Lake City, 1989-92, St. Peter Hosp., Olympia, Wash., 1992—; clin. instr. U. Utah, 1989-92; chmn. dept. thoracic surgery USAF Med. Ctr., Keesler AFB, Miss., 1983-86. Fellow Am. Coll. Surgeons, Am. Coll. Chest Surgeons; mem. Am. Heart Assn., Intermnt. Thoracic Soc., Soc. Thoracic Surgeons, Air Force Soc. Clin. Surgeons. Office: Olympia Cardiac Surgery Inc 525 Lilly Rd NE Ste 200 Olympia WA 98506

QUINTOS, ELIAS RILLORAZA, cardiac surgeon, thoracic surgeon; b. Manila, Apr. 29, 1955; s. Melanio and Aurora (Rilloraza) Q.; m. Augusta Madarang, Mar. 17, 1985; children: Melanie, Amanda, Elias Joseph. BS in Biochemistry, SUNY, Stony Brook, 1978; MD, Tulane U., 1982. Diplomate Am. Bd. Thoracic Surgery, Am. Bd. Surgery. Resident in surgery SUNY, Stony Brook, 1982-87; resident in thoracic surgery SUNY, Syracuse, 1987-89; cardiac surgeon Arnot-Ogden Med. Ctr., Elmira, N.Y., 1989-91; resident in surgery Orlando (Fla.) Regional med. Ctr., 1991-92, asst. dir. surg. edn. and thoracic surgery attending, 1992-93; cardiac surgeon Arnot-Ogden Med. Ctr., 1993—. Recipient Attending Surgeon of Yr. award, 1992-93, Physician Recognition award AMA, 1994—. Fellow Am. Coll. Surgeons, Am. Coll. Chest Physicians, Am. Coll. Cardiology; mem. Soc. Thoracic Surgeons, Upstate Soc. Thoracic Surgeons, Med. Soc. State of N.Y. Roman Catholic. Office: Ctrl NY Cardiac Surg Group 600 Ivy St Ste 101 Elmira NY 14905

QUIROZ, CAROLE ELIZABETH, critical care nurse; b. Passaic, N.J., Mar. 20, 1961; d. Masami Okada and Bette (Shizuko) Masuda; m. Richard Quiroz, Oct. 19, 1985; children: Richard Sean, Danielle Elizabeth, Bryan David. AAS, Fashion Inst. Tech., N.Y.C., 1980; BSN, Seton Hall U., 1985, MSN, 1994. ACLS; cert. med. surg. clin. nurse specialist. Staff nurse Overlook Hosp., Summit, N.J., 1985-86; ICU staff nurse Lenox Hill Hosp., N.Y.C., 1986-88; charge nurse Montclair (N.J.) Cmty. Hosp., 1989-93; critical care nurse Lenox Hill Hosp., N.Y.C., 1988-93; nurse CPACU Morristown Meml. Hosp., $, 1992-93; nurse Critical Care Assocs., Montclair, N.J., 1990-93; adminstrv. supr. The Gen. Hosp. Ctr. at Passaic, Passaic, N.J., 1993-94; adj. prof. Seton Hall U., South Orange, N.J., 1994—; presenter in field. Recipient Nursing Rsch. award Jersey Shore Med. Ctr., 1992. Mem. AACN, N.J. State Nurses Assn., Sigma Theta Tau. Office: Seton Hall U S Orange Ave South Orange NJ 07079

QUISMORIO, FRANCISCO P., JR., physician, medical educator, researcher; b. San Fernando, The Philippines, Jan. 21, 1941; s. Francisco N. Sr. and Cristina (Parpana) Q.; m. Violeta Consolacion; children: James Patrick, Anne Violet. BS, U. Philippines, Quezon City, 1960, MD, 1964. Fellow in rheumatology U. Pa., Phila., 1966-68; fellow in immunology L.A. County and So. Calif. Med. Ctr., L.A., 1969-70; chief clin. rheumatology lab. LAC and U. So. CAlif. Med. Ctr., L.A., 1978—; assoc. prof. sch. med. U. So. Calif., L.A., 1976-83, prof. med., 1983—, prof. pathology, 1986—, vice chief div. rheumatology and immunology, 1986—; counselor Am. Fedn. Clin. Rsch., 1980; mem. Scientific and Med. Com. Arthritis Found., 1979-83; dir. Clin. Immunology Lab., L.A., 1984—; commnr. oral exams. Calif. Med. Bd., 1981—. Contbr. articles to profl. jours. Recipient rsch. award Am. Lupus Soc., 1980, svc. award Arthritis Found., 1980, Borie Fibrositis Rsch. award, 1989, Fleur de Lis award, 1991; named Outstanding Alumnus, U. Philippines, 1990. Fellow Am. Coll. Rheumatology, Am. Coll. Physicians; mem. So. Calif. Rheumatism Soc. (pres. 1969, 70), Am. Assn. Immunologists, N.Y. Acad. Sci., Clin. Immunology Soc., Philippine Med. Soc. So. Calif. (rsch award). Office: Sch Medicine 2025 Zonal Ave Los Angeles CA 90033-4526

QUITMAN, JEFFREY ADRIAN, ophthalmologist, educator; b. N.Y.C., Nov. 13, 1954. BS in Biology magna cum laude, Brown U., 1975; MD, Stanford U., 1981. Diplomate Am. Bd. Ophthalmology, Nat. Bd. Med. Examiners. Internship Santa Clara Valley Med. Ctr., Stanford Tchg. Hosp., San Jose, Calif., 1982; chief resident ophthalmology Stanford U. Med. Ctr., 1985; pvt. practice Nashville, 1985-86; ophthalmologist Permanente Med. Group, Walnut Creek, Calif., 1986-87; pvt. practice Walnut Creek, Calif., 1987-96; asst. clin. prof. Stanford U., 1987—; ophthalmologist Wisconsin Rapids (Wis.) Eye Ctr., 1996—; sci. adv. bd. Insite Pharm., 1988, clin. investigator, 1994, Alameda, Calif.; cons. Medlabs-Alcon, 1985-88, Coherent Radiation, 1983, Ciba Vision Ophthalmics, 1993; specialty reviewer Med. Bd. Calif., Sacramento, 1991, Calif. Med. Review Inc., San Jose, 1991—. Recipient Chemistry prize Chem. Rubber Co., 1972. Fellow Am. Acad. Ophthalmology (Lifetime Edn. Achievment award 1995); mem. Am. Soc. Cataract and Refractive Surgery, Calif. Med. Assn. (alt. del. young physicians sect. 1991), Calif. Assn. Ophthalmology (mentor program 1993). Office: Wisconsin Rapids Eye Ctr 710 E Grand Ave Wisconsin Rapids WI 54494

QUITTELL, MURIEL GOLDBERG, social worker; b. North Tarrytown, N.Y., Mar. 16, 1916; d. Max and Goldie Goldberg; m. Jules Quittell, Nov. 15, 1942; children: Glenn, Frederic, Lynne. BA cum laude, SUNY, Albany, 1938; MSW, NYU, 1968. Cert. social worker, N.Y. Social worker Westchester County Dept. Social Svcs., White Plains, N.Y., 1938-42, St. Agnes Children's Rehab. Ctr., White Plains, 1968-95. Mem. NASW. Republican. Jewish. Home: 101 Hilary Cir New Rochelle NY 10804-1805

QUON, MICHAEL JAMES, medical scientist, physician; b. Oakland, Calif., Apr. 26, 1960; s. Jimmie Earl and Helen (Tang) Q.; m. Huison Kim, June 22, 1985; children: Hana, James. BS in Biomed. Engring., Northwestern U., 1982, PhD in Biomed. Engring., 1987, MD, 1988. Diplomate Nat. Bd. Med. Examiners, Am. Bd. Internal Medicine. Resident in internal medicine U. Chgo., 1988-90; fellow in endocrinology NIH, Bethesda, Md., 1990-93, sr. clin. investigator, 1993-95, sr. investigator Nat. Heart, Lung and Blood Inst., 1995—. Contbr. over 30 articles to profl. jours. Comdr. USPHS, 1990—. Mem. Am. Diabetes Assn. (Rsch. award grant 1994—), Am. Coll. Physicians, Am. Heart Assn., Coun. for High Blood Pressure, Juvenile Diabetes Found. Internat. Office: NIH NHLBI HEB Bldg 10 Rm 8C-103 Bethesda MD 10892

QUON, WANDA ANN, physician; b. Los Angeles, Mar. 2, 1967; d. Bill Jack and So Fa (Ng) Q. BS, Univ. Southern Calif., 1989; DO, Univ. Health Scis., 1996. Mem. Am. Osteopathic Assn., Am. Coll. General Practitioners, Am. Coll. Osteopathic Family Physicians, Mo. Assn. Osteopathic Physicians, Phi Sigma Soc. Home: 805 Juarez St Montebello CA 90640

QURAISHI, MOHAMMED SAYEED, health scientist, administrator; b. Jodhpur, India, June 23, 1924; came to U.S., 1946, naturalized, 1973; s. Mohammed Latif and Akhtar Jahan Q.; m. Akhtar Imtiaz, Nov. 12, 1953; children: Rana, Naveed, Sabah. B.Sc., St. John's Coll., 1942; M.Sc., Aligarh Muslim U., 1944; Ph.D., U. Mass., 1948. Sr. mem. UN, WHO Team to Bangladesh, 1949-51; entomologist Malaria Inst. Pakistan, 1951-55; sr. rsch. officer Pakistan Council Sci. and Indsl. Rsch., 1955-60; sr. sci. officer Pakistan AEC, 1960-64; assoc. prof. entomology U. Man., 1964-66; assoc. prof. entomology N.D. State U., Fargo, 1966-70, prof., 1970-74; chief scientist biology N.Y. State Sci. Svc., Albany, 1974-75; entomologist, toxicologist, chief pest control and consultation sect. NIH, Bethesda, Md., 1976-84; health scientist adminstr., exec. sec. microbiology and infectious disease rsch. com. Nat. Inst. Allergy and Infectious Diseases, Bethesda, Md., 1984-88, sci. rev. adminstr. spl. revs., 1988—; sr. scientist Cen. Treaty Orgn., Inst. Nuclear Sci., Tehran, Iran, 1960-64; program mgr. interdepartmental contract Project THEMIS, Dept. Def., 1968-74; vis. scientist Harvard Sch. of Pub. Health, 1995. Author: Biochemical Insect Control: Its Impact on Economy, Environment and Natural Selection, 1977; mem. editorial bd. Jour. Environ. Toxicology and Chemistry, 1981-84; author numerous sci. papers. Chmn. NIH Asian-Am. Cultural Assn., 1980-81. Recipient Sustained High Quality Performance award, 1980, Merit Pay Performance awards, 1984, 86, 87, Recognition and Appreciation of Spl. Achievement award NIH, 1988, Spl. Recognition award for Svcs. to NIH, Asian Am. Cultural Com., 1989, Appreciation in Recognition of Outstanding Support for Combined Fed. Campaign, 1991. Mem. Am. Chem. Soc., Soc. Environ. Toxicology and Chemistry (mem. publs. com. in charge spl. publs. 1982-84), Sigma Xi, Phi Kappa Phi. Home: 19813 Cochrane Way Gaithersburg MD 20879-1637 Office: NIH Rm 4C22 Solar Bldg 6003 Executive Blvd Bethesda MD 20892

QURAISHI, NISAR ALI, internist; b. Rawalpindi, Punjab, Pakistan, May 15, 1946; came to U.S., 1970; s. Jehan Dad and Sahib Jan (Qureshi) Q.; m. Shahida Parveen, June 25, 1970; children—Abid, Zahid. M.B., B.S. Dacca (Pakistan) Med. Coll., 1969. Diplomate Am. Bd. Internal Medicine. House surgeon Dacca Med. Coll., 1969, sr. house physician, 1969-70; intern Beekman Downtown Hosp., N.Y.C., 1970-71, resident, 1971-74; assoc. attending N.Y. Infirmary-Beekman Downtown Hosp., N.Y.C., 1982—; physician in charge exercise EKG, Mobil Oil Corp., N.Y.C., 1977-86. Mem. N.Y. County Med. Soc., N.Y. State Med. Soc., AMA, ACP, Am. Soc. Internal Medicine. Office: 303 Greenwich St New York NY 10013 Office: 1 Chopin Ct Jersey City NJ 07302-3240

RAAB, EDWARD LEON, ophthalmologist, educator, lawyer; b. N.Y.C., Jan. 26, 1933; m. Rosanne Brody Raab, Aug. 28, 1955; children: Barbara G., Renee J., Steven B. BA, Columbia U., 1954; MD, NYU, 1958; JD, Fordham U., 1994. Diplomate Am. Bd. Ophthalmology. Intern Montefiore Med. Ctr., N.Y.C., 1958-59; resident Mt. Sinai Hosp., N.Y.C., 1961-64; pvt. practice ophthalmology N.Y.C., 1964-66; prof. ophthalmology, prof. pediatrics Mt. Sinai Sch. Medicine, CUNY, N.Y.C., 1967—; cons. ophthalmology USPHS, S.I., N.Y., 1968-81; mem. Am. Orthoptic Coun., 1982—, v.p., 1994—; advisor Nat. Soc. to Prevent Blindness, N.Y.C., 1974-88, Children's Eye Care Found., Washington, 1973-79. Contbr. articles on ophthalmology to profl. jours., chpts. to books. Capt. U.S. Army, 1959-61. Pediatric Ophthalmology fellow Children's Hosp. Nat. Med. Ctr., Washington, 1966-67. Fellow ACS, Am. Ophthalmol. Soc., Am. Acad. Ophthalmology, Am. Coll. Legal Medicine; mem. ABA, Am. Assn. Pediatric Ophthalmology and Strabismis (bd. dirs. 1996—), N.Y. Soc. Pediatric Ophthalmology (pres. 1991-92), N.Y. State Bar Assn., Assn. of Bar City of N.Y. Home: 167 E 61st St New York NY 10021-8128 Office: Mt Sinai Med Ctr Dept Ophthalmology 5 E 98th St Fl 7 New York NY 10029-6501

RAAM, SHANTHI, cancer researcher; b. Madras, India, Nov. 26, 1941; came to U.S. 1964, naturalized 1977; BSc in Zoology, U. Madras, 1960, MS in Parasitology, 1962; PhD in Immunology, Immunochemistry, U. Ga., 1973. Rsch. asst. dept. zoology U. Madras, India, 1962-64, U. Tenn., Knoxville, 1964-65; teaching asst. Med. Coll. Ga., Augusta, 1968-70; teaching asst. then rsch. asst. U. Ga., Athens, 1970-73; postdoctoral rsch. fellow then rsch. assoc. Cancer Rsch. Ctr. Sch. Medicine Tufts U., Boston, 1973-85; dir. oncology lab. Lemuel Shattuck Hosp., Boston, 1976-92; assoc. prof. (rsch.) Sch. Medicine Tufts U., Boston, 1986-94; ind. sales rep. Equinox Internat. Inc., Las Vegas, 1995—; real estate agent Jack Conway & Co. Inc. Realtors, Norton, Mass., 1996—; chmn. ad hoc peer rev. com. NIH, 1989-90, adv. com. for clin. trials and cancer interventions, 1990—; mem. program com. Internat. Congress on Breast Diseases, 1990. Author, editor: Immunology of Steroid Hormone Receptors, 1988. Recipient Kenneth Dodgson Meml. Lectr. award U. Ga., Athens, 1992. Office: Jack Conway & Co Inc Realtors 140 E Main St Norton MA 02766

RABAZA, JORGE R., surgeon; b. Miami, Fla., Oct. 14, 1959; s. Fernando and Lobelia (Ballester) R.; m. Maria Victoria Rabaza, Aug. 3, 1985; children: Jorge Luis, Christina, Anoela. BS, U. South Fla., 1982; MD, U. Miami, 1986. Diplomate Am. Bd. Surgery. Intern U. Miami/Jackson Meml. Hosp., 1986-87, resident, 1987-91; pvt. practice gen. surgery Miami, 1991—; clin. instr. dept. surgery U. Miami, 1992—, dept. surgery Vets. Hosp., Miami, 1995. Recipient Upjohn award for outstanding resident of the yr. U. Miami, 1991. Fellow ACS, Southeastern Surg. Congress; mem. Soc. Am. Gastrointestinal and Endoscopic Surgeons. Republican. Office: Ste B-210 7800 SW 87th Ave Miami FL 33173

RABE, RICHARD FRANK, dentist, lawyer; b. Crystal Lake, Iowa, May 19, 1919; s. Otto Henry and Agnes Marie (Juhl) R.; m. Barbara Jean McNeal, Mar. 15, 1946; children: Richard Frank, Mary Elizabeth, Kathleen Ann, Michelle. AA, Waldorf Coll., 1938; DDS, U. Iowa, 1942; JD, Drake U., 1952. Bar: Iowa 1952. Practice dentistry, Des Moines, 1946—; sole practice law, Des Moines, 1952—; cons. Nat. Bd. Dental Examiners, 1955-60; chmn. Iowa Bd. Dental Examiners, 1962-63, Iowa Bd. Nursing Home Examiners, 1980-84; lectr. dental assns. throughout U.S., Contbr. articles to profl. jours. Fellow Am. Coll. Dentists; mem. ADA (Vice chmn. council on legis. 1977-78), Am. Acad. Dental Practice Adminstrn., Iowa Dental Study Club (past pres.), Iowa Dental Assn. (pres. 1972, trustee 1960-71), ABA, Iowa Bar Assn., Des Moines Dist. Dental Soc. (past pres.), Milw. Dental Research Group, Central Regional Dental Testing Agy., Am. Inst. Parliamentarians., Psi Omega, Delta Theta Phi. Episcopalian. Clubs: Des Moines Golf and Country. Lodge: Masons, Shriners. Avocations: sailing, flying. Home & Office: 5709 N Waterbury Rd Des Moines IA 50312-1337

RABIN, AARON, neurologist; b. Bklyn., July 4, 1945; s. Mordecai and Rachel (Kopelowitz) R.; m. Abigail Teitz, Dec. 15, 1970; children: Aliza, Ariel, Moriah. BA summa cum laude, Yeshiva U., 1967; PhD, Rockefeller U., 1974; MD, Albert Einstein Coll. Medicine, 1976. Diplomate Am. Bd. Psychiatry and Neurology; cert. Am. Soc. Neurorehabilitation. Resident in medicine Brookdale Hosp., Bklyn., 1976-77; resident in neurology Albert Einstein Coll. Medicine, Bronx, 1977-80; attending physician Englewood (N.J.) Hosp., 1981—, chief emeritus, sect. neurology, 1995—; asst. clin. prof. neurology Columbia Presbyn. Med. Ctr., N.Y.C., 1984—, asst. attending physician Neurol. Inst., 1984—. Author: The Vestibular System and Motor Control, 1974. Fellow Stroke Coun. Am. Heart Assn. Fellow Am. Acad. Neurology; mem. Am. Acad. Clin. Neurophysiology, Am. Soc. Clin. Evoked Potentials, Am. Assn. Electromyography and Electrodiagnosis, Am. Electroencephalographic Soc., Am. Med. Electroencephalographic Assn., Am. Assn. Anatomists, Soc. Neurosci., Brit. Brain Rsch. Assn. (hon.), European Brain and Behavior Soc. (hon.), The Neuropathy Assn. (dir. clin. neuropathy ctr. affiliate 1995—), Am. Soc. Internal Medicine, N.J. Soc. Internal Medicine (mem. coun., trustee, treas.). Office: 177 N Dean St Englewood NJ 07631-2527

RABIN, MONROE STEPHEN ZANE, physicist; b. Bklyn., Dec. 19, 1939; s. Louis and Helen (Haspel) R.; m. Joan Greenblatt, Feb. 27, 1965; children: Elaine Judith, Carolyn Sandra. AB, Columbia Coll., 1961; PhD, Rutgers, 1967. Physicist Lawrence Berkeley (Calif.) Lab., 1967-72; assoc. prof. physics U. Mass., Amherst, 1972-81, prof. physics, 1981—; vis. physicist Stanford Linear Accelerator Ctr., Palo Alto, Calif., 1979-80; vis. scholar Physics Dept. Harvard U., Cambridge, Mass., 1986-87; Soriano scholar in radiol. physics, radiation therapy dept. Mass. Gen. Hosp., Boston, 1986-87; mem. oversight panel Proton Therapy Med. Facility, Mass. Gen. Hosp., Boston, 1991—. Contbr. articles to Physical Rev., Physical Rev. Letters, Physics Letters, Nuclear Instruments and Methods. Mem. Am. Phys. Soc., Sigma Xi. Home: 21 Atwater Cir Amherst MA 01002-3205 Office: U Mass Dept Physics & Astronomy Amherst MA 01003

RABINO, ISAAC, biology and health science educator, researcher; b. Haifa, Israel, Dec. 2, 1938; came to U.S., 1963; s. Jacob and Natalia (Besser) R.; m. Linda Lurie, June 28, 1970; 1 child, Tahli Jeanne. BS, Hebrew U., Jerusalem, 1962; MS, Cornell U., 1965; PhD, SUNY, Stony Brook, 1976. Asst. prof. St. Peter's Coll., Jersey City, N.J., 1977-81; assoc. prof. biol. and health scis. Empire State Coll., SUNY, N.Y.C., 1985—; asst. prof. biol. scis. CUNY, N.Y.C., 1983-85; NSF rsch. assoc. Columbia U., N.Y.C., summers 1978-81, asst. prof. SUNY, 1981-82, St. Peter's Coll., Jersey City, N.J., 1977-81. Contbr. numerous articles to profl. jours. Grantee Lounsbery Found., NSF. Mem. AAAS, Assn. for Politics and the Life Scis., Soc. for Social Studies of Sci., Am. Inst. of Biological Scis. Office: SUNY Empire State Coll 225 Varick St New York NY 10014-4304

RABKIN, MITCHELL THORNTON, physician, hospital administrator, educator; b. Boston, Nov. 27, 1930; s. Morris Aaron and Esther (Quint) R.; m. Adrienne M. Najarian, June 24, 1956; children: Julia Margaret, David Gregory. A.B. magna cum laude, Harvard U., 1951, M.D. cum laude, 1955; D.Sc. (hon.), Brandeis U., 1983; D.Pharm. (hon.), Mass. Coll. Pharmacy, 1983; D.Sc. (hon.), Curry Coll., 1989, Northeastern U., 1994; D in Hum. Let. (hon.), Salem (Mass.) State Coll., 1995. Intern Mass. Gen. Hosp., Boston, 1955-56; resident in internal medicine Mass. Gen. Hosp., 1956-57, 59-60, chief resident, 1962, mem. staff, 1963-72, bd. consultation, 1972-80, hon. physician, 1981—; clin. fellow NIH, Bethesda, Md., 1957-59; gen. dir. Beth Israel Hosp., Boston, 1966-80; pres. Beth Israel Hosp., 1980—; asst. prof. medicine Harvard U., 1969-70, assoc. prof., 1971-83, prof., 1983—; mem. Health Care Adv. Coun. U.S. Gen. Acctg. Office, 1991—. Served with USPHS, 1957-59. Fellow ACP, AAAS; mem. Am. Fedn. Clin. Rsch., Mass. Med. Soc., Soc. Med. Adminstrs., Assn. Am. Med. Colls. (past chmn. coun. teaching hosps., chmn. elect. 1995-96), Conf. Boston Teaching Hosps. (past chmn.), Inst. Medicine, NAS, Century Assn. (N.Y.C.), Harvard Club of Boston. Jewish. Office: Beth Israel Hosp 330 Brookline Ave Boston MA 02215-5400

RABSON, ALAN SAUL, physician, educator; b. N.Y.C., July 1, 1926; s. Abraham and Florence (Shulman) R.; m. Ruth L. Kirschstein, June 11, 1950; 1 son, Arnold B. BA, U. Rochester, 1948; MD, SUNY, Bklyn., 1950. Intern Mass. Meml. Hosp., Boston, 1951-52; resident in pathology NYU Hosp., 1952-54, USPHS Hosp., New Orleans, 1954-55; pathologist Nat. Cancer Inst., Bethesda, Md., 1955—; prof. pathology Georgetown U. Med. Sch., 1974—, Uniformed Services U. Health Scis., 1978—, George Washington U., 1978—. Contbr. articles to med. jours. Mem. Am. Assn. Pathologists, Phi Beta Kappa, Sigma Xi, Alpha Omega Alpha. Address: NIH-National Cancer Institute Bldg 31-Cancer Biology 9000 Rockville Pike Bethesda MD 20892-0001

RABUFFO, JEFFREY VINCENT, urologist; b. Bklyn., June 16, 1939; s. Vincent Michael and Bernadette (Terhune) R.; m. Judith Moore, Aug. 11, 1963 (div. Feb. 1990); children: Paul, Mark, Courtney. B.S., Georgetown U., 1961, MD, 1965. Lic. physician, Va., Conn.; diplomate Am. Bd. Urology. Intern Mercy Hosp., Buffalo, 1968-69; resident gen. surgery Porvidence Hosp., Washington, 1968-69; resident urology Georgetown U., Washington, 1969-73; v.p. Middletown (Conn.) Surg. Group, 1976—; pres. med. staff Middlesex Hosp., Middletown, 1980-82; mng. ptnr. Kaimar Realty, Middletown, 1985—; pres. Conn. Surgicenter Inc., Middletown, 1985-96; chmn. com. on bioethics Middlesex Hosp., Middletown, Conn., 1992—, dir. outpatient svcs., 1995—; sr. attending physician sect. urology dept. surgery Middlesex Hosp.; assoc. physician dept. surgery div. urology U. Conn. Health Ctr.; mem. staff Rocky Hill Vets. Hosp., Elmcrest Psychiat. Inst., Student Health Svcs., Wesleyan U.; assoc. mem. dept. surgery U. Conn. Health Ctr.; clin. instr. dept. surgery U. Conn.; mng. ptnr. Middletown Profl. Park Ltd. Partnership I, II; med. bus. cons. Cromwell Imaging Ctr. Regional chmn. Lt. Gov.'s State Com. for U. Conn. for devel. Noether chair in Italian history. Named Physician of Yr., Family Practice Residency Program, Middlesex Hosp., Middletown, 1989. Fellow ACS; mem. AMA, Am. Urol. Assn., Am. Soc. Law Medicine and Ethics, Am. Coll. Physician Execs., Conn. State Med. Soc., Conn. Hosp. Assn. (state chmn. ethics working group on futility policies), Middlesex County Med. Soc. Home: 107 Skunk Misery Rd Higganum CT 06441-4435 Office: Middletown Surg Group 520 Saybrook Rd Middletown CT 06457-4700

RABUN, JOHN BREWTON, JR., criminal justice agency administrator; b. Augusta, Ga. Nov. 16, 1946; s. John Brewton and Alsie Imor (Bateman) R.; m. Anna Betsy Park, Dec. 27, 1967; children: Kerry Kristin, John Candler. B.A., Mercer U., 1967; postgrad. So. Bapt. Theol. Sem., 1967-70; M.S. in Social Work, U. Louisville, 1971. Cert. social worker, Ky., D.C. Exec. dir. Ky. Civil Liberties Union, Louisville, 1971-72; dir. Community Residential Treatment Services, Louisville, 1973-78; program mgr. Field Services, Louisville, 1978-80; program mgr. Exploited and Missing Child Unit, Louisville, 1980-84; v.p., chief oper. officer Nat. Ctr. for Missing & Exploited Children, Washington, 1984—; mem. Alderman's Task Force on Social Svcs., Louisville, 1982, Mayor's City Youth Commn., Louisville, 1983-84; trainer and/or cons. to numerous agys. in U.S., U.K., Can., Mex. Contbr. articles to criminal justice and healthcare publs. and books. Recipient Key to City of Louisville, 1983, Disting. Alumnus award U. Louisville, 1985, Russell L. Colling lit. award Internat. Assn. for Healthcare Security and Safety, 1991, Russell Colling Lit. award Internat. Assn. for Healthcare Security and Safety, 1991; named hon. chief of police, City of Louisville, 1982. Mem. ACLU, Nat. Assn. Social Workers, Nat. Sheriff's Assn., Nat. Coun. Juvenile and Family Ct. Judges, Internat. Juvenile Officers Assn., Acad. Cert. Social Workers, Internat. Assn. Chiefs of Police. Baptist (deacon). Avocations: photography, hunting, fishing, Internet. Home: 13519 Oak Ivy Ln Fairfax VA 22033-1230 Office: Nat Ctr for Missing and Exploited Children 2101 Wilson Blvd Ste 550 Arlington VA 22201-3062

RABY, PAUL L., orthopaedist; b. N-D de la Salette, Que., Can., Aug. 14, 1939; came to the U.S., 1983; s. Joseph and Orize (Malette) R.; m. Linda Mary Fitzpatrick, Sept. 14, 1963; children: Steven, Pierre, Michel, Carolyn. BL, St. Alexander Coll., Que., 1958; BA, St. Joseph Coll., 1960; MD, Laval U., Que. Diplomate Am. Acad. Orthopaedic Surgeons. Intern St. Sacrement Hosp., Laval U., Que., 1964-65; surg. resident gen. surgery Nat. Def. med. Ctr., Ottawa, Ont., 1968-69; orthopaedic resident U. Montreal, Que., 1969-72; med. staff Sacred Heart Hosp., Montreal, 1972-84, St. Eustache (Que.) Med. Ctr., 1973-80, Notre-Dame de L'Esperance Hosp., Town of St. Laurent, Que., 1974-83; prof. U. Montreal, 1974-84, sec. orthopaedic tchg. program, 1978-82; cons. in orthopaedics Marie-Clarac Inst. Rehab., Montreal, 1975-80, Rehab. Inst. Montreal, 1975-77. Capt. Med. Corps-Royal Can. Air Force, 1965-69. Fellow Am. Acad. Orthopaedic Surgeons; mem. AMA, Ark. Orthopaedic Soc., Ark. Med. Soc., So. Orthopaedic Assn., So. Med. Assn., Royal Coll. Surgery Can., Que. Orthopaedic Assn., Med. Coun. Can., Can. Med. Assn., Can. Orthopaedic Assn., Coll. Physicians and Surgeons of the Province of Que. Office: Raby & Martimbeau Ortho Clinic 2713 74th St Ste 301 Fort Smith AR 72903

RACE, GEORGE JUSTICE, pathology educator; b. Everman, Tex., Mar. 2, 1926; s. Claude Ernest and Lila Eunice (Bunch) R.; m. Annette Isabelle Rinker, Dec. 21, 1946; children: George William Daryl, Jonathan Clark, Mark Christopher, Jennifer Anne (dec.), Elizabeth Margaret Rinker. M.D., U. Tex., Southwestern Med. Sch., 1947; M.S. in Pub. Health, U. N.C., 1953; Ph.D. in Ultrastructural Anatomy and Microbiology, Baylor U., 1969. Intern Duke Hosp., 1947-48, asst. resident pathology, 1951-53; intern Boston City Hosp., 1948-49; asst. pathologist Peter Bent Brigham Hosp., Boston, 1953-54; pathologist St. Anthony's Hosp., St. Petersburg, Fla., 1954-55; staff pathologist Children's Med. Center, Dallas, 1955-59; dir. labs. Baylor U. Med. Center, Dallas, 1959-86; chief dept. pathology Baylor U. Med. Center, 1959-86, vice chmn. exec. com. med. bd., 1970-72; cons. pathologist VA Hosp., Dallas, 1955-71; adj. prof. anthropology and biology So. Meth. U., Dallas, 1969; instr. pathology Duke, 1951-53, Harvard Med. Sch., 1953-54; asst. prof. pathology U. Tex. Southwestern Med. Sch., 1955-58, clin. assoc. prof., 1958-64, clin. prof., 1964-72, prof., 1973-94, prof. emeritus, 1994—, dir. Cancer Center, 1973-76, assoc. dean for continuing edn., 1973-94, emeritus assoc. dean, 1994—; pathologist-in-chief Baylor U. Med. Ctr., 1959-86, prof. biomed. studies Baylor Grad. sch., 1989-94; chmn. Baylor Rsch. Found., 1986-89; prof. microbiology Baylor Coll. Dentistry, 1962-68, prof. pathology, 1964-68, prof., chmn. dept. pathology 1969-73, dean A. Webb Roberts Continuing Edn., 1973-94; spl. advisor on human and animal diseases to gov. State of Tex., 1979-83. Editor: Laboratory Medicine (4 vols.), 1973, 10th edit., 1983; Contbr. articles to profl. jours., chpts. to textbooks. Pres., Tex. div. Am. Cancer Soc., 1970; chmn. Gov.'s Task Force on Higher Edn., 1981. Served with AUS, 1944-46; flight surgeon USAF, 1948-51, Korea. Decorated Air medal. Fellow Coll. Am. Pathologists, Am. Soc. Clin. Pathologists, AAAS; mem. AMA (chmn. multiple discipline research forum 1969), Am. Assn. Pathologists, Internat. Acad. Pathology, Am. Assn. Med. Colls., Explorer's Club (dir., v.p. 1993—), Sigma Xi. Home: 3429 Beverly Dr Dallas TX 75205-2928

RACHANOW, GERALD MARVIN, lawyer; b. Balt., Aug. 7, 1942; s. Louis and Lillyan (Binstock) R.; m. Sally Davis, July 26, 1964; children: Mindy, Shelly, Gary. BS in Pharmacy, U. Md., 1965; JD, U. Balt., 1972. Bar: Md. 1973, U.S. Dist. Ct. Md. 1977, U.S. Supreme Ct. 1977. Consumer safety officer FDA, Rockville, Md., 1973-96, dep. dir. divsn. OTC drug evaluation, 1978-96, regulatory counsel divsn. OTC drug products, 1996—; ptnr. Rachanow & Wolfson, Randallstown, Md., 1975—; contbr. fed. drug law exam. Nat. Assn. Bds. Pharmacy, 1985. Contbr. articles to profl. jours. Bd. dirs. parent tchr. student orgn. Md. Sch. for Blind, Balt., 1985—; mem. Community Living for Multihandicapped Blind, Balt., 1984—, adv., 1984—, Spina Bifida Assn. Md., Balt., 1985—. Fellow Am. Soc. Pharmacy Law; mem. ABA, Soc. FDA Pharmacists, Heusler Honor Soc. Home: 8817 Allenswood Rd Randallstown MD 21133-4111 Office: US FDA 5600 Fishers Ln Rockville MD 20857-0001

RACHELSON, MORTON HERMAN, pediatrician; b. Bklyn., Dec. 31, 1927; s. William and Ethel (Peltz) R.; A.B. magna cum laude, Syracuse U., 1946; M.D., Tulane U., 1950; m. Natalie Gutterman, May 25, 1952; children—Marjorie, Barbara. Intern, Queens Gen. Hosp., Jamaica, N.Y., 1950-51; resident Willard Parker Hosp., N.Y.C., 1951-52, Jewish Hosp., Bklyn., 1952, Children's Med. Center, Boston, 1955; fellow pediatrics Babies Hosp., N.Y.C., 1955-56; practice medicine, specializing in pediatrics, Caldwell and Morris Plains, N.J., 1956-93; clin. asst. prof. Columbia U., 1956-93 ; clin. asst. prof. pediatrics CMDNJ-NJMS, 1978-93 ; clin. chief pediatrics St. Barnabas Med. Ctr., Livingston, N.J., 1985-87. Served to capt. M.C., USAF, 1953-55. Mem. Am. Acad. Pediatrics, AMA, Am. Heart Assn., N.J. Acad. Medicine, AAAS, Soc. Adolescent Medicine, Juvenile Conf. Com. of North Caldwell (N.J.), Am. Physicians Fellowship, Phi Lambda Kappa. Jewish. Club: B'nai B'rith. Contbr. articles to profl. jours. Office: 10384 Sunset Blvd Dr Boca Raton FL 33428 also: 2839 State Route 10 Morris Plains NJ 07950-1200

RACHLIN, STEPHEN LEONARD, psychiatrist; b. N.Y.C., Mar. 6, 1939; s. Murray and Sophie (Rodnitsky) R.; m. Florence Einsidler, Nov. 22, 1962; children: Michael Ira, Robert Alan. BA, NYU, 1959; MD, Albert Einstein Coll. Medicine, 1963. Diplomate Nat. Bd. Med. Examiners, Am. Bd. Forensic Psychiatry, Am. Bd. Psychiatry and Neurology with added qualifications in forensic psychiatry. Internship UCLA, 1963-64; resident, chief resident in psychiatry Mt. Sinai Hosp., N.Y., 1964-67; staff psychiatrist Bronx Psychiat. Ctr., Bronx, N.Y., 1969-72; asst. chief svc. Bronx Psychiat. Ctr., 1970-72, chief svc., 1972-74; dep. dir. Meyer-Manhattan Psychiat. Ctr., N.Y.C., 1974-76; acting dir. Meyer-Manhattan Psychiat. Ctr., 1976-77; dep. dir. Manhattan Psychiat. Ctr., N.Y.C., 1977; clin. dir. dept. psychiatry & psychology Nassau County Med. Ctr., E. Meadow, N.Y., 1978-80; assoc. chmn. dept. psychiatry & psychology Nassau County Med. Ctr., 1979-80, chmn. dept. psychiatry & psychology, 1980-94; assoc. prof. clin. psychiatry sch. medicine SUNY, Stony Brook, 1978-87, prof. clin. psychiatry, 1987-94; spl. prof. law Hofstra U., Hempstead, N.Y., 1983-95. Editor in chief Psychiat. Quar., 1990—; assoc. editor Bull. of the Am. Acad. os Psychiatry of the Law, 1989—; contbr. articles to profl. jours. Lt. comdr. USNR, 1967-69. Mem. Am. Psychiat. Assn. (chmn. com. adminstrv. psychiatry 1987-92, mem. assembly 1991-94, mem. com. confidentiality 1993-96), N.Y. State Psychiat. Assn. (chmn. com. on pub. psychiatry 1986-94), Am. Assn. Psychiat. Adminstrs. (pres. 1989-90), Am. Acad. Psychiatry and Law (pres. tri-state chpt. 1988-90), Am. Assn. Gen. Hosp. Psychiatrists (pres. 1993-94), Am. Bd. Forensic Psychiatry (dir. 1990-94, treas. 1992-93), Am. Hosp. Assn. (gov. coun. sect. psychiat. and substance abuse 1991-92), Hosp. Assn. N.Y. State (chmn. mental health 1992, 93). Office: PO Box 117 H Scarsdale NY 10583

RACHLIN, WILLIAM SELIG, surgeon; b. Hartford, Conn., May 13, 1929; s. Irving I. and Rose (Szke) R.; m. Joy B. Loitman; children: Faye, Marge. AB, Princeton U., 1948; MD, Harvard Med. Sch., 1952. Diplomate Am. Bd. Surgery. Intern in surgery Beth Israel Hosp., Boston, 1952-53, asst. resident in surgery, 1953-54, 58-59, chief resident in surgery, 1959-60; pvt. practice surgery Brookline, Mass., 1960—. Capt. USAF, 1954-56. Fellow ACS, Am. Coll. Gastroenterology; mem. Mass. Med. Soc. (trustee 1980—), Norfolk Dist. Med. Soc. (pres. 1977-79). Democrat. Jewish. Office: 1 Brookline Pl Ste 302 Brookline MA 02146

RACHMAN, BRADLEY SCOTT, chiropractic physician; b. Reading, Pa., July 23, 1961; s. Roger Stuart Rachman and Lanie Brenda (Chertok) Stuart; m. Amy Sue Rachman, Oct. 14, 1994; children: Nicole, Carly, Mackie. D of Chiropractic, Palmer U., 1986. Diplomate Nat. Bd. Chiropractic Examiners. Asst. dir. student affairs Palmer U., Davenport, Iowa, 1984-86; dir. Rachman Chiropractic, Ft. Myers, Fla., 1986—; dir. Multi-Disciplinary Symposium, Sanibel, Fla., 1989—; keynote speaker Am. Holistic Nurses Assn., Gainsville, Fla., 1988. Author: American Red Cross-Backtalk, 1987; (textbook) Peripheral Neurology Workbook, 1986. Dir. spinal health program ARC, Ft. Myers, 1987, also bd. dirs. H. Neilsen scholar, 1985. Mem. Fla. Chiropractic Assn. (dir. 1990-92), Tri-County Chiropractic Soc. (pres. 1990-91). Home: 8721 Cajuput Cv Fort Myers FL 33919-1843 Office: Rachman Chiropractic 12734 Kenwood Ln Ste 84 Fort Myers FL 33907-5638

RACHMILEWITZ, ELIEZER AVIVA, hematologist; b. Jerusalem, Israel, Mar. 23, 1935; s. Moses and Eve (Pomerantz) R.; m. Brachma Budik, July 1963; children: Dalit, Guy, Aviad. MD, Hebrew U., Jerusalem, Israel, 1961. Resident internal medicine Hadassah U. Hosp., Jerusalem, Israel, 1961-64; resident hematology Hadassah U. Hosp., Jerusalem, 1964-66; sr. lectr. in Intern. Medicine Hadassah Med. Sch., Jerusalem, 1970; permanent chief physician hematology dept. Hadassah Hosp., Jerusalem, 1970-74; lectr. in Internal Medicine, postgrad. fellow Hematology Dept. Tufts Med. Sch., Boston, Mass., U.S., 1966; assoc. prof. in Internal Medicine Hebrew U. Hadassah Med. Sch., Jerusalem, 1974-76, Albert Einstein Coll. Medicine, N.Y.C., 1967-69; head Hematology Hadassah U. Hosp. Mt. Scopus, Jerusalem, 1976-78, prof. Medicine, 1978; head Dept. Hematology Hadassah Med. Orgn., Jerusalem, 1981—; vis. prof. Ministry of Health Med. Assn., Rangoon, Burma, 1985, Ministry of Health Med. Assn., Singapore, 1985, Ministry of Health Med. Assn., Sri Lanka, 1986, U. Shanghai, China, 1987, Meml. Sloan Kettering Hosp., N.Y.C., 1988; cons. Donolo Govt. Hosp., 1978-80, Hillel Yafe Govt. Hosp., 1987—; editorial bd. Hemoglobin, 1983—; chmn. U. Hadassah Med. Sch. Admission Com., 1980-84, Prize Com., 1983, Teaching Div. Internal Med., 1983-87, Rsch. Com. of the Faculty of Med., 1988—. Nat. Ombudsman for Citizen's Complaints, 1979-86; chmn. Com. for Experimental Trials, 1983—; mem. Nat. Com. of Health Problems, 1984-88, Treinin Com. for Establishing Health Policy in Israel, 1987-88; mem., chmn. coms. Hadassah Hosp., 1970—; organizer Internat. Symposium Abnormal Hemoglobins, Jerusalem, 1981. Mem. Internat. Soc. of Hematology (nat. counselor 1988—, sec. congress of European African Div., Jerusalem, 1989) Am. Soc. Hematology, Internat. Soc. Experimental Hematology, Burmese Med. Assn. (hon. mem.), Israeli Med. Assn., Israeli Soc. of Hematology (sec. 1975-76, pres. 1986—). Home: 10 Semadar St, Yfe Noff, Jerusalem Israel Office: Hadassah Hosp Hematology, PO Box 12000, Jerusalem 91120, Israel

RACKERS, PATRICK DAVID, healthcare administrator; b. Jefferson City, Mo., Nov. 29, 1943; s. Michael Anthony and Geraldine Mae (Mathoney) R.; m. Claudia Marie Swenson, Mar. 6, 1969; children: Janelle, Joseph, John Paul, Jacob. AA, Lincoln U., 1974, BS, 1974; MS, Ctr. Mo. State U., 1975. Program chief Mo. Coun. in Criminal Justice, Jefferson City, 1972-77; dir. corrections City of Lincoln (Nebr.)/Lancaster County, 1977-84; adminstr. Hillhaven of Wichita, 1984-85; exec. dir. Boeing Employees' Assn., Wichita, 1985-86, Cath. Care Ctr., Wichita, 1986-93, Boone Retirement Ctr., Columbia, Mo., 1993—; bd. dirs. Mo. Assn. Holmes for Aging, Jefferson City, HopeNet, Wichita. Founder Dismas Soc., Cath. Charities, Wichita, 1990, founder Harbor House, 1990; active Anthony Family Shelter Cath. Diocese Wichita, 1990-93. Recipient Bishop's Crest award Cath. Diocese Wichita, 1990. Fellow Am. Coll. Health Care Execs.; mem. Am. Soc. Aging, Mo. League Nursing Home Adminstrs. (edn. com. 1993—, Adminstr. of Yr. 1995), KC. Independent. Home: 1321 English Dr Columbia MO 65201 Office: Boone Retirement Ctr 1623 Anthony St Columbia MO 65201

RACKOVER, MICHAEL AARON, physician assistant; b. May 23, 1948; m. Eileen T. Rackover. BS, Hahnemann U., 1990; MS, U. Pa., 1995. Radiology dept. adminstr. Rancocas Valley Hosp., Willingboro, N.J., 1975-79; radiology cons. Humana Inc., Louisville, 1979-80; dept. radiation oncology Hahnemann U. Hosp., 1984-85; physician asst. program, didactic coord., prof. Phila. Coll. of Textiles and Sci., 1995—; chairperson cancer prevention, screening and detection com. Pa. Cancer Control Prevention and Rsch. Adv. Bd., Pa. Dept. of Health, 1990. With USAF, 1967-70. Mem. Am. Acad. of Physician Assts., Pa. Soc. of Physicians Assts., Assn. of Physicians Assts. in Oncology. Office: Phila Coll Textiles and Sci Schoolhouse Ln & Henry Ave Philadelphia PA 19144-5497

RACUSIN, ROBERT JERROLD, psychiatry educator; b. Dayton, Ohio, Mar. 14, 1946. MD cum laude, Georgetown U., 1971. Cert. psychiatry, child psychiatry Am. Bd. Psychiatry and Neurology. Internship in psychiatry Georgetown U. Affiliated Hosp., Washington, 1971-72, resident in psychiatry, 1972-73; child psychiatry fellow Dartmouth Med. Sch., Hanover, N.H., 1973-75, adj. asst. prof. clin. psychiatry, 1976-78, asst. prof., 1978-84, assoc. prof., 1984—, dir. child psychiat. tng., 1988—. Contbr. articles to profl. jours. Fellow Am. Psychiat. Assn. (rep. assembly dist. brs. 1981-89),

Am. Acad. Child and Adoelscent Psychiatry, Am. Coll. Psychiatrists. Office: Dartmouth Hitchcock Med Ctr One Medical Ctr Dr Lebanon NH 03756

RACZKOWSKI, LIANE CATHERINE, physician assistant; b. Buffalo, Feb. 17, 1972; d. James Paul and Diana Jean (Basinski) R. BS, Gannon U., 1994. Pharmacy tech. Health Care Plan, West Seneca, N.Y., 1990-94; physician asst. emergency dept. Sisters of Charity Hosp., Buffalo, 1994—. Mem. Am. Assn. Physician Assts., N.Y. Soc. Physician Assts. Roman Catholic. Home: 48 Midway Orchard Park NY 14127 Office: Sisters of Charity Hosp 2157 Main St Buffalo NY 14214

RADEL, EVA, pediatrician, hematologist; b. Vienna, Austria, Apr. 10, 1934; came to U.S., 1939; d. Ernest O. and Marian (Feiks) Grossman; m. Stanley Robert Radel, May 31, 1954; children: Carol, Laura. AB, N.Y. U., 1954, MD, 1958. Pediatric intern, resident Bronx Mcpl. Hosp. Ctr., 1958-61; pediatric hematology rsch. fellow Albert Einstein Coll. Medicine, Bronx, 1961-63; pediatrician, head pediatric hematology Morrisania city Hosp., Bronx, 1963-76; assoc. dir. pediatrics North Cen. Bronx Hosp., 1978-82; attending physician pediatric hemetology out patients Montefiore Med. Ctr., Bronx, 1965-79, svc. head pediatric hematology-oncology, 1979—; head pediatric hematology North Cen. Bronx Hosp., 1976—; responsible investigator Children's Cancer Study Group, 1980—; dir. pediatric hematology-oncology Albert Einstein Coll. Medicine, Bronx, 1981—. Fellow Am. Acad Pediatrics; mem. Am. Soc. Hematology, Am. Soc. Pediatric Hematology-Oncology, Soc. for the Study of Blood. Office: Dept Pediatrics Montefiore Med Ctr 111 E 210th St Bronx NY 10467-2490

RADENHAUSEN, RUSSELL ALAN, clinical psychologist; b. Mineola, N.Y., Oct. 26, 1950; s. Paul Henry and Evelyn (Reynolds) R.; m. Kathleen Ann Fitzpatrick, June 26, 1982. BA, L.I. U., 1977, MA, 1982; PhD, U. South Fla., 1984. Lic. clin. psychologist. Psychology intern VA Med. Ctr., Palo Alto, Calif., 1982-83; asst. prof. psychology Morehead (Ky.) State U., 1984-86; psychologist Comprehensive Care Ctr. No. Ky., Ft. Wright, 1986—; cons. psychologist Pathways, Morehead, 1985; chmn. rsch. rev. com. for Childrens Psychiat. Hosp., Ft. Wright, Ky., 1990—, Comprehensive Care Ctr. No. Ky., Ft. Wright, 1990—. Contbr. articles to profl. jours. Mem. Mental Health Task Force Subcom. for Cin. AIDS Coalition, 1990. Grad. fellow U. South Fla., 1981; faculty rsch. grantee Morehead State U., 1985. Mem. APA, Cin. Psychol. Assn., Sierra Club. Democrat. Office: Comprehensive Care Ctr North Ky 722 Scott St Covington KY 41011-2436

RADER, TINA LOUISE, pathology technologist; b. Allentown, Pa., Apr. 9, 1959; d. Marlin Robert and Gioconda Maria (Alpago) R. BS in Med. Tech., Bloomsburg U., 1981; M Health Sci., Quinnipiac Coll., 1987. Med. technologist Lehigh Valley Hosp. Ctr., Allentown, Pa., 1981-84, Brigham & Womens Hosp., Boston, 1984-85; pathologists' asst. Dartmouth-Hitchcock Med. Ctr., Lebanon, N.H., 1987-89, New Eng. Med. Ctr., Boston, 1989-91, R.I. Hosp., Providence, 1991-94, Fox Chase Cancer Ctr., Phila., 1994—. Fellow Am. Assn. Pathologists' Assts. (edn. com. chairperson 1990—). Office: Fox Chase Cancer Ctr Dept Pathology 7701 Burholme Ave Philadelphia PA 19111-2412

RADFORD, DIANE MARY, surgeon, surgical oncologist; b. Irvine, Ayrshire, Scotland, Nov. 14, 1957; came to U.S., 1985; d. Sidney and Mary Margery (Parr) R. BSc with honors, Glasgow U., Scotland, 1978, MBChB, 1981; MD, Glasgow U., 1991. Jr. house officer Gartravel Gen. Hosp., Glasgow, 1981-82, Monklands Dist. Gen. Hosp., Airdrie, Scotland, 1982; sr. house officer Western Infirmary, Glasgow, 1982-83, Royal Infirmary, Edinburgh, Scotland, 1983-84; registrar Crosshouse Hosp., Kilmarnock, Scotland, 1984-85; fellow in surg. oncology Roswell Park Meml. Inst., Buffalo, 1985-87; resident in surg. St. Louis U. Hosp., 1987-91; instr. in surgery Wash. U., St. Louis, 1991-92; asst. prof. surgery Washington U., St. Louis, 1992—. Contbr. articles to profl. jours. Recipient 1st prize residents competition Mo. chpt. ACS, 1989. Fellow Am. Coll. Surgeons (bd. cert. gen. surgery), Royal Coll. Surgeons (Edinburgh); mem. Brit. Assn. Surg. Oncology, Am. Assn. Cancer Rsch., Assn. Acad. Surgery, Mo. State Med. Assn., Mo. Acad. Sci., St. Louis Met. Med. Soc., Roswell Pk. Surg. Soc. Office: 9901 Wohl Hosp 660 S Euclid Ave Saint Louis MO 63110

RADHAKRISHNAN, JAI, nephrologist, educator, researcher; b. Kanpur, India, Aug. 8, 1962; s. Karumathil Pullara and Leela (Methil) R.; m. Jolly-Banerjee, Nov. 23, 1985; 1 child, Nikhil. MBBS, U. Madras, India, 1984, MD, 1987. Resident in internal medicine Lincoln Hosp.-N.Y. Med. Coll., Bronx, 1988-90; fellow in nephrology Presbyn. Hosp./ Mass. Gen. Hosp.-Harvard Med. Sch., Boston, 1990-91; fellow in nephrology Columbia U., N.Y.C., 1991-94, asst. prof. clin. medicine, 1994—; clin. rschr. in lupus and diabetes, Presbyn. Hosp., N.Y.C., 1991—. Mem. Am. Soc. Nephrology, Royal Coll. Physicians (U.K.). Office: Presbyn Hosp 622 W 168th St Rm Ph4124 New York NY 10032

RADIGAN, FRANK XAVIER, pharmaceutical company executive; b. Paterson, N.J., Apr. 13, 1933; s. John Joseph and Susan Clair (Brett) R.; m. Julia Lou Smith, Aug. 27, 1960 (div. Nov. 1988); children: Francis Gregory, Patricia Louise, Brett Frasier; m. Carol E. Berkley, June 26, 1992; children: Dana, Trici. AB in Sociology, Seton Hall U., 1955; MBA Mktg., U. Hartford, 1968. Asst. mgr. Beneficial Fin. Co., Newark, 1955-57; hosp. rep. Becton-Dickinson Co., Rutherford, N.J., 1957-58; dist. mgr. Merck Sharp & Dohme, West Point, Pa., 1958—. Chmn. St. John the Baptist Social Justice, New Freedom, Pa., 1981-85; mem. Passaic County Dem. Com., 1985-86. Capt. USAR, 1956. Mem. Am. Mktg. Assn., Md. Pharmacists Assn. (chmn. indsl. rels. com.), W.Va. Pharm. Soc., Balt. Pharm. Assn. (hon. pres. 1989), Hopewell Fish and Game Assn., Bon Air Country Club, Elk, Lion (pres. Glen Rock 1975-76, 86-88). Roman Catholic. Home and Office: 2440 Bradenbaugh Rd White Hall MD 21161-9661

RADINSKY, ALLAN MICHAEL, human services adminstrator, behavior consultant, mental health services professional; b. Canonsburg, Pa., Feb. 28, 1950; s. Andrew Michael and Joanna Delores (Retzel) R.; m. Sophia Beckich, Oct. 7, 1978; 1 child, Brian Scott. BA, Wittenberg U., 1972; MEd, U. Pitts., 1973, PhD, 1984. Tchr. spl. edn. Western State Sch. and Hosp., Canonsburg, 1972, Canon-McMillan Sch. Dist., Canonsburg, 1973-75; program dir., corp. v.p. Citizen Care, Inc. Robinson Devel. Ctr., McKees Rocks, Pa., 1975-82; assoc. dir. psychology, adminstr. active treatment program Polk (Pa.) Ctr., 1984-85; psychology discipline coord. Western Ctr., Canonsburg, 1985-86, 87-88, acting facility dir., 1986-87; facility dir. Rosewood Ctr., Owings Mills, Md., 1988-92, regional dir., 1989-91; dir. cmty. based programs Nat. Ctr. on Instns. and Alternatives, Balt., 1992; exec. dir., corp. pres. Human Svcs. Assocs., Inc., Pitts., 1992—; pres., bd. dirs. Quality of Life Assocs., Inc.; corp. v.p., mem. bd. dirs., dir. of program and clin. svcs. Other Options, Inc., 1996—. Mem. Am. Assn. on Mental Deficiency, Coun. for Exceptional Children, Assn. for Person with Severe Handicaps. Home: 2437 Berkshire Dr Pittsburgh PA 15241 Office: Human Svcs Assocs Inc 186 Castle Shannon Blvd Pittsburgh PA 15228

RADMACHER, MANFRED, physicist; b. Kirchheimbolanden, Germany, June 10, 1962; came to U.S., 1993; Diploma in physics, Tech. U., Munich, 1990, PhD in Biophysics, 1993. Postdoctoral rschr. U. Calif., Santa Barbara, 1993-95; rsch. asst. Ludwig Maximilians U., Munich, 1995—. Contbr. articles to profl. jours. Mem. Biophys. Soc., Deutsche Physikalische Gesellschaft. Office: Ludwig-Maximilians U, Amalien strasse 54, D-80799 Munich Germany

RADOMIROV, RADOMIR GEORGIEV, pharmacologist, researcher; b. Sofia, Bulgaria, Apr. 1, 1942; s. Georgi Petkov and Anetta Atanassova (Tetevenska) R.; m. Albena Radoslavova Ivanova, July 30, 1967; children: Georgi, Roslana, Albena. MS, MD, Med. U., Sofia, Bulgaria, 1967; PhD, Bulgarian Acad. Scis., 1975, DSc, 1982. Physician Dist. Hosp., Blagoevgrad, Bulgaria, 1968; asst. Inst. Physiology, Sofia, 1969-71, rsch. fellow, 1972-82, asst. prof., 1983-87, prof., 1988—; head lab. Inst. Physiology, 1979—, sci. sec., 1989-92, dir., 1993—. Editor: Trends in the Pharmacology of Neurotransmission, 1987, Central and Peripheral Peptidergic Regulation, 1991. Mem. Bulgarian Acad. Scis., N.Y. Acad. Scis. Home: Burel str Bl.72-A Entr 2, 1408 Sofia Bulgaria Office: Inst Physiology, Acad G Bonchev str bl 23, 1113 Sofia Bulgaria

RADOMISLI, MICHEL, psychologist; b. Istanbul, Turkey, Dec. 29, 1931; came to U.S., 1957; s. Hirsch and Sol (Leon) R.; children: Gregory, Timothy. BS, Robert Coll., Istanbul, 1951; AM, Columbia U., 1958; PhD, NYU, 1962. Clin. coord. Lincoln Inst. for Psychotherapy, N.Y.C., 1962-65; pvt. practice N.Y.C., 1964—; asst. clin. prof. Albert Einstein Coll. of Medicine, N.Y.C., 1968-76; assoc. clin. prof. Med. Coll. Cornell U., N.Y.C., 1976—; Lic. psychologist, N.Y. Author chpt. in book; reviewer various jours.; contbr. articles to profl. jours. Eugene Higgins fellow Columbia U., 1957-58, Rockefeller Found. fellow, 1958-62. Fellow Am. Bd. Med. Psychotherapists; mem. APA, N.Y. State Psychol. Assn. Office: 55 E End Ave New York NY 10028-7928

RADOMSKI, JACK LONDON, toxicology consultant; b. Milw., Dec. 10, 1920; s. Joseph Elwood and Evelyn (Hansen) R.; BS, U. Wis., 1942; PhD, George Washington U., 1950; m. Margery Dodge, Feb. 1, 1947 (dec. Nov. 1970); m. Teresa Pascual, Feb. 19, 1971; children—Mark, Linda, Eric, Janet, Mayte. Chemist, Gen. Aniline & Film Corp., Binghamton, N.Y. 1942-44; pharmacologist FDA, Washington, 1944-52, acting chief acute toxicity br., 1952-53; prof. pharmacology U. Miami, Coral Gables, Fla., 1953-82; pres. Covington Tech. Services, Andalusia, Ala., 1982-88; pvt. practice cons. in toxicology, Hudson, Fla., 1988—; cons. WHO, IARC, GAO, EPA, HEW, NIOSH. Contbr. articles to profl. jours. Recipient Spl. award Commr. FDA, 1952; diplomate in gen. toxicology Acad. Toxicol. Scis., 1982. Mem. Am. Soc. Pharmacology and Exptl. Therapeutics, Soc. Toxicology, Am. Assn. Cancer Research, N.Y. Acad. Scis., Am. Bd. Forensic Examiners. Home and Office: 6432 Driftwood Dr Port Richey FL 34667-1018

RADOSEVIC, JON DOUGLAS, microbiologist; b. Greenfield, Ind., Oct. 8, 1953; s. Harry Triffin and Bertha May (Barnard) R.; m. Norma Kay Barrett, May 16, 1987; children: Keely Anne, Jon Matthew. BS, Purdue U., 1977. Microbiologist Med. Lab., Indpls., 1977-79; microbiologist II Ind. State Bd. Health, Indpls., 1979—. Office: Ind State Bd Health 1330 W Michigan St Indianapolis IN 46202-2829

RADOVANOVIC, ZORAN, epidemiologist; b. Belgrade, Yugoslavia, Apr. 17, 1940; s. Milutin and Danica (Grujic) R.; m. Ruzica Slobodanovic, Oct. 28, 1965; children—Vera, Milutin. M.D., Belgrade Sch. Medicine, 1965, Diploma in Epidemiology, 1973; Diploma in Tropical Pub. Health, London Sch. Hygiene and Tropical Medicine, 1970; D.Sc., U. Belgrade, 1977. Asst. prof. U. Belgrade, 1967-77, assoc. prof., 1977-83, prof. epidemiology, 1983-88, dir. Inst. Epidemiology, 1983-88, sec.-gen. Yugoslav Med. Assn., 1988, prof. epidemiology Kuwait U., 1988—, chair dept. cmty. medicine, 1991-95. Co-author, editor: General Epidemiology, 1979; co-author: Epidemiology of Infectious Diseases, 1980. Mem. Royal Soc. Tropical Medicine and Hygiene, Sci. Soc. History of Medicine, Internat. Epidemiol. Assn., Am. Pub. Health Assn., European Assn. for Cancer Research. Home: Sindjeliceva 4/I, 11000 Belgrade Yugoslavia Office: Kuwait U Comm Med Fac Med, PO Box 24923, Safat Kuwait

RADVANY, CRAIG JOSEPH, pharmaceuticals company executive, accountant; b. Trenton, N.J., Apr. 20, 1949; s. Joseph D. and Marjorie I. (Balla) R.; m. Barbara Ann Prevatil, Aug. 28, 1970; children: Kerry Ann, Kevin Scott. BBA, Rider Coll., 1971, postgrad., 1977. Acct. Princeton (N.J.) Applied Research Corp., 1970-71, Thiokol Chem. Corp., Trenton, 1971-72; acct. Carter-Wallace, Inc., Cranbury, N.J., 1972-74, sr. acct., 1974-77, fin. coordinator, 1977-81, mgr. fin., 1981-88; dir. fin. and adminstrn. research and devel. div. Carter Products, 1988—. Co-rep. Thiokol United Way Campaign, Trenton, 1971; mem. bd. of Session 1st Presbyn. Ch. of Hamilton Sq., N.J., 1982-84, utilities adv. com. Hopewell Twp., 1988-93; mgr., coach Nottingham Little League, Trenton, 1982-83, Hamilton Twp. Recreation Soccer Assn., Trenton, 1982-83; mgr. Hamilton Lassies Basketball League, Trenton, 1984, Hamilton Police Athletic League Basketball, Trenton, 1985. Mem. Nat. Assn. Accts. (Trenton chpt. pres. 1985-86, nat. adv. panel to subcom. of mgmt. acctg. practices com. 1986, nat. com. on pub. rels. 1986-90, com. on acad. rels. 1990-92), Am. Mgmt. Assn. Home: PO Box 646 Cranbury NJ 08512-0646 Office: Carter-Wallace Inc PO Box 1 Cranbury NJ 08512-0001

RAEBURN, SUSAN DELANEY, clinical psychologist; b. N.Y.C., Dec. 1, 1950; d. Boyd Raeburn and Ginnie Powell; m. William Phillip Delaney, May 25, 1991. BA in Psychology, UCLA, 1972; MA in Rsch. Psychology, San Francisco State U., 1974; PhD in Social-Clin. Psychology, The Wright Inst., 1984. Lic. psychologist, Calif. Asst. faculty San Francisco State U., 1973-74; evaluation specialist Model Cities Agy., Office of Mayor, San Francisco, 1975-76; spl. studies coord. Alameda County Health Care Scis. Agy., Oakland, Calif., 1977-78; pub. health planner Alameda County Health Care Svcs. Agy., Oakland, 1980-87; staff psychologist Behavioral Medicine Clinic Dept. Psychiatry Stanford U. Med. Ctr., 1986-92; clin. psychologist pvt. practice Berkeley, Calif., 1987—; clin. assoc. U. Calif., San Francisco, Health Program for Performance Artists, 1988—; psychologist Kaiser Permanente, 1992—. Contbr. articles to profl. jours. Mem. NOW, 1991—, Amnesty Internat., 1991—. Named Calif. State scholar, 1968-72. Mem. APA, Calif. Psychol. Assn., Alameda County Psychol. Assn., Performing Arts Medicine Assn. Democrat. Office: 2576 Shattuck Ave Berkeley CA 94704-2724

RAEDER, MORTEN GUSTAV, surgeon, educator; b. Porsgrunn, Norway, Jan. 22, 1939; s. Aksel Gustav and Kate (Juel) R.; m. Joan Adele Willis, 1964 (div. 1967); m. Unn Gripsrud, Jan. 5, 1968; children: Karen, Morten Marius. MB, BChir, U. Durham, Newcastle Upon Tyne, Eng., 1964; PhD, U. Oslo, Norway, 1976. Surgical house officer Surgical Dept., Ullevaal Hosp., Oslo, 1967-69, jr. registrar, 1974-78, sr. registrar, 1978-82, cons. surgeon, 1982—; rsch. fellow Inst. for Exptl. Med. Rsch., Ullevaal Hosp., Oslo, 1967-69, prof. medicine surgical pathophysiology, 1982—. Contbr. articles to profl. jours. Mem. Norwegian Acad. Sci. and Letters. Physiol. Soc. London. Home: Claus Borchs Vei 1, N-0853 Oslo 8, Norway Office: Ullevaal Hosp Surgical Dept, Kirkeveien 166, 0407 Oslo 4, Norway

RAEL, HENRY SYLVESTER, retired health administrator; b. Pueblo, Colo., Oct. 2, 1928; s. Daniel and Grace (Abyeta) R.; m. Helen Warner Loring Brace, June 30, 1956 (dec. Aug. 1980); children: Henry Sylvester, Loring Victoria. AB, U. So. Colo., 1955; BA in Bus Adminstrn., U. Denver, 1957, MBA, 1958. Sr. boys counselor Denver Juvenile Hall, 1955-58; adminstrv. asst. to pres. Stanley Aviation Corp., Denver, 1958-61; Titan III budget and fin. control supr. Martin Marietta Corp., Denver, 1961-65; mgmt. adv. services officer U. Colo. Med. Center, Denver, 1965-72; v.p. fin., treas. Loretto Heights Coll., Denver, 1972-73; dir. fin. and adminstrn. Colo. Found. for Med. Care, 1973-86, Tri-County Health Dept., Denver, 1986-96; instr. fin. mgmt., mem. fin. com. Am. Assn. Profl. Standards Rev. Orgn., 1980-85; speaker systems devel., design assns., univs., 1967-71. Mem. budget lay adv. com. Park Hill Elem. Sch., Denver, 1967-68, chmn., 1968-69; vol. worker Boy and Girl Scouts, 1967-73; bd. dirs. Community Arts Symphony, 1981-83, 85-87; controller St. John's Episcopal Cathedral, 1982-83; charter mem. Pueblo (Colo.) Coll. Young Democrats, 1954-55; block worker Republican party, Denver, 1965-68, precinct committeeman, 1978-84 ; trustee Van Nattan Scholarship Fund, 1974-96; bd. dirs. Vis. Nurse Assn., 1977-84, treas., 1982-84. Served with USAF, 1947-53; res. 1954-61. Recipient Disting. Service award Denver Astron. Soc., 1968, Citation Chamberlin Obs., 1985; Stanley Aviation masters scholar, 1957; Ballard scholar, 1956. Mem. Assn. Systems Mgmt. (pres. 1971-72), Hosp. Systems Mgmt. Soc., Budget Execs Inst. (v.p. chpt. 1964-65, sec. 1963-64), Colo. Pub. Employees Retirement Assn. (bd. dirs. 1993), Denver Astron. Soc. (pres. 1965-66, bd. dirs. 1982-94), Am. Assn. Founds. for Med. Care (fin. com. 1981-82), Nat. Astronomers Assn. (exec. bd. 1965—). Epsilon Xi, Delta Psi Omega. Episcopalian. Home: 4600 E Kentucky Ave A-511 Denver CO 80222-2641

RAETZ, CHRISTIAN R. H., biochemistry educator; b. Berlin, Germany, Nov. 17, 1946. B.S. in Chemistry, Yale U., 1967; M.D., Harvard U., 1973, Ph.D., %. House officer Peter Bent Brigham Hosp., Boston, 1973-74; research assoc. Nat. Inst. Gen. Med. Scis., USPHS, Bethesda, Md., 1974-76; asst. prof. biochemistry U. Wis.-Madison, 1976-79, assoc. prof., 1979-82, prof., dir. Ctr. for Membrane Biosynthesis Research, 1982—; mem. biochemistry study sect. NIH. Contbr. numerous articles to profl. jours. Mem. editorial bd. Jour. Biol. Chemistry. Recipient James Tolbert Shipley Research prize Harvard U. Med. Sch., 1973, Harry and Evelyn Steenbock Career Advancement award, 1976, Research Career Devel. award NIH, 1978-83, Dreyfus Tchr.-Scholar award, 1979; H. I. Romnes Faculty fellow U. Wis., 1984; NIH grantee. Mem. Am. Soc. Biol. Chemists, Japanese Soc. Promotion Sci., Phi Beta Kappa, Alpha Omega Alpha. Office: U Wis-Madison Dept Biochemistry 420 Henry Mall Madison WI 53706-1502

RAFF, SANDRA BETH, internist; b. N.Y.C., June 9, 1947; d. Edward and Claire (Barcham) R. BA, NYU, 1967; MD, N.Y. Med. Coll., 1971. Diplomate Am. Bd. Internal Medicine; fellow Am. Coll. Physicians, 1991. Rotating intern Beth Israel Med. Ctr., N.Y.C., 1971-72, resident-in-internal medicine, 1972-74; fellow in diabetes and metabolism Sch. Medicine NYU, N.Y.C., 1974-76; asst. prof. internal medicine U. Ala. Sch. Medicine, Tuscaloosa, 1976-77, U. Conn. Sch. Medicine, Hartford, 1977-79; practice medicine specializing in diabetes and endocrinology Cromwell, Conn., 1980-84, Middletown, Conn., 1984-90; assoc. med. dir. Aetna Life & Casualty, Hartford, 1990-91; dir. provider connectivity Aetna Health Plans Aetna Life & Casualty, Hartford, 1991-93; assoc. med. dir. Nat. Med. Rsch. Corp., Hartford, Conn., 1993-94; asst. prof. medicine U. Conn., 1994—; attending physician Middlesex Meml. Hosp., Middletown, 1978-90, physician emeritus, Middlesex Hosp., 1990—; instr. clin. medicine NYU Sch. Medicine, 1974-76; cons. Elmcrest Psychiat. Hosp., Portland, Conn., 1983-90; physician advisor Conn. Peer Rev. Orgn., 1984-90; bd. dirs. M.D. Health Plan, New Haven, 1987-90; med. dir. Joslin Ctr. for Diabetes New Britain Gen. Hosp., 1996—, dir. endocrinology and metabolism, 1994—. Contbr. articles to med. jours. Fellow ACP; mem. AMA, Am. Coll. of Physician Execs., Am. Diabetes Assn. (diabetic camp com. 1980—), Psi Chi, Delta Phi Epsilon. Office: 100 Grand Sheet Aetna MC 54 New Britain CT 06050

RAFFIN, THOMAS A., physician; b. San Francisco, Jan. 25, 1947; s. Bennett L. and Carolyn M. Raffin; m. Michele Raffin, June 19, 1987; children: Elizabeth S., Ross Daniel, Jake Bennett, Nicholas Ethan. AB in Biol. Sci., Stanford Med. Sch., 1968, MD, 1973. Diplomate Am. Bd. Pulmonary Medicine, Am. Bd. Internal Medicine (also in Critical Care Medicine). Intern Peter Bent Brigham Hosp., 1973-75; fellow in respiratory medicine sch. medicine Stanford U., Stanford, Calif., 1975-78, med. fiberoptic bronchoscopy service dir. med. ctr., 1978—, acting asst. prof. sch. medicine, 1978-80, assoc. dir. med. ctr. intensive care units, med. dir. dept. respiratory therapy hosp., 1978—, assoc. prof. medicine sch. medicine, 1986-95, acting chief div. respiratory medicine, 1988—; chief div. pulmonary and critical care Stanford U., 1990—, prof. medicine sch. of medicine, 1995—; co-dir. Stanford U. Ctr. for Biomed. Ethics, 1989—; chmn. ethics com. Stanford U. Med. Ctr., 1987—. Author: Intensive Care: Facing the Critical Choices, 1988; contbr. articles to profl. jours. V.p. lung cancer com., No. Calif. Oncology Group, 1983-85; com. mem. NIH Workshop, 1984. Recipient Henry J. Kaiser Found. award, 1981, 84, 88, Arthur L. Bloomfield award, 1981. Fellow ACP (rep. coun. subsplty. socs. 1986), Am. Coll. Chest Physicians (program com. mem. 1985—); mem. AAAS, Am. Fedn. for Clin. Rsch., Am. Thoracic Soc., Santa Clara County Lung Assn. and Med. Soc., Calif. Med. Assn. (chmn. sect. chest diseases 1984-85), Soc. for Critical Care Medicine, Calif. Thoracic Soc. Jewish. Home: 13468 Three Forks Ln Los Altos CA 94022-2404 Office: Stanford U Med Ctr Dept Medicine Div Pul & Crit Care Med # H3151 Stanford CA 94305

RAFIE, SEYED, medical physicist, cancer center administrator; b. Qazvin, Iran, Oct. 30, 1957; arrived in U.S., 1975; s. Tahere and Zia Rafie. AA, Marymount Coll., Palos Verdes, Calif., 1977; BS, Loyola Marymount U., 1979; MS, Calif. State U., Carson, 1982; MBA, U. Leverne, 1991; devel. mgmt. cert., U. So. Calif., 1995. Instr. Calif. State U., Carson, 1982-84; researcher Allergy Med. Group, Los Angeles, 1983; hyperthermia physics coordinator Long Beach (Calif.) Meml. Med. Ctr., 1983—; research cons. Long Beach Arthritis Ctr., 1983—; clin. cons. UCI Med. Ctr., Orange, Calif., 1983—, Hoag Meml. Med. Ctr., Newport Beach, Calif., 1987, Pacific Radiation Oncology Group, Orange, 1988; adj. prof. Calif. State U., Long Beach. Computer Cons. Endocurietherapy/Hyperthermia Jour., 1984—, editor, 1985—; contbr. articles to profl. jours. Vol. med. lab. technician Manhattan Beach (Calif.) Free Clinic, 1977-81. Mem. Am. Endocurietherapy Soc., Internat. Clin. Hyperthermia Group. Home: 1834 Bentley # 106 Los Angeles CA 90025 Office: Long Beach Meml Med Ctr 2801 Atlantic Ave Long Beach CA 90806-1737

RAGHOEBAR, MAIKEL, pharmaceutical industry executive; b. Paramaribo, Suriname, Oct. 16, 1957; arrived in The Netherlands, 1974; s. Maximiliaan Wilfried and Hildagonda (Monsch) R.; m. Marcorette Marinus Elisabeth Maria Caminada, June 5, 1987; children: Marc (dec.), Sanne. M. in Pharmacy, U. Groningen, The Netherlands, 1981, pharmacy's diploma, 1983; PhD, U. Nijmegen, The Netherlands, 1987. Clin. pharmacology rschr. U. Nijmegen, 1983-87; group mgr. clin. pharmacokinetics Solvay Duphar B.V., Weesp, The Netherlands, 1987-92, head nonclin. pharmacokinetics, 1992-93; project mgr. Solvay Duphar B.V., 1992-94; internat. project dir. Solvay Pharma R&D, 1994—; sci. cons. KNMP, Den Haag, The Netherlands, 1990-95. Editor: Eltoprazine: A Serenic Compound, 1990; contbr. over 30 articles to profl. jours. Mem. Royal Dutch Soc. Assn. for Advancement of Pharmacy in The Netherlands (chmn. exec. team organizing com. of nat. 1995 congress). Office: Solvay Duphar BV, Van Houtenlaan 36, 1381 CP Weesp The Netherlands

RAGINS, HERZL, surgeon, educator; b. Tel Aviv, July 27, 1929; came to U.S., 1929; s. Aaron and Ida (Kraus) R.; m. Karen Anderson, Sept. 16, 1979; 1 child, Jonathan Daly. BS, U. Ill., 1949; MS, MD, U. Ill., Chgo., 1951; PhD, U. Chgo., 1956. Intern Cook County Hosp., Chgo., 1951-52; surg. resident U. Chgo. Clinics, 1952-53, 55-60; gastrointestinal endoscopy fellowship Beth Israel Hosp., N.Y.C., 1972-73; clin. prof. surgery A. Einstein Coll. Medicine, Bronx, N.Y., 1973—. Contbr. articles to profl. jours. Capt. USAF, 1953-55, Korea. Mem. ACS, Am. Soc. Gastrointestinal Endoscopy, Am. Gastroent. Assn., Am. Physiol. Soc., Soc. Surgery Alimentary Tract, Soc. Am. Gastrointestinal Endoscopic Surgeons, Am. Soc. Colorectal Surgeons. Office: Med Office 1601 Tenbroeck Ave Bronx NY 10461-2030

RAGLAND, TERRY EUGENE, emergency physician; b. Greensboro, N.C., June 14, 1944; s. Terry Porter and Virginia Lucile (Stowe) R.; m. Marguerite Elizabeth Morton, May 15, 1976; children: Kenneth John McConnell, Ryan Lee Ragland. Student, Cen. Mich. U., 1962-66; MD, U. Mich., 1970. Diplomate Am. Bd. Internal Medicine, Am. Bd. Emergency Medicine. Intern St. Joseph Mercy Hosp., Ann Arbor, Mich., 1970-71, internal medicine resident, 1974-77, chief resident internal medicine, 1975-76; emergency physician St. Joseph Mercy Hosp., Ann Arbor, 1977—; med. dir. emergency ctr. St Joseph Mercy Hosp., Ann Arbor, 1985—; clin. asst. prof. U. Mich., Ann Arbor, 1981—; chief of staff St. Joseph Mercy Hosp., 1996—; pres., CEO Secure Care, Inc., 1992—; examiner Am. Bd. Emergency Medicine, 1983—; med. dir. Life Support Services, Ann Arbor, 1983—. Contbr. chpts. to book. Bd. dirs. Emergency Physicians Med. Group, Ann Arbor. Lt. USN, 1972-74. Fellow Am. Coll. Emergency Physicians; mem. Am. Coll. Physicians, Nat. Assn. Emergency Med. Technicians, Mich. State Med. Soc. (alt. del. 1982-84, 89-90, del. 1991-94), Mich. Emergency Med. Technicians Assn., Washtenaw County Med. Soc. (pres. 1993—). Democrat.

RAGLAND, WILLIAM LAUMAN, III, educator, pathologist; b. Richmond, Va., Aug. 24, 1934; s. William Lauman Jr. and Alma Josephine (Tatum) R.; m. Lois Camilla Witcher, July 16, 1961 (div.); children: Karen Renee, Alexander Shelton, Amy Elizabeth. BS in Biology, Coll. William and Mary, 1956; postgrad. Va. Poly Inst., summer 1956; DVM, U. Ga., 1960; postgrad. in med. pathology, Tulane U., 1961-62; PhD in Pathology and Biochemistry, Wash. State U., 1966. Instr. Tulane U. dept. pathology, New Orleans, 1961-62; NIH postdoctoral fellow dept. vet. pathology Wash. State U., Pullman, 1962-66; NIH spl. rsch. fellow depts. oncology and pathology U. Wis., Madison, 1966-68, asst. prof. dept. pathology, 1968-70; assoc. prof. depts. avian medicine, med. microbiology, and vet. pathology U. Ga., Athens, 1970-76, prof., 1976—; pathologist Wis. Regional Primate Research Ctr., Madison, 1968-70; pres., chmn. Ragland Research, Inc., Athens, 1980-86; adj. prof. dept. pathology and lab. medicine Emory U., Atlanta, 1984—, vet. faculty U. Zagreb, Croatia, 1991—; dir. Custom Adjuvants, Inc., Atlanta, 1980-86, Vetrepharm Research, Inc., Detroit, 1985-86. Patentee Flourescence gel scanner, 1974, Antiviral Agent and Preparation, 1988, Method of Immunizing Poultry, 1991, (with R.L. Hunter) Method of Stimulating the Immune System, 1993. Traveling fellow Brit. Horserace Betting Levy Bd., 1968. Mem. AAAS, Internat. Acad. Pathology, Biochem. Soc., Soc. Toxicology, Am. Assn. Cancer Research, Am. Assn. Avian Pathologists, Am. Assn. Investigative Pathology, Am. Assn. Immunologists. Avocation: swimming. Office: U Ga Dept Avian Medicine Athens GA 30602 also: Veterinarski Fakultet Sveučilišta u Zagrebu, Heinzelova 55, 41000 Zagreb Croatia

RAGNARSSON, THORIR STURLA, neurosurgeon; b. Isafiordur, Iceland, July 18, 1952; s. Asgeirsson and Mariasdottir (Laufey) Ragnar; m. Sigridur Hjaltadottir, Oct. 4, 1974; children: Hjalti, Arnar, Ragnar. MD, U. Iceland, 1978. Diplomate Am. Bd. Neurol. Surgeons. Resident in neurosurgery Dartmouth-Hitchcock Med. Ctr., Hanover, N.H., 1981-87; pvt. practice Reykjavik (Iceland) City Hosp., 1987—. Mem. Am. Assn. Neurol. Surgeons, Congress Neurol. Surgeons, Icelandic Med. Assn. Home: Birkigrund 34, 200 Kopavogur Iceland Office: Reykjavik City Hosp, Dept Neurosurgery, 108 Reykjavik Iceland

RAGNI, MARGARET VICTORIA, hematologist; b. Columbus, Ohio, Mar. 13, 1949; d. Victor Francis and Margaret Johanna (Coners) R.; m. Frederick Lewis Porkolab, Apr. 23, 1977; children—Christopher, Caroline. B.S., Chatham Coll., 1971; M.D., U. Pitts., 1975. Med. intern. Presbyn. U. Hosp., Pitts., 1975-76, resident, 1976-78, fellow in hematology, 1978-82, research asst. prof. medicine, 1982-87, asst. prof. medicine, 1987-90, assoc. prof., 1990—; dir. Hemophilia Ctr. Western Pa., Pitts., 1987—. Contbr. articles to profl. jours. Fellow ACP; mem. Am. Soc. Hematology, Am. Soc. Clin. Investigation. Home: 581 Moorhead Pl Pittsburgh PA 15232-1426 Office: Hemophilia Ctr Western Pa 812 5th Ave Pittsburgh PA 15219-4701

RAGNOTTI, GIOVANNI, biomedical educator; b. Milan, Lombardia, Italy, July 21, 1936; s. Ercole and Margherita (Zambeletti) R.; m. Laura Iachello, June 24, 1965; 1 child, Luca. MD, U. Milan, 1961. Asst. vol. capacity U. Milan, 1961-63, asst. prof. gen. pathology, 1964-74, assoc. prof., 1974-80, prof. gen. pathology, 1980-82; prof. gen. pathology U. Brescia, 1982-91, dean med. faculty, 1982-88; prof. gen. pathology U. Milan, 1991—. Mem. English Biomed. Soc., Gentlemen Riders of Italy, Rotary. Roman Catholic. Home: Rita Tonoli 1, Milan Italy 20145 Office: Univ of Milan, G Colombo 46, 2133 Milan Italy

RAGSDALE, REX H., health facility administrator, physician; b. Henderson, Ky., July 31, 1957; s. Carl Wilkes and Sue Ann (Hart) R.; m. Sally E.; children: Leslie D'Anne, Kellen Edward. BSBA, U. Evansville, 1978; MD, St. Louis U., 1982. Diplomate Am. Bd. Family Practice. Resident St. Mary's Med. Ctr., Evansville, Ind., 1982-85; pvt. practice Newburgh, Ind., 1985-89; v.p. med. affairs Deaconess Hosp., Evansville, 1989—; bd. dirs. Ohio Valley Hospice, Evansville, 1990—, Impact Ministries Healthcare Ctr., Evansville, 1991—; mem. VHA Nat. Physician Leadership Coun., 1993—. Pres. 1st Dist. Med. Soc., Evansville, 1993-94; state del. Ind. State Med. Assn., Indpls., 1992—; med. advisor United Parents Support for Downs Syndrome, Newburgh, 1990, 91, 92; med. dir. Arts coun. Fun Run, Evansville, 1988. Mem. AMA, Am. Coll. Physician Execs., Am. Acad. Family Practice, Aircraft Owners and Pilots Assn., Phi Mu Alpha. Office: Deaconess Hosp Inc 600 Mary St Evansville IN 47747-0002

RAGSDALE, RICHARD ELLIOT, healthcare management executive; b. St. Louis, Dec. 20, 1943; s. Billie Oscar and Isabelle (Roques) R.; m. Anne Elizabeth Ward, Aug. 20, 1968; children: Richard, Kevin, Bethany. B.B.A., Ohio U., 1965; M. in Internat. Commerce, Am. Grad. Sch. Internat. Mgmt., 1968. Asst. treas. Chase Manhattan Bank, N.Y.C., 1968-73; v.p., treas. Hosp. Affiliates Internat., Nashville, 1973-80; v.p., treas., chief fin. officer INA Health Care Group, Dallas, 1980-81; sr. v.p., chief fin. officer, dir. Republic Health Corp., Dallas, 1981-83, sr. exec. v.p., dir., 1983-85; chmn. Community Health Systems Inc., Brentwood, Tenn., 1985—, Great No. Health Mgmt., Ltd., London, 1986-89; bd. dirs. RehabCare Group, Inc., St. Louis; chmn. ProMed Co., Inc. Ft. Worth, Tex., 1994—. Coach Spring Valley Athletic Assn., Dallas, 1985; trustee Watkins Inst., 1988-94; trustee Benton Hall Sch., 1988—, chair, 1991—; trustee Maryville Coll., 1990—, chair, 1992—. Recipient Thunderbird Disting Alumni award Entrepreneurship, 1990, Jonas Meyer Disting. Alumni award, 1993. Mem. Fedn. Am. Hosps. (legis. commn. 1984-95). Republican. Office: Community Health Systems Inc 155 Franklin Rd Ste 400 Brentwood TN 37027-4646

RAGUCCI, JOHN ALBERT, family practice physician; b. Medford, Mass., Feb. 8, 1960; s. Emilio A. and Ann Marie (Russo) R.; m. Kristin A. Spiro, Oct. 26, 1991; 1 child, Rachel K. BS in Biology cum laude, Boston Coll., 1982; MS in Health Sci., Northeastern U., 1985; MD, Tufts U., 1991. Diplomate Am. Bd. Family Medicine, Nat. Bd. Med. Examiners. Resident in family medicine Brown U./Meml. Hosp., Pawtucket, R.I., 1991-94, asst. chief resident for scheduling, 1993-94, asst. instr. in family medicine, 1993-94; mem. staff Norwood Hosp./Neponset Valley Health System, 1993-94; mem. staff Dept. Family Practice Beverly Hosp., 1994—; substitute tchr. Newton Cath. H.S., 1984-85; tchg. fellow Northeastern U., 1982-83, tchg. asst. microbiology labs., 1983-84; instr. microbiology Emmanuel Coll., New Eng. Bapt. Hosp. Sch. Nursing, 1985, 86, Anna Maria Coll., Malden Hosp. Sch. Nursing, 1986, 87, Middlesex C.C., 1985, 88; instr. anatomy and physiology dept. clin. lab. scis. U. Lowell, 1986; preceptor/tchg. attending physician Beverly Hosp. Family Practice Residency; presenter in field. Vol. mgr. Little League Baseball, 1977-81; vol. recreational program for retarded children, 1976-78. Mem. AMA, Mass. Med. Soc., Am. Acad. Family Physicians, Soc. Tchrs. of Family Medicine, Nat. Assn. Residents and Interns, Mass. Chess Fedn., U.S. Chess Fedn., Sierra Club, Planetary Soc., Alpha Omega Alpha, Phi Sigma.

RAGUSEA, STEPHEN ANTHONY, psychologist, educator; b. N.Y.C., Mar. 26, 1947; s. Anthony S. and Marie (Giampietro) R.; m. Kathleen Fox, Aug. 14, 1971; children: Anthony, Adam. AA, Nassau Coll., Garden City, N.Y., 1967; BS, Bowling Green (Ohio) State U., 1969; D of Psychology, Baylor U., Waco, Tex., 1980. Lic. psychologist, Pa.; diplomate Am. Bd. Profl. Psychology in Family Psychology, Am. Bd. Profl. Neuropsychology. Tchr. Dayton (Ohio) then Cedar Rapids (Iowa) Community Schs., 1969-76; mem. cons. team for local sch. system Waco, Tex., 1976-77; therapist Meth. Home Children's Guidance Ctr., Waco, 1977-79, Heart of Tex. Mental Health/Mental Retardation Ctr., Waco, 1977-79; intern in psychol. svcs. Norristown (Pa.) State Hosp., 1979-80; cons. Altoona (Pa.) Hosp. Community Mental Health Ctr., 1981-82; interim dir. psychol. svcs. Nittany Valley Rehab. Hosp. for Spl. Svcs., Pleasant Gap, Pa., 1983-84; pres., chief exec. officer Centre Valley Mgmt., Inc., 1981-85; exec. dir. Psychol. Forensics, P.C., State College, Pa., 1984—; clin. dir. The Medows Psychiat. Ctr., 1984-85; psychologist, dir. ops. Child, Adult, & Family Psychol. Ctr., State College, 1980—; asst. prof. Dept. Individual and Family Studies, Pa. State Univ.; adj. faculty dept. psychology Pa. State U.; mem. cons. psychol. staff The Meadows Psychiat. Ctr.; mem. cons. staff Nittany Valley Rehab. Hosp.; psychol. staff rep. to med. staff, mem. allied staff Centre Community Hosp.; bd. dirs. Penn PsyPac; numerous presentations in field. Del. from Pa., Coun. of Representatives, 1994-98. Fellow Am. Coll. Forensic Psychology, Cen. Pa. Psychol. Assn. (past-pres., chmn. profl. affairs com.), Pa. Psychol. Assn. (past-pres. clin. div., chmn. hosp. practice com., fellow and pres. 1993-94); mem. Am. Psychol. Assn. (exec. coun. 1994—), Am. Soc. Clin. Hypnosis, Nat. Acad. Neuropsychologists.

RAHAL, PARAMVIR SINGH, physician; b. Jalandhar, Punjab, India, Feb. 14, 1964; came to U.S., 1991; s Shangara Singh and Joginder (Kaur) R.; m. Simrita Minhas, Jan. 7, 1990; 1 child, Harman K. Diploma in pre-med., Guru Nanak Dev U., Amritsar, India, 1981; MD, Med. Coll., Amritsar, 1986. Diplomate Am. Bd. Internal Medicine; lic. physician, Calif., Mich., Punjab. House officer dept. medicine and surgery Med. Coll., Amritsar, 1987-88; med. officer Ruby Nelson Hosp., Jalandhar, Punjab, India, 1990-91; intern U. Louisville, Ky., 1991-92; resident in internal medicine U. Louisville, 1992-94; fellow in gastroenterology Providence Hosp. and Med. Ctrs., Southfield, Mich., 1994-96; presenter in field. Contbr. articles and abstracts to publs. Mem. AMA, ACP, ACG, AGA, Ky. Med. Assn. Home: 901 Mohawk St # 52 Bakerswfield CA 93309

RAHE, RICHARD HENRY, psychiatrist, educator; b. Seattle, May 28, 1936; s. Henry Joseph and Delora Lee (Laube) R.; m. Laurie Ann Davies, Nov. 24, 1960 (div. Dec. 1990); children: Richard Bradley, Annika Lee. Student, Princeton U., 1954-57; MD, U. Wash., 1961. Diplomate Am. Bd. Psychiatry and Neurology. Chief resident in psychiatry U. Wash. Sch. Medicine, Seattle, 1965; rsch. psychiatrist USN, San Diego, 1965-75; commdg. officer Naval Health Rsch. Ctr., San Diego, 1976-80; exec. officer Long Beach (Calif.) Naval Hosp., 1980-82; commdg. officer Guam Naval Hosp., Agana, 1982-84; prof. psychiatry U.S. Univ. Health Scis. Mil. Med. Sch., Bethesda, Md., 1984-86, U. Nev. Sch. Medicine, Reno, 1986—; dir. Mil. Stress Studies Ctr., Bethesda, 1984-86, Nev. Stress Ctr., Reno, 1986—. Contbr. numerous articles to sci. jours., chpts. to books; photographer prints and video. Med. dir. Nev. Mental Health Inst., Sparks, 1991-94. Capt. USN, 1965-86. Recipient Humanitarian award Vietnamese Refugee Com., 1974, Dept. of State award for treatment of Am. hostages held in Iran, 1981. Fellow Am. Psychiat. Assn.; mem. Am. Psychosomatic Soc. (past pres.), World Psychiat. Assn. (past. pres. mil. sect.). Home: 638 Saint Lawrence Ave Reno NV 89509-1440 Office: VA Med Ctr Code 151-C 1000 Locust St Reno NV 89520-0102

RAHHAL, DONALD K., obstetrician, gynecologist; b. Clinton, Okla., 1942. MD, U. Okla. Coll. Medicine, 1971. Diplomate Am. Bd. Ob.-Gyn. (bd. dirs.). Resident Indiana U. Hosp., Indpls., 1971-74; obstetrician-gynecologist Mercy Health Ctr., Okla. City, 1981—, Deaconess Hosp., Okla. City, 1981—; clin. prof. U. Okla. Coll. Medicine, Okla. City, 1981—. Mem. ACOG, AMA, Am. Bd. Med. Specialties (del.), Coll. Acad. Obstetricians, Gynecologists. Office: 4200 Memorial Dr Ste 410 Oklahoma City OK 73120-9349*

RAHM, ADOLF EUGEN, JR., gastroenterologist; b. Miami, Fla., Sept. 21, 1938; s. Adolf Eugen and Sarah Fort (Montgomery) R.; m. Antoinette Lee Warburg, 1961; children: Mark, Tracy, Ashley. BA, U. Cin., 1960, MD, 1964; MPH, Harvard U., 1966. Diplomate Am. Bd. Pub. Health, Am. Bd. Internal Medicine, Am. Bd. Infectious Diseases, Am. Bd. Gastroenterology. Commd. 2d lt. U.S. Army, 1960, advanced through grades to col., 1979; physician U.S. Army, Tex., Calif., Fla., Mass., Vietnam, 1964-85, San Antonio, 1991-92; pvt. practice Victoria, Tex., 1985-89; Mem. Victoria City-County Bd. of Health, 1987-89, dir., 1989. Contbr. articles to profl. jours. Decorated Bronze Star, Legion of Merit, Army Commendation medal with 2 oak leaf clusters. Fellow Am. Coll. Preventive Medicine. Home: PO Box 3548 Victoria TX 77903-3548

RAHMAN, RAFIQ UR, oncologist, educator; b. Mirali, Pakistan, Mar. 3, 1957; came to U.S., 1985; s. Rakhman and Bibi (Sana) Gul; m. Shamim Ara Bangash; children: Maryam, Hassan, Haider. BS, MB, U. Peshawar, Pakistan, 1980. Bd. cert. internal medicine, med. oncology; lic. physician Pa., Ala., Ky. House officer in internal medicine Khyber Teaching Hosp.-U. Peshawar, Pakistan, 1980-81, house officer in gen. surgery, 1981, jr. registrar med. ICU, 1983-84; jr. registrar internal medicine Khyber Teaching Hosp., 1981-82; sr. registrar internal medicine Khyber Teaching Hosp.-Lady Reading Hosp. & Postgrad. Inst., Peshawar, 1984-85; Audrey Meyer Mars fellow in med. oncology Roswell Park Cancer Inst., Buffalo, 1985-86; resident in internal medicine SUNY-Buffalo Gen. Hosp.-Erie County Med. Ctr.-VA Med. Ctr., 1986-88; chief resident in internal medicine SUNY-Buffalo-Erie County Med. Ctr., 1988; fellow in hematology and med. oncology SUNY-Buffalo-Roswell Park Cancer Inst., 1989-90; hematologist, med. oncologist Daniel Boone Clinic and Harlan A.R.H., 1991-92; clin. asst. prof. medicine U. Ky., 1991—; attending physician, hematology/med. oncologist Hardin Meml. Hosp., Elizabethtown, 1993—, chief medicine, 1996; tchr. med. students Med. Sch., SUNY; participant CALGB protocol studies Roswell Park Cancer Inst., investigator. Editor English sect. Cenna mag. Cenna; contbr. articles to profl. jours. Mem. Pakistan Med. & Dental Coun., Ky. Med. Assn., Harlan County Med. Soc., Hardin-LaRue County Med. Soc. Home: 400 Briarwood Cir Elizabethtown KY 42701-8913 Office: 1107 Woodland Dr Ste 105 Elizabethtown KY 42701-2749

RAHMING, ETTA LORRAINE, social worker, consultant, psychotherapist; b. Bronx, Mar. 6, 1957; d. Henry Lewis and Irene (Linen) R. BA in Sociology, CCNY, 1979; MSW, Howard U., 1981. Lic. social worker, N.Y.; lic. counselor, N.Y. Investigative probation officer N.Y.C. Dept. Probation, 1981-85; social worker E.N.T.E.R. Alcoholism O.P.D., 1985-86; psychiat. social worker Bronx Lebanon Alcoholism O.P.D., 1986-88; clin. supr. residential treatment program E.N.T.E.R. Inc., 1988-89; supr. Comprehensive Employment Opportunity Support Ctr. Fedn. Employment Guidance Ctr., 1989-92; therapist Our Lady of Mercy Mental Health Clinic, Bronx, 1994—. Mem. NASW, Nat. Assn. Black Social Workers, Inc., N.Y. Fedn. Alcoholism Counselors, Nat. Black Alcoholism Coun., N.Y. Women in Criminal Justice. Home: PO Box 682 Bronx NY 10462-0542

RAHTZ, ROGER ADAM, psychiatrist; b. N.Y.C., Nov. 16, 1947; s. Robert and Henrietta (Barenblatt) R.; m. Laura Fay Rubinstein, Apr. 24, 1983; children: Joshua Charles, David Jesse. BA, Yale U., 1969; MD, Albert Einstein Coll. Medicine, 1973. Diplomate Am. Bd. Psychiatry & Neurology. Clin. instr. child psychiatry Albert Einstein Coll. Medicine, Bronx, N.Y., 1977-82, N.Y. Med. Coll., Valhalla, N.Y., 1982-86; tng. coordinator, child psychiatry Metro. Hosp., N.Y.C., 1982-84; coord., child and adolescent psychiatry svcs. Lenox Hill Hosp., N.Y.C., 1984-92; clin. dir. Riverdale Mental Health Ctr., Bronx, N.Y., 1992—; practice medicine specializing in psychiatry, child psychiatry and psychoanalysis, 1977—. Mem. N.Y. Psychoanalytic Soc., Am. Psychoanalytic Assn., Am. Acad. Child and Adolescent Psychiatry. Office: 1349 Lexington Ave New York NY 10128-1511

RAICHE, BERNARD MARCEL, mental health program administrator; b. Manchester, N.H., Sept. 5, 1944; s. Marcel L. and Therese (Norman) R.; m. Jean Adams, Aug. 25, 1979. BS, Springfield Coll., 1967; MSW, U. Wis., Milw., 1982; MBA, Marquette U., 1986; EdD, U. Maine, 1977; JD, Cath. U. Am., 1996. Tchr. Milford (N.H.) Area Jr./Sr. H.S., 1967-68; counselor, tchr. Parkside Jr. High Sch., Manchester, 1968-71; sch. counselor Bow (N.H.) Meml. Sch., 1971-75; tech. coord. U. Maine Tchr. Corps Project, Orono, 1977-79; coord. counseling and pers. svc. Marquette U., Milw., 1981-85, dir. edn. clinic, 1983-87, dir. tchr. edn., 1985-87; exec. dir. Richie McFarland Children's Ctr., Stratham, N.H., 1987-88; dir. child and adolescent psychiat. svcs. Brookside Hosp., Nashua, N.H., 1988-91; assoc. adminstr. Psychiat. Ctr. of Mich. Hosp., New Baltimore, Mich., 1991-92; dir. spl. projects northeast region Nat. Med. Enterprises, 1992-94; health care cons., 1994; dir. partial hosp. programs Psychiat. Inst. Washington, 1994—; pvt. practice psychotherapist, 1996—; psychotherapist Lakeside Family Counseling, Mt. Clemens, Mich., 1992, Inner Dynamics, Milw., 1983-87; outpatient therapist Seacoast Mental Health Ctr., Exeter, N.H., 1988-91; counselor Maine Maritime Acad., Cartine, Maine, 1976-77. Contbr. articles to profl. jours. Mem. NASW, ABA, ATLA, Am. Assn. Marriage and Family Therapists, Am. Coll. Healthcare Execs., Am. Health Lawyers Assn. Home: 3440 Hidden Meadow Dr Fairfax VA 22033-1114

RAICHLE, MARCUS EDWARD, radiology, neurology educator; b. Hoquiam, Wash., Mar. 15, 1937; m. Mary Elizabeth Rupert, 1964; children: Marcus Edward, Timothy Stephen, Sarah Elizabeth, Katherine Ann. BS, U. Wash., 1960, MD, 1964. Diplomate Am. Bd. Psychiatry and Neurology. Intern Balt. City Hosps., 1964-65, resident, 1965-66; asst. neurologist N.Y. Hosp. Cornell Med. Ctr., N.Y.C., 1966-68, neurologist, chief resident, 1968-69; clin. instr. dept. medicine divsn. neurosci. U. Tex. Med. Sch., San Antonio, 1969-70; rsch. instr. Washington U. Sch. Med., St. Louis, 1971-72, from asst. prof. neurology to assoc. prof. neurology, 1972-78, from asst. prof. radiology (radiation scis.) to assoc. prof. radiology Edward Mallinckrodt Inst. Radiology, 1972-79, from asst. prof. to assoc. prof. biomedical engring., 1974-79, prof. neurology, 1978—, prof. radiology Edward Mallinckrodt Inst. Radiology, 1979—, prof. biomedical engring., 1979—; instr. dept. neurology Cornell U. Med. Coll., N.Y.C., 1968-69; asst. neurologist Barnes Hosp., St. Louis, 1971-75, assoc. neurologist, 1975-78, neurologist, 1978—; cons. neurologist St. Louis Children's Hosp., 1975—; neurologist Jewish Hosp., St. Louis, 1984—, St. Louis Regional Hosp., 1985—; mem. neurology study sect. A NIH, 1975-79; mem. com. cerebrovascular diseases Nat. Inst. Neurol. Diseases and Stroke, long range planning effort, 1978, basic sci. task force, 1978; mem ad hoc adv. panel, Nat. Inst. Neurol. Diseases and Stroke, 1983, chmn. PET grants spl. rev. com., 1983, chmn. brain imaging ctrs. spl. rev. com., 1985; mem. adv. bd. McDonnell-Pew Program cognitive neuroscience, 1989; other coms. Editorial bds. Stroke, 1974-82, Neurology, 1976-82, Annals of Neurology, 1979-86, Journal Cerebral Blood Flow and Metabolism, 1983-86, dep. chief editor, 1981-83, Brain, 1985-90, Human Neurobiology, 1985-87, Brain Research, 1985-90, Synapse, 1987-90, Journal Neuroscience, 1989—, Journal Cognitive Neuroscience, 1989—, Cerebral Cortex, 1990—, Journal Nuclear Medicine, 1990—, Biological Psychiatry, 1993—, Learning and Memory, 1993—; over 120 pub. papers; contbr. over 75 book chpts., revs. Major USAF, 1969-71. Recipient numerous awards, lectrs., fellows; sr. McDonnell fellow McDonnell Ctr. Studies Higher Brain Function, Washington U., St. Louis, 1982—. Mem. AAAS, Am. Heart Assn. (stroke coun. 1974—, cardiovascular D rsch. study com. 1975-78, Academia Rodinensis Pro Remediatione (acting), Am. Acad. Neurology, Am. Neurological Assn. (councillor 1986-88, nom. com. 1990-91), Am. Physiological Soc., Assn. Rsch. Nervous and Mental Disease, Birmingham Med. Rsch. Expeditionary Soc., Explorers Club (N.Y.), Internat. Soc. Cerebral Blood Flow and Metabolism (sec. 1985-89, pres. elect 1989-91, pres. 1991-93), Inst. Medicine/NAS, Internat. Double Reed Soc., Soc. Neuroscience (pub. rels. com. 1988—), St. Louis Soc. Neurological Scis., Soc. Nuclear Medicine.

RAIDER, LOUIS, physician, radiologist; b. Chattanooga, Sept. 7, 1913; s. Leaha Reevin; m. Emma Silberstein, Oct. 19, 1940; children: Lynne Dianne, David Bernard, Paula Raider Olichney. BS, Bklyn. Coll., 1935; MD, Dalhousie U., 1941. Diplomate, cert. Am. Bd. Radiology. Intern Met. Hosp., N.Y.C., 1940-41, resident in radiology, 1941-42; resident in radiation therapy Bellevue Hosp., N.Y.C., 1942-43; fellow in cancer therapy NIH, N.Y.C., 1943-44; chief of radiology Vets. Hosp., New Orleans, 1947-50; radiologist, chief radiology Providence Hosp., Mobile, Ala., 1950-76; clin. prof. Med. Sch. U. South Ala., Mobile, 1987—. Contbr. articles to profl. jours. Maj. AUS, 1944-47. Fellow Am. Coll. Radiology, Am. Coll. Chest Physicians; mem. Radiol. Soc. N.Am., Am. Roentgen Ray Soc., AMA, Ala. Acad. Radiology (pres. 1970-71, Silver medal 1989), So. Med. Assn. (chmn. sect. radiology 1973-74), Soc. Thoracic Radiology, So. Radiol. Conf., Am. Soc. Emergency Radiology. Democrat. Jewish. Home: 1801 S Indian Creek Dr Mobile AL 36607-2309 Office: Hosp U South Ala 2451 Fillingim St Mobile AL 36617-2238

RAIJMAN, ISAAC, gastroenterologist, endoscopist, educator; b. Empalme, Sonora, Mex., July 6, 1959; came to U.S., 1985; s. Jose and Amalia (Langsam) R. MD, Nat. Autonomous U., Mexico City, 1985; postgrad., Nat. U. Houston, U. Wis., 1985. Diplomate Am. Bd. Internal Medicine, Am. Bd. Gastroenterology. Resident in medicine Mt. Sinai Hosp., Milw., 1986-88, chief resident, 1989; clin. fellow in therapeutic endoscopy Wellesley Hosp., Toronto, Ont., Can., 1992-93; rsch. fellow in gastroenterology U. Tex., Houston, 1989-90, clin. fellow, 1990-92, asst. prof. medicine, 1993—, dir. therapeutic endoscopy, 1993—, asst. prof. M.D. Anderson Cancer Ctr., 1993—. Author: Pancreas, 1993, Bockus Textbook of Gastroenterology, 1993; also numerous articles. Mem. Am. Coll. Gastroenterology, Am. Gastroenterology Assn., Internat. Assn. Pancreatology, Am. Soc. Gastrointestinal Endoscopy, Am. Soc. Internal Medicine. Office: 6414 Fannin Ste G125 Houston TX 77030-1501

RAINE, MOLLIE RUTH, director of medical records; b. Emporia, Kans., Mar. 17, 1972; d. Arthur Marion and Tamara Jane (Tincher) R. BS cum laude, Ark. Tech. U., 1994. Coder/abstractor Washington Regional Med. Ctr., Fayetteville, Ark.; dir. med. records North Ark. Med. Ctr., Harrison; cons. NAMC Clinics, Harrison, 1995—. Mem., co-leader C. of C. Leadership Class, Harrison, 1995—; med. post advisor, Explorer's Boy Scouts of Am. Mem. Am. Health Info. Mgmt. Assn., Ark. Health Info. Mgmt. Assn. Republican. Baptist.

RAINER, JOHN DAVID, psychiatrist, educator; b. N.Y.C., July 13, 1921; s. Louis W. and Daisy (Harris) Rosen; m. Barbara Antin, Dec. 23, 1944; children: Jeff, Peter. AB, Columbia Coll., N.Y.C., 1941; MA, Columbia U., 1944, MD, 1951; DLitt (hon.), Gallaudet U., 1968. Rotating intern Mt. Sinai Hosp., N.Y.C., 1951-52; resident psychiatry N.Y. State Psychiat. Inst., N.Y.C., 1952-55; rsch. assoc. in psychiatry Columbia U., N.Y.C., 1956-59; asst. clin. prof. psychiatry Columbia U., 1959-67; chief psychiat. rsch. (genetics) N.Y. State Psychiat. Inst., N.Y.C., 1965-91; assoc. clin. prof. psychiatry Columbia U., N.Y.C., 1967-70; assoc. prof. clin. psychiatry Columbia U., 1970-72, prof. clin. psychiatry, 1972—; tng. and supervising analyst Columbia Psychoanalytic Ctr., N.Y.C., 1972—; attending psychiatrist Presbyterian Hosp., N.Y.C., 1972—. Editorial bd. mem. Am. Annals of the Deaf, Neuropsychobiology, Jour. Preventive Psychiatry; contbr. over 150 articles to profl. jours. Pres. Lake Isle Civic Assn., Eastchester, N.Y., 1989-91. With U.S. Army, 1945-46. Recipient Samuelson award N.Y. League for Hard of Hearing, 1974. Fellow Am. Psychiat. Assn. (life), Am. Psychoanalytic Assn. (life), Am. Coll. Psychoanalysts; mem. Am. Soc. Human Genetics, Am. Psychopathol. Assn. (life), Eastern Psychiat. Rsch. Assn. (pres. 1971-73), Westchester Psychoanalytic Soc. (pres. 1975-76), Phi Beta Kappa, Alpha Omega Alpha. Home: 9 Innisfree Pl Eastchester NY 10707-1207 Office: NY State Psychiat Inst 722 W 168th St New York NY 10032-2603

RAINER, WILLIAM GERALD, cardiac surgeon; b. Gordo, Ala., Nov. 13, 1927; s. Jamie Flournoy and Lula (Davis) R.; m. Lois Sayre, Oct. 7, 1950; children: Vickie, Bill, Julia, Leslie. Student, Emory U., Atlanta, Ga., 1943-44, U. Ala., 1944-45; MD, U. Tenn., Memphis, 1948; MS in Surgery, U. Colo., Denver, 1958. Diplomate Am. Bd. Surgery, Am. Bd. Thoracic Surgery. Intern Wesley Hosp., Chgo., 1949; gen. practice medicine Blue Island, Ill., 1950-52; resident Denver VA Hosp., 1954-59; practice medicine specializing in cardiac surgery Denver, 1960—; bd. dirs. St. Joseph Hosp. Found., Denver. Contbr. articles to profl. jours. Lt. U.S. Army, 1952-54. Decorated Bronze Star; recipient Disting. Alumnus award U. Tenn. Health Sci. Ctr., 1992. Mem. Soc. Thoracic Surgeons (sec. 1980-85, pres. 1989), Colo. Med. Soc. (pres. 1984-85), Denver Med. Soc. (pres. 1984), Am. Coll. Chest Physicians (pres. 1984), Am. Bd. Thoracic Surgeons (bd. dirs. 1982-88), Am. Surg. Assn., Am. Assn. Thoracic Surgery, Societé Internationale de Chirugie, Denver Athletic Club. Office: 2005 Franklin St Ste 380 Denver CO 80205-5408

RAINESS, ALAN EDWARD, psychiatrist; b. N.Y.C., Sept. 24, 1935; s. George W. and Ida Rainess; m. Alice Maree Haber, June 5, 1968; children: Alice Jeanne Rainess Kules, James Alan (dec.). AB, Columbia Coll., 1957; MD, U. Paris, 1965. Diplomate Am. Bd. Psychiatry and Neurology. Intern Meadowbrook Hosp., East Meadow, L.I., 1965-66; resident in psychiatry N.Y. VA Hosp., N.Y.C., 1966-67; teaching fellow in psychiatry Harvard Med. Sch., Boston, 1967; chief resident in psychiatry Boston City Hosp., 1967; resident in psychiatry Walter Reed Med. Ctr., Washington, 1970-72; clin. dir. St. Elizabeth's Hosp., Washington, 1973-76; asst. chief psychiatry Andrews AFB Hosp., Camp Springs, Md., 1976-80, chief neurology, 1989-91; resident in neurology Wilford Hall USAF Med. Ctr., San Antonio, 1980-83; chief medicine and neuropsychiatry Air Univ. Hosp., Maxwell AFB, Ala., 1983-89, chief neurology, 1991-94; psychiatrist Manhattan Psychiat. Ctr., N.Y.C., 1994—; asst. clin. prof. psychiatry Georgetown U. Med. Sch., Washington, 1974-79; assoc. prof. neurology and psychiatry Uniformed Svcs. U. Health Scis., Bethesda, Md., 1989-94. Maj. U.S. Army, 1968-73, col. USAF, 1976-94, ret. Fellow Am. Psychiat. Assn.; mem. Am. Soc. Psychoanalytic Physicians (pres. N.Y. chpt. 1996), Am. Acad. Psychoanalysis (psychiat. assoc.), Masons. Home: 345 E 93rd St Apt 22H New York NY 10128-5522 Office: Manhattan Psychiat Ctr New York NY 10035

RAINEY, JOHN BRUCE, surgeon; b. Belfast, May 18, 1952; s. John Stanley and Ann Margaret (Slipper) R.; m. Linda Margaret King, Feb. 23, 1980; children: Anna, Michael, Thomas. BS with honors, U. Edinburgh, 1972, MBChB, 1976, ChM, 1985. Cert. ATLS. Registrar in surgery Southmead Hosp., Bristol, United Kingdom, 1981-84; lectr. in surgery U. Edinburgh, United Kingdom, 1984-87, sr. lectr., 1988; sr. registrar St. Mark's Hosp., London, 1987; cons. surgeon West Lothian NHS Trust, Edinburgh, 1988—, dir. surgery, 1996—; examiner in surgery U. Edinburgh, 1983—, hon. sr. lectr. in surgery, 1989—; examiner Royal Coll. Surgeons Edinburgh, 1989—; vice chmn. Lothian Divsn. Surgery, 1993—. Contbr. chpts. to books in field; contbr. articles to profl. jours. Fellow Assn. Surgeons Great Britain and Ireland, Assn. Coloproctologists of Great Britain and Ireland, Brit. Assn. Surg. Oncologists. Home: 9 Blackford Hill View, Edinburgh EH9 3HD, Scotland Office: Saint Johns Hosp Hewden, Livingston West Lothian, Edinburgh EH54 6PI, Scotland

RAINWATER, AVIE JAMES, III, clinical psychologist, family medicine educator; b. Florence, S.C., Sept. 6, 1955; s. Avie James Jr. and Leila Mae (Drake) R.; m. Karen Lurie Gadberry, June 17, 1978; children: Chelsea Lurie, Seth Avie James IV, Joshua Morris Wayne. BA, Oral Roberts U., 1978; MSc, Northeastern State U., 1984; MS, Okla. State U., 1986, PhD,

1989. Lic. clin. psychologist, S.C.; diplomate Am. Bd. Profl. Psychology, Am. Acad. Pain Mgmt. Career counselor Oral Roberts U., Tulsa, 1978-79; rsch. assoc. Children's Med. Ctr., Tulsa, 1979-83, resident in clin. psychology, 1989; coord. counseling svcs. City of Faith Med. Ctr., Tulsa, 1983-85, intern in counseling psychology, 1984; psychol. assoc. Okla. State U., Stillwater, 1985-88; fellow in psychology Dartmouth Med. Sch., Hanover, N.H., 1988-89; dir. biofeedback svcs. McLeod Regional Med. Ctr., Florence, S.C., 1989-93; pvt. practice clin. psychology, 1990—; dir. behavioral medicine McLeod Family Medicine Ctr., Florence, 1989—; assoc. prof. family medicine and psychiatry Med. U. S.C., Charleston, 1989—; mem. med. staff McLeod Regional Med. Ctr., 1989—, Carolinas Hosp. Sys., 1990—; mem. gen. staff Florence Gen. Hosp., 1990—; mem. cons. staff Dartmouth-Hitchcock Meml. Hosp., 1988-89, City of Faith Hosp., 1983-85; chief psychologist pain mgmt. program McLeod Regional Med. Ctr., 1989-93; cons. in psychology, 1988, consulting psychol. assoc. United Clinics of Counseling, Inc., Tulsa, 1986; consulting biofeedback specialist pain mgmt. program City of Faith Hosp., 1982-85; mediator landlord/tenant disputes renters' adv. coun. Okla. State U., 1986; reviewer grants Am. Acad. Family Physicians Found., 1990—; apptd. by Gov. of S.C. to bd. dirs. Foster Care Rev. Bd., State of S.C.; sec. Bd. Examiners in Psychology of the State of S.C. Reviewer manuscripts and books for Jour. Family Practice, 1990—; assoc. editor Jour. Psychology and Christianity, 1989—; contbr. numerous rsch. articles to profl. jours. Recipient Pres.'s Travel award Biofeedback Soc. Am., 1981; Indian Edn. Program doctoral tng. fellow U.S. Dept. Edn., 1985-89, minority tng. fellow Am. Psychol. Assn., 1986-88; Carrie Jacobi Ednl. Found. grant, 1988, Okla. Regents grant, 1985-89, Regents scholar, 1976-78. Fellow Biofeedback Cert. Inst. Am. Office: McLeod Family Medicine Ctr 555 E Cheves St Florence SC 29506-2617

RAISZ, LAWRENCE GIDEON, medical educator, consultant; b. N.Y.C., Nov. 13, 1925; s. Erwin Joseph and Marie Georgette (Patai) R.; s. Helen Martin, June 5, 1948; children: Stephen, Matthew, Jonathan, Katherine, Nicholas. Student, Harvard U., 1943, MD, 1947; DOdontology (hon.), U. Umea, Sweden, 1990. Diplomate Am. Bd. Internal Medicine, Nat. Bd. Med. Examiners. Intern Harvard Med. Svc., Boston City Hosp., 1947-48; resident in medicine Cushing VA Hosp., 1950, Boston VA Hosp., 1952-54; asst. and instr. in physiology NYU-Bellevue Med. Ctr., 1948-50; asst. and instr. in medicine sch. medicine Boston U., 1953-56; chief renal sect. Boston VA Hosp., 1954-56; asst. chief radioisotope svc. Syracuse VA Hosp., 1956-57; asst. prof. medicine Coll. Medicine SUNY, Syracuse, 1956-61; assoc. prof. pharmacology and medicine Sch. Medicine U. Rochester, 1961-66, assoc. prof. medicine Sch. Medicine, 1966-68, prof. pharmacology, toxicology, and medicine Sch. Medicine, 1966-74, chief div. of clin. pharmacology Sch. Medicine, 1961-74; prof. medicine, head div. of endocrinology and metabolism Sch. Medicine U. Conn., Farmington, 1974—; program dir. Gen. Clin. Rsch. Ctr. U. Conn Health Ctr., Farmington, 1993—; sr. assoc. physician Strong Meml. Hosp., Rochester, 1961-68, physician, 1968-74; acting chmn. dept. pharmacology Sch. Medicine, U. Rochester, 1962-63, vis. prof. pharmacology, toxicology and medicine Sch. Medicine and Dentistry, 1974-76; vis. assoc. prof. pharmacology Sch. Medicine Stanford U., 1966; vis. prof. Coll. Medicine U. Lagos, Nigeria, 1973; mem. gen. B study sect. NIH, 1986-88; mem. subspecialty bd. on endocrinology and metabolism Am. Bd. Internal Medicine, 1990—; mem. U.S.-Japan Malnutrition Panel, 1985-91; clin. investigator Syracuse VA Hosp., 1957-60; William N. Creasy Vis. Prof. Clin. Pharmacology Med. Sch. Dartmouth Coll., 1977; chmn. Gordon Conf. on Bones and Teeth, 1980; Edwin B. Astwood lectr. Endocrine Soc., 1983. Mem. numerous editorial bds.; contbr. more than 300 articles to profl. jours. With USNR, 1943-45; capt. AUS, 1950-52. Spl. Rsch. fellow Nat. Inst. Arthritis and Metabolic Disease, Strangeways Rsch. Lab., 1960-61, Nat. Inst. Dental Rsch. NIH, 1971-72; Burroughs-Wellcome scholar in Clin. Pharmacology, 1963-68; recipient Prix Andre Lichtwitz, 1980, Class of 1947 Disting. Prof. award Med. Sch. U. Wis., 1988. Mem. AAAS, Am. Fedn. for Clin. Rsch., Am. Soc. for Clin. Investigation, Am. Soc. for Pharmacology and Exptl. Therapeutics, Endocrine Soc., Assn. Am. Physicians, Conn. Endocrine Soc. (pres. 1976), Am. Soc. for Bone and Mineral Rsch. (pres. 1980-81, William F. Neuman award 1986), Conn. Acad. Sci. and Engring., Sigma Xi. Home: 118 Waterville Rd Farmington CT 06032-1624 Office: U Conn Health Ctr 263 Farmington Ave Farmington CT 06030-1850

RAJA, JAY MOHAN, physician; b. Madras, India, July 5, 1950; came to U.S., 1977; s. Jan and Padmini (Raja) Hohan; m. Premala, Dec. 11, 1976; children: Deepak, Harish. MBBS, U. Madras, 1975. Attending physician Venice (Fla.) Hosp., 1985—, Englewood (Fla.) Hosp., 1985—; chief staff Englewood CMty. Hosp., 1990, chief medicine, 1994; cons. in field. Fellow Am. Coll. Gastroenterology; mem. Am. Soc. Gastrointestinal Endoscopy, Fla. Gastrointestinal Soc., Critical Care Medicine. Office: 900 E Pine St #215/218 Englewood FL 34223

RAJADURAI, PATHMANATHAN, pathologist, researcher, educator, consultant; b. Klang, Malaysia, Aug. 13, 1953; s. Rajadurai Arumugam and (Sivapackiadevi) Sangarapillai; m. Prema Pathmanathan, Mar. 11, 1984; children: Rohini Pathmanathan, Gayathiri Pathmanathan. MB BS, U. Malaya, Malaysia, 1978, M in Pathology, 1982; MRC in Pathology, Royal Coll. Pathologists, Eng., 1986. Cert. Malaysian Med. Coun., Gen. Med. Coun. U.K. Med. officer U. Hosp., Kuala Lumpur, Malaysia, 1978-79; trainee pathologist dept. pathology U. Malaya, 1979-82, lectr., clin. specialist, 1982-86, cons. pathologist, 1986—, assoc. prof. pathology, 1986-92, chmn. dept., 1991—, prof., dep. dean postgrads., 1992—; sr. cons. histopathologist dept. pathology Univ. Hosp., Kuala Lumpur, 1986—; cons. Tumorzentrum Regensburg, Germany, 1991—, dept. microbiology and tumor immunology U. Regensburg, 1991—. Contbr. over 100 articles to profl. jours. Recipient Pathology prize U. Malaya, 1974, 82. Fellow Acad. Medicine Malaysia, Internat. Coll. Tropical Medicine, Royal Australasian Coll. Pathologists; mem. Malaysian Med. Soc., Malaysian Soc. Pathologists, Royal Coll. Pathologists U.K., N.Y. Acad. Scis., Internat. Acad. Cytology. Hindu. Home: No 14 Lorong Siputih, Kuala Lumpur 58000, Malaysia Office: Univ Hosp Dept Pathology, Kuala Lumpur 59100, Malaysia

RAJEWSKY, MANFRED FEDOR, cell biologist, educator, cancer researcher; b. Frankfurt on Main, Germany, July 24, 1934; s. Boris N. and Olga (Kromm) R.; m. Helga Keilholz, 1964; children: Gregor P., Irina O. Student U. Paris, U. Frankfurt on Main, U. Freiburg; MD, U. Freiburg, Fed. Republic Germany, 1962; dozent biophysics and tumor biology U. Tübingen. Germany, 1971. Mem. rsch. staff Max Planck Inst. Biophysics, Frankfurt, 1962-68, Max Planck Inst. Virus Rsch., Tübingen, 1968-75; rsch. fellow Inst. Cancer Rsch., London, 1964-65; Eleanor Roosevelt internat. cancer rsch. fellow Stanford U. Sch. Medicine, Palo Alto, Calif., 1966-67; prof., dir. Inst. Cell Biology, U. Essen, Germany, 1975—; lectr. Princess Takamatsu Cancer Rsch., Japan, 1985; vis. prof. Harvard U. Sch. Pub. Healtht, 1983, Shanghai Inst. Cell Biology, Academia Sinica, China, 1986. Mem. editl. bds., sci. bds. sci jours. and book series; contbr. articles to profl. jours. Mem. adv. coun. Gen. Motors Cancer Rsch. Found., 1991—. Recipient Gerhard Domagk award for cancer rsch., 1970; Salzer award for cancer rsch. State of Baden-Württemberg, 1974; Warner award for cancer rsch., 1976, German Cancer prize, 1989. Mem. Am. Assn. Cancer Rsch. (corr.), Japanese Assn. Cancer Rsch. (hon.), European Assn. Cancer Rsch., European Orgn. Rsch. and Treatment of Cancer (chmn. rsch. br. 1988-91), European Molecular Biology Orgn., Deutsche Forschungsgemeinschaft (chmn. senate commn. for cancer rsch. 1983-91), German Soc. for Cell Biology (pres. 1985-87), others. Office: Inst Zellbiol (Tumorforschung) U, Essen Med Sch Hufelandstrasse 55, D-45122 Essen Germany

RAJU, PADMA, surgeon; b. Bangalore, India, Aug. 19, 1939; came to the U.S., 1963; m. Jaya Raju, Apr. 26, 1963; children: Jyothsna, Tara. MBBS, U. Med. Coll., Mysore, India, 1961. Intern and resident in surgery Deaconess Hosp., Buffalo, N.Y., 1963-67; resident in thoracic surgery St. Francis Hosp., Roslyn, N.Y., 1967-69; also Miss. State Sanatorium, Mt. Vernon, Mo., 1967-69; fellow in surgery Bklyn.-Cumberland Med. Ctr., 1970-71; staff surgeon VA Med. Ctr., Fort Meade, S.D., 1971-73, Topeka, 1973-82; pvt. practice Topeka, 1982—; cons. in surgery VA Med. Ctr., Topeka, 1982—. Fellow ACS, Southwestern Surg. Congress; mem. AMA, Kans. Med. Soc., Shawnee County Med. Soc., Am. Assn. Physicians from India (patron). Hindu. Office: Surg Assocs Topeka 1516 SW 6th St Topeka KS 66606

RAKEL, ROBERT EDWIN, physician, educator; b. Cin., July 13, 1932; s. Edwin J. and Elsie (Machino) R.; m. Peggy Klare; children: Barbara, Cindy, Linda, David. BS in Zoology, U. Cin., 1954, MD, 1958. Diplomate: Charter diplomate Am. Bd. Family Practice (v.p., dir.). Intern St. Mary's Hosp., Cin., 1958-59; resident in internal medicine USPHS Hosp., Seattle, 1959-61; resident in gen. practice Monterey County Hosp., Salinas, Calif., 1961-62; practice medicine Newport Beach, Calif., 1962-69; chmn. family practice program U. Calif., Irvine, 1969-71; prof., head dept. family practice U. Iowa, 1971-85; assoc. dean acad. and clin. affairs, Richard M. Kleberg, Sr. prof., chmn. dept. family medicine Baylor Coll. Medicine, Houston, 1985—; dir. family practice residency program Hoag Meml. Hosp., Newport Beach, 1969-71; med. staff Mercy Hosp., Iowa City, 1971-85; chief family practice service St. Luke's Episc. Hosp., The Meth. Hosp., Houston, 1985—; trustee The Hospice of Tex. Med. Ctr., 1986—, Inst. of Religion Tex. Author: Selected References in Family Medicine, 1973, (with H.F. Conn & T.W. Johnson) Family Practice, 1973, (with H.F. Conn.) Textbook of Family Practice, 1978, editor 3d edit., 1984, 5th edit., 1995, Principles of Family Medicine, 1977; author foreword Neurology for the Everyday Practice of Medicine, R.G. Feldman, 1984; contbr. Dictionary of Am. Med. Biography Vols. I and II, 1984; editor: Conn's Current Therapy, 1984—, Yearbook of Family Practice, 1977-90, (series) Procedures for Your Practice Patient Care, Vol. 18, Essentials of Family Practice, 1992, Saunders Manual Med. Practice, 1996; mem. 13 editorial bds. med. jours.; contbr. articles to med. jours.; contbr. Encyclopedia Britannica, 1995. Served with USPHS, 1959-61. Recipient Mead-Johnson Scholar award in Gen. Practice, 1971. Fellow Am. Acad. Family Physicians (pres. Orange County chpt. Calif. 1969, commn. on edn. 1970-76, Thomas W. Johnson award 1973); mem. AMA (sect. on med. schs. 1985—, gov. council of sect. 1986-88), Tex. Med. Assn., Am. Bd. Family Practice (bd. dirs. 1973-79, v.p. 1977-79, chmn. exam. com. 1974-79, recert. com. 1973-79, others), Am. Bd. Med. Spltys. (com. splty. evaluation 1978-81), Nat. Bd. Med. Examiners (bd. dirs. 1975-79), Soc. Tchrs. Family Medicine (dir. 1971-79, sec. 1971-73), Council Acad. Socs., Assn. Am. Med. Colls., History of Medicine Soc. (founder, chmn. U. Iowa 1978-85, founder, chmn. Baylor Coll. Medicine 1986—), Am. Osler Soc. (bd. dirs. 1989—, pres. 1994), Cosmos Club. Home: 2420 Underwood St Houston TX 77030-3506 Office: Baylor Coll Medicine 1 Baylor Plz Houston TX 77030-3411

RAKHMAN, JACOB, urologist; b. Riga, Latvia, June 17, 1947; s. Josif and Liuba (Lautsen) R.; m. Susan Ann Small; children: Joshua, Benjamin, Joana. Degree, Riga Med. Inst., 1970. Diplomate Am. Bd. Urology. Pvt. practice N.Y.C., 1985—; clin. instr. Albert Einstein Sch. of Medicine, 1994—. Mem. Am. Urologic Assn., Am. Urologic Assn. (N.Y. sect.), Am. Assn. of Clin. Urologists, N.Y. State Med. Soc. Home: 8 Arleigh Rd Great Neck NY 11021 Office: 307 East 49th St New York NY 10017

RAKIC, PASKO, neuroscientist, educator; b. Ruma, Yugoslavia, May 15, 1933; came to U.S., 1969; m. Patricia Goldman, 1969. MD, U. Belgrade, Yugoslavia, 1959, ScD in Neuroembryology, 1969. With inst. path. physiology Med. Sch. U. Belgrade, 1959-61, resident in neurosurgery, 1961-62; NIH research fellow neuropathology Harvard Med. Sch., Boston, 1962-66; asst. prof. Inst. Biol. Rsch., Belgrade, 1967-68; from asst. prof. to assoc. prof. neuropathology and neuroscience Harvard Med. Sch., 1969-77; prof. neurosci. Yale Med. Sch., New Haven, 1977-78, Dorys McConnell Duberg prof. neurosci., 1978—, also chmn. neurobiology sect. Author of 200 sci. papers and gen. books on brain orgn. and devel. Recipient Henry Gray award Am. Assn. Anatomists, 1996. Mem. NAS, Am. Acad. Arts and Sci., Soc. Neurosci. (pres. 1996—). Office: Yale U Sch Medicine Sect Neurobiology 333 Cedar St New Haven CT 06510-3206

RAKIĆ, SRDJAN, surgeon; b. Belgrade, Serbia, Yugoslavia, Aug. 8, 1951; arrived in The Netherlands, 1992; s. Cvetko and Hristina (Gajić) R.; m. Eveline Désirée Mantel, Aug. 18, 1984; children: Stefanie, Melanie, Alexander. MD, Belgrade U. Sch. Medicine, 1975, MS, 1979, specialist gen. surgery, 1982, PhD, 1987. Surgeon, chief esophageal surgery divsn. Inst. Digestive Diseases, Belgrade, Yugoslavia, 1982-93; surgeon Leyenburg Hosp., The Hague, The Netherlands, 1993—; asst. prof., assoc. prof. surgery Belgrade U. Sch. Medicine, 1982-93. Author: Rob & Smith's Operative Surgery, 1994; assoc. editor Archives of Gastroenterohepatology, 1991-95; contbr. articles to profl. jours. Recipient Icrett award, Internat. Union Against Cancer, 1992; scholarship Insternat. Soc. for Diseases of the Esophagus, 1988; rsch. fellow Creighton U., Omaha, 1991. Fellow ACS; mem. Dutch Surg. Assn., N.Y. Acad. Scis. Home: Noorderbrink 46, 2553 GC The Hague S Holland The Netherlands Office: Leyenburg Hosp, Leyweg 275, 2545 CH The Hague S Holland The Netherlands

RAKOV, ROBERT WILLIS, surgeon; b. Goshen, N.Y., Nov. 12, 1926; s. Daniel and Helen Ernestine (Buckheit) R.; m. Beatrice Emily, July 8, 1951; children: Kathryn Lynn, Lisa Helen, Robert Daniel. MD, Syracuse (N.Y.) U., 1949. Diplomate Am. Bd. Surgery. Intern Pa. Hosp., Phila., 1949-51, resident, 1951-54, 56-57; ret. chief of surgery Arden Hill Hosp., Goshen, N.Y., 1986. Chmn. Orange County Aviation Bd., Goshen. Lt. USN, 1954-56. Mem. Mid-Hudson Surg. Soc. (former pres.), Goshen Rotary Club. Episcopalian. Home: 711 Homestead Ave Maybrook NY 12543-1307

RAKSAKULTHAI, VINAI, obstetrician, gynecologist; b. Rayong, Thailand, Mar. 20, 1942; came to U.S., 1968; s. Choosak and Ngo (Koc) R.; m. Vullapa Raksakulthai, Sept. 20, 1968; children: Vipavull, Vivian, Vipat. MD, ChiengMai Med. Sch., Thailand, 1966. Diplomate Am. Bd. Ob-Gyn. Intern New Britain (Conn.) Gen. Hosp., 1969; resident St. Joseph Mercy Hosp., Pontiac, Mich., 1970-72; practice medicine specializing in ob-gyn. Fredericktown, Mo., 1973—. Mem. Mo. Med. Assn., Mineral Area Med. Soc. Buddhist. Home: 201 Williams St Fredericktown MO 63645-1317 Office: 703 N Main Fredericktown MO 63645

RALL, DAVID PLATT, pharmacologist, environmentalist; b. Aurora, Ill., Aug. 3, 1926; s. Edward Everett and Nell (Platt) R.; children: Jonathan D., Catharyn E.; m. Mary Gloria Monteiro, Apr. 22, 1989. BS, North Ctrl. Coll., Naperville, Ill., 1946; MS, Northwestern U., 1948, MD, PhD, 1951. Intern Bellevue Hosp., N.Y.C., 1952-53; officer USPHS, 1953-90, asst. surgeon gen., 1971-90; sr. investigator Lab. Chem. Pharmacology, Nat. Cancer Inst., NIH, Bethesda, Md., 1953-55, Clin. Pharmacology and Exptl. Therapeutics Service, 1956-58, head service, 1958-63; chief Clin. Pharmacology and Exptl. Therapeutics Service (Lab. Chem. Pharmacology), 1963-69; assoc. sci. dir. for exptl. therapeutics Nat. Cancer Inst., 1966-71; dir. Nat. Inst. Environ. Health Scis., 1971-90, dir. Nat. Toxicology Program, 1978-90; adj. prof. pharmacology U. N.C., Chapel Hill, 1972-90, Foreign Sociology NAS Inst. Medicine, 1994—. Trustee Environ. Def. Fund, 1991—; treas. Ramazzini Soc., 1992—. Fellow AAAS; mem. Am. Assn. Cancer Rsch., Am. Soc. Clin. Investigation, Am. Soc. Pharmacology and Exptl. Therapeutics, Inst. Medicine, Soc. Toxicology. Home and Office: 5302 Reno Rd NW Washington DC 20015-1908

RALL, WILFRID, neuroscientist; b. Los Angeles, Aug. 29, 1922; s. Udo and Doris (Keiser) R.; m. Ava Lou Freed, 1946 (dec.); children: Sara E., Madelyn Rall Badger; m. Mary Ellen Condon, 1983. B.S. summa cum laude, Yale U., 1943; M.S., U. Chgo., 1948; Ph.D., U. N.Z., 1953. Jr. physicist Manhattan Project, U. Chgo., 1943-46; biophysics fellow U. Chgo., Woods Hole, Mass., 1946-48; lectr., sr. lectr. physiology, biophysics U. Otago, Dunedin, N.Z., 1949-56; head biophysics div. Naval Med. Research Inst., Bethesda, Md., 1956-57; biophysicist, office math. research. Nat. Inst. Arthritis and Metabolic Diseases, Bethesda, 1957-67, sr. research physicist math. research br. Nat. Inst. Diabetes and Digestive and Kidney Diseases, 1967-94; scientist emeritus Nat. Insts. Health, 1994—; mem. NRC Com. on Brain Scis., 1968-73. Contbr. articles to profl. jours. Rockefeller Found. fellow, 1954-55. Mem. Soc. Neurosci. (nat. council 1970-72, chpt. pres. 1981-82), Internat. Brain Research Orgn. (central council 1968-73, U.S. nat. com. 1972-76), Biophys. Soc., Am. Physiol. Soc., Physiol. Soc. U.K., AAAS, Wilderness Soc. Office: Math Rsc Br NIDDK NIH 9190 Wisconsin Ave Ste 350 Bethesda MD 20814-3807

RALPH, GERTRUDE ELIOT, medical and surgical nurse, administrator; b. Greenfield, Mass., Nov. 14, 1938; d. John Alden Eliot and Elizabeth (Perry) Eliot Blakslee; m. John Anthony Ralph, Apr. 9, 1960; 1 child, Ian Armstrong. Diploma, Mary Hitchcock Sch. Nursing, Hanover, N.H., 1959; BSN summa cum laude, Fitchburg (Mass.) State Coll., 1984. Crt. nurse adminstr., trauma nurse specialist. Head nurse Mary Hitchcock Meml. Hosp.; staff nurse 249th Gen. Hosp., Camp Drake, Japan; sr. nursing supr. Franklin Med. Ctr., Greenfield. Mem. Mass. Coun. Nurse Mgrs., Sigma Theta Tau.

RALPH, JAMES R., physician; b. Lowell, Mass., Mar. 23, 1933; s. Richard Henry and Alice Claire (Walwood) R.; m. Edith Marquerite Aeschliman, June 7, 1958; children—James R., Lee P., Jon D., David G. BA Middlebury Coll., 1954; MD Yale U., 1959. Diplomate Nat. Bd. Med. Examiners, Am. Bd. Family Practice. Intern, Akron Gen. Med. Ctr., Ohio, 1959-60, resident Akron Gen. Hosp. and Akron Children's Hosp., 1960-61; staff physician Univ. Health Services, U. Mass., Amherst, 1963-72; team physician dept. intercollegiate athletics, U. Mass., 1965—, asst. med. dir. Univ. Health Services, 1971—, coordinator Sports Medicine U. Health Services, 1987—; assoc. family practice community medicine U. Mass. Med. Sch.-Ctr., Worcester, 1980—; attending physician U.S. VA, Florence, Mass., 1964-69; attending staff active Wing Meml. Hosp., Palmer, Mass., 1967-70. Contbr. articles to profl. jours. Bd. dirs. Inter-Faith Housing, Amherst, 1984—, Boston Med. Library, 1985—. Served to capt. USAF, 1961-67. U. Mass. Faculty research grantee, 1967-69; recipient Chancellors Citation award, 1991. Fellow Am. Acad. Family Physicians, Am. Med. Soc. Sports Medicine, 1991; mem. Mass. Acad. Family Physicians (bd. govs. 1980-89), Mass. Med. Soc. (exec. bd., bd. dirs. postgrad. med. inst.), Hampshire Dist. Med. Soc. (pres. elect 1984-86, pres. 1986-88), Am. Coll. Sports Medicine, Sigma Xi. Democrat. Roman Catholic. Avocations: tennis; hiking; camping; coin and stamp collecting. Home: 66 Hills Rd Amherst MA 01002-1839 Office: U Mass Univ Health Svcs Amherst MA 01003

RALSTON, DEBORAH ANN, rehabilitation service professional; b. Berkeley, Calif., Feb. 13, 1952; d. Hershall Robert and Natalene Ruth (Miller) R.; 1 child, Rafael. BA in Art and Psychology, San Francisco State U., 1979; MCAT in Creative Arts Therapy, Antioch U. West, 1982; MPA, Calif. State U., Hayward, 1986. Lic. nursing home adminstr., Calif. Art therpist State Hosp. System, Napa, Calif., 1980-82; spl. projects dir. Children's Hosp., San Francisco, Calif., 1986-90; art therapist Telecare Corp., San Leandro, Calif., 1982-86; dir. rehab., dir. spl. treatement program Telecare Corp., Hayward, Calif., 1990—; acting adminstr. Telecare Corp., Hayward, 1995—; cons. San Francisco Comty. Mental Health, 1986-90, Telecare Corp., Alameda, 1995—; bd. dirs. Comty. Vocational Enterprises, San Francisco, 1987-91. Vol. Health Care Clinics Afya Bora Mobile Med. Units, Arusha, Tanzania, E. Africa, 1995-96. Recipient Mayoral commendation City of San Francisco, 1990. Mem. Am. Coll. Health Care Adminstrs. Office: Telecare Corp Morton Bakar Ctr 494 Blossom Way Hayward CA 94541

RALSTON, HENRY JAMES, III, neurobiologist, anatomist, educator; b. Berkeley, Calif., Mar. 12, 1935; s. Henry James and Sue Harris (Mahnke) R.; m. Diane Cornelia Daly, Oct. 29, 1960; children: Rachel Anne, Amy Sue. BA, U. Calif., Berkeley, 1956, MD, 1959. Intern Mt. Sinai Hosp., N.Y.C., 1959-60; resident in medicine U. Calif., San Francisco, 1960-61, prof., 1973—, chmn. dept. anatomy, 1973—, chair acad. senate, 1986-88; spl. postdoctoral fellow Univ. Coll., London, 1963-65, Univ. lectr., 1981; asst. prof. anatomy Stanford (Calif.) U., 1965-69; assoc. prof. U. Wis., Madison, 1969-73; cons. NIH; mem. com. for future of anat. scis., Macy Found., 1977-80; vis. prof. French Med. Rsch. Inst.-INSERM, Paris, 1981-82; chair step I U.S. Med. Lic. Examination Com. Nat. Bd. Med. Examiners, 1992-96. With M.C. U.S. Army, 1961-63. Recipient Henry J. Kaiser award for excellence in tchg., 1978, Jacob Javits Neurosci. Investigator award NIH, 1988-95; USPHS grantee, 1966—. Mem. AAAS, Soc. Neurosci., Soc. Study Pain, Am. Pain Soc., Am. Assn. Anatomists (pres. 1987-88, chair publs. com. 1989-91), Anat. Assn. Gt. Britain, Phi Beta Kappa, Anat. Assn. Gt. Britain, Phi Beta Kappa. Office: U Calif Dept Anatomy PO Box 0452 San Francisco CA 94143

RALSTON, MICHAEL ALAN, pediatric cardiologist; b. Dayton, June 19, 1959; s. Billy Gene and Emma Jean (Morgan) R.; m. Jacqueline Kay Thomes, Dec. 19, 1982. BA, Miami U., 1981; MD, Ohio State U., 1985. Rsch. asst. Ohio State U., Columbus, 1988-89; staff pediatrician Columbus Pediatric Svcs., 1988-89; pediatric cardiologist Dayton (Ohio) Children's Cardiology, 1992—. Contbr. articles to profl. jours. Fellow Am. Coll. Cardiology, Am. Acad. Pediatrics (sect. pediatric cardiology); mem. Am. Heart Assn., Coun. Cardiovascular Disease in the Young. Office: Dayton Childrens Cardiology 705 Valley St Dayton OH 45404

RALSTON, PAULA JANE, nurse; b. Cedar Rapids, Iowa, Feb. 2, 1960; d. Paul Raymond and Martha Jane (Salato) R. BSN, Morningside Coll., Sioux City, Iowa, 1982; MA in Human Resource Devel., Webster U., 1994. Cert. med.-surg. nurse; cert. EMT. Commd. 2d lt. USAF, 1984, advanced through grades to maj., 1995; staff nurse Cass County Meml. Hosp., Atlantic, Iowa, 1982-84; staff nurse male med. USAF, Scott AFB, Ill., 1984-85, staff nurse female surg., 1985-86, staff nurse 1st Aeromed. Staging Flight, 1986-88, flight nurse, flight nurse instr, quality improvement coord. 57AES/37SAES, 1991-95; officer in charge nursing staff devel. 10TFW Clinic USAF, RAF, Alconbury, 1988-90, charge nurse acute care clinic and 24 hour ambulance svc., 1988-90; ob-gyn. asst. charge nurse 50 TFW Hosp. USAF, Hahn AB, Fed. Republic Germany, 1990-91; nurse mgr. multi-svc. unit, officer in charge hosp. dietary dept, USAF, Misawa AB, Japan, 1995—, exercise evaluation team chief, 1995—; group edn., tng. coord. USAF, 1996—; mem. coord Air Tatto USAF Air Show, RAF Alconbury, 1990; air festival coord. Misawa AFB, Japan, 1995, 96; mem. hyperbaric med. team USAF, 1988-90, 10 T.F.W. Hosp. Desert Storm USAF, Incirlik, Turkey, 1991; instr. ARC, Preparation for Parenthood, Health Baby, Health Pregnancy, Cmty. First Aid & Safety, CPR, ACLS, PALS. USAF rep. for hosp. Fete Hinchingbrooke Hosp., Huntington, U.K., 1988-90; mem. Bury Ch. Eng. Band, U.K., 1988-90, Belleville (Ill.) Philharm. Orch., 1984-88, 91-95; bd. govs. Nebr.-Iowa Circle K Dist., 1981-82, sec.-treas., 1980-81; 35th med. group change of command coord., USAF, 1995. Decorated Achievement medal, 1995, Commendation medal with two oak leaf clusters, Meritorious medal, Joint Svc. medal, 1991, Recipirnt of the 15th Air Force Air Crew of Excellent award. Mem. Assn. Women's Health, Obstetrics & Neonatal Nurses, AACN, Morningside Coll. Circle K Club (v.p. 1979-80), Sigma Theta Tau. Methodist. Home: 8952 Audubon Ct Longmont CO 80503-8668 Office: USAF, 35th Med Group, Misawa AFB Japan

RAMANI, ANANTHAKRISHNAN, epidemiologist; b. Kadayanallur, India, Oct. 23, 1956; arrived in U.S., 1993; s. Pathai Ramier and Janaki Ananthakrishnan; m. Rama Narayan, Mar. 17, 1986; children: Ahsok A., Rohini A. MBBS, J.N. Med. Coll., 1979, Md, 1983. Diplomate Nat. Bd. Med. Examiners. House physician AJN Med. Coll., 1980-81, registrar in medicine, 1981-84; lectr. in medicine Kasturba Med. Coll., Karnataka, India, 1984-85, asst. prof., 1985-88, reader, 1988-90, assoc. prof., 1990-92, prof. medicine, 1992-93; fellow divsn. of infectious diseases Albany (N.Y.) Med. Coll., 1993—. Contbr. articles to profl. jours. Recipient Best Paper award Indian Soc. of Gastroenterology, 1990. Fellow Internat. Coll. of Angiology. Home: 115 B Wellington Ave Albany NY 12203 Office: Albany Med Coll 47 New Scotland Ave Albany NY 12208

RAMETTA, C. S., physician; b. Solarino, Italy, Oct. 5, 1945; s. Sebastian and Lucy R.; came to U.S., 1953, naturalized, 1955; A.B., Seton Hall U., 1967; M.D., Georgetown U., 1971; children—Thomas, Rachel, Benjamin, Robert, Michael Matthew; m. Lisa Ann Garibian. Diplomate Am. Bd. Internal Medicine, Geriatric Medicine. Intern, U. Va., Charlottesville, 1971-72, resident, 1972-74; chief dept. clinics Kimbrough Hosp., Fort Meade, Md., 1974-76; attending Horton Hosp., Middletown, N.Y., 1976—, chmn. dept. medicine, 1984-90, chief of staff, 1990-91. Pres., Orange-Rockland-Sullivan Counties, Am. Heart Assn.; bd. dirs. Am. Cancer Soc. Orange County. Served to maj., M.C., U.S. Army, 1974-76. Fellow Am. Coll. Angiology, Internat. Coll. Angiology, Am. Coll. Utilization Rev. Physicians; mem. ACP, Am. Soc. Internal Medicine. Club: Elks. Office: 22 Grove St Middletown NY 10940-4806

RAMIREZ, MAGDALENA, hospital administrator. BS, Cornell U., Ithaca, N.Y., 1975; MPA, NYU, 1978. Resident N.Y.C. Health and Hosp. Corp., N.Y.C., 1977-78, asst. dir. ops., 1978-81; resident Bellevue Hosp., N.Y.C., 1978; assoc. exec. dir. Queens Hosp. Ctr., Jamaica, N.Y., 1981-86; asst. dir. N.Y. State Dept. Health, Albany, 1986-89; CEO Helen Hayes Hosp., West Haverstraw, N.Y., 1989—; advisor N.Y. State Tech. Adv. Group on Traumatic Brain Injuries. Bd. dirs. Rockland Subarea Health

Coun. Mem. Am. Hosp. Assn., Health Care Exec. Forum (pres.), Am. Rehab. Assn., No. Met. Hosp. Assn. (bd. dirs.). Office: Helen Hayes Hosp Rt 9W West Haverstraw NY 10993

RAMIREZ, PAUL MICHAEL, psychology educator, researcher, neuropsychologist; b. N.Y.C., May 15, 1951. BA, CUNY, 1973; MPhil, CCNY, 1987, PhD, 1990; MA, NYU, 1976, CCNY, 1980. Lic. psychologist, N.Y. Clin. asst. N.Y. Hosp.-Cornell Med. Ctr., N.Y.C., 1978-79; psychology assoc. Downstate Med. Ctr., Bklyn., 1979-81; clin. psychology intern Hutchings Psychiat. Ctr., Syracuse, N.Y., 1981-82; dir. neuropsychology New Medico TBI Program, Milford, Conn., 1983-84; dep. chief of svc. neuropsychiatry svc. Bronx Psychiat. Ctr., 1984-88; sr. clin. neuropsychologist Columbia-Presbyn. Med. Ctr., N.Y.C., 1988-94; mem. med. sch. faculty Coll. of Physicians and Surgeons Columbia U., N.Y.C., 1990-94; assoc. prof. clin. psychology L.I. U., 1993—; mem. adj. psychology faculty Hunter Coll., CUNY, 1982—; dir. psychiat. svcs. Woodstock '94 Festival; guest reviewer Jour. of Reading, 1987-88, Jour. Ednl. Psychology, 1991-92; clin. tng. cons. N.Y. State Office Vocat. Rehab., N.Y.C., 1983-84; rsch. cons. SUNY Coll. Optometry, 1989-90; clin. and rsch. cons. N.Y. State Psychiat. Inst., N.Y.C., 1990-91. Editor Jour. Ednl. Neuropsychology, 1981-88; contbr. articles to profl. jours. NSF fellow CUNY, 1978-81; recipient Recognition award N.Y. State Head-Injury Assn., 1984. Mem. APA, Internat. Neuropsychol. Soc., N.Y. Acad. Scis., Internat. Reading Assn. (chmn. neuropsychol. issues SIG 1980-91), N.Y. Neuropsychology Group (bd. dirs. 1990—), Brain Injury Assn. N.Y. (bd. dirs. 1993-96), Internat. Soc. for Profl. Hypnosis (bd. dirs. 1995—).

RAMIREZ, PAUL ROBERT, obstetrician, gynecologist; b. Bronx, N.Y., Nov. 18, 1950; s. Luciano and Maria Emilia (Gonzalez) R.; m. Carolyn Marie Longhi, Nov. 11, 1972; children: Leah Marie, Elyssa Anne, Nathan Paul, Adam Paul. BA in Psychology, Yale U., 1972, MD, 1976. Diplomate Am. Bd. Ob-Gyn. Intern, resident, then chief resident in ob-gyn. Yale-New Haven Hosp., 1976-80; pvt. practice New Haven, Guilford and Essex, Conn., 1980-84; clin. instr. ob-gyn. Sch. Medicine Yale U., 1981-84, asst. prof. clin. ob-gyn. Sch. Medicine, 1993—; asst. prof. clin. ob-gyn. Sch. Medicine U. Conn., 1992—; asst. prof. ob-gyn., residency program coord., med. dir. outpatient clinics, chief div. gynecology Case Western Res. U., Cleve., 1984-86; chmn. dept. ob-gyn., attending physician St. Vincent's Med. Ctr., Bridgeport, Conn., 1986-91; chief dept. ob-gyn., attending physician Middlesex (Conn.) Hosp., 1992—; med. dir. families and infants Together Program Cleve. Regional Perinatal Network, 1985-86; pediatric and adolescent gynecologic cons. Rainbow Babies and Children's Hosp., Cleve., 1985-86; cons., mem. plan devel. com. Bridgeport Mayor's Select Com. on Infant Mortality, 1987-91; cons., mem. health profls. adv. com. Fairfield County chpt. March of Dimes Birth Defects Found., Norwalk, Conn., 1988—; mem. bd. dirs. St. Vincent's Physicians IPA, 1988-91; mem. Am. Bd. Ob-Gyn Dist. I Adv. Coun., 1988—; rep. com. on underserved women Am. Coll. Ob-Gyn Dist. I, 1990—; mem. EPSDT program adv. com. State of Conn. Dept. of Income Maintenance, 1989-90; ob-gyn cons. div. Family Reproduction, Dept. of Health Svcs. State of Conn. Sports coach Lakewood-Trumbull (Conn.) YMCA, 1987-88. Co-asst. chmn. Greater Bridgeport Adolescent Pregnancy Task Force, 1990-91; mem. Bridgeport Child Advocacy Colaition Com. on Substance Abuse in Pregnancy, 1990-91; rep. ob-gyn. to Mayor's Health Task Force City of Bridgeport, 1991; bd. dirs. Middlesex County United Way, 1995—. Fellow Am. Coll. Ob-Gyn (adv. com. dist. I, 1988—, maternal morality rev. com. 1990—, perinatal/morbidity/mortality com. 1991—); mem. Conn. Med. Soc. (com. on statewide med planning 1988—), Fairfield County Med. Assn. (com. on Legis. 1987—), Conn. Hosp. Assn. (cons., mem. clinician panel for obstetrics 1989—), Yale Club Ea. Fairfield County (sec. 1989-90). Democrat. Roman Catholic. Office: Middlesex Hosp 28 Crescent St Middletown CT 06457-3654

RAMIREZ, RALPH HENRY, nurse, corporate executive; b. Oakland, Calif., Sept. 25, 1949; s. Hector Ramirez and Genevieve (Figueroa) Ingraham. BS in Nursing, San Jose State U., 1974. RN; cert. critical care nurse. DON nursing Chgo. Ctr. Hosp., 1980-84; adminstr. Med. Profls. Supplemental Staffing, Chgo., 1984-85; pres. Progressive Svcs., Chgo., 1985-92; v.p. Seville Internat. Tours, Inc., 1990—; pres. Progressive Health Svcs. Ctrs., Inc., 1992-94, Merchants Nat. Fin. and Mgmt., Houston, 1994-96; ops. dir. Ravenswood Home Care, Chgo., 1996—. Contbr. articles to profl. jours. Sponsor nursing symposium, Chgo., 1991—; bd. dirs. AIDS Found. of Chgo., 1991—, chmn. Gala com., 1993, 94; co-chair Bonaventure House Benefit, 1993. Mem. Am. Biog. Inst. (Disting. Leadership award for Outstanding Svc. to Nursing Profession, Golden Acad. award), Chgo. Nurses Assn., Ill. Nurses Assn., Sigma Theta Tau. Democrat. Roman Catholic. Home: 4334 N Hazel St Apt 1708 Chicago IL 60613-1444 Office: Ravenswood Home Care 4600 N Ravenswood Ave Chicago IL 60640-3218

RAMIREZ, SALVADOR MANUEL, orthopedic surgeon; b. N.Y.C., Mar. 17, 1936; s. Salvador H. and Providencia (Torres) R.; m. Janis Tarpo, Nov. 26, 1960; children: Sally Ann, Robert, Elena, Elizabeth. BS, St. John's U., 1956; MD, Chgo. Med. Sch., 1960. Intern Kings County Hosp., Bklyn., 1960-61; resident Jewish Hosp. and Med. Ctr., Bklyn., 1963-67; chief orthopedics Mercy Hosp., Miami, Fla., 1980-83, pres. med. staff, 1983—, chief orthopedic surgery, 1995-96. Served with USN, 1961-63. Mem. AMA, ACS, Internat. Coll. Surgeons, Am. Acad. Orthopedic Surgeons. Republican. Roman Catholic. Address: 1797 Coral Way Miami FL 33145-2728

RAMLOW, WILLIAM A., orthodontist; b. Grosse Pointe, Mich., Oct. 9, 1940; s. William mcGrery and Lois Mildred (Fowler) R.; m. Jeanne Anne Prettyman, Sept. 7, 1961 (div. June 1975); children: Kristin, Alec, Andrew; m. Juanita Claire Meyers, Aug. 16, 1980; 1 child, John. BA, U. Mo., 1962; DDS, U. Mo., Kansas City, 1966; postgrad., U. Mo., 1973. Bd. eligible Am. Bd. Orthodontics. Pvt. practice, orthodontics Columbia, Mo., 1973—; instr. Sch. of Dentistry U. Mo., Kansas City, 1969-71; pvt. practice, dentistry Kansas City, Mo., 1968-69; mil. dentist U.S. Army, Ft. Huachucha, Ariz., 1966-68; cons. orthodontics dept. plastic surgery, U. Mo. Health Svcs., Columbia, 1973—, Divsn. Med. Svcs., State of Mo., Jefferson City, 1991—. Bd. dirs. Advent Enterprises, Columbia, 1990-93. Col. U.S. Army. Mem. Mo. Dental Assn. (bd. govs. 1969-96), Am. Assn. Orthodontists, Columbia Dental Soc. (pres. 1977-78), Rotary (pres. Columbia club 1988-89), Psi Omega, Theta Nu Epsilon. Office: 1400 Forum Blvd Columbia MO 65203

RAMMLER, LINDA HOPE, human services consultant; b. Bklyn., July 10, 1955; d. Walter and Helen (Shymanski) R.; m. Paul Gionfriddo, Aug. 7, 1982; children: Timothy James, Larissa Ellen, Elizabeth Kay, Benjamin Michael. BA, U. Conn., 1975; MEd, U. Hartford, 1982; MS, Yale U., 1989. Tchr. aide Hartford Regional Ctr., Newington, Conn., 1974; human rights aide, recreation program instr. Mansfield (Conn.) Tng. Sch., 1976-78; instr. Manchester (Conn.) Community Coll., 1978-79; substitute tchr., program specialist John N. Dempsey Regional Ctr., Putnam, Conn., 1979-80; planning analyst then dir. planning and evaluation Dept. Mental Retardation, East Hartford, Conn., 1980-85; exec. asst. Univ. Affiliated Program, Storrs, Conn., 1986-87; coord. CARC v. Thorne study Rsch. Project on Deinstitutionalization, Phila., 1987-88; project co-dir. Consumer Survey Devel. Disabilities Coun., East Hartford, 1988-89; human svcs. cons. in disability issues and inclusive edn. Conn., 1985—; ptnr. Rammler & Wood Cons., LLC, 1995—; part-time instr. Yale U., New Haven, 1989—, Ctrl. Conn. State U., 1994; staff devel. instr. N.E. Area Regional Edn. Svc., Putnam, 1979; presenter programs to various orgns., including Conn. Psychol. Assn., Young Adult Inst. N.Y.C., New England Ednl. Rsch. Orgn., others. Mem. Middletown Co. Concerning People with Disabilities, Conn., 1990-91. Mem. Acad. Mental Retardation, Am. Assn. Mental Retardation (adminstrn. div.), Nat. Assn. Dual Diagnosis, Assn. Retarded Citizens of Conn., Conn. Coalition for Inclusive Edn., Coun. for Exceptional Children (mental retardation, tchr. perparation divs.), Manchester Assn. for Retarded Citizens (bd. mem.), Assn. for Persons with Severe Handicaps (nat. and New Eng. chpts.). Home: 454 Ballfall Rd Middletown CT 06457-2331 Office: 6 Way Rd Ste 301 Middlefield CT 06455

RAMOS, ELEANOR LACSON, internist; b. Quezon City, The Philippines, Mar. 26, 1956; d. Pol and Evelyn (Manahan) Ramos. BS, Tufts U., 1977; MD, Tufts Med. Sch., Boston, 1981. Diplomate Am. Bd. Internal Medicine, Am. Bd. Nephrology. Resident in internal medicine N.E. Med. Ctr., Boston, 1981-84; fellow in nephrology Brigham & Women's Hosp., Boston, 1984-88, med. dir. renal transplant svc., 1988-90; med. dir. renal transplant svc. U. Fla., Gainesville, 1990-94; assoc. dir. immunology clin. rsch. Bristol-Myers Squibb Pharm. Rsch. Inst., Wallingford, Conn., 1994-96; asst. clin. prof. medicine Yale U., 1995-96; dir. med. rsch. Roche Global Devel., Palo Alto, Calif., 1996—. Mem. Am. Soc. Transplant Physicans (chairperson patient care and edn. com. 1994-95, Young Investigator award 1988), Am. Soc. Nephrology, Internat. Soc. Nephrology, Alpha Omega Alpha. Office: Roche Golbal Devel 3401 Hillview Ave Palo Alto CA 94304

RAMOS, HAROLD SMITH, health science facility administrator; b. Atlanta, July 20, 1928; s. Ralph Molena and Louise (Price) R.; m. Barbara T. Lavendar, Aug. 21, 1993; children: Mary Catherine, Ralph Samuel, Steven Michael. AB, The Johns Hopkins U., 1948; MD, Med. Coll. Ga., 1954. Commd. 1st lt. U.S. Air Force, 1954, advanced through grades to maj., 1963; intern, resident, fellow Walter Reed Army Hosp., Washington (D.C.), 1954-58; from asst. prof. to prof. of medicine Emory U., Atlanta, 1963—, chief of medicine, Crawford W. Long Meml. Hosp., 1963-85, asst. dean Sch. Medicine, 1975-85, assoc. dean, Sch. of Medicine, 1985—, med. dir., Crawford Long Hosp., 1985—. Mem. Atlanta Hist. Soc. Fellow ACP; mem. AMA, Am. Soc. Internal Medicine, Assn. Hosp. Med. Edn., Am. Acad. Med. Dirs., Capitol City Club (Atlanta). Methodist. Home: 4114 E Brookhaven Dr NE Atlanta GA 30319-2862 Office: Crawford W Long Meml Hosp 550 Peachtree St Atlanta GA 30308-3512

RAMOS, JUAN SARASA, internist; b. Madrid, Sept. 29, 1933; s. Juan Fernandez Ramos and Eulalia Arrieta Sarasa; m. Emilia Benitez Ruiz, 1958 (dec. 1982); m. Isabel Padrón Lopez, 1983; children: Emilia, Palmia, Eva. B Medicine, U. Madrid, 1950, MD cum laude, 1956. Head internal medicine svc. Social Security Hosp. W.S. Pino, Las Palmas, Spain, 1970-76, head dept. internal medicine, 1974—, chair tng. unit family medicine, 1980—; assoc. prof. La Lapuca, 1979. Subdir. Gen. Health Ministry, Madrid, 1983.

RAMOS, JULIO ANTONIO, ophthalmologist, educator; b. Buenos Aires, July 13, 1939; s. Jose Antonio and Anita (Garcia) R.; m. Martha Beatriz Bueno; children: Diana, Julio, Pablo. MD, U. Buenos Aires, 1961. Cert. Argentine Acad. Medicine. Adj. prof. Faculty of Medicine, Buenos Aires, 1988—; chief of svc. ophthalmology dept. Hosp. Español, Buenos Aires, 1976. Mem. Rotary Club. Roman Catholic. Home & Office: Ave de la Riestra 5644, 1439 Buenos Aires Argentina

RAMOS, MANUEL ANTONIO, JR., pulmonologist; b. Lima, Peru, Dec. 17, 1959; arrived in U.S., 1962; s. Manuel and Rosa (Palao) R. BS with Hons., cum laude, U. Miami, 1980; MD, Tulane U., 1984. Diplomate Am. Bd. Internal Medicine, diplomate Subspecialty of Pulmonary Disease. Intern Tulane Hosps., New Orleans, 1984-85; resident in medicine Jackson Meml. Hosp., Miami, Fla., 1985-87, fellow in pulmonology, 1987-90; pvt. practice in pulmonology Plantation, Fla., 1990—; sec. dept. medicine Plantation Gen. Hosp. Contbr. articles to profl. jours. Active Archbishops of Miami Charity Drive Guild. Fellow Am. Coll. Chest Physicians; mem. AMA (Physicians Recognition award 1990, 95), ACP, Am. Thoracic Soc., Am. Soc. Internal Medicine, Broward County Med. Assn. (Salvation Army Clinic, Ft. Lauderdale 1991—), Plantation C. of C. Office: 7050 NW 4th St Ste 301 Plantation FL 33317-2247

RAMOSO, ROBERTO BAYLOR, medical examiner; b. San Isidro, Philippines, Nov. 9, 1941; s. Wenceslao Pingol and Irene Magno (Baylor) R.; m. Ladestate de Belen Esquiuel, June 20, 1970; children: Gary Robert, Wesley Theodore, Ryan Lawrence. MD, Far Eastern U., 1966. Intern United Hosp. Newark, 1967; resident Christ Hosp., Jersey City, N.J., 1968-70, Morristown (N.J.) Meml. Hosp., 1970-73; asst. pathologist Christ Hosp., 1973-74; staff pathologist Charleston (S.C.) Naval Med. Ctr., 1975-78; assoc. pathologist Northwest Hosp., Des Moines, 1978-84; deputy med. examiner Park County Med. Examiner, Des Moines, 1978-84; asst. med. examiner N.J. Med. Examiner's Office, Newark, 1985, Essex County Med. Examiner's Office, Newark, 1986-92; assoc. med. examiner Pierce County Med. Examiner's Office, Tacoma, 1992—. Lt. comdr. USN, 1975-78. Fellow Am. Coll. Pathologists, Am. Soc. Clin. Pathologists; mem. Nat. Assn. Med. Examiners. Roman Catholic. Office: Pierce County Med Examiners 3619 Pacific Ave Tacoma WA

RAMPELL, NANCY, neurologist, electromyographer; b. N.Y.C., Jan. 2, 1954; d. Edward Samuel and Naomi (Bachman) R. BS, U. Fla., 1975; M of Med. Sci., Emory U., 1978, MD, 1984. Intern Emory U. Sch. Medicine, Atlanta, 1984-85, resident in neurology, 1985-88, fellow in neurophysiology, 1988, asst. prof. neurology, 1988; pvt. practice neurology and electromyography Decatur, Ga., 1989—; clin. rschr. on strokes Cambridge Neurosci., Decatur, 1995; dir. stroke unit DeKalb Med. Ctr., Decatur, 1995—; mem. adv. bd. on neurology Blue Cross Blue Shield Metro Atlanta, 1995—; mem. adv. bd. DeKalb Physician Hosp. Authority, Decatur, 1996—. Vol. med. svcs. Physicians Care Clinic, DeKalb Med. Ctr. Family Care, 1995—. Mem. AMA, Am. Acad. Neurology, Med. Assn. Ga. Office: Emory U Sch Med Specialists of Atlanta Neurology & Headache Decatur GA 30033

RAMSAY, DAVID L., physician, dermatologist, medical educator; b. Rochester, N.Y., Apr. 25, 1943; s. Joseph Walter and Jean (Eastwood) R. AB in English with honors, Ind. U., 1965, MD, 1969; MEd, U. Ill., 1973. Diplomate Am. Bd. Dermatology. Assoc. prof. English Ind. U., Indpls., 1965-69; dir. dermatology residency tng. Nat. Naval Med. Ctr., Bethesda, Md., 1973-75; asst. prof. medicine Georgetown U., Washington, 1974-75; asst. prof. dermatology NYU, 1974-78, assoc. prof. dermatology, 1978-95, prof. dermatology, 1995—, senator, 1986-94, pres. faculty coun., 1988-90, dir. ednl. affairs dermatology, 1975—, dir. cutaneous lymphoma sect., 1975—. Author: Simulations in Dermatology, 1974; contbg. author: Adolescent Dermatology, Basic Mechanisms of Physiologic and Aberrant Lymphoproliferation in the Skin, Hematology and Oncology Clinics in North America; contbr. more than 25 articles to profl. jours. Pres., bd. dirs. One Fifth Ave. Apt. Corp., N.Y.C., 1978-80; trustee Bklyn. Acad. Music, 1989—. Lt. comdr. USN, 1973-75. Fellow ACP, Internat. Soc. Cutaneous Lymphomas, Am. Acad. Dermatology; mem. Am. Dermatologic Assn. Roman Catholic. Home: One Fifth Ave New York NY 10003 Office: NYU Med Ctr 530 Fifth Ave New York NY 10016

RAMSEY, NANCY LOCKWOOD, nursing educator; b. L.A., Jan. 26, 1943; d. Jack Thanke and Virginia Lee (Slaughter) Lockwood; m. Gordon S. Ramsey, June 24, 1972; children: Douglas Lockwood, Kathryn Anne. BSN, Loma Linda U., 1966; MS in Nursing, Duke U., 1969; postgrad., Calif. State U., L.A., 1974. Staff nurse various hosps., 1966-82, 91-92; clin. instr. Azusa (Calif.)-Pacific U., 1966-93; instr. U. N.C., Chapel Hill, Calif. State U., L.A.; acting dir. nursing edn. Children's Hosp. L.A.; prof. nursing L.A. City Coll., East L.A. Coll., Monterey Park, Calif.; instr. advanced pediatric nursing State Bd. Rev. Classes, L.A. and San Francisco; instr. statewide nursing program Calif. State U., Dominguez Hills. Author, editor: Child and Family Concepts of Nursing Practice, 1982, 87; contbr. articles to profl. jours. Mem. Sigma Theta Tau. Home: 1561 N Berenice Dr Brea CA 92621-1802 Office: East LA Coll Dept Nursing 1301 Cesar Chavez Monterey Park CA 91754-6099

RAMSEY, PAMELA YVETTE, physician assistant, health educator; b. Welch, W.Va., July 25, 1954; d. Albert V. and Betty Ann (Bland) Vineyard; m. Robert Ramsey (div. Dec. 1986); children: Nekeha Marie, Robyne Lynette. BS in Med. Sci., Alderson Broadus Coll., 1991. Cert. NCCPA, W.Va. Bd. Med., W.Va. Bd. Osteo. Analytical acctg. clk. U.S. Steel Corp., Gary, W.Va., 1976-79; radiology coord. Logan Gen. Hosp., Logan, W.Va., 1979-87; physician asst., health educator Tug River Health Assn., Gary, W.Va., 1991—; sch. health educator Tug River Health Assn, Gary, 1991—, CPR instr., 1995—. Fellow McDowell County ALIC Coalition, 1993—; mem. Am. Cancer Soc.,1993—. Fellow Am. Assn. Physician Assts., Adult Reproductive Health Assn., W.Va. Assn. Physician Assts. (membership com. chair. 1995). Baptist. Home: PO Box 886 Gary WV 24836-0886

RAMSEY, PAUL GLENN, internist; b. Pitts., 1949. MD, Harvard U., 1975. Diplomate Am. Bd. Internal Medicine. Intern Cambridge Hosp., 1975-76; resident in medicine Mass. Gen. Hosp., Boston, 1976-78; resident in medicine U. Wash., Seattle, 1980-81, fellow infectious diseases, 1978-80, prof., 1991—, chmn. dept. medicine, 1992—; physician-in-chief U. Wash. Med. Ctr., 1992—. Mem. ACP, AFCR, AAP, ADA, APM, SGIM. Office: U Wash Hosp RG-20 Dept Medicine Seattle WA 98165

RAMSEY, SANDRA LYNN, psychotherapist; b. Camp LeJeune, N.C., Feb. 7, 1951; d. Robert A. and Lola J. (Hann) R.; m. Edward G. Schmidt, July 9, 1988; children: Seth, Sarah, Anna, Rachel. Student, U. Calif., Long Beach, 1969-70, Orange Coast Coll., Costa Mesa, Calif., 1971-72; BA in Psychology with distinction, U. Nebr., 1987, MA in Counseling Psychology, 1989. Vol. coord., client adv. Rape/Spouse Abuse Crisis Ctr., Lincoln, 1989-90; mental health therapist Health Am., HMO, Lincoln, 1991-94; pvt. practice, Lincoln, 1994—; adj. faculty S.E. Cmty. Coll; contract therapist Lincoln Pediatric Group, 1990-91, Family Svc. Assn., Lincoln, 1990-91, Cmty. Preservation Assocs., Lincoln, 1991-94. Mem. Nebr. Domestic Violence Sexual Assault Coalition; vol. ARC Disaster Mental Health Svcs.; mem., vol. Nebr. Critical Incident Stress Debriefing team. Portenier scholar U. Nebr., 1986-87. Mem. APA (assoc., divsn. 50 addictions), Am. Assn. Sex Educators, Counselors and Therapists, Assn. Pvt. Practice Therapists, Nebr. Assn. for Counseling and Devel., Sex Info. and Edn. Coun. of the U.S., Am. Mental Health Counselors Assn. (clin.), Golden Key, Psi Chi.

RAMSEY, THEODORE F., physician assistant; b. Detroit, May 7, 1940; s. Woodward H. and Gertrude F. (Madajewski) R.; m. Gladys Aviles, Nov. 6, 1971; children: Michael, Sandra, Douglas. AA, Coll. of the Redwoods, Eureka, Calif., 1970; BS, Alderson-Broaddus Coll., 1973. Physician asst. U.S. Coast Guard, various locations, 1973-90, Dept. VA, Mobile, Ala., 1990—. Mem. Am. Acad. Physician Assts. Republican. Baptist. Home: 7461 Creekwood Dr Mobile AL 36695-4059 Office: VA Outpatient Clinic 2359 Springhill Ave Mobile AL 36604

RAMSEY-GOLDMAN, ROSALIND, physician; b. N.Y.C., Mar. 22, 1954; d. Abraham L. and Miriam (Colen) Goldman; m. Glenn Ramsey, June 29,1 975; children: Ethan Ramsey, Caitlin Ramsey. BA, Case Western Res. U., 1975, MD, 1978; MPH, U. Pitts., 1988, DPH, 1992. Med. resident U. Rochester (N.Y.), 1978-81; chief resident Rochester Gen. Hosp., 1981-82; staff physician Univ. Health Svc., Rochester, 1982-83; rheumatology fellow U. Pitts., 1983-86, instr. medicine, 1986-87, asst. prof., 1987-91, co-dir. Lupus Treatment and Diagnostic Ctr., 1987-91; asst. prof. medicine Northwestern U., Chgo., 1991-96; assoc. prof. medicine Northwestern U., 1996—; dir. Chgo. Lupus Registry, Northwestern U., Chgo., 1991—. Contbr. rsch. articles to profl. jours. Recipient Finkelstein award Hershey (Pa.) Med. Ctr., 1986. Fellow Am. Coll. Rheumatology; mem. Am. Coll. Physicians, Soc. for Epidemiologic Rsch., Ctrl. Soc. Clin. Rsch. Office: Northwestern U Ward 3-315 303 E Chicago Ave Chicago IL 60611-3008

RANCK, SANDRA ANN, nurse; b. Ashtabula, Ohio, Apr. 16, 1962; d. Robert Jay Sr. and Sarah Alice (Hakala) Halman; m. Charles Thomas Ranck II, Sept. 26, 1987. BSN, Kent State U., 1985; postgrad., Gannon U., 1993—. RN, Ohio; cert. EMT. Nurse Huron Rd. Hosp., East Cleveland, Ohio, 1985-87, St. Joseph Riverside Hosp., Warren, Ohio, 1987-88; head nurse emergency svcs. Ashtabula (Ohio) County Med. Ctr., 1988—; co-chair critical incident stress mgmt. steering com. Ashtabula County, 1994-95. Mem. Local Emergency Planning Com., Ashtabula County, 1990—, Sexual Assault Team Ashtabula County, 1990—, chairperson, 1992-95. Recipient AMA award Explorers/Boy Scouts Am., Cleve., 1980. Mem. AAUW (sec. 1990-92), Emergency Nurses Assn. (pres. North Coast chpt. 1990-91, 92-93, 96—, legis. chair 1988—, treas. 1994-95), Women's Evening Fellowship (chmn. core com. 1989-91), Order Ea. Star, Ali Baba Caldron, Sigma Theta Tau (Eta Xi chpt. scholar 1995). Mem. United Church of Christ. Home: 4207 Lake Rd W Ashtabula OH 44004-2105 Office: Ashtabula County Med Ctr 2420 Lake Ave Ashtabula OH 44004-4954

RANCOURT, JOHN HERBERT, pharmaceutical company executive; b. Troy, N.Y., Aug. 10, 1946; s. Charles Dennis and Helen Mary (Keadin) R.; BS in Mgmt., Rensselaer Poly. Inst., 1968, MS in Mgmt., 1972, MBA, 1981. CPA, Ill.; cert. mgmt. acct.; m. Susan Jane Koneski, Feb. 14, 1970; children: Karen Mary, John Herbert, Alison Jane, Elizabeth Anne, Maureen Ellen. Asst. to dir. rsch. Rensselaer Poly. Inst., 1968-69; mgmt. trainee, buyer/purchasing agt., contr. rsch. div. Huyck Corp., Rensselaer, N.Y., 1969-74, corp. internat. project mgr., Wake Forest, N.C., 1974-76, adminstrv. svc. mgr. Formex div., 1976-77; sr. fin. analyst Abbott Labs., North Chicago, Ill., 1977-79, sect. mgr. sales acctg., 1979-80, mgr. fin. analysis, materials mgmt. div., 1980-82, mgr. fin. planning and analysis, pharm. products div., 1982-84; contr. TAP Pharms subs. Abbott Labs., North Chicago, Ill., 1984—; instr. acctg. Coll. of Lake County, Grayslake, Ill., part-time, 1981—. Indian Guide/Princess Tribal leader YMCA, 1980—; solicitor United Way, 1981, 83, 85, 87, 88-89, 90-91, mem. allocation panel, 1990-92 Mem. Nat. Assn. Accts., Am. Acctg. Assn., Am. Inst. CPA's, Ill. CPA Soc., Fin. Execs. Inst., Liberty Road and Track Club. Roman Catholic. Home: 826 Furlong Dr Libertyville IL 60048-3721 Office: Tap Pharms 2355 Waukegan Rd Deerfield IL 60015-1586

RAND, JACOB HARRY, hematology and blood coagulation physician and researcher; b. Fürth, Fed. Republic of Germany, July 5, 1948; came to U.S., 1949; s. David and Eva (Stamler) R.; m. Margaret Moss; children: Freya, Gabriel, Ethan, Nathaniel. BA, Yeshiva U., 1970; MD, Albert Einstein Coll. Medicine, 1973. Diplomate Am. Bd. Internal Medicine, Am. Bd. Hematology. Resident in pathology Montefiore Hosp., Bronx, N.Y., 1973-74, hematology fellow, 1976-78, vis. scientist, 1980-82; med. resident Mount Sinai Med. Ctr., N.Y.C., 1974-76; faculty, prof. medicine Mount Sinai Sch. Medicine, N.Y.C., 1978-80, 82—; dir. Mount Sinai Blood Coagulation Lab. Author: (book chpt.) Hemorrhagic Disorders in Pregnancy, 1985, 91, Disseminated Intravascular Coagulation, 1991; contbr. articles to medical and profl. jours. Recipient Clinician Scientist award Am. Heart Assn., 1980; NIH traineeship, 1977, prin. investigator, 1983-93. Mem. Am. Soc. Hematology, Internat. Soc. Thrombosis and Hemostasis, Soc. for the Study of Blood. Office: Mt Sinai Med Ctr 5 East 98th St Box 1079 New York NY 10029

RAND, MARTHA ELIZABETH, clinical social worker, consultant; b. N.Y.C., Nov. 30, 1950; d. Arthur and Jean (MacNeish) R.; m. David Louis Ryzman, Apr. 20, 1986. BA, CUNY, 1972; cert. in dance and movement therapy, Inst. of Sociotherapy, N.Y.C., 1978; MA, New Sch. for Social Rsch., N.Y.C., 1982; diploma, Swedish Inst., 1985; MSW, Fordham U., 1990. Lic. social worker. Adj. prof. yoga and dance Queensborough Community Coll., Queens, N.Y., 1978, 80; dep. dir. communications and spl. projects N.Y. State Spl. Prosecutor for Health, Social Svc. and Welfare, N.Y.C., 1978-79; instr. phys. edn. YWCA., N.Y.C., 1981-82, Human Rels. Ctr. New Sch. for Social Rsch., 1980-82; ptnr. Help Yourself Assocs., N.Y.C. and Montclair, N.J., 1981—; recreation dir. Coler Hosp., N.Y.C., 1985-86; ptnr. Lively Earth Yoga Studio, N.Y.C., 1984-85; staff clinician inpatient and intermediate care program eating disorders unit St. Clare's Hosp., Boonton, N.J., 1986-90; adult and family svcs. St. Clare's Hosp., Boonton, 1990—; cons. Inst. Complementary Medicine, Northwest Covenant Care Med. Ctr., 1995—; cons. behavioral medicine-infertility program Mind/Body Inst. Morristown Meml. Hosp., 1995—; ptnr. Lively Earth Yoga Studio, N.Y.C., 1984-85; dance therapist Very Spl. Arts N.J., 1989; cons. Inst. Complementary Medicine Northwest Care Med. Ctr., 1995—, Mind-Body Inst. Morristown Meml. Hosp., 1996, Behavioral Medicine Program for Infertility. Mem. Am. Massage Therapy Assn., Internat. Assn. Eating Disorder Profls. (cert. eating disorder therapist), Am. Group Psychotherapy Assn., Nat. Assn. Social Workers, Am. Anorexia/Bulimia Assn. (bd. dirs. N.J. chpt.).

RAND, WILLIAM MEDDEN, biostatistics educator; b. Seneca Falls, N.Y., June 26, 1938; s. Austin Loomer and Rheua Vaughn (Medden) R.; m. Patricia Ann Gooding, Oct. 7, 1967; 1 child, Toby Stewart. BA, Ind. U., 1959; MA, Brandeis U., 1961; PhD, UCLA, 1969. Rsch. engr. Jet Propulsion Lab., Pasadena, Calif., 1962-65; rsch. assoc. U. So. Calif., L.A., 1965-67; asst. prof. MIT, Cambridge, 1969-74, assoc. prof., 1974-76, lectr., 1976-88; prof. biostats. Tufts U. Sch. Medicine, Boston, 1988—, dir. biometry div., 1988—; rsch. coord. world hunger program UN U., Tokyo, 1979-82. Editor: Protein-Energy Requirement Studies in Developing Countries, 1984, Food Composition Data, 1987. Mem. Am. Statis. Assn., Biometric Soc., Am. Inst. Nutrition, Am. Soc. for Clin. Nutrition. Home: 17 Belmont St Newton MA 02158 Office: Tufts U Sch Medicine 136 Harrison Ave Boston MA 02111-1800

RANDALL, HENRY BERNARD, physician and surgeon; b. Gordonsville, Ala., July 29, 1960; s. Robert Lee and Fannie R.; m. Mechelle Auguste, July 3, 1993. BS, Mich. State U., 1983; postgrad., Wayne State U., 1983-86, MD, 1990. Resident in surgery U. Calif. Davis-East Bay, Oakland, 1990—; rsch. fellow in liver transplant U. Calif., San Francisco, 1993—. Med. dir. Cmty. Care Svcs., Oakland, 1994—; active Big Bros./Big Sisters Program, Oakland, 1995—. NIH fellow 1993—, Henry Halliday fellow, 1986-87, Henry Ford Hosp. rsch. fellow, 1987-90. Mem. ACS, AMA, AAAS, Black Med. Assn. (pres. 1987-88), Internat. Liver Transplant Soc., Soc. Black Acad. Surgeons, Nat. Med. Assn. Office: U Calif San Francisco M-896 Box 0780 505 Parnassus Ave San Francisco CA 94143

RANDALL, JEFFREY WORTH, medical records adminstrator; b. Kalamazoo, Mich.. BS in Med. Records, Ill. State U., 1986. Cert. profl. in healthcare quality; registered record adminstr. Dir. med. records Otis Bowen Ctr., Warsaw, Ind., 1986; supr. med. records Mercy Hosp., Des Moines, 1987, Mid-Mo. Mental Health, Columbia, Mo., 1988; med. record adminstr. N.E. Guidance Ctr., Detroit, 1989-91; field mgmt. rep. Smart Corp., Florissant, Mo., 1992; dir. med. records Sikeston (Mo.) Regional Ctr., 1993-94; med. record coord. Barnes Extended Care, St. Louis, 1994—; med. record cons. Jersey Cmty. Hosp., Jerseyville, Ill., 1992—, Greenwood Manor, Jerseyville, 1992—, St. Louis Dialysis Ctr., Bridgeton, Mo., 1993—, Bio-Med. Application, St. Louis, 1993—. Home: Apt A 8143 Grant Colonial Dr Saint Louis MO 63123 Office: Barnes Extended Care 401 Corporate Park Dr Clayton MD 63105

RANDALL, NEIL WARREN, gastroenterologist; b. White Plains, N.Y., Mar. 24, 1957; s. Leroy Bruce and Libby Cynthia (Brandt) R.; m. Linda Ilene Zell, Oct. 31, 1992. BA, U. Va., 1978; MD, U. Md., 1983. Diplomate Am. Bd. Internal Medicine with subspecialty in gastroenterology, geriatrics. Resident in internal medicine Ochsner Clinic, New Orleans, 1983-86; fellow in gastroenterology Tufts U., Boston, 1986-88; staff gastroenterologist Cleve. Clinic Fla., Fort Lauderdale, 1988-92, Geisinger Clinic, Danville, Pa., 1992—; Fellow ACP, Am. Coll. Gastroenterology; mem. Am. Gastroent. Assn., Am. Soc for Gastroent. Endoscopy. Office: Geisinger Med Ctr Dept Gastroenterology Danville PA 17822

RANDALL, PETER, plastic surgeon; b. Phila., Mar. 29, 1923; s. Alexander and Edith Tilghman (Kneedler) R.; m. Rose Gordon Johnson, May 1, 1949; children: Deborah K., Peter G., Julia B., Susanna T. BA, Princeton U., 1944; MD, Johns Hopkins U., 1946; MS (hon.), U. Pa., 1969. Diplomate Am. Bd. Plastic Surgery. Intern Union Meml. Hosp., Balt., 1946-47; asst. resident in surgery Hosp. of U. of Pa., Phila., 1949-50; fellow in plastic surgery Barnes Hosp.-St. Louis Childrens Hosp., 1950-52, resident in plastic surgery, 1952-53; asst. instr. plastic surgery Washington U., St. Louis, 1950-53; from asst. prof. to assoc. prof. plastic surgery U. Pa. Hosp., Phila., 1953-69, prof. plastic surgery, 1969-92; emeritus prof. plastic surgery, 1992—; chief div. plastic surgery sch. medicine U. Pa., Phila., 1979-87; sr. surgeon Children's Hosp. Phila., 1965—. Contbr. articles to profl. jours. Lt. (j.g.) USNR, 1947-48. Fellow ACS (bd. govs., chmn. 1982-84, 1st v.p. 1985-86), Am. Assn. Plastic Surgeons (hon., clinician of yr. award 1987); mem. AMA, Am. Cleft Palate Assn. (pres. 1965-66, Honors award 1986), Am. Cleft Palate Ednl. Found. (founder, pres. 1972-73), Am. Bd. Plastic Surgery (vice-chmn. 1976-77), Am. Soc. Plastic and Reconstructive Surgery (pres. 1978-79, Spl. Achievement award 1987), Am. Coll. Physicians of Phila., Am. Surg. Assn., Northeastern Soc. Plastic Surgery (founder), Phila. County Med. Soc., Phila. Acad. Surgery, Plastic Surgery Rsch. Coun. (founder, chmn. 1964-65), Halsted Soc., Sigma Xi, others. Office: U Pa Hosp 3400 Spruce St Philadelphia PA 19104

RANDALL, RICHARD WILLIAM, optometrist; b. Jamestown, N.Y., Nov. 29, 1931; s. Harry William and Claudia (Thompson) R.; m. Diane Nowak; children: David, Deborah, Douglas, Dawne, Allan, Kimberly. OD, Ill. Coll. Optometry, 1963. Optician House of Vision Inc., Chgo., 1960-63; pvt. practice optometry Geneseo, N.Y., 1963—; chief optometry sect. No. Livingston Health Ctr., Geneseo, 1974-77, Red Jacket Med. Ctr., Dansville, N.Y., 1975-77; pres. Lad-Nar Realty, Inc.; pres., gen. mgr. Ladco Internat.; exec. dir. Ladco Rental Property, Geneseo Profl. Bldg. (all Geneseo); CEO, pub. Sr. Press, Fla., 1995—; pres. TRACS, Fla., 1996—; clin. investigator Bausch & Lomb; lectr. OptiFair East, N.Y.C., 1982, 86, OptiFair West, Calif., 1985; cons. in field. Contbr. articles to profl. jours. Exec. dir. Livingston County (N.Y.) Traffic Safety Bd., 1976-82; bd. dirs. Rochester (N.Y.) Safety Coun., 1982-94; mem. Geneseo Ambulance Squad, N.Y. State Emergency Med. Technicians, 1981-88; bd. dirs. Geneseo Fire Dept., 1982-84; dep. coord. STOP-DWI Adv. Com., Livingston County, 1982; dep. sheriff County of Livingston, 1966-95, County of Hillsborough, Fla., 1995—. With USAF, 1951-53, Korea. Recipient scholarship award Am. Bd. Opticianry, 1960, Clin. Optometry award Ill. Coll. Optometry, 1963. Fellow Am. Acad. Optometry; mem. APHA, Am. Optometric Assn. (practice enhancement adv. task force 1982-83), N.Y. State Optometric Assn. (chmn. master plan com. 1976-78), Optometric Ctr. N.Y., Better Vision Inst., Coun. Sports Vision. Methodist. Office: 1727 Flamingo Ln Sun City Center FL 33573-5705

RANDEL, RONALD DEAN, physiologist, educator; b. Lewis, Kan., May 22, 1938; s. Emery Howard and Pauline (Mahan) R.; m. Colleen Kay O'Brien, Sept. 4, 1966; 1 child, Lowell Warren. BS in Animal Sci., Washington State U., 1965; PhD in Animal Physiology, Purdue U., 1971. Research fellow Purdue U., West Lafayette, Ind., 1965-71; visiting scientist U.S. Range Livestock Experiment Station, Miles City, Mont., 1971-72; research physiologist USDA, Agrl. Rsch. Svc., Miles City, 1972-74; assoc. prof. Texas A & M U., Overton, Tex., 1974-78, prof., 1978—; cooperating scientist USDA-Office Internat. Coop. and Devel./Taiwan Livestock Rsch. Inst., Ping Tung, 1987—; presenter in field. Mem. editl. bd. Jour. Animal Sci., 1990-93, 95—, Theriogeneology, 1994—; contbr. numerous papers to profl. jours., 2 chpts. to books, also numerous paper presentations, misc. papers, and symposia. Adult leader 4-H, Rusk County Riding Club Overton, 1981-90. With USN, 1958-62. Named Alpha Zeta agrl. hon. Wash. State U., 1964, Phi Kappa Phi scholastic hon. Wash. State U., 1964, Sigma Xi rsch. hon. Purdue U., 1970, Award in Excellence for Rsch. Tex. A&M U., 1987, 90, Svc. award Dept. Animal Sci., 1994; sr. Fulbright rsch. fellow James Cook U. of N. Queensland, Townsville, Australia, 1984; Donald Henry Barron lectr., 1995. Mem. Am. Soc. of Animal Sci. (Physiology and Endocrinology award 1996), Soc. for the Study of Reproduction, Assn. Latino Americana de Prodn. Animal, Reproductive Performance of Domestic Ruminants (W-112Reg. Proj. Com.; pres. 1986). Protestant. Home: 604 W Patricia Dr Overton TX 75684-1526 Office: Tex A&M U Agrl Rsch & Extension Drawer E Overton TX 75684

RANDINITIS, EDWARD JOHN, pharmacokineticist; b. Scranton, Pa., Apr. 7, 1940; s. Frank and Adella (Verbus) S.; m. Georgia Marie Wasilewski, Sept. 30, 1972; children: Karen, Joanne. BS in Pharmacy, Wayne State U., 1962, MS in Pharm., 1964, PhD, 1969. Registered pharmacist, Mich. Pharmacist Harper Hosp., Detroit, 1962-64; rsch. pharmacist Parke-Davis, Detroit, 1969-72; rsch. assoc. Parke-Davis, Detroit and Ann Arbor, Mich., 1972-90; sr. rsch. assoc. Parke-Davis, Ann Arbor, 1991—. Mem. Am. Assn. Pharm. Scientists, Am. Pharm. Assn., Sigma Xi. Office: Parke-Davis 2800 Plymouth Rd Ann Arbor MI 48105-2430

RANDISH, JOAN MARIE, dentist; b. Seattle, Oct. 2, 1954; d. Matthew John and Margaret Cecelia (Waham) R. DDS, U. Wash., 1981. Dentist S.E. Dental Clinic, Seattle, 1981-82, Indian Health Bd., Seattle, 1982-84, Joe Whiting Dental Clinic, Seattle, 1984-85, Georgetown Dental Clinic, Seattle, 1981-88, King County Pub. Health, Seattle, 1987—; pvt. practice dentist Bellevue, Wash., 1981—. Recipient Women of Yr. award Bellevue Bus. and Profl. Women, Seattle, 1987. Mem. ADA, Seattle King County Dental Soc., Soroptimist Club of Bellevue (del. 1983-91). Office: 25 102nd Ave NE Bellevue WA 98004-5622

RANDOLPH, HARRY FRANKLIN, III, health facility administrator; b. Vallejo, Calif., Nov. 5, 1946; s. Harry Franklin Jr. and Viola Vinnie (Snyder) R.; m. Candice Patricia Garrison, Dec. 30, 1970; 1 child, Brandon Todd. BS in Zoology, San Diego State U., 1969; BS, Baylor Coll. Med., 1977. Cert. physician asst., Nat. Commn. Cert. Physician Assts. Staff rsch. assoc. U. Calif. San Diego, La Jolla, 1969-72; med. mach. Technitian VA Hosp., San Diego, 1972-75; physician asst. So. Calif. Permenente Med. Group, San Diego, 1977-79, Mt. Health Ctr., Boulevard, Calif., 1979-81, So. Calif. HMO, San Diego, 1981-82, Scripps Clin. Med. Group, La Jolla, 1982—; chief physician extender sect. Scripps Clin. Med. Group, La Jolla, 1991—, expert witness/pysician asst. practice, 1992—, chief physician assts. Green Hosp., 1994—; med. legal cons. Contbr. articles to profl. jours. editor Surg. Physician Asst., 1994-96. Mem. Health Sys. Agency Sub-area Coun. VI, El Cajon, Calif., 1980-81, San Diego Zool. Soc., 1985—. Fellow Am. Acad Physician Assts., Am. Assn. Surgeon Assts. (treas. 1994-96), Calif. Acad. Physician Assts. (dir. at large 1984, chmn. continuing med. edn. com. 1984-86, v.p. 1985, chmn. prof. practice com. 1996, Outstanding Achievement award 1985, Outstanding Svc. award, 1994). Democrat. Office: Scripps Clin Med Group Mail Drop MS 213 10666N Torrey Pines Rd La Jolla CA 92037

RANDOLPH, JUDSON GRAVES, pediatric surgeon; b. Macon, Ga., July 19, 1927; s. Milton Fitz and Abigail Theresa (Graves) R.; m. Susan Comfort Adams, June 14, 1952; children: Somers, Garrett, Judson, Adam, Comfort. BA, Vanderbilt U., 1950, MD, 1953. Intern in surgery U. Rochester, N.Y., 1953-54; asst. resident in pathology Vanderbilt U., 1954-55; asst. resident, then sr. resident in surgery Mass. Gen. Hosp., Boston, 1956-58; asst. resident in surgery Children's Hosp., Boston, 1955-56, sr. resident, then chief resident, 1958-61, asst. surgeon, 1961-63; teaching fellow to instr. surgery Med. Sch. Harvard U., 1960-63; jr. assoc. in surgery Peter Bent Brigham Hosp., Boston, 1961-63; surgeon-in-chief Children's Hosp., Washington, 1964-91; mem. faculty Med. Sch. George Washington U., 1964-91, prof. surgery and child health, 1968-91; prof. surgery Meharry Med. Coll., 1992—; cons. Nat. Naval Med. Ctr., NIH, Walter Reed Army Med. Ctr.; trustee Children's Hosp. Nat. Med. Ctr., 1972-84, Vanderbilt U., 1980—. Editor: Pediatric Surgery, 3d edit., 2 vols., 1979, 4th edit., 2 vols., 1985, The Injured Child, 1980; mem. editl. bd. Surgery, 1978-92; contbr. numerous articles to med. jours. With USNR, 1945-46, PTO. Mem. ACS (gov. 1969-75), AMA, Am. Acad. Pediats. (chmn. exec. com. surg. sect. 1974-75), Am. Assn. Thoracic Surgery, Am. Pediat. Surg. Assn. (gov. 1980—, pres. 1984), Washington Acad. Surgery (pres. 1989), Soc. U. Surgeons, Am. Surg. Assn., So. Surg. Assn., Am. Bd. Surgery (bd. dirs. 1973-79, diplomate), Alpha Omega Alpha (faculty), Cosmos Club (Washington). Methodist.

RANDOLPH, LILLIAN LARSON, medical association executive; b. Spokane, Wash., May 3, 1932; d. Charles P. and Juanita S (Parrish) Larson; m. Philip L. Randolph, Nov. 12, 1952; children: Marcus, Andrew. BA, U. Wash., 1954, MA, 1956; PhD, U. Calif., Berkeley, 1966; EdD, N.Mex. State U., 1979. Researcher U. Wash., Seattle, 1954-59; asst. prof. Calif. State U., Hayward, 1964-68, U. Tex., El Paso, 1972-74; dir. S.W. Conservatory of Music, El Paso, 1972-74; adj. prof. Loyola U. and DePaul U., Chgo., 1974-78; asst. prof. DeVry Inst. Tech., Lombard, Ill., 1982-84; mgr. AMA, Chgo., 1985—; cons. Weber Co., Chgo., 1979-85. Author: Fundamentals of Government Organizations, 1971, Third Party Settlement of Disputes, 1973. Mem. AAUP, Phi Beta Kappa. Home: 408 W Wilshire Dr Wilmette IL 60091-3154

RANGEL-GUERRA, RICARDO ALBERTO, neurologist; b. Monterrey, Nuevo Leon, Mexico, Mar. 3, 1934; s. Enrique Rangel-Estrella and Dolores Guerra de Rangel; m. Minerva Carolina Flores, Sept. 26, 1958; children: Carolina, Ricardo, Roberto, Rodrigo. MD, Universidad de Nuevo Leon, Monterrey, 1958. Resident in internal medicine Hosp. Enf de la Nutricion, Mexico, 1958-60; resident in neurology U. Fla., Gainesville, 1961-64; fellow in internal medicine 2d Cornell Med. Div. Bellevue Hosp., N.Y.C., 1960. Contbr. over 200 articles to profl. jours. Internal Medicine fellow Bellevue Hosp., N.Y.C., 1960. Fellow ACP, Am. Heart Assn. (stroke coun.), Am. Acad. Neurology, Am. Neurol. Assn. (corr. fellow); mem. So. Clin. Neurol. Soc. (pres. 1992-94), Academia Nac de Medicina Academia Mexicana de Cirugia. Roman Catholic. Home: Col Miravalle, Rio San Juan # 221, 64660 Monterrey Nuevo Leon, Mexico Office: Centro de Esp Medicas U Monterrey Hosp, Jose Benitez 2704, 64460 Monterrey Mexico

RANGNEKAR, VIVEK MANGESH, molecular biologist, researcher; b. Bombay, Dec. 17, 1955; s. Mangesh Vithal and Sanjivani (Dewoolkar) R.; m. Vidya Vivek Varsha Kulkarni, May 15, 1981; children: Vidyuta, Viraj. MSc, U. Bombay, 1979, PhD, 1983. Postdoctoral fellow U. Chgo., 1983-86; rsch. assoc. Rush Med. Ctr., Chgo., 1986-87; asst. prof. U. Chgo., 1988-91; asst. prof. U. Ky., Lexington, 1992-96, assoc. prof., 1996—. Contbr. articles to profl. jours. including Jour. Biol. Chemistry, Nucleic Acids Rsch., Molecular Cell Biology. Mem. AAAS, Am. Soc. Microbiology. Office: U Ky 800 Rose St Lexington KY 40536-0001

RANKIN, DAVID K., physician; b. East Liverpool, Ohio, Mar. 16, 1959; s. Earl and Louise (Graham) R. BS in Biology, U. Tex., 1986; DO, U. North Tex. Coll. Osteo., Medicine, 1990. Diplomate Am. Bd. Family Practice. Resident East Tenn. State U. - Kingsport Family Practice, 1990-93; physician Tri-City Med. Plaza, South Pittsburg, Tenn., 1993-95, Mid. Ga. Family Health, North, Macon, Ga., 1995—. Mem. Am. Acad. Family Practitioners, Tenn. Osteo. Med. Assn., Ga. Osteo. Med. Assn., Tenn. Med. Assn., Bibb County Med. Assn., AMA, Am. Osteo. Assn. Office: Mid Ga Family Health North 2614 Riverside Dr Macon GA 31204

RANKIN, ELIZABETH ANNE DESALVO, nurse, psychotherapist, educator, consultant; b. Wurtzburg, Germany, Sept. 30, 1948; d. William Joseph and Elizabeth Agnes (Faraci) DeSalvo; m. Richard Forrest Rankin, June 5, 1971; children: William Alvin, David Michael. BSN, U. Md., Balt., 1970, MS, 1972; PhD., U. Md., College Park, 1979. Cert. health edn. specialist, specialist stress mgmt. edn., master hypnotherapist, master practitioner neurolinguistic programmer, nonquatic exercise instrn.; cert. Nat. Bd. Cert. Clin. Hypnotherapists. Prof. U. Md.; mem. dept. psychiat. mental health/ community health nursing U. Md. at Balt. Sch. Nursing, dir. div. bus. and industry; prof. U. Md.; cns. Ctr. for Alternative Medicine, Pain Rsch. and Evaluation; cons. various pubs. Co-author of books; contbr. chpts. to books, articles to profl. jours.; editor: Network Independent Study; mem. editl. bd. Md. Nurse, Delmarva Found. Newsletter. Advisor U. Md. chpt. Nat. Student Nurses Assn. Recipient Twila Stinecker Leadership award, 1987, Leadership Excellence award Md. Assn. Nursing Students, 1990-92. Mem. ANA, Md. Nursing Assn. (bd. dirs., exec. com., 2d v.p., appointments mgr.), U. Md. Assn. Nursing Students (chpt. Nat. Student Nurses Assn. advisor), Nat. Coun. Family Rels., Coun. Nurse Rschrs., Nat. Assn. Cert. Health Educators (charter), Am. Assn. Profl. Hypnotherapists, Milton H. Erickson Found., Washington Soc. Clin. Hypnosis, Aquatic Exercise Assn., Capital Area Roundtable on Informatics in Nursing, Sigma Theta Tau, Phi Epsilon Alpha, Phi Kappa Phi, Alpha Xi Delta.

RANKIN, GARY O'NEAL, pharmacology educator; b. Little Rock, Oct. 6, 1949; s. Leroy Emmett and Robbie Jean (Loyd) R. BS in Chemistry, U. Ark., 1972; PhD in Medicinal Chemistry, U. Miss., 1976. Teaching assoc. Med. Coll. Ohio, Toledo, 1976-78; asst. prof. dept. pharmacology Marshall U. Sch. Medicine, Huntington, W.Va., 1978-82, assoc. prof., 1982-86, prof., chmn. dept. pharmacology, 1986—; assoc. dean rsch. devel. and grad. edn., 1989-92; mem. rsch. com. VA Hosp., 1981-35, mem. animals and equipment subcoms., 1981-85, dean's com., 1984—; mem. pharmacy and therapeutics com. Family Care Outpatient Clinic Inc., 1978-79; ad hoc reviewer toxicology study sect. NIH, 1987, mem. toxicology study sect., 1994—. Assoc. editor Toxicology and Applied Pharmacology, 1995—; mem. editorial bd. Toxicology, 1994—; contbr. articles to profl. jours. Mem. research com. W.Va. affiliate Am. Heart Assn., 1979-82, vice chmn. research com., 1981-82, chmn. research pub. info., 1980-81, mem., 1982-88, mem. research grant peer rev. com., 1980-84, bd. dirs., 1981—; mem. nature and sci. com. Huntington Mus. Art, 1984-86, mem. NSF grant subcom., 1984-87, mem. archeol. subcom., 1984-85, mem. sci. adv. subcom., 1985-86, mem. edn. com., 1987-94. NDEA fellow U. Miss., 1973-74; grantee W.Va. affiliate Am. Heart Assn., 1981-82, 84-85, 86-87, NIH, 1983—. Mem. Am. Soc. for Pharmacology and Exptl. Therapeutics (profl. utilization and tng. subcom. 1986-93, chair com. profl. affairs 1993—), AAAS, Internat. Soc. for Study Xenobiotics, Soc. for Exptl. Biology and Medicine, Soc. Toxicology, Am. Soc. for Pharmacology and Exptl. Therapeutics (div. drug metabolism 1985—, divsn. toxicology 1992—), W.Va. Acad. Sci., Assn. for Med. Sch. Pharmacology, Genetic Toxicology Assn., Sigma Xi (program com. 1982-85, chmn. program com. 1984-85, outstanding researcher com. 1986, pres. elect 1986-87, pres. 1987-88, admissions com. 1987-88), Alpha Omega Alpha, Rho Chi, Phi Kappa Phi. Baptist. Office: Marshall U Dept Pharmacology 1542 Spring Valley Dr Huntington WV 25704-9388

RANKIN, JAMES SCOTT, cardiothoracic surgeon; b. San Francisco, June 9, 1947; s. James J. and Bonevie E. R.; m. Sue Dean Batson; children: James Scott, Jr., John Todd, Alan, Susan, Anne, Robert, Helen. BS, Midd. Tenn. State U., 1966; MD, U. Tenn., Memphis, 1969. Diplomate Am. Bd. Surgery, Am. Bd. Thoracic Surgery. Gen. surgeon USAF, Wurtsmith, Mich., 1972-74; rsch., resident dept. surgery Duke U., Durham, N.C., 1974-80, tchg. scholar, 1980-81, asst. prof. surgery, 1981-86, asst. prof. physiology, 1981-90, assoc. prof. surgery, 1986-90; chief, prof. surgery U. Calif., San Francisco, 1990-93; assoc. clin. prof. Vanderbilt U., Nashville, 1993—; attending surgeon St. Thomas & Centennial Hosp., Nashville, 1993—. Contbr. articles to profl. jours. and chpts. to books. Maj. USAF, 1972-74. Recipient fellowship Whitaker Found., 1980-83, fellowship John A. Hartford Found., 1981-84; NIH Rsch. grantee, 1982—. Republican. Office: Cardiothoracic Surgery Assoc 4230 Harding Rd Nashville TN 37205

RANNEY, HELEN MARGARET, physician, educator; b. Summer Hill, N.Y., Apr. 12, 1920; d. Arthur C. and Alesia (Toolan) R. AB, Barnard Coll., 1941; MD, Columbia U., 1947; ScD, U. S.C., 1979. Diplomate: Am. Bd. Internal Medicine. Intern Presbyn. Hosp., N.Y.C., 1947-48, resident, 1948-50, asst. physician, 1954-60; practice medicine specializing in internal medicine, hematology N.Y.C., 1954-70; instr. Coll. Phys. and Surg. Columbia, N.Y.C., 1954-60; assoc. prof. medicine Albert Einstein Coll. Medicine, N.Y.C., 1960-64, prof. medicine, 1965-70; prof. medicine SUNY, Buffalo, 1970-73; prof. medicine U. Calif., San Diego, 1973-90, chmn. dept. medicine, 1973-86, Disting. physician vet. adminstr., 1986-91; mem. staff Alliance Pharm. Corp., San Diego, 1991—. Master ACP; fellow AAAS; mem. NAS, Inst. Medicine, Am. Soc. for Clin. Investigation, Am. Soc. Hematology, Harvey Soc., Am. Assn. Physicians, Am. Acad. Arts and Scis., Phi Beta Kappa, Sigma Xi, Alpha Omega Alpha. Office: Alliance Pharm Corp 3040 Science Park Rd San Diego CA 92121-1102

RANNEY, RICHARD RAYMOND, dental educator, researcher; b. Atlanta, July 11, 1939; s. Russell Ballou and Maureen Joan (Bannon) R.; m. Beverly Anne Toton, June 10, 1961 (div.); children—Christine Marie, Kathleen Anne; m. 2d, Patricia Marie DeNoto, Feb. 22, 1969; children—Maureen Frances, Russell Christopher. D.D.S., U. Iowa, 1963; M.S., U. Rochester, 1969. Asst. prof. periodontology U. Oreg., 1969-72; assoc. prof. periodontics Va. Commonwealth U., Richmond, 1972-78, prof., 1978-86, dir. grad. periodontics, 1972-76, chmn. dept. periodontics, 1974-77, asst. dean research and grad. affairs, 1977-84, asst. dean research, 1984-86; dir. Clin. Research Ctr. for Periodontal Diseases, 1978-86. Served with USPHS, 1963-66. Nat. Inst. Dental Research grantee, 1970-86; prof. Sch. of Dentistry, U. Ala., Birmingham, 1986-91, dean, 1986-89; prof., dean U. Md., Balt., 1991—. Fellow AAAS, Internat. Coll. Dentists, Am. Coll. Dentists; mem. ADA, Am. Acad. Periodontology, Internat. Assn. Dental Research (pres. 1995-96, basic research in periodontology award 1985), Am. Assn. Dental Rsch. (pres. 1990-91), Am. Assn. Dental Schs., Am. Soc. Microbiology, Sigma Xi, Omicron Kappa Upsilon. Contbr. chpts. to books, articles to profl. jours. Office: U Md 666 W Baltimore St Baltimore MD 21201

RANSIL, BERNARD J(EROME), research physician, methodologist, consultant, educator; b. Pitts., Nov. 15, 1929; s. Raymond Augustine and Louise Mary (Berhalter) R. BS, Duquesne U., 1951; PhD in Phys. Chemistry, Cath. U. Am., 1955; MD, U. Chgo., 1964. NRC-NAS postdoctoral fellow Nat. Bur. Stds., Washington, 1955-56; cons. heat div. thermodynamics sect. Nat. Bur. Standards, Washington, 1956-62; cons. NASA exobiology project, Washington, 1962-68; rsch. assoc. and dir. diatomic molecule project Lab. Molecular Structure and Spectra, physics dept. U. Chgo., 1956-63; intern Harbor Gen. Hosp., UCLA, Torrance, 1964-65, Guggenheim fellow, 1965-66; from rsch. assoc. in medicine to assoc. prof. in medicine Harvard Med. Sch., Boston, 1966—; from rsch. assoc. and clin. fellow to clin. assoc. Harvard II and IV Med. Svcs., 1966-74; core lab. scientist clin. rsch. ctr. Thorndike Meml. Lab Boston City Hosp., Boston, 1966-74; asst. physician Beth Israel Hosp., Boston, 1974-96, sr. physician, 1996—; dir. Core Lab. Clin. Rsch. Ctr., 1974-89, Data Analysis Lab., 1989-94; cons. statistical computing Boston City Hosp., Beth Israel Hosp., 1966—; cons. Prophet project NIH, Bethesda, Md., 1971-88, exec. com., 1986-91, Howard Hughes Med. Inst., Boston, 1979-80, Coop. Cataract Rsch. Group, Boston, 1981-83, Mass. Alzheimer's Disease Rsch. Ctr., Boston, 1992-94; guest lectr. Seton Hall U., 1970—; vis. scientist Rockefeller U., 1985, Scripps Rsch. Found., 1986, Calif. State U., 1986, U. Pitts. Med. Sch., 1987. Author: Abortion, 1969, Background to Abortion, 1979; editor: Life of a Scientist: Autobiography of Robert S. Mulliken, 1989 (videocassettes) Elements of Statistics and Data Analysis, 1985, diatomic molecule studies (computational chemistry), 1960-80; contbr. numerous articles and book revs. in sci. jours., non-sci. periodicals in many fields. Recipient alumni rsch. award Cath. U. Am., 1969, Duquesne U. centennial award, 1978. Mem. numerous profl. socs. Home: 226 Calumet St Boston MA 02120-3303

RANSLER, CHARLES W., urologist; b. Covington, Ky., Feb. 1, 1951; s. Charles W. and Barbara (Lutes) R.; m. Gail Della Findley, June 11, 1977; children: Charles, Findley, Abigail, Anna Catherine. BS, U. Va., 1973; MD, U. Ky., 1977. Diplomate Am. Bd. Urology. Intern, resident in surgery Parkland Meml. Hosp., Dallas, 1977-79; resident in urology U. Tex. Southwestern, Dallas, 1989-83; pvt. practice Paducah, Ky., 1983—; bd. trustees Western Bapt. Hosp., Paducah, 1991-95, chief surgery, 1987-89, chief of staff, 1992-93. Bd. dirs. Citizens Bank & Trust, Paducah, 1993—; vestryman, sr. warden Grace Episcopal Ch., Paducah, 1994—. Fellow Am. Bd. Urology; mem. AMA, Ky. Med Assn., Ky. Urol. Assn. Republican. Home: 4025 Buckner Ln Paducah KY 42001 Office: 220 Loan Oak Rd Paducah KY 42001

RANSOHOFF, JOSEPH, neurosurgeon; b. Cin., July 1, 1915; s. J. Louis and Doris (Kauffman) R.; m. Rita Mayer, June 1, 1941 (div. Apr. 1984); children: Joan, Joe; m. Lori Cohen, Apr. 7, 1984; children: Jake, Jade. BS, Harvard U., 1938; MD, U. Chgo., 1942. Diplomate Am. Bd. Neurosurgery. Neurosurgeon Columbia Presbyn. Hosp., N.Y.C., 1949-61; chmn. dept. neurosurgery NYU, N.Y.C., 1962-92; prof. neurosurgery U. South Fla., Tampa, 1992—. Contbr. articles to neurosurg. jours. Capt. U.S. Army, 1944-46, ETO. Home: 915 Woodul Circle Tampa FL 33602 Office: Tampa VA 13000 Bruce Downs Blvd Tampa FL 33612

RANSOHOFF, RICHARD MILTON, neurologist, researcher; b. Cin., Aug. 18, 1946; s. Jerry Nathan and Sue (Westheimer) R.; m. Margaret Seidler, Mar. 26, 1988; children: Amy Julia, Lena Jane. BA, Bard Coll., 1968; MD, Case Western Reserve U., 1978. Diplomate Am. Bd. Psychiatry and Neurology, Am. Bd. Internal Medicine. Resident in internal medicine Mt. Sinai Hosp., Cleve., 1978-81; resident in neurology The Cleve. Clinic Found., 1981-83, chief resident in neurology, 1983-84, mem. assoc. staff in neurology, 1984-93, mem. asst. staff in molecular biology Rsch. Inst., 1989-94, mem. staff neurology dept., 1993—, mem. assoc. staff in molecular biology Rsch. Inst., 1994—, mem. assoc. staff in neuroscis. Rsch. Inst., 1994—; postdoctoral fellow in molecular biology Case Western Reserve U., Cleve., 1984-89; mem. neurology C study sect., Washington, 1995—; adj. prof. dept. biology Cleve. State U., 1994—. Editor: Cytokines in the CNS, 1996; contbr. articles to profl. jours. Chair profl. adv. com. Nat. Multiple Sclerosis Soc., Northeast Ohio, 1985-95, trustee, 1985—, mem. med. adv. bd. Nat. Multiple Sclerosis Soc., N.Y.C. 1996—; mem. rsch. allocation com. Am. Heart Assn., Cleve., 1995—. Grantee NIH, Washington, 1988, Harry Weaver Neurosci. scholar Nat. Multiple Sclerosis Soc., N.Y.C., 1987-92; recipient Physicians Rsch. Tng. award Am. Cancer Soc., N.Y.C., 1984-86, Clin. Investigator Devel. award Nat. Inst. Neurol. and Communicative Diseases and Stroke, Washington, 1988-93. Mem. Am. Neurol. Assn., Am. Assn. Neurology. Office: Rsch Inst NC-30 Cleve Clinic Found 9500 Euclid Ave Cleveland OH 44195

RANSOM, SCOTT BRIAN, obstetrician and gynecologist; b. Orange, Calif., Sept. 6, 1962; s. John and Peggy R.; m. Elizabeth R. Ransom, Dec. 20, 1987; children: Kelly, Christopher, Sarah. BA, Pacific Luth. U., 1984; DO, U. Health Sci., Kansas City, Mo., 1988; MBA, U. Mich., 1996. Resident ob-gyn. Oakwood Hosp., Dearborn, Mich., 1988-92; ob-gyn. physician Adian Ob/Gyn., P.C., Adrian, Mich., 1992-94; assoc. med. dir. Hutzel Hosp., Detroit, 1994-95; asst. prof. Wayne State U., Detroit, 1994—; divsn. head-med. dir. Henry Ford Health System, Detroit, 1996—; chmn. ob-gyn. Henry Ford Cottage Hosp., Grosse Point, Mich., 1996—. Author: Gynecology for Primary Care Providers, 1996; contbr. numerous articles to profl. jours. Fellow ACS, Am. Coll. Ob-Gyn., Am. Coll. Physician Execs., Assn. of Profs. in Gynecology and Obstretrics, Am. Coll. Health Care Execs. (diplomate). Home: 528 Covington Bloomfield Hills MI 48301

RANU, HARCHARAN SINGH, biomedical scientist, administrator, orthopaedic biomechanics educator; b. Lyallpur, India; came to U.S., 1976; s. Jodh Singh and Harnam Kaur R. BSc, Leicester Poly., Eng., 1963; MSc, U. Surrey, Guilford, Eng., 1967, Cambridge (Eng.) U., 1972; PhD, Middlesex Hosp. Med. Sch. and Poly. of Cen. London, 1975; diploma, MIT, 1984. Chartered engr., Eng. Med. scientist Nat. Inst. Med. Rsch. of the Med. Rsch. Coun., London, 1967-70; rsch. fellow Middlesex Hosp. Med. Sch. and Poly. of Cen. London, 1971-76; rsch. scientist Plastics Rsch. Assn. of Great Britain, Shawbury, Eng., 1977; asst. prof. Wayne State U., Detroit, 1977-81; prof. biomed. engring./orthopaedic biomechanics biomaterials La. Tech. U., Ruston, 1982—; prof., chmn. dept. biomechanics N.Y. Coll. Osteo. Medicine, Old Westbury, 1989-93; prof., asst. to pres. and dir. doctoral program Life Coll., Marietta, Ga., 1993—; dir. tng. Rehab. Rsch. and Devel. Ctr., 1983-85; mem. La. Tech. U. Libr. Com., 1983-85; chmn. design competition Assn. Biomed. Engrs.; mem. steering com. So. Biomed. Engring. Confs., 1983—; chmn. tech. in health care conf. U. Cambridge, 1985; chmn. Internat. Symposium on Bioengring., Calcutta, India, 1985; dir. orthopaedic biomechanics rsch. labs., staff Nassau County Med. Ctr., Long Island, 1989—; prof., asst. to pres., dir. doctoral program Life Coll., Marietta, Ga., 1993—; mem. biomed. engring. faculty com. La. Tech. U., faculty com., rsch. awards com., grad. studies com., grad. faculty, acad. bd. dirs; vis. scientist Dryburn Hosp., Durham, Eng., 1985-87, cons., 1988—; vis. prof. U. Istanbul, 1982, Lab. de Recherch Orthopediques, Paris, 1985—, Kings Coll. Med. Sch. U. London, 1989—, Indian Inst. Tech., New Delhi, Postgrad Inst. Med. Edn. and Rsch., Chandigarh, India, 1989—, Inst. Biol. Physics USSR Acad. Sci., Moscow, 1990, Polytech. Ctrl. London, 1991—; adj. prof. Coll. Physicians and Surgeons Columbia U., N.Y.C., 1988—, Inst. Biol. Physics USSR Acad. Sci., Moscow, 1990, N.Y. Coll. Podiatric Medicine, 1991—, CUNY, 1992—; cons. Lincoln Gen. Hosp., Ruston, La., 1982-85, La. State U. Med. Ctr., Shreveport, 1982—, St. Luke's and Roosevelt Hosp. Ctr., N.Y., 1988—, Foot Clinics N.Y., 1991—, Vets. Affairs Med. Ctr., N.Y., 1992—, various biomed. rsch. & legal corps., U.S., United Kingdom; mem. media resource svc. Inst. Pub. Info., N.Y., 1989—; med. scientist, cons. NATO, 1982—; presenter, lectr., dir. organizer numerous sci. orgns. and nat. & internat. confs.; external examiner for doctoral candidates All India Inst. Med. Scis., New Delhi, Indian Inst. of Tech., New Delhi, Banaras Hindu U., Varanasi, India, 1994—. Author: Rheological Behavior of Articular Cartiliage Under Tensile Loads, 1967, Effects of Ionizing Radiation on the Mechanical Properties of Skin, 1975, Effects of Fractionated Doses of X-irradiation on the Mechanical Properties of Skin--A Long Term Study, 1980, Effects of Ionizing Radiation on the Structure & Physical Properties of the Skin, 1983, 3-D Model of Vertebra for Spinal Surgery, 1985, Application of Carbon Fibers in Orthopaedic Surgery, 1985, Relation Between Metal Corrision & Electrical Polarization, 1989, The Distribution of Stresses in the Human Lumbar Spine, 1989, Medical Devices & Orthopaedic Implants in the United States, 1989, Spinal Surgery by Modeling, 1989, Multipoint Determination of Pressure-Volume Curves in Human Intervertebral Discs, 1993, Evaluation of Volume-Pressure Relationship in Lumbar Discs Using Model and Experimental Studies, 1994, A Mechanism of Laser Nuclectomy, 1994, Microminiaturization in Laser Surgery in Vivo Intradiscal Pressure Measurements in Lumbar Intervertebral Discs, 1994, An Experimental and Mathematical Simulation of Fracture of Human Bone Due to Jumping, 1994; editor The Lower Extremity, 1993—; guest editor IEEE Engring. in Medicine & Biology, 1991; mem. editorial bd. Med. Instrumentation, 1988—, Jour. Biomed. Instrumentation & Tech., 1988—, Jour. Med. Engring. & Tech., 1989—, Joul, 1990—, Jour. Long-Term Effects Med. Implants, 1991—, Biomed. Sci. & Tech., 1991—; reviewer Jour. Biomechanics, 1981—, Clin. Biomechanics, 1984—, Jour. Biomed. Engring., 1981, Phys. Therapy, 1990—, IEEE Biomed. Transactions, 1991—, Jour. Engring. in Medicine, 1989—; contbr. articles to profl. jours. Faculty advisor India Students Assn. Wayne State U., 1980. Recipient Edwin Tate award U. Surrey, 1968, Third Internat. Olympic Com. World Congress On Sprots Sci. award, Atlanta, 1995; numerous rsch. grants. Fellow ASME (bioengring. com. 1990—, award L.I. chpt. 1991), Biol. Engring. Soc. (London) (President's prize 1984), Instn. Mech. Engrs. (chmn. revv. bd. for corp. memberships, James Clayton awards 1974-76); mem. Am. Soc. Biomechanics (edn. com. 1990—), Orthopaedic Rsch. Soc., Biomed. Engring. Soc., India Assn., India Assn. North La. Sikh. Office: Sch of Grad Studies Life Coll Marietta GA 30060

RAO, DABEERU C., epidemiologist; b. Santhabommali, India, Apr. 6, 1946; came to U.S., 1972; s. Ramarao Patnaik and Venkataratnam (Raghupatruni) R.; m. Sarada Patnaik, 1974; children: Ravi, Lakshmi. BS in Stats., Indian Statis. Inst., Calcutta, 1967, MS, 1968, PhD, 1971. Research fellow U. Sheffield, Eng., 1971-72; asst. prof., geneticist U. Hawaii, Honolulu, 1972-78, assoc. prof.-geneticist, 1978-80; assoc. prof., dir. div. biostats. Washington U. Med. Sch., St. Louis, 1980-82, prof. depts. biostats., psychiatry and genetics, 1982—, adj. prof. math., 1982—, dir. div. biostats., 1980—. Author: A Source Book for Linkage in Man, 1979, Methods in Genetic Epidemiology, 1983, Genetic Epidemiology of Coronary Heart Disease, 1984; editor-in-chief Genetic Epidemiology jour., 1984-91; contbr. articles to profl. jours. Grantee NIH, 1978—. Mem. Am. Statis. Assn., Am. Soc. Human Genetics, Internat. Genetic Epidemiology Soc. (pres. 1996), Behavior Genetics Assn., Soc. Epidemiol. Res., Biom. Soc. Office: Washington U Sch Medicine Div Biostatistics 660 S Euclid Ave Saint Louis MO 63110

RAPAPORT, FELIX THEODOSIUS, surgeon, editor, researcher, educator; b. Munich, Germany, Sept. 27, 1929; s. Max W. and Adelaide (Rathaus) R.; m. Margaret Birsner, Dec. 14, 1969; children: Max, Benjamin, Simon, Michel, Adelaide. AB, NYU, 1951, MD, 1954. Diplomate Am. Bd. Surgery. Intern Mt. Sinai Hosp., N.Y.C., 1955-56; resident, chief resident NYU Surg. Services, 1958-62, USPHS postdoctoral fellow in pathology, 1956; exec. officer Naval Med. Rsch. Unit No. 1, U. Calif., Berkeley, 1956-58; trainee in allergy and infectious diseases NYU, 1958-61; head, transplantation and immunology div. NYU Surg. Svcs., 1965-77; dir. rsch. Inst. Reconstrn. and Plastic Surgery, NYU, 1965-77; assoc. prof. surgery NYU Med. Ctr., 1965-70, prof., 1970-77; prof. surgery, prof. pathology, dir. transplantation svc. SUNY, Stony Brook, 1977-95, disting. prof., 1995—, chmn. dept. surgery, 1989-91; guest investigator Hosp. St. Louis, Paris, 1963-79; Claude Bernard vis. prof. exptl. medicine Coll. de France, Paris, 1985; sr. attendingsurgeon SUNY Hosp., 1980—, surgeon-in-chief, 1989-91; pres. bd. dirs. regional N.Y. Transplant Program, 1972-89; cons. VA Hosp., N.Y.C., 1963-77, Northport, N.Y., 1977—; adv. panel on medicine and dentistry U.S. Office of Naval Res., 1974-78; adv. com. NIAID, 1964-68; merit review bd. immunology V.A. Dept. of Medicine and Surgery, 1974-78. Editor in chief Transplantation Proc., 1968—; assoc. editor Am. Jour. Kidney Diseases, 1981-86, Am. Jour. Craniofacial Genetics and Developmental Biology, 1980-85, Cellular Immunology, 1980—; contbr. over 500 articles to profl. jours.; author, editor 20 books on transplantation. Bd. dirs. United Network for Organ Sharing, 1986-88. Served to lt. comdr. M.C. USNR, 1956-58. Decorated comdr. Order Sci. Merit, chevalier Ordre National du Merite, France, 1970, officer Legion of Honor (France), 1990; recipient Gold medal Societe d'Encouragement au Bien, 1979, Gold medal City of Paris, France, 1980, Commandeur Ordre des Palmes Academiques, France, 1981, Samuel L. Kountz award Howard U., 1989, Lester Hoenig award Nat. Kidney Found., 1990, Sol Berson award NYU, 1990, Disting. Achievement in Med. Scis. award Touro Coll. B. Levine Sch. Health Scis., 1991, USPHS Res. Career Devel. award, NIAID, 1961-62, Career Scientst award Health Rsch. Coun., 1963-72, Maimonides Physician award, new Skwere Institutions, 1995. Mem. ACS, French Acad. Scis., Soc. Univ. Surgeons, N.Y. Surg. Soc., Am. Burn Assn., Am. Surg. Assn., Am. Assn. Immunologists, Soc. Exptl. Biology and Medicine, Harvey Soc., Am. Soc. Transplant Surgeons, Am. Soc. Transplant Physicians, Soc. for Organ Sharing (hon. pres.), Am. Assn. Clin. Histocompatibility Testing, Internat. Soc. Exptl. Hematology, Transplantation Soc. (founding sec., v.p., treas., councillor, historian, pres. 1986-88), Alpha Omega Alpha. Jewish. Current Work: induction of specific tolerance to major transplantable organs in man; research concerned with effects of irradiation and bone marrow transplantation in the production of host unresponsiveness to tissue allografts. Office: SUNY Stony Brook Dept Surgery Health Sc Ctr Stony Brook NY 11794

RAPAPORT, JONATHAN L., psychologist; b. Hackensack, N.J., Jan. 28, 1957; s. Morris and Rachel (Berz) R.; m. Sheila I. Rapaport. BA, Rutgers U., 1978; PhD, U. Ala., 1984. From staff clin. psychologist to prin. psychologist State of N.J./Trenton Psychiat. Hosp., 1984—; pvt. practice, Trenton, N.J., 1989—. Mem. APA (divsn. ind. practice), N.J. Psychol. Assn., Soc. for Personality Assessment. Home: 71 Summer Dr Southampton PA 18966-2734

RAPAPORT, SAMUEL I., educator, physician; b. Los Angeles, Nov. 19, 1921; s. Hyman and Bertha (Krupnick) R.; m. Joyce Mildred Cooperman, Oct. 3, 1950; children: Susan Rapaport Braunwald, Sally Rapaport Hartinian, Mark Hyman, Bruce Allen. Student, UCLA; MD, U. So. Calif., 1945. Diplomate: Am. Bd. Internal Medicine (mem. bd. 1973-80, bd. govs. 1976-80, sec.-treas., chmn. hematology subcom. 1978-80). Intern Los Angeles County Hosp., 1945; resident medicine VA Hosp., Long Beach, Calif., 1948-50; chief hematology sect. VA Hosp., 1950-57; asso. prof. medicine U. Calif. at Los Angeles Med. Center, 1957-58; mem. faculty U. So. Calif. Sch. Medicine, 1958-74, head hematology div. dept. medicine, 1958-74, prof. medicine, 1964-74; head hematology div. Los Angeles County-U. So. Calif. Med. Center, 1958-74; chief med. service San Diego VA Hosp., 1974-78; prof. medicine U. Calif., San Diego, 1974-96; prof. emeritus, 1996—; vice chmn. dept. medicine U. Calif., 1974-78, co-head hematology-oncology div., 1978-87, prof. pathology, 1980-93; dir. Hematology Lab., U. Calif.-San Diego Med. Ctr., 1980-87; cons. hematology tng. grants study sect. Nat. Inst. Arthritis and Metabolic Diseases, 1968-71; mem. med. adv. coun. Nat. Hemophilia Found., 1970, 77—; chmn. adv. com., div. blood diseases and resources Nat. Heart, Lung and Blood Inst., 1980-82, mem. adv. coun., 1989—; mem. hematology study sect. NIH, 1984-88, chmn. study sect., 1977-88. Author: Introduction to Hematology, 1971, 2d edit., 1987; also papers in field. Served with USAAF, 1946-48. Spl. fellow Nat. Heart Inst., U. Oslo, 1964-65; Fulbright research scholar U. Oslo, 1953-54; fellow Sackler Inst. for Advanced Study, Tel Aviv U., 1983. Master ACP; mem. Assn. Am. Physicians, Am. Soc. Hematology (pres. 1977), Western Soc. Clin. Rsch. (pres. 1966), Am. Fedn. Clin. Rsch. (chmn. Western sect. 1960), Am. Soc. Clin. Investigation, Western Assn. Physicians (pres. 1973). Home: 7887 Lookout Dr La Jolla CA 92037-3951

RAPHAEL, CHESTER MARTIN, physician; b. Rockaway Beach, N.Y., Oct. 7, 1912; s. Jack and Lena (Schoenfeld) R.; A.B. cum laude, U. Mich., 1933, M.D., 1937; m. Margaret Mary Hubbert, Aug. 15, 1943; children—Maura Ann, Barbara Lynn. Intern, Monmouth Meml. Hosp., Long Branch, N.J., 1937-39; resident physician N.J. State Hosp., Marlboro, N.J., 1939-42, 46-48; practice medicine specializing in psychiatry and orgonomy, Forest Hills, N.Y., 1948—; sec. Wilhelm Reich Found., 1949-54; co-dir. Orgone Energy Clinic, 1949-54. Bd. dirs. Guide Dog Found. for Blind, Friends of Wilhelm Reich Mus. Served with AUS, 1942-46. Fellow Am. Geriatric Soc., Acad. Psychosomatic Medicine; mem. Queens County Med. Soc., AMA, Am. Psychiat. Assn., Am. Assn. Med. Orgonomy, AAAS, Wilhelm Reich Inst. Orgonomic Studies (dir.), Assn. for Advancement Psychotherapy, Tau Delta Phi. Club: University of Michigan (N.Y.C.). Author: (with Helen E. MacDonald) Orgonomic Diagnosis of the Cancer Biopathy, 1952; Wilhelm Reich: Misconstrued-Misesteemed; Some Questions and Answers About Orgone Therapy; assoc. editor: Jour. Orgonomic Medicine, 1955-56, Orgonomic Functionalism, 1989—; editor: (with Mary Higgins) Reich Speaks of Freud, The Cancer Biopathy (Wilhelm Reich); Passion of Youth-An Autobiography (Wilhelm Reich), Early Writings (Wilhelm Reich); The Bion Experiments on The Origin of Life (Wilhelm Reich); Character Analysis (Wilhelm Reich); Genitality (Wilhelm Reich); Bioelectrical Investigation of Sexuality and Anxiety (Wilhelm Reich); Children of the Future (Wilhelm Reich). Home and Office: 69-17 Fleet St Forest Hills NY 11375-5165

RAPHAEL, HUGH ALEXANDER, surgeon; b. N.Y.C., Sept. 11, 1930; s. Louis Julian and Emma Amy (Roseman) R.; m. Jo Ann Hollingshead, Dec. 29, 1956; children: Scott, Stacy, Stuart. AB, Harvard U., 1952; MD, McGill U., 1956; MS, U. Minn., 1965. Diplomate Am. Bd. Surgery. Intern Highland Hosp., Oakland, Calif., 1956-57; resident Mayo Clinic, Rochester, Minn., 1961-65; assoc. clin. prof. surgery U. So. Calif., L.A., 1975—. Contbr. articles to profl. jours. Capt., flight surgeon USAF, 1957-59. Fellow ACS; mem. Soc. for Clin. Vascular Surgery, So. Calif. Vascular Surg. Soc., L.A. Surg. Soc. Office: # 105 18433 Roscoe Blvd Northridge CA 91325

RAPHAELY, RUSSELL C., anesthesiology, pediatrician, educator; b. Bridgeport, Conn., Mar. 31, 1937; m. Marianne Raphaely, Aug. 1961; m. Marianne Carrano; children: R. Christopher, James Scott. BA, U. Conn., 1959; MD, N.Y. Med. Coll., 1963. Intern St. Vincent's Hosp., Bridgeport, Conn., 1964-66; resident Hosp. of Univ. Pa., Phila., 1966-67; asst. instr. anesthesiology U. Pa. Sch. Medicine, Phila., 1964-66, clin. instr. anesthesiology, 1966-67, instr. anesthesiology, 1968-74, asst. prof. anesthesiology and pediat., 1974-77; asst. prof. anesthesiology and pediat. The Children's Hosp. Phila., 1977-79, assoc. prof. anesthesiology and pediat., 1979-88, prof. anesthesiology and pediat., 1988—. Mem. AMA, Am. Coll. Chest Physicians, Am. Soc. Critical Care Anesthesiologists, Am. Soc. Anesthesiologists, Am. Acad. Pediatrics, Soc. Critical Care Medicine (pres. 1992-94), Assn. U. Anesthesiologists. Office: The Childrens Hosp Phila 34th St & Civic Ctr Blvd Philadelphia PA 19104-4399

RAPHLING, DAVID L., psychiatrist; b. Washington, June 8, 1937; s. Joseph Jacob and Sylvia (Topol) R.; m. Lois Susan Hassan, July 19, 1959; children: Elizabeth Britt, John Lawrence. BA, George Washington U., 1959, MD, 1962. Cert. in psychiatry and psychoanalysis. Intern Barnes Hosp., St. Louis, 1962-63; resident Barnes Hosp., 1963-64; psychiatry resident Mass. Gen. Hosp., Boston, 1966-69; candidate in psychoanalysis Washington Psychoanalytic Inst., 1969-76; psychiat. cons. D.C. Rehab., Washington, 1969—; pvt. practice psychiatry and psychoanalysis Washington, 1969—; tng. and supervising analyst Washington Psychoanalytic Inst., 1984—; assoc. clin. prof. psychiatry George Washington U. Med. Sch., 1984—; clin. prof. psychiatry Uniformed Svcs. U. of Health Scis., Bethesda, Md. 1989—. Editl. reader Psychoanalytic Quar., 1996—; contbr. articles to profl. jours. Capt. USAF, 1964-66. Fellow Am. Psychiat. Assn.; mem. Am. Psychoanalytic Assn. (cert., editl. bd. 1992-95), Internat. Psychoanalytic Assn., Ctr. for Advanced Psychoanalytic Studies, Alpha Omega Alpha. Office: 5225 Connecticut Ave NW Washington DC 20015-1845

RAPKIN, ROBERT MICHAEL, psychiatrist; b. N.Y.C., Jan. 14, 1940; s. Bernard David and Rose (Suprin) R.; m. Bonnie Stark, June 5, 1971; children: Jonathan Daniel, Meredith Colwell. AB in English Lit., Lafayette Coll., 1961; MD, Tufts U., 1965. Diplomate, Am. Bd. Psychiatry and Neurology. Intern Mt. Auburn Hosp.-Harvard U., Boston, 1965-66; resident in psychiatry Univ. Hosp.-Boston U., 1966-69; dir. drug treatment unit Fed. Correctional Unit, Danbury, Conn., 1969-71; assoc. dir. Yale Drug Dependence Unit, New Haven, 1971-76; dir. tardive dyskinesia unit Lawrence & Meml. Hosp., New London, Conn., 1976-81; pvt. practice Guilford, Conn., 1981-94; staff psychiatrist Penn Found., Sellersville, Pa., 1994—; cons. psychiatrist East Ctrl. Mental Health, Branford, Conn., 1988-92. Contbr. to profl. publs. Lt. comdr. USPHS, 1969-71. Grantee, NIMH, 1971-81. Mem. AAAS, Am. Psychiat. Assn., Am. Assn. Geriatric Psychiatry, Physicians for Social Responsibility, Fedn. Am. Scientists, Amnesty Internat. Democrat. Jewish. Office: Penn Found PO Box 32 Sellersville PA 18960

RAPOPORT, JUDITH, psychiatrist; b. N.Y.C., July 12, 1933; d. Louis and Minna (Enteen) Livant; m. Stanley Rapoport, June 25, 1961; children: Stuart, Erik. BA, Swarthmore Coll., 1955; MD, Harvard U., 1959. Lic. psychiatrist. Cons., child psychiatrist NIMH/St. Elizabeth's Hosp., Washington, 1969-72; clin. asst. prof. Georgetown U. Med. Sch., Washington, 1972-82, clin. assoc. prof., 1982-85, clin. prof. psychiat., 1985—; med. officer biol. psychiatry br. NIMH, Bethesda, Md., 1976-78, chief, child mental illness unit, biol. psychiat. br., 1979-82, chief, child psychiatry lab. of clin. scis., 1982-84, chief, child psychiatry div. intramural rsch. programs, 1984—; prof. psychiatry George Washington U. Sch. Med., Washington, 1979—; prof. pediatrics Georgetown U., Washington, 1985—; cons. in field. Author: (non-fiction) The Boy Who Couldn't Stop Washing, 1989 (best seller literary guild selection 1989), Childhood Obsessive Compulsive Disorder, 1989. Fellow Am. Psychiat. Assn., Am. Acad. Child Psychiat.; mem. D.C. Psychiat. Assn., Inst. Medicine. Home: 3010 44th Pl NW Washington DC 20016-3557 Office: NIMH Bldg 10 Rm 6N240 Bethesda MD 20892

RAPOPORT, ROBERT MORTON, medical educator; b. Oakland, Calif., Nov. 20, 1952; married; 2 children. BA in Biological Scis., U. Calif., Santa Barbara, 1974; PhD in Pharmacology, U. Calif., L.A., 1980; postdoc. studies in Pharmacology, U. Va., 1980-81, Stanford U., 1981-83. Rsch. pharmacologist VA Med. Ctr., Palo Alto, Calif., 1983-84, Cin., 1984—; asst. prof. dept. pharmacology and cell biophysics U. Cin., 1984-91, assoc. prof., 1991—; asst. dir. med. pharmacology, 1994; spkr. in field. Reviewer manuscripts. various jours., grants various assns.; contbr. over 100 articles to profl. publs. Grantee U. Calif., 1977, VA, 1983-86, 85-86, 87-90, NIH, 1985-87, 88-93, Am. Heart Assn. S.W. Ohio, 1985-86, 86-87, 88-89, 89-91, 91-92, U. Cin., 1985-86, Am. Heart Assn., 1987-90, 1995—, Veterans Affairs, 1994-95, 95—, Univ. Rsch. Coun., 1994-95, Parke-Davis, 1994, 95; recipient Rsch. Career Devel. award, 1986-91. Office: Dept Pharmacology Univ Cincinnati 231 Bethesda Ave Cincinnati OH 45267

RAPOZA, PETER AUGUSTUS, ophthalmologist; b. New Bedford, Mass., Sept. 6, 1956; s. Augustus and Mary (Faria) R. BA in Biol. Scis., Northwestern U., Evanston, Ill., 1978; MD, U. Chgo., 1982. Diplomate Am. Bd. Ophthalmology. Intern internal medicine U. Chgo. Hosps. and Clinics, 1982-83; resident ophthalmology Johns Hopkins Hosp., Balt., 1983-86; fellow cornea and external disease U. Wis., Madison, 1986-87, clin. asst. prof., 1987-92; clin. asst. prof. Harvard Med. Sch., Boston, 1993—; ptnr. Cornea Cons., Boston, 1992—; clin. rsch. adv. bd. Schepens Eye Rsch. Inst., Boston, 1995—; cons. Ministry of Health, Tanzania, 1986, Indonesia, 1990, United Arab Emirates, 1995-96. Contbr. chpts. to books. Mem. med. com. Boston-N.Y. AIDS Ride, 1995; ann. auction vol. UNICEF, Boston, 1996. Fellow ACS, Am. Acad. Ophthalmology; mem. Phi Beta Kappa, Alpha Omega Alpha. Democrat. Home: 99 Pinckney St Boston MA 02114 Office: Cornea Cons 100 Charles River Plz Boston MA 02114

RAPP, FRED, virologist; b. Fulda, Germany, Mar. 13, 1929; came to U.S., 1936, naturalized, 1945; s. Albert and Rita (Hain) R.; children: Stanley I., Richard J., Kenneth A.; m. Pamela A. Miles, Aug. 28, 1988. BS, Bklyn. Coll., 1951; MS, Albany Med. Coll., Union U., 1956; PhD, U. So. Calif., 1958. Jr. bacteriologist to bacteriologist divsn. labs. and rsch. N.Y. State Dept. Health, 1952-55; from teaching asst. to instr. dept. med. microbiology Sch. Medicine U. So. Calif., 1956-59; cons. supervisory microbiologist Hosp. Spl. Surgery, N.Y.C., 1959-62; also virologist div. pathology Philip D. Wilson Research Found., N.Y.C.; asst. prof. microbiology and immunology Cornell U. Med. Coll., N.Y.C., 1961-62; assoc. prof. Baylor U. Sch. Medicine, Houston, 1962-66, prof., 1966-69; prof., chmn. dept. microbiology and immunology Pa. State U. Coll. Medicine, Hershey, Pa., 1969-90; Evan Pugh prof. microbiology Pa. State U. Coll. Medicine, University Park, 1978-90, prof. emeritus, 1990—, assoc. provost, dean health affairs, 1973-80, sr. mem. grad. faculty, assoc. dean acad. affairs, research and grad. studies, 1987-90, professor emeritus, 1990—; researh career prof. of virology Am. Cancer Soc., 1966-69, prof. virology, 1977-90; dir. Coll. Med. Pa. State U. (Specialized Cancer Research Ctr.), 1973-84; mem. del. on viral oncology, U.S./USSR Joint Com. Health Cooperation; chmn., Gordon Rsch. Conf. in Cancer, 1975; virology Task Force, 1976-79; chmn. Atlantic Coast Tumor Virology Group, Nat. Cancer Insts. Health, 1971-77; mem. council for projection and analysis Am. Cancer Soc., 1976-80; chmn. standards and exam. com. on virology Am. Bd. Med. Microbiology, 1977, 80; chmn. subsect. on virology program com. Am. Assn. Cancer Research, 1978-79; mem. adv. council virology div. Internat. Union Microbiol. Socs., 1978-84; referee Macy Faculty Scholar Award Program, 1979-81; mem. programme com. Fifth Internat. Congress for Virology, Strasbourg, France, 1981; mem. basic cancer rsch. group U.S.-France Agreement for Cooperation in Cancer Research, 1980-84; mem. organizing com. Internat. Workshop on Herpes viruses, Bologna, Italy, 1980-81, NATO Internat. Advanced Study Inst., Corfu Island, Greece, 1981; mem. Herpes viruses Study Group, 1981-84; mem. sci. adv. com. Wilmot Fellowship Program, U. Rochester Med. Ctr., 1981-90 ; mem. scientific rev. com. Hubert H. Humphrey Cancer Research Ctr., Boston U., 1981; mem. fin. com. Am. Soc. Virology, 1982-89, mem. council, 1984-88; mem. adv. com. persistent virus-host interactions research program R.J. Reynolds Scientific Bd./Wistar Inst., 1983-90; mem. med. adv. bd. Herpes Resource Ctr., Am. Social Health Assn., 1983-90; bd. dirs. U.S.-Japan Found. Biomedicine, 1983-90; mem. council Soc. Exptl. Biology and Medicine, 1983-87; mem. scientific adv. com. Internat. Assn. Study and Prevention of Virus-Associated Cancers, 1983-90; mem. Basil O'Connor Starter Research Adv. Com., 1984-90; mem. council for research and clin. investigation awards Am. Cancer Soc., 1984-90; mem. recombinant DNA adv. com. NIH, 1984-87; mem. outstanding investigator grant rev. com. Nat. Cancer Inst., 1984-90; mem. organizing com. Fourth Symposium Sapporo Cancer Seminar, Japan, 1984, Second Internat. Conf. Immunobiology and Prophylaxis of Human Herpes virus Infections, Ft. Lauderdale, Fl., 1984-85, Internat. Congress of Virology, Sendai, Japan, 1984; mem. internat. sci. com. Internat. Meeting on Adv. in Virology, Catania, Italy, 1984-85; mem. adv. bd. Cancer Info., Dissemination and Analysis Ctr. Carcinogenesis and Cancer Biology, 1984-89; mem. internat. programme com. 7th Internat. Congress of Virology, Edmonton, Can., 1985-87; councilor div. DNA viruses Am. Soc. Microbiology, 1985-87; mem. adv. com. rsch. on etiology, diagnosis, natural history, prevention and therapy of multiple sclerosis Nat. Multiple Sclerosis Soc., 1985-89; mem. sci. adv. bd. Tampa Bay Rsch. Inst., 1985-91; mem. sci. adv. coun. Pitts. Ctr. AIDS Rsch. U. Pitts., 1988; mem. recombinant DNAdv. com. Working Group on Transgenic Animals NIH, 1988; mem. adv. com. 15th Internat. Herpes Virus Workshop, Washington, 1989-90. Sect. editor on oncology: Intervirology, 1972-84, assoc. editor, 1978-84, editor-in-chief, 1985-90; mem. ed. bd. Archives Virology, 1976-81; editorial bd. Jour. Immunology, 1966-73, Jour. Virology, 1968-88; assoc. editor Cancer Research, 1972-79; editorial bd. Virology, 1979-83, editor, 1983-90; mem. adv. bd. Ency. Americana, 1992—. Recipient 1st CIBA-Geigy Drew award for biomed. research, 1977, Nat. award for teaching excellence in microbiology, U. Medicine and Dentistry N.J. Med. Sch., 1988; Wellcome vis. professorship in microbiology, 1989-90; Disting. fellow Inst. Advanced Biotech., 1991. Mem. AAAS, AAUP, Am. Acad. Microbiology (fellow, diplomate), Soc. Microbiology (mem. com. med. microbiology and immunology, bd. pub. sci. affairs 1979-88, chmn. DNA viruses div. 1981-82, divsn. councilor DNA viruses), Am. Soc. Virology (chmn. fin. com. 1987-88, emeritus 1991), Am. Assn. Immunologists, The Harvey Soc., Soc. Exptl. Biology and Medicine (emeritus 1993), Am. Assn. Cancer Rsch. (emeritus 1991), Assn. Med. Sch. Microbiology Chmn. (pres. 1980-81), Sigma Xi (Monie A. Ferst award 1990, nat. lectr. 1977-79), Alpha Omega Alpha. Home: 68 Azalea Dr Hershey PA 17033-2602

RAPPA, MICHAEL GEORGE, occupational and environmental medicine physician; b. Milw., Mar. 26, 1960; s. Raymond Anthony and Carol Kathleen (McKenzie) R.; m. Adriana D'Angelo, June 1, 1985; children: Walter, Brian, Erik, Christine. BS, U. West Fla., 1982, MBA, 1984; DO, Southeastern U., Miami, 1988; MPH with honors, Johns Hopkins U., 1992. Diplomate Am. Bd. Preventive Medicine; cert. chemist Am. Chem. Soc. Commd. 2d lt. US Army, 1984, advanced through grades to maj., 1994; intern William Beaumont Army Med. Ctr./Ft. Bliss, El Paso, Tex., 1988-89, occupational health physician, 1989-91; occupational medicine resident U.S. Army Environ. Hygiene Agy., Aberdeen Proving Ground, Md., 1991-93; occupational and environmental medicine cons. U.S. Army Ctr. Health Promotion & Preventive Medicine, Aurora, Colo., 1993-95; assoc. med. dir. occupational and preventive health BroMenn Healthcare, Bloomington, Ill., 1995—. U.S. Army scholar, 1984-88. Mem. APHA, Am. Chemical Soc., Am. Coll. Occupational and Environ. Medicine, Am. Coll. Preventive Medicine, Assn. Mil. Osteo. Physicians and Surgeons, Am. Osteo. Assn., Delta Omega Alpha. Home: 1917 Redbud Ln Bloomington IL 61704 Office: BroMenn Healthcare 807 N Main St Bloomington IL 61701

RAPPAPORT, ALAN FRED, clinical psychologist; b. N.Y.C., Nov. 20, 1946; s. Sol and Edith (Drutman) R.; m. Liza E. Peguero, Dec. 27, 1981. B.A., Seton Hall U., 1968; M.A., U. Conn., 1969; Ph.D., Pa. State U., 1971. Clin. psychologist, marital therapist, N.J. Assoc. prof. Montclair State Coll., N.J., 1971-73; psychotherapist, N.Y.C., 1973-78; clin. dir. Community Mental Health Assocs., Parsippany, N.J., 1978—; cons. psychologist Stress Release Ltd., N.Y.C., 1972-75; adj. prof. Montclair State Coll., 1973-75; psychol. cons. Youth Services Bur., Pequannock, N.J., 1978-79. Author: (with others) Marriage and Family Therapy, 1974; Couples in Conflict, 1975; Treating Relationships, 1976. Program dir. Holistic Health Inst. N.J., 1983-85. Fellow Am. Coll. Psychology; mem. Am. Psychol. Assn., Am. Assn. Martial and Family Therapy, Phi Kappa Phi, Alpha Kappa Delta. Office: Cmty Mental Health Assoc 3599 Rt 46 E Parsippany NJ 07054

RAPPAPORT, HERBERT, clinical psychologist, educator; b. N.Y.C., Sept. 19, 1940; s. Isaac I. and Ida Rappaport; B.A., Queens Coll., 1964; Ph.D., SUNY at Buffalo, 1969; m. Margaret M. Williams, Oct. 20, 1967; children—Amanda, Alexander. Psychologist, Ft. Logan Mental Health Center, Denver, 1969-71, NIMH grantee, 1969-71; Fulbright scholar U. of Dar es Salaam, Inst. of Edn. grantee Republic of Tanzania, 1971-73; dir. psychol. services center Temple U., Phila., 1973-78, dir. clin. tng., 1978-84, NIMH grantee, 1979-82, assoc. prof., 1984—; pvt. practice clin. psychology; cons. in field. Author books. Mem. Am. Psychol. Assn., Eastern Psychol. Assn., Phila. Soc. Clin. Psychologists. Club: Phila. Cricket. Contbr. articles to profl. jours. Home: 509 E Sedgwick St Philadelphia PA 19119-1327 Office: Temple U Psychology Dept Philadelphia PA 19122

RAPPAPORT, MARGARET M., psychologist, physician, author, aviation consultant; b. Nov. 16, 1947; d. Leo J. and Marie L. (Fischle) Williams; m. Herbert Rappaport; children: Amanda, Alexander. BA, U. Buffalo; MA, SUNY; PhD, MD, U. Colo. Prof., researcher Univ. Dar es Salaam, Tanzania; with Rappaport Assocs., Phila., 1974-94; exec. dir. Inst. for Parent/Child Svcs., Phila., 1978-94; mem. adj. faculty Temple U., Phila., 1974-94. Mem. AAUP, AOPA, NOW, Inter Seaplane Pilots Assn., Ninety-Nines Internat. Orgn. Women Pilots, Soaring Soc. Am., Aero Club New Eng., Women in Aviation Internat., Exptl. Aircraft Assn., Phila. Cricket Club, Cosmopolitan Club. Republican. Avocation: pilot of airplanes, seaplanes and sailplanes. Home: PO Box 1845 Orleans MA 02653-1845

RAPPAPORT, MARTIN PAUL, internist, nephrologist, educator; b. Bronx, N.Y., Apr. 25, 1935; s. Joseph and Anne (Kramer) R.; BS, Tulane U., 1957, MD, 1960; m. Bethany Ann Mitchell; children: Karen, Steven. Intern, Charity Hosp. of La., New Orleans, 1960-61, resident in internal medicine, 1961-64; pvt. practice medicine specializing in internal medicine and nephrology, Seabrook, Tex., 1968-72, Webster, Tex., 1972—; mem. courtesy staff Mainland Ctr. Hosp. (formerly Galveston County Meml. Hosp.), Houston, 1968-96, Bapt. Meml. System, 1969-72, 88—; mem. staff Clear Lake Regional Med. Ctr., 1972—; cons. staff St. Mary's Hosp., 1973-79; cons. nephrology St. John's Hosp., Nassau Bay, Tex.; fellow in nephrology Northwestern U. Med. Sch., Chgo., 1968; clin. asst. prof. in medicine and nephrology U. Tex., Galveston, 1969—; lectr. emergency med. technician course, 1974-76; adviser on respiratory therapy program Alvin (Tex.) Jr. Coll., 1976-82; cons. nephrology USPHS, 1979-80. Served to capt. M.C., U.S. Army, 1961-67. Diplomate Am. Bd. Internal Medicine, Nat. Bd. Med. Examiners. Fellow ACP, Am. Coll. Chest Physicians; mem. Internat., Am. Socs. Nephrology, So. Med. Assn., Tex. Med. Assn., Tex. Soc. Internal Medicine (bd. govs. 1994-96), Am. Soc. Artificial Internal Organs, Tex. Acad. Internal Medicine, Harris County Med. Soc., Am. Geriatrics Soc., Bay Area Heart Assn. (bd. govs. 1969-75), Clear Lake C. of C., Phi Delta Epsilon, Alpha Epsilon Pi, Tulane Alumni Assn. Lodge: Rotary. Home: 1818 Linfield Way Houston TX 77058-2324 Office: PO Box 57609 Webster TX 77598-7609

RAPPAPORT, ZVI HARRY, neurosurgeon; b. Munich, Fed. Republic Germany, June 25, 1949; arrived in Israel, 1980; s. Aron and Sarah (Silberberg) R.; m. Isabelle Klein, Dec. 19, 1978; children: Yael, Maya, Ron. BA, Columbia Coll., 1969; MD, U. Pa., 1973. Diplomate Am. Bd. Neurol. Surgery. Surg. resident Columbia-Presbyn. Med. Ctr., N.Y., 1973-74; resident in neurosurgery NYU Med. Ctr., 1974-78; fellow in physiol. neurosurgery Westchester County Med. Ctr., Valhalla, N.Y., 1979; sr. neurosurgeon Sheba Med. Ctr., Tel Hashomer, Israel, 1980-83, Hadassah U. Med. Ctr., Jerusalem, 1983-89; chmn. dept. neurosurgery Rabin Med. Ctr., Petach Tikva, Israel, 1989—; asst. prof. neurosurgery NYU Med. Sch., 1978-79; sr. lectr. in neurosurgery Hebrew U., Jerusalem, 1985-90; assoc. prof. neurosurgery Tel Aviv U., 1991—. Contbr. articles to profl. jours. Served as med. officer Israel Def. Forces, 1985—. Recipient research prize Am. Heart Assn., 1970. Mem. Israel Surg. Soc. (governing body), Israel Neurosurg. Soc. (pres. 1993—), Am. Assn. Neurosurgery, Congress Neurol. Surgery, Internat. Assn. for Study Pain, European Assn. Neurosurgery (tng. and ethico-legal com.). Jewish. Office: Rabin Med Ctr, Dept of Neurosurgery, Petah Tikva 49100, Israel

RAPPEL, ROBERT, osteopathic physician, educator; b. Newark, N.J., June 23, 1936; s. Louis and Celia (Radowitz) R.; m. Sandra Bernice Shechtman, Aug. 16, 1959 (div. 1988); children: Michael Blair, Craig Marc, Michele Elise Rappel Best, Danielle Ashley Rappel; m. Josette Marie Martini, Dec. 22, 1990. BS in Chemistry, Fairleigh Dickinson U., 1959; DO, Kirksville Coll., Mo., 1962; postgrad., inst. Osteo. Medicine, 1967-68; JD, Nova Southeastern U., 1991. Lic. osteopath, N.Y., N.J., Fla., Mo., Ky., Calif.; bar: Fla., U.S. Ct. Appeals (11th cir.), U.S. Dist. Ct. (mid. dist.) Fla. Fellow NIH, 1959-63; intern Kirksville Osteo. Hosp., 1962-63, resident in internal medicine, gen. surgery and urology, 1963-66; instr. surgery Kirksville Coll. Osteo. Medicine, 1963-66, assoc. prof. surgery, 1966-68; dean academic affairs Coll. Osteo. Medicine of The Pacific, Pamona, Calif., 1977-78; assoc. prof. urology Coll. Osteo Medicine Nova Southeastern U., North Miami Beach, Fla., 1980—; mng. dir. health law divsn. Ronian, Narrell, Mitchell & Wattwood, P.A., Melbourne, Fla., 1994-96; mng. atty. Rappel & Assocs., P.A., Vero Beach, Fla., 1996—; dir. med. edn. Universal Med. Ctr., Plantation, Fla., 1986-88, chmn. dept. surgery, 1985-88, mem. staff; mem. staff Westside Regional Med. Ctr., Plantation, Fla. Med. Ctr., Lauderdale Lakes; dir. med. edn. Wellington Regional Med. Ctr., West Palm Beach, Fla., 1991-93; mng. dir. Healthlaw divsn. Reinnan & Wattwood, PA, 1993—; bd. dirs. Fellsmere Med. Ctr. Coalition; bd. dirs. Broward Collier Profl. Svcs. Rev. Orgn., vice chmn. data com., mem. peer rev. and coord. com., mem. by-laws com.; cons. Profl. Rev. Orgn. Tampa; lectr. in field. Contbr. articles to profl. jours. Stewart scholar, 1962. Fellow Am. Coll. Legal Medicine; mem. AMA, ABA (health law forum), Am. Coll. Osteo. Surgeons (ast chmn. urology sect., legis. com. to Congress 1990—), Am. Soc. Law and Medicine, Nat. Health Lawyers Assn., Am. Bd. Quality Assurance and Utilization Rev. Physicians, Am. Coll. Physician Execs., Am. Judicature Soc., Am. Osteo. Assn., Fla. Med. Assn., Fla. Urol. Soc., Fla. Osteo. Med. Assn. (co-chmn. legis. comms. com.), Acad. Osteo. Med. Dirs., Palm Beach County Med. Assn., Palm Beach County Health Care Dist. (med. adv. com.), Fla. Bar Assn. (health law sect.), Am. Acad. of Health Law Attys., Fla. Acad. of Health Law Attys., Fla. Hosp. Assn., Fed. Bar Assn., Broward County Med. Assn., Broward County Bar Assn., Indian River County Bar Assn. Republican. Home: 1110 Bounty Blvd Vero Beach FL 32963-2553 Office: Ste 307 2770 Indian River Rd Vero Beach FL 32960

RAPPERPORT, ALAN SHERWIN, plastic surgeon; b. St. Louis, Nov. 14, 1933; s. Carl and Rose (Wool) R.; m. Sue Louise Heimovics; children: Jill Ellen, Karen Ann, David Andrew. BA cum laude, Harvard U., 1955; MD, Tulane U., 1959. Diplomate Am. Bd. Plastic Surgery. Intern, then resident in gen. surgery Jackson Meml. Hosp., Miami, 1959-61; resident in general, plastic and reconstructive surgery U. Tex. Med. Br., Galveston, 1961-66; assoc. prof. U. Miami (Fla.) Sch. Medicine, 1967—; plastic surgeon Rapperport Plastic Surgery Assn., Miami; dir. Sunset Surgicenter, Miami, 1977—; chief of plastic surgery South Miami Hosp., 1983; examiner Am. Bd. Plastic Surgeons, 1979; chmn. internal rev. bd. Larkin Gen. Hosp., 1993-94; cons. Fla. Dept. Profl. Regulations, 1990-96; spkr. in field. Contbr. articles to profl. publs., chpt. to book. Fellow Am. Cancer Soc., 1964-65; rsch. grantee Edl. Found. Am. Soc. Plastic Surgeons, 1980. Fellow ACS; mem. Am. Coll. Plastic Surgeons, Am. Soc. Aesthetic Surgeons, Fla. Soc. Plastic Surgeons (pres. 1979), Greater Miami Soc. Plastic Surgeons (pres. 1977, 79), Singleton Surg. Soc., Coconut Grove C. of C. Home: 13645 Deering Bay Dr # 154 Miami FL 33158 Office: Rapperport Plastic Surgery 6280 Sunset Dr # 501 Miami FL 33143

RASBERRY, KERRY WORTH, physician; b. Houston, Dec. 26, 1943. AA, Tyler Jr. Coll., 1965; BS, North Tex. State U., 1968; DO, Coll. Osteo. Medicine/Surgery, Des Moines, 1972. Radiologic technologist Am. Assn. Radiologic Technologists, various locations, 1964-72; gen. practice medicine Whitehouse, Tex., 1972-78, Troup, Tex., 1978-84; gen. practice medicine Tex. Dept. Criminal Justice, Tennessee Colony, 1984-87; staff physician No. Region Health Authority/Tex. Dept. Criminal Justice, Tennessee Colony, 1987-94; no. region med. dir. U. Tex. Med. Br./TDCJ-Managed Care, Tennessee Colony, 1994—; instr. instnl. and correctional health U. Tex. Med. Br., Galveston, 1996—; chmn. pharmacy and therapeutics com. U. Tex. Med. Br./TDCJ, Huntsville, 1994-96, off-line EMS med. dir., 1992—, liaison physician for legal affairs Office of Atty. Gen. of Tex., 1994—. Mem. Tex. Osteo. Med. Assn. Republican. Baptist. Home: 306 Dove Ridge Palestine TX 75801 Office: Univ Tex Med Br Divsn Instnl Correct Health 1 116 Ewing Hall Rt 1150 Galveston TX 77555-1150

RASCATI, KAREN LEWIS, pharmacy educator; b. Alexandria, Va., Dec. 23, 1956; d. Richard David and Glenna Louise (Rupp) L.; m. E. Joseph Rascati, June 14, 1980; children: Maria Elizabeth, Michelle Renee. BS in Pharmacy, U. Fla., 1979, PhD in Pharmacy, 1986. Registered pharmacist, Fla. Pharmacist Walgreens Drugs, Orlando, Fla., 1979-82; pharmacy supr. Shands Teaching Hosp., Gainesville, Fla., 1982-84; grad. teaching asst. Coll. of Pharmacy U. Fla., Gainesville, 1984-85; asst. prof. U. Tex., Austin, 1986-92, assoc. prof., 1992—; cons. Tex. Dept. Mental Health and Retardation, Austin, 1986-88. Contbr. articles to Am. Jour. Hosp. Pharmacy, Am. Jour. Pharm. Edn., Jour. Pharm. Mktg. and Mgmt., Am. Pharmacy. grantee in field. Mem. Am. Pharm. Assn. (Presentation Merit award 1990, nat. officer 1992—), Am. Assn. Colls. of Pharmacy, Phi Kappa Phi, Rho Chi. Office: U Tex PHR 3.209 Coll Pharmacy Austin TX 78712-1074

RASCH, ELLEN MYRBERG, cell biology educator; b. Chicago Heights, Ill., Jan. 31, 1927; d. Arthur August and Helen Catherine (Stelle) Myrberg; m. Robert W. E. Rasch, June 17, 1950; 1 son, Martin Karl. PhB with honors, U. Chgo., 1945, BS in Biol. Sci., 1947, MS in Botany, 1948, PhD, 1950. Asst. histologist Am. Meat Inst. Found., Chgo., 1950-51; USPHS postdoctoral fellow U. Chgo., 1951-53, rsch. assoc. dept. zoology, 1954-59; rsch. assoc. Marquette U., Milw., 1962-65, assoc. prof. biology, 1965-68, prof. biology, 1968-75, Wehr Disting. prof. biophysics, 1975-78; rsch. prof. biophysics East Tenn. State U., James H. Quillen Coll. Medicine, Johnson City, 1978-94, interim chmn. dept. cellular biophysics, 1985-94, prof. anatomy and cell biology, 1994—. Mem. Wis. Bd. Basic Sci. Examiners, 1971-75, sec. bd., 1973-75. Recipient Post-doctoral fellowship USPHS, 1951-53, Research Career Devel. award, 1967-72; Teaching Excellence and Disting. award Marquette U., 1975; Kreeger-Wolf vis. disting. prof. in biol. sci. Northwestern U., 1979. Mem. Royal Microscopic Soc., Am. Soc. Cell Biology, Am. Soc. Zoologists, Am. Soc. Ichthyologists and Herpetologists, The Histochem. Soc., Phi Beta Kappa, Sigma Xi. Contbr. articles to various publs. Home: 1504 Chickees St Johnson City TN 37604-7103 Office: East Tenn State U Dept Anatomy & Cell Biology PO Box 70 421 Johnson City TN 37614-0421

RASCH, ROBERT WILLIAM, medical educator; b. Chgo., Nov. 19, 1926; s. William Edward and Florence (Siebert) R.; m. Ellen M. Myrberg, June 17, 1950; 1 child, Martin Karl. Ph.B., U. Chgo., 1946, M.D., 1951, Ph.D., 1959; B.S., Northwestern U. Sch. Medicine, 1951. Instr. to asst. prof. physiology Coll. Medicine, Marquette U., Milw., 1959-71; assoc. prof. Med. Coll. Wis., Milw., 1971-77; prof., chmn. physiology dept. Quillen Dishner Coll. Medicine, East Tenn. State U., Johnson City, 1977-87, prof. emeritus, 1987—, 1987—. Contbr. sci. papers and revs. to profl. publs. Served with M.C., U.S. Army, 1951-53. Decorated Bronze Star; grantee USPHS; grantee NSF. Mem. Am. Soc. Cell Biology, AAAS, Wis. Acad. Scis., N.Y. Acad. Scis., Tenn. Acad. Scis., Nat. Speliol. Soc., Phi Gamma Delta, Phi Chi. Home: 1504 Chickees St Johnson City TN 37604-7103 Office: Quillen-Dishner E Tenn State U Johnson City TN 37614

RASCH, STUART GARY, emergency physician; b. Rochester, N.Y., Aug. 2, 1958; s. Stanley Alvin and Lore (Mane) R.; m. Carolynn Gold; 1 child, Erica Danielle. BS in Biology, SUNY, New Paltz, 1980; MD, St. George's U., Grenada, West Indies, 1988. Emergency med. technician II The N.Y. Hosp./Empire State Ambulance, N.Y.C., 1977-82; computer cons. Goldman Sachs & Co., N.Y.C., 1986-87; intern, resident Maimonides Med. Ctr., Bklyn., 1988-90; resident in Emergency Medicine The Greenwich (Conn.) Hosp., 1990—; physician Emergency dept. The Nyack (N.Y.) Hospital/Rockland Critical Care, 1991—; tchg. asst., vis. prof. internal medicine St. George's U. Sch. Medicine, Grenada, 1990—. Mem. postal adv. com. U.S. Postal Svc., Pearl River, N.Y.; police surgeon Pearl River Fire Dept. Mem. AMA, Conn. Med. Soc., Fairfield County Med. Soc., Rockland County Med. Soc., N.Y. State Med. Soc. Home: 40 Sickletown Rd Pearl River NY 10965-2858

RASCHKA, CHRISTOPH JOSEF, sports physician, internist, anthropologist; b. Fulda, Hessen, Germany, Jan. 8, 1961; s. Herbert Helmut and Marga Rosa (Herget) R. Dr.Medicine cum laude, Justus-Liebig U., Giessen, Germany, 1987; Dr.rer.nat. magna cum laude, Johannes-Gutenberg U., Mainz, 1988; Dr.Sci. of Sports, Ruhr-U., Bochum, Germany, 1994. Cert. in sports medicine, acupuncture, chiropractic, homeopathy, tropotherapy. Asst. Inst. Anthropology, Mainz, 1987-88; resident Frankenklinik, Bad Neustadt/Saale, Germany, 1988-89, St. Markus-Krankenhaus, Frankfurt, 1989, KVB-Klinik, Koenigstein/Taunus, 1989, Klinikum Fulda, 1990—; lectr. Acad. for Sch. Nurses, Fulda, 1992-93; tchr. Sch. for Nurses of Klinikum Fulda, 1991—; lectr. spl. evening course in anthropology Fulda, 1992-93; lectr. in field. Book reviewer Jour. Comparative Human Biology, 1995—, Jour. Naturarzt, 1995—. Johannes-Gutenberg U. Postgrad. scholar, 1987. Mem. German Soc. Sports Physicians, German Soc. Physicians for Acupuncture. Roman Catholic. Home: Edith-Stein-Strasse 34, 36100 Petersberg Hessen, Germany Office: Klinikum Fulda-Med Klinik II, Pacelliallee 4, 36043 Fulda Hessen, Germany

RASKIN, NOEL MICHAEL, thoracic surgeon; b. Bklyn., May 29, 1947; s. Rubin and Pauline (Sturm) R.; m. Deborah M. Axelrod, Feb. 27, 1987; children: Max, Ben. BA, NYU, 1969; MD, N.Y. Med. Coll., 1977. Intern St. Vincent's Hosp., N.Y.C., 1977-78; resident SUNY, Stony Brook, 1978-82; fellow in cardio-thoracic surgery U. Miami, Fla., 1982-84, fellow in thoracic oncology, 1984-85; attending surgeon Beth Israel Med. Ctr. and Cabrini Med. Ctr., N.Y.C., 1985—; chief thoracic surgery Cabrini Med. Ctr.; thoracic surgeon Kriser Lung Cancer Ctr., N.Y.C., 1989; attending surgeon Dover (N.J.) Gen. Hosp., 1989-91; surgeon pvt. practice N.Y.C., 1992—. Fellow ACS, Am. Coll. Chest Physicians; mem. AMA, Soc. Thoracic Surgeons, Gen. Thoracic Surg. Club. Office: 41 5th Ave New York NY 10003-4319

RASMASON, FREDERICK C., III, emergency nurse; b. Evergreen Park, Ill., May 10, 1958; s. Frederick C. Jr. and Kathleen M. R.; m. Concepcion A. Rasmason, Nov. 14, 1981; children: F. Charlie IV, Randy. Diploma, Clin. Specialist Sch., 1977; BS in Nursing, Chgo. State U., 1988; postgrad., Spertus Coll. Staff nurse Holy Family Hosp., Des Plaines, Ill., Mt. Sinai Med. Ctr., Chgo.; RN, CEN, TNS, certification in edn. nursing, ACLS, PALS and PHTLS King Drew Med. Ctr., Calif.; e.d. staff Provident Hosp. Cook County, Chgo. Sgt. U.S. Army, 1976-82, 86-88. Named Nightingale Soc. Honors Mem.; recipient U.S. Achievement Acad. Scholastic All-Am. award, U.S. Achievement Acad. Nat. Collegiate Nursing award. Mem. Am. Assn. Critical Care Nurses, Emergency Nurses Assn., Ill. Nurses Assn. Home: 13260 Windward Trl Orland Park IL 60462-1860

RASMUSSEN, CAREN NANCY, hospital executive; b. Fort Riley, Kans., July 7, 1950; d. Stanley Junior and Katherina Wilhelmina (Wagner) R. AAS, Grand Rapids Jr. Coll., 1970; BS, U. Md., 1977. Cert. profl. contracts mgr. Med. sec., Walter Reed Army Med. Ctr., Washington, 1970-72, sec. procurement, 1972-76, contract specialist, 1976-79, 81-84; contract specialist Kadena Air Base, Okinawa, 1979-81; procurement analyst Walter Reed Med. ctr., 1984—, sr. contracting specialist, 1988—. Fellow NAFE; mem. Nat. Contract Mgmt. Assn. Democrat. Avocations: photography, stamp collecting, gardening, travel. Home: 18632 Clovercrest Cir Olney MD 20832-3057 Office: Walter Reed Army Med Ctr Directorate of Contracting Washington DC 20307

RASMUSSEN, GAIL MAUREEN, critical care nurse; b. Can., Feb. 22, 1941; d. Thomas Alfred and Bernice Hilda (Sayler) Salisbury; m. Byron Karl Rasmussen, June 28, 1964; children: Stephen, Carla, Wade, Gregory. AS, Riverside City Coll., 1961; BSN, U. Phoenix, 1987; MS in Health Professions Edn., Osteo. Coll. the Pacific, 1991. RN, Calif.; CCRN. Staff nurse Meml. Med. Ctr., Long Beach, Calif., 1961-63, UCLA Med. Ctr., 1963-64; clin. nurse critical care unit Intercomty. Med. Ctr. (name changed to Citrus Valley Health Ptnrs.- Intercomty. Campus), Covina, Calif., 1964-71, 78-95, 96; instr. ACLS, Los Angeles County, 1991—. Mem. AACN.

RASMUSSEN, KATHLEEN MAHER, nutritional sciences educator; b. Dayton, Ohio, Mar. 1, 1948. AB, Brown U., 1970; MSc, Harvard U., 1975, DSc, 1978. Registered dietitian. Tchr. sci. Cape Elem. Sch., Buxton, N.C., 1971-72; analytical chemist Berkeley Machine Works, Foundry Co., Norfolk, Va., 1972-73; rsch. assoc. dept. nutrition Harvard U., Boston, 1978; instr. div. nutritional scis. Cornell U., Ithaca, N.Y., 1981-83, asst. prof., 1983-88, assoc. prof., 1988—, assoc. dir. grad. affairs, 1992-95; com. mem. NAS, Washington, 1988—; Pew faculty scholar in nutrition Nat. Ctr. Sci. Rsch., Meudon-Bellevue, France, 1989-90. NIH trainee, 1974-80; NIH grantee, 1984-90, 87—, 93—, various other grants and awards, 1982-85, 88-89, 89-92, 92-94, 93-95. Mem. Am. Inst. Nutrition, Am. Soc. Clin. Nutrition, Brit. Nutrition Soc., Internat. Soc. for Rsch. in Human Milk and Lactation. Office: Cornell U Div Nutritional Sci 111 Savage Hall Ithaca NY 14853-6301

RASPER, DEBORAH YOUNG, hospital administrator; b. Bluffton, Ind., Dec. 24, 1950; d. Jacques Edward and Eleanor (Shafer) Young; m. Alan Frank Rasper, Apr. 5, 1975; 1 child, Alison. BS, U. Cin., 1973; MHA, Xavier U., 1980. Dietitian's asst., dietetic trainee Provdence Hosp., Cin., 1973-74; adminstrv. dietitian The Christ Hosp., Cin., 1974-79; exec. asst., dir. transition St. Fancis, St. George Hosp. Inc., Cin., 1979-82; adminstrv. dir. Mgmt. Dynamics, Inc., Cin., 1982-84; asst. adminstr. Univ. Cin. Hosp., Cin., 1984-88, CareUnit Hosp. Cin., 1988-90; v.p. clin. svcs. Margaret Mary Community Hosp., Batesville, Inc., 1990-91; v.p. ops. Cmty. Hosp. Indpls., Indpls., 1991-95; adminstr. Cmty. Hosp., South Indpls., Ind., 1995—. Mem. Adv. Com. Dietetic Internship Christ Hosp., 1980-91; mem. chmn. St. John's Learning Ctr. Bd., 1985-91; mem. fin. com. Southport United Meth. Ch. Fellow Am. Coll. Healthcare Exec.; mem. Tri State Health Adminstr. Forum, Am. Hosp. Assn. Home: 6460 Pheasant Dr Indianapolis IN 46237-2959

RASSIN, BARRY JONATHAN, health science facility administrator; b. London, June 28, 1947; arrived in Bahamas, 1947; s. Meyer and Rosetta (House) R.; children: Pascale, Michele, Anthony; m. Esther Knowles, Nov. 24, 1990. BBA, U. Miami, 1971; MBA, U. Fla., 1973. Adminstrv. intern Miami Heart Inst., Miami Beach, Fla., 1971; asst. dir. Mt. Sinai Med. Ctr., Miami Beach, Fla., 1973-77; adminstr.-at-large Am. Medicrop, Inc., Pompano Beach, Fla., 1977; adminstr. Doctors' Hosp. of Hollywood, Fla., 1978, Doctors' Hosp., Nassau, Bahamas, 1979—; founding pres. Nat. Health Edn. Coun., Nassau, 1980-82, 86. Mem. Nat. Commn. for Physically Disabled, Nassau, 1981, adv. bd. St. Augustines, Nassau, 1983-88, Bahamas Employers Confedn., Nassau, 1987-88. Mem. Am. Coll. Healthcare Execs. (diplomate), Am. Hosp. Assn., Nassau C. of C. (com. chmn. 1980-82), Rotary (pres. East Nassau 1987-88, dist. gov. 1991-92). Office: Doctors Hosp, PO Box N972, Nassau Bahamas

RASSIN, DAVID KEITH, nutrition educator, researcher; b. Liverpool, Eng., Dec. 1, 1942; came to U.S., 1974; s. Meyer and Ella Rosetta (House) R.; m. Mildred Glennda McConnell, Feb. 5, 1965; children: Meya Glynne, Keith David, Heather Kareen. AB, Columbia U., 1965; PhD, CUNY, 1974. Rsch. scientist IV Inst. Basic Rsch. in Mental Retardation, Staten Island, N.Y., 1977-79, rsch. scientist V, 1979-80; with U. Tex. Med. Br., Galveston, 1980—, dir. devel. nutrition and metabolism, 1980—, prof. perinatal pediatrics, 1985—, dir. div. med. edn. and rsch. facilitation, 1991—. Editor: Basic and Clinical Aspects of Nutrition and Brain Development, 1987, Neural Control of Reproductive Function, 1988; mem. editl. bd. Jour. Neurosci. Rsch., Internat. Jour. Devel. Neurosci. Mem. Soc. Pediatric Rsch., Am. Inst. Nutrition, Am. Soc. for Neurochemistry, Soc. for Neurosci., Am. Soc. Pharmacology and Exptl. Therapeutics, Internat. Soc. for Devel. Neurosci., Am. Soc. for Clin. Nutrition. Home: 1318 Sealy St Galveston TX 77550 Office: U Tex Med Br Dept Pediatrics RTC-44 Galveston TX 77555-0344

RASSULO, DONNA MARIE, nurse, poet, writer, TV producer; b. Boston, Jan. 18, 1951; d. Donald and Eleanor (Kadish) Guay; m. John A. Rassulo, June 20, 1981; children: Garret John, Nicole Darcy. Diploma, Shepard-Gill Sch. Practical Nursing, 1978; cert., Inst. Children's Lit., 1990. LPN, Mass. Model, cons. Reflections Unlimited, Amherst, Mass., 1974; med. sec. Mass. Gen. Hosp., Boston, 1969-78, staff nurse, acute medicine, 1978-1990, staff nurse, pediatric intermediate care, 1990-94; staff nurse Commonwealth Care, Inc., Newton, Mass., 1994—, Quantum Care Network, Inc., Newton, Mass., 1995—; mem. Long Ridge Writers Group, West Redding, Conn., 1991—. Author numerous poems and articles; co-producer (with Marjorie Harrison) Clay Pit Pond Prodns., 1991—, Parent 2 Parent Show. Mem. Neonatal ICU Parent Support Inc., Newton, Mass., 1989—, Parent Care, Inc., Alexandria, Va., 1990—. Recipient Disting. Poet award Sparrowgrass Poetry Forum, 1990, Golden Poet award World of Poetry Press, 1990. Mem. LPNs Mass., Nat. Fedn. LPNs. Democrat. Roman Catholic. Home: 65A Trowbridge St Belmont MA 02178-4001

RATCLIFF, CHRIS ARNOLD, optometrist; b. Charleston, W.Va., June 24, 1965; s. William Arnold and Vonya Lee (Bott) R.; m. Gena Gail Webb, Sept. 22, 1990; 1 child, Chandler Elizabeth. OD, So. Coll. Optometry, 1990. Nat. bd. cert. Internat. Assn. Bds. of Examiners in Optometry in treatment and mgmt. of ocular disease. Optometrist Drs. Ratcliff and Ratcliff, P.A., Huntington, W.Va., 1990—. Office: Drs Ratcliff & Ratcliff PA 1001 Fifth Ave Huntington WV 25701

RATCLIFF, DAVID GRADY, internist, educator; b. Little Rock, Ark., Oct. 17, 1958; s. Grady Frank and Martha Lorraine (Springer) R.; m. Cynthia Kaye Dillon, July 18, 1981; children: Jonathan Alan, Kathryn Elizabeth, Jason David, Adam Dillon. BA, Hendrix Coll., 1981; MD, Vanderbilt Med. Sch., 1985. Diplomate Am. Bd. Internal Medicine, Nat. Bd. Med. Examiners. Intern in internal medicine U. Colo. Health Sci. Ctr., Denver, 1985-86, resident in internal medicine, 1986-88, chief med. resident, 1988-89; asst. prof. medicine Vanderbilt Med. Ctr., Nashville, 1989-91; attending physician Fayetteville (Ark.) Diagnostic Clinic, 1991—; clin. asst. prof. medicine U. Ark. Med. Ctr., Fayetteville, 1991—. Petroleum Rsch. scholar, 1979, NSF scholar, 1980, Justin Potter Found. med. scholar, 1981-85. Mem. ACP. Office: Diagnostic Clinic 3344 N Futrall Dr Fayetteville AR 72703

RATH, DAVID RUSSELL, physical therapist; b. Garfield Heights, Ohio, Mar. 13, 1953; s. Robert Russell and Kathleen (Nicholas) R.; m. Christy Sommakio, Dec. 15, 1990. BA in Phys. Therapy, Cleve. State U., 1977; MS, Ohio State U., 1987. Staff phys. therapist Riverside Meth. Hosp., Columbus, Ohio, 1978-83; owner, pres., therapist Worthington Phys. Therapy, Columbus, 1984—; editor Phys. Therapy Briefings, Anadem Pub., Columbus, 1992—. Mem. Am. Phys. Therapy Assn. (cert. orthopedic specialist), Am. Acad. Orthopedic Manual Phys. Therapists, Ohio Phys. Therapy Assn. (pub. rels. com. 1994—). Home: 5910 Sinclair Rd Columbus OH 43229 Office: Worthington Phys Therapy 7100 N High St Ste 101 Worthington OH 43085

RATHAUSER, VLADIMIRO, health organization administrator; b. Bucharest, Romania, Oct. 24, 1934; s. Josef and Ita (Podgaetzky) R.; m. Sara Bekering, Nov. 19, 1969; children: Michael, Natalie. MD, U. Buenos Aires, 1962; MPH, Harvard U., Boston, 1968. Diplomate Am. Bd. Pediatrics. Gastarzt Kinderspital, Bern, Switzerland, 1963-64; sr. resident U. Louisville, 1965-66; chief resident in pediatrics Maimonides Hosp., N.Y.C., 1966-67; resident rep. Pan Am. Health Orgn./WHO, Port-au-Prince, Haiti, 1974-79, LaPaz, Bolivia, 1979-83, Montevideo, Uruguay, 1983-92, Belize, 1992-95; ret., 1995. Home: Guayaqui 3428/801, 11300 Montevideo Uruguay

RATHBONE, ISABEL SERVICI, psychiatrist, educator; b. Comodoro-Rivadavia, Argentina, Jan. 26, 1954; m. R. Rodion Rathbone; children: Taryn, Daniel. BA, Yale U., 1975, MD, 1979. Rotating intern Hosp. of St. Raphael, New Haven, 1979-80; resident in psychiatry Yale U., New Haven, 1980-83, asst. clin. prof., 1985—; substance abuse fellow West Haven (Conn.) VA Med. Ctr., 1983-85, med. dir. alcoholism ambulatory svc., 1985-87, dir. alcoholism ambulatory svc., 1987-89, med. dir. substance abuse rehab. unit, 1989-92; staff psychiatrist Yale Psychiatric Inst., 1995—. Mem. AMA, Am. Psychiat. Assn., Conn. Psychiat. Soc., Am. Med. Women's Assn. Home: 1800 Whitney Ave Hamden CT 06517-1404

RATHBUN, JESSE EARL, JR., ophthalmologist; b. San Francisco, Sept. 7, 1940; s. Jesse Earl and Iris Vivian (Smitheram) R.; m. Mary Lou Cantu, June 23, 1963 (div. 1973); children: Lisa, Mary Beth, Debra, Carolyn, Robert; m.

Kathleen Ann Walkowiak, Nov. 1, 1975; children: Christopher, Thomas, Sara. B.A., Stanford U., 1962; M.D., U. Calif.-San Francisco, 1965. Diplomate Am. Bd. Ophthalmology. Resident in ophthalmology U. Calif. Sch. Medicine, San Francisco, 1965-69, fellow in ophthalmic plastic and reconstructive surgery, 1969-70, instr., 1970-72, asst. clin. prof., 1972-80, assoc. clin. prof., 1980-87, clin. prof., 1987—; cons. Ft. Miley VA Hosp., San Francisco, 1970—. Contbr. articles to ophthal. jours., 1969-84. Cubmaster Sonoma-Mendocino council Boy Scouts Am., 1983-87. Fellow Am. Acad. Ophthalmology (bd. councillors) 1982-84, Am. Soc. Ophthalmic Plastic and Reconstructive Surgery (treas. 1980-81, pres. 1983), ACS; mem. AMA, Calif. Med. Assn. Office: 100 Brookwood Ave Santa Rosa CA 95404-5202

RATHKAMP, WALTER ROBERT, biology educator; b. Williamsburg, Va., Sept. 5, 1942; s. Walter Frank and Helen Martha (Seostrom) R.; divorced; children: W. Thad, Samuel Martin, Joshua Raymond. BS, Cornell U., 1964; MA, Ind. U., 1968, PhD, 1972. Biology tchr. U.S. Peace Corps, Ethiopia, 1964-66; teaching asst. Ind. U., Bloomington, 1967-70; asst. prof. Ind. U. Purdue, Indpls., 1973, Saginaw Valley State U., University Center, Mich., 1973-77; assoc. prof. biology Saginaw Valley State Coll., University Center, Mich., 1977-83, prof. biology, 1983—; vis. asst. prof. Ind. U., Bloomington, 1976; dir. regional math. sci. ctr. Saginaw Valley State U., University Center, Mich., 1989—; exec. dir. Ctr. Sci. and Math Edn., 1995—; rsch. assoc. Ind. U., 1972-73; prin. investigator Dow Corning Corp., Freeland, Mich., 1985; chmn. all coll. judiciary Saginaw Valley State U., 1977-78. Contbr. articles to profl. jours. Active Boy Scouts Am., Saginaw, 1976-78, Career Day All Saints Cen. High Sch., 1987, 89; presenter Am. Diabetes Assn., Mich., 1980; judge Acad. Olympics, Saginaw, 1984. Recipient Landee award for excellence in teaching; Can Doer awrd MIch. Tech. Coun. Sci. Quest, 1989. Mem. Big Bros. Am., Ind. Acad. Sci., Am. Assn. Advisors for Advancement Sci., Cen. Assn. Advisors for Health Professions Inc., Mich. Acad. Sci., Mich. Sci. Tchrs. Assn., Nat. Sci. Tchrs. Assn., Sigma Xi. Office: Saginaw Valley State U 7400 Bay Rd University Center MI 48710

RATHLESBERGER, JAMES HOWARD, medical board executive; b. Pitts., May 2, 1948; s. Howard Erwin and Jean Edna (Heiden) R.; m. M. Elizabeth Ware, Jan. 2, 1988. BA, U. Calif., Berkeley, 1971; MPA, NYU, 1986. Staff dir. environ. study conf. U.S. Congress, Washington, 1974-75; v.p. Nat. Limestone Inst., Washington, 1975-76; mem. Carter-Mondale Transition Team, Atlanta and Washington, 1976-77; spl. asst. to the asst. sec. U.S. Dept. of the Interior, Washington, 1977-81; spl. asst. to dean of the faculty of arts and scis. NYU, 1981-85; asst. exec. v.p. Nat. Health Coun., N.Y.C., 1985-89; exec. officer Bd. of Podiatric Medicine, Sacramento, Calif., 1989—. Editor: Nixon and the Environment, 1972; contbr. articles to profl. jours. Vol. VISTA, Charleston, W.Va., 1968-69. Named Hon. Citizen Paola, Kans., 1968. Home: 2757 11th Ave Sacramento CA 95818-4420 Office: Bd of Podiatric Medicine 1420 Howe Ave Ste 8 Sacramento CA 95825-3229

RATLIFF, LEIGH ANN, pharmacist; b. Long Beach, Calif., May 20, 1961; d. Harry Warren and Verna Lee (Zwink) R. D in Pharmacy, U. Pacific, 1984. Registered pharmacist, Calif., Nev. Pharmacist intern Green Bros. Inc., Stockton, Calif., 1982-84, staff pharmacist Thrifty Corp., Long Beach, Calif., 1984-85, head pharmacist, 1986-87, pharm. buyer, 1987-92; pharmacy. mgr. Kmart Pharmacy, Long Beach, Calif., 1992—; mem. joint mktg. com. Calif. Pharmacist's Assn. Mem. Pacific Alumni Assocs., Nat. Trust for Hist. Preservation, Friends of Rancho Los Cerritos; treas. Bixby Knolls Ter. Homeowners Assn., 1988-92, pres. 1992-96; vol. Docent Rancho Los Cerritos Hist. Site, 1988—; vol. preceptor U. So. Calif. Sch. Pharmacy; vol. Fairfield YMCA, Long Beach. Mem. Am. Pharm. Assn., Am. Inst. History Pharmacy, Calif. Pharmacist Assn., Lambda Kappa Sigma. Republican. Methodist. Avocations: raising African cichlids, growing herbs, collecting Hull pottery, antiquing. Home: 3913 N Virginia Rd Unit 301 Long Beach CA 90807-2670 Office: Kmart Pharmacy 5450 Cherry Ave Long Beach CA 90805-5502

RATNER, HAROLD, pediatrician, educator; b. Bklyn., June 19, 1927; s. George and Bertha (Silverman) R.; BS, Coll. City N.Y., 1948; MD, Chgo. Med. Sch., 1952; m. Lillian Gross, Feb. 4, 1961; children—Sanford Miles, Marcia Ellen. Intern, Jewish Hosp., Med. Center Bklyn., 1952-53, resident in pediatrics, 1953-55; practice medicine specializing in pediatrics, Bklyn.; clin. instr. pediatrics SUNY Downstate Med. Center, N.Y.C., 1955-67, clin. asst. prof., 1967-69, clin. assoc. prof., 1969-87; lectr. pediatrics, 1987—; chief of pediatrics Greenpoint Hosp., Bklyn., 1967-80, pres. med. staff, 1970-71, 74-80; dir. ambulatory services Woodhull Med. and Mental Health Center, Bklyn., 1980-83; clin. assoc. prof. pediatrics SUNY-Bklyn., 1983-87, lectr., 1987—; clin. assoc. prof. pediatrics, N.Y.U., 1987-90; med. specialist Nathan Kline Inst. for Psychiat. Research, Orangeburg, N.Y., Rockland Psychiat. Ctr., Orangeburg, N.Y., 1986-88, unit chief med. services, 1988-90; assoc. clin. dir. and dir. medicine Manhattan Psychiat. Ctr., N.Y.C., 1990—; mem. adv. council to pres. N.Y.C. Health and Hosp. Corp., 1970-71, 74-80, 81-83, sec., 1975, v.p., 1976-80; mem. med. bd., dir. Camp Sussex, camp for underprivileged children; bd. dirs. Kings County Health Care Rev. Orgn., Bklyn., 1976-84, past co-chmn. hosp. rev. com., continuing med. edn., med. care evaluation com. Trustee Village of Saddle Rock (N.Y.), 1980—. Served with AUS, 1945-47. Diplomate Nat. Bd. Med. Examiners, Am. Bd. Pediatrics. Fellow Am. Pediatric Soc., Am. Soc. Clin. Hypnosis, Bklyn. Pediatric Soc., Kings County Med. Soc., Royal Soc. Health; mem. AMA, Soc. Clin. and Exptl. Hypnosis, Am. Pub. Health Assn., Am. Soc. Clin. Hypnosis, N.Y. State Soc. Clin. Hypnosis, Kings County Med. Soc., Pan-Am. Med. Socs. Democrat. Jewish. Contbr. articles to med. jours. Home: 55 Blue Bird Dr Great Neck NY 11023-1001

RATNER, JAMES HENRY, dermatologist; b. El Paso, Tex., Mar. 31, 1945; s. Alfred A. and Adelaide M. (Moye) R.; m. Janice Dimenstein, June 30, 1968; children: Derek J., Andrea E. BS, Yale U., 1967; MD, Baylor U., 1971. Diplomate Am. Bd. Dermatology, Am. Bd. Pathology. Intern in internal medicine St. Luke's Episcopal Hosp., Houston, La., 1971-72; resident in dermatology Dartmouth Med. Sch. Affiliated Hosps., Hamover, N.H., 1972-75; chief of dermatology U.S. Army Hosp., Ft. Polk, La., 1976-77; pvt. practice in dermatology Amherst, Mass., 1977—. Bd. dirs. Amherst (Mass.) Youth Hockey Assn., 1985-91, Greater Springfield (Mass.) Jr. Amateur Hockey Assn., 1989-91. Major, U.S. Army, 1976-77. Fellow Am. Acad. Dermatology, Mass. Acad. Dermatology (bd. dirs. 1989-93); mem. New Eng. Dermatol. Assn., Internat. Soc. Dermatology, Mass. Med. Soc. (alt. exec. councilor 1983-84), So. Med. Assn. Office: 196 N Pleasant St Amherst MA 01002

RATNER, RICHARD A., psychiatrist, educator; b. N.Y.C., July 20, 1941; s. Oscar Joshua and Marguerite Pearl (Weiss) R.; m. Linda Helene Fein, May 18, 1969; children—Carolyn, Lauren. B.A. with honors, U. Chgo., 1962; M.D., U. Pa., 1966. Diplomate Am. Bd. Psychiatry and Neurology. Intern Montefiore Hosp., Bronx, N.Y., 1966-67; resident Albert Einstein Coll. Medicine, N.Y.C., 1967-70; adolescent staff psychiatrist Psychiatric Inst. D.C., Washington, 1972-75; psychiatric cons. Fairfax County Drug Program, Va., 1972-74; dir. psychiat. svcs. George Washington U. Sch. Medicine Polydrug Abuse Project, Washington, 1973-74; pvt. practice psychiatry, Washington and Bethesda, Md., 1971—; ptnr. Forensic Psychiatry Assocs., Washington, 1978-89; cons. forensic div. St. Elizabeth's Hosp., Washington, 1972—; attending physician Dominion Hosp., Falls Church, Va., 1984—; assoc. clin. prof. psychiatry George Washington U., 1973-88, clin. prof. psychiatry, 1988—; adj. prof. Georgetown U. Law Ctr., Washington, 1978—. Author chpts. to book; contbr. articles to profl. jours. Liaison from adolescent psychiatry to ad hoc coalition for juvenile justice; liaison to ABA, Washington, 1984-88; liaison AMA Coalition for Adolescent Health, 1992—, mem. steering com. Healthy Youth By 2000, 1992—. Served to maj. M.C., U.S. Army, 1970-72, Vietnam. Decorated Bronze Star, Army Commendation medal. Fellow Am. Psychiatric Assn. (mem. panel on treatment of impulse disorders, corrs. mem. com. juvenile justice issues, chair com. 1993-95, mem. coun. children adolescents and their families 1996—), Am. Soc. Adolescent Psychiatry (chmn. juvenile delinquency com. 1982-89, sec. 1988-90, v.p. 1990-92, pres.-elect 1992-93, pres. 1993-94); mem. Washington Psychiatric Soc. (pres. D.C. chpt. 1985-86, coun. mem. 1989-91), Med. Soc. D.C. (vice chmn. mental health com. 1984-86; editor-in-chief monthly newsletter MSDC Physician), Am. Acad. Psychiatry and Law (chmn. nominating com. Chesapeake Bay chpt., 1986-88). Jewish. Home: 5210 Elliott Rd Bethesda MD 20816-2909 Office: 5301 Wisconsin Ave NW # 220 Washington DC 20015-2015

RATNER, ROBERT EDWARD, internist, researcher; b. El Paso, Tex., Dec. 18, 1951; s. Alfred Alexander and Adalaide (Moye) R.; m. Nancy Elizabeth Bernstein, Oct. 24, 1981; children: Jamie Alexis, Adam Ross. BS, Tufts U., 1974; MD, Baylor Coll. Medicine, 1977. Diplomate Am. Bd. Internal Medicine, Am. Bd. Endocrinology and Metabolism. Intern St. Luke's Episcopal Hosp.-Baylor Affiliated Programs, Houston, 1977-78; resident in internal medicine Baylor Affiliated Programs, Houston, 1978-80; chief clin. fellow Joslin Diabetes Ctr., Boston, 1981-82; dir. Diabetes Ctr., George Washington U., Washington, 1982-92, assoc. prof. medicine, 1988-96; dir. sect. endocrinology Washington Hosp. Ctr., 1992-94, dir. sect. diabetes, 1994—; dir. Medlantic Clin. Rsch. Ctr., Washington, 1992—. Editor Diabetes Spectrum, 1992-95; contbr. articles to med. jours., chpts. to books. Grantee NIH, 1992—. Fellow ACP, Am. Assn. Clin. Endocrinologists; mem. Endocrine Soc., Am. Assn. Diabetes Educators (nat. cert. bd. 1985-88, bd. dirs. 1989-92), Am. Diabetes Assn. (pres. Washington affiliate 1984-85, vice chmn. pregnancy coun. 1995-96, Maurice Protas award 1985). Office: Medlantic Clin Rsch Ctr 650 Pennsylvania Ave SE Washington DC 20003

RATNOFF, OSCAR DAVIS, physician, educator; b. N.Y.C., Aug. 23, 1916; s. Hyman L. and Ethel (Davis) R.; m. Marian Foreman, Mar. 31, 1945; children: William Davis, Martha. AB, Columbia U., 1936, MD, 1939; LLD (hon.), U. Aberdeen, 1981; ScD (hon.), Case Western Res. U., 1996. Intern Johns Hopkins Hosp., Balt., 1939-40; Austin fellow in physiology Harvard Med. Sch., Boston, 1940-41; asst. resident Montefiore Hosp., N.Y.C., 1942; resident Goldwater Meml. Hosp., N.Y.C., 1942-43; asst. in medicine Columbia Coll. Physicians and Surgeons, N.Y.C., 1942-46; fellow in medicine Johns Hopkins, 1946-48, instr. medicine, 1948-50, instr. bacteriology, 1949-50; asst. prof. medicine Western Res. U., Cleve., 1950-56; assoc. prof. Case Western Res. U., 1956-61, prof., 1961—; asst. physician (Univ. Hosp.), Cleve., 1952-56; assoc. physician (Univ. Hosp.), 1956-67, physician, 1967—. Author: Bleeding Syndromes, 1960; mem. editorial bd. Jour. Lab. Clin. Medicine, 1956-62, assoc. editor, 1986-91, bd. rev. editors 1991-95, editl. adv. bd. 1995—; editor: Treatment of Hemorrhagic Disorders, 1968, (with C. D. Forbes) Disorders of Hemostasis, 1984, 3d edit., 1996; mem. editorial bd. Circulation, 1961-65, Blood, 1963-69, 78-81, Am. Jour. Physiology, 1966-72, Jour. Applied Physiology, 1966-72, Jour. Lipid Rsch., 1967-69, Jour. Clin. Investigation, 1969-71, Circulation Rsch., 1970-75, Annals Internal Medicine, 1973-76, Perspectives in Biology and Medicine, 1974—, Thrombosis Rsch., 1981-84, Jour. Urology, 1981-88, Internat. Jour. Hematology, 1991—; contbr. articles to med. jours. Career investigator Am. Heart Assn., 1960-86. Served to maj. M.C., 1943-46, Ind. Recipient Henry Moses award Montefiore Hosp., 1949, Disting. Achievement award Modern Medicine, 1967, James F. Mitchell award, 1971, Murray Thelin award Nat. Hemophilia Found., 1971, H.P. Smith award Am. Soc. Clin. Pathology, 1975, Joseph Mather Smith prize Columbia Coll. Physicians and Surgeons, 1976, Disting. Achievemtn in Med. Sci. award U. Hosps. of Cleve, 1992, Saltzman award Mt. Sinai Hosp. of Cleve., 1994; named to Heart Hall of Fame, N.E. Ohio Heart Assn., 1989. Master ACP (John Phillips award 1974); fellow AAAS; mem. NAS (Kovalenko award 1985), AMA, Am. Fedn. Clin. Rsch., Soc. Scholars Johns Hopkins U., Am. Soc. Clin. Investigation, Ctrl. Soc. Clin. Rsch. (Disting. Svc. award 1992), Assn. Am. Physicians (Kober lectr. 1985, Kober medal 1988), Am. Soc. Hematology (Dameshek award 1972), Internat. Soc. Hematology, Internat. Soc. Thrombosis (Grant award 1981, spl. award 1993), Am. Physiol. Soc., Am. Soc. Biol. Chemists. Home: 2916 Sedgewick Rd Cleveland OH 44120-1840 Office: Univ Hosps of Cleve Dept Pysicians Cleveland OH 44106

RAUCH, RONALD ARTHUR, neuroradiologist, educator; b. Camden, N.J., Apr. 11, 1953; s. Eldon Lloyd and Joan Lurene (Jay) R.; m. Jill Shari Mestel, Dec. 20, 1984 (div. Sept. 1995); children: Gregory Lloyd, Bradley Daniel. BA in Biochemistry, U. Kans., 1975; MD, Baylor Coll. Medicine, 1979. Bd. cert. diagnostic radiology with added qualifications in neuroradiology; bd. cert. neurology. Intern internal medicine Baylor Coll. Medicine, Houston, 1979-80; staff physician U. Houston, 1980-81; resident neurology Stanford U., Palo Alto, Calif., 1981-84; neurologist Kaiser Permante Hosps., L.A., 1984-85; resident radiology U. Calif., Irvine, 1985-88; neuroradiology fellow Long Beach (Calif.) Meml. Hosp., 1988-89, U. Calif., L.A., 1989-90; asst. prof. U. Tex. Health Sci. Ctr., San Antonio, 1990—. Mem. jour. rev. bd. Neurology, 1992-93, Am. Jour. Neuroradiology, 1995—; contbr. chpts. to book and articles to profl. jours. Summerfield scholar U. Kans., Lawrence, 1971-75. Mem. Am. Soc. Neuroradiology, Radiol. Soc. N.Am., Western Neuroradiology Soc., Soc. for Magnetic Resonance Imaging, Alpha Omega Alpha, Phi Beta Kappa. Home: 5 Tanner Woods San Antonio TX 78248 Office: U Tex Health Sci Ctr Radiology Dept 7703 Floyd Curl Dr San Antonio TX 78284-7800

RAUÏS, ANDRE L., orthopedist, surgeon; b. Brussels, June 11, 1939; s. Leopold C. and Berthe S. (Wallet) R.; m. Michele S. Morret, Aug. 17, 1972; children: Antoine, Bruno. MD, Free U., Brussels, 1966, cert. surgeon, 1975, cert. expert in corporal damage, 1980. Registrar IMC Bracops, Brussels, 1968-76; cons. Chu Tivoli, La Louviere, Belgium, 1976-90, IM Edith Cavell, Brussels, 1983—; chief orthopedist Shape Med. Ctr., 196th U.S. Army Hosp., 1990-93; organizer bone bank IM Cavell, Brussels, 1993—. Mem. Internat. Soc. Fracture Repair, Internat. Soc. Arthroscopic Surgery. Home: Ave FD Roosevelt 186, B 1050 Brussels Belgium Office: IM Edith Cavell, Rue E Cavell 32, B 1180 Brussels Belgium

RAULIN, MICHAEL LOUIS, psychological services administrator; b. Chippewa Falls, Wis., June 2, 1950; s. Delton Leo and Florence Juanita (Ritzinger) R.; m. Sheryl Ann Olson, June 25, 1977. BA in Psychology, U. Wis., 1972, MS, 1975, PhD in Clin. Psychology, 1977. Lic. psychologist, N.Y. Psychology intern VA Med. Ctr., Milw., 1977-78; asst. prof. psychology SUNY, Buffalo, 1978-84; pvt. practice psychology Buffalo, 1984—; adminstrv. dir. Psychol. Svcs. Ctr., Buffalo, 1984—; dir. clin. tng. psychology SUNY, Buffalo, 1989-94; Adventure Bound program evaluator Baker Hall, Lackawanna, N.Y., 1981-84; contbg. content specialist for coll. proficiency exam. N.Y. State Dept. Edn., SUNY, 1982-83; cons. to psychology tng. com. psychology svc. VA Med. Ctr., Buffalo, 1979—; rsch. cons. to CMG Health Western N.Y., 1992—; mem. com. to develop regents coll. exam. in abnormal psychology N.Y. State Dept. Edn.; presenter in field. Author: (with A.M. Graziano) Research Methods: A Process of Inquiry, 1989, 2d edit., 1993, Study Guide to Accompany Research Methods, 1989, 2d edit., 1993, Instructor's Manual/Test Bank to Accompany Research Methods, 1989, 2d edit., 1993; cons. editor Jour. Cons. and Clin. Psychology, 1987-88; editorial reviewer for profl. publs.; contbr. articles to profl. jours. Mem. AAAS, APA, Am. Psychol. Soc., Assn. for Advancement of Psychology, Soc. for Personality Assessment, Soc. for Rsch. on Psychopathology, Assn. for Advancement of Behavior Therapy, Am. Assn. Applied and Preventive Psychology, Ea. Psychol. Assn., Psychology Assn. Western N.Y., Erie County Mental Health Assn., Assn. Dirs. of Psychology Tng. Clinics (nat. chmn. 1991-93), Coun. Univ. Dirs. of Clin. Psychology, Assembly Scientist-Practitioner Psychologists, Phi Kappa Phi. Home: 526 Linwood Ave Buffalo NY 14209-1404 Office: SUNY Psychology Dept Buffalo NY 14260-4110

RAUSCH, JEFFREY LYNN, psychiatrist, psychopharmacologist; b. Butler, Pa., Jan. 10, 1953; s. John Kenneth and June Alice (Morrow) R.; m. Catherine Rebecca Montgomery, Aug. 24, 1974; children: Jeffrey David, Caroline Rebecca, Lauren Elizabeth. BS in Biology summa cum laude, Mercer U., Macon, Ga., 1974; MD, Med. Coll. Ga., 1978. Resident in psychiatry U. S.C., 1978-80; clin. psychopharmacology rsch. fellow U. Calif., San Diego, 1980-82; staff psychiatrist San Diego VA Med. Ctr., La Jolla, 1980-91; asst. prof. U. Calif., San Diego, 1982-89; assoc. prof. U. Calif., 1989-91, dir. psychoneuroendocrinology lab., 1990-91; acting assoc. chief psychiatry San Diego VA Med. Ctr., 1989-90; prof., vice chmn. dept. psychiatry Med. Coll. Ga., Augusta, 1991—; dir. lab. clin. neurosci. Augusta VA Med. ctr., 1991—; sci. cons. NIMH Study Sect. Contbr. articles to profl. jours. NIMH First award, 1987. Mem. AAAS, Am. Assn. Chairs Depts. Psychiatry, Nat. Alliance Mentally Ill, N.Y. Acad. Sci., Soc. Biol. Psychiatry, Psychiat. Rsch. Soc. Presbyterian. Office: Med Coll Ga Dept Psychiatry Health Behavior 1515 Pope Ave Augusta GA 30912-3800

RAUSCHER, ELIZABETH ANN, physics educator, researcher; b. Berkeley, Calif., Mar. 18, 1943; d. Philip Jenkins and Claire Elsa (Soderblom) Webster; m. Warren Carleton Rauscher, Oct. 5, 1962 (div. June 1965); 1 child, Brent Allen; m. William Lloyd Van Bise, Mar. 1, 1995. BS in Chemistry and Physics, U. Calif., Berkeley, 1962, MS in Nuclear Engring., 1964, PhD in Nuclear Sci., 1979. Staff rschr. Lawrence Berkeley Lab. U. Calif., 1963-79; staff rschr. Lawrence Livermore Nat. Lab., Livermore, Calif., 1966-69; prof., instr. U. Calif., 1971-74; instr., rschr. Stanford (Calif.) Linear Accelerator Ctr., 1971-72; rschr. SRI Internat., Menlo Park, Calif., 1974-76; dir. Tecnic Rsch. Labs., San Leandro, Calif., 1979—; v.p. Magtek Labs, Inc., Reno, 1988-94; prof. physics U. Nev., Stanford, 1990-96; cons. McDonnell-Douglass, L.A., 1978, 80, Learned Soc. Can., Montreal, 1981, USN, Silver Spring, Md., 1983, NASA, Martin-Marietta, New Orleans, 1988-89; adviser Engring. Inst., Provo, Utah, 1979. Patentee in field. Del. UN, N.Y.C., 1979, mem. UN com., 1989; adviser Congress Office Tech. Assessment, Washington, 1979-81; adviser, cons. City Coun., Reno, 1993. Recipient Outstanding Contbn. award Am. Astron. Soc., 1978, Honor award Rosebridge Grad. Sch., 1988; grantee USN, 1970-74, 82-83, PF Found., 1978, 79, 81; Delta Delta Delta scholar, 1960; Iota Sigma Pi Woman's fellow, 1961. Mem. IEEE, Am. Phys. Soc. (chair), Am. Chem. Soc. (v.p.), Lawrence Berkeley Lab. Fundametal Physics (chair, pres.), Psychology Rsch. Group San Franciso (bd. dirs., pres.). Address: 85 3rd St Ste 113 Ottawa IL 61350

RAUSHER, DAVID BENJAMIN, internist; b. Bklyn., Sept. 15, 1952; s. Herbet and Shirley Ruth R.; m. Judy A. Steinlaus, Aug. 8, 1976; children: Scott, Michael, Steven. BA, Hamilton Coll., 1973; MD, SUNY, Bklyn., 1977. Diplomate Am. Bd. Internal Medicine, Am. Bd. Gastroenterology. Resident Emory U. Hosp., Atlanta, 1977-80, fellow in gastroenerology, 1980-82; resident Atlanta Ctr. for Gastroenterology, Decatur, Ga., 1982—; resident, med. dir. Atlanta Endoscopy Ctr., Decatur, 1994—; chmn. diagnostic treatment ctr. De Kalb Med. Ctr., Decatur, Ga., 1985—, co-chief gastroenterology, 1995—. Office: Atlanta Ctr Gastro 2801 N Decatur Rd Decatur GA 30033

RAVICH, LAWRENCE, nursing home administrator, urologist; b. N.Y.C., Sept. 14, 1924; s. Samuel and Dorothy (Maran) R.; m. Sally Ann Miller, June 26, 1949; children: Peggy Ann, Steven Jay, George Mark. BS, CCNY, 1945; MB, MD, Chgo. Med. Sch., 1950; MPS in Health Care Adminstrn., L.I. U., 1979. Diplomate Am. Bd. Urology. Intern Morrisania Hosp., Bronx, N.Y., 1950-51; resident in urology Beth Israel Hosp., N.Y.C., 1951-54; pvt. practice, Bethpage, N.Y., 1956-90; co-exec. dir. St. James (N.Y.) Nursing Home, also bd. dirs.; asst. prof. clin. surgery (urology) SUNY, Stony Brook; pres. Ctrl. L.I. Med. Network, Inc., Plainview, N.Y., 1994-96; mem. Nassau County Bd. Health; mem. health care planning and policy com. Nassau-Suffolk Health Sys. Agy.; bd. dirs. Nassau PSRO, 1974-82; pres. med. staff Mid-Island Hosp., Bethpage, 1968-69, mem. med. bd., 1983-85, 87-90; mem. Nassau County coun. Health Sys. Agy., 1971-74; bd. dirs. Cmty. Health Plan Suffolk, 1981-83, Ctrl. Gen. Hosp., Inc., 1982-94; v.p., bd. dirs. United Med. Svc. (Blue Shield) N.Y., 1969-74; vice chmn., bd. dirs. Blue Cross & Blue Shield Greater N.Y., 1974-82; assoc. med. dir. PruCare N.Y., 1986-93; mem. N.Y. Gov.'s Health Care Adv. Bd., 1993-94; bd. dirs. Nat. Assn. Blue Shield and Blue Cross Plans, 1981-82. Chmn., mem. Oyster Bay (N.Y.) Planning Adv. Bd., 1970-74. With U.S.Army, 1945-46; capt. M.C., USAF, 1954-56. Fellow ACS, Internat. Coll. Surgeons, Nassau Acad. Medicine, N.Y. Acad. Medicine, Am. Geriatric Soc.; mem. AMA, Am. Urol. Assn. (vice chmn., mem. profl. rels. com.), Am. Urol. Assn. N.Y. Sect. (chmn. profl. rels. com.), Med. Soc. State N.Y. (chmn. hosp. and profl. rels. com. 1982-84, del. from N.Y. State Urol. Soc. to ho. of dels. 1980-87, pres. 2d dist. br. 1983-85), N.Y. State Urol. Soc. (pres. 1980-82), Nassau County Med. Soc. (pres. 1979-80), Am. Assn. Clin. Urologists, Nassau Surg. Soc., Pi Alpha Alpha. Office: St James Nursing Home 275 Moriches Rd Saint James NY 11780-2150

RAVICH, STEVEN JAY, orthopedic surgeon; b. N.Y.C., Mar. 16, 1954; s. Lawrence and Sally Ann R.; m. Rachel Solomon, Sept. 4, 1982; children: Danielle, Solomon. BS, Muhlenberg Coll., 1976; MD, Chgo. Med. Sch., 1981. Intern, resident orthopedics Maimonides Med. Ctr., Bklyn., 1981-86; pvt. practice Bklyn., 1986—; clin. instr. surgery Univ. Health Svcs. Downstate, Bklyn., 1986—. Fellow Am. Coll. Surgeons, Am. Coll. Orthopedic Surgeons. Office: 520 Franklin Ave Garden City NY 11530

RAVID, KATYA, medical educator; m. Shmuel Ravid; children: Yinon Arie, Noga Leah, Jonathan David. BSc, Technion-Israel Inst. Tech., Haifa, Israel, 1979, PhD, 1985. Postdoctoral fellow dept. biochemistry Brandeis Univ., Waltham, Mass., 1986-88; postdoctoral assoc. dept. biology Mass. Inst. Tech., Cambridge, 1988-91; instr. molecular medicine Harvard Medical Sch., Boston, 1992; asst. prof. biochemistry Boston Univ. Sch. Medicine, Boston, 1993-95, assoc. prof. biochemistry rsch. assoc. prof. medicine, 1993—, investigator Whitaker Cardiovascular Inst., 1993—, scientific dir. Core Transgenci facility, 1993—; peer reviewer Am. Heart Assn. 1995—. Contbr. articles to profl. jours. With Israeli Def. Forces, 1977-79. Recipient numerous rsch. grants. Mem. The Am. Soc. Hematology, Am. Soc. Cell Biology, Am. Soc. Biochemistry and Molecular Biology, Am. Assn. Advancement of Sci. Office: Boston Univ Sch Medicine Dept Biochemistry 80 East Concord St Boston MA 02118*

RAVITZ, LEONARD, JR., physician, scientist, consultant; b. Cuyahoga County, Ohio, Apr. 17; s. Leonard Robert and Esther Evelyn (Skerball) R. BS, Case Western Res. U., 1944; MD, Wayne State U., 1946; MS, Yale U., 1950. Diplomate Am. Bd. Psychiatry and Neurology, 1952; bd. cert. forensic examiner. Rsch. asst. EEG to A.J. Derbyshire, PhD Harper Hosp., Detroit, 1943-46; electromagnetic field measurement project office dep. asst. Sec. Defense in Charge of Health & Medical E.H. Cushing, 1958; spl. trainee in hypnosis to Milton H. Erickson MD Wayne County Gen. Hosp., Eloise, Mich., 1945-46, 46-80; rotating intern St. Elizabeth's Hosp., Washington, 1946-47; jr./sr. asst. resident in psychiatry Yale-New Haven Hosp.; asst. in psychiatry and mental hygiene Yale Med. Sch., 1947-48, assoc. in psychiatry and mental hygiene, 1948-49, rsch. fellow to Harold S. Burr, PhD, sect. neuro-anatomy, 1949-50, sr. resident in neuropsychiatry Richard S. Lyman svc., 1950-51; instr. Duke U. Med. Sch., Durham, 1950-51; assoc. to R. Burke Suitt, MD, Pvt. Diagnostic Clinic, Duke Hosp., Durham, 1951-53; assoc. Duke U. Med. Sch., 1951-53; vis. asst. prof. neuropsychiatry and asst. to vis. prof. Richard S. Lyman, MD, Meharry Med. Ctr., Nashville, 1953; asst. dir. profl. edn. in charge tng. U. Wyo. Nursing Sch. affiliates; chief rsch. rehab. bldg. Downey VA Hosp. (now called VA Hosp.), N. Chicago, Ill., 1953-54; assoc. psychiatry Sch. Medicine and Hosp., U. Pa., Phila., 1955-58; electromagnetic field measurement project office dep. asst. sec. def. in charge health & med. E.H. Cushing M.D. Dept. Def., Pentagon, 1958; dir. tng. and rsch. Ea. State Hosp., Williamsburg, Va., 1958-60; pvt. practice neuropsychiatry specializing in hypnosis Norfolk, Va., 1961—; psychiatrist, cons. Divsn. Alcohol Studies and Rehab. Va. Dept. Health (later Va. Dept. Mental Health and Mental Retardation), 1961-81; psychiatrist Greenpoint Clinic, Bklyn., 1983-87, 17th St. Clinic, N.Y.C., 1987-92, Downstate Mental Hygiene Assocs., Bklyn., 1983—; sec.-treas. Euclid-97th St. Clinic, Inc., Cleve., 1957-63, pres., 1963-69; spl. tng. in epistemology and methodologic foundations of sci. knowledge F.S.C. Northrop, PhD, 1973-92; electrodynamic field rschr. with Harold S. Burr, PhD, sect. neuro-anatomy Yale Med. Sch., 1948-73; cons. hypnosis with Milton H. Erickson, MD, 1945-80; clin. asst. prof. psychiatry SUNY Health Sci. Ctr. Med. Sch., 1983—; pvt. cons., Cleve., 1961-69, Upper Montclair, N.J., 1982—; lectr. sociology Old Dominion U., Norfolk, 1961-62, cons. nutrition rsch. project Old Dominion U. Rsch. Found., 1978-90; spl. med. cons. Frederick Mil. Acad., Portsmouth, Va., 1963-71; cons. Tidewater Epilepsy Found., Chesapeake, Va., 1962-68, USPH Hosp. Alcohol Unit, Norfolk, 1980-81, Nat. Inst. Rehab. Therapy, Butler, N.J., 1982-83; participant 5th Internat. Congress Hypnosis and Psychosomatic Medicine, Gutenburg U., Mainz, Germany, 1970; organizer symposia on hypnosis in psychiatry and medicine, field theory as office practice, history of certain forensic and psychotherapeutic aspects of the study of man, Eastern State Hosp., Coll. William and Mary, James City County Med. Soc., Va. Soc. Clin. Hypnosis, Williamsburg, Va., 1959-60; founding pres. Found. for Study Electrodynamic Theory of Life, 1989—. Asst. editor Jour. Am. Soc. Psychosomatic Dentistry and Medicine, 1980-83; mem. editorial bd. Internat. Jour. Psychosomatics, 1984—; contbr. sects. to books, articles, book revs., abstracts to profl. publs. Sr. v.p. Willoughby Civic League, 1971-75. 1st lt. AUS, 1943-46. Lyman Rsch. Fund grantee, 1950-53. Fellow AAAS, Am. Psychiat. Assn. (life), N.Y. Acad. Scis., Am.

Soc. Clin. Hypnosis (charter, cons. cert. program), Royal Soc. Health (London); mem. Va. Soc. Clin. Hypnosis (founding pres. 1959-60), Norfolk Acad. Medicine, Soc. for Investigation of Recurring Events, Va. Med. Soc., Sigma Xi, Nu Sigma Nu. Office: SUNY Health Sci Ctr Med Sch Dept Psychiatry 450 Clarkson Ave Box 1203 Brooklyn NY 11203-2012 also:x 9409 Norfolk VA 23505-0409

RAVITZ, S. PETER, plastic surgeon; b. N.Y.C., July 18, 1935; s. Harry and Grace (Ginsburg) R.; m. J. Gail Livingston, Mar. 2, 1963; children: Amy, Ashley, Alyson, Adrian. BA, Vanderbilt U., 1956, MD, 1960. Diplomate Am. Bd. Plastic Surgery. Intern Albany Med. Ctr. Hosp., 1960-61, resident, 1961-64, 64-66; chief plastic surgery Kessler Air Force Base Hosp., Biloxi, Miss., 1966-68; attending chief plastic surgery Mid-Inland Hosp., Bethpage, N.Y., 1968—, Huntington (N.Y.) Hosp., 1968—; assoc. attending North Shore Univ. Hosp., Syosset, N.Y., 1984—; mem. med. bd. Mid-Inland Hosp., 1990—. Capt. USAF, 1966-68. Fellow Am. Coll. Surgery; mem. AMA, Am. Soc. Plastic and Reconstructive Surgeons, N.Y. Regional Soc. Plastic Surgeons. Office: Plastic & Reconstructive Surgeons 8243 Jericho Tpke Woodbury NY 11797

RAVNIKAR, VERONIKA A., medical educator; b. Bklyn., Jan. 16, 1950; m. Dr. Leonard Sicilian; 3 children. AB in premedicine magna cum laude, Immaculata (Pa.) Coll., 1971; MD, SUNY Upstate, 1975. Diplomate Am. Bd. Ob-gyn. Resident in ob-gyn Prentice Women's Hosp. of Northwestern Med. Ctr., Chgo., 1975-79; fellow in reproductive endocrinology and infertility Brigham and Women's Hosp.-Harvard Med. Sch., Boston, 1979-81, obstetrician-gynecologist, 1981-89; asst. prof. ob-gyn, and reproductive biology Harvard Med. Sch., 1987-92, part-time lectr., 1992—; prof. U. Mass. Med. Ctr., 1992—, obstetrician-gynecologist, 1993—, dir. divsn. reproductive endocrine and infertility, 1992—; cons. in field. Mem. editl. bd. Women's Health Digest Med., 1994, Prevention Mag., 1994. Recipient rsch. paper award Dist. VI meeting, Milw., 1979, rsch. paper award Boston Obstetrical Soc., 1981; Bristol Myers grantee, NIH grantee; Grace La Gendre fellow Com. of Nat. Bus. and Profl. Women's Club in N.Y., 1973. Fellow Am. Coll. Obstetricians and Gynecologists; mem. Am. Fertility Soc., Soc. Reproductive Endocrinologists, The Endocrine Soc., Assn. Gynecologic Laparoscopists, Am. Heart Assn., North Am. Menopause Soc. (founding mem.), others. Home: 423 Commonwealth Ave Newton MA 02159*

RAWLINGS, SAMUEL CRAIG, psychologist; b. Wichita, Kans., Sept. 7, 1938; s. Roy Bird and Virginia (Kinsley) R.; children from a previous marriage Megan Malinda, Chainy Anne; m. Kathy J. Bowers, June 6, 1981; 1 child, Jamison Ryan. BS, Calif. State U., Fullerton, 1964; MS, U. Miami, 1968, PhD, 1970, postgrad., 1971. Rsch. asst./assoc. U. Miami, Coral Gables, Fla., 1966-71; sch. psychologist Dade County Pub. Schs., Miami, 1969-70; asst. prof. U. Houston, 1971-74; program dir. Nat. Eye Inst., NIH, Bethesda, Md., 1975-77; asst. prof., dir. rsch. dept. ophthalmology U. Tex. Health Sci. Ctr., San Antonio, 1977-80; sci. review adminstr. NIH, Bethesda, 1980-86, chief behavioral/neuro scis. rev. sect., 1986—; NIH rep. Fedn. of Behavior, Psychol. and Cognitive Scis., Washington, 1989—. Contbr. articles to profl. jours.; co-editor: Methodological Issues in Aging Research, 1985; chair editorial bd. NIH Peer Rev. Notes, 1992—. With U.S. Army, 1960-61. NSF sci. reviewer, 1970-78, Vision Rsch sci. reviewer, 1968-71; Nat. Soc. to Prevent Blindness grantee, 1979-80, Fight for Sight grantee, 1979-80. Home: 6536 Farmingdale Ct Rockville MD 20855-1505 Office: NIH Westwood Bldg Rm 310 Rockledge Bldg 2 Rm 5160 Bethesda MD 20892

RAWLINGS, SHANNON MARIE, nurse, naval officer; b. Vicksburg, Mich., June 27, 1969; d. Alfred Edward and Ruby Anna Smith; m. Brent Elgin Rawlings, Aug. 1, 1987. BSN, Mich. State U., 1995. Nurse, officer U.S. Navy, Great Lakes, Ill., 1993—. Mem. Sigma Theta Tau. Republican. Home: 2801 Brisbane Dr Lake In The Hills IL 60102 Office: Great Lakes Naval Hosp 5E Great Lakes IL 60088

RAWLINS, RICHARD GRAHAM, obstetrics, gynecology educator; b. Joliet, Ill., Jan. 15, 1950; s. Herbert Lee and Eleanore (Graham) R. BA, Northwestern U., Evanston, Ill., 1972; MA, Northwestern U., 1973; PhD, Mich. State U., 1984. Diplomate Am. Bd. Bioanalysis. Instr. Northwestern U., Evanston, Ill., 1975-76; scientist in charge Caribbean Primate Rsch. Ctr. U. P.R. Med. Sch., San Juan, 1976-82, instr. dept. anatomy, 1976-82; asst. to assoc. prof. dept. ob-gyn. Rush Med. Coll., Chgo., 1984-96, prof. dept. ob-gyn., 1996—, asst. prof. dept. anatomy, 1988—; assoc. scientist Rush-Presbyn.-St. Luke's Med. Ctr., Chgo., 1984-88, dir. in vitro fertilization labs., 1984—, assoc. scientist, 1988—; adj. prof. U. Ill. Biological Resources Lab., Chgo., 1988—. Author: The Cayo Santiago Macaques, 1986; inventor in field; contbr. articles to profl. jours. Fellow NSF; mem. Am. Soc. Primatologists (treas. 1984-90, pres.-elect 1990-92, pres. 1992-94), Internat. Primatological Soc. (treas. 1988-92), Am. Fertility Soc., Soc. for Study of Reproduction, Soc. for Assisted Reproduction, Sigma Xi (pres. 1990-92). Office: Dept Ob-Gyn Rush Presbyn St Lukes Med Ctr 1653 W Congress Pky Chicago IL 60612-3833

RAWNSLEY, HOWARD MELODY, physician, educator; b. Long Branch, N.J., Nov. 20, 1925; s. Walter A. and Elizabeth (Melody) R.; m. B. Eileen Fiddes, Sept. 5, 1967; children—Virgilia Ingram, Elizabeth Sue. A.B., Haverford Coll., 1949; M.D., U. Pa., 1952. Diplomate Am. Bd. Pathology (trustee 1988—). Intern Hosp. U. Pa., 1952-53, resident, 1953-57; practice medicine, specializing in pathology Phila., 1957-75; mem. Wm. Pepper Lab., U. Pa., 1957-75, asst. dir., 1960-68, dir., 1968-75; assoc. dir. Clin. Research Ctr., 1962-67, acting dir., 1969—70, asst. prof. pathology and medicine, 1960-65, assoc. prof., 1965-69, prof., 1969-75; prof. pathology Dartmouth Hitchcock Med. Ctr., Hanover, N.H., 1975-95, chmn. dept., 1980-87, sr. v.p. med. affairs, 1987-94, emeritus, 1995—; cons. VA Hosp. Served with AUS, 1944-46. Woodward fellow in chemistry, 1953-55. Mem. AMA, ARC (biomed. svcs. com. 1990-92), Pathology Soc. Phila. (pres.), Coll. Am. Pathologists (bd. govs. 1985-93), Am. Soc. Clin. Pathologists. Home: 7 Haskins Rd Hanover NH 03755-2204

RAWSON, ROBERT ORRIN, physiologist; b. East St. Louis, Apr. 25, 1917; s. Orrin Garfield and Mabel Estelle (Casteel) R.; m. Barbara Ellis, Nov. 19, 1966; children—David Garfield, Mary Ellen, Judith Ann. Student, Ill. State Normal U., 1935-37; B.S. in Psychology, U. Ill., 1940; Ph.D. in Physiology, Loyola U., 1961. Broadcaster radio and TV St. Louis and Chgo., 1941-56; instr. biology U. Ill., Chgo., 1956-58; instr. physiology Yale U. Sch. Medicine, 1961-68, asst. prof., 1968-75, sr. research asso., lectr., 1975-82; asst., then asso. fellow John B. Pierce Found. of Conn., New Haven, 1961-69, fellow, 1969-83, fellow emeritus, 1982. Contbr. articles to profl. jours. Mem. Inland Wetlands Commn., Guilford, Conn., 1980-86; mem. Mcpl. Preservation Bd., Guilford, 1980-86;sec. Madison Planning and Zoning Commn., 1987—. NIH grantee. Mem. Am. Physiol. Soc. Republican. Episcopalian. Home: 273 Legend Hill Rd Madison CT 06443-1864 Office: 290 Congress Ave New Haven CT 06519-1403

RAY, ALBERT, family physician; b. N.Y.C., Aug. 8, 1948; s. Herman and Stella (Meritz) R.; m. Cheryl Antecol, Oct. 8, 1977; children: Heather, Erin, Samantha. BA, Bklyn. Coll., 1969; MD, Catholic U. of Louvain, Belgium, 1976. Diplomate Am. Bd. Family Practice, Canadian Coll. Family Physicians. Intern Meml. U. of NFLD, Saint John's, Canada, 1976; resident McGill U., Montreal, Canada, 1978; family physician SCPMG, San Diego, 1978—; assoc. clin. prof. U. Calif., San Diego, 1978—; mem. cmty. faculty UCLA, USD, U. Calif., Davis, USC; mem. clerkship cmty. adv. bd. U. Calif., San Diego, 1995—; pres. profl. staff Kaiser Found. Hosp. Author: Lecons d'Histologie, 1973. Program chair adult edn. Cong. Beth Israel, 1995; mem. bd. dirs. Temple Emanuel, San Diego, 1990; expert reviewer Med. Bd. Calif., 1995; bd. dirs. Agy. for Jewish Edn. Fellow Am. Acad. Family Physicians; mem. Calif. Med. Assn., San Diego County Med. Soc. (mem. profl. conduct com. 1994), San Diego Acad. Family Physicians (pres.), Calif. Acad. Physicians (trustee found.). Office: Kaiser Permanente 4405 Vandever Ave San Diego CA 92120

RAY, ALBERT BARTOW, psychologist, psychotherapist, consultant, educator; b. Washington, July 2, 1946; s. Albert B. and Virginia Lee (Young) R.; m. Barbara McGarity, Oct. 8, 1994; 1 child, Albert Bartow II; stepchildren: Tripp Stripling, Holly Stripling, Lynn Stripling. BS in Psychology, U. Ga., 1969, MS, 1971, PhD, 1976. Lic. psychologist, Fla., Ga.; cert. addiction counselor. Rsch. asst. Animal Behavior Lab., U. Ga., Athens, 1968-69, equipment coordinator, 1969-70, teaching asst., 1970-71; rsch. asst. to the dir. Athens Unit, Ga. Retardation Ctr., 1970-75; neuroanatomy, neurophysiology and neurology instr. Emergency Med. Tech. Courses and guest instr. practical nursing Athens Area Vocat. Tech. Sch., 1973-75; instr. dept. psychology U. Ga., Athens, 1974; asst. prof. biol. psychology SUNY, Brockport, 1975-77; asst. and assoc. prof. psychology Ga. Southwestern Coll., Americus, 1977-81; staff Sumter Regional Hosp. dir., pres. Alcoholism Recovery Svcs., Inc., Americus, 1979-82; instr. Sumter County Driver Improvement Clinic, 1980-82; substance abuse/addiction and mental health counselor, cons. Peach County Hosp., Ft. Valley, Ga., 1981-82; program co-dir. Ithical Place, Treatment Ctr. for Chem. Dependence, Golcenrod, Fla., 1981-82; adj. counselor Pastoral Inst. of Americus, 1981-82; owner, dir. Horizons Unltd. Counseling and Enrichment Ctr., Americus, 1982—; adj. faculty, San Francisco Theol. Sem., 1983—; pvt. practice, Americus, 1984—; cons. psychologist, Internat. Hqr. of Habitat for Humanity, Americus, 1985—; co-owner Blackshear Psychiat. and Psychol. Svcs., Americus, 1986—; founder, prin. Excelsys Inc., Americus, 1993; co-owner Assocs. for Mental & Behavioral Health, Americus, 1996; co-owner Disability Assistance, Americus, 1996; lectr. in field; conductor workshops. Meritorious scholar, Dept. Psychology, SUNY, Brockport, 1975-76, 76-77. Mem. Ga. Psychol. Assn., Fla. Psychol. Assn., Sumter County Mental Health Assn. (dir. 1979-80, Cert. of Appreciation 1980), Ga. Citizens Council on Alcoholism (Cert. of Appreciation 1981), Ga. Addiction Counselors Assn. (bd. dirs., statewide chmn. cert. bd.), Nat. Assn. Alcoholism and Drug Abuse Counselors, Fla. Assn. Practicing Psychologists, So. Soc. for Philosophy and Psychology, Psi Chi (pres. 1969), Aircraft Owners and Pilots Assn., Mooney Aircraft and Pilots Assn. Contbr. articles to profl. jours.; presenter numerous papers profl. meetings, workshops, civic and community groups. Office: 902 Elmo St Americus GA 31709-3709

RAY, BARBARA ANN, psychologist; b. N.Y.C., Dec. 17, 1937; d. Frederick Goodrich and Marjorie (Lawrence) Street. BA, Barnard Coll., 1958; MA, Columbia U., 1959, PhD, 1966. Rsch. psychologist Mass. Gen. Hosp., Harvard Med. Sch., Boston, 1961-75, asst. prof., sr. scientist, pres. sci. sport, 1975-79; dir. staff devel. Mass. Dept. Mental Health, Boston, 1979-81; dir. spl. projects Advanced Health Inc., Irvine, Calif., 1981-84; rsch. psychologist Nat. Inst. on Drug Abuse, Rockville, Md., 1984-86; sr. policy analyst ADAMHA/OA, Rockville, 1986—, Health Svcs. Rsch. SAMHSA/OAS, Rockville, 1992—. Fellow Am. Psychol. Assn.

RAY, CHARLES JOSEPH, dentist; b. South Sioux City, Nebr., June 4, 1911; s. Charles Joseph and Katherine Frances (Bridgeford) R.; m. Cecilia Estelle Radlinger, Nov. 22, 1933; children: Carole, Margie, Kathy, Jeane, Rita, Charles, Chrystal. EE, S.D. Sch. of Mines, 1932; DDS, U. Minn., 1936; postgrad. Forsythe Dental Infirmary, Boston, 1936-37. Eastman Dental Dispensary, 1937-38. Pvt. practice dentistry, 1938—, with Ray Dental Group, Rapid City, S.D., 1953—; mem. S.D. Med. Adv. Bd., 1958-65, S.D. Dental Legis. Com., 1985—, chmn. 1985-86. Active USO, 1959, pres. Rapid City chpt. 1952-60; pres. S.D. Crippled Children's Assn. Mem. ADA (life), S.D. Dental Assn. (Gold Tooth award 1980, pres. 1964), Am. Prosthodontic Soc. (pres. 1980-81, exec. coun. 1981-82, life mem.), Fedn. Prosthodontic Orgn. (sec. 1976-80), Am. Assn. Hosp. Dentists, Am. Soc. Psychosomatic Dentistry and Medicine, Pierre-Fauchard Acad. (award 1980), Am. Acad. Periodontology, Acad. Internat. Dentistry and Medicine, Internat. Coll. Dentistry, Am. Acad. Practice Adminstrn., Am. Acad. Gen. Dentistry, Am. Acad. Dental Group Practice, Colo. Prosthodontic Soc., Rapid City Dental Soc., Black Hills Dist. Dental Soc., Dental Group Mgmt. Assn., Chgo. Dental Soc. (assoc.), Internat. Coll. Dentists, Rapid City C. of C., Omicron Kappa Upsilon. Roman Catholic. Clubs: International Cosmopolitan (pres. 1972), Rapid City Cosmopolitan (pres. 1962; Disting. Service award 1977), Sioux Land Study, KC, Elks. Home: 250 Timberline Ct Rapid City SD 57702-2708 Office: Ray Dental Group PO Box 9625 Rapid City SD 57709-9625

RAY, DAVID GILBERT, psychologist; b. Hazleton, Pa., Oct. 18, 1952; s. Eugene and Martha Lorraine (Gilbert) R.; m. Kathleen Ruth Meachum, Dec. 31, 1973 (div. Apr. 1990); children: David Jr., Jennifer, Anne; m. Virginia Maclay Madden. BS, Pa. State U., 1974, MEd, 1975. Cert. clin. mental health counselor. Counselor Juniata Valley MH/MR Partial Hospitalization Program, Lewistown, Pa., 1975-77; dir. Juniata Valley MH/MR Partial Hospitalization Program, Lewistown, 1977-81, Out-Patient Psychiat. Svc. of Lewistown (Pa.) Hosp., 1981-86; pvt. practice Lewistown, 1986—; cons. Hospice The Bridge Lewistown Hosp., 1981—. Mem. Am. Assn. Counseling Devel., Pa. Psychol. Assn. Republican. Lutheran. Home: 71 Shelly Dr Reedsville PA 17084-9749 Office: 43 Chestnut St Lewistown PA 17044-2202

RAY, GERALD LEON, medical student; b. Tomball, Tex., Dec. 19, 1950; s. James O. and Louise (Cotton) R. BSME, Lamar U., 1975; student, North Harris County Coll., Houston, 1988-90, U. North Tex. Health Sci. Ctr., 1991—. Power plant engr. Gulf States Utilities, Beaumont, Tex., 1977-80; sr. design engr. Wellhead divsn. FMC Corp., Houston, 1981-87, quality assurance mgr., 1987-89, contract engr., 1990-91; undergrad. tchg. fellow U. North Tex. Health Sci. Ctr., 1993—. Contbr. articles to profl. jours. Vol. Ctr. for Creative Living, Ft. Worth, 1995—. Mem. Am. Osteo. Assn., Am. Acad. Osteopathy, Am. Coll. Gen. Practitioners, Undergrad. Am. Acad. Osteopathy (pres. 1991-96), Tex. Osteo. Med. Assn. Home: 3636 Eldridge Fort Worth TX 76107

RAY, JAMES ALEXANDER, physician assistant; b. N.Y.C., Nov 9, 1942; m. Martha Annette Washington, July 16, 1977; children: Deborah, Sonja, Tanya, Cherise, Alexandria, Randy, Robert, Terry (dec.), James, Joseph. BS, U. Nebr., 1978. Cert. physician assistant NCCPA, Bd. Med. Examiners. Founding pastor True Love Baptist Ch., Fairfield, Calif., 1993—; pastor First Bapt. Ch., Dixon, Calif., 1990-93; asst. pastor Mt. Calvary Bapt. Ch., Suisin City, Calif., 1984-93; pres. Tri-City NAACP, Fairfield, 1990-92; mem. Ryan White AIDS Consortium, Fairfield, 1993. Served to capt. USAF, 1961-88. Decorated bronze star USAF, 1971, commendation medals, 1974, 83, meritorious svc. medal, 1988. Fellow Soc. Air Physician Assts., Am. Acad. Physician Assts., Calif. Acad. Physician Assts. Home: 1406 Prospect Way Suisun City CA 94585 Office: Northbay Healthcare 1900 Pennsylvania Ave Fairfield CA 94533

RAY, JOHN WALKER, otolaryngologist, educator, broadcast commentator; b. Columbus, Ohio, Jan. 12, 1936; s. Kenneth Clark and Hope (Walker) Ray; m. Susanne Gettings, July 15, 1961; children: Nancy Ann, Susan Christy. AB magna cum laude, Marietta Coll., 1956; MD cum laude, Ohio State U., 1960; postgrad. Temple U., 1964, Mt. Sinai Hosp. and Columbia U., 1964, 66, Northwestern U., 1967, 71, U. Ill., 1968, U. Ind., 1969, Tulane U., 1969. Intern, Ohio State U. Hosps., Columbus, 1960-61, clin. rsch. trainee NIH, 1963-65, resident dept. otolaryngology, 1963-65, 1966-67, resident dept. surgery 1965-66, instr. dept. otolaryngology, 1966-67, 70-75, clin. asst. prof., 1975-82, clin. assoc. prof., 1982-92, clin. prof., 1992—; active staff, past chief of staff Bethesda Hosp.; active staff, past chief of staff Good Samaritan Hosp., Zanesville, Ohio, 1967—; courtesy staff Ohio State U. Hosps., Columbus, 1970—; hon. active staff Meml. Hosp., Marietta, Ohio, 1992—; radio-TV health commentator, 1982—. Past pres. Muskingum chpt. Am. Cancer Soc.; trustee Ohio Med. Polit. Action Com.; bd. dirs. Zanesville Art Ctr. Capt. USAF, 1961-63. Recipient Barraquer Meml. award, 1965; named to Order of Ky. Col., 1966, Muskingum County Country Music Hall of Fame. Diplomate Am. Bd. Otolaryngology. Fellow ACS, Am. Soc. Otolaryn. Allergy, Am. Acad. Otolaryngology-Head and Neck Surgery (gov.), Am. Acad. Facial Plastic and Reconstructive Surgery; mem. Nat. Assn. Physician Broadcasters, Muskingum County Acad. Medicine (past pres.), AMA (del. hosp. med. Staff sect.), Ohio Med. Assn. (del.), Columbus Ophthalmol. and Otolaryngol. Soc. (past pres.), Ohio Soc. Otolaryngology (past pres.), Pan-Am. Assn. Otolaryngology and Bronchoesophagology, Pan-Am. Allergy Soc., Am. Acad. Invitro Allergy, Am. Auditory Soc., Am. Soc. Contemporary Medicine and Surgery, Acad. Radio and TV Health Communicators, Fraternal Order Police Assocs., Phi Beta Kappa, Alpha Tau Omega, Alpha Kappa Kappa, Alpha Omega Alpha, Beta Beta Beta. Presbyterian. Contbr. articles to sci., med. jours; collaborator with surg. motion picture: Laryngectomy and Neck Dissection, 1964. Office: 2945 Maple Ave Zanesville OH 43701-1733

RAY, ROBERT D., physician, educator; b. Cleve., Sept. 21, 1914; s. Clifford A. and Edna (Durant) R.; m. Genevieve Triau, Dec. 19, 1953; children—Frances Carol, Robert Triau, Esten Bernard, Gisele Antoinette, Charles Alexander. B.A. cum laude, U. Calif., 1936, M.A., 1938, Ph.D., 1948; M.D., Harvard U., 1943; Hon. H.D. (Docent), Umeö, Sweden. Diplomate Am. Bd. Surgery. Teaching asst. in anatomy U. Calif. Med. Sch., 1937-38, Carnegie research fellow, 1938-40, instr. anatomy, 1947-48; postgrad. tng. U. Calif. Hosp., San Francisco, 1949; intern Peter Bent Brigham Hosp., Boston, 1943; resident orthopaedic surgery Children's Hosp., Boston, 1944-45; asst. orthopaedic surgery Harvard U. Med. Sch., 1944-45; asst. prof. surgery, head orthopaedic surgery U. Wash. Sch. Medicine, 1948-51, asso. prof. surgery, 1954-56; prof., chmn. dept. orthopaedic surgery Presbyn.-St. Luke's Hosp., 1956-70; also U. Ill. Med. Sch., Chgo., 1956-85; ret., 1985; chief surgery 61st Sta. Hosp.; theatre cons. orthopaedic surgery MTOUSA, 1945-47. Contbr. articles to profl. publs. Recipient ann. award for outstanding orthopaedic research Kappa Delta, Chgo., 1954. Mem. Am. Orthopaedic Assn., Orthopaedic Research Soc., Soc. Nuclear Medicine, Internat. Assn. Orthopaedics and Traumatology, AAAS, Am. Assn. Anatomists, Am. Acad. Orthopaedic Surgery, A.C.S., Sigma Xi, Phi Sigma. Home: 2200 Laguna Vista Dr Novato CA 94945-1523

RAY, SUSANNE GETTINGS, counselor; b. Marietta, Ohio, July 20, 1937; d. Lewis B. and Reina Ashton Gettings; m. John W. Ray; children: Nancy Ann, Susan Christy. BS in Nursing, Case Western Res. U., 1960; MEd in Community Counseling, Ohio U., 1987. Staff nurse Cleve. Vis. Nurse Assn., 1960-61; sr. nurse Columbus (Ohio) Pub. Health Nursing Svc., 1962-64; founder, mgr. healthcare program Muskingum County (Ohio) Children's Svcs., 1972-76; spl. svcs. coord. Muskingum County Head Start, Zanesville, Ohio, 1979-85; clin. counselor Six County Mental Health Ctr., Zanesville, 1987-94; edn. coord. Safe/Response, Zanesville, 1995—. Stephen Min. Ch. Sch. tchr. Ctrl. Presbyn. Ch., elder, 1996—; founder, coord. SAFE; bd. dirs. Ohio Head Start Handicap Assn., Cmty. Against Rape Edn. and Svc., Eastside Cmty. Ministry, Grads. and Headstart Health Adv. Bd.; mem., legis. chair Ohio Coalition of Sexual Assualt. Recipient various profl. and community awards. Mem. Am. Counseling Assn., Ohio Counseling Assn., Sigma Theta Tau, Chi Sigma Iota. Office: Safe/Response 38 N 4th Rm 314 Zanesville OH 43701

RAY, TIMOTHY BRITT, social worker, lawyer, administrator; b. New Orleans, June 13, 1939; s. Archibald Cole and Eliza Owen (Britt) R.; m. Constance Helen Abbott, Nov. 27, 1964; children: Michael Gregory Owen, Mary Eliza Rebecca. BA, Davidson Coll., 1961; MA, La. State U., 1963; MSW, W. Va. U., 1968; JD, U. Santa Clara, 1976. Bar: Ohio 1981. Chief psychiatric social worker Alameda County, Oakland, Calif., 1974-77; exec. dir. Toledo Legal Aid Soc., 1977-82, Concept House Inc., Miami, 1982-83; counselor youth Fla. Health and Rehabilitative Svcs., Miami, 1983-84; exec. dir. Dist. III Mental Health Bd., Gainesville, Fla., 1984, Older Americans Coun., Gainesville, 1984-90; elderly housing mgr. Gainesville Housing Authority, 1990-92, med. social work supr. Olsten-Kimberly Quality Care, 1993-94; med. social worker Hospice of Marion County, Gainesville, 1994—; chmn. health care services adv. com. Upjohn Co., Gainesville, 1986. Contbr. articles in profl. jours. Chmn. United Way Exec. Dirs. Coun., Gainesville, 1985; appointee Dist. III Alcohol, Drug Abuse and Mental Health Planning Coun.; chmn. Adult and Elderly Svcs. Com., 1987-88; pres. Interagy. Coun., Gainesville, 1986; pres. bd. Bread of Mighty Food Bank, Inc., 1987-90; elder 1st Presbyn. Ch., Gainesville; bd. dirs. Alzheimers Assn., 1989-90, Cmty. with a Heart, Ocala, Fla., 1995; active Fla. Coun. on Aging, Gainesville Human Rels. Adv. Bd., 1989-91. Bd. govs. fellow, 1967. Mem. ABA, Acad. Cert. Social Workers, Nat. Assn. Social Workers, Gainesville Area C. of C., Phi Alpha Delta. Democrat. Presbyterian. Home: 3321 NW 45th Ave Gainesville FL 32605-1459

RAY, WAYNE ALLEN, epidemiologist; b. Yakima, Wash., July 2, 1949; s. Allen and Patsy (McKay) R.; m. Janine Elise Thorson, June 11, 1972; children: Lily Amelia, Lea Camille. BS, U. Washington, 1971; MS, Vanderbilt U., 1974, PhD, 1981. Research assoc. Vanderbilt U. Sch. Medicine, Nashville, 1974-75, research instr., 1975-78, research asst. prof., 1979-83, asst. prof., 1984-85, dir. div. pharmacoepidemiology, 1984—, assoc. prof., 1985-90, prof., 1991—. Contbr. articles to profl. jours. Recipient Burroughs Wellcome scholar in Pharmacoepidemiology Am. Coll. Preventive Medicine, 1984. Mem. Am. Statis. Assn., Assn. Computing Machinery, Computer Soc. of IEEE, Soc. Epidemiologic Research, Am. Pub. Health Assn., Phi Beta Kappa. Office: Vanderbilt Univ Sch Medicine Nashville TN 37232

RAY, WILLIAM JACKSON, psychologist; b. Birmingham, Ala., Sept. 3, 1945; s. Norman M. and Mary K. Agnew; m. Judith Mebane, Aug. 22, 1987; children from previous marriage: Adam, Lauren. BA, Eckerd Coll., 1967; MA, Vanderbilt U., 1969, PhD, 1971; Fellow in med. psychology, Langley Porter Neuropsychiat. Inst., U. Calif. Med. Center, San Francisco, 1971-72. Prof., dir. clin. psychology tng. program Pa. State U., 1972—, dir. clin. trng., 1991—. Author: (with R.M. Stern) Biofeedback, 1977, (with others) Evaluation of Clinical Biofeedback, 1979, (with R.M. Stern and C.M. Davis) Psychophysiological Recording, 1980, Methods Toward a Science of Behavior and Experience, 1981, 4th edit., 1992, (with E. Susman & L. Feajous) Emotion, Cognition, Health and Development in Children and Adolescents, 1992, (with L. Michelson) Handbook of Dissociation, 1996; series editor: Plenum Series in Behavioral Psychophysiology and Medicine. Recipient Nat. Media award Am. Psychol. Found., 1976, 78. Mem. AAAS, APA, APS, Soc. Psychophysiol. Rsch. Office: Dept Psychology Pa State U University Park PA 16802

RAYBECK, MICHAEL JOSEPH, surgeon; b. Danbury, Conn., Oct. 5, 1945; s. Michael Thomas and Edythe Caroline (Tomaino) R. BS, Mt. St. Mary's Coll., Emmitsburg, Md., 1967; MD, Tulane U., 1971. Diplomate Am. Bd. Surgery, Am. Bd. Quality Assurance Utilization Rev. Physicians. Intern in surgery St. Vincent's Hosp. and Med. Ctr., N.Y.C., 1971-72; resident in gen. and vascular surgery Ochsner Found. Hosp., New Orleans, 1974-78; ptnr. Burshan, Raybeck, MD, P.A., Pompano Beach, Fla., 1978-82, Lauderdale Surg. Group, P.A., Ft. Lauderdale, 1982—; med. adv. com. Dept. Profl. Regulation, State of Fla.; pres. med. staff Holy Cross Hosp., 1995, vice chmn. PHO. Bd. dirs. Am. Heart Assn., Ft. Lauderdale, 1988-91. Fellow ACS, Internat. Coll. Surgeons, Soc. Am. Gastrointestinal Endoscopic Surgeons; mem. Am. Soc. Colon-Rectal Surgeons. Republican. Roman Catholic. Office: Lauderdale Surg Group 4701 N Federal Hwy Fort Lauderdale FL 33308-4608

RAYBURN, CAROLE (MARY AIDA) ANN, psychologist, researcher, writer; b. Washington, Feb. 14, 1938; d. Carl Frederick and Mary Helen (Milkie) Miller; m. Ronald Allen Rayburn (dec. Apr. 1970). BA in Psychology, Am. U., 1961; MA in Clin. Psychology, George Washington U., 1965; PhD in Ednl. Psychology, Cath. U. Am., 1969; MDiv in Ministry, Andrews U., 1980. Lic. psychologist, Md., Mich. Psychometrician Columbian Prep. Sch., Washington, 1963; clin. psychologist Spring Grove State Hosp., Catonsville, Md., 1966-68; pvt. practice, 1969, 71—; staff clin. psychologist Instl. Care Svcs. Div. D.C. Children's Ctr., Laurel, Md., 1970-78; psychologist Md. Dept. Vocat. Rehab., 1973-74; psychometrician Montgomery County Pub. Schs., 1981-85; lectr. Strayer Coll., Washington, 1969-70; forensic psychology expert witness, 1973—; guest lectr. Andrews U., Berrien Springs, Mich., 1979, Hood Coll., Frederick, Md., 1986-88; instr. Johns Hopkins U., 1986, 88-89; adj. faculty Profl. Sch. Psychology Studies, San Diego, 1987; adj. asst. prof. Loyola Coll., 1987; cons. Julia Brown Montessori Schs., 1972, 78, 82—, VA Ctr., 1978, 91-93. Editor: (with M.J. Meadow) A Time to Weep and a Time to Sing, 1985; contbg. author: Montessori: Her Method and the Movement (What You Need to Know), 1973, Drugs, Alcohol and Women: A National Forum Source Book, 1975, The Other Side of the Couch: Faith of the Psychotherapist, 1981, Clinical Handbook of Pastoral Counseling, 1985, An Encyclopedic Dictionary of Pastoral Care and Counseling, 1990, Religion Personality and Mental Health, 1993; author copyrighted inventories Religious Occupational and Stress Questionnaire, 1986, Religion and Stress Questionnaire, 1986, Organizational Relationships Survey, 1987, Attitudes Toward Children Inventory, 1987, State-Trait Morality Inventory, 1987, Body Awareness and Sexual Intimacy Comfort Scale (Basics), 1993; cons. editor Profl. Psychology, 1980-83; assoc. editor Jour. Pastoral Counseling, 1985-90, guest editor, 1988; contbr. numerous articles to profl. jours. Recipient Svc. award Coun. for

Advancement Psychol. Professions and Scis., 1975, cert. D.C. Dept. Human Resources, 1975, 76, cert. recognition D.C. Psychol. Assn., 1976, 1985; AAUW rsch. grantee, 1983. Fellow APA (pres. divsn. psychology of religion 1995-96, psychology of women, clin. psychology, cons. psychology, psychotherapy, state assn. affairs, chair equal opportunity affirmative action divsn. clin. psychology 1980-82, mem. editl. bd. Jour. Child Clin. Psychology 1978-82, pres. clin psychology women's sect. 1984-86, program chair 1991-94, divsn. psychology women chair task force on women and religion 1980-81, divsn. psychology issues in grad. edn. and clin. tng. 1988—, pres. 1995-96), Am. Orthopsychiat. Assn., Md. Psychol. Assn. (editor newsletter 1975-76, chpt. recognition 1978, chair ins. com. 1981-83, pres. 1984-85, exec. adv. com. 1985—), Am. Assn. Applied & Preventive Psychology (sec. 1992-93, chair fellows com. 1992-93); mem. Assn. Practicing Psychologists Montgomery-Prince George's Counties (pres. 1986-88, editor newsletter 1990—), Balt Assn. Cons. Psychologists (pres. D.C. chpt. 1991-92), Psi Chi (hon.). Address: 1200 Morningside Dr Silver Spring MD 20904-3149

RAYMER, MARY ANNE, social worker, psychotherapist; b. Lincoln, Nebr., Sept. 4, 1954. BA, Doane Coll., 1976; MSW, Wayne State U., 1980. Outreach worker, cmty. organizer Sr. Citizen Outreach, Detroit, 1976-80; outpatient therapist North Ctrl. Mich. Mental Health Svcs., 1980-82; dir. Grand Traverse Area Hospice, Traverse City, Mich., 1982-87, Raymer Psychotherapy and Consultation, Acme, Mich., 1987—. Author: (with others) The Art of Grief, 1986, Federal Pediatric Manual of Hospice Care, 1989. Lifetime bd. dirs. Am. Cancer Soc., Traverse City, 1996—, No. Mich. Mental Health Corp., Traverse City, 1996—. Mem. NASW (del to del. assembly 1996—), Nat. Hospice Orgn. (social work chair 1996—, disting. lectr. series), Mi. Hospice Orgn. (pub. rels. chair 1993—), Nat. Assn. Social Workers Del. Assembly, Assn. for Death Edn. Counselling. Office: Raymer Psychotherapy and Consultation Svcs PO Box 105 Acme MI 49610

RAYMOND, DENINE SUE, critical care nurse, educator; b. Pincher Creek, Alta., Can., May 23, 1967; came to U.S., 1991; d. Albert Tyoshi Tatebe and Jean Miyeko Okutake Armstrong; m. Glenn Allen Raymon, Oct. 9, 1993. BN, U. Calgary, Alta., 1990. RN, Tex.; CCRN; cert. ACLS, BLS, TNCC. Staff nurse Meth. Hosp., Lubbock, Tex., 1992; staff nurse U. Tex. Med. Br., Galveston, 1991-92, 92-94, clin. educator, 1994—. Home: 5918 Maco Ave Galveston TX 77551 Office: U Tex Med Br 303 University Blvd Galveston TX 77555

RAYMOND, JOHN RICHARD, medical educator; b. Akron, Ohio, Aug. 31, 1956; s. John Francis and Patricia Arline (Redmond) R.; m. Kathryn Ann Boll; children: John Richard Jr., Krisanna Marie. BS, Ohio State U., 1978, MD, 1982. Resident Duke U., Durhan, N.C., 1986-87, assoc., 1988-89, asst. prof. medicine, 1989-93, assoc. prof. medicine, 1994-96; chief nephrology VA Med. Ctr., Durhan, N.C., 1991-96; prof. medicine Med. U. S.C., Charleston, 1996—. Recipient Henry Christian award AFCR, 1991, 95. Mem. AMA, AAAS, ACP, ASCI, Am. Soc. Nephrology, Am. Heart Assn., Nat. Kidney Found. Office: Med U SC Rm 829 CSB 171 Ashley Ave Charleston SC 29425

RAYNOR, RICHARD BENJAMIN, neurosurgeon, educator; b. N.Y.C., Aug. 16, 1928; s. Murray and Mildred (Pitt) R.; m. Barbara Golob; children: Geoffrey, Michele. BSME, U. Mich., 1950; MD, U. Vt., 1955. Diplomate Am. Bd. Neurol. Surgery. Intern Mt. Sinai, N.Y.C., 1955-56; residency Neurol. Inst. Presbyn. Hosp., N.Y.C., 1956-57, Nat. Hosp., London, 1957; residency neurosurgery Neurol. Inst. Presbyn. Hosp., 1958-62; assoc. in neurosurgery Coll. Physicians and Surgeons Columbia U., N.Y.C., 1965-77; clin. assoc. prof. NYU, N.Y.C., 1977-84, clin. prof., 1984—; pvt. practice neurosurgery, N.Y.C., 1965—. Consulting editor Spine; contbr. more than 40 articles to profl. jours., chpts. to books. Served as capt. U.S. Army, 1962-64. Fellow Am. Coll. Surgeons; mem. Cervical Spine Research Soc. (pres. 1986-87), Am. Assn. Neurol. Surgeons, Congress Neurol. Surgeons. Club: University (N.Y.C.). Office: 112 E 74th St New York NY 10021-3562

RAYPORT, MARK, neurological surgery educator; b. Kharkov, Ukraine, Sept. 6, 1922; came to U.S., 1940.; s. Gregory Abraham and Zinaida Moiseievna (Berman) R.; m. Shirley Martha Ferguson, Jan. 28, 1951; children: Stephen Gregory, Jeffrey Ferguson, Jennifer Susan. BA, Earlham Coll., 1943; MD CM, McGill U., Montreal, PQ, Can., 1948, PhD, 1958, diploma in Neurosurgery, 1958. Diplomate Nat. Bd. Med. Examiners, Am. Bd. Neurol. Surgery. Postdoctoral rsch. fellow U.S. Pub. Health Svc., 1955-58; spl. sr. post doctoral fellow interdisciplinary program NIMH, 1958-60; career scientist Health Rsch. Coun., N.Y.C., 1962-68; asst. prof. neurol. surgery Albert Einstein Coll. Medicine, N.Y.C., 1958-61, assoc. prof. neurol. surgery, asst. prof. physiology, 1961-68; from asst. visiting to visiting neurosurgeon Bronx Mcpl. Hosp. Ctr., N.Y.C., 1958-68; asst. chief of neurol. surgery Mt. Zion Hosp. and Med. Ctr., San Francisco, 1968-69; prof. neurol. surgery Med. Coll. Ohio, Toledo, 1969-93, prof. emeritus, 1993—, founding chmn. neurol. surgery, 1969-89; dir. neurosurgery Med. Coll. Ohio Hosps., Toledo, 1969-89; dir. neurosurgery svc. Mercy Hosp., Toledo, 1975-80; mem. planning and adv. coun. Ohio Devel. Disabilities, 1971-74; mem. med. adv. com. Bur. Children with Med. Handicaps, State of Ohio Dept. Health, 1977—, chmn. epilepsy standards subcom.; founding dir., neurosurgeon Epilepsy Comprehensive Program, Med. Coll. Ohio, 1971-93, dep. dir., 1993—. Editor: L.M. Davidoff Festschrift, 1968; pantentee isometric muscle biopsy clamp. Sr. asst. surgeon, USPHS, 1951-53. Recipient First Lamplighter award Epilepsy Ctr. Northwestern Ohio, 1980; named Neurosurgeon of Yr. Ohio State Neurol. Soc., 1987. Fellow ACS, Am. Electroencephalographic Soc.; mem. Am. Assn. Neurol. Surgeons, Am. Epilepsy Soc., Am. Soc. Biol. Psychiatry, Soc. for Neurosci., Applied Neurophysiology (editorial bd. 1975-86), N.Y. Acad. Sci., Neuropsychiat. Assn., Sigma Xi, Alpha Omega Alpha (founding pres. Delta chpt. Ohio 1974-80, 94-95). Office: Med Coll of Ohio 3000 Arlington Ave Toledo OH 43614-2595

RAYSON, GLENDON ENNES, internist, preventive medicine specialist, writer; b. Oak Park, Ill., Dec. 2, 1915; s. Ennes Charles and Beatrice Margaret (Rowland) R. AB, U. Rochester, 1939; MD, U. Ill., Chgo., 1948; MPH, Johns Hopkins U., 1965; MA, Northwestern U., 1965. Diplomate Am. Bd. Internal Medicine, Am. Bd. Preventive Medicine. Resident in internal medicine Presbyn.-St. Luke's Hosp., Chgo., 1953-56; physician-in-charge Contagious Disease Hosp., Chgo., 1956-58, asst. med. supt., 1958-64; rsch. assoc. Sch. Hygiene and Pub. Health Johns Hopkins U., Balt., 1966-71; internist Johns Hopkins Hosp., 1971-82, Columbia Free State Health Plan, Balt., 1984-91; pvt. practice Balt., 1984—; with Neurodiagnostics Assocs., 1990—; attending internist emergency rm. South Balt. Gen. Hosp., 1982-84; asst. prof. health sci. U. Ill., Chgo., 1958-64; fellow in gastroenterology and endocrinology Presbyn.-St. Luke's Hosp., 1956-58. Contbr. articles to med. jours., chpt. to book. Vol. physician, Vietnam, 1968, 71, 72, 73; mem. Citizens Amb. Program Delegation to Vietnam, 1993. Capt. M.C., USAF, 1951-53. Fellow Am. Coll. Preventive Medicine, Am Geriatrics Soc.; mem. AMA, Am. Pub. Health Assn. Home: 337 Poplar Point Rd Perryville MD 21903-1803 Office: 218 N Charles St Apt 1407 Baltimore MD 21201-4027

RAZAK, MOHAMAD, orthopaedic surgeon, educator; b. Johor, Malaysia, Nov. 16, 1953; s. Abdullah and Hamidah (Asari) R.; m. Rokiah Yahya; children: Faizal, Firdaus, Iman, Nurul Aimi. MD, Nat. U. Malaysia, 1979, MS in Orthop., 1985. House officer Ministry of Health, Kuala Lumpur, 1979-80; trainee lectr. UKM, Kuala Lumpur, 1980-85, lectr., 1985-91, head dept. orthop., 1993—, sr. orthop. cons., 1993—; registrar Southport Spinal Ctr., Eng., 1991-93. Editor Jour. of Sean Orthop. Assn., 1995. Fellow Western Pacific Orthop. Assn.; mem. Acad. Medicine, Malaysian Orthop. Assn. (sec. 1994-96). Home: 6B Kamsis Tun Dr Ismail, Kuala Lumpur 53200, Malaysia Office: UKM, Dept Orthopaedics, Kuala Lumpur 50300, Malaysia

REA, RUTH EMILY, retired military officer; b. Champaign, Ill., Dec. 30, 1949; d. Ike Davis and Eleanor Z. R. BSN, U. Md., 1972; MS, U. Colo., 1978; PhD, U. Tex. at Austin, 1987. Cert. emergency nurse, staff devel. and edn. nurse. Commd. 1st lt. U.S. Army, 1972, advanced through grades to col., 1993; nurse educator U.S. Army, Tacoma, 1990-95; ret.; health svcs. and edn. cons., 1995—. Co-author: Challenges in Emergency Nursing, 1992. Recipient Surgeon Gen.'s Silver medal, 1972, Phyllis J. Venhonick Rsch. award, 1988, Emergency Nurses Rsch. award, 1988. Mem. Emergency Nurses Assn. Home: 1616 63rd Ave NE Tacoma WA 98422-3642 Office: 1911 SU Campus SDr Ste 111 Federal Way WA 98023

REACH, REBECCA M., nursing educator, university dean. BSN, No. Ill. U., 1964; MSN in Cmty. Health Nursing, U. Evansville, 1978. RN, Ark. Cmty. health nurse Peoria (Ill.) City and County Health Dept., 1964-65, Jackson County Health Dept., Murphysboro, Ill., 1972-74; staff nurse Proctor Hosp., Peoria, 1965-66; charge nurse Herrin (Ill.) Hosp., 1966-72; DON, Franklin-Williamson Bi-County Health Dept., Johnston City, Ill., 1975-77, Egyptian Health Dept., Eldorado, Ill., 1977-79; coord. allied health related occupations John A. Logan Coll., Carterville, Ill., 1979-81; mem. faculty, chmn. nursing and health scis. dept. U. N.Mex., Gallup, 1981-86; prof. nursing, chmn. dept. Sinclair C.C., Dayton, Ohio, 1986-94; prof. nursing, chmn. dept. U. Ark., Little Rock, 1994—, also dean nursing; presenter in field; nurse specialist accreditation teams Am. Coun. Ind. Colls. and Schs., 1989—; coord. educator exch. visits to Russia, 1990, 92, 94; mem. new program site visit team Ohio Bd. Regents,1991, 93. Former mem. editl. bd. ADvancing Clin. Care (formerly AD Nurse); contbr. articles to nursing jours. Recipient cert. of appreciation Navajo C.C., 1982, excellence in writing award Am. Jour. Nursing and N.Mex. Nurses Assn., 1983, 84, 85; grantee FITNE, 1992. Mem. ANA, Nat. League for Nursing, Nat. Orgn. for Advancement ADN, Ark. Nurses Assn., Nursing Adminstrs. in Nursing Edn. Programs in Ark., Clin. Experience Planning and Coordinating Coun. (chnn.), Ark. for Nursing, Fuld Inst. Tech. in Nursing, Sigma Theta Tau. Office: Sinclair Comm Coll Dept of Nursing 444 W 3rd St Dayton OH 45402-1421*

READ, GEORGE WESLEY, pharmacology educator, researcher; b. Los Angeles, June 24, 1934; s. Earl George Read and Gertrude Louise (Mason) McNeil; m. Dorothy Leonie Davis, Aug. 22, 1954 (div. Nov. 1981); children: Gregory Cecil, Lani Louise (dec.), Bonnie Alice; m. Carol Ann Malfer, Aug. 2, 1986 (div. Sept. 1991). AA, Menlo Coll., 1956; BA in Biology, Stanford U., 1959, MS in Physiology, 1962; PhD in Pharmacology, U. Hawaii, 1969. Instr., U. Hawaii, Hilo, 1963-64, asst. prof., Honolulu, 1969-74, assoc. prof. dept. pharmacology, 1974-86, prof., 1986—; vis. pharmacologist U. Tex. Med. Sch., Dallas, 1975, 83, U. Wash., Seattle, 1976, St. Louis U., 1983; vis. scientist NIH, Research Triangle Park, N.C., 1978, Inst. Med. Exp., Rome, 1990. Patentee in field. Stanford U. scholar, 1960-61; research grantee NIH, Heart Assn., Lung Assn. Mem. state task force substance abuse, 1994-95, Gov. Commn. Drug Abuse, 1992—. Mem. AAUP, Am. Soc. Pharmacology and Exptl. Therapeutics, Western Pharmacology Soc. Office: Pharmacology Dept John A Burns Sch Medicine Honolulu HI 96822

READ, VIRGINIA HALL, biochemistry educator; b. Louisville, Miss., Oct. 15, 1937; d. Angus R. and Hassie (Bowie) Hall; m. Dale Gilbert Read Sr., Mar. 5, 1960; children: Laura Read Sprabery, Dale Gilbert Jr., Eva Read Warden. BS, U. Miss., 1959; MS, U. Miss., Jackson, 1962, PhD, 1964. Instr. biochemistry U. Miss., Jackson, 1965-66, asst. prof. biochemistry, 1966-68, 70-74, assoc. prof. biochemistry, 1974—, assoc prof. pathology, 1979—; asst. prof. medicine U. Ala., Birmingham, 1968-70. Contbr. articles to Jour. Clin. Investigation, Jour. Clin. Endocrinology and Metabolism, Nature, Biochem. Pharmacology. Grantee U.S. Pub. Health Svc., 1960-62, fellow, 1966-70. Mem. Am. Assn. Clin. Chmeistry, Acad. Clin. Biochemistry, Endocrine Soc., Sigma Xi. United Methodist. Home: 311 Hand Dr Brandon MS 39042-8309

READER, GEORGE GORDON, physician, educator; b. Bklyn., Feb. 8, 1919; s. Houston Parker and Marion J. (Payne) R.; m. Helen C. Brown, May 23, 1942; children: Jonathan, David, Mark, Peter. BA, Cornell U., 1940, MD, 1943; DSc (hon.), Drew U., 1988. Diplomate Am. Bd. Internal Medicine. Intern N.Y. Hosp., N.Y.C., 1944; resident N.Y. Hosp., 1947-49, attending physician, 1962-92; hon. staff, 1992—; dir. comprehensive care and teaching program N.Y. Hosp., 1952-66, chief med. clinic, 1952-72; practice medicine specializing in internal medicine N.Y.C., 1949-93; chief div. ambulatory and community medicine N.Y. Hosp.-Cornell Med. Center, N.Y.C., 1969-72; prof. medicine Cornell U. Med. Coll., 1957-89, Livingston Farrand prof. pub. health, 1972-89, prof. emeritus pub. health and medicine, 1989—, chmn. dept. pub. health, 1972-92; chmn. human ecology study sect. NIH, 1961-65; chmn. med. adv. com. Vis. Nurse Svc., N.Y., 1963—; mem. med. control bd. Health Ins. Plan Greater N.Y., 1964—; mem. Gov.'s Health Adv. Coun., N.Y., 1974-79. Author: (with R. Merton, P. Kendall) The Student Physician, 1957, (with Goss) Comprehensive Medical Care and Teaching, 1967, (with Goodrich and Olendzki) Welfare Medical Care: An Experiment, 1969; mem. editorial bd. Medical Care, 1969-70, Jour. Med. Edn, 1975-79; editor-in-chief Milbank Meml. Fund Quar.: Health and Society, 1972-76. Bd. dirs. N.Y.C. Vis. Nurse Svc., The Osborn Retirement Community, Health Ins. Plan Greater N.Y., 1983-93, Helen Keller Internat.; trustee Cornell U., 1982-87. Lt. USNR, 1944-46, PTO. Fellow ACP, APHA (governing coun. 1968-69), AAAS, Am. Coll. Preventive Medicine; mem. AMA, N.Y. Acad. Medicine (chmn. com. med. edn. 1968-71, v.p. 1978-80), Am. Sociol. Assn., Harvey Soc., Internat. Sociol. Assn., Internat. Epidemiol. Assn., N.Y.C. Pub. Health Assn. (pres. 1956), Inst. Medicine Nat. Acad. Scis. (sr. mem.), Sigma Xi, Alpha Omega Alpha. Home: 155 Stuyvesant Ave Rye NY 10580-3112

READER, SYDNEY RALPH, health science association administrator, director; b. Brisbane, Queensland, Australia, June 6, 1918; s. Sydney Robert and Nellie Vera (Magub) R.; m. Hazel Jean Scanlan; children: Brian, Caroline, Jeremy. B in Medicine and Surgery, U. Sydney, 1941; PhD, U. Oxford, Eng., 1951. Marian Clare Reddall rsch. scholar U. Sydney, 1946-48; Nuffield Dominions fellow U. Oxford, 1948-51; hon. physician Royal Prince Alfred Hosp., Sydney, 1951-61; med. dir., dir. Nat. Heart Found., Australia, 1961-80, ret., 1980; pvt. practice cons., 1951-61; chmn. liaison com. on mild hypertension WHO, 1975-80. Author: National Heart Foundation and Heart Disease in Australia, 1996. Mem. coun., pres. Friends of Canberra (A.C.T., Australia) Sch. Music, 1980-83. Fellow Royal Coll. Physicians London, Royal Australasian Coll. Physicians, Internat. Soc. Hypertension (emeritus); mem. Cardiac Soc. Australia and New Zealand (life, Ralph Reader Young Investigator award). Home: PO Box 4513, 36/15 Howitt St, Kingston Canberra ACT 2604, Australia

REAGAN, JANET THOMPSON, psychologist, educator; b. Monticello, Ken., Sept. 15, 1945; d. Virgil Joe and Carrie Mae (Alexander) Thompson; m. Robert Barry Reagan, Jr., Aug. 7, 1977; children: Natalia Alexandria, Robert Barry. B.A. in Psychology, Berea Coll., 1967; Ph.D. in Psychology, Vanderbilt U., 1972. Mgr. research and eval. Nashville Mental Health Center, 1971-72; mgr. eval. Family Health Found., New Orleans, 1973-74; asst. prof. dept. health systems mgmt. Tulane U., New Orleans, 1974-77; dir. eval. Project Heavy West, Los Angeles, 1977-78; asst. prof. health adminstrn. Calif. State U.-Northridge, 1978-83, assoc. prof., director health adminstrn., 1983-87, prof., dir. health adminstrn., 1987—; cons. in field. Mem. Am. Pub. Health Assn., Am. Coll. Health Care Adminstrn., Assn. Health Svcs. Rsch., Am. Coll. Health Care Execs. (com. on higher edn. 1987, chmn. 1991), Assn. Univ. Programs in Health Adminstrn. (task force on undergrad. edn. 1985-90, chmn. 1988-90, mem. bd. dirs. 1995), Psi Chi, Phi Kappa Phi. Mem. editorial adv. bd. Jour. of Long Term Care Adminstrn.; contbr. to books, articles to profl. jours., papers to profl. assns. Home: 9354 Encino Ave Northridge CA 91325-2414 Office: Calif State U Dept Health Sci Northridge CA 91330

REALE, VINCENT FRANCIS, plastic surgeon; b. New Brunswick, N.J., Apr. 24, 1942; s. Nicholas Paul and Ann (Saladino) R.; m. Nancy Jane Fisher, Nov. 1, 1969; children: Stephen, William, David. AB, Princeton U., 1963; MD, Harvard U., 1968. Diplomate Am. Bd. Surgery, Am. Bd. Plastic Surgery. Intern Johns Hopkins Hosp., Balt., 1968-69, resident in surgery, 1969-70; resident in surgery Harvard Affiliated Hosp., Boston, 1972-76; resident in plastic surgery U. Rochester, N.Y., 1976-78; pvt. practice Rochester, 1978—; plastic surgeon Genesee Hsop., Rochester, 1978—, chief divsn. plastic surgery, 1988—; assoc. clin. prof. plastic surgery U. Rochester, 1991—, pres. med. staff, 1989—; med. adv. bd. Rochester Blue Cross/Blue Shield, 1982-93, pres., 1991-93; mem. Blue choice HMO, 1993-96. Maj. U.S. Army, 1970-72. Fellow ACS; mem. Am. Soc. Plastic Surgeons, Am. Assn. Hand Surgery. Office: 220 Alexander St #511 Rochester NY 14607

REAM, SHERYL STANFORD, internist, pediatrician; b. St. Louis, Aug. 1, 1960; d. Don Lowell and Janet Irma (Waser) Stanford; m. Robert S. Ream, June 27, 1992; children: Stephen, Matthew. BA in Chemistry, St. Louis U., 1982, MD, 1986. Diplomate Am. Bd. Internal Medicine, Am. Bd. Pediatrics. Intern, resident St. Louis U. Hosps., 1986-90, instr., 1990-91; pvt. practice Brandywine Med. Assocs., Kennett Square, Pa., 1991-94; chief of staff Group Health Plan, Arnold, Mo., 1994—. Mem. ACP, Am. Acad. of Pediatrics. Office: Group Health Plan 2132 Tenbrook Arnold MO 63010

REAMAN, GREGORY HAROLD, pediatric hematologist, oncologist; b. Akron, Ohio, Sept. 9, 1947; s. Harold J. and Margaret U. (D'Alfonso) R.; m. Susan J. Pristo, Sept. 7, 1974; children: Emily Margaret, Sarah Elizabeth. BS in Biology, U. Detroit, 1969; MD, Loyola U., Chgo., 1973. Diplomate Nat. Bd. Med. Examiners, Am. Bd. Pediatrics. Pediatric intern Loyola U. Med. Ctr., 1973-74; resident in pediatrics Montreal Children's Hosp., McGill U., 1974-76; clin. assoc. pediatric oncology br. Nat. Cancer Inst., NIH, Bethesda, Md., 1976-78, investigator pediatric oncology br., 1978-79; assoc. dept. hematology/oncology, attending physician Children's Nat. Med. Ctr., Washington, 1979-87, chmn. dept. hematology/oncology, 1987—; asst. prof. pediatrics Sch. Medicine and Health Scis., George Washington U., 1979-82, assoc. prof. pediatrics, 1982-87, prof. pediatrics, 1987—; mem. immunology devices panel FDA; assoc. chmn. Children's Cancer Group; bd. dirs., mem. med. affairs com., chmn., strategic planning com. Children's Oncology Scs. of Met. Washington. Mem. editorial bd. Cancer Physicians Data Query, Nat. Cancer Inst.; reviewer Cancer Treatment Resports, Blood, Jour. Clin. Oncology; contbr. articles to profl. publs. Trustee Nat. Childhood Cancer Found., Arcadia, Calif.; bd. dirs. Am. Cancer Soc., Atlanta; trustee, chmn. patient care and profl. edn. coms. Leukemia Soc. Am. Lt. comdr. USPHS, 1976-79, Res., 1979—. Folger Summer scholar Am. Cancer Soc.; recipient Spl. Fellowship Rsch. award Leukemia Soc. Am., 1980-82; grantee DHHS, Nat. Cancer Inst., 1987—. Mem. Soc. Pediatric Rsch., Am. Fedn. Clin. Rsch., Am. Soc. Clin. Oncology, Am. Assn. Cancer Rsch., Am. Soc. Pediatric Hematology/Oncology, Children's Cancer Group, Washington Blood Club, Alpha Omega Alpha. Democrat. Roman Catholic. Home: 7306 Brennon Ln Chevy Chase MD 20815-4064 Office: Children's Nat Med Ctr 111 Michigan Ave NW Washington DC 20010-2970

REARDEN, CAROLE ANN, clinical pathologist, educator; b. Belleville, Ont., Can., June 11, 1946; d. Joseph Brady and Honora Patricia (O'Halloran) R. BSc, McGill U., 1969, MSc, MDCM, 1971. Diplomate Am. Bd. Pathology, Am. Bd. Immunohematology and Blood Banking. Resident and fellow Children's Meml. Hosp., Chgo., 1971-73; resident in pediatrics U. Calif., San Diego, 1974, resident then fellow, 1975-79, asst. prof. pathology, 1979-86, dir. histocompatibility and immunogenetics lab., 1979-94, assoc. prof., 1986-92, prof., 1992—, head divsn. lab. medicine, 1989-94; dir. med. ctr. U. Calif. Thornton Hosp. Clin. Labs., San Diego, 1993—; prin. investigator devel. monoclonal antibodies to erythroid antigens, recombinant autoantigens; dir. lab. exam. com. Am. Bd. Histocompatibility and Immunogenetics. Contbr. articles to profl. jours. Mem. Mayor's Task Force on AIDS, San Diego, 1983. Recipient Young Investigator Rsch. award NIH, 1979; grantee U. Calif. Cancer Rsch. Coordinating Com., 1982, NIH, 1983. Mem. Am. Soc. Investigative Pathology, Acad. Clin. Lab. Physicians and Scientists, Am. Soc. Hematology, Am. Assn. Blood Banks (com. organ transplantation and tissue typing 1982-87), Am. Soc. Histocompatibility and Immunogenetics. Office: U Calif San Diego Dept Pathology 0612 9500 Gilman Dr La Jolla CA 92093-5003

REAVES, CHARLES EDWIN, dermatologist; b. Gulfport, Miss., July 16, 1942; s. Thomas Boyd and Jessie Adair (Roberts) R.; m. Sandra Joyce Carter, July 5, 1965 (div. 1983); children: Valerie C., Charles E. Jr.; m. Ruth Ann Pruett, Sept. 24, 1983; 1 child, Thomas Hall. BS in Chemistry and Medicine, U. Miss., 1964; MD, U. Miss., Jackson, 1967; cert. in laser surgery, U. Cin., 1982. Diplomate Am. Bd. Dermatology, Am. Bd. Dermatopathology. Intern USAF Med. Ctr., Biloxi, Miss., 1967-69; resident in dermatology USAF Med. Ctr., San Antonio, 1971-74; commd. lt. col. USAF, 1967; chief outpatient svc., dir. laboratories USAF, Moron AFB, Spain, 1968-69; chief profl. svcs., interim hosp. comdr. Zweibrucken AFB, Fed. Republic of Germany, 1969-71; chief dermatology and medicine USAF Regional Hosp., Riverside, Calif., 1974-76; pvt. practice Pine Bluff, Ark., 1976-78, Galesburg, Ill., 1978-87, Charlotte, N.C., 1987—; asst. clin. prof. U. Ark. Sch. Med., Little Rock, 1976-78, U. Ill. Sch. Med., Peoria, 1978-86, U. N.C. Sch. Med., Charlotte, 1987—; chmn. dept. medicine St. Mary's Hosp., Galesburg, 1986-87, v.p., pres.-elect. med. staff, Cottage Hosp., Galesburg, 1986-87; cons. Charlotte Meml. Med. Ctr.; staff Charlotte Meml. Hosp., Presbyn. Hosp., Mercy Hosp. Contbr. articles to profl. jours. bd. dirs. Am. Cancer Soc., chmn. profl. edn., med. cons. Mecklenburg County chpt. prog. Named Outstanding Med. Intern, Keesler AFB Med. Ctr., 1968. Fellow Am. Soc. Dermatopathology, Am. Acad. Dermatology (govt. liason, consumer affairs com., continuing edn. com.); mem. AMA, ACP, Am. Acad. Cosmetic Surgery, Am. Soc. for Dermatologic Surgery, Am. Venereal Disease Assn., Ill. Dermatological Soc., N.C. State Dermatological Soc. (v.p., pres.-elect 1996), North Am. Soc. Phlebology, So. Med. Assn., Ark. Med. Soc., N.C. State Med. Soc., Mecklenburg County Med. Soc., Charlotte Dermatological Soc. Republican. Office: 435 N Wendover Rd Charlotte NC 28211

REAVES, TROY ALBERT, JR., pharmaceutical executive; b. Ft. Worth, Aug. 7, 1945; s. Troy Albert and Emalyn (Sumner) R.; m. Antha Ruth May, June 2, 1984. BS, West Tex. State U., 1969; MS, North Tex. State U., 1971; PhD, U. Ill., 1976. Asst. prof. dept. neurology U. N.C., Chapel Hill, 1976-82; ptnr. WCC Inc., Ft. Worth, 1982-84; mgr. clin. rsch. Alcon Labs. Inc., Ft. Worth, 1984-89; dir. clin. and regulatory affairs Xenon Vision Inc., Alachua, Fla., 1989-91; dir. clin. rsch. Ciba Vision Ophthalmics, Atlanta, 1991—. Contbr. 50 articles to profl. jours. NIH postdoctoral fellow, 1976; Rsch. grantee N.C. Heart Assn., 1977, SBIR-Nat. Eye Inst., 1990. Mem. Am. Acad. Ophthalmology, Assn. for Rsch. in Vision and Ophthalmology, Assocs. Clin. Pharmacology, Drug Info. Assn., Regulatory Affairs Profl. Soc. Office: Ciba Vision Ophthalmics 11460 Johns Creek Pky Duluth GA 30136-1518

REBIK, JAMES MICHAEL, otolaryngologist; b. Marshalltown, Iowa, July 10, 1953; s. Hubert James and Donna Jean (Grandgeorge) R.; m. Sue Ellyn Primmer, Dec. 22, 1979; children: Christopher James, Kristin Leigh, Robert James, Jonathan Michael. BA summa cum laude, U. No. Iowa, 1981; DO, Kirksville Coll. Osteo. Med., 1985. Diplomate in otorhinolaryngology and facial plastic surgery Am. Osteo. Bd. Ophthalmology and Otorhinolaryngology; diplomate Nat. Bd. Med. Examiners for Osteo. Physicians and Surgeons; lic. physician, Mo., Iowa, Minn., Tex. Intern Kirksville (Mo.) Osteo Med. Ctr., 1985-86, resident otorhinolaryngology/oro-facial plastic surgery, 1986-90; otolaryngologist Landstuhl (Germany) Army Regional Med. Ctr., 1990-92; chief otolaryngology-head and neck surgery svc. Reynolds Army Community Hosp., Ft. Sill, Okla., 1992-94; with Primary Med. Clinic, Midland, Tex., 1996—. Maj. M.C. U.S. Army, 1990-94. Recipient 1st degree brown belt Gup U.S. Tang Soo Do Moo Duk Kwan Fedn., 1979. Fellow Soc. Mil. Otolaryngologists; mem. AMA, Am. Osteo. Assn., Am. Coll. Ophthalmology and Otolaryngology-Head and Neck Surgery, Assn. Mil. Surgeons U.S., Am. Acad. Otolaryngic Allergy, Am. Acad. Otolaryngology-Head and Neck Surgery, Christian Soc. Otolaryngology-Head and Neck Surgery, Freeborn County Med Soc., Minn. Med. Assn., Pan-Am. Assn. Otorhinolaryngology-Head and Neck Surgery, Tex. Osteo. Med. Assn., Tex. Med. Found., Mensa. Baptist. Home: 7005 Chadwick Ct Midland TX 79707 Office: Ste 100 4214 Andrews Hwy Midland TX 79703

REBORA, ALFREDO ENRICO, dermatology educator; b. Genoa, Italy, Dec. 15, 1935; s. Pietro and Maria (Repetto) R.; m. Paola Staricco, May 29, 1965; 1 child, Valentina. MD, U. Genoa, 1959. Resident in dermatology U. Genoa, 1959-61, asst. ordinario dept. dermatology, 1962-80, prof. dermatology, chmn. dept., 1980—; fellow dept. dermatology Pa. U., 1971-72. Contbr. over 350 articles to profl. publs. Recipient Hans Schwarzkopf Forschungspreis, 1971. Mem. Soc. Italiana Dermatologia e Venereologia, Am. Acad. Dermatology, N.Y. Acad. Scis., German-Italian Soc. Dermatology, Italian Soc. Tropical Dermatology, German Dermatologische Gesellschaft (hon.). Office: U Genoa Dept Dermatology, Viale Benedettoxv 7, Genoa Italy

RECHSTEINER, CHARLES WILLIAM, II, school psychologist; b. Danville, Pa., Feb. 28, 1954; s. Charles William and Doris Elizabeth (Kleymeyer) R. BA in Interdisciplinary Studies, U. N.C., Chapel Hill, 1976; MS in Sch. Psychology, Bucknell U., Lewisburg, Pa., 1978; postgrad., Lehigh U., Bethlehem, Pa., 1981-84. Cert. sch. psychologist, Pa., Md., Del., Calif.

Intern Cen. Susquehanna Intermediate Unit, Lewisburg, 1976-78; sch. psychologist Kent County Pub. Schs., Chestertown, Md., 1979-81, Sch. Dist. of City of Allentown (Pa.), 1981-85, Indian River Sch. Dist., Millsboro, Del., 1985—; co-chair eligibility criteria com. for mental disabilities Del. Dept. Pub. Instrn., Dover, 1989-91. Grantee U.S. Dept. Edn., Washington, 1984, Allentown Sch. Dist., 1984. Mem. Nat. Assn. Sch. Psychologists (cert.), Del. Assn. Sch. Psychologists, Coun. Exceptional Children (presenter state conv. 1992), Sussex Assn. Sch. Psychologists (pres. 1989-90, 94-95). Democrat. Home: 1442B Ocean Pnes Berlin MD 21811-7113 Office: Lord Baltimore Elem Sch Bethany Beach DE 19975

RECHTINE, GLENN ROY, orthopaedic surgeon; b. Germany, Jan. 3, 1952; s. Glenn and Roberta Rechtine; m. Brenda Rechtine (dec.); m. Joann Crogan, May 11, 1991. BA, U. S. Fla., 1973, MD, 1975. Diplomate Am. Bd. Orthop. Surgery; lic. Calif., Fla. Intern U.S. Navy, San Diego, 1975-76; gen. med. officer U.S. Navy, USS Hunley, 1976-77; resident U.S. Navy, Portsmouth, Va., 1977-80; fellow spine surgery Case Western Reserve U., Cleve., 1980-81, instr., 1980-81; staff orthop. svc. Naval Regional Med. Ctr., Portsmouth, Va., 1981-83; chief orthop. svc. VA Ctr., Cleve., 1983-85; asst. prof. dept. orthop. U. S. Fla., Tampa, 1984-86, asst. prof. dept. surgery, divsn. neurosurgery, assoc. prof. dept. orthop., 1986-89, assoc. prof. dept. surgery, divsn. neurosurgery, 1986-89, clin. assoc. prof. dept. surgery, divsn. orthop., 1989-94, clin. assoc. prof. dept. surgery, divsn. neurosurgery, 1989—; owner, physician Fla. Orthop. Inst., Tampa, 1989—; chmn. spinal cord injury com. Tampa Gen. Hosp., 1986—; mem. brain and spinal cord injury adv. coun., State of Fla., 1994—; mem. edtl. bd. Spine Rehab.; edtl. adv. bd. Spine. Contbr. 40 articles to profl. publs., 4 chpts to med. texts; author of over 160 presentations for sci. workshops, confs., seminars, co-author more than 30. Bd. dirs. Tampa YMCA, 1993—. Fellow Am. Acad. Orthop. Surgeons, Am. Coll. Surgeons, Scoliosis Rsch. Soc. (cand.); mem. AMA, Am. Orthop. Soc., Am. Spinal Injury Assn., Cervical Spine Rsch. Soc., Groupe Internat. CD, Fla. Med. Assn., Hillsborough County Med. Assn., N. Am. Spine Soc., Orthop. Rehab. Assn., So. Med. Assn. So. Orthop. Assn., SICOT., Va. Orthop. Soc. (hon. mem.). Office: Fla Orthop Inst 4175 E Fowler Ave Tampa FL 33617

RECK, DONNA LOUISE, nursing administrator; b. Bklyn., Jan. 22, 1959; d. Joseph Leonard and Virginia Louise (Peck) Hart; m. William George Reck June 25, 1988. BSN, Trenton State Coll., 1981; MSN, Univ. Pa., 1985. RN, CRNP, Pa.; CNA, ANCC. Staff nurse in renal transplant Hosp. Univ. Pa., Phila., 1981-83, staff nurse in post anesthesia care, 1983-86, nurse practitioner in lithotripsy, 1986-88; nurse mgr. Hershey (Pa.) Med. Ctr., 1988—; nurse cons. dbi, Harrisburg, Pa., 1992. Campaign coord. United Way, Hershey Med. Ctr., 1995-96. Recipient Centennial Leadership award Nat. League for Nursing, 1993. Mem. Am. Soc. Post Anesthesia Nurses, Assn. Operating Room Nurses (Ctrl. Pa. Chpt.), Sigma Theta Tau. Home: 5 Oakhill Dr Etters PA 17319 Office: Hershey Med Ctr PO Box 850 Hershey PA 17033

RECTOR, FLOYD CLINTON, JR., physiologist, physician; b. Slaton, Tex., Jan. 28, 1929; s. Floyd Clinton and Faye Elizabeth (Tucker) R.; m. Marjory L. Bullen, May 27, 1950; children—Lynn, Ruth, Janet. BS, Tex. Tech. Coll., 1950; MD, U. Tex. Southwestern Med. Sch., 954. Instr. U. Tex. Southwestern Med. Sch., Dallas, 1958-59; asst. prof. medicine U. Tex. Southwestern Med. Sch., 1959-63, assoc. prof., 1963-66, prof., 1966-73; prof. medicine and physiology, sr. scientist Cardiovascular Research Inst.; dir. div. nephrology U. Calif., San Francisco, 1973-89, chmn. dept. medicine, 1989—. Editor: (with B.M. Brenner) The Kidney, 1976, 81, 85, 90-91, 94. Served with USPHS, 1956-58. NIH grantee, 1973—. Mem. Am. Soc. Nephrology, Am. Soc. Clin. Investigation, Am. Assn. Physicians, Am. Physiol. Soc. Office: U Calif PO Box 0120 San Francisco CA 94143

REDDING, BARBARA J., nursing administrator, occupational health nurse; b. Youngstown, Ohio, Jan. 5, 1938; d. Richard Howard and Helen N. (Price) Sterling; m. Philip L. Redding, Nov. 7, 1957; children: Cheryl L., Jeffrey A., Scott P. Diploma in nursing, Miami Valley Hosp., Dayton, Ohio, 1959; AA in Sociology, Miami U., Oxford, Ohio, 1984; postgrad., U. Cin. RN, Ohio; cert. EMT, CPR, BLS. Office nurse Dr. Stewart Adam, Dayton; primary nurse Miami Valley Hosp; adminstr. employee health Armco Steel Co., L.P., Middletown, Ohio; v.p. Redding Ins. Agy., Inc., Middletown, Ohio, 1993—. Instr. CPR, ARC. Mem. NAFE, Am. Assn. Occupational Health Nurses, Ind. Ins. Agts. Am., Inc. Home: 4501 Riverview Ave Middletown OH 45042-2938

REDDING-STEWART, DEBORAH LYNN, psychologist; b. Miami, Fla., Feb. 16, 1953; d. Sidney Douglas and Lois May (Tily) R.; m. John Thomas Stewart, Aug. 19, 1978; children: Garrett Lorne, Tyler Douglas, Kelly Lynn. BA in Psychology, San Diego State U., 1975; MA in Psychology, U. Calif., Santa Barbara, 1980. Instr. Allan Hancock Coll., Lompoc, Calif., 1980-86; adminstr., dir. clin. svcs. Mary Lou Stewart Learning Ctr., Lompoc, Calif., 1982—; prin. Pacific Health and Fitness, Lompoc, 1994—; owner Pacific Health and Fitness. Author: The Soft Voice of the Rain, 1993. State Coun. Devel. Disabilities PDF grantee, 1990, Instructional Deve. grantee U. Calif., 1979. Home: 1019 Onstott Rd Lompoc CA 93436-2342 also: 1019 Onstott Rd Lompoc CA 93436

REDDY, ERAGAM PREMKUMAR, medical educator; b. Madanapalli, India, Jan. 2, 1944; married; 2 children. BS in Chemistry, Botany, Zoology, Osmania U., India, 1962, MS in Chemistry, 1965, PhD in Molecular Biology, 1971. Rsch. scholar Indian Coun. Sci. and Indsl. Rsch., Hyderabad, 1965-72; NIH postdoctoral fellow UCLA, 1972-73; Fogarty Internat. postdoctoral fellow Nat. Cancer Inst., 1974-75; head viral immunology program Microbiol. Assocs., Bethesda, Md., 1975-78; vis. scientist Lab. Cellular and Molecular Biology, Nat. Cancer Inst., 1978-82, chief molecular genetics sect., 1982-84; rsch. leader dept. molecular oncology Hoffman-LaRoche, Inc., Nutley, N.J., 1984-85; full mem. Roche Inst. Molecular Biology, Nutley, 1985-86; prof. The Wistar Inst., Phila., 1986-91; Wister prof. pathology U. Pa., Phila., 1987-91; dep. dir. Wistar Inst., Phila., 1991-92; dir. Fels Inst. for Cancer Rsch. and Molecular Biology, Phila., 1992—; bd. dirs. Nat. Inst. Environ. Health Scis., NIH, 1990-95, mem. cell biology, physiology study sect.-2, 1984-89; invited participant nat. and internat. sci. meetings, workshops and symposia; Laura H. Carnell prof. medicine Temple U., Phila., 1993—. Editor: Oncogene, 1987—, The Oncogene Handbook, 1988; assoc. editor Jour. Cellular Biochemistry, 1994. Adv. com. State of N.J. Commn. on Cancer Rsch., 1987—; adv. com. on cell and developmental biology Am. Cancer Soc., 1984. Recipient Sci. Achievement award Am. Cancer Soc., 1993. Mem. AAAS, Internat. Assn. for Comparative Rsch. on Leukemia and Related Diseases. Office: Fels Inst Cancer Rsch 3420 N Broad St Philadelphia PA 19140*

REDDY, JANARDAN K., medical educator; b. Moolasaal, India, Oct. 7, 1938. MB, BS, Osmania U., Hyderabad, India, 1961; MD in Pathology, All India Inst. Med. Scis., 1965. Lic. physicain, Mo., Kans., Ill.; diplomate Am. Bd. Pathology. Rotating house officer Osmania Gen. Hosp., 1961-62; instr. pathology Kakatiya Med. Coll., Warangal, India, 1962-63, asst. prof., 1965-66; resident fellow pathology U. Kans. Med. Ctr., 1966-68, rsch. fellow pathology, 1968-70, asst. prof., 1970-73, assoc. prof., 1973-76, prof., 1976; prof. pathology Northwestern U. Med. Sch., Chgo., 1976—; dir. med. scientist tng. program Northwestern U. Med. Sch., 1990-93, chmn. pathology, 1993—; dir. anatomic pathology Northwestern Meml. Hosp., 1978-81, mem. med. staff, 1976—; mem. Northwestern U. Cancer Ctr., 1976—; mem. med. staff VA Lakeside Hosp., 1990—; group leader Chem.Carcinogenesis Rsch. Group, Northwestern U. Cancer Ctr., 1990—, assoc. dir. cancer edn., 1991—; mem. Task Force on an Environ. Sci./Policy Initiative, Northwestern U., 1991—; chmn. NIH clin. scis. study sect., 1990-91; mem. NIH spl. study sect., 1992; mem. com. on comparative toxicity of naturally occurring carcinogens, 1993—; mem. Nat. Toxicology Program Rev. Com., 1992—; mem. monograph com. WHO, Internat. Agy. on Cancer Rsch., Lyon, France, 1994. Mem. editl. bds. Jour. Histochemistry and Cytochemistry, 1973-76, Exptl. Pathology, 1982—, Toxicologic Pathology, 1983—, Internat. Jour. Pancreatology, 1986—, Lab. Investigation, 1988—, Carcinogenesis, 1989—, The Jour. Northwestern U. Cancer Ctr., 1990—, Gene Expression, 1990—, Internat. Jour. Toxicology, Occupational and Environ. Health, 1992—, Life Sci. Advanced, Oncology, 1991—; assoc. editor Jour. Toxicology and Environ. Health, 1984—, Cancer Rsch., 1985-90. Grantee Joseph Mayberry Endowment Fund, Cancer Rsch. Found., 1991-93, NIEHS, 1995—, NIGMS, 1992-97, NIDDK, 1995—, NIGMS, 1992-97; merit scholar Osmania U., 1954-61, Govt. of Andhra Pradesh merit scholar, 1963-65; WHO Yamagiwa-Yoshida Internat. Cancer fellow in Japan, 1985; recipient NIH merit award, 1987, UN Devel. Programme-Tckten award, 1988, Fletscher scholar award, 1991; named George H. Joost Outstanding Basic Sci. Tchr., 1995. Mem. AAAS, Assn. Scientists of Indian Origin in Am. (pres. 1983-84, sr. scientist award 1991), Soc. Toxicology (v.p. molecular toxicology speciality sect. 1990-91, pres. 1991-92, pres. carcinogenesis specialty sect. 1990-91, Kenneth P. Dubois award 1990), Am. Pancreatic Assn., Am. Assn. Pathologists (mem. program com. 1989-93), Am. Assn. Cancer Rsch. (mem. program com. 1990-91), Internat. Acad. Pathology, Am. Soc. Cell Biology, Histochem. Soc., Soc. Exptl. Biology and Medicine, Biochem. Soc. London, Soc. Toxicology Pathologists, Internat. Assn. Pancreatology, N.Y. Acad. Scis. Home: 1212 Asbury Ave Evanston IL 60202 Office: Northwestern U Med Sch Dept Pathology Ward 6-204 303 E Chicago Ave Chicago IL 60611-3008*

REDDY, KALLURU JAYARAMI, molecular biologist, educator; b. Andhra Pradesh, India, Apr. 15, 1953; came to U.S., 1980; s. Subba and Venkatamma R.; m. Satya Cheekireddy, May 12, 1984; children: Gowtham, Divya. BSc, Sri Venkateswara U., 1972; MSc, S. V. U., 1974; PhD, U. Miami, 1984. Jr. rsch. fellow Indian Inst. Tech., Kharagpur, India, 1974-76; jr. plant physiologist Indian Agrl. Rsch. Inst., New Dehli, 1976-80; grad. rsch. asst. Univ. Miami, Fla., 1980-84; postdoctoral fellow Univ. Mo., Columbia, 1985-89; rsch. scientist Purdue Univ., West Lafayette, Ind., 1989-90; asst. prof. SUNY, Binghamton, N.Y., 1990—. Mem. Am. Soc. for Microbiology. Office: SUNY-Binghamton Dept Biol Scis Binghamton NY 13902

REDDY, PRATAP CHANDUPATLA, cardiologist, educator, researcher; b. Laxmipur, Andhra Pradesh, India, Apr. 12, 1944; came to U.S., 1969; s. Chandra C. and Butchamma (Kota) R.; m. Shobha Katangur, May 15, 1971; children: Ashutosh, Kirthi. MBBS, Osmania U., Hyderabad, India, 1968. Diplomate Am. Bd. Internal Medicine, Am. Bd. Cardiovascular Diseases. Resident in internal medicine St. Vincent Med. Ctr., S.I., N.Y., 1969-73; fellow in cardiology Maimonide Med. Ctr., Bklyn., 1973-74; rsch. assoc. USPHS Hosp., S.I., 1974-76; asst. prof. medicine U. Ky., Lexington, 1976-81, dir. cardiac electrophysiology, 1976-84, assoc. prof., 1981-84; prof. medicine La. State U. Med. Ctr., Shreveport, 1984—, assoc. dir. cardiology, 1984—, dir. cardiac electrophysiology program, 1984—; attending cardiologist VA Med. Ctr., Shreveport, La. Editor: Tachycardia, 1984; contbr. articles to profl. jours. Named Kentucky Colonel Gov. Ky., 1983. Fellow ACP, Am. Coll. Cardiology; mem. AMA, Am. Heart Assn. (v.p. La. affiliate 1988-89, pres. 1991-92, mem. coun. clin. cardiology), Cen. Soc. for Clin. Rsch., N.Am. Soc. Pacing and Electrophysiology. Office: La State U Med Sch 1530 Kings Hwy Shreveport LA 71103-4229

REDER, ROBERT F., physician; b. Verwyn, Ill., Mar. 31, 1947; s. Robert and Bernice (Jordan) R.; divorced; 1 child, Robert S. BA, U. Wis., 1969; MD, Mt. Sinai Sch. Medicine, 1973. Asst. prof. pediatrics Columbia-Presbyn. Hosp., N.Y.C., 1979-80, Mt. Sinai Hosp., N.Y.C., 1980-83; assoc. dir. cardiovascular & clin. rsch. Bristol Myers, Evansville, Ind., 1983-84; v.p. med. affairs Knoll Pharm. Co., Whippany, N.J., 1984-90; v.p. clin. rsch. Sanote Pharm. Co., N.Y.C., 1990-91; v.p., med. dir. Purdue Frederick Co., Norwalk, Conn., 1992—. Fellow Am. Acad. Pediatrics, N.Y. Acad. Medicine; mem. Am. Acad. Pharm. Physicians. Office: Purdue Frederick Co 100 Connecticut Ave Norwalk CT 06850

REDICAN, KERRY JOHN, health education educator; b. Chgo., May 1, 1950; s. Albert and Catherine (Locelsc) Quintiliani; m. Barbara Lee Willman, June 26, 1982; children: Kelly Nicole, Kyle James. BA, Calif. State U., 1971; MS in Pub. Health, UCLA, 1972; PhD, U. Ill., 1975; MPH, U. N.C., 1986. Cert. pub. health specialist. Asst. prof. U. Nebr., Lincoln, 1975-78, Ariz. State U., Tempe, 1978-81; assoc. prof. Va. Tech., Blacksburg, 1981—; cons. Aramco, Saudi Arabia, 1978-80, ABT Assocs., Cambridge, Mass., 1980-82. Co-author: Health Today, 1986, Organization of School Health Program, 1986. Bd. dirs. Med. Clinic of New River Valley, Christiansburg, Va., 1984-86, Crisis Pregnancy Ctr., Blacksburg, 1983-91, Am. Lung Assn., Richmond, Va., 1989—. Mem. APHA, Am. Alliance Health Edn., Am. Sch. Health Assn., Va. Pub. Health Assn. Republican. Home: 2503 Manchester St Blacksburg VA 24060-8225 Office: Va Tech 104 WMH Blacksburg VA 24061

REDIG, DALE FRANCIS, dentist, association executive; b. Arcadia, Iowa, Mar. 24, 1929; s. Philip F. and Clara (Bohnenkamp) R.; m. Diane Marie Murphy, June 13, 1953; children: Mary Catherine, John Francis, Ann Bennett. Student, U. Iowa, 1949-51, DDS, 1955, MS, 1965. Pvt. practice specializing in pediatric dentistry Des Moines, 1955-61; mem. faculty U. Iowa Coll. Dentistry, Iowa City, 1961-69; assoc. prof. pedodontics U. Iowa Coll. Dentistry, 1968-69, head dept., 1964-69; Fulbright lectr. U. Baghdad, 1963-64; dean Sch. Dentistry U. Pacific, San Francisco, 1969-78; exec. dir. Calif. Dental Assn., Sacramento, 1978—; bd. dirs. CDA Holding Co., chmn., 1993—; mem. dental health rsch. and edn. adv. com. USPHS, 1972-74; UN devel. program cons. to Quatar Ministry of Health, 1991. Dir dental div. Des Moines United Campaign, 1958; bd. dirs. Des Moines Health Ctr., 1956-61, pres., 1961; bd. dirs. Am. Fund for Dental Health, 1976-84, pres., 1980-83; regent U. Pacific, 1986—, chmn. bd. dirs., 1994; mem. adv. bd. Golden Gate U., 1992—; bd. dirs. Sacramento Theater Co., 1994—; mem. corp. cabinet Sacramento AIDS Found., 1994—. With USAAF, 1946-49. Mem. ADA (ednl. cons. Vietnam 1968, mem. coun. on dental edn. 1974-78), Am. Soc. Dentistry for Children, Am. Acad. Pediatric Dentistry (bd. dirs. 1972-75), Am. Coll. Dentists, Internat. Coll. Dentists, Am. Soc. Constituent Dental Execs. (pres. 1989-90). Office: Calif Dental Assn PO Box 13749 Sacramento CA 95853-4749

REDLICH, FREDRICK CARL, psychiatrist, educator; b. Vienna, Austria, June 2, 1910; married; 2 children. MD, U. Vienna, 1935. Intern Allgem Krankenhaus, Vienna, 1935-36; resident Univ. Psychiat. Clin. U. Vienna, 1936-38; asst. physician State Hosp. Iowa, 1938-40; resident Neurol. Unit Boston City Hosp., 1940-42; from instr. to assoc. prof. psychiat. Yale U., New Haven, Conn., 1942-50, exec. officer, 1947-50, prof. psychiat., chmn. dept., 1950-67, assoc. provost med. affairs. dean, 1967-72, prof. psychiat. Sch. Medicine, 1972-77, dir. Behavioral Sci. Study Ctr., 1973-77, emeritus prof. psychiat. and neuropsychiat., 1977—; assoc. chief of staff edn. VA Med. Ctr., Brentwood, 1977-82; mem. staff Neuropsychiat. Inst. UCLA, 1982—; tchg. fellow Harvard Med. Sch., 1941-42; dir. Conn. Mental Health Ctr., 1964-67; cons. NIMH and Office Surgeon Gen., U.S. Army. Fellow Am. Psychiat. Assn., Am. Orthopsychiat. Assn., AAAS; mem. Inst. Medicine-NAS, Am. Psychosomatic Soc. Office: UCLA Dept of Psychiatry Neuropsychiat Inst. Los Angeles CA 90024*

REDMOND, DONALD EUGENE, JR., neuroscientist, educator; b. San Antonio, June 17, 1939; s. Donald Eugene and Viola (Kellum) R.; m. Patricia Welder Robinson, Dec. 22, 1972; 1 child, Andy J. BA, So. Meth. U., 1961; MD, Baylor U., 1968; MAH, Yale U., 1987. Diplomate Am. Bd. Psychiatry and Neurology. With Lab. of Clin. Sci., NIMH, Bethesda, Md., 1973-74; assoc. chief clin. neurosci. unit Conn. Mental Health Ctr., New Haven, 1974-87; asst. prof. psychiatry Yale U., New Haven, 1974-77; assoc. prof. psychiatry Yale U., 1978-87, prof. psychiatry, dir. neurobehavior lab., 1987—, dir. neural transplant program for neurol. diseases, 1987—; pres. St. Kitts Biomed. Rsch. Found., St. Kitts, W.I., 1983—, Axion Rsch. Found., Hamden, Conn., 1985—; prof. neurosurgery, 1993—. Contbr. articles to profl. jours.; patentee in field. With USPHS, 1972-74. Recipient Rsch. Scientist award NIMH, 1980— Founds. Fund prize, 1981; grantee NIMH, 1974-91, Nat. Inst. Neurol. Diseases and Stroke, 1986—, others. Mem. Am. Psychiat. Assn., Am. Coll. Neuropsychopharmacology, Am. Soc. Neural Transplantation (coun. mem. 1994—), Internat. Med. Soc. Motor Disturbances. Office: Neurobehavior Lab PO Box 3333 New Haven CT 06510-0333

REDMOND, FRANCES HARRIETTA, psychologist; b. Akron, Ohio, Apr. 8, 1921; m. John F. Redmond, Nov. 15, 1941; children: Kerry Shawn, Timothy Michael, Kimberly Diane, Debra Lynn. BS in Edn., Kent State U., 1961, MA, 1962, PhD, 1966. Cert. tchr., speech, counselor, psychologist, supr. pupil personnel, Ohio; lic. psychologist, Ohio. Intern psychologist Summit County Bd. Edn., Akron, 1963-64; instr. Kent (Ohio) State U., 1965-71; sch. psychologist Portage County Bd. Edn., Ravenna, 1965-66; asst. prof., edn. Hiram (Ohio) Coll., 1966-67, assoc. prof., 1967-69, dean of students, assoc. prof., 1969-70; assoc. dir., counseling svc. Southwestern Tenn. U. (now Rhodes Coll.), Memphis, 1970-71; chmn., dept. edn. Hiram Coll., 1971-75; psychologyst pvt. practice, Ravenna, Ohio, 1975-88, 91-94, Chagrin Falls, Ohio, 1964-75; staff mem. Ribonson Meml. Hosp., Ravenna, 1986-94; pvt. practice Redmond Cons., 1990—; adj. prof. Union Grad. Sch., 1971-77; cons. to sch. psychologists Portage County Bd. Edn., 1966-68, Reach Out Crisis Intervention Ctr., Solon, Ohio, 1974-76, Portage County Alcohol & Drug Abuse Svcs., 1991-94, Redmond Cons., 1994—. Contbr. articles to profl. jours. Bd. dirs. Unity-Clearwater Ch., 1990-94, Spouse Abuse Shelter, 1989-91, Unity-Progressive Coun., 1990—. Mem. Am. Psychol. Assn., Ohio Psychol. Assn., Alpha Psi Omega, Kappa Delta Pi, Delta Kappa Gamma.

REDMOND, LULA MOSHOURES, family therapist; b. Asheville, N.C., Feb. 3, 1929; d. Christopher John and Rosa Marie (Blankenship) Moshoures; m. John Gerald Redmond, Oct. 9, 1949 (dec. Aug. 1974); children: John Christopher, Thomas Michael, Anne Redmond Fishel. Student, Coker Coll., 1945-46; RN, Duke U., 1949; BSN, George Mason U., 1976; MS, U. Md., 1978; postgrad. Georgetown Family Ctr., Georgetown U., 1978-81. Counselor Navy Relief Soc., Hawaii, Guam, Brunswick, Maine, Washington, 1957-68; psychiat./pediatric instr. Arlington (Va.) Hosp., 1975-76; coord. cmty. adult edn. program Mt. Vernon Cmty. Mental Health, Alexandria, Va., 1978-80; family therapist, edn. dir. Hospice Care Inc., Seminole, Fla., 1980-81; pvt. practitioner family therapy Clearwater, Fla., 1980—; exec. dir. Ctr. for Crime Victims and Survivors, Inc., 1987—; mem. faculty Assn. for Death Edn. and Counseling Inc., Washington, 1979-83, bd. dirs., 1981—, coord. internat. conf., 1979-81; program case cons. Hospice Programs, 1980-83; founder, dir. Homicide Survivors Group Treatment program, 1985; lectr. Nat. Orgn. for Victim Assistance, Nat. Victim Ctr., 1988, 89. Author: Surviving When Someone You Love Was Murdered: A Professional's Guide to Group Grief Therapy for Families and Friends of Murder Victims, 1989. Chmn. edn. com. Mental Health Assn. Pinellas County, Clearwater, 1981-82, v.p., 1982-84; bd. dirs. Homicide Survivors Group Inc. Pinellas County, 1986—. Recipient Victim Services award Pinellas County Victims Rights Coalition, 1987, Nat. Service award Assn. for Death Edn. and Counseling, Inc., 1988, Tribute to Women in Bus. and Industry award, 1989; NIMH fellow, 1976. Mem. ANA, Assn. Death Edn. and Counseling (1st v.p. 1996-97), Crime Victims Rights, Fla. Bar Assn., Internat. Soc. for Traumatic Stress Studies Inc., Am. Assn. for Marriage and Family Therapy, Am. Inst. Life-Threatening Illness and Loss, Am. Orthopsychiat. Assn., Fla. Group Psychotherapy Soc., Fla. Network of Victim Witness Svcs., Fla. Soc. Psychotherapists, Menninger Found., Nat. Orgn. Victim Assistance, Nat. Victim Ctr., Sigma Theta Tau., Alpha Chi, Phi Kappa Phi. Republican. Roman Catholic. Office: Psychol Cons & Edn Svcs PO Box 6111 Clearwater FL 34618-6111

REDO, MARIA ELAINE, gerontologist, educator; b. N.Y.C., Jan. 12, 1925; d. Ernest and Mary C. Lappano; B.S. in Edn., Fordham U., 1945; cert. in gerontology, Brookdale Sch. Social Sci., 1979; m. S. Frank Redo, June 27, 1948; children—Philip L., Martha Maria. Tchr. pvt. sch., N.Y.C., 1946-56; dir. Child Service League, Queens, N.Y., 1949-57; founder, dir. Community Concern for Sr. Citizens, Inc., N.Y.C. Dept. for the Aging, 1971-85; dir. N.Y.C. Silver Pages Directory, Silver Savers' Passport. Bd. dirs. Escort Service of Yorkville (N.Y.), 1977—, Sr. Citizen Outreach Program for Elderly, N.Y.C., 1970—; mem. Community Planning Bd., N.Y.C., 1970-77; del. Nat. Republican Conv., N.Y.C., 1976, N.Y. State White House Conf. on Aging, 1981, Nat. White House Conf. on Aging, N.Y.C., 1981; del. N.Y. State Conf. on Mid-Life and Older Women, 1983. Recipient Mayor's Cert. of Appreciation N.Y.C., 1975; Hon. Sec. of State of Mont., 1975; Franny award WPIX-TV, 1974. Mem. LWV, Roman Catholic. Club: Met. Rep. (pres. 1975-77). Contbr. tng. manuals, brochures for dept. on aging., 1973-85. Home: 435 E 70th St New York NY 10021-5342

REDO, S(AVERIO) FRANK, surgeon; b. Bklyn., Dec. 28, 1920; s. Frank and Maria (Guida) R.; m. Maria Lappano, June 27, 1948; children—Philip, Martha. B.S., Queens Coll., 1942; M.D., Cornell U., 1950. Diplomate: Am. Bd. Thoracic Surgery, Am. Bd. Surgery (pediatric surgery). Intern in surgery N.Y. Hosp., N.Y.C., 1950-51; asst. resident surgeon N.Y. Hosp., 1951-56, resident surgeon, 1956-57, asst. attending surgeon, 1958-60, assoc. attending surgeon, 1960-66, surgeon in charge pediatric surgery, 1960, attending surgeon, 1966—; practice medicine specializing in surgery; clin. asso. prof. surgery Cornell U. Med. Coll., 1963-72, prof., 1972—. Author: Surgery in the Ambulatory Child, 1961, Principles of Surgery in the First Six Months of Life, 1976, Atlas of Surgery in the First Six Months of Life, 1977; contbr. articles to profl. jours. Served to capt. USAAF, 1942-46. Fellow A.C.S., Am. Coll. Chest Physicians; mem. Harvey Soc., Pan Am. Med. Assn., Soc. Univ. Surgeons, Am. Acad. Pediatrics, Am. Fedn. for Clin. Research, Internat. Cardiovascular Soc., Am. Surg. Assn., Am. Assn. Thoracic Surgery, Soc. for Surgery Alimentary Tract, Am. Soc. Artificial Internat. Organs, Am. Acad. Pediatrics, Assn. Advancement Med. Instrumentation, Soc. Thoracic Surgeons, Internat. Soc. Surgery, N.Y. Gastroent. Soc., N.Y. Acad. Sci., N.Y. Cardiovascular Soc., N.Y. Acad. Medicine, N.Y. Soc. Thoracic Surgery, N.Y. Pediatric Soc., Med. Soc. County N.Y., Queens Coll. Alumni Assn. (gov. 1962—), Sigma Xi. Home: 435 E 70th St New York NY 10021-5342 Office: 525 E 68th St New York NY 10021-4873

REDWINE, JOHN NEWLAND, physician; b. Pratt, Kans., Oct. 28, 1950; s. Albert Herold and Joyce Nadean (Durall R.; m. Barbara Ann Bomgaars, Dec. 27, 1975; children: John Newland II, William Merritt, Adam Boone. BA with honors, U. Kans., 1972; cert. med. technology, U. Tex. at Houston, 1974; DO, U. Health Scis., Kansas City, Mo., 1978. Diplomate Am. Bd. of Family Practice. Intern U. Hosp., Ctr. for Health Scis., Kansas City, Mo., 1978-79; family practice resident Siouxland Med. Edn. Found., Sioux City, Iowa, 1979-81; med. dir. Morningside Family Practice, Sioux City, Iowa, 1981-95; sr. v.p. med. affairs St. Luke's Health Sys., Inc., Sioux City, Iowa; sr. aviation med. examiner FAA, 1979-95; clin. lectr. Iowa U. Coll. Medicine, Iowa City, 1983—; past pres. Siouxland Med. Edn. Found., 1982—; past chmn. family practice St. Luke's Regional Med. Ctr., Sioux City, Iowa, pres. elect, 1993-95. Contbr. articles to profl. jours. V.p. program Prairie Gold Area coun. Boy Scouts Am., Sioux City; bd. dirs. Sioux City Cmty. Sch. Dist. Recipient achievement award, Upjohn Pharm. Co., Kansas City, 1978. Fellow Am. Acad. Family Physicians; mem. AMA, Iowa Med. Soc., Woodbury Med. Soc. (past pres.), Flying Physicians Assn. Republican. Methodist. Office: St Luke's Health Sys Inc 2720 Stone Park Blvd Sioux City IA 51104

REDWINE, MICHAEL DWAIN, radiologist, army officer; b. Kirksville, Mo., Dec. 16, 1946; s. Alfred Austin and Herma Alma (Duke) R.; m. Shirley Jean Lawson, June 14, 1974. BA in Zoology, Tex. Tech U., 1969; MD, U. Tex., Galveston, 1973. Diplomate Am. Bd. Internal Medicine, Am. Bd. Radiology, Am. Bd. Nuclear Medicine. Commd. officer U.S. Army, 1973, advanced through grades to col., 1987; nuclear medicine fellow Wm. Beaumont Army Med. Ctr., El Paso, Tex., 1978-81; staff nuclear medicine Letterman Army Med. Ctr., San Francisco, 1981-83, resident in radiology, 1983-87; staff mem radiology Brooke Army Med. Ctr., San Antonio, 1987-89, chief of diagnostic imaging, 1989-93; asst. prof. radiology U. Tex. Health Sci. Ctr., Houston, 1993—. Home: 4818 Beech St Bellaire TX 77401-3403 Office: Univ of Tex Health Sci Ctr Dept Radiology 6431 Fannin St Ste 2 100 Houston TX 77030-1501

REECE, CHERI DODSON, nurse, educator; b. Altoona, Pa., Apr. 17, 1946; d. Paul Francis and Evelyn Pearl (Brown) Dodson; diploma in nursing Western Pa. Hosp. Sch. Nursing, Pitts., 1967; BS in Nursing, Cedar Crest Coll., Allentown, Pa., 1969; MSN in Perinatal Nursing, Case Western Res. Univ., 1987; postgrad. in nursing Kent State U., 1979-83; 1 dau., Michelle Lynn. Nurse coll. infirmary, 1967-69; staff nurse Western Pa. Hosp., 1968; pvt. duty nurse, 1969, 78, 84-85; staff nurse Nason Hosp., Roaring Spring, Pa., 1969; instr. in-svc. edn. N.D. State Hosp., Jamestown, 1969-71; staff nurse Santa Clara Valley Med. Ctr., San Jose, Calif., 1971-72; instr. nursing San Jose Hosps. and Health Ctr., 1972-74; instr. nursing Kent State U., 1974-75, 78-84; instr. nursing Ohio Valley Hosp., Steubenville, Ohio, 1975-77; staff nurse Ashtabula (Ohio) Medicare Ctr., 1977-78; instr. adult edn. Ashtabula County Joint Vocat. Sch., 1978-79; phys. exam. nurse Phys. Measurements, Inc., Ashtabula, 1978; grad. asst. Case Western Res. U.,

1985-86; continuing edn. instr.; cons. well-baby care; staff and clin. nurse Home Health Svcs. of Ashtabula County, 1986-87; clin. nursing faculty Cleve. State U., 1987; perinatal clin. nurse specialist, perinatal case mgr. Cape Fear Valley Med. Ctr., Fayetteville, N.C., 1987—. Guest lecturer, active in campaign U.S. Rep., Am. Cancer Soc., Am. Heart Fund; patron Straw Hat Theatre; councilmatic aide Ashtabula City Council, 1981-83; head Center Shop at Ashtabula Arts Center, also patron; mem. panel of content experts Nat. Coun. Licensure Examinations; mem coms. Fayetteville YMCA, Westminster Presbyterian Ch.; mem. Gov. Commn. on Reduction Infant Mortality, N.C. PTA. Mem. Coastal Area Perinatal Assn. (sec.- treas.), AAUW (sec. chpt. 1980-82, treas. 1983-85), AWHONN, Nat. League Nursing, Neonatal Resuscitation Program (regional trainer), Cedar Crest Coll. Alumnae Assn., Alumnae Assn. Claysburg-Kimmel High Sch., East Carolina U. Parent's Assn., Douglas Byrd Sr. High Band Booster (pres.), U.S. Masters Swimming, Sigma Theta Tau. Office: Cape Fear Valley Med Ctr PO Box 2000 Fayetteville NC 28302-2000

REECE, DAVID BRYSON, health facility administrator, research administrator, nurse consultant, nurse educator; b. Phoenix, Aug. 5, 1953; s. Frank Williams and Margaret Leonora (Bryson) W.; div.; children: Ashley Cambridge, Christopher David. ADN, Phoenix C.C., 1974; Baccelaurette Sci. Wholistic Nursing, Westbrook U., 1991, Master Sci. Wholistic Nursing, 1992, PhD, 1993. V.p. Young Nursing Svc., Kingman, Ariz., 1987-89; CEO No. Ariz. Cons., Phoenix, 1987-92, Butterfield Health Systems, Phoenix, 1990—; v.p. United Submersible Sys., Phoenix, 1990-94; dean of nursing, co-founder Sch. Wholistic Nursing Westbrook U., Aztec, N.Mex., 1991—; v.p. R&D, grant procurement and various rsch. projects Am. Minority Bus. for Engring. and Rsch., Chadler, Ariz., 1993-96; alternative health nurse practitioner. Rsch. includes homeopathic proving aspartame, ethnobotany, ancient botanical database, ancient medicine database, alternative therapeutics database; cofactor for HIV and Ebola. Mem. Ariz. Assn. Healthcare Agys. (bd. dirs. 1988-90). Office: AMBER Inc PO Box 3323 Chandler AZ 85224-3323

REECE, JULIETTE M. STOLPER, community health and mental health nurse; b. Muskogee, Okla., Oct. 4, 1926; d. Joseph Harry and Marie (Duquesne) Stolper; m. Warren Crane, Apr. 12, 1947; children: Warren Crane, Judith Gayle Crane Cox Fitzpatrick, Janice M. Crane Sharp, Cathy L. Crane Hubble; m. Roy M. Reece Jr., July 16, 1970 (dec.). Diploma, Muskogee Gen. Hosp., 1947; BS in Psychology, Cameron Coll., Lawton, Okla., 1993, postgrad., 1993; student, U. Okla. Cert. pub. health nurse. ICU nurse Southwestern Hosp., Lawton, 1976-77; psychiat. nurse Taliaferro Community Mental Health Ctr., 1977-86; cons. nurse Cedar Crest Manor, Lawton, 1985-86, dir. nursing svc., 1986-87; asst. head nurse Reynolds Family Practice Clinic, Ft. Sill, Okla., 1987-91, head nurse, 1991—, also diabetes educator, 1991—; patient/staff edn. coord. dept. family practice Reynolds Army Cmty. Hosp., Ft. Sill, 1996—; vis. mem. Pub. Health Nursing Study Group, USSR, 1979. Vol. for Am. Cancer Soc., Am. Heart Assn., Am. Diabetes Assn., Am. Lung Assn., Am. Assn. Diabetes Educators, Assn. Western Okla. Diabetes Educators, ARC, Easter Seal Programs; tchr. classes for home health care aides, ARC; tchr. med. terminology to hosp. receptionists. Recipient nursing grants. Home: 1601 NW Pollard Ave Lawton OK 73507-2048 Office: Reynolds Family Practice Clinic # 4 Thomas St Bldg # 4300 Fort Sill OK 73503

REECE, STACEY LYNN, neonatal nurse; b. Meridian, Miss., Dec. 10, 1970; d. Ronald William Reece and Jo Ann (Threatt) Oubre. ADN, Meridian C.C., 1992. RN, Miss. Neonatal ICU nurse Rush Found. Hosp., Meridian, 1992—. Republican. Baptist. Home: PO Box 464 Marion MS 39342

REECE, THOMAS HOWARD, physician; b. Takoma Park, Mo., July 25, 1955; s. Howard C. and Elaine Florence (Ross) R. BS in Chemistry, Tulane U., 1977; BS in Human Biology, Kans. Newman Coll., Wichita, 1980; D in Natoropathic, Nat. Coll. Natoropathic Med., Portland, Oreg., 1982; DO, Kirksville Coll. Osteo. Med., Mo., 1990. Intern Mesa (Ariz.) Gen. Hosp., 1990-91; resident Cmty. Hosp., Mesa, Ariz.; pvt. practice specializing in natoropathic medicine Phoenix, 1982-86, pvt. practice specializing in osteo. medicine, 1990—; clin. tchr. S.W. Coll. Natoropathic Medicine, 1995; med. dir. Southwest Naturopathic Med. Ctr. Mem. Am. Osteo. Med. Assn., Am. Coll. Osteo. Family Practitioners, Am. Osteo. Acad. Sports Medicine, Am. Assn. Natoropathic Physicians, Ariz. Osteo. Medicine Assn., Nat. Hon. Osteo. Fraternity. Home: 6818 E Fanfol Paradise Valley AZ 85253 Office: SW Natoropathic Med Ctr 8010 E McDowell Scottsdale AZ 85257

REED, CON SCOTT, consultant physician; b. Palmerston, New Zealand, June 4, 1928; s. Roy James and Jean Bowie (Scott) R.; m. Judith Ann Routley, Dec. 28, 1953; children: Michael James, Barbara Jean, Sandra Jane, Iain Geoffrey. Student, Scots Coll., Sydney, 1942-46; MB, BS, U. Sydney, 1953. Jr. resident med. officer Sydney Hosp., 1953, hon. physician, 1961—; Basser fellow Royal Prince Alfred Hosp., Sydney, 1954; registrar Clin. Rsch. Unit, R.P.A.H., Sydney, 1955; Leverhulme lectr. U. Hong Kong, 1967; Centenary lectr. Mater Hosp., Brisbane, 1970; Ciba-Geigy lectr. Post Grad. Fedn., New Zealand, 1973; area med. cons. Bristol-Myers Ltd., Sydney, 1970-82; mem. N.S.W. State Cancer Coun., Sydney, 1978—; mem. East Sydney Area Hosp. Bd., 1990-95; mem. various state and fed. govt. coms. Contbr. numerous papers and articles to profl. jours. Fellow Australian Med. Assn. (councilor 1970-85, pres. 1978-79, fed. councilor 1975-86), Royal Australian Coll. Physicians; mem. Australian Jockey Club, Australian Golf Club. Presbyterian. Home: 127 Wallis St, Woollahra NSW 2025, Australia Office: 183 Macquarie St, Sydney NSW 2000, Australia

REED, DIANE MARIE, psychologist; b. Joplin, Mo., Jan. 11, 1934; d. William Marion and Olive Francis (Smith) Kinney; married; children: Wendy Robison, Douglas Funkhouser. Student, Art Ctr. Col., L.A., 1951-54; BS, U. Oreg., 1976, MS, 1977, PhD, 1981. Lic. psychologist. Illustrator J.L. Hudson Co., Detroit, 1954-56; designer, stylist N.Y.C., 1960-70; designer, owner Decor To You, Inc., Stamford, Conn., 1970-76; founder, exec. dir. Alcohol Counseling and Edn. Svcs., Inc., Eugene, Oreg., 1981-86, clin. supr., 1986; clin. supr. Christian Family Svcs., Eugene, 1986-87; pvt. practice Eugene, 1985-94; founder Reed Consulting, Bend, Oreg., 1995—. Evaluator Vocat. Rehab. Div., Eugene, 1982—; alcohol and drug evaluator and commitment examiner Oreg. Mental Health Div., 1981-86; life mem. Rep. Presdl. Task Force. Mem. APA, Oreg. Psychol. Assn., Lane County Psychol. Assn. (pres. 1989-90), Ctrl. Oreg. Mental Health Profls., C2 Investors (treas. 1987-88), Altair Ski and Sport, Oreg. Track, Rotary Internat.

REED, DWAYNE MILTON, medical epidemiologist, educator; b. Kinsley, Kans., Dec. 10, 1933; s. John Milton and Margaret (Reger) R.; m. Leslie Smith, June 28, 1962 (div. 1968); children: Colin, Heather. BA, U. Calif., Berkeley, 1956; MD, U. Calif., San Franciso, 1960; MPH, U. Calif., 1962, PhD in Epidemiology, 1968. Dep. chief epidemiology Nat. Inst. Neurol. Disease NIH, Bethesda, Md., 1962-64; chief epidemiology Arctic Health Ctr. USPHS, 1964-66; assoc. prof. Sch. Pub. Health R. Tex., Houston, 1968-70; chief epidemiology NIH Neurology Field Ctr., Agana, Guam, 1970-72; epidemiologist South Pacific Commn., New Caledonia, 1972-75; chief epidemiology br. Nat. Inst. Child Health, NIH, Bethesda, 1975-78; dir. environ. epidemiology Calif. Dept. Health, Berkeley, 1978-79; dir. Honolulu health program Nat. Heart Lung Blood Inst. NIH, 1980-93; sr. epidemiologist Buck Ctr. for Rsch. in Aging, Novato, Calif., 1993—; adj. prof. epidemiology Sch. Pub. Health U. Calif., Berkeley, 1978-78, Sch. Pub. Health U. Honolulu, 1980—; cons. WHO-Pacific, Manila, 1983, 86-87, 89, Hawaii State Dept. Health, Honolulu, 1988—. Editor: The Epidemiology of Premature, 1977; contbr. chpts. to books and over 150 sci. articles on med. epidemiology to profl. jours. Recipient Commendation medal USPHS, 1987. Fellow Am. Heart Assn.; mem. Am. Pub. Health Assn., Am. Coll. Epidemiology, Am. Epidemiology Soc., Soc. Epidemiologic Rsch., Delta Omega. Office: Buck Ctr for Rsch in Aging 505 San Marin Dr Novato CA 94945-1309

REED, ELIZABETH ANN, nurse practitioner; b. Phila., July 14, 1943; d. Thomas B. and Ann B. (Kuzmann) R. Diploma, Thomas Jefferson U. Hosp. Sch. Nursing, Phila., 1961-64; student Temple U., 1964-68, U. Calif., Davis, 1991-93. R.N., Pa., Calif., nurse practitioner, Calif. Various nursing positions Thomas Jefferson U. Hosp., Phila., 1964-68, head nurse cardiac surgery, 1972; head nurse cardiovascular surgery Cooper Hosp., Camden, N.J., 1968-72, clin. coordinator cardiac surgery, 1972-75; head nurse clin. perfusion U. Calif.-San Francisco, 1975-76, quality assurance coordinator, 1976-78, clin. supr., 1978-86, Pacific Presbyn. Med. Ctr., San Francisco, 1986-91, dir. operating room services; pvt. practice, 1993—; speaker numerous profl. meetings. Mem. Assn. Oper. Rm. Nurses (dir. 1977-81, dir. San Francisco chpt. 1980-84, various other offices), Am. Acad. Nurse Practitioners, Calif. Coalition of Nurse Practitioners, Nurse's Alumnae Assn. Thomas Jefferson U. Hosp. Sch. Nursing. Contbg. author Alexander's Care of the Patient in Surgery, 1978, 7th edit., 1983; contbr. numerous articles and papers to profl. jours. Home: 77 Blanca Dr Novato CA 94947

REED, GEORGE ELLIOTT, surgery educator; b. N.Y.C., Aug. 4, 1923; s. Morris and Mary R.; children: Elizabeth E., George E. Jr.; m. Anne Miller Moore, 1995. DVM, Cornell U., 1944; MD, NYU, 1951. Diplomate Am. Bd. Surgery, Am. Bd. Thoracic Surgery. Successively intern, resident, chief resident NYU Bellevue Med. Ctr., N.Y.C., 1951-56, Berg fellow in cardiovascular surgery, 1956-58; from asst. prof. to assoc. prof. surgery NYU, N.Y.C., 1959-69, prof., 1969-77; prof. N.Y. Med. Coll., Valhalla, 1977—; pres. med. staff Westchester County Med. Ctr., Valhalla, N.Y., 1989-92; med. dir. acting Westchester County Med. Ctr., Valhalla, 1992-95, med. dir., 1995—, dir. George E. Reed Heart Ctr., 1994—; pres. Med. Coll. Health Alliance, Valhalla, 1994—; vice dean N.Y. Med. Coll., 1995—; cons. surgery N.Y. State Dept. Health, Albany, 1963-90, VA, N.Y.C., 1969-77, Lennox Hill Hosp., N.Y.C., 1971-91, Kingston (N.Y.) Hosp., 1971-90; pres. Federated Faculty Practise Plan, 1996—; presenter in field. Contbr. articles to profl. jours., chpts. to books. Capt. U.S. Army, 1944-47. Fellow ACS, Am. Coll. Cardiology; mem. Am. Assn. Thoracic Surgery, Soc. Thoracic Surgeons, Alpha Omega Alpha (faculty). Office: Westchester County Med Ctr Macy 203 Valhalla NY 10595

REED, J. CRAIG, biochemistry and molecular genetics researcher; b. Anniston, Ala., Jan. 25, 1967; s. George W. and Elizabeth E. Reed. BS in Molecular Biology, Vanderbilt U., 1988; PhD in Biochemistry/Molecular Biology, U. Ga., 1995. Biochemist divsn. bacteriology U.S. Army Med. Rsch. Inst. Infectious Diseases, Ft. Detrick, Frederick, Md., 1995—; cons. to various govt. agys. 1996—; presenter in field. Contbr. articles to profl. jours. Asst. scoutmaster Boy Scouts Am., Frederick, 1996—. Capt. Med. Svc. Corps, U.S. Army, 1995—. ROTC scholar, 1984-88. Mem. AAAS, Nat. Eagle Scout Assn., Sigma Xi. Home: 5731 Magnolia Ct B43 Frederick MD 21703 Office: USAMRIID Divsn Bacteriology Fort Detrick Frederick MD 21701-5011

REED, JAMES WHITFIELD, physician, educator; b. Pahokee, Fla., Nov. 1, 1935; s. Thomas Reed and Chineater (Grey) Whitfield; married; children: David M., Robert A., Mary I., Katherine E. BS, W.Va. State Coll., 1954; MD, Howard U., 1963. Diplomate Am. Bd. Internal Medicine, Am. Bd. Endocrinology and Metabolism. Commd. U.S. Army, 1963; advanced through grades to col., 1981; resident in internal medicine Madigan Army Med. Ctr., Tacoma, Wash., 1966-69, chief endocrinology and metabolism, 1971-76, chief dept. clin. rsch., 1976-78; chief dept. medicine Eisenhower Army Med. Ctr., Augusta, Ga., 1978-81; assoc. prof. internal medicine edn. for FP program U. Tex. at Dallas, 1981-84; prof. medicine Morehouse Sch. Medicine, Atlanta, 1985—, chmn. dept., 1985-92, chmn. grad. med. edn., 1992—, activity chmn., 1986-88; postdoctoral fellow in endocrinology and metabolism U. Calif. Med. Ctr., San Francisco, 1969-71; dir. endocrinology, fellow Madigan Army Med. Ctr., 1976-78; dir. internal medicine residency program Eisenhower Army Med. Ctr., 1978-81, chmn. directorate of clin. investigation, 1978-81, dir. endocrinology fellowship program; med. cons. Tuskgee (Ala.) VA Hosp., 1985—; mem. nat. high blood pressure edn. com. NHLBI/NIH, Nat. Diabetes Mellitus Adv. Coun., Nat. Diabetes Adv. Bd., NHLBI working Com. on Hypertension and Diabetes; chmn. Sub Com. Special Population and Situations, chmn. subcom., mem. exec. com. Joint Nat. Commn. for Detection Evaluation and Treatment of High Blood Pressure. Author: Black Man's Guide to Good Health, 1994; contbr. articles to profl. publs. Med. advisor, chmn. March of Dimes, Pierce County, Tacoma, 1976-78; pres. Charles Drew Sickle Cell and Health Bd., Tacoma, 1976-78; mem. task force on cardiovascular risk reduction Am. Heart Assn. Decorated Legion of Merit; recipient Disting. Alumni award Nat. Assn. for Equal Opportunity in Higher Edn., 1988, Nat. Alumnus of Yr. award W.Va. State Coll., 1987; inducted into ROTC Hall of Fame, W.Va. State Coll., 1987. Fellow ACP, Am. Coll. Clin. Endocrinologist; mem. Assn. Profs. Medicine, Endocrine Soc., Internat. Soc. Hypertension in Blacks (v.p. 1986, pres. 1992—), Assn. of Program Dirs. in Internal Medicine, Am. Heart Assn. Task Force on Cardiovascular Risk, Alpha Phi Alpha. Democrat. Home: 380 Mcgill Pl NE Atlanta GA 30312-1069 Office: Morehouse Sch Medicine 720 Westview Dr SW Atlanta GA 30310-1458

REED, JENNIFER LYNN, public helath nurse; b. Rochester, Pa., Dec. 15, 1971; d. John Bernard and Deborah Lee (Simmons) Hojdila; m. Michael David Reed, Apr. 15, 1994. LPN, Lanier Tech., Oakwood, Ga., 1993. Sec., LPN Ga. Poultry Lab., Oakwood, 1990—; LPN Hall County Health Dept., Gainesville, Ga., 1995—. Salvation Army Med. fellow, 1993. Democrat. Roman Catholic.

REED, KATHLYN LOUISE, occupational therapist, educator; b. Detroit, June 2, 1940; d. Herbert C. and Jessie R. (Krehbiel) R. BS in Occupational Therapy, U. Kans., 1964; MA, Western Mich. U., 1966; PhD, U. Wash., 1973; MLS, U. Okla., 1987. Occupational therapist in psychiatry Kans. U. Med. Center, Kansas City, 1964-65; instr. occupational therapy U. Wash., Seattle, 1967-70; assoc. prof. dept. occupational therapy U. Okla. Health Scis. Ctr., Oklahoma City, 1973-77, prof., 1978-85; chmn. dept. occupational therapy U. Okla. Health Scis. Ctr., 1973-85; libr. edn. info. svcs. Houston Acad. Medicine Tex. Med. Ctr. Libr., 1988—; cons. to Okla. State Dept. Health, 1976-77, Children's Convalescent Ctr., Oklahoma City, 1977-80, Oklahoma City pub. schs., 1980-81; vis. scholars program Tex. Woman's U., 1991-94, adj. prof. Sch. Occupational Therapy, Tex. Woman's U., 1992—. Author: (with Sharon Sanderson) Concepts of Occupational Therapy, 1980, 2d edit., 1983, 3rd edit., 1992, Models of Practice in Occupational Therapy, 1983, Quick Reference to Occupational Therapy, 1991, (with Julie Pauls) Quick Reference to Physical Therapy, 1996. Vol. crisis counselor Open Door Clinic, Seattle, 1968-72; mem. exec. bd. Seattle Mental Health Inst., 1971-72; Mem. Citizen Participation Liaison Council, Seattle, 1970-72. Recipient Award of Merit, Can. Assn. Occupational Therapists, 1988. Fellow Am. Occupational Therapy Assn. (Merit award 1983, Slagle lecture award 1985, Svc. award 1985); mem. ALA, World Fedn. Occupational Therapists, Coun. Exceptional Children, Okla. Occupational Therapy Assn. (pres. 1974-76), Tex. Occupational Therapy Assn., Med. Libr. Assn. (Rittenhouse award 1987, Acad. Health Info. Professions), Nat. Rehab. Assn., Am. Occupational Therapy Found., Assn. Advancement Rehab. Tech., Sensory Integration Internat., Sigma Kappa (Colby award 1994). Democrat. Home: 6699 De Moss Dr Houston TX 77074-5003

REED, KENNETH PAUL, industrial hygienist, consultant; b. Covington, Ky., Aug. 30, 1937; s. George Anderson and Alice Martha (Spritzky) R.; m. Carol Irene Luken, May 21, 1966; children: Ann E., Susan L., Pamela N. AB, Thomas More Coll., 1957; MS, Xavier U., 1959; PhD, La. State U., 1968. Cert. indsl. hygienist Am. Bd. Indsl. Hygiene. Prof. chemistry Thomas More Coll., Ft. Mitchell, Ky., 1959-78, dir. devel., 1975-78, chmn. dept., 1969-75, asst. dean freshman & gen. studies, 1972-75; gen. mgr. Actus Environ. Service, Florence, Ky., 1978-80; pres., founder Kenneth P. Reed and Assocs., Covington, 1980—; cons. Nat. Inst. Occupational Safety and Health, Cin., 1975—, U.S. Geol. Survey, Doraville, Ga., 1980-82, No. Ky. Bd. Health, Covington, 1980—, Hamilton County Bd. Health, 1996—. Author: Venture, 1975, (with others) Quantitative Chemistry, 1965; contbr. articles to profl. jours. NSF fellow, 1966-67. Mem. ASHRAE, Am. Chem. Soc., Am. Indsl. Hygiene Assn., Am. Conf. Govtl. Indsl. Hygienists, Greater Cin. Area Safety Coun. (founder), Kenton (Ky.) Fish and Game Club, Rotary (bd. dirs. Covnnington 1982-87, pres. 1986-87). Republican. Roman Catholic. Home: 609 Oak Ridge Dr Edgewood KY 41017-3231 Office: 3027 Dixie Hwy Ste 117 Covington KY 41017-2361

REED, MICHAEL JOHN, dentist, college dean, oral biology educator; b. Wednesbury, Eng., Dec. 25, 1940; came to U.S., 1967, naturalized, 1972; s. Harry Ernest and Ida Veva (Heywood) R.; m. Pamela Twycross, July 4, 1965 (div. Feb. 1976); children: Justine Marianne, Helena Clare; m. Ingrid Liepins, Sept. 8, 1978; children: Kathryn Anne, Matthew Harrison. BS with honors, U. Durham, Eng., 1963; B in Dental Surgery, U. Newcastle-Upon-Tyne, Eng., 1967; PhD, SUNY, Buffalo, 1971. Lic. dentist U.K., N.Y., Miss. Instr. oral biology SUNY, Buffalo, 1971-72, asst. prof. oral biology, 1972-77, assoc. prof., 1977-79; asst. dean Sch. Dentistry, U. Miss., Jackson, 1980-85, assoc. dean, 1985; dean, prof. oral biology Sch. Dentistry, U. Mo., Kansas City, 1985—; cons. Nat. Inst. Dental Rsch., Washington, 1975-85. Contbr. numerous articles to profl. jours. Recipient rsch. career devel. award NIH, 1975-80. Fellow Acad. Dentistry Internat., Internat. Coll. Dentists, Am. Coll. Dentists; mem. ADA (cons. 1982—, joint com. on nat. dental exam., 1988-93, chair 1992-93), Am. Assn. Dental Schs. (sect. chair 1985-86. chmn. schs. coun. of deans, 1992-93), Am. Assn. Dental Rsch. (councillor 1974-76), Fedn. Dentaire Internat., Am. Assn. for Microbiology, Mid-Am. Masters Club, Omicron Kappa Upsilon. Episcopalian. Home: 12812 Delmar St Leawood KS 66209-3319 Office: U Mo-Kansas City Sch Dentistry 650 E 25th St Kansas City MO 64108-2716

REED, SHELDON CLARK, human genetics educator; b. Barre, Vt., Nov. 7, 1910; s. George Albert and Nellie Abigail (Colburn) R.; m. Elizabeth Cleland Wagner, Aug. 20, 1946; children: Catherine Cleland Westhoff, William George. BS, Dartmouth Coll., 1932; MA, Harvard U., 1933, PhD, 1935; DS, Gustafus Adolphus Coll., 1986. Instr. McGill U., Mont., Can., 1936-40; asst. prof. Harvard U., Cambridge, Mass., 1940-47; assoc. prof. U. Minn., Mpls., 1947-51, prof., 1951-77, emeritus prof., 1977—. Author: Counseling in Medical Genetics, 1955, 2d edit. 1963, 3d edit. 1980, (with E.W. Reed) Mental Retardation A Family Study, 1965. Democrat. Congregationalist. Home: 1588 Vincent Ave Saint Paul MN 55108-1323

REED, WILLIAM PIPER, JR., surgeon, educator; b. Melrose, Mass., May 24, 1942; s. William Piper and Gertrude Harriet (Irons) R.; m. Martine Francoise Valentine Billet, Oct. 16, 1963; children: Antoinette Elsa, Christopher Llewellyn. AB, Harvard U., 1964, MD, 1968; diploma head, neck, cancer surgery, U. Paris (Villejuif), 1977. Diplomate Am. Bd. Surgery; diplomate Nat. Bd. Med. Examiners. Resident in surgery Stanford Med. Ctr., Stanford, Calif., 1976; dir. surgical ICU U. Md. Hosp., Balt., 1979-81, dir. tumor registry, 1981-86; asst. prof. surgery Sch. Medicine U. Md., Balt., 1978-83, assoc. prof. surgery, 1983-86; dir. surgical oncology Baystate Med. Ctr., Springfield, Mass., 1986—, dir. breast health ctr., 1992-94; assoc. prof. surgery Tufts U., Boston, 1986-92, prof. surgery, 1992—; mem. admissions com. Tufts U. Sch. Medicine, 1988—, mem. promotion com., 1995—; mem. admissions, promotions com., Tufts. U.; pres. Balt. County Unit Am. Cancer Soc., Balt., 1983-86; med. v.p. Springfield (Mass.) Unit Am. Cancer Soc., 1987-93, v.p. 1993-95, pres., 1995—; bd. dirs. Mass. div. Am. Cancer Soc., Boston, 1989—. Contbr. articles to profl. jours. Mem. Conservation Commn. Longmeadow, Mass., 1989-95. Capt. U.S. Army, 1970-72, Vietnam. Recipient Golden Apple award Baystate Med. Ctr., Springfield, 1988; grantee NIHA 1973-75, Am. Cancer Soc. Md. Div., 1983-85, Margery Sadowski Found., Springfield, 1988-91, Mass. Dept. Pub. Health Access to Breast Care, 1993—; recipient Lifesaver award Am. Cancer Soc., 1994. Fellow ACS, Soc. Surg. Oncology (mem. issues com.); mem. Soc. for Surgery of Alimentary Tract, Soc. of Univ. Surgeons, Soc. Head and Neck Surgeons, New Eng. Surg. Soc., Soc. Am. Gastrointestinal Endoscopic Surgeons (credentials com., ethics com.), New Eng. Cancer Soc. (exec. com.). Office: Baystate Med Ctr 759 Chestnut St Springfield MA 01199-1001

REEDY, JOHN JOSEPH, biologist; b. Buffalo, May 14, 1927; s. Frank A. and Margaret (Bunce) R.; m. Joann Elizabeth Walsh, Jan. 19, 1952; children: Kerry Francis, Susan Margaret, Mary Ann, Timothy John. BS, Niagara U., 1948; MS, U. Notre Dame, 1950, PhD, 1952; MEd, Bridgewater State Coll., 1960. Instr. St. Mary's Coll., South Bend, Ind., 1951-52, Detroit Dental Sch., 1952-53; prof. Stonehill (Mass.) Coll., 1953-60; prof. emeritus biology Niagara (N.Y.) U., 1960—; instr. Niagara County Community Coll., part-time, 1969-75. Contbr. articles to profl. jours. Mem. Congressman's Environ. Oversight Com., 1978—, Gov.'s Environ. Siting Bds., 1986, 89. With U.S. Army, 1945-46. U. Notre Dame teaching fellow, 1949-52; postdoctoral fellow U. Minn., summer, 1958, U. Mich., summer, 1959, MIT, summer 1960, Harvard U., summer 1962. Mem. AAAS, Am. Genetic Soc., Soc. Study Evolution, Soc. Systematic Zoology, Albertus Magnus, Am. Inst. Biol. Scis., Torrey Bot. Soc., Sigma Xi, Delta Epsilon Sigma, Sigma Alpha Sigma. Office: Niagara U PO Box 121 Niagara University NY 14109-0121

REELING, GLENN EUGENE, psychology educator, researcher; b. Dover, Pa., Aug. 21, 1930; s. Irvin Roy and Dora lMay (Swartz) R.; m. Patricia ann Glueck, Aug. 18, 1962; children: Craig, Aimée. BS, Pa. State U., 1952; MS, U. N.Mex., 1958; postgrad., U. Cin., 1958-59; EdD, Ind. U., 1962. Tchr. math. and sci. Kennard-Dale Jr. and Sr. High Sch., Fawn Grove, Pa., 1954-55; tchr. 5th grade Newberrytown (Pa.) Elem. Sch., 1955-56; tchr. gen. math. grade 9 Albuquerque Pub. Schs., 1956-59; tchr. math. and sci. jr. and sr. high schs. Cin. Pub. Schs., 1959-60; teaching assoc. Ind. U., Bloomington, 1960-62; test editor Houghton Mifflin Co., Boston, 1962-63; dir. testing and rsch. Montclair (N.J.) Pub. Schs., 1963-66; prof. psychology and edn. Jersey City State Coll., 1966—. Cpl. U.S. Army, 1952-54, Korea. Mem. AACD, Am. Edn. Rsch. Assn., Am. Psychol. Assn., Am. Assn. Higher Edn., New Jersey Edn. Assn. Higher Edn. (bd. dirs. 1978—), Phi Delta Kappa. Lutheran. Home: 4 Cutlass Way Waretown NJ 08758-2105 Office: Jersey City State Coll Kennedy Blvd Jersey City NJ 07305

REEMELIN, ANGELA NORVILLE, dietitian consultant; b. Pitts., Apr. 28, 1945; d. Richard Gerow and Kathleen Taylor (Brannen) Norville; m. Philip Barrows Reemelin, Nov. 17, 1973; children: Richard Barrows, Kathleen Easson. BS, U. Tenn., 1967; dietetic intern, Emory U., 1968. Cert. water safety instr. Adminstr. dietitian Servomation of Atlanta, 1968-70; food svc. dir. ARA Food Svcs., Norfolk, Va., 1970-80; cons. Jacksonville, Fla., 1980—; cons. William T. Hall Convalescent Home, Portsmouth, Va., 1975-79. Recipient Outstanding Young Dietitian award Tidewater Dietetic Assn., 1974; Best of Show in sewing FFWC State Arts Festival, 1985, 86, 87. Mem. ARC (30 yr. Vol. award), ADA, Am. Soc. Hosp. Food Svc. Adminstrs., Jr. Womans Club Orange Park (pres. 1986-87, v.p., fundraiser, membership chair, Outstanding Dist. Pres. 1987), U. Tenn. Alumni Assn. (pres. 1982-84, bd. govs. 1984-85), Omicron Nu. Roman Catholic. Home: 601 Lorn Ct Orange Park FL 32073-4228

REEMTSMA, KEITH, surgeon, educator; b. Madera, Calif., Dec. 5, 1925; children: Lance Brewster, Dirk Van Horn. BS, Idaho State Coll., 1948; MD, U. Pa., 1949; D in Med.Sc., Columbia U., 1958. Diplomate Am. Bd. Med. Examiners, Am. Bd. Surgery (planning com. 1968-70, nominating com. 1970, com. on certification for spl. competence 1971), Am. Bd. Thoracic Surgery. Intern Presbyn. Hosp., N.Y.C., 1950-51, asst. resident in surgery, 1951-55, resident in surgery, 1956, chief resident in surgery, 1957; asst. surgery Columbia Coll. Physicians and Surgeons, N.Y.C., 1957; mem. faculty Tulane U. Sch. Medicine, New Orleans, 1957-66, prof. surgery, 1966—; head dept. surgery U. Utah Coll. Medicine, Salt Lake City, 1966-71; chmn. dept. surgery, Valentine Mott prof. surgery, Johnson and Johnson disting. prof. surgery Columbia U., N.Y.C., 1971-94; dir. surg. svc. U. Utah, 1966-71, Presbyn. Hosp., 1971-94. Contbr. articles to profl. jours. Lt. (j.g.) USNR, 1951-53; lt. MC USN, 1953. Mem. AMA, ACS, Soc. Clin. Surgery, Am. Surg. Assn., Soc. U. Surgeons (treas. 1962-75), So. Soc. for Clin. Rsch., Am. Fedn. for Clin. Rsch., Am. Assn. for Thoracic Surgery, Soc. for Vascular Surgery, Internat. Cardiovascular Soc., So. Thoracic Surg. Assn., New Orleans Surg. Soc., Surg. Assn. La., La. Med. Soc., Orleans Parish Med. Soc., Surg. Biology Club II, Western Surg. Assn., Alpha Omega Alpha. Office: Columbia University Dept Surgery 630 W 168th St New York NY 10032-3702

REEPING, JANICE CAROL, health services administrator; b. Johnstown, Pa., July 12, 1939; d. John David and Adele Grace (Irwin) Niesner; m. John Francis Ziants, Aug. 31, 1963 (dec. Aug. 1970); children: John Jeffrey Ziants, James Francis Ziants; m. Theodore V. Reeping Jr., June 8, 1976. BSEd, Indiana U. of Pa., 1975. Co-owner M&R Vocat. Inst., Greensburg, Pa., 1984-85; dir. nursing Mt. View Ctr., Greensburg, 1980-86, adminstr., 1987-89; corp. nurse cons. Integrated Health Svcs. Inc., Hunt Valley, Md., 1986-87; regional dir. Integrated Health Svcs. Inc., Pa., 1989-91; adminstr. VHA/LTC, Venice, Fla., 1991-93, Health Care and Retirement Corp., Brooksville, Fla., 1993—; advisor Area Agy. on Aging, Venice, Fla., 1991-93, Econ. Devel. Com., Hernando County, Fla., 1995—. Mem., participant Leadership Hernando Program, Brooksville, Fla., 1994—. Mem. NAFE, Kappa Delta Pi. Office: Heartland Health Care Ctr 575 Lamar Ave Brooksville FL 34601

REES, ALLAN HUGH, pediatrician, educator; b. Santiago, Chile, Dec. 16, 1940; came to U.S., 1973; s. Charles Henry and Sara Jane (Jones) R.; m. Vivian Frances Liscombe, Apr. 26, 1968; children: Bryan, Jennifer. MD, U. Chile, Santiago, 1968. Diplomate Am. Bd. Pediatrics and Pediatric Cardiology. Resident in pediat. U. Chile Children's Hosp., 1968-70, fellow in pediat. cardiology, 1971-72; instr. in pediatrics U. Chile, 1972-73; resident in pediat. U. Louisville, 1973-74, asst. prof., 1977-83, assoc. prof., 1983-89, prof., 1989—, dir. med. edn. divsn. pediatric cardiology, 1978—, dir. preventive pediatric cardiology, 1990—; fellow in pediat. cardiology Med. Coll. Ga., 1975-77; pediatric cardiologist Pediatric Cardiology Assocs., Louisville, 1977—; mem. med. staff Pres. Kosair Children's Hosp., Louisville, 1986; cons. in pediatric cardiology Ireland Army Hosp., Ft. Knox, Ky., 1980—. Co-author: Innovations Congenital Heart Surgery; editor: Handbook of Pediatric Cardiology, 1987. Active Sister Cities of Louisville, 1993—. Recipient Humanitarian award Mayor of City of Louisville, 1993, Republic of Ecuador, 1994. Fellow Am. Acad. Pediatrics, Am. Coll. Cardiology; mem. Am. Heart Assn. (mem. coun. cardiovascular diseases of young 1990—). Home: 3705 Gaston Ct Louisville KY 40241 Office: Pediatric Cardiology Assocs 601 S Floyd St Louisville KY 40202

REES, JOSEPH RICHARD, physician, surgeon; b. Salt Lake City, Apr. 8, 1938; s. Don Merrill and Norma Josephine (Anderson) R.; m. Patricia Anne Long, June 29, 1963; children: Wendi, Kelly, Richard. BS, U. Utah, 1959, MD, 1962. Intern in surgery N.Y. Hosp.-CUMC, N.Y.C., 1962-63, resident in surgery, 1963-70, asst. clin. prof. in surgery, 1970-71; asst. clin. prof. surgery U. Utah, Salt Lake City, 1971—; attending surgeon McKay-Dee Hosp., Ogden, Utah, 1971—. Contbr. numerous articles to profl. jours. 2d lt. VANG, 1956-62. Office: 924 24th St Ogden UT 84401

REESE, ANDY CLARE, immunology and microbiology educator; b. Coffeyville, Kans., June 22, 1942; s. Clarence William and Rubye (Miller) R.; m. Alice Lucille Burt, Aug. 7, 1965. Student, Coffeyville Coll., 1960-61; BS in Chemistry, U. Okla., 1964; PhD in Biochemistry, U. Mo., 1970; MBA, Augusta Coll., 1991. Chemist Skelly Oil Co., Eldorado, Kans., 1964-66; rsch. assoc. Case Western Res. U., Cleve., 1970-74; asst. rsch. prof. Mt. Sinai Sch. Medicine, CUNY, 1974-75; asst. prof. cell biology and anatomy Med. Coll. Ga., Augusta, 1975-81, assoc. prof., 1981—, dir. MD-PhD program, 1991-94; pres. Multimedia Learning Resources Inc., 1995—. Editor-in-chief Ga. Jour. Sci., 1988-92; contbr. chpts. to books and articles to profl. jours. Mem. Wyche Fowler Senatorial Campaign Com., Augusta, 1986, Greater Augusta Arts Coun., 1987—, Hist. Augusta, 1990—; mem. Augustans Together, chmn. bd. trustees, 1994-95; chmn. bd. trustees Augusta Players, Inc., 1988, 93-94; mem. exec. com. Imperial Theatre, Inc., Augusta, 1988-89; chmn. Grad. Faculty, 1990-91; bd. dirs. Unitarian Universalist Assn., Augusta, 1993-95, pres.-elect, 1996—; mem. organizing com. Don Johnson (U.S.) Congrl. Campaign, 1994. Mem. AAUP (pres. Med. Coll. Ga. chpt. 1983-84, 90-92, exec. coun. Ga. Conf. 1991-94), Ga. Acad. Sci. (exec. com. 1988—, pres.-elect 1994-95, pres. 1995-96), Soc. for Leukocyte Biology (teller's com. 1984-94, constn. and bylaws com. 1987-94), Am. Assn. Immunologists, Sigma Xi (program chmn. CSRA chpt 1996—), Phi Kappa Phi. Democrat. Office: Med Coll Ga Dept Immunology Microb Augusta GA 30912

REESE, DAVID, physician, pediatric ophthalmologist; b. Akron, Ohio, Aug. 6, 1943; s. Paul O. and Dorothy (Engle) R. BA, Earlham Coll., 1966; MD, U. Ky., 1971. Diplomate Am. Bd. Ophthalmology. Intern Wesley Hosp., Wichita, Kans., 1971-72; resident in ophthalmology U. Iowa Hosp., Iowa City, 1980-84, pediat. ophthalmology fellow, 1985; pediat. ophthalmology fellow Johns Hopkins Hosp., Balt., 1986, Smith-Settlewell Eye Rsch. Inst., San Francisco, 1986; asst. prof. New Eng. Med. Ctr., Boston, 1987-93; dir. The Children's Strabismus Ctr., Walthm, Mass., 1993—; dir. The Mass. Presch. Vision Screening Initiative, 1995—; cons. Nat. Birth Defects Ctr., Waltham, 1994—; spkr. in field. Editor (newsletter) Straight Talk, 1994—; prodr. (ednl. video) Before Your Child's Surgery, 1995; contbr. chpts. to books, articles to profl. jours. Mem. Waltham Head Start Health Adv. Com., 1995—. Recipient Leinfelder award U. Iowa Hosp., 1984, Fellowship grant, Heed Found., 1986, Fellowship grant Nat. Children's Eye Care Found., 1986, Residents' award for tchg. excellence New Eng. Med. Ctr., 1993. Fellow Am. Acad. Ophthalmology, Am. Acad. Pediat.; mem. AMA, Am. Assn. for Pediat. Ophthalmology, Mass. Soc. Eye Physicians, Mass. Med. Soc. (com. sch. health and sports medicine 1995—), New Eng. Ophthal. Soc. Methodist. Office: Childrens Strabismus Ctr 40 Second Ave Ste 510 Waltham MA 02154

REESE, JEFFREY HURN, urologic surgeon; b. Apple Valley, Calif., Nov. 27, 1957; s. Dudley Lake and Lydia (Hurn) R.; m. Linda Margaret Waters, May 19, 1984; children: Stephen, Jennifer, Ashley. BS, Johns Hopkins U., 1979, MD, 1982. Diplomate Am. Bd. Urology. Resident in surgery/urology Stanford (Calif.) U., 1982-88; chief urology divsn. Palo Alto (Calif.) Vets. Hosp., 1988-90; asst. prof. urology Stanford U., 1988-94, assoc. prof., 1994—; assoc. chief urology Santa Clara Valley Med. Ctr., San Jose, Calif., 1990-96, chief urology, 1996—; mem. urology adv. bd. Laserscope Inc., San Jose, 1993-94. Patentee direct vision surg. probe. Mem. AMA, Am. Urol. Assn., Am. Soc. Clin. Oncologists. Office: Santa Clara Valley Med Ctr Dept Urology 751 S Bascom Ave San Jose CA 95128

REESE, JON ALLEN, surgeon; b. Poteau, Okla., Jan. 31, 1955; s. Homer Calvin and Patricia (Hively) R.; m. Kimberly Kay Sullivan, Nov. 12, 1983; children: Jon Michael, Matthew Steven, Samuel Clayton. BS in Biochemistry, U. North Tex., Denton, 1977; MD, Southwestern Med. Sch., Dallas, 1981. Diplomate Am. Bd. Surgery, S.W. Surg. Congress. Intern surgery U. Okla., Oklahoma City, 1981-82, resident, 1982-85, chief resident, 1985-86; surgeon Med. Arts Clinic, Ardmore, Okla., 1986-88, Smith-Glynn-Callaway, Springfield, Mo., 1988-94, Springfield Clinic, 1994—; med. dir. vascular lab. St. John's Regional Health Ctr., Springfield, 1991—, chmn. surgery sect., 1995—. Fellow ACS, Am. Coll. Angiology; mem. Soc. Laparosopic Surgery. Office: Springfield Clinic 3231 S National Springfield MO 65807

REESE, LAWRENCE, ophthalmologist; b. Bklyn., Jan. 18, 1948; s. Samuel Isaac and Miriam (Bernstein) R.; 1 child, Michael. BA in Chemistry, NYU, 1969; MD, Cornell U., 1973. Intern Bellevue Hosp., N.Y.C., 1973-74; resident N.Y. Hosp.-Cornell, N.Y.C., 1974-77; chief resident N.Y. Hosp., 1977; fellow Bascom Palmer Eye Inst., Miami, Fla., 1977-78; clin. asst. prof. U. Miami Sch. Medicine, 1979—; ophthalmologist specializing in retinal and macular disease Retinal and Macular Cons., Aventura, Fla., 1979—; presenter in field. Contbr. articles to profl. jours. Maj. ARNG, 1974-80. Fellow ACS, Am. Acad. Ophthalmology. Office: Retinal & Macular Cons 21110 Biscayne Blvd Aventura FL 33180

REESE, NORMA CAROL, psychologist; b. Biloxi, Miss., Oct. 26, 1946; d. Virgil Stephen and Lila Mae (Shelton) Tatom; m. John Jay Reese, June 5, 1965 (div. Mar. 1983); children: Cher LeAnne, James Steven. AA in Psychology, Dade County Jr. Coll., Kendall, Fla., 1971; BS in Psychology, U. Miami, 1973; MS and PhD in Psychology, U. So. Miss., 1976. Lic. psychologist, Minn., N.D. Rsch. asst. NASA Lang. Rsch. Lab., Coral Gables, Fla., 1971-73; psychology instr. U. So. Miss., Hattiesburg, 1975-76, Grambling (La.) State U., 1976-78; clin. psychologist II Lake Charles (La.) Mental Health Ctr., 1979-83; tng. cons. Human Rels. Cons., Lake Charles, 1983-86; clin. dir. Grafton (N.D.) State Sch., 1986-89; dir. psychol. svcs. State Devel. Ctr., Grafton, 1989-95; ind. contractor, cons. psychol. svcs. Harley Residential Svcs. (name changed to Applied Behavioral Cons., Inc. 1990), Roseville, Minn., 1990-91; pvt. practice MYNDAK Moblie Cons., Minn. and N.D., 1990-95; program dir. for spl. needs Saint Coletta Sch., Jefferson, Wis., 1995—, mem. human rights and sexual health curriculum coms., 1995—; dir. sexual health project for devel. disabled and mentally retarded N.D. Dept. Human Svcs., Grafton, 1989-95, dir. sex offender and treatment program devel. disabled offenders, 1986-87; mem. adj. faculty grad. clin. psychology dept. U. N.D., Grand Forks, 1994—. Author: The Bulletin of the Psychonomic Soc., 1975-76; author/cartoonist The Worm Runner's Digest, 1975-80. Freedom writer Amnesty Internat., Midwest, 1989; founding mem. Sexual Health Coalition Steel of N.D., 1990; nat. disaster mental health technician, chpt. family svc. worker Red River Valley chpt. ARC, 1993—; mentor Am. Assn. Mental Retardation, 1992—; vol. Red Cross Nat. Disaster Mental Health Team, 1993, Emilys List, 1993. Named Silver Knight candidate, art, Miami (Fla.) Herald News, 1965; nominated Profl. of the Yr., La. Assn. Retarded Citizens, Lake Charles, 1983. Mem. APA (Div. 10), N.D. Psychol. Assn. (legis. action com. 1990-91, mem. disaster action com. 1993-94, mem. women in psychology 1995), Am. Assn. Mental Retardation (sec.-treas. N.D. chpt. 1991), Women in Networking, Assn. for Advancement of Psychology, Assn. for Sexual Abuse Prevention, Assn. for Play Therapy, Century Club. Republican Methodist. Office: St Coletta Sch Hwy 18 Jefferson WI 53719-2428

REESE, RONALD CRAIG, physician; b. Harrisburg, Pa.; s. Earl Joseph and Catherine Elizabeth (Hughes) R.; divorced; children: Brian Alexander, Daniel Tyler, Melanie Elizabeth. BA in Physics, Franklin & Marshall Coll., 1979; MD, Pa. State U., 1983. Diplomate Nat. Bd. Med. Examiners. Intern Nassau County Med. Ctr., East Meadow, N.Y., 1983-84; radiology resident NYU Med. Ctr., N.Y.C., 1984-88, chief resident, 1987-88; ptnr. Montclair (N.J.) Radiol. Assocs. P.A., 1992—; med. advisor Mountainside Hosp. Sch. Radiography, 1990-95, treas. med. staff, 1995—; co-dir. MR imaging ctr. Mountainside Hosp., 1993; trifounder, treas., bd. dirs. Intelliquest Internat. Corp., 1991. Inventor fiber optic connector, 1983. Trustee Park United Meth. Ch., 1995—. Kershner physics scholar Franklin & Marshall Coll., Lancaster, Pa., 1979; recipient Dr. Aaron B. Chausmer award Nat. Student Research Forum, Galveston, Tex., 1985. Mem. Radiol. Soc. N.Am., Am. Coll. Radiology, Radiol. Soc. of N.J., Radiology Quality Assurance Com. (chmn. 1990—), Med. Records Com. Republican. Home: 15 Wesley Pl Nutley NJ 07110-3353 Office: Montclair Radiol Assocs PA 116 Park St Montclair NJ 07042-2930

REESE, RONNIE L., medical technologist, consultant; b. Banana River, Fla., Oct. 7, 1945; s. Herman Andrew and Mary Emma (Burrows) R.; m. Linda Sue Taylor, Nov. 15, 1969; 1 child, Wendy Dawn. BS, U. Okla., 1967, M in Bus. Mgmt., 1981; postgrad., Lasalle U., 1994—. Chemistry supr. Bone and Joint Hosp., Oklahoma City, 1978-84; outpatient lab. dir. Northwest Labs., Oklahoma City, 1984-86; dean of allied health United Tech. Inst., Oklahoma City, 1986-88; clin. lab. mgr. LHS Diagnostics Svcs., Oklahoma City, 1988-92; pvt. practice Midwest City, Okla., 1992-93; lab. mgr., cons. Preferred Healthcare Mgmt., Hugoton, Kans., 1993-94; mng. lab. dir. Lake Tahoe Med. Ctr., Incline Village, Nev., 1994—; adv. bd. Draughan Coll., Oklahoma City, 1987-92; owner POL Consulting Bus., Crystal Bay Nev., 1992—. Contbr. articles to profl. pubs. Bd. dirs. Young Reps., Oklahoma City, 1984-92, Okla. AIDS Found., Oklahoma City, 1984-93, Lake Tahoe AIDS Found., Incline Village, 1995—; organizing com. Northern Lights, Incline Village, 1994—; host com. Walk the Lake AIDS Walk, Incline Village, 1995—. Named Med. Tech. of Yr., Okla. Soc. for Med. Technologists, 1981, Allied Health Profl. of Yr., Okla. Gov., 1982, Tech. of Yr., Am. Soc. for Med. Technologists, 1983, Vol. of Yr., Okla. AIDS Found., 1986. Fellow Royal Acad. Medicine; mem. Am. Med. Technologist (student councillor), Clin. Lab. Mgrs. Assn. (state pres., bd. dirs.), Am. Soc. Clin. Lab. Scis. (all offices). Home: PO Box 1117 Crystal Bay NV 89402

REESE, TED M., dentist; b. Dayton, Ohio, Jan. 21, 1959; s. Virgil Marion and Elizabeth June (Holmes) R.; m. Lisa M. Hein, Sept. 3, 1988. Student, Anderson (Ind.) Coll., 1977-80; DDS with distinction, Ind. U., Indpls., 1984. Gen. practice dentistry Clinton, Ind., 1984-87; practice specializing in implant dentistry Indpls., 1987—; co-founder, pres. Med./Dental Missions, Inc., 1988; treas. Ctrl. Ind. Dental Implant Study Group, v.p., 1990-91, pres., 1991-92; co-chmn. Ind. Acad. Gen. Dentistry. Vol. Project Ptnr. in Christ, Middletown, Ohio, 1984, Good Shepherd Ministries, Rockledge, Fla., 1985, Orphans, Inc., 1984, Dayspring Ministries; chmn. profl. edn. Am. Cancer Soc., Vermillion County, Ind., 1986; mem. River Oaks Presbyn. Ch. Fellow Am. Acad. Implant Dentistry, Midwest Implant Inst., Internat. Congress of Oral Implantology; mastership Acad. Gen. Dentistry; mem. ADA, Ind. Dental Assn., Indpls. Dist. Dental Soc. (past editor), Indpls. Gen. Dental Study Club (v.p.). Republican. Office: 7218 Us Highway 31 S Indianapolis IN 46227-8539

REESE, WILLIAM ALBERT, III, psychologist; b. Tabor, Iowa, Nov. 23, 1932; s. William Albert and Mary-Evelyn Hope (Lundeen) R.; B.A., U. Washington Reed Coll., 1955; M.Ed., U. Ariz., 1964, Ph.D., 1981; m. Barbara Diane Windermere, Dec. 22, 1954; children: Judy, Diane, William IV, Sandra-Siobhan, Debra-Anne, Robert-Gregory, Barbara-Joanne. Diplomate Am. Bd. Christian Psychology. Clin. Psychology cons. Nogales Pub. Schs., Nogales-Tucson, Ariz., 1971-79; clin. psychologist Astra Found., N.Y.C., 1979-86, chief psychology svc., neuropsychiatry, 1980-89; chief psychologist Family Support Ctr. Community-Family Exceptional Mem. Svcs., Sonoita, Ariz., 1986-89, Psychol. Svc. Ctr., Mount Tabor, Iowa, 1989-95, Calif. Ctr., 1995—; dir. religious Marriage and Family Life Wilderness Ctr., Berchtesgaden, W.Ger., summer 1981-82; exec. sec. Astra Ednl. Found., 1975-79, bd. dirs., 1979—, EEO officer, 1978—. Served with USAF, 1967-71: Vietnam. Decorated Bronze Star. Fellow in cons. psychology and holistic medicine Clin. Services Found., Ariz., 1979—. Fellow Am. Psychol. Soc.; mem. Calif. Psychol. Assn., Ariz. Psychol. Assn., Am. Counseling Assn., Iowa Psychol. Assn. Clubs: Los Padres Wilderness Center. Outdoor, Sierra, Skyline Estates Golf and Country (Tucson), K.C. Author: Developing a Scale of Human Values for Adults of Diverse Cultural Backgrounds, 1981, rev. edit., 1988. Office: Psychol Service Ctr Integrated Med Ctr-Wellness Clin 225 Crossroads Blvd Ste 417 Carmel CA 93923-8649 also: Box 1089 Bellevue NE 68005-1089

REEVE, ANTHONY EDMUND, biochemist; b. Christchurch, New Zealand, Aug. 30, 1946; s. Northleigh Frank Edmund and Patricia Clarice (Rose) R.; m. Shona Margaret Plowman, Jan. 19, 1971; children: Katharine Anna, Charlotte Helen. BSc, Canterbury U., Christchurch, 1968; MSc, Otago U., Dunedin, New Zealand, 1971, PhD, 1975. Postdoctoral fellow Johns Hopkins U., Balt., 1975-79; rsch. fellow U. Otago, 1980-84, sr. rsch. fellow, 1985-90, dir. cancer genetics lab., 1989—, professorial rsch. fellow, 1991—; vis. fellow Australian Nat. U., 1993; vis. investigator U. Mich., Ann Arbor, 1987-88; mem. sci. com. Cancer Soc. New Zealand, 1994; convenor forward planning rsch. com. U. Otago Med. Sch., 1992. Contbr. 52 articles to profl. jours. Bd. dirs. Dunedin Sinfonia Orch., 1983-86, 87-90. Fogarty Internat. Postdoctoral fellow, NIH, 1975-79. Fellow Royal Soc. N.Z. Office: Univ of Otago Dept Biochemistry, PO Box 56, Dunedin New Zealand

REEVE, HAROLD RANDOLPH, urologist; b. Vernal, Utah, June 9, 1945; s. Eldrow and Marjorie (Seely) R.; m. Marie Christine Olsen, June 11, 1976; children: Sarah, Kimberly, David, Andrew. BS, Colo. State U., 1968; MD, U. Pa., 1972. Diplomate Am. Bd. Urology. Urologist Urology Physicians PA, Mt. Holly, N.J., 1979—; bd. trustees Meml. Hosp. Burlington County, Mt. Holly, 1994-95; pres. med. staff Meml. Hosp. Burlington County, Mt. Holly, 1994-95. Maj. USAF, 1974-76. Fellow ACS; mem. AMA, Am. Urol. Assn., Med. Soc. N.J., Burlington County Med. Soc. (pres. 1987-88). Mem. LDS Ch. Office: Urology Physicians PA 217 Madison Ave Mount Holly NJ 08060

REEVE, THOMAS SMITH, surgeon; b. Queanbeyan, NSW, Australia, Nov. 23, 1923; s. Thomas Carlisle and Laura Margaret (MacLennan) R.; m. Mary Jo Bradley, Apr. 17, 1953; children: Thomas Carlyle, Anne Bradley, Graham Douglas. MB, BS, U. Sydney (Australia), 1947, MD (hon.), 1991. Lic. surgeon. Sr. resident fellow thoracic surgery Albany Hosp. Med. Coll., N.Y., 1954-55; sr. lectr. U. Sydney, 1961-64, assoc. prof. surgery, 1964-73, prof., 1973-88, emeritus prof., 1989—; chmn. No. Sydney Area Health Svc., 1988—; exec. officer The Australian Cancer Network, 1994—. Contbr. articles to profl. jours. Mem. Royal Australasian Coll. Surgeons (pres. 1989-91), Internat. Assn. Endocrine Surgeons (pres. 1985-87), Com. Pres. Med. Colls. (pres. 1989-92). Home: 84 Sutherland Rd, Sydney Beecroft 2114, Australia Office: 43 Palmerston Rd, Hornsby NSW 2077, Australia

REEVES, A. SUE WINDSOR, healthcare administrator; b. Oxford, Miss., Mar. 1, 1947; d. Alton Eugene and Mary Emma (Haney) Windsor; m. Johnny Lafayette Reeves Jr., Nov. 1, 1969; children: Ashley Renee, Lesley Windsor, Douglas Stephens. BA in Edn., U. Miss., 1969; MEd, La. State U., 1972. Cert. tchr., La. Tchr. Jackson (Miss.) Pub. Schs., 1969-71; profl. vol. Nat. Assn. Jr. Aux., Slidell, La., 1979-87; tchr. St. Tammany Parish Schs., Slidell, 1981-83; dir. infant youth services Slidell Meml. Hosp., 1984, dir. community relations, 1984-85, dir. women's ctr., 1985-87, dir. physician recruitment, 1985-87, dir. physician services, 1987-90; exec. dir. Women's Health Found. Am. Med. Internat., New Orleans, 1986-88; asst. chair for adminstrn. dept. ob/gyn. U. N.C. Sch. Medicine, Chapel Hill, 1990-91; asst. adminstr. Highland Med. Ctr., Lubbock, Tex., 1991-94; physician recruitment dir. Tex. Tech. U. Health Sci. Ctr. and Univ. Med. Ctr., 1994-95; adminstr. Lubbock Ind. Physician Assn., 1995—; mem. com. Women's Health Found. La.; healthcare cons., 1989-96; cons. Pro-Active Mgmt., 1995—; ind. rep. Excel Telecomms. Project designer Vol. Coord. Ctr., 1983, bd. dirs., 1983-88; exec. dir. Women's Health Found., 1987-88; mem. gala com. Leukemia Soc. Am., 1989; founding bd., v.p. Women's Health Care Exec. Network, New Orleans, 1988-90, West Tex. Speakers, 1992; sec. Lubbock Mentor Coun., 1993-96, Exec. Forum, 1994—, Women's Fin. Forum, 1995—; speaker Ann. Women's Wellness Conf., Lubbock, 1992—, 94, Teen Health Conf., Lubbock, 1994. State La. grantee, 1982; recipient Tex. Vol. award Tex. Dept. of Human Svcs., 1994, Commendation award Lubbock Mentoring Coun., 1995. Mem. NAFE, Am. Assn. Med. Colls., Nat. Assn. Jr. Aux. (Martha Wise award 1984, nat. com. woman 1982-87), Am. Coll. Healthcare Execs., Assn. for Mgrs., Ob-Gyn. Med. Group Mgmt. Assn., Assn. for Profl. Women Medicine, Slidell Panhellenic, Univ. Women's Club, Nat. Assn. Women's Health Profls., Lubbock C. of C. (healthcare com.), Phi Kappa Phi, Phi Mu. Republican. Home: 3504 84th Lubbock TX 79423-2025 Office: PO Box 53104 Lubbock TX 79453

REEVES, BILLY DEAN, obstetrics and gynecology educator emeritus; b. Franklin Park, Ill., Jan. 17, 1927; s. Barney William and Martha Dorcus (Benbrook) R.; m. Phyllis Joan Faber, Aug. 25, 1951; children: Philip, Pamela, Tina, Brian, Timothy. BA, Elmhurst (Ill.) Coll., 1953; BS, U. Ill., Chgo., 1958, MD, 1960; post grad., UCLA, N.Mex. State U., 1953-54, 75-76. Diplomate Am. Bd. Ob-Gyn. Intern Evanston (Ill.) Hosp., 1960-61, resident ob-gyn., 1961-64; NIH fellow in reproductive endocrinology Karolinska Hosp. and Inst., Stockholm, 1968-69; pvt. practice Evanston, 1964-71, Las Cruces, N.Mex., 1972-77; from instr. to asst. prof. Dept. Ob-gyn. Northwestern U. Med. Sch., 1964-71; assoc. prof. Dept. Ob-gyn. Rush Med. Coll., Chgo., 1971-72; clin. assoc. in ob-gyn. U. N.Mex. Med. Sch., Albuquerque, 1972-77; clin. assoc. U. Ariz. Sch. Medicine, Tucson, 1975-78; from clin. prof. to prof. emeritus Tex. Tech. Med. Sch., El Paso, 1976-91. Contbr. 70 articles and chpts. to med., profl. jours., 1958-93. Adv. bd. Associated Home Health Svcs., Inc., Las Cruces; adv. com. N.Mex. State U. Nursing Sch.; community adv. com. Meml. Gen. Hosp., Las Cruces; tech. advisor on health edn. N.Mex. Health Systems Agy.; mem. N.Mex. State U. Task Force 88; bd. dirs. Meml. Med. Ctr, Los Cruces, 1989-91, Parenthood Edn. Assn. of El Paso, Inc., Planned Parenthood of South Ctrl. N.Mex. (chmn. med. adv. com.). With USNR, 1945-46, 82-88, U.S. Army, 1946-47. Recipient Elmhurst Coll. Alumni Merit award, 1990, William W. Fry award for profl. excellence Tex. Tech. U. Sch. Medicine, 1979. Mem. AMA, ACS, AAAS, ACOG, Am. Coll. Physician Execs., Am. Assn. Advancement Humanities, Am. Fertility Soc., Assn. Profs. Ob-Gyn., North Am. Ob-Gyn. Soc., Ctrl. Assn. Ob-Gyn., Chgo. Gyn. Soc., Com. for Philosophy in Medicine, Dona Ana County Med. Soc. (assoc.), El Paso County Med. Soc., El Paso Surg. Soc., Endocrine Soc., Inst. Medicine in Chgo., Hasting Ctr., N.Mex. Med. Soc. (assoc.), N.Mex. Ob-Gyn. Soc., Soc. for Health and Human Values, Tex. Med. Assn., Tex. Assn. Ob-Gyn., U.S.-Mexico Border Health Assn. Home: 1620 Altura Ave Las Cruces NM 88001-1532

REEVES, CARLA MARIANNE, women's health, nurse midwife; b. San Francisco, June 25, 1949; d. Robert Dwight and Irma Marianne (Nelson) R. BS in Nursing, U. Md., Balt., 1971; MS in Nursing, U. Ky., 1975. RN, Ariz., Calif.; cert. nurse midwife, Ariz., Calif. Commd. officer U.S. Army, 1967-77; commd. officer USAF, 1978, advanced through grades to maj., 1971-83; nurse, midwife USAF Hosp. Luke, Luke AFB, Ariz., 1978-84, sr. nurse, midwife, 1985-88; sr. nurse, midwife Regional Med. Ctr., Clark Air Base, The Philippines, 1984-85; ret., 1988; nurse midwife S.W. Women's Health Svcs., Phoenix, 1988-94, Loma Vista Med. Group, San Jose, Calif., 1994-96, Palo Alto Med. Found., Fremont, Calif., 1996—; pvt. duty-clinic nurse Homemakers Upjohn, Santa Maria, Calif., 1978; ob-gyn nurse practitioner Planned Parenthood Santa Barbara (Calif.), Inc., 1978. Decorated Meritorious Svc. medal with oak leaf cluster; named Ariz. Outstanding Achievement-PMH Physician Office Nurse of Yr., 1992. Mem. Am. Coll. Nurse Midwifes (cert.), Assn. of Women's Health, Obstetric and Neonatal Nurses, Soc. of Retired Air Force Nurses, World Wildlife Fund, Ariz. Humane Soc., Doris Day Animal League, Cousteau Soc. Home: 882 Bedford St Fremont CA 94539 Office: Palo Alto Med Found 39500 Liberty St Fremont CA 94538-2211

REEVES, JUDY SHERRILL, medical record technician; b. Clarksville, Tenn., Feb. 11, 1961; d. Alfred M. Sherrill and Betty H. Sherrill Robertson; m. Donnie R. Reeves, May 11, 1979; 1 child, Craig. Bus. degree, U. Ky., 1980, liberal arts degree, 1985. Accredited record technician. Quality improvement dir. Jennie Stuart Med. Ctr., Hopkinsville, Ky., 1981-93; quality improvement dir., risk mgr. Cumberland Hall Psychiat. Hosp., Hopkinsville, 1993-95; med. record scvs. project mgr. Blanchfield Army Cmty. Hosp., Ft. Campbell, Ky., 1995—; cons., project mgr. BMAR & Assocs., Hopkinsville, 1995—; cons. in accreditation Ky. Hosp. Assn., Louisville, 1995. Author in field. V.p. PTA, Hopkinsville, 1993, pres., 1994. Mem. Nat. Assn. for Healthcare Quality (state rep.), Ky. Assn. for Healthcare Quality (pres. 1994-95, bd. dirs. 1993-96), Western Ky. Assn. for Healthcare Quality (pres. 1993-96), Ky. Health Info. Mgmt. Assn. (com. 1989—), Am. Health Info. Mgmt., Pennyrile Health Info. Assn. (pres. 1988-90). Home: 3708 Dale Hollow Hopkinsville KY 42240 Office: BMAR & Assocs 933 W 9th St Hopkinsville KY 42240

REEVES, NANCY ALICE, critical care nurse; b. Manhasset, N.Y., Aug. 19, 1965; d. Kenneth George and Jean Adele (Reineke) Leib. BSN, Hartwick Coll., 1988. RN, N.Y. Staff nurse intermediate care unit Mercy Med. Ctr., Rockville Center, N.Y., 1988-92, staff nurse CCU, 1992—; office nurse Gary Friedman, MD, Rockville Center, 1993—. Mem. AACN, N.Y. State Nurses Assn., Alpha Omicron Pi.

REFINETTI, ROBERTO, physiological psychologist; b. Sao Paulo, Brazil, Nov. 19, 1957; came to U.S., 1988; s. Renato and Maria Stella (Barroso) R.; m. Kathleen Diane Zylan, Mar. 5, 1988 (div. Aug. 1991); 1 child, Lauren Lynne. BA in Philosophy, Pontifical Cath. U., Sao Paulo, 1981; BS in Psychology, U. Sao Paulo, 1981, MA in Psychology, 1983; PhD in Psychology, U. Calif., Santa Barbara, 1987. Asst. prof. U. Sao Paulo, 1986-88; postdoctoral fellow U. Calif., Santa Barbara, 1988-89, U. Ill., Champaign, 1989-90, U. Va., Charlottesville, 1990-92; asst. prof. Coll. William and Mary, Williamsburg, Va., 1992—. Contbr. over 90 articles to profl. jours. Area grantee NIH, 1996; recipient Nat. Rsch. Svc. Individual award NIMH, 1991, Career award NSF, 1995. Mem. Am. Physiol. Soc., Am. Psychol. Soc., Soc. Neuroscience, Soc. Rsch. on Biol. Rhythms. Office: Coll of William and Mary Dept Psychology Williamsburg VA 23187

REGAL, ROBERT DENIS, radiologist, oncologist; b. Arles, Provence, France, Jan. 31, 1941; s. Rene Germain and Madeleine (Belin) R.; m. Simone Marie Louise Trouche, Feb. 3, 1966; children: Olivier, Jerome, Caroline. Cert. electro-radiology, Montpellier Med. Faculty, 1969, cert. rhumatology, 1971, MD in legal reparation for phys. injury, 1972, diploma medicine and biology related to sport, 1975. Resident Montpellier Hosps., 1965; hosp. asst., head hosp. svc. Monpellier Med. Faculty, 1970-74; radiologist, oncologist Clementville Pvt. Hosp., Montpellier, France, 1974—; advisor Montpellier Ct. Appeals. Editor, contbr. Resonance annual med. mag.; contbr. articles to profl. jours. Pres., Montpellier-Lodeve Med. Union, 1982-85, regional Union Qualified Electro-Radiologists, Languedoc-Roussillon, Héraultais Med. Com. for Breast Cancer Detection; bd. dirs. Nat. Fedn. Qualified Electro-Radiologists Languedoc-Roussillon; mem. directing com. Languedoc-Roussillon Regional Coun. for Further Med. Tng. Lt. Health Svc., 1967-68. Decorated Silver Cross for French Award for Merit and Dedication, Languedoc Com., 1989. Mem. French Oncology Assn. (sec.), French Soc. Med. Radiology, European Soc. for Therapeutic Radiology and Oncology, French Soc. Legal Medicine and Criminology, Assn. Doctors, Biologists and Chemists, Order of Doctors of Hérault (dept. coun.). Roman Catholic. Home: 74 Rue de la farigoule, 34090 Montpellier France Office: Clinique Clementville, 25 rue de Clémentville, 34000 Montpellier France

REGAN, DAVID MICHAEL, health care administrator; b. Phila., Oct. 3, 1955; s. James Rodman and Dorothy Marie (Jones) R.; m. Cathy Jean Aspril, June 13, 1981; children: Bethany Ann, Sarah Kathleen. BA,

Franklin and Marshall Coll., 1977; MS in Health Planning and Adminstrn., Pa. State U., 1984. Cert. med. practice exec. Adminstrv. asst. York (Pa.) Hosp., 1983; asst. dir. office emergency med. services Pa. State U., University Park, 1983-84; adminstrv. asst., research analyst L.I. Jewish Med. Ctr., New Hyde Park, N.Y., 1984-85; asst. adminstr. Geisinger Clinic, Lewistown, Pa., 1985-88, mgr. of revenue, reimbursement, 1987-90, adminstrv. dir. primary care svcs., 1990-93; dir. HealthAm., 1993-96; COO Lexington Clinic, Ky., 1996—; bd. dirs. Geisinger Fed. Credit Union. Mem. Pa. Med. Group Mgmt. Assn. (pres. 1995-96), Pa. Med. Soc., Med. Group Mgmt. Assn., Juniata Area C. of C. (bd. dirs. 1987-88), Nat. Health Lawyers Assn., Rotary Club. Office: Lexington Clinic 1221 S Broadway Lexington KY 40504

REGAN, ELLEN FRANCES (MRS. WALSTON SHEPARD BROWN), ophthalmologist; b. Boston, Feb. 1, 1919; d. Edward Francis and Margaret (Moynihan) R.; AB, Wellesley Coll., 1940; MD, Yale U., 1943; m. Walston Shepard Brown, Aug. 13, 1955. Intern, Boston City Hosp., 1944; asst. resident, resident Inst. Ophthalmology, Presbyn. Hosp., N.Y.C., 1944-47, asst. ophthalmologist, 1947-56, asst. attending ophthalmologist, 1956-84; instr. ophthalmology Columbia Coll. Physicians and Surgeons, 1947-55, asso. ophthalmology, 1955-67, asst. clin. prof., 1967-84. Mem. Am. Ophthal. Soc., AMA, Am. Acad. Ophthalmology, N.Y. Acad. Medicine, N.Y. State Med. Soc., Mass. Med. Soc., River Club. Office: PO Box 632 Tuxedo Park NY 10987-0632

REGAN, JAMES ARTHUR, physician assistant, medical tecbnologist; b. North Babylon, N.Y., Mar. 30, 1960; s. Harold John Charles and Ruth Anne Howe R.; m. Melanie Lynne Mead, Mar. 15, 1980; children: Kara Anne, James Arthur Jr. AS in Biology, New River C.C., Dublin, Va., 1981; AAS in Biology, Med. Tech., Wytheville (Va.) C.C., 1983; BS in Biology, Chemistry (microbiology), Va. Polytech. and State U., 1987; physician asst., Wake Forest U., 1993. Med. technologist Roche Biomed., Richmond, Va., 1987-89; microbiologist NAVCARE, Jacksonville, N.C., 1989-91, Bapt. Hosp., Winston Salem, N.C., 1991-93; physician asst. James Crosswell, Beaufort, N.C., 1993—; mem. bd. dirs. Health Effectiveness Coun., N.C., 1992—, monitor, peer contact, 1994—; lab. supr. James Crosswell MD, P.A., Beaufort, N.C., 1992—; cons. Cateret Sch. System, 1994. Fellow Am. Soc. Clin. Pathologists (med. tech. 1983, microbiology specialist 1988); mem. Am. Acad. Physician Assts., Nat. Commn. on Cert. Physician Assts. (cert.), N.C. Assn. Physician Assts., Rotary Club Beaufort. Roman Catholic. Home: 704 Comet Dr Beaufort NC 28516 Office: James Crosswell MD PA 97 Campen Rd Beaufort NC 28516

REGAN, PETER FRANCIS, III, physician, psychiatry educator; b. Bklyn., Nov. 11, 1924; s. Peter Francis Jr. and Veronica (Tierney) R.; m. Laurette Patricia O'Connor, June 18, 1949; children: Peter, Stephen, William, Elizabeth, John, Carol. MD, Cornell U., Ithaca, N.Y., 1949. Diplomate Am. Bd. Psychiatry and Neurology, Nat. Bd. Med. Examiners. Intern in medicine N.Y. Hosp., 1949-50; asst. resident psychiatry Payne Whitney Psychiat. Clinic, 1950, 53-54, resident, 1954-56; asst. prof. psychiatry Cornell U. Med. Coll., 1956-58; prof., head dept. psychiatry U. Fla. Coll. Medicine, chief psychiat. svc. Univ. Teaching Hosp., 1958-64; prof. psychiatry SUNY, Buffalo, 1964-84, v.p. health affairs, 1964-67, exec. v.p. univ., 1967-69, exec. v.p., acting pres. univ., 1969-70, vice chancellor acad. programs, 1970-71; assoc. chief staff for edn. Buffalo VA Med. Ctr., 1979-84; prof. psychiatry U. Tex. Health Sci. Ctr., San Antonio, 1984-87, assoc. dean Sch. Medicine, 1986-87; assoc. chief staff for edn. San Antonio VA Med. Ctr., 1984-86, chief staff, 1986-87; dep. assoc. chief med. dir. for acad. affairs VA Cen. Office, Washington, 1987-88, assoc. chief med. dir. for acad. affairs, 1988-92; prof. emeritus / sen. cons. dept. psychiatry SUNY, Buffalo, N.Y., 1992—; project dir. Ctr. for Ednl. Rsch. and Innovation, OECD, 1972-74. Author: (with F. Flach) Chemotherapy in Emotional Disorders, 1960, (With E. Pattishall) Behavioral Science Contributions to Psychiatry; contbr. articles to profl. jours. Capt. M.C. AUS, 1951-52. Fellow Am. Psychiat. Assn., Am. Coll. Psychiatrists (bd. regents 1986-95, 2d v.p. 1988, 1st v.p. 1989, pres.-elect 1990, pres. 1991); mem. AMA, Alpha Omega Alpha. Home: 900 Delaware Ave # 504 Buffalo NY 14209-2012 Office: SUNY Dept Psychiatry 462 Grider St Buffalo NY 14215-3075

REGECOVÁ, VALÉRIA, biologist, researcher; b. Trenčín, Slovak Republic, Dec. 25, 1954; d. Milan Peter and Valéria (Talamonová) Petrová; m. Miroslav Regec, Oct. 22, 1977; children: Milan, Vojtech, Adam. RNDr, Komensky U., Bratislava, Slovakia, 1980. Asst. prof. Faculty of Natural Science, Bratislava, Slovakia, 1980-81; rsch. asst. Slovak Acad. of Science, Bratislava, 1981—. coord. Soroptimist Internat., Bratislava, 1995—. Mem. Slovak Physiological Soc., Anthropological Soc. of Slovakia. Home: Klemensova str Nr 7, 81109 Bratislava Slovak Republic Office: Inst Normal & Pathological Physiology, Sienkiewiczova 1, 81371 Bratislava Slovak Republic

REGELSON, WILLIAM, physician, educator; b. N.Y.C., July 12, 1925; s. Joseph and Anna (Wolfson) R.; m. Sylvia Phillips, Nov. 28, 1948; children: Rachel, Jessica, Miriam, Esther, Naomi, Isaac. AB, U. N.C., 1948; MD, SUNY, Bklyn., 1952. Intern Maimonides Hosp., Bklyn., 1952-53; resident Meml. Hosp./Sloan Kettering, N.Y.C., 1953-55; fellow cancer rsch., sr. cancer rsch., assoc. chief medicine Roswell Park Meml. Inst., Buffalo, N.Y., 1955-67; prof. medicine Med. Coll. Va./Va. Commonwealth U., Richmond, 1967—, adj. prof. microbiology and biomed. engring., 1978—; cons. in field. Author: Melatonin Miracle, 1995; editor: Biologic Action of DHEA (Pehtdroepirndrostgrone), 1990, Intervention in the Aging Process, 1983. Sgt. U.S. Signal Corps, 1943-46. Office: Med Coll Va/Va Commonwealth Box 980273 Richmond VA 23298

REH, THOMAS EDWARD, radiologist, educator; b. St. Louis, Sept. 12, 1943; s. Edward Paul and Ceil Anne (Golden) R.; m. Benedette Texada Gieselman, June 22, 1968; children: Matthew J., Benedette T., Elizabeth W. BA, St. Louis U., 1965, MD, 1969. Diplomate Am. Bd. Radiology, Nat. Bd. Med. Examiners. Intern St. John's Mercy Med. Ctr., St. Louis, 1969-70; resident St. Louis VA Hosp., 1970-73; fellow in vascular radiology Beth Israel Hosp., Boston, 1973-74; radiologist St. Mary's Health Ctr., St. Louis, 1974—, chmn. dept. radiology, 1986—; clin. asst. prof. radiology St. Louis U. Sch. Medicine, 1978—; clin. assoc. prof. radiology, 1989—. Mem. Am. Coll. Radiology, AMA, Radiol. Soc. N.Am., St. Louis Met. Med. Soc., Alpha Omega Alpha, Alpha Sigma Nu, Delta Sigma Phi. Republican. Roman Catholic. Clubs: St. Louis, Confrerie des Chevaliers du Tastevin. Home: 9850 Waterbury Dr Saint Louis MO 63124-1046 Office: Bellevue Radiology Inc 1699 S Hanley Rd Saint Louis MO 63144-2913

REHANI, MADAN MOHAN, physicist, researcher; b. Panipat, Haryana, India, Oct. 14, 1950; s. S. L. and L. W. Rehani; m. Usha Malik, Nov. 30, 1979; children: Bhavya, Navya. MS, Kurukshetra U., Haryana, 1972; PhD, All India Inst. Med. Sci., New Delhi, 1976. Lectr. Punjab U., Chandigarh, India, 1976-77, Postgrad. Inst. Med. Edn. & Rsch., Chandigarh, 1977-81; cons., asst. prof. S. K. Inst. Med. Sci., Srinagar, India, 1981-88; additional prof. All India Inst. Med. Sci., New Delhi, 1988—; expert panel mem. in Radiation of WHO, expert Internat. Atomic Energy Agy., UN, Mulago Hosp., Kampala, Uganda, 1993; vis. scientist Forschungzentrum, Jülich, Germany, 1991; chmn. U.P.-Delhi chpt. Assn. Med. Physicists of India, 1990-95. Editor: Physics of Medical Imaging, 1991, Radiation Safety in Medicine, 1992, Diagnostic Imaging: Quality Assurance, 1995; mem. editl. bd.: Jour. Nuclear Medicine, 1988, 89, Jour. Med. Physics, 1992-95; contbr. numerous rsch. papers and editls. to profl. jours. and books. Rsch. grantee WHO, Atomic Energy Regulatory Bd., Indian Coun. of Med. Rsch. Mem. Am. Assn. Physicists in Medicine, Internat. Orgn. Med. Physics (mem. edn. and tng. com. 1990—, Soc. Nuclear Medicine (life), Assn. Med. Physicists India. Office: All India Inst Med Scis, Inst Rotary Cancer Hosp, 110 029 New Delhi India

REHM, LYNN PAUL, psychologist, educator; b. Chgo., May 20, 1941; s. Stanley Franklin and Bernice Agnes (Stiebler) R.; m. Susan Hanson Higginbotham, Feb. 28, 1964; children: Elizabeth Susan, Sarah Ann. BA, U. So. Calif., 1963; MA, U. Wis., 1966, PhD, 1970. Asst. prof. neuropsychiat. inst. UCLA, 1968-70; assoc. prof. U. Pitts., 1970-79; prof. U. Houston, 1979—; cons. tex. Dept. Corrections, Huntsville, 1986-93. Editor: Behavior Therapy for Depression, 1981, (with others) Psychology Research, Public Policy and Practice, 1985. Fellow APA; mem. Assn. for Advancement Behavior Therapy, Soc. for Psychotherapy Rsch., Soc. for Rsch. in Psychopathology, Tex. Psychol. Assn., Phi Beta Kappa. Office: U Houston Dept Psychology Houston TX 77204

REHNKE, ERNEST CURT, physician; b. Tuscaloosa, Ala., Mar. 3, 1953; m. Linda Rehnke; 1 child, Elizabeth. MD, St. George's U., 1981. Diplomate Am. Bd. Surgery; ACLS. Resident Downstate Med. Ctr., Bklyn., 1983; resident in gen. surgery Meth. Hosp., Bklyn., 1981-85, chief resident in gen. surgery, 1985-86; cardiovascular surgery fellow Tex. Heart Inst., Houston, 1986-87; asst. prof. U. S. Fla. Coll. of Medicine, 1986-96; chief of surgery Edward White Hosp., 1992-94, chief of staff, 1993-96; hosp. affiliations included St. Anthony's Hosp., Bayfront Med. Ctr., Edward White Hosp., Palms of Pasadena Hosp., St. Petersburg Gen. Hosp., Northside Hosp., St. Petersburg Surgery Ctr., all in Fla. Fellow Am. Coll. Surgeons; mem. Am. Soc. Laser Medicine and Surgery, Denton A. Cooley Cardiovascular Surg. Soc., Fla. Med. Assn., Pinellas County Med. Soc., Southeastern Surg. Congress, Fla. Vascular Soc., Omicron Delta Kappa. Home: 7800 Second Ave South Saint Petersburg FL 33707 Office: 1615 Pasadena Ave S Ste 460 Saint Petersburg FL 33707

REHORN, LOIS M(ARIE), nursing administrator; b. Larned, Kans., Apr. 15, 1919; d. Charles and Ethel L. (Canaday) Williamson; m. C. Howard Smith, Feb. 15, 1946 (dec. Aug. 1980); 1 child, Cynthia A. Huddleston; m. Harlan W. Rehorn, Aug. 25, 1981. RN, Bethany Hosp. Sch. Nursing, Kansas City, Kans., 1943; BS, Ft. Hays Kans. State U., Hays, 1968, MS, 1970. RN, N.Mex. Office nurse, surg. asst. Dr. John H. Luke, Kansas City, Kans., 1943-47; supr. nursing unit Larned (Kans.) State Hosp., 1949-68, dir. nursing edn., 1968-71, dir. nursing, 1972-81, ret., 1981. Named Nurse of Yr. DNA-4, 1986. Mem. Am. Nurses Assn., Kans. Nurses Assn. (dist. treas.), N.Mex. Nurses Assn. (dist. pres. 1982-86, dist. bd. dirs. 1992-94). Home: 1436 Brentwood Dr Clovis NM 88101-4602

REIBER, GREGORY DUANE, forensic pathologist; b. Loma Linda, Calif., May 25, 1955; s. Clifford D. and Anna M. (Field) R.; m. Faustina Mae Davis, Feb. 10, 1980; children: Jenessa Anne, Zachary Duane. BS magna cum laude, Andrews U., Berrien Springs, Mich., 1977; MD, Loma Linda (Calif.) U., 1981. Diplomate Am. Bd. Pathology. Resident in pathology Loma Linda U. Med. Ctr., 1981-85; fellow in forensic pathology Root Pathology Lab., San Bernardino, Calif., 1985-86; assoc. pathologist Root Pathology Lab., 1986-90, No. Calif. Forensic Pathology, Sacramento, 1990—; asst. clin. prof. pathology Loma Linda U. Sch. Medicine, 1987-90, U. Calif., Davis, 1990—; program dir., forensic pathology fellowship NCFP/ U. Calif. Davis, 1994—; apptd. Calif. SIDS Autopsy Protocol Com. Contbr. articles to profl. jours. Fellow Am. Soc. Clin. Pathologists, Am. Coll. Forensic Examiners; mem. Am. Bd. Forensic Examiners, AMA, Internat. Wound Ballistics Assn., Nat. Assn. Med. Examiners, Am. Acad. Forensic Scis., Calif. Med. Assn., Sacramento-El Dorado Med. Soc., Alpha Omega Alpha. Republican. Seventh-day Adventist. Office: No Calif Forensic Pathology 2443 Fair Oaks Blvd Ste 311 Sacramento CA 95825-7684

REICH, JAMES HARRY, psychiatrist; b. N.Y.C., Oct. 25, 1950; s. Stanley Benjamin and Adelle Edith (Axelrod) R. BS, U. Calif., Berkeley, 1973; MD, U. Colo., 1978; MPH, Yale U., 1984. Diplomate Am. Bd. Psychiatry and Neurology. Resident in psychiatry U. Calif., Sacramento, 1978-82; fellow Yale U., New Haven, 1982-84; instr. in psychiatry Yale U. Med. Sch., New Haven, 1982-84; asst. prof. psychiatry U. Iowa Med. Sch., Iowa City, 1984-87, Harvard U., Cambridge, 1987—; assoc. prof. psychiatry Brown U., Providence, 1992-94; dir. ambulatory psychiatry St. Mary's Hosp., San Francisco, 1995-96, Kaiser of No. Calif., 1996—. Contbr. numerous articles to profl. jours. Mem. Am. Psychiat. Assn., Am. Psychopathologic Assn., found. treas. Assn. rsch. in Personality Disorders. Republican. Home and Office: 2255 N Point St #102 San Francisco CA 94123

REICH, NATHANIEL EDWIN, physician, poet, author, artist, educator; b. N.Y.C., May 19, 1907; s. Alexander and Betty (Feigenbaum) R.; m. Joan Finkel, May 22, 1943; children: Andrew, Matthew. B.S., NYU, 1927; student, Marquette U. Coll. Medicine, 1927-29; M.D., Rush Med. Coll., U. Chgo., 1932. Diplomate Am. Bd. Internal Medicine. Intern, resident pathologist City Hosp., N.Y.C., 1931-33; emeritus attending physician Kingsbrook Jewish Med. Center Hosp.; vis. physician Kings County Hosp., Bklyn.; attending physician State U. Hosp.; faculty SUNY Downstate Med. Center, 1938—, asso. clin. prof. medicine, 1952-74, clin. prof., 1974-77, emeritus prof., 1977—; vis. prof. San Marcos U. Coll. Medicine, Lima, Peru, 1968, U. Afghanistan, 1970, U. Indonesia, 1972, U. Sri Lanka, 1975; asst. attending physician N.Y. Postgrad. Hosp., Columbia U., 1940; cons. Dept. H and HS; cardiac cons. U.S. R.R. Retirement Bd., 1965—; program cons. Acad. Family Physicians, 1973, N.Y. State Disability Determinations; lectr. univs., Rome, Moscow, Rijeka, Haiti, Jerusalem, Cairo, Athens, Bangkok, Bucharest, Manila, Lisbon, Beijing, Shanghai, Romania, Taiwan, Cairo, Athens, Tunis, Triente, Madras, Dakar, Senegal, Durban, Witwatersrand, Capetown, Natal, Lima, Buenos Aires, Rio de Janeiro, Quito; 1st Am. physician invited to lecture in USSR, 1956; lectr. univs. U. Madras (India), 1969, Spain, 1971, Auckland, N.Z., Sydney, Australia, Senegal, Portugal; lectr. Japan Med. Assn., Philippine Heart Assn., Royal Thai Air Force Med. Svc., China Med. Assn., Shanghai, 1978, Nat. Taiwan U., Taipei, 1978, Beijing Cardiac Inst., 1986; chmn. internat. cardiology sect. Congress Chest Diseases, Cologne, Germany, 1956; impartial specialist U.S. Fed. Employees; cons. N.Y. State Bur. Disability Determinations, N.Y.C., Office Vocat. Rehab., Dept. Health and Human Svcs., 1965—; chief med. examiner SSS, 1942-44 (Presdl. commendation). One-man shows include L.I. U., 1961, NYU Loeb Ctr., 1962, 72, 74, Greer Gallery, 1962, 64, St. Charles, La., 1964, Nyack, N.Y., 1986, Prospect Park Ctrl. Art Show, 1966, Art Inst. Boston, 1970, 76, George Wiener Gallery, 1972; exhibited in group shows at Little Studio, 1952, Mus. Modern Art, Paris, 1970, Bodley Gallery, 1965, 69, Nyack, N.Y., 1987, others; represented in permanent collections at Huntington Hartford collection N.Y. Cultural Ctr., 1969, Washington County Mus. of Fine Arts, Hagerstown, md.; author 3 textbooks on cardiology; author chpts. in 3 encys.; author: A Renaissance Man at Large; author: (collected poems) Reflections, 1993. Served from 1st lt. to maj. M.C., AUS, 1944-47. Recipient St. Gaudens award, 1923, 1st prize Art Assn. AMA, 1948, 1st prize Art Assn. Literary Soc., 1949, Disting. Achievement award Boys' H.S. Alumni Assn., 1988, Am. Poetry Assn. Hon. mention World of Poetry, 1990; named Best New Poets of 1989, 94, 95. Fellow ACP, Royal Soc. Medicine (London), Am. Coll. Cardiology, Am. Coll. Angiology (med. honor award 1956, 59), Am. Coll. Legal Medicine (founder), Am. Coll. Chest Physicians (chmn. exhibits com. 1961, cardiovascular rehab. com. 1965, coronary disease com. 1968, pres. N.Y. state chpt. 1970); mem. N.Y. State Med. Soc. (vice chmn. space med. sect. 1967, 75, chmn. chest sect. 1972), Internat. Soc. Internal Medicine, World Med. Assn., Am. Heart Assn. (coun. on thrombosis), N.Y. Heart Assn., N.Y. Cardiol. Soc. (exec. bd., pres.), Explorers Club (4 explorations described in jour. 1966—), Temple Club (v.p.), Doctors Club Bklyn. (vice chmn. bd. govs.), Circumnavigators. Home: 1620 Avenue I Brooklyn NY 11230-3050

REICHEN, JÜRG, pharmacology educator; b. Aarau, Switzerland, Jan. 23, 1946; s. Hans A. and Susi (Aeberhard) R.; m. Suzi Graden, may 29, 1970; children: Hansjakob, Annemarie, Katharina. BA, Gymnasium City, Burgdorf, Switzerland, 1964; MD, U. Bern, Switzerland, 1971. Diplomate medicine. Fellow dept. exptl. medicine Hoffmann LaRoche, Basel, Switzerland, 1972; fellow dept. clin. pharmacology U. Bern, 1973-76, prof. medicine, clin. pharmacologist, 1986-94, dir. clin. pharmacologist and clin. rsch. depts., 1994—; intern, resident Georgetown U. and V.A. Med. Ctr., Washington, 1978-79; fellow div. GI UCHSC, Denver, 1980; asst. prof. div. GI and Clin. Pharmacology USHSC, Denver, 1980-84, assoc. prof., 1984-85; guest scientist Liver Unit, NIH, Bethesda, Md., 1976-78; mem. rsch. com. AASLD, Chgo., 1984-85; sec. scientific com. EASL, 1988-91. Editl. bd. Hepatology, 1988-94, Hepatol, 1994—; assoc. editor Jour. Hepatology, 1989-94, Hepatology, 1994-96; contbr. articles to profl. jours., chpts. to books. Mem. Fed. Commn. for MDPhD, Bern, 1994; referee SNF, DFG, NIH, INSERM and others. Recipient Prize of Faculty award U. Bern, 1976, Faculty Devel. award Pharm. Mfg. Assn., 1981-83, Rsch. Career Devel. award NIH, 1983-88, Swiss Nat. Found. Sci. Rsch. award, 1986-91, prize Swiss Soc. for Internal Medicine, 1987, Cloëtta award Cloëtta Found., Zurich, 1995. Mem. European Assn. Study of the Liver, Am. Assn. Study of Liver Disease, Am. Gastroenterology Assn., Western Soc. Clin. Investigators, Internat. Assn. Study of the Liver (counselor 1992-94), United European Gastroenterologists Fedn. (counselor 1991-95), European Soc. Biochem. Pharms. Office: Univ Bern Dept Clin Pharmacology, Murtenstrasse 35, CH-3010 Bern Switzerland

REICHENBACH, DENNIS DALE, physician, pathology educator; b. Billings, Mont., Sept. 14, 1933; s. Ernest A. and Lilli (Stockland) R.; m. Jean Karen Hickey, Feb. 27, 1960; children: Stephen, Laura. BS in Basic Med. Sci., U. Wash., 1955, MD, 1958. Intern King County (Wash.) Hosp., Seattle, 1958-59; resident in pathology U. Wash., Seattle, 1959-63, asst. prof. pathology, 1966-70, assoc. prof., 1970-75, prof., 1975—; dir. pathology residency program, U. Wash., 1981-88; pathologist in chief Harvorview Med. Ctr., Seattle, 1982—. Contbr. articles to profl. jours. Served with USPHS, 1963-65. Mem. Am. Assn. Pathologists (cert.), Soc. Cardiovascular Pathologists, King County Med. Assn. Home: 6548 49th Ave NE Seattle WA 98115-7733 Office: Harborview Med Ctr 325 9th Ave Seattle WA 98104-2420

REICHERT, CHERYL MCBROOM, pathologist, research consultant; b. Great Falls, Mont., Sept. 4, 1946; d. Harold and Arlyne (Cohn) R.; m. Sherwood McBroom Jr., 1964 (div. 1971); children: Scott, Cari. BS, Coll. of Great Falls, 1969; MS, U. Mich., 1971, PhD, 1974, MD, 1976. Diplomate Am. Bd. Med. Examiners, Am. Bd. Pathology. Tching fellow dept. biochemistry U. Mich., Ann Arbor, 1969-74; resident in anatomic pathology Nat. Cancer Inst., Bethesda, Md., 1977-79; resident in clin. pathology NIH, Bethesda, 1979-80, surgical pathologist, chief autopsy service, 1981-85; pathologist Sibley Meml. Hosp., Washington, 1985-86; cons. Digene Corp., College Park, Md., 1985-90, Nat. Cancer Inst., Bethesda, 1985-92; pathologist Columbus Hosp., Great Falls, 1987—, dir. labs., 1990-91, 94—; assoc. rsch. scientist McLaughlin Research Inst., Great Falls, 1987—; clin. assoc. prof. Uniformed Svcs. U. Health Scis., Bethesda, 1983-86; presenter President's Nat. Cancer Adv. Bd., Washington, 1983. Contbr. 50 articles to profl. jours. Trustee Coll. of Gt. Falls, 1991-94; mem. profl. edn. com. Am. Cancer Soc.; bd. dirs. Ann Arbor Child Care and Devel.; charter mem., bd. dirs. Project Heal Montana, 1993-96. Lt. comdr. USPHS, 1977-80. Named Outstanding Young Women of Yr., State of Mich., 1993, Great Falls Profl. Women of Yr., YMCA, 1991. Mem. U.S. Acad. Pathologists, Mont. Pathologists Soc. (pres. 1989-90, sec.-treas. 1990-91), Galens Med. Soc., Alpha Omega Alpha. Home: 51 Prospect Dr Great Falls MT 59405-4123

REICHERT, RICHARD WILLIAM, physician; b. Panama City, Fla., May 28, 1959; s. Wallace Alfred and Mary Edna (Hoskns) R.; m. Jill Elizabeth Heath, Nov. 1, 1986; children: Katherine, Molly, Sarah, Christine. AA, Univ. Fla., 1978, BS, 1980, MD, 1985; MBA, Univ. S.C., 1994. Diplomate Am. Bd. Ophthalmology. Internship medicine Boston Univ. Malden Hosp., Malden, Mass., 1985-86; residency, ophthalomlogy Duke Univ., Durham, N.C., 1986-89; fellowship The Eye Inst., Gainesville, Fla., 1989-90; pvt. practice Lake City, Jasper, Starke, Fla., 1990—; CEO North Fla. Surgery Ctr., Lake City, Fla., 1996—; con. VA. Hosp., Lake City, 1994—; externship St. Bartholomew's Hosp., London, 1986; mission physician Kamakwie Mission Hosp., Sierra Leone, Africa, 1985; tech. North Fla. Lions Eye Bank, 1979-84. Contbr. articles to profl. jours. Pres. Club Mem. Rep. Nat. Com., Washington, 1995—; scholarship ptnr., Univ. Fla. Gator Boosters, 1994—. Recipient Rsch. grant Southern Medical Assn., 1982, Annual Rsch. award Alpha Omega Alpha, 1986, rsch. fellowship Fight for Sight, 1979-81. Fellow Am. Acad. Ophthalmology, Am. Coll. Surgeons, Am. Soc. Ophthalmology Adminstrs., Rocky Mountain Trauma Soc., Fla. Soc. Ophthalmology. Republican. Presbyterian. Office: North Fla Surgery Ctr 1385 South First St Lake City FL 32025

REICHGOTT, MICHAEL JOEL, medicine educator, dean, physician; b. Newark, July 26, 1940; s. Leo and Gertrude (Millman) R.; m. Lynn Gay Haar, Dec. 22, 1962; children: Jay Howard, Seth Alan, Douglas Jordan. AB, Gettysburg (Pa.) Coll., 1961; MD, Albert Einstein Coll. Medicine, 1965; PhD, U. Calif., San Francisco, 1973. Diplomate Am. Bd. Internal Medicine. Fellow in clin. pharmacology U. Calif., 1969-72; asst. prof. medicine U. Pa., Phila., 1973-81, assoc. prof., 1981-84; assoc. prof. Albert Einstein Coll. Medicine, Bronx, N.Y., 1984-94, prof., 1994—, assoc. dean of students and grad. med. edn., 1989—; med. dir. Bronx Mcpl. Hosp. Ctr., 1984-89; bd. dirs. Holy Cross Care Systems, Inc., South Bend, Iowa; presenter in field. Contbr. articles to profl. jours. V.p. Larchmont (N.Y.) Temple, 1990-92, pres., 1992-94. Maj. M.C., U.S. Army, 1967-69, Vietnam. Fellow ACP (com.); mem. Assn. Am. Med. Colls. (com. 1990—), N.Y. Acad. Medicine, Phila. Acad. Medicine, Soc. for Gen. Internal Medicine (com.). Office: Albert Einstein Coll of Medicine 1300 Morris Park Ave Bronx NY 10461-1926

REICHLE, FREDERICK ADOLPH, surgeon, educator; b. Neshaminy, Pa., Apr. 20, 1935; s. Albert and Ernestine R. BA summa cum laude, Temple U., 1957, MD, 1961, MS in Biochemistry, 1961, MS in Surgery, 1966. Diplomate Am. Bd. Surgery. Intern Abington Meml. Hosp., 1962; resident Temple U. Hosp., Phila., 1966, surgeon, 1966—; practice medicine specializing in surgery Phila., 1966—; assoc. attending surgeon Epis. Hosp., St. Mary's Hosp., St. Christopher's Hosp. for Children, Phoenixville Hosp.; cons. VA Hosp., Wilkes Barre, Pa., Germantown Dispensary and Hosp.; site vis. Can. Dept. Health and Welfare Program Br., 1977; clin. prof. surgery Presbyn. -U. Pa. Med. Ctr., 1980; prof. clin. surgery U. Pa., 1980—, prof. clin. surgery Med. Coll. of Pa.; prof. surgery Temple U. Sch. Medicine; chmn. dept. surgery John F. Kennedy Meml. Hosp. Contbr. articles to profl. jours. Recipient Surg. Residents Rsch. Paper award Phila. Acad. Surgery, 1964, 66, Gross Essay prize, 1976; Am. Heart Assn. grantee, 1973. Fellow ACS, Coll. Physicians Phila.; mem. AMA, AAAS, Am. Surg. Assn., Soc. Univ. Surgeons, Pa. Med. Soc., Assn. Acad. Surgery, Chilean Surg. Soc., Royal Soc. Medicine, N.Y. Acad. Sci., Am. Fedn. Clin. Research, Nat. Assn. Professions, Am. Gastroent. Assn., Am. Assn. Cancer Rsch., Am. Heart Assn., Phila. Acad. Surgery, Heart Assn. Southeastern Pa., Internat. Soc. Thombosis and Haemostasis, Nat. Kidney Found., Soc. for Surgery Alimentary Tract, Soc. Vascular Surgery, Colleguim Internationale Chirurgie Digestivae, Am. Soc. Pharmacology and Exptl. Therapeutics, Am. Inst. Ultrasound in Medicine, Am. Physiol. Soc., Soc. Internationale de Chirurgie, Am. Soc. Abdominal Surgeons, Surg. Hist. Soc., Am. Aging Assn., Am. Geriatrics Soc., Gerontol. Soc., Am. Diabetes Assn., Surg. Biology Club, Omega Alpha, Sigma Xi, Phi Rho Sigma. Office: Cheltenham And Langdon St Philadelphia PA 19124

REICHMANN, HEINZ, physician, neurologist, educator; b. Friedrichshafen, Germany, Mar. 15, 1953; s. Hans Karl and Maria Reichmann; m. Hiltrud Jrmgard Langer, Mar. 7, 1979; children: Philipp Christopher, Kristina Ann. MD, Freiburg U., Germany, 1979. Rsch. fellow dept. biochemistry U. Konstanz, 1980-83; rsch. fellow Neurol. Inst. Columbia U., N.Y.C., 1983-84; med. asst. neurology U. Würzburg, 1984-88, cons. neurology, 1988-90, prof. neurology, vice chmn., 1990-95; chmn. dept. neurology U. Dresden, 1996—. Author: Mitochondrial Myopathies, 1988. Recipient Young Histochem. award Inst. for Histochemistry, 1984, Muscle Rsch. prize German Muscular Dystrophy Assn., 1991, Aging Studies rsch. prize Merck Co., 1993. Mem. Am. Neurol. Assn., Royal Soc. Medicine, N.Y. Acad. Scis., European Neurol. Soc., Soc. for Histochemistry, German Neurol. Soc. (Heinrich Pette prize 1988), German Biochem. Soc. Office: Univ Dresden Dept Neurology, Fetscherstr 74, D-01307 Dresden Germany

REID, HELEN VERONICA, dean; b. Reading, Eng., Sept. 25, 1956; d. Alan A. and Teresa H. (Thatcher) Ware; m. Gary B. Reid, May 29, 1976; children: Robert, Jennifer, Kristen. BA in Biolgoy, U. Tex., Austin, 1976; BSN, U. Tex., Arlington, 1978; MSN, Tex. Women's U., Denton, 1983. CCRN; cert. CPR instr. Asst. nurse coord., staff nurse, float pool nurse Parkland Meml. Hosp., Dallas, 1979-83, float pool nurse, 1987-93; instr. Trinity Valley Community Coll., Kaufman, Tex., 1983-86, freshman team leader, 1986-90; dean health occupations Trinity Valley C.C., Kaufman, Tex., 1990—. Mem. Nursing Network on Violence Against Women, Tex. Assn. Vocat. Nurse Educators, Orgn. for ADN (sec. 1988-92, nom. com. chair 1995-96), Tex. Jr. Coll. Tchrs. Assn., Tex. Assn. of Jr. and C.C. Instructional Adminstrs., Sigma Theta Tau. Home: 4332 Crestover Dr Mesquite TX 75150-4452

REID, JOHN LOW, pharmacologist, educator; b. Glasgow, Scotland, Oct. 1, 1943; s. James and Irene Margaret (Dale) R.; m. Randa Pharaon, May 2, 1964; children: James, Rebecca Louise. MA, Oxford (Eng.) U., 1965, BM BCh, 1967, DM, 1973. Rsch. fellow R.P.M.S., London, 1970-73, reader,

1975-78; vis. fellow MRC, Bethesda, Md., 1973-74; vis. scientist USPHS/NIMH, Bethesda, 1974-75; prof. U. Glasgow, Scotland, 1978—. Author: Lecture Notes in Clinical Pharmacology, 1981, 5th edit., 1996,. Fellow Royal Coll. Physicians;mem. European Soc. Hypertention (pres. 1991-93), Brit. Hypertension Soc. (pres. 1989-91). Office: U Glasgow Dept Medicine, Western Infirmary, Glasgow G11 6NT, Scotland

REID, JOHN MITCHELL, biomedical engineer, researcher; b. Mpls., June 8, 1926; s. Robert Sherman and Meryl (Mitchell) R.; m. Virginia Montgomery, Dec. 31, 1949 (div.); children: Donald, Kathryn, Richard; m. Shadi Wang, June 30, 1983. BS, U. Minn., 1950, MS, 1957; PhD, U. Pa., 1965. Engring. assoc. U. Minn., Mpls., 1950-54; rsch. engr. St. Barnabas Hosp., Mpls., 1954-57; assoc. U. Pa., Phila., 1957-66; rsch. asst. prof. U. Wash., Seattle, 1966-72; rsch. engr. Providence Hosp., 1972-74; dir. bioengring. Inst. of Applied Physiology & Medicine, 1973-81; Calhoun prof. Drexel U., Phila., 1981-94, prof. emeritus, rsch. prof., 1994; adj. prof. radiology Thomas Jefferson Med. Sch., Phila., 1982—; affiliate prof. U. Washington, 1995—; cons. Inst. Applied Physiology and Medicine, Seattle. Contbr. over 100 articles to profl. jours.; 5 U.S. patents on devel. of ultrasonic med. imaging. Scoutmaster Boy Scouts Am., Mpls., 1955-57, Phila., 1960-65, cub and scoutmaster, Seattle, 1965-70. With USN, 1950-52, World War II. Recipient Pioneer award Soc. of Vascular Technologists, 1994; grantee NIH. Fellow IEEE, Am. Inst. Ultrasound in Medicine (bd. govs., Pioneer award), Acoustical Soc. Am., Engring. in Medicine and Biology Soc. (Lifetime Achievement award 1993), Am. Inst. Med. and Biol. Engrs. Home: 16711 254 Ave SE Issaquah WA 98027-7262 also: Inst Applied Physiology and Medicine 701 16th Ave Seattle WA 98122-4525

REID, LAWRENCE H., physician, dermatologist; b. Tenn., Feb. 22, 1945; m. Donna Good. BS, U. Tenn., 1967, MD, 1970. Diplomate Am. Bd. Dermatology, Am. Bd. Pathology for Dermatopathology. Intern UCLA Harbor Gen. Hosp., Torrance, 1971-72; resident in dermatology U. Colo., Denver, 1972-75; assoc. clin. prof. U. Hawaii, 1975-77; physician Lodi (Calif.) Meml. Hosp.; physician Lodi Outpatient Surg. Ctr., pres. med. exec. com., 1992—. Contbr. articles to profl. jours. With U.S. Army, 1975-77. Mem. Calif. Med. Assn., San Joaquin Med. Soc., Am. Acad. Dermatology, Sacramento Valley Dermatologic Soc., Pacific Dermatologic Assn., Am. Soc. Dermatologic Surgery, Internat. Soc. for Dermatologic Surgery. Office: 421 S Ham Ln Ste A Lodi CA 95242-3523

REID, NANCI GLICK, health care professional; b. Brookline, Mass., Sept. 22, 1941; d. Robert Louis and Esther (Shostack) Green; m. Ronald Jay Coleman, July 5, 1962 (div. Sept. 1969); 1 child, Lori Sue; m. Alan Marshall Glick, Jan. 12, 1976 (div. Oct. 1978); 1 child, Staci Alison; m. Raymond Augustus Reid, Feb. 15, 1985. AS, Garland Jr. Coll., Boston, 1960; student, Harvard U. Extension, 1961, 64, 65; BS, Northeastern U., 1983, postgrad., 1989—; postgrad., Ecole Superieure de Commerce, Reims, France, 1990-91; MBA, Northeastern U., 1991. Cert. clin. lab. sci., clin. lab. specialist in cytogenetics. Rsch. technician Children's Hosp., Boston, 1961-63; sr. rsch. technician, med. technician New England Med. Ctr., Boston, 1963-65, 67-69; cytogeneticist supr. Carney Hosp., Boston, 1969-84; instr. medicine Med. Sch. Tufts U., Boston, 1969-86; systems analyst Cognos/Coulter Corp., Waltham, Mass., 1976-77; med. technologist Milton (Mass.) Hosp, 1978-83, Mass. Eye and Ear, Boston, 1983-84; lab. mgr. Harvard Cmty. Health Plan, Braintree, Mass., 1985-88; chairperson com. continuing edn. Harvard Cmty. Health Plan, Boston, 1986-88; quality control mgr. Oncolab Inc., Boston, 1988-90; supr. Park Med. Lab., Inc., 1990-91; clin. lab. adminstrn. Dept. Health and Hosp. Mattapan, Boston, 1991—; labo. coord. New England regional newborn screening program State Lab. Inst., Jamaica Plain, Mass., 1993-95; presenter abstracts at 12th and 13th Internat. Hematology Soc. confs. Contbr. articles to profl. jours. Vol. human body discovery space program Mus. Sci., 1990; adv. bd. trustees Jordan Hosp., 1993—. Mem. Assn. Cytogenetic Technologists (pres. 1976-78), Am. Soc. Med. Tech. (lectr.), Mass. Ski Club (supr. 1989—), Plymouth Yacht Club, Pythian Sisters Club (sec., editor 1966-67), Sigma Epsilon Rho (pres. 1994-96, v.p. 1987-88, former treas.). Republican. Jewish. Home: 10 Woodbine Dr Plymouth MA 02360-3525

REID, SUSAN JO, medical, surgical nurse, nursing administrator; b. Mansfield, Ohio, Oct. 17, 1953; d. James Harvey and Shirley Mae (Greving) Hawkins; m. Henry James Reid, April 1, 1971; children: Andrea Susan Reid Bell, Paul William, Jennifer Lynd. Student, Tyler (Tex.) Jr. Coll., 1989-91; BSN magna cum laude, U. Tex., Tyler, 1993. RN, Tex. Nurse asst. Hamlet Manor Nursing Home, Chagrin Falls, Ohio, 1980-81; nurse extern Mother Frances Hosp., Tyler, 1992-93, staff nurse, relief charge nurse, preceptor - new nurses, 1993—; peer tutor, lab asst. Tyler Jr. Coll., 1990-91; dept. safety officer Mother Frances Hosp., Tyler, 1993—, presenter extern orientation, preceptor nursing students, 1994. Sunday sch. tchr. Southside Baptist Ch., Tyler, 1990-93; first aid instr. ARC, Tyler, 1991-93. Mem. ANA, Tex. Nurses Assn., Sigma Theta Tau. Baptist. Home: 4320 County Rd 325 Lindale TX 75771

REID, WILLIAM HOWARD, psychiatrist; b. Dallas, Apr. 10, 1945; s. Howard Clinton and Lucile (Lattanner) R. BA, U. Minn., 1966, MD, 1970; MPH, U. Calif.-Berkeley, 1975. Diplomate Am. Bd. Psychiatry and Neurology, Am. Bd. Forensic Psychiatry, cert. in adminstrv. psychiatry. Intern, U. Calif.-Davis, 1970-71, resident in psychiatry, 1973-75; with Nebr. Psychiat. Inst., Omaha, 1977-86; med. dir. Colonial Hills/Hosp., San Antonio, 1986-89; med. dir. Tex. Dept. Mental Health and Retardation, Austin, 1989-96; prof. psychiatry U. Tex. Med. Sch., 1989—, Tex. A&M Coll. Med., 1991—. With M.C., AUS, 1971-73. Mem. Am. Psychiat. Assn., AMA, Am. Acad. Psychiatry and the Law (pres. 1988-89). Author: The Psychopath: A Comprehensive Study of Antisocial Disorders and Behaviors, 1978, Psychiatry for the House Officer, 1979, Basic Intensive Psychotherapy, 1980, The Treatment of Antisocial Syndromes, 1981, Treatment of the DSM-III Psychiatric Disorders, 1983, The Treatment of Psychiatric Disorders, 1989, Training Guide for the DSM-III-R, 1989; Editor-in-chief: Psychiatric Update Ser., 1995—; co-editor: Terrorism: Interdisciplinary Perspectives, 1983, Assaults Within Psychiatric Facilities, 1983, Unmasking the Psychopath, 1986, DSM IV Training Guide, 1995, Treatment of Psychiatric Disorders, 3rd edit., 1996; contbr. articles to sci. jours.; composer 25 mus. compositions. Office: PO Box 49817 Austin TX 78765

REIDA-ALLEN, PAMELA ANNE, healthcare consultant and administrator; b. Fitchburg, Mass., June 8, 1944; d. Alvah Michael Reida and Sirkka Margaret (Anttila) Kao; m. Dennis Alan Joaquin, 1967 (div. 1973); children: Joshua, Amy, Sebastian; m. Yahya Radazar, Oct. 1983 (dec. Sept. 1987); m. Loyall C. Allen. BA in English, Philosophy, Calif. State U., Los Angeles, 1966; RN diploma with honors, Leominster (Mass.) Hosp., 1976; BS in Nursing cum laude, Fitchburg (Mass.) State Coll., 1982; MS magna cum laude, Lesley Coll., 1986. Substitute tchr. Fitchburg Pub. Schs., 1966-67; social worker N.Y.C. Dept. Social Services, N.Y.C., 1967-68; news correspondent The Lowell (Mass.) Sun, 1969-71; nurse lab., delivery Leominster Hosp., 1976-77A; inservice coordinator Birchwood Manor Nursing Home, Fitchburg, 1977, asst. dir. nursing, 1977-78, dir. nursing, 1978-80; dir. nursing Naukeag Hosp., Ashburnham, Mass., 1980-84; asst. dir. nursing Beech Hill Hosp., Dublin, N.H., 1984-87, dir nursing, 1987-90, chair utilization rev. com., 1985-95; clin. coord. Hospice of Cape Cod, Yarmouthport, Mass., 1995—; mem. adv. council allied health majors Mass. Regional Vocat. Sch., Fitchburg, Mass., 1977-84; with Area Speakers Bur., Fitchburg, 1980-84, vice chair Quality Assurance Program, 1988; cons. Quality Healthcare Resources, Inc. subs. Joint Commn. on Accreditation of Hosps., 1988—, Joint Commn. on Accreditation of Healthcare Orgns., Chgo., 1988-95. Vol. Family Planning, Fitchburg, 1981-82; del. Intercity Mgmt. Council, Fitchburg, 1980-84; clin. coord. Hospice Cape Cod, 1995—. Mem. NAFE, Tri-City Nursing Home Assn. (pres. 1978-80), Nat. Nurses Assn., N.H. Nurses Assn. (program com. 1985—), Greater Fitchburg C. of C., N.H. Orgn. Exec. Nurses, N.H. Quality Assurance Assn. Office: Hospice of Cape Cod 962 Rt 6A Yarmouthport MA

REIDENBERG, MARCUS MILTON, physician, educator; b. Phila., Jan. 3, 1934; s. Leon and Adeline Reidenberg; m. June Wilson, July 14, 1957; children: Bruce, Joel, Julie. Student, Cornell U., 1951-54; MD, Temple U., 1958. Diplomate Am. Bd. Internal Medicine. Intern Community Gen. Hosp., Reading, Pa., 1958-59; resident Temple U. Hosp., Phila., 1962-65; from instr. to assoc. prof. Temple U. Med. Sch., Phila., 1962-75; assoc. prof. Cornell U. Med. Coll., N.Y.C., 1975-76, prof. pharmacology, head div. clin. pharmacology, 1976—, prof. medicine, 1980—, acting assoc. dean, 1981-82, asst. dean, 1988—; attending physician N.Y. Hosp., 1980—; vis. physician Rockefeller U. Hosp., N.Y.C., 1980—; mem. project adv. group FDA, Rockville, Md., 1977-82; vice chmn. Joint Commn. on Prescription Drug Use, Washington, 1977-80; mem. study sect. NIH, Bethesda, Md., 1980-86; del. U.S. Pharmacopeal Conv., 1975-80. Author: Renal Function and Drug Action, 1971; editor various books; editor Clin. Pharmacology and Therapeutics, 1985—; contbr. articles to profl. jours. Served to lt. M.C., USNR, 1960-62. Recipient Research Career Devel. award NIH, 1970, Julius Sturmer award Phila. Coll. Pharmacy and Sci., 1982. Fellow ACP; mem. Am. Soc. Clin. Investigations, Assn. Am. Physicians, Am. Soc. Clin. Pharmacology and Therapeutics (pres. 1984-85, Rawls Palmer award 1981), Am. Soc. Pharmacology and Exptl. Therapeutics (award 1983), Internat. Union Pharmacology (vice chmn. sect. clin. pharmacology 1984-87, chmn. 1987-89). Office: Cornell U Med Coll Dept Clin Pharmacology 1300 York Ave New York NY 10021-4805

REIDER, CARROLL ANN, nutritionist, consultant; b. Phoenix, Feb. 28, 1960; d. John Jerome and Patricia Elaine (Heath) Reider. BS in Nutrition, Calif. State U., Long Beach, 1983; Advanced MS in Nutrition, Inst. Health Professions, Mass. Gen. Hosp., Boston, 1989. Registered dietitian, cert. nutrition support dietitian. Clin. dietetic technician Hoag Hosp., Newport Beach, Calif., 1982-84; dietetic intern U. Calif., San Francisco, 1984-85; chief clin. dietitian, nutrition support specialist St. Mary's Med. Ctr., San Francisco, 1986-88; nutrition support team dietitian, surg. rsch. dietitian Mass. Gen. Hosp., Brigham & Women's Hosp., Harvard U., Boston, 1988-89; critical care nutritionist UCLA Med. Ctr., 1989-92, associated faculty, instr., 1989-94; corp. mgr. nutritional support svcs. Salick Health Care/INFUSX, Inc., Beverly Hills, 1992-95; cons., lectr., 1986—; home care nutrition cons. Am. Dietetic Assn., Chgo., 1993—. Contbr. articles to profl. jours. Mem. Am. Dietetic Assn. (excellence/leadership award 1993, 96, cert. of recognition 1992, 95, cabinet mem. dietitians in nutrition support practice group), Am. Soc. Parenteral and Enteral Nutrition. Home: 1521 Centinela Ave Apt A Santa Monica CA 90404-3206

REID-ROBERTS, DAYL HELEN, mental health counselor; b Rochester, N.Y., Oct. 15, 1941; d. Russell Harrison and Elizabeth Spencer (Page) Ferrey; m. David Alan Reid, July 16, 1960 (div. 1982); children: Deborah Elizabeth, Patricia Anne, David Alan Jr. (dec.), Matthew Stephen; m. David Gillies Roberts, Aug. 9, 1985. BA, Salisbury (Md.) State U., 1988, MEd, 1990. Lic. profl. counselor; cert. group psychotherapist. Clinician Community Svcs. Bd., Eastern Shore, Nassawadox, Va., 1990—; clinician substance abuse svc. Community Svcs. Bd., Eastern Shore, Onancock, Va., 1990—; clinican, mental social worker, psychiat. Northampton Accomack Meml. Hosp., Nassawadox, 1992-93; v.p. Humanitec, Inc., Accomac, Va., 1993—; instr. philosophy, psychology Ea. Shore Cmty. Coll., 1995—; asst. dir. Literacy Coun. of No. Va., Annandale, 1980-85. Contbr. articles to profl. jours. Treas., co-founder Ea. Shore Literacy Coun., 1986. Mem. Am. Counseling Assn., Am. Psychologists Assn. (student), Phi Sigma Tau, Kappa Delta Phi. Republican. Presbyterian. Home: The Oliver House Onancock VA 23417 Office: Humanitec Inc Front St PO Box 580 Accomac VA 23301-0580

REIF, MARY ELLEN, neurologist; b. Rock Island, Ill., Oct. 10, 1953; m. H.B. Edwards, Oct. 31, 1988; children: Conner, Lauren. BS, U. Iowa, 1975, MD, 1978. Resident U. Utah, Salt Lake City, 1979-82; neurologist pvt. practice, Seattle, 1982—. Mem. Am. Acad. Neurology. Office: 1229 Madison #1110 Seattle WA 98104

REIFF, JAMES STANLEY, addictions physician, psychiatric physician, osteopathic physician, surgeon; b. Chgo., Mar. 17, 1935; s. Nathan Edgar and Freda Matilda (Imhoff) R.; m. Sharon Ann Kraybill, June 9, 1956 (div. Apr. 1970); children: Gregory James, James Stanley II, Cynthia Diane, Jeffery Cameron. B.A. in Chemistry, Goshen Coll., 1957; D.O., Chgo. Coll. Osteo. Medicine, 1961. Biochemist Miles/Ames Pharm. Co., Elkhart, Ind., 1955-57; gen. practice medicine, Michigan City, Ind., 1962-69; addictions physician Oaklawn Psychiat. Ctr., Elkhart, Ind. 1974-84; clin. team leader, addictions team Oaklawn Ctr., Elkhart, 1980-83. Alcohol Anonymous Cen. Service Area Inc., 1984-87; med. dir., Life Recovery Cen., Elkhart, 1987-90; med. dir., Substance Abuse Coun. St. Joe County, Mich., 1990-95; med. dir. Am. Plasma Mgmt., Inc, Kalamazoo and East Lansing, Mich., 1991—; staff psychiatrist Community Mental Health Svcs. St. Joe County, 1993—; bd. dirs. Home for Runaway Kids - Victory House, Elkhart, Ind., 1974-76, 12 Step House Meth. Ch.-Halfway House, Elkhart, 1974-77; bd. dirs., treas. Caldwell Home Corp.-Social Rehab. Ctr. for Alcoholism, Elkhart, 1984-87; bd. dirs. Hope House, Jonesville, Mich.; organist First Presbyn. Ch., Sturgis, Mich., 1993—. Mem. AMA, Am. Osteopathic Assn., Am. Soc. Addiction Medicine (com. on addiction medicine in correctional facilities 1993—), Am. Med. Soc. on Alcoholism, Soc. Correctional Physicians, Nat. Coun. on Alcoholism and Drug Dependence in Mich., Mich. State Med. Soc., St. Joe County Med. Soc., Am. Osteopathic Assn. Avocations: organ and piano playing. Home: 1301 E Congress St Sturgis MI 49091-2326 Office: Cmty Mental Health St Joe County 210 S Main St Three Rivers MI 49093

REIFFEL, JAMES, physician; researcher, educator; b. N.Y.C., Sept. 20, 1943; s. Martin Lawrence and Roslyn (Siskind) R.; m. Bonnie Geffen, Mar. 18, 1967; children—Gabrielle, Jamie. B.A., Duke U., 1965; M.D., Coll. of Physicians and Surgeons, Columbia U., 1969. Intern, Presbyn. Hosp., N.Y.C., 1969-70, resident, 1970-72; fellow in cardiology, 1972-74, asst. physician, 1974-76, asst. attending physician, 1976-80, assoc. attending physician, 1980-88, attending physician, 1988—, assoc. dir. electrophysiology lab., 1979—, dir electrophysiology programs College of Physician and Surgeons. Columbia U. N.Y.C. 1991—; assoc. in clin. medicine College of Physicians and Surgeons, Columbia U., N.Y.C., 1974-76, asst. prof. clin. medicine, 1976-80, assoc. prof. clin. medicine, 1980-88, prof. clin. medicine, 1988—. Diplomate Am. Bd. Internal Medicine, subsplty. bd. Cardiovascular Disease; cert. Nat. Bd. Examiners. Author numerous abstracts, sci. papers. Contbr. numerous articles to profl. jours. Served with USAR, 1970-76, chief of medicine, 1972-76. Fellow ACP, Am. Heart Assn. Council on Clin. Cardiology, Am. Coll. Cardiology, N.Y. Cardiol. Soc.; mem. N.Y. Heart Assn., Med. Soc. County of N.Y., Med. Soc. State of N.Y., Am. Fedn. for Clin. Research, Cardiac Electrophysiologic Soc., N.Am. Soc. Pacing & Electrophysiology. Office: 161 Ft Washington Ave New York NY 10032-3713

REIFLER, CLIFFORD BRUCE, psychiatrist, educator; b. Chgo., Dec. 28, 1931; s. Eugene Alan and Harriet (Offer) R.; m. Barbara Karnuth, Sept. 11, 1954; children: Margery Sue, Cynthia Jean, Angela Harriet. AB, U. Chgo., 1951; BS, Northwestern U., 1953; MD, Yale U., 1957; MPH, U. N.C., 1967. Intern Univ. Hosps., Ann Arbor, Mich., 1957-58; resident in psychiatry Strong Meml. Hosp., Rochester, N.Y., 1958-61; mem. faculty U. N.C. Med. Sch., 1963-70, assoc. prof. psychiatry, 1969-70, assoc. prof. mental health Sch. Pub. Health, 1969-70, sr. psychiatrist, chief mental health sect., student health svc., 1963-70; prof. health svcs., psychiatry and community and preventive medicine U. Rochester Med. Sch., 1970-94, dir. univ. health svc., 1970-80, 81-94, prof. emeritus of psychiatry and health svcs., dir. emeritus, 1994—, interim v.p. student affairs, 1980-81, sr. assoc. dean for clin. affairs Sch. Medicine and Dentistry, acting chmn. dept. health svcs., 1983-85; med. dir. Strong Meml. Hosp., 1983-85; bd. dirs. Genesee Valley Group Health Assn., 1972-82; cons. in field; vis. prof. of psychiatry, Harvard U. Med. Sch., 1987; Dana L. Farnsworth hon. cons. Harvard U. Health Service, 1987. Coauthor: Mental Health on the Campus-A Field Study, 1973; co-author: The Alternative Services: Their Role in Mental Health, 1975, Old Folks at Home-A Field Study of Nursing and Board-and-Care Homes, 1976; exec. editor Jour. Am. Coll. Health, 1983—; mem. editorial bd. Jour. of Coll. Student Psychotherapy, 1986—; contbr. profl. jours. Bd. dirs. Am. Coll. Health Found., 1994—, chair 1995—; bd. dirs. Rochester Meml. Soc., 1971-74; mem. med. adv. com., bd. dirs. Planned Parenthood Rochester and Monroe County, 1973-74; mem. devel. com. Seneca Zool. Soc., 1990-95, chair 1993-95, trustee, 1991—; mem. mem. com. Rochester Philharm. Orch. Inc., 1981-83. With M.C., USAF, 1961-63. Fellow Am. Coll. Health Assn. (pres. 1976-77, Edward Hitchcock award 1981, Ruth C. Boynton award 1988), Am. Psychiat. Assn. (life), Am. Coll. Physician Execs. (disting.); mem. N.Y. State Coll. Health Assn. Home: 143 Palmerston Rd Rochester NY 14618-1247 Office: U Health Svc 250 Crittenden Blvd Box 617 Rochester NY 14642-8617

REIJNEVELD, SIJMEN ANNE, epidemiologist; b. Kamerik, The Netherlands, Mar. 13, 1960; d. Dirk Reijneveld and Jansje M. Korver. Med. degree, Utrecht Med. Sch., The Netherlands, 1985; degree in pub. health, Vrije U., Amsterdam, The Netherlands, 1991; PhD, U. Amsterdam, 1995. Cert. comty. physician. Asst. surgeon-tchr., 1986-87; rschr. Utrecht Med. Sch., 1987-88, Vrye U., Amsterdam, 1988-90; epidemiologist Amsterdam Mcpl. Health Svc., 1990—, U. Amsterdam, 1995—. Author: The Measurement of Local Public Health, 1995. Mem. Netherlands Epidemiol. Soc. (bd. dirs. 1992—), Dutch Assn. GPs (cons. 1995—), European Pub. Health Assn. Office: Amsterdam Mcpl Health Svc, PO Box 20244, 1000 HE Amsterdam The Netherlands

REIK, RITA ANN FITZPATRICK, pathologist; b. Cleve., Mar. 9, 1951; d. Charles Robert Sr. and Rita Mae (Wilke) Fitzpatrick; m. Curtis A. Reik, Oct. 19, 1974. BA in Chemistry, Fla. Internat. U., 1985; MD, U. Miami, 1989. Diplomate Am. Bd. Anatomic and Clinical Pathology. Resident in pathology Jackson Meml. Hosp., Miami, Fla., 1989-95; mem. faculty dept. pathology U. Miami Sch. Medicine, 1995—; attending physician transfusion med. svcs. U. Miami/Jackson Meml. Hosp., 1996—; dir. immunogentics & cryopreservation lab. U. Miami Sch. Medicine/Jackson Meml. Hosp.; dir. lab. svcs. Jackson U. Maternity Ctr., Miami; dir. lab. svcs. North Dade Amb. Care Ctr. Fellow Coll. Am. Pathologists; mem. AMA, NOW, U. Miami Med. Women (pres. 1988-89), Am. Soc. Clin. Pathologists, Alpha Omega Alpha, Phi Kappa Phi. Office: U Miami Jackson Meml Hosp Dept Pathology 1611 NW 12th Ave Miami FL 33136-1015

REIK, WOLF ULRICH, geneticist; b. Aachen, Fed. Republic Germany, Aug. 22, 1957; arrived in Eng., 1985; s. Helmut Gottlieb and Rosemarie (Heiles) R.; m. Cristina Antonia Rada, July 21, 1989. MD, U. Hamburg, Fed. Republic Germany, 1985. Fellow EMBO Inst. Animal Physiology, Cambridge, Eng., 1985-87, fellow of the Lister Inst. Preventive Medicine, 1987—, prin. sci. officer, group leader, 1989—, head lab. of devel. genetics & imprinting, 1992—. Contbr. articles to profl. jours. Recipient Wellcome prize in physiology, 1994; grantee AFRC, 1988, 92, Combat Huntington's Chorea, 1989, Brit. Coun., 1990, Ministry Agr., Fisheries and Food, 1994, Action Rsch., 1995, European Cmtys., 1996. Fellow Lister Inst. Preventive Medicine (grantee 1987). Home: Bay Cottage, Little Shelford CB2 5ES, England Office: The Babraham Inst, Babraham, Cambridge CB2 4AT, England

REILLY, JAMES FRANCIS, health facility administrator; b. July 24, 1953; m. Michelle Reilly, Aug. 1, 1981; children; Jonathan, Melissa, Michael. MD, Georgetown U., 1979; MBA, U. So. Calif., 1991. Diplomate Am. Bd. Family Practice. Family practice physician Fairview Gen. Hosp., Cleve., 1979-82; with USPHS, Ark., 1982-84; family practice physician CIGNA Health Plan, 1984-91; med. dir. CareAmerica, 1991-95, sr. med. dir., sr. v.p. quality improvement. Fellow Am. Acad. Family Practice; mem. Am. Coll. Physician Execs., Beta Gamma Sigma. Roman Catholic. Office: CareAmerica Inc 6300 Canoga Ave Woodland Hills CA 91367

REILLY, JEFFREY MICHAEL, vascular surgeon; b. Albany, N.Y., Jan. 30, 1959; s. John Joseph and Barbara Ann (Smith) R.; m. Barbara McKinley, July 31, 1982; children: Jeffrey Michael Jr., Anna Claire, Caroline Virginia. AB cum laude and high distinction, Dartmouth Coll., 1981; MD with honors, 1985. Diplomate Am. Bd. Surgery. Resident in gen. surgery Yale-New Haven (Conn.) Hosp., 1988-91; fellow in vascular surgery Washington U., St. Louis, 1991-93; attending surgeon Barnes-Jewish Hosp., St. Louis, 1993—, Children's Hosp., St. Louis, 1993—, VA Med. Ctr., St. Louis, 1993—. Mem. Assn. Acad. Surgery, Internat. Soc. Endovascular Surgery, Midwestern Vascular Surgery Soc., St. Louis Vascular Soc., St. Louis Surg. Soc., Alpha Omega Alpha. Office: Washington U Sch Medicine 216 S Kingshighway Saint Louis MO 63110

REILLY, LAURA KATHERINE, account supervisor; b. Bronx, N.Y., Aug. 18, 1957; d. Michael F. and Winfred K. (Lynch) R. BS, Molloy Coll., 1979; MBA, NYU, 1993. Pediatric antiemetic rsch. nurse Meml. Sloan Kettering Cancer Ctr., N.Y.C., 1979-84; med. sales rep. Pennwalt Pharms., Rochester, N.Y., 1984-86; asst. securities analyst Morgan Stanley & Co. Inc., N.Y.C., 1986-89; rsch. nurse Meml. Sloan Kettering Cancer Ctr., N.Y.C., 1989-93; acct. supr.-oncology Integrated Comm., Inc., Parsippany, N.J., 1993, account supr., 1993-96; v.p., group acct. supr. NCI Pharma, Princeton, N.J., 1996—. Mem. Assn. Pediatric Oncology Nurses, Oncology Nursing Soc., Sigma Theta Tau (chpt. pres. 1979-80). Home: 8350 Kennedy Blvd North Bergen NJ 07047-4264

REILLY, LINDA V., academic administrator; b. Sea Isle City, N.J., July 31, 1950; d. Robert F. and Madelyn E. (Ciufo) Prow; m. Juan R. Villazon, Feb. 14, 1977 (div. Aug. 1991); m. Richard V. Reilly, Jan. 7, 1994. BS in Med. Tech., Gwynedd-Mercy Coll., 1973; MS in Clin. Microbiology, Thomas Jefferson U., 1978; EdD in Ednl. Adminstrn., Temple U., 1992. Cert. med. technologist Am. Soc. Clin. Pathologists. Med. technologist Suburban Gen. Hosp., Norristown, Pa., 1973-74; rsch. technologist Thomas Jefferson U., Phila., 1974-75, microbiologist, 1975-78; microbiologist Roxbourgh Meml. Hosp., Phila., 1978-79; acad. program dir. Gwynedd-Mercy Coll., Gwynedd Valley, Pa., 1979-85; chairperson Allied Health Divsn. Gwynedd-Mercy Coll., Gwynedd Valley, 1990—. Mem. subcom. on women's health issues Montgomery County Commn. on Women & Families, Norristown, 1993—. Mem. Am. Coun. on Edn.-Nat. Identification Program (spring regional conf. com. 1994-96), Am. Assn. for Higher Edn., Assn. Schs. Allied Health, Am. Assn. for Microbiology. Office: Gwynedd-Mercy Coll Gwynedd Valley PA 19437

REILLY, ROBERT JOSEPH, counselor; b. Spokane, Wash., Mar. 7, 1936; s. John Francis and Vivian Helen (White) R.; m. Joan Steiner, June 20, 1960; children: Sean Michael, Patrick Joseph, Bridget Colleen. BA in Psychology, Seattle U., 1985; postgrad., Infantry Officer Candidate Sch, Ft. Benning, 1960, EOAC, Ft. Belvoir, 1968, Leadership Inst. Seattle/City U., 1991-92. Ordained Congl. Ch. Practical Theology. Enlisted U.S. Army, 1953, advanced through grades to maj., 1981, ret., 1981; with U.S. Army, Korea, 1961-62, Vietnam, 1966-67, 68-69; counselor Schick Shadel Hosp., Seattle, 1984-89; dir. Canyon Counseling, Puyallup, Wash., 1987-92, 95—; social worker Wash. State Employee Adv. Svc., Olympia, 1992—; dir. Nat. Bd. for Hypnotherapy and Hypnotic Anaesthesiology, v.p. 1991—, pres. Wash. chpt. 1991-94; exec. v.p. Coll. Therapeutic Hypnosis, Puyallup, 1989-94; mem. adj. faculty Pierce Coll., Tacoma, 1991-92. Pres. Irish Cultural Club, Tacoma, 1983-85, 93-94; sec. Tacoma chpt. Ret. Officers Assn., 1983-87, pres., 1993-95. Decorated Vietnamese Cross of Gallantry with silver star, Bronze Star with oak leaf cluster, Meritorious Svc. medal, Army Commendation medal with 2 oak leaf clusters; named Profl. of Yr. Chem. Dependency Profls. Wash., 1994. Mem. Nat. Bd. Hypnotherapy and Hypnotic Anesthesiology (v.p. 1991—, Mem of Yr. 1994, pres. Wash. chpt. 1991-94), Internat. Med. and Dental Hypnotherapy Assn., Nat. Assn. Alcohol and Drug Abuse Counselors (mem. del. Russia & Czech Rep. 1996), Am. Congress Hypnotist Examiners, Army Engr. Assn., Nat. 4th Inf. Divsn. Assn. (sec.-treas. N.W. chpt. 1993—), Employee Assistance Profls. Assn. Office: Wash State Employee Adv Svc PO Box 47540 Olympia WA 98504-7540

REIM, BRUCE E., psychotherapist; b. Bklyn., Mar. 14, 1947; s. George and Rose Sherrey (Friedman) R.; m. Maia Coven, Aug. 4, 1974; children: Aviva, Jordana. BA, Rutgers U., 1968; MA, NYU, 1971; MSW, Rutgers U., 1979. Lic. clin. social worker, N.J.; cert. group psychotherapist. Pvt. practice Montgomery Township, N.J.; dir. clin. svc. Family and Children's Svc. of Ctrl. N.J.; dir. profl. svc. Jewish Family and Vocat. Svc. of Middlesex County, Edison, N.J.; dir. of groups, psychiat. social worker Cath. Welfare Bur., Trenton, N.J. Contbr. articles to profl. jours. Mem. Mcpl. Youth Svc. Commn. Woodbridge, N.J.; mem. crisis intervention team Norty Brunswick Sch. Dist.; mem. Inst. for Group Work Edn. Mem. NASW, Am. Bd. of Examiners in Clin. Social Wk., Community Childhood Suicide Prevention Task Force.

REIMER, LARRY GENE, physician, pathology educator; b. Greeley, Colo., Jan. 24, 1949; s. Isaac R. and Opal M. (Nikkel) R.; m. Becky Lou Chesnut, Aug. 3, 1969; 1 child, Brendon Hollis. BA, Harvard U., 1971; MD, U. Colo., 1975. Asst. prof. medicine and pathology, dir. clin. microbiology W.Va. U., Morgantown, 1981-84, U. Utah, Salt Lake City, 1984—; bd. dirs. postgrad. tng. program clin. microbiology U. Utah VA Med. Ctr., Salt

Lake City, 1984—. Contbr. articles to profl. jours. Mem. AAAS, ACP, Am. Soc. Microbiology, Infectious Diseases Soc. Am. Office: VA Med Ctr Dept Pathology # 113 Salt Lake City UT 84148

REINA, CHARLES RICCA, orthopedic surgeon; b. N.Y.C., May 27, 1949; s. Vincent F. and Mildred (Ricca) R.; m. Mary E. Walpole, Mar. 5, 1977; children: Christopher Robert, Patricia Carmel. AS, CUNY, 1968, BS in Chemistry, 1970; MD, N.Y. Med. Coll., 1974. Diplomate Am. Bd. Orthopedic Surgery. Intern St. Vincents Hosp., N.Y.C., 1974-75, resident in surgery, 1975-76, resident in orthopedic surgery, 1976-79; asst. prof. orthopedic surgery Hahnemann Med. Coll., Phila., 1983—; pvt. practice orthopedic surgery; cons. pediatric orthopedist, State of N.J., Clinton, 1982—; attending surgeon Easton (Pa.) Hosp., 1982—, Warren Hosp., Phillipsburg, N.J., 1982—. Named. UNICO Man of Yr., UNICO Nat., Pottsville, Pa., 1980. Fellow ACS, Am. Coll. Orthopedic Surgeons; mem. Pa. Med. Soc., Conn. Med. Soc., LeHigh Valley Orthopedic Soc. Roman Catholic. Office: 3311 Northwood Ave Easton PA 18045

REINER, MARK ROBERT, physician assistant; b. Bklyn., Oct. 21, 1951; s. Seymour R. and Ruth (Victorine) R.; m. Paula Deene Lee, June 26, 1983. BS, Marietta Coll., 1973; PA, U. Cin. Coll. of Medicine, 1975. Cert. procurement transplant coord. Procurement coord. Tenn. Donor Svc., Knoxville, 1976-79; dir. organ procurement Dept. of Surgery U. Fla. Coll. of Medicine, Gainesville, 1979-86; v.p. nat. svcs. Musculoskeletal Transplant Found., Holmdel, N.J., 1986-89; exec. dir. Golden State Transplant Svcs., Sacramento, Calif., 1989-91, Transplant Resource Ctr. of Md., Balt., 1991-93; dir. program devel. U. Fla., Gainesville, 1994—; mem. bd. dirs. United Network for Organ Sharing, Richmond, Va., 1986-88; pres. NAm. Transplant Coords. Orgn., 1985-86; grant reviewer Divsn. of Organ Transplantation, Health and Human Svcs., Washington, 1987-88; mem. N.J. Transplant Adv. Coun., Trenton, 1988-89; mem. med. adv. com. on anatomical transplants Dept. Health Svcs., Sacramento, Calif., 1990-91. Contbr. articles to profl. jours. Mem. bd. trustees Nat. Kidney Found., Fla. chpt., 1994—, North Fla. Lions Eye Bank, Gainesville, 1995. Mem. Am. Acad. Physician Assts., North Am. Transplant Coords. Orgn., Fla. Acad. Physician Assts., Am. Assn. Tissue Banks. Office: Jacksonville Organ Retrieval Program 655 W 8th St Jacksonville FL 32209

REINER, ORLY YAEL, molecular geneticist, researcher; b. Jaffo, Israel, Feb. 24, 1958; d. Shmuel Barly and Miriam (Segalovitz) Yaacovi; m. Natan Reiner, Aug. 12, 1975; children: Noit, Talli. BSc, Hebrew U., Rehovot, Israel, 1978, MSc, 1985; PhD, Weizmann Inst. Sci., Rehovot, 1990. Postdoctoral fellow Baylor Coll. Medicine, Houston, 1990-93; sr. scientist Weizmann Inst. Sci., Rehovot, 1993—. Contbr. articles to profl. publs. (award Israel Kennesset 1990, Fulbright travel award 1991). Mem. Am. Soc. Human Genetics, European Soc. Human Genetics, Israeli Soc. Devel., Israel Acad. Scis. Jewish. Office: Weizmann Inst Sci, Dept Molecular Genetics, Rehovot 76100, Israel

REINERTSEN, JAMES LUTHER, internist; b. Pietermaritzburg, South Africa, 1947. MD, Harvard U., 1973. Diplomate Am. Bd. Internal Medicine. Intern San Francisco Gen. Hosp., 1973-74; resident internal medicine U. Calif., 1974-76; resident in rheumatology NIH, Bethesda, Md., 1976-78; with Meth. Hosp., Mpls.; pvt. practice HealthSys. Minn., Mpls. Mem. ACP, ARA, Alpha Omega Alpha. Office: Healthsys Minn PO Box 650 Minneapolis MN 55440*

REINERTSON, JAMES WAYNE, pediatrician; b. Des Moines, Jan. 25, 1927; s. A. Jennings and Bonnie V. (Wald) R.; m. Beverly E. Sampson, June 6, 1958; children: Mark W., Merilee Reinertson Torres. BA, Luther Coll., 1948; MS in Pub. Health, U. N.C., 1949; MD, U. Iowa, 1959. Diplomate Am. Bd. Pediatrics. Rsch. asst. in parasitology U. Iowa Med. Coll., Iowa City, 1954-59; intern Mercy Hosp., Cedar Rapids, Iowa, 1959-60; resident pediatrics Raymond Blank Hosp., Des Moines, 1960-62; assoc. rsch. parasitologist Parke Davis & Co., Detroit; pvt. practice, Cedar Rapids, Iowa, 1962—; pres. med. staff St. Lukes Hosp., Cedar Rapids, 1979, mem. staff Mercy Hosp.; instr. Cedar Rapids Med. Edn. Program; bd. Luther Coll. Alumni Coun., 1988—. Bd. dirs. Linn County Assn. Retarded Citizens, 1972-78; commr. Iowa Substance Abuse Commn., Des Moines, 1984, chmn., 1988-90. Wyeth Pediatric fellow, 1960-62. Mem. AMA, Am. Acad. Pediatrics, Iowa Med. Soc. Lutheran. Office: 855 A Ave NE Cedar Rapids IA 52402-5064

REINHARD, ARTHUR ELLIOT, physician; b. Bklyn., Sept. 3, 1933; s. David and Anne (Sackstein) R. BA, Cornell U., 1954; MD, NYU Med. Sch., 1958. Intern Montefiore Hosp., Bronx, N.Y., 1958-59, resident in medicine, 1959-60; resident in medicine VA Hosp., Bronx, 1960-61; fellow in gastroenterology U. Pa., Phila., 1961-62, Kings County Hosp., Bklyn., 1962-63; dep. dir. medicine Kingsbrook Jewish Med. Ctr., Bklyn., 1963-67, 69—; asst. prof. medicine Downstate Med. Ctr., Bklyn., 1963-67, 69—. Lt. col. U.S. Army, 1967-69, Vietnam. Mem. AMA, ACP, Bklyn. Gastroenterology Assn., Kings County Med. Soc., N.Y. State Med. Soc. Jewish. Office: Kingsbrook Jewish Med Ctr 585 Schenectady Ave Brooklyn NY 11203-1854

REINHARD, DAVID WILLARD, psychologist; b. Sept. 28, 1936; s. Willard J. and Irene (Keefer) R.; married; children: Scott. Lisa, Jodi, Alexander. AB, Muhlenberg Coll., 1958; MA, Temple U., 1961; EdD, U. Pa., 1971. Psychologist, State Correctional Instn., Graterford, Pa., 1958-61, Elwyn Inst., 1961-65, Wallingford Home, 1962-65, Wren Evaluation Center, Lansdowne, Pa., 1962-67, Carson Valley Sch., 1963-68, Marriage Council U. Pa., 1970-71, Mental Health Clinics Delaware County, Media, Pa., 1968-71, Cabrini Coll., Radnor, Pa., 1971-73, Bapt. Children's Home, Phila., 1973-75, Intermediate Unit Delaware County, 1975-77, Child and Youth Services Montgomery County, Pa., 1978-79; assoc. Human Svcs. Ctr., Phila. Soc. Clin. Psychologists; pvt. practice, Media, 1971—. Trustee, Unitarian Ch. Delaware County, Media, pres. bd. trustees, 1969-70. Fellow Phila. Soc. Clin. Psychologists; mem. APA, Pa. Psychol. Assn., Phila. Soc. Clin. Psychologists (exec. bd., treas. human svcs. ctr.), Am. Assn. Marital and Family Therapists, Assn. Advancement Psychology. Unitarian. Contbr. articles to profl. jours. Home: 200 E Fifth St Media PA 19063-3012 Office: PO Box 1049 Media PA 19063-0849

REINHARD, KENNETH EDWARD, clinical psychologist; b. Bklyn., Mar. 12, 1953; s. Edward Leo and Theresa Reinhard; B.S. in Psychology magna cum laude with honors, CCNY, 1975; M.A., L.I. U., 1977, Ph.D., 1979. Diplomate in clin. psychology Am. Bd. Profl. Psychology. Co-dir. F.D.R. Anxiety Disorders Clinic, Montrose, N.Y., 1984—; staff clin. psychologist Roosevelt VA Hosp., Montrose, 1979—, Center Applied Clin. Research, N.Y.C., 1979-81; pvt. practice, 1981—; mem. aux. med. staff Northern Westchester Med. Ctr., Mt. Kisco, N.Y. Mem. Am. Psychol. Assn., N.Y. Soc. Clin. Hypnosis (treas. 1979-81), N.Y. Soc. Clin. Psychologists, Westchester Psychol. Assn., Phi Beta Kappa. Author articles in field. Home: 17 Dailey Dr Croton On Hudson NY 10520

REINHARDT, HERBERT PAUL, physician; b. Little Rock, Oct. 16, 1932; s. Herbert Paul and Cleffie Ritchie (Brewer) R.; m. Mary Jane Jackson, Sept. 6, 1958; 1 child, Rece Jane Reinhardt Hanoch. MD and BS in Medicine, U. Ark., 1957. Diplomate Am. Bd. Internal Medicine. Intern U. Ark. Med. Ctr., Little Rock, 1957-58, resident in internal medicine, 1958-61; pvt. practice Oklahoma City, 1963—; clin. instr. internal medicine U. Okla. Med. Sch., Oklahoma City, 1963-89, clin. asst. prof., 1989—. Commander Oklahoma City Power Squadron, 1987. With USPHS, 1961-63. Fellow Am. Coll. Physicians. Republican. Mem. Ch. of Christ. Office: 6424 N Portland Ave Oklahoma City OK 73116-2028

REINHARDT, KURT, retired radiologist and nuclear physician; b. Limbach, Saar, Feb. 18, 1920; s. Friedrich and Elisabeth (Hock) R.; m. Maria Lefeber, Dec. 29, 1951. Student U. Berlin, 1939-40, U. Heidelberg, 1940-45; med. diploma U. Innsbruck, 1945. Resident dept. radiology U. Homburg, 1951-58; head physician dept. radiol. nuclear medicine Kreiskrankenhaus Volklingen, 1958—, habilitation, 1958, prof., 1964—, now ret. Decorated Cross of Merit 1st class Fed. Republic Germany. Mem. Deutsche Roentgengesellschaft, Internat. Skeletal Soc. Author 10 monographs and med. books including Krankhafte Haltungsänderungen Skoliosen und Kyphosen, and hist. books Gedanken über Erinnerungen an dem RuBlandkrieg, 1991, Quellen der Geschichte des deutschen Nobobs von Sardhana, 1994, Ein Justizverbrechen, 1995, Mr. Dyce Sombres Refutation, 1995; contbr. 200 articles to med. jours. Home: 32 am Kirschenwaldchen, Volklingen Germany

REINHART, JOHN BELVIN, child and adolescent psychiatrist, educator; b. Merrill, Wis., Dec. 22, 1917; s. Dabney Belvin and Ann (Toomey) R.; m. Helen Elsen Reinhart, Jan. 3, 1994; children: Peter, Catherine, Ann, John, Frederick, Andrew. BA, Duke U., 1939; MD, Bowman Gray Sch. Medicine, Winston-Salem, N.C., 1943. Diplomate Am. Bd. Pediatrics, Am. Bd. Psychiatry in child and adolescent psychiatry. Instr. pediatrics Bowman Gray Sch. Medicine, Winston-Salem, 1950-52; asst. prof., assoc. prof., prof. pediatrics and psychiatry U. Pitts. Sch. Medicine, 1956-83, emeritus prof. pediatrics, 1983—; clin. prof. psychiatry Bowman Gray Sch. Medicine, Winston-Salem, 1986—. Co-Author: A Baby's First Year, 1956. Capt. M.C. AUS, 1946-48. Roman Catholic. Home: 34 Hunter's Ln Hendersonville NC 28791 Office: Trend MHS Cons Hendersonville NC 28791

REINHART, MARY ANN, medical board executive; b. Jackson, Mich., Aug. 14, 1942; d. Herbert Martin and Josephine Marie (Keyes) Conway; m. David Lee Reinhart, Dec. 28, 1963; children: Stephen Paul, Michael David. MA, Mich. State U., 1983, PhD, 1985. Rsch. asst. Mich. State U., East Lansing, 1979-82, 85, teaching asst. dept psychology, 1982-84, asst. prof. Office Med. Edn. R&D, Coll. Human Medicine, 1985-88; assoc. exec. dir. Am. Bd. Emergency Medicine, East Lansing, 1988-95, dep. exec. dir., 1995—; cons. Am. Bd. Emergency Medicine, 1985-88; chairperson collegewide evaluation com. Coll. Human Medicine, Mich. State U., East Lansing, 1985-88; adj. asst. prof. Office Med. Edn. Rsch. and Devel., Coll. Human Medicine, 1988—. Reviewer Annals of Emergency Medicine, 1987-95, Acad. Emergency Medicine, 1995—. Bd. dirs. Neahtawanta Rsch. and Edn. Ctr., Traverse City, Mich., 1991—. Mem. APA (divsn. indsl./orgnl. psychology, health psychology), Phi Kappa Phi. Office: Am Bd Emergency Medicine 3000 Coolidge Rd East Lansing MI 48823-6319

REINHOLD, RANDOLPH B., general surgeon; b. Balt., Nov. 2, 1938; m. Rita Berkson; 4 children. AB, Princeton U., 1960; MD, Johns Hopkins U., 1964. Diplomate Am. Bd. Surgery. Dir. cmty. medicine New Eng. Deaconess Hosp., Boston, 1971-77, med. dir. ambulatory svc., 1971-77, vice chair dept. surg., dir. oper. rms., 1982-92, coord. surg. residence, 1982-92; program dir. surg. residency Hosp. St. Raphael, New Haven, 1992—, chmn. dept. surgery, 1992—; clin. prof. surgery Yale Med. Sch., New Haven, 1993—; vis. prof. surgery U. Zimbabwe Med. Sch., Harare, 1992; from assoc. prof. to prof. surgery Tufts U. Med. Sch., Boston., 1982-92. Editor: Consultation in General Surgery, 1985. Bd. dirs. Physicians for Human Rights, 1989. Fellow ACS; mem. AMA, New Eng. Surg. Soc., Assn. Program Dirs. in Surgery, Soc. Surgery Alimentary Tract (rep.), Pancreas Club, World Assn. HPB Surgery. Office: Hosp St Raphael 1450 Chapel St New Haven CT 06511

REINHOUDT, JOHAN FEIKE, nurse anesthetist; b. Kamperland, Zeeland, The Netherlands, Nov. 24, 1962; s. Isaak and Atje (Van Netten) R.; m. Miep Apolonia Huige; 1 child, Jurgen Raymond. Student nursing, Sch. voor Verplergkundigen, The Netherlands, 1984; Nurse Anesthetist, Acad. Hosp. Leiden, The Netherlands, 1987. RN, RN anesthetist. Nurse trainee Found. Oosterschelde Hosps., Goes, The Netherland, 1980-85; nurse anesthetist trainee Acad. Hosp. Leiden (The Netherlands), 1985-88; rsch. nurse Pharma Bio-Rsch. Internat., Assen, The Netherlands, 1988; product specialist Rhône-Poulenc Pharma B.V., Amstelveen, The Netherlands, 1988-89; CRA CRA-mgr. Rhône-Poulenc Rorer B.V., Amstelveen, The Netherlands, 1989-92; area rsch. cons. Medinet V.O.F., Breda, The Netherlands, 1992-93; mgr. affiliate liaison, coordination Rhône-Poulenc Rorer SA, Antony, France, 1993—; initiator GCP platform Nefarma, Utrecht, The Netherlands, 1991-92. Mem. Drug Info. Assn. Office: Rhône-Poulenc Rorer, 20 Avenue Raymond Aron, 92165 Antony France

REINISCH, JOHN FERDINAND, plastic surgeon, educator; b. Holyoke, Mass., July 4, 1944. AB, Dartmouth Coll., 1966, BS, 1968; MD, Harvard U., 1970. Intern U. Mich., Ann Arbor, 1970-71, resident, 1971-73; resident Tulane U., New Orleans, 1975-76, U. Va., Charlottesville, 1976-78; asst. prof. U. Mo., Columbia, 1978-82; asst. prof. U. So. Calif., L.A., 1983-85, assoc. prof., 1985—; chmn. plastic surgery divsn. U. So. Calif., 1985-94. Contbr. articles to profl. jours., chpts. to books. Home: 654 S Rimpau Blvd Los Angeles CA 90005-3841 Office: U So Calif 4650 Sunset Blvd Los Angeles CA 90027-6016

REINITZ, ELIZABETH, rheumatologist, internist; b. Budapest, Hungary, May 26, 1952; came to U.S., 1956; d. George and Eva (Frater) Reinitz; m. Robert I. Weinberger; children: Julie D., Jeremy F. BS, Cornell U., 1973; MD, Albert Einstein Coll. Medicine, 1976. Intern/resident in internal medicine Boston City Hosp., 1976-79; fellow in rheumatology Albert Einstein Coll. Medicine/Montefiore Hosp., Bronx, 1981-89; pvt. practice Scarsdale (N.Y.) Med. Group, 1989—; chief sect. rheumatology White Plains (N.Y.) Hosp., 1992—. Office: 250 Heathcote Rd Scarsdale NY 10583

REINKER, DALE L., osteopath; b. St. Louis, Feb. 17, 1943; s. Harold Leo and Evelyn Marie (Beinke) R.; m. Joan Ann Brehm, July 1, 1967; children: Conni, Brad, Carolyn. BS, Northeast State U., 1965; DO, U. Health Scis., 1969. Intern Bayview Hosp., Cleve., 1969-70; resident Coffey County Hosp., Burlington, Kans., 1970-72, 72-75, chmn. dept. surgery, 1975-85; attending dept. surgery Lincoln County Meml. Hosp., Troy, Mo., 1985-96, med. staff exec. com., 1989—. Bd. trustees Coffey County Hosp., Burlington, Kans., 1978-84, Lincoln Cmty. Meml. Hosp., Troy, 1991—; bd. edn. Burlington Sch. System, 1982-85; bd. elders Trinity Luth. Ch., Troy, 1988—. Fellow Am. Acad. Osteo. Surgeons (pres. 1980); mem. Am. Osteo. Assn., Am. Assn. Physician Specialists, Mo. Assn. Osteo. Physicians & Surgeons, St. Louis Soc. Osteo. Physicians, Troy City C. of C. Republican. Lutheran. Office: Surg Assocs 1175 E Cherry St Troy MO 63379

REINWALD, KEITH CONRAD, physician assistant, educator; b. Marion, Ohio, Aug. 19, 1947; s. Eugene Karl and Velma Gertrude (Hartman) R.; m. Mary Lou Kincaid, Feb. 24, 1985; children: Kyle Aaron, Kendra Kay, Kamela Erin. Student, Ohio State U., Marion, 1965-66, Marion Tech. Coll., 1971-72; B in Med. Scis., Alderson-Broaddus Coll., Philippi, W.Va., 1982. Cert. NCCPA, Ohio State Med. Bd. Oper. room tech. Cmty. MedCtr. Hosp., Mariion, 1962-66, 71-77; pvt. oper. room tech. Grady Meml. Hosp., Deleware, Ohio, 1977-78; physician asst. F.C. Smith Clinic, Marion, 1982—; clin. prof. Alderson-Braddus Coll., Philippi, 1986—; on-site coord. physician asst. students, F.C. Smith Clinic, Marion, 1986—; provider ann. athletic physicals Marion County and other county schs., 1993—. Judge local and dist. sci. fairs, Marion, 1990—; v.p. Salem United Ch. Christ, Marion, 1995—. With USN, 1966-71, Vietnam. Mem. Am. Assn. Physician Assts., Ohio Assn. Physician Assts. Republican. Home: 307 Belmont St Marion OH 43302 Office: FC Smith Clinic 1040 Delaware Ave Marion OH 43302

REIS, DONALD JEFFERY, neurologist, neurobiologist, educator; b. N.Y.C., Sept. 9, 1931; s. Samuel H. and Alice (Kiesler) R.; m. Cornelia Langer Noland, Apr. 13, 1985. A.B., Cornell U., 1953, M.D., 1956. Intern N.Y. Hosp., N.Y.C., 1956; resident in neurology Boston City Hosp.-Harvard Med. Sch., 1957-59; Fulbright fellow, United Cerebral Palsy Found. fellow London and Stockholm, 1959-60; rsch. assoc. NIMH, Bethesda, Md., 1960-62; spl. fellow NIH, Nobel Neurophysiology Inst., Stockholm, 1962-63; asst. prof. neurology Cornell U. Med. Sch., N.Y.C., 1963-67; assoc. prof. neurology and psychiatry Cornell U. Med. Sch., 1967-71, prof., 1971—, First George C. Cotzias Disting. prof. neurology, 1982—; mem. U.S.-Soviet Exch. Program; mem. adv. coun. NIH; bd. sci. advisers Merck, Sharpe & Dohm, Sterling Rsch. Group; cons. Eli Lilly, Servier Pharms.; bd. dirs. China Seas, Inc., Charles masterson Burke Rsch. Found. Contbr. articles to profl. jours.; mem. editorial bd. various profl. jours. Recipient CIBA Prize award Am. Heart Assn. Fellow AAAS, ACP; mem. Am. Physiol. Soc., Am. Neurol. Assn., Am. Pharmacol. Soc., Am. Assn. Physicians, Telluride Assn., Am. Soc. Clin. Investigation, Century Assn., Ellis Island Yacht Club (commadore), Phi Beta Kappa, Sigma Xi, Alpha Omega Alpha. Home: 190 E 72nd St New York NY 10021-4370 also: 73 Water St Stonington CT 06378-1433 Office: 1300 York Ave New York NY 10021-4805

REISBERG, BARRY, geropsychiatrist, neuropsychopharmacologist; b. Bklyn., Dec. 3, 1947; s. Harry and Claire (Cohen) R.; m. Rosalie DePaola, Feb. 23, 1974 (dec. Oct. 1975); m. Nancy A. Minich, May 7, 1988. BA, CUNY, Bklyn., 1968; MD, N.Y. Med. Coll., 1972. Diplomate Am. Bd. Psychiatry and Neurology, Am. Bd. Geriatric Psychiatry. Intern N.Y. Med. Coll./Met. Hosp., N.Y.C., 1972-75, resident in psychiatry, 1972-75; fellow dept. psychiatry Middlesex Hosp. Med. Sch. U. London, 1975; staff psychiatrist Franklin D. Roosevelt VA Hosp., Montrose, N.Y., 1975-78; staff psychiatrist Neuropsychopharmacology Rsch. Unit NYU Med. Ctr., N.Y.C., 1978-80, clin. dir. Aging and Dementia Rsch. Ctr., 1978—; adj. prof. Ctr. for Studies in Aging McGill U., Montreal, Que., Can., 1993—; clin. instr. dept. psychiatry N.Y. Med. Coll., Valhalla, 1975-78; asst. prof. NYU Sch. Medicine, N.Y.C., 1978-84, assoc. prof., 1984-90, prof., 1990—; rsch. collaborator, vis. clinician Brookhaven Nat. Labs., Upton, N.Y., 1979-80; dir. clin. core NIMH Clin. Rsch. Ctr., 1989—, Nat. Inst. Aging Alzheimer's Disease Ctr., 1990—; dir. Zachary and Elizabeth M. Fisher Alzheimer's Disease Edn. and Resources Program NYU Med. Ctr., 1995—; med. and sci. adv. bd. Alzheimer's Assn., Chgo., 1993—; cons. psychiatrist N.Y. VA Hosp., 1980-89; chmn. work group WHO, Copenhagen, 1984; mem. aging sect. NIH, 1986-90; vis. prof. Palmerston North Postgrad. Med. Soc., New Zealand, 1991. Author: Brain Failure, 1981; editor: Alzheimer's Disease, 1983; (with others) Diagnosis and Treatment of Senile Dementia, 1989; mem. editl. bd. Jour. Am. Aging Assn., 1985—, Alzheimer's Disease and Associated Disorders, 1985—, Jour. Geriat. Psychiatry and Neurology, 1986—, Am. Jour. Alzheimer's Care, 1986—, Internat. Psychogeriat., 1989—, Am. Jour. Geriat. Psychiatry, 1992—, Integrative Psychiatry, 1994—; contbr. over 150 articles to med. and sci. jours. Fellow NSF, 1963, Coun. on Internat. Ednl. Exch.-Japan Soc., Tokyo, 1968; grantee NIH, 1979-81, 82-85, 87, 90, 92—, NIMH, 1983-85. Mem. Internat. Psychogeriat. Assn. (bd. dirs. 1985-93, treas. 1993-95, pres.-elect 1995—), Am. Aging Assn. (bd. dirs. 1990—), Alzheimer's and Related Disorders Soc. India (hon.), Am. Assn. Geriat. Psychiatry (sec. 1991-92, bd. dirs. 1992-96), Am. Coll. Neuropsychopharmacology. Office: NYU Med Ctr Aging and Dementia Rsch Ctr 550 1st Ave New York NY 10016-6481

REISCHL, UDO MICHAEL, biochemist, researcher; b. Deggendorf, Bavaria, Fed. Republic Germany, Dec. 1, 1963; s. Helfried and Leonore (Groebner) R.; m. Michaela Franziska Seitz, Sept. 11, 1993. D of Natural Scis., U. Munich, 1992. Group leader, lectr. Univ. Hosp., Regensburg, Germany, 1992—; cons. DNA-based amplification sys., DNA diagnostics, Boehringer Mannheim GmbH, Penzberg, Germany, 1989-92. Author: DNA Amplification Techniques, 1992; editor: Molecular-Biology Based Methods, 1995; mem. editl. bd. (jour.) Molecular Biotech., 1994—; contbr. articles to sci. publs. Rescue asst. DLRG, Regensburg, 1992-95. Roman Catholic. Home: Gertrud-von-Le-Fort Str 5, 93051 Regensburg Germany Office: Univ Regensburg, Franz-Josef-Strauss-All 11, 93053 Regensburg Germany

REISER, LYNN WHISNANT, psychiatrist; b. Charlotte, N.C., July 28, 1944; d. Ward William and Susan (Richardson) Whisnant; m. Morton F. Reiser, Dec. 19, 1976. BS, Duke U., 1966; MD, Yale U., 1970; Diplomate Am. Bd. Psychiatry and Neurology (examiner). Intern, Hosp. of St. Raphael, New Haven, Conn., 1970-71; resident in psychiatry, Yale U., 1971-74, asst. clin. prof., 1975-83, assoc. clin. prof., 1983-94, clin. prof. 1994—, assoc. dir. undergrad. edn., 1978-85, dir. undergrad. edn., 1985—. Fellow Am. Psychiat. Assn.; mem. Am. Psychoanalytic Assn., Western New Eng. Psychoanalytic Soc. Contbr. articles in field to profl. jours. Home: 200 Todd St Hamden CT 06518-1511 Office: Yale Medical School Dept Psychiatry New Haven CT 06511

REISER, MORTON FRANCIS, psychiatrist, educator; b. Cin., Aug. 22, 1919; s. Sigmund and Mary (Roth) R.; m. Lynn B. Whisnant, Dec. 19, 1976; children: David E., Barbara, Linda. B.S., U. Cin., 1940, M.D., 1943; grad., N.Y. Psychoanalytic Inst., 1960. Diplomate Am. Bd. Psychiatry and Neurology. Intern King's County Hosp., Bklyn., 1944; resident Cin. Gen. Hosp., 1944-49; practice medicine, specializing in psychiatry Cin., 1947-52, Washington, 1954-55, N.Y.C., 1955-69; mem. faculty Cin. Gen. Hosp., also U. Cin. Coll. Medicine, 1949-52, Washington Sch. Psychiatry, 1953-55; faculty Albert Einstein Coll. Medicine, Yeshiva U., N.Y.C., 1955-69; prof. psychiatry Albert Einstein Coll. Medicine, Yeshiva U., 1958-69, dir. research dept. psychiatry, 1958-65; chief div. psychiatry Montefiore Hosp. and Med. Center, N.Y.C., 1965-69; chmn. dept. psychiatry Yale Med. Sch., 1969—, prof., 1969-78, chmn. dept., 1969-86, Charles B.G. Murphy prof., 1978-86, Albert E. Kent prof., 1986-90, Albert E. Kent prof. emeritus, 1990—; cons. Walter Reed Army Inst. Research, 1957-58, High Point Hosp., Port Chester, N.Y., 1957-69; com. WHO, 1963; mem. profl. adv. com. Jerusalem Mental Health Center, 1972—; mem. clin. program projects rev. com. NIMH, 1970—, chmn., 1973-74. Author: (with H. Leigh) The Patient: Biological, Psychological, and Social Dimensions of Medical Practice, 1980, Mind, Brain, Body: Toward a Convergence of Psychoanalysis and Neurobiology, 1984; (with H. Leigh) The Patient, 3d edit., 1992; Memory in Mind and Brain: What Dream Imagery Reveals, 1990; editor: American Handbook of Psychiatry, vol. IV, 1975; editor in chief Psychosomatic Medicine, 1962-72; mem. editorial bd. AMA Archives of Gen. Psychiatry, 1961-71, (with H. Leigh) Psychiatry Medicine and Primary Care, 1978; contbr. articles to profl. jours. and books. Fellow Am. Coll. Psychiatrists, Am. Psychiat. Assn. (Seymour Vestermark award 1986); mem. Am. Soc. Clin. Investigation, Am. Psychosomatic Soc. (pres. 1960-61), Am. Fedn. Clin. Research, Am. Assn. Chairmen Depts. Psychiatry (exec. com. 1971—, pres. 1975-76), Acad. Behavioral Medicine Research (exec. council 1978), Am. Psychoanalytic Assn. (pres.-elect 1980-82, pres. 1982-84), Internat. Psycho-Analytical Assn., Assn. Psychophysiol. Study of Sleep, Internat. Coll. Psychosomatic Medicine (pres. 1975), Psychiat. Research Soc., A. Graeme Mitchell Undergrad. Pediatric Soc., Benjamin Rush Soc., Rapaport-Klein Study Group, World Psychiat. Assn. (organizing com. sect. psychosomatic medicine 1967), Sigma Xi, Phi Eta Sigma, Pi Kappa Epsilon, Alpha Omega Alpha. Home: 200 Todd St Hamden CT 06518-1511 Office: 255 Bradley St New Haven CT 06510-1105

REISIN, EFRAIN, nephrologist, researcher, educator; b. Cordoba, Argentina, Feb. 25, 1943; came to U.S., 1979; s. Maximo and Elisa Reisin; m. Ilana Hershkovitz, Sept. 6, 1971; children: Eyal, Thalia Alexis. MD, Nat. U., Cordoba, 1966. Intern internal medicine Nat. U. Cordoba-Clinicas Hosp., 1966; resident Jimenes Diaz Found., Madrid, 1966-68; resident Chaim Sheba Med. Ctr., Tel Hashomer, Israel, 1968-71, fellow in nephrology, 1971-74, staff physician nephrology, 1974-77; rsch. fellow in hypertension Health Sci. Ctr., Winnipeg, Man., Can., 1977-78; vis. scientist in hypertension Nat. Health Welfare Can., Winnipeg, Man., 1978-79; Ochsner vis. scientist in hypertension Ochsner Found. Hosp., New Orleans, 1979-82; from asst. prof. to assoc. prof. medicine La. State U., New Orleans, 1982-89, prof. medicine, 1989—; dir. dept. nephrology Med. Ctr. Charity Hosp., New Orleans, 1985—; panelist Consensus Conf., NIH, Bethesda, Md., 1991. Author numerous articles and book chpts. on hypertension and nephrology; conducted 1st research study documenting positive effects of weight reduction in treatment of hypertension, 1978 (citation classic Inst. Sci. Info. 1988). 1st lt. Israel Army, 1971-72. Grantee Nat. Health and Welfare Can., 1978-79, Am. Heart Assn., 1980-81, also several pharm. cos., 1984—. Fellow ACP, Am. Coun. High Blood Pressure Rsch., Am. Heart Fund, Am. Coll. Clin. Pharmacology (counselor south ctrl. regional chpt. 1991-92), Am. Fedn. Clin. Rsch., So. Soc. for Clin. Investigation; mem. Internat. Soc. Nephrology, Internat. Soc. Hypertension, Am. Soc. Nephrology, Am. Soc. Hypertension, Coun. Nephrology, Am. Heart Assn., Inter-Am. Soc. Hypertension, Orleans Parish Med. Soc. Office: La State U Sch Medicine 1542 Tulane Ave New Orleans LA 70112-2825

REISINE, GEORGE MARTIN, psychologist; b. N.Y.C.. BA, SUNY, Stony Brook, MA; PhD, Hofstra U. Lic. psychologist, N.Y. Psychologist Fed. Grant Evaluation Team/Willow Brook Devel. Ctr., N.Y.C., 1973-74; staff psychologist N.Y. Med. Coll., N.Y.C., 1974-75; assoc. psychologist Pilgrim Psychiat. Ctr., Brentwood, N.Y., 1975—; psychologist, pvt. practice Northport, N.Y.; adj. prof. Suffolk Community Coll., Brentwood, 1987—. Mem. Am. Psychol. Assn. Office: 299 Main St Northport NY 11768-1730

REISMAN, SCOTT, clinical psychologist, neuropsychologist; b. N.Y.C., Oct. 9, 1951; s. Emanuel and Myra L. (Deutch) R.; m. Susan Greenberg Levy, Apr. 3, 1982; children: Ian M., Megan B. BA, Ohio U., 1974; MSc in Counseling, Nova U., 1978, MSc in Psychology, 1982, PhD in Clin.

Psychology, 1988. Lic. psychologist, Fla., N.Y. Mental health technician Dade County Pub. Health Trust, Miami, Fla., 1974-76; program evaluator Nova U. Clinics, Inc., Ft. Lauderdale, Fla., 1980-82; clin. psychology intern VA Med. Ctr., Miami, Fla., 1984-85; psychologist Fla. Med. Ctr. Hosp., Ft. Lauderdale, 1990-91; dir. neuropsychol. svcs. Alan Jaffe PhD & Assocs., P.A., Coral Springs, Fla., 1988-90; pvt. practice Plantation, Fla., 1990—; adj. prof. Nova U. Ctr. Psychol. Studies, Ft. Lauderdale, 1989—, Fla. Atlantic U., Ft. Lauderdale, 1992—, Miami Inst. Psychology; workshop instr. Acad. Rev., Inc., N.Y., 1990—; S.O.A.R. of Am., Inc., Melbourne, Fla.; clin. dir. NeuroCare Inst., Inc., North Miami Beach, Fla., 1992—; co-dir. The Psychometric Inst., Inc., 1995—. Contbr. articles to prof. jours. Recipient Dissertation Rsch. award APA, 1988; fellow Clin. Neuropsychology, U. Miami Med. Ctr., 1988-90. Mem. APA, Nat. Head Found., Am. Acad. Neurology, Nat. Acad. Neuropsychology, Internat. Neuropsychol. Soc., Fla. Psychol. Assn., Nat. Stroke Assn., Nat. Register Health Svc. Providers in Psychology, Broward Mental Health Assn., Am. Statis. Assn. Jewish.

REISNER, ANDREW DOUGLAS, psychologist, chief clinical officer, educator; b. Ithaca, N.Y., Dec. 28, 1955; s. Gerald Seymour and Estelle Ruth (Siegel) R.; m. Deborah Kay Dermen, Aug. 1, 1981; children: David Aaron, Alyssa Danielle. BA, Allegheny Coll., 1977; MA, Edinboro (Pa.) State U., 1978; D of Psychology, Baylor U., 1987. Lic. psychologist, Ohio. Psychology asst. Tiffin (Ohio) Devel. Mental Health Ctr., 1979-80; psychology asst. Community Counseling Svcs., Galion, Ohio, 1980-83, chief clin. officer, 1990—; psychologist, 1990—; intern in clin. psychology Mich. State U., East Lansing, 1986-87; postdoctoral fellow in clin. psychology Harding Hosp., Worthington, Ohio, 1987-88; psychologist Ctr. for Individual Family Svcs., Mansfield, Ohio, 1988-90; psychology cons. Crestline (Ohio) Meml. Hosp., 1989—; adj. faculty Ashland U., 1993—. Contbr. articles to Phobia Practice and Rsch. Jour., Pastoral Psychology, Psychoanalytic Psychology, The Psychol. Record. Mem. APA. Office: Community Counseling Svcs PO Box 954 Galion OH 44833-0954

REISNER, MILTON, psychiatrist, psychoanalyst; b. N.Y.C., Jan. 30, 1934; s. Maximillian and Dora Reisner; m. Linda Ellis, Mar. 3, 1959 (div. 1975); children: Margaret Ann, Amanda Lee. BA, NYU, 1954; MD, Downstate Med. Ctr., 1958. Diplomate Am. Bd. Forensic Examiners, Nat. Bd. Med. Examiners, Am. Bd. Forensic Medicine, N.Y. State Bd. Psychiat. Examiners. Resident in psychiatry Kings County Hosp., Bklyn., 1959-62; sr. psychiatrist Manhattan VA Hosp., N.Y.C., 1962-66; assoc. dir. psychiatry Westchester Community Mental Health Bd., White Plains, N.Y., 1966-69; dir. psychiatry Westchester Mental Health Bd., White Plains, 1969-74; pvt. practice N.Y.C., 1976—; cons. Cath. Charities, N.Y.C., 1965-66, H.I.P., N.Y.C., 1973-74, NYU Med. Ctr., 1963-68. Contbr. articles to profl. jours. Lt. j.g. USPHS, 1958-59. Fellow Am. Soc. Psychoanalytic Physicians; mem. Am. Assn. Psychoanalytic Physicians (pres. 1985-86, 87-88, Plaque 1988), Nat. Arts Club, Phi Beta Kappa. Office: 200 E 84th St New York NY 10028-2906

REISS, GEORGE RUSSELL, JR., physician; b. Phila., Dec. 25, 1928; s. G. Russell Sr. and Mary Ellen (Brogan) R.; m. Rosemarie Theresa Curcillo, Sept. 19, 1959; children: Mary Elizabeth, Stephanie, G. Russell III, Charlene. BA, LaSalle U., 1953; MD, Temple U., 1957. Diplomate Am. Bd. Pediatrics. Intern Misericordia Hosp., Phila., 1957-58; resident pediatrics St. Christopher Hosp. for Children, Phila., 1958-60; pvt. practice Glenside, Pa., 1960—. With USCG, 1946-49. Mem. Montgomery County Med. Soc., Pa. Med. Soc., Am. Acad. Pediatrics, AMA, Am. Assn. Pro-Life Pediatricians. Roman Catholic. Office: 2220 Mt Carmel Ave Glenside PA 19038

REISS, MICHAEL, medical oncologist, researcher; b. Addis Ababa, Ethiopia, Sept. 22, 1950; came to U.S., 1982; s. Willy and Lies (Gerzon) R.; m. Elisabeth Meta Souget, Mar. 15, 1977; children: Kim, Daniel J. Student, U. Amsterdam Med. Sch., The Netherlands, 1968-73; MD, U. Amsterdam, 1976. Cert. Bd. Internal Medicine, The Netherlands; fed. licensing exam.; lic. physician Conn. Clk., subintern U. Amsterdam Hosps. and Affiliated Hosps., 1974-76; rsch. assoc. Cen. Lab. Netherlands Red Cross Blood Trans. Lab. for Immunology, U. Amsterdam, 1976-77; intern in internal medicine Med. Coll. Ohio, Toledo, 1977-78; resident in internal medicine U. Hosp. Binnengasthuis, Amsterdam, 1978-82; rotation in med. oncology Netherlands Cancer Inst., Amsterdam, 1980; postdoctoral fellow in med. oncology Yale U. Sch. Medicine, 1982-85, instr. in med. oncology, 1985-87, asst. prof. dept. internal medicine Yale Comp. Cancer Ctr., 1987-91, assoc. prof. dept. internal medicine Yale Comp. Cancer Ctr., 1991—; attending physician Yale New Haven Hosp., 1985—; med. oncologist Yale Comprehensive Breast Care Ctr., 1989—, co-dir., 1992—; dir. breast cancer rsch. program Yale Cancer Ctr., 1995—; chmn. rsch. com. sect. med. oncology Yale U. Sch. Medicine, 1986—, fellowship com. sect. med. oncology, 1986—, cancer edn. com. Yale Comprehensive Cancer Ctr., 1989—, funds and fellowships com., 1991-95; mem. instnl. grant rev. com. Am. Cancer Soc., 1988-94; invited mem. Sec.'s Spl. Conf. on Breast Cancer, NIH, 1993; reviewer Netherlands Cancer Found. Rsch. Grants. Reviewer: Cancer Rsch., Blood, Jour. Cell Physiology, Cancer Comms., European Jour. Cancer Clin. Oncology; contbr. articles to profl. jours. 2d lt. Dutch Army, 1975-77. Recipient Swebilius Cancer Rsch. award, 1985-86; clin. fellow Queen Wilhelmina Cancer Found., Amsterdam, 1982-84; rsch. grantee numerous orgns. Mem. AAAS, Am. Assn. for Cancer Rsch., Am. Soc. Clin. Oncology, Am. Soc. Cell Biology, Am. Fedn. for Clin. Rsch.

REITEMEIER, RICHARD JOSEPH, physician; b. Pueblo, Colo., Jan. 2, 1923; s. Paul John and Ethel Regina (McCarthy) R.; m. Patricia Claire Mulligan, July 21, 1951; children: Mary Louise, Paul, Joseph, Susan, Robert, Patrick, Daniel. A.B., U. Denver, 1944; M.D., U. Colo., 1946; M.S. in Internal Medicine, U. Minn., 1954. Diplomate: Am. Bd. Internal Medicine (gov. 1971-79, chmn. 1978-79, rep. to Federated Council Internal Medicine 1977-80, 83-84, accreditation council grad. med. edn. 1979-85, chmn. 1982-83). Intern Corwin Hosp., Pueblo, 1946-47; resident Henry Ford Hosp., Detroit, 1949-50, Mayo Found., Rochester, Minn., 1950-53; cons. internal medicine and gastroenterology Mayo Clinic, Rochester, 1954-87; chmn. dept. internal medicine Mayo Clinic (Mayo Clinic and Mayo Med. Sch.), 1967-74, prof., 1971—; bd. govs. Mayo Clinic, 1970-74; bd. dirs. Sisters of Mercy Health System, St. Louis, 1986-92; mem. governing bd. Am. Bd. Med. Specialties, 1983-86; sci. and med. dir. Ludwig Inst. Cancer Rsch., 1987-88; cons. Kaiser Family Med. Found., 1989-90; med. dir. Phoenix Alliance Inc., 1990-93. Author: (with C. G. Moertel) Advanced Gastrointestinal Cancer, Clinical Management and Chemotherapy, 1969; contbr. numerous articles to med. jours. Trustee Mayo Found., 1970-74; trustee St. Mary's Hosp., Rochester, 1976-82. Served with U.S. Army, 1947-49. Recipient Alumni award U. Colo. Sch. Medicine; Irving Cutter award Phi Rho Sigma, 1986. Master ACP (regent 1979-82, gov. for Minn. 1975-79, pres. 1983-84, Alfred Stengel Meml. award 1990); fellow Am. Gastroenterol. Assn., AMA, Am. Clin. and Climatol. Assn., Am. Fedn. Clin. Rsch., Am. Soc. Clin. Oncology, Coun. Med. Splty. Socs., Inst. Medicine, Am. Assn. Cancer Rsch., Am. Assn. Study Liver Disease, Nat. Bd. Med. Examiners (treas. 1987-89), Alpha Omega Alpha. Republican. Roman Catholic. Home: 707 12th Ave SW Rochester MN 55902-2027 Office: 200 1st Ave SW Rochester MN 55902-3129

REITH, MARIANNE, nurse, educator, researcher; b. N.Y.C., Nov. 15, 1955; d. Edward John and Adamina (Kieliszek) R. BA in Religion, U. Fla., 1976; BS in Nursing, Cornell U., 1978; MSN, Oreg. Health Scis. U., 1988, postgrad., 1988—. R.N., N.Y., Wash., Oreg. Staff nurse Cornell U.-N.Y. Hosp. Med. Ctr., N.Y.C., 1978-79, Providence Med. Ctr., Seattle, 1979-80, U. Wash. Hosp., Seattle, 1981-84, Group Health Hosp., Seattle, 1984-85, St. Vincent Hosp. and Med. Ctr., Portland, Oreg., 1985-87; grad. asst., sr. grad. asst. Sch. Nursing Oreg. Health Scis. U., Portland, 1985-92; rsch. analyst Oreg. Health Divsn., Portland, 1992-95; dir., nurse scientist Northwest Health Rsch., Milwaukie, Oreg., 1995—. Mem. Oreg. Nurses Assn., ANA, Union Concerned Scientists, Amnesty Internat., Am. Statis. Assn., Sigma Theta Tau. Office: NW Health Rsch 9884 SE 50th Ave Milwaukie OR 97222

REITINGER, THOMAS ANTHONY, hospital administrator; b. Freeport, Ill., July 12, 1944; married. BA, U. Wis., 1967; MA, Washington U., 1971. Adm. resident Jewish Hosp. St. Louis, 1970-71; asst. admin. St. John's Regional Health Ctr., Springfield, Mo., 1971-73, assoc. dir., 1973-75; exec. dir. Waupun (Wis.) Meml. Hosp., 1975-77, Fort Atkinson (Wis.) Meml. Hosp., 1977-83; v.p. St. Joseph's Hosp., Milw., 1983-84, sr. v.p., 1984-86, exec. v.p., COO, 1986-90, pres., 1990-93; pres., CEO Mercy Hosp. Med. Ctr., Des Moines, 1993—. Home: 5554 Beechwood Ter West Des Moines IA 50266-6620 Office: Mercy Hosp Med Ctr 400 University Des Moines IA 50313

REITZ, ALLEN BERNARD, organic chemist; b. Alameda, Calif., Apr. 7, 1956; s. Arnold Benno and Ruth Hazel (Stillings) R.; m. Evelyn June McCullough, Nov. 24, 1978; children: Darryl, Meredith. BA in Biochemistry and Molecular Biology, U. Calif., Santa Barbara, 1977; MS in Chemistry, U. Calif., San Diego, 1979, PhD in Chemistry, 1982. Postdoctoral rsch. fellow McNeil Pharm., Spring House, Pa., 1982-83, rsch. scientist, 1983-84, sr. scientist, 1984-87; prin. scientist Janssen Rsch. Found., Spring House, 1987-89; rsch. fellow R.W. Johnson Pharm. Rsch. Inst., Spring House, 1990—; reviewer Jour. Organic Chemistry, Tetrahedron Letters, Heteroatom Chemistry, Carbohydrate Rsch. Editor symposium series Inositol Phosphates and Derivatives, 1991; contbr. articles to profl. publs., chpt. to books; expert analyst Chemtracts-Organic Chemistry. Recipient Johnson & Johnson Achievement award, 1990, Philip B. Hofmann Rsch. award, 1994. Mem. AAAS, N.Y. Acad. Sci., Am. Chem. Soc. Phila. Organic Chemists Club (sec. 1986-88, chmn. 1996), Sigma Xi. Home: 109 Greenbriar Rd Lansdale PA 19446-1519 Office: RW Johnson Pharm Rsch Inst Welsh And Mckean Rd Spring House PA 19477

REITZ, BRUCE ARNOLD, cardiac surgeon, educator; b. Seattle, Sept. 14, 1944; s. Arnold B. and Ruth (Stillings) R.; m. Nan Norton, Oct. 3, 1970; children: Megan, Jay. BS, Stanford U., 1966; MD, Yale U., 1970. Diplomate: Am. Bd. Surgery, Am. Bd. Thoracic Surgery. Intern Johns Hopkins Hosp., Balt., 1970-71, cardiac surgeon-in-charge, 1982-92; resident Stanford U. Hosp., (Calif.), 1971-72, 74-78; clin. assoc. Nat. Heart Lung Blood Inst., NIH, Bethesda, Md., 1972-74; asst. prof. Stanford U. Sch. Medicine, 1977-81, assoc. prof., 1981-82; prof. surgery Johns Hopkins U. Sch Medicine, Balt., 1982-92; prof., chmn. Sch Medicine Stanford (Calif.) U., 1992—. Developer heart-lung transplant technique, 1981. Office: Stanford U Sch Medicine Dept Cardiothoracic Surgery Stanford CA 94305

REITZ, JOANNE BELLAM, health information manager; b. Rochester, N.Y., Dec. 26, 1950; d. Ernest Wilson and Anne (Hasenhno) Bellam; 1 child, Stephen Ernest Reitz. AS in Applied Scis., Monroe C.C., 1971; BS in Bus. Mgmt. and Econs., SUNY, 1993. Accredited Med. Records Technician. Med. records technician Genesee Meml. Hosp., Batavia, N.Y., 1971-76, St. Jerome Hosp., Batavia, 1976-79; dir. med. records and health info. mgmt. LeRoy (N.Y.) Village Green Nursing Home; health info. mgr., 1995; cons. health info., med. records Scottsville, N.Y., 1996—; cons. Livingston County SNF, Geneseo, N.Y., 1987—, Norloch Nursing Home, Rochester, N.Y., 1991—, Brae Loche Nursing Home, Rochester, 1991—, Livingston County HRF, Mt. Morris, N.Y., 1992—, Rochester Rehab. Ctr., 1995—; instr. Bryant & Stratton Coll. for Med. Programs, 1996. Mem. Am. Health Info. Mgmt. Assn., N.Y. State Health Info. Mgmt. Assn., Rochester Health Info. Mgmt. Assn., greater Rochester chpt. Assn. Records Mgrs. and Adminstrs. Home and Office: 949 Scotts Mumford Rd Scottsville NY 14546

REKATE, ALBERT C., physician; b. Buffalo, June 12, 1916; s. Gustave E. and Fannie (Hummell) R.; m. Elizabeth Foster, June 12 1943 (dec. 1985); 1 child, Suzanne (Mrs. R. Willis Post); m. Linda Ann Holt, Aug. 1, 1992. M.D., U. Buffalo, 1940. Diplomate Am. Bd. Internal Medicine. Intern E.J. Meyer Meml. Hosp., Buffalo, 1940-41, med. resident, 1941-44; asst. prof. medicine SUNY-Buffalo, 1954-61, assoc. prof., 1961-65, prof., 1965-86, prof. emeritus, 1986—; dir. rehab. medicine SUNY, Buffalo, 1965-72, acting dean Sch. Health Related Professions, 1965-66, assoc. dean, 1966-74, acting chmn. dept. rehab. medicine, 1972-75; assoc. dir. medicine E.J. Meyer Meml. Hosp., Buffalo, 1957-63, head dept. rehab. medicine, 1964-69, dir. primary rehab. center, 1965-69, acting head cardiology, 1966-69, dir., 1970-72; bd. dirs. Buffalo Hearing and Speech Ctr., 1973—; mem. adv. bd. Coastal Empire Mental Health Ctr., S.C., 1980-81, bd. dirs., 1981-93; mem. dean's adv. coun. SUNY-Buffalo Sch. Medicine and Biomed. Scis., 1995—. Contbr. articles to profl. jours. Served with M.C. AUS, World War II. Mem. Am. Heart Assn., Western N.Y. Heart Assn. (pres. 1954-55), Assn. Am. Med. Colls., N.Y. State Heart Assembly, N.Y. Acad. Scis., Med. Union (pres. 1974-75), Buffalo Acad. Medicine (pres. 1969-70), Erie County Med. Soc., Med. Alumni Assn. U. Buffalo (pres. 1960-61), Beaufort-Jasper Mental Health Assn. (dir. 1980-86). Home: PO Box 3164 Hilton Head Island SC 29928-0164 Office: 462 Grider St Buffalo NY 14215-3075

REKUC, GREGORY MATTHEW, physician; b. Trenton, Mich, Jan. 1, 1957; s. Walter Stephen and Barbara Teresa (Olszewski) R.; m. Jill Frances Callahan, Oct. 12, 1985; children: Caroline Christine, Brian Gregory. AA, U. Fla., 1975, BS, 1978, MD with honors, 1981. Intern, resident U. N.C. Meml. Hosp., Chapel Hill, 1981-84; staff internist Kaiser Permanente, Raleigh, N.C., 1985-87; internist Raleigh Internal Medicine, 1987—. Mem. Am. Coll. Physicians, Phi Beta Kappa, Alpha Epsilon Delta, Alpha Omega Alpha. Home: 4105 John S Raboteau Wynd Raleigh NC 27612 Office: Raleigh Internal Medicine 3320 Wake Forest Rd Raleigh NC 27609

RELLE, ATTILA TIBOR, dentist, geriodontist; b. Columbus, Ohio, Aug. 31, 1959; s. Ferenc Matyas and Trudi (Tubach) R.; m. Kim Ann McDonald, Apr. 26, 1986; 1 dau., Ilona. DDS, Case Western Reserve U., 1985; BS, Ohio State U., 1985, postgrad., 1985-88, 93; postgrad., Wright State U. Sch. Medicine, 1988-93. Dentist Mobile Care Corp., Dublin, Ohio, 1985; assoc. dentist Richard P. Deed, D.D.S. and Assocs., Columbus, 1985-86; dentist Family Dental and Denture Ctr. II, Dayton, Ohio, 1986-87; geriodontist Midwest Mobile Dental Care, Inc., Hamilton, Ohio, 1988-91, Mobile Dental Care, Inc., Hamilton, Ohio, 1991-92; dentist/owner Attila T. Relle, DDS and Assocs., Columbus, 1985—, Attila T. Relle, DDS & Assocs., Hilliard, 1995—; dentist Jerry Owens, D.D.S. and Assocs., Lancaster, Ohio, 1989-92; state dir. Ohio Residentcare dental geriatric program Meridian Svc. Care Corp. of Ohio, 1992-94, dentist/geriodontist, 1992-94; co-chmn. Ohio Dental Careers Day, Columbus, 1980-81; regional dir. Midwest Mobile Dental Care, Inc., 1988-89; mem. adv. com. N.Am. Health Corp., 1989-92; sci. judge Ohio Acad. Sci., Delaware, 1985—. Mem. Civitan Internat. (pres. Eastern Columbus Club 1986-87). Presbyterian. Home: 5203 Carifa Ct Hilliard OH 43026-9589 Office: Attila T Relle DDS & Assocs 5203 Carifa Ct Hilliard OH 43026-9589 also: Ste 100 4984-A Scioto Darby Rd Hilliard OH 43026-1550

RELMAN, ARNOLD SEYMOUR, physician, educator, editor; b. N.Y.C., June 17, 1923; s. Simon and Rose (Mallach) R.; m. Harriet Morse Vitkin, June 26, 1953; children: David Arnold, John Peter, Margaret Rose. A.B., Cornell U., 1943; M.D., Columbia U., 1946; LLD (hon.), U. Pa.; ScD (hon.), Med. Coll. Wis., Union U., Med. Coll. Ohio, CUNY; DMSc (hon.), Brown U.; DLH (hon.), SUNY; LittD (hon.), Temple U. Diplomate Am. Bd. Internal Medicine. House officer New Haven Hosp., Yale, 1946-49; NRC fellow Evans Meml., Mass. Meml. hosps., 1949-50; practice medicine, specializing in internal medicine Boston, 1950-68, Phila., 1968-77; asst. prof., prof. medicine Boston U. Sch. Medicine, 1950-68; dir. Boston U. Med. Services, Boston City Hosp., 1967-68; prof. medicine, chmn. dept. medicine U. Pa.; chief med. services Hosp. of U. Pa., 1968-77; editor New Eng. Jour. Medicine, Boston, 1977-91, editor emeritus, 1991—; sr. physician Brigham and Women's Hosp., Boston, 1977—; prof. medicine and social medicine Harvard Med. Sch., 1977-93, prof. medicine and social medicine emeritus, 1993—; cons. NIH, USPHS.; mem. bd. registration in medicine Commonwealth of Mass., 1995—. Editor: Jour. Clin. Investigation, 1962-67, (with F.J. Ingelfinger and M. Finland) Controversy in Internal Medicine, Vol. 1, 1966, Vol. 2, 1974; contbr. articles to profl. jours. Trustee Columbia U., 1990—; bd. dirs. Hastings Ctr., 1981-83. Recipient Columbia Alumni Gold medal, 1980, Disting. Svc. award Am. Coll. Cardiology, 1987, McGovern award Cosmos Club Washington, 1991, John Peters award Am. Soc. Nephrology, 1992. Fellow ACP (master, John Phillips medal 1985), Am. Acad. Arts and Scis.; mem. AMA, Assn. Am. Physicians (coun., pres. 1983-84, Kober medal 1993), Am. Physiol. Soc., Mass. Med. Soc., Inst. Medicine of NAS (coun. 1979-82), Am. Soc. Clin. Investigation (past pres.), Am. Fedn. Clin. Rsch. (past pres.), Phi Beta Kappa (senator 1991—), Alpha Omega Alpha. Office: Brigham and Women's Hosp Dept of Medicine 75 Francis St Boston MA 02115-6110

REMBAR, JAMES CARLSON, psychologist; b. N.Y.C., May 4, 1949; s. Charles Isaiah and Billie Ann (Olsson) R.; m. Jill Bailin, June 4, 1988; 1 child, Lilianna. BA, Sarah Lawrence Coll., 1972; MA, U. Mich., 1976, PhD, 1978. Lic. psychologist, psychoanalyst, N.Y. Clin. psychologist U. Mich. Med. Ctr., Ann Arbor, 1978-80; instr. psychology in psychiatry N.Y. Hosp. Cornell U. Med. Coll., White Plains, 1980-84, clin. asst. prof., 1984—, coord. child and adolescent psychology Westchester div., 1982-87; pvt. practice clin. psychologist Irvington, White Plains, N.Y., 1981—; faculty Westchester Ctr. for Study of Psychoanalysis and Psychotherapy, 1989—, dir. continuing edn., 1992—; mem. adv. bd. Veritas Young Mothers Program; cons. Andrus Children's Home, Yonkers, N.Y., 1987—. Contbr. articles to profl. jours., chpt. in book. Mem. Am. Psychol. Assn., N.Y. State Psychol. Assn., Westchester County Psychol. Assn., Psychoanalytic Assn. Westchester Ctr. Home and Office: 9 Sunnyside Pl Irvington NY 10533-1300 Office: 510 N Broadway White Plains NY 10603-3217

REMENCHIK, ALEXANDER PAVLOVICH, internist; b. Chgo., Sept. 13, 1922; s. Paul Samuelovich and Irina Alexandra (Babich) R.; m. Mary Margaret Mays, Apr. 19, 1947; children: Alex Kevin, Ellen Jean, Karen Ann, Margaret Lynn. BS in Physics, U. Chgo., 1943, MD, 1951. Diplomate Am. Bd. Internal Medicine. Intern Cook County Hosp., Chgo., 1951-52; resident U. Ill. Research and Ednl. Hosps., 1952-53, fellow, 1953-54; clin. investigator VA Hosp., Hines, Ill., 1960-62; practice medicine specializing in internal medicine, Chgo., 1953-72, Montclair, N.J., 1972-74, Houston, 1974—; asst. med. supt. Mcpl. Contagious Disease Hosp., Chgo., 1953-59; instr. medicine U. Ill., Chgo., 1954-59; asst. prof. medicine Stritch Sch. Medicine, Loyola U., Maywood, Ill., 1960-63, assoc. prof., 1964-67, prof., 1967-72, pres. Faculty Collegium, 1970-71, asst. chmn. dept. medicine, 1964-70; dir. dept. nuclear medicine Loyola U. Hosp., 1969-71; attending physician Cook County Hosp., 1959-72; attending physician Mountainside Hosp., Montclair, 1972-74, dir. med. edn., chmn. dept. medicine, 1972-74; attending mem. active staff Parkway Hosp., 1974-79, Citizens Gen. Hosp., 1974-86, chief med. service, 1977, chief of staff, 1979, 82-83, mem. governing bd., 1977-86; mem. staff Eastway Gen. Hosp., 1974—, chmn. dept. medicine, 1976-80; pres. East Loop Emergency Med. Clinic, Houston, 1979-82, East Loop Cardio Pulmonary Ctr., Inc., 1979-85; bd. dirs. Seminars and Symposia Inc.; chmn. continuing med. edn. com., 1988—; mem., bd. dirs. Mt. Everest Granite Corp.; med. expert Office of Hearings and Appeals, Dept. Health and Human Svcs. Social Security Adminstrn., 1993—. Editor: (with P.J. Talso) Mechanisms of Disease, 1968; contbr. over 50 articles on internal medicine to profl. jours. Mem. Zoning Commn. Oak Park (Ill.), 1969-72; trustee Unitarian-Universalist Ch. of Oak Park, 1969-70; vice chmn., bd. dirs. Bounty of Sea, Inc. Lt. (j.g.) USN, 1943-46. Fellow ACP; mem. AMA, Soc. Exptl. Biology and Medicine, Am. Fedn. Clin. Research, Harris County Med. Soc., Tex. Med. Assn., Am. Heart Assn., Am. Diabetes Assn., Sigma Xi. Home: 9330 Oakford Ct Houston TX 77024-3615 Office: 8799 North Loop E Houston TX 77029-1250

REMETTA, JANET, pharmaceutical company executive, veterinarian; b. Camden, N.J., July 11, 1952; d. John Matthew and Marie Stella (Klemaszewski) R.; m. Neal Robert Frank, Oct. 19, 1974. BA, Trenton State Coll., 1974; MSW, Rutgers U., 1975; postgrad., Delaware Valley Coll., 1977-79; VMD, U. Pa., 1985. Lic. vet. medicine, Pa., N.J. Program specialist N.J. Dept. Health, Trenton, 1975-77, labor/mgmt. cons., 1977-79, supervising program specialist, 1979-81; clin. vet. Emerson Vet. Clinic, Buckingham, Pa., 1985-86, Ewing Vet. Hosp., Trenton, 1986-88; mgr. issues mgmt. Sandoz Pharm. Corp., East Hanover, N.J., 1988-90, assoc. dir. issues mgmt., 1990-91, dir. issues mgmt., 1992, interim dept. head sci. and external affairs, 1992-93, exec. dir. site ops., 1993-95; exec. dir. internat. pub. policy Rhône-Poulenc Rorer Pharms., Collegeville, Pa., 1995—. Mem. policy and legis. com. N.J. Chem. Industry Coun., Trenton, 1988-92, chairperson-biotech. com., 1989-91; legis. com. N.J. Bus. and Industry Assn., Trenton, 1988-92; apptd. mem. N.J. Commn. on Smoking and Health, 1991-92; exec. chairperson N.J. Lung Assn., 1994; mem. bus. adv. bd. Women in Govt., 1994—; mem. steering com. Ctr. for the Am. woman, 1995; bd. dirs. YWCA, 1994-95. Recipient Tribute to Women in Industry award, 1992. Mem. AVMA, European Women's Mgmt. Devel. Network, Pa. Vet. Med. Assn. (legis. com. 1990—, long range planning com. 1995), Am. Mgmt. Assn., Am. Lung Assn. (exec. chairperson 1994), Assn. Indsl. Vets. Healthcare Businesswomen's Assn., N.J. Health Products Coun. (chairperson elect 1989-91, chairperson 1991-93), Nat. Pharm. Coun. (pub. affairs com. 1988-91, sci. affairs com. 1989-90), Pharm. Rsch. and Mfrs. Assn. (govt. affairs com. 1989-93, internat. com. 1995, exec. com. internat. sect. 1995—, econ. policy task force 1995—), Greater Valley Forge Rhodesian Ridge Back Club (founding mem.), Internat. Pharm. Aerosol Consortium (corp. rep. 1996—), Internat. Bus. Coun. (corp. rep. 1996—). Home: 379 Sweetbriar Rd Perkasie PA 18944-3868

REMINE, WILLIAM HERVEY, JR., surgeon; b. Richmond, Va., Oct. 11, 1918; s. William Hervey and Mabel Inez (Walthall) ReM.; m. Doris Irene Grumbacher, June 9, 1943; children: William H., Stephen Gordon, Walter James, Gary Craig. B.S. in Biology, U. Richmond, 1940, D.Sc. (hon.), 1965; M.D., Med. Coll. Va., Richmond, 1943; M.S. in Surgery, U. Minn., Mpls., 1952. Diplomate Am. Bd. Surgery. Intern Doctor's Hosp., Washington, 1944; fellow in surgery Mayo Clinic, Rochester, Minn., 1944-45, 47-52; instr. surgery Mayo Grad. Sch. Medicine, Rochester, Minn., 1954-59, asst. prof. surgery, 1959-65, assoc. prof. surgery, 1965-70, prof. surgery, 1970-83, prof. surgery emeritus, 1983—; surg. cons. to surgeon gen. U.S. Army, 1965-75; surg. lectr., USSR, 1987, 89, Japan, 1988, 90, Egypt, 1990; lectr. Soviet-Am. seminars, USSR, 1987, 89. Sr. author: Cancer of the Stomach, 1964, Manual of Upper Gastro-intestinal Surgery, 1985; editor: Problems in General Surgery, Surgery of the Biliary Tract, 1986; mem. editorial bd. Rev. Surgery, 1965-75, Jour. Lancet, 1968-77; contbr. 200 articles to profl. jours. Served to capt. U.S. Army, 1945-47. Recipient St. Francis surg. award St. Francis Hosp., Pitts., 1976, disting. service award Alumni Council, U. Richmond, 1976. Mem. ACS, AAAS, Am. Assn. History of Medicine, AMA, Am. Med. Writers Assn., Am. Soc. Colon and Rectal Surgeons, Soc. Surgery Alimentary Tract (v.p. 1983-84), Am. Surg. Assn., Assn. Mil. Surgeons U.S., Internat. Soc. Surgery, Digestive Disease Found., Priestley Soc. (pres. 1968-69), Central Assn. Physicians and Dentists (pres. 1972-73), Central Surg. Assn., Soc. Med. Cons. Armed Forces, Mayo Clinic Surg. Soc. (chmn. 1964-66), Soc. Head and Neck Surgeons, Soc. Surg. Oncology, So. Surg. Assn., Western Surg. Assn. (pres. 1979-80), Minn. State Med. Assn., Minn. Surg. Soc. (pres. 1966-67), Zumbro Valley Med. Soc., Sigma Xi; hon. mem. Colombian Coll. Surgeons, St. Paul Surg. Soc., Flint Surg. Soc., Venezuelan Surg. Soc., Colombian Soc. Gastroenterology, Dallas So. Clin. Soc., Ga. Surg. Soc., Soc. Postgrad. Surgeons Los Angeles County, Japanese Surg. Soc., Argentine Surg. Digestive Soc., Bassanese Surg. Assn. (Italy), Tex. Surg. Soc., Omicron Delta Kappa, Alpha Omega Alpha, Beta Beta Beta, Kappa Sigma. Methodist. Home: Sawgrass Players Club 8212 Seven Mile Dr Ponte Vedra Beach FL 32082-3129

REMLEY, THEODORE PHANT, JR., counseling educator, lawyer; b. Eustis, Fla., Feb. 7, 1947; s. Theodore Phant Sr. and Era Annie (Forehand) R. BA, U. Fla., 1969, EdS, 1971, PhD, 1980; JD, Catholic U., 1980. Bar: Va. 1981, Fla. 1982. lic. profl. counselor, Va., Miss., La. Exec. dir. Am. Counseling Assn., Alexandria, Va., 1990-94; prof. counseling U. New Orleans, 1994—. Contbr. articles to profl. jours., chpts. to books. Mem. Am. Counseling Assn., Am. Assn. State Counseling Bds. Democrat. Roman Catholic. Home: 3800 Camp St New Orleans LA 70115-2629 Office: Dept Edn Leadership Counseling & Founds U New Orleans New Orleans LA 70148

REMO, JOHN WILLIAM, radiologist; b. Fond du Lac, Wis., July 11, 1936; s. Maynard William and Vivian Lucille (Leininger) R.; m. Jean Fletcher Steadman, July 12, 1969; children: Jessica Jean, Jeremy John. BA in Biology, Ill. Wesleyan U., 1958; MD, U. Calif., San Francisco, 1967. Cert. diagnostic radiology. Intern Wayne County Gen. Hosp., Eloise, Mich., 1967-68; resident in radiology U. Mich., Ann Arbor, 1968-71; radiologist Home Hosp., Lafayette, Ind., 1971—. Bd. trustee Ill. Wesleyan U., Bloomington, 1985. Served to lt. USNR, 1961-65. Mem. AMA, Ind. State Med. Assn. Presbyterian. Home: 1230 S River Rd West Lafayette IN 47906-4311 Office: Radiologic Specialists Ind 2400 South St Lafayette IN 47904-3027

REMPEL, ARTHUR GUSTAV, biology educator; b. Marinskaya, Ukraine, Jan. 5, 1910; came to U.S., 1923; s. Gustav Aron and Elisabeth Electra

(Dirks) R.; m. Lucile Elma Sommerfield, June 19, 1934; children: Robert Arthur (dec.), Herbert Frank, Paul Leonard (dec.), Margaret Louise, Roland Richard. Cert., Pasadena Jr. Coll., 1931; AB, Oberlin Coll., 1934; PhD, U. Calif., Berkeley, 1938; DSc (hon), Whitman Coll., 1987. Acting curator Mus. Anthropology and Zoology Oberlin (Ohio) Coll., 1931-34; teaching asst. U. Calif., Berkeley, 1934-38; mem. faculty biology Whitman Coll., Walla Walla, Wash., 1938—, prof., 1949-75, prof. emeritus, 1975—; vis. prof. biology U. Calif., Berkeley, summer 1949, U. Wash., Seattle, summer 1957, 58, 66, 67; rsch. assoc. Wash. State U., Pullman, summer 1956; ranger, historian Nat. Park Svc., summer 1953, 54; ranger, naturalist Nat. Park Svc., Yosemite, Calif., summer 1955. Fellow AAAS; mem. Phi Beta Kappa, Sigma Xi. Home: 635 University St Walla Walla WA 99362-2338

REMSBERG, RICHARD J., retired osteopath; b. Alma, Mich., June 13, 1930; s. Emory Richard and Ruth Aileen (Aldrich) R.; m. Molly Rae Engle, Oct. 12, 1956; children: Susan Marie, Kathryn Rae, Lee Ann. BS, Alma Coll., 1952; DO, Chgo. Coll. Osteo Medicine, 1955. Intern Grand Rapids (Mich.) Osteopathic Hosp., 1955-56; asst. med. dir. Mich. Masonic Home, Alma, 1964-84, med. dir., 1985-92; ret., 1992. Mem. Masons (Worshipful Master 1964), Rotary (pres. 1971), Elks. Home: 519 Fairlane Dr Alma MI 48801-2105

RENAUD, REGINA MARIA RYBARSKI, critical care nurse; b. Worcester, Mass., June 10, 1953; d. Tadeus and Dorothy (Dietz) Rybarski; m. Richard H. Renaud, Aug. 18, 1995; 1 child, Michael T. Chesnis; stepchildren: Joseph P., Jeffrey R. Diploma in nursing, St. Vincent Hosp., 1974; BSN magna cum laude, Worcester State Coll., 1981; MSN, Anna Maria Coll., Paxton, 1990. RN, Mass.; CCRN, CEN, ACLS instr., BCLS instr. Hemodialysis staff nurse St. Vincent Hosp., Worcester, Mass., 1978-80, critical care charge nurse, staff nurse, float, 1974-80, critical care instr., 1981-87, critical care clin. nurse specialist, 1987-91, cardiovasc. clin. nurse specialist, 1991—, instr. ADN and BSN programs, 1991-96; researcher in field. Contbr. articles to profl. jours. Mem. AACN (Worcester chpt.), Emergency Nurses Assn., Worcester Area Insvc. Group, St. Vincent Hosp. Alumni Assn., Am. Heart Assn.

RENDIN, ROBERT WINTER, environmental health officer; b. Jamaica, N.Y., Oct. 21, 1949; s. Anthony and Gertrude Helen (Winter) R.; m. Janet Elizabeth Meyer, Apr. 8, 1972; children: Cheryl, Valerie, Scott. BS, Rutgers U., 1971; MS in Environ. Health, E. Tenn. State U., 1974; postgrad., U.S. Marine Corps Command & Staff Coll., 1985-86, Tulane U., 1994-95. Commd. lt. (j.g.) USN, 1974, advanced through grades to comdr.; environ. health officer U.S. Naval Hosp., San Diego, 1988; chief preventive medicine U.S. Naval Hosp., Taipei, Taiwan, 1976-78; chief occupational and preventive medicine U.S. Naval Hosp., Great Lakes, Ill., 1978-81; environ. health officer U.S. Navy Atlantic Fleet, Norfolk, Va., 1981-84; chief environ. health svc. Navy Environ. & Preventive Medicine Unit, Virginia Beach, Va., 1984-85; med. planner 1st Marine Force Svc. Support Group, Camp Pendleton, Calif., 1986-87, 4th Marine Div., New Orleans, 1987-90; exec. officer Naval Biodynamics Lab., New Orleans, 1990-92, comdg. officer, 1992-95; dep. dir. preventive medicine and health promotion Navy Environ. Health Ctr., Norfolk, Va., 1995-96, dep. dir. Preventive Medicine and Health Promotion, 1996—. Contbr. articles to profl. jours. Decorated Navy Commendation award (2), Meritorious Svc. medal (2); recipient Combined Svc. Hon. award Republic of China, 1977. Mem. U.S. Naval Inst., Nat. Environ. Health Assn. (registered sanitarian), Uniformed Svcs. Environ. Health Assn., Phi Kappa Phi. Lutheran. Home: 646 Edgewood Arch Chesapeake VA 23320 Office: Navy Environ Health Ctr 2510 Walmer Ave Norfolk VA 23513-2617

RENDON, MARIO IVAN, psychiatrist; b. Medellin, Antioquia, Colombia, May 9, 1938; came to U.S., 1966; s. Jairo and Melania (Cardona) R.; m. Diane Cristine Courchesne, Oct. 4, 1969; children: Adan, Renata. MD, U. Antioquia, 1963. Diplomate Am. Bd. Psychiatry and Neurology, Am. Bd. Child Psychiatry. Intern Hosp. St. Vicente De Paul, Medellin, 1962-63; med. dr. Hosp. Urrao and Andes, 1963-66; resident in psychiatry Fairfield Hills Hosp., Newtown, Conn., 1966-67; resident, fellow in child psychiatry Bellevue Hosp., N.Y.C., 1967-70, mem. faculty, 1970-79; clin. dir. Leake and Watts Children's Home, Yonkers, N.Y., 1979-89; dir. bilingual-bi-cultural Hispanic svc. Bronx Mcpl. Hosp. Ctr., N.Y.C., 1989-90; dir. dept. psychiatry Lincoln Hosp., N.Y.C., 1990; mem. attending faculty Aecom-Montefiore, N.Y.C., 1981-86; clin. assoc. prof. psychiatry NYU Med. Ctr., 1982-89, AECOM, 1989—; prof. clin. psychiatry N.Y. Med. Coll., 1989—. Editor: Am. Jour. of Psychoanalysis, 1984-91. Fellow Am. Acad. Psychoanalysis; mem. Soc. for Rsch. in Child Devel., Am. Orthopsychiat. Assn., Am. Psychiat. Assn., Am. Inst. for Psychoanalysis, Assn. for Advancement of Psychoanalysis (pres. 1979-81). Home: 333 E 30th St Apt 8L New York NY 10016-6472 Office: Lincon Hosp 234 E 149th St Bronx NY 10451-5589

RENDON-PELLERANO, MARTA INES, dermatologist; b. Sept. 19, 1957; d. Uriel and Rosa Rendon. BA and Scis., U. P.R., Mayaquez, 1977; postgrad., Autonoma U., Santo Domingo, Dominican Republic, 1977-79; MD, U. P.R., San Juan, 1982. Diplomate Am. Bd. Internal Medicine, Am. Bd. Dermatology; lic. physician, Fla., Tex., Pa., ACLS, Drug Enforcement Adminstrn. Intern and resident in internal medicine Albert Einstein Med. Ctr., Phila., 1982-85; resident in dermatology Parkland Meml. Hosp., Southwestern Med. Sch., Dallas, 1985-88; emergency rm. physician Pottsborough (Tex.) Med. Clinic, 1985-86; coord. dermatology clinic Kayser Permanente Med. Assn. Tex., Dallas, 1986-88; dermatology assoc. Dermatology Ctr., Dallas, 1988-89; staff physician Southwestern Med. Sch., Vets. Hosp., Dallas, 1988-89; clin. asst. prof. dept. deramtology U. Miami (Fla.) Sch. Medicine, 1989—; chief dept. dermatology Cleveland Clinic Fla., Ft. Lauderdale, 1989—; mem. adv. bd. South Fla. Vis. Lectureship Series, 1991-92; mem. rsch. bd. advisors Medecis Corp. Featured on TV shows and in popular mags.; contbr. articles to profl. jours., chpts. to books. Recipient Radio Klaridad award for best sci. work, Miami, 1990. Fellow Am. Acad. Dermatology; mem. ACP (assoc.), AAUW, Womens Med. Assn., Womens Dermatol. Soc., Cuban-Interam. Dermatol. Soc., Women of Spanish Origin, Tex. Med. Assn., Miami Dermatology Soc., Fla. Med. Assn., Broward Dermatology Soc., Broward County Med. Assn., Etta Gamma Delta. Roman Catholic. Office: Cleveland Clinic Fla 3000 W Cypress Creek Rd Fort Lauderdale FL 33309-1710

RENFORD, EDWARD J., hospital administrator; b. July 16, 1943; married. AA, L.A. City Coll., 1969; BA, Calif. State U., 1971; MA, Pepperdine U., 1983. Asst. fiscal officer Martin Luther King Jr., Drew Med. Ctr., L.A., 1974-75, assoc. adminstr. fin. svcs., 1984-86, hosp. adminstr., 1990—; dir. fiscal svcs. LAC Harbor UCLA Med. Ctr., Torrance, Calif., 1975-77, asst. adminstr. fin., 1977-79, assoc. adminstr., 1979-82; asst. adminstr. Centinela Hosp. Med. Ctr., Inglewood, Calif., 1982-84; assoc. exec. dir. LAC Rancho Los Amigos Med. Ctr., Downey, Calif., 1986-89; chief staff Hosp. Adminstrn./ Dept. Health Svcs., L.A., 1989-90; CEO, pres. Grady Meml Hosp, Atlanta, GA. Recipient numerous awards. Home: PO Box 54221 Atlanta GA 30308-0221 Office: Grady Meml Hosp 80 Butler St Atlanta GA 30335*

RENICK, JOHN T., physician; b. New Albany, Miss., Aug. 2, 1939; m. Jane Willis; children: Lanette, John T., III. BS, Stetson Coll., 1962; Doctorate, Emory U., 1966. Med. dir. Rivendell Psychiat. Ctr., Panama City, Fla.; pvt. practice Panama City; dir. inpatient unit U. South Ala. Med. Ctr., 1979-81; assoc. clin. tchr. psychiatry, family practice South Ala. Med. Ctr., 1978-81, profl. resident tng. program, 1982-84; various med. staff positions to pres. med. staff Southland Hosp., Mobile, Ala., 1984-85, mem. exec. med. com., 1982-85; med. exec. com. Doctor's Hosp., Mobile, 1985-89. Mem. fin. bd. St. John's Ch., Panama City, minister of communion, lectr. Recipient Acad. Coun. award Stetson U.; fellow Emory U., 1963-65. Mem. AMA, APA, Am. Assn. Gestalt-Therapists, Med. Assn. State of Ala., Mobile County Med. Soc., Am. Soc. Psychosomatic Ob/Gyn., AAAS, Am. Acad. Clin. Psychiatrists, Am. Acad. Med. Dirs., Ala. Anti-Drug Commn., Ind. Physicians Assn. of Psychiatry (chmn.), Cancer Inst., Sigma Phi Epsilon. Office: 2739 Jenks Ave Panama City FL 32405

RENNERT, OWEN MURRAY, physician, educator; b. N.Y.C., Aug. 8, 1938; s. David Rennert and Frieda (Weinsteiner) Sommer; m. Sandra Serota, Mar. 22, 1964; children: Laura, Rachel, Ian. BS, BA, U. Chgo., 1957, MD, 1961, MS in Biochemistry, 1963. Diplomate Am. Bd. Pediatrics, Am. Bd. Genetics, Am. Bd. Med. Genetics. Assoc. prof. pediatrics U. Fla., Gainesville, 1968-71, prof. pediatrics and biochemistry, 1971-78; prof. biochemistry, prof. and head dept. pediatrics U. Okla., Oklahoma City, 1977-88; chief pediatrics service and head genetics, endocrinology and metabolics Okla. Children's Mem. Hosp., Oklahoma City, 1977-88; prof., chmn. dept. pediatrics Georgetown U. Sch. Medicine, Washington, 1988—. Co-author: Metabolism of Trace Metals in Man: Developmental Biology and Genetic Implications (2 vols.), 1983; contbr. articles to profl. jours. Bd. dirs. Children's Med. Research, Oklahoma City, 1984-88. Served to sr. surgeon USPHS, 1964-66. Named Clin. Scientist of Yr., Am. Assn. Clin. Scientists, 1978. Mem. Am. Pediatric Soc., Am. Acad. Pediatrics, Soc. Pediatric Research, Am. Coll. Clin. Nutrition, Biochem. Soc., Am. Soc. Molecular Biology and Biochemistry. Office: Georgetown U Childrens Med Ctr Dept Pediatrics 3800 Reservoir Rd NW Washington DC 20007-2196

RENO, JOSEPH HARRY, retired orthopedic surgeon; b. Allentown, Pa., Mar. 5, 1915; s. Harvey Luther and Olive May (Wilson) R.; m. Maude Olivia Mutchler, June 27, 1942; children: Joseph David, Sally Jo, Diana Jane, Deborah Marion. Student, Temple U., 1934-37, MD, 1941. Intern. Chester (Pa.) Hosp., 1941-42; residency Tex. Scottish Rite Hosp. for Crippled Children, Dallas, 1942-43, 44-45, Robert Packer Hosp., Sayre, Pa., 1943-44; assoc. Homer Stryker, M.D., Kalamazoo, 1945-46; pvt. practice Bethlehem, Pa., 1946-71, Flagstaff, Ariz., 1971-93; team physician Lehigh U., Bethlehem, 1946-70, No. Ariz. U., Flagstaff, 1971-77, Ariz. State U., Tempe, 1977-84; chief surg. staff Flagstaff Hosp., 1975. Contbr. articles to profl. jours.; prodr. surg. films for Am. Acad. Ortho. Surgeons and others, 1952-70. Pres. Coconino County Easter Seal Soc., 1973; bd. dirs., med. advisor Ariz. Easter Seal Soc., 1974-84. Recipient Pioneer award Ariz. Med. Assn., 1981, Cert. of Appreciation, Pa. Dept. Health Crippled Children's Div., 1971; Dr. Joseph Reno Sports Medicine award named in honor, No. Ariz. State U. and Blue Cross Blue Shield, 1986. Fellow Am. Acad. Ortho. Surgeons, Am. Assn. for Surgery of Trauma, Am. Coll. Sports Med., Am. Coll. Surgeons (chmn. Lehigh Valley subcom. on trauma 1954-66, Ea. Pa. chpt. pres. 1969); mem. NRA, Am. Bd. Ortho. Surgery (cert., diplomate 1948), Coconino County Med. Soc. (pres. 1976), Western Ortho. Assn., Babcock Surg. Soc., Phi Chi, Alpha Tau Omega. Home: 621 Beal Rd Flagstaff AZ 86001-3008

RENSON, JEAN FELIX, psychiatry educator; b. Liège, Belgium, Nov. 9, 1930; came to U.S., 1960; s. Louis and Laurence (Crahai) R.; m. Gisèle Bouillenne, Sept. 8, 1956; children: Marc, Dominique, Jean-Luc. MD, U. Liege, 1959; PhD in Biochemistry, George Washington U., 1971. Diplomate Am. Bd. Psychiatry. Asst. prof. U. Liège, 1957-60; rsch. fellow U. Liege, 1966-72; clin. assoc. prof. dept. psychiatry U. Calif., San Francisco, 1978—; vis. asst. prof. Stanford U., Palo Alto, Calif., 1972-77. Assoc. editor: Fundamentals of Biochemical Pharmacology, 1971. NIH fellow, 1960-66. Democrat.

RENTAS, ROBERTO ANTONIO, hospital administrator; b. Ponce, P.R., Oct. 20, 1962; s. Carlos and Hilda (Ramos) R.; m. Eva C. Ramos, Aug. 12, 1989; children: Roberto Jean Carlos, Ann Maria Cristina. BBA in Acctg., Cath. U. P.R., 1984; M.Health Svcs. Adminstrn., U. P.R., San Juan, 1986. HMO adminstr. Dr. Pila Hosp., Ponce, 1986-87, asst. exec. dir., 1987-88; v.p. adminstrn., assoc. adminstr. Damas Hosp., Ponce, 1989, adminstr., 1989—. Sponsor Muscular Dystrophy Assn., Ponce, 1989—. Mem. Coll. Health Svcs. Adminstrs. (bd. dirs. 1993-95), P.R. Hosp. Assn. (bd. dirs. 1995-96). Home: Villas Sagrado Corazon A St #29 Ponce PR 00731 Office: Hospital Damas Ponce By Pass Ponce PR 00731

REPA, GEORGE, hospital administrator; b. Chgo., Aug. 14, 1955; s. Gregory and Josephine (Danyliw) R.; m. Donna Elaine Bromiel, Aug. 26, 1978. BS highest honors, U. Ill., 1977; MHA, Duke U., 1981. Asst. adminstr. Bladen County Hosp., Elizabethtown, N.C., 1981-82, Lea Regional Hosp., Hobbs, N.Mex., 1982-85; adminstr. Doctors Hosp., Jackson, Mich., 1985—, Hoots Meml. Hosp., Yadkinville, N.C., 1986-91; chief exec. officer Lincoln County Health Facilities, Fayetteville, Tenn., 1991-95; CEO Delta Regional Med. Ctr., Greenville, Miss., 1995—; mem. Fayetteville Telecomms. Project, 1993; bd. dirs. The Regional Health Network, 1995—. Mem. Study on Aging Task Force, Water Resources Steering Com., Yadkin County, N.C. 1988-89; active United Way. Named Ill. state scholar, 1973, Edmund James scholar, 1975; recipient Cert. of Appreciation, Task Force on Aging, Yadkin County, 1990, THA Recognition of Excellence, 1994. Mem. Am. Coll. Healthcare Execs. (assoc.), Sertoma, Rotary (bd. dirs. 1993-94), Beta Gamma Sigma, Phi Kappa Phi, Phi Eta Sigma. Home: 1761 Lance Cove Greenville MS 38701 Office: Delta Regional Med Ctr 1400 E Union Greenville MS 38704

REPASKE, ROY, molecular biologist; b. Cleve., Mar. 17, 1925; s. Matthew and Irene (Zajatz) R.; m. Anne Christine Colm, July 29, 1950; children: David Roy, William Allen, Carol Anne. B.S., Western Res. U., 1948; M.S., U. Mich., 1950; Ph.D., U. Wis., 1953. Instr. to assoc. prof. Ind. U., Bloomington, 1954-59; biochemist NIH Bethesda, Md., 1959-78, molecular biologist, 1978-92, dep. lab. chief LMM, 1991-92; retired, 1992; cons. Martin-Marietta Co., Balt., 1961, NASA, Washington, 1962-65; mem. com. on Detection of Extra-terrestrial life, USPHS, 1965; asst. program dir. U. Mich. summer program, Interlocken, 1963, 64; vis. rsch. assoc. Naval Med. Rsch. Inst., Bethesda, Md., 1989-90; mem. editorial bd. Jour. of Microbiology, 1962-67; instr. Found. for Advanced Studies in Scis., Bethesda, 1966-73; program dir. NSF Biochemistry, 1973-74. Active Boy Scouts Am., Bethesda, U.S. AEC fellow, 1951-53. Fellow AAAS; mem. Am. Soc. Biol. Chemists, Am. Soc. Microbiology (chmn. gen. div. 1963-64), Am. Soc. Virology, Fedn. of Am. Socs. for Exptl. Biology, Sigma Xi, Beta Theta Pi. Club: Am. Recorder Soc. (pres. 1968, 71-73). Avocations: amateur string quartet and recorder playing, gardening.

REPLOGLE, ROBERT L., cardiovascular and thoracic surgeon; b. Ottumwa, Iowa, Sept. 30, 1931; s. Ralph Ruby and Edith Dorothy (Swartz) R.; m. Carol A. Heeschen, Aug. 24, 1958; children: Robert E., Jennifer Bremer, Edith. MD cum laude, Cornell Coll., 1956, DSc (hon.), 1972; postgrad., Harvard U., 1956-60. Diplomate Am. Bd. Surgery, Am. Bd. Thoracic Surgery, Am. Bd. Pediat. Surgery. Intern in surgery U. Minn. Hosp., 1960-61; asst. resident in surgery Peter Bent Brigham Hosp., Boston, 1961-63, Mass. Gen. Hosp., Boston, 1965-66; sr. resident in surgery Children's Hosp. Med. Ctr., Boston, 1966; asst. in surgery Children's Hosp. Med. Ctr. and Harvard Med. Sch., Boston, 1966-67; asst. prof. surgery Pritzker Sch. Medicine U. Chgo., 1967-70, assoc. prof. surgery and head, sect. pediat. surgery, 1970-73, prof. surgery and head, sect. pediat. surgery, 1973-74, prof. surgery and head, sect. cardiac surgery, 1973-80, prof. surgery, sect. cardiac surgery, 1973—; mem. med. staff, divsn. cardiac surgery Humana Michael Reese Hosp. and Med. Ctr., Chgo., 1977—; med. dir. cardiac surgery unit Ingalls Meml. Hosp., 1989—; chief divsn. cardiac surgery Columbus Hosp., Chgo., 1987—; vis. prof. Albany Med. Coll., 1974, Dalhousie Sch. of Medicine, Halifax, 1975, Walter Reed Army Med. Ctr., 1978, U. Miami Med. Sch., 1992, Philippine Heart Ctr. for Asia March, 1979, Health Inst. Japan, Tokyo, 1982, Creighton Med. Sch., 1988, Brooke Army Med. Ctr., 1993, U. Heidelberg, 1995, Kerkoff Clinic/Max Planct Inst., Bad Nanheim, Germany, 1995, German Heart Ctr., Munich, 1995, Peter Bent Brigham Hosp. Harvard Med. Sch., 1996; mem. surgery and bioengrng. study sect. HHS, NIH, 1979-83; mem. ad hoc adv. com. bypass angioplasty revascularization investigation, NIH, 1993-94; mem. subcom. on quality N.Y. State Dept. Health, 1989-93, mem. subcom. on resources and facilities, 1993—, mem. cardiac adv. com., 1989—. Author: (with others) Microcirculation, Perfusion, and Transplantation of Organs, 1970, The Critically Ill Child, 1972, Surgical Clinics in North America, 1976, Biprosthetic Vardiac Valves, 1979, Year Book of Nuclear Medicine, 1981, among others; mem. editl. bd. Jour. Cardiac Surgery, 1982—; contbr. more than 125 articles to profl. jours. With USN, 1951-54. Recipient Merit award Philippine Heart ctr. for Asia, Manila, 1985, Friendship award Shanghai Chest Hosp., 1987. Mem. AMA (diagnostic and therapeutic tech. assessment panel 1995—, ho. of dels. 1992—, joint rev. com. on ednl. programs for physicians assts. 1979-84), ACS (com. on allied health pers. 1979-84, chmn. 1983-84, com. on med. motion pictures 1979-85, com. on membership 1988—, residency rev. com. for thoracic surgery of the accreditation com. for grad. med. edn. 1992-95, 96—), Ill. State Med. Soc., Chgo. Med. Soc., Am. Surg. Assn., European Assn. for Cardiothoracic Surgery, Soc. for Acad. Surgery, Am. Heart Assn. (adv. coun. cardiovasc. surgery 1968-71), Soc. Univ. Surgeons, Internat. Cardiovasc. Soc., Societe Internationale de Chirurgie (N.Am. chpt.), Am. Assn. for Thoracic Surgery (del. AMA 1992—, com. on soc. responsibility 1991—), Soc. Thoracic Surgeons (program com. 1978-81, chmn. 1981, com. on medico-legal affairs, chmn. 1985-88, ad hoc fin. adv. com. 1987-89, ad hoc exhibitors adv. com. 1988-89, ad hoc com. on social responsibility 1992-95, ad hoc database liaison com. 1993-94, database liaison com. 1994—, ad hoc com. on physician-specific mortality for cardiac surgery 1993-96, stds. and ethics com. 1984-88, treas. 1986-92, exec. com. 1986—, pres.-elect. 1995-96, pres. 1996-97, rep. to the coun. of med. specialty socs. 1990—, annals of thoracic surgery liaision com. 1992—, com. on grad. edn. in thoracic surgery 1992—, com. on major issues in thoracic surgery 1993, chmn. 1994, 95). Home: 1160 E 56th St Chicago IL 60637 Office: Ingalls Meml Hosp One Ingalls Dr West 536 Harvey IL 60426

REPLOGLE, STEPHEN PATRICK, osteopath, health facility administrator; b. L.I., Apr. 29, 1957; s. Fred W. and Wilma E. (Fuhrman) R.; m. Jan A. Smith, May 12, 1979; children: Joy S., Benjamin D. BA with honors, Temple U., 1984; DO, Kirksville Coll. Osteo. Med., 1990. Intern Philips County Regional Med. Ctr., Rolla, Mo.; physician Indian Health Svc., Yuma, Ariz., 1991-92, 16th St. Med. Clinic, Yuma, 1992-94; med. dir., physician Yuma (Ariz.) Urgent Care, 1994-96, Replogle Osteo. Med. Ctr., Yuma, 1996—. Founder, dir. Manna Ministries, Phila., 1982-86. Lt. Indian Health Svc. Commn. Corps, 1991-92. Republican. Home: 8300 Shannon Way Yuma AZ 85365 Office: Yuma Urgent Care 3939 Ave 3E Yuma AZ 85365

REPPEL, PETER DIRK, dental educator, dentist; b. Lüdenscheid, Germany, July 2, 1949. Dr. Med. Dent., FU Berlin, 1979, PhD, 1987. Prof. dental sch. Free U., Berlin, 1994—. Author: Resin-Bonded Bridges in Prosthetic Dentistry, 1988; translator Resin-Bonded Bridges, 1995. Mem. Deutsch Gesellschaft Zahn, Deutsche Gesellschaft zahnärztl, European Prosthodontik Assn.

REPPUCCI, NICHOLAS DICKON, psychologist, educator; b. Boston, May 1, 1941; s. Nicholas Ralph and Bertha Elizabeth (Williams) R.; m. Christine Marlow Onufrock, Sept. 10, 1967; children: Nicholas Jason, Jonathan Dickon, Anna Jin Marlow. BA with honors, U. N.C., 1962; MA, Harvard U., 1964, PhD, 1968. Lectr., rsch. assoc. Harvard U., Cambridge, Mass., 1967-68; asst. prof. Yale U., New Haven, 1968-73, assoc. prof., 1973-76; prof. psychology U. Va., Charlottesville, 1976—, dir. grad. studies in psychology, 1984-95; originator biennial conf. on community rsch. and action, 1986. Assoc. editor Law and Human Behavior, 1986—; mem. editl. bd. Am. Jour. Cmty. Psychology, 1974-83, 88-91; author: (with J. Haugaard) Sexual Abuse of Children, 1988; editor: (with J. Haugaard) Prevention in Community Mental Health Practice, (with E. Mulvey, L. Weithorn and J. Monahan) Mental Health, Law and Children, 1984; contbr. over 100 articles to profl. publs., chpts. in books. Adv. bd. on prevention Va. Dept. Mental Health, Mental Retardation and Substance Abuse Svcs., Richmond, 1986-92. Disting. scholar in psychology Va. Assn. Social Sci., 1991. Fellow APA (chair task force on pub. policy 1980-84), Am. Psychol. Soc., Soc. for Community Rsch. and Action (pres. 1986), Phi Beta Kappa. Office: U Va Dept Psychology Charlottesville VA 22903

REPSHER, LAWRENCE HARVEY, pulmonologist; b. Louisville, Aug. 1, 1939; s. Leonard Elton and Helen Margaret (Junge) R.; m. Diane Marie Bishop, Dec. 19, 1989; children: James Merrill, David Lawrence. BA, Harvard Coll., 1961; MD, U. Rochester, 1965. Intern Univ. Colo. Hosp., 1965-66, resident, 1966-67, 70, fellow in pulmonary diseases, 1970-72; pvt. practice pulmonary diseases and critical care medicine Luth. Med. Ctr., Wheat Ridge, Colo., 1972—; med. dir. Occptl. & Environ. Lung Disease Prog., Wheat Ridge, 1980—, Pulmonary Drug Evaluation Prog., 1974-91, Pulmonary Rsch. Cons., 1991—. Maj. USAR, 1968-70. Fellow Am. Coll. Chest Physicians; mem. Am. Thoracic Soc., Colo. Pulmonary Physicians Soc. (pres. 1978-88). Office: 3555 Lutheran Pky Ste 330 Wheat Ridge CO 80033-6039

REQUARTH, WILLIAM HENRY, surgeon; b. Charlotte, N.C., Jan. 23, 1913; s. Charles William and Amelia (George) R.; m. Nancy Charlton, 1948 (div. 1966); children—Kurt, Betsy, Jeff, Jan, Tim, Suzanna; m. Connie Harper, 1977. AB, Millikin U., 1934, LLD, 1996; MD, U. Ill., 1938, MS, 1939. Diplomate: Am. Bd. Surgery. Intern St. Luke's Hosp., Chgo., 1938-39; resident Cook County Hosp., Chgo., 1940-42, 46-48; pvt. practice medicine, specializing in surgery Decatur, Ill., 1950—; clin. prof. surgery U. Ill. Med. Sch., from 1962, now emeritus; Mem. Chgo. Bd. Trade. Author: Diagnosis of Abdominal Pain, 1953, The Acute Abdomen, 1958; also contbg. author chpts. books. Chmn. trustees Millikin U.; chmn. James Millikin Found.; bd. dirs. Decatur Meml. Hosp. Served to comdr. USNR, 1941-46. Mem. ACS, Cen. Surg. Assn., Western Surg. Assn., Chgo. Surg. Soc., Ill. Surg. Soc. (pres. 1970-71), Am. Soc. Surgery Hand (founder), Am. Soc. Surgery Trauma, Soc. Surgery Alimentary Tract, Warren Cole Soc., Societe Internationale Chirurgie, Nat. Pilots Assn. (pres. 1960-61), Soaring Soc. Am., Sportsman Pilot Assn. (pres. 1966-67), Aerobatic Club Am., Internat. Aerobatic Club. Home: 1860 S Spitler Dr Decatur IL 62521-4417 Office: 158 W Prairie Ave Decatur IL 62523-1230

REQUÉNEZ, EUNICE L., medical/surgical and community health nurse; b. Tex., Oct. 31, 1938; d. Thomas and Mary (Gonzalez) Requénez; children: Jonathan Warmkessel, Ethan Warmkessel. BSN, Loma Linda U., 1960; diploma in audiometry, Fullerton State Coll., 1965. Cert. myofunctional therapist, home nutritionist, oncology nurse, home health nurse. Community health nurse Washoe County Health Dept., Reno; med.-surg. staff nurse Taho Forest Hosp., Truckee, Calif.; pub. health nurse North Tahoe-Placer County Health Dept., Tahoe City, Calif.; sch. nurse Tahoe Truckee Unified Sch. Dist., Truckee. Vol. ARC; instr. Basic First Aid/CPR, B.S.E. facilitator Am. Cancer Soc.; mem. Tahoe Truckee Children's Netowrk. Mem. ANA, CSNO, No. Calif. CSNO (mktg. chair).

RESANO, FERNANDO, anesthesiologist; b. Buenos Aires, Mar. 24, 1947; s. Justino and Ana Maria (Lassalle) R. Bs, Colegio del Salvador, Buenos Aires, 1964; MD with honors, U. Buenos Aires, 1970. Diplomate Am. Bd. Anesthesiology. Cons. VA Hosp., N.Y.C., 1970-79; attending anesthesiologist NYU Med. Ctr., N.Y.C., 1976-79; attending anesthesiologist Washington Hosp. Ctr., 1979-85, vice chmn. dept. anesthesiology, 1989, sr. attending, 1985—; asst. prof. anesthesiology George Washington U., Washington, 1987—. U. Buenos Aires scholar, 1966-69. Fellow Am. Coll. Anesthesiologists; mem. AMA, Am. Soc. Anesthesiologists, Internat. Anesthesia Rsch. Soc., Med. Soc. D.C., Soc. Cardiovascular Anesthesiologists, Md.-D.C. Soc. Anesthesiologists (v.p. 1985-86, pres. 1989, chmn. ann. sci. symposium 1984). Democrat. Roman Catholic.

RESCH, KLAUS, pharmacology educator; b. Berlin, June 28, 1941; s. Johann and Gertrud (Pöche) R.; m. Silke Bollhagen, July 11, 1969; children: Julia, Philipp. MD, U. Freiburg, Germany, 1967. Intern, 1966-67; rsch. fellow Max Planck Inst. for Immunobiology, Freiburg, Germany, 1968-74; asst. prof. U. Heidelberg, Germany, 1974-79; Heisenberg fellow German Cancer Rsch. Ctr., Heidelberg, 1979-81; prof. pharmacology Med. Sch. Hannover, Germany, 1981—; vis. scientist NIH, Bethesda, Md., 1977-78. Editor sci. books and rsch. jours.; also over 250 articles. Recipient Heinrich Wieland award, 1975; rsch. grantee German Rsch. Coun., numerous others. Mem. Am. Assn. Immunologists, German Soc. for Pharmacology and Toxicology (v.p. 1991-93), German Soc. for Immunology, German Soc. for Biochemistry. Office: Med Sch Hannover Inst Molec Pharm, Carl-Neubert-Str 8, D-30623 Hannover Germany

RESCH, MARY LOUISE, social services administrator; b. David City, Nebr., Oct. 26, 1956; d. Ernest John and Mary Jean (Roelandts) Cermak; m. Eugene Joseph Resch, Apr. 28, 1979. BS in Psychology, SUNY, Albany, 1984; MS in Counseling and Edn. with high honors, U. Wis., Platteville, 1986. Enlisted U.S. Army, 1974, advance through ranks to sgt., 1982; bomb disposal tech. U.S. Army, Ft. Riley, Kans., 1977-79; bomb disposal instr. U.S. Army, Indian Head, Md., 1979-80; resigned U.S. Army, 1985; instr., intern family advocacy Army Community Svc., U.S. Army, Ft. Belvoir, 1986; sr. counselor, child therapist Community Crisis and Referral Ctr., Inc., Waldorf, Md., 1986-87; adminstr. Walter Reed Army Med. Ctr. USDA Grad. Sch., Washington, 1987-88; contract mgr. USDA Grad. Sch., Ft. Jackson, S.C., 1988-91; pres. Athena Cons., Columbia, S.C., 1991-93; dir. spl. programs Newberry (S.C.) Commn. on Alcohol and Drug Abuse, 1993-95; resource devel. coord. Cities in Schs.-SC, Inc., Columbia, 1995—; human svcs. cons., Washington, 1986-87; adj. instr. Coker Coll., Ft. Jackson, 1989-

95. Mem. NAFE, ACA, Nat. Contract Mgmt. Assn. (fellow, former pres., mentor), Mil. Educators and Counselors Assn., Com. Mil. Edn. S.C. Republican. Lutheran. Home: 1016 Harvey Killian Rd Chapin SC 29036-7807 Office: Cities in Schs SC Inc PO Box 773 1200 Catawba St Columbia SC 29202

RESCH, SYLVIA, orthopedic surgeon, educator; b. Mainz, Germany, Feb. 7, 1948; came to U.S., 1957; arrived in Sweden, 1969; d. Johan Heinrich and Eleonore Susanne (Stenzel) R.; m. Peter A. Thomason, 1969 (div. 1981); children: Christopher, Timothy, Jens, Emily. AB, Bryn Mawr Coll., 1968; MD, Uppsala U., Sweden, 1977; PhD, Lund U., Sweden, 1995. Staff physician Univ. Lund Hosp., 1983-95, asst. prof., 1995—; adminstrv. chief Orthopedic Emergency Svcs. Univ. Lund Hosp., 1990—. Author: Hallus Valgus Surgery, 1995. Mem. Am. Orthopedic Foot and Ankle Soc., European Soc. Foot and Ankle Surgeons, Scandinavian Orthopedic Soc. Office: Dept Orthopedics, University Hosp, 221 85 Lund Sweden

RESCORLA, ROBERT ARTHUR, psychology educator; b. Pitts, May 9, 1940; s. Arthur R. and Mildred J. (Jenkins) R.; m. Shirley Steele; children: Eric, Michael. BA, Swarthmore Coll., 1962; PhD, U. Pa., 1966; MA, Yale U., 1974. Successively asst. prof., assoc. prof., prof. Yale U., New Haven, 1966-80; prof. psychology U. Pa., Phila., 1981—, James Skinner prof. sci., 1986—, dean of coll. Sch. of Arts and Scis., 1994—. Author: Pavlovian Second-Order Conditioning, 1980; editor: Animal Learning and Behavior, 1995—; contbr. articles to profl. jours. Mem. APA (pres. div. 3 1985, Disting. Sci. Contbn. award 1986), Am. Psychol. Soc. (William James fellow 1988), NAS, AAAS (pres. sect. J., psychology 1988-89), Soc. Exptl. Psychologists (Warren medal 1991), Psychonomic Soc. (mem. governing bd. 1979-85, chmn. publ. bd. 1985-86), Ea. Psychol. Assn. (bd. dirs. 1983-86, pres. 1986-87). Office: U Pa Dept Psychology 3815 Walnut St Philadelphia PA 19104-3604

RESDEN, RONALD EVERETTE, medical devices product development engineer; b. Littleton, N.H., Oct. 27, 1944; s. Lawrence A. and Rita Mae (Bowen) R.; m. Dee Kronenburg, Apr. 20, 1974 (div.); children: Philip, Alison; m. Louise Simons, June 18, 1994. Cons. Franklin Mfg. Co., Norwood, Mass., 1984—, Boston Sci. Co., Watertown, Mass., 1985—, Via Med, Easton, Mass., 1986—, White Marsh Labs., Balt., 1989—, Spectraphos Malmo Sweden, 1991—, Vision Scis. Inc., Natick, Mass., 1991—, Cordis Corp., Miami, Fla., 1993—; cons. Cardiology Catheter Lab. Mass. Hosp. Cardiology, Boston, 1993—; Active MIT Enterprise Forum. Author: Hologram Control Transfer, 1984; inventor, patentee in field; mem. rev. bd. Medica Plastics and Biomaterials mag. Mem. NRA (life), Soc. Plastics Engrs. (mem. med. plastics and biomaterials mag. rev. bd.), Soc. Mfg. Engrs., Nat. Geog. Soc., Mass. Chiefs of Police Assn., Citizens for Ltd. Taxation. Home and Office: Resden Rsch Inc 44 Arrowhead Rd Weston MA 02193-1707

RESNICK, DEBRA BETH, clinical psychologist; b. Montreal, June 30, 1955; came to U.S., 1981; d. Frank and Sorryl (Cohen) Hoffer; m. Jerome H. Resnick, Aug. 5, 1981; children: Justin, Jonathan. BA, McGill U., 1977; MA, Temple U., 1979; D in Psychology, Hahnemann U., 1986. Lic. psychologist Que., Pa. Staff psychologist Allan Meml. Inst., Montreal, 1980-81; sr. clin. instr. Hahnemann U., Phila., 1986-89, staff psychologist, 1986-89; attending psychologist Eugenia Hosp., Lafayette Hill, Pa.; pvt. practice Elkins Pk., Pa., 1989—, Ft. Washington, Pa., 1995—; psychology cons. Inpatient Psychodiagnostic Assessment, 1988—; adj. clin. asst. prof. Widener U., Chester, Pa., 1989—. Ad Hoc adv. com. to supt. Sch. Dist. of Cheltenham Twp., Elkins Pk., 1988. Mem. Am. Psychol. Assn., Pa. Psychol. Assn., Que. Corp. Psychologists, Phila. Soc. Clin. Psychologists. Jewish. Home: 328 Marvin Rd Elkins Park PA 19207 Office: Psychol Svcs and Human Devel Ctr 220 Commerce Dr Ste 210 Fort Washington PA 19034

RESNICK, EUGENE VICTOR, psychiatrist; b. Passaic, N.J., Mar. 11, 1923. BS cum laude, Franklin and Marshall Coll., Lancaster, Pa., 1943; MD, Georgetown U., 1946; postgrad., SUNY, Bklyn., 1951-53. Diplomate Am. Bd. Psychiatry and Neurology. Intern Beth Israel Hosp., Newark, 1946-47; resident Brooke Army Med. Ctr., San Antonio, 1947-48, VA Hosp., Northport and Bklyn., N.Y., 1949-51; pvt. practice psychiatry N.Y.C., Teaneck, Paramus, N.J., 1951-91; clin. asst. to assoc. attending psychiatrist dept. psychiatry Mt. Sinai Hosp., N.Y.C., 1953-62; attending psychiatrist U. Medicine and Dentistry Community Mental Health Ctr., Newark, 1984—; adj. attending to assoc. dir. emeritus dept. psychiatry Hackensack (N.J.) Univ. Med. Ctr., 1958—; med. dir., psychiat. cons. Hackensack Hosp. Community Mental Health Ctr., 1968-75; psychiat. cons. Prospect House, East ORange, N.J., 1971-84, Friendship House, Hackensack, 1981—; asst. prof. clin. psychiatry U. Medicine and Dentistry N.J., N.J. Med. Sch., Newark, 1975—; student Psychoanalytic Inst., SUNY; mem. Downstate Med. Ctr., 1951-53. Mem. editorial bd. Hosp. and Community Psychiatry, 1970-76; contbr. articles and book revs. to profl. jours. Mem. Profl. Adv. Com. Bergen County Health Bd., Hackensack, 1964-69; bd. trustees Bergen-Passaic Health Systems Agy., 1979-83. Fellow Am. Psychiat. Assn. (life); mem. Med. Soc. N.J. (coun. mental health 1968-78), N.J. Psychiat. Assn. (pres. 1971-72), North Jersey Psychiat. Soc. (pres. 1964-65), Bergen County Med. Soc. (jud. com. 1977-82). Office: 640 Blauvelt Dr Oradell NJ 07649-1205

RESNICK, HENRY ROY, pharmacist; b. N.Y.C., Dec. 12, 1952; s. Samuel and Miriam (Jacobson) R.; m. Mary Lee Monroe. Sept. 13, 1981; children: Jacob Monroe, Aaron Leo. BS in Pharmacy, L.I. U., 1975, MS in Drug Info. & Communication, 1978. Pharmacist Sagamore Childrens Ctr., Melville, N.Y., 1976-77; staff pharmacist Montefiore Hosp. and Med. Ctr., N.Y.C., 1977-80; mgr. clin. pharmacy svcs. Beth Israel Med. Ctr., N.Y.C., 1980-82, asst. dir. pharmacy, 1982-87, supervising pharmacist methadone maintenance treatment program, 1982-90, sr. assoc. dir., 1987-90; dir. pharmacy New Rochelle (N.Y.) Hosp. Med. Ctr., 1990-94; asst. dir. pharmacy Allied Pharmacy Mgmt. Inc., Lantana, Fla., 1994-95; pharmacy supr. Delray Cmty. Hosp., Delray Beach, Fla., 1995—; adj. clin. instr. Arnold and Marie Schwartz Coll. Pharmacy Health Scis., N.Y.C., 1980-82. Mem. Am. Soc. Hosp. Pharmacists, Am. Soc. Pharmacy Law, Fla. Soc. Hosp. Pharmacists, N.Y. State Coun. Hosp. Pharmacists (monitoring com. on legislation 1989-90, joint com. with industry 1989-90, govt. affairs com. 1991-94), Westchester Soc. Hosp. Pharmacists (chmn. legis., constn. and bylaws com. 1991-94, exec. com. 1991-94, pres.-elect 1992-93, pres. 1993-94, del. N.Y. State coun. hosp. pharmacists 1992-94). Office: Delray Cmty Hosp 5352 Linton Blvd Delray Beach FL 33484

RESNICK, JAQUELYN LISS, psychology educator; b. Miami Beach, Fla., Feb. 23, 1946; d. Morris Joseph and Gertrude (Yagoda) L.; m. Michael Bruce Resnick, Aug. 20, 1967; children: Aaron René, Jeremy Ben. Student, Boston U., 1962-63; BA in Math. with honors, U. Fla., 1966, MEd in Counselor Edn., 1967, PhD in Counselor Edn., 1972. Asst. prof. Counseling Ctr., U. Fla., Gainesville, 1973-78, assoc. prof., 1978-83, prof., 1983—, dir. affiliate dept. behavioral studies, 1974-78, affiliate dept. counselor edn., 1976—, affiliate dept. psychology, 1988—, coord. women's svcs. Counseling Ctr., 1974-94, dir. Counseling Ctr., 1994—; cons. on sexual harassment, women's devel. and eating disorders to numerous orgns., Gainesville, 1972—; pvt. practice, Gainesville; mem. bd. dirs. Internat. Assn. Counseling Svcs., Inc., 1995—. Co-author: Rape Crisis Center Training Manual, 1976; co-editor: Para-professional Counseling, 1976. Bd. dirs. Sexual and Phys. Abuse Ctr., Alachua County, 1978-81; pres. Kirkwood Environ. Assn., Gainesville, 1981-82; mem. Gainesville Mayor's Task Force on Violence, 1985-88; chmn. Gainesville Commn. on Status of Women, 1988-90. Recipient Outstanding Contbns. award div. student affairs U. Fla., 1984, Superior Accomplishment award, 1990; Martha Varnes award Gainesville Commn. on Status of Women, 1988. Mem. APA (chmn. com. for women psychotherapy divsn. 1978-80, mem. exec. coml. psychology of woemn divsn. 1990, Jack Krasner award psychotherapy divsn. 1994), SE Psychol. Assn. (chmn. commn. on status of women 1977-78, com. on equal profl. opportunity 1978-79, mem. exe. com. 1981-84), Assn. for Women Faculty (pres.-elect 1994—), Mortar Bd., Phi Beta Kappa, Phi Kappa Phi. Office: U Fla 301 Peabody Hall Gainesville FL 32611-4100

RESNICK, MARK JEFFREY, psychologist; b. Balt., Mar. 3, 1955; s. Martin Ronald and Thalia Ann (Dragon) R. BA, Oglethorpe U., 1977; MA, Loyola Coll., Balt., 1980; PhD, U. Kans., 1987. Nat. cert. sch. psychologist. Sch. psychologist Shawnee Mission (Kans.) Pub. Schs., 1980-84, Gardner-Edgerton-Antioch Unified Sch. Dist. 231, 1984-85; behavioral cons. Responsive Mgmt. Clinic, Overland Park, Kans., 1982-84; sch. psychologist Carroll County Pub. Schs., Westminster, Md., 1985-92; sch. psychologist Howard Pub. Schs., Ellicott City, Md., 1993—; pvt. practice psychology, Balt., 1986—; fellow dept. pediatrics Kennedy Inst., Johns Hopkins Hosp., Balt., 1989-90; Mem. Nat. Assn. Sch. Psychologists, Md. Sch. Psychologists' Assn. Jewish. Home: 16 Beecham Ct Owings Mills MD 21117 Office: The Howard County Pub Sch System 1 Mall N Ste 309 10910 Rte 108 Ellicott City MO 21042

RESNICK, OSCAR, neuroscientist; b. Bayonne, N.J., Apr. 27, 1924; s. Samuel and Rebecca (Rubinstein) R.; m. Janice Zelda Ravitz, July 13, 1949; children—Sandra, Scott. A.B., Clark U., Worcester, Mass., 1944; M.A., Harvard U., 1945; Ph.D., Boston U., 1955. Research fellow U. Iowa Med. Sch., 1945-46; instr. St. Petersburg Jr. Coll., 1946-47; research fellow U. Kans., 1947-49; instr. U. Minn., 1949-50; editorial asst. Biol. Abstracts, U. Pa., 1950-51; scientist Nat. Drug Co., Phila., 1951-53, Worcester Found. Exptl. Biology, Shrewsbury, Mass., 1953—; now sr. scientist, lectr. Boston U., 1961—, Clark U., 1965—; dir. research Worcester County Rehab. and Detention Ctr., West Boylston, Mass., 1965-76; cons. Medfield State Hosp., Mass., Norwich State Hosp., Conn. Contbr. articles to profl. jours. Mem. mental retardation research com. NIH, 1975-78. NIH grantee, 1957—. Fellow Am. Coll. Neuopsychopharmacology; mem. AAAS, Soc. Biol. Psychiatry, Am. Psychopath. Soc., N.Y. Acad. Sci., Soc. Neurosci., Sigma Xi. Office: Boston U Sch Medicine Ctr Behavioral Dev Mental Retardation 85 E Newton St Roxbury MA 02118-2340 Address: 270 E Douglas Ave El Cajon CA 92020-4534

RESNICK, RICHARD BOYCE, psychiatrist; b. N.Y.C., Apr. 18, 1931; s. Albert and Barbara (Jaffe) R.; m. Elaine Bernstein; children: Deborah, Demian, Jesse, Nora. BS, CCNY, 1953; MD, N.Y. Med. Coll., 1958. Diplomate Am. Bd. Psychiatry and Neurology. Chief, psychiatric outpatient unit Montefiore Hosp., Bronx, N.Y., 1962-65; dir., narcotic addiction treatment program Met. Hosp. Med. Ctr., N.Y.C., 1966-72; dir., div. drug abuse rsch., treatment N.Y. Med. Coll., 1973-82, asst. clin. prof. psychiatry, 1966-72, asst. prof. psychiatry, 1972-74, assoc. prof. clin. psychiatry, 1974-83; clin. assoc. prof. psychiatry NYU Sch. Medicine, 1983—; rsch. psychiatrist N.Y. State Psychiatric Inst., 1987; exec. dir. Ctr. for Psychiatry and Family Therapy, N.Y.C., 1988—; clin. asst. attending psychiatrist Bellevue Hosp. Ctr., N.Y.C., 1977—; attending psychiatrist Gracie Square Hosp., 1989—; cons. N.Y.C. Dept. Social Svcs., 1966-83; cons. com. on clin. evaluation of narcotic antagonists Nat. Acad. Scis., 1973-84; mem. med. rev. com. Phase III Naltrexone Studies, Nat. Inst. on Drug Abuse, 1979-81; cons. rsch. N.Y. VA Med. Ctr., Psychiat. Svc., N.Y.C., 1983-86, 89-92; dir. buprenorphine rsch. program NYU Med. Ctr., 1989-93. Contbr. articles to profl. jours. Fellow Am. Psychiat. Assn., Am. Coll. Neuropsycholopharmacology, Am. Assn. Social Psychiatry; mem. Am. Assn. Psychiatrists in Alcoholism and Addictions, Alpha Omega Alpha. Home: 43 W 94th St New York NY 10025-7113 Office: Ctr for Psychiatry and Family Therapy 43 W 94th St New York NY 10025-7113

RESNICK, STEVEN IVES, psychiatrist, educator; b. N.Y.C., July 15, 1956; s. Sam Louis and Sylvia (Friedman) R. BA Psychology cum laude, Princeton U., 1977; MD, N.Y. Med. Coll., 1981. Med. intern Med. Coll. Pa., Phila., 1981-82; house physician Jewish Meml. Hosp., N.Y.C., 1982-83, White Plains (N.Y.) Hosp., 1982-83; resident in psychiatry St. Luke's Hosp., N.Y.C., 1983-86; staff psychiatrist Carrier Found., Belle Mead, N.J., 1986—; pvt. practice, Princeton Somerville, Hamilton, N.J.; on-call psychiatrist Bapt. Med. Ctr., Bklyn., 1984-85; session psychiatrist Gracie Square Hosp., N.Y.C., 1984-86; vis. clin. fellow Columbia U., N.Y.C., 1983-86; asst. clin. prof. Robert Wood Johnson Med. Sch., U. Medicine and Dentistry N.J., Piscataway, N.J., 1986—; lectr. on stress mgmt. to various orgns. Contbr. articles to med. jours. Light therapy coord. Carrier Found. Mem. Am. Psychiat. Assn., Am. Group Psychotherapy Assn., N.J. Psychiat. Assn. (media rels. com.), Physicians for Social Responsibility, Internat. Physicians for Prevention Nuclear War, Coalition for Nuclear Disarmament, Soviet-Am. Rels. Com., Sigma Xi. Democrat. Jewish. Office: Ste 162 CN 5256 Princeton NJ 08543

RESNICK, TRINA LYNNE SCHNEIDER, nurse, educator; b. Camden, N.J., Dec. 13; d. Frederick and Evelyn Leona (Sprenkel) Schneider; m. Michael Arthur Resnick, Oct. 4, 1968; children: Elizabeth, Catherine. Student, George Mason U., Arlington, Va., 1987-88; BA, George Washington U., 1973; BSN, George Mason U., Fairfax, Va., 1991, MSN, 1994. RN, Va., Washington. Program analyst, rschr. NAS, Washington, 1972-74; cons. Resnick & Assocs., Fairfax, 1977-87; clinc asst. surgery and urology Kaiser Permanente HMO, Falls Church, Va., 1988-1990; medical-surgical night staff nurse Arlington (Va.) Hosp., 1991-92. circulating and scrub nurse, 1992-93; rsch.-drug trials Kunitz & Assocs., Bethesda, Md., 1993; instr. medical-surgical and comty. health nursing George Mason U. Coll. of Nursing and Health Scis., Fairfax, 1994-95; diabetes case mgr., educator Diabetes treatment Ctrs. of Am., Washington, 1995—; CEO and pres. Resnick & Assocs., Fairfax, 1982-87, 93. Writer, prodr. ednl. films Alzheimer's Patients in Emergency Room, 1993, Diabetes: How to Heal Yourself, 1995. Chair county heart assn. fund drive, AHA, Loudoun County, Va., 1976; magisterial chair County Political Party, Loudown County, 1977-79; mem. bd. Kids for Kids, Fairfax County, 1986-87; v.p. PTA, 1986-87. CHANGE Program graduate fellow HHS, Washington, 1993-94. Mem. ANA, Am. Diabetes Assn., Am. Assn. Diabetes Educators, Assn. Operating Room Nurses, Capitol Assn. Diabetes Educators (fed. legis. liaison for no. Va.), Va. Nurses Assn., Epsilon Zeta chpt. Sigma Theta Tau (editor newsletter, bd. dirs, 1994-96). Home: 632 Springvale Rd Great Falls VA 22066-3304

RESNIK, HARVEY LEWIS PAUL, psychiatrist; b. Buffalo, Apr. 6, 1930; s. Samuel andCelia (Greenberg) R.; m. Audrey Ruth Frey, Aug 30, 1964 (dec. 1993); children: Rebecca Gabrielle. Henry Seth Maccabee, Jessica Ruth. B.A. magna cum laude, U. Buffalo, 1951; M.D., Columbia, 1955; grad., Phila. Psychoanalytic Inst., 1967. Diplomate: Am. Bd. Psychiatry and Neurology. Intern Phila. Gen. Hosp., 1955-56, resident in surgery, 1956-57; resident in psychiatry Jackson Meml. Hosp., Miami, Fla., 1959-61; fellow U. Pa. Hosp., 1961-62, mem. staff, 1962-67; instr; Sch. Medicine, U. Pa., 1962-66; instr. med. hypnosis Sch. Medicine, U. Pa. (Grad. Sch. Medicine), 1963-65; clin. dir. psychiatry E. J. Meyer Meml. Hosp., Buffalo, 1967; dir. psychiatry E. J. Meyer Meml. Hosp., 1968; assoc. prof. psychiatry Sch. Medicine, SUNY at Buffalo, 1967, prof., 1968-70, dep. dir., chmn. dept. psychiatry, 1968-69; chief Nat. Center for Studies of Suicide Prevention, NIMH, 1969-74, chief mental health emergencies sect., 1974-76; with Reproductive Biology Research Found., St. Louis, 1971; clin. prof. psychiatry Sch. Medicine, George Washington U., 1969—; dir. Human Behavior Found., 1975—; lectr. Sch. Medicine, Johns Hopkins, 1969-74; adj. prof. Johns Hopkins U. Sch. Pub. Health, 1981-82; prof. cmty. health Fed. City Coll., 1971-75; med. dir. Human Behavior Found., 1975—, Johns Hopkins U. Compulsive Gambling Ctr. (now Washington Ctr. for Pathol. Gambling); mem. dir. Univ. Alcohol and Substance Abuse Program, 1986—; CEO Assoc. Mental Helath Profls.; instr. Delaware Valley Group Therapy Inst.; vis. prof. Katholieke U., Leuven, Belgium, 1986—; cons. to Sec.-Gen. Ministry of Health, Belgium, 1986-95, NATO, 1986-87, also fellow Ten Kerselaere Psycho-Geriatric Hosp.; bd. dirs. Internat. Helath Ctr., Belgium, Human Behavior Found.; cons. various hosps. and orgns. Author: Suicidal Behaviors: Diagnosis and Management, 1968, 2d edit., 1994, (with M. E. Wolfgang) Treatment of the Sexual Offender, 1971, Sexual Behaviors: Social, Clinical and Legal Aspects, 1972, (with B. Hathorne) Suicide Prevention in the Seventies, 1973, (with H.L. Ruben) Emergency Psychiatric Care, 1974, (with others) The Prediction of Suicide, 1974, Emergency and Disaster Management, 1976; (with J.T. Mitchell) Emergency Response to Crisis, 1981; Editor: Bull. Suicidology, 1969-74; Contbr. (with others) articles on hypnosis, sexual offenders, marriage and sexual dysfunction treatment, suicide, death and dying, emergency psychiatric care. Mem. Addictions Adv. Bd. Prince Georges County, 1980-85. Served to capt. USAF, 1957-59, ETO-Middle East; capt. USNR; ret. Decorated officer in the Order King Leopold, Belgium, 1990. Fellow Am. Coll. Psychiatrists, Am. Psychiat. Assn. (life); mem. Med-Chi of Md., Prince Georges County Med. Assn., Phila. Psychoanalytic Soc., Columbia Med. Alumni Assn. (bd. dirs. 1993-95), Phi Beta Kappa, Beta Sigma Rho (grand vice warden 1963), Cosmos Club (Washington). Jewish. Office: Air Rights Ctr # 1300W 7315 Wisconsin Ave Bethesda MD 20814-3202 also: Univ Profl Ctr 4700 Berwyn House Rd # 201 College Park MD 20740-2474

RESNIK, ROBERT, medical educator; b. New Haven, Dec. 7, 1938; s. Nathan Alfred and Elsie (Hershman) R.; m. Lauren Brahms, Oct. 29, 1966; children: Andrew Scott, Jamie Layne. BA, Yale U., 1960; MD, Case Western Res. U., 1965. Intern in internal medicine Mt. Sinai Hosp., Cleve., 1965-66; resident in ob-gyn. Yale U. Sch. Medicine, 1966-70; asst. prof. Sch. Medicine U. Calif., San Diego, 1974-78, assoc. prof., 1978-82, prof. reproductive medicine, 1982—, chmn. dept., 1982-95, dean clin. affairs, 1988-90, dean admissions, 1995—; cons. Nat. Heart, Lung and Blood Inst. NIH, Washington, 1987; mem. exec. com. Coun. Residency Edn. Ob-Gyn, Washington, 1988-94, residency rev. com., 1988-94. Editor: (textbook) Maternal-Fetal Medicine: Principles and Practice, 1984, 3d edit., 1994; contbr. numerous articles to profl. jours. Major U.S. Army, 1970-72. Rsch. grantee Nat. Found., NIH. Fellow Am. Coll. Obstetrics and Gynecology, Pacific Coast Obstet. and Gynecol. Soc.; mem. Soc. Gynecologic Investigation (coun. 1983-88), Perinatal Rsch. Soc. (pres. 1985), Am. Gynecologic and Obstet. Soc., San Diego Gynecol. Soc. (pres. 1982), Yale Club. Office: U Calif Sch Medicine Dept 0621 9500 Gilman Dr La Jolla CA 92093-0621

RESSLER, DAVID RONALD, hospital administrator; b. West Chester, Pa., Apr. 30, 1964; s. Ronald Roy and Susan Joy (Trouant) R.; m. Laurie Bacon, May 25, 1985 (div. Nov. 89); m. Julia Lynn Perkich, July 20, 1991. BS in Bus. Adminstrn., U. Ariz., 1986; student, Westminster Coll., Salt Lake City, 1991-93. Mktg. coord. TMCare Health Network, Tucson, 1986-87; account exec. Ptnrs. Health Plan, Tucson, 1987-89, mktg. mgr., 1989-91; v.p. Associated Health Plan, Salt Lake City, 1991-92; plan mgr. FHP, Inc., Salt Lake City, 1992-93; COO Sierra Vista (Ariz.) Cmty. Hosp., 1992-96. Chmn. bd. dirs. Cochise County March of Dimes, Sierra Vista, 1994-96. Republican. Lutheran. Office: Sierra Vista Cmty Hosp 300 El Camino Real Sierra Vista AZ 85635

RESTAK, RICHARD MARTIN, neurologist, educator; b. Washington, Feb. 4, 1942; s. Lewis Joseph and Alice (Hynes) R.; m. Carolyn Serbert, Oct. 12, 1968; 3 children. BS, Gettysburg Coll., 1962; MD, Georgetown U., 1966. Diplomate Am. Bd. Psychiatry and Neurology. Rotating intern St. Vincent's Hosp., N.Y.C., 1966-67; resident in psychiatry Mt. Sinai Hosp., N.Y.C., 1967-68, Georgetown U. Hosp., Washington, 1968-69; resident in neurology George Washington Hosp., Washington, 1970-73; pvt. practice neuropsychiatry, Washington, 1973—; clin. prof. neurology George Washington U. Sch. Medicine and Health scis.; clin. asst. prof. Georgetown U. Sch. Medicine, dir. Adult Neurobehavioral Ctr., 1983-87, cons., 1987—; mem. clin. faculty St. Elizabeths Hosp., Washington; cons. Coun. for Sci. and Society, London, 1976, Ency. Bioethics, Kennedy Inst. for Study Reprodn. and Bioethics, 1978, World Book, 1992; commentator Nat. Pub. Radio, 1987—; mem. adv. panel on new devels. in neurosci. U.S. Congress, Office Tech. Assessment, 1989-92; mem. adv. panel Franklin Inst. Sci. Mus., Phila., 1991-92; mem. rsch. adv. com. NIH, 1974-75; mem. vis. com. Rsch. Ctr. for Lang. and Semiotic Studies, Ind. U., 1985-87; bd. dirs. Washington Found. for Psychiatry, 1989-92; mem. sci. adv. com. Nat. Brain Tumor Found., San Francisco, 1990-91; mem. adv. coun. Nat. Found. for Brain Rsch., 1990-92. Author: Premeditated Man: Bioethics and the Control of Future Human Life, 1975, The Brain: The Last Frontier: Explorations of the Human Mind and Our Future, 1979, The Self Seekers, 1982, The Brain, 1984, The Infant Mind, 1986, The Mind, 1988, The Brain Has a Mind of Its Own, 1991, Receptors, 1994, Brainscapes, 1995; contbr. numerous articles and book revs. to med. jours., anthologies, mags., and newspapers, chpts. to books. Recipient Claude Bernard sci. journalism award Nat. Soc. for Med. Rsch., 1976, Disting. Alumni award Gettysburg Coll., 1985, Decade of Brain award Chgo. Neurosurg. Ctr., 1992; fellow NEH, Stanford U., summer 1976. Fellow Am. Psychiat. Assn., Am. Acad. Neurology, Academia, Medicinae and Psychiatriae Found. (charter); mem. Am. Soc. Clin. Psychopharmacology, Assn. for Rsch. in Nervous and Mental Disease, Am. Neuropsychiat. Assn. (program com. 1991—), Am. Acad. Psychiatry and Law, Behavioral Neurology Soc., N.Y. Acad. Scis., Royal Soc. Medicine (London), Semiotic Soc. Am., Internat. Neuropsychol. Soc., Nat. Book Critics Circle, Internat. Brotherhood Magicians, Philos. Soc. Washington, Internat. Platform Assn., Reality Club, Nat. Press Club, Cosmos Club, Vineyard Haven Yacht Club. Office: Neurology Assocs PC 1800 R St NW Ste C-3 Washington DC 20009

RESTIFO, MARY, physician; b. Cleve., Aug. 28, 1941; d. Samuel Joseph and Valerie (Stark) R. BA, Lawrence Coll., 1963; MD, Western Reserve U., 1967. Intern, resident U. N.C., Chapel Hill, 1967-70; physician pvt. practice, Washington, 1973—. Cardiology fellow Brompton Hosp., London, 1970-71, Georgetown U., Washington, 1971-73. Fellow Am. Coll. Cardiology; mem. AMA, Am. Coll. Phusicians, Am. Soc. Internal Medicine, Am. Women Physicians Assn., D.C. Med. Soc. Office: 3301 New Mexico Ave NW Washington DC 20016

RETSAS, SPYROS, oncologist; b. Thessaloniki, Greece, Dec. 4, 1942; arrived in U.K., 1969; s. Stylianos and Panaghiota (Alexandri) R.; m. Diana Gillian Rees, July 8, 1972; 1 child, Philip-Alexander. MD, Aristotle U., Thessaloniki, 1967, U. Athens, 1978. Accredited specialist. Sr. house officer Royal Marsden Hosp., Surrey, Eng., 1971-72; registrar in medicine Whipps Cross Hosp., London, 1973-75; sr. lectr. Westminster Hosp., London, 1978-85; cons. med. oncologist Chelsea & Westminster Hosp., Charing Cross Hosp., London, Charing Cross & Westminster Med. Sch., London, 1985—; tchr. U. London, 1979—; chmn. adv. com. on cancer svcs. Riverside Health Authority, 1990; vis. prof. U. Ioannina (Greece) Med. Sch., 1991-92; lectr. cancer med. instns. in Europe, N.Am. S.Am. and China. Editor: Palaeoncology-The Antiquity of Cancer, 1986. Contbr. articles to profl. jours. Founder, pres. Hellenic Med. Soc. Gt. Britain, 1987. 2d lt. M.C. Greek Army, 1967-69. Fellow RCP (London), Royal Soc. Medicine, Hunterian Soc.; mem. Royal Coll. Physicians (U.K.), British Assn. Cancer Physicians, British Assn. Cancer Rsch., European Soc. Med. Oncology, Am. Soc. Clin. Oncology. Home: Parnassus Park Hill, Essex Loughton IG10 4ES, England Office: Med Oncology Unit, Charing Cross Hosp, London W6 8RF, England

RETSEMA, JAMES ALLAN, microbiologist; b. Muskegon, Mich., Feb. 27, 1942; s. Jay and Christine Retsema; m. Arija Bets, Oct. 13, 1969; children: Anna Aria, Andrew James. BS, Mich. State U., 1964; MS, U. Iowa, 1967, PhD, 1969. Postdoctoral fellow U. Wis., Madison, 1969; rsch. scientist cen. rsch. div. Pfizer, Inc., Groton, Conn., 1969-75, sr. rsch. scientist, 1975-79, project leader, 1979-83, mgr., 1983-90, rsch. advisor on antibacteria discovery and devel., 1990—. Fellow Am. Acad. Microbiology. Office: Pfizer Inc Cen Rsch Eastern Point Rd Groton CT 06340

RETTERSTOL, NILS, retired psychiatrist; b. Oslo, Norway, Oct. 3, 1924; s. Kittel and Kathrine (Steen) R.; M.D., U. Oslo, 1950, Dr.med., 1966; m. Kirsten Christensen, Aug. 16, 1958; children: Trine Lise, Kjetil, Lars Jorgen. Med. officer Dikemark Hosp., Ulleval Hosp., Oslo, 1952-56, Runwell Hosp., Eng., 1956-57; resident in psychiatry Ullevål Hosp., Oslo, 1957-58; asso. prof., dep. dir. Univ. Psychiat. Clinic, Oslo, 1959-68; prof. psychiatry U. Bergen, head dir. Neevengarden Hosp., Bergen, 1969-73; prof. psychiatry U. Oslo, 1973-94; head dir. Gaustad Hosp., Oslo, 1973-94; ret., 1995; head Norwegian Info. Bank for Narcotic problems; chmn. Norwegian Commn. for Forensic Pschiatry, 1983; cons. in field. Served to capt. Norwegian Army. Recipient gold medal for psychiat. research, H.M. The King of Norway; prize for research Norwegian Council Humanities and Sci., 1978; comdr. The Royal St. Olav Order, 1984. Mem. Norwegian Acad. Sci. (hon.), Swedish Psychiat. Assn., German. Assn. Neurology and Psychiatry, Finnish Assn. Psychiatry, Norwegian Med. Soc., Norwegian Psychiat. Soc., French Assn. Psychiatry, Assn. European Psychiatrists, Internat. Assn. Suicide Prevention and Crisis Intervention (pres. 1989-91). Author: 30 books including Paranoid and Paranoiac Psychoses, 1966, (with A. Sund) Drug Dependence, 1967, Suicide, 1970, 5th edit., 1995, Prognosis in Paranoid Psychoses, 1970 (with L. Eitinger and A. A. Dahl) Crisis and Neuroses, 5th edit., 1990, (with L. Eitinger) Forensic Psychiatry, 4th edit., 1990, (with Eitinger and U. Malt) Psychoses, 4th edit., 1984, Suicide A European Perspective, 1993, (with A.A. Dahl, L. Eitinger and U. Malt) Textbook of Psychiatry, 1994; editor Scand. Med. Yearbook, 1972-94, Eur. Archives of Phychiatry and Neurological Scis., 1975-89; European editor Jour. Drug Issues, 1980; co-editor Psychopathology, 1983. Home: Nordseterveien 20 A, Oslo 11, Norway Office: Gaustad Hosp, Boks 24 Gaustad, 0320 Oslo 3, Norway

REUBEN, GLORIA WHITEHEAD, family practice physician, educator; b. Goldsboro, N.C., Nov. 26, 1947; d. Oscar and Emma (McCoy) Hooper; m. Wylie Jewell Robinson, Nov. 26, 1964 (div. July 1969); children: Shaun Robinson, Kwame Mali Robinson Yvahkeia, Brent Robinson; m. Anthony Glenn Reuben, Nov. 26, 1990; 1 child, Lisa. BA in Sci., Wayne State U.; DO, Mich. State U. Intern Mich. Osteo. Med. Ctr., 1986-87; physician Park Health Care Sys., Detroit, 1987—; cons., Detroit. Recipient grant Wayne State U., 1978. Mem. Am. Assn. Osteopathy, Nat. Assn. Aging, Physicians of the Future (pres. 1987-96), Wayne County Med. Soc. Home: 26307 Franklin Point Southfield MI 48234

REUDER, MARY E(ILEEN), retired psychology and statistics educator; b. Mpls., Mar. 12, 1923; d. Leo Aloysius and Mary Agnes (McGuire) R.; m. Marvin Alvin Iverson, July 11, 1953 (dec. Dec. 1979); children: Carol Mary, Kent Gery. BA, Coll. St. Catherine, St. Paul, 1944; MA, Brown U., 1945; PhD, U. Pa., 1951. Lic. psychologist, N.Y. Asst. instr. psychology U. Pa., Phila., 1946-51; work mgmt. specialist U.S. Naval Ammunition Depot, Ft. Mifflin, Pa., 1951-52; rsch. psychologist pers. br. Adj. Gen.'s Office, Dept. Army, Washington, 1952-54; instr. psychology Queens Coll., CUNY, Flushing, 1957-62, asst. prof., 1962-66, assoc. prof., 1966-71, prof., 1971-86, chmn. dept., 1984-85, chmn. acad. senate, 1982-85, prof. emerita, 1986—; mem. grad. faculty CUNY, 1977-86; mem. adv. bd. Dushkin Press, Guilford, Conn., 1975-84; cons. NATO postdoctoral fellowships NSF, Washington, 1978; cons., manuscript peer reviewer Acad. Psychology Bull., 1980-85, Jour. Profl. Psychology, 1986-88, Am. Psychologist, 1987-88, Psychol. Reports, 1995-96. Contbr. articles to profl. jours. and encys., also monographs, chpt. to book. Cons. com. on rsch. and evaluation Nassau coun. Girl Scouts U.S., 1971-74; bd. dirs. Walker Lake Community Assn., 1993—. Grantee NSF, 1964, Sigma Xi, 1962. Fellow APA (pres. divs. 1 and 36 1987-88, exec. com. div. 1 1981-87, div. 36 1979—, coun. reps. div. 36 1980-83, 91—, award for exceptional svc. to divsn. gen. psychology, disting. svc. award by divsn. of psychology of religion, 1996, accreditation site visitor 1996—), Am. Psychol. Soc., N.Y. Acad. Scis., Am. Assn. Applied and Preventive Psychology (charter); mem. AAAS, Ea. Psychol. Assn. (adminstrv. coord. 1961-67, 70), Psychometric Soc., Biometric Soc., Am. Statis. Assn., Queens Coll. Faculty Club (past bd. dirs., v.p.), U. Pa. Club L.I. (bd. govs. 1980—, Jack White award), Brown U. Club L.I., N.Am. Lake Mgmt. Soc., Pa. Lake Mgmt. Soc., Sigma Xi (grantee 1962, regional lectr. 1977-86, nat. bd. dirs. 1972-75, 77), Alpha Sigma Lambda, Pi Gamma Mu, Delta Phi Lambda, Kappa Gamma Pi, Alpha Pi Epsilon, Psi Chi. Democrat. Roman Catholic. Home: PO Box C Shohola PA 18458-0080 Office: CUNY Queens Coll Dept Psychology Flushing NY 11367

REUL, GEORGE JOHN, cardiovascular and vascular surgeon, educator; b. Milw., Apr. 19, 1937; s. George John and Anne Rose (Klune) R.; m. Kay Ross (div. Oct. 1987); children: George John III, Ross Michael, David Kevin, Darren Sean; m. Susan Kay Kister, July 19, 1988; children: Thomas Douglas, John Taylor. BS, Marquette U., 1958, MS, 1962, MD, 1966. Diplomate Am. Bd. Surgery, Am. Bd. Thoracic Surgery, Am. Bd. Vascular Surgery. Intern U. Chgo. Clinics, 1962-63; resident in gen. surgery Marquette U. Sch. Medicine Affiliated Hosps., Milw., 1963-66, 68-69; clin. instr. dept. surgery Marquette U. Sch. Medicine Affiliated Hosps., 1963-69; resident in thoracic surgery Baylor Coll. Medicine, Houston, 1969-71, instr., then asst. prof. dept. surgery, 1971-73, clin. prof., 1994—; pvt. practice Houston, 1971—; clin. assoc. prof. divsn. thoracic and cardiac surgery U. Tex. Med. Sch., Houston, 1977-87, clin. prof., 1987—; hon. cons. prof. thoracic surgery Shanghai 2d Med. Coll., 1985; dep. chief surgery Ben Taub Hosp., Houston, 1971-73; cons. in cardiovasc. surgery Tex. Children's Hosp., Houston, 1973—; cons. in cardiovasc. surgery St. Luke's Episcopal Hosp., Houston, 1973—, dir. Peripheral Vascular Lab., 1981—; assoc. chief surgery Tex. Heart Inst., Houston, 1983—; mem. Vietnam Vascular Registry; chmn. Ethicon Cardiovasc. Surgery Adv. Panel. Contbr. over 150 articles to med. jours. Capt. M.C., U.S. Army, 1966-68, Vietnam. Fellow NIH, 1960, Allen Bradley Rsch. Lab., 1965-6, Am. Cancer Soc., 1966, Nat. Tobacco Inst., 1969. Mem. AMA, ACS, Am. Heart Assn., Am. Coll. Cardiology, Am. Coll. Chest Physicians, Soc. for Vascular Surgery, Soc. Thoracic Surgery, Am. Assn. Thoracic Surgery, Assn. Clin. Cardiac Surgeons, Am. Surg. Assn., Internat. Coll. Angiology, Internat. Soc. Cardiovasc. Surgery, N.Am. Soc. Pacing and Electrophysiology, Southwestern Surg. Congress, Western Surg. Assn., So. Assn. Vascular Surgery, So. Thoracic Surg. Soc., Pan Pacific Surg. Assn., Denton A. Cooley Cardiovasc. Surg. Soc. (past pres.), Colombian Soc. Cardiology (hon.), Tex. Med. Assn., Harris County Med. Assn., Houston Surg. Soc., Houston Cardiology Soc., N.Y. Acad. Scis., Broward County Heart Assn. (hon.), USU Surg. Assocs., Alpha Omega Alpha. Office: Surg Assocs Tex PA 1101 Bates Ave Houston TX 77030

REULAND, PETER, nuclear medicine physician, researcher; b. Gürzenich, Nordrhein-Westfalen, Ger., Oct. 3, 1953; s. Heinz Jakob and Hanni (Müller) R.; m. Marietta Antonia Anspach, Sept. 29, 1977; children: Anna-Kristina, Milena, Irina. MD, Tech. H.S., Aachen, Ger., 1984; PhD, Eberhard-Karls U., Tübingen, Ger., 1991. Physicist Inst. Theor. Physics Tech. H.S., Aachen, Ger., 1977-79, physiologist Inst. Cardiac Physiology, 1979-84; fellow dept. nuclear medicine Eberhard-Karls U., Tübingen, Ger., 1985-89, resident dept. nuclear medicine, 1989-91; tech. dir. Inst. Nuclear Medicine, Freiburg, Ger., 1992—; dir. Euro-PET Ctr., Freiburg, 1995—; assoc. prof. U. Tübingen, 1992—, Eberhard-Karls U., 1991; head PET Group. Author: Skeletal Scintigraphy, 1989; contbr. articles to profl. jours. Mem. So. W. Ger. Soc. Nuclear Medicine (v.p. 1993—), Soc. Nuclear Medicine, Soc. European Nuclear Medicine, Assn. German Nuclear Physicians (head 1995—).

REUTER, HARALD, pharmacologist; b. Düsseldorf, Germany, Mar. 25, 1934; s. Rudolf and Else (Koerfer) R.; m. Lieselotte Speckmann, Aug. 10, 1960; children: Kirsten, Andreas, Sabine. Diploma, U. Freiburg, Germany, 1959; MD, U. Mainz, Germany, 1960. Asst. dept. pharmacology U. Mainz, 1960-65, privatdozent, 1965-69; prof. pharmacology U. Bern, Switzerland, 1969—, dean med. faculty, 1983-85, chmn. dept. pharmacology, 1971—; vis. prof. various univs. in Eng., Israel, U.S., Japan and China. Co-author: Calcium Movement in Excitable Cells, 1975; editor: Sodium-Calcium Exchange, 1989; mem. editorial bd. numerous sci. jours.; contbr. over 120 articles to internat. jours. Recipient Outstanding Rsch. award Internat. Soc. Heart Rsch., 1984, Ciba-Geigy-Drew award Drew U., 1984, Marcel-Benoist prize Swiss Govt., 1985, Schmiedeberg-Plakette award German Pharmacology Soc., 1987, K.S. Cole award Biophys. Soc., 1993. Mem. Academia Europea, Deutsche Akademie der Naturforscher Leopoldina, Swiss Acad. Med. Scis. Home: Hofenstrasse 15, CH 3032 Hinterkappelen Switzerland Office: Dept Pharmacology U Bern, Friedbühlstrasse 49, CH 3010 Bern Switzerland

REUTER, HELEN HYDE, psychologist; b. McGehee, Ark.; d. John Lloyd and Sallie Elizabeth (Holcomb) Hyde; m. George S. Reuter Jr.; children: Don N., M. Allan, K.L. BA, Westmar U., 1968; AM, U. S.D., 1969; PhD, Westgate U., 1976; LHD (hon.), Sioux Empire Coll.; LLD (hon.), St. John U., New Orleans; DD (hon.), Temple Bapt. Coll. Ordained So. Bapt. minister. Postmaster U.S. Post Office, College Heights, Ark.; sch. counselor various pub. sch. systems, Mo., Iowa; sch. psychologist Oak Park (Ill.) and River Forest High Sch.; v.p., sec. Internat. Assocs. for Christians, Holden, Mo.; cons. in field. Co-author: One Blood, 1964, 2d edit., 1988, Democracy and Quality Education, 1965, 2d edit., 1986. Named Mother of Yr., City of Monticello, 1960; cited as Psychologist of Yr., Internat. U., Lagos, Nigeria, 1992. Mem. P.E.O. (v.p.), Shakespeare Club (v.p.), Garden Club (v.p.). Democrat. Baptist. Home: 406 S Olive St Holden MO 64040-1438 Office: Iac Bldg Holden MO 64040

REUTER, STEWART RALSTON, radiologist, lawyer, educator; b. Detroit, Feb. 14, 1934; s. Carl H. and Grace M. R.; m. Marianne Ahlfeldt, June 6, 1966. B.A., Ohio Wesleyan U., 1955; M.D., Case Western Res. U., 1959; J.D., U. San Francisco, 1980. Diplomate: Am. Bd. Radiology. Bar: Tex. 1981. Intern U. Calif., San Francisco, 1959-60, resident in radiology, 1960-63; instr. radiology Stanford (Calif.) U., 1963-64; asst. prof. U. Mich., Ann Arbor, 1966-69, prof., 1972-76; assoc. prof. U. Calif., San Diego, 1969-72; prof. U. Calif., San Francisco and Davis, 1976-80; prof., chmn. dept. radiology Health Scis. Ctr., U. Tex., San Antonio, 1980—. Co-author: Gastrointestinal Radiology, 3d edit., 1986; mem. editorial bd. Am. Jour. Roentgenology, 1975-91, Iatrogenics, 1990-93; contbr. articles to profl. jours. Picker fellow, 1964-66. Fellow Am. Coll. Radiology, (councillor, 1996—), Am. Coll. Legal Medicine (bd. govs. 1985-91, 92-94, sec. 1994, pres.-elect 1995, pres. 1996); mem. ABA, Assn. Univ. Radiologists, Am. Roentgen Ray Soc., Tex. Radiol. Assn. (trustee 1989-92, pres. 1994), Soc. Cardiovascular and Interventional Radiologists (pres. 1979), Soc. Gastrointestinal Radiologists, Tex. Bar Assn. Home: 3923 Morgans Crk San Antonio TX 78230-1945 Office: U Tex Health Sci Ctr Dept Radiology 7703 Floyd Curl Dr San Antonio TX 78284-6200

REUTHER, JÜRGEN FRIEDRICH, maxillo-facial surgeon, educator; b. Heidelberg, Germany, Nov. 19, 1940; s. Friedrich and Elisabeth (Schaurer) R.; m. Birgit Gebwill, June 25, 1969; children: Tobias, Susanne. Grad., Coll. Abiturkurfürst, Heidelberg, Germany, 1960; DMD, U. Heidelberg, 1965, MD, 1969; PhD, U. Mainz, Germany, 1977. Asst., fellow in maxillo-facial surgery U. Mainz, 1970-74, head asst., 1974-78; prof. U. Frankfurt, Germany, 1978-81; prof. maxillo-facial surgery U. Würzburg, Germany, 1981—. Inventor small bowel transplant technique. Maj. med. unit German mil., 1969-70. Recipient Wassmund prize, 1981. Mem. German Soc. Maxillofacial surgery (pres. 1991), European Soc. Cranio-maxillo-facial Surgery, Internat. Soc. Microsurgery. Evangelical Lutheran. Office: Univ Würzburg, Pleicherwall 2, 8700 Würzburg Germany

REVELL, DOROTHY EVANGELINE TOMPKINS, dietitian; b. Rugby, N.D., Dec. 22, 1911; d. Clarence Herbert and Regina Andrea (Bergh) Tompkins; m. Eugene Allen Revell, Sept 17, 1935; children: Eugene Allen II, Dorothy Ann. BS in Food and Nutrition, U. N.D., Grand Forks, 1933. Lic. registered dietitian, N.D. Dietetic intern Harper Hosp., Detroit, 1933-34; staff dietitian, 1934-35; nutrition instr. student nurses Mercy Hosp., Valley City, N.D., 1958; dietitian Dakota Clinic, Fargo, N.D., 1958-76; pvt. practice Revell's Diet Svc., Fargo, 1977—; home nursing chmn. ARC, Fargo, 1952-54; participant at internat. dietetic meetings. Author 8 books; contbr. articles to profl. jours. Invitee Dietetic Assn. South Africa, Cape Town, 1974, Nutrition and Health Care Study, China, 1984; del. People to People, China, 1987; mem. nutrition study to former USSR, 1974. Recipient Sioux Award to Alumni U. of N.D., named Outstanding Alumni of U. N.D. Mem. Am. Dietetic Assn. (registered dietitian), N.D. Affiliate of Am. Diabetic Assn. (pres. 1950-59), Daughters Am. Colonists, Pi Beta Phi. Republican. Episcopalian. Home: 2407 E Country Club Dr Fargo ND 58103-5730 Office: Revell's Diet Svc 2407 E Country Club Dr Fargo ND 58103-5730

REVELL, JOHN HAROLD, dentist; b. Lead, S.D., Dec. 12, 1906; s. Aris LeRoy and Margaret (O'Donnell) R.; AB in Engring., Stanford, 1930; postgrad. McGill Med. Sch., 1930; DDS summa cum laude, U. So. Calif., 1941; postgrad. in Maxillo Facial and Plastic Surgery, Mayo Found., U. Minn., 1944; m. Catherine Cecelia Gerrard, Sept. 14, 1936; children: Mary Margaret, Kathleen Dianne Revell, Timothy John, Maureen Frances Brown, Dennis Cormac. Engaged as instr. U. So. Calif. Dental Coll., L.A., 1941-42; practice oral surgery, maxillo facial-plastic surgery, Shafter, Calif., 1946—; mem. staff Mercy Hosp., Bakersfield, Calif., 1948—, chmn. dental sect., 1955-60, 70-71; mem. surg. staff San Joaquin Hosp., Bakersfield; lectr. on applied nutrition; internat. pioneer lectr. surg. orthodontics. Served with AUS, 1932-37, 42-46; now maj. ret. Recipient of Special Clinic award Am. Soc. Dentistry for Children, 1964; Rotary Internat. Presdl. citation, 1982. Diplomate Internat. Bd. Applied Nutrition. Fellow Internat. Coll. Applied Nutrition; mem. ADA (life), Calif. Dental Assn. (life), Ventura Dental Soc. (life), So. Calif., Kern County (dir.), Los Angeles County (award 1941), Santa Barbara-Ventura County dental assns., Am. Acad. Dental Medicine, Am. Acad. Applied Nutrition, Am. Soc. Dentistry for Children (life), Pierre Fauchard Acad., Shafter C. of C. (dir. 1948-50), Alpha Tau Epsilon, Omicron Kappa Upsilon, Phi Kappa Phi, Theta Xi. Republican. Roman Catholic. Rotarian (pres. Shafter 1950-51, dir. 1951-52). Patentee precisioner. Rsch. on maxillary dental papilloma, rotation unerupted impacted teeth, channeling for extensive movement of teeth; also clin. rsch. in cleft palate surgery; inventor rapid fabrication device for infant feeding; pioneer in prefab. bldgs. and homes while constrn. officer U.S. Army, 1932-37; developer prototype WW-2 Jeep machine gun mount. Author publs. in field; all rsch. data presented to and housed at La. State U. Dental Coll., New Orleans. Home: Eighty One 620 Ave 49th Indio CA 92201

REVER, BARBARA L., medical educator, consultant, researcher; b. Bklyn., Dec. 18, 1947. B.A., Barnard Coll., 1969; M.P.H., U. Calif.-Berkeley, 1970; M.D., N.Y. Med. Coll., 1974. Diplomate Am. Bd. Internal Medicine, Splty. Nephrology. Intern, Los Angeles County Hosp., U. So. Calif., 1974-75; resident in internal medicine, Los Angeles County Hosp., 1975-76, Kaiser Found. Hosps., Los Angeles, 1976-77; fellow in nephrology U. Calif., L.A. Sch. Medicine, 1978-80, founder and specialist in Nephrology, Salinas Valley Dialysis Services, Inc., 1982—, also chmn. bd.; spl. cons. Calif. State Dept. Pub. Health, summer 1970; research assoc. Dept. Community and Preventive Medicine, N.Y. Hosp. Coll., summer 1971; instr. biology and physiology Community Health Medic Tng. Program, Indian Health Service Hosp., N. Mex., summer 1972; asst. prof. medicine, asst. dir. renal transplantation div. nephrology UCLA, 1980-81; founder Salinas Valley Dialysis Svcs., Inc., 1983; pvt. practice nephrology, 1981—. Office: 951 Blanco Cir # D Salinas CA 93901-4451

REVER, GEORGE WRIGHT, psychiatrist, health facility administrator; b. Balt., May 18, 1928; s. William Benjamin and Amy Blanche (Wright) R.; m. Bridget Valerie Hanley, 1961 (dec. 1988); children: Kurt, Maeve Rever Raedle; m. Ann Roe, Feb. 4, 1994. BS, U. Md., 1950; MD, U. Md., Balt., 1957. Rotating intern Mercy Hosp., Balt., 1957-58; resident psychiatry and neurology VA Hosp., Boston, 1958-60; fellow Harvard Med. Sch., Cambridge, Mass., 1960-64, clin. instr. psychiatry, 1964—; psychiatrist divsn. legal medicine Cambridge Ct., 1960-71; psychiatrist Cambridge Ct. Clinic Divsn. of Legal Medicine, Mass., 1960-71; pvt. practice Cohasset, Mass., 1963-90, Easton, Md., 1990-93; psychiatric cons. Travelers Aid Soc., Boston, 1966-74; psychiatrist Eunice Kennedy Shriver Ctr., Waltham, Mass., 1967-90; fellow child psychiatry Mass. Gen. Hosp., Boston, 1960-61, 62-63, fellow community mental health, 1963-64, staff psychiatrist, 1964-90, dir. child psychiatry tng. program neuropsychiatry devel. disabilities sect., 1967-90, asst. pediatrician, 1969-71, psychiat. cons. social svc. dept., 1970-74, psychiatrist Chelsea Health Ctr., 1974-77, hon. psychiatrist, 1991—; med. dir. Brockton (Mass.) Family and Community Rsch., 1979-90; child and adolescent psychiatrist Wicomico County Health Dept., Salisbury, Md., 1990-91, Queen Anne County Mental Health, Centreville, Md., 1990-92; child and adolescent psychiatrist Talbot County Mental Health, Easton, 1990-92, med. dir., 1992—; psychiatric cons. Benedictine Sch., Ridgely, Md., 1990—; part-time fellow child psychiatry Mass. Gen. Hosp., Boston, 1961-62, James Jackson Putnam Children's Ctr., Roxbury, Mass., 1961-62; cons. Am. Heritage Dictionaries, 1992. Editl. cons. The Am. Jour. of Child and Adolescent Psychiatry, 1994—. Sgt. U.S. Army, 1950-52, Korea. Decorated Bronze Star medal; Recipient Talbot County Assn. Retarded Citizens award, 1993. Mem. AMA, Am. Acad. Child and Adolescent Psychiatry, Am. Psychiatric Assn., Md. Psychiatric Soc., Med. and Chirurg. Faculty Md., Talbot County Med. Soc. Home: 104 W Chestnut St PO Box D Saint Michaels MD 21663-2980

REVERE, VIRGINIA LEHR, clinical psychologist; b. Long Branch, N.J.; d. Joseph and Essie Lehr; m. Robert B. Revere; children: Elspeth, Andrew, Lisa, Robert Jr. PhB, U. Chgo., 1949, MA, 1959, PhD, 1971. Lic. cons. clin. psychologist, Va. Intern, staff psychologist Ea. Mental Health Reception Ctr., Phila., 1959-61; instr. Trenton (N.J.) State Coll., 1962-63; staff psychologist Trenton State Hosp., 1964-65, Bucks County Psychiat. Ctr., Phila., 1965-67; assoc. prof. Mansfield (Pa.) State U., 1967-77; clin. rsch. psychologist St. Elizabeth Hosp., Washington, 1977-81, tng. psychology coord., 1981-83, staff psychologist, 1985-91; child psychologist Community Mental Health Ctr., Washington, 1983-85; pvt. practice Alexandria, Va., 1980—; cons., lectr. in field. Author: Applied Psychology for Criminal Justice Professionals, 1982; contbr. articles to profl. jours. Recipient Group Merit award St. Elizabeth's Hosp., 1983, Community Svc. award D.C. Psychol. Assn., 1978, Outstanding Educator award, 1972; traineeship NIH, USPHS, Chgo., 1963-65; fellow Family Svcs. Assn., 1958-59. Mem. APA, No. Va. Soc. Clin. Psychologists, Va. Acad. Clin. Psychologists. Home: 9012 Linton Ln Alexandria VA 22308-2733 Office: 5021 Seminary Rd Ste 110 Alexandria VA 22311-1923

REY, ALIX CHARLES, psychiatrist; b. Port-Au-Prince, Haiti, Nov. 4, 1940; came to U.S., 1965; s. Stenon and Luce (St. Gerard) Rey; m. Phyllis Ann Harris, Oct. 24, 1969; children: David Alix, Marc Christopher. Baccalaureate, St Louis De Gonzague, Port-Au-Prince, 1960; physician and surgeon, Facultad De Medicina, Mex. City, 1968. Resident in psychiatry Med. Coll. of Ohio, 1973-75; clin. research assoc. NIMH, Bethesda, Md., 1975-76; sr. research assoc. Hispano Health Ctr. Md. Psychiat. Research Ctr., 1976-78; clin. dir. psychiat. svc. Howard County Gen. Hosp., 1979-85, chmn. dept. psychiatry, 1985-91, pres. med. staff, 1989—. Lt. comdr. USPHS, 1975-81. Fellow Am. Psychiat. Assn.; mem. AMA, Med. & Chirurgical Facility Md., Md. Psychiat. Soc., Soc. Biol. Psychiatry, Black Psychiatrists Am. Roman Catholic. Office: 10808 Hickory Ridge Rd Columbia MD 21044-3622

REYBROUCK, TONY, physical medicine and rehabilitation educator; b. Oostduinkerke, Belgium, July 19, 1948; s. Albert and Andrea (Vanbillemont) Reybrouck; m. Odette Teyssen, Dec. 2, 1972; children: Stefaan, Annick, Frank. MS in Phys. Edn. with distinction, U. Leuven, Belgium, 1972, MS in Physiotherapy with gt. distinction, 1972, D in Phys. Rehab., 1975. Lectr. phys. medicine and rehab. U. Leuven, 1976, rsch. asst., 1979, assoc. prof., 1979, prof., 1985—; clin. exercise physiologist Gasthuisberg U. Hosp., Leuven, 1979—. Author books, book chpts; contbr. numerous articles to sci. jours., 1972—. Officer Belgian Med. Svc., 1973-74. Co-recipient Sports prize Belgian Soc. Sports Medicine, Luik, 1978, Sci. prize Belgian Soc. Hypertension, Brussels, 1979. Mem. European Working Group on Pediat. Work Physiology, Brit. Physiol. Soc. (fgn. mem.). Home: Sterrenlaan 32, 3360 Korbeek-Lo Belgium Office: Gasthuisberg Univ Hosp, Herestraat 49, Dep Phys Med, 3000 Leuven Belgium

REYES, ANDRES JESUS, priest, family therapist; b. Santiago, Cuba, May 20, 1943; s. Andres and Ernestina (Aguiar) R.; 1 adopted child. Postgrad., Roman Cath. Sem., Tegucigalpa, Honduras, 1966, U. Javeriana, Bogota, Colombia, 1970; MSW, Yeshiva U., N.Y.C., 1988. Ordained priest Roman Cath. Ch., 1970. Counselor Union Exiled Cubans, Union City, N.J., 1963-64; tchr. religious edn. dept. Instituto Tecnico Cen. High Sch., Bogota, Colombia, 1968-69; counselor Latin Am. Pastoral Team, Bogota, 1967-70; tchr. social sci. electronic engring. dept. Universidad Javeriana, Bogota, 1970; counselor Roman Cath. Archdiocese Newark, 1975; nat. dir. family life for Honduras Bishops' Nat. Conf., 1977-78; convener, chmn. Cuban prisoner refugee program Roman Cath. Archdiocese Newark, 1978-79; therapist psychiat. dept. Elizabeth (N.J.) Gen. Med. Ctr., 1986-88; pvt. practice individual and family therapy Bergenfield, N.J., 1988—; parish priest Roman Cath. Archdiocese Newark, 1971—; mem. bd. Welfare Dept., Borough of Bergenfield, 1987-90. Roman Catholic. Office: 155 William St Belleville NJ 07109

REYES, DAVID CENTENO, cardiovascular surgeon; b. Tegucigalpa, Honduras, July 3, 1934; came to U.S., 1964; s. Manuel and Rosa (Centeno) R.; m. Anna Marie West, June 21, 1969. MD, U. Nat. Autonoma de Honduras, Tegucigalpa, 1964. Diplomate Am. Bd. Surgery, Am. Bd. Thoracic Surgery, spl. qualification in vascular surgery, Am. Bd. Med. Mgmt. Intern Presbyn. Hosp., Phila., 1964-65; resident in gen. surgery Rochester (N.Y.) Gen. Hosp., 1965-66, Harlem Hosp., N.Y.C., 1966-68; chief resident in gen. surgery Ohio Valley Med. Ctr., Wheeling, W.Va., 1968-69; resident in thoracic surgery St. Vincent Hosp., Cleve., 1969-70; chief resident in thoracic surgery U. S.C., Charleston, 1970-71; surgery officer Weirton (W.Va.) Gen. Hosp., 1971-73; emergency room physician Mercy Hosp., Columbus, Ohio, 1973-75; fellow in cardiovascular surgery Tex. Heart Inst., Houston, 1975-76; mem. med. staff Bay Med. Ctr., Bay City, Mich., 1976—. Fellow ACS; mem. Soc. Thoracic Surgeons, Bay County Med. Soc. (pres. 1995). Roman Catholic. Office: 2110 16th St Bay City MI 48708

REYES, HERNAN MACABALLUG, pediatric surgeon; b. Isabela, Philippines, Apr. 5, 1933; came to U.S., 1958; s. Leonor Bulacan and Anacleta (Macaballug) R.; m. Dolores L. Cruz, Feb. 27, 1960; children: Cynthia, Michael, Maria, Patricia, Catherine. Student, U. Philippines, 1949-51; AA; MD, U. Santo Tomas Sch. Medicine, Manila, 1957. Diplomate Am. Bd. Surgery, Am. Bd. Pediatric Surgery. Intern Cook County Hosp., Chgo., 1958-59, resident, 1959-65; clin. asst. dept. surgery Stritch Sch. Medicine, Loyola U., Maywood, Ill., 1964-65, 68, clin. assoc., 1969); acting pediatric surgeon Cook County Children's Hosp., Chgo., 1965; instr. surgery, chief sect. pediatric surgery U. Santo Tomas Faculty Medicine and Surgery, Manila, 1966-67; attending surgeon, chief pediatric surgery U. Santo Tomas Hosp., Manila, 1966-67; attending surgeon Little Co. of Mary Hosp., Evergreen Park, Ill., 1968-85; asst. prof. dept. surgery Pritzker Sch. Medicine, U. Chgo., 1969-73, assoc. prof., 1973-76, acting chief sect. pediatric surgery, 1973-74; attending surgeon Wyler Children's Hosp., U. Chgo., 1969-76, dir. emergency surg. services, 1973-74; prof. dept. surgery U. Ill. Coll. Medicine, Chgo., 1976-94, prof. surgery Rush U./Rush Med. Coll., 1994—; dir. surg. acad. programs, 1994—, prof. clin. pediatrics, 1982—; chief div. pediatric surgery U. Ill. Hosp., Chgo., 1976-90, chmn. div. pediatric surgery Cook County Hosp., 1976-92, chmn. dept. surgery, 1986—. Contbr. articles to profl. publs., chpts. to books. Recipient Tchr. of Yr. award Little Co. Mary Hosp., 1969, Disting. Physician award Philippine Med. Assn. Chgo., 1972, Class recognition Pritzker Sch. Medicine, 1974-75, Leadership award Soc. Philippine Surgeons, 1976, cert. of Appreciation Philippine Med. Assn., 1977; Distg. Recognition award U. Ill, 1987, 89. Mem. AAAS, ACS (Chgo. com. on trauma, chmn. 1994—), Am. Acad. Pediatrics (mem. surgery and oncology sect.), Am. Assn. Surgery Trauma, AAUP, AMA, Am. Pediatric Surg. Assn., Assn. Acad. Surgery, Cen. Surg. Assn., Chgo. Med. Soc. (councilor 1975-76, pres. Wood St. br. 1993-94), Chgo. Surg. Soc. (v.p. 1989-90), Ill. Pediatric Surg. Assn. (sec.-treas 1976-77, pres. 1978-79), Ill. State Med. Soc., Ill. Surg. Soc. (pres. 1995—), Inst. Medicine Chgo., N.Y. Acad. Scis., Soc. Philippine Surgeons Am. (founding pres.), Western Surg. Assn., Am. Trauma Soc., Ea. Assn. for Surgery of Trauma, Societe Internationale de Chirurgie, Internat. Assn For Surgery of Trauma and Surgical Intensive Care, Sigma Xi. Avocation: tennis. Office: Cook County Hosp Dept Surgery M 2201 1835 W Harrison St Chicago IL 60612-3701

REYES, MARCIA STYGLES, medical technologist; b. Winchester, Mass., July 15, 1950; d. Bernard Francis and Eleanore Cecilia (Nicgorska) Stygles; B.S. in Med. Tech., Merrimack Coll., North Andover, Mass., 1972; M.S. in Health Scis. (Kellogg Found. grantee), SUNY, Buffalo, 1977; m. Carlos Reyes, Aug. 5, 1978. Sr. med. technologist Symmes Hosp., Arlington, Mass., 1970-73; sr. microbiologist and serologist Mt. Auburn Hosp., Cambridge, Mass., 1973-75; asst. prof., clin. coordinator Quinnipiac Coll., Hamden, Conn., 1976-81; lab. supr. Canberra Clin. Labs., Meriden, Conn., 1981-86; lab. supr. Hill Health Ctr, New Haven, Conn., 1984—; cons. in med. tech. mgmt., allied health edn. Mem. Am. Soc. Clin. Pathologists, Am. Soc. Med. Tech., Conn. Soc. Med. Tech. (Speaker awards), Am. Soc. Microbiology, Am. Soc. Allied Health Profls. Home: 199 Dover St New Haven CT 06513-4818

REYES, RAUL GREGORIO, surgeon; b. Tegucigalpa, Morazan, Honduras, June 18, 1928; came to U.S., 1939; s. Julio Gregorio and Mercedes Ofelia (Mazzoni) Reyes-Zelaya; m. Blanca Lidia Milla, Apr. 2, 1993; children: Tyra, Kimberly. BS, Georgetown U., 1945; MD, George Washington U., 1950. Diplomate Nat. Bd. Med. Examiners, Am. Bd. Surgery. Intern Charity Hosp., New Orleans, 1950-51; resident Emergency Hosp./George Washington U., Washington, 1951, Charity Hosp., New Orleans, 1952-55; chief thoracic surgery San Felipe Hosp., Tegucigalpa, 1955-56; assoc. to ptnr. Browne-McHardy Clinic, New Orleans, 1955-60, 60-73; med. dir. New Orleans Indsl. Clinic, 1956-58; chief of surgery and orthopedics Lallie Kemp Regional Hosp., Independence, La., 1987-89, med. dirs., 1988-89; owner, pres. Raul G. Reyes, A Med. Corp., New Orleans, 1973—; owner, pres. Internat. Maritime Med. Svcs., New Orleans, 1978—, Catracho Enterprises, New Orleans, 1975—, Phys. Therapy Svcs. of New Orleans, 1975—; faculty La. State Univ. Sch. Medicine, 1953—, others. Inventor in field; contbr. articles to profl. jours. Chmn. Rep. Hispanic Assembly, New Orleans, 1983; pre-cand. Nat. Party, Honduras, 1985; founder Literacy Ctrs. of Honduras, 1991; presdl. candidate Christian Dem. Party of Honduras, 1994. Named to Hon. Consul of Honduras, Hon. Citizen, City of New Orleans. Mem. Am. Coll. Surgeons, AMA, So. Med. Assn., La. State Med. Soc., Orleans Parish Med. Soc., Colegio Medico de Honduras. Roman Catholic. Office: PO Box 15379 New Orleans LA 70175-5379

REYES, RODOLFO CONTANTINO, internist; b. Plaridel, Philippines, Oct. 22, 1956; came to U.S., 1981; s. Alfonso Reyes and Pilar Constantino. BS in Gen. Sci., Manuel L. Quezon U., 1975; BS in Preparatory Medicine, U. of the East, 1977; BS in Medicine, U. East Ramon Magsaysay, Meml. Med. Ctr., 1981; MD with high honors, Ross U. Sch. of Medicine, 1989. Internal medicine resident Edgewater Med. Ctr., Chgo., 1989-92, chief resident in internal medicine, 1991-92; pvt. practice Lillington, N.C., 1995—; lab. technician Bay Harbor Hosp., 1981-82, Damon Clin. Lab., 1983; med.-surg. externship Peninsula Hosp. Ctr., Far Rockaway, N.Y., 1983-84; med. rsch. asst. Southwestern Heart Surgery, Torrance, Calif., 1984; med. historian Kenneth Geiger MD, Neurology, Hawthorne, Calif., 1984-86; med. examiner UCLA, 1986-88; med. rsch. asst. Southwestern Heart Surgery, Torrance, 1987-88. Maj. USAF, 1992-95. Mem. AMA, Rotary Club of Lillington. Home & Office: PO Box 1935 Lillington NC 27546

REYES-NOYLA, JOSE GODOY, pediatrician, endocrinologist; b. Comayaguela, Honduras, June 25, 1945; s. Ricardo and Ann Mary (Essley) R.; m. Feb. 24, 1979; children: Gabriela Maria, Ana Felicidad. MD, U. Honduras, 1972. Diplomate Am. Bd. Pediatrics. Intern U. Honduras, 1970-71; physician Health Ministry, Honduras, 1972; pediatric resident Children's Hosp., Honduras, 1972-73, U. Miss., Jackson, 1973-76; fellow in pediatric endocrinology U. Miami, Fla., 1976-78; attending and chief pediatrics Children's Hosp., 1978—, chief med. ward, 1987—, chief pediatric endocrinology divsn., 1978—, cons. in pediatric endocrinology, 1978—; vis. prof. Children's Hosp., 1978—. Contbr. articles to profl. jours. Fellow Am. Acad. Pediatrics; mem. Endocrine Soc., Lawson Wilkins Pediatric Endocrinology Soc. Office: PO Box 113, Comayaguela Honduras

REYNA, TROY MICHAEL, surgeon; b. Ft. Hood, Tex., July 10, 1950; s. Trinidad and Brigitte (Stuber) R. BS in Chemistry, U.S. Mil. Acad., 1972; MD, Georgetown U., 1977. Diplomate Am. Bd. Surgery, Am. Bd. Pediatric Surgery. Commd. 2d lt. U.S. Army, 1972, advanced through grades to col., 1992; intern Walter Reed Army Med. Ctr., Washington, 1977-78; resident in surgery Tripler Army Med. Ctr., Honolulu, 1978-82; staff surgeon 5th Gen. Hosp., Stuttgart, Fed. Republic Germany, 1982-84, chief surgery, 1984-85; chief trauma services William Beaumont Army Med. Ctr., El Paso, Tex., 1985-88; fellow pediatric surgery Columbus (Ohio) Children's Hosp., 1987-89; chief pediatric surgery svc. William Beaumont Army Med. Ctr., El Paso, 1989-93; ret., 1993; clin. instr. surgery Uniformed Svcs. U. of Health Scis., Bethesda, Md., 1982-85; asst. prof. Tex. Tech. U., El Paso, 1985—; cons. Emergency Med. Svcs., Office of the Mayor of El Paso, 1986-87. Contbr. numerous articles to profl. jours. Lectr. on medicine Explorer Scouts, El Paso, 1986—; mem. exec. com. ARC, El Paso; mem. Las Vegas Suspected Child Abuse & Neglect, 1994—; bd. dirs. Greater Las Vegas Ronald McDonald House, 1994—. Fellow Am. Acad. Pediatrics; mem. AMA, ACS, Assn. Mil. Surgeons, Hawaiian Surg. Assn., Tex. Med. Assn., El Paso Med. Soc., Acad. Surgery, Soc. Am. Gastrointestinal Endoscopic Surgeons, Clark County Med. Soc., Clark County Pediatric Soc. Roman Catholic. Home: 1968 Troon Dr Henderson NV 89014-1039

REYNIAK, J. VICTOR, gynecologist; b. Piekary Slaskie, Poland, Nov. 6, 1936; s. Wiktor W. and Wania Eleanor (Pokutynska) R.; m. Sibylle Maria Reyniak, Nov. 18, 1963; children: Andrew, Stefan. BS, Bielsko-Biala, 1953; MD, Med. Acad., 1960; MA, Jagiellonian U., 1962. Diplomate Am. Bd. Ob-Gyn., Am. Bd. Reproductive Endocrinology. Dir. divsn. reproductive-endocrinology N.Y. Med. Coll., 1967-78; dir. divsn. reproductive-endocrinology Mount Sinai Med. Ctr., N.Y.C., 1979-91, dir. reproductive surgery, 1991—. Editor: Principles of Microsurgical Techniques Infertility, 1982; contbr. numerous articles to profl. jours. Fellow ACS, Am. Coll. Ob-Gyn.; mem. N.Y. Obstet. Soc., N.Y. Gynecol. Soc. (pres. 1990-91). Republican. Roman Catholic. Office: 1107 Fifth Ave New York NY 10128

REYNOLDS, CHARLES PATRICK, pediatric oncologist, researcher; b. El Paso, Tex., Aug. 8, 1952; s. Charles Albert and Lallah Elizabeth (Munro) R.; m. Debra Dawn Adams, Feb. 3, 1979; children: Amy Elizabeth, Jennifer Ann. BA in Biology, U. Tex., 1974; MD, U. Tex. Southwestern Med. Sch., Dallas, 1979; PhD, U. Tex., 1979. Lic. Tex., Calif. Postdoctoral fellow U. Tex. Southwestern Med. Sch., Dallas, 1979-80; pediatric intern Nat. Naval Med. Ctr., Bethesda, Md., 1980-81; battalion surg. Third Marine Div., Okinawa, Japan, 1981-82; rsch. med. officer Naval Med. Rsch. Inst., Bethesda, 1982-87; asst. prof. UCLA, 1987-89; assoc. prof. U. So. Calif., L.A., 1989—; head devel. therapeutics sect. divsn. hematology-oncology Children's Hosp. L.A., L.A., 1993—; dir. Neuroblastoma Marrow Purging Lab. Childrens Cancer Group, L.A., 1988—; team physician U.S. Shooting Team, 1991—. Patentee in field; contbr. articles to profl. jours. Mem. 1992 USA Olympic Shooting Team, Barcelona, Spain. Grantee Nat. Cancer Inst., Am. Inst. Cancer Rsch., Am. Cancer Soc. Mem. Am. Soc. Clin. Oncology, Am. Assn. Cancer Rsch., Soc. Analytical Cytology. Roman Catholic. Office: Childrens Hosp LA Div Hematology Oncology PO Box 54700 Los Angeles CA 90054-0700

REYNOLDS, DEAN R., oral surgeon; m. Alice D. Bovard, 1956; children: Julie Boyard Nugent, Dean Lee Reynolds. AA, Santa Monica City Coll., 1949; student, U. So. Calif., 1949-50; DDS, U. Calif., 1954; MS, Mayo Grad. Sch. Medicine, 1961. Sr. surgical staff St. John's Hosp., 1961—; clin. assoc. prof. oral surgery, U. So. Calif., 1961-81;; chief sect. oral surgery St. Joseph's Hosp., 1967-73, libr. com., 1986-88; staff Santa Monica Hosp., 1961—, med. record com., 1968-69; cons. oral surgery VA Hosp. San Fernando, Calif., 1964-72; tumor bd. U. So. Calif. Sch. Dentistry, 1962-80; com. disaster med. care L.A. County Med. Assn., 1973-78, sub-com. modernization of treatment on field and hosp., 1973-78; lectr., rschr. in field. Contbr. articles to profl. jours. Mem. com. new dimensions, Calif. Luth. Coll.; vol. children's dental clinics St. John's Hosp., Santa Monica Hosp.; vol. profl. svc. Delancey St. Found. Recipient Disting. Svc. award YMCA, Outstanding and Dedicated Svc. plaque, Santa Monica Hosp., 1990, Cert. Appreciation, St. John's Hosp., 1975; Mayo Grad. Sch. Medicine sect. oral surgery fellow, 1958-61. Fellow Am. Assn. Oral Maxillofacial Surgeons, Royal Soc. Health; mem. ADA, Calif. Dental Assn., Western Dental Soc., Beverly Hills Acad. Dentistry (pres. 1986), Inst. Nutritional Rsch. (exec. bd. 1970-75), Western Soc. Oral Maxillofacial Surgeons, Marsh Robinson Acad. Oral Pathology, Am. Acad. Oral maxillofacial Radiology, Internat. Assn. Oral Maxillofacial Surgery, Westwood Acad. Medicine and Dentistry (pres. 1968), Am. Dental Soc. Anesthesiology (life), OKU, Am. Cutting Horse Assn., Les Voyageurs Travel Club. Address: Ste 216 11633 San Vincente Blvd Los Angeles CA 90049-6513

REYNOLDS, DONNA BETH, nursing administrator; b. Waurika, Okla., Mar. 10, 1956; d. Floyd Doil and Eileen Janet (Spears) Park; m. Doyle Thomas Reynolds, May 17, 1975; children: Spence T., Chance J., Chelsey B. LPN, Red River Area Vo-Tech, 1976. LPN, Okla. From aide to LPN Jefferson County Hosp., Waurika, 1974-77; office nurse Dr. W.A. Heflin, Ryan, Okla., 1977-79, Dr. Harry Spence, Dallas, 1979-80; from LPN to LPN svcs. coord. Jefferson County Hosp., 1990—; quality assurance JCH Home Health, Waurika, 1993—. Vol. Ryan Sch., 1990—. Democrat. Mem. Ch. of Christ. Home: Rt 1 Box 77B Ryan OK 73565 Office: Jefferson County Hosp PO Box 90 Waurika OK 73573

REYNOLDS, ELLEN A., pediatrics and trauma nurse; b. Sleepy Eye, Minn., Sept. 3, 1957; d. O. A. and M. Helene (Gerhardsen) Aaker; m. Richard C. Reynolds, Jan. 19, 1980; children: Christopher, Brett. BSN magna cum laude, St. Olaf Coll., 1979; MS in Maternal-Child Nursing, U. Maryland, 1985. Cert. emergency nurse. Clin. nurse Children's Hosp. of the King's Daughters, Norfolk, Va., 1981-82; nurse ICU Jacksonville (Fla.) Children's Hosp., 1982-83; primary nurse critical care float pool Children's Hosp. Nat. Med. Ctr., Washington, 1983-85, clin. nurse, 1985-86; head nurse pediatric ICU U. S. Ala. Med. Ctr., Mobile, 1986-87, pediatric trauma coord., 1987-89, pediatric nursing instr., 1989-90; trauma clin. nurse specialist Children's Hosp. of Pitts., 1990-92, clin. rsch. nurse specialist, 1992—; adj. nursing faculty U. Pitts., 1992—. Contbr. articles to profl. jours. Mem. Phi Kappa Phi, Sigma Theta Tau.

REYNOLDS, HERBERT YOUNG, physician, internist; b. Richmond, Va., Aug. 20, 1939; s. George Audney and Pearle Maupin (Young) R.; m. Anne Browning Leavell, July 11, 1964; children: Nancy, George, William Stuart. BA in English, U. Va., 1961, MD, 1965; MA (hon.), Yale U., 1979. Diplomate Am. Bd. Internal Medicine, Am. Bd. Allergy and Immunology. Intern in medicine The N.Y. Hosp., Cornell Med. Ctr., N.Y.C., 1965-66, asst. physician, fellow in medicine, 1966-67; clin. assoc., lab. clin. investigation Nat. Inst. Allergy and Infectious Diseases, NIH, Bethesda, Md., 1967-70, chief clin. assoc. lab. clin. investigation, 1968-69; sr. investigator lab. of clin. investigation Nat. Inst. Allergy and Infectious Diseases, NIH, 1971-76; chief resident, instr. medicine U. Hosp. U. Wash., Seattle, 1970-71; assoc. prof. internal medicine, head pulmonary div. Sch. Medicine Yale U., New Haven, 1976-79, prof., 1979-88; J. Lloyd Huck prof. medicine, chmn. dept. Pa. State U.-Milton S. Hershey Med. Ctr., 1988—; mem. exec. com. Coll. Medicine Pa. State U.-Hershey Med. Ctr., 1988—, mem. exec. bd. U. Hosp., 1988, mem. fin. bd. acad. enrichment fun, 1988-95, mem. dean's adv. com., 1988-96, mem. diversity task force, 1995—, others; cons. in infectious diseases Nat. Naval Med. Ctr. NIH, Bethesda, 1971-76, mem. clin. rsch. com., 1971-76, chmn., 1974-76, med. bd., 1974-76, pulmonary disease adv. com. divsn. of lung diseases Nat. Heart, Lung and Blood Inst., 1978-82, mem. sci. counselors bd., 1984-88, mem. data and safety monitoring bd. registry of patientss with deficiency of Alpha-1 Antitrypsin, 1989-96. Assoc. editor, mem. editl. bd. Lung, 1978-96, Am. Jour. Medicine, 1979-89, Jour. Clin. Investigation, 1980-86, Am. Rev. Respiratory Disease, 1980-87, Jour. Applied Physiology, 1981-89, Resident Physician, 1981-95; contbr. over 260 articles and revs. to profl. jours. Mem. parent com. Troop 1 Boy Scouts Am., Madison, 1979-82; bd. dirs. Neighborhood Music Sch., Guilford, Conn., 1978-87, Music at Gretna, 1994—; bd. dirs. Harrisburg Symphony, 1996—; active All Saints Episc. Ch., Hershey; mem. pulmonary infections com. Cystic Fibrosis Found., Bethesda, 1980-86; mem. coun. sci. advisors Parker B. Francis Found., Kansas City, Kans., 1983-87; mem. internat. com. World Orgn. for Sarcoidosis and other Granulomatous Disorders, 1987-95; bd. dirs., mem. coun. Am. Lung Assn., 1989-93, bd. govs. 1990-93, various com. positions, 1990—; coach Guilford Soccer League, 1985-88. Surgeon USPHS, 1967-70. John Edward Nobel fellow, 1961-65; named Outstanding Med. Specialist in USA, Town and Country Mag., 1989, The Best Med. Specialists, Town & Country mag., 1995, One of 400 Best Drs. in U.S. Good Housekeeping Mag., 1991, named in The Best Doctors in America, 1st edit. 1992-93, 2d edit. 1994-95. Fellow ACP (coun. subsplty. socs. 1983—), Am. Coll. Chest Physicians (program com. 1978-84), Infectious Disease Soc. Am., Coll. Physicians Phila.; mem. Am. Thoracic Soc. (sec.-treas. 1987-88, bd. dirs. 1989-93, v.p. 1988-89, pres. 1992-93), Am. Soc. Clin. Investigation, Assn. Am. Physicians, Am. Assn. Immunologists, Am. Fedn. Clin. Rsch., Am. Clin. and Climatological Soc., Interurban Clin. Club (emeritus 1989), Assn. Profs. Medicine, Country Club of Hershey, Farmington Country Club, Raven Soc., Phi Beta Kappa, Alpha Omega Alpha, Omicron Delta Kappa. Republican. Home: 226 E Caracas Ave Hershey PA 17033-1309 Office: Pa State U Milton S Hershey Med Ctr 850 University Dr Hershey PA 17033

REYNOLDS, JOHN WESTON, pediatric medicine educator; b. Portland, Oreg., Aug. 5, 1930; s. Lloyd Jay and Virginia (Bliss) R.; m. Phyllis Cantrell, Sept. 19, 1954. BA, Reed Coll., 1951; MD, U. Oreg., 1956. Diplomate Am. Bd. Pediatrics. Asst. prof. pediatrics U. Minn., Mpls., 1961-66, assoc. prof., 1966-70, prof., 1970-77; prof. Oreg. Health Scis. U., Portland, 1977-92, prof. emeritus, 1992—. Contbr. numerous articles to profl. jours. Bd. dirs. Planned Parenthood of Portland, 1984-88, Friends of Columbia Gorge, 1993—. Recipient Research Career Devel. award NIH, 1964-74 Fellow Am. Acad. Pediatrics (nutrition com. 1981-87); mem. Am. Pediatric Soc., Soc. Pediatric Research, Endocrine Soc. Home: 4471 SW Fairview Circus Portland OR 97221-2715 Office: Oreg Health Scis U 3181 SW Sam Jackson Park Rd Portland OR 97201-3011

REYNOLDS, LAWRENCE PAUL, physiology educator; b. Winslow, Ariz., May 31, 1953; s. Charles W. and Patricia A. Reynolds; m. Lavona K. Cleaver, July 6, 1976; children: Shaun Michael, Scott Patrick. BS in Zoology, Ariz. State U., 1977, MS in Agriculture, 1980; PhD in Reproductive Physiology, Iowa State U., 1983. Postdoctoral fellow in nutrition USDA, Clay Center, Nebr., 1983-85; asst. prof. N.D. State U., Fargo, 1985-88, assoc. prof., 1988-94, prof., 1994—, dir. cell biology ctr., 1990—; invited speaker XVII Biennial Symposium on Animal Reprodn., Athens, Ga., 1985, Symposium on Local Sys. in Reprodn., Paris, 1992, 3d NATO ASI on Molecular, Cellular and Clin. Aspects on Angiogenesis, Porto Carras, Greece, 1995. Contbr. articles to profl. jours., including jour. of Fed. Am. Soc. Exptl. Biology, Endocrinology, Biol. Reprodn., Jour. Animal Sci., Jour. Agrl. Sci., Jour. Reprodn. Fertility. Grantee NIH, 1987—, USDA, 1987—, NSF, 1988—. Mem. AAAS, Am. Physiol. Soc., Am. Soc. Animal Sci. (chair physiology program Midwest sect. 1988-90), Soc. for Study Fertility, Soc. for Study Reproduction. Evangelical. Office: ND State U Dept Animal & Range Sci & Cell Biol Ctr Hultz Hall Fargo ND 58102

REYNOLDS, LOUISE MAXINE KRUSE, retired school nurse; b. Waynesboro, Va., May 28, 1935; d. Emil Herman and Cora Lee (Hammer) Kruse; m. Elbert B. Reynolds Jr., June 13, 1964; children: David Emil, Jane Marie. Diploma, Rockingham Meml. Hosp., 1956; student, Madison Coll., Tex. Tech U. RN, Tex., Va, cert. sch. nurse. Head nurse orthopedic, opthalmology dept. surgery Duke U., Durham, N.C., 1961-62; head nurse surg. fl. Waynesboro (Va.) Hosp., 1962-64; sch. nurse Lubbock (Tex.) Ind. Sch. Dist., 1974-94, ret., 1994. Mem. Va. Nurses Assn. (dist. sec., chair), Tex. Assn. Sch. Nurses (sec., treas. dist. 17, program chair 1989 state conv.).

REYNOLDS, MARJORIE LAVERS, educator; b. Collingwood, Ont., Can., Jan. 10, 1931; d. Henry James and Laura (Wilson) Lavers; m. John Horace Reynolds, Aug. 17, 1963; children: Steven, Mark. BA, U. Toronto, 1953; MS, U. Minn., 1957; PhD, U. Wis., 1964; AS, State Tech. Inst. Knoxville, 1982. Registered dietitian. Rsch. dietitian Mayo Clinic, Rochester, Minn., 1957-59; rsch. dietitian Cleve. Met. Gen. Hosp., 1959-60; rsch. assoc. U. Tenn., Knoxville, 1963-66; instr. Ft. Sanders Sch. Nursing, Knoxville, 1967-76, State Tech. Inst., Knoxville, 1982-88; substitute secondary sch. tchr. Knox County Schs., Knoxville, 1989-93. Contbr. articles to biochem. and nutrition jours.; newsletter editor Juvenile Diabetes Found., Knoxville, 1985-93. Sec. Midway Rehab. Ctr., Knoxville, 1987—; mem. LWV, Knoxville, 1965—. Mem. Knoxville Dist. Dietetic Assn. (pres. 1971-72, Outstanding Dietitian 1973-1974), Tenn Dietetic Assn. (pres. 1973-74, Outstanding Dietitian 1973-74), Omicron Nu. Democrat. Presbyterian. Home: 7112 Stockton Dr Knoxville TN 37909-2534

REYNOLDS, REBECCA BARRON, medical record administrator; b. Memphis, Sept. 2, 1971; d. Ed and Glenda (Williamson) Barron; m. Jeremy Reynolds, Sept. 4, 1993. BS in Health Info. Mgmt. with honors, U. Tenn., 1993. Registered record adminstr. Supr. med. records VNA, Memphis, 1993-94; asst. dir. med. records U. Tenn. Bowld Hosp., Memphis, 1994—; clin. site instr. U. Tenn. HIM Students, 1993—, recruitment com. treas. 1995, scholarship com. 1994. Mem. Memphis Health Info. Mgmt. Assn. (program dir. 1993), Am. Health Info. Mgmt. Assn., Tenn. Health Info. Mgmt. Assn. Office: U Tenn Bowld Hosp Med Record Dept 951 Court Memphis TN 38103

REYNOLDS, RONALD DAVISON, physician; b. Boston, July 31, 1958; s. Orland Bruce and Moira (Davison) R.; m. Diana May Prieur; children: Brittany, Andrew, Avery. BS in Biochemistry, No. Mich. U., 1980; MD, U. Mich., 1984. Bd. cert. family practice. Resident family practice Flower Meml. Hosp., Sylvania, Ohio, 1984-87; family physician, ctr. dir. So. Ohio Health Svcs. Network New Richmond (Ohio) Family Practice, 1987—; asst. prof. family medicine U. Cin. Coll. Medicine, 1987—; mem. quality assurance com. So. Ohio Health Svcs. Network, Cin., 1993—; presenter in field. Reviewer Am. Family Physician, Jour. Family Practice, Mosby-Year Book Publishers; contbr. chpts. to books and articles to profl. jours. Fellow Am. Acad. Family Physicians; mem. Ohio Acad. Family Physicians, Southwestern Ohio Soc. Family Physicians, Assn. for Voluntary Surg. Contraception. Office: New Richmond Family Practice 1050 Old US 52 New Richmond OH 45157

REYNOLDS, SCARLETT RENEE, physician assistant; b. Amarillo, Tex., Sept. 7, 1956; d. Robert Warren and Lavora Jean (Miller) Miller; m. Carl Jewel Reynolds Jr., Feb. 18, 1978; children: Reagan Renee, Brittany Dawn. BS in Sci., U. Tex./Southwestern Med. Ctr., Dallas, 1993. Cert. physician asst. with honors. Physician asst. Inova Health Care, Plano, Tex., 1993—. Leader Girl Scouts U.S., Lewisville, 1986-94; deaconess Ch. of Christ. Fellow Am. Acad. Physician Assts., Tex. Assn. Physician Assts. Republican. Ch. of Christ. Home: 1375 Forest Hill Cir Lewisville TX 75062 Office: Inova 2200 Spring Creek Pky Plano TX 75028

REYNOLDS, TIMOTHY MARK, pathologist, researcher; b. Solihull, West Mid, Eng., Apr. 12, 1960; s. Leonard and Pamela Ann (Pascall) R.; m. Jane Elizabeth Oldfield. BSc with honors, Leeds (Eng.) U., 1981, MBChB, 1984, MD, 1994. Registrar Birmingham (Eng.) Rotation, 1985-88; sr. registrar South Wales Rotation, Newport and Cardiff, 1988-93; cons. chem. pathology Burton Hosp., Burton Upon Trent, Eng., 1993—; b. dirs. Klinchem Svcs., Cardiff; cons. in fied. Author: (with others) Screening for Donn's Syndrome, 1994; contbr. articles to profl. jours. Grantee Nat. Kidney Rsch. Found., 1993, Scotia Pharms., Ltd., 1993. Mem. Brit. Med. Assn., Assn. Clin. Biochemists (mem. regional com. 1993—), Royal Coll. Pathology, Med. Rsch. Soc. Office: Burton Hosp Clin Chem Dept, Belvedere Rd, Stafford Burton Upon Trent DE13 0RB, England

REYNOLDS, VERNON DANIEL, plastic surgeon, pharmacist; b. Lorain, Ohio, Feb. 14, 1965; s. Vernon Reynolds and Madalaine Karen (Bomback) Thornsberry. BS in Pharmacy, Ohio State U., 1988; MD, Ohio U., 1996. Diplomate Am. Bd. Surgery; registered pharmacist, Ohio. Pharmacy subcontracor Columbus, Ohio, 1994-96; E.N.T./oro-facial plastic surgery resident Doctors Hosp., Columbus, 1996—; rschr. drug project State Bd. Pharmacy, Columbus, 1987; pharmacy cons., Columbus, 1988-92; tchg. asst. in chemistry Ohio State U., Columbus, 1985-86. Recipient Rsch. award Ohio State Bd. Pharmacy, 1987; Nickles Med. scholar, 1991-95. Mem. AMA, Ohio State Med. Assn., Ohio PhHarmacists Assn., Am. Pharm. Assn. Home: 5336 Firebush Ln Columbus OH 43235

REZNICK, RICHARD HOWARD, pediatrician; b. Chgo., Oct. 31, 1939; s. Louis and Mae (Roth) R.; m. Barbara Ann Glantz, June 20, 1965; children: Steven L., Alicia T., Scott M., Stacey R. BS, U. Ill., 1961; MD, Loyola U., Chgo., 1965. Diplomate Am. Bd. Pediatrics. Pediatrician USAF, Homestead AFB, Fla., 1968-70; pediatrician pvt. practice Winnetka, Ill., 1970-71, Scottsdale, Ariz., 1971—; pres. med. staff Phoenix Children's Hosp., 1990-93, bd. dirs. 1990-94. Capt. USAF, 1968-70. Fellow Am. Acad. Pediatrics (treas. Ariz. chpt. 1982-84); mem. AMA, Ariz. Med. Assn., Phoenix Pediatric Soc. (treas. 1976-77), Maricopa County Med. Soc. Office: Papago Buttes Pediatric Ctr 6390-3 E Thomas Rd Ste 130 Scottsdale AZ 85251

REZNIK, ANDREA ISABELLE, neurologist; b. Bound Brook, N.J., Oct. 3, 1952; d. Andrew and Isabelle (Schaub) R.; m. Richard Hall III, Apr. 24, 1982; 1 child Richard IV. BS, Rutgers U., 1973; MD, Tufts U., 1977. Diplomate Am. Bd. Psychiatry and Neurology. Intern Mt. Sinai Hosp., N.Y.C., 1977-78, resident, 1978-82; asst. prof. Robert Wood Johnson Med. Sch., New Brunswick, N.J., 1982—; pvt. practice, Somerset, N.J., 1984—. Mem. Am. Acad. Neurology. Office: 201 Union Ave Bridgewater NJ 08807

RHAME, RICHARD COLEMAN, physician; b. Bklyn., June 16, 1929; s. Harold Ellis and Clara (Dunagan) R.; m. Karen Carsel, Feb. 8, 1965 (div. 1980); m. Jean Graham, Feb. 4, 1989; children: Helen, Alexander, Laura, Scott. AB, Princeton U., 1950; MD, George Washington U., 1954. Diplomate Am. Bd. Urology. Intern Johns Hopkins Hosp., Balt., 1954-55; resident Yale Med. Ctr., New Haven, Conn., 1957-62; asst. prof. urology George Washington U., Washington, 1965-80; chief urology Alexandria (Va.) Hosp., 1970-80; pres. Alexandria Urol. Assocs., 1980—; instr. surgery Yale Med. Ctr., New Haven, 1961-62; cons. D.C. Vets. Hosp., 1968-78; mem. staff Alexandria Hosp., Mount Vernon Hosp., Fairfax Hosp., Vencor Hosp. Contbr. articles to profl. jours. Lt. USN, 1955-57. Fellow ACS; mem. Am. Urol. Assn., Washington Urol. Soc. (treas. 1985-86), No. Va. Acad. Surgery, Johns Hopkins Med. and Surg. Soc., N.Y. Yacht Club, Royal Bermuda Yacht Club, Annapolis Yacht Club. Office: Alexandria Urol Assocs PC 1707 Osage St Alexandria VA 22302-2611

RHEE, YANG HO, radiologist; b. Kunsan, Republic of Korea, Mar. 22, 1943; came to U.S., 1973; s. Young Whan and Ae Wol (Rah) R.; m. Shin Ae Kang; children: Hoyeon, Thomas, Karen. MD, Chonnam Med. Sch., Kwangju, Republic of Korea, 1968. Diplomate Am. Bd. Radiology. Intern Seoul Adventist Hosp., Republic of Korea, 1972-73, Cook County Hosp., Chgo., 1973-74; resident Hines (Ill.) VA Hosp., 1974-77; staff physician Illini Hosp., Silvis, Ill., 1977—. Chmn. bd. trustees Quad City Korean Assn., Ill. and Iowa, 1986-88, v.p., 1980-81; mem. adv. coun. on peaceful unification policy Republic of Korea, 1984-93; chmn. dept. radiology Ilini Hosp., Silvis, Ill., 1988—. Capt. Korean Army, 1968-72, Korea and Vietnam. Mem. AMA, Am. Coll. Radiology, Radiol. Soc. N.Am., Soc. Nuclear Medicine, Am. Inst. Ultasound in Medicine, Am. Roentgen Ray Soc. Office: 801 Hospital Rd Silvis IL 61282-1804

RHEINSTEIN, PETER HOWARD, government official, physician, lawyer; b. Cleve., Sept. 7, 1943; s. Franz Joseph Rheinstein and Hede Henrietta (Neheimer) Rheinstein Lerner; m. Miriam Ruth Weissman, Feb. 22, 1969; 1 child, Jason Edward. BA with high honors, Mich. State U., 1963, MS, 1964; MD, Johns Hopkins U., 1967; JD, U. Md., 1973. Bar: Md., D.C.; diplomate Am. Bd. Family Practice, Am. Bd. Geriatrics; cert. added qualifications in geriatric medicine. Intern USPHS Hosp., San Francisco, 1967-68; resident in internal medicine USPHS Hosp., Balt., 1968-70; practice medicine specializing in internal medicine Balt., 1970—; instr. medicine U. Md., Balt., 1970-73; med. dir. extended care facilities CHC Corp., Balt., 1972-74; dir. drug advt. and labeling div. FDA, Rockville, Md., 1974-82, acting dep. dir. Office Drugs, 1982-83, acting dir. Office Drugs, 1983-84, dir. Office Drug Standards, 1984-90; dir. medicine staff, Office Health Affairs FDA, 1990—; chmn. Com. on Advanced Sci. Edn., 1978-86, Rsch. in Human Subjects Com., 1990-92; adj. prof. forensic medicine George Washington U., 1974-76; WHO cons. on drug regulation Nat. Inst. for Control Pharm. and Biol. Products, People's Republic of China, 1981—; advisor on essential drugs WHO, 1985—; FDA del. to U.S. Pharmacopeial Conv., 1985-90. Co-author: (with others) Human Organ Transplantation, 1987; spl. editorial advisor Good Housekeeping Guide to Medicine and Drugs, 1977—; mem. editorial bd. Legal Aspects Med. Practice, 1981-89, Drug Info. Jour., 1982-86, 91-95; contbr. articles to profl. jours. Recipient Commendable Svc. award FDA, 1981, Group award of merit, 1983, 88, Group Commendable Svc. award 1989, 92, 93, 95, Commr.'s Spl. citation, 1993. Fellow Am. Coll. Legal Medicine (bd. govs. 1983-93, treas., chmn. fin. com. 1985-88, 90-91, chmn. publs. com. 1988-93, jud. coun. 1993—; Pres.'s awards 1985, 86, 89, 90, 91, 93), Am. Acad. Family Physicians; mem. AMA, ABA, Drug Info. Assn. (bd. dirs. 1982-90, pres. 1984-85, 88-89, v.p. 1986-87, chmn. ann. meeting 1991, 94, steering com. Ams. 1991—, Outstanding Svc. award 1990), Fed. Bar Assn. (chmn. food and drug com. 1976-79, Disting Svc. award 1977), Med. and Chirurgical Faculty Md., Balt. City Med. Soc., Johns Hopkins Med. and Surg. Assn., Am. Pub Health Assn., Md. Bar Assn., Math. Assn. Am., Soc. Indsl. and Applied Math., Mensa (life), U. Md. Alumni Assn. (life), Johns Hopkins U. Alumni Assn. (life), Chartwell Golf and Country Club, Annapolis Yacht Club, Johns Hopkins Club, Delta Theta Phi. Home: 621 Holly Ridge Rd Severna Park MD 21146-3520 Office: FDA Office of Health Affairs Dir Medicine Staff 5600 Fishers Ln Rockville MD 20857-0001

RHIEW, FRANCIS CHANGNAM, physician; b. Korea, Dec. 3, 1938; came to U.S., 1967, naturalized, 1977; s. Byung Kyun and In Sil (Lee) R.; m. Kay Kyungja Chang, June 11, 1967; children: Richard C., Elizabeth. BS, Seoul Nat. U., 1960, MD, 1964. Intern, St. Mary's Hosp., Waterbury, Conn., 1967-68; resident in radiology and nuclear medicine L.I.U.-Queens Hosp. Ctr., N.Y., 1968-71; instr. radiology W. Va. U. Sch. Medicine, Morgantown, 1971-73; mem. staff Mercy Hosp. and Moses Taylor Hosp., Scranton, Pa., 1973—, also dir. nuclear medicine; clin. instr., Temple U., 1987—; pres. Radiol. Consultants, Inc., 1984—. Served with M.C., Korean Army, 1964-67. Recipient Minister of Health and Welfare award, 1963; certified Am. Bd. Nuclear Medicine. Mem. AMA, Soc. Nuclear Medicine, Radicl. Soc. N.Am., Am. Coll. Nuclear Medicine, Am. Coll. Radiology, Am. Inst. Ultra Sound, Country Club Scranton, Pres.'s Club U. Scranton, Elks. Home: 14 Lakeside Dr Clarks Summit PA 18411-9419 Office: 746 Jefferson Ave Scranton PA 18510-1624

RHOADES, RODNEY ALLEN, physiologist, educator; b. Greenville, Ohio, Jan. 5, 1939; s. John H. and Floris L. Rhoades; m. Judith Ann Brown, Aug. 6, 1961; children: Annelisa, Kirsten. BS, Miami U., 1961, MS, 1963; PhD, Ohio State U., 1966. Asst. prof. Pa. State U., State College, 1966-72, assoc. prof., 1972-75; rsch. scientist NIH, Bethesda, Md., 1975-76; prof. Ind. U. Sch. Medicine, Indpls., 1976-81, prof., chmn., 1981—; dir. Indpls. Ctr. for Advanced Rsch. Author: Physiology, 1984; contbr. articles to profl. jours. Recipient NASA fellow, 1964-66, Rsch. Career Devel. award NIH, 1975-80.

Mem. Am. Physiol. Soc., Am. Heart Assn., Am. Thoracic Soc., Biophysics Soc., Sigma Xi. Home: 1768 Spruce Dr Carmel IN 46033-9025 Office: Ind U Sch Medicine 635 Barnhill Dr Indianapolis IN 46202-5126

RHOADS, JONATHAN EVANS, surgeon; b. Phila., May 9, 1907; s. Edward G. and Margaret (Ely Paxson) R.; m. Teresa Folin, July 4, 1936 (dec. 1987); children: Margaret Rhoads Kendon, Jonathan Evans Jr., George Grant, Edward Otto Folin, Philip Garrett, Charles James; m. Katharine Evans Goddard, Oct. 13, 1990. BA, Haverford Coll., 1928, DSc (hon.), 1962; MD, Johns Hopkins U., 1932; D. Med. Sci., U. Pa., 1940, LLD (hon.), 1960; DSc (hon.), Swarthmore Coll., 1969, Hahnemann Med. Coll., 1978, Duke U., 1979, Med. Coll. Ohio, 1985; DSc (Med.) (hon.), Med. Coll. Pa., 1974, Georgetown U., 1981, Yale U., 1990; LittD (hon.), Thomas Jefferson U., 1979. Intern Hosp. of U. Pa., 1932-34, fellow, instr. surgery, 1934-39; assoc. surgery, surg. research U. Pa. Med. Sch., Grad. Sch. Medicine, 1939-47, asst. prof. surg. research, 1944-47, asst. prof. surgery, 1946-47, assoc. prof., 1947-49; J. William White prof. surg. research U. Pa., 1949-51; prof. surgery Grad. Sch. Medicine, U. Pa., 1950—; prof. surgery and surg. research U. Pa. Sch. Med., 1951-57, prof. surgery, 1957-59; provost U. Pa., 1956-59, provost emeritus, 1977—, John Rhea Barton prof. surgery, chmn. dept. surgery, 1959-72, prof. surgery, 1972—, acting dir. Harrison dept. surg. research, 1944-46, asst. dir., 1946-59, dir., 1959-72; chief surgery Hosp. U. Pa., 1959-72, chmn. med. bd., 1959-61; dir. surgery Pa. Hosp., 1972-74; surg. cons. Pa. Hosp., Germantown (Pa.); mem. staff Hosp. of U. Pa.; mem. bd. pub. edn., City of Phila., 1965-69; co-chmn. Phila. Mayor's Commn. on Health Aspects of Trash to Steam Plant, 1986, chief justice Pa. Com. on Phila. Traffic Ct.; former mem. bd. mgrs. Haverford Coll., chmn., 1963-72, pres. corp., 1963-78, emeritus bd. mgrs. 1989—; bd. mgrs. Friends Hosp. of Phila.; trustee Coriell Inst. Med. Rsch., 1957-90, v.p. sci. affairs, 1964-76, life trustee, 1990—; trustee GM Cancer Rsch. Found.; chmn. bd. trustees Measey Found.; trustee emeritus Bryn Mawr Coll.; mem. com. in charge Westtown Sch., 1962-94, emeritus, 1994; treas. Germantown Friends Sch.; cons. Bur. State Services, VA, 1963; cons. to divsn. med. scis. NIH, 1962-63; nat. adv. gen. medical scis. council USPHS, 1963; adv. council Life Ins. Med. Research Fund., 1961-66; Pres. Phila. div., 1955-56; chmn. adv. commn. on research on pathogenesis of cancer Am. Cancer Soc., 1956-57, del., 1956-61, dir. at large, 1965—, pres., 1969-70, past officer dir., 1970-77, hon. life mem., 1977—; chmn. surgery adv. com. Food and Drug Adminstrn., 1972-74; chmn. Nat. Cancer Adv. Bd., 1972-79; Mem. Am. Bd. Surgery, 1963-69, sr. mem., 1969—. Author, co-editor: Surgery: Principles and Practice, 1957, 61, 65, 70; author: (with J.M. Howard) The Chemistry of Trauma; mem. editl. bd. Jour. Surg. Rsch., 1960-71, Oncology Times, 1979—; co-editor: Accomplishments in Cancer research, 1979-94; editor Jour. Cancer, 1972-91, editor emeritus, 1991—; editl. bd. Annals of Surgery, 1947-77, emeritus, 1977-95, sr. 1995—, chmn. 1971-73; editl. adv. bd. Guthrie Bull., 1986—; contbr. articles to med. jours., chpts. to books. Trustee John Rhea Barton Surg. Found. Recipient Roswell Park medal, 1973, Papanicolaou award, 1977, Phila. award, 1976, Swanberg award, 1987, Benjamin Franklin medal Am. Philos. Soc., Medal of the Surgeon Gen. of U.S., Disting. Alumnus award U. Pa., 1993, Russell W. Richie award Friends Hosp. Phila., 1994, Presdl. award Nat. Assn. Psychiat. Health Systems, 1994; hon. Benjamin Franklin fellow Royal Soc. Arts; Patient Care Pavilion at Hosp. U. Pa. named in honor of Jonathan Evans Rhoads, 1994, Clarence E. Shaffrey S.J. medal 1996. Fellow Am. Med. Writers Assn., Am. Philos. Soc. (sec. 1963-66, pres. 1977-84), ACS (regent, chmn. bd. regents 1967-69, pres. 1971-72), Royal Coll. Surgeons (Eng.) (hon.), Royal Coll. Surgeons Edinburgh (hon.), Deutsches Gesellschaft für Chirurgie (corr.), Assn. Surgeons India (hon.), Royal Coll. Physicians and Surgeons Can. (hon.), Coll. Medicine South Africa (hon.), Polish Assn. Surgeons (hon.), Royal Coll. Seons in Ireland (hon.), AAAS (sec. med. sci. sect. 1980-86); mem. Hollandsche Maatschappij der Wetenschappen (fgn.), Am. Public Health Assn., Assn. Am. Med. Colls. (chmn. council acad. socs. 1968-69, disting. service mem. 1974—), Fedn. Am. Socs. Exptl. Biology, Am. Assn. Surgery Trauma (Fitts lectr., 1995), Am. Soc. Clin. Nutrition, Am. Trauma Soc. (founding mem., chmn. bd. dirs. 1986-94, Curtis Artz award 1996), AMA (co-recipient Goldberger award 1970, Dr. Rodman and Thomas G. Sheen award 1980), Pa. Med. Soc. (mem. jud. coun. 1991-94, vice chmn. 1994-96, chmn. 1996—, Disting. Svc. award 1975), Phila. County Med. Soc. (pres. 1970, Strittmater award 1968), Coll. Physicians Phila. (v.p. 1954-57, pres. 1958-60, Disting. Svc. award 1987), Phila. Acad. Surgery (pres. 1964-66, Ann. Oration named for Jonathan E. Rhoads 1985), Phila. Physiol. Soc. (v.p. 1945-46), Am. Surg. Assn. (pres. 1972-73, Disting. Service medal, trustee found., vice chmn. 1992-96), Pan Pacific Surg. Assn. (v.p. 1975-77), So. Surg. Assn., The Internat. Surg. Group (pres. 1958), Internat. Fedn. Surg. Colls. (v.p. 1972-78, pres. 1978-81, hon. pres. 1987—), Fellows of Am. Studies, Soc. of U. Surgeons, Soc. Clin. Surgery (pres. 1966-68), Am. Assn. for Cancer Research, Am. Chem. Soc., Am. Physiol. Soc., Coun. Biology Editors, Internat. Soc. Surgery (hon.) N.Y. Acad. Scis., Surg. Infection Soc. (pres. 1984-85), Surgeons Travel Club (pres. 1976, hon. mem.), Am. Inst. Nutrition, World Med. Assn., Am. Acad. Arts and Scis. (mem. coun. 1977-81), Inst. of Medicine (sr.), Soc. for Surgery Alimentary Tract (pres. 1967-68), Southeastern Surg. Congress, Soc. Surg. Chmn. (pres. 1966-68), Buckingham Mountain Found. (sec., treas., pres., 1996—), James IV Soc. (hon.), Phi Beta Kappa, Alpha Omega Alpha, Sigma Xi. Clubs: Rittenhouse, Union League, Philadelphia; Cosmos (D.C.). Office: 3400 Spruce St Philadelphia PA 19104

RHODES, EDDIE, JR., medical technologist, phlebotomy technician; b. Memphis, Apr. 14, 1955; s. Eddie Sr. and Mabel (Payne) R. AS, Shelby State C.C., Memphis, 1979; BS, Memphis State U., 1981. Cert. med. technologist. Rsch. technologist St. Jude's Children Rsch. Hosp., Memphis, Ga., 1980-81; med. lab. asst. Roche Biomedical Lab., Tucker, Ga., 1991-92; med. technologist Damon / MetPath Clin. Lab., Smyrna, Ga., 1992-93, ARC, Norcross, Ga., 1993-95, Ga. Bapt. Med. Ctr., Atlanta, 1994—; instr. microbiology Atlanta Area Tech., 1995-96; adv. bd. mem. Atlanta Area Tech., Atlanta, 1995—; blood donor specialist Civitan Regl. Blood Sys., Atlanta, 1996—; program coord. W. Ga. Tech., LaGrange, 1996—. Named one of the Outstanding Young Men of Am., Atlanta, 1989. Mem. Am. Soc. Microbiology, Am. Soc. of Phlebotomy Technicians. Home: 410 Park Pl LaGrange GA 30240 Office: West Ga Technical 303 Fort Dr Lagrange GA 30240

RHODES, IDA ELIZABETH, human services professional; b. Ansonia, Conn., May 26, 1942; d. Samuel Lee and Beersheba Queen (London) R. AS in Human Svcs., South Ctrl. C.C., 1977; BS in Human Svcs., N.H. Coll., 1982. Asst. housing dir., counselor Urban League Greater New Haven (Conn.), 1978-83; mental health worker Conn. Mental Health Ctr., New Haven, 1984-86; social worker trainee Bridgeport (Conn.) Community Mental Health, 1986-87; psychiatric social worker asst. Bridgeport (Conn.) Community Mental Health, New Haven, 1987-88, Conn. State Mental HEalth Ctr., New Haven, 1988-89; resident advocate, social worker Conn. AIDS Residence Program, New Haven, 1989-90; social worker NIH AIDS Rsch. Program, Hill Health Ctr., New Haven, 1990; corrections psychiatric treatment worker State of Conn. Dept. Corrections, Bridgeport, 1990—; membership coord. Community Housing Resource Bd., Dept. Housing & Urban Devel. & New Haven Bd. Realtors, 1979-80; asst. coord. N.H. Coll. Student Community Svc. Group, 1980-82. Author of poems. Mem. East Coast Affirmative Action Com., 1978-79; v.p. Urban League Guild-Urban League Greater New Haven, Inc., 1979-83; mem. Mayor's Task Force on AIDS, New Haven, 1989-90; sec. bd. dirs. Afro-Am. Hist. Soc., New Haven, 1979; nominated honoree Women in Leadership-YWCA, New Haven, 1983. Address: PO Box 7733 New Haven CT 06519-0733

RHODES, JAMES DEVERS, psychotherapist; b. Midland, Tex., Apr. 28, 1955; s. James Ireland and Loys Ruth (McElrath) R.; m. Moira Sheelagh Josephine Fox Elmore, June 21, 1986. BS, Tex. Christian U., 1978; MEd, U. North Tex., 1991. Lic. profl. counselor, Tex.; lic. chem. dependency counselor, Tex.; nat. cert. addictions counselor II.; nat. cert. clin. hypnotherapist. Substance abuse technician Tarrant Coun. Mental Health-Mental Retardation, Ft. Worth, 1986; substance abuse counselor CPC Millwood Hosp., Arlington, Tex., 1986-89; family therapist Parkside Lodge-Westgate, Denton, Tex., 1989-90; co-dependence therapist, dir. Parkside Outpatient Svcs., Ft. Worth, 1990-91; psychotherapist Behavioral Health Unit La Hacienda Treatment Ctr., Hunt, Tex.; pvt. practice Kerrville, Tex., 1991—; peer evaluator Tex. Bd. Alcoholism and Drug Counselors, Austin, 1988—; allied staff La Hacienda, Charter Hosp., Hill Country Crisis Coun.; practicum supr. Hill Country Coun. on Alcoholism, Hill Country Ind. House, Sid Peterson Regional Hosp.; ct. cons. 216th Dist. Ct., Kerrville, Tex.; clin. supr. Youth Habitat Tex.; adj. psychology faculty San Antonio Coll. Author: Adult Recovery Handbook, 1988. Cmty. liaison Mid-South Redevel. Assn., Ft. Worth, 1979-83; mem. Fairmount Assn., Ft. Worth, 1979-84; bd. dirs. Mid-South Housing Coop. Study, Ft. Worth, 1983, Ctr. Point Alliance for Progress. Mem. ACA, Tex. Assn. Alcoholism and Drug Counselors, Nat. Assn. Alcoholism and Drug Abuse Counselors, Tex. Counseling Assn., Tex. Mental Health Counselors Assn. (treas.), Matt Talbot Retreat Movement (sec. 1989-91), Nat. Assn. Eagle Scouts, Order of Arrow, Rotary, Hill Country Men's Rehab. House (dir.). Episcopalian. Office: The Comfort Zone 180 Guadalupe Plz Kerrville TX 78028

RHODES, MARLENE RUTHERFORD, counseling educator, educational consultant; b. St. Louis; d. Odie Douglas and Helen (Ward) Rutherford; m. David L. Rhodes, Nob. 18, 1961; children: Jay David, Michael Stanford, John David, Mark Stanford. BS in Psychology cum laude, Washington U., St. Louis, 1973, MA in Counseling Edn., 1975; postgrad., St. Louis U., 1987—. Registered med. record libr. Caseworker I and II, Mo. Div. Family Svcs., St. Louis, 1961-65, supr. caseworker II's, 1965-70; personal effectiveness trainer women's program U. Mo., St. Louis, 1974-77; assoc. prof. counseling, chair counseling St. Louis C.C. at Forest Park, 1975—, chmn. dept., 1993—, dir. step up coll. program, 1990-93; developer, coord. crisis intervention facilitation tng. St. Louis Pub. Schs., 1987-88; ednl. project cons. Project Achievement, Ralston Purina Co., 1993-94; developer, presenter over 80 ednl. project consultations for area colls., profl. orgns. and bus. groups, 1975—. Author: Crisis Intervention Facilitation Training Manual, 1988. Chmn. Ft. Louis Friends of Arts, 1984—; coord. for coun. of elders for Better Family Life Orgn., 1995—; com. co-chmn. for black dance and unity ball Better Family Inc., St. Louis, 1990—; panelist for counseling support svcs. for families United Way Greater St. Louis, 1993—; mem. fin. com. St. Thomas Archdiocese, 1995—; bd. dirs. Bishop Hearly Cath. Sch. Recipient Disting. Svc. as Am. Educator award Alpha Zeta chpt. Iota Phi Lambda, 1990, role model award St. Louis Pub. Schs., 1993, cert. of achievement Nat. Orgn. for Victim Assistance, 1993. Mem. NEA (co-coord. polit. action com. St. Louis 1985-90, bargaining negotiator 1987—), ACA (nat. chair orgn., adminstrn. and mgmt. com. 1994-95), Assn. Multicultural Counseling and Devel. (nat. pres. 1994-95), Nat. Assn. for Multicultural Counseling and Devel. (rep. for 13 states 1990-92, pres. 1994-95, Exemplary Svc. award 1992, 94), Mo. Assn. Multicultural Counseling and Devel. (chpt. pres. 1977-78). Democrat. Roman Catholic. Home: 5935 Pershing Ave Saint Louis MO 63112-1513 Office: St Louis CC at Forest Park 5600 Oakland Ave Saint Louis MO 63110-1316

RHODES, PATRICIA ANNE, health information officer; b. Lincoln, Nebr., May 23, 1963; d. Billy Dean Inbody and Juliana (Mestl) Inbody-Buller; m. Thomas Eugene Rhodes, June 22, 1985; children: Julia Anne, Jordan Thomas. BS in Med. Record Adminstrn., Coll. of St. Mary, Omaha, 1985. Med. record abstractor St. Francis Med. Ctr., Grand Island, Nebr., 1985, diagnostic related groups/utilization review coord., 1985-87; diagnostic related groups coord. VA Med. Ctr., Grand Island, Nebr., 1987-88, chief health info. mgmt., 1988—; mem. health info. mgmt. adv. coun. Dept. Vet. Affairs, VA Ctrl. Office, Washington, 1994—. Mem. Am. Health Info. Mgmt. Assn. (registered records adminstr.), Nat. Hemophilia Found. (Nebr. chpt. sec., bd. dirs. 1993—), Nebr. Health Info. Mgmt. (1st and 2d yr. dir. 1992-93, del. 1993-95, pres.-elect 1994—). Home: 3571 Summer Dr Grand Island NE 68803-6517 Office: VA Med Ctr 2201 N Broadwell Grand Island NE 68803

RHODES, RONDELL HORACE, biology educator; b. Abbeville, S.C., May 25, 1918; s. Leslie Franklin and Pearl Lee (Clinkscales) R.; B.S., Benedict Coll., Columbia, S.C., 1940; M.S., U. Mich., 1950; Ph.D., N.Y.U., 1960. Instr. biology Lincoln U., Jefferson City, Mo., 1947-49; asst. prof. Tuskegee (Ala.) Inst., 1950-55; teaching fellow N.Y.U., 1955-61; mem. faculty Fairleigh Dickinson U., Teaneck, N.Y., 1961—, prof. biol. scis., 1968-88, prof. emeritus, 1988—; chmn. dept., 1966-70, 73-76, 79-82. Served with AUS, 1942-46. Mem. AAAS, Am. Inst. Biol. Scis., Am. Soc. Zoologists, AAUP, Nat. Assn. Biology Tchrs., N.Y. Acad. Scis., Sigma Xi. Democrat. Episcopalian. Home: 122 Ashland Pl Apt 5H Brooklyn NY 11201-3910 Office: Fairleigh Dickinson U Teaneck NJ 07666

RHONEY, DALE V., orthodontist; b. Hickory, N.C., Aug. 28, 1945; s. Otis Lee and Perry Lea (Propst) R.; m. Kay Susan Moffat, June 1, 1968; children: Suzanne, Michelle. BS in Dentistry, U. N.C., 1967, DDS, 1970. Orthodontist pvt. practice, Lake Oswego, Oreg., 1975—; clin. instr. orthodontic dept. U. Oreg. Sch. Dentistry, Portland, 1976-81, asst. prof., 1981—. Dir. Lake Oswego Sch. Dist. Found., 1995. Capt. USAF, 1970-73. Named Eagle Scout Boy Scouts Am., Harlingen, Tex., 1959. Fellow Am. Coll. Dentistry; mem. Am. Assn. Orthodontists, Am. Dental Assn., Pacific Coast Soc. Orthodontists, Oreg. State Soc. Orthodontists, Oreg. Dental Soc., Clackamas Dental Soc. (pres. 1985), Angle ORthodontic Soc. (pres. 1996—), Rotary (pres. 1985), Pi Kappa Phi (pledge master 1966-67), Xi Psu Phi (pres. 1970). Office: 507 A Ave Lake Oswego OR 97034

RHOTON, ALBERT LOREN, JR., neurological surgery educator; b. Parvin, Ky., Nov. 18, 1932; s. Albert Loren and Hazel Arnette (Van Cleve) R.; m. Joyce L. Moldenhauer, June 23, 1957; children: Eric L., Albert J., Alice S., Laural A. BS, Ohio State U., 1954; MD cum laude, Washington U., St. Louis, 1959. Diplomate Am. Bd. Neurol. Surgery (bd. dirs. 1985-91, vice chmn. 1991). Intern, Columbia Presbyn. Med. Ctr., N.Y.C., 1959; resident in neurol. surgery Barnes Hosp., St. Louis, 1961-65; cons. neurol. surgery Mayo Clinic, Rochester, Minn., 1965-72; chief div. neurol. surgery U. Fla., Gainesville, 1972-80, R.D. Keene prof. and chmn. dept. neurol. surgery, 1980—; developer microsurg. tng. ctr.; guest lectr. Neurol. Socs. Switzerland, Japan, Venezuela, France, Columbia, Middle East, Brazil, Japan, Mex., Can., Costa Rica, Uruguay, Korea, Australia, Egypt, Argentina, Hong Kong, UK, Turkey; invited faculty and guest lectr. Harvard U., Washington U., Emory, U., UCLA, U. Calif., San Francisco, U. Miami, U. Okla., U. So. Calif., U. Mich., Northwestern U., U. Chgo., U. Pa., Johns Hopkins U., Ohio State U., Temple U., Duke U., Cornell U., NYU, U. Cin., Tulane U., Vanderbilt, U. Minnesota, U. Md., U. Pa., Albany Med. Coll., Cleve. Clin. Found., St. Louis U., Henry Ford Med. Found., Med. Coll. N.Y., Jefferson Med. Coll., Hahnemann Med. Coll., U. P.R., U. Calif., Irvine, U. Hong Kong, La. State U., U. Ky., U. Louisville, Singapore Nat. U. Recipient Disting. Faculty award U. Fla., 1981, Alumni Achievement award Washington U. Sch. Medicine, 1985, Jones award for outstanding spl. med. exhibit of yr. Am. Assn. Med. Illustrators, 1969; grantee NIH, VA, Am. Heart Assn.; awarded hon. memberships neurosurg. socs. of Brazil, Japan, Mex., Can., Uruguay, Venezuela, Tex., Okla., Wis., Ga., Rocky Mountain. Mem. ACS (bd. govs. 1978-84), Congress Neurol. Surgeons (pres. 1978, honored guest 1993), Nat. Found. Brain Rsch. (bd. dirs. 1990-94), Nat. Coalition for Rsch. in Neurol. Disorders (bd. dirs. 1990-94), Fla. Neurosurgical Soc. (pres. 1978), Am. Assn. Neurol. Surgeons (chmn. vascular sect., treas. 1983-86, v.p. 1987-88, pres. 1989-90, exec. com. 1993), Soc. Neurol. Surgeons (treas. 1975-81, pres. 1993), So. Neurol. Soc. (v.p. 1976), Alachua County Med. Soc. (exec. com. 1978), AMA (Billings Bronze medal for sci. exhibit 1969), Fla. Med. Assn., Am. Surg. Assn., Soc. Univ. Neurosurgeons, Am. Heart Assn. (stroke coun., Outstanding Achievement award 1971), North Am. Skull Base Soc. (pres. 1993-94), Am. Acad. Neurol. Surgery, Neurol. Soc. Am., Acoustic Neuroma Assn. (med. adv. bd. 1983—, chmn. 1992—), Trigeminal Neurol. Assn. (med. advisor bd. 1992—). Designed over 200 microsurgery instruments. Author: Orbit and Sellar Region, 1996; contbr. numerous articles to profl. jours.; mem. editorial bd. Neurosurgery, Jour. Microsurgery, Surgical Neurology, Jour. Fla. Med. Assn., Am. Jour. Otology, Skull Base Surgery. Home: 2505 NW 22nd Ave Gainesville FL 32605-3819 Office: U Fla Shands Hosp Gainesville FL 32610

RHYNE, DENNIS ALFRED, orthopedic surgeon; b. N.Y.C., Mar. 21, 1943; s. Elbert Alfred and Florence Ann (Klein) R.; m. Linda Lee Forsey; children: Cheryl, Laura, Mathew, Dennis Jr., Pegeen. BS, Fordham U., 1964; MD, N.J. Coll. Medicine, 1968. Diplomate Am. Bd. Orthopaedic Surgery; cert. qualified med. evaluator. Intern U.S. Naval Hosp., St. Albans, N.Y., 1969-72; resident U.S. Naval Hosp., Oakland, Calif., 1969-72, A.I. duPont Inst., Wilmington, Del., 1972-73; staff orthopaedic surgeon U.S. Naval Regional Med. Ctr., Long Beach, Calif., 1974-76; pvt. practice orthopaedic surgery Laguna Hills, Calif., 1976—; chief orthopedics Mission Hosp., 1982-83; sec.-treas. med. staff Saddleback Hosp. 1981-82, vice chief of staff, 1982-84, chief of staff, 1985-86, bd. dirs., 1985-87; mem. staff Mission Regional Med. Ctr., Mission Viejo, Calif., 1976—, Saddleback Meml. Ctr., Laguna Hills, 1976—, Irvine (Calif.) Med. Ctr., 1990-92; bd. dirs. Orange County PSRO, 1981-82. V.p. Calif. Dept. Res. Officers Assn., 1989-90. Capt. USN, 1967-76, res., 1990-91, Operation Desert Shield/Storm. Fellow ACS, Am. Acad. Orthopaedic Surgeons; mem. AMA, Calif. Med. Assn. (alternate del. 1988-91, 91-92, del. 1992—), Soc. Mil. Orthopaedic Surgeons, Western Orthopaedic Assn., Soc. Mil. Orthopaedic Surgeons. Office: Ste 420 24411 Health Center Dr Laguna Hills CA 92653

RIBAR, DIXIE LEE, nursing administrator; b. Albia, Iowa, June 22, 1938; d. Eugene Guy Clark and Margaret Ellen (Edwards) De Joode; m. John David Ribar, Aug. 22, 1959 (div. 1981); children: Michael, Christopher, Patrick. Diploma, St. Joseph Hosp. Sch. Nursing, Ottumwa, Iowa, 1959; BSN, U. Dubuque, 1987, MSN, 1991. RN, Iowa; cert. emergency room nurse; cert. emergency med. technician, Iowa. Staff nurse Ottumwa Hosp., 1959-60; surg. staff nurse Jane Lamb Hosp., Clinton, Iowa, 1960-67; dir. nursing ICU-CCU Jane Lamb Health Ctr., Clinton, Iowa, 1967-79, dir. cardiac rehab., 1980-86; instr. edn. Samaritan Health Ctr., Clinton, 1986-91; nurse mgr. Asbury-Salina (Kans.) Regional Med. Ctr., 1991-92; assoc. chief nursing svc. ambulatory care VA Med. Ctr., Knoxville, Iowa, 1992-93, chief ambulatory care svcs., 1993—; internat. edn. cons. Am.-Mideast Ednl. and Tng. Svcs., 1989-90; contractual instr. med. svcs. Emergency Learning Resources Ctr., Univ. Iowa Hosp., Iowa City, 1976-90, Ea. Iowa Community Coll., Davenport, Iowa, 1978-90, Marycrest Coll., Davenport, 1986-90; parmedic River Cities Ambulance Co., Clinton, 1987-90; presenter in field. Contbr. articles to profl. jours. Bd. dirs. Clinton County Heart Assn., 1976-90; coord. emergency med. tech. program Clinton Fire Dept., 1980-88; med. missionary 1st Congl. Ch. Clinton, Ghana, 1983. Mem. ANA, Emergency Nurses Assn., Kans. Emergency Nurses Assn., Iowa Nurses Assn. Republican. Roman Catholic. Home: 905 W Robinson St Knoxville IA 50138-2822 Office: VA Med Ctr 1515 W Pleasant St Knoxville IA 50138-3354

RIBBLE, RONALD GEORGE, psychologist, educator, writer; b. West Reading, Pa., May 7, 1937; s. Jeremiah George and Mildred Sarah (Folk) R.; m. Catalina Valenzuela (Torres), Sept. 30, 1961; children: Christina, Timothy, Kenneth. BSEE cum laude, U. Mo., 1968, MSEE, 1969, MA, 1985, PhD, 1986. Cert. psychologist, Tex. Enlisted man USAF, 1956-60, advance through grades to lt. col., 1976; rsch. dir. Coping Resources, Inc., Columbia, Mo., 1986; pres., co-owner Towers and Rushing Ltd., San Antonio, 1986—; referral devel. Laughlin Pavilion Psychiat. Hosp., Kirksville, Mo., 1987; program dir. Psychiat. Insts. of Am., Iowa Falls, Iowa, 1987-88; lead psychotherapist Gasconade County Counseling Ctr., Hermann, Mo., 1988; lectr. U. Tex., San Antonio, 1989—, Trinity U., San Antonio, 1995—; assessment clinician Afton Oaks Psychiat. Hosp., San Antonio, 1989-91; psychologist Olmos Psychol. Svcs., Inc., San Antonio, 1991-93; vol. assessor Holmgreen Children's Shelter, San Antonio, 1992-93; condr. seminars, revs. for maj. pubs. Author: Apples, Weeds, and Doggie Poo, 1995; contbr. essays to psychol. reference books and poetry to anthologies periodicals, lyrics to popular music; columnist Feelings, 1993—; public access TV appearances, 1991—. Del. Boone County (Mo.) Dem. Conv., 1984; vol. announcer pub. radio sta., Columbia, 1993; contbg. mem. Dem. Nat. Com., 1983—, Presdl. Congl. Task Force, 1994; vol. counselor Cath. Family and Children's Svc., San Antonio, 1989-91; chpt. advisor Rational Recovery Program for Alcoholics, San Antonio, 1991-92; mem. Pres. Leadership Cir., 1994-95. Recipient Roberts Meml. Prize in Poetry, 1995. Mem. APA, AAUP, NEA, ACLU, Am. Coll. Forensic Examiners, Internat. Soc. for Study of Individual Differences, Internat. Platform Assn. (Poetry award 1995), Bexar County Psychol. Assn., Air Force Assn., Ret. Officers Assn, People for the Am. Way, Poetry Soc. Am., Acad. Am. Poets. Roman Catholic. Home: 14023 N Hills Village Dr San Antonio TX 78249-2531 Office: U Tex Divsn Cultural and Sci San Antonio TX 78249 also: Towers and Rushing Ltd San Antonio TX 78249

RIBBY, ALICE MARIE, nurse; b. Lowell, Mich., Oct. 16, 1943; d. Merle Levi and Merleen Maude (Gooden) Bickford; children: Bobette Morgan, Mylie Wasylewski, Joseph R. Ribby, Barbara A. Cupp. AD in Gen. Edn. cum laude, Lansing (Mich.) Community Coll., 1975, AS in Nursing cum laude, 1976; BA in Family Life Edn., Spring Arbor Coll., 1992. Nurse ICU Ingham Med. Ctr., Lansing, Mich., 1976-81; nurse acute and chronic hemo and peritoneal dialysis Sparrow Hosp., Lansing, Mich., 1983-84; head nurse, alternate CEO Community Dialysis Ctr., Jackson, Mich., 1984-87, dir. Continuous Ambulatory Peritoneal Dialysis Program; dialysis cons. Cmty. Dialysis Ctr.; nursing supr. Doctor's Hosp., Jackson, Mich., 1987-90; co-founder, co-owner, nurse therapist St. Lawrence Hosp., Diamondale and Lansing, Mich., 1990-95, Ptnrs. Psychol. Svcs., Lansing, 1994—; nurse cons., mental health therapist OBRA program Cmty. Mental Health-Older Adults Svcs., Lansing, 1996—; lectr. in field, preenter workshops and seminars on childhood sexual abuse; founder One Another's Support Group. Mem. Am. Assn. Christian Counselors, Profl. Staff Devel. Orgn. Republican. Address: 301 Ann St Mason MI 48854-1203

RIBET, MICHEL ELIE, surgery educator; b. Dunkirk, Nord, France, June 28, 1928; s. Daniel Leon Ribet and Jeanne Henriette Degand; m. Beatrice Jane Foster, Aug. 4, 1951; children: Marc Daniel, Michel Alexis, Carole Jane. MD, U. Lille, France, 1952. Diplomate Bd. Surgery. Agrégé des universités Lille, France, 1958-67; prof. semiology U. Lille, Lille, France, 1967-70, prof. surgery, 1970-96. Co-author: (with P. Razemon) Chirurgie du Mediastin, 1970; author: Chirurgie Thoracique Générale, 1989; contbr. articles to profl. jours. Served with French Navy Reserve. Decorated Legion of Honor, Palmes Academiques Ministry Edn. (France); recipient Prix Nat. for med.-surg. film Cannes Festival, 1959, Prix Dubar, 1956. Mem. Acad. Surgery (pres. 1992-93), European Assn. Cardiothoracic Surgery (v.p. 1993), French Coll. Thoracic and Cardiovasc. Surgery (pres. 1993-96), Am. Soc. Thoracic Surgery, N.Y. Acad. Scis. Roman Catholic. Home: 2 Rue de Condé, 59110 La Madeleine France Office: Ctr Hosp Reg & U Lille, Bd Pr J Leclercq, 59037 Lille France

RICCA, JOSEPH JOHN, internist, gastroenterologist; b. Bklyn., Nov. 26, 1925; s. John F. and Josephine C. (Ingegno) R.; m. Heather Moira Dorman, Dec. 11, 1965; children: Gerald, Laurie Ellen, Joseph Patrick. BS, Fordham U., 1949; MD, SUNY, Bklyn., 1953. Diplomate Am. Bd. Internal Medicine, Am. Bd. Gastroenterology. Intern L.I. Coll. Hosp., Bklyn., 1953-54, resident, 1954-56; chief resident Bklyn. VA Hosp., 1956-57; gastroenterology fellow L.I. Coll. Hosp., 1972-73, chief gastroenterology, 1979-84; chief gastroenterology Victory Meml. Hosp., Bklyn., 1984-94; attending staff Victory Meml. Hosp., 1984—; pvt. practice Bklyn., 1957—; cons. medicine, L.I. Coll. Hosp., 1991—; clin. asst. prof. SUNY, Bklyn., 1972-89. Contbg. author: Prevention of Kidney Disease and Long Term Survival, 1982; contbr. articles to profl. jours. Recipient Physicians Recognition award AMA, 1969-73, 73-77, 77-83. Fellow ACP, Am. Coll. Gastroenterology. Office: 235 Bay Ridge Pkwy Brooklyn NY 11209

RICCI, JOHN LAWRENCE, surgical oncologist; b. Bklyn., Sept. 9, 1953. BS magna cum laude, Lehigh U., 1975; MD, N.Y.U., 1979. Surgical oncologist Northshore U. Hosp., Manhasset, N.Y., 1987—; gen. surgeon U. Pa., 1985; oncologist Meml. Sloan Kettering, 1987. Contbr. articles to profl. jours. Fellow Am. Cancer Soc., ACS; mem. Met. Breast Cancer Group, Assn. Acad. Surgery. Office: NorthShore U Hosp 300 Community Dr Manhasset NY 11030

RICCIARDI, ANTONIO, prosthodontist, implantologist, educator; b. Jersey City, June 5, 1922; s. Frank and Eugenia (Izzo) R.; m. Lucy DePalma, June 21, 1945; children: Eugenia, Lynda. Student Upsala Coll., 1941-42, BA in Chemistry, 1951; DDS, Temple U., 1958. Diplomate Am. Bd. Oral Implantology, Am. Bd. Implant Dentistry. Purchasing agt. Dade Bros., Newark, Airport, 1951-52; asst. work mgr. Cooper Alloy Steel Co., Hillside, N.J., 1954; chemist White's Pharm. Co., Union, N.J., 1954; practice gen. dentistry, Westfield, N.J., 1958—; dentist Westfield Public Schs., 1958-60; mem. staff Mountainside Hosp., Montclair, N.J., St. Elizabeth's Hosp., Elizabeth, N.J.; implant staff John F. Kennedy Hosp., Edison, N.J., chief of prosthetics, 1980—; clin. chmn. implant study Columbia U. Sch. Oral Surgery and Dentistry; implant cons. Columbia Presbyn. Sch. Oral Surgery and Dentistry, N.Y.C.; cons. Implants Internat., N.Y.C., 1971—; pres. Universal Dental Implements, Inc., 1979—. Pres. Nat. Gymnastics Clinic, Sarasota, Fla., 1968—; v.p. rebound tumbling center Welmarick Inc., Plainfield, 1958—. Gymnastics ofcl. Eastern Coll. Conf., 1954—. Served to lt. col. USMCR, figter pilot, 1942-48, jet fighter pilot, 52-54, Korea. Fellow Acad. Gen. Dentistry, Royal Soc. Health (Eng.), Internat. Coll. Oral Implantology (founding mem.), Am. Acad. Gen. Dentistry, Am. Acad. Implant Dentistry (program chmn. nat. conv. 1974, sec. 1976, pres. N.E. sect. 1978, chmn. ethics com. 1980, ethics chmn. 1981, credentialling mem. 1985—), Acad. Dentistry Internat., Am. Acad. Implant Dentistry, Fedn. Dentistry Internat.; hon fellow Italian and German implant socs.; mem. Inst. Endosseous Implants, Inst. for Advance Dental Research, ADA, Middlesex County Dental Assn., Union County and Plainfield Dental Soc. Fedn. Prosthodontics Orgns., Internat. Research Com. on Oral Implantology (pres. U.S. chpt.), Am. Acad. Oral Implantology, Nat. Gymnastics Judges Assn. (pres. Eastern div.; named to Gymnastic Hall of Fame 1978), Delta Sigma Delta. Writer, tchr. on implantology. Address: 1450 Fernwood Rd Mountainside NJ 07092-2503

RICCULLI, NICHOLAS PATRICK, cardiologist; b. Jersey City, N.J., Mar. 28, 1958; s. Joseph M. and Louise M. (Mango) R.; m. Anne M. Johnson, June 26, 1983. BA, NYU, 1980; DO, U. Medicine & Dentistry N.J., 1985. Diplomate Am. Bd. Internal Medicine; cert. medicine and cardiology. Pvt. practice Morristown (N.J.) Med. Cardiology Assn., 1991—. Fellow Am. Coll. Cardiology. Office: 95 Madison Ave Morristown NJ 07960-6092

RICE, ANNIE L. KEMPTON, medical, surgical and rehabilitation nurse; b. West Fairlee, Vt., Oct. 26, 1932; d. James Warren and Lena May (Bower); m. Abbott Eames Rice, Aug. 29, 1959; children: James W., Beverly A., Abbott Jr., David K. Diploma, Mary Hitchcock Sch. Nursing, Hanover, N.H., 1955; student, U. R.I., 1956-57; BSN, Boston U., 1959; postgrad., St. Anthlems Coll., Manchester, N.H. RN. Staff nurse spl. care unit R.I. Hosp., 1955; staff nurse New Eng. Deaconess Hosp., Boston, 1957; head nurse Jordan Hosp, Plymouth, Mass., 1960; staff nurse ICU/emergency Lakes Region Hosp., Laconia, N.H., 1968; staff nurse Pine Hill Nurses Registry, Nashua, N.H., 1976; charge nurse Greenbriar Terr., Nashua, 1985—. Past mem. Arthritis Found. Mem. Mary Hitchcock Sch. Nursing Alumnae, Boston U. Alumnae, Ea. Star, Grange, Women's Club. Home: 28 Sunland Dr Hudson NH 03051-3209

RICE, CHARLES LANE, surgical educator; b. Atlanta, May 22, 1945; s. Marion Jennings and Molly Black (Moore) R.; m. Lynn Carol Inscoe, Dec. 27, 1968 (div. 1976); m. Judith Josephine Bousha, July 9, 1977; children: Aaron Nicholas, Patrick Marion. AB, U. Ga., 1964; MD, Med. Coll. Ga., 1968. Commd. ensign USN, 1966, advanced through grades to comdr., 1976, ret., 1977; intern Bowman Gray Sch. Medicine, Winston-Salem, N.C., 1968-69; resident Nat. Naval Med. Ctr., Bethesda, Md., 1969-73; asst. prof. surgery U. Chgo., 1977-80, assoc. prof. surgery, 1980-84; dir. intensive care unit Michael Reese Hosp., Chgo., 1977-84; prof., vice chmn. dept. surgery U. Wash., Seattle, 1985-92; surgeon-in-chief Harborview Med. Ctr., Seattle, 1985-92; Dr. Lee Hudson- Robert R. Penn prof., chmn., divsn. gen. surgery U. Tex. Southwestern Med. Ctr., Dallas, 1992-93; prof. surgery U. Ill., Chgo., 1993—; sr. assoc. dean Coll. Medicine, 1994—; Robert Wood Johnson Health Policy fellow, 1991-92; legis. asst. to U.S. senator Tom Daschle, 1991-92; vice chmn. Com. Trauma, Am. Coll. Surgeons, Chgo., 1992-93; ann. lectr. U. Wash., Soc. U. Surgeons. Assoc. editor Jour. of Surg. Rsch., 1983-90; contbr. articles to profl. jours. Fellow ACS (gov. 1992—. vice chmn. com. on trauma 1992-93), Am. Surg. Assn., Am. Assn. for Surgery of Trauma (com. chair 1989-91); mem. Soc. Univ. Surgeons, Am. Physiol. Soc., Shock Soc. (pres. 1991-92). Democrat. Episcopalian. Office: U of IL Com Office of the Dean 1819 W Polk St # C 784 Chicago IL 60612-7331

RICE, CYNTHIA ANN, critical care nurse; b. Lakewood, Ohio, Feb. 4, 1968; d. Charles Foster and Olga Ann (Hilder) Palmer; m. Andrew D. Rice, Febr. 29, 1992. AA, Cuyahoga C.C., 1988; BSN, Cleve. State U., 1991. CCRN. Staff nurse Aristocrat Berea (Ohio) Nursing Facility, 1991-92; staff nurse CCU Southwest Gen. Hosp., Middleburg Heights, Ohio, 1992—, chair CCU-patient & family advocacy coun., 1994—, ACLS instr., 1995. Mem. AACN. Republican. Home: 445 Laurel Dr Berea OH 44017

RICE, DOROTHY PECHMAN (MRS. JOHN DONALD RICE), medical economist; b. Bklyn., June 11, 1922; d. Gershon and Lena (Schiff) Pechman; m. John Donald Rice, Apr. 3, 1943; children: Kenneth D., Donald B., Thomas H. Student, Bklyn. Coll., 1938-39; BA, U. Wis., 1941; DSc (hon.), Coll. Medicine and Dentistry N.J., 1979. With hosp., and med. facilities USPHS, Washington, 1960-61; med. econs. studies Social Security Adminstrn., 1962-63; health econs. br. Community Health Svc., USPHS, 1964-65; chief health ins. rsch. br. Social Security Adminstrn., 1966-72, dep. asst. commr. for rsch. and statistics, 1972-75; dir. Nat. Ctr. for Health Stats., Rockville, Md., 1976-82; prof. Inst. Health & Aging U. Calif., San Francisco, 1982-94, prof. emeritus, 1994—; developer, mgr. nationwide health info. svcs.; expert on aging, health care costs, disability, and cost-of-illness. Contbr. articles to profl. jours. Recipient Social Security Adminstrn. citation, 1968, Disting. Service medal HEW, 1974, Jack C. Massey Found. award, 1978. Fellow Am. Public Health Assn. (domestic award for excellence 1978, Sedgwick Meml. medal, 1988), Am. Statis. Assn.; mem. Inst. Medicine, Assn. Health Svcs. Rsch. (President's award 1988), Am. Econ. Assn., Population Assn. Am., LWV. Home: 13895 Campus Dr Oakland CA 94605-3831 Office: U Calif Sch Nursing Calif San Francisco CA 94143-0646

RICE, EILEEN MARIE, physician, neurologist; b. Pitts., June 8, 1950; m. Marc Rice; children: David, Heather, Lori, Mara, Natalie. MD, U. Pitts., 1974. Diplomate Am. Bd. Neurology. Intern Montefiore U. Hosp., Pitts., 1974-75; neurologist Neurol. Neurosurg. Assocs., Pitts., 1979—; resident in neurology Montefiore U. Hosp., Pitts., 1976-79. Mem. AMA, Am. Acad. Neurology, Pa. Med. Soc., Allegheny County Med. Soc. Office: Neurol Neurosurg Assocs 3471 5th Ave Pittsburgh PA 15213

RICE, EMANUEL, psychiatrist, educator; b. N.Y.C., July 26, 1927; s. Samuel and Minnie (Feder) R.; m. Harriet T. Nahum, May 8, 1966. BA, Bklyn. Coll., 1951; MA, Columbia U., 1955; MD, Howard U., 1961. Diplomate Am. Bd. Psychiatry and Neurology. Rotating intern Lenox Hill Hosp., N.Y.C., 1961-62; resident Manhattan State Hosp., 1962-65; pvt. practice N.Y.C., 1965—; attending in psychiatry Mt. Sinai Hosp., N.Y.C., 1965—; clin. prof. psychiatry Mt. Sinai Sch. Medicine, N.Y.C., 1965—. Author: Freud and Moses - The Long Journey Home, 1990; contbr. articles to profl. jours. Mem. Am. Psychiat. Assn. Office: 19 E 88th St New York NY 10128-0557

RICE, JAMES PHILIP, surgeon; b. Richland, Wash., Dec. 2, 1956; s. James Edward and Elizabeth Agnus (O'Leary) R. BS, Wash. State U., 1979; MD, St. Louis U., 1983. Diplomate Am. Bd. Surgery. Commd. officer USN, 1983, advanced through grades to comdr., 1994; intern in gen. surgery Nat. Naval Med. Ctr., Bethesda, Md., 1983-84; resident gen. surgery Nat. Naval Med. Ctr., Bethesda, 1985-89; med. dept. head USS Nassau, 1984-85; staff surg. privileges Naval Hosp., Jacksonville, 1989-90; ship's surgeon USS Saratoga, 1989-90; staff surgeon Naval Hosp. Bremerton, 1991-93, head dept. surgery, 1992-93; staff surgeon Naval Hosp. Jacksonville, 1993—, asst. dept. head, 1995—; asst. prof. Uniformed Svcs. U. of the Health Scis., 1995—. Decorated Navy Commendation medals USN, 1985, 90, Navy Achievement medals, 1992. Fellow ACS; mem. AMA, Am. Bd. Surgery, ACS (Jacksonville chpt.), Soc. Laparoendoscopic Surgeons, Bethesda Surg. Soc., Assn. Mil. Surgeons of the U.S., St. Louis U. Sch. Medicine Alumni Assn., Phi Chi Med. Fraternity Alumni Assn. Office: Naval Hosp Dept Surgery Jacksonville FL 32214

RICE, JERRY MERCER, biochemist; b. Washington, Oct. 3, 1940; s. John Earle Rice and Leona (Mercer) Greiner; m. Mary Jane Janocha, Jan. 10, 1978; children: Stacey Lynn, Stephen Mark. BA, Wesleyan U., 1962; PhD, Harvard U., 1966. Commd. officer USPHS, 1966; rsch. scientist Nat. Cancer Inst., Bethesda, Md., 1966-81, chief Lab. of Comparative Carcinogenesis, Frederick, Md., 1981-94, 96; assoc. dir. Frederick Cancer Rsch. and Devel. Ctr., Nat. Cancer Inst., Frederick, Md., 1994-95, acting dir. divsn. cancer etiology, 1994-95; sr. scientist WHO, 1996—; chief Unit of Carcinogen Identification and Evaluation Internat. Agy. for Rsch. on Cancer, Lyons, France, 1996—; lectr. univs., profl. groups, med. socs. Editor: Perinatal Carcinogenesis, 1979. Co-editor: Organ and Species Specificity in Chemical Carcinogenesis, 1983, Perinatal and Multigeneration Carcinogenesis, 1989; contbr. rsch. articles and revs. in mechanisms of chem. carcinogenesis to profl. jours. Mem. Am. Soc. Microbiology, Am. Assn. Cancer Research, Internat. Soc. of Differentiation, Teratology Soc., Phi Beta Kappa, Sigma Xi. Avocation: viticulture. Home: 3213 Coquelin Ter Bethesda MD 20815-4840 Office: Internat Org Rsch Cancer, 150 Cours Albert Thomas, 69372 Cedex 08 Lyon France

RICE, JOHN DILLARD, ophthalmologist; b. Columbus, Ohio, June 23, 1940; s. Harvey M. and Dorothy (Dillard) R.; m. Mary Elizabeth Hulings, July 13, 1963 (div.); children: Mary Elizabeth, Katherine Dillard; m. Barbara Jean Olson, July 20, 1982; 1 child, Alison. BA, Carleton Coll., 1962; MD, U. Minn., 1966. Diplomate Am. Bd. Ophthalmology. Pvt. practice Highland Eye Clinic, St. Paul, 1982—. Major U.S. Army, 1967-70. Mem. AMA, Am. Acad. Ophthalmology, Minn. Med. Assn., Minn. Acad. Ophthalmology. Home: 1807 Hillcrest Ave Saint Paul MN 55116 Office: Highland Eye Clinic 2221 Ford Pkwy Saint Paul MN 55116

RICE, JOHN OSCAR, oral-maxillofacial surgeon; b. Waukegan Ill., Mar. 12, 1945; s. Maurice Gregory and Elizabeth Louise (Weber) R.; m. Janna Lou Nelson, July 29, 1972; children: Sonja, Kristin, Natalie. BS, U. Iowa, 1967, DDS, 1971. Diplomate Am. Bd. Oral and Maxillofacial Surgery; lic. dentist, Iowa, Wis. Resident U. Chgo. Hosps., 1971-74; pvt. practice Spring Park Oral and Maxillofacial Surgery, Davenport, Iowa, 1974—. Divsn. chmn. United Way of QCA, Rock Island, Ill., 1984; dir. Cmty. Health Care, Davenport, 1980-83; treas. Bettendorf (Iowa) Presbyn. Ch., 1979-81, 87-90. Fellow Am. Assn. Oral and Maxillofacial Surgery (del. 1982-83), Iowa Soc. Oral and Maxillofacial Surgeons (sec.-treas. 197682, pres. 1990-91), Am Dental Soc. of Anesthesiology; mem. ADA, Iowa Dental Soc. (trustee 1971—), Scott County Dental Soc., Davenport Dist. Dental Soc. (prs. 1991), Am. Assn. Oral Surgery (del. 1982-87), Midwest Soc. Oral and Maxillofacial Surgery. Office: Spring Park Oral/Max Surg 3319 Spring St #204 Davenport IA 52807

RICE, JOHN RUSSELL, physician; b. Pensacola, Fla., Mar. 8, 1942; s. George Frank and Rosa (Russell) R.; m. Celia Ann Lawrence, June 10, 1964; children: Timothy Russell, Christian Cameron, Matthew Dana. BS in zoology, Duke Univ., 1964; MD, Univ. Miami, 1968. Diplomate Am. Bd. Internal Medicine. Major U.S. Army Medical Corps., Docheim, Germany, 1970-73; internship Duke Univ. Medical Ctr., Durham, N.C., 1968-69, residency JAR/SAR, 1969-70, 73-74, fellowship rheumatology, 1974-76, clinical assoc., 1976-78, asst. prof., 1978-86, assoc. prof., 1986—. Fellow Am. Coll. Rheumatology; mem. AMA, N.C. Medical Soc., Orange County Medical Soc. Republican. Methodist. Office: Duke Univ Medical Ctr Box 3383 Med Ctr Durham NC 27710

RICE, JON RICHARD, state health officer, physician; b. Grand Forks, N.D., July 10, 1946; s. Harry Frazer and Marian (Lund) R.; m. Roberta Jane Lindbergh, June 7, 1969; children: Kristen, Jennifer. BA, U. N.D., 1969, BS, 1970; MD, U. Tex., San Antonio 1972; MS in Health Adminstrn., U. Colo., 1991. Intern U.S. Naval Hosp., San Diego, 1972-73; resident U. N.D. Sch. Medicine, Minot, 1975-77; physician Valley Med., Grand Forks, 1977-93; state health officer N.D. Dept. Health, Bismarck, 1993—. Contbg. author: Pilots, Personality and Performance. Lt. USN, 1972-75. Recipient Outstanding Vol. award Dakota Heart Assn., 1989, YMCA, 1992, Outstanding Health Care Provider Grand Forks C. of C., 1992. Mem. AMA, Am. Acad. Family Physicians, Am. Coll. Physician Execs., Rotary, Alpha Omega Alpha. Office: ND Dept Health 600 E Boulevard Ave Bismarck ND 58505-0200

RICE, KENNER CRALLE, medicinal chemist; b. Rocky Mount, Va., May 14, 1940; s. Kenner Cralle Jr. and Annie Grace (Early) R. BS, Va. Mil. Inst., 1961; PhD, Ga. Inst. Tech., 1966. Sr. scientist Ciba-Geigy Corp., Summit, N.J., 1969-72; sr. staff fellow NIH, Bethesda, Md., 1972-76, rsch. chemist, 1977-86; chief sect. drug design and synthesis Nat. Inst. Diabetes, Digestive and Kidney Diseases, Bethesda, Md., 1987-88; chief lab. medicinal chemistry NIDDK, NIH, Bethesda, Md., 1989—; adj. prof. pharmacology U. Md., Balt., 1985—; mem. fed. sr. exec. svc. U.S. Govt., Bethesda, 1989—; affiliate prof. Va. Commonwealth U., Richmond, 1995—; vis. prof. pharmacology, U. Ill., Peoria, 1995—; adj. prof. medicinal chemistry Comprehensive Drug Rsch. Ctr., U. Miami, 1995—. Author: (with others) Pharmalogical Reviews, 1987; editor: NIDA Research Monograph, 1990; contbr. articles to Jour. Medicinal Chemistry. Capt. U.S. Army, 1966-68. Recipient Internat. Sato Meml. award Japanese Pharm. Soc., 1983, Rsch. Achievement award Am. Pharm. Assn., 1987, Hillebrand prize Chem. Soc. Washington, 1986, award Am. Chem. Soc., 1996. Fellow Coll. on Problems of Drug Dependence (bd. dirs. 1988-92); mem. Am. Coll. Neuropsychopharmacology, Cosmos Club. Office: NIH NIDDK Lab Medicinal Chemist Bldg 8 Rm B1 23 Bethesda MD 20892

RICE, MICHAEL JOHN, psychiatric mental health nurse; b. Neligh, Nebr., Jan. 12, 1953; s. Arlo and Mary Maceline (Conger) R.; children: Erin Marie, Michael John Jr., Colleen Kay. BSN, Mt. Marty Coll., 1974; MSN, U. Nebr., 1976; PhD, U. Ariz., 1988. Student health nurse Mt. Marty Coll., Yankton, S.D., 1973-74; nurse trainee adolescent svcs. Nebr. Psychiat. Inst.-U. Nebr. Med. Ctr., Omaha, 1975, staff nurse adult acute care svcs., 1976; clin. nurse specialist, sr. staff Crisis Svcs. Langley Porter Neuro-Psychiat. Inst., U. Calif. Med. Ctr., San Francisco, 1977-80; asst. clin. prof. Sch. Nursing U. Calif. Med. Ctr., San Francisco, 1979-80; grad. rsch. assoc., psychiat. nurse liaison U. Ariz., Tucson, 1980-84; staff nurse Rincon Nurses Profl. Registry, Tucson, 1984-85; dir. acute care treatment teams, asst. to chmn. psychiatry Kino Community Hosp., Tucson, 1985-89; founder, mgr. Omega Care Nursing Svcs., Tucson, 1987-91; assoc. prof. psychiat nursing Intercollegiate Ctr. Nursing Edn., Spokane, Wash., 1989—; mem. mental health awareness planning com. So. Ariz. Mental Health Coun., 1986-87; mem. dist. community task force on alcoholism Community Mental Health Ctr., San Francisco, 1978; cons., therapist Ogden Hall Shelter for Women and Children, Spokane, 1990—; rsch. cons., head trauma force Sacred Heart Med. Ctr., Spokane, 1992-93; founder, dir. Spokane Therapy and Art Resource Svcs., 1991—; therapist YWCA Sch. for Homeless Children, Spokane, 1992—; presenter at profl. confs. Contbr. chpts. to nursing textbooks, articles to profl. jours.; author conf. procs. Mem. tech. adv. com. on community needs assessment, Pima County, Ariz., 1984-85, data collection com. Human Svcs. Coordinating Coun., Pima County, 1984-85. Nursing rsch. emphasis rsch. assoc. and div. nursing fellow HHS, 1981-84. Mem. ANA (coun. nurse rschrs. 1982-86, 90—), Nurses Against Violence, Western Inst. Nursing (membership and fin com. 1992-93, chmn. 1994-95, bd. govs. 1993—), Western Soc. Nursing Rsch., Wash. States Nurses Assn., Inland Empire Nurses Assn., Sigma Xi, Sigma Theta Tau. Home: 9610 N Wichiup Ct Spokane WA 99208 Office: Intercollegiate Ctr Nursing 2917 W Fort George Wright Dr Spokane WA 99204-5202

RICE, RONALD JAMES, hospital administrator; b. Springfield, Mo., Feb. 5, 1944; s. Glen Elwood and Alice Jeanett (Robinson) R. BSBA, Cen. Mo. State U., 1966, MABA, 1969, Specialist, 1972. Lic. nursing home adminstr.; lic. risk mgr. Unit mgr. Bapt. Med. Ctr., Kansas City, Mo., 1970-71; dir. unit mgmt. Ind. Health Ctr., Independence, Mo., 1971-72; adminstr. officer Meth. Hosp., Jacksonville, Fla., 1972-73, dir. personnel, 1973-74; assoc. adminstr. Humana Hosp. Orange Park (Fla.), 1974-77; adminstr. Cathedral Rehab. Hosp., Jacksonville, 1977-79, Marion County Gen. Hosp., Hamilton, Ala., 1979-80, Nassau Gen. Hosp., Fernandina Beach, Fla., 1980-85. Reception Med. Ctr., Lake Butler, Fla., 1985-91; regional adminstr. health svcs. Dept. Corrections, Gainesville, Fla., 1991—; cons. Clay Meml. Hosp., Green Cove Springs, Fla., 1976-77, Allied Health Care, Jacksonville, 1989. Mem. Polit. Action Com., Fla. Hosp. Assn., 1990, Coun. on Crime and Delinquency, Gainesville, 1990, Human Resources Com., Orlando, 1991. With U.S. Army, 1967-69. Decorated Army Commendation medal. Fellow Am. Coll. Health Care Execs.; mem. Am. acad Med. Adminstrs., Am. Coll. Health Care Adminstrs., Am. Soc. Personnel Adminstrs., Fla. Hosp. Assn., Rotary (pres. 1984-86). Democrat. Unity Sch. Christianity. Home: 1744 Horton Dr Orange Park FL 32073-2757

RICE, SHARON MARGARET, clinical psychologist; b. Detroit, Sept. 4, 1943; d. William Christopher and Sylvia Lucille (Lawecki) R.; m. John Robert Speer, Aug. 14, 1977 (dec. Mar. 1994). AB, Oberlin Coll., 1965; MA, Boston U., 1968, PhD, 1977. Clin. psychologist Los Angeles County Juvenile Probation, L.A., 1969-75, Las Vegas (Nev.) Mental Health Ctr., 1976-81, Foothills Psychol. Assn., Upland, Calif., 1981—; pvt. cons., Claremont, Calif., 1984—. NIMH grantee, 1967-69; recipient Good Apple award Las Vegas Tchrs. Ctr., 1978-80. Mem. APA, Calif. Psychol. Assn., Internat. Soc. for Study of Dissociation, Inst. Noetic Scis., Sigma Xi. Office: Foothills Psychol Assn 715 N Mountain Ave # G Upland CA 91786-4364

RICE, STANLEY ARTHUR, biology educator; b. Cushing, Okla., May 30, 1957; s. Arthur John and Nina Irene (Hicks) R.; m. Althea Lisette Clarkston, June 9, 1984; 1 child, Anita. BA, U. Calif., Santa Barbara, 1979; PhD, U. Ill., 1987. Vis. teaching specialist Univ. Ill., Urbana, 1986-87; asst. prof. The King's Coll., Briarcliff Manor, N.Y., 1987-90; vis. faculty Sarah Lawrence Coll., Bronxville, N.Y., 1989-90; asst. prof. Huntington (Ind.) Coll., 1990-93, S.W. State U., Marshall, Minn., 1993—; vis. faculty mem. Wheaton (Ill.) Coll. Sci. Sta., 1993—, Taylor U., Upland, Ind., 1993. Contbr. articles to Oecologia, Perspectives on Sci. and Christian Faith, Creation/Evolution. Predoctoral fellowship NSF, Univ. Ill., 1980. Mem. Ecol. Soc. Am., British Ecol. Soc., Bot. Soc. Am., Am. Sci. Affiliation. Office: SW State Univ Dept Biology Marshall MN 56258

RICE, STEPHEN GARY, medical educator; b. Bklyn., Dec. 21, 1945; s. Abraham S. and Anne (Shelling) R.; m. Hilary Jo Turett, May 10, 1987; children: Adam, Bryan. AB, Columbia Coll., 1967; MD, PhD, NYU, 1974; MPH, U. Wash., 1983. Intern, resident Children's Hosp. & U. Wash., Seattle, 1974-77; faculty mem. sports medicine U. Wash., Seattle, 1977—; sec. Am. Bd. Sports Medicine, Inc., 1991; developer, dir. Athletic Health Care Sys., Seattle, 1978—; cons. in field. Author: Athletic Health Care System, 1988. Team physician U. Wash., 1977-81, Garfield H.S., Seattle, 1975—. Fellow Am. Acad. Pediatrics, Am. Coll. Sports Medicine; mem. Am. Alliance Health, Phys. Edn., Recreation and Dance, Nat. Strength & Conditioning Assn., Am. Med. Soc. Sports Medicine. Home: 220 26th Ave E Seattle WA 98112 Office: U Wash Box 354060 Seattle WA 98195-4060

RICE, STEPHEN RAY, optometrist; b. St. Louis, May 14, 1961; s. Jackie Ray Rice and Patricia Ann (Linkey) Beil; m. Karen Leslie O'Neil, Sept. 11, 1982; children: Kevin, Stephanie. BS in Biology, So. Ill. U., 1983; OD, U. Mo., 1987. Optometrist E.J. Mobley & Assoc., Overland, Mo., 1987-89, O'Donnell Eye Inst., St. Louis, 1987-89; optometrist, ptnr. Vision Clinic/Nixa Vision Clinic, Springfield, Mo., 1989—. Telethon V.I.P. chmn. Easter Seals Soc., Springfield, 1993-95; optometry chair, profl. divsn. United Way, Springfield, 1992, 93. Recipient Gift of Time award Coun. of Chs., 1993. Mem. Rotary Club of Sringfield S.E. (pres. 1995—), Mo. Optometric Assn. (trustee), Greater Ozarks Optometric Soc. (pres. 1992-93). Roman Catholic. Home: 4156 E Oak Knoll Springfield MO 65809 Office: The Vision Clinic 1211 S Glenstone Springfield MO 65804

RICE, SUSAN JOETTE, nurse; b. Topeka, Nov. 15, 1946; d. Claude Harvey and Martha May (McClellan) R.; student Pasadena Nazarene Coll., 1964-66; BS in Nursing, Calif. State U., L.A., 1969, MSN, 1982; PhD in Clin. Psychology, Cambridge Grad. Sch., L.A., 1992. Staff nurse Children's Hosp. L.A., 1969-72, asst. head nurse, 1972-74, nurse mgr., 1974-75; nursing unit coord. newborn and neonatal intensive care nurseries, perinatal clinician Glendale (Calif.) Adventist Med. Center, 1976-78; neonatal clin. specialist Huntington Meml. Hosp., Pasadena, 1981-85; staff nurse mental health unit Glendale Adventist Med. Ctr., 1985—; practicum field placement Treatment Ctrs. Am. Panorama City, Calif., 1988-89; intern Life PLUS Treatment Ctr., Panorama City, 1988-89, Wright Inst., L.A., 1989-91; psychol. asst. to Shirley C. Geller, Arcadia, 1991-93; pvt. practice, Arcadia, 1993—; clin. instr. psychiat. nursing Glendale Community Coll., 1992-94. Vol. counselor Pasadena Mental Health Ctr., 1985-88. Mem. Calif. State Psychol. Assn., Pasadena Area Psychol. Assn. Republican. Mem. Nazarene Ch. Home: 133 Pamela Rd Monrovia CA 91016-5034

RICE, THOMAS BOTHWELL, research management executive; b. Washington, July 18, 1946; s. Thomas Edwin and Louise Eleanor (Arsenault) Rice Dandelske; m. Frances Alana Newton, June 15, 1968 (div. 1986); children: Kevin, Jessica; m. Barbara Jean Long, Jan. 19, 1990. B.A., Amherst Coll., 1968; Ph.D., Yale U., 1973. Postdoctoral fellow Brookhaven Nat. Lab., Upton, L.I., N.Y., 1973-74; research assoc. Mich. State U., East Lansing, 1974-76; sr. research scientist Pfizer Central Research Lab., Groton, Conn., 1976-78, project leader, 1978-80, mgr., 1980-81, dir. plant genetics research, 1981-85, v.p. research and devel. DeKalb-Pfizer Genetics, 1985-86, exec. v.p., 1986-90; pres., COO DeKalb (Ill.) Plant Genetics, 1990—; sr. v.p. DeKalb Genetics Corp., 1993-95; cons., 1995—; adj. assoc. prof. Conn. Coll., New London, 1982-83, 83-84; adj. prof., 1985-86. Contbr. articles to profl. jours. Pres. Pheasant Run Homeowners Assn., Gales Ferry, Conn., 1981, 82. NIH grantee, 1968-72. Mem. AAAS, Crop Sci. Soc. Am., Internat. Assn. Plant Cell and Tissue Culture, Phi Beta Kappa, Sigma Xi (assoc.). Avocations: bridge, golf, racquetball, fishing.

RICE, V. LIANE, optometrist; b. Santa Cruz, Calif., Nov. 6, 1956. BS, U. Calif., Davis, 1979; OD, Pacific U., Forest Grove, Oreg., 1983. Dir. Vision Care Clinic, San Jose, 1987—; chmn. San Jose Vision Therapy Conf., 1984—; state dir. Coll. of Optometrists in Vision Devel., 1990—; dir. paraoptometric divsn. Optometric Ext. Program, 1993—. Named Young Optometrist of the Yr., Calif. Optometric Assn., 1987; COVD fellow, 1989. Mem. Kiwanis (program vice chair). Office: Vision Care Clinic 2730 Union Ave San Jose CA 95124

RICE, VALERIE JEANETTE BERG, occupational therapist, ergonomist; b. Sept. 1, 1953. BA, Salve Regina Coll., 1975; MS, U. Puget Sound, 1978; M Health Care Adminstrn., Baylor U., 1984; PhD, Va. Polytech. Inst./State U., 1990. Lic. occupational therapist; cert. profl. ergonomist. Commd. 2d lt. U.S. Army, 1977, advanced through grades to lt. col.; clin. intern occupational therapy Walter Reed Army Med. Ctr., Washington, 1977-78; asst. chief occupational therapy Womack Army Community Hosp., Ft. Bragg, N.C., 1978-82, dir. psychiat. and pediatric occupational therapy, 1978-82; resident U.S. Army-Baylor Master's Program in Health Care, Landstuhl, Germany, 1983-84; chief occupational therapy 97th Gen. Hosp., Frankfurt, Germany, 1984-86; spl. project officer U.S. Army Environ. Hygiene Agy., Indsl. Hygiene Divsn., Aberdeen Proving Ground, Md., 1992; prin. investigator, rsch. team leader U.S. Army Rsch. Inst. of Environ. Medicine, Natick, Mass., 1990-92, 93-95, acting dep. comdr., chief mil. performance/neurosci. divsn., 1995—; presenter in field. Contbr. articles to profl. jours. including Human Factors Bull., Work Jour. of Prevention, Assessment, and Rehab., Mil. Medicine, Aviation, Space and Environ. Medicine, Internat. Jour. Indsl. Ergonomics, Internat. Jour. Safety and Ergonomics, Rehab. Mgmt. Mem. Am. Occupational Therapy Assn., Army Med. Spcialists Corps, Assn. for the Advancement of Med. Instrumentation (mem. human engrng. com.), Bd. of Certification in Profl. Ergonomics (bd. dirs., v.p.), Dept. of Def. Ergonomics Working Group, Human Factors and Ergonomics Soc., The Ergonomics Soc., Sigma Xi, Alpha Pi Mu.

RICH, CLAYTON, university administrator; b. N.Y.C., May 21, 1924; s. Clayton Eugene and Leonore (Elliot) R.; m. Mary Bell Hodgkinson, Dec. 19, 1953 (div. May 2, 1974); 1 son, Clayton Greig.; m. Rosalind Rich, Apr. 1987. Grad., Putney Sch., 1942; student, Swarthmore Coll., 1942-44; M.D., Cornell U., 1948. Diplomate Am. Bd. Internal Medicine. Intern Albany (N.Y.) Hosp., 1948-49, asst. resident, 1950-51; research asst. Cornell U. Med. Coll., 1949-50; asst. Rockefeller U., 1953-58, asst. prof., 1958-60; asst. prof. medicine U. Wash. Sch. Medicine, 1960-62, assoc. prof., 1962-67, prof., 1967-71, assoc. dean, 1968-71; chief radioisotope service VA Hosp., Seattle, 1960-70; assoc. chief staff VA Hosp., 1962-71, chief staff, 1968-70; v.p. med. affairs, dean Sch. Medicine; prof. medicine Stanford U., 1971-79, Carl and Elizabeth Naumann prof., 1977-79; chief staff Stanford U. Hosp., 1971-77, chief exec. officer, 1977-79; sr. scholar Inst. Medicine, Nat. Acad. Sci., Washington, 1979-80; mem. gen. medicine B study sect. NIH, 1969-73, chmn., 1972-73; mem. spl. med. adv. group VA, 1977-81; provost U. Okla. Health Scis. Ctr., Oklahoma City, 1980—, v.p. for health scis., 1983—; also exec. dean, prof. U. Okla. (Coll. Medicine), 1980-83. Editorial bd.: Calcified Tissue Research, 1966-72, Clin. Orthopedics, 1967-72, Jour. Clin. Endocrinology and Metabolism, 1971-72; Contbr. numerous articles to med. jours. Bd. dirs. Children's Hosp. at Stanford, Stanford U. Hosp., 1974-79; chmn. Gordon Research Conf. Chemistry, Physiology and Structure of Bones and Teeth, 1967; bd. dirs. Okla. Med. Research Found.; bd. dirs. Leadership Oklahoma City, 1981—, v.p., 1985—; bd. dirs. Okla. Blood Inst., 1982—, Oklahoma City Chpt. ARC, 1983—. Served to lt. USNR, 1951-53. Fellow ACP; mem. Assn. Am. Physicians, Western Assn. Physicians, Am. Soc.

Mineral and Bone Research (adv. bd. 1977-80), Am. Soc. Clin. Investigation, Assn. Am. Med. Colls. (exec. council 1975-79), Inst. of Medicine, Western Soc. Clin. Research (v.p. 1967-68), Endocrine Soc., Assn. Acad. Health Ctrs. (bd. dirs. 1984—), Sigma Xi, Alpha Omega Alpha. Office: Provost Office U Okla PO Box 26901 Oklahoma City OK 73126*

RICH, DONNA CAROL, surgeon; b. Houston, Nov. 10, 1960; d. June David and Dorothy Faye (Devers) R.; m. Glen Joseph Cullinane, Nov. 21, 1987. BS in Biomed. Sci., Tex. A&M U., 1983, MS in Genetics, 1986; MD, U. Tex. Med. Sch., Galveston, 1993. Intern U. Tex. Health Sci. Ctr., Houston, 1993-94, resident in gen. surgery, 1994—. Contbr. articles to profl. pubis. Recipient Herman Barrett award for scholarly performance in anesthesiology/surgery, 1993. Mem. AMA, ACS, Am. Med. Women Assn., Tex. Med. Assn., Am. Assn. Women Surgeons. Home: 2023 Cutter Dr League City TX 77513 Office: U Tex Health Sci Ctr Dept Surgery 6431 Fannin Houston TX 77030

RICH, LEONARD STEVEN, ophthalmology educator; b. Dover, Ohio, Mar. 1, 1950; m. Bess C.; children: Michael, Lauren. BS, Ohio State U., 1972; MD, Ohio State Coll. Medicine, 1975. Resident Cleve. Clinic, 1979; pediat. ophthalmology fellow Bascom Palmer Eye Inst., 1979-80; cons. ophthalmologist Ocshner Found., New Orleans, 1982-96; dir. ophthalmology dept. surgery U. So. Ala., Mobile, 1982-86, assoc. prof., dir. ophthalmology dept. surgery, 1986-88; chmn. USA Ophthalmology, Mobile, 1988—, prof., 1992—. active Rep. Exec. Com., Mobile, 1995-96; founder Lions/USA Eye Rsch. Inst., Mobile, 1990. Mem. AMA, Am. Acad. Ophthalmology, Assn. Univ. Profs. Ophthalmology, Lions, Leadership Mobile Alumni Assn. (dean class 1996—), Mobile Lions Club (pres. 1995-96). Home: 625 Cumberland Rd E Mobile AL 36608 Office: USA Ophthalmology 304 Univ Blvd HSB 2500 Mobile AL 36688

RICH, ROBERT REGIER, immunology educator, physician; b. Newton, Kans., Mar. 7, 1941; s. Eldon Stahly and Margaret Joy (Regier) R.; m. Susan Jepson Solliday, Mar. 22, 1974; children from previous marriage: Kenneth Eldon, Cathryn Louise. A.B., Oberlin Coll., 1962; M.D., U. Kans., 1966. Diplomate Am. Bd. Internal Medicine (bd. dirs. 1990-93), Am. Bd. Allergy and Immunology (bd. dirs. 1987-93, chmn. 1991); cert. spl. qualification Diagnostic Lab. Immunology. Intern, resident in internal medicine U. Wash., Seattle, 1966-68; clin. asso., chief clin. asso., sr. staff fellow NIH, Bethesda, Md., 1968-71; research asso. Harvard Med. Sch., Boston, 1971-73; asst. in medicine Peter Bent Brigham Hosp., 1972-73; asst. prof., assoc. prof. microbiology, immunology and internal medicine Baylor Coll. Medicine, Houston, 1973-78, prof., 1978-95, Disting. Svc. prof., 1995—, head immunology sect., 1978—, chief clin. immunology, 1979-91, v.p., dean rsch., 1990—; investigator Howard Huges Med. Inst., Bethesda, Md., 1977-91; mem. immunobiology study sect. NIH, 1977-81; mem. med. staff Harris County Hosp. Dist., Meth. Hosp., Houston; mem. transplantation biology and immunology com. Nat. Inst. Allergy and Infectious Disease, 1982-86, chmn., 1984-86; mem. nat. ctr. grants com. Arthritis Found., 1983-86, chmn., 1984-86, nat. rsch. com., 1984-89, chmn., 1986-89, ho. of dels., 1985-91; mem. rsch. adv. com. Nat. Multiple Sclerosis Soc., 1989-94, chmn., 1993-94. Assoc. editor: Jour. Immunology, 1978-82, sect. editor, 1991-96; assoc. editor: Jour. Infectious Diseases, 1984-88; adv. editor: Jour. Exptl. Medicine, 1980-84; mem. editl. bd. Jour. Clin. Immunology, 1989—, Clin. and Exptl. Immunology, 1995—; editor-in-chief Clin. Immunology: Principles and Practice; contbr. articles to profl. jours. Served with USPHS, 1968-70. Recipient Research Career Devel. award NIH, 1975-77, Merit award NIH, 1987. Fellow ACP, Am. Acad. Allergy, Asthma, and Immunology (chmn. basic and clin. immunology interest sect. 1992-93, chmn. profl. edn. coun. 1996—), Infectious Diseases Soc. Am., Molecular Medicine Soc.; mem. AMA, AAAS, Am. Bd. Internal Medicine (diplomate, bd. dirs. 1990-93), Am. Bd. Allergy and Immunology (diplomate, bd. dirs. 1987-93), Assn. Am. Physicians, Am. Soc. Clin. Investigation, Am. Soc. Histocompatibility and Immunogenetics, Am. Assn. Immunologists (chmn. pub. affairs com. 1994—), Am. Assn. Investigative Pathology, Transplantation Soc., Am. Soc. Microbiologists, So. Soc. Clin. Investigation, Am. Fedn. Clin. Rsch., Am. Clin. Climatological Assn., Harris County Med. Soc., Tex. Med. Assn., Clin. Immunology Soc. (coun. 1990—, pres. 1995), Alpha Omega Alpha, Sigma Xi. Office: Baylor Coll Medicine One Baylor Pla Houston TX 77030

RICHARDS, ARNOLD DAVID, psychiatrist; b. Bklyn., Aug. 2, 1934; s. Samuel and Lillian (Ehrenberg) R.; m. Arlene Doris Kramer, Mar. 21, 1954; children: Stephen, Rebecca, Tamar. AB, U. Chgo., 1951; MD, SUNY, Bklyn., 1958. Diplomate Am. Bd. Psychiatry and Neurology. Intern USPHS, Balt., 1959-60; resident in psychiatry Topeka VA Hosp., 1960-63; Psychiatrist, chief med. officer Fed. Reformatory, Petersberg, Va., 1962-64; pvt. practice psychiatry N.Y.C., 1964—. Editor: Psychoanalysis: The Science of Mental Conflict, 1987, Fantasy, Myth and Reality, 1988, The Spectrum of Psychoanalysis; editor Newsletter of the Am. Psychoanalytic Assn., 1989, The Am. Psychoanalyst, 1989-93, The Jour. of Am. Psychoanalytic Assn., 1994—; contbg. book rev. editor P.A.N.Y. Bull., 1984—; contbr. articles to profl. jours. Bd. dirs. YIVO-Inst. for Jewish Rsch., 1986-88, 91—, chmn. bd. dirs., 1988-91. With USPHS, 1962-64. Fellow Am. Psychiat. Assn. (life); mem. APA, Am. Psychoanalytic Assn. (cert. mem., councilor), N.Y. Psychoanalytic Soc. (sec., chmn. community edn. and outreach div.), Psychoanalytic Assn. N.Y. Jewish. Office: 200 E 89th St New York NY 10128-4300

RICHARDS, DIANA LYN, psychologist; b. Baton Rouge, Dec. 8, 1944; d. William Allen Richards and Julia Viola (Hamilton) Richards Hamilton. AA, Stephens Coll., 1964; BA, U. Colo., 1966; MA, Miami U., Oxford, Ohio, 1969, PhD, 1974. Lic. psychologist, Mo. Dir. community psychol. svcs. Malcolm Bliss Mental Health Ctr., St. Louis, 1975-77; mem. staff Women's Counseling Ctr., St. Louis, 1976-78; mem. faculty Gestalt Inst., St. Louis, 1977-80; instr. Washington U., St. Louis, 1977; dir. psychology Lindenwood Coll. for Individualized Edn., St. Louis, 1978-80, core faculty in psychology, 1984-94; psychologist in pvt. practice St. Louis, 1977—; career cons. Stephens Coll., Columbia, Mo., 1994—; mem. Psychoanalytic Study Group, St. Louis, 1980—; supr. psychology clinic, clin. doctoral program U. Mo., St. Louis, 1994—; facilitator Coun. of All Beings Workshops, 1995—; presenter in field. Contbr. articles to profl. jours. and conf. presentations. Mem. Operation Food Search, Defenders of Wildlife, Humane Soc., People for Ethical Treatment of Animals, Arts and Edn. Fund, Mo. Bot. Garden, Digit Fund, Earth Island Inst., World Wildlife Fund, Nature Conservancy, Audubon Soc., Humane Farming Assn.; founding mem. The Pleiades; vol. food ministry, chair fellowship dinners, edn. com. Trinity Episcopal Ch.; vol. Wildbird Rehab. Ctr. Mem. APA, Mo. Psychol. Assn., St. Louis Psychol. Assn. (program chair 1988-89, pres.-elect 1995-96, pres. 1996—), Network of Women Psychologists (program chair 1986), St. Louis Psychoanalytic Inst. Democrat. Home: 2014 S Mason Rd Saint Louis MO 63131-1619 Office: 7396 Pershing Ave Saint Louis MO 63130-4206

RICHARDS, GARY PAUL, microbiologist, researcher; b. Springfield, Mass., June 4, 1950; s. Norman Raymond and Irene Elizabeth (Clarkin) R.; m. Brenda Grace Allen, Aug. 18, 1973; children: David, Kevin, Brian. BA in Microbiology, U. N.H., 1973; PhD in Molecular and Cellular Biology, Med. U. S.C., 1995. Lic. fed. fishery products inspector. Dir. quality control and rsch. Rockland (Maine) Shrimp Corp., 1973-75; food inspector U.S. Dept. Commerce Inspection Office, Gloucester, Mass., 1975-77; microbiologist Nat. Marine Fisheries Svc., College Park, Md., 1977-78; dir. Bio Rsch. & Testing Lab., Charleston, S.C., 1978-85; rsch. microbiologist Nat. Marine Fisheries Svc., Charleston, S.C., 1978—; rsch. scientist on viruses in shellfish and serine proteinases, 1978—. Contbr. articles to profl. jours. Cubmaster Boy Scouts Am., Charleston, 1989-90, mem. troop com., 1990—; mem. ch. coun. St. Mary's Cath. Ch., Yonges Island, S.C., 1989-91. Mem. Am. Soc. for Microbiology, Sigma Xi (Charleston chpt.). Home: 4391 Cloudmont Dr Hollywood SC 29449 Office: Nat Marine Fisheries Svc Charleston Lab 219 Fort Johnson Lab Charleston SC 29412-9110

RICHARDS, JAMES CARLTON, microbiologist, business executive; b. Storm Lake, Iowa, Aug. 19, 1947; s. Jack M. and June G. Richards; m. Lois Ruth Rebbe, July 22, 1974 (div. Sept. 1986); 1 child, Kimberly Ann; m. Susan M. Wos, Aug. 27, 1988; children: Derek Anthony, Kristin Marie. BS in Microbiology, U. Ill., 1970; PhD in Microbiology, So. Ill. U., 1977. Postdoctoral fellow Pa. State U. Med. Ctr., Hershey, Pa., 1977-79; sr. scientist E.I. duPont de Nemours, Wilmington, Del., 1979-85; program mgr. Amoco, Naperville, Ill., 1985-86; dir. bus. Gene-Trak Systems, Framingham, Mass., 1986-90; mng. dir. Carlton BioVenture Ptnrs., Sudbury, Mass., 1990—; pres., CEO, bd. dirs. Symbollon Corp., Sudbury, Mass., 1991-95; pres., CEO, bd. dirs. IntelliGene, Ltd., Sudbury, Mass., 1995—, Jerusalem, Israel, 1995—; invited lectr. on genetic analysis and advances in gene amplification and detection. Contbr. chpt. to books, articles to sci. jours.; patentee in field. Deacon United Ch. of Christ, Framingham, 1988—. Mem. AAAS, Am. Soc. for Microbiology, Am. Chem. Soc., Inst. Food Technologists, N.Y. Acad. Scis., Clin. Ligand Soc., Sigma Xi, others. Home and office: 44 Codman Dr Sudbury MA 01776-1745

RICHARDS, JANE AILEEN, family nurse practitioner; b. Oakland, Calif., Oct. 19, 1948; d. John Donald and Mary Dolores (Peters) R. BS in Nursing, U. San Francisco, 1970; MS in Nursing, San Jose State U., 1976, FNP, 1995. RN; cert. FNP. Staff nurse ICU Mills Meml. Hosp., San Mateo, Calif., 1970-73; asst. head nurse ICU, 1973-76, edn. specialist, 1976-80, mgr. acute rehab. ctr., 1980-83; case mgr. J.R. Assocs., San Mateo, 1983-95; nurse cons. Calif. State Dept. Corps., 1989—, FNP Seneca Hosp. Dist., Lake Almanor Clinic, Chester, Calif., 1995—. Pres. United Cerebral Palsy Assn., Mt. View, Calif., 1979-85, 93-94, bd. dirs. N.Y.C. chpt., 1983-91, vice chmn. vol. devel. com., N.Y.C., 1989-91. Mem. Rehab. Ins. Nurse Group (pres. 1987-89), Sigma Theta Tau (Alpha Gamma chpt.), PEO (chpt. BO-Calif.). Republican. Avocations: golf, camping. Home: PO Box 1743 Chester CA 96020-1743 Office: Lake Almanor Clinic PO Box 737 Chester CA 96020

RICHARDS, JOHN WILLIAM, JR., family physician, consultant; b. Kershaw, S.C., Aug. 18, 1950; s. John William Sr. and Dorothy Mae (Thompson) R.; m. Nancy Ann Neef, Mar. 7, 1987. BS, Clemson U., 1972; MD, Med. U. of S.C., 1976. Diplomate Am. Bd. Family Practice. Intern, then resident in family practice Spartanburg (S.C.) Gen. Hosp., 1976-79; with U.S. Army, 1979-83; asst. prof. dept. family medicine Med. Coll. Ga., Augusta, 1983-88, assoc. prof. dept. family medicine, 1988-89, clin. assoc. prof., 1989-94; pvt. practice Univ. Family Medicine, Evans, Ga., 1994—; pes. Innovative Health Strategies, Evans, 1987—; cons. on cancer prevention and cost-effective medicine; reviewer N.Y. Jour. Medicine, 1983-85, JAMA, 1987—. Assoc. editor Jour. Family Practice, 1990—; mem. editl. bd. Managed Care. With USAR, 1971-79, maj. M.C., U.S. Army, 1979-83. Leroy Spring Med. scholar, 1972-76, John T. Stevens Found. scholar, 1976; recipient Am. Nat. Cancer award, 1980, Surgeon Gen.'s Medallion, 1988. Fellow Am. Acad. Family Physicians (del. 1979, chmn. subcom. on awards 1987, pub. rels. and mktg. com. 1986-87); mem. AMA (Disting. Svc. to Am. Youth award 1990), Drs. Ought To Care (nat. v.p. 1980-81, nat. pres. 1982-91), Ga. Acad. Family Physicians (alt. bd. dirs. 1985-87, various coms. 1983—), Med. Assn. Ga., Ga. Physicians Assn. for AIDS Care (pharms. com. 1989-91), Richmond County Med. Assn., Soc. Tchrs. Family Medicine (various coms.), Nat. Assn. Managed Care Physicians (pubs. com. 1992—). Presbyterian. Office: University Family Medicine 447 N Belair Rd Evans GA 30809

RICHARDS, LORIE GAGE, occupational therapist, educator; b. Ilion, N.Y., May 22, 1961; d. Gerald LaMont and Doris Jean (Wilcox) Gage; m. Thomas Edward Richards, May 20, 1989; children: Alia Irene, Ian Andrew. BS in Occupational Therapy, Elizabethtown Coll., 1983; MS in Exptl. Psychology, Syracuse U., 1989, PhD, 1992. Cert. occupational therapist. Staff occupational therapist Plaza Health & Rehab. Ctr., Syracuse, N.Y., 1983-85, The Neurologic Ctr. at Cortland, N.Y., 1985-86; teaching and rsch. asst. dept. psychology Syracuse U., 1986-92; asst. prof. U. Kans. Med. Ctr., Kansas City, 1992—, assoc. scientist ctr. on aging, 1993—; courtesy asst. prof. dept. psychology U. Kans., Kansas City, 1993—. Contbr. articles and revs. to profl. jours. Recipient Dissertation award Am. Psychol. Assn., 1991-92. Mem. Am. Occupational Therapy Assn., Psychonomics Soc. (assoc.), Midwestern Psychol. Assn., Kans. Occupational Therapy Assn. (co-chair conf. program 1995-96), Am. Psychol. Soc. Methodist. Home: 7411 Booth Prairie Village KS 66208 Office: U Kans Med Ctr Dept Occupational Therapy 3033 Robinson 3901 Rainbow Kansas City KS 66160-7602

RICHARDS, MARK GEORGE, physician; b. Indpls., Mar. 2, 1955; s. George Leon and Imogene (Kessler) R.; m. Cyndi Adomatis, July 9, 1977; children: Bethany, Zachary, Hannah. BS, Marion Coll., 1977; MD, Ind. U., 1981. Diplomate Am. Bd. Family Practice. Resident in family practice St. Vincent's Hosp., Indpls., 1982-85; pvt. practice Carmel, Ind., 1985—. Named Alumnus of Yr., Ind. Wesleyan U., 1995. Fellow Am. Acad. Family Practice; mem. U.S. Tennis and Lawn Assn., Nat. Right to Life Com. Baptist. Home: 14200 Cherry Tree Rd Carmel IN 46033-9612 Office: 1120 Triple A Way Carmel IN 46032

RICHARDS, NELSON GLASGOW, neurologist; b. Orange, N.J., Aug. 15, 1924; s. Nelson and Annette (Glasgow) R.; m. Sara Jean Raudenbush, Sept. 4, 1953; children: Linda, Janis, Nelson Scott, Karen, John, Tom. Nelson G. II. BA in biology, U. Va., 1948, MD, 1952. Diplomate Am. Bd. Psychiatry and Neurology; cert. Neurology and Child Neurology. Asst. resident in medicine N.Y. Hosp.-Cornell Med. Ctr., N.Y.C., 1952-55, resident in neurology, 1955-57; clin. fellow in neurology NIH, Bethesda, Md., 1957-58; neurologist Cleve. Clinic Found., 1958-69; pvt. practice Roanoke, Va., 1969-72, Richmond, Va., 1972—; attending neurologist McGuire VA Hosp., Richmond, 1972—; cons. AMA/RBRVS Harvard, Boston, 1987—. Editor: ICD-9 for Neurologists, 1991, 3d edit., 1993; mem. editl. panel AMA/CPT, 1992-95. With USNR, 1944-46. Fellow ACP, Am. Acad. Neurology (asst. sec.-treas. 1972-73, sec.-treas. 1973-77, pres. 1983-85); mem. AMA (alt. del. 1985—), Am. Soc. Internal Medicine (del. 1987—), AMA/SSS (chmn. 1995-96), Am. Med. Peer Rev. Assn. (bd. dirs. 1992-94), Va. Soc. Internal Medicine (pres. 1994-95). Home: 11820 Wakehurst Dr Richmond VA 23236-4142 Office: Associated Neurologists PC Ste 5300 The Atrium 1401 Johnston Willis Dr Richmond VA 23235-4730

RICHARDS, ROY JOHN, biology educator; b. Delabole, Cornwall, Eng., Sept. 13, 1944; s. John Gordon and Olive Ruth (Dawe) R.; m. Susan Grace Mayson, Mar. 25, 1967; children: Dax Jonathan, Zöe Grace. BSc in Zoology with honors, Univ. Coll., Swansea, Wales, 1966; PhD in Parasitology, Univ. Coll., Swansea, Eng., 1969; DSc in Biochem. Toxicology, U. Wales, 1991. Med. Rsch. Coun. fellow biochemistry dept. Univ. Coll. Cardiff, Wales, 1969-71, lectr. in biochemistry, 1971-78, sr. lectr. biochemistry dept., 1978-86, reader biochemistry dept., 1986—; mem. adv. group in pollution episodes Dept. of Health, London, 1990—; mem. com. on effects of air pollutants Dept of Environment/Dept of Health. Contbr. numerous articles to profl. jours. Mem. Brit. Assn. Lung Rsch. (chmn. 1989-94), Brit. Soc. for Cell Biology.

RICHARDS, WILLIAM H., urologist; b. Ironwood, Mich., Sept. 22, 1958; s. William H. and Kathleen Marie (Nelson) R.; m. Sherri Lynne Cottrell, Dec. 20, 1980; children: Heather, Ryan, Kristi. BS, Mich. Tech. U., 1980; MD, U. Mich. Med. Sch., 1984. Diplomate Am. Bd. Urology. Resident urology U. Wis. Hosp. and Clinics, Madison, 1984-89; chief urology Langley Air Force Base, Hampton, Va., 1989-93; staff urologist Heartland Hosp. East/West, St. Joseph, Mo., 1993-95; pvt. practice urology Escanaba, Mich., 1995—. Mem. Am. Coll. Surgeons, Am. Urology Assn. Office: Great Northern Urology 3403 Ludington Ste 100 Escanaba MI 49829

RICHARDS-KORTUM, REBECCA RAE, biomedical engineering educator; b. Grand Island, Nebr., Apr. 14, 1964; d. Larry Alan and Linda Mae (Hohnstein) Richards; m. Philip Ted Kortum, May 12, 1985; children: Alexander Scott, Maxwell James. BS, U. Nebr., 1985; MS, MIT, 1987, PhD, 1990. Assoc. U. Tex., Austin, 1990—. Named Presdl. Young Investigator NSF, Washington, 1991; NSF presdl. faculty fellow, Washington, 1992; recipient Career Achievement award Assn. Advancement Med. Instrumentation, 1992, Dow Outstanding Young Faculty awd., Am. Soc. for Engineering Education, 1992. Mem. AAAS, Am. Soc. Engring. Edn. (Outstanding Young Faculty award 1992), Optical Soc. Am., Am. Soc. Photobiology. Office: U Tex Dept Elec & Computer Engring Austin TX 78712

RICHARDSON, ANDREW, orthodontist, educator; b. Dundee, Angus, Scotland, Jan. 23, 1933; arrived in Northern Ireland, 1960.; s. Andrew Phillips Richardson and Williamina Mitchell; m. Margaret Elizabeth Sweeney, Feb. 13, 1961; 1 child, Lindsay. B in Dental Surgery, U. St. Andrew, Scotland, 1955, diploma in Pub. Dentistry, 1960; MSc, Queens U., Belfast, Ireland, 1965; D in Orthodontics, Royal Coll. Surgeons, London, 1961. House surgeon Dundee (Scotland) Dental Hosp., 1955-56; sr. dental officer Ghana Army, 1956-59; registrar Sch. of Dentistry, Belfast, Northern Ireland, 1960-62, sr. registrar, 1962-64; lectr., sr. lectr. Queens U., Belfast, 1964-83, prof., cons., 1984—; examiner Royal Coll. Surgeons, London, 1974-80, U. London, 1994—. Author: Interceptive Orthodontics, 3rd edit., 1996. Capt. Ghana Army, 1956-59. Fellow Royal Coll. Surgeons in Ireland (examiner 1992-94). Home: 33 Cherryvalley Park, BT5 6PN Belfast Northern Ireland Office: Roayl Victoria Hosp Ortho Dept, Sch of Dentistry, BT12 6BP Belfast Northern Ireland

RICHARDSON, A(RTHUR) LESLIE, former medical group consultant; b. Ramsgate, Kent, Eng., Feb. 21, 1910; s. John William and Emily Lilian (Wilkins) R.; came to U.S., 1930, naturalized, 1937; student spl. courses U. So. Calif., 1933-35; m. B. Kathleen Sargent, Oct. 15, 1937. Mgr., Tower Theater, Los Angeles, 1931-33; accountant Felix-Krueper Co., Los Angeles, 1933-35; indsl. engr. Pettengill, Inc., Los Angeles, 1935-37; purchasing agt. Gen. Petroleum Corp. Los Angeles, 1937-46; adminstr. Beaver Med. Clinic, Redlands, Calif., 1946-72, exec. cons. 1972-75, 95; sec.-treas. Fern Properties, Inc., Redlands, 1955-75, Redelco, Inc., Redlands, 1960-67; pres. Buinco, Inc., Redlands, 1956-65; vice chmn. Redlands adv. bd. Bank of Am., 1973-80; exec. cons. Med. Adminstrs. Calif., 1975-83. Pres., Redlands Area Community Chest, 1953; volunteer exec. Internat. Exec. Service Corps; mem. San Bernardino County (Calif.) Grand Jury, 1952-53. Bd. dirs. Beaver Med. Clinic Found., Redlands, 1961—, sec.-treas., 1961-74, pres., 1974-75, chmn. bd. dirs. 1992—. Served to lt. Med. Adminstrv. Corps., AUS, 1942-45. Recipient Redlands Civic award Elks, 1953. Fellow Am. Coll. Med. Practice Execs. (life, disting. fellow 1980, pres. 1965-66, dir.); mem. Med. Group Mgmt. Assn. (hon. life; mem. nat. long range planning com. 1963-68, pres. western sect. 1960), Kiwanis (pres. 1951), Masons. Episcopalian. Home: 1 Verlie Dr Redlands CA 92373-6943

RICHARDSON, BETTY KEHL, nursing educator, administrator, counselor, resear; b. Jacksonville, Ill., Mar. 24, 1938; d. Alfred Jason and Hilda (Emmons) Kehl; m. Joseph Richardson, June 27, 1959 (div. 1980); children: Mark Joseph, Stephanie Elaine. BA in Nursing, Sangamon State U., 1975, MA in Adminstrn., 1977; MSN, Med. Coll. Ga., 1980; PhD in Nursing, U. Tex., 1985. Cert. advanced nursing adminstrn., clin. specialist child and adolescent psychiat. nursing ANCC; lic. profl. counselor, marriage and family counselor. Instr. nursing Lincoln Land Community Coll., Springfield, Ill., 1978-79; acting dir. nursing MacMurray Coll., Jacksonville, Ill., 1979-81; asst. prof. Sangamon State U., Springfield, 1981-82; adminstr. children and adolescent programs Shoal Creek Hosp., Austin, 1989-90; nursing dir. Austin State Hosp., 1983-89; therapist San Marcos (Tex.) Treatment Ctr., 1989-90; instr. Austin C.C., 1990—; pvt. practice psychotherapy, Austin, 1990—. Advising editor: Parenting in the 90s jour.; contbr. articles to profl. jours. Pres. PTA, 1968. Named Outstanding Nurse, Passavant Hosp., 1958, Nurse of Yr., Tex. Nurses Assn., 1994-95; recipient Plaque for Outstanding Leadership, Austin State Hosp., 1989, plaque for svc. to the poor people of Mexico and C.Am. Internat. Good Neighbor Coun. (Austin chpt.) and U. Area Rotary Club, 1995. Mem. ANA, DAR, Southwest Group Psychotherapy Assn., Tex. Counseling Assn., Assn. Play Therapy, Rotary (Good Neighbor Coun./Univ. award 1995), Sigma Theta Tau, Phi Kappa Phi. Methodist. Home: 5207 Doe Valley Ln Austin TX 78759-7103 Office: Austin C C 1020 Grove Blvd Austin TX 78759-3300

RICHARDSON, DAVID WALTHALL, cardiologic educator, consultant; b. Nanking, China, Mar. 22, 1925; s. Donald William and Virginia (McIlwaine) R.; m. Frances Lee Wingfield, June 12, 1948; children—Donald, Sarah, David. B.S., Davidson Coll., 1947; M.D., Harvard U., 1951. Diplomate Am. Bd. Internal Medicine, Am. Bd. Cardiology. Intern, resident Yale New Haven Hosp., Conn., 1951-53; resident, fellow Med. Coll. Va., Richmond, 1953-56, assoc. prof. to prof. medicine, 1962-95, prof. emeritus, 1995—, chmn. div. cardiology, 1972-87; interim chmn. dept. medicine, 1973-74; chief cardiology, assoc. chief staff for rsch. VA Hosp., Richmond, 1956-61, dir. cardiology tng. program, 1990-95; vis. scientist Oxford U., Eng., 1961-62; vis. prof. U. Milan, Italy, 1972-73. Contbr. articles to profl. jours. Moderator Hanover Presbytery, Presbyterian Ch. U.S., Richmond, 1970; chmn. events com. NHLBI Cardiac Arrhythmia Suppression Trial, 1983-92. Served with USN, 1944-46. Fellow. Am. Coll. Cardiology (gov. VA. 1970-72), Am. Heart Assn. (coun. clin. cardiology and high blood pressure rsch.); mem. Am. Soc. Clin. Investigation, Am. Clin. and Climatol. Assn. Home: 5501 Queensbury Rd Richmond VA 23226-2121

RICHARDSON, DEANNA RUTH, microbiologist; b. Columbus, Ohio, Jan. 7, 1956; d. Raymond and Anna Mary (Underwood) R. BS, Ohio State U., 1978. Lab tech. Ohio Dept. Agr., Reynoldsburg, Ohio, 1978-81, lab technologist, 1981-86, microbiologist, 1986—. Active East Columbus Christian Ch.; mem. Neighborhood Civic Assn., 1983-87. Mem. Ohio Valley Inst. Food Technologists, Vet. Microbiologists Assn., Ohio State U. Alumni Assn., Franklin County Alumni Club, Smithsonian Instn., Nat. Wildlife Fedn., Internat. Wildlife Fedn., World Wildlife Fund, African Wildlife Found., Columbus Zoo, Ohio State U. Century Club, Ohio State U. Friend of the Wexner Art Ctr. Home: 6267 Barberry Holw Columbus OH 43213-3308 Office: Ohio Dept Agr Labs 8995 E Main St Reynoldsburg OH 43068-3398

RICHARDSON, DONALD EDWARD, neurosurgery educator; b. Vicksburg, Miss., Oct. 5, 1931; s. Edward K. and Ina Mae (Cooper) R.; children: Donna Richardson Boas, Scott, David, W. Jeffrey, Cooper E.H. BS in Chemistry, Millsaps Coll., 1953; MD, Tulane U., 1957. Diplomate Am. Bd. Neurol. Surgery. Intern in surgery Charity Hosp., New Orleans, 1957-58, resident in neurosurgery, 1961-62; resident in neurosurgery Ochsner Found. Hosp., New Orleans, 1958-60, VA Hosp., New Orleans, 1960-61; instr. Dept. Neurosurgery, Tulane U., New Orleans, 1962-64, asst. prof., 1964-67, assoc. prof., 1967-74, prof., chmn., 1980—, adj. prof. dept. biomed. engring., 1984—; clin. assoc. prof. dept. neurosurgery La. State U., New Orleans, 1974-80; dir. Pain Treatment Ctr. Hotel Dieu Hosp., New Orleans, 1978-93, mem.-at-large exec. com., 1978-84, chmn. spl. procedures com., 1984-93; chief neurosurgery sect. Charity Hosp. La. New Orleans, 1980—, VA Hosp. New Orleans, 1980—; mem. neurosurgery staff, Toure Infirmary, So. Bapt. Hosp., Pendelton Meml. Meth. Hosp., St. Jude Med. Ctr.; chmn. Neurosurgery dept. Tulane U. Med. Ctr. Hosp., 1980—, oper. rm. and exec. coms., 1980—; lectr. in field. Contbr. articles to profl. jours. Fellow ACS; mem. AAAS, Am. Assn. Neurol. Surgeons, AMA, Am. Pain Soc., Am. Soc. for Stereotactic and Functional Neurosurgery, Assn. for Acad. Surgery, Congress Neurol. Surgeons, Internat. Assn. for Study Pain, Internat. Neurosurg. Soc., La. Neurol. Soc. (pres. 1979), La. State Med. Soc., Neuroelectric Soc., N.Y. Acad. Sci., Orleans Parish Med. Soc., Research Soc. Neurol. Surgeons, Royal Soc. Medicine, Soc. for Neurosci., So. Med. Assn., So. Neurosurg. Assn., Oscar Creek Surg. Soc., Midwest Pain Soc., Can. Neurosurg. Soc., Am. Acad. Pain Medicine, Alton Ochsner Med. Found. Soc., Soc. Neurol. Surgeons, La. Med. Rev. Found., Am. Acad. Clin. Neurophysiology, Alpha Omega Alpha. Lodge: Rotary. Office: Tulane U Sch of Medicine Dept of Neurosurgery 1430 Tulane Ave New Orleans LA 70112-2699

RICHARDSON, J. DAVID, surgeon; b. Morehead, Ky., 1945. MD, U. Ky., 1970. Diplomate Am. Bd. Surgeons, Am. Bd. Vascular Surgery, Am. Bd. Thoracic Surgery, Am. Bd. SCC. Intern U. Ky. Med. Ctr., Lexington, 1970, resident, 1971-72; resident U. Tex., San Antonio, 1972-76; surgeon Norton Kosair Children's Hosp., Louisville, Ky., 1977—; prof. surgery U. Louisville, 1979—. Fellow ACS; mem. AMA, AAST, SSAT, Alpah Omega Alpha. Office: U Louisville Dept Surgery 530 S Jackson St Louisville KY 40292*

RICHARDSON, JAMES MATTHEW, medical organization administrator; b. Ft. Leonard Wood, Mo., Feb. 28, 1966; s. James Joseph Richardson and Sheila (Dineen) Foster; m. Maria S. Garza, Nov. 30, 1991; 1 child, Jacob Matthew. B.Health Care Adminstrn., Fla. Atlantic U., 1988. Human resource specialist Humana, Inc., Pompano Beach, Fla., 1989-90; asst. adminstr. Humana Health Care Plans, Brandon, Fla., 1990, adminstr., 1990-91; adminstr. Humana Health Care Plans, San Antonio, 1991-92, network devel. specialist, 1992-94; dir. managed care NDP Inc., San Antonio, 1994-95; dir. managed care S.W. ORNDA, Inc., San Antonio, 1995, regional dir. managed care, mem. adv. bd., 1995—; cons. in field. Mem. Am. Coll. Healthcare Adminstrs., Group Health Assn. Am. Roman Catholic. Home: 7522 Silent

Rain San ANTONIO TX 78250 Office: Medpartners Inc 9150 Huebner Rd #210 San Antonio TX 78240

RICHARDSON, JOSEPH HILL, physician, medical educator; b. Rensselaer, Ind., June 16, 1928; s. William Clark and Vera (Hill) R.; m. Joan Grace Meininger, July 8, 1950; children: Lois N., Ellen M., James K. MS in Medicine Northwestern U., 1950, MD, 1953. Intern, U.S. Naval Hosp., Great Lakes, Ill., 1953-54; fellow in medicine Cleve. Clinic, 1956-59; individual practice medicine specializing in internal medicine and hematology, Marion, Ind., 1959-67, Ft. Wayne, Ind., 1967—; assoc. clin. prof. medicine, Ind. U. Sch. Medicine, 1993—; med. dir. emeritus The Med. Protective Co., Ft. Wayne, 1995—. Served to lt. MC USNR, 1953-56. Diplomate Am. Bd. Internal Medicine. Fellow ACP, AAAS; mem. AMA, Masons. Contbr. articles to med. jours. Home and Office: 8726 Fortuna Way Fort Wayne IN 46815-5725

RICHARDSON, KENNETH T., JR., psychotherapist, consultant, educator, author; b. Santa Monica, Calif., Sept. 16, 1948; s. Kenneth T. Richardson and Florence (Wheeler) Neal; m. Mary L. Nutter, Dec. 31, 1983; children: Kenneth T. III, Russell A., Shad Martin, Cheralyn Martin. BA, Prescott (Ariz.) Coll., 1985; postgrad., Antioch (Ohio) Coll., 1987-88. Cert. addictions counselor, Ariz.; nat. cert. NCRC/ADOA. Program dir. Calvary Rehab. Ctr., Phoenix, 1979-82; clin. dir. Friendship House Comprehensive Recovery Ctr., San Francisco, 1982-84; dir. treatment The Meadows, Wickenburg, Ariz., 1984-87; co-founder, dir. The Orion Found., Phoenix, 1989—; owner, dir. Phoenix Cons. and Counseling Assocs., 1987—; cons. Addictions Svcs., The Hopi Tribe, Kykotsmoni, Ariz., 1989—, Baywood Hosp., Houston, 1988-89; advisor Nat. Coun. on Co-Dependence, Phoenix, 1990—, Recourse Found., Phoenix, 1989-93; faculty instr. Rio Salado C.C., Phoenix, 1987-90, The Recovery Source, Houston, 1989-90; co-chair Nat. Conv. of Men., Relationships and Recovery, Phoenix, 1990, 91. Creator, presenter audiotape series: Codependence and the Development of Addictions, 1991, Your Spiritual Self: The Child Within, 1991, Relationship Recovery, 1992, Men's Sexuality and Relationships, 1993-96, Body Mind and Spirit, 1994-96; creator edn. and support materials related to addictions, relationships and family sys., 1987—. Mem. Nat. Assn. Alcoholism and Drug Counselors, Am. Counseling Assn., Am. Mental Health Counselors Assn., Nat. Certification Reciprocity Consortium, Nat. Platform Assn. Office: Phoenix Cons and Counseling 5333 N 7th St Ste A202 Phoenix AZ 85014

RICHARDSON, MARY LOU, psychotherapist; b. Topeka, Oct. 4, 1953; d. Darrell and Beverly Nutter; m. Kenneth T Richardson Jr. children: Shad Martin, Cheralyn Pasbrig, Kenneth T Richardson III, Russ Richardson. Cert. addictions counselor, Ariz.; cert. Nat. Assn. of Alcolism and Drug Abuse Counselors. Counselor Compcare Alcoholism Ctr. The Meadows Treatment Ctr., Phoenix, 1986-88; co-dir. Phoenix Cons. & Counseling Assocs., Ariz., 1989—; founder and adminstr. The Orion Found., Ariz.; project mem. The Hutoomkhum Com. and Support Program, Hopi Reservation, Ariz.; cons. Baywood Hosp., 1988-89; faculty instr. The Recovery Source, 1989-90; chair Nat. Conv. Women, 1992. Author: Women's Acts of Power, 1991-93, Relationship Recover, 1992—, Women's Empowerment, 1992—, Body, Mind & Spirit, 1994—. Mem. Am. Mental Health Counselors, Am. Counseling Assn., Nat. Assn. Alcoholism & Drug Abuse Counselors, Nat. Reciprocity Consortium. Office: Phoenix Cons & Counseling Assocs 5333 N 7th St Ste A202 Phoenix AZ 85014

RICHARDSON, MILDRED TOURTILLOTT, psychologist; b. North Hampton, N.H., May 8, 1907; d. Herbert Shaw and Sarah Louise (Fife) Tourtillott; m. Harold Wellington Richardson, June 25, 1932; children: Elizabeth Fern Ruben, Constance Joy Van Valer, Carol Louise Dennis. AB, Bates Coll., 1930; MA, U. Mich., 1948; EdS, Butler U., 1961; PhD, Ind. U., 1965. Diplomate Am. Bd. Profl. Psychology, Nat. Register Health Svc. Providers in Psychology, hosp. staff mem.; cert. clin. and sch. psychologist, Ind. Tchr. math. and sci. Norwich (Conn.) Free Acad., 1930-32, Port Huron (Mich.) High Sch., 1943-45; dir. intermediate girls Interlochen Nat. Music Camp, Mich., 1953, asst. dean univ. women, 1954; tchr., guidance counselor Community Sch. Corp., Franklin, Ind., 1956-64; supr. tng. Devereux Found., Devon, Pa., 1965-78, cons. clin. tng. in sch. and clin. psychology, 1975-78; tchr. psychology of spl. edn. Pa. State U.ext., King of Prussia, 1966-68; sch. psychologist Johnson County (Ind.) Spl. Svcs., 1979-82; head clin. psychology Community Psychiat. Ctrs. Valle Vista Hosp., Greenwood, Ind., 1983-88; pvt. practice psychol. health svc. Greenwood, 1985-95; clin. psychologist St. Francis Hosp., Indpls., 1988-95; clin. assoc. prof. Hahnemann Med. Coll., Phila., 1973-78; part-time dir. psychodiagnostics seminar; assoc. prof. sch. psychology, condr. grad. seminar, practicum Ind. U., Bloomington, 1982, lectr., 1987; mem. bd. examiners Midwest Regional Bd. Am. Bd. Profl. Psychology, 1988-95, Ind.Tchrs. Assn., Ind. Psychol. Assn.; cons. Valle Vista Guidance Ctr., 1991-94; adj. prof. psychology Ind. U., 1992-94, U. Indpls., 1992-94; cons. clin. psychologist Am. Stress Ctr., Inc., 1993-95; pvt. practice, Pa., 1970-78. Contbr. articles to profl. jours. Active Johnson County Commn. on Child Abuse, 1988-89, Gov.'s Drug-Free Ind. Coun. on Alcoholism; bd. dirs. Greater Johnson County Cmty. Found., 1990-95. Recipient Headliner award Theta Sigma Phi, 1964, Disting. Svc. award Bates Coll. Alumni Assn., 1990. Mem. APA (fellow sch. psychology, clin. psychology), Inst. Clin. Tng. Devereux Found. (hon.), Internat. Coun. Psychologists, Internat. Sch. Psychology Com., Exec. Svc. Corps (mem. mentor program), Franklin Coll. Alumnae (hon., assoc. 1988), Ben Franklin Soc., Phi Kappa Phi. Republican. Baptist. Address: Marquette Manor Apt 5302 8140 Township Line Rd Indianapolis IN 46260

RICHARDSON, PATRICE ANN, medical, surgical nurse, consultant; b. Providence, Feb. 5, 1952; d. Louis A. and Caroline M. (Zimmer) Giroux; m. John White Richardson III, Sept. 18, 1977; children: Ian G., Trevor A. BSN, U. R.I., 1974, MA in Edn., 1989. Staff nurse John E. Fogarty Meml. Hosp., Woonsocket, R.I., 1974-76; nursing coord. John E. Fogarty Meml. Hosp., Woonsocket, 1976-79; triage nurse Brown U. Health Svcs., Providence, 1989-90; case magr. Meml. Hosp. of R.I., Pawtucket, 1990-94; patient care coord. Coop. Care of R.I., Providence, 1994—; cons. Personal Health Care Records, Barrington, R.I., 1989—. Author: Personal Health Care Records, 1989. Exec. bd. Parents Reaching Out of R.I., Providence, 1989—. Recipient Nursing Excellence award Hosp. Assn. R.I., Providence, 1994. Mem. Internat. Urological Sci., Nat. Orgn. for Rare Disorders, Ehlers Danlos Nat. Found., Assn. for the Care of Children's Health, Sigma Theta Tau. Home: 5 Quincy Adams Rd Barrington RI 02806-5030 Office: Coop Care RI 2 Dudley St Providence RI 02903

RICHARDSON, STEPHEN GILES, biotechnology company executive; b. Mpls., Sept. 17, 1951; s. Richard Giles and Constance Bernice (Krieg) R.; m. Maureane Hoffman, Mar. 21, 1981. BA cum laude, Wartburg Coll., 1972; MS, U. Iowa, 1974, PhD, 1981; postdoctoral, Duke U., 1982-84. Territory mgr. Wyeth Labs., Phila., 1974-76; research asst. U. Iowa, Iowa City, 1976-82; research assoc. Duke, Durham, N.C., 1982-84; scientist Becton Dickinson Rsch. Ctr., Research Triangle Park, N.C., 1984-86; devel. group leader Dade (formerly div. Baxter Healthcare), Miami, Fla., 1986; research group leader Organon Teknika Corp., Durham, N.C., 1987-89; R&D sect. head, internat. R&D area mgr., 1989-90; program mgr. divsn. Akzo Nobel, N.V. Organon Teknika Corp., Durham, N.C., 1990-94, assoc. dir., head product devel., 1994—. Contbr. articles to profl. jours.; patentee in field. Co-founder Libertarian Party Minn., Mpls., 1972; exec. sec. Iowa Council to Repeal Conscription, Waterloo, 1971. Mem. Am. Chem. Soc., Am. Assn. Blood Banks, Am. Assn. for Clin. Chemistry, Royal Soc. Chemistry (U.K.), N.Y. Acad. Sci., Sigma Xi. Home: 5408 Sunny Ridge Dr Durham NC 27705-8552 Office: Organon Teknika Corp Divsn Akzo Nobel NV 100 Akzo Ave Durham NC 27712-9402

RICHARDSON, WILLIAM CHASE, foundation executive; b. Passaic, N.J., May 11, 1940; s. Henry Burtt and Frances (Chase) R.; m. Nancy Freeland, June 18, 1966; children: Elizabeth, Jennifer. BA, Trinity Coll., 1962; MBA, U. Chgo., 1964, PhD, 1971. Rsch. assoc., instr. U. Chgo., 1967-70; asst. prof. health services U. Wash., 1971-73, assoc. prof., 1973-76, prof., 1976-84, chmn. dept. health services, 1973-76, assoc. dean Sch. Pub. Health, 1976-81, acting dean, 1977, 78, dean Grad. Sch., vice provost, 1981-84; exec. v.p., provost, prof. dept. family and community medicine Pa. State U., 1984-90; pres. Johns Hopkins U., Balt., 1990-95, pres., prof. emeritus, 1995, prof. dept. health policy, mgmt., 1990-95, prof. emeritus, 1995—; pres., CEO W.K. Kellogg Found, Battle Creek, Mich., 1995—; cons. in field; bd. dirs. Kellogg Co., CSX Corp., Mercantile Bankshares Corp., Mercantile-Safe Deposit & Trust Co. Author: books, including Ambulatory Use of Physicians Services, 1971, Health Program Evaluation, 1978; contbr. articles to profl. jours. Mem. external adv. com. Fred Hutchinson Cancer Rsch. Ctr. Kellogg fellow, 1965-67. Fellow Am. Public Health Assn.; mem. Inst. Medicine, Nat. Acad. Scis. Office: WK Kellogg Found One Michigan Ave E Battle Creek MI 49017

RICHENBACHER, WAYNE EDWARD, cardiothoracic surgeon; b. Akron, May 2, 1954. BS with high honors, Case Western Res. U., 1976; MD, U. Cin., 1980. Resident Pa. State U., Hershey, 1980-88, instr., 1988-89; asst. prof. U. Utah, Salt Lake City, 1989-93; assoc. prof. U. Iowa, Iowa City, 1993—. Rsch. fellow Pa. State U., 1982-83, 85-86. Fellow ACS mem. Am. Soc. Artificial Internal Organs (travel fellow 1986, Graphic Forum award 1986), Internat. Soc. Heart and Lung Transplant, Internat. Soc. Artificial Organs, Assn. Acad. Surgery, Soc. Thoracic Surgeons, Am. Assn. Thoracic Surgery. Office: U Iowa Hosps & Clinics 1613-B JCP 200 Hawkins Dr Iowa City IA 52242

RICHENS, MURIEL WHITTAKER, AIDS therapist, counselor and educator; b. Prineville, Oreg.; d. John Reginald and Victoria Cecilia (Pascale) Whittaker; children: Karen, John, Candice, Stephanie, Rebecca. BS, Oreg. State U.; MA, San Francisco State U., 1962; postgrad., U. Calif., Berkeley, 1967-69, U. Birmingham, Eng., 1973, U. Soria, Spain, 1981. Lic. sch. adminstr., tchr. 7-12, pupil personnel specialist, Calif., marriage, child and family counselor, Calif. Instr. Springfield (Oreg.) High Sch., San Francisco State U.; instr., counselor Coll. San Mateo, Calif., San Mateo High Sch. Dist., 1963-86; therapist AIDS Health Project U. Calif., San Francisco, 1988—; pvt. practice MFCC San Mateo; guest West German-European Acad. seminar, Berlin, 1975. Lifeguard, ARC. postgrad. student Ctr. for Human Communications, Los Gatos, Calif., 1974, U. P.R., 1977, U. Guadalajara (Mex.), 1978, U. Durango (Mex.), 1980, U. Guanajuato (Mex.) 1982. Mem. U. Calif. Berkeley Alumni Assn., Am. Contract Bridge League (Diamond Life Master, cert. instr., tournament dir.), Women in Comm., Computer-Using Educators, Commonwealth Club, Pi Lambda Theta, Delta Pi Epsilon. Republican. Roman Catholic. Home and Office: 847 N Humboldt St Apt 309 San Mateo CA 94401-1451

RICHERT, HARVEY MILLER, II, ophthalmologist; b. Weatherford, Okla., Aug. 25, 1948; s. Harvey Miller and Catherine Cornelia (Ryan) R.; m. Diana Dee Sisney, Nov. 23, 1966; children: Ronald Lance, Rachelle Lea. BS, Southwestern Okla. State U., 1970; MD, U. Okla., Oklahoma City, 1974. Intern St. Anthony Hosp., Oklahoma City, 1974-75; resident in ophthalmology Tulane U., New Orleans, 1975-78; physician Tucker & Walker Ophthalmology Assocs., Abilene, Tex., 1978-80; ptnr. Tucker, Walker & Richert, Abilene, 1980-86; pvt. practice Abilene, 1986—; med. dir. Lions Eye Bank, Abilene, 1979—; head opthalmology sect. Humana Hosp., 1984-90, Hendrick Med. Ctr., 1984-92. V.p. Chisholm Trail coun. Boy Scouts Am., 1984-89, 92—, dist. chmn., 1990-92, asst. scoutmaster, 1982-85, scoutmaster, 1985-88. Recipient Scoutmaster of Merit award, Silver Beaver award, Dist. award of Merit, Boy Scouts Am., 1988. Fellow Am. Acad. Ophthalmology, Castroviejo Soc. (assoc.); mem. AMA, Tex. Ophthal. Assn., Tex. Med. Assn., Lions (founders club), Abilene C. of C. Republican. Baptist. Home: 15 Glen Abbey St Abilene TX 79606-5023 Office: 950 N 19th St Ste 200 Abilene TX 79601-2413

RICHICHI-CHIANESE, JOANN, obstetrician, gynecologist; b. Bklyn., Dec. 30, 1957; d. John B. and Helen M. (Lobriaco) R.; m. Anthony Chianese, Mar. 1, 1986; children: Alex, Nicholas. Wagner Coll., 1978; MD, Coll. Oseto Med Pacific, 1984. Internship Kennedy Meml. Hosp. Stratford, N.J., 1984-85, ob/gyn residency, 1985-89; prof. Univ. Medicine & Dental of N.J., Stratford, 1991-92, mem. admissions com., 1990-92, mem. intern & resident selection com., 1989-94. Contbr. articles to profl. jours. Fellow Am. Coll. Osteopathic Obstetricians & Gynecologists. Office: SDR OB& GYN Assoc 106 King's Way W Sewell NJ 08080

RICHIE, RODNEY CHARLES, critical care and pulmonary medicine physician; b. Big Springs, Tex., Aug. 17, 1946; s. Howard Mouzon and Gloria (Hollingshead) R.; m. Sara Lee Dilley, July 13, 1968; children: Megan Kathryn, Paul Nathan. BA in Chemistry, So. Meth. U., 1968; MD cum laude, Baylor Coll., 1972. Diplomate in Internal Medicine, Pulmonary, Crit. Care and Ins. Medicine. Resident in medicine Baylor Affiliated Hosps., Houston, 1973-75, chief med. resident, 1975, fellow in pulmonary medicine, 1976-77; pvt. practice, pres. Waco (Tex.) Lung Assocs., 1977—; med. dir. Tex. Life Ins., Waco, 1985—. Chmn. med. staff Hillcrest Bapt. Med. Ctr., Waco, 1993; chmn. bd. dirs. GH Pape Found., Waco, 1993. Fellow Am. Coll. Chest Physicians; mem. ACP, AMA, Am. Thoracic Soc., Tex. Club Internists. Episcopalian. Home: 3509 Lake Heights Dr Waco TX 76708-1005 Office: Waco Med Group 2911 Herring Ave Ste 212 Waco TX 76708-3244

RICHMAN, DAVID PAUL, neurologist, researcher; b. Boston, June 9, 1943; s. Harry S. and Anne (Goodkin) R.; m. Carol Mae von Bastian, Aug. 31, 1969; children—Sarah Ann, Jacob Charles. A.B., Princeton U., 1965; M.D., Johns Hopkins U., 1969. Diplomate Am. Bd. Psychiatry and Neurology. Intern, asst. resident in medicine Albert Einstein Coll. Medicine, N.Y.C., 1969-71; resident in neurology Mass. Gen. Hosp., Boston, 1971-73, chief resident in neurology, 1973-74; instr. neurology Harvard Med. Sch., Boston, 1975-76; asst. prof. neurology U. Chgo., 1976-80, assoc. prof. dept. neurology, mem. immunology and neurobiology coms., 1981-85, prof. dept. neurology and com. on immunology, 1985-91, Straus prof. neurol. scis., 1988-91; prof., chair dept. neurology U. Calif., Davis, 1991—; mem. com. Nat. Inst. Aging, NIH, 1984-85, mem. immunological scis. study sect., 1986-90. Mem. AAAS, Am. Assn. Immunologists, Am. Acad. Neurology, Am. Neurol. Assn., Phi Beta Kappa, Sigma Xi. Office: U Calif Davis Neurology Dept Davis CA 95616-8603

RICHMAN, JOSEPH HERBERT, public health services official; b. Balt., Aug. 13, 1941; s. Samuel and Beatrice R. BS, Howard U., 1962, MD, 1966; MPH, Johns Hopkins U., 1974. Intern Maimonides Med. Ctr., Bklyn., 1966-67; resident pediats. Sinai Hosp. of Balt., 1967-69; chief sch. health P.G. Health Dept. of Md., Cleve., 1972-75; dir. area health svcs. Montgomery County Health Dept., Bethesda, Md., 1975-82; county chief pub. health physician State of Del., Dover, 1982—. Fellow Am. Acad. Pediatrics, Am. Coll. Preventive Medicine; mem. Masons, Rotary, Phi Beta Kappa. Democrat. Jewish. Home: PO Box 386 Dover DE 19903-0386 Office: Divsn Pub Health of Del 805 River Rd Dover DE 19901-3753

RICHMAN, JUSTIN LEWIS, physician; b. Providence, Apr. 12, 1925; s. Sydney and Rose Lillian (Cohen) R.; m. Susan Kadison, May 19, 1957; children: Donna, Vicki, Toby. AB, Brown U., 1946; MD, Tufts U., 1949. Diplomate Am. Bd. Internal Medicine. Assoc. prof. medicine Tufts U., Boston, 1982—. Lt. sgt. USNRA 1954-55. Fellow Am. Coll. Cardiology, Am. Soc. Internal Medicine. Home: 14 Ledgewood Rd Newton MA 02161 Office: 25 Boylston St Chestnut Hill MA 02167

RICHMAN, MARC HERBERT, forensic engineer, educator; b. Boston, Oct. 14, 1936; s. Samuel and Janet (Gordon) R.; m. Ann Raeshel Yoffa, Aug. 31, 1963. BS, MIT, 1957, ScD, 1963; MA, Brown U., 1967. Registered profl. engr., Conn., Mass., R.I.; cert. forensic examiner. Cons. engr., 1957—; engr. shipbldg. div. Bethlehem Steel Corp., Quincy, Mass., 1957; instr. metallurgy MIT, Cambridge, 1957-60, research asst. dept. metallurgy, 1960-63; instr. metallurgy div. univ. extension Commonwealth of Mass., 1958-62; asst. prof. engring. Brown U., Providence, 1963-67, assoc. prof., 1967-70, prof., 1970—, dir. central electron microscopy facility Materials Research program, 1971-86, dir. undergrad. program in engring. 1991—; pres. Ednl. Aids of Newton Inc., Providence, 1968-71, Marc H. Richman Inc., Providence, 1981—; guest scientist Franklin Inst., Phila., 1959; vis. prof. U. R.I., Kingston, 1970-71; biophysicist dept. medicine Miriam Hosp., Providence, 1974-87; biogengr. dept. orthopaedics R.I. Hosp., 1979-93. Author: Introduction to Science of Metals, 1967; also articles; editor Soviet Physics: Crystallography, 1970-94; mem. editorial adv. bd. Metallography, 1970—; mem. editorial adv. bd. Jour. Forensic Engring., 1985-88. Maj. Ordnance Corps, U.S. Army, 1963. Served to maj. Ordnance Corps, U.S. Army, 1963. Recipient Engr. of Yr. award R.I. Soc. Profl. Engrs., 1993. Fellow Nat. Acad. Forensic Engrs. (cert.), Am. Coll. Forensic Examiners (cert.), Am. Inst. Chemists, Inst. Materials (U.K.); mem. ASCE, AIME, NSPE, ASEE (Outstanding Young Faculty award 1969), NAFE (bd. cert. diplomate in forensic engring.), Am. Acad. Forensic Scis., Am. Soc. Metals (sec.-treas. 1965-68, chmn. R.I. chpt. 1968-69, Albert Sauveur Meml. award 1968, 69), Providence Engring. Soc. (pres. 1991-92, Freeman award for engring. achievement 1989), B'nai B'rith, Sigma Xi, Tau Beta Pi. Home: 291 Cole Ave Providence RI 02906-3452 Office: Brown U Divsn Engring Box D Providence RI 02912 also: One Richmond Sq Providence RI 02906

RICHMAN, MONROE FRANKLIN, physician; b. Bklyn., Feb. 26, 1927; s. Samuel David and Beatrice Paula (Kasselman) R.; m. Esther Sarner, July 8, 1951; children: Keith, David, Craig, Marla. BA, NYU, 1949; MS, Syracuse U., 1951; MD, SUNY, Syracuse, 1955. Diplomate Am. Bd. Family Practice. Intern St. Joseph's Hosp., Elmira, N.Y., 1955-56; rsch. asst. Syracuse U., 1949-50; prodn. engr. GE, Syracuse, 1950, rsch. physicist, 1951; pvt. practice Sun Valley, Calif., 1956—; pres. Medco Assoc. Inc., Pacoima, Calif., 1986—; cons. space medicine, bioinstrumentation N.Am. Aviation, El Segundo, Calif., 1959-61. Contbr. articles to profl. jours. Commr. police and fire pensions City of L.A., 1964-72, AIDS Commn. County of L.A., 1988-90; trustee L.A. Community Coll., 1971-87; founding mem. Calif. Coun. on Humanities, 1978. With USN, 1945-46. Mem. Rotary (dist. gov. 1967-68, pres. 1965-67). Office: Medco Assn Inc 10325 Glenoaks Blvd Pacoima CA 91331-1607

RICHMAN, PETER SPEER, surgeon; b. Encino, Calif., July 26, 1957; s. Walter Powell and Marjorie (Speer) R.; m. Marie Martel, Aug. 5, 1990. BA, Amherst Coll., 1979; MD, UCLA, 1985. Resident Harbor-UCLA Med. Ctr., Torrance, 1985-91; surgeon Facey Med. Group, Missions Hills, Calif., 1991—. Author: (book chpt.) Current Therapy in Vascular Surgery, 1991. Fellow Am. Coll. Surgeons (liaison physician commn. on cancer 1996), Am. Soc. Gen. Surgeons, Sigma Xi. Office: Facey Med Group 11211 Sepulveda Blvd Mission Hills CA 91345-1115

RICHMAN, SELMA, microbiologist; b. Bklyn.; d. Joseph and Leah (Kennis) R. B.S., Bklyn. Coll.; M.A., Cen. Mich. U., 1979. Successively lab. technician Queens Gen. Hosp., Jamaica, N.Y.; jr. microbiologist Cumberland Hosp., Bklyn.; asst microbiologist Queens Hosp. Ctr., Jamaica; prin. microbiologist Coney Island Hosp., Bklyn., 1965-91, tech. dir. microbiology and serology, 1991—; lectr. Scientists in Sch. program N.Y. Acad. Scis.; judge sch. sci. fairs, N.Y.C.; cons. in field. Author: Case Study on Aeromonas Hydrophila, 1982. Mem. NAFE, Am. Soc. Clin. Pathologists, Am. Soc. Microbiology, Med. Mycology Soc. Am. Avocations: knitting, tennis, racquetball, swimming, music. Office: Coney Island Hosp 2601 Ocean Pky Brooklyn NY 11235-7791

RICHMAN, SIDNEY M., cardiologist; b. Providence, June 14, 1932; s. Harry and Sonia (Sklar) R.; m. Adele Richman, Nov. 10, 1955; children: Lynn, Karen, Susan, Stacy. AB, Brown U., 1954; MD, Washington U., St. Louis, 1958. Diplomat Am. Bd. Internal Medicine, Am. Bd. Cardiology. Pvt. practice, Hartford, Conn., 1962-95; chief cardiology Mt. Sinai Hosp., Hartford, 1970-72, West Palm Beach (Fla.) VA Med. Ctr., 1995—. Contbr. articles to med. jours. Chmn. Hartford Heart Assn., 1976-78. Fellow ACP, Am. Coll. Cardiology; mem. Phi Beta Kappa. Office: West Palm Beach VA Med Ctr 7305 N Military Trail West Palm Beach FL 33410

RICHMOND, ALLEN MARTIN, speech pathologist, educator; b. N.Y.C., July 24, 1936; m. Deborah Moll. BS, SUNY, Geneseo, 1958; MEd, Pa. State U., 1961; PhD, Ohio U., 1965. Instr. N.Y.S. Public Schools, 1958-60, Penn. Rehab. Ctr., 1960-62, Buffalo Hearing and Speech Ctr., 1969-88; clin. instr. dept. otolaryngology SUNY Med. Sch., 1980—; speech pathologist dept. otolaryngology SUNY, Buffalo, 1989—; vis. prof. U. Md., 1968; adj. asst. prof. comm. disorders dept., 1989—; staff Sisters of Charity Hosp.; advisor New Voice Club of Niagara Frontier, Buffalo, 1980-90; cons. Bry-Lin Hosp., Buffalo, 1989—, W.B. Saunders Co., 1988. Contbg. author: An Atlas of Head and Neck Surgery. Participant Very Spl. Arts, Niagara, 1990—. Mem. Am. Speech-Lang.-Hearing Assn. Home: 423 Walton Dr Buffalo NY 14225-1005 Office: Sisters Hosp Head and Neck Ctr 2157 Main St Buffalo NY 14214

RICHMOND, DAVID ERIC, college dean; b. Auckland, New Zealand, Jan. 1, 1938; s. Louis Eric and Dinah Wilhelmina (Green) R.; m. Pauline Reynolds, Jan. 15, 1966; children: Anthony John, Mary Elizabeth-Anne. MBChB, U. Otago, Dunedin, New Zealand, 1962, MD, 1977; MPHEd, U. New South Wales, Sydney, Australia, 1982; BD, Melbourne (Australia) Coll. Divinity, 1995. Diplomate Am. Bd. Internal Medicine, Am. Bd. Nephrology. Resident Georgetown U., Washington, 1969-70; sr. lectr. in medicine U. Auckland (New Zealand), 1970-78, Masonic prof. geriatric medicine, 1986-94, asst. dean, 1994—; med. dir. Ciba-Geigy, Auckland, 1984-86; cons. delivery med. svcs. to South Vietnam, Govt. of New Zealand, 1972-73; vis. cons. in medicine U. Papua, New Guinea, 1975-76, vis. cons. in nephrology Queen Mary Hosp., Hong Kong, 1978; con. med. edn. WHO, Singapore, 1979, New Delhi, India, 1990, Manila, 1991. Contbr. articles to profl. jours., chpts. to books. chair New Zealand Coun. Asia Pacific Christian Mission, Auckland, 1978—; active Bapt. Edn., Svc. & Tng. Bd., Auckland, 1992-94; chair bd. trustees Auckland Found. Tng. Rsch. & Edn. in the Health of Older People, 1993—; active bd. mgmt. Carey Bapt. Theol. Coll., Auckland, 1994—. Grantee in field. Fellow Royal Australian Coll. Physicians (dir. continuing med. edn. 1979-84), Royal Coll. Physicians (London); mem. New Zealand Geriatrics Soc. (pres. 1995-96), New Zealand Assn. Gerontology, Australia/New Zealand Assn. Med. Edn. Baptist. Office: U Auckland Sch Medicine & Health Scis, Pvt Bag 92019, Auckland New Zealand

RICHMOND, GLENN EUGENE, nursing administrator; b. Akron, Ohio, Sept. 19, 1949; s. Carl Eugene and Dorla Mae (Allman) R. BA in Edn., U. New Orleans, 1971; BSN, William Carey Coll., 1976; M. Nursing, La. State U., 1983. RN, La.; clin. nurse specialist. Tchr. English Jefferson Parish Sch. Bd., Gretna, La., 1972-75; dialysis nurse Hotel Dieu Hosp., New Orleans, 1976-78; DON Westbank Renal Ctr., New Orleans, 1978-81; clin. nurse specialist Tulane Univ. Hosp., New Orleans, 1981-89, mgr. quality assessment, case mgmt., infection control, 1989-95, dir. quality assessment, risk mgmt., infection control, 1995—. Office: Tulane University Hospital 1415 Tulane Ave #Hc-13 New Orleans LA 70112-2605

RICHMOND, ISABELLE LOUISE, neurosurgeon; b. N.Y.C., July 9, 1944. BS, Cornell U., 1965, PhD, 1968; MD, Duke U., 1974. Neurosurgeon pvt. practice, Norfolk, Va., 1984—; clin. prof. USUHS, Bethesda, Md., 1984—; assoc. prof. neurosurgery EUMS, Norfolk, 1984—. Chmn. peer rev. dist. V Va. State Bd. Workmen's Compensation, 1994—. Col. U.S. Army Med. Corps, 1979-84. NSF Postdoctoral grantee, 1968-70; NSF fellow, 1965-68. Fellow Am. Coll. Surgeons; mem. AANS, CNS, AMA, Norfolk Acad. Medicine (pres. 1993-94), Alpha Omega ALpha, Phi Kappa Phi. Office: 229 W Bute St 230 Norfolk VA 23510

RICHMOND, JONATHAN Y., public health administration officer. BA in Zoology, U. Conn., 1962, MS in Genetics, 1964; PhD in Genetics, Hahnemann U., 1967. Post-doctoral resident rsch. fellow Plum Island Animal Disease Ctr., Greenport, N.Y., 1967-69; rsch. microbiologist Plum Island Animal Disease Ctr., USDA, ARS, Greenport, 1969-79; biol. safety officer Plum Island Animal Disease Ctr., USDA, Greenport, 1979-83; chief safety ops. sect. Occupl. Safety and Health br., Divsn. Safety NIH, Bethesda, Md., 1983-90; dir. WHO Collaborating Ctr. Applied Biosafety and Tng., Ctrs. for Disease Control, Atlanta, 1990—, Office Health and Safety, Ctrs. for Disease Control and Prevention, Atlanta, 1990—; mem. planning com. ann. NIH Rsch. Safety Symposia, 1983-84, 88; chairperson Ctrs. for Disease Control Nat. Symposium on Biosafety, 1992, 94, 96, coord. Pub. Health Merit Badge Seminar, 1993, 95; internat. cons. lab design project San Juan, P.R., 1993—, Project RETRO-CI, Abidjan, Ivory Coast, Africa, 1994—, Plasma-derived Hepatitis B Vaccine Project, Bulandshar, Uttar Pradesh, India, 1994, Viral Diagnostic Lab., Toronto, 1995. Editor: (with R.W. McKinney) Biosafety in Mirobiological and Biomedical Laboratories, 3rd edit., 1993, Primary Containment for Biohazards: Selection and Use of Biological Safety Cabinets, 1st edit., 1995; contbr. articles to profl. jours. Fellow Am. Acad. Microbiology; mem. Am. Biol. Safety Assn. (steering com. 1979-81, pres. 1986-87, exec. coun. 1985-88, ann. conf. chairperson 1988, pres. Chesapeake Area chpt. 1989-90, Everett Hanel Jr. Meml. award

1995), Am. Soc. Microbiology (coord. biosafety workshops 1986, 89, 94, mem. lab. safety com. 1993—). *

RICHMOND, JULIUS BENJAMIN, retired physician, health policy educator emeritus; b. Chgo., Sept. 26, 1916; s. Jacob and Anna (Dayno) R.; m. Rhee Chidekel, June 3, 1937 (dec. Oct. 9, 1985); children: Barry J., Charles Allen, Dale Keith (dec.); m. Jean Rabow, Jan. 11, 1987. BS, U. Ill., 1937, MS, MD, 1939; DSc (hon.), Ind. U., 1978, Rush-Presbyn.-St. Luke Med. Ctr., 1978, U. Ill., 1979, Georgetown U., 1980, SUNY, Syracuse, 1986, U. Ariz., 1991; DMS (hon.), Med. Coll. Pa., 1980; D in Pub. Svc. (hon.), Nat. Coll. Edn., Evanston, Ill., 1980; LHD (hon.), Tufts U., 1986. Intern Cook County Hosp., Chgo., 1939-41, resident, 1941-42, 46; resident Mcpl. Contagious Disease Hosp., Chgo., 1941; mem. faculty U. Ill. Med. Sch., Chgo., 1946-53, prof. pediatrics, 1950-53; dir. Inst. Juvenile Research Inst. Juvenile Rsch., Chgo., 1952-53; prof., chmn. dept. pediatrics Coll. Medicine, SUNY at Syracuse, 1953-65, dean med. faculty, chmn. dept. pediatrics, 1965-70; prof. child psychiatry and human devel., prof., chmn. dept. preventive and social medicine Harvard Med. Sch., 1971-77, prof. health policy, 1981-88, dir. divsn. health policy rsch. and edn., 1983-88, prof. health policy emeritus, 1988—; also faculty Harvard Sch. Pub. Health; psychiatrist-in-chief Children's Hosp. Med. Center, Boston, 1971-77, adv. on child health policy, 1981—; dir. Judge Baker Guidance Center, Boston, 1971-77; asst. sec. health and surgeon gen. HHS, 1977-81; mem. Pres.'s Commn. on Mental Health, 1977. Author: Pediatric Diagnosis, 1962, Currents in American Medicine, 1969. Nat. dir. Project Head Start; dir. Office Health Affairs OEO, 1965-66. Served as flight surgeon USAAF, 1942-46. Recipient Agnes Bruce Greig Sch. award, 1966, Parents Mag. award, 1966, Disting. Service award Office Econ. Opportunity, 1967, Family Health Mag. award, 1977, Myrdal award Assn. For Evaluation Rsch., 1977, award for disting. sci. contbn. Soc. for Research in Child Devel., 1979, Dolly Madison award Inst. on Clin. Infants Programs, 1979, Public Health Disting. Service award HEW, 1980, Illini Achievement award U. Ill. Alumni Assn., 1982, Community Service award Health Planning Council Greater Boston, 1985, Lemuel Shattuck award Mass. Pub. Health Assn., 1985, 1st Ann. Ronald McDonald Children's Charities award for Outstanding Contbns. to Child Health and Welfare, 1986, Sedgwick award APHA, 1992. Fellow Am. Orthopsychiat. Assn. (Ittleson award 1994), Am. Psychiat. Assn. (disting.); mem. Am. Acad. Child Psychiatry (hon.), New Eng. Coun. Child Psychiatry (assoc.), Inst. Medicine of NAS (1st Ann. Gustav O. Lienhard award 1986), AMA (AMA-ERF award in health edn. 1988), Am. Pediatric Soc. (John Howland award 1990), Am. Acad. Pediatrics (C. Anderson Aldrich award 1966, ann. award sect. on community pediatrics 1977, Outstanding Contbn. award sect. community pediatrics 1978), Soc. Pediatric Rsch., Am. Psychosomatic Soc., APHA (Martha May Eliot award 1970, Sedgwick Medal 1992), Sigma Xi, Alpha Omega Alpha, Phi Eta Sigma.

RICHMOND, LEA, surgeon; b. Oklahoma City, Jan. 28, 1923; s. Lea and Corinne (Johnson) R.; m. Jo Sharp, Nov. 17, 1967; children: Lea III, John. BA, Emory U., 1946, MD, 1950. Diplomate Am. Bd. Surgery. Intern St. Albans Naval Hosp., 1950-51; surg. resident Grady Meml. Hosp., 1951-52; resident Atlanta VA Hosp., 1952-53; pvt. practice Atlanta, 1955—. Bd. trustees, chmn. North Side Hosp., Atlanta; chmn. north Side Hosp. Found., Atlanta; bd. mem. Holy Innocents Sch., Atlanta, 1959-67; head profl. divsn. United Way Met. Atlanta. Lt. (j.g.) USN, 1950-51. Mem. Cherokee Town and Country Club, Sandy Springs Rotary (initial pres.). Episcopalian. Home: 6690 Riverside Dr NW Atlanta GA 30328 Office: 755 Mt Vernon Hwy Atlanta GA 30328-4274

RICHMOND, ROSALIND, clinical social worker; b. Boston, May 18, 1938; d. Leonard J. and Esther (Greenberg) R. BS, Simmons Coll., MS. Clin. social worker MGH, Boston, 1962-65; clin. social worker VA Hosp., Livermore, Calif., 1966-67, San Francisco, 1967—; lic. examiner Bd. Behavioral Scis., Sacramento, 1982; chmn. patient edn. com. San Francisco Hosp., 1983-87, social work student supr. psychiat. emergency room; co-organizer psychiatric AIDS program, 1989—; co-leader substance abuse AIDS group, 1995. Recipient Dir's. Commendation, San Francisco Hosp., 1982, 83, 85, 91. Mem. Nat. Assn. Social Workers (cert.), Simmons Coll. Alumnae Assn. (v.p. 1972-73, pres. 1973-74). Democrat. Jewish. Home: 1 Summerhill Way San Rafael CA 94903-3813 Office: VA Med Ctr 4150 Clement St San Francisco CA 94121-1545

RICHSTONE, BEVERLY JUNE, psychologist; b. N.Y.C., June 8, 1952; d. Max and Rosalyn Richstone. BA summa cum laude, Queens Coll., 1975; MEd, U. Miami, 1978; PsyD, Nova U., 1982. Lic. clin. psychologist. Clin. fellow Harvard Med. Sch., 1982-83; staff psychologist Met. State Hosp., Waltham, Mass., 1983-85; asst. attending psychologist McLean Hosp., Belmont, Mass., 1983-84; asst. psychologist Cambridge Hosp./N. Charles Mental Health Rsch./Tng. Found., Cambridge, Mass., 1984-85; assoc. dir. Coastal Geriatric Svcs., Hingham, Mass., 1985-86, Alpha Geriatric Svcs., Hingham, 1986-87; rsch. assoc. Harvard Sch. Pub. Health, Boston, 1992-94; instr. psychology Harvard Med. Sch., Boston, 1983-84; consulting psychologist Coastal Geriatric Svcs., Hingham, 1985. Contbg. author: The New Our Bodies, Ourselves, 1992. Cmty. advisor Mass. Office Disability, Boston, 1992—. Mem. APA, Phi Beta Kappa.

RICHTER, HARRY MARK, dentist; b. Rutland, Vt., June 15, 1954; s. Morris and Bina R.; m. Faye J. Weintraub, June 14, 1981; children: Rebecca Lynn, Rachel Leigh. BA in Biology, Temple U., 1975; DDS, Georgetown U., 1981; Cert. in Comprehensive Dentistry, U. Fla., 1987. Sanitarian Phila. Health Dept., 1975-77; dentist USPHS, Cross City, Fla., 1981-84; dentist pvt. practice Newberry, Fla., 1985—; dental dir. Dixie Dental Unit, Cross City, 1981-84. Dir. Newberry C. of C., 1987. Lt. USPHS, 1981-84. Fellow, Acad. Gen. Dentistry, 1991. Fellow Acad. Gen. Dentistry (master); mem. Am. Dental Assn., Ctrl. Dist. Dental Assn., Alachus County Dental Soc., Suwanee River Valley Dental Study Club (program chmn. 1989, 90, 91). Home: 12 S Main St Newberry FL 32669-0455 Office: Harry M Richter DDS PO Box 455 Newberry FL 32669-0455

RICHTER, KENNETH JAMES, oral and maxillofacial surgeon; b. Neenah, Wis., Feb. 8, 1935; s. Walter William and Elizabeth Mary (Polansky) R.; m. Elia Josepha Camorlinga, Nov. 25, 1964. BA, Macalester Coll., St. Paul, Minn., 1957; DDS, U. Minn. Dental Sch., Mpls., 1960, MSD, 1969. Diplomate Am. Bd. Oral & Maxillofacial Surgery. Assoc. prof. oral surgery U. Minn. Dental Sch., Mpls., 1970-74; chief oral surgery St. Paul Ramsey Hosp., 1972-74; pvt. practice oral surgery St. Cloud, Minn., 1974-84; clin. assoc. prof. oral and maxillofacial surgery U. Minn. Sch. Dentistry, Mpls., 1985—; chief oral and maxillofacial surgery VA Med. Ctr., Mpls., 1985—. Contbr. articles to profl. jours. Lt. comdr. USPHS, 1960-65. Mem. ADA, Am. Soc. Oral & Maxillofacial Surgeons, Minn. Soc. Oral & Maxillofacial Surgeons. Home: 10 Poplar Ln North Oaks MN 55127 Office: VA Med Ctr Dental Svc 160 1 Veterans Dr Minneapolis MN 55417

RICHTER, LINDA DALE, occupational therapist, management consultant; b. Ft. Collins, Colo., Jan. 11, 1949; d. Kenneth Dale and Dorothy Lenore (Ward) R.; m. Robert Allan Manuel, Dec. 31, 1988. BS, Colo. State U., 1972, MS, 1984, PhD, 1995. Dir. occupational therapy Mercy Med. Ctr., OshKosh, Wis., 1973-74; dir. occupational therapy Poudre Valley Hosp., Ft. Collins, Wis., 1974-88, dir. work ctr., 1987-88; developer, pvt. cons. mgmt. tng. for health care mgrs. Bldg. Bridges, Ft. Collins, 1986—; owner, dir. Life Achievement Systems, Ft. Collins, 1989—, New Visions, Ft. Collins, 1994—; loaned exec. United Way campaign Poudre Valley Hosp., 1986-88; mem. affiliate faculty Colo. State U., Ft. Collins, 1985—, postgrad. field work rep., 1985-88, adj. faculty, 1992—. Mem. Am. Occupational Therapy Assn., World Fedn. Occupational Therapists, Ft. Collins Soc. of Head Injury Found. (pres. 1988), Nat. Head Injury Found. (bd. dirs. Denver chpt. 1988-91), Colo. Occupational Therapy Assn., Ptnrs. of Colo. Assn. (chairperson com. of rehab. and phys. medicine). Republican. Office: Life Achievement Systems 3030 S College Ave Unit 101 Fort Collins CO 80525-2557

RICHTER, ROBERT MARK, surgeon; b. N.Y.C., Feb. 27, 1933; s. Irving Phillip and Madeline Hortense (Margon) R.; m. Gladys Liberman, June 14, 1954; children: Sara Gruenspecht, Miriam. BS, Union Coll., 1954; MD, Albany Med. Coll., 1958. Diplomate Am. Bd. Surgery. Intern, resident surgery Mt. Sinai Hosp., N.Y.C., 1958-64; assoc. dir. surgery Greenpoint Hosp., Bklyn., 1964-68, Jewish Hosp., Bklyn., 1968-78; pvt. practice Bklyn., 1978—. Fellow Am. Coll. Surgeons, Am. Coll. Gastroenterology, N.Y. Soc. Colon & Rectal Surgeons; mem. Am. Soc. Colon & Rectal Surgeons, Sigma Xi, Phi Beta Kappa, Alpha Omega Alpha. Office: 1 Hanson Pl #1511 Brooklyn NY 11243

RICHTER, SUSAN MARY, medical and surgical nurse; b. Breese, Ill., Aug. 17, 1959; d. Jerome J. and Emilia C. (Robke) Albers; m. Michael Richter, Nov. 14, 1980; children: David, Timothy, Alicia. ADN, Kaskaskia Coll., 1979. Nurse aide St. Joseph's Hosp., Breese, Ill., 1977-79; staff nurse ICU/telemetry unit St. Joseph's Hosp., Breese, 1979—; instr. BCLS, ACLS. Com. chmn. pack 273 Boy Scouts Am., Germantown, 1993. Recipient ARC Nurse Vol. award; named Outstanding Young Women in Am., 1989. Mem. Emergency Nurses Assn. (cert. trauma nursing core course provider).

RICKABAUGH, JEFF L., orthodontist; b. Oceanside, Calif., Oct. 31, 1956; s. Thomas H. and Freida M. (Nicholas) R.; m. Yvonne Pazdalski, Aug. 31, 1985; children: Thomas J., Alexander L. BA, Wichita State U., 1978; DDS, U. Mo., Kansas City, 1982; M Dental Sci., U. Pitts., 1993. Commd. ens. USN, 1982, advanced through grades to lt. comdr.; dental officer USN, Moffett Field, Calif., 1982-84, Mcas Kaneohe, Hawaii, 1984-87; mem. staff OIC-dental detachment USN, Camp Geiger, N.C., 1987-89; dept. head USN, Camp Lejeune, 1989-90; resigned USN, 1990; orthodontic resident U. Pitts., 1990-93; pvt. practice orthodontics Winston-Salem, N.C., 1993—. Patentee orthodontic apparatus and method. Mem. ADA, Am. Assn. Orthodontists (award of spl. merit 1994), N.C. Dental Soc., N.c. Assn. Orthodontists, Forsyth County Dental Soc. (program dir. 1995, treas. 1996). Home: 218 Cedar Trail Winston Salem NC 27104 Office: 1900 S Hawthorne Rd Ste 462 Winston Salem NC 27103

RICKARD, JOSEPH CONWAY, retired psychologist; b. Weatherford, Tex., July 16, 1926; s. Joe Smith and Mattie Mae (Wright) R.; m. Dorothy June Wilson, May 29, 1948; children: Miles, Janis, Robert, Martha, Sarah. AA, San Angelo Coll., 1948; PhD, U. Chgo., 1955. Lic. clin. psychologist, Tex. Clin. psychologist VA Med. Ctr., Temple, Tex., 1955-60, chief psychology svc., 1960-89; ret., 1989; pvt. practice, Temple, 1965-85; instr. U. Tex., U. Mary Hardin Baylor, Baylor U., 1956-86; cons. Temple Ind. Sch. Dist., 1965-79, Killeen (Tex.) Ind. Sch. Dist., 1970-86; prof. Tex. A&M Coll. Medicine, Temple, 1979-89. With USAAF, 1945-46. Fellow Soc. for Personality Assessment; mem. APA, Tex. Psychol. Assn. Episcopalian. Home: 3302 Oaklawn Dr Temple TX 76502-2328

RICKE, P. SCOTT, obstetrician, gynecologist; b. Indpls., June 28, 1948; s. Joseph and Betty (Rae) R.; divorced; 1 child. BA, Ind. U., 1970; MD, Ind. U. Sch. of Medicine, 1974. Bd. cert. ob-gyn., 1981. Intern St. Lukes Hosp., Denver, 1975; resident U. Calif. at Irvine, Orange, 1977-79; pvt. practice Ob-Gyn Tucson, 1981—; pres., founder The Adv. Group; founder, dir. Inst. for Med. Weight Loss. Inventor (med. instrument) Vaginal Retractor, 1989. Bd. dirs. City of Hope, Tucson, 1981-85, Am. Cancer Soc., Tucson, 1981-83. Fellow Am. Bd. Ob-Gyn.; mem. Am. Bariatric Soc. Home: 3755 N Tanuri Dr Tucson AZ 85715-1939 Office: 3972 N Campbell Tucson AZ 85719

RICKEL, ANNETTE URSO, psychology educator; b. Phila.; d. Ralph Francis and Marguerite (Calcaterra) Urso; m. Peter Rupert Fink, July 21, 1989; 1 child, John Ralph. BA, Mich. State U., 1963; MA, U. Mich., 1965, PhD, 1972. Lic. psychologist, Mich. Faculty early childhood edn. Merrill-Palmer Inst., Detroit, 1967-69; adj. faculty U. Mich., Ann Arbor, 1969-75; asst. dir. N.E. Guidance Ctr., Detroit, 1972-75; asst. prof. psychology Wayne State U., Detroit, 1975-81; vis. assoc. prof. Columbia U., N.Y.C., 1982-83; assoc. prof. psychology Wayne State U., 1981-87, asst. provost, 1989-91, prof. psychology, 1987—; Am. Coun. on Edn. fellow Princeton and Rutgers Univs., 1990-91; dir. mental health and devel. Nat. Com. for Quality Assurance, Washington, 1995-96; clin. prof. dept. Psychiatry Georgetown U., Washington, 1995—; AAAS and APA Congl. Sci. fellow on Senate Fin. Subcom. on Health and Pres.'s Nat. Health Care Reform Task Force, 1992-93. Cons. editor Jour. of Cmty. Psychology, Jour. Primary Prevention; co-author: Social and Psychological Problems of Women, 1984, Preventing Maladjustment..., 1987; author: Teenage Pregnancy and Parenting, 1989; contbr. articles to profl. jours. Mem. Pres.'s Task Force on Nat. Health Care Reform, 1993; bd. dirs. Children's Ctr. of Wayne County, Mich., The Epilepsy Ctr. of Mich., Planned Parenthood League, Inc. Grantee NIMH, 1976-86, Eloise and Richard Webber Found., 1977-80, McGregor Fund, 1977-78, 82, David M. Whitney Fund, 1982, Katherine Tuck Fund, 1985-90; recipient Career Devel. Chair award, 1985-86; Congl. Sci. fellow AAAS, 1992-93. Fellow APA (div. pres. 1984-85); mem. Midwestern Psychol. Assn., Mich. Psychol. Assn., Soc. for Rsch. in Child Devel., Soc. for Rsch. in Child and Adolescent Psychopathology, Internat. Assn. of Applied Psychologists, Sigma Xi, Psi Chi. Roman Catholic.

RICKELS, KARL, psychiatrist, physician, educator; b. Wilhelmshaven, Germany, Aug. 17, 1924; came to U.S., 1954, naturalized, 1960; s. Karl E. and Stephanie (Roehrhoff) R.; m. Rosalind Wilson, June 27, 1964; children: Laurence Arthur, Stephen W., Michael R. M.D., U. Muenster, 1951. Intern Dortmund (Germany) Hosp., 1951-52; postgrad. tng. U. Erlangen, U. Frankfurt, City Hosp. Kassel, 1952-54; resident in psychiatry Mental Health Inst., Cherokee, Iowa, 1954-55, Hosp. U. Pa., Phila., 1955-57; from instr. to assoc. prof. U. Pa., Phila., 1957-69; prof. psychiatry U. Pa., 1969—, prof. pharmacology, 1976—, Stuart and Emily B.H. Mudd prof. human behavior, 1977—, chief mood and anxiety disorders program, 1964—; chmn. com. on studies involving human beings U. Pa., Phila., 1985—; chief psychiatry Phila. Gen. Hosp., 1975-77. Editor, author 7 books; contbr. over 500 articles to profl. publs. Fellow Am. Coll. Neuropsychopharmacology (charter), Am. Coll. Clin. Pharmacology, Am. Psychiat. Assn., Coll. Physicians Phila., Collegium INternat. Neuro-Psychopharmacologicum; mem. Arbeits Gemeinschaft Neuro-Psychopharmacology, Internat. Soc. Investigation of Stress, European Coll. Neuropsychopharmacology (corr.). Home: 1324 Youngsford Rd Gladwyne PA 19035-1231 Office: U Pa Dept Psychiatry 803 Sci Ctr 3600 Market St Philadelphia PA 19104-2611

RICKER, FRANCES MARGARET, community health nurse, educator; b. Lowell, Mass., Apr. 3, 1962; d. John E. and B. Aline (Levasseur) R. BS in Nursing, Northeastern U., 1985. Cert. diabetes educator. Staff nurse in orthopaedics Lakes Region Gen. Hosp., Laconia, N.H., 1985—, diabetes nurse educator, 1987-91; community health nurse Community Health and Hospice, Laconia, 1987—. Mem. ANA, Am. Assn. Diabetes Educators, Nat. Assn. Orthopaedic Nurses. Home: PO Box 355 Winnisquam NH 03289-0355

RICKERT, DOUGLAS EDWARD, toxicologist, pharmacologist; b. Sioux City, Iowa, Jan. 27, 1946; s. Waldo Henry Herman and Genevieve Lucille (Hahn) R.; m. Sharlene Joyce Nordblom, Sept. 2, 1967 (div. 1979); m. Terrie Sue Baker, June 27, 1981. BS in Chemistry, U. Iowa, 1968, MS in Pharmacology, 1972, PhD in Pharmacology, 1974. Diplomate Am. Bd. Toxicology. Asst. prof. pharmacology Mich. State U., East Lansing, 1974-77; scientist Chem. Industry Inst. Toxicology, Research Triangle Park, N.C., 1977-87; head drug disposition sect. dept. drug metabolism Glaxo, Inc., Research Triangle Park, 1987-95; dir. U.S. devel. bioanalysis & drug metabolism Glaxo Wellcome Inc., 1996—. Editor: Toxicity of Nitroaromatic Compounds, 1984; contbr. articles to profl. jours. Served with U.S. Army, 1969-71. NIH grantee, 1978. Mem. Soc. Toxicology, Am. Soc. Pharmacology and Exptl. Therapeutics, Am. Soc. Mass Spectrometry, Am. Chem. Soc., AAAS. Democrat. Office: Glaxo Wellcome Inc Dept Drug Metabolism 5 Moore Pl Research Triangle Park NC 27709

RICKETTS, RICHARD RANDALL, surgeon, educator; b. Sacramento, Apr. 11, 1947; s. William F. Ricketts Jr. and Alcia (Percy) Pickles; m. Sandra Kay Ramey, June 20, 1979; 1 child, Shelley Kay. BA, Stanford U., 1969; MD, Northwestern U., 1973. Intern L.A. County-U. So. Calif. Med. Ctr., 1973-74, resident, 1974-78; instr. surgery Children's Meml. Hosp., Chgo., 1978-80; asst. prof. surgery Emory U. Sch. Medicine, Atlanta, 1980-85, assoc. prof., 1985—; chief of surgery Egleston Children's Hosp., Atlanta, 1987-93. Contbr. articles to profl. jours. Fellow ACS, Am. Acad. Pediatrics, Southeastern Surg. Congress (councilor 1990—); mem. Am. Pediatric Surg. Assn. (publs. com. 1990-96), Ga. Surg. Soc., Brit. Assn. Pediatric Surgeons. Office: Emory Clinic 1365 Clifton Rd NE Atlanta GA 30307-1013

RICO, DAVID M., physician, researcher; b. Brownwood, Tex., June 6, 1951; s. Ignacio W. and Betty (Luna-Sanchez) R. BS, Okla. City U., 1981; DO, Okla. State U., 1986. Family practice intern La. State U., Shreveport/Monroe, 1986-87; family practice resident U. Ark. for Med. Scis., Little Rock, 1988-90; rsch. assoc. Dept. of Endocrinology VA Hosp., Little Rock, 1987-91; lt., commd. med. officer USPHS, 1987-90; with U. Ark. for Med. Scis., Little Rock, 1987-90; faculty devel., rsch. fellow Health Scis. Ctr. U. Ariz., Tucson, 1992-93; W.K. Kellogg-NACHC fellow in cmty. health W.K. Kellogg Nat. Assn. Cmty. Health Ctrs., 1992-94; chief med. officer USPHS Indian Health Svc., Okmulgee, Okla., 1994—; rsch. cons. U.S. Naval Rsch. Inst., Bethesda, Md., 1989. Contbr. numerous articles to profl. jours. Spokesperson/advocate Am. Indian Inst., Okla. City/Norman, 1989, Wellness & Native Men Conf., Albuquerque, 1993. Nat. Med. Fellowship Found. scholar Okla. State U., 1982-84. Mem. Am. Acad. Family Physicians, So. Med. Assn., Tri Beta. Office: Chief Med Officer USPHSIHS-Tribal Health Sys PO Box 126 Okmulgee OK 74447-0126

RICORDI, CAMILLO, surgeon, transplant and diabetes researcher; b. N.Y.C., Apr. 1, 1957; m. Valerie A. Grace, Aug. 8, 1986; children: M. Caterina, Eliana G., Carlo A. MD, U. Milan (Italy) Sch. Medicine, 1982. Trainee in gen. surgery San Raffaele Inst., Milan, 1982-85; NIH trainee Washington U. Sch. Medicine, St. Louis, 1985-88; attending surgeon San Raffaele Inst., Milan, 1988-89; asst. prof. surgery U. Pitts., Pa., 1989-91; assoc. prof. surgery U. Pitts., 1991-93; prof. surgery, chief divsn. cellular transplantation U. Miami, Fla., 1993—, scientific dir., chief acad. officer Diabetes Rsch. Inst., 1996—; reviewer of applications for grants Can. Diabetes Assn., Am. Diabetes Assn., Juvenile Diabetes Found., NIH; chmn. First Internat. Congress of Cell Transplant Soc., Pitts., 1992, 3d Internat. Congress of Cell Transplantation, Miami, 1996, 5th Internat. Congress on Pancreas and Islet Transplantation, Miami, 1995, others; mem. editl. bd. Transplantation, Transplantation Sci., Cell Transplantation, Transplantation Procs., Jour. Tissue Engrng. Editor: Pancreatic Islet Cell Transplantation, 1992, Methods in Cell Transplantation, 1995; contbr. over 200 numerous chpts. to books and articles to jours. including NEJM, Immunology Today, Jour. Clin. Investigation, Hepatology, Diabetes, Transplantation, Endocrinology, Procs. NAS, USA, Am. Jour. Physiology, World Jour. Surgery, Surgery, Nature, Lancet, many others. Recipient Juvenile Diabetes Found. Internat. Rsch. Grant award, 1988—, NIH award, 1986-88; grantee NIH-RO1, 1993—. Mem. AAAS, Cell Transplant Soc. (founder, pres. 1992-94), Am. Soc. Transplant Surgeons, Internat. Pancreas and Islet Transplant Assn. (co-founder), The Transplantation Soc., Am. Diabetes Assn. (Rsch. award 1996), Am. Fedn. Clin. Rsch., Diabetes Rsch. Internat. Network (founder, chmn. 1994—), Nat. Diabetes Coalition (co-founder 1994—). Home: 72 S Hibiscus Dr Hisbiscus Island Miami Beach FL 33139 Office: U Miami Diabetes Rsch Inst 1450 NW 10th Ave Miami FL 33136-1011

RICOTTA, JOHN JOSEPH, vascular surgeon, educator; b. Buffalo, N.Y., Sept. 13, 1949; s. Joseph J. and Joan (Tarantino) R.; m. Gloria DeSantis, July 25, 1970; children: Joseph, Genna, Lise. BA, Yale Coll., 1969; MD, Johns Hopkins U., 1973. Diplomate Am. Bd. Surgery. Intern, resident Johns Hopkins Hosp., 1973-79; instr. surgery Johns Hopkins U., Balt., 1979-80; asst. prof. surgery U. Rochester, N.Y., 1980-85, assoc. prof. surgery, 1985-88; prof. surgery, dir. vascular surgery SUNY, Buffalo, 1988—; chief surgery Millard Fillmore Hosp., Buffalo, 1988—. Fellow ACS; mem. Soc. Vascular Surgery, Internat. Soc. Cardiovascular Surgery, Soc. Univ. Surgeons, Ctrl. Surg. Assn., Ea. Vascular Soc. (recorder 1992—). Office: Millard Fillmore Hosp 3 Gates Cir Buffalo NY 14209

RIDDICK, FRANK ADAMS, JR., physician, health care facility administrator; b. Memphis, June 14, 1929; s. Frank Adams and Falba (Crawford) R.; m. Mary Belle Alston, June 15, 1952; children: Laura Elizabeth Dufresne, Frank Adams III, John Alston. BA cum laude, Vanderbilt U., 1951, MD, 1954. Diplomate: Am. Bd. Internal Medicine (bd. govs. 1973-80). Intern Barnes Hosp., St. Louis, 1954-55, resident in medicine, 1957-60; fellow in metabolic diseases Washington U., St. Louis, 1960-61; staff Ochsner Clinic (Ochsner Found. Hosp.), New Orleans, 1961—; head sect. endocrinology and metabolic disease Ochsner Clinic (Ochsner Found. Hosp.), 1976-83, asst. med. dir., 1968-72, assoc. med. dir., 1972-75, med. dir., 1975-92; clin. prof. Tulane U., New Orleans, 1977—; trustee Alton Ochsner Med. Found., 1973—, CEO, 1991—; chmn. bd. Ochsner Health Plan, 1983-92; pres. Orleans Svc. Corp., 1976-80, South La. Med. Assocs., New Orleans, 1978—; dir. Brent House Corp., New Orleans, 1980—; chmn. Accreditation Coun. on Grad. Med. Edn., 1986-87. v.p. nat. resident matching program, 1986-90, mem. accreditation coun. on med. edn., 1988-90. Trustee St. Martin's Protestant Epis. Sch., Metairie, La., 1970-84; bd. govs. Isidore Newman Sch., New Orleans, 1987-93. Recipient Disting. Alumnus award Castle Heights Mil. Acad., 1979; recipient teaching award Alton Ochsner Med. Found., 1969, Physician Exec. award Am. Coll. Med. Group Adminstrs., 1984, Disting. Alumnus award Vanderbilt U. Sch. Med., 1988. Fellow ACP, Am. Coll. Physician Execs. (pres. 1987-88); mem. AMA (ho. dels. 1971-92, chmn. coun. on med. edn. 1983-85, coun. on jud. and ethical affairs 1995—), NAS Inst. Medicine, Am. Soc. Internal Medicine (trustee 1970-76, disting. internist award), Endocrine Soc., Am. Diabetes Assn., Soc. Med. Adminstrs. (pres. 1995—), Am. Group Practice Assn. (pres. 1992-94), Boston Club, New Orleans Country Club, Cosmos Club. Home: 1923 Octavia St New Orleans LA 70115-5651 Office: Ochsner Clinic 1514 Jefferson Hwy New Orleans LA 70121-2429

RIDDLE, CHARLES DANIEL (DAN RIDDLE), biomedical educator; b. Spartanburg, S.C., Jan. 21, 1945; s. Robert Charles and Nell Grace (Eubanks) R.; 1 child, Ashley Mya. BS in Biology, Clemson U., 1967, MS in Zoology, 1969. Dir. audiovisual lab. Spartanburg Meth. Coll., 1969; tchr. Prevocat. Jr. High Sch., Spartanburg, 1970-71; biomed. instr. Greenville (S.C.) Tech. Coll., 1971—. Mem. Greenville County Coun., 1977-78; pres. Edwards Forest Recreation Assn., Taylors, 1988. 2d lt. U.S. Army, 1969-70. Recipient resolution for svc. Greenville County Coun., 1979. Mem. S.C. Soc. Radiologic Technologists, S.C. Tchrs. Assn., Human Anatomy and Physiology Soc. Baptist. Home: 3 Shelly Ln Taylors SC 29687-4844 Office: Greenville Tech Coll Pleasantburg Dr Greenville SC 29607-2510

RIDDLE, MARK ALAN, child psychiatrist; b. Huntingburg, Ind., Feb. 18, 1948; s. James G. and Louise (Burgdorf) R.; m. Clarine Carol Nardi, Aug. 15, 1971; children: Carl, Julia. BA, Ind. U., 1970, MS, 1973, MD, 1977. Intern in pediatrics Ind. U. Med. Ctr., Indpls., 1977-78; resident in psychiatry Sch. Medicine Yale U., New Haven, 1978-81; fellow in child psychiatry Yale Child Study Ctr., New Haven, 1981-83; asst. prof. child psychiatry Sch. Medicine Yale U., New Haven, 1983-89, assoc. prof. child psychiatry, 1989-93; dir. divsn. child and adolescent psychiatry Johns Hopkins Med. Inst., 1993—; mem. pediatrics panel U.S. Pharmacopea. Assoc. editor Jour. Child and Adolescent Psychopharmacology; editor Pediatric Psychopharmacology I & II, 1995; contbr. articles to profl. jours. Mem. med. com. Tourette Syndrome Assn., 1989—. Mem. Am. Acad. Child and Adolescent Psychiatry (editorial bd. Jour.). Home: 10607 Millet Seed Hl Columbia MD 21044-4150

RIDDLE, ROBBY CLARK, family practice physician; b. Cheyenne, Wyo., Mar. 11, 1961; s. Dicky Joe Riddle and Beverly Kaye (Hornbeck) Carson; m. Little Louisa Poplin, June 30, 1979; children: Robyn Louisa, Little Clarissa, Robby Clark II, Melissa Kate, Lisa Dawn, Kelly Elizabeth. BS, U. Okla., 1986; MD, Uniformed Svcs. U. Health Scis, 1995. Cert. physician asst. Nurses aide San Juan County Hosp., Farmington, N.Mex., 1978-79; USAF med. technician Wilford Hall Med. Ctr., San Antonio, 1979-84; student physician asst. USAF, Sheppard AFB, Tex., 1984-86; family practice physician asst. USAF, Fairchild AFB, Wash., 1986-91; resident in family practice USAF, Scott AFB, Ill., 1995—. Deacon So. Bapt. Assn., 1988—; mem. The Gideons Internat., Nashville, 1993—. Mem. Am. Acad. Family Practice, Assn. Mil. Surgeons U.S. (life), Christian Med. and Dental soc., Alpha Omega Alpha.

RIDEY, DOUGLAS E., orthopaedic surgeon; b. Detroit, Jan. 11, 1941; s. H. Earl and Mary Frances Ridey; m. Sherry Anderson, Dec. 27, 1965. Student, Ea. Mich. U., 1960-63; MD, U. Mich., 1967. Diplomate Am. Bd. Orthopaedic Surgery; qualified med. evaluator. Intern Santa Barbara (Calif.) Cottage and Gen. Hosp., 1967-68; pvt. practice gen. medicine, South Lake Tahoe, Calif., 1971-74; resident in orthopaedic surgery Akron (Ohoi) Gen. Med. Ctr., Akron Children's Hosp., 1974-78, N.E. Ohio

Med. Sch., Rootstown, 1974-78; pvt. practice orthopaedic surgery Pinole, Calif., 1978—; orthopaedic surgeon Doctors Hosp. Pinole, 1978—, chief orthopaedic surgeon, 1984-87; orthopaedic surgeon Brookside Hosp., San Pablo, Calif., 1978—, chief orthopaedic surgeon, 1980-84. Author: Orchids I Have Known, 1990, The Thrill of Sky Diving, 1992. Lt. comdr. N.C., USN, 1968-71. Fellow ACS, Am. Acad. Orthopaedic Surgeons; mem. AMA, Calif. Orthopaedic Assn., Animal Rescue Assn. Office: 1330 Tara Hills Dr Ste E Pinole CA 94564

RIDOUT, DANIEL LYMAN, III, physician, educator; b. Salisbury, Md., June 13, 1953; married. BA in Music, Dartmouth Coll., 1975; MD, U. Cin., 1979. Diplomate Nat. Bd. Med. Examiners, Am. Bd. Internal Medicine, Am. Bd. Gastrointestinal Bd.; lic. physician, Pa., Del; cert. ACLS, Advanced Trauma and Life Support. Intern then resident U. Pa. Hosp., Phila., 1979-82, chief med. resident, clin. instr. internal medicine, 1982-83, clin. instr., 1983-84, attending physician, teaching staff, 1986—; attending physician Crozer-Chester Med. Ctr., Upland, Pa., 1988—; pvt. practice, Upland, 1986—; chief gastrointestinal divsn. VA Hosp., Coatesville, Pa., 1987-89. Contbr. articles to profl. jours. Recipient Achievement and Svc. in Medicine award Afro-Am. Hist. Soc. Del., 1989. Mem. AMA, Am. Profl. Practice Assn., Am. Soc. Gastrointestinal Endoscopy, Pa. Med. Soc., Del. County Med. Soc. (bd. dirs.), Am. Soc. Internal Medicine, Med. Soc. Eastern Pa., Phila. County Med. Soc., Phila. Coll. Physicians, New Castle County Med. Soc. Office: Crozer Chester Med Ctr Profl Office Bldg II 1 Medical Blvd Upland PA 19013

RIDSDALE, LEONE LORNA, physician, educator; b. London, Sept. 7, 1947; arrived in Can., 1980; d. Philip and Lorna Ridsdale; 1 child, Serife. BA, Kent U., Eng., 1969; MSc, London Sch. Econs., 1970; MD, McMaster U., Eng., 1974; PhD, London U., 1994. Lectr. Manchester U., Eng., 1970-71; resident McGill, Royal Victoria Hosp., Montreal, Can., 1974-76, 77-80; registrar Nat. Hosp., London, 1977-78; trainee gen. practice surgery Surrey, Eng., 1980-81; gen. practitioner Surrey, 1981—; sr. lectr. London U., 1985—. Author: Evidence-Based General Practice, 1995. Grantee Welcome Trust, London, 1993, various rsch. funders, U.K., 1993-95. Fellow Royal Coll. Physicians Can., Royal Coll. Gen. Practitioners London; mem. Am. Acad. Neurology, Thirlingham Club, Roehautan Club. Office: UMDS Guys & St Thomas Hosp, Dept Gen Practice, 80 Kennington Rd, London SE11 6SP, England

RIEBSAME, WILLIAM EDWARD, psychologist; b. Ft. Bragg, N.C., July 20, 1955; s. William Paul and Ina (Dillman) R.; m. Susan Lyndall Skinner, Jan. 10, 1981; children: William Matthew, Patrick James, Karen Marie. BA, U. South Fla., 1977; MA, Columbia U., 1980; MS, Va. Commonwealth U., 1985, PhD, 1987. Lic. psychologist, Fla. Counselor James Madison U., Harrisonburg, Va., 1981-83; instr. Va. Commonwealth U., Richmond, Va., 1983-86; doctoral intern U. South Fla., Tampa, Fla., 1986-87; asst. prof., staff psychologist U. Md., College Park, 1987-89; psychologist Atlantic Psychiatric, Palm Bay, Fla., 1989-94; pvt. practice Palm Bay, 1994—; adj. prof. Fla. Inst. Tech., Melbourne, 1989—, Rollins Coll., Orlando, 1992—; cons. Brevard County Police Acad., Melbourne, 1989—; expert witness Office of Pub. Defender, State Atty. Parent educator BCC Lab. Sh., Palm Bay, 1990. Mem. APA, Counseling Psychology, Psychology Law Soc., Family Psychology. Office: 2123 Franklin Dr NE Palm Bay FL 32905-4022

RIEDEL, DAVID ROBERT, physician; b. St. Louis, Dec. 9, 1946; s. Harry Edward and Beulah Viola (Schlender) R.; m. Margaret T. Donnelly, Jan. 10, 1975; children: Julia Donnelly Riedel, Adam Donnelly Riedel. AB, Cardinal Glennon Coll., 1964-68; DMS, U. Mo., 1971-75. Cert. Bd. Internal Medicine, Bd. Gastroenterology. Resident in internal medicine St. Louis U. Hosp., 1975-78; gastroenterology fellowship Med. Coll. of Wis., Milw., 1978-80; pvt. practice Alton, Ill., 1980—; pres. med. staff Alton Meml. Hosp., 1989-91, bd. dirs. 1989; bd. dirs. Physician's Preferred Health, St. Louis. Fellow Am. Coll. Gastroenterology; mem. Am. Gastroent. Assn., Am. Soc. Gastro Intestinal Endoscopy. Office: 3550 College Ave Alton IL 62002-5008

RIEFKOHL, RONALD EDWARD, plastic and reconstructive surgery educator; b. Margarita, Canal Zone, Mar. 27, 1947; s. Frank Edward and Catherine (Rogdakis) R.; m. Nancy Jeane Georgiade, Mar. 4, 1978; children: Kristen, Edward. Student, Tulane U., 1965-68, MD, 1972. Cert. Am. Bd. Plastic Surgery, Am. Bd. Surgery. Resident in general surgery Ochsner Found. Hosp., New Orleans, 1972-76; resident in plastic surgery Duke U. Med. Ctr., Durham, N.C., 1976-79, assoc. prof. plastic surgery, 1979—. Fellow Am. Coll. Surgeons; mem. Am. Soc. Plastic & Reconstructive Surgeons, Am. Assn. Plastic Surgery, Aesthetic Soc. Plastic Surgery, Southeastern Soc. Plastic Surgery, Duke Davison Club. Republican. Episcopalian. Home: 816 Anderson St Durham NC 27706-2554 Office: 100 E Carver St Durham NC 27704-2700

RIEGEL, BYRON WILLIAM, ophthalmologist; b. Evanston, Ill., Jan. 19, 1938; s. Byron and Belle Mae (Huot) R.; BS, Stanford U., 1960; MD, Cornell U., 1964; m. Marilyn Hills, May 18, 1968; children—Marc William, Ryan Marie, Andrea Elizabeth. Intern, King County Hosp., Seattle, 1964-65; asst. resident in surgery U. Wash., Seattle, 1965; resident in ophthalmology U. Fla., 1968-71; pvt. practice medicine specializing in ophthalmology, Sierra Eye Med. Group, Inc., Visalia, Calif., 1972—; mem. staff Kaweah Delta Dist. Hosp., chief of staff, 1978-79. Bd. dirs., asst. sec. Kaweah Delta Dist. Hosp., 1983-90. Served as flight surgeon USN, 1966-68. Co-recipient Fight-for-Sight citation for research in retinal dystrophy, 1970. Diplomate Am. Bd. Ophthalmology, Nat. Bd. Med. Examiners. Fellow ACS, Am. Acad. Ophthalmology; mem. Calif. Med. Assn. (del. 1978-79), Tulare County Med. Assns., Calif. Assn. Ophthalmology (v.p. 3d party liaison 1994-96), Am. Soc. Cataract and Refractive Surgery, Internat. Phacoemulsification and Cataract Methodology Soc. Roman Catholic. Club: Rotary (Visalia). Home: 3027 W Keogh Ct Visalia CA 93291-4228 Office: 2830 W Main St Visalia CA 93291-4331

RIEGEL, NORMAN, physician; b. N.Y.C., Jan. 22, 1935; children: Bram, Lisa, Karyn, Daniel; m. Joan Ann Gordon, June 17, 1973. AB, Columbia Coll., 1956; MD, Einstein Coll. Med., 1960. Diplomate Am. Bd. Internal Medicine. Intern U. Chgo., 1960-61; resident Kings County Hosp., Bklyn., N.Y., 1961-62; asst. resident Bellevue Hosp., N.Y.C., 1962-63, GI fellow, 1963-64; pvt. practice Hackensack, N.J., 1966—; clin. assoc. prof. medicine Coll. Medicine and Dentistry of N.J., Newark, 1977—; chief dept. gastroeneterol. Bergen Pines County Hosp., Paramus, N.J., 1970—; dir. dept. medicine Bergen Pine County Hosp., Paramus, 1985-87, 89-96. Editor, Jour. of Med. Soc., 1983-87; contbr. numerous articles to profl jours. Served to capt. USAF, 1964-66. Fellow, Am. Coll. Gastroenterol., Am. Soc. Internal Medicine, Am. Coll. Physicians; mem., Am. Soc. Gastrointestinal Endoscopy, Bergen County Med Soc., N.J. Med. Soc. Office: 11 Elm Ave Hackensack NJ 07601-4702

RIEGER, ELAINE JUNE, nursing administrator; b. Lebanon, Pa., June 7, 1937; d. Frank and Florence (Hitz) Plasterer; m. Jere LeFever Longenecker, Sept. 13, 1958 (div. 1968); children: Julie Lynn Porto, Jere Lee Longenecker; m. Bernhard Rieger, Oct. 12, 1971. Nursing diploma, Coatesville (Pa.) Hosp. Sch. of Nursing, 1958; BA, U. Redlands, 1976; MS in Healthcare Mgmt., Calif. State U., L.A., 1984. Cert. nursing adminstr., gerontol. nurse. From staff nurse to clin. supr. to dir. of nurses St. Johns Regional Med. Ctr., Oxnard, Calif., 1966-86; dir. of nurses Motion Picture and TV Hosp., Woodland Hills, Calif., 1987-89; with Care West, Nothridge-Reseda, Calif., 1989-90; dist. nurse mgr. Hillhaven Corp., Newbury Park, Calif., 1990-91; quality mgmt. nursing cons. Beverly Enterprises, Memphis, 1991-95; DON Beverly Manor Rehab. and Nursing Ctr., Van Nuys, Calif., 1996—. Home: 1817 Shady Brook Dr Thousand Oaks CA 91362-1335 Office: Beverly Manor Rehab and Nursing Ctr 6700 Sepulveda Blvd Van Nuys CA 91411

RIEMENSCHNEIDER, PAUL ARTHUR, physician, radiologist; b. Cleve., Apr. 17, 1920; s. Albert and Selma (Marting) R.; m. Mildred McCarthy, May 12, 1945; children: Barbara Anne, Nancy Emelia, David Andrew, Paul Albert, Mary Elizabeth, Sarah Bache. BS magna cum laude, Baldwin-Wallace Coll., 1941; MD, Harvard U., 1944. Diplomate Am. Bd. Radiology (trustee 1973-85), Nat. Bd. Med. Examiners. Prof., chmn. dept. radiology SUNY, Syracuse, 1945-64; chief diagnostic radiology Santa Barbara (Calif.) Cottage Hosp., 1964-89, bd. dirs., 1984-90; vis. prof. in residence SUNY, Syracuse, 1983—; Radiology Soc. of No. Am. Internat. vis. prof. of Radiology, Univ. Malaya, 1990-91. Co-editor: N.Y. State Jour. Medicine, 1960-64; mem. editorial adv. bd. Yearbook of Cancer, 1960-64; contbr. articles to profl. jours. Mem. appropriations com. Santa Barbara Found., 1984-93; vestryman All Saints Episc. Ch., 1970-76, sr. warden, 1973; bd. dirs. ARC, Santa Barbara, 1968-72, Am. cancer Soc., Santa Barbara, 1967-70, Casa Dorinda Retirement Residence, 1975-76, 89-96, pres., 1993-96; bd. dirs. Wood Glen Hall Retirement Residence, 1980—, sec., 1987; bd. dirs. Cancer Found. Santa Barbara, 1966-82, 89-95, chmn. equipment com., 1973-82. Lt. comdr. USNR, 1945-46, 54-56. Recipient Alumni Merit award Baldwin-Wallace Coll., 1985. Fellow Am. Coll. Radiology (cancer com. 1952-54, council 1956-64, bd. chancellors 1967-73, chmn. commn. standards in radiologic practice 1968-71, v.p. 1972, pres. 1974, chmn. com. manpower 1972-86, chmn. com. manpower in armed svcs. 1975-86, Gold medal 1982); mem. AMA, Calif. Med. Assn., Santa Barbara County Med. Soc. (chmn. med. sch. com. 1967-71), Am. Roentgen Ray Soc. (mem. publs. com. 1965-75, chmn. 1970-75, exec. council 1970-75, 77-82, chmn. program com. 1977-79, pres.-elect 1977-79, pres. 1979, Gold medal award 1986), South Coast Radiol. Soc. (pres. 1967), Assn. Univ. Radiologists (sec. 1960, pres. 1961, com. resident tng. 1984-88), Radiol. Soc. N.Am. (Gold medal award 1990), Am. Soc. Neuroradiology, Soc. Pediatric Radiology, Eastern Radiol. Soc. (pres.-elect 1987, pres. 1988-89), Calif. Radiol. Soc., So. Calif. Radiol. Soc., Detroit Roentgen Soc. (hon.), Bluegrass Radiol. Soc. (hon.), Pacific N.W. Radiol. Soc. (hon.), Alpha Omega Alpha. Republican. Clubs: Birnamwood Golf (Santa Barbara); Skaneateles Country (N.Y.). Home: 112 Olive Mill Rd Santa Barbara CA 93108-2424

RIENDEAU, THERESA FRANCES, rehabilitation nurse; b. Revere, Mass., June 12, 1953; d. Samuel and Eleanor M. (Rizzo) Spinazzola; m. Armand D. Riendeau, Dec. 31, 1994; children: James, Richard, Mark. Diploma, New Eng. Bapt. Hosp. Sch., Boston, 1975. Cert. rehab. RN. Charge nurse VA Med. Ctr., West Roxbury, Mass., 1975-80; asst. nurse mgr. Braintree (Mass.) Hosp., 1981-90; supr. nursing Randolph (Mass.) Crossings Nursing Ctr., 1990-93; home health nurse, home health aide/homemaker educator Alternative Care Med. Svcs., Salem, N.H., 1990—; rehab. nurse Vis. Nurse Assocs. Inc., Dedham, Mass., 1993-94, VNA Homecare, Andover, Mass., 1994-95. Mem. Assn. Rehab. Nurses. Home: 35 Wheeler St Dracut MA 01826 Office: Vis Nurse Assoc Home Care 59 Stiles Rd Salem NH

RIENHOFF, OTTO, physician, medical informatics educator; b. Dortmund, Fed. Republic of Germany, Nov. 9, 1949; s. Otto and Lotte (Wiechers) R. Ed., Wilhelms U., Münster, Federal Republic of Germany, 1973, Hannover Med. Sch., Federal Republic of Germany, Y. Intern Hannover Med. Sch., 1974, rsch. asst. Inst. Med. Informatics, 1975-82, dep. dir. Inst. Med. Informatics, 1980-83, assoc. prof. med. informatics, 1982-85; prof., dir. Inst. Med. Informatics U. Marburg, Germany, 1985-94, U. Goettingen, Germany, 1994-96; cons. med. documentation, edn., quality mgmt., tng. and systems devel., 1977—; mem. editorial bd. various profl. jours. and publs. Editor books on med. informatics and edn.; contbr. numerous articles to profl. jours. Mem. Internat. Med. Informatics Assn. (pres. 1995—), German Soc. Med. Informetics, Biometry and Epidemiology (pres. 1993-95), South African Med. Informatics Group (corr.), Brazilian Soc. Informatics in Health (corr.), others.

RIENZO, ROBERT JAMES, radiologist; b. Jersey City, N.J., July 27, 1949; s. James Joseph and Marie Nicoletta (Bernardo) R.; m. Janice Meyer, Apr. 8, 1972 (div. Dec. 1991); 1 child, Michael Robert; m. Catherine Elizabeth Rafferty, Jan. 11, 1992; 1 child, Robert Francis. AB, Cornell U., 1971; MD, N.Y. Med. Coll., 1975. Diplomate Am. Bd. Radiology, Am. Bd. Nuclear Medicine. Resident St. Vincent's Hosp., N.Y.C., 1975-80; staff physician Jefferson Hosp., Pitts., 1980-81, Allentown (Pa.) Hosp., Lehigh Valley Hosp., Pa., 1981—. Contbr. articles to profl. jours. Mem. Exch. Club Western LeHigh, Emmaus, Pa., 1983—. Mem. AMA (Physicians Recognition award 1986—), Soc. Nuclear Medicine, Am. Coll. Nuclear Physicians, Am. Coll. Radiology, Soc. Radiologists in Ultrasound. Office: Valley Nuclear Med Assoc 5940 Hamilton Blvd Wescosville PA 18106-9648

RIES, BARBARA ELLEN, alcohol and drug abuse services professional; b. Chgo., Oct. 27, 1952; d. Laurence B. and Genieveve (Wasiek) R. AAS in Human Svcs., Coll. of DuPage, Glen Ellyn, Ill., 1973; BA in Social Work, Sangamon State U., Springfield, Ill., 1978; postgrad., U. Mo., 1987-88, U. Tex., Arlington, 1991—. Cert. social therapist, criminal justice counselor-master addiction counselor; nat., internat. cert. alcohol and drug counselor; qualified chem. dependency counselor. Counselor Ray Graham Assn. for Handicapped, Addison, Ill., 1975-76; child abuse counselor Ill. Dept. Children and Family Svcs., Springfield, 1977-78; alcoholism counselor non-med. detoxification program S.H.A.R.E., Villa Park, Ill., 1978-80; outpatient therapist Ingalls Meml. Hosp., Harvey, Ill., 1980-83; dir. aftercare Lifeline Program, Chgo., 1984-85; case mgr. Lifecenter Program, Kansas City, Mo., 1985-87; counselor, acting clin. coord. Lakeside Hosp., Kansas City, 1988-89; program mgr., dir. chem. recovery programs Two Rivers Psychiat. Hosp., Kansas City, 1989-90; dir. day program and chem. dependency program SW Hosp./Citadel, Dallas, 1990—; dir. Flexcare program Dallas Meml. Hosp., 1990-91; pvt. practice Spokane, Wash., 1991—; program coord. Advanced Clin. Svcs., Federal Way, 1992-94; spkr. in field. Recipient commendation Ingalls Hosp., 1983. Mem. APA, ACA, Am. Correctional Assn., Nat. Assn. Drug and Alcohol Counselors (cert., (NCAC II), Nat. Assn. for Relapse Prevention Counselors, Employee Assistance Profls. Am., Learning Disabilities Assn. Wash., Wash. Assocs. Alcoholism & Addictions Programs, Wash. Advs. Mentally Ill, Wash. Assn. Alcoholism and Drug Abuse Counselors, Dual Diagnosis Com.

RIES, KRISTEN M., infectious diseases physician; b. Phila., Sept. 29, 1940; d. Philip Thomas and Mildred Martha (Smith) R. BS, Pa. State U., 1962, MEd, 1963; MD, Women's Med. Coll. Pa., 1967. Diplomate Am. Bd. Internal Medicine, Am. Bd. Infectious Diseases. Asst. prof. medicine Med. Coll. Pa., Phila., 1972-75; physician Indian Health Svc., Rosebud, S.D., 1975-76, Nat. Health Svc., Vermillion, S.D.; chief adult medicine U. Utah, Salt Lake City, 1981-83, prof. internal medicine, 1994—; pvt. practice Salt Lake City, 1983—; med. dir. Cmty. Nursing Svc., Salt Lake City, 1988-94; chair ethics com. Holy Cross Hosp., Salt Lake City, 1990-94. Bd. dirs., co-founder Utah AIDS Found., Salt Lake City, 1985—. Fellow Am. Coll. Physicians, Infectious Diseases Soc. Am.; mem. Internat. AIDS Soc., Am. Soc. Microbiology, Am. Soc. Internal Medicine, Optivia. Home: 3670 S Millbrook Terr Salt Lake City UT 84106 Office: U Utah Health Scis Ctr 50 N Medical Dr Salt Lake City UT 84132

RIES, WILLIAM RUSSELL, physician, facial plastic surgeon, educator; b. Union City, Tenn., Jan. 30, 1953; s. Herbert Nelson and Marjorie (Miller) R.; m. Susan Hunter Webb, Dec. 19, 1977; children: Katherine Dossett, William Russell Jr., Robert Webb Nelson. BS, Rhodes Coll., 1975; MD, U. Tenn., 1978. Gen. surgery resident Bapt. Meml. Hosp., Memphis, 1979-81; otolaryngology resident Northwestern U. Med. Ctr., Chgo., 1981-84; facial plastic surgery fellow Tulane U. Med. Ctr., New Orleans, 1984-85; asst. clin. prof. Vanderbilt U. Med. Ctr., Nashville, 1987-88, asst. prof., 1987—, dir. div. facial plastic surgery, dept. otolaryngology, 1988—; Course co-chmn. Lasers in Head and Neck Surgery, Nashville, 1989—. Co-author: Rhinoplasty, 1986. Fellow ACS, Am. Acad. Facial Plastic and Reconstructive Surgery, Am. Soc. Laser Medicine and Surgery, Am. Acad. Otolaryngology Head and Neck Surgery. Episcopalian. Home: 6124 Hillsboro Rd Nashville TN 37215-5006 Office: Dept Otolaryngology Vanderbilt U Med Ctr S-2100 Med Ctr North Nashville TN 37232

RIETSCHEL, ROBERT LOUIS, dermatologist; b. New Orleans, Oct. 9, 1946; s. Frederick Arnt and Estelle Marie (Fleckinger) R.; m. Connie Joanne Dent, Sept. 3, 1966; children: Eric, Penny. BA, North Tex. State U., 1968; MD, U. Tex., Galveston, 1972. Diplomate Am. Bd. Dermatology. Med. intern Letterman Army Med. Ctr., San Francisco, 1972-73, dermatology researcher, 1973-74; resident in dermatology Brooke Army Med. Ctr., San Antonio, 1974-77, staff dermatologist, 1977-79; assoc. prof. dermatology Emory U. Sch. Medicine, Atlanta, 1981-85, acting chmn. dept. dermatology, 1984-85; assoc. chmn. dept. dermatology Ochsner Clinic, New Orleans, 1985-88; chmn. dept. dermatology, 1988—. Contbr. articles to profl jours. Cubmaster, Boy Scouts Am., Decatur, Ga., 1983-84. Served to maj. U.S. Army, 1971-79. NIOSH grantee, 1981-84. Fellow Am. Acad. Dermatology, Soc. for Investigative Dermatology; mem. AMA, N.Am. Contact Dermatitis Group (sec. 1985-93), Am. Contact Dermatitis Soc. (sec. 1989-93, pres. 1993-95). Republican. Lutheran. Office: Ochsner Clinic 1514 Jefferson Hwy New Orleans LA 70121-2429

RIFAS, LEONARD, cell biology educator; b. Kansas City, Mo., Sept. 20, 1946; s. Irwin and Marjorie (Postelneck) R.; m. Geraldine Bernice Shapiro, June 29, 1969; children: Joanne Alyssa, Stephanie Michelle. AB, U. Mo., 1969, MS, 1973. Sr. rsch. technician, Sch. Veterinary Medicine U. Mo., Columbia, 1969-73; rsch. asst., Albert Einstein Coll. Medicine Yeshiva U., N.Y.C., 1973-79; instr. Sch. Medicine Washington U., St. Louis, 1979-95, asst. prof. medicine, 1995—; sci. staff Shriners Hosp. for Crippled Children, St. Louis. Mem. editl. bd. Calcified Tissue Internat., 1990—; contbr. numerous articles to profl. jours. Mem. AAAS, Am. Soc. for Cell Biology, Am. Soc. for Bone and Mineral Rsch., N.Y. Acad. Scis., Fedn. Am. Socs. for Exptl. Biology, Endocrine Soc. Office: Washington U Sch Medicine Barnes-Jewish Hosp 216 S Kingshighway Blvd Saint Louis MO 63110-1026

RIFKIN, LARRY JAY, medical products executive; b. Phila., Dec. 14, 1960; s. Marvin John and Rita Vivian (Shore) R. BS in Psychology, U. Charleston, W.Va., 1982. V.p. Phone Owners Group, Cherry Hill, N.J., 1982-84; dist. mgr. Oxford Med. Corp., Fla., 1984-86; regional mgr. Puritan Bennett Med. Corp., Boston, 1986-89; co-founder, exec. v.p., chief operating officer Action Life Alert (now Pioneer Med. Corp.), Mt. Laurel, N.J., 1988-93, v.p. market devel., 1993—. Mem. Masons (master 1991). Republican. Jewish. Home: 108 Kelly Cv # A Mount Laurel NJ 08054-2735

RIGDON, DAVID TEDRICK, air force officer, geneticist, director; b. Laurel, Miss., Jan. 27, 1948; s. James T. and Marie T. (Taylor) R.; m. Elizabeth Sue Jones, June 1, 1973; children: Angela Denise, Michael David. BS in Biology, U. Ala., 1970; MD cum laude, U. Miss., 1975. Diplomate Am. Bd. Pediats., Am. Bd. Med. Genetics. Commd. USAF, 1975, advanced through grades to col., 1991; intern in pediats. USAF Med. Ctr., Keesler AFB, Miss., 1975-76, resident in pediats., 1976-78; fellow in med. genetics U. Ala., Birmingham, 1978-80; med. geneticist USAF Med. Genetics Ctr., Keesler AFB, 1980-85, dir. Air Force Med. Genetics Ctr., 1985—; cons. Surgeon Gen. USAF, Miss. State Dept. Health; clin. asst. prof. pediats. Uniformed Svcs. Univ. of Health Scis., F. Edward Herbert Sch. Medicine, Bethesda, Md. Contbr. articles to profl. jours. Recipient Physician's Recognition award AMA, 1978, 81, 84, 87, 90, 93, 96. Fellow Am. Acad. Pediats.; mem. Am. Soc. Human Genetics, So. Genetics Group, Alpha Omega Alpha. Republican. Methodist. Office: Air Force Med Genetics Ctr 81 MDOS/SGOT Rm 1A 132 301 Fisher St Keesler AFB MS 39534-2519

RIGDON, EDWARD EUGENE, general vascular surgeon; b. Union, Miss., Aug. 4, 1953; s. Lamar Keith and Betty Sue (Ridout) R.; m. Patricia Lee Kersh, May 24, 1974; children: John Michael, Anna Katherine, Ashley Elizabeth. BS, Miss. State U., 1975; MD, U. Miss., Jackson, 1978. Diplomate Am. Bd. Surgery, gen. and gen. vascular. Intern U. Ala., Birmingham, 1978-79; resident specializing in surgery U. Miss. Med. Ctr., Jackson, 1979-84; staff surgeon U.S. Naval Hosp., Keflavik, Iceland, 1984-86; practice medicine in vascular and gen. surgery Miss. Med. Ctr., 1990—. Served to lt. comdr. USNR, 1981-87. Ohio State U. fellow gen. vascular surgery, 1989-90; recipient J.W. Ward award Miss. State U., 1974, Wear scholar, 1977. Mem. ACS, AMA, Miss. Med. Assn., Peripheral Vascular Surg. Soc., So. Assn. for Vascular Surgery, Internat. Soc. for Cardiovasc. Surgery, Southeastern Surg. Congress, Alpha Omega Alpha, Phi Kappa Phi. Episcopalian. Home: 310 Sherborne Pl Jackson MS 39208-8959 Office: U Miss Med Ctr Dept Surgery 2500 N State St Jackson MS 39216-4500

RIGG, CHARLES ANDREW, pediatrician; b. Hamilton, Vic., Australia, Oct. 18, 1926; came to U.S., 1963; s. Arthur Oscar and Mary Eileen (Wingrove) R. B in Medicine, Surgery with honors, Sydney U., 1951. Staff adolescent medicine Children's Hosp., Boston, 1964-65; chief dept. adolescent medicine Children's Hosp., Washington, 1967-80, Boston City Hosp., 1981-83; med. dir. Outer Cape Health, Provincetown, Mass., 1983-88; pediatrician, med. dir. Medicenter Five, Harwich, Mass., 1988-95, pediatrician, 1995—; from asst. prof. to assoc. prof. child health George Washington U. Med. Sch., 1967-80; cons. Nat. Naval Med. Ctr., Bethesda, Md., 1973-80, Walter Reed Army Med. Ctr., Washington, 1973-80; assoc. prof. pediatrics Boston U. Med. Sch., 1981-83; courtesy staff medicine Children's Hosp., Boston, 1983—. Editor: Adolescent Medicine Present and Future Concepts, 1980; contbr. articles to profl. jours. Mem. Mus. Fine Arts, Boston, Folger Shakespeare Libr., Washington. Lt. col. USAR, 1985-91. Decorated Army Commendation medal; model tng. program in adolescent medicine grantee Maternal and Child Health Svcs.-U.S. Govt., 1967-80, Comprehensive Health Svcs. Adolescent Ctr. grantee Mass. Dept. Pub. Health, 1981-83. Fellow Am. Acad. Pediatrics, Royal Australasian Coll. Physicians, Soc. Adolescent Medicine (charter, treas., chmn., legis. com.); mem. Royal Sydney Golf Club, City Tavern Club Washington. Episcopalian. Office: Medicenter Five 525 Long Pond Dr Harwich MA 02645-1227

RIGGS, BYRON LAWRENCE, JR., physician, educator; b. Hot Springs, Ark., Mar. 24, 1931; s. Byron Lawrence and Elizabeth Ann (Patching) R.; m. Janet Templeton Brewer, June 24, 1955; children: Byron Kent, Ann Templeton. B.S., U. Ark., 1953, B.S. in Medicine, 1955, M.D., 1955; M.S. in Medicine, U. Minn., 1962. Diplomate: Am. Bd. Internal Medicine. Intern Letterman Army Hosp., San Francisco, 1955-56; resident in internal medicine Mayo Grad. Sch. Medicine Hosp., Rochester, Minn., 1958-61; asst. to staff Mayo Clinic and Found., Rochester, 1961, mem. staff internal medicine and metabolism, 1962—; mem. faculty U. Minn. Med. Sch., Rochester, 1962—, assoc. prof., 1970-72, prof., 1972—; Purvis and Roberta Tabor prof. med. rsch. Mayo Clinic and Med. Sch., Rochester, 1974—, chmn. divsn. endocrinology and metabolism, 1974-84; mem. gen. medicine B study sect. NIH, 1979-82; nat. adv. bd. NIAMS/NIH, 1987-91, disting. investigator Mayo Found., 1991—. Contbr. articles to med. jours. Dist. investigator Mayo Found., 1991—. Served with M.C. AUS, 1956-58. Recipient Mayo Found. postgrad. travel award, 1961; Kappa Delta award Am. Acad. Orthopedic Surgery, 1972; traveling fellow Royal Soc. Medicine, 1973. Fellow ACP; mem. AMA, AAAS, Assn. Am. Physicians, Am. Soc. Clin. Investigation, Endocrine Soc. (Rorer Clin. Investigator award 1989), Am. Fedn. Clin. Rsch. (councillor Midwest sect. 1969-71), Am. Soc. for Bone and Mineral Rsch. (pres. 1985-86, Bartter Clin. Investigation award 1990, Career Recognition award, 9th Workshop on Vitamin D rsch.), Ctrl. Soc. Clin. Rsch. (councillor). Home: 432 10th Ave SW Rochester MN 55902-2911 Office: Mayo Clinic 200 1st St SW Rochester MN 55905-0001

RIGGS, JACK EDWARD, neurologist, educator; b. Toledo, Oct. 6, 1949; s. Paul Henson and Bertha Jean (Terry) R.; m. Christine Marie Gunther, Sept. 18, 1978; children: Allison, Kevin, Lauren, Todd. BA, U. Toledo, 1972, BS, 1972; MD, U. Rochester, 1976. Diplomate Am. Bd. Internal Medicine. Diplomate Am. Bd. Neurology and Psychiatry. Asst. prof. neurology W.Va. U., Morgantown, W.Va., 1981-84; assoc. prof. neurology W.Va. U., 1984-87, prof. neurology, 1987—. Contbr. over 160 articles to profl. jours. Fellow Am. Acad. Neurology; mem. Am. Neurol. Assn. Home: 10 Lakeview Dr Morgantown WV 26505 Office: WVa U Dept Neurology Box 9180 Health Sci Ctr Morgantown WV 26506

RIGGS, LORRIN ANDREWS, psychologist, educator; b. Harput, Turkey, June 11, 1912; parents Am. citizens; s. Ernest Wilson and Alice (Shepard) R.; m. Doris Robinson, 1937 (dec.); children: Douglas Rikert, Dwight Alan; m. Caroline Cressman, 1994. A.B., Dartmouth Coll., 1933; M.A., Clark U., 1934, Ph.D., 1936. NRC fellow biol. scis. U. Pa., 1936-37; instr. U. Vt., 1937-38, 39-41; with Brown U., 1938-39, 41—, from asst. to assoc. prof., 1938-51, prof., 1951—, L. Herbert Ballou prof., 1960-68, E.J. Marston Univ. prof., 1968-77, prof. emeritus, 1977—; Guggenheim fellow U. Cambridge, 1971-72. Author sci. articles on vision, physiol. psychology. Recipient Kenneth Craik award Cambridge U., 1979, Prentice medal Am. Acad. Optometry, 1973. Mem. AAAS (chmn., v.p. sect. 1 1964), APA (div. pres. 1962-63, Disting. Sci. Contn. award 1974), Eastern Psychol. Assn. (pres. 1975-76), Optical Soc. Am. (Tillyer medal 1969, Ives medal 1982), Nat. Acad. Scis., Am. Physiol. Soc., Internat. Brain Rsch. Orgn., Soc. for Neurosci., Soc. Exptl. Psychologists (Howard Crosby Warren medal 1957), Assn. Rsch. in Vision and Ophthalmology (pres. 1977, Friedenwald award 1966), Am. Acad. Arts and Scis., Am. Psychol. Soc. (William James fellow 1989), Sigma Xi (chpt. pres. 1962-64). Home: Kendal at Hanover # 104 80 Lyme Rd Hanover NH 03755-1225

RIGHTER, ANNE ROBINSON, clinical social worker, psychotherapist; b. N.Y.C., July 5, 1939; d. Hamilton and Elizabeth Parker (Case) Robinson; m. James Volney Righter, June 22, 1962; children: Eliot Day Righter Ramos, Mark Hamilton Righter. BA in Sociology summa cum laude, U. New Haven, 1974; M of Social Work, U. Conn., 1976; postgrad., Yale U., 1976-77. Lic. independent social worker, Mass.; cert. Acad. of Cert. Social Workers. Clin. instr. social work Child Psychiatry Unit-Yale U., New Haven, 1977-80; staff social worker Univ. Child Study Ctr., New Haven; clin. instr., field work supr. Simmons Sch. of Social Work, Boston, 1981-82; clin. social worker, chief court clinics Mass. Mental Health Ctr., Boston, 1981-82; clin. social worker Ctr. for Counseling Family Svc. Assn., Boston, 1982-84; chief social worker Ctr. for Therapy, Boston Children's Svc., Boston, 1983-86; pvt. practice Boston, 1982-95; bd. dirs., officer Planned Parenthood Greater New Haven, 1967-75, Affiliated Children's Svcs., Brookline-Lexington, Mass., 1981-85, Island Health Project, Inc., Fishers Island, N.Y., 1991—, Trinity Hospice, Brookline, Mass., 1988—, Rutland Corner House, Inc., Brookline, 1982-96, pres. 1984-91. Vestry mem. St. Johns Ch., Fishers Island, 1990—; bd. visitors Walnut Hill Sch. Performing Arts, Natick, Mass., 1995—; bd. overseers New Eng. Conservatory, Boston, 1995—. Mem. Nat. Assn. Social Workers, Nat. Registry Health Care Providers in Clin. Social Work, Mass. Acad. Clin. Social Workers, Tuesday Club, Tavern Club. Democrat. Episcopalian. Home and Office: 72 Pinckney St Boston MA 02114

RIISE, GERDT CHRISTIAN, pulmonary physician; b. Bergen, Norway, Dec. 20, 1956; arrived in Sweden, 1969; s. Børre Merlees and Tina (Hernes) R.; m. Wilhelmina Christina Hult, Nov. 14, 1986; children: Rebecka, Christian, Hanne. BS, Göteborg U., 1978, MD, 1981, PhD, 1994. Intern Alingsås, Sweden, 1981-83; jr. registrar Dept. Pulmonary Medicine, 1983-87; specialist pulmonary medicine Göteborg U., 1987; sr. registrar pulmonary medicine Sahlgrens U. Hosp., Göteborg, 1987—. Mem. European Respiratory Soc., Swedish Med. Soc. Office: Dept Pulmonary MedSahlgrens Hosp, Bruna Str 11, 41345 Goteborg Sweden

RIKER, WILLIAM KAY, pharmacologist, educator; b. N.Y.C., Aug. 31, 1925; s. Walter Franklin and Eleanore Louise (Scafard) R.; m. Carmela Louise DePamphilis, Dec. 21, 1947 (dec. 1981); children: Eleanor Louise, Gainor, Victoria; m. Leena Mela, Aug. 13, 1983. B.A., Columbia U., 1949; M.D., Cornell U., 1953. Intern 2d Cornell med. div., Bellevue Hosp., 1953-54; practice medicine, specializing in pharmacology Phila., 1954-69, Portland, Oreg., 1969—; instr., asst. prof. dept. pharmacology U. Pa. Sch. Medicine, 1954-61; spl. fellow dept. physiology U. Utah Sch. Medicine, 1961-64; assoc. prof., prof., chmn. dept. pharmacology Woman's Med. Coll., Phila., 1964-69; prof., chmn. dept. pharmacology U. Oreg. Sch. Medicine, U. Oreg. Health Scis. Center, 1969-91, prof. emeritus, 1991—, asst. dean. for admissions, 1986-89; mem. neurol. disorders program project com. NIH, 1975-79. Editor: Jour. Pharmacology and Exptl. Therapeutics, 1969-72; contbr. articles to biomed. jours. Served with USNR, 1943-46. Recipient Christian R. and Mary F. Lindback Found. award for disting. teaching, 1968; Pa. Plan scholar, 1957-61; Nat. Inst. Neurol. Diseases and Blindness spl. fellow, 1961-64; USPHS-NIH research grantee, 1958-83. Mem. Am. Soc. Pharmacology and Exptl. Therapeutics (sec.-treas. 1978-81, pres. 1985-86), Western Pharmacol. Soc. (pres. 1976), Japanese Pharmacol. Soc., Assn. Med. Sch. Pharmacologists (sec. 1976-78), Epilepsy Assn. Am., Pharm. Mfrs. Assn. Found. (chmn. pharmacology-morphology adv. com., sci. adv. com. 1976-92), Cosmos Club. Home: 4326 SW Warrensway Portland OR 97221

RIKKERS, LAYTON FREDERICK, surgeon; b. Fond du Lac, Wis., Jan. 31, 1944; s. Judson John and Dorothy (Layton) R.; m. Diane Lynn Foster, Aug. 20, 1966; children: Steven, Kristin. BS, U. Wis., 1966; MD, Stanford U. Sch. Medicine, 1970. Diplomate Nat. Bd. Med. Examiners, Am. Bd. Surgery. Intern U. Utah Sch. Medicine, Salt Lake City, 1970-71, surgical residency, 1971-76; instr. surgery Emory U. Sch. Medicine, Atlanta, 1976-77; from asst. prof. surgery to acting chmn. div. gen. surgery U. Utah Sch. Medicine, Salt Lake City, 1977-84; prof., chmn. dept. surgery U. Nebr. Med. Ctr., Omaha, 1984-96; chmn. dept. surgery U. Wis., Madison, 1996—; interim dean Coll. Medicine, U. Nebr. Coll. Medicine, 1991-93, M.M. Musselman prof. surgery, 1990—; cons. Omaha Vet. Adminstrv. Ctr., 1984-86, NIH, 1992, Gov.'s Blue Ribbon Coalition on Health Care, Nebr., 1993-94. Editor: Surgical Clinics of North America, 1990; contbr. articles to profl. jours. Mem. Am. Surgical Assn., Am. Coll. Surgeons (com. chair 1993-95), Am. Bd. Surgery (clin. chmn. 1994-95), Soc. Clin. Surgery (pres.-elect 1994-95). Episcopalian. Office: U Wis H4/710 Clin Sci Ctr 600 Highland Ave Madison WI 53792-0001

RIKLI, ARTHUR EUGENE, physician, educator; b. Aurora, Ill., Dec. 2, 1917; s. Arthur Richard and Sarah Rebecca (Brown) R.; m. Frances Louise Mayer, Sept. 17, 1944; children: Barbara, Stephen, Ann, Robert. BS, MD, U. Ill., Chgo., 1944; MPH, Johns Hopkins U., 1948. Diplomate Am. Bd. Preventive Medicine. Commd. med. officer USPHS, advanced through grades to col., ret., 1968; regional med. cons. Denver, 1948-53, Chgo., 1953-58; dir. nat. heart disease program Pub. Health Svc. Regular Corp. Commn., Washington, 1958-68; health attache U.S. Mission, Geneva, Switzerland, 1958-68; prof. dept. family community medicine U. Mo. Coll. Medicine, Columbia, 1968-84, coord. Mo. Regional Med. Program, cons. to info. group, 1984—; cons. Nat. Libr. Medicine, Bethesda, Md., 1984-90, vis. scholar, 1994. Author: Computers As a Diagnostic Aid, 1968; contbr. articles to profl. jours.; pioneer in computerization of the electrocardiogram, 1953. Bd. dirs. Mo. Symphony Soc., pres. emeritus, 1994; pres. Mizzou Optimist Club, Columbia, Mo., 1985; founder Nat. Orgn. State Kidney Programs, 1972. Col. USPHS, 1944-68. USPHS grantee, 1968-84, Mo. Legis. Appropriation grantee, 1968-84; recipient Alumnus of Yr. North Ctrl. Coll., 1995. Mem. Mo. State Med. Assn. (state com. benefits 1989), Mid. Mo. Geneal. Soc. (bd. dirs. 1989—), U. Mo. Ret. Employees Assn. (sec. 1989). Home: 4003 Faurot Dr Columbia MO 65203-0311 Office: U Mo Lewis Hall Rm 626 Columbia MO 65203

RILEY, CHARLES LOGAN (REX RILEY), healthcare administrator; b. Toledo, Jan. 20, 1946; s. Charles Allen and Phyllis Mary (Logan) R.; m. Rosemarie Jeanette Webster, Apr. 10, 1971; children: Paul Anthony, Ross Evan. BA, U. Mich., 1968; MHA, U. New South Wales, 1976. Indsl. engr. Internat. Harvester, Melbourne, Victoria, Australia, 1972-74; with Royal Women's Hosp., Melbourne, 1974-79; chief operating officer Preston (Victoria) & Northcote Community Hosp., 1979-84, Valley Children's Hosp., Fresno, Calif., 1989—; chief exec. officer Geelong (Victoria) Hosp., 1984-89; bd. dirs. Hosp. Coun. No. and Ctrl. Calif., Calif. Hosp. Polit. Action Co.; chmn. Fresno/Madera Hosp. Conf. Mem. Leadership Fresno, 1990-91; mem. exec. com. Combined Health Appeal, 1989-90; bd. dirs. Ronald McDonald House, Fresno, 1990-92; chair Fresno-Madera Hosp. Conf., 1995. Decorated Navy Commendation medal; scholar Buehler Found., 1964, Health Dept. Victoria, 1973. Fellow Am. Coll. Healthcare Execs., Australian Coll. Healthsvc. Execs. (registrar 1983-85, v.p. 1985-87, pres. 1987-88); mem. Rotary. Home: 2287 W Pinedale Ave Fresno CA 93711-7109 Office: Valley Children's Hosp 3151 N Millbrook Ave Fresno CA 93703-1425

RILEY, DOROTHY ELAINE, nursing executive; b. Boston, July 4; d. Daniel Thomas and Josephine Marie (Durken) Horgan; m. Timothy John Riley; children: Timothy John Jr., Christopher John, Shannon Marie. BS in Nursing, Boston Coll., 1966; MS in Nursing, U. Wis., Milw., 1977. Cert. advanced nursing adminstr. Staff nurse various hosps., 1969-75; dir. nursing Samaritan Home, West Bend, Wis., 1975-76; mem. nursing faculty Marquette U., Milw., 1977-79; asst. dir. nursing Outagamie County Health Care Ctr., Appleton, Wis., 1979-80; mem. nursing faculty U. Wis., Oshkosh, 1980-83; nursing svc. adminstr. Brown County Mental Health Ctr., Green Bay, Wis., 1983-88, nursing home adminstr., 1988-93; nursing home adminstrn. Washoe Care Ctr., Sparks, Nev., 1994; DON Nev. Mental Health Inst., Sparks, 1994—. Mem. NOW, LWV, Planned Parenthood, The Feminist Majority. Lt. Nurses Corps USN, 1966-69. Named Nurse of Yr., Appleton Dist. Nurses Assn., 1984. Mem. Wis. Nurses Assn. (bd. dirs. 1984-86, sec. 1986-88, pres. 1993—), Green Bay Nurses Assn. (bd. dirs. 1986-89, pres. 1990-92), Green Bay Dist. Nurses Assn. (Svc. award 1992), Nev. Nurses Assn., Sigma Theta Tau.

RILEY, KATHLEEN ANN, healthcare industries consultant; b. Norfolk, Va., Jan. 30, 1945; d. Edward Miles and Ruth Annette (Powers) R.; m. Wendell Earl Dunn III, Mar. 29, 1981; 1 child, Elissa Brooks Dunn. Student, Tulane U., 1962-64; BS in Chemistry, Coll. William & Mary, 1967; MS, U. Ill., 1970; MBA, Northwestern U., 1977. Pharm. chemist Abbott Labs., North Chicago, Ill., 1970-73; clinical research assoc. Abbott Labs., North Chicago, 1973-75; cons. Mgmt. Analysis Ctr., Northbrook, Ill., 1975-76; mgr. strategic planning agrl. chemicals FMC Corp., Phila., 1977-81, mgr. strategic planning phosphorus chemicals, 1981-82; mgr. new compound opportunities Smith Kline French Internat. Labs., Phila., 1982-86, market planning mgr., 1986-88; assoc. dir. new product evaluation Smith, Kline & French, Phila., 1988-89; assoc. dir. new compound evaluation Smith Kline Beecham Pharms., Phila., 1989-91, dir. product evaluation and analysis, 1991-94, dir. portfolio planning, 1994; prin. The Gladstone Group, Charlottesville, Va., 1995—. Patentee in field; contbr. articles to profl. jours. Bd. dirs. Cmty. Arts Alliance, Phila., 1982-87; cons., counselor Girl Scouts Am., Haddonfield, N.J., 1986-87, leader, 1994-96, troop coord. Albemarle County, Va., 1996—. Mem. World Future Soc. (profl.), Internat. Health Futures Network, Phila. Women's Network (bd. dirs. 1980-84, treas. 1983-84, chmn. strategic planning com. 1982-87), Haddon Fortnightly Club (program speaker 1991, 93, bd. dirs. 1987-93, 95—, chmn. internat. rels. com. 1987-89, chmn. conservation and gardening com. 1987-91, internat. affairs com. 1991-93, arts/creative com. 1995—), Sigma Xi, Iota Sigma Pi. Lutheran. Office: PO Box 4313 Charlottesville VA 22901

RILEY, MATILDA WHITE (MRS. JOHN W. RILEY, JR.), sociology educator; b. Boston, Apr. 19, 1911; d. Percival and Mary (Cliff) White; m. John Winchell Riley, Jr., June 19, 1931; children: John Winchell III, Lucy Ellen Riley Sallick. BA, Radcliffe Coll., 1931, MA, 1937, DSc (hon.), 1994; DSc, Bowdoin Coll., 1972; LHD (hon.), Rutgers U., 1983. Rsch. asst. Harvard U., Cambridge, Mass., 1932; v.p. Market Rsch. Co. Am., 1938-49; chief cons. economist WPB, 1941; rsch. specialist Rutgers U., 1950, prof., 1951-73, dir. sociology lab., chmn. dept. sociology and anthropology, 1959-73, emeritus prof., 1973—; Daniel B. Fayerweather prof. polit. econ. and sociology Bowdoin Coll., 1974-78, prof. emeritus, 1978—; assoc. dir. Nat. Inst. on Aging, 1979-91, sr. social scientist, 1991—; mem. faculty Harvard U., summer 1955; staff assoc., dir. aging and society Russell Sage Found., 1964-73, staff sociologist, 1974-77; chmn. com. on life course Social Sci. Rsch. Coun., 1977-80; sr. rsch. assoc. Ctr. for Social Scis., Columbia U., 1978-80; adv. bd. Carnegie Aging Soc. Project, 1985-87; mem. Commn. on Coll. Retirement, 1982-86; vis. prof. NYU, 1954-61; cons. Nat. Coun. on Aging, Acad. Ednl. Devel.; mem. study group NIH, 1971-79, Social Sci. Rsch. Coun. Com. on Middle Years, 1973-77; chmn. NIH Task Force on Health and Behavior, 1986-91; cons. WHO, 1987—; Winkelman lectr. U. Mich., 1984, Selo lectr. U. No. Calif., 1987, Boettner lectr. Am. Coll., 1990, Claude Pepper lectr. Fla. State U., 1993, Disting. lectr. Southwestern Social Scis. Assn., 1990, Standing lectr. SUNY, 1992, Inaugural lectr. Cornell U., 1992; lectr. Internat. Inst. of Sociology, Plenary, 1993, Inter-Univ. Consortium Pol. and Social Rsch., U. Mich., 1993, Duke U., 1993. Author: (with P. White) Gliding and Soaring, (with Riley and Toby) Sociological Studies in Scale Analysis, 1954, Sociological Research, vols. I, II, 1964, (with others) Aging and Society, vol. I, 1968, vol. II, 1969, vol. III, 1972, (with Nelson) Sociological Observation, 1974, Aging from Birth to Death: Interdisciplinary Perspectives, 1979, (with Merton) Sociological Traditions from Generation to Generation, 1980, (with Abeles and Teitelbaum) Aging from Birth to Death: Sociotemporal Perspectives, 1982, (with Hess and Bond) Aging in Society, 1983; editor: (with M. Ory and D. Zablotsky) AIDS in an Aging Society: What We Need to Know, 1989; co-editor: Perspectives in Behavioral Medicine: The Aging Dimension, 1987, (with J. W. Riley) The Quality of Aging, 1989, The Annuals, 1989; sr. editor: Structural Lag, 1994; editorial com.: Ann. Rev. Sociology, 1978-81, Social Change and the Life Course, vol. 1, Social Structures and Human Lives, (with B. Huber and B. Hess) Sociological Lives, vol. II, 1988, (with R. Kahn and Anne Foner) Structural Lag, 1994; contbr. chpts. to books, articles to profl. jours. Former trustee The Big Sisters Assn. Recipient Lindback Rsch. award Rutgers U., 1970, Social Sci. award Andrus Gerontology Ctr., U. So. Calif., 1972, Radcliffe Alumnae award, 1982, Commonwealth award 1984, Kesten Lecture award U. So. Calif., 1987, Sci. Achievement award Washington Acad. Scis., 1989, Disting. Sci. award, 1989, Disting. Creative award Gerontol. Soc. Am., 1990, Presdl. Meritorious award, 1990, Stuart Rice award Columbia Sociol. Soc., 1992, Kent award Gerontol. Soc. Am., 1992; fellow Advanced Study in Behaviorial Scis., 1978-79; Matilda White Riley award in rsch. and methodology established in her honor Rutgers U., 1977; Matilda White Riley prize established Bowdoin Coll., 1987; Matilda White Riley House dedicated Bowdoin Coll., 1996. Fellow AAAS (chmn. sect. on social and econ. scis. 1977-78); mem. NAS, Inst. Medicine of NAS (sr.), Acad. Behavioral Medicine Rsch., Am. Sociol. Assn. (exec. officer 1949-60, v.p. 1973-74, pres. 1986, 91, chmn. sect. on sociology of aging 1989, Disting. Scholar in Aging 1988, Career award 1992), Am. Assn. Public Opinion Rsch. (sec.-treas. 1949-51, Disting. Svc. award 1983), Eastern Sociol. Soc. (v.p. 1968-69, pres. 1977-78, Dis. Career award 1986), Soc. for Study Social Biology (bd. dirs. 1986-92), Am. Acad. Arts and Scis., D.C. Sociol. Soc. (co-pres. 1983-84), Sociol. Rsch. Assn., Internat. Orgn. Study Human Devel., Am. Philos. Soc. (membership lectr. 1987), Phi Beta Kappa, Phi Beta Kappa Assocs. Home: 4701 Willard Ave Apt 1607 Chevy Chase MD 20815-4630 Office: NIH Nat Inst on Aging 7201 Wisconsin Ave Bethesda MD 20814-4810

RILEY, RICHARD HAYDN, anaesthetist, researcher; b. Perth, W. Aus., Australia, Nov. 11, 1955; s. Bertram Leon and Lyle Emily (Rees) R.; m. Vera Josefine Fisch, Mar. 13, 1982; children: Benjamin Aaron, Matthew Joel. MB, BS, U. of Western Australia, Perth, 1980. Diplomate Am. Bd. Anesthesiologists. Staff anaesthetist Royal Perth (Australia) Hosp., 1988—; dir. Acute Pain Svc., Royal Perth Hosp., 1994-95. Contbr. articles to profl. jours. Fellow Am. Coll. Anesthesiologists; mem. Am. Soc. Anesthesiologists, Australian Soc. Anesthetists, Australian Med. Assn. Anglican. Office: Royal Perth Hosp., Wellington St, Perth WA 6000, Australia

RILEY, WILLIAM B., JR., plastic surgeon; b. Chattanooga, Aug. 2, 1941. MD, U. N.C., 1967. Diplomate Am. Bd. Plastic Surgery. Intern Stanford (Calif.) U., 1967-68; resident in gen. surgery U. Ariz., Tucson, 1971-73; resident in plastic surgery Royal Melbourne (Australia) Hosp., 1973-74, Emory U. Affiliated Hosps., Atlanta, 1974-75, U. Miami Affiliated Hosps., 1975-76; active staff Ft. Bend Hosp., Sugar Land, 1984; staff Meml. Southwest Hosp., Houston, 1987—; clin. prof. surgery U. Tex., Houston, 1991—; pvt. practice Plastic Surgery Specialists, Houston, 1977—; courtesy staff Hermann Hosp., Houston, 1977—, St. Luke's Hosp., Houston, 1987—. Mem. AMA.

RILEY, WILLIAM J., pediatrician, educator; b. Covington, Ky., Mar. 30, 1947; s. Fleming Charles and Aileen Marcella (Frisch) R.; m. Rebecca Jane Whitfield, Sept. 27, 1967; children: Aaron, Chad. BS, Xavier U., 1967; MD, U. Ky., 1971. Diplomate Am. Bd. Pediatrics and Pediatric Endocrinology. From asst. prof. to prof. U. Fla., Gainesville, 1982-93; prof. U. Tex., Houston, 1993—. Maj. U.S. Army, 1975-78. Fellow Am. Acad. Pediatrics; mem. Lawson Wilkins Pediatric Endocrinology Soc., Am. Diabetes Assn. Office: Health Sci Ctr U Tex 6431 Fannin St Houston TX 77030

RILEY, WILLIAM JOHN, neurologist; b. Seattle, Oct. 24, 1930; s. William John and Virginia (McCarthy) R.; m. Joan Marie Weismann, 1956 (div. 1976); children: Sean, Kevan, Megan, Janeen, Michael; m. Margit Mary, 1976; children: Britta, Shane, Timothy. MS in Anatomy, U. Chgo., 1958, MD, 1960; PhD, U. Minn., 1965. Asst. chief neurology Mpls. Gen. Hosp., 1965-69; chief neurology St. Luke's Episcopal Hosp., Houston, 1970-85; pres., CEO Tex. Neurol. Clinic Assn., Houston, 1969—. Staff sgt. USAF, 1951-55. Recipient Disting. Teaching award Minn. Med. Found., Mpls., 1969. Fellow Am. Acad. Neurology, Am. Coll. Physicians; mem. AMA, Tex. Neurol. Soc. (9th dist.), Tex. Med. Assn. (pres. 1991), Alpha Omega Alpha, Sigma Xi. Roman Catholic. Office: Tex Neurol Clinic Assn 5620 Greenbriar #203 Houston TX 77005

RILLA, DONALD ROBERT, social services administrator; b. Feb. 6, 1941. AS, Berkshire Community Coll., Pittsfield, Mass., 1964; BA, U. Mass., 1967; MSW, U. Conn., 1974. Lic. clin. social worker, Conn.; diplomate Am. Bd. Clin. Social Work. Social worker Children and Youth Svcs., New Haven, Conn., 1967-73, Branford (Conn.) Counseling Ctr., 1973-74; psychiatric social worker Whiting Forensic Inst., Middletown, Conn., 1974-79; psychiatric social worker supr. Cts. Diagnostic Clinic, Hartford, Conn., 1979-87; dir. Bridgeport (Conn.) Ct. Clinic, 1987—; cons. Bridgeport Mental Health Ctr., 1990—. Contbr. articles to profl. jours. Chair Town-Bus Safety Commn., North Haven, 1975; mem. Mental Health Assn. Conn., New Haven, 1968-75; chair, mem. New Haven Halfway House, 1969-73. With USN, 1958-62. Mem. NASW, Nat. Orgn. Forensic Social Work (founding mem. 1983—, chair ethics com. 1985—, treas. 1994-95, pres.- elect 1995, pres. 1996), Acad. Cert. Social Workers, Acad. Forensic Social Workers (diplomate, bd. dirs.). Office: Bridgeport Ct Clinic 1635 Central Ave Bridgeport CT 06610-2717 also: Family Resource Assocs Stratford CT 06497

RILLING, DAVID CARL, surgeon; b. Phila., Oct. 10, 1940; s. Carl Adam and Elizabeth Barbara (Young) R.; m. Karina Sturman, Mar. 25, 1972; children: Jonathan David, Alexander Valentine, Claudia Carla. BS with honors in Biology, Dickinson Coll., Carlisle, pa., 1962; MD, Hahnemann U., 1966. Diplomate Am. Bd. Surgery. Intern Hosp. of U. Pa., Phila., 1966-67; resident Abington (Pa.) Meml. Hosp., 1967-68, 70-73; surgeon Pennridge Surg Assocs., Sellersville, Pa., 1973—; active staff Grand View Hosp., Sellersville, Pa., chmn. dept. surgery, 1985-89, pres. med. staff, 1995. Lt. col. U.S. Army, 1968-70, Vietnam, USARMC. Decorated Bronze Star medal, Nat. Def. Svc. medal, Vietnam Svc. medal. Fellow Am. Coll. Surgeons; mem. AMA, Soc. Clin. Vascular Surgery, Pa. Med. Soc., Bucks County Med. Soc., Vietnam Vascular Registry. Office: Pennridge Surg Assocs 670 Lawn Ave Sellersville PA 18960-1571

RIMOIN, DAVID LAWRENCE, physician, geneticist; b. Montreal, Nov. 9, 1936; s. Michael and Fay (Lecker) R.; m. Mary Ann Singleton, 1962 (div. 1979); 1 child, Anne; m. Ann Piilani Garber, July 27, 1980; children: Michael, Lauren. BSc, McGill U., Montreal, 1957, MSc, MD, CM, 1961; PhD, Johns Hopkins U., 1967. Asst. prof. medicine, pediatrics Washington U., St. Louis, 1967-70; assoc. prof. medicine, pediatrics UCLA, 1970-73, prof., 1973—, chief med. genetics, Harbor-UCLA Med. Ctr., 1970-86; dir. dept. pediatrics, dir. Med. Genetics and Birth Defects Ctr., 1986—; Steven Spielberg chmn. pediatrics Cedars-Sinai Med. Ctr., L.A., 1989—; chmn. coun. Med. Genetics Orgn., 1993. Co-author: Principles and Practice of Medical Genetics, 1983, 90, 96; contbr. articles to profl. jours., chpts. to books. Recipient Ross Outstanding Young Investigator award Western Soc. Pediatric Research, 1976, E. Mead Johnson award Am. Acad. Pediatrics, 1976. Fellow ACP, AAAS, Am. Coll. Med. Genetics (pres. 1991—); mem. Am. Fedn. Clin. Rsch. (sec.-treas. 1972-75), Western Soc. Clin. Rsch. (pres. 1978), Western Soc. Pediatric Rsch. (pres. 1995), Am. Bd. Med. Genetics (pres. 1979-83), Am. Soc. Human Genetics (pres. 1984), Am. Pediatric Soc., Soc. Pediatric Rsch., Am. Soc. Clin. Investigation, Assn. Am. Physicians, Johns Hopkins Soc. Scholars, Inst. Medicine. Office: Cedars-Sinai Med Ctr 8700 Beverly Blvd Los Angeles CA 90048-1804

RIMPILA, CHARLES R., physician; b. Chgo., June 28, 1945; s. Charles Einar and Verna Catherine (Swanson) R.; m. Ellen D. McSweeney; children: Charles Edward, Erica, Darren, Alison. BA, North Park Coll., 1968; MD, Chgo. Med. Sch., 1972. Emergency physician Riverview Hosp., 1987—; med. dir. Consolidated Papers, Inc., 1994—; instr. Mid. State Tech. Coll., 1992—; co-med. dir. South Wood County, Wis., 1992—. Mem. AMA, Am. Coll. Emergency Medicine, Am. Coll. Occupational Medicine & Environ. Medicine.

RINALDI, RENEE ZAIRA, physician; b. N.Y.C., Dec. 10, 1949; d. John James and Concetta (Vecchio) Rinaldi; m. Kenneth Robert Ballard, June 16, 1977; children: Claudia Michele, Celeste Noelle, Christopher Charles. B.A., Barnard Coll., Columbia U., 1971; Ed.M., Harvard, 1973; M.D., N.Y. Med. Coll., 1976. Diplomate Am. Bd. Internal Medicine and Rheumatology. Intern, Met. Hosp., N.Y.C., 1976-77; resident medicine San Fernando program UCLA, Sepulveda Campus, 1977-79, adj. asst. prof. medicine, 1982-83; staff internist Olive View Hosp., Van Nuys, Calif., 1979-80; fellow rheumatology UCLA, 1980-82; practice medicine specializing in rheumatology, Los Angeles, 1983—; asst. clin. prof. medicine UCLA, 1983—. Jane Wyman Clin. fellow, 1981. Mem. So. Calif. Rheumatology Soc., Los Angeles County Women's Med. Assn., Am. Rheumatology Assn.

RINDE, JOHN JACQUES, internist; b. Przemysl, Poland, Jan. 3, 1935; came to U.S., 1952; s. Maurice and Stella (Klein) R.; m. Toni Jgel, June 21, 1959; children: Debbie Ann, Barbara Gail. BS, MIT, 1957, MS, 1958, MME, 1959; MSEE, Poly. Inst. Bklyn., 1965; MD, U. Ark., 1975. Cert. profl. engr.; diplomate Am. Bd. Internal Medicine. Sr. engr. Sperry Gyroscope Co., Great Neck, N.Y., 1959-67, 70-71; v.p. Olson Assocs. Inc., Huntington, N.Y., 1967-69; sr. engr. Hydrosystems, Inc., Farmingdale, N.Y., 1969-70; physician Clearwater, Fla., 1978—. NSF fellow, 1958. Mem. ACP, Am. Soc. Internal Medicine, Fla. Med. Assn., Pinellas County Med. Soc. (bd. govs. 1989-92). Office: 1305 S Fort Harrison Ave Clearwater FL 34616-3301

RINDERKNECHT, ROBERT EUGENE, internist; b. Dover, Ohio, Apr. 27, 1921; s. Henry Carl and Mary Dorothy (Walter) R.; m. Janice Marie Rausch, Oct. 14, 1966; children: Mary Ellen, William A., Janis E. BS, Case Western Reserve U., 1943, MD, 1945. Diplomate Am. Bd. Internal Medicine. Intern Grasslands Hosp., Valhalla, N.Y., 1945-46; resident U. Hosps. Cleve., 1948-49, VA Hosp., Cleve., 1949-51; internist pvt. practice, Dover, Ohio, 1951-79; ret., 1979; trustee Physicians Ins. Co. Ohio, Columbus, 1978-79. Pres. Tuscarawas County (Ohio) Heart Br., 1962-64, 75-77, East Ctrl. Ohio Heart Assn., Canton, 1967-69. Fellow ACP; mem. Masons, Shriners, Elks. Republican. Presbyterian. Home: 101 Dewitt Circle Daphne AL 36526-7740

RINDFLEISCH, RALPH GERARD, physician; b. Richmond, Va., Jan. 18, 1955; s. Dorothy Theresa Rindfleisch; m. Marie Suzanne Suddreth, Jul. 11, 1981; children: Luis Cameron, Stephanie Suzanne, Christopher Gerard. BS, George Washington Univ., 1982; D in osteopathic medicine, W.Va. Sch. Osteopathic Med., 1987. Diplomate Nat. Bd. Osteopathic Medical Examiners. Intern Riverside Hosp., Wilmington, Del., 1987-88; student flight surgeon NAS, Pensacola, Fla., 1989-90; flight surgeon U.S. Naval 2nd Marine Air Wing, MCAS Cherry Point, N.C., 1990-92; resident emergency medicine Univ. Md. Medical System, Balt., 1992-95; attending physician Capital EMCARE Laurel Regional Hosp., Laurel, Md., 1995-96; reviewer Military Medicine, 1995-96. Den leader Cub Scouts Am., Laurel, Md., 1995-96. With U.S. Navy, 1988-92, Kuwait. Decorated Navy Achievement medal U.S. Navy, 1991, S.W. Asia Svc. medal, 1991, Fleet Marine Force Ribbon, 1991, Kuwaiti Liberation medal, 1991. Mem. Assn. Military Surgeons U.S., Am. Coll. Emergency Physicians. Republican. Roman Catholic. Home: 1212 Asquith Pines Pl Arnold MD 21012 Office: Capital Emcare 575 Main St Ste 355 Laurel MD 20707

RINEHART, ARTHUR MIDDLETON, psychiatrist; b. Balt., Jan. 31, 1919; s. Thomas Warden and Janet (Grimes) R.; m. Louise Gail Schmeisser, Oct. 2, 1944; children: Gail W., William Warden. BS, Trinity Coll., 1940; MD, U. Md., 1943. Intern U. Hosp., Balt., 1944, resident, 1944; resident in psychiatry VA Hosp., Perry Point, Md., 1946-48; pvt. practice Balt., 1949—. Capt. U.S. Army Med. Corps, 1944-46. Fellow Am. Psychiatric Assn.; mem. AMA, Am. Orthopsychiatric Assn., Am. Soc. for Adolescent Psychiatry, Md. Soc. for Adolescent Psychiatry, Md. Assn. Pvt. Practicing Psychiatrists (past. chmn.), Gibson Island Club. Home: 13801 York Rd N3 Cockeysville MD 21030-1899

RINELLA, JOSEPH VINCENT, JR., physical pharmacist; b. Chgo., Mar. 15, 1967; s. Joseph Vincent Sr. and Catherine (Mitchell) R.; m. Kimberly Ann Rodgers, July 21, 1990. BS summa cum laude, St. Louis Coll. Pharmacy, 1990; PhD, Purdue U., 1995. Registered pharmacist, Ill. Quality control SmithKline Beecham, St. Louis, 1987; NPC summer intern Warner Lambert, Morris Plains, N.J., 1988; Nat. Pharm. Coun. rsch. intern Merck & Co., West Point, Pa., 1989; pharmacist, medic U.S. Army Res., Indpls., 1985—; sr. scientist biopharm. product devel. Eli Lilly & Co., Indpls., 1995—. 1st lt. USAR, 1985—. Mem. Am. Assn. Pharm. Sci., Am. Chem. Soc., Res. Officers Assn., Sigma Xi, Delta Sigma Theta (scribe), Phi Kappa Phi, Rho Chi. Home: 3640 Romar Dr Brownsburg IN 46112 Office: Eli Lilly & Co Indianapolis IN 46285

RINER, RONALD NATHAN, cardiologist, consultant; b. Hot Springs, S.D., Mar. 7, 1949. AB, Princeton, 1970; MD, Cornell U., N.Y.C., 1974. Diplomate Am. Bd. Internal Medicine, Am. Bd. Cardiovascular Disease.

Resident in internal medicine N.Y. Hosp., Meml. Sloan-Kettering, Hosp. for Spl. Surgery, 1974-76; resident in cardiology Mayo Grad. Sch. Medicine, Rochester, Minn., 1976-79; chmn. dept. internal medicine, St. Mary's Health Ctr., St. Louis, 1980-83, program dir. internal medicine, 1980-83; pvt. practice cardiology, St. Louis, 1983—; sr. scientific advisor pharmaceutical divsn. BioMed. Sys., St. Louis, 1984—; asst. prof. medicine, Washington U. Med. Ctr., 1985-88, pres. Ronald N. Riner and Assocs., Ltd., 1986—, Riner Group, Inc., 1986—, Riner Heart Group, Inc., 1988-95; asst. prof. St. Louis U.; corp. dir. quality affairs SSM Health Care Sys. 1989-91; chmn. Mo. State Med. Assn. Commn. on Med. Econs., Third Party Medicine and Govt. Rels., 1990-92; v.p. clin. svcs. Daus. Charity Nat. Health Sys., 1992—; dir. Allegheny Health Sys., Tampa, Fla., 1991-94, chmn. bd. dirs., 1994—. Editor practice mgmt. and econs. sect. Jour. Invasive Cardiology, 1996—. Bd. dirs. Seton Inst. for Internat. Devel., San Francisco, 1995—. Fellow Am. Coll. Physicians, Am. Coll. Cardiology, Am. Acad. Med. Dirs.; mem. N.Y. Acad. Scis. (life), Mo. Soc. Internal Medicine (coun.), Gov. Rel. Com., Assn. for the Advancement of Scis., Am. Acad. Physician Execs., Mayo Alumni Assns., Am. Cons. League, Am. Mgmt. Assn., AAAS, Cornell U. Alumni Assn., Princeton Alumni Assn., Princeton U. Club. Office: The Riner Group Inc 1034 S Brentwood Blvd Ste 1605 Saint Louis MO 63117-1208

RING, ALICE RUTH BISHOP, physician; b. Ft. Collins, Oct. 11, 1931; d. Ernest Otto and Mary Frances (Drohan) Bishop; m. Wallace Harold Ring, July 26, 1956 (div. 1969); children: Rebecca, Eric, Mark; m. Robert Charles Deifenbach, Sept. 10, 1977. BS, Colo. State U., 1953; MD, U. Colo., 1956; MPH, U. Calif., Berkeley, 1971. Physician cons. Utah State Div. HEalth, Salt Lake City, 1960-65; med. dir., project head start Salt Lake City Community Action Program, 1965-70; resident Utah State Div. Health, 1969-71; asst. assoc. reg. health dir. U.S. Pub. Health Svc., San Francisco, 1971-75; med. cons. U.S. Pub. Health Svc., Atlanta, 1975-77, dir. primary care, 1977-84; dir. div. diabetes control Ctrs. Disease Control, Atlanta, 1984-88; dir. WHO Collabor Ctr., Atlanta, 1986-91; dir. preventive medicine residency Ctrs. Disease Control, Atlanta, 1988-93; exec. dir. Am. Bd. Preventive Medicine, 1993—; trustee Am. Bd. Preventive Medicine, 1990-92 (diplomate); lectr. Emory U. Sch. Pub. Health, 1988-94. Co-author: Clinical Diabetes, 1991. Bd. dirs. Diabetes Assn. Atlanta, 1985-90, med. adv. com., 1990-94. Fellow Am. Coll. Preventive Medicine (bd. dirs. 1990-94); mem. APHA, AMA (grad. med. edn. adv. com. 1993—), Assn. Tchrs. Preventive Medicine, Am. Acad. Pediatrics, Sigma Xi. Office: Am Bd Preventive Medicine 9950 Lawrence Ave Schiller Park IL 60176-1310

RING, JOHANNES, dermatologist, educator; b. Bad Wörishofen, Germany, June 3, 1945; s. Josef and Berta (Christ) R.; m. Susanna Pfeffer; children: Lorenz, Ludwig. MD, Ludwig-Maximillian U., Munich, 1970; DPhil, Ludwig-Maximillian U., 1979. Intern Landesärztekammer, Munich, 1970; rsch. fellow Inst. Surg. Rsch., U. Munich, 1971-76; postdoctoral rsch. fellow Scripps Clinic and Rsch. Found., La Jolla, Calif., 1977-78; resident, Dermatology Clinic Munich U., 1978-82, mem. staff Dermatology Clinic, 1982—, head allergy div., 1982—, prof. medicine, 1983—. Author: Bavarian Image in USA, 1979; author, editor books on allergy; contbr. articles to sci. publs. Fellow Collegium Internat. Allergologicum (coun. mem. 1986—), European Soc. Dermatol. Rsch. (pres. 1989-90), Deutsche Gesellschaft Allergie Immunitatsforschung (bd. dirs. 1987—), Am. Acad. Allergy and Immunology. Roman Catholic. Office: Hautklinik U Krankenhaus Eppendorf, Martinistrabe 53, 20246 Hamburg Germany

RINGEL, DAVID NEIL, osteopath; b. Hamilton, Ohio, Jan. 15, 1959; s. Erich Wolfgang and Rita Ilene (Kaplan) R.; 1 child, Aaron Michael. BS in Biology, U. Cin., 1980; DO, Ohio U. Coll. Osteo. Medicine, 1988. Diplomate Am. Bd. Family Practice. Intern Bay Med Ctr., Bay City, Mich., 1988-89; resident St. Elizabeth Med. Ctr., Dayton, Ohio, 1989-91, family practice physician, 1991-92; family practice physician Miami Valley Hosp. Enterprises, Dayton, Ohio, 1992-94, Ohio Valley Med. Group, Dayton, Ohio, 1994—. Mem. AMA, Ohio State Med. Assn., Am. Acad. Family Practice, Sigma Sigma Phi. Office: Ohio Valley Medical Group 6611 Clyo Rd Centerville OH 45459

RINGEL, RICHARD HENRY, pediatrician; b. Washington, Mar. 28, 1941; s. Samuel Joseph and June Rose (Komsky) R.; m. Marcia Esther Van Dam, June 18, 1966; children: Paul B., Deborah R. AB, Princeton U., 1963; MD, Georgetown U., 1966. Diplomate Am. Bd. Pediatrics. Intern, resident New Eng. Med. Ctr. Hosp., 1966-69; pediatrician Goddard Med. Assn., Boakton, Mass., 1971-84, Tri-County Pediat. Assoc., P.C., Stoughton, Mass., 1984—; chief pediats. Goddard Meml. Hosp., Stoughton, 1977-94; physician advisor Pilgrim Health Care, Norwell, Mass., 1990—; pres. Greater Brockton Primary Care Assn., Stoughton, 1994; v.p. Good Samaritan IPA, Stoughton, 1995. Chairperson legis. com. Mass. chpt. AAP, Boston, 1994—; treas. M-DAC, Boston, 1995. Maj. U.S. Army, 1969-91. Office: Med Office Bldg Ste M102 907 Sumner St Stoughton MA 02072-3374

RINGO, BETTY PENFOLD, hypnotherapist; b. Wheaton, Ill., Apr. 26, 1924; d. Alexander Derby and Vega Thelma (Friborg) Penfold; children: Susan K. Paul, Robert B., Richard G., Peter A. ADN, Purdue U., 1982, BLS, 1985. RN, Ind.; cert. hypnotherapist, neurolinguistic practitioner, Reiki master. Medication nurse Meml. Hosp., Michigan City, Ind., 1982-83; pvt. practice in reflexology Michigan City, 1981—, pvt. practice in hypnotherapy, reiki, reflexology and healing touch, 1985—; design human engring. I facilitator AIDS Support Group, 1990-92. Mem. AAUW (pres. 1988-89, v.p., program chair 1986-88, 90-92). Lutheran.

RINGOIR, SEVERIN MARIA GHISLENUS, medical educator, physician; b. Aalst, Belgium, June 17, 1931; s. Benoni and Mariette (Vlasschaert) R.; children: Marc, Yves. MD, U. Gent, Belgium, 1956, PhD, 1967. Resident Med. Clinic U. Gent, 1958-61, instr., 1961-71, assoc. prof., 1971-75, prof. nephrology, 1975—, chief renal div., 1971—, chmn. medicine, 1981-84; chmn. biomed engring. program U. Gent, 1991-95; pres. Inst. Biomed. Tech. Ghent U., 1995—; chmn. 1st Internat. Symposium Single Needle Hemodialysis, Tampa, Fla., 1984; co-founder Internat. Faculty Artificial Organs. Inventor pressure-pressure single needle hemodialysis; contbr. sci. articles to profl. jours. Maj. Mil. Health Svc., 1956-58, Res., 1958-89. Decorated comdr. Order of Leopold, Grand officer Order of Crown (Belgium); recipient J. Lemaire prize, 1970, Internat. Disting. medal Nat. Kidney Found. U.S.A., 1991. Fellow Royal Soc. Medicine U.K.; mem. Royal Acad. Medicine Belgium, Am. Soc. Artificial Internal Organs, Swiss, German, French and Dutch Soc. Nephrology, European Dialysis and Transplant Assn. (coun. 1981-84, pres. 1985 Congress), European Soc. for Artificial Organs (gov. 1988-92, pres. Congress 1989), Internat. Soc. Artificial Organs (v.p. 1981-85, gen. sec. 1984-90). Home: Vaderlandstraat 44, B9000 Ghent Belgium Office: Univ Gent, De Pintelaan 185, B9000 Ghent Belgium

RINKER, CHARLES FREDERICK, II, surgeon; b. Washington, Aug. 29, 1945; s. Royden Carrington and Elsie Margaret (Kilroy) R.; m. Katherine Ann Bogenreif, Oct. 10, 1982; children: Neil, Brian, Lindsay, Charles. AB, Hamilton Coll., 1967; MD, Case Western Res. U., 1971. Diplomate Am. Bd. Surgery. Intern Case Western Res U. and Affiliated Hosps., Cleve., 1971-72, resident, 1972-76; ptnr. Surg. Assoc. of Bozeman, Mont., 1976—. Co-prodr. (documentary film) Trauma Care in Montana, 1994. Trustee Intermountain Opera, Bozeman, 1985-89, Mus. of the Rockies, Bozeman, 1987-93, Polit. Economy Rsch. Ctr., Bozeman, 1988-94. Fellow ACS (pres. Mont-Wyo. chpt. 1987-88, gov. at large Mont. 1992—, chair regional com. on trauma 1994—, vice-chair com. on trauma 1994—, Trauma Achievement award 1993), Southwestern Surg. Congress. Office: Surg Assocs Bozeman Ste 2200 925 Highland Blvd Bozeman MT 59715

RINNE, PAUL WALTER, anesthesiologist; b. Washington, May 25, 1957; s. Walter William Rinne and Margaret Elizabeth (Yeager) Howard; m. Andrea Bourland, Dec. 27, 1980; children: Andrew, Nicholas, Matthew. BS, Mary Washington Coll., 1979; MD, Med. Coll. Va., 1983. Diplomate Am. Bd. Anesthesiology. Intern U. Wyo., Cheyenne, 1983-84; resident in anesthesiology Med. Coll. Va., Richmond, 1984-86; anesthesiologist United Med. Ctr., Cheyenne, 1986-87, 88—, Radford (Va.) Cmty. Hosp., 1987-88; chmn. anesthesia dept. United Med. Ctr., 1988-93; chief anesthesia svc. VA Med. Ctr., Cheyenne, 1993—. Mem. Am. Soc. Anesthesiologists, Aerospace Med. Assn., Wyo. Med. Soc. Methodist. Office: 800 E 20th St Cheyenne WY 82001

RINTA, CHRISTINE EVELYN, nurse, air force officer; b. Geneva, Ohio, Oct. 4, 1952; d. Arvi Alexander and Catharina Maria (Steenbergen) R. BSN, Kent State U., 1974; MSN, Case Western Res. U., 1979. CNOR. Staff nurse in oper. rm. Euclid (Ohio) Gen. Hosp., 1974-76, oper. rm. charge nurse, 1977-79; commd. 1st lt. USAF, 1979, advanced through grades to lt. col.; staff nurse oper. rm. Air Force Regional Hosp., Sheppard AFB, Tex., 1979-82; staff nurse oper. rm., asst. oper. rm. supr. Regional Med. Ctr. Clark, Clark Air Base, Philippines, 1982-83; chief, nurse recruiting br. 3513th Air Force Recruiting Squadron, North Syracuse, N.Y., 1983-87; nurse supr. surg. svcs. 432d Med. Group, Misawa Air Base, Japan, 1987-89; course supr./instr. oper. rm. nursing courses 3793d Nursing Tng. Squadron, Keesler Med. Ctr., Keesler AFB, Miss., 1989-92; asst. dir., then dir. oper. rm. and ctrl. sterile supply Keesler Med. Ctr., Keesler AFB, Miss., 1992-93; comdr., enlisted clin. courses flight 383d Tng. Squadron, Sheppard AFB, Tex., 1993-94; comdr., officer clin. courses flight 383rd Tng. Squadron, Sheppard AFB, Tex., 1994-95; comdr. enlisted courses flight 383rd Tng. Squadron, Sheppard AFB, Tex., 1995—. Decorated Air Force Commendation medal, Air Force Achievement medal, Meritorious Svc. medal. Mem. ANA, Ohio Nurses Assn., Assn. Operating Rm. Nurses, Air Force Assn., Sigma Theta Tau. Home: 14 Pilot Point Dr Wichita Falls TX 76306-1000 Office: 383d Tng Squadron 939 Missile Rd Ste 3 Sheppard AFB TX 76311-2262

RIOS-DALENZ, JAIME LUIS, pathologist, educator; b. Cochabamba, Bolivia, Nov. 13, 1993; s. Humberto Rios-Zambrana and Carmen H. Dalenz; m. Haydee M. Ismael, Apr. 18, 1960; children: Mauricio, Maria Eugenia. B of Humanities, La Salle Coll., La Paz, Bolivia, 1951; med. degree, San Andres U., Cochabamba, 1960. Cert. in anatomical pathology and clin. pathology Am. Bd. Pathology. Resident in pathol. anatomy Del Valle U., Cali, Colombia, 1960-61; resident in clin. pathology Ball Meml. Hosp., Muncie, Ind., 1961-64; resident in pathol. anatomy Temple U. Hosp., Phila., 1965-66; pathologist Hosp. # 1 CNS, La Paz, 1969-93, chief pathology dept., 1993—; from asst. prof. pathology to assoc. prof. pathology San Andres U., La Paz, 1968-85, prof. pathology, 1985-87, prof. emeritus, 1989—, chief of dept. pathology, 1987-94; dir. La Paz Cancer Registry, 1988—; pres. Bolivian Commn. on Smoking, La Paz, 1983—; coord. Bolivian Network on Health Info., La Paz, 1988—. Editor pathology textbook; contbr. articles to sci. publs. Recipient Gold medal WHO, 1992. Mem. Bolivian divsn. Internat. Acad. Pathology (pres. 1986-96), Bolivian Acad. Medicine, Latin Am. Soc. Pathology (pres. 1979-81). Address: PO Box 490, La Paz Bolivia Home: Calle del Aviador # 100, La Paz Bolivia Office: Hosp Metodista, Dept Pathology, La Paz Bolivia

RIPP, MICHAEL WERNER, pharmacy director; b. Waunakee, Wis., May 21, 1948; s. Roman Peter and Doris (Maden) R.; m. Kathleen Gruber, Aug. 18, 1969 (div.); 1 child, Jeffrey R.; m. Teresa Jean Geving Aug. 19, 1985. BS in Pharmacy, U. Wis., 1973. Registered pharmacist. Staff pharmacist Walgreen's, Eau Claire, Wis., 1974-75; cons. pharmacist Mike Ripp, Cons., Eau Claire, Wis., 1975-78; pres. Eau Claire Pharmacy, 1978-86; dir. pharmacy Erickson Diversified, Hudson, Wis., 1986-95; cons. pharmacist NWNL Life Ins. Co., Mpls., 1991-92; pres. Country Inn Waunakee, River Falls Properties. Mem., coord. Lions, River Falls, Wis., 1992; ambassador Eau Claire C. of C., 1980-84; sec., v.p. Westgate Sportsman's Club, Eau Claire, 1982, 84; v.p., dir. Jaycees, Eau Claire, 1980-85. Named one of Outstanding Young Men of Am., 1978. Fellow Am. Coll. Apothecaries (membership com. 1982-83); mem. Wis. Pharmacists Assn., Minn. Pharmacists Assn., Chippewa Valley Pharmacists Assn. (v.p., pres. 1982-84), Nat. Assn. Retail Druggists, Am. Pharm. Assn., Saint Croix Valley Pharmacists. Republican. Lutheran.

RIRIE, CRAIG MARTIN, periodontist; b. Lewiston, Utah, Apr. 17, 1943; s. Martin Clarence and VaLera (Dixon) R.; m. Becky Ann Ririe, Sept. 17, 1982; children: Paige, Seth, Theron, Kendall, Nathan, Derek, Brian, Amber, Kristen. AA, San Bernadino Valley Coll., 1966; DDS, Creighton U., 1972; MSD, Loma Linda U., 1978. Staff mem. Flagstaff (Ariz.) Med. Ctr., 1974—; pvt. practice dentistry specializing in periodontics Flagstaff, 1974—; assoc. prof. periodontics No. Ariz. U., Flagstaff, 1979—, chmn. dept. dental hygiene, 1980-81; med. research cons. W.L. Gore, Flagstaff, 1983—. Contbr. articles to profl. jours. Vice pres. bd. dirs. Grand Canyon coun. Boy Scouts Am., 1991—. Lt. col. USAFR. Health professions scholarship Creighton U., Omaha, 1969-71; recipient Mosby award Mosby Pub. Co., 1972; research fellowship U. Bergen, Norway, 1978-79. Mem. ADA, Am. Acad. Periodontology (cert.), Western Soc. Periodontology (chmn. com. on rsch. 1982—, bd. dirs. 1983—), No. Ariz. Dental Soc. (pres. 1994-96), Am. Acad. Oral Implantologists, Internat. Congress Oral Implantologists, Ariz. Dental Assn., Am. Cancer Soc. (bd. dirs.), Flagstaff C. of C., Rotary. Republican. Mem. LDS Ch. Home: 1320 N Aztec St Flagstaff AZ 86001-3004 Office: 1050 N San Francisco St Flagstaff AZ 86001-3259

RISELEY, MARTHA SUZANNAH HEATER (MRS. CHARLES RISELEY), psychologist, educator; b. Middletown, Ohio, Apr. 25, 1916; d. Elsor and Mary (Henderson) Heater; BEd, U. Toledo, 1943, MA, 1958; PhD, Toledo Bible Coll., 1977; student Columbia U., summers 1943, 57; m. Lester Seiple, Aug. 27, 1944 (div. Feb. 1953); 1 child, L. Rolland, III; m. Charles Riseley, July 30, 1960. Tchr. kindergarten Maumee Valley Country Day Sch., Maumee, Ohio, 1942-44; dir. recreation Toledo Soc. for Crippled Children, 1950-51; tchr. trainable children Lott Day Sch., Toledo, 1951-57; psychologist, asst. dir. Sheltered Workshop Found., Lucas County, Ohio, 1957-62; psychologist Lucas County Child Welfare Bd., Toledo, 1956-62; tchr. educable retarded, head dept. spl. edn. Maumee City Schs., 1962-69; pvt. practice clin. psychology, 1956—; instr. spl. edn. Bowling Green State U., 1962-65; instr. Owens Tech. Coll., 1973-78; interim dir. rehab. services Toledo Goodwill Industries, summer 1967, clin. psychologist Rehab. Center, 1967—; staff psychologist Toledo Mental Health Center, 1979-84. Dir. camping activities for retarded girls and women Camp Libbey, Defiance, Ohio, summers 1951-62; group worker for retarded women Toledo YWCA, 1957-62; guest lectr. Ohio State U., 1957. Health care profl. mem. Nat. Osteoporosis Found., 1988—. Mem. Ohio Assn. Tchrs. Trainable Youth (pres. 1956-57), NW Ohio Rehab. Assn. (pres. 1961-62), Toledo Council for Exceptional Children (pres. 1965), Greater Toledo Assn. Mental Health, Nat. Assn. for Retarded Children, Ohio Assn. Tchrs. Slow Learners, Am. Assn. Mental Deficiency, Am. Soc. Psychologists in Marital and Family Counseling, Psychology and Law Soc. Am. (assoc.), Ohio, NW Ohio (sec.-treas. 1974-77, pres. 1978-79), Am. Theater Orgn. Soc., Ohio Psychol. Assn. (continuing edn. com. 1978—), NEA, AAUW, Am. Soc. Psychologists in Pvt. Practice (nat. dir. 1976—), State Assn. Psychologists and Psychol. Assts., Bus. and Profl. Women's Club, (pres. 1970-72), Ohio Fedn. Bus. and Profl. Women's Clubs (dist. sec. 1970-71, dist. legis. chmn. 1972-74), Toledo Art Mus., Women's Aux. Toledo Bar Assn., League Women Voters (pres. Toledo Lucas County 1991-93), Y Matrons (pres. 1993—), Toledo Area Theater Orgn. Soc. (sec. 1991—), Zonta Internat. (local pres. 1973-74, 78-79, area dir. 1976-78, Maumee River Valley Woman of Yr. for svc to community and Zonta, 1992), Maumee Valley Hist. Soc., MBLS PEO (chpt. pres. 1950-51), Toledo Council on World Affairs, Internat. Platform Assn. Baptist. Home and Office: 2816 Wicklow Rd Toledo OH 43606-2833

RISHER, WILLIAM HENRY, cardiothoracic surgeon; b. New Orleans, Oct. 3, 1958; m. Michele Helene Risher; children: Amelia Alexandra, Jordan Prescott, Olivia Leigh. Student, U. New Orleans; BS in Biomed. Engring., Tulane U., 1981; MD, La. State U., 1985. Diplomate Am. Bd. Surgery, Am. Bd. Thoracic Surgery; lic. surgeon, N.Y.; cert. ACLS, advanced trauma life support, pediatric advanced life support provider, basic life support provider. Resident in gen. surgery Alton Ochsner Med. Found., New Orleans, 1985-90, chief resident, 1989-90, resident and fellow in cardiovascular surgery, 1990-92, chief resident, 1991-92; flight care physician Ochsner Flight Care, 1986-92; asst. prof. cardiothoracic surgery Med. Ctr. U. Rochester, N.Y., 1992—; presenter in field. Contbr. 20 articles to med. and sci. jours. T.H. Harris scholar Tulane U, 1977-79, full scholar, 1979-81. Fellow ACS, Am. Coll. Cardiology (assoc.); mem. AMA, Am. Coll. Chest Physicians, Soc. Thoracic Surgeons, Internat. Soc. Heart and Lung Transplantation, S.E. Surg. Congress, So. Med. Assn., Med. Soc. County Monroe, Rochester Acad. Medicine, Rochester Cardiovascular Soc., Upstate Soc. Thoracic Surgeons, Rochester Surg. Soc., Assn. for Advancement of Med. Instrumentation, Alton Ochsner Med. Soc., Tau Beta Pi, Alpha Omega Alpha. Home: 90 Rhinecliff Dr Rochester NY 14618-1506

RISICA, VIRGINIA JEAN, psychologist; b. Queens, N.Y., June 21, 1957; d. John Phillip and Erma Margaret (Cantus) R. BA in Psychology, St. John's U., Jamaica, N.Y., 1979, MA Explt. Psychology, 1981, PhD in Clin. Psychology, 1987. Lic. psychologist, N.Y. Extern in psychology Mercy Hosp., Rockville Centre, N.Y., 1982-83, Creedmoor Psychiat. Ctr., Queens Village, N.Y., 1982-83, Oceanside (N.Y.) Counseling Ctr., 1983-84; intern in psychology NYU Med. Ctr./Rusk Inst. Rehab. Medicine, N.Y.C., 1984-85; staff psychologist N.Y.C. Police Dept., Rego Park, N.Y., 1986-93, sr. psychologist, 1993—; pvt. practice clin. psychology Little Neck, N.Y., 1991—; presenter Oceanside Counseling Ctr., 1984; presenter colloquim at St. John's U., 1989. Recipient Cert. of Excellence, St. John's U., 1978. Mem. APA (presenter conv. 1987), N.Y. State Psychol. Assn., Nassau County Psychol. Assn., Queens County Psychol. Assn. Democrat. Roman Catholic. Home: 25426 37th Ave Flushing NY 11363-1441 Office: NYC Police Dept Psychol Svc 1 Lefrak City Plz Fl 15 Flushing NY 11368-4160

RISPO, RITA THERESA, psychotherapist; b. Phila., Apr. 27, 1953; d. Vito J. and Rita A. (Aversa) R. AS, Hahnemann U., 1983, BS, 1985, MS, 1987. Psychotherapist Horizon House Inc., Phila., 1982-83, Community Mental Health and Mental Retardation Orgn., Phila., 1985-88, Delaware Valley Psychol. Assocs., Phila., 1988-89. With U.S. Army 1973-75. Home: 3513 Braddock St Philadelphia PA 19134-2123

RISPOLI, KATHERINE KLENOTICH, optometrist; b. Sharon, Pa., Jan. 16, 1959. BS, Muhlenberg Coll., 1980, Pa. Coll. Optometry, 1981; OD, Pa. Coll. Optometry, 1984. Optometrist Laurel Eye Clinic, Brookville, Pa., 1984-86, Drs. Eudenbach & Rispoli, Middletown, R.I., 1991—, John Ferris Health Clinic, Warwick, R.I., 1987-89, 93—. Mem. Newport County Women's Network, R.I. Optometric Assn. (bd. dirs. 1995—, Vision USA chairperson 1989-92, 94—, Vol. of Yr. 1990), Safe Kids Coalition. Home: 58 E Main Rd Middletown RI 02842-4912

RISSE, GUENTER BERNHARD, physician, historian, educator; b. Buenos Aires, Argentina, Apr. 28, 1932; s. Francisco B. and Kaete A. R.; m. Alexandra G. Paradzinski, Oct. 14, 1961; children—Heidi, Monica, Alisa. MD, U. Buenos Aires, 1958; PhD, U. Chgo., 1971. Intern Mercy Hosp., Buffalo, 1958-59; resident in medicine Henry Ford Hosp., Detroit, 1960-61, Mt. Carmel Hosp., Columbus, Ohio, 1962-63; asst. dept. medicine U. Chgo., 1963-67; asst. prof. dept. history of medicine U. Minn., 1969-71; asso. prof. dept. history of medicine and dept. history of sci. U. Wis., Madison, 1971-76; prof. U. Wis., 1976-85, chmn. dept. history of medicine, 1971-77; prof., chmn. dept. history health scis. U. Calif., San Francisco, 1985—; mem. project com. Ctr. for Photog. Images in Medicine and Health Care. Author: Paleopathology of Ancient Egypt, 1964, Hospital Life in Enlightenment Scotland, 1986; editor: Modern China and Traditional Chinese Medicine, 1973, History of Physiology, 1973, Medicine Without Doctors, 1977, AIDS and the Historian, 1991; mem. editl. bd. Jour. History of Medicine, 1971-74, 90-93, Clio Medica, 1973-88, Bull. History of Medicine, 1980-94, Medizinhistorisches Jour., 1981—, Med. History, 1989-95, History of Philos. Life Scis., 1993—, Asclepio, 1995—. Served with Argentine Armed Forces, 1955. Recipient NIH grants, 1971-73, 82-84, WHO grant, 1979, named Logan Campbell Disting. Lectr., New Zealand, 1994. Mem. Am. Assn. History of Medicine (pres. 1988-90, William H. Welch medal 1988), History Sci. Soc., Internat. Acad. History Medicine, Deutsche Gesellschaft fur Geschichte der Medizin, European Assn. History of Medicine and Health, Internat. Network for History of Pub. Health, Mex. Soc. History and Philosophy of Medicine, Peruvian Assn. Med. Ethnology and History, Brit. Soc. for Social History of Medicine, Argentine Ateneo de Historia de la Medicina, AIDS History Group (co-chair 1988-94), Internat. Network for History of Hosps. (convenor 1995—), Bay Area Med. Hist. Club (pres. 1994-96). Home: 600 Noriega St San Francisco CA 94122-4616 Office: Univ of Calif Dept History Health Scis 513 Parnassus Ave San Francisco CA 94143-0726

RISSMAN, BARBARA SUSAN ZIMMER, psychotherapist; b. Copiague, N.Y., May 14, 1951; d. Samuel and Hilda (Krebs) Zimmer; m. Randall S. Rissman, June 20, 1976; children: Jesse, Dahlia. BS, Boston U., 1973; MSW, Rutgers U., 1980. Diplomate Am. Bd. Examiners. Family therapist The Children's Annex, Woodstock, N.Y., 1980-83, Catskill Family Inst., Kingston, N.Y., 1980-86; family therapist dir. Maverick Family Counseling, Woodstock, 1984—; cons. Compuserve-Human Sexuality Svc., Woodstock, 1987—. Mem. NASW. Office: Maverick Family Counseling 401 Zena Rd Woodstock NY 12498-2620

RISTICH, MIODRAG, psychiatrist; b. Belgrade, Yugoslavia, July 19, 1938; came to U.S., 1967; s. Teodosije and Gordana (Isailovic) Ristic; m. Yvonne Muriel Cunliffe, May 6, 1967; children: Katharine Alexandra, Elizabeth Victoria. MD, U. Belgrade, 1962. Diplomate Am. Bd. Psychiatry and Neurology. Resident in psychiatry Manhattan Psychiat. Ctr., NYU, 1980-83; med. dir. Cambridge (Minn.) State Hosp., 1967-72; dir. Willowbrook State Sch., Staten Island, N.Y., 1972-74; med. dir. DeWitt Nursing Home, N.Y.C., 1976—; clin. asst. prof. psychiatry NYU Med. Coll., 1996—; pvt. practice psychiatry, N.Y.C., 1973—. Mem. AMA, Am. Psychiat. Assn., Am. Assn. for Geriatric Psychiatry, Royal Coll. Psychiatrists. Republican. Home: 37 Sunrise Ln Saddle River NJ 07458-1631 Office: 201 E 79th St Apt 7J New York NY 10021-0835

RISTOW, BRUNNO, plastic surgeon; b. Brusque, Brazil, Oct. 18, 1940; came to U.S., 1967, naturalized, 1981; s. Arno and Ally Odette (von Buettner) R.; student Coll. Sinodal, Brazil, 1956-57, Coll. Julio de Castilhos, Brazil, 1957-58; M.D. magna cum laude, U. Brazil, 1966; m. Urannia Carrasquilla Gutierrez, Nov. 10, 1979; children by previous marriage: Christian Kilian, Trevor Roland. Intern in surgery Hosp. dos Estrangeiros, Rio de Janeiro, Brazil, 1965, Hospital Estadual Miguel Couto, Brazil, 1965-66, Instituto Aposentadoria Pensão Comerciarios Hosp. for Gen. Surgery, 1966; resident in plastic and reconstructive surgery, Dr. Ivo Pitanguy Hosp. Santa Casa de Misericordia, Rio de Janeiro, 1967; fellow Inst. of Reconstructive Plastic Surgery, N.Y. U. Med. Center, N.Y.C., 1967-68, jr. resident, 1971-72, sr. and chief resident, 1972-73; practice medicine specializing in plastic surgery, Rio de Janeiro, 1967, N.Y.C., 1968-73, San Francisco, 1973—; asst. surgeon N.Y. Hosp., Cornell Med. Center, N.Y.C., 1968-71; clin. instr. surgery N.Y. U. Sch. of Medicine, 1972-73; chmn. plastic and reconstructive surgery div. Presbyn. Hosp., Pacific Med. Center, San Francisco, 1974-92, chmn. emeritus, 1992—. Served with M.C., Brazilian Army Res., 1959-60. Decorated knight Venerable Order of St. Hubertus; Knight Order St. John of Jerusalem; fellow in surgery Cornell Med. Sch., 1968-71; diplomate Am. Bd. Plastic and Reconstructive Surgery. Fellow A.C.S., Internat. Coll. Surgeons; mem. Am. Soc. Aesthetic Plastic Surgery (chmn. edn.), Am Soc. Plastic and Reconstructive Surgeons, Internat. Soc. Aesthetic Plastic Surgeons, Calif. Soc. Plastic Surgeons, AMA (Physician's Recognition award 1971-83), Calif. Med. Assn., San Francisco Med. Assn. Republican. Mem. Evang. Lutheran Ch. Club: San Francisco Olympic. Contbg. author: Cancer of the Hand, 1975, Current Therapy in Plastic and Reconstructive Surgery, 1988, Male Aesthetic Surgery, 1989, How They Do It: Procedures in Plastic and Reconstructive Surgery, 1990, Middle Crus: The Missing Link in Alar Cartilage Anatomy, 1991, Surgical Technology International, 1992, Aesthetic Plastic Surgery, 1993, Mastery of Surgery: Plastic and Reconstructive Surgery, 1993; Reoperative Aesthetic Plastic Surgery of the Face and Breast, 1994, 95; contbr. articles on plastic surgery to profl. pubis. Office: Calif Pacific Med Ctr Pacific Profl Bldg 2100 Webster St Ste 502 San Francisco CA 94115-2381

RITCH, JOSEPH GEORGE, ophthalmologist, educator; b. West Palm Beach, Fla., Oct. 10, 1932. BS, U. Fla., 1952; MD, U. Tenn., 1955. Diplomate Am. Bd. Ophthalmology. Surgery intern U. Minn. Hosp., Mpls., 1955-56; ophthalmology resident Washington U., St. Louis, 1961-64; pvt. practice opthalmology St. Petersburg, Fla., 1964—; clin. asst. prof. ophthalmology U. South Fla., Tampa, 1975—; chief of surgery E.H. White Hosp., St. Petersburg, 1982-84; chmn. ophthalmology Barfront Med. Ctr., St. Petersburg, 1983-87, 91—. Fellow Am. Acad. Ophthalmology; mem. Fla. Med. Assn., Pinellas County Med. Soc. (bd. govs. 1982-85). Roman Catholic. Home: 1120 Friendly Way South Saint Petersburg FL 33705 Office: 2200-16th St N Saint Petersburg FL 33704

RITCH, ROBERT HARRY, ophthalmologist, educator; b. New Haven, May 14, 1944; s. Edward Lewis and Minerva (Grosberg) R.; BA cum laude (hon. scholar), Harvard, 1965, MA (NSF fellow), 1967; postgrad. (Harvard traveling fellow), Rice U., 1967-68; MD, Albert Einstein Coll. Medicine, 1972. Diplomate Am. Bd. Ophthalmology, Am. Bd. Laser Surgery. Intern, St. Vincent's Med. Ctr., N.Y.C., 1972-73; resident in ophthalmology Mt. Sinai Sch. Medicine, N.Y.C., 1973-75, chief resident, 1975-76, Heed Ophthalmic Found. fellow, 1976-77, NIH-Nat. Rsch. Svc. fellow, 1976-78, asst. clin. ophthalmologist, 1976-77, instr., 1977-78, asst. prof., 1978-80, assoc. prof., 1980-82; attending ophthalmologist Beth Israel Med. Ctr., N.Y.C., 1978—; cons. ophthalmologist VA Hosp., Bronx, 1978-82, Manhattan Eye, Ear and Throat Hosp., 1989—; dir. glaucoma svc. Elmhurst Hosp., 1978-82, acting dir. dept. ophthalmology, 1979-82; chief glaucoma svc. N.Y. Eye and Ear Infirmary, N.Y.C., 1983—, surgeon dir., 1991—; prof. clin. ophthalmology N.Y. Med. Coll., Valhalla, 1983—; cons. Sukhumvit Hosp., Bangkok, Thailand, 1994—; pres. Internat. Eye Cons., Ltd., 1995—; mem. adv. bd. Doctor-to-Doctor, Berkeley, Calif., 1995—; sec., treas., chmn. sci. adv. bd. Glaucoma Found., 1984—, med. dir. Children's Right to Sight, prin. investigator Collaborative Initial Glaucoma Treatment Study, 1993—; mem. glaucoma adv. com. Nat. Soc. to Prevent Blindness, 1986—; organizing chmn. Bangkok Ophthal. Cong., 1985—; external assessor U. Malaya, 1988—; spl. advisor 4th Internat. Conf. on Myopia, Singapore, 1990. Bd. dirs. Dooley Found./Intermed. U.S.A., 1991—, UN; vol. Devel. Coun., 1991-93; chmn., bd. dirs. I-Med. Devel. Corps., 1991-94. Acad. Investigator award NIH, 1978-81; Disting. Service award Internat. Ctr. N.Y., 1981, Exec. Dirs. award, 1985; Founders award Nat. Exhibits by Blind Artists, 1985. Fellow Am. Acad. Ophthalmology (edn. distbrn. subcom. 1994—, book/jour. link subcom. 1994—, Honor award 1985), Am. Ophthalmol. Soc., N.Y. Acad. Medicine, Royal Coll. Ophthalmologists (U.K.), Am. Coll. Surgeons, Internat. Coll. Surgeons, Am. Soc. Laser Surg. Medicine (chmn. ophthalmology sect. 1991-92, moderator and program chmn. joint sci. symposium on glaucoma 1991), N.Y. Acad. Medicine (sec. sect. on ophthalmology 1991-92, chmn. 1993-94); mem. AMA, AAAS, N.Y. State Med. Soc., N.Y. County Med. Soc., Assn. Rsch. in Vision and Ophthalmology (program com., glaucoma sect. 1991-93, program chmn. 1993-94), Am. Assn. Ophthalmology, Ophthal. Soc. U.K., Internat. Assn. Ocular Surgeons, Internat. Congress Ophthalmology (glaucoma com. 1994—), N.Y. Intra-Ocular Lens Implant Soc., Manhattan Ophthal. Soc., Internat. Soc. Eye Rsch., Soc. for Clin. Trials, Pan-Pacific Anterior Segment Soc. (v.p. 1985-88), N.Y. Acad. Sci., Ophthalmic Laser Surg. Soc. (sec.-treas. 1982—), N.Y. Soc. Clin. Ophthalmology (rec. sec. 1988-90, program chmn. 1990-91, pres. 1991-92), Am. Soc. Cell Biology, Am. Telemed. Assn., Internat. Soc. On-Line Ophthalmologists (mem. orgn. com., chmn. glaucoma sect. 1995—), Internat. Fedn. Cell Biologists, Philippine Soc. Ophthalmology (hon.), Thailand Ophthal. Soc. (hon.), Italian Assn. for the Study of Glaucoma (hon.), La.-Miss. Ophthal. and Otolarygol. Soc. (hon.), Can. Implant Soc. (hon.), Chinese-Am. Ophthalomology Soc., Ophthalmic Genetics Discussion Club, Harvard Club (N.Y.C.), N.Y. Glaucoma Club (pres. 1991—), N.Y. Athletic Club. Author: (with M.B. Shields) The Secondary Glaucomas, 1982, (with M.B. Shields and T. Krupin) The Glaucomas, 1988, 2d edit. 1996; spl. sect. editor Jour. of Glaucoma, 1991—; mem. editorial bd. Sightsaving, 1981-86, Ophthalmic Laser Therapy, 1984-88, Ophthalmic Resident, 1992-95, Ophthalmic Surgery and Lasers, 1995—, Microsurgery, 1994—, Ophthalmology Times, 1996—; contbg. editor Ophthalmic Practice, 1993—; contbr. to films on laser therapy, over 500 articles and abstracts in field Home: 455 E 57th St # 14D New York NY 10022-3065 Office: NY Eye and Ear Infirmary 310003-4200

RITCHIE, DAVID MALCOLM, pharmacologist; b. Woodbury, N.J., Apr. 13, 1950; s. Malcolm Wood and Ruth Maryland (Stevens) R.; m. Deborah Ann Jones, Jan. 29, 1972; children: Christopher David, Jillian Shannon. AB, Rutgers U., 1972; MSc, Hahnemann U., 1974, PhD, 1976. Rsch. assoc. Med. Coll. Pa., Phila., 1976-78; from scientist to sr. scientist Ortho Pharm., Raritan, N.J., 1978-85; prin. scientist R.W. Johnson Pharm. Rsch. Inst., Raritan, 1985-91, rsch. fellow, 1991—. Contbr. articles to profl. jours.; patentee in field. Chmn. West Windsor (N.J.) Recreation Commn., 1988-89; coach West Windsor Soccer Assn., West Windsor Little League, 1983-92. Mem. Internat. Soc. Immunopharmacology, Am. Soc. Exptl. Therapeutics, N.Y. Acad. Scis., Inflammation Rsch. Assn. Home: 15 Scott Ave Princeton Junction NJ 08550-1022 Office: R W Johnson Pharm Rsch Inst Rte 202 Raritan NJ 08869

RITCHIE, ELSPETH CAMERON, psychiatrist; b. San Francisco, Mar. 22, 1958; d. Lyell Hale and Elisavietta (Artamonoff) R.; m. James M. Curtis. BA cum laude, Harvard U., 1980; MD, George Washington U., 1986. Commd. 2d lt. U.S. Army, 1986, advanced through grades to maj., 1992; intern Walter Reed Army Med. Ctr., Washington, 1986-87, resident in psychiatry, 1987-90; div. psychiatrist 2 ID, Korea, 1990-91; attending psychiatrist Walter Reed Army Med. Ctr., Washington, 1991-93, forensic psychiatry fellow, 1993-94, chief cmty. psychiatry, 1995—; chief inpatient psychiatry U.S. Army, Republic Korea, 1994-95; rschr. for TV prodn. group Sci. Program Group, Washington, 1980-81; jr. tchg. fellow Uniformed Svcs. Univ. Health Scis., 1988-89, sr. tchg. fellow, 1989-90, clin. instr., 1990-91, asst. prof. psychiatry, 1991—. Contbr. articles to profl. publs. Recipient Albert Glass award for Outstanding Psychiat. Resident, 1990, Lewis A. Mologne award, 1990. Mem. AMA, Am. Acad. Psychiatry & Law, Am. Coll. Forensic Examiners, Assn. Mil. Surgeons U.S., Am. Psychiat. Assn. Office: Walter Reed Army Med Ctr Washington DC 20307

RITCHIE, WALLACE PARKS, JR., surgeon, educator; b. St. Paul, Nov. 4, 1935; s. Wallace Parks and Alice Ransome (Otis) R.; m. Barbara Carey Jewell, Aug. 10, 1960; children: Stephanie, David, Jessica. BA, Yale U., 1957; MD, Johns Hopkins U., 1961; PhD, U. Minn., 1971. Diplomate Am. Bd. Surgery. Intern, resident in surgery Yale U., New Haven, 1961-63; resident in surgery U. Minn. Hosps., Mpls., 1963-69, instr. in surgery, 1969-70; from asst. prof. to prof. surgery U. Va. Sch. Medicine, Charlottesville, 1973-83; prof., chmn. dept. surgery Temple U. Sch. Medicine, Phila., 1983-93; exec. dir. Am. Bd. Surgery, Phila., 1994—. Editor textbook: Essentials of Surgery, 1994; contbr. over 125 sci. articles to profl. jours. Lt. col. Med. Corps U.S. Army, 1970-73. USPHS grantee, 1974-85. Office: Am Bd Surgery Inc 1617 John F Kennedy Blvd Philadelphia PA 19103

RITCHLIN, MARTHA ANN, occupational therapist; b. Jacksboro, Tex., Oct. 20, 1953; d. Carl Alton and Julia Ann (Jones) Rumage; divorced; children: Carl Allen, Julie Marie. BS, Tex. Women's U., 1976, postgrad., 1986. Occupational therapist Wichita Gen. Hosp., Wichita Falls, Tex., 1977-79; dir. occupational therapy Red River Hosp., Wichita Falls, 1979-83, Bethania Regional Health Care Ctr., Wichita Falls, 1983-87; occupational therapist Girling Home Health, Wichita Falls, 1984-85, Wichita Home Health, Wichita Falls, 1984-86, Outreach Home Health Svcs., Seymour, Tex., 1987—, N. Tex. Easter Seal Rehab. Ctr., Wichita Falls, 1988—; owner, therapist Community Occupational Therapy Svcs., Wichita Falls, 1988—; dir. occupational therapy Wichita Falls (Tex.) State Hosp., 1991—; cons., speaker Muscular Dystrophy Assn., Wichita Falls, 1986, Advantage Sr. Citizens Club, Wichita Falls, 1988, Stroke Club, 1986; cons., activity dir. Clay County Hosp., Henrietta, Tex., 1986-87. Cons., vol. Wichita County Juvenile Detention Svcs., Wichita Falls, 1980; mem. task force State Task Force on Assistive Tech., Tex., 1989—; bus. mem. Ptnrs. in Edn. Named Notable Women of Tex., 1985. Mem. Tex. Occupational Therapy Assn., Am. Occupational Therapy Assn., World Fedn. Occupational Therapy. Baptist. Home: 107 N 12th St Jacksboro TX 76458 Office: Faith Cmty Hosp Jacksboro TX 76458

RITSCHEL, WOLFGANG ADOLF, pharmacy and medical educator; b. Trautenau, Bohemia, Jan. 10, 1933; came to U.S., 1968; s. Karl and Eleonore (Olbert) R.; m. Ingrid M. Wallner, Aug. 5, 1991; children from previous marriage: Alexander, Barbara. Mr.Pharm., U. Innsbruck, Austria, 1955; Dr.Univ., U. Strasbourg, France, 1960; PhD, U. Vienna, Austria, 1965; MD, U. Villarreal, Peru, 1989. Chief pharmacist Girol AG, Zurich, Switzerland, 1958-59; head pharmacy rsch. Biochemie AG, Kundl, Austria, 1959-61; seminar docent Teaching Hosp., Kufstein, Austria, 1959-61; head rsch. Albert David Rsch. Inst., Dacca, Pakistan, 1961-64; prof. Dacca U., 1961-64, U. Basel, Switzerland, 1965-68; prof. U. Cin., 1969—, head of div., 1985-94; numerous vis. professorships including Med. Acad. Krakow, Univ. Clermont-Ferrand, S. Marcos, Lima. Author: The Tablet, 1966, Applied Biopharmaceutics, 1973, Laboratory Manual of Biopharmaceutics and Pharmacokinetics, 1974, Handbook of Basic Pharmacokinetics, 4th revised edit., 1992, Graphic Approach to Clinical Pharmacokinetics, 1993, 2d edit., 1994, Antacids and Other Drugs in GI Diseases, 1984, Gerontokinetics, 1988, Japanese edit., 1994, (with Betzien, Kaufmann and Schneider) KINPAK: A Comprehensive Approach to Evaluating Blood Level Curves, 1985, (with Koch) Synopsis der Biopharmazie und Pharmkokinetik, 1986; editor: Clinical Pharmacokinetics: Proceedingd of An International Symposium at Salzgitter-Ringelheim, 1977; contbr. over 420 articles to profl. jours., 28 chpts. in books; 9 patents in field. Recipient Theodor-Koerner prize Austria Ministry of Edn., 1962, Cross of Honor, Pres. Fedn. Republic Austria, 1975; named Hon. Prof. U. San Marcos, 1973, U. Cayetano Heredia, 1979; Hon. Senator U. Pisa, 1978; Fulbright sr. scholar, 1993, 1996; named to Internat. Order of Merit, Cambridge, 1993. Fellow Am. Coll. Clin. Pharmacology; mem. Am. Assn. Pharm. Scientists, Acad. Am. Pharm. Assn., Fedn. Internat. Pharm., Royal Acad. Sci. (Spain), Acad. of Sci. (hon.). Roman Catholic. Home: 3436 Cornell Pl Cincinnati OH 45220-1502 Office: Univ Cin Med Ctr 3223 Eden Cincinnati OH 45267

RITTER, HENRY, JR., physician; b. N.Y.C., Apr. 14, 1920; s. Henry and Beatrice Victoria R.; m. Mary Loewe, June 10, 1949; children: Mark, Caroline. BA, Lafayette Coll., 1941; MD, NYU, 1945. Physician pvt. practice, N.Y.C., 1954-55, Redwood, Calif., 1955-94, Palo Alto, Calif., 1955-72, Menlo Park, Calif., 1972-94, Atherton, Calif., 1994—; treas. Sequia Hosp., Redwood, 1983—, chmn. urology, 1975—, chmn. credit com., 1988. Author: From Man to Man, 1979. Mem. AMA, Am. Coll. Surgeons, Am. Urological Assn. (western sect.), Northwest Med. Assn. (pres. elect 1996, bd. dirs. 1993-96), Calif. Med. Assn. (communication commn.), No. Calif. Urological Soc., N.Y.C. Med. Soc., Rotary. Office: Peninsula Urology Clinic 3351 El Camino #101 Atherton CA 94027

RITVO, EDWARD ROSS, psychiatrist; b. Boston, June 1, 1930; s. Max Ritvo; m. Riva Golan, Sept. 11, 1989; children: Deborah, Eva, Anne, Matthew, Victoria, Skylre, Max. BA, Harvard U., 1951; MD, Boston U. Sch. Medicine, 1955. Diplomate Am. Bd. Psychiatry and Neurology, Am. Bd. Child Psychiatry. Prof. UCLA Sch. Medicine, 1963—. Author 4 books; contbr. over 150 articles to profl. jours. Capt. U.S. Army, 1959-61. Recipient Blanche F. Ittleson award Am. Psychiat. Assn., 1990. Mem. Nat. Soc. for Autistic Children, Profl. Adv. Bd. (chmn.). Office: UCLA Sch Medicine Dept Psychiatry 760 Westwood Plz Los Angeles CA 90024-8300

RITZ, EUGENE FREDERICK, therapist; b. Watertown, S.D., Jan. 4, 1962; s. Donald Eugene and Darlene Margaret (Jacobs) R. BS in History and Math., S.D. State U., 1986, MS in Counseling and Human Resources, 1988. Lic. independent clin. social worker; lic. profl. counselor. In-home therapist Luth. Social Svc., Moorhead, Minn., 1989—; mem. M.W. Family Based Svc. Conf. com. Mem. Minn. Family Base Svc. Assn., N.D. Marriage and Family Assn., N.D. Family Base Svc. Assn., N.D. Counselors Assn., N.D. Mental Health Counselors Assn. Office: Lutheran Social Svc 715 11th St N Ste 401 Moorhead MN 56560

RITZE, JAMES MICHAEL, family practice physician and surgeon; b. Trenton, Mo., Oct. 16, 1948; s. Theodore Edward and Oka Marie (Rosson) R.; m. Connie Ilene, Sept. 6, 1975; children: Amity Eileen, Heidi Marie, James Michael, Kelsey. BS, Northeast Mo. State U., 1969; DO, Kirksville Coll. Osteo. Med., 1973. Diplomate Am. Bd. Family Practice; cert. med. examiner and child abuse examiner, Okla.; cert. aviation med. examiner FAA. Intern Okla. Osteo. Hosp., Tulsa, 1973-74; clin. prof. Okla. State U. Coll. Osteo. Medicine and Surgery. bd. dirs. MEND Crisis Pregnancy Ctr., Broken Arrow, Okla., 1980—, Gatesway Found., Broken Arrow, 1980-83; chmn. Tulsa County Rep. Party, 1989-91; bd. dirs. Ron Lamb Missions, Broken Arrow, 1975-77, Jim Black Prison Ministries, Broken Arrow, 1974-76, HOPE Ministries, Tulsa, 1980-82. Capt. USAR, 1975-81. Mem. Am. Osteopathic Assn., Okla. Osteopathic Assn., Christian Med. Soc., Tulsa Dist. Osteopathic Med. Soc. Republican. Baptist. Home: Rt 6 Box 3 Broken Arrow OK 74011 Office: Family Medicine Assocs 3100 S Elm Pl A Broken Arrow OK 74012

RIVA, ALESSANDRO LODOVICO, anatomy educator, scientist; b. Milan, Aug. 25, 1939; s. Giuseppe and Carolina (Ajmar) R.; m. Francesca Testa, Oct. 10, 1969; children: Laura, Giulia, Margherita. MD, U. Pavia, Italy, 1964. Prof. anatomy U. Cagliari, Italy, 1969-75, dep. chmn. Inst. Anatomy, 1971-75, prof. anatomy, 1975—, dir. dept. cytomorphology, 1987-92, prof. history of medicine, 1989—; dir. doctorate morphological scis. U. Cagliari, 1987—; curator Mus. Anatomical Waxes, U. Cagliari, 1991—. Editor: (with P. M. Motta) Ultrastructure of Extraparietal Glands of the Digestive Tract, 1990, (with L. Cattaneo) The Anatomical Waxes of Clemente Susini of the University of Cagliari, 1993, (with P. M. Motta and F. Testa-Riva) Ultrastructure of Male Urogenital Glands, 1994; contbr. articles to profl. jours. Olzai freeman, 1994; bd. govs. U. Cagliari, 1980-96. Mem. Anat. Soc. Gt. Britain and Ireland, Histochem. Soc., Am. Assn. Anatomists, Am. Assn. Andrology, Am. Fertility Soc., Am. Assn. Dental Rsch., Italian Assn. Anatomists (bd. dirs. 1993—), Italian Histochem. Soc. (mem. bd. 1989-93), Italian Soc. Electron Microscopy, Federative Com. on Anatomical Terminology. Home: Via Stampa 15, I 09131 Cagliari Sardinia, Italy Office: U Cagliari Dept Cytomorphol, via Porcell 2, I 09124 Cagliari Sardinia, Italy

RIVAS, FRANK, physician; b. Huila, Colombia, Feb. 18, 1938; s. Francisco Rivas-Lazaro and Emma Martinez de Rivas; B.S., La Salle Coll., 1958; M.D., U. Central de Venezuela, 1964; m. Carole Marie Miller, Dec. 11, 1970; children—Mary Frances, Brendan, Carole Elizabeth. Fellow in hypertension U. Mich., Ann Arbor, 1965-66; fellow in adult cardiology U. Pa., 1966-67, Temple U., Phila., 1967-68; fellow in adult and pediatric cardiology U. Fla., Gainesville, 1968-69; fellow in cardiac catheterization and coronary arteriography St. Vincent Hosp., Cleve., 1969-70; fellow in pediatric cardiology U. Kans., Kansas City, 1970-71; resident in internal medicine, chief resident St. Louis U., 1971-73; sr. fellow in cardiology Duke U., Durham, N.C., 1973-75; asst. prof. medicine and cardiology Med. Coll. Ga., Augusta, 1975-79; hemodynamist and non-invasive cardiologist VA Med. Center, Augusta, 1975-79, also dir. coronary circulation research lab. and coronary care unit, 1975-79, 1975-79; chief sect. cardiology Huntington (W.Va.) VA Med. Center, 1979-81; assoc. prof. medicine, chmn. cardiology Marshall U. Sch. Medicine, Huntington, 1979-81; pvt. practice medicine specializing in cardiology and cardiac catheterization, Huntington, 1981—; instr. in trauma U. Md.; ATLS instr. ACS; mem. rsch. com. Ga. Heart Assn., W.Va. Heart Assn.; bd. dirs. W.Va. Heart Assn. Diplomate Am. Bd. Internal Medicine (Advanced Achievement in Internal Medicine award), Am. Bd. Cardiology. Contbr. articles to med. jours. Fellow ACP, Am. Coll. Angiology, Am. Coll. Cardiology, Am. Heart Assn., Am. Coll. Chest Physicians; mem. Am. Fedn. Clin. Rsch., Internat. Soc. Heart Rsch., N.Y. Acad. Scis., Sigma Xi. Address: 16264 Whitney Rd Strongsville OH 44136-2554

RIVERA, ENRIQUE, healthcare administrator, educator; b. Moca, P.R., Feb. 1, 1960; s. Jose and Carmen (Valle) R.; m. Olga Babilonia, Sept. 8, 1985; children: Valerie, Natalie. MBA, Interam. U., 1994. Acct. Miguel A. Roman CPA, Moca, 1982, Torres, Padilla & Co., CPA, Aguadilla, P.R., 1982-85; accounts payable mgr. Bella Vista Hosp., Mayaguez, P.R., 1985-88, chief acct., 1988-94; asst. adminstr. Bella Vista Policlinic, Mayaguez, 1994—; part-time prof. Antillian U., Mayaguez, 1994—. Author: Accounting Procedures Manual, 1993. Bd. dirs. Seventh Day Adventists Ch., Mayaguez, 1993-95. Mem. Healthcare Fin. Mgmt. Assn., Am. Acad. Med. Adminstrs. Office: Policlinica Bella Vista PO Box 1750 Mayaguez PR 00681-1750

RIVERA-URRUTIA, BEATRIZ DALILA, psychology and rehabilitation counseling educator; b. Bayamón, P.R., Jan. 16, 1951; d. José and Carmen B. (Urrutia) Rivera; m. Julio C. Ribera, July 1, 1978; 1 child, Alejandra B. BA, U. P.R., 1972, MA, 1975; PhD, Temple U., 1982. Staff pscyhologist Learning Plus, Inc., Phila., 1979-80; cons. Hispanic Mental Health Inst., Phila., 1981-82; staff psychologist J.F. Kennedy Community Mental Health Ctr., Phila., 1982-83; prof. U. P.R., Rio Piedras, 1983—; cons. Jewish Employment & Vocat. Svcs., Phila., 1980; staff psychologist San Juan VA Hosp., Rio Piedras, 1990—. Contbr. articles to profl. jours. Vol. Parroquia San Juan Apóstol y Evangelista, Caguas, P.R., 1988-90, ARC, San Juan, 1990. Faculty U. P.R. instnl. rsch. grantee, 1986-87. Mem. P.R. Psychol. Assn. (bd. editors jour. 1984-89, bd. dirs. 1989-91), P.R. Lic. Bd. Psychologists (pres. ethics com. 1991-92). Home: Roble D 23 Arbolada Caguas PR 00725 Office: PO Box 22724 San Juan PR 00931-2724

RIVNER, MICHAEL HARVEY, neurologist; b. Bklyn., Sept. 26, 1950; s. Norman and Carol (Simson) R.; m. Roberta Fran Gottlieb, Aug. 13, 1978; children: Asher, Joshua, Peter, Harold. BA, Duke U., 1972; MD, Emory U., 1978. Diplomate Am. Bd. Psychiatry and Neurology, added qualifications in clin. neurophysiology; diplomate Am. Bd. Electrodiagnostic Medicine. Intern, resident in neurology Med. Coll. Ga., Augusta, 1978-82; from fellow to assoc. prof. neurology Med. Coll. Ga., 1982—; cons. neurology Eisenhower Med. Hosp., Ft. Gordon, Ga., 1982—, VA Med. Ctr., Augusta, 1982—. V.p., campaign chmn. Augusta Jewish Found., 1994, pres., 1995-96; treas. CSRA Swim League, Augusta, 1993—; treas. Augusta Jewish C.C. Fellow Am. Acad. Neurology; mem. Am. Assn. Electrodiagnostic Medicine (equipment com. 1984-87, tng. program com. 1989-92, edn. com. 1992—, chmn. edn. com. 1994—), Southeastern Neuromuscular Group (pres. 1996—). Office: Med Coll Ga EMG Lab Augusta GA 30912

RIZER, DEAN KIRBY, retired internist; b. Anaconda, Mont., May 4, 1912; s. Robert Inskeer and Ruth Muriel (Lackersteen) R.; m. Kathryn Eleanor Waitney, Sept. 4, 1939 (div. 1952); children: Ann, Dean K. Jr. AB cum laude, Princeton U., 1934; MD, Harvard Med. Sch., Boston, 1938. Diplomate Am. Bd. Internal Medicine. Prof. U. Minn., 1938; intern Peter Beut Brigham and Childrens Hosp., 1938-42; pvt. practice Mpls., 1946-86; ret., 1986; from instr. to clin. prof. medicine U. Minn., Mpls., 1946-80, prof. emeritus, 1980; cons. in field. Bd. dirs. ARC, Mpls., 1950, Viking coun. Boy Scouts Am., Mpls., 1953-58, Minn. Sci. Mus., St. Paul. Maj. M.C., U.S. Army, 1943-46, ETO. Mem. Minn. Med. Soc. (environ. resource com. 1970's). Republican. Home: 8102 Highwood Dr Apt B226 Minneapolis MN 55438-1048

RIZER, FRANKLIN MORRIS, physician, otolarynogologist; b. Gallipolis, Ohio, Aug. 13, 1953; s. Franklin Morris and Wanda Mae (Potts) R.; m. Maria Nicolette Guglielmi, Feb. 8, 1986. BS cum laude, Ohio State U., 1975; MD, U. Cin., 1979. Diplomate Am. Bd. Otolaryngology. Intern U. Calif., Davis, 1979-80; resident U. Wash., Seattle, 1980-81, Ea. Va. U. Coll. of Medicine, Norfolk, 1981-84; fellow House Ear Inst., 1984-87; chief of otology St. Joseph's Riverside Hosp., Warren, Ohio, 1989—; assoc. prof. Ea. Va. Coll. of Medicine, Norfolk, 1987—, Northeastern Ohio U. Coll. of Medicine, Rootstown, 1987—, Ohio State U., Columbus, 1995—; fellowship dir. Warren Otologic Group, Warren, 1991—. Contbr. articles to profl. jours. Trustee Makoning Valley Macintosh Users Group, Warren, 1989-92; active Leadership Warren, 1989; bd. dirs. Humility of Mary Integrated Delivery Network, 1995—. With USAF, 1971-73. Fellow Am. Acad. Otolaryngology; mem. Am. Acad. Facial Plastics, Soc. of Wilderness Medicine, Undersea and Hyperbaric Med. Soc. United Methodist. Home: 469 Country Club Dr NE Warren OH 44484-4616 Office: Warren Otologic Group 3893 E Market St Warren OH 44484-4706

RIZZA, CHARLES ROCCO, hematologist; b. Dundee, Scotland, Mar. 26, 1930; s. Domenico and Rosa (Iannetta) R.; m. Sheena Gilroy Henderson, July 4, 1956; children: Philip, Paul, Jane, Christopher. MB, ChB, St. Andrews U., Scotland, 1955, M.D., 1962; M.R.C.P., Edinburgh, 1964, F.R.C.P., 1972. House physician Dundee (Scotland) Hosp., 1955-56; clin. rsch. fellow Med. Rsch. Coun., Eng., 1958-61; lectr. in therapeutics St. Andrews U., Scotland, 1965-66; cons. physician Oxfordshire Health Authority, Eng., 1966-93, dir. Oxford Haemophilia Ctr., 1977-93; chmn. Haemophilia Ctr. Dirs. Orgn., Eng., 1987-90; med. advisor to Haemophilia Soc., 1970-93. Contbr. articles to profl. jours. Mem. British Soc. Haematology, Internat. Soc. for Thrombosis and Haemostasis. Office: Oxford Haemophilia Ctr, Old Rd, Oxford England

RIZZI, TERESA MARIE, bilingual speech and language pathologist; b. Denver, Aug. 8, 1964; d. Theophilus Marcus and Maudie Marie (Pitts) R. BA in Speech Pathology, U. Denver, 1986, BA in Spanish, 1986; MS in Speech Pathology, Vanderbilt U., 1988. Pediatric speech-lang. pathologist Rose Med. Ctr., Denver, 1988-90; pvt. practice Denver, 1990—; Spanish tchr. Temple Emanual, Denver, 1992-95; owner, operator Niños De Colo., Denver; Spanish tutor and interpreter, Denver, 1988—; bilingual pediatric speech-lang. pathologist The Children's Hosp., Denver, 1994—; presenter in field. G'arin grantee Ctrl. Agy. Jewish Edn., 1993, grantee U. No. Colo. Grad. Sch., 1994. Mem. Am. Speech-Lang.-Hearing Assn. (Continuing Edn. award 1991), Colo. Speech-Lang.-Hearing Assn., Internat. Assn. Orofacial Myology, Phi Sigma Iota. Office: Teresa M Rizzi MS CCC 695 S Colorado Blvd Ste 410 Denver CO 80222-8008

RIZZO, DONALD CHARLES, biology educator; b. Boston, June 10, 1945; s. Michael S. and Rita F. (Ward) R. BA, Boston State Coll., 1968; MS, Cornell U., 1970, PhD, 1973. Rsch. asst. Dept. Entomology Cornell U., Ithaca, N.Y., 1968-73; instr. Siena Heights Coll., Adrian, Mich., 1973-74; asst. prof. Marygrove Coll., Detroit, 1974-78, assoc. prof., 1978-95, prof., 1995—, head biology dept., 1974—, unit head math. and sci., 1975—, project dir. Minority Instns. Sci. Improvement program grants, 1983-85, 85-87. Mem. Am. Inst. Biolog. Sci., Nat. Assn. Sci. Tchrs., AAUP, Mich. Depression Glas Soc. (chmn. book com. 1985—). Democrat. Roman Catholic. Home: 41 Cambridge Blvd Pleasant Ridge MI 48069

RIZZO, GIUSEPPE, obstetrician and gynecologist; b. Cagliari, Italy, June 1, 1958; s. Giorgio and Rosanna (Lupi) R.; m. Maria Vittoria Lavaggi, Aug. 18, 1987; children: Ludovica, Giorgio. MD, Cath. U. Rome, 1983. Asst. prof. Cath. U. Rome, 1986-92; asst. prof. U. Roma Tor Vergata, Rome, 1992-95, cons. obstetrician and gynecologist, 1996—. Author: Fetal Cardiac Function, 1995. Recipient Best Rsch. award Soc. Perinatal Obstetricians, 1989, Rsch. Excellence in Prematurity, 1996. Mem. Internat. Soc. Perinatal Obstetrics, Italian Soc. Obstetricians and Gynecologists, Internat. Soc. Ultrasound in Ob-Gyn. Roman Catholic. Home: Via G Severano 5, 00161 Rome Italy Office: U Roma Tor Vergata-Policlin Nuovo S Eugenio, P Umanesimo 10, 00144 Rome Italy

RIZZO, JOANNE T., family nurse practitioner; b. Boston, Feb. 20, 1950; d. Anthony M. and Barbara A. Rizzo. BS, Northeastern U., 1972; MS, U. Colo., Denver, 1976. ACLS; cert. family nurse practitioner. RN pediatrics Mass. Gen. Hosp., Boston, 1972-75; family nurse practitioner Frontier Nursing Svc., Hyden, Ky., 1976-78; nurse practitioner migrant health program U. Colo., Alamosa, 1978-79; family nurse practitioner, clinic mgr. Plan de Salud del Valle, Ft. Lupton, Colo., 1979-82; family nurse practitioner Family Health Svc., Worcester, Mass., 1982-89; fgn. svc. nurse practitioner State Dept., Washington, 1989—; fgn. svc. nurse practitioner Am. Embassy, Bucharest, Romania, 1989-91, Lima, Peru, 1991—; nurse practitioner preceptor Robert Wood Johnson plan de salud del valle, Platteville, Colo., 1980-81, U. Lowell, Worcester, 1984-88, U. Wash., 1995. Recipient Cert. of Appreciation, Agy. Internat. Devel., Romania, 1990, Meritorious Honor award & Group Valor award, Romania, 1990, Dept. of State Health Practitioner of Yr. award, 1995. Mem. Sigma Theta Tau. Home: Am Embassy Lima Unit 3755 APO AA 34031-3750

RIZZO, THOMAS DIGNAN, orthopedic surgeon; b. N.Y.C., May 25, 1931; s. Peter-Cyrus and Rose Ann (Dignan) R.; m. Jean Foley; children: Thomas D. Jr., Peter F., James G., Kathryn Anne Marie, William J., Francis V. BS cum laude, Georgetown U., 1958, MD cum laude, 1956. Diplomate Am. Bd. Orthopedic Surgery, Nat. Bd. Med. Examiners. Intern Georgetown U. Med. Ctr., Washington, 1956-57; asst. resident surgeon St. Vincent's Hosp., N.Y.C., 1957-58; resident in orthopedic surgery Hosp. for Spl. Surgery, N.Y.C., 1958-59, fellow in orthopedic surgery, 1961-62; resident fellow in orthopedic surgery Newington Hosp. for Crippled Children, Conn., 1962; pvt. practice Bronxville, N.Y., 1962—; clin. cons. orthopedic surgery N.Y. State Dept. Health, 1965; assoc. dir. orthopedics Lawrence Hosp., Bronxville, 1970-79, attending staff, 1963—; asst. attending St. John's Riverside Hosp., Yonkers, N.Y., 1963-74, sr. attending surgeon, 1974-87, dir. dept. orthopedic surgery, 1975-86, courtesy staff, 1987—; assoc. attending Dobbs Ferry Hosp., 1970-73, cons. staff, 1973—; asst. attending Hosp. for Spl. Surgery, N.Y.C., 1963, Doctors Hosp., 1973-80; asst. attending surgeon N.Y. Hosp., 1981-83. Mem. adv. bd. Bapt. Home for Aged; trustee Fordham Prep. Sch., 1987-93; mem. Westchester Health Planning Coun., 1983—, sec., 1988-89; bd. dirs. Hudson Valley Health Sys. Agy., 1988—. Fellow ACS, Am. Acad. Orthopedic Surgeons, Am. Acad. Legal and Indsl. Medicine, N.Y. Acad. of Medicine, Westchester Acad. Medicine (bd. trustees 1968—), Am. Orthopedic Foot and Ankle Soc.; mem. AMA, N.Y. State Med. Soc. (county del. 1975-87), Westchester County Med. Soc. (bd. dirs. 1968—, pres. 1975-76), Irish Am. Orthopedic Soc., N.Y. State Soc. Orthopedic Surgeons, Ea. Orthopedic Assn., Georgetown U. Alumni Assn.

(bd. govs. 1970-73, chpt. v.p. 1970-72), KC, Knight of Malta, Knight of Holy Sepulchre, Lotos Club (N.Y.C.), Cottage Club (Sea Island, Ga.), Lawrence Beach Club (Atlantic Beach, N.Y.), Bronxville (N.Y.) Field Club, Alpha Omega Alpha. Home: 633 California Rd Bronxville NY 10708-2311 also: 349 Cook Ave Sea Island GA 31561 Office: 77 Pondfield Rd Bronxville NY 10708-3809 also: Hosp for Spl Surgery 535 E 70th St New York NY 10021-4892

RIZZO, THOMAS DIGNAN, JR., physical medicine and rehabilitation physician; b. N.Y.C., Mar. 3, 1959; s. Thomas Dignan and Jean Kathryn (Foley) R.; m. Margaret Mary Drew, June 1, 1986; children: Thomas Dignan III, Katherine Jean, Elizabeth Ann, Carolyn Drew. BA in English, Williams Coll., 1981; MD, Georgetown U., 1985. Diplomate Am. Bd. Phys. Medicine and Rehab. Sr. assoc. cons. Mayo Clinic, Rochester, Minn., 1989-92, cons., 1992-93; cons. Mayo Clinic, Jacksonville, Fla., 1993—; med. dir. rehab. svcs. St. Luke's Hosp., Jacksonville, 1993—, med. dir. subacute skilled care unit, 1996—; mem. adv. bd. St. Luke's Home Health Svcs., 1996—; co-dir. Sportsmedicine Ctr.: Mayo Clinic Rochester, 1990-93; team physician high sch., profl. level, Rochester, 1986-93. Author: (with others) Clinics of NA in PM&R Hand Injuries, 1993; contbr. articles to profl. jours.; editl. bd. Phys. and Sports Medicine, Mpls., 1992—. Med. dir. Star of the North State Games, Rochester, 1990, AAU/Jr. Olympics, Rochester, 1992. Fellow Am. Acad. of Phys. Medicine and Rehab. (chair spl. interest sports medicine 1994-96, SIG com. 1994-96, task force on fellowships 1994-95, chair 1996—); mem. AMA, Am. Coll. of Sportsmedicine, Duval County Med. Soc., Fla. Med. Assn. Office: Mayo Clinic Jacksonville 4500 San Pablo Rd Jacksonville FL 32224

RIZZONI, WALTER ENRICO, cardiovascular and thoracic surgeon; b. N.Y.C., Oct. 22, 1957; s. Eitel Manlio and Renee Suzanne (Gilbert) R.; m. Anne Marie Hall, Dec. 27, 1996; children: Michael, Catherine, Elizabeth. BA summa cum laude, Boston U., 1979, MD, 1983. Diplomate Am. Bd. Surgery. Resident gen. surgery Boston U., 1983-85; fellow in surg. oncology Nat. Cancer Inst., 1985-87; resident gen. surgery Loma Linda U., 1987-90; fellow in peripheral vascular surgery Carolinas Med. Ctr., Charlotte, N.C., 1994-95, fellow in cardiovascular and thoracic surgery, 1995—. Maj. USAF, 1990-94. Mem. ACS, AMA.

RIZZUTI, RICHARD PHILIP, plastic surgeon; b. N.Y.C., Oct. 6, 1957; s. Richard and Catherine (Keaveny) R.; m. Karen Thodes, May 7, 1983; children: Christian, Lara. BS, Boston Coll., 1979; MD, East Carolina U., 1983. Diplomate Am. Bd. Plastic Surgery. Plastic surgeon East Carolina U. Sch. Medicine, Greenville, N.C., 1991-92, Greenville Plastic Surgery, 1992—. Office: Greenville Plastic Surgery 400 Spring Forest Rd Greenville NC 27834

RIZZUTO, CARMELA RITA, nursing administrator; b. Waterbury, Conn., Aug. 26, 1942; d. Joseph Anthony and Carmella Rosa R.; m. Thomas Lee Chernesky, Aug. 28, 1982. BS, St. Joseph Coll., 1965; MS, Boston Coll., 1971; EdD, Sch. Edn., UCLA, 1983. RN, Calif. Nursing instr. Samaritan Hosp. Sch. Nursing, Troy, N.Y., 1969; med. nursing coord., clin. specialist Harvard Community Health Plan, Boston, 1971-72; instr. inservice edn. Tufts-New Eng. Med. Ctr., Boston, 1972-73; instr. inservice edn. St. John's Hosp. and Health Ctr., Santa Monica, Calif., 1974-76; asst. clin. prof. Sch. Nursing, UCLA, 1976-79; assoc. dir. nursing edn. St. Francis Hosp. of Santa Barbara, 1981-83; asst. dir. nursing edn. and rsch. Stanford U. Hosp., 1983-90, dir. geriatric patient care grant, 1990-93; rsch. coord. sch. medicine Stanford U., 1994—; instr. Calif. State U., Dominquez Hills, 1993—. Grantee USPHS, NIH, DHHS, USPHS nurse trainee, 1969-71; recipient Chancellor's Patent Fund, UCLA, 1972-73. Contbr. articles to profl. publs. Home: 925 Cascade Dr Sunnyvale CA 94087-4043

ROACH, HARRY ALLEN, cardiovascular and thoracic surgeon; b. Lake Charles, La., July 13, 1955; s. Larry Arlen and Dorothy Belle (Cormie) R. BS in Biology, McNeese State U., Lake Charles, 1976; MD, Tulane U., 1980. Diplomate Am. Bd. Surgery, Am. Bd. Thoracic Surgery; lic. MD, La. Resident in surgery Tulane U. Sch. Medicine, New Orleans, 1980-85; adminstrv. chief resident in surgery Tulane U. Sch. Medicine, 1984, resident in thoracic surgery, 1985-87; pvt. practice Barnes, Kastl Bros. Raborn, Roach, Inc., Metairie, La., 1987-94, Cardiac, Thoracic & Vascular Surgery, Inc., Metairie, 1994—; clin. asst. prof. surgery Tulane U. Sch. Medicine, 1987—; lectr. in field. Mem. The Audubon Inst., New Orleans, 1995—; staff physician Charity Hosp. Med. Ctr. La., New Orleans, 1987—. Fellow ACS (comm. on application La. Dist. I 1994—); mem. AMA, Soc. Thoracic Surgeons, Orleans Parish Med. Soc. (bd. govs. 1995), Alton Ochsner Surg. Soc., Tulane Surg. Soc. (charter). Home: 7529 St Charles Ave New Orleans LA 70118 Office: Cardiac Thoracic & Vascular Surgery Inc 3939 Houma Blvd Ste 20 Metairie LA 70006

ROACH, JOHN MICHAEL, gastroenterologist; b. Walla Walla, Wash., Feb. 28, 1947; s. John Francis and Johanna Patricia (Sullivan) R.; m. Nancy Marie Mudd, Mar. 31, 1973; children: Shannon, John, Luke, Patrick, William, Bartholomew, Michelle. BS, Seattle U., 1969; MD, U. Wash., 1973. Diplomate Am. Bd. Internal Medicine. Intern straight medicine Maricopa County Gen. Hosp., Phoenix, 1974, resident internal medicine, 1975-76, gastroenterology fellow, 1976-78; pvt. practice gastroenterology Kennewick, Wash., 1978—; pres. med. staff Kennewick Gen. Hosp., 1985. Contbr. articles to Gastrointestinal Endoscopy, Surgical Laparoscopy & Endoscopy, Gastroenterology. Mem. Tri-City Renaissance Com., Pasco, Wash., 1987-91. Mem. ACP, Am. Soc. Gastrointestinal Endoscopy, Am. Gastroent. Assn., Am. Coll. Gastroenterology, Benton-Franklin County Med. Soc. (chmn. continuing med. edn. 1987-88, pres. 1989), Wash. State Med. Assn., Pacific NW Endoscopy Soc. Republican. Roman Catholic. Office: 811 S Auburn St Kennewick WA 99336-5661

ROACH, RALPH LEE, human services and rehabilitation consultant; b. Silver Spring, Md., Mar. 27, 1957; s. William A. and Mary B. (Collins) R.; m. Susan Diane Schirmacher, Aug. 17, 1985. BA, Messiah Coll., 1982; MS, Shippensburg U., 1985; postgrad., Kennedy-We. U., 1995—. Inventory controller Messiah Coll., Grantham, Pa., 1977-85; therapist, crisis interviewer Stevens Mental Health, Carlisle, Pa., 1983-86; psychotherapist Holy Spirit Community Mental Health Inst., Camp Hill, Pa., 1986—; presentor, cons. Lebanon (Pa.) Valley Coll., 1986; vocat. tng. mgr. Ctr. for Indsl. Tng., Mechanicsburg, Pa., 1985-87; program mgr. living unltd. program univ. hosp. rehab. ctr. for children and adults Pa. U. Hosp. Milton S. Hershey Med. Ctr., Hershey, Pa., 1987-92; corp. officer, clin. dir. Avalon Affiliates Rehab. Consultants, Inc. (now MRW, Inc.), Duncannon, Pa., 1993-96, MRW, Inc., 1995—; adj. faculty Elizabethtown Coll., 1987; presenter at profl. confs. Edn. dir. Cumberland Valley Ch., Dillsburg, Pa., 1980-83; presentor Gov.'s Com. on Handicapped, Harrisburg, Pa., 1986; presentor Office of Spl. Edn. and Rehab., Harrisburg, 1987. Mem. ACA, Am. Acad. Rehab. Medicine, Pa. Specialists in Group Work, Pa. Crisis Intervention Assn., Pa. Assn. Rehab. Facilities, Keystone State Head Injury Found. Presbyterian. Home: 101 Jefferson St Duncannon PA 17020-9675 Office: MRW Inc 101 Jefferson St 101 Jefferson St Duncannon PA 17020

ROAK, SANDRA K., social worker; b. N.Y.C., Dec. 21, 1937; m. David B. Roak, Aug. 15, 1959; children: Susan, Rebecca. BA, Smith Coll., 1959; MS in Social Work, Boston U., 1976. Lic. clin. social worker. Asst. exec. dir. Greenfield (Mass.) Girls Club, 1959-60; case aid Family Svc. Assn., Stamford, Conn., 1969-70; social worker Roxbury Manor Nursing Home, W. Roxbury, Mass., 1971-72; clin social worker Goddard Meml. Hosp., Stoughton, Mass., 1976-89, clin. social work supr., 1989—; bd. dirs. Protestant Social Svc. Bur., Quincy, Mass., 1977—; mem. edn. com. Am. Cancer Soc., Stoughton, 1989-95. Mem. Assn. Hosp. Social Work Dirs. (S.E. Mass. region). Democrat. Home: 170 Centre St Milton MA 02186-3338 Office: Good Samaritan Med Ctr 235 N Pearl St Brockton MA 02401

ROARK, GLENN EARNEST, psychiatrist; b. Marfa, Tex., July 6, 1929; s. Cloyd Earnest and Lucy Elene (Lagow) R.; m. Dorothea Jean Lawler, Dec. 28, 1950; children: Carol Elaine, Lawrence Glenn, Linda Jean. BS, Stephen F. Austin State Coll., 1953; MD, U. Tex., Galveston, 1953. Intern USPHS Hosp., S.I., N.Y., 1953-54; resident Wichita Gen. Hosp., Wichita Falls, Tex., 1954-55; pvt. practice Dierks, Ark., 1955-56; dist. dir. pub. health U.S. Trust Territory of Pacific Islands, Truk, Caroline Islands, 1956-58; staff physician student health service U. Mo., Columbia, 1958-67; resident in psychiatry U. Mo. Med. Ctr., Columbia, 1967-70; psychiatrist student health ctr. U. Tex., Austin, 1970-73, chief mental health sect., 1973-85; med. dir. Counseling and Pastoral Care Ctr., Austin, 1985-88; pvt. practice Austin, 1988—; cons. psychiatrist Counseling and Pastoral Care Ctr., 1975-85, St. Matthews Family of Christ Ministry, Austin, 1989-90, Samaritan Counseling Ctr., Austin, 1989-95; psychotherapy supr. Austin State Hosp., 1985-88. With U.S. Army, 1946-48. Mem. Austin Psychiat. Soc., Am. Psychiat. Assn., Tex. Soc. Psychiat. Physicians, Travis County Med. Soc., Tex. Med. Assn., Austin Astron. Soc. (v.p. 1989-91), Internat. Occulation Timing Assn., Austin Cycling Assn. Baptist. Home: 7401 Berkman Dr Austin TX 78752-2025 Office: 3724 Jefferson St Ste 308 Austin TX 78731-6222

ROATH, KENNETH B., investment company executive. Pres., chmn. bd., CEO Health Care Property Investors, L.A., 1978—. Office: Health Care Property Investors 10990 Wilshire Blvd Los Angeles CA 90024-3913

ROATH-ALGERA, KATHLEEN MARIE, massage therapist; b. Binghamton, N.Y., Feb. 7, 1952; d. Stephen James and Virginia Mary (Purdy) Roath; m. Parker Newcomb Wheeler Jr., Sept. 18, 1971 (div. June 1976); 1 child, Colleen Marie Wheeler; m. John M. Algera, Feb. 14, 1981. AS in Phys. Edn., Dean Jr. Coll., Franklin, Mass., 1971; BS in Edn., Boston U., 1977; postgrad., U. Ctrl. Fla., Orlando, 1981-82; grad., Reese Inst. Massage Therapy, Oviedo, Fla., 1988. Lic. massage therapist; master practitioner in myofascial release. Counselor Dept. Def., Orlando, 1979-84; tchr. Divine Mercy Cath. Sch., Merritt Island, Fla., 1984-85; courier Emery Worldwide, Orlando, 1985-89; massage therapist, dir., owner Massage Therapy Clinic of Titusville, Fla., 1989—; instr., supr. clin. internship Reese Inst., 1992-95; assoc. Todd Jaffe, M.D., 1995. Mem. Am. Massage Therapy Assn., Fla. State Massage Therapy Assn. (pres. Brevard County 1992—, Therapist of Yr. 1991-92), Nat. Cert. Bd. Therapeutic Massage and Bodywork (recert. chair 1994—). Home: 5538 River Oaks Dr Titusville FL 32780 Office: Massage Therapy Clinic Titusville 3410 S Park Ave Titusville FL 32780-5139

ROBAK, ROSTYSLAW WSEWOLOD, psychologist, educator; b. Passau, Germany, Nov. 15, 1948; s. Bohdan and Maria R.; m. Loretta J. Tallon; children: Marika, Boyan. BA, Seton Hall U., 1970; MA, Fairleigh Dickinson U., 1973; PhD, Hofstra U., 1976. Lic. psychologist N.Y., Pa., Mass. Prof. Pace U., Pleasantville, N.Y., 1988—; dir. M.S. program in substance abuse counseling Pace U., 1992—; adj. prof. Orange County Community Coll., Middletown, N.Y. 1985-88; founding faculty advisor Pace U. chpt. Psi Chi Nat. Honor Soc., 1991—. Author: A Primer for Today's Substance Abuse Counselor, 1991. Mem. APA, Am. Orthopsychiat. Assn., Nat. Register Health Svc. Providers in Psychology, Assn. Death Edn. and Counseling. Office: Pace Univ Dir Substance Abuse Counseling Prog Pleasantville NY 10570

ROBB, ROY KENT, juvenile probation officer; b. Pasadena, Tex., Aug. 19, 1943; s. Roy E. and Virginia Jeanette (Wall) R.; m. Dolores Kay Robb, May 19, 1968; children: James Kent, Joel Glenn. BS in History and Edn., Howard Payne U., 1968; M in Criminal Justice, Am. Tech. U., 1977; cert., NAt. Coll. Juvenile Justice, 1981, 82. Prin. May (Tex.) Elem. Sch., 1967-69; caseworker Tex. Youth Commn., Gatesville, 1968-71; chief probation officer 52d Jud. Dist., Gatesville, 1971-85, Tom Green County, San Angelo, Tex., 1985—; mem. adv. com. Juvenile Probation Commn., 1982-85, Tex. Adult Probation Commn., 1985; mem. adv. bd. Sam Houston State U., 1973-81, 86—; appointee Juvenile Justice Delinquency Prevention Adv. Bd., Criminal Justice Div. of the Governor's Office, 1988; cons. Mott, McDonald and Assocs., Washington, 1979. Bd. dirs. Rivercrest Hosp., 1987—, Concho Valley chpt. ARC, 1987—; mem. Am. Christian T.V. Svc. Bd., San Angelo, 1987—, Gatesville, Tex., 1984; mem. Planning and Zoning Commn., Gatesville, 1985; chmn. fund drive ARC, Coryell County, Tex., 1978; pres. Gatesville Little League, 1976-77; chmn. bldg. com. Trinity Bapt. Ch., Gatesville, 1976. Recipient Award of Appreciation, Harris County Juvenile Bd., 1981, Sam Houston State U., 1980, Cert. award Tex. Inst. on Children and Youth, 1980, Tex. Jud. Coun., 1979. Mem. Tex. Probation Assn. (pres. 1979-81, chmn. awards com. 1983-87, chmn. legis. com. 1983, 85, editor newsletter 1978-86, cert. of award 1983), Tex. Corrections Assn. (chmn. probation div. 1973-75, chmn. legis. com. 1974-79). Office: Tom Green County Juvenile Probation 1253 W 19th St San Angelo TX 76903-4305

ROBBIE, BETH ANNE, medical and surgical nurse; b. Melrose, Mass., Feb. 25, 1969; d. Frederick Pierre and Anna Sulvia (Casey) Labrousse; m. Jeffrey Edwin Robbie, Dec. 31, 1989; children: James Edwin, Emily Elaine. A in Liberal Arts, Quinsigamond C.C., Worcester, Mass., 1990, ADN, 1992. Psychiat. nurse Worcester State Hosp., 1993; staff nurse Rockingham Meml. Hosp., Harrisonburg, Va., 1994—. Home: Rte 1 Box 199 Churchville VA 24421

ROBBINS, ARNOLD, psychiatrist; b. Pitts., Aug. 24, 1931; s. Oscar and Leah Vera (Ruben) R.; 1 child, Carolyn. BS in Psychology, U. Pitts., 1953; MD, Tulane U., 1957. Diplomate Am. Bd. Psychiatry. Intern Phila. Gen. Hosp., 1957-58; resident fellow Med. Ctr. Boston U., 1959-62, teaching fellow Med. Sch., 1960-62, assoc. prof. clin. psychiatry Med. Sch., 1984—; lectr. in psychiatry Med. Sch. Harvard U., Cambridge, Mass., 1978-85; dir. South Boston Ct. Clinic Tufts Bay Cove Mental Health Ctr., Boston, 1980-84; med. and clinical dir. Mystic Valley Mental Health Ctr., Arlington, Mass., 1984-87; asst. prof. clin. psychiatry Med. Sch. Tufts U., Boston, 1981—; chief mental health, Med. Assocs., Multigroup Harvard Community Health Plan Chelmsford (Mass.) Ctr., 1984-90; d. dirs. Ctr. House Found., Boston; chief psychiatrist The Somerville (Mass.) Hosp., 1990—; med. dir., chief of psychiatry The Beech Hill Hosp., N.H., 1989, 93; assoc. clin. prof. psychiatry Boston U. Med. Sch. Bd. dirs. Am. Mental Health Affiliation with Israel, 1984-88. Mem. Am. Psychiat. Assn., Mass. Med. Soc., Am. Assn. Community Psychiatrists (bd. dirs. 1987-91), Harvard Club, Alpha Omega Alpha. Home: 116 Hancock St Cambridge MA 02139-2206

ROBBINS, DARRYL ANDREW, pediatrician; b. Modesto, Calif., Sept. 16, 1945; s. Jerome and Grace (Bass) R.; m. Harriette Lee Eisenberg, June 12, 1971; children: Jennifer Lynn, Julie Ellen, Allison Beth. BS, Dickinson Coll., 1967; DO, Phila. Coll. Osteo. Medicine, 1971. Diplomate Am. Bd. Pediatrics. Intern Doctor's Hosp., Columbus, Ohio, 1971-72; resident in pediatrics Children's Hosp. Med. Ctr., Cin., 1972-75; practice medicine specializing in pediatrics Columbus, 1975—; vice chairperson Diocesan Child Guidance Ctr., Columbus, 1986, bd. dirs., 1983-88; mem. genetics svcs. adv. com. Ohio Dept. Health, 1978-86; pres. med. staff Columbus Children's Hosp., 1996. Recipient Samuel Dalinsky Meml. award for Outstanding Graduating Resident Cin. Children's Hosp., 1975; named Pediatrician of Yr., Columbus Children's Hosp., 1982, 90. Fellow Am. Acad. Pediatrics; mem. Cen. Ohio Pediatric Soc. (pres. elect 1988, pres. 1989-90). Jewish. Home: 953 Old Farm Rd Columbus OH 43213-2674 Office: 3341 E Livingston Ave Columbus OH 43227-1949

ROBBINS, DICK LAMSON, internist, educator; b. Boston, May 13, 1941; married; 3 children. BA, Lawrence U., 1963; MD, U. Vt., 1967. Diplomate Am. Bd. Internal Medicine, Nat. Bd. Med. Examiners, Am. Bd. Rheumatology. Intern Good Samaritan Hosp., Phoenix, 1967-68; resident in internal medicine U. Oreg. Med. Sch., Portland, 1968-71; research fellow rheumatology Scripps Clinic and Research Found., La Jolla, Calif., 1973-76; asst. prof. medicine dept. internal medicine sect. rheumatology U. Calif., Davis, 1976-82, assoc. prof., 1982-88, prof., 1988—; program chmn. Soc. Fellows Scripps Clinic and Research Found., 1974-75, pres., 1975-76; adminstrn. coms. held at U. Calif. Med. Ctr. include med. records 1976-78, patient care 1978-79, capital equipment 1979-80, quality assurance outpatient rev. subcom. 1985-86; chmn. patient care 1979-81; coms. held with dept. Internal Medicine include internship-residency selection 1979-80, residency rev. 1980-82, internal medicine research 1984-86, internal medicine quality assurance rev. 1984-86, chmn. 1982-84; coms. held with Sch. Medicine include grad. group immunology 1977—, comparative pathology group 1977—, faculty affairs 1977-78, faculty exec. 1984-85; exec. com. grad. group in immunology 1985-86; grade change 1979-81, chmn. 1981-85; coms. held with U. Davis include gen. ed. ad hoc 1981-82; chmn. grad. research awards 1983-84; coms. held Div. Rheumatology/Allergy and Clin. Immunology include dir. postgrad. fellowship program 1977—, dir. rheumatology-orthopedics combined clinics 1978-81, acting chmn. 1985-86; cons. San Joaquin Gen. Hosp., Stockton, Calif., 1976—, Calif. Crippled Children Services, Sacramento, 1976—, Kaiser Hosp., Sacramento, 1979—, VA Hosp., Martinez, Calif., 1979—, Woodland (Calif.) Meml. Hosp., 1979-81, David Grant Meml. Hosp., Travis AFB, Calif., 1980—; internal medicine continuous quality ins. review com., 1989-93; internal med. fin. coun., 1990—. Contbr. numerous articles to profl. jours. Recipient Earle C. Anthony award 1976-77, Faculty Rsch. award 1976-81; New Eng. Bd. Higher Edn. scholar 1963-67; NIH fellow 1974-76; rsch. grantee NIH, 1976-83, Calif. Lung Assn., 1977-79, NIH, 1978-81, Am. Heart Assn., 1980-81, NIH, 1983-87, 91-95. Fellow Am. Coll. Rheumatology (coun. we. region 1977-94, co-chair programs we. region; mem. AAAS, Am. Heart Assn. (no. Calif. affiliate rsch. peer review com. 1991-92)Am. Rheumatism Assn. (mem. western region council 1988—), Am. Soc. Zoologists (comparative immunology sect.), Western Soc. Naturalists, Internat. Soc. Devel. and Comparative Immunology.

ROBBINS, EDITH SCHULTZ, microscopy educator; b. Galveston, Tex., July 4, 1941; d. Leon and Sara (Major) Schultz; m. Peter L. Robbins, May 26, 1966; 1 child, George M. AB, Barnard Coll., N.Y.C., 1962; MS, NYU Grad. Sch. Arts & Scis., 1965, PhD, 1970. Instr. CUNY, N.Y.C., 1968-71; asst. prof. Borough Manhattan Community Coll., N.Y.C., 1973-75; assoc. prof. CUNY, N.Y.C., 1975-82, prof., 1982—; adj. instr. NYU Sch. Medicine, 1970-73, adj. asst. prof., 1973-75, adj. assoc. prof. 1975—. Recipient grants NYU Sch. Medicine, Dept. Energy. Mem. AAAS, N.Y. Soc. Exptl. Microscopists, Microscopy Soc. Am., Am. Soc. Cell Biology. Jewish. Home: 12 Myrtle Dr Great Neck NY 11021-1808 Office: NYU Sch Medicine/Cell Biol 550 1st Ave New York NY 10016-6481 also: Borough of Manhattan CC 199 Chambers St New York NY 10007-1079

ROBBINS, EDWIN SIDNEY, psychiatrist; b. N.Y.C., Nov. 5, 1925; s. Herman L. and Clara (Warm) R.; m. Lillian Cukier Robbins, Aug. 5, 1956; children: Hallie Jo, Russell Dana. BA, NYU, 1948, MD, 1952; cert. in psychoanalyst, N.Y. Med. Coll., 1965. Diplomat Am. Bd. Psychiatry and Neurology. Assoc. dir. psychiatry Bellevue Hosp. Ctr., N.Y.C., 1969-90; dir. EAP NYU Med. Ctr., 1971-95, clin. prof., 1974—; clin. prof. Albert Einstein Coll. of Medicine, N.Y.C., 1993—; cons. Vocat. Rehab., N.Y.C., 1957—. Author: (with others) Psychiatric Emergencies, 1976, Psychiatric Emergency Treatment at Bellevue Hospital Center, 1981. cons. N.Y.C. Commr., Mental Health, 1972-77; chairperson Emergency Med. Svc. Grant com., N.Y.C., 1975-76; co-chair Manhattan Mental Health Coun., N.Y.C., 1983-86. With USNR, 1942-45. Fellow Am. Psychoanalytic Assn., Am. Psychiatric Assn., N.Y. Acad. Sci.; mem. AMA, Soc. Med. Psychologists (pres. 1994-95). Home: PO Box 119 Walker Valley NY 12588-0119 Office: 49 E 96th St New York NY 10128-0782

ROBBINS, FREDERICK CHAPMAN, physician, medical school dean emeritus; b. Auburn, Ala., Aug. 25, 1916; s. William J. and Christine (Chapman) R.; m. Alice Havemeyer Northrop, June 19, 1948; children: Alice, Louise. AB, U. Mo., 1936, BS, 1938; MD, Harvard U., 1940; DSc (hon.), John Carroll U., 1955, U. Mo., 1958, U. N.C., 1979, Tufts U., 1983, Med. Coll. Ohio, 1983; LLD, U. N.Mex., 1968. Diplomate Am. Bd. Pediatrics. Intern Children's Hosp., Boston, 1941-42, resident, 1940-41, resident pediatrician, 1946-48; sr. fellow virus disease Nat. Rsch. Coun., 1948-50; staff rsch. div. infectious diseases Children's Hosp., Boston, 1948-50, assoc. physician, assoc. dir. isolation svc., asso. rsch. div. infectious diseases, 1950-52; instr., assoc. in pediatrics Harvard Med. Sch., 1950-52; dir. dept. pediatrics and contagious diseases Cleve. Met. Gen. Hosp., 1952-66; prof. pediatrics Case Western Res. U., 1950-80, dean Sch. Medicine, 1966-80, univ. prof., dean emeritus, 1980—, univ. prof. emeritus, 1987—; pres. Inst. Medicine, NAS, 1980-85; vis. scientist Donner Lab., U. Calif., 1963-64. Served as maj. AUS, 1942-46; chief virus and rickettsial disease sect. 15th Med. Gen. Lab. investigations infectious hepatitis, typhus fever and Q fever. Decorated Bronze Star, 1945; recipient 1st Mead Johnson prize application tissue culture methods to study of viral infections, 1953; co-recipient Nobel prize in physiology and medicine, 1954; Med. Mut. Honor Award for, 1969; Ohio Gov.'s award, 1971. Mem. Assn. Am. Med. Colls. (Abraham Flexner award 1987), Nat. Acad. Scis., Am. Acad. Arts and Scis., Am. Soc. Clin. Investigation (emeritus mem.), Am. Acad. Pediatrics, Soc. Pediatric Research (pres. 1961-62, emeritus mem.), Am. Pediatric Soc., Am. Philos. Soc., Phi Beta Kappa, Sigma Xi, Phi Gamma Delta. Office: Case Western Res U Sch Med 10900 Euclid Ave Cleveland OH 44106-4945*

ROBBINS, JACOB, biomedical researcher, endocrinologist; b. Yonkers, N.Y., Sept. 1, 1922; s. Samuel and Tillie (Sanoff) R.; m. Jean Adams, Sept. 4, 1949; children: Alice Elizabeth, Susan Lynn, Mark Samuel. AB, Cornell U., Ithaca, N.Y., 1944; MD, Cornell U., N.Y.C., 1947. Intern in medicine N.Y. Hosp., N.Y.C., 1947-48; resident Meml. Hosp., N.Y.C., 1948-50, rsch. fellow, 1949-53, asst. attending physician, 1953-54; commd. sr. asst. surgeon USPHS, 1954, advanced through grades to med. dir., 1963, ret., 1989; rsch. scientist NIH, Bethesda, Md., 1954—; chief clin. endocrinology br. Nat. Inst. Diabetes, Digestive and Kidney Diseas, NIH, Bethesda, 1963-92; chief endocrinology sect. genetics and biochemistry br. Nat. Inst. Diabetes, Digestive and Kidney Diseas, NIH, 1992-94; scientist emeritus NIH, 1995—; asst. Sloan Kettering Inst., N.Y.C., 1953-54; instr. Cornell U. Med. Coll., 1950-54, George Washington U. Sch. Medicine, Washington, 1955-61; vis. scientist Carlsberg Lab., Copenhagen, 1959-60; vis. prof. Stellenbosch U., Capetown, South Africa, 1967, Gumma U., Maebashi, Japan, 1970. Editor-in-chief Endocrinology, 1968-72; editor rsch. monographs; also numerous articles on thyroid rsch., chpts. on thyroidology. Recipient Meritorious Svc. medal USPHS, 1971. Mem. Am. Thyroid Assn. (pres. 1974-75, Parke Davis award 1980, Disting. Svc. award 1983), Endocrine Soc. (Ingbar Disting. Svc. award 1995), Am. Soc. for Clin. Investigation, Assn. Am. Physicians, Am. Physiol. Soc., European Thyroid Assn., Japan Endocrine Soc. (hon.), Italian Endocrine Soc. (hon.). Home: 7203 Bradley Blvd Bethesda MD 20817-2127 Office: NIH Bldg Bldg 10 Rm 8N315 Bethesda MD 20892

ROBBINS, JOHN B., medical researcher; b. Bklyn., Dec. 1, 1932. BA, NYU, 1956, MD, 1959; MD (hon.), U. Goteborg, Sweden, 1976. Intern, resident Children's Med. Svc. Mass. Gen. Hosp., Boston, 1959-60; rsch. fellow dept. pediatrics U. Fla., 1961-64; guest scientist dept. chem. immunology Weizmann Inst. Sci., Rehovot, Israel, 1965-66; asst. prof. pediatrics and microbiology U. Fla., Gainesville, 1964-67; from asst. prof. to assoc. prof. pediatrics Albert Einstein Coll. Medicine, 1967-70; clin. dir. Nat. Inst. Child Health and Human Devel. NIH, 1970-72; chief devel. immunology br. NIH, 1971-74; dir. divsn. bacterial products FDA, 1974-83; chief lab. devel. and molecular immunity Nat. Inst. Child Health and Human Devel. NIH, 1983—; Henry Bale Meml. lectr. Nat. Inst. Biol. Stds. and Control, 1979, Erwin Neter Meml. lectr. U. Buffalo, 1984, Henry L. Barnett lectr. Albert Einstein Coll. Medicine, 1985, Maxwell Finland lectr. Infectious Disease Soc. Am., 1989, Louis Weinstein lectr. Tufts U., 1989. Recipient E. Mead Johnson award Am. Acad. Pediatrics, 1975. Fellow Am. Acad. Microbiology; mem. Inst. Med.-Nat. Acad. Sci., Soc. Pediatric Rsch., Soc. Infectious Disease, Am. Soc. Clin. Investigation, Assn. Am. Physicians, Am. Assn. Immunologists. Office: Nat Inst of Child Hlth & Hum Dev Developmental Molecular Imm Lab 9000 Rockville Pike Bldg 6 Bethesda MD 20892-0001*

ROBBINS, LESTER ELISHA, JR., surgeon; b. Trenton, N.J., Sept. 17, 1936; s. Lester E. and Charlotte (Diamond) R.; m. Barbara A. Valeri; children: Sharon, Lester, Krista. AB, Princeton U., 1958; MD, Hahnemann U., 1962. Diplomate Am. Bd. of Surgery. Resident in gen. surgery Abington (Pa.) Meml. Hosp., 1963-66, 68-69; pvt practice in gen. and vascular surgery Helene Fuld Med Ctr., Trenton, N.J., 1969—; courtesy surgeon Robert Wood Johnson U. Hosp., Hamilton, N.J., 1969—; attending surgeon St. Francis Med. Ctr., Trenton, N.J., 1993—; chief sect. peripheral, vascular surgery, Helen Fuld Med. Ctr., 1978-89; chmn. dept. surgery 1982-84, 89-91, 92-94, v.p. med. staff, 1993-95, pres. med. staff, 1995—. Capt. U.S. Army Med. Corps, 1966-68, Vietnam. Fellow ACS, Acad. of Medicine of N.J.; mem. AMA (Physician's Recognition award, continuing med. edn. 1973-94), Med. Soc. N.J. (award for continuing edn. 1994—), Soc. for Clin. Vascular Surgery, Eastern Vascular Soc., Vascular Soc. of N.J., Southeastern Surgical Congress. Republican. Episcopalian. Office: 40 Fuld St Ste 202 Trenton NJ 08638

ROBBINS, LINNEA MARIE, optometrist; b. Rockford, Ill., Nov. 13, 1966; d. Richard Charles and Elizabeth (Strom) R. B of Optometry, Ind. U., 1987, OD, 1991. Resident in optometry Pa. Coll., Phila., 1992; optometrist Mich. Eye Ctr., Mishawaka, Ind., 1992—. Mem. Am. Optometric Assn., North Ctrl. Optometric Soc. (v.p. 1996—), Ind. Optometric Assn.,

Beta Sigma Kappa. Lutheran. Office: Michiana Eye Ctr 230 E Day Rd Ste 100 Mishawaka IN 46545

ROBBINS, MARK STANTON, physician; b. Phila., Feb. 20, 1951; s. William and Helene Robbins; m. Lois Jean Polak, 1977; children: Jeremy, Noah. BA, U. Pa., 1973, MD, 1977. Lic. MD Pa., N.J., Fla.; bd. cert. internal medicine 1980, medical oncology 1983, hematology 1984. Intern Temple Univ. Hosp., Phila., 1977-78, resident, 1978-80, fellow hematology/oncology, 1980-83; pvt. practice hematology, oncology, internal medicine, 1980—; clin. asst. prof. medicine Temple U., 1990—; adj. instr. Jefferson Med. Coll. Mem. ACP, Am. Soc. Clin. Oncology, Pa. Med. Soc., Philadelphia County Med. Soc. Office: 1907 S Broad St Philadelphia PA 19148-2216

ROBBINS, ROBERT R., acute care nurse; b. Torrington, Wyo., Dec. 25, 1954; s. Robert Perry and Helen Francis (Leavitt) R.; children: Stacey, Jeremy, Jeff. ADN, Laramie County Cmty. Coll., Cheyenne, Wyo., 1993. RN, Wyo. Charge nurse LHS, Torrington, Wyo., 1993—. Republican. Mem. LDS Ch.

ROBBINS, STANLEY LEONARD, pathologist, educator; b. Portland, Maine, Feb. 27, 1915. BS, MIT, 1936; MD, Tufts U., 1940. Diplomate Am. Bd. Pathology. Intern Mallory Inst. Pathology, Boston, 1940-41, resident, 1941-44, asst. pathologist, 1945-53, assoc. dir., 1953-66, dir., 1966-72; asst. prof. Sch. Medicine, Boston U., 1947-50, assoc. prof., 1950-57, prof. pathology, 1957-80, chmn. dept. pathology, 1964-80; asst. prof. Med. Sch., Tufts U., Boston, 1947-50; vis. prof. Med. Sch., Harvard U., Boston, 1980—; pathologist Brigham and Women's Hosp., Boston, 1980—; vis. prof. U. Glasgow, Scotland, 1959-60, Hebrew U., Jerusalem, 1976-77; cons. VA Hosp., Boston, 1965-80, Univ. Hosp., Boston, 1970-80. Author: Robbins Pathologic Basis of Disease, 5th edit., 1994, Basic Pathology, 5th edit., 1992, Companion Handbook to Robbins Pathologic Basis of Disease, 2d edit., 1995. Trustee Boston Med. Libr., Combined Jewish Philanthropies; bd. dirs. Jewish Family Children's Svc.; past chmn. rsch. allocation com. Mass. Heart Assn. Fellow Am. Soc. Clin. Pathologists (hon.); mem. AAAS, U.S. and Can. Acad. Pathology (designated Disting. Pathologist 1990), Mass. Med. Soc. (Disting. Leader in Am. Medicine 1980), New Eng. Soc. Pathologists (pres. 1955), Am. Assn. Pathologists (Gold-Headed Cane award 1992), Am. Assn. Med. Mus., Am. Soc. Clin. Investigation, Alpha Omega Alpha. Home: 1010 Memorial Dr Cambridge MA 02138-4859 Office: Brigham and Women's Hosp 75 Francis St Boston MA 02115-6110

ROBERGE, FERNAND ADRIEN, biomedical researcher; b. Thetford Mines, Que., Can., June 11, 1935. BAS, Engr., Poly. Sch. Montreal, Can., 1959, MScA, 1960; PhD in Control Engring., Biomedical Engring., McGill U., 1964. Devel. engr. numerical control Sperry Gyroscope Co., Montreal, 1960-61; from asst. prof. to prof. physiology faculty medicine U. Montreal, 1965-78, prof. biomedical engring., 1978—, dir. biomedical engring. inst. ecole poly., 1978-88, dir. rsch. group biomedical modeling, 1988—; mem. rsch. group neurol. sci. Med. Rsch. Coun. Can. U. Montreal, 1967-75, mem. grant com. biomedical engring., 1971-76; mem. Sci. Coun. Can., 1971-74; mem. sci. com. Can. Heart Found., 1974-77; mem. Killiam Program Can. Coun., 1974-77; mem. elec. engring. com. Nat. Sci. Engring. Rsch. Coun., Can., 1981-83, chmn., 1985-88. Recipient D. W. Ambridge award, 1964, Rousseau award Assn. Can.-France Advancement Sci., 1986, Leon Lortie award, 1987. Fellow IEEE, Can. Med. and Biol. Engring. Soc., Royal Soc. Can.; mem. AAAS, Internat. Fedn. Med. Electronics and Biol. Engring., Can. Physiol. Soc., Biomed. Engring. Soc.

ROBERGE, LAWRENCE FRANCIS, neuroscientist, biotechnology consultant, writer, bioethicist; b. Springfield, Mass., Mar. 16, 1959; s. Donald Richard and Cornelia Marie (Daly) R. BS in Zoology and Psychology cum laude, U. Mass., 1985; MS in Biomed. Sci., U. Mass., Worcester, 1989; Biotech. Studies Cert., Becker Coll., 1994. Cert. radiation safety and protection. Sr. tech. Mass. Gen. Hosp., Boston, 1988; nuclear chemist Interstate Nuclear Svc., Springfield, 1989; tech. specialist NERAC, Tolland, Conn., 1989-93; instr. Assumption Coll., Worcester, 1988-91, Quinsigamond C.C., Worcester, 1989; tchr. Prince Lifeskill Inst., Leicester, Mass., 1988-89; adj. faculty instr. Anna Marie Coll., Paxton, Mass., 1995—, Bay Path Coll., Longmeadow, Mass., 1996—. Author: The Cost of Abortion, 1995. Precinct mem. Ludlow, Mass., 1978-81; bd. dirs. Great Awakening Ministries, Inc., 1994-95. Mem. Internat. Fedn. Advancement of Genetic Engring. and Biotech., N.Y. Acad. Sci., Cath. Assn. Scientists and Engrs., Biotech West (founder), Ctr. for Bioethics and Human Dignity, Soc. Cath. Social Scientists, Mortar Board, Psi Chi. Home: 62 Hubbard St Apt 13 Ludlow MA 01056-2701

ROBERSON, WILLIAM BOYD, osteopath; b. Huntsville, Ala., Sept. 8, 1960; s. Benny Ray and Joan Vivian (Vaughn) Fuller; m. Carolyn Jeanette Eaton; children: Benjamin, Miriam, Timothy, Thomas, Deborah, Johnathan. AS in Biology, Kilgore (Tex.) Coll., 1980; BS in Biology, Stephen F. Austin State U., Nacogdoches, Tex., 1983, MBA, 1987; DO, U. North Tex., Ft. Worth, 1994. Lab. technician Meml. Hosp., Nacogdoches, 1981-90, Woodland Heights Hosp., Lufkin, Tex., 1989-90, Osteo. Med. Ctr. of Tex., Ft. Worth, 1990-94; transitional intern Dwight D. Eisenhower Army Med. Ctr., Ft. Gordon, Ga., 1994—; commd. capt. U.S. Army, 1994—. Mem. Christian Coalition, 1993-95. Recipient Michael A. Calabrese, D.O. Arrowsmith award U. North Tex. Health Sci. Ctr., 1994. Mem. AMA, Am. Osteo. Med. Assn. Republican. Ch. of God. Home: 1919 Stonehenge Dr Hinesville GA 31313

ROBERTIELLO, RICHARD CANDELA, psychiatrist, writer; b. Bklyn., June 20, 1923; s. Attilio and Eleanor (Candela) R.; m. Terril Gangier, May 28, 1990; 1 child by previous marriage, Robert A. BA, Harvard U., 1943; MD, Columbia U., 1946; cert. psychoanalyst, N.Y. Med. Coll., 1954. Diplomate in Psychiatry Am. Bd. of Psychiatry & Neurology. Intern. Morrisania City Hosp., Bronx, N.Y., 1946-47; res. N.Y. State Psychiatric Ins., N.Y.C., 1950-51; fellow N.Y.U. Bellevue, N.Y.C., 1951-52; dir. of Psychiatric Svcs. Long Isl. Consultation Ctr., Forest Hills, N.Y., 1950-75; pvt. practice N.Y.C., 1950—; chmn. bd. of trustees, Long Isl. Inst. for Mental Health, Forest Hills,; mem. adv. coun., Am. Inst. for Psychotherapy and Psychoanalysis, N.Y.C. Author: 11 books, inlcuding Voyage From Leobos, 1959, Your Own True Love, 1978, and A Man in the Making, 1979. Capt. Med. Corps., Army of the U.S., 1948-50, Ft. Knox, Ky. Fellow Am. Psychiatric Assn. (life), Am. Acad. Psychoanalysis; mem. Soc. of Med. Psychoanalysts, Nat. Psychological Assn. for Psychoanalysis, Soc for the Scientific Study of Sex (adv. bd. 1965-75). Home: 25 E 69th St New York NY 10021-4925 Office: 49 E 78th St New York NY 10021-0211

ROBERTIN, HECTOR, clinical psychologist; b. N.Y.C., June 18, 1932; s. Vincent and Maria (Jimenez) R.; m. Linda Green, June 29, 1952 (div. June 1972); 1 child, Hector; m. Thida Kumgun, Aug. 23, 1972. B of Gen. Studies, Chaminade U., 1975; MA, U. No. Colo., 1977; PhD, Union Grad. Sch., Cin., 1979. Lic. psychologist. Enlisted U.S. Army, 1951-71, advanced through grades to sgt., 1967; researcher Inst. Behavioral Sci., Honolulu, 1979-80; instr. Chaminade U., Honolulu, 1980-82; clin. psychologist Hawaii State Dept. Health, Honolulu, 1982-95; corp. exec. officer JHC Cons., Inc., Honolulu, 1985-95, bd. dirs.; instr. U. Hawaii, 1985—. Mem. APA Hawaii Psychol. Assn., Am. Mensa. Democrat. Buddhist.

ROBERTS, ALAN SILVERMAN, orthopedic surgeon; b. N.Y.C., Apr. 20, 1939; s. Joseph William and Fannie (Margolies) S.; BA, Conn. Wesleyan U., 1960; MD, Jefferson Med. Coll., 1966; children: Michael Eric, Daniel Ian. Rotating intern, Lankenau Hosp., Phila., 1966-67; resident orthopaedics Tulane U. Med. Coll., 1967-71; pvt. practice medicine, specializing in orthopedics and hand surgery, Los Angeles, 1971—; mem. clin. faculty UCLA Med. Coll., 1971-76. Served with AUS, 1961. Recipient Riordan Hand fellowship, 1969; Boyes Hand fellowship, 1971. Mem. Riordan Hand Soc., Western Orthopaedic Assn., A.C.S., AMA, Calif., Los Angeles County Med. Assns., Am. Acad. Orthopaedic Surgeons. Republican. Jewish. Contbr. articles to profl. jours.

ROBERTS, ANTHONY HOWARD NORMAN, plastic surgeon; b. Woodford Green, Essex, Eng., Nov. 15, 1938; s. Kenneth Arthur Norman and Ivy Beatrice Maude (Leggatt) R.; m. Fiona Edith Vivian Onians, Mar. 24, 1972; children: Clare, Natasha. BS in Engring., U. Leeds, Eng., 1961; BA, MA in Med. Sci., U. Cambridge, Eng., 1969; BA, MA, U. Oxford, 1969, B.M. BCh., 1972. Lectr. in chem. engring. U. Surrey, Eng., 1964-67; registrar burn unit Birmingham Accident Hosp., Eng., 1974-76; registrar plastic surgery Royal Victoria Infirmary, Newcastle Upon Tyne, Eng., 1978-80; sr. registrar plastic surgery St. James's Hosp. Leeds, St. Luke's Hosp. Bradford, Eng., 1980-85; rsch. fellow Microsurgery Rsch. Inst., Melbourne, Australia, 1981-82; dir. Nuffield Burn Unit, Microsurgery Rsch. Inst., 1985—; hon. lectr. dept. biomed. scis. U. Bradford, 1984—; advisor for a TV program, 1988. Co-author: Bander's Aid, 1986; contbr. articles to profl. jours. Rsch. scholar U. Cambridge, 1961-64. Fellow Royal Coll. Surgeons Eng. (Ethicon Travelling fellow 1981); mem. Brit. Assn. Plastic Surgeons, Brit. Soc. for Surgery of the Hand, Brit. Burn Assn., Brit. Microsurg. Assn., Brit. Ornithological Union, Hawks Club (Cambridge, Eng.). Home: The Old House, Buckinghamshire, Whitchurch HP22 4JX, England Office: stoke Mandeville Hosp, Aylesbury HP21 8AL, England

ROBERTS, CALVIN W., ophthalmologist; b. N.Y.C., Sept. 7, 1952; s. Murray M. and Joyce A. (Marcus) Warshavsky; m. Andrea Colvin Roberts, Mar. 16, 1980; children: David, Lindsay, Joanna. BA, Princeton U., 1974; MD, Columbia U., 1978. Resident in ophthalmology Edward S. Harkness Eye Inst., N.Y.C., 1978-81; fellow in corneal disease Harvard Med. Sch., Boston, 1981-82; from asst. prof. to prof. ophthalmology Cornell U. Med. Coll., N.Y.C., 1982—; med. dir. Flight for Sight, N.Y.C., 1983—; med. bd. dirs. Eye Bank for Sight Restoration, N.Y.C., 1985—; cons. in field. Author: Advances in Cataract Surgery, 1988; contbr. articles to profl. jours.; patentee in field. Fellow Am. Acad. Ophthalmology, Am. Soc. Cataract and Refractive Surgeons, Assn. for Rsch. in Vision & Ophthalmology. Office: Cornell U Med Coll 520 E 70th St New York NY 10021

ROBERTS, CATHLEEN DOMAN, developmental pediatrician, educator; b. Charleroi, Pa., Apr. 12, 1960; d. Earl Andrew and Lucille Catherine (Lucas) Doman; m. Stanley Bruce Roberts, June 1, 1990. BA, Washington and Jefferson Coll., 1982; DO, Phila. Coll. Osteopathy, 1986. Diplomate Am. Bd. Pediats. Intern Meml. Hosp., York, Pa., 1986-87; pediat. resident Geisinger Med. Ctr., Danville, Pa., 1987-90; fellow in pediat. rehab. U. So. Calif., Downey, 1990-91; fellow in devel. pediats. U. Va., Charlottesville, 1991-94; asst. prof. pediats. U. Tex. Health Scis. Ctr., San Antonio, 1994—; mem. adv. bd. Tex. Assistive Tech. Partnership, Austin, 1994—; mem. sci. adv. bd. Winston Sch., San Antonio, 1994-95. Author chpts. to books; contbr. articles to profl. jours. Vol. Children's Assn. Maximum Potential, Comfort, Tex., 1994—; mem. adv. bd. Parent Info. Exch., San Antonio, 1995—. Tng. Award fellow United Cerebral Palsy, 1992. Fellow Am. Acad. Pediats., Am. Acad. Cerebral Palsy and Devel. Medicine; mem. Am. Coll. Osteo. Pediatricians (sr.), Irish and Am. Pediat. Soc. Office: U Tex Health Sci Ctr 7703 Floyd Curl Dr San Antonio TX 78284

ROBERTS, CHRISTOPHER W., internist, hospital administrator; b. Lake City, Fla., Mar. 6, 1955; s. Edward Micreery and Joan (Warthling) R.; m. Catherine Caldarella, May 6, 1984; children: Hannah, Everett. BS, U. Cin., 1977; MD, Yale U., 1982. Diplomate Am. Bd. Internal Medicine. Resident in medicine R.I. Hosp., Providence, 1982-85; staff physician North Country Hosp., Newport, Vt., 1985-89, chief medicine, 1987-89; staff physician Cmty. Health Care Plan, New Haven, Conn., 1989-93; clin. instr. medicine Yale U., New Haven, 1989-93; dir. emergency svcs. Nanticoke Meml. Hosp., Seaford, Del., 1993—. Inventor in field. Vol. Himalayan Rescue Assn., Nepal, 1989. With USPHS, 1985-89. Mem. ACP, Am. Coll. Emergency Physicians, Am. Coll. Physician Execs. Home: 39 N Shore Dr Seaford DE 19973-1851 Office: Nanticoke Memll Hosp 801 Middleford Rd Seaford DE 19973

ROBERTS, DAVID DUNCAN, biochemist; b. Indiana, Pa., July 1, 1954; s. David and Sarah Edith (Nicely) R.; divorced; children: Benjamin Roberts, James Roberts; m. Nancy Smyth Templeton, Mar. 6, 1993; children: Lizette Templeton, Renee Templeton. BS Chemistry, MIT, 1976; PhD Biol. Chemistry, U. Mich., 1983. Sr. rsch. assoc. Clin. Assays/Div. Travenol Lab., Cambridge, Mass., 1976-79; staff fellow NIDDK, NIH, Bethesda, Md., 1984-86; sr. staff fellow NIDDK, NIH, Bethesda, 1987, rsch. chemist, 1987-88; chief, biochem. pathology sect., lab. of pathology Nat. Cancer Inst., NIH, Bethesda, 1988—; mem. NIDDK Cystic Fibrosis SCOR rev. com., NIH, 1994; ad hoc mem. pathobiochemistry study sect., NIH, 1989-95. Editorial bd.: Jour. Biol. Chemistry, 1995—; editor: Cell Surface Glycoconjugates: Structure and Function, 1993; contbr. articles to profl. jours.; patentee in field. Recipient Lee Murphy Meml. prize U. Mich., 1985, Walter J. Johnson Ann. prize for rsch. in life scis., Harcourt, Brace, Jovanovich, Phila., 1987. Mem. Am. Soc. Biochemistry and Molecular Biology, The Soc. for Glycobiology, AAAS. Office: NIH 10 Center Dr MSC 1500 Bethesda MD 20892-1500

ROBERTS, DONALD WILLIAM, orthopedic surgeon; b. L.A., Sept. 22, 1952; s. John D. and Edith M. (Johnson) R.; m. Barbara Allen, Aug. 28, 1982; children: Emily, Margaret, Heather, D. Allen. BA, Stanford U., 1975, MD, 1980. Intern U. Wash., Seattle, 1980-81; lectr. dept. anatomy Stanford (Calif.) U., 1981-82, resident in surgery, 1982; resident in surgery Harvard Combined Orthopedic Program, Boston, 1982-85; chief resident in orthopedic surgery Mass. Gen. Hosp., Boston, 1985; fellow in sports medicine Brigham & Womens Hosp., Boston, 1986; pvt. practice N.W. Surg. Specialists, Vancouver, Wash., 1986—; asst. instr. Harvard Med. Sch., Boston, 1985; team physician Portland (Oreg.) Trailblazers, 1994—. Contbr. articles to profl. jours.; reviewer Jour. Bone and Joint Surgery, 1987—, assoc. editor, 1992-95. Fellow Am. Acad. Orthopedic Surgery, ACS; mem. Am. Assn. Tissue Banking, Wash. State Med. Soc., AMA, NBA Team Physicians Soc., Phi Beta Kappa. Office: NW Surg Specialists 505 NE 87th Ave Vancouver WA 98664

ROBERTS, DORIS EMMA, epidemiologist, consultant; b. Toledo, Dec. 28, 1915; d. Frederic Constable and Emma Selina (Reader) R. Diploma, Peter Bent Brigham Sch. Nursing, Boston, 1938; BS, Geneva Coll., Beaver Falls, Pa., 1944; MPH, U. Minn., 1958; PhD, U. N.C., 1967. RN, Mass. Staff nurse Vis. Nurse Assn., New Haven, 1938-40; sr. nurse Neighborhood House, Millburn, N.J., 1942-45; supr. Tb Baltimore County Dept. Health, Towson, Md., 1945-46; Tb cons. Md. State Dept. Health, Balt., 1946-50; cons., chief nurse Tb program USPHS, Washington, 1950-57; cons. divsn. nursing USPHS, 1958-63; chief nursing practice br. Health Resources Adminstrn., HEW, Bethesda, Md., 1966-75; adj. prof. U. N.C. Sch. Pub. Health, 1975-92; cons. WHO, 1961-82. Contbr. articles to profl. jours. With USPHS, 1945-75. Recipient Disting. Alumna award Geneva Coll., 1971, Disting. Svc. award USPHS, 1971, Outstanding Achievement award U. Minn., 1983. Fellow APHA (v.p. 1978-79, Disting. Svc. award Pub. Health Nursing sect. 1975, Sedgwick Meml. medal 1979), Am. Acad. Nursing (hon. fellow); mem. Inst. Medicine of NAS, Common Cause, LWV, Delta Omega. Democrat. Episcopalian. Home: Apt 1112 9707 Old Georgetown Rd Bethesda MD 20814-1727

ROBERTS, (RUTH) ELEANOR STERETT, osteopathic physician; b. Chgo., July 6, 1921; d. Dwight and Edith (Maine) Sterett; m. Edward Morse Roberts, Oct. 9, 1948; children: Alfred D., Marjorie R. Carpenter, James R. BA, Allegheny Coll., 1943; cert. meteorology, MIT, 1944; DO, Coll. Osteo. Medicine, Kirksville, Mo., 1950. Physician pvt. practice Queen City, Mo., 1950—; mem. bd. N.E. Mo. Home Health Agy., Kirksville, Mo., 1974-87. Bd. dirs. N.E. Mo. Libr. Svcs. Kahoka, 1974-82, pres.; pres. Queen City Sr. Housing Bd., 1968-76. Lt. W (A), USNR, 1943-46. Named Woman of Yr. Schuyler Bus. and Profl. Women, Lancaster, Mo., 1972. Mem. Am. Osteo. Assn. (life), Mo. Assn. Osteo. Physicians and Surgeons (life), N.E. Mo. Osteo. Assn. (life, parliamentarian 1988—), Order Eastern Star (worthy matron 1961, 83-87, treas. 1990—), Delta Omega (nat. pres. 1961-63, nat. sec. 1984-89).

ROBERTS, ELIZABETH H., podiatrist, author; b. Bklyn. m. Nathan Wasserheit (dec.); 1 dau., Judith N. Wasserheit. D. Podiatric Medicine, L.I. U., 1943. Pvt. practice podiatry, N.Y.C., 1943-89; prof. emeritus, N.Y. Coll. Podiatric Medicine; established diabetic foot clinic N.Y. Infirmary, 1949; chairperson dept. regional anatomy, M.J. Lewi Coll. Podiatric Medicine, 1954-66, chairperson dept. practice adminstrn., 1945-51. Bd. trustee, vice chairperson N.Y. Coll. Podiatric Medicine, 1987-96. Author: Manual of Practice Administration, 1949; On Your Feet, 1975, put on cassettes for blind, 1977, N.Y. College of Podiatric Medicine--From Then to Now, 1996; contbr. articles to profl. publs. Fellow Am. Soc. Podiatric Medicine, Am. Acad. Podiatry, Am. Assn. Podiatry Adminstrn.; mem. N.Y. State Bd. Podiatry (chairperson 1979-81). Address: 210 W 90th St New York NY 10024-1243

ROBERTS, GLENN DALE, microbiologist, educator; b. Gilmer, Tex., Apr. 9, 1943; s. B. C. and Mary Fern (Baker) R.; m. Kathleen Louise Brackin, Oct. 13, 1973; children: Michael Glenn, Heather Michelle, Megan Louise. BS, North Tex. State U., 1967; MS, U. Okla., 1969, PhD, 1972. Diplomate Am. Bd. Med. Microbiology. Fellow dept. community medicine Coll. Medicine U. Ky., Lexington, 1971-72; dir. clin. mycology and mycobacteriology labs. May Clinic, Rochester, Minn., 1972—; prof. Mayo Med. Sch., Rochester, 1986—; advisor Nat. Com. for Clin. Lab. Standards, Villanova, Pa., 1985-90. Co-author: Practical Laboratory Mycology, 1985. Recipient Meridian award for Clin. Mycology, Med. Mycol. Soc. of Ams., 1988. Fellow Am. Acad. Microbiology; mem. Am. Soc. Microbiology, Am. Soc. Clin. Pathologists, Internat. Soc. Human and Animal Mycology. Lutheran. Home: 1751 Walden Ln SW Rochester MN 55902-0901 Office: Mayo Clinic 200 1st St SW Rochester MN 55905-0001

ROBERTS, HYMAN JACOB, internist, researcher, author, historian, publisher; b. Boston, May 29, 1924; s. Benjamin and Eva (Sherman) R.; m. Carol Antonia Klein, Aug. 9, 1953; children: David, Jonathan, Mark, Stephen, Scott, Pamela. M.D. cum laude, Tufts U., 1947. Diplomate Am. Bd. Internal Medicine. Intern, resident Boston City Hosp., 1947-49; resident Mcpl. Hosp., Washington, 1949-50; rsch. fellow, instr. med. Tufts Med. Sch., Boston, 1948-49, Georgetown Med. Sch., Washington, 1949-50; fellow in medicine Lahey Clinic, Boston, 1950-51; mem. active staff Good Samaritan and St. Mary's Hosps., West Palm Beach, Fla., 1955—; dir. Palm Beach Inst. Med. Rsch., West Palm Beach, 1964—, pres., Sunshine Sentinel Press, Inc. lectr. two day seminar on The New Frontiers in Legal Medicine, Seminar on Defense Against Alzheimer's Disease. U.S. rep. Council of Europe for Driving Standards, 1972. Author: Difficult Diagnosis, Spanish and Italian edits, 1958; The Causes, Ecology and Prevention of Traffic Accidents, 1971, Is Vasectomy Safe?, 1979, Aspartame (NutraSweet): Is It Safe?, 1989, Sweet'ner Dearest, 1992, Is Vasectomy Worth the Risk?, 1993, Mega Vitamin E: Is It Safe?, 1994, The Spirit of Modern Taiwan, 1994, West Palm Beach: Centennial Reflections, 1994, A Guide to Personal Peace, 1994, Defense Against Alzheimers Disease, 1995, The CACOF Conspiracy, 1996—, Health and Wealth, Palm Beach Style, 1996—; (play) My Wife, The Politician; assoc. editor: Tufts Med. Alumni Bull, Boston, 1978-87, Nutrition Health Rev.; contbr. sci. and med. articles to profl. and theol. jours. Pres. Jewish Community Day Sch., West Palm Beach, Fla., 1975-76; disting. mem. pres. council U. Fla., Gainesville, 1974—; founder, dir. Jewish Fedn. Palm Beach County, West Palm Beach, 1960-72. Served to lt. USNR, 1951-54. Named Fla. Outstanding Young Man Jr. C. of C. Fla., 1958; hon. Ky. col.; recipient Gold Share cert. and silver certs. Inst. Agr. and Food Scis., U. Fla., 1974-78; Paul Harris fellow Rotary Found., 1980. Fellow ACP, Am. Coll. Chest Physicians, Am. Coll. Nutrition, Stroke Council; mem. AMA, Am. Acad. Neurology, Endocrine Soc., Am. Diabetes Assn., Am. Heart Assn., Am. Fedn. Clin. Research, Am. Coll. Angiology (gov. 1981), Am. Coll. Legal Medicine, Pan Am. Med. Assn. (chmn. endocrinology 1982), So. Med. Assn., N.Y. Acad. Scis., Am. Physicians Fellowship of Israel Med. Assn., Confrerie de la Chaine des Rotisseurs, Alpha Omega Alpha, Sigma Xi. Club: Governors of West Palm Beach (a founder), Executive (founder). Lodges: Rotary; B'nai B'rith, Order St. George (knight of magistral grace 1992). Research in med. diagnosis, diabetes, hypoglycemia, postvasectomy state, Vitamin E metabolism, pentachlorophenol, heavy metal toxicity, narcolepsy, traffic accidents, thrombophlebitis, aspartame, Alzheimer's disease, brain tumors, nutrition and bioethics. Home: 6708 Pamela Ln West Palm Beach FL 33405-4175 Office: Palm Beach Inst Med Rsch 300 27th St West Palm Beach FL 33407-5202 also: Sunshine Sentinel Press Inc PO Box 17799 West Palm Beach FL 33416

ROBERTS, JAMES LEWIS, medical sciences educator; b. Lima, Peru, Oct. 23, 1951; U.S. citizen; s. David and Mary (Fuller) R.; m. Mariann Blum, Mar. 7, 1986. BS, Colo. State U., 1973; PhD, U. Oreg., 1977. Fellow U. Calif., San Francisco, 1977-79; asst. prof. Columbia U., N.Y.C., 1979-86, assoc. prof., 1986; dir., prof. Mt. Sinai Sch. Medicine, N.Y.C., 1986-90, prof., 1990—; cons. Calif. Biotech., Mountain View, Calif., 1986-88, NIH, Bethesda, Md., 1979—. Recipient Golden Lamport award, Excellence Basic Sci.; NIH rsch. grantee, 1979—, NSF rsch. grantee 1981-84, 95—, Mellon Found. rsch. grantee, 1980-84. Mem. AAAS, Soc. for Neurosci., Endocrine Soc., Internat. Endocrine Soc., N.Y. Acad. Scis., Am. Soc. Biochemists and Molecular Biologists. Office: Mt Sinai Sch Medicine 1 Gustave L Levy Pl New York NY 10029-6504

ROBERTS, JOHN H., physician; b. Oak Park, Ill., Mar. 10, 1929; s. Harry W. and Mary E. Roberts; m. Julianna Roberts, Sept. 28, 1963 (div. Jan. 1979); children: Linda, Sandra. DSc in Naprapathy, D in Naprapathy, Chgo. Coll. Naprapathy, 1949; AS cum laude, Wright Jr. Coll., Chgo., 1953; postgrad., U. Ill., Chgo., 1953-54; DO, Chgo. Coll. Osteo. Medicine, 1959. Bd. cert. in family medicine Am. Osteo. Bd. Family Physicians. Pvt. practice family medicine Chgo., 1960-92; clinic physician family medicine dept. Chgo. Osteo. Hosp., 1992-93; staff physician urgent care and occupl. medicine St. Francisc Hosp. Blue Island, Ill., 1993—; asst. prof. family medicine Midwestern U.-Chgo. Coll. Osteo. Medicine, Chgo. and Downers Grove, Ill., 1960-93. Recipient Cert. Appreciation, Ill. Selective Svc. Sys., 1971. Fellow Am. Osteo. Colls. Family Physicians; mem. AMA, Am. Osteo. Assn., Am. Coll. Osteo. Family Physicians, Am. Osteo. Coll. Occupl. Medicine and Preventive Medicine, Ill. Assn. Osteo. Physicians and Surgeons (pres. 1967, Disting. Svc. award 1984), Ill. State Med. Soc., Chgo. Med. Soc. Office: St Francis Family Health 13755 S Cicero Ave Crestwood IL 60445

ROBERTS, KENNETH BOYETT, pharmacy educator; b. Sharon, Tenn., Nov. 7, 1944; s. James Russell and Blanche (Boyett) R.; m. Kittye Louise Rice, Oct. 20, 1968; children: Millicent Boyett, LouAnne Rice. BS in Pharmacy, U. Tenn., Memphis, 1964-67; MBA, U. Tenn., Knoxville, 1973; PhD, U. Miss., Oxford, 1975. Prof. pharmacy U. Tenn., Memphis, 1979-89, assoc. dean, 1984-89; teaching asst. Sch. Pharmacy U. Miss., Oxford, 1973-75, prof., 1989—, dean, 1989—; asst. prof. U. Tex., Austin, 1975-77; exec. dir. Mo. Found. Pharm. Care, St. Louis, 1977-79, Am. Coll. Apothecaries, Memphis, 1981-85; pres. West Tenn. Health Edn. Ctr., Memphis, 1987-88; cons. Chapman Drug Co., 1985-92, Cardinal Health, 1992-96, Mass. Soc. Cons. Pharmacists, Boston, 1988-92. Author: Establishing a Professional Pharmacy Practice, 1980, Managing Support Personnel in Community Pharmacy, 1982, Guidelines for Marketing a Pharmacy Practice, 1983, Guidelines for Pharmacy Management by Self Study, 1984, Guidelines for Establishing Pharmacy Services for Hospice, 1987. Asst. dir. Pharmacy, U.S. Naval Hosp., Great Lakes, Ill., dir. of Pharmacy, U.S. Naval Hosp., Taipei, Taiwan. Lt. USN, 1967-71. Charles R. Walgreen Meml. fellow Am. Found. Pharm. Edn., 1974-75. Fellow Am. Coll. Apothecaries; mem. Internat. Fedn. Pharmacists, Am. Pharm. Assn., Am. Soc. Hosp. Pharmacists, Am. Assn. Pharm. Scientists, Am. Assn. Colls. Pharmacy (chmn. counsel of deans), Miss. Pharmacists Assn., Miss. Soc. Hosp. Pharmacists, Tenn. Pharmacists Assn., Sigma Xi, Pi Kappa Alpha, Kappa Psi (nat. pres. 1987-89, Citation of Appreciation 1989), Rho Chi, Phi Lambda Sigma, Phi Kappa Phi. Home: PO Box 901 Oxford MS 38655-0901 Office: U Miss Sch Pharmacy Natural Products Ctr Rm 1017 University MS 38677

ROBERTS, LANA MARCINE, hospital administrator, nurse; b. Jackson, Tenn., Feb. 5, 1945; d. Otto G. and Zula D. (Beller) Umlauf; m. James L. Roberts, June 5, 1966; children: James L. II, Jennifer L., Julie L. BSN, So. Coll. 7th-day Adventists, Colledgedale, Tenn., 1967; MPH, Loma Linda U., 198l; cert. in health svcs. adminstrn., U. Ala., Birmingham, 1983. Staff nurse U.S. Army Hosp., Ft. Knox, Ky., and Ft. Dix, N.J., 1968-70; clin. instr. So. Coll. Seventh-day Adventists, Orlando, Fla., 1970-72; dir. Sch. Practical Nursing, Fla. Hosp. Med. Ctr., Orlando, 1972-79, dir. nursing, 1979-80, v.p., 1980—; mem. adj. faculty U. Fla. Coll. Nursing, Gainesville, 1985—; mem. adj. faculty health svcs. adminstrn. U. Minn., Mpls., 1986—. Mem. Am. Nurses Assn. (cert.), Am. Coll. Healthcare Execs., Med. Group Mgmt. Assn., Am. Soc. for Hosp. Nursing Svc. Adminstrn., Am. Hosp. Assn. Soc. for Ambulatory Care Profls., Am. Bus. Women's Assn., NAFE, Sigma Theta Tau. Home: 403 N Shine Ave Orlando FL 32803-5425 Office: Fla Hosp Med Ctr 60l E Rollins Ave Orlando FL 32803

ROBERTS, LARRY SPURGEON, biological sciences educator, zoologist; b. Texon, Tex., June 30, 1935; s. E. Fowler and Frances Wray (Huggins) R.; m. Maria Elek, Feb. 7, 1962; children: Gregory Lorinc, Bruce Tibor, Teresa Margit, Eric Miklos. B.S., So. Meth. U., 1956; M.S. (NSF predoctoral fellow), U. Ill., 1958; D.Sc. (NIH predoctoral fellow), Johns Hopkins U., 1961. Cert. scuba instr. Nat. Assn. Underwater Instrs. Asst. prof. zoology U. Mass., Amherst, 1963-69, assoc. prof., 1969-75, prof., 1975-79; prof. biol. scis. Tex. Tech U., Lubbock, 1979-90; chmn. dept. Tex. Tech U., 1979-84; adj. prof. biol. scis. U. Miami, 1990—, Fla. Internat. U., 1990-93. Author: (with others) Foundations of Parasitology, 1977, 5th edit., 1996, Integrated Principles of Zoology, 1979, 10th edit., 1997, Biology of Animals, 1982, 6th edit., 1994, The Underwater World of Sport Diving, 1991, Animal Diversity, 1994. Mem. Amherst Dem. Town Com., 1968-79, vice chmn., 1972-76; mem. Amherst Town Meeting, 1966-76; mem. Amherst Zoning Bd. Appeals, 1972-75, vice chmn., 1972-75; recorder West Tex. Dems., 1985-86; mem. Dade County Dem. Exec. Com., 1991—. NIH postdoctoral trainee, 1961-63; NIH fellow, 1969-70; recipient Disting. Service cert. Mass. Tchrs. Assn., 1979. Mem. AAAS, ACLU (vice chmn. Hampshire County chpt. 1966-68, bd. dirs. Lubbock chpt. 1985-89, vice chmn. 1988-89, bd. dirs. Miami, Fla. chpt. 1991—, Fla. State bd. dirs.), Am. Soc. Parasitologists (Henry Baldwin Ward medal 1971, council mem. at large 1980-83, v.p. 1984-85, 96—), Am. Micros. Soc. (v.p. 1974-75, exec. com. 1978-81), Mass. Soc. Profs. (pres. 1977-78), Soc. Protozoologists, Am. Soc. Tropical Medicine and Hygiene, Wildlife Disease Assn., Southwestern Assn. Parasitologists (v.p. 1982, pres. 1983), Southeastern Soc. Parasitologists (pres. elect 1993, pres. 1994), Internat. Soc. Reef Studies, Crustacean Soc., Am. Acad. Underwater Scis., Sigma Xi. Home: 27700 SW 164th Ave Homestead FL 33031-2846

ROBERTS, LEIGH MILTON, psychiatrist; b. Jacksonville, Ill., June 9, 1925; s. Victor Harold and Ruby Harriet (Kelsey) R.; m. Marilyn Edith Kadow, Sept. 6, 1946; children: David, Carol Roberts Mayer, Paul, Nancy Mills. B.S., U. Ill., 1945, M.D., 1947. Diplomate: Am. Bd. Psychiatry and Neurology. Intern St. Francis Hosp., Peoria, Ill., 1947-48; gen. practice medicine Macomb, Ill., 1948-50; resident in psychiatry U. Wis. Hosps., Madison, 1953-56; staff psychiatrist Mendota (Wis.) State Hosp., 1956-58; mem. faculty U. Wis. Med. Sch., Madison, 1959-89; prof. psychiatry U. Wis. Med. Sch., 1971-89, acting chmn. dept., 1972-75; mem. spl. rev. bd. Wis. Parole Bd. Sex Crimes Law, 1962-88, forensic cons., 1988—; mem. Dane County Devel. Disabilities Bd., 1962-66, Wis. Planning Com. Mental Health, 1963-65, Wis. Planning Com. Health, 1969-71, Wis. Planning Com. Vocat. Rehab., 1966-68, Wis. Planning Com. Health Centers, 1967-71, Wis. Mental Health Adv. Com., 1973-78; bd. dirs. Methodist Hosp., Madison, Dane County Rehab. House, Dane County Assn. Mental Health; cons. in field. Editor: Community Psychiatry, 1966, Comprehensive Mental Health, 1968; contbr. articles profl. jours. Pres. Wis. Council Chs., 1976-78; bd. dirs. Madison Campus Ministry, St. Benedict Center; trustee N.Central Coll., Naperville, Ill. Served with USNR, 1943-45, 50-53. Decorated Bronze Star, Purple Heart. Fellow Am. Psychiat. Assn. (bd. trustees 1981-84), Wis. Psychiat. Assn. (pres. 1967). Methodist. Home and Office: 722A Sauk Ridge Trl Madison WI 53705-1155

ROBERTS, LLOYD EUGENE, obstetrician, gynecologist; b. Sterling, Colo., June 24, 1943; s. James Myrl and Ruby Vaye (Haynes) R.; married June 13, 1965 (div. 1985); Benjamin Andrew, Elizabeth Anne. BA, U. Colo., 1965; MD, U. Colo., Denver, 1969; postgrad., U. N.C., Wilmington, 1991—. Diplomate Am. Bd. Ob-Gyn. Intern in surgery Hartford (Conn.) Hosp., 1969-70, resident ob-gyn., 1970-73; physician Hartford (Conn.) Ob-Gyn Group, P.C., 1973-78, S.E. Ob-Gyn. Assocs., P.A., Wilmington, N.C., 1978-92; pvt. practice Wilmington, 1992—; clin. assoc. prof. U. N.C., Chapel Hill, 1980—; chmn. dept. ob-gyn. New Hanover Regional Med. Ctr., Wilmington, 1985-87. Mem. adminstrv. bd. Grace United Meth. Ch., Wilmington, 1982-83; mem. Met. Opera Guild, N.Y.C., 1961—. Fellow Am. Coll. Ob-Gyn.; mem. AMA, N.C. Med. Soc., New Hanover County Med. Soc. Republican. Methodist. Home: 914 Bayshore Dr Wilmington NC 28405-9425 Office: 1928 S 16th St Wilmington NC 28401-6611

ROBERTS, LYNNE JEANINE, physician; b. St. Louis, Apr. 19, 1952; d. H. Clarke and Dorothy June (Cockrum) R.; m. Richard Allen Beadle Jr., July 18, 1981; children: Richard Andrew, Erica Roberts. BA with distinction, Ind. U., 1974, MD, 1978. Diplomate Am. Bd. Dermatology, Am. Bd. Pediatrics, Am. Bd. Laser Surgery. Intern in pediats. Children's Med. Ctr., Dallas, 1978-79, resident in pediats., 1979-80; resident in dermatology U. Tex. Southwestern Med. Ctr., Dallas, 1980-83, chief resident in dermatology, 1982-83, asst. instr. dermatology and pediatrics, 1983-84, asst. prof., 1984-90, assoc. prof., 1990—; physician Cons. Dermatol. Specialists, Dallas, 1990-93; pres. Lynne J. Roberts, MD, PA, Dallas, 1993—; dir. dermatology Children's Med. Ctr., Dallas, 1986—; dermatology sect. chief Med. City Dallas Hosp., 1994-95, 95—. Contbr. articles to profl. jours., chpts. to books. Recipient Scholastic Achievement Citation Am. Med. Women's Assn., 1978. Fellow Am. Acad. Dermatology, Am. Acad. Pediatrics, Am. Soc. Laser Medicine and Surgery (bd. dirs. 1994—); mem. Soc. Pediatric Dermatology, Am. Soc. Dermatologic Surgery, Tex. Med. Assn., Dallas Zool. Soc., Dallas Arboretum, Kappa Alpha Theta, Alpha Omega Alpha. Office: 7777 Forest Ln Ste B314 Dallas TX 75230-2518

ROBERTS, MARGARET MARY, rehabilitation physician, educator; b. Milw., Aug. 12, 1956; d. Francis Henry and Rosemary Ann (Kleinke) P.; m. Mark A. Roberts, Dec. 27, 1985; children: Alexander Preston, Kaitlin Marie. BS summa cum laude, U. Wis., La Crosse, 1978; MS, U. Okla. Health Sci. Ctr., 1983, PhD, 1989, MD, 1989. Diplomate Am. Bd. Physical Medicine and Rehabilitation, Am. Bd. Electrodiagnostic Medicine.; lic. phys. therapist. Intern U. Okla., 1989-90; resident phys. medicine and rehab. Med. Coll. Wis., 1990-91, chief resident, 1991-92, fellow, 1993-94, asst. prof. phys. medicine and rehab., 1994—; chief, phys. medicine and rehab. Zablocki VAMC, Milw., 1994—. Contbr. articles to sci. jours. including Muscle and Nerve, Am. Jour. PM&R, others; reviewer Archives of PM&R. Dean McGee MD-PhD scholar U. Okla., 1983-89; Harris Rsch. fellow U. Okla., 1982. Fellow Amer. Acad. Phys. Medicine and Rehab., Am. Acad. Electrodiagnostic Medicine; mem. Assn. Acad. Physiatrists Am. Congress Phys. Medicine and Rehab., Am. Coll. Sports Medicine, Wis. State Phys. Medicine and Rehab. Soc. Office: Zablocki VAMC PM&RS 117 5000 West National Ave Milwaukee WI 53295

ROBERTS, MARY BELLE, clinical social worker; b. Akron, Ohio, Sept. 27, 1923; d. Joseph Gill and Inez Wilson (Garvey) Roberts; BS, U. Mich., 1948, MSW, 1950. Cert. social worker, Md., lic. clin. social worker, Fla. Instr. dept. psychiatry U. Ala. Med. Coll., 1950-53; psychiat. social worker divsn. mental hygiene Ala. Dept. Pub. Health, 1950-52, acting dir., dir., 1952-53; sr. psychiat. social worker bur. mental health divsn. cmty. svc. Pa. Dept. Welfare, 1954-55; cons. psychiat. social work cmty. svc. br. NIMH, USPHS, HEW, 1955-64; pvt. practice psychiat. social work, 1964-68; caseworker Family Svc., Miami, Fla., 1968-70, Family and Childrens Svc., Miami, 1971-75; casework cons. United Family and Childrens Svcs., Miami, 1975-85; clin. social worker Family Counseling Svcs., Miami, 1985-90; pvt. practice clin. social work, 1990—; lic. clin. social worker Apogee, Inc., 1994-96. Home: 8126 SW 105th Pl Ocala FL 34481-9132

ROBERTS, MARY LOU, school psychologist; b. Green Bay, Wis., Sept. 28, 1950; d. Elmer David and Leona Theodora (Puyleart) DeGrand. BA in Elem. Edn. and English, U. Wis., Oshkosh, 1972, student, 1977; MS in Counseling Psychology, U. Cen. Tex., 1989; student, U. Hawaii, 1988. Lic. sch. counselor, Tex.; lic. prof. counselor, Tex.; lic. marriage and family therapist, Tex.; cert. tchr., Tex., Wis., Hawaii. Kindergarten tchr. Howard-Suamico ISD, Green Bay, 1972-78; elem. tchr. St. Anthony's Sch., Kalihi, Hawaii, 1978-80, Ave. E. Copperas Cove (Tex.) ISD, 1983-85; elem. tchr. Killeen (Tex.) ISD, 1985-89, sch. psychologist, 1989—; parent teaching cons. Chpt. I Killeen ISD, 1989—, tchr. inservice training, 1989—, child psychologist, 1989—, cons. family and community counselor, 1989—, community speaker, 1988—. Author: (handbook) Counseling Sessions for Small Groups, 1990; editor, reviewer: Let's Learn More About Responsibility, 1991. Vol. Families In Crisi Inc., Killeen, 1987-89; presenter Family Fair Killeen Ind. Sch. dist., 1989; mentor for two at-risk children in Killeen; sch. bd. mem. St. Joseph Sch., Killeen. Mem. AACD, Am. Bus. Women of Am. (scholarship 1985, ways and means com. chmn. Globe chpt. 1986), Tex. Fedn. Tchrs. U. Cen. Tex. Alumni Assn., Tex. Assn. Counseling Devel., Tex. Sch. Counselor Assn., Mid-Tex. Assn. for Counseling Devel. (sec. 1990-92). Democrat. Roman Catholic.

ROBERTS, MELVILLE PARKER, JR., neurosurgeon, educator; b. Phila., Oct. 15, 1931; s. Melville Parker and Marguerite Louise (Reimann) R.; m. Sigrid Marianne Magnusson, Mar. 27, 1954; children: Melville Parker III, Julia Pell, Erik Emerson. BS, Washington and Lee U., 1953; MD, Yale U., 1957. Diplomate: Am. Bd. Neurol. Surgery. Intern Yale Med. Ctr., 1957, neurosurg. resident, 1958-60, 62-64, Am. Cancer Soc. fellow in neurosurgery, 1962-64, instr., 1964; asst. prof. surgery Sch. Medicine U. Va., Charlottesville, 1965-69; practice medicine specializing in neurol. surgery Hartford, Conn., 1970—; mem. sr. staff Hartford Hosp., John Dempsey Hosp.; asst. prof. surgery Sch. Medicine U. Conn., Farmington, 1970-71; assoc. prof. U. Conn., 1972-75, assoc. prof. neurology, 1974-77, chmn. divsn. neurosurgery, 1971-84, prof. surgery, 1975—, acting chmn. dept. neurology, 1973-77, acting chmn. dept. surgery, 1974-77, William Beecher Scoville prof. neurosurgery, 1976—; James Hudson Brown rsch. fellow Yale U., 1957. Author: Atlas of the Human Brain in Section, 1970, 2d edition, 1987; mem. editorial bd.: Conn. Medicine, 1973—; contbr. articles to profl. jours. Capt. M.C., U.S. Army, 1960-61. Fellow ACS, Royal Soc. Medicine (London); mem. AAUP, Am. Assn. Neurol. Surgeons, Soc. Neurol. Surgeons, Congress Neurol. Surgeons (bd. dirs. joint spinal sect. with Am. Assn. Neurol. Surgeons, chmn. ann. meeting 1987, sci. program chmn. ann. meeting 1988), Assn. for Rsch. in Nervous and Mental Diseases, New Eng. Neurosurg. Soc. (bd. dirs. 1976-79, pres. 1989-91), Soc. Brit. Neurol. Surgeons, Rsch. Soc. Neurol. Surgeons, Soc. Rsch. into Hydrocephalus and Spina Bifida, Conn. Acad. Arts and Sci., Vereingung Schweizer Neurochirugen, Mory's Assn., Graduate Club, Beaumont Med. Club (pres. 1988), Sloane Club, Naval Club, La Grande Mare Golf Club. Episcopalian. Office: 85 Seymour St Ste 707 Hartford CT 06106-5526

ROBERTS, MICHAEL BRUCE, surgeon; b. Augusta, Ga., Dec. 11, 1947; s. Lawrence Bruce Roberts and Mary I. (Barrett) Peck; m. Jill Gildehaus, June 3, 1983; children: Peter, Joey, Sammy. AB in Chemistry, Duke U., 1969; MS, Med. Coll. Ga., 1972, PhD, 1975, MD, 1979. Diplomate Am. Bd. Surgery. Resident in surgery U. Utah Affilited Hosps., Salt Lake City, 1979-81, Luth. Med. Ctr., Cleve., 1981-84; surgeon St. Joseph's Hosp. and Trinity Med. Ctr., Minot, N.D., 1986-88, SAC 91st Strategic Hosp., Minot AFB, 1988-89; pvt. practice, Milledgeville, Ga., 1990—. Office: Gen and Thoracic Surgery PC 750 N Cobb St Ste 8 Milledgeville GA 31061

ROBERTS, MICHAEL FOSTER, biology educator; b. Guatemala City, Guatemala, Aug. 8, 1943; s. Ralph Jackson and Arleda (Allen) R.; m. Mary Sherill Noe, Dec. 27, 1966; children: Rosemary, Amelia. BA, U. Calif., Berkeley, 1966; MA, U. Wis. (Madison), 1968, PhD, 1972. Fellow John B. Pierce Found. Lab., Yale U., New Haven, Conn., 1972-76; asst prof. Yale U., New Haven, 1976-81, Linfield Coll., McMinnville, oreg., 1981-84; assoc. prof. Linfield Coll., McMinnville, 1984-90, prof. biology, 1990—; guest referee editor Am. Physiol. Soc., Bethesda, Md., 1974—; peer rev. com. Am. Heart Assn., Portland, Oreg., 1982-87. Contbr. articles to profl. jours. Named NIH Predoctoral Fellow, 1969-72, Postdoctoral fellow, 1972-76; recipient NIH Rsch. grant, 1982-85, Am. Heart Assn. rsch. grant, 1985-86. Mem. Am. Physiol. Soc., Sigma Xi. Office: Linfield Coll Dept Biology McMinnville OR 97128

ROBERTS, MICHAEL WELLS, dentist, consultant, educator; b Prescott, Ark., July 10, 1941; s. Forest E. and Theron H. (Wells) R.; m. Sandra Beth Nance, June 2, 1964. DDS, U. Tex., 1965; MScD, Boston U., 1970. Diplomate Am. Bd. Pediatric Dentistry. Commd. lt. dental officer USPHS, 1965, advanced through grades to capt. 1975; dep. chief dental dept USPHS Hosp., San Francisco, 1970-75; chief dental dept. USPHS Outpatient Clinic, Washington, 1975-81; chief dental staff Bur. Med. Services USPHS, Washington, 1981; chief patient care, dep. clin. dir. Nat. Inst. Dental Research/NIH, Bethesda, Md., 1981-89, cons. pediatric dentistry, 1989—; cons. pediatric dentistry Nat. Naval Dental Ctr., Bethesda, 1983-90; assoc. prof. Georgetown U. Washington, 1976-90; assoc. prof., dir. grad. program. U. N.C., Chapel Hill, 1990-94, chair dept. pediatric dentistry, 1994—; cons. Nat. Inst. Environ. Health Sci. NIH, Research Triangle Park, N.C., 1990—; dir. Am. Bd. Pediatric Dentistry, 1993—. Contbg. author: Textbook of Pediatric Dentistry, 1980, 85, Pediatric Dentistry: Infancy through Adolescence, 1993, also articles. Fellow Am. Acad. Pediatric Dentistry, Am. Soc. Dentistry for Children, Am. Coll. Dentistry; mem. ADA, S.E. Soc. Pediatric Dentistry, Internat. Assn. Dental Research, Commd. Officers Assn. of USPHS (bd. dirs., nat. officer, Surgeon Gen.'s Exemplary Svc. medal, Meritorious Svc. and Commendation medals, Chief Dental Officer's Exemplary Svc. award). Avocations: flying, stamp collecting, sports. Office: U NC Sch Dentistry Brauer Hall # 205 Chapel Hill NC 27599

ROBERTS, MYRON SHELDON, urologist; b. N.Y.C., Nov. 22, 1927; s. Charles Henry and Martha (Friedland) R.; m. Lila Roberts, June 6, 1955 (div. Apr. 1972); m. Natalie Jane Roberts; children: James, Richard, Lesley. BA, Syracuse U., 1950; MD, N.Y. State Coll. Medicine, Syracuse, 1954. Diplomate Am. Bd. Urology. Intern Lenox Hill Hosp., N.Y.C., 1954-55, resident in surgery, 1955-56; resident in urology Columbia Presbyn. Med. Ctr., N.Y.C., 1956-59, assoc. prof. clin. urology, 1959—; dir. urology Mt. Vernon (N.Y.) Hosp., 1962-91. Contbr. articles to med. jours. With USN, 1945-46. Fellow ACS; mem. N.Y. Acad. Medicine (chmn. urology sect. 1973-74), Am. Urol. Assn. (pres. N.Y. sect. 1980-81), Internat. Soc. Urology, Soc. Pediatric Urology, Alpha Omega Alpha. Republican. Jewish. Office: Urol cons Columbia Presbyn Med Ctr 161 Ft Washington Ave New York NY 10032

ROBERTS, NORBERT J., JR., internist, educator in infectious diseases. BA, Haverford Coll., 1966; MD, NYU, 1971. Diplomate Am. Bd. Internal Medicine, Am. Bd. Infectious Diseases; lic. N.Y., N. Mex., Tex. Intern (internal medicine) St Luke's Hosp Ctr., Columbia U., N.Y.C., 1971-72, resident (internal medicine), 1972-74; fellow infectious disease unit, dept of medicine U. Rochester (N.Y.) Sch. Medicine; asst. prof. medicine U. Rochester (N.Y.) Sch. of Medicine, 1976-82, assoc. prof. medicine, 1982-93, assoc. prof. pediatrics, 1991-93, assoc. prof. microbiology and immunology, 1991-93, prof. medicine, pediatrics, microbiology and immunology, 1993-94; prof. internal medicine, microbiology and immunology U. Tex. Med. Br., Galveston, 1994—, mem. WHO Collaborating Ctr. for Tropical Diseases, 1994—, The Paul R. Stalnaker MD Disting. prof. of internal medicine, 1995—; mem. working group on Hematology and Immunology: com. for biolog. principles validation Am. Nat. Standards Inst., 1983-93, VA Merit Rev. Bd. in Infectious Diseases 1986-89, immunology com. Nat. Inst. Allergy and Infectious Diseases AIDS Clin. Trials Group Program (core com. 1987-94), 1987—, AIDS Vaccine Evaluation Group Program (initial chmn. 1989-92), 1989-94, microbiology and infectious diseases rsch. com. Nat. Inst. Allergy and Infectious Diseases, NIH, 1992-95; reviewer rsch. proposals, VA Merit Rev. Bd. in Infectious Diseases, VA Career Devel. Program, Nat. Scis. Found., NIH, Health Effects Inst., Ontario Ministry of Labour, Am. Fedn. for Clin. Rsch. Found; asst. physician Strong Meml. Hosp., Rochester, 1974-76, assoc. physician, 1976-82, sr. assoc. physician, 1982-93, physician, 1993-94; physician U. Tex. Med. Branch Hosps., 1994—. Contbr over 100 articles to profl. jours.; mem. editorial bd. Clin. and Diagnostic Lab. Immunology; ad hoc reviewer manuscripts for 19 sci. jours. including Science, Chest, Jour. Infectious Diseases, Annals of Internal Medicine, Am. Jour. Diseases of Children. Named Buswell Faculty fellow U. Rochester Sch. of Medicine, 1976-78; recipient Young Investigator award Nat. Inst. Allergy and Infectious Diseases, 1979-81. Fellow Am. Coll. Physicians, Infectious Diseases Soc. Am. (awards com. 1985-90, chmn. 1989-90); mem. Am. Soc. for Clin. Investigation, Am. Soc. for Virology, Soc. for Leukocyte Biology, Am. Assn. Immunologists. Am. Soc. Microbiolgy. Office: U Tex Med Br Divsn Infectious Diseases 301 University Blvd Galveston TX 77555-0835

ROBERTS, PAUL DALE, health services administrator; b. Fresno, Calif., Jan. 17, 1955; s. Paul Marceau and Rosemarie Roberts; m. Patricia Mary Mitchell, Mar. 24, 1964; 1 child, Jason Randall Porter. AA, Sacramento City Coll., 1977; diploma in pvt. investigations, Ctrl. Investigation & Security, 1984. Office asst. I Dept. Benefit Payments, Sacramento, Calif., 1976-77; firefighter Calif. Divsn. Forestry, Colfax, 1977; key data operator Dept. Justice, Sacramento, 1977-78; intelligence analyst, spl. forces instr. U.S. Army Mil. Intelligence, Seoul, Korea, 1979-84; law libr. Employment Devel. Dept., Sacramento, 1989-92; office asst. II Dept. Health Svcs., Sacramento, 1992—; disaster courier dept. social svcs. Gov.'s Office of Emergency Svcs., L.A., 1994; chief cert. support Dept. Health Svcs., Sacramento, 1992—. Author: Organization of D.E.A.T.H. (Destroy Evildoers and Teach Harmony), 1984, The Cosmic Bleeder, 1991, Madam Zara, Vampiress, 1993; (jour.) Memoirs of Paul Roberts, 1991; prodr.: (book) Villalobos Family, 1993. Sgt. U.S. Army Mil. Police, 1973-76. Democrat. Roman Catholic. Home: 60 Parkshore Cir Sacramento CA 95831-3061 Office: Dept Health Svcs Radiologic Health Br 601 N 7th St Sacramento CA 95814-0208

ROBERTS, PAUL WILLIAM, JR., medical technologist; b. Cin., Sept. 18, 1954; s. Paul William Roberts and Nancy Alice (Lockard) Overdorff; m. Cathy Ann Lawler, May 23, 1975; 1 child, Michael Paul. BS in med. tech., Midwestern State Univ., 1987. Medical tech. U.S. Army, 1977-86; co-front end supr. Gibson Discount Ctr., Wichita Falls, Tex., 1987-88; toy dept. supr. Gibson Discount Ctr., Wichita Falls, 1988; medical tech. Cozby-Germany Hosp., Grand Saline, Tex., 1988-92, St. Mary's Hosp., Galveston, Tex., 1992—; lab. dir. Cozby Germany Hosp., 1989-92. Author/editor various manuels. Mem./organizer Methodist Men, pres., 1995—. Named Best of Show East Tex. County Fair. Home: 208 17th Ave N Texas City TX 77590

ROBERTS, RICHARD JOHN, molecular biologist, consultant, research director; b. Derby, Eng., Sept. 6, 1943; came to U.S., 1969; s. John Walter and Edna Wilhelmina (Allsop) R.; m. Elizabeth Dyson, Aug. 21, 1965 (dec.); children: Alison, Andrew; m. Jean E. Tagliabue, Feb. 14, 1986; children: Christopher, Amanda. BS, Sheffield (Eng.) U., 1965, PhD, 1968. Rsch. fellow Harvard U., Cambridge, Mass., 1969-70, rsch. assoc., 1971-72; sr. staff investigator Cold Spring Harbor Lab., N.Y., 1972-87, asst. dir., 1987-92; rsch. dir. New England Biolabs, 1992—, cons. New Eng. Biolabs, Beverly, Mass., 1974-92; sci. adv. bd. Genex, Rockville, Md., 1977-85, Molecular Tool, Balt., 1994—. Contbr. articles to profl. jours. Recipient Nobel prize in Physiology and Medicine, Nobel Foundation, 1993. John Simon Guggenheim Found. fellow, 1979. Fellow Royal Soc.; mem. Am. Soc. Microbiology, Am. Soc. Biol. Chemists. Office: New Eng Biolabs 32 Tozer Rd Beverly MA 01915-5510

ROBERTS, ROBERT J., neonatologist; b. Centralia, Wash., Sept. 19, 1939; s. Waldo J. and Anna Laura (Von Behren) R.; m. Donna M. Whitney, Mar. 23, 1940; children: Robert J. Jr., LeAnn M. Wambacher. BS, Wash. State U., 1962, B.Pharmacy, 1964; MS in Pharmacology, U. Iowa, 1966, PhD in Pharmacology, 1968, MD, 1970. Diplomate Am. Bd. Pediats.; lic. physician, Iowa, Va. Intern in pediatrics U. Iowa Hosps., Iowa City, 1970-71, pediat. resident, 1971-73; instr. pharmacology U. Iowa, Iowa City, 1968-71, asst. prof., 1971-73, assoc. prof., 1973-77, chmn. divsn. pediat. clin. pharmacology, 1973-87, mem. divsn. neonatology, 1973-87, prof. pharmacology/pediats., 1977-87; prof., chmn. dept. pediats., med. dir. Children's Med. Ctr. U. Va., Charlottesville, 1987—; adj. prof. dept. pharmacology, clin. prof. dept. pediats. Tulane U. Med. Ctr., New Orleans, 1993—; vis. prof. Harvard Joint Program in Neonatology/Boston Children's Hosp., 1979; cons. in field; reviewer March of Dimes grants, Can. Heart Assn.; mem. pediat. adv. panel U.S. Pharmacopeial Conv., Inc., 1995—; bd. dirs. Health Svcs. Found., mem. exec. com., 1987—. mem. Piedmont Liability Trust bd., 1989—. Author: Drug Therapy in Infants, 1984; contbr. numerous articles to profl. jours.; editl. bd. Drug Metabolism and Disposition, 1976-82, Jour. Lab. and Clin. Medicine, 1980-84, Develop. Pharmacology and Therapeutics, 1982—; reviewer Jour. Pediats., Pediat. Rsch., New Eng. Jour. Medicine, Jour. Clin. Investigation, Jour. Pharmacology and Exptl. Therapeutics, Toxicology and Applied Pharmacology, Jour. Clin. Toxicology, Pediats., Sci., Jour. of AMA, Pediat. Pulmonology, Biochem. Pharmacology, Fedn. Procs., Can. Jour. Physiology and Pharmacology, Am. Rev. of Respiratory Disease, Neonatal Pahrmacology Quar. Recipient Faculty Devel. award in clin. pharmacology PMA Found., 1973, Herbert C. Miller Vis. lectr., U. Kans., 1981, Pfizer lectr. in clin. pharmacology Dartmouth Med. Sch., 1985, Tex. Tech. Med. Sch., 1985; grantee NIH, 1985-87, 87-92, 86-92, 86-89, 93-95, 90-95, 92—, FDA, 1985-87, Proctor and Gamble, 1985-87, 3M Co., 1985-86, IVAC Corp., 1985. Fellow Am. Acad. Pediats.; mem. Am. Soc. Pharmacology and Exptl. Therapeutics, Soc. Toxicology, Am. Acad. Clin. Toxicology, Soc. Pediat. Rsch., Am. Soc. Clin. Pharmacology and Therapeutics, Perinatal Rsch. Soc. (exec. com. 1989-91), Midwest Soc. for Pediat. Rsch., Am. Pediat. Soc., So. Soc. for Pediat. Rsch., Va. Perinatal Soc. Office: U Va Dept Pediatrics Charlottesville VA 22903

ROBERTS, ROBERT WINSTON, social work educator, dean; b. Balt., July 23, 1932; s. Kelmer Swan Roberts and Lettie Mae (Collins) Johnston; m. Helen Elizabeth Perpich, Mar. 4, 1964. BA with high honors, San Francisco State U., 1957; MSW, U. Calif., Berkeley, 1959; D in Social Welfare, Columbia U., 1970. Caseworker Edgewood Protestant Orphanage, San Francisco, 1959-62, Jewish Family Service, San Francisco, 1962-63; research assoc. U. Calif., Berkeley, 1963-65; research analyst Family Service Assn. Am., N.Y.C., 1965-69; asst. prof. U. Chgo., 1967-70; prof. U. So. Calif., Los Angeles, 1970-90, dean sch. social work, 1980-88, dean emeritus, prof. emeritus, 1990—; vis. prof. Western Australia Inst. Tech., Perth, 1976-77, Chinese U. Hong Kong and U. Hong Kong, 1980; cons. Crittenton Services, Los Angeles, 1970-72, James Weldon Johnson Community Ctr., N.Y., 1966-67; bd. dirs. El Centro, Los Angeles. Editor: The Unwed Mother, 1966; co-editor: Theories of Social Casework, 1970, Child Caring: Social Policy and the Institution, 1973, Theories of Social Work with Groups, 1976, Theory and Practice of Community Social Work, 1980; editorial bd. Social Work Jour.; contbr. articles to profl. jours. Staff sgt. USAF, 1950-54; sgt. 1st class USAR, 1956-59. Fellow NIMH, 1957-58, 65-67, Crown Zellerbach Found., 1958-59; recipient Outstanding Educator award Los Amigos de la Humanidad, 1979; named Disting. Assoc., Nat. Acad. Practice in Social Work, 1985. Mem. Nat. Assn. Social Workers (chmn. social action com. 1960-61), Council on Social Work Edn. (bd. dirs. 1970-73, del. to assembly 1971-72, commn. minority groups 1972-73). Office: Univ So Calif Sch Social Work Rm 214 Montgomery Ross Fisher Bldg Los Angeles CA 90089-0411

ROBERTS, WILBUR EUGENE, dental educator, research scientist; b. Lubbock, Tex., Nov. 16, 1942; s. Wilbur Eugene Roberts and Elva Etna (Chance) Turnwall; m. Cheryl Ann Jones, June 6, 1967; children: Jeffery Alan, Carrie Jean. DDS, Creighton U., 1967; PhD in Anatomy, U. Utah, 1969; cert. in orthodontics, U. Conn., 1974; DHC (hon.), Lille (France) U., 1994. Diplomate Am. Bd. Orthodontics. Rsch. fellow U. Utah, Salt Lake City, 1967-69; postdoctoral fellow U. Conn., Farmington, 1971-74; from asst. prof. to prof. dentistry U. Pacific, San Francisco, 1974-88; prof. chmn. dept. orthodontics Ind. U., Indpls., 1988-93, chmn. dept. oral and facial devel., 1993—, prof. physiology and biophysics Sch. Medicine, 1988—; mem. steering com. Biomechs. and Biomaterials Rsch. Ctr. Ind. U.-Purdue U., Indpls., 1990—; NRC sr. rsch. assoc. NASA Ames Rsch. Ctr., Moffett Field, Calif., 1982-83; dir. Bone Rsch. Lab., U. Pacific, 1980-88, Oral Devel. Clinic, 1980-86; rsch. cons. Neodontics Corp., Laguna Nigel, Calif., 1982-85, Denar Corp., Anaheim, Calif., 1985-87, Nobelpharma AG, Goteborg, Sweden, 1988, Dental Implant Clin. Rsch. Group, Ann Arbor, Mich., 1991—, Oral Medicine and Biology Study sect. NIH, 1992—, Rsch. Coun. ADA, 1992; adj. prof. mech. engring. Purdue U., Indpls., 1990—; assoc. prof. implantology, maxillofacial surgery U. Lille, France, 1987—; guest prof. U. Western Ont., Can., 1987; Dr. Fred West Meml. lectr. U. Pacific, 1989, Dr. George Grieve Meml. lectr. Can. Dental Assn., 1993; ptnr. Vintner for Zuperb Zinfandel, Ltd. Contbr. sci. articles to profl. jours. Rep. campaign worker, Contra Costa County, Calif., 1980-82; ch. sch. supt. San Ramon Valley Meth. Ch., Alamo, Calif., 1979-81; adult ministries council San Ramon Valley Meth. Ch., Danville, Calif., 1984-86; sci. cons. St. Isadore Sch. and San Ramon Valley High Sch., Danville, 1978-86; chmn. bldg. com. Sunrise at Geist United Meth. Ch., Indpls. Served to lt. comdr. USN, 1969-71, Vietnam. Recipient Cosmos Achievement award NASA, 1981, 88, 92, medal City of Paris, 1989, City of Rouen, France, 1991, Rsch. award Ind. U. Sch. Dentistry, 1993. Fellow Internat. Coll. Dentists, Am. Coll. Dentists; mem. Med. Dental Guild Calif. (pres. 1982-83, Gold Key award 1985), Am. Assn. Dental Rsch., Pacific Dental Rsch. Found. (pres. 1976-80), Conf. of the Company of Wine Tasters of Normandy (pres. Ind. med. chpt. 1992—), Omicron Kappa Upsilon. Home: 8260 Skipjack Dr Indianapolis IN 46236-8429 Office: Ind U Sch Dentistry Sch Dentistry Dept Orthodontics 1121 W Michigan St Indianapolis IN 46202-5211

ROBERTS, WILLIAM JAMES CYNFAB, physician; b. Liverpool, Lancashire, Eng., May 31, 1938; s. Cynfab and Ellen James (Pritchard) R.; m. Beryl Ann Davies, July 18, 1962; children: Robert Sion Cynfab, William Owain Marc Cynfab. BA in Nat. Scis., Cambridge (Eng.) U., 1960, BChir, 1963, MA, MB, 1964. Diplomate Royal Coll. Obstetricians and Gynecologists. Intern St. Marys Hosp. Med. Sch., Paddington; resident Royal Hosp., Sheffield Yorks; mng. ptnr. Roberts, Roberts, Jones and Penry, Abergrystwyth Dyfed, Wales, 1967—; chmn. com. edn. Gen. Med. Practitioners Wales; mem. Coun. for Postgrad. Edn. of Drs. and Dentists, Wales; hon. med. adviser Astra Pharm. Ltd.; vis. prof. King Saud U., Riyhad, Saudi Arabia, summer 1992; provost S.W. Wales Faculty Royal Coll. Gen. Practitioners, 1994; tutor workshops. Contbr. articles to profl. jours. Mem. Court of Nat. Libr. Wales, 1984—, Ct. and Coun. U. Coll. Wales, 1985—, Abgrystwyth; trustee Pantyfedn. Charitable Found. Fellow Royal Coll. Gen. Practitioners; mem. Brits. Med. Assn. (chmn. West Wales div.), U.K. Council Royal Coll. Gen. Practitioners; vis. fellow King Saud Univ. Methodist. Office: Roberts Roberts Jones and Penry, 26 N Parade, Aberystwyth Dyfe SY23 2NF, Wales

ROBERTS, WILLIAM MICHAEL EUGENE, hospital administrator; b. Detroit, Aug. 25, 1950; s. William Michael Eugene and Muriel (Rogers) R.; m. Robin Anne Wilkinson, Oct. 20, 1978; children: Christopher Frederick, Colin Michael, Alexander Karl. AA with honors, Macomb Coll., 1974; BA with distinction, Wayne State U., 1977; postgrad., Lawrence Tech. Coll., 1981-83. Material control supr. Chrysler Corp., Hamtramck, Mich., 1972-80; reporter Parker Publs., Highland Park, Mich., 1977; gen. stores mgr. Botsford Gen. Hosp., Farmington Hills, Mich., 1980-84; dir. purchasing Bon Secours Hosp., North Miami, Fla., 1984-95, dir. comm., 1989-95; dir. materials mgmt. Pan Am. Hosp., Miami, 1995—; Editor Outreach mag., 1984-95; contbr. articles to newspapers. Editor Outreach mag., 1984-95; contbr. articles to newspapers. Mem. Nat. Assn. Purchasing Mgmt., Internat. Assn. Cen. Svc. Mgmt., South Fla. Assn. Hosp. Purchasing and Materials Mgmt. Republican. Roman Catholic. Home: 4101 SW 84th Ter Fort Lauderdale FL 33328-2954 Office: Pan Am Hosp 5959 NW 7th St Miami FL 33126

ROBERTS, WILLIAM SMITHSON, gynecologic oncologist; b. Charlottesville, Va., Dec. 14, 1949; s. Paul Smithson and Cynthia (Larkum) R.; m. Virginia Ann Cummins, Dec. 30, 1981 (div. Apr. 1991); 1 child, William Miles; m. Sineath Gaynell Luzey, July 25, 1991; children: Seneca Leigh, Stratton Smithson. BA, Rutgers Coll., 1972; MD, Coll. of Medicine of N.J., 1976. Diplomate Am. Bd. Ob-gyn. Resident in ob-gyn. U. Fla. Coll. Medicine, Gainesville, 1976-80; fellow gynecologic oncology U. Calif. Irvine Coll. Medicine, Orange, 1980-82; asst. prof. ob-gyn. U. South Fla. Coll. Medicine, Tampa, 1982-87, assoc. prof. ob-gyn., 1987-94, prof. ob-gyn., 1995—; program leader gynecologic oncology H. Lee Moffitt Cancer Ctr., Tampa, 1993-96; chief gynecologic oncology Watson Clinic, Lakeland, Fla., 1996—; mem.-at-large bd. dirs. physicians group U. South Fla., 1992—, faculty senator, 1988-91; chief of staff H. Lee Moffitt Cancer Ctr., 1994-96. Author: (chpt.) Invasive Corcinoma of the Vulva: A Diseas of the Aged, 1987, (chpt.) Management of Malignant and Premalignant Lesion of the Female Genital Tract During Pregnancy, 1992, (chpt.) Ovarian Cancer Screening, 1996. Chmn. cancer control Hillsborough County Am. Cancer Soc., Tampa. 1991-93. Fellow Am. Coll. Ob-gyns., Am. Coll. Surgeons; mem. Soc. Gynecologic Oncologists, Fla. Soc. Gynecologic Oncologist (pres.-elect 1994—), Western Assn. Gynecologic Oncologists (v.p. 1992, James F. Nolan award 1986). Republican. Home: 4814 Highlands Place Dr Lakeland FL 33813 Office: Watson Clinic 1600 Lakeland Hills Blvd Lakeland FL 33805

ROBERTSON, ABEL L., JR., pathologist; b. St. Andrews, Argentina, July 21, 1926; came to U.S., 1952, naturalized, 1957; s. Abel Alfred Lazzarini and Margaret Theresa (Anderson) R.; m. Irene Kirmayr Mauch, Dec. 26, 1958; children: Margaret Anne, Abel Martin, Andrew Duncan, Malcolm Alexander. BS, Coll. D.F. Sarmiento, Buenos Aires, Argentina, 1946; MD suma cum laude, U. Buenos Aires, 1951; PhD, Cornell U., 1959. Fellow tissue culture div. Inst. Histoloty and Embryology, Sch. Medicine Inst. Histology and Embryology, 1947-49; surg. intern Hosp. Ramos Mejia, Buenos Aires, 1948-50; fellow in tissue culture research Ministry of Health, Buenos Aires, 1950-51; resident Hosp. Nacional de Clinicas, Buenos Aires, 1950-51; head blood vessel bank and organ transplants Research Ctr. Ministry of Health, Buenos Aires, 1951-53; fellow dept. surgery and pathology Sch. Medicine Cornell U., N.Y.C., 1953-55; asst. vis. surgery U. Hosp. N.Y., N.Y.C., 1955-60; asst. prof. research surgery Postgrad. Med. Sch. NYU, N.Y.C., 1955-56; asst. vis. surgeon Bellevue Hosp., N.Y.C., 1955-60; assoc. prof. research surgery NYU, 1956-60, assoc. prof. pathology Sch. Medicine and Postgrad Med. Sch., 1960-63; staff mem. div. research Cleve. Clinic Found., 1963-73, prof. research, 1972-73; assoc. clin. prof. pathology Case Western Res. U. Sch. Medicine, Cleve., 1966-72, prof. pathology, 1973-82, dir. interdisciplinary cardiovascular research, 1975-82; exec. head dept. pathology Coll. Medicine, U. Ill., Chgo., 1982-88; prof. pathology Coll. Medicine U. Ill., 1982-93, prof. emeritus, 1993-95; vis. prof. emeritus in cardiovascular medicine Stanford U. Coll. Medicine, 1995—; vis. prof. emeritus Stanford U. Coll. Medicine, 1995—; rsch. fellow N.Y. Soc. Cardiovasc. Surgery, 1957-58; mem. rsch. study subcom. of heart com. N.E. Ohio Regional Med. Program, 1969—. Mem. internat. editorial bd.: Atherosclerosis, Jour. Exptl. and Molecular Pathology, 1964—, Lab. Investigation, 1989—, Acta Pathologica Japonica, 1991—; contbr. articles to profl. jours. Recipient Research Devel. award NIH, 1961-63. Fellow Am. Coll. Cardiology, Am. Coll. Clin. Pharmacology, Am. Heart Assn. (established investigator 1956-61, nominating com. council on arteriosclerosis 1972), Royal Microscopical Soc., Royal Soc. Promotion Health (Gt. Britain), Am. Geriatrics Soc., N.Y. Acad. Scis., Cleve. Med. Library Assn.; mem. AMA, AAAS, AAUP, Am. Soc. for Investigative Pathology, Am. Inst. Biol. Scis., Am. Judicature Soc., Am. Soc. Cell Biology, Am. Soc. Pathologists, Am. Soc. Nephrology, Assn. Am. Physicians and Surgeons, Assn. Computing Machinery, Electron Microscopy Soc. Am., Assn. Pathology Chmn., Internat. Acad. Pathology, Soc. Cardiovascular Pathology, Internat. Cardiovascular Soc., Internat. Soc. Cardiology (sci. council on arteriosclerosis and ischemic heart disease), Internat. Fed. on Genetic Engring. and Biotechnology, Internat. Soc. for Heart Rsch., Internat. Soc. Nephrology, Internat. Soc. Stereology, Pan Am. Med. Assn. (life, councillor in angiology 1966), Ill. Registry Anatomical Pathology (treas. 1985-87), Chgo. Pathology Soc., Reticuloendothelial Soc. Leucocyte Biology, Soc. Cryobiology, Tissue Culture Assn., Ohio Soc. Pathologists, Electron Microscopy Soc. Northeastern Ohio (pres., trustee 1966-68), Heart Assn. Northeastern Ohio, N.Y. Soc. Cardiovascular Surgery, N.Y. Soc. Electron Microscopists, Cuyahoga County Med. Soc., Cleve. Soc. Pathologists, The Oxygen Soc., Sigma Xi. Home: 415 Lee Ave Half Moon Bay CA 94019-1367

ROBERTSON, BRADLEY CHARLES, plastic and reconstructive surgeon; b. Washington, July 16, 1953. BS, Emory and Henry Coll., 1975; DDS magna cum laude, U. Md., 1980; MD, Johns Hopkins U., 1987. Diplomate Am. Bd. Plastic and Reconstructive Surgery. Intern, resident in oral and maxillofacial surgery Johns Hopkins Sch. Medicine, Balt., 1980-84, gen. surgery intern, 1986-87, resident in gen. surgery, 1987-89, resident in plastic surgery, 1989-92; academic practice in shock trauma U. Md., Johns Hopkins, Balt., 1992—; asst. prof. plastic surgery U. Md., Balt., 1992—, Johns Hopkins U., Balt., 1992—, Shock Trauma, Balt., 1992—, section head plastic surgery, 1996; dir. U. Md. Cleft Palate/Craniofacial Surgery, Balt., 1992—, Kernan's Cleft Lip/Palate Ctr., Balt., 1995—. Contbr. articles to profl. jours. Bd. dirs. Operation Smile Internat., Balt., 1995—. U. Md. grantee, 1993—. Mem. AMA, Am. Soc. Maxillofacial Surgeons, Am. Soc. Plastic and Reconstructive Surgeons, John Staige Davis Soc. Office: Univ of Maryland Dept Plastic Surgery 22 S Greene St Baltimore MD 21201

ROBERTSON, DAVID, pharmacologist, educator; b. Sylvia, Tenn., May 23, 1947; s. David Herlie and Lucille Luther (Bowen) R.; m. Rose Marie Stevens, Oct. 30, 1976; 1 child, Rose. B.A., Vanderbilt U., 1969, M.D., 1973. Diplomate Am. Bd. Internal Medicine, Am. Bd. Clin. Pharmacology. Intern, Johns Hopkins U., Balt., 1973-74, asst. resident, 1974-75, asst. chief service in medicine, 1977-78; fellow in clin. pharmacology Vanderbilt U., Nashville, 1975-77, asst. prof. medicine and pharmacology, 1978-82, assoc. prof., 1982-86, prof., 1986—, prof. neurology, 1991—; dir. clin. research ctr., 1987—; dir. Ctr. for Space Physiology and Medicine, 1989—; dir. Med. Sci. Tng. Program, 1993—; pclin. rsch. specializing in gene therapy and disorders of blood pressure regulation, Nashville, 1978—; mem. staff Vanderbilt Hosp., Burroughs Wellcome scholar in clin. pharmacology, 1985-91. Author: (with B.M. Greene and G.J. Taylor) Problems in Internal Medicine, 1980, (with C.R. Smith) Manual of Clinical Pharmacology, 1981, (with Italo Biaggioni) Disorders of the Autonomic Nervous System, 1995, Primer on the Autonomic Nervous System, 1996; editor-in-chief Drug Therapy, 1991-94; editorial bds. Jour. Autonomic Nervous System, Clin. Pharm. and Therapeutics, Clin. Autonomic Rsch., Am. Jour. Med. Sci., Current Topics in Pharmacology. Recipient Research Career Devel. award NIH, 1981, Grant W. Liddle award for leadership in rsch., 1991; Adolph-Morsbach grantee Bonn, Germany, 1968; Logan Clendening fellow Reykjavik, Iceland, 1969. Fellow Am. Heart Assn. Council Hypertension and Circulation, ACP (teaching and research scholar 1978-81); mem. Am. Autonomic Soc. (pres. 1992-94), Am. Acad. Neurology, Soc. Neurosci., Am. Inst. Aeronautics and Astronautics, U.S. Pharmacopeial Conv., Nat. Bd. Med. Examiners, Aerospace Med. Assn. (space station sci. and applications com.), FDA Consortium Rare Disorders, Rare Disorder Network, Am. Fedn. for Clin. Research, Am. Soc. Clin. Investigation, Assn. Am. Physicians, So. Soc. for Clin. Investigation, Am. Soc. for Clin. Pharmacology and Therapeutics, Phi Beta Kappa, Alpha Omega Alpha (hon., bd. dirs. 1995—). Baptist. Home: 4003 Newman Pl Nashville TN 37204-4308 Office: Vanderbilt U Clin Rsch Ctr 21st Ave S Nashville TN 37232-2195

ROBERTSON, DAVID WAYNE, pharmaceutical company executive; b. Dumas, Tex., July 30, 1955; s. R.L. and N.C. R. BS, Stephen F. Austin State U., 1977; MS, U. Ill., 1978, PhD, 1981. Sr. medicinal chemist Eli Lilly and Co., Indpls., 1981-84, rsch. scientist, 1985-87, sr. rsch. scientist, 1988-89, rsch. group leader, 1988-89, dir. cen. nervous system rsch., 1990-91; v.p. medicinal chemistry Ligand Pharms., Inc., San Diego, 1991-92, v.p. rsch., 1992-93, v.p. discovery rsch., 1993—. Contbr. articles to profl. jours. Mem. Soc. for Neurosci., Am. Soc. Pharmacology and Exptl. Therapeutics, Am. Chem. Soc. Office: Ligand Pharm Inc 9393 Towne Centre Dr San Diego CA 92121-3016

ROBERTSON, EDWARD NEIL, dentist; b. Rumford, Maine, Mar. 3, 1950; s. Edward Norris and Edith Louis (Kirk) R.; m. Rosalind Siegel, May 10, 1969 (div.); children: Christie Portia, Juliet Melissa (dec.), Jenni Celia, Edward Noah, Jessica Edith. BS in Biology, Antioch Coll., Yellow Springs, Ohio, 1973; MS in Epidemiology, Ohio State U., 1977; DDS, Case Western Res. U., 1983. Faculty adv. to med. students Ohio State U., Columbus, 1975-77; rsch. cons. Ohio Dept. Health, Columbus, 1976-77; rsch. assoc. UCLA, 1977; epidemiologic/statis. cons. L.A., 1977; medic J & L Steel Corp., Cleve., 1979-84; pvt. practice Cleveland Heights, Ohio, 1983—; mem. adj. faculty Cuyahoga C.C., Cleve., 1986-88; assoc. prof. Sch. Dentistry Case Western Res. U., 1991—. Pres. Robertson Family Assn. of N.Am., 1986-88. Recipient numerous rsch. grants. Mem. Acad. Gen. Dentistry, Am. Assn. Functional Orthodontists, U.S. Dental Inst., Acad. Laser Surgery, Alpha Omega. Office: 5031 Mayfield Rd # 105 Cleveland OH 44124

ROBERTSON, EVELYN CRAWFORD, JR., healthcare executive, former county official; b. Winchester, Tenn., Nov. 19, 1941; s. Evelyn Crawford and Pearl (Brewer) R.; m. Hugholene Ellison, Oct. 13, 1963; children—Jeffrey Bernard, Sheila Yvette. B.S., Tenn. State U., 1962, M.A., 1969; postgrad. Memphis State U., 1976-77. Cert. tchr., ednl. supt. Tchr., Allen-White Elem. Sch., Whiteville, Tenn., 1962-68, prin., 1968-69; asst. prin. Central High Sch., Bolivar, Tenn., 1970-74; asst. supt. Western Mental Health Inst., Bolivar, 1974-79, supt., 1983-95; supt. Nat T. Winston Devel. Ctr., Bolivar, 1979-83; v.p. behavioral health Pathways, Jackson, Tenn., 1996—; cons. in field. Pres. Whiteville Civic League, Tenn., 1969-74, mem. Hardeman County Commn., Bolivar, 1981—; chmn. bd. dirs. Hardeman County Devel. Services Ctr., Bolivar, 1976-77; former commr. Dept. Mental Health and Mental Retardation. Named Outstanding Young Tchr. Hardeman County Jaycees, 1972; honored Evelyn C. Robertson Day, Whiteville, Tenn., 1983; Outstanding Citizens award Sigma Gamma Rho, Bolivar, 1983. Mem. Am. Assn. on Mental Deficiency, Southeastern Assn. on Mental Deficiency (chmn. adminstrv. div. 1982-83), Inst. on Hosp. and Community Psychiatry, Tenn. State U. Alumni (life, pres. Bolivar chpt. 1978-80). Baptist. Club: Civitan (pres. 1981-82) (Bolivar). Lodges: Silver Star (pres. 1968-73), Shriners (past pres.), Kappa Alpha Psi (life). Avocations: spectator sports; reading; gardening; fishing; photography. Home: 2665 Newsom Rd Whiteville TN 38075 Office: Pathways 238 Summar Dr Jackson TN 38301

ROBERTSON, FRED SHAUNE, emergency physician; b. Montgomery, W.Va., Sept. 13, 1954; s. Fred H. and Betty L. (Lundy) R.; m. Valerie J., Aug. 18, 1979. BS, Davidson Coll., 1976; MD, W.Va. U., 1980. Emergency staff physician Butler (Pa.) Meml. Hosp., 1987-88, United Cmty. Hosp., Grove City, Pa., 1988—; guest lectr. Grove City Coll., 1995—. Maj. U.S. Army, 1980-87. Fellow Am. Coll. Emergency Physicians. Home: 15 Dogwood Ln Grove City PA 16127 Office: United CMty Hosp 631 N Broad St Ext Grove City PA 16127

ROBERTSON, JAMES SYDNOR, retired nuclear medicine physician, government agency official; b. Richmond, Va., Nov. 27, 1920; s. Paul Augustus and Beth O'Ferrall (Whitacre) R.; m. Ruth Elizabeth Henrici, Jan. 15, 1944; children: Kathleen Mary, John Paul, Marion Adelle. BS, U. Minn., 1943, MB, 1944, MD, 1945; PhD in Physiology, U. Calif., Berkeley, 1949. Diplomate Am. Bd. Nuclear Medicine. Head med. physics Brookhaven Nat. Lab., Upton, N.Y., 1950-75; cons. nuclear medicine Mayo Clinic, Rochester, Minn., 1975-84; dir. human health Office Energy Rsch., U.S. Dept. Energy, Washington, D.C., 1984-91. Author, editor: Compartmental Distribution of Radiotracers, 1983; contbr. articles to profl. jours. Served to capt. USNR. Fellow AAAS; mem. Am. Physiol. Soc., Health Physics Soc., Radiation Rsch. Soc., Soc. Nuclear Medicine, Math. Assn. Am., Masons. Democrat. Methodist. Home: 18909 Tributary Ln Gaithersburg MD 20879-3409

ROBERTSON, JAMES THOMAS, neurosurgeon; b. McComb, Miss., Apr. 5, 1931; s. Clyde Aubrey and Catherine Roberta (Darville) R.; m. Valeria Ann Brower, Nov. 26, 1952; children: James T. Jr., Elizabeth, Catherine, Clay, Roberta, Daniel. BS, Southwestern U., 1951; MD, U. Tenn., 1954. Diplomat Am. Bd. Neurol. Surgeons, 1962. Intern Bapt. Meml. Hosp., Memphis, 1955; resident U. Tenn., Memphis, 1956-59, Peter Bent Brigham & Children's Hosp., Boston, 1959-60; chief neurosurgery Travis AFB, Fairfield, Calif., 1960-63; asst. chief nuerosurgery Lackland AFB, San Antonio, 1963-64; assoc. physician Semmes Murphey Clinic, Memphis, 1964-65; asst. prof. neurosurgery U. Tenn., 1964-69, assoc. prof., 1969-73, prof., chmn. dept. neurosurgery, 1973—. Editor: Subarachnoid Hemorrhage and Cerebrocascular Vasopasm, 1975; contbr. articles to mags. Vice chair Rep. Party, Shelby County, Memphis, 1980, treas., DeSoto County, Miss., 1993; pres. Shelby County chpt. Am. Heart Assn., 1996, chmn. stroke coun., 1992-94. Capt. USNR, 1982—. Recipient Disting. Alumni award U. Tenn., 1990, Rhodes Coll., 1994. Fellow Am. Coll. Surgeons (bd. govs. 1987-92); mem. Am. Assn. Neurol. Surgeons (pres. 1990-91), Congress Neurol. Surgeons (pres. 1975), Am. Acad. Neurol. Surgery (pres. 1988), Soc. Univ. Neurosurgeons (pres. 1965). Presbyterian. Home: 8570 Jones Rd Olive Branch MS 38654 Office: U Tenn 847 Monroe Ave #427 Memphis TN 38163

ROBERTSON, JOHN MARSHALL, surgeon, educator; b. San Francisco, Mar. 3, 1950; s. James MacPhearson and Pauline Jane (Lenoir) R.; m. Jill Marie Duchein, Nov. 1, 1980; children; Cheryl Pauline, Marshall James. BS with highest honors, U. Calif., Berkeley, 1972; MD cum laude, St. Louis U., 1977. Diplomate Am. Bd. Surgery, Am. Bd. Thoracic Surgery; cert. ACLS instr. Am. Heart Assn. Intern in surgery UCLA Med. Ctr., 1977-78, resident, sr. resident, then chief resident in surgery, 1978-79, 81-83, asst. rsch. surgeon divsn. thoracic surgery, 1979-81, resident in thoracic surgery, 1983-85, staff surgeon, 1994—; asst. prof. surgery UCLA, 1985-91, clin. asst. prof., 1991—; pvt. practice, Santa Monica, Calif., 1991—; asst. chief divsn. thoracic and cardiovasc. surgery Harbor-UCLA Med. Ctr., Torrance, 1985-89, chief, 1989-91; cons. St. John's Heart Inst., Santa Monica, 1987-89, dir. cardiac surgery, 1993—; staff surgeon Wadsworth VA Hosp., L.A., 1987-89; lectr., presenter local, nat. and internat. programs, confs., hosps., schs. Contbr. over 50 articles and abstracts to med. jours. Grantee NIH, 1986-87, Sandoz Rsch. Inst., 1986-88, Greater L.A. affiliate Am. Heart Assn., 1986-87, Johnson & Johnson, 1986-87, 89, Nat. Cancer Inst., 1986-90, St. John's Heart Inst., 1987-89, Internat. Cardiovasc. Medicine, Inc., 1988-89, Fenwell divsn. Baxter, 1989—, Rsch. and Edn. Inst., Inc., 1987-97, St. John's Hosp., 1993-94. Fellow ACS, Am. Coll. Chest Physicians; mem. AMA, Soc. Thoracic Surgeons, Am. Assn. for Thoracic Surgery, Western Thoracic Surg. Assn., Pacific Coast Surg. Assn., Bay Surg. Soc., L.A. Surg. Soc., Phi Beta Kappa, Alpha Omega Alpha. Office: 1301 20th St Ste 590 Santa Monica CA 90405

ROBERTSON, JOSEPH DANIEL, JR., psychologist, minister; b. Portsmouth, Va., Jan. 28, 1957; s. Joseph Daniel and Peggy Louise (Mizelle) R.; m. Angela Rose Respess, Mar. 7, 1981; children: Joseph Justus, Johanna Danielle, Jessa Rose. BA, U. N.C., 1979; MAEd, E. Carolina U., 1980; PhD, U. Tenn., 1989. Lic. psychologist, Tenn. Psychologist, campus min. Campus Christian Fellowship, Greenville, N.C., 1994—. Mem. Am. Counseling Assn., Am. Psychol. Assn., Am. Assn. of Christian Counseling. Mem. Christian Chs./Ch. of Christ. Office: Campus Christian Fellowship PO Box 2613 Greenville NC 27836

ROBERTSON, JOSEPH E., JR., ophthalmologist, educator; b. Jackson County, Ind., July 24, 1952; s. Joseph E. and Virginia Faye (Baxter) R.; m. Margaret Hewitt, Oct. 10, 1976; children: Katherine Faye, Charles Joseph. BS cum laude, Yale U., 1974; MD, Ind. U., 1978. Diplomate Am. Bd. Ophthalmology. Intern Bapt. Med. Ctr., Birmingham, Ala., 1978-79; resident Oreg. Health Sci. U., Portland, 1979-82; pvt. practice Vancouver, Wash., 1982-83; fellow Oreg. Health Sci. U./Devers Hosp./Good Samaritan Hosp., Portland, 1983-84; vitreous surgery fellow Steve Charles, M.D., Memphis, Tenn., 1984-85; asst. prof. Oreg. Health Sci. U., Portland, 1985-92, assoc. prof., 1992—. Contbr. articles to profl. jours., chpts. to books; editor videotapes. Apptd. mem. Oreg. Commn. for the Blind, 1988-94; bd. dirs. Oreg. Med. Polit. Action Com., Salem, 1994—. Mem. Am. Acad. Ophthalmology (Oreg. rep. to coun. 1992-95, COVE com. 1988-93, skills transfer adv. com. 1994—, nat. chair & state coord. Diabetes 2000), Oreg. Acad. Ophthalmology (pres. 1990-91), Oreg. Med. Assn. Democrat. Presbyterian. Office: Casey Eye Inst/OHSU 3375 SW Terwilliger Blvd Portland OR 97201-4197

ROBERTSON, JUDITH ANN, physician assistant; b. Waynesville, N.C., Mar. 8, 1947; d. Maxie Lee and Clara Mae (Chapman) Stamey; m. Larry Lee Robertson, Dec. 26, 1974; children: Diana Lynne, Larry Lee II. BS in Medicine, U. Nebr., 1975. Commd. officer USN, 1968, advanced through grades to lt. comdr.; hosp. corpsman USN, Orlando, Fla., 1969-70, Gretna, La., 1970-71, Portsmouth, Va., 1971-72; physician asst. USN, Camp Pendleton, Calif., 1973-83, Treasure Island, Calif., 1983-90, Kaneohe, Hawaii, 1990-93, Charleston, S.C., 1993—; selection mem. bd. MUSC, Charleston, 1995—. Pres. San Francisco BRAVO Vols., San Francisco Ballet, 1989-90. Fellow Naval Assn. Physician Assts. (sec. 1975-77, treas. 1980-81, pres. 1990-92), Am. Acad. Physician Assts. (ho. of dels. 1980-87), Calif. Acad. Physician Assts. Home: 1246 Hidden Lakes Dr Mt Pleasant SC 29464 Office: Naval Hosp Rivers Ave Charleston SC 29463

ROBERTSON, MICHAEL JOHN, internist, research scientist, educator; b. Morrison, Ill., Sept. 13, 1958; s. Donald L. and Doris M. (Burch) R. AB in English summa cum laude, U. Ill., 1980; MD with honors, U. Chgo., 1984. Diplomate Am. Bd. Internal Medicine, Am. Bd. Med. Oncology. Intrn in internal medicine U. Chgo. Med. Ctr., 1984-85, resident, 1985-87; fellow in med. oncology Dana-Farber Cancer Inst., Boston, 1987-90, fellow in tumor immunology, 1988-91, attending physician, 1991—; instr. medicine Harvard U. Med. Sch., Boston, 1991-93, asst. prof., 1994-96; asst. prof. medicine Ind. U. Sch. Medicine, Indpls., 1996—. Contbr. articles to med. jours. Mem. ACP, Soc. for Natural Immunity, Am. Soc. for Blood and Marrow Transplantation, Internat. Soc. for Hemotothery and Graft Engring., Am. Soc. Clin. Oncology, Am. Soc. Hematology, Am. Assn. Immunologists, Phi Beta Kappa, Alpha Omega Alpha. Office: Ind Univ Med Ctr Hematology Oncology Sect 975 W Walnut St Indianapolis IN 46202

ROBERTSON, WILLIAM WRIGHT, JR., orthopedic surgeon educator; b. Mayfield, Ky., Dec. 26, 1946; s. William Wright and Dorothy Frances (Beadles) R.; m. Karel Virginia Dierks, Jan. 26, 1974; children: Anna Elizabeth, Claire Alexandra. BA, Rhodes Coll., 1968; MD, Vanderbilt U., 1972. Intern U. Calif., San Diego, 1972-73, resident, 1975-76; resident Vanderbilt U., Nashville, 1976-79; asst. prof. orthopedics Tex. Tech U., Lubbock, 1979-86; assoc. prof. U. Pa., Phila., 1986-90; prof. orthopedic surgery George Washington U., Washington, 1990—; chair pediatric orthopedics Children's Nat. Med. Ctr., Washington, 1990—. Lt. USN, 1973-75. Fellow AMA, Am. Acad. Orthopedic Surgeons, Am. Acad. Cerebralpalsy Devel. Medicine, Am. Acad. Pediatrics, Am. Orthopedic Assn., Pediatric Orthopedic Soc. (bd. dirs. 1993—). Office: Childrens Nat Med Ctr 111 Michigan Ave NW Washington DC 20010-2970

ROBIN, MITCHELL WOLFE, psychology educator, psychotherapist; b. Bklyn., Apr. 30, 1944; s. Benjamin and Lee (White) R.; m. Regina Catherine Spires, Mar. 26, 1972; children: Elaine Dara Robin, Abigail Alice. BBA, CCNY, 1965; MA, New Sch. for Social Rsch., 1969; PhD, NYU, 1984. Lic. psychologist, N.Y.; cert. clin. supr. rational-emotive therapy, N.Y. Assoc. prof. N.Y.C. Tech. Coll., Bklyn., 1968—; mem. faculty New Sch. for Social Rsch., N.Y.C., 1970-89; fellow Inst. for Rational-Emotive Therapy, N.Y.C., 1986, staff psychotherapist, 1986-95, mem. faculty, 1986—; pvt. practice, N.Y.C., 1995—. Author: (with Rochelle Balter) Performance Anxiety: Overcoming Your Fear in the Workplace, Social Situations, Interpersonal Communications and the Performing Arts, 1994, (with Ray DiGiuseppe) (psychol. test) ASBII, 1988, (with others) (psychol. test) The Anger Response Inventory, 1993; editor Jour. Rational-Emotive and Cognitive Behavior Therapy, 1990; contbr. chpt. to book. Exec. dir. Sea View Playwright's Children's Theatre, 1984. Democrat. Jewish. Office: New York City Tech Coll Social Sci Dept 300 Jay St Brooklyn NY 11201-2902 other: Therapy Office Penthouse Ste 3 19 W 34th St New York NY 10001

ROBINS, CLIVE JUSTIN, psychology educator, researcher, psychotherapist; b. London, Apr. 5, 1953; came to U.S., 1975; s. Thomas Justin and Doris May (Yardley) R.; m. Melissa Kathleen Doyle, May 6, 1978; children: Justin, Alexander, Daniel. B.Sc., U. Sussex, Brighton, Eng., 1974; M.A., Stanford U., 1978; Ph.D., SUNY-Stony Brook, 1982. Lic. psychologist, N.Y., N.C. Asst. prof. psychology NYU, N.Y.C., 1982-87; assoc. prof. psychiatry Duke U. Med. Ctr., 1987—; instr., supr. Inst. Behavior Therapy, N.Y.C., 1983-87; pvt. practice psychology, N.Y.C., 1984-87. Contbr. chpt., articles to profl. pubs., 1974—. Rsch. Challenge Fund grantee NYU, 1984, NIMH grantee, 1986. Mem. Am. Psychol. Assn., Assn. Advancement Behavior Therapy, Soc for Rsch. in Psychopathology, Soc. Exploration Psychotherapy Integration. Avocations: tennis; jogging; cinema. Home: 28 E Bayberry Ct Durham NC 27713-9438 Office: Duke U Med Ctr Dept Psychiatry Box 3362 Durham NC 27710

ROBINS, H(ENRY) IAN, medical oncologist; b. N.Y.C., Feb. 17, 1945; s. Edwin and Matilda (Morgenstern) R. AB in Biology, Boston U., 1966, AM in Biochemistry, 1968, PhD in Molecular Biology, 1971, MD, 1976. Diplomate Am. Bd. Internal Medicine, Am. Bd. Med. Oncology, Am. Bd. Forensic Medicine, Am. Bd. Forensic Examiners. Intern in internal medicine Univ. Hosps., Madison, Wis., 1976-77, resident in internal medicine, 1977-79; fellow in clin. oncology Wis. Clin. Cancer Ctr., Madison, 1979-81, fellow in rsch. oncology, 1981-82; instr. dept. human oncology, dept. medicine Dept. Human Oncology, Dept. Medicine U. Wis. Sch. Medicine, Madison, 1982-83, asst. prof., 1983-86, assoc. prof., 1986—; chief sect. med. oncology, dir. U. Wis. Sch. Medicine, Madison, 1990-95, prof. dept. human oncology, medicine and neurology, 1992—. Contbr. numerous articles to profl. jours.; reviewer numerous sci. jours. including Biochem. Pharmacology, Internat. Jour. Radiation Biology, Jour. Clin. Oncology, New Eng. Jour. Medicine, others. Mem. N.Y. Acad. Scis., AAAS, ACP, Internat. Clin. Hyperthermia Soc. , Radiation Rsch. Soc., N.am. Hyperthermia Group, Oncology Group, Am. Fedn. clin. Rsch., Ea. Coop. Oncology Group, European Soc. Hyperthermic Oncology, Vet. Cancer Soc., Transplantation Soc., Collaborative Ocular Melanoma Study Group, Am. Soc. Clin. Hypnosis, Minn. Soc. Clin. Hypnosis, Sigma Xi. Office: Clin Sci Ctr K4/662 600 Highland Ave Madison WI 53792-0001

ROBINS, JAMES DOW, counselor; b. Athens, Ga., Oct. 17, 1952; s. Gerald Burns and Fay Ann (Kennan) R.; m. Sharon Eileen Parker, Apr. 12, 1974 (div. 1976). BA in Psychology, SUNY, Albany, 1981; BA in Comm. cum laude, Tex. A&M U., 1981, MA in Secondary Edn., 1982; ABA, cert. legal asst., Southwestern Paralegal Inst., 1984; MS in Guidance and Counseling, Tex. A&M U., 1993. Bar: Tex., 1985; cert. counselor, psychologist, English and speech tchr., legal asst., Tex. Program dir. University City, Inc.,

Athens, 1971-73; sta. mgr. Bethany Broadcasting, Houston, 1973-76; program coord. for radio and TV, Tex. A&I U., Kingsville, 1977-82; dir. pub. rels. Kleberg Meml. Hosp., Kingsville, 1983-84; legal asst., cons. Kleberg, Dyer, Redford & Weil, Corpus Christi, Tex., 1984-86; tchr. English lit. Brownsville (Tex.) Ind. Sch. Dist., 1986-90; dir. testing and assessment, dir. suicide intervention Kingsville Ind. Sch. Dist., Kingsville, 1993—; counselor Kingsville Ind. Sch. Dist., 1993—; cons. Conner Mus., Kingsville, 1981-82. Author: The School Counselor: A Profession in Transition, 1993; contbr. articles to various publs. Recipient Disting. Svc. award for Excellence in Broadcasting, Tex. A&M, 1980-81. Mem. ACA (profl.), Tex. Counseling Assn., Mensa, The Blues Found. (internat. voting mem.), State Bar of Tex. (legal asst. div. 1985), Am. Counseling Assn., Tex. Counselors Assn., Tex. Sch. Counselors Assn., Tex. Assn. for Humanistic Edn. and Devel., Tex. Assn. for Multi-Cultural Counseling and Devel., Am. Assn. Assessment in Counseling, World Wildlife Fedn., Gulf Coast Counseling Assn., Gulf Coast Assn. for Counseling and Devel., The Blues Found., Phi Delta Kappa , Alpha Chi. Methodist. Home: 515 University Blvd Kingsville TX 78363-4242 Office: 515 University Blvd Kingsville TX 78363

ROBINSON, ALEXANDER JACOB, clinical psychologist; b. St. John, Kans., Nov. 7, 1920; s. Oscar Frank and Lydia May (Beitler) R.; m. Elsie Louise Riggs, July 29, 1942; children: Madelyn K., Alicia A., David J., Charles A., Paul S., Marietta J., Stephen N. BA in Psychology, Ft. Hays (Kans.) State U., 1942, MS in Clin. Psychology, 1942; postgrad., U. Ill., 1942-44. Cert. psychologist, sch. psychologist. Chief psychologist Larned (Kans.) State Hosp., 1948-53, with employee selection, outpatient services, 1953-55; sch. psychologist County Schs., Modesto, Calif., 1955-61, Pratt (Kans.) Jr. Coll., 1961-66; fed. grantee, writer assoc. dir. Exemplary Federally Funded Program for Spl. Edn., Pratt, 1966-70; dir. spl. edn., researcher Stafford County Schs., St. John, 1970-81, ret., 1981; supr. testing and data Incidence of Exceptional Children in Kansas, Kans. State U., Ft. Hays, 1946; writer, asst. dir. Best Exemplary Federally Funded Program on Spl. Edn., Pratt, 1966-70; fed. grantee, researcher, writer, study dir. Edn. for the High-Performance Child, St. John, 1970—, Psychogenesis of the Sociopathic Personality, a longitudinal study. Minister, The Ch. of Jesus Christ. Served to 2d lt. U.S. Army, 1944-46, PTO. Mem. N.Y. Acad. Scis. Lodge: Lions (program chmn. St. John 1974-76). Home and Office: RR 1 Box 121A Saint John KS 67576-9801

ROBINSON, ANGELA TOMEI, clinical laboratory scientist; b. Bklyn., June 5, 1957; d. Leo James and Nina Angela T.; m. John C. Robinson, Sept. 27, 1987. BS, St. John's U., 1979, MS, 1985. Cert. lab. technologist Nat. Cert. Agy. for Med. Lab. Personnel. Exec. sec. Stead-fast Temporaries, Inc., N.Y.C., 1975-79; chief med. technologist Winthrop-U. Hosp., Mineola, N.Y., 1979—; coord., founder Nat. Med. Lab. Week, Mineola, N.Y., 1981—; tech. supr., lab. mgr., cons. Hilton Med. Group, Hempstead, N.Y., 1993—; staff contbr. newsletter Winthrop-U. Hosp., Mineola, 1981—, in pub. rels., 1981—, mem. numerous coms., clin. instr. for retng. personnel in lab., chmn. com. to petition salary increases, 1987-90; guest lectr. seminar C.W. Post Coll., Westbury, N.Y., 1986—, adj. prof., 1992—; guest lectr. SUNY, Stony Brook, 1995—; rep. Nassau Suffolk Health Manpower Plan, 1991. Author: (poetry) Our World's Best Loved Poems, 1984 (2d place merit cert. 1983) contbr. articles to profl. jours.; lectr. edn1. seminars and confs. Singer Blessed Sacrament Ch. Choir, Bklyn., 1971-73, coord., singer ch. folk group, 1971-79; mem. Mothers Against Drunk Driving, 1985-87, Nat. Rep. Congl. Com., 1984-86, Am. Health Found., 1986-87, DAV, 1984-87; fundraiser Statue of Liberty/Ellis Island Found., 1985-86, 95-96, Hands Across Am., 1986, U.S. Olympic Team Spirit, 1992—, U.S. English First, Nat. Mus. Am. Indians. Recipient cert. of merit N.Y. State Senate, 1985, citation Gov. N.Y. State Pres. Soc., 1975; award St. John's U. Med. Tech. Alumni, 1992. Mem. Am. Soc. Clin. Lab. Sci., Profl. Stds. Coalition Clin. Lab. Pers., Am. Soc. Clin. Pathologists (registered), Made in the U.S. Found., N.Y. State Soc. Clin. Lab. Sci. (chmn. govt. liason com., state bd. dirs. 1988—, Outstanding Med. Tech. Student award 1979, Member of Yr. award 1995, founding officer Nassau-Suffolk chpt. 1985-86, bd. dirs., seminar moderator 1985-87, pres.-elect 1986-87, 90-91, pres. 1991—, membership com. 1991, state chairperson 1993—), Profl. STDS Coalition (pub. rels. chair 1993—), Theta Phi Alpha (alumni chmn. 1976-77, alumni-collegiate rep. 1986-87).

ROBINSON, BERNARD PAHL, thoracic surgeon, educator; b. N.Y.C., Apr. 12, 1919; s. Nathaniel and Augusta (Strauss) R.; m. Gloria Joyce Rehfuss, Oct. 3, 1943; children: Lawrence, Andrew. BS, NYU, 1938; MD, L.I. Coll. Medicine, 1942. Diplomate Am. Bd. Surgery, Am. Bd. Thoracic Surgery. Intern Mount Sinai Hosp., N.Y.C., 1942-43, resident in surgery, 1946-47; resident in surgery Beth Israel Hosp., Boston, 1948-49; resident in thoracic surgery VA Hosp, Castle Point, N.Y., 1949-50; assoc. attending surgeon Mt. Sinai Hosp., N.Y.C., 1956—; asst. clin. prof. surgery Mt. Sinai Sch. Medicine, N.Y.C., 1968—. Capt. U.S. Army, 1943-46. Fellow Am. Coll. Surgeons, Am. Coll. Chest Physicians; mem. N.Y. Soc. for Thoracic Surgery. Jewish. Home: 4601 Henry Hudson Pky W Bronx NY 10471-3801 Office: 8 E 83rd St New York NY 10028-0418

ROBINSON, BEVERLY CLAIRE HARRIS, community health nurse, educator, researcher; b. Austin, Tex., Oct. 20, 1946; d. George R. and Goldie (Hodge) Harris; m. Ronald Anthony Robinson, Apr. 5, 1969; 1 child, Jon Michael. BS, U. Tex., 1968, PhD, 1989; MS, Tex. Woman's U., 1978. Team leader Bapt. Meml. Hosp., San Antonio, 1968-69; staff nurse Nashoba Community Hosp., Ayer, Mass., 1969-70; charge nurse Holy Cross Hosp., Austin, 1970-71; staff nurse, charge nurse Martin Army Hosp., Ft. Benning, Ga., 1971-73; community health nurse, cons. Harris County Health Dept., Houston, 1973-79; from instr. to assoc. prof. Sch. Nursing U. Tex. Health Sci. Ctr., San Antonio, 1979—; cons. Ella Austin Cmty. Ctr., San Antonio, 1982—; bd. dirs. numerous orgns.; charter mem., nursing rsch. initial study sect. NIH, Nat. Inst. Nursing. Rsch. Divsn. Rsch. Grants, 1994-96; rep. payment adv. com. Social Security Adminstrn., 1995-96. Co-editor: (newsletter) Assn. Community Health Nursing Educators, 1989-90; contbr. articles to profl. jours. Mem. adv. com. task force Homelessness and Severe Mental Illness, NIMH, Washington, 1991-92; mem. Leadership Tex., 1992. Recipient Rosemary McKevitt New Investigator Rsch. award, U. Tex. Health Sci. Ctr., 1992. Fellow Am. Acad. Nursing; mem. ANA (Ethnic Minority fellow 1983-88, W.K. Kellogg Found. fellow 1989-91), ANCC (cert., bd. dirs. 1991-92, 95, chairperson commn. on certification 1991-92, 95, chairperson bd. certification in gen. nursing practice 1990-92), Sigma Theta Tau. Office: U Tex Health Sci Ctr Sch Nursing 7703 Floyd Curl Dr San Antonio TX 78284-7950

ROBINSON, BRUCE, medical scientist, physician, educator; b. Perth, Australia, June 2, 1950. MBBS, U. We. Australia, 1974, MD, 1987. Registrar Guys' Hosp., London, 1976-78; vis. scientist NIH, Bethesda, Md., 1981-84; prof. medicine U. We. Australia, 1989—. Fellow Royal Australasian Coll. Physicians, Royal Coll. Physicians. Office: U Dept Medicine, Queen Elizabeth II Med Ctr, Nedlands WA 6009, Australia

ROBINSON, CHARLENE G., mental health nurse; b. Mt. Union, Pa., Jan. 10, 1932; d. Lester and Clarabelle (Parsons) Garman; m. John W. Robinson, Dec. 21, 1951 (dec.); children: John W. Jr., Susan, Cheryl, Lester, Nancy. Diploma, Temple U., 1954; BSN, U. Louisville, 1983, MSN, 1986; MEd, Western Ky. U., 1984. Asst. prof. nursing Elizabethtown (Ky.) Community Coll.; staff nurse Ireland Army Hosp., Ft. Knox, Ky.; asst. mgr. psychiatry J.C. Blair Meml. Hosp., Huntingdon, Pa.; nursing instr. Kauai Community Coll., Lihue, Hawaii; asst. mgr. psychiatry J.C. Blair Meml. Hosp., Huntingdon. Mem. Am. Psychiat. Nurses Assn. Home: 306 4th St Huntingdon PA 16652-1422

ROBINSON, CHERYL ANN, nurse; b. Buffalo, Feb. 18, 1946; d. James Erskine Robinson and Helen Marie (Tsybulsky) Applestein; m. William DeDario, Apr. 26, 1972 (div. 1981); children: Jennifer Denise, Marc Anthony. Grad., Meyer Meml. Hosp. Sch. Nursing, Buffalo, 1966; nurse practitioner, Meharry Med. Coll., Nashville, 1982-83; BS, Coll. St. Francis, Joliet, Ill., 1990; MA, Webster U., 1994. RN, N.Y., Tenn., Calif., Nev. Nurse, head nurse Erie County Med. Ctr., Buffalo, N.Y., 1966-70, So. Nev. Meml. Hosp., Las Vegas, 1970-72; field nursing supr. Upjohn Health Care Svcs., Las Vegas, 1976-80; utilization rev. coord. N. Las Vegas Hosp., N. Las Vegas, Nev., 1980-81; hosp. rev. mgr. Nev. Profl. Standards Rev. Orgn., Reno, 1981-83; claims/risk investigator Vanderbilt U. Med. Ctr., Nashville, 1983-84; mgr. health care rev. Corroon & Black Benefits, Inc., Nashville, 1984-87; dir. med. svcs. Equicor Health Plan, Inc., Nashville, 1987; nat. dir. utilization mgmt. Equicor, Inc., Nashville, 1988-90; dir. utilization mgmt. Aetna Health Plans, San Diego, 1990-92; v.p. med. mgmt. Managed Care Adminstrs., San Diego, 1992-93; v.p. med. mgmt. and MIS, Strategic Healthcare Mgmt., 1993-94; dir. utilization mgmt. group health Community Care Network, Inc., San Diego, 1994-95; ind. managed care cons. Ariston Cons., Del Mar, Calif., 1995—. Contbr. articles to profl. jours. Mem. Jacques Costeau Soc., 1975, Greenpeace, 1988; past pres. Middle Tenn. Utilization Mgmt. Quality Assurance Profls. Mem. Nat. Assn. Quality Assurance Profls., Mid. Tenn. Utilization Mgmt. Quality Assurance Profls. (v.p. 1985, pres. 1986), Calif. Assn. Quality Assurance Profls., San Diego Women in Healthcare Adminstrn. Episcopalian. Home: 14035 Mango Dr Apt E Del Mar CA 92014-2922 Office: Ste 369 2640 Del Mar Heights Rd Del Mar CA 92014

ROBINSON, DAVID MASON, cell physiologist; b. Barton, Eng., July 7, 1932; came to U.S., 1969, naturalized, 1979; s. Thomas Leon Mason and Mabel (Orr) R.; B.Sc. with 1st class honours, U. Durham, 1955, Ph.D. (Philip Buckle Meml. scholar), 1958; m. Jean Marcia Smith, Sept. 10, 1965; children—Jane Leonie Mason, Simon Henry Mason. Mem. sci. staff Namulonge Research Sta., Kampala, Uganda, 1959-61; research officer, tutor Hope Dept. Zoology, Oxford (Eng.) U., 1961-63; mem. sci. staff, biophysics group Med. Research Council, Radiobiol. Research Unit, Harwell, Eng., 1963-66; prin. sci. officer, head cell biology Microbiol. Research Establishment, Porton, Eng., 1966-69; asst. research dir., head cell biology ARC Blood Research Lab., Bethesda, Md., 1969-73; prof. biology, assoc. mem. Vincent Lombardi Cancer Research Ctr., Georgetown U., Washington, 1974-80, adj. prof. anatomy and cell biology, Sch. of Medicine, 1982-90; professorial lectr. in liberal studies Georgetown U., 1980—; assoc. dir. for sci. programs, div. heart and vascular disease Nat. Heart, Lung and Blood Inst., NIH, Bethesda, Md., 1980-94, acting dir., 1993, dir. vascular rsch. program, 1994—; mem. faculty biology and genetics NIH Grad. Sch., 1981-86; mem. faculty Brookings Inst., 1994—. Capt. 1st Royal Green Jackets, 43d and 52d, Brit. Ter. Army, 1962-65. Empire Cotton Growing Corp. postgrad. scholar, 1957. Recipient Vicennial medal Georgetown U., 1992. Mem. Biophys. Soc., Soc. Complex Carbohydrates, Soc. Cryobiology (sec. 1975), Am. Soc. Cell Biology, Sigma Xi (pres. Georgetown chpt. 1978), Alpha Sigma Nu (hon.). Democrat. Episcopalian. Club: Royal Green Jackets Officers. Author: (with G.A. Jamieson) Mammalian Cell Membranes, 5 vols., 1973-76; contbr. articles to profl. jours. Home: Stoneleigh Cottage PO Box 2164 Shepherdstown WV 25443-2164 Office: NIH Two Rockledge Ctr Ste 10193 Bethesda MD 20892-7956

ROBINSON, DEREK, medical editor; b. Manchester, Eng., May 25, 1928; came to U.S., 1957.; MBChB, Manchester U., 1952, MD, 1961; diploma in child health, London U., 1958, diploma in pub. health, 1959. Diplomate Am. Bd. Preventive Medicine. Assoc. editor Med. Jour. Australia, 1955-57; resident in pub. health Va. State Health Dept., 1957-58; dir. child health Hampshire, Eng., 1959-61; fellow Toronto Sch. Pub. Health, Can., 1961-62; instr. Harvard Sch. Pub. Health, 1962-64; assoc. pediatrics Boston Childrens Hosp., 1963-68; dep. state health commr. Mass., 1966-75; sr. clin. lectr. Liverpool Sch. Tropical Medicine, Eng., 1975-85; dir. pub. health, exec. dir. Shropshire Health Authority, 1985-93; pvt. practice med. writer, infectious disease epidemiologist. Editor, contbr.: Epidemiology and the Community Control of Disease in Warm Climate Countries, 1985; editor pub. health New Eng. Jour. Medicine and Mass. Physician; contbr. articles to profl. jours. Mem. Brit. Med. Assn., Mass. Med. Soc. Home and Office: Axland Assocs, 15 Claremont Hill, Shrewsbury SY1 1RD, England

ROBINSON, EDWARD NORWOOD, JR., physician, educator; b. Winston-Salem, N.C., Aug. 20, 1953; s. Edward Norwood and Pauline (Gray) R.; m. Pamela Martin Pittman, Apr. 22, 1978; children: Patrick Edward, Alexander Wood. BA, Duke U., 1975; MD, Bowman Gray Sch., Winston-Salem, 1979. Diplomate Am. Bd. Internal Medicine. Intern East Carolina U. Sch. Medicine, Greenville, N.C., 1979-80, resident, 1980-82; postdoctoral fellow U. Utah Sch. Medicine, Salt Lake City, 1982-85, asst. prof. medicine, 1985-86; asst. prof. medicine U. Louisville, 1986-88; chief infectious diseases Louisville VA Hosp., 1987-88; clin. assoc. prof. medicine U. N.C., Greensboro, 1988-93, clin. prof. medicine, 1994—; epidemiologist Greensboro Women's Hosp., 1990—. Contbr. articles to profl. jours. Fellow ACP, Infectious Diseases Soc. Am.; mem. Am. Soc. Microbiology, Am. Med. Infomatics Assn., Cousteau Soc. (founding mem.), Alpha Omega Alpha. Democrat. Methodist. Office: Moses H Cone Meml Hosp 1200 N Elm St Greensboro NC 27401-1004

ROBINSON, FLOYD WALTER, JR., health center director; b. Chambersburg, Pa., Dec. 22, 1947; s. Floyd Walter, Sr. and Nellie Jeanettie (Payton) R. B.S. in English and Speech, Shippensburg U., 1969. English master Mercersburg Acad., Pa., 1969-76; asst. to v.p. human resources Gulf Oil Chems., Houston, 1976-79; mgr. Am. Express Co., St. Thomas, Virgin Islands, 1979-82; assoc. dir. patient supply, processing and distbn. U. Tex. M.D. Anderson Cancer Ctr., Houston, 1982-89; mgr. supply, distbn., and processing cen. svcs. Hermann Hosp., Houston, 1989-90, adminstrv. dir. quality assurance quality control nutritional svc. ctr., 1990-91, Hermann Nutrition and Human Performance Ctr., 1992; career counselor Career Mgmt., 1978-79; bd. dirs. Body Positive, Houston, 1990-93, co-chair nominations com., chmn. polit. action com. for city coun. mem.; reader Taping for the Blind; bd. dirs. Delia Stewart Dance Co., 1991-95; dir. Wellness Ctr. Hermann Hosp., 1992-94, Health Ctr. U. Houston, 1994—, Houston Challenge Found., 1992—, Houston Met. Dance Ctr., Inc., 1995—. Trustee Montrose Clinic, 1991-92, Elliott H. Matthews Found., 1994—; mem. Mayor's Speakers Bur., 1991-92. Author short stories. Advisor Mayor's Youth Council, Houston, 1976-79; co-chmn. membership com. Community Alliance Houston, 1988-90, bd. dirs. Mental Health/Mental Retardation Central Pa., 1970-77, Community Concert Assn., Chambersburg, Pa., 1974-76; mem. Houston Grand Opera Co., 1989—, dir. youth employment program Houston Metropolitan Ministries, 1973-79; mem. Theatre Under Stars Friends Ctr., 1994—. Mem. Am. Soc. Hosp. Central Service Personnel, Am. Coll. Health Assn., Tex. Hosp. Assn., Houston Soc. for Central Service Personnel, Am. Mgmt. Assn. Democrat. Episcopalian. Avocations: traveling, reading, public speaking, acting and singing, reading. Home: 3140 Las Palmas Dr Houston TX 77027-5723 Office: Univ Houston Univ Health Ctr Houston TX 77204-3251

ROBINSON, HELENE SUSAN, pharmacist, manager; b. Cleve., July 10, 1956; d. Martin Stanley and Elaine (Steinhardt) Grumbach; children: Marie, Michelle, Michael. BS in Pharm. Scis., U. Cin., 1979; cert. Women in Mgmt., Ursuline Coll., Pepper Pike, Ohio, 1983. Cert. pharmacy, bus. Asst. mgr. Cunningham Drugs, Cleve., 1979-80; staff pharmacist St. Luke's Hosp., Cleve., 1980-84, oncology pharmacist, 1984-85; dir. of pharmacy Care Plus-Cleve., Beachwood, Ohio, 1985-87; staff pharmacist Kaiser Permanente, 1987-88; pharmacist HMSS, Cleve., 1988-94; pharmaicst Coram, Cleve., 1995—. Mem. Cleve. Soc. Hosp. Pharmacists (chmn. oncology 1984-85), Ohio Soc. Hosp. Pharmacists, Am. Soc. Hosp. Pharmacists, Kappa Epsilon. Baptist. Office: Coram 4350 Emery Indsl Pkwy Cleveland OH 44128

ROBINSON, HERBERT HENRY, III, educator, psychotherapist; b. Leavenworth, Wash., Mar. 31, 1933; s. Herbert Henry II and Alberta (Sperber) R.; m. Georgia Murial Jones, Nov. 24, 1954 (div. 1974); children: Cheri Dean Asbury, David Keith, Peri Elizabeth Layton, Tanda Rene Graff, Gaila Daire. Grad. of Theology, Bapt. Bible Coll., 1959; BA in Philosophy/Greek, Whitworth Coll., 1968; MA in Coll. Teaching, Ea. Wash. U., 1976; postgrad., Gonzaga U., 1980—. Cert. psychotherapist, perpetrator treatment program supervision. Choir dir. Twin City Bapt. Temple, Mishawaka, Ind., 1959-61; min. Inland Empire Bapt. Ch., Spokane, 1961-73; tchr. philosophy Spokane (Wash.) C.C., 1969-72; dir. Alternatives to Violence, Women in Crisis, Fairbanks, Alaska, 1985-87; tchr. pub. rels. U. Alaska, Fairbanks, 1986-87; dir. Alternatives to Violence Men Inc., Juneau, 1988-89; tchr. leadership mgmt. U. Alaska S.E., Juneau, 1988-89; min. Sci. of Mind Ctr., Sandpoint, Idaho, 1989-92; dir., therapist Tapio Counseling Ctr., Spokane, 1991—; cert. psychotherapist, supr. perpetrator treatment program Wash.; cons. Lilac Blind/Alpha Inc./Marshall Coll., Spokane, 1975-85, Alaska Placer Mining Co., Fairbanks, 1987; tchr. Spokane Falls C.C., Spokane, 1979-85; seminar, presenter Human Resource Devel., Spokane and Seattle, Wash., Pa., 1980; guest trainer United Way/Kellogg Found. Inst. for Volunteerism, Spokane, 1983. 1st trombone San Diego Marine Band, 1953-56, Spokane Symphony, 1961; bd. dirs. Tanani Learning Ctr., Fairbanks, 1987; mem. consensus bldg. team Sci. of Mind Ctr., Sandpoint, 1989-92. Cpl. USMC, 1953-56. Mem. ACA, Assn. for Humanistic Edn. and Devel., Assn. for Religious Values in Counseling, Internat. Assn. Addictions and Offender Counselors, Internat. Assn. Marriage and Family Counselors, Am. Assn. Profl. Hypnotherapists, Masterson Inst. Home: 11611 E Maxwell Ave Spokane WA 99206-4867 Office: Tapio Counseling Svcs Red Flag Bldg # 101A 104 S Freya Tapio Ctr Spokane WA 99202

ROBINSON, JERRY MASON, physician; b. Springplace, Ga., July 4, 1938; s. Henry Grady and Loise (Mashburn) R.; m. Rosemary Marshall, Feb. 22, 1957 (div. 1981), remarried Nov. 28, 1992; children: Deborah Elizabeth, Vickie Patricia, Lisa Anne; m. Karen Ann Eldridge, Aug. 1, 1981 (div. 1992); children: Melissa Renee, Matthew Grady, Mindi Kaye. MD, Emory U., 1962. Diplomate Am. Bd. Family Practice. Med. intern Grady Meml. Hosp., Atlanta, 1962-63; pvt. practice Deltona, Fla., 1967—; staff physician Volusia Med. Ctr., Orange City, Fla., 1994—; staff physician Central Fla. Regional Hosp., Sanford, 1982—, Fla. Hosp., Orlando, 1974—; chief family practice Central Fla. Hosp., 1982. Lt. USN, 1963-67, Vietnam. Mem. AMA, So. Med. Assn., Am. Assn. Family Practitioners, Fla. Acad. Family Practice, Seminole County Med. Soc. (pres. 1974), Heathrow Country Club, Deltona Country Club, Citrus Club, Masons, Shriners. Office: Med Arts Ctr 1555 Saxon Blvd Ste 301 Deltona FL 32725-5899

ROBINSON, JOHN CHARLES, surgeon; b. N.Y.C., Dec. 29, 1944; s. Benjamin Mag and Eugenie Levy Robinson; m. Fredelle Paula Gross, Nov. 26, 1970; children: Daniel, Melissa.; Student, U. Wis., 1963-66; MD, Washington U., 1970. Intern and resident in surgery Washington U., St. Louis, 1970-76; fellow Harvard, Boston, 1976-78; asst. prof. surgery Johns Hopkins U., Balt., 1978-81; pvt. practice Smithtown, N.Y. Recipient Nat. Koplar Rsch. award Jewish Hosp. of St. Louis, 1974-75. Fellow ACS, The Assn. of Acad. Surgery. Office: 222 E Main St Smithtown NY 11787-2814

ROBINSON, LARY ALLEN, cardiothoracic surgeon; b. Iola, Kans., Dec. 5, 1946; s. Leo Davis and Lillian Martha (Heuring) R.; m. Susannah L.; children: Schuyler A., Joshua D. BA in Anthropology, U. Kans., 1968; MD, Washington U., 1972. Diplomate Nat Bd. Med. Examiners, Am. Bd. Thoracic Surgery; diplomate in surgery and surg. critical care Am. Bd. Surgery. Resident in gen. and thoracic surgery Duke U. Med. Ctr., Durham, N.C., 1972-81, cardiothoracic fellowship, 1982-83; cardiac surgery clin. and rsch. fellowship St. Thomas' Hosp., London, 1981-82; assoc. prof. surgery U. Nebr. Med. Ctr., Omaha, 1983-94; assoc. prof. surgery U. South Fla., Tampa, 1994—, dir. divsn. cardiovascular and thoracic surgery, 1995—; adv. panel on surg. drugs and devices U.S. Pharmacopoeial Conv., 1985-90, chmn. adv. panel of surg. drugs and devices, 1990-95, 95—; critical care coun. Am. Coll. of Chest Physicians, 1988—; com. on applicants ACS, 1990—; assoc. examiner Am. Bd. Surgery, 1991-95; steering com. sect. on cardiac surgery Am. Coll. of Chest Physicians, 1993—; spl. rev. com. Nat. Cancer Inst., NIH, 1995. Contbr. chpts. to books and articles to profl. jours. Mem. great Am. Smokeout steering com. Am. Cancer Soc., 1984-86; spkr. for lectr. Bur. of Am. Cancer Soc., 1987-94, Am. Heart Assn., 1987-94; bd. dirs. Student Exch. Internat., 1989-90; rsch. com. Am. Heart Assn., 1990-94, bd. dirs. Douglas County divsn., 1991-94, comm. com. 1992-94. Maj. USAF, 1974-76. Grantee Am. Heart Assn., 1985-87, NIH, 1987-92, Abbott Labs., 1992-94, VA Rsch. grant, 1985-86. Fellow ACS, Am. Coll. Cardiology, Am. Coll. Chest Physicians; mem. Internat. Soc. for Heart Rsch., Am. Heart Assn., David C. Sabiston Jr. Surg. Soc., Assn. for Acad. Surgery, Southwestern Surg. Congress, Soc. of Thoracic Surgeons, Am. Assn. for Thoracic Surgery, Ea. Coop. Oncology Group. Office: H Lee Moffitt Cancer Ctr Rsch Inst 12902 Magnolia Dr Tampa FL 33612

ROBINSON, LESLIE ANNE, psychologist, educator; b. DeRidder, La., Dec. 11, 1956; d. Archie Edward Robinson and Nancy Carolyn Collins Mertens; m. William Leslie Fulliton, June 22, 1985; children: Samuel, Lucy. BA, Rhodes Coll., Memphis, 1978; MS, Fla. State U., 1981; PhD, U. Memphis, 1990. Lic. psychologist, Tenn. Psychology intern VA Med. Ctr., Memphis, 1989-90; psychologist Bapt. Meml. Hosp., Memphis, 1990-93; clin. psychologist Colonial Counseling Ctr., Memphis, 1993—; asst. prof. U. Memphis, 1993—; presenter/lectr. in field. Contbr. articles to profl. jours. VanVleet Meml. fellow U. Memphis, 1988-89; Fulbright-Hays grantee, 1978-79. Mem. APA, Tenn. Psychol. Assn., Phi Beta Kappa. Office: The Prevention Ctr Univ of Memphis Dept Psychology Memphis TN 38152

ROBINSON, LISA ANNE, health information management administrator; b. Dallas, May 2, 1971; d. Louie Nunn and Carol Marie (Miller) R. AS, Columbus Coll., 1992; BS in Med. Record Adminstrn., U. Ala., Birmingham, 1994. Clk. U. Ala. at Birmingham Hosp.; asst. dir. health info. mgmt. Montgomery (Ala.) Regional Med. Ctr., 1994, dir. health info. mgmt., 1994—. Mem. Am. Health Info. Mgmt. Assn. (registered record adminstr.), Ala. Health Info. Mgmt. Assn. Republican. Methodist. Home: 7036D Watchman Cir Montgomery AL 36116

ROBINSON, LOUISE EVETTE, marriage family child counselor; b. San Francisco, May 8, 1952; d. Ellis Hart and Doris Sonia (Morris) R.; stepmother Anita Robinson. BA in Psychology, U. Calif., Berkeley, 1973; MA in Psychology, Sonoma State U., 1976. Lic. marriage, family and child counselor. Co-therapist John Champlin M.D., Berkeley, 1976, Jonothon Gross M.D., Napa, Calif., 1976; counselor Buckelew House, Kentfield, Calif., 1975-77, Petaluma (Calif.) Peoples Svcs. Ctr., 1977; intake counselor Youth Advocates C.C. Riders Clinic, Novato, Calif., 1978-80, clin. supr., 1980-82; psychotherapist Robert Cohen M.D., Santa Rosa, Calif., 1984-85; dir., founder Sonoma County Assocs. in Drug Edn., Rohnert Park, Calif., 1982-90; pvt. practice marriage, family and child counseling Kentfield, Rohnert Park and Petaluma, Calif.; speaker Marin Gen. Hosp. Pediatricians, 1981, Chope Hosp. Psychiatry Residents, San Mateo, Calif., 1984; guest speaker Marin County Grand Jury Edn. Com., 1981; instr. Sonoma State U., 1984. Contbr. articles to profl. jours. Mem. Internat. Platform Assn. Democrat. Office: 100 Avram Ave Ste 105 Rohnert Park CA 94928-3100

ROBINSON, MALCOLM, gastroenterologist; b. Amarillo, Tex., July 25, 1942; s. H. Malcolm and Frances Pauline (Kohn) R.; m. Susan Laird Robinson, June 22, 1969. BS with honors, Tulane U., 1964; MD, Okla. U., 1968. Diplomate Am. Bd. Internal Medicine, Internal Medicine and Gastroenterology. Intern Cleve. Clinic, 1968-69; sr. resident, internal medicine U. Okla., Okla. City, 1974-75; GI fellow Duke U., Durham, N.C., 1969-71; sr. resident internal medicine U. Okla., Oklahoma City, 1974-75, asst. prof., 1975-76; chief GI Oklahoma City Clinic, 1976-89, Columbia Presbyn. Hosp., Okla. City, 1976—; pres., dir. Okla. Found. for Digestive Rsch., Oklahoma City, 1989-96; chief GI Presbyn. Hosp.; clin. assoc. prof. U. Okla., Oklahoma City, 1976-92, clin. prof., 1992—; mem. adv. bd. Glaxo, Inc., Solvay, Inc., Procter and Gamble, Inc., Merck-J&J, TAP Pharm., Inc., Eisai, Inc.; reviewer Am. Jour. Gastroenterology, Gastroenterology, Digestive Diseases and Sci., Gastrointestinal Endoscopy; bd. regents higher edn. U. Okla.; chair in dept. of medicine Digestive Diseases and Nutrition sect. Mem. internat. editl. bd. Alimentary Pharmacology and Therapeutics. Maj. M.C., U.S. Army, 1971-74. Benefactor 1 million dollar chair in Gastroenterology, U. Okla. Coll. of Medicine, 1996. Fellow ACP, Am. Coll. Gastroenterology; mem. Am. Soc. Gastrointestinal Endoscopy, Am. Gastroent. Assn. (Janssen award for outstanding achievement in clin. gastroenterology 1995). Office: Okla Found Digestive Rsch Ste 501 711 Stanton L Young Blvd Oklahoma City OK 73104 Office: Okla Found Digestive Rsch Ste 501 711 Stanton L Young Blvd Oklahoma City OK 73104-5022

ROBINSON, MARY JO, pathologist; b. Spokane, Wash., May 26, 1954; d. Jerry Lee and Ann (Brodie) R. BS in Biology, Gonzaga U., 1976; DO, Coll. Osteo. Medicine and Surgery, U. Med. Health Scis., 1987. Diplomate Nat. Bd. Osteo. Med. Examiners, Am. Osteo. Bd. Pathology. Med. technologist Whitman Comty. Hosp., Colfax, Wash., 1977-81, Madigan Army Med. Ctr., Ft. Lewis, Wash., 1981-83; intern Des Moines Gen. Hosp., 1987-88; resident in pathology Kennedy Meml. Hosp., Stratford, N.J., 1988-92; asst. prof. pathology Sch. Medicine U. Medicine and Dentistry of N.J., Stratford, 1995—; staff pathologist Kennedy Meml. Hosp., Cherry Hill, N.J., 1995—; fellow in dermatopathology Jefferson Med. Coll., Phila., 1994. Fellow Coll. Am. Pathologists; mem. AMA, Am. Osteo. Coll. Pathologists (1st prize resident paper 1992), Am. Osteo. Assn., Am. Soc. Clin. Pathologists, N.J.

Assn. Osteo. Physicians and Surgeons. Office: Kennedy Meml Hosp U Med Ctr 2201 Chapel Ave W Cherry Hill NJ 08002-2048

ROBINSON, MELISSA RICHARDSON, case manager, utilization review coordinator; b. Deer Park, Ala., Mar. 26, 1962; d. Henry Oley amd Eula Beatrice (Hearn) Richardson; m. Terry Lynn Robinson, Nov. 25, 1983; 1 child, Mallory Eliza. Diploma, Hobson State Tech. Coll., Thomasville, Ala., 1981. LPN Ala., La., Tenn. Cert. profl. in utilization rev. Staff nurse rehab. Rotary Rehab. Mobile (Ala.) Infirmary, 1981-82; staff nurse med.-surg. Washington County Hosp., Chatom, Ala., 1982-84; staff nurse rehab. St. Francis Hosp., Memphis, 1984-85; utilization rev. coord. Mid-South Found. for Med. Care, Memphis, 1985-86, La. Med. Rev. Found., Metairie, 1986-87; residential family care parent Meth. Children's Home, New Orleans, 1986-88; quality assurance data abstractor So. Bapt. Hosp., New Orleans, 1987-88; patient care coord. Prin. Health Care of La., Metairie, 1988-92; case mgr./utilization rev. coord. Slidell (La.) Meml. Hosp., 1992—. Brownie leader Girl Scouts U.S., Slidell, 1985-86. Baptist. Home: 61418 Yaupon Trail LaCombe LA 70445 Office: Slidell Meml Hosp 1001 Gause Blvd Slidell LA 70458-2939

ROBINSON, MICHAEL RICHARD, ophthalmologist; b. Chgo., Sept. 7, 1957; s. Kenneth E. and Jacqueline Robinson; m. Roberta L. Frank, Aug. 25, 1990. BS in Biology magna cum laude, Syracuse U., 1979; MD, SUNY, Syracuse, 1983. Diplomate Am. Bd. Ophthalmology, Nat. Bd. Med. Examiners. Intern St. Joseph's Hosp. and Health Ctr., Syracuse, 1983-84; resident SUNY, Syracuse, 1984-87; med. dir. Rochester Eye Ctr., 1986—; pres. Antiviral Delivery Systems, Rochester; presenter in field. Contbr. articles to profl. jours. Mem. AMA, Assn. for Rsch. in Vision and Ophthalmology, Am. Acad. Ophthalmology, Am. Coll. of Eye Surgeons, Phi Beta Kappa. Office: Rochester Eye Ctr 30 N Union St Rochester NY 14607

ROBINSON, NANCY MAYER, psychology educator; b. Houston, Aug. 30, 1930; d. Sidney L. and Bertha-Louise (Heyman) Mayer; m. Halbert B. Robinson, June 24, 1951 (dec. Mar. 1981); children: Christine Halberstadt, Laura Nicholson, David Robinson, Elizabeth Robinson. BA, Stanford (Calif.) U., 1951, MA, 1953, PhD, 1958. Lic. psychologist, Wash. Asst. prof. edn. U. N.C., Chapel Hill, 1966-69; sr. rsch. assoc. U. Wash., Seattle, 1969-74, assoc. prof. psychiatry and behavioral scis., 1974-82, prof. psychiatry and behavioral scis., 1982—, chief psychologist Child Devel. and Mental Retardation Ctr., 1974-88, dir. Ctr. for Study of Capable Youth, 1981—; cons. U.S. State Dept. Office Overseas Schs., Washington, 1986—; mem. nat. adv. bd. Nat. Inst. Child Health and Human Devel., Bethesda, Md., 1979-83; trustee Am. Psychol. Found. Author: (with H.B. Robinson) Mentally Retarded Child, 1965, 76; editor Am. Jour. Mental Deficiency, 1979-86. Recipient Edn. award Am. Assn. Mental Deficiency, 1982, Presidential award, 1986. Fellow APA, Am. Psychol. Soc.; mem. AAAS, Acad. Mental Retardation (sec. 1983-86), Am. Ednl. Rsch. Assn., Soc. Rsch. in Child Devel., Nat. Assn. Gifted Children. Home: 5005 NE 45th St Seattle WA 98105-3805 Office: Halbert Robinson Ctr Capable Youth U Wash Box 351630 Seattle WA 98195-1630

ROBINSON, NATHANIEL DAVID, physician; b. Providence, May 21, 1904; m. Dorothy Mae McLaughlin, Mar. 27, 1940; children: Nathaniel David Jr., Judith A. (Mrs. Joseph F. Baugher), Nancy L. (Mrs. Robert W. VanTuyle). BS, Tufts U., 1928, MD, 1931; postgrad. ophthalmology, N.Y.U., 1945-46. Diplomate Am. Bd. Ophthalmology. Intern Gallinger Mcpl. Hosp., Washington, 1931-32; physician gen. medicine Marine Hosp., Balt., 1935-36; gen. practice medicine Providence, 1936-40; resident ophthalmology Bellevue Hosp., N.Y.C., 1946-49; asst. to prof. ophtalmology N.Y.U., N.Y.C., 1949; practice medicine specilizing in ophthalmology Providence, 1949—; cons. staff R.I., Miriam, VA, Roger Williams, Chapin Hosps., Providence, Meml. Hosp., Pawtucket, R.I.; ophthalmologist Sr. Friendship Ctr., Naples, Fla. Served with USN, 1940-45, PTO, ret. capt. USNR, 1964. N.Y. Kiwanis Club grantee for ophthalmology. Mem. R.I., Providence, Collier County med. socs., R.I., New Eng., Pan Am. Ophthal. socs., AMA, Am. Acad. Ophthalmology, Pan. Am. Med. Assn., Soc. Eye Surgeons, R.I. Hist. Soc., English Speaking Union, Audobon Soc., Narragansett Bay Power Squadron, Ret. Officers Assn., Mil. Order Fgn. Wars, Navy League of the U.S. Unitarian. Clubs: University, Moorings Country. Home: 2880 Gulf Shore Blvd N Apt 308 Naples FL 33940-4326

ROBINSON, PATRICIA ELAINE, women's health nurse practitioner; b. St. Louis, June 30, 1955; d. Harold Winford and Robbie LaVeal (Ferguson) Hammett; m. Kenneth M. Robinson, Nov. 18, 1978 (div.); children: Barry Christopher, Emily Vanessa; m. C. gilbert, Nov. 20, 1990. ADN, St. Louis Community Coll., 1987; student, Webster U., 1990—; cert. in forensic pathology, St. Louis U., 1975; cert. in pharmacology, St. Louis Coll. Health, 1984; womens health nurse practioner, U. Mo., 1995. Per diem float nurse St. Louis U. Hosp.; court. ob-gyn. unit Group Health Plan, St. Louis; staff nurse Barnes Hosp., St. Louis; staff nurse dept. ob-gyn. Washington U. Sch. Medicine, St. Louis, 1990-93; chief exec. study coord. women's health rsch. Obstetric & Gynecologic Diagnosis & Consultation, Florissant, Mo., 1992-96; nurse practitioner and exec. study coord. women's health rsch. Women's HealthPartners, 1996—; acting dir. Nurses for Reproductive Health Svcs., St. Louis, 1990-93. Mem. NAFE, Nurse Assn. Am. Coll. Obstetrics and Gynecologists, Med. Group Mgmt. Assn., Nat. Assn. Nurse Practitioners Reproductive Health, Phi Theta Kappa. Office: OBG Diagnosis & Consultation 1150 Graham Rd Ste 105 Florissant MO 63031-8013

ROBINSON, RICHARD GARWOOD, neurosurgeon; b. Dartford, Eng., Apr. 9, 1915; arrived in New Zealand, 1951; s. William Thomas and Annie Elizabeth (Garwood) R.; m. Florence Ellen Nonk, June 12, 1941; children: Sara, Celia. MB, BS, Guy's Hosp., 1939. Sr. neurosurg. reg United Sheffield (Eng.) Hosps., 1947-51; neurosurgeon Dunedin (New Zealand) Hosp., 1951-64, dir. neurosurgery, 1964-81; prof. U. Otago, Dunedin, 1976-81, prof. emeritus, 1981—; med. advisor Accident Compensation Corp., Dunedin, 1982—. Author: (ency.) Agenesis and other Anomalies of Brain, 1971; editor: NZMA Guide to Medicines and Drugs, 1991; editor-in-chief Reader's Digest Encyclopedia of Family Health, 1995; editor New Zealand Med. Jour., 1967—. Squadron leader RAF, 1940-46. Decorated George medal (GM), Comdr. Order of the Brit. Empire. Fellow Royal Coll. Surgeons (Eng., Hunterian Prof. 1959), Royal Australian Coll. Surgeons, New Zealand Med. Assn.; mem. Neurol. Assn. New Zealand (pres. 1963-65), Neurosurg. Assn. Australasia. Home: 12A Heriot Row, Dunedin 9001, New Zealand Office: New Zealand Med Jour, PO Box 913, Dunedin 9001, New Zealand

ROBINSON, ROSCOE ROSS, nephrologist, educator; b. Oklahoma City, Aug. 21, 1929; s. Roscoe and Tennie (Ross) R.; m. Ann Allen, Aug. 24, 1952; children: Susan, Brooke. BS, U. Ctrl. Okla., 1949, MD, U. Okla., 1954, LHD, 1994. Diplomate: Nat. Bd. Med. Examiners, Am. Bd. Internal Medicine (asso. mem. bd. govs. 1975-78, mem. 1979-82, chmn. test com. on nephrology 1979-82). Intern in medicine Duke U. Med. Ctr., Durham, N.C., 1954-55, jr. asst. resident in medicine, 1955-56, chief resident, instr. medicine, 1957-58, assoc. in medicine, 1960-62, asst. prof. medicine, dir. div. nephrology, 1962-65, assoc. prof. medicine, dir. div. nephrology, 1965-69, prof. medicine, dir. div. nephrology, 1969-78, Florence McAlister prof. medicine, dir. div. nephrology, 1978-81, asso. v.p., 1976-81; chief exec. officer Duke U. Hosp., 1976-81; prof. medicine, vice chancellor health affairs Vanderbilt U. Med. Ctr., Nashville, 1981—; Am. Heart Assn. rsch. fellow, vis. fellow dept. medicine Columbia-Presbyn. Med. Ctr., N.Y.C., 1956-57; clin. investigator Durham VA Hosp., 1960-62, attending physician, 1962-81; cons. nephrology Fayetteville and Asheville, N.C.; cons. nephrology Research Triangle (N.C.) Inst., 1964-81; nat. cons. to surgeon gen. USAF, 1970-89; chmn. N.C. Kidney Coun. Region 21, Dept. HEW, 1977-81; bd. dirs. Research!America, 1993—. Mem. editorial bd. Archives Internal Medicine, 1970-80, Seminars in Nephrology, 1972-93, Mineral and Electrolyte Metabolism, 1977—; mem. editorial com. Fogerty internat. com. Monograph on Prevention of Kidney and Urinary Tract Disease; cons. editor renal diseases: Cecil Textbook of Medicine, 15th edit., 16th edit.; contbr. articles to profl. jours. Bd. dirs. SunHealth Corp., 1986-92, 1st Am. Corp., Tenn., 1992—; trustee Montgomery Bell Acad., Nashville, 1983—, Duke U., 1994—. Fellow ACP; mem. Am. Clin. and Climatol. Assn., Am. Fedn. Clin. Rsch. (councillor So. sect. 1968-71), Assn. Am. Physicians, European Dialysis and Transplant Assn., Am. Heart Assn., N.C. Heart Assn. (sr. investigator 1962-74, exec. com., bd. dirs. 1971-72), Am. Soc. Clin. Investigation, So. Soc. Clin. Investigation (councillor 1977-80), Am. Physiol. Soc., Am. Soc. Artificial Internal Organs (councillor 1968-71), Internat. Soc. Nephrology (editor Kidney Internat. jour. 1971-84, exec. com. 1972-95, v.p. 1984-87, pres.-elect 1987-90, pres. 1990-93), Am. Soc. Nephrology (councillor 1977-80, pres.-elect 1980-81, pres. 1981-82), Nat. Kidney Found. (sci. adv. bd. 1970-75), Kidney Found. N.C., Assn. Acad. Health Ctrs. (bd. dirs. 1985-91, chmn. 1989-90), Soc. Med. Adminstrs. (pres.-elect 1989-91, pres. 1991-93), Nat. Inst. Diabetes, Digestive and Kidney Diseases (nat. adv. coun. 1987-90), Alpha Omega Alpha. Home: 501 Jackson Blvd Nashville TN 37205-3427 Office: Vanderbilt U Med Center Dept Health Affairs Nashville TN 37232

ROBINSON, SAMUEL PETTIGREW, physician; b. Shreveport, La., Aug. 10, 1951; s. Benjamin Boags and Ann Young (Pettigrew) R.; m. Theresa Marie Parker; children: Laura Marie, Parker Pettigrew, Benjamin Garland. Student, Tulane U., 1969-72, MD, 1976. Diplomate Am. Bd. Otolaryngology. Intern in surgery Maricopa County Hosp., Phoenix, Ariz.; resident in otolaryngology Tulane U.; pntr. Eye, Ear, Nose & Throat Clinic, Gulfport, Miss., 1981-83, Green Clinic, Ruston, La., 1983-88; pvt. practice Gulfport, 1988—; clin. instr. ENT dept. Tulane U.-Sch. Medicine, New Orleans, 1990—; past pres. Gulf South Outpatient Ctr., Gulfport, 1991, sec., 1996—. Stewardship chmn. 1st United Meth. Ch., Gulfport, 1995—. Fellow AMA, Am. Acad. Otolaryngology (head and neck surgery), Miss. State Med. Assn., Coast Counties Med. Assn. (del.), Miss. Eye, Ear, Nose and Throat Soc. (del.), La.-Miss. Ophthal. & Otolaryn. Soc.; mem. Alpha Omega Alpha, Tau Beta Pi, Omicron Delta Kappa. Home: 1310 E Beach Blvd Gulfport MS 39501 Office: 3017 13th St Gulfport MS 39501

ROBINSON, TERRY EARL, neuroscience and psychology educator; b. Rochester, N.Y., May 22, 1949; s. Earl Leslie Robinson and Jean (Hanson) Fraser. BA, U. Lethbridge, 1972; MA, U. Sask., 1974; PhD, U. Western Ont., 1978. Postdoctoral fellow U. Calif., Irvine, 1977-78; asst. prof. then assoc. prof. U. Mich., Ann Arbor, 1978-89, prof., 1989—. Editor: Behavioral Approaches to Brain Research, 1983, Microdialysis in the Neurosciences, 1991; editor-in-chief: Behavioral Brain Research, 1996—; contbr. articles to profl. jours. Fellow AAAS, Am. Psychol. Soc. Office: Univ Mich Dept Psychology 525 E University St Ann Arbor MI 48109-1109

ROBINSON, TIMOTHY THOMAS, physician; b. Flushing, N.Y., Nov. 23, 1959; s. Theresa Antoinette (Jannaccio) R. BS, Fordham u., 1981; DO, N.Y. Coll. Osteo. Medicine, Old Westbury, L.I., 1985. Diplomate Am. Bd. Family Practice; lic. physician, N.Y. Attending physician Cath. Med. Ctr., Jamaica and Queens, N.Y., 1989—, North Shore Univ. Hosp., Manhasset, N.Y., Long Island Jewish Med. Ctr., New Hyde Park, N.Y., N.Y. Hosp. Med. Ctr. of Queens, Flushing, N.Y. Mem. AMA, Am. Acad. Family Physicians, Am. Coll. Emrgency Physicians, Am. Osteo. Assn., N.Y. Med. Soc., Queens County Med. Soc. Home and Office: 32 45 Bell Blvd Bayside NY 11361

ROBINSON, WALKER LEE, neurological surgeon; b. Balt., Oct. 13, 1941; s. Edward Findol and Wilma Lee (Walker) R.; m. Mae Elizabeth Meads, Apr. 9, 1966; children: Kimberly, Walker Jr. BSChemE, Morgan State Coll., 1962; MD, U. Md., 1970. Bd. cert. neurosurgeon. Capt. U.S. Army, El Paso, Tex., 1962-64; mgr. C & P Telephone Co., Balt., 1964-66; intern surgery Strong Meml. Hosp., Rochester, N.Y., 1970-71; resident neurosurgery U. Md., Univ. Hosp., Balt., 1971-74, 75-76; fellow neurology U. London, Eng., 1974-75; dir. neurotrauma U. Md., Shock Trauma Ctr., Balt., 1989-91, 94-95; head pediatric neurosurgery U. Md., Balt., 1978, assoc. prof. neurosurgery and pediatrics, 1989—; acting chmn. div. neurosurgery U. Md. Med. Sch., Balt., 1990-92; cons. Nat. Cancer Inst., Bethesda, Md., 1985-91, N.I.N.C.D.S., Bethesda, 1983-91; mem. editorial bd. Jour. of the Nat. Med. Assn., Washington, 1985-87; chmn. membership com. Am. Assn. Neurosurgery, Chgo., 1991-95; mem. med. exec. com. Shock Trauma Ctr., 1994-96. Contbr. articles to profl. jours. and chpts. to books. Bd.d irs. East Balt. Community Corp., 1978-85, Variety Club of Balt., 1989-90, Urban Cardiology Rsch. Ctr., Balt., 1987-91. Named Disting. alumni Fund for Edn. Excellence, 1991, Honoree, Afram Expo-Urban Svcs., 1989, Paul Harris fellow Rotary Internat., 1990; grantee NIH, 1991. Fellow ACS, Am. Acad. Pediatrics; mem. Am. Soc. Pediatric Neurosurgery (chmn. ethics & legal com. 1996—), Balt. Urban Svcs. Found. (pres. 1986-87), Clarence Green Neurosurg. Soc. (pres. 1984-88), Black Faculty and Staff Assn. (pres. 1989-90), State Med. Assn. (legis. com. 1990-92). Home: 3701 Cedar Dr Baltimore MD 21207-6357 Office: U of Maryland Med Sch 22 S Greene St Baltimore MD 21201-1544

ROBISON, CLARENCE, JR., surgeon; b. Tecumseh, Okla., Dec. 9, 1924; s. Clarence Sr. and Margaret Irene (Buzzard) R.; m. Patricia Antoinette Hagee, May 27, 1951; children: Timothy D., Paul D., John D., Rebecca A. AS, Stanford U., 1943; MD, U. Okla., 1948. Intern Good Samaritan Hosp., Portland, Oreg., 1948-49; fellow pathology and oncology U. Okla., 1949-51; pathologist USAF Hosp., Cheyenne, Wyo., 1951-53; resident in surgery Okla. U. Health Scis.-Va. Svc., Oklahoma City, 1953-56; mem. faculty surgery dept. Okla. U. Health Scis., Oklahoma City, 1956-57, clin. prof. surgery, 1957—; mem. bd. advisors Mercy Health Ctr., Oklahoma City, 1974-81, sec. of staff, 1974-84, chief surgery, 1992-95; bd. dirs. Okla. Found. for Peer Rev., Oklahoma City. Mem. Commn. on Mission Indian Nations Presbytery, 1980-91; bd. dirs. Found. Sr. Citizens, 1964—; elder Presbyn. Ch.; presdl. elector Dem. Party, 1960. Capt. USAF, 1951-53. Fellow ACS, Southwestern Surg. Soc., Am. Cancer Soc. (past pres. Okla. divsn., exec. com., bd. dirs., nat. del. dir.); mem. AMA (del. hosp. med. staff sect. Oklahoma City 1989—, alt. del. AMA from Okla. 1991-93, 96—), SAR, Okla. Med. Soc., Oklahoma County Med. Soc. (bd. dirs. 1989-93), Okla. State Med. Assn. (alt. trustee Okla. 1989-92, trustee 1993-96), Okla. Surg. Assn. (sec., treas. 1966-68), Oklahoma City Surg. Soc. (pres. 1967-69), Oak Tree Sportsman's Club, Petroleum Club, Men's Dinner Club, Masons (32d degree), Shriners. Office: 4200 W Memorial Rd Oklahoma City OK 73120-8305

ROBISON, JUDY KAY, nursing home administrator; b. Rosebud, Tex., Mar. 26, 1947; d. Edwin Jerry and Mildred Nadine (Tawater) Slovacek; m. James Harold Cunningham, Mar. 19, 1971 (div. Aug. 1976); 1 child, Jena Cassidie; m. Donnie Ray Robison, Dec. 20, 1976 (div. July 1982). Student LaSalle Extension U., 1966, U. Tex., 1976; AAS, McLennan Community Coll., 1980. Designer Green Flower Shop, Rosebud, 1961-65; exec. sec. Gary Job Corps Ctr., San Marcos, Tex., 1965-74; asst. adminstr. Rosebud Med. Services, 1975-77, adminstr., 1977-82; Community adminstr. Hosp. Assn. of Tex., Inc., Rosebud, 1982-91; adminstr., gen. mgr. Cam-Col Partnership Cameron Nursing Home, 1991—. Mem. Med. Products Research Panel, 1985—; adv. bd. Foodservice Research Ctr., 1984, Temple Jr. Coll., Tex., 1982, 85, R-L Ind. Sch. Dist., 1979—; TV telethon coord. Easter Seal Soc., 1985; mem. zoning com. City of Rosebud; com. mem. Ctrl. Tex. Hosp. Devel. Fund, 1992—. Recipient Friend to Edn. award Tex. State Tchrs. Assn., 1986. Mem. Am. Coll. Nursing Home Adminstrs., Rosebud C. of C. (bd. dirs. 1990-96, sec.-treas. 1991, treas. 1992, 93, 94). Clubs: Rosebud Ex-Students (sec., treas. 1982—), Rosebud-Lott Booster (sec. 1989). Avocations: music, horticulture, tennis, skiing, dancing. Home: 530 E Ave G Rosebud TX 76570 Office: CAM-COL Partnership Cameron Nursing Ctr 2202 N Travis PO Box 795 Cameron TX 76520

ROBISON, MARK KEVIN, health facility administrator; b. Louisville, Aug. 21, 1956; s. Aubrey B. and Lois (McLemore) R.; m. Gay Crass, Dec. 16, 1978; children: Matthew F., Kellyn Jo. BS cum laude, Murray State U., 1978. CPA, Fla. Staff auditor Coopers & Lybrand, Louisville, 1978-79; sr. auditor Citizens Fidelity Bank & Trust, Louisville, 1979-81; audit mgr. Owensboro (Ky.) Nat. Bank, 1981-83, Holiday Corp., Memphis, 1984-88; v.p., contr. Southeast Real Estate Ent., Orlando, Fla., 1988-89; contr. WorldSource Coil Coating, Inc., Hawsville, Ky., 1989-92; dir. bus. svcs. Mercy Hosp., Owensboro, 1992-94, St. Mary's Health Sys., Knoxville, Tenn., 1994-95; dir. therapy svcs. St. Mary's Health Sys., Knoxville, 1995—; adj. instr. Memphis Tech., 1989; cons. Direct Pay, Inc., Detroit, 1989-94; spkr. Inst. Healthcare Auditors, Knoxville, 1994. Coach Am. Yough Soccer Orgn., Knoxville, 1994, 95, Knoxville Youth Basketball, 1995-96. Mem. Ky. Soc. CPA, Knoxville Area Bus. Orgn. Office: St Mary's Health Sys 900 E Oak Hill Ave Knoxville TN 37917

ROBISON, ODIS WAYNE, geneticist, educator; b. Lawton, Okla., Aug. 23, 1934; s. Paul Estes and Ruby Isabel (Oswalt) R.; m. Ruth Ann Knight, Nov. 16, 1956;. AS in Animal Sci., Cameron State Agrl. Coll., 1953; BS in Animal Sci., Okla. State U., 1955; MS in Genetics, U. Wis., 1957, PhD in Genetics, 1959. Fellow Wis. Alumni Rsch. Found. U. Wis., Madison, 1955-57, fellow dept. genetics, 1957-59; from asst. to assoc. prof. animal sci. and genetics N.C. State U., Raleigh, 1959-74, prof. animal sci. and genetics, 1974—; cons. Shell Chem. Co., Kleen Leen, Inc., Aid to Internat. Devel.; mem. rsch. evaluation adv. com. NSF. Mem. editorial bd., sect. editor Jour. Animal Sci.; contbr. articles to profl. jours. Budget dir., treas., pres. PTA; treas., sec., deacon Ch. of Christ; vol. community programs. Recipient Disting. Svc. award Nat. Swine Improvement Fedn., 1985; named Grad. of distinction, Okla. State U., 1996; Fulbright scholar, 1990. Fellow Am. Soc. Animal Sci. (Rockefeller Prentice Meml. award 1982); mem. AAAS, Coun. for Agriculture and Sci. Tech., Am. Genetic Assn., Biometric Soc., Sigma Xi, Phi Kappa Phi, Gamma Sigma Delta (pres. 1991-92), Alpha Zeta. Office: NC State U Dept Animal Sci Box 7621 Raleigh NC 27695-7621

ROBISON, SUSAN MILLER, psychologist, educator, consultant; b. Chgo., Nov. 15, 1945; d. William Louis and Constance Mary (Maloney) Miller; m. Philip Dean Robison, Dec. 27, 1969; 1 child, Christine Alyssa. BS, Loyola U., Chgo., 1967; MS, Ohio U., 1969, PhD, 1971. Lic. psychologist, Md. Asst. prof. psychology Ohio U., Lancaster, 1970-72; prof. psychology Coll. Notre Dame, Balt., 1972—; pvt. practice Ellicott City, Md., 1982—; leadership cons. Nat. Coun. Cath. Women, Washington, 1987—. Author: Sharing Our Gifts, 1987, 2d edit., 1992, Discovering Our Gifts, 1989, Thinking and Writing in College, 1991. Troop leader Girl Scouts U.S.A., Ellicott City, 1982-85, mem. adv. bd. Girl Scouts Central Md., 1987-88; mem. adv. bd. Archdiocese of Balt., 1986. Mem. Am. Psychol. Assn., Am. Assn. Sex Educators, Counselors and Therapists, Assn. for Advancement Behavior Therapy. Home: 3725 Font Hill Dr Ellicott City MD 21042-4932

ROBITAILLE, MARK, health facility administrator; b. New Bedford, Mass., Apr. 29, 1951; children: Kari, Lauren. BA, U. Fla., 1973, MBA, 1976. Admissions/cachier North Fla. Regional Hosp., Gainesville, 1973-74; staff position/physician's billing Shands Teaching Hosp. and Clinic, Gainesville, Fla., 1971-74; adminstrv. resident Manatee Meml. Hsop., Bradenton, Fla., 1976; asst. adminstr. Martin Meml. Hosp., Stuart, Fla., 1976-81, West Orange Manor, Winter Garden, Fla., 1982-84; S.E. regional mgr., v.p. Ziegler Securities, Orlando, Fla., 1987-91; v.p., COO Martin Meml. Health Systems, Stuart, Fla., 1991—. Mem. Tri-County Tec, Stuart, Econ. Coun. Martin County. Mem. Am. Hosp. Assn., Am. Coll. Healthcare Execs., Am. Cancer Soc., Fla. Hosp. Assn., Healthcare Fin. Mgmt. Assn., Rotary. Home: 53 S River Rd Stuart FL 34996 Office: Martin Meml Health Systems 300 SE Hospital Dr Stuart FL 34994

ROBSON, MARTIN CECIL, surgery educator, plastic surgeon; b. Lancaster, Ohio, Mar. 8, 1939; children: Karen Iredell, Douglas Spears, Martin Cecil III. Student, Northwestern U., 1957-59; B.A., Johns Hopkins U., 1961, M.D., 1964. Diplomate Am. Bd. Surgery, Am. Bd. Plastic Surgery. Intern U. Chgo. Hosps. and Clinics, 1964-65; resident in surgery Balt. City Hosp., 1965-67, Brooke Gen. Hosp., Ft. Sam Houston, Tex., 1967-69; resident in plastic surgery Yale-New Haven Hosp., 1971-73; instr. dept. surgery Yale U. Sch. Medicine, New Haven, 1973-74, asst. prof. plastic surgery, 1973-74, assoc. prof., 1974; assoc. prof., chief plastic surgery U. Chgo., 1974-77, prof. and chief plastic surgery, 1977-83, dir. Burn Center, 1976-83; prof., chmn. divsn. plastic and reconstructive surgery Wayne State U., Detroit, 1983-88; dir. Detroit Med. Ctr. Burn Ctr., 1983-88; Truman Blocker Disting. prof., chief divsn. plastic surgery U. Tex. Med. Br., 1988-93; dir. surg. svcs. Shriners' Burn Inst., Galveston, Tex., 1988-93; prof. surgery, chair divsn. surg. rsch. U. South Fla., Tampa, 1993—; chair surg. svc. Bay Pines (Fla.) VA Med. Ctr., 1993—. Mem. editl. bd. Jour. Burn Care and Rehab.; editl. cons. bd.: Jour. Trauma. Served to maj. M.C. U.S. Army, 1967-71; col. USAR Med. Corps, 1991—. Recipient Writing award Am. Med. Technologists, 1979, 80, 81, 82; recipient Lancer Authors' award, 1981, 82, Fisher award, 1982. Fellow ACS, Royal Australian Coll. Surgeons (hon.); mem. Plastic Surgery Rsch. Coun. (chmn. 1983-84), Am. Burn Assn. (pres. 1985-86, Disting. Svc. award), Am. Surg. Assn., Am. Assn. Plastic Surgery, Am. Soc. Plastic and Reconstructive Surgeons, Nu Sigma Nu, Phi Delta Theta, Alpha Omega Alpha. Office: Bay Pines VA Med Ctr Bay Pines FL 33504

ROCA, JOSÉ RAMÓN, invasive cardiologist; b. San Juan, P.R., Mar. 28, 1956; s. Fernando and Angelina (Saavedra) R.; m. Francine Monroy; children: Nikiel and Michèle. BS, U. P.R., San Juan, 1981, MD, 1981. Intern Wayne State U., Detroit, 1981-82, resident in internal medicine, 1982-84, fellow in cardiology, 1984-87; staff Garper-Grace Hosp., Detroit, 1987-88; pvt. practice specializing in invasive cardiology Tarpon Springs, Fla., 1988—. Fellow Am. Coll. Cardiology, Am. Coll. Chest Physicians; mem. Pinellas County Med. Soc. Office: 34911 US Hwy 19 N Ste 508 Palm Harbor FL 34684

ROCHA, MARILYN EVA, clinical psychologist; b. San Bernardino, Calif., Oct. 23, 1928; d. Howard Ray Gonding and Laura Anne (Johanson) Walker; m. Hilario Ursala Rocha, Mar. 25, 1948 (dec. Feb. 1971); children: Michael, Sherry, Teri, Denise. AA, Solano Jr. Coll., 1970. BA, Sacramento State U., 1973, MA, 1974; PhD, U.S. Internat. U., 1981. Psychologist, Naval Drug Rehab. Ctr., U.S. Navy, San Diego, 1975-85, chief psychologist, 1983-84; staff clin. psychologist Calif. Youth Authority No. Reception Ctr. Clinic, 1985-92, El Paso de Robles Sch., 1992—; dir. Self-Help Agys., San Diego. Author short story. Vol. counselor Hamonium, San Diego, 1976-77; SMRC Planning Group Scripps/Miramar Ranch, 1982-85; leader Vacaville council Cub Scouts Am., Calif., 1957-62, 4-H, also Brownie's. Recipient Outstanding Svc. award CYA, 1993, Woman of the Yr. award CYA, 1995. Mem. APA, PTA (hon., life), Calif. Scholastic Fedn., Am. Assn. Suicidology, Friends of the Libr. (sec.), Bus. and Profl. Women, Kiwanis Internat., Delta Zeta. Democrat. Unitarian. Home: Morning Glory Ranch 4625 Ross Dr Paso Robles CA 93446-9379

ROCHE, JAMES RICHARD, pediatric dentist, university dean; b. Fortville, Ind., July 17, 1924; s. George Joseph and Nelle (Kinnaman) R.; m. Viola Marie Morris, May 15, 1949; 1 child, Ann Marie Roche Potter. DDS, Ind. U., 1947, MS in Dentistry, 1983. Diplomate Am. Bd. Pediat. Dentistry (exec. sec.-treas. 1982—). Prof. emeritus Ind. U. Sch. Dentistry, Indpls., 1968—, chmn. divsn. grad. pediat. dentistry, 1969-76, asst. dean faculty devel., 1976-80, assoc. dean faculty devel., 1980-87, assoc. dean for acad. affairs, 1987-88; cons. Coun. Dental Edn., Hosp. Dental Svc. and Commn. Accreditation, Chgo., 1977-83. Capt. U.S. Army, 1952-54. Recipient Disting. Teaching Recognition award Ind. U., 1976. Fellow Internat. Coll. Dentists, Am. Coll. Dentists, Am. Acad. Pediat. Dentistry (bd. dirs. 1967-70), Pierre Fauchard Acad.; mem. ADA (cons. Bur. Dental Health Edn. 1977), Am. Soc. Dentistry for Children (award of excellence 1993), Ind. Dental Assn. (v.p. 1973-74, chmn. legis. com. 1968-77, lobbyist 1970-77), Indpls. Dist. Dental Assn. (pres. 1967-68), Ind. U.-Purdue U. Indpls. Sr. Acad. (charter), Masons, Omicron Kappa Upsilon. Home and Office: 1193 Woodgate Dr Carmel IN 46033-9232

ROCHEN, DONALD MICHAEL, osteopathic physician; b. Buffalo, Apr. 15, 1943; s. Leo Kant and Phoebe (Elkan) R.; m. Phyllis Helene Been, Aug. 15, 1971; children: Steven, Douglas, Deborah, Andrew. B.A., Northwestern U., 1964; D.O., Coll. Osteo. Medicine and Surgery, Des Moines, 1968. Intern, Detroit Osteo./Bi County Cmty. Hosps., 1968-69, resident in otorhinolaryngology, 1969-73; practice otorhinolaryngology otolaryngic allergy oro-facial plastic surgery, Madison Heights, Warren, Farmington Hills and Mt. Clemens, Mich., 1973—; program dir. residency and chmn. dept. otolaryngology and orofacial plastic surgery Bi County Cmty. Hosp., Warren, Mich.; past chmn. dept. otolaryngology Mt. Clemens Gen. Hosp.; mem. staff Mt. Clemens Gen. Hosp. (Mich.), Oakland Gen. Hosp., Botsford Gen. Hosp., Bi County Community Hosp.; assoc. prof. Mich. State U. Coll. Osteo. Medicine and Surgery, 1975—; adj. prof. Coll. Osteo. Medicine and Surgery, Des Moines, 1981—. Fellow Osteo. Coll. Ophthalmology and Otorhinolaryngology (diplomate), Am. Acad. Otolaryngology, Head and Neck Surgery, Am. Acad. Otolaryngic Allergy; mem. Am. Osteo. Assn., Mich. Assn. Osteo. Physicians and Surgeons, Am. Acad. Otolaryngic Allergy, N.Y. Acad. Scis., Mich. Otolaryngol. Soc., Oakland County Osteo. Assn., Macomb County Osteo. Assn. Home: 4808 Tyndale Ct West Bloomfield MI 48323-3351 Office: 27483 Dequindre Rd Madison Heights MI 48071-3491

ROCHLIN, GREGORY, psychiatrist, educator; b. Balt., Oct. 19, 1912; s. Howard and Marie (Ross) R.; m. Helen Louise Buker, Dec. 17, 1938; children: Gregory Martin Rochlin, Martha Bayard Kapos. BS, U. Md., 1932, MD, 1936. Cert. Diplomate Am. Bd. Psychiatry and Neurology. Intern Sinai Hosp., Balt., 1936-37; resident in psychiatry Worcester (Mass.) State Hosp., 1937-38; asst. resident in psychiatry Inst. Human Relations Yale U., New Haven, 1938-39, sr. asst. resident in psychiatry, 1939-40; psychiatrist Mass. Gen. Hsop., 1944-45; judge Baker Guidance Ctr., 1945-47; tng. analyst Boston Psychoanalytic Inst., 1950-87; chief child psychiatrist Mass. Mental Health Ctr., 1950-75; pres. Boston Psychoanalytic Soc. and Inst., 1960-63; assoc. clin. prof. psychiatry Harvard U. Med. Sch., 1963-75; pres. Inst. Continuing Edn. Child Psychiatry, 1975-81; lectr. psychiatry Harvard U. Med. Sch., Cambridge, 1978—. Author: Griefs and Discontents, the Forces of Change, 1965, Man's Aggression, the Defense of the Self, 1973, The Masculine Dilemma, 1980. Mem. Am. Psychiat. Assn. (life), Boston Psychoanalytic Soc. (life, pres. 1960-63), Am. Psychoanalytic Assn. (bd. profl. standards 1960-63, cert., life), Acad. Child Psychiatry (charter mem.). Democrat. Home and Office: 200 Brattle St Cambridge MA 02138-3347

ROCHON, ROY BERNARD, surgeon, educator; b. Houston, Dec. 2, 1956; s. Lonnie Bernard Rochon and Carrie Lee (Hampton) McAfee; m. CArol Elizabeth Joyce, Aug. 2, 1986; children: Preston Bernard, Hilliary Ann. BS, U. Houston, 1978; MDMeharry Med. Coll., 1982. Diplomate Am. Bd. Surgery. Internship in gen. surgery William Beaumont Am. Med. Ctr., El Paso, Tex., 1982-83, residency in gen. surgery, 1984-88; fellowship in trauma, critical care Parkland Meml. Hosp., Dallas, 1988-90; staff surgeon Brooke Army Med. Ctr., San Antonio, 1990-91; asst. prof. surgery U. Tex. Southwestern Med. Ctr., Dallas, 1991-93; attending surgeon Med. and Surg. Clinic Irving, Tex., 1993—; Fellow Am. Coll. Surgeons. Author: (chpt.) Surgical Clinics of North America, 1991, (chpt.) General Thoracic Surgery, 1994. Fellow Am. Coll. Surgeons, Southwestern Surg. Congress; mem. Nat. Med. Assn., Tex. Med. Assn., Dallas County Med. Soc., Dallas Soc. Gen. Surgeons, Alpha Omega Alpha. Roman Catholic. Office: Med and Surg Clinic Irving 1923 West Park Dr Irving TX 75061

ROCK, GAIL ANN, obstetrical/gynecological nurse; b. Maquokela, Iowa, Mar. 24, 1960; d. Robert William and Mary Anne (Franzen) Scheckel; m. William Beale Rock III, June 6, 1981; 1 child, William Beale IV. Chiropractic Asst., Palmer Coll. Chiropractic, Davenport, Iowa, 1979; AAS in Nursing, North County Community Coll., Saranac Lake, N.Y., 1987; BSN, SUNY, Plattsburg, 1992-95. Cert. resolve thru sharing counselor, inpatient obstet. nurse; cert. childbirth educator. Staff nurse ob-gyn. Adriondack Med. Ctr., Saranac Lake, N.Y., 1987-90, nurse mgr. ob-gyn., 1990-95; nurse mgr. birth ctr. Preston Meml. Hosp., Kingwood, W.Va., 1995—; group educator sibling and new parent classes, Saranac Lake, 1991-95; mem. Garrett County Pub. Health Childbirth Edn., 1995—. Mem. Assn. Women's Health Obstetric & Neonatal Nurses, NAFE, Sigma Theta Tau. Home: 880 Trap Run Rd Friendsville MD 21531 Office: Preston Meml Hosp 300 S Price St Kingwood WV 26537

ROCK, JOHN AUBREY, gynecologist and obstetrician, educator; b. Corpus Christi, Tex., Oct. 21, 1946; s. William A. and Burta (Wheeler) R.; m. Barbara McAlpine, Oct. 8, 1976; children: John Aubrey Jr., Deborah Ellen, Daniel Authur. BS in Zoology, La. State U., Baton Rouge, 1968; MD, La. State U., New Orleans, 1972. Asst. prof. Johns Hopkins U. Sch. Medicine, Balt., 1978-80, assoc. prof., 1980-87, prof. ob-gyn, 1987-92, prof. pediatrics, 1988-92, dir. reproductive endocrinology, 1979-91, dep. dir. med. sch., 1985-88; chmn. Union Meml. Hosp., Balt., 1991-92; James Robert McCord prof., chmn. dept. ob-gyn. Emory U. Sch. Medicine, Atlanta, 1992—; cons. Dept. Army, Washington, 1982-93, NASA, Houston, 1988—; chmn. ad hoc com. on in vitro fertilization State of Md., 1985. Author: Reparative and Constructive Surgery of the Female Generative Tract, 1983, Endometriosis, 1988, TeLinde's Operative Gynecology, 1991, 95; mem. editl. bd. Fertility and Sterility jour., 1986-94, Gynecology Surgery, 1989—. Fellow ACOG; mem. Am. Gynecol. and Obstet. Soc., Soc. Gynecol. Surgeons, Am. Fertility Soc. (bd. dirs. 1989-92), Soc. Gynecologic Investigation, Soc. Reproductive Surgeons (pres. 1986), Am. Soc. for Reproductive Medicine (pres. 1996—), Rotary Club, Phi Kappa Phi. Methodist. Office: Emory U Sch Medicine Dept OBGYN Atlanta GA 30303-9999

ROCKEMANN, DAVID DOUGLAS, health services administrator; b. Jefferson City, Mo., Mar. 9, 1954; s. Raymond William and Irene Pauline (Strobel) R.; m. Margaret Ann Perkinson, June 20, 1986. BA in Sociology, U. Mo., 1976, MS in Community Devel., 1978. State health planner State Health Planning Devel. Agy., Jefferson City, 1978; health cons., research assoc. Syncaredian Health Assn., Walnut Creek, Calif., 1978-79; asst. dir. day care Jewish Home for the Aged, San Francisco, 1979; adminstr. St. Regis Retirement Ctr., Hayward, Calif., 1979-82; dir. aging services Community and Econ. Devel. Assn., Chgo., 1982-86; exec. dir., chief exec. officer Community Nutrition Network, Chgo., 1986-87; dir. of bus. devel. Health Services div. John Knox Village, Lee's Summit, Mo., 1987-89; adminstr. Ctr. on Rural Elderly, U. Mo., Kansas City, 1989-90; dir. program devel. geriatric svcs. Chestnut Hill Hosp. Healthcare, Phila., Pa., 1991-92; adminstr. Twining Village Continuing Care Retirement Ctr., South Hampton, Pa., 1992-95, Riddle Village Continuing Care Retirement Cmty., Media, Pa., 1995-96, Health Care Recovery Group, Quakertown, Pa., 1996—; cons. Wade West Inc., San Francisco, 1979; researcher Calif. Dept. Health Svcs., San Francisco, 1978-79; rsch. asst. Ctr. for Rsch. in Social Behavior, Columbia, Mo., 1977-79; gerontology rsch. cons. Ctr. for Aging, U. Mo., Kansas City, 1987-90; cons. Diversified Health Svcs., Plymouth Meeting, Pa., 1990-91. Author: Outreach to the Elderly, 1983; (with others) Health Care Trends, 1978, Consumer's Guide to Nursing Homes, 1978. Mem. adv. coun. Suburban Cook County Area Agy. on Aging, Chgo., 1983-84; legis. adv. State of Ill. Spl. Com. on Aging, Chgo., 1985; presenter XIV meeting Internat. Assn. Gerontology, Acapulco, Mex., 1989, presenter XV meeting, Budapest, Hungary, 1993; coord., moderator Mid-Am. Congress on Aging, Kansas City, Mo., 1985; mem. planning com. Mid-Am. Congress on Aging, Chgo., 1986; bd. mem. Elder Abuse Coun., Kansas City, Mo. Adminstrn. on Aging scholar U. Mo., 1977-78; Older Americans Act grantee, 1982-87. Mem. Gerontol. Soc. Am. (presenter ann. sci. meeting 1992, 93, 94, 95), Am. Soc.on Aging (presenter ann. meeting 1989, 90, 94), Am. Coll. Health Care Administrs. Lutheran. Office: Health Care Recovery Group 2100 Quakerpoint Dr Ste 242 Quakertown PA 18951

ROCKETT, IAN RICHARD HILDRETH, epidemiologist, medical educator; b. Perth, Australia, Oct. 3, 1943; m. Sandra L. Putnam. BA, U. Western Australia, Perth, 1965; MA, U. Western Ont., London, Can., 1973; PhD, Brown U., 1978; MPH, Harvard U., 1986. Sr. rsch. fellow U. Melbourne, Australia, 1981-83; vis. asst. prof. Brown U., Providence, R.I., 1983-84; epidemiologic cons. R.I. Dept. Health, Providence, 1984-88; assoc. prof. pub. health U. Tenn., Knoxville, 1988-91, prof. pub. health, 1991-94, prof. epidemiology, 1994—; epidemiologic cons. Tenn. Dept. Health, City of Knoxville, Johns Hopkins U., Yaffe Found. Contbr. articles to profl. jours. Ont. Grad. fellow, 1972-73, Can. Coun. fellow, 1973-74, Population Coun. fellow, 1974-76. Mem. APHA, Soc. for Epidemiologic Rsch., Internat. Epidemiol. Assn., Population Assn. Am., Internat. Union for the Sci. Study of Population. Office: Univ Tenn 1914 Andy Holt Ave Knoxville TN 37996-2700

ROCKOFF, S. DAVID, radiologist, physician, educator; b. Utica, N.Y., July 21, 1931; s. Samuel and Sarah (Rattinger) R.; m. Jacqueline Garsh; children—Lisa E., Todd E., Kevin D. A.B., Syracuse U., 1951; M.D., Albany Med. Coll., 1955; M.Sc. in Medicine, U. Pa., 1961. Diplomate: Am. Bd. Radiology. Intern U.S. Naval Hosp., Bethesda, Md., 1955-56; resident and fellow in radiology, USPHS trainee dept. radiology p. of U. Pa., Phila., 1958-61; staff radiologist NIH, Bethesda, Md., 1961-65; asst. prof. radiology Yale U. Sch. Medicine, New Haven, 1965-68; assoc. prof. Yale U. Sch. Medicine, 1968; asst. attending radiologist Yale-New Haven Med. Center, 1965-68; assoc. prof. radiology Washington U. Sch. Medicine, St. Louis, 1968-71; asst. radiologist Barnes and Allied Hosps., St. Louis, 1969-71; cons. radiologist VA Hosp., St. Louis, 1969-71, Homer G. Phillips Hosp., St. Louis, 1968-71; prof. radiology George Washington U. Sch. Medicine, Washington, 1971—; chmn. dept. radiology George Washington U. Sch. Medicine, 1971-77, head pulmonary radiology, 1978—, interim chmn. dept. radiology, 1989-90, prof. emeritus radiology, 1993—; cons. NIH, 1972—; vis. prof. Hadassah U., Beersheba U., Rambam Hosp., Israel, 1977; cons. in radiology VA Hosp., Washington, 1972-77, U.S. Naval Med. Center, Bethesda, 1973-77; mem. diagnostic radiology adv. com. NIH, 1973-76; mem. Cancer Research Manpower Rev. Com., NIH, 1978. Editor-in-chief: Investigative Radiology, 1965-76; editor-in-chief emeritus, 1976—; editor Jour. Thoracic Imaging, 1985; Contbr. numerous articles to med. jours. Served with USN, 1955-58; Served with USPHS, 1961-63. Recipient numerous USPHS grants. Fellow Am. Coll. Radiology (pres.-elect D.C. chpt. 1976), Am. Coll. Chest Physicians; mem. Am. Fedn. Clin. Research, D.C. Med. Soc. (mem. med.-legal com. 1975-78), AMA, Radiol. Soc. N.Am., Assn. Univ. Radiologists, Soc. Thoracic Radiology (pres. 1983-84, exec. dir. 1984-87). Home: PO Box 675650 Rancho Santa Fe CA 92067-5650

ROCKOFF, SHEILA G., nursing and health facility administrator, educator, college administrator; b. Chgo., Mar. 15, 1945; d. Herbert Irwin and Marilyn (Victor) R.; divorced. ADN, Long Beach City Coll., 1966; BSN, San Francisco State U., 1970; MSN, Calif. State U.-L.A., 1976; EDD , South Ea. Nova U., 1993. RN, pub. health nurse, nursing instr., prof., health facility supr., Calif. Staff nurse Meml. Hosp., Long Beach, Calif., 1966-67, Mt. Zion Med. Ctr., San Francisco, 1967-69; instr. nursing Hollywood Presbyn. Med. Ctr., L.A., 1970-74; nursing supr. Orthopedic Hosp., L.A., 1974-76; instr. nursing Ariz. State U., Tempe, 1976-78; nurse supr. Hoag Meml. Hosp., Newport Beach, Calif., 1977-78; nurse educator U. Calif.-Irvine and Orange, Calif., 1978-80, Rancho Santiago Coll. (Calif.), 1980-89, dir. health svcs., 1989-95; dir., chair Health Occupations, 1995—; nursing prof. Rancho Santiago C.C., Santa Ana Campus; nurse cons. Home Health Care Agy., Irvine, 1983; educator, cons. Parenting Resources, Tustin, Calif., 1985-89. Contbr. articles to profl. jours. Mem. Nat. Assn. Student Personal Adminstrs., Am. Coll. Health Assn., Calif. Nurses Assn. (chmn. com. 1970-73), Assoc. of Calif. C.C. Administr., Calif C.C. Health Occpl. Educators, Assn. (bd. dirs.), Pacific Coast Coll. Health Assn., Phi Kappa Phi. Democrat. Jewish. Office: Rancho Santiago CC 1530 W 17th St Santa Ana CA 92706-3315

ROCKWELL, DON ARTHUR, psychiatrist; b. Wheatland, Wyo., Apr. 24, 1938; s. Orson Arthur and Kathleen Emily (Richards) R.; m. Frances Pepitone-Arreola, Dec. 23, 1965; children: Grant, Chad. BA, Wash. U., 1959; MD, U. Okla., 1963; MA in Sociology, U. Calif., Berkeley, 1967. Diplomate Am. Bd. Psychiatry and Neurology. Intern in surgery San Francisco Gen. Hosp., 1963-64; resident in psychiatry Langley-Porter Neuropsychiatric Inst. U. Calif. Med. Ctr., San Francisco, 1964-67; instr. dept. psychiatry U. Calif. Sch. Medicine, Davis, 1969-70, asst. prof., 1970-74, assoc. prof., 1974-80, acting. assoc., dean curricular affiars, 1979-80, acting assoc. dean student affairs, 1980, assoc. dean student affairs, 1980-82, prof., 1980-84; career tchr. NIMH, 1970-72; assoc. psychiatrist Sacramento Med. Ctr.; med. dir. U. Calif. Med. Ctr., Davis, 1982-84; prof., vice chmn. dept. psychiatry and biobehavioral scis. UCLA, 1984-96; dir. of profl. svcs., 1996—; chief profl. staff Neuropsychiat. Inst., UCLA, 1984-85, also dir. outpatient svcs.; chmn. U. Calif. Hosp. Dirs. Council, 1988-89; cons. Nat. Commn. on Marijuana, Washington, 1971-73. Co-author: Psychiatric Disorders, 1982; contbr. chpts. to books; articles to profl. jours. Bd. dirs. Bereavement Outreach, Sacramento, 1974-84, Suicide Prevention, Yolo County, 1969-84; bd. visitors U. Okla. Sch. Medicine; chmn. hosp. dirs. coun. U. Calif. Hosp.; governing coun. AHA Psychiat. Hosp. Fellow Am. Psychiat. Assn., Am. Coll. Psychiatrists, Am. Coll. Mental Health Adminstrs.; mem. AMA (gov. coun. psych. hosp.), Am. Sociologic Assn., Cen. Calif. Psychiat. Assn. (sec.-pres. 1977-78), U. Okla. Alumni Assn. (trustee 1981-86), Alpha Omega Alpha. Home: 1816 E Las Tunas Rd Santa Barbara CA 93103-1744

ROCKWELL, WILLIAM JAMES, allergist; b. Port Chester, N.Y., Nov. 5, 1947; s. Clemence James and Mae (Corbo) R.; m. Margaret Mary Hayden, June 28, 1969; children: Thomas, Kelly. BA, U. Bridgeport, 1969; MD, Albany Med. Coll., 1973. Resident physician Bridgeport Hosp., 1973-76; pediatrician Birney Mcloughlin, Rockwell, Bridgeport, 1976-79; fellow in allergy L.I. Coll. Hosps., Bklyn., 1979-81; allergist, physician Allergy Assocs. of Fairfield County, Bridgeport, 1981—; chief sect. of allergy Bridgeport Hosp., 1981—; co-dir. allergy rsch. ctr., 1990—. Contbr. articles to profl. jours. Mem. Fairfield County Med. Assn., Conn. State Med. Soc. Office: Allergy Assocs of Fairfield County PC 4675 Main St Bridgeport CT 06606

ROCKWOOD, EDWARD J., ophthalmologist; b. Syracuse, N.Y., Nov. 6, 1954; m. Joann A. Rockwood; 4 children. BS in Biology, Rensselaer Poly. Inst., 1976; MD, SUNY, Buffalo, 1980. Glaucoma fellow Bascom Palmer Eye Inst., Miami, Fla., 1984-86; resident in ophthalmology Cleve. Clinic Found., 1980-84, staff ophthalmologist, 1986—. Mem. AMA, Am. Acad. Ophthalmology (self-assessment com. 1994—, Honor awad 1995), Cleve. Acad. Medicine, Assn. for Rsch. in Vision and Ophthalmology. Roman Catholic. Home: 20150 Shaker Blvd Shaker Heights OH 44122-1875 Office: Cleve Clin Found Ophthalmology 9500 Euclid Ave Cleveland OH 44195-0001

RODBELL, MARTIN, biochemist; b. Balt., Dec. 1, 1925; s. Milton William and Shirley Helen (Abrams) R.; m. Barbara Charlotte Ledermann, Sept. 10, 1950; children: Paul, Suzanne, Andrew, Phillip. BA, Johns Hopkins U., 1949; PhD, U. Wash., 1954; DSc (hon.), U. Montpelier, 1992, U. Wash., 1996, U. Geneva, 1996, Va. Commonwealth U., 1996. Nutrition and endocrinology chemist NIH, Bethesda, Md., 1956—; chief lab. nutrition and endocrinology NIAMD, Bethesda, Md., 1972-84; sci. dir. Nat. Inst. Environ. Health Scis., Rsch. Triangle Park, N.C., 1985-89, chief sect. signal transduction, 1989-94; scientist emeritus Nat. Inst. Environ. Health Scis., Rsch. Triangle Park, 1994—. Recipient Supr. Svc. award HHS, 1974, Gairdner Found. award, 1984, Jacobeus award, 1973, Nobel Prize for Physiology or Medicine, 1994. Mem. NAS (Richard Lounsbery award 1987), Am. Soc. Biol. Chemists., Am. Acad. Arts and Scis. Office: NIH Environmental Health Scis Research Triangle Park NC 27709

RODDAN, RAY GENE, chiropractor; b Springfield, S.D., Dec. 9, 1947; s. Glendon William and Marvel Grace (Brown) R.; m. Sheleth Lee, June 1, 1969; children—Erik, Kelene, Daniel. Student Oholone Coll., 1968-71, U. S.D., 1966-68, U. Calif., 1971-74; Dr. Chiropractic Medicine, Palmer Coll. of Chiropractic, 1978. Material control mgr. Guardian Packaging Corp., Newark, Calif., 1968-75; mid-states sales mgr. Agridustrial Electronic Co., Davenport, Iowa, 1975-78; gen. practice chiropractic medicine, Green Bay, Wis., 1978—; pres., clinic dir. J&R Chiropractic Office, S.C., Green Bay, 1978-85, ProCare Chiropractic Clinic, Ltd., Green Bay, Howard, Denmark, Milw. and Pulaski, 1985—; pres. ProCare Mgmt. Corp., 1995—, Talon Enterprises, 1995—; indsl. cons.; software developer Healthcare Office Mgmt. Active Green Bay Cmty. Ch. Mem. Profl. Chiropractic Soc. Am. (Chiropractor of Yr. 1983), Am. Chiropractic Assn., Wis. Chiropractic Assn., Christian Chiropractic Assn., Green Bay C. of C., Fellowship Cos. for Christ, Internat. Acad. Chiropractic Cons., Christian Athletes Outreach, Pi Tau Delta. Republican. Clubs: Businessmen's (Green Bay) (v.p. 1979-80). Home: 1414 Longtail Beach Rd Suamico WI 54173

RODDY, WILLIAM MEYER, internist, psychiatrist; b. Waco, Tex., Oct. 14, 1959; s. William Nathan and Mona (Bodansky) R.; m. Wendy Sue Walsh, Aug. 21, 1987; children: Eric Meyer, Asher Michael. BA in Psychology, U. North Tex., 1984, MS in Psychology, 1986; Do Kirksville Coll. Osteo. Med., 1991. Intern in medicine Riverside Hosp., Wichita, 1991-92; resident in psychiatry U. Kans. Sch. Medicine, Wichita, 1992-93; resident in internal medicine/psychiatry East Carolina U. Sch. Medicine, Greenville, N.C., 1993-94; chief resident in internal medicine/psychiatry East Carolina U. Sch. Medicine, Greenville, 1995—; cons. psychiatrist Edgecombe-Nash Mental Health Ctr., Rocky Mountain, N.C., 1993—; emergency room physician Our Cmty. Hosp., Scotland Neck, N.C., 1994—; cons. for state hosp. and prisons. Mem. ACP, AMA, Am. Psychiat. Assn., Am. Osteo. Assn., Soc. Critical Care Physicians. Jewish. Office: Pitt County Meml Hosp 2100 Stantonsburg Rd Greenville NC 27834

RODEN, DAN MARK, cardiologist, medical educator; b. Montreal, Can., Apr. 15, 1950; came to U.S., 1978; s. Rudolph George and Eva (Vonchovsky) R.; m. Rosemary Wetherill, Dec. 29, 1972; children: Mark McKenzie, Paul Joseph, Rosemary Claire. BSc, McGill U., 1970, MD, 1974. Diplomate Am. Bd. Internal Medicine, Am. Bd. Cardiovascular Disease, Am. Bd. Clinical Cardiac Electrophysiology, Am. Bd. Clinical Pharmacology; Lic. physician, Quebec, Canada and Tenn.; Cert. Med. Coun. of Canada, Nat. Bd. Med. Examiners. Intern Royal Victoria Hosp., Montreal, Can., 1974-75, resident, 1975-76, 77-78; pvt. practice Montreal, Can., 1976-77; rsch. fellow clin. pharmacology Vanderbilt U., Nashville, 1978-81, fellow cardiol., 1980-81, asst. prof., 1981-85, assoc. prof., 1985-89, prof. Med. and Pharmacology, 1989—, also dir. divsn. clin. pharmacology, 1992—; del. 4th U.S.-USSR Symposium on Sudden Death, Birmingham, Ala., 1985; mem. Nat. VA Merit Review Cardiovasc. Disease com., 1986-88, chmn. 1988-89; ad hoc reviewer, Pharmacology Study and Cardiovasc. and Pulmonary Study sects., NIH, mem. Cardiovasc. and Pulmonary Study sect., 1991-94, chmn. 1994-96; adv. panel cardiovasc. and renal drugs, U.S. Phamacopeial Conv., 1990-95; mem. external adv. com., Pharmacological Scis. Tng. Grant, Columbia U., 1992—; mem. Clin. Cardiac Electrophysiology Test Writing com., Am. Bd. Internal Medicine, 1992—; mem. adv. com., Vanderbilt Clin Rsch. Ctr., 1989-91, chmn. 91-92, faculty appointments and promotions, Vanderbilt U. Dept. Med., 1992-95; mem. instl. review bd., Vanderbilt U. Dept. Health Scis., 1991-93, chmn. 1993-94. Author 27 book chpts., over 150 abstracts and 130 articles to profl. jours.; mem. editl. bd. Jour. Cardiovasc. Electrophys., 1990—; mem. adv. bd. The Med. Letter (newsletter), 1991—. Fellow Am. Coll. Physicians, Am. Coll. Cardiology (annual scientific session program com. 1992-93), Royal Coll. Physicians of Can.; mem. Am. Fedn. Clin. Rsch., Am. Soc. Clin. Pharmacology Therapeutics (bd. dirs. 1994—, chmn. cardiovasc. and pulmonary sect., 1995—), North Am. Soc. Pacing and Electrophysiol., Cardiac Electrophysiol. Soc., Biophysical Soc., Am. Soc. Pharmacol. and Experimental Therapeutics, So. Soc. Clin. Investigation, Am. Soc. Clin. Investigation, Am. Heart Assn. (clinician-sci.t award, 1981-86, long-range planning com. 1995—, basic sci. coun. exec. com. 1995—). Office: Vanderbilt U 532B Medical Rsch Bldg I Nashville TN 37232-6602

RODENHIUS, SJOERD, medical oncologist; b. Eindhoven, The Netherlands, Aug. 9, 1951; s. Klaas and Jannetje (Fris) R.; m. Lucia AM Rood. MD, Groningen U., The Netherlands, 1978, PhD, 1983. Registered med. oncologist. Resident physician Roman Cath. Hosp., Groningen, 1978-79; resident in tng. Groningen U., 1979-84, internist, 1984; postdoctoral fellow Dutch Cancer Soc., 1984-86; rsch. scientist Netherlands Cancer Inst., Amsterdam, 1986-87, cons. med. oncologist, 1987-94, chief medicine, 1994—; mem. Permanent Adv. Coun. on Cancer and Oncology, The Netherlands, 1990-93; mem. Wetenschappelyke Raad voor de Kankerbestryding, The Netherlands, 1996—. Contbr. articles to profl. jours. Recipient Fulbright award U.S. Govt., 1985, Prof. Muntendam prize Dutch Cancer Soc., 1990. Mem. Am. Soc. Clin. Oncology, Am. Assn. Cancer Rsch., European Soc. Med. Oncology. Office: The Netherlands Cancer Inst, Dept Med Oncology, Plesmanlaan 121, 1066 CX Amsterdam The Netherlands

RODERICK, TRAVIS W., health services administrator; b. Dallas, July 15, 1965; s. Charles N. and Norma J. (Jackson) R.; m. Rachel Marie Troup, Mar. 14, 1992. BS in Pub. Adminstrn., U. Tex., Dallas, 1990; MHA, MBA, U. Houston Clear Lake, 1992. Exec. resident Sid Peterson Meml. Hosp., Kerrville, Tex., 1992-93; v.p. network devel. Humana Health Care Plans, San Antonio, Tex., 1993-95; adminstr., CEO Collingsworth Gen. Hosp., Wellington, Tex., 1995—; cons. TWR Solutions, Kerrville, Tex., 1992—. Bd. dirs. Econ. Devel. Coun. 1992-93, v.p. Boerne (Tex.) Optimist Soccer League, 1994-95; mem. polit. action com. Tex. Orgn. Rural Cmty. Hosps. Mem. Am. Coll. Healthcare Execs. (cert.), Kiwanis Internat. Republican. Lutheran. Home: Rt 1 Box 40 Wellington TX 79095 Office: Collinsworth Gen Hosp 1014 15th St Wellington TX 79095

RODGER, ALAN, radiation oncology educator, administrator; b. Kirkcaldy, Fife, Scotland, June 9, 1946; arrived in Australia, 1992; s. Matthew Penman and Christina Nairn (Briggs) R. BS Med. Sci. in Physiology with honors, Edinburgh (Scotland) U., 1968, MB ChB, 1971, Diploma in Med. Radiation Therapy, 1977. Tng. registrar radiotherapy Edinburgh, 1975-77; lectr. radiation oncology U. Edinburgh, 1977-80; project investigator radiotherapy M. D. Anderson Hosp., Houston, 1980-81; cons. radiation oncologist Lothian Health Bd., Scotland, 1981-92; prof. radiation oncology Monash U., Melbourne, Australia, 1992—; dir. radiation oncology Alfred Healthcare Group, Melbourne, 1992—; mem. several home and health dept. coms., Scotland; chmn. Scottish home and health dept. Rev. of Radiology Svcs.; chmn. Bd. Breast Screen, Victoria, Australia, 1995—. Co-author chpts.: ABC of Breast Cancer; editor series: Essentials of Clinical Practice: Breast Cancer, Med. Jour. Australia, 1995-96; contbr. articles to profl. jours. Fellow Royal Coll. Surgeons (Edinburgh), Royal Coll. Radiologists (bd. dirs., com. mem.), Royal Australasian Coll. Radiologists; mem. nat. Trust Scotland (life), Charles REnnie MacIntosh Soc. (life), Friends of Edinburgh Internat. Festival (life), G.H. Fletcher Soc., Clin. Oncology Soc. Australia, European Soc. Therapeutic Radiation Oncology, European Soc. Mastology, Australia New Zealand Breast Trials Group, Brit. Breast Group. Office: Alfred Hosp, William Buckland Radiother, Commercial Rd, Prahran Melbourne 3181, Australia

RODGERS, CARLA, psychiatrist, educator; b. Chgo., Apr. 18, 1949. BA in Comm. with honors, U. Ill., Chgo., 1970, postgrad., 1974-76; MD, Rush Med. Coll., 1980. Diplomate Nat. Bd. Med. Examiners, Am. Bd. Psychiatry and Neurology, Am. Acad. Pain Mgmt; cert. subspecialty in geriat. psychiatry Am. Bd. Psychiatry and Neurology. Intern Cook County Hosp., Chgo., 1980-81; dept. health physician City of Chgo., 1981-84; resident in anesthesiology Ill. Masonic Med. Ctr., Chgo., 1984-86; attending anesthesiologist Carle Found. Hosp., Champaign-Urbana, Ill., 1986-88; resident in psychiatry Thomas Jefferson U. Hosp., Phila., 1988-91, attending psychiatrist divsn. consultation/liaison, 1991—; clin. instr. dept. surgery U. Ill., Champaign-Urbana, 1987-88; instr. dept. psychiatry Jefferson Med. Coll., 1991-93, asst. prof. dept. psychiatry, 1993—, dir. psychosomatic rsch., 1994—; dir. psychiat. svcs. Jefferson Pain Ctr., Thomas Jefferson U. Hosp.; presenter in field. Reviewer Psychosomatics, Jour. Am. Med. Women's Assn., Gen. Hosp. Psychiatry; contbr. chpts. to books and articles to profl. jours. Mem. Am. Med. Women's Assn., Am. Psychiat. Assn., Assn. for Acad. Psychiatry, Acad. Psychosomatic Medicine, Phila. Psychiat. Soc., Consultation Liaison Assn. Phila., Delaware Valley Pain Soc. Home: 908 Carroll Rd Wynnewood PA 19096 Office: Thomas Jefferson Univ 1652 Thompson Bldg 11th and Walnut Sts Philadelphia PA 19107

RODGERS, JANET, nursing educator. BS in Nursing, Wagner Coll.; MA in Psychiat./Mental Health Nursing, NYU, PhD in Nursing. Dep. chair dept. nursing Lehman Coll.; chair dept. nursing Old Dominion U.; founding chair dept. nursing Lycoming Coll.; dean, prof. Philip Y. Hahn Sch. Nursing U. San Diego; pres. Am. Assn. Colls. Nursing; bd. dirs. Am. Coun. Edn. Contbr. articles to profl. jours. Fellow Am. Acad. Nursing. Office: U San Diego Office of Dean Nursing La Jolla CA 92093*

RODGERS, LYNNE SAUNDERS, women's health nurse; b. Winchester, Va., May 11, 1956; d. Ronald Otho and Anne Coleman (Grille) Saunders; m. Joseph Rodgers, Dec. 21, 1985; children: Joseph Anthony, John Robert, Stephanie Lynne. BSN, George Mason U., 1978. Cert. inpatient obstetric nursing, prenatal childbirth educator, Resolve Through Sharing counselor, perinatal grief counselor. Clin. nurse specialist in labor and delivery Bethesda (Md.) Naval Hosp., 1978-87; labor and delivery staff nurse clinician Fairfax Hosp. Assn., Falls Church, Va., 1987—; clinician, staff nurse in obstetrics Fauquier Hosp., Warrenton, Va., 1990—. Mem. Assn. Women's Health Obstetric and Neonatal Nurses. Office: Fauquier Hosp 500 Hospital Dr Warrenton VA 22186-3027

RODGERS, WILLARD LINEUS, research scientist, social psychologist; b. Omaha, Dec. 11, 1940; s. Willard L. Sr. and Genevieve A. (Robinson) R.; m. Mary Ann Swartz; children: Willard Loren, Joanna Laurel. BS in Biology, MIT, 1962; PhD in Psychology, U. Pa., 1966. Asst. prof. psychology Pahlavi U., Shiraz, Iran, 1966-67; postdoctoral fellow U. Mich., Ann Arbor, 1967-69, study dir., 1969-73, sr. study dir., 1973-90, rsch. scientist, 1990—; cons. U. at Mannheim, Fed. Republic Germany, 1982, Postal Rate Commn., Washington, 1990-91. Author: The Quality of American Life, 1976; contbr. articles to Jour. Ofcl. Stats., Jour. Labor Econs., Jour. Gerontology, Psychology and Aging Sociol. Methodology. Rsch. grantee NSF, 1977, 87, NIMH, 1977, 87, Nat. Inst. Aging, 1980, 83, 86, 91, 92, 95, U.S. Agy. Internat. Devel., Cairo, Egypt, 1986, Ford Found., 1988. Mem. AAAS, Am. Assn. Pub. Opinion Rsch. (editl. bd. Pub. Opinion Quar. 1991-94), Am. Statis. Assn. (contbr. jour.), Gerontol. Soc. Am. (cons. to editor 1994—), Population Assn. Am. Office: U Mich Inst Social Rsch 426 Thompson St Ann Arbor MI 48104-2321

RODIN, HOWARD ALAN, periodontist; b. Bronx, N.Y., Oct. 21, 1942; s. David and Edna (Fialkow) R.; m. Gail Sandra Stein, July 8, 1967; children: Dennis, Stephanie. BS, Fairleigh Dickinson U., 1964; MS in Physiology, 1966, postdoctoral fellow dept. periodontics, 1971; DDS, Howard U., 1970; cert. in periodontics, Columbia U., 1973. Intern Sydenham Hosp., N.Y.C., 1970-71; mem. staff dept. virology Mt. Sinai Hosp., N.Y.C., 1964-66; pvt. practice periodontics, Babylon, N.Y., 1973-82, Smithtown, N.Y., 1978—; mem. staff, dept. spl. surgery St. John's Hosp., Smithtown, 1979-81, 85—; cons. NYU Med. Ctr./Goldwater Meml. Hosp., 1995—; mem. planning com. Greater L.I. Dental Meeting, 1973—, gen. chmn., 1985; asst. clin. prof. periodontics, Columbia U., 1986-88; pres. L.I. Acad. Periodontists, 1986-90. Contbr. articles to profl. jours. Fellow Am. Coll. Dentists, Internat. Coll. Dentists, Pierre Fauchand Acad., N.Y. Acad. Denistry, Suffolk Acad. Medicine (pres. 1992-93, bd. trustees 1990—); mem. ADA (del., alt. del. 1989—), Internat. Assn. Dental Rsch. (Hatton award 1968, periodontal rsch. com. 1984—), Am. Acad. Periodontology, Suffolk County Dental Soc. (bd. dels. 1981—, pres. 1991), N.Y. State Soc. Periodontists (bd. dirs.), Northeastern Soc. Periodontists, N.Y. Acad. Scis., Western Soc. Periodontology, Fedn. Dentnire Internat., Suffolk Soc. Forensic Dentistry (exec. com. 1995—), Am. Acad. Osseointegration, Sigma Xi, Alpha Omega (pres. 1985-87). Jewish.

RODIN, JUDITH SEITZ, academic administrator, psychology educator; b. Phila., Sept. 9, 1944; d. Morris and Sally R. (Winson) Seitz. AB, U. Pa., 1966; PhD, U. Columbia, 1970. Asst. prof. psychology NYU, 1970-72; assoc. prof. Yale U., 1975-79, prof., dir. grad. studies, 1982-89, Philip R. Allen prof. psychology, medicine and psychiatry, 1984-94, chmn. dept. psychology, 1989-91, dean Grad. Sch., 1991-92, provost, 1992-94; pres. U. Pa., Phila., 1994—, prof. psychology, medicine and psychiatry, 1994—; chmn. John D. and Catherine T. MacArthur Found. Rsch. Network on Determinants and Consequences of Health-Promoting and Health-Damaging Behavior, 1983-93; vice chair coun. press. U. Rsch. Assn., 1994-95, chair, 1995-96; mem. Ind. Panel to Review Safety Procedures at The White House, 1994-95; chair adv. com. Robert Wood Johnson Found., 1994—; mem. Pres. Clinton's Com. Advisors Sci. and Tech., 1994—; bd. dirs. Aetna Life & Casualty Co., Air Products, Allentown, Pa. Author: (with S. Schachter) Obese Humans and Rats, 1978, Exploding the Weight Myths, 1982, Body Traps, 1992; chief editor Appetite Jour., 1979-92; contbr. articles to profl. jours. Mem. Pa. Task Force on Higher Edn. Funding, 1994; bd. dirs. Catalyst, N.Y.C., 1994—; trustee Brookings Inst., 1995—. Fellow Woodrow Wilson Found., 1966-67, John Simon Guggenheim Found., 1986-87; grantee NSF, 1973-82, NIH, 1981—. Fellow AAAS, Am. Acad. Arts and Scis., Am. Psychol. Assn. (bd. sci. affairs 1979-82), Soc. Behavioral Medicine; mem. Am. Philosophical Soc., Inst. Medicine of NAS, Acad. Behavioral Medicine Rsch., Ea. Psychol. Assn. (exec. bd. 1980-82, pres. divsn. 38 health psychology 1982-83, Outstanding Contbn. award 1980, Disting. Sci. award 1977), Phi Beta Kappa, Sigma Xi (pres. Yale chpt. 1986-87). Office: U Pa 121 College Hall Philadelphia PA 19104-6380

RODMAN, LINDA E., physician assistant; b. Cambridge, Mass., May 13, 1947; d. Melvin H. and Rosalyn S. (Silver) R. BA, Simmons Coll., 1973; cert. physician asst., Northeastern U., 1977; MPH, Boston U., 1981. RN, Mass. Operating and recovery room nurse Beth Israel Hosp., Boston, 1973-75; physician asst. Columbia U., N.Y.C., 1977-80; with Harvard Cmty. Health Plan, Boston, 1980-82; program assoc. Health Policy Inst., Boston, 1981-83; physician asst. geriatrics Urban Med. Group, Boston, 1983-90; physician asst. St. Elizabeth's Hosp., 1983-90; physician asst. detox Waltham/Weston (Mass.) Hosp., 1990-92; physician asst. AIDS Fenway Cmty. Health Ctr., Boston, 1992-95; physician asst. Mt. Sinai Hosp., N.Y.C., 1995—; mem. med. adv. bd. Bridge Over Troubled Water, Boston, 1988-90; clin. instr. Tufts Sch. Medicine, Boston, 1987-95. Mem. staff Lifespring Inc., N.Y.C.; tchr. Am. Heart Assn., Bread and Circus, 1992-94. Mem. Am. Acad. Physician Assts.

RODNE, KJELL JOHN, healthcare administrator; b. Haugesund, Norway, July 6, 1948; came to U.S., 1959; s. Johannes and Margit (Gautun) R.; m. Kathleen Anne Gordon, Sept. 21, 1966; children: Jay Robert, Lee Eric. BS, U. Minn., Duluth, 1971, MSW, 1985; cert. Univ. Assoc. Human Resources program, 1995; PMA sci. of success diploma, 1996, personal computer tng. program diploma, 1996. Asst. youth dir. YMCA, Duluth, 1967-68; counselor Northwood, Duluth, 1968-71, team leader, 1971-76, social worker, 1976-77, program dir., 1977-85; pers. dir. City of Duluth, 1985-86, adminstrv. asst. City of Duluth, 1986-92; mgmt. cons., 1992-93; adminstr. Northwood West, 1993-95, dir. quality assurance, 1995—; bd. dirs. Minn. Coun. Residential Treatment Ctrs., St. Paul, 1977-85, 93—. Mem. Duluth City Coun., 1978-85, pres., 1981; bd. dirs. United Devel. Achievement Ctr., Duluth, 1978-85, Arrowhead Regional Devel. Commn., Duluth, 1981-85, United Way of Duluth, 1981-89, Duluth Econ. Devel. Authority, 1989-92, Arrowhead Growth Alliance, 1990-92, Northspan, 1991-92. Mem. Lake Superior Assn. Labor Mgmt. (bd. dirs. 1989-92), Internat. City Mgrs. Assn. (pub. policy com. 1991—), Nat. Assn. Homes for Children. Democrat. Lutheran. Home: 1731 Kenwood Ave Duluth MN 55811

RODNICK, ELIOT HERMAN, psychologist, educator; b. New Haven, Nov. 27, 1911; s. Louis D. and Bertha (Caplan) R.; m. Helen Percival Hollander, Nov. 20, 1940; children: Jonathan Eliot, Marion Percival Rodnick Bell. AB with high oration, Yale U., 1933, PhD, 1936. Asst. research Yale U., 1934-36; research psychologist, research service Worcester (Mass.) State Hosp., 1936-46, dir. psychol. research, chief psychologist, 1946-49; acting dir. Worcester Child Guidance Clinic, 1946-47; instr. Mt. Holyoke Coll., 1939; asst. prof. psychology Clark U., 1942-46, assoc. prof., 1946-49; vis. lectr. summer session U. Wis., 1949, Harvard U., 1952, U. Colo., 1958; prof. psychology, dir. clin. tng. psychology Duke U., 1949-61, chmn. dept. psychology, 1951-61; prof. psychology, dir. clin. tng. psychology U. Calif. at Los Angeles, 1961-79, prof. emeritus, 1979—; cons. psychologist VA, 1949-79, mem. central office adv. com. to chief, dept. psychiatry and neurology, 1957-61; mem. mental health study sect. NIH, 1954-57, behavorial sci. study sect., 1957, mental health projects rev. commn., 1957-60, chmn. spl. mental health grants rev. com., 1960-62; bd. dirs. Los Angeles Psychiat. Service, 1961-66, Didi Hirsch Mental Health Center, 1973-82, Calif. Sch. Profl. Psychology, 1981-83; cons. Calif. Dept. Mental Hygiene; mem. com. on research tng. in biol. scis. Nat. Inst. Mental Health, 1962-66, chmn., 1965-66; mem. mental health council Western Commn. Higher Edn., 1961-66; adv. com. abuse of stimulant and depressant drugs FDA, 1966-68; sci. adv. com. on drug abuse U.S. Dept. Justice, 1968-75; Cons. Narcotics Control Commn. N.Y., 1969-75; cons. Calif. Sch. Profl. Psychology. Editorial bd.: Am. Jour. Orthopsychiatry, 1954-57, Jour. Personality, 1955-60, Jour. Abnormal and Social Psychology, 1957-62, Am. Jour. Community Psychology, 1972-77, Family Process, 1977-81. Trustee Calif. Sch. Profl. Psychology, 1981-83. Commd. officer USPHS Res. Recipient Stanley Dean prize for outstanding research in schizophrenia, 1967; Wilbur Lucius Cross medal for outstanding profl. performance Yale Grad. Sch. Assn., 1975. Fellow AAAS, APA (bd. dirs. 1962-65, Disting. Contbn. to Clin. Psychology award 1976), Western Psychol. Assn. (pres. 1966-67), Am. Psychol. Soc. (James McKeen Cattell fellow award), Calif. Psychol. Assn. (Disting. Sci. Contbns. in Psychology award 1975), Los Angeles County Psychol. Assn., N.C. Psychol. Assn. (past pres.), Am. Orthopsychiat. Assn. (bd. dirs. 1966-69, pres. 1967-68); mem. Cosmos Club (Washington), Phi Beta Kappa, Sigma Xi. Home: 7577 Oak Leaf Dr Santa Rosa CA 95409-6254 Office: Dept Psychology U Cal 405 Hilgard Ave Los Angeles CA 90024-1301

RODNITZKY, ROBERT LEE, neurology educator; b. Chgo., Aug. 17, 1941; s. Nathan and Ann (Orenstein) R.; m. Donna Joy Pliner, May 14, 1967; children: David, Adam, Laura. BS, U. Chgo., 1963, MD, 1966. Diplomate in neurology Am. Bd. Psychiatry and Neurology. Asst. prof. Coll. Medicine U. Iowa, Iowa City, 1972-76, assoc. prof. Coll. Medicine, 1976-82, prof. Coll. Medicine, 1982—, vice chmn. dept. neurology Coll. Medicine, 1986—; chief of staff U. Iowa Hosps. and Clinics, 1992—; examiner Am. Bd. Psychiatry and Neurology, Deerfield, Ill., 1976—; cons. Pres.' Commn. on Mental Health, Washington, 1976. Author: (textbook) Van Allen's Pictorial Manual Neurologic Tests, 1988; asst. editor: (med. jour.) Muscle and Nerve, 1988—; contbr. articles to profl. jours. Lt. comdr. USNR, 1970-72. Grantee NIH, 1987-92. Fellow Am. Acad. Neurology; mem. Am. Acad. Clin. Neurophysiology, Am. Neurolog. Assn., Am. Assn. Electrodiagnostic Medicine, Cen. Soc. Neurolog. Rsch. (pres. 1987). Office: U Hosp Dept Neurology Iowa City IA 52242

RODOS, JOSEPH JERRY, osteopathic physician, educator; b. Phila., July 7, 1933; s. Harry and Lisa (Perlman) R.; m. Bobbi Golden, Apr. 6, 1957; (div. 1974); m. Joyce L. Pennington, Sept. 26, 1981; children: Adam Justin, Nicole Ann. BS, Franklin & Marshall Coll., 1955; DO, Kirksville Coll. Medicine, Mo., 1959; DSc Pub. Health, Somerset Univ., 1993. Diplomate Am. Bd. Family Medicine, Am. Bd. Osteo, Am. Osteo. Bd. Pub., Health and Preventive Medicine, Bd. Neuro Psychiatry, Am. Bd. of Pain Mgmt, Am. Bd. Correctional Health Care, Am. Bd. Forensic Medicine. NIMH fellow in psychiatry, Brown U./Butler Hos., Providence, 1966-68; intern Grandview Hosp., Dayton, Ohio, 1959-60; gen. practice medicine, Cranston, R.I., 1960-78; exec. sec. R.I. Soc. Osteo. P/S, Cranston, 1960-78; assoc. exec. dir. Am. Osteo. Assn., 1978-79; dean New Eng. Coll. Osteo. Medicine, Biddleford, Maine, 1979-82; acting dean Chgo. Coll. Osteo. Medicine, 1982-88; spec. asst. to pres. Chgo. Osteop. Health Systems, 1987-95; chair dept. psychiatry Midwestern U.; spl. asst. to pres., interim chair dept. psychiatry Midwestern U.; prof. family medicine and psychiatry; adj. prof. U. Ill. Sch. Medicine; cons. to dir. Nat. Health Svc. Corps HHS; Disting. Practitioner Nat. Acad. Practitioners, 1990; fellow Inst. of Medicine, Chgo., 1990; clin. dir. Dept. Mental Health, Providence, R.I., 1973-78; med. dir. Dept. Corrections, Providence, 1976-78; sr. cons. medicine Pub. Sector Cons., Lansing, Mich., 1980—; prin. Health Cons. Rhodes Group, 1989—; lectr. in field. Editor, Jour. Osteo. Annals, 1982. Bd. dirs. Cranston Red Cross, R.I. Camps, Inc., Dial Dictation, Inc., Cranston Mental Health Clinic; mem. Internat. Platform Assn., ACLU; lectr. Premarital Confs., Catholic Diocese Providence. Fellow Am. Coll. Gen. Practice, Acad. Psychosomatic Medicine, Royal Soc. Health (Eng.); mem. Am. Assn. Osteo. Specialists (cert.), Am. Coll. Osteo. and Obstetrics and Gynecology, Acad. Clin. and Exptl. Hypnosis. Avocations: breeding, showing Saint Bernards and Scottish Terriers. Licenced Am. Kennel Club judge. Home: 5204 Lawn Ave Western Springs IL 60558-1844 Office: Chgo Coll Osteopathic Medicine 5200 S Ellis Ave Chicago IL 60615-4314

RODRIGUES LIMA, KRISTINE ROOP, clinical social worker; b. Norwood, Mass., Dec. 8, 1948; d. John Wesley and Emily (Lawrence) Roop; m. Otavio A. Rodrigues Lima, July 21, 1979; 1 child, Kathryn. Student, U. Manchester, Eng., 1968-69; BA in English, Allegheny Coll., 1970; MSW, Smith Coll., 1973. Lic. ind. clin. social worker; bd. cert. diplomate. Assessor and counselor adoptive applicants Family and Children's Svcs., Pitts., 1970-71; group therapist St. Jude Halfway House, Jamaica Plain, Mass., 1971-73; clin. social worker Children's Friend and Family Svc., Salem, Mass., 1973-77, Head Start, Action, Inc., Gloucester, Mass., 1977, Marlborough (Mass.)-Westborough Community Mental Health Clinic, 1977-79; pvt. practice Cambridge, Mass., 1977—; psychotherapist and counselor Health Integration Svcs., Inc., Peabody, Mass., 1979-82; dir. South End Christian Counseling Ctr., Boston, 1982-84; ptnr. Advent Counseling Assn., Cambridge, 1983—; dir. Milestone Counseling Assocs., Cambridge, 1990—. Deacon, film/discussion moderator Newton (Mass.) Presbyn. Ch.; tchr. How Families Work program Southborough (Mass.) Pub. Libr., Creative Parenting program Marlborough Pub. Libr.; co-chmn. Project Home Again and World Vision, Newton, 1990. Mem. Acad. Cert. Social Workers. Office: 144A Mt Auburn St Cambridge MA 02138-5776

RODRIGUEZ, AGUSTIN ANTONIO, surgeon; b. Hato Rey, P.R., Aug. 20, 1961; s. Agustin and Esther Rodriguez (Gonzalez) R.; m. Liana Esther Lopez, 1993; 1 child, Agustin Andrés. AB in Biology, Harvard Coll., 1982; MD, U. P.R., San Juan, 1986. Diplomate Nat. Bd. Med. Examiners, Am. Bd. Surgery. Surgical intern Boston U. Med. Ctr., 1986-87, surgical resident, 1988-93, acad. trainee surgery; vascular fellow Tufts U., N. Eng. Med. Ctr., 1993-95; asst. prof. surgery Tufts U. Sch. Medicine, Boston, 1995—; asst. prof. surgery Sch. Medicine U. P.R., San Juan, 1996—. Contbr. articles to Jour. Cardiovascular Surgery, Jour. Vascular Surgery, Archives of Surgery, Jour. Surgery Rsch. Mem. AMA, Am. Numismatic Soc., Am. Numismatic Assn., Mass. Med. Soc., N.Y. Acad. Scis., European Soc. Vascular Surgery (assoc.), Am. Venous Forum, Interam. Coll. Physicians and Surgeons, Am. Soc. Clin. Vascular Surgery, Assn. Acad. Surgery, Alpha Omega Alpha (Psi chpt.). Republican. Home: 1483 Ashford Ave #702 San Juan PR 00907-1533 Office: U PR Sch Medicine Dept Surgery San Juan PR 00936-5067

RODRIGUEZ, AURELIO, surgeon; b. Chincha Alta, Ica, Peru, July 3, 1943; came to U.S., 1971; s. Marcelino and Maria (Vitela) R.; m. Olga Catter (div. 1988); children: Samantha, Ralph, Ben, Vanessa, Ivan; m. Wendy Parker, July 7, 1988; children: Jose Antonio Marcelino, Luis Enrique. BS, San Marcos U., 1960, MD, 1968. Diplomate Am. Bd. Surgery. Intern U. Cin., 1971-72; resident surgery Henry Ford Hosp., Detroit, 1972-73, Pontiac (Mich.) Gen. Hosp., 1973-76; fellow trauma critical care U. Md., Balt., 1976-77; resident cardiothoracic Wayne State U., Detroit, 1978-79; surgeon thoracic, trauma Shock Trauma Unit U. Md., Balt., 1979—. Editor: Management Cardiothoracid Trauma, 1992, Complications in Trauma Critical Care, 1996, Critical Care Clinics of N.Am., 1994, Trauma Patient with Pre Existing Diseases, 1995; contbr. numerous articles to profl. jours. 1st lt. Peruvian Navy, 1968-71. Fellow ACS (state chmn. 1994), Am. Assn. Surgeons of Trauma, East Trauma Assocs.; mem. AMA Peru (v.p. 1993—), Critical Care Soc., Am. Trauma Soc. (charter), PanAm. Trauma Soc. (founder, pres. 1987-91, exec. dir. 1992—), Peruvian Club Md. (pres. 1992-94, Best Trauma Surgeon award 1995). Methodist. Home: 3118 Hunt Rd Fallston MD 21047 Office: Univ Md Shock Trauma Unit 22 S Greene St Baltimore MD 21201

RODRIGUEZ, CARLOS ALBERTO, pathologist; b. San Miguel de Tucuman, Argentina, Apr. 27, 1948; s. Belarmino and Blanca Rosa (Gallo) R.; m. Elean Teresa Conejos, Nov. 20, 1974; children: Sebastian A., C. Gonzalo, Santiago M. BS, Colegio Nacional Bartolome, Tucuman, 1965; MD, Faculty of Medicine, Tucuman, 1974. Diplomate Am. Bd. Pathology. Resident and chief resident dept. pathology Montefiore Hosp., N.Y.C., 1975-79; fellow orthopedic pathology Presbyn. Hosp., N.Y.C., 1978; fellow dept. pathology Meml. Sloan-Kettering Cancer Ctr., N.Y.C., 1979-80; chief dept. pathology Hosp. Avellaneda, Tucuman, 1980-90, Hosp. Maternidad, Tucuman, 1990—; prof. pathology Faculty of Medicine, Tucuman, 1990—, councillor, 1989; dir. pvt. practice Departamento de Patologia, Tucuman, 1980—. Contbr. articles to profl. jours., chpts. to books. Mem. Internat. Acad. Cytology, Internat. Acad. Pathology, Argentine Soc. Pathology, Argentine Soc. Cytology. Office: Departamento de Patologia, Laprida 802, 4000 San Miguel Tucuman Argentina

RODRIGUEZ, ERIC GIBSON, geriatrician, educator; b. San Jose, Costa Rica, Sept. 11, 1947; came to U.S., 1948; s. Alfonso and Susan (Smith) R.; m. Grace Maureen McGorrian, 1983; 2 children. BA, George Washington U., 1969, MD, 1979; MPhil, Yale U., 1973. Diplomate Am. Bd. Internal Medicine. Resident George Washington U., Washington, 1979-82, chief resident, 1982-83; staff physician Indian Health Svc., Chinle, Ariz., 1983-85; asst., prof., assoc. prof. U. Pitts., 1985—, interim chief geriatric medicine, 1994—. Office: Univ Pitts Med Ctr 200 Lothrop St Pittsburgh PA 15213

RODRIGUEZ, FRED HENRY, JR., pathologist, educator b. New Orleans, Oct. 5, 1950; s. Fred Henry and Lorraine Esther (Fitzpatrick) R.; m. Susan Marilyn Miller, Dec. 22, 1973; children: Alison Patricia, Fred Henry, Kathryn Lorraine, David Miller. BS in Biology, U. New Orleans, 1972; MD, La. State U., 1975. Diplomate Am. Bd. Pathology, immunology test com. 1988-94, cert. anatomic and clin. pathology 1979, spl. competence in immunopathology 1983. Pathology intern Charity Hosp., New Orleans, 1975-76, pathology resident, 1976-79, co-chief resident, 1978, vis. pathologist, 1979—; instr. dept. pathology La. State U. Med. Ctr., New Orleans, 1978-80, asst. prof., 1980-83, assoc. prof., 1983-93, prof., 1993—, asst. prof. dept. med. tech., 1980-83, assoc. prof., 1983-93, prof., 1993—, assoc. dir. diagnostic electron microscopy lab., 1978—; staff pathologist VA Med. Ctr., New Orleans, 1979—, dir. Sch. Med. Tech., coord.pathology residency tng., dir. serology and immunology lab. sects., assoc. dir. diagnostic electron microscopy sect., 1979—, chief lab. svc., 1984—, v.p. med. staff, 1990. Bd. dirs. Ronald McDonald House, New Orleans, 1982-89. Recipient biol. scis. faculty award U. New Orleans, 1972; Am. Cancer Soc. grantee, 1974. Fellow Coll. Am. Pathologists (VA Adminstrn. del. Ho. Dels. 1988—); mem. AMA (physician's recognition award, 1978, 81, 84, 87, 90, 93), So. Med. Assn., Am. Soc. Clin. Pathologists (immunology examination com. bd. registry 1986-92, cons. rsch. and devel. com. 1988-94, bd. govs. 1991—, adv. coun. 1991—, sec. 1995—), Internat. Acad. Pathology, U. New Orleans Alumni Assn. (awards and scholarship com. 1986—), Alpha Omega Alpha, Phi Eta Sigma, Beta Beta Beta, Phi Kappa Phi. Author, co-author sci. articles; author course manual for slides series, course manual for clin. pathology.

RODRIGUEZ, JEAN BATES, counselor; b. Haverhill, N.H., Oct. 27, 1943; d. Guy Wilbur and Rowena Jeanette (Monette) Bates. Assoc. in Bus. Sci. with honors, Champlain Coll., Burlington, Vt., 1964; BA with honors, Trinity Coll., Burlington, 1974; MS in Community Counseling, St. Michael's Coll., Winooski, Vt., 1977. Cert. profl. counselor, Ariz. Counselor Interfaith Counseling, Scottsdale, Ariz., 1980; assoc. United Campus Christian Ministry, Tempe, Ariz., 1979-82; pvt. practice counseling Scottsdale, 1982-91; pvt. counseling practice Columbia, Tenn., 1992-93; lectr. various workshops and retreats; speaker on food addiction Nat. Med. Conf., 1989. Mem. ACA, Nat. Disting. Svc. Registry for Counseling and Devel., PEO (Franklin). Republican. Presbyterian.

RODRIGUEZ, JERRY, medical technologist; b. Brownsville, Tex., July 20, 1949; s. Samuel and Berta (Rubio) R.; m. Sylvia Sanchez, Dec. 27, 1969; children: Jerry Lee, Gina Rebecca, Jason Gabriel. Student, Tex. Southwest Coll., 1967-69, George Washington U., 1973-75; cert. lab. technician, Bethesda Nat. Naval Med. Ctr. Registered med. technologist. Gen. lab. technician Mercy Hosp., Brownsville, 1968-73; hosp. corpsman USN, San Diego, 1973; med. lab. technician USN, Bethesda, Md., 1973-75, Corpus Christi, Tex., 1975-77; med. technologist Physicians and Surgeons Hosp., Corpus Christi, Tex., 1976-77; chief med. technologist Flory Lab., Harlingen, Tex., 1978-81; AIS coord. (postal clerk) US Postal Svc., Harlingen, Tex., 1981-85; allergy and x-ray dept. supr. Valley Ear/Nose/Throat Specialists, Harlingen, Tex., 1985—. Recipient Lions Club award of merit, USN, San Diego, 1973, Outstanding Recruit award USN, San Diego, 1973. Mem. Am. Soc. Allergy Technologists, Pan-Am. Allergy Soc. Roman Catholic. Home: Route 3 Box 363-R Harlingen TX 78552

RODRIGUEZ, MANUEL ALVAREZ, pathologist; b. Guantanamo, Cuba, Nov. 12, 1946; came to U.S., 1961, naturalized, 1970; s. Mauel and Maria Teresa (Alvarez) R.; divorced; children: Austin B., Matthew J. BSc in Biology, U. Nev., 1966; MT, St. Alexius Hosp., Bismarck, N.D., 1969; BSc in Medicine, U. N.D., 1971; MD, U. Tex., Galveston, 1973. Diplomate Am. Bd. Pathology. Rotating intern Meml. Med. Ctr., Corpus Christi, Tex., 1973-74; commd. USPHS, 1974, advanced through grades to comdr., 1993; gen. surgery resident USPHS Hosp., New Orleans, 1974-75, anatomic/clin. pathology resident, 1975-76; anatomic/clin. pathology resident U. N.D. Sch. Medicine, Grand Forks, 1976-77, Touro Infirmary Hosp., New Orleans, 1977-79; pvt. practice Houston, 1979-89; sr. med. officer USPHS-USCG Med. Clinic, New Orleans, 1990-92; flight surgeon, sr. med. officer USPHS-Brooks AFB, San Antonio, 1992, USPHS-USCG Air Sta. Med. Clinic, Sitka, Alaska, 1992-96, USPHS-USCG Miami Air Sta. Med. Clinic, Miami Lakes, Fla., 1996; sr. staff med. officer USPHS, San Pedro, Calif., 1996—; instr. pathology La. State U. Med. Sch., Baton Rouge, 1979-80; tchg. fellow pathology U. N.D. Med. Sch., Grand Forks, 1976-77. Contbr. articles to profl. jours. Dir. charitable donations mil. ann. drive USPHS-USCG, New Orleans, Sitka, 1990-96, Miami Lakes, Fla., 1996. Fellow Am. Acad. Family Practice, Coll. Am. Pathologists, Aerospace Med. Assn. Roman Catholic. Home: 6941 Holly Rd Miami Lakes FL 33014

RODRIGUEZ, WILLIAM JULIO, physician; b. Ponce, P.R., June 18, 1941. BS, MD, Georgetown U., Washington, 1967; PhD, Georgetown U., 1975. Intern and resident Univ. Hosp., San Juan, P.R., 1967-72; fellow Children's Hosp., Washington, 1972-75; attending in infectious disease Children's Hosp. Nat. Med. Ctr., Washington, 1975—; assoc. chief infectious disease and microbiology rsch. Children's Hosp. Med. Ctr., 1979-80, chief infectious disease and microbiology, 1980-83, chmn. infectious disease dept., 1983—; cons. staff Hosp. for Sick Children, Washington, 1985—; cons. staff Shady Grove Adventist Hosp., Rockville, Md., 1988—, Holy Cross Hosp., Silver Spring, Md., 1988—, Columbia Hosp. for Women, 1990—. contbr. articles to profl. jours. MARC fellow, XIII, 1973-76. Fellow Infectious Disease Soc.; mem. AAAS, Am. Fedn. Clin. Rsch., Am. Soc. Microbiology, Assn. of Puerto Ricans in Sci. & Engring. Office: Childrens Nat Med Ctr 111 Michigan Ave NW Washington DC 20010-2970

RODRIGUEZ ARROYO, JESUS, gynecologic oncologist; b. Arecibo, P.R., Jan. 11, 1948; s. Jesus Rodriguez and Blanca Arroyo; m. Annie Arsuaga, June 3, 1972; children: Ivan, Patricia. BS, U. P.R., San Juan, 1968, MD, 1972, postgrad., 1976. Diplomate Am. Bd. Ob-Gyn. Assoc. dir. gynecologic oncology Oncology Hosp., Rio Piedras, P.R., 1978-83; assoc. prof. ob-gyn, dir. gynecologic oncology U. Hosp. Sch. Medicine, Rio Piedras, 1978-85; gynecologic oncologist Met. Hosp., Rio Piedras, 1979-88; obstetrician, gynecologist Auxilio Mutuo Hosp., P.R., 1981-91, San Pablo Hosp., Bayamon, P.R., 1981-91, Ashford Meml. Community Hosp., 1983-91; cons. gynecologic oncology Tchrs. Hosp., Hato Rey, P.R., 1979-85, Hermanos Melendez Hosp., Bayamon, 1979-91; instr. ob-gyn. U. P.R. Sch. Medicine, 1976-78, asst. prof., 1978-83, assoc. prof., 1984, dir. gynecologic oncology sect., 1978-84. Contbr. articles to med. jours. Mem. Citizen Ambassador Cancer Mgmt. Del. to USSR, 1990. Mem. AAAS, Am. Coll. Surgeons, P.R. Med. Assn. (jud. ethical coun. 1990-91), Internat. Gynecologic Cancer Soc., Soc. Gynecologic Oncologists, Dorado Beach Hotel, Caparra Country Club. Home: 1910 Pasionaria St Urban Santa Maria Rio Piedras PR 00927 Office: Caribbean Oncology & Ob-Gyn Assn PO Box 194557 San Juan PR 00919-4557

RODRIGUEZ-SAINS, RENE S., physician, surgeon, educator; b. Santiago, Cuba, July 25, 1952; came to U.S., 1960, naturalized, 1968; s. Emilio Rene Rodriguez and Caridad Sains; m. Juanita Laszlo, Aug. 31, 1974; children: Daniel Rene, Diana. BA cum laude, CUNY, 1973; MD, NYU, 1977. Diplomate Nat. Bd. Med. Examiners, Am. Bd. Ophthalmology. Dermatology rsch. fellow NYU Med. Ctr., N.Y.C., 1973-77, intern dept. medicine, 1977-78; resident in ophthalmology Manhattan Eye, Ear and Throat Hosp., 1978-81, chief resident in ophthalmology, 1980-81, asst. attending surgeon, 1981-85, assoc. attending surgeon Ophthalmic Plastic & Reconstructive Surgery, Ocular Tumor & Orbital Clinic, 1985-89, surgeon dir. Ophthalmic Plastic & Reconstructive Surgery Clinic, 1989-93, surgeon dir., chief Ocular Tumor & Orbital Clinic, 1989-93; attending surgeon, chief Manhattan Eye, Ear And Throat Hosp., N.Y.C., 1993—, attending surgeon ophthalmic plastic and reconstructive surgery clinic, 1993—, dir. internat. fellowship program, 1991—. Heed Ophthalmic Found. fellow Manhattan Eye, Ear and Throat Hosp.-N.Y. Hosp., Cornell U. Med. Ctr., 1981-82, resident instr. dept. ophthalmology, 1983-85; adj. asst. prof. dermatology NYU, 1981-88; clin. asst. prof. ophthalmology, Mt. Sinai Med. Ctr.; attending surgeon Dept. Ophthalmology, Plastic and Reconstructive Surgery divsn., Bronx VA Hosp., 1985-88; clin. asst. prof. Dept. Ophthalmology, NYU Med. Ctr., 1988—. Mem. med. adv. bd. Skin Cancer Found., 1980—; mem. NYU Malignant Melanoma Clin. Coop. Group, 1981—; bd. dirs. Orbital Disease Found., 1994—; mem. Barraquer Inst. Barcelona, Spain, N.Y. Soc for Clin. Ophthalmology. Contbg. editor Jour. Dermatologic Surgery ad Oncology, 1980-90; co-author: Malignant Melanoma, 1979; contbr. articles to med. jours. Fellow Am. Coll. Surgeons, Am. Acad. Facial Plastic and Reconstructive Surgery, Am. Soc. Ophthalmic Plastic and Reconstructive Surgery, N.Y. Acad. Medicine; mem. AMA, N.Y. State Ophthalmol. Soc., Am. Assn. Ophthalmology, Assn. Rsch. in Vision and Ophthalmology, Manhattan Ophthalmologic Soc., N.Y. County Med. Soc., Med. Soc. State N.Y., Am. Acad. Ophthalmology. Office: 178 E 71st St New York NY 10021-5119

ROE, BENSON BERTHEAU, surgeon, educator; b. L.A., July 7, 1918; s. Hall and Helene Louise (Bertheau) R.; m. Jane Faulkner St. John, Jan. 20, 1945; children: David B., Virginia St. John. AB, U. Calif., Berkeley, 1939; MD cum laude, Harvard U., 1943. Diplomate Am. Bd. Surgery, Am. Bd. Thoracic Surgery (dir. 1971-83, chmn. bd. 1981-83, chmn. exam. com. 1978, chmn. long-range planning com. 1980, chmn. program com. 1977). Intern Mass. Gen. Hosp., Boston, 1943-44, resident, 1946-50; nat. rsch. fellow dept. physiology Med. Sch., Harvard U., Boston, Mass., 1947, instr. surgery, 1950; Moseley Traveling fellow Harvard. U. at U. Edinburgh, Scotland, 1951; asst. clin. prof. surgery U. Calif., San Francisco, 1951-58, chief cardiothoracic surgery, 1958-76, prof. surgery, 1966-89, emeritus prof., 1989—; pvt. practice medicine specializing in cardiothoracic surgery San Francisco, 1952-85; cons. thoracic surgery VA Hosp., San Francisco Gen. Hosp., Letterman Army Hosp., St. Lukes Hosp., Blue Shield of Calif., Baxter Labs., Ethicon, Inc.;

bd. dirs. Control Laser Corp.; vis. prof. U. Utah, U. Ky., U. Gdansk, Poland, Nat. Heart Hosp., London, U. Ibadan, Nigeria, Sanger Clinic, Charlotte, Rush-Presbyn. Hosp., Chgo., Penrose Hosp., Colorado Springs; bd. dirs. Internat. Bioethics Inst. Mem. editl. bd. Annals of Thoracic Surgery, 1969-82, Pharos; editor 2 med. texts; author 21 textbook chpts.; contbr. 174 articles to profl. jours. Bd. dirs. United Bay Area Crusade, 1958-70, mem. exec. com., 1964-65; bd. dirs. chmn. exec. com. San Francisco chpt. Am. Cancer Soc., 1955-57; bd. dirs. San Francisco Heart Assn., 1964-72, pres., 1964-65, chmn. rsch. com., 1966-71; mem. various coms. Am. Heart Assn., 1967-70; pres. Miranda Lux Found., 1982-94; trustee Avery Fuller Found.; bd. dirs. Internat. Bioethics Inst., Point Reyes Bird Observatory. Served with Med. Svc. Corps, USNR, 1944-46. Fellow Am. Coll. Cardiology, ACS (chmn. adv. coun. thoracic surgery, program chmn. thoracic surgery, cardiovascular com.), Polish Surg. Assn. (hon.); mem. Am. Assn. Thoracic Surgery (chmn. membership com. 1974-75), AMA (residency rev. com. for thoracic surgery), Am. Surg. Assn., Pacific Coast Surg. Assn., Calif. Acad. Medicine (pres. 1974), Calif. Med. Assn., Soc. Univ. Surgeons, Soc. Throacic Surgerons (pres. 1972, chmn. standards and ethics com.), Soc. Vascular Surgery (v.p.). Clubs: Cruising of Am, Pacific Union, St. Francis Yacht, Calif. Tennis. Office: U Calif Div Cardiothoracic Surgery U Calif M593 San Francisco CA 94143-0118

ROE, CHRISTOPHER JOHN, nephrologist; b. London, Jan. 11, 1954; s. James Joseph and Sybil Audrey R. MB BS, Monash U., Melbourne, 1978; PhD, Melbourne U., 1990. Diplomate Soc. Apothecaries, London. Intern Alfred Hosp., Melbourne, 1979, jr. resident med. officer, 1980, sr. resident med. officer, 1981, renal registrar, 1982; renal registrar St. Bartholomew's Hosp., London, 1983-85; vis. nephrologist Royal Children's Hosp., Melbourne, 1988-92; sessional nephrologist Royal Melbourne Hosp., 1989-93; renal physician Repatriation Gen. Hosp., Heidelberg, 1989—; clin. instr. U. Melbourne, 1986—. Med. postgrad. rsch. scholar Nat. Health and Med. Rsch. Coun., 1986-88; Victor Hurley Med. Rsch. grantee Royal Melbourne Hosp., 1987-88; Australian Kidney Found. grantee, 1988, Brit. Coun. overseas travel grantee, 1990, Ctrl. Health and Med. Rsch. Coun./Dept Vets. Affairs grantee, 1991-92. Fellow Royal Australian Coll. Physicians; mem. Assn. Monash Med. Grads. (pres. 1991-93), Australian Soc. Med. Rsch. (hon. sec. 1990-91), Australian and New Zealand Soc. Nephrology, European Renal Assn., Internat. Soc. Nephrology, Asian Pacific Soc. Nephrology, Nat. Kidney Found., Polycystic Kidney Rsch. Found., Australian Med. Assn., Bird Observers Club Australia. Office: Austin/Repatriaion Med Ctr, Renal Unit, Locked Bag 25, Heidelberg 3084, Australia

ROE, THOMAS LEROY WILLIS, pediatrician; b. Bend, Oreg., Sept. 1, 1936. MD, U. Oregon Health Scis. U., Portland, 1961. Diplomate Am. Bd. Pediatrics. Intern U. Calif., San Francisco, 1961-62, resident, 1962-64; physician Sacred Heart Med. Ctr., Eugene, Oreg.; pvt. practice Peace Health Med. Group, Eugene, 1985—; clin prof. pediatrics U. Oregon, Eugene, 1985—. Fellow Am. Acad. Pediatricians; mem. AMA, North Pacific Pediatrics Soc. Office: Eugene Clin 1162 Williamette St Eugene OR 97401*

ROE, WILLIAM THOMAS, behaviorial engineer, educator, researcher; b. N.Y.C., July 7, 1944; s. William T. and Harriet E. (Higgins) R.; m. Susan C. Kane, Aug. 30, 1972. BA in Enginng./Indsl. Psychology, Calif. State U.-Northridge, 1971, MA in Human Factors and Applied Exptl. Psychology, 1978; postgrad., Grad. Sch. Am. Rsch. asst. XYZYX Info. Corp., Canoga Park, Calif., 1973-74; mem. psychol. staff Manned Systems Scis. Inc., Northridge, 1974-75; rsch. psychologist Inst. Safety and Systems Mgmt., U. So. Calif., L.A., 1975-76; mgr., acct. exec. systems and data processing Mgmt. Recruiters So. Calif., Encino, 1976-79; resource evaluation analyst Samaritan Health Svc., Phoenix, 1979; sr. methods analyst Valley Nat. Bank, Phoenix, 1979-81; indsl. engr. City of Scottsdale, Ariz., 1981-84; prof. psychology Phoenix Coll., 1984—; editorial reviewer numerous major text publs. Author: Ergonomic Models of Human Performance: Source Materials for the Analyst, 1975, Behavioral Engineering: Paradigm for Human Transformation, 1988, Mind-Body Psychology: Source Materials for Medical Education, 1995; contbr. articles to profl. jours. With USN, 1961-67, Vietnam. Recipient Recognition certs. San Fernando Valley chpt. Data Processing Mgmt. Assn., 1978, Phoenix chpt. 1983, NISOD Teaching Excellence award, 1996. Mem. APA (divsn. 27), AACD, Am. Inst. Indsl. Engrs., Human Factors Soc., World Future Soc., Western Psychol. Assn., Ariz. Counselors Assn., Ariz. Mental Health Counselors Assn. Office: Phoenix Coll 1202 W Thomas Rd Phoenix AZ 85013-4208

ROEBUCK-COLGAN, KATHLEEN, health care administrator; b. St. Joseph, Mo., Mar. 22, 1949; d. Robert Kermyt and Dorothy (Hogue) R.; m. Anthony Ray Colgan, Dec. 13, 1980 (div. Sept. 1984); children: Bailey Mikél, Kristin Kathleen. BA, Mo. Western State Coll., 1972; diplomaa, Meth. Med. Ctr. of Nursing, 1979. RN, Mo. Staff nurse oper. rm. St. Joseph (Mo.) Hosp., 1979-81; staff nurse St. Joseph State Hosp., 1982-89, staff nurse quality improvement, 1989-95, dir. quality improvement, 1995—. Mem. Leadership St. Joseph United Way, 1994. Mem. Nat. Assn. of Healthcare Quality (cert.). Methodist. Home: 812 N 6th St Saint Joseph MO 64501-1602 Office: St Joseph State Hosp 3400 Frederick Saint Joseph MO 64506

ROEDER, ROBERT GAYLE, biochemist, educator; b. Boonville, Ind., June 3, 1942; s. Frederick John and Helene (Bredenkamp) R.; m. Suzanne Himsel, July 11, 1964 (div. 1981); children: Kimberly, Michael; m. Cun Jing Hong, June 2, 1990. BA summa cum laude (Gilbert scholar), Wabash Coll., 1964, DSc (hon.), 1990; MS, U. Ill., 1965; PhD (USPHS fellow), U. Wash., 1969. Am. Cancer Soc. fellow dept. embryology Carnegie Instn. Washington, Balt., 1969-71; asst. prof. biol. chemistry Washington U., St. Louis, 1971-75; assoc. prof. Washington U., 1975-76, prof., 1976-82, prof. genetics, 1978-82, James S. McDonnell prof. biochem. genetics, 1979-82; prof. lab. biochemistry and molecular biology Rockefeller U., N.Y.C., 1982—; Arnold O. and Mabel S. Beckmann prof. molecular biology and biochemistry Rockefeller U., 1985—; cons. USPHS, 1975-79, Am. Cancer Soc., 1983-86. Recipient Dreyfus Tchr.-Scholar award Dreyfus Found., 1976, molecular biology award NAS-U.S. Steel Found., 1986, outstanding investigator award Nat. Cancer Inst., 1986—, Rosensteil award for disting. work in basic med. scis. Brandeis U., 1995, Passano award Passano Found., Inc., 1995; grantee NIH, 1972—, NSF, 1975-79, Am. Cancer Soc., 1979-85. Fellow AAAS, Am. Acad. Arts & Scis., Am. Acad. Microbiology, N.Y. Acad. Scis.; mem. NAS, Am. Chem. Soc. (Eli Lilly award 1977), Am. Soc. Biol. Chemists, Am. Soc. Microbiologists, Harvey Soc. (pres. 1994), Phi Beta Kappa. Home: 504 E 63rd St Apt 36P New York NY 10021-7929 Office: Rockefeller University 1230 York Ave New York NY 10021-6307*

ROEDER, VICTOR H., optometrist; b. Waupun, Wis., Apr. 24, 1964; s. Victor H. Jr. and Beverly M. (Thull) R.; m. Cathleen M. Zimmerman, June 6, 1987; children: Andrew, John. BS, U. Wis., 1986; DO, U. Mo., St. Louis, 1991. Optometrist Thomas K. Marsh, O.D., Oconomowo, Wis., 1991-94, Kindy Optical, West Bend, Wis., 1992—, Vision Care Assocs., Ripon, Wis., 1994—. Mem. Wis. Optometric Assn., Lake Winnebago Optometric Soc., Early Bird Kiwanis, K.C. Republican. Roman Catholic. Office: Visioncare Assocs 113 Watson St Ripon WI 54971

ROEDERSHEIMER, LOUIS RICHARD, surgeon; b. Cin., Dec. 30, 1948; s. Louis and Anna R. Roedersheimer; m. Marianne Matuska; children: Melissa, Rebecca, Rich, Katie. BS, Brown U., 1971; MD, U. Cin., 1975. Diplomate Am. Bd. Surgery. Surgeon Cranley Surg. Assn., Cin., 1980—, pres., 1991—; dir. vascular surgery sect. St. Francis-St. George, Cin., 1993—, instr. dep. surgery, 1993—, dir. vascular lab., 1993—, pres.-elect med. staff, 1995—. Contbr. numerous articles to profl. jours. Recipient Good Samaritan Hosp. Teaching Faculty awards, 1981, 87, 90; Sloan Nat. scholar, 1974. Fellow ACS; mem. Internat. Soc. Cardiovascular Surgery, Midwestern Vascular Surg. Soc., Cin. Surg. Soc. (pres. 1993), Soc. Clin. Vascular Surgery. Home: 5393 Manor Tree Ln Cincinnati OH 45238 Office: Cranley Surg Assocs Inc 310 Terrace Ave Cincinnati OH 45220

ROEDLER, SUZANNE MARIA, cardiologist, educator; b. Vienna, Austria, Jan. 25, 1957; d. Friedrich Otto and Marianne Suzanne (Borbas) R. Pvt. practice, Vienna; asst. prof. U. Vienna, 1995—. Initiator Cliniclowns Austria. Mem. Internat. Soc. Heart and Lung Transplantation. Home: Perntergasse 15, 1190 Vienna Austria Office: U Vienna, Wahringergurtel 18-20, 1090 Vienna Austria

ROEHRIG, C(HARLES) BURNS, internist, health policy consultant, editor; b. Brookline, Mass., Jan. 21, 1923; s. Gilbert Haven and Helen (Burns) R.; m. Patricia Joan Orme, July 22, 1952; children—Joan Russell Roehrig Vater, Jennifer Orme Roehrig Munn, Charles Burns, Jr. Student, Amherst Coll., 1941-43, Vanderbilt U., 1943-44; M.D., U. Md., 1949; cert. in internal medicine, U. Pa. Grad. Sch. Medicine, Phila., 1953. Diplomate Am. Bd. Internal Medicine. Intern Boston City Hosp., 1949-50; resident in internal medicine and diabetes Joslin Clinic, New Eng. Deaconess Hosp., Boston, 1952-54; practice medicine specializing in internal medicine and diabetes Boston, 1954—; chief of staff, pres. med. adminstrv. bd. New Eng. Deaconess Hosp., Boston, 1972-75; dir., mem. exec. com. Blue Shield of Mass., Inc., Boston, 1977-88, dir., 1989—; mem. exec. com. Met. Boston Hosp. Coun., 1982-86; mem. physician adv. council Mass. Hosp. Assn., Burlington, 1982-86. Editor: The Internist: Health Policy in Practice, Washington, 1987—; contbr. med. articles to profl. jours. Bd. dirs. Camping Svcs. Bd., Greater Boston YMCA, 1966—; mem. physician adv. group Health Care Financing Adminstrn., Washington, 1983-88; mem. adv. panel on physician payment and med. tech. Office of Tech. Assessment, U.S. Congress, Washington, 1984-85; chmn. Federated Coun. for Internal Medicine, Washington, 1985-86; trustee New Eng. Deaconess Hosp. Capt. (flight surgeon) USAF, 1949-52. Fellow ACP; mem. AMA (chmn. coun. on long range planning and devel., Chgo.), New Eng. Diabetes Assn. (pres. 1963-64), Mass. Soc. Internal Medicine (pres. 1971-72), Am. Soc. Internal Medicine (pres. 1984-85). Republican. Episcopalian. Club: Wellesley Country (Mass.).

ROËL, LAWRENCE EDMOUND, ophthalmologist; b. Aug. 19, 1949; s. Edmond Lawrence and Leslie Adele (Gonzalez) R. AB in Biochemistry, Princeton U., 1971; PhD in Nutritional Biochemistry, MIT, 1976; MD, U. Pa., 1985. Lic. physician S.C., N.Y. Blood bank technician Boston Hosp. for Women, 1972-75; predoctoral fellow MIT, 1971-75; postdoctoral fellow U. Calif., San Diego, 1976-78; intern Montefiore Hosp., Pitts., 1985-86; resident in ophthalmology Columbia U.-Presbyn. Hosp., N.Y.C., 1986-89; pvt. practice Spartanburg, S.C., 1994—; staff ophthalmologist Mary Black Meml. Hosp., Spartanburg, S.C., Spartanburg Regional Med. Ctr.; lectr. in field. Contbr. articles to profl. jours. Fellow NIH, Muscular Dystrophy Assn.; grantee Am. Cancer Soc., Northwestern U., NIH. Mem. Am. Acad. Ophthalmology, S.C. Med. Soc., Spartanburg County Med. Soc. Office: Eastside Eye Center 735 E Main St Spartanburg SC 29302

ROELCKE, DIETER, physician, educator, blood bank director; b. Heidelberg, Germany, Dec. 28, 1936. DM, Univs. Heidelberg and Hamburg, 1962. Habilitation, 1971. Prof. immunology U. Heidelberg, 1974—. Contbr. 200 articles to profl. publs. Office: Univ Heidelberg Inst Immunologie, Im Neuenheimer Feld 305, 69120 Heidelberg Germany

ROELS, FRANK, anatomy and embryology educator; b. Antwerp, Belgium, Apr. 23, 1937; s. Rudolf and Prudence (Goddaert) R.; m. Betty Gilberte De Prest, Jan. 30, 1971; children: Sidney, Britt. MD, State U., Gent, Belgium, 1961; aggregatie HO, Free U., Brussels, 1991. Lic. MD. Asst. dept. human anatomy State U., Gent, 1961-65, first asst., 1965; vis. asst. prof. dept. pathology Einstein Coll. Medicine, Bronx, N.Y., 1971; adj. prof. dept. human anatomy U. Antwerp, Belgium, 1973-89; prof. human anatomy, embryology Free U., Brussels, 1978-92, U. Gent, 1992—; coord European Concerted Action Screening, Prevention, Treatment and Pathogenesisof Peroxisomal Leukodystrophy, 1996—. Author: Peroxisomes--A Personal Account, 1991, (with others) Diagnosis of Human Peroxisomal Disorders--A Handbook, 1995; contbr. articles to profl. jours. Chmn. Gent Mcpl. Med. Commn., 1977-89. Grantee Belgian Nat. Fund. Sci. Rsch., Ghent, 1973, Fund for Med. Sci. Rsch., Brussels, 1975, 79, 83, 86, 89, 93, Nat. Lottery, 1988, European Fedn. Biochem. Socs., 1994, European Commn. Med. Rsch., 1995—, others. Mem. AAAS, Belgian Soc. for Elctron Microscopy (pres. 1991-92), Belgian Soc. Med. Biol. Enging. and Computing (pres. 1986-88), European Soc. Analytical and Cellular Pathology (coun. 1990-94), Belgian Soc. Cell Biology (coun. 1989—), N.Y. Acad. Scis., Histochem. Soc., Am. Soc. for Cell Biology, Internat. Soc. Neonatal Screening, Soc. Study Inborn Errors of Metabolism (U.K.), Gesellschaft für Histochemie (Germany), Soc. Biol. Cell (France), Soc. Française Microscopie Electronique, Netherland Soc. Cell Biology, Belgian Soc. Biochemistry and Molecular Biology, Assn. des Anatomistes. Home: Gordunakaai 11, 9000 Gent Belgium Office: Univ Gent, Godshuizenlaan 4, 9000 Gent Belgium

ROEMER, MILTON IRWIN, physician, educator; b. Paterson, N.J., Mar. 24, 1916; s. Jacob and Mary (Rabinowitz) R.; m. Ruth Rosenbaum, Sept. 1. 1939; children: John, Beth. B.A., Cornell U., 1936, M.A., 1939; M.D., NYU, 1940; M.P.H., U. Mich., 1943. Diplomate: Am. Bd. Preventive Medicine. Intern Barnert Meml. Hosp., Paterson, 1940-41; with N.J. Health Dept., Trenton, 1941-42, USPHS, Washington, 1943-48; mem. faculty Yale U. Med. Sch., 1949-51; with WHO, Geneva, 1951-53, Sask. (Can.) Health Dept., 1953-56; mem. faculty Cornell U., 1957-61; prof. health adminstrn. U. Calif. Sch. Pub. Health, Los Angeles, 1962—; cons. in field. Author: numerous books, including Health Care Systems in World Perspective, 1976, Comparative National Policies on Health Care, 1977, Ambulatory Health Services in America, 1981, National Health Systems of the World: Vol. 1: The Countries, 1991, Vol. 2: The Issues, 1993. Mem. Inst. Medicine, Am. Pub. Health Assn. (award for excellence in internat. health 1977, Sedgwick medal 1983), Am. Coll. Preventive Medicine, Internat. Epidemiol. Assn., Physicians Forum, Group Health Assn. Am., Phi Beta Kappa, Sigma Xi, Alpha Omega Alpha, Phi Kappa Phi, Delta Omega. Home: 365 S Westgate Ave Los Angeles CA 90049-4207 Office: Univ Calif Univ Calif Sch Pub Health Los Angeles CA 90095

ROEMER, PATRICIA STREED, optometrist; b. Bemidji, Minn., Apr. 11, 1966; d. James Leroy and Joan Helen (Talbott) Streed; m. Scott William Roemer, June 30, 1990; children: Austin James, Sydney Regina. AA, Highland Coll., Freeport, Ill., 1987; BS in Visual Sci., Ind. U., 1988, OD, 1991. Staff optometrist U.S. Naval Hosp., Bremerton, Wash., 1991-94, Pacific Eye Care Ctr., Poulsbo, Wash., 1994—. Lt. USN, 1991-94. Mem. Am. Optometric Soc., Am. Optometric Assn. (contact lens sect. 1994—, low vision sect. 1994—), Wash. Assn. Optometric Physicians (v.p. 1995, sec.-treas. 1994). Office: Pacific Eye Care Ctr 20696 Bond Rd NE Poulsbo WA 98370

ROERS, CHERYL MARIE, optometrist; b. Racine, Wis., May 28, 1966; d. Wayne Joseph and Bonita Martha (Post) R. BS, U. Wis., 1988; OD, Ind. U., 1992. Lic. optometrist, Wis. Optometrist Sheboygan, Wis., 1992—. Mem. Am. Optometric Assn., Wis. Optometric Assn., Lakeshore Optometric Soc. (v.p. 1993—). Office: 1442 N 31st St Sheboygan WI 53081

ROESCH, ROBERT EUGENE, dentist; b. Falls City, Nebr., July 10, 1951; s. Wilber H. and Vivian (Reese) R.; m. Susan M. Tuttle, Aug. 25, 1973. BA, Midland Luth. Coll., 1973; DDS, U. Nebr., 1976. Pvt. practice dentistry, Fremont, Nebr., 1979—; dental cons. Dodge County Am. Cancer Soc., Fremont, Nebr. 1984—; cons. Nebr. Dental Assn., Dodge County, 1979—, third party dental care com. 1984-88, del., 1991—, dental care com. 1993-95; v.p. region 10 Acad. of Gen. Dentistry, 1990-91, dir., 1991-93, trustee, 1993—, budget & fin. com., 1994—, chm., Acad. Gen. Dentistry, budget & fin. com., Campaign chmn. Fremont United Way, 1987, v.p., 1988; pres. Sinai Luth. Ch. Coun., Fremont, 1983-84, bd. dirs. 1987-90; mem. endowment com. Sinai Luth. Ch., 1990-94; bd. dirs. Gannett Found., Ascertainment Com., Fremont, 1981-88, Dodge County Reps., Fremont, 1981-88; bd. dirs. Dodge County Hist. Soc., 1989-92. Fellow Internat. Acad. Dentistry, Internat. Coll. Dentistry; mem. ADA, Acad. Operative Dentistry, Nebr. Acad. of Gen. Dentistry (pub. info. officer 1983-85, sec., treas. 1985-88, pres. elect 1988-89, pres. 1990-92, exec. dir. 1992-94, continuing edn. chmn., 1994—), Am. Orthodontic Soc., Am. Assn. Functional Orthodontists, Am. Equilibration Soc., Omaha Dist. Dental Soc. (bd. dirs., pres.-elect 1996—), R.V. Tucker Nebr. study club Salmon Soc. Dodge County Hist. Soc., Midland Coll. Alumni (bd. dirs. 1981-87, pres. 1983-84), Fremont Wellness Coun. (bd. dirs. 1996—), Fremont C. of C. (diplomat 1985-94, bd. dirs. 1991-94, vice-chmn. memberships and membership svcs. 1989-90, vice-chmn. pub. affairs 1992-94), Optimists (bd. dirs. 1981-83, 84-88, pres. 1987, bd. dirs. Fremont club 1991-93), Fremont Indsl Found., Main St. Fremont (org. com. 1995—), Main St. Ambs. (co-chmn. 1996—), Fremont Tennis Assn., Am. Legion, Fremont Community Players, Midland Luth. Coll. Boosters Club (bd. dirs. 1988-94), Tri Valley Dental Study Club (sec.-treas. 1983, v.p. 1984, pres. 1985, v.p. 1989), Ak-Sar-Ben Dental Study Club. Republican. Avocations: tennis, racquetball, traveling. Home: 750 N Clarkson St Fremont NE 68025-5172 Office: 553 N Broad St Fremont NE 68025-4930

ROESCH, RONALD, psychology educator; b. Montclair, N.J., May 25, 1947; s. Irene (O'Donnell) Taylor; m. Kathleen Mitchell, Nov. 13, 1976; children: David, Jeremy, Stefan, Michael. BS in Psychology, Ariz. State U., 1971; PhD in Psychology, U. Ill., 1977. Prof. Simon Fraser U., Burnaby, B.C., Can., 1977—, dir. clin. tng., 1981—, dir. mental health, law and policy inst., 1991—; chair bd. dirs. Family Violence Inst., Vancouver, B.C., 1988-94. Author: Competency to Stand Trial, 1980 (ABA award 1981); editor: Family Violence, 1990, Law and Human Behavior; contbr. articles to profl. jours. Recipient Social Issues Dissertation award Soc. for Psychol. Study Social Issues, 1977. Fellow APA (cons. psychology rsch. award 1977), Can. Psychol. Assn., Baha'i. Home: 936 Peace Portal Dr PO Box 8014-153 Blaine WA 98231 Office: Simon Fraser U, Dept Psychology, Burnaby, BC Canada V5A 1S6

ROEVER, FREDERICK HENRY, internist; b. Phila., June 9, 1940; s. Henry Frederick and Irma Suzanna (Lux) R.; B.S., Haverford Coll., 1962; M.D., Hahnemann Med. Coll., 1966; m. Patricia Anne Ayars, Sept. 4, 1965; children—Christopher Paul, Cynthia Patricia. Chief med. resident Mercy Catholic Med. Center, Phila., 1972; dir. med. edn. Tarpon Springs (Fla.) Hosp., 1973—, chief dept. medicine, 1976—, also mem. staff; practice medicine, specializing in internal medicine, Tarpon Springs; lectr. U. S.Fla. Served to capt., inf., U.S. Army, 1968-69; Vietnam. Decorated Bronze Star, Air medal, Vietnamese Honor medal 1st class. Diplomate Am. Bd. Internal Medicine. Fellow ACP; mem. AMA (student teaching award 1976), Undersea Med. Soc., Christian Med. Soc., Am. Soc. Internal Medicine, Assn. U.S. Army, VFW, Am. Legion. Democrat. Lutheran. Office: 42674 US 19 N Tarpon Springs FL 34689-6902

ROFMAN, ETHAN SAMUEL, psychiatrist, educator; b. N.Y.C., July 26, 1940; s. Joseph and Clara (Ginzberg) R.; m. Barbara Elaine Johnson, July 29, 1972; children: Amy J., Julie A. AB, Columbia U., 1961, MD, 1965. Diplomate Nat. Bd. Med. Examiners. Psychiatrist Mental Health Clin. Utapao AFB, Thailand, 1969-70; psychiatrist Mental Health Clinic, Westover AFB, Mass., 1970-71; assisting physician Boston City Hosp., 1971-75, chief psychiat. cons. svc., 1971-76; chief psychiat. svc. E.N. Rogers Meml. Vets. Hosp., Bedford, Mass., 1976-80; med. dir. Charles River Hosp., Wellesley, Mass., 1980-85; dir. human svcs. New Eng. Meml. Hosp., Stoneham, Mass., 1985-89; chmn. psychiat. dept. Framingham (Mass.) Union Hosp., 1989-93; dir. cmty. psychiatry Metrowest Med. Ctr., Natick, Mass., 1993—, chmn. psychiat dept., 1995-96; med. dir. Mass. Behavioral Health Partnership, Boston, 1996—; assoc. prof. psychiatry Boston U., 1976—; lectr. psychiatry Harvard U., Cambridge, Mass., 1986-90, 95-96. Author: chpt. Emergency Psychiatry, 1977, 2d edit., 1983, Programs for Chronic Patients, 1981. Bd. dirs. Alternative Homes, Newton, Mass., 1983-85, Metrowest Mental Health Assn., 1991-95. Fellow Am. Psychiat. Assn.; mem. Mass. Med. Soc. (Pride in Medicine award 1989).

ROFSKY, JAY ELLIOT, optometrist; b. Garden Grove, Calif., Jan. 6, 1966; s. Marvin and Claire (Kantor) R. BS, U. Calif., Irvine, 1989; OD, Ill. Coll. Optometry, 1993. Lic. optometrist, Calif. Resident optometrist West L.A. VA Med. Ctr., 1993-94; optometrist Talbert Med. Group, Tustin, Calif., 1994—; continuing edn. lectr. So. Calif. Coll. Optometry, Fullerton, 1994; lectr., presenter in field. Contbr. articles to profl. publs. Wildermuth Found. scholar, 1992, 93. Fellow Am. Acad. Optometry; mem. Am. Optometric Assn. (Editor's Eagle award 1995), Calif. Optometric Assn., Los Angeles County Optometric Soc. (polit. action com. 1995—), Alpha Epsilon Pi (life, Brother of Yr. 1989). Office: Talbert Med Group 13132 Newport Tustin CA 92680

ROGALLA, CAROLYN JANETTE, nurse, consultant; b. San Francisco, Feb. 3, 1945; d. William Henry and Janette Malene (Nelsen) Bohn; m. Marion Leonard Rogalla, Sept. 8, 1973. Grad., St. Luke's Sch. Nursing, San Francisco, 1967; BA in Mgmt., Redlands U., 1986. RN, Calif. Staff nurse ICU Stanford U. Hosp., Palo Alto, Calif., 1967-69; mgr. cardiovasc. rsch. Stanford U. Hosp., 1969-71; cardiovasc. rschr. Ames Rsch. Lab., 1971-73; ICU nurse VA Hosp., Mpls., 1973; oper. rm. nurse VA Hosp., 1974-76; operating room nurse Western Med. Ctr., Santa Ana, Calif., 1977-80, 81-86; oper. rm. nurse Mt. Vernon Hosp., Alexandria, Va., 1980-81; coord. med. rels. Xanar/Coherent Laser, Colo., 1987; regional nurse cons. Candela Corp., Yorba Linda, Calif., 1987—; mem. nursing adv. bd. Minimally Invasive Surg. Nursing Jour., 1995—. Contbr. articles to profl. jours. Mem. Assn. Oper. Rm. Nurses (editor Splty. Assembly newsletter 1993—), Far West Ski Assn. (conv. chmn. 1972). Republican. Home and Office: 6052 Grandview Ave Yorba Linda CA 92686-5309

ROGALSKI, CAROL JEAN, clinical psychologist, educator; b. Chgo., Sept. 25, 1937; d. Casimir Joseph and Lillian Valentine Rogalski. BS, Loyola U., Chgo., 1961; PhD, NYU, 1968; cert. in psychoanalysis, Postgrad. Ctr. Mental Health, 1973. Lic. clin. psychologist, N.Y., Ill. Rsch. assoc. William Alanson White Inst., N.Y.C., 1961-66; rsch. asst., intern Hillside Hosp., Glen Oaks, N.Y., 1966-68; cons. Mt. Sinai Hosp., N.Y.C., 1968-73; staff psychologist Westside VA Hosp., Chgo., 1974—; clin. asst. prof. psychiatry Med. Sch. U. Ill., 1996—. Mem. editorial bd. Internat. Jour. Addictions, 1994—; contbr. articles to profl. publs. Mem. APA, Communal Studies Assn., Chgo. Soc. for Psychotherapy Rsch. (chair 1988-91). Office: Westside VA Hosp 820 S Damen Ave Chicago IL 60612-3728

ROGALSKI, LOIS ANN, speech and language pathologist; b. Bklyn.; d. Louis J. and Filomena Evelyn (Maro) Giordano; m. Stephen James Rogalski, Jun e 27, 1970; children: Keri Anne, Stefan Louis, Christopher James, Rebecca Blair, Gregory Alexander. BA, Bklyn. Coll., 1968; MA, U. Mass., 1969; PhD., NYU, 1975. Lic. speech and lang. pathologist, N.Y. Speech, lang. and voice pathologist Rehab. Ctr. of So. Fairfield County, Stamford, Conn., 1969, Sch. Health Program-P.A. 481, Stamford, 1969-72; pvt. practice speech, lang. and voice pathology Sch. Health Program-P.A. 481, Scarsdale, N.Y., 1972—; cons. Bd. Coop. Ednl. Svcs., 1976-79, Handicapped Program for Preschoolers for Alcott Montessori Sch., Ardsley, N.Y., 1978—; rsch. methodologist Burke Rehab. Ctr., 1977. Mem. profl. adv. bd. Found. for Children with Learning Disabilities, 1978—; bd. dirs. United Way of Scarsdale-Edgemont, 1988-89; instr. religious instr. CCD Immaculate Heart of Mary Ch., Scarsdale, 1991—. Fellow Rehab. Svcs. Adminstrn., 1968-69; N.Y. Med. Coll., 1972-75. Mem. N.Y. Speech & Hearing Assn., Westchester Speech & Hearing Assn., Am. Speech, Hearing & Lang. Assn. (cert. clin. competence), Coun. for Exceptional Children, Assn. on Mental Deficiency, Am. Acad. Pvt. Practice in Speech Pathology & Audiology (bd. dirs., treas. 1983-87, pres. 1987-89), Internat. Assn. Logopedics & Phoniatrics, Sigma Alpha Eta. Office: PO Box 1242 Scarsdale NY 10583-9242

ROGAN, DEBRA HOWER, intravenous specialist, nurse; b. Bloomsburg, Pa., Jan. 20, 1954; d. Edwin Eugene and Dorothy Thelma (Cotner) Hower; m. Richard M. Rogan, Jr., July 25, 1992; 1 child, Corey Michael. AAS in Nursing, No. Va. Community Coll., 1974; student, George Mason U., 1975, Northeastern U., 1985-87; St. Joseph's Coll., 1990—. Staff nurse Prince William Hosp., Manassas, Va., 1974-76; head nurse, regional blood program, D.C. chpt. ARC, Washington, 1976-80; IV nurse specialist Newton-Wellesley Hosp., Newton Lower Falls, Mass., 1980-81; IV coord. Visiting Nurses Associates, Dedham, Mass., 1981-86; clin. mktg. rep., clin. coord., mktg. rep. T.P.N. Pharmacy and Healthcare Svcs., Boston, 1986-88; IV nurse specialist New Eng. Deaconess Hosp., Boston, 1988-89; dir. nursing and quality assurance Nutritional Support Svcs., Knoxville, Tenn., 1989; dir. ops. nutritional support svcs., 1989-92; v.p. infusion svcs. Nutritional Support Svcs., Knoxville and Tampa, Fla., 1992-93; mem. PRN staff IV team St. Mary's Med. Ctr., Knoxville, TN, 1990-92; dir. nursing Bayada Nurse, Tampa, 1993-95; IV specialist Mariner Med Svcs., Longwood, Fla., 1995—; IV case mgmt. cons. in home care and long-term care facilities, 1987—; mem. IV task force on LPN scope of practice Fla. Bd. Nursing, 1996. Contbg. author: Nurse's Quick Reference; contbr. articles to mags. CPR instr. ARC, Washington, 1977-78, mem. edn. com., 1991—. Grantee No. Va. Community Coll., Annandale, Va., 1973, Prince William Hosp., Manassas, 1973, scholarship Westgate Woman's Club, Manassas, 1971. Mem. Nat. IV Nurse Soc. (cert. IV therapist, organizer IV therapy workshops, item writer cert. exams., 1989, organized first local chpt. 1990), Tenn. Assn. for Home Care (speaker), Region II Coun. Home Health Agys. (speaker, program com.),

Tenn. Valley Intravenous Nurses Soc. (chpt. pres. 1990-92). Democrat. Roman Catholic. Home: 1613 Bent Pine Way Brandon FL 33511-8355 Office: NSS Infusion Svcs 9000 Executive Park Dr Ste A20 Knoxville TN 37923-4685

ROGAN, ROBERT W., psychiatrist; s. Rudolph and Alice Rogan. BA, SUNY, Buffalo, MBA; DO, W.Va. Sch. Osteo. Medicine, 1983; JD, Regent U., 1990. Bar: Pa. 1992; Diplomate Nat. Bd. Osteo. Medicine. Assoc. prof. West Liberty State Coll., W.Va., 1976-79; chief intern Metro Health Ctr., Erie, Pa., 1983-84; resident Mich. Health Ctr., Detroit, 1991-92; gen. practice physician Oceana (W.Va.) Med. Ctr., 1992; sr. resident psychiat. medicine East Carolina U. Sch. Medicine, Greenville, N.C., 1992-96; mem. guilty but mentally ill task force N.C. Legislature, 1996—; tchr., rschr. in law St. Petersburg, Russia, 1993; tchr. forensic psychiatry, Australia, 1996. Commr. Hist. Preservation, Greenville, N.C., 1995-96; med. vol., Jamaica, 1988-89, Haiti, 1989, Calcutta, India, 1992. Recipient Hon. Sci. award Bausch and Lomb; scholar SUNY-Buffalo, Cornell U.; NSF grantee. Mem. Am. Psychiat. Assn., Am. Coll. Osteo. Family Practitioners, N.C. Psychiat. Assn. (rep. for residency 1994-96, mem. psychiatry and law com. 1995-96, mem. econ. affairs com. 1996—), N.C. Med. Soc. (coalition com. 1996—), Group for Advancement of Psychiatry (Ginsburg fellow 1994-96).

ROGATZ, PETER, physician; b. N.Y.C., Aug. 5, 1926; s. Julian and Sally (Levy) R.; m. Marjorie Plaut, June 10, 1949; children—Peggy Joy, William Peter. B.A., Columbia Coll., 1945; M.D., Cornell U., 1949; M.P.H., Columbia U., 1956. Intern Lenox Hill Hosp., N.Y.C., 1949-50; resident Lenox Hill Hosp., 1950-51, VA Hosp., Bronx, N.Y., 1951-52, N.Y. Hosp., N.Y.C., 1952-53; dep. dir. Montefiore Hosp., N.Y.C., 1960-63; dir. L.I. Jewish Med. Center, 1964-68, Univ. Hosp., SUNY, Stony Brook, 1968-71; sr. v.p. Blue Cross/Blue Shield of Greater N.Y., 1971-76; prin., founding ptnr. RMR Health and Hosp. Mgmt. Cons., Inc., Roslyn Heights, N.Y., 1976-84; v.p. med. affairs Vis. Nurse Service, N.Y., 1984-91; med. dir. Staff Builders, Inc., 1992—; prof. cmty. medicine SUNY, Stony Brook, 1968—; mem. N.Y.C. Mayor's Commn. on Delivery of Health Svcs., 1967; v.p. Health and Welfare Coun. of Nassau County, 1968-72; bd. dirs. Cmty. Coun. Greater N.Y., 1974-77; mem. Task Force on N.Y.C. Crisis, 1976-81; chmn. bd. dirs. Cmty. Health Program (affiliated with L.I. Jewish Med. Ctr.), 1989-94; chmn. bd. dirs. Managed Health Inc., 1990-94. Author: Organized Home Medical Care in New York City, 1956, (with Eli Ginzberg) Planning for Better Hospital Care, 1961; mem. editorial bd.: Preventive Medicine, 1975-81; contbr. articles to profl. jours. Bd. dirs. Choice in Dying, 1994—. Commonwealth Fund fellow, 1955; recipient Dean Conley award Am. Coll. Hosp. Adminstrs., 1975. Fellow ACP, N.Y. Acad. Medicine, Am. Public Health Assn., Am. Coll. Preventive Medicine; mem. Am. Hosp. Assn., N.Y. Public Health Assn., AMA, N.Y. State Med. Soc., N.Y. County Med. Soc. Home and Office: 76 Oakdale Ln Roslyn Heights NY 11577-1535

ROGERS, ADRIANNE ELLEFSON, physician, researcher, educator; b. Aberdeen, Wash., Feb. 18, 1933; d. Raymond Carl and Gretchen Lucille (Hodges) Ellefson; m. Hartley Rogers J.r, Aug. 6, 1954; children: Hartley Raymond, Campbell David Kinsey, Caroline Rebecca. AB magna cum laude, Radcliffe Coll., 1954; MD with honors, Harvard U., 1958. Diplomate Am. Bd. Pathology, Am. Bd. Toxicology. Intern in medicine Beth Israel Hosp., Boston, 1958-59; rsch. fellow pathology dept. Mallory Inst. Harvard U. Med. Sch., Boston, 1960-65; rsch. assoc. MIT, Cambridge, Mass., 1965-72, sr. rsch. scientist, 1972-86; assoc. pathologist Boston City Hosp., 1982; prof. pathology Boston U., 1982—, assoc. chair pathology, 1984—, dir. office med. edn., 1992—; lectr., instr. in pathology Harvard U. Med. Sch., 1964-88; staff pathologist Boston City Hosp., 1982—, U. Hosp. Boston, 1985—; toxicology cons. Brush Wellman Inc., Cleve., 1975—; chair grants rev. panel Am. Inst. Cancer Rsch., Washington, 1984-95; bd. sci. Counselors Nat. Toxicology Program Rsch., Triangle Park, N.C., 1986-90. Contbr. numerous articles to profl. jours. Mem. Mystic River Watershed Assn., Arlington, Mass., 1975—; trustee Forsyth Dental Ctr., Boston, 1987—. Mem. Am. Assn. Pathologists, Fedn. Am. Soc. for Exptl. Biology, Am. Inst. Nutrition, New Eng. Soc. Pathologists, Am. Assn. for Cancer Rsch., Soc. of Toxicology. Office: Boston U Sch of Medicine 80 E Concord St Boston MA 02118-2307

ROGERS, BRYAN ALLEN, retired hospital administrator; b. Akron, Ohio, Aug. 2, 1925; s. Jesse L. and Helen O. (Baker) R.; m. Jean E. Hoffman, Dec. 29, 1950; children—Mark, Amy. B.A., U. Akron, 1949; M.H.A., Washington U., St. Louis, 1954. Mem. adminstrv. staff Methodist Hosp., Indpls., 1954-72; exec. v.p., adminstr. Methodist Hosp., 1971-72; adminstr. Toledo Hosp., 1977-92, pres., 1977-92; ret., 1991; adj. instr. health care adminstrn. U. Toledo, Washington U.; charter mem. bus. adv. council Coll. Bus. Adminstrn., U. Toledo; mem. public health council Ohio Dept. Health, 1978-85; chmn. task force on cost-effectiveness Blue Cross, 1978-79; dir. Soc. Bank and Trust Co. Chmn. Pub. Health Council, 1984, Hosp. Council of Northwest Ohio, 1984. Served with AUS, 1943-46. Fellow Am. Coll. Hosp. Adminstrs.; mem. Am. Hosp. Assn. (ho. of dels. 1985-87), Ohio Hosp. Assn. (pres. 1984-85, chmn. 1984), Toledo Area C. of C. (trustee 1979-82). Presbyterian. Club: Toledo Rotary. Home: 4626 Corey Rd Toledo OH 43623-2610

ROGERS, BRYAN ROSS, health care facility administrator; b. Newport Beach, Calif., May 9, 1957; s. Maurice and Patricia Mary (Ross) R.; m. Linda Lee Chase, Sept. 18, 1981. AS, Orange Coast Coll., 1978; MA in Health Sci. summa cum laude, Duke U., 1983; MS in Pub. Health, UCLA, 1985. Registered respiratory therapist; cert. physician asst. Dir. program devel. Anaheim (Calif.) Meml. Hosp., 1985-86, v.p., 1985—; v.p. bd. Hosp. Cen. Lab., Orange, Calif., 1986-87. Mem. Health Care Exec. Office: Anaheim Meml Hosp 1111 W La Palma Ave Anaheim CA 92801-2804

ROGERS, CHERYLL ANN, health information administrator; b. Buffalo, Aug. 25, 1957; d. Archie W. and Rita J. (Dmochowski) Wilkowski; m. Robert R. Rogers, Aug. 24, 1979; children: Alexander, Amanda. BS, Daemen Coll., Amherst, N.Y., 1979. Reg. records adminstr.; cert. coding specialist. Asst. dir. med. records St. Joseph Hosp. Health Ctr., Syracuse, N.Y., 1979-82, Mercy Hosp., Buffalo, 1982-85; dir. med. records St. Joseph's Hosp., Cheektowaga, N.Y., 1985-92, Brooks Meml. Hosp., Dunkirk, N.Y., 1992—; Mem. adv. bd. Trocaire Coll., Buffalo, 1991—. Pres. Chautauqua Day Care Bd., Fredonia, N.Y., 1994—. Mem. Am. Health Info. Mgmt. Assn., N.Y. Health Info. Mgmt. Assn., Health Info. Mgmt. Assn. Western N.Y. (pres. 1984-86). Home: 251 Eagle St Fredonia NY 14063 Office: Brooks Meml Hosp 529 Central Ave Dunkirk NY 14048

ROGERS, DONALD ROBERT, retired pathologist, consultant; b. Tacoma, Apr. 7, 1932; s. John Robert and Thelma Ethel (Neely) R.; m. Georgia Lee Miller, June 9, 1956; children: Steven, Julie. BS, U. Puget Sound, 1954; MD, U. Wash., 1958. Diplomate Am. Bd. Pathology. Intern Mpls. Gen. Hosp., 1958-59; resident U. Wash., Seattle, 1963-66; pathologist Humana Hosp., Anchorage, 1967-94, ret., 1994; med. examiner State of Alaska, 1967-94; cons. forensic pathology. Contbr. articles to profl. jours. Bd. dirs. Am. Cancer Soc., Alaska, 1967—, nat. del. dir., 1983-84. Lt. comdr. USN, 1959-62. Fellow Coll. Am. Pathologists; mem. Ala. State Med. Assn. (pres. 1989-91), Anchorage Med. Soc. (pres. 1972), Nat. Assn. Med. Examiners, Rotary. Republican. Home and Office: 921 W Klatt Rd Anchorage AK 99515-3254

ROGERS, GREGORY AARON, surgeon; b. Ada, Okla., Oct. 25, 1956; s. Thomas Aaron and Mary Frances (Hargis) R.; m. Judy Ann Sappington, Oct. 17, 1975; children: Julie Denise, Gregory Aaron II, Mary Cynthia. BS in Biology, Northeastern State U., Tahlequah, Okla., 1979; DO, Okla. State U., 1983. Cert. flight surgeon, NASA, 1989. Pvt. practice Tacoma, Wash., 1987-89; commd. USAF, 1989—, advanced through grades to maj.; chief aerospace medicine Ea. Space and Missile Ctr., Patrick AFB, Fla., 1989-93, 71st Med. Group, Vance AFB, Okla., 1993-95; emergency rm. physician 45th Med. Group, Patrick AFB, 1995—; rescue flight surgeon Astronaut Rescue and Recovery Team, Kennedy Space Ctr., Fla., 1989-93, Hurricane Andrew, Miami, 1992. Author: (novel) Impact, 1995. Coach little league. With U.S. Army, 1984-87. Decorated Air medal. Mem. N.W. Okla. Osteo. Soc. Jewish. Home: PO Box 98 Webbers Falls OK 74470-0098 Office: USAF 45th Medical Group Patrick AFB FL 32925

ROGERS, JAMES VIRGIL, JR., retired radiologist and educator; b. Johnson City, Tenn., Oct. 7, 1922; s. James Virgil and Mary Ruth (Collins) R.; m. Mildred Vandivere, June 9, 1945 (div. 1985); children: Rebecca Jean, James V. III, Janet Marie, Susan Margaret; m. Mary Lujean Craven, Mar. 18, 1989. BS, Emory U., 1943, MD, 1945. Intern Kings County Hosp., N.Y.C., 1945-46; resident in radiology Grady Meml. Hosp., Altanta, 1947-48, Emory U. Hosp., Altanta, 1948-50; instr. Emory U. Sch. Medicine, Atlanta, 1950-51, assoc., 1950-53, asst. prof., 1954-60, assoc. prof., 1960-64, prof., 1965-93; ret.; chief radiology svc. Emory U. Hosp., Atlanta, 1971-80, vice chmn. dept. radiology 1973-78, acting chmn., 1978-80; dep. sect. head Emory Clinic, Atlanta, 1971-78, sect. head, 1978-80, chief radiology svc., 1982-91; cons. radiology 3d Army Hdqrs., Atlanta; examiner Am. Bd. Radiology, 1970-79, site inspector for residency programs, 1972-83. Contbr. articles to profl. jours. Pres. PHRC Ga., Atlanta, 1990. 1st lt. U.S. Army, 1946-47. Fellow Am. Coll. Radiology (councilor); mem. Radiol. Soc. North Am., Am. Roentgen Ray Soc., So. Radiologic Conf. (past pres.), Ga. Radiologic Soc. (past pres.), Atlanta Radiologic Soc. (past. pres.), AMA, So. Med. Assn. (past pres. radiology sect.), Druid Hills Golf Club, Am. Legion. Republican. Methodist. Home: 3810 Shore Blvd Oldsmar FL 34677

ROGERS, JO ANN, emergency nurse, educator; b. Fresno, Calif., June 6, 1955; d. Frank Bane Vandegrift and Elaine Marie (Lamoureux) Easley; m. Donald Carleton Rogers, July 19, 1975; children: Douglas Wayne, David Alan. AA, Miami-Dade C.C., 1978; diploma of Nursing, Jackson Meml. Hosp. Sch. Nursing, 1978; ASN, Miami-Dade C.C., 1978; BSN, Western Carolina U., 1992. RN, N.C.; cert. BCLS, ACLS instr., trauma nursing core course, med. intensive care nurse. Staff nurse Jackson Meml. Hosp., Miami, 1978-79; staff nurse med. ICU, Duke Hosp., Durham, N.C., 1979-81; emergency nurse clinician St. Joseph's Hosp., Asheville, N.C., 1989-91; emergency nurse Mission and St. Joseph's Health Sys., Asheville, 1981—; clin. instr. Western Carolina U., Cullowhee, N.C., 1992—; nurse vol. Asheville-Buncombe County Christian Ministry, Asheville, N.C., 1992-94. Named Special Vol. Sand-Hill Venable P.T.O., 1994. Roman Catholic. Home: 4 Singing Pines Dr Candler NC 28715

ROGERS, JOHN CHARLES, physician; b. Gillett Grove, Iowa, Aug. 18, 1949; s. Elwyn Charles and Aletharae (Thomas) R.; m. Lisa Louise Soiney, May, 1970 (div. Mar., 1976); m. Donna Lynn Raymond, May 22, 1976 (div. Nov., 1994); m. Jane Ellen Corboy, Oct., 1995. AA, Rochester (Minn.) Jr. Coll., 1969; BA, U. Iowa, 1971, MD, 1975; MPH, U. Wash., 1980. Diplomate Am. Bd. Family Practice, Am. Bd. Preventive Medicine (Pub. Health and Gen. Preventive Medicine). Resident family practice U. N.C., Chapel Hill, 1975-78; resident preventive medicine U. Wash., Seattle, 1978-80, fellow family medicine, 1978-80, acting asst. prof. family medicine, 1980; med. officer Pub. Health Svc. Hosp. Primary Care, Seattle, 1980-81; asst. prof. family medicine UMDNJ Rob Wood Johnson Med. Sch., Piscataway, N.J., 1981-87; assoc. prof. clin. family medicine UMDNJ Rob Wood Johnson Med. Sch., Piscataway, 1987; assoc. prof. family medicine Baylor Coll. Medicine, Houston, 1987-95, prof. family medicine, 1995—; rsch. mentor U. N.C., 1987-90. Contbr. to books and articles to profl. jours. Grantee Pub. Health Svc., 1981—. Fellow Am. Acad. Family Physicians, Am. Coll. Preventive Medicine; mem. Soc. of Tchrs. of Family Medicine (rsch. chair 1989-91, 93-95, bd. dirs. 1989-91, 93-95). Home: 3139 Las Palmas Houston TX 77027 Office: Baylor Family Practice Ctr 5510 Greenbriar St Houston TX 77005-2638

ROGERS, LEE FRANK, radiologist; b. Colchester, Vt., Sept. 24, 1934; s. Watson Frank and Marguerite Mortimer (Cole) R.; m. Donna Mae Brinker, June 20, 1956; children: Michelle, Cynthia, Christopher, Matthew. BS, Northwestern U., 1956, MD, 1959. Commd. 2d lt. U.S. Army, 1959, advanced through grades to maj., 1967; rotating intern Walter Reed Gen. Hosp., 1959-60; resident radiology Fitzsimons Gen. Hosp., 1960-63; ret., 1967; radiologist Baptist Meml. Hosp., San Antonio, 1967-68, U. Tex. Med. Sch., San Antonio, 1968-71; dir. residency tng., radiologist U. Tex. Med. Sch., Houston, 1972-74; prof., chmn. dept. radiology Northwestern U. Med. Sch., Chgo., 1974-95; editor-in-chief Am. Jour. Roentgenology, Winston-Salem, N.C., 1995—; prof. radiology Bowman Gray Sch. Medicine Wake Forest Univ. Fellow Am. Coll. Radiology (past pres.), Am. Roentgen Ray Soc. (past pres.); mem. Assn. U. Radiologists (past pres.), Radiol. Soc. N.Am., Am. Bd. Radiology (past pres.), Alpha Omega Alpha. Episcopalian. Office: Am Jour Roentgenology 101 S Stratford Rd #303 Winston Salem NC 27104

ROGERS, LLOYD SLOAN, surgeon; b. Waukegan, Ill., Apr. 23, 1914; s. Irvin Lloyd and Maude Elizabeth (Sloan) R. BS, Trinity Coll., Hartford, Conn., 1936; MD, U. Rochester, N.Y., 1941. Decorated Purple Heart. Intern surgery Strong Meml. Hosp., Rochester, N.Y., 1941-42; resident surgery U. Rochester (N.Y.) Hosps., 1946-50; asst. chief surgeon Crile VA Hosp., Celve., 1951-53; chief surgical svc. VA Hosp., Syracuse, N.Y., 1953-81; from asst. prof. to assoc. prof. surgery SUNY Health Sci. Ctr., Syracuse, 1953-67, prof. surgery, 1967-84, acting chmn. surgery, 1967-70, vice chmn. surgery, 1970-84, prof. emeritus, 1984—; mem. VA Surgical Oncology Group, Washington, 1960-83, NIH Surgical Study sect., Bethesda, Md., 1963-68; cancer coord. SUNY Health Sci. Ctr., Syracuse, 1967-72. Contbr 35 articles to peer reviewed surgical jours., 1957-84. Maj. U.S. Army Med. Corps, 1942-46, ETO. Decorated Purple Heart U.S. Army. Fellow ACS; mem. AMA, Assn. VA Surgeons (pres. 1967, Disting. Svc. award 1973), Ctrl. Surgical Assn., Internat. Surgical Soc., Soc. for Surgery Alimentary Tract. Office: SUNY Health Sci Ctr Dept Surgery 750 E Adams St Syracuse NY 13210

ROGERS, MARK CHARLES, physician, educator; b. N.Y.C., Oct. 25, 1942; s. Gerald and Inez (Kaufman) R.; m. Elizabeth Ann London, Dec. 30, 1972; children: Bradley, Meredith. BA, Columbia U., 1964; MD, SUNY, Syracuse, 1969; MBA, U. Pa., 1991; PhD (hon.), U. Ljubljana Slovenia, 1995. Diplomate Am. Bd. Anesthesiology (examiner 1982—), Am. Bd. Pediatrics. Intern Mass. Gen. Hosp., Boston, 1969-70, resident, 1973-75; resident Boston Children's Hosp., 1970-71; fellow Duke U. Med. Ctr., Durham, N.C., 1971-73; asst. prof. dept. anesthesiology and critical care medicine Johns Hopkins U., Balt., 1977-79, assoc. prof., 1979-80, prof., chmn. dept., 1980-93, assoc. dean Sch. Medicine, 1990-93, dir. pediatric ICU, 1977-93; CEO Duke Hosp. and Health Network, 1993-96; sr. v.p. Perkin Elmer, Wilton, Conn., 1996—; pres. Critical Care Found., Balt., 1981-96; cons. WHO, Bangkok, 1982-83. Editor in chief: Yearbook of Critical Care, 1983-96, Textbook of Pediatric Intensive Care, 1987, 91, 96, Principles and Practices of Anesthesiology, 1990; editor: Perioperative Management, 1989, dep. editor in chief Critical Care Medicine Jour., 1990-96. Maj. U.S. Army, 1975-77. Recipient Club of Mainz award, Mainz, Fed. Republic of Germany, 1981, award Assn. Univ. Anesthetists, 1980; Fulbright scholar, Ljubljana, Yugoslavia, 1990. Mem. Inst. Medicine. Home: 4406 W Cornwallis Rd Durham NC 27705-8126 Office: Perkin Elmer 50 Danbury Rd Wilton CT 06897

ROGERS, MICHAEL BRUCE, orthodontist; b. Augusta, Ga., Oct. 25, 1945; s. Bruce Latimer and Dorothy (Baird) R.; m. Elizabeth Bennett, Dec. 21, 1968; children: Bruce, Kay, Alison, Lisa. Student, Emory U., 1963-65, DDS, 1969; cert. in Orthodontics, Med. Coll. Ga., 1973. Diplomate Am. Bd. Orthodontists. Pvt. practice orthodontia, Augusta, Ga., 1973—; part-time asst. clin. prof. Sch. Dentistry, Med. Coll. Ga., Augusta, 1973—. Capt. Dental Corps U.S. Army, 1971-73. Fellow Internat. Acad. Dental Studies, Am. Coll. Dentists, Ga. Dental Assn. (hon.), Pierre Fauchard Acad., The Internat. Acad. of Dentists; mem. ADA (del.), Am. Assn. Orthodontists (Ga. del., chmn. mem., ethics and judicial concerns, spkr. of house 1996—, bd. trustees), So. Assn. Orthodontists (spokesperson, sec.-treas. 1993-95, dir. 1995), Eastern Dist. Dental Soc. (pres. 1982-83), Ga. Soc. Orthodontists (v.p. 1983-84, pres. 1984-85), Med. Coll. Ga. Orthodontic Alumni Assn. (pres. 1981-83), Augusta Dental Soc. (pres. 1986-87), Psi Omega (pres. 1967-68), Omicron Kappa Upsilon. Roman Catholic. Avocations: golf, boating. Home: 3214 Candace Dr Augusta GA 30909-3259 Office: 3545 Wheeler Rd Augusta GA 30909-6517

ROGERS, PHILO ALAN, osteopath; b. Kirksville, Mo., July 30, 1957; s. Edward A. and Joan (Scott) R.; m. Marla K. Lowe, May 26, 1979; children: Michelle, Joshua, Jessica, Sean. BS, NE Mo. State U., 1979; DO, Kirksville Coll., 1992. Diplomate Am. Bd. Osteo. Medicine; cert. ACLS, Pediat. Advanced Life Support, Am. Heart Assn., Advanced Trauma Life Support, ACS. Intern Mesa (Ariz.) Gen. Hosp., 1992-93, resident in family practice, 1993-95; physician, owner Patients' Choice, Mesa, 1995—. team physician soccer league; coach little league. mem. Am. Osteo. Assn., Christian Med. and Dental Assn., Ariz. Osteo. Med. Assn., Am. Cranial Acad. Office: Patients Choice 6336 E Brown Rd # 101 Mesa AZ 85205

ROGERS, ROBERT MARK, physician; b. Upper Darby, Pa., June 9, 1933; s. John Francis and Clara (Baumann) R.; m. Sandra Betz, Feb. 14, 1968; children: Janet Marie, Robert Mark, Linda, William Bradford, David Philip. BA cum laude, LaSalle Coll., Phila., 1956; MD, U. Pa., 1960. Intern Hosp. of U. Pa., 1960-61, chief emergency svcs., 1968-69, founder, dir. respiratory ICU, 1968-72, dir. pulmonary disease sect. tng. program, 1970-72; resident Case Western Res. U. Hosps., Cleve., 1961-63; fellow in pulmonary disease VA Hosp., Cleve., 1963-64; fellow in pulmonary disease U. Pa., 1964-65, postdoctoral trainee in physiology, 1966-68, asst. prof. medicine and assoc. in physiology, 1968-72; prof.medicine, assoc. prof. physiology Okla. Health Scis. Ctr. Coll. Medicine, 1972-80, also chief pulmonary disease sect., dept. medicine, dir. clin. pulmonary physiology lab. hosp. and clinics; prof. medicine, chief pulmonary, allergy & critical care medicine U. Pitts. Med. Sch., 1980—, dir. Comprehensive Lung Ctr., 1990—. Editor: Respiratory Intensive Care, 1977; mem. editl. bd. Current Opinion in Pulmonary Medicine and Critical Care; contbr. rsch. articles to profl. publs. Mem. ACP (U.S. rep. to Chinese Med. Assn. 1979, founding editor-in-chief audio cassettes program 1978-80), Am. Thoracic Soc. (founding dir. Learning Resources Ctr. 1971-77, Presdl. commendation 1977), Am. Fedn. Clin. Rsch., Am. Coll. Chest Physicians, Am. Physiol. Soc., Soc. Critical Care Medicine, Am. Heart Assn., Ctrl. Soc. Clin. Rsch., So. Soc. Clin. Rsch., Pa. Thoracic Soc. (pres. 1985-88), Coll. Physicians Phila. Home: 4116 Bigelow Blvd Pittsburgh PA 15213-1408 Office: U Pitts Sch Medicine 440 Scaife Hall Pittsburgh PA 15261-2004

ROGERS, R(OGER) CLAUDE, physician; b. Paris, France, June 3, 1923; arrived in U.S., 1963; s. Marcel and Renée (Pierre) R.; m. Felicia Antoinette Bessher, Oct. 27, 1954. BS, Bucharest, Romania, 1941; MD, Sch. Medicine, Bucharest, Romania, 1950. Chief cons. Phila. Gen. Hosp., 1971-78; chief dept. phys. medicine and rehab. All Saints Hosp., Springfield, Pa., 1971-78; chief phys. medicine and rehab. cons. Univ. Pa. Hosp. Medicine Ctr., Phila., 1978-88, hon. cons., 1988—; emeritus prof. U. Pa. Sch. Medicine, 1988—. Co-author: Archives of P.M.R., 1984; contbr. articles to profl. jours. Home: 161 Highland Cir Bala Cynwyd PA 19004

ROGERS, ROY STEELE, III, dermatology educator, dean; b. Hillsboro, Ohio, Mar. 3, 1940; s. Roy S. Jr. and Anna Mary (Murray) R.; m. Susan Camille Hudson, Aug. 22, 1964; children: Roy Steele IV, Katherine Hudson. BA, Denison U., 1962; MD, Ohio State U., 1966; MS, U. Minn., 1974. Cert. dermatologist, dermatopathologist and immunodermatologist. Intern Strong meml. Hosp., Rochester, N.Y., 1966-67; resident Duke U. Med. Ctr., Durham, N.C., 1969-71; resident Mayo Clinic, Rochester, Minn., 1972-73, cons., 1973—, prof. dermatology, 1983—, dean Sch. Health Related Scis., 1991—; adv. coun. Rochester Community Coll., 1991—. Contbr. over 170 sci. articles to publs. Capt. USAF, 1967-69. Recipient Alumni Achievement award Ohio State U. Coll. of Medicine, 1991, Alumni citation Denison U., 1993, Faculty Svc. award Mayo Med. Sch., 1993. Mem. Am. Acad. Dermatology (bd. dirs. 1988-91), Am. Soc. Dermatologic Allergy and Immunology (sec.-treas. 1988—), Am. Dermatologic Assn., Soc. Investigative Dermatology, Assn. Schs. Allied Health Professions, Dermatology Found. Home: 1101 7th Ave SW Rochester MN 55902-6333 Office: Mayo Clinic 200 1st St SW Rochester MN 55905-0001

ROGERS, SHERRY A., physician; b. Syracuse, N.Y., Apr. 15, 1943; d. Rodney Wellington and Hayne (Marshall) Hammond; m. Robert Hamilton Rogers, June 30, 1970. BA, Syracuse U., 1965; MD, SUNY, 1969. Pediatrician pvt. practice, Auburn, N.Y., 1970-71; emergency physician Cmty. Gen. Hosp., Syracuse, N.Y., 1971-72; family physician pvt. practice, Syracuse, N.Y., 1972-85, physician environ. medicine, 1978—. Contbr. articles to profl. jours. Office: Northeast Ctr Environ Med 2800 W Genesee St Syracuse NY 13219

ROGIN, JOANNE B., neurologist; b. Mpls., Sept. 6, 1951; m. Ron Abrams; 2 children. BA summa cum laude, U. Minn., 1973, MD, 1977. Diplomate Am. Bd. Psychiatry and Neurology. Neurologist Mpls. Clinic of Neurology, 1982—; med. dir. Midwest Ctr. for Seizure Disorders; clin. assoc. prof. dept. neurology U. Minn.; chief of staff Met. Mt. Sinai Hosp., Mpls., 1981, bd. govs., 1990-91. Bd. dirs., chair profl. adv. bd. Epilepsy Found. Minn., Mpls., 1985—; trustee Abbott Northwestern Hosp., Mpls., 1991—. Mem. Minn. Soc. Neurol. Sci. (pres. 1995-96), Phi Beta Kappa, Alpha Omega Alpha. Office: Mpls Clinic 4225 Golden Valley Rd Minneapolis MN 55422

ROGLIERI, JOHN LOUIS, health facility administrator; b. Plainfield, N.J., June 24, 1939; s. Vito and Grace Mary (DeCristofaro) R.; m. Geraldine Ann Piller, June 15, 1963; children: Maria Roglieri Friedman, Anna, John. BSChemE, Lehigh U., 1960, AB in Applied Scis., 1960; MD, Harvard U., 1966; MS in Bus., Columbia U., 1978. Diplomate Nat. Bd. Med. Examiners. Intern Bellevue Hosp., Columbia Svc., 1966-67; resident Presbyn. Hosp., N.Y.C., 1969-71, dir. divsn. ambulatory medicine, 1973-75, v.p. ambulatory svcs., 1975-82, dir. employee health svc., 1988-92; fellow Harvard Med. Sch., Boston, 1971-73; asst. dir. Lab. Computer Sci. Mass. Gen. Hosp., 1972-73, dir. Ambulatory Screening Clinic, 1972-73; med. dir. N.Y. Health Plan, Inc., N.Y.C., 1988-92; corp. med. dir. Sanus Corp. Health Sys., Ft. Lee, N.J., 1992-95, NYL Care Health Plans Inc., N.Y.C., 1996—; cons. Nat. Ctr. Health Svc. Rsch. and Devel., 1973-75; dir. clin. scholar program Columbia U., 1975-77, asst. prof. clin. medicine Coll. Physicians and Surgeons, 1973—; health edn. cons. Basic Internat. Investments, 1975-76; v.p., bd. dirs. AMARCO Internat., N.Y.C., 1975-85; mem. adv. bd. Western and Upper Manhattan Regional Perinatal Network, Coll. Physicians and Surgeons, N.Y.C., 1975-80; appeared in various TV and radio programs. Author: Odds on Your Life, 1980; mem. editorial bd. Managed Care, 1992—, Jour. Applied Rsch. in Health Adminstrn., 1979-81; book rev. cons. Acad. Press, Inc., N.Y.C.; contbr. articles to profl. publs.;. Capt. USPHS, 1967-69. Mem. APHA, Am. Fedn. Clin. Rsch., Am. Soc. Internal Medicine, N.Y. State Soc. Internal Medicine, Soc. for Rsch. and Edn. in Primary Care Internal Medicine, Nat. Assn. Managed Care Physicians. Roman Catholic. Office: NYL Care Health Plan 1 Liberty Plz New York NY 10006

ROGOFF, JEROME HOWARD, psychiatrist, psychoanalyst, forensic expert; b. Detroit, Dec. 21, 1938; s. Abraham Solomon and Sarah Riva (Epstein) R.; (div. 1983); m. Erika Kathleen Keller, Sept. 25, 1983. BA, Harvard Coll., 1960; MD, Case Western Reserve U., 1965. Diplomate Am. Bd. Psychiatry and Neurology. Physician Peace Corps USPHS, Kathmandu, Nepal, 1966-68; clin. fellow psychiatry Harvard Med. Sch., Boston, 1975-79; staff psychiatrist Westwood (Mass.) Lodge Hosp., 1972-74; assoc. clin. prof. psych. Tufts Med. Sch., Boston, 1977-86; assoc. chief, psychiatry and dir., inpatient Psychiatry, day hosp. Faulkner Hosp., Boston, 1975-94; cons. psychiatrist Mass. Parole Bd. Probate Ct. Plymouth County, Mass., LEAA, Washington, 1971-78; med. psychiat. dir. ct. diversion program Boston TASC-A, 1974-75; treas., bd. dirs. Guild for Continuing Edn., Boston, 1981-95; founding dir. Law and Psychiatry Resource Ctr., Boston, 1983—; adj. prof. Simmons Sch. Social Work, Boston, 1981-85; lectr. on psychiatry Harvard Med. Sch., Boston, 1980-81, 84-94. Chmn. psychiatry team Combined Jewish Philanthropies, Boston, 1978-83, assoc. chmn. med. team, 1984-87, mem. social planning and allocations com., 1991—; bd. dirs. Jewish Vocat. Svc., Boston, 1987-91. Fellow Am. Psychiat. Assn. (pub. affairs rep. 1988-92, 93-94); mem. Mass. Psychiat. Soc. (councillor 1988-94, chair pub. affairs com. 1988-92, 93-94, chair nominating com. 1990, budget com. 1996—), Am. Psychoanalytic Assn., Boston Psychoanalytic Soc., Am. Acad. Psychiatry and Law. Democrat. Home and Office: 659 Chestnut St Newton MA 02168-2035

ROGOW, LOUIS MICHAEL, oncologist, educator; b. Jersey City, June 20, 1944; s. Irving and Helen (Grollman) R.; m. Enid Zazeela, Jan. 24, 1982; children from previous marriage: Ilisa, Jay. BS, Trinity Coll., 1965; MD, Hahnemann U., 1969. Diplomate Nat. Bd. of Med. Examiners; cert. radiology, radiation oncology. Instr. radiology Radiation Oncology N.Y. Med. Coll., N.Y.C., 1973-75, asst. prof., 1975-77; CEO Ideal Window Mfg., Bayonne, N.J., 1980—; dir. radiation oncology, hyperthermia John F. Kennedy Med. Ctr., Edison, N.J., 1977-95; ret., 1995; clin. asst. prof. radiology, U. Medicine and Dentistry, Rutgers Med. Sch., New Brunswick, N.J., 1983—; instr. Sch. of Nuclear Medicine Technology, John F. Kennedy Med.

Ctr., Edison, N.J., 1984—. Contbr. articles to profl. jours. Bd. trustees Am. Cancer Soc. (N.J. divsn.); bd. dirs. Resource Ctr. for Women and Their Families, Somerset County, N.J., 1993—. Clin. fellow Am. Cancer Soc., 1971, 73, faculty fellow Am. Cancer Soc., 1975, 76. Fellow Am. Coll. Radiology; mem. Am. Soc. Therapeutic Radiology and Oncology, Am. Endocurie Therapy Soc., Am. Radium Soc., N.Y. Cancer Soc., Oncology Soc. N.J., Radiology Soc. N.J. (exec. com. 1994—), Somerset Hills Handicapped Riders Club. Office: Ideal Window Mfg Box 48 100 W 7th St Bayonne NJ 07002

ROHACK, JOHN JAMES, cardiologist; b. Rochester, N.Y., Aug. 22, 1954; s. John Joseph and Margaret Elizabeth (McLaughlin) R.; m. Charlotte McCown, Dec. 7, 1980; 1 child, Elisha Monique Feigle. BS, U. Tex., El Paso, 1976; MD, U. Tex., Galveston, 1980. Diplomate Am. Bd. Internal Medicine. Intern internal medicine U. Tex. Med. Br. Hosps., Galveston, 1980-81, resident internal medicine, 1981-83, chief resident internal medicine, 1983-84, fellow cardiology, 1984-86; instr. medicine U. Tex. Med. Br., Galveston, 1983-86; asst. prof. medicine Tex. A&M Coll. Medicine, College Station, 1986-95, assoc. prof., 1995—, sect. chief cardiology, 1995—; sect. chief, 1989—; assoc. med. dir. Scott and White Health Plan, 1995—; bd. dirs. Health for All Clinic, v.p., 1994-96; mem. Accreditation Coun. on Continuing Med. Edn., 1995—; med. dir. Fitlife Ctr. Tex. A&M U., College Station, 1990—. Bd. dirs. Am. Heart Assn., Brazos Valley College Station, 1987—, Tex. affiliate Austin, 1991—, 1st v.p., 1994-95, pres.-elect, 1995-96, pres., 1996-97. Fellow ACP, Am. Coll. Cardiology (bd. dirs. Tex. chpt. 1992—); mem. AMA (alt del. ho. of dels. 1984-93, del. 1993—, coun. on med. edn. 1995-98), Tex. Med. Assn. (exec. coun. med. student sect. 1981-82, ho. of dels. 1982—, trustee 1994—), U. Tex. Med. Br. Alumni Assn. (trustee 1989—, pres. 1996-97), Brazos Robertson County Med. Soc. (exec. com. 1989—, pres. 1995-96). Office: Scott and White Clinic 1600 University Dr E College Station TX 77840-2642

ROHATGI, RAJEEV, cardiologist; b. New Delhi, India, Dec. 5, 1953; married. MB, BS, Inst. Med. Scis., New Delhi, 1975. Diplomate Am. Bd. Internal Medicine. Intern All-India Inst. Med. Scis., 1976; resident in internal medicine Easton (Pa.) Hosp., 1977-80; fellow in cardiology U. Chgo. Med. Sch., 1980-82; cardiologist Easton Cardiovascular Assocs., Inc., 1982—. V.p. Am. Heart Assn., 1990-91. Mem. AMA, Am. Coll. Cardiology, Soc. Nuclear Medicine, Pa. Med. Soc., Am. Soc. Echocardiography. Home: 20 Tamarack Path Easton PA 18045-5572 Office: Easton Cardiovasular Assocs 2003 Fairview Ave Easton PA 18042-3915

ROHLF, F. JAMES, biometrician, educator; b. Blythe, Calif., Oct. 24, 1936. BS, San Diego State Coll., 1958; PhD in Entomology, U. Kans., 1962. Asst. prof. biology U. Calif., Santa Barbara, 1962-65; assoc. prof. statis. biology U. Kans., 1965-69; assoc. prof. biology SUNY, Stony Brook, 1969-72, prof., 1972—, chmn. dept. ecology and evolution, 1975-80, 90-91; statis. cons. N.Y. Pub. Svc. Commn., 1975-78, IBM, 1977-81, U.S. EPA, 1978-80; vis. scientist IBM, Yorktown Heights, N.Y., 1976-77, 80-81. Mem. Biometric Soc., Assn. Computing Machinery, Soc. Systematic Biology, Classification Soc. Office: SUNY at Stony Brook Dept Ecology and Evolution Stony Brook NY 11794-5245

ROHN, REUBEN DAVID, pediatric educator and administrator; b. Israel, Apr. 12, 1945; came to U.S., 1954; s. Aryeh and Rachel (Brenner) R.; m. Judith Semel, Sept. 6, 1971; 1 child, Karen. BA cum laude, Bklyn. Coll., 1967; MD, N.Y. Med. Coll., 1971. Diplomate Am. Bd. Pediat., Am. Bd. Pediatric Endocrinology, Am. Bd. Pediatrics-Adolescent Medicine. Intern in pediatrics Montefiore Hosp., Bronx, N.Y., 1971-72, resident in pediatrics, 1972-74; fellow in adolescent medicine U. Md. Hosp., Balt., 1974-76; preceptor in pediatrics Johns Hopkins U. Sch. Health Svcs., Balt., 1975-76; asst. prof. dept. pediatrics Ea. Va. Med. Sch., Norfolk, 1976-82; coord. pediatric clerkship Ea. Va. Med. Sch., Children's Hosp. of King's Daughters, Norfolk, 1977-90; prof. dept. pediatrics Ea. Va. Med. Sch., Norfolk, 1989—; adj. prof. chemistry Old Dominion U., Norfolk, 1984—; dir. adolescent medicine/endocrinology Children's Hosp. of King's Daughters, Norfolk, 1976—; mem. curriculum com. Ea. Va. Med. Sch., 1977-79, clerkship coords. com. 1977-90, genetics com., 1978-80, evaluation com. 1979-91, chmn. selectives com., 1981-82, ad hoc com. on consultation, 1982-83, student progress com., 1983-85, student health com., 1985-87, LCME com. on curriculum, 1990-92; mem. child abuse com. Children's Hosp. of King 's Daus., 1976-80, chmn. adolescent adv. com., 1976-80, patient care com. 1980-94, nutrition com. 1980-94, utilization rev. com., 1980-82, med. records com., 1987-89, gen. med./surg. task force com., 1987-88; bd. dirs. Pediat. Fac. Assocs., 1994—; speaker in field. Reviewer Jour. Adolescent Health Care, 1986—, mem. editorial bd., 1989-92; contbr. articles to profl. jours. Mem. Norfolk Sch. Health Coun., 1977—, mem. ad hoc com. infant screening program for hypothroidism Commonwealth of Va., 1977-79, cons., 1979—; mem. cmty. adv. bd. Norfolk Adolescent Pregnancy Prevention Svc. Project, 1981-83; bd. dirs. Elizabeth River chpt. Am. Diabetes Assn., 1982-85, South Hampton Roads chpt. 1985-93; mem. adv. com. Norfolk-Virginia Beach Jr. League, 1987-88; judge ann. Health Edn. Fair, Norfolk Pub. schs., 1980-94. Recipient grant Bressler Rsch. Fund, 1975-76, Biomed. Rsch. Devel. grant Ea. Va. Med. Sch., 1978, 78-79, 79-80. 81-82, 83-84, Children's Health Found. grant, 1988-89. Fellow Am. Acad. Pediatrics (youth and adolescence com. Va. chpt. 1978—); mem. Soc. Adolescent Medicine (abstract reviewer 1984-91), Lawson Wilkins Pediatric Endocrine Soc., Sigma Xi. Home: 4653 Larkwood Dr Virginia Beach VA 23464-5815 Office: Childrens Hosp Kings Daus 601 Childrens Ln Norfolk VA 23507-1910

ROHNER, THOMAS JOHN, JR., urologist; b. Trenton, N.J., Jan. 1, 1936; s. Thomas J. and Julia (Kanyo) R.; m. Jessie Rohner; children: Christopher, James. BA, Yale U., 1957; MD, U. Pa., 1961. Diplomate Am. Bd. Urology. Intern Hosp. U. Pa., Phila., 1961-62, resident in gen. surgery, 1962-64, resident in urology, 1964-67; asst. prof. surgery M.S. Hersey Med. Ctr., Pa. State U., Hershey, 1970-71, assoc. prof., 1971-75, prof., 1975—, chief urol. divsn., assoc. dean for clin. affairs, 1970-96; urologic cons. VA Hosp., Lebanon, Pa., 1970—; assoc. dean for clin. affairs M.S. Hersey Med. Ctr., Pa. State U., Hershey, 1996—; corp. mem. Pa. Blue Shield, 1991—, bd. dirs., 1993—. Contbr. articles to profl. jours. Served to maj. M.C., U.S. Army, 1967-69. USPHS fellow, 1969-70; grantee HEW, 1971-76, USPHS, 1971-76. Fellow ACS (pres. cen. Pa. chpt. 1983-84, bd. govs. 1991—); mem. AMA, Am. Urol. Assn. (pres. mid-Atlantic sect. 1986-87), Urol. Assn. Pa., Phila. Urol. Soc. (pres. 1980-81), Assn. Acad. Surgeons, Am. Bd. Urology (trustee 1995—), Pa. Med. Soc., Dauphin County Med. Soc., Soc. Pediat. Urology, Soc. Univ. Urologists (pres. 1990-91), Nat. Urol. Forum, Societe Internationale d'Urologie, Transamerican Urol. Rschrs., Internat. Continence Soc., Coll. Physicians of Phila. Home: 2907 Mt Gretna Rd Elizabethtown PA 17022-9689 Office: Milton S Hershey Med Ctr Pa State Univ PO Box 850 Hershey PA 17033-0850

ROHRBAUGH, JAMES RICHARD, child neurologist; b. Tiffin, Ohio, May 21, 1949; m. Jane Ellen Rohrbaugh. BA, Yale U., 1971; MD, Ohio State U. Diplomate Am. Bd. Pediatrics with subspecialty in child neurology. Pvt. practice Child Neurology Assocs., Chesterfield, Mo. Office: Child Neurology Assocs 226 S Woods Mill Rd Chesterfield MO 63017

ROHRBAUGH, ROBERT MARK, psychiatrist; b. New York, Pa., Apr. 3, 1956; s. Robert Leroy and Isabelle Elaine (Neff) R.; m. Ellen Joan Quinn, Sept. 10, 1983. BA in Biology, Franklin & Marshall Coll., 1978; MD, Yale U., 1982. Diplomate Am. Bd. Psychiatry and Neurology, Am. Bd. Geriatric Psychiatry. Intern Yale U. St. Raphael Hosp., New Haven, 1982-83; residency in psychiatry Yale U., New Yaven, 1983-86; fellow in clin. research NIMH, New Haven, 1987; fellow in geriatric psycyiatry Yale U., New Haven, 1988, asst. clin. prof. psychiatry, 1988—, dir. edn. and tng., 1995—; med. dir. Community Support Program, West Haven, Conn., 1987—; dir. consultation-liaison svc. West Haven VA Med. Ctr., 1992—. Contbr. articles to profl. jours. Bd. dirs. So. Conn. chpt. Alzheimers Disease and Related Disorders, New Haven, 1987-90. Named Fund Fellow Nat. Psychiat. Endowment, 1986; Yale Internat. Health Rsch. fellow, 1979; recipient Tchrs. award Yale Psychiat. Residents Assn., 1993, 94. Mem. Am. Psychiat. Assn., Am. Assn. for Geriatric Psychiatry. Home: 58 Vineyard Ave Guilford CT 06437-3235 Office: West Haven VA Med Ctr 950 Campbell Ave West Haven CT 06510

ROHREN, BRENDA MARIE ANDERSON, therapist, educator; b. Kansas City, Mo., Apr. 18, 1959; d. Wilbur Dean and Katheryn Elizabeth (Albright) Anderson; m. Lathan Edward Rohren, May 10, 1985; 1 child, Amanda Jessica. BS in Psychology, Colo. State U., 1983; MA in Psychology, Cath. U. Am., 1986. Lic. mental health practitioner. Mental health therapist, sr. case mgr. Rappahannock Area Community Svcs. Bd., Fredericksburg, Va., 1986-88; mental health therapist, case mgmt. supr. Rappahannock Area Community Svcs. Bd., 1988; rsch. assoc. Inst. Medicine, NAS, Washington, 1988-89; supr. adult psychiat. program Lincoln (Nebr.) Gen. Hosp., 1989, program supr. mental health svcs., 1989-91; adj. instr. S.E. Community Coll., Lincoln, 1990—; assessment & referral specialist Rivendell Psychiat. Ctr., Seward, Nebr., 1993-95; therapist Lincoln Day Treatment Ctr., Lincoln, Nebr., 1993-95; adj. inst. Coll. of St. Mary, 1994—; therapist Rape/Spouse Abuse Crisis Ctr., Lincoln, 1996—; computer cons. Syscon Corp., Washington, 1983-84. Author: (report) Bottom Line Benefits: Building Economic Success Through Stronger Families; editor: (newsletter) Alliance for Mentally Ill, Lincoln. Active Lincoln Alliance for the Mentally Ill, Nebr. Domestic Violence/Sexual Assault Coalition. Mem. NOW, APA (assoc.), Nat. Alliance for Mentally Ill, Nebr. Psychol. Assn. (assoc.). Democrat. Roman Catholic. Home: 3821 S 33rd St Lincoln NE 68506-3806 Office: SE Community Coll 8800 O St Lincoln NE 68520-1227 also: Coll of St Mary 4600 Valley Rd Rm 403 Lincoln NE 68510

ROHRER, RICHARD JEFFREY, surgeon, educator; b. Columbus, Mar. 14, 1950; s. James William and Nancy Lenore (Acheson) R.; m. Jill Ellen Stein, Nov. 29, 1981; children: Benjamin, Noah. BS, Yale U., 1973; MD, Columbia U., 1977. Surgeon New England Deaconess and Harvard Med. Sch., Boston, 1984-87; surgeon, chief transplantation New Eng. Med. Ctr., Boston, 1988—; assoc. prof. surgery Tufts Sch. Medicine, Boston, 1988—. Trustee New Eng. Organ Bank, Boston, 1988—; councillor United Network for Organ Sharing, 1996—. Fellow ACS; mem. Am. Soc. Transplant Surgeons, Transplantation Soc., Physicians for Social Responsibility, Assn. for Acad. Surgery, Assn. for Surg. Edn., Soc. Critical Care Medicine. Office: New England Med Ctr Box 40 750 Washington St Boston MA 02111-1526

ROHRS, F(REDERICK) BRUCE, clinical psychologist; b. Lansing, Mich., Dec. 24, 1960; s. Frederick W. and Jan Caroline (Van Duzer) R.; m. Melissa Lynn Phelps, Dec. 8, 1984; children: Benjamin D., Matthew L. BA, U. Rochester, 1983; MS, Ohio U., 1986, PhD, 1989. Intern in psychology Broughton Hosp., Morgantown, N.C., 1987-88, psychologist, 1988-89; staff psychologist Staunton Clinic, Sewickley, Pa., 1989—, dir. tng., 1995—, intern supr., 1989—; intern supr. Broughton Hosp., Morgantown, N.C., 1988-89. Mem. Greater Pitts. Psychol. Assn., Habitat for Humanity, Phi Beta Kappa. Office: Sewickley Valley Hosp Staunton Clinic Sewickley PA 15143

ROISEN, FRED JERROLD, neurobiologist, educator, researcher, anatomy educator; b. N.Y.C., Sept. 12, 1941; s. Israel Jacob and Louise M. (Friedman) R.; m. Maxine G. Gerson, Mar. 28, 1965; children: Kim Felice, Alexandra Suzanne. PhD, Princeton U., 1966, 69. Asst. prof. Rutgers U., New Brunswick, N.J., 1969-72; asst. prof. Med. Sch. Rutgers U., Piscataway, N.J., 1972-75, assoc. prof. Med. Sch., 1975-80; prof. Med. Sch. U. Medicine & Dentistry of N.J., Piscataway, 1980-83, acting dept. chair, prof. Med. Sch., 1983-86; chmn., prof. Sch. of Medicine U. Louisville, 1986—; chair ad hoc com. shared instrumentation NIH, Bethesda, Md., 1987-90. Author: Histology Review, 1980; contbr. over 100 articles to profl. jours. Pres., chair AAUP, Piscataway, 1977-80. Recipient numerous grants. Jewish Home: 5800 River Knolls Dr Louisville KY 40222-5863 Office: U Louisville Sch Medicine Dept Anat Sci Neurobio Louisville KY 40292*

ROIZEN, NANCY J., physician, educator; b. Hartford, Conn.; m. Michael F. Roizen; children: Jeffrey, Jennifer. BS, Tufts U., 1968, MD, 1972. Diplomate Am. Bd. Pediats. Staff physician Oakland (Calif.) Children's Hosp., 1976-84; asst. prof. clin. pediats. Johns Hopkins Hosp., Balt., 1984-85; from asst. prof. to assoc. prof. pediats. and psychiatry U. Chgo., 1985—. Fellow Am. Acad. Pediats.; mem. Soc. for Devel. Pediats. (pres. 1996—). Office: U Chgo Hosps MC 1051 5841 S Maryland Ave Chicago IL 60637-1463

ROIZMAN, BERNARD, virologist, educator; b. Chisinau, Rumania, Apr. 17, 1929; came to U.S., 1947, naturalized, 1954; s. Abram and Liudmilla (Seinberg) R.; m. Betty Cohen, Aug. 26, 1950; children: Arthur, Niels. B.A., Temple U., 1952, M.S., 1954; Sc.D. in Microbiology, Johns Hopkins, 1956; D.H.L. (hon.), Gov.'s State U., 1984; MD (hon.), U. Ferrara (Italy), 1991. From instr. microbiology to asst. prof. Johns Hopkins Med. Sch., 1956-65; mem. faculty div. biol. scis. U. Chgo., 1965—, prof. microbiology, 1969-84, prof. biophysics, 1970—, chmn. com. virology, 1969-85, 88—, Joseph Regenstein prof., 1981-83, Joseph Regenstein Disting. Svc. prof., 1984—, chmn. dept. molecular genetics and cell biology, 1985-88; convener herpes virus workshop, Cold Spring Harbor, N.Y., 1972; lectr. Am. Found. for Microbiology, 1974-75; mem. spl. virus cancer program, devel. rsch. working group Nat. Cancer Inst., 1967-71, cons. inst., 1967-73; mem. steering com. human cell biology program NSF, 1971-74, cons. found., 1972-74; mem. adv. com. cell biology and virology Am. Cancer Soc., 1970-74; chmn. herpes virus study group Internat. Commn. Taxonomy of Viruses, 1971-93; mem. Internat. Microbiol. Genetics Commn. Internat. Assn. Microbiol. Scis., 1974-81; mem. sci. adv. coun. N.Y. Cancer Inst., 1971-88; med. adv. bd. Leukemia Rsch. Found., 1972-77; mem. herpes-virus working team WHO/FOA, 1978-81; mem. bd. sci. cons. Sloan Kettering Inst., N.Y.C., 1975-81; mem. study sect. exptl. virology NIH, 1976-80; mem. task force on virology Nat. Inst. Allergy and Infectious Disease, 1976-77; mem. external adv. com. Emory U. Cancer Ctr., 1973-81, Northwestern U. Cancer Ctr., 1979-89; cons. Inst. Merieux, Lyon, France, 1979-91; mem. com. to establish vaccine priorities Nat. Inst. Medicine, 1983-85; chmn. sci. adv bd. Teiky-Showa Univs. Ctr., Tampa Bay Rsch. Inst., 1983—, chmn. bd. trustees, 1991—. Author sci. papers, chpts. in books; editor: Herpes Viruses, Vol. 1, 1982, Vol. 2, 1983, Vols. 3 and 4, 1985, The Human Herpesviruses, 1993, Infectious Diseases in an Age of Change, 1995; adv. editor Progress in Surface Membrane Science, 1972; editor-in-chief Jour. Infectious Agts. and Disease, 1992—; mem. editl. bd. Jour. Hygiene, 1985-61, Infectious Diseases, 1965-69. Jour. Virology, 1970—, Jour. Intervirology, 1972-85, Archives of Virology, 1975-81, Virology, 1976-78, 83—, Microbiologica, 1978—, Cell, 1979-80, Gene Therapy, 1994. Trustee Goodwin Inst. for Cancer Rsch., 1977—. Recipient Lederle Med. Faculty award, 1960-61, Career Devel. award USPHS, 1963-65, Pasteur award Ill. Soc. Microbiology, 1972, Esther Langer award for achievement in cancer research, 1974, Outstanding Alumnus in Pub. Health award Johns Hopkins U., 1984; named hon. prof. Shandong Acad. Med. Scis., People's Republic of China, 1985; Am. Cancer Soc. scholar cancer research at Pasteur Inst. Paris, 1961-62; ICN Internat. prize in virology, 1988; faculty research assoc., 1966-71; traveling fellow Internat. Agy. Research Against Cancer, Karolinska Inst., Stockholm, Sweden, 1970; grantee USPHS/NIH, 1958—, Am. Cancer Soc., 1962-90, NSF, 1962-79, Whitehall Found., 1966-74. Fellow Japanese Soc. for Promotion of Sci., Pan Am. Cancer Soc. (hon.); mem. Nat. Acad. Scis., Hungarian Acad. of Scis. (hon.), Am. Acad. Arts and Scis., Am. Acad. Microbiology, Am. Assn. Immunologists, Am. Soc. Microbiology, Am. Soc. Virology, Am. Soc. Biol. Chemists, Brit. Soc. Gen. Microbiology, Johns Hopkins U. Soc. Scholars, Quadrangle Club (Chgo.). Home: 5555 S Everett Ave Chicago IL 60637-1968 Office: U Chgo MB Kouler Viral Oncology Labs 910 E 58th St Chicago IL 60637-1432

ROJCEWICZ, STEPHEN JOSEPH, JR., psychiatrist; b. Worcester, Mass., July 23, 1943; s. Stephen J. and Victoria T. (Lemanski) R.; m. Mary Alice Miller, Aug. 3, 1968; children: Mary Alice, Joanne, Kristin, Gregory. BS, Holy Cross Coll., 1965; MD, Georgetown U., 1969. Diplomate in psychiatry and forensic psychiatry Am. Bd. Psychiatry and Neurology. Psychiatrist USPHS, Washington, 1969-91, pvt. practice, Silver Spring, Md., 1973—; mem. exec. com. St. Elizabeth's Hosp., Washington, 1988-91; clin. assoc. prof. Georgetown U., Washington, 1973—. Contbr. various articles in profl. jours. Recipient Outstanding Svc. Medal USPHS, 1988. Fellow Am. Psychiat. Assn.; mem. Washington Psychiat. Soc. (exec. coun.), Nat. Assn. for Poetry Therapy (pres.-elect). Democrat. Roman Catholic. Home and Office: 13808 Old Columbia Pike Silver Spring MD 20904-4554

ROJEK, KENNETH J., health facility administrator, hospital; m. Carol Rojek; 2 children. BS, U. Ill.; MBA with honors, Roosevelt U. Diplomate, cert. healthcare exec. Am. Coll. Healthcare Execs. Lab. mgr., tech. dir. Rush-Presbyn.-St. Lukes Med. Ctr., Chgo.; adminstr. Wyler Children's Hosp., dept. pediatrics U. Chgo.; v.p., exec. dir. Luth. Gen. Med. Group, S.C., Chgo.; CEO Luth. Gen. Hosp., Park Ridge, Ill.; adj. faculty U. Minn., St. Francis Coll., Joliet, Ill. Active numerous cmty. and civic orgns., cmty. devel. couns. Fellow Am. Coll. Med. Practice Execs. Med. Group Mgmt. Assn. Office: Luth Gen Hosp 1775 Dempster St Park Ridge IL 60068-1174*

ROKES, FREDERICK RALPH, JR., bioprocess engineer; b. Framingham, Mass., Nov. 12, 1968; s. Frederick Ralph and Emily Mary (Jorge) R. BSChemE, Rutgers U., Piscataway, N.J., 1992; BA in Biology, Rutgers U., New Brunswick, N.J., 1992. Registered engr.-in-tng., Del. Rsch. bioengr. Affinity Biotech Inc., Aston, Pa., 1992-94; bioprocess engr. Life Scis. Internat., Phila., 1994—. Mem. AIChE. Home: 909 F Cloister Rd Wilmington DE 19809 Office: Life Scis Internat 1818 Market St 9th Fl Philadelphia PA 19103

ROKOSZ, GREGORY JOSEPH, emergency medicine physician, educator; b. Passaic, N.J., Mar. 27, 1955; s. Ferdinand and Stella D. (Wirkowski) R.; m. Christine M. Muller, Oct. 1, 1983; 1 child, Stefanie Lee. BA in Biol. Scis. with honors, Rutgers U., 1977; DO, U. Osteo. Medicine/Health Sci., Des Moines, 1980; postgrad., Seton Hall U., 1995—. Diplomate Am. Bd. Emergency Medicine, Am. Bd. Osteo. Emergency Medicine, Am. Osteo. Bd. Family Physicians. Intern Met. Hosp., Phila., 1980-81; resident in family practice Union (N.J.) Hosp., 1981-82, emergency dept. physician, 1982-94, dir. med. edn., 1993—, v.p. med. affairs, 1994—; med. dir. N.J. Paramedic Registry Exam., 1990-94; mobile ICU insp. N.J. Dept. Health, Office EMS, Newark, 1990-94; mem. N.J. State Bd. Med. Examiners, Trenton, 1994—; clin. instr. dept. emergency medicine U. Medicine and Dentistry Sch. Osteo. Medicine, Stratford, 1992-93, asst. clin. prof., 1993—; asst. prof. emergency medicine N.Y. Coll. Osteo. Medicine/N.Y. Inst. Tech., Old Westbury, 1994—; assoc. mem. PRO of N.J., 1991—; expert witness in emergency medicine. Contbg. author: Continuous Quality Improvement for Emergency Departments, 1994, Emergent Use of Echocardiography in a Post-Myocardial Infarction Patient with Acute Dyspoea, 1996. Fellow Am. Coll. Emergency Physicians, Am. Coll. Osteo. Emergency Physicians; mem. Am. Osteo. Assn., Am. Coll. Osteo. Family Physicians, Assn. Osteo. Dirs. and Med. Educators, Am. Coll. Physician Execs., Assn. for Hosp. Med. Edn. Republican. Roman Catholic. Home: 12 Ivy Ln Parsippany NJ 07054 Office: Union Hosp 1000 Galloping Hill Rd Union NJ 07083

ROLAND, BETH NAOMI, obstetrician, gynecologist; b. N.Y.C., Feb. 17, 1964; d. Norman Martin and Marilyn Pearl Roland; m. Benjamin Coopersmith; 1 child, Amanda. BA, Brandeis U., 1985; MD, N.Y. Med. Coll., 1989. Resident ob-gyn. Mount Sinai Med. Ctr., N.Y.C., 1989-93; physician ob-gyn. Ob/Gyn Assocs., Denver, 1993—; spkr. in field. Spkr. Teen Pregnancy Prevention, Denver, 1994-95. Fellow Am. Coll. Ob-Gyn. (jr.); mem. Soc. Laparoendoscopic Surgeons, Am. Assn. Gynecol. Laparoscopists, Denver Med. Soc. Office: Ob/Gyn Assocs Rose Med Plaza 4500 E 9th Ave 6705 Denver CO 80220 also: 1550 S Potomac St Aurora CO 80012

ROLAND, JAY ALAN, psychologist; b. Bklyn., June 20, 1930; s. Jay R. and Lillian June (Suttonberg) Edelman; m. Joan Barbara Gardner, Sept. 30, 1962; children: Taraki L., Ariel Jon. BA, Antioch Coll., Yellow Springs, Ohio, 1955; PhD, Adelphi U., 1960. Cert. psychologist, N.Y. Psychology intern St. Vincent's Hosp., N.Y.C., 1957-58, N.Y. Regional Office VA, 1959-60; psychologist Jewish Bd. Guardians, N.Y.C., 1960-62, Lincoln Ctr. for Mental Health, N.Y.C., 1960-63; pvt. practice N.Y.C., 1960—; rsch. assoc. So. Asian Inst., Columbia U., N.Y.C., 1979-86; mem. faculty New Sch., N.Y.C., 1969-71, 73-74. Author: In Search of Self in India and Japan: Toward a Cross Cultural Psychology, 1988, Cultural Pluralism and Psychoanalysis: The Asian and American Experience, 1996; editor, contbr. Psychoanalysis, Creativity and Literature: A French-American Inquiry, 1978, Career and Motherhood: Struggles for a New Identity, 1978; contbr. articles to profl. jours.; nat. exhibited printmaker and artist. Pvt. USMC, 1949-50. Rsch. grantee Am. Coun. Learned Socs., 1981-82; Am. Inst. Indian Studies fellow, 1977-78, 80, 91. Mem. APA, Coun. Psychoanalytic Psychotherapists, Nat. Psychol. Assn. for Psychoanalysis (faculty bd. dirs. 1967-95),. Democrat. Jewish. Home: 274 W 11th St New York NY 10014-2494 Office: 26 W 9th St Apt 4D New York NY 10011-8919

ROLAND, MAXWELL, obstetrician, gynecologist; b. Ciechonow, Poland, Dec. 21, 1908; came to the U.S., 1928; s. Morris and Elka (Baron) R.; m. Helen L. Kaltman, Feb. 6, 1944; children: Eron Ronni, Bruce Laurence. BA, NYU, 1936; MD, U. Lausanne, 1941. Resident Morrisania City Hosp., N.Y.C., 1941-42; pvt. practice, 1944—; pres., chmn. bd. U.S. Internat. Found. for Studies in Reproduction, 1969—; prof. emeritus French Polyclinic Med. Sch. and Health Ctr., 1965—; hon. attending gynecologist N.Y. Hosp. & Med. Ctr. Queens. Editor in chief: Internat. Jour. Fertility, 1969-95; contbr. articles to profl. jours. Fellow N.Y. Acad. Medicine, ACS, Internat. Coll. Surgeons, N.Y. Gynecology Soc.; mem. Am. Coll. Ob.-Gyn. (founder), Am. Assn. Gynecol. Laparoscopists (founder). Office: Med Sci Pub Internat Inc 405 Main St Port Washington NY 11050

ROLEN, STANLEY ROBERT, pharmacist; b. Beaver Dam, Wis., Nov. 24, 1934; s. H. Wallace and Irene M. (Andrews) R.; m. Jane L. Sheehan, Jan. 21, 1961; children: Andrew, Elizabeth, Carolyn. BS in Pharmacy with honors, Union U., 1956. Product devel. pharmacist Norwich (N.Y.) Pharmacal Co., 1959-60, mfg. pharmacist, 1960-63, sr. mfg. pharmacist, 1963-69; prodn. supt. Morton-Norwich, Greenville, S.C., 1969-70; asst. mgr. pharm. ops. Wyeth-Ayerst Internat., Inc. (formerly Wyeth Internat. Ltd.), Radnor, Pa., 1970-72, mfg. products mgr., 1972-77, asst. prodn. dir., 1977-80, dir. prodn., 1980-85, asst. v.p. prodn., 1985—. Served with U.S. Army, 1956-58. Named Dist. Alumnus, Albany Coll. Pharmacy, 1981. Mem. Am. Pharm. Assn., Pharm. Mfrs. Assn. Internat. Tech. (steering com. 1991, PMA vice chmn.). Republican. Lodges: Masons, Shriners. Home: 103 Noel Cir Exton PA 19341-1752 Office: Wyeth-Ayerst Internat Inc PO Box 8616 Philadelphia PA 19101-8616

ROLLENCE, MICHELE LYNETTE, molecular biologist; b. Takoma Park, Md., Nov. 23, 1955; d. John Francis and Martha Jo (Jackson) R.; m. David H. Specht, June 3, 1978 (div. Sept. 1982). AA, Montgomery Coll., 1976; BS, U. Md., 1978; MS, Johns Hopkins U., 1995. Lab. technician Dairy and Food Labs., San Francisco, 1979-81; rsch. asst. Genex Corp., Gaithersburg, Md., 1981-82, rsch. assoc., 1982-86, sr. rsch. assoc., 1986-88, rsch. scientist, 1989-93; rsch. assoc. Genetic Therapy, Inc., Gaithersburg, Md., 1993—. Contbr. articles to profl. publs.; patentee in field. Pres. Explorer Post div. Boy Scouts Am., Gaithersburg, 1973; youth advisor Neelsville Presbyn. Ch., Germantown, Md., 1990. Recipient Nat. Exploration award TRW/Explorers Club, 1973. Mem. AAAS, Am. Soc. Microbiology, DAR, Pleasant Plains of Damascus. Republican. Presbyterian. Office: Genetic Therapy Inc 19 Firstfield Rd Gaithersburg MD 20878-1703

ROLLER, DEAN HIRAM, cardiologist; b. N.Y.C., Nov. 29, 1949; s. Paul G. and Beatrice (Bleiweiss) R.; m. Barbara Alterman, June 19, 1971 (div. June 1994); children: Shawn Everett, Bradley Curtis, Kimberly Paige. BS, MIT, 1970; MD, U. Pa., 1974. Med. intern, resident Hosp. U. Pa., Phila., 1974-77; fellow in cardiology Yale U., New Haven, 1977-79; pvt. practice Cardiovascular Assocs. South Fla., Coral Gables, 1979—; dir. Cardiac Catherization Lab., Doctors Hosp. Coral Gables, 1987—, chmn. dept.cardiology, 1990—; dir. Echocardiography Lab., South Miami (Fla.) Hosp., 1987. Mem. U. Miami Citizens Bd., 1981. C.V. Mosby med. scholar, 1974; recipient Haversfield Scholastic Achievement award Miami Med. Forum, 1988. Fellow Am. Coll. Cardiology, Clin. Coun. Cardiology Am. Heart Assn.; mem. ACP, Phi Lambda Upsilon, Alpha Omega Alpha. Republican. Home: 6525 SW 131 St Miami FL 33156 Office: 4685 Ponce DeLeon Blvd Coral Gables FL 33146

ROLLER, NEAL WALLACE, periodontist; b. Alton, Ill., Apr. 22, 1943; s. Wallace William and Bernadette A. (Hellrung) R.; m. Marilyn L. Roe, July 24, 1971; children: Julia L., Karen M. DDS, St. Louis (Mo.) U., 1968; cert. in oral medicine, U. Pa., 1973; MS, U. Mo., Kansas City, 1975. Diplomate AM. Bd. Periodontology, Am. Bd. Oral Medicine. From asst. to assoc. prof. So. Ill. U., Alton, 1975-83, prof., 1983—; dept. chmn. So. Ill. U. Sch. Dental Medicine, Alton, 1989-93. Contbr. articles to profl. jours. Pres. Am. Cancer Soc., Alton, 1991-93. Capt. U.S. Army, 1969-71. Fellow Am. Coll. Dentistry; mem. ADA, Am. Acad. Periodontology, Phi Kappa Phi, Omicron Kappa Upsilon (pres. 1987-88). Office: So Ill Univ Sch Dental Medicine 2800 College Ave Alton IL 62002

ROLLIN, WALTER JEROME, psychology educational consultant; b. N.Y.C., Nov. 27, 1932; s. Harold and Rae (Marder) R.; m. Bonnie L. Baker, Oct. 9, 1976; children: Todd, Brad; stepchildren: Hannah, Sarah. BA, Queens Coll., 1954; MS, U. Pitts., 1958; PhD, Wayne State U., 1962. Cert. clin. competence speech lang. pathology; lic. marriage, family, and child therapist. Dir. speech and hearing clinic Chico (Calif.) State Coll., 1962-67; dir., prof. communicative disorders program in spl. edn. San Francisco (Calif.) State Univ., 1967-90, prof. emeritus in spl. edn., 1990—; dean, sch. of health and human svcs. Columbia Pacific Univ., San Rafael, Calif., 1982—; family therapist, cons. San Francisco (Calif.) VA Med. Ctr., 1975-90. Author: (book) The Psychology of Communication Disorders in Individuals and Their Families, 1987; contbr. chpts. to books and articles to jours. With U.S. Army, 1954-56. Mem. Am. Assn. Marriage and Family Therapy (clin. mem.).

ROLLINS, ARLEN JEFFERY, osteopathic physician; b. Cleve., June 30, 1946; s. Lee Roy and Celia (Madorsky) R.; m. Deborah Joyce Gross, Dec. 18, 1971 (div.); children: Aaron Jason, Howard Philip, Lee Craig. AB, Miami U., Oxford, Ohio, 1968; DO, Chgo. Coll. Osteo. Medicine, 1973; MS in Occupl. Medicine, Environ. Health, U. Cin., 1984. Diplomate Am. Bd. Preventive Medicine. Intern, Phoenix Gen. Hosp., 1973-74; resident in environ. health/occupl. medicine Cin. Gen. Hosp.-U. Cin., 1974-77; plant physician Ford Motor Co., Cin., 1974-77, Walton Hills stamping plant divsn., Cleve., 1987—; assoc. med. dir. East Side Occupl. Health Ctr., Cleve., 1977-79; med. dir. Ferro Corp., Cleve., 1979—, S.K. Wellman Corp., Cleve., 1979-87, Morgan Matroc, 1979—; pres. Occupl. Health Mgmt. Cons.; cons. occupl. health Ohio Bell Telephone Co., Cleve., 1981-87; cons. Occupl. Health Ctr., Univ. Hosps. of Cleve.; dir. occupl. health program Bedford Med. Ctr. Univ. Hosps. Cleve. Fellow Am. Acad. Occupl. Medicine, Am. Occupl. Med. Assn., Am. Coll. Preventive Medicine; mem. Ohio State Med. Assn., Cleve. Acad. Medicine (pub. health and immunization com., med.-legal com.), Western Res. Med. Dirs. Assn., Am. Osteo. Assn., Am. Osteo. Acad. Pub. Health and Preventive Medicine (past bd. dirs.).

ROLLS, BARBARA JEAN, nutrition educator, laboratory director; b. Washington, Jan. 5, 1945; d. Howard Julian and Patricia Jane (Pratt) Simons; m. Edmund Thomson Rolls, Sept. 6, 1969 (div. Jan. 1983); children: Melissa May, Juliet Helen. BA, U. Pa., 1966; PhD, Cambridge (Eng.) U., 1970; MA (hon.), Oxford (Eng.) U., 1970. Mary Somerville rsch. fellow Oxford U., 1969-72, IBM rsch. fellow, 1972-74, jr. rsch. fellow Wolfson Coll., 1974-75, E.P. Abraham rsch. fellow Green Coll., 1979-82, fellow in nutrition, 1983-84; assoc. prof. psychiatry Johns Hopkins U. Sch. Medicine, Balt., 1984-91, prof. psychiatry, 1991-92, dir. Lab. for Study Human Ingestive Behavior, 1984—; Jean Phillips Shibley prof. biobehavioral health Pa. State U., State College, 1992-94, Guthrie chair nutrition, 1994—; mem. Nat. Diabetes and Digestive and Kidney Diseases Adv. Coun., 1994—; cons. to numerous large corps., 1983—. Author: Thirst, 1982; mem. editl. adv. bd. Jour. Appetite, 1981—; mem. editl. bd. Am. Jour. Physiology, 1985—, Trends in Food Sci. and Tech., 1991-93, Am. Jour. Clin Nutrition, 1992—, Obestity Rsch., 1992—, Nutrition Rev., 1993—; contbr. numerous articles to profl. jours. Recipient Rolleston Meml. prize Oxford U., 1974, Lederle award in Human Nutrition, 1995; Thouron scholar Cambridge U., 1966-69; Med. Rsch. Coun. (U.K.) grantee, 1969-84, NIH grantee, 1987—. Mem. Am. Physiol. Soc., Soc. for Study Ingestive Behavior (bd. dirs. 1986-90, pres.-elect 1990-91, pres. 1991-92), N.Am. Assn. for Study Obesity (coun. 1991-93, v.p. 1994-95, pres.-elect 1995-96, pres. 1996—), Am. Inst. Nutrition, Am. Soc. Clin. Nutrition. Office: Pa State U 226 Henderson Bldg University Park PA 16802-6501

ROLNICK, REUBEN, anesthesiologist; b. Boras, Sweden, Dec. 9, 1951; came to U.S., 1962; s. Aron and Frida Rolnick. BA, CUNY, 1974; MBA, L.I. U., 1982; MD, St. George's U. Sch. Medicine, Grenada, 1989. Resident in anesthesiology St. Luke's-Roosevelt Hosp. Ctr., N.Y.C., 1994; anesthesiologist Brooksville (Fla.) Regional Hosp., 1995—. Mem. Am. Soc. Anesthesiologists, Fla. Soc. Anesthesiologists. Home: 8247 Omaha Circle Spring Hill FL 34606

ROM, WILLIAM NICHOLAS, physician; b. San Francisco, July 6, 1945; s. William N. and Barbara J. (Berlin) R.; m. Holly Wight Meeker, Oct. 7, 1973; children: Nicole, Meredith. BA, U. Colo., 1967; MD, U. Minn., 1971; MPH, Harvard U., 1973. Diplomate Am. Bd. Internatl Medicine, Am. Bd. Pulmonary Disease, Am. Bd. Preventive Medicine, Occupational Medicine. Internship U. Calif.-Davis, 1971-72; residency, 1973-75. from asst. to assoc. prof. U. Utah, Salt Lake City, 1977-83; sr. investigator NIH, Bethesda, Md., 1983-89; chief Divsn. Pulmonary/Critical Care Medicine NYU Med. Ctr., 1989—. Author: Canoe Country Wilderness, 1987; editor: Environmental and Occupational Medicine, 1992. Capt. USAFR, 1972-77. Recipient Harriet Hardy award New Eng. Occupational Med. Assn., 1993. Fellow Explorer's Club, Pulmonary and Occupational Medicine, Mt. Sinai, N.Y., 1975-77. Democrat. Home: 4 Stanley Keyes Ct Rye NY 10580-3259 Office: NYU Med Ctr 550 1st Ave New York NY 10016-6481

ROMAGOSA, JEROME J., retired physician; b. Thibdaux, La., June 2, 1917. Student, La. State U., MD, 1943; postgrad., Tulane U., M.D. Anderson Hosp. and Tumor Inst., Houston, Curie Found., Paris, Royal Marsdon Hosp., London, Holt Radium Inst. and Christie Hosp., Manchester, Eng., St. Lukes Cancer Hosp., Dublin, Ireland. Diplomate Am. Bd. Radiology. Pvt. practice Opelousas, La., 1944-47; pvt. practice Lafayette, La., 1950-83, ret., 1983; med. vol. Hospice of Acadiana, Lafayette, 1983—, also bd. dirs.; vis. lectr. U. Southwestern La.; clin. asst. La. State U. Med. Sch., New Orleans; chief med. staff Our Lady of Lourdes Hosp.; radiol. cons. for civil def.; various hosp. staff appts. Author: Lafitte's Stowaway, 1984; contbr. articles to profl. jours. Bd. dirs. Coun. on the Aging, SW La. Edn. and Referral Ctr.; chmn. bd. dirs. Ret. Sr. Vol. Program; past mem. bd. commrs. Lafayette Natural History Mus. and Planetarium; bd. trustees Lafayette Gen. Hosp., also charter mem. Recipient Pvt. Sector Initiative Commendation Pres. Ronald Reagan, 1985. Fellow Am. Coll. Radiology; mem. AMA, Am. Radium Soc., La. State Med. Soc. (past pres.), Radiol. Soc. La. (past pres.), Am. Soc. Therapeutic Radiology and Oncology, Am. Fedn. Clin. Oncologic Socs. Office: PO Box 53387 Lafayette LA 70505-3387

ROMAN, ELIZABETH, nursing educator; b. Chgo., Nov. 26, 1959; d. Jesus and Angela (Rivera) R. ADN with honors, P.R. Jr. Coll., 1980; BSN magna cum laude, Inter Am. U. P.R., 1983; MS in Nursing, U. P.R., 1988. RN, P.R. Staff nurse Met. Hosp., San Juan, P.R.; educator Caribbean U., Bayamon. Mem. Nursing Profession Assn. P.R. Home: S3 #9 Carretera 21 Las Lomas Rio Piedras PR 00921

ROMAN, STANFORD AUGUSTUS, JR., medical educator, dean; b. N.Y.C.; s. Stanford Augustas and Ivy L. (White) R.; children: Mawiyah Lythcott, Jane E. Roman-Brown. AB, Dartmouth Coll., 1964; MD, Columbia U., 1968; MPH, U. Mich., 1975. Diplomate Nat. Bd. of Med. Examiners. Intern in medicine Columbia U.-Harlem Hosp. Ctr., 1966-69, resident in medicine, 1969-71, chief resident in medicine, 1971-73; assoc. dir. ambulatory care Columbia U. Harlem Hosp., N.Y.C., 1972-73; instr. in medicine Columbia U., N.Y.C., 1972-73; asst. physician Presbyn. Hosp., 1972-73; clin. dir. Healthco, Inc., Soul City, N.C., 1973-74; dir. ambulatory care, asst. prof. medicine/sociomed. scis. Boston City Hosp., 1974-78; asst. prof. medicine U. N.C., Chapel Hill, 1973-74; asst. dean Boston U. Sch. Medicine, 1974-78; med. dir. D.C. Gen. Hosp., Washington, 1978-81; assoc. dean acad. affairs Dartmouth Med. Sch., Hanover, N.H., 1981-86, assoc. prof., 1981-87, dep. dean, 1986-87; dean, v.p., prof. medicine Morehouse Sch. Med., Atlanta, 1987-89; sr. v.p., med. and profl. affairs Health and Hosps. Corp., N.Y.C., 1989-90; dean med. sch., prof. community health and social medicine CUNY, 1990—; dir. Boston Comprehensive Sickle Cell Ctr., 1975-78; bd. dirs. Nat. Bd. Med. Examiners, Phila., 1988-92, Winifred Masterson Burke Rehab. Hosp., White Plains, N.Y.; mem. Dartmouth Hitchcock Med. Ctr. Bd. of Medicine, N.Y.; trustee Dartmouth Coll., Hanover, N.H. Contbr. to book chpts. and profl. jours. and editls. Fellow N.Y. Acad. Medicine; mem. AMA, APHA, Nat. Med. Assn., N.Y. State Coun. Grad. Med. Edn., N.Y. State Dept. Edn. Bd. Medicine. Democrat. Episcopalian. Office: CUNY Med Sch J 909 Convent Ave and 138th St New York NY 10031

ROMANIUK, ANDRZEJ, neurophysiologist, educator; b. Stanisławów, Poland, Aug. 13, 1931; s. Włodzimierz and Janina (Kaszubiak) R.; m. Maria Majdanska, Dec. 28, 1952; 1 child, Halina. BSc, Ul Łódź, Poland, 1956, PhD, 1960, ScD, 1965. Rsch. fellow U. Łódź, 1955-60, sr. rsch. fellow, 1960-65, prof., 1965—, head dept. neurophysiology, 1966—, dir. Inst. Physiology and Cytology, 1973-81, dean faculty of biology, 1978-81. Mem. Polish Acad. Scis. (mem. physiol. sci. com. 1978). Home: Matejki 12, 91-402 Łódź Poland Office: U Łódź, Rewolucji 1905 r 66, 90-222 Łódź Poland

ROMANO, JOHN FRANCIS, physician; b. S.I., N.Y., July 4, 1948; s. Francis John and Grace (Ferris) R.; m. Catherine Theresa Marino, Mar. 5, 1977; children: Francesca, Caterina. BS in Biology, St. Peter's Coll., 1969; MD, Cornell U., 1973. Diplomate Am. Bd. Dermatology. Pratice medicine specializing in dermatology N.Y.C., 1979—; dir. dermatology Queens (N.Y.) Hosp. Ctr., 1980-83; attending St. Vincent's Hosp., N.Y.C., 1979—; clin. asst. prof. dermatology N.Y. Hosp.-Cornell, N.Y.C., 1979—; dermatology cons. Walsh Home, N.Y.C., 1983-92. Contbr. articles to profl. jours. Mem. Columbus Citizen's Found. Fellow Am. Acad. Dermatology, Manhattan Dermatology Soc. (pres., sec.), N.Y. Acad. Medicine, Am. Soc. Dermatol. Surgery, Soc. for Pediat. Dermatology, N.Y. State Dermatology Soc., Am. Order Malta. Club: N.Y. Athletic. Office: 36 7th Ave New York NY 10011-6609

ROMANO, PAUL EDWARD, pediatric ophthalmologist, educator, strabologist; b. N.Y.C., Oct. 30, 1934; s. Paul Salvatore and Mary Elizabeth (Simms) R.; m. Judith Ann Robinson, Oct. 18, 1969. A.B., Cornell U., 1955, M.D., 1959; M.S. with distinction in Ophthalmology, Georgetown U., 1967. Diplomate Am. Bd. Ophthalmology. Intern in surgery Albany Med. Ctr. Hosp., N.Y., 1959-60, residency in gen. surgery, 1960-61; residency in ophthalmology Georgetown U. Hosp., Washington, 1964-67; fellow in ophthalmology Armed Forces Inst. Pathology, Washington, 1967, Wilmer Ophthal. Inst., Johns Hopkins Hosp., Balt., 1967-69; dir. ophthalmology Children's Meml. Hosp., Chgo., 1970-80; asst. prof. Northwestern U. Med. Sch., Chgo., 1969-73, assoc. prof., 1973-80; prof. ophthalmology U. Fla. Coll. Medicine, Gainesville, 1980-89; cons. VA Med. Ctr., Gainesville, 1980-89, Naval Regional Med. Ctr., Jacksonville, Fla., 1981-89. Founding editor, pub. Binocular Vision and Strabismus Quar. Jour., 1985—. Contbr. over 250 articles to sci. jours. Served to capt. U.S. Army, 1961-64. Fellow Heed Found., 1968, NIH, 1968-69. Fellow Am. Acad. Ophthalmology, Am. Acad. Pediatrics; mem. Internat. Assn. Ocular Surgeons (charter), Internat. Strabismus Assn., Am. Assn. for Pediatric Ophthalmology (charter), Assn. for Research in Vision and Ophthalmology, European Strabismus Assn., Von Noorden Fellows Assn., Soc. Heed Fellows, Wilmer Residents' Assn. Home and Office: PO Box 3727 740 Piney Acres Cir Dillon CO 80435-3727

ROMANOFF, JULIUS SAMUEL, psychologist; b. Trenton, July 16, 1922; s. Morris and Mary (Green) R.; BA, Bklyn. Coll., 1943; MA, George Washington U., 1951; EdD (Univ. scholar), Temple U., 1976; m. Dorothy Owen, Feb. 23, 1950; 1 son, Barry. Rehab. counselor Tb Assn., Washington, 1949-51; mgr. Romanoff's Products, Newark, 1951-64; rehab. counselor East Orange (N.J.) Bd. Edn., 1964-66; vocat. counselor Jewish Family Service, Columbus, Ohio, 1966-68; exec. dir. B'nai B'rith Career and Counseling Service, Phila., 1968-90; pvt. practice psychology; vocat. expert Bur. Hearings and Appeals, Social Security Adminstrn., Phila. and Jenkintown, Pa., 1969—; chmn. Franklin County (Ohio) Employ the Handicapped Com., 1967-68; bd. dirs. Gratz Cmty. H.S. Served with USAAF, 1943-46. Lic. psychologist, Pa.; cert. sch. psychologist, Pa., N.J. Mem. Am. Psychol. Assn., Pa. Psychol. Assn., Phila. Soc. Clin. Psychologists, Am. Assn. Counseling and Devel., Nat. Career Devel. Assn., Assn. Measurement and Evaluation in Counseling and Devel., Am. Rehab. Counselors Assn., Psi Chi. Jewish. Clubs: Ashton Golf, Northampton Valley Golf, Quaker City Lodge, B'nai B'rith. Home and Office: 41 Union St Newtown PA 18940-1460

ROMANOWSKI, RICHARD RONALD, physician, gynecologist, educator; b. Buffalo, N.Y., Apr. 19, 1932; s. Ignatius Marion and Michaelena (Rockna) R.; m. Mary Anne Michalski, June 11, 1958; children: Roslyn, Ronda Lee Yeomans, Marcus, Richard Michael. BS cum laude, Canisius Coll., 1954; MD, U. Buffalo, 1958. Diplomate Am. Bd. Ob-gyn. Intern San Francisco Gen. Hosp., 1958-59; resident Millard Fillmore Hosp., 1959-62, Roswell Pk. Inst., 1962-63; pres. Med. Assocs. in Gynecology and Obstetrics, Buffalo and Williamsville, N.Y., 1980—; clin. asst. prof. in ob-gyn. SUNY, Buffalo; attending staff dept. ob-gyn. Millard Fillmore Hosp., Sister's Hosp., Children's Hosp. Past bd. mem. Ask Women, Buffalo, Millard Fillmore Hosp. Mem. AMA, Am. Coll. Ob-Gyn., Am. Assn. Gynecol. Laparoscopists, Erie County Med. Soc., Cath. Physicians Guild (exec. com., past pres., nat. del.), Buffalo Ob-Gyn. Soc. (past pres., v.p.), Tri Beta (past pres.). Office: Med Assocs in Ob-Gyn 1000 Youngs Rd Williamsville NY 14221-2644

ROMANSKY, MONROE JAMES, physician, educator; b. Hartford, Conn., Mar. 16, 1911; s. Benjamin and Henrietta (Levine) R.; m. Evelyn Muriel Lackman, Jan. 10, 1943; children: Stephen, Gerald, Michael, Richard. A.B., U. Maine, 1933; M.D., U. Rochester, 1937. Diplomate: Am. Bd. Internal Medicine. Intern Strong Meml. Hosp.-U. Rochester, N.Y., 1937-38; asst. resident Strong Meml. Hosp.-U. Rochester, 1938-39, James Gleason Research fellow studies on relationship of kidneys to hypertension, 1939-40, chief resident, 1940-41, instr. in medicine, 1941-42; investigator Office Sci. Research and Devel., Surgeon Gen. U.S., 1941-42; chief biochemistry and antibiotic research Walter Reed Army Hosp., 1942-46; asso. prof. Sch. Medicine, George Washington U., Washington, 1946—; prof. medicine Sch. Medicine, George Washington U., 1957—; dir. George Washington U. med. div. D.C. Gen. Hosp., 1950-69; dir. infectious diseases research lab. and infectious diseases div. D.C. Gen. Hosp., 1950-69; cons. internal medicine antibiotics Walter Reed Army Hosp., Washington, 1946—; Cons. internal medicine antibiotics VA Hosp., Washington, 1952—, NIH, Bethesda, Md., 1953—, Surgeon Gen. USAF, 1966—; mem. Asian influenza adv. com. D.C., 1956-61; mem. ad hoc adv. com. Bur. Medicine FDA, 1966-67; examiner Am. Bd. Internal Medicine, 1965, 67, 69. Editorial bd.: Antimicrobial Agts. and Chemotherapy, 1961-72; Contbr. to profl. jours. Trustees council U. Rochester, 1965—. Served with M.C., AUS, 1942-46. Decorated Legion of Merit; recipient Founders award Tau Epsilon Phi, Disting. Career award U. Maine. Fellow ACP (adv. bd. to gov. D.C. 1969—); mem. Am. Soc. Internal Medicine, Am. Fedn. Clin. Research, Soc. Exptl. Biology and Medicine, Am. Soc. Microbiology, Infectious Diseases Soc. (founding council 1963-66), Soc. Med. Cons. to Armed Forces, Sigma Xi, Alpha Omega Alpha. Club: Woodmont Country. Home: 5600 Wisconsin Ave Chevy Chase MD 20815-4408

ROMAN-UNFER, SUSAN, hematologist, oncologist; b. Cedar Rapids, Iowa, June 25, 1959; d. George V. Roman and Cecelia (Zieser) Roman; m. Robert Charles Unfer, June 13, 1987. BS in Microbiology, Iowa State U., 1984, MS in Molecular Biology, 1989; DO, U. Osteo. Med. & Health Scis., 1993. Rsch. asst. Nat. Animal Disease Ctr., Ames, Iowa, 1984-88; tchg. asst. in biology Iowa State U., Ames, 1988, rsch. asst., 1988-89; rsch. asst. Garst Seed Co., Slater, Iowa, 1989; resident in medicine Luth. Gen. Hosp., Park Ridge, Ill., 1993-96; fellow in hematology and oncology U. Colo., Denver, 1996—. Author rsch. papers, abstracts in field. Recipient rsch. award Am. Leptospirosis Rsch. Com., 1985, 87, Donald E. Kahn Meml. award Am. Assn. Vet. Microbiologists, 1987. Mem. Am. Osteo. Assn., Sigma Xi. Roman Catholic. Home: 600 W County Line Rd #12003 Highlands Ranch CO 80126 Office: Univ Colo Health Scis Ctr Box B-170 4200 E 9th Ave Denver CO 80262

ROMEIS, RONALD ALAN, retirement and nursing home executive; b. Ft. Myers, Fla., May 13, 1947; s. Ludwig and Elizabeth Mina (Perry) R.; m. Margaret Elizabeth Whitworth, Oct. 19, 1968; children: Margaret Elizabeth, Sara Ellen. BA, Eckerd Coll., 1969; MDiv, Vanderbilt U., 1973. Assoc. pastor Towson (Md.) Presbyn. Ch., 1973-77; asst. to pres. Phila. Presbytery Homes, Villanova, Pa., 1977-83, v.p., 1984—; trustee Presbytery Phila., 1985-96, pres., 1991-96; pres. Presbyn. Assn. Homes for Aging, 1987-88. Editor: Directory of Presbyterian Homes In The United States, 1978—. Minister The Presbytery of Phila., 1977—, The Presbytery of Balt., 1973-77. Mem. Union League Phila. Republican. Office: Phila Presbytery Homes 2000 Joshua Road Lafayette Hill PA 19444-2430

ROMEO, JAMES JOSEPH, retired army nurse corps officer, nursing researcher; b. Tuckahoe, N.Y., Apr. 16, 1935; m. Roberta Hardy McNeill, May 6, 1961; children: Bennett J., Karin M. Diploma, Creedmoor State Hosp. Sch. Nsg, Queens Village, N.Y., 1956; BA in Nursing, San Francisco State Coll., 1961; MS in Nursing, Boston U., 1967. Commd. 2d lt. U.S. Army, 1958, advanced through grades to col., 1978; chief clin. nursing svc. Walter Reed Army Med. Ctr., Washington, 1979-80; chief dept. nursing U.S. Army Community Hosp., Seoul, Korea, 1980-81, Evans Army Community Hosp., Colorado Springs, Colo., 1981-84, Walter Reed Army Med. Ctr., Washington, 1987-88; ret., 1988; protocol coord. HIV rsch. Henry M. Jackson Found. Walter Reed Army Med. Ctr., Washington, 1988-90. Mem. ANA/Calif., Sigma Theta Tau.

ROMEO, RICHARD MICHAEL, chiropractor, researcher; b. Bklyn., Apr. 9, 1968; s. Richard G. and Anna (Modafferi) R. BS in Applied Computer Math., St. Joseph's Coll., Bklyn., 1988; MS in Applied Computer Math., Hofstra U., 1989; DChiropractic cum laude, Life Coll., Marietta, Ga., 1993, M in Sports Medicine magna cum laude, 1994. Asst. physician Krantz Chiropractic Ctr., Marietta, 1989-94; pvt. practice, Bklyn., 1994—. Author: Abuse of Recreational Drugs,1994. Mem. Graeff Assn. (pres. 1992-95). Office: Sunset Park Physician Group 916 39th St Brooklyn NY 11219

ROMEO, VINCENT DOMINICK, pharmacologist, researcher, researcher; b. Bklyn., Oct. 26, 1956; s. Salvatore and Louise (Amendola) R.; m. Daria Lynn Senaldi, Aug. 23, 1986. BS in Pharmacy, St. John's U., Jamaica, N.Y., 1980, MS in Pharm. Scis., 1981, PhD in Pharm. Scis., 1985. Registered pharmacist, N.Y. Sr. scientist Nastech Pharm. Co., Inc., Hauppauge, N.Y., 1985-87, dir. R & D, 1987-91, pres., CEO, 1991—; adj. prof. pharmacology St. John's U., 1986—. Contbr. articles to sci. jours. Mem. Am. Assn. Pharm. Scientists (presenter 1993), Am. Coll. Clin. Pharmacology (presenter 1994), Am. Pharm. Assn., N.Y. Acad. Scis., St. John's U. Pharmacology Alumni Assn. (pres. 1989—), KC, Rho Chi. Roman Catholic. Home: 104 Harbor Ln Massapequa Park NY 11762 Office: Nastech Pharm Co Inc 129 Oser Ave Hauppauge NY 11788

ROMERO, DENNIS O., counselor; b. Quito, Ecuador, Nov. 5, 1963; came to U.S., 1971; s. Hector Raul and Cecilia (Baca) R. BA in Psychology and Philosophy, Cathedral Coll., 1987; MA in Counseling Psychology, Manhattan Coll., 1990; postgrad., 1992—. Tchr. Our Lady of Fatima, Jackson Heights, N.Y., 1987-88, St. Agnes Acad. High Sch., College Park, N.Y., 1988-89; psychol. counselor Highbridge Community Life Ctr., Bronx, N.Y., 1989-90; clin. counselor Beth Israel Med. Ctr., N.Y.C., 1990-91; acad. advisor Regents Coll., Albany, N.Y., 1991-94; psychol. coun. Counseling for Unity, Albany, N.Y., 1993—; clinic supr. psychiatry Ellis Hosp., Schenectady, N.Y., 1994—; counselor Our Lady of Sorrows Parish, Corona, N.Y., 1990-94,. EMT Corona Vol. Ambulance Corps., 1985-94. Mem. Chi Sigma Iota. Roman Catholic. Office: Ellis Hosp Dept Psychiatry Mental Health Clinic 216 Lafayette St Schenectady NY 12305

ROMERO, EMILIO FELIPE, psychiatry educator, psychotherapist, hospital administrator; b. Havana, Cuba, Nov. 12, 1946; came to U.S., 1960; s. Emilio Jose and Isela Maria (Correoso) R. BA cum laude, U. Miami, Coral Gables, Fla., 1966; MD, U. Zaragoza (Spain), 1972. Diplomate Am. Bd. Psychiatry and Neurology (examiner 1987—). Resident in psychiatry U. Tex. Health Sci. Ctr., San Antonio, 1976; assoc. dir. Therapeutic Community for Schizophrenics Audie L. Murphy VA Hosp., San Antonio, 1976-78, staff psychiatrist outpatient psychiatry svcs., 1978-81, dir. outpatient psychiatry svcs., 1981-89, acting chief psychiatry svc., 1989-90, chief psychiatry svc., 1990—; asst. prof. psychiatry U. Tex. Health Sci. Ctr., San Antonio, 1976-87, assoc. prof. psychiatry, 1987-93, prof., 1993—; psychoanalytical cons. Med. Ctr. Hosp., San Antonio, 1981-87; lectr. on dream interpretation, U.S., Can., Europe, S.Am., 1977—; judge Internat. Film Festival on Culture and Psychiatry, 1976, 78; cons. to Donald Sutherland on film Lost Angels, 1988. Co-author: Psiquiatria Clinica Para Estudiantes de Medicina, 1993, Psiquiatria Para No Psiquiatras, 1995; contbr. articles to nat. and internat. profl. jours. Active local TV and radio stas., San Antonio Express News & Light, San Antonio and Diario del las Americas, Miami, Fla., 1973—; mem. art com. San Antonio Mus. Assn., 1988—, mayor's Com. to Receive the King of Spain, San Antonio, 1987; mem. Mex. Rels. Com. to Receive His Holiness Pope John Paul II, San Antonio, 1987. Knighted Sovereign Order of Malta, Rome, 1987; recipient Silver plaque U. Salamanca (Spain), 1982; recognized with proclamation of day in his honor, Dade County, Fla., 1992; named to Austrian Order of Mil. Medicine and Pharmacy, 1994. Fellow Am. Psychiat. Assn., Am. Assn. Social Psychiatry, Am. Coll. Psychiatrists; mem. Tex. Soc. Psychiat. Physicians (chmn. internat. grads. 1985—), Assn. Mil. Surgeons U.S. (internat. com. 1986—, chair 1996), Bexar County Psychiat. Soc. (pres. 1987-88, Leadership award 1988), Sociedad Española de Psiquiatria (Mem. of Honor 1988, Disting. Guest and Citizen City of Salamanca Spain 1990), Austrian Order Mil. Medicine and Pharmacy. Roman Catholic. Home: 141 Twinleaf Ln San Antonio TX 78213-2516 Office: Audie Murphy VA Hosp 7400 Merton Minter St San Antonio TX 78284-5700

ROMERO, JORGE ANTONIO, neurologist, educator; b. Bayamon, P.R., Apr. 15, 1948; s. Calixto Antonio Romero-Barcelo and Antonia (de Juan) R.; m. Helen Mella, June 20, 1970 (div. 1983); children: Sofia, Jorge, Alfredo, Isabel; m. Cheryl Raps, Aug. 1994; 1 child, Jessica. SB, MIT, 1968; MD, Harvard U., 1972. Diplomate Am. Bd. Psychiatry and Neurology. Intern U. Chgo. Hosp. and Clinics, 1972-73; resident Mass. Gen. Hosp., Boston, 1975-78; rsch. fellow in pharmacology NIMH, Bethesda, Md., 1973-75; asst. prof. neurology Harvard Med. Sch., Boston, 1979-92; mem. staff VA Med. Ctr., Brockton, Mass., 1979-92; assoc. physician Brigham and Women's Hosp., Boston, 1980-92; chmn. dept. neurology Ochsner Clin. Baton Rouge, 1993—; cons. Mass. Mental Health Ctr., Boston, 1987-92. With USPHS, 1973-75. Recipient Career Devel. award VA, 1979. Mem. Am. Acad. Neurology. Office: Ochsner Clin Baton Rouge 16777 Medical Center Dr Baton Rouge LA 70816-3228

ROMICH, BARRY A., health products company executive; b. Dec. 13, 1945; s. Benjamin A. Jr. and Marian R.; children: Jennifer, Kathryn. BS in Engring., Case Western Res. U., 1967. Registered profl. engr., Ohio. Staff engr. med. engring. rsch. program Case Western Res. U., Cleve., 1967-70; pvt. cons., 1970-73; pres. Prentke Romich Co., Wooster, Ohio, 1966-91, chmn., chief exec. officer, 1991—; presenter seminars in field. Contbr. articles to profl. jours. Bd. dirs. Found. for Exceptional Children, Goodwill Industries Wayne County, Wayne Ctr. Arts; hon. mem. bd. dirs. Nat. Spl. Children's Fund. Recipient Goldenson award United Cerebral Palsy Assn., 1986; named Small Bus. Person of Yr., Wooster Area C. of C., 1990; named to Buckeye Boys State Hall of Fame, 1992; Switzer scholar Nat. Rehab. Assn., 1990. Fellow RESNA, Am. Inst. Med. and Biol. Engring., Am. Assn. for Advancement Rehab. Tech. (founding, exec. com. 1987-90, bd. dirs.); mem. IEEE Engring. in Medicine and Biology Soc., Internat. Soc. for Augmentative and Alternative Comm. (founding, exec. com. 1987-90), U.S. Soc. for Augmentative and Alternative Comm. (organizing com., founding bd. dirs.), Comm. Aid Mfrs. Assn. Office: Prentke Romich Co 1022 Heyl Rd Wooster OH 44691-9786

ROMM, JOHN DAVID, physician, educator; b. N.Y.C., May 27, 1930; s. Murray and Blanche (Gordon) R.; m. Helen Cavas, June 17, 1956; children: David Michael, Stephanie Friduss. BS, Kalamazoo U., 1951; MD, Wayne state U., 1956. Diplomate Am. Bd. Internal Medicine. Intern then resident Cedars Sinai Med. Ctr., L.A., 1956-59; fellow in gastroenterology Wodsworth VA Hosp., West L.A., 1961-62; mem. staff Cedars Sinai Med. Ctr., 1962—; assoc. prof. medicine UCLA, 1962—. Capt. USAF, 1959-61. Office: 8631 W 3d St # 725E Los Angeles CA 90048

ROMMER, JAMES ANDREW, physician; b. Newark, Aug. 22, 1952; s. Thomas Colman and Hortense (Marsh) R.; m. Linda Joan Anderson, Oct. 7, 1979; children: Elizabeth Anne, Nicole Marie. BS, Haverford Coll., 1974; MD, Cornell U., 1978. Diplomate Am. Bd. Internal Medicine. Intern N.Y. Hosp., Cornell Med. Ctr., N.Y.C., 1978-79; resident in internal medicine N.Y. Hosp., Cornell Med. Ctr., 1978-81; fellow in internal medicine Johns Hopkins Med. Sch., Balt., 1981-82; pvt. practice internal medicine Livingston, N.J., 1982—; attending physician St. Barnabas Med. Ctr., Livingston, 1984—, mem. exec. com., 1990, 94, 96; assoc. chief sect. of internal medicine, clinical chief dept. medicine, 1996; asst. clin. prof. Univ. Medicine and Dentistry N.J. Med. Sch., Newark, 1983—. Fellow Am. Coll. Physicians; mem.

AMA, Am. Soc. Internal Medicine, Alpha Omega Alpha. Office: 349 E Northfield Rd Livingston NJ 07039-4802

ROMRELL, LYNN JOHN, anatomy and cell biology educator, dean; b. Idaho Falls, Idaho, Oct. 20, 1944; s. Milton A. and Helen (Wadsworth) R.; m. Deanne Barlow, Jan. 28, 1980; children: Janet, David, Jaime, Robert, Devin, Jacob. BS, Idaho State U., 1967; PhD, Utah State U., 1971. Postdoctoral fellow Med. Sch. Harvard U., Boston, 1971-73, instr. Med. Sch., 1973-75; asst. prof. Coll. of Medicine, U. Fla., Gainesville, 1975-79, assoc. prof., 1979-87; prof., assoc. dean Coll. Medicine U. Fla., Gainesville, 1987—; exec. dir. anatomical bd. State of Fla., Gainesville, 1983—. Co-author: Visible Human Body, 1990, Histology: A Text and Atlas, 1994, Sectional Anatomy of the Head and Neck with Correlative Diagnostic Imaging, 1994, Human Anatomy—Video Guide to Dissection, 1994; assoc. editor Anat. Record, 1980—. Mem. Am. Assn. Anatomists, Soc. for Study of Reprodn., Soc. for Cell Biology, Clin. Assn. of Anatomists, U. Fla. Coll. Medicine Faculty Assn. (v.p. 1985-86, pres. elect 1986-87). LDS. Home: 3901 NW 33rd Pl Gainesville FL 32606-6159

ROMSA, DONALD EDWARD, oral and maxillofacial surgeon; b. Berwyn, Ill., Apr. 18, 1950; s. Arnold Edwin and Gladys Helen (Holub) R.; m. Colleen Hannah Owens, Sept. 14, 1974; children: Scott, Amanda, Bradley. BS, Ill. State U., 1971; DDS, U. Ill., Chgo., 1975; postgrad., Northwestern U., Chgo., 1980. Diplomate Am. Bd. Oral and Maxillofacial Surgery. Pvt. practice Racine (Wis.) Oral and Maxillofacial Surgery Assocs., 1980—; asst. clin. prof. dept. oral and maxillofacial surgery Northwestern U. Med. Ctr., Chgo., 1980—. Bd. dirs., pres. Racine Health Care Network, Inc., 1989—. Capt. U.S. Army, 1975-77. Fellow Am. Assn. Oral and Maxillofacial Surgeons; mem. ADA, Ill. Soc. Oral and Maxillofacial Surgeons, Chgo. Soc. Oral and Maxillofacial Surgeons, Wis. Soc. Oral and Maxillofacial Surgeons, Racine County Dental Soc. (pres.). Roman Catholic. Office: Racine Oral/Maxill Surg 5801 Washington Racine WI 53406-4057

ROMSDAHL, MARVIN MAGNUS, surgeon, educator; b. Hayti, S.D., Apr. 2, 1930; s. Conrad Magnus and Hilda Johanna (Shelsta) R.; m. Virginia McElvany; children: Christine Ann, Laura Marie. AB, U. S.D., 1952, BS, 1954; MD, U. Ill., Chgo., 1956; PhD, U. Tex., Houston, 1968. Diplomate Am. Bd. Surgery. Clin. assoc. NIH, NCI, Bethesda, Md., 1958-60; instr. surgery U. Ill., Chgo., 1963-64; asst. surgeon, asst. prof. surgery U. Tex./M.D. Anderson Cancer Ctr., Houston, 1967-69; assoc. grad. faculty mem. Grad. Sch. Biomed. Sci., U. Tex., Houston, 1969-72; assoc. surgeon/asso. prof. surgery U. Tex./M.D. Anderson Cancer Ctr., Houston, 1969-75; dep. dept. head U. Tex./M.D. Anderson Cancer Ctr., 1979-85; grad. faculty mem. U. Tex. Health Sci. Ctr., Houston, 1972—; prof. surgery U. Tex. Med. Sch., Houston, 1975—; surgeon, prof. surgery U. Tex./M.D. Anderson Cancer Ctr., Houston, 1975—; lectr. in field. Contbr. articles to profl. jours. Pfizer scholar, 1953; recipient Sr. Clin. Traineeship award, USPHS, 1963, Spl. Fellowship award, 1964; ACS Mead Johnson award, 1965, Ann. Outstanding Tchr. award, Dept. Gen. Surgery, U. Tex. M.D. Anderson Cancer Ctr., 1988. Mem. ACS, AMA, Am. Assn. Cancer Rsch., Am. Radium Soc., Assn. for Acad. Surgery, Collegium Internationale Chirugiae Digestivae, Harris County Med. Soc., Houston Acad. Medicine, Houston Philos. Soc., Soc. for Surgery of Alimentary Tract, Soc. of Surg. Oncology, S.W. Sci. Forum, Tex. Med. Assn., Tex. Surg. Soc., Houston Surg. Soc., W.H. Cole Soc., Western Surg. Assn., Sigma Xi. Republican. Home: 4530 Verone St Bellaire TX 77401-5514 Office: UT M D Anderson Cancer Ctr 1515 Holcombe Blvd Houston TX 77030-4009

RONAGHAN, CATHERINE ANN, surgeon; b. Clark AFB, The Philippines, Mar. 1, 1959; d. James Thomas and Evelyn Bertha (Frey) Ronaghan; m. William Augustus Nolan, July 30, 1993; 1 child, Mairead Evelyn Nolan. BS in Biology and Chemistry, Miss. U. for Women, Columbus, 1981; MD, Tex. Tech. U., 1986. Intern in gen. surgery New York Hosp./Cornell U., N.Y.C., 1986, resident in gen. surgery, 1987-91; instr. dept. surgery Tex. Tech. U., Lubbock, 1991-92, asst. prof. surgery, 1992—; med. dir. Dimensions Ctr. for Women's Health, Lubbock, 1992—; asst. med. dir. surg. ICU Univ. Med. Ctr., Lubbock, 1992—, med. dir. trauma ICU, 1993—; cons. gen. surgery VA Med. Ctr., Lubbock, 1993—; mem. task force Tex. Med. Assn. Women's Health Rsch. Task Force, Austin, 1994—. Bd. dirs. Am. Cancer Soc., Lubbock, 1993—, Koman Found., Lubbock, 1994—. Fellow ACS; mem. AMA, AAUW, AAAS, Soc. Critical Care Medicine, Tex. Med. Assn., Assn. Women Surgeons, Soc. Laparoendoscopic Surgeons, Am. Soc. for Parenteral and Enteral Nutrition, Soc. Am. Gastrointestinal Endoscopic Surgeons, Lubbock, Crosby, GArza Med. Soc., Am. Soc. Gen. Surgeons, Tex. Tech. Assn. for Advancement of Women in Higher Edn., Univ. Quar. Club., Chirurgio, Alpha Omega Alpha. Roman Catholic. Office: Medical Arts Clinic 4102 24th St ste 100 Lubbock TX 79410

RONAGHAN, JOSEPH EDWARD, surgeon; b. Astoria, N.Y., May 4, 1950; s. James Thomas and Evelyn Bertha (Frey) R.; m. Cynthia Ann Hein, Nov. 27, 1976; 1 child, Kelly Elizabeth. BA in Biol. Scis., U. Colo., Colorado Springs, 1972; MD, Tulane U., 1977. Diplomate Am. Bd. Surgery. Surg. intern Miami Valley Hosp., Dayton, Ohio, 1977-78; resident in surgery Wright State U., Dayton, 1982-86; chief surg. svcs. 27th Med. Group, Cannon AFB, N.Mex., 1986-90; gen. surgeon The Harbin Clinic, Rome, Ga., 1990-91; asst. prof. dept. surgery Tex. Tech Health Scis. Ctr., Amarillo, 1991-92, regional chmn. dept. surgery, 1992—; mem. regional bd. dirs. Am. Cancer Soc., Amarillo, 1994—; bd. dirs. Regional Adv. Com. on Trauma, Amarillo, 1993—. Contbr. chpt. to book, articles to profl. jours. Lt. col. USAF, 1978-90. Fellow ACS, Internat. Coll. Surgeons, Southeastern Surg. Congress (assoc.), Southwestern Surg. Congress. Office: Tex Tech Health Scis Ctr 1400 Wallace Blvd Amarillo TX 79106

RONAN, GEORGE F., psychology educator; b. Salem, Mass., Dec. 13, 1953; s. Leo E. and Dorothy (DeVarennes) R.; m. Donna M. Wollerman, Aug. 9, 1986. BA, Salem State Coll., 1979; PhD, Fairleigh Dickinson U., 1985. Lic. clin. psychologist, N.Y., Mich. Postdoctoral fellow divsn. psychol. svcs. Fairleigh Dickinson U., Hackensack, N.J., 1984-85; asst. prof. Alfred (N.Y.) U., 1985-89; assoc. prof. psychology Ctrl. Mich. U., Mt. Pleasant, Mich., 1989—. Contbr. articles to profl. jours. Mem. APA, Am. Psychol. Soc., Assn. for Advancement of Behavior Therapy. Home: 612 S Kinney Mount Pleasant MI 48858 Office: Ctrl Mich U Dept Psychology Mount Pleasant MI 48859

RONCHETTI, ROBERTO, pediatrics educator, pneumologist; b. Rome, Aug. 5, 1935; s. Artemio and Fernanda (Calmanti) R.; m. Giuliana Gentili, Sept. 9, 1967 (dec. Nov. 1980); children: Francesco, Maria Paola; m. Maria Pia Villa, July 21, 1990; 1 child, Beatrice. MD, U. Parma, Italy, 1959. Resident in pediatrics U. Parma, 1959-63; resident in allergy and clin. immunology U. Florence, Italy, 1971; pvt. practice, Rome; prof. pediatrics U. Lapienza, Rome, 1980—; dir. Inst. Pediatrics, U. Rome, 1991-92. Editor Rivista Italiana Broncopneumologia Pediatrics, 1988, Pediatra, 1991. Home: Piazza Bainsizza 3, 00195 Rome Italy Office: Via Asiago 6, 00195 Rome Italy

RONGO, LUCILLE LYNN, medical center executive; b. N.Y.C., Sept. 15, 1958; d. Vincent Frank and Lucy Ann (Guilano) R. BS, Mercy Coll., Dobbs Ferry, N.Y., 1984. Asst. supr. accounts receivable Montefiore Med. Ctr., Bronx, 1978-81, asst. mgr. accounts payable, 1981-83, payroll mgr., 1983-87, spl. funds mgr., 1987-91, asst. controller spl. funds/payroll, 1991—. Mem. NAFE, Am. Mgmt. Assn., Am. Payroll Assn., Healthcare Fin. Mgmt. Assn. Avocations: drying, preserving and framing flowers; collecting miniatures; art; dance, skiing. Home: 12 Fountain Ln Scarsdale NY 10583 Office: Montefiore Med Ctr 111 E 210th St Bronx NY 10467-2490

RONIS, MARTIN JORN JANIS, pediatrics researcher and educator; b. Huddersfield, Yorkshire, Eng., Apr. 8, 1961; came to U.S., 1985; s. Fritz and Helga (Nicks) R.; m. Lisa Ricketson, May 16, 1992. BA in Natural Scis., Cambridge U., Eng., 1982; PhD in Biochemistry and Physiology, Reading (Eng.) U., 1985. Teaching asst., instr. biochemistry Reading U., 1982-85; postdoctoral rsch. assoc. toxicology program N.C. State U., Raleigh, 1985-87; vis. rsch. assoc. dept. physiol. chemistry Karolinska Inst., Stockholm, 1987-89; instr. dept. pediatrics U. Ark. Med. Scis., Little Rock, 1989-90, asst. prof., 1990-96, tenured assoc. prof. Ark. Children's Hosp. Rsch. Inst., 1996—; ad hoc reviewer sea grant instl. program Hancock Inst. Marine Studies, U. So. Calif., 1990, La. Bd. Regents, LEQSF Grant Program, 1992. Ad hoc reviewer Alcohol: Clin. and Exptl. Rsch., Gastroenterology, others; contbr. articles to profl. jours. Grantee Nat. Inst. Alcohol Abuse and Alcoholism, 1990—, Nat. Inst. Drug Abuse, 1992-95, Nat. Inst. Environ. Health Sci., 1994—, EPA, 1995-96, USDA, 1995—. Mem. Internat. Soc. Study of Xenobiotics, Soc. Toxicology, N.Y. Acad. Sci., Sigma Xi. Democrat. Home: 7214 Apache Rd Little Rock AR 72205-5002 Office: U Ark Med Scis Dept Pediats Slot 512B Little Rock AR 72205

RONK, PATRICIA, operating room nurse; b. Camden, N.J., June 21, 1961; d. Thomas R. and Mary A. (Vaughan) Conlon; m. William Ronk; children: Katilyn Anne, Ryan Patrick. AA, Orange County Community Coll., Middletown, N.Y., 1986; BA, Mt. St. Mary Coll., Newburgh, N.Y., 1983. RN, N.Y. Med./surg. unit nurse Good Samaritan Hosp., Suffern, N.Y., 1986-87; med./surg. unit nurse St. Francis Hosp., Beacon, N.Y., 1987-88, oper. rm. nurse, 1988-89; recovery rm. nurse Vassar Bros. Hosp., Poughkeepsie, N.Y., 1989-90, oper. rm. nurse, 1990—. Mem. N.Y. State Nurses Assn. Home: PO Box 218 Rhinecliff NY 12574

RONKAINEN, ANTTI, physician; b. Tuupovaara, North Carelia, Finland, Mar. 30, 1960; s. Väinö and Raisa (Rojc) R.; m. Ritva Pulkkinen, June 19, 1993; children: Tero, Aino. MD, Kuopio U., Finland, 1985 Cert. of specialization in neurosurgery, 1993. Resident physician, ear, nose and throat dir. U. of Kuopio, Finland, 1987-88; resident in surgery Cen. Hosp. Savonlinna, 1989; resident in neurosurgery U. Kuopio, Finland, 1989-93, specialist, 1993-94; rsch. asst. Dept. Biochemistry and Molecular Biology Thomas Jefferson U., 1994-95; rsch. asst. Ctr. for Molecular Medicine and Genetics Wayne State U., Detroit, 1995-95; specialist Dept. Neurosurgery U. Kuopio, 1996—. Author: (book) Manual of Neurosurgery, 1995. 2d Lt. Finnish Armed Forces, 1986-87. Mem. European Assn. of Neurosurgical Socs., Scandinavian Neurological Soc., Finnish Neurosurgical Soc. Office: Dept Neurosurgery, PL 1777, 70210 Kuopio Finland

RONNER, HILARY, pediatric ophthalmologist; b. N.Y.C., Jan. 12, 1954; d. Irving and Gladys (Braunheim) R.; m. Ronald Feiman, Jan. 7, 1984; 1 child, Jed Ronner Feiman. BA, Barnard Coll., 1975; MD, Columbia U., 1979. Diplomate Am. Bd. Ophthalmology. Intern Overlook Hosp., Summit, N.J., 1979-80; resident Edward Harkness Eye Inst., N.Y.C., 1980-83; fellow U. Toronto, 1983-84; asst. attending Lenox Hill Hosp., N.Y.C., 1986—; asst. attending Manhattan Eye, Ear & Throat Hosp., N.Y.C., 1986—. Recipient Mary Putnam award Women's Med. Assn. N.Y., 1983; Ewart Angus fellow, U. Toronto, 1983. Fellow Am. Coll. Surgeons, Am. Acad. Ophthalmology.

RONQUIST, GUNNAR, physician; b. Visby, Gotland, Sweden, Mar. 23, 1938; s. Nils Henrik and Ingrid (Weidenhaijn) R.; m. Birgitta Lundqvist Ronquist, Dec. 30, 1966; children: Stefan, Daniel, Göran, Ingela PhD, U. Uppsala, 1968, MD, 1971. Lic. physician, U.S. Lectr. med. chemistry U. Uppsala, 1968-71; vis. lectr. U. Mich. Med. Sch., 1971-73; head physician Gen. Hosp., Eskilstuna, Sweden, 1976-77, U. Hosp., Uppsala, 1977—. Editor-in-chief Upsala Jour. Med. Scis., 1982—; contbr. over 250 articles to profl. jours.; discoverer of prostasomes-a new type of organelles in man. Mem. Swedish Soc. Physicians, Swedish Soc. Clin. Chemistry, Am. Fertility Soc. Home: Kälkvägen 51, S-756 47 Uppsala Sweden Office: U Hosp, Dept Clin Chemistry, S-751 85 Uppsala Sweden

ROODIN, PAUL A., psychology educator; b. Brookline, Mass., June 1, 1943; s. Harry and Blossom (Sugarman) R.; m. Marlene Linda Lubarsky, Aug. 27, 1967; children: Neal D., Pamela L. AB, Boston U., 1965; MS, Purdue U., 1968, PhD, 1970. Asst. prof. psychology SUNY, Oswego, 1969-75, assoc. prof., 1975-81, prof., 1981—, assoc. dean, 1989-91, assoc. provost, 1991-95, dir. experience-based edn., 1996—. Co-author: Developmental Psychology, 1980, Adult Cognition and Aging, 1986, Adult Development and Aging, 1991; contbr. articles on devel. psychology to profl. jours. Jewish. Home: 122 Stanwood Ln Manlius NY 13104-1412 Office: SUNY Coll at Oswego Oswego NY 13126

ROODMAN, STANFORD TRENT, immunologist; b. St. Louis, Sept. 17, 1939; s. Robert and Dorothy (Burjoski) R.; m. Estelle Renee Knight, June 25, 1961; children: Aaron Jay, Allison Anne. BS in Chemistry, Purdue U., 1961; PhD in Biochemistry, U. Mich., 1968. Postdoctoral fellow dept. biology U. Calif., La Jolla, 1968-70; asst. prof. dept. biochemistry St. Louis U., 1970-74, from asst. prof. to assoc. prof. dept. pathology, 1974—, dir. grad. program in pathology, 1977—, dir. flow cytometry rsch. lab., 1981—; cons. Sigma Chem., St. Louis, 1990-92. Contbr. articles to Jour. Cancer Rsch., Jour. Med. Primatology, Internat. Jour. of Immunology Pathology & Immunology Pharm., Jour. Toxicology Environ. 1st lt. U.S. Army, 1962-63. NIH fellow, 1969-70. Mem. Am. Assn. Immunologists, Internat. Soc. Analytical Cytology. Home: 1034 Dutch Mill Dr Ballwin MO 63011-3682 Office: St Louis U Dept Pathology 1402 S Grand Blvd Saint Louis MO 63104-1004

ROONEY, CAROL BRUNS, dietitian; b. Milw., Dec. 20, 1940; d. Edward G. and Elizabeth C. (Lemke) Bruns; m. George Eugene Rooney Jr., July 1, 1967; children: Steven, Sean. BS, U. Wis., 1962; MS, U. Iowa, 1965. Registered dietitian; cert. nutrition specialist; disting. health care food svc. adminstr. Intern VA Med. Ctr., Hines, Ill., 1962-63; resident in nutrition and food svc. VA Med. Ctr., Iowa City, 1963-65; dietitian nutrition clinic VA Med. Ctr., Hines, 1965-67, 69-70, chief clin. dietetics, 1970-71, chief adminstrv. dietetics, 1971-73; clin. dietitian VA Med. Ctr., Memphis, 1967-68; asst. chief nutrition and food svc. Zablocki VA Med. Ctr., Milw., 1974-85, chief nutrition and food svc., 1985-96, divsn. mgr., cons. care, 1996—, cons. nutrition and food svc. mgmt., 1995—; adj. lectr. Loyola U. Coll. Dentistry, Maywood, Ill., 1969-72; investigator nutrition VA/Med. Coll. Wis., Milw., 1975—, co-dir. ann. clin. nutrition symposium, Milw., 1979—; chmn. task force on ration allowance VA, Washington, 1977-84, mem. nutrition and food svc. spl. interest users group Washington, 1983-85, chmn. tech. adv. group region IV, 1986; mem. Dept. Vets. Affairs Mktg. Ctr. Subsistence Task Force, 1991—, dietetic internship adv. bd. St. Luke's Hosp., Milw., 1983-87; mem. Dept. Vets. Affairs Nat. Cost Containment Ctr. Nutrition & Food Svc. Benchmarking Tech. Adv., 1995—; lectr. in field, 1965—; mem. Dept. Vets. Affairs, Nutrition and Food Svc. Policy Manual Rev. Task Force, 1992-96, Dept. Vets. Chiefs, Food and Nutrition Svc. Mentor Group, 1992—. Author: (videocassette) VA Ration Allowance as a Management Tool 1976; editor: Nutrition Principles and Dietary Guidelines for Patients Receiving Chemotherapy and Radiation Therapy, 1980; contbr. articles to profl. jours., 1978—. Mem. profl. edn. com. Milw. South unit Am. Cancer Soc., 1976-86, bd. dirs. Milw. South unit, 1984-86, Milw. div., 1986-87, Wis. div., 1987-91, media spokesperson, 1983-91, del. to Milw. div., 1984-85, mem. organizational and expansion com. Milw. div., 1986-87, profl. edn. com. Milw. div., 1986-87, Wis. div., 1987-91, mem. taking control Wis. div., 1987-91, chmn. nutrition Wis. div., 1989-91; mem. med. adv. com. YMCA Met. Milw., 1985—; mem. Marquette U. High Sch. Mothers Guild, 1990-94. Recipient Disting. Svc. award Am. Cancer Soc. Milw. South unit, 1980, Women of Achievement award Girl Scouts USA Milw. area, 1987, Leadership award VA, 1989, Dept. Vets. Affairs Dietitian of Yr., 1994, Dept. Vets. Affairs Fed. Women's Program cert. merit for outstanding profl. leadership, 1994, Paralyzed Vets. Am. rsch. grantee, 1981-83. Fellow Am. Dietetic Assn. (registered, practice groups in mgmt. responsibilities in health care delivery, gerontology nutrition 1980—, dietetics in phys. medicine and rehab. 1983—, clin. nutrition mgmt. 1987—, amb. nat. media spokesperson 1983-89, Resource Amb. 1991—, Outstanding Svc. award 1983-89), FADA; mem. Am. Soc. Health Care Food Svc. Adminstrs. (dir.-at-large Wis. chpt. 1993-95, pres.-elect Wis. chpt. 1995-96, pres. 1996-97, Disting. Health Care Food Svc. Adminstr. 1995—), Wis. Dietetic Assn. (co-chmn. divsn. mgmt. practice 1976-77, chmn. 1977-78, bd. dirs. 1981-83, coord. cabinet 1984-91, pres. 1988-89, chmn. nominating com. 1989-90, chmn. long-range planning com. 1989-90, legis. com. 1988—, Wis. Medallion award 1986), Milw. Dietetic Assn. (cmty. nutrition and clin. dietetics and rsch. coms. 1975-76, chair ad hoc com. for nutrition and oncology patients 1976-79, clin. dietetics and rsch. study group 1981-90, chair 1983-85, pres. 1982-83, by-laws com. 1983-84, chair policies and procedures com. 1983-87, pub. rels. com. 1983-87, chair nominating com. 1984-85), Fed. Execs. Assn., Leadership Vets. Affairs Alumni Assn. (charter, life), Phi Upsilon Omicron, Kappa Delta. Home: 18230 Le Chateau Dr Brookfield WI 53045-4922 Office: Zablocki VA Med Ctr 5000 W National Ave Milwaukee WI 53295-0001

ROONEY, PEG (MARGARET E. ROONEY), vocational education administrator; b. Pueblo, Colo., Nov. 23, 1944; d. Joseph and Margaret Pugel; children: Kate, Sean. Diploma, St. Mary Corwin Sch. Nursing, 1965; BS, U. So. Colo., 1968; MSN, Colo. U., 1975; PhD, Colo. State U., Ft. Collins, 1993. Nursing coord. Pikes Peak Community Coll., Colorado Springs, Colo.; instr. Beth El Coll. of Nursing, Colorado Springs; asst. prof. U. So. Colo., Pueblo; health programs mgr. Colo. C.C. Sys., Denver. Mem. Colo. Orgn. for ADN (pres.).

ROOS, PHILIP, psychologist; b. Brussels, Belgium, Jan. 24, 1930; came to U.S., 1939, naturalized, 1945; s. Maurice and Berthe (Matthyssens) R.; m. Susan Morgan, June 4, 1958; 1 child, Valerie Gail. B.S. in Biology and Psychology with highest distinction, Stanford, 1949, postgrad., 1950-51; Ph.D. in Clin. Psychology, U. Tex., 1955. Psychology trainee VA Hosp., Waco, Tex., 1953-55; staff psychologist USPHS Hosp., Ft. Worth, 1955-57; assoc. prof. psychology Tex. Christian U., 1957-59; chief psychologist Timberlawn Sanitarium, Dallas, 1959-60; dir. psychol. services Tex. Dept. Mental Health and Mental Retardation, 1960-63; supt. Austin (Tex.) State Sch., 1963-67; asso. commr. div. mental retardation N.Y. State Dept. Mental Hygiene, 1967-68; nat. exec. dir. Assn. Retarded Citizens, Arlington, Tex., 1969-83; pres. Roos & Assocs., Arlington, Tex., 1980—; nat. exec. dir. Mothers Against Drunk Driving, Hurst, Tex., 1983-84; asst. clin. prof. Baylor Med. Sch., 1963-67; lectr. U. Tex., 1966-67; pvt. practice psychology; cons. in field, 1957—. Contbr. numerous articles to profl. jours. and books. Mem. Gov. Tex. Com. Mental Retardation, 1964-65, Pres.'s Com. on Employment Handicapped, 1969-86; trustee Mental Health Law Project, 1978-87; bd. dirs. Nat. Industries for Severely Handicapped, 1977-83; Squadron comdr. CAP, 1959, group comdr., 1960; bd. dirs. Sunny Von Bulow Victim Advocacy Ctr., 1986-94. Fellow Am. Assn. Mental Deficiency, Am. Orthopsychiat. Assn.; mem. Am. Psychol. Assn., Am. Soc. for Clin. Hypnosis, Phi Beta Kappa, Sigma Xi, Psi Chi. Home: 6100 Tiffany Park Ct Arlington TX 76016-2037 Office: Roos & Assocs 4025 Woodland Park Blvd Ste 290 Arlington TX 76013-4301

ROOT, ALLEN WILLIAM, pediatrician, educator; b. Phila., Sept. 24, 1933; s. Morris Jacob and Priscilla R.; m. Janet Greenberg, June 15, 1958; children: Jonathan, Jennifer, Michael. AB, Dartmouth Coll., 1955, postgrad. Med. Sch., 1954-56; MD, Harvard U., 1958. Diplomate Am. Bd. Pediatrics (mem. bd. 1986—), Am. Pediatric Endocrinology (mem. bd. 1985-90, chmn. 1990). Intern Strong Meml. Hosp., Rochester, N.Y., 1958-60; resident in pediatrics Hosp. U. Pa., Phila., 1960-62; fellow in pediatric endocrinology Children's Hosp. of Phila., 1962-65; assoc. physician in pediatrics U. Pa. Sch. Medicine, 1964-66, asst. prof. pediatrics, 1966-69; assoc. prof. pediatrics Temple U. Sch. Medicine, Phila., 1969-73; prof. Temple U. Sch. Medicine, 1973; asst. physician in endocrinology Children's Hosp. Phila., 1965-69; chmn. divsn. pediatrics Albert Einstein Med. Center., Phila., 1969-73; prof. pediatrics U. South Fla. Coll. Medicine, Tampa, 1973—, prof. biochemistry, 1987—, assoc. chmn. dept. pediatrics, 1974—, dir. sect. pediatric endocrinology, 1973-96; dir. univ. tchg. svcs. All Children's Hosp., St. Petersburg, 1973-89; mem. Fla. Infant Screening Adv. Coun., 1979—, chmn., 1994—; mem. Hillsborough County Thyroid Adv. Com., 1980; mem. adv. com. Nat. Pituitary Agy., 1974-78, mem. growth hormone subcom., 1972-79, 81-85. Author: Human Pituitary Growth Hormone, 1972; editor: (with C. La Cauza) Problems in Pediatric Endocrinology, 1980; mem. editl. bd. Jour. Pediats., 1973-81, Jour. Adolescent Health Care, 1979-95, Jour. Pediat. Endocrinology and Metabolism, 1985—, Jour. Clin. Endocrinology and Metabolism, 1993—, Growth, Genetics and Hormones, 1993—, Pediats. in Rev., 1995—; assoc. editor Adolescent and Pediat. Gynecology, 1992—. USPHS grantee; Birth Defects Found. grantee. Mem. AAAS, Am. Pediatric Soc., Soc. Pediatric Rsch., Lawson Wilkins Pediatric Endocrine Soc. (treas. 1979-88, pres. 1988-89), Endocrine Soc., Am. Acad. Pediatrics, Am. Fedn. Clin. Rsch., Soc. Exptl. Biology and Medicine, Soc. Nuclear Medicine, N.Y. Acad. Scis., Phila. Coll. Physicians, Phila. Endocrine Soc. (bd. dirs. 1971-72, treas. 1973), Dartmouth Coll. Alumni Coun., Dartmouth Club. Office: 801 6th St S Saint Petersburg FL 33701-4816

ROPER, DANIEL LEONARD, ophthalmologist; b. Dallas, June 7, 1945; s. Leonard Bouman and Marjorie (Ferrell) R.; m. Ann Ledbetter, June 17, 1967; children: Eric, Jonathan. BA, USAF Acad., 1967; MD, U. Tex., 1971. Intern Johns Hopkins Hosp.; resident U. Tex. Med. Br.; commd. 2d lt. USAF, 1967, advanced through grades to col., 1988; flight surgeon USAF, Eglin AFB, Fla., 1972-74; ophthalmologist, flight surgeon USAF, Barksdale AFB, La., 1977-79; ophthalmologist USAF, Eglin AFB, 1979-81; discharged USAF, 1981; ophthalmologist White-Wilson Med. Ctr., Ft. Walton Beach, Fla., 1981—. Author: (novel) Eye of the Hurricane, 1995. Bd. dirs. USAF Armament Mus., Ft. Walton Beach, 1986-96. Fellow ACS, Am. Acad. Ophthalmology; mem. Fla. Soc. Ophthalmology, Fla. Med. Assn. Republican. Methodist. Home: 59 Meigs Dr Shalimar FL 32579 Office: White-Wilson Med Ctr 1005 Mar Walt Dr Fort Walton Beach FL 32547

ROPER, PHILIP A., physician; b. San Diego, Calif., Sept. 27, 1944. BA, DePauw U., 1966; MD, Ind. U., 1970. Diplomate Am. Bd. Internal Medicine and Cardiology. Physician Escondido (Calif.) Cardiology Assocs., 1972-73, Affiliated Cardiologists, Phoenix, 1973—.

ROPER, STEPHEN DAVID, medical researcher, consultant; b. Rock Island, Ill., May 30, 1945; s. Wesley S. and Ruth M. (Tilley) R.; m. Kathleen Ann Herburger, Sept. 2, 1967 (div. 1983); children: Anna, Peter; m. Nirupa Chaudhari, May 5, 1983. BA, Harvard U., 1967, postdoctoral, 1970-73; PhD, U. Coll., London, 1970. Instr., Harvard U., Cambridge, Mass., 1971-73; asst. prof. U. Colo. Med. Sch., Denver, 1973-79, assoc. prof., 1979-85, prof. 1985; prof., chmn. dept. anatomy and neurobiology, Colo. State U., Ft. Collins, 1985-90, prof., 1990-95; prof. dept. physiology and biophysics U. Miami Sch. Medicine, 1995—; cons. NIH, Bethesda, Md., 1978-86. Fellow Fulbright Found., NSF, NIH; recipient Research and Career Devel. award NIH, 1978-82. Mem. Rocky Mountain Region Neurosci. Group (founder, chmn. 1979-80), Neurosci. Soc. (chpts. com. 1981-84, pub. rels. com. 1992-96), Am. Physiol. Soc., Assn. Chemoreception Scis. (councillor 1989-91), Am. Assn. Anatomists. Office: U Miami Sch Medicine Dept Physiology and Biophysics Miami FL 33101

RORER, GERALD BARCROFT, health care company executive; b. Phila., Apr. 10, 1942; s. Gerald Francis and Mary Amelie (Runk) R.; m. Elizabeth Anne Keator, Dec. 20, 1973; children: Jonathan Barcroft, Carrie Amelie, Christopher Keator, Elizabeth Crawley. AB, Princeton U., 1964; MBA, Harvard U., 1966. Area mgr. Middle East, William H. Rorer, Fort Washington, Pa., 1968-69, treas., 1969-76; asst. treas. Rorer Group, Inc., Fort Washington, Pa., 1977-78, controller, 1978-80, v.p. fin., 1980-82, v.p. planning, 1982-84, v.p. planning and devel., 1984-87, v.p. community affairs, 1987-88; dir. Rorer Group Inc., Fort Washington, 1976-90. Trustee Montgomery Sch., treas., 1987-93; trustee Wistar Inst. Anatomy and Biology, Phila., 1974—, vice chmn., 1984-94; trustee Presbyn. U. Pa. Med. Center, Phila., 1976-95, Presbyn. Found. Phila., 1995—; bd. dirs. Inst. on Aging U. Pa., 1982—; mem. bd. trustees Acad. Natural Scis., 1993—, Beaver Coll., 1990—, chair acad. affairs com., 1995—; mem. bd. dirs. Upper Main Line YMCA, 1994—. Mem. Fin. Execs. Inst. Republican. Episcopalian. Clubs: Merion Cricket, Merion Golf, Corinthian Yacht (trustee 1992-94, chmn. mem. com. 1995—), Gulf Stream Bath and Tennis.

RORER, LEONARD GEORGE, psychologist, writer; b. Dixon, Ill., Dec. 24, 1932; s. Leonard Gleason and Marion Emma (Geyer) R.; m. Gail Evans, Apr. 30, 1958 (div. May 11, 1964); children: Liat, Eric Evans; m. Nancy McKimens, Jan. 9, 1969 (div. Jan. 19, 1976); 1 child, Mya Noelani. BA, Swarthmore Coll., 1954; PhD, U. Minn., 1963 . Rsch. assoc., then assoc. dir. Oreg. Rsch. Inst., Eugene, 1963-75; prof. psychology Miami U., Oxford, Ohio, 1975-93, dir. clin. psychology tng. program, 1976-86; pres. Oreg. Psychol. Assn., 1973-75. NIMH spl. rsch. fellow, 1967-68; fellow Netherlands Inst. Advanced Study, 1971-72; postdoctoral fellow Inst. for Rational-Emotive Therapy, 1982-83. Fellow APA (coun. reps. 1968-72), Am. Psychol. Soc. (charter), We. Psychol. Assn.; mem. Midwestern Psychol. Assn., Assn. Advancement Behavior Therapy, Soc. Multivariate Exptl. Psychology. Author articles in field, mem. editorial bds. profl. jours. Home: 116 Adobe St Santa Cruz CA 95060-3721

RORKE, LUCY BALIAN, neuropathologist; b. St. Paul, June 22, 1929; d. Aram Haji and Karzouhy (Ousdigian) Balian; m. Robert Radcliffe Rorke,

June 4, 1960. A.B., U. Minn., 1951, M.A., 1952, B.S., 1955, M.D., 1957. Diplomate Am. Bd. Pathology. Intern Phila. Gen. Hosp., 1957-58, resident anat. pathology and neuropathology, 1958-62, asst. neuropathologist, 1963-67, chief pediat. pathologist, 1967-68, chief neuropathologist, 1968-69, chmn. dept. anat. pathology and chief neuropathologist, 1969-73, chmn. dept. pathology, 1973-77, pres. med. staff, 1973-75; practice medicine specializing in neuropathology Phila., 1962—; neuropathologist Children's Hosp., Phila., 1965—, pres. med. staff, 1986-88, acting pathologist-in-chief, 1995—; cons. neuropathologist Wyeth Rsch. Labs., Radnor, Pa., 1961-87, Wistar Inst. Anatomy and Biology, Phila., 1967-93; assoc. prof. pathology U. Pa. Sch. Medicine, Phila., 1970-73, prof., 1973—, clin. prof. neurology, 1979—; forensic neuropathologist Office of Med. Examiner, Phila., 1977—. Author: Myelinization of the Brain in the Newborn, 1969, Pathology of Perinatal Brain Injury, 1982; mem. editl. bd. Jours. Neuropathology Exptl. Neurology, 1980-85, 93—, Pediatric neurosurgery, 1984—, Child's Nervous System, 1984-88, Brain pathology, 1990-95; contbr. articles to profl. jours. NIH fellow in neuropathology, 1961-62; NIH grantee for study of neonatal brain, 1963-68. Fellow Coll. Am. Pathologists; mem. Phila. Gen. Hosp. Med. Staff (pres. 1973-75), Phila. Neurol. Soc. (v.p. 1971-72, editor Transactions 1973, pres. 1975-76), Am. Assn. Neuropathologists (exec. council 1976-85, v.p. 1979-80, pres. 1981-82), Am. Neurol. Assn., AMA, Burlington County Med. Soc., Phila. Coll. Physicians. Home: 120 Chestnut St Moorestown NJ 08057-2937 Office: Children's Hosp of Philadelphia 324 S 34th St Philadelphia PA 19104-4301

ROS, PABLO RIERA, physician, radiologist; b. Barcelona, Spain, May 4, 1955; came to U.S., 1980; s. Juan Nicolau and Maria Mercedes (Riera) R.; m. Ana Mara Viamonte, Dec. 2, 1982; children: Pablo Manuel, Cristina Mercedes. MD, U. Autonoma de Barcelona, 1978. Resident in diagnostic radiology Mt. Sinai Med. Ctr./U. Miami, Miami Beach, Fla., 1980-83, fellow in diagnostic imaging, 1983-84; asst. prof. radiology U. Miami, 1984-85; chief gastrointestinal radiology Armed Forces Inst. Pathology, Washington, 1984-87; asst. prof. radiology Uniformed Svcs. U. Health Scis., Bethesda, Md., 1985-87; assoc. prof. radiology U. Fla., Gainesville, 1987-90, prof., 1990—, dir. divsn. body imaging, 1987—, assoc. chmn. radiology, 1994—; advisor in health Barcelona Organizing Olympic Com., 1988-92; advisor in radiology Pan Am. Devel. Found., Washington, 1984-88; vis. prof. Armed Forces Inst. Pathology, 1987—, Harvard U., Boston, 1996. Author, editor: Abdominal Magnetic Resonance, 1993; contbr. articles to profl. jours.; patentee in field. Asst. scoutmaster Boy Scouts Am., Gainesville, 1995; lithurgy min. Queen of Peace Cath. Ch., Gainesville, 1990. Fellow Am. Coll. Radiology; mem. Radiol. Soc. N.Am. (program com. 1992-96), Am. Roentgen Ray Soc., Soc. Gastroenterol. Radiologists (program com. 1993, 95-96, Rsch. award 1990, Traveling Professorship award 1992), Soc. Computed Body Tomography and Magnetic Resonance (credentials com. 1996). Roman Catholic. Office: U Fla Dept Radiology 1600 SW Archer Rd Gainesville FL 32610

ROSA, DEBORAH MARIA, surgeon; b. Ft. Campbell, Ky., Aug. 22, 1955; d. August and Bernice (Wheeler) R.; m. John Jacob Flanagan, Jr., June 1, 1991; children: Lauren Ashley, Brandon Scott. BSN, U. Tenn., Chattanooga, 1977; MD, Med. Coll. Pa., 1991. Diplomate Am. Bd. Surgery. Intern U. Med. and Dentistry of N.J., Newark, 1985-91; surgical residency U. Medicine and Dentistry of N.J., Newark, 1986-91; surgeon, lectr. Phoenixville (Pa.) Hosp., 1991—; pvt. practice Phoenixville, 1991—. Fellow ACS; mem. AMA, Assn. Women Surgeons, Soc. Am. Gastrointestinal Endoscopic Surgeons, Pa. Med. Assn. Roman Catholic. Office: Valley Forge Surg Assn 750 S Main St Ste 300 Phoenixville PA 19460

ROSADO, RODOLFO JOSE, psychologist, educator; b. N.Y.C., Jan. 9, 1959; s. Rodolfo Jose and Maria (Gonzalez) R.; m. Ruth Laura Morrison, June 11, 1982; children: Emily Hope, Adam Philip. BS in Psychology, Fordham U., Bronx, N.Y., 1979, MA in Clin. Psychology, 1986, PhD in Clin. Psychology, 1992. Lic. psychologist, N.Y., Conn. Psychology tng. fellow N.Y. Med. Coll., Valhalla, 1979-81; clin. psychology intern Hall-Brooke Hosp., Westport, Conn., 1982-83; therapist Child Guidance Ctr., Bridgeport, Conn., 1983-85, office coord., 1985-90, program dir., 1990-93; asst. prof. Fairfield (Conn.) U., 1993—, program dir. coll. access, 1995—; IRG profl. reviewer USPHS, Rockville, Md., 1990-95; regional adv. com. Dept. Children & Families, Bridgeport, 1995—; oversight collaborative Bridgeport Futures, 1994-95; faculty co-sponsor SALSA Hispanic Students Assn.,Fairfield U., 1995—. Author, moderator TV show Conversation in Edn., 1994; co-author proposal Empowerment Zone Grant, 1994; author proposal Comprehensive Child & Adolescent Svc., 1993. Mem. Youth Svc. Bur., City of Bridgeport, 1991-93; family preservation initiative Conn. Dept. Children& Families, Bridgeport, 1995—. Recipient N.Y. Regents scholarship, 1975-79, scholarship Fordham U., Bronx, 1975-79, Appreciation award for collaborative support State of Conn. Dept. Children & Families, 1995. Mem. APA, Hispanic Assn. Mental Health and Allied Professions (exec. com., treas. 1988-92), Conn. Coalition for Children of Alcoholics (steering com. 1986-87), Sigma Xi. Office: Fairfield U Grad Sch Edn and Allied Professions N Benson Rd Fairfield CT 06430

ROSAL, MARCIA LUISA, art therapy educator, art therapist; b. Pitts., Apr. 14, 1951; d. Enrique Rafael and Ellie (Monfredo) R. BS, Pa. State U., 1973; MA, U. Louisville, 1977; PhD, U. Queensland, Australia, 1986. Art therapist E. La. State Hosp., Jackson, 1977-78, Tulane U., New Orleans, 1978-79; asst. prof. Buffalo (N.Y.) State Coll., 1979-81; art therapist East Baton Rouge Sch. Dist., 1981-83; rsch. scholar U. Queensland, 1983-85; asst. prof. U. Louisville, 1985-91, assoc. prof., 1991—; adj. prof. Vt. Coll. Norwich, 1987-89, Fla. State U., Tallahassee, 1989-90. Contbr.: Art for All the Children, 1990; contbr. articles to profl. jours. Chmn. Louisville Network in Solidarity with the People of Guatemala, 1987—; mem. com. in solidarity with the People Cen. Am., Louisville, 1988—. Mem. Internat. Assn. Imagery, Am. Art Therapy Assn. (chmn. honors com. 1985-87, edn. and tng. bd. mem. 1988—), Australian Nat. Art Therapy Assn., Kentuckiana Expressive Art Therapy Assn., Coun. for Exceptional Children.

ROSALES, OSCAR R., cardiologist; b. Barranquilla, Colombia, Mar. 17, 1959; s. Oscar and Grace (Cepeda) R.; m. Marguerite F. Miranne, Jan. 11, 1960; children: Andrew Daniel, Sophie Marguerite. MD, Javeriana U., 1983. Diplomate Am. Bd. Internal Medicine. Intern, chief med. resident Tulane U., New Orleans, 1984-88; fellow in cardiology Yale U., New Haven, 1988-91; fellow in interventional cardiology U. Tex., Houston, 1991-92; asst. prof. medicine Yale U., 1993-96; dir. critical care quality assurance program West Haven VA Med. Ctr., 1993-96; dir. coronary care unit Ochsner Clinic, New Orleans, 1996—. Author: Hemodynamic Forces and Vascular Cell Biology, 1993. Fellow Am. Coll. Cardiology; mem. Am. Fedn. Clin. Rsch., Am. Heart Assn. Roman Catholic. Office: Oschner Clinic 1516 Jefferson Hwy New Orleans LA 70121

ROSALES, SUZANNE MARIE, hospital coordinator; b. Merced, Calif., July 23, 1946; d. Walter Marshall and Ellen Marie (Earl) Potter; children: Anita Carol, Michelle Suzanne. AA, City Coll., San Francisco, 1966. Diplomate Am. Coll. Utilization Review Physicians. Utilization review coord. San Francisco Gen. Hosp., 1967-74; mgr. utilization review/discharge planning UCLA Hosp. and Clinics, 1974-79; nurse III Hawaii State Hosp., Kaneohe, 1979-80; review coord. Pacific Profl. Std. Review Orgn., Honolulu, 1980-81; coord. admission and utilization reviewq The Rehab. Hosp. of the Pacific, Honolulu, 1981-85; coord. Pacific Med. Referral Project, Honolulu, 1985-87; dir. profl. svcs. The Queen's Healthcare Plan, Honolulu, 1987-88; utilization mgmt. coord. Vista Psychiat. Physician Assocs., San Diego, 1989; admission coord. utilization review San Francisco Gen. Hosp., 1989-91, quality improvement coordinator, 1991—; cons. Am. Med. Records Assn. Contbr. articles to profl. jours. Mem. Nat. Assn. Utilization Review Profls. Home: 505 Hanover St Daly City CA 94014-1351 Office: San Francisco Gen Hosp 1001 Potrero Ave San Francisco CA 94110-3518

ROSARIO-GUARDIOLA, REINALDO, dermatologist; b. Santurce, P.R., Sept. 17, 1948; s. Tomas and Aurea (Guardiola) Rosario; m. Fe Milagros Rivera, Aug. 19, 1972; children: Amarillis, Reinaldo, Gadiel. BS, U. P.R., 1968, MD, 1972. Rsch. fellow photobiology Harvard Med. Sch., Boston, 1976-77; asst. prof. U. P.R. Sch. of Medicine, Rio Piedras, 1979—; chief, dermatology sect. San Juan VA Hosp., Rio Piedras, 1979—. Bd. dirs. Wesleyan Acad. Guaynabo, P.R., 1990—. Grantee Dermatology Found., 1978. Fellow Am. Acad. Dermatology; mem. P.R. Dermatol. Soc. (pres. scientific com. 1978-79), Harvard-MGH House Officers Club, Alpha Omega Alpha. Office: El Monte Mall Ste 33A San Juan PR 00918

ROSATI, SHARON WETMORE, social worker; b. Montpelier, Vt., Feb. 19, 1963; d. Duane Paul and Ann Jeannette (Hoadley) Wetmore; m. Paul David Rosati, Sept. 19, 1986. AS with honors, Suny, Delhi, 1983; BS cum laude, Suny, Brockport, 1985; MSW, U. Buffalo, 1993. Sociotherapist, asst. supr., social worker Hillside Children's Ctr., Rochester, N.Y., 1985—. Mem. NASW, Assn. Child Care Workers. Home: 24 Portage St Rochester NY 14621-4212 Office: Hillside Childrens Ctr 1183 Monroe Ave Rochester NY 14620-1662

ROSBROW-REICH, SUSAN R., psychologist; b. Wilmington, Del., Apr. 1, 1946; d. James Manuel and Miriam Faith (Berger) Rosbrow; m. Kenneth I. Reich; children: Elizabeth, Jennifer. BA cum laude, U. Pa., 1968; MS, Columbia U., 1970; PhD, Adelphi U., 1974; grad., Psychoanalytic Inst. New Eng. Lic. psychologist, Mass. Dir. Ednl. Program on Drugs, New Hyde Park, N.Y., 1972-73; family therapist therapeutic instrn. ctr. Bronx State Hosp., Albert Einstein Med. Coll., N.Y., 1972-73; intern in clin. psychology Harvard U. Health Svcs. Ctr./Cambridge (Mass.) Guidance Ctr., 1973-74; psychologist Chelsea Clinc, Erich Lindemann Mental Health Ctr., Boston, 1974-75; asst. in psychology Dept. Psychiatry Mass. Gen. Hosp., Boston, 1975-77; cons. psychologist Harvard U. Health Svcs., Cambridge, 1976—; pvt. practice Cambridge, 1974-81, Belmont, Mass., 1981—; cons. supr. Harvard U. Health Svcs., Cambridge, 1976—, Mass. Gen. Hosp., Boston, 1988-91; cons. psychologist Women's Counseling and Resource Ctr., Cambridge, 1974-75; advising faculty Mass. Inst. Psychoanalysis, 1991—; mem. faculty Psychoanalytic Inst. of New Eng., East, 1993—. cons. psychologist Women's Counseling and Resource Ctr., Cambridge, 1974-75. Bela Williams scholarship U. Pa., 1964-68. Fellow Mass. Psychol. Assn.; mem. Am. Psychol. Assn., Am. Psychoanalytic Assn., Internat. Psychoanalytic Assn., Mass. Assn. for Psychoanalytic Psychology, Nat. Register Health Care Providers in Psychology.

ROSCH, PAUL JOHN, physician, educator; b. Yonkers, N.Y., June 30, 1927; s. Samuel Joseph and Mary (Gang) R.; m. Lorraine Marie Hunt, June 27, 1951; children: David Carl, Jonathan Hunt, Jane Ellen, Michael Edward, Richard Joseph, Donna Marie; m. Marguerite Delamater, Sept. 12, 1972. AB, Brown U., NYU, 1948; MA, NYU, 1950; MD, Albany Med. Coll., 1954. Diplomate Am. Bd. Internal Medicine. Fellow Inst. Exptl. Medicine and Surgery, U. Montreal, Que., Can., 1951-52; intern, asst. resident in medicine Johns Hopkins Hosp., 1954-56; resident in medicine, then chief dept. metabolism Walter Reed Med. Ctr., 1956-58; physician-in-charge nuclear medicine St. John's Riverside Hosp., Yonkers, 1959-67, dir. endocrine clinic, sr. attending physician, 1959-96, vice chief of staff, 1977; chief endocrine clinic St. Joseph's Hosp., 1959, sr. cons. in medicine, 1980—; pres. Am. Inst. Stress, Yonkers, 1978—, sr. cons. in medicine, 1980—; clin. prof. medicine and psychiatry N.Y. Med. Coll., 1980—; asst. clin. prof. medicine Mt. Sinai Hosp. Sch. Medicine, 1963-67; former adj. prof. medicine in psychiatry U. Md. Sch. Medicine. From asst. to assoc. editor Health Comm. and Informatics; editor-in-chief Stress Medicine, 1990—; mem. editorial bd. AMA Archives Internal Medicine, Folia Clinica Internat, Jour. Human Stress, Internat. Jour. Psychosomatics, Am. Jour. Health Promotion, Cardiovascular Revs. & Reports, Internat. Jour. Stress Mgmt., Comprehensive Therapy, Jour. Human Behavior; contbg. editor Creative Living; contbr. articles to profl. jours. Bd. govs. Jewish Community Ctr.; bd. dirs. Family Svc. Soc., Mensana Clinic, 1980—; chmn. bd. Internat. Found. Biosocial Devel. and Human Health, 1980—; mem. adv. bd. Image Inst., 1980—. Capt. AUS, 1956-58. Fellow ACP, Internat. Stress Mgmt. Assn. (hon. v.p. 1991—), Am. Coll. Cardiology, Internat. Acad. Medicine, Am. Coll. Angiology, N.Y. Diabetes Assn.; mem. Westchester Diabetes Assn. (pres. 1968), Internat. Law Enforcement Stress Assn. (adv. bd. 1980—), Yonkers Acad. Medicine (bd. govs., pres. 1971), N.Y. Cardiology Soc., Acad. Psychosomatic Medicine, Soc. Behavioral Medicine, N.Y. Acad. Scis., Endocrine Soc., Am. Diabetes Assn., Westchester Soc. Internat. Medicine (past pres.), Stress Mgmt. Assn. (hon. v.p.), N.Y. State Soc. Internal Medicine (pres. 1974), Soc. Nuclear Medicine (bd. dirs.), Am. Fedn. Clin. Rsch., Am. Soc. Internal Medicine, Am. Geriatrics Soc., Elmwood Country Club, Atlantis Golf Club, Breakers Golf Club, St. Andrews Golf Club, La Coquille Club (Palm Beach, Fla.). Home: 10 Old Jackson Ave Hastings On Hudson NY 10706 also: 221 N Country Club Dr Atlantis FL 33462-1113

ROSE, BEVERLY ANNE, pharmacist; b. Lewiston, Idaho, June 11, 1950; d. Burton Roswell and Nell Dora (Greenburg) Stein; m. Fred Joseph Rose, July 21, 1973 (div. Aug. 1980). BS in Pharmacy, Ohio No. U., 1973; MBA, Cleve. State U., 1987. Registered pharmacist, Ohio, N.Y. Staff pharmacist Lorain (Ohio) Community Hosp., 1973-79, dir. pharmacy, 1979-91; dir. dept. pharmacy svcs. The House of the Good Samaritan Health Care Complex, Watertown, N.Y., 1991-93; adj. faculty, clin. tng. specialist U. Toledo Coll. Pharmacy, 1980-91; computer cons. Hosp. Pharmacy Network; mem. State Bd. Legis. Rule Rev., Ohio State Bd. Pharmacy, 1987, 88; mem. pres. adv. bd. Ohio No. U., Ada, 1990—. Mem. editl. bd. Aspen Publs., 1992—. Mem. Am. Soc. Health Sys. Pharmacists (apptd. coun. legal and pub. affairs 1988-89, 89-90, state del. ho. of dels. Ohio 1984, 85, 86, 87, 88, 89, mem. psychotherapeutics-spl. practice group 1990—), Adminstrs. Practice Mgmt. Group, Am. Pharm. Assn., Ohio Soc. Hosp. Pharmacists (pres. 1985-89, Squibb Leadership award 1988, Ciba-Geigy Svc. award 1988, Evlyn Gray Scott award 1987), N.Y. State Coun. Hosp. Pharmacists, Am. Soc. Parenteral and Enteral Nutrition, Fedn. Internat. Pharmaceutique, N.Y. Chpt. Am. Coll. Clin. Pharmacy, others. Home: 20 Cambridge Dr Apt 4 Georgetown OH 45121-9746

ROSE, CHERYL ROMPREY, counseling psychologist; b. Laconia, N.H., Nov. 15, 1949; d. Thomas Adrian Romprey and Vera Irene (Swift) Curry; m. Clinton Richard Rose, Nov. 27, 1981; children: Cydney Ryanne, Chandler Randall. BS, Plymouth State Coll., 1971; MEd, Wayne State U., 1974; PhD, Brigham Young U., 1981. Lic. profl. counselor, Ala. Treatment adminstr. Odyssey House, Salt Lake City, 1975-76; dir. counseling and guidance Jordan Sch. Dist., Copperton, Utah, 1976-81; counselor Family Counseling Ctr., Mobile, Ala., 1982—; counselor Lyons Park Evaluation and Counseling Ctr., Mobile, Ala., 1983-84; supr. practice and grad. students U. South Ala., Auburn, 1983—, instr. edn. svc., 1985—; staff mem. Doctors Hosp., Mobile, 1990; bd. dirs. Child Study Ctr., 1990—, Epilepsy Found. Contbr. articles to profl. jours. Trainer, instr. Contact Mobile, 1985—; presentor Barton Acad.-Mobile Sch. Dist., 1984; pres. Community Health Fairs, Mobile, 1982—; group leader Community Activities Workshop, Mobile, 1982—. Bd. dirs. Epilepsy Found., 1992—. Capt. U.S. Army, 1971-74. Decorated Army Commendation medal; Lakes Region scholar, 1967. Mem. Am. Psychol. Assn., Mobile Assn. Psychologists. Democrat. Roman Catholic. Clubs: New Mobilians, St. Andrews County. Avocations: golf, creative writing, sports. Home: 105 Claridge Rd E Mobile AL 36608-1754 Office: Family Counseling Ctr 705 Oak Circle Dr Mobile AL 36609

ROSE, DAVID ALAN, psychologist, management consultant; b. N.Y.C., Mar. 9, 1949; s. Alfred and Mildred (Rothfeld) R.; m. Patricia Huff; children: Alexandra, Jordan. BA, Rutgers U., 1972; MA, Fairleigh Dickinson U., 1975; PhD, Vanderbilt U., 1984. Dir. planning & evaluation Multicounty Comprehensive Mental Health Ctr., Tullahoma, Tenn., 1977-80; corp. psychologist DeMann Ltd., Mpls., 1984-86, RHR Internat., Phila., 1986-90; dir. clin. svcs. Greenleaf Outpatient Svcs., Chattanooga, 1990-94; corporate/ family bus. cons. Rose & Assocs., 1990—; pvt. practice Chattanooga, 1992—. Bd. dirs. AIM Ctr. Fellow Fairleigh Dickinson U., 1973-75; NIMH grantee Vanderbilt U., 1975-77. Mem. APA, Family Firm Inst., Chattanooga Area Psychol. Assn. Jewish. Home: 6 Highdown Ct Signal Mountain TN 37377-3120 Office: 7405 Shallowford Rd # 160 Chattanooga TN 37421-2662

ROSE, EDWARD LEE, JR., dentist; b. Birmingham, Ala., Mar. 16, 1934; s. Edward Lee Sr. and Margaret Hooker (Brown) R.; m. Mitzi Carol Fisher, Aug. 19, 1955; children: Rachel Lee, Edward Lee III. BS, Auburn U., 1957; DMD, U. Ala., 1961. Pvt. practice restorative dentistry Vero Beach, Fla., 1962-88; ptnr. Ocean Oaks Dental Group, Vero Beach, 1988—. Past pres. So. Acad. Clin. Nutrition; past pres., bd. dirs. Beach Bus. Bur.; past co-chmn. beautification com. Indian River C. of C. Capt. USAF NG. Fellow Acad. Dental Materials, Am. Soc. Clin. Hypnosis; mem. ADA, Fla. Acad. Dental Practice Adminstrn. (past pres.), Tri-County Dental Soc. (1st pres., past chmn. dental study club), Atlantic Coast Dist. Dental Soc., Fla. Dental Assn. (past trustee), Fla. Soc. Clin. Hypnosis (past pres.), Am. Equilibration Soc. (past pres.), Fla. Prosthodontic Group, Southeastern Acad. Prosthodontics, Indian River Dental Rsch. Clinic (treas., past chmn. crown and bridge sect.), Clan Rose Soc. Am. (life), Vero Beach Country Club. Republican. Office: Ocean Oaks Dental Group 979 Flamevine Ln Vero Beach FL 32963

ROSE, ERIC ALLEN, cardiac surgeon, organ transplant research scientist, educator; b. Bronx, N.Y., Jan. 25, 1951; s. Herb and Myra (Morgenstern) R.; m. Ellise Delphin; children: Adam, Sydney, Zachary, Gabriel. BA summa cum laude, Columbia Coll., 1971; MD, Columbia U., 1975. Diplomate Am. Bd. Surgery, Am. Bd. Thoracic Surgery. Intern in surgery Presbyn. Hosp., N.Y.C., 1975-76, resident in surgery, 1976-79, resident thoracic surgery, 1980-81; NIH Surg. Rsch. fellow Columbia U., N.Y.C., 1977; asst. prof. surgery Coll. Physicians and Surgeons, Columbia U., 1982-88, assoc. prof., 1988-93, prof. surgery, 1993—; dir. cardiac transplantation svc. Columbia Presbyn. Med. Ctr., 1982-93, dir. surg. cardiac intensive care unit, 1982-86, dir. clin. perfusion svc., 1986-95, dir. cardiothoracic surg. svc., 1990-96, asst. attending surgeon Presbyn. Hosp., 1982-88, assoc. attending surgeon, 1982-93, attending surgeon, 1993—, chmn. dept. surgery, 1994—; bd. dirs. N.Y. Regional Transplant Program; mem. com. on heart transplantation United Network for Organ Sharing. Mem. editorial bd. Jour. Heart Transplantation, 1982-86, Jour. Thoracic Cardiovascular Surgery, 1993—; author numerous articles and book chpts.; patentee in field. NIH grantee, 1987. Fellow ACS, Am. Coll. Cardiology; mem. AMA, Am. Assn. Thoracic Surgery, Soc. Thoracic Surgery, N.Y. Soc. Thoracic Surgery, Am. Soc. Transplant Surgeons (com. on heart transplantation), Soc. Univ. Surgeons, Am. Heart Assn. (exec. com. of coun. cardiovascular surgery), Internat. Soc. for Lung Heart Transplantation (bd. councillors 1990—, pres. 1993), N.Y. County Med. Soc., N.Y. Heart Assn., Phi Beta Kappa, Alpha Omega Alpha. Home: 96 Oxford Dr Tenafly NJ 07670-3114 Office: Columbia U 622 W 168th St New York NY 10032-3702

ROSE, FRANK CLIFFORD, neurologist, medical facility administrator, consultant; b. London, Aug. 29, 1926; m. Angela Juliet Halsted, Sept. 16, 1963; children—Sebastian, Jolyon, Fabian. M.B.B.S., Westminster Med., London, 1949. Resident med. officer Nat. Hosp., London, 1957-60; sr. registrar St. George's Hosp., London, 1961-65; cons. neurologist St. Thomas Hosp., London, 1963-85; cons. neurologist Charing Cross Hosp., London, 1965-91; dir. acad. unit neurosci. Charing Cross Hosp. and Westminster Med. Sch., 1985-91; dir. London Neurol. Ctr., 1991—; prin. med. officer Allied Dunbar Assurance Co., London, 1970-96 ; trustee Migraine Trust, London, 1980-95 , chmn., 1989-95. Author: Basic Neurology of Speech, 3d edit., 1983; Hypoglycaemia, 2d edit., 1982. Editor: Migraine: Clinical and Research Advances, 1985; Modern Approaches to the Dementias, 2 vols., 1985. Chmn. sci. adv. com. Internat. Als. MND Research Found., 1987-90—, Assn. for Research into Multiple Sclerosis, 1987-90. Recipient Harold Wolff award Am. Assn. for Study of Headache, 1981, 84, also Disting. Clinician award, 1986. Fellow Royal Coll. Physicians (councillor 1985-88), Med. Soc. London (pres. 1983-84, treas. 1984-89—), Assn. Brit. Neurologists (council 1984-86); mem. Assurance Med. Soc. (pres. 1983-85), World Fedn. Neurology (chmn. migraine research group 1975-95, sec.-treas. gen. 1989—), chmn. history of neuroscis. research group 1980—). Clubs: Savile, Royal Soc. Medicine (London). Avocations: travel; reading.

ROSE, GILBERT JACOB, psychiatrist, writer, psychoanalyst; b. Malden, Mass., May 9, 1923; s. M. Edward and Sara (Freedman) R.; m. Anne Kaufman, Mar. 10, 1946; children: Renee Rose Shield, Daniel Asa, Cecily Rose Itkoff, Aron Dana. AB, Harvard U., 1944; MD, Boston U., 1947. Diplomate Am. Bd. Psychiatry and Neurology. Asst. clin. prof. psychiatry Med. Sch. Yale U., New Haven, 1961-67; assoc. clin. prof. psychiatry Yale U. Med. Sch., New Haven, 1967-83, lectr. in psychiatry Med. Sch., 1983-87; instr. Western New Eng. Psychoanalytic Inst., New Haven, 1970-76; pvt. practice Rowayton, Conn., 1955—. Author: Power of Form: A Psychoanalytic Approach to Aesthetic Form, 1980, expanded edit., 1992, Trauma & Mastery in Life & Art, 1987, expanded edit., 1996, Necessary Illusion: Art as Witness, 1996. Capt. USAF, 1953-55. Fellow Am. Psychiat. Assn. (life), Am. Coll. Psychoanalysts; mem. Am. Psychoanalytic Assn. (life), Yale U. Muriel Gardiner Program for Psychoanalysis and the Humanities. Home and Office: PO Box 215 Norwalk CT 06853-0215

ROSE, NOEL RICHARD, immunologist, microbiologist, educator; b. Stamford, Conn., Dec. 3, 1927; s. Samuel Allison and Helen (Richard) R.; m. Deborah S. Harber, June 14, 1951; children: Alison, David, Bethany, Jonathan. BS, Yale U., 1948; MA, U. Pa., 1949, PhD, 1951; MD, SUNY, Buffalo, 1964; MD (hon.), U. Cagliari, Italy, 1990; ScD (hon.), U. Sassari, Italy, 1992. From instr. to prof. microbiology SUNY Sch. Medicine, Buffalo, 1951-73; dir. Center for Immunology SUNY Sch. Medicine, 1970-73, dir. Erie County Labs., 1964-70; dir. WHO Collaborating Center for Autoimmune Disorders, 1968—; prof. immunology and microbiology, chmn. dept. immunology and microbiology Wayne State U. Sch. Medicine, 1973—82; prof., chmn. dept. immunology and infectious diseases Johns Hopkins U. Sch. Hygiene and Pub. Health, Balt., 1082-93, prof. medicine and environ. health scis., 1982—, prof. molecular microbiology and immunology, 1993—; prof. pathology, dir. immunology Johns Hopkins U. Sch. Medicine, 1994—; cons. in field. Editor: (with others) International Convocation on Immunology, 1969, Methods in Immunodiagnosis, 1973, 3d rev. edit., 1986, The Autoimmune Diseases, 1986, 2d edit., 1992, Microbiology, Basic Principles and Clinical Applications, 1983 Principles of Immunology, 1973, 2d rev. edit., 1979, Specific Receptors of Antibodies, Antigens and Cells, 1973, Manual of Clinical Laboratory Immunology, 1976, 2d rev. edit., 1980, 4d edit. 1992, Genetic Control of Autoimmune Disease, 1978, Recent Advances in Clinical Immunology, 1983, Clinical Immunotoxicology, 1992; editor in chief Clin. Immunology and Immunopathology, 1988—; contbr. articles to profl. jours. Recipient award Sigma Xi, 1952, award Alpha Omega Alpha, 1976, Lamp award, 1975, Faculty Recognition award Wayne State U. Bd. Govs., 1979, Pres.'s award for excellence in teaching, 1979, Disting. Service award Wayne State U. Sch. Medicine, 1982, U. Pisa medal, 1986; named to Acad. Scholars Wayne State U., 1981; Josiah Macy fellow, 1979. Fellow APHA, Am. Acad. Allergy and Immunology, Am. Acad. Microbiology; mem. AAAS, Acad. Clin. Lab. Physicians and Scientists, Am. Assn. Immunologists, Am. Soc. Investigative Pathology, Am. Soc. Clin. Pathologists, Am. Soc. Microbiology (Abbott Lab. Clin. and Diagnostic Immunology award 1993), Brit. Soc. Immunology, Coll. Am. Pathologists, Sociètè Française d'Immunologie, Can. Soc. Immunology, Soc. Exptl. Biology and Medicine Coun., Clin. Immunology Soc. (sec., treas., pres. 1993), Austrian Immunology Soc. (hon. mem.), Sigma Xi (pres. Johns Hopkins U. chpt. 1988), Alpha Omega Alpha, Delta Omega. Office: Johns Hopkins U Sch Hygiene & Pub Health Dept Molecular Microbiology & Immunology 615 N Wolfe St Baltimore MD 21205-2103

ROSE, ROBERT A., surgeon. BS, Queen's Coll., 1942; MD, NYU Sch. Medicine, 1945. Diplomate Am. Bd. Surgery. Intern U.S. Naval Hosp., Corona, Calif., 1945; chief dept. anesthesiology U.S. Naval Hosp., 1947-48; resident in surgery VA Med. Tchg. Group, 1948-52; fellow in cardiovascular surgery Hahnemann Hosp., Phila., 1953; attending pediatric surgery Children's Hosp., 1955; fellow in peripheral vascular surgery L.A. County Hosp., 1955-56. Fellow Am. Coll. Surgeons; mem. Am. Profl. Practice Assn., Am. Soc. Gastro-Intestinal Endoscopy, Am. Soc. Colon-Rectal Surgeons, Assn. Am. Physicians and Surgeons, Bowers Surg. Assn., Hawaii Surgical Assn. (pres. 1962-65, regent 1965-75), Pan-Pacific Surg. Assn. (trustee 1957-75, ad hoc bylaws com. 1962-63, program chmn. 1966, chmn. bd. trustees 1966-69, sec. scientific programs 1969-75, chmn. gen. surg. program com. 1972-76), Royal Soc. Medicine (London), Soc. Grad. Surgeons, Soc. Surgery Alimentary Tract, Am. Cancer Soc. (chmn. Hawaii div. tech. adv. subcom. colorectal task force). Home: PO Box 420332 San Francisco CA 94142-0332

ROSEBAUM, PETER ANDREW, biology educator; b. N.Y.C., Sept. 11, 1952; s. Salo Rosenbaum and Selma (Stein) Cohen; m. Robin Edelstein, Sept. 15, 1979; children: Samantha, Sophia. BS, Tulane U., 1974, MS, 1976, PhD, 1980. Instr. Tulane U., New Orleans, 1979-80; rsch. assoc. La. State U. Med. Ctr., New Orleans, 1980-82, asst. prof., 1982-85; asst. prof. SUNY, Oswego, 1985-91, assoc. prof., 1991—. Contbr. articles to profl. jours. Pres., bd. dirs. Rice Creek Assocs., Oswego, N.Y., 1988-91, v.p., 1987-88,

91—, pres., 1991—. Democrat. Jewish. Home: 250 CR 24 Oswego NY 13126-9230 Office: Biology Dept SUNY-Oswego Oswego NY 13126

ROSEFSKY, JONATHAN BENENSOHN, pediatrician; b. Johnson City, N.Y., June 28, 1939; s. I.J. and Elsie S. Rosefsky; m. Sue Perel, 1964; children: Katherine, Douglas, Matthew. AB, Cornell U., 1960; B in Med. Sc., Dartmouth U., 1962; MD, Harvard U., 1964. Diplomate Am. Bd. of Pediatrics; lic. Pa., Va. Intern in surgery Vanderbilt Univ. Hosp., Nashville, 1964-65; resident in pediatrics Children's Hosp. Med. Ctr., Boston, 1965-67; pediatrician USAF Med. Corps, Langley AFB, Va., 1967-69; dir. neonatal ICU United Health Svcs. Hosp., Johnson City, N.Y., 1969-74; pvt. practice pediatrics Binghamton, N.Y., 1969-86; pres. Notation Systems, Inc., Binghamton, 1981-89; asst. dir. clin. devel. McNeil Consumer Products Co., Ft. Washington, Pa., 1986-89; sr. dir. med. affairs Wyeth-Ayerst Labs., St. David's, Pa., 1990—; cons. in pediatrics, N.Y. State Dept. Social Svcs., Albany, 1976-86, FDA adv. com. on Gen. Hosp. and Personal Use Devices, Rockville, Md., 1986; industry rep. FDA adv. com. on immunology devices, Rockville, 1987-93; asst. prof. pediatrics, Jefferson Med. Sch., Phila., 1987—. Inventor: back wedge, 1981, mole marker, 1982; contbr. articles to profl. jours. Chmn. Citizen's Adv. Com. to Mayor of Binghamton, N.Y., 1971; Captain USAF Med. Corps, 1967-69. Recipient Physician's Recognition award AMA, 1995. Fellow Am. Acad. Pediatrics, Am. Coll. Nutrition, Am. Coll. Physician Execs., Am. Acad. Pharm. Physicians; mem. Harvard Club (N.Y.C.), Green Valley Country Club. Home: 251 W Montgomery Ave Haverford PA 19041

ROSEMBERG, EUGENIA, physician, educator, medical research administrator; b. Buenos Aires, Argentina, Apr. 25, 1918; came to U.S., 1948, naturalized, 1956; d. Pedro and Fanny (Hestrin) R. BS, Liceo Nacional de Senoritas, Buenos Aires, 1936; MD, U. Buenos Aires, 1944. Intern Hosp. Pirovano, Buenos Aires, 1940-41; resident Hosp. Nacional de Clinicas, U. Hosp., U. Buenos Aires, 1941-44, assoc. in pediatrics, 1943-48; instr. in anatomy Hosp. Nacional de Clinicas, U. Hosp., U. Buenos Aires (Med. Sch.), 1940-46, instr. pediatrics, 1946-48; practice medicine specializing in pediatrics, 1946-48; research in endocrinology Balt., 1948-51, Worcester, Mass., 1955—; Mead Johnson fellow dept. endocrinology Johns Hopkins Med. Sch., Balt., 1948-49; vis. scientist Med. Sch., U. Montevideo, Uruguay, 1950; research fellow NIH, Bethesda, Md., 1951-53, Nat. Inst. Arthritis and Metabolic Diseases, 1951-53, Med. Research Inst. and Hosp., Oklahoma City, 1953; mem. staff Worcester Found. Exptl. Biology, Shrewsbury, Mass., 1953-62; research dir. Med. Research Inst. of Worcester, Inc., 1962—; cons. Center for Population Research, Nat. Inst. Child Health and Human Devel., NIH, 1969-70, chief contraceptive devel. br., 1970-71; prof. pediatrics U. Md. Hosp., Balt., 1970-73; prof. medicine U. Mass. Med. Sch., Worcester, 1972—; mem. staff Worcester City Hosp., 1955-85, sec. human experimentation com., 1965-83, chmn., 1984-85, dir. clin. research, 1972-85; Sec. subcom. on gonadotropins Nat. Hormone and Pituitary Program, Nat. Inst. Arthritis, Diabetes, Digestive and Kidney Diseases, 1965-69, chmn., 1969-85, mem. med. adv. bd., 1969-72, 73-85, sec. subcom. on standards endocrinology study sect., 1968. Author: Gonadotropins, 1968, (with C.A. Paulsen) The Human Testis, 1970, Gonadotropin Therapy in Female Infertility, 1973, (with C. Gual) Hypothalamic Hypophysiotropic Hormones—Physiological and Clinical Studies, 1973; Mem. editorial bd.: Giner, 1970—, Procs. 1st Ann. Meeting Am. Soc. Andrology, supplement, Vol. 8, 1976, Andrologia, 1978—, Jour. Andrology, 1979-82, Internat. Jour. Andrology, 1978—; assoc. editor: Reproduccion, 1970—, Andrologia jour, 1974-77; Contbr. articles and book chpts. on research in endocrinology to med. texts and jours.; Translator: from Spanish Diagnosis and Treatment of Endocrine Disorders in Childhood and Adolescence (L. Wilkins). Patentee in field, U.S., Can., Europe. Fellow AAAS; mem. Am. Med. Women's Assn., Endocrine Soc. U.S. (mem. com. pub. affairs 1971, v.p. 1975-76), Soc. for Research in Biology of Reproduction, Soc. for Study of Reproduction, Am. Fertility Soc., Peru Fertility Soc. (fgn. corr.), N.Y. Acad. Scis., New Eng. Cardiovascular Soc., Am., Mass. heart assns., Argentine Endocrine Soc., Argentine Pediatric Soc., Sociedad Argentine Para El Estudio de la Esterilidad., Pan Am. Med. Women's Alliance, Am. Soc. Andrology (program chmn. 1975-76, exec. council 1976-78, chmn. publ. com. 1975-80, Disting. Andrologist award 1982), Internat. Com. for Study Andrology (exec. council 1976-79).

ROSEMBLAT, ALDO MARIO, neurosurgeon; b. Buenos Aires, Argentina, Mar. 30, 1948. MD, U. Buenos Aires, 1973. Diplomate Am. Bd. Neurol. Surgery. Postdoctoral tng. Hosp. Base de Avellaneda, Buenos Aires, 1973-76; intern Union Meml. Hosp., Balt., 1976-77; resident, chief resident Georgetown U. Hosp., Washington, 1977-82; pvt. practice as neurosurgeon Falls Church, Va., 1982—; forensic examiner, Falls Church, 1996—. Author: Clinic-Pathological Corr. in the Tumors of Lateral Ventricles, 1973; contbr. articles to profl. jours. Fellow Am. Acad. Disability Evaluating Physicians. Jewish. Office: 6316 Castle Pl # 200 Falls Church VA 22044

ROSEN, ARTHUR DAVID, neurology educator; b. Bklyn., Sept. 19, 1935; s. Elihu and Gertrude (Simonson) R.; children: Jody L., Matthew S. BA, Columbia U., 1956; MD, SUNY, Bklyn., 1960. Diplomate Am. Bd. Psychiatry and Neurology. Intern Bklyn. Jewish Hosp., 1960-61; fellow in neurophysiology SUNY, Bklyn., 1961-62; resident in neurology Kings County Hosp., Bklyn., 1962-64; asst. prof. medicine SUNY, Bklyn., 1966-73; assoc. prof. neurology SUNY, Stony Brook, 1973-80, prof. neurology, 1980—; NIH/NRSA fellow in neurobiology, 1993-94; mem. adv. bd. Nat. Amyotrophic Lateral Sclerosis Soc., 1974—. Contbr. articles to Jour. Neurophys., Exptl. Neurology, Jour. Neurol. Sci., Am. Jour. Physiology. Lt. comdr. USNR, 1964-66. Grantee NINDB, 1971, NIH, 1973, VA, 1974, 77, Haemoneties Inst., 1985, KROC Found., 1985. Fellow Am. Acad. Neurology; mem. Am. Neurol. Assn., Am. Epilepsy Soc., Bioelectromagnetics Soc., Sigma Xi. Office: SUNY Dept Neurology Stony Brook NY 11794-8121

ROSEN, BERNARD, psychologist, consultant; b. N.Y.C., Feb. 16, 1934; s. Samuel and Lillian Pearl (Bloom) R.; m. Elizabeth Catherine Flynn, Aug. 18, 1963; children: Delores Judith, Sara-Ann. BA in psychology, Bklyn. Coll., 1961; MA in psychology, Columbia U., 1966; PhD in psychology, Hofstra U., 1979. Rsch. psychologist Kings County Hosp. Ctr., Bklyn., 1960-66, rsch. assoc., 1975-77; rsch. assoc. L.I. Jewish - Hillside Med. Ctr., Glen Oaks, N.Y., 1967-77; cons. Kings County Hosp. Ctr., Bklyn., 1977-82; dir. program evaluation Kingsboro Psychiat. Ctr., Bklyn., 1982-91, acting dir. quality assurance, 1987-88, facility info. coord., 1987-91; dir. program evaluation Creedmoor Psychiat. Ctr., Queens Village, N.Y., 1991-96; dir. program evaluation Central Islip (N.Y.) Psychiat. Ctr., 1977-82; clin. asst. prof. SUNY Downstate Med. Ctr., Bklyn., 1975-77; lectr. Adelphi U., Garden City, N.Y., 1970-75; cons. League Sch. for Seriously Disturbed Children, N.Y.C., 1967-77; co-project dir. Med. and Health Rsch. Assn., N.Y.C., 1964-66. Contbr. articles to profl. jours. Home: 51 S Oxford St Brooklyn NY 11217-1304 : Queens Vlg NY 11427-2147

ROSEN, BERTRAM HOWARD, psychiatrist; b. N.Y.C., Mar. 16, 1933; s. Morris and Tillie (Roseman) R. AB, Cornell U., 1954; MD, Chgo. Med. Sch., 1958. Asst. resident in psychiatry Mt. Sinai Hosp., N.Y.C., 1959-60; resident in adolescent psychiatry Hillside Hosp., Glen Oaks, N.Y., 1960-61; resident in adult psychiatry Hillside Hosp., 1961-62, staff psychiatrist, 1962-65; staff psychiatrist Riverside Hosp., Bronx, 1962-64; attending psychiatrist Mt. Sinai Hosp., N.Y.C., 1962—; sr. instr. Mt. Sinai Med. Sch., 1969—; staff psychiatrist N.Y.C. Bd. Edn., 1964—; chair Forum for the Psychoanalytic Study of Film, N.Y. Group, 1990—; bd. dirs. Nat. Forum for the Psychoanalytic Study of Film. Comdr. USN, 1967-69. Fellow N.Y. Acad. Medicine; mem. Am. Psychiat. Assn., Soc. for Adolescent Psychiatry (bd. dirs. 1987—, sec. 1990-93, chair Forum for the Psychoanalytic Study 1990-94, bd. dirs. Forum for the Psychoanalytic Study of Film 1994, co-chair AP Group for Applied Psychoanalysis 1991—), N.Y. Soc. for Adolescent Psychiatry (sec. 1991-93, v.p. 1993-94, pres. 1994-96), Med. Soc. N.Y. Office: 4 E 95th St New York NY 10128-0705

ROSEN, ELLEN FREDA, psychologist, educator; b. Chgo., Jan. 28, 1941; d. Samuel Aaron and Clara Laura (Pauker) R. BA, Carleton Coll., 1962; MA, U. Ill., 1965, PhD, 1968. Instr. psychology U. Ill., Urbana, 1966-67; prof. Coll. William and Mary, Williamsburg, Va., 1967—; cons. Ctr. for Teaching Excellence Hampton (Va.) U., 1988-94. Author: Ednl. Computer Software, (with E. Rae Harcum) The Gatekeepers of Psychology, 1993; contbr. articles to profl. jours. Mem. Soc. for Computers in Psychology (bd. dirs.), Psychonomic Soc., Va. Psychol. Assn., Ea. Psychol. Assn., C.G. Jung Soc. of Tidewater (treas.), Am. Psychol. Soc., Assn. for Anorexia and Bulimia of Va. Office: Coll of William and Mary Dept of Psychology Williamsburg VA 23187

ROSEN, FRED SAUL, pediatrics educator; b. Newark, May 26, 1930; s. Philip and Amelia (Feld) R. AB, Lafayette Coll., 1951; MD, Western Res. U., 1955; MA (hon.), Harvard U., 1970; DSc (hon.), Lafayette Coll., 1978. From asst. to assoc. prof. pediatrics Harvard Med. Sch., Boston, 1966-72, James L. Gamble prof. pediatrics, 1972—; chief. div. immunology Children's Hosp., Boston, 1968-85, program dir. Gen. Clin. Rsch. Ctr., 1977-91; pres. Ctr. for Blood Rsch., Boston, 1987—; chmn. sci. com. on immunodeficiencies WHO, Boston, 1988—. Author: Dictionary of Immunology, 1989. Pres. Am. Friends of Jenner Appeal, Boston, 1985—; Sr. asst. surgeon USPHS, 1957-59. Recipient E. Mead Johnson award for pediatric rsch. Am. Acad. Pediatrics, 1970, Gen. Clin. Rsch. Ctrs. Program 4th Ann. award NIH, 1992; John Simon Guggenheim Meml. Found. fellow, 1974. Mem. Am. Assn. Immunology, Am. Soc. Clin. Investigation, Am. Pediatric Soc., Assn. Am. Physicians, NAS Inst. Medicine, St. Botolph Club, Harvard Club, Somerset Club. Home: 101 Chestnut St Boston MA 02108 Office: The Ctr for Blood Rsch 800 Huntington Ave Boston MA 02115-6303*

ROSEN, HENRY, physician, educator; b. Germany, Nov. 26, 1946; came to U.S., 1949, naturalized, 1954; s. Arthur and Helen (Solomonovitch) R.; m. Sara Eilenberg, Aug. 6, 1979; children: Lindsay Michel, Suzanne Elizabeth. AB, Yale U., 1968; MD, U. Rochester, 1972. Intern U. Wash. Hosp., Seattle, 1972-73, resident in internal medicine, 1973-74, fellow in infectious diseases, 1974-77, univ. asst. prof., 1977-83, assoc. prof. medicine, 1983-91; prof. medicine, 1991—; dir. edn. in medicine Swedish Hosp. Med. Ctr., Seattle, 1983-93; assoc. chmn. dept. of medicine U. Wash., 1993—; cons. NIH, Bethesda, Md., 1980-84. Contbr. articles to profl. jours. Recipient Nat. Research Service award NIH, 1975-77, Research Career Devel. award, 1979-84. Mem. Am. Fedn. for Clin. Research, Infectious Diseases Soc. Am., Western Soc. Clin. Investigation (pres. 1996—), Western Assoc. of Physicians, Am. Soc. for Clin. Invest, Assoc. of Am. Physicians Office: U Wash Dept Medicine Box 356420 Seattle WA 98195

ROSEN, HOWARD, orthopaedic surgeon; b. N.Y.C., Feb. 17 1925; m. Constance; children: Terry, Aileen. BA, NYU, 1944, MD, 1947. Diplomate Nat. Bd. Med. Examiners, Am. Bd. Orthopaedic Surgery. Chief problem trauma svc. Hosp. Joint Diseases/Orthopedic Inst., N.Y.C., 1952—; clin. prof. of orthopaedics Mt. Sinai Sch. Medicine, 1980-93, NYU Sch. Medicine, 1993—; instr. Columbia U. Coll. Physicians & Surgeons, N.Y.C., 1952-55; adj. surgeon, Montefiore Hosp., N.Y.C., 1952-58; assoc. surgeon Grand Ctrl. Hosp., N.Y.C., 1952-63; cons. surgeon Leroy Hosp., N.Y.C. 1971-79, Gracie Square Hosp., N.Y.C., 1972-87. Fellow Am. Coll. Surgeons, Am. Acad. Orthopedic Surgeons, N.Y. Acad. Medicine; mem. Orthopedic Trauma Assn. Office: 70 E 10th St New York NY 10003

ROSEN, IRVING LOUIS, internist; b. New Orleans, Mar. 28, 1928; s. Ulrich and Jeanette Blanche (Cohen) R.; m. Carol Lise Brenner, Mar. 9, 1957; children: Elizabeth Lynn, Edith Louise. BS, Tulane U., 1947, MD, 1949. Diplomate Am. Bd. Internal Medicine. Intern Touro Infirmary, New Orleans, 1949-50, resident, 1950-51; resident Charity Hosp., New Orleans, 1952-54; intern, resident Touro Infirmary, New Orleans; resident Charity Hosp., New Orleans; pvt. practice internal medicine New Orleans; mem. staff Elmwood Hosp., New Orleans, East Jefferson Gen. Hosp., New Orleans, Touro Infirmary. Capt. USAF, 1951-52. Fellow Am. Coll. Physicians, Am. Coll. Cardiology, Am. Coll. Chest Physicians. Office: Tulane University Hospital and Clinics 200 Broadway New Orleans LA 70118

ROSEN, JAMES CARL, psychology educator; b. L.A., July 30, 1949; s. Robert Bert and Sandra (Brysha) R.; m. Julie Weston, Aug. 22, 1976; children: Emilia, Alexander. AB, U. Calif., Berkeley, 1971; PhD, U. Nev., 1976. Prof. psychology U. Vt., Burlington, 1976—. Contbr. articles to profl. publs. Office: U Vt Dept Psychology Burlington VT 05405-5000

ROSEN, KAREN SCHNEIDER, psychologist, educator; b. N.Y.C., Jan. 31, 1958; d. Laurence Ashley and Audrey Sydelle (Asher) Schneider; m. Ronald Edward Rosen, July 1, 1979; children: Emily, Gabriel, Rebecca. BA summa cum laude, Brandeis U., 1979; PhD, Harvard U., 1984. Prof. psychology Boston Coll., Chestnut Hill, Mass., 1984—; staff psychologist Brookline (Mass.) Psychol. Services, 1985—; cons. editor Child Devel., Chgo., 1984—, Infant Mental Health Jour., 1987—, Little, Brown and Co., Boston, 1984—, McGraw Hill, 1987—, Holt, Rinehart & Winston, Inc., 1987—. Co-editor (book) Childhood Depression, 1984; contbr. book chpts., articles in field. Fellow NSF, 1979-82, Merit, Harvard U., 1982-83. Mem. Am. Psychol. Assn., Nat. Ctr. Clin. Infant Programs, Soc. Research Child Devel., Phi Beta Kappa, Sigma Xi. Jewish. Office: Boston Coll Dept Psychology Chestnut Hill MA 02167

ROSEN, MARK JEFFREY, critical care physician, educator; b. N.Y.C., Aug. 26, 1951. BA, Brown U., 1972, MD, 1975. Diplomate, Am. Bd. Internal Medicine, Am. Bd. Pulmonary Medicine, Am. Bd. Critical Care Medicine. Intern medicine Mt. Sinai Med. Ctr., N.Y.C., 1975-76, resident medicine, 1976-78, fellow pulmonary disease, 1978-80; fellow critical care medicine St. Vincent's Med. Ctr., N.Y.C., 1980; instr. medicine Mt. Sinai Sch. Medicine, N.Y.C., 1981-82; asst. to assoc. prof. clin. medicine Mt. Sinai Sch. Medicine, N.Y.C., 1982-88; clin. asst. Mt. Sinai Hosp., N.Y.C., 1981-83, asst. attending, 1983-86, dir. Med. Spl. Care Unit, 1981-90, assoc. dir. divsn. pulmonary and critical care medicine, 1986-90, dir. critical care dept. medicine, 1986-90; attending physician Beth Israel Med. Ctr., N.Y.C., 1990—, chief divsn. pulmonary and critical care medicine, 1990—; prof. medicine Albert Einstein Coll. Medicine, N.Y.C., 1994—; presenter in field. Contbr. chpts. to books including Intensive Care Medicine, 1996, Textbook of Bronchoscopy, 1995, Infectious Disease Teaching Atlas, 1995, others; contbr. over 100 articles to profl. pubs including Clin. Chest Med., European Respirptory Rev., Am. Jour. Respiratory Critical Care Medicine, others; editl. reviewer. NIH grantee, 1986-87, NHLBI grantee, 1987-92, 92-96; named in "The Best Doctors in New York", New York mag., 1991, "The Best Doctors in America", Woodward/White, 1994, "The Best Doctors in North America", Town & Country, 1995. Fellow ACP, Am. Coll. Critical Care Medicine, Am. Coll. Chest Physicians; mem. Sigma Xi. Office: Beth Israel Med Ctr Divsn Pulm Crit Care Med New York NY 10003

ROSEN, PETER, health facility administrator, emergency physician, educator; b. Bklyn., Aug. 3, 1935; s. Isadore Theodore and Jessie Olga (Solomon) R.; m. Ann Helen Rosen, May 16, 1959; children: Henry, Monte, Curt, Ted. BA, U. Chgo., 1955; MD, Washington U., St. Louis, 1960. Diplomate Am. Bd. Surgery, Nat. Bd. Med. Examiners, Am. Bd. Emergency Medicine; cert. Advanced Cardiac Life Support Instr., Advanced Trauma Life Support Provider. Intern U. Chgo. Hosps. & Clinics, 1960-61; resident Highland County Hosp., Oakland, Calif., 1961-65; assoc. prof. divsn. emergency medicine U. Chgo. Hosps. & Clinics, 1971-73, prof. divsn. emergency medicine, 1973-77; dir. divsn. emergency medicine Denver City Health & Hosps., 1977-86, 87-89; asst. dir. dept. emergency medicine U. Calif., San Diego Med. Ctr., 1989—, dir. edn. dept. emergency medicine, 1989—, dir. emergency medicine residency program, 1991—; attending physician Hot Springs Meml. Hosp., Thermopolis, Wyo., Worland (Wyo.) County Hosp., Basin-Graybull Hosp., Basin, Wyo., 1968-71, U. Chgo. Hosps. & Clinics, 1971-77; dir. emergency medicine residency program, divsn. emergency medicine U. Chgo. Hosps. & Clinics, 1971-77; emergency medicine med. advisor State of Colo., 1977-85; dir. emergency medicine residency program Denver Gen. Hosp., St Anthony Hosp. Systems, St. Joseph Hosp., 1977-88; clin. prof. divsn. emergency medicine Oreg. Health Scis. U., Portland, 1978-89; prof. sect. emergency medicine, dept. surgery U. Colo. Health Scis. Ctr., 1984-89; dep. mgr. med. affairs Denver Dept Health & Hosps., 1986-87; med. dir. life flight air med. svc. U. Calif., San Diego Med. Ctr., 1989-91; mem. hosp. staff U. Calif., San Diego Med. Ctr., Tri-City Med. Ctr., Oceanside, Calif., 1989—; base hosp. physician, adj. prof. medicine & surgery U. Calif., San Diego Med. Ctr., 1989—; chair med. ethics com., mem. ethics consult team U. Calif., San Diego Med. Ctr., 1990—, mem. recruitment and admissions com., 1992—; lectr. in field; cons. in field. Author: (with others) Case Reports in Emergency Medicine: 1974-76, 1977, Encyclopedia Brittannica, 1978, 85, Principles and Practice of Emergency Medicine, 1978, 86, Protocols for Prehospital Emergency Care, 1980, 84, Cardiopulmonary Resuscitation, 1982, An Atlas of Emergency Medicine Procedures, 1984, Critical Decisions in Trauma, 1984, Emergency Pediatrics, 1984, 86, 90, Controversies in Trauma Management, 1985, Standardized Nursing Care Plans for Emergency Department, 1986, Emergency Medicine: Concepts and Clinical Practice, 1988, 92, The Clinical Practice of Emergency Medicine, 1991, Essentials of Emergency Medicine, 1991, Current Practice of Emergency Medicine, 1991, Care of the Surgical Patient, 1991, Diagnostic Radiology in Emergency Medicine, 1992, Pediatric Emergency Care Systems: Planning and Management, 1992, The Airway: Emergency Management, 1992; contbg. editor, editor abstracts sect. Jour. Am. Coll. Emergency Physicians, Annals of Emergency Medicine, 1976-83; mem. editorial bd. Topics in Emergency Medicine, 1979-82, ER Reports, 1981-83; consulting editor Emergindex Microindex, 1980—; editor in chief Jour. Emergency Medicine, 1983—; contbr. articles to profl. jours. Capt. USMC, 1965-68, lt. col. Res. inactive. Recipient AMA award, 1970, Am. Hosp. Assn. award, 1973. Fellow Am. Coll. Surgeons, Am. Burn Assn., Am. Coll. Emergency Physicians (chmn. edn. com. 1977-79, bd. dirs. Colo. chpt. 1977-80, pres. Colo. chpt. 1981-82, N.C. chpt. award 1976, Outstanding Contbns. and Leadership in Emergency Medicine award 1977, Silver Tongue Debater award 1980, John. D. Mills Outstanding Contbn. to Emergency Medicine award 1984); mem. Am. Trauma Soc. (founding), Soc. Acad. Emergency Medicine (Leadership award 1990), Alpha Omega Alpha Honor Med. Soc. (grad.), Coun. Emergency Medicine Dirs. Office: U of California-San Diego 200 W Arbor Dr San Diego CA 92103-1911*

ROSEN, RICHARD ALAN, pediatrician; b. Valparaiso, Ind., May 28, 1945; m. Jani Rosen, June 15, 1969; children: Leslie, Russell, Leon, Toby. BS, CCNY, 1966; MD, St. Louis U. Med. Sch., 1970. Pediatrician Harvard Comty. Health Plan-NE, Providence, R.I., 1975—; assoc. med. dir. R.I. Group Health Assn., 1984-90; quality cons. Nat. Com. for Quality Assurance, Washington, 980—. Author: (book) Primary Care Pediatrics, 1984; editor and author (jour) HMO Practice, 1987—. Capt. USAF, 1973-75. Mem. Providence Radio Assn. (sec.), R.I. Aeromodelers. Office: Harvard Comty. Health Plan New Eng 1 Commerce St Lincoln RI 02865-1149

ROSEN, RICHARD JAMES, physician; b. Bklyn., July 11, 1930; s. John Nathaniel and Hazel (Geismar) R.; m. Eva Clare Smith, Oct. 8, 1960 (div. May 1982); children: Alexander, Margaret, Sally; m. Mabelle Whitfield Burnham, Oct. 29, 1994. Student, Dartmouth Coll., 1948-51; MD, George Washington U., 1955. Diplomate Am. Bd. Internal Medicine. Resident in internal medicine Stanford U. Program, San Francisco, 1958-59, Mass. Meml. Hosp., Boston, 1959-61; pvt. practice internal medicine Los Altos, Calif., 1962-64; fellow in hematology Duke U. Med. Ctr., Durham, N.C., 1965; med. dir. Physicians Health Plan, Greensboro, N.C., 1985-88; pvt. practice internal medicine Greensboro, 1966—; chmn. cmty. bd. for project assist Guilford County, Greensboro, 1992-94; clin. prof. medicine U. N.C. Sch. Medicine, 1991—. Mem. Greensboro Com. to Alleviate Smoking Pollution, Greensboro, 1988-91. Lt. (s.g.) USN, 1956-58. Recipient award N.C. Pub. Health Assn., 1994. Mem. Greater Greensboro Soc. Medicine (pres. 1991), Greensboro Heart Assn. (pres. 1984—. Home: 8 Sommerton Dr Greensboro NC 27408 Office: 1032 Professional Village Greensboro NC 27401

ROSEN, STEVEN TERRY, oncologist, hematologist; b. Bklyn., Feb. 18, 1952; married, 1976; 4 children. MB, Northwestern U., 1972, MD, 1976. Genevieve Teuton prof., med. sch. Northwestern U., 1989—, dir. cancer ctr., 1989—; dir. clin. programs Northwestern Meml. Hosp., 1989—. Editor-in-Chief Jour. Northwestern U. Cancer Center, 1989—, Contemporary Oncology, 1990-95. Mem. AAAS, ACP, AMA, Am. Soc. Hematology, Am. Soc. Clin. Oncology, Ctrl. Soc. Clin. Rsch. Office: Northwestern U Robert H. Lurie Cancer Ctr Olson Pavilion Rm 8250 303 E Chicago Ave Chicago IL 60611-3008

ROSENBAUM, DAVID MARK, engineering executive, consultant, educator; b. Boston, Feb. 11, 1935; s. Frederick and Elizabeth (Gelman) R.; m. Karen Jeanne Smith, Dec. 27, 1964; children: Benjamin Micah, Shoshana Elizabeth. BSc, Brown U., 1956; MS, Renessaler Polytech. Inst., 1958; PhD, Brandeis U., 1964. Asst. rsch. prof. Boston U., 1964-65; assoc. prof. Polytech. U., Bklyn., 1969-70; pres. Network Analysis Corp., Glen Cove, N.Y., 1970-72; asst. dir. Office of Nat. Narcotics Intelligence, Washington, 1973-74; cons. to compt. gen. GAO, Washington, 1975-78; dir. Office of Radiation Programs EPA, Washington, 1978-81; pres. Tech. Analysis Corp., McLean, Va., 1981—; cons. Dir. of Licensing, AEC, Washington, 1972-73. Author: Super Hilbert Space and the Quantum Time Operator, 1969, Liquefield Energy Gases Safety, 1978, A Statistical Procedure for Testing Pacemakers, 1978, Health Effects of Low-Level Radiation, 1981, A Statistical Procedure for Cluster Recognition with Application to Atlanta Leukemia Data, 1983. Mem. IEEE (sr.), Am. Phys. Soc. Office: Tech Analysts Corp # 202 6723 Whittier Ave Mc Lean VA 22101-4533

ROSENBAUM, DONALD HERMAN, JR., orthopaedic surgeon; b. Gary, Ind., Dec. 30, 1951; s. Donald Herman and Jane Rae (Bond) R.; m. Lola Sicard; 1 child, Christine. BA in Zoology and Pre-Med. Scis., DePauw U., 1974; MHA, Washington U., 1977; DO, Phila. Coll. Osteo. Medicine, 1986. lic., Fla., Pa. Commd. ensign USN, 1979; advanced through grades to comdr. USN, 1993, 1979, 1993; chief ops. mgmt. svc., asst. mil. constrn. liaison officer Naval Regional Med. Ctr., Orlando, Fla., 1977-80; outpatient dept. adminstr., fleet liaison officer Naval Regional Med. Ctr., Naples, Italy, 1980-82; surg. intern, lt. comdr. Naval Hosp., Oakland, Calif., 1986-87; flight surgeon VMFA-451 MAG 31 Marine Corps Air Station, Beaufort, S.C., 1987-90; resident in orthopedics Nat. Naval Med. Ctr., Bethesda, Md., 1990-94; chief dept. orthopedic surgery Jacksonville (Fla.) Naval Hosp., 1994—. Contbr. articles to profl. jours. Named Second Marine Airwing Flight Surgeon of Yr., 1990; recipient Navy Commendation medal, 1982, Humanitarian medal, 1980, Medal of Merit by Italian Govt., 1983, Meritorious Unit Commendation Ribbon 5 stars, 1988, 89, 90, Nat. Def. medal, 1990, Navy Commendation medal, 1990. Mem. AMA, Am. Assn. Orthopaedic Surgeons, Am. Coll. Health Care Execs., Assn. Mil. Surgeons of U.S., Am. Osteo. Assn., Assn. Mil. Osteopathic Physicians and Surgeons, Soc. of U.S. Naval Flight Surgeons. Home: 1847 Commodore Point Orange Park FL 32073 Office: Jacksonville Naval Hosp Dept Orthopedic Surgery 2013 Child St Jacksonville FL 32224

ROSENBAUM, HOWARD STEWART, podiatrist; b. N.Y.C., Nov. 9, 1949; s. Benjamin andEsther (Cohen) R.; m. Donna Mae Sint, June 10, 1972; children: Elyssa Jill, Jamie Beth. BA cum laude, SUNY, Albany, 1971; DPM cum laude, N.Y. Coll. Podiatric Medicine, 1976. Diplomate Am. Bd. Podiatric Surgery, Am. Bd. Podiatric Orthopedics. Pvt. practice Bergen Podiatry Group, Rutherford, N.J., 1979—, Hillsdale, N.J., 1982—; mem. podiatric residency selection com. Englewood (N.J.) Hosp., 1988-90. Active Temple Emmanuel, Woodcliff Lake, N.J. Fellow Am. Coll. Foot Surgeons; mem. Am. Podiatric Med. Assn., N.J. Podiatric Med. Soc. (trustee 1981-84, chmn. no. divsn. 1987-88, mem. peer rev. com.1992—, long range strategic planning com. 1992-93, membership com. 1993-94, sec. 1994-95, v.p. 1995-96, pres.-elect 1996—). Office: 31 Park Ave Rutherford NJ 07070-1711 also: 185 Broadway Hillsdale NJ 07642-2031

ROSENBAUM, RALPH STEVE, physician; b. Houston, June 14, 1951; s. Max and Helen (Krakowsky) R.; m. Adriana Engel, Dec. 30, 1972; children: Sean Max, Alec Todd. BA in Psychology, U. Tex., Austin, 1972; MD, U. Tex., Galveston, 1976. Diplomate Am. Bd. Internal Medicine. Intern U. Tex. Health Sci. Ctr., Houston, 1976-77, resident, 1977-79, instr., 1988—; staff physician, sr. ptnr. Diagnostic Clinic of Houston, 1979—; instr. U. Tex. Med. Br., Galveston, 1995—. Mem. AMA, ACP, Am. Soc. Internal Medicine, Tex. Med. Assn., Harris County Med. Soc. Office: Diagnostic Clinic of Houston 6448 Fannin St Houston TX 77030

ROSENBAUM, ROBERT LEON, endocrinologist, internist; b. Bklyn., Oct. 28, 1949; s. Max and Peggy Rosenbaum; m. Debra Borut, Oct. 12, 1975; children: Sarah, Seth. BS, Columbia U., 1970, MD, 1975; MSChemE, U. Pa., 1971. Diplomate Am. Bd. Internal Medicine, Am. Bd. Endocrinology, Diabetes and Metabolism. Intern, then resident in internal medicine Montefiore Med. Ctr., Bronx, N.Y., 1975-78, fellow in endocrinology, 1978-80; pvt. practice, Summit, N.J., 1980—; mem. staff Overlook Hosp., Summit, 1980—. Contbr. articles to med. jours. Mem. Summit Bd. Health, 1984-88, pres., 1986-88. Fellow ACP; mem. Am. Diabetes Assn., Endocrine Soc., Am. Assn. Clin. Endocrinologists. Office: Summit Med Group 120 Summit Ave Summit NJ 07901

ROSENBAUM, STANLEY H., physician, educator; b. N.Y.C., Dec. 26, 1946; s. Isidore and Belle (Geiger) R.; m. Paula E. Hyman, June 7, 1969; children: Judith, Adina. BA, Columbia U., 1967; MA, Harvard U., 1969; MD, Cornell U., N.Y.C., 1973. Asst. prof. Columbia Univ., N.Y.C., 1978-85; assoc. prof. Columbia Univ., 1985-87, Yale U., New Haven, Conn., 1987-92; prof. Yale U., New Haven, 1992—. Democrat. Jewish. Office: Yale School of Medicine 333 Cedar St New Haven CT 06510-3206

ROSENBERG, CHARLES HARVEY, otorhinolaryngologist; b. N.Y.C., June 10, 1919; s. Morris and Bessie (Greditor) R.; m. Florence Rich, Dec. 27, 1942; children: Kenneth, Ina Garten. BA cum laude, Alfred U., 1941; MD, U. Buffalo, 1944. Intern Jewish Hosp. Bklyn., 1944-45; resident otolaryngology Mt. Sinai Hosp., N.Y.C., 1945-46, 48-50; teaching faculty, sr. clin. asst. Mt. Sinai Hosp. and Med. Sch., N.Y.C., 1950-72; attending surgeon Stamford (Conn.) Hosp., St. Joseph's Hosp., 1953—; dir. dept. otolaryngology Stamford Hosp. and St. Joseph's Hosp., 1973-79. Campaign chmn. United Jewish Fedn., Stamford, 1978-81, pres., 1981-83, exec. com., 1978—; mem. pres.'s coun. Alfred (N.Y.) U., 1990—. Capt. U.S. Army, 1945-46. Fellow ACS; mem. AMA, Stamford Med. Soc., Fairfield Med. Soc., Conn. State Med. Soc., Am. Bd. Otolaryngology, Am. Acad. Ophthalmology and Otolaryngology. Democrat. Jewish. Home: 304 Erskine Rd Stamford CT 06903-1001 Office: 810 Bedford St Stamford CT 06901-1115

ROSENBERG, IRWIN HAROLD, physician, educator; b. Madison, Wis., Jan. 6, 1935; s. Abraham Joseph and Celia (Mazursky) R.; m. Civia Muffs, May 24, 1964; 1 child, Ilana. BS, U. Wis., 1956; MD, Harvard U., 1959. Diplomate Am. Bd. Internal Medicine. Intern Mass. Gen. Hosp., Boston, 1959-60, resident, 1960-61; instr. medicine Harvard Med. Sch., Boston, 1965-66, assoc. in medicine, 1966-68, asst. prof., 1968-70; assoc. prof. medicine U. Chgo., 1970-75, prof., 1975-86, Sarah and Harold Lincoln Thomson prof. medicine, 1983-86; prof., dir. USDA Human Nutrition Rsch. Ctr. on Aging Tufts U., Boston, 1986—, Jean Mayer prof., 1993; mem. food and nutrition bd. Nat. Acad. of Scis., 1971-83, chmn., 1981-83; W.O. Atwater lectr. USDA, 1993. Co-chair local br. Med. Com. on Human Rights, Boston, 1967; mem. adv. bd. Hebrew Coll., Boston, 1987, 91; chmn. bd. dirs. Hillel Found., U. Chgo. With USPHS, 1961-64. Recipient Josiah Macy Faculty award Macy Found., 1974, Goldsmith award Am. Coll. Nutrition, 1984. Fellow AAAS; mem. Am. Soc. for Clin. Nutrition (pres. 1983-84, Herman award 1989), Internat. Life Sci. Inst. (editor nutrition revs. 1989—), Inst. of Medicine, Nat. Acad. Scis. Jewish. Office: Tufts U USDA Human Nutrition Rsch Ctr 711 Washington St Boston MA 02111-1524

ROSENBERG, JACOB, surgeon; b. Copenhagen, Aug. 15, 1964; s. Bent and Ellis (Rasmussen) R.; m. Bettina Palmkvist, Feb. 19, 1994; 1 child, Natasha. MD, U. Copenhagen, 1991, DMSc, 1994. Resident U. Copenhagen, 1991-94, chief resident, 1994—. Contbr. articles to profl. jours. and chpts. to books. Home: Folkets Alle 22, DK-2000 Frederiksberg Denmark Office: U Copenhagen, Hvidovre Hosp, Dept 235, DK-2650 Hvidovre Denmark

ROSENBERG, JACOB JOSEPH, orthodontist; b. N.Y.C., July 15, 1947; s. Louis and Pearl (Flaster) R.; m. Marylynn Borteck; children: Jonathan, Carolyn, Hilary. BA, U. Vt., 1968; MS, Colo. State U., 1970; DDS with honors, SUNY, Buffalo, 1975; cert. in Orthodontics, Columbia U., 1977. Diplomate Am. Bd. Orthodontics. Practice dentistry specializing in orthodontics Bethesda, Md., 1977—; alumni admission rep. U. Vt. Mem. ADA, Md. State Soc. Orthodontists (pres. 1986-87), Am. Assn. Orthodontists, Am. Bd. Orthodontics (mem. Coll. Diplomates), Orthodontic Edn. of Research Found., Alpha Omega. Office: 4405 E West Hwy Bethesda MD 20814-4522

ROSENBERG, MARK L., health facility administrator; b. Newark, July 30, 1945; m. Jill Rosenberg; children: Julie, Ben. BA in Biology magna cum laude, Harvard Coll., 1967, MD cum laude, 1972, M of Pub. Policy, 1972. Diplomate Am. Bd. Internal Medicine, Am. Bd. Psychiatry and Neurology. Intern Mass. Gen. Hosp., Boston, 1972-73, resident in medicine, 1973-74; resident in preventive medicine Ctrs. for Disease Control, Atlanta, 1975-76; resident in psychiatry Beth Israel Hosp., Boston, 1980-83; clin. assoc. prof. dept. cmty. medicine & family practice Morehouse Sch. Medicine, Atlanta, 1984-93; clin. prof. psychiatry Emory U. Sch. Medicine, Atlanta, 1993—; dir. Nat. Ctr. for Injury Prevention and Control, Atlanta, 1994—, acting assoc. dir. for public health practice, 1992-93; dir. divsn. injury control Ctr. for Environ. Health and Injury Control, 1989-92; spl. asst. for behavioral sci. office of dep. dir. Ctrs. for Disease Control, Atlanta, 1989, advisor to dep. dir., 1988, asst. dir. for sci. divsn. injury epidemiology and control, 1986-88, liaison officer office program planning and evaluation, 1979-80; assoc. dir. office extramural health programs Harvard Sch. Pub. Health, Boston, 1979-80; clin. fellow in psychiatry Harvard Med. Sch., Boston, 1980-83; vis. prof. dept. cmty. health Emory U. Sch. Medicine, Atlanta, 1984-91, clin. asst. prof. psychiatry, 1985-87, clin. assoc. prof., 1988-93; adj. prof. Emory U. Sch. Public Health, Atlanta, 1991—; clin. prof. dept. cmty. health and preventive medicine Morehouse Sch. Medicine, Atlanta, 1993; staff physician Womens Med. Clinic, Atlanta, 1974-76, Harvard St. Neighborhood Health Ctr., Boston, 1976-77, Winchester (Mass.) Hosp., 1978-83; emergency rm. physician Burbank Hosp., Fitchburg, Mass., 1976-77, Harrington Hosp., Southbridge, Mass., 1976-77; vis. physician dept. psychiatry Grady Meml. Hosp., Atlanta, 1985—; lectr. and cons. in field. Mem. editl. bd. Violence and Victims, 1985-88, Violence, Aggression and Terrorism, 1986—; contbr. articles to profl. jours. Bd. dirs. southeastern divsn., sci. adv. coun. Am. Suicide Found., 1990—; active Calif. Wellness Found., 1993—. Mass. Gen. Hosp. fellow, 1977-78, Mead-Johnson fellow, 1982; John Harvard scholar, 1964; recipient Coulter Lecture award Am. Congress Rehab. Medicine, 1991, William S. Stone award Am. Trauma Soc., 1991, Outstanding Achievement award, 1994, World Health Day award Am. Assn. for World Health, 1993, Disting. Svc. award Ga. Assn. Family and Marital Therapists, 1994. Mem. Phi Beta Kappa, Alpha Omega Alpha. Home: 972 Oakdale Rd Atlanta GA 30307*

ROSENBERG, RABEN, psychiatrist; b. Copenhagen, Feb. 21, 1946; s. Abraham and Karla (Sommer) R.; m. Annie Lehrmann, Aug. 10, 1968 (div.); children: Tanja, Lajla; m. Nicole K. Gremaud Kristjansen, May 31, 1985; children: Ahn Cecilie, Josephine, Gabrielle. MD, U. Copenhagen, 1970. Instr. Psychochemistry Inst. U. Copenhagen, 1975-79, asst. prof., 1979-82; resident U. Hosp. Copenhagen, 1982-87, med. dir. Dept. Psychiatry, 1989-91; prof. biological psychiatry, psychopharmacology U. Aarhus, Denmark, 1991—; med. dir. dept. clin. biochemistry Inst. Biol. Psychiatry, Aarhus, 1991—. Author books; contbr. articles to profl. jours. Mem. Danish Psychiat. Assn. (pres. 1996—). Office: Inst Biol Psychiatry, Psychiat Hosp, Skovagervej 2, 8240 Risskov Denmark

ROSENBERG, RICHARD ALAN, ophthalmologist; b. Queens, N.Y., Jan. 1, 1959; s. Robert Simon and Roberta Hyla (Goodman) R.; m. Cindy Robin Brofsky, Nov. 30, 1986 (div.); children: Lisa Beth, Erica Sara, Marisa Jill. BS with distinction, Cornell U., 1979; MD, SUNY, Bklyn., 1983. Diplomate Am. Bd. Ophthalmology. Intern L.I. Jewish Hosp., New Hyde Park, N.Y., 1983-84; resident in ophthalmology Interfaith Med. Ctr., Bklyn., 1984-87; assoc. Steuben Ophthalmic Assocs., Corning, N.Y., 1987-89, Guthrie Med. Group P.C., Corning, 1990-94; ptnr., owner Twin Tiers Eye Care Assocs., Elmira and Corning, 1994—; pres. med. staff Corning Hosp., 1995, chmn. surgery, 1993. Bd. dirs. Temple B'nai Israel, Elmira, N.Y., 1989—, v.p., 1991-95, pres., 1996. Fellow Am. Acad. Ophthalmology; mem. N.Y. State Med. Soc., N.Y. Ophthalmol. Soc., Chemung County Med. Soc., Rotary Club. Jewish. Office: Twin Tiers Eye Care 15 E Pulteney St Corning NY 14830

ROSENBERG, RICHARD F., physician, radiologist; b. N.Y.C., June 13, 1942; s. Henry J. and Sylvia (Harris) R.; m. Judith Wolf, May 5, 1985; 1 child, Glen. BA, Colgate U., 1964; MD, N.Y. Med. Coll., 1968. Diplomate Am. Bd. Radiology. Intern Met. Hosp., N.Y.C., 1968-69; resident Montefiore Hosp. and Med. Ctr., Bronx, N.Y., 1969-70, 72-74, chief resident, 1974; radiologist Lipsay & Rosenberg, Great Neck, N.Y., 1974-78; dir. gastrointestinal radiology North Shore U. Hosp., Manhasset, N.Y., 1978-82; radiologist, owner Great Neck Radiologists, 1982—; mem. adv. bd. Bank of Great Neck, 1990-94. Contbr. articles to profl. jours. Lt. comdr. USN, 1970-72. Fellow Am. Coll. Gastroenterology; mem. Am. Coll. Radiology, Alpha Omega Alpha. Republican. Office: Great Neck Radiologists 935 Northern Blvd Great Neck NY 11021

ROSENBERG, ROBERT ALLEN, psychologist, educator, optometrist; b. Phila., July 31, 1935; s. Theodore Samuel and Dorothy (Bailes) R.; m. Geraldine Bella Tishler, Sept. 3, 1961; children: Lawrence David, Ronald Joseph. BA, Temple U., 1957, MA, 1964; BS, Pa. Coll. Optometry, 1960, OD, 1961. Lic. optometrist, psychologist, Pa. Instr. Pa. Coll. Optometry, Phila., 1962-65, asst. prof., 1965-67; asst. prof. psychology Community Coll. Phila., 1967-76, assoc. prof., 1976—; pvt. practice optometry, Roslyn, Pa., 1965-95; assoc. in practice optometry, Huntingdon Valley, Pa., 1995—. Contbr. articles to profl. jours. Named Humanitarian Chapel of Four Chaplains Bapt. Temple, 1980. Fellow Am. Acad. Optometry; mem. Am. Optometric Assn., Pa. Optometric Assn., Bucks-Montgomery Optometric Assn., Alumni Assn. Pa. Coll. Optometry (v.p. 1991—, sec. 1992—). Home: 970 Corn Crib Dr Huntingdon Valley PA 19006-3304 Office: Community Coll Phila 1700 Spring Garden St Philadelphia PA 19130-3936

ROSENBERG, ROGER NEWMAN, neurologist, educator; b. Milw., Mar. 3, 1939; s. Sol J. and Cora D. (Newman) R.; m. Adrienne Turick, June 24, 1962; children—Jennifer, Lara. Student, Tufts U., 1957-60; BS, Northwestern U., 1961, MD with distinction, 1964. Diplomate Am. Bd. Psychiatry and Neurology. Intern Harvard Med. Service, Beth Israel Hosp., Boston, 1964-65; resident in neurology Neurol. Inst., Columbia U., N.Y.C., 1965-67, instr. neurology, 1967-68; research assoc. Lab. of Biochem. Genetics, NIH, Bethesda, Md., 1968-70; clin. instr. Howard U. Med. Sch., Washington, 1969-70; asst. prof. neuroscis. Sch. Medicine, U. Calif.-San Diego, 1970-71; assoc. prof. neuroscis. and pediatrics, attending neurologist Univ. Hosp., U. Calif.-La Jolla, 1971-74; prof., chmn. dept. neurology U. Tex. Southwestern Med. Ctr., Dallas, 1973-91, prof. physiology, 1976—, Zale Disting. chair, prof. neurology, 1990—, dir. Alzheimer's Disease Rsch. Ctr., 1989—; attending neurologist Parkland Meml. Hosp. and Children's Med. Ctr., Dallas, 1974—, Zale Lipshy Univ. Hosp., 1990—; mem. staff Presbyn. Hosp., Dallas, 1974—, St. Paul's Hosp., Dallas, 1974—; cons. staff VA Hosp., Dallas, 1974—; mem. nat. med. adv. bd. Nat. Ataxia Found., Mpls., 1971—, Myasthenia Gravis Found., 1973; chmn. med. adv. bd., dir. med. sci. research Internat. Joseph Diseases Found., Livermore, Calif., 1977—; lectr. Japanese Soc. Neurology, 1987, 94, Chinese Neurol. Soc., 1987, Spanish Neurol. Soc., 1992; chmn. bd. sci. councilors NIH, 1984-86; pres. (hon.), Intl. French Soc. of Neurology Charcot Centenary Symposium, 1993. Editor Jour. Neurogenetics; mem. editorial bd. Neurology, 1977-82, 91—, Trends in Neurosci., 1980-86, Current Opinion in Neurology & Neurosurgery, 1990—; contbr. articles to med. jours. Bd. dirs. Winston Sch., Dallas, 1974-80. 1st Woody Guthrie scholar, 1971; USPHS grantee; recipient Disting. Alumnus award Neurol. Inst., N.Y., 1994. Fellow AAAS; mem. Am. Acad. Neurology (chmn. sci. program com. nat. meetings 1979-84, elected councillor exec. bd. 1984-89, pres. 1991-93), Am. Neurochem. Soc., Tissue Culture Soc., Soc. Neurosci., Am. Fedn. Clin. Rsch., Soc. Pediat. Rsch., Internat. Child Neurology Assn., Am. Neurol. Assn. (1st v.p. 1987), Ctrl. Soc. Neurol. Rsch., Can. Congress Neurol. Scis. (hon.), Spanish Neurol. Soc. (hon. 1994), Sigma Xi, Alpha Omega Alpha (Merit award Northwestern U. Alumni Assn. 1986). Home: 4425 Wildwood Rd Dallas TX 75209-2801 Office: U Tex Southwestern Med Ctr Dallas TX 75235

ROSENBERG, SAUL ALLEN, oncologist, educator; b. Cleve., Aug. 2, 1927. BS, Western Res. U., 1948, MD, 1953. Diplomate Am. Bd. Internal Medicine, Am. Bd. Oncology. Intern Univ. Hosp., Cleve., 1953-54; resident in internal medicine Peter Bent Brigham Hosp., Boston, 1954-61; research asst. toxicology AEC Med. Research Project, Western Res. U., 1948-53; asst. prof. medicine and radiology Stanford (Calif.) U., 1961-65, assoc. prof., 1965-79, chief div. oncology, 1965-93, prof., 1970-95; prof. emeritus, 1995—; Am. Cancer Soc. prof. Stanford (Calif.) U., 1983-89, assoc. dean, 1989-92; chmn. bd. No. Calif. Cancer Program, 1974-80. Contbr. articles to profl. jours. Served to lt. M.C. USNR, 1954-56. Master ACP; mem. Am. Assn. Cancer Research, Inst. Medicine Nat. Acad. Sci., Am. Assn. Cancer Edn., Am. Fedn. Clin. Research, Am. Soc. Clin. Oncology (pres. 1982-83), Assn. Am. Physicians, Calif. Acad. Medicine, Radiation Research Soc., Western Soc. Clin. Research, Western Assn. Physicians. Office: Stanford U Sch Medicine Div Oncology M-211 Stanford CA 94305

ROSENBERG, SELIG, psychologist; b. N.Y.C., Oct. 9, 1914. BA, Bklyn. Coll., 1936; MLitt, U. Pitts., 1944; PhD, NYU, 1952. Staff psychologist VA Clinic, N.Y.C., 1945-58; chief clin. psychologist VA Hosp., Northport, N.Y., 1958-74; chief psychologist L.I. Devel. Ctr., Melville, N.Y., 1974-84; pvt. practice psychology Woodbury, N.Y., 1984—; lectr. Bkyn. Coll., 1952-65, NYU, N.Y.C., 1965-68; supr. doctoral interns Hofstra U., Uniondale, N.Y., 1965-69. Contbr. articles to profl. jours. Sgt. U.S. Army, 1941-45. Home and Office: 43 Joyce Ln Woodbury NY 11797-2124

ROSENBERG, SEYMOUR, psychologist, educator; b. Newark, Sept. 7, 1926; s. Morris and Celia (Weiss) R.; children: Harold Stanley, Michael Seth. B.S., The Citadel, 1948; M.A., Ind. U., 1951, Ph.D., 1952. Research psychologist USAF, San Antonio, 1952-58, U. Kans., Lawrence, 1958-59, Bell Telephone Labs., Murray Hill, N.J., 1959-65; vis. prof. psychology Columbia, N.Y.C., 1965-66; prof. psychology Rutgers U., New Brunswick, N.J., 1966—; chmn. dept. psychology Rutgers U., 1981-83, 94-95; adj. prof. Rutgers U. Med. Sch., 1974—; vis. scholar U. Leuven, Belgium, 1983, 92, Université de Provence, France, 1990; panel mem. NSF, 1970-72. Cons. editor Jours. Personality and Social Psychology, 1968-69; assoc. editor, 1970-73; contbr. articles to profl. jours. Served with USN, 1945-46. NSF grantee, 1965—; NIMH, 1966-68; NIMH research scientist grantee, 1968-73; Social Sci. Research Council fellow, 1973-74. Fellow Am. Psychol. Assn.; mem. Soc. Exptl. Social Psychology, Psychometric Soc., Classification Soc., N.Y. Acad. Sci., Eastern Psychol. Assn. Home: 689 Canal Rd Somerset NJ 08873-7327 Office: Rutgers U Dept Psychology ED Livingston Campus New Brunswick NJ 08903

ROSENBERG, STANLEY ERNEST, urologist, surgeon, educator; b. N.Y.C., Mar. 13, 1933; s. David Irwin and Jeanette (Strausberg) R.; m. Irene Marcia Kaplan, June 27, 1957 (div. Aug. 20, 1974); children: James Allen, Drew Ann; m. Betsy Layne Hatch, Aug. 30, 1974. BA magna cum laude, Dartmouth Coll., 1954; MD, Columbia, 1957. Intern Bellevue Hosp., N.Y.C., 1957-58, resident in surgery, 1958-59; resident in urology Columbia Presbyn. Med. Ctr., N.Y.C., 1961-64; founder, pres. Urology Group, Princeton, N.J., 1965—; lectr., clin. prof. Robert Wood Johnson Med. Sch. (formerly Rutgers Med. Sch.), Piscataway, N.J., 1966—. Scoutmaster Boy Scouts Am. Explorer Troop, Princeton H.S., 1966-68. Capt. USAF, 1954-61. Fellow Am. Coll. Surgeons; mem. Am. Urol. Assn. (N.Y. sect.), Phi Beta Kappa. Jewish. Office: Urology Group Princeton 281 Witherspoon St Princeton NJ 08540

ROSENBERG, STEVEN AARON, surgeon, medical researcher; b. N.Y.C., Aug. 2, 1940; s. Abraham and Harriet (Wendroff) R.; m. Alice Ruth O'Connell, Sept. 15, 1968; children—Beth, Rachel, Naomi. B.A., Johns Hopkins U., 1960, M.D., 1963; Ph.D., Harvard U., 1968. Resident in surgery Peter Bent Brigham Hosp., Boston, 1963-64, 68-69, 72-74; resident fellow in immunology Harvard U. Med. Sch., Boston, 1969-70; clin. assoc. immunology br. Nat. Cancer Inst., Bethesda, Md., 1970-72; chief surgery Nat. Cancer Inst., 1974—, assoc. editor Jour., 1974—; mem. U.S.-USSR Coop. Immunotherapy Program, 1974—, U.S.-Japan Coop. Immunotherapy Program, 1975—; clin. assoc. prof. surgery George Washington U. Med. Ctr., 1976—; prof. surgery Uniformed Services U. Health Scis. Contbr. articles to profl. jours. Author: The Transformed Cell: Unlocking the Mysteries of Cancer, 1992. Served with USPHS, 1970-72. Recipient Meritorious Service medal Pub. Health Service, 1981; co-recipient Armand Hammer Cancer prize, 1985; named 1990 Scientist of the Yr., R&D magazine. Mem. Soc. Univ. Surgeons, Am. Surg. Assn., Soc. Surg. Oncology, Surg. Biology Club II, Halsted Soc., Transplantation Soc., Am. Assn. Immunologists, Am. Assn. Cancer Research, Phi Beta Kappa, Alpha Omega Alpha. *

ROSENBERG, THOMAS FREDERICK, physician; b. St. Louis, June 17, 1941; s. William Lawrence Rosenberg and Gertrude Lubens; m. Adrienne Merle France, July 3, 1966; children: Lisa Jill, Jason Gregory. AB, Washington & Jefferson U., 1963. Physician Alergy and Asthma Ctr., Kans., 1974—; clin. asst. prof. pediatrics Sch. of Medicine U. Kans., Wichita, 1975-87, clin. assoc. prof. pediatrics Sch. of Medicine, 1987—; clin. asst. prof. Wichita State U., 1987-90. Maj. USAF, 1970-74. Fellow Am. Acad. Pediatrics, Am. Coll. Allergy & Immunology; mem. NASW (Citizen of the Yr. Kans. chpt. 1983). Office: Allergy and Asthma Ctr 8110 E 32d St N Wichita KS 67224-4608

ROSENBERG, VICTOR I., plastic surgeon; b. N.Y.C., Nov. 15, 1936; s. Leonard C. and Sarah G. (Berger) R.; AB, NYU, 1957; MD, Chgo. Med. Sch., 1961; m. Deborah Iskoe, Jan. 2, 1966; children: Spencer, Ria. Intern, Beth Israel Hosp., N.Y.C., 1961-62, resident, 1962-63, 64-66; resident Beckman Downtown Hosp., 1963-64, Bronx Mcpl. Hosp., 1966-67, Mt. Sinai Hosp., N.Y.C., 1967-68; practice medicine specializing in plastic surgery, N.Y.C., 1968—; assoc. attending surgeon Beth Isreal Hosp., 1968—; assoc. attending surgeon Beekman Downtown Hosp., 1968—, chief plastic surgery, 1976-80; attending surgeon N.Y. Infirmary-Beekman Downtown Hosp., 1980—, dir. cosmetic surgery, 1984—; asst. attending surgeon Mt. Sinai Hosp., N.Y.C., 1968—; asst. clin. prof. Mt. Sinai Sch. Medicine CUNY. Served to comdr. USN, 1968-70. Diplomate Am. Bd. Plastic Surgery. Fellow ACS, Internat. Coll. Surgeons; mem. Am., N.Y. Regional socs. plastic and reconstructive surgeons, Am. Soc. Aesthetic Plastic Surgery, AMA, Am. Cleft Palate Assn., N.Y. Acad. Medicine, N.Y. State, N.Y. County Med. Socs., Pan Am. Med. Assn. (diplomate sect. plastic surgery). Club: Friars. Office: 4 Sutton Pl New York NY 10022-3056

ROSENBERG, ZACHARY, surgeon; b. N.Y.C., July 26, 1935; s. Carol and Rose (Dermer) R.; m. Judith Karen Gerber, July 29, 1968; children: Jonathan, Matthew. BA, Ind. U., 1957; MD, Chgo. Med. Sch., 1966; MA, U. Minn., 1975. Bd. cert. Am. Bd. Otolaryngology. Intern, resident U. Minn. Hosps., 1966-67, resident dept. otolaryngology, 1970-75; surg. fellow in cardiovascular surgery, 1967, surg. fellow otolaryngology, 1970-75; physician, surgeon Shea Clinic, Memphis, 1975, Memphis Otolaryngology Group, 1975-81, ZRMD, Memphis, 1981—; presenter in field. Contbr. articles to profl. jours. With U.S. Army, 1967-69. Decorated Bronze and Silver stars U.S. Army, 1967-68. Fellow ACS; mem. AAAS, AMA, Am. Bd. Otolaryngology-Head and Neck Surgery, Am. Coun. Otolaryngology, Internat. Fedn. Otorhinolaryngol. Socs., Nat. Acad. Scis., N.Y. Acad. Scis., So. Med. Assn., Memphis Soc. Otolaryngology, Memphis and Shelby County Med. Assn., Med. Jour. Club, Alumni Assn. Ind. U., Alumni Assn. U. Minn., Alumni Assn. Chgo. Med. Sch. Office: Ste 600 6005 Park Ave Memphis TN 38119

ROSENBERGER, JANICE WHITEHILL, speech and language pathologist; b. Newport, Vt., Sept. 27, 1943; d. Clarence Arthur and Doris Martha Jordan; children: Gregory, Karen, Andrew. AA, Orange Coast Coll., 1974; student, Portland (Oreg.) State U., 1974-75; BS, No. Ill. U., 1977; MS, Marquette U., 1978; postgrad., U. Vt., 1981-82, cert., 1990. Accounts receivable clk. Yankton (S.D.) Coll., 1963-66; libr. researcher Microwave Instruments Co., Corona del Mar, Calif., 1973; tchr. ESL Libertyville (Ill.) Sch. Dist., 1978-80; tchr. GED Mundelein (Ill.) High Sch., 1979-80; speech-lang. pathologist Barre (Vt.) City Schs., 1981-83, Orleans Essex Vis. Nurses Assn. and Hospice, Inc., Newport, Vt., 1983—; workshop presenter Coll. Lake County, Grayslake, Ill., 1980; exec. sec. Paul Rosenberger Appraiser, North Troy, Vt., 1982—; recorder, auditor, mem. profl. health adv. com., 1984-94, support group facilitator, 1992-93; facilitator, time keeper Newport Early Action Team, 1986—; speech-lang. pathologist Orleans and Essex North Supervisory Union, Derby, Vt., 1987-90, mem. infectious control com., 1996—. Editor 4 publs. in field. Pres. ch. women's group, North Troy, 1987-89; election judge state govt., Mundelein, 1978-79; supr., mem. United Ch. Christ, 1984—; mem. Hosp. Aux., 1986—; sec. Friendly Class Union, 1986-88; mem. Vt. Conf. Christian Edn. Cluster, 1984-82. Recipient Jr. Women's Club award, 1974, Editing Internat. award, 1981, Activity Achievement award, 1985, Outstanding Contbn. award, 1990, Award Continuing Edn., 1993, Pres.'s award, 1980, Dedicated Svc. plaque for commitment to provision of speech svcs. in N.E. kingdom, 1995, cert. for constant "can do" attitude, loyalty and cheerfulness, 1995. Mem. Am. Speech-Lang.-Hearing Assn., Vt. Speech-Lang.-Hearing Assn., After 5 Club (telephone chmn. 1984-85, bible coord. 1985-90, 93-94, chmn. 1992-93, area rep. 1994—). Home: West Rd PO Box 631 North Troy VT 05859-0631

ROSENBLATT, KARIN ANN, community health educator; b. Chgo., Apr. 22, 1954; d. Murray and Adylin Rosenblatt. BA, U. Calif., Santa Cruz, 1975; MPH, U. Mich., 1977; PhD, Johns Hopkins U., 1988. Postdoctoral fellow U. Wash., Seattle, 1987-89; staff scientist Fred Hutchinson Cancer Rsch. Ctr., Seattle, 1989-91; asst. prof. U. Ill., Champaign, 1991—. Mem. APHA, Internat. Genetic Epidemiology Soc., Am. Coll. Epidemiology, Soc. for Epidemiologic Rsch. Home: 1603-A1 Valley Rd Champaign IL 61820 Office: Dept Comty Health 121 Huff Hall MC 588 1206 S 4th St Champaign IL 61820

ROSENBLATT, MICHAEL, medical researcher, educator; b. Lund, Sweden, Nov. 27, 1947; s. Arthur Rosenblatt and Jean (Strosberg) Bialer; m. Patricia Ellen Regenbogen, Aug. 23, 1969; children: Anna Miriam, Adam Richard. AB summa cum laude, Columbia U., 1969; MD magna cum laude, Harvard U., 1973. Diplomate Am. Bd. Internal Medicine. Intern then resident Mass. Gen. Hosp., Boston, 1973-75, clin. rsch. fellow in endocrinology and metabolism, 1975-77, chief endocrine unit, 1981-84; instr. in medicine Harvard U., Boston, 1976-78, asst. prof. medicine, 1978-82, assoc. prof. medicine, 1982-85; v.p. for biol. rsch. Merck Sharp & Dohme Rsch. Labs., 1984-87, v.p. for biol. rsch. and molecular biology, 1987-89; sr. v.p. rsch. Merck Sharp & Dohme Rsch. Labs., West Point, Pa., 1989-92; Ebert prof. molecular medicine Harvard Med. Sch., Boston, 1992—; dir. div. health scis. and tech. Harvard-MIT, 1992—; chief div. bone and mineral metabolism Beth Israel Hosp., Boston, 1992-96; faculty dean acad. programs Beth Israel Hosp., Harvard Med., 1996; sr. v.p. acad. affairs Beth Israel Hosp., 1996; exec. dir. Harvard Med. Sch./Beth Israel Healthcare Found. for Rsch. and Edn., 1996. Editor: Atrial Natriuretic Factor Endocrinology and Metabolism Clinics of N.Am., 1987; contbr. numerous sci. articles on parathyroid hormone and calcium metabolism to leading sci. jours. Recipient Vincent du Vigneaud award Gordon Confs., Kingston, R.I., 1986, Fuller Albright award Am. Soc. for Bone and Mineral Rsch., 1986, citation Japan Endocrine Soc., Tokyo. Fellow AAAS; mem. The Endocrine Soc., Am. Soc. for Biochemistry and Molecular Biology, Am. Soc. for Clin. Investigation, Am. Soc. Bone and Mineral Rsch. (pres.-elect 1996), Assn. Am. Physicians, Inter-Urban Clin. Club. Home: 130 Lake Ave Newton MA 02159-2108 Office: Harvard Med Sch HST MEC 213 Bldg 260 Longwood Ave Boston MA 02115-5701

ROSENBLATT, ROGER ALAN, physician, educator; b. Denver, Aug. 8, 1945; s. Alfred Dreyfus and Judith Ann (Ginsburg) R.; m. Fernne Schnitzer, Sept. 23, 1942; children: Eli Samuel, Benjamin. BA magna cum laude, Harvard U., 1967, MD cum laude, M in Pub. Health, 1971. Diplomate Am. Bd. Family Practice, Nat. Bd. Med. Examiners. Intern internal medicine U. Wash., Seattle, 1971-72, resident in family medicine, 1974; regional med. cons. region X Pub. Health Service, Seattle, 1974-76, dir. Nat. Health Services Corps., 1976-77; asst. prof. dept. family medicine U. Wash., Seattle, 1977-81, assoc. prof. dept. family medicine, 1981-85, prof., vice chmn. dept. family medicine, 1985—; cons. U.S. Agy. for Internat. Devel., 1978, Western Interstate Commn. Higher Edn., 1981-82; vis. prof. medicine U. Auckland, New Zealand, 1983-84, Royal Australia Coll. Gen. Practitioners, Victoria, 1984, U. Calgary, 1988, U. Mo., 1988; vis. prof., Fogarty Ctr. Sr. Internat. fellow dept. ob-gyn. NIH, Coll. Medicine, U. Wales, Cardiff, 1992-93. Author: Rural Health Care, 1982; contbr. numerous articles on healthcare to profl. jours. Mem. Beyond War, Physicians for Social Responsiblity. Served with USPHS, 1974-77. Recipient Hanes Rsch. award North Am. Primary Care Rsch. Group, 1996. Mem. Am. Acad. Family Physicians (Hanes Rsch. award 1996), Am. Pub. Health Assn., Soc. Tchrs. Family Medicine (Hanes Rsch. award 1996), Nat. Rural Health Assn., Nat. Council Internat. Health, Nat. Acad. Sci. (elected inst. medicine 1987), Am. Rural Health Assn. (Research award 1985), Phi Beta Kappa. Office: U Wash Dept Family Medicine # Hq-30 Dept Family Medicine Seattle WA 98195

ROSENBLATT, WILLIAM BENNETT, plastic surgeon; b. N.Y.C., June 27, 1947; s. Philip and Miriam Rosenblatt; children: Rachel, Steven. BS,

Trinity Coll., Hartford, Conn., 1969; MD, N.Y. Med. Coll., 1973. Diplomate Am. Bd. Plastic and Reconstructive Surgery, Am. Bd. Otolaryngology. Surg. resident Lenox Hill Hosp., 1973-74; otolaryngology resident Met. Hosp., 1974-77, chief resident ear/nose/throat, 1976-77; resident in plastic surgery Lenox Hill Hosp., 1977-79, chief resident, 1978-79; pvt. practice plastic and reconstructive surgery N.Y.C., 1979—; attending physician, resident instr. in plastic surgery Lenox Hill Hosp., Manhattan Eye, Ear and Throat Hosp.; appeared in various TV and radio programs, including Regis Philbin, Maury Povich, Geraldo Rivera, Lifetime, CNBC, Today Show, ABC News, CBS News, Medstar. Bd. dirs. N.Y. Med. Polit. Action Com., 1988-93. Fellow ACS, N.Y. Acad. Medicine; mem. AMA (N.Y. State del. young physicians sect. 1987, alternate del. 1993—), Med. Soc. of State of N.Y. (vice chmn. med. liability def. bd. 1993, mem. fed. legis. com. 1988—, New York County Med. Soc. (sec. 1988-89, v.p. 1989-90, pres.-elect 1990-91, pres. 1991-92, vice chmn. legis. com. 1986-88, chmn. 1986-88), Lipoplasty Soc. N.Am., Northeastern Soc. Plastic Surgeons, N.Y. Regional Soc. Plastic and Reconstructive Surgery, Am. Acad. Otolaryngology and Head and Neck Surgeons, Am. Soc. Plastic and Reconstructive Surgeons, Inc., Physicians Attending Assn. Lenox Hill Hosp. (vice chmn. 1992-96). Office: 308 E 79th St New York NY 10021-0904

ROSENBLITH, JUDY FRANCIS, psychology educator; b. Salt Lake City, Mar. 20, 1921; d. John Edward and Mary Louise (Slack) Francis; m. Walter A. Rosenblith, Sept. 27, 1941; children—Sandra Y., Ronald F. Student Occidental Coll., 1938-40; A.B., UCLA, 1942; M.A., Radcliffe Coll., 1950, Ph.D., 1958. Asst. prof. psychology Simmons Coll., 1951-52; New Eng. supr. Nat. Opinion Research Center, 1953-57; teaching fellow social relations Harvard U., 1948-50, Grad. Sch. Edn., 1953-56, instr., 1956-57, lectr., 1962-63; asst. prof. psychology Brown U., 1957-61, asst. mem. to mem. Inst. Life Scis., 1961-75, sr. research investigator div. biol. and med. scis., 1975-77; assoc. psychology dept. psychiatry Harvard Med. Sch., 1961-64, clin. assoc., 1965-67; assoc. prof. Wheaton Coll., Norton, Mass., 1965-68, prof. psychology, 1968-84, prof. emerita, 1984—; vis. prof. Fla. Internat. U., 1992; mem. maternal and child health research adv. com. Nat. Inst. Child Health and Human Devel., 1974-78. Author: (with Judith Sims-Knight) In the Beginning: Development in the First Two Years, 1985, In the Beginning: Development from Conception at Age Two, 2d edit., 1992, (with M. Rands and B. Myers) Student Manual for In the Beginning, 1992. Adv. editor Contemporary Psychology, 1979-80; sr. editor: The Causes of Behavior: Readings in Child Development and Educational Psychology, 3 edits., 1962, 66, 72. Named Meneely Prof., Wheaton Coll., 1972-74; N.Y. Acad. Scis. fellow, 1976; grantee NIMH, 1958-60, Neurol. Diseases and Blindness, 1961-64, Child Health and Human Devel., 1966-70, Grant Found., 1971-77. Fellow Am. Psychol. Assn. (mem. bd. social and ethical responsibility for psychology 1977-81, mem. pub. info. com. 1981-84) mem. Soc. for Research in Child Devel. (sec. 1965-69, chmn. conv. arrangements 1979-81, chmn. history com. 1993-95), Am. Psychol. Soc., Internat. Conf. Infant Studies, Internat. Assn. Cross-Cultural Psychology, Internat. Assn. Applied Psychology, Internat. Soc. Study of Behavioral Devel., Psychonomic Soc., Eastern Psychol. Assn. Home: 4000 Towerside Terr # 2309 Miami FL 33138 also: 54 Devolder Rd Marstons Mills MA 02648

ROSENBLUM, BERNARD FRANK, retired physician; b. Chgo., Mar. 1, 1909; s. Frank Abraham and Bessie (Levitis) R.; m. Edna Fox, June 1, 1937 (div. Jan. 1942); m. Elizabeth Jane Gilmore, May 13, 1942; children: Douglas, Frank, Bessie. BS, U. Ill., 1933; MD, Chgo. Med. Sch., 1938; MPH, Johns Hopkins U., 1954. Lic. physician, Ill., Tex. Pvt. practice Chgo., 1940-42; commd. Lt. comdr. USPHS, 1950, advanced through grades to capt., 1970; veneral disease cons. USPHS, Atlanta, 1950-51, Balt., 1951-53, Tallahassee, 1953-54, Santa Fe, N.Mex., 1954-56, N.C., 1956-57, L.A., 1957-63, El Paso, Tex., 1963-70; dir. El Paso City/County Health Dist., 1970-83; retired, 1983. Contbr. articles, monographs to profl. jours. Capt. U.S. Army, 1942. Recipient Honor Recognition, City of L.A., 1963, Conquesdor award City of El Paso, 1983. Mem. AMA, Tex. Med. Assn., El Paso County Med. Soc., Assn. Mil. surgeons, Am. Legion, Rotary. Democrat. Jewish. Home: 507 Crown Point Dr El Paso TX 79912

ROSENBLUM, DAVID STEVEN, physician; b. N.Y.C., June 28, 1961; m. Marcia Ellen Rosenblum, July 13, 1989; 2 children. BS, SUNY, Albany, 1983; MD, SUNY, Buffalo, 1987. Intern Millard Filmore Hosp., Buffalo, 1987-88; resident Columbia-Presbyn. Med. Ctr., N.Y.C., 1988-92; med. dir. sci. program, dir. multiple sclerosis clinic Gaylord Hosp., Wallingford, Conn., 1992—. Contbr. articles to profl. jours. Bd. dirs. Greater Conn. chpt. Nat. Multiple Sclerosis Soc., 1994—. Mem. Alpha Omega Alpha, Phi Beta Kappa. Office: Gaylord Hosp PO Box 400 Gaylord Farm Rd Wallingford CT 06492

ROSENBLUM, ESTELLE HELENE, retired dean, nursing educator; b. Davenport, Iowa, Feb. 8, 1933; d. Dan and Cecil (Spiewak) Masters; m. Sidney Rosenblum, Aug. 30, 1953 (dec. 1988); children: Jay Douglas, Gail Rae, Paul Mitchell; m. Jack Grevey, Mar. 31, 1996. Student U. Iowa, 1950-53; BSN, Wayne State U., Detroit, 1956; MSN, U. Tex., El Paso, 1981; PhD, U. N.Mex., 1979, MA in Audiology, 1971. Head nurse Northville (Mich.) State Hosp., 1956; head nurse, supr. Sister Kenny Polio/Rehab. Hosp., 1957-60; pub. health nurse Englewood County Health Dept., 1961-62; nursing supr. Bernalillo County Indian Hosp., Albuquerque, 1962-63; asst. dir. nursing Bernalillo County Indian Hosp., 1963-64; clin. tchr. U. N.Mex. Coll. Nursing, Albuquerque, 1964-65, inst. to prof., 1972-86; dean and prof. nursing U. N.Mex. Coll. Nursing, 1986-93, dean and prof. emerita, 1993—; sch. nurse West Mesa High Sch., Albuquerque, 1967-69; internat. nursing cons.; dir. ANA Approved CE program, Profl. Seminar Cons., 1979-89; speaker Hong Kong Nurse Educators Soc., 1985; bd. dirs. U. N.Mex. Found. Contbr. articles to profl. jours., chpts. to book. USPHS grantee, 1989; recipient Centennial Disting. Alumni award, U. N.Mex., 1989, Helene Fuld award to Coll. Nursing, U. N.Mex., 1987, Sigma Delta Tau Nat. Disting. Alumni award, 1988, Gov. Disting. Pub. Svc. award State of N.Mex., 1993, State N.Mex. Gov.'s Disting. Svc. award, 1993, Estelle H. Rosenblum Thesis award U. N.Mex. Coll. Nursing, 1995. Fellow Am. Acad. Nursing; mem. Am. Assn. Colls. of Nursing (emeritus, exec. devel. series 1988-92), Am. Colls. Nursing (bd. dirs. 1990-92, Membership award 1994), N.Mex. Nurses Assn. (pres. 1975), N.Mex. Health Resources (bd. dirs. 1986—), Sigma Theta Tau (founder, pres. Gamma Sigma chpt. 1974-76, Mentor award).

ROSENBLUM, LILA, psychotherapist; b. Youngstown, Ohio, Dec. 14, 1925; d. Simon Maurice and Gladys (Frank) R. BS in Rehab. Svcs., NYU, 1971, MA in Rehab. Counseling, 1972. Exec. asst. Nat. Coun. on Alcoholism, 1952-55; assoc. editor Indsl. Rels. News, 1955-57; dir. pub. info. Nat. Com. Employment of Youth, 1957-61; mng. editor Clin. Notes on Respiratory Diseases, Am. Lung Assn., 1961-69; head ancillary svcs. Speech and Hearing Inst., N.Y.C., 1971-74; supr. counseling svc. Speech and Hearing Inst., Internat. Ctr. for Disabled, N.Y.C., 1974-78; pvt. practice psychotherapy N.Y.C., 1975—; tchr. Am. Inst. for Psychotherapy and Psychoanalysis, N.Y.C., 1986-88; mem. adv. com. rehab. counseling dept. NYU. Fellow Am. Inst. Psychotherapy and Psychoanalysis (cert.); mem. Soc. for Advancement of Self Psychology, Assn. Psychoanalytic Self Psychology.

ROSENBLUM, MARTIN JEROME, ophthalmologist; b. N.Y.C., Apr. 7, 1948; s. Philip and Rita (Steppel) R.; m. Zina Zarin, May 31, 1975; children: Steven David, Richard James. BS, Bklyn. Coll., 1968; MD, U. Ariz., 1973. Diplomate Am. Bd. Ophthalmology, Nat. Bd. Med. Examiners. Intern Cornell U., N.Y.C., 1974-75; resident N.Y. Med. Coll., 1975-78, instr., 1978-79; resident Columbia U., 1977; practice medicine specializing in eye surgery, St. Petersburg, Fla., 1979—; chief ophthalmology, chief surgery Edward White Hosp.; asst. clin. prof. ophthalmology, U. So. Fla.; attending surgeon Columbia St. Petersburg Med. Ctr., St. Anthony's Bayfront Med. Ctr., Palms of Pasadena Amer Soc. for Cataract and Refractive Surgery. Fellow ACS, Am. Acad. Ophthalmology; mem. AMA, Am. Soc. Ophthalmic Plastic and Reconstructive Surgery, Fla. Med. Assn., Fla. Soc. Ophthalmology, Pinellas County Med. Soc. Republican. Jewish. Club: Seminole Lake Country. Avocation: tennis, golf, travel. Home: 9035 Baywood Park Dr Largo FL 33777-4630 Office: 2200 16th St N Saint Petersburg FL 33704-3106

ROSENBLUM, ROBERT, cardiologist; b. N.Y.C., Oct. 21, 1926; s. Jacob and Pauline (Feldman) R.; m. Lila S. Silverstein, Dec. 24, 1953; children: Naomi Lee Rosenblum Remes, Mark B. AB, Johns Hopkins U., 1946; MD, NYU, 1949. Diplomate Nat. Bd. Med. Examiners, Am. Bd. Internal Medicine with subspecialty cardiovascular diseases (examiner 1967). Intern Bellevue Hosp., N.Y.C., 1949-50; asst. resident in medicine Goldwater Meml. Hosp., N.Y.C., 1950-51; resident in medicine Kings County Hosp., Bklyn., 1953-54; hon. asst. registrar Inst. Cardiology, London, 1954-55; rsch. fellow Montefiore Hosp., N.Y.C., 1955-57, rsch. asst., asst. attending in medicine, 1957-59, assoc. cardiac catheterization lab., 1957-83, rsch. assoc., adj. attending physician in cardiology, 1959-60, tchg. and rsch. coord. cardiology svc., med. divsn., 1963—, investigator-supr. cardiovascular metabolic rsch. labs., 1965-72, electrocardiographer, 1966—, assoc. attending in cardiology, rsch. assoc., 1967-74; asst. in medicine Univ. Hosp., N.Y.C., 1958-89; asst. in medicine NYU Sch. Medicine, N.Y.C., 1959-60, asst. prof. clin. medicine, 1968-89, assoc. clin. prof. medicine, 1989; assoc. medicine Tish Hosp., 1989; assoc. attending physician in medicine Morrisania Hosp., Bronx, 1963—; asst. clin. prof. medicine Albert Einstein Coll. Medicine, N.Y.C., 1966-72, vis. assoc. prof. medicine, 1972—; med. officer N.Y.C. Fire Dept., 1971-86; mem. courtesy staff Doctors Hosp., N.Y., 1978-87, assoc. attending dept. medicine, 1987—; cons. in field. Contbr. numerous articles to profl. publs. Fellow Nat. Found. for Infantile Paralysis, 1955-56, Am. Heart Assn., 1956-57; rsch. grantee NIH-Nat. Heart Inst., 1959-63, 63-68, Ayerst and Co., 1965-67, Arnar-Stone Labs., Inc., 1967-74, Westchester Heart Assn., Inc., 1968-70, N.Y. State Heart Assembly, Inc., 1970-71. Fellow ACP, Am. Coll. Cardiology, Clin. Coun. of Am. Heart Assn., N.Y. Acad. Medicine; mem. AMA, AAAS, N.Y. County Med. Soc. (mem. com. for govtl. affairs 1989—, com. on health planning 1988-89), N.Y. State Med. Soc., Am. Fedn. for Clin. Rsch., N.Y. Heart Assn. (coun. on profl. edn. 1978-81, rsch. grantee 1959-60), Am. Heart Assn. Home: 365 West Bend Ave New York NY 10024 Office: 889 Lexington Ave New York NY 10021

ROSENBLUTH, MARION HELEN, educator, consultant, psychotherapist; b. Chgo., Apr. 4, 1928; d. Edwin William and Louise (Sulzberger) Eisendrath; m. Paul Richard Rosenbluth, June 16, 1950 (dec. Nov. 1972); children: Daniel, Jane Baldwin, Thomas, James, Catherine Rothschild. BA, Harvard U., 1949; MSW, Cath. U. of Am., 1951; PhD, U. Ill., 1986. Lic. clin. social worker, Ill. Clin. therapist Chgo. Dept. of Health, 1973-80; pvt. practice Chgo., 1980—; prof. Loyola U., Chgo., 1986—; cons. Inst. for Clin. Social Work, Chgo., 1988—; cons. student health Loyola U., 1978-80. Bd. dirs. Chgo. Area Project, 1978—, Rec. for the Blind, Chgo., 1980—, Inst. Psychiatry Northwestern U. Mem. NASW, Coun. on Social Work Edn., Bd. Examiners Clin. Social Work (diplomate), Ill. Soc. Clin. Social Work, Arts Club of Chgo., Cliff Dwellers, Friday Club. Office: 676 N Saint Clair St Chicago IL 60611

ROSENBURG, JEFFREY MICHAEL, cardiovascular and thoracic surgeon; b. L.A., Jan. 6, 1955; s. Marvin Joseph and Janis Faye (Moss) R.; m. Jeanette Renee Lewey, May 29, 1988; children: Mathew, Michael. BS, U. So. Calif., 1979, MD, 1983. Diplomate Am. Bd. Surgery, Am. Bd. Thoracic Surgery. Resident in gen. surgery Harbor-UCLA Med. Ctr., Torrance, 1983-85, Kaiser Permanente Med. Ctr., Oakland, Calif., 1985-89; fellow in cardiothoracic surgery Kaiser Permanente Med. Ctr., San Francisco, 1989-90; resident in cardiopulmonary surgery SUNY, Syracuse, 1990-92; pvt. practice, San Diego, 1992-95, Chula Vista, Calif., 1995—; asst. chief surgery Sharp Chula Vista Med. Ctr., 1996—. Fellow ACS, Am. Coll. Chest Physicians, Am. Coll. Cardiology; mem. AMA, Am. Heart Assn. (bd. dirs. Chula Vista 1996—), Calif. Med. Assn. (alt. del. 1995—), San Diego County Med. Assn. Office: 450 4th Ave Ste 200 Chula Vista CA 91910

ROSENBUSH, STUART WILLIAM, cardiologist; b. Chgo., Jan. 31, 1951; s. Walter and Rena R.; m. Miriam Strilky, Jan. 19, 1974; children: Eric, Lara, Aaron. BS, U. Ill., 1972, MD, 1976. Diplomate Am. Bd. Internal Medicine, Am. Bd. Cardiovascular Diseases. Intern in internal medicine Michael Reese Med. Ctr., Chgo., 1976-77, resident in internal medicine, 1977-79; fellow in cardiology Rush Presbyn. St. Luke's Med. Ctr., Chgo., 1979-81, attending cardiologist, 1981—; asst. prof. medicine Rush Med. Coll., Chgo., 1982—. Fellow Soc. for Cardiac Angiography and Interventions. Fellow ACP, Am. Coll. Cardiology, Am. Heart Assn. (clin. coun.). Home: 6643 N LeMai Ave Lincolnwood IL 60646 Office: Assocs in Cardiology 1725 W Harrison Chicago IL 60612 Office: 9669 Kenton Ave Skokie IL 60076

ROSENFELD, ALVIN A., psychiatrist; b. Bklyn., May 9, 1945; s. Jack and Sara Lee (Gold) R.; m. Dorothy Ann Levine, Sept. 8, 1985; children: Lisa Claire, Samuel Aaron, Michael Daniel. BA, Cornell U., 1966; MD, Harvard U., 1970. Diplomate Am. Bd. Psychiatry & Neurology; cert. adult and adolescent/child psychiatrist. Intern in medicine R.I. Hosp., Providence, 1970-71; resident in psychiatry Harvard U. Med. Sch., Boston, 1971-73, clin. fellow in child psychiatry, 1973-75, clin. instr., 1975-77; dir. child psychiatry tng. Stanford (Calif.) U. Med. Sch., 1977-83; sr. rsch. scholar Columbia U. Tchrs. Coll., N.Y.C., 1984-92; dir. psychiat. svcs. Jewish Child Care Assn. N.Y., N.Y.C., 1984-96; acad. advisor Coun. Better Bus. Burs., Washington, 1988—; scholar-in-residence Rockefeller Found.-Bellagio (Italy) Ctr., 1985. Author: the Somatizing Child, 1987, Healing the Heart, 1990, A Dissenter in the House of God, 1990, The Art of the Obvious, 1993; mem. editorial bd. adv. bd. First Child mag., 1989-90; Parenting Q's and A's columnist Am. Baby mag., 1989-90; contbr. articles to profl. jours. Bd. dirs. Met. Coll. Mental Health Assn., N.Y.C., 1985-88; pres. Com. Physicians Voluntary Care Agys., N.Y.C., 1988-91, bd. dirs. U. Chgo. Sonia Shankman Orthogenic Sch., Inwood House, N.Y.C. Lt. comdr. USMC, USNR, 1975-77. Recipient Outstanding Tchr. award Stanford U., 1978. Fellow Am. Psychiat. Assn.; mem. Am. Acad. Child and Adolescent Psychiatry, N.Y.. Coun. on Child Psychiatry. Office: 4 East 89th St Ste 1/F New York NY 10128

ROSENFELD, CHARLES RICHARD, physician; b. Atlanta, Aug. 25, 1941; s. Bernard and Tillye Beatrice (Bach) R.; m. Ann Marie Christina Anderson, Aug. 21, 1971; children: Evan Louis, Scott Bernard, Jason Anders. MD, Emory U., 1966; postgrad., U. Colo. Med. Ctr., Denver, 1971-73. Diplomate Am. Bd. Pediatrics. Asst. clin. instr. Albert Einstein Coll. Medicine, Bronx, 1969-70, clin. instr., 1970-71; asst. prof. U. Tex., Southwestern Med. Sch., Dallas, 1973-77, assoc. prof., 1977-81; prof. U. Tex., Southewestern Med. Sch., Dallas, 1981—, dir. neonatal medicine, 1980—; George L. MacGregor prof. pediatrics, 1993—; v.p. Upper Trinity Perinatal assocs., 1981-82. Editor: The Uterine Circulation, 1989; assoc. editor Early Human Development, 1986—, Jour of Soc. for Gynecologic Investigation, 1994—; mem. editorial bd. Am. Jour. Physiology: Integrative and Comparative Physiology, 1996—; contbr. over 100 articles to profl. jours. Bd. dirs. Am. Lung Assn., Dallas, 1975-82, Dallas Aquatic Club, 1988-96; chmn. Health Profl. Adv. Com., March of Dimes, 1981-84; task force on perinatal care N. Ctrl. Tex. Coun. Govts., 1974-75. Stipes scholar, 1961; NIH grantee, 1974—, 86-89. Mem. AAAS, Am. Pediatric Soc., Endocrine Soc., Soc. for Gynecologic Investigation, Soc. for Pediatric Rsch., Am. Physiologic Soc., Perinatal Rsch. Soc., Alpha Kappa Alpha. Office: UT Southwestern Med Ctr 5323 Harry Hines Blvd Dallas TX 75235-7200

ROSENFELD, IRWIN IRA, psychiatrist; b. Bklyn., Feb. 26, 1951; s. Rubin Robert and Mildred (Kashtan) R.; m. Sheryl Tally Schwaber, June 24, 1973; children: Elayna Fern, Ethan Seth. BA in Biology, Cornell U., 1972; MD, Med. Coll. of Wis., 1976. Diplomate Am. Bd. Psychiatry and Neurology. Asst. clin. prof. U. Calif., Irvine, 1982—; pvt. practice Laguna Hills, Calif., 1980—; chief of staff Capistrano-By-the-Sea Hosp., Dana Point, Calif., 1986-88; vice chmn. dept. psychiatry South Coast Med. Ctr., South Laguna, Calif., 1990-95; chmn. dept. psychiatry , Saddleback Hosp., Laguna Hills, 1980—, Samaritan Hosp. San Clemente, Calif., 1990—; co-chmn. Calif. Medicare Carrier Adv. Com., 1992—. Group leader Orange County Alliance for the Mentally Ill, Tustin, Calif., 1986—; mem. physician's adv. bd. Manic-Depressive Assn. of Orange County, Dana Point, 1989—. Recipient Exemplary Psychiatrist award, 1994. Fellow Am. Psychiat. Assn.; mem. AMA, Am. Assn. for Geriatric Psychiatry (rep. 1987—), Calif. Psychiat. Assn. (chmn. com. 1988—), Calif. Med. Assn., Orange County Med. Assn. Democrat. Jewish. Office: 24022 La Plata #540 Laguna Hills CA 92653

ROSENFELD, ISADORE, medical educator, cardiologist, lecturer; b. Montreal, Que., Can., Sept. 7, 1926; came to U.S., 1958; s. Morris and Vera (Friedman) R.; m. Camilla Master, Aug. 19, 1956; children: Arthur, Stephen, Hildi, Herbert. BS, McGill U., 1947, M.D.C.M., 1951, diploma internal medicine, 1956. Intern Royal Victoria Hosp., Montreal; also resident Balt. City Hosp.; clin. asst. prof. medicine Cornell Med. Coll., N.Y.C., 1964-71, clin. assoc. prof., 1971-79, clin. prof., 1979—; Rossi Disting. prof. clin. medicine, 1993—; now hon. fellow; attending N.Y. Hosp., N.Y.C., 1989—; pres. Rosenfeld Heart Found., N.Y.C., 1974—; juror Lasker Sci. Awards, 1974-92; ; dir. Rsch. Am., 1990; lectr., TV commentator.; vis. prof. Baylor U. Coll. Medicine, 1982; mem. practicing physicians adv. coun. to U.S. Sec. Health and Human Svcs., 1992-96, practicing physician. Author: ECG and X-Ray in Diseases of the Heart, 1963, The Complete Medical Exam, 1978, Second Opinion, 1981; Modern Prevention, 1986, Symptoms, 1988, The Best Treatment, 1991, Doctor, What Should I EAT?, 1995. Bd. dirs. N.Y. Heart Assn., 1979-82; mem. nat. adv. com. Harriman Inst. Advanced Study of Soviet Union, 1982—; bd. overseers Cornell U. Med. Coll., 1980—; bd. visitors U. Calif. Sch. Medicine, Davis, 1983—. Recipient Vera award The Voice Found., 1981, Inaugural award N.Y. Heart Assn., 1996. Fellow ACP, Am. Coll. Chest Physicians, Am. Coll. Cardiology, Royal Coll. Physicians Can., N.Y. County Med. Soc. (bd. censors 1979-83, v.p. 1983-84, pres. 1984-85, trustee 1985—), Am. Physician's Fellowship for Israel (hon. nat. pres. 1975—), Cornell Alumni Assn. (hon.). Jewish. Research on hypertension, angina pectoris, sudden cardiac death, arteriosclerosis. Office: 125 E 72nd St New York NY 10021-4250

ROSENFELD, JOEL, ophthalmologist, lawyer; b. Jan. 27, 1957; s. Jacques Maurice and Mazal (Attia) R.; m. Amy Beth Garon. BS with high honors, U. Mich., 1976, MD, 1980; JD cum laude, U. Detroit, 1993. Diplomate Nat. Bd. Med. Examiners, Am. Bd. Ophthalmology; bar: Mich. 1994. Intern Baylor Coll. Medicine, Houston, 1980-81; resident in ophthalmology Kresge Eye Inst./Wayne State U., Detroit, 1981-84; fellow in ultrasound U. Iowa, Iowa City, 1984; chief of ophthalmology Wheelock Hosp., Goodrich, Mich., 1984—, Huron Meml. Hosp., Bad Axe, Mich., 1988—; St. Joseph Mercy Hosp., Pontiac, Mich., 1989—; co-founder, pres., gen. counsel Mktg. Systems, Inc., 1994—. Author rsch. reports. Supporting mem. Boys and Girls Club Am., Pontiac, Mich., 1984—, Pontiac Rescue Mission, 1988—. Recipient Man of Yr. award Boys and Girls Clubs Am., 1988; named Hon. Citizen, Father Flanagan Boys Home, Boys Town, Nebr., 1991, Ptnr. of Conscience, Amnesty Internat., N.Y.C., 1991. Fellow AMA, Am. Acad. Ophthalmology, Am. Coll. Legal Medicine; mem. ABA, FBA, Am. Soc. Law, Medicine and Ethics, Mich. State Med. Soc., Nat. Health Lawyers Assn. Jewish. Home: 4612 W Maple Rd Bloomfield Hills MI 48301-1415

ROSENFELD, MICHAEL G., medical educator. Prof. dept. medicine U. Calif. Med. Sch., La Jolla. Mem. NAS. Office: U Calif San Diego Sch Medicine M-013 Dept Medicine La Jolla CA 92093*

ROSENFELD, RONALD NORMAN, orthopaedic surgeon; b. Phila.; m. Amy Biener; children, Jonathan, Scott, Carl. AB, Temple U., 1968; DO, Phila. Coll. Osteopathy, 1973; MD, Med. Coll. Pa., 1974. Diplomate Am. Bd. Orthopaedic Surgery. Intern in surgery Med. Coll. Pa., Phila., 1975; resident in orthopaedics Einstein Med. Ctr., Phila., 1975-79; pvt. practive Orthopaedic Surgery, Ltd., Swarthmore, Pa.; mem. staff Crozer Chester Med. Ctr., Mercy Haverford Hosp., Fitzgerald Mercy Hosp., Del. County Meml. Hosp.; chief of staff, chief orthop. svc. Springfield Divsn. Office: Orthopaedic Surgery Ltd 623 S Chester Rd Swarthmore PA 19081-2315

ROSENFELD, STEVEN IRA, ophthalmologist; b. N.Y.C., Nov. 18, 1954; s. Frederick and Pearl (Stern) R.; m. Lisa Allyson Klar, June 24, 1978; children: Michael, Julie. BA, Johns Hopkins U., 1976; MD, Yale U., 1980. Diplomate Am. Bd. Ophthalmology, Nat. Bd. Med. Examiners. Intern Yale-New Haven Hosp., 1980-81; resident Barnes Hosp., St. Louis, 1981-84; fellow Bascom Palmer Eye Inst., Miami, Fla., 1984-85; ptnr. in pvt. practice Delray Eye Assocs., Delray Beach, Fla., 1985—; clin. instr. Bascom Palmer Eye Inst., 1985-90, asst. clin. prof., 1990—; assoc. examiner Am. Bd. Ophthalmology, Phila., 1993—. Author: Lens and Cataract: The Eye in Systemic Disease; contbr. articles to profl. jours. Recipient Harry Rosenbaum Rsch. award Washington U. Sch. Medicine, 1984; named one of Best Doctors in Am., 1996; Heed Ophthalmic Found. fellow, 1984. Fellow ACS, Am. Acad. Ophthalmology, Soc. Heed Fellows; mem. Castroviejo Corneal Soc., Eye Bank Assn. Am., Fla. Med. Assn., Fla. Soc. Ophthalmology, Assn. for Rsch. in Vision and Ophthalmology, Ocular Microbiology and Immunology Group, Phi Beta Kappa, Alpha Omega Alpha. Office: Delray Eye Assocs 16201 S Military Trl Delray Beach FL 33484-6503

ROSENFIELD, ALLAN, physician; b. Cambridge, Mass., Apr. 28, 1933; s. Harold Herman and Beatrice (Garber) R.; m. Clare Stein, July 31, 1966; children: Paul Allan, Jill Emilie. BA cum laude, Harvard U., 1955; MD, Columbia U., 1959. Diplomate Am. Bd. Ob-Gyn. Intern, surgical resident Beth Israel Hosp., Boston, 1959-61; resident in ob-gyn Boston Hosp. for Women (now Brigham and Woman's Hosp.), Boston, 1963-66; rep., med. advisor The Population Council and Ministry Pub. Health, Bangkok, 1967-73; asst. dir. tech. assistance div. The Population Council, N.Y.C., 1973-75; prof. ob-gyn Columbia U., N.Y.C., 1975-88, prof. pub. health, 1975-86, DeLamar Prof. pub. health, 1986—, dir. ctr. for population and family health, 1975-88, acting chmn. dept. ob-gyn., 1984-86, dean sch. pub. health, 1986—. Contbr. over 100 articles to profl. jours. Capt. USAF, 1961-63. Fellow Am. Coll. Obstetricians and Gynecologists; mem. Inst. Medicine of NAS (several coms. and bds.), Am. Pub. Health Assn. Jewish. Home: 4 Crosshill Rd Hartsdale NY 10530-3014 Office: Columbia U Sch Pub Health 600 W 168th St New York NY 10032-3702

ROSENFIELD, ARTHUR TED, radiology educator; b. Waterbury, Conn., Dec. 7, 1942; s. Harry Nathan and Selina Sylvia (Glasser) R.; m. Nancy Schulkind, May 26, 1968; children: Wendy, Jonathan, Eric. BA cum laude, Brandeis U., 1964; MD, NYU, 1968; MA (hon.), Yale U., 1983. Diplomate Am. Bd. Radiology, Nat. Bd. Med. Examiners. Med. intern Montefiore Hosp., Pitts., 1968-69; instr. in medicine U. Pitts., 1968-69; resident, diagnostic radiology Beth Israel Hosp., Boston, 1971-73, chief resident, radiology, 1973-74; clin. fellow, radiology Harvard Med. Sch., Boston, 1971-74; various to attending radiologist Yale-New Haven Hosp., New Haven, Conn., 1975—; assoc. prof. diagnostic radiology Yale U. Sch. Medicine, New Haven, 1978-83, prof. diagnostic radiology, 1983—, prof. diagnostic radiology and surgery (urology), 1987-92; asst. resident internal medicine USPHS Hosp., Balt, 1969-70; affiliated resident, Armed Forces Inst. of Pathology, Washington, 1972, Children's Hosp. Med. Ctr., Boston, 1973, Tufts U. New Eng. Med. Ctr., Boston, 1973, Mass. Eye and Ear Infirmary, Boston, 1973; attending radiologist VA Hosp. West Haven, Conn., 1976—; cons. Norwalk (Conn.) Hosp., 1979—, The Yale Hereditary Renal Disease Clinic, New Haven, 1991; other. Contbg. author books in field; contbr. numerous articles to profl. jours. Recipient Editor's Recognition awards Radiology, 1986, 87, 90; grantee Squibb Med. Rsch. Found., Winthrop Labs., Gen. Electric Corp., others. Fellow Soc. Uroradiology (award-winning paper 1988, 95); mem. New Eng. Roentgen Ray Soc., Mass. Med. Soc., Yale Soc. Urol. Surgeons, Am. Coll. Radiology, Assn. Univ. Radiologists, Radiol. Soc. N.Am., Am. Inst. Ultrasound in Medicine, Am. Roentgen Ray Soc., Am. Urol. Assn. (guest mem.), Sigma Xi. Office: Yale Univ Sch Medicine 300 Cedar St New Haven CT 06519-1612

ROSENFIELD, LORNE KING, surgeon; b. Winnipeg, Man., Can., Jan. 24, 1956; children: Lauren, Ian, Michael. BS in Medicine, U. Man., Winnipeg, 1976; MD, U. Man., 1980. Diplomate Am. Bd. Surgery, Am. Bd. Plastic Surgery. General surgery resident St. Mary's Hosp., San Francisco, 1985-87; plastic surgery fellow Baylor Coll. Medicine, 1987; chmn. dept. plastic surgery Mills-Peninsula Hosp., Burlingame, Calif., 1995—; past chmn. St. Mary's Hosp., San Francisco, 1992-95. Fellow Am. Coll. Surgeons; mem. San Francisco Med. Soc. (mem. ethics com. bd. 1990-95). Office: Peninsula Plastic Surgery Inc 1750 El Camino Real Ste 405 Burlingame CA 94010-3225

ROSENFIELD, LOUIS, cardiologist; b. Waterbury, Conn., Nov. 22, 1951; s. Samuel Alfred and Charlotte June (Dorfman) R. BA in Chemistry, George Wash. U., 1973, MD, 1982. Diplomate Am. Bd. Internal Medicine. Dir. Cardiovasc. Lab. Med. Ctr. Hosp., Punta Gorda, Fla., 1984-89; dir. Gulf Coast Med. Imaging, Port Charlotte, Fla., 1990-95; pres. Cardiology Assocs., Port Charlotte, Fla., 1996—. Office: Cardiology Assocs 4130 Tamiami Tr Port Charlotte FL 33952

ROSENFIELD, ROBERT LEE, pediatric endocrinologist, educator; b. Robinson, Ill., Dec. 16, 1934; s. Irving and Sadie (Osipe) R.; m. Sandra L. McVicker, Apr. 14, 1973. BS, Northwestern U., 1956, MD, 1960. Diplomate Am. Bd. Pediatric Endocrinology. Intern, Phila. Gen. Hosp. and Children's Hosp., Phila., 1960-63, 65-68; practice medicine specializing in pediatric endocrinology; prof. pediatrics, medicine U. Chgo., 1968—. Contbr. research articles to profl. jours. Served to capt. USMC, 1963-65. Fogarty Sr. Internat. fellow, USPHS, Weizmann Inst., Israel, 1977-78. Mem. Am. Bd. Pediatrics (sub.-bd. pediatric endocrinology 1983-86), Am. Pediatric Soc., Lawson Wilkins Pediatric Endocrinology Soc., Endocrine Soc., Soc. Gynecol. Investigation, Chgo. Pediatric Soc. (pres. 1981). Democrat. Jewish. Avocation: photography. Home: 5474 S Greenwood Ave Chicago IL 60615-5104 Office: U Chgo Med Ctr 5841 S Maryland Ave Chicago IL 60637-1463

ROSENHEIM, CHRISTINE LABODA, health management consultant; b. N.Y.C., June 22, 1952; d. Henry Oliver and Olga Caroline (Chupurdy) Laboda; m. Thomas Rosenheim, May 19, 1973; children: Brad Erik, Randy Thomas. AA in Nursing, Queensborough C.C., 1972; BS in Health Care Adminstrn., Stockton State Coll., 1976. RN, N.J., N.Y.; cert. med. case mgr., case mgr. Staff nurse N. Shore Med. Ctr., Manhassett, N.Y., 1972-73, W. Jersey Hosp., Voorhees, N.J., 1973-79; nurse Everett R. Curran Jr. M.D., Cherry Hill, N.J., 1979-83, Valley Rehab. Co., Hammonton, N.J., 1983-85; nurse auditor Consolidated Rehab. Co., Haddon Heights, N.J., 1986-87; pres. Medi Fax Cons., Atco, N.J., 1987—; presenter case mgmt. tng. Nursing Spectrum, 1994-95. Editor: Pediatric Press, 1982. Chairperson Cub Scouts Am., Atco 1986-87; v.p. Waterford Twp. Home and Sch. Assn., Atco 1985-87. Mem. NAFE, Emergency Dept. Nurses Assn., South Jersey Claims Assn., Profl. Rehab. Network (pres. 1994—, instr. nursing spectrum bus. network case mgmt. training), Nat. Assn. Rehab. Profls. Home: 2271 Linden Ave Atco NJ 08004-1210 Office: Medi-Fax Cons 639 Jackson Rd Atco NJ 08004-1108

ROSENMAN, KENNETH D., medical educator; b. N.Y.C., Feb. 25, 1951. AB, Cornell U., 1972; MD, NYU, 1975. Bd. cert. internal medicine; bd. cert. occupational and preventive medicine. Asst. prof. U. Mass., Amherst, 1979-81; dir. occupational and environ. health N.J. Dept. Health, Trenton, 1981-86; pvt. practice Plainsboro, N.J., 1986-88; assoc. prof. Mich. State U., East Lansing, 1988-93, prof., 1993—. Office: Mich State U 117 W Fee East Lansing MI 48864

ROSENMAN, STANLEY, psychologist; b. N.Y.C., May 29, 1923; s. Sigmund Zanvel and Bryna (Gross) R.; m. Muriel Cecile Zimmerman, 1952; 1 child, Peter. PhD, Harvard U., 1953. Lic. psychologist, N.Y. Pvt. practice clin. psychology and marital therapy, N.Y.C., 1955—. Sgt. inf. AUS, 1945. Mem. APA, Nat. Psychol. Assn. for Psychoanalysis, Internat. Psychohist. Assn. Home and Office: 55 E 86th St 6A New York NY 10028-1059

ROSENMAN, STEPHEN DAVID, physician, obstetrics, gynecology; b. Bklyn., Sept. 4, 1945; s. Bernard and Theresa (Marks) R. m. Arlette de Greef, Dec. 26m 1970; children: Burt, Joelle. BA in Biology, Hofstra U., 1967; MD magna cum laude, Cath. U. of Louvain (Belgium), 1972. Diplomate Am. Bd. Ob-Gyn., voluntarily re-cert. 1991; lic. N.Y., Conn. Rotating intern Dalhousie U., Canada, 1972-73; ob-gyn. resident Bridgeport (Conn.) Hosp., 1973-75, chief resident, 1976-77, sr. attending physician ob-gyn., 1986—; pvt. practice Fairfield, Stratford, Trumbull, Bridgeport, Conn., 1978—. Named Tchr. of Yr., Bridgeport (Conn.) Hosp. 1977, '78, '80. Fellow Am. Bd. Obstetrics, Am. Coll. Ob.-Gyn. Office: Ob-gyn of FFLD County PC 1725 Post Rd Fairfield CT 06430-5715 also: 2499 Main St Stratford CT 06497-5843 also: 15 Corporate Dr Trumbull CT 06611

ROSENQUIST, CARL JOHN, radiologist, educator; b. Austin, Tex., Nov. 9, 1935; s. Carl Martin and Helen E. (Barrett) R.; m. Grace D. Link, Dec. 30, 1960; children: Kerstin, Marta. BA, U. Tex., 1956; MD, Washington U., St. Louis, 1960. Diplomate Am. Bd. Radiology. Asst. prof. radiology Stanford (Calif.) U., 1966-71; prof. radiology U. Calif., Davis, 1972—; hon. cons. Royal Free Hosp., London, 1981. Contbr. articles to profl. jours. Capt. USAF, 1964-66. PEW Found. fellow, 1986. Mem. Am. Coll. Radiology, Radiol. Soc. N.Am., Assn. Univ. Radiologists. Office: Univ of Calif Dept Radiology 2516 Stockton Blvd Sacramento CA 95817

ROSENQUIST, ROBERT CHARLES, retired internist; b. Madison, Wis., Jan. 7, 1921; s. Carl Philip and Ellen June (Hickok) R.; m. Betty Alfarata Oliver, Jan. 8, 1945; children: Ellen Dianne Rosenquist-Rice, Nancy Lynn Rosenquist-Wernick, Janine Sue Rosenquist-Cochrane, Robert Charles Jr. BS, Pacific Union Coll., 1943; MD, Loma Linda U., 1946. Diplomate Am. Bd. Internal Medicine, Am. Bd. Endocrinology and Metabolism. From instr. to prof. internal med. Loma Linda (Calif.) U. Sch. Medicine, 1951-86, prof. emeritus, 1990—; chief endocrinology and metabolism Jerry L. Pettis Meml. VA Hosp., Loma Linda, 1977-86; chmn. dept. internal medicine Sir Run Run Shaw Hosp., Hangzhou, China, 1993-95. Contbr. articles to profl. jours. Advisor Diabetes Soc., San Bernardino, Calif., 1964-65. Capt. U.S. Army, 1946-49. Fellow ACP. Republican. Adventist. Home: 36246 Golden Gate Dr Yucaipa CA 92399

ROSENSCHEIN, GUY RAOUL, pediatric and visceral surgeon, airline pilot; b. Paris, July 28, 1953; s. Maurice and Caroline (Meller) R. M.D., Lariboisiere-St. Louis, Paris, 1977. Qualified airline transport pilot, 1992, flight instr., 1993—. Intern, Hôpital Saint-Louis, 1973-74, Hôpital Lariboisière, 1975-76; resident Hôpitaux de Paris, 1977-80, Hôpital Bretonneau, 1977-78, Hôpital Lariboisière, 1979-80; resident Hôpital de Monaco, Monte Carlo, 1980-81; resident Hôpital St. Vincent de Paul, Paris, 1981-82, attache, 1982-84, asst., 1984-86, asst. prof. pediat. surgery; chef de clinique U. Paris, 1984-86; attache Hôpital de Villeneuve St Georges, 1987-94; attache C.H.S. Saine Anne, Paris, 1982-94; maitre de stage hospitalier Faculté de Médecine de Creteil, 1987-92; pilot 1981; profl. transport. instr., 1993; attending pediat. surgery Maimonides Med. Ctr. and S.I. Univ. Hosp., 1994—. Author: Pancreatite non traumatique et non infectieuse de l'enfant, 1982. Capt., M.C., French Armed Forces, 1977. Mem. Nat. Assn. Flight Instrs., TEFC Club TEFC (chief flight instr.). Jewish. Home: 351 Marine Ave Brooklyn NY 11209-8045 Office: 8520 Ridge Blvd Brooklyn NY 11209

ROSENSON, ROBERT SIDNEY, cardiologist, researcher; b. Chgo., Oct. 31, 1956; s. Ronald Howard and Arlene Rosenson. BA, Drake U., 1978; MD, Tulane U., 1983. Intern Brigham and Women's Hosp., Boston, 1983-84, resident in medicine, 1984-86; fellow in cardiology U. Chgo., 1986-89, rsch. assoc., 1989-90; asst. prof. Rush Med. Coll., Chgo., 1990—; bd. dirs. Preventive Cardiology Ctr., Cardiac Rehab., Lipoprotein and Hemorheology Rsch. Facility. Contbr. articles to Jour. Physiology, Chest, Biochem. Biophys. Rsch., Am. Jour. Cardiology, Gastroenterology, Jour. Am. Coll. Cardiology, Archives Internal Medicine, Arteriosclerosis and Thrombosis. Mem. epidemiology and atherosclerosis couns. Am. Heart Assn., Dallas, 1990—. Fellow ACP, Am. Coll. Cardiology (mem. prevention cardiovascular disease com.), Am. Coll. Chest Physicians (fellowship grantee 1991—), Am. Coll. Physicians; mem. AAAS, Mended Hearts (med. liaison). Office: Rush-Presbyn-St Lukes Med Ctr 1653 W Congress Pky Chicago IL 60612-3833

ROSENSPIRE, KAREN CHERYL, biomedical researcher; b. Phila., Dec. 10, 1951; d. James Joseph and Ruth Arlene (Ridge) Lawless; m. Allen Jay Rosenspire, Aug. 20, 1977; children: Joshua, David. BA, Eastern Coll., St. Davids, Pa., 1973; PhD, SUNY, Buffalo, 1980. Diplomate Am. Bd. Sci. in Nuclear Medicine. Rsch. assoc. SUNY, Buffalo, 1979; postdoctoral fellow Sloan-Kettering Inst., N.Y.C., 1979-82, rsch. assoc., 1982-86; rsch. assoc. U. Mich., Ann Arbor, 1986-89; rsch. investigator Bristol-Myers Squibb, New Brunswick, N.J., 1989-91; sr. fellow U. Mich., Ann Arbor, 1992-94; reviewer jours. Applied Radiation and Isotopes, 1990—, Jour. Nuclear Medicine and Biology, 1990—, Jour. Nuclear Medicine, 1987—. Contbr. articles to profl. jours. Recipient Nat. Rsch. Svc. award NIH, 1979-82, New Investigator Rsch. award NCI/NIH, 1983-86, sr. fellowship award NIH, 1992-94. Mem. AAAS, Soc. Nuclear Medicine (Edn. and Rsch. Found. grantee 1977), Am. Chem. Soc., Internat. Assn. Radiopharmacology, Am. Coll. Nuclear Physicians. Home: 3221 Lockridge St Ann Arbor MI 48108-1721

ROSENSTEIN, BERYL JOEL, physician; b. Boston, Jan. 5, 1937; s. Benjamin and Doris (Goldhagen) R.; m. Carolyn S., Aug. 31, 1958; children: Susan Eileen, Jonathan David. BA, Boston U., 1957; MD, Tufts U., 1961; M Adminstrv. Sci., Johns Hopkins U., 1987. Diplomate Am. Bd. Pediatrics. Intern in pediatrics Johns Hopkins Hosp., Balt., 1961-62, resident in pediatrics, 1962-64, dir. cystic fibrosis clinic, 1972—, v.p. med. affairs, 1994—; prof. pediatrics Johns Hopkins Sch. Med., Balt., 1989—; med. dir. Mt. Washington Pediatric Hosp., Balt., 1988-93; med. adv. coun. Cystic Fibrosis Found., Bethesda, Md., 1980-88, trustee, 1986—. Author: Pediatric Pearls: Handbook of Pediatrics, 1989, Primary Care of the Newborn, 1992; contbr. over 100 articles to profl. jours. and chpts. to books. Lt. comdr. USPHS, 1964-66. Fellow Am. Acad. Pediatrics, Ambulator Pediatric Assn.; mem. Am. Thoracic Soc., Am. Pediatric Soc., Alpha Omega Alpha. Office: Johns Hopkins Hosp Park 315 Baltimore MD 21287-2533

ROSENSTEIN, HENRI, cardiologist; b. Paris, June 3, 1941; s. Eljasz and Chana (Stobiecki) R.; m. Marie-Laure Adida, Dec. 5, 1969; children: Florence, Lucile. Degree in Physics, Chemistry and Biology, Faculte de Scis, Paris, 1960; student, Faculte de Medecine de Paris, 1961-66; MD, Med. Sch. Paris XIII, 1973. Externe Hopitaux de Paris, 1962-67, interne, 1968-73; worked in S. Renaud Lab., Inst. de Cardiologie de Montreal, Quebec, Can., 1972; chef de clinique, asst. Hopitaux de Paris, 1973-77, attache, 1977—; mem. staff Dr. Volter Hosp. Jean-Verdier, Bondy, France. Jewish. Office: 45 Rue Jean Jaures, 94500 Champigny Sur Marn France

ROSENSTEIN, MARVIN, public health administrator; b. Sept. 5, 1939. BSChemE, U. Md., 1961; MS in Environ. Engring., Renssselaer Poly. Inst., 1966; PhD in Nuclear Engring., U. Md., 1971. Rschr. U.S. Bur. Mines/College Park (Md.) Metall. Rsch. Sta., 1961; commd. ensign Commd. Corps Pub. Health Svc., 1962, advanced through grades to capt., 1983; with N.E. Radiological Health Lab., Winchester, Mass., 1962, program coord. analytical quality control svc. divsn. radiological health, 1962; with data collation and analysis sect. radiation surveillance ctr. Divsn. Radiological Health, Washington, 1966; chief radiation exposure intelligence sect. standards and intelligence br. Nat. Ctr. for Radiological Health, Rockville, Md., 1967; dep. chief radiation measurements and calibration br. divsn. electronic products Bur. Radiological Health, Rockville, 1971, spl. asst. to dir. divsn. electronic products, 1972, dep. dir. divsn. electonic products, 1973; dep. assoc. commr. for policy coordination office policy coordination FDA, Rockville, 1978; sr. sci. advisor, 1979; dir. office health physics Ctr. for Devices and Radiological Health, Rockville, 1982-95; sr. staff fellow Ctr. for Devices and Radiol. Health, Rockville, Md., 1995—; mem. USASI Standards Com. N101, 1968-69; guest worker Ctr. for Radiation Rsch., Nat. Bur. Standards, 1969-74; faculty rsch. assoc. lab. for polymer and radiation sci. dept. chem. engring. U. Md., 1971-74; asst. clin. prof. radiology sch. medicine and scis. George Washington U., 1977-90. Contbr. over 70 publs. to profl. and sci. jours. Recipient Fed. Engr. of Yr. award NSPE/Dept. Health and Human Svcs., 1987. Mem. Nat. Coun. on Radiation Protection and Measurements (coun. 1988—, sci. com. 44 1976—, sci. com. 62 1980-85, chmn. sci. com. 46-12 1992-96), Health Physics Soc. (publs. com. 1967-77, del. to 4th internat. congress Internat. Radiation Protection Assn. 1977, contbg. editor newsletter 1982—), Com. on Interagy. Radiation Rsch. and Policy Coord. (alt. HHS policy panel 1984-95, vice chmn. sci. panel 1985-94, exec. com. 1985-94, chmn. subpanel on use NAS com. on biol. effects of ionizing radiation report V and UN sci. com. on the effects of atomic radiation 1988, report in risk assessment 1989-92), Internat. Commn. on Radiol. Protection (com. 3 on radiol. protection in medicine 1985—, corr. mem. task group on rev. publ. 21 1979-88), Internat. Commn. on Radiation Units and Measurements (report com. on dosimetry in diagnostic radiology for the patient 1994—), Commd. Officers Assn., Sigma Xi. Office: FDA Ctr Devices & Radiol Health 16071 Industrial Dr Rockville MD 20850

ROSENSTEIN, RICHARD KENNETH, physician; b. Louisville, July 31, 1951; s. Abraham Sydney and Ruth Florence (Tanenhaus) R.; m. Lynn Marla Cook, May 9, 1977; children: Yitzhok, Yehoshua, Tova, Golda, Shmuel, Hayim. BA, Washington U., St. Louis, 1973; MD, U. Louisville, 1977. Resident ob-gyn SUNY, Buffalo, 1977-81; ob-gyn house physician Marymount Hosp., Garfield Heights, Ohio, 1981-90, Wyandotte (Mich.) Hosp. and Med. Ctr., 1990—; cons. obstetrician Womankind, Inc., Cleve., 1985-90. V.p. Cong. Zemach Zedek, Cleveland Heights, 1984-90, Russian Immigrant Aid Soc., Cleveland Heights, 1982-90; coord. Israeli Widows and Orphans Fund, Cleve., 1985-90; v.p. Congr. Bais Chabad of North Oak Park, Mich., 1990-94. Assoc. fellow ACOG; mem. Mich. State Med. Soc., Wayne County Med. Soc. Jewish. Home: 25321 Gardner St Oak Park MI 48237-1346 Office: Wyandotte Hosp Med Ctr 2333 Biddle St Wyandotte MI 48192-4668

ROSENSTEIN, ROBERT NATHAN, optometrist. BS, OD, New Eng. Coll. Optometry, 1974. Pvt. practice optometry Durham, N.C., 1974—; clin. examiner N.C. Bd. Examiners in Optometry, 1993-96; chmn. dept. optometry N.C. Eye & Ear Hosp., 1994-96; instr. Pa. Coll. Optometry, 1990; lectr. in field. Bd. dirs. Beth-el Synagogue, 1975-77, 92-93; bd. dirs. B'nai B'rith Hillel Found., 1977-79, pres. Nanthan Rosenstein Lodge, 1977-78, pres. N.C. Assn., 1978, mem. dist. 5 bd. govs., 1977-79; apptd. adv. bd. N.C. Vis. Israel Scholar Program, 1978; mem. USA Delegation 5th World Conf. YMCA's, Nottingham, England, 1969; pres. Durham YMCA, 1986, bd. dirs. 1979-94; bd. dirs. Durham Bd. Health, 1986-90, vice chmn., 1989-90; bd. dirs. N.C. Symphony, 1992-95. Fellow Am. Acad. Optometry (admission exam. com. 1993—); mem. N.C. State Optometric Soc. (ins. chmn. 1992-94), Eastern Dist. Optometric Soc. Office: 2901 N Duke St Durham NC 27704

ROSENSTOCK, HARVEY ALLAN, psychiatrist; b. Michigan City, Ind., May 24, 1940; s. Arnold and Leona (Cohen) R.; m. Judith D. Naistadt, May 9, 1982; children: Amara Biro, Aaron, Marc, Benjamin, Debbie. BA in Chemistry, Ariz. State U., 1962; MD, U. Oreg. Med. Sch., 1966. Diplomate Am. Bd. Med. Examiners, Am. Bd. Psychiatry and Neurology. Resident in adult psychiatry Baylor Coll. of Medicine, Houston, Tex., 1969-73; med. dir. adolescent ctr. Houston Internat. Hosp., 1974-90; pvt. practice Rosenstock Clinic, Bellaire, Tex., 1982—; assoc. clin. prof. of psychiatry and behavioral sciences U. Tex. Med. Sch., Houston, 1990—; intern Good Samaritan Hosp., Phoenix, 1966-67; assoc. med. dir. Intracare Hosp., Houston, 1990-91, chief of staff, 1991—, med. dir., 1995-96; cons., co-med. dir. Lake Jackson Mental Health Clinic; cons. in child psychiatry med. clinic Tex. Rsch. Inst. Mental Sci., 1972-73; bd. dirs. Sexuality Info. Edn. Coun. U.S. Author: Your Hospital Stay: It'll Be Okay, 1984, (with Rosenstock and Weiner) Journey Through Divorce: Five Stages Toward Recovery, 1988, Tu Estadia en el Hospital...Va a Ser Buena, Spanish edit., 1990; contbr. articles to profl. jours. Bd. dirs. Sexuality Info. and Edn. Coun. U.S., 1995-96, Houston Hillel Orgn., Houston Action for Soviet Jewry, S.W. region Anti-Defamation League of B'nai B'rith. Lt. USN, 1967-69. Child fellow Baylor Coll. of Med., 1971-73; Falk fellow Am. Psychiat. Assn., 1971. Mem. Internat. Group Psychotherapy Assn., World Psychiat. Assn., Am. Psychiat. Assn., The Am. Coll. Psychiatrists, Am. Group Psychotherapy Assn., Am. Assn. Sex Educators, Counselors and Therapists, Tex. Dist. Br. Am. Psychiat. Assn., Tex. Med. Assn., Harris County Med. Soc., Houston Group Psychotherapy Soc., Houston Psychiat. Soc. Jewish. Office: 4747 Bellaire Blvd Ste 550 Bellaire TX 77401

ROSENSTOCK, LINDA, medical educator; b. N.Y.C., Dec. 20, 1950. AB in Psychology, Brandeis U., 1971; student, U. B.C., Vancouver, Can., 1971-72; MD, Johns Hopkins U., 1977, MPH, 1977. Diplomate Am. Bd. Internal Medicine, Am. Bd. Preventive Medicine; lic. physician and surgeon, Wash. Med. resident then chief resident U. Wash., Seattle, 1977-80, resident in preventive medicine, instr. medicine, 1980-82, asst. prof., 1982-83, 83-87, lectr. environ. heatlh, 1982-83, adj. asst. prof., 1983-86, mem. grad. sch. faculty, 1985—, assoc. prof., 1987-93, prof. medicine and environ. health, 1993—, also dir. programs; dir. Harborview Med. Ctr., Seattle, 1981-87, acting sect. head, 1992-94; dir. Nat. Isnt. Occupational Safety and Health, Washington, 1994—. Assoc. editor Internat. Jour. Occupational Medicine and Toxicology, 1991—; mem. editorial bd. Am. Jour. Indsl. Medicine, 1985-94, Jour. Gen. Internal Medicine, 1987-90, Environ. Rsch., 1987—, Western Jour. Medicine, 1990—; contbr. numerous articles to profl. jours. Mem. exec. bd. Physicians for Human Rights, 1990—; mem. occupl. health adv. bd. United Auto Workers GM, 1990-94, chair, 1993-94; mem. task force on pneumoconioses Am. Coll. Radiology, 1991-94; mem. external adv. panel Agrl. Health and Safety Ctr., 1992-93; mem. adv. com. Ctrs. for Disease Control, 1992-94; mem. com. to survey health effects of mustard gas and lewisite Inst. Medicine, 1992, mem. bd. health promotion and disease prevention, 1993-94; mem. bd. sci. counselors HHS, 1993-94, mem. exec. com. nat. toxicology program, 1994—; mem. med. adv. bd. Teamsters Internat., 1993-94. Recipient Upjohn Achievement award Harborview Med. Ctr., 1978, Jean Spencer Felton MD award Western Occupational Med. Assn., 1988, Environ. and Occupational Medicine award Nat. Isnt. Environ. Health Scis., 1991-94; Robert Wood Johnson scholar, 1980-82, Henry j. Kaiser scholar, 1984-89. Fellow ACP (health promotion subcom. 1989-90, clin. practicie subcom. 1990-91), Collegium Ramazzini; mem. APHA (chair membership com. 1983-85, chairperson occupational helath and safety sect. 1985-86, gov. coun. 1986-88), Am. Coll. Occupational Medicine (mem. jud. com. 1989-94), Am. Thoracic Soc. (com. health care policy and clin. practice 1990-93), Internat. Commn. Occupational Health (sci. com. epidemiology in occupational health 1989—), Soc. Gen. Internal Medicine (program planning com. 1987, Glaser award com. 1993-94), Western Assn. Physicians, Pacific Interurban Clin. Club. Office: Nat Inst Occupational Safety & Health 200 Indpendence Ave SW Washington DC 20201

ROSENSTREICH, DAVID LEON, medical educator, immunologist, allergist; b. N.Y.C., Nov. 16, 1942; s. Joseph S. and Gertrude (Tankenbaum) R.; m. Victoria Abokrek, June 13, 1965; children: Jonathan, Peter, Rebecca. BS in Chemistry, CCNY, 1963; MD, NYU, 1967. Internship, residency Bronx (N.Y.) Mcpl. Hosp. Ctr., 1967-69; clin. assoc. NIAID, NIH, Bethesda, Md., 1969-72; sr. investigator NIDR, NIH, Bethesda, 1972-78; vis. assoc. prof. Rockefeller U., N.Y.C., 1978-80; prof. medicine Albert Einstein Coll. Medicine, N.Y.C., 1980—, dir. div. allergy and immunology, 1980—. Editor: Mitogens in Immunobiology, 1975, Cellular Functions in Immunity and Inflamation, 1980; assoc. editor Clin. Revs. in Allergy, 1987—, Annals of Allergy, 1994—. Comdr. USPHS, 1969-78. Fellow Am. Soc. Clin. Investigation, Am. Acad. Allergy and Immunology, Am. Coll. Allergy, Am. Assn. Physicians. Office: Albert Einstein Coll Med 1300 Morris Park Ave Bronx NY 10461-1926

ROSEN-SUPNICK, ELAINE RENEE, physical therapist; b. N.Y.C., May 7, 1951; d. Oscar Arthur and Sydell (Zimmerman) R.;m. Jed Supnick, Apr. 21, 1985. BS, CUNY-Hunter Coll., 1973; MS, L.I. U., Bklyn., 1977. Cert. orthop. specialist. Phys. therapy cons. Lenox Hill Hosp. Home Care, N.Y.C., 1977-83, Group Health Ins., Queens, N.Y., 1977-83, Vis. Nurse Assn., Bklyn., 1977-83; sr. phys. therapist Bird S. Coler Hosp., Roosevelt Island, N.Y., 1973-77; assoc. prof. Hunter Coll. CUNY-Hunter Coll., 1977—; ptnr. Queens Phys. Therapy Assocs., Forest Hills, N.Y., 1982—. Mem. Am. Phys. Therapy Assn. (dist. dir. greater N.Y. dist. 1984-88, dir. orthop. sect. 1994—, Merit award 1985, Outstanding Svc. award 1986, Disting. Svc. award 1988), Am. Acad. Orthop. Manual Therapists, Am. Assn. Orthop. Medicine, N.Y. State Assn. Coords. Clin. Edn. (treas. 1985-88). Democrat. Jewish. Office: Queens Phys Therapy Assocs 6940 108th St Flushing NY 11375-3851

ROSENTHAL, ALBERT LESTER, dermatologist; b. New Bedford, Mass., July 25, 1926; s. Myer and Ruth Naomi (Gourse) R.; m. Carol Ash, July 30, 1969; children—Robert, Jill, Bruce. BA magna cum laude, Tufts U., 1946, MD, 1951. Intern, R.I. Hosp., Providence, 1951-52, asst. resident surgery, 1952-53; asst. resident dermatology Mass. Gen. Hosp., Boston, 1955-56; asst. in dermatology N.Y. U., 1958-60; practice medicine specializing in dermatology, Trenton, N.J., 1958—; attending dermatologist Mercer Hosp., 1958—, chief dermatologist, 1958-93; chief dermatologist Helene Fuld Hosp., 1973-85; asso. in dermatology U. Pa., Phila., 1969-73; asso. prof. dermatology Hahnemann Med. Coll., Phila., 1973-87, clin. prof., dermatology, 1987— ; mem. staff Grad. Hosp. of Pa., 1969-73; mem. staff Hamilton Hosp., chief dermatologist, 1972-76. Contbr. numerous articles on dermatology to med. jours. Trustee, Friends of the N.J. State Mus., 1972—, chmn. bd. trustees, 1980-82, v.p. fine arts, 1978-80; gov. appointee adv. coun. N.J. State Mus., 1994—; mem. Mercer County Cultural and Heritage Commn., 1982—, chmn., 1984—; mem. Mercer County Open Space Preservation Commn., 1992—. Served to capt., M.C., USAF, 1953-55. Diplomate Am. Bd. Dermatology. Mem. Am. Acad. Dermatology, Pa. Acad. Dermatology, Noah Worcester Dermatology Soc., Phila. Dermatology Soc. (pres. 1984-85), N.J. Dermatology Soc., N.J. Med. Soc., Mercer Med. Soc., AMA. Jewish. Office: 74 Franklin Corner Rd Trenton NJ 08648-2102

ROSENTHAL, DAVID, physician; b. Phila., Sept. 30, 1929; m.; Suzanne Rosenthal; children: Michael, Samuel, Abrielle. Student, Julliard Sch. Music, 1948-49, George Washington U., 1953-54, Temple U., 1954-56; DO, Phila. Coll. Osteopathic Med., 1960. Diplomate Am. Bd. Osteopathic Rehabilitation Medicine. Internship Youngstown (Ohio) Osteopathic Hosp., 1960-61; resident VA Hosp. U. Pa., 1970-73; asst. medical dir. Moss Rehabilitation Hosp., Phila., 1974-77; gen. practice Phila., 1960-70; chmn. div. physical medicine & rehabilitation Suburban Gen. Hosp., Norristown, Pa., 1977—; medical dir. Medical Ctr. Performing Artists, Norristown, Pa., 1984—; medical dir. The Rehab Station, Norristown, Pa., 1988—, exec. dir., 1994—; asst. instr. in phys. medicine and rehab. U. Pa., 1972-73; asst. prof. Temple U., 1973-77, asst. clin. profl., 1977—; asst. clin. prof. Phila. Coll. Osteopathic Medicine, 1978-81; adj. clin. prof. N.Y. Coll., 1980-84; clin. assoc. prof. Phila. Coll., 1981—; hosp. affiliation Moss Rehab. Hosp., Grad. Hosp. City Ave. and Parkview Divsns., Albert Einstein Med. Ctr., Frankford Hosp., Suburban Gen. Hosp.; chmn. med. audit com. Moss Rehab. Hosp., 1974-77, chmn. med. records com., 1974-77; surveyor Commn. on Accreditation of Rehab. Facilities, 1994—. Contbr. articles to profl. jours. Profl. Standards Review Orgn. Health Systems of South Eastern Pa., 1977-82; cons. to com. Rehabilitation and Spl. Devices Food and Drug Adminstrn., 1979-84, panel mem. com., 1979-84. Mem. Am. Osteopathic Assn., Pa. Osteopathic Medical Assn., Dist. X Pa. Osteopathic Medical Assn., Am. Osteopathic Coll. Rehabilitation Medicine (trustee 1975-79, vice chmn., 1977-78, pres. 1979-80, past pres. 1980-81), Am. Congress Rehabilitation Medicine, Phila. Soc. Physical Medicine and Rehabilitation (sec.-treas. 1975-76, v.p. 1975-77, pres. 1977-78), Am. Geriatrics Soc., Pan-Am. Medical Assn., Am. Coll. Sports Medicine, Am. Osteopathic Acad. Sports Medicine, Am. Acad. Clinical Neurophysiology. Home: 210 W Rittenhouse Sq Apt 2506 Philadelphia PA 19103 Office: Physiatric Assn Ltd 2705 Dekalb Pike Norristown PA 19401-1852

ROSENTHAL, ELIZABETH ROBBINS, physician; b. Bklyn., Feb. 10, 1943; d. Marc and Ruth Jackson (Oginz) Robbins; m. Samuel Leonard Rosenthal, June 26, 1940; children: Thomas, Benjamin, Marc. AB, Smith Coll., 1963; MD, NYU, 1967. Diplomate Am. Bd. of Dermatology. Intern in pediatrics Upstate Med. Ctr., Syracuse, N.Y., 1967-68; resident in dermatology Henry Ford Hosp., Detroit, 1968-69, Roosevelt Hosp., N.Y.C., 1969-70, Boston U. Med. Ctr., 1972-74; pvt. practice Mamaroneck, N.Y., 1976—; chief dermatology, attending United Hosp., Pt. Chester, N.Y., 1994—; asst. clin. prof. Albert Einstein Coll. Medicine, Bronx, 1978—. Bd. dirs. Community Counseling Ctr., Mamaroneck, N.Y., 1982—. Fellow Am. Acad. Dermatology; mem. N.Y. State Med. Soc., NOW, Westchester County Med. Soc., Am. Med. Women's Assn. Office: 1600 Harrison Ave Mamaroneck NY 10543-3124

ROSENTHAL, HAROLD MYRON, internist; b. Bklyn., Sept. 12, 1949. BS in Biology cum laude, CUNY, Bklyn., 1970; MD, Georgetown U., 1974. Diplomate Am. Bd. Internal Medicine with subspecialty in cardiovascular diseases. Intern Georgetown U. Hosp., Washington, 1974-75, resident in internal medicine, 1975-77; fellow in cardiology N.C. Meml. Hosp., Chapel Hill, 1977-79; cardiologist Doctor's Clinic, Webster, Tex., 1979-80; cardiologist, pres. Bay Area Cardiology, P.A., Webster, 1980—; clin. instr. medicine Baylor Coll. Medicine, Houston, 1980—; med. dir., chief cardiologist Clear Lake Cardiac Rehab. Ctr., Webster, 1982-92; med. staff Clear Lake Regional Med. Ctr., Webster, 1979—, St. John Hosp., Nassau Bay, Tex., 1982—, S.E. Meml. Hosp., Houston, 1987—, Mainland Ctr. Hosp., Texas City, 1980—; lectr. in field. Contbr. articles to profl. jours. Fellow Am. Coll. Cardiology, Am. Heart Assn. (sci. coun. on clin. cardiology), Houston Cardiology Soc.; mem. AMA (Physician's Recognition award 1991—), ACP. Office: Bay Area Cardiology PA #2 Professional Park Dr Webster TX 77598

ROSENTHAL, J. WILLIAM, ophthalmologist; b. New Orleans, Oct. 30, 1922; s. Jonas William and Marjorie Florence (Oppenheimer) R.; m. Harriet Beth Stern, Mar. 27, 1945; children—Paul William, Susan Ann Rosenthal

Farrell. B.S., Tulane U., 1942, M.D., 1945; M.Sc., U. Pa., 1952, D.Sc., 1956. Diplomate Am. Bd. Ophthalmology. Intern, Charity Hosp., New Orleans, 1945-46, resident, 1948-51; practice medicine specializing in ophthalmology, New Orleans, 1951—; pres. New Orleans Eye Specialists, 1981—; curator Am. Acad. Ophthalmology Found. Mus.; past pres. med. staff Eye, Ear, Nose and Throat Hosp. Editor: New Orleans Acad. Ophthalmology Series, 1962-65. Contbr. articles to profl. publs. Served to lt. (j.g.) USNR, 1945-48. Fellow ACS, Internat. Coll. Surgeons (regent 1981—), Am. Acad. Ophthalmologists (1st Service award 1985, Honor award 1990), Royal Soc. Medicine, French Ophthal. Soc., Orleans Parish Med. Soc., New Orleans Acad. Ophthalmology (past pres. 1961), La. State Med. Soc., Optical Heritage Soc., Am. Ophthalmic History Soc., Beta Mu. Lodge: Lions (pres. 1984, sec. 1984—). Avocations: collecting edged weapons and visual aids, fishing. Home: 1320 Valence St New Orleans LA 70115-3934 Office: New Orleans Eye Specialists 3434 Prytania St Ste 250 New Orleans LA 70115-3532

ROSENTHAL, JOHN DAVID, dentist; b. Portland, Oreg., Feb. 26, 1950; s. Lawrence A. and H. Bertha (Klein) R.; m. Barbara J. Loomis, Apr. 1, 1977; children: Kristin, Benjamin. BS, U. Oreg., 1973; DMD, U. Oreg. Health Sci. U., 1976. Dentist Rosenthal & Rosenthal, DMD, Portland, 1976-79; pvt. practice Portland, 1979—; ptnr. Downtown Dental Assocs., 1995—. Dental chmn. United Way of Oreg., Portland, 1985; mem. membership com. Temple Beth Israel, Portland, 1984-87; mem. adv. com. Robison Retirement Home, Portland, 1986—. Fellow Am. Coll. Dentists, Acad. Gen. Dentistry, Acad. Dentistry Internat.; mem. Oreg. Soc. Dentistry for Children, Western Soc. Periodontology, Multnomah Dental Soc. (b.d dirs. 1979-81, pres. 1986), Oreg. Dental Assn. (membership chmn. 1984-88, chmn. mem. svcs. coun. 1988-91, Svc. award 1991), Oreg. Acad. Gen. Dentistry (bd. dirs. 1986-90, sec.-treas. 1990-91, pres. 1991-92, regional dir. 1995—), Oreg. Health Sci. U. Sch. Dentistry Alumni Assn. (bd. dirs. 1987-90), Theta Chi. Home: 6565 SW 88th Pl Portland OR 97223-7273 Office: 1221 SW Yamhill St # 310 Portland OR 97205-2009

ROSENTHAL, KATHRYN AYRES, nursing administrator and educator; b. Kansas City, Mo., July 2, 1953; d. William C. and Allie Jo (Hackett) Ayres; m. Lowell Thomas Rosenthal, Oct. 13, 1979; children: Alicia Nicole, Thomas William. BSN, Creighton U., 1975; CVNS, Meth. Hosp., 1977; MSN, U. Colo., 1988, PhD in Nursing, 1996. RN, Colo.; CCRN. Nursing supr. AMI St. Lukes's Hosp., Denver; instr. nursing program Regis Coll., Denver; clin. specialist, coord. Colo. campus U. Phoenix; DON/asst. adminstr. Estes Park Med. Ctr. Mem. ANA, CNA, AACN, Denver Assn. Critical Care Nursing (past pres.), Nebr. Nurses' Assn., Estes Park Nurses' Assn., Sigma Theta Tau. Home: 690 Pinewood Dr Estes Park CO 80517

ROSENTHAL, MARK JAY, physician; b. L.A., Dec. 15, 1951; s. Edwin Marshall and Rosalie Jayne (Newport) R.; m. Katherine Leigh Rosenthal. BA, Claremont Men's Coll., 1973; MD, Univ. Pa., 1977. Diplomate Am. Bd. Internal Medicine. Internship internal medicine L.A. County/USC Medical Ctr., 1978, residency internal medicine, 1978-80; fellowship geriatrics and endocrinology Palo Alto VA Medical Ctr., 1980-82; assoc. prof. UCLA, L.A., 1982—; co-chmn. internat. Congress Physiologic Scis., 1995-97; dir. and initiator Geriatric Sexuality Clinic Sepulveda VA Medical Ctr., 1993—, dir. geriatric grand rounds, 1991-94, co-dir. and initiator wheelchair cushion sizing clinic, 1991—; assoc. prof. in residence Univ. Calif., 1990—, asst. prof., 1986-89; cons. New Mex, Medical Review Assn., 1984-86; asst. prof. Univ. New Mex. Medical Ctr., 1983-86, dir.and initiator, 1983-86; medical dir. nursing home care unit Albuquerque VA Medical Ctr., 1984-85, medical dir. geriatric evaluation clinic, 1983-84; acting dir. geriatric evaluation clinic Palo Alto VA Medical Ctr., 1982-83. Contbr. articles to profl. jours. Recipient numerous rsch. grants. Mem. Gerontological Soc. Am., Am. Geriatrics Soc., Am. Fedn. Clinical Rsch., Endocrine Soc., Am. Assn. Advancement Sci., Am. Diabetes Assn. Home: 13000 SKy Valley Rd Los Angeles CA 90049 Office: Geriatric Rsch Ctr 16111 Plummer St Sepulveda CA 91343

ROSENTHAL, MARVIN BERNARD, pediatrician, educator; b. Bklyn., Jan. 1, 1930; s. Robert Rosenthal and Elizabeth (Gartner) Rosenthal Dreyfuss; m. Janet H. Swerlick, dec. 31, 1959; 1 child, Robert G. BA, Alfred U., 1951; MD, Leiden U., The Netherlands, 1957. Diplomate Nat. Bd. Med. Examiners, Am. Bd. Pediatrics. Intern Kings County Hosp., Bklyn., 1957-58; resident in pediatrics SUNY Downstate Med. Sch., Bklyn., 1958-60; fellow in hematology Children's Hosp. Phila., 1962; pediatrician Somerset Pediatric Group, Bridgewater, N.J., 1963-84; chief pediatrics Somerset Hosp., Somerville, N.J., 1983-84; assoc. dir. family practice residency Warren Hosp., Phillipsburg, N.J., 1984—, chief pediatrics, 1991—, dir. med. edn., 1989—; mem. cons. staff Morristown (N.J.) Meml. Hosp. 1989—; clin. assoc. prof. Robert W. Johnson Med. Sch., UMDNJ, New Brunswick, N.J., 1980—; mem. adj. faculty U. New Eng. Coll. Osteopathics, Biddeford, Maine, 1988—. Capt. USAF, 1960-62. Recipient Silver medallion Am. Heart Assn., 1976, 78. Fellow Am. Acad. Pediatrics, Am. Acad. Family Practice; mem. N.J. Med. Soc., Acad. Medicine N.J., N.J. Pediatric Soc., Soc. Tchrs. Family Medicine, Ambulatory Pediatric Assn., Assn. Hosp. Med. Educators, Fagle Scout Assn. Home: 500 Spring Valley Rd Easton PA 18042-6872 Office: Warren Hosp Roseberry St Phillipsburg NJ 08865-1628

ROSENTHAL, MITCHELL, healthcare executive; b. Newark, N.J., Mar. 13, 1949; s. Morris Robert and Edythe (Kurtz) R.; m. Margaret Fridel, Aug. 18, 1974; children: Michelle Sara, David Joseph. BA in Psychology, Rutgers U., 1970; MA in Psychology, Fairleigh Dickinson U., 1972; PhD in Clin. Psychology, U. Cin., 1975. Staff psychologist Children's Psychiat. Ctr., Cin., 1974-75; dir. rehab. psychology Med. Coll. of Va., Richmond, 1975-79, New Eng. Med. Ctr., Boston, 1979-86; dir. psychol. medicine Marianjoy Rehab. Ctr., Wheaton, Ill., 1986-89; prof., assoc. chmn. of phys. medicine and rehab. Wayne State U., Detroit, 1990—; v.p. rsch. and edn. Rehab. Inst. of Mich., Detroit, 1990——; trustee Comm. on Accreditation of Rehab. Facilities, Tuscon, Ariz., 1991—. Editor: (book) Rehabilitation of Adult and Child With Trauma Brain Injury, 1990; editor: Jour. of Head Trauma Rehab., 1985—. Recipient 1st Clin. Svc. award Nat. Head Injury Found., Washington, 1988; long-term tng. grantee in rehab. psychology Rehab. Svcs. Adminstrn., Washington, 1994, grantee Nat. Inst. on Disability and Rehab. Rsch., Washington, 1993. Fellow Am. Psychol. Assn. (pres. divsn. of rehab. psychology 1991-92); mem. Am. Congress of Rehab. Medicine, Internat. Neuropsychol. Soc. Office: Rehab Inst of Mich 261 Mack Blvd Detroit MI 48201

ROSENTHAL, MYER H., anesthesiologist; b. Boston, July 11, 1941. MD, U. Vt., 1967. Intern Naval Hosp. Bethesda, Md., 1967-68; resident Fell Critical Care Medicine Naval Hosp. San Diego, 1968-70; attending anesthesiologist Stanford (Calif.) Med. Ctr., 1975—; prof. Stanford U., 1975—. Office: Med Dir Intensive Care Stanford U Med Ctr 300 Pasteur Dr Palo Alto CA 94304-2203*

ROSENTHAL, PHILIP, gastroenterologist; b. Bayshore, N.Y., Oct. 18, 1949; m. Sherrin Jean Packer; children: Seth, Aaron. BS, SUNY, Albany, 1971; MD, SUNY, Bklyn., 1975. Asst. prof. pediatrics Coll. of Physicians and Surgeons Columbia U., N.Y.C., 1981-83; asst. prof. pediatrics U. So. Calif., L.A., 1983-89, tenured assoc. prof. pediatrics, 1989; dir. pediatrics and nutrition, med. dir. pediatric liver transplant program Cedars-Sinai Med. Ctr., L.A., 1989-95; assoc. prof. UCLA, 1989-95; prof. pediat. and surg. U. Calif. San Francisco Med. Ctr., 1995—; asst. attending physician Presbyn. Hosp./Vanderbilt Clinic, N.Y.C., 1981-83, Babies Hosp./Columbia U., 1981-83, Children's Hosp. of L.A., 1983-89; with Vanderbilt Clinic/Columbia U., 1981-83; attending physician Harlem Hosp. and Med. Ctr., N.Y.C., 1981-83, L.A. County/U. So. Calif. Med. Ctr., 1988-89. Vol. City of L.A. Marathon, 1989-90; v.p. Westside Jewish Community Ctr., L.A., 1989-92, bd. dirs. program com., 1987, Children's Liver Found., 1986; mem adv. bd. Jewish Activities Mus., 1990-95. Nat. Inst. Arthritis grantee, 1978-81, Children's Hosp. of L.A. grantee, 1984-86, 86-87, Abbott Labs. grantee, 1984-85, Children's Liver Found. grantee, 1985-86. Mem. Am. Acad. Pediatrics, N.Am. Soc. Pediatric Gastroenterology and Nutrition. Office: U Calif San Francisco Med Ctr MU4 East 500 Parnassus Ave San Francisco CA 94143-0136

ROSENTHAL, ROBERT, psychology educator; b. Giessen, Germany, Mar. 2, 1933; came to U.S., 1940, naturalized, 1946; s. Julius and Hermine (Kahn) R.; m. Mary Lu Clayton, Apr. 20, 1951; children: Roberta, David C., Virginia. A.B., UCLA, 1953, Ph.D., 1956. Diplomate: clin. psychology Am. Bd. Examiners Profl. Psychology. Clin. psychology trainee Los Angeles Area VA, 1954-57; lectr. U. So. Calif., 1956-57; acting instr. UCLA, 1957; from asst. to assoc. prof., coordinator clin. tng. U. N.D., 1957-62; vis. assoc. prof. Ohio State U., 1960-61; lectr. Boston U., 1965-66; lectr. clin. psychology Harvard U., Cambridge, Mass., 1962-67, prof. social psychology, 1967—, chmn. dept. psychology, 1992-95, Edgar Pierce prof. psychology, 1995—. Author: Experimenter Effects in Behavioral Research, 1966, enlarged edit., 1976; (with Lenore Jacobson) Pygmalion in the Classroom, expanded edit., 1992, Meta-analytic Procedures for Social Research, 1984, rev. edit., 1991, Judgement Studies, 1987; (with others) New Directions in Psychology 4, 1970, Sensitivity to Nonverbal Communication: The Pons Test, 1979; (with Ralph L. Rosnow) The Volunteer Subject, 1975, Primer of Methods for the Behavioral Sciences, 1975, Essentials of Behavioral Research, 1984, 2d edit., 1991, Understanding Behavioral Science, 1984, Contrast Analysis, 1985, Beginning Behavioral Research, 1993, 2d edit., 1996; (with Brian Mullen) BASIC Meta-analysis, 1985; editor: (with Ralph L. Rosnow) Artifact in Behavioral Research, 1969, Skill in Nonverbal Communication, 1979, Quantitative Assessment of Research Domains, 1980, (with Thomas A. Sebeok) The Clever Hans Phenomenon: Communication With Horses, Whales, Apes and People, 1981; (with Blanck and Buck) Nonverbal Communication in the Clinical Context, 1986; (with Gheorghiu, Netter and Eysenck) Suggestion and Suggestibility: Theory and Research, 1989. Recipient Donald Campbell award Soc. for Personality and Social Psychology, 1988, James McKeen Cattell Sabbatical award, 1995-96, Golden Anniversary Monograph award Speech Comm. Assn., 1996; Guggenheim fellow, 1973-74, fellow Ctr. for Advanced Study in Behavioral Scis., 1988-89; sr. Fulbright Scholar, 1972. Fellow AAAS (co-recipient Sociopsychol. prize 1960, co-recipient Behavioral Sci. Rsch. prize 1993), APA (co-recipient Cattell Fund award 1967), Am. Psychol. Soc.; mem. Soc. Exptl. Social Psychology (Disting. Scientist award 1996), Ea. Psychol. Assn. (Disting. lectr. 1989), Mid-western Psychol. Assn., Mass. Psychol. Assn. (Disting. Career Contbn. award 1979), Soc. Projective Techniques (past treas.), Phi Beta Kappa, Sigma Xi. Home: 12 Phinney Rd Lexington MA 02173-7717 Office: Harvard U 33 Kirkland St Cambridge MA 02138-2044

ROSENTHAL, SAMUEL GERSON, plastic surgeon; b. N.Y.C., May 28, 1939; m. Elaine Rosen Rosenthal, June 24, 1962; children: Caryn Beth, Bradley David, Pamela Jill. BA, Yeshiva U., 1960, BHL, 1960; MD, SUNY, Syracuse, 1964. Intern Kings County Hosp., N.Y.C., 1964-65, resident combined gen. and plastic surgery, 1965-71; head plastic surgery svc. dept. surgery Naval Hosp., Jacksonville, Fla., 1971-73; asst. instr. plastic surgery SUNY-Coll. Medicine, 1965-69, instr. plastic surgery, 1969-71; clin. instr. plastic surgery U. Fla. Sch. Medicine, 1973-78, clin. asst. prof. plastic surgery, 1979-83, clin. assoc. prof. plastic surgery, 1984-87; attending plastic surgeon SUNY-Downstate Med. Ctr., N.Y.C., 1987—; pres. house staff Kings County Hosp., 1968-69, 69-70; cons. plastic surgeon USN, Jacksonville, 1973—; chmn. dept. plastic surgery Humana Hosp., Orange Park, Fla., 1975-87, Meml. Hosp. Jacksonville, 1983—; sec. med. staff Meml. Med. Ctr., 1984-86, v.p. med. staff, 1986-88. Contbr. articles to profl. jours. Lt. comdr. USN, 1971-73. Mem. Am. Soc. Plastic and Reconstructive Surgery, Am. Soc. for Aesthetic Plastic Surgery, Lipoplasty Soc. N.Am., Fla. Soc. Plastic and Reconstructive Surgery, N.E. Fla. Soc. Plastic and Maxillofacial Surgery, Fla. Med. Soc., Duval County Med. Soc., Soc. Former Residents and Assocs. Plastic Surgery of Kings County Hosp. Office: Ste 403 3599 University Blvd S Jacksonville FL 32216

ROSENTHAL, SUSAN LESLIE, psychologist; b. Washington, Sept. 27, 1956; d. Alan Sayre and Helen (Miller) R. BA, Wellesley Coll., 1978; PhD, U. N.C., 1986. Postdoctoral fellow Yale Child Study Ctr., New Haven, 1986-88; asst. prof. clin. pediatrics U. Cin., 1988-93, dir. psychology div. adolescent medicine, 1988—, assoc. prof. clin. pediatrics, 1993—; adj. faculty dept. psychology Miami U., Oxford, Ohio, 1992—. Contbr. articles to profl. jours. Grantee NIH, 1994—, Merck & Co. Inc., 1995, Wyeth-Ayerst Labs., 1995-96. Mem. APA (program chair divsn. 37 1992, sec. 1996—), Cin. Soc. Clin. Child Psychologists (treas. 1992-94, pres. 1994-96), Ohio Psychol. Assn., Soc. Behavioral Pediatrics, Soc. Rsch. on Adolescence, Cin. Acad. Profl. Psychology. Office: Children's Hosp Med Ctr Div Adolescent Medicine 3333 Burnet Ave Cincinnati OH 45229-3026

ROSENWASSER, LARRY JEFFREY, allergist, immunologist; b. N.Y.C., Mar. 3, 1948. MD, NYU, 1972. Cert. in allergy and immunology; cert. in internal medicine. Intern U. Calif.-HC Moffitt Hosp., San Francisco, 1972-73; resident U. Calif. Affiliated Hosps., San Francisco, 1973-74 Mem. Alpha Omega Alpha, Sigma Xi. Office: Nat Jewish Ctr Im/Resp Med 1400 Jackson St San Francisco CA 80206-2761*

ROSENZWEIG, ROBERT ERWIN, physician; b. N.Y.C., Oct. 18, 1927. Grad., Adelphi U., 1952, Chgo. Med. Sch., 1957. Diplomate Am. Bd. Orthop. Surgery. Intern Hosp. for Joint Diseases, 1957-58, resident in gen. surgery, 1958-59, resident in orthops., 1959-61, chief resident in orthop. surgery, 1961-62; pvt. practice Highland Park, Ill., 1962—; asst. clin. prof. orthop. surgery Chgo. Med. Sch., 1967-72, assoc. clin. prof. orthop. surgery, 1972—, mem. Orthop. Residency Tng. Program, 1972-79, coord. Orthop. Tng. Program at Highland Park Hosp., 1972-79; instr. Chemonucleolysis Course, 1983; examiner aux. bd. Am. Bd. Sports Medicine, Atlanta, 1991; attending staff Cook County Hosp., 1966-85; active staff Highland Park Hosp., 1962—; cons. Am. Internat. Hosp., 1975-77; clin. investigator Waldemar Found., 1965, Abbott Labs., 1977, 91, Wallace Labs., 1981, Smith Labs., 1981, Ciba-Geigy, 1986; cons., lectr. in field. Contbr. articles to profl. jours. Bd. dirs. Dad's Club, Highland Park H.S., football team physician; team physician Chgo. Sting Soccer Team, 1978-87; vol. physician U.S. Olympic Tng. Ctr., Sports Medicine Clinic, Colorado Springs, summer 1990. With U.S. Med. Corps, 1945-48. Fellow Am. Coll. Surgeons, Am. Acad. Orthop. Surgeons, Chgo. Orthop. Soc., AMA; mem. Alpha Epsilon Delta. Home and Office: 873 Fairview Rd Highland Park IL 60035-4817

ROSES, ALLEN DAVID, neurologist, educator; b. Paterson, N.J., Feb. 21, 1943. BS in Chemistry summa cum laude, U. Pitts., 1963; MD, U. Pa., 1967. Diplomate Am. Bd. Psychiatry and Neurology. Intern Hosp. of the U. Pa., Phila., 1967-68; resident in neurology N.Y. Neurol. Inst., Columbia U., N.Y.C., 1968-70; chief resident divsn. neurology Duke U. Med. Ctr., 1970-71, assoc. in medicine divsn. neurology, 1970-73, asst. prof. medicine divsn. neurology, 1973-76, assoc. prof. medicine divsn. neurology, 1976-79, asst. prof. biochemistry, 1977-89, prof. neurology dept. medicine, 1979—, prof. neurobiology, 1989—, Jefferson-Pilot Corp. prof. neurobiology and neurology, 1990—, chief divsn. neurology dept. medicine, 1977—; fellow Nat. Multiple Sclerosis Soc., Lab. Neurochemistry, Divsn. Neurology, Duke U. Med. Ctr., Lab. Virology, Divsn. Pediat. Neurology, Duke U. Med. Ctr., 1971-73, dir. Duke Neuromuscular Rsch. Clinic, 1974—, dir. neurosciences study program Sch. Medicine, 1975-85, investigator Howard Hughes Med. Inst., 1977-81, dir. Duke Muscular Dystrophy Assn. Clinic, 1979—, Joseph and Kathleen Bryan Alzheimer's Disease Rsch. Ctr., 1985— ; cons. neurologist N.C. State Hosp. Sys., Cherry Hosp., Goldsboro, 1973-76, N.C. State Hosp. Sys., Lenox Baker Hosp., Durham, 1974—; chmn. internat. sci. adv. com. Australian Neuromuscular Rsch. Inst., 1989-92; sci. adv. Cyprus Isnt. Neurology and Genetics, 1990—; mem. external adv. com. Neonatal Neurology Ctr., SUNY, Stonybrook, Epidemiology of Dementia in an Urban Cmty. Program Project Renewal. Assoc. editor Molecular and Cellular Neuroscis., 1989-94; mem. editl. bd. Amyloidosis Jour., An Internat. Jour. Exptl. and Clin. Investigation, 1993—, Neurobiology of Disease, 1993—, Fondation Ipsen, Rsch. and Perspectives in Neuroscis., 1994—, Alzheimer's Rsch., 1995—, Contemporary Neurology, 1995—, Alezheimer's Disease Rev., 1995—; contbr. articles to profl. jours. Capt. USAFR, 1967-72. Recipient Rsch. Career Devel. award Nat. Inst. Neurol. and Communicative Disorders and Stroke, 1976, Best in the Triangle-Aerobics Instr. award Spectator Mag., 1986, Leadership in Excellence in Alzheimer's Disease award Nat. Inst. Aging, 1988, Met.-Life Found. prize for outstanding med. rsch., 1994, Potamkin prize for Alzheimer's Disease Rsch., 1994; Basil O'Connor Starter Rsch. grantee Nat. Found. March of Dimes. Fellow Am. Acad. Neurology; mem. Am. Soc. for Clin. Investigation, Am. Soc. for Clin. Rsch., Am. Neurol. Assn. (trustee 1982-84), Assn. Univ. Profs. Neurology, Assn. Brit. Neurologists (hon. fgn. mem.), Muscular Dystrophy Assn. (genetics task force and rev. com. 1989—, med. adv. com. 1990—, nat. v.p. nat. hdqrs. 1994—), Alzheimer's Assn. (med. sci. adv. com. 1989—, vice chair 1991—, Sigma Tau award 1990, Rita Hayward Gala award 1994), Phi Beta Kappa. Office: Duke Univ Med Ctr Durham NC 27710-7599 also: Divsn Neurology Box 2900 Durham NC 27710*

ROSEWARNE, ANNE, health science association administrator; b. Columbus, Ohio, Sept. 21, 1939; d. Hugh Clifton and Mary Claire (Janssen) Wear; m. Philip James Rosewarne, Aug. 19, 1961 (div. 1983); children: Amy, Stephen, Katherine, Brian. BS, U. Mich., 1961. Tchr. Belleville, Mich., 1961-64, Lansing, Mich., 1964-66; owner Crossroads, East Lansing, Mich., 1977-83; exec. dir. Am. Cancer Soc., Lansing, 1987-91; pres. Mich. Health Coun., Okemos, 1991—. Bd. dirs. Lansing Art Gallery, 1993—, also membership chair; bd. dirs. Mich. Non-Profit Forum, 1991—, exec. com.; bd. dirs. Health Occupational Students Am., 1993—. Home: 4442 Greenwood Dr Okemos MI 48864 Office: Mich Health Coun 3410 Woodlake Dr Okemos MI 48864

ROSEWATER, ANN, federal official; b. Phila., July 30, 1945; d. Edward and Maxine (Friedmann) R. BA with distinction, Wellesley Coll., 1967; MA, Columbia U., 1969. Rsch. editl. asst. Tchrs. Coll. Columbia U., N.Y.C., 1969; rsch. asst. to pres., v.p. rsch. Met. Applied Rsch. Ctr., N.Y.C., 1969-70; asst. to v.p. Nat. Urban Coalition, Washington, 1970-73; nat. edn. staff Childrens Def. Fund, Washington, 1973-77; assoc. prodr. Smithsonian World Nat. Pub. TV Series, Washington, 1977-78; sr. legis. asst. U.S. Ho. of Reps., Washington, 1979-83, dep. staff to staff dir. com. on children, youth and families, 1983-90; sr. assoc. Chapin Hall Ctr. for Children/U. Chgo., 1990-93; dep. asst. sec. Dept. Health & Human Svcs., Washington, 1993—; pub. policy and found. cons. in field, 1977-79, 90-93; grad. instr. Harvard Sch. Pub. Health, Nova U., George Washington U., 1977-79; mem. Nat. Adv. Com. on Svcs. for Families with Infants and Toddlers, Washington, 1994, Nat. Adv. Com. for Campaign Against Domestic Violence, 1992-93. Contbr. articles to profl. jours. Bd. dirs. Family Resources Coalition, Chgo., 1990-93, Youth Law Ctr., San Francisco, 1990-93, Jewish Fund for Justice, N.Y.C., 1990-93, Georgians for Children, Atlanta, 1990-93. Recipient Leadership award Leadership Atlanta, 1992-93, Pres. cert. for outstanding svc. Am. Acad. Pediat., 1990, Leadership in Human Svc. award Am. Pub. Welfare Assn., 1989-90. Mem. D.C. Bar Assn. (mem. citizens adv. com. 1974-79, fee conciliation svc., panel bd. on profl. responsibility). Office: Admin for Children & Families 370 L'Enfant Plz Washington DC 20447-0001

ROSHEL, JOHN ALBERT, JR., orthodontist; b. Terre Haute, Ind., Apr. 7, 1941; s. John Albert and Mary M. (Griglione) R.; B.S., Ind. State U., 1963; D.D.S., Ind. U., 1966; M.S., U. Mich., 1968; m. Kathy Roshel; children—John Albert III, James Livingston, Angela Kay. Individual practice dentistry, specializing in orthodontics Terre Haute, 1968—. Mem. ADA, Am. Assn. Orthodontists, Terre Haute C. of C., Lambda Chi Alpha, Delta Sigma Delta, Omicron Kappa Upsilon. Clubs: Terre Haute Country, Lions, Elks, K.C. Roman Catholic. Home: 15 E Wedgeway Dr Terre Haute IN 47802-4983 Office: 4241 S 7th St Terre Haute IN 47802-4367

ROSHKIND, DAVID MICHAEL, dentist; b. N.Y.C., June 10, 1950; s. Stanley and Marian (Weill) R.; children: Corey Beth, Lindsay Anne. BA, Cornell U., 1972; DMD, U. Pa., 1975, MBA, 1976. Pvt. practice dentistry Phila., 1975-76; dentist, pres. Flagler Dental Assocs., West Palm Beach, Fla., 1976—; instr. Palm Beach C.C., Lake Worth, Fla., 1982-87; sr. clin. instr. Inst. for Laser Dentistry, 1991—. Recipient Community Svc. award, Am. Legion, 1968, Award of Merit, Am. Soc. Dentistry for Children, 1976, Award of Merit, U. Pa., 1976. Fellow Acad. Gen. Dentistry; mem. ADA, Fla. Dental Assn., Atlantic Coast Rsch. Clinic, Acad. Laser Dentistry (charter, master, pres.), Cornell Club Ea. Fla. (bd. dirs.), Wharton Club South Fla., U. Pa. Club of the Palm Beaches, Omicron Kappa Upsilon. Office: Flagler Dental Assocs 901 N Flagler Dr West Palm Beach FL 33401-3707

ROSIAK, JOHN PAUL, drug abuse prevention administrator; b. Trenton, N.J., Dec. 19, 1955; s. Valentine Joseph and Ann (Poinsett) R.; m. Kathleen Margaret Higgins, June 28, 1980; children: Luke Higgins, Daniel Higgins, Paul Higgins. BA in Religious Edn., Cath. U., 1978, MA in Religious Edn., 1979, MA in Edn. Adminstrn., 1986. Tchr. Stone Ridge County Day Sch., Bethesda, 1979-80; rsch. writer Saudi Press Agy., Washington (D.C.), 1980-81; fin. aid officer Cath. U., Washington (D.C.), 1981-83, admissions counselor, 1983-84, asst. dir. admissions, 1984-86; assoc. dir. Am. Coun. Drug Edn., Rockville, Md., 1986-87; dir. substance abuse prevention and children's initiatives Nat. Crime Prevention, Washington (D.C.), 1987—; cons. U.S. Ctr. for Substance Abuse Preventino, Rockville, 1988, U.S. Dept. Edn., Washington, 1989—, Office Nat. Drug Control Policy, 1995—, UN Drug Control Program, 1996—. Contbr. articles to profl. jours. Mem. Citizens Com. to Nominate Mems. Bd. Trustees, Montgomery Coll., Md., 1985-88, St. Patrick's Alcohol and Other Drug Task Force, Rockville, 1989-90; grad. Leadership Montgomery, Montgomery County, Md., 1995-96. Mem. APHA, Nat. Assn. Prevention Profls. and Advs. (charter), Mental Health Assn. Montgomery County (v.p. 1988-90, pres. 1990-92, past pres. 1992-94, voices vs. violence com. Montgomery County 1992-94, vcl. youth sports coach 1990—). Roman Catholic. Office: Nat Crime Prevention Coun 1700 K St NW Washington DC 20006-3817

ROSICK, EDWARD RUDOLPH, physician; b. Lincoln Park, Mich., Aug. 16, 1960; s. John Edward and Evelyn Helen (Chick) R.; m. Pamela Stewart, Mar. 16, 1996. BS cum laude, Mich. Tech. U., Houghton, 1983; MS, U. North Tex., 1985; DO, Mich. State U., 1993; MPH, Loma Linda U., 1997. Teaching asst. U. North Tex., Denton, 1983-85; rsch. asst. Wayne State U., Detroit, 1985-86; rsch. assoc. U. Mich., Ann ARbor, 1986-88; rsch. asst. Mich. State U., East Lansing, 1988-91; intern Mich. Capitol Med. Ctr., Lansing, 1993-94; physician Redicare Urgent Care Clinic, Lansing, 1994-95; resident in preventive medicine Loma Linda (Calif.) U., 1995—. Contbr. articles to profl. jours. Rsch. fellow Mich. State U., 1988. Mem. Am. Osteo. Assn. (recipient Glaxo Wellcome Resident Leadership award 1996), Easter Island Found.

ROSIELLO, ARTHUR PETER, neurosurgeon; b. N.Y.C., Jan. 13, 1954; s. Arthur and Theresa (Pellegrino) R.; m. Leslie Ann Wessler, Aug. 19, 1995; 1 child, Rachele Ann. BS, MIT, 1975; MD, U. Buffalo, Buffalo, 1979. Postdoctoral assoc. MIT, Cambridge, Mass., 1979; resident Boston U., 1979-80, Harvard-Longwood Area, Boston, 1980-81, NYU, N.Y.C., 1981-87; instr. neurosurgery Boston U. Sch. Medicine, 1988-90, asst. prof. neurosurgery, 1990—; rsch. assoc. MIT, Cambridge, 1976, 77; acting chief neurosurgery Carney Hosp., 1990-93. Contbr. articles to profl. jours. Spine and cranial base fellow NYU, 1987-88. Mem. AAAS, Am. Assn. Neurol. Surgeons, Mass. Med. Soc., Mass. Neurosurg. Soc., New England Neurosurg. Soc., Boston Soc. Neurology & Psychiatry. Office: Dept Neurol Surgery 720 Harrison Ave Ste 710 Boston MA 02118

ROSIN, ELAINE Y., internist, cardiologist; b. Cin., Sept. 11, 1940; children: Paul, Julie, Marci. Student, U. Mich., 1958-60; pre-med. student, Ohio State U., 1960-61, MD cum laude, 1965. Diplomate Am. Bd. Internal Medicine, Am. Bd. Cardiovascular Disease. Intern Jewish Hosp., Cin., 1965-66; resident in internal medicine Cin. Gen. Hosp., 1966-68, resident in cardiology, 1968-70; pvt. practice in cardiology and internal medicine Florence, Ky., 1970—; asst. clin. prof. medicine U. Cin. Med. Ctr., 1970—; physician chief coronary care unit Jewish Hosp., Cin., 1975-78; staff: Jewish Hosp., Cin., Univ. Hosps., Cin., Bethesda Hosp., Cin., St. Luke E. & W., Florence, Ky., St. Elizabeth Med. Ctrs., Edgewood, Ky. Mem. exec. bd. Jewish Hosp., Cin., 1980-83. Fellow Am. Coll. Cardiology, Am. Coll. Angiology; mem. AMA, Cin. Acad. Medicine, Ohio State Med. Assn., Cin. Soc. Internal Medicine, No. Ky. Med. Soc. Office: Cardiology and Internal Medicine 7388 Turfway Rd Ste 203 Florence KY 41042

ROSIN, HANRY DAVID, physician; b. Bklyn., Apr. 1, 1931; s. Morris Bernard and Esther Harriet (Auerbach) R.; m. Nancy Claire Perkin; children: Diane, Matthew, Laura, Robert. BA, Syracuse U., 1951; MD, SUNY, Syracuse, 1956. Diplomat Am. Bd. Otolaryngology. Intern Mt. Sinai Hosp., N.Y.C., 1956-57, resident, 1959-63; dir. dept. otolaryngology & head & neck surgery Valley Hosp., Ridgewood, N.J., 1963-64; med. dir. Northwest Bergen Hospice, Ridgewood, N.J., 1982-90; otolaryngologist pvt. practice, 1990—. Pres. Physician Polit. Com., Midland Park, N.J. Capt. USAF, 1957-59. Fellow Am. Acad. Ophthalmology and Otolaryngology, Am. Coll. surgeons, Am. Acad. Facial, Plastic and Reconstructive Surgery; mem.

AMA, N.Y. Head and Neck Surgery, Med. Soc. N.J., N.J. Hospice Orgn. (past pres.), Bergen County Med. Soc. (trustee 1980-81), Soc. Fellows, Tower Club. Home: PO Box 647 Franklin Lakes NJ 07417 Office: 44 Godwin Ave Midland Park NJ 07432

ROSIN, LINDSAY ZWEIG, clinical psychologist; b. San Antonio, Oct. 28, 1954; s. Morris and Ethel (Rosenberg) R.; m. Susana Aceituno, Sept. 3, 1981; children: Lauren, Melanie. BA, U. Tex., 1975; MA, Xavier U., 1979; PhD, Fla. Inst. Tech., 1985. Lic. psychologist, Tex. Psychology assoc. Dayton (Ohio) Mental Health Ctr., 1980-81, Cin. Neurological Assocs., Cin., 1981-82; intern VA Med. Ctr., Houston, 1982-83; coord. outpatient services Houston Child Guidance Ctr., Houston, 1983-84; fellow Med. Ctr. del Oro Hosp., Houston, 1984-85; staff psychologist Mid-City Mental Health Mental Retardation, Houston, 1985-89; clin. asst. prof. psychology Baylor Coll. Medicine, Houston, 1985—; pvt. practice Houston, 1986—; psychologist St. Joseph Hosp., Houston, 1987—; psychologist cons. Mid-City Mental Health Mental Retardation, Houston, 1989—, Tex. Children's Hosp., 1993—. Contbr. articles to profl. jours. Recipient Outstanding Contbn. to Psychology award, Ohio Assn. Psychologists, 1982. Mem. Am. Psychol. Assn., Tex. Psychol. Assn., Houston Psychol. Assn., Internat. Neuropsychological Soc., Gerontological Soc. Am. Home: PO Box 20671 Houston TX 77225-0671 Office: 3730 Kirby Dr Ste 825 Houston TX 77098-3927

ROSLANSKY, PRISCILLA FENN, retired microbiologist; b. Rochester, N.Y., Nov. 24, 1925; d. Wallace Osgood and Clara Bryce (Comstock) Fenn; m. John Dale Roslansky, June 20, 1953; children: Louise, John Wallace, William Fenn, Clara Ruth. BA, Smith Coll., 1947; MA, Radcliffe Coll.-Harvard U., 1948; PhD, U. Rochester, 1952. Clin. lab. technician, Calif., N.J., part-time, 1952-59; research assoc. U. Calif., Berkeley, 1953-55; NIH fellow, Copenhagen, 1959-60; research assoc. U. Ill., Urbana, 1960-63; research assoc. Marine Biol. Lab., Woods Hole, Mass., 1964-68, 75-79, research on ultrastructure of nerves, 1987—; research assoc. U. Saarlandes, Homburg-Saar, Fed. Republic Germany, 1968-69; clin. lab. technician Falmouth Med. Assocs., 1969-75, fellow Bunting Inst. of Radcliffe Coll., 1981-83; dir. research Assocs. of Cape Cod, 1983-86, resident scientist, 1986-93; ret., 1993; bd. dirs. MBL Assoc. V.p. Woods Hole Community Assn., 1976; active Falmouth Zoning Bd. Appeals, 1990—; mem. Woods Hole Civic Assn., 1967-68. Contbr. articles to profl. jours. Mem. Am. Soc. Microbiology, LWV (bd. dirs. 1979—), Sigma Xi. Club: Woods Hole Women's. Home: 57 Buzzards Bay Ave Woods Hole MA 02543-1108

ROSMARIN, LEONARD ALAN, dermatologist; b. Bronx, May 29, 1950; s. Jack and Dorothy (Blumenstein) R.; m. Wendy Nevard, June 13, 1976; children: David, Deborah. BA, SUNY, Stony Brook, 1972; MD, NYU, 1976. Intern Montefiore Hosp., Bronx, 1976-77, resident, 1977-80; dermatologist pvt. practice, Whitestone, N.Y., 1981—; instr. dermatology Montefiore Hosp., Bronx, 1980-90; attending physician, cons. dermatology N.Y. Hosp. Med. Ctr. Queens County, 1980—. Fellow Am. Acad. Dermatology; mem. L.I. Dermatologic Soc., Greater N.Y. Dermatologic Soc., Soc. Tropical Dermatology. Jewish. Office: 18-15 Francis Lewis Blvd Whitestone NY 11357

ROSNER, BENNETT LEONARD, psychiatrist, educator; b. N.Y.C., Oct. 31, 1936; s. Herman and Dorothy (Elster) R.; m. Sarelle Ruth Ferster, June 4, 1961; children: Marc Allen, Beverly Eden, Daniel Gregory. BA, U. Rochester, 1957; MD, SUNY, Syracuse, 1961. Diplomate Am. Bd. Psychiatry and Neurology. Intern and resident in psychiatry SUNY, Syracuse, 1962-65; tng. in psychoanalysis Columbia U., N.Y.C., 1967-72; assoc. prof. psychiatry Albert Einstein Coll. Medicine, Yeshiva U., N.Y.C., 1972—; dir. inpatient svc. Montefiore Med. Ctr., Bronx, N.Y., 1972-77, clin. dir., 1977-83; med. dir. Hall-Brooke Hosp., Westport, Conn., 1983-90; dir. Mental Health Ctr. Stamford (Conn.) Hosp., 1991—; pvt. practice N.Y.C., 1967—. Sec., trustee August Aichorn Ctr., N.Y.C., 1979—. Surgeon USPHS, 1965-67. Fellow Am. Psychiat. Assn., Am. Psychoanalytic Assn.; mem. AMA, Am. Acad. Psychoanalysis, Am. Soc. Adolescent Psychiatry, Conn. Psychiat. Soc. (pres. 1995-96). Democrat. Jewish. Home: 205 Devoe Ave Yonkers NY 10705-2738 Office: 231 E 76th St New York NY 10021-2134

ROSNER, RICHARD, psychiatrist; b. N.Y.C., May 1, 1941; s. Henry J. and Rose L. Rosner; m. M. Bernice Horner. AB cum laude, Princeton U., 1962; MD, NYU, 1966. Intern Jewish Hosp., Bklyn., 1967; resident in psychiatry Mount Sinai Hosp., N.Y.C., 1967-70; pvt. practice N.Y.C., 1970—; med. dir. Forensic Psychiatry Clinic, N.Y.C., 1974—; clin. asst. prof. dept. psychiatry NYU Sch. Medicine, 1976-81, clin. assoc. prof., 1981-88, clin. prof., 1988—; pres. Am. Acad. Psychiatry and Law, Inc., Balt., 1987-88; dir. for psychiatry Am. Acad. Foresnic Scis., Inc., Colorado Springs, 1984-90. Editor: Critical Issues in American Psychiatry and the Law, 1982, (with others) Geriatric Psychiatry and the Law, 1988, Juvenile Psychiatry and the Law, 1989, (with R. Harmon) Criminal Court Consultation, 1989, (with R. Weinstock) Ethical Practice in Psychiatry and the Law, 1990, Principles and Practise of Forensic Psychiatry, 1994. Recipient Maier Tuchler award Am. Acad. Forensic Scis., Inc., 1986, Silver Apple award Am. Acad. Psychiatry and Law, Inc., 1988. Fellow Am. Psychiat. Assn., Am. Acad. Forensic Scis. (pres.-elect 1995, pres. 1996—), Am. Soc. for Adolescent Psychiatry (accreditation coun. on fellowship tng. programs in adolescent psychiatry pres. 1993—); mem. Am. Coll. Psychiatrists. Office: Forensic Psychiatry Clinic 100 Centre St Ste 124 New York NY 10013-4308

ROSNER, STANLEY, psychologist; b. Yonkers, N.Y., July 6, 1928; s. David Jacob and Rose (Meyers) R.; m. Blanche Muriel Altman, Feb. 20, 1955; children: David, Elisa, Adam, Jennifer. BA, NYU, 1950; MA, Boston U., 1951; PhD, New Sch. for Social Rsch., 1956. Diplomate Am. Bd. Profl. Psychology; cert. psychoanalysis; cert. neuropsychology. Psychology intern Grasslands Hosp., Valhalla, N.Y., 1951-52, jr. psychologist, 1952-55; clin. psychologist Manhattan State Hosp., N.Y.C., 1955-56; chief clin. psychologist Child Guidance Clinic of Greater Bridgeport, Conn., 1956-60; pvt. practice Fairfield, Stamford, Conn., 1958—; adj. med. staff Hall Brooke Hosp., Westport, Conn., 1959-84, Norwalk (Conn.) Hosp., 1978—; neuropsychol. cons., neuro-rehab. unit Park City Hosp., Bridgeport, Conn., 1985-93; mem. allied health profl. staff Bridgeport Hosp., 1994. Co-author: The Marriage-Gap, 1974; co-editor: The Creative Experience, 1970, The Creative Expression, 1976, Essays in Creativity, 1974; contbr. articles to profl. jours. Fellow Am. Psychol. Assn. (state psychol. affairs 1980), Am. Orthopsychiat. Assn., Soc. for Personality Assessment; mem. Conn. Psychol. Assn. (pres. 1972-73), Am. Group Psychotherapy Assn., Conn. Soc. of Psychoanalytic Psychologists (pres. 1984-88), Internat. Neuropsychol. Soc. Office: Counseling & Psychotherapy 1305 Post Rd Fairfield CT 06430-6016

ROSNOW, RALPH LEON, psychology researcher and educator; b. Balt., Jan. 10, 1936; s. Irvin and Rebecca (Faber) R.; m. Mimi Quin Medinger, Aug. 12, 1963. BS, U. Md., 1957; MA, George Washington U., 1958; PhD, Am. U., 1962. Asst. prof. Boston U., 1963-67; assoc. prof. Temple U., Phila., 1967-70, full prof., 1970—; vis. prof. London Sch. Econs., 1973; visiting prof. Harvard U., Cambridge, Mass., 1978, 1988-89; Bolton prof. Temple U., 1982—, dir social and orgnl. psychology, dept. psychology, 1988—; cons. editor jours. and encys. in psychology and comm.; cons. on rsch. methods and data analysis, 1976—. Author: Paradigms in Transition, 1981, (with Robert Rosenthal) The Volunteer Subject, 1975, Essentials of Behavioral Research, 1984, 2d edit., 1991, Contrast Analysis, 1985, Beginning Behavioral Research, 1993, 2d edit., 1996, (with Gary Fine) Rumor and Gossip, 1976, (with Mimi Rosnow) Writing Papers in Psychology, 1986, 2d edit., 1992, 3d edit., 1995, others; editor: (with Robert Rosenthal) Artifact in Behavioral Research, 1969, (with Marianthi Georgoudi) Contextualism and Understanding in Behavioral Science; assoc. editor: Encyclopedia of Psychology. Fellow AAAS, APA (mem. com. standards in rsch., chair 1992-93), Am. Psychol. Soc.; mem. Soc. Exptl. Social Psychology. Office: Temple U Psychology Dept 517 Weiss Hall Philadelphia PA 19122

ROSOFF, LEONARD, SR., retired surgeon, medical educator; b. Grand Forks, N.D., May 5, 1912; s. Albert and Sophie (Koblin) R.; m. Marie Louise Aronsfeld, June 1, 1935; 1 son, Leonard. BA, U. So. Calif., 1931; MD, U. Tex., 1935. Diplomate: Am. Bd. Surgery (dir. 1970-76). Intern, then resident gen. surgery Los Angeles County Hosp., 1935-40; from instr. to prof. surgery U. So. Calif. Sch. Medicine, 1946-80, emeritus, 1980—, chmn. dept., 1969-79; chief surg. services, dir. surgery Los Angeles County-U. So. Calif. Med. Center, 1955-77, sr. attending surgeon, 1977-80, ret., 1980; clin. prof. surgery U. Tex. Health Ctr., San Antonio, 1992—; hon. staff Hosp. Good Samaritan, Cedars-Sinai, Los Angeles Children's, Huntington Meml. hosps.; lectr. in field. Contbr. articles to med. jours., textbooks. Served with M.C., AUS, 1942-45. Recipient Outstanding Alumnus award U. Tex. Med. Br., 1971. Fellow ACS (bd. govs. 1975-81, 2d v.p. 1981), Tex. Surg. Soc. (hon.); mem. Am. Surg. Assn. (1st v.p. 1984), Western Surg. Assn. (2d v.p.), Pacific Coast Surg. Assn., L.A. Surg. Assn. (pres. 1970), Am. Assn. Endocrine Surgeons (bd. councilors 1980-87, pres. 1984), Am. Assn. Surgery Trauma, Soc. Surgery Alimentary Tract (pres. 1979-80), Internat. Soc. Surgery, L.A. Acad. Medicine, L.A. Athletic Club, Giraud Club (San Antonio). Home: One Towers Park Ln # 1115 San Antonio TX 78209

ROSS, AMY ANN, experimental pathologist; b. Glendale, Calif., Apr. 28, 1953; d. William F. Ross and Joyce V. (Stuart) Ruygrok. BA, Calif. State U., Northridge, 1981; PhD, U. So. Calif., 1986. Assoc. dir. rsch. Inst. Cancer and Blood Rsch., Beverly Hills, Calif., 1986-89; dir. R & D Biologic and Immunologic Sci. Labs., Reseda, Calif., 1989-94; dir. diagnostic applications Cell Pro Inc., Bothell, Wash., 1995—; rsch. asst. Sch. Medicine U. So. Calif., L.A., 1975-80, rsch. assoc., 1982-86. Mem. AAAS, Am. Soc. Clin. Pathology, Assn. of Women in Sci. (pres. L.A. chpt. 1979-80). Office: Cell Pro Inc 22215 26th Ave SE Bothell WA 98021

ROSS, DOUGLAS STERLING, physician, medical educator; b. Boston, Aug. 9, 1951; s. Melvin J. and Shirley (Sterling) R.; m. Anne E. Person. BS, MIT, 1973, MS, 1973; MD, Harvard U., 1977. Cert. internal medicine, endocrinology and metabolism Am. Bd. Internal Medicine. Internal medicine resident Mass. Gen. Hosp., Boston, 1977-80, endocrine fellow, 1980-83, instr., 1983-85, co-dir. Thyroid Assocs., 1985—; instr. Harvard Med. Sch., Boston, 1983-85, asst. prof. medicine, 1985—; pub. affairs com. Am. Thyroid Assn., 1989-90, devel. com., 1990-93; cons. AMA, 1992—; spkr. in field. Mem. editl. bd. Jour. Clin. Endocrinology and Metabolism, 1995. Mem. Phi Lambda Upsilon, Alpha Omega Alpha. Office: Thyroid Unit ACC-730 Mass Gen Hosp 15 Parkman St Boston MA 02114

ROSS, ELLIOTT DANIEL, neurology educator, researcher; b. N.Y.C., Mar. 1, 1945; s. Robert and Beatrice (Simon) R.; m. Stephanie Nina Silverman, July 1, 1970; children: Benjamin A., Rebecca L. BA, MD, Boston U., 1968. Diplomate Am. Bd. Psychiat. and Neurology. Clin. fellow in neurology Med. Sch. Harvard U., Boston, 1972-75; asst. prof. neurology U. Tex. Southwestern Med. Ctr., Dallas, 1975-81, asst. prof. psychiatry, 1979-81, assoc. prof. neurology and psychiatry, 1982-88; prof., chmn. neurology, dept. neurosci. U. N.D., Fargo, 1988—; chief neurol. svc. VA Med. Ctr., Fargo, 1990—; dir. clin. rsch. program Neuropsychiat. Rsch. Inst., Fargo, 1990—; Gralnik disting. lectr. Soc. for Biol. Psychiatry, 1985; Plenary lectr. Can. Coll. Neuropsychopharmacology, Vancouver, B.C., 1986. Author: Archives Neurology, 1979, 80, 81, Archives General Psychiatry, 1981, Brain and Langauge, 1988, Neuropsychiatry, Neuropsychology and Behavioral Neurology, 1994; assoc. editor Neuropsychiatry, Neuropsychology and Behavioral Neurology, 1993—. Lt. comdr. USN, 1970-72, Vietnam. Mem. Am. Acad. Neurology, Am. Neurol. Assn., Internat. Neuropsychology Soc., Behavioral Neurology Soc. (sec.-treas. 1981-91, pres. 1991-93). Office: U ND Dept Neuroscience 1919 Elm St Fargo ND 58102-2416

ROSS, ELLIOTT M., pharmacology educator; b. Stockton, Calif., Jan. 16, 1949; married; 1 child. Instr. sect. biochemistry, molecular & cell biology Cornell U., 1974; postdoctoral fellow dept. pharmacology Sch. Medicine U. Va., 1975-77, asst. prof. depts. biochemistry & pharmacology, 1978-81; assoc. prof. dept. pharmacology U. Tex. Southwestern Grad. Sch. Biomed. Scis., 1981-86, chmn. grad. program pharmacology, 1982-89, mem. grad. programs cell regulation, 1991—, mem. grad. program molecular biophysics, 1991-93, 95—, mem. grad. program biochemistry & molecular biology, 1993—, mem. grad. program pharmacology, 1981-91, mem. grad. program cell & molecular biology, 1981-91; prof. dept. pharmacology U. Tex. Southwestern Med. Ctr., Dallas, 1986—; vis. asst. prof. dept. pharmacology U. Va. Sch. Medicine, 1977-78. Recipient Goodman & Gikman Drug Receptor Pharmacology award Am. Soc. Pharmacology & Exptl. Therapeutics, 1996. Office: U Tex Southwestern Med Ctr Dept Pharmacology 5323 Harry Hines Blvd Dallas TX 75235-9041*

ROSS, JAMES B., optometrist; b. Chgo., July 9, 1959; s. Charles Edward and Rosie Pearl (Wright) R.; m. Gwendolyn Pullen, June 20, 1987; children: Crystal, Byron. BS, Bradley U., Peoria, Ill., 1981; Med. Technologist, St. Francis Hosp., Peoria, Ill., 1982; DO, Ill. Coll. Optometry, Chgo., 1989. Lic. optometrist, Ill., Wis. Med. technologist Oak Park (Ill.) Hosp.; optometrist Concept II, Chgo. Spkr. for Career Day, People's Ch. of God in Christ, Chgo., 1993. Named to Outstanding Young Men of Am. Mem. Am. Optometric Assn., Nat. Optometric Assn., Ill. Optometric Assn. Home: 1411 S 13th Ave Maywood IL 60153 Office: Concept II 3844 W Fillmore St Chicago IL 60624-4203

ROSS, JEFFREY ALAN, research biologist; b. Thayer, Mo., Oct. 19, 1955; s. Ralph and Naomi June (Jacobs) R.; m. Lisa Lynn Pnazek, Apr. 23, 1977; children: Trillian Elise, Jennifer Ariane, Marissa Kerowyn. BS, U. Dallas, 1977; PhD, U. Tex., Dallas, 1982. Predoctoral fellow Robert A. Welch Found., 1979-82; postdoctoral fellow Cancer Ctr. Rsch. div. U. Tex., Smithville, 1982-85; NRC fellow U.S. EPA, Research Triangle Park, N.C., 1985-86, rsch. biologist, 1986—. Contbr. articles to profl. jours. Bd. dirs. 1st Environments Early Learning Ctr., Research Triangle Park, 1989-90, 94-96, 94-96. John B. O'Hara Found. fellow, 1973-76. Mem. AAAS, Am. Assn. Cancer Rsch., N.Y. Acad. Scis., Genotoxicity and Environ. Mutagen Soc. (bd. dirs. 1991-94). Office: US EPA MD-68 Research Triangle Park NC 27711

ROSS, JOSEPH COMER, physician, educator, academic administrator; b. Tompkinsville, Ky., June 16, 1927; s. Joseph M. and Annie (Pinckley) R.; m. Isabelle Nevins, June 15, 1952; children: Laura Ann, Sharon Lynn, Jennifer Jo, Mary Martha, Jefferson Arthur. BS, U. Ky., 1950; MD, Vanderbilt U., 1954. Diplomate Am. Bd. Internal Medicine (bd. govs. 1975-81), with added qualifications in pulmonary disease. Intern Vanderbilt U. Hosp., Nashville, 1954-55; resident Duke U. Hosp., Durham, N.C., 1955-57, rsch. fellow, 1957-58; instr. medicine Ind. U. Sch. Medicine, Indpls., 1958-60, asst. prof., 1960-62, assoc. prof., 1962-66, prof., 1966-70; prof., chmn. dept. medicine Med. U. of S.C., Charleston, 1970-80; vis. prof. Vanderbilt U. Sch. Medicine, Nashville, 1979-80, prof. medicine, 1981—, assoc. vice chancellor for health affairs, 1982—; mem. cardiovascular study sect. NIH, 1966-70, program project com., 1971-75; mem. adv. coun. Nat. Heart, Lung and Blood Inst., 1982-86; mem. ad hoc coms. NAS, 1966, 67; mem. Pres.'s Nat. Adv. Panel on Heart Disease, 1972; mem. merit rev. bd. in respiration VA Rsch. Svc., 1972-76, chmn., 1974-76. Mem. editorial bd. Jour. Lab. and Clin. Medicine, 1964-70, Chest, 1968-73, Jour. Applied Physiology,1968-73, Archives of Internal Medicine, 1976-82, Heart and Lung, 1977-86; contbr. articles to profl. jours. Bd. dirs., past pres. Nashville Ronald McDonald House; bd. dirs. Agape, Leadership Nashville; mem. adv. com. Davidson County Cmty. Health Agy.; active Tenn. Lung Assn. With U.S. Army, 1945-47. Fellow ACP, Am. Coll. Chest Physicians (gov. S.C. 1970-76, vice chmn. bd. govs. 1974-75, chmn. bd. govs. 1975-76, exec. council 1974-80, pres.-elect 1976-77, pres. 1978-79, chmn. sci. program com. 1973), Am. Coll. Cardiology; mem. AMA (sect. on med. schs.), Am. Fedn. Clin. Rsch. (chmn. Midwest sect.), Am. Physiol. Soc., Am. Soc. Clin. Investigation, Assn. Am. Physicians, Assn. Profs. Medicine, Cen. Soc. Clin. Rsch., S.C. Med. Soc., Am. Thoracic Soc. (nat. councillor 1972-76), So. Soc. Clin. Rsch., S.C. Lung Assn. (v.p. 1974-75), Am. Soc. Internal Medicine, Phi Beta Kappa, Alpha Omega Alpha. Mem. Ch. of Christ (elder). Office: Vanderbilt University 2000 Village at Vanderbilt Nashville TN 37232

ROSS, JOSEPH FOSTER, physician, educator; b. Azusa, Calif., Oct. 11, 1910; s. Verne Ralph and Isabel Mills (Bumgarner) R.; m. Eileen Sullivan, Dec. 19, 1942; children: Louisa, Elisabeth, Joseph, Jeanne, Marianne. AB with great distinction, Leland Stanford Jr. U., 1933; MD cum laude with spl. honors in Physiology, Harvard U., 1936. Diplomate Am. Bd. Internal Medicine (mem. 1973-83), Am. Bd. Nuclear Medicine (founding, sec. 1971-72, 79, chmn. 1973-77, pres., chief exec. officer 1980—). Asst. topographical anatomy Harvard U. Sch. Medicine, 1934-37, research fellow biochemistry, 1943-46; med. house officer Harvard cancer commn. Huntington Meml. Hosp., 1934-35; Palmer Meml., New Eng. Deaconess hosps., 1935-36; resident pathology Mallory Inst. Pathology, 1936-37; intern Harvard Med. Svc. Boston City Hosp., 1937-39; asst. pathology U. Rochester Sch. Medicine, 1939-40; resident pathology Strong Meml. Hosp., Rochester, N.Y., 1939-40; physician, dir. hematology and radioisotope divs. Mass. Meml. Hosp., 1940-54; instr., asst. prof., assoc. prof. medicine Boston U., 1940-54; dir. radioisotope unit Cushing VA, Boston VA hosps., 1948-54; prof. medicine UCLA, 1954—, prof. radiobiology, 1954-59, assoc. dean, 1954-58, chmn. dept. nuclear med. and radiation biology, 1958-60, dir. Lab. Nuclear Med. and Radiation Biology, 1958-65, prof., chmn. dept. biophysics and nuclear medicine, 1960-65, chief div. hematology, 1969-76; chief staff U. Calif. Hosp., Los Angeles, 1954-58; attending physician U. Calif. Hosp., 1954—; U.S. del. Internat. Conf. Peaceful Uses Atomic Energy, Geneva, 1955; mem. U.S. Atoms for Peace mission to Latin Am., 1956, U.S. AEC Life Scis. Mission to, Greece, Turkey, 1961; mem. USA AEC sci. mission to USSR, 1966; mem. Calif. Adv. Council on Cancer, 1959-84, chmn., 1963-66, 74-77; mem. CENTO Sci. Mission Iran, Turkey, Pakistan, 1963; mem. nat. adv. cancer council Nat. Cancer Inst., 1956-60; Research preservation whole blood OSRD, World War II. Editorial bd.: Blood, Jour. Hematology, 1946-76, Annals Internal Medicine, 1960-70, Jour. Nuclear Medicine, 1968; med. book div., Little Brown Co., 1958-68, med. book series, U. Calif. Press, 1962-70; Contbr. articles to profl. jours. Recipient cert. of merit Pres. U.S., 1948, Van Meter award Am. Goiter Soc., 1953, Dorothy Kirsten French Meml. award for disting. contbn. to medicine French Found. for Alzheimer's Disease Rsch., 1994; Wilson medalist, lectr. Am. Clin. and Climatol. Assn., 1964; Disting. fellow Am. Coll. Nuclear Physicians, 1994. Fellow Am. Coll. Nuclear Medicine (Disting. fellow 1988); mem. ACP, AMA, Am. Soc. Exptl. Pathology, Am. Soc. Clin. Investigation, Assn. Am. Physicians, Am. Acad. Arts and Scis., Biophys. Soc., Radiation Research Soc. (council 1964-65), Internat. Soc. Hematology, Am. Soc. Hematology (pres. 1961-62), Western Assn. Physicians (pres. 1962-63), Am. Bd. Nuclear Medicine (co-founder 1972, sec. 1972-75, chmn., pres. 1975-78, exec. dir. 1978-79, pres. 1980—), Soc. Nuclear Med. (trustee 1962-72, pres. So. Calif. chpt. 1964-65, Nuclear Pioneer lectr. 1971, 77, Disting. Scientist award Western. sect. 1977, Disting. Svc. award 1984, Spl. Presdl. Recognition award 1991, Hevesy Nuc. Pioneer award and lectr., 1995), L.A. County Med. Assn. (dist. v.p. 1976-77, 78-79, del. to Calif. Med. Assn. 1978-79), Am. Bd. Med. Spltys. (exec. com. 1982-84), Council Med. Splty. Socs. (sec. 1981-82, dir. 1980-82), World Fedn. Nuclear Medicine and Biology (chmn. statutes com. 1980-84), Phi Beta Kappa, Sigma Xi, Alpha Omega Alpha, Theta Xi, Nu Sigma Nu. Presbyterian (exec. com. Westminster Found. So. Calif. 1962-72, pres. 1968). Clubs: Harvard (Boston); Cosmos (Washington). Home: 11246 Cashmere St Los Angeles CA 90049-3503 Office: Am Bd Nuclear Med 900 Veteran Ave Rm 12-200 Los Angeles CA 90024

ROSS, JOYCE ADAMS, gerontological clinical specialist; b. Phila., June 29, 1944; d. Thomas Grandville and Dorothy (Anglea) Adams; m. Jerome Samuel Ross, June 8, 1963; children: Mary Teresa, Dorothy, Jerome Jr., Michael, Erin. ADN, Gwynedd Mercy Coll., 1987, BSN cum laude, 1988, MSN, 1992. RN Pa.; cert. gerontol. nurse., nurse practitioner/CRNP. Gerontol. nurse clinician Franklin Sq. Hosp. Ctr., Balt., 1988-89; instr. Fair Acres Geriatric Ctr., Lima, Pa., 1989; dir. staff devel., cert. gerontol. clin. specialist Dunwoody Village Continuing Care Retirement Cmty., Newtown Square, Pa., 1989—, mem. speakers bur., 1989—; with med. genetics dept. Hosp. of U. of Pa., Phila.; nursing home adminstr., mem. speakers bur.; long term care consortium Main Line, Inc.; evaluator continuing care accreditation Am. Assn. Homes for the Aged, 1993—, nursing home adminstr., 1994—. Nurst of Hope Am. Cancer Soc., Media, Pa., 1981, mem. edn. com., 1990-92. Mem. Delaware Valley Geriatric Soc., Sigma Theta Tau (Iota Kappa chpt.). Roman Catholic. Home: 347 Sussex Blvd Broomall PA 19008-4153 Office: Hosp U Pa Maloney Bldg Philadelphia PA 19104

ROSS, LEABELLE ISAAC (MRS. CHARLES R. ROSS), retired psychiatrist; b. Lorain, Ohio, Feb. 11, 1905; d. Charles E. and Harriet (Dobbie) Isaac; AB, Western Res. U., 1927, MD, 1930; m. Charles R. Ross, Sept. 23, 1941; children: Charles R., John Edwin. surg. intern Lakeside Hosp., Cleve., 1931-32; resident in ob-gyn. Iowa State U. Hosp., 1932-33; resident obstetrics and surgery N.Y. Infirmary, N.Y.C., 1933-34; pvt. practice, Cleve., 1935-40; staff physician Cleve. State Hosp., 1938-42; dir. student health Bowling Green (Ohio) State U., 1942-45; psychiatrist Bur. Juvenile Rsch., Columbus, Ohio, 1946-47; psychiat. cons., 1948-51; psychiatrist Mental Hygiene Clinic, Columbus, Va., 1951-55; dir. med. svcs. Juvenile Diagnostic Ctr., 1955-59, acting supt., 1958, 61-62, dir. psychiat. svcs., 1959-62, clin. dir., 1962-70. Mem. Am. Psychiat. Assn., Ohio Psychiat. Assn., Am. Group Psychotherapy Assn., Tri-State Group Psychotherapy Soc., Neuropsychiat. Assn. Ctrl. Ohio, Assn. Physicians Divsn. Mental Hygiene and Correction (pres. 1963-64), Soroptomist, Alpha Sigma Rho, Nu Sigma Phi. Home: 1085 Tasman Dr #200 Sunnyvale CA 94089

ROSS, LEONARD LESTER, anatomist; b. N.Y.C., Sept. 11, 1927; s. Aaron Theodore and Shirley (Smolen) R.; m. Marcella Gamel, June 23, 1951; children: Jane, Jill. A.B., NYU, 1946, Ph.D., 1954. Asst. prof. U. Ala. Med. Coll., 1954-57; assoc. prof. Cornell U. Med. Coll., 1957-69, prof., 1969-73; vis. prof. Cambridge U., 1967-68; prof., chmn. dept. anatomy Med. Coll. Pa., Phila., 1973-89; exec. v.p., Annenberg dean Med. Coll. Pa., 1989-93, pres. and Annenberg dean, 1993-94; provost Allegheny U., Phila., 1994; exec. v.p. Allegheny Health, Edn. and Rsch. Found. Assoc. editor: Anat. Record, 1976. Served with M.C., U.S. Army, 1946-47. Recipient Lindback award for teaching, 1976; NIH sr. research fellow, 1967-68. Mem. Am. Assn. Anatomists (exec. com. 1984-88), Soc. Neurosci., Soc. Cell Biology, N.Y. Soc. Electron Microscopists (pres. 1975-76), Assn. Anatomy Chairmen (pres. 1983-84), AAUP (nat. council 1974-77), Sigma Xi. Office: Broad and Vine St Philadelphia PA 19102-5087

ROSS, MALCOLM, mineralogist, crystallographer; b. Washington, Aug. 22, 1929; s. Clarence Samuel and Helen Hall (Frederick) R.; m. Daphne Dee Virginia Riska, Sept. 1, 1956; children: Christopher A., Alexander MacC. BS in Zoology, Utah State U., 1951; MS in Chemistry, U. Md., 1959; PhD in Geology, Harvard U., 1962. Rsch. mineralogist U.S. Geol. Survey, Washington, 1954-5, 61-74, Reston, Va., 1974—; prin. investigator lunar sci. program NASA, 1969-74. Author: Asbestos and Other Fibrous Minerals, 1988; contbr. numerous articles to profl. jours. First Lt. U.S. Army, 1952-54. Recipient Disting. Svc. award, U.S. Dept. Interior, 1986. Fellow Mineral. Soc. Am., Geol. Soc. Am., AAAS; mem. Am. Geophys. Union, Clay Minerals Soc., Mineral Soc. Am. (bd. dirs. treas. 1976-80, v.p. 1990, pres. 1991, Pub. Svc. award, 1990). Home: 1608 44th St NW Washington DC 20007-2025 Office: US Geol Survey MS # 955 Reston VA 22092

ROSS, MARK ALFRED, neurologist, educator; b. Iowa City, Sept. 24, 1956. BA, U. Calif., Berkeley, 1978; MD, Northwestern U., 1982. Diplomate Nat. Bd. Med. Examiners, Am. Bd. Neurology and Psychiatry, Am. Bd. Electrodiagnostic Medicine, Am. Bd. Neurology and Psychiatry Clin. Neurophysiology. Intern Evanston (Ill.) Hosp., 1982-83; resident in neurology U. Iowa, Iowa City, 1983-86, fellow in neurophysiology, 1986-87, fellow in neuropathology, 1987-88, neurology assoc., 1988-90, asst. prof. neurology, 1990-96, assoc. prof., 1996—; electroencephalographer dept. neurology U. Iowa, Iowa City, 1988-94, dir. electromyography lab., 1989—, dir. adult Muscular Dystrophy Assn. clinic, 1991—, dir. neuromuscular divsn., 1991—; dir. Neurophysiology Fellowship Tng. Program, 1995—. Contbr. articles to profl. jours. Recipient Physician's Recognition award AMA, 1988, 91, 94. Mem. Am. Acad. Neurology, Am. Assn. Electrodiagnostic Medicine, Ctrl. Electroencephalographic Soc., Iowa-Midwest Neurol. Soc., Am. Acad. Clin. Neurophysiology. Office: U Iowa Dept Neurology Iowa City IA 52242

ROSS, MATHEW, psychiatry educator; b. Boston, July 29, 1917; s. Abraham and Frances (Lampke) R.; m. Brenda Boynton, Dec. 24, 1946; children: Douglas Ross, Gail Ross, Craig Ross, Bruce Ross. BS, Tufts U., 1938, MD, 1942. Diplomate Am. Bd. Psychiatry and Neurology. Intern Kings County Hosp., N.Y.C., 1942-43, VA Med. Ctr., L.A., 1946-48, L.A. Psychoanalytic Inst., 1949-53; Prof. Sch. Medicine UCLA, 1953-58; prof. Sch. Medicine George Washington U., Washington, 1958-73; resident psychiat. adminstrn. U. Chgo., 1959; prof. Sch. Medicine Harvard U., Boston, 1963-73, Brown U., Providence, 1964-65, R.I. U., Providence, 1964-65, U. Calif., Irvine, 1974—; resident sch. alcoholism U. Utah, 1977; Fulbright prof., rsch. scholar U. Gronigen and U. Amsterdam, The Netherlands, 1962-63; med. dir. Am. Psychiat. Assn., Washington, 1958-62. Editor:

Newsletter Am. Psychiat. Assn., 1958-62, Mental Hosp. & Community Psychiatry, 1958-62, PDE Scientific Journal, 1975—. Sr. legislator State of Calif., 1985-86; commr. Newport Beach (Calif.) Arts Commn., 1989—. Maj. U.S. Army, 1943-46, ETO. Fellow ACP, Am. Psychiat. Assn., Am. Assn. Psychiatrists, Am. Pub. Health Assn., So. Calif. Psychiat. Soc. (founding pres. 1953-60); hon. fellow Australia-New Zealand Coll. Psychiatrists. Home: Unit 1163 24055 Paseo Del Lago Laguna Hills CA 92653-7313

ROSS, PATTI JAYNE, obstetrics and gynecology educator; b. Nov. 17, 1946; d. James J. and Mary N. Ross; B.S., DePauw U., 1968; M.D., Tulane, U., 1972; m. Allan Robert Katz, May 23, 1976. Asst. prof. U. Tex. Med. Sch., Houston, 1976-82, assoc. prof., 1982—, dir. adolescent ob-gyn., 1976—, also dir. phys. diagnosis, dir. devel. dept. ob-gyn.; speaker in field. Bd. dirs. Am. Diabetes Assn., 1982—; mem. Rape Coun. Diplomate Am. Bd. Ob-Gyn, Children's Miracle Network Hermann's Children's Hosp; Olympic torch relay carrier, 1996; founder Women's Med. Rsch. Fund, U. Tex. Med. Sch., Houston. Mem. Tex. Med. Assn., Harris County Med. Soc., Houston Ob-Gyn. Soc., Assn. Profs. Ob-Gyn., Soc. Adolescent Medicine, AAAS, Am. Women's Med. Assn., Orgn. Women in Sci., Sigma Xi. Roman Catholic. Clubs: River Oak Breakfast, Profl. Women Execs. Contbr. articles to profl. jours. Office: 6431 Fannin St Houston TX 77030-1501

ROSS, RICHARD STARR, medical school dean emeritus, cardiologist; b. Richmond, Ind., Jan. 18, 1924; s. Louis Francisco and Margaret (Starr) R.; m. Elizabeth McCracken, July 1, 1950; children: Deborah Starr, Margaret Casad, Richard McCracken. Student, Harvard U., 1942-44, M.D. cum laude, 1947; Sc.D. (hon.), Ind. U., 1981; LHD (hon.), Johns Hopkins U., 1994. Diplomate: Nat. Bd. Med. Examiners, Am. Bd. Internal Medicine. (subsplty. bd. cardiovascular disease). Successively intern, asst. resident, chief resident Osler Med. Service, Johns Hopkins Hosp., 1947-54; research fellow physiology Harvard Med. Sch., 1952-53; instr. medicine Johns Hopkins Med. Sch., 1954-56, asst. prof. medicine, 1956-59, assoc. prof., 1959-65, assoc. prof. radiology, 1960-71, prof. medicine, 1965—, Clayton prof. cardiovascular disease, 1969-75; dir. Wellcome Research Lab., Johns Hopkins; physician Johns Hopkins Hosp.; dir. cardiovascular div. dept. medicine, adult cardiac clinic Johns Hopkins Sch. Medicine and Hosp., dir. myocardial infarction research unit, 1967-75; dean med. faculty, v.p. medicine Johns Hopkins U., 1975-90, dean. emeritus, 1990—; Sir Thomas Lewis lectr. Brit. Cardiac Soc., 1969; John Kent Lewis lectr. Stanford U., 1972; bd. dirs. emeritus Johns Hopkins Hosp., Francis Scott Key Med. Ctr.; mem. cardiovascular study sect. Nat. Heart and Lung Inst., 1965-69, chmn. cardiovascular study sect., 1966-69, mem. tng. grant com., 1971-73, chmn. heart panel, 1972-73, adv. coun., 1974-78; mem. Inst. of Medicine, 1976—; chmn. vis. com. Harvard Med. and Dental Sch., 1979-86; bd. overseers Harvard U., 1980-86. Editor Modern Concepts Cardiovascular Disease, 1961-65, The Principles and Practice of Medicine, 17th-22nd edits., 1968-88; mem. editorial bd. Circulation, 1968-74; mem. editorial com. Jour. Clin. Investigation, 1969-73; contbr. numerous articles on cardiovascular disease and physiology to profl. jours. Served as capt. M.C. AUS, 1949-51. Flexner award, Assn Am. Med. Coll., 1994; hon. fellow UMDS, Guy's and St. Thomas' Hosps., London, 1996. Fellow Am. Coll. Cardiology; mem. ACP (master 1979), Boylston Med. Soc., Am. Fedn. Clin. Research, Am. Physiol. Soc., Assn. Am. Physicians, Am. Soc. Clin. Investigation (councillor 1967-69), Am. Clin. and Climatol. Assn. (pres. 1978-79, councillor 1979-83, Metzger lecture 1986), Assn. Univ. Cardiologists (councillor 1972-75), Am. Heart Assn. (chmn. sci. sessions program com. 1965-67, chmn. publs. com. 1970-73, pres. 1973-74, dir. 1974-77, Connor lectr. 1979, Gold Heart award 1976, James B. Herrick award 1982), Heart Assn. Md. (pres. 1967-68), Sigma Xi, Alpha Omega Alpha; corr. mem. Brit. Cardiac Soc., Sociedad Peruana de Cardiologie, Cardiac Soc. Australia and New Zealand. Clubs: Peripatetic, Interurban (pres. 1978), Elkridge, Blue Hill Country Club (Maine). Home: 901 Drohomer Pl Baltimore MD 21210 Office: Johns Hopkins U 1830 E Monument St Baltimore MD 21205-2100

ROSS, ROBERT E., psychologist, clergyman, counselor. ThB in Pastoral Counseling, BD, MA, PhD in Religion; postgrad. in Clin. Psychology, Alfred Adler Inst. of Counseling and Psychotherapy, Chgo. Ordained clergyman. Counselor psychiat. unit of the neuropsychiatry br. profl. div. of Dept. of Medicine and Surgery U.S. Navy; dir. Counseling Ctr. for Effective Living, Indpls.; participant in grad. rsch. program in Substance Abuse and the Family, Substance Abuse in Bus. and Industry, and the Psychology and Physiology of Substance AbuseNova U.; speaker in field; workshop leader; numerous appearances radio and TV shows. Author: Beyond the Rope's End. Lt. commdr. USNR. Fellow Am. Assn. of Pastoral Counselors; mem. Nat. Assn. Sch. Psychologists, Am. Counseling Assn., Am. Mental Health Counselors Assn. Office: Counseling Ctr for Effective Living 4321 E 82nd St Indianapolis IN 46250-1676

ROSS, RUSSELL, pathologist, educator; b. St. Augustine, Fla., May 25, 1929; s. Samuel and Minnie (DuBoff) R.; m. Jean Long Teller, Feb. 22, 1956; children: Valerie Regina, Douglas Teller. A.B., Cornell U., 1951; D.D.S., Columbia U., 1955; Ph.D., U. Wash., 1962; DSc (hon.P, Med. Coll. of Pa., 1987. Intern Columbia-Presbyn. Med. Ctr., 1955-56, USPHS Hosp., Seattle, 1956-58; spl. research fellow pathology sch. medicine U. Wash., Seattle, 1958-62, asst. prof. pathology and oral biology sch. medicine and dentistry, 1962-65, assoc. prof. pathology Sch. Medicine, 1965-69, prof. Sch. Medicine, 1969—, adj. prof. biochemistry Sch. Medicine, 1978—, assoc. dean for sci. affairs sch. medicine, 1971-78, chmn. dept. pathology sch. medicine, 1982-94; dir. Ctr. for Vascular Biology, 1991—; vis. scientist Strangeways Rsch. Lab., Cambridge, Eng.; mem. rsch. com. Am. Heart Assn.; mem. adv. bd. Found. Cardiologique Princess Liliane, Brussels, Belgium; life fellow Clare Hall, Cambridge U.; mem. adv. coun. Nat. Heart, Lung and Blood Inst., NIH, 1978-81; vis. prof. Royal Soc. Medicine, U.K., 1987, 95. Editorial bd. Procs. Exptl. Biology and Medicine, 1971-86, Jours. Cell Biology, 1972-74, Exptl. Cell Rsch., 1982-92, Jour. Exptl. Medicine, Growth Factors, Am. Jours. Pathology, Internat. Cell Biology Jour., Circulation, Arteriosclerosis & Thrombosis, Growth Regulation; assoc. editor Arteriosclerosis, 1982-92, Jours. Cellular Physiology, Jours. Cellular Biochemistry; exec. editor Trends in Cariovascular Medicine; reviewing editorial bd. Sci. mag., 1987-90; contbr. articles to profl. jours. Trustee Seattle Symphony Orch. Recipient Birnberg Rsch. award Columbia U., 1975, Nat. Rsch. Achievement award Am. Heart Assn., 1990, Rous-Whiple award Am. Assn. Pathologists, 1992, Glorney-Raisbeck award N.Y. Acad. Medicine, 1995, Gordon Wilson medal Am. Clin. and Climatol. Assn., 1981; named to Inst. Medicine, Nat. Acad. Scis., Japan Soc. Promotion of Sci. fellow, 1985, Guggenheim fellow, 1966-67. Fellow AAAS, Am. Acad. Arts and Scis.; mem. Am. Soc. Cell Biology, Tissue Culture Assn., Am. Assn. Pathologists (Rous-Whipple award 1992), Internat. Soc. Cell Biology, Electron Microscope Soc. Am., Am. Soc. for Investigative Pathology (pres. 1994-95), Am. Heart Assn. (fellow Coun. on Arteriosclerosis, Nat. Rsch. Achievement award 1990), Royal Micros. Soc., Harvey Soc. (hon.), Am. Soc. Biochemistry and Molecular Biology, Romanian Acad. Med. Scis. (hon.), Royal Belgian Acad. Scis. (fgn. corr. mem.), Sigma Xi. Home: 3812 48th Ave NE Seattle WA 98105-5227 Office: U Wash Sch Medicine 1959 NE Pacific St Seattle WA 98195-0004

ROSS, SHERMAN, psychologist, educator; b. N.Y.C., Jan. 1, 1919; s. Max R. and Rachel (Khoutman) R.; m. Jean Goodwin, Aug. 18, 1945; children: Norman Kimball, Claudia Lisbeth (Mrs. Overway), Michael Lachlan. B.S., CCNY, 1939; A.M., Columbia U., 1941, Ph.D., 1943. Asst. psychology, research psychologist Columbia U., 1941-44; asst., then assoc. prof. psychology Bucknell U., 1946-50; research fellow N.Y. Zool. Soc., 1948; guest investigator, sci. asso. Jackson Lab., 1947-77; assoc. prof., then prof. psychology U. Md., 1950-60; spl. cons. Psychopharmacology Svc. Ctr. NIMH, 1956-63; asst. chief NIMH, 1956-57; exec. sec. edn. and tng. bd., sci. affairs officer APA, 1960-68; prof. psychology Howard U., 1968-89, emeritus, 1989—; exec. sec., staff assoc., assembly of behavioral and social scis. Nat. Acad. Scis.-NRC, 1968-76; lectr. Himmelfarb Mobile U., 1994—; cons. VA, Human Ecology Fund, Stanford Research Inst., Office Naval Research, U.S. Sci. Exhibit, Am. U., HRB-Singer, Inc.; bd. dirs. Interdisciplinary Communications Assocs., Washington; adv. council Woodrow Wilson Rehab. Center Found.; mem. Md. Bd. Examiners Psychology, 1957-58, 84-89; chmn. bd. dirs. Inst. for Research, State Coll., Pa.; mem. Montgomery County Health Planning Commn.; mem. Md. Statewide Health Coordinating Coun., Met. Washington Area Council of Health Planning Agys., Emergency Med. Svcs. Adv. Council; commr. health emeritus Montgomery County, Md. Trustee Carver Research Found., Tuskegee U. Served to lt. (j.g.) USNR, 1944-46; capt. USNR (ret.). Fellow APA, Am. Coll. Neuropsychopharmacology, Royal Soc. Health, Washington Acad. Scis.; mem. Aerospace Med. Assn., Am. Soc. Zoologists, Ecol. Soc., Ergonomics Rsch. Soc., Md. Psychol. Assn. (pres. 1973-74), D.C. Psychol. Assn. (pres. 1982), Cosmos Club (Washington), Sigma Xi (pres. U. Md. 1957-58, pres. Howard U. 1983-84), Phi Kappa Phi, Psi Chi (nat. pres. 1964-68). Home: 382 Russell Ave Gaithersburg MD 20877-2863 also: Glen Mary Rd Bar Harbor ME 04609-1301

ROSS, STEPHEN ADDISON, physician; b. Neptune, N.J., Jan. 2, 1940; s. Delbert Amos Ross and Evelyn Ernestine (Hutchinson) Bradway; m. Pamela Schrader Jensen, June 8, 1974. AB, Williams Coll., 1960; MD, Cornell U., 1964. Diplomate Am. Bd. Internal Medicine, Am. Bd. Hematology, Am. Bd. Med. Oncology. Intern in internal medicine Yale-New Haven Hosp., New Haven, 1964-65, resident in internal medicine, 1965-66, 68-69; fellow in hematology Yale U., New Haven, 1969-70 chief resident in internal medicine VA Hosp., West Haven, Conn., 1970-71, fellow in hematology/oncology, 1971-73; mem. staff in internal medicine, hematology, oncology Community Health Care Ctr. Plan, New Haven, 1973-76; pvt. practice Rockland, Maine, 1976—; instr. Medicine Yale U., New Haven, 1970-72, asst. prof. Medicine, 1972-76; asst. clin. prof. Community Health Tufts U., Boston, 1983—, pres. med. staff, 1983—. Del. U.S. Pharmacopeial Conv., Washington, 1980-85; mem. adv. bd. Coastal Family Hospice, Rockland, 1984-92. Capt. USAF, 1966-68. Fellow ACP; mem. Maine Med. Assn., Knox County Med. Soc., Am. Soc. of Clin. Oncology. Home: HC 60 Box 3170 Camden ME 04843-9504 Office: Ste 103 4 Glen Cove Dr Bldg 103 Rockport ME 04856-4236

ROSS, STEVEN GARY, psychiatrist; b. N.Y.C., Mar. 6, 1954; s. Robert and Mildred (Davis) R.; m. Patricia Colletta, Oct. 29, 1989. BA, U. Pa., 1975; MD, Autonomous U. of Guadalajara, Jalisco, Mexico, 1980. Subintern L.I. Jewish/Queens Hosp. Ctr., N.Y.C., 1981-82; intern in surgery Flushing Hosp., N.Y.C., 1982-83; resident in psychiatry Maimonides Med. Ctr., N.Y.C., 1983-86, chief resident in psychiatry, 1985-86; asst. unit chief, asst. prof. psychiatry Cornell U. Med. Coll., N.Y.C., 1986-92; attending physician Burke Rehab. Ctr., White Plains, N.Y., 1987-92; unit chief geropsychiat. day programs L.I. Jewish Hosp., 1992—; ass.t prof. Albert Einstein Med. Coll., 1992—. Mem. Am. Psychiat. Assn., Am. Assn. Geriatric Psychiatrists. Democrat. Jewish. Home: 448 Abbey Rd Manhasset NY 11030-2143

ROSS, WESLEY FREDERICK, clinical psychologist; b. Erie, Pa., Feb. 23, 1941; s. Wesley K. and Lucille (Schurz) R.; m. Shirley Ann Cody, Apr. 7, 1962; 1 child, Wesley Charles. AB, U. Ky., 1962, MA, 1964, PhD, 1969. Commd. 2d lt., USPHS, 1963, advanced through grades to col., 1983; psychologist VA Hosp., Lexington, Ky., 1964-66; instr. U. Ky., Lexington, 1964—; psychologist, unit chief NIMH Clinic Research Ctr., Lexington, 1966-74; unit mgr. Fed. Correction Inst., Lexington, 1974—. Contbr. articles to profl. publs., chpt. to book. Mem. allocations panel United Way, Lexington, 1982-91, mem. campaign panel, 1983, 86, 91, mem. Speakers Bur., 1982-84; instr. wellness program YMCA, Lexington, 1983—, bd. dirs., 1981—; pres. Fayette County Leaders Coun., 1985-87; v.p. Bluegrass Area 4-H Leaders Coun., 1987-89—. Decorated Commendation medal; recipient Superior Performance award USPHS Hosp., 1962, Vocat. Rehab. award Vocat. Rehab. Adminstrn., 1964, Outstanding Svc. award Pub. Health Svc. & Bur. Prisons, 1989, Outstanding Ky. Vol. award United Way, 1992. Mem. Psyhcologists in Pub. Service, Am. Psychol. Assn., Central Ky. Psychol. Assn. (sec. 1965-66, v.p. 1966-67), Antique Automobile Club (bd. dirs. 1971-73), Bluegrass R.R. Club (pres. 1975, 82), Nat. Ry. Hist. Soc. (pres., nat. dir. Ky. Cen. chpt. 1988—, regional v.p. Ohio Valley region 1992—), Kappa Delta Pi (pres. 1963). Lutheran. Avocations: collecting antique automobiles, collecting railroadiania, photography. Home: 1749 Bahama Rd Lexington KY 40509-9536

ROSSA, PETER PAUL, healthcare facility administrator; b. Milw., July 12, 1949; s. Peter Paul and Agnes (Stolpa) R.; m. Rae Ann Ryder, Nov. 17, 1978; children: David Mark, Angela Rena Rossa Scoggin. BS, U. Wis.-Milw., 1977; MA, U. Philippines, 1980, PhD, 1982. Quality assurance coord. U.S. Naval Shipyard, Portsmouth, N.H., 1985-89; chief quality assurance N.H. Dept. Corrections, Concord, 1990-92; quality assurance mgr. Melrose (Mass.) Wakefield Hosp., 1992-94; quality assurance coord., safety officer Sun Coast Hosp., Largo, Fla., 1994-95; dir. quality assurance Seacoast Healthcare, Hampton, N.H., 1995-96; project mgr. Blue Cross/ Blue Shield Maine, South Portland, 1996—; del. China healthcare quality mgmt. issues; con. in field. Mem. Senate Re-election Com., Washington, 1993. Mem. N.H. Assn. Healthcare, Shriners, Scottish Rite, Masons. Methodist. Office: Blue Cross/ Blue Shield Maine 2 Gannett Rd South Portland ME 04106

ROSSARO, LORENZO, medical educator; b. Trento, Italy, Mar. 25, 1956; came to U.S., 1993; s. Enrico and Carla (Linardi) R.; m. Debra Lynn Adams, Aug. 12, 1989. MD, U. Pabova, 1982. Asst. prof. medicine U. Padova (Italy), 1989-93, Pa. State U., Hershey, 1993—. Fulbright scholar, 1986-88. Office: Hershey Med Ctr PO Box 850 Hershey PA 17033

ROSSAVIK, IVAR KRISTIAN, obstetrician, gynecologist; b. Stavanger, Rogaland, Norway, Nov. 3, 1936; came to U.S., 1982; s. Andreas and Bergit (Berge) R.; divorced; children: Line, Anne Britt, Kirsten, Solveig; m. Claudia Lagos, May 23, 1987; children: Claudia Kristina, Eevar Benjamin. MD, U. Oslo, 1962, PhD, 1982. Pvt. practice, medicine Stavanger, 1974; asst. chief, acting chmn. U. Tromsoe, Norway, 1974-76; clin. fellow Nat. Hosp. of Norway, Oslo, 1976-81, Norwegian Radium Hosp./U. Oslo, 1981-82; pvt. practice Oslo, 1977-82; rsch. asst. prof. Baylor Coll. Medicine, Houston, 1983-86; assoc. prof. U. Okla., Oklahoma City, 1987-93, prof., 1993—; dir. Ultrasound Svcs., Dept. Ob/Gyn., U. Okla. Inventor Rossavik Growth Equation, 1980; author: (textbook) Practical Obstetrical Ultrasound: With and Without A Computer, 1991. Lt. Royal Norwegian Navy, 1964-65. Mem. AMA, Am. Fertility Soc., Am. Inst. Ultrasound in Medicine, Okla. State Med. Assn., Irish and Am. Paediatric Soc., Internat. Perinatal Doppler Soc., So. Med. Assn., AAAS. Lutheran. Office: Univ Oklahoma Dept Ob-Gyn PO Box 26901 Oklahoma City OK 73126-0901

ROSSDEUTSCHER, REINHARD KURT PAUL, JR., radiologist, educator; b. Wiesbaden, Germany, June 25, 1953; s. Reinhard Kurt Alfred and Ingeburg (Liese) R. MD, Free U., Berlin, 1979. Cert. radiologist. Resident in radiology Klinikum Charlottenburg, Free U., Berlin, 1986; mem. staff dept. radiology Heckeshorn Chest Hosp., Berlin, 1986—; vice dir. dept. radiology Heckershorn Chest Hosp., Berlin, 1987; instr. Roentgen Diagnostic Postgrad. Course, Neuss, Germany, 1994—. Author: Manual of Radiology, 1996, (with others) Memorix Innere Medizin, 1996. Recipient Film Quiz 2nd Place award Internat. Diagnostic Course Davos, 1989, 1st Place award, 1991, 95. Fellow Berlin Roentgen Soc., German Roentgen Soc. (Film Quiz 2nd Place award 1991, 92); mem. Radiological Soc. North Am. (corr.), Berlin-Brandenburg Soc. Nuclear Medicine. Mem. Social Dem. Party. Home: Tuebinger Str 4, D-10715 Berlin Germany Office: Lungenklinik Heckeshorn Dept Radiology, Zum Heckeshorn 33, D-14109 Berlin Germany

ROSSER, RHONDA LANAE, psychotherapist; b. Champaign, Ill., Aug. 29, 1953; d. Neill Albert and Grace Lee (Byers) R.; (div. June 1, 1993); children: Anthony Neill Williams, Joseph Neill Jackson Hogan. BS in Psychology, Guilford Coll., 1975; MEd in Edn., U. N.C., Greensboro, 1979, PhD in Counseling, 1991. Joined 3rd Order of Secular Franciscans/Order of St. Francis. Instr. U. N.C., Greensboro, 1985-88; dir. Montagnard Program Luth. Family Svcs., Greensboro, 1985-88; psychotherapist pvt. practice, Greensboro, 1989—. Contbr. articles to profl. jours. Recipient Presdl. citation U.S. Govt., 1987. Mem. Am. Counseling Assn. (Outstanding Rsch. award 1991), Chi Sigma Iota. Democrat. Roman Catholic (3d order of Secular Franciscans/Order of St. Francis). Home and Office: 2318 W Cornwallis Dr Greensboro NC 27408-6802

ROSSI, ENNIO C., internist, educator; b. Madison, Wis., Apr. 3, 1931; s. Joseph and Esther (D'Amelio) R.; m. Anna Maria Bianchi, June 22, 1957; children: Roberta, Marco. BA, U. Wis., 1951, MD, 1954. Diplomate Am. Bd. Internal Medicine. Intern Ohio State U. Hosps., 1954-55; resident medicine U. Wis. Hosps., 1958-61, fellow, 1961-63; instr. medicine Marquette U., Milw., 1963-64, asst. prof. medicine, 1964-66; assoc. prof. medicine Northwestern U., Chgo., 1966-72, prof. medicine, 1972—, chief hematology, 1967-84, chief transfusion medicine, 1984—; v.p. med. affairs Life Source Blood Ctr., Glenview, Ill., 1988-93; vis. scientist Mario Negri Inst., Milan, 1977. Co-editor: Haemostasis and the Kidney, 1989; sr. editor: Principles of Transfusion Medicine, 1991, 2d edit., 1996. Capt. U.S. Army, 1956-58. Fulbright scholar, U.S. Dept. State, U. Rome, 1955; Nat. Heart, Lung Blood Inst. Transfusion Medicine Acad. awardee, 1983; WHO travelling fellow, 1985. Fellow ACP; mem. Am. Soc. Hematology, Am. Soc. Pharmacology and Exptl. Therapeutics, Am. Assn. Blood Banks (chmn. acad. transfusion medicine com. 1988-93), Internat. Soc. Blood Transfusion. Office: Northwestern U 303 E Chicago Ave Chicago IL 60611-3008

ROSSI, MICHAEL A., cardiologist; b. Bklyn., July 3, 1959; m. Barbara Rossi; 4 children. BS, Brown U., 1980, MD, 1984. Resident in internal medicine Robert Wood Johnson Univ. Hosp., New Brunswick, N.J., 1984-87; chief resident Robert Wood Johnson Univ. Hosp., New Brunswick, 1987; attending physician Med. Ctr. at Princeton, N.J., 1987-89; cardiology fellow The Grad. Hosp., Phila., 1989-91; advanced cardiology fellow Temple Univ. Hosp., Phila., 1991-92; attending cardiologist Cardiology Care Specialists, Lehigh Valley Hosp., Allentown, Pa., 1992—. Office: Cardiology Care Specialists 3340 Hamilton Blvd Allentown PA 18103

ROSSI, MICHAEL ANDREW, cardiologist; b. Waterbury, Conn., June 27, 1936; s. Anthony and Mary (Castaldi) R.; m. Virginia Louise Brello, Aug. 20, 1960; children: Mary, Christin, Michael, Anthony, Peter. BS in Biology, Fairfield U., 1958; MD, St. Louis U., 1962. Diplomate Am. Bd. Internal Medicine, Am. Bd. Cardiovascular Diseases. Intern St. Louis City Hosp., 1962-63; resident in internal medicine Hartford (Conn.) Hosp., 1963-64; fellow in cardiology NIH and Peter Bent Brigham Hosp., 1964-66; instr. in medicine Washington U. Med. Sch., St. Louis, 1962-63, Harvard Med. Sch., Boston, 1964-66; chief divsn. medicine U.S.N. Naval Submarine Base, New London, Conn., 1966-68; instr. divsn. cardiology U. Conn. Med. Sch., Farmington, 1970-80, asst. prof. medicine, 1980-90, assoc. clin. prof. medicine, 1990—; chief dept medicine Johnson Meml. Hosp., Stafford Springs, Conn., 1968-74; chief cardiac svcs. to cardiac surgery Hartford (Conn.) Hosp., 1970—; cons. cardiology Winsted (Conn.) Meml. Hosp., 1968-88, Johnson Meml. Hosp., Stafford Springs, 1968-88, Inst. of Living, Hartford, 1990-95; sr. attending physician U. Conn. Med. Sch., John Dempsey Hosp., Hartford Hosp., 1968—; mem. exec. com. cardiology divsn., Hartford Hosp., 1972—. Contbr. articles to profl. jours. including Jour. Am. Coll. Cardiology, Chest Diseases, Conn. Medicine., 1966—. Lt. cmmdr. USN, 1966-68. Fellow Am. Coll. Cardiology; mem. Am. Heart Assn., Conn. State Med. Soc., Hartford County Med. Soc., Am. Heart Assn., Hartford Club, Hartford Canoe Club. Office: Consulting Cardiologists PC 85 Seymour St Hartford CT 06106

ROSSIER, JEAN PIERRE, neuropharmacologist, biochemist; b. Brussels, June 18, 1944; s. Michel Pierre and Anne Marie (Van der Heyde) R.; m. Florence M. Baut, Apr. 14, 1972; children: Ombeline, Olivier. MD, U. Brussels, 1969; DSc, U. Paris, 1975. Intern City Hosp., Brussels, 1966-69; rsch. asst. Coll. France, Paris, 1969-75; asst. prof. Tufts U. Med. Sch., Boston, 1975-76; scientist Salk Inst., San Diego, 1976-78, Roche Inst., Nutley, N.J., 1979; dir. neurophysiology Nat. Ctr. Sci. Rsch. (CNRS), Gif sur Yvette, France, 1980-95, dir. neurobiology of cellular diversity, 1995—; prof. biology Higher Sch. Indsl. Phys. Chemistry, Paris, 1994—; dir. rsch. 1st class Inst. Nat. Health and Med. Rsch., Paris, 1971—; cons. French Ministry Higher Edn. and Rsch., 1993—; cons. Human Frontier Sci. Program, 1995—. Editor: Neurochemistry Internat., 1987—, Neuropeptides, 1987—. Fellow Internat. Soc. for Neurochemistry, Internat. Brain Rsch. Orgn., Soc. Française Neuroendocrinologie Experimentale, Collegium Internat. Neuropsychopharmacologie. Office: ESPCI, 10 rue Vauquelin, 75231 Paris Cedex 5, France

ROSSIGNOL, JEAN LUC, geneticist, educator; b. Paris, Feb. 20, 1939; s. Yves Marie and Magdeleine (Crombe) R.; m. Michele Therese Fleureau, July 20, 1961; children: Charles-Henri, Emmanuelle. Lic. in Scis. Naturelles, Faculte des Scis., Paris, 1960; Dr. D'Etat, Faculte des Scis., Orsay, France, 1967. Maitre asst. Faculte des Scis., Osray, 1964-69; maitre de confs. Ctr. Exptl. Montrouge, France, 1969-71; prof. Faculte des Scis., Orsay, 1971—; bd. dirs. Inst. de Genetique et Microbiologie, Orsay, 1991. Author: Abrege de Genetique, 1975. Mem. French Soc. Cell Biology, French Soc. Genetics, European Molecular Biology Orgn. Office: Inst Genetics & Microbiology, Bât 400 U Paris Sud, 91405 Orsay France

ROSSKOTHEN, HEINZ DIETER, engineer; b. Duisburg, Germany, Sept. 19, 1936; came to U.S., 1959; naturalized, 1965; s. Bernhard and Hedwig Rosskothen; m. Ilse Meyer, Oct. 26, 1963; children: Norman, Susan. Diploma tool and die maker, Bloomfield (N.J.) Tech., 1964. Elec. engr. Niederheinische Hutte, Duisburg, 1957-59; instrument designer Buders Tool Co., Caldwell, N.J., 1959-60; mgr. Monach Tool & Mfg., Coldwell, N.J., 1960-64; engr. Columbia U., N.Y.C., 1964-72, sr. st. assoc., 1972—, dir. instrumentation, 1974—; cons. Kreske Eye Inst., Detroit, 1983—. Elder Presbyn. Ch., 1991—. Mem. SME (sr.), MTA/SME (charter mem.). Home: 293 Carlton Ter Teaneck NJ 07666-3403 Office: Columbia U 635 W 165th St New York NY 10032-3701

ROSSMAN, ISADORE, physician; b. Elizabeth, N.J., Mar. 29, 1913; s. Abraham and Lena (Roshonik) R.; m. Sylvia Weiner; 1 child, Paul Gordon. BA, U. Wis., 1933; PhD, U. Chgo., 1937, MD, 1942. Diplomate internal medicine. Rsch. assoc. anatomy U. Chgo., 1935-42; physician pvt. practice, N.Y.C., 1947—; med. dir. Montefiore Home Health Agy., N.Y.C., 1948—; assoc. clin. prof. medicine Einstein Coll. Medicine, 1970-84; commr. N.Y. State Moreland Commn., 1974-76; adv. coun. Nat. Inst. Aging, 1978-81; bd. dirs. Am. Geriatrics Soc., 1975-85, pres., 1982-83; asst. dir. Bur. Chronic Disease Control, N.Y.C. Dept. Health, 1971-75. Author: Looking Forward, 1989; editor: Clinical Geriatrics, 1970, 2d edit. 1979, 3d edit. 1986; contbr. articles to profl. jours. Capt. U.S. Army, 1943-46. Recipient Freeman award, Gerontologic Soc. Am., 1980, Leavitt award, Am. Geriatrics Soc., 1987. Fellow N.Y. Acad. Medicine, Phi Beta Kappa, Sigma Xi. Democrat. Jewish. Home: 50 W 96th St New York NY 10025-6526

ROSSMAN, PEGGY EYRE ELROD, retired nursing administrator, gerontology nurse; b. Hooven, Ohio, Mar. 6, 1928; d. Lloyd Estell and Leah Ann (Haworth) Elrod; m. William N. Rossman, Oct. 1, 1949; 1 child, Robert W. Diploma, Christ Hosp. Sch. Nursing, Cin., 1949. RN, Ohio, Ind. Staff med.-surg. nurse Christ Hosp., 1949-53; recovery room nurse Dearborn County Hosp., Lawrenceburg, Ind., 1959-65, head med.-surg. nurse, 1959; dir. nursing Terrace View Health Care Ctr., Lawrenceburg, 1970-90. Mem. ANA, Ind. Nurses Assn. (pres. dist. 9, 1977, coun. on practice gerontol. nursing 1971-75).

ROSSMAN, TOBY GALE, genetic toxicology educator, researcher; b. Weehawken, N.J., June 3, 1942; d. Norman N. and Sylvia Betty (May) Natowitz; m. Neil I. Rossman, Sept. 16, 1962 (div. Sept. 1980); m. Gordon Rauer, Aug. 19, 1990. AB, NYU, 1964, PhD, 1968; postgrad., Brandeis U., 1964-65. Instr. Polytech. Inst. of N.Y., N.Y.C., 1968-69; postdoctoral dept. pathology NYU, N.Y.C., 1969-71; from asst. to assoc. prof. Inst. for Environ Medicine NYU Med Ctr, N.Y.C., 1974-85; prof. Inst. for Environ. Medicine, 1985—; dir. molecular and genetic toxicology Nelson Inst. Environ. Medicine, NYU Med. Ctr., N.Y.C., 1995—. Mem. editorial bd. Molecular Toxicology, 1989-91, Teratogenesis, Carcinogenesis, Mutagenesis, 1990-91, Environmental and Molecular Mutagenesis, 1994—, Mutation Research, 1994—; contbr. numerous articles to profl. jours. EPA grantee, NIH grantee. Mem. AAAS, Assn. for Women in Sci., Am. Assn. for Cancer Rsch., Am. Soc. for Microbiology, Environ. Mutagen Soc. (councilor 1990-93). Office: NYU Inst Environ Medicine Long Meadow Rd Tuxedo Park NY 10987

ROSSMANN, CHARLES BORIS, obstetrician, gynecologist; b. Brno, Moravia, Czechoslovakia, Nov. 19, 1945; came to U.S., 1988; s. Milos and Vlasta Boudna (Cernochova) Lota; m. Tatiana Elenka Hajossy, Oct. 19, 1979; children: Nathalie Nissa Cora, Nadine Nicole. MD, Purkyne U., Brno, Czechoslovakia, 1969. Bd. cert. ob-gyn., ACLS. Intern, resident Valtice Gen. Hosp., Czechoslovakia, 1969-73; resident pathology Sunnybrook and Toronto Gen. Hosp., 1981-82; resident in ob/gyn. Grace and St. Clare Gen. Hosp., St. John's, Can., 1982-83; ob-gyn. specialist Skalica Gen. Hosp., Czechoslovakia, 1973-74; gen. practice Fed. Republic Germany,

1974-80; med. officer Fogo Island Hosp., Can., 1983-84, Baragwanath Hosp., Johannesburg, South Africa, 1984-85, Edendale Hosp., Pietermaritzburg, South Africa, 1985-86; ob-gyn. specialist Western Mem. Regional Hosp., Corner Brook, Can., 1986-88; ob-gyn. gen. practice Deuel County Mem. Hosp., Clear Lake, S.D., 1988-89; ob-gyn. specialist Bullock County Hosp., Union Springs, Ala., 1989, St. Joseph's Hosp., Huntingburg, Ind., 1989-94; Smith Hosp., Hahira, Ga., 1994—. Contbr. articles to profl. jours.; inventor in field. Mem. AMA, Am. Assn. Gyncecol. Laparoscopists, Am. Coll. Internat. Physicians (Ky. chpt.), Ga. Med. Assn. Office: 2301 N Ashley St Valdosta GA 31602

ROSS MEEHAN, JEAN M., occupational health and safety management consultant; b. Chgo., Mar. 16, 1954; d. A. Ronald Gonzalez and Barbara Marx Shipley; m. John J. Meehan, 1993; 1 child, Jenna A.; 1 child from previous marriage, Justin L. Ross. Diploma in Nursing with high honors, St. Mary of Nazareth Hosp., Chgo., 1974; BS in Health Arts, Coll. St. Francis, 1988. Staff nurse St. Mary of Nazareth Hosp., Chgo., 1973-75; head nurse ambulatory care Edgebrook Med. Diagnostic Ctr., Chgo., 1975-76; occupl. health nurse Williams Electronics, Inc., Chgo., 1976-84; adminstr. safety and benefits Reliable Power Products, Franklin Park, Ill., 1984-90; corp. dir. risk and benefits MacLean-Fogg Co., Mundelein, Ill., 1990—; pres., cons. Auriel Mgmt. Sys., Island Lake, Ill., 1992—; gov., apptd. mem. Ill. Pollution Prevention Adv. Coun., Springfield, Ill., 1993—, mem. coun., 1993—; bd. dirs. Gt. Lakes Health Care Alliance, 1996—; spkr. in workshops. Guest speaker local schs. and environ. groups, also I.E.P.A. and U.S. E.P.A. workshops; corp. campaign chmn. Charitable Preference Drives, Mundelein, Ill., 1991-94. Recipient Leadership Civic citation United Way Charities of Lake County, 1993, 94. Mem. Am. Assn. Occupational Health Nurses, Ill. Assn. Occupational Health Nurses, Suburban Chgo. Occupational Health Nurses, Fedn. Environ. Technologists, Lake County Violence Intervention and Prevention. Office: MacLean-Fogg Co 1000 Allanson Rd Mundelein IL 60060

ROSSNER, CHARLES WILLIAM, ophthalmologist; b. New Orleans, July 4, 1942; s. Charles William and Helen Louisa (Gates) R.; m. Donna Jane Ardoin, July 20, 1978; children: Ryan Joseph, Carter Wade. MD, Tulane U., 1967. Diplomate Am. Bd. Ophthalmology. Intern Tulane program Charity Hosp., New Orleans, 1967-68, resident, 1971-74; ophthalmologist Browne-McHardy Clinic, Metairie, La., 1974—. Capt. USAF, 1968-70, Vietnam. Fellow ACS, Am. Acad. Ophthalmology, Am. Soc. Cataract and Refractive Surgeons, New Orleans Acad. Ophthalmology. Home: 5124 Folse Dr Metairie LA 70006 Office: Browne-McHardy Clinic 4315 Houma Blvd Metairie LA 70006-2981

ROSSON, BARRY, physician; b. Memphis, Tenn., Aug. 16, 1946; s. Walter and Eleanor (Arbetter) R.; m. Susan Patty Silverman; 1 child, Steven. MD, Univ. Tex. Southwestern, 1971. Pvt. practice Dallas, 1976-95. Office: Medication Cons Svc 8210 Walnut Hill Ln LB27 Dallas TX 75231

ROST, PETER, pharmaceutical company executive; b. Bollebygd, Sweden, May 31, 1959; came to U.S., 1987; s. Siegfrid and Kathie (Zerne) R.; m. Tina Forssten, Apr. 21, 1984. MD, U. Gothenburg, Sweden, 1984. Intern anesthesiology dept. Ea. Hosp., Gothenburg, 1984, practice medicine specializing in anesthesiology, 1984; pres., CEO Bus. Lit. Inc., Gothenburg, 1985-87; copywriter Ehrenstrahle & Co., Gothenburg, 1985, Ogilvy & Mather, Gothenburg, 1985; account supr., copywriter Grey Gothenburg, Gothenburg, 1985-87; med. dir., account supr. Maher Kaump & Clark, Inc., L.A., 1987-92; assoc. dir. med. edn. Lederle Labs. divsn. Am. Cyanamid Co., Wayne, N.J., 1992, dir. med. edn., 1993; product mgr. Lederle Labs. divsn. Am. Cyanimid Co., Wayne, N.J., 1993-94; mkt. planning mgr. Wyeth-Ayerst Internat., St. Davids, Pa., 1995, dir. mktg internal medicine products, 1995—; chmn., chief exec. officer W. Swedish Model Group, Gothenburg, 1985. Author: Emergency Surgery, 1985, The Art of Driving a Car Free, 1985. Mem. AMA, Am. Coll. Physician Execs., Pharm. Advt. Coun. Office: Wyeth-Ayerst Internat Inc PO Box 8616 Philadelphia PA 19101-8616 also: 150 Radnor-Chester Rd Saint Davids PA 19087

ROSTECK, PAUL ROBERT, JR., molecular biologist; b. Decatur, Ill., July 6, 1949; s. Paul Robert Sr. and Erma Evelyn (Bernard) R.; m. Donna Lynn Rozanski, Apr. 22, 1972; 1 child, Erica Lynn. BA, Millikin U., 1976; MS, U. Cin., 1979. Assoc. microbiologist Eli Lilly & Co., Indpls., 1980-81, microbiologist, 1982-83, asst. sr. microbiologist, 1983-89, assoc. sr. microbiologist, 1989-91, sr. microbiologist, 1991-94; rsch. scientist Eli Lilly & Co, Indpls., 1995—. Contbr. articles to profl. jours., chpts. to books. With U.S. Army, 1969-71, Vietnam. Mem. AAAS, Am. Chem. Soc., Am. Soc. for Biochemistry and Molecular Biology, Am. Soc. Microbiology, Sigma Xi. Republican. Lutheran. Office: Eli Lilly & Co Lilly Corp Ctr Indianapolis IN 46285

ROTBART, ABRAHAM, internist; b. Havana, Cuba, Sept. 30, 1944; came to U.S., 1960; s. Azriel and Dina (Zelesniak) R.; m. Shelly Macy Sharpe, June 18, 1970; children: Brandon, Abby. MD, U. Kans., Kansas City, 1970. Diplomate Am. Bd. Internal Medicine. Pres. Pulmonary Medicine Assn., Miami Beach, Fla., 1975—; dir. pulmonary dept. and respiratory medicine dept. Miami Heart Inst., Miami Beach, 1991—; assoc. prof. U. Miami, Fla. Patentee surgical instrument; contbr. articles to profl. publs. Fellow Am. Coll. Chest Physicians; mem. AMA, Fla. Med. Assn., Dade County Med. Assn., Soc. Am. Inventors. Office: Pulmonary Medicine Assocs 4701 Meridian Ave Miami Beach FL 33140

ROTERT, DENISE ANNE, occupational therapist, army officer, educator; b. Sioux Falls, S.D., Nov. 18, 1949; d. Leonard Joseph and Irene Winnifred (Jennings) R. BS, U. Puget Sound, 1971; MA, U. No. Colo., 1975. Commd. 2d lt. Med. Specialist Corps, U.S. Army, 1970, advanced through grades to lt. col. , 1990; staff occupational therapist Tripler Army Med. Center, Honolulu, 1973-76, officer in charge occupational therapy sect. Ireland Army Hosp., Fort Knox, Ky., 1976-77; clin. supr. occupational therapy sect. Letterman Army Med. Center, Presidio of San Francisco, 1977-79; chief instr. occupational therapy asst. course Acad. Health Scis., Ft. Sam Houston, Tex., 1979-84; chief occupational therapy Tri-Service Alcohol Recovery Dept., Naval Hosp., Bethesda, Md., 1984-89, Womack Army Hosp., Ft. Bragg, N.C., 1989-90, ret., 1990; mem. faculty U. S.D., 1991—. Recipient Myra McDaniel Writer's award, 1989. Mem. Am. Occupational Therapy Assn., World Fedn. Occupational Therapists, S.D. Occupational Therapy Assn. Roman Catholic. Home: 2609 S Prairie Ave Sioux Falls SD 57105-4626 Office: USDSM OT Dept 414 E Clark St Vermillion SD 57069-2307

ROTH, DAVID, nephrologist, educator; b. N.Y.C., Sept. 7, 1951; s. Reubin and Ruth (Wunderlich) R.; m. Patricia Marie Byers, Dec. 7, 1985; children: Joshua Reubin, Jonathan Albert. BS in Chemistry, SUNY, 1973, MD, 1977. Diplomate Am. Bd. Internal Medicine, Nat. Bd. Med. Examiners, Am. Bd. Nephrology. Intern and resident in internal medicine U. Miami (Fla.)-Jackson Meml. Med. Ctr., 1977-80, fellow in nephrology, 1980-82, asst. prof. medicine, 1982-83, assoc. prof. medicine and surgery, 1988-94, prof., 1994—, med. dir. renal transplant clinic, transplant nephrologist, 1985—; intern selection com. U. Miami, 1985—, housestaff adv. com. 1985, chmn. nephrology trainee evaluation com, deans ad hoc com. on child care, 1989-90, JMH/UM dialysis com., 1989-91, chmn. Jackson Meml. Hosp. Pharmacy and Therapeutics com., 1991—; governing bd. U. Miami Med. Group, 1994; scientific adv. bd. Nat. Kidney Found.; scientific studies com. Am. Soc. of Transplant Physicians. Editl. bd. Tranplantation and Immunology Letter; contbr. chpts. to books and numerous articles to profl. jours. Fellow ACP; mem. Am. Soc. of Nephrology, Internat. Soc. of Nephrology, Am. Soc. of Transplant Physicians, Am. Fedn. of Clin. Rsch., Transplantation Soc. (med. rev. bd. ESRD Network of Fla.). Office: U Miami Divsn of Nephrology 1600 NW 10th Ave R-126 Miami FL 33136

ROTH, HARRY, ophthalmologist; b. Dayton, Ohio, Nov. 1, 1937; s. Louis and Sophia (Froug) R.; m. Karen Margretha Ebstrub, Aug. 23, 1963; children: Sara Ann, Julie Margaret. Student, Ohio State U., 1955-58; MD, Case Western Res., 1962. Diplomate Am. Bd. Ophthalmology. Intern Cin. Gen. Hosp., 1962-63; resident U. Wisc. Hosp., Madison, 1965-68; fellow in glaucoma U. Calif., San Francisco, 1969-70; pvt. practice Davis Dueher Dean Eye Clinic, Madison, 1970—; assoc. clin. prof. ophthalmologist U. Wis., Madison, 1970—. Capt. USAF, 1963-65. Decorated Air medal, Bronze star. Mem. AMA, Am. Acad. Ophthalmology, Am. Glacouma Soc. Office: Davis Duehr Dean Eye Clinic 1025 Regent St Madison WI 53715

ROTH, JACK ALAN, thoracic surgeon; b. Jan. 29, 1945; s. Richard and Bernice (Saperstein) R.; m. Elizabeth Ann Grimm, Nov. 24, 1978; children: Johanna, Katherine. BA, Cornell U., 1967; MD, Johns Hopkins U., 1971. Diplomate Am. Bd. Surgery, Am. Bd. Thoracic Surgery. Surg. intern Johns Hopkins Hosp., Balt., 1971-72, resident in surgery, 1972-73; postgrad. rsch. fellow div. surg. oncology UCLA Ctr. for Health Scis., 1973-75; resident in gen. surgery UCLA Sch. Medicine, 1975-77, resident, chief resident in thoracic surgery, 1977-79, chief resident in gen. surgery, 1979-80; sr. investigator surgery br. div. cancer treatment Nat. Cancer Inst., NIH, Bethesda, Md., 1980-86, head thoracic oncology sect., 1982-86; prof. tumor biology U. Tex.-M.D. Anderson Cancer Ctr., Houston, 1986—, Bud S. Johnson prof. thoracic surgery, chmn. dept., 1986—; prof. dept. surgery U. Tex., Houston, 1986—; apptd. faculty grad. sch. biomed. scis. U. Tex. Health Sci. Ctr., Houston, 1987—; tng. Ctr. for Advanced Tng. in Cell and Molecular Biology, Washington, 1985; lectr. surgery Johns Hopkins U. Sch. Medicine, 1980-86; clin. asst. prof. Georgetown U. Sch. Medicine, Washington, 1982-86; cons. cardiothoracic surgery svc. Walter Reed Army Hosp., Washington, 1984-86; cons. rsch. microbiology dept. George Washington U. Grad. Sch. Arts and Scis., 1986. Editor: Thoracic Oncology, 1989; contbr. more than 500 articles to publs. including Cancer Rsch., Jour. Clin. Oncology. Recipient Mead Johnson Excellence of Rsch. award Nat. Rsch. Forum, 1980, spl. achievement award HHS, 1981, Lucy Wortham James Basic Rsch. award, E.J. Tabah award, Cosbie lectr.; grantee NIH, 1987—. Office: Anderson Cancer Ctr 1515 Holcombe Blvd Houston TX 77030-4009

ROTH, JEROME ALLAN, pharmacology educator; b. N.Y.C., Aug. 20, 1943; s. Fred and Lillian Roth; divorced; children: Rachel, Evan; m. Patricia A. Kowal, Jan. 26, 1984; children: Chrissy A., Lyndsey B. BS, SUNY, New Paltz, 1965; M Nutritional Sci., Cornell U., 1967, PhD, 1971. Rsch. assoc. Vanderbilt U. Sch. Medicine, Nashville, 1971-72; asst. prof. Yale U. Sch. Medicine, New Haven, 1972-76; asst. prof. SUNY, Buffalo, 1976-80, assoc. prof., 1980-85, prof., 1985—, dir. med. scientist tng. program, 1990—. Mem. editorial bd. Biochem. Pharmacology. Office: SUNY Dept Pharmacology & Therapeutics Buffalo NY 14214

ROTH, LOREN H., psychiatrist; b. May 9, 1939; m. Ellen A. Roth; children: Jonathan, Alexandra, Elizabeth. BA in Philosophy, Cornell U., 1961; MD cum laude, Harvard U., 1966, MPH, 1972; postgrad., Am. U., 1972-73. Diplomate Am. Bd. Psychiatry and Neurology; lic. physician, Conn., Md., Mass., Pa. Med. intern Univ. Hosps., Western Res. U., Cleve., 1966-67; resident psychiatry Yale U., New Haven, 1969-70, Mass. Gen. Hosp., Boston, 1970-72; staff psychiatrist Ctr. for Studies Crime and Delinquency, NIMH, Rockville, Md., 1972-74; co-dir., dir. law and psychiatry program Western Psychiat. Inst. and Clinic/U. Pitts., 1974—, chief adult clin. svcs., 1983-87, 88-89, chief clin. svcs., 1989-95, co-dir., dir. law and psychiatry program, 1974-94; vice-chmn. dept. psychiatry U. Pitts., 1988—, asst. prof., 1974-78, assoc. prof., 1978-82, prof., 1982—; v.p. for Managed Care U. Pitt. Med. Ctr., 1993—; assoc. vice chancellor for edn., health scis. U. Pitts. Sch. Medicine, 1995—; med. staff Presbyn.-Univ. Hosp., Pitts., 1983—; gen. med. officer Fed. Penitentiary, Lewisburg, Pa., 1967-69; William E. Schumacher disting. lectr. Maine Dept. Mental Health and Mental Retardation, Portland, 1982; mem. commn. on mentally disabled ABA, Washington, 1987; cons. law and psychiatry Dept. Welfare, Commonwealth Pa., 1974; cons. reviewer, site visitor crime and delinquency sect. NIMH, 1977; examiner Am. Bd. Psychiatry and Neurology, 1985. Author: (with others) Informed Consent: A Study of Decisionmaking in Psychiatry, 1984; editor: (with others) Psychiatry, Social, Epidemiologic and Legal Psychiatry, Vol. 5, 1986; contbr. articles to profl. jours., chpts. to books; editorial bd. Criminology, 1974-78, Law and Human Behavior, 1980-85, Internat. Jour. Law and Psychiatry, 1980-88, Behavioral Scis. and the Law, 1987-95; assoc. editor Am. Jour. Psychiatry, 1982-90; cons. editor Criminal Justice and Behavior, 1982-85. Lt. comrd. USPHS Res., 1967—. Recipient Steve Allen award United Mental Health, Inc., 1990; grantee NIMH, 1979, 80-81, 89, Founds. Fund for Rsch. in Psychiatry, 1980-82. Fellow Am. Psychiat. Assn. (Isaac Ray award 1988), Am. Coll. Utilization Rev. Physicians, Am. Coll. Psychiatrists; mem. AMA, Am. Acad. Psychiatry and Law (pres. 1983-84), Group for Advancement Psychiatry (com. on psychiatry and law 1979-80, chmn. 1981-84), Am. Soc. Criminology, Am. Soc. Law and Medicine (bd. dirs. 1982-85), Internat. Acad. Law and Mental Health (bd. dirs.), Am. Psychopath. Assn., Phi Beta Kappa, Phi Kappa Phi. Home: 6820 Edgerton Ave Pittsburgh PA 15208-2803 Office: Western Psychiat Inst 3811 Ohara St Pittsburgh PA 15213-2593

ROTH, NANCY LOUISE, former nurse, veterinarian; b. Cin., June 24, 1955; d. Jack Leopold Jr. and Elsie Harriet (Shemin) R. BS in Agr., U. Mo., 1977, DVM, 1989; BSN, Avila Coll., 1980. Critical care RN. Staff nurse St. Louis Univ. Hosp., 1980-81, Barnes Hosp., St. Louis, 1981-85, U. Mo. Hosp. and Clinic, Columbia, 1985-89; assoc. veterinarian Ill. Equine Field Svc., North Aurora, 1989-95; proprietor Cedar Ln. Equine Clinic, New Haven, Mo., 1995—. Contbr. articles to profl. jours. Vol. instr. U.S. Pony Club, Wayne, Ill., 1991-95, 4-H Club, Wheaton, Ill., 1991-95; bd. dirs. Ill. Dressage and Combined Tng. Assn. Mem. AVMA, Am. Assn. Equine Practitioners (trails and events com.), Sigma Theta Tau, Phi Zeta. Home: 3134 Hwy E New Haven MO 63068 Office: Cedar Ln Equine Clinic PO Box 108 New Haven MO 63068-0108

ROTH, OLIVER RALPH, radiologist; b. Cumberland, Md., Nov. 30, 1921; s. DeCoursey Andrew and Mabel (Lathrum) R.; BS, Frostburg (Md.) State Coll., 1942, DSc (hon.), 1980; MD, U. Md., 1950; m. Virginia McBride, June 2, 1943; 1 child, Tiija. Diplomate Am. Bd. Radiology. Resident, Johns Hopkins Hosp., Balt., 1954-57; cancer research fellow Middlesex Hosp., London, 1957-58; founder dept. radiation oncology Presbyn. Hosp., Charlotte, N.C., 1958-62; attending radiologist King's Daus. Hosp., Ashland, Ky., 1962-80; radiologist Our Lady of Bellefonte Hosp., 1981-86; mem. faculty Sch. of Allied Health Shawnee State U., Portsmouth, Ohio, 1986-90; prof. radiology Sch. Medicine Marshall U., Huntington, W.Va., 1990—; mem. adv. com. Ky. Cancer Commn., 1978; bd. dirs. Boyd County chpt. Am. Cancer Soc., 1978. With USN, 1942-45. Commanded to Buckingham Palace, June 17, 1958; recipient Disting. Alumni award Frostburg State U., 1979. Mem. AMA, Am. Coll. Radiology, Radiol. Soc. N.Am., Am. Radium Soc., Royal Faculty Radiology, Brit. Inst. Radiology. Democrat. Lutheran. Club: Shriners (Cumberland, Md.). Book reviewer Radiology, 1954-55. Home: 2912 Cogan St Ashland KY 41102-5230

ROTH, PAUL B., emergency medicine physician; b. Glen Ridge, N.J., Oct. 7, 1947; s. Jerome M. and Selma (Leitner) R. BS, Fairleigh Dickinson U., 1969, MS, 1972; MD, George Washington U., 1976; postgrad., U. N.Mex., 1976-79. Owner, pres. EMS of N.Mex., Albuquerque, 1978-82; owner, mem. of bd. Heights Urgent Care Ctr., Albuquerque, 1980-82; dir. divsn. emergency medicine U. N.Mex. Sch. Medicine, Albuquerque, 1982-91, chair dept. emergency medicine, 1991—; interim chief med. officer U. N.Mex. Med. Ctr., Albuquerque, 1992—; dir. Ctr. for Disaster Medicine U. N.Mex. Sch. Medicine, Albuquerque, 1990—; co-chair NDMS-Med. Response Steering Com., Rockville, Mass., 1991—; chair sect. on disaster medicine Nat. ACEP, Dallas, 1991—. Contbr. articles to Annals of EM, Current Practice of EM-Disaster Medicine, Jour. of AMA. Recipient Outstanding Individual Svc. award Nat. Disaster Med. System, 1986. Fellow Am. Coll. Emergency Physicians; mem. AMA, Soc. for Acad. Emergency Medicine, Am. Coll. Physician Execs., Am. Acad. Family Physicians. Office: U NMex Sch Medicine Dept Emergency Medicine Ambulatory Care Ctr 4 West Albuquerque NM 87131-5246

ROTH, REGINA SARAH, psychologist; b. Lake Forest, Ill., Mar. 6, 1950; d. Richard James and Shirley R.; A.B. with honors, Conn. Coll., 1972; M.A., NYU, 1974, Ph.D. (NIMH trainee), 1976; postdoctoral student Northwestern U. Med. Hosp. Inst. Psychiatry, 1978-79. Staff cons. clin. div. Worthington Hurst & Assocs., Chgo., 1977-78; psychology postdoctoral trainee Hines (Ill.) VA Hosp., 1979; psychology postdoctoral trainee West Side VA Hosp., Chgo., 1979-80; pvt. practice clin. psychology, 1980—. Mem. Am. Psychol. Assn., Ill. Psychol. Assn., Nat. Register Mental Health Service Providers, Am. Group Psychotherapy Assn. Home: 3001 S King Dr Apt 902 Chicago IL 60616-3328 Office: 1701 E Lake Ave Ste 445 Glenview IL 60025-2097

ROTH, SANFORD IRWIN, pathologist, educator; b. McAlester, Okla., Oct. 14, 1932; s. Herman Moe and Blanche (Brown) R.; m. Kathryn Ann Corliss, Sept. 3, 1961; children: Jeffrey Franklin, Elisabeth Francyne, Gregory James, Suzannah Joan. Student, Vanderbilt U., 1949-52; MD, Harvard U., 1956. Intern Mass. Gen. Hosp., Boston, 1956-57; resident in pathology Mass. Gen. Hosp., 1957-60, pathologist, 1962-75; pathologist Armed Forces Inst. Pathology, 1960-62; asst. prof. Med. Sch. Harvard U., 1962-69, assoc. prof. Med. Sch., 1969-75; pathologist, prof., chmn. dept. Coll. Medicine U. Ark., Little Rock, 1975-81; prof. Med. Sch. Northwestern U., Chgo., 1981—; chief lab. svc. VA Lakeside Med. Ctr., Chgo., 1981-86; attending pathologist Northwestern U. Hosp., 1981—. With M.C. U.S. Army, 1960-62. Mem. AMA, AAAS, Am. Soc. Cell Biology, Coll. Am. Pathology, U.S.-Can. Acad. Pathology, Soc. for Investigative Dermatology, Ill. Med. Soc., Mass. Med. Soc. Home: 920 Forest Glen Dr W Winnetka IL 60093-1430 Office: 303 E Chicago Ave Chicago IL 60611-3008

ROTH, STEPHEN L., cardiologist; b. N.Y.C., Feb. 20, 1949; s. Joel and Pauline (Wolf) R.; m. Susan E. Katz, Dec. 24, 1974 (div. Nov. 1994); children: Mark, Jason. BA, NYU, 1970; MD, U. Pa., 1974, PhD, 1976. Intern Bellevue-NYU Med. Ctr., 1976-77, resident in internal medicine, 1977-79, fellow in cardiology, 1979-81; pres. Cardiology Cons. of Hollywood, Fla., 1981—; sr. attending physician Hollywood (Fla.) Meml. Hosp., Hollywood Med. Ctr.; lectr. in field. Recipient AMA Physician Recognition award, 1983, 86, 89, 92, 95. Fellow Am. Heart Assn., Am. Coll. Cardiology, Phi Beta Kappa. Office: Cardiology Cons Hollywood 4700F Sheridan St Hollywood FL 33021

ROTH, WILLIAM STANLEY, hospital foundation executive; b. N.Y.C., Jan. 12, 1929; s. Sam Irving and Louise Caroline (Martin) R.; m. Hazel Adcock, May 6, 1963; children: R. Charles, W. Stanley. AA, Asheville-Biltmore Jr. Coll., 1948; BS, U. N.C., 1950. Dep. regional exec. Nat. council Boy Scouts Am., 1953-65; exec. v.p. Am. Humanics Found., 1965-67; dir. devel. Bethany Med. Ctr., Kansas City, Kans., 1967-74; exec. v.p. Geisinger Med. Ctr. Found., Danville, Pa., 1974-78; found. pres. Baptist Med. Ctrs., Birmingham, Ala., 1978—; sec. Western Med. Systems, Cherokee Cmty. Homes, Cullman Sr. Housing, Dekalb Sr. Housing, Limestone Sr. Housing, Oxford Sr. Housing. Mem.-at-large Nat. council Boy Scouts Am., 1972-86; chmn. NAHD Ednl. Fund, 1980-82; ruling elder John Knox Kirk, Kansas City, Mo., Grove Presbyn. Ch., Danville, Pa. Recipient Silver award United Methodist Ch., 1970, Mid-West Health Congress, 1971; Seymour award for outstanding hosp. devel. officer 1983. Fellow Assn. for Healthcare Philanthropy (life, nat. pres. 1975-76); mem. Nat. Soc. Fund Raising Execs. (pres. Ala. chpt. 1980-82, nat. dir. 1980-84, mem. ethics bd. 1993—, advanced cert. fund raising exec., Outstanding Fund Raising Exec., Ala. chpt. 1983), Mid-Am.Hosp. Devel. Assn. (pres. 1973-74), Mid-West Health Congress (devel. chmn. 1972-74), Am. Soc. for Healthcare Mktg. and Pub. Rels., Ala. Soc. for Sleep Disorders, Ala. Heart Inst., Ala. Assn. Healthcare Philanthropy (pres. 1991-93, chmn. bd. 1993-94), Ala. Planned Giving Coun. (bd. dirs. 1991—, pres. 1994-95), Alpha Phi Omega (nat. pres. 1958-62, dir. 1950—, Nat. Disting. Service award 1962), Delta Upsilon (pres. N.C. Alumni 1963-65). Clubs: Rotary (pres. club 1976-77), Relay House, Summit, Green Valley (bd. govs.), Elks, Order Holy Grail, Order Golden Fleece, Order of The Arrow (Nat. Disting. Service award 1958). Editor Torch and Trefoil, 1960-61. Home: 341 Laredo Dr Birmingham AL 35226-2325 Office: 3500 Blue Lake Dr Ste 101 Birmingham AL 35243-1908

ROTHBERG, HARVEY D., internist, oncologist; b. Plainfield, N.J., Nov. 17, 1928; s. Harvey Rothberg and Helen Rosenberg; m. Mary Ann Powell (div. 1973); m. Nancy Mundy; children: Elizabeth, Marjorie, Nancy. BA, Princeton U., 1949; MD, Harvard U., 1953. Diplomate Am. Bd. Internal Medicine, Am. Bd. Med. Oncology, Am. Bd. Hematology. Attending physician The Med. Ctr. at Princeton, N.J.; clin. prof. medicine U. Medicine & Dentistry N.J.- Robert Wood Johnson Sch. of Medicine, Piscataway, N.J.; pres. Princeton Regional Bd. of Edn., 1968, pres. med. staff Med. Ctr. at Princeton, 1975. Author: The First Seventy-Five Years: A History of the Medical Center at Princeton, 1995; contbr. articles to profl. jours. Capt. U.S. Army, 1956-58. Fellow ACP; mem. AMA, Am. Soc. Clin. Oncology, Oncology Soc. N.J. (pres. 1984). Office: Princeton Med Group 419 N Harrison St Princeton NJ 08540

ROTHENBERG, ALBERT, psychiatrist, educator; b. N.Y.C., June 2, 1930; s. Gabriel and Rose (Goldberg) R.; m. Julia C. Johnson, June 28, 1970; children: Michael, Mora, Rina. A.B., Harvard U., 1952; M.D., Tufts U., 1956. Diplomate: Am. Bd. Psychiatry and Neurology. Intern Pa. Hosp., Phila., 1956-57; resident in psychiatry Yale U., West Haven (Conn.) VA Hosp., 1957-58, Grace-New Haven Hosp., 1958-59; resident in psychiatry Yale Psychiat. Inst., New Haven, 1959-60, chief resident, 1960-61; practice medicine specializing in psychiatry New Haven, 1960-61, 1963-75; chief neuropsychiatry Rodriguez U.S. Army Hosp., San Juan, P.R., 1961-63; practice medicine specializing in psychiatry Farmington, Conn., 1975-79, Stockbridge, Mass., 1979-94, Chatham, N.Y., 1994—, Great Barrington, Mass., 1994—; dir. rsch. Austen Riggs Center, Stockbridge, Mass., 1979-94; asst. dir. Yale Psychiat. Inst., 1963-64, sr. staff mem., 1964-83; mem. staff Yale-New Haven Med. Ctr., West Haven VA Hosp., U. Conn. Health Ctr., Farmington; cons., mem. editorial bd. various jours. in psychiatry and psychology; instr. dept. psychiatry Yale U. Sch. Medicine, 1960-61, 63-64, asst. prof., 1964-68, assoc. prof., 1968-74, clin. prof., 1974-84; prof. psychiatry U. Conn. Sch. Medicine, Farmington, 1975-79, dir. residency tng., 1976-78, dir. clin. svcs., 1975-78; prin. investigator Studies in the Creative Process, 1964—; vis. prof. Pa. State U., 1971, adj. prof., 1971-78; vis. prof. dept. Am. studies Yale U., 1974-76; lectr. dept. psychiatry Harvard U. Med. Sch., 1982-86, clin. prof., 1986—; researcher in psychotherapy. Author: (with B. Greenberg) Index of Scientific Writings on Creativity: Creative Men and Women, 1974, Index of Scientific Writings on Creativity: General 1566-1974, 1976; (with C.R. Hausman) The Creativity Question, 1976; The Emerging Goddess: The Creative Process in Art, Science and Other Fields, 1979; The Creative Process of Psychotherapy, 1988; Adolescence: Psychopathology, Normality, and Creativity, 1990; Creativity and Madness: New Findings and Old Stereotypes, 1990; contbr. numerous articles on the creative process, schizophrenia, anorexia nervosa, and psychotherapy to profl. and popular jours. Researcher on creativity in the arts, sci. and tech. Served with M.C. U.S. Army, 1961-63. Recipient Tufts Med. Alumni award 1956, Rsch. Scientist Career Devel. award NIMH 1964, 69, Golestan Found. award 1991, 92; Guggenheim Meml. fellow 1974-75, Ctr. Adv. Study in Behavioral Studies fellow 1986-87, Netherlands Inst. for Adv. Study in Humanities and Social Scis. fellow, 1992-93. Fellow Am. Psychiat. Assn. (life), Am. Coll. Psychoanalysts; mem. AAAS, Mass. Psychiat. Soc., Am. Soc. Aesthetics, Sigma Xi. Democrat. Home: PO Box 236 52 Pine Ridge Rd Canaan NY 12029

ROTHENBERG, MIRA KOWARSKI, clinical psychologist and psychotherapist; b. Wilno, Poland; came to U.S., 1938; d. Jacob and Rosa (Joffe) Kowarski; m. Tev Goldsman, Dec. 7, 1960 (div. June 1974); 1 child, Akiva. BA, Bklyn. Coll., 1943; MA, Columbia U., 1957, Yeshiva U., 1959; ABD, Yeshiva U., 1962. Lic. psychologist, N.Y. Therapist, tchr.ir. Hawthorne (N.Y.) Cedar Knolls, 1952-53, League Sch., Bklyn., 1953-58; founder, clin. dir. Blueberry Treatment Ctrs., Bklyn., 1958-90; staff psychologist L.I. Coll. Hosp., Bklyn., 1966—; cons. Beachbrook Nursery, Bkyn., 1969-70, San Felipe Del Rio, Santa Fe, 1980—, Children's House Montessori Nursery, Bklyn., 1982-89, Austrlia Dept. Edn., Carynia, New South Wales; adj. prof. L.I. U., Bklyn., 1976-78; internat. speaker in field; worker with psychotic and autistic children, Croatia, 1994, Lithuania, 1994-95. Author: Children with Emerald Eyes, 1977, (with others) Pet Oriented Psychotherapy, 1980, The Outsiders, 1989; contbr. to books and articles to profl. jours. Mem. APA, World Fedn. Mental Health, N.Y. State Psychol. Assn., Inter. Soc. Child Abuse and Neglect (Hamburg, Germany), Physicians for Social Responsibility, N.Y. Acad. Scis., Amnest Internat., ACLU, NOW, Anti Defamation League, Yivo, Nat. Register Svc. Providers in Psychology. Home and Office: 160 State St Brooklyn NY 11201-5610

ROTHENBERG, PETER JOHN, psychologist, psychotherapist, mental health services administrator, consultant; b. N.Y.C., Nov. 26, 1941; s. Benjamin J. Rothenberg and Emma (Rubin) Shulman; m. Judith D. Cohen; children: Karen L. Gersten-Rothenberg, Sara B. Gerstein-Rothenberg. BA, Lehigh U., 1963; PhD, Washington U., St. Louis, 1968. Lic. psychologist, Conn.; cert. Nat. Registry group psychothrapists. Postdoctoral fellow dept.

psychiatry Med. Sch. Yale U., New Haven, 1970-72; asst. prof. So. Conn. State U., New Haven, 1970-72; clin. dir. Shoreline Mental Health Svc., Clinton, Conn., 1972-81; dir. Shoreline Ctr. for Counseling & Psychotherapy, Madison, Conn., 1981—; cons. Chrysalis Counseling Ctr., Niantic, Conn., 1985—, Shoreline Assn. for Retarded and Handicapped Citizens, Guilford, Conn., 1985—; mem. field faculty Union U. Grad. Sch., N.Y.C., 1985—. Contbr. articles to profl. jours. Capt. U.S. Army, 1968-70. USPHS fellow, 1963-67, NIMH fellow, 1970-72. Fellow Am. Orthopsychiat. Assn.; mem. APA, Conn. Psychol. Assn., Nat. Assn. for the Dually Diagnosed, Pvt. Practice Assn. of Conn. Home: 53 Lanes Pond Rd Northford CT 06472-1125 Office: Shoreline Ctr Counseling & Psychotherapy 230 Boston Post Rd Madison CT 06443-2225

ROTHENBERG, ROBERT EDWARD, physician, surgeon, author; b. Bklyn., Sept. 27, 1908; s. Simon and Caroline A. (Baer) R.; m. Lillian Lustig, 1933 (dec. 1977); m. Eileen Fein, 1977 (dec. 1987); children: Robert Philip, Lynn Barbara Rothenberg Kay; m. Florence Richman, 1989. A.B., Cornell U., 1929, M.D., 1932. Diplomate Am. Bd. Surgery. Intern Jewish Hosp., Bklyn., 1932-34; attending surgeon Jewish Hosp., 1955-82; postgrad. study Royal Infirmary, Edinburgh, 1934-35; civilian cons. U.S. Army Hosp., Ft. Jay, N.Y., 1960-66; attending surgeon French Polyclinic Med. Sch. and Health Center, N.Y.C., 1964-76; pres., 1973-76, trustee, 1972-76; attending surgeon Cabrini Health Care Center, 1976-86; cons. surgeon Cabrini Med. Ctr., 1986—, dir. surg. research, 1981—; clin. asst. prof. environ. medicine and community health State U. Coll. Medicine, N.Y.C., 1950-60; clin. prof. surgery N.Y. Med. Coll., 1981-86, prof. emeritus, 1986—; pvt. practice, 1935-86; chmn. Med. Group Coun. Health Ins. Plan of Greater N.Y., 1947-64; cons. Office and Profl. Employees Internat. Union (Local 153) Health Plan, 1960-82, United Automobile Workers (Local 259) Health Plan, 1960-86, Sanitationmen's Security Benefit Fund, 1964-83; dir. Surgery Internat. Ladies Garment Workers Union, 1970-85; med. adv. bd. Hotel Assn. and Hotel Workers Health Plan, 1950-60, Hosp. Workers Health Plan, 1970-76; past bd. dirs. Health Ins. Plan of Greater N.Y. Author and/or editor: Group Medicine and Health Insurance in Action, 1949, Understanding Surgery, 1955, New Illustrated Med. Ency., 4 vols., 1959, New Am. Med. Dictionary and Health Manual, 1962, Reoperative Surgery, 1964, Health in Later Years, 1964, Child Care Ency., 12 vols., 1966, Doctor's Premarital Medical Adviser, 1969, The Fast Diet Book, 1970, The Unabridged Medical Encyclopedia, 20 vols., 1973, Our Family Medical Record Book, 1973, The Complete Surgical Guide, 1973, What Every Patient Wants to Know, 1975, The Complete Book of Breast Care, 1975, Disney's Growing Up Healthy, 4 vols., 1975, First Aid—What to Do in an Emergency, 1976, The Plain Language Law Dictionary, 1980; contbr. articles to med. jours. Served to lt. col. M.C., AUS, 1942- 45. Recipient Cabrini Gold medal, 1986. Fellow ACS; mem. AMA, Bklyn. Surg. Assn., N.Y. County Med. Soc., Alpha Omega Alpha. Home: 35 Sutton Pl New York NY 10022-2464 also: Monterosso, Camaiore Italy

ROTHENBERGER, DAVID ALBERT, surgeon; b. Sioux Falls, S.D., 1947. MD, Tufts U., 1973. Cert. colon and rectal surgery. Intern St. Paul-Ramsey Med. Ctr., 1973-74, resident gen. surgery, 1974-78; fellow colon rectal surgery U. Minn., Mpls., 1978-79; mem. staff United Hosp., St. Paul; cln. prof. surgery U. Minn., Mpls., chief divsn. colon and rectal surgery. Fellow ACS; mem. Am. Soc. Colon and Rectal Surgeons (exec. coun.), CICD, SSAT, WSA. Office: 299 Fort Rd Med Bldg Minneapolis MN 55102-2409*

ROTHFIELD, NAOMI FOX, physician; b. Bklyn., Apr. 5, 1929; d. Morris and Violet (Bloomgarden) Fox; m. Lawrence Rothfield, Sept. 18, 1954; children—Susan, Lawrence, John, Jane. B.A., Bard Coll., 1950; M.D., N.Y. U., 1955. Intern Lenox Hill Hosp., N.Y.C., 1955-56; instr. N.Y. U. Sch. Medicine, 1956-62, asst. prof., 1962-68; assoc. prof. U. Conn. Sch. Medicine, Farmington, 1968-72; prof., chief div. rheumatic diseases U. Conn. Sch. Medicine, 1972—. Contbr. chpts. to books; contbr. articles to med. jours. Mem. Am. Soc. Clin. Investigation, Am. Rheumatism Assn., Assn. Am. Physics. Jewish. Home: 540 Deercliff Rd Avon CT 06001-2859 Office: U Conn Sch Medicine Div of Rheumatic Diseases Farmington CT 06030

ROTHMAN, FRANK GEORGE, biology educator, biochemical genetics researcher; b. Budapest, Hungary, Feb. 2, 1930; came to U.S., 1938; s. Stephen and Irene Elizabeth (Manheim) R.; m. Joan Therese Kiernan, Aug.22, 1953; children: Michael, Jean, Stephen, Maria. BA, U. Chgo., 1948, MS, 1951; PhD, Harvard U., 1955. Postdoctoral fellow NSF, U. Wis., MIT, 1956-58, Am. Cancer Soc., MIT, Cambridge, 1958-59; postdoctoral assoc. MIT, Cambridge, 1957-61; asst. prof. Brown U., Providence, 1961-65, assoc. prof., 1965-70, prof., 1970—, dean of biology, 1984-90, provost, 1990-95. Contbr. articles to profl. jours. Served with U.S. Army, 1954-56. Spl. fellow USPHS, U. Sussex, Eng., 1967-68; NSF grantee, 1961-84. Fellow AAAS; mem. Genetics Soc. Am. Office: Brown U Box G-J119 Providence RI 02912

ROTHMAN, GAIL ANN, counseling services administrator; b. Rochester, N.Y., June 25, 1944; d. Herman Tony and Grace Helen (Fortuna) Giancola; m. Michael Frederick Rothman, Feb. 6, 1967 (div. 1977); m. Gerald Francis Marshall, Feb. 26, 1995. BA, SUNY, Albany, 1970; MS, SUNY, Brockport, 1976; PhD, SUNY, Buffalo, 1989. Cert. clin. mental health counselor, cert. fitness profl. Dance and drama instr. Baden St. Settlement, Rochester, N.Y., 1968-69; day care ctr. instr. Action for a Better Community, Rochester, N.Y., 1968-70; sr. residential counselor Rochester Sch. for the Deaf, 1970-74; interpreter Rochester Inst. of Tech., 1974-75, counselor, 1975-79, chairperson of counseling svcs., 1979—, diagnostician learning assessment team, 1987-90; sign and content expert Nat. Tech. Inst. for the Deaf, Rochester, 1983; part-time adj. prof. psychology Coll. Liberal Arts Rochester Inst. Tech., 1990-93, 94—, part-time adj. prof. aerobics dept. phys. edn. and recreation, 1992—; mem. activity faculty Am. Jour. Health Promotion Conf., 1994. Contbr. articles to profl. jours. Vol. Drug and Alcohol Coun., Rochester, 1987-89; program com. co-chmn. Niagara Assn. for Psychol. Type, Rochester, 1986-88; chaperone, vol. Spl. Olympics, Rochester, 1989, 90, tenure com. chmn., 1991-94. Sch. of Visual Comms. grantee, 1986, 89, 93, Ctr. for Student Resources grantee, 1994. Mem. Am. Counseling Assn., Assn. for Psychol. Type, Am. Coll. Pers. Assn., Assn. for Counselor Edn. and Supervision, Am. Mental Health Counselors Assn., Nat. Career Devel. Assn., Monroe County Assn. for the Hearing Impaired, Aerobic Fitness Assn. Am. Home: 61 Marquette Dr Rochester NY 14618-5613 Office: Rochester Inst of Tech Johnson Bldg 52 Lomb Memorial Dr Rochester NY 14623-5604

ROTHMAN, HOWARD BARRY, acoustic phonetician; b. N.Y.C., July 17, 1938; s. Zoltan and Mary (Farkas) R.; m. GloryAnn May Coomer, Dec. 23, 1979; children: Rachel, Gabrielle, Aviva. BA, CCNY, 1961; MA, NYU, 1964; PhD, Stanford U., 1971. Asst. prof. U. Fla., Gainesville, 1971-76, assoc. prof., 1976-88, prof., 1988—, cons. dept. neurology, 1980-86; cons. Conquest Mktg. Co., Costa Mesa, Calif., 1978-79, Tallahassee Police Dept., 1977-80; expert witness in fed. cts. Tenn., Fla., Calif.; held seminars on singing voice and acoustics of voice. Author: (with others) The Artificial Larynx Handbook, 1978, Electroacoustic Analysis and Enhancement of Laryngeal Speech, 1982; contbr. articles to Jour. Voice, The NATS Jour. Chmn. B'nai Brith Hillel Found., Gainesville, 1976-79, 90—, Pro Arte Musica Concert Selection, Gainesville, 1971-88. With U.S. Army, 1961-63. Mem. Acoustical Soc. Am., Am. Speech, Lang., and Hearing Assn., Internat. Soc. Phonetic Scis., Medart Internat. Democrat. Jewish. Office: U Fla 336 Dauer Gainesville FL 32611

ROTHMAN, MARC IRWIN, psychiatrist; b. Bklyn., Jan. 3, 1952. BA, Bklyn. Coll., 1972; MD, Upstate Med. Ctr., 1976. Diplomate Am. Bd. Psychiatry and Neurology with qualifications in geriatric psychiatry. Resident psychiatry Thomas Jefferson U. Hosp., Phila., 1976-80; dir. inpatient psychiat. svcs. Cooper Hosp., Camden, N.J., 1980-82; med. dir. Guidance Ctr. Camden County, Cherry Hill, N.J., 1982-84; dir. older adults program Phila. Psychiat. Ctr., 1984-85; dir. med. student edn. in psychiatry Cooper Hosp., Camden, 1986-96, head divsn. geriatric psychiatry, 1990-96; med. dir. Hampton Hosp., Rancocas, N.J., 1996—; assoc. prof. clin. psychiatry U. Medicine and Dentistry N.J., Robert Wood Johnson Med. Sch., Camden, 1987—.. Mem. AMA, Am. Psychiat. Assn., N.J. Psychiat. Assn. (chmn. geriatrics com. 1987—), Camden County Med. Soc. (co-chmn. com. on aging 1989). Office: Cooper Hosp Dept Psychiatry 3 Cooper Plz Camden NJ 08103-1438

ROTHMAN-BERNSTEIN, LISA J., operating room nurse; b. Toledo, Dec. 29, 1949; 1 child, Daniel Karvinen. Diploma, Mercy Hosp. Sch. Nursing, Toledo, 1974; B Individualized Studies magna cum laude, Lourdes Coll., Sylvania, Ohio, 1989; AS in Bus., U. Toledo, 1970; student, U. Florence, Italy, 1972. Buyer Lamson's of Toledo; owner/designer FUNKtional Art, Inc.; owner/baker Tres Bon Cheesecakes, Inc., Margate, Fla.; cruise ship nurse Costa Cruise Line, Miami, Fla.; home health nurse Upjohn, Ft. Lauderdale, Fla.; patient svcs. coord. Fla. Med. Ctr., Lauderdale Lakes, Fla.; vol. nurse in ob-gyn. Yoseftal Hosp., Eilat, Israel; staff nurse in ob-gyn. Mt. Sinai Med. Ctr., Miami Beach, Fla.; staff nurse on eye svc., oper. rm. St. Vincent Med. Ctr., Toledo; nursing and healthcare recruiter, customer svc. advocate emergency dept. Co-chmn. Lourdes Coll. Red Cross Blood Drive, 1988-89; publicity chairperson St. Vincent Med. Ctr. 1993 Nurses' Week. Mem. Assn. Operating Rm. Nurses, Nat. Assn. of Health Care Recruiters, Kappa Gamma Pi.

ROTHMANN, BRUCE FRANKLIN, pediatric surgeon; b. Akron, Ohio, July 11, 1924; s. Edwin Franklin Rothmann and Mary Madoline Policy; m. Lola May Secor, June 14, 1947; children: Susan Ann, Pamela Jane, Elizabeth Rothmann Rusnak. Student, Case Western Reserve U., 1942-45, Wesleyan U., 1943-44; MD, NYU, 1948. Diplomate Am. Bd. Surgery. Intern Akron City Hosp., 1948-49, from resident in surgery to chief resident surgeon, 1949-55; from resident pediatric surgeon to chief staff Children's Hosp., Akron, 1953-74; pvt. practice in surgery Akron, 1955, pvt. practice in pediatric surgery, 1968—; clin. instr. Case Western Reserve U., Cleve. 1962-64, asst. clin prof, 1967--, assoc. clin. prof. pediatric surgery, 1983--, asst. surgeon Univ. Hosp., Cleve. 1962--; cons. in pediatric surgery Akron City Hosp.; v.p. devel. Nat. Invention Ctr., Inc. Contbr. med. articles to profl. jours. Dir. Med. Outreach Children Hosp. Med. Ctr. of Akron, 1986; bd. mgmt. Cuyahoga Falls Cmty. YMCA, 1957-63; trustee Akron Symphony Orch., 1959-85, Akron Jr. Achievement, 1980—, First Congl. Ch. Akron, 1960-64; mem. adv. bd. Children's Concert Soc., Akron, 1970—; bd. trustees Children's Family Care, 1984-86, Cuyahoga H.S. Found., 1988—; v.p fin., mem. exec. bd. Gt. Trail coun. Boy Scouts Am.; mem. Nat. Inventors Hall of Fame, Cleve. Inst. Music. With USN, 1942-45, 50-52. Home: 3020 Kent Rd Cuyahoga Falls OH 44224-3044 Office: 330 Locust St Akron OH 44302-1801

ROTHROCK, ROBERT WILLIAM, physician assistant; b. Phila., Apr. 21, 1955; s. Arthur Andrew and Margaret (Pilkington) R.; m. Maria Donna Marinelli, May 10, 1980; children: Matthew Robert, Tara Nicole. AS with honors, Cmty. Coll. Phila., 1979; BS, Hahnemann U., 1982. Cert. physician asst.; cert. pain mgmt. specialist. Respiratory therapist Jefferson U. Hops., Phila., 1979-80; physician asst. Pennsbury Family Med. Ctr., Morrisville, Pa., 1982-83, Pennsbury Orthop. Medicine Assocs., Morrisville, Pa., 1983—; mem. admissions com. Physician Asst. Program, Hahnemann U., 1985; cons. World Boxing Assn. Edo Aragua, Venezuela, 1990—. Author: Chronic Pain, 1991, 2d edit., 1992; contbg. author Minor Head Trauma. 1993, Innovations of Pain Management, 1993; contbg. editor Bucks Fortune Mag., 1988-89; peer reviewer Jour. Am. Acad. Physician Assts., 1992—; contbr. articles to profl. jours. Fellow Am. Acad. Physician Assts.; mem. Am. Acad. Pain Mgmt. (site reviewer 1992—), Phila. Pain Soc., Pa. State Soc. Physician Assts., N.J. State Soc. Physician Assts., Pa. State Soc. Physician Assts., Phi Theta Kappa. Home: 2 Creek Rd Sewell NJ 08080 Office: Pennsbury Orthop Medicine Assocs PO Box 909 Morrisville PA 19067

ROTHSCHILD, HENRY, physician, anatomist, educator; b. Horstein, Germany, June 5, 1932; naturalized Am. citizen, 1945; s. William and Fanny (Hahn) R.; m. Joy C. Lesser; children: Shoshana, Jamin. BA, Cornell U., 1954; MD, U. Chgo., 1958; PhD, Johns Hopkins U., 1968. Instr. Mass. Gen. Hosp., Boston, 1970-71; assoc. prof. medicine La. State U. Med. Ctr., New Orleans, 1971-75, assoc. prof. anatomy, 1972-75, assoc. grad. faculty, 1973—, prof. anatomy, 1975-92, prof. medicine, 1975—. Editor: Human Disease Caused by Virus, 1978, Biocultural Aspect of Disease, 1981, Risk Factors for Senility, 1984, Virology in Medicine, 1986. Fellow ACP; mem. Am. Soc. for Exptl. Pathology, Am. Fedn. for Clin. Rsch., So. Soc. for Clin. Investigation, Soc. for Exptl. Biology and Medicine, Am. Assn. for Cancer Rsch., Sigma Xi. Office: La State U Med Ctr 1542 Tulane Ave Rm 317A New Orleans LA 70112-2825

ROTHSCHILD, HERBERT BERNARD, retired pediatrician; b. Columbus, Ga., Oct. 16, 1904; s. Herman and Flora (Wise) R.; m. Leonie Weiss Davis, Oct. 18, 1934; children: Ann, Herbert Jr. BA, U. Ga., 1925; MD, Johns Hopkins U., 1929. Diplomate Am. Bd. Pediats. Pvt. practice New Orleans, 1933-88; chief of pediatrics Touro Infirmary, 1972-84; clin. prof. pediats. La. State U. Med. Sch., New Orleans, 1988-94, vis. prof., 1936-88; author laws of La. on child abuse; emeritus mem. staff Touro Infirmary, Children's Hosp., New Orleans, 1988—, Bapt.-Mercy Hosp., East Jefferson Hosp., Lakeside Hosp. Contbr. articles to profl. jours. Fellow Am. Acad. Pediats. (emeritus); mem. Greater New Orleans Pediat. Soc. (pres. 1980-84), Am. Acad. Ret. Persons (chmn. cmty. svc. adv. bd.). Home: 1425 Eleonore St New Orleans LA 70115

ROTHSCHILD, JANICE GITA, surgery educator; b. N.Y.C., June 23, 1958; d. Jacob and Mildred (Bonchek) R.; m. Andrew Jay Wiener, July 1, 1990; children: Michelle, Alexander. BA, CUNY, 1978; MD, NYU, 1982. Diplomate Am. Bd. Surgeons; diplomage Nat. Bd. Med. Examiners. Intern, then resident New Eng. Med. Ctr., Boston, 1982-87, asst. prof. surgery, 1987—. Contbr. articles to med. jours. Fellow ACS; mem. Mass. Med. Soc. (med. svcs. com. 1992—), Suffolk Dist. Med. Soc. (councillor 1990-91). Office: New Eng Med Ctr 750 Washington St Boston MA 02111

ROTHSTEIN, MANFRED SHELDON, dermatologist; b. Balt., Mar. 9, 1949; s. Leonard and Marcia R.; m. Sonja Kendrick; children: Nitza, Dana. BA, Johns Hopkins U., 1970; MD, Duke U., 1974. Intern Med. Coll. Va., Richmond, 1974-75; resident Duke U. Med. Ctr., Durham, N.C., 1975-78; dermatologist pvt. practice, Fayetteville, N.C., 1978—; clin. assoc. Duke U. MEd. Ctr., 1979—; staff mem Cape Fear Valley Med. Ctr., Fayetteville, 1978—, Betsy Johnson Meml. Hosp., Dunn, N.C., 1978—, Highsmith Rainey Meml. Hosp., Fayetteville, 1978-83, 85—; lectr in field. Contbr. articles to profl. jours. Fellow Am. Coll. Physicians; mem. AMA, Am. Acad. Dermatology, Am. Coll. Cryosurgery, N.C. Med. Soc. (sec./treas. dermatology sect. 1985-86), Cumberland County Med. Soc., Internat. Soc. Pediatric Dermatology, Soc. Pediatric Dermatology. Office: 1308 MEdical Dr Fayetteville NC 28304

ROTHSTEIN, RUTH M., hospital adminstrator. Dir. Cook County Hosp., Chgo.; chief Cook County Bur. of Health Svcs. Office: Cook County Hosp 1835 W Harrison St Chicago IL 60612-3701*

ROTOLO, VILMA STOLFI, immunology researcher; b. Villa Diego, Argentina, Jan. 27, 1930; d. Eduardo and Manuela (Gallego) Stolfi; m. Jose Jaime Rotolo, Dec. 6, 1957; children: Gloria Claudia, Alejandro Claudio. Degree in pharmacology, U. Litoral Med. Sch., Rosario, Argentina, 1953, Lic. in Biochem. Sci., 1956, PhD in Biochem. Sci., 1966. Asst. dir., rsch. mem. oncology lab. Oncology Inst., Nat. Ministry Pub. Health, Rosario, 1956-67; rsch. mem. dept. pathology-tissue culture div. U. Rosario Med. Sch., 1967-72, chief Exptl. Immunopathology Inst., 1972-89, dir. immunotoxicology program, 1989-91; sr. rsch. scientist Prodinar Co., Rosario, 1991—; pres. internat. symposium Assn. Allergy and Immunopathology, Argentina, 1981; rapporteur internat. seminar Commn. European Communities and IPCS, WHO, ILO, UNEP, EPA, NIEHS, Luxembourg, 1984; cons. Fed. Justice, Argentina, 1989. Guest editor: African Jour. Clin. and Exptl. Immunology, 1982; contbr. paper to Triduo Sci. Ann. (hon. diploma award 1965). Active For the Life Found., Neuquén, Argentina, 1987-90; pres. Found. Nature and Sci., 1990—. Recipient rsch. visitor travel award WHO, 1983, expert immunotoxicology travel award Commn. European Communities and UNEP, ILO, IPCS, WHO, EPA, NIEHS, Luxembourg, 1984; WHO travel award fellow, 1973, 78; Nat. Coun. Sci. Investigation grantee, 1974-77, 79-81, 82-83. Mem. Internat. Soc. Immunopharmacology (mem. internat. coun.), Argentine Assn. Immunopharmacology and Immunotoxicology (pres. 1987), Argentine Environ. Protection Assn., Latin Am. Assn. Immunology, Argentine Soc. Ecology, Sigma Delta Epsilon. Home: Mendoza 2435, Santa Fe, 2000 Rosario Argentina

ROTTON, JAMES, psychology educator, researcher; b. Black Oak, Ark., Feb. 14, 1944; s. Mett L. and Viola (Forbes) R.; m. Cheryl R. Allen, Mar. 11, 1968; children—Allen, Mischele. B.S., Purdue U., 1965, M.S., 1971, Ph.D., 1973. Vis. instr. Miami U., Oxford, Ohio, 1972-73; asst. prof. U. Dayton, Ohio, 1973-77; prof. psychology Fla. Internat. U., North Miami, Fla., 1977—. Contbr. articles to profl. jours. Fellow Am. Psychol. Assn.; mem. Psychonomic Soc., Environ. Design Research Assn., Com. for Sci. Investigation of Claims of Paranormal, Soc. Exptl. Social Psychology, Sigma Xi. Democrat. Avocations: biking; canoeing. Office: Fla Internat U North Miami FL 33181

ROUDIER, JEAN ALEX, medical educator; b. Lyons, France, Mar. 10, 1953; s. Robert and Marie Louise (Alexandre) R.; m. Chantal Thivolet, June 23, 1978; children: Felix, Paul, Antoine. MD, Lyons Coll., 1983; PhD, Marseilles (France) U., 1992. Resident fellow Lyons U. Hosps., 1978-83; asst. prof. medicine Marseilles U. Med. Sch., 1984-86; rsch. assoc. Scripps Clinic and Rsch. Found., LaJolla, Calif., 1986-88, sr. rsch. assoc., 1988-89; asst. prof. medicine U. Calif.-San Diego, La Jolla, 1990-91, prof. medicine U. Marseilles Med. Sch., 1991—; adj. assoc. prof. UCSD Sch. Medicine, 1995—. Contbr. sci. articles to profl. jours. Recipient Investigator award Arthritis Found., 1989, Andar prize for rheumatology rsch., 1990. Mem. Am. Coll. Rheumatology (award 1990), Am. Assn. Immunologists, Am. Assn. Immunogenetics and Histocompatability. Office: Immuno Rheumatology Lab, 27 Blvd Jean Moulin, 13005 Marseilles France

ROUKOS, DIMITRIOS, surgeon, consultant; b. Korydallos, Attiki, Greece, Mar. 31, 1953; s. Heraclis and Evagelia (Efstathiou) R.; m. Paraskevi Parashou, June 26, 1992; children: Athina, Heraclis. Student, U. Athens, Greece, 1980; MD, J.W. Goethe U., Frankfurt, Germany, 1988. Trainee in surgery dept. orthopedics U. Ioannina, Greece, 1982-83, lectr. surgery, 1990—; trainee in surgery Hosp. Offenbach, Germany, 1983-84, U. Frankfurt, 1984-89; surgeon Med. Ctr., Athens, 1989-90. Contbr. articles to profl. jours. With Greek Army, 1981-82. German Acad. Svc. scholar, 1983-84, 96—, U. Athens, 1983-85. Mem. AAAS, N.Y. Acad. Scis., active mem. Internat Soc. of Surgery. Home: Roma 19, 452 21 Ioannina Greece Office: Univ of Ioannina, Dept of Surgery, 453 32 Ioannina Greece

ROULET, NORMAN LAWRENCE, psychiatrist, educator; b. Toledo, Mar. 23, 1932; s. Norman Lawrence and Clara Matilda (Whistinghausen) R.; m. Ann Edelen, June 26, 1954; children: Laura, Norman, III. AB, Harvard U., 1954; MD, U. Pa., 1958. Diplomate Am. Bd. Psychiatry and Neurology. Pvt. practice Cleve., 1962—; faculty mem. to asst. clin. prof. psychiatry Case Western Res. Sch. Medicine, Cleve., 1962—; faculty mem. Cleve. Psychoanalytic Inst., 1976—. Author: (book with others) The Specialties in General Practice, 1964, Illegitimacy Today, 1969; contbr. articles to psychiat. jours. Fellow Am. Psychiat. Assn.; mem. Am. Psychoanalytic Assn., various local med., psychiat. and psychoanalytic socs. Republican. Presbyterian. Home: 17400 Shaker Blvd Cleveland OH 44120-1742 Office: Univ Suburban Health Ctr 1611 S Green Rd Cleveland OH 44121-4128

ROUMAS, JAMES CHARLES, health and safety executive, consultant, engineer; b. Salem, Mass., Jan. 20, 1926; s. Charles James and Catherine (Danas) R.; m. Angela Tzanakos, June 16, 1957; children: Charles, John. BS, Tufts U., 1948, MS, U. Tenn., 1951; SM in Hygiene, Harvard U., 1952. Registered profl. engr., Calif., health officer, N.J. Indsl. hygiene engr. Western Electric Co., Allentown, Pa., 1952-56; dir. rsch. Assn. Casualty & Surety Cos., N.Y.C., 1956-65; dir. dept. health and safety Lead Industries Assn., N.Y.C., 1965-70; dep. exec. dir. N.Y. State Health Planning Commn., N.Y.C., 1970-71; pres. J.C. Roumas & Assocs., Ridgefield, N.J., 1971-73, 88—; dir. Northwest Bergen Regional Health Commn., Waldwick, N.J., 1973-77; chief dept. occupational health and safety N.J. State Dept. Labor, Trenton, 1977-81; mgr. safety adminstrn. Lever Bros. Co., N.Y.C., 1981-88. Vol. Tomorrow's Children's Fund Hackensack U. Med. Ctr. With USNR, 1944-46, ETO. Fellow APHA; mem. Am. Acad. Sanitarians (diplomate), Am. Indsl. Hygiene Assn. (profl.), Am. Soc. Safety Engrs. (profl.). Home and Office: 895 Linden Ave Ridgefield NJ 07657-1142

ROUS, STEPHEN NORMAN, urologist, educator; b. N.Y.C., Nov. 1, 1931; s. David H. and Luba (Margulies) R.; m. Margot Woolfolk, Nov. 12, 1966; children: Benjamin, David. A.B., Amherst Coll., 1952; M.D., N.Y. Med. Coll., 1956; M.S., U. Minn., 1963. Diplomate: Am. Bd. Urology. Intern Phila. Gen. Hosp., 1956-57, resident, 1959-60; resident Flower-Fifth Ave. and Met. Hosp., N.Y.C., 1957-59, Mayo Clinic, Rochester, Minn., 1960-63; practice medicine specializing in urology San Francisco, 1963-68; assoc. prof. urology N.Y. Med. Coll., N.Y.C., 1968-72; assoc. dean N.Y. Med. Coll., 1970-72; prof. surgery, chief div. urology Mich. State U., East Lansing, 1972-75; prof., chmn. dept. urology Med. U. S.C., Charleston, 1975-88; urologist-in-chief Med. U. S.C. and County hosps., Charleston, 1975-88; editorial dir. Norton Med. Books div. W.W. Norton and Co., 1988-94, editorial cons., 1994—; clin. prof. surgery Uniformed Svcs. U. of Health Scis., Bethesda, Md., 1992—; adj. prof. urology Med. U. S.C., 1988—, adj. prof. surgery Dartmouth Med. Sch., 1988-91, prof. surgery (urology), 1991—; staff urologist Dartmouth-Hitchcock Med. Ctr., 1991—; cons. urologist Saginaw VA Hosp., 1971-75, Charleston VA Hosp., 1975-88; hon. cons. St. Peter's Hosp., London, 1981-82; sr. vis. fellow Inst. Urology, London, 1981-82; mil. cons. in urology USAF Surgeon Gen., 1982-85; chmn. alumni devel. com. Mayo Clinic, 1979-82; hon. staff The Exeter Hosp., N.H., 1988—; mem. nat. bd. visitors N.Y. Med. Coll., 1988—; chief urology VA Med. Ctr., White River Junction, Vt., 1991—. Author: Understanding Urology, 1973, Urology in Primary Care, 1976, Spanish edit., 1978, Russian edit., 1979, Urology: A Core Textbook, 1985, 2d edit., 1996, The Prostate Book, 1988, latest rev. edit., 1995, (with Judge Hiller B. Zobel) Doctors and the Law: Defendants and Expert Witnesses, 1993; editor Urology Ann., 1987-97, Stone Disease: Diagnosis and Management, 1987; mem. editl. bd. Mil. Medicine, 1984-94; contbr. articles to med. jours. Mem. East Lansing (Mich.) Planning Commn., 1974-75; vestryman, jr. warden All Saints Episcopal Ch., East Lansing, 1973-75, lay reader, mem. diocesan com. on continuing edn., 1975-86; vestryman St. Michael's Episc. Ch., 1979-82, Charleston, S.C., chmn. every mem. canvas, 1979-80, chmn. lay readers, 1983-86; mem. fin. com., lay reader Christ Episc. Ch., Exeter, N.H., 1989-91; lector St. Thomas Episc. Ch., Hanover, N.H., 1991—, vestryman, 1992-96, stewardship chmn., 1992-94, jr. warden, 1994-96; mem. selectman's alt. Hampton Falls Planning Bd., 1989-91. Col. USAFR, 1981-85, col. USAR, 1985—. Recipient "A" designator in urology, U.S. Army Surgeon Gen., 1986. Fellow ACS, Am. Acad. Pediatrics; mem. AMA, Soc. Univ. Urologists, Internat. Soc. Urology, Am. Urol. Assn., Nat. Urologic Forum, Soc. Pediatric Urology, Brit. Assn. Urol. Surgeons, German Urol. Assn. (hon.), Mayo Alumni Assn. (v.p. 1979-81, pres. 1983-85), Army and Navy Club (Washington), Lotos Club (N.Y.C.), Sigma Xi, Alpha Omega Alpha (hon.). Republican. Home: 6 Partridge Rd Etna NH 03750-0354 Office: Dartmouth Hitchcock Med Ctr Sect Urology Lebanon NH 03756

ROUSE, DORIS JANE, physiologist, research administrator; b. Greensboro, N.C., Oct. 3, 1948; d. Welby Corbett and Nadia Elizabeth (Grainger) R.; m. Blake Shaw Wilson, Jan. 6, 1974; children: Nadia Jacqueline, Blair Elizabeth. B.A. in Chemistry, Duke U., 1970, Ph.D. in Physiology and Pharmacology, 1980. Tchr. sci. Peace Corps, Tugbake, Liberia, 1970-71; research scientist Burroughs Wellcome Co., Research Triangle Park, N.C., 1971-76; sr. physiologist Rsch. Triangle Inst., 1976-83, ctr. dir., 1980—, also dir. NASA tech. application team, 1980—; adminstr. ANSI Tech. Adv. Group for Wheelchairs, N.Y.C., 1982-86; adj. asst. prof. Sch. Medicine U. N.C., 1983—; chair Instl. Rev. Bd., Profl. Devel. Award Com., Rsch. Triangle Inst.; mem. adv. bd. Assistive Tech. Rsch. Ctr., 1994—. Mem. adv. bd. Assn. Retarded Citizens, Arlington (Tex.), 1981-88. Western Gerontology Soc., San Francisco, 1982-85; bd. dirs. Simon Found., Chgo. 1983—; mem. spl. rev. com. small bus. applications; Nat. Forum on Tech. and Aging. Recipient Group Achievement award NASA, 1979. Mem. Rehab. Engrng. Soc. N.Am. (chmn. wheelchair com. 1981-86), Am. Soc. on Aging, Rehab. Engrng. Soc. N.Am., Tech. Transfer Soc., Assn. Fed. Tech. Transfer Execs., Nat. Space Soc. Club: Triangle Dive. Home: 2410 Wrightwood Ave Durham NC 27705-5802 Office: Research Triangle Inst PO Box 12194 Durham NC 27709-2194

ROUSE, KATRINA L., medical records coordinator; b. El Paso, Tex., July 7, 1966; d. Peter George Mann and Linda Lee (Toohey) Kramer; m. Robert E. Rouse, Jr., Apr. 22, 1989; 1 child, Bryan Edward. BS in Med. Records

Adminstrn., Ohio State U., 1988. Med. records coord. Canton (Ohio) Health Care Ctr., 1988—; quality circle leader Canton Health Care Ctr., 1993-95. Mem. Ohio Health Info. Mgmt. Assn., Am. Health Info. Mgmt. Assn. Roman Catholic. Office: Canton Health Care Ctr 1223 Market Ave N Canton OH 44714

ROUSE, RICHARD GEORGE, cardiac and thoracic surgeon; b. Oak Park, Ill., 1947. MD, Loyola U., Chgo., 1973. Diplomate Am. Bd. Thoracic Surgery. Resident U. Ala. Hosps., Birmingham, 1973-80; pvt. practice San Antonio, 1981—. Office: South Tex Cardiovasc Ctr 4330 Medical Dr Ste 325 San Antonio TX 78229-3326

ROUSELL, RALPH HENRY, pharmacologist, immunologist; b. Johannesburg, South Africa, Jan. 7, 1933; s. Henry Reginald John and Olive Agnes (Neilson) R.; came to U.S., 1979. M.B., B.Ch., Witwatersrand U., South Africa, 1958; M.Sc., U. London, 1976; diploma in pharm. medicine Royal Colls. Physicians, Edinburgh, Glasgow and London, 1976. Intern in medicine and surgery Johannesburg Gen. Hosp., 1959, resident in surgery and anesthesiology, 1960-63; practice medicine specializing in anesthesiology London Teaching Hosps., 1963; fellow in pharmacology St. Thomas' Hosp., London, 1964-65; med. dir. Pharmacia (Gt. Britain) Ltd., London, 1965-70; head med. svcs. Hoechst U.K., London, 1970-79; dir. clin. rsch. biol. and intravenous nutritionals div. Miles Pharms., Berkeley, Calif., 1979-86, dir. internat. clin. rsch. and spl. projects Cutter div. Miles Pharms., Berkeley, 1986-93, dir. safety assurance biological products Bayer Corp., Berkeley, 1993—; mem. sci. coun. Am. Blood Resources Assn., 1980-88. Fellow faculty pharm. medicine Royal Coll. Physicians U.K., 1990. Mem. Brit. Med. Assn., Brit. Soc. Immunology, Royal Inst. Biology, Am. Soc. Clin. Pharmacology, Am. Assn. Clin. Scientists. Methodist. Clubs: Hammersmith Rugby (life), Brockley (London). Editor: Streptokinase in Clinical Practice, 1973, Antilymphocyte Globulin in Clinical Practice, 1976, Intravenous Immune Globulin: Its Use and Potential, 1981, Antibody Purification From Plasma, 1990. Home: 14 Emery Bay Dr Emeryville CA 94608 Office: 800 Dwight Way Berkeley CA 94710

ROUSON, VIVIAN REISSLAND, alcohol and drug abuse services professional; b. New Orleans, July 18, 1929; d. Albert Isaac and Ophelia (Scott) Reissland; m. W. Ervin Rouson, June 22, 1953 (dec. May 1979); children: Lizette Hélène, Darryl Ervin, Brigette Maria, Janine Patrice, Damian William. BA, Xavier U., 1951; MS, Nova U., 1979; postgrad., U. Ky., 1965, U. South Fla., 1970. Tchr., cons. Gibbs Jr. Coll., St. Petersburg, Fla., 1958-60; tchr., cons. Pinellas County Schs., St. Petersburg,, Clearwater, Fla., 1960-78; freelance opinion editorial columnist U.S. newspaper, 1976-82; columnist Evening Independent, Pinellas County, Fla., 1976-78, Palm Beach (County, Fla.) Post, 1979-82; tchr., cons. Palm Beach County Sch., Lake Worth, W. Palm Beach, Fla., 1978-82; editorial writer St. Petersburg Times, 1979; program coord., interim dir. Women's Resource Ctr. Normandale C.C., Bloomington, Minn., 1986-89; interim dir. Women's Resource Ctr., Normandale Community Coll., Bloomington, Minn., 1989; vol., intern program coord. Inst. on Black Chem. Abuse, Mpls., 1989-90; assoc. editor Nat. Black Media Coalition, Washington, 1991—; V.I.P. coord. Inst. on Black Chem. Abuse, Mpls., 1989-90; writing and fgn. lang. cons. Pinellas County and Palm Beach County, fla., 1960-82; bd. dirs. Carroll Pub. Co. Author: The Hummingbird Within Us, 1980, Like a Mighty Banyan, 1982, Alcohol and Drug Abuse in Black America, 1988; editor conf. proceedings; editorial writer-columnist; editorial bd. St. Petersburg Times, 1979. Bd. dirs. St. Petersburg Cath. High Sch., 1976, Minn. divsn. Am. Cancer Soc., Mpls., 1983-90, Ind. Sch. Dist. 191, Burnsville, Eagan, Savage, Minn., 1984-87, Minn. Valley YMCA, Dakota County, Minn., 1987-90; pres. D.C. chpt. Hook-Up Plack Women, 1992—; sec., bd. dirs. Ionia Whipper Home, Inc., 1992—; mem. D.C. chpt. Nat. Urban League. Named Outstanding Journalist south Atlantic region Alpha Kappa Alpha, 1978, 79, 80; recipient Appreciation Pub. Svc. cert. Nat. Assn. Black Accts., 1992. Mem. AAUW, Twin Cities Black Journalists (co-chair 1985-86, v.p. 1989-90), Minn. Polit. Congress Black Women (charter), Nat. Urban League (subscribing life, Washington chpt.), Minn. Elected Women Ofcls., Dakota County Soc. Black Women (founder 1983, v.p. 1983-84), Pinellas County Fgn. Lang. Tchrs. (treas., pres.), The Links (sec. Capital City chpt.), Alpha Kappa Alpha (life). Roman Catholic. Home: 2311 N Capitol St NE Washington DC 20002-1105 Office: One Church-One Addict Ste 630 1101 14th St NW Ste 630 Washington DC 20005

ROUTH, JOSEPH ISAAC, biochemist; b. Logansport, Ind., May 8, 1910; s. William Arthur and Ethel Marie (Etnire) R.; m. Dorothy Francis Hayes, Sept. 4, 1937 (widowed May 1972); children: Joseph Hayes, John Michael; m. Elizabeth Marie Hayes, Dec. 4, 1976 (widowed Feb. 1990). BSChemE, Purdue U., 1933, MS, 1934; PhD, U. Mich., 1937. Diplomate Am. Bd. Clin. Chemistry. Instr. dept. biochemistry U. Iowa, Iowa City, 1937-42, asst. prof., 1942-46, assoc. prof., 1946-51, prof., 1951-78; dir. clin. biochemistry lab. Univ. Hosps., 1952-64; prof. pathology U. Iowa, 1970-78, dir. spl. clin. chem. lab., 1970-78; pres. Am. Bd. Clin. Chemistry, Washington, 1957-73; cons. VA Hosp., Iowa City, 1952-78. Sect. editor Chem. Abstracts, Clin. Chemistry; contbr. articles to profl. jours. Fellow Am. Inst. Chemists; mem. Am. Assn. Clin. Chemists (past pres., award for outstanding efforts in edn. and tng. 1973). Republican. Roman Catholic. Home: PO Box 712 Cherokee Vlg AR 72525-0712 Office: Dept Biochemistry Univ Iowa Iowa City IA 52242

ROUTLEY, LOWELL R., social services administrator, therapist; b. South Milw., Wis., June 7, 1945; s. Raymond W. and Laura S. (Orloff) R.; m. Terry L. Routley, June 3, 1967; children: Ramona S., Paula A. Diploma, Moody Bible Inst., 1966; BA, Greenville Coll., 1968; postgrad., U. Iowa, 1974; PhD, Walden U., 1978. Lic. counselor, Iowa. Dir., counselor Quad City Counseling Svc., Davenport, Iowa; adj. prof. Emmaus Bible Coll., Dubuque, Iowa; pvt. practice counselor Dubuque; employee assistance counselor Northwestern Bell, Davenport; assoc. prof. psychology Blackhawk Coll., Moline, Ill.; founder, pres. study group for MPD, Iowa. Mem. AACD, Am. Mental Health Counselors Assn. Home: 1017 Aspen Ct Dubuque IA 52001-3108

ROUTMAN, BURTON NORMAN, medical educator; b. Youngstown, Ohio, Apr. 21, 1941; s. Samuel Leonard and Beatrice Roberta (Epstein) R.; m. Teri Lisa Laybourn, June 12, 1964; children: Stephanie Lynn Routman Leverage, Leslie Gail. BA, Johns Hopkins U., 1963; DO, U. Osteo. Med. & Health Sci., 1968. Intern Cuyahoga Falls (Ohio) Gen. Hosp., 1968-69; asst. prof. clin. scis. U. Osteo. Med. & Health Sci., Des Moines, 1972-76; asst. chief primary care unit Ben Gurion U., Beer Sheva, Israel, 1980-81; assoc. prof. clin. scis. U. Osteo. Medicine & Health Sci., Des Moines, 1981-82, assoc. prof. family practice, 1990-94; assoc. prof. family practice Coll. Osteo. Medicine of Pacific, Pomona, Calif., 1995—. Capt. USAFMC, 1969-71. Mem. Am. Osteo. Assn., Am. Coll. Osteo. Family Physicians, Iowa Osteo. Med. Assn., Calif. Soc. Osteo. Physicians, Nat. Alumni Assn. Coll. Osteo. Medicine & Surgery, Israel-Am. Physicians Fellowship Assn., Sigma Sigma Phi, Lambda Omicron Gamma. Jewish. Office: Coll Osteo Medicine Pacific 309 E 2d St Pomona CA 91766

ROUW, CARLA SUE ROBERTS, medical nurse; b. Chariton, Iowa, June 5, 1968; d. Glen Marlin and Phyllis Darlene (Allison) Roberts. ADN, Indian Hills C.C., 1988. RN, Iowa. Float med.-surg. LPN; lic. practical nurse med.-surg. float Ottumwa (Iowa) Regional Health Ctr., 1987-88; adolescent and children's charge nurse Laughlin Pavilion, Kirksville, Mo., 1988-89; charge nurse, dir. med. records Monroe Care Ctr., Albia, 1989-91; gen. surgery/urology nurse, office nurse Dr. Edeliro A. Escobar, Fort Madison, Iowa, 1991-96; nursing svc. supr. Homestead Living & Learning Ctr.-Serving Iowans with Autism, Runnells, Iowa, 1996—.

ROUZBAHANI, LOTFOLLAH, cytogeneticist; b. Tehran, Iran, June 20, 1949; came to U.S., 1985; s. Hossein Rouzbahani and Mahjabin Faryadras; m. Mansooreh Shadkamian, Sept. 21, 1975; children: Ashkan, Faraz. DVM, Tehran U., 1979, PhD in Cytology, 1981; postgrad., Pasteur Inst., Lyon, France, 1979, Razi Inst., Tehran, 1982, The Genetics Inst., 1992. Lab. dir. Terhan Cytogenetics Ctr., 1979-85, Biogene, Riverside, Calif., 1991-92; dir. cytogenetics lab. Iranian Ministry Pub. Health, Tehran, 1980-85; tchr. Paramed. Inst. Tehran, 1980-85, Shafa, Farah Nursing Colls., Tehran, 1980-85; asst. prof. Iranian Med. Assn. Ctr., Tehran, 1982-85, Terhan U. Med. Sch., 1982-85; cytogeneticist Genetics Inst., Pasadena, Calif., 1986—; genetics cons. several hosps., Tehran, 1982-85; lab. dir. Genetics Clinic of Dr. Farhud, Tehran, 1982-85; chmn. Sci., Tech. Med., Aids of Tehran, 1983-85; cytogeneticist Genetic Ctr., Orange, Calif., 1988-90, Loma Linda (Calif.) U., 1989-92, Corning Nichols Inst., 1995, Alfigen/The Genetics Inst., 1995—. Author: Human Genetic Counseling, 1981 (award 1984, 88), Hereditary, Environment and Child Health, 1985 (awards 1988, 91), Genetics and Woman Disease, 1986 (award 1990), Techniques of the Chromosome Laboratory, 1990; contbr. over 50 articles to profl. jours. Sec. Persian Cultural and Social Soc., 1988-91, Nat. Iranian Resistance Movement, Claremont, Calif., 1985—; mem. Sci. Tchg. Bd. of Inst. of Mothers and Newborns, 1979-85. Named to Honor Bd., Sci. Mag. of Iran, 1983. Mem. So. Calif. Profl. Group, Am. Soc. Human Genetics, Assn. Cytogenetic Technologists, Med. Lab. Workers Soc., Internat. Sterility Soc., Ancient Iran Cultural Soc. Home: 443 Lewis Ct Claremont CA 91711-5132 Office: Alfigen/The Genetics Inst 111 W Del Mar Blvd Pasadena CA 91105

ROVEN, MILTON DEAN, podiatrist; b. Bklyn., Feb. 25, 1916; s. Harry and Ida R.; m. Ruth Katz, Dec. 18, 1955; children: Glen, Janice. DPM, L.I. U., 1938. Diplomate Am. Bd. Ambulatory Foot Surgery. Pvt. practice Bklyn., 1938—; spl. lectr. N.Y. Coll. Podiatric Medicine, Ohio Coll. Podiatric Medicine. Author: Non-Disabling Surgical Rehabilitation of the Forefoot, 1976; asst. editor Jour. Podiatric Medicine, Jour of Hosp. Podiatrists; editorial cons. Current Podiatry Jour.; contbr. numerous book revs. With USNR, 1942-46. Mem. Am. Podiatric Med. Assn., Acad. Podiatric Medicine (past pres.), Am. Podiatry Coun. (past pres.), Acad. Ambulatory Foot Surgery (past regional dir.). Home: 5 Caldwell Ter Marlboro NJ 07746-1778 Office: 1331 E 16th St Brooklyn NY 11230-6042

ROVIS, CHRISTOPHER PATRICK, clinical social worker; b. N.Y.C., Dec. 2, 1950; s. Del Patrick and Patricia Joan (Martin) R.; m. Lorraine Theresa LaPanna, July 26, 1985; children: Lauren Christine, Vincent Christopher. BS, George Mason U., 1973; MSW, Va. Commonwealth U., 1975; cert., Cath. U., 1985; PsyD, Newport U., 1988; cert. in family therapy, Family Therapy Inst., 1984. Lic. clin. social worker, Va., Md. D.C.; diplomate Am. Bd. Examiners in Clin. Social Work. Sr. staff psychotherapist N.W. Ctr. for Community Mental Health, Reston, Va., 1976-84; pvt. practice Tysons Corner Psychotherapy Assocs., Vienna, Va., 1982-91, Ctr. Psychotherapy at Tyson's Corner, Vienna, Va., 1991—. Mem. NASW, Acad. Cert. Social Workers, Greater Washington Soc. for Clin. Social Work. Roman Catholic. Home: 3189 Mary Etta Ln Herndon VA 22071-1620 Office: Ctr Psychotherapy at Tysons Corner 8308 Old Courthouse Rd # B Vienna VA 22182-3809

ROVIT, RICHARD LEE, neurological surgeon; b. Boston, Apr. 3, 1924; s. Samuel and Frances (Ehrenberg) R.; m. Barbara Sayre Margolis, Mar. 29, 1953; children: Sandra Amy Golze, Adam John, Hugh Russel. Grad., U. Mich., 1944; MD, Jefferson Med. Coll., 1950; MSc, McGill U., 1961. Diplomate Am. Bd. Neurol. Surgery (dir. vice chmn. 1986-92). Intern in surgery Beth Israel Hosp., Boston, 1950-51; resident, then chief resident Mass. Gen. Hosp., Boston, 1951-58; sr. fellow in neurosurgery Lahey Clinic, Boston, 1957; fellow in neurophysiology and EEG Montreal (Can.) Neurol. Inst., 1958-59; prof. clin. neurosurgery NYU, 1967—; chmn. neurosurgery St. Vincent's Hosp. and Med. Ctr., N.Y.C., 1967-92, past chmn. neurosurgery, 1992—. Editor, author: Trigeminal Neuralgia, 1991; contbr. articles to profl. jours. Lt. USN, 1952-54. Fellow ACS (v.p. 1994-95), Am. Assn. Neurol. Surgeons (v.p. 1980-81); mem. N.Y. Soc. Neurosurgeons, Soc. Neurol. Surgeons, N.Y. State Soc. Neurosurgeons, Harvard Club of N.Y. Home: 42 Brite Ave Scarsdale NY 10583 Office: Manhattan Neurosurg 153 W 11th St New York NY 10011

ROWAN, JOHN ROBERT, medical center director; b. Joliet, Ill., Aug. 19, 1919; s. Hugh Hamilton and Elizabeth Margaret (Maloney) R.; m. Ruth Elaine Boyle, June 17, 1944; 1 child, Robert J. Student, Butler U., 1952-53, Ind. U., 1953-54. Personnel specialist VA Br. Office 7, Chgo., 1946; personnel officer VA Hosp., Ft. Benjamin Harrison, Ind., 1946-51, Indpls., 1951-56; asst. dir. VA Hosp., 1960-67; asst. mgr. VA Hosp., Iron Mountain, Mich., 1956-60; hosp. adminstrn. specialist VA Central Office, Washington, 1967-69; dir. VA Hosp., Manchester, N.H., 1969-71, Buffalo, 1971-72; dir. VA Med. Center, Lexington, Ky., 1972-88, Montgomery, Ala., 1988—, VA Med. Dist. 11, 1975-86. Bd. dirs. Marion County (Ind.) unit Am. Cancer Soc., 1960-67, pres., 1964-66, bd. dirs. Ind. div., 1966-67; bd. dirs. Western N.Y. Regional Med. Program, 1971-72, Eastern Ky. Health Systems Agy., 1976-79, United Way of Bluegrass, 1976-79, 82-85; mem. regional advisory council Ohio Valley Regional Med. Program, 1972-76; mem. State Health Planning Bd., 1982-88; bd. dirs. Hosp. Hospitality House of Lexington, 1981; mem. adv. coun. Cen. Ala. Aging Consortium, 1991; chmn. Montgomery Area Combined Fed. Campaign, 1991. Served in USAAF, 1942-46. Decorated Bronze Star; recipient Meritorious Svc. citations Ind. dept. DAV, 1964, Meritorious Svc. citations Ky. dept. Am. Legion, 1975, Meritorious Svc. citations Ky. dept. VFW, 1976, Meritorious Svc. citations Eastern Ky. U., 1974, Meritorious Svc. citations Ky. dept. DAV 1978, Spl. Recognition award VFW, 1982, cert. of Merit, DAV, 1982; recipient Dedicated Svc. to Vets. award DAV, 1984, Meritorious Svc. to Vets. award, Am. Legion, 1985, Meritorious Svc. award, Chpt. I, Ky. DAV, 1988, VA Performance award, 1990, Joint Fed. Campaign Meritorious Svc. award, 1990, Dedicated Svc. award DAV, 1992, McClusky award Ala. State Nurses Assn., 1993. Fellow Am. Coll. Healthcare Execs.; mem. Am. Hosp. Assn., Ala. Hosp. Assn. (profl. standards and quality assurance com. 1991—), Ctrl. Ala. Hosp. Coun., Ala. Assn. Hosp. Execs., Assn. Mil. Surgeons U.S., Fed. Hosp. Inst. Alumni Assn. Roman Catholic. Home: 2213 Walbash Dr Montgomery AL 36116-2220 Office: Va Med Ctr 215 Perry Hill Rd Montgomery AL 36109-3725

ROWBOTHAM, TIMOTHY JOHN, research microbiologist; b. London, Aug. 16, 1948; s. John Anthony and Georgina Bella (Parks) R.; m. Daphne Elizabeth Churms, Dec. 17, 1970; children: Christopher James, Jennifer Louise. BSc in Med. Microbiology with honors, U. Leeds, Eng., 1971; PhD, U. Bradford, Eng., 1975. Sci. officer Leeds (Eng.) Regional Pub. Health Lab., 1979-80, sr. sci. officer, 1980-90, clin. scientist B15, 1990-94, clin. scientist B19, 1994—; discoverer that freshwater amoebae were natural hosts for legionellae, the bacteria that cause legionnaires' disease. Contbr. articles to profl. jours. Mem. Am. Soc. for Microbiology. Office: Leeds Reg Pub Health Lab, Bridle Path York Rd, Leeds LS15 7TR, England

ROWE, BRIAN PETER, physiologist, educator; b. Shoreham, Sussex, Eng., May 13, 1953; came to U.S., 1977; s. Edward George and Nellie Leonora (Dillard) R.; m. Rebecca L. Bowser, May 23, 1987. PhD, Southampton U., U.K., 1978. Rsch. assoc. U. Mo., Columbia, 1977-79, U. Tenn., Memphis, 1979-81; asst. prof. East Tenn. State U., Johnson City, 1981-86, assoc. prof., 1986-93, prof., 1993—. Contbr. articles to profl. jours. Recipient awards Am. Heart Assn., 1979, 82, 89, 90, NIH, 1991. Mem. Am. Physiol. Soc., Soc. for Neurosci. Office: East Tenn State U Physiology Dept Johnson City TN 37614

ROWE, GENEVA LASSITER, psychotherapist, former counseling center administrator, consultant; b. Atlanta, Aug. 11, 1927; d. Hoyt Cleveland and Tinie (Gresham) Lassiter; m. Fred Earnest Rowe, May 3, 1958; children: Carol, Vickie, Randall. BA, Oglethorpe U., 1968; MSW, U. Ga., 1970; PhD, Fla. State U., 1978. Accredited Acad. Cert. Social Workers; lic. marriage and family therapist, Ga.; approved AAMFT supr., 1986. Alcohol and drug counselor Georgian Clinic, Atlanta, 1968; outpatient counselor DeKalb Guidance Clinic, Atlanta, 1969; protective services supr. DeKalb Family and Children Services, Decatur, Ga., 1970-72; outpatient therapist Cen. DeKalb Mental Health Ctr., 1972-75; marriage and family therapist Fla. State U., 1977; lectr. sociology Oglethorpe U., 1978-81; psychotherapist, clin. supr., dir., owner N.E. Counseling Ctr., P.C., Atlanta and Lawrenceville, Ga., 1978-92; clin. supr. master's students in practicum Ga. State U., 1980-92; approved AAMFT supr., 1986-92; allied health profl. CPC Parkwood Hosp., 1987-96; mem. adminstrv. bd. Peachtree Rd. United Meth. Ch., High Mus. Art, Atlanta Symphony. Fellow Am. Orthopsychiat. Assn., Internat. Coun. Sex Edn. and Parenthood; mem. AAUW, Am. Assn. Marriage and Family Therapy (clin. mem., approved supr.), Nat. Speaker's Assn., Ga. Speaker's Assn., Ga. Assn. Marriage & Family Therapy (pub. relations chmn. 1984-86). Home and Office: 2005 Woodsdale Rd NE Atlanta GA 30324-2762

ROWE, GEORGE LEE, optometrist; b. Madison, Wis., Nov. 23, 1951; s. George G. and Patsey R. (Barnett) R.; m. Debra A. Rowe, June 5, 1976; children: Laina Marie, Krista Elin. BS, U. Wis., Platteville, 1974; OD, Ill. Coll. Optometry, 1986. Lic. optometrist, Wis. Pvt. practice, Waukesha, Wis., 1986-94, Milw., 1994—; optometrist Herslof Nursing Home Eye Care Svc., Milw., 1994-96. Elder Kettle Moraine Evang. Free Ch., Delafield, Wis., 1990—. Mem. Am. Optometric Assn., Wis. Optometric Assn., Kettle Moraine Optometric Assn. (v.p. 1987-88). Office: Herslof Opticians 12000 W Carmen Ave Milwaukee WI 53225

ROWE, JOHN WALLIS, medical school president, hospital administrator; b. Jersey City, June 20, 1944; s. Albert Wallis and Elizabeth (Lynch) R.; m. Valerie Ann DelTufo, Aug. 10, 1968; children: Meredith, Abigail, Rebecca. BS with honors, Canisius Coll., 1966; MD with distinction, U. Rochester, 1970. Diplomate Am. Bd. Internal Medicine, Am. Bd. Nephrology. Resident in internal medicine Harvard Med. Sch., Beth Israel Hosp., Boston, 1970-72; clin. assoc. Nat. Inst. Child Health and Human Devel., Balt., 1972-74; rsch., clin. fellow Harvard Med. Sch., Mass. Gen. Hosp., Boston, 1974-75; from instr. to prof. Harvard Med. Sch., Boston, 1976-88; pres. Mt. Sinai Sch. Medicine and Mt. Sinai Hosp., N.Y.C., 1988—, prof. geriatrics and medicine, 1988—; trustee N.Y. Acad. Medicine, 1989—, Buck Ctr. for Rsch. in Aging, Marin, Calif., 1989—. Editor: Health and Disease in Old Age, 1982, Geriatric Medicine, 1988, Handbook of the Biology of Aging, 1990, Geriatric Neurology, 1991; contbr. articles to jours. in field. Lt. comdr. USPHS, 1972-74. MacArthur Found. grantee, 1985—. Mem. NAS Inst. Med., Gerontol. Soc. Am. (pres. 1988), Am. Fedn. for Aging Rsch. (pres. 1988), N.Y. Yacht Club, Century Assn. Roman Catholic. Home: 300 Central Park W New York NY 10024-1513 Office: Mt Sinai Med Ctr Fifth Ave & 100th St New York NY 10029

ROWE, JOSEPH SAMUEL, JR., surgeon; b. Balt., Nov. 6, 1940; s. Joseph Samuel and Carolyn (Carleton) R.; m. Jamie Peppers, Apr. 21, 1949; 1 child, Jack Samuel. MD, Northwestern U., 1966. Diplomate Am. Bd. Surgery. Intern Memphis, 1966-67; resident Atlanta, 1969-73; physician IndeCare, Inc., Key Largo, Fla., 1973-75; med. dir. home care program VA Med. Ctr., Atlanta, 1975—. Author: Anatomical Complications in General Surgery, 1983. Co-pres. Holy Innocents Sch. Parents Assn., Atlanta, 1994-95. Capt. U.S. Army, 1967-69, Korea. Mem. Am. Acad. Home Care Physicians, Acad. Hospice Physicians, Phi Beta Kappa, Alpha Omega Alpha. Roman Catholic. Home: 3889 Foxford Dr NE Atlanta GA 30340

ROWE, MARJORIE DOUGLAS, retired social services administrator; b. Bklyn., July 29, 1912; d. Herbert Lynn and Mary Manson (Hall) Douglas; m. Richard Daniel Rowe, July 29, 1937; 1 child, Richard Douglas. AB cum laude, Whitman Coll., 1933; MS in Social Adminstrn., Case Western Res. U., 1936. Caseworker Children's Svcs., Cleve., 1933-36, supr., 1937-39; dir. Adoption Svc. Bur., Cleve., 1940-41; social work supr., psychiat. social work cons. Ea. State Hosp., Medical Lake, Wash., 1962-67; dir. social svcs. Interlake Sch.for Developmentally Disabled, Medical Lake, 1967-74, supt., 1975-82. Pres. chpt. R.P.E.O., Spokane, Wash., 1949, Spokane Alumnae chpt. Delta Delta Delta, 1955-57; chpt. mem. ARC, Orofino, Idaho, 1941-45, Orofino chpt. chmn., 1945-46; sec. Idaho state chpt. AAUW, 1945-46. Mem. Am. Assn. for Mental Deficiency (region I chmn. 1976-77, social work chmn. 1971-73), NASW (gold card mem.), P.E.O. (pres. Spokane Reciprocity 1950), Acad. Cert. Social Workers, Spokane Women of Rotary (pres. 1960-61), Phi Beta Kappa, Delta Sigma Rho, Mortar Bd. Episcopalian. Home: 946 E Thurston Ave Spokane WA 99203-2948

ROWE, MELINDA GRACE, public health service officer; b. Decatur, Ala., Aug. 18, 1953; m. Dana Calvin Craig Jr., Jan. 1, 1994. MD, U. Ala., 1978, MPH, 1985, MBA, 1987. Bd. cert. Am. Bd. Pediatrics, Am. Bd. Preventive Medicine. Pediatrics intern U. Ky., Lexington, 1978-79; pediatrics resident Lloyd Nolan Hosp., Fairfield, Ala., 1979-81; physician Columbus (Miss.) Children's Clinic, 1981, pvt. practice, Winfield, Ala., 1982-84; pediatric medicine resident U. Ala., Birmingham, 1984-85; asst. state health officer Pub. Health Area III, Pelham, Ala., 1985-95; dir. health Jefferson County Health Dept., Louisville, 1995—; asst. prof. U. Ala., Birmingham, 1988—, U. Louisville, 1995—. Bd. dirs. Cahaba Riyer Soc., Birmingham, 1988-95, UAB Nat. Alumni Soc., 1988-93. Mem. Ky. Med. Assn., Ky. Pub. Health Assn., Ky. Pediatric Soc., Jefferson County Med. Soc., Louisville/Jefferson County Primary Care Assn. (bd. dirs.), Health Ky. Methodist. Office: Jefferson County Health 400 E Gray St PO Box 1704 Louisville KY 40201-1704

ROWEN, MARSHALL, radiologist; b. Chgo.; s. Harry and Dorothy (Kasnow) R.; m. Helen Lee Friedman, Apr. 5, 1952; children: Eric, Scott, Mark. AB in Chemistry with highest honors, U. Ill., Urbana, 1951; MD with honors, U. Ill., Chgo., 1954, MS in Internal Medicine, 1954. Diplomate Am. Bd. Radiology. Intern Long Beach (Calif.) VA Hosp., 1955; resident in radiology Los Angeles VA Hosp., 1955-58; practice medicine specializing in radiology Orange, Calif., 1960—; chmn. bd. dirs. Moran, Rowen and Dorsey, Inc., Radiologists, 1969—; asst. radiologist L.A. Children's Hosp., 1958; assoc. radiologist Valley Presbyn. Hosp., Van Nuys, Calif., 1960; dir. dept. radiology St. Joseph Hosp., Orange, 1961—, v.p. staff, 1972; dir. dept. radiology Children's Hosp. Orange County, 1964—, chief staff, 1977-78, v.p., 1978-83, v.p., trustee, 1990-91, 92-95; asst. clin. prof. radiology U. Calif., Irvine, 1967-70, assoc. clin. prof., 1979-72, clin. prof. radiology and pediatrics, 1976-95, pres. clin. faculty assn., 1980-81; trustee Choc. Padrinos; sec. Choco Health Svcs., 1987-89, v.p., 1990-93, trustee, 1995—; trustee Found. Med. Care Orange County, 1972-76, Calif. Commn. Adminstrn. Svcs. Hosp., 1975-79, Profl. Practice Systems, 1990-92, Med. Specialty Mgrs., 1990—, St. Joseph Med. Corp., 1993—; v.p. Found. Med. Care Children's Hosp., 1988-89; v.p., sr. v.p., bd. dirs. St. Joseph Med. Corp. IPA, 1995-96; bd. dirs. Orange Coast Managed Care Svcs., 1995, sr. v.p., 1995-96, Paragon Med. Imaging, 1993—, Calif. Managed Imaging, 1994—, Alliance Premier Hosps., 1995-96; chmn. bd. dirs. Children's Healthcare of Calif., 1995-96; corp. mem. Blue Shield Calif., 1995-96. Mem. editorial bd. Western Jour. Medicine; contbr. articles to med. jours. Founder Orange County Performing Arts Ctr., mem. Laguna Art Mus., Laguna Festival of Arts, Opera Pacific, S. Coast Reportory, Am. Ballet Theater, World Affairs Council. Served to capt. M.C., U.S. Army, 1958-60. Recipient Rea sr. med. prize U. Ill, 1953; William Cook scholar U. Ill., 1951. Fellow Am. Coll. Radiology; mem. AMA, Am. Heart Assn., Soc. Nuclear Medicine (trustee 1961-62), Orange County Radiol. Soc. (pres. 1968-69), Calif. Radiol. Soc. (pres. 1978-79), Radiol. Soc. So. Calif. (pres. 1976), Pacific Coast Pediatric Radiologists Assn. (pres. 1971), Soc. Pediatric Radiology, Calif. Med. Assn. (chmn. sect. on radiology 1978-79), Orange County Med. Assn. (chmn. UCI liaison com. 1976-78), Cardioradiology Soc. So. Calif., Radiol. Soc. N.Am., Am. Roentgen Ray Soc., Am. Coll. Physician Execs., Soc. Chmn. Radiologists Children Hosp., Center Club, Phi Beta Kappa, Phi Eta Sigma, Omega Beta Phi, Alpha Omega Alpha. Office: 1201 W La Veta Ave Orange CA 92668-4213

ROWLAND, FRANK SHERWOOD, chemistry educator; b. Delaware, Ohio, June 28, 1927; m. Joan Lundberg, 1952; children: Ingrid Drake, Jeffrey Sherwood. AB, Ohio Wesleyan U., 1948; MS, U. Chgo., 1951, PhD, 1952, DSc (hon.), 1989; DSc (hon.), Duke U., 1989, Whittier Coll., 1989, Princeton U., 1990, Haverford Coll., 1992; LLD (hon.), Ohio Wesleyan U., 1989, Simon Fraser U., 1991. Instr. chemistry Princeton (N.J.) U., 1952-56; asst. prof. chemistry U. Kans., 1956-58, assoc. prof. chemistry, 1958-63, prof. chemistry, 1963-64; prof. chemistry U. Calif., Irvine, 1964—, dept. chmn., 1964-70, Aldrich prof. chemistry, 1985-89, Bren prof. chemistry, 1989-94, Bren rsch. prof., 1994—; Humboldt sr. scientist, Fed. Republic of Germany, 1981; chmn. Dahlem (Fed. Republic of Germany) Conf. on Changing Atmosphere, 1987; vis. scientist Japan Soc. for Promotion Sci., 1980; co-dir. western region Nat. Inst. Global Environ. Changes, 1989-93; del. Internat. Coun. Sci. Unions, 1993—; fgn. sec. NAS, 1994—; lectr., cons. in field. Contbr. numerous articles to profl. jours. Mem. ozone commn. Internat. Assn. Meteorology and Atmospheric Physics, 1980-88, mem. commn. on atmospheric chemistry and global pollution, 1979-91; mem. acid rain peer rev. panel U.S. Office of Sci. and Tech., Exec. Office of White House, 1982-84; mem. vis. com. Max Planck Insts., Heidelberg and Mainz, Fed. Republic Germany, 1982-96; ozone trends panel mem. NASA, 1986-88; chmn. Gordon Conf. Environ. Scis.-Air, 1987; mem. Calif. Coun. Sci. Tech., 1989-94, Exec. Com. Tyler Prize, 1992—. Recipient numerous awards including John Wiley Jones award Rochester Inst. of Tech., 1975, Disting. Faculty Rsch. award U.

Calif., Irvine, 1976, Profl. Achievement award U. Chgo., 1977, Billard award N.Y. Acad. Sci., 1977, Tyler World Prize in Environment Achievement, 1983, Global 500 Roll of Honor for Environ. Achievement UN Environment Program, 1988, Dana award for Pioneering Achievements in Health, 1987, Silver medal Royal Inst. Chemistry, U.K., 1989, Wadsworth award N.Y. State Dept. Health, 1989, medal U. Calif., Irvine, 1989, Japan prize in Environ. Sci., 1989, Dickson prize Carnegie-Mellon U., 1991; Guggenheim fellow, 1962, 74, Albert Einstein prize of World Cultural Coun., 1994, Nobel Prize in Chemistry, 1995. Fellow AAAS (pres. elect 1991, pres. 1992, chmn. bd. dirs. 1993), Am. Phys. Soc. (Leo Szilard award for Physics in Pub. Interest 1979), Am. Geophys. Union (Roger Revelle medal 1994); mem. NAS (bd. environ. studies and toxicology 1986-91, com. on atmospheric chemistry 1987-89, com. atmospheric scis., solar-terrestial com. 1979-83, co-DATA com. 1977-82, sci. com. on problems environment 1986-89, Infinite Voyage film com. 1988-92, Robertson Meml. lectr. 1993, chmn. com. on internat. orgns. and programs 1993—, chmn. office of internat. affairs 1994—, co-chmn. interacad. panel 1995—), Am. Acad. Arts and Scis., Am. Chem. Soc. (chmn. divsn. nuclear sci. and tech. 1973-74, chmn. divsn. phys. chemistry 1974-75, Tolman medal 1976, Zimmerman award 1980, E.F. Smith lectureship 1980, Environ. Sci. and Tech. award 1983, Esselen award 1987, Peter Debye Phys. Chem. award 1993), Am. Philos. Soc., Inst. Medicine. Home: 4807 Dorchester Rd Corona Del Mar CA 92625-2718 Office: U Calif Irvine Dept of Chemistry 571 PS1 Irvine CA 92697-2025

ROWLAND, LEWIS PHILLIP, neurologist, medical editor, educator; b. Bklyn., Aug. 3, 1925; s. Henry Alexander and Cecile (Coles) R.; m. Esther Edelman, Aug. 31, 1952; children: Andrew Simon, Steven Samuel, Joy Rosenthal. B.S., Yale U., 1945, M.D., 1948; hon. doctorate, U. Aix-Marseilles, France, 1986, U. Padua, 1996. Diplomate: Am. Bd. Psychiatry and Neurology. Intern New Haven Hosp., 1949-50; asst. resident N.Y. Neurol. Inst., 1950-52, fellow, 1953; clin. assoc. NIH, Bethesda, Md., 1953-54; practice research medicine, specializing in neurology N.Y.C., 1954-67, Phila., 1967-73, N.Y.C., 1973—; asst. neurologist Montefiore Hosp., N.Y.C., 1954-57; vis. fellow Nat. Inst. Med. Research, London, 1956; from asst. prof. to prof. neurology Columbia Coll. Physicians and Surgeons, 1957-67, prof., chmn. dept. neurology, 1973—; prof., chmn. dept. neurology U. Pa., Med. Sch., 1967-73; from asst. neurologist to attending neurologist Presbyn. Hosp., 1957-67; co-dir. Neurol. Clin. Research Center, 1961-67, dir. neurology service, 1973—, pres. med. bd., 1991-94; cons. Harlem Hosp., 1973—; mem. med. adv. bd. Myasthenia Gravis Found., pres., 1971-73; med. adv. bd. Muscular Dystrophy Assocs., Nat. Multiple Sclerosis Soc., Com. to Combat Huntington's Disease; pres. Parkinson's Disease Found., 1979—; mem. tng. grants com. Nat. Inst. Neurol. Diseases and Stroke, NIH, 1971-73, bd. sci. counselors, 1978-83, chmn., 1981-83, nat. adv. council, 1986-90. Editorial bd.; Archives of Neurology, 1968-76, Advances in Neurology, 1969—, Italian Jour. Neurol. Sci., 1979—, Handbook of Clin. Neurology, 1982—, New England Jour. Medicine, 1990—, Medical Letter, 1990—, Jour. Neurol. Sci., 1991—, Jour. Neuromuscular Disorders, 1991—; editor-in-chief: Neurology, 1977-87. Served with USNR, 1942-44; with USPHS, 1953-54. Mem. Am. Neurol. Assn. (pres. 1980, hon. mem. 1989—), Am. Acad. Neurology (pres.-elect 1987-89, pres. 1989-91), Phila. Neurol. Soc. (pres. 1972), Assn. Research Nervous Mental Disease (pres. 1969, trustee 1976—, v.p. 1980, chmn. bd. trustees 1992—), Assn. Univ. Profs. Neurology (sec. 1971-74, pres. 1978), Eastern Pa. Multiple Sclerosis Soc. (chmn. med. adv. bd. 1969-73); hon. mem. Neurol. Socs. France, Poland, Can., Europe, Italy, Gt. Britain, Spain, Japan; mem. N.Y.C. Multiple Sclerosis Soc. (chmn. med. adv. bd. 1977-92). Home: 404 Riverside Dr New York NY 10025-1861 Office: Columbia-Presbyn Med Ctr Neurological Inst 710 W 168th St New York NY 10032-2603

ROWLAND, ROBERT CHARLES, clinical psychotherapist, writer, researcher; b. Columbus, Ohio, Jan. 18, 1946; s. Charles Albert and Lorene Bernadine (Friedlinghaus) R.; m. Saundra Marie Gardner, Dec. 21, 1968 (div. Mar. 1987); children: Carrie Ann, Marcus Jules Harrad, Heather Renée. BS in Physiol. Psychology, Ohio State U., 1971, MSW, 1981. Cert. marital and family therapist; cert. in drug and alcohol treatment; cert. sex therapist; cert. hypnotist. Respiratory therapist Mt. Carmel Med. Ctr., Columbus, Ohio, 1965-68; adj. prof. Columbus Ctr. Sci. and Industry, Columbus, Ohio, 1968-71; researcher in tetrahydrocannabinol/learning experiments Ohio State U. Rsch. Ctr., 1970-71; secondary tchr. Columbus (Ohio) Pub. Schs., 1971-73; case cons. Bur. Disability Determination, Columbus, 1973-80; clin. social worker Clarke County Out-Patient Mental Health Ctr., Springfield, Ohio, 1979-80, Upham Hall, Ohio State U. Hosps., 1980-81; clin. psychotherapist Psychol. Systems, Inc., Columbus, 1981-84; psychotherapist, cons. Columbus, 1974-87, 94—, Delray Beach, Fla., 1987-93; dir. social svc. and cmty. rels. Apple Creek (Ohio) Devel. Ctr., 1981-82; pres., rsch. dir. Neurosocial Scis. Inst., Delray Beach, 1987-93, Columbus, 1994—. Author: Brain Wars-The End of the Drug Game, 1991; contbr. articles to profl. jours. Advisor Neighbor to Neighbor, Delray Beach, 1991-93. Recipient scholarship grant, Ohio State U. Coll. of Social Work, 1980-81. Mem. AAAS, NASW (chmn. Ohio Pace chpt., lobbyist 1980-81, Excellence award 1981, mem. Fla. chpt.), Archaeol. Soc. Ohio, Archaeol. Soc. Fla., Fla. Freelance Writer's Assn., Union of Concerned Scientists, Palm Beach County Scis. Jour. Club, Alpha Delta Mu. Home: 6378 Busch Blvd Apt 386 Columbus OH 43229

ROWLAND, TIMOTHY NORWOOD, psychiatrist; b. Hanover, N.H., July 21, 1947; s. Rufus Story and DeLette (Norwood) R. BA, U. Vt., 1969, MD, 1974. Diplomate Am. Bd. Psychiatry and Neurology with added qualification in geriatric psychiatry. Resident in psychiatry Dartmouth Coll., Hanover, 1985-88; pvt. practice Enosburg Falls, Vt., 1976-78; staff physician Vt. State Hosp., Waterbury, 1978-80, clin. dir., 1980-85; staff psychiatrist West Cen. Svcs., Lebanon, N.H., 1988-90; med. dir. mental health unit Valley Regional Hosp., Claremont, N.H., 1990-92; assoc. med. dir. mental health unit Cheshire Med. Ctr., Keene, N.H., 1992-94; staff psychiatrist Brattleboro (Vt.) Retreat, 1994—. Mem. Vt. State Med. Soc., N.H. State Med. Soc., Am. Psychiatric Assn., Am. Med. Assn., Windham County Med. Soc., Vt. Psychiat. Assn. Home: PO Box 790 Putney VT 05346-0790 Office: PO Box 803 Brattleboro VT 05302-0803

ROWLANDS, BRIAN JAMES, surgeon and educator; b. Bebington, Wirral, U.K., Mar. 18, 1945; s. Arthur Leslie and Lillian Grace (Allan) R.; m. Judith Thomas, Oct. 16, 1971; 1 child, Rachel Jane. M.B.B.S., U. London, 1968; MD, U. Sheffield, U.K., 1978. Surg. trainee Sheffield Hosp., 1971-73; lectr. surgery U. Sheffield, 1974-77; fellow in gastrointestinal surgery U. Tex., Houston, 1978, assoc. prof. surgery, 1978-86; prof. surgery and head dept. surgery Queen's U. of Belfast, No. Ireland, 1986—; chmn. No. Ireland Surg. Tng. Com., 1992—; Marjorie Budd vis. prof. U. Bristol, 1992. Coun. of Europe Travelling fellow, 1990. Fellow ACS, Royal Coll. Surgeons Eng., Royal Coll. Surgeons Ireland (Robert Adams Lectr. 1987), Royal Coll. Surgeons Edinburgh (hon.), Royal Coll. Physicians and Surgeons Glasgow (hon.); mem. ATLS No. Ireland (chmn. 1990-92), Assn. Profs. of Surgery U.K. (sec. 1990-93), Internat. Assn. Trauma and Surg. Intensive Care (sec.-treas. 1995—).

ROWLEY, BEVERLEY DAVIES, medical sociologist; b. Antioch, Calif., July 28, 1941; d. George M. and Eloise (DeWhitt) Davies; m. Richard B. Rowley, Apr. 1, 1966 (div. 1983). BS, Colo. State U., 1963; MA, U. Nev., 1975; PhD, Union Inst., 1983. Social worker Nev. Dept. Pub. Welfare, Reno, 1963-65, Santa Clara County Dept. Welfare, San Jose, Calif., 1965-66; field dir. Sierra Sage Council Camp Fire Girls, Sparks, Nev., 1966-70; program coord. div. health scis. sch. medicine U. Nev., 1976-78, program coord., health analyst office rural health, 1978-84, acting dir. office rural health, 1982-84; exec. asst. to pres. Med. Coll. of Hampton Rds., Norfolk, Va., 1984-87; rsch. mgr. Office Med. Edn. Info. AMA, Chgo., 1987-88, dir. dept. data systems, 1988-91; dir. med. edn. Maricopa Med. Ctr., Phoenix, 1992—; v.p. Med. Edn. and Rsch. Assocs., Inc., Phoenix, Chgo., 1992—; various positions as adj. prof. and lectr. in health scis. U. Nev. Sch. of Medicine, 1972-75; lectr. Dept. of Family and Community Medicine, U. Nev., 1978-84, asst. dir., evaluator Health Careers for Am. Indians Programs, 1978-84; cons. Nev. Statewide Health Survey, 1979-84; interim dir. Health Max, 1985-86; asst. prof. dept. of family and community medicine Med. Coll. of Hampton Rds., Norfolk, Va., 1985-87; v.p., treas. Systems Devel. Assocs., Reno, 1981-84. Editor of five books; contbr. numerous articles to profl. jours; developer three computer systems including AMA-FREIDA. Mem. Am. Sociol. Assn., Nat. Rural Health Assn. (bd. dirs. 1986-88), Assn. Behavioral Sci. and Med. Edn. (pres. 1986), Assn. Am. Med. Colls. (exec. coun. 1993-95), Coun. Acad. Scis. (adminstrv. bd. 1992—), Delta, Delta, Delta. Office: Maricopa Med Ctr Dept Acad Affairs 2601 E Roosevelt St Phoenix AZ 85008-4973

ROWLEY, JANET DAVISON, physician; b. N.Y.C., Apr. 5, 1925; d. Hurford Henry and Ethel Mary (Ballantyne) Davison; m. Donald A. Rowley, Dec. 18, 1948; children: Donald, David, Robert, Roger. PhB, U. Chgo., 1944, BS, 1946, MD, 1948; DSc (hon.), U. Ariz., 1989, U. Pa., 1989, Knox Coll., 1991, U. So. Calif., 1992. Cert. Am. Bd. Med. Genetics. Rsch. asst. U. Chgo., 1949-50; intern Marine Hosp., USPHS, Chgo., 1950-51; attending physician Infant Welfare and Prenatal Clinics Dept. Pub. Health, Montgomery County, Md., 1953-54; rsch. fellow Levinson Found., Cook County Hosp., Chgo., 1955-61; clin. instr. neurology U. Ill., Chgo., 1957-61; USPHS spl. trainee Radiobiology Lab. The Churchill Hosp., Oxford, Eng., 1961-62; rsch. assoc. dept. medicine and Argonne Cancer Rsch. Hosp. U. Chgo., 1962-69, assoc. prof. dept. medicine and Argonne Cancer Rsch. Hosp., 1969-77, prof. dept. medicine and Franklin McLean Meml. Rsch. Inst., 1977-84; Blum-Riese Disting. Svc. prof., dept. medicine and dept. molecular genetics and cell biology, 1984—; mem. Nat. Cancer Adv. Bd., 1979-84; bd. sci. counsellors Nat. Ctr. for Human Genome Rsch., NIH, 1994—, chmn., 1994—; Bernard Cohen Meml. lectr. U. Pa., 1993, Katherine D. McCormick Disting. lectr. Stanford U., 1994; Donald D. Van Slyke lectr. Brookhaven Nat. Lab., 1994. Co-founder, co-editor Genes, Chromosomes and Cancer; mem. editl. bds. Oncology Rsch., Cancer Genetics and Cytogenetics, Internat. Jour. Hematology, Genomics, Internat. Jour. Cancer, Leukemia; past mem. editorial bd. Blood, Cancer Rsch., Hematol. Oncology, Leukemia Rsch.; contbr. chpts. to books, articles to profl. jours. Mem. Bd. Sci. Counsellors, Nat. Inst. Dental Rsch., NIH, 1972-76, chmn., 1974-76; mem. Nat. Cancer Adv. Bd. Nat. Cancer Inst., 1979-84; mem. adv. com. Frederick Cancer Rsch. Facility, 1983-85; mem. adv. bd. Leukemia Soc. Am., 1979-84; mem. MIT Corp. vis. com. Dept. Applied Biol. Scis., 1983-86; mem. selection com. scholar award in Biomed. Sci., Lucille P. Markey Charitable Trust, 1984-87; trustee Adler Planetarium, Chgo., 1978—; bd. dirs. am. Bd. Med. Genetics, 1982-83, Am. Bd. Human Genetics, 1985-88; bd. sci. cons. meml. Sloan-Kettering Cancer Ctr., 1988-90; nat. adv. com. McDonnell Found. Program for Molecular Medicine in Cancer Rsch., 1988—; adv. com. Ency. Britannica U. Chgo., 1988—; mem. adv. bd. Howard Hughes Med. Inst., 1989-94; adv. com. for career awards in biomed. scis. Burroughs Wellcome Fund, 1994—. Recipient First Kuwait Cancer prize, 1984, Esther Langer award Ann Langer Cancer Rsch. Found., 1983, A. Cressy Morrison award in natural scis. N.Y. Acad. Scis., 1985, Past State Pres.' award Tex. Fedn. Bus. and Profl. Women's Clubs, 1986, Karnofsky award and lecture Am. Soc. Clin. Oncology, 1987, prix Antoine Lacassagne Lique Nationale Francaise Contre le Cancer, 1987, King Faisal Internat. prize in medicine (co-recipient), 1988, Katherine Berkan Judd award Meml. Sloan-Kettering Cancer Ctr., 1989, (co-recipient) Charles Mott Prize GM Cancer Rsch. Found., 1989, Steven C. Beering award U. Ind. Med. Sch., 1992, Robert de Villiers award Leukemia Soc. Am., 1993, Kaplan Family prize for cancer rsch. excellence Oncology Soc. Dayton, 1995, Cotlove award and lecture Acad. Clin. Lab. Physicians and Scientists, 1995, Nilsson-Ehle lecture Mendelian Soc. and Royal Physiograhic Soc., U. Lund, 1995, The Gardner Found. award, 1996. Mem. NAS (chmn. sect. 41 1995—), Am. Acad. Arts and Scis., Am. Philos. Soc., Am. Soc. Human Genetics (pres.-elect 1992, pres. 1993, Allen award and lectr. 1991), Genetical Soc. (Gt. Britain), Am. Soc. Hematology (Presdl. Symposium 1982, Dameshek prize 1982, Ham-Wasserman award 1995), Am. Assn. Cancer Rsch. (G.H.A. Clowes Meml. award 1989), Inst. Medicine (coun. 1988-90), Sigma Xi (William Proctor prize for sci. achievement 1989), Alpha Omega Alpha Alumnus. Episcopalian. Home: 5310 S University Ave Chicago IL 60615-5106 Office: U Chgo 5841 Maryland Ave MC 2115 Chicago IL 60637

ROWLEY, PETER TEMPLETON, physician, educator; b. Greenville, Pa., Apr. 29, 1929; s. George Hardy and Susan Mossman (Templeton) R.; m. Carol Stone, Mar. 19, 1967; children: Derek Stone, Jason Templeton. AB magna cum laude, Harvard U., 1951; MD, Columbia U., 1955. Diplomate: Am. Bd. Internal Medicine. Intern med. service N.Y. Hosp.-Cornell Med. Center, 1955-56; clin. assoc. Nat. Inst. Neurol. Disease and Blindness, NIH, 1956-58; asst. resident, then resident Harvard Med. Service, Boston City Hosp.; asst. in medicine Harvard U. Med. Sch. and researcher Thorndike Meml. Lab., 1958-60; hon. research asst. dept. eugenics, biometry and genetics Univ. Coll., U. London, 1960-61; postdoctoral fellow dept. microbiology NYU Sch. Medicine, 1961-63; asst. prof. medicine Stanford U., 1963-70; assoc. prof. medicine pediatrics and genetics U. Rochester, 1970-75, prof. medicine, pediatrics, genetics and microbiology, 1975—, prof. oncology, 1991—, chmn. div. genetics, 1990—; physician, pediatrician Strong Meml. Hosp., 1970—; mem. N.Y. State Exec. and Adv. Coms. on Genetic Disease, 1979—; WHO vis. scholar Inst. Biol. Chemistry, U. Ferrara, Italy, 1970. Editor: (with M. Lipkin Jr.) Genetic Responsibility: On Choosing Our Children's Genes, 1974. With USPHS, 1956-58. Recipient Excellence in Teaching award U. Rochester Class of 1976, 1973; NRC fellow, 1960-63; Buswell research fellow, 1970-71, 71-72. Fellow ACP, Am. Coll. Genetics; mem. Am. Fedn. Clin. Rsch., Am. Soc. Hematology, Am. Soc. Human Genetics (social issues com. 1980-89, program com. 1993-96). Office: U Rochester Med Sch Div Genetics PO Box 641 601 Elmwood Ave Rochester NY 14642-0001

ROWLINGSON, JOHN CLYDE, anesthesiologist, educator, physician; b. Syracuse, N.Y., Aug. 3, 1948; s. John Winthrop and Genevieve Estelle (Mahan) R.; m. Rosemary Colette Laney, Oct. 26, 1974 (div. 1992); children: Kristen, Andrew. BS, Allegheny Coll., 1970; MD, SUNY, Buffalo, 1974. Intern Millard Fillmore Hosp., Buffalo, 1974-75; resident in anesthesiology U. Va., Charlottesville, 1975-77; fellow in anesthesia pain mgmt. U. Va. Med. Ctr., 1977-78; asst. prof. anesthesiology U. Va. Sch. Medicine, Charlottesville, 1978-82, assoc. prof., 1982-86, prof., 1986—, tenured prof., 1995—; assoc. dir. Pain Mgmt. Ctr., U. Va. Health Sci. Ctr., 1978-79, dir., 1980—. Author: Regional Anesthesia, 1984; co-editor: Handbook of Critical Care Pain Management, 1993. Nat. Inst. Handicapped Rsch. fellow, 1983-87, Pain fellow 1977-78. Felllow Am. Coll. Anesthesiology; mem. Am. Soc. Anesthesiologists, Am. Soc. Regional Anesthesia (rsch. grantee 1977, pres. 1996—), Am. Pain Soc., Internat. Assn. Study of Pain, Am. Acad. Pain Medicine (editl. bd. Anesthesia Analog 1996—). Methodist. Home: 1255 Hunters Ridge Ln Earlysville VA 22936-9571 Office: U Va Health Sci Ctr Anesthesiology PO Box 238 Charlottesville VA 22908-0238

ROWSEY, NORA KATHLEEN, management consultant; b. Ypsilanti, Mich., July 1, 1954; d. Eldron Carpenter and Vivian Irene (Fouty) R. LPN, Oakland Community Coll., Royal Oak, Mich., 1980; ASN, U. State N.Y., Albany, 1986; BS in Applied Organizational Mgmt. cum laude, Tusculum Coll., 1989. RN, lic. practical nurse. Staff nurse orthopedics, med. surg. Pontiac (Mich.) Osteo. Hosp., alternate charge nurse ICU, 1987-91; DON nursing Superior Home Health Care, Inc., Maryville, Tenn.; home care cons. Alpha Med., Chattanooga, 1991-94; exec. dir. of profl. svcs. Putnam Home Health Care, Inc., Palatka, Fla., 1994—, Superior Home Care, Jacksonville, Fla., 1994—. Home: 390 A1A Beach Blvd Apt 59 Saint Augustine FL 32084-5992

ROY, CATHERINE ELIZABETH, physical therapist; b. Tucson, Jan. 16, 1948; d. Francis Albert and Dorothy Orme (Thomas) R.; m. Richard M. Johnson, Aug. 31, 1968 (div. 1978); children: Kimberly Anne, Troy Michael. BA in Social Sci. magna cum laude, San Diego State U., 1980; MS in Phys. Therapy, U. So. Calif., 1984. Staff therapist Sharp Meml. Hosp., San Diego, 1984-89, chairperson patient and family edn. com., 1986-87, chairperson sex edn. and counselling com., 1987-89, chairperson adv. bd. for phys. therapy, asst. for edn. program, 1987-89; mgr. rehab. phys. therapy San Diego Rehab. Inst., Alvarado Hosp., 1989-91; dir. therapeutic svcs. VA Med. Ctr., San Diego, 1991—; lectr. patient edn., family edn., peer edn.; mem. curriculum rev. com. U. So. Calif. Phys. Therapy Dept., 1982; bd. dirs. Ctr. for Edn. in Health; writer, reviewer licensure examination items for phys. therapy Profl. Examination Services.. Tennis coach at clinics Rancho Penasquitos Swim and Tennis Club, San Diego, 1980-81; active Polit. Activities Network, 1985; counselor EEO, 1992-95. Mem. Am. Phys. Therapy Assn. (rsch. presenter nat. conf. 1985, del. nat. conf. 1986-94, rep. state conf. 1987-89, 92-94, Mary McMillan student award 1984, mem. exec. bd. San Diego dist. 1985-88, 92-94), AAUW, NAFE, Am. Congress Rehab. Medicine, Phi Beta Kappa, Phi Kappa Phi, Chi Omega. Home: 5067 Park West Ave San Diego CA 92117-1048 Office: San Diego VA Med Ctr Spinal Cord Injury Svc 3350 La Jolla Village Dr San Diego CA 92161-0002

ROY, CHUNILAL, psychiatrist; b. Digboi, India, Jan. 1, 1935; came to Can., 1967, naturalized, 1975; s. Atikay Bandhu and Nirupama (Devi) R.; m. Elizabeth Ainscow, Apr. 15, 1967; children: Nicholas, Phillip, Charles. MB, BS, Calcutta Med. Coll., India, 1959; diploma in psychol. medicine, Kings Coll., Newcastle-upon-Tyne, Eng., 1963. Intern Middlesborough Gen. Hosp., Eng., 1960-61; jr. hosp. officer St. Luke's Hosp., Middlesborough, Eng., 1961-64, sr. registrar, 1964; sr. hosp. med. officer Parkside Hosp., Macclesfield, Eng., 1964-66; sr. registrar Moorehaven Hosp., Ivybridge, Eng., 1966; reader, head dept. psychiatry Maulana Azad Med. Coll., New Delhi, 1966; sr. med. officer Republic of Ireland, County Louth, 1966; sr. psychiatrist Sask. Dept. Psychiat. Services, Can., 1967-68; regional dir. Swift Current, Can., 1968-71; practice medicine specializing in psychiatry Regina, Sask., Can., 1971-72; founding dir., med. dir. Regional Psychiat. Ctr., Abbotsford, B.C., Can., 1972-82; with dept. psychiatry Vancouver Gen. Hosp., 1987—; cons. to prison adminstrs.; hon. lectr. psychology and clin. prof. dept. psychiatry U. B.C.; ex-officio mem. Nat. Adv. Com. on Health Care of Prisoners in Can.; cons. psychiatrist Vancouver Hosp.; advisor Asian chpt. Psychosomatic Medicine, World Congress of Law and Medicine, New Delhi, 1985. Author: (with D.J. West and F.L. Nichols) Understanding Sexual Attacks, 1978; co-author: Oath of Athens, 1979; ; assoc. editor Internat. Jour. Offender Therapy and Comparative Criminology, 1978—; field editor Jour. of Medicine and Law; corr. editor Internat. Jour. Medicine; mem. bd. Internat. Law Medicine, 1979—; mem. editl. rev. bd. Evaluation, 1977—; contbr. articles to profl. jours. Recipient merit awards Dept. Health, Republic of Ireland, 1966, Can. Penitentiary Svc., 1974, Correctional Svcs. Can., 1983, citation by pres. U. B.C., 1983, Lahenf. Scuagstrand Found. prize, Holland, 1995; knighted by Order of St. John Ecumenical Found., 1993. Fellow Royal Coll. Psychiatry (Can.), Royal Coll. Psychiatry (Eng.), Pacific Rim Coll. Psychiatrists (founder); mem. World Psychiat. Assn. (sec., vice chmn. forensic psychiatry 1983), World Fedn. Mental Health, Internat. Coun. Prison Med. Svcs. (founding sec.-gen. 1977), Can. Med. Assn., Can. Psychiat. Assn., Amnesty Internat., Internat. Acad. Legal Medicine and Social Medicine, Indian Psychiat. Assn. (life), Can. Assn. Profl. Treatment Offenders (founding dir. 1975), Assn. Physicians and Surgeons Who Work in Can. Prisons (founding pres. 1974), Internat. Found. for Tng. in Penitentiary Medicine and Forensic Psychiatry (founding pres. 1980, vice chmn., sec.), World Psychiatry Assn., Australian Acad. Forensic Sci. (corr.), Can. Physicians Interested in South Asia (v.p. 1989, pres. 1990), Internat. Coll. Psychosomatic Medicine (adv. Asian chpt.), Internat. Conf. on Health, Culture and Contemporary Soc. (chief advisor Bombay 1989, v.p. 1989, pres. 1990), Internat. Coun. Penitentiary Medicine (founding sec., bd. dirs.), World Psyciat. Assn. (vice chmn. forensic psychiat. sect. 1989), World Assn. Health, Culture and Environ. (sec.-gen. 1995, award 1995), Order of St. John (knight 1992), Vancouver MultiCultural Soc. (bd. dirs. 1992-93), B.C. Psychiat. Assn. (pres.-elect 1995). Home: 2439 Trinity St, Vancouver, BC Canada V5K 1C9 Office: 1417-750 W Broadway, Vancouver, BC Canada V5Z 1J4

ROY, RAYMOND CLYDE, anesthesiologist; b. 1944. PhD in Chemistry, Duke U., 1971; MD, Tulane U., 1974. Resident Hosp. U. Pa.; prof., chair dept. anesthesia & perioperative medicine Med. U. S.C.; dir. Am. Bd. Anesthesiology. Office: 171 Ashley Ave Chapel Hill SC 29425-2207*

ROY, ROB J., biomedical engineer, anesthesiologist; b. Bklyn., Jan. 2, 1933; m. Carole Ann Roy, Aug. 1, 1959; children: Robert Bruce, David John, Bruce Glenn. BSEE, Cooper Union, N.Y.C., 1954; MSEE, Columbia U., 1956; DEngSc, Rensselaer Poly. Inst., 1962; MD, Albany (N.Y.) Med. Coll., 1976. Profl. engr., N.Y.; diplomate Am. Bd. Anesthesiology. Prof. elec. engrin. dept. Rensselaer Poly. Inst., Troy, N.Y., 1962, prof. elec. engring. dept., 1980—, head biomed. engring. dept., 1985-94; prof. anesthesiology Albany (N.Y.) Med. Ctr., 1979—. Author: State Variables for Engineers, 1965; author 150 papers in field. Sr. mem. IEEE; mem. Am. Soc. Anesthesiologists, Sigma Xi. Home: 565 Highwood Cir Albany NY 12203 Office: Albany Med Ctr Dept Anesthesiology 47 New Scotland Ave Albany NY 12208

ROY, ROBERT RUSSELL, toxicologist; b. Mpls., Sept. 14, 1957; s. Rudolph Russell and Arlene Charlotte (Miller) R.; m. Barbara Jane Richie, Oct. 10, 1987; children: Andrew, Katherine. BA cum laude, Augsburg Coll., 1980; MS, U. Minn., 1986, PhD, 1989. Bd. cert. in toxicology. Rsch. asst. U. Minn., Mpls., 1986-88; toxicologist, project mgr. Pace Labs., Inc., Mpls., 1989-90; toxicologist Minn. Dept. Health, Mpls., 1990-93, Minn. Regional Poison Ctr., St. Paul, 1990—; lectr. U. Minn., Mpls., 1986-90, Midwest Ctr. Occupl. Health and Safety, St. Paul, 1990—, instr., 1989; clin. asst. prof. U. Minn., 1993—; mem. grad. faculty in toxicology U. Minn.; adj. asst. prof. emergency medicine Oreg. Health Sci. U., Portland. Tutor Mpls. Pub. Schs., 1982; vol. U. Minn. Hosps., Mpls., 1983; mem. Waite Pk. Community Coun., Mpls., 1977-80, Mt. Carmel Luth. Ch. Coun., Mpls., 1983-85. Mem. Am. Coll. Toxicology, Soc. Toxicology, Am. Indsl. Hygiene Assn., Minn. Acad. Sci., Sigma Xi, Delta Omega. Home: 6201 Near Mountain Blvd Chanhassen MN 55317-9117 Office: Minn Regional Poison Ctr St Paul-Ramsey Med Ctr 640 Jackson St Saint Paul MN 55101-2502

ROY, WILLIAM ROBERT, physician, lawyer, former congressman; b. Bloomington, Ill., Feb. 23, 1926; s. Elmer Javan and Edna Blanche (Foley) R.; m. Jane Twining Osterhoudt, Sept. 1947; children: Robin Jo, Randall Jay, Richelle Jane, William Robert, Renee Jan, Rise Javan. B.S., Ill. Wesleyan U., 1946; M.D., Northwestern U., 1949; J.D. with honors, Washburn U., 1970. Mem. 92d-93d congresses from 2d Dist. Kans.; dir. Sentry Ins.; Democratic candidate for U.S. Senate, 1974, 78. Mem. Inst. Medicine of Nat. Acad. Scis. Democrat. Methodist. Home: 6137 SW 38th Ter Topeka KS 66610-1307

ROYAL, DANIEL FULLER, physician; b. Winston-Salem, N.C., July 25, 1959; s. Flemming Fuller and Madge Marie (Snipes) R.; m. Cheryl Marie Ohrn, May 9, 1981; children: Brittany, McKay, Lindsey, Karley. BS, U. Nev., Las Vegas, 1985; DO, Coll. Osteo. Medicine Pacific, Pomona, Calif., 1989. Physician Nev. Clinic, Los Vegas, 1990-92; med. dir. Madsion Rejuvenation Ctr., Madison, Wis., 1992-93, E. Drumore Family Health Ctr., Quarryville, Pa., 1993-94; physician Nev. Clinic, Los Vegas, 1994-96; med. dir. Royal Ctr. Advanced Medicine, 1996—. Contbr. articles to profl. jours.; dir. TV show For the Health of It, 1991-93, Radio: The Royal Treatment, 1996—. Brigham Young U. scholar, 1977. Mem. Am. Osteo. Assn., Am. Inst. Homeopathy, Am. Coll. Advancement of Medicine, Great Lakes Assn. Clin. Medicine (bd. dirs. 1994—, editor newsletter 1994—), Callif. Homeopathic Med. Soc. (tres. 1990-92). LDS. Home: 38 Diplomat Ct Henderson NV 89014 Office: 2501 N Green Valley Pkwy Ste D-132 Henderson NV 89014

ROYAL, HENRY DUVAL, nuclear medicine physician; b. Norwich, Conn., May 14, 1948. MD, St. Louis U., 1974. Diplomate Am. Bd. Internal Medicine; Am. Bd. Nuclear Medicine. Intern R.I. Hosp., Providence, 1974, resident internal medicine, 1975-76; resident nuclear medicine Harvard Med. Sch., Boston, 1977-79; assoc. Barnes Hosp., St. Louis, 1987—, Children's Hosp., St. Louis, 1987—, Jewish Hosp., St. Louis, 1993—; prof. Washington U., St. Louis, 1993—; co-team leader health effects sect. Internat. Atome Energy Agy. Internat. Chernobyl Project, 1990; bd. dirs. Am. Bd. Nuclear Medicine; mem. com. on assessment of CDC radiation studies NRC/NAS, 1993—; mem. sci. com. Nat. Coun. on Radiation Protection and Measurements, 1993—; mem. coun. Nat. Coun. on Radiation Protection, 1996—. Contbr. more than 100 articles to profl. jours. Mem. Soc. Nuclear Medicine (chair tech. and outcomes assessment com. 1994—), Alpha Omega Alpha. Office: Acad Faculty Mallinkrodt Inst Radiology 510 S Kingshighway Blvd Saint Louis MO 63110

ROYCE, ROBERT KILLIAN, physician; b. Greenville, Miss., Mar. 18, 1917; s. Owen and Eda (Luhm) R.; widowed; children: Corinne Elizabeth Royce Ulbright, Margaret Anne Royce Chida. BS, U. Miss., 1939; MD, Washington U., 1942. Diplomate Am. Bd. Urology. Rotating intern U. Chgo. Clinics, 1942-43; intern, asst. resident in gen. surgery Barnes Hosp.-Wash. U. Sch. Medicine, St. Louis, 1945-47, resident in urology, 1947-49; asst. prof. Washington U., St. Louis, 1949-55, assoc. prof., 1955-70, prof. surgery, 1970—, chmn. divsn. urology, 1975-78; cons. U.S. Vet.'s Hosp., St. Louis, 1953—. Maj. Med. Corps, 1943-46, ETO. Decorated Bronze Star. Fellow Am. Coll. Surgeons; mem. Am. Urol. Assn., Soc. Univ. Urologists, Univ. Club, Country Club at The Legends, Old Warson Country Club,

Alpha Omega Alpha. Republican. Roman Catholic. Home: 766 High Hampton Rd Saint Louis MO 63124 Office: Washington Univ Divsn Urology 4960 Childrens Pl Saint Louis MO 63110

ROYDS, ROBERT BRUCE, physician; b. Harrogate, England, Oct. 3, 1944; came to U.S., 1974; s. John Edmund and Ailsa Dorothea (Williams) R.; m. Marilyn Maria Valerio, Apr. 28, 1948; children: Elizabeth Caroline, Leslie Alexandra. M.B., B.S., U. London, 1967, M.R.C.P., 1970. Sr. house officer Royal Northern Hosp., London, 1968; sr. house officer Luton and Dunstable Hosp., Beds, England, 1968-69; registrar St. Albans City Hosp., Herts, England, 1969-70; research fellow clin. pharmacology dept. St. Bartholomew's Hosp., U. London, London, 1970-72; chief asst., sr. registrar med. professorial unit St. Bartholomew's Hosp., U. London, 1972-74; assoc. dir. Merck, Sharp & Dohme, Inc., Rahway, N.J., 1974-75; sr. research physician Hoffmann-La Roche Inc., Nutley, N.J., 1976-78; v.p. Besselaar Assocs., Princeton, N.J., 1979-82; pres. Theradex Sys., Inc., Princeton, 1982-94, chmn. bd. dirs., 1994—; cons. Ctr. for Rsch. Mothers/Infants Nat. Inst. Child Health & Human Devel., Washington, 1983. Bd. trustees Chapin Sch., Princeton, 1984-89, pres. bd. trustees, 1986-89; pres. Riverside Condominium Assn., Cranford, N.J., 1978-79. Fellow Royal Soc. Medicine; mem. Royal Coll. Physicians, Am. Coll. Clin. Pharmacology Therapeutics, Am. Soc. for Clin. Research (sr. mem.), Am. Soc. Microbiology. Home: 5 Quick Ln Plainsboro NJ 08536-1424

ROYKO, M. DAVID, mediation services administrator, psychologist; b. Chgo., June 8, 1959; s. Mike and Carol Joyce (Duckman) R.; m. Karen Miller, Aug. 27, 1959; children: (twins) Jacob Isaac and Benjamin Frederick. BA in Psychology, Lake Forest Coll., 1981; D of Psychology, Ill. Sch. Profl. Psychology, 1989. Lic. clin. psychologist, Ill. Staff therapist/supr. Michael Reese Hosp., Chgo., 1984-86; group therapist Ravenswood Hosp., Chgo., 1986-88; mediator Marriage and Family Counseling Svc. Circuit Ct. Cook County, Chgo., 1988-94, clin. dir. Marriage and Family Counseling Svc., 1994—; pvt. practice Chgo., 1986—. Contbr. articles on music to newspapers, mags. Recipient Sterling Price Williams prize in psychology Lake Forest Coll., 1981. Mem. AFCC, IBMA, Mediator Coun. Ill. Home: 2956 W Birchwood Ave Chicago IL 60645-1220

ROZBRUCH, JACOB D., surgeon; b. Bari, Italy, June 7, 1948; s. Max and Frieda (Einhorn) R.; m. Marsha Beth Golub, Aug. 15, 1971; children: Josh, Jenny. BA cum laude, CUNY, Bklyn., 1969; MD, SUNY, Buffalo, 1973. Intern pediatrics N.Y. Hosp. Cornell Med. Ctr., N.Y.C., 1973-74, resident in gen. surgery, 1974-76; orthopedic surgeon Hosp. for Spl. Surgery/Cornell Med. Ctr., N.Y.C., 1976-79; attending orthopedic surgeon Hosp. for Joint Disease, N.Y.C., 1979—; attending orthopedic surgeon Beth Israel Med. Ctr. North, N.Y.C., 1980—, chief of orthopedic surgery, 1987-95. Contbr. articles to profl. jours. Fellow Am. Acad. of Orthopedic Surgeons, Am. Acad. Pediatrics, Arthoscopy Assn. of N. Am., Arthritic Hip and Knee Soc. (charter mem.).

ROZELL, DANIEL WILLIS, medical educator; b. Neenah, Wis., Feb. 9, 1936; s. Vernon Jesse Rozell and Marion Cathrine Newstub Butler; m. Joann Lorene Ausherman, June 14, 1959; children: Florence Kay Rozell Sutherland, Kenneth Daniel. BSBA, So. Missionary Coll., Collegedale, Tenn., 1961; MA, Ctrl. Mich. U., 1972; BS in Long-Term Health Care Adminstrn., So. Coll., Collegedale, Tenn., 1986. Cert. nursing home adminstr., Tenn. Dean of boys, tchr. Mt. Pisgah Acad., Candler, N.C., 1961-64; tchr. bus. Sunnydale Acad., Centralia, Mo., 1964-65; registrar, tchr. Sunnydale Acad., 1965-66, treas., tchr., 1966-69; registrar, tchr. Cedar Lake (Mich.) Acad., 1969-72; asst. prof. bus. Southwestern Union Coll., Keene, Tex., 1972-76; asst. prof. bus., chmn. bus. adminstrn. Southwestern Union Coll., 1976-78; asst. prof. bus. So. Missionary Coll., Collegedale, Tenn., 1978-79; assoc. prof. bus., dir. long-term health care So. Coll., Collegedale, 1979—; charter mem. bd. dirs. Sunbelt Health Care Ctrs., Orlando, Fla., 1981—; mem. adv. bd. long-term care adminstrn. So. Coll., 1985—; test item writer Nat. Assn. Bds., Washington, 1995—; reviewer Nat. Continuing Edn. Rev. Svc., Washington, 1995—. Author, editor: Long-Term Care Internship Manual, 1986—; contbr. AIT Manual for Nat. Health Care, 1995. Treas. Tenn. Assn. Gerontology/Geriat. Edn., 1984—; v.p. Tenn. Fedn. Aging, Nashville, 1995. Recipient William E. Cole Meml. award Tenn. Assn. Gerontology/Geriat. Edn., 1993. Mem. Am. Coll. Health Care Adminstrn., Nat. Assn. Bds. of Examiners for Nursing Home Adminstrs. Seventh Day Adventist. Home: 7729 Royal Harbour Cir Ooltewah TN 37363 Office: So Coll PO Box 370 Collegedale TN 37315

ROZZELL, JAMES DAVID, JR., biotechnology company executive, consultant; b. Humboldt, Tenn., Dec. 9, 1955; s. James David Rozzell and Lois Anne (Nicholson) Jones; m. Francoise Solange Thomas, Dec. 28, 1985; children: Alexander, Nicolas. BS, U. Va., 1978; PhD, Harvard U., 1983. Sr. scientist Genetics Inst. Inc., Cambridge, Mass., 1983-88; dir. R & D, Celgene Corp., Warren, N.J., 1988-91; v.p. R & D, Exogene Corp., Monrovia, Calif., 1991-92, pres., 1992-94; pres. Sulfonics, Inc., Pasadena, Calif., 1995—, Biocatalytics, Inc., Pasadena, 1996—. Editor: Biocataltyic Production of Amino Acids, 1992; patentee in field. Mem. Am. Chem. Soc. Office: Sulfonics Inc Ste 207 1021 S Orange Grove Blvd Pasadena CA 91105

RUBAYI, SALAH, surgeon, educator; b. Baghdad, Iraq, Oct. 1, 1942; came to U.S., 1981; s. Abdulla Mossa Rubayi and Fatma (Ibriham) Al-Jarah; m. Cecile-Rose, June 23, 1985. MD, U. Baghdad, Iraq, 1966; LRCP and LRCS, Royal Coll. Surgeons and Physicians, Scotland, 1974. Surgeon burn and reconstructive surgery Birmingham Accident Hosp., Eng., 1978-81; fellow burn unit Los Angeles County/U. So. Calif. Med. Ctr., 1981-82; fellow plastic surgery Rancho Los Amigos Med. Ctr., Downey, Calif., 1982-85, mem. attending staff in plastic and reconstructive surgery, chief pressure ulcer mgmt. service, 1985—; chmn. Laser Safety Com. Rancho Los Amigos Med. Ctr., 1985—; asst. prof. surgery U. So. Calif. Contbr. articles to profl. jours. Fellow ACS, Internat. Coll. Surgeons, Am. Soc. Laser Medicine and Surgery; mem. Internat. Soc. Burn Injury, Am. Burn Assn., Internat. Soc. Paraplegia. Office: Rancho Los Amigos Med Ctr HB121 7601 Imperial Hwy # Hb121 Downey CA 90242-3456

RUBELL, BONNIE LEVINE, occupational therapist; b. Bklyn., Aug. 6, 1957; d. Seymour and Gladys Levine; m. Paul Rubell, June 3, 1990. BS in Occupational Therapy, NYU, 1979. Staff occupational therapist Main Campus Vocat. Workshop United Cerebral Palsy, Bklyn., 1980-83; sr. occupational therapist N.Y.C. Bd. Edn. Office Related and Contractual Svcs., 1983-86, supr. occupational therapy, 1986-87; sr. staff occupational therapist United Cerebral Palsy Treatment and Rehab. Ctr., Roosevelt, N.Y., 1987-89; master profl. occupational therapist The Sch. for Lang. and Communication Devel., North Bellmore, N.Y., 1987-92; staff occupational therapist Nassau Bd. Coop. Ednl. Svcs., The Lewis Ames Sch., 1992—; cons. On Your Mark program Staten Island Jewish Community Ctrs., 1984-85. Author: Big Strokes for Little Folks, 1995. Mem. Assn. Occupational Therapists Am., N.Y. Met. and L.I. Dists. Occupational Therapy Assn.

RUBEN, HARVEY L., psychiatrist; b. St. Louis, July 25, 1941; s. Milton Eugene Ruben and Freda Frances (Leuin) Abramson; m. Diane Sherry Daskal, Aug. 15, 1965; children: Adam, Justin, Marc. BS, U. Pitts., 1963; MD, Northwestern U., Chgo., 1966; MPH, Harvard U., 1968. Diplomate Nat. Bd. Med. Examiners, Am. Bd. Psychiatry and Neurology. Resident psychiatry Walter Reed Gen. Hosp., Washington, 1968-71; asst. prof. psychiatry Yale U. Sch. Medicine, New Haven, 1973-76, assoc. clin. prof. psychiatry, 1978-94, clin. prof., 1994—, dir. continuing edn. dept., 1987—; program dir. alcohol and drug svcs. Conn. Dept. Mental Health, New Haven, 1976-79; assoc. clin. prof. psychiatry U. Conn. Sch. Med., 1978-86; exec. dir. Home Health Care Conn., Inc., New Haven, 1976-78; acting dir. psychiat. emergency svc. Yale New Haven Hosp., 1982-83; host TalkNet NBC Radio Network, N.Y.C., 1982-93; presdl. councilor Enoch Pratt Hosp., Towson, Md., 1987-89; mem. bd. alumni counselors Northwestern U. Med. Sch., Chgo., 1986-94, chmn., 1991. Author: C.I.: Crisis Intervention, 1976, Competing, 1980, Super Marriage, 1986; author, co-editor: Emergency Psychiatric Care, 1975. Chmn. bd. dirs. Conn. Assn. Mental Health and Aging, Hartford, 1977-85; bd. dirs. Alzheimers Disease Assn. Conn., New Haven, 1986-88, Cornerstone Found., Inc., New Haven, 1974-88. Maj. U.S. Army, 1968-73. Recipient Mission award Nat. Mental Health Assn., 1992. Fellow Am. Psychiat. Assn. (pub. affairs chmn. 1986-92, Robinson Electronic Media award 1989, Braceland award for pub. svc. 1992), Am. Coll. Psychiatrists); mem. AMA, APHA, Group for Advancement of Psychiatry (bd. dirs. 1989). Democrat. Jewish. Home and Office: 77 Knollwood Dr New Haven CT 06515-2413

RUBEN, JAMES BRADFORD, ophthalmology physician; b. Rye, N.Y., Dec. 21, 1958; s. Robert Joseph and Audrey Hazel (Zweig) R.; m. Linda Joyce Rochlin, May 22, 1983; children: Eric, Elisa, Michelle. BA, Univ. Colo., 1980; MD, Wash. Univ. Sch. Medicine, 1984. Internship internal medicine U. Calif. Medical Ctr., Sacramento, 1984-85, resident opthalmology, 1985-88; fellowship pediatric opthalmology Univ. Iowa, Iowa City, 1989-90; dir. pediatric ophthalmology and ocular mobility svc. The Permanente Medical Group, Sacramento, 1990—; asst. clin. prof. U. Calif. Davis Dept. Ophthalmology, 1992—; dir. residency training Kaiser Ophthalmology, 1995—; chairperson ophthalmology quality assurance com. The Permanente Med. Group, 1994—. Author (book chpts.): Diseases of the Eye and Skin; contbr. articles to profl. jours. Fellow Am. Acad. Ophthalmology; mem. Am. Ophthalmology (pres. 1995—, program dir. 1994, sec. 1992), Am. Assn. Pediatric Ophthalmology, Sacramento El Dorado Med. Soc., Calif. Assn. of Ophthalmology. Office: The Permanente Medical Group 10725 International Dr Rancho Cordova CA 95670

RUBEN, MONIQUE LOUISE, health care specialist; b. Indpls., Mar. 31, 1964; d. Gary A. and Irene (Jehle) R. BS, Ind. U., 1984; MBA, Baker U., 1995, CPHQ, 1996. Nat. accounts, mktg. mgr. Physio Tech., Topeka, 1984-89; adminstrv. dir. mktg. Mid-Am. Rehab. Hosp., Overland Park, Kans., 1989-91; exec. dir. Surgix, Shawnee Mission, Kans., 1991-92; resource utilization/outcome specialist Shawnee Mission Med. Ctr., 1992-96; cons. Blue Cross Blue Shield, KCDS, Kansas City, Mo., Lane Sales, Inc., Overland Park, VHA, Inc., Overland Park. Mem. Nat. Assn. for Healthcare Quality (cert.), Inst. for Healthcare Improvement, Am. Coll. Healthcare Execs. Office: Shawnee Mission Med Ctr 9100 W 74th St Shawnee Mission KS 66201

RUBEN, ROBERT JOEL, physician, educator; b. N.Y.C., Aug. 2, 1933; s. Julian Carl and Sadie (Weiss) R.; children—Ann, Emily, Karin, Arthur. A.B., Princeton U., 1955; M.D., Johns Hopkins U., 1959. Intern Johns Hopkins Hosp., Balt., 1959-60; resident Johns Hopkins Hosp., 1960-64, dir. neurophysiology lab., div. otolaryngology, 1958-64; practice specializing in pediatric otorhinolaryngology N.Y.C., 1964—; asst. prof. otorhinolaryngology N.Y. U. Sch. Medicine, 1966-68; mem. staff hosps. Montefiore Med. Ctr., Bronx Med. Hosp. Ctr., N. Cen. Bronx Hosp., Montefiore Med.; prof., chmn. Montefiore Med. Ctr., Bronx Mcpl. Hosp. Ctr., N. Cen. Bronx, Bronx, N.Y., 1979—; prof. pediatrics Albert Einstein Coll. Medicine, Bronx, 1983—; assoc. prof. otorhinolaryngology Albert Einstein Coll. Medicine, N.Y.C., 1968-70, prof., chmn. dept. otolaryngology, 1970—; prof. pediatrics Albert Einstein Coll. Medicine and Montefiore Med. Ctr., 1983—; chmn. Nat. Com. for Rsch. and Neurol. and Communicative Disorders, pres., 1982-84; bd. dirs. Am. Bd. Otolaryngology-Head and Neck Surgery, 1989—; chmn. ENT devices com. FDA, 1993-96. Editor-in-chief: Internat. Jour. Pediatric Otorhinolaryngology, 1979—. Bd. dirs. N.Y. League Hard of Hearing, 1969-75, 76-85. Served to surgeon USPHS, 1964-66. Recipient Rsch. award Am. Acad. Ophthalmology and Otolaryngology, 1962, Edmund Prince Fowler award Am. Rhinological-Laryngological-Otological Assn., 1973, Gold medal Best Didactic Film, IX World Congress Otorhinolaryngology, 1977, Pres.'s award Am. Acad. Otolaryngology-Head and Neck Surgery, 1992, Johns Hopkins U. Soc. of Scholars, 1993, George E. Schambaugh Otology prize, 1996. Fellow ACS, N.Y. Acad. Medicine; mem. AMA, Am. Assn. Anatomists, Audiology Study Group N.Y. (pres. 1964-66), Acoustical Soc. Am., Am. Acad. Ophthalmology and Otolaryngology, Soc. Univ. Otolaryngologists, Am. Otol. Soc. (sec.-treas. rsch. fund 1979—), Soc. for Ear, Nose and Throat Advances in Children (pres. 1973), Assn. for Rsch. in Otolaryngology (pres. 1985-86), Am. Acad. Pediat. (chmn. otol. bronchoesphology 1983-85), Am. Soc. Pediat. Otolaryngology (historian 1986-95), Am. Soc. Pediat. Otolaryngologists (historian 1986-93, pres.-elect 1993-94, pres. 1994-95), Nat. Inst. Deafness and Other Comm. Disorders (adv. coun. 1989-93), Am. Laryngol. Soc. Home: 1025 Fifth Ave Apt 12C S New York NY 10028-0134 Office: Montefiore Med Ctr 111 E 210th St Bronx NY 10467-2401

RUBENOWITZ, SIGVARD, psychology educator; b. Lund, Sweden, Oct. 1, 1925; s. Salomo and Rebecka (Juvall) R.; m. Ulla Jacobson; children: Ann, Eva, Astrid. MS, Chalmers U. Tech., Gothenburg, Sweden, 1950; diploma in occupational psychology, London U., 1954; PhD in Psychology, Gothenburg U., 1963. Sect. head Swedish Coun. for Personnel Adminstrn., 1954-62; assoc. prof. applied psychology U. Gothenburg, 1963-70, prof. applied psychology, 1970—; v.p. faculty social sci. Gothenburg U., 1970-78, chmn. bd. behavioral scis., 1985—; guest prof. Hangzhou U., China, 1983. Home: Frodings alle 11, S-44331 Lerum Sweden

RUBENS, ROBERT, physician; b. Gent, Belgium, Jan. 20, 1943; s. Michel and Hilda (Van Hoeywegen); m. Hedwig De Wilde, Dec. 2, 1967; children: Kitty, Joop. MD, State U., Ghent, Belgium, 1967; MSc, Leeds U., Eng., 1972. Asst. U. Gent, 1967-72, 1st asst., 1972-78, sr. lectr., 1978-91, prof. endocrinology, 1991—; endocrinologist Polikliniek Rerum Novarum, Gent, 1972—; lectr. physiology Hoger Inst. Paramedische Beroepen, Gent, 1968-83, med. advisor., 1983—. Mem. Soc. Endocrinology (v.p. 1989-92), Orde van de Prince Gent II. Office: U Gent Dept Endocrinology, 185 De Pintelaan 9000, Belgium

RUBENSTEIN, ARTHUR HAROLD, physician, educator; b. Johannesburg, South Africa, Dec. 28, 1937; came to U.S., 1967; s. Montague and Isabel (Nathanson) R.; m. Denise Hack, Aug. 19, 1962; children: Jeffrey Lawrence, Errol Charles. MB, BChir, U. Witwatersrand, 1960. Diplomate Am. Bd. Internal Medicine. Intern, then resident Johannesburg Gen. Hosp., 1961, 63-65, 66-67; fellow in endocrinology Postgrad. Med. Sch., London, 1965-66; fellow in medicine U. Chgo., 1967-68, asst. prof., 1968-70, assoc. prof., 1970-74, prof., 1974—, Lowell T. Coggeshall prof. med. sci., 1981—, assoc. chmn. dept. medicine, 1975-81, chmn., 1981—, dir. Diabetes Rsch. and Tng. Ctr., 1986-91; attending physician Mitchell Hosp., U. Chgo., 1968—; mem. study sect. NIH, 1973-77, Hadassah Med. Adv. Bd., 1986—, adv. council Nat. Inst. Arthritis, Metabolism and Digestive Diseases, 1978-80; chmn. Nat. Diabetes Adv. Bd., 1982, mem., 1981-83. Mem. editorial bd. Diabetes, 1973-77, Endocrinology, 1973-77, Jour. Clin. Investigation, 1976-81, Am. Jour. Medicine, 1978-81, Diabetologia, 1982-86, Diabetes Medicine, 1987-91, Annals of Internal Medicine, 1991—, Medicine, 1992—; contbr. articles to profl. jours. Mem. Gov.'s Sci. Adv. Coun. State of Ill., 1989-94. Recipient David Rumbough Meml. award Juvenile Diabetes Found., 1978. Master ACP (John Phillips Meml. award 1995); fellow South African Coll. Physicians, Royal Coll. Physicians (London); mem. Am. Soc. for Clin. Investigation, Am. Diabetes Assn. (Eli Lilly award 1973, Banting medal 1983, Solomon Berson Meml. lectr. 1985), Brit. Diabetes Assn. (Banting lectr. 1987), Endocrine Soc., Am. Fedn. Clin. Rsch., Ctrl. Soc. Clin. Rsch. (v.p. 1988, pres. 1989), Assn. Am. Physicians (treas. 1984-89, councillor 1989-94, v.p. 1994-95, pres. 1995-96), Am. Bd. Internal Medicine (bd. govs. 1985-93, exec. com. 1990-93, chmn. 1992-93), Residency Rev. Com., Am. Acad. Arts and Scis., Inst. Medicine (coun. 1991—), Assn. Profs. Medicine (councillor 1991-94, v.p. 1994-95, pres. 1995-96). Home: 5517 S Kimbark Ave Chicago IL 60637-1618 Office: U Chgo Dept of Medicine 5841 S Maryland Ave Chicago IL 60637-1463

RUBENSTEIN, EDWARD, physician, educator; b. Cin., Dec. 5, 1924; s. Louis and Nettie R.; m. Nancy Ellen Millman, June 20, 1954; children: John, William, James. MD, U. Cin., 1947. House staff Cin. Gen. Hosp., 1947-50; fellow May Inst., Cin., 1950; sr. asst. resident Ward Med. Service, Barnes Hosp., St. Louis, 1953-54; chief of medicine San Mateo County Hosp., Calif., 1960-70; assoc. dean postgrad. med. edn., prof. medicine Stanford (Calif.) U., 1971—, emeritus, active; mem. faculty Stanford Photon Research Lab.; affiliated faculty mem. Stanford Synchortron Radiation Lab., 1971—; mem. maj. materials facilities com. Nat. Research Council, 1984-85, Nat. Steering Com. 6 GeV Electron Storage Ring., 1986—. Author: (textbook) Intensive Medical Care; editor-in-chief: (textbook) Sci. Am. Medicine, 1978-94; editor: Synchotron Radiation Handbook, 1988, vol. 4, 1991; editor Synchotron Radiation in the Biosciences, Molecular Medicine; mem. editorial adv. bd. Sci. Am., Inc., 1991-94. Served with USAF, 1950-52. Recipient Kaiser award for outstanding and innovative contbns. to med. edn., 1989, Albion Walter Hewlett Award, 1993. Fellow AAAS, Royal Soc. Medicine; mem. APS, ACP (master), Inst. Medicine, Calif. Acad. Medicine, Western Assn. Physicians, Soc. Photo-Optical Engrs., Am. Clin. and Climatol. Assn., Alpha Omega Alpha. Office: Stanford Medical Center Dept of Medicine Stanford CA 94305

RUBENSTEIN, MARK ALLEN, physiatrist; b. Syracuse, N.Y., Feb. 14, 1963; s. Harold and Judith (Allen) R. BSE in Biomed. Engring., Tulane U., New Orleans, 1985; MD, SUNY, Syracuse, 1989. Diplomate Am. Bd. Phys. Medicine and Rehab. Intern St. Joseph's Hosp., Syracuse, N.Y., 1989-90; resident Johns Hopkins U., Balt., 1990-93; physician Rehab. Med. Cons., Norfolk, 1993-95, Gold Coast Orthopedics, West Palm Beach, Fla., 1995—; med. dir. rehab. svcs. Hillhaven Health Care, Virginia Beach, Va., 1993-95. Bd. dirs. Jewish Fedn. Young Leadership Divsn., West Palm Beach, 1995-96. Fellow Am. Acad. Phys. Medicine and Rehab.; mem. AMA, Internat. Spinal Injection Soc., Am. Assn. Electrodiagnostic Medicine, Am. Med. Athletic Assn., Am. Running and Fitness Assn. Office: Gold Cost Orthopedics 1411 N Flagler Dr Ste 8800 West Palm Beach FL 33401

RUBENSTEIN, MARK M., pediatrician; b. Pittsburgh, Calif., Dec. 21, 1935; s. Myer W. and Belle (Barsky) R.; m. Yvonne L. LaLanne, Feb. 8, 1988; children: Rebecca, Matthew, Lean, Seth. BS, U. Pitts., 1957, MD, 1961. Pediatrician Ross Valley Med. Clinic, Green Bras, Calif., 1968-70, Diablo Valley Pediatric Med. Group, Concord, Calif., 1970—. Lt. comdr. USN, 1965-68. Fellow Am. Acad. Pediatrics. Democrat. Jewish. Home: 147 Los Altos Ave Walnut Creek CA 94598

RUBERG, ROBERT LIONEL, surgery educator; b. Phila., July 22, 1941; s. Norman and Yetta (Wolfman) R.; m. Cynthia Lief, June 26, 1966; children: Frederick, Mark, Joshua. BA, Haverford (Pa.) Coll., 1963; MD, Harvard U., 1967. Diplomate Am. Bd. Surgery, Am. Bd. Plastic Surgery. Instr. surgery U. Pa., Phila., 1972-75; asst. prof. Ohio State U., Columbus, 1975-81, assoc. prof., 1981-88, prof., 1988—; bd. dirs. Am. Bd. Plastic Surgery, 1991—, vice-chair, 1996—; chmn. curriculum com. Coll. Medicine, Ohio State U., 1984—; chief plastic surgery Ohio State U. Hosps., 1985—. Plastic Surgery Ednl. Found. research grantee, 1976, 78. Fellow ACS; mem. Am. Assn. Plastic Surgeons, Assn. Acad. Chairmen of Plastic Surgery (sec.-treas. 1990-93, pres. 1994-85). Home: 100 Walnut Woods Ct Gahanna OH 43230-6200 Office: Ohio State U Hosps 410 W 10th Ave # 809 Columbus OH 43210-1240

RUBIN, BERNARD, pharmacologist, biomedical writer, consultant; b. N.Y.C., Feb. 15, 1919; s. Charles and Ann (Slutskin) R.; m. Betty R. Schindler, June 15, 1945; children: Stefi Gail, Robert Henry. BA, Bklyn. Coll., 1939; PhD, Yale U., 1951. Rsch. asst. various orgns., N.Y., 1940-48; rsch. pharmacologist E.R. Squibb & Sons, Inc., New Brunswick, N.J., 1951-65; group leader, pharmacology E.R. Squibb & Sons, Inc., Princeton, N.J., 1965-84; cons., licensing Bristol-Myers Squibb Co., Princeton, 1984—. Contbr. over 100 rsch. articles to profl. jours., 1948-85. With U.S. Army, 1942-43. Recipient A.E.C. pre-doctoral fellowship, Washington, 1949-50. Home: 2 Pin Oak Dr Trenton NJ 08648-3134

RUBIN, BRIAN GREGORY, surgeon, educator; b. N.Y.C., June 24, 1958; s. Joel and Lucille (Schutmaat) R.; m. Susan Margaret Brown, Aug. 1, 1987; children: Rachel, Brian, Julia. AB, Colgate U., 1979; MD, U. Vt., 1984. Resident Yale-New Haven Hosp., 1985-89; clin. fellow Washington U. Sch. Medicine, St. Louis, 1990-91, asst. prof. surgery, 1991—. Contbr. articles to profl. jours. Recipient Lifeline Found. award. Mem. ACS (Mo. chpt.), Soc. Clin. Vascular Surgery, Internat. Soc. Cardiovascular Surgery (N.Am. chpt.), Am. Heart Assn. (Stroke coun.), Peripheral Vascular Surg. Soc., Soc. of Vascular Technology, Southwestern Surg. Congress, Assn. Academic Surgery, Am. Venous Forum, Midwestern Vascular Surgery Soc., St. Louis Met. Med. Soc., St. Louis Surg. Soc., St. Louis Vascular Soc. Office: Washington U Sch Medicine 216 S Kings Hwy Saint Louis MO 63110

RUBIN, DAVID ALBERT, physician; b. Longbranch, N.J., Apr. 1, 1950; s. Samuel Harold and Audrey (Arndt) R.; m. Lorna Sacks, Dec. 23, 1973; children: Elizabeth, Geoffrey. AB, Brown U., 1971; MD, Columbia U., 1975. Resident in medicine Columbia-Presbyn. Med. Ctr., N.Y.C., 1975-78; fellow in cardiology Mount Sinai Hosp., N.Y.C., 1978-80; assoc. prof. medicine N.Y. Med. Coll., 1980-94; assoc. prof. clin. medicine Columbia U., 1994—; dir. clin. electrophysiology Westchester Med. Ctr., Valhalla, 1980-94; attending physician Presbyn. Hosp., N.Y.C., 1994—. Contbr. articles to profl. jours. Fellow Am. Coll. Cardiology; mem. N.Am. Soc. of Pacing and Electrophysiology, Phi Beta Kappa, Sigma Xi, Alpha Omega Alpha.

RUBIN, EMANUEL, pathologist, educator; b. N.Y.C., Dec. 5, 1928; s. Jacob and Sophie R.; m. Barbara Kurn, Mar. 27, 1955 (div. 1985); children: Raphael, Jonathan, Daniel, Rebecca; m. Linda A. Haegele, Oct. 13, 1985; children: Ariel, Ethan. B.S., Villanova U., 1950; M.D., Harvard U., 1954. Intern Boston City Hosp., 1954-55; resident Children's Hosp. of Phila., 1957-58; research fellow in pathology Mt. Sinai Hosp., N.Y.C., 1958-62, asst. attending pathologist, 1962-64, assoc. attending pathologist, 1964-68; attending pathologist, dir. hosp. pathology services Mt. Sinai Hosp., 1968-72, pathologist-in-chief, 1972-76; dir. labs. Hahnemann Hosp., Phila., 1977-86; physician-in-chief pathology Thomas Jefferson U. Hosp., 1986—; prof. pathology Mt. Sinai Sch. Medicine, CUNY, 1966-72, Irene Heinz and John LaPorte Givien prof. pathology, chmn. dept., 1972-76; prof., chmn. dept. pathology and lab. medicine Hahnemann U. Sch. Medicine, Phila., 1977-86; Gonzalo Aponte prof. pathology, chmn. dept. pathology and cell biology Thomas Jefferson U. Coll. Medicine, Phila., 1986-94, chmn. dept. pathology, anatomy and cell biology, 1994—; adj. prof. biochemistry and biophysics U. Pa. Sch. Medicine, Phila., 1977-88. Author: (with J.L. Farber) Pathology, 1988, 94; (with K.W. Miller and S.H. Roth) Cellular and Molecular Mechanisms of Alcohol and Anesthetics, 1991; editor-in-chief Lab. Investigation, 1982-96; pathology editor: Fedn. Proc., 1982-86, J. Stud Alc, 1982-94. Served with USN, 1955-57. Mem. ACP, Am. Soc. Investigative Pathology, Internat. Acad. Pathology, U.S.-Can. Acad. Pathology, Am. Soc. Biol. Chemists and Molecular Biology, Am. Assn. Study of Liver Diseases, Am. Gastroent. Assn., Internat. Assn. Study of the Liver, Am. Coll. Toxicology. Home: 1505 Monk Rd Gladwyne PA 19035-1316 Office: 1020 Locust St Philadelphia PA 19107-6731

RUBIN, GUSTAV, orthopedic surgeon, consultant, researcher; b. N.Y.C., May 19, 1913; s. William and Rose (Strongin) R.; m. Mildred Synthia Holtzer, July 4, 1946 (dec. Dec. 1964); m. Esther Rosenberg Partnow, July 23, 1965; 1 stepchild, Michael Partnow. B.S., NYU, 1934; M.D., SUNY-Downstate Med. Ctr., 1939. Diplomate Am. Bd. Orthopedic Surgery. Intern Maimonides Hosp., Bklyn., 1939-41; resident in orthopedics Hosp. for Joint Diseases, N.Y.C., 1941-42, 1946; practice medicine specializing in orthopedics Bklyn., 1947-56; from orthopedic surgeon to dir. clinic VA Clinic, Bklyn., 1956-70; chief Spl. Prosthetic Clinic VA Prosthetics Ctr., N.Y.C., 1970-85, dir. spl. team for amputations, mobility, prosthetics/orthotics, 1985-87, mem. chief med. dir. adv. group on prosthetics services, rehab. research and devel., 1985-87, orthopedic cons., 1970-87, ret., 1987; pvt. practice N.Y.C., 1987—; med. advisor prosthetic rsch. com. N.Y. State DAV, 1970—; lectr. prosthetics NYU, 1972-89; clin. prof. orthopedics N.Y. Coll. Podiatric Medicine, 1980—; orthopedic cons. Internat. Ctr. for the Disabled, N.Y.C., 1987—. Contbr. book chpts., articles to profl. jours.; contbr. article on amputations Ency. for Disability and Rehab., 1995. Capt. U.S. Army, 1943-46. Recipient Nat. Comdrs. award DAV, 1968, Amvets award for outstanding service, 1969, award for Service to Veterans Allied Veterans Meml. Com., 1970, Eastern Paralyzed Veterans Assn. award, 1977, award for Service to Israeli Wounded Israeli Govt. Dept. Rehab., 1981, Cert. of Merit, Nat. Amputation Found., 1972, Olin E. Teague award VA, 1984, Physician of Yr. award Pres.'s Commn. on Employment of People with Disabilities, 1984. Fellow Am. Acad. Orthopedic Surgeons, ACS, Am. Acad. Neurol. and Orthopedic Surgeons; mem. Alumni Assn. Hosp. Joint Disease, Sigma Xi. Jewish. Home: PO Box 572 15 Circle Dr Moorestown NJ 08057 Office: 304 E 24th St New York NY 10010

RUBIN, IRVING, pharmaceutical editor; b. N.Y.C., Apr. 7, 1916; s. Julius and Sadie (Seidman) R.; m. Florence Podolsky, Mar. 12, 1949; children: Joanne, Saul Robert. PhG, Bklyn. Coll. Pharmacy, 1936; BA, Bklyn. Evening Coll., 1948; PharmD (hon.), Mass. Coll. Pharmacy, 1973; DSc (hon.), Union U., 1986; DHL (hon.), L.I. U., 1986; DSc (hon.), St. John's U., 1989. With retail pharmacies N.Y.C., 1933-38; assoc. editor, then mng.

editor Pharmacy, Am. Druggist mag.; editorial dir. Blue Price Book, 1938-60; editor, v.p., publ. dir. Pharmacy Times (and predecessors), Port Washington, N.Y., 1960-86; pub. Pharmacy Times (and predecessors), Port Washington, 1984, editor-in-chief, pub., 1987, editor-at-large, 1988-93; pharmacy cons. Resident and Staff Physician mag., 1978—; mem. consumer interest/health edn. panel U.S. Pharmacopeial Conv., Inc., 1991-95; mem. dean's adv. bd. steering com. Coll. Pharmacy and Allied Health Professions, St. John's U. Author: The Pharmacy Graduate's Career Guide, 1970; editor Wellcome Trends in Pharmacy, 1990-93; editor-in-chief emeritus Pharmacy Times, 1994—; chmn. editl. adv. bd. Glaxo Wellcome Trends in Pharmacy, 1996—. Trustee Arnold and Marie Schwartz Coll. Pharmacy, Bklyn.; del. leader People to People Internat., People's Republic China, 1988, USSR, 1990, Great Britain and Ireland, 1992; also addressed about 150 mems. of the Supreme Soviet in the Kremlin about the Chernobyl disaster, 1990. With AUS, 1941-46, ETO. Decorated Bronze Star; recipient Alumni Achievement award Alumni Assn. Bklyn. Coll. Pharmacy, 1963, Editorial Achievement award Alpha Zeta Omega, 1968, Am. Cancer Soc., 1964, Gold medal Nicholas S. Gesoalde Pharm. Econ. Research Found., 1972, J. Leon Lascoff award Am. Coll. Apothecaries, 1977, Presdl. citation ADA, 1982, Disting. Journalism award Pharm. Soc. State N.Y., 1984, Citation Merit, Nat. Assn. Chain Drug Stores, 1986, Spl. Journalism award Nat. Assn. Chain Drug Stores, 1987; named Man of Yr. Pharmacy, B'nai B'rith, 1973, Man of Yr., Empire State Pharm. Soc., 1985; established Irving Rubin scholarship Arnold and Marie Schwartz Coll. of Pharmacy and Health Scis., L.I. U., 1988. Fellow N.Y. Acad. Pharmacy; mem. Am. Coll. Pharmacists (hon. life), Am. Inst. History of Pharmacy (coun. 1982-88), Nat. Assn. Retail Druggists (award 1987), Am. Pharm. Assn. (prs. N.Y. chpt. 1955-56, ho. of dels., Remington Honor medal 1986), NARD Found. (John W. Dargavel Outstanding Svc. medal 1995), Am. Soc. Hosp. Pharmacists, Am. Found. for Pharm. Edn. (exec. com., bd. dirs. 1988—), Okla. Pharm. Assn. (hon.), Alumni Assn. Bklyn. Coll. Pharmacy (prs. 1946-48), Alpha Zeta Omega, Rho Pi Phi, Delta Sigma Theta, Rho Chi, Kappa Psi, Phi Delta Chi (hon.), Phi Lambda Sigma (hon., Nat. Leadership award 1993). Jewish. Home: 39 Ruxton Rd Great Neck NY 11023-1514 Office: Irv Rubin Assocs 39 Ruxton Rd Great Neck NY 11023-1514

RUBIN, ISADORE RUBIN, medical educator; b. Phila., July 18, 1909; s. Alexander Leon and Ida (Godelsky) R.; m. Ann G.; children, Aug. 17, 1937: Barbara Rottenberg, Carol Newman. MD, U. Pa., 1935. Assoc. prof.ophthalmology U. Pa. Med. Sch., Phila., 1950—. Mem. Ophthalmology Club Phila. Home: Apt 2505 1801 J F Kennedy Blvd Philadelphia PA 19103 Office: 255 S 17th Ste 1509 Philadelphia PA 19103

RUBIN, JAMES MILTON, allergist, educator; b. N.Y.C., Dec. 23, 1935; s. Emanuel and Annette (Tischenkel) R.; m. Phyllis Getz, Oct. 28, 1961; children: Felicia Rubin Engel, Andrea. AB, Columbia U., 1956; MD, N.Y. Med. Coll., 1960. Intern Mt. Sinai, 1960-61; resident Beth Israel, 1962-64, Jewish Hosp. Bklyn., 1964-65; pvt. practice N.Y.C.; chief allergy and immunology Beth Israel Med. Ctr., N.Y.C., 1971—, pres. med. bd., 1993-95; assoc. prof. medicine Mt. Sinai Med. Sch., N.Y.C., 1972-94, Yeshiva U. Albert Einstein Coll. Medicine, N.Y.C., 1994—. Capt. M.C., U.S. Army, 1961-63. Office: Allergy and Asthma Assocs Murray Hill 35 E 35th St New York NY 10016

RUBIN, JEFFREY MICHAEL, psychologist; b. N.Y.C., Sept. 29, 1948; s. Sidney and Lillian (Meyer) R.; m. Felice Berman, Apr. 3, 1971 (dec. July 1988); children: Mitchell, Stephanie; m. Barbara Levine, Mar. 17, 1990. BA, CCNY, 1970, MS in Edn., 1973, advanced cert., 1975; MEd, Columbia U., 1979, EdD, 1986. Cert. sch. psychologist; lic. psychologist, N.Y. Tchr. N.Y.C. Bd. Edn., 1971-74, sch. psychologist in tng., 1974-75, sch. psychologist, 1979; vocat. counselor Fed. Manpower Planning Project, N.Y.C., 1976-77; vocat. rehab. specialist Internat. Rehab. Assn., N.Y.C., 1977-79; sch. psychologist City of Newburgh, N.Y., 1980—; adj. prof. edn. Mt. St. Mary Coll., Newburgh, N.Y.; pvt. practice; cons. for Blind and Visually Impaired, Office of Vocat. Rehab., Devel. Learning Ctr., Craig House Hosp., various pub. and pvt. sch. dists., various state and local depts. of social svcs. Mem. Menninger Found., Topeka, 1990, patron, 1991; trustee Temple Beth Jacob, Newburgh, 1988, pres., 1996, bd. dirs. religious sch., 1988; mem. Family Counseling Svc., Orange County, N.Y., 1981-85. N.Y.C. Dept. of Labor scholar, 1975-77. Mem. APA, Nat. Assn. Sch. Psychologists. Home: 27 Pacer Dr Newburgh NY 12550-3837

RUBIN, JUDITH DIANE, medical educator; b. Pitts., 1944. MD, U. Pa., 1969. Diplomate Am. Bd. Pediatrics, Am. Bd. Preventive Medicine. Intern in pediats. Children's Hosp., Phila., 1969-70; resident in pediats. Pahlavi U., Shiraz, Iran, 1970-71; resident in pediats. U. Md. Hosp., Balt., 1975-76, resident preventive medicine, 1973-77; fellow in pub. health Johns Hopkins Sch. Pub. Health, Balt., 1974-75; assoc. prof. U. Md. Sch. Medicine. Contbr. numerous articles to profl. jours. Fellow Am. Acad. Pediatrics, Am. Coll. Preventive Medicine; mem. Am. Bd. Preventive Medicine (trustee). Office: U Md Sch Med Epid & Prev Medicine 132 E Howard Hall 660 W Redwood St Baltimore MD 21201-1596

RUBIN, MARK STEPHEN, ophthalmic surgeon; b. Syracuse, N.Y., Dec. 22, 1946; s. Max Leon and Ruth (Dworski) R.; m. Patrizia Silvestri, May 1, 1994; 1 child, Jonathan C. BA, SUNY, Buffalo, 1968; MD summa cum laude, U. Bologna, Italy, 1974. Diplomate Am. Bd. Ophthalmology. Intern Deaconess Hosp., Buffalo, 1976; resident in ophthalmology Wettlauffer Eye Clinic, Buffalo, 1979; chief ophthalmology Augsburg (Fed. Republic Germany) Army Hosp., 1979-80; pvt. practice Modena, Italy, 1980-88; head dept. ophthalmology Fla. Health Care Plan, Daytona Beach, 1988-90; pvt. practice Daytona Beach, Fla., 1990—; cons. USAF, Aviano Air Base, Italy, 1982-88; cons. surgeon Hesperia Hosp., Modena, 1980-88. Author: (with others) Extracapsular Cataract Surgery, 1988; translator: Lasers and Microsurgery, 1986, Ophthalmic Lasers, 1986. Pres., bd. dirs. Ctr. for Visually Impaired, Daytona Beach; cons. Volusia County Health Dept. Fellow Am. Coll. Internat. Physicians, Am. Coll. Surgeons; mem. Italian Order Physicians and Surgeons, Internat. Assn. Ocular Surgeons, Am. Acad. Ophthalmology, Am. Soc. Cataract and Refractive Surgery, Fla. Med. Soc., European Soc. Refractive Surgery, Italian Ophthalmologic Soc., Italian Soc. Profl. Ophthalmologists, Volusia County Med. Soc., Cen. Fla. Soc. Ophthalmology, Volusia County Reef Rsch. Dive Team. Jewish. Home: 891 N Beach St Ormond Beach FL 32174-4002 Office: 570 Memorial Cir Ormond Beach FL 32174-5070 also: 402 N Halifax Ave Daytona Beach FL 32118-4016

RUBIN, MARVIN JOSEPH, podiatrist, educator; b. Jersey City, June 27, 1928; s. Eli Lazarus and Doris (Epstein) R.; m. Sherry Carrol, Oct. 1957 (div. July 1959); 1 child, Deidre Solonge; m. Barbara Ruth Goldberg Luers, Aug. 16, 1970; children: Robert Daniel, Evan Brian. D of Podiatric Medicine, Chgo. Coll. Podiatric Medicine, 1949. Diplomate Am. Bd. Podiatric Orthopedics. Intern Foot Clinics of Chgo., 1950; assoc. prof. podiatric medicine Pa. Coll. Podiatry Medicine, Phila., 1968-75; pvt. practice Hasbrouck Heights, N.J., 1953—; staff mem. South Bergen Hosp., 1975-87; asst. attending Hackensack Med. Ctr., 1988-91; mem. podiatry staff Kennedy Meml. Hosp., Saddle Brook, N.J., 1984-93; cons. Bergen County Dept. on Aging, Hackensack, 1968-88, Patient Care mag., 1970, 73; mem. profl. com. United Jewish Cmty. Assn. Developmentally Disabled, Tenafly, N.J., 1988—; resource person Office Minority Pub. Health Svc. U.S. Dept. Health Human Svc., 1989—; mem. planning com. Project LEAP, 1992—, Foot Aware Coalition Am. Diabetes Assn., 1995—; assoc. attending podiatrist Bergen Pines County Hosp., 1996. Vice chmn. bd. govs., 1978, exec. com. Bergen-Passaic Health Systems Agy., Rochelle Park, N.J., 1976-79; bd. dirs. Jewish Family Svcs. Bergen County, Hackensack, 1972-77, Jewish Fedn. Community Svc., Hackensack. Recipient Yr. of Miracles award Friends of Lubavitch of Bergen County, 1990; Appreciation award United Jewish Community Assn. Developmentally Disabled, 1988, 91, United Jewish Community of Bergen County, 1986, United Cerebral Palsy citation, 1961. Fellow Am. Coll. Foot Orthopedics (pres. 1968-69), Am. Assocs. Hosp. Podiatrists; mem. APHA (sects. podiatric health and community health planning and policy devel. Stephen P. Toth award 1991, governing coun. 1994—), Am. Podiatric Med. Soc., N.J. Podiatric Med. Soc. (bd. trustees, pres. No. divsn. 1964-66, Resolution award 1991, Ralph Zigler award 1966), N.J. Pub. Health Assn. (pres. 1992, 93), Young Israel Ft. Lee (bd. dirs., pres. 1979-81, Men of Achievement). Office: 169 Boulevard Hasbrouck Heights NJ 07604-1937

RUBIN, MELVIN LYNNE, ophthalmologist, educator; b. San Francisco, May 10, 1932; s. Morris and May (Gelman) R.; m. Lorna Isen, June 21, 1953; children: Gabrielle, Daniel, Michael. AA, U. Calif., Berkeley, 1951, BS, 1953; MD, U. Calif., San Francisco, 1957; MS, State U. Iowa, 1961. Diplomate Am. Bd. Ophthalmology (bd. dirs. 1977-83, chmn. 1984). Intern U. Calif. Hosp., San Francisco, 1957-58; resident in ophthalmology State U. Iowa, 1958-61; attending surgeon Georgetown U., Washington, 1961-63; asst. prof. surgery U. Fla. Med. Sch., Gainesville, 1963-66; assoc. prof. ophthalmology U. Fla. Med. Sch., 1966-67, prof. ophthalmology, 1967—, chmn. dept. ophthalmology, 1978-95; eminent scholar U. Fla. Med. Sch., Gainesville, 1989—; research cons. Dawson Corp.; ophthalmology cons. VA Hosp., Gainesville. Author: Studies in Physiological Optics, 1965, Fundamentals of Visual Science, 1969, Optics for Clinicians, 1971, 2d edit., 1974, 25th ann. edit., 1995, The Fine Art of Prescribing Glasses, 1978, 2d edit., 1991; editor: Dictionary of Eye Terminology, 1984, 3d edit., 1996, Eye Care Notes, 1989; mem. editorial bd. Survey Ophthalmology; contbr. more than 100 articles to profl. jours. Co-founder Gainesville Assn. Creative Arts, Citizens for Pub. Schs., Inc., ProArteMusica Gainesville, Inc., 1969, pres., 1971-73; mem. Thomas Ctr. Adv. Bd. for the Arts, 1978-84, nat. sci. adv. bd. Helen Keller Eye Rsch. Found., 1989—; bd. dirs. Hippodrome State Theater, 1981-87; bd. trustees U. Fla. Performing ARts Ctr., 1995—, Friends of Photography Ansel Adams Ctr., 1991—. With USPHS, 1961-63. Recipient Best Med. Book for 1978 award Am. Med. Writers Assn., 1979, Shaler Richardson award for svc. to medicine Fla. Soc. Ophthalmology, 1995; M.L. Rubin Ann. Lectureship established in his honor by Fla. State Ophthalmology, 1993. Fellow ACS, Am. Acad. Ophthalmology (sec., dir. 1978-92, pres. 1988, Sr. Honor award 1987. Guest of Honor 1992), Found. Am. Acad. Ophthalmology (bd. trustees, 1988-95, chmn., 1992-94), Joint Commn. on Allied Health Pers. in Ophthalmology (Statesman of Yr. award 1987); mem. Assn. Rsch. in Vision and Ophthalmology (trustee 1973-78, pres. 1979), Retina Soc., Macula Soc., Club Jules Gonin, N.Y. Acad. Sci., Fla. Soc. Ophthalmology, Am. Ophthal. Soc., Pan Am. Soc. Ophthalmology, Ophthalmic Photographers Soc., Alachua County Med. Soc., Fla. Med. Assn., AMA (editorial bd. Archives of Ophthalmology 1975-85), Sigma Xi, Alpha Omega Alpha., Phi Kappa Phi. Office: U Fla Med Ctr PO Box 100284 Gainesville FL 32610-0284

RUBIN, MICHAEL HOTELLING, physician; b. Lansdowne, Pa., Aug. 10, 1944; s. Ernest and Mary Louise (Villon) R.; m. Denorah Kahn, Sept. 4, 1966; children: Nicholas, Jennifer, Benjamin. AB, U. Pa., 1965, MS in Biology, 1966; MD, Med. Coll. Va., 1970. Sect. chief Forsyth Meml. Hosp., Winston-Salem, N.C., 1990-93, divsn. chief medicine, 1994—. Capt. U.S. Army, 1971-73. Liver Disease flelow. 1975-76. Fellow Am. Coll. Physicians, Am. Coll. Gastroenterologyl mem. ASGE, Am. Soc. Study Lime Disease. Home: 2928 Buena Vista Rd Winston Salem NC 27106 Office: Salem Gastroenterology 1830 S Hawthorne Rd Winston Salem NC 27103

RUBIN, PATRICIA, internist; b. Apr. 27, 1962. MD, Wright State U., 1988. Cert. internal medicine. Resident in internal medicine U. Cin., 1988-91; fellow in cardiology U. Hosp., Cleve., 1991; rsch. fellow in cardiology U. Wash. Sch. Medicine, Seattle, 1993—. Recipient Clinician Scientist award Am. Heart Assn., 1995-96. Mem. ACP, AMA, ACC. Office: U Wash Sch Medicine Box 8086 660 S Euclid Seattle WA 63119

RUBIN, ROBERT TERRY, physician, researcher; b. Los Angeles, Aug. 26, 1936; s. Joseph Salem and Lorraine Grace (Baum) R.; m. Lynne Esther Mathews, Mar. 10, 1962 (div. Dec. 1980); children: Deborah, Sharon, Rachel; m. Ada Joan Mickas, Jan. 18, 1985. AB, UCLA. 1958. MD, U. Calif., San Francisco, 1961; PhD, U. So. Calif., Los Angeles, 1977. Diplomate Am. Bd. Psychiatry and Neurology. Asst. prof. psychiatry UCLA, 1965-71, prof. psychiatry, 1972—; prof. Pa. State U., Hershey, 1972-93; Blue Cross of Western Pa. prof. neuroscis., prof. psychiatry, dir. neurosci. rsch. ctr. Allegheny campus Med. Coll. Pa., Hahnemann Sch. Medicine, Allegheny U. Health Scis., Pitts., 1992—; cons. Naval Health Rsch. Ctr., San Diego, 1969-70; mem. Brain Rsch. Inst. UCLA, 1969—; trustee Kinsey Inst. Sex Rsch., Ind. U., 1986-90. Contbr. articles to profl. jours. With USNR, 1967-69. Recipient Rsch. Sci. Devel. awards NIMH, 1972-77, Rsch. Scientist award, 1982, 87, 93. Fellow AAAS, Am. Psychiat. Assn., Am. Coll. Psychiatrists; mem. World Psychiat. Assn. (sec. sect. biol. psychiatry 1983-88, chmn. sect. biol. psychiatry 1988-93), Internat. Soc. Psychoneuroendocrinology (pres. 1984-87). Office: Allegheny Gen Hosp 8 ST Neurosci Rsch Ctr 320 E North Ave Pittsburgh PA 15212-4772

RUBIN, STEPHEN CURTIS, gynecologic oncologist, educator; b. Phila., May 24, 1951; s. Alan and Helen (Metz) R.; m. Anne Loughran, May 30, 1985; children: Michael, Elisabeth. BS, Franklin & Marshall U., 1972; MD, U. Pa., 1976. Diplomate Am. Bd. Ob-Gyn., Nat. Bd. Med. Examiners. Intern in ob.-gyn. Hosp. of Univ. of Pa., Phila., 1976-77, residency in ob.-gyn., 1977-80, fellow in gynecologic oncology, 1980-82; asst. prof. of ob-gyn Med. Coll. of Pa., Phila., 1982-85, dir. surg. gynecology, 1982-85, chief gynecol. oncology, 1984-85; asst. mem. gynecol. staff Meml. Sloan-Kettering Hosp., N.Y.C., 1985-90, assoc. mem., 1990-93; asst. prof. ob-gyn Cornell U. Med. Coll., N.Y.C., 1985-90, assoc. prof., 1990-93; prof. ob-gyn., dir. gynecologic oncology U. Pa., Phila., 1993—. Editor: Ovarian Cancer, Cervical Cancer, Chemotherapy of Gynecologic Cancer; contbr. over 150 articles to profl. publs. Recipient Career Devel. award Am. Cancer Soc., 1987, Boyer award Meml. Sloan-Kettering; Nat. Cancer Inst. grantee, 1991, 96. Mem. ACS, Am. Coll. Ob-Gyn., Am. Soc. Clin. Oncology, Soc. Gynecol. Oncologists (Pres.'s award 1993), Soc. Gynecologic Investigation, Soc. Pelvic Surgeons, Gynecol. Cancer Found. (Karin Smith award 1996). Office: U Pa Med Ctr 3400 Spruce St Philadelphia PA 19104

RUBIN, THEODORE ISAAC, psychiatrist; b. Bklyn., Apr. 11, 1923; s. Nathan and Esther (Marcus) R.; m. Eleanor Katz, June 16, 1946; children: Jeffrey, Trudy, Eugene. B.A., Bklyn. Coll., 1946; M.D., U. Lausanne, Switzerland, 1951; grad., Am. Inst. Psychoanalysis, 1964. Resident psychiatrist Los Angeles VA Hosp., 1953, Rockland (N.Y.) State Hosp., 1954, Bklyn. State Hosp., 1955, Kings County (N.Y.) Hosp., 1956; chief psychiatrist Women's House of Detention, N.Y.C., 1957; mem. faculty Downstate Med. Sch., N.Y. State U., 1957-59; pvt. practice N.Y.C., 1956—; tng. and supervising psychoanalyst Am. Inst. for Psychoanalysis of Karen Horney Clinic and Ctr.; mem. faculty Am. Inst. Psychoanalytic Psychoanalysis, 1962—; pres. emeritus bd. trustees Am. Inst. Psychoanalysis. Author: Jordi, 1960, Lisa and David, 1961, Sweet Daddy, 1963, In The Life, 1964, Platzo and the Mexican Pony Rider, 1965, The Thin Book by a Formerly Fat Psychiatrist, 1966, The 29th Summer, 1966, Cat, 1966, Coming Out, 1967, The Winner's Note Book, 1967, The Angry Book, 1969, Forever Thin, 1970, Emergency Room Diary, 1972, Doctor Rubin Please Make Me Happy, 1974, Shrink, 1974, Compassion and Self-Hate, An Alternative to Despair, 1975, Love Me, Love My Fool, 1976, Reflections in a Goldfish Tank, 1977, Alive and Fat and Thinning in America, 1978, Reconciliations, 1980, Through My Own Eyes, 1982, One to One, Understanding Personal Relationships, 1983, Not to Worry, The American Family Book of Mental Health, 1984, Overcoming Indecisiveness, 1985, Lisa and David, The Story Continues, 1986, Miracle at Bellevue, 1986, Real Love, 1990, Child Potential, 1990, Anti-Semitism: A Disease of the Mind, 1990; mem. editorial bd. Am. Jour. Psychoanalysis; also articles, columns. Served as officer USNR, World War II. Recipient Adolf Meyer award Assn. Improvement Mental Health, 1963. Fellow Am. Acad. Psychoanalysis; mem. N.Y. County Med. Soc., Am. Psychiat. Assn., Assn. Advancement Psychoanalysis, Authors Guild. Office: 219 E 62nd St New York NY 10021-7685

RUBINO, FRANK AUGUST, neurologist; b. Chgo., Feb. 19, 1933; s. Frank and Lena Lorraine (Casello) R.; m. Nancy A. Mulcahey, June, 1962 (div. 1973); children: Dorothy Ann, Patricia Louise. BA in Chemistry, Bradley U., 1955; MD, U. Ill., Chgo., 1962. Cert. Am. Bd. Psychiatry and Neurology (examiner 1972—). Resident in psychiatry Ill. State Psychiat. Inst., Chgo., 1967; resident in neurology Northwestern U., Chgo., 1969; acting chief neurology Hines (Ill.) VA Hosp., 1969-70, chief of neurology, 1970—; asst. prof. Loyola U., Maywood, Ill., 1970-74; assoc. prof. Loyola U., Maywood, 1974-79, prof., assoc. chmn. dept., 1979—; cons. neurology Mayo Clinic, Jacksonville, 1989—. Contbr. numerous articles to profl. jours. Served with U.S. Army, 1956-58, lt. col. Res., 1985—. Named Tchr. of Yr., Loyola U., 1978. Fellow Am. Acad. Neurology; mem. AMA, Am. Epilepsy Soc., Chgo. Neurol. Soc. (sec.-treas. 1976-77, v.p./pres. 1977-79) Alpha Omega Alpha. Clubs: Meadow (Rolling Meadows, Ill.). Home: 1520 Birkdale Lane Ponte Vedra Beach FL 32082 Office: Mayo Clinic Jacksonville 4500 San Pablo Rd Jacksonville FL 32224

RUBINOFF, M. LAWRENCE, physician and surgeon; b. Detroit, Feb. 24, 1936; s. Charles and Margaret Rose (Fleiss) R.; m. Carole Irene Hammond Saslow, June 3, 1960 (div. Apr. 1968); children: Marla Jeanette, Tamara Elise, Danita Beth; m. Virginia Leigh Innes, July 31, 1981; 1 child, Charles Joseph. BS in Math., Wayne State U., 1956; DO, Coll. Osteo. Medicine/Surgery, Des Moines, 1960; MD, U. Calif., Irvine, 1962. Diplomate Am. Bd. Surgery, Am. Bd. Family Practice. Intern Flint (Mich.) Osteo. Hosp., 1960-61; resident in gen. surgery L.A. County Gen. Hosp., L.A., 1961-65; physician and surgeon in pvt. practice Woodland Hills/West Hills, Calif., 1965-85; physician and surgeon Your Family Med. Group, Garden Grove, Calif., 1985—. Lt. col. USAFR, 1981-91. Mem. AMA, Am. Assn. Physician Specialists, Calif. Med. Assn., L.A. County Med. Assn. Office: Your Family Med Group 12828 Harbor Blvd Ste 300 Garden Grove CA 92640

RUBINSTEIN, ARYE, pediatrician, microbiology and immunology educator; b. Tel Aviv, Oct. 2; came to U.S., 1971; s. Reuven and Kathe (Samson) R.; m. Orna Eisenstein, Dec. 7, 1965 (div. 1982); children: Ran, Yair, Avner, Noam; m. Charline Nezri, Dec. 27, 1983; children: Reuven, Rena, Rachel. MD, U. Berne, Switzerland, 1962. Diplomate Am. Bd. Pediatrics; bd. cert. in pediatrics, Israel, Switzerland; Am. Bd. Allergy and Immunology cert. in allergy and immunology. Intern, pediatrics resident, fellow U. Tel Aviv, 1962-67; rsch. assoc. divsn. immunology Med. Sch. Harvard Coll., 1971-73; dir. divsn. immunology and bone marrow transplantation U. Berne, 1969-71; asst. prof. cell biology Albert Einstein Coll. Medicine, Bronx, 1973-80, asst. prof. pediatrics, 1973-77, assoc. prof., 1977-82, assoc. prof. microbiology and immunology, 1981-85, prof. pediatrics, 1982—, prof. microbiology and immunology, 1985—; dir. divsn. clin. allergy and immunology Albert Einstein Coll. Medicine, dir. tng. program for allergy and immunology; dir. divsn. clin. allergy and immunology Montefiore Med. Ctr.; attending pediatrician Bronx Mcpl. Med. Ctr., Hosp. Albert Einstein Coll. Medicine; mem. study sect. on AIDS rsch. NIH. Mem. editl. bd. Annals of Allergy; reviewer New England Jour. Medicine, Jour. for Clin. Investigation, Jour. Pediatrics, Am. Jour. Diseases of Children; contbr. over 165 articles to profl. publs. Lt. armed svcs., Israel, 1955-57. Recipient Lifetime award in Immunology, Humanitarian award DIFFA, Birch Svcs. for Children, Annual award U.S. Asst. Sec. of Health for excellence in AIDS rsch. and treatment, 1990; AIDS Rsch. Program grantee NIH, Bronx. Fellow Am. Acad. Allergy and Immunology, Am. Coll. Allergy & Immunology; mem. N.Y. Acad. Scis., Soc. Pediatric Rsch., The Harvey Soc., Am. Coll. Allergy, Clin. Immunology Soc., Clin. Immunology Soc. Office: Albert Einstein Coll Medicine 1300 Morris Park Ave Bronx NY 10461-1926

RUBIO, PEDRO A., cardiovascular surgeon; b. Mexico City, Dec. 17, 1944; came to U.S., 1970; s. Isaac and Esther; m. Debra Rubio; children: Sandra, Edward, MD, U. Nacional Autónoma de Méx., 1968; MS in Surg. Tech., Pacific Western U., 1981, PhD in Biomed. Tech., 1982. Diplomate Am. Bd. Surgery, Am. Bd. Abdominal Surgery, Am. Bd. Laser Surgery, Am. Bd. Quality Assurance and Utilization Rev. Physicians, Am. Acad. Pain Mgmt., Am. Bd. Forensic Medicine, Am. Bd. Forensic Examiners, Diplomate Mexican bd. Angiology and Vascular Surgery, Infectious Diseases and Gen. Surgery; profl. cert. law enforcement sci., Nat. Com. Profl. Law Enforcement Standards, 1972. Prof. neurology Escuela Normal de Especialización, Secretaría de Educación Publica, Mexico City, 1968-69; asst. instr. dept. surgery Baylor Coll. Medicine, Houston, 1971-76; clin. instr. dept. surgery U. Tex. Med. Sch. Houston, 1978-91; clin. assoc. prof. surgery dept. surgery U. Tex. Med. Sch., Houston, 1991—, prof.l vascular surgery, Nat U. Mexico Med. Sch., clin. supr. psychiatry residency tng. program Tex. Research Inst. Mental Scis., Houston, 1979-85; surgeon, dir. Cardiovascular Surg. Ctr., Houston, 1976-85, Houston Cardiovascular Inst., 1985-89, Laser Gallbladder Surgery Ctr. of Houston, 1990-94; course dir. Laser Tng. Inst., 1991—, Houston Laser Inst., 1989-91; chmn. surgery dept. Med. Ctr. Hosp., Houston, 1978-94, chmn. emeritus dept. surgery Med. Ctr. Hosp., Houston, 1994—; nat. med. dir. Nat. Assn. Preferred Providers, Houston, 1995—, pres. CEO, chmn., bd. Nat. Assn., Preferred Providers, Houston, 1996—; research projects with FDA, NCI, HEW, VA ; pres. exec. com. Houston Chamber Singers, 1982-83. Decorated Palms Honor Cross (hon.), Mex. Army; recipient Recognition diploma bachelor's class Universidad Nacional Autonoma de Mex., 1961, Facultad de Medicina, 1966; named Outstanding Surg. Intern, Baylor Coll. Medicine, 1970-71.Doctor of Humane Letters Loudou Inst. Applied Rsch., Fellow Academia de Ciencias Medicas del Instituto Mexicana de Cultura, Academia Mexicana de Cirugia, ACS (Best Paper award South Tex. chpt. 1976), Am. Coll. Angiology, Am. Coll. Chest Physicians, Assn. Surgeons India (hon.), Soc. Surgeons Nepal (hon.), Internat. Coll. Surgeons (hon.), Knight Grand Cross, The Sovereign and Military Order of Saint John of Jerusalem, Houston Acad. Medicine. Internat. Coll. Angiology, Internat. Coll. Surgeons (N.Am. fedn. sec. 1991-92, pres. U.S. sect. 1988-89, pres. Tex. div. 1983-85, world pres.-elect 1993-94, world pres. 1995, historian 1985-94, chmn. membership com. U.S. sect. 1984-86, 3d pl. sci. motion picture 1980), Israel Med. Assn. USA, Royal Soc. Medicine, Am. Heart Assn. (stroke council), Am. Geriatrics Soc., AMA (Recognition award 1972-95), Am. Trauma Soc., Denton A. Cooley Cardiovascular Soc., Harris County (Tex.) Med. Soc., Houston Surg. Soc. (1st pl. essay 1973, 75), Internat. Assn. Study Lung Cancer, Internat. Cardiovascular Soc., Internat. Soc. Laser Medicine and Surgery, Sociedad Mexicana de Angiologia (1st pl. nat. essay contest 1974), Soc. Internat. Chirurgie, Soc. Am. Gastrointestinal Endoscopic Surgeons, Soc. Laparoendoscopic Surgeons, Soc. for Minimally Invasive Surgery, Southwestern Surg. Congress, Tex. Med. Assn., World Med. Assn., Internat. Coll. Surgeons (world pres.), Phi Beta Delta. Lodge: Rosicrucian. Author: Atlas of Angioaccess Surgery, 1983; Atlas of Stapling Techniques, 1986; contbr. 260 sci. articles to publs.; patentee med. instrumentation. Office: 20682 SweetGlen Dr Porter TX 77365-6385

RUBIS, LORRAINE JOYCE, surgeon; b. Mpls., Aug. 23, 1943; m. Cornelius S. Franckle Jr., Sept. 14, 1991. BA, U. Minn., 1964, MD, 1968. Intern Cleve. Metro Gen. Hosp., 1968-69; gen. surg. resident Case Western Res. U. Hosps., Cleve., 1969-73; thoracic surgery resident U. Toronto (Can.) Hosps., 1973-76; pvt. practice Cardiovascular Thoracic Surgery, Inc., Huntington, W.Va., 1980-92, St. Petersburg, Fla., 1992—; assoc. clin. prof. surgery Marshall U., Huntington, 1979-91; asst. clin. prof. surgery U. South Fla., Tampa, 1996. Home: 106 4th St E Tierra Verde FL 33715 Office: 5800 49th St N Saint Petersburg FL 33709

RUBNITZ, MYRON ETHAN, pathologist, educator; b. Omaha, Mar. 2, 1924; s. Abraham Srol and Esther Molly (Jonich) R.; m. Susan Belle Block, Feb. 9, 1952; children: Mary Ly Rubnitz Roffe, Peter, Thomas (dec.), Robert. BSc, U. Nebr., 1945; MD, U. Nebr., Omaha, 1947. Diplomate Am. Bd. Pathology. Intern Mt. Sinai Hosp., Cleve., 1947-48; fellow Mt. Sinai Hosp., N.Y.C., 1948-49; resident in pathology Michael Reese Hosp., Chgo., 1949-51; pathologist VA Hosp., Hines, Ill., 1953-56, chief labs., 1956-93, cons., 1993—; assoc. prof. pathology Loyola U. Med. Sch., Maywood, Ill., 1963-70, prof., 1970—; adj. prof. Ill. State U., Normal, 1979—, Coll. St. Francis, Joliet, Ill., 1989—, Ea. Ill. U. Charleston, 1991—, Western Ill. U., Macomb, 1991—; adj. assoc. prof. No. Ill. U., DeKalb, 1979-92; clin. instr. Augustana Coll., Rock Island, Ill., 1991—. Chmn. candidates com. Village Caucus, Winnteka, Ill., 1969-70; bd. dirs. Chgo. Commons Assn., 1968—; mem. New Trier High Sch. Caucus, Winnetka, 1972-74. With AUS, 1943-46, PTO; lst lt. M.C., U.S. Army, 1951-53. Fellow Am. Soc. Clin. Pathologists, Coll. Am. Pathologists; mem. Internat. Acad. Pathology, Assn. VA Pathologists (pres. 1982-84), Chgo. Pathology Soc., Lake Shore Country Club (Glencoe, Ill.), North Shore Racquet Club, Mich. Shores Club (Wilmette, Ill.). Republican. Jewish.

RUBY, STEPHEN GERARD, pathologist; b. Detroit, July 4, 1956. BS in Biology, Wayne State U., 1977, MD, 1981. Diplomate Nat. Bd. Med. Examiners Anatomic and Clin. Pathology; med. lic., Mich., Ill. Resident in pathology St. John Hosp., Detroit, 1981-85, chief resident, 1984-85; fellow in surg. pathology William Beaumont Hosp., Royal Oak, Mich., 1985-86; mem. staff in pathology Hinsdale (Ill.) Hosp., 1986—, med. dir. surg. pathology and molecular pathology, 1986—, asst. med. dir. cytology, 1987—, v.p. DuPage Pathology Assocs., S.C., 1988—, med. dir. anatomic pathology, 1989—; presenter in field. Contbr. articles to Clin. Genet., Clin. Chemist, Am. Jour. Pathology, Ann. Clin.Lab. Sci, Am. Jour. Clin. Pathology; abstract pubs. reviewed: reviewer AMA Drug Evaluations Ann., 1991. Mem. AAAS, Internat. Acad. Pathologists, Internat. Soc. Gynecol. Pathologists, Am. Soc. Clin. Pathologists, Coll. Am. Pathologists, Ill. Soc. Pathology, Chgo. Pathology Soc. Office: Hinsdale Hosp Dept Pathology 120 N Oak St Hinsdale IL 60521-3829

RUBY, STEVEN TODD, surgeon; b. Boston, May 11, 1952; s. Norman I. and Lois Ruby; m. Gaile Marie Barresi; children: Matthew, Jordan. BA, Brandeis U., 1974; MD, Columbia U., 1978. Diplomate Am. Bd. Surgery, Sub-bd. Vascular Surgery. Intern, resident Columbia Presbyn. Med. Ctr., N.Y.C., 1978-83; John Homans fellow in vascular surgery Brigham and Women's Hosp., Boston, 1983-84; asst. prof. surgery Columbia U., N.Y.C., 1984-86; asst. prof. surgery U. Conn., Farmington, 1987-91, assoc. prof., 1991—. Recipient Whipple award Columbia U., 1978. Mem. Alpha Omega Alpha. Hme: 77 Beverly Dr Avon CT 06001 Office: U Conn Health Ctr 263 Farmington Ave Farmington CT 06032

RUCH, TERESA DAHLMAN, neurosurgeon; b. Cin., Apr. 25, 1949; m. Edward Ruch, Dec. 27, 1969; children: Christopher, Leslie, Paul, Leah. BA, Miami U., Oxford, Ohio, 1971; MD, Case Western Res. U., 1979. Diplomate Am. Bd. Neurol. Surgery. Lab technician, spl. chemistry Good Samaritan Hosp., Dayton, Ohio, 1971; lab technician, spl. chemistry Christ Hosp., Cin., 1972; lab technician, pediatric chemistry Rainbow Babies & Childrens Hosp., Cleve., 1972-75; rsch. technician, pediatric metabolism Rainbow Babies & Childrens Hosp., 1975-79; intern, gen. surgery Univ. Hosps., Cleve., 1979-80; resident in neurol. surgery Univ. Hosps., 1980-86; pvt. practice Northeastern Ohio Neurol. Assocs., Cleve., 1986—; chief neurosurgery Meridia Hillcrest Hosp., Mayfield Heights, Ohio, 1991—. Co-contbr. articles to profl. jours. Mem. AMA, Ohio State Med. Assn., Am. Assn. Neurol. Surgeons, Congress Neurol. Surgeons, Ohio State Neurol. Soc., Northeast Ohio Neurol. Soc. (treas. 1988—), Alpha Omega Alpha. Office: Northeastern Ohio Neurosurg Assn 34900 Chardon Rd Ste 107 Willoughby OH 44094

RUCHMAN, ISAAC, microbiologist; b. N.Y.C., July 2, 1909; s. Nathan Leib and Rose Naomi (Schaffro) R.; m. Marietta Duke, Sept. 6, 1940; 1 child, Reed. BS, CUNY, 1937; MS, U. Cin., 1941, PhD, 1944. Lab technician Rockefeller Inst., N.Y.C., 1930-39; grad. asst. U. Cin., 1939-44; asst. prof. U. Cin. Coll. of Medicine, 1946-55; head microbiology Wm. S. Merrell Co., Cin., 1955-63; prof. U. Ky., Lexington, 1963-74, adj. prof., 1976-86; adj. prof. Transylvania U., Lexington, 1976—. Contbr. articles to profl. jours. Grantee NIH, Lederle. Mem. Optimist, Sigma Xi, Am. Soc. Mircrobiologists, Am. Acad. Microbiologists, Am. Bd. Microbiologists, Am. Assn. Immunologists, Soc. Exptl. Biology & Medicine. Home: 365 Garden Rd Lexington KY 40502-2417

RUCKDESCHEL, JOHN CHARLES, oncologist, researcher; b. Newport, R.I., Jan. 5, 1946; s. John Adam and Rita Frances (Riley) R.; m. Maureen Cassidy, June 26, 1986; children: Daniel, Emily. BSc, Rensselaer Poly. Inst., 1967; MD, Albany Med. Coll., 1971. Intern Johns Hopkins U., Balt., 1971-72; fellow Nat. Cancer Inst., Balt., 1972-75; resident Beth Israel Hosp., Boston, 1975-76; asst. prof. medicine Albany (N.Y.) Med. Coll., 1976-79, assoc. prof. medicine, 1979-85, prof. medicine, 1985-91, head div. med. oncology, 1987-91, dir. joint ctr. for cancer and blood disorders, 1989-91; dir., chief exec. officer H. Lee Moffitt Cancer Ctr. and Rsch. Inst., Tampa, 1991—; prof. Univ. South Fla. Coll. Medicine, 1991—. Co-editor: (textbook) Thoracic Oncology, 1989, 95; contbr. articles to med. jours. Recipient Physicians Recognition award AMA, 1994. Fellow Am. Coll. Physicians, Am. Coll. Chest Physicians; mem. Am. Assn. for Cancer Rsch., Am. Soc. Clin. Oncology, Am. coll. Physician Execs., Internat. Assn. for the Study of Lung Cancer, Alpha Omega Alpha. Home: 2506 Mistic Point Way Tampa FL 33611-5061 Office: H Lee Moffitt Cancer Ctr 12902 Magnolia Dr Tampa FL 33612-9416

RUCKMAN, ROGER NORRIS, pediatric cardiologist; b. Washington, Dec. 15, 1944; s. Norris Elliott and Eugenia (Campbell) R.; m. Kathleen Anne Smith; children: Robert, Karen, Stephen, Jonathan. BA in Chemistry, Williams Coll., Williamstown, Mass., 1966; MD, U. Va., 1970. Intern Peter Bent Brigham Hosp., 1970-71; resident Med. Ctr. Hosp. of Vermont, 1973-75; fellow in cardiology Children's Hosp., Boston, 1975-77; asst. prof. pediatrics U. Nebr., Omaha, 1977-79; asst. prof. pediatrics George Washington U., Washington, 1980-82, assoc. prof. pediatrics, 1982-90, prof. pediatrics, 1990—; pediatric cardiologist Children's Hosp. Nat. Med. Ctr., Washington, 1980—, chmn. cardiology, 1986-89. Contbr. articles to profl. jours. Served to capt. U.S. Army, 1971-73. Recipient Disting. Service award, Am.-Korea Found., 1972; NIH grantee, 1982—. Fellow Am. Acad. Pediatrics, Am. Coll. Cardiology; mem. Am. Heart Assn., Teratology Soc., Soc. Pediatric Research. Republican. Presbyterian. Club: University (Washington). Office: CNMC Dept Cardiology 111 Michigan Ave NW Washington DC 20010-2970

RUDAN, VINCENT THADDEUS, nursing administrator; b. N.Y.C., June 19, 1955; s. Vincent and Vera (Palma) R. BSN, SUNY, Stony Brook, 1977; MA, NYU, 1979; postgrad., Villanova U., 1984-85. RN, N.Y., N.J.; CNAA. Staff nurse N.Y. Hosp., N.Y.C., 1977-79; asst. dir. nursing Downstate Med. Ctr., Bklyn., 1979-80; instr. Rutgers U., Newark, N.J., 1980-83; asst. dir. nursing Manhattan Eye, Ear & Throat Hosp., N.Y.C., 1983-84, assoc. dir nursing, 1984-94, dir. nursing/patient care svcs., 1994—. Mem. ANA, Am. Orgn. Nurse Execs., Sigma Theta Tau, Kappa Delta Pi. Office: Manhattan Eye Ear Throat 210 E 64th St New York NY 10021-7480

RUDBERG, MARK AARON, internist, medical researcher. BS, U. Wis., Milw., 1981; MD, Med. Coll. Wis., Milw., 1984; MPH, Boston U., 1989. Diplomate Am. Bd. Internal Medicine with added qualification in geriatrics. Intern in medicine Evans Meml. Dept. Clin. Rsch. Dept. Medicine Boston U. Med. Ctr., 1984-85, resident in medicine, 1985-87, fellow in geriatrics, 1987-89; asst. prof. medicine Pritzker Sch. Medicine, Divsn. Biol. Scis., U. Chgo., 1989-96; attending physician Oak Park (Ill.) Hosp., 1989-91; med. dir. Montgomery Place, Chgo., 1991-94; assoc. faculty Com. on Human Nutrition/Nutritional Biology U. Chgo., 1993—, faculty assoc. Ctr. Health Policy Rsch., 1993—, tng. faculty com. on demographic tng. Population Rsch. Ctr., 1994—, rsch. assoc., 1994—, assoc. prof. medicine Pritzker Sch. Medicine, 1996—; lectr. in field. Contbr. numerous articles and abstracts to profl. jours.; reviewer Jour. of AMA, Gerontol. Soc. Am., Annals of Internal Medicine, Am. Jour. Medicine, Alzheimer's Assn., Nursing Home Medicine, Jour. of Am. geriatrics Soc., Jour. Aging and Health, Ency. of Bioethics, Jour. of Gerontology: Med. Scis. Grantee NIA, 1989-90, 93-95, 94-95, 94—, John A. Hartford Found., 1990-91, 95, NIDDK and Diabetes Rsch. and Tng. Ctr. of U. Chgo., 1991-93, U. Chgo. Home Health Care, 1993-94, 95-96, NICHD, 1996-96, Population Rsch. Ctr., U. Chgo. and NIA, 1996. Mem. Am. Geriatrics Soc. (New Investigator award 1994, ethics com. 1995—), Ctrl. Soc. for Clin. Rsch. (planning com. mem. geriatrics coun. 1996), Soc. Gen. Internal Medicine (mentor for One-on-One mentoring program 1995), Gerontol. Soc. Am. (co-chmn. epidemiology interest group 1994—), Am. Med. Dirs. Assn. (ho. of dels. 1994—, abstract chmn. nat. meeting 1994), Am. Diabetes Assn. (task force on feasibility for recognizing diabetes treatment program 1991-93), Internat. Network on Health Expectancy, The Gray Panthers (bd. dirs. Chgo. chpt. 1990-91), Alpha Omega Alpha. Office: U Chgo Dept Med, Sect Gen Internal Med 5841 S Maryland Ave Chicago IL 60637-1463 Office: University of Chicago Dept Medicine 5841 S Maryland Ave MC6098 Chicago IL 60637*

RUDD, EUGENE GREGORY, obstetrician and gynecologist, educator; b. Tallahassee, May 29, 1951; s. Herbert Eugene and Esther Elizabeth (Till) R.; m. Brenda Caddell, Dec. 18, 1976; children: Jonathan, Deborah, Joshua, David. BS, U. Ga., 1973; MD, U. S.C., 1977; ob/gyn. residency program, U.S. Army, Honolulu, 1981. Diplomate Am. Bd. Ob-Gyn. Assoc. clin. prof. Tex. Tech. U., El Paso; bd. dirs. Marion (N.C.) Christian Acad.; pvt. practice Marion. Maj. U.S. Army, 1977-85. Mem. Am. Coll. Ob-gyn., Christian Med. & Dental Soc. (assoc. dir.), Alpha Omega Alpha. Home: 305 Glenway Rd Bristol TN 37620

RUDDLE, NANCY HARTMAN, microbiology educator; b. St. Louis, Apr. 3, 1940; d. David Eugene and Josephine (Odell) Hartman; m. Francis Hugh Ruddle, Aug. 1, 1964; children: Kathlyn, Amy. BA, Mt. Holyoke Coll., 1962; PhD, Yale U., 1968. Rsch. assoc. Yale U., New Haven, 1968-71, postdoctoral fellow, 1971-74, rsch. assoc., 1974-75, asst. prof., 1975-80, assoc. prof., 1980-91, prof. microbiology, 1991—, head microbiology div., 1990—; panel mem. Am. Cancer Soc., 1987-91; study sect. mem. NIH, 1991—. Contbr. over 100 articles to profl. jurs. Am. Cancer Soc. postdoctoral fellow, Damon Runyon postdoctoral fellow; recipient Am. Cancer Soc. Faculty Rsch. award; NIH grantee, Am. Cancer Soc. grantee, others. Office: Yale Univ Sch Medicine 60 College St New Haven CT 06510-3210

RUDE, GILBERT ARTHUR, physician; b. Columbus, Nebr., May 4, 1951; s. Gilbert Otis and Dorothy Dean (Morlan) R.; m. Belinda Jane Rude; children: Michael, Matthew. BA, Kearney State Coll.; MD, U. Nebr. Diplomate Am. Bd. Family Practice. Ptnr. Family Practice Assocs., P.C., Kearney, Nebr., 1979—. Bd. dirs. Good Samaritan Hosp., Kearney, 1987, Sentinel Health Care, Kearney, 1993. Mem. AMA, AAFA, Shriners (Ft. Kearney noble 1993—). Office: Family Practice Assocs PC 3907 Sixth Ave Kearney NE 68847

RUDERMAN, ANNE TULLY, hypnoanalyst; b. Wilmington, Del., June 26, 1927; d. James Joseph and Adeline (Van Buren) Tully; BA, Antioch Coll., 1948; postgrad. Yale U., 1949-50; MSW, Smith Coll., 1952; m. S.G. Ruderman, July 23, 1947; children: James Michael, Dan Tully. Diplomate Nat. Assn. Social Workers. Clin. social work psychotherapist Westchester County Divsn. Mental Hygiene, 1952-54; pvt. practice psychotherapy, 1954—; sr. staff therapist, practicum supr. Morton Prince Ctr., Inst. Rsch. in Hypnosis, N.Y.C., 1970-77; co-founder, co-dir. Cancer Counseling and Tng. Ctr. of Westchester, Scarsdale, N.Y., 1977—, clin. dir. Somamente group; disting. lectr., guest lectr. orgns., colls. and univs. Cert. in hypnotherapy and hypnoanalysis Inst. Rsch. in Hypnosis; cert. clin. social worker N.Y.; lic. social worker, N.J., Conn.; cert. masterpractitioner in Neuro-Linguistic Programming; cert. Acad. Cert. Social Workers; cert. Nat. Bd. Examiners. Fellow Soc. Clin. Social Work Psychotherapists; mem. Soc. Clin. and Exptl. Hypnosis, Internat. Soc. Hypnosis, Am. Soc. Clin. Hypnosis (approved cons.), N.Y. Soc. Ericksonian Psychotherapy and Hypnosis (bd. dirs., past pres., sr. faculty tng. inst.). Home and Office: 29 Quentin Rd Scarsdale NY 10583-4518

RUDERMAN, JEANNE WENDY, pediatrician, neonatologist; b. Los Angeles, June 30, 1953; d. George Lawrence and Ruth (Bornstein) Ruderman. B.S. in Biol. Scis., U. So. Calif., 1974; M.D., UCLA, 1978. Diplomate Am. Bd. Pediatrics. Intern, resident in pediatrics Los Angeles County-U. So. Calif. Med. Ctr., Los Angeles, 1978-81; fellow in neonatology Cedars-Sinai Med. Ctr., Los Angeles, 1981-83, attending staff neonatologist, 1983-91; asst. prof. pediatrics UCLA Sch. Medicine, 1984-91; attending staff neonatologist Encino-Tarzana (Calif.) Regional Med. Ctr., 1991—; assoc. prof. pediatrics U. Calif., Irvine, 1991—. Contbr. articles to med. jours. Fellow Am. Acad. Pediatrics; mem. We. Soc. Pediatric Rsch., Calif. Perinatal Assn., Phi Beta Kappa. Office: Encino-Tarzana Regional Med Ctr Dept Neonatology 18321 Clark St Tarzana CA 91356-3501

RUDERMAN, ROBERT, internist, hematologist; b. Bklyn., Aug. 1, 1938; s. Israel Irving and Rebecca (Kochman) R.; m. Elaine Savatsky, June 9, 1962; children—Mindy Lisa, Marchelle Ann. BS cum laude in Chemistry Bklyn. Coll., 1959; MD, SUNY-Syracuse, 1963. Diplomate Am. Bd. Internal Medicine. Intern Syracuse Med. Ctr. Hosp., N.Y., 1963-64; resident Kings County Hosp. Ctr., Bklyn., 1964-65, V.A. Hosp., Washington, 1967-69; fellow hematology, 1969-70; practice medicine specializing in internal medicine-hematology College Park, Md., 1970-84, Riverdale, 1984—; chief, div. hematology-oncology Med. Ctr. of Prince George Gen. Hosp., Cheverly, Md, 1974-86; v.p. Prince George Found. Med. Care, Landover, Md., 1981-84, pres. 1984-87; chmn. utilization rev. dept. Leland Meml. Hosp., Riverdale, Md., 1986-93; pres. Nat. Frozen Blood Svcs., Inc., 1986-87; med. dir. utilization mgmt. Dr.'s Community Hosp., Lanham, Md., 1992-94, treas., 1993-95. Mem. steering com. ARC (Prince George chpt.) Hyattsville, Md., 1983-87, 94; bd. dirs. Mishkan Torah Synagogue, Greenbelt, Md., 1980; Capt., AUS, 1965-67. Army Commendation medal; recipient Gubernatorial citation State of Md., 1990, Exec. citation Prince George's County, 1990, Citation Senate of State of Md., 1990; N.Y. State Regents scholar, 1955. Mem. Prince George County Med. Soc. (bd. dirs. 1984, treas. 1986, sec. 1987, pres. elect 1988, pres. 1989-90), Med. Surg. Faculty Md., Am. Physician Fellowship, Am. Soc. Internal Med., D.C. Soc. Internal Medicine, Jaycees, Upsilon Lambda Phi (nat. sec. 1956-58, reg. pres. 1955-56). Democrat. Jewish. Club: Prospect Bay Yacht (commodore 1986-87, past-commodore 1988). Office: 6510 Kenilworth Ave Riverdale MD 20737-1339

RUDERT, CYNTHIA SUE, gastroenterologist; b. Cin., Mar. 17, 1955; d. John Wayne and Hilda Wanda (Loftus) R.; children: Ronald Lamar Hilley II, Henry Byron Hilley. BS with honors, U. Ky., 1975; MD, U. Louisville, 1979. Diplomate Am. Bd. Internal Medicine, Am. Bd. Gastroenterology. Intern internal medicine Emory U., Atlanta, 1979-80, resident, 1980-82, fellow gastroenterology, 1982-84, asst. prof. medicine, Emory U., Atlanta, 1984-91; guest speaker Alcoholism Conf., Kanasawa, Japan, 1987; nat. and internat. speaker in gastroenterology; author: Medicine for the Practicing Physician, 3rd rev. edition, 1991, (chpts.) Acute Pancreatitis, Chronic Pancreatitis, Ischaemic Hepatitis, Rudert, C.S. Alcohol Related Symptons. Recipient Newburg award U. Louisville, 1979. Fellow ACP; mem. AMA, Am. Med. Women's Assn., Am. Assn. for Study Liver Disease, Am. Gastroent. Assn., Am. Assn. for Study Liver Diseases, So. Med. Assn., Am. Liver Found., Am. Acad. Scis., Ga. Gastroent. Soc., Med. Assn. Ga., Med. Assn. Atlanta, Atlanta Women's Med. Alliance (founder). Office: 2500 Hospital Blvd Ste 210 Roswell GA 30076-4918

RUDIN, ROBERT LAWRENCE, internist; b. Phila., Dec. 18, 1956; s. Norman and Elinor (Klass) R. BA, U. Pa., 1980; MD, Hahnemann U., 1986. Intern, resident in pediatrics William Beaumont Army Med. Ctr., Fort Bliss, Tex., 1986-88; gen. med. officer U.S. Army, 1989-93; intern, resident internal medicine Grad. Hosp., Phila., 1993—. Mem. AMA, Am. Coll. Physicians, Pa. Med. Soc.

RUDIS, GARY KEITH, medical equipment company executive; b. Lawrence, Mass., May 2, 1952; s. Alphonse and Norma Irene (Hines) R.; m. Linda Denise Martel, July 24, 1971; children: Keith, Todd, Glen, Alex. AS with high honors, No. Essex Coll., Haverhill, Mass., 1974; BS with high honors, Franklin Pierce Coll., Rindge, N.H., 1990. Registered respiratory therapist, Mass. Regional mgr. Inhalation Therapy Svcs., Lexington, Mass., 1974-83; pres., owner Home Care Specialists, Inc., Haverhill, Mass., 1979—; bd. dirs. No. Essex Respiratory Adv. Com., Haverhill, 1986—; mem. Nat. Bd. Respiratory Therapy, 1974-90. Grantee Mass. Soc. Respiratory Therapists, 1976; recipient Innovator award Greater Haverhill C. of C. Mem. Nat. Assn. Med. Equipment Suppliers, New Eng. Med. Equipment Dealers, Alpha Sigma Lambda. Democrat. Home: 21 Singing Wood Dr Haverhill MA 01830-1452

RUDISILL, GEORGE DANIEL, physical therapist; b. Gettysburg, Pa., Apr. 9, 1961; s. Lester Elvin and Cleone Larue (Hohman) R.; m. Joanna Joyce Moyer, Aug. 10, 1985; children: Daniel Wayne, Hanna Joyce, Weston George. BA in Biology, Susquehana U., Selinsgrove, Pa., 1983; BS in Phys. Therapy, Thomas Jefferson U., Phila., 1983-85. Lic. phys. therapist, Pa. Staff phys. therapist Lancaster (Pa.) Gen. Hosp., 1985-86, Phys. Therapy Svcs. P.C., Lancaster, 1986-87, Hershey Phys. Therapy Svcs., Lancaster, 1987-88, Willow Lakes Health Ctr., Willow Street, Pa., 1988-96, Genesis Elder Care-Maple Farm Nursing Ctr., Akron, Pa., 1996—. Mem. Am. Phys. Therapy Assn., Am. Running and Fitness Assn., Pa. Phys. Therapy Assn. Republican. Lutheran. Home: 329 Main St Akron PA 17501-1212 Office: Maple Farm Nursing Ctr 204 Oak St Akron PA 17501

RUDKIN, GEORGE HENRY, plastic surgeon; b. Wilmington, Del., July 29, 1964; s. George Osborne and Helene Rita (De Sanctis) R.; m. Jill Christine Brittenham, Sept. 30, 1995. BA, Johns Hopkins U., 1986; MD, Columbia U., 1990. Resident in gen. surgery UCLA Med. Ctr., 1990-96, resident in plastic surgery, 1996—. Mem. Alpha Omega Alpha, Phi Beta Kappa. Office: UCLA Med Ctr 10833 Le Conte Ave Los Angeles CA 90024

RUDLAND, PHILIP SPENCER, biochemist, educator; b. Birmingham, Eng., Jan. 2, 1946; s. Frederick William and Margaret Doms (Phillips) R.; m. Suzete de Almeida Silva, July 24, 1993. BA in Natural Scis. 1st class, Cambridge (Eng.) U., 1966, BA in Chemistry 1st class, 1967, PhD in Molecular Biology, 1971, MA (hon.), 1986. Postgrad. fellow unit molecular biology Med. Rsch. Ctr., Cambridge, 1970-71; Helen Hay Whitney fellow Salk Inst., La Jolla, Calif., 1971-73; staff mem. Imperial Cancer Rsch. Fund, London, 1974-79; head dept. cell and molecular biology Ludwig Inst. for Cancer Rsch., London, 1979-86; prof. biochemistry U. Liverpool, Eng., 1987—, head dept. biochemistry, 1988-90, head cancer and polio rsch. fund labs., 1986—; dir. Cancer and Polio Rsch. Fund, Wirral, U.K., 1994—; chmn. sci. adv. com. Clatterbridge Cancer Rsch. Trust, U.K., 1993—. Author: Medical Perspectives in Cancer Research, 1985; editor: Mammary Development and Cancer, 1996; contbr. articles to profl. publs. Gonville and Caius Coll. scholar, 1966, Salteleis Inst. Indsl. Chemistry scholar, 1967-71. Fellow Royal Soc. Sci. and Arts, Royal Coll. Pathologists, Inst. Biology. Mem. Ch. of England. Office: U Liverpool Dept Biochem, PO Box 147, Liverpool L69 3BX, England

RUDLEY, LLOYD DAVE, psychiatrist; b. Phila., Aug. 7, 1955; s. John Frank and Ida (Rthmann) R. BA summa cum laude, U. Pa., 1977; MD, Hahnemann U., 198l. Diplomate Am. Bd. Psychiatry and Neurology. Resident in psychiatry Med. Coll. Pa., Phila., 198l-85; pvt. practice Phila., 1985—, Elmer, N.J., 1986—; staff psychiatrist N.E. Community Mental Health Ctr., Phila., 1985-87, Counseling Program N.J., Marlton, 1987-88; attending psychiatrist Hosp. U. Pa., Phila., 1985—; attending psychiatrist Inst. of Pa. Hosp., Phila. Psychiat. Ctr.; cons. psychiatrist Horizon Ho, Phila, 1989—; mem. med. adv. bd. Juvenile Diabetes Found., Phila., 1986—. Mem. jr. com. Scheie Eye Inst., Phila., 1985—. Mem. AMA, Am. Psychiat. Assn., Pa. Psychiat. Soc., Pa. Med. Soc., Philadelphia County Med. Soc. (mental health subcom. 1988—), Phi Beta Kappa. Republican. Office: Inst of Pa Hosp Lll N 49th # 49th St Philadelphia PA 19139

RUDNICK, ELLEN AVA, health care executive; b. New Haven; d. Harold and C. Vivian (Soybel) R.; children from previous marriage: Sarah, Noah; m. Paul W. Earle. BA, Vassar Coll., 1972; MBA, U. Chgo., 1973. Sr. fin. analyst Quaker Oats, Chgo., 1973-75; various positions Baxter Internat., Deerfield, Ill., 1975-80, dir. planning, 1980-83, corp. v.p., 1985-1990; pres. Baxter Mgmt. Svcs., Deerfield, 1983-1990, HCIA, Balt., 1990-92, CEO Advs., Northbrook, Ill., 1992—; prin., chmn. Pacific Biometrics, Irvine, Calif., 1993—; bd. dirs. NCCI. Chief crusader Met. Chgo. United Way, 1982-85; pres. coun. Nat. Coll. Edn., Evanston, Ill., 1983—; cir. of friends Chgo. YMCA, 1985-89; bd. dirs. Highland Park Hosp., 1990—, NCCI. Mem. Chgo. Network, Econs. Club Chgo. (officer, bd. dirs.). Office: CEO Advs 255 Revere Dr Ste 111 Northbrook IL 60062-1595

RUDNICKI, MAREK, surgeon; b. Łańcut, Poland, Jan. 2, 1948; came to U.S., 1987; s. Stanisław Rudnicki and Aniela Wawrzkiewicz; m. Joanna, May 27, 1972; children; Anna Maria, Jacek Damian. MD, Silesian Sch. of Medicine, Katowice, Poland, 1972, PhD, 1980, D.Sc., 1993. Lic. MD, Poland, N.Y. State. Intern, then resident in surgery Univ. Hosp., Silesian Sch. of Medicine, 1972-79; asst. prof., surgeon Silesian Sch. of Medicine, 1980-1987; postdoctoral fellow U. Cin., 1987-1990; attending surgeon Mary Imogene Bassett Hosp., Cooperstown, N.Y., 1990—; assoc. prof. clin. surgery Columbia U., 1992—; dir. surg. rsch. Mary Imogene Basset Hosp., 1990—. Author (with others): General Surgery Board Review, 1992; contbr. articles to profl. jours. Co-founder Solidarity, Silesian Sch. of Medicine, 1980. Recipient 1st prize European Assn. for Gastroenterology and Endoscopy, 1987, Polish Assn. for Gastroenterology, 1985; grantee Steven C. Clark Found., 1992-95. Fellow ACS; mem. AMA, Assn. for Acad. Surgery, Soc. for Surgery of Alimentary Tract, Collegium Internat. Chirurgiae Digestivae, European Soc. for Surg. Rsch., Plish Assn. for Surgery. Roman Catholic. Home: 286 Murphy Hill Rd Cooperstown NY 13326 Office: Bassett Healthcare 1 Atwell Rd Cooperstown NY 13326

RUDO, NEIL DENNIS, surgeon; b. White Plains, N.Y., Mar. 15, 1947; s. Milton and Roslind (Mandel) R.; m. Sandra Sandberg, Jan. 19, 1974; children: Kimber, Abraham. BA, Stanford U., 1969; MD, U. Chgo., 1975, PhD, 1975. Intern U. Calif., San Francisco, 1980-81, resident in surgery, 1975-80; fellow in vascular surgery Northwestern U., Chgo., 1980-81; attending surgeon Sequoia Hosp., Redwood City, Calif., 1981-88; clin. surgeon Stanford VA Hosp., Palo Alto, Calif., 1981-88; attending surgeon Salinas (Calif.) Valley Meml. Hosp., 1988—; Please verify info. in CAR 005 especially the date of employment. Mem. Alpha Omega Alpha. Office: 110 John St Salinas CA 93901

RUDOLPH, ABRAHAM MORRIS, physician, educator; b. Johannesburg, Republic of South Africa, Feb. 3, 1924; s. Chone and Sarah (Feinstein) R.; m. Rhona Sax, Nov. 2, 1949; children: Linda, Colin, Jeffrey. M.B.B.Ch. summa cum laude, U. Witwatersrand, Johannesburg, 1946, M.D., 1951. Instr. Harvard Med. Sch., 1955-57, assoc. pediatrics, 1957-60; assoc. cardiologist in charge cardiopulmonary lab. Children's Hosp., Boston, 1955-60; dir. pediatric cardiology Albert Einstein Coll. Medicine, 1960-66; prof. pediatrics, assoc. prof. physiology Albert Einstein Coll. Medicine, N.Y.C., 1962-66; vis. pediatrician Bronx Mcpl. Hosp. Ctr., N.Y.C., 1960-66; prof. pediatrics U. Calif., San Francisco, 1966—, prof. physiology, 1974-88, Neider prof. pediatric cardiology, prof. ob-gyn and reproductive scis., 1974—, chmn. dept. pediatrics, 1987-91; practice medicine, specializing in pediatric cardiology San Francisco.; mem. cardiovascular study sect. NIH, 1961-65, mem. nat. adv. heart council, 1968-72; established investigator Am. Heart Assn., 1958-62; career scientist Health Research Council, City N.Y., 1962-66; Harvey lectr., Oxford, Eng., 1984; inaugural lectr. 1st Nat. Congress Italian Soc. Perinatal Medicine, 1985. Mem. editorial bd. Pediatrics, 1964-70; assoc. editor Circulation Research, 1965-70; mem. editorial bd. Circulation, 1966-74, 83—; Am. Assoc. editor Pediatric Research, 1970-77; contbr. articles profl. jours. Recipient Merit award Nat. Heart, Lung and Blood Inst., 1986, Arvo Yllpo medal Helsinki U., Finland, 1987, Jonxis medal Children's Hosp. Groningen, 1993. Fellow Royal Coll. Physicians (Edinburgh), Royal Coll. Physicians (London); mem. NAS Inst. Medicine, Am. Acad. Pediatrics (E. Mead Johnson award for research in pediatrics 1964, Borden award 1979, past chmn. sect. on cardiology, Lifetime Med. Edn. award 1992, Joseph St. Geme leadership award Pediatrics 1993), Am. Phys. Soc., Soc. for Clin. Investigation, Soc. for Pediatric Research (coun. 1961-64), Am. Pediatric Soc. (coun. 1985-92, v.p. 1992-93, pres. 1993-94), Am. Heart Assn. (Rsch. Achievement award 1991). Office: U Calif Cardiovascular Rsch Inst Calif Rm 1403 Hse San Francisco CA 94143

RUDOLPH, ANDREW HENRY, dermatologist, educator; b. Detroit, Jan. 30, 1943; s. John J. and Mary M. (Mizesko) R.; children: Kristen Ann, Kevin Andrew. MD cum laude, U. Mich., 1966. Diplomate Am. Bd. Dermatology. Intern, Univ. Hosp., U. Mich. Med. Center, Ann Arbor, 1966-67, resident dept. dermatology, 1967-70; practice medicine specializing in dermatology, 1972—; asst. prof. dermatology Baylor Coll. Medicine, Houston, 1972-75, assoc. prof., 1975-83, clin. prof., 1983—; chief dermatology svc. VA Hosp., Houston, 1977-82; mem. staff Meth. Hosp., Tex. Children's Hosp., St. Luke's Episcopal Hosp. Served as surgeon USPHS, 1970-72. Regent's scholar U. Mich., 1966. Fellow Am. Acad. Dermatology; mem. Am. Dermatol. Assn., AMA, So. Med. Assn., Tex. Med. Assn., Harris County Med. Soc., Houston Dermatol. Soc. (past pres.), Tex. Dermatol. Soc., Assn. Mil. Dermatologists, Internat. Soc. Tropical Dermatology, Royal Soc. Health, Royal Soc. Medicine, Dermatology Found., Skin Cancer Found., Am. Venereal Disease Assn. (past pres.), Assn. Mil. Surgeons U.S., Am. Soc. for Dermatol. Surgery, Soc. for Investigative Dermatology, S. Central Dermatologic Congress, Mich. Alumni Assn. (life), Alpha Omega Alpha, Phi Kappa Phi, Phi Rho Sigma, Theta Xi. Mem. editorial bd. Jour. of Sexually Transmitted Diseases, 1977-85. Contbr. to med. jours., periodicals and textbooks. Office: 6560 Fannin St Ste 724 Houston TX 77030-2725

RU DUSKY, BASIL MICHAEL, cardiologist; b. Wilkes-Barre, Pa., July 27, 1933; s. Michael and Anne RuD.; m. Bernadine RuDusky, 1957; children: Daryl, Bryan. B.A., Va. Mil. Inst., 1955; M.D., U. Pitts., 1959. Diplomate Am. Bd. Forensic Medicine. Intern, Martin Army Hosp., Ft. Benning, Ga., 1959-60; resident Youngstown (Ohio) Hosp. Assn., 1962-63, Temple U. Hosp., 1963-66; practice medicine specializing in internal medicine, cardiovascular medicine and forensic medicine, Wilkes-Barre, Pa., 1966—; mem.

staff Mercy Hosp., 1966—, chief of medicine, 1966-70, dir. ICU AND CCU, 1966-70, dir. phonocardiography lab., 1966-70; dir. N.E. Cardiovascular Clinic and Research Inst.; mem. staff Wilkes-Barre Gen. Hosp.; cons. cardiology Armed Forces Examining Service; sr. cons. Social Security Adminstrn., HEW; sr. cons. physician Met. Ins. Co. Am., Liberty Mut. Ins. Co., Aetna Ins. Co.; cons. internal medicine and cardiology Retreat State Hosp.; dir. Northeast Cardiovascular Clinic and Research Inst.; clin. instr. medicine Temple U., 1966-70. Served to capt. M.C., U.S. Army, 1959-62. Diplomate Am. Bd. Internal Medicine, Am. Bd. Forensic Medicine, Am. Bd. Forensic Examiners (fellow). Fellow ACP, Am. Coll. Angiology (bd. govs. Eastern Pa.), Am. Coll. Chest Physicians, Am. Coll. Cardiology; mem. Am. Soc. Internal Medicine, AMA, Am. Coll. Occupl. and Environ. Medicine, Nat. Rehab. Assn., N.Y. Acad. Scis., Am. Geriatrics Soc., Assn. Mil. Surgeons U.S., Pan-Am. Med. Assn., Amateur Fencers League Am. Home: 7 Pine Tree Rd Wilkes Barre PA 18707-1707 Office: Bicentennial Bldg 15 Public Sq Wilkes Barre PA 18701-1702

RUDY, ELLEN BEAM, nursing educator; b. Moundsville, W.Va., May 5, 1936; d. William Henry and Mary Ellen Beam; m. Theodore Rudy, June 13, 1959; children: Richard, Alan, William. BSN, Ohio State U., 1958; MPA, U. Dayton, 1974; MSN, U. Md., 1977; PhD, Case Western Res. U., 1980. Cmty. health staff nurse Columbus (Ohio) Pub. Health Nursing Svc., 1958-60; supr. in-svc. instr. Henry County Hosp., New Castle, Ind., 1960-66; emergency room staff nurse St. Elizabeth Med. Ctr., Dayton, Ohio, 1970-73; instr. critical care Johns Hopkins Hosp., Balt., 1975-76; assoc. prof., program dir. Kent (Ohio) State U. Adult Program, 1978-84; adminstrv. assoc. U. Hosp. Cleve., 1985-90; assoc. prof., chmn. MSN Case Western Res. U., Cleve., 1985-88, prof., chair acute care nursing, 1988-90, assoc. dean rsch., 1990-91; dean, prof. U. Pitts., 1991—. Author: (with others) Critical Care Nursing, 1992 (Am. Jour. Nursing Book of Yr. 1993); contbr. articles to profl. jours. grant reviewer NIH Nursing Student Sect., Washington, 1990-93; provider expert testimony Senate Appropriations Com., Washington, 1993, Health Care Forum, Washington, 1993. Edward J. and Louise Mellen Endowed Chair in Acute Care Nursing, 1989-91; fellow Am. Acad. Nursing, 1988; rsch. grantee NIH Nat. Ctr. for Nursing Rsch., 1989-91, 91-94. Mem. ANA, AACN, Am. Heart Assn., Nat. Kidney Found. (co-chair critical care task force 1988-91), Coun. Nurse Researchers. Home: 130 Radcliff Dr Pittsburgh PA 15237 Office: Univ Pitts Sch Nursing 350 Victoria Bldg Pittsburgh PA 15261*

RUDZKI, EDWARD ZYGMUNT, dermatologist, educator; b. Wilno, Poland, May 2, 1925; s. Apolinary and Eugenia (Skriabin) R. MD, Sch. Medicine Warsaw, 1951, PhD, 1960, habil., 1964. Asst., asst. prof., assoc. prof. Sch. Medicine Warsaw, Poland, 1951-79; prof. Sch. Medicine Warsaw, 1979-95; ret., 1995; head allergologic unit Dept. Dermatology, Sch. Medicine Warsaw, 1995—. Author: Allergy, 1961, Problems of Clinical Allergology, 1970, Contact Dermatitis, 1976, Occupational Skin Diseases, 1986, European Porcelain of the 18th Century, 1981, Polish Queens I: Wives of Piasts and Jagiellons, 1985, 2d edit., 1988, Polish Queens II: Wives of Elected Kings, 1987, 2d edit., 1988, Delfina Potocka, 1990. 1st lt. Polish Army, 1944-46. Mem. Polish Assn. Dermatology (pres. allergologic sect. 1971—), Dermatitis Rsch. Group in Ctrl. and East European Countries (organizer 1974-76), Capitula of Polish medal Gloria Medicine, Polish Acad. Scis. (hed commn. environ. alergens, human ecology com. 1986—), Assotiatio Medicorum Bohemioslovacorum J.E. Purkyne Societas Bohenoslovaca Allergologiae atque Immunologica (hon.), Societas Medica Polonorum (hon.), Bulgarian Soc. Dermatology (hon.), Polish Soc. Allergology (hon.), Societas Scienciarum Varsoviensis (corr.). Roman Catholic. Home: Zlota 79 m 11, 00 819 Warsaw Poland Office: Dept Dermatology, Koszykowa 82 a, 02 008 Warsaw Poland

RUE, LORING WASHINGTON, III, surgeon, educator; b. Portsmouth, Va., Oct. 10, 1957; s. Loring Washington Rue, Jr. BA with high distinction, U. Va., 1979, MD, 1983. Diplomate Am. Bd. Surgeons. Intern in surgery U. Ala., Birmingham, 1983-84, resident in surgery, 1984-88; assoc. Hampton (Va.) Gen. Hosp., 1988-89, Mary Immaculate Hosp., Newsport, Va., 1988-89; clin. asst. prof. surgery U. Tex., San Antonio, 1989-91; clin. assoc. prof. surgery F. Edward Herbert Sch. Medicine, Bethesda, Md., 1991; asst. prof. surgery, dir. surg. critical care/intensive care U. Ala., Brimingham, 1992-95, dir. undergrad. surg. edn., 1994-95, assoc. prof. surgery, chief trauma, 1995—. Contbr. articles to profl. jours. Maj. U.S. Army, 1990-92. Fellow ACS; mem. Am. Assn. for the Surgery of Trauma, Surg. Infection Soc., Soc. of Critical Care Medicine, Am. Burn Assn., Am. Trauma Soc., Phi Beta Kappa. Office: U Ala 701 S 19th St LHR 112 Birmingham AL 35294

RUEBNER, BORIS HENRY, pathologist, educator; b. Dusseldorf, Germany, Aug. 30, 1923; came to U.S., 1959, naturalized, 1965; s. Fred and Martha (Klein) R.; m. Susan Mautner, Sept. 20, 1957; children: Sally, Anthony. MB, Edinburgh U., Scotland, 1946, MD, 1956. Diplomate Am. Bd. Anatomic Pathology, Am. Bd. Clin. Pathology. Intern, Royal Infirmary, Edinburgh, 1946-47; resident Bristol Royal Infirmary, Eng., Hammersmith Hosp., London, 1950-56; asst. prof. pathology Dalhousie U., Halifax, N.S., Can., 1957-59; assoc. prof. Johns Hopkins U., Balt., 1959-68; prof. U. Calif.-Davis, 1968—. Author: Diagnostic Pathology of the Liver, 1982, 2nd edit., 1991, The Gastrointestinal System, 1983. Served to capt. M.C., Brit. Army, 1947-49. Recipient Career Devel. award NIH, 1962-68. Fellow Coll. Am. Pathologists; mem. Internat. Acad. Pathologists, Assn. Am. Pathologists. Office: U Calif Sch Medicine Dept Med Pathology Davis CA 95616

RUECKERT, FREDERIC, plastic surgeon; b. Boston, Oct. 24, 1921; s. Frederic and Elizabeth (Howe) R.; m. Joan Dodge, May 31, 1947; children: Nancy Lee, Patricia, William Dodge, Carolyn. AB, Hamilton Coll., 1945; MD, Columbia U., 1947. Diplomate Am. Bd. Plastic Surgery, Nat. Bd. Med. Examiners; lic. physician, N.Y., N.H. Intern internal medicine Bellevue Hosp., N.Y.C., 1947-48; resident gen. surgery Am. U. Hosp., Beirut, 1948-50; fellow surg. pathology Columbia-Presbyn. Hosp., N.Y.C., 1950-51; resident gen. surgery Dartmouth-Hitchcock Med. Ctr., Hanover, N.H., 1953-54, staff surgeon, 1956-86; resident plastic surgery, teaching fellow plastic surgery U. Pitts. Med. Ctr., 1954-56; mem. faculty Dartmouth Med. Sch., Hanover, 1956—, prof. plastic surgery, 1974-86, prof. plastic surgery emeritus, 1986—; cons. VA Hosp., White River Junction, Vt., 1956—. Contbr. articles to profl. jours., chpts. to books. Mem. Sch. Bd. Edn., Hanover, N.H., 1964-67; bd. trustees Northfield (Mass.) Mt. Hermon Sch., 1969-71, 80-90. Capt. USAF, 1951-53. Recipient Lamplighter award Northfield Mt. Herman Sch., 1991. Mem. AMA, ACS, Am. Assn. Plastic Surgeons, Am. Assn. Med. Colls., Am. Soc. Plastic and Reconstructive Surgeons (bd. dirs. 1980-83, 84-86), Plastic Surgery Ednl. Found. (pres. 1985-86), Plastic Surgeons Assn. Am. (pres. 1984-85), Internat. Confederation Plastic, Reconstructive and Aesthetic Surgeons, Am. Soc. Aesthetic Plastic Surgeons, New Eng. Surg. Soc., Northeastern Soc. Plastic Surgeons, New Eng. Soc. Plastic and Reconstructive Surgeons (pres. 1969-71), N.H. State Med. Soc., Grafton County Med. Soc. (pres. 1974-75). Republican. Home: 18 Berrill Farms Ln Hanover NH 03755-3213

RUEDEMAN, CANDACE FENIMORE, legal nurse consultant; b. Akron, Ohio, Feb. 15, 1947; d. Edward David Fenimore and Fern (Morgan) Kaufman; m. George A. Ruedeman, Mar. 15, 1974; children: Geoffrey, Daniel. RN, Deaconess Hosp. Sch. Nursing, Evansville, Ind., 1968; student, U. New Mex. RN mgr. Humana, Louisville, 1972-82, Prowers Med. Ctr., Lamar, Colo., 1982-87; hosp. assoc. adminstr. Prowers Med. Ctr., Lamar, 1988-92; staff nurse/paralegal Am. Assn. Nurse Legal Cons., Lamar, 1992—. Mem. sch. adv. com. Lamar Pub. Schs., 1989—. Mem. Am. Assn. Nurse Legal Cons. Home: 311 W Park St Lamar CO 81052-3149 Office: PO Box 83 Lamar CO 81052

RUEGSEGGER, DONALD RAY, JR., radiological physicist, educator; b. Detroit, May 29, 1942; s. Donald Ray and Margaret Arlene (Elliot) R.; B.S., Wheaton Coll., 1964; M.S., Ariz. State U., 1966, Ph.D. (NDEA fellow), 1969. Diplomate Am. Bd. Radiology; m. Judith Ann Merrill, Aug. 20, 1965; children—Steven, Susan, Mark, Ann. Radiol. physicist Miami Valley Hosp., Dayton, Ohio, 1969—, chief med. physics sect., 1983—; physics cons. X-ray dept. VA Hosp., Dayton, 1970—; adj. asst. prof. physics Wright State U., Fairborn, Ohio, 1973—, clin. asst. prof. radiology, 1976-81, clin. assoc. prof. radiology, 1981—, group leader in med. physics, dept. radiol. scis. Med. Sch., 1978—. Mem. Am. Assn. Physicists in Medicine (pres. Ohio River Valley chpt. 1982-83, co-chmn. local summer sch. arrangements com. 1986), Am. Coll. Radiology, Am. Coll. Med. Physics (founding chancellor), Am. Phys. Soc., AAAS, Ohio Radiol. Soc., Health Physics Soc. Baptist. Home: 1613 E Mars Hill West Carrollton OH 45449 Office: Radiation Therapy Miami Valley Hosp 1 Wyoming St Dayton OH 45409-2722

RUEHLE, CHARLES JOSEPH, pathologist, military officer; b. Boone, Iowa, May 26, 1943; s. John Donald and Alta (Brown) R. DVM, Iowa State U., 1967; MD, U. Iowa, 1973, MS, 1973; m. Nellie Backus, Aug. 5, 1972. Commd. 2d lt. USAF, 1964, advanced through grades to col., sr. flight surgeon, 1984, chief flight surgeon, 1987; chief Vet. Service, Grissom AFB, Ind., 1967-69; resident in aerospace medicine Brook AFB, Tex., 1973-75; resident in pathology Wilford Hall USAF Med. Ctr., Lackland AFB, Tex., 1975-79, with div. aerospace pathology Armed Forces Inst. Pathology, Washington, 1979-88, chief div. aerospace pathology, 1982-85, chmn. dept. forensic scis., 1985-88, sec. Joint Com. Aviation Pathology, 1984-88, exec. asst. to fed. air surgeon FAA, Washington, 1988—, sr. aviation med. examiner, 1989—; adj. asst. prof. preventive medicine Uniformed Services U. Health Scis. lectr. aerospace pathology; cons. USAF Sugeon Gen., 1987. Diplomate Am. Bd. Preventive Medicine, Am. Bd. Pathology. Fellow Am. Soc. Clin. Pathologists, Aerospace Med. Assn.; mem. Am. Acad. Forensic Scis. AMA, USAF Flight Surgeons, Nat. Sojourners, Assn. Mil. Surgeons U.S., Internat. Soc. Air Safety Investigators, Air Force Assn., Alpha Zeta, Gamma Sigma Delta, Omega Tau Sigma (gov. 1967-75), Cosmos Club, Masons. Republican. Presbyterian. Home: 1000 Lower Pindell Rd Lothian MD 20711-2704 Office: Fed Air Surgeon FAA 800 Independence Ave SW Washington DC 20591-0002

RUFF, ROBERT LOUIS, neurologist, physiology researcher; b. Bklyn., Dec. 16, 1950; s. John Joseph and Rhoda (Alpert) R.; m. Louise Seymour Acheson, Apr. 26, 1980. BS summa cum laude, Cooper Union, 1971; MD summa cum laude, U. Wash., 1976, PhD in Physiology, 1976. Diplomate Am. Bd. Neurology and Psychiatry. Asst. neurologist N.Y. Hosp., Cornell Med. Sch., N.Y.C., 1977-80; asst. prof. physiology and medicine U. Wash., Seattle, 1980-84; assoc. prof. neurology Case Western Res. Med. Sch., Cleve., 1984-92, prof. neurology and neuroscis., 1993—, vice chair neurology dept., 1995—; chief dept. neurology Cleve. VA Med. Ctr., 1984—; adv. Child Devel. and Mental Retardation Ctr., Seattle, 1980-84, Burien Devel. Disability Ctr., Wash., 1982-84; mem. med. adv. bd. Muscular Dystrophy Assn., Seattle, 1984, NE Ohio chpt. Multiple Sclerosis Soc., 1986—; mem. adv. bd. for Neurology Dept. Vets. Affairs, 1989—; chmn. med. adv. bd. N.E. Ohio chpt. Myasthenia Gravis Found., 1987—, bd. trustees, 1993—, nat. med. adv. bd., 1988—, grant and fellowship com., 1990—. Assoc. editor: Neurology, 1994—; ad hoc reviewer various profl. and sci. jours.; contbr. articles to profl. jours. and chpts. to books. Nat. bd. dirs. Myasthenia Gravis Found., 1994—. Recipient Tchr. Investigator award NIH; NSF fellow, 1971; NIH grantee, Muscular Dystrophy Assn. grantee, Dept. Vets. Affair grantee; N.Y. State Regents med. scholar, 1971. Fellow Am. Heart Assn. (stroke coun.), Am. Acad. Neurology (scientific issues com., legis. action com.); mem. AMA, Am. Physics Soc., Neurosci. Soc., Biophys. Soc., Am. Neurol. Assn., N.Y. Acad. Sci., Am. Geriatrics Soc., Sigma Pi Sigma (v.p. 1970-71), Alpha Omega Alpha (v.p. 1975-76). Home: 2572 Stratford Rd Cleveland OH 44118-4063 Office: VA Med Ctr 10701 East Blvd Ste 127W Cleveland OH 44106-1702

RUFF, RONALD MARK, neuropsychologist; b. San Jose, Calif., May 28, 1949; s. Siegmund Richard and Carola Paula (Lindroos) R.; m. Ann Marie Richardson, Aug. 29, 1992; children: David, Saralyn. PhD magna cum laude, U. Zürich, 1978. Diplomate Am. Bd. Med. Psychotherapists; cert. clin. psychologist. Clin. neuropsychologist U. Med. Ctr., Zürich, 1974-78; chief of psychology U. of Calif., San Diego, 1980-87, head of neuropsych unit, 1980-87, program dir., 1987-88, dir. head injury ctr., 1988-90; dir. neurorehab. St. Mary's Med. Ctr., San Francisco, 1990—; adj. assoc. prof. U. Calif., San Francisco, 1990—. Contbr. articles to profl. jours. Pres. San Diego Head Injury Found., 1983-90; mem. Athletic Commrs. Com., 1991-93. Grantee IBM, NIH, Robert Wood Johnson Found. Fellow Nat. Acad. of Neuropsychology (N. Butters award for Rsch. 1993); mem. Am. Psychol. Assn., Internat. Neuropsychology Assn. Democrat. Presbyterian. Office: St Mary's Med Ctr 450 Stanyan St San Francisco CA 94117-1079

RUFF, TILMAN ALFRED, physician; b. Adelaide, Australia, Mar. 23, 1955; s. Dietrich Paul and Irene (Wagner) R.; m. Charlotte Laemmle, Dec. 21, 1982; children: Ingrid Lara Laemmle-Ruff, Kristan Thomas Laemmle-Ruff. M.B.B.S. with 1st class/honors, Monash U., Melbourne, 1980. Intern, jr., sr. registrar, clin. supr. Prince Henry's Hosp., Melbourne, 1981-85; med. registrar Fairfield Infectious Diseases Hosp., Melbourne, 1986-87; sr. lectr. Monash Med. Sch., Melbourne, 1988—; dir. travel health Fairfield Infectious Diseases Hosp., Melbourne, 1990-96; physician Macfarlane Burnet Centre for Med. Rsch., Melbourne, 1989—; med. advisor Overseas Svc. Bur., Melbourne, 1988—; head travel medicine svc. Royal Melbourne Hosp., 1996—. Editor Pulse Jour., 1987-89; contbr. to books: Radioactive Heaven and Earth, 1991, A Textbook of Preventive Medicine, 1990; contbr. articles to profl. jours. Victorian com. mem. Amnesty Internat., Melbourne, 1972-73; co-organizer Save Life on Earth Internat. Art Exhbn., Melbourne, 1986; mem. Victorian Internat. Yr. of Peace Com., 1986; mem. Moonee Creek Coop. Ltd. Fellow Royal Australasian Coll. Physicians; mem. Australasian Soc. Infectious Diseases, Pub. Health Assn. Australia, Amnesty Internat. Med. Group, Victorian Found. for Survivors of Torture, Internat. Soc. Infectious Diseases, Internat. Soc. Travel Medicine, Internat. Physicians for Prevention of Nuclear War (v.p. Asia Pacific 1989-93), Med. Assn. for Prevention War (Australia) Inc. (v.p. 1989—). Office: Macfarlane Burnet Ctr Med, Internat Health Unit, PO Box 254, Fairfield VIC 3078, Australia

RUGGERA, PAUL STEPHEN, biomedical engineer; b. Rock Springs, Wyo., Aug. 30, 1944; s. David Joe and Anna Eva (Ribovich) R.; m. Doris Ann Hankins, July 10, 1971. BSEE, U. Wyo., 1966, MS in Bioengring., 1968. Registered profl. engr., Va. Commd. officer USPHS, 1968, advanced through grades to capt., 1986; staff engr. Nat. Ctr. for Radiol. Health, Rockville, Md., 1968-72; spl. med. products engr. Bur. Radiol. Health, Rockville, 1972-82; spl. product engr. Ctr. for Devices and Radiol. Health, Rockville, 1982—; com. on Electromagnetic Compatibility, subcom. methods of measurement Am. Nat. Stds. Inst., N.Y.C., 1984—. Contbr. articles to IEEE EMC Soc. Proc., IEEE Trans. on Biomed. Engring., Internat. Jour. Hyperthermia, Cryobiology. Recipient commendation medal USPHS, 1980, 91, Outstanding Unit citation, 1991, PHS citation, 1991, 92, Unit citation USPHS, 1995, U.S. FDA Group award, 1996. Mem. IEEE (sr.), Assn. for Advancement Med. Instrumentation (electromagnetic compatability com. 1995—), Soc. Automotive Engrs. (AE-4 com. on electromagnetic compatibility 1972—), Eagles. Democrat. Roman Catholic. Home: 1609 Woodmoor Ln Mc Lean VA 22101-5160 Office: Ctr for Devices and Radiol Health HFZ-133 12721 Twinbrook Pky Rockville MD 20852-1719

RUGGERI, ZAVERIO MARCELLO, medical researcher; b. Bergamo, Italy, Jan. 7, 1945; came to U.S., 1978; s. Giovanni and Anna (Dolci) R.; m. Rosamaria Carrara, June 12, 1971. MD magna cum laude, U. Milan, 1970; degree in Clin. and Exptl. Hematology magna cum laude, U. Pavia, Italy, 1973, degree in Internal Medicine magna cum laude, 1981. Asst. clin. prof. hematology U. Milan, 1972-80; assoc. dir. hemophilia ctr. Policlinico Hosp., Milan, 1980-82; vis. investigator Scripps Clinic and Research Found., La Jolla, Calif., 1978-80, asst. mem., 1982-89; assoc. mem. Scripps Clinic and Rsch. Found., La Jolla, Calif., 1989-93; mem. Scripps Rsch. Inst., 1993—; dir. Roon Ctr. for Arteriosclerosis and Thrombosis, 1989—; head div. Exptl. Thrombosis and Hemostasis, 1989—; vis. investigator St. Thomas/St. Bartholomews Hosps., London, 1974-76. Editor: Clinics in Haematology, 1985; mem. editl. bds. Blood, 1988-92, Peptide Rsch., 1988—, Haematologica, 1990—, Jour. Biol. Chemistry, 1993—; assoc. editor: Jour. Clin. Investigation, 1993—; contbr. articles to profl. jours., chpts. to books. Research scholar Italian Ministry of Edn., 1970, Italian Hemophilia Found., 1970-72. Mem. AAAS, Assn. Am. Physicians, Italian Hemophilia Found., Am. Soc. Clin. Investigation, Italian Soc. Thrombosis and Hemostasis, Internat. Soc. Thrombosis and Hemostasis, Am. Heart Assn. (council on thrombosis), World Fedn. Hemophilia, Am. Fedn. Clin. Research, N.Y. Acad. Scis., Am. Soc. Hematology. Office: Scripps Rsch Inst 10550 N Torrey Pines Rd La Jolla CA 92037-1027

RUGGERO, MARIO ALFREDO, physiologist, educator; b. Resistencia, Argentina, Nov. 7, 1943; came to U.S., 1961; s. Juan M. and Carolina F. (Volpe) R.; m. Elsa L. Statzner, Apr. 2, 1973. BA, Cath. U. Am., 1965; PhD, U. Chgo., 1972. Rsch. assoc. U. Wis., Madison, 1975; asst. prof. otolaryngology U. Minn., Mpls., 1975-87, assoc. prof., 1987-92, prof., 1992-93; Hugh Knowles prof. hearing sci. dept. comm. scis. and disorders Northwestern U., Evanston, Ill., 1993—; mem. communication disorders rev. com. Nat. Inst. on Deafness and Other Communication Disorders, NIH, Bethesda, Md., 1990-94. Assoc. editor Jour. of Neurosci., 1989-95; co-editor: The Mechanics and Biophysics of Hearing; contbr. articles to profl. jours. including Nature Jour. Neurophysiology, Jour Acoustical Soc. Am. Grantee NIH, 1975—, NSF, 1983-87. Mem. Soc. for Neurosci., Acoustical Soc. Am., Assn. for Rsch. in Otolaryngology. Home: 1209 Central St # A Evanston IL 60201-1611 Office: Northwestern U Dept Comm Scis and Disorders 2299 N Campus Dr Evanston IL 60208-3550

RUGGIERI, PAMELA JOY, psychologist; b. Chgo., Mar. 25, 1944; d. Armand Rudolph and Ruth Joy (Hildebrand) R. BS, Butler U., 1965; postgrad., L'Ecole des Beaux Arts, Aix-en-Provence, France, 1969-70; MA, U. Chgo., 1975, Calif. Sch. Profl. Psychology, San Diego, 1981; PhD, Calif. Sch. Profl. Psychology, San Diego, 1984. Lic. psychologist, Ind., Ill.; cert. tchr., Ill. Vol. Peace Corps, Tanzania, 1965-67; caseworker Luth. Child & Family Svcs., River Forest, Ill., 1968-69; tchr. Chgo. Bd. of Edn., 1970-71, Sch. Dist. 150, South Holland, Ill., 1971-74; rsch. asst. Ctr. for Ednl. Devel., Coll. of Medicine U. Ill., Chgo., 1975-76; social worker Oak Community Ctr., Oak Park, Ill., 1976-79; psychologist CMHS, Muncie, Ind., 1984-87; supr., psychologist Southlake Ctr. for Mental Health, Merrillville, Ind., 1987—; pvt. practice Ctr. for Personal and Family Life, Matteson, Ill., 1991—. Mem. Nat. Wildlife Fedn., 1984—, Friends of the Ind. Dunes, 1988—. Mem. APA, Ind. Psychol. Assn., NOW, ACLU. Home: 7647 Hemlock Ave Gary IN 46403-2160 Office: Ctr for Personal and Family Life 3624 216th St Matteson IL 60443-2713

RUGGIERO, DOMINIC, JR., medical technologist; b. Bridgeport, Conn., Oct. 11, 1953; s. Dominic and Jean Rose (Mastriano) R.; m. Kathleen Ann Rote, Oct. 20, 1979; children: Dillon Edward, Jennifer Rose. AA in Life Sci., Mesa Coll., San Diego, 1983; cert. in lab. technology, Mesa Coll., 1988. Med. lab. technician St. Luke's Med. Ctr., Phoenix, 1989-91, Nat. Health Labs., Phoenix, 1990-91; med. technologist Bradshaw Mountain Labs., Prescott, Ariz., 1991—. Vol. Libertarian Party, Ariz., 1994—. Mem. Am. Med. Technologists (cert.). Home: 2145 Eldred Rd Chino Valley AZ 86323 Office: Bradshaw Mountain Labs 907 Ainsworth Dr Prescott AZ 86301

RUGGIERO, KATHLEEN ANN, cardiology nurse; b. Niagara Falls, N.Y., Jan. 22, 1952; d. Frank Paul and Mary Elizabeth (Paonessa) Taibi; children: Kevin Douglas, Kristian Francis, Kenneth Joseph Jr. BSN, Niagara U., 1974. RN. RN staff Niagara Falls Meml. Med. Ctr., 1974-87, patient care coord. intermediate care unit, 1987-88; clin. cardiology nurse Buffalo (N.Y.) Cardiology Pulmonary Assn., 1989—; quality assurance role Buffalo Cardiology Pulmonary, Buffalo, 1993—. Contbr. Educational Guidelines Pacing and Electrophysiology, 1994. Mem. Nat. Assn. Healthcare Quality. Roman Catholic.

RUGGILL, SOLOMON P., psychologist; b. N.Y.C., Sept. 29, 1906; s. Abraham and Sarah (Silverberg) R.; m. Sophie Stock, June 8, 1938; children: Robert Zachary, Peter Alan. BS, CCNY, 1927; MA in Edn., Columbia U., 1930, PhD in Psychology, 1934. Lic. psychologist, N.Y. Tchr. elem. and jr. high sch. Bd. of Edn. of N.Y.C., 1929-59, psychologist, Bur. of Child Guidance, 1959-62; psychologist Baro Civic Ctr. Clinic, Bklyn., 1961-62; assoc. prof. L.I. U., Bklyn., 1962-69, prof., 1969-79, prof. emeritus, 1979—, acting chmn. dept. guidance and counseling, 1972-73; dir. Flatback Progressive Sch., Bklyn., 1943-45, Camp Kinderwelt, Fraternal Order Farband, N.Y.C., 1959-60; lectr. in gerontology to various orgns., Tucson, 1980—, Keeping Mentally Alert classes Sr. Day Ctrs., 1985—. Pres. Chancy Meml. Found., N.Y.C., 1961-63; mem. adv. council Pima Council on Aging, Tucson, 1987—. Mem. N.Y. Acad. Pub. Edn., N.Y. State Guidance Assn., Jewish Tchrs. Assn. (life). Jewish. Home: 425 W Paseo Redondo Apt 7E Tucson AZ 85701-8262

RUH, DENNIS ROBERT, physical therapist; b. Buffalo, Oct. 24, 1957; m. Judith Cameron, June 14, 1986; children: Haley, Dana, Jamie, Eric. Lic. phys. therapist. Staff therapist Our Lady of Victory Hosp., Buffalo, 1979-81; phys. therapist Vis. Nursing Assn., Buffalo, 1981-83; dir., owner Southtowns Phys. Therapy Group, Buffalo, 1983—; pres., CEO Buffalo Indsl. Work Harding. Treas. Western N.Y. Forum, Buffalo, 1990. Mem. Coun. Lic. Phys. Therapists (sec. 1987), N.Y. Am. Phys. Therapy Assn. (mem. ins. com.). Office: Southtowns Phys Therapy Group PC 100 Union Rd West Seneca NY 14224-4630

RUIZ, GERARD, alcohol and drug abuse services professional; b. Jackson Heights, N.Y., Oct. 6, 1959; s. Pedro and Reine Marie (Lambot) R.; m. Dana Schaefer, July 8, 1990. BA, Cathedral Coll., Douglaston, N.Y., 1981; MA, Immaculate Conception Sem., Huntington, N.Y., 1983; Cert., NYU, 1982, Molloy Coll., Rockville Centre, N.Y., 1988. Credentialled alcoholism counselor, 1991. Tchr. Immaculate Conception Sch., Jamaica, N.Y.; tchr. 6th-8th grade reading, lang. arts Bklyn. Diocese; tchr. Our Lady of Loreto Sch., East New York, N.Y.; alcoholism counselor Nassau County Dept. Drug and Alcohol Addiction, Hempstead, N.Y.; clin. supr. Manhattan Alcoholism Treatment Ctr., mem. faculty Acad. Addiction Studies, asst. dir., 1995, asst. dir. Home: 99 Kraemer St Hicksville NY 11801-4359

RUIZ, PEDRO, psychiatrist; b. Cuba, Dec. 31, 1936. MD, U. Paris VI, 1964. Intern Jackson Meml. Hosp., Miami, Fla., 1965, resident in psychiatry, 1966-68; prof. psychiatry U. Tex./Houston Health Sci. Ctr. Office: U Tex-Houston Health Sci Ct Mental Sci Inst 1300 Moursund Houston TX 77030*

RUIZ FERRAN, JULIAN, managed healthcare company executive; b. Vitoria, Alava, Spain, Mar. 4, 1953; s. Julian Ruiz Aranda and Roser Ferran Gayet; m. Irini Mandyla, July 4, 1985; children: Adrian, Alexis. MD, Complutense U., Madrid, 1977, specialist in clin. pharmacology, 1984, specialist in pharm. medicine, 1989. Head med. mktg. liaison Antibioticos, S.A., Madrid, 1977-81; regional med. dir. Robapharm, A.G., Basel, Switzerland, 1982-84; med. dir. Pfizer, S.A., Madrid, 1984-88, Antibioticos-Farma, S.A., Madrid, 1988-91; pharm. ind. mgmt. cons. Madrid, 1992-93; med. dir. Sanitas, S.A. BUPA Group, Madrid, 1993—; pres. Spanish Assn. Pharm. Physicians, Madrid, 1989-91; mem. Bd. Sanitas. Editor: Communication in Pharmaceutical Medicine, 1991. Fellow Faculty Pharm. Medicine of the Royal Colls. of Physicians of the U.K. Office: Sanitas SA, Serrano 88, 28006 Madrid Spain

RULIN, MARVIN CALVIN, obstetrics and gynecology educator, physician; b. Youngstown, Ohio, July 21, 1928; s. Harry B. and Rhoda B. (Malkin) R.; m. Steffi G. Goldman, July 4, 1954; children: Renee, Elliott, Edye, Judy. BA, Ohio State U., 1949; MD, Chgo. Med. Sch., 1953. Diplomate Am. Bd. Ob-Gyn. Intern Cook County Hosp., Chgo.; resident Magee Womens Hosp-U. Pitts.; med. dir. outpatient dept. Magee-Women's Hosp., Pitts., 1985—; prof. ob-gyn. U. Pitts., 1979—, interim chmn. ob-gyn., 1988-92, dir. ambulatory care, 1992—; examiner Am. Bd. Ob-Gyn., 1974-94; ednl. cons. in ob-gyn., 1985—; mem. in-tng. exam com. Coun. on Resident Edn. in Ob-Gyn., 1979-88; mem. exam com. Nat. Bd. Med. Examiners, Phila., 1982-85. Author: (with others) Health Care for the Older Woman, 1966; guest editor: Clinical Obstetrics and Gynecology, 1993; contbr. articles to profl. jours. Mem. Mayors Commn. on Families, Pitts., 1987-90. Capt. USAF, 1954-56. Democrat. Jewish. Home: 552 Neville St PH # 1 Pittsburgh PA 15213 Office: Magee-Womens Hosp 300 Halket St Pittsburgh PA 15213

RUMBLE, THOMAS REID, psychiatrist; b. Atlanta, Sept. 1, 1943; s. Charles Taylor and Eddie Mae (Clark) R.; m. Barbara Friday, May 29, 1971; children: Thomas Reid, Elizabeth Lynn. BA, Emory U., 1965, MD, 1969. Diplomate Am. Bd. Psychiatry and Neurology; cert. in geriatric psychiatry, 1991. Intern medicine Western Pa. Hosp., 1969-70; resident psychiatry Western Psychiat. Inst. and Clinic, 1970-73; staff psychiatrist, chief, somatic therapies Oakland VA Med. Ctr., Pitts., 1975-82; psychiat. physician I Dixmont State Hosp., Pitts., 1975-77; psychiat. cons. Greensburg Community Mental Health/Mental Retardation, Greensburg, Pa., 1977-82; ptnr. Clin. Psychiatry Assocs., PC, Pitts., 1982—; chief, div. psychiatry The Western Pa. Hosp., Pitts., 1983—; teaching fellow U. Pitts., Western Psychiat. Inst. and Clinic, Pitts., 1970-73; clin. instr., 1975—. Major USAF, 1973-75. Mem. AMA, Allegheny County Med. Soc., Pa. Med. Soc., Pitts. Psychiat. Assn. (membership chmn. 1982), Psychiat. Physicians of Pa., Am. Psychiat. Assn. Office: Clinical Psychiatry Assocs 4815 Liberty Ave Ste 127 Pittsburgh PA 15224-2156

RUMMERFIELD, PHILIP SHERIDAN, medical physicist; b. Raton, N. Mex., Feb. 27, 1922; s. Lawrence Lewis and Helen Antoinette (Roper) R.; m. Mary Evelyn Kubick, Dec. 29, 1978; children: Casey Regan, Dana Jay. BSME, Healds Coll., 1954; MSc, U. Cin., 1964, DSc, 1965. Registered profl. engr., safety, nuclear, Calif. Piping engr. Morrison Knudsen Co., Surabaja, E. Java, 1956-57; civil engr. State of Calif., San Francisco, 1957-59, constn. and radiation engr., 1959-63; hosp. physicist and radiation safety officer U. Calif., San Diego, 1966-73; prin. Applied Radiation Protection Svc., Encinitas, Calif., 1973—. Contbr. articles to Science, Bull. Atomic Scientists, Occupational Health Nursing, Health Physics Jour., Internat. Jour. Applied Radiation & Isotopes. Cpl. C.E. U.S. Army, 1943-46. Grantee Teaching grant NSF, 1969-71. Mem. Am. Nuclear Soc., Calif. Soc. Profl. Engrs., Am. Indsl. Hygiene Assn., Am. Assn. Physicists in Medicine (pres. So. Calif. chpt. 1971-72), Calif. Soc. Profl. Engrs., Health Physics Soc. (pres. So. Calif. chpt. 1973-74). Democrat. Home: 3303 Dorado Pl Carlsbad CA 92009-7706 Office: Applied Radiation Protection Svcs 700 2nd St Ste C Encinitas CA 92024-4459

RUMORE, MARTHA MARY, pharmacist, educator; b. N.Y.C., Feb. 29, 1956; d. Barney B. and Frieda A. (Sinacore) R. BS in Pharmacy, St. John's U., Jamaica, N.Y., 1978, PharmD, 1980; JD, Thomas Jefferson Coll., L.A., 1986; MS in Drug Info., Arnold & Marie Schwartz Coll., 1990. Registered pharmacist, N.Y., Fla., Conn.; cert. in drug regulatory affairs. Lab. asst. St. John's U., 1973-77; pharmacy intern Queens Hosp. Ctr., Jamaica, 1977-78; sr. info. scientist Richardson-Vicks, Inc., Shelton, Conn., 1981-84; assoc. dir. profl. svcs. Sterling Drug Inc., N.Y.C., 1984-90; assoc. prof. pharmacy adminstrn. Arnold & Marie Schwartz Coll. Pharmacy, Bklyn., 1990—; clin. pharmacist Lenox Hill Hosp., N.Y.C., 1990-93, Beth Israel Hosp.-North, 1993—; lectr., presenter in field. Contbr. over 70 articles to jours. Pharmacoepidemiology, Drug Info., Pharmacy Law, Drug Regulatory Affairs, Pharmacotherapeutics; mem. several jour. editl. adv. bds. Recipient Hosp. Pharmacy Achievement award L.I. Soc. Hosp. Pharmacists, 1978, Vis. Scientist award Pharm. Mfrs. Assn., 1990, 91; named Outstanding Young Women Am., 1988. Fellow Am. Pharm. Assn. (trustee, ho. of dels. 1988—, vice chmn. publs. 1988-89, polit. action com. 1990—, policy com. on sci. affairs), Acad. Pharm. Practice and Mgmt., Am. Soc. Pharmacy Law (bd. dirs. 1996—); mem. Drug Info. Assn., Regulatory Affairs Profls. Soc. (mem. specialty coun. on nuclear pharmacy 1993-96), Pharm. Soc. of State of N.Y., Am. Inst. on History of Pharmacy, Am. Assn. Colls. of Pharmacy. Republican. Roman Catholic. Office: Arnold and Marie Schwartz Coll Pharmacy 75 Dekalb Ave Brooklyn NY 11201-5497

RUND, DOUGLAS ANDREW, emergency physician; b. Columbus, Ohio, July 20, 1945; s. Carl Andrew and Caroline Amelia (Row) R.; m. Sue E, Padavana, 1980; children: Carie, Emily, Ashley. BA, Yale U., 1967; MD, Stanford U., 1971. Lic. physician, Ohio; Diplomate Nat. Bd. Med. Examiners, Am. Bd. Family Practice, Am. Bd. Emergency Medicine (pres., 1995—). Intern in medicine U. Calif., San Francisco-Moffett Hosp., 1971-72; resident in gen. surgery Stanford U., 1972-74; Robert Wood Johnson Found. clin. scholar in medicine Stanford U., 1974-76; med. dir. Mid-Peninsula Health Svc., Palo Alto, Calif., 1975-76; clin. instr. dept. medicine and preventive medicine Stanford U. Med. Sch., 1975-76; assoc. prof., dir. div. emergency medicine Ohio State Coll. Medicine, 1982-87; dir. emergency medicine residency program, assoc. prof. dept. family medicine, 1976-87, prof., chmn. dept. preventive medicine, 1988-90, prof., chmn. dept. emergency medicine, 1990—, prof., interim chmn. dept. family medicine, 1994-95; attending staff Ohio State U. Hosps., 1976—; med. dir. CSCC, Emergency Med. Svcs. Dept.; pres. Internat. Rsch. Inst. Emergency Medicine; med. dir. Internat. Soc. for Emergency Med. Svcs.; sr. rsch. fellow NATO: Health and Med. Aspects of Disaster Preparedness, 1985-87; bd. dirs. ABEM, 1988—, sr. editor in tng. exam., 1989—; on profl. leave epidemiology and injury control, U. Edinburgh, Scotland, 1987. Fellow Am. Coll. Emergency Physicians (task force on substance abuse and injury control); Mem. Nat. Inst. on Alcohol Abuse and Alcoholism, IAAA, Assn. Acad. Chairs Emergency Medicine (pres. 1992-93), Soc. Acad. Emergency Medicine (chmn. internat. com. 1991—), Columbus Medical Forum (pres. 1993), Alpha Omega Alpha. Author: Triage, 1981; Essentials of Emergency Medicine, 1982, 2nd edit., 1986; Emergency Radiology, 1982; Emergency Psychiatry, 1983; Environmental Emergencies, 1985; editor: Emergency Medicine Ann., 1983, 84; Emergency Medicine Survey, Annals of Emergency Medicine; editor-in-chief Ohio State Series on Emergency Medicine, Emergency Medicine Observer, 1986-87; guest editor Annals of Emergency Medicine Symposium, 1986; mem. editorial bd. Physician, Sports Medicine, Emergency Med. Svcs.; contbr. chpt. to Family Medicine Principles and Practice, 1978, 2d edit., 1983; contbr. articles to profl. jours. Office: Ohio State U Rm 005 Upham Hall 473 W 12th Ave Columbus OH 43210-1228

RUNFOLA, JOAN FRAMO, social services administrator; b. Austin, Tex., May 30, 1950; d. James Lawrence and Mary (D'Adamo) Framo; m. Daniel Ralph Runfola; children: Matthew, David, Jonathan. BA, Pa. State U., 1972; MS, U. Tex., 1975. Lic. social worker, N.J. Social worker Child and Family Svc., Austin, 1975-77; social worker Cancer Care, N.Y.C., 1977-85, coord. community edn. program, 1985; social work supr. Cancer Care, Millburn; dir. social svc. cancer care Cancer Care, Millburn, N.J., 1990—; pvt. practice Livington, N.J., 1985—. Mem. NASW, Assn. Oncology Social Workers. Home: 47 Lincoln Ave Livingston NJ 07039-2110 Office: Cancer Care 241 Millburn Ave Ste 241C Millburn NJ 07041-1700

RUNG, GEORGE W., physician; b. Altoona, Pa., Dec. 18, 1957; s. Wilbur Karl and Emma May (Peterson) R.; m. Catherine Ann Kline, June 9, 1979; children: Katrina, Allison, Jonathan, Christopher. BS, Juniata Coll., 1978; MD, Pa. State U., 1982. Diplomate Am. Bd. Anesthesiology; cert. in pain mgmt. Intern Pa. State U. Hosp., Hershey, 1983, anesthesia resident, 1984-85; asst. prof. Pa. State U., 1986, assoc. prof., 1993—; anesthesia/crit. care fellow U. Western Australia, Perth, 1985-86; vis. scientist and univ. sabbatical, U. Copenhagen, Denmark, 1995; fellow Project Hope, Guayaquil, Equador, 1992. Author: A Practice of Cardiac Anesthesia, 1991, 95, Anesthesia for Vascular Surgery, 1993; contbr. articles to profl. jours. vis. scientist, Pa. State U., Denmark, 1995. Mem. Am. Soc. Anesthesiologists, Am. Soc. Regional Anesthesiologists, Internat. Anesthesia Rsch. Soc. Home: 222 East Granada Ave Hershey PA 17033 Office: Pa State Coll of Medicine 500 University Dr Hershey PA 17033

RUNGE, LORNE ARTHUR, physician; b. Winnipeg, Man., Can., Aug. 3, 1940; s. Gustave A. and Eileen (Pepper) R.; m. Ellen K. Fitzpatrick; children: Christopher, Timothy, Margaret, Anne. BS, McGill U., Montreal, Que., Can., 1961, MDCM, 1965. Diplomate internal medicine, rheumatology, sports medicine Am. Bd. Internal Medicine. Asst. prof. U. Ottawa, Ont., 1972-75; assoc. prof. SUNY, Syracuse, 1975-87; pvt. practice Syracuse, 1987—. Fellow Am. Coll. Rheumatology; mem. Am. Coll. Sports Medicine. Home: 214 Standish Dr Syracuse NY 13224 Office: 310 S Crouse Ave Syracuse NY 13210

RUNGE, MARY MUNSON, pharmacist; b. Donaldsonville, La., July 25, 1928; d. John Harvey and Mary Leona (Brown) Lowery; m. Wilbert Percy Munson, Dec. 7, 1946 (div.); 1 dau., Katherine Marie; m. Alfred Joseph Runge, Sept. 4, 1976. B.S., Xavier U., 1948; Sc.D. (hon.), Mass. Coll. Pharmacy, 1980; D.Pharmacy, Ohio No. U., 1984. Pharmacist Roddick Pharmacy, Richmond, Calif., 1949-51, Contra Costa County Hosp., Martinez, Calif., 1951-65, Brookside Hosp., San Pablo, Calif., 1965-71; assoc. pharmacist The Apothecary, Oakland, Calif., 1971-91; corp. mem. Calif. Blue Shield, San Francisco, 1981-92; apptd. mem. Prescription Drug Rev. Commn., 1988; preceptor-intern advisor U. Pacific, Stockton, Calif., 1972-75; mem. Am. Coun. Pharm. Edn., Chgo., 1972-82. Recipient Pharmacist of Yr., 1968; recipient Geigy Pharm. Leadership, 1963. Mem. Am. Pharm. Assn. (pres. 1979, chmn. bd. dirs. 1980), Calif. Pharmacist Assn. (pres. 1979, chmn. bd. dirs. 1980, Hugo H. Schaefer award 1996), Calif. Pharmacist Assn. (pres. 1974-75), Calif. State Bd. Pharmacy (v.p. 1986-88, treas. 1988-91), Calif. Soc. Hosp. Pharmacist (pres. 1967-68). Home and Office: 1825 Saint Andrews Dr Moraga CA 94556-1056

RUNYAN, THOMAS EARL, retired opthalmologist; b. Mpls., Sept. 18, 1932; s. Earl John and Marguerite (Haugstad) R.; m. Carol Levier Bell, Aug. 26, 1961; children: Scott, Mark, Thomas K., David, Pamela. BS, U.S. Mil. Acad., 1957; MD, Duke U., 1963. Commd. 2d lt. U.S. Army, 1957, resigned, 1977; ophthalmologist U.S. Army, various locations, 1968-77, U. Tenn., Memphis, 1977-79, Scott and White Clinic, Temple, Tex., 1979-93; ret., 1993; cons. U.S. Army Darnall Army Hosp. Ft. Hood, Killeen, Tex., 1979-90; med. dir. Cen. Tex. Eye Bank, Temple, 1979-90. Author: Concussive and Penetrating Injuries to Eye and Optic Nerve, 1977; contbr. articles to profl. jours. Fellow ACS, Am. Acad. Ophthalmologists; mem. AMA, Tex. Med. ASsn. Home: RR 2 Box 2322 Belton TX 76513-9607

RUNYON, JOHN CHARLES, psychologist; b. Annapolis, Md., Aug. 17, 1944; s. Charles Fredrick and Dorothy (Swift) R.; m. Anna Lee Cox, June 10, 1967 (div. 1987); m. Susan Marie Bard, July 15, 1989; children: Nicole Marie, Christian Fredrick, Aaron Samuel. BS, Murray State U., 1967, MS, 1973. Psychologist-supr. Western Ky. Mental Health/Mental Retardation Bd. Inc., Paducah, 1974-80; psychologist Kelley Psychiat. Clinic, Paducah, 1980-83; psychologist, pres. Psychol. Assocs. Paducah, Inc., 1983—, also chmn. bd. Bd. dirs. Mayfield/Graves County (Ky.) Sr. Citizens, 1976-78, Mayfield-Graves County United Way, 1976-78, Parents Anonymous, Paducah, 1985-87, Childwatch, Paducah, 1987-90; mem. Ky. Post Trauma Response team, 1992—. Named Ky. Col. Gov. Ky., 1987, Duke Paducah, Mayor City of Paducah, 1987. Mem. APA (assoc.), Ky. Psychol. Assn. (legis. com. 1990-94, West Ky. rep., bd. dirs.), Ky. C. of C. (small bus. council 1994—), Psi Chi. Office: Psychol Assocs Paducah Inc 2204 Kentucky Ave Paducah KY 42003-3242

RUOFF, MICHAEL, internist, gastroenterologist, educator; b. N.Y.C., Nov. 28, 1938; s. Charles and Matilda (Kelner) R.; children: Shari, Craig; m. Natalie Fisher, Jan. 12, 1992. AB, Columbia Coll., 1959; MD, NYU, 1963. Diplomate Am. Bd. Internal Medicine, Am. Bd. Gastroenterology. Intern in medicine NYU Bellevue Hosp., N.Y.C., 1963-64, resident in medicine, 1964-66, gastroenterology fellow, 1966-67; instr. clin. medicine NYU Sch. Medicine, 1967-71, asst. prof. clin. medicine, 1971-86, clin. assoc. prof. medicine, 1986-94, clin. prof. medicine, 1994—; dir. student health svc. NYU Sch. Medicine and Postgrad. Med. Sch., 1968-81. Assoc. editor Am. Jour. Gastroenterology, 1979-86. Fellow Am. Coll. Gastroenterology, N.Y. Acad. Gastroenterology (pres. 1976-77), Am. Coll. Physicians; mem. N.Y. Gastroent. Assn., Am. Gastroent. Assn., Am. Soc. Gastroent. Endoscopy, Phi Beta Kappa, Alpha Omega Alpha. Office: 530 First Ave New York NY 10016

RUOHO, ARNOLD EINO, pharmacology educator; b. Thunder Bay, Ont., Can., Nov. 26, 1941; s. Eino Armas and Toini Helen (Kuusisto) R.; m. Marjorie Denise Anderson, Aug. 21, 1965; children—David, Daniel, Jonathon. B.S. in Pharmacy, U. Toronto, Ont., Can., 1964; Ph.D. in Physiol. Chemistry, U. Wis.-Madison, 1970. Helen Hay Whitney postdoctoral fellow U. Calif.-San Diego, 1971-74; asst. prof. pharmacology U Wis.-Madison, 1974-80, assoc. prof., 1980-84, prof., 1984—, acting chair dept. pharmacology Med. Sch., 1994-95, chair, 1995—; cons. NIH, Bethesda, Md., 1984—. Contbr. articles to profl. jours., chpts. to books. Den leader local council Boy Scouts Am., Madison, 1975-77, mem. at large, 1979—; hockey coach, 1983—. Grantee March of Dimes, 1975-78, Pharm. Mfrs., 1975-76, NIH, 1975—. Mem. AAAS. Lutheran. *

RUOSLAHTI, ERKKI, medical research administrator; b. Puumala, Finland. B.Medicine, U. Helsinki, Finland, 1961, MD, 1965, Dr.Medicine, 1967; Dr.Medicine (hon.), U. Lund, Sweden, 1991. Rsch./teaching asst. dept. serology and bacteriology U. Helsinki, 1964-66; head blood group dept. State Serum Inst., Helsinki, 1966-68; NIH rsch. fellow Calif. Inst. Tech., 1968-70; asst. prof., acting assoc. prof. dept. serology U. Helsinki, 1970-75; prof. bacteriology and serology U. Turku, Finland, 1975-76; sr. rsch. scientist dept. immunology City of Hope, Duarte, Calif., 1976; dir. immunobiology divsn. immunology City of Hope Nat. Med. Ctr., Duarte, 1978-79; assoc. sci. dir. La Jolla (Calif.) Cancer Rsch. Found., 1979-80, v.p., COO, 1982-89, sci. dir., 1980—, pres., CEO and dir. Cancer Ctr., 1989—; adj. prof. dept. pathology U. Calif., San Diego, 1980—; mem. sci. adv. bd. Helen Keller Eye Rsch. Found., Birmingham, Ala., 1989—; mem. pathobiochemistry study sect. Nat. Cancer Inst., 1981-85; Robert and Estelle Stadtler lectr. U. Tex., Sys. Cancer Ctr., 1984, Burton L. Baker Meml. lectr. U. Mich., Ann Arbor, 1987, Harvey Soc. lectr., 1988, Jeanette Piperno Meml. lectr. Temple U., Phila., 1989, G.H.A. Clowes award and lectr. Am. Assn. Cancer Rsch., 1990, Karl H. Beyer lectr. U. Wis., 1990, Walter Hubert lectr. 33d Ann. Meeting, Brit. Assn. for Cancer Rsch., 1992. Contbr. over 300 articles to profl. jours.; editl. bd. mem. Matrix, 1991—, Internat. Jour. Cancer, 1979—, Ann. Rev. of cell Biology, 1987-90, Jour. Cell Biology, 1987-89, Jour. Biol. Chemistry, 1985-88, Cancer Rsch., 1979-82; reviewing editor Science, 1989—; editor-in-chief Cell Regulation, 1989-91. Recipient Barbara Robert Meml. medal French Soc. of Connective Tissue, 1988, Outstanding Investigator award Nat. Cancer Inst., 1986-93, Robert J. and Claire Pasarow Found. award, 1991, Lella Gruber Cancer Rsch. award Am. Acad. Dermatology, 1993, Abbott award Internat. Soc. for Oncodevelopmental Biology and Medicine, 1995. Fellow Am. Acad. Arts and Scis.; mem. Finnish Acad. Scis. Office: LaJolla Cancer Res Fnd 10901 N Torrey Pines Rd La Jolla CA 92037-1005*

RUPNIK, JOHN KENYON, physician; b. Tulsa, Feb. 21, 1947; s. John Joseph and Dorothy Beryl (Baugher) R.; m. Lauren Achor, Sept. 12, 1971; children: Brian Kenyon, Carolyn Lauren. BA cum laude, Stanford U., 1969; MD, U. Calif., San Francisco, 1973. Diplomate Am. Bd. Internal Medicine, Am. Bd. Infectious Diseases, Am. Bd. Geriatrics. Extern occupational medicine USPHS, Cin., 1972; intern U. Calif., Irvine, 1973-74; resident in internal medicine U. Calif., 1974-75; fellow in infectious diseases U. Calif., Irvine, 1975-77; staff physician internal medicine and infectious diseases So. Calif. Permanent Med. Group, Bellflower, 1977-80; cons. med. staff. Vallejo (Calif.) Gen. Hosp., 1980-84, Sonoma Valley (Calif.) Hosp., 1980-84, St. Helena Med. Ctr., 1980—; staff physician Queen of the Valley Hosp., Napa, Calif., 1980—; practice internal medicine Napa, 1980—; asst. clin. prof. U. Calif.-Irvine, 1977-79, assoc. clin. prof., 1979-80; cons., lectr. in field; chmn. infection control com. Kaiser-Permanente Hosp., Bellflower, 1979-80; treas. Napa Valley Physician's Plan, Inc., 1986-88; mem. utilization rev. com. Napa Nursing Ctr., 1985—; mem. ad hoc com. on AIDS policy Napa City Bd. Edn., 1987; med. dir. Silverado Nursing Ctr., Napa, 1985-86. Mem. AMA, AAAS, Am. Coll. Physicians, Am. Soc. Microbiology, Napa County Med. Soc. (community health liaison com. 1985—), Calif. Med. Assn., Am. Soc. Internal Medicine, Calif. Soc. Internal Medicine, Stanford Alumnus Club. Democrat. Presbyterian. Office: 3443 Villa Ln Apt 9 Napa CA 94558-6417

RUSCHE, HERMAN FREDERICK, gastroenterologist; b. Evansville, Ind., Oct. 20, 1935; s. Herman Frederick and Eleanor Clementine (Schu) R.; m. Dorisann Branen, July 24, 1965; children: Kristin Marie, Herman Frederick, Michael Branen, Karen Elizabeth. BS in Optometry, Ind. U., 1957, MO in Optometry, 1958, MD, 1963. Bd. cert. Rotating intern Phila. Gen. Hosp., 1963-64; resident in internal medicine Mayo Clinic, Rochester, Minn., 1964, 67; resident in internal medicine Ind. U. Med. Ctr., Indpls., 1967-89, fellow in gastroenterology, 1969-71; pvt. practice, founder Gastroenterology Assoc., Evansville, 1971—; pres., bd. dirs. Vanderburgh County Med. Soc., Evansville. Capt. U.S. Army M.C., 1965-66. Fellow Am. Coll. Gastroenterology; mem. Am. Soc. Gastrointestinal Endoscopy. Office: Gastroenterology Assocs # 110 W 801 St Mary's Dr Evansville IN 47714

RUSE, WILLIAM ELLIOTT, healthcare administrator; b. Cleve., Dec. 3, 1934; s. Ollie and Mary (Vinsek) R.; m. Donna Ruse, June 23, 1956; children: William, Rebecca, Robert. BSc in Pharmacy, Ohio No. U., Ada, 1957; MBA, Xavier U., Cin., 1963; JD, U. Toledo, 1972. Registered pharmacist, Ohio; lic. atty., Ohio. Dir. pharmacy Lima (Ohio) Meml. Hosp., 1957-60; chief pharmacist Blanchard Valley Hosp., Findlay, Ohio, 1960-61, dir. pers. and purchasing, 1961-63, asst. adminstr., 1963-64, pres., CEO, 1964—; mem., vice chair Ohio Health Care Bd., Columbus, 1993—; sec. Ohio Hosp. Ins. Co., Columbus, 1993—; chair Ohio Hosp. Assoc. Bd., Columbus, 1991; mem. adv. bd. Ohio No. U. Coll. Pharmacy. Contbr. articles to profl. jours. Sec.-treas. Cmty. Devel. Found., Findlay; campaign chmn., pres. United Way, Findlay; pres. ARC, Findlay; chmn. adv. bd. Salvation Army, Findlay; trustee U. Findlay. Named to Outstanding Young Men of Am.; recipient Am. Jurisprudence awards, 1971, 72, Service to Mankind award Sertoma Internat., 1978, others. Fellow Am. Coll. Healthcare Execs. (regent for Ohio); mem. ABA, Ohio Bar Assn., Soc. Hosp. Attys. (past pres.), Am. Acad. Hosp. Attys., Findlay Rotary Club (pres. 1994-95). Republican. Roman Catholic. Home: 13456 SR 68 Findlay OH 45840 Office: Blanchard Valley Hosp 145 W Wallace St Findlay OH 45840

RUSH, DAVID, medical investigator, epidemiologist; b. N.Y.C., May 3, 1934; s. Samuel Hersh and Fannie (Dubin) R.; m. Catharine Ireland Dawson, June 24, 1957; children: Naomi Rush Olson, Hannah M., Leah D. BA cum laude, Harvard U., 1955, MD, 1959. Diplomate Am. Bd. Pediatrics. Resident in medicine U. Ill. Hosp., Chgo., 1959-61; resident in pediatrics Children's Hosp., Boston, 1963-65; registrar in pediatrics St. Mary's Hosp. Med. Sch., London, 1964-65; rsch. fellow, Harvard U. Med. Sch., Boston, 1965-66; asst. prof. preventive medicine and pediatrics, U. Rochester (N.Y.), 1967-69; asst. prof. pub. health (epidemiology) and pediatrics Columbia U., N.Y.C., also dir. prenatal project, 1969-76, assoc. prof., 1976-82; prof. pediatrics, social medicine and ob-gyn Albert Einstein Coll. Medicine, Bronx, N.Y., 1983-88; dir. epidemiology program USDA, Human Nutrition Research Ctr. on Aging, 1988-96, prof. nutrition, community health, pediatrics Tufts U., Boston, 1988—; mem. human devel. and aging study sect. NIH, USPHS, 1982-86; prin. investigator nat. evaluation of spl. supplemental food program for women, infants and children U.S. Dept. Agr., 1981-86. Author: Diet in Pregnancy, 1980, Dead Reckoning, 1992; assoc. editor Medicine and Global Survival; mem. editorial bd. Am. Jour. Pub. Health; contbr. articles to profl. jours. Trustee, chmn. health services com. Children's Aid Soc., N.Y.C., 1971-86. Served as surgeon USPHS, 1961-63; capt. Res. Recipient career investigator award N.Y.C. Health Research Council, 1977; sr. internat. fellow Fogarty Ctr., NIH, USPHS, U. Bristol, Eng., 1977-78, U. Paris, 1984-85; research grantee Nat. Inst. Child and Human Devel., NIH, 1979-86. Fellow Am. Pub. Health Assn. (governing council 1976-79); mem. Soc. for Epidemiologic Research (pres. 1980-81), Soc. for Pediatric Research, Internat. Epidemiologic. Assn., Am. Epidemiol. Soc., Am. Pediatric Soc., Perinatal Research Soc., Am. Inst. of Nutrition, Am. Soc. Clin. Nutrition, Am. Coll. of Epidemiology. Office: Human Nutrition Rsch Ctr 711 Washington St Boston MA 02111-1524

RUSH, DOMENICA MARIE, health facilities administrator; b. Gallup, N.Mex., Apr. 10, 1937; d. Bernardo G. and Guadalupe (Milan) Iorio; m. W. E. Rush, Jan. 5, 1967. Diploma, Regina Sch. Nursing, Albuquerque, 1958. RN N.Mex.; lic. nursing home adminstr. Charge nurse, house supr. St. Joseph Hosp., Albuquerque, 1958-63; dir. nursing Cibola Hosp., Grants, 1960-64; supr. operating room, dir. med. seminars Carrie Tingley Crippled Children's Hosp., Truth or Consequences, N.Mex., 1964-73; adminstr. Sierra Vista Hosp., Truth or Consequences, 1974-88, pres., 1980-89; clin. nursing mgr. U. N.Mex. Hosp., 1989-90; adminstr. Nor-Lea Hosp., Lovington, N.Mex., 1990-94; with regional ops. divsn. Presbyn. Healthcare Svcs., Albuquerque, 1994—, regional ops., 1994—; adminstr. Sierra Vista Hosp., Truth or Consequences, N.Mex., 1995—; bd. dirs. N.Mex. Blue Cross/Blue Shield, 1977-88, chmn. hosp. relations com., 1983-85, exec. com. 1983—; bd. dirs. Region II Emergency Med. Svcs. Originating bd. SW Mental Health Ctr., Sierra County, N.Mex., 1975; chmn. Sierra County Personnel Bd., 1983—. Named Lea County Outstanding Woman, N.Mex. Commn. on Status of Women; Woman of Yr. for Lea County, N.Mex., 1993. Mem. Am. Coll. Health Care Adminstrs., Sierra County C. of C. (bd. dirs. 1972, 75-76, svc. award 1973, Businesswoman of the Yr. 1973-74), N.Mex. Hosp. Assn. (bd. dirs., sec.-treas., pres.-elect, com. chmn., 1977-88, pres. 1980-81, exec. com., 1980-83, 84-85, recipient meritorius svc. award 1988), N.Mex. So. Hosp. Coun. (sec. 1980-81, pres. 1981-82), Am. Hosp. Assn. (N.Mex. del. 1984-88, regional adv. bd. 1984-88). Republican. Roman Catholic. Home: 1100 N Riverside Truth or Consequence NM 87901 Office: 800 E 9th Truth or Consequence NM 87901

RUSHING, PHILIP DALE, retired social worker; b. Carbondale, Ill., Mar. 15, 1932; S. Paul and Beulah Myrl (Benton) R.; m. Linda North, July 5, 1958 (div. July 1964); 1 child, Lisa Ann Rushing Burrow; m. Rosalie Anne Sturm, Aug. 20, 1966. BA, So. Ill. U., 1958; MSW, Washington U., St. Louis, 1960. Bd. cert. diplomate, ACSW; lic. social worker, Ill. Child welfare worker Ill. Dept. Pub. Welfare, Salem, E. St. Louis, 1958-60; child welfare supr. Ill. Dept. Pub. Welfare, E. St. Louis, 1960-63; field rep. Nat. Assn. for Retarded Children, Dallas, Denver, 1963-65; dir. social svcs. A.L. Bowen Children's Ctr., Harrisburg, Ill., 1965-68; asst. zone dir. for mentally retarded Ill. Dept. of Mental Health, Harrisburg, 1968-74; regional coord. for devel. disabilities Ill. Dept. of Mental Health & Dev. Disabilities, Marion, 1974-83; social work adminstr. Choate Mental Health & Devel. Ctr., Anna, Ill., 1983-95; ret., 1995; adj. asst. prof. So. Ill. U. Rehab. Inst., Carbondale, Ill., 1968-78. Bd. cert. diplomate ACSW; lic. clin. social worker. Bd. deacons First Presbyn. Ch., Harrisburg, 1974-77, bd. trustees, 1978-80, bd. elders, 1980-83, 96—. With USN, 1951-55, Korea. Fellow Am. Assn. on Mental Retardation (life, chmn. social work divsn. Ill. chpt. 1973-74); mem. NASW (chmn. East St. Louis br. 1962). Home: 6542 Highway 13 W Harrisburg IL 62946-4142

RUSIN, WILLIAM ALOYSIUS, otolaryngologist; b. Wilkes-Barre, Pa., Jan. 16, 1938; s. Steven and Catherine (Halupka) R.; m. Elaine A. Jatkowski, June 24, 1961; children: William A. Jr., Christopher J. BS in Biology, King's Coll., Wilkes-Barre, 1959; MD, Temple U., 1963. Diplomate Am. Bd. Otolaryngology. Med. intern Geisinger Med. Ctr., Danville, Pa., 1963-64; otolaryngology resident Geisinger Med. Ctr., Danville, 1964-68; otolaryngologist E.N.T. Surg. Group, Wilkes-Barre, 1972—; pres. med. staff Wilkes-Barre Gen. Hosp. Maj. U.S. Army, 1968-71. Fellow Am. Acad. Otolaryngology, Head and Neck Surgery. Republican. Roman Catholic. Office: ENT Surg Group 35 W Linden St Ste 320 Wilkes Barre PA 18702-2619

RUSKIN, HOWARD MARK, neurologist; b. Bklyn., May 8, 1942; s. Oscar Straus and Thelma (Freiberg) R.; m. Paula Harriet Cohen, Aug. 22, 1965; children: Stacie, Joshua, Ryan. Student, U. Fla., 1959-62; MD, U. Miami, 1966. Diplomate Am. Bd. Psychiatry and Neurology. Intern U. Miami, Jackson Meml. Hosp., 1966-67, resident, 1967-70; chief neurology svc. USPHS, San Francisco, 1970-72; clin. instr. U. Calif., San Francisco, 1970-72; instr. neurology U. Miami, Fla., 1972, clin. asst. prof. neurology, 1972-81, clin. assoc. prof. neurology, 1981-94, clin. prof. neurology, 1994—; pvt. practice; chief of staff Humana Hosp. Bennett, Plantation, Fla., 1988-91, chief of medicine, 1986-87; chief of medicine Plantation (Fla.) Gen. Hosp., 1977-79. With USPHS, 1970-72. Fellow Am. Acad. Neurology; mem. AMA, Fla. Med. Assn., Broward County Med. Assn., Fla. Soc. Neurology, Phi Kappa Phi, Alpha Omega Alpha. Jewish. Office: 8251 W Broward Blvd Plantation FL 33325

RUSOFF, IRVING ISADORE, industrial food scientist, consultant; b. Newark, Jan. 29, 1915; s. Max and Rachel (Dodin) R.; m. Perle Greenspan, Sept. 12, 1941 (dec. Nov. 1986); children: Susan, Arnold; m. Lillian Louise Skora, Sept. 6, 1987. BS, U. Fla., 1937, MS, 1939; PhD, U. Minn., 1943. Dairy chemistry instr. U. Fla., Gainesville, 1939-40; Nat. Def. Coun. fellow U. Minn., Mpls., 1944-46; head of nutritional rsch. Standard Brands, Inc., N.Y.C., 1946-47; head of nutrition, fats and oils Gen. Foods Corp., Hoboken and Tarrytown, N.Y., 1947-62; mgr. rsch. DCA Food Industries, N.Y.C., 1962-63; dir. nutritional biochemistry Beech Nut Life Savers, N.Y.C., 1963-66; dir. basic studies Nabisco, Inc., Fairlawn, N.J., 1966-76; sr. scientist Nabisco Brands, Inc., East Hanover, N.J., 1976-85; cons. Brick, N.J., 1985—; membership chmn. indslo. liaison panel NRC, Washington, 1979-83; liaison chmn. of IFT, Nat. Inventors Hall of Fame, Akron, Ohio, 1980-95; chmn. Gordon Rsch. Conf. on Food and Nutrition, 1981-82; rep. Grocery Mfrs. Assn.; mem. tech. com. for Nabisco, 1975-82; rep. to nutrition com. Biscuit and Crackers Mfrs. Assn., 1978-82. Contbr. articles to profl. jours.; patentee in field. Pres. Park Ridge (N.J.) Bd. Health, 1968. Nat. Found. for Infantile Paralysis fellow, 1943. Fellow Inst. Food Technologists (chmn. 1979-80); mem. Am. Assn. of Cereal Chemists (Charles N. Frey award 1984), Am. Chem. Soc., Am. Inst. Nutrition, Am. Oil Chemists Soc. (assoc. editor 1960-62), N.Y. Acad. Scis., Sigma Xi, Phi Tau Sigma. Jewish. Home: 65 Central Blvd Brick NJ 08724-2451

RUSS, JOSEPH EDWARD, surgeon; b. LaPorte, Ind., Feb. 24, 1946; s. Joseph Edward and Ann Leone (Fail) R.; m. Patricia Marie Surjan, Mar. 25, 1972; children: Matthew Joseph, Andrew Edward, Jennifer Susan. BS, Northwestern U., Evanston, Ill., 1968; MD, Northwestern U., Chgo., 1970. Diplomate Am. Bd. Surgery. Resident in surgery Northwestern U., Chgo., 1977; surg. oncology fellow M.D. Anderson Hosp., Houston, 1978; pvt. practice Midwest Surgery, S.C., St. Charles, Ill., 1978—. Contbr. articles to profl. jours. Maj. USAF, 1971-77. Fellow ACS; mem. Soc. Surg. Oncology, Chgo. Surg. Soc., Am. Radium Soc. (Resident Award Paper 1978), Am. Soc. Colon and Rectal Surgeons, Soc. Head and Neck Surgeons (Resident Award Paper 1979). Republican. Roman Catholic. Office: Midwest Surgery SC 2210 Dean St #B Saint Charles IL 60175

RUSSAC, RANDALL JOSEPH, psychology educator; b. Perth, Australia, Jan. 8, 1947; came to U.S., 1948; s. Joe Russac and Billie Patricia (Hunt) Flynn; m. Julie Ann Bush, Nov. 22, 1971 (div. Sept. 1980); children: Megan, Beth, Adam, Emily; m. Janet Lynn Harris, Aug. 22, 1985. BA in Psychology, U. Wash., 1972; PhD in Psychology, Ariz. State U., 1977. Cert. sch. psychologist, Fla. Assoc. prof. psychology U. North Fla., Jacksonville, 1977—, chmn. dept., 1986-87, dir. Lab. for Rsch. in Noncognitive Devel., 1985—; ptnr. Weaver and Russac, Cons.; co-owner Tots to Teens Book Orders, Inc., Jacksonville, 1988—. Author Memory Assessment Battery test, 1988. Bd. dirs. Mandarin Libr. Assn., Jacksonville, 1989-90; mem. Jacksonville Community Coun., Inc., 1988—, Greater Jacksonville Families in Action, 1988—. With U.S. Army, 1967-70, Vietnam. Decorated Purple Heart. Mem. Am. Psychol. Soc., SE Psychol. Assn., Cognitive Neurosci. Group Jacksonville (founder, pres. 1987-90). Home: 2057 River Oaks Dr Jacksonville FL 32259-8330 Office: U North Fla 4567 Saint Johns Bluff Rd S Jacksonville FL 32224-2646

RUSSELL, BRIAN KEITH, neurologist; b. Herrin, Ill., Jan. 19, 1957; m. Kimberly Ann Burgess, 1984; children: Wesley Ryan, Patrick Scott, Kevin Lee, Sara Elizabeth. BA in Psychology, So. Ill. U., 1980, MD, 1983. Diplomate Am. Bd. Neurosurgery; lic. Ill. Intern So. Ill. U. Affiliated Hosps., Springfield, 1983-84; resident U. Kans. Med. Ctr., Kansas City, 1984-89; pvt. practice Springfield, 1989—; staff physician St. John's Hosp., Springfield, Meml. Med. Ctr., Springfield, Doctors Hosp., Springfield. Presenter in field; contbr. articles to profl. jours. Rsch. fellow Mayo Found., 1979. Fellow ACS; mem. AMA, Am. Assn. Neurol. Surgeons, Congress Neurol. Surgeons, Ill. State Med. Soc., Sangamon County Med. Soc. Home: 1250 Rachel Ln Springfield IL 62707 Office: 455 W Carpenter Springfield IL 62702

RUSSELL, DAVID P., urologist; b. Evansville, Ind., June 4, 1952; s. Kenneth and Louise (Powell) R.; m. Betsy Curran, July 1977. BS, U. Ky., 1974, MD, 1978. Pvt. practice, Owensboro, Ky., 1983—. Fellow ACS; mem. AMA, Ky. Med. Assn., Ky. Urol. Assn. Office: 2211 Mayfair Dr Owensboro KY 42301

RUSSELL, DOUGLAS CAMPBELL, cardiologist; b. Oxford, Eng., July 26, 1945; came to U.S., 1989; s. David Syme and Marion Hamilton (Campbell) R.; m. Mercedes Dumas, Nov. 16, 1975; 1 child, Georgina Mercedes. BA with 1st class honors, Cambridge U., 1966, MB, BChir, 1969, MD, 1981; PhD, Edinburgh (Scotland) U., 1979. House officer Charing Cross Hosp. Med. Sch., London, 1970-71, sr. house officer, 1971-73; sr. house officer Hammersmith Hosp., London, 1973; registrar cardiology London Chest Hosp., 1973-75; rsch. asst. Med. Rsch. Coun. Edinburgh U., 1975-77, Brit. Heart Found. fellow, 1977-79, lectr. medicine, 1979-83, sr. lectr., sr. rsch. fellow cardiovascular rsch. unit, 1983-89; prof. medicine, chief cardiology U. Va. Sch. Medicine, Salem (Va.) VA Med. Ctr., Roanoke, 1989—; cons. cardiologist Royal Infirmary Edinburgh, 1983-89. Contbr. articles to med. jours. Rsch. grantee British Heart Found., Chest Heart and Stroke Assn., Thyssen Found., Scottish Home & Health, Pharm. Cos., 1976-89; John French Meml. lectr. Arterosclerosis Discussion Grop, Oxford, 1979. Fellow Am. Coll. Cardiology, Royal Coll. Physicians; mem. British Cardiac Soc., British Soc. Cardiovascular Rsch. (treas. 1984-87), Internat. Soc. Heart Rsch., British Med. Assn. Baptist. Home: 6315 Spring Run Dr Roanoke VA 24018-5417 Office: U Va Dept Cardiology Salem VA 24157

RUSSELL, ELBERT WINSLOW, neuropsychologist; b. Las Vegas, N.Mex., June 4, 1929; s. Josiah Cox and Ruth Annice (Winslow) R.; children from previous marriage: Gwendolyn Marie Harvey, Franklin Winslow, Kirsten Nash, Jonathan Nash; m. Sally Lynn Kolitz, Apr. 2, 1989. BA, Earlham Coll., Richmond, Ind., 1951; MA, U. Ill., 1953; MS, Pa. State U., 1958; PhD, U. Kans., 1968. Clin. psychologist Warnersville (Pa.) State Hosp., 1959-61; clin. neuropsychologist VA Med. Ctr., Cin., 1968-71; dir. neuropsychology lab. VA Med. Ctr., Miami, Fla., 1971-89, rsch. psychologist, 1989—; adj. prof. Nova U., Ft. Lauderdale, 1980-87, U. Miami Med. Sch., 1980-94, U. Miami, 1979—. Author: (with C. Neuringer and G. Goldstein) Assessment of Brain Damage, 1970; (with R.I. Starkey) Halstead Russell Neuropsychology Evaluation System (manual and computer program), 1993; contbr. articles to profl. jours. Fellow APA, Am. Psychol. Soc., Nat. Acad. Neuropsychology; mem. Sigma Xi. Democrat. Soc. of Friends. Home: 6091 SW 79th St Miami FL 33143-5030 Office: 6262 Sunset Dr Ste PH 228 Miami FL 33143

RUSSELL, FINDLAY EWING, physician; b. San Francisco, Sept. 1, 1919; s. William and Mary Jane (Findlay) R.; m. Marilyn Ruth Jenkins, Apr. 12, 1975; children—Christa Ann, Sharon Jane, Robin Emily, Constance Susan, Mark Findlay. BA, Walla Walla (Wash.) Coll., 1941; MD, Loma Linda (Calif.) U., 1950; postgrad. (fellow), Calif. Inst. Tech., 1951-53; PhD, U. Santa Barbara, Calif., 1974, LLD (hon.), 1989. Intern White Meml. Hosp., Los Angeles, 1950-51; practice medicine specializing in toxinology and toxicology Los Angeles, 1953—; mem. staff Los Angeles County-U. So. Calif. Med. Center, Loma Linda U. Med. Center, U. Ariz. Med. Ctr.; physiologist Huntington Inst. Med. Research, 1953-55; dir. lab. neurol. research Los Angeles County-U. So. Calif. Med. Center, 1955-80; mem. faculty Loma Linda U. Med. Sch., 1955—; prof. neurology, physiology and biology U. So. Calif. Med. Sch., 1966-81; prof. pharmacology and toxicology U. Ariz., 1981—; cons. USPHS, NSF, Office Naval Rsch., WHO, U.S. Army, Walter Reed, USAF, Brooks AFB. Author: Marine Toxins and Venomous and Poisonous Marine Animals, 1965, Poisonous Marine Animals, 1971, Snake Venom Poisoning, 1980; co-author: Bibliography of Snake Venoms and Venomous Snakes, 1964, Animal Toxins, 1967, Poisonous Snakes of The World, 1968, Snake Venom Poisoning, 1983, Bibliography of Venomous and Poisonous Marine Animals and Their Toxins, 1984; editor: Toxicon, 1962-70. Served with AUS, 1942-46. Decorated Purple Heart, Bronze Star; recipient award Los Angeles County Bd. Suprs., 1960; award Acad. Medicine Buenos Aires, 1966; Skylab Achievement award, 1974; Jozef Stefan medal Yugoslavia, 1978. Fellow A.C.P., Am. Coll. Cardiology, Royal Soc. Tropical Medicine, N.Y. Acad. Scis.; mem. Internat. Soc. Toxinology (pres. 1962-66, Francisco Redi medal 1967), Royal Soc. Medicine, Am. Soc. Physiology, Western Soc. Pharmacology (pres. 1973). Office: U Ariz Coll Pharmacy Tucson AZ 85721

RUSSELL, GEORGE KEITH, biology educator, editor; b. Bronxville, N.Y., Dec. 13, 1937; s. Donald Keith and Anna (Kibitz) R.; m. Leonore Diane deSylva, Mar. 29, 1970. A.B., Princeton U., 1959; Ph.D., Harvard U., 1963. Asst. prof. biology Princeton U., 1965-67; asst. prof. Adelphi U., Garden City, N.Y., 1967-70, assoc. prof., 1970-77, prof. biology, 1977—. Editor ORION mag., 1982—. Author sci. monograph and lab. manual. Chmn. bd. trustees The Waldorf Sch. of Garden City, 1983-95; bd. dirs. Am. Council for Drug Edn., N.Y.C., 1978-94, The Myrin Inst., N.Y.C., 1977— . Mem. Am. Soc. Plant Physiologists. Avocations: gardening; hiking; reading. Office: Adelphi U Dept Biology South Ave Garden City NY 11530

RUSSELL, GERALD EDWARD, social worker, retired army officer; b. Monticello, Miss., Apr. 7, 1933; s. Jessie Edward and Lavert Virdew (Franklin) R.; m. Nina Merle Holmes, Dec. 17, 1955; children: Tina, Aprile, Glen, Eric. MSW, Tulane U., 1962. Cert. social worker, La.; diplomate Am. Bd. Examiners and NASW in Clin. Social Work. With Dept. Pub. Welfare, Jackson, Miss., 1958-64, supr. child welfare, 1962-64; commd. 1st lt. U.S. Army, 1964, advanced to grade of lt. col., 1979; ret., 1982; chief social work U.S. Army Hosp., Ft. Jackson, S.C., 1964-66; mem. child fellowship program Walter Reed Hosp., Washington, 1966-68; asst. chief social work Brooke Gen. Hosp., Ft. Sam Houston, Tex., 1968-72; chief social work U.S. Army Hosp., Ft. Polk, La., 1972-82, supr. child protection, 1982—. Mem. NASW (cert.), Acad. Cert. Social Workers, La. Assn. Substance Abuse, La. Conf. Social Welfare, La. Soc. Clin. Social Workers. Home: 136 Russell Cir Leesville LA 71446-9011

RUSSELL, JAMES CRAIG, general surgeon; b. Niagara Falls, Ont., Can., Apr. 23, 1952; m. Barbara Jane Russell, June 9, 1984; children: Alex, Sam, Jeremy. BA, Colgate U., 1975; postgrad., Waterloo U.; MD, McMaster U., Hamilton, Ont., 1979. Diplomate Am. Bd. Surgery. Resident in surgery McMaster U., Hamilton, Ont., 1984; pvt. practice gen. surgery Brantford, Ont., 1985-92; with trauma svc. Baystate Med. Ctr., Springfield, Mass., 1992-93; solo practice gen. surgery Phoenix, 1993—; with trauma svc. St. Joseph's Hosp., Phoenix, 1994—. Mem. ACS, Am. Soc. Gen. Surgeons, Soc. Critical Care Medicine, Maricopa County Med. Soc., Phoenix Surg. Soc. Office: 2720 N 20th St # 310 Phoenix AZ 85006

RUSSELL, JOAN DELIGHT, hospital administrator, realtor, investor; b. Youngstown, Ohio, July 20, 1933; d. Jack Leonard and Pauline Frances (Cox) Burris; m. Herbert A. Cook, Dec. 12, 1964 (div. May, 1981); children—Scott, Vicki, Todd, Herbert, Jr., Tami, Susan; m. Camp Wells Russell, May 16, 1981. Student St. Paul Bible Coll., Minn., 1951-56; diploma in nursing Grant Hosp., Columbus, Ohio, 1955. Registered nurse; cert. nursing home administrator. Post-operative specialist open heart surgery various hosps., 1956-61; in-service coordinator I.V. therapist various hosps., 1962-64; owner, dir. of nurses, hops. adminstr. Convalescent Hosp., Long Beach, Calif., 1964-72; v.p. Circle Convalescent Hosp., Calif., 1972-82, Leisure Convalescent Hosp., Calif., 1972-82, Hac-Con Corp., Long Beach, 1972-82; sec. Pacific Coast Convalescent Hosp. Corp., Long Beach, 1972-82; pvt. practice investments, real estate, office bldg. mgmt., Long Beach, 1972-84; pres. Delight Investment, Inc., Long Beach, 1981—; owner, operator Calif. Convalescent Hosp., Long Beach, 1984—; pres., chmn. Jurupa Hills Enterprises, 1987—; speaker schs. and seminars. Weekly radio broadcast, 1965-72. Del., Am. Nurses Assn., Calif. Nurses Assn.; organist West Lakewood Baptist Ch., Sunday sch. tchr.; mem. Campus Crusade, Campus Life; pres. Point Loma Coll. Women's Aux. Mem. Nursing Home Adminstrs., Registered Nurses Assn., Real Estate Assn., Concerned Women Am. Republican. Club: Youth for Christ (exec. bd.). Avocations: music, boating, motor home camping. Home: PO Box 10549 Scottsdale AZ 85271-0549 Office: Calif Convalescent Hosp 3850 E Esther St Long Beach CA 90804-2009

RUSSELL, LAWRENCE, physician's assistant; b. Jersey City, Mar. 29, 1942; s. Arthur and Rita (Auer) R.; m. Barbara M. Russell, Nov. 29, 1938; children: Denise M. Russell Walker, Dale J., Renee A., Lawrence Jr. BS, U. Nebr., 1974; MA in Health Svc. Adminstrn., Webster U., 1983. Cert. physician asst. Commd. USAF, 1959-88, advanced through grades to maj., ret. 1988; physician asst. USAF Regional Hosp., Sheppard AFB, Tex., 1973-74; cons. for computer assisted edn. devel. Sch. Health Care Scis., Sheppard AFB, Tex., 1974-76, instr. supr. for physician asst. course, 1976-31; cons. to USAF surgeon gen., assoc. chief biomed. corp USAF Med. Svc. Ctr., Brooks AFB, Tex., 1981-84; physician asst. USAF Regional Hosp., Sheppard AFB, 1984-88, Wichitan Falls (Tex.) Clinic, 1988-90; physician asst. neurology North Tex. Neurology, Wichita Falls, 1990—. Vice pres. Little League; team trainer Burburnett H.S. Decorated Air Force Commendation medal (4), Air Medal with 2 oak leaf clusters. Fellow Am. Acad. Physician Assts., Soc. of Air Force Physician Assts., Vietnam Vets of Am.; mem. Tex. Acad. Physician Asst., Rotary (dir.). Republican. Roman Catholic. Office: North Texas Neurology 1722 9th St Wichita Falls TX 76301

RUSSELL, LAWRENCE B., JR., physician assistant, x-ray technologist; b. Stevens Point, Wis., Dec. 19, 1946; s. Lawrence B. and Berniece (Kostubuski) R.; m. Marcia M. Russell. Student, U. Wis., Stevens Point, 1968-70, U. Wis., Madison, 1970-72, Pa. State U., Hershey, 1973-75. Radiologic technologist U. Wis., Madison, 1970-72; mgr. emergency room St. Anthony's Hosp., Chgo., 1972-73; physician asst. Charles Yoder, M.D., McAlisterville, Pa., 1974-75, Elk Valley Med. Ctr., Girard, Pa., 1975—; clin. instr. Gannon U., Erie, Pa., 1975—, nat. clin. examiner phys. assts., 1988—. Chmn., mgr. West County YMCA, 1975-86; bd. dirs., sec. Girard Civil Svc. Police, 1985-95; softball coach Girard Girls Softball, bd. dirs., 1984-95; chmn. athletic boosters Villa H.S., Erie, 1992—. With U.S. Army, 1966-68. Recipient President's award West County YMCA, 1985. Mem. Pa. Acad. Phys. Assts. (bd. dirs. 1975-80, Pa. Pa. Acad. X-Ray Technologists, KC (grand knight, pres. 1976, Knight of Yr. award). Republican. Roman Catholic. Office: Elk Valley Med Ctr 5165 Imperial Pky Girard PA 16417

RUSSELL, LILLIAN, medical, surgical nurse; b. N.Y.C., Feb. 21, 1942; d. Joserelle Russell; 1 child, Evan Gregory. AAS, N.Y.C. Community Coll., 1973; BS, St. Xavier Coll., Chgo., 1986; MS, Spertus Coll. of Judaica, Chgo., 1989. Staff/charge nurse Beth Israel Med. Ctr., N.Y.C., 1973-76; charge nurse Roosevelt Hosp., N.Y.C., 1977-78; staff/charge nurse U. Ill. Hosp., Chgo., 1979-90; asst. adminstrv. coord. Bethany Hosp., Chgo., 1990-91; adminstv. nurse I Mile Square Health Ctr. & U. Ill. Hosp., Chgo., 1991-95; asst. dir. nursing Mile Square Health Ctr., Chgo., 1995—; mem. instnl. rev. com. Bethany Hosp., 1987—; adj. asst. prof. Trinity Christian Coll., Palos Heights, Ill., 1996—. Mem. Great Cities Com., Chgo., 1994—. Mem. ANA, NAFE, AAUW, Ill. Nurses Assn., Res. Officers Assn. Home: 1342 N Oakley Blvd Chicago IL 60622-3048

RUSSELL, MARLOU, psychologist; b. Tucson, June 2, 1956; d. William Herman and Carole Eleanor (Musgrove) McBratney; m. Jan Christopher Russell, Sept. 9, 1989. BA U. Ariz., 1981; MA Calif. Grad. Inst., 1983, PhD, 1987. Lic. psychologist, marriage, family and child counselor. Asst. to pres. Western Psychol. Svcs., L.A., 1978-81; crisis counselor Cedars-Sinai Med. Ctr., L.A., 1980-84; counselor South Bay Therapeutic Clinic, Hawthorne, Calif., 1982-84; psychotherapist PMC Treatment Systems, L.A., 1984-85, Beverly Hills Counseling Ctr., 1984-85, Comprehensive Care Corp., L.A., 1985-86; pvt. practice, L.A., 1986—; counselor Brotman Med. Ctr., L.A., 1982-83, Julia Ann Singer Ctr., L.A., 1984; bd. dirs. Los Angeles Commn. Assualts Against Women, 1987-89. Author: Adoption Wisdom: A Guide to the Issues and Feelings of Adoption. Mem. Internat. Assn. Eating Disorders Profls, Women in Health (bd. dirs. 1993-94), Women's Referral Svc., Calif. State Psychol. Assn., Calif. Assn. Marriage & Family Therapists (bd. dirs. 1993-94), Am. Adoption Congress, Westside Bus. Womens Assn. (bd. dirs. 1993-94). Democrat. Office: 1452 26th St Ste 103 Santa Monica CA 90404-3042

RUSSELL, MICHAEL WILLIAM, immunologist, educator; b. Epsom, Surrey, Eng., July 12, 1944; s. Harold William and Mary Louisa Frances (Parker) R. BA, U. Cambridge, Eng., 1966, MA, 1970; PhD, U. Reading, Eng., 1973. Rsch. asst., lectr. Guy's Hosp. and Med. Dental Schs., London, 1972-79; rsch. asst. prof. U. Ala., Birmingham, 1982-86, rsch. assoc. prof., 1986-92, rsch. prof., 1992—; vis. investigator U. Ala., Birmingham, 1979-82; vis. assoc. prof. Royal Dental Coll., Aarhus, Denmark, 1987-88. Patentee, U.S., Eng., Japan; contbr. articles to profl. jours. Pres. Birmingham Audubon Soc., 1986-87. Open scholar St. John's Coll., Cambridge, 1963; rsch. grantee NIH, 1984—, 91—, 94—. Mem. British Soc. Immunology, Internat. Assn. Dental Rsch., Am. Soc. Microbiology, Am. Assn. Immunologists, Soc. Mucosal Immunology. Office: U Ala UAB Sta Birmingham AL 35294

RUSSELL, PAUL SNOWDEN, surgeon, educator; b. Chgo., Jan. 22, 1925; s. Paul Snowden and Carroll (Mason) R.; m. Allene Lummis, Sept. 24, 1952; children—Katherine Swift, Paul Snowden, Allene, Laura Rice. Student, Groton (Mass.) Sch., 1939-41; Ph.B., U. Chgo., 1944, B.S., 1945, M.D., 1947; M.A. (hon.), Harvard U., 1962. Diplomate: Am. Bd. Surgery, Am. Bd. Thoracic Surgery. From surg. intern. to resident Mass. Gen. Hosp., 1948-56, asst. surgery, 1957-60, chief gen. surg. services, 1962-69, vis. surgeon, 1969—, chief transplantation unit, 1969-90, chmn. com. on research, 1973-76; postdoctoral fellow USPHS, 1954-55; successively teaching fellow, instr., clin. asso. surgery Harvard Med. Sch., 1956-60, John Homans prof. surgery, 1962—; asso. prof. surgery Columbia Coll. Phys. and Surg., 1960-62; asso. attending surgeon Presbyn. Hosp., N.Y.C., 1960-62; assoc. vis. surgeon Francis Delafield Hosp., N.Y.C., 1960-62, 74-94; mem. com. tissue transplantation NRC-Nat. Acad. Scis., 1963-71, com. trauma, 1963-68; ad hoc com. to study clin. investigation and edn. in USN, 1971-73; allergy and immunology study sect. USPHS, 1963-65, chmn. allergy and immunology study sect. B, 1965-67; mem. transplantation and immunology com. Nat. Inst. Allergy and Infectious Diseases, 1967-69, chmn., 1970; mem. com. on cancer immunotherapy Nat. Cancer Inst., 1974-79. Contbr. papers in field.; Editorial bd.: Archives Surgery, 1963-72, Surgery, 1963-71, Transplantation, 1965-79, Annals of Surgery, 1966—, Transplantation Procs, 1966—, Jour. Immunology, 1977-80. Trustee Pine Manor Coll., Chestnut Hill, Mass., 1963-76, Groton Sch., 1964-79; bd. dirs. Boston Fulbright Com., 1968, pres., 1980—; bd. governing trustees Jackson Lab.; bd. trustees Worcester Found. for Biomed. Rsch. With USAF, 1951-53. Fellow ACS, Royal Soc. Medicine; mem. AAAS, Am. Acad. Arts and Scis., Assn. Immunologists, N.Y. Acad. Scis., Mass. Med. Soc., New Eng. Surg. Soc., Boston Surg. Soc. (pres. 1994), Soc. Univ. Surgeons, Soc. Exptl. Biology and Medicine, Halsted Soc., Whipple Soc., Internat. Soc. Surgery, Am. Surg. Assn., Transplantation Soc. (pres. 1970), Polish Acad. Sci. (fgn.), Sigma Xi. Home: 32 Lawrence Rd Chestnut Hill MA 02167-1230 Office: Dept Surgery Mass Gen Hosp Boston MA 02114

RUSSELL, PAULA L., geriatrics nurse; b. Dallas, June 18, 1965; d. Maurine S. Russell. Student, Hill Coll., Cleburne, Tex., 1992-93. Lic. vocat. nurse, Tex. With Kemp (Tex.) Care Ctr.; geriatrics nurse West Place, Athens, Tex. Mormon. Home: 401 S Carroll St Apt 219 Athens TX 75751-2846

RUSSELL, ROBERT C., plastic surgeon; b. Mansfield, Ohio, July 13, 1945. MD, Ind. U., 1972. Diplomate Am. Bd. Plastic Surgery. Intern Wishard Meml. Hosp., Indpls., 1972; resident gen. surgery Ind. U. Sch. Medicine, Indpls., 1973-75, resident plastic surgery, 1975-76; fellow plastic surgery St. Vincent's Hosp., Indpls., 1974, 76-77; resident Southern Ill. U. Sch. Medicine, Springfield, Ill., 1977-79; plastic surgeon St. John's Hosp., Springfield, Ill.; prof surg. divsn. plastic surgery Southern Ill. U., Springfield. Mem. AMA, Am. Assn. Hand Surgeons, Am. Soc. Plastic and Reconstructive Surgery, Am. Soc. Surgery for the Hand. Office: So Ill Sch Medicine PO Box 19230 747 N Rutledge St 3d Fl Springfield IL 62781*

RUSSELL, ROBERT MITCHELL, gastroenterology educator; b. Boston, Apr. 9, 1941; s. Stanley Gordon and Martha Lillian (Johnson) R.; m. Sharon Stanton, Aug. 28, 1965; children: Kimberley, Brooke. BA cum laude, Harvard U., 1963; MD, Columbia U., 1967. Intern U. Chgo., 1967-69, resident, 1971-73, NIH fellow gastroenterology, 1973-75; from asst. to assoc. prof. medicine U. Md. Sch. Medicine, Balt., 1974-81; assoc. prof. medicine Tufts U., Boston, 1981-88, dir. human studies USDA Human Nutrition Rsch. Ctr. on Aging, 1981—, assoc. dir. USDA Human Nutrition Rsch. Ctr. on Aging, 1983—, sr. scientist USDA Human Nutrition Rsch. Ctr. on Aging, 1987—, prof. medicine and nutrition, 1988—; staff physician dept. medicine sect. gastroenterology and clinical nutrition New England Med. Ctr. Hosps., Boston, 1981—; chmn. sci. adv. bd. Nat. Dairy Coun., Chgo., 1987-91; mem. pretest com. Am. Bd. Internal Medicine, Phila., 1990—. Author: Nutritional Status of Boston Elderly, 1991, Chronic Gastritis and Hypochlorhydria in the Elderly, 1992; contbr. articles to profl. jours. Mem. Hyde Park Community Conf., Chgo., 1972-74, Famine Policy Ctr. Com., Boston, 1985-88; mem. So. Iraq cons. team UNICEF, N.Y.C., 1991. Major U.S. Army, 1969-71, Vietnam. Recipient Global Medicine award Assn. U.S. Army, 1971, rsch. award Chgo. Soc. Gastroenterology, 1974, Rsch. Devel. award VA Career Devel. Program, 1975-78. Fellow ACP; mem. Am. Gastroent. Soc., Am. Inst. Nutrition (grad. nutrition edn. com. 1989-90), Am. Coll. Nutrition (Grace Goldsmith award 1994), Am. Soc. Clin. Nutrition, Soc. for Internat. Nutrition Rsch. Democrat. Christian. Office: Tufts U USDA Human Nutrition Rsch Ctr Aging 711 Washington St Boston MA 02111-1524

RUSSELL, ROBERT PRITCHARD, ophthalmologist; b. Columbia, S.C., Apr. 30, 1945; s. Austin Henderson and Ruby Mae (Pritchard) R.; m. Olivia Louise Walker, Jan. 22, 1972; children: Robert Pritchard Jr., Denise Olivia. BA with distinction, U. Miss., 1967; MD, U. Miss., Jackson, 1971. Intern Miss. Bapt. Hosp., Jackson, 1971-72; resident U. Med. Ctr., Jackson, 1974-77; pvt. practice ophthalmologist Jackson, 1977—; mem. surg. staff St. Dominic Health Svcs., Jackson, 1977—; cons. Miss. Bapt. Med. Ctr., Jackson, 1977—, River Oaks Hosp., Flowood, Miss., 1981—; attending teaching staff mem. U. Med. Ctr., Jackson, 1977—. Lt. USNR, 1972-74. Mem. Am. Assn. Ophthalmology, Am. Soc. Contemporary Ophthalmology, Internat. Glaucoma Congress, Am. Intraocular Implant Soc., Contact Lens Assn. Ophthalmologists, Am. Acad. Ophthalmology, Phi Kappa Phi, Alpha Epsilon Delta, Phi Eta Sigma, Phi Chi, Sigma Chi. Republican. Home: 139 Royal Lytham Jackson MS 39211-2516 Office: Watkins Med Bldg 1421 N State St Ste 501 Jackson MS 39202-1658

RUSSELL, ROGER ALLEN, psychology educator; b. Brownsville, Tex., July 23, 1952; s. C.W. and Ola Faye (White) R.; m. Terri Jane Brown, Aug. 17, 1985; 1 child, Ryan Christopher. BA, S.W. Tex. State U., San Marcos, 1974, MEd, 1975; PhD, Tex. A&M U., 1983. Lic. psychologist, marriage and family therapist, Tex. Assoc. psychologist Killeen (Tex.) Ind. Sch. Dist., 1975-77, Abilene (Tex.) Ind. Sch. Dist., 1977-79; counselor Tex. A&M U., College Station, 1979-82; clin. psychologist USAF, Wilford Hall, USAF Med. Ctr., 1982-83, Tinker (Okla.) AFB, 1983-85; assoc. prof. psychology Hardin-Simmons U., Abilene, 1985-93, U. Houston-Victoria, 1993-95; pvt. practice psychologist Abilene, 1988—; Victoria, 1995—; clinical psychologist/clinical supervisor Abilene (Tex.) Regional MH/MR Ctr., 1995—; pvt. practice Abilene, Tex., 1995—. Editor counseling sect. Jour. Family Ministry, 1989-92; edtl. bd. The Family Jour., 1992—; contbr. articles to profl. jours.. Me. ACA, APA, Tex. Psychol. Assn., Abilene Psychol. Assn., Am. Assn. Marriage and Family Therapy, Tex. Assn. Marriage and Family Therapy. Baptist. Office: Big Country Family Therapy Assn 1049 N 3d Ste 505 Abilene TX 79601

RUSSELL, THOMAS J., critical care supervisor; b. Meriden, Conn., July 30, 1954; s. Joseph George and Anna M. (Ruszczek) R. BS in Immunology, Kans. State U., 1977; BS in Microbiology, U. New Haven, 1981; MS, Yale U., 1984; cert. EMT-P, Norwalk Community Coll. Instr. in biology U. New Haven, West Haven, Conn., So. Conn. State U., New Haven; PALS instr, ACLS instr., PHTLS instr. Yale U.; ops. supr. New Eng. Ambulance, Shelton, Conn., New Haven Ambulance; instr. EMS, Conn.; EMS coord. Bradley Meml. Hosp., Southington, Conn.; mem. pre-hosp. pediatric task force State of Conn. Mem. Nat. Assn. EMT's, Nat. Paramedic Assn., N.Y. Acad. Scis., Nat. Acad. Scis., Am. Soc. Microbiology, Am. Soc. Immunology, Conn. Soc. Paramedics, Conn. CISD Team, Conn. EMS-C Com., Conn. Spl. Olympics World Games Med. Team Leader, Phi Beta Kappa, Tau Kappa Epsilon (Teke of Yr.), Beta Beta Beta. Home: 129 Tuttle Rd Durham CT 06422-2208

RUSSELL, WILLIAM BLANTON, physician; b. Paducah, Ky., June 29, 1934; s. Blanton Everett and Nell (Brown) R.; m. Anna Judd Russell, Oct. 4, 1958; children: Karen Leigh, Bryan Blanton, Timothy Scott. Student, U. Mich., 1951-54, MD, 1958. Intern Baptist Hosp., Nashville, 1958-59, resident in pediatrics, 1961-62; resident in internal medicine Veterans Hosp., Memphis, 1959-61; assoc. physician, dir. Graves-Gilbert Clinic, PSC, Bowling Green, Ky., 1962—; chmn. medical records The Med. Ctr., Bowling Green, 1970-95; pres. Clinic Bldg., Inc., Bowling Green, 1989-90. Coauthor: (musical comedy) Film Flam, 1955; author-lyricist: Look at Us, 1968, Land O' My Own, 1970, High and Rising, 1984. Bd. dirs. Commonwealth Health Corp., Bowling Green, 1988—; vestryman Christ Episcopal Ch., Bowling Green, 1970-72, 80-82, 93-96. Capt. U.S. Army, 1967-68. Recipient Citizenship award Am. Legion, 1951. Mem. AMA, Bowling Green-Warren County Med. Soc., Ky. Medical Assn., Southern Med. Assn., Mimes Soc., Phi Eta Sigma. Republican. Episcopalian. Home: 719 Sherwood Dr Bowling Green KY 42103-1422 Office: Graves-Gilbert Clinic PSC PO Box 90007 Bowling Green KY 42102-9007

RUSSELL, WILLIAM LAWSON, geneticist; b. Newhaven, Eng., Aug. 19, 1910; came to U.S., 1932; s. Robert Lawson and Ellen Frances (Frost) R.; m. Elizabeth Buckley Shull, Aug. 29, 1936 (div.); children—Richard L., John S., James J., Ellen M.; m. Liane Ruth Brauch, Sept. 23, 1947; children—David L., Evelyn R. B.A., Oxford U., Eng., 1932; Ph.D., U. Chgo., 1937. Sherman Pratt fellow Amherst Coll., Mass., 1932-33; fellow, asst. U. Chgo., 1933-36; research assoc. Jackson Lab., Bar Harbor, Maine, 1937-47; prin. geneticist Oak Ridge Nat. Lab., 1947-77, cons., 1977—; del. UN Confs. on Peaceful Uses Atomic Energy, 1955, 58, 71, UN Sci. Com. on Effects Atomic Radiation, 1962—; mem. coms. on biol. effects of atomic (ionizing) radiation Nat. Acad. Scis., 1955-80; adviser Fed. Radiation Council, 1964-70. Contbr. numerous articles to profl. jours., chpts. to books. Founder Tenn. Citizens for Wilderness Planning, 1971, pres., 1971-73, 81-85. Recipient Roentgen medal, 1973, Enrico Fermi medal, 1976. Fellow Health Physics Soc.; mem. Nat. Acad. Scis., Genetics Soc. Am. (sec. 1959-61, pres. 1965, Disting. Achievement award 1976), Environ. Mutagen Soc. (councilor), Nat. Council on Radiation Protection and Measurements (hon.). Home: 130 Tabor Rd Oak Ridge TN 37830-5537 Office: Oak Ridge Nat Lab Biology Div PO Box Y Oak Ridge TN 37831*

RUSSO, ALVIN LEON, obstetrician, gynecologist; b. Buffalo, Dec. 2, 1924; s. Anthony Joseph and Sarah (Leone) R.; m. Mary Rose Hehir, Sept. 19, 1953; children: Mary B., Sally A. Silvestri, Daniel J., Jeanne Wotherspoon, Margaret Battaile, Terri A., Anthony A. Student, Baylor U., Waco, Tex., 1943-44, U. Iowa, 1944; MD, U. Kans., Kansas City, 1949. Diplomate Am. Bd. Obstetrics and Gynecology. Intern, then resident E. J. Meyer Meml. Hosp., Buffalo, 1949-55; Fellow in gynocological oncology Roswell Park Meml. Inst., Buffalo, 1955; pvt. practice ob/gyn. San Bernardino, Calif., 1955-89; med. dir. San Bernardino Community Hosp., 1989-92; ret., 1992; bd. dirs. San Bernardino Community Hosp., 1982-89, chmn. bd., 1982-85. Pres. San Bernardino unit Am. Cancer Soc., 1961-62; bd. dirs. More Attractive Community Found. Capt. USAF, 1951-53. Knight, St. John of Jerusalem, 1986--; recipient Distinguished Member award Boy Scouts Am., 1987. Fellow Am. Coll. Ob-Gyns.; mem. AMA, Calif. Med. Assn., N.Y. Acad. Scis., S.W. Ob-Gyn. Soc. (coun. mem. 1989—, v.p. 1992), San Bernardino-Riverside Ob-Gyn. Soc. (pres. 1966), Lions Internat. (dep. dist. gov. 1962-63), Serra Club (pres. San Bernardino chpt.), Arrowhead Country Club (bd. dirs., pres.). Republican. Roman Catholic. Home: 3070 Pepper Tree Ln San Bernardino CA 92404-2313

RUSSO, DENNIS CHARLES, psychologist; b. Cleve., Feb. 11, 1950; s. Charles Martin and Helen Marie (Watrt) R.; m. Deborah Jillson, Oct. 26, 1985; children: Nicholas Charles, Amelia DeBogory. BA with honors, U. Calif., Santa Barbara, 1972, PhD, 1975. Diplomate Am. Bd. Profl. Psychology. Asst. prof. pediatrics and med. psychology Johns Hopkins U. Sch. Medicine, Balt., 1975-79; assoc. dir., dept. behavioral psychology John F. Kennedy Inst., Balt., 1975-79; assoc. prof. psychology Harvard Med. Sch., Boston, 1979—; dir. behavioral medicine The Children's Hosp., Boston, 1979-89; dir. behavioral & pediatric programming New Medico Assocs. Inc., Boston, 1989-92; v.p. health and rehab. svcs. May Inst., Chatham, Mass., 1992—; assoc. attending psychologist McLean Hosp., Norwood, Mass., 1994—; cons. in psychology Mass. Gen. Hosp., Spaulding Rehab. Hosp., Norwood, 1994—. Editor: Behavioral Pediatrics, 1982, Behavioral Medicine with the Developmentally Disabled, 1988; contbr. articles to profl. jours. Fellow APA, Am. Psychol. Soc., Mass. Psychol. Assn., Soc. Behavioral Medicine, Soc. Pediat. Psychology (pres. 1994); mem. Assn. Advancement Behavior Therapy (pres. 1988-89). Office: May Inst Ste 204 220 Norwood Park South Norwood MA 02062

RUSSO, ETHAN BUDD, neurologist, educator; b. Plymouth, Mass., Mar. 14, 1952; s. Raymond and Mildred (Bromberg) R.; m. Kay Annette Frey, Nov. 18, 1983; chlidren: Sarah Lynne, Colin Elliot. BS, U. Pa., 1973; postgrad., Faculte Libbe de Medicine, Lille, France, 1974-75; MD, U. Mass., 1978. Bd. cert. neurology/child neurology. Intern in pediat. Phoenix Hosps. Affiliated Pediat. Program, 1978-80; resident in neurology Univ. Wash. Neurology Program, Seattle, 1980-83; staff neurologist Western Mont. Clinic, Missoula, 1983—; dir. Western Mont. Muscular Dystrophy Clinic, Missoula, 1983—; clin. instr. medicine U. Wash., Seattle, 1988-94, clin. asst. prof. medicine, 1994—; expert witness Vaccine Injury Compensation Program, Washington, 1990—; sci. advisor Shaman Pharmaceuticals, San Carlos, Calif., 1991; seminar leader Pharmacy From the Rainforest, Internat. Expeditions, Iquitos, Peru, 1995; ethnobotanical rschr. Manu (Peru) Nat. Pk., 1995. Contbr. chpt. to book. Bd. mem. Big Bear, Missoula, Head Start, Missoula. Mem. Am. Acad. Neurology, Am. Assn. for the Study of Headache, Am. Epilepsy Soc., Child Neurology Soc. Democrat. Jewish. Office: Western Mont Clinic 515 W Front St Missoula MT 59807

RUSSO, JOSE, pathologist; b. Mendoza, Argentina, Mar. 24, 1942; came to U.S., 1971; s. Felipe and Teresa (Pagano) R.; m. Irma Haydee, Feb. 8, 1969; 1 child, Patricia Alexandra. BS, Agustin Alvarez Nat. Coll., 1959; MD, U. Nat. Cuyo, 1967. Instr. Inst. Gen. and Exptl. Pathology Med. Sch., Mendoza, 1961-66; asst. prof. Inst. Histology and Embryology, 1967-71; Rockefeller Found. postdoctoral fellow Inst. Molecular and Cellular Evolution U. Miami, 1971-73; chief exptl. pathology lab. Mich. Cancer Found., Detroit, 1973-81; assoc. clin. prof. pathology Wayne State U., Detroit, 1979-91, chmn. dept. pathology, 1981-91; chmn. dept. pathology, sr. mem. Fox Chase Cancer Ctr., Phila., 1991-94, sr. mem., dir. Breast Cancer Rsch. Lab., 1994—; mem. Mich. Cancer Found., 1982-91; adj. prof. pathology Jefferson Sch. Medicine, Univ. Penn. Sch. Medicine, Phila. Author: Tumor Diagnosis by Electron Microscopy, vol. 1, 1986, vol. 2, 1988, vol. 3, 1990, Immunocytochemistry in Tumor Diagnosis, 1985; contbr. over 200 articles to profl. jours. USPHS grantee, 1978, 80, 84, 88, 90, 93, 94, 95, grantee Am. Cancer Soc., 1982; NRC Argentina fellow, 1967-71. Mem. Am. Assn. Cancer Rsch., Am. Soc. Cell Biology, Soc. Exptl. Biology and Medicine, Tissue Culture Assn., Am. Soc. Clin. Pathology, Internat. Acad. Pathology, Am. Coll. Pathology, Sigma Xi. Roman Catholic.

RUSSO, PIERANTONIO, pediatric cardiac surgeon; b. Bergamo, Italy, Apr. 5, 1954; came to U.S., 1988; s. Vincenzo and Bianca (Raneri) R. Classic Liceum, Collegio San Luigi, Bologna, Italy, 1972; MD cum laude, Bologna U., 1978. Lic. physician, Italy, Pa., Eng. Intern in gen. surgery Castel-San Pietro Hosp., Bologna, 1979-80; intern in emergency medicine Univ. Hosp., Bologna, 1980-81; asst. dept. surgery Bologna Med. Sch., 1981-82; surg. fellow Cardiothoracic Inst., U. London, 1982-84; rsch. fellow dept. pediatrics Cardiothoracic Inst., Brompton Hosp., London, 1982-84; fellow cardiothoracic and cardiovascular surgery Mayo Clinic and Mayo Found., Rochester, Minn., 1984-86; surg. sr. registrar Cardiothoracic Unit Hosp. for Sick Children, London, 1986-87; dir. CICU and dir. heart transplant program St. Christopher's Hosp. for Children, Phila., 1988—; dir. surg. divsn. Pediatric Heart Inst. Temple U., Phila., 1988—, chief pediatric cardiothoracic surgery and assoc. prof., 1988—; surgical dir.heart ctr. for children St. Christopher Hosp. for Children; dir. fetal rsch. lab. Temple U., 1989—; attending surgeon cardiothoracic surgery Temple U. Hosp.; hon. mem. acad. staff dept. physiology U. Reading, U.K., 1987-88; hon. fellow pediatric cardiology Inst. of Child Health, U. London, 1987-88; vis. prof. cardiothoracic surgery U. Ark., Little Rock, 1992, Bologna Med. Sch., 1992; vis. prof. Baltic Soc. of Cardiac Surgery, Riga, Latvia, 1993; vis. surgeon cardiothoracic surgery, Riga, 1993; lectr. in field; assoc. prof. Cardiothoracic Surgery Med. Coll. Hahnemann U., 1995. Contbr. numerous articles, abstracts to profl. jours., chpts. to books. Recipient Princeps Studiorium aaward in Classic Studies, Bologna, Italy, 1972, Award Gran Croce Al Merito della Sanita, Acad. Internat. Sci. Econ. Sociali, and others, 1986; grantee Brit. Heart Found., 1987, Temple U., 1982. Fellow Internat. Coll. Surgeons, Soc. Acad. Surgeons, Am. Coll. Angiology; mem. AAAS, AMA, Internat. Soc. Heart and Lung Transplantation, Greater Delaware Valley Soc. Transplant Surgeons, N.Y. Acad. Sci., STS, Mayo Alumni Assn., Italian Med. Soc. Roman Catholic. Office: St Christophers Hosp Front St and Eric Ave Philadelphia PA 19134-1095

RUSSO-BILISKI, MICHELE, pediatric radiology nursing coordinator; b. Chester, Pa., Feb. 15, 1954; d. Michael John and Frances Agnes (DiMatteo) Russo; m. Charles John Biliski, Jr., July 2, 1977; children: Sarah, Christan, Ryan Ann. Diploma in nursing, Nursing Sch. Wilmington, Del., 1974; BSN magna cum laude, Wilmington (Del.) Coll., 1995; postgrad., Wilmington Coll., 1995—. Cert. Pediatric Advanced Life Support. Mem. nursing staff Wilmington (Del.) Med. Ctr., 1974-76; mem. nursing staff A.I. duPont Inst., Wilmington, 1976—, mem. rehab. nursing staff, 1982-84, coord. sexuality edn., 1984-90, coord. radiology nurses, 1989—; mem. Sedation Data Base Com., A.I. duPont Inst., 1994—, Quality Assurance Com., 1994-95, Day Medicine Task Force Com., Take Our Daughters to Work Day Com., Employee Coun., Dress Code Com., spkr., presenter profl. confs., faculty Del. Tech. and C.C., clin. instr. Pediatrics and Neurology. Pres. St. Elizabeth Home and Sch. Assn., Wilmington, 1992-94, St. Elizabeth Elem. Sch. Computer Edn. Com., 1993—, McDonald's Children's Charities, Wilmington, 1992-95, chmn. LPGA Med./1st Aid com.; med. NOW; rep. Union Pk. Garden Neighborhood Assn. Nursing Acad. scholar Wilmington Rotary Club, 1973-74. Mem. Am. Radiology Nurses Assn., Delta Epsilon Rho. Democrat. Roman Catholic. Home: 603 S Union St Wilmington DE 19805 Office: Alfred I duPont Inst Childrens Hosp PO Box 269 Wilmington DE 19899

RUSSO-MARIE, FRANCOISE, biologist; b. Neuilly, France, Sept. 15, 1945; d. René and Marie-Josèphe (Malbet) Russo; m. Jean Pierre Marie, Sept. 6, 1973; children: Hélène, Olivier-Emmanuel. MD, u. Paris, 1971, PhD in Biochemistry, 1984. Nephrologist Hosp. Necker, Paris, 1973-76; rsch. fellow Inserm U 90, Paris, 1976-84, Inst. Pasteur (Inserm U 285), Paris, 1984-89; sr. scientist Cochin Inst. Molecular Genetics (Inserm U 332), Paris, 1989—; dir. rsch. Inserm, Paris, 1990—. Home: 105 rue des Bruyères, 92310 Sevres France Office: Cochin Inst Molecular, Genetics, 22 rue Méchain, 22 rue Méchain, 75014 Paris France

RUSSOMONDO-MOREHEAD, ANNETTE MARIE, disabled children's facility administrator, child advocate; b. San Diego; d. Michael Peter and Katherine Helen (Keegan) Russomondo; m. Peter James Morehead; children: Bradley Michael Caloca, Katherine Dana. Student, Southwestern Coll., Grossmont Coll. Dir. Rayito Day Care Ctr., San Diego, 1981-85; instrnl. asst. for children with disabilities San Diego City Schools, 1985-88; owner, operator Scripps Ranch Childcare Ctr. for Disabled Children, San Diego, 1990—; child advocate; speaker San Diego Bd. Edn., 1986, News Eight Local TV News, 1989, Miramar Coll., 1991, Scottish Rite Charities, 1992, Exceptional Parents Found., 1993. vol. Schweitzer Ctr. for Disabled Children, San Diego, 1985, Stein Edn. Ctr. fof Autistic Children, San Diego, 1987-88. Mem. Autism Soc. Am. (bd. dirs.), Mensa. Democrat. Home and Office: 7230 Blaisdell Ave S Minneapolis MN 55423

RUST, JAMES HENRY, JR., epidemologist; b. Lykens, Pa., Aug. 9, 1928; s. James Henry and Drucilla (Davey) R.; m. Nancy Elizabeth Hipple, Aug. 21, 1949; children: James Henry, Nancy Elizabeth, Mary Suzanne, David Hipple. BS, Franklin & Marshall Coll., 1954; MS, George Washington U., 1955, PhD, 1958. Chief, microbiological chemistry Walter Reed Army Inst. Rsch. Dept., Washington, 1958-66, rsch. assoc., 1966-70; dep. chief epidemology and spl. studies SEATO Med. Rsch. Lab., Bangkok, Thailand, 1970-72; advisor epidemiology WHO, Saigon, Vietnam, 1972-74; advisor WHO, Manila, Phillipines, 1974-75; epidemologist WHO, smallpox eradication team, Bangladesh, 1975-76; regional advisor WHO Pan American Health Orgn., Washington, 1976-89; pvt. practice cons. Rockville, Md., 1989—; cons. in field. Contbr. articles to many profl. jours. With U.S. Navy, 1946-48, 1950-52, Korea. Mem. Am. Soc. Tropical Medicine & Hygiene, Soc. Am. Microbiology, N.Y. Acad. Sci., AAAS, Am. Pub. Health Assn. Home: 13711 Ashby Rd Rockville MD 20853-2904

RUTAN, THOMAS CARL, nurse; b. El Paso, Tex., May 18, 1954; s. Robert Judson and Louisa Almeria Elizabeth (Niccolls) R.; m. Randi Lee Watson, Sept. 17, 1980; children: Thomas Caleb, Susannah Christine, Rebecca Abigail. BSN, U. Tex., 1977, MSN, 1987. RN. Staff nurse U. Burn Ctr., U. Tex. Med. Br. Hosp., Galveston, 1977, U.S. Army Inst. Surg. Rsch., Ft. Sam Houston, Tex., 1978-81; flight nurse U.S. Army Inst. Surg. Rsch., 1979-81; staff nurse Burn Intensive Care Unit, U. Tex. Med. Br. Hosp., Galveston, 1981-83; clin. rsch. nurse Shriners Burns Inst., Galveston, 1983-94, project leader clin. info. systems, 1988-91; asst. dir. med. staff and rsch. adminstrn. Shriners Burn Inst., Galveston, 1991-94; nurse clinician III Blocker Burn Ctr., U. Tex. Med. Br., Galveston, 1994; clin. nurse specialist-Burns U. Hosp. UMDNJ, Newark, 1994—. Capt. U.S. Army, 1978-81. Mem. AAAS, ANA, N.Am. Burn Soc., Tex. Nurses Assn., Am. Burn Assn., N.Y. Acad. Sci., Planetary Soc., Consumers Union, Nature Conservancy. Methodist. Office: UMDNJ 150 Bergen St Newark NJ 07103-2406

RUTGERS, JOANNE K.L., pathologist; b. Glendale, Calif., Aug. 19, 1955; d. Donald Lee and Edna Katherine (Hauenstein) Licking; m. Richard Peter Rutgers, Apr. 12, 1982; children: Alexander, Eric. BA cum laude, Pomona Coll., 1977; MD, U. Calif., San Diego, 1981. Diplomate Am. Bd. Pathology. Intern in pathology U. So. Calif. Med. Ctr., L.A., 1981-82; resident in pathology Montefiore Med. Ctr., Bronx, N.Y., 1982-83, NYU Med. Ctr., N.Y.C., 1983-85; pathologist, instr. Mass. Gen. Hosp., Boston, 1985-88; pathologist Harbor-UCLA Med. Ctr., Torrance, Calif., 1988-89, 90-96; asst. prof. Harbor-UCLA Med. Ctr., Torrance, 1990-96; pathologist Saddleback Hosp., Laguna Hills, Calif., 1989-90, Long Beach (Calif.) Meml. Med. Ctr., 1996—; mem. expert diagnostic panel on testicular tumors Coll. Am. Pathologists, 1986-87. Contbr. over 60 articles and abstracts to profl. pubs. Sponsor Bonding in Love, Hawthorne, Calif., 1993—. Mem. AAAS, Am. Soc. Clin. Pathology, Internat. Soc. Gynecol. Pahtologists, Internat. Acad. Pathology, Soc. Study Reproduction, Calif. Soc. Pathologists, Phi Beta Kappa. Office: Dept Pathology Long Beach Meml Med Ctr 2801 Atlantic Ave PO Box 1428 Long Beach CA 90801

RUTH, RICHARD, psychologist. BA, New Sch. for Social Rsch., 1974; MA, Yeshiva U., 1977, PhD, 1986. Lic. psychologist. Rsch. psychologist dept. preventive medicine Cornell U., Ithaca, N.Y., 1979-80; staff psychologist Gouverneur Hosp., N.Y.C., 1980-82, Elizabeth (N.J.) Gen. Med. Ctr., 1982-84; clin. coord. emergency svc. Arlington (Va.) Mental Health Ctr., 1984-88; dir. Puerto Rico Rsch. Inst., Washington, 1983—; lectr. Trinity Coll., Washington, 1986—; cons. psychologist Cmty. Psychiat. Clinic, Gaithersburg, Md., 1988-93, sr. psychologist, 1993-94, acting chief psychologist, 1994-96, dir. psychology, 1996—; psychologist Wheaton, Md., 1988—; cons. Montgomery County Pub. Schs., Rockville, Md., 1987—, Prince George's County Pub. Schs., Upper Marlboro, Md., 1989—, Arlington (Va.) County Pub. Schs., 1988—, Washington County Health Dept., Hagerstown, Md., 1989—. Contbr. articles to profl. jours. Recipient Cert. Recognition Pres.'s Com. on Employment of the Handicapped, 1984. Fellow Am. Orthopsychiat. Assn.; mem. APA, Va. Psychol. Assn., Md. Psychol. Assn., Internat. Assn. Cross-Cultural Psychology. Office: 11303 Amherst Ave Ste 1 Silver Spring MD 20902-4600

RUTHERFORD, LINDA MARIE, hospital official; b. Chgo., Sept. 13, 1947; d. Allen A. and Marie (Romano) Gregory; children: Jason Alan Hunt, Lisa Marie Hunt; m. John H. Rutherford; stepchildren: Maury, Helena. BS, U. Phoenix, 1987. Adminstrv. asst. Old Tucson/Old Vegas, 1975-78; asst. mgr. W & W Mktg. Corp., Houston, 1978-83; adminstr. profl. rels. Tucson Gen. Hosp., 1983-84; mgr. Romero Road Med. Clinic, Tucson, 1984-89; mgr. physician svcs. El Dorado Hosp. and Med. Ctr., Tucson, 1989—; with N.W. Hosp., Tucson, 1994—. Bd. dirs. Flowing Wells Community Effort Coun., 1988; mem. Concerned Women for Am., 1986—. Mem. NAFE, Med. Group Mgmt. Assn. Baptist. Office: NW Hosp 6200 N La Cholla Blvd Tucson AZ 85741-3529

RUTHERFORD, ROBERT BARRY, surgeon; b. Edmonton, Alta., Can., July 29, 1931; s. Robert Lyon and Kathleen Emily (Gunn) R.; m. Beulah Kay Folk, Aug. 20, 1955; children: Robert Scott, Lori Jayne, Holly Anne, Trudy Kaye, Jay Wilson. BA in Biology, Johns Hopkins U., 1952, MD, 1956. Surgeon U. Colo. Health Sci. Ctr., Denver; cons. EndoVascular Techs., Menlo Park, Calif., 1989; mem. adv. bd. Med. Edn. Collaborative, Lakewood, Colo., 1989; bd. dirs. Am. Bd. Surgery. Editor: (texts) Management of Trauma, 1968, 4 edits., Vascular Surgery, 1978, 4 edits, An Atlas of Vascular Surgery, 1993; editor quar. rev. Seminars in Vascular Surgery. Mem. Internat. Soc. for Cardiovascular Surgery, Phi Beta Kappa, Alpha Omega Alpha. Republican. Unitarian. Office: U Colo Dept Vascular Surgery 4200 E 9th Ave # C-312 Denver CO 80220-3706

RUTHERFORD, WARREN LOYD, healthcare administrator; b. Omaha, Nebr., May 22, 1936; s. Loyd Aldwin and Veola Agda Theresea (Magnusson) R.; m. Barbara Jean Gruendemann, Nov. 20, 1993. BBA, U. Minn., 1958, MHA, 1961. Diplomate Am. Coll. Healthcare Execs. Assoc. adminstr. U. Tex. Sys. Cancer Ctr./M.D. Anderson Hosp., Houston, 1969-76, adminstr., 1976-82, dir. hosp./clinic, 1979-80, assoc. v.p. patient care ops., 1980-82; pres., CEO Boone Hosp. Ctr., Columbia, Mo., 1982-85; sr. v.p., exec. dir. Meth. Hosps. of Dallas, 1985-86, sr. v.p. corp. svcs., 1986-91, sr. v.p. for development/pub. rels., 1991—; exec. v.p., COO Dallas Meth. Hosps. Found., 1991—; chmn. Greater Houston Hosp. Coun., 1980-81; chmn. bd. dirs. Greater Houston Hosp. Svc. Corp., 1979-80. Vice chmn. United Way of Met. Dallas, 1995, 96; bd. dirs. Gateway Tax Increment Fin. Dist., Dallas, 1994—. Mem. Assn. for Healthcare Philanthropy, Nat. Soc. Fundraising Execs., Oak Cliff C. of C. (bd. dirs. 1987—), Tex. Hosp. Assn. (ho. of dels. 1980-82), Mo. Hosp. Assn. (pres. ctrl. dist. coun. 1983-84), Rotary (pres. 1992-93), Masons, Shriner. Methodist. Home: 8611 Breakers Point Dallas TX 75243

RUTHVEN, COURTNEY LEWIS, mental health services professional; b. Chattanooga, May 16, 1936; d. Joseph Darwin and Harriet Agnes (Courtney) L.; n. Leslie Ruthven, July 16, 1955; children: Harriet Elizabeth, LEslie Darwin, Laura Ann. BS, U. Tenn., 1963; M, Wichita State U., 1973; DPhil, Okla. State U., 1977. Psychologist pvt. practice, Wichita, 1979-93; asst. prof. Wichita U., 1979-81; v.p. The Ruthven Group, Wichita, 1979—; owner, gen. mgr. Ctrl. Box Co., Newton, Kans., 1983-85; assoc. prof. Kans. Newman Coll., Wichita, 1986-90; exec. v.p. Preferred Mental Health, Wichita, 1988—; mem. adv. bd. Preferred Mental Health, 1988-96, March Tenn., 1994-96; cons. in field. Mem. Downtown Bus. Assn., Wichita, 1995-96. Mem. Soc. Neurosci., Nat. Assn. Neuropsychology, Kans. Assn. Profl. Psychologists, Kans. Psychologist Assn. (pres. 1975), Wichita Soc. Neurosci., Wichita C. of C., Phi Gamma Nu, Psy Chi. Office: Preferred Mental Health Mgmt Inc 401 E Douglas Ste 3 Wichita KS 67202

RUTKAUSKAS, JOHN SVAJUNAS, dental association administrator; b. Rockford, Mar. 22, 1961; s. Kazys and Paulina R.; m. Charmaine Rutkauskas; 1 child, Gabrielle. BA, U. Chgo., 1983, MS, 1989; BS in Dentistry, U. Ill., Chgo., 1988, DDS, 1990. Gen. practice resident U. Chgo., 1990-91; account exec. Am. Med. Internat., L.A., 1985-86; exec. dir. Fedn. Spl. Care Orgns. in Dentistry, Chgo., 1991—. Mng. editor Spl. Care in Dentistry, 1991—. Recipient Arm and Hammer dental award, 1987, Cert. of Merit Pierre Fauchard Acad., 1990, award of merit Am. Coll. Dentists, 1990. Mem. ADA, Am. Assn. Hosp. Dentists (exec. dir. 1991—), Acad. Dentistry for Persons with Disabilities, Am. Soc. Geriatric Dentistry, Ill. State Dental Soc., Chgo. Dental Soc., Nat. Alliance Oral Health (pres. 1995—). Home: 212 E Chicago Ave Hinsdale IL 60521 Office: Fedn Spl Care Orgns to Dentistry 211 E Chicago Ave Chicago IL 60617

RUTTAN, CINDY GAIL, physician; b. Kansas City, Mo., Dec. 15, 1963. BS in Biology and Chemistry, Rockhurst Coll., 1985; DO, U. Health Sci. Coll. of, Osteo. Medicine, Kansas City, 1989. Rotating intern Kansas City, 1989-90; internal medicine physician U. Mo. Kansas City/St. Luke's Hosp., 1990; adult psychiatrist Western Mo. Mental Health, Kansas City, 1991-93; child-adolescent psychiatrist Washington U. Sch. of Medicine, St. Louis, 1993-95; staff psychiatrist Hawthorn State Children's Psych. Hosp., St. Louis, 1993-95. Mem. AMA, Am. Osteo. Assn., APA, Am. Acad. Child-Adolescent Psychiatry, Am. Soc. Addiction Medicine.

RUVOLO, LOUIS SALVATORE, surgeon; b. Bayonne, N.J., Aug. 1, 1940; s. Frank H. and Victoria (LaPilusa) R.; m. Clara A. Darcy, June 9, 1962; children: Loretta, Louis, Christine. BS, U. Notre Dame, 1962; MD, Ind. U., 1966. Chmn. dept. surgery Rancocas Hosp., Willingboro, N.J.; pres. Rancocas Valley Surgical Assocs., Willingboro, N.J. Capt. U.S. Army, 1969. Fellow Am. Coll. Surgeons; mem. Ea. Vascular Soc., N.J. Oncol. Soc., Soc. for Laparoscopic Surgery, AMA.

RUYBALID, LOUIS ARTHUR, social worker, community development consultant; b. Allison, Colo., Apr. 6, 1925; s. Mike Joseph and Helen Mary (Rodriguez) R.; m. Seraphima Alexander, June 12, 1949; children: Mariana, John. BA, U. Denver, 1946-49, MSW, 1951; PhD, U. Calif., Berkeley, 1970; Professor Ad-Honorem (hon.), Nat. U., Caracas, Venezuela, 1964. Social worker Ariz., Calif., Colo., 1951-62; advisor community devel. Unitarian Service Com., Caracas, 1962-64, U.S. Agy. for Internat. Devel., Rio de Janeiro, Brazil, 1964-66; area coordinator U.S. Office Econ. Opportunity, San Francisco, 1966-68; prof., dept. head U. So. Colo., Pueblo, 1974-80; licensing analyst State of Calif., Campbell, 1984—; prof. sch. of social work Highlands U., Las Vegas, N.Mex., 1988-89; cons. UN, Caracas, 1978, Brazilian Govt., Brazilia, 1964-66, Venezuelan Govt., Caracas, 1962-64. Author: (books) Favela, 1970, Glossary for Hominology, 1978, (research instrument) The Conglomerate Hom., 1976. Mem. exec. com. Pueblo (Colo.) Regional Planning Com., 1974-79, Nat. Advisory com. The Program Agy. United Presbyn. Ch., 1978-79. Served with USN, 1944-46. Recipient Pro Mundo Beneficio medal Brazilian Acad. Human Sci., Sao Paulo, 1976; United Def. Fund fellow U. Calif., Berkeley, 1961-62, Cert. World Leadership Internat. Leaders of Achievement, 1988-89. Mem. NASW (cert.), Ethnic Minority Commn., IMAGE (nat. edn. chair), Am. Hominol. Assn. (nat. pres. 1975-79), U. Calif. Alumni Assn., AARP (minority spokesperson), Phi Beta Kappa, Phi Sigma Iota. Democrat. Home and Office: Ruybalid Assoc Inc 129 Calle Don Jose Santa Fe NM 87501-2364

RUZICKA, MARY FRANCES, psychologist, educator; b. Balt., Dec. 4, 1943; d. Francis Frederick Jr. and Mary Margaret (Kernan) R. BA cum laude, Georgian Ct. Coll., 1966; PhD, Fordham U., 1975. Diplomate Am. Bd. Disability Analysts; lic. psychologist, N.J. Guidance counselor N.J. Pub. Schs., Sayreville, 1971-73; tchr. Cath. schs., South Amboy and Edison, N.J., 1966-71; prof. psychology, dept. chair Seton Hall U., S. Orange, N.J., 1973—; pvt. practice psychology Maplewood, N.J., 1978—; conductor workshops, cons. and ad hoc reviewer in field. Co-author: A Manual Teaching the Use of APA Style, 1976; contbr. articles to profl. jours. Fellow Am. Acad. Sexology; mem. Am. Psychol. Assn. (cert. in alcoholism and substance abuse), Am. Bd. Sexology (diplomate), Internat. Coun. Psychologists, Am. Assn. Sex Edn. Therapists and Counselors, Am. Coll. Forensic Examiners (bd. cert., diplomate), Am. Acads. Practice (Disting. Practitioner). Roman Catholic. Home: 12 Northview Ter Maplewood NJ 07040-3606 Office: Seton Hall U Dept of Profl Psychiatry and Family Therapy South Orange NJ 07079

RYALL, JO-ELLYN M., psychiatrist; b. Newark, May 25, 1949; d. Joseph P. and Tekla (Paraszczuk) R.; BA in Chemistry with gen. honors, Douglass Coll., Rutgers U., 1971; MD, Washington U., St. Louis, 1975. Diplomate Am. Bd. Psychiatry and Neurology. Resident in psychiatry Washington U., 1975-78, psychiatrist Student Health, 1980-84, clin. instr. psychiatry, 1978-83, clin. asst. prof. psychiatry, 1983—; inpatient supr. Malcolm Bliss Mental Health Ctr., St. Louis, 1978-80, psychiatrist outpatient clinic, 1980-82; pvt. practice medicine specializing in psychiatry, St. Louis, 1980—. Bd. dirs. Women's Self Help Ctr., St. Louis, 1980-83. Fellow APA, Soc. (pres. Ea. Mo. Dist. Br. 1983-85, sect. coun. AMA 1986—, dep. rep. to assembly 1994—); mem. AMA (alt. del. Mo. 1988-90, 93-94, del. 1995—), Am. Med. Women's Assn. (pres. St. Louis Dist. br. 1981-82, 92, regional gov. VIII 1986-89, spkr. house of dels., 1993—), St. Louis Met. Med. Soc. (del. to state conv. 1981-86, 93—, councilor 1985-87, v.p. 1989), Mo. State Med. Assn. (vice speaker ho. of dels. 1986-89, speaker 1989-92), Manic Depressive Assn. St. Louis (chmn. bd. dirs. 1985-89), Washington U. Faculty Club. Office: 9216 Clayton Rd Saint Louis MO 63124-1560

RYAN, ALLAN JAMES, publishing executive, editor; b. Bklyn., Dec. 9, 1915; s. Lorne McDonnell and Valerie (Britton) R.; m. Agnes Louise Nelson, July 4, 1942; children: Brendan Michael, James Allan, Robert Edward. BA, Yale U., 1936; MD, Columbia U., 1940; D in Sports Sci., U.S. Sports Acad., 1983. Diplomate Am. Bd. Gen. Surgery. Intern in gen. surgery Kings County Hosp., Bklyn., 1940-42, research fellow surgery, 1942-43; asst. resident surgery Grace New Haven (Conn.) Hosp., 1943-45; chief resident surgery Long Island (N.Y.) Coll. Hosp., Bklyn., 1945-46; attending surgeon Meriden (Conn.) Hosp., 1947-1965; assoc. prof. U. Wis., Madison, 1965-70; prof. U. Wis., 1970-76; editor-in-chief Postgrad. Medicine, Mpls., 1976-79, The Physician & Sports Medicine, Mpls., 1973-85; dir. Sports Medicine Enterprise, Edina, Minn., 1985-95; editor-in-chief Fitness in Bus. mag., 1986-90; athletic teams physician U. Wis., Madison, 1965-76. Author: Medical Care of Athlete, 1962, Guide to Running, 1980; co-author: The Healthy Dancer's Complete Guide to Health Care, 1989; editor: Sports Medicine, 1974, Dance Medicine, 1986; co-editor: Sports Medicine, 2d edit., 1989, The Healthy Dancer, 1989. Mem. Commn. Mil. Accidents, Washington, 1964-69; med. examiner City of Meriden, 1947-65; trustee U.S. Sports Academy, Mobile, 1985-87; mem. Minn. Gov.'s Coun. on Phys. Fitness and Sports, 1986—. Recipient Silver Medal award City of Paris, 1983, Nat. Phys. Fitness Leadership award Jr. C. of C., 1971. Fellow Am. Coll. Sports Medicine (pres. 1963—), Am. Orthopaedic Soc. Sports Medicine (assoc.); mem. Am. Alliance Health, Phys. Edn. Recreation and Dance, Council Phys. Fitness and Sports (cons., pres. 1960—), AMA (commn. on med. aspects of athletics), Internat. Fedn. Sports Medicine (sec. gen. 1980-86), Phi Beta

Kappa, Sigma Xi. Republican. Roman Catholic. Office: 5800 Jeff Plz Edina MN 55436-1938

RYAN, ARTHUR FREDERICK, insurance company executive; b. Bklyn., Sept. 14, 1942; s. Arthur Vincent and Gertrude (Wingert) R.; m. Patricia Elizabeth Kelly; children: Arthur, Kelly Ann, Kevin, Kathleen. BA in Math., Providence Coll., 1963. Area mgr. Data Corp., Washington, 1965-72; project mgr. Chase Manhattan Corp. and Bank, N.Y.C., 1972-73, 2d v.p., 1973-74, v.p., 1974-75, from 1978, former ops. exec., from 1978, former exec. v.p., from 1982, former vice-chmn., then pres., chief operating officer, 1990-94; chmn., CEO Prudential Ins. Co. Am., Newark, N.J., 1994—; mem. policy and planning com.; bd. dirs., chmn. audit com. Depository Trust Co.; past mem. exec. com., Cedel (European Depository); past chmn. steering com., program mgr. CHIPS Same Day Settlement, N.Y. Clearing House. Past bd. dirs. Urban Acad. N.Y.C. Lt. U.S. Army, 1963-65. Mem. Am. Bankers Assn. (vice chmn. ops. and automation div. and govt. rels. coun., past chmn. internat. ops. com.). Home: 144 The Helm East Islip NY 11730-2918 Office: Prudential Ins Co Am 751 Broad St Newark NJ 07102-3777

RYAN, CATHERINE STUART, rheumatologist; b. Mineola, N.Y., Mar. 19, 1952; m. Edward Ryan, June 28, 1980; 1 child, Christine. AB, Cornell U., 1974; MD, Washington U., 1979. Intern, residency George Washington U. Hosp., 1979-82; fellow in rheumatology Hosp. U. Pa., 1982-85. Mem. AMA, Am. Womens Med. Assn., N.J. Med. Soc. Home: 69 Portland Rd Summit NJ 07901

RYAN, CHARLOTTE MURIEL, oncology nurse; b. Beedeville, Ark., Sept. 2, 1939; d. Eugene Sanford and Edith Elizabeth (Goforth) Breckenridge; children: Russell Kent, Cary Randall, Molly Renee. BSN cum laude, Calif. State U., Fresno, 1991, MSN, 1996. OCN cert. nurse. Psychiat. technician Porterville (Calif.) State Hosp., 1959-67; tchr. developmentally disabled Ariz. Tng. Ctr., Coolidge, 1967-71; Montessori tchr. Tucson, 1972-77; tchr. developmentally disabled Heartland Opportunity Ctr., Madera, Calif., 1977-79; med. office mgr. office of orthopedic surgeon, Madera, 1979-83, office mgr., x-ray technician, 1983-87; staff nurse in oncology St. Agnes Med. Ctr., Fresno, 1991—; instr. nursing dept. Calif. State U., Fresno, 1992, 93, 95. Treas. Hospice of Madera County, 1990-92, bd. dirs., 1992; peer counselor Calif. State U., Fresno, 1989-91; pres. bd. dirs. Easter Seals Soc., Madera, 1981. Mem. Oncology Nursing Soc., Nightingale Soc., Golden Key, Sigma Theta Tau (chair pub. com., editor MUNEWS newsletter 1994-95). Republican. Home: 4544 N Barton Fresno CA 93726 Office: St Agnes Med Ctr 1303 E Herndon Ave Fresno CA 93720-3309

RYAN, DANIEL MARTIN, rehabilitation physician; b. Royal Oak, Mich., Feb. 21, 1963; s. Jack and Lois (Patterson) R.; m. Shannon O'Mara, Aug. 7, 1994. BA, Kalamazoo Coll., 1985; MD, Wayne State U., 1989. Diplomate Am. Bd. Phys. Medicine and Rehab. Med. dir. phys. medicine and rehab. Detroit Riverview Hosp., 1994—; med. dir. sports medicine Macomb Hosp. Ctr., Warren, Mich., 1995—; clin. asst. prof. Wayne State U. Sch. Medicine, Detroit, 1994—. Contbr. chpt. to book, articles to profl. jours.; inventor in field. Recipient Disting. Svc. award Wayne State U. Sch. Medicine, 1989. Fellow Am. Acad. Phys. Medicine, Assn. Acad. Physiatrists; mem. AMA, Am. Coll. Sports Medicine, Mich. Acad. Phys. Medicine and Rehab. (sec.-treas. 1996). Office: Neurorehab Assocs 11900 Twelve Mile Rd Warren MI 48093

RYAN, DAVID THOMAS, chiropractor; b. Columbus, Ohio, Sept. 1, 1960; s. John Robert and Mary Louise R.; m. Cherie Marie Coyne; children: Cassie, Makenzie. BS, Ohio State U., 1985; D of Chiropractoc, Palmer Coll. Chiropractic, 1988. Chiropractor, owner Columbus Chiropractic Ctrs., Columbus, Ohio, 1989—; mem. staff Columbus Cmty. Hosp.; mem. med. bd. USA Fibroymalgia Assn., Columbus, 1991-96; med. dir. World Powerlifting Championships, 1994, 95. V.p. Woodstone Civic Assn., Lewis Center, Ohio, 1994-96. Recipient 3 Gold medals Panamerica Games, 1988, 3 world weight lifting records Amatur Athlete Union, 1984-88, Cecil award, Arthritis Found., Atlanta, 1995. Mem. Am. Chiropractic Assn., Ohio State Chiropractic Assn. (labor legis.). Republican. Methodist. Office: Columbus Chiropractic Ctr 5870 Cleveland Ave Columbus OH 43231

RYAN, DIANE PHYLLIS, nurse; b. Buffalo, June 19, 1954; d. Edward John and Helen (Pasko) Vnuk; m. Terrance Patrick Ryan, May 14, 1977; children: Kevin Daniel, Jaclyn Nicole, Amanda Leigh, Scott Michael. BSN, D'Youville Coll., 1976; MS in Nursing, SUNY, 1980. Cert. adult nurse practitioner. Staff nurse Buffalo VA Med. Ctr., 1976-79, nurse practitioner, 1980-83, community referral nurse coordinator, 1983-92, nurse practitioner, 1992—. Contbr. articles to profl. jours. Recipient continuing edn. award Homemaker's Upjohn, Buffalo, 1976, Carol Sinicki manuscript award Am. Diabetes Educators, 1984, 1st place award 11th Ann. Discharge Planning Symposium, Soc. Hosp. Social Work Dirs., Am. Hosp. Assn. Mem. Western N.Y. Nurse Practitioners, Sigma Theta Tau. Office: Buffalo VA Med Ctr 3495 Bailey Ave Buffalo NY 14215-1129

RYAN, EDWARD FRANCIS, JR., physician; b. Darby, Pa., Jan. 6, 1954; s. Edward Francis and Regina Cecelia (Fellona) R.; m. Jane Drueding, Apr. 29, 1988; children: Christopher, Jeffrey, Timothy. BS, Boston Coll., 1975; DO, Phila. Coll. Osteo. Medicine, 1979. Diplomate Am. Bd. Dermatology. Intern Suburban Gen. Hosp., Norristown, Pa., 1979-80; resident in internal medicine Byrn Mawr Hosp., 1980-82; resident in dermatology Univ. Hosp., Phila., 1982-85; asst. prof. medicine Hahnemann U., Phila., 1985—; pvt. practice Edward F. Ryan, Jr., Drexel Hill, Pa., 1986—. Contbr. articles to profl. jours. Recipient Residents Forum award Pa. Acad. Dermatology, 1984. Fellow Am. Acad. Dermatology; mem. Pa. Med. Soc., Phila. Dermatol. Soc. (sec./treas. 1990-92, pres. 1992-93), Pa. Med. Soc., Del. County Med. Soc. Office: 2100 Keystone Ave Ste 205 Drexel Hill PA 19026-1129

RYAN, ELEANORE A., clinical psychologist; b. Chgo.; children: Robert, James, Mark, John, Christopher, Marynel. BS with honors in Chemistry, Mundelein Coll.; PhD in Clin. Psychology, Northwestern U., 1978. Cert. psychologist, Ill., Ind. Staff psychologist Porter-Starke Svcs., Valparaiso, Ind., 1978-80; psychol. cons. Gary (Ind.) Cmty. Mental Health Ctr., 1980-81; pvt. practice clin. and cons. psychology, Clarendon Hills, Ill., 1981—; cons. Francenter, Darien, Ill., 1988—; dir. Assocs. in Clin. Therapy, 1987—; psychologist Hines VA Hosp., Ill., 1983-88, Oak Park (Ill.) Vet. Ctr., 1988-95; mem. allied health staff Riveredge Hosp., 1992—, Westlake Cmty. Hosp., 1992—, Loyola U. Med. Ctr., 1995—. Mem. APA, Ill. Psychol. Assn. (chmn. Disaster Response Network, Humanitarian award 1995), Assn. DuPage Psychologists (pres. 1993, 96—), Soc. for Clin. and Exptl. Hypnosis, Soc. for Traumatic Stress Studies, Chgo. Psychologists in Addictive Behavior, Consortium Vietnam Vet. Svc. Providers. Roman Catholic. Home and Office: 215 Coe Rd Clarendon Hills IL 60514-1001

RYAN, JAMES WALTER, physician, medical researcher; b. Amarillo, Tex., June 8, 1935; s. Lee W. and Emma E. (Haddox) R.; children: James P.A., Alexandra L.E., Amy J.S. A.B. in Polit. Sci., Dartmouth Coll., 1957; M.D., Cornell U., 1961; D.Phil., Oxford U. (Eng.), 1967. Diplomate: Nat. Bd. Med. Examiners. Intern, Montreal (Que.) Gen. Hosp., McGill U., Can., 1961-62; asst. resident in medicine Montreal (Que.) Gen. Hosp., McGill U., 1962-63; USPHS research asso. NIMH, NIH, 1963-65; guest investigator Rockefeller U., N.Y.C., 1967-68; asst. prof. biochemistry Rockefeller U., 1968; asso. prof. medicine U. Miami (Fla.) Sch. Medicine, 1968-79, prof. medicine, 1979-95; prof. anesthesiology, pharmacology and toxicology Med. Coll. Ga., Augusta, 1995—; sr. scientist Papanicolaou Cancer Rsch. Inst., Miami, 1972-77; hon. med. officer to Regius prof. medicine Oxford U., 1965-67; vis. prof. Clin. Rsch. Inst. Montreal, 1974; mem. vis. faculty thoracic disease divsn., dept. internal medicine Mayo Clinic, 1974; cons. Hycor, Inc., Chugai Pharm. Co., Ltd., Tokyo, Apotex, Inc., Toronto. Contbr. numerous articles on biochem. research and pathology to sci. jours.; patentee in field. Rockefeller Found. travel awardee, 1962; William Waldorf Astor travelling fellow, 1966; USPHS spl. fellow, 1967-68; Pfizer travelling fellow, 1972; recipient Louis and Artur Luciano award for research of circulatory diseases McGill U., 1984-85. Fellow Am. Inst. Chemists; mem. Am. Chem. Soc., Biochem. Soc., Am. Soc. Biol. Chemists, Am. Heart Assn. (mem. council cardiopulmonary diseases 1972—, Council for High Blood Pressure Research 1976—), Microcirculatory Soc., So. Soc. Clin. Investigation, AAAS, N.Y. Acad. Scis., Sigma Xi. Baptist. Club: United Oxford and Cambridge U. (London). Home: 3047 Lake Forest Dr Augusta GA 30909-3027 Office: Med Coll Ga Vascular Biology Ctr Augusta GA 30912

RYAN, JUDITH ANDRE, health care executive, hospital administrator, nurse; b. Vermillion, S.D., Sept. 11, 1936; d. Hugo Carl and Nelle Marie (Schultz) Andre; m. Darrell Richard Yates, Sept. 13, 1958 (div. June 1975); m. Gerald Odin Ryan, Dec. 22, 1982; children: Allison Marie, Matthew Andre. BSN, St. Olaf Coll., 1958; PhD in Hosp. and Health Care Adminstrn., U. Minn., 1983. Registered nurse, Minn. Staff nurse Mower County Pub. Health Nursing Services, Family Nursing Service, St. Paul, 1958-62; asst. exec. dir. govtl. and pub. relations Minn. Nurses Assn., Mpls., 1964-68; instr. St. Mary's Jr. Coll., Mpls., 1975-76; dir. nursing edn. Rochester Meth. Hosp., Minn., 1976-80; dep. exec. dir. Am. Nurses' Assn., Kansas City, Mo., 1980-81, exec. dir., 1982-89; v.p. Luth. Gen. Health Care System, Park Ridge, Ill., 1989-91, sr. v.p., 1991—; bd. govs. EcuMed, N.Y.C.; bd. dirs. The Kendall Co.; cons. in field. Author: Moving and Lifting Patients, 1970; assoc. editor Minn. Nursing Accent, 1964-68; contbr. articles to profl. jours., chpts. to books. Mem. exec. com. Minn. Comprehensive Health Planning Adv. Coun., 1968-76; trustee St. Olaf Coll. Bush Leadership fellow, 1978-79; recipient Disting. Alumnae award St. Olaf Coll., 1984. Mem. Am. Acad. Nurses, Am. Soc. Assn. Execs., Nat. League for Nursing, Nat. Commn. on Nursing, Sigma Theta Tau. Republican. Lutheran. Office: Luth Gen Health Sys 1775 Dempster St Park Ridge IL 60068-1173

RYAN, JULIE MAE, optometrist, educator, researcher; b. Des Moines, Sept. 3, 1951; d. Albert Boyd and A. Gretchen (Manderscheid) Berg; m. Patrick D. Ryan, June 27, 1976. AA, Southwestern C.C., Creston, Iowa, 1971; BS in Visual Sci., Ill. Coll. Optometry, Chgo., 1975, OD, 1975; MS, Calif. State U., Fullerton, 1986. Diplomate Am. Acad. Optometry. Pvt. practice assoc. Champaign, Ill., 1976-77; instr. So. Calif. Coll. Optometry, Fullerton, 1977-81, asst. prof., 1981-86, assoc. prof., 1986—, chief pediatric vision svcs., 1986-88; co-owner, ptnr. Irvine (Calif.) Optometric Group, 1988—; bd. dirs. Irvine Child Devel. Ctr., 1991-93. Contbr. chpt. to book, articles to profl. jours. Named to Outstanding Young Women of Am., 1979. Fellow Am. Acad. Optometry (vice chair binocular vision and perception sect. 1986-88, coord. written exam. 1991-96), Coll. Optometrists in Vision Devel.; mem. Am. Optometric Assn. (primary care com. 1988-90, long range planning com. 1990-92, mem. membership com. 1992-94, mem. binocular vision com. 1994—), Orton Dyslexia Soc. (bd. dirs. 1994—), Orange County Optometric Soc. (trustee 1995—). Home: 5510 Avenida Del Tren Yorba Linda CA 92887 Office: Irvine Optometric Group 4950 Barranca Pkwy Ste 310 Irvine CA 92604

RYAN, KAREN MARIE, physician assistant; b. N.Y.C., Jan. 5, 1957; d. Edward Francis and Rosemarie (Duffy) R.; m. Burdette V. Polk, Apr. 17, 1989. BS, Spring Hill Coll., 1979, Baylor U., 1982. Physician asst. Tex. Urology Clinic, Houston, 1982-86, Mayo Clinic, Jacksonville, Fla., 1986—; supr. physician asst., mem. coord. com. Mayo Clinic, 1988—. Fellow Am. Acad. Physicians Assts., Fla. Acad. Physicians Assts. Home: 237 Charlemagne Cir Ponte Vedra Beach FL 32082 Office: Mayo Clinic 4500 San Pablo Rd Jacksonville FL 32224

RYAN, KENNETH JOHN, physician, educator; b. N.Y.C., Aug. 26, 1926; s. Joseph M. R.; m. Marion Elizabeth Kinney, June 8, 1948; children: Alison Leigh, Kenneth John, Christopher Elliot. Student, Northwestern U., 1946-48; MD, Harvard U., 1952. Diplomate Am. Bd. Ob-Gyn. Intern, then resident internal medicine Mass. Gen. Hosp., Boston, also Columbia-Presbyn. Med. Center, N.Y.C., 1952-54, 56-57; resident in ob-gyn. Boston Lying-in Hosp., also Free Hosp. for Women, Brookline, Mass., 1957-60; prof. ob-gyn., dir. dept. Med. Sch. Western Res. U., 1961-70; prof. reproductive biology, dept. ob-gyn. U. Calif. San Diego, La Jolla, 1970-73; chief of staff Boston Hosp. for Women, 1973-80; chmn. dept. ob-gyn. Brigham Women's Hosp., Boston, 1980-93; instr. ob-gyn. Harvard U., also dir. Fearing Rsch. Lab., 1960-61, Kate Macy Ladd prof., chmn. dept. ob-gyn. Med. Sch., 1973-93, dir. Lab. Human Reprodn. and Reproductive Biology, 1974-93, Disting. prof., 1993-96, prof. emeritus, 1996—; chief staff Boston Hosp. for Women, 1973-80; chmn. dept. ob-gyn. Brigham Women's Hosp., Boston, 1980-93. Chmn. Nat. Commn. for Protection of Human Subjects Biomed. and Behavioral Rsch., 1974-78. Recipient Schering award Harvard Med. Sch., 1951, Soma Weis award, 1952, Bordon award, 1952; Ernst Oppenheimer award, 1964; Max Weinstein award, 1970; fellow Mass. Gen. Hosp., 1954-56. Fellow Am. Cancer Soc.; mem. ACOG, Am. Soc. Biol. Chemists, Endocrine Soc., Soc. Gynecol. Investigation, Am. Gynecol. Soc., Am. Soc. Clin. Investigation, Mass. Med. Soc., Alpha Omega Alpha. Office: Brigham & Women's Hosp 75 Francis St Boston MA 02115-6110

RYAN, KEVIN GUDE, radiologist; b. N.Y.C., July 4, 1934; s. Eric James and Catherine (Gude) R.; m. Susan Leach, Aug. 24, 1957; children: Christopher Gordon, Eric Cook. BA, Dartmouth Coll., Hanover, N.H., 1956; MD, Harvard U., 1959. Diplomate Am. Bd. Radiology, Am. Bd. Nuclear Medicine. Med. intern Mass. Gen. Hosp., Boston, 1959-60; radiology resident Peter Bent Brigam Hosp., Boston, 1963-66; radiologist Temple U. Hosp., Phila.. 1966-68, Woodland (Calif.) Clinic, 1968—; clin. prof. radiology U. Calif.-Davis Sch. Medicine, 1973—; pres. med. staff Woodland Meml. Hosp., 1983-84. Contbr. articles to profl. jours. Capt. USAF, 1963-66. Picker scholar in radiol. rsch., 1966. Mem. AMA, Calif. Med. Assn., Calif. Radiol. Soc. (pres. 1979-80), No. Calif. Radiol. Soc. (pres. 1972-73), Yolo County Med. Soc. (pres. 1996—), Western Angiographic and Interventional Soc., Woodland Sunrise Rotary, Phi Beta Kappa, Alpha Omega Alpha. Office: Woodland Clnic Med Group 1207 Fairchild Ct Woodland CA 95695

RYAN, MARY C., oncology and hematology nurse; b. Harvey, Ill., Sept. 30, 1971; d. James Edward and Barbara Jean (Gyenge) R. AAS, South Suburban Coll., South Holland, Ill., 1992, AS, 1993; BSN, No. Ill. U., 1994. RN, Ill. Staff nurse oncology/hematology U. Chgo., 1992—. Team mem. The Happening in Christianity, Kankakee, Ill., 1988-91. Mem. Ill. Nurses Assn., Golden Key. Roman Catholic.

RYAN, MICHAEL G., hospital executive; b. Washington, Jan. 19, 1960; s. John Lawrence and Anne Marguerite (Herkins) R.; m. Martha Jeanne Carrick, Sept. 22, 1984; children: Taylor Kathleen, Michael Spencer. BA cum laude, Regis U., 1981, BA Commns. cum laude, 1981; MA, Georgetown U., 1984. Diplomate Am. Coll. Healthcare Execs. Rsch. asst. Ryan Advisors, Inc., Washington, 1975-81; from fellow to v.p. adminstrn. St. Vincent's Health Sys., Jacksonville, Fla., 1983-87; ceo Ryan Adv., Inc., Jacksonville, 1987-88; v.p. ops. Providence Hosp., Washington, 1988-92; from v.p. ancillary to pres., ceo St. Francis Specialty Hosp., Monroe, La., 1992—; sec./treas. Ryan Adv., 1987; pres. MGR Holdings, Inc., Monroe, 1994; v.p. News Group Comms., Washington, 1986; bd. dirs. NELA Children's Mus., Monroe, 1994. Allocations com. United Way, Monroe, 1994-95; bd. dirs., capital funds ARC, Monroe, 1993-95. Mem. Am. Acad. Med. Adminstrn., Catholic Health Assn. La. (bd. dirs., pres. 1995), Capital Area Soc. Plan (pres. 1992, founding bd. dirs.), St. Vincent de Paul Soc. (bd. dirs., Good Samaritan award 1992), Leadership Ouachita. Home: 505 Loop Rd Monroe LA 71201 Office: St Francis Specialty Hosp 309 Jackson St Monroe LA 71201

RYAN, SHEILA A., dean, nursing educator. Dean Sch. Nursing, U. Rochester, N.Y., dir. Med. Ctr. Nursing. Mem. NAS. Office: U Rochester Med Sch 601 Elmwood Rochester NY 14642*

RYAN, STEPHEN J., academic dean. Dean U. So. Calif. Sch. Medicine, L.A. Office: U So Calif Sch Medicine 1450 San Pablo St Los Angeles CA 90033*

RYAN, STEPHEN JOSEPH, JR., ophthalmology educator, university dean; b. Honolulu, Mar. 20, 1940; s. S.J. and Mildred Elizabeth (Farrer) F.; m. Anne Christine Mullady, Sept. 25, 1965; 1 dau., Patricia Anne. A.B., Providence Coll., 1961; M.D., Johns Hopkins U., 1965. Intern Bellevue Hosp., N.Y.C., 1965-66; resident Wilmer Inst. Ophthalmology, Johns Hopkins Hosp., Balt., 1966-69, chief resident, 1969-70; fellow Armed Force Inst. Pathology, Washington, 1970-71; instr. ophthalmology Johns Hopkins U., Balt., 1970-71, asst. prof., 1971-72, assoc. prof., 1972-74; prof., chmn. dept. ophthalmology Los Angeles County-U. So. Calif. Med. Ctr., L.A., 1974-95, prof. dept. ophthalmology, 1974—; acting head ophthalmology div., dept. surgery Children's Hosp., L.A., 1975-77; med. dir. Doheny Eye Inst. (formerly Estelle Doheny Eye Found.), L.A., 1977-86; chief of staff Doheny Eye Hosp., L.A., 1985-88; dean U. So. Calif. Sch. Medicine, L.A., 1991—; mem. advisory panel Calif. Med. Assn., 1975—. Editor: (with M.D. Andrews) A Survey of Ophthalmology--Manual for Medical Students, 1970, (with R.E. Smith) Selected Topics on the Eye in Systemic Disease, 1974, (with Dawson and Little) Retinal Diseases, 1985, (with others) Retina, 1989; assoc. editor: Ophthalmol. Surgery, 1974-85; mem. editorial bd. Am. Jour. Ophthalmology, 1981—, Internat. Ophthalmology, 1982—, Retina, 1983—, Graefes Archives, 1984—; contbr. articles to med. jours. Recipient cert. of merit AMA, 1971; Louis B. Mayer Scholar award Research to Prevent Blindness, 1973; Rear Adm. William Campbell Chambliss USN award, 1982. Mem. Wilmer Ophthal. Inst. Residents Assn., Am. Acad. Ophthalmology and Otolaryngology (award of Merit 1975), Am. Ophthal. Soc., Pan-Am. Assn. Ophthalmology, Assn. Univ. Profs. of Ophthalmology, L.A. Soc. Ophthalmology, AMA, Calif. Med. Assn., Los Angeles County Med. Assn., Pacific Coast Oto-Ophthal. Soc., L.A. Acad. Medicine, Pan Am. Assn. Microsurgery, Macula Soc, Retina Soc., Nat. Eye Care Project, Rsch. Study Club, Jules Gonin Club, Soc. Scholars of Johns Hopkins U. (life). Office: U So Calif Sch of Medicine 1450 San Pablo St Los Angeles CA 90033

RYAN, SUZANNE IRENE, nursing educator; b. Yonkers, N.Y., Mar. 13, 1939; d. Edward Vincent and Winifred E. (Goemann) R. BA in Biology, Mt. St. Agnes Coll., Balt., 1962; BSN, Columbia U., 1967, MA in Nursing Svc., 1973, MEd in Nursing Edn., 1975; MS in Oncology, San Jose (Calif.) State Coll. U., 1982. RN, N.Y.; cert. AIDS educator, N.Y. Prof. nursing Molloy Coll., Rockville Centre, N.Y., 1970—, co-dir. health svcs., dir. edn. programs, 1987-94, dir. health svcs., 1994—, health educator, 1992—, co-dir. mobile health van, adminstr. health edn., 1992—; pres., CEO SIR Enterprises, Inc., 1982—; photographer Molloy Coll. Pubs., 1991—; photographic dir. Bali-Art, Inc., 1992—; mem. N.Y. State AIDS Coun., 1987—, L.I. Alcohol Consortium, 1987—; educator Nassau County Dept. Sr. Citizens Health, 1991—; photographer-in-residence Molloy Coll., 1992—; lectr. on landscape, wildlife and flower photography, L.I., N.H., Can., 1993—. Represented in permanent collections in photographic galleries in Carmel, Calif., Laconia, Wolfboro and Moultonboro, N.H., 1963—; one-woman shows include Mollay Coll., Rockville Ctr. Library; photographer 4 books on Monterey Peninulsa, New Eng. and N.H.; writer, editor Health News Letter Molloy Coll., 1990—. Health educator Nassau County Dept. of Sr. Citizens Outreach Program, Molloy Coll., AIDS educator, 1991—; adminstr., chief AIDS counselor Interaction AIDS Counseling, Babylon, N.Y., 1992—; lic. AIDS educator N.Y. Metro Area; chairperson of grants com. in higher edn. Nassau U. USPHS fellow, 1962, Nat. Cancer Inst. fellow, 1981-82. Mem. AAUP, AAUW, Nat. Congress Oncology Nurses, N.Y. State Fedn. Health Educators, Inc., Nurses Assn. Counties L.I. Dist. 14, N.Y. State Nurses Assn., World Wildlife Orgn., Audubon Soc., Internat. Ctr. Photography, Nature Conservancy, Sierra Club, Sigma Theta Tau (Epsilon Kappa chpt., rsch. grantee 1985, 87), Zeta Epsilon Gamma. Roman Catholic. Home: 16 Walker St Malverne NY 11565-1829

RYAN, TERESA WEAVER, obstetrical nurse; b. Dallas, July 18, 1956; d. J.E. and Mary (Davis) Weaver; m. Patrick Hallaron Ryan, Apr. 7, 1991. BS, Troy State U., 1983; BSN, Tex. Christian U., 1987; MSN, U. South Ala., 1994; postgrad., La. State U. RN, Fla.; cert. maternal-newborn nurse ANCC. Intelligence analyst USN, Dallas, 1983-87; enlisted USAF, 1987, advanced through grades to capt. (obstetrical nurse), 1987—; childbirth educator USAF, 1988—. Mem. NOW, Assn. Women's Health, Obstetrical and Neonatal Nurses, Nat. Humane Soc. Educators, People for the Ethical Treatment of Animals, Sigma Theta Tau (sec. 1987—, rsch. grant 1987), Phi Kappa Phi. Roman Catholic. Home: 35 Imperial Woods Dr Harahan LA 70123

RYAN, WILLIAM GEORGE, psychiatrist; b. Berkeley, Calif., Jan. 7, 1951; s. William George and Natalie Elizabeth (Harris) Ryan. Student, Princeton U., 1969-71; A.B., Ind. U., 1974, M.D., 1978. Diplomate Am. Bd. Psychiatry and Neurology. Resident in psychiatry N.C. Meml. Hosp., Chapel Hill, 1978-82; asst. prof. psychiatry U. Ala., Birmingham, 1982-87, assoc. prof., 1987— ; attending physician Univ. Hosp., Birmingham, 1982—. NSF grantee, 1972. Mem. Am. Psychiat. Assn., Soc. Biol. Psychiatry, Ala. Conservacy, Phi Beta Kappa, Alpha Omega Alpha. Episcopalian. Office: 390 N 422 Comm Care Bldg UAB Birmingham AL 35294-2050

RYBOUCHKIN, ANDREI VASILIEVICH, obstetrician, gynecologist; b. Petrozavodsk, Russia, Mar. 11, 1962; s. Vasily Nicolaevich and Valentina Ivanovna (Chistyakova) R.; m. Goulnara Anusovna Reziapova, Feb. 10, 1990; 1 child. MS, U. St. Petersburg, 1983. Rschr. Inst. Animal Genetics, Russia, 1989-94; embryologist IVF Ctr., Russia, 1993-94, Belgium, 1994—. Contbr. articles to profl. jours. Scholar Ghent U., 1994-97. Home: Zuijnoardseesteenweg 435, B-9000 Ghent Belgium Office: U Hosp Ghent-Dept Ob-Gyn, De Pintelaan 185, B-9000 Ghent Belgium

RYDHSTROEM, HAKAN, obstetrician, gynecologist; b. Kalmar, Sweden, Nov. 8, 1946; s. Olle and Rose (Rydell) R.; m. Karin Behrens; children: Erica, Jenny. MD, Lund U., 1976, PhD, 1990. Intern Ctrl. Hosp., Helsingborg, Sweden, resident in ob-gyn.; cons. Hosp. Karls Krona, Sweden, 1990-93, U. Lund, Sweden, 1994; head dept. ob-gyn. Trelleborg, Sweden, 1995—; workshop dir. 8th Internat. Workshop on Multiple Pregnancy, 1993; mem. expert Nat. Bd. Health and Welfare, 1994—. Co-author: Multiple Pregnancy, 1995; contbr. articles to profl. jours. Home: Per Jacobs V 10, S-26352 Hoeganas Sweden Office: U Lund, S-22185 Lund Sweden

RYGNESTAD, TARJEI, anesthesiologist, consultant, educator; b. Trondheim, Sø-Trøndelag, Norway, July 26, 1954; s. Knut Olavsson and Inger Mathilde (Hoel) R.; m. Tone Kristin Smistad, Apr. 20, 1992; children: Tina, Knut Olav, Ingrid. MD, U. Trondheim, Norway, 1981, PhD, 1990; M. Pub. Health, U. Tromsø, Norway, 1996. Diplomate European Acad. Anaesthesiology; specialist clin. pharmacology; specialist anesthesiology. Resident anesthesiology U. Hosp., Trondheim, Norway, 1983-88, 89-90, jr. resident clin. pharmacology, 1988-90, cons. anesthesiology, 1991-92, 94—, lectr., 1994—; dist. med. officer Min. Health and Child Welfare, Zimbabwe, 1992-94; co-organizer WHO rsch. program internat. multicenter study on parasuicide, 1988-91. Author: Deliberate Self Poisoning in Trondheim, 1990; contbr. chpt. to book. Rsch. fellow Norwegian RSch. Coun. Sci. and Humanities, 1977-78; grantee Med. Assn. Sør-Trøndelag, 1987, 88, 89, 91, 94, U. Hosp. Mem. Am. Assn. Regional Anesthesia, Norwegian Soc. Clin. Pharmacology, Scandinavian Soc. Anaesthesiology, European Soc. Intensive Care Medicine. Office: U Trondheim Faculty Medicine, Dept Pharmacology and Toxicology, N-7005 Trondheim Norway

RYHÄNEN, PAULI TAAVETTI, anesthetist; b. Kajaani, Oulu, Finland, Oct. 19, 1939; s. Lauri and Irma Alice (Korhonen) R.; m. Elsi Kaarina Kalaja, June 24, 1962; children: Jorma, Tapio. MD, U. Oulu, 1966, PhD, 1977. Lectr. anesthesia U. Oulu, 1972-74, acting prof. anesthesiology, 1992-94; rsch. asst. Med. Rsch. Coun. of Acad. Finland, Oulu, 1974-77; specialist in anesthesia Univ. Ctrl. Hosp., Oulu, 1977-81; chief paediatric anesthetist Children's Hosp./Univ. Ctrl. Hosp., Oulu, 1981—; cons. anesthetist Päivärinne Hosp., Oulu, 1972-87. Contbr. articles to profl. jours. Mem. Finnish Soc. Anesthetists (vice chmn. 1986-88), Assn. of Paediatric Anesthetists of Gt. Britain and Ireland. Lutheran. Home: Uistintie 3, 90550 Oulu Finland Office: Oulu Univ Ctrl Hosp, Dept Anesthetists, 90220 Oulu Finland

RYMOND, CLAES GORAN, health care executive; b. Vetlanda, Sweden, Mar. 8, 1956; s. Bertil and Carin (Lundmark) R.; m. Anita C. Darmanian, Aug. 27, 1989. BA, Harvard U., 1977; MD, NYU, 1981. Diplomate Nat. Bd. Med. Examiners, Am. Bd. Internal Medicine. Resident Columbia U./ Presbyn. Med. Ctr., N.Y.C., 1981-84, chief resident, 1984-85; pvt. practice N.Y.C., 1985-87; dir. Merck & Co., Inc., Rahway, N.J., 1987-90; pres., CEO BioCarb Group, Lund, Sweden, 1990-91, Medicon Internat., Fort Lee, N.J., 1991—; bd. dirs. MicroCarb, Inc., Gaithersburg, Md. Recipient scholarships Harvard Coll., Cambridge, Mass., 1974, 75, John Harvard Hon. scholarship, 1976-77, Samuel Spiegel Med. award NYU, N.Y.C., 1981. Mem. Alpha Omega Alpha. Office: Medicon Internat 1350 15th St Apt 4H Fort Lee NJ 07024-2012

RYPKA, EUGENE WESTON, microbiologist; b. Owatonna, Minn., May 6, 1925; s. Charles Frederick and Ethel Marie (Ellerman) R.; m. Rosemary Speeker, June 1, 1967. Student, Carleton Coll., 1946-47; BA, Stanford U., 1950, PhD, 1958. Prof. microbiology, systems, cybernetics U. N.Mex., Albuquerque, 1957-62; bacteriologist Leonard Wood Meml. Lab. Johns Hopkins U., Balt., 1962-63; sr. scientist Lovelace Med. Ctr., Albuquerque, 1963-71, chief microbiologist, 1971-93; adj. prof. U. N.Mex., 1973—; cons. Hoffmann-LaRoche Inc., 1974—, Airline Pilots Assn., Washington, 1976, Pasco Lab., Denver, 1983—; advisor Nat. Com. Clinic Lab. Standards, Pa., 1980-84. Contbr. articles to profl. jours. and chpts. in books. Served with USNR, USMC 1943-46. Fellow AAAS; mem. IEEE, Internat. Soc. Systems Sci. Republican. Presbyterian. Home: PO Box 8345 Highland Sta Albuquerque NM 87198

RYSER, STEFAN, molecular biologist, healthcare company executive; b. Brugg, Aargau, Switzerland, Dec. 3, 1959; s. Markus Hermann and Edith (Waelti) R.; m. Marion Sylvia Kienzler, Aug. 3, 1985; children: Nathalie, Jennifer. Degree in biochemistry at Biocenter, U. Basel, Switzerland, PhD, 1988. Info. officer biotech. F. Hoffmann-LaRoche Ltd., Basel, 1989-92; mgr. pub. policy and comm. Hoffmann-LaRoche Inc., Nutley, N.J., 1992-93; sci. asst. to pres. internat. R&D Hoffmann-LaRoche Inc., Nutley, 1993-95; chmn. steering com. to lead pub. rels. campaign for biotech. F. Hoffmann-LaRoche Ltd. and Interpharma, Basel, 1995-96, mem. internat. pharm. rsch. staff, 1996—; vice chmn. Sr. Adv. Group Biotech., Bruxelles, 1989—, Internat. Rels. Com. Bioindustry Orgn., Washington, 1992-95. Editor various books; contbr. articles to profl. jours. Office: F Hoffmann-LaRoche Ltd, 4070 Basel Switzerland

RYU, KYOO-HAI LEE, physiologist; b. Seoul, Republic of Korea, Sept. 5, 1948; came to U.S., 1972; d. Hee Soon and Jung Ock Lee; m. David Tai-Hyung Ryu, May 13, 1978; children: Eugenia, Christina, John. BS, Yonsei U., Seoul, 1971; PhD, U. Minn., 1981. Postdoctoral fellow U. Minn., Mpls., 1980-81, staff scientist, 1981-82; sr. rsch. assoc. Wright State U., Dayton, Ohio, 1985-91; adminstr. Ohio Ctr. of Cosmetic Surgery, Bellefontaine, Ohio, 1991—. Mem. Am. Physiol. Soc., Biophys. Soc., Soc. Gen. Physiologists. Home: 15 Bexley Ave Springfield OH 45503-1103

SAADEH, CONSTANTINE KHALIL, internist, medical educator; b. Beirut, Sept. 6, 1957; came to U.S., 1982; s. Khalil Constantine and Angel Janet (Iskendarian) S.; m. Vivian Camille Novni, June 28, 1988 (div. Apr. 1993); 1 child, Charles; m. M. Celeste Gaylor, 1996; 2 children: Charles, McKenzie. BS in Biology-Chemistry, Am. U. Beirut, 1978, MD, 1982. Diplomate Nat. Bd. Med. Examiners, Am. Bd. Internal Medicine, Am. Bd. Allergy and Immunology, Am. Bd. Internal Medicine, Am. Bd. Rheumatology, Am. Bd. Geriatrics, Am. Acad. Pain Mgmt. Intern dept. of medicine U. Miami, Jackson Meml. Hosp., Fla., 1982-83, resident dept. of medicine, 1983-85; fellow in clin. immunology Baylor Coll. of Medicine, Houston, 1985-87; fellow in rheumatology U. Colo. Health Sci. Ctr., Denver, 1987-88, instr. dept. internal medicine, 1988-89; acting chief med. svc. VA Med. Ctr., Amarillo, Tex., 1989, med. svc. staff physician, 1989—; asst. prof. dept. internal medicine Tex. Tech U. Health Scis. Ctr., Amarillo, 1989-91, assoc. prof. internal medicine and pediatrics, dir., 1991—, regional chair internal medicine, dir. residency program, 1992—, assoc. prof. dept. microbiology and immunology, 1992—; mem. grad. med. edn. com. Tex. Tech. U. Health Sci. Ctr.; mem. pharmacy and therapeutics com. N.W. Tex. Hosp.; mem. pharmacy and therapeutics com., R&D com. VA Med. Ctr., faculty appointments com., MPIP com. Tex. Tech. U., program dir., chmn. residency evaluation com., 1992—; lectr. in field. Contbr. articles to profl. jours. Fellow ACP, Am. Acad. Allergy and Immunology, Am. Coll. Rheumatology; mem. AMA, So. Med. Assn. (chmn. rheumatology sect. 1996-97). Home: 7100 Canterbury Amarillo TX 79109 Office: Tex Tech U Health Scis Ctr 1400 Wallace Blvd Amarillo TX 79106-1708

SAADEH, PETER BOUTROS, physiatrist, educator; b. Beirut, Aug. 8, 1930; came to U.S., 1975; s. Beshara B. and Edma A. Saadeh; m. Genevieve L. Verbrugghen, Apr. 27, 1968; children: Pierre, Kris. BA, Coll. de Sagesse, Beirut, 19849; MD, St. Joseph French U., Beirut, 1957. Diplomate Am. Bd. Phys. Medicine and Rehab. Intern Elizabeth (N.J.) Gen. Hosp., 1957-58; resident in neurology Montefiore Hosp., Bronx, N.Y., 1958-60; resident in phys. medicine and rehab. NYU Hosp., N.Y.C., 1960-62; assoc. Am. U. Hosp., Beirut, 1962-75; pvt. practice, N.Y.C., 1978—; asst. clin. prof. NYU, N.Y.C. Contbr. articles to med. jours. Mem. AMA, Am. Acad. Phys. Medicine and Rehab., Am. Assn. Electromyography, Assn. Acad. Physiatrists, Am. Coll. Occpl. and Environ. Medicine, N.Y. Soc. Phys. Medicine Rehab. (pres. 1989-90), N.Y. Acad. Medicine. Republican. Office: 5 World Trade Ctr Ste 367B New York NY 10048

SAADIA, ROGER, surgery educator; b. France, Apr. 4, 1951; arrived in South Africa, 1981; s. Emile and Linda (Hazan) S; m. Vivien Paynter, Mar. 1, 1995. MD, U. Grenoble, 1977; BA, U. South Africa, 1992. Cons. surgeon U. Witwatersrand, Johannesburg, South Africa, 1985-93, prof. surgery, 1993—. Contbr. articles to profl. jours.; mem. editorial bd. South African Jour. Surgery, 1993—, Trauma and Emergency Medicine, 1993—. Lt. French Army, 1977-78. Fellow Royal Coll. Surgeons; mem. Assn. Surgeons South Africa, N.Y. Acad. Scis. Jewish. Home: 17 Killarney Manor 8th St, 2193 Killarney Johannesburg South Africa Office: Dept Surgery Med Sch, 7 York Rd Parktown, 2193 Johannesburg South Africa

SAAG, KENNETH GARY, medical educator; b. Chgo., Mar. 13, 1960; s. James Burton and Gloria Hariet (Speyer) S.; m. Leah Ann Waller; children: Jennifer Ruth, Lauren Ann. BS, U. Mich., 1982; MD, Northwestern U., 1986; MS, U. Iowa, 1993. Diplomate Am. Bd. Internal Medicine. Resident Evanston (Ill.) Hosp./Northwestern U., 1986-89, 1989-90; assoc. U. Iowa Dept. Internal Medicine, Iowa City, 1993-94, asst. prof., 1994—. Contbr. articles to profl. jours. Tng. grantee NIH, 1993; fellow U. Iowa Dept. Internal Medicine, 1990-93; recipient rsch. award U. Iowa, Coll. Medicine, 1994. Fellow Am. Coll. Rheumatology, Am. Coll. Medicine; mem. Am. Fedn. Clin. Rsch., Soc. Gen. Internal Medicine, Assn. Health Svcs. Rsch., Ctrl. Soc. Clin. Rsch. Office: U Iowa Hosp Dept Internal Medicine SE 615 Gh Iowa City IA 52242

SAAH, ALFRED JOSEPH, epidemiology educator; b. Washington, Aug. 16, 1947; m. Marylou Dooley, Jan. 1977 (div. 1990); children: Victoria, Emily; m. Andrea Imredy, June 18, 1994; 1 child, Michael. BS, Mt. St. Mary's Coll., Emmitsburg, Md., 1969; MD, U. Md., Balt., 1973; MPH, Johns Hopkins U., 1981. Diplomate Am. Bd. Internal Medicine, Am. Bd. Infectious Diseases, Am. Bd. Epidemiology. Resident in internal medicine U. Md. Hosp., 1973-76, fellow in infectious diseases, 1978-80; commd. lt. comdr. USPHS, 1976, advanced through grades to commdr.; epidemic intelligence officer Ctrs. for Disease Control, Atlanta, 1976-78; with epidemiology tng. program Nat. Inst. Arthritis and Infectious Diseases, NIH, Bethesda, Md., 1980-83, med. epidemiologist, 1983-87; assoc. prof. epidemiology Johns Hopkins U. Sch. Pub. Health, Balt., 1987—, dir. infectious diseases program, 1989-92; cons., tchr. Nat. Basketball Players Assn., N.Y.C., 1991—; cons. Inst. Medicine, NAS, Washington, 1991—; mem. sexually transmitted dieseases guidelines com. Ctrs. for Disease Control, 1994—. Contbr. articles to med. jours. Grantee Nat. Inst. Arthritis and Infectious Diseases, 1990. Fellow ACP; mem. Infectious Diseases Soc. Am. Am. Soc. for Microbiology, Am. Soc. Tropical Medicine. Office: Johns Hopkins U Sch Pub Health 615 N Wolfe St Baltimore MD 21205

SAAKVITNE, KAREN WINSLOW, psychologist; b. Aug. 13, 1957. BA in Psychology/English magna cum laude, Yale Coll., 1979; MA in Clin. Psychology, U. Mich., 1984, PhD in Clin. Psychology, 1986. Lic. clin. psychologist, Mass., Conn.; lic. secondary sch. tchr., Mass. Tchr. Cedarhurst Sch., Yale Psychiat. Inst., New Haven, 1980-82; psychology intern Children's Psychiat. Hosp., U. Mich., Ann Arbor, 1983-85, U. Mich. Psychol. Clinic, Ann Arbor, 1986; postdoctoral fellow in psychology Austen Riggs Ctr., Stockbridge, Mass., 1986-90; vis. counselor Smith Coll. Counseling Svcs., Northampton, Mass., 1989-90; clin. dir. Traumatic Stress Inst. Ctr. for Adult and Adolescent Psychotherapy, South Windsor, Conn., 1990—; author, presenter 1st Internat. Congress on Disorders of Personality, Copenhagen, 1988. Author: (with L.A. Pearlman) Trauma and the Therapist, 1995, (with L.A. Pearlman and staff) Transforming the Rain: A workbook on Various Traumatization, 1996; contbr. chpts. to books and articles to profl. jours. Mem. APA (author, presenter conv. 1984, 85, 87, 90, 91, 93, 96, author, presenter divsn. psychoanalysis 1988, 96), Mass. Psychol. Assn., Conn. Psychol. Assn., Conn. Soc. for Psychoanalytic Psychology, Internat. Soc. for Traumatic Stress Studies (author, presenter 1991, 92, 93, 94, 95).

SAARI, JOY ANN, family nurse practitioner, geriatrics and medical/surgical nurse; b. Chippewa Falls, Wis., July 14, 1953; d. Harry R. and Hilda R. (Christianson) Harwood; m. Allan A. Saari, Dec. 31, 1973 (dec.); children: Christopher, Erik. BSN summa cum laude, U. Wis., Eau Claire, 1978; postgrad., Blue Ridge Community Coll., Verona, Va., 1987; MSN, FNP, George Mason U., 1995; MSN. RN, Mich., Wis., Va.; FNP, Va.; cert. BLS instr., ACLS. Staff nurse Portage View Hosp., Hancock, Mich., 1979-80; evening supr., asst. dir. nursing Chippewa Manor, Chippewa Falls, 1980-86; staff nurse Bridgewater (Va.) Home, Inc., 1986-90; p.m. charge nurse Medicalodge Leavenworth, Kans., 1990-91; outdoor edn. nurse Montgomery County (Md.) Schs., 1991-93; FNP Leesburg/Sterling Family Practice, 1995—. Capt. USAR Nurse Corps. Mem. Am. Acad. Nurse Practitioners, Nat. League of Nursing, No. Va. Nurse Practitioner Assn., Res. Officer Assn., Am. Legion Aux., Phi Kappa Phi.

SAATHOFF, PATRICIA LEE, hospital administrator; b. Ann Arbor, Mich., Feb. 11, 1954; d. Stuart Meese Jr. and Betty Ann (Reske) Gould; m. David Roger Saathoff, Nov. 3, 1990. BSN, Ariz. State U., 1979, MS, 1982. RN, Ariz. Staff nurse Good Samaritan Hosp., Phoenix, 1979-80, VA Med. Ctr., Phoenix, 1980-82; crisis nurse Presbyn. Svc. Agy., Phoenix, 1981-83; psychiat. clin. specialist Mesa (Ariz.) Luth. Hosp., 1983-85; nurse mgr. West Valley Camelback Hosp., Glendale, Ariz., 1985; psychiat. clin. specialist Vis. Nurse Svc., Phoenix, 1985-87, Pvt. Practice-Dr. Gould, Phoenix, 1984-87; asst. adminstr. Charter Med. Corp., Chandler, Ariz., 1987-92; v.p. clin. svcs. St. Luke's Health Sys., Phoenix, 1993-96; dir. patient care svcs. Westbridge Treatment Ctrs., Phoenix, 1996—. Edn. grantee NIMH, 1982. Mem. Ariz. Coun. Ctrs. for Children and Adults, ANA (cert.), Ariz. Nurses Assn. (pub. rels. chairperson 1982-84, legis. com.), Sigma Theta Tau. Democrat. Methodist. Office: Westbridge Treatment Ctrs 1830 E Roosevelt Phoenix AZ 85006

SABANAYAGAM, MUTHUKRISHNA, neuropsychiatrist; b. Chidambaram, Tamilnadu, India, Jan. 15, 1940; came to U.S., 1967; s. Muthukrishna and Marimuthu (Krishnan) S.; m. Cheryl Braun (div. 1985); 1 child, Mari Suzanne. MD, U. Madras, 1965. Diplomate Am. Bd. Psychiatry and Neurology. Med. intern St. Francis Hosp., Poughkeepsie, N.Y., 1967-68; resident in psychiatry Central Islip (N.Y.) Psychiat. Ctr., 1968-72; postgrad. N.Y. Sch. Psychiatry, N.Y.C., 1969-72; resident in neurology N.Y. Med. Coll., N.Y.C., 1972-74; pvt. practice Bayshore, N.Y., 1974—; assoc. med. dir. Kings Park (N.Y.) Psychiat. Ctr., 1983—; cons. in neurology N.Y. Med. Devel. Inst., N.Y.C., 1974-77; psychiat. cons. Hoch Psychiat. Ctr., Brentwood, N.Y., 1975-78; psychiatrist II univ. svc. SUNY, Stony Brook, Central Islip, 1978-82, psychiatrist III, 1081-83. Mem. Am. Acad. Neurology, Am. Psychiat. Assn., Am. Geriatric Soc., Am. Neurophysiology Soc., N.Y. Med. Soc., Suffolk County Med. Soc. Home: 1 Northwood Ct Dix Hills NY 11746 Office: 270 E Main St Bay Shore NY 11706-8403

SABANEGH, EDMUND SAMI, JR., urologist; b. Boston, Oct. 30, 1958; s. Edmund S. and Marlowe (Farnum) S.; m. Amy Wilburn, June 1, 1985; 1 child, Emily Wilburn. BSChemE summa cum laude, Princeton (N.J.) U., 1981; MD, U. Va., 1985. Diplomate Am. Bd. Urology. Urology resident Wilford Hall Med. Ctr., San Antonio, 1986-92, staff urologist, 1992-93, 1994-95, chmn. dept. urology, 1996—; male infertility/microsurgery fellowship Cleve. Clinic, 1993-94. Author: (with others) Atlas, Male Infertility, 1995; contbr. articles to profl. jours. Maj. USAF, 1985—. Mem. Soc. of Air Force Clin. Surgeons, Soc. of Govt. Svc. Urologists, Am. Urol. Assn., Am. Fertility Soc. Office: Wilford Hall Med Ctr Dept Urology 2200 Bergquist Dr Ste 1 Lackland AFB TX 78236-5300

SABATELLA, ELIZABETH MARIA, clinical therapist, educator, mental health facility administrator; b. Mineola, N.Y., Nov. 9, 1940; d. D. F. and Blanche M. (Schmetzle) S; 1 child, Kevin Woog. BS, SUNY, Brockport, 1961; MA, SUNY, Stony Brook, 1971, MSW, 1983. Lic. social worker, N.Y., N.Mex., tchr., N.Y., N.Mex.; registered clin. social worker, Calif. Tchr. physical edn. Comseqogue Sch. Dist., Port Jefferson, N.Y., 1968-73, 84-87, 88-91; clin. therapist Cibola Counseling Svcs., Grants, N.Mex., 1991-95, regional dir., 1993-95; clin. therapist Family Growth Counseling Ctr., Encinitos, Calif., 1995—; clin. social worker Family Advocacy, San Diego, 1995—; therapist for abused children Farmingville Mental Health Clinic; therapist for adolescents Comsewogue Sch. Dist.; therapist for alcoholics Lighthouse Ctr.; mem. Family Systems Network for Continuing Edn., Calif., Colo., 1978-80; mem. biofeedback and mediation com. McLean Hosp., Boston, 1978; mem. therapeutic touch team East and West Ctr., N.Y.C., 1980-84, sexual abuse treatment coord., 1992-95. Art and photographs exhibited at group show N.Mex. Art League, 1991; contbr. poetry and children's story to various publs. Recipient Editor's Choice award and Best New Poet award Nat. Libr. Poetry, 1988, Merit award and Place Winner for Poetry, Iliad Press, 1993. Mem. NASW, N.Y. State United Tchrs., Writers Assn., Sierra Club. Home: 3852 Jewell St Apt 208 San Diego CA 92109

SABATH, LEON DAVID, physician, educator; b. Savannah, Ga., July 24, 1930; s. Sholom and Sarah (Cherkas) S.; children: Natasha Roxanne, Joanna Tamara, Rachel Tatiana. AB, Harvard Coll., 1952; MD, Harvard Med. Sch., 1956. Diplomate Am. Bd. Internal Medicine, Am. Bd. Infectious Diseases. Intern in medicine Peter Bent Brigham Hosp., Boston, 1956-57; jr. resident in medicine Bellevue Hosp., N.Y.C., 1959-60; rsch. fellow Harvard Med. Sch., Boston, 1960-62, asst. in medicine, 1965-71, asst. prof. medicine, 1968-71, assoc. prof. medicine, 1971-74; sr. resident in medicine Peter Bent Brigham Hosp., Boston, 1962-63; rsch. assoc. U. Oxford, Eng., 1963-65; prof. medicine U. Minn., Mpls., 1974—; adj. faculty Rockefeller U., N.Y.C., 1990-91; trustee EPA Cephelosporin Trust, Oxford, 1970—. Contbr. 170 articles to profl. pubs. and chpts. to books. Capt. U.S. Army Med. Corps., 1957-59, Korea. Special fellow NIH, 1961-63; recipient Career Devel. award NIH, 1969-74. Fellow ACP, Infectious Disease Soc. Am.; mem. Am. Soc. Clin. Investigation, Am. Fedn. Clin. Rsch., Mass. Med. Soc., Am. Soc. Microbiology (pres. sect. antimicrobial chemotherapy, 1975-76). Jewish. Home: 2504 Washburn Ave S Minneapolis MN 55416 Office: U Minn Hosp Box 489 Minneapolis MN 55455

SABATINI, DAVID DOMINGO, cell biologist, biochemist; b. Bolivar, Argentina, May 10, 1931; m. Zulema Lena Sabatina, 1960; children: Bernardo L., David M. MD, Nat. U. Litoral, 1954; PhD in Biochemistry, Rockefeller U., 1966. Instr., lectr., assoc. prof. histiology Inst. Gen. Anatomy and Embryology, U. Buenos Aires, 1957-60; dir. admissions Med. Sch. U. Buenos Aires, 1957-60; Rockefeller Found. fellow Med. Sch. Yale U., 1961, Rockefeller Inst., 1961-62; rsch. assoc. cell biol. lab Rockefeller U., N.Y.C., 1961-63, from asst. prof. to assoc. prof. cell biology, 1960-72; prof. cell biology and biochemistry NYU, 1972-74, Frederick L. Ehrman prof., chmn. dept. cell biol. Sch. Med., 1975—, dir. MD-PhD program, 1987—; Wendell Griffith Meml. lectr. St. Louis U., 1977; Mary Peterman Meml. lectr. Meml.-Sloan Kettering Inst., N.Y., 1977; 25th Robert J. Terry lectr. Wash. U., 1978; 7th Ann. Kenneth F. Naidorff Meml. lectr. Columbia U., 1989; fellow Nat. Acad. Medicine, Argentina, 1956; UNESCO fellow Biophysics Inst., Rio de Janeiro, 1957; Pfizer traveling fellow, 1972; mem. molecular biology study sect. NIH, 1973-77, chmn., 1976-77; mem. bd. basic biology Nat. Rsch. Coun., 1986—. Editor Jour. Cellular Biochemistry, 1980-84, Molecular & Cellular Biology, 1980-82, Biol. Cell, 1986—, Current Opinions Cell Biology, 1990—. Recipient Samuel Roberts Noble Rsch. Recognition award, 1980. Fellow AAAS, N.Y. Acad. Sci.; mem. NAS, Am. Soc. Cell Biology (pres. 1978-79, coun. mem. 1974-77, E. B. Wilson award 1986), Harvey Soc. (v.p. 1985-86, pres. 1986-87). *

SABATINI, SANDRA, physician; b. N.Y.C.; Dec. 1, 1940. BS in Chemistry, Millsaps Coll., 1962; MS in Pharmacology, Marquette U., 1966; PhD in Pharmacology, U. Miss., 1968; MD in Internal Medicine, Tex. Med. Sch., 1974. Lic. physician, Ill., Tex. Intern in medicine U. Ill. Hosp., Chgo., 1974-75; asst. prof. U. Tex. Med. Sch., San Antonio, 1968-70; assoc. dir. U. Ill. Hosp., Chgo., 1977-78; asst. prof. U. Ill. Coll. of Medicine, Chgo., 1977-83, assoc. prof. medicine and physiology, 1983-84; attending physician in nephrology VA, Chgo., 1977-84; med. dir. Dialysis Unit U. Ill., Chgo., 1978-84; prof. internal medicine and physiology Tex. Tech. U. Health Sci. Ctr., Lubbock, 1985—, chmn. dept. physiology, 1993—; attending physician in nephrology U. Med. Ctr., Lubbock, 1985—; lab. instr. Millsaps Coll., Jackson, Miss., 1961-62; instr. in pharmacology, Bapt. Hosp. Sch. Nursing, Jackson, 1966-68; merit rev. mem. NSF, 1987, 91, 92; rev. mem. several orgns. including Chgo. Heart Assn., 1984, NIH, 1982, 86, 89-93, Nat. Kidney Found., 1987, 89—, Am. Heart Assn., 1981-84, others. Editorial referee Am. Jour. Kidney Disease, Am. Jour. Physiology, Am. Jour. Nephrology, Annals of Internal Medicine, others; editorial bd. Am. Jour. Nephrology, 1989-93, Seminars in Nephrology, 1984—; ; author numerous publs. and abstracts in field; contbr. articles to profl. jours. Recipient predoctoral fellowship grant, Marquette U., 1963-66, pub. health predoctoral fellow U. Miss. Med. Sch., 1967-69, gen. medicine sci. rsch. grant U. Tex. Med. Sch., 1968-70, post-grad. fellowship award Karolinska Inst., Swedish Med. Coun., 1971, 73, NIH grants, 1979-82, 1984—, Chgo. Heart Assn. grant-in-aid, 1979-85, Nat. Eye Inst. grant, 1979-80, Banes Charitable Trust award U. Ill.,1984-85, U.S. Olympic Com. Rsch. Found. Clin. Study, 1986-87, numerous others awards in field. Fellow Am. Coll. Physicians; mem. AAAS, AAUP, AOA (hon.), Am. Fedn. Clin. Rsch., Am. Heart Assn., Am. Physiol. Soc., Am. Soc. Nephrology, Am. Soc. Pharmacology and Exptl. Therapeutics, Am. Soc. Renal Biochemistry and Metabolism (pres. elect 1994), Cen. Soc. Clin. Rsch., Ill. Kidney Found., Internat. Soc. Nephrology, Italian-Am. Nephrologists, Inc., Nat. Kidney Found. (numerous offices including chmn. several coms.), Nat. Kidney Found. of West Tex. (bd. dirs. 1993—, Outstanding Vol. 1995). Office: Tex Tech U Health Sci Ctr 3601 4th St Lubbock TX 79430-0001

SABIDO, ALMEDA ALICE, mental health facility administrator; b. Blairsville, Pa., Sept. 24, 1928; d. George Jackson and Dora Irene (Byrd) McClellen; m. Frederick Lionel Harrison, Feb. 1, 1963; children: Frederick L.H., Derek M. BS in Secondary Edn., Indiana U. of Pa., 1950; MSW cum laude, U. Pitts., 1958. Staff psychiat. social worker S.I. Mental Health Soc., 1958-63, supr. psychiat. social worker, 1963-66, asst. dir. psychiat. social work, 1967-69, dir. psychiat. social work, 1969-81, acting dir. Children's Community Mental Health Ctr., 1981, dir. Children's Community Mental Health Ctr., 1982—. Mem. NAACP, NASW, N.Y. Urban League, Nat. Coun. Negro Women, S.I. Com. on Child and Adolescent Mental Health (pres. 1984-86), S.I. Mental Health Coun. (sec. 1982-84), S.I. Mental Health Soc. (Richard M. Silberstein award 1991). Presbyterian. Home: 142 Benedict Ave Staten Island NY 10314-2315 Office: SI Mental Health Soc 669 Castleton Ave Staten Island NY 10301-2028

SABINO, JEFFER Y., family nurse practitioner; b. Baguio City, Philippines, Feb. 15, 1949; came to U.S., 1964; s. Nicanor and Victoria (Ymson) S.; m. Ellen Regoso, June 4, 1972; children: Alan Dale, Jeniffer Ellen. Diploma, East Los Angeles Coll., 1972; BS in Hosp. Adminstrn., Pacific Christian Coll., Fullerton, Calif., 1981; student, U. Calif., Davis, 1987-89. RN, Calif., Hawaii; cert. family nurse practitioner. Nurse, orthopedic dept. Valley Med. Ctr., Fresno, Calif., 1986-92; family nurse practitioner to pvt. physician Fresno, 1993; orthopedic family nurse pracitioner Madera (Calif.) Orthopedic Med. Ctr., 1993—; surgery first asst. with privileges at Fresno Cmty. Hosp., St. Agnes Med. Ctr., Fresno Surgery Ctr., others, 1986—; guest lectr. orthopedics and wound mgmt. U. Calif., Davis, 1987—. Served to lt. col. USAR, 1980—. Mem. Assn. Mil. Surgeons U.S., Assn. Oper. Rm. Nurses, Am. Acad. Physician Assts., Calif. Coalition Nurse Practitioners. Seventh-day Adventist. Home: 16307 Austin Ave Madera CA 93638 Office: 41969 Hwy 41 Oakhurst CA 93644

SABISTON, DAVID COSTON, JR., surgeon, educator; b. Onslow County, N.C., Oct. 4, 1924; s. David Coston and Marie (Jackson) S.; m. Agnes Foy Barden, Sept. 24, 1955; children: Anne Sabiston Leggett, Agnes Sabiston Butler, Sarah Coston. BS, U. N.C., 1944; MD, Johns Hopkins U., 1947; DSc (hon.), U. Madrid. Diplomate: Am. Bd. Surgery (chmn. 1971-72). Successively intern, asst. resident, chief resident surgery Johns Hopkins Hosp., 1947-53; successively asst. prof., assoc. prof., prof. surgery Johns Hopkins Med. Sch., 1955-64, Howard Hughes investigator, 1955-61; Fulbright research scholar U. Oxford, Eng., 1960; research assoc. Hosp. Sick Children, U. London, Eng., 1961; James B. Duke prof. surgery, chmn. dept. Duke Med. Sch., 1964-94; chief of staff Duke U. Med. Ctr., Durham, N.C., 1994-96, dir. internat. programs, 1996—; chmn. Accreditation Council for Grad. Med. Edn., 1985-86. Editor: Textbook of Surgery, Essentials of Surgery, Atlas of General Surgery, Atlas of Cardiothoracic Surgery, A Review of Surgery; co-editor: Gibbon's Surgery of the Chest, Companion Handbook to Textbook of Surgery; chmn. editl. bd. Annals of Surgery; mem. editl. bd. Annals Clin. Rsch., ISI Atlas of Sci.: The Classics of Surgery Libr., Surgery, Gynecology and Obsetrics, Jour. Applied Cardiology, Jour. Cardiac Surgery, World Jour. Surgery, Jour. Served to capt., M.C. AUS, 1953-55. Recipient Career Rsch. award NIH, 1962-64, N.C. award in Sci., 1978, Disting. Achievement award Am. Heart Assn. Sci. Coun., 1983 Michael E. DeBakey award for Outstanding Achievement, 1984, Significant Sigma Chi award, 1987, Coll. medalist Am. Coll. Chest Physicians, 1987, Disting. Tchr. award Alpha Omega Alpha, 1992; named Disting. Physician, U.S. VA, 1995. Mem. ACS (chmn. bd. govs. 1974-75, regent 1975-82, chmn. bd. regents 1982-84, pres. 1985-86), NAS Inst. Medicine, Am. Surg. Assn. (pres. 1977-78), So. Surg. Assn. (sec. 1969-73, pres. 1973-74), Am. Assn. Thoracic Surgery (pres. 1984-85), Soc. Clin. Surgery, Internat. Soc. Cardiovascular Surgery, Soc. Vascular Surgery (v.p. 1967-68), Soc. Univ. Surgeons (pres. 1968-69), Halsted Soc., Surg. Biology Club II, Soc. Thoracic Surgery, Soc. Surgery Alimentary Tract, Johns Hopkins U. Soc. Scholars, Soc. Surg. Chairmen (pres. 1974-76), Soc. Thoracic Surgeons Great Britain and Ireland, Soc. Internat. De Chirurgie, James IV Assn. Surgeons (bd. dirs. U.S. chpt.), Ill. Surg. Soc. (hon.), Phila. Acad. Surgery (hon.), Royal Coll. Surgeons Edinburgh (hon., editl. bd. jour.), Royal Coll. Surgeons Eng. (hon.), Asociación de Cirugía del Litoral (Argentina) (hon.), Royal Coll. Physicians and Surgeons Can. (hon.), Royal Coll. Surgeons Ireland (hon.), Royal Australasian Coll. Surgeons (hon.), German Surgical Soc. (hon.), Colombian Surg. Soc. (hon.), Brazilian Coll. Surgeons (hon.), Japanese Coll. Surgeons (hon.), French Surg. Assn. (hon.), Surg. Congress Assn. Espanola de Cirujanos (hon.), Philippine Coll. Surgeons (hon.), Phi Beta Kappa, Alpha Omega Alpha. Clubs: Cosmos (Washington), Hope Valley Country Club (Durham), Treyburn City Club (Durham). Home: 1528 Pinecrest Rd Durham NC 27705-5817 Office: Duke U Med Ctr PO Box 2600 MSRB Durham NC 27710

SABLE, ROBERT ALLEN, gastroenterologist; b. Bklyn., June 21, 1948; s. Benjamin and Sara (Dickstein) S.; m. Valerie P. Kubie Kopelman, July 1, 1969 (div. Mar. 1982); 1 child, Jesse; m. Ellen Sue Finer, May 29, 1982; children: Scott, Eric. BS, MIT, 1969; MD, Albert Einstein U., 1973. Bd. cert. in internal medicine, gastroenterology and geriatrics Am. Bd. Internal Medicine. Staff physician N.Y. Telephone Co. Mid Manhattan Med. Dept., N.Y.C., 1978-81; physician Riverdale Gastroenterology Cons., Bronx, N.Y., 1981—; chief gastroenterology St. Barnabas Hosp., Bronx, 1982—, pres. med. bd., 1985-90. Contbr. articles, reports, revs. to profl. jours. Fellow ACP, Am. Coll. Gastroenterology; mem. AMA, Am. Gastroenterologic Assn., Am. Soc. for Gastrointestinal Endoscopy. Office: Riverdale Gastroenterol Con 3765 Riverdale Ave Bronx NY 10463

SABOE, GERALD WAYNE, osteopath; b. Waterloo, Iowa, June 30, 1953; s. Orville Lawrence and Ione Norma (Thoresen) S.; m. Julie Ann Miller, Aug. 13, 1977; children: John Michael, Kristin Nicole. BA, Luther Coll., 1975; DO, Coll. Osteo. Medicine/Surgery, 1978; MPH, Johns Hopkins U., 1984. Diplomate Am. Bd. Preventive Medicine, Am. Osteo. Bd. Preventive Medicine, Nat. Bd. of Med. Examiners. Commd. 2d lt. USAF, 1975, advanced through grades to col.; chief aeromed. and clin. svcs. USAF Clinic, Vance AFB, Okla., 1979-83; comdr. 49th tactical hosp. 833rd Med. Group, Holloman AFB, N.Mex., 1985-87, chief aerospace medicine svcs., 1985-87; resident aerospace medicine USAF Sch. Aerospace Medicine, Brooks AFB, Tex., 1984-85; chief aeromed. advisor Life Support Systems Program Office, Wright-Patterson AFB, Ohio, 1987-91; resident diagnostic radiology Wilford Hall Med. Ctr., Lackland AFB, Tex., 1991-92; chief profl. svcs. Clin. Scis. divsn.-Armstrong Lab., Brooks AFB, Tex., 1992—; asst. clin. prof. Wright State U. Sch. of Medicine, Dayton, Ohio, 1988—; faculty USAF Sch. of Aerospace Medicine, Brooks AFB, Tex., 1992—; vice chair Adv. Com. Human Experimentation, 1992-96; USAF Aeromed. rep. NASA Aerospace Medicine Bd., Houston, 1993—. Contbr. articles to profl. jours. Named Air Tng. Command Flight Surgeon of the Yr. Soc. USAF Flight Surgeons, 1982. Fellow Am. Osteo. Coll. Preventive Medicine (bd. trustees 1988-91), Am.

Coll. Preventive Medicine, Aerospace Med. Assn. Office: Armstrong Lab Clin Scis Divsn 2507 Kennedy Circle Brooks AFB TX 78235-5117

SABOKBAR, NASSER, pediatric allergist; b. Teheran, Iran, June 18, 1927; s. Shamsedin and Ghamar S.; M.D., U. Geneva (Switzerland), 1956; children—Julie M., Karen L. House physician St. Peters Hosp., Chertsey, Eng., 1956-57; sr. house officer Childrens Hosp., Nottingham, Eng., 1957-58, Childrens Hosp., Derby, Eng., 1958-59; resident in pediatrics Strong Meml. Hosp., Rochester, N.Y., 1961-62; practice medicine specializing in pediatrics, Lansdale, Pa., 1962-66, specializing in pediatric allergy, Sellersville, Pa., 1967—; fellow in pediatric allergy St. Christophers Hosp., Phila., 1966-67; clin. asst. prof. pediatrics Temple U. Sch. Medicine. Diplomate Am. Bd. Pediatrics (sub-bd. in pediatric allergy), Am. Bd. Allergy and Immunology. Fellow Am. Coll. Allergy, Am. Acad. Pediatrics, Am. Acad. Allergy, Am. Coll. Chest Physicians; mem. AMA, Brit. Med. Assn., Phila., Pa. allergy socs. Clu Rotary. Home: 605 Ederer Ln PO Box 388 Gwynedd PA 19436-0388 Office: 711 Lawn Ave PO Box 190 Sellersville PA 18960-0190

SACCENTE, VINCENT ULYSSES, dentist; b. N.Y.C., Oct. 16, 1946; s. John and Mary Dolores (Acciavatti) S.; m. Regina Marie Heuerman, Oct. 30, 1971; children: Kenneth, Carolyn. BS, Rensselaer Poly., 1968; MBA, Xavier U. Ohio, 1971; DDS, SUNY, Buffalo, 1976; cert. in prosthodontics, NYU, 1991; cert. in endodontics, Nassau County Med. Ctr., 1980, cert. in oral surgery, 1981. Engr. Procter & Gamble, Cinn., 1968-72; pvt. practice N.Y.C., 1976—; attending dentist Eger Nursing Home, S.I., N.Y., 1976-93, dir. dental svcs., 1977-87; clin. asst. dentistry Seaview Hosp., S.I., 1978-80; jr. attending dentist Nassau County Med. Ctr., S.I., 1982-83; mem. med. bd. Eger Nursing Home, S.I., 1977—. Com. mem. Boy Scouts Am., S.I., 1988—. Fellow Acad. Gen. Dentistry; mem. ADA, Richmond County Dental Soc. Roman Catholic. Office: 1896 Richmond Rd Staten Island NY 10306-2552

SACCO, FRANK VINCENT, hospital administrator; b. Akron, Ohio, June 28, 1947; married. BA, U. Miami, 1970; MA, Fla. Internat. U., 1978. Various positions Meml. Hosp., Hollywood, Fla., 1973-78, adminstrv. asst., 1978-79, asst. adminstr., 1979-84, sr. assoc. adminstr., 1984-85, sr. assoc. adminstr., COO, 1985-87, adminstr., CEO, 1987—; adj. educator in field. Home: 3120 Peachtree Cir Fort Lauderdale FL 33328-6705 Office: Meml Hosp 3501 Johnson St Hollywood FL 33021-5421*

SACHAR, DAVID BERNARD, gastroenterologist, medical educator; b. Urbana, Ill., Mar. 2, 1940; s. Abram Leon and Thelma (Horwitz) S.; m. Joanna Maud Belford Silver, Aug. 29, 1961; children: Mark Benson, Kenneth Hulbert Belford (dec.). AB magna cum laude, Harvard U., 1959, MD cum laude, 1963. Diplomate Bd. Gastroenterology Am. Bd. Internal Medicine. Intern medicine Beth Israel Hosp., Boston, 1963-65, resident, 1967-68; asst. chief clin. rsch. Pakistan-SEATO Cholera Rsch. Lab., Dhaka, Bangladesh, 1965-67; resident in gastroenterology Mt. Sinai Hosp., N.Y.C., 1968-70; from instr. to prof. medicine Mt. Sinai Sch. Medicine, CUNY, N.Y.C., 1970-92, 1st Burrill B. Crohn prof. medicine, 1992—; dir. div. gastroenterology Mt. Sinai Hosp., N.Y.C., 1983—, vice chmn. dept. medicine, 1992—; co-chmn. work group on inflammatory bowel disease NIH, 1973-75; expert adv. panel on gastroenterology and nutrition U.S. Pharmacopeial Conf., 1980-85; chmn. rsch. devel. com. Nat. Found. for Ileitis and Colitis, 1984-89; co-founder, sec.-treas. Burrill B. Crohn Rsch. Found., N.Y.C., 1984—; K.H. Koster meml. lectr. Danish Soc. of Gastroenterology, 1992; Internat. State of the Art lectr. Brit. Soc. Gastroenterology, 1995 and Falk Symposium, Germany, 1996; mem. Gastroenterology Leadership Coun. Task Force on Fellowship Curriculum, 1994. Author over 130 articles and chpts. on natural history and treatment of inflammatory bowel disease; editor 7 books and monographs on gastroenterology. Trustee Bangladesh Coun. of the Asia Soc., N.Y.C., 1972-75, Bd. Edn., Englewood Cliffs, N.J., 1973-75. Sr. surgeon, comdr. USPHS,1965-67. Recipient Jacobi medallion for Disting. Achievement, Mt. Sinai Alumni Assn., 1994, Alexander Richman Commemorative award for humanism in medicine, 1996. Fellow ACP, Am. Coll. Gastroenterology (program dirs. com. 1991—, Henry Baker Presdl. lectr. 1989); mem. Am. Gastroent. Assn. (chmn. subcom. on cert. 1987, 1st chmn. clin. tchg. project 1984-90, nominating com., chmn. Immunology-Microbiology-Inflammatory Disorders sect. 1995, Disting. Educator award 1996), Crohn's and Colitis Found. Am. (grants rev. com. and coun. 1990-94, Disting. Svc. award 1991, N.Y. Govs. medal 1992, chmn. clin. rsch. subcom. Disease Classification and Measurement 1994), Internat. Orgtn. for Study of Inflammatory Bowel Disease (1st Am. elected chmn. 1989-92), Phi Beta Kappa, Alpha Omega Alpha. Office: Mt Sinai Med Ctr One Gustave L Levy Pl New York NY 10029

SACHDEV, VED PARKASH, neurosurgeon; b. Mitranwali, India, Feb. 22, 1932; came to the U.S., 1969; s. Girdhari Lal and Amar Kaur Sachdev; m. Ranjit Kaur Sachdev, Apr. 17, 1970; children: Ulka, Rivka. MB BS, Govt. Med. Coll., Amritsar, Panjab, India, 1955. Diplomate Am. Bd. Neurosurgery. Asst. prof. neurosurgery Med. Inst., Chandigarh, India, 1964-69; intern St. Josephs Hosp., Lorain, Ohio, 1969-70; resident in neurosurgery Mt. Sinai Med. Ctr., N.Y.C., 1970-73, from asst. to assoc. clin. prof. dept. neurosurgery, 1974-88, clin. prof. dept. neurosurgery, 1988—; vice chmn. dept. neurosurgery Mt. Sinai Med. Ctr., N.Y.C., 1988-92. Author chpts. in 7 med. books. Surgeon lt., Indian Navy, 1957-60. Fellow ACS, Royal Coll. Surgeons Eng. (diplomate laryngology and otology). Home: 128 Moorland Dr Scarsdale NY 10583-1937 Office: Mt Sinai Med Ctr Dept Neurosurgery 1148 5th Ave New York NY 10128-0807

SACHERE, ANDREW B., physician; b. Cleve.. BS, MIT, 1979; MD, Rutgers U., 1983. Diplomate Am. Bd. Family Practice; lic. N.J. Bd. Med. Examiners, N.Y. Bd. Med. Examiners, N.H. Bd. Registration, Commonwealth of Pa. Clin. instr. family medicine Robert Wood John Med. Sch. Rutgers U. Med. and Dentistry of N.J., 1986—; pvt. practice family medicine. Fellow Am. Acad. Family Physicians; mem. Am. Acad. Family Physicians, Physicians for Social Responsibility, N.Y. Acad. Scis., Union of Concern Scientists, MIT Alumni of Princeton (bd. dirs.). Office: 87 Brunswick Woods Dr East Brunswick NJ 08816-5601

SACHS, DAVID HOWARD, surgery and immunology educator, researcher; b. N.Y.C., Jan. 10, 1942; s. Elliot and Elsie (Hurvitz) S.; m. Kristina Olsson, Mar. 15, 1969; children: Michelle, Jessica, Karin, Teviah. AB, Harvard U., 1963; DES, U. Paris, 1964; MD, Harvard U., Boston, 1968. Intern in surgery Mass. Gen. Hosp., Boston, 1968-69, resident in surgery, 1969-70, dir. transplantation biology rsch. ctr. surgery dept., 1991—; chief immunology br. Nat. Cancer Inst., Bethesda, Md., 1982-90; prof. surgery and immunology Harvard U. Med. Sch., 1991—. Capt. PHS, 1970-91. Office: Mass Gen Hosp East Bldg 149-9019 13th St Boston MA 02129

SACHS, MURRAY B., audiologist, educator. BS, MIT, 1962, MS, 1964, PhD in Elec. Engring., 1966. From asst. prof. to assoc. prof. biomed. engring. Johns Hopkins U., Balt., 1970-80, dir. Ctr. Hearing Sci., 1986-91, Massey prof., dir. dept. biomed. engring., 1991—; mem. com. communication and control Internat. Union Pure and Applied Biophysics, 1975-80; mem. communication disease panel and basic sci. task force Nat. Inst. Neurol. and Communicative Disorders and Stroke NIH, 1977-78, chmn. communicative disease rev. com., 1977-79, ad hoc adv. com., 1979-86, sci. program adv. com., 1984-86; prof. biomed. engring. Johns Hopkins U., 1980—, prof. neurosci., 1981—, prof. otolaryngology-head and neck surgery, 1982-85. Mem. Inst. Medicine-Nat. Acad. Sci., Sigma Xi. Office: Johns Hopkins U Sch Medicine Ctr for Hearing Scis 720 Rutland Ave Baltimore MD 21205-2109*

SACHSE, GUENTHER, health facility administrator, medical educator; b. Zeitz, Sachsen, Fed. Republic of Germany, Feb. 21, 1949; s. Gerhard and Johanna (Waitz) S.; m. Regina Haas, Mar. 5, 1982; 1 child, Juliane Elisabeth. Medizinisches Staatsexamen, Georg-August U., Göttingen, Fed. Republic of Germany, 1974; MD, U. Göttingen, 1975. Leitender arzt in diabetes and medicine German Diagnostic Clinic, Wiesbaden, Fed. Republic of Germany, 1987—, med. dir., 1991—; chmn. cons. group Wyeth Pharms, Münster, Fed. Republic of Germany, 1991—. Author: Diabetologié, 1989. Mem. Internat. Diabetes Fedn., European Assn. Study of Diabetes, German Diabetes Assn. Office: German Diagnostic Clinic, Aukammallee 33, 65191 Wiesbaden Germany

SACK, CONRAD J., dentist; b. Camden, N.J., Dec. 15, 1952; s. Harvey Conrad and Elizabeth Ann (Power) S.; 1 child, Kevin Austin. BS in Biology magna cum laude, Fitchburg (Mass.) State Coll., 1979; DMD, Boston U., 1983; MS in Oral Biology, UCLA, 1986, Cert. of Specialty Pediatric Dentistry, 1986. Lectr., clin. instr. orthodontics UCLA, 1988—; pvt. practice pediatric dentistry, orthodontics L.A.; lectr. in field; vis. lectr. UCLA Sch. Dentistry Dept. Continuing Edn., Dept. Orthodontics, Loma Linda U.; clin. instr. U. So. Calif./UCLA Mobile Dental Clinic; resident Neuropsychiat. Inst., UCLA Med. Ctr.; resident pedodontist City of Hope Nat. Med. Ctr., Duarte, Calif.; dental hygienist, oral health ctr. coord. Ft. Devens, Mass. Mem. ADA, Calif. Dental Assn., San Fernando Valley Dental Soc., Am. Assn. Orthodontists, Pacific Coast Soc. Orthodontists, Calif. Soc. Orthodontists, Am. Assn. for Functional Orthodontics, Am. Acad. Gnathologic Orthop., Am. Acad. Pediatric Dentistry, Am. Soc. of Dentistry for Children (exec. coun. So. Calif. unit 1993-95, sec.-treas. 1995—), San Fernando Valley Orthodontic Study Club, L.A. Orthop.-Gnathologists Study Club, UCLA Orthodontic Alumni Assn. (pres. 1990-91). Office: 9201 Sunset Blvd #202 West Hollywood CA 90069

SACK, FRED DAVID, biology educator; b. N.Y.C., May 22, 1947; s. Irving F. and Matilda G. Sack. BA, Antioch Coll., Yellow Springs, Ohio, 1969; PhD, Cornell U., 1982. Postdoctoral rsch. assoc. Boyce Thompson Inst. Plant Rsch., Cornell U., 1982-84; asst. prof. biology Ohio State U., Columbus, 1984-90, assoc. prof. biology, 1990—. Mem. space biology and medicine com. NRC, 1993-95. Mem. Am. Soc. for Gravitational and Space Biology (bd. dirs. 1990-92). Office: Ohio State U 1735 Neil Ave Columbus OH 43210-1220

SACK, GEORGE HENRY, JR., molecular geneticist; b. Balt., Apr. 17, 1943; s. George Henry and Sophia Ann (Philippi) S. BA, Johns Hopkins U., 1965, MD, 1968, PhD, 1974. Diplomate Am. Bd. Med. Examiners, Md. Bd. Med. Genetics. Intern Johns Hopkins Hosp., Balt., 1968-69, asst. resident, 1969-70, fellow genetics, 1975-76; rsch. fellow Johns Hopkins Sch. Medicine, Balt., 1970-73; asst. prof. dept. medicine Johns Hopkins U., Balt., 1976-84, assoc. prof. dept. medicine and biological chemistry, 1984—; molecular biologist Kennedy Inst., Balt., 1982-93. Contbr. articles to profl. jours. Maj. USAR, 1973-75. Andrew W. Mellon scholar Johns Hopkins U., 1976, Kennedy Found. scholar, 1982. Fellow Am. Coll. Med. Genetics; mem. AMA, AAAS, Am. Soc. Human Genetics, Phi Beta Kappa. Office: Johns Hopkins Hosp Blalock 1008 600 N Wolfe St Baltimore MD 21287-3914

SACK, KENNETH EDWARD, rheumatologist, educator; b. N.Y.C., July 5, 1942; s. Harold Meyer and Lauretta Anita (Dorn) S.; m. Suzanne Elizabeth Sack, June 9, 1978; children: Elizabeth Anne, Allison Michelle, Jennifer Nicole. AB, Dartmouth Coll., 1964; MD, Tufts U., 1968. Instr. U. Tex. Med. Sch., Houston, 1974-75, dir. in-patient teaching, 1974-76, asst. prof. medicine, 1975; asst. prof. medicine rheumatology U. Calif., San Francisco, 1978-81; dir. profl. edn. U. Calif. San Francisco Med. Ctr., 1981-83, from asst. clin. prof. to assoc. clin. prof., 1983-88, dir. clin. program rheumatology, 1983-88, prof. clin. medicine, 1995—. Contbr. articles to profl. jours. and chpts. to books. Major U.S. Army, 1970-72. Decorated Commendation medal. Office: U Calif San Francisco Sch Medicine 400 Parnassus Ave Rm A 540 San Francisco CA 94143

SACKASH, WANDA SUE, medical technologist; b. Du Bois, Pa., Jan. 7, 1942; d. Harry William and Joy Prudence (Salada) Whaling; m. George Sackash, June 17, 1967; children: Georgeanne Joy, William Michael (dec.), Christine Joyce, Sonya Sue. AS, Carnegie Coll. Med. Tech., 1960. Cert. med. technologist. Med. technologist, supr. Maple Ave. Hosp., Du Bois, 1960-73; med. technologist Du Bois Hosp., 1973-86, Agape Family Health Ctr., Du Bois, 1986—. Leader Girl Scouts U.S., 1977-83. Mem. Am. Med. Technologists (v.p. N.W. regl. chpt.). Republican. Methodist.

SACKEIM, HAROLD, psychologist; b. Hackensack, N.J., July 13, 1951; s. Alexander and Ruth (Frymer) S.; m. Donna Zucchi, Oct. 9, 1977. BA, Columbia U., 1972; BA, MA, Oxford (Eng.) U., 1974; PhD, U. Pa., 1977. Asst. prof. psychology Columbia U., N.Y.C., 1977-79, lectr. psychiatry Coll. Physicians and Surgeons, 1980-87; asst. prof. psychology N.Y.U., N.Y.C., 1979-81, assoc. prof., 1981-87; assoc. prof. dept. psychiatry Columbia U., N.Y.C., 1987-90, prof. dept. psychiatry, 1990—, chief dept. biol. psychiatry, 1991—; assoc. attending psychologist N.Y. State Psychiat. Inst., N.Y.C., 1980—, rsch. sci. and dep. chief dept. biol. psychiatry, 1980-91, chief dept. biol. psychiatry, 1991—; cons. WNET, 1978, 85; pvt. practice psychology, N.Y.C., 1977—. NIMH grantee, 1981—, NYU Rsch. Challenge Fund grantee, 1981-82, McGraw-Hill grantee, 1979-80, NIA grantee, 1985—; recipient Rsch. Excellence award N.Y. Office Mental Health, 1995. Fellow Am. Psychiat. Assn. (hon.); mem. AAAS, APA, Am. Coll. Neuropsychopharmacology (Joel Elkes Internat. award 1994), Am. Psychopathol. Assn., Internat. Neuropsychol. Soc., Soc. Biol. Psychiatry. Assoc. editor Jour. Social and Clin. Psychology, 1982-87; cons. editor jour. Imagination, Cognition and Personality, 1981—, Convulsive Therapy, 1985—, Neuropsychiatry, Neuropsychol. and Behavior Neurology, 1987—; contbr. numerous articles to profl. jours. Office: Columbia U Dept Psychiatry 722 W 168th St # 72 New York NY 10032-2603

SACKEL, STEPHEN GARY, gastroenterologist; b. Lawrence, Mass., Feb. 20, 1953; s. Sol and Lillian (Selinger) S.; m. Madeline Traurie, July 2, 1978; children: Shelley, Jodi. BA magna cum laude, Brown U., 1975; MD, Tufts U. Med. Sch., 1979. Diplomate Am. Bd. Internal Medicine and Gastroenterology. Intern Albany (N.Y.) Med. Ctr., 1979-80; resident Tufts NE Med. Ctr. Hosp., Boston, 1980-82; fellow Boston U., 1982-84; pvt. practice Digestive Disease Cons., Fort Lauderdale, Fla., 1984—. Contbr. articles to profl. jours. Fellow ACP, Am. Gastroenterology Assn.; mem. Sigma Xi. Office: 5601 N Dixie Hwy # 306 Fort Lauderdale FL 33334

SACKELLARES, JAMES CHRIS, neurology educator; b. Savannah, Ga., July 30, 1948; s. James and Doris Evelyn (Parks) S.; m. Dalma Kalogjera, Dec. 14, 1991; children: Stephanie, Chiara. BS in Chemistry, U. Ga., 1970; MD, Med. Coll. Ga., 1973. Cert. neurology, clin. neurophysiology. Intern in internal medicine U. Louisville, Ky., 1973-74; resident in neurology Med. Coll. Ga., Augusta, 1974-77; fellow in epilepsy U. Va., Charlottesville, 1977-79, rsch. asst. prof., 1979; asst. prof. neurology U. Mich., Ann Arbor, 1979-84, assoc. prof. neurology, 1984-91, prof. neurology, 1991-93; faculty bioengring. program dept. computer & elec. engring. U. Mich., 1984-93; prof. neurology U. Fla., Gainesville, 1993-95, affiliate prof. neurosci., 1995—; chief neurology svcs. VA Med. Ctr., Gainesville, 1993-96; dir. epilepsy program U. Mich., Ann Arbor, 1979-93; cons. neurologist Ann Arbor (Mich.) VA, 1982-93; dir. Clin. Neurophysiology Labs., U. Mich., Ann Arbor, 1984-87. Editor: Psychological Disturbances in Epilepsy, 1995; sect. editor Clin. Neuropharmacology, 1992—; contbr. chpts. to books and articles to profl. jours. Mem. adv. bd. Epilepsy Found. Am., 1981-84; mem. anticonvulsant drug use com. Mich. Dept. Mental Health, 1991-92; participant NIH workshop on Antiepileptic Drug Trials in Children, 1994; mem. task force health care reform State of Fla., 1994-95; mem. faculty senate U. Fla., 1994—. Fellow Am. Acad. Neurology, Am. Electroencephalographic Soc.; mem. AAAS, Am. Epilepsy Soc., Am. Neurol. Assn., N.Y. Acad. Scis., Royal Soc. Medicine.

SACKETT, JOSEPH FREDERIC, radiologist, educator, administrator; b. Cleve., Jan. 16, 1940; s. George Leslie and Cora Lenore (Hurst) S.; children: Joseph Frederic, Samson Occom, Penelope Cora. B.A., Dartmouth Coll., 1962; M.D., Tulane U., 1966. Diplomate Am. Bd. Radiology. Intern Mary Hitchcock Meml. Hosp., Hanover, N.H., 1966-67; resident Dartmouth Coll.-Hitchcock Hosp., Hanover, 1969-72; fellow in neuroradiology Ulleval Hosp., Oslo, 1972-73, N.Y. Hosp.-Cornell U., N.Y.C., 1973-74; asst. prof. radiology U. Wis.-Madison, 1974-78, assoc. prof., 1978-81, chmn. dept., prof., 1981—; vis. prof. U. Nebr.-Omaha, 1977, Dartmouth Med. Sch., 1977, 82, U. Calif.-San Francisco, 1977, Med. Coll. Wis., Milw., 1977, Cleve. Clinic, 1978, Case Western Res. Sch. Medicine, 1978, UCLA, 1978, U. Kans., 1979, U. Cin., 1979, Rutgers Med. Sch., New Brunswick, N.J., 1979, Cornell U. Med. Ctr., 1980, U. Louisville, 1981, others; lectr. in field. Author: New Techniques in Myelography, 1979; editor: Digital Subtraction Angiography, 1981; contbr. numerous articles to profl. jours. Served to capt. M.C., U.S. Army, 1967-69, Vietnam. Fellow Am. Coll. Radiology; mem. Assn. Univ. Radiologists (fin. chmn. 1984—), Radiol. Soc. N.Am., Am. Soc. Neuroradiology, Rotary Internat. Republican. Home: 3100 Lake Mendota Dr Madison WI 53705-1481 Office: Clin Sci Ctr 600 Highland Ave Madison WI 53792-0001

SACKIN, CLAIRE, social work educator; b. N.Y.C., Oct. 1, 1925; d. Harry and Diana (Mednick) Gershfeld; m. Milton Sackin, Feb. 4, 1955; children: William, Daniel, David. BA, Hunter Coll., 1946; MEd, U. Pitts., 1968, MSW, 1972, PhD, 1976. Tenured tchr. jr. high sch. Bronx, N.Y., 1947-57; rsch. asst. U. Pitts., 1973, instr. dept. urban mgmt., 1974; rsch. assoc. U. Pitts. Sch. of Social Work, 1975-76, Health & Welfare Planning Assn., 1974; prof. social work, dir. social work program St. Francis Coll., Loretto, Pa., 1976—; registered trainer alcoholism specialists cert. program; mem. adv. bd. Cedar Manor Treatment Ctr., Cresson, Pa., 1994-95; mem. Pa. Gov.'s Coun. Alcoholism, 1980, Nat. Assn. People with AIDS; presenter in field. Contbr. articles to jours. Mem. NASW (social action com. Pa. chpt. 1983-85, mem. Del. Assembly 1984, eastern regional coalition liaison 1984), Coun. on Social Work Edn., Alpha Delta Mu (nat. bd. dirs.). Home: 531 Sandrae Dr Pittsburgh PA 15243-1727 Office: St Francis Coll Loretto PA 15940

SACKS, HERBERT SIMEON, psychiatrist, educator, consultant; b. N.Y.C., Nov. 29, 1926; s. Maxwell Lawrence and Anne (Edelstein) S.; m. Helen Margery Levin, Dec. 26, 1948; children—Eric Livingston, Katharine Bird, Douglas Lowell, Russell Avery. A.B. magna cum laude, Dickinson Coll., 1948; M.D., Cornell U., 1952. Diplomate Am. Bd. Psychiatry and Neurology and subspecialty Child and Adolescent Psychiatry. Clin. assoc. Western New Eng. Psychoanalytic Inst., New Haven, 1955-63; intern in pediatrics Yale-New Haven Med. Ctr., 1952-53; jr. asst. resident in psychiatry Yale Psychiat. Inst., 1953-54; sr. asst. resident in psychiatry, USPHS fellow Yale-New Haven Med. Ctr., psychiat. out patient dept., 1954-55; USPHS fellow in child psychiatry Yale U. Child Study Ctr., 1955-57; clin. dir. Mid-Fairfield Child Guidance Ctr., Norwalk, Conn., 1957-59; cons. Expt. in Internat. Living, Putney, Vt., 1962-69; sr. cons. U.S. Peace Corps, Washington, 1962-69; cons. AID, U.S. Dept. State, Office of Sahel, West Africa, 1974-84, Neurosci. Consultation Group, Grosse Point Farms, Mich., 1984-94; clin. prof. child and adolescent psychiatry Child Study Ctr., Yale U. Sch. Medicine, New Haven; co-investigator, co-dir. Senegal River pilot health research program, New Haven and West Africa, 1976-78, co-investigator, co-dir. health sector, design team Senegal River integrated devel. project, 1981-83; vis. lectr. Yale Coll., 1969-71; mem. com. reviewers Dept. Commerce Nat. Bur. Standards, Inst. for Computer Scis. and Tech., Washington, 1975-77; mem. exec. com. Nat. Commn. on Confidentiality of Health Records, 1975-80. Author: Hurdles: The Admissions Dilemma in American Higher Education, 1978; contbg. author chpts. in books, articles on confidentiality, juvenile justice, higher edn., issues of youth in transition, other topics; author monographs. Mem. Conn. Juvenile Justice Commn., Hartford, 1975-80; bd. advisors Dickinson Coll., Carlisle, Pa., 1980-85. Served to lt. (j.g.) U.S. Navy, 1944-46; PTO. Fellow AMA, ACPO, Am. Psychiat. Assn. (trustee 1988-94, v.p. 1994-96, pres.-elect 1996—), Am. Acad. Child and Adolescent Psychiatry, Am. Orthopsychiat. Assn., Am. Coll. Psychiatrists; mem. Conn. Psychiat. Soc. (pres. 1976-77), Conn. Coun. Child and Adolescent Psychiatrists (pres. 1972-73), World Fedn. for Mental Health, Phi Beta Kappa. Home: 110 Laurel Rd New Haven CT 06515-2426 Office: 260 Riverside Ave Westport CT 06880-4804 also: Yale U Child Study Ctr PO Box 207900 New Haven CT 06520

SACKS, JOEL GERALD, ophthalmologist, educator; b. Chgo., Sept. 14, 1939; s. Louis and Rose S.; m. Cynthia Ann Dana, June 10, 1967; children: Charles, David, Martha. BA, Northwestern U., 1960, MS, 1962, MD, 1963; MBA, U. Cin., 1986. Diplomate, Am. Bd. Ophthalmology. NIH spl. fellow Md. Med. Legal Found., Balt., 1967-68; rsch. fellow Johns Hopkins Sch. Medicine, Balt., 1968-69; asst. prof., then assoc. prof. Northwestern U., Chgo., 1969-77; prof., dir. dept. ophthalmology U. Cin., 1977-94; pres. Ophthalmic Cons., Inc., Cin., 1977-94; clin. prof. surgery Mich. State U., 1994—; v.p. med. affairs, dir. med. edn. Butterworth Hosp., Grand Rapids, Mich., 1994—; pres. Med. Ctr. Fund Cion., 1985-88, Univ. Health Plan, Inc., Cin., 1987-89. Co-author: Neuropathology of Vision: an Atlas, 1973; contbr. articles to sci. jours. Founder, Beth Adam: The Cin. Congregation Humanistic Judaism, 1980. Capt. U.S. Army, 1967-74. Fellow Am. Acad. Ophthalmology (Honor award 1982); mem. Assn. Am. Med. Coll.s, Phi Beta Kappa, Alpha Omega Alpha, Delta Mu Delta. Office: Butterworth Hosp 100 Michigan St NE Grand Rapids MI 49503

SACKS, LEE BERNARD, physician; b. Chgo., Feb. 24, 1951; s. Philip and Floradahl (Gladstone) S.; m. Joan Sue Lewenstein, Aug. 17, 1975; children: Steven, Lisa, Jeffrey. BSChemE, U. Pa., 1973; MD, U. Ill., Chgo., 1977. Diplomate Am. Bd. Family Practice. Family practice resident Luth. Gen. Hosp., Park Ridge, Ill., 1977-80; chief resident family practice Luth. Gen. Hosp., 1979-80; ptnr. Metro Family Practice, Des Plaines, Ill., 1980-92; physician Luth. Gen. Med. Group, Park Ridge, 1992—; med. dir. Luth. Gen. Health Plan, Park Ridge, 1990-94; v.p. Luth. Gen. Health Plan, 1994-95; v.p. primary care devel. Luth. Gen. Health Sys., Park Ridge, 1994-95; pres. Advocate Health Ptnrs., Oak Brook, Ill., 1995—; mem. continuum of care design team Luth. Gen. Health Sys., 1993-94. mem. Dist. 225 H.S. Bd. Edn. caucus, Glenview, Ill., 1995. Fellow Am. Acad. Family Physicians (del. 1990-95); mem. Ill. Acad. Family Physicians (president 1979-80), Am. Coll. Physician Execs. Office: Advocate Health Ptnrs 2025 Windsor Dr Oak Brook IL 60521-1586

SACKS, STEPHEN ARNOLD, urologic surgeon; b. Phila., Jan. 5, 1942; s. Albert and Rae (Fingerman) S.; children: Rachael Elizabeth, Lisa Michelle. BA, UCLA, 1963; MD, U. So. Calif., 1967. Diplomate Nat. Bd. Med. Examiners, Am. Bd. Urology. Intern in medicine, surgery UCLA, 1967-68, resident in surgery, 1968-69; surgeon U.S. Navy USS Dibuke, Vietnam, 1969-70; urologist U.S. Navy Hosp., Long Beach, Calif., 1970-71; resident in urology UCLA/Wadsworth VA Hosp., 1971-74, Sepulveda VA Hosp., Harber Gen. Hosp., L.A., 1971-74; pvt. practice urol. surgery L.A., 1974—; attending urol. surgeon Cedars Sinai Med. Ctr., 1974—, Midway Hosp., L.A., 1974—, Century City Hosp., L.A., 1974—; med. dir. So. Calif. Sexual Function Ctr., L.A., 1994; from lectr. to assoc. clin. prof. UCLA Ctr. for the Health Scis., 1974-85; panelist in urology Calif. Crippled Children's Svcs., 1975. Grantee NIH, 1975; decorated Navy commendation medal, 1970. Fellow Am. Coll. Surgeons; mem. Assn. Acad. Surgery, AMA, L.A. Med. Assn., Am. Geriatric Assn., L.A. Urol. Soc., Am. Urol. Assn., Am. Assn. Clin. Urologists, Calif. Urol. Assn., So. Calif. Transplant Soc., Western Assn. Transplant Surgeons, Am. Assn. Tissue Banks, Alpha Omega Alpha, Phi Delta Epsilon. Office: Cedars Sinai Med Ctr Office Towers 8631 W 3d St #915E Los Angeles CA 90048

SACKTOR, NED CHARLTON, physician; b. Balt., Feb. 28, 1963; s. Bertram and June Dale (Charlton) S. AB, Harvard Coll., 1984; MD, U. Pa., 1988. Diplomate Am. Bd. Psychiatry and Neurology. Resident in neurology Neurol. Inst. N.Y., N.Y.C., 1989-92, fellow in behavioral neurology, 1992-94; asst. prof. neurology Sch. Medicine Johns Hopkins U., Balt., 1996—. Author: (with others) Current Therapy in Neurologic Disease, 1993, Alzheimer Disease, 1994, Merritt's Textbook in Neurology, 9th edit., 1995. Office: Johns Hopkins Bayview Med Ctr 4940 Eastern Ave Baltimore MD 21224

SACKTOR, TODD CHARLTON, neurologist; b. Balt., Jan. 11, 1957; s. Bertram and June (Charlton) S.; m. Bette Clark, May 28, 1988; children: Rose, Clark. AB, Harvard Coll., 1978; MD, Albert Einstein U., 1982. Diplomate Am. Bd. Psychiatry and Neurology. Assoc. prof. SUNY, Bklyn., 1995—. Grantee NIH, 1990, 95. Mem. Am. Acad. Neurology, Soc. for Neurosci. Office: SUNY Health Sci Ctr Dept Pharmacology Box 29 450 Clarkson Ave Brooklyn NY 11203

SADI, MARCUS VINICIUS, urologist; b. Sao Paulo, Brazil, Aug. 18, 1956; s. Afiz and Leila (Maluli) S.; m. Angela Chofhi Atala, May 12, 1983; children: Amanda and Rodrigo. MD, Escola Paulista de Medicina, Sao Paulo, 1979; hosp. adminstr. degree, Faculdades Sao Camilo, Sao Paulo, 1992. Resident Escola Paulista Medicina, Sao Paulo, 1979-82; fellow Harvard Med. Sch., Boston, 1983-85; asst. prof. Escola Paulista Medicina, Sao Paulo, 1986-88; fellow Johns Hopkins Sch. Medicine, Balt., 1989-90; assoc. prof. Escola Paulista Medicina, Sao Paulo, 1991—, chief urologic oncology surgeon, 1986—; chief divsn. urology Fed. U. of Sao Paulo, 1995—. Mem. editorial bd. Urology Ency.; contbr. 23 book chpts., 36 articles to profl. jours. Mem. Internat. Soc. Urology, Am. Urological Assn., Am. Soc. Andrology, Am.

Inst. Ultrasound in Medicine, Brazilian Med. Assn. (jour. editorial bd. mem. 1989—), Brazilian Coll. Surgeons, Brazilian Urological Assn. (bd. dirs. 1988-89, 94-95), Sao Paulo State Med. Assn. (sec. 1988-89), N.Y. Acad. Scis. Home: Rua Honduras 1108, 01428-001 São Paulo Brazil Office: Escola Paulista Medicina, Rua Napoleão de Barros 715, 04063 São Paulo Brazil

SADLACK, FRANK J., health service administrator, consultant; b. Jersey City, Sept. 24, 1941; s. Frank John and Marion A. (Sawicki) S.; m. Patt Lucas, Apr. 3, 1989. AB in Psychology, East Carolina U., 1964, MA in Psychology, 1965; PhD in Neurobiology, U. Fla., 1973; postgrad., Duke U., 1973-74. Programs specialist Rep. Health Corp., Dallas, 1984-88; assoc. adminstrv., clin. dir. Starlite Village Hosp., Center Point, Tex., 1988-93; exec. dir. Esperanza Health Sys., Hunt, Tex., 1993—; psychiat. constituency counselor Tex. Hosp. Assn., Austin, 1992-93; mem. ad hoc criteria com. Tex. Legis., Austin, 1991; cons. Hacienda del Lago, Ajijic, Mex., 1994—. Contbr. articles to profl. jours. Fellow NIH, 1967-72, Duke U., 1973. Mem. Am. Assn. Health Care Providers in Addictive Disorders (cert. addictions specialist), Tex. Rsch. Soc. on Chem. Addictions, Kerrville C. of C. Home: 805 Bluebonnet Dr Kerrville TX 78028 Office: La Hacienda Treatment Ctr FM 1740 Box 1 Hunt TX 78024

SADLER, JAMES BERTRAM, psychologist, clergyman; b. Albuquerque, Mar. 29, 1911; s. James Monroe and Mary Agnes (English) S.; m. Vera Ellen Ahrendt, Apr. 10, 1938. AB, U. N.Mex., 1938; BD, Crozer Theol. Sem., 1941, ThM, 1948; MA, U. Pa., 1941, EdD, 1959. Lic. psychologist, S.D.; ordained to ministry Baptist Ch., 1941. Pastor First Bapt. Ch., Mt. Union, Pa., 1941-42; chaplain USAF, 1943-48; pastor Hatboro (Pa.) Bapt. Ch., 1948-61; chmn. dept. psychology Sioux Falls (S.D.) Coll., 1961-75; pvt. practice psychology, Sioux Falls, 1975—; cons. in psychology and religion. Contbr. articles to profl. jours. Mem. ministers coun. Am. Bapt. Conv. Mem. APA, ACA, Soc. for Sci. Study Religion, Masons, Rotary (pres. 1960). Home: 4312 Glenview Rd Sioux Falls SD 57103-4935

SADLER, KENNETH MARVIN, dental healthcare company administrator, dentist; b. Gastonia, N.C., Oct. 12, 1949; s. Edward DeWitt Sr. (dec.) and Mildred Augustina (Jackson) S.; m. Brenda Arlene Latham, Sept. 24, 1983. BA, Lincoln U., 1971; DDS, Howard U., 1975; M Pub. Adminstrn., Golden Gate U., 1978. Lectr. Howard U. Coll. Dentistry, Washington, 1972-76, instr., dir., 1975; dir. quality assurance Winston-Salem (N.C.) Dental Care, 1978—. Mem. Town Coun. Lewisville, mayor pro tempore, 1991-93; mem. Forsyth County Indsl. Pollution Financing Authority, Winston-Salem Forsyth County Appearance com.; speaker East Winston Noon Optimists, 1983, Srs.-Winston-Salem Urban League, 1984; participant Nat. Alliance of Bus., Washington, 1983, Am. Cancer Soc., Winston-Salem, 1983; trustee, chmn. bd. Lincoln U., Pa.; trustee Forsyth Tech. C.C. Capt. U.S. Army, 1975-78. Capt. U.S. Army, 1975-78, lt. col. Res. Recipient Internat. Coll. of Dentistry award, 1975, Silver Beaver award Old Hickory chpt. Boy Scouts Am., 1994; named One of Outstanding Coll. Athletes of Am., 1971, Disting. Alumni of Yr. Nat. Assn. Equal Opportunity, 1986. Fellow Am. Coll. Dentistry, Acad. Gen. Dentistry; mem. ADA, Nat. Dental Assn., N.C. Dental Soc. (Citizenship award 1994), Am. Soc. Clin. Hypnosis (cert.), Omega Psi Phi (life), Omicron Kappa Upsilon. Democrat. Methodist. Office: Winston-Salem Dental Care Plan 201 Charlois Blvd Winston Salem NC 27103-1507

SADOCK, BENJAMIN JAMES, psychiatrist, educator; b. N.Y.C., Dec. 22, 1933; s. Samuel William and Gertrude S.; m. Virginia Alcott, Oct. 20, 1963; children: James William, Victoria Anne. A.B., Union Coll., 1955; M.D., N.Y. Med. Coll., 1959. Rotating intern Albany (N.Y.) Hosp., 1959-60; resident Bellevue Psychiat. Hosp., N.Y.C., 1960-63; instr. psychiatry Southwestern Med. Sch., Dallas, 1964-65, N.Y. Med. Coll., N.Y.C., 1965-67; asst. prof. N.Y. Med. Coll., 1967-71, assoc. prof., 1972-74, prof., 1975-80, dir. student health psychiatry, 1980—; prof. psychiatry NYU Sch Medicine, 1981—, vice chmn. dept. psychiatry, 1984—; attending psychiatrist Tisch Univ. Hosp. of NYU Med. Ctr., Bellevue Hosp.; cons. psychiatrist Franklin Delano Roosevelt VA Hosp., 1970-78, U.S. Dept. State, 1980-81, P.R. Inst. Psychiatry, 1976-80; examiner Am. Bd. Psychiatry and Neurology, 1970—; mem. conf. on recert. Am. Bd. Med. Spltys.-Am. Psychiat. Assn., 1974; mem. Commn. on Continuing Edn. in Psychiatry, NIMH-Am. Psychiat. Assn., 1974-75. Co-author: Comprehensive Group Psychotherapy, 1971, 3d edit., 1993, Synopsis of Psychiatry, 1972, 4th edit., 1985, 5th edit., 1989, 6th edit., 1991, 7th edit., 1994, The Sexual Experience, 1976, Study Guide Modern Synopsis of Psychiatry, 1983, 2d edit., 1985, 3d edit., 1989, 4th edit., 1991, 5th edit., 1994, Comprehensive Textbook of Psychiatry, 5th edit., 1988, 6th edit., 1995, Pocket Handbook of Clinical Psychiatry, 1991, 2d edit., 1995, Comprehensive Glossary of Psychiatry and Psychology, 1991, Pocket Handbook of Drug Treatment in Psychiatry, 1992, 2d edit., 1995, Pocket Handbook of Psychiatric Emergency Medicine, 1993; contbr. articles on psychiat. edn., individual and group psychotherapy, diagnosis and treatment psychiat. and sexual disorders to med. jours.; contbr. to Ency. Americana. Fellow Am. Psychiat. Assn. (treas. N.Y. County dist. br. 1973-76, mem. conf. on psychiatry and med. edn. 1967), N.Y. Acad. Medicine, A.C.P.; mem. AMA, Med. Soc. County and State N.Y., N.Y. Acad. Scis., AAAS, Am. Group Psychotherapy Assn., World Psychiat. Assn., Am. Public Health Assn., Royal Soc. Medicine (London), Psychiat. Soc. N.Y. Med. Coll. (founder, pres. 1975-79), N.Y. Med. Coll. Alumni Assn. (gov. 1965-90), NYU-Bellevue Psychiat. Soc. (pres. 1981—), Alpha Omega Alpha. Office: 4 E 89th St New York NY 10128-0636 also: NYU Med Ctr 550 1st Ave New York NY 10016-6481

SADOCK, VIRGINIA ALCOTT, psychiatrist; b. Sofia, Bulgaria, Nov. 25, 1938; came to U.S., 1941; d. Fred and Rica (Boni) Alcott; m. Benjamin James Sadock, Oct. 20, 1963; children: James, Victoria. AB, Bennington Coll., 1960; MD, N.Y. Med. Coll., 1970. Diplomate Am. Bd. Psychiatry and Neurology. Instr. N.Y. Med. Coll., N.Y.C., 1973-75, dir. program in human sexuality, 1973-80, asst. prof., 1975-80; assoc. prof. psychiatry NYU Med. Ctr., N.Y.C., 1980-88, clin. prof. psychiatry, 1988—, dir. human sexuality and sex therapy program, 1980—; mem. attending staff Bellevue Hosp., N.Y.C., 1980—, Tisch Hosp., NYU Med. Ctr., 1980—. Contbg. editor Comprehensive Textbook of Psychiatry, author, asst. to editors, 6th edit., 1995; contbg. editor Kaplan and Sadock's Synopsis of Psychiatry, 7th edit., 1995. Fellow Am. Psychiat. Assn., N.Y. Acad. Medicine; mem. AMA, Soc. for Sex Therapy and Research (founding 1976), Am. Assn. Sex Educators, Counselors, and Therapists. Avocations: travel; theatre. Office: 4 E 89th St New York NY 10128-0636

SADOFF, ROBERT LESLIE, psychiatrist; b. Mpls., Feb. 8, 1936; s. Max and Rose C. (Karroll) S.; m. Joan A. Handleman, June 21, 1959; children—Debra, David, Julie, Sherry. B.A., U. Minn., 1956, B.S., 1957, M.D., 1959; M.S., UCLA, 1963. Intern Los Angeles VA Hosp., 1959-60; resident UCLA, 1960-63; asst. prof. psychiatry Temple U., Phila., 1966-72; clin. prof. psychiatry U. Pa., Phila., 1972—; lectr. in law Villanova U., 1972-85. Author: (with Marvin Lewis) Psychic Injuries, 1975; Forensic Psychiatry, 1975, 2d edit., 1988; Legal Issues in the Care of Psychiatric Patients, 1982, Violence and Responsibility, 1988; (with Robert I. Simon) Psychiatric Malpractice, 1992; editor: Psychiatric Clinics of North America, 1984. Bd. dirs. Joseph T. Peters Inst., Phila., 1980-92 . Served to capt. U.S. Army, 1963-65. Recipient Earl Bond award U. Pa., 1979, VIIth Annual Nathaniel Winkelman award Phila. Psychiat. Ctr., 1988, Manfred Guttmacher award Am. Psychiat. Assn., 1992. Fellow Am. Psychiat. Assn., Am. Coll. Psychiatrists, Am. Coll. Legal Medicine; mem. AMA, Am. Acad. Psychiatry and Law (pres. 1971-73), Internat. Soc. for Philos. Enquiry (mentor 1987—), Am. Red Magen David for Israel (nat. pres. 1987—), Internat. Acad. Law and Mental Health (bd. dirs. 1989—, Philippe Pinel award 1995) . Avocation: collecting antique books in law and medicine. Office: Benjamin Fox Pavilion Ste 326 Jenkintown PA 19046

SADOW, HARVEY S., health care company executive; b. N.Y.C., Oct. 6, 1922; s. Nat. and Frances Donna (Saveth) S.; m. Sylvia June Riber, Dec. 22, 1944 (div. 1966); children: Harvey Jr., Suzanne Gail, Todd Forrest, Gay Summer; m. Jacqueline Lucille Clavel, Jan. 24, 1969 (div. 1993); 1 adopted child, Daniel Jean marie; m. Mary Morrissey McSwiggan, July 13, 1995. BS, Va. Mil. Inst., Lexington, 1947; MS, U. Kans., 1949; PhD, U. Conn., 1953. Intelligence officer CIA, Washington, 1951-53; assoc. dir. rsch. Lakeside Labs., Inc., Milw., 1953-56; med. rsch. cons. Milw., 1956; dir. clin. rsch. U.S. Vitamin & Pharm. Corp., N.Y.C., 1957-64, v.p. rsch. and devel., 1964-68; sr. v.p. scientific affairs USV Pharm./Revlon Corp., N.Y.C., 1969-71; pres., CEO Boehringer Ingelheim, Ltd. (named changed to Boehringer Ingelheim Pharms., Inc. 1984), Ridgefield, Conn., 1971-88; pres., CEO Boehringer Ingelheim Corp., Ridgefield, 1984-88, chmn. bd., 1988-90; chmn. bd. Roxane Labs., Inc., Columbus, Ohio, 1981-88, Boehringer Ingelheim Animal Health, Inc., St. Joseph, Mo., 1981-88, Henley Co., N.Y.C., 1986-88, U. Conn. Rsch. and Devel. Corp., Storrs, 1984-87; bd. dirs. Cortex Pharms., Inc., Irvine, Calif., 1989—, chmn. bd., 1991—; bd. dirs. Cholestech Corp., Hayward, Calif., chmn. bd. 1992—; bd. dirs. Cytel Corp., San Diego, Anika Rsch. Corp.; mem. adv. bd. Salk Inst. Biotechnology-Indsl. Assocs., Inc., La Jolla, 1988-90. Co-author: Oral Treatment of Diabetes, 1967; author, co-author 23 papers on intermediary metabolism, diabetes, obesity and cardiovascular disease., 1963-72. Bd. dirs. Pharm. Mfrs. Assn., 1983-90; chmn. Pharm. Mfrs. Assn. Found., 1988-90; bd. dirs. Conn. Bd. Higher Edn., Hartford, 1977-83, Govs. Tech. Adv. Bd., Hartford, 1984-87; mem. Conn. Commn. on Bus. Opportunity, Def. Diversification and Indsl. Policy, 1991-93; mem. bd. visitors Va. Mil. Inst., Lexington, 1987—, pres. bd., 1991-95; chmn. bd. Comm. Law Enforcement Found., Hartford, 1981-86, 92—, U. Conn. Found., Storrs, 1984-87; chmn., pres.' coun. Am. Lung Assn., N.Y.C., 1986-87, York Sch., Monterey, Calif., 1988-89; trustee Conn. Coll., Groton, 1991-96, ALdrich Mus. Contemporary Art, Ridgefield, Conn., 1991—. Decorated Disting. Svc. Cross, Fed. Republic of Germany, 1987; recipient Univ. medal U. Conn., 1987, Recognition award Nat. Hypertension Assn., 1990, Humanitarian award Am. Lung Assn. Conn., 1993, Disting. Svc. award Conn. Innovatins, Inc., 1996. Mem. Am. Soc. for Clin. Pharmacology and Therapeutics, Am. Fedn. for Clin. Rsch., Am. Diabetes Assn., Danbury C. of C. (Abraham Ribicoff Community Svc. award City of Danbury 1987, bd. dirs. 1978-81), Union League (N.Y.C.), Landmark Club (Stamford, Conn.), Masons, Sigma Xi, Sigma Pi Sigma, Phi Lambda Upsilon. Home and Office: 120-36 Prospect St Ridgefield CT 06877-4648

SADUN, ALFREDO ARRIGO, neuro-ophthalmologist, scientist, educator; b. New Orleans, Oct. 23, 1950; s. Elvio H. and Lina (Ottoleghi) S.; m. Debra Leigh Rice, Mar. 18, 1978; children: Rebecca Eli, Elvio Aaron, Benjamin Maxwell. BS, MIT, 1972; PhD, Albert Einstein Med. Sch., Bronx, N.Y., 1976, MD, 1978. Intern Huntington Meml. Hosp. U. So. Calif., Pasadena, 1978-79; resident Harvard U. Med. Sch., Boston, 1979-82, HEED Found. fellow in neuro-ophthalmology Mass. Eye and Ear Inst., 1982-83, instr. ophthalmology, 1983, asst. prof. ophthalmology, 1984; dir. residential tng. U. So. Calif. Dept. Ophthalmology, L.A., 1984-85, 90—; asst. prof. ophthalmology and neurosurgery U. So. Calif., L.A., 1984-87, assoc. prof., 1987-90; full prof. U. So. Calif., 1990—, mem. internal review bd.; prin. investigator Howe Lab. Harvard U., Boston, 1981-84, E. Doheny Eye Inst., L.A., 1984—; examiner Am. Bd. Ophthalmology; mem. internal rev. bd. U. So. Calif.; mem. sci. exec. bd. K. Rasmussen Found.; mem. sci. adv. bd. Internat. Found. for Optic Nerve Diseases. Author: Optics for Opthalmologists, 1988, New Methods of Sensory Visual Testing, 1989; contbr. articles to profl. jours. and chpts. to books. James Adams scholar, 1990-91; recipient Pecan D. award, 1988-92. Fellow Am. Acad. Ophthalmology Neuro-Ophthalmologists; mem. NIH (Med. Scientists Tng. award 1972-78), Am. Assn. Anatomists, Assn. Univ. Prof. Ophthalmology (assoc.), Am. Bd. Ophthalmology (rep. to residency rev. com. 1994—), Soc. to Prevent Blindness, Nat. Eye Inst. (New Investigator Rsch. award 1983-86, rsch. grants 1988-91, 93—), Soc. Neuroscis., Assn. Rsch. in Vision and Ophthalmology, N.Am. Neuro-Ophthal. Soc. (chmn. membership com. 1990—, v.p. 1994—). Home: 2478 Adair St San Marino CA 91108-2610 Office: U So Calif E Doheny Eye Inst 1450 San Pablo St Los Angeles CA 90033-4615

SADWIN, ARNOLD, neuropsychiatrist; b. Woonsocket, R.I., Nov. 12, 1926; m. Sue Matney, 1955; children: Donna Liane, Stuart Glenn, Lori Sheryl. BA, Boston U., 1948; postgrad., Brown U., 1948-49, Northwestern U., 1951-52; MD, Chgo. Med. Sch., 1956. Diplomate Nat. Bd. Med. Examiners; cert. in psychiatry Am. Bd. Psychiatry and Neurology. R.I. Cancer Soc. rsch. fellow R.I. Hosp., Providence, 1949-50; rotating intern Jackson Meml. Hosp., U. Miami, Fla., 1956-57; resident in psychiatry Lafayette Clinic, Wayne State U., Detroit, 1957-60; staff psychiatrist Phila. Psychiat. Ctr., 1960-85; staff psychiatrist Inst. of Pa. Hosp., Phila., 1960-79, sr. staff psychiatrist, 1979—; asst. psychiatrist Presbyterian-U. Pa. Med. Ctr., 1967-75, med. dir. neighborhood community mental health ctr., 1967-75, assoc. in psychiatry, 1977-79; chief neuropsychiatry Grad. Hosp., U. Pa., Phila., 1982-93; attending psychiatrist, attending neurologist Grad. Hosp., U. Pa., 1960-93; cons. in neurology and psychiatry Gen. Hosp. Monroe County, East Stroudsburg, Pa., Bridgeton (N.J.) Hosp., 1977-79; acting chmn. dept. psychiatry Grad. Hosp., U. Pa., Phila., 1978-81; appointed lifetime hon. cons. psychiatrist and neurologist Pocono Med. Ctr., East Stroudsburg, 1983—; sr. staff psychiatrist Phila. Psychiat. Ctr. (now Belmont), 1985—; asst. clin. prof. psychiatry U. Pa. Sch. Medicine, 1972-87; asst. clin. prof. neurology U. Pa., 1972-86; asst. clin. prof. family medicine UMDNJ Sch. Medicine, 1993—; lectr. in field. Contbr. articles to Am. Jour. Psychiatry, 1958, Psychosomatics, 1968; abstractor in field; contbr. chpts. to books. Program chmn. Willowdale Civic Assn., Cherry Hill, N.J., 1963-66; active DaVinci Art Alliance, Phila., 1987—. With USN, 1945-46. Recipient Humanitarian of Yr. award, 1971, cert. merit, 1976, Multiple Sclerosis Assn., Physician's Recognition award AMA, 1975, 78, 81, 84, 87, 90, 93, 96. Fellow Am. Acad Forensic Examiners, Am. Acad. Psychosomatic Medicine, Phila. Coll. Physicians, Behavioral Neurology Internat.; mem. AMA (Physicians Recognition award 1993, 96), Am. Psychiat. Assn., Am. Inst. Bio-Med. Climatology (v.p. 1980-83), Phila. County Med. Soc., Pa. Med. Soc., South Jersey Psychiat. Soc., Phila. Psychoanalytic Soc. (postgrad. psychosomatic study group), Phila. Med. Club, Phil-Mont Mobile Amateur Radio Club (Franklin Inst., Phila., past pres.), Willowdale Gourmet Club (Cherry Hill), 25 Yr. Club of U. Pa. Home: 1205 Heartwood Dr Cherry Hill NJ 08003-2739 Office: 313 S 17th St Philadelphia PA 19103-6726 also: 11-A E Laurel Rd Stratford NJ 08084

SAEV, STOYAN KONSTANTINOV, anesthesiologist, surgeon; b. Sofia, Bulgaria, Sept. 20, 1928; s. Konstantin Gueorguiev and Dora Nikolova (Ivanova) S.; m. Milka Lubenova Mincheva, July 12, 1953; 1 child, Dora Stoyanova Stefanova. MD, Higher Med. Sch., Sofia, Bulgaria, 1952; DA, WHO Ctr. Univ., Copenhagen, 1960; MSc, Med. Acad., Sofia, 1963, PhD, 1973; academician (hon.), European Acad. Anesthesiology, 1980. Cert. MD; specialist in surgery and anesthesiology. Surgeon, anesthetist Postgrad. Inst., Sofia, 1952-63, asst. prof., head of chair, 1963-72; prof., head of sect. Inst. Cardiovascular Disease, Sofia, 1972-87; prof., head of chair med. faculty, Sofia, 1987-90; pres. Bulgarian Red Cross, Sofia, 1992—; short-term cons. WHO, 1976-85; lectr. WHO courses, Copenhagen, 1970-72. Contbr. 30 chpts. to med. textbooks, over 320 articles to profl. jours. Pres. Lifesaving Svc. Bulgarian Red Cross, 1964-90; pres. Bulgarian Soc. Anesthesiologists, 1969-73; life mem. Fedn. Internat. de Sauvetage Aquatique, 1993—, mem. directional com., 1980-95; life mem., v.p. Internat. Lifesaving Fedn., 1995—; mem. Internat. Com. Red Cross Internat. Fedn. Red Cross/Red Crescent Socs., Geneva, 1994—. Named honored mem. Socs. Anesthesiologists Romania, 1976, Poland, 1985, USSR, 1989, Vietnam, 1989, Bulgaria, 1993; decorated State of Bulgaria, DRLG Germany, Lifesaving of Poland, Bulgarian Red Cross, Turkish Red Crescent. Fellow Royal Coll. Anaesthetists. Home: Bd Tzarigradsko Chaussee 35, 1124 Sofia Bulgaria Office: Bulgarian Red Cross, Bd Dondukov 61, 1527 Sofia Bulgaria

SAFER, DANIEL J., psychiatrist; b. Milw., June 29, 1934; s. Mendel and Belle (Rottman) S.; children: Debra, Alan, Judith. BS, U. Wis., 1956, MD, 1959. Diplomate in psychiatry and child psychiatry Am. Bd. Psychiatry and Neurology. Rotating intern D.C. Gen. Hosp., Washington, 1959-60; resident psychiatry Cleve. Psychiat. Inst., 1960-63; fellow in child psychiatry Inst. for Juvenile Rsch., 1963-64; asst. attending psychiatrist Children's Meml. Hosp., Chgo., 1964-66; fellow in child psychiatry Johns Hopkins Hosp., Balt., 1968-69; pychiat. cons. Balt. City Hosps., 1966-68; co-dir. sch. child mental health scs. Balt. County Dept. Health, 1969-72, dir. child pschiatry svcs., ea. region, 1972-95; med. dir. Ea. Community Mental Health Ctr. Balt. County Dept. Health, Rosedale, Md., 1983-92; staff psychiatrist Southeastern Cmty. Mental Health Ctr., Balt., 1995—; psychiat. cons. Franklin Sq. Hosp., Rosedale, 1970-73, Delaware Guidance Svcs. for Children, 1981-82; instr. psychiatry dept. neurology and psychiatry Northwestern U. Sch. Medicine, 1964-66; instr. dept. psychiatry and pediatrics Johns Hopkins Hosp., 1969-70; asst. prof. dept. psychiatry and pediatrics Johns Hopkins U. Sch. Medicine, 1970-79, assoc. prof., 1979—. Co-author: Hyperactive Children: Diagnosis and Management, 1976, School Programs for Disruptive Adolescents, 1982, numerous other chpts.; contbr. articles to profl. jours. Capt. med. corps U.S. Army, 1966-68. NIH fellow in pharmacology U. Wis. Med. Sch., 1956; grantee CIBA Labs, 1970-72, Merrell Lab., 1971-74, NIMH, 1974-77, Law Enforcement Assistance Adminstrn., 1977-80. Fellow Am. Psychiat. Assn. (life); mem. Md. Psychiat. Soc., Am. Orthopsychiat. Assn. Home: 301 Radcliffe Dr Newark DE 19711-3150 Office: 7702 Dunmanway Baltimore MD 21222

SAFFITZ, JEFFREY ERNEST, experimental cardiovascular pathologist, educator; b. Washington, Mar. 19, 1949; m. Sharon Epstein, June 13, 1971; children: Emily, Jane, Claire. BA, MS, Case Western Res. U., 1971, PhD, 1977, MD, 1978. Intern and resident in pathology Washington U., St. Louis, 1978-82, rsch. fellow cardiology, 1979-81; fellow pathology br. Nat. Heart, Lung, Blood Inst., NIH, Bethesda, Md., 1982-83; asst. prof. pathology and medicine Washington U., St. Louis, 1983-89, assoc. prof. pathology and medicine, 1989-94, prof. pathology and medicine, 1994—; Contbr. articles to profl. jours. Office: Washington Univ Med Sch Dept Pathology 660 S Euclid Ave Saint Louis MO 63110-1093

SAFFRA, NORMAN A., ophthalmologist; b. Ky., Sept. 19, 1963; s. Rafael and Martha Saffra. BA magna cum laude, Yeshiva U., 1984; MD, Albert Einstein Coll. Medicine, 1988. Bd. cert. Am. Bd. Ophthalmology; diplomate Nat. Bd. Med. Examiners. Intern in internal medicine Maimonides Med. Ctr., Bklyn., 1988-89; resident in internal medicine Albert Einstein Coll. Medicine/Montefiore Med. Ctr., Bronx, 1989-92; fellow in med. and surg. diseases of the retina and vitreous SUNY Health Sci. Ctr., Bklyn., 1992-93; assoc. dir. ophthalmology, dir. retina-vitreous svc. Maimonides Med. Ctr., Bklyn., 1993—, dir. regional ocular trauma svc., 1993—; clin. asst. prof. ophthalmology SUNY HSCB/Univ. Hosp., Bklyn., 1993—; dir. retina-vitreous svc. Coney Island Hosp., Bklyn., 1993—, Luth. Med. Ctr., Bklyn., 1994—; attending physician retina-vitreous svc. L.I. Coll. Hosp., Bklyn., 1993—, Manhattan Eye and Ear Hosp., N.Y.C., 1995—, N.Y. Eye and Ear Infirmary, N.Y.C., 1995—; acting dir. ophthalmology Coney Island Hosp., Bklyn., 1993-94; presenter in field. Contbr. articles to profl. jours. Albert Einstein Geriat. Rsch. grantee, 1985; Albert Einstein Student Rschr. Travel fellow, 1987, ARVO/Nat. Eye Inst. Travel fellow, 1988. Fellow Am. Acad. Ophthalmology, Am. Soc. for Laser Medicine and Surgery; mem. AMA, Vitreous Soc., N.Y. State Ophthalmologic Soc. Office: Maimonides Med Ctr 921-49 St Brooklyn NY 11219

SAFFRAN, MURRAY, biochemist; b. Montreal, Oct. 30, 1924; s. Isidore Irving and Rebecca Reva (Elimelech) S.; m. Judith Cohen, June 8, 1947; children—Michael David, Wilma Anne, Arthur Martin, Richard Eli. B.Sc., McGill U., 1945, M.Sc., 1946, Ph.D., 1949. Mem. faculty depts. psychiatry and biochemistry McGill U., Montreal, 1948-69; prof. McGill U., 1966-69; prof. biochemistry Med. Coll. Ohio, Toledo, 1969—, chmn. dept., 1969-80, asst. dean Med. Edn., 1992—; Dozor vis. prof. biochemistry Ben Gurion U., Israel, 1981; vis. prof. Inst. Biochemistry, Armenian Acad. Scis., Yerevan, 1988, U. Automon, Guadalajara, 1991-94. Mem. editl. bd. Biochem. Edn., Med. Biochemistry Question Bank, Drug Delivery; contbr. articles to profl. jours. Recipient Ayerst-Squibb award Endocrine Soc., 1968. Fellow AAAS, Ohio Acad. Sci.; mem. Am. Soc. Biochemistry and Molecular Biology, Endocrine Soc., Internat. Brain Rsch. Orgn., Alpha Omega Alpha. Home: 2331 Hempstead Rd Toledo OH 43606-2447 Office: Med Coll Ohio PO Box 10008 Toledo OH 43699

SAFIAN, LEROY SCHELLER, radiologist; b. N.Y.C., Dec. 15, 1916; s. Harry Markus and Frances (Scheller) S.; m. Renée Morgenstern Bonis, June 15, 1946 (div. Feb. 1952); m. Helen Hoffman, Jan. 25, 1953 (div. Nov. 1962). BS, NYU, 1938; MD, Med. Coll. Va., 1943. Diplomate Am. Bd. Radiology. Instr. radiology N.Y. Med. Coll., N.Y.C., 1962-64; asst. radiologist Coney Island Hosp., Bklyn., 1965-69, assoc. radiologist, 1969-70; asst. radiologist Maimonides Med. Ctr., N.Y.C., 1966-70; attending radiologist Golden Isles Hosp., Hallendale, Fla., 1970-71; instr. radiology Columbia Coll. Physicians & Surgeons, 1972-75, Montefiore Med. Ctr., Bronx, 1975-87; asst. prof. radiology Albert Einstein Coll. Medicine, Bronx, 1975-88; asst. attending radiologist North Cen. Hosp., Bronx, 1975-84, assoc. attending radiologist, 1984-91; hon. radiologist North Cen. Hosp., Bronx, 1992—. Author articles on radiology and plastic surgery. Recipient Cert. of Merit, Mallinckrodt Pharms., 1981. Fellow Royal Soc. Medicine; mem. Am. Coll. Legal Medicine (assoc.), N.Y. Med. Soc. (grievance com.), Fla. Med. Soc., Univ. Club, various radiol. socs. Home: 301 E 66th St New York NY 10021-6205

SAGE, ELDERIA FRANCKLING, social worker; b. Hartford, Conn., Feb. 9, 1942. BA, Beaver Coll., 1964; MSW, U. Conn., 1968. Lic. clin. social worker, Conn. Program dir. YWCA of Wilkes-Barre, Pa., 1964-66; sch. social workers Hartford Bd. of Edn., 1968-72; social work cons. Chesterfield Convalescent Home, Chester, Conn., 1977-85; social worker Colchester (Conn.) Convalescent Home, 1985-89; clin. social worker Middlesex Meml. Hosp., Middletown, Conn., 1989—. Sec., bd. dirs. Vis. Nurses of the Lower Valley, Centerbrook, Conn., 1978-80; bd. dirs. Nat. Kidney Found. Conn., 1993-95. Mem. NASW, Acad. Cert. Social Workers, Conn. Coun. Nephrology Social Workers (sec. 1989-90, 91—, chairperson 1990-92.). Office: Middlesex Meml Hosp Dialysis Unit 28 Crescent St Middletown CT 06457-3654

SAGE, JACOB I., neurologist, educator; b. Sept. 26, 1946; s. Joseph and Fern (Ginsburg) S.; m. Cynthia Fox; children: Naomi, Rebecca, Abigail. AB, U. Chgo., 1968; MD, U. Pitts., 1972. Intern Yale-New Haven Hosp., 1972-73; resident in neurology U. Pitts., 1976-78; fellow in neurochemistry Cornell Med. Coll., N.Y.C., 1978-80; asst. prof. neurology U. Medicine and Dentistry of N.J., New Brunswick, 1980-86, assoc. prof., 1986-90, prof. neurology, 1990—, dir. movement disorders divsn., 1995—; mem. sci. adv. bd. Am. Parkinsons Disease Assn., N.Y.C., 1995—. Author: Parkinson's Disease: A Guide for Patients, 1996; editor: Practical Neurology of the Elderly, 1996; contbr. articles to profl. jours. Fellow Am. Neurol. Assn.; mem. Acad. of Neurology. Office: UMDNJ Robert Wood Johnson Med Sch Dept Neurology New Brunswick NJ 08903

SAGEBIEL, RICHARD WALLACE, pathologist; b. Dayton, Ohio, Jan. 18, 1934. BA, Yale U., 1956; MD, Harvard U., 1961. Diplomate Am. Bd. Pathology, Am. Bd. Dermatopathology. Clin. prof. pathology and dermatology U. Calif., San Francisco, 1986—; dir. melanoma ctr. Mt. Zion Hosp., U. Calif. San Francisco, 1988—. Office: Univ Calif Melanoma Ctr 2356 Sutter St 4th Fl San Francisco CA 94115

SAGER, CLIFFORD J(ULIUS), psychiatrist, educator; b. N.Y.C.; s. Max and Lena (Lipman) S.; m. Anne Scheinman; children by previous marriage: Barbara L., Philip T., Rebecca J., Anthony F. BS, Pa. State U., 1937; MD, NYU, 1941; cert. in psychoanalysis, N.Y. Med. Coll., 1949. Diplomate: Am. Bd. Psychiatry and Neurology. Rotating intern Montefiore Hosp., N.Y.C., 1941-42; resident in psychiatry Bellevue Hosp., N.Y.C., 1942, 46-48; practice medicine specializing in psychiatry N.Y.C., 1946—; dir. therapeutic services, asso. dean Postgrad. Ctr. Mental Health, 1948-60; vis. psychiatrist, med. bd. Flower and Fifth Ave Hosp., 1960-71, Met. Hosp., 1960-71; dir. psychiat. tng. and edn. N.Y. Med. Coll., 1960-71; attending psychiatrist Bird S. Coler Hosp., 1960-71; clin. dir. N.Y. Med. Coll., 1960-63, assoc. prof. psychiatry, 1960-65, prof., 1966-71, dir. partial hosp. programs and family treatment and study unit, 1964-71; clin. prof. psychiatry Mt. Sinai Sch. Medicine, 1971-80; assoc. dir. psychiatry Beth Israel Hosp. for Family and Mental Therapy; chief of psychiatry Gov.'s Hosp., 1970-74; dir. family therapy Mt. Sinai Sch. Medicine, 1974-80; clin. prof. psychiatry N.Y. Hosp.-Cornell Univ. Med. Ctr., 1980—; attending psychiatrist N.Y. Hosp.-Payne Whitney Clinic, 1980—; dir. marital and family clinic N.Y. Hosp., 1991—; attending psychiatrist Mt. Sinai Hosp., 1971-80; chief behavioral scis. Gouverneur Hosp.; chief family treatment unit Beth Israel Med. Ctr., 1970-74, assoc. dir. psychiatry family and group therapy, 1971-74; psychiat. dir. Jewish Family Svc., 1974-77; dir. family psychiatry Jewish Bd. Family and Childrens Svcs., 1978-90; dir. Remarried Consultation Svc., 1976-90; dir. Tng. and Sex Therapy Clinic, 1974-90; founder The Relationship Inst., N.Y.C., 1990—; psychiat. dir. Employee Consultation and Corp. Health Programs, JBFCS, 1980—; faculty , supr. Contemporary Ctr. Advanced Psychoanalytic Studies; chief neuropsychiatry 42d and 312th Gen. Hosp. Author: Marriage Contracts and Couple Therapy, 1976, Intimate Partners, 1979, Treating the Remarried Family, 1983; 4 other books; mem. editorial bd. Am. Jour.

Orthopsychiatry, 1960-69, Internat. Jour. Group Psychotherapy, 1968—, Family Process, 1969-92, Divorce and Remarriage, 1977—, Comprehensive Rev. Jour. Family and Marriage, 1978—; cons. Sexual Medicine, 1974-82; co-editor, founder Jour. Sex and Marital Therapy, 1974—; mem. editorial bd.: Jour. Marriage and Family Counseling, 1977—, Internat. Jour. Family Counseling, 1977—; author or contbr. over 88 sci. articles to jours. Capt. M.C. AUS, 1942-46, chief neuropsychiatry 42d and 312th Gen. Hosp. Recipient Am. Family Therapy Assn. award for Outstanding Contribution to Family Therapy 1983, Assn. Marriage and Family Therapists award for Outstanding Contributions to the field of Marital and Family Therapy, 1984. Fellow Am. Psychiat. Assn. (life), Am. Orthopsychiat. Assn. (life), Acad. Psychoanalysis (charter), Am. Group Psychotherapy Assn. (pres. 1968-70, dir. 1962-74), Soc. Med. Psychoanalysts (pres. 1960-61, dir. 1958-62), Am. Assn. Marital and Famiy Therapists; mem. AMA, Am. Soc. Advancement Psychotherapy (dir. 1954-67), N.Y. Soc. Clin. Psychiatry, Soc. for Sex Therapy and Rsch. (pres. 1976-77, bd. dirs. 1953-58) PAIRS Found. (bd. dirs. 1985—). Office: 65 E 76th St New York NY 10021-1844 also: 33 Breeze Hill Rd East Hampton NY 11937-4505

SAGER, NEIL, obstetrician, gynecologist; b. Bklyn., Nov. 12, 1946; s. Joseph and Frances (Goldberg) S.; m. Gaye Swan Mergner, Jan. 18, 1970; children: Jennifer, Todd. BA cum laude, Hofstra U., 1969; DO, Univ. Osteo. Medicine & Surg., DesMoines, 1973. Intern Interboro Gen. Hosp., Bklyn.; resident ob-gyn U. Fla. Med. Sch.; clin. prof. dept. ob-gyn., 1977—; bd. mem. Planned Parenthood, Jacksonville, Fla., Child Edn. Assn., Jacksonville, River Garden Home for Aged, Jacksonville. Fellow Am. Coll. Ob-Gyn. Office: Ste 17 4131 University Blvd Jacksonville FL 32216

SAGER, PHILIP TRAVIS, academic physician, cardiac electrophysiologist; b. N.Y.C., Jan. 23, 1956; s. Clifford Julius and Ruth (Levy) S.; m. Jodi Lauren Halpern, Nov. 29, 1986. BS in Chemistry and Biology, MIT, Cambridge, Mass., 1977; MD, Yale U., New Haven, Conn., 1982, resident, cardiology fellow, 1982-88. Diplomate Am. Bd. Internal Medicine, Am. Bd. Cardiology, AM. Bd. Cardiac Electrophysiology. Asst. prof. medicine Sch. Medicine, U. So. Calif., L.A., 1988-90, asst. dir. electrophysiology, 1988-90, dir. Pacemaker Ctr., 1988-90; asst. prof. medicine Sch. Medicine, UCLA, 1990-96, assoc. prof. of medicine, 1996—; dir. cardiac electrophysiology West L.A. VA Med. Ctr., 1990-96; mem. cardiology adv. com. VA Adminstrn., Washington, 1990-94; cons. electrophysiology ACGME, Chgo., 1995—; vis. prof. Kern Med. Ctr., Bakersfield, Calif., 1991, 94, U. Iowa Sch. Medicine, 1994, Northwestern U. Sch. Medicine, 1994, Yale U. Sch. Medicine, 1995; invited lectr. Contbr. chpts. to books, numerous articles to profl. jours. grantee Am. Heart Assn., 1996. Fellow Am. Coll. Cardiology, Am. Coll. Physicians; mem. Am. Fedn. Clin. Rsch., Nat. Assn. Pacing and Electrophysiology (program dirs. com. 1992—, govt. com. 1994—), Phi Beta Kappa, Alpha Omega Alpha. Office: W LA VAMC-UCLA Dept 111E 11301 Wilshire Blvd Los Angeles CA 90073

SAGHIR, JAWAID, surgeon; b. Hyderabad, Sind, Pakistan, Oct. 18, 1952; s. Syed Saghirul Hasan and Sarwar Jehan; m. Nuwayrah Jawaid Rehman, Sept. 2, 1985; children: Naaimah, Saarim. HSC, Govt. Coll., Hyderabad, 1979; MB BS, Dow Med. Coll., Karachi, Pakistan, 1976. Jr. house surgeon Jinnah Postgrad. Med. Ctr., Karachi, 1976-77, sr. house physician, 1977; R.M.O. in gen. surgery Abbasi Shaheed Hosp., Karachi, 1977-82; med. officer Sohar (Oman) Ctrl. Hosp., 1982-85, Tanam Ctrl. Hosp., Ibri, Oman, 1991—; med. officer-in-charge Suwaiq/Wadi Fidai Dhank Health Ctr., Oman, 1985-91. Recipient Gold medal Bd. Intermediate and Secondary Edn., Hyderabad. Fellow ICA. Muslim. Office: Tanam Hosp, PO Box 3, Ibri Al Dhahira 511, Oman

SAGUNSKY, BYRON THOMAS, surgeon; b. Butte, Mont., June 30, 1944; s. Walter Gustav and Edith Sagunsky; m. Katherine Leone, May 6, 1972; children—David Lee, Anita Marie. B.A., Ripon Coll., 1966; M.D., U. Utah, 1970. Diplomate Am. Bd. Surgery. Intern Good Samaritan Hosp., Phoenix, 1970-71; resident in surgery U. Calif. Med. Ctr., Sacramento, 1974-78; practice medicine specializing in gen. surgery, Klamath Falls, Oreg., 1978—. Served as capt. USAF, 1971-74. Fellow ACS. Home: 1973 Benson Ave Klamath Falls OR 97601-1507 Office: 2300 Clairmont Dr Klamath Falls OR 97601

SAHA, ASIS KUMAR, cardiologist; b. Calcutta, West Bengal, India, June 14, 1941; came to U.S., 1966; s. Asoke Kumar and Swarna Prabha Saha; m. Barbara Ann Bialy, June 23, 1968; children: Kamala, Tiara, Michael, Stephen. MBBS, Calcutta U., 1963. Diplomate Am. Bd. Internal Medicine and Cardiovascular Diseases. Intern Med. Coll., Calcutta U., 1963; rotating intern Willingdon Hosp., New Delhi, India, 1964-65; rotating resident Safdarjung Hosp., New Delhi, 1965-66; rotating intern St. Peter's Gen. Hosp., Rutgers U., New Brunswick, N.J., 1966-67; med. resident St. Peter's Gen. Hosp., Rutgers U., New Burnswick, N.J., 1967-69, chief med. resident, 1969-70; cardiology fellow Mt. Sinai Med. Ctr., Miami Beach, Fla., 1970-72; staff cardiologist Kissimmee (Fla.) Meml. Hosp., 1973—, chmn. dept. medicine, 1973-87, 90—, dir. cardiopulminary dept., 1974-80, trustee, 1978—; practice medicine specializing in cardiology Kissimmee, 1973—; mem. active staff Fla. Hosp. Kissimmee and Orlando, Orlando Regional Healthcare Sys. at St. Cloud and Orlando, Osceola Regional Hosp., Columbia Pk. Med. Ctr., Orlando, Heart of Fla. Hosp., Haines City, Fla. Fellow Am. Coll. Cardiology, Am. Coll. Chest Physicians, Coun. Clin. Cardiology, Am. Coll. Angiology, Internat. Coll. Angiology; mem. ACP, Am. Soc. Echocardiology, Am. Soc. Geriatric Medicine, Am. Soc. Nuclear Cardiology (founding), Am. Heart Assn. (pres. Ctrl. Fla. chpt. 1980, lic. in nuclear cardiology), Com. of 100, Kissimmee C. of C. Democrat. Hindu. Office: 201 Hilda St Kissimmee FL 34741-2320

SAHAI, HARDEO, medical statistics educator; b. Bahraich, India, Jan. 10, 1942; m. Lillian Sahai, Dec. 28, 1973; 3 children. BS in Math., Stats. and Physics, Lucknow U., India, 1962; MS in Math., Banaras U., Varanasi, India, 1964; MS in Math. Stats., U. Chgo., 1968; PhD in Stats., U. Ky., 1971. Lectr. in math. and stats. Banaras U., Varanasi, India, 1964-65; asst. stats. officer Durgapur Steel Plant, Durgapur West Bengal, India, 1965; statistician Rsch. and Planning div. Blue Cross Assn., Chgo., 1966; statis. programmer Cleft Palate Ctr., U. Ill., 1967, Chgo. Health Rsch. Found., 1968; mgmt. scientist Mgmt. Systems Devel. Dept. Burroughs Corp., Detroit, 1971-72; from asst. prof. to prof. dept. math. U. P.R., Mayaguez, 1972-82; vis. research prof. Dept. Stats. and Applied Math. Fed. U. of Ceara, Brazil, 1978-79; sr. research statistician Travenol Labs., Inc., Round Lake, Ill., 1982-83; chief statistician U.S. Army Hqrs., Ft. Sheridan, Ill., 1983-84; sr. math. statistician U.S. Bur. of Census Dept. of Commerce, Washington, 1984-85; sr. ops. rsch. analyst Def. Logistics Agy. Dept. Def., Chgo., 1985-86; prof. Dept. Biostats. and Epidemiology U. P.R. Med. Scis., San Juan, 1986—; cons. P.R. Univ Cons., P.R. Driving Safety Evaluation Project, Water Resources Rsch. Inst., Travenol Labs., Campo Rico, P.R., U.S. Bur. Census, Washington, Lawrence Livermore Nat. Lab., Calif., others; vis. prof. U. Granada, Spain, U. Veracruzana, Mex., U. Nacional de Colombia; vis. prof. U. Nacional de Trujillo, Peru, 1993-94, hon. prof. dept. stats., 1994—; adj. prof. dept. math. U. P.R. Natural Scis. Faculty, 1995—. Author: Statistics and Probability: Learning Module, 1984; author: (with Jose Berrios) A Dictionary of Statistical Scientific and Technical Terms: English-Spanish and Spanish-English, 1981, (with Wilfredo Martinez) Statistical Tables and Formulas for the Biological Social and Physical Sciences, 1996, (with Anwer Khurshid) Statistics in Epidemiology: Methods, Techniques and Applications, 1996, (with Satish C. Misra and Michael Graham) Quotations on Probability and Statistics with Illustrations, 1996; mem. editl. bd. Sociedad Colombiana de Matematicas, P.R. Health Scis. Jour.; contbr. editor Current Index to Stats.; reviewer Collegiate Microcomputer, Comm. in Statistics, Indian Jour. Stats., Jour. Royal Statis. Soc. (series D, The Statistician), New Zealand Statistician, Biometrics, Can. Jour. Stats., Technometrics, Problems, Resources and Issues in Math. Undergrad. Studies; contbr. more than 100 articles and papers to profl. and sci. jours., numerous articles to tech. mags. Active Dept. Consumer Affairs Svcs. Commonwealth of P.R., San Juan, Dept. Anti-Addiction Svcs., Commonwealth of P.R., San Juan., Inst. of AIDS, Municipality of San Juan, VA Med. Ctr. of San Juan, Caribbean Primate Rsch. Ctr., Ctr. Addiction Studies Caribbean Ctrl. U. Recipient Dept. Army Cert. Achievement award, 1984, U. Ky. Outstanding Alumnus award, 1993, medal of honor U. Granada, 1994, plaque of honor U. Nacional de Trujillo, 1994; fellow Coun. Sci. and Indsl. Rsch., 1964-65, U. Chgo., 1965-68, Harvard U., 1979, Fulbright Found., 1982; U.P. Bd. Merit scholar, 1957-59, Govt. India Merit scholar, 1959-64; grantee NSF, 1974-77, NIMH, 1987-90, 91—, NIDA, 1991—. Fellow AAAS, Inst. Statisticians (charter statistician), Inst. Math. and Its Applications (charter mathematician), N.Y. Acad. Scis., Royal Statis. Soc.; mem. Internat. Statis. Inst., Internat. Assn. Teaching Stats., Soc. Epidemiol. Rsch., Inst. Math. Stats., Bernouilli Soc. for Math. Stats. and Probability, Internat. Biometric Soc., Am. Soc. for Quality Control, Am. Stats. Assn., Japan Statis. Soc., Can. Statis. Soc., Inter-Am. Statis. Inst., Internat. Assn. Statis. Computing, Sch. Sci. and Math. Assn., Sigma Xi. Home: Street Dr Gaudier Texidor K-5-B Terrace Mayaguez PR 00680-9998 Office: U PR Grad Sch Pub Health Med Scis Campus Dept Biostats & Epid PO Box 365067 San Juan PR 00936-5067

SAHATJIAN, MANIK, nurse, psychologist; b. Tabris, Iran, July 24, 1921; came to U.S., 1951; d. Dicran and Shushanig (Der-Galustian) Maatzaganian; m. George Sahatjian, Jan. 21, 1954; children: Robert, Edwin. Nursing Cert., Am. Mission Hosps.-Boston U., 1954; BA in Psychology, San Jose State U., 1974, MA in Psychology, 1979. RN, Calif., Mass. Head nurse Am. Mission Hosp., Tabris, 1945-46; charge nurse Banke-Melli Hosp., Tehran, 1946-51; vis. nurse Vis. Nurse Assn., Oakland, Calif., 1956-57; research asst. Stanford U., 1979-81, Palo Alto (Calif.) Med. Research Found., 1981-84; documentation supr. Bethesda Convalescent Ctr., Los Gatos, Calif., 1985-86; sr. outreach worker City of Fremont (Calif.) Human Svcs., 1987-90, case mgr., 1990—; guest rsch. asst. NASA Ames Lab., Mountain View, Calif., summers 1978, 79. Author (with others) psychol. research reports. Fulbright scholar, 1951; Iran Found. scholar, 1953. Mem. AAUW, Western Psychol. Assn. Democrat. Mem. St. Andrew Armenian Church. Home: 339 Starlite Way Fremont CA 94539-7642

SAIDMAN, LAWRENCE JAY, anesthesiologist; b. Detroit, 1936. MD, U. Mich., 1961. Diplomate Am. Bd. Anesthesiology (v.p. 1992-93, pres. 1993-94). Intern Sinai Hosp., Detroit, 1961-62; resident in anesthesiology U. Calif., San Francisco, 1962-65; fellow Cardiovascular Rsch. Inst., San Francisco, 1963-64; anesthesiologist U. Calif. Med. Ctr., San Diego; prof. U. Calif., San Diego. Editor-in-chief Anesthesiology, 1985—. Mem. Am. Bd. Anesthesiology (bd. dirs.). Office: U Calif at San Diego Sch Medicine T-015 San Diego CA 92110

SAIFER, MARK GARY PIERCE, pharmaceutical executive; b. Phila., Sept. 16, 1938; s. Albert and Sylvia (Jolles) S.; m. Phyllis Lynne Trommer, Jan. 28, 1961 (dec.); children: Scott David, Alandria Gail; m. Merry R. Sherman, June 26, 1994. AB, U. Pa., 1960; PhD, U. Calif., Berkeley, 1966. Acting asst. prof. zoology U. Calif., Berkeley, 1966, postdoctoral fellow, 1967-68; sr. cancer research scientist Roswell Park Meml. Inst., Buffalo, 1968-70; lab. dir. Diagnostic Data Inc., Palo Alto, Calif., 1970-78; v.p. DDI Pharms., Inc., Mountain View, Calif., 1978-94, Oxis Internat., Inc., 1994-95; sci. dir. Mountain View Pharms., Inc., San Carlos, Calif., 1996—. Patentee in field. Mem. AAAS (life), Am. Assn. Pharm. Scientists, Parenteral Drug Assn. Home: 1114 Royal Ln San Carlos CA 94070 Office: Mountain View Pharms Inc 871-L Industrial Rd San Carlos CA 94070

SAIN, RONALD ARCHIE, mental health services administrator; b. Missoula, Mont., Apr. 3, 1945; s. Archie C. and Mabel F. (Martin) S.; m. Esther A. Warford, Sept. 5, 1970; 1 child, Erin. BA, U. Mont., 1969; MSW, U. Denver, 1976. Lic. social worker, Pa. Social worker Warm Springs (Mont.) State Hosp., 1970-74; chief social worker Warm Springs State Hosp. Child Program, 1976-80; dir. partial hosp. Pathways Inc., Greenup, Ky., 1981-82; dir. partial hosp. adult and adolescent programs Indiana (Pa.) County Guidance Ctr., 1983—; cons. mental health svcs. Head Start, Indiana, 1986-87. Mem. Am. Contract Bridge League (life master, treas. local chpt. 1977-78), Moose. Home: 201 Forest Dr Indiana PA 15701-8709 Office: Indiana County Guidance Ctr 699 Philadelphia St Ste 201 Indiana PA 15701-3916

SAINSOUS, JOEL, cardiologist; b. Zinder, Niger, Apr. 19, 1955; s. Guy and Janine (Legrand) S.; m. Anne-Marie Maurer, Sept. 2, 1978; children: Adrien, Raphael, Benjamin. Cert. in cardiology, France. Intern Hosp. Marseille, France, 1978-82, asst., 1982-85; pvt. practice Avignon, France, 1986—; dir. Cardiac Catheterization Lab., Avignon, 1995—. Contbr. articles to profl. jours. Mem. French Soc. Cardiology. Office: Clinique Rhone Durance, Chemin du Lavarin, 84000 Avignon France

ST. CLAIR, BARBARA LOUISE, healthcare facility administrator; b. Green Bay, Wis., Sept. 14, 1947; d. Francis Joseph and Esther (Morris) Bergeron; m. John Frederick St. Clair, June 28, 1969; children: Thomas William, Elizabeth Grace, Maria Bethany. Liberal arts, U. Wis., 1969; postgrad., Western Internat. U., 1996—. Social worker AZ Physicians IPA, Phoenix, 1987-90; quality assurance supr. Thunderbird Health Care Ctr., Phoenix, 1990-92, dir. admissions, 1992-93; dir. mktg. Phoenix Mtn. Nursing Ctr., Phoenix, 1993-94; dir. admissions and mktg. Grancare Med. Ctr., Phoenix, 1994-95; adminstr. Mimosa Springs Plaza Health Care, Scottsdale, Ariz., 1995—; programs co-chair Human Svcs. Profls., Phoenix, 1994-95. Participant Alzheimers Walk Alzheimer's Assn., 1994. Mem. Am. Coll. Health Care Adminstrs., Delta Mu Delta. Office: Plaza Health Care Mimosa Springs 8435 E McDowell Rd Scottsdale AZ 85257

ST. CYR, JOHN ALBERT, II, cardiovascular and thoracic surgeon; b. Mpls., Nov. 26, 1949; s. John Albert and Myrtle Lavira (Jensen) St. C.; m. Mary Helen Malinoski, Oct. 29, 1977. BA summa cum laude, U. Minn., 1973, BS, 1975, MS, 1977, MD, 1980, PhD, 1988. Teaching asst. dept. biochemistry U. Minn., Mpls., 1973, rsch. asst. dept. surgery, 1977-78, intern surgery dept. surgery, 1980-81, resident surgery, 1981-88, cardiovascular rsch. fellow dept. surgery, 1983-86, with dept. surgery, 1991-92; rsch. assoc. fellow Cardiovasular Pathology, United Hosp., St. Paul, 1987-88; cardiovascular surg. resident U. Colo., Dept. Cardiovascular Surgery, Denver, 1988-91; med. advisor Organetics, Ltd., Mpls., 1992, med. dir., 1992; med. advisor Aor Tech., Inc., St. Paul, 1992; bd. dirs. Minn. Acad. Sci.; pres. Virotech, Inc., 1993-94; ind. rsch., 1992—; dir. R&D Medcorp Internat., 1996—. Contbr. more than 60 articles to profl. jours. Recipient NIH Rsch./Fellowship award, 1983-86, Grant in Aid Rsch. award Minn. Heart Assn., 1983-85, Med. Student Rsch. award Minn. Med. Found., 1980, Acad. Excellence award Merck Found., 1980. Mem. AAAS, ACS, AMA, Assn. Acad. Surgeons, Soc. Thoracic Surgeons, Am. Physiol. Soc., Am. Fedn. and Clin. Rsch., N.Y. Acad. Scis., Phi Kappa Phi. Republican.

ST. JOHN, CHARLES VIRGIL, retired pharmaceutical company executive; b. Bryan, Ohio, Dec. 18, 1922; s. Clyde W. and Elsie (Kintner) St. J.; m. Ruth Ilene Wilson, Oct. 27, 1946; children: Janet Sue St. John Arny, Debra Ann St. John Mishler. AB, Manchester Coll., 1943; MS, Purdue U., 1946. Asst. gen. mgr., dir. ops. Eli Lilly and Co., Clinton, Ind., 1971-75; gen. mgr. Eli Lilly and Co., Lafayette, Ind., 1975-77, v.p. prodn. ops. divsn., 1977-89; bd. dirs. Bank One of Lafayette, Lafayette Life Ins. Co., Lafayette Cmty. Found., Bioanalytical Sys., Inc., West Lafayette, Ind. Past pres. bd. dirs. United Way Greater Lafayette and Tippecanoe County; bd. trustees Lafayette Symphony Found.; past chmn. lay adv. coun. St. Elizabeth Hosp.; mem. pres.'s coun. Purdue U.; trustee Manchester (Ind.) Coll.; bd. dirs. Lafayette Cmty. Found.; bd. dirs. Jr. Achievement of Greater Lafayette. Recipient Elizabethan award, St. Elizabeth Hosp., Lafayette, 1985; named Cmty. Hero Olympic Torch Bearer, 1996. Mem. Am. Chem. Soc., Purdue Rsch. Found., Greater Lafayette C. of C. (past bd. dirs.), Lafayette Country Club, Rotary. Republican. Methodist. Home: 321 Overlook Dr West Lafayette IN 47906-1249

ST. JOHN, KENNETH RAYMOND, bioengineer, educator, consultant; b. Montpelier, Vt., July 26, 1953; s. Stanley Arthur and Marjorie Irene (Holmes) St.J.; m. Susan Ilene Stark, Aug. 7, 1982; children: Matthew Paul, Jessica Marie. BS in Biomed. Engring., Rensselaer Poly. Inst., 1975; MS in Bioengring., Clemson U., 1977. Biomed. engr. Abcor, Inc., Wilmington, Mass., 1977-79; rsch. project leader Hexcel, Inc., Dublin, Calif., 1979-87, Osteonics Biomaterials, Livermore, Calif., 1987-89; asst. prof U. Miss. Med. Ctr., Jackson, 1989—. Editor: Biocompatibility of Particulate Debris, 1992; contbr. articles to jours. Mem. ASTM (chmn. biocompatibility 1986—, gen. interest vice chmn. 1994—, chmn. com. on pubs. 1996—, Moses award 1987, Sci. Am. award 1992, Symposium and Pubs. Mgmt. Excellence award 1993), Soc. for Biomaterials, Orthopaedic Rsch. Soc., Nat. Soc. for Histotech. United Methodist. Home: 123 Post Hill Cv Brandon MS 39042-2037 Office: U Miss Med Ctr 2500 N State St Jackson MS 39216-4505

ST. PIERRE, CATHY M., family nurse practitioner; b. Manchester, N.H., Mar. 23, 1954; d. Roland J. and Beatrice A. (Devine) St. P. BS in Nursing, Northeastern U., Boston, 1977; MS in Nursing, U. Pa., Phila., 1981; PhD, Boston Coll., 1995. Cert. family nurse practitioner. Staff nurse St. Elizabeth's Hosp., Brighton, Mass., 1977-78, VA Med. Ctr., Manchester, N.H., 1978-79, Boston Vis. Nurse Assn., 1979-80, Grad. Hosp., Phila., 1980-82; family nurse practitioner Dorchester (Mass.) House Health Ctr., 1982-85; instr., lectr. U. Lowell (Mass.), 1985-88; adolescent nurse practitioner Child Health Svcs., Manchester, 1988-89; family nurse practitioner Valley Med. Assocs. HMO, Methuen, Mass., 1989—; asst. prof. Rivier Coll., Nashua, N.H., 1994—; instr., lectr. U. Pa., Phila., 1981-82; clin. instr. Northeastern U., Boston, 1984-85, U. Mass., Boston, 1982-84; mem. nurse practitioner liaison com. Bd. Nursing in N.H., 1986-88. Bd. mem. Family Svcs. Greater Lowell, 1987-88. Mem. ANA, N.J. Nurses Assn., N.H. Nurse Practitioner Assn. (co-pres. 1986-88, v.p. 1992-94).

SAITO, HIDEHIKO, internal medicine educator; b. Nagoy, Japan, Feb. 8, 1939; s. Shoichi and Mitsu (Kawamoto) S.; m. Yuko Terada, July 7, 1969; children: Taro, Shoji. MD, Nagoya U., 1963, PhD, 1968. Asst. prof. medicine Case Western Res. U., Cleve., 1976-79, assoc. prof., 1979-82; prof. Saga (Japan) Sch. Medicine, 1982-84; prof., dept. chmn. Sch. Medicine Nagoya U., 1984—; dean Sch. Medicine Nagoya U., 1991—. Editor: Vitamin K Dependent Proteins and their Metabolic Roles, 1989. Office: Nagoya U Sch Medicine, 65 Tsurumai-cho Showa-ku, Nagoya 466, Japan

SAITO, TAIICHI, pharmacology educator; b. Osaka, Japan, Jan. 14, 1931; s. Masaichi and Yoshiko (Asaka) S.; m. Mitsuko Fujita, July 29, 1960; children: Koichi, Masami. MD, Jikeikai Med. Sch., Tokyo, 1955, DMSc, 1961. Intern St. Luke's Internat. Hosp., Tokyo, 1955-56; rsch. fellow, Dept. Pharmacology Jikeikai Med. Sch., 1956-60, instr., 1962-63; staff scientist Worcester Found. Exptl. Biology, Shrewsbury, Mass., 1960-62; chief med. officer Nat. Sanatorium Kofuen, Yamagata, 1963-64; prof. Iwate Med. Sch., Morioka, Iwate, 1964-76; prof. dept. pharmacology Kawasaki Med. Sch., Kurashiki, Okayama, 1976-96, prof. emeritus, 1996—; prof. dept. nursing Kawasaki U. Med. Welfare, 1996—; prof. emeritus Kawasaki U. Med. Welfare, Kurashiki, Okayama, Japan, 1996—. Author: Essential Pharmacology, 1994, Medical Diagnosis Using Fuzzy Sets, 1994, Sanmenkyo (a triple glass), 1994. Home: Amakidai 4-7-19, Kurashiki Okayama 710-01, Japan Office: Kawasaki U Med Welfare, Med Welfare, Matsushima 288, Kurashiki Okayama 710-01, Japan

SAITOH, SATORU, orthopaedist; b. Suzaka, Nagano, Japan, July 10, 1952; s. Toshio and Michiko Saitoh; m. Michiko Sakurai; children: Aya, Tomoya. MD, Niigata U., 1978; PhD (hon.), Shinshu U., 1987. Asst. prof. dept. orthopaedics Sch. Medicine Shinshu U., 1984-93, lectr. dept. orthopaedics Sch. Medicine, 1993—. Contbr. articles to profl. jours. Mem. Japanese Soc. Surgery Hand (councilor), Japanese Orthopaedic Assn. (travelling fellow). Buddhist. Office: Shinshu U Sch Medicine, Dept Orthopaedics Asahi 3-1-1, Matsumoto 390, Japan

SAITZ, RICHARD, physician, researcher; b. Mass., Nov. 13, 1963; s. Robert and Linda Saitz. BA, Boston U., 1987, MD, 1987; MPH, Harvard U., 1993. Intern, resident in internal medicine Boston City Hosp., Boston U. Sch. Medicine, 1987-91; fellow Deaconness Hosp., Boston, 1991-93; asst. prof. medicine Boston City Hosp.-Boston U., 1993—. Mem. ACP, Soc. Gen. Internal Medicine, Assn. for Health Svcs. Rsch., Assn. for Med. Edn. and Rsch. in Substance Abuse (Young Investigator award 1995), Alpha Omega Alpha. Home: 175 Islington Rd Auburndale MA 02166 Office: Boston City Hosp-Boston U Rsch Unit Gen Internal Med 91 E Concord St Ste 200 Boston MA 02118

SAKAGAMI, MASAFUMI, otolaryngologist, educator; b. Ibaraki City, Osaka, Japan, Apr. 18, 1954; s. Tomoya and Ikuko (Shimizu) S.; m. Michiko Suchi, Nov. 29, 1980; children: Kumiko, Masaharu. MD, Osaka U., 1980, PhD, 1984. Med. lic., Japan; specialist of otolaryngology, Japan. Instr. Kagawa Med. Sch., Takamatsu, Japan, 1984-86; instr. Osaka U. Med. Sch., 1986-94, asst. prof., 1994; prof., chmn. Hyogo Coll. Medicine, Nishinomiya, Japan, 1994—; part-time asst. prof. Osaka U. Med. Sch., 1995—; dir. Hyogo Ear Bank, Nishinomiya, 1996—. Recipient Award for Young Rschrs., Clin. Electron Microscopic Soc. Japan, 1991. Mem. Am. Assn. for Rsch. Otolaryngology, Oto-Rhino-Laryngol. Soc. Japan (councilor 1995—), Japan Soc. Electron Microscopy (councilor), Barany Soc., Politzer Soc. Home: 4-6-15 Kitakasugaoka, 567 Ibaraki City Osaka, Japan Office: Hyogo Coll Medicine, Dept Otolaryngology, 1-1 Mukogawa-cho, 663 Nishinomiya Hyogo, Japan

SAKAGUCHI, KAZUSHIGE (KEN SAKAGUCHI), scientist, physician; b. Wakayama, Japan, Jan. 21, 1953; s. Tokuji and Hideko (Akamatsu) S.; m. Akiko Ueno, May 2, 1981; children: Yoshiki, Mayu, Yusuke. MD, Wakayama Medical Sch., Wakayama, Japan, 1977; PhD, Kobe Univ. Sch. Medicine, Kobe, Japan, 1984. Resident Toranomon Hosp., Tokyo, 1977-80; chief dept. internal medicine North Hyogo Medical & Orthopedic Ctr., Hyogo, Japan, 1984-85; asst. prof. Kobe Univ. Sch. Medicine, Kobe, 1985; vis. fellow NIDDK, NIH, Bethesda, 1986-89; vis. assoc. NIDDK NIH, Bethesda, 1989-93, vis. scientist, 1993—. Author: The Parathyroids, 1994; contbr. articles to profl. jours. Recipient Young Investigator award Am. Soc. Bone & Mineral Rsch., New Orleans, 1988, Advances in Mineral Metabolism, Colo., 1993. Mem. The Endocrine Soc., The Am. Soc. Bone and Mineral Rsch. Office: Nat Inst Health Bldg 30 Rm 106 9000 Rockville Pike Bethesda MD 20892

SAKANASHI, MATAO, pharmacology educator; b. Kumamoto, Japan, Oct. 16, 1943; s. Hidefumi and Mine Sakanashi; m. Yukiko Sakanashi, Nov. 30, 1970; children: Mayuko, Makiko. B in Medicine and MD, Kumamoto U., 1968, PhD, 1972. Asst. prof. Sch. of Medicine Kumamoto U., Kumamoto-City, 1973-75, instr. Sch. of Medicine, 1975-82; prof. pharmacology U. Ryukyus Sch. Medicine, Nishihara-cho, Okinawa, Japan, 1982—. Author: Peripheral Dopaminergic Receptors, 1979, Vascular Neuroeffector Mechanisms, 1983, Progress in Hypertension, 1988, Cardiovascular Disease in Diabetes, 1992. Ministry of Edn. grantee, 1979-80, 89-90; recipient Kanae Fund awards, 1983. Mem. Japanese Circulation Soc., Japanese Pharmacol. Soc., Japanese Coll. of Angiology, Japanese Soc. Circulation Rsch., Japanese Soc. Clin. Pharmacology and Therapeutics, Internat. Soc. Toxinology, Japanese Soc. Pharmacoanesthesiology, Internat. Soc. Heart Rsch., N.Y. Acad. Scis. Home: 2-96-1-2-302 Shuri-ishimine-cho, Naha Okinawa 903, Japan Office: U Ryukyus Sch Medicine, 207 Uehara, Nishihara-cho, Okinawa 903-01, Japan

SAKELLARIOS, GERTRUDE EDITH, retired office nurse; b. Lowell, Mass., Mar. 14, 1929; d. William V. and Eileen E. (Hale) Yoachimciuk; m. Angelos D. Sakellarios, Dec. 30, 1966. Diploma, Lowell Gen. Hosp., 1949; student, Boston U., 1949-53, Boston Coll./St. Josephs Hosp., Lowell, 1951. Gen. duty med.-surg. nurse Lowell Gen. Hosp., 1949-50, operating room nurse, 1950-52; office nurse gen. practitioner's office, Lowell, 1952-83. Home: 124 Cashin St Lowell MA 01851-2004

SAKHEIM, DAVID KURT, psychologist; b. Brockton, Mass., July 24, 1956; s. George A. and Ilse H. (Oschinsky) S.; m. Susan E. Devine, May 7, 1988. BS, Brown U., 1978; PhD, SUNY, Albany, 1984. Lic. psychologist, Mass., Conn. Inpatient team leader Bay State Med. Ctr., Springfield, Mass., 1984-85, cons. psychologist, 1985-86; dir. edn. and tng. Traumatic Stress Tx Program, South Windsor, Conn., 1986-87; pvt. practice South Windsor, 1987—. Co-editor: Out of Darkness: Exploring Satanism and Ritual Abuse, 1991. Mem. Am. Psychol. Assn., Internat. Soc. Study Multiple Personality and Dissociative Disorders. Office: Maple Hill Psychology Assoc 852 Main St South Windsor CT 06074-3305

SAKKAL, SAAD, endocrinologist, geriatrician; b. Aleppo, Syria, Nov. 5, 1947; came to U.S., 1972; s. Mohamed Loutfy and Durie (Khatib) S.; m. Maysa Mounla, 1981; children: Luna, Mohammed. PCB, Damascus U., Syria, 1966; MD, Damascus Med. Sch., Syria, 1972. Diplomate Am. Bd. Internal Medicine, Am. Bd. Endocrinology and Metabolism, Am. Bd. Geriatrics. Intern Luth. Med. Ctr., Bklyn., 1972-73; resident internal medicine St. Joseph's Hosp. Med. Ctr., Paterson, N.J., 1973-74, Phila. Gen. Hosp., 1974-75; chief resident internal medicine Conemaugh Valley Meml. Hosp., Johnstown, Pa., 1975-76; fellow in endocrinology and metabolism George

Washington U. Med. Ctr., Washington, 1976-78, asst. in medicine, 1979-80; guest worker NIH NICHD, Bethesda, Md., 1979-81; med. dir. Metabolic Care Ctr., Greenville, Pa., 1982—; acting dir. endocrinology and metabolism Youngstown (Ohio) Hosp. Assn., 1984-86; asst. clin. prof. medicine Northeastern Ohio U. Coll. Medicine, Rootstown, 1984; med. dir. Regional Diabetes Ctr., Greenville, 1991—; pres. med. staff Greenville Regional Hosp., Horizon Hosp. Sys., 1993-94; rep. Managed Care Leader, Horizon Hosp. Sys., 1984—; sec.-treas. Physicians Orgn. for Mercer County, Pa., 1993—; bd. dirs. Pa. Physicians Healthcare Plan, 1994—. Contbr. articles to profl. jours. Trustee Mahoning, Shenango Area Health Edn. Network, Youngstown, 1985-90; pres. Mercer County Med. Soc., 1991. Recipient Govt. award for Best Med. Student, Damascus Med. Sch., 1966-72, The Eudowood award Am. Coll. Chest Physicians, 1976, AMA Physicians Recognition award AMA, 1975-93. Fellow ACP, Am. Coll. Internat. Physicians, Am. Coll. Endocrinology; mem. The Endocrine Soc., Soc. for Clin. Densitometry, Islamic Med. Assn., Assn. Insulin Pump Therapists. Muslim. Office: Metabolic Care Ctr 81 N Main St Greenville PA 16125-1781

SAKLAD, STEPHEN ROSS, clinical pharmacist, researcher; b. L.A., Apr. 7, 1953; s. J. Jay and Elizabeth (Ravich) S.; m. Judith Marie Jamieson, Mar. 12, 1982. B in Bacteriology, UCLA, 1974; PharmD, U. So. Calif., 1978. Clin. instr. Coll. of Pharmacy U. Nebr., Omaha, 1978-79; clin. asst. prof. U. Tex., Austin, 1979-84, clin. assoc. prof., 1984—; clin. pharmacology coord. San Antonio State Hosp., 1979—; co-dir. Psychiat. Pharmacy Program, San Antonio, 1980—, Webmaster Coll. of Pharmacy, 1995—; cons. pharm. mfrs., 1982—. Author software: Pharmacotherapy DB, 1989, Drug Education, 1989, Prometheus Clozapine Monitoring System, 1991; editor newsletter NeuralNetwork and Webmaster of Neural Network Online; contbr. articles to profl. jours. Mem. Named Neill B. Walsdorf fellow Coll. of Pharmacy U. Tex., 1986—; recipient Harrison cert. Tex. Dept. Mental Health and Mental Retardation, 1986, clin. rsch. unit Tex. Legislature, 1989. Mem. AAAS, ACLU, Am. Soc. Healthsystem Pharmacists, Am. Assn. Colls. of Pharmacy, Union of Concerned Scientists, Alliance for Mentally Ill, Planetary Soc. Democrat. Jewish. Office: U Tex Health Sci Ctr 7703 Floyd Curl Dr San Antonio TX 78284-6200

SAKUTA, MANABU, neurologist, educator; b. Ichikawa, Japan, Oct. 31, 1947; s. Jun and Shizuko (Tsuji) S.; m. Yuko Fukushi, June 17, 1973; children: Akiko, Junko, Ken-Ichi. MD, U. Tokyo, 1973, PhD, 1978; MS in Neurology, U. Minn., 1981. Med. diplomate. Diplomat Japanese Bd. Neurology, Japanese Bd. Internal Medicine. Asst. Dept. Neurology U. Tokyo, Japan, 1980; rsch. fellow Dept. Neurology U. Minn., Mpls., 1980-81, asst. prof., 1981-82; head Dept. Neurology Japanese Red Cross Med. Ctr., Tokyo, 1982—; prof. Japanese Red Cross Women's Coll. Sch. Nursing, Tokyo, 1983-85, instr. 1986-88; lectr. dept. neurology, U. Tokyo, 1984—, dept. medicine U. Kobe, 1990—; cons. Nakayama Hosp., Ichikawa, Japan, 1980—. Contbr. articles to profl. jours. Fellow Royal Soc. Medicine (London); mem. AAAS, N.Y. Acad. Sci., Japanese Soc. Internal Medicine (pres. Kanto br. 1992), Japanese Soc. Neurology (mem. coun., 1985—, mem. coun. Kanto Br., 1984—, pres. Kanto Br. 1984, mem. editorial bd. 1988—), Japanese Soc. Diabetology, Japanese Soc. Electroencephalography and Electromyography, Japanese Soc. Autonomic Nervous System (mem. coun.), Clinical Neurology Club, Chevalier Club (pres. internat. com. 1995—), U. Minn. Alumni Club, Tetsumon Club. Democrat. Buddhist. Office: Japanese Red Cross Med Ctr, 4-1-22 Hiroo Shibuya-ku, Tokyo 150, Japan

SALA, LUIS FRANCISCO, surgeon, educator; b. N.Y.C., Dec. 13, 1919; s. Luis and Josefina (Goenaga) S.; m. Judith Colon, June 5, 1943; children: Luis E., Francisco A., Jorge P., Jose M. BS cum laude, Georgetown U., 1939, M.D., 1943; M.Sc. in Surgery, U. Pa., 1951. Diplomate: Am. Bd. Surgery. Intern, resident Presbyn. Hosp., San Juan, P.R., 1943-45; resident Presbyn. Hosp., 1944-45; chief resident Grad. Hosp. U. Pa., 1947-51, instr. surgery, 1950-51; clin. asst. surgery Med. Coll. Pa.; practice medicine, specializing in surgery Ponce, P.R., 1951-91; chmn. dept. surgery Damas Hosp., Ponce, 1955-88; prof. surgery U. P.R. Sch. Medicine, 1968-88; pres., dean, prof. surgery Ponce Sch. of Medicine, 1988-94; del. P.R. Med. Assn., 1960-93, pres., 1965-66; apptd. mem. Med. Examining Bd. by Gov. of P.R., 1995. Author: Consideraciones Basicas para la Acreditacion de Hospitales, 1978; contbr. chpts. to books, articles to profl. jours. Active Boy Scouts Am., 1955-74; pres. adv. com. to pres. Cath. U. P.R., 1963-72; bd. dirs. Boys Home of Ponce, 1966-76; bd. regents Amigos Museo de Arte de Ponce, 1968-73, Cath. U., 1972-93; pres. bd. regents Ponce Med. Sch. Found., 1980-92. Served with M.C. U.S. Army, 1945-47. Recipient Silver Beaver award, 1965, Acad. Médica, Dto. Sur, 1st. Dr. Luis F. Sasa medal, 1995; named lt. P.R. Equestrian Order of Holy Sepulchre of Jerusalem, 1982—. Fellow ACS (gov. for P.R. 1965-74, Disting. Svc. award 1989), Internat. Soc. Surgery, P.R. Med. Assn. (so. dist., Dr. Pila medal for disting. svc. 1991), Indsl. Med. Coun. of SIF (apptd. pres. by Gov. of P.R. 1993-95), P.R. Mfrs. Assn. (Profl. of Yr. in area of svcs. 1994), C. of C. (Profl. of Yr. 1990), State Med. Examining Bd. (appt. by Gov. of P.R. 1995—). Republican. Roman Catholic. Home: 6 Almena Alhambra Ponce PR 00731 Office: 43 Calle Concordia Ponce PR 00731-4984

SALAMA, SHEILA RACHEL, child psychiatrist; b. Cairo, Oct. 22, 1943; d. Simeon and Victoria (Levy) S. MD, SUNY-Downstate Med. Ctr., Bklyn., 1969. Diplomate Am. Bd. Psychiatry and Neurology. Staff child psychiatrist Manhattan Children's Psychiatric Ctr., N.Y., 1974-76, Vincent's Hosp., N.Y.C., 1976-78; cons. Jewish Bd. Families and Children's Svcs., N.Y.C., 1983-86; chief child psychiatrist Postgrad. Ctr. of NYU, 1986-90; child psychiatrist HIP HMO, N.Y.C., 1974—. Office: 372 CPWWashington Sq S New York NY 10025

SALAMON, ITAMAR, psychiatry educator; b. Nov. 12, 1934; m. Linda Frank, 1959; children: Margaret, Elizabeth, Thomas. BS with high honors, Queens Coll., Flushing, N.Y., 1955; MD, Albert Einstein Coll. of Medicine, Bronx, N.Y., 1959. Intern Montefiore Hosp., Bronx, 1959-60; assoc. resident, chief resident psychiatry Strong Meml. Hosp. U. Rochester, 1960-63; surgeon St. Elizabeth's Hosp. USPHS, Washington, 1963-65; instr. psychiatry, attending psychiatrist Albert Einstein Coll. of Medicine and Bronx Mcpl. Hosp. Ctr., 1965-67, asst. prof. psychiatry, dir. inpatient psychiatry, 1967-70, asst. clin. prof. psychiatry, dir. geriatric psychiatry, 1970-71, asst. clin. prof., dir. psychiatry emergency svcs., 1971-77; assoc. clin. prof., dir. Sound View-Throg's Neck Community Mental Health Ctr. Albert Einstein Coll. Medicine, 1977-92; pvt. practice Hartsdale, N.Y., 1970—; chmn. computer com. Dept. Psychiatry Albert Einstein Coll. of Medicine, 1985—. Contbr. articles and presentations to profl. jours. Mem. Nat. Coun. Community Mental Health Ctrs. (coun. on svcs.), Am. Psychiat. Assn. (steering com. to plan conf. on recruitment into psychiatry), Am. Assn. Geriatric Psychiatrists. Home: 1217 Colony Dr Hartsdale NY 10530-1723

SALAMON, MICHAEL JACOB, psychologist, health care and psychology educator, researcher; b. Bklyn., Oct. 18, 1951; s. Milton and Bessie (Kessler) S. BA, Queens Coll., 1974, MA, 1977; MA, Hofstra U., 1981, PhD, 1983. Project dir. Nat. Coun. Sr. League, Far Rockaway, N.Y., 1974-78; dir., founder Adult Devel. Ctr., Hewlett, N.Y., 1978—; dir. rsch. Gustave Hartman YM-YWHA, Far Rockaway, 1978-82; asst. prof. psychology L.I. U., 1981-83; gerontology cons. St. Johns Hosp., Far Rockaway, 1980-83; adult devel. cons. CSE, Far Rockaway, 1980-83, N.Y. State Dept. of Labor, Far Rockaway, 1978-80; dir. rsch. div. Hebrew Home for Aged at Riverdale, 1983-85; dir. psychology St. John's Home and Hosp., 1986-88; dir. rsch., clin. supr. New Hope Guild Ctrs., Bklyn., 1989—; vis. scholar Brookdale Found., Jerusalem, 1985. Author: Adult Assessment Scale, 1982; textbooks on gerontology, nursing homes; editor: Jour. Clin. Gerontology; contbr. articles to profl. jours. Assoc. bd. dirs. Dem. Club of Rockaways, 1981; bd. dirs. Young Israel of Woodmere, 1982; mem. bd. edn. Hebrew Acad. of the Five Towns and Rockaways, 1991, chmn., 1995—; mem. bd. edn. PTACH Ctrs. for Learning Disabilities, 1991. Bruner Found. grantee, 1979; N.Y. State Dept. Social Svcs. grantee, 1982. Mem. APA, Gerontol. Soc. Am. (rsch. fellow 1983), Northeastern Gerontol. Soc., Psychologists in Long-Term Care Network (bd. dirs.), Assn. Jewish Scientists, Am. Psychiat. Assn. Democrat. Jewish. Office: Adult Devel Ctr 1728 Broadway Hewlett NY 11557

SALANDRA, JOHN A., health facility financial administrator; b. N.Y.C., June 3, 1952; s. Michael R. and Ida C. (Cannata) S.; m. Kathryn A. Tota, Oct. 12, 1975; children: Justin, Erika, Lindsay. BBA in Acctg., Iona Coll., 1974. CPA, N.Y. Sr. mgr. Peat Marwick Co., N.Y.C., 1974-84; v.p. fin. Nyack (N.Y.) Hosp., 1984-85; dir. fin. ops. Cath. Med. Ctr. of Bklyn. and Queens, Inc., Queens, N.Y., 1985—; trustee, chmn. fin. com. Dominican Sisters Family Health Svcs., Ossining, N.Y., 1986—; trustee St. Jerome's Health Svcs., Inc., bd. dirs., chmn., treas., 1989—; trustee Bishop Francis J. Mugauero Ctr. for Geriatric Care Inc. Lt., vol. firefighter and EMT Hawthorne (N.Y.) Fire Co. No. 1, 1985. Mem. AICPA, N.Y. State Soc. CPA's, Am. Hosp. Assn., Fin. Mgmt. Assn. (pres. N.Y.C. 1996-97). Republican. Roman Catholic. Office: Catholic Med Ctr 88 25 153rd St Jamaica NY 11432

SALANGER, MATTHEW JOSEPH, health services administrator; b. Syracuse, N.Y., May 11, 1955; s. James F. and Dolores H. (Huvar) S.; m. Mary Ellen O'Connor, Nov. 12, 1983; children: Connor, Nora, Maeve, Shane. BA, SUNY, Albany, 1977; MHA, Xavier U., Cin., 1982. Diplomate Am. Coll. Healthcare Execs.; lic. nursing home adminstr., N.Y. Social worker St. Camillus Health and Rehab. Ctr., Syracuse, 1979-80; adminstrv. resident Rochester Meml. Hosp., N.Y., 1981-82, adminstrv. asst., 1982; asst. adminstr. Univ. Hosp., Syracuse, 1983-85; asst. v.p., hosp. dir. United Health Svcs. Hosp., Binghamton, N.Y., 1985-89, assoc. v.p., hosp. dir., 1989-91, v.p. ops., hosp. dir., 1991-93, exec. v.p., chief oper. officer, 1993-94, pres., CEO, 1994—. Vol. Make-A-Wish Found., Binghamton, 1990-94; bd. dirs. Am. Cancer Soc., Binghamton, 1986-92, Broome County Mental Health Assn., Binghamton, 1990-94; bd. dirs., treas. Leadership Broome, Binghamton, 1990-94. Mem. Am. Coll. Healthcare Execs., N.Y. State Assn. Long Term Care, Rotary Club of Binghamton. Home: 805 River Rd Binghamton NY 13901 Office: United Health Svcs Hosp 33-57 Harrison St Binghamton NY 13790

SALAS, RAFAEL ANGEL, psychologist, army officer; b. Isabela, P.R., Oct. 24, 1956; s. Ramon S. and Ignacia (Cubero) S.; m. Ileana Soto, June 20, 1981; children: Amarilis, Rafael Omar. BA magna cum laude, Inter Am. U. P.R., 1981; MA, Indiana U. Pa., 1986, D Psychology, 1988. Lic. psychologist, Ga. Bilingual mental health worker Family Svc. Assn., Absecon, N.J., 1983-84; bilingual psychologist Ventura Mental Health Svcs., Oxnard, Calif., 1988-90; commd. 2d lt. USAF, 1981; commd. capt. U.S. Army, 1990; psychologist U.S. Army, Ft. Gordon, Ga., 1990—. Mem. APA (fellow 1984). Roman Catholic. Home: 403 Gina Dr Harker Hts TX 76543-6088

SALATICH, JOHN SMYTH, cardiologist; b. New Orleans, Nov. 28, 1926; s. Peter B. and Gladys (Malter) S.; BS cum laude, Loyola U., New Orleans, 1946; MD, La. State U., 1950; m. Patricia L. Mattison, Sept. 26, 1959; children: John Smyth, Elizabeth, Allison, Stephanie. Intern Charity Hosp., New Orleans, 1950-51, resident, 1951-54; practice medicine, specializing in cardiology and internal medicine, New Orleans, 1954-92, Gen. Internal Med. Clinic Tulane Med. Sch., 1992—; dir. EKG dept. Southeastern La. Hosp., Mandeville, La.; prof. clin. medicine La. State U., 1994; mem. staff Touro Infirmary, St. Charles Gen. Hosp.; chmn. dept. medicine Hotel Dieu, 1974-86 pres., New Orleans Emergency Room Corp., Physician Supplemental Services; adv. bd. Bank La., 1960-89; mem. Pres.'s Coun. Loyola U., 1990-92. Bd. dirs. La. Regional Med. Program, 1972. Served to capt. M.C., AUS, 1954-56; Korea. Decorated Medallion of Greek Army. Diplomate Am. Bd. Internal Medicine. Fellow Am. Coll. Chest Physicians, ACP; mem. Am. Heart Assn., La. Heart Assn., New Orleans Acad. Internal Medicine, La. Soc. Internal Medicine, AMA, La. Med. Soc., Orleans Parish Med. Soc., Theta Beta, Alpha Sigma Nu, Delta Epsilon Sigma. Club: New Orleans Country. Contbr. articles to profl. and bus. jours. Home: 433 Country Club Dr New Orleans LA 70124-1038 Office: Nola 70112 144 Elk Pl Ste 1100 New Orleans LA 70112-2636

SALBER, HUBERT WILHELM, psychologist, educator; b. Aachen, Germany, Mar. 9, 1928; s. Johannes and Elisabeth (Wehrens) S.; m. Christa Roericht (div. 1968); children: Daniel, Susanne; m. Linde Wangemann, Aug. 7, 1968. PhD, U. Bonn, Germany, 1952. Prof. psychology U. Cologne, Germany, 1959-61, dir. Inst. Psychology, 1963-93, prof. psychology, 1952—; prof. U. Wurzburg, Germany, 1961-63. Author: Describing Character, 1955, Working-Units, 1969, Psychology of Literature, 1972, Developments of S. Freud's Psychology, 3 vols., 1973, Art-Psychology-Therapy, 1977, Turning Figures, 1978, Fairy-Tales Analyzed, 1987, Psychology of Every-Day Life, 1989, Gestalt on Journey, 1991, Soul-Revolution, 1993, Unthings—Goya's Black Paintings, 1994, Working - Analysis, 1995. Office: U Cologne, Herbert-Lewin-Str 2, Cologne Germany

SALCEDO, JOSE RODOLFO, nephrologist; b. Guadalajara, Jal, Mex., June 15, 1945; came to U.S., 1971; s. Rodolfo Salcedo-Moreno and Sara (Contreras) Moya; m. Uma T. Salcedo, Nov. 8, 1974; children: Nicholas A., Jonathan E. BA, U. Guadalajara, 1964, MD, 1970. Diplomate Am. Bd. Pediatrics, Pediatric Nephrology. Resident Martland Hosp., Newark, 1971-74; fellow, acting dir. pediatric nephrology, dir. dialysis unit Children's Hosp., Washington, 1976-87; dir. pediatric nephrology divsn. N.J. Med. Sch., Newark, 1987-96; chief pediat. nephrology Children's Hosp. St. Joseph's, Paterson, N.J., 1996—. Contbr. chpts. in books and articles to profl. jours. Office: Children's Hospital St Joseph's Paterson NJ

SALCEDO-DOVI, HECTOR E., anatomist, educator; b. Cordoba, Argentina, Apr. 3, 1993; s. Domingo and Rosa (Dovi) Salcedo; m. Adriana Gomez, Apr. 3, 1993. MD, U. Nat. Cordoba, 1984; DO, N.Y. Coll. Osteopathic Medicine, 1995. Asst. prof. anatomy, histology N.Y. Coll. Osteopathic Medicine, Old Westbury, 1990-93, prof. anatomy, physiology, 1993; chie intern Good Samaritan Hosp., 1996—. Mem. Am. Med. Student Assn., Am. Osteopathic Assn. Roman Catholic. Home: 2 Manchester Rd Huntington NY 11743

SALEH, SUHAYL SHUKRI, cardiac surgeon, educator; b. Jaffa, Palestine, Israel, Jan. 20, 1937; s. Shukri Ibrahim Saleh and Anastasia Christophorides; m. Umayma Izzeddine Abzakh, Apr. 25, 1980; children: Shukri, Omar, Tamara. BSc, Am U. Beirut, 1957, MD, 1961. Diplomate Am. Bd. Surgery, Am. Bd. Thoracic Surgery. Resident in gen. surgery Am. U., Beirut, 1961-65; resident in thoracic surgery U. Miss. Med. Ctr., Jackson, 1965-67; cons. in surgery Royal Med. Svcs., Amman, Jordan, 1968-83, Khalidi and Islamic Hosp., Amman, 1983—; vis. prof. Am. U. Beirut Sch. Medicine, 1980-82; chief staff Queen Alia Heart Inst., Amman, 1981-83; clin. prof. Jordan U. Sch. Medicine, Jordan, 1985—. Mem. Alpha Omega Alpha. Home: PO Box 5151, Amman Jordan

SALEME, SALVATORE ALPHONSE, pharmacist; b. Revere, Mass., Apr. 21, 1923; s. Rosario and Clorinda M. (Filadoro) S.; m. Orlinda A. Imperiali, Aug. 1, 1954; children: Carol Anne Saleme Brent, Paul E. BS in Pharmacy, Mass. Coll. Pharmacy, 1943. Registered pharmacist, Mass., Va., Md. Pharmacist, 1942-50, owner, pharmacist, 1950-61; owner, pharmacist Cataldo Pharmacy, Wakefield, Mass., 1961-63; exec. dir. Mass. Pharm. Assn., Boston, 1963-67; dir. profl. svcs. Henry B. Gilpin Co., Washington, 1967-72, 74-78; dir. pharmacy and cen. supply Potomac Hosp., Woodbridge, Va., 1972-74; v.p. Pracon Inc., Heath Info., Fairfax, Va., 1978-81; dir. drug info. systems Med. Econs. Co., Oradell, N.J., 1981-84; dir. mktg. and electronic drug info. systems U.S. Pharmacopeia, Rockville, Md., 1984-87; dir. devel. Drug Data Systems, Fairfax, 1987—. Author electronic database Patient Medication Adv. Electronic Drug Reference. Mem. Am. Pharm. Assn. Home and Office: 4630 Luxberry Dr Fairfax VA 22032-1927

SALETTA, JOHN DANIEL, surgeon; b. Chgo., May 20, 1937; s. Frank John and Genevieve Margaret (Halton) S.; m. Suzanne Norberta Shay, July 9, 1960; children: John, Thomas, Suzanne, Mary, Michael. BS, U. Notre Dame, 1959; MD, Loyola U., 1962. Intern Cook County Hosp., Chgo., 1962-63, resident, 1965-69, attending surgeon, 1969-76, chief gen. surgery, 1972-76; attending surgeon Holy Cross Hosp., Chgo., 1976-82; chmn. dept. surgery Luth. Gen. Hosp., Park Ridge, Ill., 1982-89, chief gen. surgery, dir. surg. resident edn., 1989—; asst. prof. surgery U. Ill., Chgo., 1970-72, assoc. prof., 1972-76, clin. prof., 1982-93; clin. prof. surgery U. chgo., 1993—. Capt. USAF, 1963-65. Mem. Am. Coll. Surgeons (credentials com. 1982—, com. applicants 1982—), Ill. Surg. Soc. (pres. 1985-86), Chgo. Surg. Soc. (pres. 1988-89). Roman Catholic. Office: Luth Gen Hosp 1775 Dempster Park Ridge IL 60068

SALGADO, ANTONIO VASCO, neurologist, researcher; b. Lisbon, Portugal, June 27, 1955; s. Antonio Maria and Maria Ines (Sande e Castro) S.; m. Raffaella Dintino, Sept. 21, 1992. Degree in medicine, Faculdade de Medicina de Lisboa, Lisbon, 1980. Diplomate Am. Bd. Psychiatry and Neurology; cert. Ordem dos Médicos. Intern Hosp. de S. Maria, Lisbon, 1981-82; resident Mt. Sinai Hosp., N.Y.C., 1983-86; fellow Cleve. Clinic, 1986-88; instr. in neurology FML, 1989-96; dir. neurology HFF, Amadora, Portugal, 1996—. Home: Rua Cecilio Sousa 23 3 Esq, 1200 Lisbon Portugal Office: Hosp Fernando da Fonseca, Dept Neurology, Amadora Portugal

SALGANICOFF, LEON, pharmacology educator; b. Buenos Aires, Sept. 11, 1924; came to U.S., 1964; s. Marcos Salganicoff and Ana Rosa Zelicson; m. Matilde Saffier, Dec. 11, 1957; children, Alina, Marcos. MSc in Pharmacy, U. Buenos Aires, 1948, DSc in Biochemistry, 1955. Instr. U. Buenos Aires, 1947-49; chief clin. pathologist Hosp. Mil. Cen., Buenos Aires, 1955-59; chief lab. Conicet, Buenos Aires, 1959-64; rsch. asst. Nat. Coun. Investigation, Buenos Aires, 1959-64; rsch. fellow Johnson Found., U. Pa., Phila., 1965-68, Nat. Multiple Sclerosis Soc., 1968-71; assoc. prof. pharmacology Temple U., Phila., 1972-84, sect. leader, 1971—, prof. pharmacology Med. Sch., 1976-95, prof. emeritus, 1995—; vis. prof. U. Rome la Sapienza, 1976—, NATO vis. prof., 1992; dir. rsch. Barnett Found. for Mitochondrial Diseases. Grantee NIH, 1984-87; recipient W.W. Smith Charitable Trust award, 1992. Mem. AAAS, Fedn. Am. Socs. Exptl. Biology, Sigma Xi. Home: 556 N 23rd St Philadelphia PA 19130-3117 Office: Temple U Sch Medicine 3400 N Broad St Philadelphia PA 19140-5196

SALIBELLO, COSMO, business executive, optometrist; b. N.Y.C., Sept. 21, 1943; s. Joseph and Maria (Patalano) S.; m. Jane Susan Wilde Crawford, July 1, 1984. B Mgmt. Engring., Rensselaer Poly. Inst., 1965; BA in Biology summa cum laude, Ctrl. Wash. U., 1979; B Visual Sci., Pacific U., Forest Grove, Oreg., 1981, OD, 1983. Lic. optometrist, Oreg., Wash. Mgmt. devel. assoc. Bendix Corp., Elmira, N.Y., 1965-66; dep. aircrew tng. mgr. Grumman Aerospace, Tehran, Iran, 1974-76; pvt. practice, Salem, Oreg., 1983-91; pres., chmn. Applied Vision Concepts, Inc., Portland, Oreg., 1991-93; v.p. tech. PRIO Corp., Lake Oswego, Oreg., 1993—, also bd. dirs.; cons. on VDT workplace, Salem, 1983-91; mem. bd. optometry advisors Pacific U., 1986-93. Contbr. articles to profl. jours.; inventor VDT prescription sys. Mem., baritone Ellensburg (Wash.) Cmty. Choir, 1977-79; pres. Laurel West Homeowners Assn., Forest Grove, 1979-82. Lt. comdr. USN, 1966-74, Vietnam. Fellow Am. Acad. Optometry; mem. Am. Optometric Assn., Human Factors and Ergonomics Soc., Oreg. Optometric Assn., Portland Met. Optometric Soc. Office: PRIO Corp 4000 Kruse Way Pl Ste 2-355 Lake Oswego OR 97035

SALINGER, CHARLES, dermatologist; b. N.Y.C.; s. Ernest and Mae (Brenner) S.; m. Donna Marcia Gafford, May 14, 1974; children: Jennifer, Jeffrey. BS, U. Wis., 1965; MD, SUNY, Syracuse, 1968. Lic. M.D., Calif. Intern Charity Hosp., La. State U., New Orleans, 1968-69, resident in dermatology, 1969-72; chief of dermatology USAF Maxwell Hosp., Montgomery, Ala., 1972-74; pvt. practice, dermatology La Mirada, Calif., 1974—; chief med. staff La Mirada (Calif.) Cmty. Hosp., 1987-88; clin. assoc. prof. dermatology, Coll. Osteo. Medicine, Pomona, Calif., 1977—; trustee Med. Ctr. La Mirada, 1985-90. Major USAF, 1972-74. Fellow Am. Acad. Dermatology, Am. Soc. Dermatologic Surgery, Internat. Soc. Dermatologic Surgery, Pacific Dermatologic Assn., L.A. Met. Dermatologic Soc. (pres. 1994-95, bd. dirs. 1987—); mem. AMA, Calif. Med. Assn., L.A. County Med. Assn. Jewish. Home: 5440 Emerywood Dr Buena Park CA 90621 Office: 12625 La Mirada Blvd La Mirada CA 90638

SALITERMAN, LAURA SHRAGER, pediatrician; b. N.Y.C., June 26, 1946; d. Arthur M. and Ida (Wildman) Shrager; m. Richard Arlen Saliterman, June 15, 1975; 1 child, Robert Warren. AB magna cum laude, Brandeis U., 1967; MD, NYU, 1971. Intern Montefiore Hosp. and Med. Ctr., Bronx, N.Y., 1971-72, resident in pediatrics, 1972-74; pediatrician Morrisania Family Care Ctr., N.Y.C., 1974-75; pediatrician Share Health Plan, St. Paul, 1975-85, dir. pediatrics, 1976-82; pediatrician Aspen Med. Group, St. Paul, 1985-91, South Lake Clinic, Minnetonka, 1991—; clin. asst. prof. U. Minn. Med. Sch. Mem. Am. Acad. Pediatrics (chair accident prevention com. Minn. chpt. 1985-89), Phi Beta Kappa. Club: Oak Ridge. Home: 11911 Live Oak Dr Hopkins MN 55305-2597 Office: 17705 Hutchins Dr Minnetonka MN 55345-4145

SALKIN, PAUL, psychiatrist; b. Bklyn., Dec. 22, 1932; s. Bernard David and Evelyn Salkin; m. Nesrin Bignöl, Nov. 20, 1959; 1 child, David. BA, NYU, 1954, MD, 1956. Intern Kings County Hosp., Bklyn., 1956-57; resident Bronx (N.Y.) Mcpl. Hosp., 1957-60; staff psychiatrist Hillside Hosp., Queens, N.Y., 1960-66; pvt. practice N.Y.C. and South Salem, N.Y., 1960—; co-dir. Assn. for Male Sexual Dysfunction, N.Y.C.; med. dir. Ctr. for Therapeutic Arts, Patterson, N.Y., 1991—. Author: Assessment of Current Knowledge in Psychiatry, 1976. Fellow Am. Psychiat. Assn., N.Y. Acad. Medicine; mem. Am. Acad. Psychoanalysis, Westchester Psychiat. Soc. (chmn. pvt. practice com. 1988), Am. Acad. Psychiatry and Law, Publicity Lodge, Masons. Jewish. Office: 200 E End Ave New York NY 10128-7831

SALKIND, GENE ZACHARY, neurosurgeon; b. Phila., Sept. 29, 1953; m. Catherine P. Malloy; 1 child, Julian R. BA cum laude, Univ. Pa., 1974; MD, Temple Univ. Sch. Medicine, 1979. Diplomate Am. Bd. Neurological Surgery. Attending physician Jeanes Hosp., Phila., 1985-95, Germantown Hosp. & Medical Ctr., Phila., 1985—, Albert Einstein, Phila., 1986-94; chief divsn. neurosurgery Jeanes Hosp., 1995—; assoc. chief Albert Einstein, 1994-95, chief divsn. neurosurgery, 1995—; attending physician Allegheny U. Hosps., 1996—, co-dir. divsn. cmty. neurosurgical, 1996—; assoc. prof. neurosurgery Med. Coll. Pa./Hahnemann U.; bd. dirs. Temple Univ. Sch. Medicine, 1993—. Mem. Am. Assn. Neurosurgical Surgeons, AMA, Congress of Neurological Surgeons, Mid-Atlantic Neurosurgical Soc., Pa. Neurosurgical Soc., Phila. County Medical Soc., Phila. Neurosurgical Soc., The Medical Club Phila. Office: Allegheny U. Hosps 1601 Walnut St Ste 908 Philadelphia PA 19103

SALLEY, JOHN JONES, university administrator, oral pathologist; b. Richmond, Va., Oct. 29, 1926; s. Thomas Raysor and Kathryn (Josey) S.; m. Jean Gordon Cunningham, Dec. 21, 1950; children: Katharine Gordon, John Jones, Martha Cunningham. DDS, Med. Coll. Va., 1951; PhD, U. Rochester, 1954; DSc, Boston U., 1975. Research fellow U. Rochester, 1951-54; from instr. to prof., chmn. dept. oral pathology Med. Coll. Va., 1954-63, prof. emeritus, 1991—; prof. pathology, dean Sch. Dentistry U. Md., 1963-74, dean emeritus Sch. Dentistry, 1977—, ret., 1991; v.p. research and grad. affairs Va. Commonwealth U., Richmond, 1974-85; acting pres. Va. Ctr. for Innovative Tech., 1985, v.p., 1985-87; cons. div. research grants NIH, 1962-66; cons. U.S. Naval Dental Sch., Bethesda, Md., 1966-75; spl. cons. Nat. Inst. Dental Research, NIH, 1957-64; cons. USPHS Hosp., Balt., 1963-74, U.S. Naval Hosp., Portsmouth, Va., VA Hosp., Balt., 1964-74; dental health div. USPHS; mem. Md. Adv. Council Comprehensive Health Planning, 1968-74, Nat. Health Council, 1970-71; pres. Am. Assn. Dental Schs., 1971-72, Conf. So. Grad. Schs., 1983-84; sr. program cons. Robert Wood Johnson Found., 1978-84; mem. career devel. rev. com. VA, 1974-78; mem. com. health care resources in VA, NRC, 1974-77; cons. WHO, 1969-75; mem. Va. Gov.'s Task Force Sci. and Tech., 1982-83, sci. advisor to Gov. of Va., 1984-86; mem. research com. Va. State Council Higher Edn., 1974-84; chmn. task force Council Grad. Schs. in U.S., 1979-82. Contbr. articles in field; editorial rev. bd.: Jour. Dental Edn, 1974-78. Bd. dirs. Md. divsn. Am. Cancer Soc., 1963-70, Am. Fund Dental Health, Nat. Found. Dentistry for the Handicapped, 1986, pres., 1992-94; mem. adv. bd. Va. Inst. for Devel. Disabilities, 1987-91; bd. trustees Middlesex County Pub. Libr., 1994—, pres., 1995—. With USAAF, 1944-46. Recipient Outstanding Civilian Service medal Dept. Army, 1961, Disting. Citizenship award State Md., 1974. Fellow AAAS, Am. Coll. Dentists; mem. ADA, Nat. Conf. Univ. Research Adminstrs., Am. Acad. Oral Pathology, Internat. Assn. Dental Research (Novice award 1953), Internat. Med. Informatics Assn. (chmn. working group 1989-92), Sigma Xi, Sigma Zeta, Omicron Kappa Upsilon. Episcopalian (vestryman). Home and Office: PO Box 838 Urbanna VA 23175-0838

SALLMAN, ALAN L., physician; b. Phila., June 26, 1951; s. Bennett and Eileen Virginia (Ellsworth) S.; m. Nancy Lee Sereda, May 22, 1973; children:

Jennifer Lynn, Jonathan Michael. BA, Johns Hopkins U., 1973; MD, U. Fla., 1977. Intern, resident Eastern Va. U., Norfolk, 1977-80; instr. medicine U. Ky., Lexington, 1982-84; asst. prof. medicine U. Ark., Little Rock, 1984-88; physician pvt. practice, Winter Haven, Fla., 1988—. Contbr. articles to profl. jours. Renal fellow U. Miami, 1982. Fellow Am. Coll. Physicians. Office: Bond Clinic 500 E Central Ave Winter Haven FL 33880

SALMAN, JENAN AL-YAZDI, pharmacist, small business owner; b. Basrah, Iraq, May 3, 1948; came to U.S., 1973; d. Mahmood M. Al-Yazdi and Sadeeka Sh. Ridha; m. Kadhim N. Salman, July 17, 1968, Feb. 21, 1969; children: Ayser, Zaid, Lameace. BA in Pharmacy, Bagdad, Iraq, 1969; PharmD, U. Ky., 1990. Pharmacist pvt. drug store, Bagdad, 1970-73; research technician Ohio State U. Sch. Pharmacy, Columbus, 1974-75; research asst. Ohio State U. Vet. Sci., Columbus, 1975-77; rsch. analyst Coll. Pharmacy U. Ky., Lexington, 1977-78, Agriculture Sta. U. Ky., Lexington, 1978-79; sci. demonstrator Coll. Medicine King Saud U., Saudi Arabia, 1980-85; pres., owner J.J. Gazelle Ltd., Lexington, 1985-88; clin. coord. Merrillville, Ind., 1990-92; clin. pharmacy mgr. Valley Hosp. Med. Ctr., Las Vegas, 1992—. Contbr. articles to profl. jours. Home: 9720 Trail Rider Dr Las Vegas NV 89117-6624 Office: Valley Hosp Med Ctr 620 Shadow Ln Las Vegas NV 89106

SALMOIRAGHI, GIAN CARLO, physiologist, educator; b. Gorla Minore, Italy, Sept. 19, 1924; came to U.S., 1952, naturalized, 1958; s. Giuseppe Carlo and Dina (Rinetti) S.; m. Eva Tchoukourlieva, Dec. 5, 1970; 1 child, George Charles. MD, U. Rome, 1948; PhD, McGill U., 1959; DSc (hon.), Hahnemann U., 1995. Sr. med. officer Internat. Refugee Orgn., Naples, Italy, 1949-52; research fellow Cleve. Clinic Found., 1952-55; lectr. dept. physiology McGill U., Montreal, Que., Can., 1956-58; from neurophysiologist to dir., div. spl. mental health research NIMH, Washington, 1959-73; assoc. commr. research N.Y. State Dept. Mental Hygiene, Albany, 1973-77; assoc. dir. for research Nat. Inst. Alcohol Abuse, HHS, Bethesda, Md., 1977-84; prof. neurology and physiology Hahnemann U., Phila., 1984-85, vice provost for research affairs, 1984-85, chmn. dept. physiology, asst. v.p sci. affairs, 1986-94; clin. prof. psychiatry George Washington U., 1966-73. Contbr. articles to profl. jours. Recipient Superior Service award HEW, 1970. Fellow Am. Coll. Neuropsychopharmacology; mem. AAAS, Am. Physiol. Soc., Am. Soc. Pharmacology and Exptl. Therapeutics, Internat. Brain Research Orgn., Internat. Soc. Psychoneuroendocrinology, Am. Psychiat. Assn., Soc. Neurosci., Royal Soc. Medicine, Soc. Biol. Psychiat., Assn. Research Neurol. and Mental Disease, Research Soc. Alcoholism, Assn. Chmn. Dept. Physiology, Sci. Research Soc., Sigma Xi. Club: Cosmos (Washington). Home: 8216 Hamilton Spring Ct Bethesda MD 20817-2714

SALMON, J. WARREN, pharmacy educator; b. Phila., Apr. 28, 1947; s. John Warren and Florence (McGrath) S.; m. Agatha Marie Gallo, May 24, 1981; children: Christopher John, Bethany Rose. BS, Drexel U., 1970; MS, Cornell U., 1972, PhD, 1978. Asst. to adminstrv. asst. Presbyn.-U. Pa. Med. Ctr., Phila., 1967; adminstrv. asst. to treas. Hahnemann U., Phila., 1968-69, asst. adminstr. for ambulatory care, 1970, orgn. devel. cons., 1970-72; program dir. Greater Del. Valley Regional Med. Program Arthritis Control, Phila., 1974-76; asst. prof. dept. community medicine Hahnemann Med. U., Phila., 1972-79, assoc. prof., 1979-83; prof., coord. health policy and planning specialization U. Ill., Chgo., 1984-90, prof., head dept. pharmacy adminstrn., 1990—; cons. Chilton Rsch. Svcs., Radnor, Pa., 1983, Am. Inst. for Rsch., Cambridge, Mass., 1983-84; cons. on conservation human resources Columbia U., N.Y.C., 1987-90. Editor: Alternative Medicines: Popular and Policy Perspectives, 1984 (award Am. Jour. Nursing 1984), Symposium and Public Hearings on Corporation of Health Care, 1987, Community Empowerment in Health Promotion Strategies, 1989, Corporate Transformation of Health Care, Part I, 1990, Part II, 1994. Mem. health com. Met. Planning Coun., Chgo., 1987-91; co-chmn. health needs com. United Way Chgo., 1990-91; past bd. dirs. Planned Parenthood Chgo., United Cerebral Palsy Phila. Fellow Inst. Medicine Chgo.; mem. APHA, Am. Assn. Coll. Pharmacy, Health and Medicine Policy Rsch. Group (bd. dirs., sec. 1989-91), Acad. Managed Care Pharmacy, Ill. Pub. Health Assn., Alpha Kappa Psi (life). Home: 348 Forest Ave River Forest IL 60305-2008 Office: U Ill Coll Pharmacy M C # 871 Chicago IL 60612

SALMON, VINCENT, acoustical consultant; b. Kingston, Jamaica, Jan. 21, 1912; came to U.S., 1914; s. Albert James and Ethlin (Baruch) S.; m. Madeline L. Giuffra, June 11, 1937 (dec. 1977); children—Margaret Elizabeth, Jean Louise. B.A., Temple U., 1934, M.A., 1936; Ph.D., MIT, 1938. Registered profl. engr., Calif. Physicist research and devel. Jensen Mfg. Co., Chgo., 1939-49; mgr. sonics sect. Stanford Research Inst., Menlo Park, Calif., 1949-65; staff scientist SRI Internat., Menlo Park, Calif., 1965-94; acoustical cons., Chgo., 1946-49, Menlo Park, 1949-71, 76—; dir. Acoustical Svcs., v.p., sec. Indsl. Helath, Inc., 1971-76; cons. prof. dept. aeronautics and astronautics Stanford U., Calif., 1977-95. Contbr. articles to profl. jours.; inventor new family of horns, 1942, 46. Pres. Palo Alto Sr. Housing Project, Calif., 1966; v.p. Stebbins Found. for Community Facilities, San Francisco, 1966; pres. Planned Parenthood Assn. of Santa Clara County, 1967, Sr. Coordinating Council of Palo Alto, 1971. Recipient Disting. Alumnus award Temple U., Phila., 1964. Fellow Acoustical Soc. Am. (pres. 1970-71, Biennial award 1946, Silver Medal in engring. acoustics 84), Audio Engring. Soc. (life charter, western v.p. 1958-59); mem. Chgo. Audio and Acoustical Group (founder, pres. 1948), Inst. Noise Control Engring. (pres. 1974-75), Nat. Council of Acoustical Cons. (pres. 1969-71). Democrat. Unitarian. Club: Stanford Faculty. Home: 765 Hobart St Menlo Park CA 94025-5705

SALMON, WATT THOMAS, psychiatrist; b. Erath County, Tex., Jan. 30, 1927; s. Thomas Harvey and Katie (Knick) S.; BS, So. Meth. U., 1950; MD, U. Tenn., Memphis, 1954; m. Barbara Jean Smith, 1962; children: Amelia Gail, Thomas Harald. Fellow, Menninger Sch. Psychiatry, Topeka, 1957-60, mem. faculty, 1960-77; chief outpatient services Topeka VA Hosp., 1965-69; staff Menninger Meml. Hosp. and Menninger Found., 1969-77; pvt. practice medicine specializing in psychiatry, Amarillo, Tex., 1977-81; med. dir. outpatient services Amarillo Psychiat. Pavilion, 1978-81; asso. prof. Tex. Tech. Med. Sch., 1978-92, dir. residency tng., 1982-87, chief psychiatry Amarillo VA Ctr., 1988-94; dir. Psychiat. Ambulatory Clinic, 1978-82. Diplomate Am. Bd. Psychiatry. Mem. Am. Acad. Psychiatry and Law, Am. Psychiat. Assn., Tex. Soc. Psychiatric Physicians, Alumni Assn. Menninger Sch. Psychiatry. Office: 3418 Rutson Dr Amarillo TX 79109-3930

SALO, HARRY A., health care executive; b. Rahway, N.J., Jan. 27, 1944; s. E. Arthur and Nina (Hill) S.; m. Karen Waugh, Sept. 7, 1964 (div. 1972); 1 child, Jannine; m. Carol Ann Vath, Mar. 17, 1973; children: Jessica, Adam. BA, Cornell U., 1967; MA, Barry U., 1974; postgrad., Columbia U., 1974, NYU, 1974-75. Tchr. Miami (Fla.) Country Day Sch., 1967-69, Fairfield (Conn.) Country Day Sch., 1968-74; MA Barry U., 1969; dir. admissions Fairfield (Conn.) Country Day Sch., 1972-74; adminstr. Med. Pers. Pool, Cin., 1975-77; v.p. Salo Inc., Cin., 1977-79; v.p., founder T.S.O. Mgmt. Corp., Media, Pa., 1979-84, pres., 1984-90, chmn., 1990—; chmn. bd. dirs. Ind. Franchise Assn., San Francisco; mem. Owners Adv. Coun., Ft. Lauderdale, Fla., 1981-82, chmn., 1993—. Bd. dirs. Women Against Rape, Delaware County, Pa., 1985-88; mem. leadership group, exec. dir.'s adv. coun. Amnesty Internat., N.Y.C., 1989—; fundraiser Berkshire Sch., Sheffield, Mass., 1990; vol. Oxfam Am., N.Y.C., 1991—. Recipient L.E. Dettman Founders award Pers. Pool Am., 1981, Raymond Herrighes Mgmt. award, 1986. Office: TSO Mgmt Corp 113 N Olive St Media PA 19063-2809

SALO, JONATHAN, surgeon; b. Mpls., Jan. 24, 1959; s. Melvin F. and Alice (Bell) S.; m. Victoria Kohlstadt, Sept. 15, 1990; children: Daniel, Emily. BS in Biology, Stanford (Calif.) U., 1981; MD, U. Calif., San Francisco, 1985. Diplomate Am. Bd. Surgery. Resident in gen. surgery U. Calif., San Francisco, 1985-93; med. staff fellow Nat. Cancer Inst., Bethesda, Md., 1988-91; clin. assoc. NIH, Bethesda, 1993-96; surg. oncology fellow Meml. Sloan-Kettering, N.Y.C., 1996—. Office: Memorial Sloan-Kettering Dept Surgery 1275 York Ave New York NY 10021

SALOMON, DAVID SCOTT, oncology researcher; b. N.Y.C., Sept. 30, 1947; s. Leicester and Elizabeth (Scott) S.; m. Jane Foran, May 7, 1984 (div.); 1 chld, Matthew; m. Kathy Chestnutt, July 3, 1994; children: Robin, Christopher. BS, Clark U., 1969; PhD, SUNY, Albany, 1973. Postdoctoral fellow Roche Inst. Molecular Biology, Nutley, N.J., 1973-75; with Lab. Devel. Biology NIDR/NIH, 1975-79; with Lab. of Pathophysiology Nat. Cancer Inst./NIH, Bethesda, Md., 1979-83, chief tumor growth factor sect. Lab. Tumor Immunology, 1983—. Assoc. editor Breast Cancer Rsch. and Treatment, 1993—, Internat. Jour. Oncology, 1994—, Topics in Mammary Gland Biology and Neoplasia, 1995—, Cancer Reports Bull., 1995—; contbr. chpts. to books, some 150 articles to profl. jours.; patenteecloned human cripto gene and applications thereof, human cripto-related gene. Mem. Am. Assn. Cancer Rsch., Am. Soc. for Biochemistry and Molecular Biology. Home: 604 Sunnybrook Terrace Rd Gaithersburg MD 20877 Office: Nat Cancer Inst Lab Tumor Immunology Wisconsin Ave Bethesda MD 20892

SALOMON, JACK BARRY, family medicine; b. Highland Park, Mich., July 5, 1945; s. William and Minnie Deborah (Salzberg) S.; m. Audrey Ruth Blautz, Nov. 12, 1974; children: Mark, Garret, Jessica. BA, Wayne State U., 1969, MD, 1971. Instr. family medicine Wayne State U., Detroit, 1974-75; sr. staff Met. Med. Group, Dearborn, Mich., 1975-77, Plymouth Gen. Hosp., Detroit, 1977-79, Group Health Plan of S.E. Mich., Warren, 1979-83; chmn. Somerset Med. Group, Troy, Mich., 1983-85; sr. staff Selectcare, Warren, 1985-89; sr. staff Henry Ford Med. Group, Sterling Heights, Mich., 1989—, chmn. managed care com. N.E., 1993—; cons. Health Alliance Plan, Detroit, 1989-91. Mem. Am. Coll. Physician Execs. Office: Henry Ford Medical Group 3500 15 Mile Rd Sterling Heights MI 48310

SALOMONE, JOSEPH ANTHONY, III, emergency medicine physician; b. Reno, June 5, 1958; s. Joseph Anthony and Peggy Ruth (Crompton) S.; m. Cynthia Amelia Douglas, Aug. 10, 1980; children: Joseph Kenneth, Christopher Anthony. BS, U. Nev., 1979, MD, 1983. Diplomate Am. Bd. Emergency Medicine. Intern in gen. surgery Truman Med. Ctr., Kansas City, 1983-84, resident in emergency medicine, 1984-86, fellow in emergency medicine, 1986-87, rsch. dir. emergency medicine, 1987-88, assoc. residency dir., 1990—, assoc. prof. emergency medicine, 1994—; med. dir. Met. Ambulance Svcs., Kansas City, 1988-89; staff physician Bapt Med. Ctr., Asheville, N.C., 1989-90; chmn. Emergency Physicians Adv. Bd., Kansas City, 1992-94. Author: Toxicology Guide for Emergency Medicine, 1988, Emergency Medicine, 1995; editor: Critical Decision in Emergency Medicine, 1995. Cubmaster Pack 397 Boy Scouts Am., Kearney, Mo., 1994—, webelos leader, 1993-95, den leader, asst. adminstr., 1991-93. Fellow Am. Coll. Emergency Medicine; mem. Am. Coll. Emergency Physicians (mem. emergency med. svcs. com. Mo. chpt. 1990-94), Soc. for Acad Emergency Medicine, Coun. Residency Dirs., Nat. Assn. Emergency Med. Svc. Physicians (state liaison 1988-90). Baptist. Office: Truman Med Ctr Dept Emergency Medicine 2301 Holmes Rd Kansas City MO 64108

SALTER, DAVID ROBERT, cardiac surgeon, educator; b. St. Anthony, Nfld., Jan. 28, 1950; s. Robert Bruce and Agnes Robina (McGee) S.; m. Margita Ibergs, June 28, 1973. MD, U. Toronto, 1974; fellow gen. surgery, U. Toronto, Ont., Can., 1981, fellow cardiac surgery, 1983. Family practice N.S., Can., 1975-77; surgical pathology Auckland U., New Zealand, 1977; gen. surgery resident U. Toronto, 1977-81; cardiovascular and thoracic surgery U. Toronto, Ont., Can., 1981-83; assoc staff ct surgeon Toronto Western Hosp., 1983-84; Duke Surg. Rsch. fellow Duke U., Durham, N.C., 1984-86; asst. prof. surgery Toronto Western Hosp., 1986-89, Med. Coll. Va., Richmond, 1989-96; assoc. prof. surgery Med. Coll. of Va., Richmond, 1996—, dir. undergrad. surg. edn., 1993—; chief cardiac and thoracic surgeon McGuire VA Med. Ctr. McGuire VA Med. Ctr., Richmond, 1989—. Contbr. articles Circulation, Jour. Thoracic Medicine, Cardiovascular Surgery. Recipient Humeris award rsch. fellow MC Humeris Soc., Richmond, 1991, 93. Fellow ACS, Royal Coll. Surgeons of Can., Am. Coll. Cardiology; mem. Can. and Ontario Med. Assns. Office: Med Coll of Va PO Box 68 1200 E Broad St Richmond VA 23298

SALTER, EDWIN CARROLL, physician; b. Oklahoma City, Jan. 19, 1927; s. Leslie Ernest and Maud (Carroll) S.; m. Ellen Gertrude Malone, June 30, 1962; children—Mary Susanna, David Patrick. B.A., DePauw U., 1947; M.D., Northwestern U., 1951. Intern Cook County Hosp., Chgo., 1951-53; resident in pediatrics Children's Meml. Hosp., Chgo., 1956-58, Cook County Hosp., Chgo., 1956-58; practice medicine specializing in pediatrics Lake Forest, Ill., 1958—; attending physician Lake Forest Hosp., 1958—, pres. med. staff, 1981-82; attending physician Children's Meml. Hosp., Chgo.; clin. faculty mem. dept. pediatrics Northwestern U. Med. Sch. Served to capt. M.C., U.S. Army, 1954-56. Mem. AMA, Ill. State Med. Soc., Lake County Med. Soc. (pres. 1984), Phi Beta Kappa. Republican. Methodist. Home: 19 N Maywood Rd Lake Forest IL 60045-3233 Office: 900 N Westmoreland Rd Ste 110 Lake Forest IL 60045-1688

SALTER, LEO GUILFORD, mental health services professional; b. Atlanta, Nov. 12, 1937; s. Robert Franklin and Era Mae (Mask) S.; m. Evelyn Sue Clements. BA, Ga. State U., 1962; MEd, U. Ga., 1966; PhD, U. So. Miss., 1972. Lic. clin. psychologist, Fla.. Exec. dir. Human Resources Ctr., Daytona Beach, Fla., 1975-80; asst. dir. ACT Corp., Daytona Beach, 1980-85, dir. psychology svcs., 1986-91; pres. Behavioral Health Svcs., Daytona Beach, 1988—; adj. prof. Stetson U., Deland, Fla., 1980-91; clin. cons. West Volusia Meml. Hosp., Deland, 1988—; bd. dirs. AFCC Corp., Daytona Beach. Author: Labor Research Project, 1968. Del. Fla. State Dem. Conv., Hollywood, 1984; mem. Dem. Exec. Com., Volusia County, 1991. With USN, 1958-62. Recipient Excellence in Crime and Drug Intervention award ARP, Daytona Beach, 1987, Spl. Commendation award Nat. Coun. Cmty. Mental Health, Washington, 1980, Outstanding Svc. award Dist. Mental Health Bd., Volusia County, 1978, Outstanding Vol. Svc. award State of Fla., 1978, Spl. Commendation award Fla. Coun. for Cmty. Mental Health, 1993, Clinician of Yr. award ACT Corp., 1995. Mem. Am. Psychol. Assn., Fla. Psychol. Assn. Home: 1980 Reynolds Rd De Leon Springs FL 32130-3262 Office: ACT Corp 1220 Willis Ave Daytona Beach FL 32114-2810

SALTZBERG, EUGENE ERNEST, physician, educator; b. Chgo., Feb. 2, 1947; s. Samuel and Florence (Weiner) S.; m. Roberta Rice, Apr. 28, 1984; children: Noah Edward, Evan Hale, Paige Erica. BA in Psychology cum laude, U. Ill., 1968; MD, Chgo. Med. Sch. U. Health Scis., 1972. Diplomate Am. Bd. Emergency Medicine, Am. Bd. Med. Examiners. Resident Children's Meml. Hosp., Chgo., 1974; health officer Pitkin County, Aspen, Colo., 1975-79; clin. instr. dept. medicine Northwestern U., Chgo., 1981—; chief of staff Condell Med. Ctr., Libertyville, Ill., 1996-97; med. dir. The Lambs Farm, Libertyville, 1986—; asst. clin. prof. U. Health Svcs. Chgo. Med. Sch., 1988—. Fellow Am. Coll. Emergency Physicians; mem. Univ. Assn. for Emergency Medicine, Soc. for Critical Care Medicine, Physicians for Social Responsibility, Am. Coll. Physicians. Jewish. Home: 620 Euclid Ct Highland Park IL 60035-1271

SALTZMAN, MELVIN BORIS, physician; b. Bronx, N.Y., Oct 22, 1950; s. Jonas Ernest and Marion (Severs) S.; m. Louise F. Sobel, June 10, 1973; children—Sarah, Stephanie, Samantha, Michael. B.A. in Biology, CUNY, 1972; D.O., Mich. State U. Coll. Osteo. Medicine, 1975. Diplomate Nat. Bd. Examiners Osteo. Physicians and Surgeons, Am. Osteo. Bd. Internal Medicine, Am. Bd. Internal Medicine with subsplty. in gastroenterology. Intern Zieger-Botsford Osteo. Hosp., Detroit, Farmington Hills, 1975-76, resident in internal medicine, 1976-79; clin. fellow in gastroenterology Yale U. Sch. Medicine, New Haven, 1979-81; staff physician Deaconess West, 1981—. North and South, St. Louis, 1981—, DePaul Med. Ctr., St. Louis, 1984—, St. Peters (Mo.) Community Hosp., 1985, Christian Hosps., 1987, St Anthony's Hosp, 1989—, Missouri Bapt. Hosp, 1996—, chief staff Deaconess West Hosp 1993-1995; del. numerous sci. meetings. Contbr. articles to profl. jours. Fellow Am. Coll. Osteopathic Internists; mem. Am. Osteo. Assn., Am. Soc. Parenteral and Enteral Nutrition, Mo. Assn. Osteo. Physicians and Surgeons, St. Louis Assn. Osteo. Physicians and Surgeons, Am. Soc. Gastrointestinal Endoscopy. Avocation: photography, computers. Office: 12277 DePaul Dr Ste 404 Bridgeton MO 63044

SALVADOR, RICHARD ANTHONY, pharmaceutical company executive; b. Albany, N.Y., May 19, 1927; s. Domenico and Irma Ida Salvador; m. Carole Snarski, Sept. 17, 1966; children: Barbara, Diana. BS in Chemistry-Biology, Siena Coll., 1951; AM in Pharmacology, Boston U., 1953; PhD in Pharmacology, George Washington U., 1956. Rsch. fellow Boston U. Sch. Medicine, 1951-53, George Washington U. Sch. Medicine, Washington, 1953-57; postdoctoral fellow NIH, Bethesda, Md., 1957-58; rsch. instr. Sch. U. Wash. U., St. Louis, 1958-60; sr. pharmacologist Burroughs Wellcome & Co., Tuckahoe, N.Y., 1960-69; group chief biochem. nutrition Hoffmann-La Roche Inc., Nutley, N.J., 1970-73, sect. head pharmacology, 1973-75, asst. dir. pharmacology, 1975-79, dir. exptl. therapeutics, 1979-83, asst. v.p. exptl. therapeutics, 1983-85, v.p. preclin. devel., 1985-94, v.p. internat. preclin. devel., 1984—. With U.S. Army, 1945-47. Mem. AAAS, Am. Assn. Pharmaceutics Scientists, Am. Soc. Pharmacology and Exptl. Therapeutics, Am. Soc. Clin. Pharmacology and Therapeutics, N.Y. Acad. Sci. Office: Hoffmann-La Roche Inc 340 Kingsland St Nutley NJ 07110

SALVATIERRA, OSCAR, JR., physician; b. Phoenix, Apr. 15, 1935; s. Oscar and Josefine S.; m. Donna J. Meyer, June 9, 1962; children: Mark, Lisa Marie. B.S., Georgetown U., 1957; M.D., U. So. Calif., 1961. Intern, resident in surgery and urology U. So. Calif.-Los Angeles County Med. Center, 1961-66; practice medicine Pomona, Calif., 1968-72; chief staff Casa Colina Hosp., 1972; post doctoral fellow in transplantation U. Calif.-San Francisco, 1972-73, asst. prof. surgery and urology, 1973-75, assoc. prof., 1975-81, prof., 1981—, chmn. transplant service, 1974—; attending surgeon and urologist Moffitt Hosp., 1973—; mem. study sect. NIH, 1981-85, nat. adv. bd. kidney and urologic diseases NIH, 1986—. Contbr. over 170 articles and chpts. to med. lit.; bd. clin. editors Transplantation procs., 1982—; mem. editorial bd. Transplantation and Immunology, 1984—, Transplantation, 1987—; assoc. editor Am. Jour. Kidney Diseases, 1987—. Served with M.C., U.S. Army, Vietnam, 1966-68. Decorated Army Commendation medal; recipient Chancellor's award for pub. service U. Calif., 1986; NIH grantee, 1974-76; USPHS grantee, 1986-89. Fellow ACS (bd. govs. 1986—); mem. Am. Soc. Transplant Surgeons (bd. dirs. 1977—, pres. 1983-84, chmn. adv. com. on issues 1984—), Soc. Univ. Surgeons, Soc. Univ. Urologists, N.Y. Acad. Scis., Am. Soc. Nephrology, Transplantation Soc. (bd. dirs. 1984—), Soc. Pediatric Urology, Am. Urol. Assn., Nat. Kidney Found., Renal Physicians Assn. (bd. dirs. 1984—), Pacific Coast Surg. Assn., San Francisco Surg. Soc., United Network Organ Sharing (bd. dirs. 1984—, pres. 1985-86), Nafzigger Surg. Soc., AMA, Calif. Med. Assn., San Francisco Med. Soc. Office: U Calif Kidney Transplant Svc San Francisco CA 94143

SALZANO, FRANCISCO MAURO, geneticist; b. Cachoeira do Sul, Brazil, July 27, 1928; s. Francisco and Onelia (Pertille) S.; m. Thereza Torres, Mar. 20, 1952; children: Felipe, Renato. Sci. Lic. in Natural History, Fed. U. RGS, Porto Alegre, 1952; PhD in Biology, U. São Paulo, Brazil, 1955; Private Docent Genetics, Fed. U. RGS, Porto Alegre, 1960. Instr. Fed. U. Rio Grande Sul, Porto Alegre, 1952-60, asst. prof., 1960-67, assoc. prof., 1967-81, prof. genetics, 1981—, head genetics dept., 1963-68, dir. Natural Sci. Inst., 1968-71, head dept. genetics, 1973-75. Author 11 books and 3 monographs; contbr. articles to profl. jours. Recipient Sci. Tech. Nat. award Brazilian Govt., 1994, Nat. Order of Scientific merit Great-Cross Class, 1995. Mem. Brazilian Assn. Advancement Sci. (v.p. 1977-79, 93-95), L.Am. Assn. Biol. Anthropology (pres. 1990-92), Internat. Union Anthropol. Ethnol. Sci. (v.p. 1978-88), Internat. Assn. Human Biologists (sec.-gen. 1974-80), Royal Anthropol. Inst. Gt. Britain and Ireland (hon.), Soc. Genética de Chile (hon.). Home: Apto 11, Venancio Aires 1092, 90040192 Porto Alegre Brazil Office: UFRGS Dept Genetics, Caixa Postal 15053, 91501970 Porto Alegre Brazil

SALZINGER, FRED HOWARD, health services administrator; b. Alexandria, Va., Sept. 8, 1948; s. Emanuel M. and Ida (Gordon) S.; m. Lynn B. Schrader, Feb. 14, 1986; children: Ben, Sam, Kyle. BA, U. Va., 1970; MS, Va. Commonwealth U., 1979. Tchr. Mathews (Va.) County Schs., 1970-72, Richmond (Va.) Pub. Schs., 1972-75; contr. MCV Associated Physicians, Richmond, 1976-83; assoc. dean Creighton U., Omaha, Nebr., 1983-88, assoc. v.p., 1988—; dir. Truckee (Calif.) Tahoe Lumber Co., 1991—, Amicare, Omaha, Nebr., 1986-88; fin. cons. ADA, Chgo., 1992—. Contbr. articles to profl. jours. Pres. Girls, Inc., Omaha, 1992; v.p. Landmarks, Omaha, 1986; mem. United Way Allocation Com., 1992—; mem. curriculum com. Leadership Omaha, 1988-91. Mem. Med. Group Mgmt. Assn., Nebr. Med. Group Mgmt. Assn., Assn. of Am. Med. Colls., Va. Med Group Mgmt. Assn. (pres.), Acad. Health Ctrs. (chmn. 1993), Nat. Health Lawyers Assn. Jewish. Home: 5620 Howard St Omaha NE 68106 Office: Creighton U 2500 California Plaza Omaha NE 68178

SAMAAN, SELIM TAWFICK, surgeon; b. Alexandria, Egypt, Jan. 23, 1932; s. Tawfick Elias and Eva Nichola (Hamoui) S.; came to U.S., 1960, naturalized, 1971; M.B.B.Ch., Alexandria U., 1951, M.D., 1958; m. Judith Lane Watson, Dec. 29, 1962; children—Eva, Peter, Andrew, Catherine. Intern, Harlem Hosp., N.Y.C., 1960-61, resident surgery Union Meml. Hosp., Balt., 1961-63, chief resident in surgery, 1964-65; resident in colon and rectal surgery Lahey Clinic, Boston, 1965-66, asst. staff, 1966-67; practice medicine specializing in colon and rectal surgery, Garden City, N.Y., 1967—; chief colon and rectal surgery Mercy Hosp., 1975—; asst. clin. prof. SUNY. Diplomate Am. Bd. Surgery, Am. Bd. Colon and Rectal Surgery. Fellow ACS, Internat. Soc. Univ. Colon and Rectal Surgeons; mem. N.E. Soc. Colon and Rectal Surgeons (pres. elect), N.Y. Med Soc., Nassau County Med. Soc., N.Y. Soc. Surgeons, N.Y. Soc. Colon and Rectal Surgery, Pa. Soc. Colon and Rectal Surgery. Republican. Greek Orthodox. Club: North Fork Country Club. Office: 520 Franklin Ave Garden City NY 11530-5801

SAMACH, MICHAEL ALAN, gastroenterologist; b. N.Y.C., Mar. 10, 1947; s. Samuel and Rae (James) S.; m. Alice Blumberg, Nov. 27, 1969; children: Julie, David, Laurie. AB, Cornell U., 1967; MD, NYU, 1971. Diplomate Am. Bd. Internal Medicine, Am. Bd. Gastroenterology. Intern in internal medicine Montefiore Hosp., Bronx, N.Y., 1971-72, resident in internal medicine, 1972-74, fellow in gastroenterology, 1976-78; pvt. practice Denville, N.J., 1978-87; physician Affiliates in Gastroenterology, Morristown, N.J., 1987—; asst. clin. prof. Columbia U. Coll. Physicians and Surgeons, N.Y.C., 1989—. Contbr. articles to profl. jours. Trustee United Jewish Fedn., Metrowest, 1991-92, Temple B'nai Or, Morristown, 1986. Maj. USAF, 1974-76. Fellow Am. Coll. Physicians, Am. Coll. Gastroenterology; mem. Am. Gastroenterol. Assn., Am. Soc. Gastrointestinal Endoscopy, N.J. Gastro Soc. (pres. 1987-88), Morris County Med. Soc. (pres. 1989-90), AMA. Office: 101 Madison Ave Morristown NJ 07960-7305

SAMAHA, FRANCIS JOSEPH, periodontist; b. Washington, Apr. 16, 1928; s. Toufig Nickolas and Edna (George) S.; D.D.S., Georgetown U., 1951; m. Lili Ann Sheahin, July 4, 1951; children—Jeffrey F., Gary M., Lisa M., Richard G.; m. 2d, Gina A. Rota, Sept. 15, 1973; 1 dau., Nina M. Commd. 2d lt. USAF, 1950, advanced through grades to col., 1968; intern Fitzsimmons Army Hosp., Denver, 1951-52; assigned Bergstrom AFB, Tex., 1952-56; resident Tufts U., Boston, 1956-58; assigned Ramey AFB, P.R., 1958-61, Andrews AFB, Md., 1961-69, Clark Air Base, Philippines, 1969-70; ret., 1970; practice dentistry, 1970—; asso. prof., dir. grad. periodontics Georgetown U., Washington, 1970-72, U. Md., 1972-73. Cons. to surgeon gen. USAF, 1961-69; nat., internat. lectr. in field. Pres., Holy Name Soc., Bergstrom AFB, 1955-56; coach, mgr. Little League Baseball, Andrews AFB, 1961-64. Bd. dirs. Prince Georges County Boys Club, 1965-67. Decorated Legion of Merit, Commendation medal; diplomate Am. Bd. Periodontology. Fellow Am. Coll. Dentists, Va. Dental Assn., Am. Acad. Occlusodontia; mem. ADA, Am. Acad. Oral Medicine, Am. Acad. Periodontology, Am. Acad. Oral Pathology, No. Va. Dental Soc. (pres. 1984-85), Greater Washington Soc. Periodontology (pres. 1967-68), Omicron Kappa Upsilon. Melkite Catholic. Home: 4741 Rock Spring Rd Arlington VA 22207-4241 Office: 6845 Elm St Ste 607 Mc Lean VA 22101-3822

SAMAHA, RICHARD JOHN, oncologist; b. Boston, June 7, 1938; s. John Rosseller and Agnes (Maloof) S.; m. Christine Gonis. BS, MIT, 1960; MD, PhD in Biochemistry, Boston U., 1966. Diplomate Am. Bd. Internal Medicine, Am. Bd. Hematology and Med. Oncology. Intern Boston U. Sch. Medicine, 1966-67; resident Cornel Med. Coll., N.Y.C., 1967-68; clin. assoc. Nat. Cancer Inst., NIH, Bethesda, Md., 1968-70; asst. prof. medicine U. Mo. Sch. Medicine, Columbia, 1970-74; Good Samaritan Hosp. (formerly Cardinal Cushing Hosp.) Cardinal Cushing Hosp., Brockton, Mass., 1974—, chief, div. oncology and hematology, 1981—. Contbr. articles to profl. jours. With USPHS, 1968-70. Mem. Am. Soc. Clin. Oncology, Am. Soc. Hematology, New Eng. Cancer Soc., Internat. Soc. Hematology. Mem. Eastern Orthodox Ch. Office: Med Oncology & Hematology 225 Quincy Ave Brockton MA 02402-2864

SAMAJA, MICHELE, physiology and biochemistry researcher; b. Milan, Italy, Italy, Apr. 13, 1951; s. Ugo and Lucilla (Gobbo) S.; m. Ilaria Vannini Parenti, Oct. 3, 1980; 1 child, Martina. PhD, Univ., Milan, Italy, 1975.

Internal fellow Univ. Milan, 1974-75; grantee Nat. Rsch. Coun.-Italy, Milan, 1975-76, 77-81; vis. fellow NIH, Bethesda, Md., 1976-77; scientist Italian Himalayan Expdns., 1975, 91, 94; scientist Am. Med. Rsch. Expedition to Everest, 1981, sr. investigator, 1991—; scientist Himalayan Andes Rsch. Program, 1986; asst. prof. Univ. Milan, 1981—, Univ. Brescia, 1995—. Reviewer internat. jours.; contbr. over 190 articles to profl. jours. Recipient Milano Medicina award, 1986, 3d award. Cong. Clin. Chemistry, 1987, Medicine award Milano, 1992; NATO grantee, 1990, 95. Mem. Am. Soc. Physiology, Internat. Soc. Mountain Medicine, Internat. Soc. Heart Rsch., Internat. Soc. Oxygen Transport Tissue. Home: 1 CSo Sempione, 20145 Milan Italy

SAMENFELD, HERBERT WILLIAM, retired psychology educator; b. Newark, Mar. 7, 1924; s. Herbert and Estelle Bertha (Andrew) S.; m. Melanie Marie Maxwell, Jan. 21, 1948; children: Herbert Scott, Lisa Gae. BA, Drew U., 1949; MA, U. Minn., 1951, PhD, 1954. Lic. psychologist N.J. Asst. prof. psychology So. Conn. State U., New Haven, 1953-57; counselor Vocat. Counseling Svc., New Haven, 1953-57; assoc. prof. Kean Coll., Union, N.J., 1957-62, dean students, 1962-69, prof. psychology, 1969-77, chmn., 1977-89, prof. emeritus, 1989—. Pres. Am. Cancer Soc. Union County Unit, Elizabeth, N.J., mem. exec. com. 1964-91; pres. Assn. Good Schs., Scotch Plains, 1959-61; v.p. (Kean Coll. chpt.) Am. Fedn. Tchrs. Union, 1969-89. With USAF, 1943-46. Rose Honor scholar, Drew U., 1942; Rsch. fellow U. Minn., 1950-53. Mem. APA, N.J. Acad. Psychology, Heather Gardens Assn. (bd. dirs. 1993-96, pres. 1994, 95, treas. 1996). Democrat.

SAMET, JONATHAN MICHAEL, epidemiologist, educator; b. Newport News, Va., Mar. 26, 1946; s. H. Arthur and Dorothy (Helene) S.; m. Shirley Murphy, Jan. 21, 1990; 1 child, Matthew. AB in Chemistry and Physics, Harvard Coll., 1966, MS in Epidemiology, 1977; MD, U. Rochester, 1970. Diplomate Nat. Bd. Med. Examiners, Am. Bd. Internal Medicine. Intern in medicine U. Ky. Med. Ctr., Lexington, 1970-71; anesthesiologist U.S. Army, Gorgas Hosp., Balboa Heights, Canal Zone, 1971-73; asst. resident in medicine U. N.Mex. Affiliated Hosps., Albuquerque, 1973-74, sr. resident in medicine, 1974-75; rsch. fellow in clin. epidemiology Channing Lab. Harvard Med. Sch., Boston, 1975-78, rsch. assoc. in medicine, 1978-83; asst. prof. medicine U. N.Mex., Albuquerque, 1978-82, epidemiologist N.Mex. Tumor Registry, Cancer Rsch. and Treatment Ctr., 1980—, assoc. prof. medicine, 1982-86, assoc. prof. family, cmty. and emergency medicine, 1985-86, chief hosp. pulmonary divsn., 1985-94, chief pulmonary and critical care divsn. Dept. Medicine, 1986-94, prof. medicine, 1986-94, prof. family, cmty. and emergency medicine, 1994—, clin. prof. dept. medicine Health Scis. Ctr., 1994—; prof., chmn. dept. epidemiology Sch. Hygiene and Pub. Health Johns Hopkins U., Balt., 1994—, joint appointment dept. medicine Sch. of Medicine, 1994—, secondary appointment Oncology Ctr., 1995—, co-dir. Risk Scis. and Pub. Policy Inst., Sch. Hygiene and Pub. Health, 1995—; sci. adv. bd. EPA, 1987—; chmn. biol. effects of ionizing radiation com. VI Nat. Rsch. Coun., 1992—. Mem. editl. bd. Annals of Sports Medicine, 1982-88, Am. Rev. Respiratory Diseases, 1988-89, assoc. editor, 89-94; mem. editl. bd. EPIDEMIOLOGY, 1988—; assoc. editor Am. Jour. Epidemiology, 1986-91, editor, pro tem, 1991-92, editor, 1992—; sr. sci. editor Report of the Surgeon Gen.: The Health Benefits of Smoking Cessation, 1989-90; assoc. editor Tobacco Control: An Internat. Jour., 1991—, Am. Jour. Respiratory and Critical Care Medicine, 1994; mem. editl. adv. bd. Cancer Epidemiology, Biomarkers and Prevention, 1991—; editor Epidemiologic Revs., 1994—; contbr. articles to profl. jours., chpts. to books. Capt. U.S. Army, 1971-73. Recipient Career Devel. award Divsn. Lung Diseases, Nat. Heart, Lung, and Blood Inst., 1981-86, Clinton P. Anderson award Am. Lung Assn. N.Mex., 1986, Surgeon Gen.'s medallion, 1990; award for Excellence in Environ. Health Rsch. The Lovelace Inst., Albuquerque, 1996. Fellow AAAS, Am. Coll. Epidemiology; mem. Am. Thoracic Soc. (steering com. EPA-Am. Lung Assn. Project, Physician Seminars on Health Effects of Air Pollution 1979-82, program com. Environ. and Occupl. Health Assembly 1980-85, sec. 1981-83, chmn. 83-84, program com. 1987-88, long range planning com. 1992—, annual meeting com. 1984, chmn. Workshop Environ. Control and Lung Disease 1987-88, program com. Behavioral Scis. Sect. 1994-95), Internat. Epidemiol. Assn., Internat. Soc. Indoor Air Quality and Climate, Md. Thoracic Soc., N.Mex. Thoracic Soc. (sec.- treas. 1982-83, v.p. 83-84, pres. 84-85), Soc. Epidemiologic Rsch. (pres.- elect 1988-89, pres. 89-90, exec. com. 88-91), Alpha Omega Alpha, Delta Omega (Alpha chpt.). Office: Johns Hopkins U Dept Epidemiology 615 N Wolfe St Ste 6039 Baltimore MD 21205-2179*

SAMET, KENNETH ALAN, hospital administrator; b. Bklyn., Mar. 17, 1958; married. BA, Old Dominion U., 1990; MA, U. Mich., 1982. Adminstrv. intern Mt. Vernon Hosp., Fairfax, Va., 1981; adminstrv. resident Washington Hosp. Ctr., 1982-83, pres., 1991—; asst. to pres. Washington Health Care Corp., 1983-85, dir. system devel., 1985-86; v.p. system devel. Medlantic Health Care Group, Washington, 1986-88, exec. v.p. systems, bus. devel., 1988-91; pres. Medlantic Enterprises, Washington, 1988-91. Mem. D.C. Hosp. Assn., Md. Hosp. Assn., Va. Hosp. Assn. (bd. dirs.). Home: 9041 Holly Leaf Ln Bethesda MD 20817-2657 Office: Washington Hosp Ctr 110 Irving St NW Rm 2A2 Washington DC 20010-2979*

SAMET, MARC KRANE, pharmacologist; b. Chgo., Apr. 30, 1950; s. Herman and Nora (Krane) S. BS, No. Ill. U., 1973; MS, Northwestern U., 1975; PhD, Kans. U., 1983. Mem. faculty U. Calif., Berkeley/San Francisco, 1983-85 with Applied Immune Scis., Menlo Park, Calif., 1985-87, Glenwood Mgmt., Menlo Park, 1987; cons. Vitaphore Corp., Menlo Park, 1988-90, Van Med Venture Capital, Palo Alto, Calif., 1990; prin. strategic planning and mktg. firm, 1991, Merck & Co., 1992-95, Vanguard Ventures, 1995—. Contbr. articles to profl. jours. NIH fellow, 1983-84, 84-85. Mem. N.Y. Acad. Sci., Am. Assn. Immunologists, Controlled Release Soc., Am. Assn. Pharm. Scientists. Jewish. Home: 2113 Caminito del Barco Del Mar CA 92014

SAMII, ABDOL HOSSEIN, physician, educator; b. Rasht, Iran, June 20, 1930; came to U.S., 1947; s. Mehdi Ebtehaj and Zahra (Mojdehi-Akbar) S.; m. Shahla Khosrowshahi; children: Ali, Golnaz. Student, Stanford U., 1947-49; BA, UCLA, 1950, MA, 1952; MD, Cornell U., 1956. Intern N.Y. Hosp., N.Y.C., 1956, asst. in medicine, 1956-58; asst. in physiology Cornell U. Med. Sch., N.Y.C., 1958-59; resident and sr. resident N.Y. Hosp., Peter Bent Brigham Hosp. and Mass. Gen. Hosp., Boston, 1959-61; adj. prof. medicine Cornell U. Med. Sch., 1973-79, prof. clin. medicine, 1979—; rsch. fellow Harvard U., Boston, 1959-60; prof. medicine Nat. Univ. Iran, Tehran, 1963-68; med. dir. Pars Hosp., Tehran, 1968-73; dir. div. medicine N.Y. Hosp.-Cornell Med. Coll., White Plains, 1979—; chancellor Reza Shah Kabir Grad. Univ., Tehran, 1973-78; cons. med. rsch. WHO, Geneva, 1973-79; v.p. Imperial Acad. Sci., Tehran, 1974-78. Gen. editor: International Textbook of Medicine, 1981; author, editor: Medical Clinics of North America, 1983, Textbook of Diagnostic Medicine, 1987. Dep. minister, Ministry of Health, Tehran, 1963-65; minister, Ministry Sci. and Higher Edn., Tehran, 1973-75. Fellow Rockefeller Found., Helen Hay Whitney Found. Fellow Royal Soc. of Medicine; mem. N.Y. Acad. Medicine, Harvey Soc., Internat. Soc. Nephrology, Am. Fed. Clin. Rsch. Office: NY Hosp CMC WD 21 Bloomingdale Rd White Plains NY 10605-1504 also: 14 E 63d St New York City NY 10021

SAMMAD, MOHAMED ABDEL, cardiovascular surgeon, consultant; b. Misurata, Libya, Nov. 30, 1953; arrived in Austria, 1985; s. Makhzoum A. Sammad and Mabrouka Ahmed; m. Moufeda A. Fituri, Feb. 5, 1981; children: Manal M., Sara M., Basma, Moad M. MD, Alfateh Med. Sch., Tripoli, Libya, 1980. House officer surgery Tripoli (Libya) U. Hosp., 1980-81, sr. house officer, 1981-83; sr. resident Tajour U. Hosp., Tajoura, Libya, 1983-85; resident in cardiovascular surgery U. Hosp. Vienna (Austria), 1985-87, sr. resident in cardiovascular surgery, 1987-89, fellow in cardiovascular surgery, 1989-91. Author: Hypertension and Related Illness Risk Factors and Prevention, 1989, Arteriosclerosis & Sudden Death. Fellow Austrian Bd. Surgery; mem. Internat. Soc. Heart Transplantation, N.Y. Acad. Scis., Am. Assn. for Advancement Sci. Home: Leystr 106/3/6, 1190 Vienna 1200, Austria Office: Vienna Univ Hosp 2d Surg, Spitalgasse 23, 1090 Vienna Austria

SAMMAN, GEORGE, obstetrician, gynecologist; b. Syria, Dec. 12, 1946; came to U.S., 1971; naturalized, 1982; s. Nicolaki and Antoinette (Charaoui) S.; M.D., Damascus U., 1971; m. Husn Massouh, July 4, 1971; children—Fadi, Luna Miriam. Intern, Washington Hosp. Center, 1971-72, resident in ob-gyn., 1972-75, mem. hosp. staff, 1975—, vice chmn. dept. gynecology, 1980, teaching faculty, 1985-88; practice medicine specializing in ob-gyn, Washington, 1975—, Fairfax, Va., 1980—; mem. staff Providence Hosp., 1975—, Columbia Hosp. for Women. Recipient Best Teaching award Washington Hosp. Ctr., 1985, 88. Diplomate Am. Bd. Ob-Gyn. Fellow Am. Coll. Obstetricians and Gynecologists, Am. Fertility Assn.; mem. Med. Soc. D.C. (maternal health com. 1978-80). Melkite Catholic. Home: 10400 Bit & Spur Ln Potomac MD 20854 Office: 2021 K St NW Washington DC 20006-2104

SAMMAN, JUAN M., prosthodontist; b. Damascus, Syria, Nov. 4, 1953; s. Moukhtar and Souha S; m. Angela Mignone, Oct. 3, 1983 (div. July, 1989). BS, Am. U., Beirut, 1976; DDS, NYU, 1981; MSc, London U., 1983. Hon. clin. asst. to the Dental Hosp. Univ. Coll. Hosp., London, 1983; scientific rschr. NYU, N.Y.C., 1984-87, clin. asst. prof., 1987-93; pvt. practice Manhattan, N.Y., 1988—; assoc. N.Y. Dental Implant Restorative and Cosmetic Dentistry Ctr., 1985-87, Sam Weber, DDS, 1987-88; lectr. NYU. Contbr. articles to profl. publs. Fellow Brit. Soc. for Study of Prosthetic Dentistry; mem. Internat. Assn. Dental Rsch., European Prosthodontic Assn., Acad. Ossolintegration, Am. Dental Assn. Office: 200 Central Park South New York NY 10019

SAMMONS, LUCY NEWMARK, nursing educator, researcher, administrator, clinician; m. Timothy J. Sammons; children: Julie, Andrew. BSN, Stanford U., 1973; MS, U. Calif., San Francisco, 1979, D of Nursing Sci., 1985. RN, Calif.; cert. childbirth educator, Am. Soc. for Psychoprophylaxis in Obstetrics. Health rsch. cons., San Ramon, Calif.; guest scientist, H.M. Jackson Found. for Advancement of Mil. Medicine, first reserve specialty to Navy Surgeon Gen. on Women's Health/Maternal-Child Nursing, 1992-96. Author: Ambulatory Obstetrics: Protocols for Nurse Practitioners and Nurse Midwives; numerous editl. bds.; ocntbr. articles to nursing jours. Officer Nurse Corps, Calif. USNR. Mem. ANA, AWHONN (cert. ob-gyn. nurse practitioner), Sigma Theta Tau. Home: 2608 Campeche Ct San Ramon CA 94583-2016

SAMOJLIK, EUGENIUSZ, administrator, medical educator; b. Kuchmy-Bialystok, Poland, Aug. 20, 1933; s. Michael and Anastazia S.; m. Anna Morozewicz, Apr. 10, 1965; children: Dorothy, Michael. BS in Biomedicine, U. Warsaw, 1958, PhD in Reproductive Endocrinology, 1964. Rsch. asst. Maternity Inst. Dept. Pharmacology, Warsaw, 1958-62, sr. asst., 1962-66; asst. prof., chief reproductive pharmacology & toxicology Inst. Pharmacy Dept. Pharmacology, Warsaw, 1966-70; assoc. prof., chief hormone rsch. lab. Med. Acad. Dept. Clin. Endocrinology, Warsaw, 1970-73; staff researcher II Syntex, Inc. Rsch. Divsn., Palo Alto, Calif., 1974-75; asst. prof. physiology, dir. radioimmunoassay lab. Milton S. Hershey (Pa.) Med. Ctr., Divsn. Endocrinology, 1975-80; staff endocrinologist VA Med. Ctr. Dept. Medicine, Sect. Endocrinology, East Orange, N.J., 1980-82; dir. endocrine lab. Newark Beth Israel Med. Ctr., Dept. Medicine, 1982-92; assoc. prof. medicine U. Medicine & Dentistry-N.J. Med. Sch., Newark, 1982—; chief endocrine lab. dept. Labs. NBIMC, 1994-96; vis. researcher UCLA Sch. Medicine, Torrance, Calif., 1973; vis. scientist Nat. Inst. Child Health Human Devel., Reproductive Br., Bethesda, Md., 1973-74; lectr. in field. Mem. internat. adv. bd. Jour. Assisted Reproductive Tech. and Andrology, mem. editorial bd., 1996; contbr. articles to profl. jours. Grantee WHO, 1973-74, Ciba-Geigy, 1982-83, Nat. Cancer Inst., 1983-86, 85-88; tng. program fellow Worcester Found. Experimental Biology, Shrewsbury, Mass., 1967-69. Mem. Am. Soc. Andrology, Am. Assn. Clin. Chemistry, Nat. Acad. Clin. Biochemistry, Acad. Medicine N.J., Endocrine Soc. Home: 73 Sykes Ave Livingston NJ 07039-1318 Office: Newark Beth Israel Med Ctr Endocrine Lab Newark NJ 07112

SAMOUILIDIS, LEONIDAS, psychoanalyst; b. Zagazig, Egypt, Dec. 15, 1930; came to U.S., 1957; s. Telemachus and Antigone (Calogeropoulou) S.; m. Alexandra Mantzorou, Nov. 12, 1967; children: Leo, Paul. MD, Athens U., 1956. Cert. psychoanalayst; cert. sex therapist. Gen. intern Deaconess Hosp., Cleve., 1957-58; resident in psychiatry St. Lawrence State Hosp., Ogdensburg, N.Y., 1958-59, Buffalo State Hosp., 1959-61, Pilgrim State Hosp., West Brentwood, N.Y., 1961-63; therapist Lincoln Inst. for Psychotherapy, N.Y.C., 1963-70; therapist Karen Horney Clinic, N.Y.C., 1962-70, clin. asst. physician in-charge, 1965-72; med. dir. N.J. Mental Health Ctr., Passaic, 1970-76, Ctr. for Creative Living, Allendale, N.J., 1976—; pvt. practice Glen Roch, River Edge, N.J., 1970-85; attending psysician St. Joseph's Hosp., Paterson, N.J., 1970-75, Lincoln Park (N.J.) Nursing Home, 1972-74. Contbr. articles to profl. jours. Mem. Masons. Home: 4 Lookout Dr Saddle River NJ 07458-3314

SAMPINO, ANTHONY F., physician, obstetrician and gynecologist; b. Bklyn., Jan. 13, 1965; s. Frank Paul-Joseph and Lillian Katherine (Cucinotta) S. D Osteopathic Medicine, N.Y. Coll. Osteopathic Medicine, 1991. Rotating intern St. Barnabas Hosp., Bronx, N.Y., 1991-92; resident ob/gyn St. Vincents Med. Ctr. of Richmond, Staten Island, N.Y., 1992-96; with dept. ob/gyn Good Samaritan Hosp., West Islip, N.Y., 1996—; adj. clin. instr. N.Y. Coll. Osteo. Medicine, 1996—. Fellow Am. Coll. Obstetricians/Gynecologists (jr., sect. chmn. 1992-94); mem. AMA, Am. Osteopathic Assn., Am. Assn. Gynecologic Laparoscopists (Outstanding Resident in Gyn. Endoscopy 1996), Med. Soc. State of N.Y., L.I. Soc. Osteo. Physicians & Surgeons, Richmond County Med. Soc. Home: 69 Wildwood Dr Dix Hills NY 11746

SAMPSON, HERSCHEL WAYNE, anatomy educator; b. Greenville, Tex., June 28, 1944; s. Clyde Edwin and Wanda Ruth (Brandon) S.; m. Patricia Janell Hudson, Nov. 27, 1965; children: Nathan Paul, Susan Diane. BS, Arlington State Coll., 1967; PhD, Baylor U., 1970. Asst. prof. of anatomy Creighton U. Sch. Medicine, Omaha, 1970-72; asst to assoc. prof. of Anatomy Baylor Coll. Dentistry, Dallas, 1972-77; assoc. prof. Oral Roberts U. Sch. Dentistry, Dallas, 1977-78; prof. Tex. A&M U. Coll. Medicine, College Station, Tex., 1979—; adjunct prof. Dallas Bible Coll., 1972-79; exec. sec. Anatomical Bd., State of Tex., Dallas, 1974-77; coord. Med. Electron Microscope Facility Coll. Station, Tex., 1982-95; nutrition faculty Tex. A&M U., Coll. Station, 1989—. Co-author: Atlas of the Human Skull, 1991; contbr. articles to profl. jours. Bd. dirs. Greenville (Tex.) Christian Sch., 1976-77, Brazos Valley Rehab. Ctr., Bryan, Tex., 1979-85, Dallas Bible Coll., 1979-83; deacon Cen. Bapt. Ch., Bryan, 1984—. Mem. Am. Assn. Anatomy, Am. Physiol. Soc., Am. Soc. for Bone and Mineral Rsch., Internat. Conf. on Calcium Regulating Hormones, Tex. Soc. for Electron Microscopy (pres. 1984-90), Tex. Mineralized Tissue Soc., Rsch. Soc. Alcoholism, Tex. Soc. on Alcoholism. Home: 902 Briar Bend St Bryan TX 77802-2401 Office: Coll of Medicine Tex A&M U College Station TX 77843-1114

SAMPSON, ROBERT CARL, JR., psychiatrist; b. Concord, N.H., June 6, 1948; s. Robert Carl Sr. and Alice May (Bedor) S. BA magna cum laude, Yale U., 1970; MD, U. Pa., 1974; CAc, New Eng. Sch. Acupuncture, Watertown, Mass., 1984. Diplomate Nat. Bd. Med. Examiners, Am. Bd. Psychiatry and Neurology, Child Psychiatry. Intern Bryn Mawr (Pa.) Hosp., 1974-75; resident in psychiatry U. Mich., Ann Arbor, 1975-77; resident in child psychiatry New Eng. Med. Ctr., Boston, 1977-79; staff psychiatrist Beaverbrook Guidance Ctr., Waltham, Mass., 1979-89, med. dir., 1989-92; med. dir. Sino-U.S. Qi Gong Health Scis. Devel. Ctr., Cambridge, Mass., 1985-87; psychiatrist Ctr. for Health, Newton Centre, Mass., 1986-89; instr. psychiatry Harvard U. Med. Sch., Boston, 1987-90; assoc. med. dir. Family Counseling and Guidance Ctrs., Inc., Marshfield, Mass., 1987-89; rsch. cons. Cambridge Hosp.-Psychiatry Dept., 1987-90; founder, cons. Stress Transformation Systems, Newton, Mass. and Londonderry, N.H., 1987—. Contbr. articles to profl. jours. Fellow Am. Acad. Child and Adolescent Psychiatry; mem. New Eng. Coun. Child and Adolescent Psychiatry, Internat. Soc. Study of Subtle Energies and Energy Medicine, Human Ecology Action League, Nat. Ctr. Environ. Health Strategies, Phi Beta Kappa. Home: PO Box 940 Londonderry NH 03053-0940 Office: 1647 Washington St Newton MA 02165

SAMS, W(ILEY) MITCHELL, JR., dermatologist; b. Ann Arbor, Mich., Apr. 15, 1933; s. Wiley Mitchell and Elizabeth (Hastings) S.; m. Marion Ruth Yount, June 7, 1959; children—Robert, Margery, Hunter. B.S., U. Mich., 1955; M.D., Emory U., 1959. Intern Emory U. Hosp., Atlanta, 1959-60; resident in dermatology Duke U., Durham, N.C., 1960-64; clin. asst. prof. U. Calif., San Francisco, 1964-66; asst., asso. prof. Mayo Grad. Sch. Medicine, Mpls., 1966-72; prof., chmn. dept. dermatology U. Colo., Denver, 1972-76; prof. dermatology U. N.C. Sch. Medicine, Chapel Hill, 1976-80; prof., chmn. dept. dermatology U. Ala., Birmingham, 1981—. Served to capt. M.C. U.S. Army, 1964-66. NIH research fellow, 1962-64; grantee, 1972. Mem. Am. Acad. Dermatology, Soc. Investigative Dermatology, Am. Dermatol. Assn., So. Med. Assn. Office: U Ala University Sta Dept Dermatology Kracke Bldg Rm 101 Birmingham AL 35294

SAMUEL, PAUL, cardiologist; b. Janoshaza, Hungary, Feb. 17, 1927; came to U.S., 1954, naturalized, 1960; s. Adolf and Magda (Zollner) S.; m. Gabriella R. Zeichner, Mar. 27, 1954; children: Robert Mark, Adrianne Jill. Baccalaureat, Kemeny Zsigmond Gymnasium, Budapest, 1945; MD, U. Paris, 1953. Intern Queens Hosp. Ctr., N.Y.C., 1954-55; resident L.I. Jewish Med. Ctr., New Hyde Park, N.Y., 1959-61; adj. prof. Rockefeller U., N.Y.C., 1971-81; adj. prof. medicine Cornell U., N.Y.C., 1979—; clin. prof. medicine Albert Einstein Coll. Medicine, Bronx, 1981—; dir. Arteriosclerosis Rsch. Lab., L.I. Jewish-Hillside Med. Ctr., New Hyde Park, 1962—; chmn. N.Y. Lipid Rsch. Club, Rockefeller U., 1977-78. Contbr. articles to profl. jours. Pres. Am. Heart Assn., Nassau County, 1980. Fellow Am. Coll. Cardiology; mem. Am. Heart Assn. (fellow coun. on arteriosclerosis, Disting. Achievement award 1975), Am. Fedn. Clin. Rsch., Harvey Soc., ACP. Home: 25 Nassau Dr Great Neck NY 11021-2163 Office: LI Jewish Med Ctr 1554 Northern Blvd Manhasset NY 11030-3006 also: 110-20 71st Rd Forest Hills NY 11375

SAMUEL, ROBERT THOMPSON, optometrist; b. Kansas City, Mo., June 27, 1944; s. Manlius Thompson and Helen Evelyn (Syverson) S. B.A., William Jewel Coll., 1966; postgrad. U. Mo.-Kansas City, 1967, M.S. U. Mo., 1968; D. Optometry, U. Tenn.-Memphis, 1971. Cert. optometrist, Mo. Buyer Recco, Inc., Kansas City, Mo., 1963-67; histology lab. instr. William Jewell Coll., Liberty, Mo., 1965-66; pvt. practice optometry Gladstone, Mo., 1972—; panel Dr. Ford Motor Co., Claycomo, Mo., 1985—, Union Pacific R.R., Kansas City, 1985—, TWA Airlines, 1990, Union Carbide, 1990. Publicity coord. Rep. Party, Kansas City, Mo., 1975-76; chmn. Save Your Vision Week, Kansas City, 1977; mem. Theatre League of Kansas City, 1976—, Kansas City Mus., 1986—, Friends of Art, 1985, Friends of Mo. Town 1855, 1980—. Recipient Outstanding Young Men of Am. award Jaycees, 1978, Good Citizens award DAR, 1962. Mem. Am. Optometric Assn., Mo. Optometric Assn., Optometric Soc. Greater Kansas City, Heart of Am. Contact Lens Congress, Am. Acad. Sports Vision, Vol. Optometric Svcs. for Humanity, Smithsonian Assocs, Kappa Alpha Order (treas. 1966). Republican. Lutheran. Lodge: Lions (exec. bd. dirs. Lions Eye Clinic 1974-84, bd. dirs. Lions Eye Clinic 1982—, Outstanding Svc. award 1973, 74, editor Lions Optometric Ctr. Quar., 1974-84). Avocations: photography, music, piano, swimming, travel. Home: 6325 N Monroe Ave Kansas City MO 64119-1923 Office: 2700 NE Kendallwood Pky Ste 109 Kansas City MO 64119-2071

SAMUELS, DAVID PAUL, physician; b. Seattle, Wash., Aug. 20, 1944; s. Milton Sidney and Patricia Athlone (Carrigan) S.; m. Barbara Gail Bergman, Aug. 9, 1969; children: Kevin Michael, Owen Michael. AB in Human Biology, Brown U., 1966; MD, Tufts U., 1970. Diplomate Am. Acad. Pediatris; subspeciality Neonatal Periantal Medicine. Neonatologist Webster Clinic, Green Bay, Wis., 1976-90; dir. NICU Stuincent Hosp., Green Bay, 1978—; neonatologist Neonatal Cons., Green Bay, 1990—; bd. dirs. N.E. Wis. Cerebral Palsy, Green Bay. Lt. comdr. USN, 1972-74. Fellow Am. Acad. Pediatrics (mem. sect. perinatal neonatal medicine); mem. Wis. Assn. Perinatal Medicine, Wis. State Med. Soc., Phi Beta Kappa, Sigma Xi. Home: 200 Rosemont Dr Green Bay WI 54301 Office: Neonatal Cons 2941 S Ridge Rd Green Bay WI 54303

SAMUELS, SHARON BETH, surgeon, educator; b. N.Y.C., Oct. 20, 1959; d. Leonard and Sandra (Litman) S.; m. Mark D. Sklar, May 23, 1993; 1 child, Aaron Benjamin. BS, U. Md., 1981, MD, 1985. Diplomate Am. Bd. Surgery. Resident surgery Hartford (Conn.) Hosp., 1985-88; rsch. fellow U. Conn., Farmington, 1988-90; resident surgery U. Mass., Worcester, 1990-93; fellow Hartford Hosp., 1993-94; co-dir. SICU, asst. prof. surgery Albany (N.Y.) Med. Ctr., 1994—. Mem. AMA, Soc. Critical Care Medicine, N.Y. Med. Soc. Office: Albany Med Ctr A-162 47 New Scotland Ave Albany NY 12208

SAMUELS, SHIRLEY CHASINS, psychotherapist; b. Bronx, N.Y., Dec. 6, 1930; d. Rubin and Clara (Traub) Chasins; B.S., Syracuse U., 1952, M.S., 1957; Ed.D., Columbia U., 1969; postgrad. Child Psychoanalysis, Center for Preventive Psychiatry, 1977; m. Stanley Samuels, Sept. 9, 1951; children—Jeffrey, Nita, Mark. Tchr., Syracuse (N.Y.) U. Nursery Sch., 1955-57, Maywood Nursery Sch., Hartsdale, N.Y., 1961-63; dir. Mt. Vernon (N.Y.) YM-YWHA Nursery Sch., 1963-65; dir. early childhood program Conservative Synagogue of Riverdale, Bronx, N.Y., 1966-68; adj. asst. prof. Hunter Coll., N.Y.C., 1968-74; assoc. prof. edn. Manhattanville Coll., Purchase, N.Y., 1969-80; child psychotherapist Ctr. for Preventive Psychiatry, White Plains, N.Y., 1974-80, clin. coord., 1980-94; asst. clinic dir., 1994—. adj. prof. Coll. New Rochelle (N.Y.), 1978—, Pace U., 1986—; pvt. practice psychotherapy, White Plains, 1977—; cons., lectr. in field. Bd. dirs. Union Day Care, Greenburgh, N.Y., 1981—, Westchester Assn. Young Children, White Plains, 1974—; mem. Youth Bd. Westchester County, 1975-91, pres. 1981-83; chmn. Westchester County Internat. Youth, 1985; mem. adv. bd. therapeutic activity program Grasslands Hosp., Valhalla, N.Y., 1981—, chmn., 1992—; mem. health adv. bd. Westchester Community Action Program, 1990—; mem. task froce on sexual abuse Westchester County, 1987—. Recipient award Youth Bd. Westchester County, 1981, Proclamation Service award, 1981. Mem. Assn. Marriage and Family Therapy (corr. sec. 1983-85); mem. Assn. Child Psychoanalysis, Am. Psychol. Assn., Am. Orthopsychiat. Assn. Democrat. Jewish. Author: Enhancing Self-Concept in Early Childhood, 1977, Disturbed Exceptional Children: An Integrated Approach, 1981, 2d edit., 1986, Ideal Adoption, 1990. Mem. editorial bd. Jour. Preventive Psychiatry, 1981-94. Home: 10 Crest Dr White Plains NY 10607-2702 Office: 19 Greenridge Ave White Plains NY 10605-1201

SAMUELSON, EMILY MEG, psychologist; b. Balt., May 5, 1952; divorced; 1 child, Allison Kara. BA, Tufts U., 1970; MEd, Temple U., 1978, PhD, 1989. Coord. creative arts therapy Thomas Jefferson U. Hosp., Phila., 1978-85; dir. day treatment svcs. for children and adolescent Vance, Franklin, Warren & Granville Counties, N.C., 1985-87; pvt. practice consultation and forensic testimony, 1987—; sr. psychologist Children's Guild, Balt., 1989-90, therapy supr., 1990-94; faculty Thomas Jefferson U., Phila., 1980-85; adj. faculty Antioch New Eng., Vt., 1980-83; sr. clin. faculty Hahnemann U., Phila., 1980-85. Author: (with others) Primer for Dance/Movement Therapy, 1979. Mem. Am. Psychol. Assn. Office: 28 Allegheny Ave Unit 1305 Baltimore MD 21204-3919

SAMUELSSON, BENGT INGEMAR, medical chemist; b. Halmstad, Sweden, May 21, 1934; s. Anders and Stina (Nilsson) S.; m. Inga Karin Bergstein, Aug. 19, 1958; children: Bo, Elisabet, Astrid. DMS, Karolinska Inst., Stockholm, 1960, MD, 1961; DSc (hon.), U. Chgo., 1978, U. Ill., 1983. Asst. prof. Karolinska Inst., 1961-66, prof. med. and physiol. chemistry, 1972—, chmn. physiol. chemistry dept., 1973-83, dean Med. Faculty, 1978-83, pres., 1983-95; rsch. fellow Harvard U., 1961-62; prof. med. chemistry Royal Vet. Coll., Stockholm, 1967-72; Harvey lectr., N.Y.C., 1979; mem. Nobel Com. Physiology and Medicine, 1984—, chmn. com., 1987-89; mem. rsch. adv. bd. Swedish Govt., 1985-88; mem. Nat. Commn. Health Policy, 1987-90; mem. European Sci. and Tech. Assembly, 1994—; spl. adv. to commr. rsch. and edn. European commn., 1995—; chmn. Nobel Found., 1993—. Contbr articles to profl. jours. Recipient A. Jahres award Oslo U., 1970, Louisa Gross Horwitz award Columbia U., 1975, Albert Lasker basic med. research award, 1977, Ciba-Geigy Drew award in biomed. research, 1980, Lewis S. Rosenstiel award in basic med. research Brandeis U., 1981, Gairdner Found. award, 1981, Heinrich Wieland prize, 1981, Nobel prize in physiology or medicine, 1982, award medicinal chemistry div. Am. Chem. Soc., 1982, Waterford Bio-Med. Sci. award, 1982, Internat. Assn. Allergology and Clin. Immunology award, 1982, Abraham White sci. achievement award, 1984, Gregory Pincus Meml. award, 1984, Charles E. Culpepper award, 1985, Supelco award Am. Oil Chemists Soc., 1985, Chilton lectureship award, 1986, Abraham White Disting. Sci. award, 1991,

City of Medicine award, 1992. Mem. AAAS (hon.), Royal Swedish Acad. Scis., Mediterranean Acad. Sci., Acad. Europaea (founding mem.), French Acad. Scis., Assn. Am. Physicians, Swedish Med. Assn., Am. Soc. Biol. Chemists, Italian Pharm. Soc., Acad. Nat. Medicina de Buenos Aires, Internat. Soc. Hematology, Fgn. Assn. U.S. Nat. Acad. Scis., Royal Soc. London (fgn. mem.), Spanish Soc. Allergology and Clin. Immunology, Royal Nat. Acad. Medicine Spain (hon.), Internat. Acad. Sci. (hon.). Office: Karolinska Inst, Dept MMB Divsn Physiol Chemistry II, S-171 77 Stockholm Sweden

SAN, NGUYEN DUY, psychiatrist, educator; b. Langson, Vietnam, Sept. 25, 1932; s. Nguyen Duy and Tran Tuyet (Trang) Quyen; came to Can., 1971, naturalized, 1977; MD, U. Saigon, 1960; postgrad. U. Mich., 1970; m. Eddie Jean Ciesielski, Aug. 24, 1971; children: Thuan Le, Megan Thuloan, Muriel Mylinh, Claire Kimlan, Robin Xuanlan, Baodan Edward. Intern, Cho Ray Hosp., Saigon, 1957-58; resident Univ. Hosp., Ann Arbor, Mich., 1968-70, Lafayette Clinic, Detroit, 1970-71, Clarke Inst. Psychiatry, Toronto, Ont., Can., 1971-72; chief of psychiatry South Vietnamese Army, 1964-68; sr. psychiatrist Queen St. Mental Health Ctr., Toronto, 1972-74; unit dir. Homewood San., Guelph, Ont., 1974-80; cons. psychiatrist Guelph Gen. Hosp., St. Joseph's Hosp., Guelph; practice medicine specializing in psychiatry, Guelph, 1974-80; unit dir. inpatient svc. Royal Ottawa (Ont., Can.) Hosp., 1980-84, dir. psychiat. rehab. program, 1985-87; asst. prof. psychiatry U. Ottawa Med. Sch., 1980-85, assoc. prof. psychiatry, 1985-87; bd. dirs. Hong Fook Mental Health Svc., Toronto, 1987—, dir. East-West Mental Health Ctr., Toronto, 1987—; chmn., bd. dirs. Access Alliance Multicultural Health Ctr., Toronto, 1988—; cons. UN High Commr. for Refugees, 1987—. Served with Army Republic of Vietnam, 1953-68. Mem. Can. Med. Assn., Can., Am. psychiat. assns., Am. Soc. Clin. Hypnosis, Internat. Soc. Hypnosis, N.Y. Acad. Scis. Buddhist. Author: Etude du Tetanos au Vietnam, 1960; (with others) The Psychology and Physiology of Stress, 1969, Psychosomatic Medicine, theoretical, clinical, and transcultural aspects, 1983, Uprooting, Loss and Adaptation, 1984, 87, Southeast Asian Mental Health, 1985, Ten Years Later: Indochinese Communities in Canada, 1988, Refugee Resettlement and Well-Being, 1989. Office: 2238 Dundas St W Ste 306, Toronto, ON Canada M6R 3A9

SANANMAN, MICHAEL LAWRENCE, neurologist; b. Bklyn., Oct. 11, 1939; s. Jack and Sarey (Bykofsky) S.; m. Elisa Joan Freeman, Apr. 12, 1964; children: Amy, Peter. AB, Swarthmore Coll., 1960; MD, Columbia U., 1964. Diplomate Am. Bd. Psychiatry and Neurology. Intern, Univ. Hosp., San Francisco, 1964-65; resident in neurology N.Y. Neurol. Inst., N.Y.C., 1966-69; practice medicine specializing in neurology, Elizabeth, N.J., 1972—; cons. neurologist St. Elizabeth's Hosp., Elizabeth Gen. Hosp., Rahway (N.J.) Hosp.; instr. neurology Columbia U., N.Y.C., 1971-75; asso. clin. prof. neurology U. Medicine and Dentistry N.J., Newark, 1975—; mem. adv. coun. N.J. chpt. Multiple Sclerosis Soc. Served to lt. comdr. M.C., USNR, 1969-71. Mem. AMA, Am. Acad. Neurology, Am. Epilepsy Soc. (adv. coun. N.J. chpt.), N.J. Acad. Medicine (chmn. neurology sect.), Am., Eastern EEG socs., Am. Assn. EMG and Electrodiagnosis. Office: 700 N Broad St Elizabeth NJ 07208-2310

SANBE, CHARLES A., osteopath; b. Chester, Pa., Mar. 4, 1931; m. Margaret Nugent; children: Charles A. Jr., Stephanie Ann Kasuboski. BS, Villanova U., 1953; DO, Kansas City Coll. Osteo. Med., 1962. Diplomate Am. Osteopathic Bd. Gen. Practice. Intern Doctor's Hosp., Columbus, Ohio, 1962-63; staff Tri-County Hosp., Springfield, Pa., 1963-76, Cmty. Hosp. Chester, Pa., 1969—. Mem. Am. Osteopathic Med. Assn., Am. Coll. Gen. Practitioners and Osteopathic Medicine and Surgery, Pa. Gen. Practitioners Soc., Phila. County Osteopathic Med. Soc., Am. Osteopathic Soc. Sports Medicine. Home: 310 Donnelly Ave Aston PA 19014 Office: 3125 Pennell Rd Media PA 19063

SAN-BLAS, GIOCONDA, microbiology educator, researcher; b. Caracas, Venezuela, Dec. 14, 1943; d. Biagio and Luisa (Domínguez) Cunto; m. Felipe San-Blas, Aug. 23, 1969; children: Agustín, Ernesto, Felipe. Lic. in chemistry, Ctrl. U. Venezuela, Caracas, 1967; PhD in Biochemistry, Heriot-Watt U., Edinburgh, Scotland, 1972. Rsch. assoc. Venezuelan Inst. Investigative Sci., Caracas, 1967-69, assoc. rschr., 1972-84, prof. microbiology, 1984—. Contbr. over 80 articles to sci. jours. Decorated Orden Andrés Bello, Venezuelan Ministry Edn., 1982. Mem. Acad. Medicine (Córdoba, Argentina), Assn. Rschrs. (sec. gen. 1983-85). Office: IVIC, Apartado Postal 21827, Caracas 1020A, Venezuela

SANBORN, JEANNIE CELLANA, medical nurse; b. Athol, Mass., Aug. 25, 1953; d. Remo Guido and Helen (Deyo) Cellana; m. Wayne Farrel Sanborn, Aug. 10, 1974; 1 child, Haley Marie. AS, Mt. Wachusett C.C., Gardner, Mass., 1978; BS in Mgmt., Lesley Coll., 1991; postgrad. student, Emmanuel Coll. RN, Mass.; cert. in infection control. Asst. head nurse ICU Heywood Hosp., Gardner, 1979-84, coord. infection control, 1984-90, mgr. infection control dept., 1990—; dir. health ctr. Cushing Acad., Ashburnham, Mass., 1986-91; cons. Infection Control and Sch. Health, 1986—; pres., co-founder AIDS-Free Am. Found., Westminster, Mass., 1994—; bd. dirs. Gardner Area Mental Health Assn., Common Sensitivity. Prin. author: AIDS Facts, 1994. Past facilitator and HIV pre/post test counselor No. Worcester County AIDS Consortium, Gardner, 1980—. Mem. Assn. Infection Control Profls. Office: Heywood Hosp 242 Green St Gardner MA 01440

SÁNCHEZ, BERTA, immunologist; b. Madrid, Apr. 21, 1960; d. Carlos and Berta S. Grad. in biology, Autonoma U. Madrid, 1982, degree in biology, 1984; PhD in Biology, U. Seville (Spain), 1990. Rsch. scientist Supr. Coun. for Scientific Rsch., Madrid, 1983-84, Hosp. for Joint Diseases, N.Y.C., 1987; resident Hosp. Univ. Virgen del Rocio, Seville, 1985-89, immunologist, 1990—. Author: (with others) Immunobiology of HLA, 1989; contbr. articles to profl. jours. Fellow NYU, 1987, Fundacion Juan March, Madrid,1989. Mem. Spanish Soc. Immunology, European Found. for Immunogenetics, Internat. Soc.for Analytical Cytology, N.Y. Acad. Scis. Office: Hosp U Virgen del Rocio, Av Manuel Siurot s/n, 41013 Seville Spain

SANCHEZ, JANICE PATTERSON, psychotherapist, educator; b. Indpls., Nov. 5, 1948; d. Jack Downey and Elizabeth (Evard) Patterson; m. Adel Sanchez, Sept. 20, 1972; children: Christina, Alison. BS in Edn., Ind. U., 1970; MSW, Cath. U. Am., 1983; grad. adv. psychotherapy tng. prog., Washington Sch. Psychiatry, 1988-91, grad. nat. group psychotherapy tng., 1994-96. Lic. clin. social worker, Va., Washington. Tchr. Fairfax County Pub. Schs., McLean, Va., 1970-76; psychotherapist D.C. Inst. Mental Hygiene, Washington, 1984-89; pvt. practice Arlington, Va., 1989—. Vol. tchr. Jr. Gt. Books, Taylor Elem. Sch., Arlington, Va., 1987-89; active Columbia Bapt. Ch. Mem. Am. Group Psychotherapy Assn., Inst. Contemporary Psychotherapy, Greater Washington Soc. for Clin. Social Workers, Jr. League No. Va. Office: Ste 14 3801 Fairfax Dr Arlington VA 22203-1762

SANCHEZ, JOSÉ R., psychiatric center executive; b. Rio Piedras, P.R., Jan. 10, 1953; s. José and Aura (Santana) S.; m. Arlene Gonzalez, July 4, 1981; 1 child, Lizamar D. BA, CCNY, 1977; MSW, Adelphi U., 1979. Team leader Brookdale Hosp., Bklyn., 1979-84; dir. on-site program Bronx (N.Y.)-Lebanon Hosp., 1984-92; chief staff N.Y.C. Dept. Mental Health, 1992-93; CEO, Bronx Psychiat. Ctr., 1993—; cons. Queens County (N.Y.) Clinic, 1982—. Mem. bd. visitors Queens Children's Hosp., 1988. Mem. Profl. Mental Health Assn. (treas. 1987). Office: Bronx Psychiat Ctr 1500 Waters Pl Bronx NY 10456

SANCHEZ, MIGUEL RAMON, dermatologist, educator; b. Havana, Cuba, May 5, 1950; came to the U.S., 1962; s. Rodolfo and Maria Sanchez. BS, CCNY, 1971; MD, Albert Einstein Coll. Medicine, 1974. Instr. Montefiore Dept. Family Medicine, Bronx, N.Y., 1978-79; sr. med. specialist Kingsborough Psychiat. Ctr., Bklyn., 1979-80; med. dir. Ten Communities Health Ctr., Tulare, Calif., 1980-82; teaching asst. dept. dermatology NYU, N.Y.C., 1982-83, asst. prof., 1983—; attending-in-chief dept. dermatology Bellevue Hosp., N.Y.C., 1983—; mem. Tulare County Mental Health Bd., 1980-81; mem. med. bd. Bellevue Hosp., 1990—. Contbr. articles to profl. jours. and chpts. to books; editor: (software) Derm-Rx, 1986-90, (book) Dermatology Educational Review Manual, 1993. Bd. dirs. Community Health Project, N.Y.C., 1993; mem. patient care com. community bd. Bellevue Hosp., 1990-93; co-founder, pres. Assn. Latino Faculty and Students. Recipient Testimonial of Appreciation So. Tulare County, 1981, 1st Place award Scientific Forum N.Y. Acad. Dermatology, 1985. Mem. Am. Acad. Dermatology, Acad. for Advancement Sci., Dermatologic Found. Democrat. Roman Catholic. Office: NYU Dept Dermatology 562 1st Ave New York NY 10016-6402

SAND, DONALD WAYNE, physician; b. Rugby, N.D., Feb. 1, 1943; s. Stranford A. and Lucille A. (Hartvickson) S.; married, 1966; children: Laura, Sara. BS, Jamestown Coll., 1965, U. N.D., 1967; MD, U. Wash., 1969. Diplomate Am. Bd. Internal Medicine. Practice medicine specializing in internal medicine Grants Pass, Oreg., 1975—. Served to maj. U.S. Army, 1969-75. Mem. Josephine County Med. Soc. (pres. 1987). Office: 124M NW Midland Ave Grants Pass OR 97526-1267

SAND, RAYMOND MICHAEL, health facility administrator; b. Wilmette, Ill., Sept. 4, 1951; s. Henry and Genevieve (Benck) S.; m. Marilyne Evenson Keyser, Mar. 24, 1990 (div. Jan. 1994); 1 child, Eric Michael. BA in Bus. Adminstrn., No. Ill. U., 1973; MA in Health Adminstrn., U. Iowa, 1975. Diplomate Am. Coll. Healthcare Execs. Chief project rev. Western Wis. Health Systems Agy., LaCrosse, 1975-86; planning coord. Franciscan Skemp Healthcare, LaCrosse, 1986—; coord. FSH, LaCrosse-Dubna (Russia) Health Partnership, 1993—. Mem. State Health Planning and Mktg. Soc. Wis., Greater LaCrosse Area C. of C. (chair bus. coun. 1989-93, 95—), Am. Hosp. Assn. Office: Franciscan Skemp Healthcare 700 West Ave South La Crosse WI 54601

SANDAHL, BONNIE BEARDSLEY, pediatric nurse practitioner, clinical nurse specialist, nurse manager; b. Washington, Jan. 17, 1939; d. Erwin Leonard and Carol Myrtle (Collis) B.; m. Glen Emil Sandahl, Aug 17, 1963; children: Cara Lynne, Cory Glen. BSN, U. Wash., 1962, MN, 1974, cert. pediatric nurse practitioner, 1972. Dir. Wash. State Joint Practice Commn., Seattle, 1974-76; instr. pediatric nurse practitioner program U. Wash., Seattle, 1976, course coordinator quality assurance, 1977-78; pediatric nurse practitioner/health coordinator Snohomish County Head Start, Everett, Wash., 1975-77; clin. nurse educator (specialist), nurse manager Harborview Med. Ctr., Seattle, 1978—, dir. child abuse prevention project, 1986—; speaker legis. focus on children, 1987; clin. assoc. Dept. of Pediatrics, U. Wash. Sch. medicine, 1987—, clin. faculty Sch. Nursing. Mem. Task Force on Pharmacotherapeutic Courses, Wash. State Bd. Nursing, 1985-86; Puget Sound Health Systems Agy., 1975-88, pres., 1980-82; mem. child devel. project adv. bd. Mukilteo Sch. Dist., 1984-85; mem. parenting adv. com. Edmonds Sch. Dist., 1985—; chmn. hospice-home health task force Snohomish County Hospice Program, Everett, 1984-85, bd. dirs. hospice, 1985-87, adv. com. 1986-88; mem. Wash. State Health Coordinating, Council. 1977-82, chmn. nursing home bed projection methodology task force, 1986-87; mem., interim chair Nat. Council Health Planning and Devel., HHS, 1980-87; mem. adv. com. on uncompensated care Wash. State Legislature, 1983-84; mem. Joint Select Com., Tech. Adv. Com. on Managed Health Care Systems, 1984-85. Pres., Alderwood Manor Community Council, 1983-85; treas. Wash. St. Women's Polit. Caucus, 1983-84; mem. com. to examine changes in Wash. State Criminal Sex Law, 1987; appointee county needs assessment com. Snohomish County Govt. United Way, 1989; chair human svcs. adv. coun. Snohomish County Human Svcs. Dept., chair adv. com., 1992-96. Recipient Golden Acorn award Seattle-King County PTA, 1973, Katherine Rickey Vol. Participation award, 1987. Mem. Am. Nurses Assn. (chmn. pediatric nurse practitioner subcom. Com. Examiners Maternal-Child Nursing Practice, 1986-92, chair Com. Examiners Maternal-Child Nursing Practice 1988-90), Wash. State Nurses Assn. (hon. leadership award 1981, chair healthcare reform task force 1992—), King County Nurses Assn. (Nurse of Yr. 1985, 1st v.p. 1992—, pres. 1996—), Wash. State Soc. Pediatrics, Sigma Theta Tau. Democrat. Methodist. Home: 1814 201st Pl SW Lynnwood WA 98036-7060 Office: Harborview Med Ctr 325 9th Ave # Za-53 Seattle WA 98104-2420

SANDALA, MARTIN WILLIAM, podiatric physician, surgeon; b. N.Y.C., Aug. 14, 1954; s. Josef S. and Lily K. (Klein) S.; m. Karen Leigh Gordon, May 29, 1976 (div. May 1992); children: Bryan Craig, Brett Andrew. BS magna cum laude, Wagner Coll., 1976; BS in Basic Med. Scis., Calif. Coll. Podiatric Medicine, 1978; D of Podiatric Medicine, Calif. Coll. Podiatric Medicin, 1980. Diplomate Am. Bd. Podiatric Medicine. Founding v.p. Juvenile Diabetes Fedn., San Francisco, 1978-80; pvt. practice West Palm Beach, Fla., 1981—; med. dir. Palm Beach Ctr. for Pathology and Surgery, West Palm Beach, Fla., 1990—. Co-author: (textbook) Compendium of Biomechanics, 1977; contbr. articles to profl. jours. Pres. bd. dirs. Am. Diabetes Assn., Palm Beach., 1986—. Office: Crosstown Med Plz 2885 N Military Tr Ste J West Palm Beach FL 33409

SANDER, LARRY JOSEPH, health facility administrator; b. Boca Raton, Fla., Mar. 22, 1946; s. Larry Edward and Jean E. (Ezzell) S.; m. Nancy W. Sander, Jan. 30, 1971. Bachelors, Southeastern U., 1970; Masters, Frostburg State Coll., 1973. Pers. mgmt. specialist VA Med. Ctr., Washington, 1972-75; supr. pers. mgmt. specialist VA Med. Ctr., Richmond, Va., 1975-77; asst. pers. officer VA Med. Ctr., Miami, Fla., 1977-79; pers. officer VA Med. Ctr., Richmond, 1979-81; assoc. dir. trainee VA Med. Ctr., Asheville, N.C., 1981-82; assoc. dir. VA Med. Ctr., Perry Point, Md., 1982-85, Lexington, Ky., 1985-87; dep. regional dir. VA Ctrl. Office S.E. Region, Washington, 1987-89; med. ctr. dir./CEO VA Med. Ctr., Louisville, Ky., 1989—. Chmn. Combined Fed. Campaign, Louisville, 1993. Recipient Hammer award V.p. Gore Nat. Performance Review, 1994, Excellence in Pub. Affairs award Va. Under Sec. for Health, 1993, Excellence in Pub. Affairs award Va. Chief Med. Dir., 1991. Fellow Am. Coll. Healthcare Execs.; mem. Fed. Exec. Assn. (pres. 1994—), Metro. Hosp. Coun., Nat. Sr. Exec. Assn., Va. Exec. Assn. Office: VA Med Ctr 800 Zorn Ave Louisville KY 40206

SANDER, LOUIS WILSON, psychiatry educator, researcher b. San Francisco, July 31, 1918; s. Louis Francis and Emily (Wilson) S.; m. Betty Estelle Thorpe, Apr. 25, 1953; children—Mark, Rebecca, David. A.B., U. Calif.-Berkeley, 1939; M.D., U. Calif.-San Francisco, 1942. Diplomate Am. Bd. Psychiatry and Neurology. Intern U. Calif. Hosp., San Francisco, 1942-43; resident psychiatry Worcester State Hosp., Mass., 1947, Judge Baker Guidance Ctr., Boston, 1949-50; resident psychiatry Mass. Meml. Hosps., Boston U. Sch. Medicine, 1947-49, resident in neurology, 1950; from instr. to assoc. prof. psychiatry Boston U. Sch. Medicine, 1949-68, prof., 1968-78; prof. psychiatry U. Colo. Sch. Medicine, Denver, 1978-87; prof. emeritus, 1987—; prin. investigator 25 yr. longitudinal study Boston U. Sch. Medicine-U. Colo. Sch. Medicine, 1981—; prin. investigator research Boston U. Sch. Medicine, 1954-78; vis. prof. U. Calif., Davis, 1979; Simpson vis. prof. U. Calif., San Francisco, 1984. Editor: (with others) Infant Psychiatry: A New Synthesis, 1976. Inventor/developer non-invasive infant bassinet monitor, 1958, infant state and infant caregiver systems regulation monitor, 1987. Contbr. articles, book chpts., and revs. to profl. publs., 1962-83. Served to maj. USAAF, 1943-46. Recipient Research Career Devel. awards USPHS, 1963-78; research grantee USPHS, March of Dimes, W. Grant Found., MacArthur Found., Spencer Found., Developmental Psychobiology Research Group-Colo. U., Nat. Coun. on Alcoholism, Univ. Hosp., Boston. Fellow Am. Coll. Psychoanalysts, Denver Psychoanalytic Soc.; mem. Am. Psychiat. Assn., Am. Acad. Child Psychiatry (sec. 1960-61), Boston Psychoanalytic Soc., AAAS, Soc. for Rsch. in Child Devel. (governing coun. 1975-77), World Assn. of Infant Mental Health, Phi Beta Kappa, Alpha Omega Alpha. Home and Office: 2525 Madrona Ave Saint Helena CA 94574-2300

SANDERLIN, TERRY KEITH, counselor; b. Ashland, Oreg., Aug. 5, 1950; s. Calvin Carney and Myrtle Estell (Cope) S.; m. Theresa Emma Garcia, Jan. 19, 1969 (div. Feb. 1976); 1 child, Sean Eric; m. Margaret Lillian Lutz, Dec. 26, 1987. B in Bus., U. N.Mex., 1982, M in Counseling, 1983, EdD, 1993. Lic. clin. mental health, N.Mex.; cert. hypnotherapist Internat. Assn. Counselors and Therapists. Unit supr. Bernalillo County Juvenile Detention Ctr., Albuquerque, 1978-80; counselor Independence Halfway House, Albuquerque, 1980-81; mental health worker Bernalillo County Mental Health Ctr., Albuquerque, 1981-82; probation parole officer N.Mex. Probation/Parole, Albuquerque, 1982-87; dist. supr. N.Mex. Probation/Parole, Gallup, 1987-88; vocat. counselor Internat. Rehab. Assn., Albuquerque, 1989-91; counseling psychologist VA, Albuquerque, 1991—; owner, dir. Counseling and Tng. Specialist, Albuquerque, 1988—; counselor Albuquerque (N.Mex.) Counseling Specialist, 1983-86; guest lectr. sociology dept. U. N.Mex., Albuquerque, 1992; presenter 5th Annual S.W. Substance Abuse Conf., Albuquerque, 1992; presenter N.Mex. Corrections Dept., Santa Fe, 1993. Author: (video tapes) Breathing Free & Good, 1991, Understanding Adolescent Satanism, 1991, (manual) Social Skills and Anger Management, 1993. Vol. counselor Adult Misdemeanor Probation, Albuquerque, 1974-76; panel mem. Cmty. Corrections Selection Panel, Albuquerque, 1987-90. With U.S. Army, 1969-72, Vietnam. Recipient Outstanding Citizenship, Albuquerque (N.Mex.) Police Dept., 1974. Mem. ACA, Am. Corrections Assn., Am. Legion. Democrat. Office: Counseling & Tng Specialist 5215 Grand Albuquerque NM 87108

SANDERS, AUGUSTA SWANN, retired nurse; b. Alexandria, La., July 22, 1932; d. James and Elizabeth (Thompson) Swann; m. James Robert Sanders, Jan. 12, 1962 (div. 1969). Student, Morgan State U., 1956. Pub. health nurse USPHS, Washington, 1963-64; mental health counselor Los Angeles County Sheriff's Dept., 1972-79; program coordinator Los Angeles County Dept. Mental Health, 1979-88; program dir. L.A. County Dept. Health Svcs., 1989-92; ret., 1992; apptd. by Calif. Gov. Jerry Brown to 11th Dist. Bd. Med. Quality Assurance, 1979-85; health cons., legal, 1994—. Mem. Assemblyman Mike Roo's Commn. on Women's Issues, 1981—, Senator Diane Watson's Commn. on Health Issues, 1979—; chmn. Commn. Sex. Equity Los Angeles Unified Sch. Dist., 1984-90. Mem. NAFE, L.A. County Employees Assn. (v.p. 1971-72), So. Calif. Black Nurses Assn. (founding mem.), Internat. Fedn. Bus. and Profl. Women (pres. L.A. Sunset dist. 1988-89, dist. officer 1982-89), Internat. Assn. Chemical Dependency Nurses (treas. 1990-92), Chi Eta Phi. Democrat. Methodist.

SANDERS, BARBARA LOUISE, physical therapist; b. Covington, Ky., Mar. 31, 1950; d. Nicholas S. and Emily Louise (Winchester) Furnish; m. Douglas Ragland, Aug. 1970 (div. Aug. 1974); m. Michael T. Sanders, June 3, 1978; 1 child, Whitney. BS, U. Ky., 1972, MS, 1976; PhD, U. Tex., 1991. Lic. phys. therapist, Tex., Ky. Phys. therapist Good Samaritan Hosp., Lexington, Ky., 1972-74; pvt. practice Lexington, Ky., 1974-76; instr. U. Ky., Lexington, Ky., 1976-77; phys. therapist St. Cloud (Minn.) Hosp., 1977-78; instr. U. Wis., Lacrosse, 1978-83; phys. therapist Ft. Sanders Regional Med. Ctr., Knoxville, Tenn., 1983-86; asst. prof. S.W. Tex. State U., San Marcos, 1986-90, assoc. prof., 1990-96, prof., 1996—. Editor: Sports Physical Therapy, 1990; contbr. articles to profl. jours. Mem. AAUW, Am. Phys. Therapy Assn. (Mary McMillan scholar 1990, Excellence in Edn. award 1994), Tex. Phys. Therapy Assn. (pres.-elect 1995, pres. 1996—). Home: 8206 Cache Dr Austin TX 78749 Office: SW Tex State U 601 University Dr San Marcos TX 78666

SANDERS, CHARLES ADDISON, physician; b. Dallas, Feb. 10, 1932; s. Harold Barefoot and May Elizabeth (Forrester) S.; m. Elizabeth Ann Chipman, Mar. 6, 1956; children: Elizabeth, Charles Addison, Carlyn, Christopher. MD, U. Tex., 1955. Intern, asst. resident Boston City Hosp., 1955-57, chief resident, 1957-58; clin. and rsch. fellow in medicine Mass. Gen. Hosp., Boston, 1958-60; chief cardiac catheterization lab. Mass. Gen. Hosp., 1962-72, gen. dir., 1972-81, physician, 1973-81, program dir. myocardial infarction rsch. unit, 1967-72; exec. v.p. E.R. Squibb and Sons, 1981-84; exec. v.p. Squibb Corp., 1984-88, vice chmn., 1988-89; chief exec. officer Glaxo Inc., Research Triangle Park, N.C., 1989-94, chmn., 1992-95; assoc. prof. medicine Harvard U. Med. Sch., 1969-80, prof., 1980-83; candidate U.S. Senate, 1996; bd. dirs. Mt. Sinai Med. Ctr., N.Y.C.; chmn. Commonwealth Fund N.Y.C.; mem. Inst. Medicine. Mem. editorial bd. New Eng. Jour. Medicine, 1969-72. Chmn. Project Hope; bd. dirs. U. N.C., Chapel Hill. Capt. USAF, 1960-62. Mem. ACP, Am. Heart Assn., Mass. Med. Soc. Office: 100 Europa Dr Ste 170 Chapel Hill NC 27514

SANDERS, DONALD BENJAMIN, neurologist, educator; b. Sumter, S.C., Aug. 3, 1938; s. Colclough E. and Frances Ann Sanders; m. Lynda Louise Frank, July 19, 1976; children: Colclough Allison, Kathleen Chatterton. BS, Univ. of the South, 1959; MD, Harvard Med. Sch., 1964. Diplomate Am. Bd. Neurology, Am. Bd. Electrodiagnostic Medicine. Asst. prof. neurology U. Va. Med. Sch., Charlottesville, 1973-77, assoc. prof. neurology, 1978-80; prof. medicine Duke U. Med. Sch., Durham, N.C., 1980—. Contbr. articles to profl. jours. Maj. USAF, 1969-72. Fellow Am. Acad. Neurology; mem. Am. Neurol. Assn., Am. Assn. Electrodiagnostic Medicine (bd. dirs. 1993-95, pres.-elect 1995-96). Office: Duke U Med Ctr Box 3403 Durham NC 27710

SANDERS, GILBERT OTIS, health and addiction psychologist, consultant, educator, motivational speaker; b. Oklahoma City, Aug. 7, 1945; s. Richard Allen and Evelyn Wilmoth (Barker) S.; m. Lidia Julia Grados-Ventura; 1 child, Lisa Dawn Sanders-Coker. AS, Murray State Coll, 1965; BA, Okla. State U., 1967, U. State of N.Y.; MS, Troy State U., 1970; EdD, U. Tulsa, 1974; postdoctoral studies St. Louis U., Am. Tech. U.; grad. U.S. Army Command and Gen. Staff Coll., Ft. Leavenworth, Kas., 1979. Diplomate Am. Bd. Med. Pschotherapist, Am. Bd. Forensic Examiners. Dir. edn. Am. Humane Edn. Soc., Boston, 1975; chmn. dept. computer sci., dir. Individual Learning and Counseling Ctr., asst. prof. pscholgy and law enforcement Calumet Coll., Whiting, Ind., 1975-78; rsch. psychologist U.S. Army Rsch. Inst., Ft. Hood, Tex., 1978-79; pvt. practice counseling, Killen, Tex., 1978-79; psychologist U.S. Army Tng. and Doctrine Command Sys. Analysis Activity, White Sands Missile Range, N.Mex., 1979-80; project dir. psychologist Applied Sci. Assocs., Ft. Sill, Okla., 1980-81; pvt. practice counseling, Lake St. Louis, 1981-83; assoc. prof. Pittsburg State U., Kans., 1983-85; pres. Applied Behavioral Rsch. Assocs. (formerly Southwestern Behavioral Rsch.), Oklahoma City, 1985-94; pvt. practice counseling Christian Family Counseling Ctr., Lawton, Okla., 1986-87; psychologist, systems analyst U.S Army Field Artillery Sch.-Directorate of Combat Devels., Ft. Sill, Okla., 1987; psychologist U.S. Army Operational Test and Evaluation Agy., Washington, 1988-89; psychologist, drug abuse program dir. Fed. Bur. of Prisons-Fed. Correctional Inst. El Reno, Okla., 1989-91; psychologist, clin. dir. drug abuse program U.S. Penitentiary, Leavenworth, Kans., 1991-95; pvt. practice psychologist MacArthur Med. and Psychotherapy, Inc. and Acad. Christian Counseling Okla., Oklahoma City, 1992—; adj. prof. bus. and psychology Columbia Coll.-Buder Campus, St. Louis, 1982-84; adj. prof. U.S. Army Command Staff and Gen. Coll., 1983-89, Columbia Pacific U., 1984—, Greenwich U., 1990—, U. Alaska S.E., 1995—. Editor: Evaluation for a Manual Backup System for TACFIRE (ARI), 1978, Training/Humane Factors Implications--Copperhead Operational Test II Livefire Phase, 1979, TRADOC Training Effectiveness Analysis Handbook, 1980, Cost and Training Effectiveness Analysis/TEA 8-80/Patroit Air Defense Missile System, 1980, Cost and Training Analysis/Infantry Fighting Vehicle (Bradley), 1980, Human Factors Implications for the Howitzer Improvement Program, 1989, The Drug Education Handbook, 1995, Therapist Handbook for Drug Treatment, 1996; author research reports. Recipient Kavanough Found. Community Builder award, 1967; named Hon. Col. Okla. Gov. Staff, 1972, Hon. Amb., 1974. Fellow Am. Assn. Psychologists Treating Addictions (diplomate), Am. Forensic Counselors Assn.; mem. APA, ACA, Am. Assn. Marriage and Family Therapists, Am. Mental Health Counselors Assn., Res. Officers Assn., Commd. Officers Assn., U.S. Pub. Health Svc., Pi Kappa Phi, Alpha Phi Omega. Home: 5404 NW 65th St Oklahoma City OK 73132-7747 Office: Mac Arthur Med Inst 7317 N Mac Arthur Blvd Oklahoma City OK 73132

SANDERS, JAMES NORMAN, marriage, family, individual and group counselor; b. Benington, Okla., Nov. 13, 1930; s. James C. Sanders and Bella (Hodges) Welch; m. Patricia J. Dews, May 27, 1955; children: James Norman Jr., Timothy W. DD, Clarksville Sch. Theology, 1979, ThD, 1980; PhD, ZOE Internat. Coll., Jacksonville, Fla., 1989; Cert. Addiction Profl., Am. Coll. Addictionology and, Maladaptive Behavior, Miami, 1995. Cert. Christian counselor; diplomate Am. Bd. Christian Psychology. Enlisted man USAF, 1948, advanced through grades to master sgt., 1963, manpower systems engr., 1948-68; ret., 1968; asst. adminstrs. Johns Hopkins Hosp., Balt., 1968-73; cons., 1973-78; exec. v.p. Fla. Beacon Coll., Largo, 1979-82; dir. Christian Counseling Svcs., Vero Beach, Fla., 1983—; cons. health div. Westinghouse Co., Pitts., 1970-72. Co-author: Supervisory Development for Hospital Employees, 1972. Bd. dirs. ZOE Internat. Coll., 1986. Recipient cert. of appreciation State of Md., 1952. Office: The Charles Parker Found for HHS Rsch & Devel 2213 Highland Ave Melbourne FL 32935

SANDERS, JEFF DAVIS, biology educator; b. Brownfield, Tex., Dec. 27, 1931; s. Aaron Benjamin and Ida Faye (Ball) S.; m. Marcie Jane Mitchell, Mar. 3, 1953; children: Karl F., Chris. AA, Del Mar Coll., 1951; BS, S.W. Tex. State U., 1958, MA, 1962. Instr. Tex. A&I U., Kingsville, 1959-66; instr. biology S.W. Tex. Jr. Coll., Uvalde, 1966—; mem. Bd. Voc. Nurse Examiners, Austin, 1984; mem. Tchrs. Profl. Practice Commn., Tex., 1984-88; pres. Honey Capital Fed. Credit Union, 1974-78; cons. in field. Author/editor various newsletters in field; author lab manual: Zoology Lab Manual, 1963, 72. Campaign worker Dem. Party cand., 1964—; mem. various county bds., 1994—; bd. dirs. El Progreso Meml. Libr., 1994—. With USAF, 1951-55. NSF fellow, 1965, 70, others. Mem. NEA, Am. Soc. Microbiology, Nat. Assn. Biology Tchrs., Tex. Faculty Assn., Tex. United Faculty (local pres., bd. dirs. 1983-87), N.Y. Acad. Sci., Tex. Orgn. Endangered Species, Greenpeace, World Wildlife Fund, Sierra Club, Nature Conservancy, Amnesty Internat. Democrat. Baptist. Office: SW Tex Jr Coll Garner Field Rd Uvalde TX 78801

SANDERS, SANDRA JO, medical technologist, educator; b. Marfrance, W.Va., Dec. 5, 1946; d. Clinton Billings and Lorene (Pittsenbarger) Billings McClung; m. Darrell Leroy Sanders, Nov. 15, 1965; children: Clifton Lee, Darrell Leroy Jr., Tina Marie. BA magna cum laude, W.Va. State U., 1986; postgrad., Marshall U. Cert. med. technologist. Med. technologist Boone Meml. Hosp., Madison, W.Va., 1965-74, Logan (W.Va.) Gen. Hosp., 1989—; tchr. vocat. health Boone County Bd. Edn., Madison, 1974—; adj. instr. S. W.Va. C.C., Boone and Logan, 1990-92; mem. Boone County Adv. Bd. on Vocat. Edn., Madison, 1973; cons. Bur. Vocat., Tech. and Adult Edn., Charleston, W.Va., 1975. Mem. Am. Med. Technologists Assn. (Disting. Achievement award 1983), Am. Vocat. Assn., Internat. Soc. Clin. Lab. Technologists, W.Va. Edn. Assn. Democrat. Mem. Ch. of Christ. Home: 813 Greenwood Dr Madison WV 25130-1611 Office: Boone County Career and Tech Ctr HC 81 Box 50B Danville WV 25053

SANDERS, STEVEN LOUIS, surgeon; b. Atlanta, Jan. 4, 1939; s. Abe L. and Betty Ruth (Lipman) S.; m. Linda Ellen Schapiro, Dec. 27, 1963; children: Mark I., David B. Student, Emory U., 1956-59, MD, 1963. Diplomate Am. Bd. Surgery. Intern surgery Yale-New Haven (Conn.) Med. Ctr., 1963-64; asst. resident, chief resident dept. surgery Emory U.-VA and Grady Meml. Hosps., Atlanta, 1966-70; pvt. practice gen. surgery Atlanta, 1970—. Capt. U.S. Army, 1964-66. Fellow ACS; mem. AMA, Med. Assn. Ga., Med. Assn. Atlanta (sec. 1981-84), Southeastern Surg. Congress, Soc. for Laparoendoscopic Surgery, Am. Soc. for Gen. Surgery. Office: Ste 380 5667 Peachtree Dunwoody Rd Atlanta GA 30342

SANDERSON, MARY LOUISE, medical association administrator; b. Fairmont, W. Va., Oct. 29, 1942; d. Lawrence Oliver and Frances Evelyn (Shuttleworth) Shingleton; m. William W. Olmstead III, Dec. 1966 (div. June 1974); children: William W. IV, Happy; m. Lester F. Davis, III, Oct. 1979 (div. Dec. 1986); m. David S. Sanderson, Sept. 1992. Student, Vassar Coll., 1960-62, Carnegie Mellon, 1962-63. Real estate broker, N.C. Exec. sec. Creative Dining, Raleigh, N.C., 1980-83, Sea Pines Plantation Co., Hilton Head, S.C., 1973-79; adminstr. Am. Bd. Neurological Surgery, Houston, 1983—. Vol. Interact, Raleigh, 1984-86, M.D. Anderson Cancer Ctr./Camp Star Trails, 1994—; docent Mordicai House Hist. Preservation, Raleigh, 1981-83; mem. Reach to Recovery, 1995—. Recipient Vol. award N.C. State Gov., 1986. Mem. Am. Soc. Assn. Execs. Democrat. Episcopalian. Office: Am Bd Neurol Surgery 6550 Fannin St Ste 2139 Houston TX 77030-2722

SANDESC, DOREL, anesthesiologist, intensivist, consultant; b. Orastie, Hunedoara, Romania, July 13, 1959; s. Ioan and Ana (Petrescu) S.; m. Matilda Badea, Mar. 1, 1986; 1 child, Mihai Alexandru. MD, U. Medicine, Cluj Napoca, Romania, 1985; postgrad., U. Medicine, Timisoara, Romania, 1993. Gen. medicine physician County Hosp., Deva, Romania, 1985-88; gen. medicine physician Village Health Unit, Chiochis, Romania, 1988-89, Geoagiu, Romania, 1989-90; anesthesiology trainee # 1 Clin. Hosp., Timisoara, 1991-93, cons. in anesthesiology, 1994; cons. anesthesia and intensive care Univ. Medicine, Timisoara, 1994. Contbr. articles to profl. jours. Corp. Romanian Army, 1978-79. Fellow Soc. Anesthesia and Intensive Care; mem. Romanian Soc. Anesthesia, Romanian Profl. Assn. Anesthetists (pres. 1993). Home: L Rebreanu 148A Ap 13, 1900 Timisoara Timis, Romania Office: # 1 Hosp, L Rebreanu 156, 1900 Timisoara Timis, Romania

SANDLOW, LESLIE JORDAN, physician, educator; b. Chgo., Jan. 7, 1934; s. Harry H. and Rose (Ehrlich) S.; m. Joanne J. Fleischer, June 16, 1957; children: Jay, Bruce, Lisa. BS, U. Ill., 1956; MD, Chgo. Med. Sch., 1960. Intern Michael Reese Hosp. and Med. Ctr., Chgo., 1961, med. resident, rsch. fellow gastrointestinal rsch., 1961-64, physician-in-charge clin. gastroenterology lab., 1963-74, asst. attending physician, 1964-67, assoc. attending physician, 1967-72, vice chmn. divsn. gastroenterology, dir. ambulatory medicine, 1968, dir. ambulatory care, 1969-76, attending physician, 1972—, assoc. med. dir., 1972-73; clin. asst. Chgo. Med. Sch., 1963-68, clin. instr., 1966; asst. prof. dept. medicine Pritzker Sch. Medicine, U. Chgo., 1973-76, assoc. prof., 1976-85, prof., 1985-90; prof. clin. medicine and med. edn. U. Ill. Coll. Medicine, Chgo., 1990-91, prof. medicine and med. edn., 1992—, sr. assoc. dean for grad. and continuing med. edn., 1993—, head dept. med. edn., 1993—, sr. assoc. dean for med. edn., 1994—; dep. v.p. profl. affairs Michael Reese Hosp. and Med. Ctr., 1973-78, dir. Office Ednl. Affairs, 1976-81, assoc. v.p. acad. affairs, 1978-82, dir. quality assurance program, 1981-91, v.p. planning, 1982-83, v.p. profl. affairs and planning, 1983-88, dir. divsn. internal medicine, 1986-93, v.p. profl. and acad. affairs, 1988-91, med. dirs. acad. and med. affairs, 1992-94; med. dir. Michael Reese Health Plan, Inc., 1972-74, interim exec. dir., 1976-77; cons. gastroenterologist Ill. Ctrl. Hosp., 1978-80; vis. prof. Pontifica U. Catolica Rio Grande do Sul, Brazil, 1978, U. Fed. Espirito Santo, Brazil, 1978, Nordic Fedn. for Med. Understanding, Akureyri, Iceland, 1978, Seoul Nat. U. Sch. Medicine, 1981, Coll. Physicians and Surgsons, Kharachi, Pakistan, 1994, U. Tex., Ft. Worth, 1977, U. Ariz., Tucson, 1977, Loyola U. Med. Sch., Maywood, Ill., 1979; cons. in field; coord. Health Scis. Librs. in Ill.; mem. Midwest Med. Libr. Network; mem. subcom. on delivery of ambulatory med. care Inst. Medicine Chgo.; mem. cmty. resources task force Interinstnl. Cardiovascular Ctr.; chmn. steering group Ill. Regional Med. Program; past co-chmn. curriculum com. U. Chgo. Reviewer Rsch. in Med. Edn./Assn. Am. Med. Colls., 1985—, Acad. Medicine/Assn. Am. Med. Colls., 1989; contbr. numerous articles to profl. publs. Mem. Skokie (Ill.) Bd. Health, 1973-85, chmn., 1976-85; bd. dirs. Group Health Assn. Am., 1976-78, Portes Ctr., 1980—; bd. dirs. Good Health Program Skokie Valley Hosp., 1978-80; bd. dirs., exec. com. Rsch. and Edn. Found. of Michael Reese Hosp. Med. Staff, 1992—. Recipient numerous grants, including NIH, 1988, Michael Reese Hosp. Found., 1994-95, Chgo. Cmty. Trust, 1994-95. Fellow Am. Coll. Gastroenterology; mem. N.Y. Acad. Scis., Inst. Medicine, Assn. Am. Med. Colls., Am. Coll. Physician Execs. (co-chair resource mgmt. com. of quality assurance forum), Soc. Dirs. Med. Coll. Continuing Med. Edn., Soc. Dir. Rsch. in Med. Edn. Home: 2314 Lincoln Park West Chicago IL 60614 Office: U Ill Coll Medicine Med Edn MC 784 1819 W Polk St Chicago IL 60612

SANDMAN, DAVID EDWARD, JR., rehabilitation nurse; b. Cin., Mar. 14, 1959; s. David Edward and Jean Marie (Thiemann) S. Diploma in nursing, Christ Hosp., Cin., 1984; BS in Communication Sci. and Disorders, U. Cin., 1981. RN, Ohio. Rehab. nurse Jewish Hosp., Cin., 1984-86, U. Hosp., Cin., 1986-87; pvt. duty home rehab. nurse RN Registry, Cin., 1987-91; rehab. nurse No. Ky. Rehab. Hosp., Edgewood, 1991—; contract co-statis. analyst rehab. medicine dept. Good Samaritan Hosp., Cin., 1986; presenter in field. Contbr. articles to profl. jours.

SANDMEYER, E. E., toxicologist, consultant; b. Winterthur, Zurich, Switzerland, Aug. 9, 1929; came to U.S., 1955; d. Fritz Henry and Aline (Schoch) S. BSChemE, Technikum, Winterthur, 1951; MS in Organic Chemistry, Ohio State U., 1960, PhD in Biochemistry, 1965. Cert. civil svc. chemist II, Nev., biochemist II, Pa., clin. lab. dir. Ctrs. for Disease Control. Head corp. toxicology Gulf Oil Corp., Pitts., 1971-75; div. head organic analysis Barringer Labs., Denver, 1986-88; pres., toxicologist, owner Transcontec, Inc., Kelseyville, Calif., 1976—; Contbg. author: Patty's Industrial Hygiene and Toxicology, 1981, A Guide to General Toxicology, 1983. Mem. AAAS, Am. Chem. Soc., Soc. Environ. Health, Sigma Xi, Sigma Delta Epsilon. Office: Transcontec Inc 7305 Live Oak Dr Kelseyville CA 95451-9677

SANDOK, BURTON ALAN, medical educator, neurologist, dean of faculty; b. N.Y.C., Nov. 28, 1937; s. Raymond and Helen S.; m. Florence Bobrove, Aug. 14, 1960; children: Evan Kendall, Douglas Phillip. BA, Iowa U., Iowa City, 1958, MD, 1961. Diplomate Am. Bd. Psychiatry and Neurology. Intern U.S. Naval Hosp., Oakland, Calif., 1961-62; resident in neuropsychiatry U.S. Naval Hosp., Phila., 1962-63; fellow in neurology Mayo Grad. Sch. Medicine, Rochester, Minn., 1966-69; assoc. dir. med. and lab. specialties Mayo Grad. Sch. Medicine, Rochester, 1984-88; cons. neurology Mayo Clinic, Rochester, 1969, prof., chmn. neurology, 1980, 81-88; asst. prof. then assoc. prof. neurology Mayo Med. Sch., Rochester, 1972-80; assoc. dean academic affairs Mayo Med. Sch., Rochester, Minn., 1989—. Served to lt. comdr. USN, 1963-66. Recipient Outstanding Teacher awards Mayo Grad Sch., 1971, 72, 77, 86, Mayo Med. Sch., 1982, 84. Fellow Am. Acad. Neurology, Stroke Council Am. Heart Assn.; mem. AMA, Assn. Univ. Profs. Neurology, Am. Neurologic Assn. Office: Mayo Med Sch 200 1st St SW Rochester MN 55905-0001*

SANDS, DOLORES S., dean, nursing educator. BSN, Wayne State U., MSN; PhD, Ariz. State U. Prof., dir. Ctr. Health Care Rsch. and Evaluation U. Tex., Austin, 1984-89, dir. grad. program nursing adminstrn., 1989—, former acting dean, asst. dean rsch. and resources, asst. dean baccalaureate program, now dean, Laura Lee Blanton chair in nursing, also now Joseph H. Blades Centennial Meml. prof. in nursing; mem. nursing sci. rev. com. Exploratory Rsch. Ctr. Grants; mem. adv. coun. on nurses edn. and practice divsn. nursing Health Resources and Svcs. Adminstrn. U.S. Dept. Health and Human Svcs., 1991-93, co-chair adv. coun., 1993-95, mem. adv. group nat. task force for workforce projections of nurse practitioners and nurse-midwives, 1993, now mem. joint coun. primary care workforce workgroup; active Nat. Ctr. for Nursing Rsch., NIH. Contbr. articles to profl. jours. Grantee USPHS, 1986-89; recipient Alumni Achievement award Ariz. State U., 1987. Mem. ANA, Coun. Nurse Rschrs., Soc. Rsch. in Nursing Edn., Phi Kappa Phi, Sigma Theta Tau. Office: U Tex Austin Sch Nursing Austin TX 78712*

SANDS, JUDITH R., healthcare quality professional; b. Buffalo, May 30, 1960; d. Henry and Anita (Zatz) Dallman; m. Louis Allan Sands, Mar. 16, 1985; children: Daniel Aaron, Seth Adam. BSN, U. Fla., 1981. Lic. healthcare risk mgmt., Fla.; cert. profl. in healthcare quality; cert. case mgr. Staff nurse Broward Gen. Med. Ctr., Ft. Lauderdale, Fla., 1982; cons. Med. Personnel Pool, Ft. Lauderdale, 1983-85; flight nurse Nat. Jet, Ft. Lauderdale, 1984-86; staff nurse Humana Hosp. Cypress, Pompano Beach, Fla., 1982-85; risk mgr., quality assurance coord. CIGNA HealthPlan of South Fla., Inc., Ft. Lauderdale, 1985-87; mgr. risk control and quality rev. N.W. Regional Hosp., Margate, Fla., 1988-92, dir. quality resource mgmt.HCA, 1992-94; owner Healthcare Initiatives, 1995—. Mem. Nat. Assn. Healthcare Quality (mem. edn. team com. 1996—), Am. Assn. Legal Nurse Cons., Broward Assn. Health Care Profls. (v.p. 1995-96), Women in Healthcare.

SANDS, MICHAEL EUGENE, osteopathic physician; b. Frederick, Okla., Dec. 11, 1961; s. Earl Eugene and Janice Jean (Herring) S. BS in Biology, U. Nebr., 1985; ADN, Riverside (Calif.) C.C., 1988; DO, Univ. Health Scis.-COM, Kansas City, Mo., 1993. RN, Calif.; cert. physician and surgeon Calif. Osteo. Med. Bd.; cert. BCLS instr., ACLS instr.; ordained to ministry World Christianship Ministries. With environ. svcs. Mercy Hosp., Omaha, 1984-85; nursing asst. Parkview Cmty. Hosp., Riverside, 1987-88; nurse Riverside Gen. Hosp., 1988-89; resident in family practice Pacific Hosp. of Long Beach, Calif., 1993—. Recipient R.R. Hannah MD award Mo. chpt. Am. Coll. Emergency Physicians, 1993. Mem. Am. Osteo. Assn., Am. Acad. Osteopathy, Am. Coll. Osteo. Family Physicians, Mensa, NRA, Pi Sigma Alpha, Sigma Sigma Phi.

SANDSTEDT, PETER IVAR, oral surgeon; b. Stockholm, July 5, 1947; s. Stig Karl Ingemar Sandstedt and Eva Birgitta (Berg) Lindgren. BSc in Behavioural Scis., U. Stockholm, 1970; DDS, Karolinska Inst., Stockholm, 1974. Diplomate in Oral Surgery Nat. Swedish Bd. of Health and Welfare. Private dental practitioner Stockholm, 1975-80; asst. oral surgeon Dept. Dental and Jaw Diseases Karolinska Hosp., Stockholm, 1981; resident Dept Oral Surgery Danderyd Hosp., Sweden, 1982-85; assoc. dir. Dept. Oral Surgery Norrköping (Sweden) Hosp., 1986, Dept. Oral Surgery Västeras (Sweden) Hosp.; assoc. dir. dept. of oral and maxillofacial surgery Stockholm Söder Hosp., Stockholm, 1991—. Mem. Acad. Osseointegration, Scandinavian Assn. Oral and Maxillofacial Surgeons. Home: Värtavägen 23, 115 53 Stockholm Sweden Office: Stockholm Söder Hosp, Oral & Maxillofacial Surg, Ringvägen 52, 118 83 Stockholm Sweden

SANDSTRÖM, GUNNAR EMANUEL, microbiologist; b. Lycksele, Sweden, June 1, 1951; s. Lars Åke Emanuel and Maj Dovi Helena (Holmgren) S.; m. Elsa Lillemor Johansson, May 30, 1986; children: Jörgen, Sandra. D. in Med. Sci., U. Umeå (Sweden), 1988. Asst. U. Umeå, 1970-80; asst. Nat. Def. Rsch. Establishment, Umeå, 1980-85, sr. rsch. officer, 1985-89; postdoctoral fellow US Army Med. Rsch. Inst., Ft. Detrick, Frederick, Md., 1989-90; head div. microbiology Nat. Def. Rsch. Establishment, Umeå, 1990, assoc. prof., 1991; prof. Nat. Def. Rsch. Establishment and U. Umeå, Umeå, 1994—; dir. rsch. Nat. Def. Rsch. Establishment, Umeå, 1995—, dir., 1997—; sr. rsch. officer NRC, Frederick, 1989-90. Contbr. tularemia articles to profl. jours.; inventor-patentee rapid diagnosis of bacteria. Chmn. Local Community Coun., Umeå, 1979-88. Mem. Lion Club (Umeå, Sweden). Home: Vallmovägen 33, S 90352 Umeå Sweden Office: Nat Def Rsch Establishment, Cementvägen 20, S 901 82 Umeå Sweden

SANDSTROM, ROBERT EDWARD, physician, pathologist; b. Hull, Yorkshire, Eng., Apr. 4, 1946; came to U.S., 1946; s. Edward Joseph and Ena Joyce (Rilatt) S.; m. Regina Lois Charlebois (dec. May 1987); children: Karin, Ingrid, Erica. BSc, McGill U., Montreal, 1968; MD, U. Wash., 1971. Diplomate Am. Bd. Pathology, Am. Bd. Dermatopathology. Internship Toronto (Can.) Gen. Hosp., 1971-72; resident pathologist Mass. Gen. Hosp., Boston, 1974-78; clin. fellow Harvard U. Med. Sch., Boston, 1976-78; cons. King Faisel Hosp., Riyadh, Saudi Arabia, 1978; pathologist, dir. labs. St. John's Med. Ctr., Longview, Wash., 1978—; v.p. Intersect Systems Inc., Longview, Wash., 1990—; chmn. bd. Cowlitz Med. Svc., Longview, 1988; participant congl. sponsored seminar on AIDS, Wash., 1987. Script writer movie Blood Donation in Saudi Arabia, 1978; contbr. articles to profl. jours. Surgeon USPHS, 1972-74. Fellow Coll. Am. Pathologists, Royal Coll. Physicians; mem. Cowlitz-Wahkiakum County Med. Soc. (past pres.). Roman Catholic. Home: 49 View Ridge Ln Longview WA 98632-5556 Office: Lower Columbia Pathologists 1606 E Kessler Blvd Ste 100 Longview WA 98632-1841

SANDT, JOHN JOSEPH, psychiatrist, educator; b. N.Y.C., June 29, 1925; s. John Jacob and Victoria Theodora Sandt; m. Mary Cummings Evans, Sept. 14, 1946; children: Christine, Karen, John K., Kurt, Colin, Carol; m. Mary W. Griswold, July 10, 1992. BA, Vanderbilt U., 1948; MA, Yale U., 1951; MD, Vanderbilt U., 1957. Instr. English Vanderbilt U., Nashville, 1951-52, Syracuse (N.Y.) U. Coll., 1960-61; intern SUNY Upstate Med. Ctr., Syracuse, 1957-58, resident, 1958-61; instr. psychiatry Southwestern Med. Sch., Dallas, 1961-63; chief psychiatry VA Med. Ctr., Dallas, 1961-63; chief outpatient clinic Dept. Mental Health, Springfield, Mass., 1963-66; asst. prof. psychiatry U. Rochester (N.Y.) Med. Sch., 1966-75, clin. assoc. prof. psychiatry, 1975—; chief psychiatry Clifton Springs (N.Y.), 1985-88, VA Med. Ctr., Bath, N.Y., 1988—; cons. psychiatry VA Med. Ctr., Northampton, Mass., 1965-66, Springfield Coll., 1964-66, Brockport (N.Y.) State Coll., 1966-75, Fairport (N.Y.) Bapt. Home, 1966-88; asst. dir. ind. study program U. Rochester Med. Sch., 1971-75. Author: Clinical Supervision of Psychiatric Resident, 1972; contbr. articles on psychiat. consultation and treatment to profl. jours. Vestryman All Saints Episcopal Ch., South Hadley, Mass., 1963-66. With USNR 1944-46, PTO. Nathaniel Currier fellow Yale Grad. Sch., 1948-49. Mem. Am. Psychiat. Assn., Am. Assn. Geriatric Psychiatry, AAAS, Med. Soc. N.Y. State. Office: VA Med Ctr Bath NY 14810

SANETO, RUSSELL PATRICK, pediatrician, neurobiologist; b. Burbank, Calif., Oct. 10, 1950; s. Arthur and Mitzi (Seddon) S.; m. Kathleen D. Saneto. BS with honors, San Diego State U., 1972, MS, 1975; PhD, U. Tex. Med. Br., 1981; DO U. Osteo. Medicine and Surgery, 1994. Teaching asst. San Diego State U. 1969-75; substitute tchr. Salt Lake City Sch. Dist., 1975; teaching and rsch. asst. U. Tex. Med. Br., 1976-77, NIH predoctoral fellow, 1977-81, postdoctoral fellow, 1981; Jeanne B. Kempner postdoctoral fellow UCLA, 1981-82, NIH postdoctoral fellow, 1982-87; asst. prof. Oreg. Regional Primate Rsch. Ctr. div. Neurosci., Beaverton, 1987-89; asst. prof. dept. cell biology and anatomy Oreg. Health Scis. U., Portland, 1988-90, U. Osteo. Medicine & Surgery, 1991-94, Cleve. Clinic, 1994—; lectr. rsch. methods Grad. Sch., 1982; vis. scholar in ethics So. Baptist Theol. Sem., Louisville, 1981. Contbr. articles to profl. jours. Recipient Merit award Nat. March of Dimes, 1978; named one of Outstanding Young Men in Am., 1979, 81, one of Men of Significance, 1985. Mem. AAAS, Am. Acad. Pediats., Bread for World, Save the Whales, Sierra Club, Am. Soc. Human Genetics, Winter Confs. Brain Rsch., Neuroscis. Study Program, N.Y. Acad. Scis., Am. Soc. Neurochem., Soc. Neurosci., Am. Soc. Neurochemistry, Soc. Neurosci., World Runners Club, Sigma Sigma Phi. Democrat. Mem. Evangelical Free Ch.

SANFORD, HOWARD S., physician; b. Floral Park, N.Y., Jan. 10, 1933; s. Abraham H. and Celia Y. Sanford; m. Margery Ruth Taub, June 15, 1960; children: Allan, Steven. BS, Columbia U., 1954; MD, Northwestern U., Chgo., 1958. Diplomate Am. Bd. Internal Medicine. Intern Phila. Gen. Hosp., 1958-59; resident U. Mich. Hosp., Ann Arbor, 1960-62; fellow in cardiology Jackson Meml. Hosp., Miami, Fla., 1962-63; pvt. practice North Miami Beach, 1963—; chief med. staff Parkway Regional Med. Ctr., North Miami Beach, 1989-90, chmn. bd. dirs. Lt. col. U.S. Army, 1967-69. Mem. Alpha Omega Alpha. Home: 18740 NE 19th Ave N Miami Bch FL 33179-4313 Office: 18620 NE 19th Ave North Miami Beach FL 33162-3149

SANFORD, JAY PHILIP, internist, educator; b. Madison, Wis., May 27, 1928; s. Joseph Arthur and Arlyn (Carlson) S.; m. Lorraine Burklund, Apr. 7, 1950; children—Jeb, Nancy, Sarah, Philip, Catherine. M.D., U. Mich., 1952; D of Mil. Medicine (hon.), Uniformed Svcs. U. Health Sci., 1991. Intern Peter Bent Brigham Hosp., Boston, 1952-53; research fellow Harvard Med. Sch., Boston, 1953-54; resident Duke U. Hosp., Durham, N.C., 1956-57; practice medicine specializing in internal medicine Dallas, 1957-75; mem. faculty U. Tex. Southwestern Med. Sch. at Dallas, 1957-75; prof. internal medicine, 1965-75; dean F. Edward Hebert Sch. Medicine, Uniformed Services U. Health Scis., Bethesda, Md., 1975-90; pres. Uniformed Services U. Health Scis., 1981-90, dean emeritus, 1990—; clin. prof. internal medicine U. Tex. Southwestern Med. Sch., 1992—; chief microbiology lab. Parkland Meml. Hosp., Dallas, 1957-75, pres. med. staff, 1968-69, mem. attending staff; mem. adv. coun. Dallas Health and Sci. Mus., 1968-75; chmn. Am. Bd. Internal Medicine, 1978-79, Gov.'s Commn. Phys. Fitness, 1971-75; bd. regents Nat. Libr. Medicine, 1984-90; mem. Accreditation Coun. on Grad. Med. Edn., 1987-92, chmn. transitional year residency rev. com., 1989-92, chmn., 1990-91; mem. bd. on army sci. and tech. NRC, 1995—; cons. Dallas VA Ctr. Contbr. articles to profl. jours. With M.C., U.S. Army, 1954-56; col. Res., 1983—. Decorated Medal of Honor du Service de Sante des Armees, France, 1991; recipient cert. of award Div. Health Moblzn. USPHS, 1963, 64, Prizer award for CD, 1965, Presdl. citation for Health Moblzn. Planning, 1970, Disting. Pub. Svc. medal Dept. Def., 1982, 91. Fellow Am. Acad. Microbiology, ACP (master); mem. Inst. Medicine of NAS, Assn. Am. Physicians, Nat. Inst. Allergy and Infectious Diseases (chmn. tng. grant com. 1971, adv. coun. 1979-90), Am. Fedn. Clin. Research (pres. 1968-69), Am. Soc. Microbiology, Central Soc. Clin. Rsch., Soc. Exptl. Biology and Medicine, Am. Soc. Clin. Investigation, Soc. Med. Consultants to Armed Forces (pres. 1976-77, John R. Seal award 1988, 91), Am. Thoracic Soc., Infectious Disease Soc. Am. (pres. 1978-79, Bristol award 1981, E.H. Kass lectr. 1994), Sigma Xi, Alpha Omega Alpha, Phi Kappa Phi. Home: 4509 Edmondson Ave Dallas TX 75205-2605 Office: 5910 N Central Expy Ste 1955 Dallas TX 75206-5151

SANFORD, JULIE ROSE TANNER, nursing consultant, nursing educator; b. Lucedale, Miss., Aug. 7, 1962; d. Eugene Joseph and Lena Marie (Eubanks) Tanner; m. Robert Roy Sanford Jr., Feb. 21, 1987; children: Joseph Robert, Brannan Terrell. BSN, U. Ala., Tuscaloosa, 1984; MSN, U. South Ala., 1990. RN, Ala.; cert. ACLS instr., Am. Heart Assn.; cert. BCLS instr., Am. Heart Assn.; cert. CCRN. Nurse in ICU Mercy Hosp., New Orleans, 1984-85; office nurse Pulmonary Assocs., Mobile, Ala., 1987-88; staff nurse in emergency dept. U. So. Ala. Med. Ctr., Mobile, 1985-87, 1987-88, critical care cons., 1988-90, staff nurse in emergency dept., 1990-91; staff develop. inservice specialist, patient edn. U. So. Ala. Knollwood Pk. Hosp., Mobile, 1991-92; staff nurse emergency dept. U. So. Ala. Med. Ctr., Mobile, 1992-93; clin. asst. prof., 1993—; lectr. numerous presentations in field. Mem. AACN (Mobile Bay area pres. 1990), Am. Heart Assn., Sigma Theta Tau. Republican. Baptist. Home: 6871 Walter Tanner Rd Wilmer AL 36587-3303

SANFORD, MARILYN KING, physical therapist, educator; b. Ash Grove, Mo., Sept. 24, 1943; d. William Howard and Helen Elizabeth (Moore) King; m. Michael Ross Sanford, Aug. 29, 1964; children: Melinda, Matthew. BS in Phys. Therapy, U. Mo., 1965, MEd in Higher Adult Edn., 1978, PhD in Higher Edn., 1987. Registered phys. therapist, Mo. Staff phys. therapist Boone County Hosp., Columbia, Mo., 1965-70, Univ. Hosp., Columbia, Mo., 1971-72; mem. phys. therapy faculty U. Mo., Columbia, 1972-93, phys. therapy program dir. Sch. Health Related Professions, 1993—. Mem. Presybn. Manors of Mid-Am., 1987-93, bd. dirs. pres., 1991-92. Mem. Mo. Phys. Therapy Assn. Home: 3100 Hill Haven Ln Columbia MO 65202 Office: Phys Therapy Program 106 Lewis Hall Columbia MO 65211

SANFORD, ROBERT STANLEY, physician, urologist; b. N.Y.C., July 5, 1938; s. Emanuel and Ruth (Rosen) S.; children: Michael, Meredith, Melissa. BS, Bklyn. Coll., 1959; MD, N.Y. Med. Coll., 1964. Diplomate Am. Bd. Urology. Commd. 2d lt. U.S. Army, 1966, advanced through grades to capt., 1971; intern Cedars of Lebanon, L.A., 1964-65; resident Jewish Hosp. & Med. Ctr., Bklyn., 1965-71; urologist Beverly Hills, Calif., 1971—; chief urology Cedars Sinai Med. Ctr., L.A., 1983-87; clin. asst., prof. urology U. So. Calif. Sch. of Medicine, 1993—; attending staff mem. Cedars Sinai. Fellow Am. Coll. Surgeons. Office: 414 N. Camden Dr Ste 650 Beverly Hills CA 90210-4532

SANGSTER, JOHN FRASER, medical practitioner; b. Adelaide, Australia, Jan. 21, 1942; m. Verity Kerridge Elix, Jan. 8, 1964; children: James Hugo, Joanna Mary, Thomas Bagot. MB, BS, U. Adelaide, 1965. Intern Royal Adelaide Hosp., 1966-67, registrar, 1968-72; Nat. Heart Found. clin. fellow Royal Postgrad. Med. Sch., London, 1972-73; sr. vis. cardiologist Royal Adelaide Hosp., 1974—; bd. dirs. Nat. Heart Found., 1980—; clin. lectr. U. Adelaide, 1980—. Contbr. articles to profl. jours. Fellow Royal Australian Coll. Physicians; mem. Cardiac Soc. Australia-New Zealand, Royal Automobile Assn. South Astralia, Inc. (coun. 1984—), Royal Adelaide Golf Club (capt. 1992-94). Office: 270 Wakefield St, Adelaide 5000 South Australia, Australia

SANKEY, NOEL EDWIN, urologist; b. Trinidad, Colo., Aug. 2, 1934; s. Daniel A. and Ruth Ann (Coates) S.; children: Kimberley, Kevin, Colin. BA, Dartmouth Coll., 1956; MD, U. Colo., 1961. Diplomate Am. Bd. Urology. Intern Ohio State U., 1961-62; pvt. practice Englewood, Colo., 1966-94; resident U. Colo., 1962-66; CEO, med. dir. Kidney Stone Ctr., Denver, 1986—. Capt. U.S. Army, 1967-69. Mem. Am. Urol. Soc., Am. Lithotripsy Soc. (pres. 1988-89, sec. 1994-96), Colo. Med. Soc. Office: Kidney Stone Ctr 1721 E 19th Ave Ste 172 Denver CO 80218

SAN MIGUEL, SANDRA BONILLA, social worker; b. Santurce, P.R., May 23, 1944; d. Isidoro and Flora (Carrero) Bonilla; m. Manuel San Miguel, July 12, 1969. BA, St. Joseph's Coll., 1966; MS in Social Work, Columbia U., 1970. Case worker Dept. Labor, Migration Div., N.Y.C., 1966-68; clin. social worker N.Y.C. Housing Authority, N.Y.C., 1968-69, Children's Aid Soc., N.Y.C., 1969-71; sr. social worker Traveler's Aid Soc., San Juan, P.R., 1971-74; coord., supr. Dept. Addiction Control Svcs., San Juan, P.R., 1974-77; substance abuse div. dir. Seminole County Mental Health Ctr., Altamonte Springs, Fla., 1978-81; cons. pvt. practice Hispanic Cons. Svcs., Winter Springs, Fla., 1982—; adj. prof. Seminole Community

Coll., Lake Mary, Fla., 1986-90; sch. social worker I Seminole County Pub. Schs., Sanford, Fla., 1986-91, lead sch. social worker, 1991—; mem. pres.'s minority adv. coun. U. Ctrl. Fla., 1982—, vice chair, 1982-86, chair, 1986-90; mem. bd. regents EEP adv. com. State Univ. System Fla., 1985-89; bd. dirs. Seminole Cmty. Mental Health Ctr., 1986-94, 95—, v.p., 1988-90, pres., 1990-91; adv. bd. Nat. Devereux Found. Ctrl. Fla., 1993—, women's adv. bd. South Seminole Hosp., Fla., 1994—; v.p.; mem. Fla. Consortium on Tchr. Edn. for Am. Minorities, 1990—; mem. local com. Hispanic Info. and Telecomms. Network, 1990; mem. Seminole County (Fla.) Juvenile Justice Coun., 1993—; mem. statewide student svcs. adv. com. Dept. Edn., Fla., 1993—. Mem. NASW, Fla. Assn. Sch. Social Workers (co-founder minority caucus 1988, columnist quar. newsletter Minority Corner 1988-92, bd. dirs. 1989—, sec. 1990-92, v.p. 1992-93, pres. 1993-94), Sch. Social Work Assn. of Am., Fla. Assn. Student Svcs. Adminstrs., Collegiate Social Workers P.R., Columbia U. Alumni Assn., St. Joseph's Coll. Alumni Assn. Home: 1214 Howell Creek Dr Winter Springs FL 32708-4516 Office: Seminole County Pub Schs 1401 S Magnolia Ave Sanford FL 32771-3400

SANNER, JOHN HARPER, retired pharmacologist; b. Anamosa, Iowa, Apr. 29, 1931; s. Lee Michael and Helen (Grace) S.; m. Marilyn Joan Eichorst, Dec. 28, 1958; children: Linda Leigh Costanzo, Steven Bradley. BS, U. Iowa, 1954, MS, 1961, PhD, 1964. Rsch. investigator G.D. Searle & Co., Skokie, Ill., 1963-69, sr. rsch. investigator, 1969-75, rsch. fellow, 1975-86, ret., 1986—. Conducted pioneering rsch. in prostaglandin antogonists; contbr. articles to profl. jours. Mem. Cable and Telecom. Commn., Deerfield, Ill. 1st lt. USAFR, 1955-57. Republican. Home: 959 Appletree Ln Deerfield IL 60015-2734

SANO, KEIJI, neurosurgeon; b. Shizuoka Prefecture, Japan, June 30, 1920; s. Takeo and Haru (Sase) S.; m. Yaeko Sano. M.D., U. Tokyo, 1945, DMS, 1951. Asst., U. Tokyo, 1945-56, lectr., chief out patient clinic, 1956-57, assoc. prof. neurosurgery, 1957-62, prof. neurosurgery, 1962-81; emeritus prof. U. Tokyo, 1981—; prof. neurosurgery Teikyo U., 1981-96; dir. Fuji Brain Inst., 1986—; pres. 5th Internat. Congress Neurol. Surgery, 1973; pres. Internat. Conf. on Cerebral Vasospasm, 1990; chmn., dir Nat. Com. for Brain Rsch., Sci. Coun. of Japan, 1987-91. Mem. Japan Neurosurg. Soc. (pres. 1965), Japanese Assn. Rsch. in Stereo-ancephalotomy (pres. 1966), Asian and Australasian Soc. Neurol. Surgeons (pres. 1967-71, hon. life pres. 1971—), World Fedn. Neurosurg. Socs. (pres. 1969-73, hon. life pres. 1973—), Japanese Soc. CNS CT (pres. 1978—), Am. Assn. Neurol. Surgeons (hon.), Deutsche Gesellschaft für Neurochirurgie (hon.), Academia Eurasiana Neurochirurgica (pres. 1986); Soc. Neurol. Surgeons (hon.), Am. Acad. Neurol. Surgery (hon.), Congress Neurol. Surgeons (hon.), Scandinavian Neurosurg. Soc. (corr.), Am. Surg. Assn. (sr.), Am. Neurol. Assn. (corr.), ACS (hon.). Research on treatment of brain tumors, aneurisms, stereo-encephalotomy, vascular lesions. Home: 4-22-6 Den-en-chofu, Ota-ku Tokyo 145, Japan

SANSING, DIANA MARIE TODD, pediatric critical care nurse; b. Balt., Dec. 3, 1963; d. Robert Franklin Jr. and Christina Adrian (Tamburo) Todd; m. Michael Ritchie Sansing, Mar. 1, 1986; children: Erica Michele, Caitlin Marie. BSN, Johns Hopkins U., 1993. RN, Md. Med.-surg. nurse Sinai Hosp., Balt., 1994-96; pediat. ICU nurse Shady Grove Adventist Hosp., Rockville, Md., 1996—. Mem. AACN, Sigma Theta Tau. Roman Catholic. Home: 5560 Watson Ct Eldersburg MD 21784 Office: Shady Grove Adventist Hosp 9901 Medical Ctr Dr Rockville MD 20850

SANSONE, THOMAS CHRISTIAN, urologist, educator; b. New Brunswick, N.J., June 25, 1939; s. Thomas John and Helene Meredith (Straub) S.; m. Brenda Elena Stabile, Aug. 10, 1963; children: Elena, Lisa, Linda, Thomas Jr., Christy. AB, Princeton U., 1961; MD, U. Pa., 1965. Diplomate Am. Bd. Urology. Fellow Harrison dept. surg. rsch. U. Pa., Phila., 1968-69, instr. urology, 1969-72; chief svc. of urology Bryn Mawr (Pa.) Hosp., 1984—; assoc. clin. prof. urology Thomas Jefferson U., Phila., 1988—; cons. Minh Hien Co., Ho Chi Minh City, Vietnam, 1995—. Capt. USAF, 1965-67. Fellow ACS; mem. AMA, Am. Urologic Assn. (membership com. Mid-Atlantic sect.), Aronomink Golf Club.

SANSONETTI, DIANE J., surgeon; b. Hinsdale, Ill., Apr. 14, 1952; m. John W. Batty. BA, Hollins (Va.) Coll., 1974; MD, Med. Coll. Va., Richmond, 1977. Diploamte Nat. Bd. Med. Examiners, Am. Bd. Surgery; lic. surgeon, N.Mex., Calif., Va. Intern then resident U. Calif., San Diego, 1977-85; asst. prof. surgery Med. Coll. Va., Richmond, 1985-87; pvt. practuce Albuquerque, 1987—. Author: (with others) Pathophysiology and Techniques of Cardiopulmonary Bypass, vol. 1, 1982; contbr. articles to profl. jours. Fellow ACS, Am. Coll. Cardiology; mem. AMA, New Mex. Med. Soc., New Mex. Cardiovascular Soc., N.Am. Transplant Coords. Orgn., Internat. Soc. Heart Transplantation, Greater Albuquerque Med. Assn. Home: 38 Cedar Hill Pl NE Albuquerque NM 87122 Office: New Mex Heart Inst 201 Cedar sE Ste 810 Albuquerque NM 87106

SANTACANA, GUIDO E., physiology educator; b. Placetas, Las Villa, Cuba, Dec. 25, 1952; came to U.S., 1964; s. Guido and Concepcion (Sanchez) S.; m. Maria E. Laffitte, May 27, 1978; 1 child, Guido E. BS, Coll. Agrl. and Mech. Arts, Mayaguez, P.R., 1975; PhD, Med. Sci. Campus, San Juan, P.R., 1982. Instr. dept. nat. sci. Sacred Heart U., Santurce, P.R., 1976-84, asst. prof. dept. natural sci., 1982-84; instr. dept. physiology S.J.B. Sch. Med., Hato Rey, P.R., 1981-83; asst. prof. dept. physiology Universidad Central del Caribe Sch. Medicine, Bayamon, P.R., P.R., 1984-86; prof., chmn. dept. physiology Universidad Central del Caribe Sch. Medicine, Bayamon, P.R., 1986-95, dir. grad. program, 1994-95; chmn. dept. physiology Ponce Sch. Medicine, 1995—. Contbr. articles to sci. jours. Recipient Sci. award Bausch & Lomb, San Juan, P.R., 1971, Rsch. Ctr. for Minority Instns. rsch. grant NIH, Bayamon, P.R., 1986—, Minority Access to Rsch. Careers Program faculty fellowship NIH, San Juan, 1979-82. Mem. AAVSO Assn. (Boston), Am. Physiol. Soc. (Porter physiology devel. grants com.), Am. Assn. Chmn. Depts. Physiology, Soc. Exptl. Biology and Medicine, Alpha Omega Alpha. Roman Catholic.

SANTIAGO, JULIO VICTOR, medical educator, researcher, administrator; b. San German, Puerto Rico, Jan. 13, 1942. BS, Manhattan Coll., 1963; MD, U. Puerto Rico, 1967. Diplomate Am. Bd. of Internal Medicine, 1975. Fellow in metabolism and endocrinology Washington U., St. Louis, 1972-74; chief resident Barnes Hosp., St. Louis, 1974-75; dir. divsn. of endocrinology and metabolism Dept. of Pediatrics, 1984—; program dir., Diabetes Rsch. and Tng. Ctr. Wash. U. Sch. Medicine, 1987—, prof. of medicine, pediatrics, 1983—. Assoc. editor Diabetes, 1977-79, 91-95, editor, 1995—. Mem. Am. Soc. for Clin. Investigation, Soc. for Pediatric Rsch., Am. Diabetes Assn. Home: 4 Forest Parkway Dr Ballwin MO 63021-5553 Office: Washington U Sch Medicine St Louis Hosp 1 Childrens Place Saint Louis MO 63110

SANTIAGO-NAZARIO, ROSALIE M., medical records administrator, consultant; b. Ft. Dix, N.J., Oct. 9, 1957; d. Gliserio Santiago and Maria Del R. Santiago Nazario; m. Rey P. Castellano Calderon, July 5, 1980; children: Rey Y., Jonathan, Giancarlo. BA in Edn., U. P.R., 1979, postgrad., 1979-80. Registered record adminstr. Med. record adminstr. State Psychiat. Hosp., Rio Piedras, P.R., 1984-87, Dr. José Ramos Lebrón Hosp., Fajardo, P.R., 1988—; cons. in coding Arecibo (P.R.) Regional Hosp., 1985; cons. in med. record dept. Caguas (P.R.) Surgicenter, 1989, Ambulatory Care Ctrs., Fajardo, 1995—; cons. Sec. Aux. Regulation and Accreditation of Med. Facilities, Bayamón, P.R., 1993. Mem. Am. Health Info. Mgmt. Assn., P.R. Health Info. Mgmt. Assn. (com. pres.). Office: Dr Jose Ramos Lebron Hosp Ave Gen Valero Fajardo PR 00773

SANTILLI, STEVEN MICHAEL, physician; b. Steubenville, May 12, 1959; s. Anthony Joseph and Millicent Elaine (Lecko) S.; m. Jamie Doreen Tollefson, Sept. 17, 1983; children: Bethany Lynn, Ashley Rebecca, Christopher Michael. BS in Chemistry, Bethany Coll., 1981; MD, Med. Coll. of Ohio, 1985; PhD, U. Minn., 1994. Diplomate Am. Bd. Surgery. Surgery resident U. Minn., Mpls., 1985-93, asst. prof. dept. surgery, 1995—; staff surgeon VAMC, Mpls., 1993-94; fellow vascular surgery U. Calif. San Francisco, 1994-95; presenter in field. Contbr. articles to profl. jours., chpts. to books in field. Grantee NIH, 1988-91, Inst. of Basic and Applied rsch. in Surgery, 1988-89, Diabetes Rsch. and Edn. Found., 1989-90, Minn. Med. Foun., 1994-95. Mem. AMA, Minn. Med. Assn., Hennepin County Med. Soc., Am. Coll. Surgeons (assoc. fellow), United Cerebral Palsy of Minn., AAAS, Peripheral Vascular Surgery Soc., Soc. for Clin. Vascular Surgery, Alpha Sigma Phi (Man of Yr. in Sci. 1979), Beta Beta Beta, Kappa Sigma Mu, Gamma Sigma Kappa, Alpha Omega Alpha, Phi Kappa Phi. Office: Univ Minn Dept Surgery-Med Sch 516 Delaware St SE Box 195 Minneapolis MN 55455

SANTONI-RUGIU, PAOLO, plastic surgeon; b. Rome, Apr. 14, 1928; s. Angelo and Antonietta Castiglia S.-R.; m. Ingegerd Maj Borgman, Jan. 3, 1960 (dec. 1993); 1 child, Eric Angelo. MD, U. Pisa, 1956, PhD, 1969; specialist in plastic surgery, U. Hosp., Uppsala, Sweden, 1960. 1st asst. in surgery U. Hosp., Uppsala, 1958-60; asst. prof. U. Hosp., Pisa, 1960-66, cons. plastic surgeon, 1970-82; assoc. prof. plastic surgery U. Pisa, 1969—; sr. surgeon Interplast Internat. in Africa, Tanzania, 1988, Zambia, 1995, 96; chief svc. plastic surgery San Rossore Hosp., Pisa, 1982—; vis. prof. plastic surgery U. Ill., Chgo., 1974, vis. prof. microsurgery, 1978, U. Calif., Irvine, 1982. Author: Le Plastiche Cutanee, 1988; co-author: Tecnica Chirurgia, Vol. 9, 1986, Microchirurgia, 1989; contbr. articles to profl. jours. With British Army, 1944-45. Paul Harris fellow Rotary, 1987. Mem. Italian Soc. Plastic Surgery (coun. mem. 1971-77), Am. Soc. Plastic Reconstructive Surgery (corr. 1988—), Svensk Plastikkiurirgisk Forening (corr. 1973—), Soc. Belgieque de Chirurgie Plastique (corr. 1975—), European Assn. Plastic Surgeons (founding, pres. 1992), Tord Skoog Soc. Plastic Surgery (pres. 1966-72). Home: Via Giovanni di Simone 12, 56127 Pisa Italy Office: Clinica San Rossore, Viale Delle Cascine 152-F, 561222 Pisa Italy

SANTOS, ARTHUR DWAYNE, thoracic cardiovascular surgeon; b. L.A., Dec. 8, 1953; s. Frank Antonio and Hughenna Louise (Gauntlett) S. BS, MD, Loma Linda (Calif.) U., 1976. Resident in gen. and critical care surgery U. Minn., Mpls., 1976-83; resident in cardiothoracic surgery U. Utah, Salt Lake City, 1983-85; pvt. practice cardio-thoracic surgery Encinitas, Calif., 1986-89; thoracic-cardiovascular surgeon So. Colo. Heart and Lung, Pueblo, 1990-94, Cedarwood Med. Ctr., St. Joseph, Mich., 1994-96, Laredo (Tex.) Med. Group, 1996—. Fellow ACS; mem. Soc. Thoracic Surgeons, Soc. Critical Care Medicine, Soc. Vascular Tech. Seventh-Day Adventist. Office: Laredo Med Group 1420 Logan Laredo TX 78040

SANTOS, ARTHUR MAGNO, thoracic cardiovascular surgeon; b. Pasay City, Philippines, May 15, 1946; s. Regalado T. and Lily Santos; m. Lorna Perez Pantangco, Mar. 26, 1973; 1 child, Vladimir Allen Santos. BS in Premedicine, Far Eastern U., Manila, Philippines, 1967; MD, U. of the East, 1972. Diplomate Am. Bd. Surgery, Am. Bd. Thoracic Surgery. Intern St. Francis Gen. Hosp., Pitts., 1973-74, resident in gen. surgery, 1974-77; resident McKeesport (Pa.) Hosp., 1977-79; resident in thoracic and cardiovascular surgery Shadyside Hosp., Pitts., 1979-81; pvt. practice Assn. of Thoracic Surgeons, Pitts., 1981—. Mem. AMA, Pa. Med. Soc., Soc. Philippine Surgeons in Am., Pa. Thoracic Soc., Allegheny County Med. Soc. Seventh-day Adventist. Office: Assn of Thoracic Surgeons 532 S Aiken Ave Pittsburgh PA 15232-1521

SANTOS, EUGENIO MIGUEL, molecular biologist, researcher; b. Salamanca, Spain, May 5, 1953; came to U.S., 1979; s. Julian Santos and Angela De Dios; m. Isabel Santos, Jan. 3, 1982; children: Miguel, Javier, Isabel. BSc, U. Salamanca, Spain, 1975, MSc, 1975, PhD, 1978. Postdoctoral fellow Roche Inst. Molecular Biology, Nutley, N.J., 1979-81; vis fellow Nat. Cancer Inst., Bethesda, Md., 1981-84; prof. microbiology Salamanca U., Spain, 1984; staff scientist Nat. Cancer Inst., Frederick, Md., 1984-85; vis. scientist lab cellular and molecular biology NIH, Nat. Cancer Inst., Bethesda, 1985—. Contbr. articles to profl. jours. and books. Spanish-N. Am. Com. Sci. Coop. fellow, 1981; Fundacion Juan March, fellow, 1982; recipient medal U. Salamanca, 1983; Annual Monographic award Spanich Assn. against Cancer, 1984; 1st Severo Ochoa award for biomed. research, 1985. Mem. Am. Soc. Microbiology, Spanish Biochem. Soc., Spanish Soc. Microbiology, AAAS, Royal Acad. Medicine (Salamanca, Spain). Roman Catholic.

SANTOS, FRANCISCO JAVIER, gastroenterologist; b. Zamora, Spain, July 30, 1964; s. Felipe Santos and Maria Concepcion Vicente; m. Maria Luisa Briones, May 15, 1992; 1 child, Javier. MD, U. Navarra, Spain, 1988; PhD, U. Barcelona, Spain, 1996. Fellow in gastroenterology U. Barcelona, 1989-92, staff rschr. digestive sys. rsch. unit, 1992—; staff gastroenterologist Hosp. Valle Hebron, Barcelona, 1995—. Traveling scholar, Cambridge, 1995. Mem. Acad. Scis. Catalonia, Spanish Soc. Gastroenterology, N.Y. Acad. Sci. Office: Gen Hosp Vall Hebron, Paseo Valle Hebron 119-129, 08035 Barcelona Spain

SANTOS, GEORGE WESLEY, physician, educator; b. Oak Park, Ill., Feb. 3, 1928; s. George and Emma (Gast) S.; m. Joanne Agnes Corrigan, June 7, 1952; children: Susan Elizabeth, George Wesley II, Kelly Anne, Amy Coburn. SB, MIT, 1951, MS in Phys. Biology, 1951; MD, Johns Hopkins U., 1955; Doctoris Medicinae Gradum Honoris Cause, U. Munich, 1989. Intern Johns Hopkins Hosp., Balt., 1955-56, asst. resident, 1958-60; scholar Leukemia Soc., N.Y.C., 1961-66; mem. faculty Johns Hopkins Sch. Medicine, Balt., 1962—, assoc. prof. medicine, 1968-73, prof. oncology and medicine, 1973-94; prof. emeritus, 1994—; asst. physician in chief Balt. City Hosp., 1963-77; mem. Cancer Clin. Investigative Rev. Com., 1969-73; mem. extramural sci. adv. bd. Meml. Sloan-Kettering Cancer Ctr., 1977-79; mem. Immunology-Epidemiology Spl. Virus Cancer Program, 1969-73; chmn. bone marrow transplant registry ACS, 1969-73; mem. Internat. Com. Organ Transplant Registry ACS, 1969-73; mem. cell biology-immunology-genetics rsch. evaluation com. VA, 1969-71. Assoc. editor Cancer Rsch., 1978-81; mem. bd. editl. advisors Jour. Immunopharmacology, 1978—; mem. editl. bd. Blood, 1983—. With USNR, 1956-58. Recipient Disting. Achievement in Cancer Rsch. award Bristol Meyers, 1988. Mem. Am. Soc. Hematology, Transplantation Soc. (counselor 1971-73), Am. Assn. Immunologists, Leukemia Soc. Am. (bd. dirs. 1973—), Internat. Soc. Exptl. Hematology (councillor 1973, pres. 1981), Am. Assn. Cancer Rsch., Am. Soc. Clin. Investigation, Nat. Multiple Sclerosis Soc. (chmn. adv. com. on drug devel. 1981-82, mem. adv. com. on drug devel. 1981—). Home: Mariners Point # 308B Hilton Head Island SC 29926-1213

SANTOS, LISA WELLS, critical care nurse; b. Richardson, Tex., Oct. 25, 1963; d. Malcolm R.N. and Maitland Anne (MacIntyre) Wells; m. Ignacio Santos, Jr., Dec. 17, 1988. Cert. med. asst., x-ray-lab. technician, Tex. Coll. Osteopathy, 1983; ASN, El Centro Coll., 1988; postgrad., U. North Tex.; BS in Bus. Mgmt., Le Tourneau U., 1993; postgrad., U. Phoenix, 1995—. RN, Tex.; cert. in CPR; cert. case mgr., cert profl. in health care quality; advanced competency certification in continuity of care; assoc. cert. mgr. Med. technologist Family Med. Ctr., Dallas, 1984-85, Beltline Med. Clinic, Dallas, 1985-86; nurse, lab. technician Primacare, Dallas, Plano, Richardson, Tex., 1986-88; charge nurse telemetry unit NME Hosp.-RHD Meml. Hosp., Denton, Tex., 1988-89; nurse ICU Denton (Tex.) Regional Med. Ctr.; nurse Angel Touch, Dallas, 1989; nurse cons. Travelers Ins., Richardson, Tex., 1990-91; med. rev. specialist Nat. Group Life, Las Colinas, Tex., 1991-94; mgr. coordinated care Nat. Group Life, 1994-95; pres. San Cal Health Care Options, Lewisville, Tex., 1994-95; clin. dir. PRN Associated Care/ Am. Care Source, Dallas, 1995—. Contbr. articles to profl. jour. Mem. AACN, NAFE, Nat. Assn. Health Care Quality, Nat. Assn. Quality Assurance Profls., Assn. Nurses in AIDS Care, Case Mgmt. Soc. Am., Am. Assn. Law Ethics and Medicine, Am. Assn. Continuity of Care, Alpha Epsilon Delta, Alpha Beta Kappa, Gamma Beta Phi.

SANTOS, OMAR DA ROSA, educator, medicine; b. Rio De Janeiro, May 20, 1940; s. Homero Da Fonseca and Zilmar Da Rosa (Pereira) S.; married; children: Omar, Otilia Helena, Olimpia Maria, Lupi. MD, Sch. Medicine Surgery, Rio De Janeiro, 1964; JD, Brazilian Faculty Legal Svcs., Rio De Janeiro, 1977. Intern numerous univs. abd pub. hosps., Rio De Janeiro, 1961-64; attending physician numerous univs. abd pub. hosps., 1965-80; dir., med. div. Justice Tribunal of Rio De Janeiro, 1972-91; chief nephrology Andarai Hosp., Rio De Janeiro, 1977—; prof., nephrology Inst. Carlos Chagas, Rio De Janeiro, 1980—; from asst. prof. to prof. Uni-Rio, Rio De Janeiro, 1966-83; chief medicine and nephrology Gaffree & Guinle U. Hosps., Rio De Janeiro, 1981—; prof., medicine U. Rio De Janeiro, Sch. Medicine & Surgery, 1983—, dir., 1988—; cons. in field; 1st sec. Nat. Acad. Medicine, Rio De Janeiro, 1991-93. Author: Diseases of the Kidney, 1988, Acute Renal Failure, 1991; contbr. articles to profl. jours. Diplomate Defense High Studies Superior Sch., Rio De Janeiro, 1984, 89, spl. studies activities, 1990-91. 1st lt. Brazilian Air Force, 1968-69. Fellow Brazilian Coll. Surgeons, Otium Cum Dignitate, High Studies Sch. Diplomate Assn.; mem. Brazilian Soc. Nephrology (pres. 1981-82), Internat. So. Nephrology, Brazilian Soc. Rheumatology, Brazilian Ned. Assn., Soc. Medicine and Surgery Rio De Janeiro. Roman Catholic. Home: 71 Botucatu, 20541 Rio De Janeiro Brazil Office: Mariz e Barros # 775, Rio de Janeiro Brazil

SANTOS-MARTÍNEZ, JESÚS, physiology and pharmacology educator, researcher; b. Vieques, P.R., Mar. 5, 1924; s. Jesús Santos and Ignacia Martínez; m. Maria F. de Jesús, 1955; children: Josè A., Miguel A., Josè R., Magali P. BS, U. P.R., 1946; MS, U. Ill., Chgo., 1948; PhD, Purdue U., 1954; postgrad., Ind. U., Indpls., 1966-67. Asst. instr. Sch. Pharmacy, U. P.R., Rio Piedras, 1946, instr. to assoc. prof., 1947-58; asst. prof. to prof. Sch. Medicine U. P.R., San Juan, 1954-79, prof., chmn. basic scis. dept. Sch. Dentistry,, 1972-76; prof., chmn. dept. physiology U. Cen. Caribe Sch. Medicine, Cayey, P.R., 1979-87, prof. pharmacology, 1979-94, chmn. dept. pharmacology, 1987-94; prof. emeritus U. Cen. Caribe Sch. Medicine, Cayey, P.R., 1994—; vis. prof. U. Nicaragua Sch. Medicine, Leon, 1960, Univ. Coll. W.I., Mona, Jamaica, 1962, Ind. U. Sch. Medicine, 1966-67; mem. P.R. Bd. Drug Bioequivalence, San Juan, 1977-87. Sec. steering com. P.R. Heart Assn., San Juan, 1970-71. Recipient Favorite Son award Vieques Mcpl. Assembly, 1947. Fellow Internat. Soc. Nephrology (travel grantee 1969); mem. Am. Physiol. Soc. (Porter devel. com. 1981-84), Am. Soc. Nephrology, AAAS, P.R. Med. Assn. (sect. nephrology). Roman Catholic. Home: 1184 Verona St San Juan PR 00924 Office: U Cen Caribe Sch Medicine Call Box 60-327 Bayamon PR 00960

SANTOSO-PHAM, JULIA CECILIA, dermatologist; b. Jakarta, Indonesia, July 20, 1962; d. Limjadi and Lili (Darmasaputra) Santoso; m. Trinh Cong Pham, June 1, 1991; 1 child, Celia Lilian Pham. BS, U. Pitts., 1984; DO, Kans. City Coll. Osteo. Med., 1989. Family practitioner Parkview Hosp., Toledo, 1990-93; dermatologist, clin. asst. prof. dermatology St. Vincent Med. Ctr., Toledo, 1994—; clin. asst. prof. dermatology Ohio U. Coll. Osteo. Med., 1993—. Mem. Am. Acad. Dermatology, Am. Osteopathic Assn., Am. Osteopathic Coll. Dermatology. Roman Catholic. Office: Franklin Park Dermatology 4607 W Sylvania Ave Ste 202 Toledo OH 43623

SANTULLI, THOMAS VINCENT, surgeon; b. N.Y.C., Mar. 16, 1915; s. Frank and Amalia (Avagliano) S.; m. Dorothy Muriel Beverly, Apr. 10, 1941 (dec.); children: Thomas Vincent Jr., Robert B.; m. Patricia Rita, May 28, 1982. B.S., Columbia, 1935; M.D., Georgetown U., 1939. Intern N.Y. Polyclinic Hosp., 1939-41, resident, 1941-44; prof. surgery Columbia U., N.Y.C., 1967-81, prof. emeritus, 1981—; chief pediatric surg. service emeritus Babies Hosp., Columbia-Presbyn. Med. Center, N.Y.C., 1955-81; attending surgeon emeritus Presybn. Hosp., Columbia-Presbyn. Med. Center. Mem. Am. Surg. Assn., Am. Pediatric Surg. Assn. (pres. 1980-81), A.C.S., British Assn. Pediatric Surgeons, N.Y. Pediatric Surg. Soc. (pres. 1967-69). Office: Babies Hosp 3959 Broadway New York NY 10032-3784

SANUA, VICTOR DAVID, psychologist, educator; b. Cairo, July 22, 1920; came to U.S., 1950; s. David V. and Marie F. (Simon) S.; m. Stella G. Sardell, Jan. 29, 1956; children: David, Marianne. BA, Am. U., Cairo, 1945; MA, Mich. State U., 1953, PhD, 1956. Lic. psychologist, N.Y. Rsch. psychologist NYU-Bellevue Med. Ctr., 1956-57; rsch. fellow Payne-Whitney Clinic of N.Y. Hosp., 1957-58, Harvard U., Cambridge, 1958-60; assoc. prof. Yeshiva U., N.Y.C., 1960-67; prof. CUNY, 1967-76, Adelphi U., Garden City, N.Y., 1976-80, St. John's U., Queens, N.Y., 1980—. Contbr. articles and revs. to profl. jours. Fulbright lectr., France, 1964-65. Fellow Am. Psychol. Assn., Interam. Soc. Psychology (v.p. 1970-75), Internat. Coun. Psychology Inc. (pres. 1972-74), N.Y. State Psychol. Assn. (pres. acad. div. 1984-85, Wilhelm Wundt award 1989). Home: 2416 Quentin Rd Brooklyn NY 11229-2416 Office: St Johns U Dept Psychology Jamaica NY 11439

SAPADIN, LINDA ALICE, psychologist, writer; b. N.Y.C., Mar. 20, 1940; d. Samuel Miles and Helen Leah (Bogen) Fink; m. Seymour Sapadin, Nov. 10, 1962 (div. 1980); children: Brian, Glenn, Daniel; m. Ronald J. Goodrich, May 15, 1983. BA, Bklyn. Coll., 1960; MA, Temple U., 1961, CUNY, 1986; PhD, CUNY, 1986. Lic. psychologist, N.Y. Sch. psychologist N.Y.C. Bd. Edn., 1962-66, rsch. cons., 1985-87; tchr. Hewlett-Woodmere (N.Y.) Adult Edn., 1975-84; devel. dir. Ctr. for Women and Achievement, Island Park, N.Y., 1984-89; dir. Biofeedback and Stress Reduction Ctr., Valley Stream, N.Y., 1990—; pvt. practice Valley Stream, 1987—; forum leader, adj. prof. Hofstra U., N.Y. Inst. Tech., Five Towns Coll., Nassau Community Coll., L.I., 1974-90; cons. Nassau County Town of Hempstead, N.Y., 1986; adj. prof. continuing edn. Hofstra U., Uniondale, N.Y., 1985—; talk show host Sta. WGBB Radio, Merrick, N.Y., 1987. Author: It's About Time! The 6 Styles of Procrastination and How to Overcome Them, 1996; columnist Chanry Communications, 1987-90, Richner Publs., 1992; contbr. articles to profl. jours. Chmn. psychology com. Nassau County NOW, Uniondale, 1983; spkr. Smithsonian Assocs., Learning Annex, L.I. Assn. Planned Parenthood, Econ. Opportunities Coun., L.I. Libr. Sys., B'nai Brith, Women's Forum, Nat. Coun. Jewish Women, 1984—. Recipient Outstanding Community Svc. award State Senator Carol Berman, 1984. Mem. APA (media div., psychology of women div.), Nassau County Psychol. Assn. (women's studies com.). Home and Office: Biofeedback and Stress 19 Cloverfield Rd Valley Stream NY 11581-2421

SAPEGA, ALEXANDER A., sports medicine physician, orthopedic surgeon; b. Chgo., Oct. 23, 1953; s. Andrew Samuel and Ludmila (Loboy) S.; m. Sally Sapega, 1977; children: Marissa, Danielle. BS with distinction, Cornell U., 1975; MD, Temple U., 1980. Diplomate Am. Bd. Orthopaedic Surgery; lic. physician, Phila., N.J. Intern, residency, fellowship U. Pa. Sch. of Medicine, Phila., 1982-85; fellow in sports medicine Temple U., Phila., 1985-86; asst. instr. orthopaedic surgery U. Pa. Sch. Medicine, Phila., 1982-85; clin. instr. orthopaedic surgery Temple U. Sch. Medicine, Phila., 1985-86; asst. prof. U. Pa. Sch. Medicine, Phila., 1986-92; asst. prof., clin. educator Hosp. U. Pa., Phila., 1992-95, assoc. prof., clin. educator, 1995—; dir. post-grad. fellowship Knee Surgery Program Hosp. U. Pa., Phila., 1995—; chief sports medicine svc. Hosp. U. Pa., Phila., 1995—; faculty lectr. for symposia and ednl. groups; invited lectr. to med. and sci. meetings, 1983—; clin. rsch. assoc. Inst. of Sports Medicine and Athletic Trauma, 1975-76; attending surg. staff Dept. Orthopaedic Surgery, Temple U., Phila., 1985-86; attending staff dept. orthopaedic surgery Hosp. Univ. Pa., Phila, 1986—, dept. orthopaedic surgery The Grad. Hosp., Phila, 1986—; chief of sports medicine svc., Phila. VA Hosp., 1986-92; attending staff dept. orthopaedic surgery, Mt. Sinai Hosp., Phila., 1989—, dir. U. Pa. Sports Medicine Ctr., Phila., 1995. Contbr. about 40 articles to profl. jours. including Am. Jour. Bone and Joint Surgery, Am. Jour Sports Medicine, Jour. Orthopaedic Rsch.; also revs., monographs and chpts. in books; mem. edtl. bd. Am. Jour. Knee Surgery, 1988-95. Post Grad. Advances in Sports Medicine, 1988-91; cons. reviewer Medicine and Sci. in Sports and Exercise, 1983-86, The Am. Jour. of Bone and Joint Surgery, 1988-95, Jour. of Orthopaedic Rsch., 1988-91; mem. editl. bd. for rsch. Am. Jour. Bone and Joint Surgery; inventor: Apparatus for Reconstructive Knee Ligament Surgery, 1988, Method for Reconstructive Knee Ligament Surgery, 1990. Recipient N. Am. Traveling fellowship Am. Orthopaedic Assn.; grantee: NIH, 1982-85, VA, 1985-86, 88-90. Advanced Tech. Ctr. S.E. Pa., 1986. Fellow Am. Acad. Orthpædic Surgeons (Elizabeth Winston Lanier award 1986); mem. Orthopaedic Rsch. Soc., Can. Assn. Applied Sports Scis., Arthroscopy Assn. N. Am., Am. Orthopaedic Soc. for Sports Medicine, Herodicus Soc. Office: Penn Sports Medicine Ctr 235 S 33rd St Phiadelphia PA 19104

SAPEIKA, RAPHAEL JOHN, ophthalmologist; b. Cape Town, South Africa, Nov. 28, 1946. MBChB, U. Cape Town Med. Sch., South Africa, 1970. Diplomate Am. Bd. Ophthalmology. Intern U. Cape Town Groote Schuur Hosp., 1971, ophthalmology resident, 1974-77; corneal fellow SUNY Downstate Med. Ctr., Bklyn., 1979; sr. ophthalmologist Henry Ford Health Sys., Dearborn, Mich., 1980—. Office: Henry Ford Hosp Fairlane 19401 Hubbard Dr Dearborn MI 48126

SAPER, CLIFFORD BAIRD, neurobiology and neurology educator; b. Chgo., Feb. 20, 1952; s. Julian and Susan Menkin S.; m. Barbara Susan Farby, Aug. 26, 1973; children: Rebecca Michelle, Leah Danielle, Sean Zachary. BS, U. Ill., 1972, MS, 1972; MD, Washington U., 1977, PhD, 1977. Diplomate Am. Bd. Psychiatry and Neurology. Intern Jewish Hosp., St.

Louis, 1977-78; resident New York Hosp., N.Y.C., 1978-81; asst. prof. Washington U., St. Louis, 1981-84, assoc. prof., 1984-85; assoc. prof. U. Chgo., 1985-88, prof., 1988-92, chmn. com. on neurobiology, 1987-92; James Jackson Putnam prof. neurology and neurosci. Harvard Med. Sch., 1992—; chmn. dept. neurology Beth Israel Hosp., Boston, 1992—. Editor-in-chief Jour. of Comparative Neurology, 1994—; contbr. articles to profl. jours. Mem. Am. Neurol. Assn., Am. Acad. Neurology, Am. Physiol. Soc., Soc. for Neurosci. Office: 330 Brookline Ave Boston MA 02215-5400

SAPER, JOEL R., neurologist, educator; b. Joliet, Ill., Feb. 6, 1943; s. Leonard and Jeanette (Kristal) S.; m. Renee L. Pergament; children: Lisa, Justin, Lauren. BS in History, U. Wis., 1965; MD, U. Ill., Chgo., 1969. Diplomate Am. Bd. Psychiatry and Neurology, Am. Bd. Pain Medicine. Intern Michael Reese Hosp., Chgo., 1969-70; resident U. Mich. Med. Ctr., Ann Arbor, 1970-73; instr. U. Mich. Med. Sch., Ann Arbor, 1973-75, asst. prof., 1975-78; dir. Mich. Head, Pain and Neurol. Inst., Ann Arbor, 1978—, Head Pain Treatment Program, Chelsea, Mich., 1979—; clin. prof. neurology Mich. State U., Lansing, 1989—. Author: Help for Headaches, 1983, Headache Disorders, 1983, Handbook of Headache Management, 1993, Clinical and Basic Neurology for Health Professionals, 1981, Controversies and Clinical Variants of Migraine, 1987; editor in chief (newsletter) Topics in Pain Mgmt., 1985—; contbr. chpt. to book. Chair physicians' subcom. State of Mich. House Health Care Task Force, 1993-94; chair Mich. Coun. on Pain, 1995-96. Fellow ACP; mem. Am. Acad. Pain Medicine (bd. mem. 1992, cons. to bd. 1995—, Phillip M. Lippe MD award 1996), Am. Acad. Neurology (edn. com. 1992—), Am. Assn. for the Study of Headache (bd. mem., pres. 1992-94), Am. Pain Soc. (cons. to bd. 1992—), Am. Coun. on Headache Edn. (chmn. 1994-95). Office: Mich Head Pain & Neurol 3120 Professional Dr Ann Arbor MI 48104

SAPHIR, RICHARD LOUIS, pediatrician; b. N.Y.C., May 1, 1933; s. Samuel and Grace (Greenberg) S.; m. Judith Schwartz, Dec. 6, 1958; 1 child, Steven. BA, NYU, 1954; MD, SUNY, N.Y.C., 1958. Diplomate Nat. Bd. Med. Examiners, Am. Bd. Pediatrics. Asst. attending physician Mt. Sinai Hosp., N.Y.C., 1965-71; chief, pediatric svcs. U.S. Naval Hosp., Newport, R.I., 1967-69; asst dir., pediatrics acute care clinic Mt. Sinai Hosp., 1970-78, asst. clin. prof. pediatrics, assoc. attending physician, 1971-82, assoc. clin. prof. pediatrics, 1982-88, attending physician, 1982—, clin. prof. pediatrics, 1988—; mem. bd. dirs. Mt. Sinai Childrens Ctr. Found., N.Y.C., 1987—. Contbr. articles to profl. jours. Chmn. community and adv. com. N.Y.C. Info. and Counseling Program for Sudden Infant Death Syndrome, 1979-81; med. bd. YMHA, N.Y.C., 1982-86. Comdr. USNR, 1967-69. Fellow N.Y. Acad. Medicine (treas. 1987-89), Am. Acad. Pediatrics (ednl. program rep. ambulatory care quality improvement program, com. sci. meetings 1985-96); mem. Am. Acad. Pediatrics (chmn. prep course 1991-96), N.Y. Pediatric Soc. (pres. 1978-79), N.Y. County Med. Soc. (vice chmn. com. child welfare 1974-85). Office: BSM Pediatrics PC 55 E 87th St New York NY 10128-1043

SAPICO, FRANCISCO LEJANO, internist, educator; b. Manila, July 18, 1940; came to U.S., 1967; s. Urbano Loyola and Asuncion Limon (Lejano) S.; m. Margaret Mary Armstrong, Nov. 7, 1969; children: Erica Anne, Derek Armstrong. AA, U. Philippines, 1960, MD, 1965. Diplomate Am. Bd. Internal Medicine, Am. Bd. Infectious Diseases. Rotating intern, resident in internal medicine Philippine Gen. Hosp.-U. Philippines, Manila, 1964-67; resident in internal medicine SUNY Upstate Med. Ctr., Syracuse, 1967-69; fellow in infectious diseases UCLA Ctr. for Health Scis., 1969-71; fellow in infectious diseases Wadsworth VA Hosp., L.A., 1971-72, staff physician dept. medicine, 1972-77; physician specialist dept. medicine Rancho Los Amigos Med. Ctr., Downey, Calif., 1977—, chief infectious diseases, 1995—; adj. asst. prof. medicine UCLA Sch. Medicine, 1972-77; asst. prof. medicine U. So. Calif. Sch. Medicine, L.A., 1977-82, assoc. prof., 1982-90, prof., 1990—. Contbr. articles to med. jours., chpts. to books. Judge Fullerton (Calif.) Youth Sci. Fair, 1982-86, Orange County Sci. and Engring. Fair, Fullerton, 1984; coach, asst. coach Fullerton Rangers Youth Soccer Club, 1982-89. Fellow ACP, Infectious Diseases Soc. Am.; mem. Am. Soc. Microbiology, Am. Fedn. Clin. Rsch., Am. Soc. Tropical Medicine and Hygiene, Infectious Disease Assn. Calif. Republican. Office: Rancho Los Amigos Med Ctr 7601 Imperial Hwy Downey CA 90242-3456

SAPIR, SELMA GUSTIN, psychologist, educator; b. N.Y.C., Aug. 6, 1916; s. Max and Sally F. (Lookstein) Gustin; m. Robert I. (dec. July 1973); children—Marc, Judith Sapir. B.S., NYU, 1935; M.A., Sarah Lawrence Coll., 1956; Ed.D., Columbia U., 1984. Cert. sch. psychologist, guidance counselor, tchr., adminstr., N.Y. Research asst. Columbia U., 1963-70; psychologist Bd. Coop. Ednl. Services, West County #2, Ardsley, N.Y., 1956-60; psychologist Mamaronack Pub. Sch., N.Y., 1965-70; prof. psychology Bank St. Coll., N.Y.C., 1968—; research lectr. Belgium Research Scientists, 1979; Fulbright prof. U. Anahuac, Mexico City, 1980; psychology cons. Alcott Sch., Ardsley, N.Y., 1982—; lectr. N.Y. Acad. Scis., 1984. Author: A Professionals Guide, 1978; Children with Special Needs, 1983; Clinical Teaching Model, 1985; Editor: Children With Learning Problems, 1973. Co-pres. Congregation M'Vakshe Derekh; v.p. Interfaith Coun. Scarsdale. Recipient Study award Ford Found., 1955. Mem. Internat. Council Psychologists (bd. dirs. 1985-87, pres.-elect 1996—, UN del. 1982—), Am. Psychol. Assn., Multidisciplinary Acad. Educators (mem. council 1983, past pres.). Jewish. Avocations: theatre, art, travel. Home: 60 Biltmore Ave Yonkers NY 10710-3104 Office: Bank Street Coll Edn 610 W 112th St New York NY 10025-1898

SAPONARA, EDUARDO MILLIGAN, hematologist, oncologist, internist; b. Lima, Peru, Mar. 6, 1948; s. Carlos Alberto Saponara and Norah (Milligan) Thaine; children: Eduardo Carlos, Fiorella Karina. MD, Peruvian U., Lima, 1973. Diplomate Am. Bd. Internal Medicine, Am. Bd. Hematology, Am. Bd. Med. Oncology. Intern medicine N.Y. Med. Coll., N.Y.C., 1973-74, resident medicine, 1974-76, fellow hematology/oncology, 1976-78; fellow neoplastic diseases Mt. Sinai Hosp., N.Y.C., 1978-79, clin. asst. attending neoplastic diseases, 1979—; sr. clin. instr. neoplastic diseases Mt. Sinai Sch. Medicine, N.Y.C.; asst. attending in neoplastic diseases Mt. Sinai Med. Ctr., N.Y.C.; clin. asst. prof. medicine, hematology, hemostasis N.Y. Med. Coll., Valhalla, N.Y., 1979—; chief hematology/oncology Lawrence Hosp., Bronxville, N.Y., 1985-95; co-chmn. prof. edn. So. Westchester divsn. Am. Cancer Soc., 1987; lectr. in medicine Columbia U. Fellow ACP; mem. Am. Soc. Med. Oncology, Am. Soc. Hematology. Office: 77 Pondfield Rd Bronxville NY 10708-3809

SAPORTA, JACK, psychologist, educator; b. N.Y.C., Oct. 21, 1927; s. David and Victoria (Fils) S.; m. Judith Hammond, May 28, 1967 (div. 1979); child: David, Victoria. AB cum laude, Adelphi U., 1951; PhD, U. Chgo., 1962. Diplomate Am. Bd. Profl. Psychology; lic. clin. psychologist. Pvt. practice, 1962—; supt. Tinley Park (Ill.) Mental Health Ctr., 1975-78; chief manpower tng. and devel. Ill. Dept. Mental Health, Chgo., 1978-82; dean, prof. Forest Inst. Profl. Psychology, Des Plaines, Ill., 1982-85; coord. studies Fielding Inst., Santa Barbara, Calif., 1984—; prof. Ill. Sch. Profl. Psychology, Chgo., 1985—; mem. adj. faculty psychology Lake Forest Grad. Sch. Mgmt., 1987—; mem. Ill. State Clin. Psychology Lic. and Disciplinary Com., Springfield, 1984-93; profl. staff Forest Hosp., Des Plaines, 1977-96; mem. staff Luth. Gen. Hosp., Park Ridge, Ill., 1986—. Served with U.S. Army, 1946-47, Germany. Named Educator of Yr., Forest Inst., 1982, Outstanding Faculty Mem. Lake Forest Grad. Sch. Mgmt. Fellow Acad. Clin. Psychology, NTL-Inst. (faculty); mem. APA (accreditation site vis. team), Ill. Psychol. Assn., Chgo. Psychol. Assn. Home: 3201 California Ave Rolling Meadows IL 60008-2226

SAQUET, ROGER, health association administrator; b. Boston, Sept. 28, 1942; s. Aurel Raymond and Hanna (Labeebee) S.; m. Margaret Matheson, July 24, 1964 (div. 1984); children: Christopher, Eric; m. Joanne Onorato, June 30, 1984. BA in English Lit., Boston U., 1963. Dir., founder Non-Circumcision Info. Ctr., Waverly, Mass., 1972—. Lance cpl. USMCR, 1961-67. Mem. Ipswich Men's Group (group leader 1974—). Home: 82 Lexington St Belmont MA 02178-1338 Office: Non-Circumcision Info Ctr PO Box 31 Waverly MA 02179-0031

SARAL, TULSI B., psychology educator, marriage and family therapist; b. Pano Akil, Sind, India, Mar. 16, 1928; came to U.S., 1964; s. Shewa Ram and Mani Bai Bhatia; m. Asha Bhatia, Sept. 9, 1953 (div. 1977); children: Chhavi, Taru, Kamal, Kumud. BA, Punjab U., India, 1953; MA, Lucknow U., India, 1959, U. Pa., 1965; PhD, U. Ill., 1969. Diplomate Am. Bd. Sexology; lic. clin. psychologist, Ill.; lic. marriage and family therapist, Tex.; cert. group psychotherapist, sex therapist. Prof. Govs. State U., University Park, Ill., 1971-83; prof. clin. psychology U. Houston-Clear Lake, 1983—; dir. intercultural communication div. Internat. Communication Assn., 1977-79; sec. So. Intercultural Edn. Tng. and Rsch., 1973-75. Recipient Outstanding New Citizen award Citizenship Coun., Chgo., 1977-78; Devel. fellow Inst. Internat. Edn., 1967-68; Acad. Leadership fellow Assn. Innovation in Higher Edn., 1977-78; East-West Sr. fellow East-West Communication Inst., Honolulu, 1979. Fellow Am. Acad. Clin. Sexology (life); m. APA, Assn. Transpersonal Psychology, Am. Assn. Sex Educators Counselors and Therapists, Am. Assn. for Study of Mental Imagery (past pres.). Democrat. Hindu. Home: 16451 Cavendish Dr Houston TX 77059-4712 Office: U Houston Clear Lake Dept Clinical Psychology Houston TX 77058

SARAN, BRUCE ROBERT, surgeon; b. Kenmore, N.Y., Mar. 24, 1962; s. Leonard Arya and Marcia Ann (Goldman) S.; m. Robin Ilene Kauffman, Oct. 9, 1988; children: Allison, Stephanie, Jesse. BS in biochemistry, U. Rochester, N.Y., 1984; MD, SUNY, Buffalo, 1988. Diplomate Am. Bd. Ophthalmology. Resident in surgery U. Ill., Chgo., 1989-92; fellow in surgery U. Pa., 1992-94; cons., surgeon Retina Assocs. PC, Annapolis, Md., 1994-96, Chester Co. Eye Care Assoc., Pa., 1996—; cons., rschr. Allergan Pharms., Irvine, Calif., 1994—. Reviewer The Jour. Retina, 1992—, The Jour. Ophthalmology, 1993, Ophthalmic Surgery and Laser, 1995; inventor in field. Fellow Am. Acad. Ophthalmology; mem. Am. Diabetes Assn. (bd. dirs. 1995). Office: Chester County Eye Care 606 E Marshall St Ste 104 West Chester PA 19830

SARASON, IRWIN G., psychology educator; b. Newark, Sept. 15, 1929; s. Max and Anna Sarason; m. Barbara June Ryrholm, Sept. 19, 1953; children: Suzanne, Jane, Donald. BA, Rutgers U., Newark, 1951; MS, U. Iowa, 1953; PhD, Ind. U., 1955. Lic. psychologist, Wash. Intern clin. psychology VA Hosp., West Haven, Conn., 1955-56; asst. prof. psychology U. Wash., Seattle, 1956-59, assoc. prof., 1959-65, prof., 1965—. Co-author: Abnormal Psychology, 1972, 8th edit., 1996; editor: Jour. Personality and Social Psychology, 1985-91; author over 250 articles. The Netherlands Inst. for Advanced Study fellow, Wassenaar, 1975, 85. Fellow APA, Japan Soc. for Promotion of Sci., AAAS, Western Psychol. Assn. (pres. 1978-79), Wash. State Psychol. Assn. (pres. 1965). Home: 13516 42nd Ave NE Seattle WA 98125-3826 Office: U Wash Dept Psychology Seattle WA 98195

SARAZEN, JEFFREY MICHAEL, optometrist; b. Milw., Jan. 4, 1962; s. Gilbert Warren and June Adeline (Gunderson) S.; m. Cherri Ann Boettcher, Aug. 8, 1987; children: Sean Mykel, Marni Rae. D of Optometry, Ill. Coll. Optometry, 1987. Lic. optometry doctor. Optometrist Pearle Vision Express, Wausau, Wis., 1987-89; pvt. practice Wausau, 1989—. Mem. Am. Optometric Assn., Wis. Optometric Assn., Tomb and Key. Republican. Lutheran. Home: 4501 Stettin Dr Wausau WI 54401-3928 Office: Jeff Sarazen and Assocs D460 Wausau Ctr Wausau WI 54403-5508

SAREMBOCK, IAN JOSEPH, internist; b. Cape Town, Republic of South Africa, June 9, 1951; m. Ghita Marueen Sarembock; children: Craig Murray, Kerri Lauren. MD, U. Cape Town, 1975, PhD, 1988. Diplomate Am. Bd. Internal Medicine, Am. Bd. Cardiovascular Medicine. Sr. house officer dept. internal medicine U. Cape Town and Groote Schuur Hosp., Cape Town, 1979-80, resident in internal medicine, 1980-83; sr. registrar Cardiac Clinic U. Cape Town and Groote Schuur Hosp., 1985-86; Velva Schrire meml. rsch. fellow Cardiac Clinic Groote Schur Hosp., 1983-85; postdoctoral rsch. assoc. divsn. cardiology Yale U., New Haven, 1986-88; attending cardiologist divsn. cardiology VA Ctr., West Haven, Conn., 1987-88; asst. prof. internal medicine cardiovascular divsn. U. Va. Health Scis. Ctr., Charlottesville, 1988-93, assoc. prof. internal medicine cardiovascular divsn., 1993—, dir. coronary care unit, cardiac catheterization lab., 1988—; cardiology cons. Salem (Va.) VA Med. Ctr., 1988—; lectr., presenter in field; invited prof. Heart-Lung Inst., Utrecht, The Netherlands, 1992; mem. faculty restenosis summits, Cleve. Clinic, 1992, 93; mem. sports edicine applied to football Italian Internat. Symposium, Rome, 1990. Contbr. articles to profl. publs. Mem. policy working com., house staff supervision Commonwealth of Va., 1990—. Grantee U. Va. Sch. Medicine, 1989, Beecham Labs., 1989-90, Am. Heart Assn., 1989-91, 91-92, NIH, 1991-94. Fellow ACP, Coll. Physicians South Africa, Am. Coll. Cardiology (allied health profls. com. 1993—); mem. AAAS, Am. Heart Assn. (bd. dirs. Charlottesville/Albermarle divsn. 1991—, mem. Va. affiliate rsch. peer rev. subcom. 1992—, thrombosis coun. 1987, fellow coun. on clin. cardiology 1989), South African Med. and Dental Coun. Office: U Va Dept Cardiology PO Box 158 Charlottesville VA 22902-0158

SARFATY, SUZANNE, internist and educator; b. Irvington, N.Y., Apr. 11, 1962; d. Sam and Pat (Petrovich) S. BS, Boston U., 1984, MD, 1988, MPH, 1994. Diplomate Am. Bd. Internal Medicine. Intern and resident Boston City Hosp., 1988-91; attending/clin. instr. Boston U., 1991-93, asst. prof. medicine and pub. health, 1995—, asst. dean of student affairs, 1995—. Mem. prof. com. Am. Cancer Soc., Boston, 1991—; mentor Boston Ptnrs. for Edn., 1991—. Recipient Cmty. Svc. award CIBA Geigy, 1986; Dana Farber cancer prevention fellow, 1993-94. Fellow ACP. Home: 11 Verndale St Brookline MA 02146-2423

SARGENT, ARLENE HONDL, nursing educator; b. Little Falls, Minn., Jan. 11, 1944; d. Anton Clarence and Eleanor (Buerman) Hondl; m. Kenneth William Sargent, June 16, 1972; children: Lisa, Michelle. BS, Coll. St. Catherine, St. Paul; MS, U. Minn., 1972; EdD, No. Ill. U., 1980. Staff nurse U. Wash. Hosp., Seattle, 1969-70; asst. head nurse U. Minn. Hosp., Mpls., 1970-72; instr. nursing Loyola U., Chgo., 1972-75; asst. prof. No. Ill. U., De Kalb, 1975-79; chmn. dept. nursing U. Dubuque, Iowa, 1980-83; prof. Holy Names Coll., Oakland, Calif., 1983-89, chairperson of nursing, 1989—, coord. of BSN teleconf. program, 1994—; cons. Mercy Health Ctr., Dubuque, 1980-83; reviewer textbooks Mosby & W.B. Saunders Pub. Co., vis. prof. Kumomoto U., Japan, 1994. Chmn. bioethics com., Lafayette, Calif., 1985—. Mem. Am. Nurses Assn., Calif. Nurses Assn., Am. Assn. Adult Continuing Edn., Sigma Theta Tau, Kappa Delta Pi, Pi Lambda Theta. Presbyterian. Home: 15 Sessions Rd Lafayette CA 94549-3124 Office: Holy Names Coll 3500 Mountain Blvd Oakland CA 94619-1627

SARGENT, PETER BRADLEE, neurobiologist, educator; b. Boston, Dec. 30, 1947; s. L. Manlius and Joan Comly (Harvey) S.; m. Margie McCuskey, Sept. 13, 1969; children: Kimberly, Jonathan. AB, Amherst Coll., 1969; PhD, Harvard U., 1975. NIH postdoctoral fellow U. Calif., San Francisco, 1975-78; Muscular Dystrophy Assn. postdoctoral fellow Stanford (Calif.) U., 1978-79; prof. neurobiology U. Calif., San Francisco; mem. NIH study sect., 1987-91. Assoc. editor Jour. Neurosci., 1990—; contbr. articles to sci. jours. Grantee NSF, 1979-85, 89—, NIH, 1985—. Mem. Soc. Neurosci., Am. Soc. Cell Biology, Soc. Developmental Biology. Office: U Calif Div Oral Biology HSW-604 San Francisco CA 94143-0512

SARIBALAS, MICHAEL GEORGE, physician; b. Columbus, Ohio, June 28, 1963; s. George Michael and Jeanette (Chakeres) S. BS in Genetics, Ohio State U., 1985, grad. student, 1986; DO, Kirksville Coll. Osteo. Med., 1992. Physician psychiatry and sleep disorders Mayo Clinic, Rochester, Jacksonville, Minn., 1992-96, U. Chgo., 1996—; physician urgent care NowCare Med. Ctr., Eagan, Minn., 1993-96, Minnetonka, Minn, 1993-96, Mankato, Minn., 1993-96, Roseville, Minn., 1993-96; chief resident Mayo Clinic, Rochester, 1995-96; instr. ACLS KCOM, Kirksville, 1990; mem. cmty. psychiatry com. Mayo Clinic Quality Improvement, 1995; instr. clin. psychiatry U. Chgo., 1996—; mem. staff THC Hosp., Chgo. Author: KCOM Peripheral Brain, 1990. Sleep Medicine fellow U. Chgo. Med. Ctr., 1996. Mem. AMA, Am. Psychiat. Assn., Minn. Psychiat. Assn., Minn. Med. Assn. (del., Ohio Osteo. Assn., Am. Osteo. Assn. Greek Orthodox. Home: 1350 N Wells St # D403 Chicago IL 60610

SARINO, EDGARDO FORMANTES, physician; b. Laoag City, Ilocos Norte, Philippines, Nov. 6, 1940; s. Epafrodito Cruz and Esperanza Raval Formantes S.; m. Milagros Felix Ona, Dec. 6, 1965; children: Edith Melanie, Edgar Michael, Edenn Michele; came to U.S., 1965, naturalized, 1983. MD, U. of the East, 1964. Rotating intern St. Clare's Hosp., N.Y.C., 1965-66; resident in anatomical pathology Coney Island Hosp., N.Y.C., 1966; resident in gen. surgery Manhattan VA Hosp., N.Y.C., 1966-67, N.Y. U.-Bellevue Med. Ctr., N.Y.C., 1967-68; resident in radiology Manhattan VA Hosp., N.Y.C., 1968-71, fellow in diagnostic radiology, 1971-73; staff radiologist Mercer Med. Ctr., Trenton, N.J., 1973-83; chief nuclear medicine service Louis Johnson VA Med. Ctr., Clarksburg, W.Va., 1983—, acting chief radiology svc., 1988-92; chief imaging svc., 1993—; clin. assoc. prof. radiology U. W.Va. Sch. Medicine, 1989—; teaching asst. in gen. surgery N.Y. U.-Bellevue Med. Ctr., N.Y.C., 1967-68. Recipient Certificate of Merit, Mallinkrodt Pharm., 1969. Diplomate Am. Bd. Radiology. Mem. Am. Coll. Physician Execs., Soc. Nuclear Med., Am. Coll. Radiology, Radiol. Soc. N.Am., Harrison County Med. Soc., W.Va. Radiol. Soc., Assn. Philippine Practicing Physicans in Am., Philippine Radiol. Soc. Am. Contbr. articles to med. jours. Home: 96 Garden Cir Bridgeport WV 26330-1367 Office: Louis Johnson VA Med Ctr Clarksburg WV 26301

SARLE, CHARLES RICHARD, health facility executive; b. Saratoga Springs, N.Y., Sept. 21, 1944; s. John Robert and Marjorie Elizabeth (Swick) S.; m. Marion D. Wallace, June 21, 1968; children: Richard Charles, Robert Edmond. BBA cum laude, Northea. U., 1968; MBA, Babson Coll., 1973. CPA, Mass., Vt.; cert. mental health adminstr. Assn. Mental Health Adminstrs. Staff acct. Price Waterhouse & Co., Boston, 1968-70, George Kanavich, CPA, Wellesley, Mass., 1970-72; controller Human Resource Inst., Boston, 1972-73, adminstr., 1973-77; controller Brattleboro (Vt.) Retreat, 1977-78, dir. adminstrn., 1978-85, v.p., 1985-88, chief exec. officer, 1988—; bd. dirs., treas. Prouty Child Devel. Ctr., Brattleboro, 1983—; speaker in field. Mem. commn. Vt. Health Bldg. Fin. Agy., 1978-90; trustee Austine Sch. for Deaf and Hard of Hearing, 1990—, pres., 1994—; trustee Winston Prouty Ctr. for Child Devel., 1982—, treas., 1983-90, sec., 1991—. Recipient recognition award Brattleboro C. of C., 1985. Fellow AICPA, Mass. Soc. CPAs, Am. Coll. Healthcare Execs. (regent Va. br. 1991-95); mem. Am. Hosp. Assn. (del.-at-large 1988-92, del.-at-large to regional policy bd.), Nat. Assn. Pvt. Psychiat. Hosps. (bd. dirs. polit. action com. 1983-93), Nat. Psychiat. Alliance (trustee 1989-96, pres. 1994-96), Vt. Soc. CPAs (Comty. Svc. award 1984), Hosp. Fin. Mgmt. Assn. (mem. hosp. cost com. 1985—), Rescue, Inc. (trustee 1982-83), New Eng. Healthcare Assembly (trustee 1995—). Republican. Home: PO Box 104 Brattleboro VT 05302-0104 Office: Brattleboro Retreat 75 Linden St Brattleboro VT 05301-4807

SARNACKI, CLIFFORD TEOFIL, urologist, renal transplant surgeon; b. Cleve., Oct. 30, 1936; s. Henry Lenard and Sophie Marie (Jablonowski) S.; married; children: Kemper, Kerry. BA, Western Reserve U., Cleve., 1959; MD, Ohio State U., 1963. Advanced through grades to col. USAF, 1964-85; chief urology USAF Hosp., Clark AFB, The Philippines, 1970-73, March AFB, Calif., 1973-76; chief surgery, urology USAF Hosp., Wiesbaden, Germany, 1976-80; chief urology Wefer Hall Med. Ctr., Lackland AFB, 1980-85; renal transplant surgeon Cmty. Hosp., San Antonio, Tex., 1985-96; assoc. prof. urology U. Tex. Health Sci. Ctr., San Antonio. Contbr. numerous articles to profl. jours. Fellow ACS, Am. Urologic Assn.; mem. San Antonio Urologic Soc. Roman Catholic. Office: 4499 Medical Dr #222 San Antonio TX 78229

SARNAT, BERNARD GEORGE, plastic surgeon, educator, researcher; b. Chgo., Sept. 1, 1912; s. Isadore M. and Fanny (Sidran) S.; m. Rhoda Elaine Gerard, Dec. 25, 1941; children: Gerard, Joan. SB, U. Chgo., 1933, MD, 1937; MS, DDS, U. Ill., 1940. Diplomate Am. Bd. Plastic Surgery. Intern Los Angeles County Gen. Hosp., 1936-37; resident oral and plastic surgery Cook County Hosp., Chgo., 1940-41; asst. to Dr. Marshall Davison (gen. surgery), Chgo., 1942-43, Drs. Vilray P. Blair and Louis T. Byars (plastic and reconstructive surgery), St. Louis, 1943-46; practice medicine specializing in plastic surgery Chgo., 1946-56, Beverly Hills, Calif., 1956-91; asst. histology U. Ill. Coll. Dentistry, 1937-40, prof., head dept. oral and maxillofacial surgery, 1946-56; asst. dept. surgery Washington U. Sch. Medicine, St. Louis, 1944-46; prof., dir. dept. oral and plastic surgery St. Louis U. Coll. Dentistry, 1945-46; clin. asst. prof. surgery (plastic surgery) U. Ill. Coll. Medicine, 1949-56; adj. prof. oral biology Sch Dentistry UCLA, 1969—, mem. Dental Rsch. Inst., 1974-95, adj. prof. plastic surgery Sch. Medicine, 1974—; attending staff Cedars-Sinai Med. Ctr., L.A., 1956-91, emeritus, 1991—, mem. staff, sr. rsch. scientist, chief plastic surgery, 1961-81; cons. in gen., plastic and maxillofacial surgery VA Regional Office, Chgo., until 1956; lectr. in field. Sr. author: (with Dr. Isaac Schour) Oral and Facial Cancer, 2d edit., 1957, (with Dr. Daniel Laskin) Surgery of the Temporomandibular Joint, 1964; editor: (with Daniel Laskin) The Temporomandibular Joint A Biological Basis for Clinical Practice, 4th edit., 1991, (with Andrew D. Dixon) Factors and Mechanisms Affecting Growth of Bone, 1982, Normal and Abnormal Bone Growth: Basic and Clinical Research, 1985, Fundamentals of Bone Growth: Methodology and Applications, 1991; contbr. chpts. to textbooks, articles to surg. and sci. jours., other pubs. Co-winner Joseph A. Capps prize for med. rsch., 1940, Frederick B. Noyes prize, 1940; recipient Kerbs award for rsch. plastic and reconstructive surgery, 1950, 1st prize, sr. award Found. Am. Soc. Plastic and Reconstructive surgeons, 1957, Beverly Hills Acad. of Medicine award, 1959, Nat. Achievement award medicine Phi Epsilon Pi, 1964, 1st prize Am. Rhinologic Soc., 1980, medal Hebrew U., Jerusalem, 1985, medal Tel Aviv U., 1985, Disting. Svc. Alumni award U. Chgo. Pritzker Sch. Medicine, 1987, hon. award Am. Soc. Maxillofacial Surgeons, 1990, Dallas B. Phemister Profl. Achievement award Dept. Surgery U. Chgo., 1993, Disting. Alumnus award U. Ill. Coll. Dentistry, 1994, Craniofacial Biology Rsch. award Internat. Assn. for Dental Rsch., 1995, Disting. Scientist award. Fellow ACS, AAAS, Am. Assn. Plastic Surgeons (hon.); mem. Calif. Med. Soc., L.A. Med. Soc., Am. Soc. Plastic and Reconstructive Surgeons, Plastic Surgery Rsch. Coun. (founding mem. 1955, chmn. 1957), Calif. Soc. Plastic Surgeons, Beverly Hills Acad. Medicine (pres. 1962-63), Internat. Assn. Craniofacial Biology, Am. Assn. Phys. Anthropologists, Internat. Assn. Study Dento-Facial Abnormalities (hon.), Sigma Xi, Omicron Kappa Upsilon, Zeta Beta Tau, Phi Delta Epsilon, Alpha Omega (Internat. Achievement medal 1988). Home: 1875 Kelton Ave Apt 301 Los Angeles CA 90025-4576

SARNO, MARTHA TAYLOR, speech and language pathologist, educator; b. N.Y.C., Nov. 25, 1927; d. Edward and Milagros Abril-Lamarque; m. John Ernest Sarno, Jan. 8, 1967; 1 child, Christina. BA, Mich. State Univ., 1949; MA, N.Y. Univ., 1954; D in medicine honoris causa, Univ. Goteborg, Goteborg, Sweden, 1982. Diplomate Am. Bd. Neurogenic Communication Disorders in Adults & Children; cert. in clin. competence. Speech-language pathologist Goldwater Meml. Hosp., N.Y.C., 1949-50; dir. speech language pathology dept. Rusk Inst. Rehabilitation Medicine, N.Y.C., 1950—; instr. prof. dept. rehab. medicine N.Y. Univ. Sch. Medicine, 1957-65, asst. prof. dept. rehab. medicine, 1965-78, assoc. prof., 1978-90, prof., 1990—; asst. prof. dept. speech-language pathology N.Y. Univ. Sch. Edn., 1964-73; faculty Kurt Goldstein Inst. Neuropsychological, Straubing, Bavaria, 1995—; chmn. tech. adv. com. speed & lang. disorder Dept. of Health, N.Y.C., 1967-77; mem. task force to study ethics in rehab. medicine Hastings Ctr., Briarcliff Manor, N.Y., 1985-88; cons. editor, Jour. Communication Disorders, 1967-91. Co-author: Stroke: The Condition and The Patient, 1979; editor: Acquired Aphasia, 1981, 2nd edit., 1991; editor: Topics in Stroke Rehabilitation, 1995. Founder, pres. Nat. Aphasia Assn., 1987—; founder, charter mem. Acad. Aphasia, 1962—, bd. govs., 1979-83, 90-96. Recipient Gold Key award Am. Congress of Rehabilitation Medicine, 1974, Outstanding Alumni award Mich. State Univ., 1976, Rusk award Howard A. Rusk Inst. Rehabilitation Medicine, 1985. Fellow Am. Speech Language Hearing Assn.; mem. Am. Congress Rehabilitation Medicine, Acad. Aphasia (chmn. sci. program com. 1969-72), Acad. Neurologic Communication Disorders & Scis., Internat. Assn. Logopedics & Phoniatrics, Soc. Hosp. Dirs. of Communicative Disorders. Office: New York Univ Sch Medicine Dept Rehab Medicine 400 E 34th St New York NY 10016

SARNO, PATRICIA ANN, biology educator; b. Ashland, Pa.; d. John Thomas and Anna (Harvest) S. BS, Pa. State U., 1966, MEd, 1971; postgrad. Bucknell U., 1967, Bloomsburg U., 1970. Programmer planetarium, tchr. sci. Pottsville (Pa.) High Sch., 1967; tchr. biology Schuylkill Haven (Pa.) Area High Sch., 1967-91, sci. chmn., coord. dist., 1973-91; lead tchr. sci. Pa. Acad. Suprs. and Curriculum Devel. Dist. Pa. Sch., 1991—; cons. Contbr. to profl. jours. Pa. Edn. Dept., career program Pottsville Hosp. Dow Chem. Co. grantee, 1971. Mem. AAAS, AAUW, NEA, Pa. Edn. Assn. (exec. bd.), Nat. Assn. Biology Tchrs., Nat. Tchrs. Assn., Pa. Assn. Supervision and Curriculum Devel., N.Y. Acad. Scis., Pa. Tchrs. Assn., Am. Inst. Biol. Scis., Pa. Acad. Scis., Pa. State U. Alumni Assn., Schuylkill Haven Edn. Assn., Phi Sigma, Delta Kappa Gamma. Discoverer spider species Atypus snetzingeri, 1973. Home: 49 S Balliet St Frackville PA 17931-1703 Office: Schuylkill Haven HS Schuylkill Haven PA 17972

SAROFF, MARIE, physician; b. Hyderabad, India, Apr. 16, 1928; came to U.S., 1958; d. Syed Abdul and K. Hy (Guha) Jabbar; m. Jack Saroff (dec. Nov. 1977); children: David, Rahel Kitty. MB BS, Christian Med. Coll., Vellore, South India, 1952; MD, SUNY, Buffalo, 1967. Diplomate Am. Bd. Pediatrics. Rotating intern Christian Med. Coll. Hosp., 1952-53; intern straight pediatrics Ottawa (Can.) Gen. Hosp., 1954-55; resident in pediatrics Children's Mercy Hosp., Kansas City, Mo., 1955-57; asst. dir. Salt Lake County Hosp., Salt Lake City, 1958-59; pediatric coord. child devel. program Children's Hosp. of Buffalo, 1959-64, mem. courtesy staff, 1966—; staff pediatrician Children's Neuromuscular Diagnostic Clinic, Cin., 1967; instr. dept. pediatrics Coll. Medicine U. Cin., 1967-72; mem. attending staff Erie County Med. Ctr., 1972-90; attending physician West Seneca Devel. Ctr., 1985—; physician well baby clinic Erie County Health Dept., Buffalo, 1990—; asst. dir. cerebral dysfunction program U. Affiliated Clin. Program for Mentally Retarded, U. Cin., 1967-72; mem. courtesy staff Children's Hosp., Cin., 1967, asst. attending staff mem., 1969-72; attending pediatrician Erie County Med. Ctr., 1972-85, mem. med. records, 1980-85, Senecca Devel. Ctr., 1985-90, Erie County Health Dept., 1991—, Sisters of Charity Hosp.; pediat. cons. infant stimulation program, 1975—, N.Y. State Disability Bd. Mem. Buffalo Pediatric Soc., Am. Acad. Pediatrics, Women Physician's League, Am. Women Med. Assn., Am. Women's Med. Assn., Am. Pub. Health Assn., Ambulatory Pediatric Assn. Home: 501 Woodland Dr Buffalo NY 14223-1724

SARRAFZADEGAN, NIZAL, cardiologist; b. Baghdad, Iraq, May 7, 1959; d. Hamed and Fatemah (Sharif) S.; m. Homayoon Ranjbar, Oct. 22, 1983; children: Parvin, Jasmine. MD, Med. Sch., Isfahan, Iran, 1985. Gen. physician Health Ctr., Isfahan, 1985-86; asst. prof. internal medicine Isfahan U. Med. Scis., 1989-91, asst. prof. cardiology, 1993—; dir. Cardiovascular Rsch. Ctr., Isfahan, 1992—; cons. Dep. of Rsch. Sch., Isfahan, 1991—, Dep. of Rsch. Ministry of Health, tehran, Iran, 1991-93. Editl. bd. Jour. U. Med. Scis., 1993-95; contbr. articles to profl. jours. Recipient Medal Minister of Health Treatment and Med. Scis., 1993, Cons. for Women for Pres. of Iran, 1994, Pres. of Isfahan U. of Med. Scis., 1991-95. Fellow World Health Assn.; mem. Internat. Soc. and Fedn. Cardiology, Am. Heart Assn., Iranian Orgn. Internists, Iranian Soc. Cardiologists (dir. 1995—). Home: Charbagbala, Hedayat-Shahrokh 47, Isfahan Iran Office: Cardiovascular Rsch Ctr, Amin Hosp Ibnsina St, 81465-1148 Isfahan Iran

SARRETT, SHEILA, research utilization coordinator, grant coordinato; b. Bklyn.; d. Bernard and Helen (Gitlin) Weitz; m. Matthew Sarrett, Nov. 9, 1957; children: Wendy Ellen, Jeffrey Evan. BA in Social Sci., Adelphi U., 1976, MS in Adult Learning and Devel., 1986. Asst. to dir.. special events Abraham & Strauss, Hempstead, N.Y., 1978-80; dir. continuing edn. Lynbrook (N.Y.) Sch. Dist., 1980-87; asst. dir. rsch. utilization PEER reg. Network/Nat. Ctr. for Disability Svcs., Albertson, N.Y., 1988—, project dir., 1994; dir. Rehab. Tech. Info. Exch., 1990—; cons. Nat. Coun. Jewish Women, N.Y.C., 1986-87. Editor Am. Heart Assn., 1983-88, Oceanside-Island Park Herald, 1980-83; columnist Pyramid Publs. 1987. Leadership Conf. scholar N.Y. Assn. Continuing Community Edn., 1989. Mem. ASTD (pres. com. employment people with disabilities), Nassau Assn. Continuing Community Edn. (pres.). Office: Nat Ctr for Disability Svcs 201 I U Willets Rd Albertson NY 11507-1516

SARSHAR, MIR AHMAD, surgeon; b. Jan. 22, 1932; came to U.S., 1958; s. Seyed Taghi and Robabeh (Hassali) S.; m. Roslyn Kronenberg, Feb. 27, 1960; children: Maryam, Farah, Kamran. Diploma, Sharaf, Tehran, Iran, 1948; MD, U. Tehran, 1955. Diplomate Am. Bd. Surgery; cert. hand surgeon. Intern South Balt. Gen. Hosp., 1958, resident, 1959-63; pvt. practice Balt., 1964—. 2d lt. M.C. Iranian Imperial Army, 1955-57. Fellow ACS, Southeastern Surg. Congress; mem. Med. and Chirugical Faculty State of Md., Balt. City Med. Soc. Moslem. Office: 3455 Wilkens Ave Baltimore MD 21229-5213

SARTIN, JAMES LEWIS, JR., physiologist; b. Jacksonville, N.C., Feb. 15, 1952; s. James Lewis and Exa (Halford) S.; m. Eva Ann Martin, Dec. 29, 1976; children: Matthew McCullough, Scott Kelly. B.A., Auburn U., 1973, M.S., 1976; Ph.D., Okla. State U., 1978. Teaching assoc. Okla. State U., Stillwater, 1978-79; postdoctoral fellow Temple U., Phila., 1979-81, staff biologist, 1981-82; asst. prof. physiology Auburn (Ala.) U., 1982-87, assoc. prof., 1987-92, prof., 1992—. Mem. AAAS, Internat. Soc. Neuroendocrinology, Am. Physiol. Soc., Am. Soc. Animal Sci., Endocrine Soc. Democrat. Baptist. Editor: Domestic Animal Endocrinology. Office: Auburn Univ Dept Physiology Auburn AL 36849

SARTORELLI, ALAN CLAYTON, pharmacology educator; b. Chelsea, Mass., Dec. 18, 1931; m. Alice C. Anderson, July 7, 1969. B.S., New Eng. Coll. Pharmacy Northeastern U., 1953; M.S., Middlebury (Vt.) Coll., 1955; Ph.D., U. Wis., 1958; M.A. (hon.), Yale U., 1967. Rsch. chemist Samuel Roberts Noble Found., Ardmore, Okla., 1958-60; sr. rsch. chemist Samuel Roberts Noble Found., 1960-61; mem. faculty dept. pharmacology Yale Sch. Medicine, New Haven, Conn., 1961—, prof., 1967—, head devel. therapeutics program Comprehensive Cancer Center, 1974-90, chmn. dept. pharmacology, 1977-84, dep. dir. Comprehensive Cancer Ctr., 1982-84, dir. Comprehensive Cancer Ctr., 1984-93, Alfred Gilman prof. pharmacology, 1987—, prof. epidemiology, 1991—; Charles B. Smith vis. rsch. prof. Meml. Sloan-Kettering Ctr., 1979; William N. Creasy vis. prof. clin. pharmacology Wayne State U., 1983; Mayo Found. vis. prof. oncology Mayo Clinic, 1983; Walter Hubert lectr. Brit. Assn. Cancer Rsch., 1985; Pfizer lectr. in clin. pharmacology U. Conn. Health Ctr., 1985; William N. Creasy vis. prof. clin. pharmacology Bowman Gray Sch. Medicine, 1987; Wellcome vis. prof. basic sci. U. Pitts. Sch. Medicine, 1990; mem. sci. adv. bd. ImmunoGen, Inc., 1981—, U. Ind. Cancer Ctr., 1992, Cancer Inst. N.J., 1993—, Cell Pathways, Inc., 1993—; chmn. cancer sci. adv. bd. ViraChem., Inc., 1986-93, The Liposome Co., 1986—, Vion Pharms., 1993—, bd. dirs.; chmn. vis. sci. adv. com. Columbia U. Comprehensive Cancer Ctr., 1986—; chmn. pres.'s cancer adv. bd. Fox Chase Cancer Ctr., 1992—; mem. cancer clin. investigation rev. com. Nat. Cancer Inst., 1968-72, mgmt. cons. to dir. divsn. cancer treatment, 1975-77, bd. sci. counselors, divsn. cancer treatment, 1978-81, chmn. com. to establish nat. coop. drug discovery groups, 1982-83, chmn. special review com. Outstanding Investigator grant applications, 1992, chmn. ad hoc contracts tech. rev. group, 1993; mem. instl. rsch. grants com. Am. Cancer Soc., 1971-76, coun. analysis and projection, 1978-79; cons. in biochemistry U. Tex. M.D. Anderson Hosp. and Tumor Clinic, Houston, 1970-76; cons. Sandoz Forschungs-Institut, Vienna, Austria, 1977-80; mem. exptl. therapeutics study sect. NIH, 1973-77, working cadre nat. large bowel cancer project, 1973-76; mem. adv. com. Cancer Rsch. Ctr., Washington U. Sch. Medicine, 1971-75, SLSB Partners, L.P., 1992—; mem. sci. adv. com. U. Iowa Cancer Ctr., 1979-83; mem. external adv. com. Wis. Clin. Cancer Ctr., 1978-79, Duke Comprehensive Cancer Ctr., 1983-94; mem. external adv. bd. U. Ariz. Cancer Ctr., 1982-92, U. So. Calif. Cancer Ctr., 1983-93, Clin. Cancer Rsch. Ctr., Brown U., 1980-86; mem. nat. program com. 13th Internat. Cancer Congress, 1979-81; cons. Bristol-Myers Co., 1982-93, mem. selection com. prize in cancer rsch., 1977-85, chmn., 1979-81, chmn. selection com. award for disting. achievement in cancer rsch., 1989-92; bd. advisors Drug and Vaccine Devel. Corp. (Ctr. for Pub. Resources), 1980-81, Specialized Cancer Ctr., Mt. Sinai Med. Ctr., 1981-90, Grace Cancer Drug Ctr., Roswell Park Meml. Inst., 1986-89; mem. med. and sci. adv. com. grants rev. subcom. Leukemia Soc. Am., 1984-88; bd. dirs. Metastasis Rsch. Soc., 1984-90; mem. program planning com. Mary Lasker-Am. Cancer Soc. Conf., 1986; mem. external sci. rev. com. Massey Cancer Ctr., 1989-94; bd. visitors Moffit Cancer Ctr. U.S. Fla., 1989-94; mem. ad hoc cons. group for cancer ctrs. program Nat. Cancer Adv. Bd., 1989-92; dep. dir. Cancer Prevention Rsch. Unit for Conn., 1989-93, acting dir., 1991-93; mem. nat. bd. Cosmetic Toiletry and Fragnance Assn.'s Look Good...Feel Better Program, 1989-91; mem. organizing com. Conf. on Bioreductive Drug Activation, 1993-94; chmn. bd. special cons. Inst. for Cancer Therapeutics, 1993—. Regional editor Am. Continent Biochem. Pharmacology, 1968—, exec. editor, 1993—; editor-in-chief Cancer Comm., 1969-91, Oncology Rsch., 1993—; editor Handbuch der experimentellen Pharmakologie vols. on antineoplastic and immunosuppressditor series on cancer chemotherapy Am. Chem. Soc. Symposium, 1976; exec. editor Pharmacology and Therapeutics, 1975—; mem. editl. bd. Internat. Ency. Pharmacology and Therapeutics, 1972—, Seminars in Oncology, 1973-83, Chemico-Biol. Interactions, 1975-78, Jour. Meldicinal Chemistry, 1977-82, Cancer Drug Delivery, 1982-85, Jour. Enzyme Inhibition, 1984—, Anti-Cancer Drug Design, 1984—, Jour. Liposome Rsch., 1986-92, In Vivo, 1990—, Cancer Biotherapy, 1992, Cancer Rsch., Therapy, and Control, 1993—, Oncology Reports, 1995—, Molecular and Celleular Differentiation, 1995—; mem. adv. bd. Advances in Chemistry Series, ACS Symposium Series, 1977-80; mem. editl. adv. bd. Cancer Rsch., 1970-71, assoc. editor, 1971-78; assoc. editor Current Awareness in Biol. Scis., Current Advances in Pharmacology and Toxicology, 1983—, Cancer Cells, 1989-91, Jour. Exptl. Therapeutics and Oncology, 1995—; mem. exec. adv. bd. Ency. of Human Biology, 1987-90, Dictionary of Sci. and Tech., 1989-91; editl. cons. Biol. Abstracts, 1984—; contbr. articles to profl. jours. Bd. dirs. Shubert Performing Arts Ctr., 1992—, Shubert Opera Bd., 1991—, chmn., 1993—. Recipient Outstanding Alumni award Northeastern U., 1987, Mike Hogg award M.D. Anderson Cancer Ctr., U. Tex., 1989, Alumni Achievement award Middlebury Coll., 1990. Fellow AAAS, N.Y. Acad. Scis.; mem. Am. Assn. Cancer Rsch. (dir 1975-78, 84-87, chmn. publs. com. 1981-88, v.p. 1985-86, fin. com. 1985-88, exec. com. 1985-89, chmn. exec. com. 1987, pres. 1986-87, chmn. awards com. 1987, chmn. nominating com. 1993-95, mem. devel. com. 1995—), Am. Chem. Soc., Am. Soc. Microbiology, Am. Soc. Biochemistry and Molecular Biology, Am. Soc. Cell Biology, Am. Soc. Pharmacology and Exptl. Therapeutics (award in exptl. therapeutics 1986, award com. 1988, chmn. 1992), Assn. Am. Cancer Insts. (v.p. 1986, bd. dirs. 1986-89, liaison rep. to Nat. Cancer Inst. 1986, pres. 1987-88, chmn. bd. dirs. 1989), Inst. of Medicine of NAS (com. on govt. industry collaboration in biomed. rsch. and edn. 1989, mem. Forum on Drug Devel. and Regulation 1989—), Conn. Acad. Sci. and Engring., Coun. Biology Editors. Home: 4 Perkins Rd Woodbridge CT 06525-1616 Office: Yale U Dept Pharmacology 333 Cedar St New Haven CT 06510-3206

SARWER-FONER, GERALD JACOB, physician, educator; b. Volkovsk, Grodno, Poland, Dec. 6, 1924; arrived in Can., 1932, naturalized, 1935; s. Michael and Ronia (Caplan) Sarwer-F.; m. Ethel Sheinfeld, May 28, 1950; children: Michael, Gladys, Janice, Henry, Brian. B.A., Loyola Coll. U., Montreal, 1945, M.D. magna cum laude, 1951; D.Psychiatry, McGill U., 1955. Diplomate: Am. Bd. Psychiatry and Neurology. Intern. Univ. Hosps. U. Montreal Sch. Medicine, 1950-51; resident Butler Hosp., Providence, 1951-52, Hosps. Western Res. U., Cleve., 1952-53, Queen Mary Vets. Hosp., Montreal, 1953-55; lectr. psychiatry U. Montreal, 1953-55; lectr., assoc. prof. McGill U., 1955-70; prof. psychiatry U. Ottawa, Ont., 1971—, prof., chmn. psychiatry, 1974-86; dir. dept. psychiatry Ottawa Gen. Hosp., 1971-87; dir. Lafayette Clinic, Detroit, 1989-92; prof. psychiatry Wayne State U., Detroit, 1989—; cons. in psychiatry Ottawa Gen. Hosp., Royal Ottawa Hosp., Nat. Def. Med. Ctr., Children's Hosp. of Eastern Ont., Ottawa, Windsor (Ont.) Western Hosp. Ctr., Ottawa Sch. Bd.; Z. Lebensohn lectr. Sibley Meml. Hosp. Cosmos Club, Washington,. 1991. Editor: Dynamics of Psychiatric Drug Therapy, 1960, Research Conference on the Depressive Group of Illnesses, 1966, Psychiatric Crossroads-the Seventies, Research Aspects, 1972; editor in chief Psychiat. Jour. U. Ottawa, 1976-90, emeritus editor in chief, 1990—; mem. editorial bds. of numerous internat. and nat. profl. jours.; editor numerous audio-video tapes; contbr. numerous articles to profl. jours. Bd. govs. Queen Elizabeth Hosp., Montreal, 1966-71; life gov. Queen Elizabeth Hosp. Found.; cons. Protestant Sch. Bd., Westmount, Que., 1966-71; advisor Com. on Health, City of Westmount, 1969-71. Served to lt. col. Royal Can. A Med. Corps, 1949-62. Recipient Sigmund Freud award Am. assn. Psychoanalytic Physicians, 1982, William V. Silverberg Meml. award Am. Acad. Psychoanalysis, 1990, Poca award Assn. Psychiat. Out Patient Ctrs. Am., 1990; Simon Bolivar lectr. Am. Psychiat. Assn., New Orleans, 1981; Can. Decoration Knight of Malta. Fellow AAAS, Royal Coll. Physicians and Surgeons (Can., mem. spl. psychiat. com. 1958-64, exec. sec. test psychiat. com. 1987-89), Royal Coll. Psychiatry (Found. fellow), Am. Coll. Neuropsychopharmacology (charter, life), Can. Coll. Neuropsychopharmacology (life, hon. found.), Internat. Coll. Psychosomatic Medicine (sec.-gen. 1979-83), Am. Psychiat. Assn. (life), Am. Orthopsychiat. Assn. (life), Am. Coll. Psychiatrists (bd. regents 1978-80, emeritus fellow), Am. Psychopathol. Assn., Am. Coll. Psychoanalysts (pres. elect 1983, pres. 1984-85, Henry Laughlin award 1986), Am. Coll. Mental Health Adminstrn. (life), Benjamin Rush Soc. (founding mem., councillor), World Psychiat. Assn. (chair Sci. program VI World Congress 1974, v.p. sect. on edn. 1989—, mem. internat. adv. com. 9th World Congress Rio de Janeiro 1993, mem. nominating com.), Collegium Internat. Neuropsychopharmacology; mem. Am. Acad. Psychiatry and the Law (sr., pres. 1977, Silver Apple award), Soc. Bio.. Psychiatry (sr. mem., H. Azina Meml. lectr. 1963, pres. 1983-84), Can. Psychoanalytic Soc. (pres. 1977-81), Can. Assn. Profs. of Psychiatry (pres. 1976-77, 82-86), Am. Assn. for Social Psychiatry (v.p. 1987-89, pres. elect 1990, pres. 1992-94), Mich. Psychoanalytic Soc., Cosmos Club, Royal Can. Mil. Inst. Club. Home and Office: 3220 Bloomfield Shore Dr West Bloomfield MI 48323-3300

SASAHARA, ARTHUR ASAO, cardiologist, educator, researcher; b. Del Rey, Calif., May 11, 1927; s. Harold Hango and Blanche (Takayama) S.; m. Alice Ann Guenther, Apr. 2, 1955; children: Ann Mariko, Claire Michiko, Ellen Reiko, Karen Hideko, Mark Tadao. AB, Oberlin Coll., 1951; MD, Case Western Res. U., 1955; AM (hon.), Harvard U., 1974. Diplomate Am. Bd. Internal Medicine. Intern Boston City Hosp., 1955-56; jr asst. med. resident Mass. Gen. Hosp., Boston, 1956-57; fellow in cardiology West Roxbury VA Med. Ctr., Mass., 1957-58, Children's Hosp. Med. Ctr., Boston, 1958-59; sr. resident in medicine Yale-New Haven Med. Ctr., 1959-60; asst. chief med. svc., dir. cardiopulmonary lab., dep. chmn. rsch. and edn. com. VA Hosp. West Roxbury, 1960-70, chief cardiopulmonary sect., 1971-74, assoc. chief staff for rsch. and edn., 1970-76, chief med. svc., 1974-82; chief med. svc. West Roxbury-Brockton VA Hosp., 1982-87; prof. medicine Harvard Med. Sch., Boston, 1974-93; prof. emeritus Harvard Med. Sch., 1993—; cons. cardiovascular-pulmonary diseases Boston, 1965-87; cons. pediatric cardiology Children's Hosp. Med. Ctr., Boston, 1976-85; physician Brigham and Women's Hosp., Boston, 1979-82, sr. physician, 1982—; dir. Thrombolytics Rsch. Pharm. Products Divsn. Abbott Labs., Abbott Park, Ill., 1987-95, sr. med. dir., 1995—. Author-editor: Pulmonary Embolic Disease, 1965, Pulmonary Emboli, 1975; contbr. articles to profl. jours.; designer constant infusion med. pump, Harvard Apparatus Co., 1973; editorial bd. Jour. Nuclear Medicine, 1981-83, Am. Jour. Medicine, 1971-72, Circulation, 1973-78, VASA, 1978-85, Jour. Cardiovascular Medicine, 1980-86, Primary Cardiology, 1986-89. With U.S. Army, 1945-47. NIH grantee, 1963-82; VA grantee, 1961-87. Fellow ACP, Am. Coll. Chest Physicians, Am. coll. Cardiology; mem. AAAS, Am. Fedn. Clin. Rsch., Internat. Soc. Thrombosis and Thrombolysis, Alpha Omega Alpha. Democrat. Episcopalian. Home: 1094 Linda Ln Glencoe IL 60022-1147 Office: Abbott Labs R&D D48N AP9 Abbott Park IL 60064

SASAKI, CLARENCE TAKASHI, surgeon, medical educator; b. Honolulu, Jan. 24, 1941; s. Tsutomu and Carla Harumi (Mirikitani) S.; m. Carolyn Elizabeth Lindahl, June 26, 1967; children: Peter Gordon, John Eric. B.A., Pomona Coll., 1962; M.D., Yale U., 1966. Diplomate: Am. Bd. Otolaryngology. Intern San Francisco Hosp., U. Calif., 1966-67; resident in surgery Dartmouth Med. Sch., 1967-68; resident in otolaryngology Yale U. Med. Sch. Hosps., New Haven, 1970-73, faculty mem., 1973—, assoc. prof., 1977-82, prof. surgery, 1982—, chief sect. otolaryngology, 1981—; Charles Ohse prof. surgery Yale U. Med. Sch. Hosps., 1988—, vice chmn. dept. surgery, 1996. Author: Surgery of the Skull Base, Head and Neck Surgery, Vol. 1 Atlas Otolarynogology, Vocal Fold Physiology, Laryngeal Function in Phonation and Respiration, Neurological Diseases of the Larynx; mem. editorial bd. profl. jours. Served to maj. M.C. U.S. Army 1968-70. Recipient award Fowler Triological Soc., 1979. Mem. Am. Acad. Otolaryngology (1st prize clin. rsch.), Am. Soc. Head and Neck Surgery (coun.), Assn. Rsch. Otolaryngology, Am. Laryngol. Rhinol. and Otol. Soc. (coun., sec. ea. sect. 1990), New Eng. Otolaryngology Soc. (pres. 1987, coun.), Assn. Acad. Depts. Otolaryngology (coun.), Am. Laryngol. Assn., Pan Pacific Surg. Assn., Soc. for Neurosci., Soc. Neurovascular Surgery, Soc. for Head and Neck Surgeons, Am. Neurotolog. Soc., Pan Am. Assn. Oto-rhinolaryngology and Bronchoesophagology, Conn. Med. Soc., N.Y. Acad. Scis., Soc. Univ. Otolaryngologists, Collegium ORLAS, Cartesian Soc., Am. Bronchoesophagological Assn., N.Am. Skull Base Soc., Laryngeal. Cancer Assn. (Padua), Am. Otol. Soc., Dysphagia Rsch. Soc. (treas., pres.), Lawn Club, Mory's Club, Yale Club, Phi Beta Kappa, Sigma Xi. Office: Yale U Med Sch Dept Surgery PO Box 208041 333 Cedar St New Haven CT 06520-8041

SASENICK, JOSEPH ANTHONY, health care company executive; b. Chgo., May 18, 1940; s. Anthony E. and Caroline E. (Smicklas) S.; m. Barbara Ellen Barr, Aug. 18, 1962; children: Richard Allen, Susan Marie, Michael Joseph. BA, DePaul U., 1962; MA, U. Okla., 1966. With Miles Labs., Inc., Elkhart, Ind., 1963-70; product mgr. Alka-Seltzer, 1966-68, dir. mktg. grocery products div., 1968-70; with Gillette Corp., Boston, 1970-79; dir. new products/new ventures, personal care div. Gillette Corp., 1977; v.p. diversified cos. and pres. Jafra Cosmetics Worldwide, 1977-79; mktg. dir. Braun AG, Kronberg, W. Ger., 1970-73; chmn. mng. dir. Braun U.K. Ltd., 1973-77; with Abbott Labs., North Chicago, 1979-84; corp. v.p., pres. consumer products div. Abbott Labs., 1979-84; pres., chief exec. officer Moxie Industries, 1984-87, Personal Monitoring Technologies, Rochester, N.Y., 1987; pres. Bioline Labs., Ft. Lauderdale, Fla., 1988; mng. dir., ptnr. Vista Resource Group, Newport Beach, Calif., 1988-90; pres., CEO, Alcide Corp., Redmond, Wash., 1991-92, CEO, 1992—. Mem. Columbia Tower Club, El Niguel Club, Wash. Athletic Club. Home: 1301 Spring St Seattle WA 98104-1354 Office: Alcide Corp 8561 154th Ave NE Redmond WA 98052-3557

SASHIN, DONALD, physicist, radiologist, educator; b. N.Y.C., Dec. 11, 1937; s. David and Pearl (Taub) S.; m. Kathleen Flaherty, July 24, 1967; children: Deirdae Moira, Courtenay Aileen. BS in Physics, MIT, 1960; MS in Physics, Carnegie Inst. Tech., 1962; PhD in Physics, Carnegie Mellon U., 1968. Instr. radiation health Dept. of Radiology U. Pitts., 1967-70, asst. prof. radiology, 1970-74, 77-89; asst. prof. Dept. of Indsl. and Environ. Health Sci. U. Pitts., 1970-77; assoc. prof. Dept. of Radiology U. Pitts., 1989—. Contbr. articles to profl. jours., patentee in field. Recipient Cum Laude award sci. exh., RSNA, 1977, cert. of merit sci. exh., RSNA, 1979. Mem. APS, AAPM, SNM, HPS, IEEE, Sigma Xi. Democrat. Roman Catholic. Home: 4360 Centre Ave Pittsburgh PA 15213 Office: PET Facility B 938 PUH 200 Lothrop St Pittsburgh PA 15213

SASLOW, GEORGE, psychiatrist, educator; b. N.Y.C., Dec. 5, 1906; s. Abram and Becky (Zinkoff) S.; m. Julia Amy Ipcar, July 28, 1928; children: Michael G., Rondi, Steven, Marguerite. ScB magna cum laude, Washington Sq. Coll. NYU, 1926; postgrad., U. Rochester, 1926-28; PhD in Physiology, NYU, 1931; MD cum laude, Harvard U., 1940. Instr., asst. prof. biology N.Y. U., 1928-37; vis. research assoc. physiology Cornell Med. Coll., 1935-36, U. Rochester Sch. Medicine, 1936-37; research assoc. physiology Harvard Sch. Pub. Health, 1937-40; neurology-neurosurgery intern Boston City Hosp., 1940-41; resident Worcester State Hosp., 1941-42; chief resident psychiatry Mass. Gen. Hosp., Boston, 1942-43; staff Mass. Gen. Hosp., 1955-57; instr., successively asst., assoc. prof., prof. pychiatry Washington U. Sch. Medicine, 1943-55; staff Barnes Hosp., St. Louis, 1943-55; practice of psychiatry, 1943—; clin. prof. psychiatry Harvard, 1955-57; prof. psychiatry U. Oreg. Med. Sch., Portland, 1957-74; head dept. U. Oreg. Med. Sch., 1957-73, prof. emeritus, 1979—; chief mental health and behavioral sci. edn., chief psychiatry service VA Hosp., Sepulveda, Calif., 1974-79; prof. psychiatry in residence UCLA, 1974-79; mem. Psychiat. Security Rev. Bd., 1983—. Nat. Tng. Labs. fellow. Fellow Am. Psychiat. Assn. (life; mem. task force on nomenclature and stats.), Am. Coll. Psychiatrists (charter); mem. AMA, Assn. for Advancment of Behavioral Therapy, Delta Soc. (bd. dirs. 1986-89). Home: 02403 SW Greenwood Rd Portland OR 97219-8394

SASS, HENNING, psychiatry educator; b. Kiel, Germany, Dec. 4, 1944; s. Friedrich and Alida (Lehmbeck) S.; m. Ulrike Zabransky, Nov. 19, 1976; children: Christian, Vera. Med. diploma, U. Kiel, 1968; MD, U. Mainz, Germany, 1971. Physician U. Kiel, 1972-75; resident in psychiatry U. Heidelberg, Germany, 1976-87; prof. psychiatry U. Munich, 1987-90; prof., head dept. and chair psychiatry U. Aachen, Germany, 1990—, dir. Univ. Clinic, 1990—, dean Faculty of Medicine, 1994—. Author: Psychopathy, 1987, Unitary Psychosis, 1991, Crimes of Passion, 1993; editor: Nervenarzt, 1990—, Methodology in Psychopathology, 1996. Office: U Aachen Psychiat Clinic, Pauwelsstrasse 30, 52057 Aachen 1, Germany

SASS, NEIL LESLIE, toxicologist; b. Balt., Oct. 24, 1944; s. Samuel and Blanche (Radoon) S.; m. Anita Paige Hoswell, June 29, 1984. BS, Wake Forest Coll., 1966; MS, W.Va. U., 1969, PhD, 1971; MS, Johns Hopkins U., 1984. Commd. officer USPHS, 1966, advanced through grades to capt., 1988, cmdr. Preventive Medicine Unit, 1989; served as rsch. toxicologist med. labs. U.S. Army, Edgewood Arsenal, Md., 1971-74; chief clin. investigations William Beaumont Med. Ctr., El Paso, Tex., 1974-77; toxicologist Bur. of Foods FDA, Washington, 1977-82; spl. asst. to dir. Ctr. for Food Safety & Applied Nutrition, Washington, 1982—. Jewish. Home: 12900 Fork Rd Baldwin MD 21013-9345 Office: CFSAN/FDA 200 C St SW Washington DC 20204-0001

SASS, PAIGE MUNNIKHUYSEN, health facility administrator; b. Marysville, Calif., Nov. 11, 1943; d. Joseph Kirby and Anita Jacqueline (Dandy) Munnikhuysen; m. James G. Hoswell, Sept. 29, 1962 (div. June 1983); m. Neil L. Sass, June 29, 1983; 1 child, Bryarly Paige. BS, Johns Hopkins U., 1983, MS, 1985. Internal auditor, clin. mgr. neuro Johns Hopkins U., Balt., 1982-84; assoc. adminstr. ambulatory care Wyman Park Hosp., Balt., 1984-89; dir. renal Bon Secours Hosp., Balt., 1994—; bd. trustees Harford Jewish Ctr., Havre de Grace, Md., 1993-95; budget, audit com. Columbia (Md.) Assocs., 1988-89. Mem. Nat. Renal Adminstrs. Assn., Md. Group Mgmt. Assn., Johns Hopkins U. Alumni Assn. Democrat. Home: 12900 Fork Rd Baldwin MD 21013 Office: 2000 W Baltimore St Baltimore MD 21223

SASS, RONALD LEWIS, biology and chemistry educator; b. Davenport, Iowa, May 26, 1932; s. Erwin Leese and Flora Alice (Puck) S.; m. Joyce R. Moorhead, 1951 (div. 1968); children: Dennise, Andria; m. Margaret Lee Macy, Apr. 4, 1969; children: Hartley, Dennis. BA, Augustana Coll., Rock Island, Ill., 1954; PhD, U. So. Calif., L.A., 1957. Chemist U.S. Army, Rock Island (Ill.) Arsenal, 1951-54; asst. prof. Rice U., Houston, 1958-62, assoc. prof., 1962-66, prof., 1966—, chmn. biology, 1981-87; co-dir. Rice Ctr. for Edn., Houston, 1988—; chair Rice Earth Sys. Inst., Houston, 1990—, Ecology and Evolutionary Biology, 1995—; cons. EPA, Washington, 1990—, Coll. Bd., N.Y.C., 1988—. Contbr. articles on chemistry, biology and biochemistry to profl. jours. NSF predoctoral fellow U. So. Calif., 1954-57, fellow AEC, 1957-58, Guggenheim fellow, 1965, sr. rsch. fellow NRC, 1988. Mem. Internat. Geospher-Biosphere Program (com. chair 1990—). Home: 2406 Wordsworth St Houston TX 77030-1834 Office: Rice U Ecology & Evolutionary Biology Houston TX 77251

SASSER, WILLIAM DUDLEY, surgeon; b. Goldsboro, N.C., Dec. 2, 1945; s. Roy Monroe and Freida Joy (Farthing) S.; m. Marinda Lou Fariss, June 5, 1971; children: Kristen Meredith, Kevin Bradford. BA in Chemistry, U. N.C., 1967, MD, 1971. Diplomate Am. Bd. Surgery. Intern, resident in surgery U. Va., Charlottesville, 1971-76; surgeon Mary Washington Hosp., Fredericksburg, Va., 1978—. Maj. USAF, 1976-78. Fellow ACS; mem. Va. Surg. Soc., Va. Vascular Soc., Soc. Am. Gastrointestinal Endoscopic Surgeons, Southeastern Surg. Congress. Office: Tompkins Martin Med Plz 1101 Sam Perry Blvd Fredericksburg VA 22401

SASTRY, KEDARNATH NANJUND, microbiologist, educator; b. Mysore, Karnataka, India, Apr. 28, 1955; came to U.S., 1986; s. N. Nanjund and N. Ratnamma (Rao) S.; m. T.S. Rajeswari, Feb. 16, 1987; 1 child, Omkar Kedarnath. BSc in Biology, U. Mysore, 1973, MSc in Microbiology, 1976; PhD in Microbiology, U. Pune, India, 1984. Rsch. asst. Nat. Inst. Virology, Pune, 1978-81, asst. rsch. officer, 1981-86; asst. prof. pathology and lab. medicine Boston U., 1990—; lectr. in field. Contbr. abstracts and articles to profl. jours. Fellow Indian Coun. Med. Rsch., 1977-78, Children's Hosp., 1986-90. Mem. AAAS. Office: Boston U 80 E Concord St Rm S301 Boston MA 02118-2307

SATA, LINDBERGH SABURO, psychiatrist, physician, educator; b. Portland, Oreg., Jan. 6, 1928; s. Charles Kazuo and Ito (Kojima) S.; m. Yuriko Kodama, Aug. 19, 1956; children: Roberta, Camille, Holly, John. BS, U. Utah, 1951, MD, 1958, MS, 1964. Intern U. Utah Coll. Medicine, Salt Lake Gen. Hosp., 1958-59, resident in psychiatry, 1959-62, chief resident in psychiatry, 1961-62; adminstrv. chief resident neurology U. Utah Coll. Medicine, VA Hosp., Salt Lake City, 1960-61; fellow Inst. for Mental Retardation, Letchworth Village, Thiells, N.Y., 1962; intern Behavioral Sci. Intern Program Nat. Tng. Labs., Bethel, Maine, 1966; instr. U. Utah, 1962-

64; asst. prof. The Psychiat. Inst. U. Md., Balt., 1964-67, assoc. prof., 1967-68; assoc. prof. U. Wash., Seattle, 1968-77, asst. dean, 1969-70, prof., 1977-78; prof., chmn. St. Louis U. Sch. Medicine, 1978-94, prof. emeritus, chmn. emeritus, 1994—. Fellow Am. Coll. Psychiatrists, Am. Psychiat. Assn., Pacific Rim Coll. Psychiatrists (founding); mem. Am. Assn. for Social Psychiatry. Office: 1606 Riverview Dr NE Auburn WA 98002-3054

SATALINE, LEE ROY, physician; b. New Britain, Conn., Oct. 31, 1929; s. Andrew James and Irene (Mongillo) S.; m. Therese Jane Reckmack, Aug. 2, 1956; children: Laura, Suzanne. BA, BS, Georgetown Univ., 1950; MS, Wesleyan Univ., 1951; MD, Bologna Univ., 1956. Diplomate Am. Bd. Internal Medicine. Intern Hosp. St. Raphael, New Haven, 1956-57; resident St Raphael's Yale-New Haven, 1957-59; chief resident in medicine Hosp. St. Raphael, 1959-60; fellow in gastroenterology Ohio State U./Dayton VA Hosp., 1960-62, chief resident in medicine, 1961-62; dir. med. edn. Lakewood and Toledo Hosps., 1963-68; staff physician Maumee Valley County Hosp., 1965-68; chief of medicine St. Luke's Hosp., Bethlehem, Pa., 1968-72; staff physician Waterbury (Conn.) Hosp., 1972-93; staff physician Bradley Meml. Hosp., Southington, Conn., 1972—, chief gastroenterology, 1978—; asst. clin. prof. medicine U. Conn., 1972—; instr. in medicine Ohio State Univ., 1960-63, sr. instr. in medicine Western Res. Univ., 1964-66, asst. clinical prof. of medicine, 1966-67; cons. V.A. Hosp., 1964-66; assoc. in medicine Cleve. Met. Gen. Hosp., 1964-67, assoc. clinical profl of medicine Jefferson Medical Coll., 1968-71. Contbr. numerous articles to profl. jours. Fellow ACP; mem. AMA, Am. Fedn. Clin. Rsch., Ohio State Med. Assn. (sec.-treas.), Am. Soc. Gastrointestinal Endoscopy, Am. Gastroenterology Assn. Office: 366 S Main St Cheshire CT 06410

SATCHER, DAVID, public health service officer, federal official; b. Anniston, Ala., Mar. 2, 1941; s. Wilmer and Anna S; m. Nola; children: Gretchen, David, Daraka, Daryl. BS, Morehouse Coll., 1963; MD, PhD, Case Western Reserve Univ., 1970. Pres. Meharry Med. Coll., Nashville, 1982-93; now dir. Centers for Disease Control and Prevention, Atlanta, 1993—. Office: Ctr Disease Control & Prevention 1600 Clifton Rd NE Bdlg 16 Atlanta GA 30333

SATHER, JOHN HENRY, biologist, educator, university dean; b. Presho, S.D., July 12, 1921; s. Anton and Anna (Imster) S.; m. Shirley M. Johnson, Aug. 21, 1948; children: Kristi, Signe, Ingrid. B.S., U. Nebr., 1943, Ph.D., 1952; M.A., U. Mo., 1948. Research biologist Nebr. Game, Forestation and Parks Commn., Lincoln, 1948-55; prof. biol. scis. Western Ill. U., Macomb, 1955—; dean Western Ill. U. (Grad. Sch.), 1964-79, emeritus grad. dean, 1979—; Tech. advisor on nat. wetland inventory, 1975-87, mem. Nat. Wetlands Tech. Coun., 1976—; mem. environ. adv. bd. U.S. Army Chief Engrs., 1978-82; pres. Central States Univs. Inc., 1978-79; leader U.S. team to establish hydrobiol. research sta., India, 1981; mem. N.Am. Riparian Coun., 1984—; wetlands cons. U.S. EPA, 1988—, Bombay Nat. History Soc., 1988—, USSR, 1991. Edward K. Love fellow, 1946-48; recipient Wildlife Soc. Spl. Recognition award, 1987, Gaylord Donnelley-Nature of Ill. Found. award, 1994. Mem. AAAS, Ecol. Soc. Am., Explorers Club, Sigma Xi. Home: 103 Oakland Ln Macomb IL 61455-1219

SATINOVER, JEFFREY B., psychiatrist, health science facility administrator, lecturer, author; b. Chgo., Sept. 4, 1947; s. Joseph and Sena (Rotman) S.; m. Julie Rachel Leff, June 10, 1982; Sarah Katherine, Anne-Rebecca, Jenny Leigh. BS, MIT, 1971; EdM, Harvard U., 1973; MD, U. Tex., 1982; Diplomate, C.G Jung Institute, Zurich, Switzerland, 1976. Diplomate Am. Bd. Psychiatry and Neurology, added qualifications in geriatric psychiatry. Fellow dept. psychiatry and child psychiatry Yale U., New Haven, 1982-86; founder, exec. dir. Sterling Inst., Stamford, Conn., 1985-92; med. dir. Temenos Inst., Westport, Conn., 1984—; pvt. practice, Westport, 1992—; mem. pastoral care ministries, pres., bd. dirs. C.G. Jung Found. N.Y., 1988-92; bd. dirs., mem. catchment area coun. S.W. Regional Mental Health Bd., 1988-92; William James lectr. psychology and religion Harvard U., 1975; mem. Lower Fairfield County Regional Action Coun. Against Substance Abuse, 1990-92. Author: Homosexuality and the Politics of Truth, 1994, The Empty Self: Gnostic Foundations of Modern Identity, 1994, Feathers of the Skylark, 1996; contbg. author: Jungian Psychotherapy, 1984, Science and the Fragile Self, 1990, Jungian Analysis, 1993; contbr. articles to profl. and pub. policy jours. Founder, mem. exec. bd. com. Save Our Schs., 1994—; bd. dirs. Towrd Tradition; trustee, pres. Family Inst. Conn., 1994-96; active nat. physician's resource coun. Focus on Family; bd. dirs. Klingberg Family Ctrs., 1994-96. Capt. USAR N.G., 1989-94; maj. USAR, 1995—. Recipient Seymour Lustman Rsch. 2d place award Yale U. psychology dept., 1983, 85. Mem. Am. Psychiat. Assn. (Burroughs-Wellcome fellow 1983-85), Am. Psychosomatic Soc., Am. Acad. Psychomatics, Internat. Assn. Analytical Psychology (diplomate), Aspetuck Valley Country Club, Alpha Omega Alpha. Republican. Jewish. Home: 38 Steep Hill Rd Weston CT 06883-1822 Office: 29 E Main St Westport CT 06880-3749

SATIR, BIRGIT H., medical educator, medical researcher; b. Copenhagen, Mar. 22, 1934. Magistra in Biochemistry, U. Copenhagen, 1961. Rsch. assoc. dept. zoology U. Chgo., 1962-66; asst. rsch. physiologist U. Calif. Dept. Physiology-Anatomy, Berkeley, 1967-74, assoc. rsch. physiologist, 1974-76, adj. assoc. prof., 1976-77; sci. dir. Analytical Ultrastructure Ctr., Cancer Rsch. Inst. Albert Einstein Coll. of Medicine, Bronx, N.Y., 1977-84, prof. dept. anatomy and structural biology, 1977—; rschr. Phys.- Chem. Inst. Copenhagen, 1956-57, Biol. Inst., Copenhagen, 1958-61; mem. Cellular and Molecular Basis of Disease Rev. Com., Nat. Inst. Gen. Med. Scis., 1977-79; vis. prof. divsn. biology Calif. Inst. Tech., 1984-85. Mem. editl. bd. Jour. Ultrastructural Rsch., 1975-80, Jour. Cell Biology, 1979-81, Modern Cell Biology, 1980-90, Jour. Eukaryotic Microbiology, 1989-95. Rsch. fellow U. Geneva, 1965-66, Spl. fellow USPHS, 1972-73; recipient Outstanding Women Scientist award N.Y. chpt. Assn. Women in Sci., 1990, Rsch. award Am. Diabetes Assn., 1995. Fellow AAAS; mem. Am. Soc. Cell Biology (coun. 1975-78, minority affairs com. 1987-90, fin. com. 1993—), Am. Assn. Anatomists, Am. Soc. Biochemistry and Molecular Biology, Electron Microscopy Soc. Am. (program vice-chairperson 38th Meeting 1980, program chairperson 39th Meeting 1981), Royal Danish Acad. Scis. and Letters (fgn.), NYSEM (pres. 1979-80), N.Y. Acad. Sci., Biophys. Soc. Office: Albert Einstein Coll of Medicine 1300 Morris Park Ave Bronx NY 10461*

SATLIN, ANDREW, psychiatrist, researcher; b. N.Y.C., May 18, 1954; s. Sheldon and Doris Claire (Flatow) S.; m. Lisa Wendy Cooper, June 3, 1979; children: Leah, Zachary. BA, Yale U., 1975; MD, Harvard U., 1979. Intern in medicine N.Y. Hosp., N.Y.C., 1979-80; with McLean Hosp., 1980—; asst. dir. geriatric psychiatry McLean Hosp., Belmont, Mass., 1985-89, dir. geriatric psychiatry, 1989—; asst. prof. psychiatry Harvard Med. Sch.; dir. Memory Diagnostic Clinic, cons. Recuperative Ctr., Roslindale, Mass., 1988—; vis. scientist MIT, Cambridge, Mass., 1988—; bd. dirs. The Community Family, Everett, Mass., Alzheimers Assn. Ea. Mass., Cambridge. Contbr. articles to profl. jours. Class rep. Yale U., New Haven, 1987-90; support group leader Alzheimers Assn., Cambridge, Mass., 1989-92. Am. Psychiat. Assn. fellow, 1981-82. Mem. Boston Soc. for Gerontol. Psychiatry (pres. 1991-95), Am. Psychiat. Assn., Gerontol. Soc., Am. Assn. Geriatric Psychiatry, Am. Geriatric Soc. Office: McLean Hosp 115 Mill St Belmont MA 02178-1041

SATLOFF, AARON, psychiatrist; b. N.Y.C., Dec. 10, 1934; s. Nathan Maximillian and Edna Belkin S.; m. Annette Bernstein, June 29, 1958; children: James E., Ellen S., Cynthia J. BA, Columbia U., 1956; MD, Albert Einstein, 1960. Diplomate Am. Bd. Psychiatry and Neurology, Am. Bd. of Quality Assurance and Utilization Review Physicians. Intern Greenwich (Conn.) Hosp., 1960-61; resident in psychiatry U. Rochester (N.Y.) Sch. of Medicine, 1961-64, asst. prof. psychiatry, 1966-68, assoc. prof. psychiatry, 1968-70, prof., 1991—; pvt. practice Pittsford, N.Y., 1970—; quality assurance cons. U. Rochester Sch. Medicine, 1989; sr. examiner Am. Bd. Psychiatry and Neurology, Chgo., 1974—. Contbr. articles to profl. jours. Merit badge counselor Boy Scouts Am., Rochester, 1970—; patron Meml. Art Gallery, Rochester, 1970—; bd. dirs. Rochester Cmty. Individual Practice Assn., 1989-95. Lt. comdr. USN, 1964-66. Fellow Am. Psychiat. Assn. (vice-chmn. quality assurance com. 1986-91), Am. Coll. Med. Quality; mem. AMA, N.Y. State Med. Soc., Monroe County Med. Soc., Genesee Valley Psychiat. Assn. (chmn. quality assurance com. 1970—), Ski Valley Club, Cobblestone Creek Country Club. Home: 6 Pondview Dr Pittsford NY 14534-9501 Office: Aaron Satloff MD PC 24A Grove St Pittsford NY 14534-1326

SATO, KAZUYOSHI, pathologist; b. Shibata, Niigata, Japan, Apr. 3, 1930; came to U.S., 1968; s. Katsueita and Kyo (Sakagawa) S.; m. Ann Marie Farrenkopf, July 5, 1964 (dec. Aug. 1983); children: P.T. Sachiko, P. Miyoko, Michael T., Phillip K. Student, Niigata U., Japan, 1954, MD, 1958. Diplomate Am. Bd. Pathology, Anatomic and Clin. Pathology. Intern USAF Hosp., Tachikawa, Japan, 1958-59; intern Ellis Hosp., Schenectady, N.Y., 1959-60, asst. resident in pathology, 1960-61; resident in pathology Free Hosp. for Women, Brookline, Mass., 1961-62; resident in pathology The Children's Med. Ctr., Boston, 1962-63, resident in neuropathology, 1963-64; resident fellow in pathology Mayo Grad. Sch. Medicine, Rochester, Minn., 1968-70; dir. labs. Falmouth (Mass.) Hosp., 1972-96; dir. Falmouth Hosp. Service Lab., Sandwich, Mass., 1986-93; pathologist and rsch. assoc. Atomic Bomb Casualty Commn., Nagasaki, Japan, 1964-68; pathologist, chief of pathology USPHS Hosp., Norfolk Va., 1970-72, Falmouth (Mass.) Hosp., 1972-96. Recipient Fulbright scholarship, 1959. Fellow Coll. Am. Pathologists, Am. Soc. Clin. Pathologists; mem. Assn. Mil. Surgeons U.S. Home: 88 Two Ponds Rd Falmouth MA 02540-2225 Office: Falmouth Hosp 100 Ter Heun Dr Falmouth MA 02540-2503

SATO, PAUL HISASHI, pharmacologist; b. Mt. Vernon, N.Y., Mar. 22, 1949; s. Yoshio and Lury (Shiogi) S.; m. Jeanne Ellen Courville, June 29, 1996. BS, Jamestown Coll., 1971; MS, NYU, 1972, PhD, 1975. Rsch. assoc. Roche Inst. Molecular Biology, Nutley, N.J., 1975-77; assoc. prof. Mich. State U., East Lansing, 1977—. Office: Mich State U Dept Pharmacology/Toxicol East Lansing MI 48824

SATOYOSHI, EIJIRO, neurologist; b. Tokyo, Feb. 11, 1924; s. Mitsuo and Tsunee S.; m. Mitsuko Nakamura, Oct. 1959; 1 child, Akihiko. MD, Keio U., 1946, PhD, 1955. Asst. prof. medicine Toho U. Sch. Medicine, Tokyo, 1957-68, prof. medicine, neurology, 1968-78; dir. neurology ctr. Nat. Musashi Hosp., Tokyo, 1978-86; dir. Nat. Inst. Neurosci., Tokyo, 1986-88; pres. Nat. Ctr. Neurology and Psychiatry, Tokyo, 1989-91, pres. emeritus, 1992—; bd. dirs. Japan Found. Neurosci. and Mental Health, chmn., 1991—. Pres. VIII Internat. Congress Neuromuscular Diseases, 1994; v.p. XII World Congress of Neurology, Kyoto, Japan, 1981, World Fedn. Neurology, 1993—. Mem. Japanese Soc. Neurology (hon., pres. 19th ann. meeting 1978, v.p. 1993—), Am. Neurological Assn. (corr. mem.), French Soc. Neurology (fgn. hon. mem.), Royal Soc. Medicine. Buddhist. Home: 4-20-33 Shimomeguro, Tokyo 153, Japan Office: Nat Ctr Neurology, 4-1-1 Ogawa-Higashi, Tokyo 187, Japan

SATTEN, NEAL RICHARD, psychiatrist; b. Topeka, Kans., Mar. 23, 1949; s. Joseph and Norma Frances (Goldstein) S.; m. Rona Cordish, Aug. 18, 1973; children: Matthew Cordish, Susanna Cordish. BSc, MIT, 1971; MD, Harvard U., 1975. Diplomate, Am. Bd. Psychiatry and Neurology. Intern Mass. Gen. Hosp., 1975-76; resident in psychiatry Inst. Pa. Hosp., Phila., 1976-79; pvt. practice Phila., 1979—; area med. dir. Medco Behavioral Care, 1994; regional med. dir. Merit Behavioral Care, 1995—; mem. staff, Inst. Pa. Hosp. Mem. Am. Psychiat. Assn., Am. Group Psychotherapy Assn. Am. Soc. Adolescent Psychiatry, Am. Orthopsychiat. Assn., Am. Anorexia Bulimia Assn. Phila. (bd. dirs. 1986—), Phi Beta Kappa. Office: Merit Behav Care 3 Friends Ln Newton PA 18940

SATTERFIELD, TERRY LEE, psychology educator; b. Kosciusko, Miss., Aug. 28, 1948; s. Cicero and Freda Lee (Terry) S.; m. Brenda Travers, Sept. 15, 1971 (div.); 1 child, Terry Jr.; m. Nellie Erma Kerr, Sept. 3, 1981; 1 child, Dallas Allen. BS, Bowie State U., 1974; MA, U. No. Colo., 1982; EdD, George Washington U., 1990. Nat. cert. counselor. Instr. D.C. Pub. Schs., Washington, 1974—; counselor AACD, Nat. Bd. Cert. Counselors, Washington, 1983—. Author: Post-traumatic Stress Disorder in African-American Vietnam Veterans, 1990. Chmn. Order of Knights Pythagarus, Washington, 1987-91; sponsor Little League Athletics, Washington, 1987. Staff sgt. U.S. Army, 1978—. Mem. ASCD, Am. Mental Health Counselors Assn., D.C. Mental Health Counselors Assn. (past-pres.), D.C. Counseling Assn. (pres. 1996—, Emerging Leader honor 1991), Phi Delta Kappa, Omega Psi Phi. Baptist. Home: 5906 Bost Ln Clinton MD 20735-4722

SATTI, VENKATA SUBBIREDDY, psychiatrist; b. Veereswarapuram, India, Apr. 4, 1939; came to U.S., 1974; s. Surreddy and Manikyam (Gudimetla) S.; m. Savithri Ambur; children: Srinivasa Dinakar Reddy, Krishna Priya, Sudhakar Reddy. Student, Andhra Vet. Coll., India, 1958-60; MB, BS, Andhra Med. Coll., 1965. Pvt. practice India, 1965-74; resident in psychiatry Utica (N.Y.) Psychiat. Ctr., 1975-76, Mt. Sinai Hosp., N.Y.C., 1976-78; staff psychiatrist Willard (N.Y.) Psychiat. Ctr., 1978-95, unit chief, 1986-95, chief psychiatrist psychogeriatric svcs., 1989-95; pvt. practice, Ithaca, N.Y., 1989-90; consulting psychiatrist Auburn (N.Y.) Correctional Facility, 1981-90, Seneca Community Mental Health Clinic, Waterloo, N.Y., 1986-95, Elmira Correctional Facility, 1992—, Schuyler County Med. Health Ctr., Watkins Glen, N.Y., 1996—. Mem. AMA, Am. Psychiat. Assn. Democrat. Hindu. Home: 17 Rosina Dr Ithaca NY 14850-9766 Office: Elmira Psychiatric Ctr 100 Washington St Elmira NY 14902-1527

SATUR, NANCY MARLENE, dermatologist; b. Philipsburg, Pa., Apr. 12, 1953; d. Nicholas and Marlene (Kutzer) S.; m. John David Lortscher, Oct. 20, 1979; children: David Nicholas, Glenn William, Stephen John. BS magna cum laude, Pa. State U., 1974; MD, Thomas Jefferson U., 1976. Diplomate Am. Bd. Dermatology. Intern Allentown (Pa.) Gen. Hosp., 1976-77; resident in pathology U. Ill. Hosp., Chgo., 1978-79; resident in dermatology Case Western Res. U. Hosp., Cleve., 1979-82; dermatologist Encinitas, Calif., 1985—; sr. instr. dermatology Case Western Res. U. Hosp., 1982-83, sr. clin. instr. dermatology, 1983-84. Fellow Am. Acad. Dermatology; mem. Am. Soc. Dermatologic Surgery, Am. Soc. Laser Medicine and Surgery, N.Am. Soc. Phlebology, San Diego Dermatologic Soc., Pacific Dermatologic Assn. Office: Ste C308 477 N El Camino Real #C308 Encinitas CA 92024-1331

SAUER, GORDON CHENOWETH, physician, educator; b. Rutland, Ill., Aug. 14, 1921; s. Fred William and Gweneth (Chenoweth) S.; m. Mary Louise Steinhilber, Dec. 28, 1944; children: Elisabeth Ruth, Gordon Chenoweth, Margaret Louise, Amy Kieffer.; m. Marion Green, Oct. 23, 1982. Student, Northwestern U., 1939-42; B.S., U. Ill., 1943, M.D., 1945. Diplomate: Am. Bd. Dermatology and Syphilology. Intern Cook County Hosp., Chgo., 1945-46; resident dermatology and syphilology N.Y. U.-Bellevue Med. Center, 1948-51; dermatologist Thompson-Brumm-Knepper Clinic, St. Joseph, Mo., 1951-54; pvt. practice Kansas City, Mo., 1954—; mem. staff St. Luke's, Research, Kansas City Gen. hosps.; asso. instr. U. Kans., 1951-56, vice chmn. sect. dermatology, 1956-58, asso. clin. prof., 1960-64, clin. prof., 1964-93; clin. prof. emeritus, 1993—; head sect. dermatology U. Kans., 1958-70; clin. asso., acting head dermatology sect. U. Mo., 1955-59, cons. dermatology, 1959-67, clin. prof., 1967—; cons. Munson Army Hosp., Ft. Leavenworth, Kans., 1959-68; Mem. dermatology panel, drug efficacy panel Nat. Acad. Sci.-FDA, 1967-69. Author: Manual of Skin Diseases, 1959, 7th edit., 1995, Teen Skin, 1965, John Gould Bird Print Reproductions, 1977, John Gould's Prospectuses and Lists of Subscribers to His Work on Natural History: With an 1866 Facsimile, 1980, John Gould The Bird Man, 1982; editor Kansas City Med. Bull., 1967-69; contbr. articles to profl. jours. Bd. dirs. Kansas City Area coun. Camp Fire Girls Am., 1956-59, Kansas City Lyric Theatre, 1969-74, Kansas City Chamber Choir, 1969-74, Chouteau Soc., 1985—, U. Mo.-Kansas City Friends of Libr., 1988-92, bd. dirs. Mo. br. The Nature Conservancy, 1984-91. Sr. asst. surgeon USPHS, 1946-48. Named Dermatology Found. Practitioner of Yr., 1992. Fellow Am. Acad. Dermatology and Syphilology (dir. 1975-79, v.p. 1980); mem. Mo., Jackson County med. socs., Mo. Dermatol. Soc. (pres. 1974-75), Dermatology Found. (trustee 1978-83), Am. Ornithol. Union, Wilson Ornithol. Soc., Royal Australasian Ornithologists Union, Soc. Bibliography Natural History, Am. Dermatol. Assn., Alpha Delta Phi, Nu Sigma Nu. Presbyterian. Office: 6400 Prospect Ave Kansas City MO 64132-1181 Home: 422 E 55th St Kansas City MO 64110

SAUL, GEORGE BRANDON, II, biology educator; b. Hartford, Conn., Aug. 8, 1928; s. George Brandon and Dorothy (Ayers) S.; m. Sue Grau Williams, Mar. 28, 1953. A.B., U. Pa., 1949, A.M., 1950, Ph.D., 1954. From instr. to assoc. prof. Dartmouth, 1954-67; prof. biology Middlebury (Vt.) Coll., 1967—, chmn. dept., 1968-76, 91-93, v.p. acad. affairs, 1976-79; Research asso. Calif. Inst. Tech., 1964-65; NSF postdoctoral fellow U. Zurich, Switzerland, 1959-60; vis. scientist Boyce Thompson Inst. for Plant Research, Yonkers, N.Y., 1972-73. Author papers in field. Fellow AAAS; mem. Pa. Acad. Sci., Genetics Soc. Am., Am. Genetics Assn., N.Y. Acad. Scis., Sigma Xi. Club: Lion. Home: Munger St RR 3 Box 2575 Middlebury VT 05753 Office: Middlebury Coll Dept Biology Middlebury VT 05753

SAUL, SHURA, gerontologist, educator; b. N.Y.C., July 8, 1920; d. Froim Camenir and Rose (Lisenco) Rudin; m. Sidney R. Saul, Dec. 14, 1941; children: Mark, Jonathan, Jennifer. BA, Hunter Coll., 1940; MSW, Columbia U., 1963, EdD, 1972. Tchr. kindergarten N.Y.C. Bd. Edn., 1943-48; dir. Bronx River Child Care Ctr., 1948-49; group worker Jewish Guild for Blind, N.Y.C., 1954-61; cons. social worker United Hosp. Fund, N.Y.C., 1964-67; mem. faculty Sch. Social Work NYU, N.Y.C., 1967-69; mem. faculty Brookdale gerontology program Adelphi U., Garden City, N.Y., 1975-83; mem. faculty Wurzweiler Sch., N.Y.C., 1981-88, Sch. Pub. Health Columbia U., N.Y.C., 1988-93; dir. student unit Self Help Community Svcs., N.Y.C., 1969-71; coord. profl. svcs. Kingsbridge Heights Nursing Home, Bronx, 1971-78, ednl. coord., 1978-87; tng. cons. N.Y. State Ombuds Program Westchester County, 1982—; cons. psychogeriatrics and edn. Borders Health Bd., others, Scotland, 1974-85, Chaim Sheba Med. Ctr., Israel, 1982—; ednl. cons. and psychotherapist, 1987—. Author: The Right To Be Different, 1962, 2d edit., 1966, Aging: An Album of People Growing Old, 1974, 2d edit., 1983 Sophia Moses Robison, Woman of the Twentieth Century, 1981; co-author: (docudrama) Somewhere A Door Blew Shut, 1986; editor: Social Group Work for Frail Elderly, 1982; (with B. MacLennan and M. B. Weiner) Group Psychotherapies for the Elderly, 1988; producer, editor: (with Sidney Saul) (videotape series) Enhancing the Quality of Life for Institutionalized Elderly, Scotland, 1980, We'll Help You Think, 1982, other videotapes on aging, 1976, 82; contbr. articles to profl. publs. Founder, chmn. bd. dirs. Bronx-North Manhattan Coalition for Elderly and Long Term Care, 1981-84, chmn. edn. com., 1984—, editor newsletter; observer, del. White House Conf. on Aging, 1981, editor several oral history pubs.; mem. history com. Goldens Bridge Community Assn., 1978—. Recipient Woman of Yr. award Jewish Welfare Bd., Bronx, 1954. Mem. Nat. Assn. Social Workers, Nat. Coun. on Aging, Am. Group Psychotherapy Assn., Am. Soc. of Aging, N.Y. State Soc. of Aging. Home: PO Box 431 Goldens Bridge NY 10526-0431

SAULS, BARBARA LYNN, physician assistant; b. Norristown, Pa., Dec. 5, 1958; d. Andrew Joseph and June Darlene (Phillippy) Yakscoe; m. Frederick Charles Sauls, Dec. 15, 1990; 1 child, Allisia Lynn Gennetts. BS in Biology, King's Coll., 1982, BS Physician Asst., 1984, MS in Health Care Adminstrn., 1995. Cert. physician asst. Physician asst. family medicine Rural Health Corp., Shickshinny, Pa., 1984-92; physician asst. homeless care Rural Health Corp., Wilkes-Barre, 1988—; faculty/clin. coord. physician asst. program King's Coll., Wilkes-Barre, 1992—; instr. EKG technicians Allied Med. Careers, Kingston, Pa., 1986-88; preceptor for physician asst. students Rural Health Corp./King's Coll., 1988-92. Recipient Recognition for Rural and Migrant Health Care, Nat. Assn. Cmty. Health Ctrs., 1990. Fellow Am. Acad. Physician Assts.; mem. Assn. of Physician Asst. Programs, Am. Coll. Healthcare Execs. Home: 295 Morio Dr Mountain Top PA 18707-9414 Office: Kings College Physician Asst Program 133 N River St Wilkes Barre PA 18711

SAUNDERS, IRIS ELAINE, social work administrator; b. N.Y.C.; d. Sidney Denison and Viola (Francis) Simon. BA, CUNY, 1946, MSW with honors, 1993. Cert. social worker, N.Y. Case mgr. Dept. Social Svcs., N.Y.C., 1949-51, supr., 1952-60; case supr. Divsn. Employment and Rehab., N.Y.C., 1960-70; dir. programs Human Resources Adminstrn., N.Y.C., 1970-92, ret., 1993; notary public N.Y. Bd. dirs. Tioga Carver Found., N.Y.C., 1989—; mem. Dem. Club; active M.L. Wilson Boys and Girls Club, N.Y.C., 1986—, Schomburg Ctr. for Rsch. in Black Culture, 1993—. Recipient cert. of achievement Am. Soc. Profl. and Exec. Women, 1987, Vol. Leadership award United Negro Coll. Fund, 1987, Vol. Recognition cert., 1988, 89, 90, Outstanding Fund Raising award M.L. Wilson Boys and Girls Club Harlem, 1991, Recognition for Cmty. Svc., N.Y. Newsday, 1992, cert. of merit Tioga Carver Cmty. Found., 1993, citation Hunter Coll. Alumni Assn. Pub., 1994, 95. Mem. NASW, NAACP, AAUW, Assn. Black Social Workers, Hunter Coll. Alumni Assn., Nat. Caucus and Ctr. on Black Aged, Coalition 100 Black Women, Area 145, Inc., Smithsonian Instn., Studio Mus. in Harlem. Democrat. Baptist.

SAUNDERS, RICHARD AMES, ophthalmologist, educator; b. N.Y.C., Nov. 9, 1946; s. Dero Ames and Beatrice (Nair) S.; m. Anne Elizabeth Leslie, Oct. 20, 1973; children: Jean, Carter. AB, Dartmouth Coll., 1969; MD, Columbia U., 1973. Intern, St. Luke's Hosp. Ctr., N.Y.C., 1973-74; resident in ophthalmology Presbyn. Hosp., N.Y.C., 1974-77; fellow Ind. U. Sch. Medicine, Indpls., 1977-78; asst. prof. ophthalmology Med. U. S.C., Charleston, 1978-81, assoc. prof., 1981-90, prof. 1990—. Mem. AMA, Am. Acad. Ophthalmology, Am. Assn. Pediatric Ophthalmology and Strabismus. Avocations: athletics, fishing. Home: PO Box 1431 Folly Beach SC 29439-1431 Office: Med U SC Storm Eye Inst Dept Ophthalmology 171 Ashley Ave Charleston SC 29425-2236

SAUNDERS, TIMOTHY ROBERT, prosthodontics educator; b. San Diego, Calif., Aug. 14, 1947; s. George Thomas and Barbara Jane (Ryan) S.; m. Marsha Lynn Bernet, May 29, 1971; children: Todd Bernet, Meghan Lyndsey. DDS, Creighton U., 1972. Diplomate Am. Bd. Prosthodontics. Commd. capt. USAF, 1972, advanced through grades to col., 1987; dental intern USAF Med. Ctr., Scott AFB, Ill., 1972-73; dental officer USAF Med. Ctr., Craig AFB, Ala., 1973-74; resident in prosthodontics-maxillofacial prosthetics Mayo Clinic, Rochester, Minn., 1974-77; asst. chmn. dept. prosthodontics Wilford Hall Med. Ctr., Lackland AFB, Tex., 1977-84; dir. prosthodontic residency programs U. Ala., Birmingham, 1984-85; chief prosthodontic dentistry USAF Regional Hosp., Elmendorf AFB, Alaska, 1985-89; asst. chmn. dept. prosthodontics David Grant USAF Med. Ctr., Travis AFB, Calif., 1989-91; chmn. dept. David Grant USAF Med. Ctr., Travis AFB, 1991-93, asst. dir. dental svcs., 1993-94; chmn. dept. prosthodontics 2d Med. Group, Barksdale AFB, La., 1994-95; ret. USAF, 1995; pvt. practice prosthodontic dentistry, Green Bay, Wis., 1995-96; assoc. prof. U. So. Calif. Sch. Dentistry, L.A., 1996—; cons. on prosthodontics to surgeon gen. USAF, Washington, 1981-95. Contbg. author: Reconstructive Preprosthetic Oral and Maxillofacial Surgery; contbr. articles to profl. jours. Fellow Am. Acad. Maxillofacial Prosthetics (bd. dirs. 1982-95, v.p. 1996—), Am. Coll. Prosthodontists; mem. ADA. Calif. Dental Assn. Office: U So Calif Sch Dentistry University Park Campus Los Angeles CA 90029

SAUNIER, JACQUES, physician; b. Bienne, Berne, Switzerland, July 13, 1948; s. René and Jacqueline (Pasche) S.; m. Bernadette Noery; children: Andréanne, Grégoire, Julien. Maturity cert., Coll. Geneva, 1968. Undergrad. Faculty of Medecine, Geneva, 1968-75; resident Dept. Surgery, Geneva, 1975-80; chief resident Orthopaedic div., Geneva, 1981-85, cons., 1985-88; resident Orthopedie Infantile, Montpellier, 1980-81, Orthopaedic FMH Specialty, Geneva, 1984; cons. Unité Médecine Du Sport, 1987—, De La Clinique Generale-Beaulieu, Geneva, 1987—. Mem. European Soc. Knee Surgery, Société Suisse de Médecine du Sport, Société française de pathologie traumatique du Sport, Internat. Musculoskeletal Law Soc. (adv. com.), Orthopaedic Laser Soc. N.Am. (fgn.), Am. Soc. Laser Medicine and Surgery. Office: FMH Chirurgie Orthopedique, 12 Chemin Beau-Soleil, 1206 Geneva Switzerland

SAUTE, ROBERT EMILE, drug and cosmetic consultant; b. West Warwick, R.I., Aug. 18, 1929; s. Camille T. and Lea E. (Goffinet) S.; m. Arda T. Darnell, May 18, 1957; children: Richard R., Steven N., Allen K. BS, R.I. Coll. Pharmacy, 1950; MS, Purdue U., 1952, PhD, 1953. Registered pharmacist. Tech. asst. to pres. Lafayette (Ind.) Pharmacal, 1955-56; sr. rsch. and devel. chemist H.K. Wampole Denver Chem. Co., Phila., 1956-57; supt. Murray Hill (N.J.) plant Strong Cobb Arner Inc., 1957-60; adminstrv. dir. rsch. and devel. Avon Products Inc., Suffern, N.Y., 1960-68; dir. rsch. and devel. toiletries div. Gillette Co., Boston, 1968-71; group v.p. Dart Industries, L.A., 1972-75; pres. Saute Cons., Inc., L.A., 1975—; bd. dirs. Joico Labs., Inc., Cosmetics Enterprises, Ltd. Contbr. to books; patentee in field. With U.S. Army, 1953-55. Fellow Soc. Cosmetic Chemists (bd. dirs. 1987-89, chmn. Calif. chpt. 1986); mem. AAAS, N.Y. Acad. Scis.,

Soc. Investigative Dermatology, Am. Assn. Pharm. Scientists, Sigma Xi, Rho Chi.

SAUTTER, SCOTT WILLARD, neuropsychologist; b. Quantico, Va., Apr. 28, 1957; s. Mel H. and Jane L. (Willard) S.; m. Sarah Adams Prescott, Aug. 1, 1981; children: Katherine Gilbert, Michael Cornell. BA in Psychology, Lafayette Coll., Easton, Pa., 1979; MEd, James Madison U., 1981, EdS, 1983; PhD in Clin. Psychology, Vanderbilt U., 1988. Lic. clin. psychologist, Va. Postdoctoral fellow Clin. Neuropsychology, U. Va. Sch. Medicine, 1988-89; dir. div. behavioral medicine Western State Hosp., Staunton, Va., 1989-90; asst. prof. U. Va. Sch. Medicine, Charlottesville, 1989-90; clin. asst. prof. U. Va. Sch. Medicine, 1991—; asst. prof. Ea. Va. Med. Sch., 1992—; pvt. practice clin. neuropsychology Hampton Roads Neuropsychology, Inc., Virginia Beach, Va., 1991—; chair med./sci. com., bd. dirs. Hampton Roads Alzheimers Assn., 1993—. Contbr. articles to profl. publs. Mem. Am. Psychol. Assn., Nat. Acad. Neuropsychology, Internat. Neuropsychological Soc., Va. Psychol. Assn. Episcopalian. Office: 621 Lynnhaven Pky Ste 366 Virginia Beach VA 23452-7300

SAUVAGE, TIMOTHY RAYMOND, nurse anesthetist; b. Bay City, Mich., Sept. 22, 1953; s. Raymond C. and Leonarda E. (Haidysz) S.; m. Gail M. De Meyer, June 26, 1982; children: Eric Raymond, Matthew Carl. BSN, Murray (Ky.) State U., 1980; postgrad., Mpls. Sch. Anesthesia; MS, St. Mary's Coll., Winona, Minn., 1986. RN, Iowa. Chief nurse anesthetist VA, Des Moines, Iowa; dir. nurse anesthesia clin. specialization Drake U., Des Moines; chief anesthesia sect. VA Med. Ctr., Des Moines, N.D. Mem. AANA, Sigma Theta Tau.

SAVAGE, ALFRED DAVID, osteopathic physician; b. Burlington, Iowa, Sept. 21, 1943; s. David Fairlee and Lena Florence (McCracken) S.; m. Debra Jeanne Deierling, Mar. 17, 1975; children: Andria Noelle, David Frank. BS, Iowa Wesleyan Coll., 1965; MS, N.E. Mo. State U., 1967; DO, Des Moines U. Health Scis., 1972. Instr. physics Centerville C.C. (Iowa), 1967-68; resident in internal medicine Davenport Osteo. Hosp., 1973-76; emergency room physician Burlington Med. Ctr. (Iowa), 1976-78; pvt. practice osteo. internal medicine, Mt. Pleasant, Iowa, 1978—; med. dir. Henry County Emergency Med. Services, 1980—. Mem. Am. Osteo. Assn., AMA, Am. Heart Assn., Henry County Med. Soc. Mem. Soc. Friends. Home: 410 Broadway St Mount Pleasant IA 52641-1608 Office: 107 E Madison St Mount Pleasant IA 52641

SAVAGE, CHRISTINE LANDREY, health services administrator, researcher; b. N.Y.C., Nov. 4, 1949; d. Leo Raymond and Mary Josephine (Ryan) Landrey; m. Joseph W. Savage, March 9, 1974; children: Timothy William, Geoffrey Joseph, James Francis. BS magna cum laude, Boston Coll. Sch. Nursing, Chestnut Hill, Mass., 1974; MS, U. Md., Balt., 1993. RN, Pa. Staff nurse New Eng. Deaconess Hosp., Boston, 1972-74; staff nurse Beverly (Mass.) Hosp., 1974; vis. nurse Salem (Mass.) Vis. Nurse Assn., 1974-76, Gardner (Mass.) Vis. Nurse Assn., 1981-82; owner/pub. Winchendon (Mass.) Courier Newspapers, 1985-88; vis. nurse Red Lion (Pa.) Vis. Nurse Assn., 1988-89; dir. nursing LGH Susquehanna Divsn., Columbia, Pa., 1989-95; dir. pvt. care svcs. VNA of Lancaster County, Lancaster, Pa., 1995—. Chair HIV/AIDS Task Force, Lancaster County, 1993; chair HIV/AIDS Coun., 1994; mem. steering com. Lancaster County Health Partnership, 1994—; pres. Winchendon LWV, 1981-84. Recipient Cynthia Ellen Northrop award U. Md. Sch. Nursing, Balt., 1993. Mem. Nat. Nurses Soc. on Addictions, Boston Coll. Nurse Assn., Sigma Theta Tau, Phi Kappa Phi. Home: 2 Klines Run Rd RD 2 Box 7 Wrightsville PA 17368 Office: VNA of Lancaster County PO Box 3232 Lancaster PA 17604

SAVAGE, ELDON PAUL, retired environmental health educator; b. Bedford, Iowa, Apr. 4, 1926; s. Paul and Nora (Arthur) S.; m. Ella May, June 5, 1948; children: Steven P., Michael D. BS, U. Kans., 1950; MPH, Tulane U., 1958; PhD, Okla. U., 1968. Coordinator environ. sanitation demonstration projects USPHS, Kans., Iowa and Pa., 1950-64; chief state aids sect. pesticide ctr. Ctr. for Disease Control, Atlanta, 1964-70; chief chem. epidemiology sect. Inst. Rural Environ. Health, Colo. State U., Ft. Collins, 1970-84, prof., dir. environ. health div., 1984-85, head dept. environ. health, 1985-90, dir. environ. health services, 1987-93, prof. emeritus, 1993—. Contbr. articles to profl. jours. Mem. Am. Acad. Sanitarians (sec., treas., diplomate), Nat. Environ. Health Assn., Sigma Xi, Gamma Sigma Delta. Home: 5220 Apple Dr Fort Collins CO 80526-4302 Office: Colo State U Inst Rural Envrion Health Fort Collins CO 80523

SAVAGE, JOHN E., gynecologic oncologist; b. Monticello, Iowa, July 17, 1948; s. Robert E. and Josephine (Ricklefs) S.; m. Marcia Kae Whitter, Sept. 15, 1979; children: Johanna and Erica (twins). BS, U. Iowa, 1970, MD, 1974. Diplomate Am. Bd. Ob-Gyn., sub-bd. gynecologic oncology. Resident in ob-gyn. U. Iowa, Iowa City, 1974-78, fellow in gynecologic oncology, 1978-81; dir. gynecologic oncology St. Paul Ramsey Med. Ctr., 1981-85, Hennepin County Med. Ctr., Mpls., 1981-86; asst. prof., assoc. dir. gynecologic oncology U. Minn. Med. Sch., Mpls., 1981-88, clin. asst. prof. dept. ob-gyn., 1988—. Contbr. articles to profl. jours.; presenter in field. Fellow ACS, Am. Coll. Ob-Gyn.; mem. AMA, Soc. Gynecologic Oncologists, Assn. Profs. Ob-Gyn., Ctrl. Assn. Ob-Gyn., Gynecology Oncology Group, Minn. Med. Assn., Minn. Ob-Gyn. Soc., Ramsey County Med. Soc., Hennepin County Med. Soc., Internat. Gynecologic Cancer Soc., Phi Beta Kappa, Alpha Omega Alpha, Phi Eta Sigma. Office: Minn Hematology Oncology 310 N Smith # 430 Saint Paul MN 53702

SAVAGE, JOSEPH SCOTT, physician, career officer; b. Malden, Mass., Dec. 30, 1958; s. Joseph Edward and Arlene Barbara (Piniarski) S.; m. Gwendolyn Kieko Uezu, July 4, 1979; 1 child, Colin Eric. BA, Wheaton Coll., 1983; DO, Kirksville Coll. Osteopath. Medicine, 1987. Diplomate Am. Bd. Osteopathic Medical Examiners. Commd. maj. USAF, 1988; attending physician Hosp. USAF Hosp., RAF Lakenheath, Eng., 1988-91, asst. dir. emergency dept., 1990-91; dir. emergency trng. we. Europe divsn. USAF, RAF Lakenheath, Eng., 1990-91; flight surgeon USAF Hosp., Holloman AFB, N. Mex., 1991-92; flight surgeon Space Shuttle contingency opers. USAF, Holloman AFB, N. Mex., 1991-92; resident physician Wright State U./USAF, Dayton, Ohio, 1992-95; staff physician, instr. tactical medicine USAF Hosp., Wright Patterson AFB, 1995—; spl. asst. Dept. Health and Human Svcs., Rockville, Md., 1986; health policy fellow U.S. Senate, Washington, 1988; chief cons. Dayton (Ohio) SWAT Team, 1994—; keynote spkr. Ohio State EMS, Columbus, 1995. Spl. lectr. Unitarian Universalist Ch., Oakwood, Ohio, 1993. Decorated Commendation medal USAF, 1993; recipient Dir.'s award USPHS U.S. Surgeon Gen., 1987. Mem. Am. Coll. Emergency Physicians. Home: 4142 Idle Hours Cir Dayton OH 45415 Office: USAF Dept Emergency Svcs Dayton OH 45433

SAVAGE, ROBERT C., plastic surgeon, educator; b. Wilkes Barre, Pa., May 2, 1951; s. Peter J. and Olga J. Savage; m. Diane C. Savage; children: Kristin L., Stephanie. BA, Wesleyan U., Middletown, Conn., 1973; MD, Jefferson Med. Coll., 1977. Diplomate Am. Bd. Plastic Surgery. Resident gen. surgery Brown U., R.I. Hosp., Providence, 1977-80, resident in plastic surgery, 1980-82; hand microsurgery fellow Mass. Gen. Hosp., Boston, 1982-83; pvt. practice plastic surgery Boston, 1983—; asst. clin. prof. surgery Harvard U., Boston, 1983—. Fellow ACS; mem. Am. Soc. Plastic and Reconstructive Surgery, New Soc. Plastic and Reconstructive Surgery, Am. Assn. for Hand Surgery, Mass. Med. Soc. Office: 111 Lincoln St Needham MA 02192

SAVAGEAU, MICHAEL ANTONIO, microbiology and immunology educator; b. Fargo, N.D., Dec. 3, 1940; s. Antonio Daniel and Jennie Ethelwin (Kaushagen) S.; m. Ann Elisa Birky, July 22, 1967; children—Mark Edward, Patrick Daniel, Elisa Marie. B.S., U. Minn., 1962; M.S., U. Iowa, 1963; Ph.D., Stanford U., 1967, postgrad., 1968-70; postgrad., UCLA, 1967-68. Research fellow UCLA, Los Angeles, 1967-68; lectr. Stanford U., Calif., 1968-69; from asst. to full prof. U. Mich., Ann Arbor, 1970—; sr. research fellow Max Planck Inst., Göttingen, Fed. Republic of Germany, 1976-77; fellow Australian Nat. U., Canberra, 1983-84; prof. microbiology and immunology U. Mich., Ann Arbor, 1978—, chmn. dept., 1982-85, 92—, prof. chem. engring., dir. cellular biotech. labs., 1988-91; dir. NIH trng. program in Cellular Biotechnology, 1991-92; cons. Upjohn Co., Kalamazoo, 1979-81, NIH, Bethesda, Md., 1981-82, 94-95, Synergen, Boulder, Colo., 1985-87; Found. for Microbiology lectr., 1993-95; vis. prof. dept. biochemistry U. Ariz., Tucson, 1994. Author: Biochemical Systems Analysis, 1976; mem. editl. bd. Math. Scis., 1976-95, editor, 1995—; mem. editl. bd. Jour. Theoretical Biology, 1989-96, mem. adv. bd., 1996—; mem. editl. bd. Nonlinear World, 1992—, Nonlinear Digest, 1992—; co-editor Math. Ecology, 1986—; contbr. articles to profl. jours. Australian Nat. U. fellow, 1983-84; Guggenheim Found., fellow N.Y.C., 1976-77; Fulbright Found., sr. research fellow, Washington, Fed. Republic of Germany, 1976-77; sr. fellow Mich. Soc. Fellows, 1990-94; grantee NIH, NSF, 1964—. Mem. AAAS, Am. Chem. Soc., Am. Soc. Microbiology, IEEE (sr.), Soc. Indsl. and Applied Math., Biophys. Soc., Soc. Gen. Physiologists, Soc. Math. Biology (bd. dirs. 1987-90). Office: U Mich Dept Microbiology and Immunology 5641 Med Sci II Ann Arbor MI 48109-0620

SAVAR, DAVID EDWARD, ophthalmic plastic surgeon; b. Balt., June 28, 1948. BA, Johns Hopkins U., 1969; MD, Boston U., 1973. Diplomate Am. Bd. Ophthalmology. Intern Michael Reese Med. Ctr., Chgo.; resident Jules Stein Eye Inst.-UCLA; fellow U. Toronto; clin. chief ophthalmology Cedars-Sinai Med. Ctr., L.A., 1990-94; assoc. prof. UCLA, 1986—. Mem. Profl. Club L.A. Office: 433 N Camden Dr # 1150 Beverly Hills CA 90210

SAVELLANO, LETICIA A., psychiatrist; came to U.S., 1963; d. Maximo and Carmen (A.) S. MD, U. Philippines, 1962. Lic. psychiatrist, N.Y.; Diplomate Am. Bd. Psychiatry and Neurology. Chief outpatient psychiatry Bronx (N.Y.) Hosp., 1962-79. Home: 750 Kappock St Bronx NY 10463-4612 Office: 1285 Fulton Ave Bronx NY 10456-3401

SAVER, JEFFREY LAWRENCE, neurologist; b. Boston, June 5, 1959; s. Harry Norman Saver and Esther Rosenbloom; m. Kay R. Young, Aug. 20, 1983. AB, Harvard Coll., 1981; MD, Harvard U., 1986. Intern Brigham and Women's Hosp., Boston, 1986-87; resident Longwood neurology program Harvard U., Boston, 1987-89, chief resident, 1989-90; fellow cognitive neurology U. Iowa Hosps. and Clinics, Iowa City, 1990-91; fellow cerebrovascular disorders Brown U., Providence, 1991-92; asst. prof. Northwestern U., Chgo., 1992-94; asst. prof. UCLA, 1994—, co-dir. Stroke Ctr.; cons. Little, Brown, Boston, 1989. Editor: Of Flame and Clay, Dialogues on Mind-Body Interaction, 1986. Mem. Am. Acad. Neurology, Am. Heart Assn., (stroke coun.), Nat. Stroke Assn. Office: Reed Neurologic Rsch Ctr UCLA 710 Westwood Plaza Los Angeles CA 90095

SAVIC, STANLEY DIMITRIUS, physicist; b. Belgrade, Yugoslavia, Dec. 30, 1938; came to the U.S., 1958; s. Dimitrius and Zorka (Vuckovic) S. BS, Roosevelt U., 1962; MS, U. Ill., 1969. Staff scientist Argonne Cancer Rsch. Hosp., Chgo., 1962-63; with radiology staff U. Chgo., 1963-64; v.p. Zenith Electronics Corp., Glenview, Ill., 1964—; chief U.S. del. Internat. Electrotech. Commn., Geneva, 1986-90; lectr. in field, 1984-91; mem. com. FDA, Washington, 1978-81; mem. faculty N.Y. Acad. Fire Scis., Albany, 1991. Author: X-Ray Conference Proceedings, 1968, co-author, 1968; contbr. chpt.: Standards Management, 1990. Apptd. by sec. Dept. Health & Human Svcs. to Tech. Electronic Products Radiation Safety Standards Com., Washington, 1978-81, 93; sec. Holy Resurrection Cathedral, Chgo., 1978-79; divsn. chmn. Crusade of Mercy, United Way, 1988. Mem. IEEE (sr.), N.Y. Acad. Scis., Nat. Fire Protection Assn., ASTM, Electronic Industries Assn. (chmn. safety com. 1983-87, mem. engring. policy coun. 1992—, Disting. Svc. award 1987). Republican. Serbian-Orthodox. Office: Zenith Electronics Corp 1000 Milwaukee Ave Glenview IL 60025-2423

SAVIN, JOHN ANDREW, dermatologist, consultant, educator; b. London, Jan. 10, 1935; s. Lewis Herbert and Mary Helen (Griffith) S.; m. Patricia Margaret Steel, Oct. 31, 1959; children: Penelope, William, Rosemary, Charles. BA, Trinity Hall, Cambridge, Eng., 1956, MA, 1959, MB BChir, 1960; MD, Cambridge U., 1978. Resident St. Thomas' Hosp., London, 1959-60; sr. house officer St. John's Hosp., London, 1965-66; registrar St. George's Hosp., London, 1966-68; sr. registrar St. John's and St. Thomas' Hosps., London, 1968-71; cons. dermatologist Royal Infirmary, Edinburgh, Scotland, 1971—. Co-author: Common Diseases of the Skin, 1984, (textbooks) Clinical Dermatology, 2d edit., 1995, Dermatology and the New Genetics, 1995; editor: Recent Advances in Dermatology, 1980. Surgeon lt. Royal Navy, 1960-64. Fellow Royal Coll. Physicians (London), Royal Coll. Physicians (Edinburgh), Royal Soc. Medicine (pres. dermatology sect. 1988-89); mem. Brit. Assn. Dermatologists (pres. 1993-94), Can. Dermatology Soc. (hon. mem.), French Dermatology Soc. (hon. mem.), Dowling Club (pres. 1992-93). Anglican. Office: The Royal Infirmary, Lauriston Pl, Edinburgh EH3 9YW, Scotland

SAVINO, MICHAEL ANTHONY, surgeon; b. Queens, N.Y., May 8, 1953; s. Daniel Joseph and Lucille Savino; m. Debra Graffeo, July 9, 1977; children: Arielle, Jared, Troy. BS, Richmond Coll., Staten Island, N.Y., 1975; MD, U. Guadalajara, Mex., 1979. Diplomate Am. Bd. Urology. Intern Coney Island Hosp., 1979-80; resident in surgery Maimonides Med. Ctr., 1980-82, resident in urology, 1982-85; surgeon in group practice Staten Island, 1985—. Fellow ACS; mem. Am. Assn. Clin. Urologists, Am. Urologic Assn. Office: Todt Hill Urologic Group PC 71 Todt Hill Rd Staten Island NY 10314

SAVITZ, MARTIN HAROLD, neurosurgeon; b. Boston, Jan. 20, 1942; s. Nathan and Bernice Beatrice (Segal) S.; m. Susan Rayna Gordon, June 23, 1968 (div. Sept. 1977); 1 child, Sean Isaac; m. Harmony Gwynne Keys, Oct. 28, 1979; 1 child, Ariel Austryn. AB, Harvard U., 1963; MD, Hahnemann, 1969. Diplomate Am. Bd. Neurol. Surgery, Am. Bd. Clin. Neurosurgery, Nat. Bd. Med. Examiners, Am. Bd. Forensic Medicine. Intern Boston City Hosp., 1969-70; resident Mount Sinai Hosp., N.Y.C., 1970-74; clin. instr. dept. neurosurgery Mt. Sinai Sch. Medicine, N.Y.C., 1974-82, asst. clin. prof., 1982-86, assoc. clin. prof., 1986—; attending neurosurgeon Nyack (N.Y.) Hosp., Good Samaritan Hosp., Rockland County, N.Y., Cmty. Hosp., Dobbs Ferry, N.Y.; mem. pres.'s coun. Harvard Coll., 1991—, marshal of commencement, 1993—; mem. alumni bd. trustees Hahnemann U., 1991-94; 16 vis. lectureships in 8 different countries; head exam com. Am. Bd. Clin. Neurosurgery, 1995—. Contbg. editor Mt. Sinai Jour. Medicine, 1976-90, asst. editor, 1990—; mem. editl. bd. Jour. Orthopaedic Neurol. Medicine and Surgery, 1991—; contbr. 2 chpts. to textbooks, over 75 articles to profl. jours. Mem. pres.'s coun. Harvard Coll., 1991—, marshal of commencement, 1993—; mem. alumni bd. trustees Hahnemann U., 1991-94. Fellow ACS, Am. Biog. Assn., Internat. Coll. Surgeons (chmn.-elect U.S. sect. neurosurgery, 1992, chmn., 1993, exec. com. 1994, chmn.-elect 1995, chmn. 1996), N.Y. Acad. Medicine, Phila. Coll. Physicians, Am. Acad. Neurol. Orthopaedic Surgery (bd. dirs. 1994—) Am. Forensic Examiners Coll. (ethics com. 1995—), Internat. Biog. Assn., Am. Biographical Inst.; mem. AMA, AAAS, Am. Assn. Neurol. Surgeons, N.Y. Soc. Neurosurgery, Congress Neurol. Surgeons, N.Y. State Neurosurg. Soc., Internat. Fedn. of Surg. Colls., Internat. Soc. Minimal Intervention in Spinal Surgery, Hastings Ctr., N.Y. Acad. Scis., Alpha Omega Alpha, Phi Delta Epsilon. Jewish. Home: Hobbit Holw New City NY 10956 Office: 55 Old Turnpike Rd Ste 101 Nanuet NY 10954-2449

SAVLOV, EDWIN DAVID, surgeon, oncologist, educator; b. Carbondale, Pa., July 11, 1924; s. Hyman and Ruth (Stone) S.; m. Peggy Weisberg, 1951 (div. 1962); children: Meg, John; m. Jean Kams; 1 child, Marc. BA, U. Rochester, 1946, MD, 1948. Diplomate Am. Bd. Surgery. Assoc. prof. surgery U. Rochester, 1968-80; prof. surgery Texas Tech, Amarillo, Tex., 1980-88, U. Nevada, Reno, 1989—. Home: 4850 Golden Springs Dr Reno NV 89509 Office: VAMC 1000 Locust St Reno NV 89520

SAVOJE, FELIX HENRY, III, orthopaedic surgeon; b. Paincourtville, La., Oct. 11, 1956; s. Felix Henry J. and Coralie Lucille (Dolese) S.; m. Barbara Coast Shanley, May 27, 1978; children: Christopher, Robert, John Reagan. BS in biochem., La. State Univ., 1978, MD, 1982. Orthopaedic resident U. Miss. Medical Ctr., Jackson, 1982-87; fellow in hand surgery Medical Coll Wis., Milw., 1987-88; fellow in arthroscopy & sports medicine Orthopaedic Rsch. of Va., Richmond, 1988; asst. prof. orthopaedics U. Miss. Medical Ctr., Jackson, 1989-90; dir. upper extremity svc. Miss. Sports Medicine, Jackson, 1990—; editorial bd. Arthoscopy, Wake Forest, N.C., 1993—. Author, editor: Arthroscopy of the Elbow, 1995; chpts. in book: Arthroscopic Reconstruction of the Shoulder, 1995, McGinty et al: Arthroscopy, 1995, Orthopaedic Clinics N. Am. Recipient Charles Nee award Am. Shoulder & Elbow Soc., 1992. Fellow Am. Acad. Orthopaedic Surgeons; mem. Arthroscopy Assn. N.Am. (mem. edn.com. 1995—), Am. Shoulder & Elbow Soc. (CPT coding com. 1994—). Roman Catholic. Office: Miss Sports Medicine 1325 E Fortification Jackson MS 39202

SAVONA, MICHAEL RICHARD, physician; b. N.Y.C., Oct. 21, 1947; s. Salvatore Joseph and Diana Grace (Menditto) S.; m. Dorothy O'Neill, Oct. 18, 1975. BS summa cum laude, Siena Coll., 1969; MD, SUNY, Buffalo, 1973. Diplomate Am. Bd. Internal Medicine. Intern in internal medicine Presbyn. Hosp. Columbia U., N.Y.C., 1973-74, resident in internal medicine, 1974-76; vis. fellow internal medicine Delafield Hosp./Columbia U. Coll. Physicians and Surgeons, N.Y.C., 1974-76; practice medicine specializing in internal medicine Maui Med. Group, Wailuku, Hawaii, 1976-87, gen. practice medicine, 1987—; dir. ICU, Maui Meml. Hosp., also dir. respiratory therapy, CCU., chmn. dept. medicine, 1980—; clin. faculty John A. Burns Sch. Medicine, U. Hawaii, asst. prof. medicine, 1985—, asst. rsch. prof., 1989—. Bd. dirs. Maui Heart Assn.; dir. profl. edn. Maui chpt. Am. Cancer Soc.; mem. Maui County Hosp. Adv. Commn.; mem. coun. Community Cancer Program of Hawaii. Recipient James A. Gibson Wayne J. Atwell award, 1970, physiology award, 1970, Ernest Whitebsky award, 1971, Roche Lab. award, 1972, Pfizer Lab. award, 1973, Phillip Sang award, 1973, Hans Lowenstein M.D. Meml. award, 1973. Mem. AMA, Am. Thoracic Soc., Hawaii Thoracic Soc., Maui County Med. Assn. (past pres.), Hawaii Med. Assn., Hawaii Oncology Group, ACP, SW Oncology Coop. Group, Alpha Omega Alpha, Delta Epsilon Sigma. Office: 1830 Wells St Wailuku HI 96793-2365

SAWADA, TOSHIO, colorectal surgeon, consultant; b. Sapporo, Hokkaido, Japan, Jan. 10, 1947; s. Minoru and Rei (Fujii) S.; m. Eiko Yamaki, Feb. 17, 1953; 2 children. Grad., U. Tokyo, 1973, DMS, 1981. Jr. resident dept. surgery U. Tokyo, 1973-75, sr. resident dept. surgery, 1975-86; staff mem. dept. colorectal surgery Nat. Cancer Ctr., Tokyo, 1986-88; lectr. dept. surgery U. Tokyo, 1988-95; v.p. Gunma Prefectural Cardiovasc. Ctr., Maebashi, Japan, 1995—; vis. prof. dept. colorectal surgery Cleve. Clin. Found., Cleve., 1986. Author: Bailliere's Clinical Gastroenterology, 1989; contbr. articles to med. jours. Mem. Internat. Soc. Univ. Colon and Rectal Surgeons, Japan Soc. Coloproctologists (exec.), Am. Soc. Colon and Rectal Surgeons. Democrat. Buddhist. Home: 2-13-7 Ote-Machi, 371 Maebashi City Gunma, Japan Office: Gunma Prefect Cardiovasc Ct, 3-12 Ko Kameizumi-Machi, 371 Maebashi City Gunma, Japan

SAWAI, TERUO, biology educator; b. Ichinomiya, Aichi, Japan, July 15, 1917; s. Denzaburo and Asano Sawai; m. Hideko Sawai, Mar. 18, 1945 (dec. Nov. 1979); 1 adopted child, Chieko; m. Fumi Sawai, June 14, 1980. BSc, Tokyo Bunrika U., 1942, DSc, 1961. Lectr. Aichi Kyoiku U., Nagoya, 1949-51, asst. prof., 1951-66, prof., 1966-81, prof. emeritus, 1981—; lectr. Aichi Woman's Jr. Coll., Nagoya,1981-88; prof. Kansai Woman's Jr. Coll., Minoo, 1983-87; lectr. Takarazuka Arts Coll., Japan, 1987-91. Contbr. articles to profl. jours.; discovered yeast transglucosyl-amylase, bacterial gluco- and isomalto-dextranases. 2d lt. Airdrome, 1943-45, North Korea. Mem. Agrl. Chem. Soc. Japan (life). Buddhist. Home: 2-18-5 Obata, Moriyama-ku, Nagoya 463, Japan

SAWAYA, RAYMOND, neurosurgeon; b. Latakia, Syria, May 5, 1949; s. Emile and Josephine (Boulos) S.; m. Kristin Tveit; children: Marc-Emile, Corinne Marguerite. MD, St. Joseph U., Beirut, 1974. Diplomate Am. Bd. Neurol. Surgery. Intern Beeckman-Downtown Hosp., N.Y.C., 1974-75; resident in surgery SUNY, Syracuse, 1975-76; resident in neurosurgery U. Cin., 1976-80, Johns Hopkins Hosp., Balt., 1981; vis. scientist NIH, Bethesda, Md., 1981-82; assoc. prof. U. Cin., 1983-90, dir. div. neuro-oncology, 1983-90; neurosurgeon Mayfield Neurol. Inst., Cin., 1983-90; prof., chmn. dept. neurosurgery U. Tex. M.D. Anderson Cancer Ctr., Houston, 1990—. Contbr. numerous articles on neurosurgery to profl. jours. research Adv. Group grantee VA Med. Ctr., 1984. Mem. AMA, Am. Radium Soc., Tex. Med. Assn., Am. Assn. Neurol. Surgeons, Congress of Neurosurgeons, Soc. Surg. Oncology, Assn. Brain Tumor Rsch., Houston Neurol. Soc. (pres.), Johns Hopkins Alumni Assn. Roman Catholic. Office: 1515 Holcombe Blvd # 64 Houston TX 77030-4009

SAWH, LALL RAMNATH, urologist; b. Couva, Trinidad and Tobago, June 1, 1951; s. Ramnath Rooplal and Ramkumaria (Sinanan) S.; m. Sylvia Sheila Ragobar, Dec. 22, 1973; children: Sean Lall, Shane Stefan. MBBS, U. W.I., Mona, Jamaica, 1975. Intern Gen. Hosp. San Fernando, Trinidad, 1975-76, sr. housr officer, 1976-77, sr. registrar in urology, 1980-86, acting cons. urologist, 1987—; clin. asst. Royal Infirmary Edinburgh, Scotland, 1978-79; clin. attachment Inst. Urology, London, 1979; examiner Nursing Coun., Trinidad, 1984-86, examiner surgery U. of the West Indies, 1991—, assoc. lectr. surgery, 1990—; cons. urologist Gen. Hosp., Port of Spain, Trinidad, 1988, Eric Williams Med. Scis. Complex, Mt. Hope, Trinidad; head local kidney transplant team, 1990; chmn. sci. com. Trinidad and Tobago Kidney Found., 1989-93; lectr. in urology to various Caribbean countries; surgeon Gen. Hosp., San Fernando, Port of Spain; cons. Eric Williams Med. Sci. Complex, 1994—, Mt. Hope, Trinidad. Author: Renal Hypothermic Surgery, 1982, Button-Hole Kidney Surgery, 1986; contbr. articles to profl. jours. Recipient award for Outstanding and Meritorious Svc. to Trinidad and Tobago, Caroni County Coun., 1989, Chaconia Gold medal Trinidad and Tobago, 1993; honored by city coun. for contbn. to medicine in San Fernando, 1989, Chamber of Commerce award Point Lisas/Couva, 1995; Rotary Club awards, Chaguanas, Tobago. Fellow Royal Coll. Surgeons; mem. Am. Urol. Assn. (corr. mem.), Med. Assn. Trinidad and Tobago (chmn. 1984-85), Endo-urol. Soc. U.S., Med. Bd. Trinidad and Tobago (specialist, med. officer), Caribbean Assn. of Nephrologists & Urologists, Caribbean Prostatic Health Coun. (Trinidad rep.), Surg. Edn. Com. (founder), Soc. Surgeons (treas. 1986-93). Club: Lawn Tennis (Point a Pierre, Trinidad). Office: Med Day Ctr, 15 Prince of Wales St, San Fernando Trinidad and Tobago also: So Med Clinic, 26-34 Quenca St, San Fernando Trinidad

SAWTELLE, CARL S., psychiatric social worker; b. Boston, July 14, 1927; s. Carl Salvador and Martha (Bellamacina) S.; BA, Suffolk U., Boston, 1951; MSW, Simmons Sch. Social Work, 1953; m. Thelma Florence Ramsay, Aug. 20, 1950; children: Tracy Lynn, Lisa June. Social worker Tewksbury (Mass.) State Hosp., 1952; psychiat. social worker, head psychiat. social worker, dir. clin. social work Taunton (Mass.) State Hosp., 1953-74; 1st dir. clin. social work, Plymouth, Mass., 1974-78; co-founder, v.p. 1st legally established War On Poverty program Triumph, Inc., Taunton; co-founder 1st Greater Taunton Coun. on Alcoholism, 1972. With USCG, 1944-46. 1st lic. social worker in Mass., 1980. Mem. Nat. Assn. Social Workers (co-founder Southeast Mass. chpt. 1957, pres. 1957, Spl. Mass. Chpt. award 1978), Acad. Cert. Social Workers (chmn. 1962-72), Am. Legion, Mass. Mental Health Social Workers Assn. (co-founder, pres. 1972-74, other offices). Created innovated programs, resources, opportunities, svcs. to state mental hosp. patients and their families; mentor to young social workers; contbr. advancement of knowledge, practice quality and standards of psychiat. social work; father of licensing and registration of Social Workers in Mass. Home: 9 Tracywood Rd Canton MA 02021-3501

SAWYER, HOWARD JEROME, physician; b. Detroit, Nov. 17, 1929; s. Howard C. and Dorothy M. (Risley) S.; m. Janet Carol Hausen, July 24, 1954; children: Daniel William, Teresa Louise. BA in Philosophy, Wayne State U., 1952, MD, 1962, postdoctoral, 1969-72. Diplomate Am. Bd. Preventive Medicine in Occupational and Environ. Medicine. Intern William Beaumont Hosp., Royal Oak, Mich., 1962-63, resident in surgery, 1963-64; chief physician gen. parts div. Ford Motor Co., Rawsonville, Mich., 1964-66; med. dir. metall. products dept. Gen. Electric Co., Detroit, 1966-73; chem. and metal div. Gen. Electric Co., 1972-73; staff physician Detroit Indsl. Clinic, Inc., 1973-74; pres., med. dir. OccuMed Assocs., Inc., Farmington Hills, Mich., 1974-84; dir. OccuMed div. Med. Service Corp. Am., Southfield, Mich., 1984-86; dir. occupational, environ. and preventive medicine Henry Ford Hosp., 1987-91; pres. Sawyer Med. Cons., P.C., 1991—; adj. asst. prof. occupational and environ. health scis. Wayne State U., 1974—; lectr. Sch. Pub. Health, U. Mich., Ann Arbor, 1977—; cons. med. dir. St. Joe Minerals Corp., 1976-87, Chesbrough Pond's Inc., 1979-83; cons. Anaconda, Bendix, Borg Warner Chems., Fed. Mogul, Gen. Electric, Gt. Lakes Chems., other corps. Contbr. articles to profl. jours., chpts. to textbooks. Fellow Am. Coll. Preventive Medicine, Am. Occupational and Environ. Med. Assn., Mich. Occupational and Environ. Med. Assn. (pres. 1986), Am. Acad. Occupational Medicine; mem. AMA, Detroit Occupational Physicians Assn. (pres. 1984), Mich. State Med. Soc., Oakland County Med. Soc., Am. Indsl. Hygiene Assn., Mich. Indsl. Hygiene Soc. Office: Sawyer Med Cons PC 7072 Edinborough Dr West Bloomfield MI 48322-4025

SAWYER, MARY CATHERINE, hospital administrator; b. Borger, Tex., Dec. 8, 1931; d. Andrew Rodgers and Mary Elizabeth (Slater) Hill; m. Edmond Eugene Sawyer, Aug. 26, 1963; children: Slater Shane, Anthony Barrett, Maronda Rae. BBA, Tex. Tech U., 1956; cert. in med. records, U. Tex. Med. Br., Galveston, 1957. Registered med. adminstr.; cert. coding specialist. Med. record adminstr. Taylor Hosp., Inc., Lubbock, Tex., 1957-63; pvt. practice cons. Paris, Tex., 1963-79; med. record adminstr., coding specialist St. Joseph's Hosp., Paris, 1979—. Mem. DAR (corr. sec. 1989-91, treas. 1991-93, 1st vice regent 1994-96, def. chmn. 1990-96), Gordon Country Club, Phi Gamma Nu. Methodist. Home: PO Box 128 Deport TX 75435-0128 Office: St Joseph's Hosp PO Box 9070 Paris TX 75461-9070

SAWYER, PHILIP NICHOLAS, surgeon, educator, health science facility administrator; b. Bangor, Maine, Oct. 25, 1925; s. Frank S. and Linda (Makanna) S.; m. Grace Makla, June 13, 1953; children: Margaret Ann, Elizabeth Lynn, Susan Jean, Philip Michael. BS, Harvard U., 1947; MD, U. Pa., 1949. Diplomate Am. Bd. Surgery, Am. Bd. Thoracic Surgery. Intern Hosp. of U. Pa., Phila., 1949-50, resident in surgery, fellow, 1953-56; chief resident in surgery, fellow in pathology St. Luke's Hosp., N.Y.C., 1953-57; instr., asst. prof. surgery SUNY Downstate Med. Ctr., Bklyn., 1957-62, assoc. prof., 1962-66, prof., head vascular surgery svc., 1966-84, prof. emeritus, 1985—; pres. Interface Biomed. Labs. Corp.; prof. surgery N.Y. Med. Coll., 1991—; vis. surgeon, head vascular surg. svcs. Kings County Hosp., Bklyn., 1972—; cons. Meth. Hosp., Bklyn.; assoc. attending, head vascular surg. svcs. St. John's Episcopal Hosp., Far Rockaway, N.Y.; attending surgery VA Hosp., Bklyn.; cons. cardiovascular and thoracic surgeon Norwalk (Conn.) Hosp.; cons. vascular surgeon Caledonian Hosp., Bklyn., Pocono Hosp., East Stroudsburg, Pa.; prin. investigator Office Naval Rsch., NIH, Am. Heart Assn., 1953-84, NIH, 1957-86; disting. lectr. worldwide. Founding editor Jour. Investigative Surgery; assoc. editor: Am. Jour. Med. Electronics, Jour. Biomed. Rsch. Engring.; editor: Biophysical Mechanisms in Vascular Homeostasis & Intravascular Thrombosis, 1965, Vascular Grafts, 1976, Modern Vascular Grafts, 1987; co-editor: Surgical Resident's Manual, 1980, Vascular Diseases, Current Controversies, 1981; contbr. over 300 articles to med. jours.; numerous patents on heart valves, vascular grafts, hemostatic agts., vascular wall protective agts. Recipient Clemson award for basic biomaterials rsch. Soc. for Biomaterials, 1985; Markle scholar, 1959-64. Mem. Acad. Surg. Rsch. (Jacob Markowitz award 1986), AAAS, Am. Assn. for Thoracic Surgery, Am. Chem. Soc., Am. Coll. Cardiology, ACS, Am. Coll. Chest Physicians, AMA, Am. Heart Assn., Am. Nuclear Soc., Am. Soc. for Artificial Internal Organs, IEEE, Internat. Cardiovascular Soc., Soc. for Thoracic Surgeons, Soc. Univ. Surgeons, Soc. for Vascular Surgery, European Soc. for Microcirculation, Fedn. Am. Socs. for Exptl. Biology, Cardiovascular Soc. (pres.), Harvard Club (N.Y.C.), Sigma Xi, others. Home and Office: 7600 Ridge Blvd Brooklyn NY 11209-3008

SAWYER, WILBUR HENDERSON, pharmacologist, educator; b. Brisbane, Australia, Mar. 23, 1921; s. Wilbur Augustus and Margaret Henderson S.; m. Marian Gholson Kittredge, Nov. 14, 1942 (dec. Mar. 1982); children: Wilbur Kittredge, Robert Kittredge, Thomas Kittredge, Richard Kittredge; m. Pomona Jean Mitchell, Aug. 28, 1982. A.B., Harvard U., 1942, M.D., 1945, PhD, 1950; DSc, Med. Coll. Ohio, Toledo, 1994. Instr. biology Harvard U., Cambridge, Mass., 1950-53; asst. prof. physiology NYU Med. Sch., N.Y.C., 1953-57; asso. prof. pharmacology Columbia U. Coll. Physicians and Surgeons, N.Y.C., 1957-64; prof. Columbia U. Coll. Physicians and Surgeons, 1964-78, Gustavus A. Pfeiffer prof., 1978-90, prof. emeritus, 1991—, spl. lectr., 1993—. Contbr. articles on exptl. endocrinology, physiology and pharmacology to profl. jours. Served to lt. (j.g.) M.C., USN, 1946-48. Recipient Lederle Med. Faculty award NYU, 1955-57; Fulbright-Hays Sr. scholar, 1974; Commonwealth Fund travelling fellow, 1965. Fellow AAAS; mem. Am. Soc. Zoologists, Am. Physiol. Soc., Soc. Gen. Physiologists, Soc. Exptl. Biology and Medicine, Endocrine Soc., Am. Soc.. Pharmacology and Exptl. Therapeutics, Harvey Soc., Soc. Endocrinology, Am. Peptide Soc., Alpha Omega Alpha. Home: 1490 Kings Ln Palo Alto CA 94303-2836

SAWYERS, JOHN LAZELLE, surgeon; b. Centerville, Iowa, July 26, 1925; s. Francis Lazelle and Almira (Baker) S.; m. Julia Edwards, May 25, 1957; children: Charles Lazelle, Al Baker, Julia Edwards. A.B., U. Rochester, 1946; M.D., Johns Hopkins U., 1949. Diplomate: Am. Bd. Surgery (dir. 1981-87), Am. Bd. Thoracic Surgery. House officer surgery Johns Hopkins Hosp., Balt., 1949-50; asst. resident, resident in surgery Vanderbilt U. Hosp., Nashville, 1953-58; practice medicine specializing in surgery Nashville, 1958—; surgeon Edwards-Eve Clinic, 1958-60; chief surg. service Nashville Gen. Hosp., 1960-77; surgeon-in-chief St. Thomas Hosp., Nashville, 1977-82; prof. surgery Vanderbilt U., Nashville, chmn. dept. surgery, dir. sect. surg. scis., 1983-94. Bd. dirs. Davidson County unit Am. Cancer Soc. Served from lt. (j.g.) to lt. M.C. USNR, 1950-52. Fellow A.C.S. (gov. 1974-80, pres. Tenn. chpt. 1974); mem. Am. Surg. Assn. 1st v.p. 1994), Southeastern Surg. Congress (pres. 1980), So. Surg. Assn. (pres. 1987), Halsted Soc. (pres. 1981). Home: 403 Ellendale Ave Nashville TN 37205-3401 Office: Vanderbilt U Dept Surgery 1001 Oxford House Nashville TN 37232-4730

SAX, MARY RANDOLPH, speech pathologist; b. Pontiac, Mich., July 13, 1925; d. Bernard Angus and Ada Lucile (Thurman) TePoorten; m. William Martin Sax, Feb. 7, 1948. BA magna cum laude, Mich. State U., 1947; MA, U. Mich., 1949; cert. clin. competence in speech and language pathology. Supr. speech correction dept. Waterford Twp. Schs., Pontiac, 1949-69; lectr. Marygrove Coll., Detroit, 1971-72; pvt. practice in speech and lang. pathology, Wayne and Oakland Counties, Mich., 1973—; co-investigator Support Personnel Profl. Practice of Speech-Lang. Pathology; counselor to divsn. stroke liaisons Am. Heart Assn. Mich.; liaison, staff Scientific Coun. Stroke AHA Mich. and Dallas, 1996—; adj. speech pathologist Southfield, Mich.; lectr. on stroke Mich. Speakers Bur., Am. Heart Assn., 1990—; pub. speaking coach, 1989—; adj. faculty SS. Cyril and Methodius Sem., Orchard Lake, Mich., 1989-90, St. Mary's Preparatory Sch., Orchard Lake, Mich., 1990—; founder, mem. Stroke Project Task Force for Detroit, 1993—; com. mem. Charrette, study Architecture and Design for physical restructuring Franklin, Mich., 1993. Mem. sci. coun. stroke Am. Heart Assn. Grantee Inst. Articulation and Learning, 1969, others, project choices and funding Meadow Lake Cmty. Coun., Birmingham, Mich., 1989—; christian svc. commn. St. Owen, Birmingham co-chmn. blood drive Red Cross, Franklin, Mich., 1991—. Mem. Am. Speech-Lang.-Hearing Assn. (clin. competence cert.), Mich. Speech-Lang.-Hearing Assn. (com. cmty. and hosp. svcs., pvt. practitioner liaison 1991—), Am. Heart Assn. of Mich. (mem. stroke awareness seminar, planning and operation ednl., liaison sci. coun. stroke 1996—, counselor divsn. stroke liaisons), Stroke Com. of Am., Internat. Assn. Logopedics and Phoniatrics (Switzerland), Franklin Found. (mem. natural resources adv. coun. 1991—, bd. dirs. 1994—), Founders Soc. of Detroit Inst. Arts, Mich. Humane Soc., Theta Alpha Phi, Phi Kappa Phi, Kappa Delta Pi, Gamma Phi Beta Internat. Contbr. articles to profl. jours. including Language and Language Behavior Abstracts, Language Speech & Hearing Services, Speech Language Hearing Jour. Achievements include research in language and speech acquisition in children in reference to the development of and prediction of biological speech change; research interests developmental phonatory voice disorders in adult acquisition of language and speech relative to central and autonomic nervous systems. Home and Office: 31320 Woodside Dr Franklin MI 48025-2027

SAXE, ANDREW WARREN, surgeon; b. N.Y.C., Jan. 5, 1944; s. David H. and Caroline Saxe; married; children: Adam, Benjamin, Sarah. BA, U. Mich., 1965, MD, 1969. Diplomate Am. Bd. Surgery. Resident in surgery U. Mich., Ann Arbor, 1969-75; asst. prof. surgery U. Calif.-Davis, Sacramento, 1977-85; sr. surgeon Cance Inst., NIH, Bethesda, Md., 1979-81; chief endocrine surgery Sinai Hosp., Detroit, 1985—; program dir. surg. residency, 1995—. Author: (with others) Current Opinion in General Surgery, 1993; contbr. articles to World Jour. Surgery, Archives of Surgery, Surgery. Lt. comdr. USPHS, 1975-77. Fellow ACS, Am. Bd. Surgery; mem. Am. Assn. Endocrine Surgery, Detroit Surg. Assn. (pres. 1992-93), Coller Surg. Assn., Internat. Assn. Endocrine Surgeons, Endocrine Soc., Assn. for Acad. Surgery, Internat. Coll. Surgeons, Western Surg. Assn. Office: Sinai Hosp 14800 W McNichols Detroit MI 48235

SAXE, DAVID H., surgeon, educator; b. Passaic, N.J., Apr. 24, 1913; s. S.M. and Sophia (Jaffe) S.; m. Caroline Sculnick, Feb. 19, 1939; children: Andrew W., Elizabeth Andoh. BA, U. Mich., 1933, MD, 1937. Cert. Am. Bd. Colon and Rectal Surgery. Pvt. practice surgery N.Y.C., 1946—; clin. prof. surgery NYU, N.Y.C., 1946—. Lt. col. U.S. Army-Med. Corps, 1941-46. Fellow AMA, Am. Soc. Colon and Rectal Surgery, N.Y. Soc. Colon and Rectal Surgery. Home: 50 Sutton Place South New York NY 10022 Office: 120 E 36th St New York NY 10016

SAXE, LEONARD, social psychologist, educator; b. N.Y.C., June 12, 1947; s. Theodore and Majorie (Mayers) S.; m. Marion Gardner, Aug. 9, 1970; 1 child, Daniel. BS in Psychology, U. Pitts., 1969, MS in Psychology, 1972, PhD in Social Psychology, 1976. Asst. instr. U. Pitts., 1973-75; asst. then assoc. prof. psychology Boston U., 1976-88, assoc. dir. Ctr. Applied Social Sci., 1982-84, dir., 1984-87; rsch. prof. Heller Sch. Social Welfare Brandeis U., Waltham, Mass., 1988-90, adj. prof. psychology, adj. rsch. prof., 1990—; prof. psychology Grad. Ctr. CUNY, 1991—; head social-personality psychology, 1991-95; Fulbright sr. lectr. U. Haifa, Israel, 1981-82; mem. task force Children's Mental Health Rsch. Inst. Medicine-NAS, 1988-89; rev. coms. HHS-Healthcare Fin. Adminstr. NIMH, Nat. Inst. Drug Abuse, Dept. Edn.; cons., contractor Office Tech. Assessment, U.S. Congress, 1980-88. Author: (with others) Children's Mental Health: Problems and Treatment, 1987, (with M. Fine) Social Experiments: Methods for Design and Evaluation, 1981; editor: (with M.J. Saks) Advances in Applied Social Psychology, Vol. 3, 1986, (with D. Koretz) New Directions for Program Evaluation, 1982, (with D. Bar-Tal) The Social Psychology of Education: Theory and Research, 1978; contbr. chpts. to books, articles to profl. jours.; assoc. and mng. editor Personality and Social Psychology Bull., 1978-81; ad hoc reviewer various jours., book reviewer various pubs. Congl. fellow Office Tech. Assessment, 1979. Fellow APA (bd. dirs. sect. social and ethical responsibility 1985-88, Disting. Contbn. award 1989), AAAS, Soc. Psychol. Study Social Issues (coun. 1982-84, 87-89). Office: CUNY Grad Ctr 33 W 42nd St New York NY 10036-8003

SAXENA, AMOL, podiatrist, consultant; b. Palo Alto, Calif., June 5, 1962; s. Arjun Nath and Veera Saxena; m. Karen Ann Palermo, Aug. 11, 1985; children: Vijay, Tara Ann. Student, U. Calif., Davis, 1980-82; BA, Washington U., St. Louis, 1984; D in Podiatric Medicine, William Scholl Coll. Podiatric Medicine, 1988. Diplomate Am. Bd. Podiatric Surgery; lic. podiatrist, Calif., Ill. Resident in podiatric surgery VA Westside Br., Chgo., 1988-89; cons. Puma U.S.A., Inc., Framingham, Mass., 1986—; pvt. practice Mountain View, Calif., 1989-93; with dept. sports medicine Palo Alto Med. Found., 1993—; dir. Puma Sports Medicine, Framingham; mem. podiatry team St. Frances/Gunn Los Altos (Calif.) High Sch., Palo Alto, 1989—, Stanford (Calif.) U., 1989—; mem. med. staff El Camino Hosp., 1989—, team podiatrist Stanford U., 1989—. Guest editor Lower Extremity; mem. editl. bd. Jour. Foot and Ankle Surgery; contbr. articles to profl. jours. Vol. coach Gunn High Sch. Track and Cross County, Palo Alto, 1989—; podiatrist U.S. Olympic Track and Field Trials, New Orleans, 1992, 1993. Fellow Am. Acad. Podiatric Sports Medicine, Am. Coll. Foot and Ankle Surgeons; mem. Am. Podiatric Med. Assn., Calif. Podiatric Med. Assn., Am. Med. Soccer Assn., Aggie Running Club. Republican. Office: 1197 E Arques Ave Sunnyvale CA 94086-3904 also: 913 Emerson St Palo Alto CA 94301-2415

SAXON, ANDREA MARY, ophthalmologist; b. Harrisburg, Pa., Apr. 6, 1956; d. Joseph George and Donna Louise (Ebert) S.; m. Vincent Richard McGuinness, Oct. 19, 1985; children: Trevor, Andrew. BS, Pa. State U., 1978; MD, Hahnemann U., 1984. Diplomate Am. Bd. Ophthalmology. Ophthalmologist Crozer Chester Med. Ctr., Upland, Pa. Contbr. articles to profl. publs. Mem. Am. Diabetes Assn. (mem. patient edn. com.), Phila. Club of Med. Women (v.p. 1993-95). Office: 1 Medical Center Blvd Upland PA 19013

SAXON, FRANCES SHIVER, retired feminist counselor, womens center director; b. Walhalla, S.C., Jan. 12, 1928; d. Noble Calhoun and Caroline (Ansel) Shiver; m. James Hendricks Saxon, Sept. 3, 1949; children: James, Frank, Scott, Suzanne, Carol, Andrew, Dorothy, David. Student, U. N.C., Greensboro, 1946-49; BA in Psychology with honors, U. N.C., Charlotte, 1975, MEd, 1981. Commuter life coordinator U. N.C., Charlotte, 1974-77; exec. dir. The Women Reach Ctr., Charlotte, 1977-89; cons. Handicapped Organized Women, Charlotte, 1983-84, Women's Concerns program Mecklenburg Presbytery, Charlotte, 1985. Recipient Outstanding Svc. award U. N.C., Charlotte, 1975, Cert. of Appreciation, Internat. Woman's Day, 1989, Commendation, N.C. Coun. on the Status of Women, 1989, Women's Equality Day award, 1989. Mem. NAFE, N.C. Assn. Counseling and Devel., Southeastern Women's Studies Assn., Nat. Assn. Bus. and Profl. Women, Nat. Assn. Group Work, Nat. Assn. Women's Centers. Home: 3120 Libeth St Charlotte NC 28205-3222

SAXON, JAMES, physician, actor; b. N.Y.C., Apr. 6, 1954; s. Peter Edward and Shelagh Maureen (Meenan) S.; m. Abby Lynn Levine, May 13, 1989; children: Tyler James, Adriana Milicent. BFA, NYU, 1977; MD, Columbia U., 1987. Actor, 1974—; intern Roosevelt Hosp., N.Y.C., 1987-88; resident in internal medicine St. Vincent's Hosp., N.Y.C., 1988-90, fellow in critical care medicine, 1990-92; fellow in pulmonary medicine St. Luke's-Roosevelt Hosp., N.Y.C., 1992-94; dir. pulmonary medicine Kingston (N.Y.) Hosp., 1994—. With USN, 1972-73.

SAXTON, LLOYD, psychologist and author; b. Loveland, Colo., Sept. 28, 1929; s. Oliver George and Alice Augusta (Andersen) S.; m. Nancy Alison Roberts, Dec. 17, 1955; children: Perry Brent, Jay Ronald, Barbara Jean. AB in English, U. Calif., Berkeley, 1950, BS in Psychology, 1954; MS in Psychology, San Francisco State U., 1955; PhD in Psychology, U. of the Pacific, Stockton, Calif., 1957. Lic., bd. cert. psychologist, Calif.; bd. cert. forensic psychologist; diplomate Am. Bd. Forensic Examiners. Intern in clin. psychology Childlren's Hosp., San Francisco, 1955-56; teaching fellow U. Pacific, San Francisco, 1955-57, instr. psychology, 1957-58, asst. prof. psychology, 1958-60; assoc. prof. psychology Am. Acad. of Asian Studies, San Francisco, 1960-62, prof. psychology, 1962-65; chmn. dept. psychology Coll. of San Mateo, Calif., 1965-75, prof. psychology, 1975-92; pvt. practice San Francisco/Larkspur, 1958—; emeritus, 1995. Author: Individual, Marriage and the Family, 1968, Individual, 9th edit., 1996; author/editor: A Marriage Reader, 1970, The American Scene, 1970. Mem. APA, AAAS, AAUP, Am. Assn. Marriage and Family Therapists, Western Psychol. Assn., Am. Coll. Forensic Examiners, Mensa. Democrat. Home and Office: 57 Hatzic Ct Larkspur CA 94939-1971

SAYK, JOHANNES, physician; b. Hirschen, OstpreuBen, Germany, Sept. 28, 1923; s. Johann and Ida Sayk; m. Dora Pfund, Feb. 17, 1947; children: Octavia, Juliane; children by previous marriage: Ruth, Philipp, Johannes. MD, U. Jena (Germany), 1950; MD (hon.), Med. Acad. of U.), Poznan, Poland, 1989. Med. asst. surg. clinic U. Jena, 1950-51, med. asst. neurol. clinic, 1952-55, head asst. docent, 1956-58, docent, head dept., 1958-61; prof., dir. neurology clinic U. Rostock (Germany), 1961-89; cons. dir. Med. Acad. Physician for Postgrad. Edn., Berlin, 1961-81; mem. med. adv. bd. Internat. Socs. Multiple Sclerosis, 1968. Author: Cytology of Cerebrospinal Fluid, 1960; inventor sediment chamber of cell enrichment, 1954, sorption chamber of cell enrichment, 1979. Lt. German Air Force, 1941-45. Recipient Rudolf Virchow prize Minister Pub. Health, Berlin, 1965, Carl Bonhoeffer medal German Soc. Neurology and Psychiatry, Berlin, 1989, Honor Needle, U. Rostock, 1989. Fellow Royal Soc. Medicine (mem. sect. neurology); mem. CSF Rsch. Group of World Fedn. Neurology, German Acad. Nature Researcher, German CSF Rsch. Group, German Soc. Neurology (hon. mem.), Brasileira Acad. Neurology (hon. mem.). Home: Lewarkweg 4, D-18147 Rostock Germany Office: U Rostock Clinic Neurology, Gehlsheimer Strasse 20, D-18147 Rostock Germany

SAYLOR, JEANNIE WATSON, pharmacist; b. Rusk, Tex., Aug. 19, 1967; d. Phillip Roy and Faye (Sargent) Watson; m. Joseph Rice Saylor III, May 21, 1988; children: Sarah Katherine, James Shackelford II. BS in Pharmacy, U. Tex., 1989. Registered pharmacist, Tex. Clin. pharmacist Harris Meth. Hosp. Ft. Worth, Ft. Worth, 1990-92, Parkland Meml. Hosp., Dallas, 1992—; cons. Drug Prevention Resources, Inc., Irving, Tex., 1991—. Mem. Tex. Soc. Hosp. Pharmacists (bd. dirs. 1991-93). Home: 7016 Timberlane Dr Fort Worth TX 76180-3526 Office: Parkland Meml Hosp 5201 Harry Hines Blvd Dallas TX 75235-7708

SAYLOR, JOHN S., human resources manager; b. Elizabeth, N.J., Sept. 4, 1945; s. John Seltzer and Margaret (Harrell) S.; m. Vivian Sholder, Nov. 13, 1974 (div. July 1992); m. Sherry Brackin, Nov. 11, 1994; children: Joshua, Caleb, Michael. BA, Yale U., 1967; MA, NYU, 1973. Cert. psychologist, employee assistance profl. From therapist to dir. therapy The Caron Found., Warnersville, Pa., 1974-82; exec. dir. Parkside Health Sys., Park Ridge, Ill., 1982-90; mgr. employee assistance programs Am. Airlines, Dallas/Ft. Worth, 1990—. Bd. dirs. Rainbow Days, Dallas, 1992-96. Mem. Am. Coll. Addictions Treatment Adminstrn., Employee Assistance Profl. Assn. (pres. Lone Star chpt. 1993-95). Home: 5203 Shadow Glen Grapevine TX 76051 Office: Am Airlines MD 5187 PO Box 619616 Dallas TX 75261-9616

SAZ, HOWARD JAY, biology educator; b. N.Y.C., Sept. 29, 1923; s. Michael and Molly (Perlmutter) S.; m. Rosalyn Pollack, Apr. 7, 1946; children: Daniel, Marjory, Wendy. BS, CCNY, 1948; PhD, Western Res. U., 1952. Rsch. assoc. Western Res. U., Cleve., 1952-53; postdoctoral fellow Nat. Found. Infantile Paralysis, Sheffield, Eng., 1953-54; rsch. assoc. La. State U., New Orleans, 1954-55, asst. prof., 1955-58, assoc. prof., 1958-60; assoc. prof. Johns Hopkins U., Balt., 1960-69; prof. biology U. Notre Dame, Ind., 1969—; cons. Army Med. Rsch. and Devel. Group, Washington, 1973-77; mem., chmn. tropical medicine and parasitology NIH, Washington, 1965-69, 69-70, 91-95; mem. study sect. NSF, 1984-86, cons. WHO, Geneva, Switzerland, 1980. Contbr. articles on biochemistry to profl. jours. Sgt. U.S. Army, 1943-45, ETO. Recipient Bronze Star, P.O.W.; NSF postdoctoral fellow La. State U., 1955. Fellow AAAS; mem. Am. Soc. Microbiology, Am. Soc. Biol. Chemistry, Am. Soc. Parasitologists (Bueding & von Brand meml. award 1989), British Biochem. Soc. Office: U Notre Dame Dept Biol Scis Notre Dame IN 46556

SAZIMA, HENRY JOHN, oral and maxillofacial surgery educator; b. Cleve., Dec. 25, 1927; s. Henry Charles and Frances (Masin) S.; m. Carol Ann Watson, Sept. 10, 1955; 1 child, Holly Ann Sazima Davani. BS, Case Western Res. U., 1948, DDS, 1953; grad. sch. medicine, U. Pa., 1956-57; grad. sch. edn., Chapman Coll., 1967-69. Diplomate Am. Bd. Oral and Maxillofacial Surgery. Chief maxillfacial div. Naval Support Act, Saigon, Republic of Viet Nam, 1969-70; chmn. dental dept. Naval Med. Ctr., Phila., 1971-73, San Diego, 1979-80; spl. asst. dentistry Sec. Def. Health Affairs, Washington, 1973-77; comdg. officer Naval Dental Ctr., Parris Island, S.C., 1977-79; dep. chief dental div. Bur. Medicine and Surgery, Washington, 1980-82; comdg. officer Nat. Naval Dental Ctr., Bethesda, Md., 1982-83; dir. resources div. Chief Naval Ops., Washington, 1983-84; dep. commdr. for readiness and logistics Naval Med. Command, Washington, 1984-87, ret. rear admiral, 1987; now clin. assoc. prof. oral and maxillofacial surgery Georgetown U. Med. Ctr.; exec. dir. Acad. Dentistry Internat., 1988—; emeritus, 1995; cons., lectr., researcher in field. Co-author: Management of War Injuries, 1977; contbr. articles to profl. jours. Recipient Residents award St. Vincent Charity Hosp., 1957. Fellow Am. Coll. Dentists, Assn. Oran and Maxillofacial Surgeons, Internat. Assn. Oral and Maxillofacial Surgeons, Acad. Dentistry Internat. (Blue Cloud award 1995); mem. Brit. Soc. Oral and Maxillofacial Surgeons, European Assn. Maxillofacial Surgery, Assn. Mil. Surgeons of U.S. (chmn. internat. com. 1984-86, Margetis award 1971), Internat. Coll. Dentists (dep. regent 1971-87), Omicron Kappa Upsilon, Delta Tau Delta, Psi Omega. Republican. Roman Catholic. Club: Mil. Order of CARABAO. Home: 4924 Sentinel Dr Apt 105 Bethesda MD 20816-3506 Office: Acad Dentistry Internat Office of Exec Dir Ste 50 5125 Macarthur Blvd NW Washington DC 20016-3300

SBRIGLIO, ROBERT PATRICK, psychiatrist; b. New Haven, Nov. 16, 1953; s. Robert and Margaret Sbriglio; m. Catherine Burton Kraft, May 30, 1993. BA, Boston U., 1976; MD, Rush Med. Coll., 1981; MPH, Yale U., 1989. Resident in psychiatry St. Vincent's Hosp. and Med. Ctr., N.Y.C., 1981-84; fellow in psychiatry and pub. health N.Y. Hosp.-Cornell Med. Ctr., N.Y.C., 1984-86; postdoctoral fellow in psychiatry Sch. Medicine Yale U., New Haven, 1987-88; pvt. practice, Bridgeport, Conn., 1989—. Mem. AMA, Am. Psychiat. Assn., Phi Beta Kappa. Office: PLEXUS Health Svcs Conn World Trade Plz 350 Fairfield Ave Bridgeport CT 06604-6001

SBUTTONI, MICHAEL JAMES, orthodontist, building contractor; b. Albany, N.Y., Aug. 6, 1953; s. Michael Francis and Mary Susan (Walsh) S.; m. Karen Sbuttoni, Aug. 9, 1975; children: Michael Louis, Ashley Ryan. BS, SUNY, Albany, 1975; DDS, SUNY, Buffalo, 1979; cert. in orthodontics, Eastman Dental Ctr., Rochester, N.Y., 1981. Real estate salesman Tri City Realty-Albany Bd. Realtors, 1971—; bldg. contractor M. Sbuttoni Constrn., Albany, 1972-86; practice dentistry specializing in orthodontics Dr. Serling and Decker DDS. P.C., Albany, 1981—; bldg. contractor The Craftsmens Guild, Albany, 1987—; staff orthodontist St. Peter's Hosp., Albany, 1984—. Mem. ADA, Am. Assn. Orthodontists Coun. on Govt. Rels., Internat. Coll. Dentists, Am. Assn. Lingual Orthodontists (charter), Dental Soc. State of N.Y. (pub. rels. 1985-88, coun. on edn. 1992-93), 3d Dist. Dental Soc. (bd. dirs. 1985-89, v.p. 1987-88, pres. 1988-90, ADA rep. 1990—), Kiwanis (fund raising dir. 1985-87), Elks. Republican. Roman Catholic. Home: 92 Middlesex Ct Slingerlands NY 12159-9636 Office: Drs Serling & Decker DDS PC 1004 Western Ave Albany NY 12203-2743

SCACCIA, LEO RALPH, III, nurse; b. Scranton, Pa., Sept. 30, 1959; s. Leo S. and Grace V. (Summa) S.; m. Dawn M. Scaccia, May 19, 1984; children: Morgan, Christian. BS in Edn., East Stroudsburg U., 1981; cert., Williamsport Paramedic Inst., 1982; diploma, Brandywine Sch., 1987; postgrad., West Chester U. RN, Pa.; CEN; CCRN; cert. flight nurse, EMT-paramedic, affiliate faculty BTLS; cert. ACLS affiliate faculty. Paramedic Brandywine Hosp., Coatesville, Pa., 1982-89, nurse, paramedic, 1989—, supr. advanced cardiac life support. Mem. AACN. Home: PO Box 18 39 Furnace Rd Bart PA 17503

SCALA, JAMES, health care industry consultant, author; b. Ramsey, N.J., Sept. 16, 1934; s. Luigi and Lorene (Hendrickson) S.; m. Nancy Peters, June 15, 1957; children: James, Gregory, Nancy, Kimberly. B.A., Columbia U., 1960; Ph.D., Cornell U., 1964; postgrad., Harvard U., 1968. Staff scientist Miami Valley Labs., Procter and Gamble Co., 1964-66; head life scis., dir. fundamental research Owens Ill. Corp., 1966-71; dir. nutrition T.J. Lipton Inc., 1971-75; dir. health scis. Gen. Foods Corp., 1975-78; v.p. sci. and tech. Shaklee Corp., San Francisco, 1978-85, sr. v.p. sci. affairs, 1986-87; lectr. Georgetown U. Med. Sch., U. Calif.-Berkeley extension. Author: Making the Vitamin Connection, 1985, The Arthritis Relief Diet, 1987, 89, Eating Right for a Bad Gut, 1990, 92, The High Blood Pressure Relief Diet, 1988, 90, Look 10 Years Younger, Feel 10 Years Better, 1991, 93, Prescription for Longevity, 1992, 94, If You Can't/Won't Stop Smoking, 1993; editor: Nutritional Determinants in Athletic Performance, 1981, New Protective Roles for Selected Nutrients, 1989; columnist Dance mag.; contbr. articles on nutrition and health scis. to profl. publs. With USAF, 1953-56. Disting. scholar U. Miami, Fla., 1977, Fla. Atlantic U., 1977. Mem. AAAS, Am. Inst. Nutrition, Am. Coll. Nutrition, Brit. Nutrition Soc., Sports Medicine Coun., Am. Soc. Cell Biology, Inst. Food Technologists, Astron. Soc. Pacific (bd. dirs., chmn. devel. coun.), Am. Dietetic Assn., Olympic Club (San Francisco), Oakland Yacht Club, Sigma Xi. Republican.

SCALES, DONALD KARL, dentist, army officer; b. Jacksonville, Fla., Apr. 7, 1960; s. Kenneth Ira and Marjorie Kathleen (Lahr) S. BS in Biology, The Citadel, 1982; DDS, Ind. U., 1989; postgrad., U. North Fla., 1982-85. Mem. affiliate faculty Ind. U. Dental Sch., Indpls., 1988-89; resident advanced edn. program in gen. dentistry MEDDAC student detachment U.S. Army, Ft. Carson, Colo., 1989-90; gen. dentistry officer 92d med. detachment, infection control officer U.S. Army, Hanau, Germany, 1990-94; chief oral surgery Hanau Dental Clinic, 1990-91; dental surgeon 4th Brigade, 3d Inf. Divsn., 1991-92; clinic chief Aschaffenburg Dental Clinic, 1992; preventive dentistry officer/pub. health dentist 92d Med. Detachment, 1992-93; clinic chief U.S. Army Dental Clinic, Buedingen, Germany, 1993-94; dep. comdr. 92d Med. Detachment, 1994; dentist 86th Combat Support Hosp., Ft. Campbell, Ky., 1995; sr. med. officer Zone IV, UN Mission in Haiti (U.S. Army Operatiton Uphold Democracy), 1995-96; dental surgeon 1st Brigade, 101st Airborne Divsn., 1995-96; dental surgeon 5th Spl. Forces Group (Airborne), 1996—;

dental cons. Westside Dental Care Ctr., Jacksonville, 1982—; lectr. and presenter in field; mem. exec. coun., mem. quality assurance com. 92nd Med. Detachment, 1991-92, Frankfurt (Germany) Dental Activity, 1993-94, Heidelburg (Germany) Dental Activity, 1994; rep. 7th Med. Command and U.S. European Command Dept. of Def. African Hosp. Project, 1993. Com. chmn. Panther edn. assistance program Hanau Am. H.S., 1990-94; CPR instr. Am. Heart Assn., Hanau, 1990-94; instr. dental asst. program ARC, Hanau, 1990-94. Mem. ADA, Acad. Gen. Dentistry, Assn. Mil. Surgeons U.S., Assn. U.S. Army, The Citadel Alumni Assn. (life), Ind. U. Alumni Assn. (life), N.E. Fla. Citadel Club. Home: USA DENTAC W2L8DC Fort Campbell KY 42223 Office: US Army Dentac Fort Campbell KY 42223

SCANDALIOS, JOHN GEORGE, geneticist, educator; b. Nisyros Isle, Greece, Nov. 1, 1934; s. George John and Calliope (Broujos) S.; m. Penelope Anne Lawrence, Jan. 18, 1961; children: Artemis Christina, Melissa Joan, Nikki Eleni. B.A., U. Va., 1957; M.S., Adelphi U., 1960; Ph.D., U. Hawaii, 1965; D.Sc. (hon.), Aristotelian U. Thessaloniki, Greece, 1986. Assoc. in bacterial genetics Cold Spring Harbor Labs., 1960-62; NIH postdoctoral fellow U. Hawaii Med. Sch., 1965; asst. prof. Mich. State U., East Lansing, 1965-70; assoc. prof. Mich. State U., 1970-72; prof., head dept. biology U. S.C., Columbia, 1973-75; prof., head dept. genetics N.C. State U., Raleigh, 1975-85; disting. univ. research prof. N.C. State U., 1985—; mem. Inst. Molecular Biology and Biotechnology, Research. Ctr. Crete, Greece; vis. prof. genetics U. Calif., Davis, 1969; vis. prof. OAS, Argentina, Chile and Brazil, 1972; mem. recombinant DNA adv. com. NIH. Author: Physiological Genetics, 1979; editor: Developmental Genetics, Advances in Genetics, Current Topics in Medical and Biological Research; co-editor: Isozymes, 4 vols., 1975, Monographs in Developmental Biology, 1968-86; molecular biology editor Physiol. Plant, 1988—. Served with USAF, 1957. Alexander von Humboldt travel fellow, 1976; mem. exchange program NAS, U.S.-USSR. Fellow AAAS; mem. Genetics Soc. Am., Am. Soc. Biochemistry and Molecular Biology, Am. Genetic Assn. (pres.), Soc. Devel. Biology (dir.), Am. Inst. Biol. Scis., Am. Soc. Plant Physiologists, N.Y. Acad. Scis., Sigma Xi. Office: NC State U Dept Genetics PO Box 7614 Raleigh NC 27695

SCANLAN, DONNA ROBIN, epidemiologist; b. Portsmouth, Va., Nov. 25, 1962; d. David S. and Elaine Sandra (Firester) Lesser; m. Barry A. Scanlan, Dec. 29, 1985; children: Lauren Nicole, Jason Brendan. BA, Skidmore Coll., 1984; DO, C.O.M.P., Pomona, Calif., 1989. Intern in internal medicine L.I.J. Med. Ctr., New Hyde Park, N.Y., 1989-90; resident in internal medicine L.I.J. Med. Ctr., New Hyde Park, 1990-92, fellowship infectious disease, 1992-94; physician Carolinas Infectious Disease, Gastonia, N.C., 1994—. Office: Carolinas Infectious Disease 1034 X Ray Dr Gastonia NC 28054

SCANLON, DERALEE ROSE, registered dietitian, educator, author; b. Santa Monica, Calif., Aug. 16, 1950; d. Stanley Ralph and Demba (Runkle) S.; m. Alex Spataru, July 20, 1970 (div. 1974). AA, Santa Monica Coll., 1968; accred. med. record tech., East L.A. Coll., 1980; BS, U. Calif., L.A., 1984. Registered Dietitian. V.p. corp. sales, nutrition dir. LIfeTrends Corp., Carlsbad, Calif., 1984-86; dir. media, nutrition Irvine Ranch Farmers Markets, L.A., 1987-88; spokesperson for media Calif. Milk Adv. Bd., San. Diego, 1986; nutrition reporter Med-NIWS, L.A., 1990-91; dietitian Sta. ABC-TV The Home Show, L.A., 1991-92, Sta. NBC-TV David Horowitz Fight Back, L.A., 1991-92; dietitian, nutrition reporter Sta. KTTV-TV Good Day L.A., 1994-95; nutritionist Sta. KABC-TV Kids View, 1994—; co-host talk radio show Light and Lively, KABC, 1994—; mgr. Nutrition Svcs. Vitex Foods, Inc., 1995-96; spokesperson Sandoz Nutrition, 1995-96; host nat. cable TV health show To Your Health, 1996—; media spokesperson Lifetime Food Co., Seaside, Calif., 1992—, Interior Design Nutritionals, Provo, Utah, 1993—, Weight Watchers, 1993-94; contbr. writer L.A. Parent Mag., Burbank, Calif., 1991—; syndicated nutrition reporter Live N'Well TV Series, Utah, 1992-93; nutrition educator Emeritus Coll. Sr. Health, Santa Monica, 1990-92; nutrition lectr. Princess Cruises, L.A., 1987; nutrition video host AMA Campaign Against Cholesterol, 1989; lectr. on nutrition and health to various orgns., 1993—; leader seminar series on I.B.S. UCLA Med. Ctr., 1994-95, others. Author: The Wellness Book of IBS, 1989, Diets That Work, 1991, rev. edit., 1992, 93; newspaper columnist: Ask the Dietitian, 1990-94; columnist Natural Way Mag.; Ask the Dietitian column in The Natural Way Mag., 1995; contbr. articles to profl. jours. Mem. AFTRA, Dietitians in Bus./Comms. (regional rep. 1990-92, So. Calif. chairperson 1991-92, editor nat. newsletter 1994-96), Am. Dietetic Assn. (pub. rels. chair 1985-87), Calif. Dietetic Assn. (Dietitian of Yr. in Pvt. Practice, Bus. and Comm. 1993), Soc. for Nutrition Edn., Nat. Speakers Assn. Home and Office: 10613 Eastborne Ave Los Angeles CA 90024-5920

SCANLON, EDWARD CHARLES, clinical psychologist; b. Bradford, Pa., Dec. 3, 1931; s. Edward John Scanlan and Martha (Karlous) Charles; m. Constance Morgan, May 19, 1962 (div. Jan. 1976); 1 child, Heather Marie. AB cum laude, SUNY, Buffalo, 1954; EdM, Harvard U., 1958, EdD, 1961; postgrad., Columbia U. Lic. psychologist, Pa. Assoc. prof. Lehigh U., Bethlehem, Pa., 1961-66; acad. dean Montgomery County C.C., Conshahoken, Pa., 1966-69; acting. dir. home sch. Wilkes Coll., Wilkes Barre, Pa., 1968-71; clin. psychologist dept. human svcs. mental health and mental retardation Northampton County Dept. Human Svcs., Easton, Pa., 1972—; vis. prof. clin. psychology Clinic Mental Health and Mental Retardation, Pottsville, Pa., 1971-72. Capt. USAF, 1954-57. Thayer scholar Harvard U. Mem. APA, Pa. Psychol. Assn., Harvard Club of Phila., Lehigh Country Club, Masons, Phi Beta Kappa. Democrat. Anglican. Office: Bridal Path Woods D-2 Bethlehem PA 18017

SCANLON, JOHN CHARLES, internist, pulmonary and critical care specialist; b. Cleve., Jan. 25, 1940; s. Charles Patrick and Mary Abigail (Bahm) S.; m. Phyllis Catherine Steinker, May 8, 1965; children: Matthew, Lisa, Susan, Daniel. HAB, Xavier U., 1961; MD, Loyola U., Chgo., 1965. Diplomate Am. Bd. Internal Medicine. Intern St. Vincent Charity Hosp., Cleve., 1965-66; resident Cleve. Clinic, 1968-71; pulmonary and criticial care and internal medicine physician Arnett Clinic, Lafayette, Ind., 1971—; med. dir. respiratory svcs., St. Elizabeth Hosp., Lafayette, Ind., 1971—, Lafayette Home Hosp., 1976—. Capt. U.S. Army, 1966-68. Fellow Am. Coll. Chest Physicians; Am. Thoracic Soc., Ind. State Med. Assn., Tippecanoe County Med. Assn. Roman Catholic. Home: 1713 Sandpiper West Lafayette IN 47906 Office: Arnett Clinic 1500 Salem St Lafayette IN 47904

SCANLON, SHAUN JAMES, healthcare executive; b. Holyoke, Mass., Apr. 14, 1939; s. Henry James and Alida Juliette (Blais) S.; m. Linda Entwistle, Dec. 31, 1963; children: Bruce, Stuart. AB, Harvard U., 1960; MBA, Columbia U., 1966. Asst. bus. mgr. Time, Inc., N.Y.C., 1966-69; sr. cons. mgmt. Touche Ross & Co., Detroit, 1969-70; mgr. acctg. systems Jacobson Stores, Jackson, Mich., 1970-71; fin. adminstr. Henry Ford Hosp., Detroit, 1971-83; v.p. fin., chief fin. officer Michael Reese Hosp. and Med. Ctr., Chgo., 1983-87; cons. Naperville, Ill., 1987-88; v.p. fin., chief fin. officer Bay State Med. Ctr., Springfield, Mass., 1988—; mem. fin. com. Baystate Health Sys. Ins. Co., 1989—; adj. lectr. Grad. Sch. Pub. Health U. Mich., Ann Arbor, 1981-83. Chmn. medicaid task force Ill. Hosp. Assn., Naperville, 1985-86, mem. fin. com., 1984-87. Capt. U.S. Army, 1960-64. Mem. Mass. Hosp. Assn. (mem. fin. com. 1994—, chmn. fin. subcom. Mass. payment issues 1994—), Am. Legion, Harvard Varsity Club. Home: 7 Hilltop Dr Wilbraham MA 01095-1742 Office: Bay State Med Ctr 759 Chestnut St Springfield MA 01199-1001

SCARLATA, PAUL ANTHONY, oral surgeon; b. McKeesport, Pa., Apr. 3, 1935; s. Joseph Mario and Josephine Gloria (Battaglia) S.; B.S., U. Pitts., 1957, D.D.S., D.M.D., 1961; m. Mary Jane Parks, June 15, 1963 (dec. 1982); children: Stephanie, Anthony, Christopher, Matthew, Sarah; m. Darla K. Hosler, May 27, 1988 (div. 1994). Resident in oral surgery Western Pa. Hosp., Pitts., 1962-63, St. Luke's Hosp., N.Y.C., 1963-64; practice gen. dentistry and oral surgery, Chambersburg, Pa., 1967—; chief dental service Chambersburg Hosp., 1974-76, 82-84. Treas., Franklin County (Pa.) Heritage, 1971—, pres., 1977-78. Served with AUS, 1964-67. Recipient Buhl Planetarium Sci. award 1st prize Astronomy 6" Newtonian Reflector, 1952. Fellow Am. Assn. Oral and Maxillofacial Surgeons; mem. ADA, Pa., Western Pa., Gt. Lakes socs. oral surgeons, N.Y. Soc. Clin. Oral Pathologists, Am. Dental Soc. of Anesthetists, Cumberland Valley Dental Soc. (pres. 1982-83). Clubs: Chambersburg, South Penn Chess, Cumberland Valley Railroad Enthusiasts, Cumberland Valley Torch (Chambersburg), Antique Studebakers Club, Lions Greater Washington Mercedes Benz. Home: 444 Franklin Square Dr Chambersburg PA 17201-1465 Office: 556 E Queen St Chambersburg PA 17201-2942

SCARNATI, RICHARD ALFRED, psychiatrist; b. Pitts., Dec. 18, 1940. Diploma in Phys. Therapy, D.T. Watson Sch. Physiatrics, Leetsdale, Pa., 1966; BS in Phys. Therapy, U. Pitts., 1966; MA in Health and Safety, Calif. State U., L.A., 1969; DO, Chgo. Coll. Osteo. Medicine, 1976. Diplomate Am. Bd. Psychiatry and Neurology. Psychiatrist Monroe Ctr. for Mental Health, Richmond, Va., 1979; prison psychiatrist Ohio Dept. Mental Health, Columbus, 1979-81; psychiatrist VA Hosp., Hampton, Va., 1981-82, VA Outpatient Clinic, Harrisburg, Pa., 1982-83, Harrisburg (Pa.) Hosp., Cin., 1984; prison psychiatrist Ohio Dept. Mental Health, Cin., 1985-91; psychiatrist North Ctrl. Mental Health Svcs., Columbus, 1992—; clin. asst. prof. psychiatry U. cin., 1985-92, Tex. Coll. Osteo. Medicine, Ft. Worth, 1990-94, Ohio State U., Columbus, 1992—, Ohio U. Coll. Osteo. Medicine, Athens, 1993-96, vol. faculty, 1987—, clin. assoc. prof. psychiatry, 1996—. Contbr. articles to profl. jours. With U.S. Army, 1960-63, Korea. Recipient Hon. Mention for Disting. Svcs., Spl. Olympics, 1979. Mem. Am. Psychiatrist Assn., Am. Acad. Psychiatry and the Law, Am. Osteo. Assn., Am. Coll. Neuro Psychiatrists (assoc.), World Psychiat. Assn., Physicians for Human Rights, Physicians for Social Responsibility, Ohio Psychiat. Assn., Psychiatrist Soc. Cen. Ohio, Christian Med. Dental Soc., Amnesty Internat., Common Cause, Sierra Club (life), Pub. Citizen. Roman Catholic. Home: PO Box 20203 Columbus OH 43220 Office: North Ctrl Mental Health Svcs 1301 N High St Columbus OH 43201

SCAROLA, JOHN MICHAEL, dentist, educator; b. N.Y.C., Nov. 18, 1934; s. Michael Fidelis and Filomena Mary (Turso) S.; m. Theodora Mary Marty, June 15, 1963; children: Michael A., John P., Stephen A., Robert M., Mary E. BS, Fordham Coll., 1956; DDS, Columbia U., 1960. Instr. Columbia Dental Sch., N.Y.C., 1962-68, asst. clin. prof., 1969-72, course dir. fixed partial dentures, 1969-72, assoc. clin. prof., 1973-86, course dir. prosthodontic elective, 1977-91, clin. prof., 1986—; lectr. postgrad. prostodontics Columbia U., N.Y.C., 1986—, AEGD-Columbia U., N.Y.C., 1990-92, Luth. Med. Ctr., Bklyn., 1993—; cons. in prosthodontics Northport VA Hosp., East Northport, N.Y., 1970-91. Scoutmaster Boy Scouts Am., Port Washington, N.Y., 1976-78; chmn. spl. gifts Bishop's Annual Appeal, St. Peter's Port Washington, 1977-78; Cath. Youth Orgn. sports coach St. Paul The Apostle, Brookville, N.Y., 1980-83; fundraising com. The Yard, Martha's Vineyard, Mass., 1990; concert com. Musician's Emergency Fund, N.Y.C., 1992. Lt. USNR, 1960-62. Fellow Am. Coll. Dentists (chmn. N.Y. sect. 1994), N.Y. Acad. Dentistry (pres. 1939-90), Greater N.Y. Acad. Prosthodontics (dir. 1993-95); mem. Greater N.Y. Acad. Prosthodontics Found. (dir., pres. 1989-95), N.Y. Acad. Dentistry Endowment Fund (dir., pres. 1992-93). Republican. Roman Catholic. Home: 83 Fruitledge Rd Brookville NY 11545 Office: 501 Madison Ave New York NY 10022

SCARPATI, DANIELE FRANCESCO, radiotherapist; b. Genoa, Italy, Aug. 26, 1947; s. Ferrante and Eloisa (Bemporad) S.; m. Andreina Avalle, Apr. 7, 1973; children: Francesco, Giovanni Battista, Maria Clementina. Degree in med. surg., U. Genoa, 1972, fellow Radiol., 1976, fellow Oncology, 1980. Asst. prof. Inst. Radiol. U. Genoa (Italy), 1976-92; assoc. prof. radiobiolgy U. Genoa, 1992. Office: Institute Radiology, Via le Benedetto XV 10, 16132 Genoa Italy

SCARR, SANDRA WOOD, psychology educator, researcher; b. Washington, Aug. 8, 1936; d. John Ruxton and Jane (Powell) Wood; m. Harry Alan Scarr, Dec. 26, 1961 (div. 1970); children: Phillip, Karen, Rebbecca, Stephanie; m. James Callan Walker, Aug. 9, 1982 (div. 1994). AB, Vassar Coll., 1958; AM, Harvard U., 1963, PhD, 1965. Asst. prof. psychology U. Md., College Park, 1964-67; assoc. prof. U. Pa., Phila., 1967-71; prof. U. Minn., Mpls., 1971-77, Yale U., New Haven, 1977-83; Commonwealth prof. U. Va., Charlottesville, 1983-95, chmn. dept. psychology, 1984-90; CEO, chmn. bd. dirs. KinderCare Learning Ctr., Inc., 1995—; mem. nat. adv. bd. Robert Wood Johnson Found., Princeton, N.J., 1985-91; coord. coun. psychology SUNY Bd. Regents, N.Y.C., 1984-92; prof. Kerstin Hesselgren, Sweden, 1993-94. Author: Race, Social Class and Individual Differences in IQ, 1981, Mother Care/Other Care, 1984 (Nat. Book award APA 1985), Caring for Children, 1989; editor Jour. Devel. Psychology, 1980-86, Current Directions in Psychol. Sci., 1991-95. Fellow Ctr. for Advanced Studies, Stanford U., Calif., 1976-77; grantee NIH, NSF, others, 1967—. Fellow AAAS, APA (chmn. com. on human rsch. 1980-83, coun. of reps. 1984—, bd. dirs. 1988—, pres.-elect 1995—, Award for Disting. Contbn. to Rsch. on Pub. Policy 1988), Am. Psychol. Soc. (bd. dirs. 1991—, James McKeen Cattell award 1993); mem. Am. Acad. Arts and Scis., Behavior Genetics Assn. (pres. 1985-86, mem. exec. coun. 1976-79, 84-87), Soc. for Rsch. in Child Devel. (governing coun. 1974-76, 87-93, chmn. fin. com. 1987-89, pres. 1989-91), Internat. Soc. for Study of Behavioral Devel. (exec. bd. 1987-94). Democrat. Home: 1243 Maple View Dr Charlottesville VA 22902-8779 Office: U Va Dept Psychology Charlottesville VA 22903

SCARROW, PAMELA KAY, health care manager; b. Washington, Nov. 4, 1949; d. Edward Charles and Elsie Lorine (Kay) Scarrow; m. Antonio Joseph Franz, Sept. 4, 1979; 1 child, Vanessa Motil Franz. AA, Navarro Coll., Tex., 1981; BS, Golden Gate U., 1983. Cert. med. staff coordinator, 1986, cert. profl. healthcare quality, 1996. Adminstrv. asst. Trust Ter. of the Pacific Islands, Saipan, Mariana Islands, 1976-79; adminstrv. asst. Navarro Coll., Corsicana, Tex., 1979-81; staff asst. San Francisco Symphony, 1981-82; med. staff liaison Calif. Med. Assn., San Francisco, 1982-87; provider, practitioner cons. Calif. Med. Rev., Inc., San Francisco, 1987-90; med. rev. specialist Am. Med. Peer Rev. Assn., Washington, 1990-93; adminstr. quality assessment Am. Coll. Ob-gyn., 1993—. Democrat. Roman Catholic. Office: Am Coll Ob-gyn 409 12th St SW Washington DC 20024-2125

SCARSE, OLIVIA MARIE, cardiologist, consultant; b. Chgo., Nov. 10, 1950; d. Oliver Marcus and Marjorie Ardis (Olsen) S. BS, North Park Coll., 1970; MD, Loyola U., Maywood, Ill., 1973. Diplomate Am. Bd. Internal Medicine, Am. Bd. Cardiovascular Diseases. Surg. intern Resurrection Hosp., Chgo., 1974; resident in internal medicine Northwestern U., Chgo., 1974-77; cardiovascular disease fellow U. Ill., Chgo., 1977-80; dir. cardiac catherization lab. Cook County Hosp., Chgo., 1981; dir. heart sta. MacNeal Hosp., Berwyn, Ill., 1983; dir. electrophysiology Hines VA Hosp., Maywood, Ill., 1984-85; dir. progressive care Columbus Hosp., Chgo., 1985-88, pvt. practice, 1984—; pvt. practice Ill. Masonic Hosp., Chgo., 1989—; founder Physician Cons. for Evaluation of Clin. Pathways, Practice Parameter and Patient Care Outcomes, 1991. Dir. continuous quality improvement Improvement Columbus, 1990-95. Pillsbury fellow Pillsbury Fund, 1980. Fellow Am. Coll. Cardiology; mem. AMA, ACP, Chgo. Med. Assn., Ill. State Med. Assn., Am. Heart Assn., Crescent Countries Found. for Med. Care, Physicians Health Network, Cen. Ill. Med. Review Orgn. Home and Office: 2650 N Lakeview Ave Apt 4109 Chicago IL 60614-1833

SCASTA, DAVID LYNN, psychiatrist; b. Austin, Tex., Dec. 13, 1949; s. Albert Ray and Helen Pearl (Hennessy) S. BA, Baylor U., 1972; MD, Baylor Coll. of Medicine, 1977. Diplomate Am. Bd. Psychiatry and Neurology. Staff physician U. Houston, 1977-78; adminstr. Temple U. Med. Sch., Phila., 1982-83; residency in psychiatry Temple U. Hosp., Phila., 1982; dir. consultation svcs. Grad. Hosp., Phila. 1983-84; dir. outpatient programs Phila. Psychiat. Ctr., 1983-84; pvt. practice Grad. Hosp. Phila. Psychiat. Ctr., 1984-89; med. dir. Phila. Consultation Ctr., 1987-89; attending psychiatrist, chair dept. psychiatry Hunterdon Med. Ctr., Flemington, N.J., 1989—, chair dept. menatl health, 1989—; pvt. practice forensic psychiatry New Hope, Pa., 1989—; clin. assoc. prof. dept. psychiatry Temple U. Med. Sch., Phila., 1983—; researcher Assn. Gay and Lesbian Psychiatrist, Phila., 1989—. Editor Jour. of Gay & Lesbian Psychotherapy, 1987-94. Dist. rep. Rep. Party of Tex., Houston, 1977, precinct sec., 1975-77; rep. Phila. Bapt. Assn., bd. dirs. Named Ginsberg Fellow Group for Advancement of Psychiatry, 1980-82. Mem. Assn. Gay and Lesbian Psychiatrists (pres., newsletter editor 1987-94), Am. Psychiat. Assn., Parents and Friends of Lesbians and Gays, Am. Acad. Psychiatry and the Law. Republican. Office: Hunterdon Med Ctr Dept Mental Health 2100 Wescott Dr Flemington NJ 08822-4603

SCEATS, D. JAMES, JR., neurological surgeon; b. Pueblo, Colo., Aug. 15, 1956; s. Donald James Sr. and Marsha (Marsh) S.; m. Deborah Anne Jalowiec, May 22, 1988 (div. Dec. 1994); children: Lindsey Anne, Hunter James. BA in Chemistry summa cum laude, Waitman Coll., 1978; MD with honors, U. Colo., 1982. Diplomate Am. Bd. Neurol. Surgery, Nat. Bd. Med. Examiners. Intern U. Colo., Denver, 1982-83; resident in neurol. surgery U. Fla., Gainesville, 1989; neurol. surgeon Colorado Springs (Colo.) Neurol. Assoc., 1989-96; v.p. Colo. Springs Neurol. Assoc. Contbr. articles to profl. jours. Recipient Analytical Chemistry award Am. Chem. Soc., 1977. Mem. Am. Assn. Neurol. Surgeons, Congress Neurol. Surgeons, Colo. Med. Soc., El Paso County Med. Soc., Phi Beta Kappa. Republican. Office: Colorado Springs Neurol 2125 La Salle Colorado Springs CO 80909

SCHAAF, BERNARD, urologist; b. Durham, N.C., Nov. 24, 1936; s. Bernard J. and Helen (Drennon) S.; m. Madeleine lyne Carignan, Aug. 24, 1985; children: Gisèle Hélène, Renée Carignan. BA magna cum laude, Washington and Lee U., 1957; MD, Wash. U., St. Louis, 1962. Diplomate Am. Bd. Urology. Mixed med.-surg. intern Upstate N.Y. Med. Ctr., Syracuse, 1962-63, surg. resident, 1963-67; urology resident Presbyn. Med. Ctr., San Francisco, 1966-69; ptnr. Med. Assocs., Dubuque, Iowa, 1969-76; pvt. practice Lafayette, Ind., 1976-87; HMO practitioner CIGNA Healthplan, L.A., 1987-90; pvt. practice Georgetown, Ky., 1991-93, Pioneer Med. Ctr., Brawley, Calif., 1993—. Lt. USNR med. corps., 1964-66. Office: Pioneer Med Ctr 205 W Legion Rd Brawley CA 92227

SCHACHAR, RONALD A., ophthalmologist; b. Bklyn., Dec. 28, 1941. BS in Physics, CUNY, 1963; MD, SUNY, Bklyn., 1967; PhD in Ophthalmology, U. Chgo., 1975. Diplomate Am. Bd. Ophthalmology, Nat. Bd. Med. Examiners. Intern Sinai Hosp. Balt., 1967-68; resident in ophthalmology U. Chgo., 1970-74, asst. prof., 1974-76; adj. asst. prof. dept. biophysics and physiology U. Tex. Health Sci. Ctr., Dallas, 1975-78; adj. prof. depts. life scis. and physics Bishop Coll., Dallas, 1978-79; adj. prof. dept. physics U. Tex., Arlington, 1979—; vis. prof. dept. ophthalmology U. Ohio, Columbus, 1983; chmn. infectious disease control Meml. Hosp. Denison, 1976; utilization com. Madonna Hosp., 1976; continuing edn. com. Texoma Med. Ctr., 1978; pres., founder Diabetic Retinopathy Found. Contbr. chpts. to books and articles to profl. jours.; patentee in field; author: Intraocular Lenses, 1979, Keratorefraction, 1980, Radial Keratotomy, 1980, Refractive Modulaiton of the Cornea, 1981, Understanding Radial Keratotomy, 1981, Refractive Keratoplasty, 1983, Keratorefractive Surgery, 1989. With USPHS, 1968-70. Grantee Nat. Soc. for Prevention Blindness, 1973, NIH, 1976-80. Fellow ACS; mem. AAAS, Am. Soc. Contemporary Ophthalmology, Ill. Ophthal. Soc., Assn. Rsch. Vision and Ophthalmology, Chgo. Ophthal. Soc., Am. Acad. Ophthalmology and Otolaryngology, Am. Intraocular Lens Soc., Grayson County Med. Soc., Dallas Ophthalm. Soc., Am. Assn. Ophthalmology, Kerato-Refractive Soc., Sigma Xi, Phi Beta Kappa. Office: Presby Corp PO Box 796728 Dallas TX 75379-6728

SCHACHTEL, BARBARA HARRIET LEVIN, epidemiologist, educator; b. Rochester, N.Y., May 27, 1921; d. Lester and Ethel (Neiman) Levin; m. Hyman Judah Schachtel, Oct. 15, 1941; children: Bernard, Ann.Mollie. Student Wellesley Coll., 1939-41; BS, U. Houston, 1951, MA in Psychology, 1967; PhD, U. Tex.-Houston, 1979. Psychol. examiner Meyer Ctr. for Devel. Pediatrics, Tex. Children's Hosp., Houston, 1967-81; instr. dept. pediatrics Baylor Coll. Medicine, Houston, 1967-81, asst. prof. dept. medicine, 1982—; asst. dir. biometry and epidemiology Sid W. Richardson Inst. for Preventive Medicine, Meth. Hosp., Houston, 1981-88, dir. quality assurance, 1988-93; retired 1993; mem. instl. rev. bd. for human rsch. Baylor Coll. Medicine, Houston, 1981-87; mem. devel. bd. U. Tex. Health Sci. Ctr., Houston, 1987—; mem. dean's adv. bd. Sch. Architecture U. Houston, 1987; bd. dirs. Tex. Medical Ctr, 1990-93. Contbr. articles to profl. jours. Vice pres., bd. dirs. Houston-Harris County Mental Health Assn., 1966-67; vice-chmn. bd. mgrs. Harris County Hosp. Dist., Houston, 1974-90, chmn. 1990-92, bd. dirs., 1970-93; trustee Inst. Religion in Tex. Med. Ctr., 1990— bd. mem. Planned Parenthood of Houston, Inc., 1994—, Houston Ind. Sch. Dist. Found., 1993—; sec. Bo Harris County Hosp. Dist. Found. Bd., 1993—. Named Great Texan of Yr., Nat. Found. for Ilietis and Colitis, Houston, 1982, Outstanding Citizen, Houston-Harris County Mental Health Assn., 1985; recipient Good Heart award B'nai Brith Women, 1984, Women of Prominence award Am. Jewish Com., 1991, Mayor's award for outstanding vol. svc., 1994. Mem. APA, APHA, Wellesley Club of Houston (pres. 1968-70). Avocations: golf, tennis, books. Home: 2527 Glen Haven Blvd Houston TX 77030-3511

SCHACHTER, EDWIN NEIL, medical educator; b. N.Y.C., May 10, 1943; s. Franz and Feiga (Zeltzman) S.; m. Deborah Anne Chase, Nov. 15, 1969; children: Karen, Lauren. AB, Columbia U., 1964; MD, NYU, 1968. Intern Bellevue Hosp., 1968-69, resident, 1969-73; asst. prof. Yale U., New Haven, 1973-78, assoc. prof., 1978-84, med. dir. respiratory care, 1974-84; prof., med. dir. respiratory care Mt. Sinai Med. Ctr., N.Y.C., 1984—. Contbr. articles to profl. jours., chpts. to books. Pres. Conn. Respiratory Assn., 1983, Nat. Assn. Med. Dirs. of Respiratory Care, Washington, 1990-92; bd. dirs. Lung Assn. N.Y., N.Y.C., 1994. Lt. comdr. USN, 1970-72. Grantee Nat. Inst. Occpl. Safety and Health, 1987—. Mem. ACP, Am. Thoracic Soc., Am. Assn. Respiratory Care, Am. Physiological Soc. Office: Mt Sinai Med Ctr 1 Gustave L Levy Pl New York NY 10029

SCHACHTER, JOEL BARRY, pharmacologist; b. Lancaster, Pa., Mar. 21, 1959; s. Bernard Zechariah and Rita (Berson) S. BA, Boston U., 1981; PHD, U. Pa., 1992. Postdoctoral rsch. NIH, Bethesda, Md., 1992-94, U. N.C., Chapel Hill, 1994—. Coach gymnastics Arlington YMCA, Arlington, Va., 1990-94. Mem. Soc. Neurosci. Office: U NC Dept Pharmacology Chapel Hill NC 27599

SCHADE, STANLEY GREINERT, JR., hematologist, educator; b. Pitts., Dec. 21, 1933; s. Stanley G. and Charlotte (Marks) S.; m. Sylvia Zottu, Mar. 24, 1966; children: David Stanley, Robert Edward. BA in English, Hamilton Coll., 1955; MD, Yale U., 1961. Diplomate Am. Bd. Internal Medicine, Am. Bd. Hematology, Am. Bd. Oncology. Intern, resident, hematology fellow U. Wis., Madison, 1962-66; chief hematology Westside VA Hosp., Chgo., 1971-77; prof. medicine, chief hematology U. Ill., Chgo., 1978—. Contbr. articles to profl. jours. Served to maj. U.S. Army, 1967-69. Fulbright fellow Tubingen, Fed. Republic of Germany, 1956. Fellow Am. Coll. Physicians; mem. Am. Soc. Hematology. Presbyterian. Home: 189 N Delaplaine Rd Riverside IL 60546-2060 Office: Westside VA Med Ctr Hematology Sect 820 S Damon St Chicago IL 60612-7317

SCHAECHTER, MOSELIO, microbiology educator; b. Milan, Italy, Apr. 26, 1928; children: Judy, John. Student Central U., Ecuador, 1947-49; MA, U. Kans., 1952; PhD, U. Pa., 1954. Postdoctoral fellow State Serum Inst., Copenhagen, 1956-58; instr., asst. prof., assoc. prof. U. Fla., Gainesville, 1958-62; from assoc. prof. to disting. prof. dept. microbiology Tufts U., Boston, 1962-95, prof. emeritus 1995—; adj. prof. San Diego State U., 1995—. Editor: Molecular Biology Bacterial Growth, 1985, Escherichia coli and Salmonella Typhimurium, 1987, 95, Mechanisms of Microbiol. Disease, 1989, 92. Mem. Am. Soc. Microbiology (pres. 1985-86, chmn. internat. activities), Am. Soc. Med. Sch. Microbiology Chmn. (pres. 1984-85, chair internat. activities 1986-94), Soc. Gen. Microbiology, Boston Mycol. Club, Sigma Xi. Avocations: field mycology; hiking. Office: San Diego State U Dept Biology San Diego CA 92182

SCHAEFER, FRANK WILLIAM, III, microbiologist, researcher; b. Dayton, Ohio, Sept. 1, 1942; s. Frank William Jr. and Irene Josephine (Krouse) S. BA, Miami U., Oxford, Ohio, 1964; MS, U. Cin., 1970, PhD, 1973. Rsch. assoc. parasitologist U. Notre Dame, South Bend, Ind., 1973-78; U.S. EPA EPA, Cin., 1978—. Mem. AAAS, Am. Soc. Parasitology, Am. Soc. Microbiology, Am. Water Works Assn., Soc. Protozoologists, Sigma Xi. Home: 9948 McCauley Woods Dr Sharonville OH 45241-1489 Office: US EPA 26 W Martin Luther King Dr W Cincinnati OH 45268

SCHAEFER, LEWIS GEORGE, physicians assistant; b. Flint, Mich., July 23, 1937; s. John George Schaefer (dec.) and Lucile Marie (Burk) Branam; children: Gregory Lewis, Janet Marie. LPN, Letterman Gen. Hosp., San Francisco, 1966; BS, Baylor U., 1974; A in Criminal Justice, Ctrl. Carolina Coll., 1984. Lic. N.C. Physician's asst. U.S. Army, Ft. Bragg, N.C., 1974-78, U.S. Army Civil Svc., Ft. Bragg, N.C., 1978-86, Dept. of Corrections,

McCain, N.C., 1994. With U.S. Army, 1954-78. Mem. Corvettes of Am. Roman Catholic. Home: 736 Carnegie Dr Fayetteville NC 28311

SCHAEFER, ROBERT EARL, retired radiologist and educator; b. Denver, Mar. 29, 1932; s. Samuel Howard and Jenny (Wilan) S.; m. Doris Marti, Feb. 12, 1962. AB, Columbia U., 1954, MD, 1958. Diplomate Am. Bd. Radiology. Intern Stanford U. Hosps., San Francisco, 1958-59; resident Stanford Palo Alto (Calif.) Hosp. Ctr., 1962-65; instr. radiology U. Wash., Seattle, 1965-72, clin. assoc., prof. radiology, 1972-82; radiologist pvt. practice Eastside Radiology Assocs., Bellevue, Wash., 1973-93; cons. in field. Capt. USAF, 1959-61. Mem. Am. Coll. Radiology, Radiol. Soc. North Am., AMA, King County Med. Soc. Home: 2239 W Viewmont Way W Seattle WA 98199-3951

SCHAEFER, ROBERT MARTIN, obstetrician and gynecologist; b. Bklyn., Dec. 26, 1951; s. Jerome and Rebecca (Rosenberg) S.; m. Barbara Lynn Bilotto, July 3, 1994; children: Anthony, Lance. BS, CUNY, 1973; MD, Jefferson Med. Coll., 1980. Diplomate Am. Bd. Ob-Gyn. Intern in medicine NYU Med. Ctr., N.Y.C., 1980-81, resident in anesthesia, 1981-83; fellow in obstet. anesthesia U. Calif.-Irvine Med. Ctr., Orange, 1983-84; resident in ob-gyn. L.I. Coll. Hosp., Bklyn., 1985-89, attending ob-gyn., 1992-94; attending ob-gyn. Brookdale Hosp., Bklyn., 1991-92, S.I. (N.Y.) Hosp., 1991-92, Wabash County Hosp., Wabash, Ind., 1994—. Fellow ACOG. Office: Wabash County Hosp 710 N East St Wabash IN 46992-0548

SCHAEFER, ROLAND MICHAEL, nephrologist, consultant; b. Wuerzburg, Germany, May 18, 1954; s. Gregor and Mathilda (Schaefer) S.; m. Liliana Barbara Denek Schaefer, Mar. 28, 1991; 1 child, Piotr. DMed, Sch. Med., Wuerzburg, Germany, 1973-80. Fellow internal med. and nephrology U. Hosp. Wuerzburg, Germany, 1982-90, asst. prof., 1991-94, prof., 1994—; cons. freelance in fields of biomaterials and genetechnology. Roman Catholic. Home: Moellmannsweg 11, D-48161 Muenster Germany Office: U Muenster, Albert-Schweitzer-Str 33, D-48149 Muenster Germany

SCHAEFFER, DONALD THOMAS, psychologist; b. San Francisco, Oct. 24, 1926; s. Frances and Olive Bernice (Flynn) S.; m. Kathryn Jane Jongewaard, Sept. 4, 1949; children: Donna Louise, Kenneth Conrad, Thomas Bernard. AB, San Jose State U., 1950; MA, San Francisco State U., 1952; EdD, U. Md., 1968. Tchr. Calif. Youth Authority, San Andreas, 1951-53; tchr., counselor Stockton (Calif.) Sch. Dist., 1953-57; psychologist, dir. guidance Lincoln Sch. Dist., Stockton, 1957-61; psychologist, program supr., intern prin. Montgomery County (Md.) Pub. Schs., 1962-88; pvt. psychologist, cons. DeLand, Fla., 1988—. Guardian 7th Cir. Ct., Volvsia County, Fla., 1991—. With USNR, 1944-46. W. T. Grant fellow, 1961-62; Nat. Drug Abuse Tng. Ctr. scholar, 1971-72. Mem. Md. Sch. Psychologists Assn. (state bd. dirs. 1980-81), Audubon Soc., Fla. Trails Assn. Home and Office: 8 Oak Ln De Land FL 32724-4822

SCHAEFFER, LEONARD DAVID, health care executive; b. Chgo., July 28, 1945; s. David and Sarah (Levin) S.; m. Pamela Lee Sidford, Aug. 11, 1968; children: David, Jacqueline. BA, Princeton U., 1969. Mgmt. cons. Arthur Andersen & Co., 1969-73; dep. dir. mgmt. Ill. Mental Health/Devel. Disability, Springfield, 1973-75; dir. Ill. Bur. of Budget, Springfield, 1975-76; v.p. Citibank, N.A., N.Y.C., 1976-78; asst. sec. mgmt. and budget HHS, Washington, 1978; adminstr. HCFA, 1978-80; exec. v.p., COO Student Loan Mktg. Assn., Washington, 1980-82; pres., CEO Group Health, Inc., Mpls., 1983-86; chmn., CEO Blue Cross of Calif., Woodland Hills, 1986—, WellPoint Health Networks Inc., 1992—; bd. dirs. Allergan, Inc., Irvine, Calif., Metra Biosystems; bd. councilors U. So. Calif. Sch. Pub. Adminstrn., 1988—; bd. dirs. exec com. Blue Cross-Blue Shield Assn., Chgo., 1986—; mem. Congl. Prospective Payment Assessment Commn., 1987-93; mem. Pew Health Professions Com., Phila., 1990-93; chmn. bd. trustees Nat. Health Found., L.A., 1992—; chmn. Nat. Inst. Health Care Mgmt., 1993—. Mem. editorial adv. bd. Managed Healthcare, 1989—. Bd. govs. Town Hall of Calif., L.A., 1989—. Kellogg Found. fellow, 1981-89, Internat. fellow King's Fund Coll., London, 1990—; recipient Citation-Outstanding Svc., Am. Acad. Pediats., 1981, Disting. Pub. Svc. award HEW, Washington, 1980. Mem. Cosmos Club, Princeton Club, Regency Club. Office: Blue Cross of Calif 21555 Oxnard St Woodland Hills CA 91367-4943

SCHAEFFER, MARK ALLEN, internist; b. Rochester, N.Y., Feb. 6, 1958; s. Thomas Allen and Marilyn (Boel) S.; m. Amy Hope Freedman, July 25, 1982; children: Jessica Molley, Rachel Leigh. BS, Syracuse U., 1980; MD, N.Y. Med. Coll., 1984. Diplomate Am. Bd. Internal Medicine, Nat. Bd. Med. Examiners. Pvt. practice Princeton (N.J.) Internal Medicine Assocs., 1989—; clin. instr. U. Medicine and Dentistry N.J., New Brunswick, 1993—. Mem. AMA, ACP, Mercer County Med. Soc. Office: Princeton Internal Med Ste 220 281 Witherspoon St Princeton NJ 08550

SCHAFER, MICHAEL DAVID, health care administrator; b. Jamestown, N.D., Feb. 26, 1963; s. Duane Lester and Shirley Ann (Borderud) S.; m. Karina J. Dienstl, Dec. 31, 1992. BA in Bus. Adminstrn./Hosp. Adminstrn., Concordia Coll., 1985; postgrad., U. Minn., 1986-88. Adminstr. Roosevelt Meml. Hosp., Culbertson, Mont., 1985-88; CEO/adminstr. Mille Lacs Health Sys., Onamia, Minn., 1988-90, Cmty. Meml. Hosp., Spooner, Wis., 1990—; mem. nursing home adv. com. Mont. Hosp. Assn., Helena, 1986-88; chair polit. action com. Franciscan Sisters Health Care, Little Falls, Minn., 1989-90. Bd. dirs. Onamia (Minn.) Civic Club, 1989-90; alternate trustee Wis. Hosp. Assn., Madison, 1995—. Mem. Spooner Area C. of C. (bd. dirs. 1992—, pres. 1995), Spooner/Trego Lions Club, Wis. Hosp. Assn. (rural health coun. 1991-94, coun. on pub. policy 1996—, alt. trustee 1995—). Office: Cmty Meml Hosp & NH 819 Ash St Spooner WI 54801

SCHAFER, MICHAEL FREDERICK, orthopedic surgeon; b. Peoria, Ill., Aug. 17, 1942; s. Harold Martin and Frances May (Ward) S.; m. Eileen M. Briggs, Jan. 8, 1966; children—Steven, Brian, Kathy, David, Daniel. B.A., U. Iowa, 1964, M.D., 1967. Diplomate: Am. Bd. Orthopedic Surgery. Intern Chgo. Wesley Meml. Hosp., 1967-68; resident in orthopedic surgery Cook County Program, Northwestern U., Chgo., 1968-72; practice medicine specializing in orthopedic surgery Chgo., 1974—; asst. prof. orthopedic surgery Northwestern U., 1977—; Reyerson prof. and chmn. dept. orthopedic surgery; asso. attending orthopedic surgeon Northwestern Meml. Hosp., 1974—; adj. staff Children's Meml. Hosp., Chgo., 1974—; cons. VA Lakeside Hosp., 1974—; adv. bd. Center Sports Medicine, Northwestern U., 1976—; panelist Bur. Health Manpower, HEW, 1976; sec.-treas. Orthopedic Research and Edn. Found. Contbr. articles to med. jours. Served to maj. U.S. Army, 1973-74. Fellow Am. Orthopaedic Assn., Am. Acad. Orthopaedic Surgeons, Assn. Bone and Joint Surgeons; mem. AMA, Am. Orthopedic Soc. Sports Medicine, Ill. Med. Soc., Chgo. Med. Soc., Internat. Soc. Study of Pain, Scoliosis Rsch. Soc. Roman Catholic. Home: 1815 Ridgewood Ln W Glenview IL 60025-2205 Office: 303 E Chicago Ave Chicago IL 60611-3008

SCHAFER, MICHAEL MOORE, healthcare administrator; b. Springfield, Ill., Feb. 25, 1957; s. Robert Joseph and Harriet (Moore) S.; m. Freda Goff, May 30, 1981; children: Carlyn, Logan, April. BA in Acctg., U. Mo., Columbia, 1980; BSN summa cum laude, Creighton U., 1984; M in Health Care Adminstrn., St. Louis U., 1987. CPA, Mo., RN, Mo. Staff CPA Ingham White and Scherle, St. Louis, 1980-81, Hill, Goerke, Schafer, and Goerke, Scottsbluff, Nebr., 1981-82; evening charge nurse John Cochran VA Hosp., St. Louis, 1984-86; v.p. St. Edward Mercy Med. Ctr., Fort Smith, Ark., 1987-92; adminstr. of clin. svcs. Holt Krock Clinic, Ft. Smith, 1992—. Republican.

SCHAFER, JOEL LANCE, dentist; b. Bklyn., Oct. 13, 1945; s. Martin Alter and Irene Natalie (Shore) S.; m. Susan Anne Swearingen, Feb. 14, 1980 (div.); 1 child, Jericho Katherine. BS, L.I. U., 1967; DDS, Howard U., 1971. Dental intern Eastman Dental Ctr., Rochester, N.Y., 1971-72; gen. practice dentistry, Boulder, Colo., 1973—; evaluator Clin. Rsch. Assocs.; lectr. in field, 1972—. Contbr. articles to dental jours; patentee in field. Advisor Boulder Meals on Wheels; mem. Boulder County Com. for Persons with Disabilities. Named outstanding clinician Boulder County Dental Forum, 1979. Fellow Am. Soc. Dental Aesthetics; mem. ADA, Am. Acad. Oral Implantology, Boulder County Dental Soc., Tau Epsilon Phi, Alpha Omega. Jewish. Home: 4171 S Hampton Cir Boulder CO 80301-1793 Office: 2880 Folsom St Boulder CO 80304-3739

SCHAFFERT, DAVID A., neurologist; b. Asheville, N.C., May 14, 1958; m. Denise. BS with high honors, Mich. State U., 1980, MD, 1985. Neurologist pvt. practice, Midland, Mich., 1989—. Office: 555 W. Wackerly Ste 3625 Midland MI 48640

SCHAFFLER, MITCHELL BARRY, research scientist, anatomist, educator; b. Bronx, N.Y., Apr. 10, 1957; s. Walter and Shirley (Balter) S. BS, SUNY, Stony Brook, 1978; PhD, W.Va. U., 1985. Rsch. fellow in radiobiology U. Utah, Salt Lake City, 1985-87; asst. prof. U. Calif., San Diego, 1987-90; assoc. prof. and sect. head anatomy Bone and Joint Ctr. Henry Ford Health Scis. Ctr., Detroit, 1990—, Case Western Res. U., 1990—; adj. prof. Anatomy U. Mich., Ann Arbor, 1990—. Mem. editl. bd. Bone, Jour. Orthop. Rsch.; contbr. articles to profl. jours. Grantee Whitaker Found., 1988, NIH, 1991—, NASA, 1996—. Mem. Am. Assn. Anatomists, Am. Assn. Phys. Anthropology, Am. Soc. Bone Mineral Rsch., Orthop. Rsch. Soc., Sigma Xi, Phi Kappa Phi. Office: Henry Ford Hlth Scis Ctr Bone and Joint Ctr 2799 W Grand Blvd Detroit MI 48202-2608

SCHAFFNER, ROBERT JAY, JR., nurse practitioner; b. Mechanicsburg, Pa., Feb. 25, 1949; s. Robert J. Sr. and Bertha May (Books) S.; m. Ellen Gail Hirsch, Sept. 7, 1974 (div.). BA in English, Edn., U. Mass., 1972; BSN, SUNY, Albany, 1986, DD (hon.), 1986; MS, U. Rochester, 1989; MBA, Simon Grad. Sch. Bus. Adminstr, 1992. RN, N.Y., Mass.; cert. dietitian-nutritionist, N.Y. Head of math. Lear Sch. Inc., Miami, Fla., 1974-81; critical care nurse Strong Meml. Hosp. U. Rochester, N.Y., 1983-86, asst. clinician burn ICU, 1986-89, clin. specialist, nurse practitioner, 1990—; clin. assoc. faculty U. Rochester, 1992—; nurse practitioner J.L. Norris Clinic, Rochester, 1993—; exec. com. profl. Nursing Orgn., Rochester, 1988-90, chair-elect, 1989; co-founder Men in Nursing Orgn., Rochester, chair, 1991-92, v.p. Am. assembly, 1993—; mem. nursing faculty com. Regents Coll., 1992—; presenter in field; ceo RSA Assocs., 1986—. Author: poetry (A Best New Poet of 1988, Golden Poet award 1989, Poet of Merit, Am. Poetry Assn. 1989); contbr. articles to profl. jours. CPR instr., disaster action team vol., ARC, 1987—; blood pressure monitor ARC, Boston, 1982-83. Recipient Eleanor Hall award, 1989, Outstanding Svc. award SUNY; Mary Riddle scholar Newton Wellesley Sch. Nursing, 1983; Commonwealth Exec. Nurse fellow, 1989; named Internat. Citizen of Yr. Hutt River Province, 1996. Mem. AACN, Am. Burn Assn., Am. Soc. Parenteral and Enteral Nutrition, N.Y. State Nurses Assn., Genesee Valley Nurses Assn. (bd. dirs. 1995—), SUNY-Albany Alumni Assn. (v.p., trustee 1989-95), U. Mass. Alumni Assn. (nominations com.), Sigma Theta Tau (fin. com.). Home: 71 S Estate Dr Webster NY 14580-2809 Office: U Rochester Med Ctr 601 Elmwood Ave PO Box 667 Rochester NY 14642

SCHAFRANK, MICHAEL STEVEN, ophthalmologist; b. N.Y.C., Oct. 11, 1935; s. Benjamin and Betty (Alper) S.; m. Phyllis T. Solomon, June 7, 1958; children: Scott, Francine. BS, Queen's Coll., 1956; MD, SUNY, 1960. Internship internal medicine Jewish Hosp. Bklyn., 1960-61; resident ophthalmology NYU Med. Ctr., N.Y.C., 1961-64; chief ophthalmology John Moses Meml. Hosp., Minot, N.D., 1964-66; attending ophthalmology, clin. instr. ophthalmology NYU, 1966—; clin. instr. in ophthalmology NYU, 1966—, Bellevue Med. Ctr. Hosp., N.Y.C., 1966—; attending physician in ophthalmology, teaching staff North Shore U. Hosp., Manhasset, N.Y., 1970—. Fellow Am. Acad. Ophthalmology, ACS. Office: 72-35 112th St Forest Hills NY 11375-5469

SCHAIBLE, STEVEN REINHOLD, mental health professional; b. Elgin, N.D., July 10, 1958; s. Reinhold and Helen (Lorenz) S.; 1 child from previous marriage, Rian Rita; m. Natalie Marker, 1994. BA in Sociology, U. N.D., 1981; MS in Pub. Adminstrn., Sage Coll., 1991; MS in Counseling, SUNY, Plattsburgh, 1991. Employment coord. Adirondack House, Westport, N.Y., 1986-87; family support worker Assn. Retarded Children, Plattsburgh, 1986-88; clinician Franklin Grand Isle Mental Health Inst., St. Albans, Vt., 1987-88; asst. mgr. Electronics Boutique, Plattsburgh, 1988-90; cons. Dept. Social Svcs., Plattsburgh, 1990—; ombudsman, client advocate Sunmount Devel. Ctr., Tupper Lake, N.Y., 1988—; coord., cons. Child Abuse Prevention Coun., Plattsburgh, 1990-91. Mem. AACD, Pub. Offender Counseling Assn., Am. Rehab. Assn., Am. Assn. Mental Retardation. Home and Office: PO Box 690741 Orlando FL 32869-0741

SCHAIE, K(LAUS) WARNER, human development and psychology educator, researcher; b. Stettin, Germany (now Poland), Feb. 1, 1928; came to U.S., 1947, naturalized, 1953; s. Sally and Lottie Louise (Gabriel) S.; m. Coloma J. Harrison, Aug. 9, 1953 (div. 1973); 1 child, Stephan; m. Sherry L. Willis, Nov. 20, 1981. A.A., City Coll. San Francisco, 1951; B.A., U. Calif.-Berkeley, 1952; M.S. U. Wash., 1953, Ph.D., 1956. Lic. psychologist, Calif., Pa. Postdoctoral fellow Washington U., St. Louis, 1956-57; asst. prof. psychology U. Nebr., Lincoln, 1957-1964, assoc. prof., 1964-68; prof., chmn. dept. psychology W.Va. U., Morgantown, 1964-73; prof. psychology, dir. Gerontology Research Inst., U. So. Calif., 1973-81; Evan Pugh prof. human devel. and psychology, dir. Gerontology Ctr., Pa. State U., University Park, 1981—; mem. devel. behavior study sect. NIH, Bethesda, Md., 1970-72, chmn., 1972-74, chmn. human devel. and aging study sect., 1979-84, mem. expert panel in comml. airline pilot retirement, 1981, data and safety bd. shep project, 1984-91. Author: Developmental Psychology; A Life Span Approach, 1981; Adult Development and Aging, 1982, 4th rev. edit., 1996, Older Adults-Decision Making and the Law, 1996; editor: Handbook of Psychology of Aging, 1977, 4th rev. edit., 1996, Longitudinal Studies of Adult Development, 1983, Cognitive Functioning and Social Structure over the Life Course, 1987, Methodological Issues in Research on Aging, 1988, Social Structure and Aging: Psychological Processes, 1989, Age Structuring in Comparative Perspective, 1989, The Course of Later Life, 1989, Self-Directedness: Cause and Effects Throughout the Life Course, 1990, Aging, Health Behaviors and Health Outcomes, 1992, Caregiving Systems: Formal and Informal Helpers, 1993, Societal Impact on Aging: Historical Perspectives, 1993, Adult Intergenerational Relations: Effects of Societal Change, 1995, Older Adults Decision Making and the Law, 1996; editor Ann. Rev. Gerontology and Geriatrics vol. 7, 1987, vol. 11, 1991; contbr. articles to profl. jours. Fellow APA (coun. reps. 1976-79, 83-86, Disting. Contbn. award 1982, Disting. Scientific Conbns. award, 1992), Gerontol. Soc. (Kleemeier award 1987), Am. Psychol. Soc.; mem. Psychometric Soc., Internat. Soc. Study Behavioral Devel. Unitarian. Avocations: hiking; stamps. Home: 425 Windmere Dr # 3A State College PA 16801 Office: Pa State U Dept Human Devel & Family Studies University Park PA 16802

SCHALLER, JANE GREEN, pediatrician; b. Cleve., June 26, 1934; d. George and May Alice (Wing) Green; children: Robert Thomas, George Charles, Margaret May. A.B., Hiram (Ohio) Coll., 1956; M.D. cum laude, Harvard U., 1960. Diplomate Am. Bd. Pediatrics, Am. Bd. Med. Examiners. Resident in pediatrics Children's Hosp.-U. Wash., Seattle, 1960-63; fellow immunology Children's Hosp. U. Wash., 1963-65; mem. faculty U. Wash. Med. Sch., 1965-83, prof. pediatrics, 1975-83; head div. rheumatic diseases Children's Hosp., Seattle, 1968-83; prof., chmn. dept. pediatrics Tufts U. Sch. Medicine/New Eng. Med. Ctr., 1983—; pediatrician-in-chief Boston Floating Hosp., 1983—; vis. physician Med. Rsch. Coun., Taplow, Eng., 1971-72; tech. advisor UN Study on the Impact of Armed Conflict on Children. Author articles in field.; Editorial bds. profl. jours. Bd. dirs. Seattle Chamber Music Festival, 1982-85; trustee Boston Chamber Music Soc., 1985—; mem. Boston adv. coun. UNICEF. Mem. Inst. Medicine of NAS, AAAS (sci. and human rights program), Soc. Pediatric Rsch., Am. Pediatric Soc., Am. Acad. Pediatrics (chmn. subcom. on children and human rights 1989—, com. on internat. child health 1990—), Am. Coll. Rheumatology, New Eng. Pediatric Soc. (pres. 1991-93), Assn. Med. Sch. Pediatric Chmn. (exec. com. 1986-89, rep. to coun. on govt. affairs and coun. of acad. socs.), Com. Health in So. Africa (exec. com. 1986—), Physicians for Human Rights (exec. com. 1986—, founding pres. 1986-89), Aesculapian Club (pres. 1988-89), Harvard U. Med. Sch. Alumni Coun. (v.p. 1977-80, pres. 1982-83), Internat. Rescue Com. (med. adv. com., women's commn. for refugee women and children), Mass. Women's Forum, Internat. Women's Forum, Tavern Club, Saturday Club. Office: Floating Hosp for Children 750 Washington St # 286 Boston MA 02111-1533

SCHALLY, ANDREW VICTOR, endocrine oncologist, researcher; b. Poland, Nov. 30, 1926; came to U.S., 1957; s. Casimir Peter and Maria (Lacka) S.; m. Ana Maria Comaru, Aug., 1976; children: Karen, Gordon. B.Sc., McGill U., Can., 1955, Ph.D. in Biochemistry, 1957; 16 hon. doctorates. Research asst. biochemistry Nat. Inst. Med. Research, London, 1949-52; dept. psychiatry McGill U., Montreal, Que., 1952-57; research assoc., asst. prof. physiology and biochemistry Coll. Medicine, Baylor U., Houston, 1957-62; assoc. prof. Tulane U. Sch. Medicine, New Orleans, 1962-67, prof., 1967—; chief Endocrine Polypeptide and Cancer Inst. VA Med. Ctr., New Orleans; sr. med. investigator VA, 1973—. Author several books; contbr. articles to profl. jours. Recipient Van Meter prize Am. Thyroid Assn., 1969; Ayerst-Squibb award Endocrine Soc., 1970; William S. Middletown award VA, 1970; Ch. Mickle award U. Toronto, 1974; Gairdner Internat. award, 1974; Borden award Assn. Am. Med. Colls. and Borden Co. Found., 1975; Lasker Basic Research award, 1975; co-recipient Nobel prize for medicine, 1977; USPHS sr. research fellow, 1961-62. Mem. NAS, AAAS, Endocrine Soc., Am. Physiol. Soc., Soc. Biol. Chemists, Soc. Exptl. Biol. Medicine, Internat. Soc. Rsch. Biology Reprodn., Soc. Study Reprodn., Soc. Internat. Brain Rsch. Orgn., Mex. Acad. Medicine, Am. Soc. Animal Sci., Nat. Acad. Medicine Brazil, Acad. Medicine Venezuela, Acad. Medicine Poland, Acad. Sci. Hungary, Acad. Sci. Russia, Acad. Medicine Poland. Home: 5025 Kawanee Ave Metairie LA 70006-2547 Office: VA Hosp 1601 Perdido St New Orleans LA 70112-1207

SCHAMBRA, PHILIP ELLIS, federal agency administrator, radiobiologist; b. Saginaw, Mich., Nov. 8, 1934; s. William Philip and Gwendolyn Maude (Leister) S.; m. Uta Gertrude Bossel, Mar. 30, 1967 (div. Aug. 1981); children: Eric William Philip, Kirsten Uta, Heidi Maren; m. Donita Bartels Feldman, Aug. 15, 1990. BA, Rice U., 1956; PhD, Yale U., 1961. Examiner Office of Mgmt. and Budget Exec. Office of Pres., Washington, 1968-71, staff mem. Coun. on Environ. Quality, 1971-74; assoc. dir. Nat. Inst. Environ. Health Scis., Research Triangle Park, N.C., 1974-81; chief internat. coordination Fogarty Internat. Ctr. NIH, Bethesda, Md., 1981-84; sci. attache U.S. Embassy, New Delhi, 1984-88; dir. Fogarty Internat. Ctr. NIH, Bethesda, Md., 1988—. Contbr. articles on radiobiology to profl. jours. Recipient Superior Svc. award USPHS, 1989; Nat. Cancer Inst. fellow, 1958, Rsch. fellow NASA, 1964. Mem. AAAS. Home: 9104 Drumaldry Dr Bethesda MD 20817-3341

SCHANBERG, SAUL MURRAY, pharmacology educator; b. Clinton, Mass., Mar. 22, 1933; m. Rachel Weinbaum, Dec. 18, 1956; children: Laura E., Linda S. B.A., Clark U., 1954, M.A., 1956; Ph.D., Yale U., 1961, M.D., 1964. Cons. Calif. Dept. Mental Health, 1962-65; intern in pediatrics Albert Einstein Med. Ctr., N.Y.C., 1964-65; rsch. assoc. NIMH, 1965-67; asst. prof. Duke U. Med. Ctr., Durham, N.C., 1967-69, assoc. prof., 1969-73, prof. of pharmacology, 1973—; prof. psychiatry Duke U. Med. Ctr., 1983—; assoc. dean Duke U. Med. Ctr. Sch., 1987-93, chair pharmacology, 1987-92. Cons. USPHS, Rockville, Md., 1983-84. NIMH grantee, 1968; NIH grantee, 1967. Fellow Am. Coll. Neuropsychopharmacology. Home: 1604 Pinecrest Rd Durham NC 27705-5832 Office: Duke U PO Box 3813 Durham NC 27710-3813

SCHANFIELD, MOSES SAMUEL, geneticist, educator; b. Mpls., Sept. 7, 1944; s. Abraham and Fanny (Schwartz) S. BA in Anthropology, U. Minn., 1966; AM in Anthropology, Harvard U., 1969; PhD in Human Genetics, U. Mich., 1971. Postdoctoral fellow in immunology U. Calif. Med. Ctr., San Francisco, 1971-74, rsch. geneticist, 1974-75; head of blood bank Milw. Blood Ctr., 1975-78; asst. dir. ARC, Washington, 1978-83; exec. dir. Genetic Testing Inst., Atlanta, 1983-85; lab. dir. Analytical Genetic Testing Ctr., Atlanta and Denver, 1985—; adj. asst. prof. Med. Coll. Wis., Milw., 1976-78; adj. assoc. prof. George Washington U., Washington, 1979-83, Emory U., Atlanta, 1984-89; adj. assoc. prof. Univ. Kans., 1992—; affiliated faculty Colo. State Univ., Fort Collins, 1992—. Author, editor: Immunobiology of the Erythrocyte, 1980, International Methods of Forensic DNA Analysis, 1996; contbg. author: Immunogenetic Factors and Thalassaemia of Hepatitis, 1975; contbr. articles to profl. publs. Recipient Gold medal Latin Am. Congress Hemotherapy and Immunohematology, 1979, R&D 100 award, 1993. Fellow Am. Acad. Forensic Sci.; mem. Am. Soc. Crime Lab. Dirs., Am. Soc. Human Genetics, Human Biology Coun., Phi Kappa Phi. Office: Analytical Genetic Testing Ctr 7808 Cherry Crk South Dr # 201 Denver CO 80231-3218

SCHANZER, HARRY, vascular transplant surgeon; b. Santiago, Chile, Mar. 27, 1942; came to U.S., 1971; s. Joaquin and Regina (Rappaport) S.; m. Helena Sobocki, June 9, 1968; children: Karen, Andres. MD, U. Chile, 1968. Intern and resident Mt. Sinai Med. Ctr., N.Y.C., 1971-76; sect. chief VA Med. Ctr., Bronx, N.Y., 1976—; dir. vascular lab. The Mt. Sinai Hosp., N.Y.C., 1980—; prof. The Mt. Sinai Sch. Medicine, N.Y.C., 1985; assoc. attending The Mt. Sinai Hosp., 1981-85, attending dept. surg., 1985; dir. transplant lab. The Mt. Sinai Sch. Medicine, 1977—, dir. surg. rsch., 1989. Author: Use of the Superficial Femoral Vein, 1991, Chronic Venous Stasis, 1990, New Dialysis Access Graft, 1989, Adverse Effect of Penicillin 1M, 1981, 85, Transplant Tolerance, 1987. Active B'Nei Brith, Westchester, N.Y., 1989—; dir. Brotherhood Larchmont Temple, Westchester, 1989—. Recipient Ralph Colp Prize Mt. Sinai Jour., 1985-86, 1989-90, Small Bowel Transplant award Ileitus and Colitis Found., 1987; Devel. Dialysis Access grantee WL Gore, Flagstaff, Ariz., 1984-86. Mem. N.Y. Soc. for Cardiovascular Surg. (sec. 1988-90, pres. 1990—). Office: Mt Sinai Med Ctr One Gustave L Levy Pl New York NY 10029

SCHAPIRA, HANS ERWIN, retired urologist; b. Vienna, Austria, Aug. 1, 1925; s. Paul and Felicitas (Mayer) S.; m. Ruth Jelinek, Aug. 31, 1957; children—Ralph Mark, Paul Victor. M.D. cum laude, U. Rome, 1955; came to U.S., 1956, naturalized, 1960. Intern, The Bronx Hosp., N.Y.C., 1957-58; resident in gen. surgery Beth Israel Hosp., N.Y.C., 1958-59; resident urology Mt. Sinai Med. Center, N.Y.C., 1959-62, clin. asst. urology, 1962-64, now attending in urology, asst. prof. urology, 1965-71, assoc. prof., 1971-81; ret., 1996; clinical prof. urology, 1981; acting chief of service-urology, 1982-84; practice medicine specializing in urology, N.Y.C., 1962—; mem. staffs Mt. Sinai Med. Center. Diplomate Am. Bd. Urology. Fellow A.C.S.; mem. Am. Fertility Soc., N.Y. Acad. Medicine, Am. Urol. Assn. Jewish. Contbr. articles to profl. jours. Home: 335 W 246th St Bronx NY 10471-3333 Office: 157 E 72nd St New York NY 10021-4331

SCHARFF, MATTHEW DANIEL, immunologist, cell biologist, educator; b. N.Y.C., Aug. 28, 1932; s. Harry and Constance S.; m. Carol Held, Dec. 19, 1954; children—Karen, Thomas, David. AB, Brown U., 1954, DrMedSci (hon.), 1994; MD, NYU, 1959. House officer II and IV med. service Boston City Hosp., 1959-61; research asso. NIH, 1961-63; asst. prof. Albert Einstein Coll. Medicine, Yeshiva U., Bronx, N.Y., 1963-67; asso. prof. Albert Einstein Coll. Medicine, Yeshiva U., 1967-71, prof. dept. cell biology, 1971—, chmn. dept., 1972-83, dir. div. biol. scis., 1975-81; asso. dir. Cancer Center, 1975-86, dir., 1986-95. Served with USPHS, 1961-63. Recipient Alumni Achievement award NYU Sch. Medicine, 1980, N.Y. Acad. Medicine medal, 1990, Commemorative award Albert Einstein Coll. Medicine, 1993, hon. Dr. Med. Sci., Brown U., 1994. Mem. Am. Assn. Immunologists, Am. Soc. Clin. Investigation, Nat. Acad. Scis., Am. Acad. Arts and Sci., Phi Beta Kappa, Sigma Xi, Alpha Omega Alpha. Office: Albert Einstein Coll Med Cancer Ctr 1300 Morris Pk Ave Bronx NY 10461-1926

SCHARLACH, ANDREW EDMUND, geriatrics educator; b. San Francisco, July 4, 1951; s. Adrian Edmund and Marilynn Lorraine (Lustig) S.; m. Ilene Benita Conison, Aug. 20, 1983; children: Rebecca Anne, Emily Joelle. BA, U. Calif., Berkeley, 1972; MS, Boston U., 1976; PhD, Stanford U., 1985. Lic. clin. social worker. Dir. adolescent svcs. Jewish Community Ctr., San Francisco, 1976-77; social worker Jewish Home for the Aged, San Francisco, 1977-79; pvt. practice specializing in geriatric cons. San Francisco and L.A., 1979—; teaching fellow Stanford (Calif.) U., 1980-83; asst. prof. U. So. Calif., L.A., 1983-90; assoc. prof. U. Calif., Berkeley, 1990-91, Eugene and Rose Kleiner prof. aging, 1991—, prof., 1995—; bd. dirs. Alzheimer's Disease Assn., 1981-83, Calif. Coun. on Gerontology and Geriatrics; faculty mem. Pacific Geriatric Edn. Ctr., L.A., 1983-90; rsch. assoc. Andrus Gerontology Ctr., L.A., 1984-91; cons. Jewish Fedn., L.A., 1985-90; commr. Lic. Clin. Social Workers Exam., Calif., 1984; dir. Ctr. for Advanced Study of Aging Svcs., 1996—. Author: Elder Care and the Work Force: Blueprint for

Action, 1991, Controversial Issues in Aging, 1996; contbr. articles to profl. jours. Mem. Gerontol. Soc. of Am., Am. Soc. Aging., Am. Psychol. Assn., Nat. Assn. Social Workers, Am. Orthopsychiat. Assn., Nat. Assn. Social Workers (mem. long term care coun. 1985-86), Jewish Fedn. Com. on Aging, Respite Planning Com. Democrat. Jewish. Home: 3032 Oakraider Dr Alamo CA 94507-1436 Office: U Calif Haviland Hall Berkeley CA 94720

SCHAROLD, MARY LOUISE, psychoanalyst, educator; b. Wichita Falls, Tex., Mar. 3, 1943; d. Walter John and Louise Helen (Hartman) Baumgartner; m. William Ballew McCollum, Aug. 23, 1964 (div. 1981); m. Harry Karl Scharold, June 19, 1982; children: Margaret Louise, Walter Ballew. BA with highest distinction, U. Kans., 1964; MD, Baylor Coll. Med., 1968; postgrad. Topeka Inst. for Psychoanalysis, 1981. Diplomate Am. Bd. Psychiatry and Neurology. Intern Meml. Baptist. Hosp., Houston, 1968-69; resident in psychiatry Baylor Coll. Med., Houston, 1969-72, chief resident, 1971-72; practice of medicine specializing in psychoanalysis, Houston, 1972—; asst. prof. Baylor Coll. Med., Houston, 1973-76, asst. clin. prof., 1981-84, assoc. clin. prof., 1984—; dir. Baylor Psychiat. Clinic, Houston, 1973-76; co-dir. Rice U. Psychiat. Service, Houston, 1981-82; asst. clin. prof. U. Kans. Sch. Medicine, Kansas City, 1977-81; teaching assoc. Topeka Inst. Psychoanalysis, 1980-81; instr. Houston-Galveston Psychoanalytic Inst., 1984-86, teaching analyst, 1986-90, tng. and supervising analyst, 1990—, v.p., 1994—; Adv. bd. Leavenworth Mental Health Assn., Kans., 1977-81. Watkins scholar U. Kans., 1961-64. Fellow Am. Psychiatric Assn. (chmn. Tex. peer review 1984-88); mem. Am. Psychoanalytic Assn. (cert. 1982, peer rev. com. 1985-90, prof. ins. commn. 1986-93, bd. profl. stds., 1994—, CME com., 1994—, mem. exec. coun. 1994-96, cert. com. 1994—), Am. Group Psychotherapy Assn., Houston Psychiatric Soc. (v.p. 1984-85, pres. elect 1985-86, pres. 1986-87), Houston-Galveston Psychoanalytic Soc. (sec.-treas. 1984-86, pres.-elect 1986-88, pres. 1988-90, alter councillor 1994-96), Psychiat. Assn. (quality assurance com. 1986-87), Houston Group Psychotherapy Soc. (adv. bd. 1984-85), Mortar Bd., Phi Beta Kappa, Delta Phi Alpha, Alpha Omega Alpha, Hilltopper, Pi Beta Phi Alumni Assn. Republican. Lutheran. Office: 3400 Bissonnet St Ste 170 Houston TX 77005-2153

SCHATTEN, GERALD PHILLIP, cell biologist, reproductive biologist, educator; b. N.Y.C., Nov. 1, 1949; s. Frank and Sylvia Schatten; m. Heather Aronson, July 4, 1994; 1 child, Daniel. BS, U. Calif., Berkeley, 1971, PhD, 1975. Instr. U. Calif., Berkeley, 1975; postdoctoral fellow Rockefeller Found., 1976-77; from asst. prof. to prof. Fla. State U., Tallahassee, 1979-86; prof. molecular biology, zoology and obstetrics gynecology U. Wis., Madison, 1986—, dir. integrated microscopy resource for biomed. rsch., 1986-92, dir. gamete and embryo biol. tng. program, 1989—; dir. gamete and embryo biol. tng. program U. Wis., Madison, 1989—; exec. bd. UNESCO Internat. Cell Rsch. Orgn., 1995—. Recipient Rsch. Career Devel. award NIH, 1981-86. Office: Univ Wis 1117 W Johnson St Madison WI 53706-1705

SCHATZ, ALICE MARIE, nurse, physician assistant; b. Linton, N.D., Apr. 8, 1958; d. Raymond Joseph and Mildred Elizabeth (Kippes) Splonskowski; m. Bruce James Schatz, Aug. 31, 1985; children: Carmen Jane, Craig James. BA, Bismarck State Coll., 1978; B of Nursing, Mary U., 1980; Cert. Physician Asst., U. N.D., 1995. RN, N.D. RN ICU/emergency room/telemetry St. Alexius Med. Ctr., Bismarck, N.D., 1980-86; floor RN Linton Hosp., 1987-90, operating rm. RN, 1987-94; RN/dist. supr. St. Alexius Med. Ctr., 1990-94; physician asst. Linton Hosp., 1995—. EMT program tchr. Linton Ambulance Squad, 1987-90. Fellow Am. Assn. Physican Assts. (cert.). Home: RR 1 Box 135 Linton ND 58552

SCHATZ, ARTHUR JAY, obstetrician, gynecologist; b. Phila., Nov. 30, 1940; s. Sidney and Charlotte (Shestack) S.; m. Elinor Kress, July 26, 1964 (div. 1976); m. Irene Molner, Aug. 26, 1976; children: Laura, Erin, Jennifer. BA, U. Pa., 1962; MD, Jefferson Med. Coll., 1966. Diplomate Nat. Bd. Med. Examiners, Am. Bd. Ob-gyn. Intern Pa. Hosp., Phila., 1966-67, resident in ob-gyn, 1967-70; pvt. practice ob.-gyn. Miami, Fla.; dept. chmn. Parkway Regional Med. Ctr., Miami, 1984-88; med. dir. Ladies Ctr. S. Fla., Miami, 1987—. Major U.S. Army, 1970-72. Fellow Am. Coll. Ob-gyn., Am. Coll. Surgery, Am. Fertility Soc.; mem. Am. Coll. Cryosurgery, N. Am. Menopause Soc., Fallopius Internat., William Little Ob-Gyn. Soc., Fla. Ob-gyn Soc., Fla. Med. Assn., Dade County Med. Assn. Jewish. Office: 20801 Biscayne Blvd Ste 100 Aventura FL 33180

SCHATZ, IRWIN JACOB, cardiologist; b. St. Boniface, Man., Can., Oct. 16, 1931; came to U.S., 1956, naturalized, 1966; s. Jacob and Reva S.; m. Barbara Jane Binder, Nov. 12, 1967; children: Jacob, Edward, Stephen and Brian (twins). Student, U. Man., Can.), Winnipeg, 1951, M.D. with honors, 1956. Diplomate: Am. Bd. Internal Medicine. Intern Vancouver (B.C.) Gen. Hosp., 1955-56; resident Hammersmith Hosp., U. London, 1957, Mayo Clinic, Rochester, Minn., 1958-61; head sec. peripheral vascular disease Henry Ford Hosp., Detroit, 1961-68; asso. prof. medicine Wayne State U., 1968-71, chief sect. cardiovascular disease, 1969-71; assoc. prof., asso. dir. sect. cardiology U. Mich., 1972-73, prof. internal medicine, 1973-75; prof. medicine John A. Burns Sch. Medicine, U. Hawaii, 1975—, chmn. dept. medicine, 1975-90. Author: Orthostatic Hypotension, 1986; contbr. numerous articles to med. jours. Rockefeller Found. scholar, 1991. Master ACP (bd. govs. 1984-89, Laureate award Hawaii chpt. 1992); fellow Am. Coll. Cardiology (bd. govs. 1980-84); mem. Am. Heart Assn. (fellow couns. cardiology and circulation), Am. Fedn. Clin. Rsch., Asian-Pacific Soc. Cardiology (v.p. 1987-91), Accreditation Coun. for Grad. Med. Edn. (chmn. residence rev. com. internal medicine 1993-95), Hawaii Heart Assn. (pres.), Western Assn. Physicians, Am. Autonomic Soc. (chmn. bd. govs., pres.-elect), Pacific Interurban Club. Jewish. Home: 4983 Kolohala St Honolulu HI 96816-5126 Office: 1356 Lusitana St Honolulu HI 96813-2421

SCHATZ, MONA CLAIRE STRUHSAKER, social worker, educator; b. Phila., Jan. 4, 1950; d. Milton and Josephine (Kivo) S.; m. James Fredrick Struhsaker, Dec. 31, 1979 (div.); 1 child, Thain Mackenzie. BA, Metro State Coll., 1976; postgrad., U. Minn., 1976; MSW, U. Denver, 1979; D in Social Work/Social Welfare, U. Pa., 1986. Teaching fellow U. Pa., Phila., 1981-82; asst. prof. S.W. Mo. State U., Springfield, 1982-85; assoc. prof. Colo. State U., Ft. Collins, 1985—, field coord., 1986-88, dir. non-profit agy. adminstrn. program, 1995—, project dir. Edn. and Rsch. Inst. for Fostering Families, 1987—, dir. youth agy. adminstrn. program Am. Humanics, 1988-90; cons. Mgmt. and Behavioral Sci. Ctr., The Wharton Sch. U. Pa., 1981-82; resource specialist So. N.J. Health Sys. Agy., 1982; adj. faculty mem. U. Mo., Springfield, 1994; med. social worker Rehab. and Vis. Nurse Assn., 1985-90; mem. Colo. Child Welfare Adv. Com., Family Conservation Initiative; internat. cons. and trainer Inst. for Internat. Connections, Russia, Latvia, Albania, U.S., Hungary, Ukraine, Romania, 1992—. Contbr. articles to profl. jours. Cons., field rep. Big Bros./Big Sisters of Am., Phila., 1979-83; acting dir., asst. dir. Big Sisters of Colo., 1971-78; owner Polit. Cons. in Colo., Denver, 1978-79; active Food Co-op, Ft. Collins, Foster Parent, Denver, Capitol Hill United Neighbors, Adams County (Denver) Social Planning Coun., Co., Colo. Justice Coun., Denver, Regional Girls Shelter, Springfield; bd. dirs. Crisis Helpline and Info. Svc. Scholar Lilly Endowment, Inc., 1976, Piton Found., 1978; recipient Spl. Recognition award Big Bros./Big Sisters of Am., 1983, Recognition award Am. Humanics Mgmt. Inst., 1990. Mem. Inst. Internat. Connections (bd. dirs.), Coun. Social Work Edn., Group for Study of Generalist Social Work, Social Welfare History Group, Nat. Assn. Social Workers (nominating com. Springfield chpt., state bd. dirs., No. Colo. rep.), Student Social Work Assn. Colo. State U. (adv. 1986-89), Permanency Planning Coun. for Children and Youth, NOW (treas. Springfield chpt. 1984-85), Student Nuclear Awareness Group (advisor), Student Social Work Assn. (advisor), Har Shalom, Alpha Delta Mu. Democrat. Office: Colo State U Social Work Dept Fort Collins CO 80523

SCHATZ, NORMAN J., ophthalmologist, neurologist; b. Phila., May 28, 1936; s. David and Anna (Kale) S.; children: Jodi E., Schatz-Jerrehian, Amy L., Jill S. Schatz-Pinover. BS, Dickinson Coll., Carlisle, Pa., 1957; MD, Hahnemann Med. Coll., Phila., 1961. Neurology-ophthalmology fellow U. Miami-Bascom Palmer Hosp., Fla., 1966; dir. dept. neurology-ophthalmology Wills Eye Hosp., Phila., 1975-86; prof. neurology and ophthalmology U. Pa., 1976—; prof. U. Miami, 1982—; neuro-opthalmologist Mercy Neuro Sci. Inst., Miami, 1995—. Fellow Am. Acad. Ophthalmology, N. Am. Opthalmologic Soc., BINOS, Walsh Soc. Home: 200 Ocean Ln Dr Ste 305 Key Biscayne FL 33149 Office: Mercy Neurosci. Inst. 3661 S Miami Ave Ste 209 Miami FL 33133

SCHATZ, PAULINE, dietitian; b. Sioux City, Iowa, Sept. 25, 1923; d. Isaac and Haya (Kaplan) Epstein; m. Hyman Schatz, Sept. 2, 1951; children: Barbara, Larry. BS, UCLA, 1945, MS, 1950, MS in Public Health, 1963; EdD, U. So. Calif., 1984. Head dietitian VA, 1946-54; assoc. prof. L.A. City Coll., 1958-68; prof. home econs. Calif. State U., L.A., 1968-83, prof. emeritus, 1983—, dir. ctr. dietetic edn., 1979—, Calif. State U., Northridge, 1988-90. Author: Manual for Clinical Dietetics, 1978, 3d edit., 1983; contbr. articles to profl. jours. Grantee VA, Kellogg Found., HEW. Mem. Am. Dietetic Assn. (Disting. Svc. award 1986), Calif. Dietetic Assn. (Zellmer grantee 1966-69, Disting. Svc. award 1986, Excellence in Education, 1993), L.A. Dietetic Assn., Kappa Omicron Nu. Office: Calif State U Dept Health and Nutritional Scis Los Angeles CA 90032

SCHATZBERG, ALAN FREDERIC, psychiatrist, researcher; b. N.Y.C., Oct. 17, 1944; s. Emanuel and Cila (Diamond) S.; m. Nancy R. Silverman, Aug. 27, 1972; children: Melissa Ann, Lindsey Diamond. BS, NYU, 1965, MD, 1968; MA (hon.), Harvard U., 1989. Diplomate Nat. Bd. Med. Examiners, Am. Bd. Psychiatry and Neurology. Intern Lenox Hill Hosp., N.Y.C., 1968-69; resident in psychiatry Mass. Mental Health Ctr., Boston, 1969-72; clin. fellow in psychiatry Harvard Med. Sch., Boston, 1969-72, asst. prof. psychiatry, 1977-82, assoc. prof., 1982-88, prof., 1988-91; interim psychiatrist-in-chief McLean Hosp., Belmont, Mass., 1984-86, dir. depression rsch. facility, 1985—, svc. chief, 1982-84, 86-88; psychiatrist adv. panel Eli Lilly & Co., Indpls., 1986-93; clin. dir. Mass. Mental Health Ctr., Boston, 1988-91; Kenneth T. Norris, Jr. prof. psychiatry and behavioral scis. Stanford U., 1991—, chmn. dept. psychiatry and behavioral scis. Sch. Medicine, 1991—; cons. AMA Videoclinics, Chgo., 1979-83; mem. AMA/FAA panel on health regulations, Chgo., 1984-86; mem. NIH Biol. Psychopathology and Clin. Neuroscis. Initial Rev. Group, 1991-95, chmn., 1993-94. Co-author: Manual of Clinical Psychopharmacology, 1986, 2d edit., 1991; contbr. more than 170 articles, book chpts. to profl. publs.; co-editor: Depression: Biology, Psychodynamics and Treatment, 1978, Hypothalamic-Pituitary-Adrenal Axis, 1988, Textbook of Psychopharmacology, 1995; mem. editl. bd. McLean Hosp. Jour., 1975-88, Jour. Psychiat. Rsch., 1986—, Integrative Psychiatry, 1990—, Harvard Rev. Psychiatry, 1993—, Archives of Gen. Psychiatry, 1995—, Psychoneuroendocrinology, 1995—, Annals Psychiatry, 1992—, Anxiety, 1993; assoc. editor-in-chief Depression, 1992—. Maj. USAF, 1972-74. Rsch. grantee NIMH, 1984-87, 94—, Poitras Charitable Found., 1985-93. Fellow Am. Psychiat. Assn., Am. Coll. Neuropsychopharmacology (coun. 1995—), Am. Psychopath. Assn.; mem. Am. Coll. Psychiatrists, Mass. Psychiat. Soc. (coun. 1987-90), No. Calif. Psychiat. Soc. Office: Stanford U Sch Medicine 401 Quarry Rd Rm 300 Stanford CA 94305-5548

SCHAUWECKER, DONALD STEVEN, radiologist; b. Greencastle, Ind., Jan. 15, 1945; s. Cleon Marion and Lois Lee (Moyer) S.; m. Brenda Kay Wright, Dec. 21, 1985; 1 child, Anastasia Elizabeth. BA, DePauw U., 1967; PhD, U. Wis., 1972; MD, Ind. U., 1977. Diplomate Am. Bd. Radiology, Am. Bd. Nuclear Medicine. Resident in radiology Ind. U., 1977-81, resident in nuclear medicine, 1980-81; from asst. prof. radiology to prof. radiology Ind. U., Indpls., 1981—. Grantee NIH, 1986, 89. Fellow Am. Coll. Nuclear Physicians (treas. 1993-94); mem. Radiol. Soc. N.Am., Soc. Nuclear Medicine (pres. ctrl. chpt. 1996—, trustee 1994—). Office: Wishard Meml Hosp 1001 W 10th St Indianapolis IN 46202

SCHECHTER, MARSHALL DAVID, psychiatrist, educator; b. Chgo., Sept. 4, 1921; s. Joseph and Bessie (Czapler) S.; m. Ann Binder, June 8, 1973; children by previous marriage: Judi, Cid, Nicole, Paul. BS, U. Wis., 1942; MD, U. Cin., 1944; MS, U. Pa., 1950. Diplomate Am. Bd. Psychiatry and Neurology, subspecialty in child psychiatry. Assoc. clin. prof. psychiatry UCLA, L.A., 1953-64; prof. child and adolescent psychiatry U. Okla., Oklahoma City, 1964-73, prof. biol. psychiatry, 1964-73, prof. pediatrics, 1964-73; prof. child and adolescent SUNY Upstate Med. Ctr., Syracuse, 1973-76; prof. child and adolescent U. Pa., Phila., 1976-86, prof. emeritus child and adolescent psychiatry, 1986—; Author, editor: Psychology of Adoption, 1990, Being Adopted, 1991. Capt. USMC, 1945-47. Named Disting. profl. Wilford Hall USAF, San Antonio, 1966-89. Fellow APA (life), Am. Acad. Child and Adolescent Psychiatry (life); mem. Am. Psychoanalytic Assn. (life), Soc. for Rsch. in Child Devel., Soc. Profl. Child and Adolescent Psychiatry, Alpha Omega Alpha. Home and Office: 1142 Morris Rd Wynnewood PA 19096-2313

SCHECKLER, WILLIAM EDWARD, physician, educator; b. Kenosha, Wis., Aug. 22, 1938; s. Edward William and Bernice Julia (Rhode) S.; m. Rolliana Antoinette Binder, Aug. 18, 1962; children: Edward William, Megan Marie, Gregory Joseph, Mara Catherine. BS magna cum laude, U. Notre Dame, 1960; MD, U. Pa., 1964. Diplomate Am. Bd. Internal Medicine. Intern then resident U. Wis. Hosp., Madison, 1964-68, chief resident in medicine, 1967-68, mem. med. sch. faculty dept. family medicine, 1974—; intern medicine, infectious disease East Madison Clinic St. Mary's Hosp., Madison, 1970-74; pvt. practice East Madison Clinic, 1970-74; cons. practice dept. family medicine and practice U. Wis., St. Mary's Hosp. Med. Ctr., Madison, 1974—; hosp. epidemiologist St. Mary's Hosp. Med. Ctr., Madison, 1971—. Contbr. articles to profl. jours. Pub. health rep. Ctr. Disease Control State of Wis., Dane County, 1970—; troop com., coun. bd. Boy Scouts Am., Dane County, 1976-88; pres., founder Newport Wilderness Soc., Door County, Wis., 1985—. Surgeon USPHS, 1968-70. Recipient Family Practice Educator of Yr. award Wis. Acad. Family Practitioners, 1982, Bd. Trustees award Dane County Med. Soc., 1988, Physician Citizen of Yr. award Wis. State Med. Soc., 1991, Disting. Svc. to Pub. Health award Wis. Pub. Health Assn., 1992, Ptnrs. in Pub. Health award State of Wis. Divsn. of Health, 1993. Fellow Infectious Disease Soc. Am.; mem. AMA, Soc. for Hosp. Epidemiology Am. (pres. 1987), Southcen. Wis. Notre Dame Club (Mem. of Yr. 1988). Roman Catholic. Office: U Wis Dept Family Medicine 777 S Mills St Madison WI 53715-1849

SCHECTER, ARNOLD JOEL, preventive medicine educator; b. Chgo., Dec. 1, 1934; s. Benjamin and Leonore Natalie (Lyon) S.; m. Martha-Jean Berenson, Feb. 14, 1964; children: Benjamin, David, Anna. BA in Liberal Arts, U. Chgo., Chgo., 1954, BS in Physiology-Neurophysiology, 1957; MD, Howard U., 1962; MPH, Columbia U., 1975. Diplomate Am. Coll. Preventive Medicine; med. lic., Ky., N.Y., N.J. Postdoct. Harvard Med. Sch., Boston, 1962-65, instr. dept. medicine, 1964-65; intern Beth Israel Hosp., Boston, 1966; gen. practitioner, sr. aviation med. examiner West Point, Ky., 1969-70; dir. inpatient rehab. ctr., drug and alcohol rehab. program Region Eight Mental Health and Mental Retardation Bd., Inc., Louisville, 1971-72; asst. prof. dept. psychiatry drug and alcohol programs SUNY, Bklyn., 1973-75; clin. assoc. prof. dept. preventive medicine N.J. Med. Sch., Newark, 1975-79; prof. dept. preventive medicine SUNY, Binghamton, 1979—; cons. U.S. EPA, Washington, 1985-86, WHO, 1986-90; dir. clin. rsch. in drug abuse, coord., faculty mem. Career Tchr. Tng. Ctr., 1972-75; assoc. dir. office primary health care edn., office of the dean N.J. Med. Sch., 1976-79; advisor Environ. Defense Fund, 1991—, Nat. Vets. Legal Svcs. Project, 1991—; co-founder assoc. editor The Am. Jour. Drug and Alcohol Abuse, N.Y.C., 1973-78, editorial bd. 1978—; editorial adv. bd. Substance and Alcohol Actions/Misuse, Elmsford, N.Y., 1979—; presenter in field. Author: Rehabilitation Aspects of Drug Dependence, 1977, Treatment Aspects of Drug Dependence, 1978, Biomedical Issues in Drug Abuse, 1981, Sociological Issues in Drug Abuse, 1981; author (with H. Alksne, E. Kaufman) Drug Abuse: Modern Trends, Issues and Perspectives, 1978, Critical Concerns in the Field of Drug Abuse, 1978; editor: Dioxins and Health, 1994; contbr. over 120 articles to profl. jours. including Organo-Halogen Compounds, Chemosphere, Women & Health, Toxicology and Applied Pharmacology, Am. Jour. Physiology, Am. Jour. Pub. Health, Jour. Occupl. and Environ. Health, Occupl. and Environ. Health, Environ. Health Perspectives; editor: Dioxins and Health, 1994. Major M.C., U.S. Army, 1967-69. Recipient Pacesetter award Commonwealth Mass., 1990. Fellow ACP, Am. Coll. Preventive Medicine, Am. Coll. Occupational Medicine; mem. APHA, AAAS, Assn. Tchrs. Preventive Medicine, Am. Coll. Epidemiology, Microscopy Soc. Am., Am. Soc. for Cell Biology, Am. Occupational Medicine Assn., Soc. for Epidemiologic Rsch., N.Y. Acad. Scis., N.Y. State Occupational Medicine Assn., N.Y. State Med. Soc., Broome County Med. Soc. Home: 88 Aldrich Ave Binghamton NY 13903-1451 Office: SUNY Health Sci Clin Campus PO Box 1000 Binghamton NY 13902-1000

SCHECTER, WILLIAM PALMER, surgeon; b. N.Y.C., Dec. 14, 1947; s. Benjamin Robert and Ann Georgina (Saunders) S.; m. Gisela Franziska Fohlmeister, Sept. 1, 1974; children: Samuel Chaim, Anna Ruth. AB in Polit. Sci., Harpur Coll., Binghamton, N.Y., 1968; MD, Albany Med. Coll., 1972. Diplomate Am. Bd. Surgery, Am. Bd. Anesthesiology. Rotating intern San Francisco Gen. Hosp., 1972-73; resident in anesthesiology Mass. Gen. Hosp., Boston, 1973-75; resident in surgery U. Calif., San Francisco, 1976-79; pvt. practice San Francisco, hand surgery fellow, 1975-80; chief of surgery San Francisco Gen. Hosp., 1994—; prof. clin. surgery U. Calif., San Francisco, 1994—. Office: San Francisco General Hosp Dept of Surgery 3-A Potrero St San Francisco CA 94110

SCHEELE, PAUL DRAKE, former hospital supply corporate executive; b. Elgin, Ill., Aug. 6, 1922; s. Arthur R. and Helen M. (Christiansen) S. B.A., Coe Coll., 1944; M.B.A., Harvard, 1947. With Am. Hosp. Supply Corp., 1947—; pres. Harleco div., Phila., 1966-68; group v.p. Am. Hosp. Supply Corp., 1968-70; exec. v.p., also pres. internat. group Am. Hosp. Supply Corp., Evanston, Ill., 1970-74, v.p., asst. to chmn. bd., 1974-81. Chmn. bd. trustees Coe Coll. Served to 1st lt., inf. AUS, 1943-46. Mem. Harvard Bus. Sch. Club, Harvard Club Fla., Econ. Club (Chgo.), Tau Kappa Epsilon, Pi Delta Epsilon.

SCHEER, R. SCOTT, physician; b. N.Y.C., Oct. 24, 1938; s. Leonard and Josephine (Holtschl) S.; m. Beverly Joan Henry Scheer, Dec. 27, 1940; children: Kirsten Leigh, Laura Lynn. AB, Cornell U., 1960; MD, SUNY, Buffalo, 1965. Diplomate Am. Bd. Radiology, Am. Bd. Nuclear Medicine. Intern Santa Barbara (Calif.) Cottage Hosp., 1965-66; resident Cornell Univ.-N.Y. Hosp., 1966, Phila. Gen. Hosp., 1968-71; staff radiologist Meth. Hosp., Phila., 1971-72; assoc. dir. radiology Coatesville (Pa.) Hosp., 1972-77; dir. dept. radiology Norristown (Pa.) State Hosp., 1973-93; dir., chief exec. officer Med. Imaging Svcs., Exton, Pa., 1977—; dir. radiology Scranton (Pa.) Imaging Ctr., 1993-94; cons. radiologist Oxford Valley Imaging Ctr., 1992-95, mng. ptnr., 1995—; cons. radiol. expert, 1981—; attending radiologist Pottstown Meml. Med. Ctr., 1977-93; cons. in magetic resonance imaging Fonar Corp., 1990-92. Capt. U.S. Army Med. Corps, 1966-68. Recipient N.Y. State Regents Med. scholarship, 1961. Mem. AMA, Am. Coll. Radiology, Radiol. Soc. N.Am., Pa. Med. Soc., Pa. Radiol. Soc., soc. of Magnetic Resonance in Medicine, Chester County Med. Soc., Am. Inst. of Ultrasound in Medicine, Pa. Coll. Nuclear Medicine, Union League of Phila., Valley Forge Mountain Racquet Assn. Republican. Presbyterian. Office: Med Imaging Svcs 486 Thomas Jones Way Ste 130 Exton PA 19341-2528

SCHEIBE, KARL EDWARD, psychology educator; b. Belleville, Ill., Mar. 5, 1937; s. John Henry and Esther Julia (Friesen) S.; m. Elizabeth Wentworth Mixter, Sept. 10, 1961; children: David Sawyer, Robert Daniel. B.S., Trinity Coll., 1959; Ph.D., U. Calif.-Berkeley, 1963; M.A. (hon.), Wesleyan U., 1973. Faculty mem. Wesleyan U., Middletown, Conn., 1963—, prof. psychology, 1973—, chmn. dept., 1973-76, 79-81, 86-88; v.p. Stonington Inst., 1984-91; dir. Saybrook Counseling Ctr., 1990—; vis. prof. U. So. Calif., 1974; dir. rev. panels NSF Sci. Profl. Devel. Program, 1975-81; cons. Am. Council Edn., 1975-81. Author: Beliefs and Values, 1970, Mirror, Masks, Lies and Secrets, 1979, Studies in Social Identity, 1983, Self Studies: The Psychology of Self and Identity, 1995. Trustee Trinity Coll., Hartford, Conn., 1977-83; moderator congregation First Ch. of Christ, Middletown, 1981-82. Woodrow Wilson fellow, 1959; NSF fellow, 1961; NIMH research grantee, 1964-68; Fulbright fellow Cath. U. Sao Paulo, Brazil, 1972-73, 84. Mem. Am. Psychol. Assn., New Eng. Psychol. Assn., Eastern Psychol. Assn., Conn. Acad. Arts and Scis., Phi Beta Kappa. Congregationalist. Home: 11 Long Ln Middletown CT 06457-4046 Office: Wesleyan U Dept Psychology Middletown CT 06459

SCHEIBEL, LEONARD WILLIAM, physician, pharmacologist, educator; b. Hays, Kans., Jan. 18, 1938; s. Raymond Philip and Thelma (Bane) S.; m. Melania Parada Valdes, May 1, 1976; children: Leonard William Jr., Raymond Philip. BS, Creighton U., 1960, MS, 1962; DS, Johns Hopkins U., 1967; MD, U. Fla., 1973. Diplomate Am. Bd. Clin. Pharmacology, Am. Bd. Preventive Medicine, Nat. Bd. Medical Examiners. Rotating intern Gorgas Hosp., Balboa Heights, Canal Zone, 1973-74, resident internal medicine, 1974-77; rsch. biochemist, capt. U.S. Army Walter Reed Army Inst. Rsch., Washington, 1967-70; rsch. assoc. dept. pharmacology U. Fla., Gainesville, 1970-73; asst. prof., lab. parasitology and staff physician Rockefeller U. and Hosp., N.Y.C., 1977-81; adj. assoc. prof. dept. microbiology U. Md., Balt., 1982-86; assoc. dept. immunology and infectious diseases Johns Hopkins U., Balt., 1982-94; asst. prof. dept. preventive medicine and biometrics Uniformed Svcs. U. of the Health Scis., Bethesda, Md., 1981-82, assoc. prof. dept. preventive medicine and biometrics, 1982-86, prof. preventive medicine, biometrics, pharmacology depts., 1986-94; dir. clin. pharmacology, prof. medicine U. Ill., Peoria, 1994—; cons. Pan American Health Orgn., Panama City, Panama, 1979, Environ. Applications Rsch., San Antonio, Tex., 1984-94, Med. Svc. Cons., Inc., Arlington, Va., 1978, various other orgns. Contbr. over 50 articles to profl. jours. Recipient Cert. of Achievement Walter Reed Army Inst. of Rsch., 1970, Faculty Rsch. award U. Fla., 1973, Igor I. Sikorsky Helicopter Rescue award Republic of Panama, 1973, Creighton U. Disting. Alumni award, 1993. Fellow Infectious Diseases Soc. Am., Am. Coll. Physicians, Am. Coll. Preventive Medicine; mem. AMA (physicians recognition award 1979-93), Fedn. Am. Soc. Exptl. Biology, Am. Soc. Pharmacology and Exptl. Therapeutics (div. clin. pharmacology and drug metabolism), Am. Soc. Clin. Pharmacology and Therapeutics, Am. Soc. Tropical Medicine, Am. Soc. Parasitologists, N.Y. Soc. Tropical Medicine, numerous other orgns. Office: U Ill Coll Medicine Coll Medicine at Peoria PO Box 1649 Peoria IL 61656-1649

SCHEIDT, DAVID A., medical optometrist; b. Rockford, Ill., Oct. 26, 1959; s. Robert A. and Mary K. Scheidt; m. Margaret A. O'Brien, Nov. 28, 1987; children: Meghan M., Michael D. BS in Biology, Marquette U., 1981; OD with honors, Ill. Coll. of Optometry, 1985. Lic. optometrist, Wis. Student externship Westside VA Hosp., Chgo., 1985; med. optometrist Med. Eye Clinic, Milw., 1986-92, Eye Care Specialists, S.C., Milw., 1992—; clin rsch. study coord. Eye Care Specialists, S.C. Mem. Am. Optometric Assn., Wis. Optometric Assn. (bd. dirs. 1990-95, Legis. Achievement award 1990), Am. Coll. Optometric Physicians, Milw. Optometric Assn. (pres. 1990-91), Am. Diabetes Assn. Roman Catholic. Office: Eye Care Specialists SC 10150 W National Ave Ste 100 West Allis WI 53227

SCHEINBAUM, SANDRA LYNN, psychologist; b. Chgo., Mar. 24, 1950; d. Raymond and Faye (Deitch) Pecken; m. Alan C. Scheinbaum, June 18, 1972; children: Laura, Carly. BS, Northwestern U., 1970, MA, 1972; PhD, Fielding Inst., 1984. Lic. clin. psychologist, biofeedback. Spl. edn. tchr. Sch. Dist. 72, Skokie, Ill., 1972-77; faculty mem., supr. clin. practicums Nat. Coll. Edn., Evanston, Ill., 1977-84; pvt. practice in psychology Biofeedback Tng. Ctr, Northbrook, Ill., 1984—, dir., 1991—; staff psychologist Highland Park (Ill.) Hosp., 1985—, CPC Old Orchard Hosp., Skokie, 1985—, Rush North Shore Med. Ctr., Skokie, 1986—. Mem. APA, Ill. Psychol. Assn., Soc. Behavioral Medicine (pres.), Biofeedback Soc. Ill., Assn. for Applied Psychophysiology and Biofeedback, Soc. for Personality Assessment, Profls. in Learning Disabilities (pres. 1982-83). Office: Biofeedback Tng Ctr 1535 Lake Cook Rd Northbrook IL 60062-1447

SCHEINBERG, LABE CHARLES, physician, educator; b. Memphis, Dec. 11, 1925; m. Louise Goldman, Jan. 6, 1952: children: Susan, David, Ellen, Amy. AB, U. N.C., 1945; MD, U. Tenn., 1948. Intern Wesley Meml. Hosp., Chgo., 1949; resident psychiatry Elgin (Ill.) State Hosp., 1950; resident, asst. neurology Neurol. Inst., N.Y., 1952-56; mem. faculty Albert Einstein Coll. Medicine, 1956-93, prof. neurology, asst. dean, 1968-69, assoc. dean, 1969-70, prof. rehab. medicine and psychiatry, dean, 1970-72; dir. neurology Hosp., 1966-73; dir. dept. neurology and psychiatry St. Barnabas Hosp., Bronx, N.Y., 1974-79; prof. neurology Mt. Sinai Med. ctr., N.Y.C., 1993—. Cons. editor: N.Y. Acad. Scis., 1964, 84; founding editor-in-chief Jour. Neurologic Rehab., Rehab. Reports, Multiple Sclerosis Rsch. Reports. Served as capt. M.C. USAF, 1951-52. Fellow Am. Acad. Neurology; mem. Am. Neurol. Assn., Am. Assn. Neuro-pathology, Am. Soc. Exptl. Pathology, Phi Beta Kappa, Alpha Omega Alpha. Home: 9 Oak Ln Scarsdale NY 10583-1621

SCHEINBLUM, ANITA FRANUSISZIN, pediatrics nurse; b. Durham, N.C., Aug. 22, 1965; d. Alfred John and Nancy A. (Atkins) F. BSN, Emory U., 1988. RN Fla.; cert. pediatric advanced life support. Staff nurse Children's Hosp. Med. U. of S.C., 1988-89; clin. nurse II, charge nurse pediatric ICU N.C. Children's Hosp., Chapel Hill, 1989-92; pediatric home care nurse Interim Healthcare, N.Y.C., 1993-95; pediat. and neonatal ICU nurse Fla. Hosp., Orlando, Fla., 1995—; chmn. primary nursing com. pediatric ICU; instr. in field. Altrusa Women's Club scholar, 1984-88. Mem. Alpha Chi Omega, Sigma Theta Tau, Rho Lambda.

SCHEINMAN, JON ISAAC, pediatrician, researcher; b. Chgo., Nov. 20, 1940; s. Daniel and Esther (Sweet) S.; m. Margarita Scheinman, May 23, 1966; children: Daniel, Rachael. AB in Biology, Wesleyan U., Middletown, Conn., 1962; MD, U. Ill., Chgo., 1966. Diplomate Am. Bd. Pediats. Intern in pediats. U. Colo. Hosp., Denver, 1966-67; resident in pediats. U. Iowa Hosp., Iowa City, 1967-68, U. Wis. Hosp., Madison, 1968-69; staff physician William Beaumont Gen. Hosp., El Paso, Tex., 1969-71; asst. prof. U. Minn., Mpls., 1974-77, assoc. prof., 1977-83; assoc. prof. Duke U. Med. Ctr., Durham, 1983-93; pediat. nephrologist Med. Coll. Va., Richmond, 1993—; med. advisor Hyperoxolwial Oxalosis Found., Maynard, Mass., 1985—. Contbr. articles to profl. jours., chpts. to books. Maj. USAF, 1969-71. Mem. Am. Soc. Nephrology, Am. Soc. Pediat. Nephrology, Internat. Soc. Nephrology, Internat. Soc. Pediat. Nephrology. Jewish. Office: Med Coll of Va Box 980498 12th & Marshall St 12-024 Richmond VA 23298-0498

SCHEINMAN, STEVEN JAY, medical educator; b. Monticello, N.Y., Oct. 22, 1951; married; 2 children. AB summa cum laude, Amherst Coll., 1973; MD cum laude, Yale U., 1977. Diplomate Am. Bd. Internal Medicine in nephrology; lic. physician, N.Y., Conn. Resident internal medicine Yale-New Haven Hosp., 1977-80; chief resident internal medicine Upstate Med. Ctr., Syracuse, N.Y., 1980-81, fellow nephrology, 1981-83; fellow nephrology Yale-New Haven Hosp., 1983-84; asst. prof. medicine SUNY Health Sci. Ctr., Syracuse, 1984-90, asst. prof. pharmacology, 1988-90, assoc. prof. medicine and pharmacology, 1990-94, prof. medicine and pharmacology, 1994—, chief nephrology sect. dept. medicine, 1994—; vis. scientist MRC Molecular Medicine Group, Royal Postgrad. Med. Sch., Hammersmith Hosp., London, 1992, 95; vis. scholar dept. biochemistry U. Oxford, 1985; attending physician U. Hosp., Syracuse, Crouse-Irving Meml. Hosp., Syracuse, VA Med. Ctr., Syracuse; dir. Nephrology Fellowship Program, 1993—; spkr. seminars, confs., orgns. Mem. editl. bd. Yale Jour. Biology and Medicine, 1975-77; contbr. articles to profl. jours. Recipient Lange award Yale U. Sch. Medicine, 1976, Resident Merit award Conn. chpt. ACP, 1980, NIH Nat. Rsch. Svc. award, 1981-83, NIH clin. investigator award, 1985-90, Charles R. Ross Rsch. award SUNY-Health Sci. Ctr., 1992; grantee Nat. Inst. Arthritis Diabetes Digestive and Kidney Diseases, 1981-83, 85-90, 95—, Am. Heart Assn., 1985, 88-90, 90-91, 92-95, 95—, NATO, 1995—. Mem. Am. Soc. Clin. Investigation, Am. Fedn. Clin. Rsch., Am. Soc. Nephrology, Internat. Soc. Nephrology, Am. Physiol. Soc., Am. Soc. Bone and Mineral Rsch., Am. Heart Assn. Coun. on Kidney, Assn. Subspecialty Profs., Phi Beta Kappa. Home: 24 University Ave Hamilton NY 13346 Office: SUNY Health Sci Ctr 750 E Adams St Syracuse NY 13210*

SCHELBERT, HEINRICH RUEDIGER, nuclear medicine physician; b. Wuerzberg, Germany, Nov. 5, 1939. MD, J. Maximillian U., Wuerzburg, Germany, 1964. Diplomate Am. Bd. Nuclear Medicine. Intern Mercy Med. Ctr., Phila., 1966-67; resident Mercy Med. Ctr., 1967-68, 70-71; resident cardiology U. Dusseldorf, Germany, 1971-72; fellow cardiology, resident nuclear medicine U. Calif., San Diego, 1968-69, 72-73; hosp. assoc. UCLA Med. Ctr., 1977—; prof. radiol. scis. UCLA Sch. Medicine, L.A., 1980-93, prof. pharmacol. and radiol. scis., 1993—. Recipient Georg von Hevesy prize 2d Internat. Congress World Fedn. Nuclear Medicine and Radiation Biology, 1978, 3d Internat. Congress World Fedn. Nuclear Medicine and Radiation Biology, 1982. Fellow Am. Coll. Cardiology; mem. Am. Heart Assn. (disting. scientific achievement award 1989), Soc. Nuclear Medicine (Herrman L. Blumgart pioneer lectr. award 1989). Office: UCLA Sch Medicine Dept Molecular & Med Pharm 23-148 CHS Los Angeles CA 90024-1735*

SCHELBLE, DANIEL TIMOTHY, emergency medicine physician; b. LaCrosse, Wis., July 9, 1946; s. Robert Martin and Pearl Elizabeth (Newman) S.; m. Susan Jean Sadler, Oct. 27, 1973; children: Anita Marie, Dana Marie. BS in Biology, Loras Coll., Dubuque, Iowa, 1968; MD in Medicine, U. Wis., 1972. Diplomate Am. Bd. Emergency Medicine, recert. Surgery intern Meth. Hosp., Dallas, 1972-73; emergency medicine resident Akron (Ohio) Gen. Med. Ctr., 1975-77, emergency medicine residency dir., 1978-80, emergency medicine dept. chmn., 1980—, emergency medicine svcs. staff, 1977—; prof. clin. emergency medicine Northeastern Ohio Univ. Coll. Medicine, 1994—. Contbr. numerous articles and chpts. to med. publs. Mem. mayor's adv. com. on emergency med. svcs. City of Akron, 1980—; med. advisor Mogadore (Ohio) Fire Dept., 1991—. Lt. USN M.C., 1973-75. Fellow Am. Coll. Emergency Physicians (mem. Ohio chpt., bd. dirs., mem. reimbursement com. 1977—), Soc. Tchrs. of Emergency Medicine (bd. dirs., pres.-elect, pres., chmn. pub. rels. 1980—), Summit County Med. Soc. Republican. Office: Akron Gen Med Ctr 400 Wabash Ave Akron OH 44307

SCHELL, CATHERINE LOUISE, family practice physician; b. Niskayuna, N.Y., Jan. 27, 1948; m. Richard J. Rathe, Jan. 7, 1986. BA, Ind. U., 1970, MA, 1974; MLS, Simmons Coll., 1975; MD, AUC Coll. Medicine, Montserrat, 1983. Diplomate Am. Bd. Family Practice. Libr. Calder Med. Libr., U. Miami, Fla., 1975-78; libr., dir. Mercy Hosp., Miami, 1978-79; libr. Miami-Dade C.C., 1978-80; intern Med. Coll. Ga., Rome, 1983; resident U. Wyo., Cheyenne, 1985-87; staff physician Vets. Hosp., Cheyenne, 1986-88, Dept. of Army, U.S. Dept. Def., Ft. Devens, Mass., 1988-90, Vets. Hosp., Lake City, Fla., 1990-93; staff physician, fellow Vets. Hosp., Gainesville, Fla., 1993-95; physician Dept. of Navy, 1996—. Tchr. ESL YMCA Internat., Taipei, Taiwan, 1970-71. Title IIB fellow Simmons Coll., 1974-75; Ford Found. grantee, Ind. U., 1969-70. Fellow Am. Acad. Family PRactice; mem. Acad. Health Sci., Med. Libr. Assn. Office: Naval Air Sta Br Clinic Jacksonville N A S FL 32212

SCHELL, GERALD RUSSELL, neurological surgeon; b. Phila., July 16, 1954. MD, Mich. State U., 1981. Diplomate Am. Bd. Neurol. Surgery. Intern McLaren Gen. Hosp., Flint, Mich., 1981; resident SUNY Health Sci. Ctr., Syracuse, 1982-87; group practice Saginaw Valley Neurosurgery, P.C., Saginaw, Mich., 1989—; med. dir. Mich. Spine and Rehab., Saginaw, 1993—. Mem. Am. Assn. Neurol. Surgeons, Am. Spine Injury Assn., Congress Neurol. Surgeons. Office: Saginaw Valley Neurosurgery 4677 Towne Saginaw MI 48604

SCHELL, NANCY MARIE, medical and surgical nurse; b. Melrose, Mass., Feb. 23, 1944; d. William John Jr. and Lillian Marie (Gartland) S. Student, Danbury State Coll., 1962; diploma, Greenwich Hosp. Sch. Nursing, 1966. RN, Conn. Staff and asst. head nurse med.-surg. unit Greenwich (Conn.) Hosp., 1966-67; staff and charge nurse Nat. Naval Med. Ctr., Bethesda, Md., 1967-77; asst. head nurse Holy Cross Hosp., Silver Spring, Md., 1978-79; charge nurse CCU Ormond Meml. Hosp., Ormond Beach, Fla., 1980-83; charge and supervising nurse Golden Age Nursing Home, South Daytona, Fla., 1985-86; charge nurse Peninsula Med. Ctr., Ormond Beach, 1986, Ormond in the Pines, Ormond Pines, 1987; hospice nurse Halifax Home Care, Daytona Beach, Fla., 1988; nurse for four agys., 1990; nurse Volusia Home Care, 1992, Oceanview Nursing Home, New Smyrna Beach, Fla., 1993, Stewart-Marchman Treatment Ctr., 1994—. Democrat. Roman Catholic. Home: 716 Jane Ave New Smyrna Beach FL 32168

SCHELL, NORMAN BARNETT, physician, consultant; b. N.Y.C., May 25, 1925; s. Jack and Ada Sylvia (Rosen) S.; m. Lila Barbara Mendelsohn, Aug. 27, 1950; children: Martin, Judith, Steven. AB cum laude, NYU, 1946, MD, 1950; MPH, Harvard U., 1971. Diplomate Am. Bd. Pediats., Am. Bd. Preventive Medicine, Nat. Bd. Med. Examiners. Rotating intern Beth Israel Hosp., N.Y.C., 1950-51; asst. resident in pediats. Mt. Sinai Hosp., N.Y.C., 1951-52; clin. fellow in pediats. N.Y.-Cornell Med. Ctr., N.Y.C., 1952-53; pvt. practice Jericho and Hicksville, N.Y., 1956-69; pub. health physician Nassau County Health Dept., Mineola, N.Y., 1969-76, dep. commr., 1976-90; asst. prof. preventive medicine SUNY, Stony Brook, 1974-90; pediat. cons. N.Y. State Health Dept., Albany, 1959-59, HEW Project Head Start, N.Y.C., 1968-75. Author: Keys to Childhood Illnesses, 1992; contbr. articles to profl. jours. Lt., M.C., USN, 1953-55, capt. Res., 1981-85. Recipient Physician Recognition award AMA, Grade 1A Health Officer N.Y. State Health Dept., 1973. Fellow Am. Acad. Pediats. (com. on sch. health 1971-77, citation com. on med. edn. 1977), Am. Coll. Preventive Medicine, N.Y. Acad. Medicine; mem. Am. Coll. Legal Medicine (assoc.), Nassau County Med. Soc. (chmn. sch. health com.), Harvard Club N.Y.C., West Point Club. Home and Office: 63 Birchwood Park Dr Jericho NY 11753-2238

SCHELLING, FRANZ ALFONS, physician; b. Linz, Austria, Mar. 31, 1945; s. Albert and Pauline (Filnkössl) S.; m. Elisabeth Anna Schaller, Aug. 8, 1970; children: Michaela, Bernhard, Barbara, Mathias. MD, U. Innsbruck, Austria, 1970. Author: The Image of Multiple Sclerosis, 1996, Multiple Sclerosis, 1984; contbr. papers to profl. jours. Roman Catholic. Home: Arlbergstr 3, A-6850 Dornbirn Austria

SCHEMMEL, JANET ELEANOR, endocrinologist, educator; b. Beaver Dam, Wis.; d. Harold Carl and Edith Louise (Rettig) S.; m. Douglas Schauer, Aug. 26, 1961; children: Joann, Luise. BA, U. Colo., 1949; MD, U. Colo., Denver, 1954. Intern Denver Gen. Hosp., 1954-55; resident St. Joseph Hosp., Denver, 1955-56; resident U. Colo., Denver, 1956-57, fellow in endocrinology, 1957-59; pvt. practice Denver, 1961—; coun. mem. Colo. Found. Med. Care, Denver, 1988—, bd. dirs. 1988-95. Contbr. chpts. in books and articles to profl. jours. Fellow ACP (Internist of Yr. Colo. br. 1995); mem. AMA, ADA, AAUW, Am. Soc. Internal Medicine, Colo. Soc. Internal Medicine (sec. 1980), Am. Assn. Clin. Endocrinologists, Endocrine Soc., Colo. Med. Soc. (del. 1979—), Colo. Diabetes Assn. (pres. 1979), Denver Med. Soc. (del. 1979—, award 1954), Denver Clin. and Pathology Soc. Office: 2005 Franklin St Ste 460 Denver CO 80205-5401

SCHEMMEL, RACHEL ANNE, food science and human nutrition educator, researcher; b. Farley, Iowa, Nov. 23, 1929; d. Frederic August and Emma Margaret (Melchert) Schemmel. BA, Clarke Coll., 1951; MS, U. Iowa, 1952; PhD, Mich. State U., 1967. Dietitian, Children's Hosp. Soc., L.A., 1952-54; instr. Mich. State, U., East Lansing, 1955-63, from asst. prof. to prof. food sci., human nutrition, 1967—. Author: Nutrition Physiology and Obesity, 1980. Contbr. articles on obesity, clin. nutrition to profl. jours. Recipient Disting. Alumni award Mt. Mercy Coll., 1971, Borden award for rsch. in applied nutrition, 1986. Mem. Am. Inst. Nutrition, Inst. Food Technologists, Am. Diet Assn. (pres. Mich. 1975-76, Lansing 1960), Brit. Nutrition Soc., Soc. for Nutrition Edn., Sigma Xi (sr. rsch. award 1986, pres. Mich. State U. chpt. 1983-84), Phi Kappa Phi (pres. 1994-95). Roman Catholic. Home: 1341 Red Leaf Ln East Lansing MI 48823-1339 Office: Mich State U Dept Food Sci Nutrit East Lansing MI 48824

SCHEMNITZ, SANFORD DAVID, wildlife biology educator; b. Cleve., Mar. 10, 1930; s. David Arthur Schemnitz; m. Mary Margaret Newby, July 8, 1958; children: Ellen Kay, Steven, Stuart. Student, U. Wis., 1948-50; BS in Wildlife, U. Mich., 1952; MS in Wildlife, U. Fla., 1953; PhD in Wildlife, Olka. State U., 1958. Cert. wildlife biologist. Conservation aide State of Mich. Dept. Conservation, Ann Arbor, 1951-52; game research biologist State of Minn. Dept. Conservation, St. Paul, 1958-59; asst. prof. wildlife Pa. State U., University Park, 1960-61; prof. wildlife resources U. Maine, Orono, 1962-75; dept. head fish and wildlife sci. N.Mex. State U., Las Cruces, 1975-81, prof. wildlife scis., 1981—. Editor: Wildlife Management Techniques Manual, 1980; contbr. articles to profl. jours. Fulbright Prof. Council for Internat. Exchange Scholars, Kathmandu, Nepal, 1983, Kenya, 1990. Mem. Am. Soc. Mammalogists, The Wildlife Soc. (life, S.W. regional rep. 1979-80), Ecol. Soc. Am., Wilson Ornithol. Soc., N.Mex. Wildlife Fedn. (bd. dirs. 1983—), Sigma Xi. Home: 8105 Dona Ana Rd Las Cruces NM 88005-6307

SCHENCK, JOHN FREDERIC, physician; b. Decatur, Ind., June 7, 1939; s. John C. Schenck and Mildred Blosser; m. Jane Stark, Oct. 12, 1962 (div. 1982); children: Brooke, Kimberly, David; m. Susan J. Kalia, Oct. 8, 1994; 1 stepchild, Tania. BS in Physics, Rensselaer Poly. Inst., 1961, PhD in Physics, 1965; MD, Albany Med. Coll., 1977. Intern Albany (N.Y.) Med. Ctr. Hosp., 1977-78; staff scientist electronics lab GE, Syracuse, N.Y., 1965-73; staff mem., sr. scientist corp. R & D ctr. GE, Schenectady, N.Y., 1973—; assoc. prof. electrical engring. Syracuse U., 1970-73; mem. med. staff Ellis Hosp., Schenectady, 1981—; adj. asst. prof. dept. radiology U. Pa., 1983—; chmn. Workshop on Advances in MR Safety and Compatibility, McLean, Va., 1996. Contbr. articles to profl. jours; 12 patents in field of magnetic resonance imaging. Recipient S.S. Greenfield award Am. Assn. Physicists in Medicine, 1993; Nat. Merit Scholar, 1957-61; NSF fellow, 1962-63;. Mem. IEEE, AAAS, Internat. Soc. Magnetic Resonance in Medicine, Am. Phys. Soc., N.Y. Acad. Sci., Sigma Xi. Home: 4914 Ravine Ct Ann Arbor MI 48105 Office: GE Corp Rsch Devel Bldg K1 NMR Schenectady NY 12309

SCHENDEL, STEPHEN ALFRED, plastic surgery educator, oral surgeon; b. Mpls., Oct. 10, 1947; s. Alfred Reck and Jeanne Shirley (Hagquist) S.; m. Susan Elizabeth Brown, Aug. 15, 1969; children: Elliott, Mélisande. BA, St. Olaf Coll., Northfield, Minn., 1969; BS with high distinction, U. Minn., 1971, DDS, 1973; diplome asst. etranger with high honors, U. Nantes, France, 1980; MD, U. Hawaii, 1983. Diplomate Am. Bd. Plastic Surgery, Nat. Bd. Med. Examiners, Nat. Bd. Dental Examiners, Am. Bd. Oral and Maxillofacial Surgery (adv. com., bd. examiner 1991-95). Fellow in oral pathology U. Minn. Sch. Dentistry, Mpls., 1972; pvt. practice gen. dentistry, then oral-maxillofac. surgery, Honolulu, 1974-75, 80-83; resident in gen. dentistry Queen's Med. Ctr., Honolulu, 1973-74; intern, then resident in oral and maxillofacial surgery Parkland Meml. Hosp., Dallas, 1975-79; resident in gen. surgery Baylor U. Med. Ctr., Dallas, 1983-84; resident in gen. surgery Stanford (Calif.) U. Med. Ctr., 1984-86, resident in plastic surgery, 1986-89, acting assoc. prof. surgery, 1989-91, assoc. prof., 1991-95, head div. plastic and reconstructive surgery, 1992—, dir. residency tng., 1992—, chmn. dept. functional restoration, 1994, chmn., 1994—, prof., 1995—; head plastic surgery, dir. Craniofacial Ctr. Lucile Salter Packard Children's Hosp., Stanford; asst. to Dr. Paul Tessier, Paris, 1987-88; asst. dept. stomatology and maxillofacial surgery Centre Hospitalier Regional Nantes, 1979-80; referee Annals Plastic Surgery, 1989—, Am. Jour. Orthodontics and Dentofacial Orthopedics, 1990—; presenter in field; mem. staff John Peter Smith Hosp., Ft. Worth, 1979; asst. clin. prof. surgery U. Hawaii John A Burns Sch. Medicine, Honolulu, 1980-84; chief plastic surgery svc., mem. med. bd. Lucile Salter Packard Children's Hosp. at Stanford, 1991—; mem. organizing com. 1st Hawaii-Pacific Cleft Palate Program, 1983; mem. in-svc. exam. com. Plastic Surgery Ednl. Found., 1992-93. Assoc. editor Selected Readings in Oral and Maxillofacial Surgery, 1989—; contbr. articles and abstracts to med. and dental jours., chpts. to books. Recipient Disting. Alumnus award St. Olaf Coll., 1993; Fulbright fellow, Nantes, 1979-80, Chateaubriand fellow Govt. of France, 1987-88. Fellow ACS, Am. Acad. Pediat.; mem. European Assn. Cranio-Maxillofacial Surgeons (mem. craniofacial com. 1989-91), Am. Soc. Pediat., Soc. Baylor Surgeons (founding), French Assn. Maxillofacial Surgeons (fgn.), Am. Cleft Palate-Craniofacial Assn., Am. Soc. Plastic and Reconstructive Surgeons (mem. sci. program com. 1992—), Am. Soc. Maxillofacial Surgeons (mem. basic course syllabus com. 1991-93, mem. membership com. 1991—, mem. sci. program com. 1991—, mem. Best Paper award com. 1991—, mem. craniofacial and maxillofacial com. 1993—, bd. dirs.-at-large 1993—, mem. Calif. carriers adv. com. 1993—, liaison to Am. Assn. Orthodontics 1994), Assn. Acad. Chairmen Plastic Surgery, Zedplast (bd. dirs., mem. surgery com. 1993—), Calif. Med. Assn. (mem. sci. adv. panel on plastic surgery 1992—), Omicron Kappa Upsilon. Office: Stanford U Med Ctr NC-104 Div Plastic-Reconstr Surg Stanford CA 94305

SCHENK, ROY U., health science and technology executive, writer; b. Ind., Nov. 18, 1929; s. Joseph W. and Marie A. (Neff) S.; m. Martha Wathen, 1950 (div. 1971); children: Christopher, David, M. Rebecca, Michael, Thomas, Benedict, Judith, Francis, Stephen, Katherine. BS, Purdue U., 1951; MS, Cornell U., 1953, PhD, 1954. Dir. biochem. rsch. Bjorksten Rsch. Labs., Madison, Wis., 1970-90; CEO Bioenergetics, Inc., Madison, 1973—, Domestic Abuse Project, Madison, 1992—; lectr. gender issues. Author: The Other Side of the Coin Causes and Consequences of Men's Oppression, 1982, We've Been Had: Writings on Men's Issues, 1989, Thoughts of Dr. Schenk on Sex and Gender, 1991; editor: Men Healing Shame, 1995; contbr. 30 articles to profl. jours. Candidate Dane County (Wis.) Bd., 1967, 69, Dane County Exec., 1973. Mem. Nat. Ctr. for Men, Nat. Coalition of Free Men. Office: Domestic Abuse Project PO Box 259173 Madison WI 53725-9173

SCHENK, SUSAN KIRKPATRICK, geriatric psychiatry nurse; b. New Richmond, Ind., Nov. 29, 1938; d. William Marcius and Frances (Kirkpatrick) Gaither; m. Richard Dee Brown, Aug. 13, 1960 (div. Feb. 1972); children: Christopher, David, Lisa; m. John Francis Schenk, July 24, 1975 (widowed Apr. 1995). BSN, Ind. U., 1962; postgrad., U. Del., 1973-75. RN, PHN, BCLS; cert. community coll. tchr., Calif. Staff nurse, then asst. dir. nursing Bloomington (Ind.) Hosp., 1962-66; charge nurse Newark (Del.) Manor, 1967-69; charge nurse GU Union Hosp., Terre Haute, Ind., 1971-72; clin. instr. nursing Ind. State U., Terre Haute, 1972-73; clin. instr. psychiatric nursing U. Del., Newark, 1974-75; psychiatric nursing care coord. VA Med. Ctr., Perry Point, Md., 1975-78; nurse educator Grossmont Hosp., La Mesa, Calif., 1978-90, cmty. rels. coord., 1990-91; dir. psychiat. svcs. Scripps Hosp. East County, El Cajon, Calif., 1991—; tech. advisor San Diego County Bd. Supervisors, 1987; tech. cons. Remedy Home and Health Care, San Diego, 1988; expert panelist Srs. Speak Out, KPBS-TV, San Diego, 1988; guest lectr. San Diego State U., 1987. Editor: Teaching Basic Caregiver Skills, 1988; author, performer tng. videotape Basic Caregiver Skills, 1988. Mem. patient svcs. com. Nat. Multiple Sclerosis Soc., San Diego, 1986-89; bd. dirs. Assn. for Quality and Participation, 1989. Adminstrn. on Aging/DHHS grantee, 1988. Mem. Am. Psychiat. Nurses Assn., Ind. U. Alumni Assn. (life), Mensa, Sigma Theta Tau. Home: 9435 Carlton Oaks Dr # D Santee CA 92071-2588 Office: Scripps Hosp East County 1688 E Main St El Cajon CA 92021-5204

SCHENKEL, SUSAN, psychologist, educator, author; b. Wroclaw, Poland, Apr. 21, 1946; came to U.S., 1949; d. Leon and Siddi (Fiedleholz) S.; m. Alvin Helfeld, Apr. 8, 1984. BA, U. Wis., 1967; MA in Clin. Psychology, SUNY, Buffalo, 1970, PhD in Clin. Psychology, 1973. Lic. psychologist, Mass. Psychologist Fitchburg (Mass.) State Coll., 1972-75, instr. in psychology, 1973-74; staff psychologist div. of alcoholism Boston City Hosp., 1975-76; chief psychologist Cambridge (Mass.) Ct. Clinic, 1976-80; instr. in psychology dept. psychiatry Med. Sch. Harvard U., 1976-80; pvt. practice psychology Cambridge, 1976—; instr. in psychology U. Mass., Boston, 1978; speaker in field. Author: Giving Away Success, 1984, German edit., 1986, Brazilian edit., 1988, rev. edit. 1991, Chinese edit., 1991; contbr. articles to profl. jours. USPHS fellow, 1967-70; N.Y. State Regents scholar, 1968-70; SUNY Rsch. Found. grantee, 1971-72. Mem. Am. Psychol. Assn., Mass. Psychol. Assn., Am. Soc. Tng. and Devel., Assn. for Advancement of Behavior Therapy.

SCHENKER, MARC BENET, preventive medicine educator; b. L.A., Aug. 25, 1947; s. Steve and Dosella Schenker; m. Heath Massey, Oct. 8; children: Yael, Phoebe, Hilary. BA, U. Calif., Berkeley, 1969; MD, U. Calif., San Francisco, 1973; MPH, Harvard U., Boston, 1980. Instr. medicine Harvard U., Boston, 1980-82; asst. prof. medicine U. Calif., Davis, 1982-86, assoc. prof., 1986-92, prof., 1992—, chmn. dept. epidemiology and preventive medicine, 1995—. Fellow ACP; mem. Am. Coll. Occupl. Medicine, Am. Thoracic Soc., Am. Pub. Health Assn., Soc. Epidemiologic Rsch., Am. Coll. Epidemiology, Soc. Occupl. Environ. Health, Internat. Commn. Occupl. Health, Phi Beta Kappa, Alpha Omega Alpha. Office: Dept Epidemiology and Preventive Medicine TB 168 Davis CA 95616-8638

SCHENKMAN, JOHN BORIS, pharmacologist, educator; b. N.Y.C., Feb. 10, 1936; s. Abraham and Theresa (Moses) S.; m. Deanna Owen, June 5, 1960; children: Jeffrey Alan, Laura Ruth. BA in Chemistry, Bklyn. Coll., 1960; PhD in Biochemistry, SUNY Upstate Med. Ctr., Syracuse, 1964. Postdoctoral fellow U. Pa. Johnson Found., Phila., 1964-67, Inst. Protein Research Osaka U., Japan, 1967-68, Inst. Toxicology Tübingen U., Fed. Republic Germany, 1968; asst. prof. Yale U. Sch. Medicine, New Haven, 1968-71, assoc. prof., 1971-78; prof., dept. head. U. Conn. Health Ctr., Farmington, 1978-87; prof. U. Conn., Farmington, 1987—, dir. grad. program cellular and molecular pharmacology, 1995—. Contbr. articles to profl. jours. Served as sgt. U.S. Army, 1953-55. Research grantee NIH, NSF; recipient Research Career Devel award NIH, 1971-76. Mem. Am. Soc. Biochemists and Molecular Biologists, AM. Soc. Pharmacology Exptl. Therapeutics, Brit. Biochemistry Soc., Soc. Toxicology, Am. Med. Sch. Pharmacologists (councilor 1987-88). Jewish. Office: U Conn Sch Medicine Dept Phamacology Farmington CT 06030-1505

SCHER, ALLAN JOSEPH, oncologist, consultant; b. Bklyn., June 2, 1935; s. David E. and Helen (Elbogen) S.; m. Linda Ronni Tash, Apr. 2, 1966; children: Michael B., Lauren J. BA, Yeshiva U., 1957; MD, Albert Einstein Coll. of Medicine, 1962. Diplomate Nat. Bd. Med. Examiners, 1963, Am. Bd. Radiology, 1967; lic. N.Y. 1963, Calif. 1966, N.J. 1968. Intern Bronx-Lebanon Hosp. Ctr., N.Y., 1962-63; resident in radiology Kings County Hosp., Bklyn., 1963-66; asst. chief radiation therapy USNR, San Diego, 1966-68; chief radiation oncology Morristown (N.J.) Meml. Hosp., 1968-86; cons. in radiation therapy Hackettstown (N.J.) Community Hosp., 1973-91; asst. adj. radiologist Beth Israel Hosp. Ctr., N.Y.C., 1966; clin. asst. instr. Kings County Hosp., 1969-71; clin. asst. prof. radiology Rutgers Med. Sch., 1974—; adj. asst. prof. allied health Fairleigh Dickinson U., Teaneck, N.J., 1975-85; cons. in radiation therapy Community Med. Ctr., Morristown, 1970-80. Presented numerous papers at various medical symposia. Mem. Coun. on Cancer, N.J., 1972-73, med. com. Riverside Hospice, 1976-79. State of N.Y. Med. Edn. and Rsch. Found. fellow, 1966-67. Fellow N.J. Acad. Medicine (sec. radiation therapy sect. 1975-76, chmn. 1976-77), Am. Coll. Radiology (alternate councillor 1981-84, councillor 1984-87); mem. AMA, Am. Soc. Therapeutic Radiologists, N.J. Oncology Soc. (co-founder, treas. 1975-77, trustee 1984-86, treas. 1987-88, sec. 1988-89, v.p. 1989-90, pres. 1990-91), N.J. Med. Soc. (sec. radiology sect. 1971-72, chmn. 1972-73, mem. ad hoc com. on atomic energy plants 1976), Radiology Soc. N.J. (sec. 1977-78, v.p. 1978-79, pres.-elect 1979-80, pres. 1980-81, mem. exec. com. 1982-94, chmn. radiotherapy sect. 1972-94, 96), Morris County Med. Soc., Albert Einstein Coll. Medicine Alumni Assn. (mem. bd. govs. 1975-78), N.J. Assn. Med. Specialty Socs. (v.p. 1980, pres. 1981), Acad. Medicine of N.J. (mem. exec. com. 1991). Jewish. Office: Radiation Oncologists of NW NJ 100 Madison Ave Morristown NJ 07960-6013

SCHER, RICHARD KEMPNER, dermatologist, eductor; b. N.Y.C., Sept. 2, 1929. AB, NYU, 1949; MA, Bklyn. Coll., 1951; MD, Howard U., 1955; MS, NYU, 1960; MA, Brown U., 1985. Diplomate Am. Bd. Dermatology. Prof. dermatology NYU, N.Y.C., 1977-83; prof. medicine Brown U., Providence, R.I., 1983-87; prof. dermatology Columbia U., N.Y.C., 1987—. Author: Nails: Treatment, Diagnosis, Surgery, 1990, 2d edit., 1996; contbr. articles to profl. jours. Lt. Comdr. USN, 1959-61. Fellow Am. Coll. Physicians, Am. Acad. Dermatology, Am. Coll. Allergists, Am. Acad. Allergy and Immunology. Office: Columbia/Presbyn Med Ctr 630 W 168 St New York NY 10032

SCHERER, HARVEY DANIEL, psychiatrist; b. Bronx, N.Y., Jan. 4, 1944; s. Benjamin and Pearl (Aropf) S.; m. Happy Levin, Sept. 25, 1981; children: Julie, Shannon, Robyn. BA, Queens Coll., 1964; MD, Albany Med Sch., 1969. Diplomate Am. Bd. Psychiatry and Neurology, Am. Bd. Child Psychiatry. Pvt. practice Albany, N.Y., 1974—; team leader adolescent unit Capital Dist. Psychiatric Ctr., Schenectady, N.Y., 1974-76; staff psychiatrist Capital Dist. Psychiatric Ctr., 1982-86; dir. adolescent svcs. Four Winds-Saratoga, 1986-89; pvt. practice child psychiatry Albany, N.Y., 1990—; clin. assoc. prof. Albany Med. Coll., 1974—; cons. in field. Bd. dirs. Bethlehem Tomboys, Delmar, N.Y., 1989. Fellow Am. Psychiatric Assn. (pres. Capital dist. br. 1989); mem. Am. Acad. Child Psychiatry, Capital Dist. Coun. Child Psychiatry (pres. 1987-89).

SCHERER, JEANNE CATHERINE, nurse, author; b. Buffalo, Apr. 8, 1928; d. Albert and Florence Rose (Steinman) Scherer. RN, Buffalo Gen. Hosp. Sch. Nursing, 1954; BSN, D'Youville Coll., 1966; MS, Canisius Coll., 1972. Staff nurse various hosps., 1954-66; clin. instr. Sisters Hosp. Sch. Nursing, Buffalo, 1966-68, 78-86, asst. dir., med. surg. nursing coord., 1968-78, cons., 1986-90. Author: Introductory Clinical Pharmacology, 1975, 3d edit., 1987, 4th edit., 1991, 5th edit., 1996; Introductory Medical-Surgical Nursing, 1977, 4th edit., 1986, 5th edit., 1991, 6th edit., 1995; Student Work Manual for Introductory Medical-Surgical Nursing, 1977, 6th edit., 1995; Student Work Manual for Introductory Clinical Pharmacology, 1982, 3d edit., 1987, 4th edit., 1991, 5th edit., 1996; Lippincott's Nurses' Drug Manual, 1985, Lippincott's Review for NCLEX-PN, 4th edit., 1994. Republican. Roman Catholic. Office: PO Box 763 West Seneca NY 14224-0763

SCHERER, KLAUS RAINER, psychologist, educator; b. Leverkusen, NRW, Germany, Mar. 18, 1943; m. Ursula Zündorf, Jan. 3, 1967. Diplom-Volkswirt, U. Cologne, Germany, 1967; PhD, Harvard U., 1970. Asst. prof. U. Pa., Phila., 1970-72; assoc. prof. U. Kiel, Germany, 1972-73; prof. U. Giessen, Germany, 1973-85, U. Geneva, 1985—; dir. psychol. assessement ctr. U. Geneva, 1989—. Author: Human Aggression and Conflict, 1975, Die Stressreaktion, 1985; editor: Handbook of Methods in Nonverbal Behavior Research, 1982, Approaches to Emotion, 1984, Psychologie der Emotion, 1990, Justice: An Interdisciplinary Perspective, 1992. Resident fellow Rockefeller Found., 1982, Netherlands Inst. Advanced Studies, 1984; recipient Akademie Stipendium, Volkswagenstiftung, 1982-83. Fellow APA; mem. Acad. Europea, Acoustical Soc. Am., German Psychol. Assn., Internat. Soc. for Rsch. on Emotion. Office: U Geneva, 9 route de Drize, CH-1227 Geneva Switzerland

SCHERER, RONALD CALLAWAY, voice scientist, educator; b. Akron, Ohio, Sept. 11, 1945; s. Belden Davis and Lois Ramona (Callaway) S.; children: Christopher, Maria. BS, Kent State U., 1968; MA, Ind. U., 1972; PhD, U. Iowa, 1981. Research asst. U. Iowa, Iowa City, 1979-81, asst. research scientist, 1981-83, adj. asst. prof., 1983-88, adj. assoc. prof., 1988—; adj. asst. prof. U. Denver, 1984-86; asst. adj. prof. U. Colo., Boulder, 1984-93, adj. assoc. prof., 1993—; research scientist The Denver Ctr. for the Performing Arts, 1983-88, sr. scientist, 1988—; lectr. voice and speech sci. Nat. Theatre Conservatory, Denver, 1990-94; asst. clin. prof. Sch. Medicine U. Colo., Denver, 1988—; adj. assoc. prof. U. Okla., 1992—; affiliate clin. prof. U. No. Colo., 1993—; mem. exec. and legis. bd. Nat. Ctr. for Voice and Speech, 1990—. Author: (with Dr. I. Titze) Vocal Fold Physiology: Biomechanics, Acoustics and Phonatory Control, 1983; contbr. articles to profl. jours. Nat. Inst. Dental Research fellow, 1972-76. Fellow Internat. Soc. Phonetic Scis. (auditor 1988-91); mem. Internat. Arts Medicine Assn., Am. Speech-Lang.-Hearing Assn., Acoustical Soc. Am., Internat. Assn. Logopedics and Phoniatrics, Am. Assn. Phonetic Scis. (nominating com. 1985-87), Collegium Medicorum Theatri, Sigma Xi, Pi Mu Epsilon. Office: Denver Ctr for Performing Arts 1245 Champa St Denver CO 80204-2104

SCHERGER, JOSEPH E., family physician, educator; b. Delphos, Ohio, Aug. 29, 1950; m. Carol M. Wintermute, Aug. 7, 1973; children: Adrian, Gabriel. BS summa cum laude, U. Dayton, 1971; MD, UCLA, 1975. Family practice residency U. Wash., Seattle, 1975-78; clin. instr. U. Calif. Sch. Medicine, Davis, 1978-80, asst. clin. prof., 1980-84, assoc. clin. prof., 1984-90, clin. prof., 1990—, dir. predoctoral program, 1991-92; med. dir. family practice and community medicine Sharp Healthcare, San Diego, 1992—. Recipeient Hippocratic Oath award UCLA, Calif. Physician of Yr. award Am. Acad. Family Physicians. Mem. Inst. Medicine of NAS, Am. Acad. Family Physicians, Soc. Tchrs. Family Medicine. Home: 3205 Rim Rock Cir Encinitas CA 92024-5718 Office: Sharp Healthcare 3571 Corporate Ct San Diego CA 92123*

SCHERICK, KENNETH JAY, optometrist; b. N.Y.C., Sept. 27, 1949; s. Sidney and Sylvia Scherick; m. Barbara Louise Klein, July 24, 1972; children: Adam, Scott, Heather. BS, Pa. Coll. Optometry, 1971, OD, 1974. Pvt. practice N.Y.C., 1974—; instr. contact lens clinic Bellvue Hosp., N.Y.C., 1987—; cons. Bausch/Lomb, 1985—, Carrera Optical, 1983-89. Mem. Optometric Coun. N.Y. (pres. 1987-89). Home: 608 2d Ave New York NY 10016

SCHERL, DELLA L., nursing administrator; b. Trenton, Oct. 16, 1951; d. Richard Stauffer and Jessie Mae (Beck) White; 1 child from previous marriage: Jessica Leigh; m. Mario M. Scherl, May 3, 1996. Diploma Helene Fuld Sch. Nursing, Trenton, 1972; B.S.N., Trenton State Coll., 1980; M.S.N., U. Pa., 1983. Lic. nursing home adminstr., N.J. Dir. nursing Lakewood House, Burlington, N.J., 1972-73, Moorestown Nursing Home, N.J., 1973-78; staff nurse Burlington County Meml. Hosp., N.J., 1978-80, head nurse, 1980-81; dir. nursing Mt. Holly Ctr., N.J., 1981-82; assoc. dir. nursing Hamilton Hosp., Trenton, 1983-85; nursing supr. Hickory House Nursing Home, Honeybrook, Pa., 1986-87, asst. dir., 1987-88; owner, mgr. Marsh Creek Campground, Lyndell, Pa., 1984-94; owner Star Nursing Home Staffing Svc., Lyndell, 1988-91; DON St. Martha Manor, Downingtown, Pa., 1991—. Home: 1307 Glenside Rd Downingtown PA 19335 Office: St Martha Manor 470 Manor Ave Downingtown PA 19335-2545

SCHERMAN, SUSAN LOUISE, nurse; b. Hoboken, N.J., Apr. 20, 1953; d. Everett Harold and Louise Annetta (Becker) S.; m. John Alfred Pendenza, Oct. 6, 1979. Student, St. Mary Hosp. Sch. Nursing, 1974, Katharine Gibbs Secretarial Sch., N.Y.C., 1976; BA, Sch. Nursing and Health Edn., Jersey City State Coll., 1978. RN, N.Y.; Lic. Real Estate Sales Rep., N.J., 1994. Sr. Staff NYU Med. Ctr., N.Y.C., 1974-78; nurse Christ Hosp., Jersey City, 1975-78; pub. health nurse Retarded Infants Svcs., Inc., N.Y.C., 1978-80; pub. health nursing supr. Hoboken Pub. Health Nursing Service, N.J., 1980-83; nurse cons. New York County Health Services Rev. Orgn., N.Y.C., 1983-86; cons. risk mgmt. Bower & Gardner, N.Y.C., 1986-91; nurse cons. Group Health, Inc., 1992; risk mgr. Jersey City Med. Ctr., 1992; sch. nurse/health edn. tchr. T. Roosevelt Sch., N.J., 1992-95; realtor Ray Fiore Real Estate, Hoboken, N.J., 1994; nurse cons. McAloon & Friedman, P.C. Attys., N.Y.C., 1995—, real estate agent P.J. Miller Assocs., Secaucus, N.J. Author: Community Health Nursing Care Plans: A Guide for Home Health Care Professionals, 1984. Mem. N.Am. Nursing Diagnosis Assn., N.J. Bd. Realtors, Nat. Assn. Realtors, Hudson County Bd. of Realtors, Inc., Soc. Scribes, Intravenous Nurses Soc. (N.J. chpt.), N.J. State Bd. Realtors. Roman Catholic. Avocations: calligraphy, swimming, needlepoint, parasailing. Office: McAloon & Friedman PC 116 John St New York NY 10038

SCHERMER, VICTOR L., psychologist, psychotherapist; b. Bklyn., Feb. 1, 1941; s. Matthew and Jean (Polansky) S. BA in Psychology, Bklyn. Coll., 1964; MA in Psychology, U. Pa., 1965; postgrad., U. N.H., 1972; cert., Inst. for Psychoanalytic Psychotherapy, 1980. Lic. psychologist, Pa; cert. addictions Counselor, Pa. Psychology instr. Upsala Coll., East Orange, N.J., 1965-66, Clarkson Coll., Potsdam, N.Y., 1966-67; asst. prof. psychology Glassboro (N.J.) State Coll., 1967-71; counselor Voyage House, Phila., 1972-73; psychologist Jefferson Hosp., Phila., 1973-75, Help Inc., Phila., 1975-84, INTERAC Community Mental Health Ctr., Phila., 1984-86, PATH Community Mental Health Ctr., Phila., 1987-88; outpatient dir. Mirmont Treatment Ctr., Lima, 1988-92; mental health/mental retardation coord. Action AIDS, 1992-94; psychologist Northwest Ctr., 1994-95, Harmony Mental Health Svcs., 1994—; pvt. practice as psychologist and psychotherapist, 1988—; exec. dir. Study Group for Contemporary Psychoanalytic Process, 1985—; mem. faculty Inst. for Psychoanalytic Psychotherapy, Bryn Mawr, Pa., 1984-93; bd. dirs., mem. faculty Inst. for Spiritual and Psychol. Healing, Bala Cynwyd, Pa., 1989—; dir. Inst. for Study of Human Conflict, Pa., 1991—. Co-author: Object Relations, The Self, and the Group, 197; co-editor: Ring of Fire, 1994; contbr. articles to profl. jours. Mem. Am. Group Psychotherapy Assn., Del. Valley Group Psychotherapy Soc., Phila. Soc. for Psychoanalytic Psychology. Home: 735 S 9th St Philadelphia PA 19147-2838 Office: The Lincoln Rittenhouse 222 W Rittenhouse Sq Philadelphia PA 19103-5705

SCHERR, LAWRENCE, physician, educator; b. N.Y.C., Nov. 6, 1928; s. Harry and Sophia (Schwartz) S.; m. Peggy L. Binenkorb, June 13, 1954; children: Cynthia E., Robert W. AB, Cornell U., 1950, MD, 1957. Diplomate Am. Bd. Internal Medicine (bd. dirs., sec.-treas. 1979-86). Intern Cornell Med. divsn. Bellevue Hosp. and Meml. Ctr., 1957-58, asst. resident, 1958-59, rsch. fellow cardiorenal lab., 1959-60, chief resident, 1960-61, co-dir. cardiorenal lab., 1961-62, asst. vis. physician, 1961-63, assoc. vis. physician, 1963-65, dir. cardiology and renal unit, 1963-67, assoc. dir., 1964-67, vis. physician, 1966-68; physician to out-patients N.Y. Hosp., 1961-63, asst. attending physician, 1963-66, assoc. attending physician, 1966-71, attending physician, 1971—; asst. attending physician Sloan-Kettering Cancer Ctr., 1962-71, cons., 1971—; chmn. dept. medicine North Shore Univ. Hosp., 1967—, dir. acad. affairs, 1969-93, sr. v.p. med. affairs, 1993—; asst. in medicine Med. Coll. Cornell U., 1958-59; rsch. fellow N.Y. Heart Assn., 1959-60, instr. medicine, 1960-63, asst. prof., 1963-66, assoc. prof., 1966-71, David J. Greene Disting. prof., 1971—, assoc. dean, 1969—; career scientist Health Rsch. Coun., N.Y.C., 1962-66; tchg. scholar Am. Heart Assn., 1966-67; pres. N.Y. State Bd. Medicine, 1974-75; bd. dirs. Nat. Bd. Med. Examiners, 1976-80; chmn. Accreditation Coun. for Grad. Med. Edn., 1988, N.Y. State Coun. on Grad. Edn., 1987-92. Contbr. articles to profl. jours. Lt. USNR, 1950-53. Fellow N.Y. Acad. Medicine, Am. Heart Assn. (coun. on clin. cardiology); mem. ACP (master, chmn. and gov. Downstate N.Y. region II 1975-80, regent 1980-86, chmn. bd. regents 1985-86; nat. pres.-elect 1986-87, pres. 1987-88, pres. emeritus), AMA, Am. Fedn. Clin. Rsch., Harvey Soc., N.Y. Med. Soc., Nassau County Med. Soc., Assn. Am. Med. Colls., Am. Clin. and Climatologic Assn. Home: 19 Doral Dr Manhasset NY 11030-3907 Office: No Shore Univ Hosp Manhasset NY 11030

SCHERY, TERIS KIM, communication disorders educator; b. St. Louis, Apr. 15, 1943; d. Robert W. and Lois J. (Keller) Schery; m. Mark W. Lipsey, Aug. 14, 1980; children: Loren Christopher, Marisa Kim. BA, Stanford U., 1965, MA, 1966; PhD, Claremont Grad. Sch., 1980. Clinician, research asst. Inst. for Childhood Aphasia, Palo Alto, Calif., 1966-70; program specialist for communication disorders Los Angeles County Superintendent of Schs. Office, 1970-80; assoc. prof. communication disorders Calif. State U., Los Angeles, 1981-84, prof. communication disorders, 1984-92; rsch. prof. edn. and human devel. Vanderbilt U., Nashville, 1992—; rsch. prof. edn. divsn. hearing and speech scis. Vanderbilt U. Med. Sch., 1992—; cons. in field, 1970—. Contbr. articles to profl. jours. and chpt. to books. Fulbright Teaching grantee U.S. Ednl. Found., 1985-86, grantee Office of Spl. Edn. and Calif. State U. Sys., 1978-90. Fellow Am. Speech-Lang.-Hearing Assn. (v.p. clin. affairs 1988-91); mem. Calif. Speech-Lang.-Hearing Assn. (cert.), Tenn. Assn. Audiologists and Speech-Lang. Pathologists, Coun. for Exceptional Children, Soc. Rsch. in Child Devel., Am. Ednl. Rsch. Assn., Phi Beta Kappa, Phi Kappa Phi. Home: 303 Fairfax Ave Nashville TN 37212-4006 Office: Vanderbilt U Box 90 GPC Nashville TN 37202

SCHERZER, JOSEPH MARTIN, dermatologist; b. Newark, July 2, 1946; s. Louis and Gertrude (Brodnick) S.; m. Anna Stella Meed, June 24, 1971; children: Jeanine Rebecca and Michael Ira. BA cum laude, Rutgers U., 1968; MD, Albert Einstein Med. Coll., 1972. Diplomate Am. Bd. Dermatology; spl. cert. in Dermopathology. Owner, president Scottsdale (Ariz.) Skin and Cancer Ctr., Ltd., 1976—; asst. instr. Bellevue (N.Y.) Med. Ctr., 1976 (fall). Founding mem. Nat. Orgn. Physicians Who Care, 1985; mem. B'nai Brith, Phoenix, 1993—; mem. Scottsdale C.C. Jazz Ensemble, 1989. Recipient Outstanding Svc. award Scottsdale C.C. Jazz Ensemble, 1989, 1990; named Jazz Performer of Yr., 1992, Jazz Instrumentalist of Yr., 1993. Mem. AMA, Am. Acad. Dermatology; Phoenix Dermatology Soc. (v.p. 1978-79, sec.-treas. 1983-84, pres. 1984-85), Ariz. Med. Assn., Assn. Am. Physician/Surgeons, (founding pres. Ariz. 1995-96), Maricopa County Med. Soc., Internat. Soc. Dermatopathology, Am. Soc. Dermatopathology. Home: 5238 E Via Los Caballos Paradise Valley AZ 85253 Office: Scottsdale Skin Cancer Ctr Ste # 502 10900 N Scottsdale Rd Scottsdale AZ 85254

SCHETKY, DIANE HEISKELL, psychiatrist; b. N.Y.C., Feb. 8, 1940; d. Andrew Heiskell and Cornelia (Scott) Chapin; m. Charles H. Browning, Aug. 3, 1963 (div. June 1977); children: James Andrew, Scott Hamilton; m. L. McDonald Schetky, Nov. 26, 1977 (div. Jan. 1986). BA, Sarah Lawrence Coll., 1961; MD, Case Western Reserve U., 1966. Diplomate Am. Bd. Psychiatry and Neurology with subspecialties in adult psychiatry, child psychiatry, and forensic psychiatry. Intern Babies and Children's Hosp., Cleve., 1966-67; resident Dept. Psychiatry U. Hosp., Cleve., 1967-69, fellow in child psychiatry, 1969-73; dir. child psychiat. clinic U. Oreg. Health Scis. Ctr., Portland, Oreg., 1974-77; pvt. practice Wilton, Conn., 1978-86, Rockport, Maine, 1986—; assoc. univ. clin. prof. psychiatry Yale Child Study Ctr., New Haven, 1978-86. Co-author: Child Sexual Abuse: A Guide for Health care and Legal Professionals, 1988; co-editor Child Psychiatry and The Lawy, 1980, Emerging Issues in Child Psychiatry and The Law, 1985, Clinical Handbook of Child Psychiatry and the Law, 1991; contbr. articles to profl. jours. Mem. chorus Surry (Maine) Opera Co., 1988; bd. dirs. Bay Chamber Concerts; mem. Hospice Vol. Bd., 1994—. Fellow Am. Acad. Child and Adolescent Psychiatry (mem. coun. 1996—), Am. Psychiat. Assn.; mem. Am. Acad. Psychiatry and Law, Maine Psychiat. Assn. (chair ethics com.). Democrat.

SCHEURING, RICHARD ANTHONY, physician; b. Chgo., Aug. 30, 1964; s. Robert Norman and Judith Marie (Puttin) S.; m. Michelle C. Scheuring, Sept. 24, 1994; children: Joshua, Caitlin Marie. BA, Ea. Ill. U., 1987; DO, Chgo. Coll. Osteo. Medicine, 1993. Intern in family medicine Presbyn./St. Luke's Med. Ctr., Denver, 1993-94, resident in family medicine, 1994—. Keyman Promise Keepers, Aurora, Colo., 1994—. Recipient Med. Student Rsch. scholarship NIH, 1993. Mem. AMA, Am. Acad. Family Physicians, Am. Osteo. Assn., Colo. Med. Soc., Aircraft Owners and Pilot Assn., Sigma Sigma Phi (sec. 1985-86). Republican. Southern Baptist. Home: 2993 S Revere St Aurora CO 80014 Office: Presbyn St Lukes Med Ctr 830 Potomac Ste 310 Aurora CO 80011

SCHIAVI, RAUL CONSTANTE, psychiatrist, educator, researcher; b. Buenos Aires, Argentina, Jan. 7, 1930; came to U.S. 1956; s. Constantino and Maria (Acquier) S.; m. Michelle deMiniac, Aug. 26, 1960; children; Isabelle, Nadine, Viviane. MD, U. Buenos Aires, 1953. Diplomate Am. Bd. Psychiatry and Neurology. Fgn. asst. psychiatry U. Paris, 1955-56; resident in psychiatry U. Pa., Phila., 1956-59; instr. psychiatry U. Pa., 1959-61; assoc. College de France, Paris, 1961-63; asst. prof. psychiatry Cornell U., N.Y.C., 1963-66; assoc. prof. psychiatry SUNY, Downstate Med. Ctr., Bklyn., 1966-71, Mt. Sinai Sch. Medicine, N.Y.C., 1971-78; prof. psychiatry Mt. Sinai Sch. Medicine, 1978-96, emeritus prof. psychiatry, 1996—; fellow Found. Fund for Rsch. in Psychiatry, 1958-63; cons. NIMH, 1966-70, 77-81 (Rsch. Sci. Devel. award 1966, grantee 1976-95); dir. human sexuality program Mt. Sinai Sch. Medicine, 1973-96; advisor WHO, 1989. Contbr. articles to profl. jours., chpts. to books; co-editor Jour. Sex and Marital Therapy; mem. editl. bd. Archives of Sexual Behavior, Hormones and Behavior, Psychosomatic Medicine, Revista Latinoamericana de Sexologia, Quaderni de Sessuologia Clinica, Revista Argentina de Sexualidad Humana, Annual Rev. Sex Rsch. Recipient Masters and Johnson award Soc. for Sex Therapy and Rsch., 1991; grantee NIH, 1977-80, 87-95, others. Fellow Am. Psychopathol. Assn., Psychiat. Rsch. Soc., Am. Psychiat. Assn. (life fellow, cons. 1989. Excellence in Edn. award 1992); mem. AAAS, Am. Psychosomatic Soc. (coun. 1985-88), Internat. Acad. Sex Rsch. (pres. 1995-96), Soc. Sex Therapy and Rsch. (pres. 1984-86), Sex Info and Edn. Coun. of U.S. (bd. dirs. 1979-83), Internat. Soc. Psychoneuroendocrinology, Sigma Xi. Office: Mt Sinai Sch Medicine 1 Gustave L Levy Pl New York NY 10029-6504

SCHICK, AUGUST, psychologist, educator; b. Baustetten, Fed. Republic of Germany, Sept. 20, 1940; s. August and Kreszentia (Guter) S.; m. Kunigunde Norz, Apr. 9, 1969; children: Monika, Christoph Ivo. Diploma in Psychology, Univ. TÜbingen, München, 1966; PhD, Univ. Münster, 1969. Rsch. asst. Tchrs. Training Coll., Osnabrück, 1966-69, Univ. Psychology Inst., Tübingen, 1969-74; prof. Univ., Oldenburg, 1974—; dir. Univ. Inst. for Rsch. into Man-Environment-Rels., Oldenburg, 1985—, mem. grad. sch. psychoacoustics, 1992—; cons. Fed. Environ. Agy. and Fed. Health Office, Berlin, 1987—. Editor Oldenburg Symposia into Psychol. Acoustics; editor-in-chief Zeitschrift f'4r Lärmbek. Bd. dirs. German Soc. for Noise Control, Düsseldorf, 1985—. Recipient Satô prize Acoustical Soc. Japan, 1986, Japanese-German Rsch. award Japan Soc. for Promotion of Sci., 1994. Mem. Rotary. Roman Catholic. Office: U Oldenburg Dept Psych, Amerländer Heerstr 114, D 26111 Oldenburg Germany

SCHIDLOW, DANIEL, pediatrician, medical association administrator; b. Santiago, Chile, Oct. 23, 1947; m. Sally Rosen; children: David, Michael, Jessica. Grad., U. Chile, 1972. Diplomate Am. Bd. Pediatrics, Am. Bd. Pediatric Pulmonology; lic. in D.C., Pa., N.J. Rotating intern U. Chile Hosp., U. Chile Sch. Medicine, 1971-72, resident in internal medicine, instr. phys. diagnosis, 1972-73; resident, emergency rm. physician in pediatrics E.G. Cortes Hosp. Children, U. Chile, 1973-74; resident in pediatrics Albert Einstein Coll. Medicine Bronx (N.Y.)-Lebanon Hosp. Ctr., 1974-76; fellow pediatric pulmonary medicine St. Christopher's Hosp. Children, Phila., 1976-78; chief sect. pediatric pulmonology dept. pediatrics St. Christopher's Hosp. Children, 1983-94, sr. v.p. clin. affairs, 1994—; from asst. to assoc. prof. pediatrics sch. medicine Temple U., Phila., 1978-90, prof., 1990-94, dep. chmn. dept. pediatrics, 1991-94; prof., sr. vice chmn. dept. pediatrics Allegheny U. of Health Scis., Phila., 1994—, Med. Coll. Pa., Phila., 1994—, Hahnemann Sch. Medicine, Phila., 1994—; attending physician St. Christopher's Hosp. Children, 1978—, dir. fellowship tng. and edn. program sect. pediatric pulmonology, 1979-91, assoc. dir. pediatric pulmonary and cystic fibrosis ctr., 1981-83, med. dir. dept. respiratory therapy, 1982-88, project dir. Phila. pediatric pulmonary ctr., 1983-86, dir. cystic fibrosis ctr., 1983—, chair capital campaign com. dept. pediatrics, 1987, mem. exec. com. med. staff, 1988—, mem. various coms.; courtesy staff Lancaster (Pa.) Gen. Hosp., 1980-82; cons. divsn. rehab. Pa. Dept. Health, 1983—; mem. promotions com. dept. pediatrics sch. medicine Temple U., 1986—, chmn. com. appointments clin.-educator track 1991—; attending staff no. divsn. Albert Einstein Med. Ctr., 1987—; cons. Nat. Ctr. Youth Disabilities, 1987—; mem. med. adv. coun. Cystic Fibrosis Found., Bethesda, Md., 1987—, trustee, 1990—, med. dir. home care svcs., 1991—, various other positons; consulting staff Temple U. Hosp., 1988—; mem. organizing com. N.Am. Cystic Fibrosis Conf., 1990-93, co-chmn., 1992—; co-chmn. Nat. Concensus Conf. Pulmonary Complications Cystic Fibrosis, McLean, Va., 1992; mem. adv. bd. Phila. Parenting Assocs., 1992—. Reviewer Jour. Pediatrics, Am. Jour. Diseases Children, others. Named Illustrious Guest, City of LaPlata, Argentina, 1992. Fellow Am. Acad. Pediatrics (Pa. chpt., sect. diseases chest), Am. Coll. Chest Physicians (sect. cardiopulmonary diseases children); mem. AAAS, Am. Thoracic Soc. (mem. nominating com. 1993—), Am. Fedn. Clin. Rsch., Chilean Pediatric Soc. (hon.), Pa. Thoracic Soc., Ea. Soc. Pediatric Rsch., Phila. Pediatric Soc. Home: 315 N Bowman Ave Merion Station PA 19066-1523 Office: St Christopher's Hosp Chldn Office Med and Acad Affairs Erie Ave at Front St Philadelphia PA 19134

SCHIEBEL, HERMAN MAX, retired surgeon; b. Balto, Md., Jan. 18, 1909; s. Max Herman and Elizabeth Martha (Schmiedicke) S.; m. Barbara Fish, Oct. 12, 1941 (dec. 1968; m. Nancy Anderson Alyea, Dec. 26, 1968; 1 child, Elizabeth Dinsmore. AB, Johns Hopkins U., 1929, MD, 1933. Diplomate Am. Bd. Surgery. Intern in surgery Duke U. Hosp., Durham, N.C., 1933-34; resident in surgery Duke U., Durham, N.C., 1933-39; instr. surgery Duke U., 1935-39; asst. prof. Sch. Medicine, Duke U., 1940-70; assoc. clin. prof. Duke U., 1970-85; asst. clin. prof. Med. Sch., U. N.C., Chapel Hill, 1941-52, assoc. clin. prof., 1952-80, clin. prof., 1980-88; sr. staff mem. Durham county Gen. Hosp. (formerly Watt Hosp., now Durham Regional Hosp.), Durham, 1940-85, chief of staff, 1949-54; chief of surgery Lincoln Hosp., Durham, 1941-68; dir. surgery Dorothea Dix Hosp., Raleigh, N.C., 1980-88. Contbr. surg. papers to profl. jours. Bd. dirs. N.C. divsn. Am. Cancer Soc., 1944—, pres., 1958-59; bd. dirs. Nat. Am. Cancer Soc., 1959-76; founder group N.C. Cancer Hosp., Lumberton, 1960—, pres., 1962-64; organizer, dir. Cancer Detection Clinic, Durham, 1949-87. Recipient Disting. Svc. medal N.C. chpt. Am. Cancer Soc., 1960, Disting. Alumnae award N.C. Med. Sch., 1980, Disting. Svc. award Dorothea Dix Hosp., 1989. Mem. AMA, So. Med. Soc., So. Thoracic Soc., S.E. Surg. Assn., N.C. Surg. Assn. (pres. 1967-68), Am. Coll. Surg., United Flying Octogenerians, Kiwanis. Republican. Episcopalian. Home: 1020 Anderson St Durham NC 27705-5804

SCHIEBLER, GEROLD LUDWIG, physician, educator; b. Hamburg, Pa., June 20, 1928; s. Alwin Robert and Charlotte Elizabeth (Schmoele) S.; m. Audrey Jean Lincourt, Jan. 8, 1954; children: Mark, Marcella, Kristen, Bettina, Wanda, Michele. BS, Franklin and Marshall Coll., 1950; MD, Harvard U., 1954. Intern pediatrics and internal medicine Mass. Gen. Hosp., Boston, 1954-55, resident, 1955-56; resident pediatrics U. Minn. Hosp., Mpls., 1956-57, fellow pediatric cardiology, 1957-58, rsch. fellow, 1958-59; rsch. fellow sect. physiology Mayo Clinic and Mayo Found., 1959-60; asst. prof. pediatric cardiology U. Fla., 1960-63, assoc. prof., 1963-66, prof., 1966-92, Disting. Svc. prof., 1992—, chmn. dept. pediatrics, 1968-85, assoc. v.p. for health affairs for external rels., 1985—; dir. div. Children's Med. Svcs., State of Fla., 1973-74. Author: (with L.P. Elliott) The X-ray Diagnosis of Congenital Cardiac Disease in Infants, Children and Adults, 1968, 2d edit., 1979, (with L.J. Krovetz and I.H. Gessner) Pediatric Cardiology, 2d edit., 1979. Mem. AAAS, Inst. Medicine NAS, Am. Acad. Pediatrics (Abraham Jacobi award 1993), AMA (Benjamin Rush award 1993), Am. Coll. Cardiology, Soc. Pediatric Rsch. (emeritus), Fla. Pediatric Soc. (exec. com.), Fla. Heart Assn. (past pres.), Fla. Med. Assn. (past v.p., bd. govs., pres. 1991-92), Phi Beta Kappa, Alpha Omega Alpha. Home: 2115 NW 15th Ave Gainesville FL 32605-5216

SCHIEFER, HANS GERD, microbiology educator; b. Wuppertal, Germany, Dec. 17, 1935. MD, Med. Akademie, Düsseldorf, Germany, 1962; Habilitation, U. Giessen, Germany, 1974. Prof. U. Giessen, 1975—. Contbg. author papers and books on membrane biology and cell physiology of mycoplasmas and chlamydiae, sexually transmitted diseases, urinary tract infections, prostatitis, and zoonoses. Mem. Gesellschaft Deutscher Naturforscher und Ärzte, Internat. Orgn. for Mycoplasmology, Am. Soc. for Microbiology, Deutsche Gesellschaft für Hygiene und Mikrobiologie, Robert Koch Stiftung. Office: Med Mikrobiologie, Schubertstr 1, D 35392 Giessen Germany

SCHIEKEN, RICHARD MERRILL, physician; b. Phila., May 6, 1939; s. Benjamin B. and Edythe (Lesser) S.; m. Barbara Lynn Newman, Aug. 23, 1964; children: Julia, William, Shira. AB, LaSalle U., 1961; MD, U. Pa., 1965. Diplomate Am. Bd. Pediatrics. Intern, then resident in pediatrics Children's Hosp. of Pa., Phila., 1965-68, fellow in pediatric cardiology, 1968-70; asst. instr. pediatrics U. Pa., Phila., 1966-67; clin. asst. prof. Sch. Medicine Georgetown U., Washington, 1971-73; with U. Iowa, Iowa City, 1973-82, prof. pediatrics Sch. Medicine, 1980-82, prof. preventive medicine Sch. Medicine, 1981-82; prof., chmn. pediatric cardiology dept. Med. Coll. of Va., Richmond, 1982—; mem. exec. com. Nat. Cholesterol Edn. Program, Bethesda, 1986-96. Contbr. articles to profl. jours. Chmn. epidemiology disease control study sect. NIH, Bethesda, Md. Maj. U.S. Army, 1970-73. Fellow Am. Coll. Cardiology (chmn. preventive cardiovascular disease com. 1984-86), Am. Acad. Pediatrics, Am. Heart Assn. (epidemiology coun.); mem. Nat. Acad. Sci. (diet and health coms. 1986-88). Jewish. Home: 422 September Dr Richmond VA 23229-7318

SCHIESSL, KATHERINE LYNN, child and adolescent clinical social worker; b. Sanford, Maine, July 5, 1963; d. Wayne L. Williams and Elaine a. (Gagne) Sullivan; m. Gary G.Schiessl, May 24, 1986; children: Courtney, Jonathan. BSW, St. Joseph Coll., West Hartford, Conn., 1985; MSW, Boston U., 1988. Lic. clin. social worker. Caseworker Gary Lodge Residential Facility, Hartford, Conn., 1986-87; clin. therapist North Cen. Conn. Mental Health, Enfield, 1988—. Mem. NASW. Democrat. Roman Catholic. Office: N Cen Conn Mental Health 47 Palomba Dr Enfield CT 06082-3641

SCHIFF, DONALD WILFRED, pediatrician, educator; b. Detroit, Sept. 11, 1925; s. Henry and Kate (Boesky) S.; m. Rosalie Pergament; children: Stephen, Jeffrey, Susan, Douglas. Student, Wayne State U., 1943-44, Oberlin Coll., 1944-45; MD, Wayne State U., 1949. Diplomate Am. Bd. Pediatrics. Intern Detroit Receiving Hosp., 1949-50; resident in pediatrics U. Colo., 1954-55, chief resident in pediatrics, 1955-56; instr. U. Colo. Health Scis. Ctr., Denver, 1956-59, asst. clin. prof., 1959-69, assoc. clin. prof., 1969-78, clin. prof., 1978-87, prof., 1987—; pvt. practice Littleton (Colo.) Clinic, 1956-86, chmn. bd., 1973-79; med. dir. HMO Colo., Denver, 1980-86; med. dir. Child Health Clinic The Children's Hosp., Denver. Contbr. articles to profl. jours. Bd. dirs. Sch. Dist. VI, Colo., 1962; pres. Arapahoe Mental Health Clinic, Denver, 1968-70, bd. dirs., 1964-70; adv. coun. State of Colo. Medicaid, Denver, 1981—. With USN, 1944-46, USPHS, 1952-54, Turtle Mountain Indian Reservation, N.D. Recipient 25 Yrs. Teaching award U. Colo. Sch. Medicine, 1981. Mem. Am. Acad. Pediatrics (chmn. Colo. chpt. 1973-79, alternate dist. chmn. 1977-81, chmn. dist. 8 1981-86, nat. pres. 1988-89), Rocky Mountain Pediatric Soc., Colo. Med. Soc. Home: 600 Front Range Rd Littleton CO 80120-4052 Office: The Children's Hosp Child Health Clinic Box BO32 1056 E 19th Ave Denver CO 80218-1007

SCHIFF, ELLIOT DONALD, clinical psychologist; b. Dubuque, Iowa, June 22, 1957; s. Solomon and Shirley (Miller) S.; m. Alisa Tannenbaum, Dec. 25, 1986. A in Hebrew Lit., Hebrew Theol. Coll., 1978; BA, Northeastern Ill. U., 1978; MA, Roosevelt U., 1982; MS, Nova U., 1987, D in Psychology, 1988. Lic. psychologist. Psychology intern NYU Med. Ctr., N.Y.C., 1981-82; psychology trainee Nova U. Mental Health Ctr., Coral Springs, Fla., 1983-84, North Miami Community Mental Health Ctr., Miami, Fla., 1984-85; psychology intern Bklyn. VA Med. Ctr., 1985-86; clin. psychologist Ctrs. for Psychol. Growth, Miami, 1987-93, Family Workshop Miami Heart Inst. North Campus, Miami Beach, 1987-93, Adult Day Treatment Ctr., Miami Beach, 1987-93; clin. psychologist clin. neurosci. unit Miami Heart Inst., North Campus, Miami Beach, 1987-93; pvt. practice

Woodmere, N.Y., 1993—; cons. Pvt. Psychologists, Miami, 1987-93. Mem. safety com. City of Miami Beach, 1987-93. Mem. APA, Nassau County Psychol. Assn., Psi Chi. Office: North Campus 999 Central Ave # 208 Woodmere NY 11598-9999

SCHIFF, ROBERT, health care consultancy company executive; b. N.Y.C., Jan. 7, 1942; s. Henry and Jeanette (Levine) S.; m. Adrianne Bendich, Aug. 16, 1964 (div. July 1979); children: Jorden, Debra; m. Joann McTaggart, Aug. 24, 1986. BS, CCNY, 1964; MS, Iowa State U., 1966; PhD, U. Calif., Davis, 1968. Asst. prof. anatomy Tufts U. Sch. Medicine, Boston, 1969-72; mgr. serology rsch. Hyland divsn. Baxter Labs., Costa Mesa, Calif., 1972-74; dir. R & D J.T. Baker Diagnostics, Bethlehem, Pa., 1974-77; dir. diagnostic R & D Hoffmann-LaRoche, Nutley, N.J., 1977-80; group v.p. Warner Lambert Co., Morris Plains, N.J., 1980-82; pres., CEO Schiff & Co., Inc., West Caldwell, N.J., 1982—; Del. Nat. Commn. for Clin. Lab. Stds., 1979-80; vice chmn. R & D Coun. N.J., 1980-82; bd. dirs. E.P.I. subs. E-Z-EM, Westbury, N.Y., 1991—. Contbr. numerous articles to profl. jours.; patentee in field. Aid to Cancer Rsch. grantee, Mass., 1970. Mem. N.Y. Acad. Sci., Regulatory Affairs Profl. Soc. (cert.), Am. Soc. Quality Control (cert. quality auditor), Am. Assn. Clin. Chemistry, Sigma Xi. Office: Schiff & Co 1129 Bloomfield Ave West Caldwell NJ 07006-7123

SCHIFFMAN, GERALD, microbiologist, educator; b. N.Y.C., May 22, 1926; s. Samuel and Mollie (Brookner) S.; m. Lillian Ebert, July 12, 1951; children: Stewart, Howard. B.A. cum laude, NYU, 1948, Ph.D., 1954. Asst. prof. and disting. prof. microbiology Coll. Physicians and Surgeons, Columbia U., N.Y.C., 1960-63; asso. prof. dept. research medicine and microbiology U. Pa., Phila., 1963-70; prof. SUNY Health Sci. Ctr., Bklyn., 1970—, disting. svc. prof., 1995—; cons. Contbr. articles to profl. jours. Served in U.S. Army, 1943-45, ETO. Decorated Bronze Star; recipient Nichols award, 1947; Atomic Energy fellow, 1948-52; NIH grantee, 1974-94. Mem. Am. Assn. Immunologists, Am. Chem. Soc., Am. Soc. Microbiology, AAAS, Harvey Soc., Soc. Complex Carbohydrates, Sigma Xi, Phi Beta Kappa, Mu Chi Sigma, Pi Mu Epsilon. Jewish. Office: 450 Clarkson Ave Brooklyn NY 11203-2012

SCHIFFMAN, LAWRENCE STEVEN, internist, rheumatologist; b. Mineola, N.Y., Dec. 8, 1950; s. Carl Schiffman and Claire (Lynn) Baron; m. Susan Vera Friedman, Aug. 16, 1975; children: Theodore Carl, Celia Rose, Lucille Lynn. BA, SUNY, Stony Brook, 1973; MD, SUNY, Bklyn., 1977. Diplomate Am. Bd. Internal Medicine, Am. Bd. Rheumatology. Intern St. Vincent Hosp., Worcester, MA, 1977-78, resident in internal medicine, 1978-80; fellow rheumatology and immunology U. Mass. Med. Ctr., 1980-82; Practice medicine specializing in rheumatology Northampton, Mass., 1982—; mem. staff Cooley Dickinson Hosp., Northampton, 1982—; cons. in rheumatology VA Med. Ctr., Northampton, 1982—. Rheumatology Immunolgy fellow U. Mass. Med. Ctr., 1980-82. Fellow Am. Coll. Rheumatology; mem. New Eng. Rheumatism Soc. Jewish. Office: Northampton Internal Medicine PC 190 Nonotuck St Northampton MA 01060-1911

SCHIFFMAN, LEONARD E., oral-maxillofacial surgeon; b. Bklyn., Dec. 22, 1948; s. Samuel and Miriam Schiffman; m. Ivi Rene Navarre, Feb. 5, 1983; children: Michael, Lauren, Lindsey. BS, Bklyn. Coll., 1969; DMD, Tufts U., 1973. Diplomate Am. Bd. Oral-Maxillofacial Surgery. Gen. practice resident Peninsula Hosp. Ctr., Far Rockaway, N.Y., 1973-74; oral-maxillofacial surgery resident Montefiore Hosp. and Med. Ctr., Bronx, N.Y., 1974-76, chief resident oral-maxillofacial surgery, 1976-77; assoc. dir. dept. dentistry and oral-maxillofacial surgery Peninsula Hosp. Ctr., Far Rockaway, 1994—, pres. med. bd., 1996-97; coord. Peninsula Hosp. Dental Soc., Far Rockaway, 1982—. Bd. mem. Peninsula Hosp. Nursing Home, Far Rockaway, 1986—. Fellow Am. Dental Soc. Anesthesiology, Am. Assn. Hosp. Dentists, Am. Coll. Oral-Maxillofacial Surgeons, Am. Assn. Oral-Maxillofacial Surgeons; mem. ADA, Internat. Assn. Oral-Maxillofacial Surgeons. Office: 141 Franklin Pl Woodmere NY 11598

SCHIFFMAN, MINDY RAE, psychologist; b. N.Y.C., Mar. 31, 1952; d. William Louis and Barbara (Teck) S. BS, Simmons Coll., 1973, MBA, 1975; PhD, Columbia U., 1985. Lic. psychologist; cert. sex therapist. Psychotherapist Bklyn. Community Counseling Ctr., 1982-85; psychologist N.Y.C. Bd. Edn., 1983-86, Bronx Psychiat. Ctr., 1984-85; rsch. assoc. Meml. Sloan-Kettering, N.Y.C., 1985-86; pvt. practice N.Y.C., 1985—; psychologist IVF Australia, 1988-91; adj. asst. prof. Columbia U., N.Y.C., 1983-89; cons. in field. Psychology fellow Sloan-Kettering, 1986-88; Biomed. Sci. Rsch. grantee, N.Y.C. Psychiat. Inst., 1980. Mem. Am. Psychol. Assn., Am. Bd. Sexology, Am. Fertility Soc., N.Y. State Psychol. Assn. (mem. steering com. AIDS task force 1990—). Office: 1 Milligan Pl New York NY 10011-8304

SCHIFFMANN, ROBERT FRANK, research and development executive; b. N.Y.C., Feb. 11, 1935; s. Franz and Sophie (Bohling) S.; m. Marilyn Thelma Schneider, Aug. 20, 1987; children: Carla, Erica, Robert Franz. BS, Columbia U., 1955; MS, Purdue U., 1959. Rsch. scientist DCA Food Ind., N.Y.C., 1959-63; v.p. rsch. Nucleonics Corp. Am., Bklyn., 1963-64; sr. project mgr. DCA Food Ind., N.Y.C., 1964-71; ptnr. Bedrosian & Assocs., Alpine, N.J., 1971-78; pres. R.F. Schiffmann Assocs., N.Y.C., 1979—, Innovative Opportunities Ltd., Mpls., 1985—. Patentee in field; contbr. articles to profl. jours., chpts. to books. Pres. Cadman Towers Cooperators Assn., Bklyn., 1970-73. Fellow, Internat. Microwave Power Inst., 1985; recipient Putnam award, Putnam Pub., 1973. Mem. Microwave Power Inst. (pres. 1973-83), Inst. Food Technologists (sci. lectr. 1988-91), Soc. Plastics Industry, N.Y. Acad. Sci., Sigma Xi. Office: RF Schiffman Assocs 149 W 88th St New York NY 10024-2401

SCHIFFRIN, MILTON JULIUS, physiologist; b. Rochester, N.Y., Mar. 23, 1914; s. William and Lillian (Harris) S.; m. Dorothy Euphemia Wharry, Oct. 10, 1942; children: David Wharry, Hilary Ann. AB, U. Rochester, 1937, MS, 1939; PhD cum laude, McGill U., 1941. Instr. physiology Northwestern U. Med. Sch., Chgo., 1941-45; lectr. pharmacology U. Ill. Med. Sch., 1947-57, clin. asst. prof. anesthesiology, 1957-61; with Hoffmann-La Roche, Inc., Nutley, N.J., 1946-79, dir. drug regulatory affairs, 1964-71, asst. v.p., 1971-79; pres. Wharry Rsch. Assn., Seattle, Wash., 1979—; chmn. Everglades Health Edn. Ctr., 1986-87. Author: (with E.G. Gross) Clinical Analgesics, 1955; editor: Management of Pain in Cancer, 1957. Capt. USAAF, 1942-46. Mem. Am. Med. Writers Assn. (bd. dirs. 1967-70, pres. N.Y. chpt. 1967-68, nat. pres. 72-73), Am. Physiol. Soc., Internat. Coll. Surgeons, Am. Therapeutic Soc., Coll. Clin. Pharmacology and Therapeutics, Am. Chem. Soc. Home and Office: Unit 401 1001 2nd Ave W Seattle WA 98119-3560

SCHIFLETT, MARY FLETCHER CAVENDER, health facility executive, researcher, educator; b. El Paso, Tex., Sept. 23, 1925; d. John F. and Mary M. (Humphries) Cavender; 1 son, Joseph Raymond. BA in Econs. with honors, So. Meth. U., 1946, BS in Journalism with honors, 1947; MA in English, U. Houston, 1971. Writer, historian Office Price Adminstrn., Dallas, 1946-47; asst. editor C. of C. Publs., Dallas, 1947-48; bus. writer Houston Oil, 1948-49; market analyst Cravens-Dargan, Ins., Houston, 1949-52; bus. writer Bus. Week and McGraw-Hill Pub. Co., Houston, 1952-56; freelance writer in bus. econs., banking and ins., 1956-68; spl. projects coord. Ctr. for Human Resources, Houston, 1969-73; dir. publs. Energy Inst., U. Houston, 1974-78; sr. rsch. assoc. Inst. Labor and Indsl. Rels., 1973-80, mem. adj. faculty Coll. Architecture, 1976-85, dir. Ctr. for Health Mgmt., Coll. Bus. Adminstrn., 1980-83; assoc. dir. rsch. and planning Tex. Med. Ctr., Inc., Houston, 1984; dir. spl. projects and pub. affairs Tex. Med. Ctr., 1985-92, asst. v.p., 1993-95, assoc. v.p., 1995—. Bd. dirs. Third Ward Redevelopment Coun., 1993—, Houston Acad. Motion Pictures, 1986-90, Houston World Trade Assn., 1988-91, Friends Hermann Pk., 1995—. Pres., Houston Ct. Humanities, 1978-80; project dir. Houston Meets Its Authors I-IV, 1980-84; pub. program dir. Houston: Internat. City, 1980-83. Named One of Houston's Women of Yr. YMCA, 1988. Mem. Internat. Coun. Indsl. Editors, World Future Soc., Tex. Folklore Soc., Friends of Libr., Houston C. of C. (future studies com. 1975-84, small bus. coun. 1981-83), Nat. Assn. Bus. Economists, AIA (profl. affiliate), Mortar Bd., Theta Sigma Phi, Alpha Theta Phi, Delta Delta Delta. Methodist. Club: Downtown (pres. 1987-89), River Oaks Rotary (bd. dirs. 1996—). Lodge: Rotary. Author: (with others) Dynamics of Growth, 1977, Applied Systems and Cybernetics, 1981, The Ethnic Groups of Houston, 1984, Names and Nicknames of Places and Things, 1986. Office: Tex Med Ctr 406 Jesse H Jones Libr Bldg Houston TX 77030

SCHILDKRAUT, JOSEPH JACOB, psychiatrist, educator; b. Bklyn., Jan. 21, 1934; s. Simon and Shirley (Schwartz) S.; m. Elizabeth Rose Beilenson, May 22, 1966; children—Peter Jeremy, Michael John. A.B. summa cum laude, Harvard U., 1955, M.D. cum laude, 1959. Intern medicine U. Calif. Hosp., San Francisco, 1959-60; resident in psychiatry Mass. Mental Health Center, Boston, 1960-63; dir. neuropsychopharmacology lab., sr. psychiatrist, 1967—; research psychiatrist NIMH, Bethesda, Md., 1963-67; cons. NIMH, 1967-68; asst. prof. psychiatry Harvard Med. Sch., Boston, 1967-70; assoc. prof. Harvard Med. Sch., 1970-74, prof., 1974—; dir. psychiat. chemistry lab. Mass. Mental Health Ctr., 1977—; bd. dirs. The Med. Found., Boston, chair clin. rsch. com., 1994—; bd. trustees Mind/Body Med. Inst., Deconess Hosp., Harvard U. Med. Sch., Boston, also chair sci. adv. bd., 1988—. Author: Neuorpsychopharmacology and the Affective Disorders, 1970; editor-in-chief Jour. Psychiat. Rsch., 1982-92; mem. editorial bd. Psychophysiology, 1968-74, Jour. Psychiat. Rsch., 1968-82, Psychopharmacology, 1970-84, Sleep Revs., 1972-79, Communications in Psychopharmacology, 1974-81, Psychotherapy and Psychosomatics, 1974-91, Rsch. Communications in Psychology, Psychiatry and Behavior, 1976—, Jour. Clin. Psychopharmacology, 1980, Integrative Psychiatry, 1982-89, 91—, others. Bd. dirs. Med. Found., Boston, chair clin. rsch. com., 1994—; trustee Mind/Body Med. Inst. Deaconess Hosp., Harvard Med. Sch., Boston, chair sci. adv. bd., 1988—. Served as surgeon USPHS, 1963-65. Recipient Anna-Monika Found. prize, 1967, Hofheimer award Am. Psychiat. Assn., 1971, hon. mention award, 1968; McCurdy-Rinkel prize No. New Eng. Dist. br. Am. Psychiat. Assn., 1969; William C. Menninger award ACP, 1978. Mem. World Psychiat. Assn. (sec. sect. biol. psychiatry 1972-77), Psychiat. Research Soc., Am. Coll. Neuropsychopharmacology, Am. Psychiat. Assn., Am. Psychosomatic Soc., AAAS, Soc. Biol. Psychiatry, N.Y. Acad. Scis., Am. Psychopath. Assn., Am. Coll. Psychiatrists, Am. Soc. Pharmacology and Exptl. Therapeutics, Am. Soc. Neurochemistry, Group Without a Name, Assn. for Research in Nervous and Mental Disease, Collegium Internationale Neuropsychopharmacologicum, Soc. for Neurosci., Phi Beta Kappa. Home: 35 Jefferson Rd Chestnut Hill MA 02167-2341 Office: Mass Mental Health Ctr 74 Fenwood Rd Boston MA 02115-6113

SCHILLER, HERBERT MILES, pathologist; b. N.Y.C., Mar. 19, 1943; s. Jack David and Dorothy (Coe) S.; m. Patricia Annette Fields, July 3, 1965; children: Anne Bothwell, Stephen Miles, Richard William. BS, Wake Forest Coll., 1964; MD, Bowman Gray Sch. Medicine, 1968; BA in History, Wake Forest U., 1987. Diplomate Am. Bd. Pathology. Assoc. pathologist St. Francis Hosp., Columbus, Ga., 1972-75, St. Lukes Hosp./McGuir Clinic, Richmond, Va., 1976-77; pathologist, lab. dir. Nat. Health Labs., Inc., Winston-Salem, N.C., 1977-95, v.p. anatomic pathology, 1991-95; v.p. anatomic pathology Lab. Corp. of Am., Inc., Winston-Salem, N.C., 1995—. Author: The Bermuda Hundred Campaign, 1988, Sumter is Avenged: The Siege and Conquest of Fort Pulaski, 1995; author, editor: Autobiography of Maj. Gen. Wm. F. Smith: 1861-64, 1989, A Captain's War: The Letters and Diaries of William H.S. Burgyn 1861-65, 1994. Lt. comdr. USNR, 1969-79. Mem. Am. Soc. Clin. Pathologists, Coll. Am. Pathologists, Phi Beta Kappa, Alpha Omega Alpha. Office: Lab Corp of America 2540 Empire Dr Winston Salem NC 27103-6710

SCHILLER, JEFFREY DAVID, surgeon; b. Newark, N.J., June 1, 1949; s. Leroy Edward and Barbara Jane (Fishkind) S.; 1 child, Matthew. BA, U. Oreg., 1974; MD, U. Medicine Dentistry N.J., 1979. Intern in internal medicine St. Michael's Med. Ctr., Newark, 1979-80; resident in ophthalmology U. Medicine and Dentistry N.J.-N.J. Med. Sch., Eye Residency, 1981-84; fellow in internat. ophthalmology Project Orbis, N.Y.C., 1984-85; founding ptnr. Firstcare Med. Group, Verona, N.J., 1986-90; fellow in oculoplastic surgery N.Y.C., Paris, 1990; pvt. practice Staten Island, N.Y., 1991—, Roseland, Edison, N.J., 1991—. Fellow Am. Acad. Ophthalmology. Home: 452 W 19th St Apt 3C New York NY 10011 Office: 245 N Gannon Ave Staten Island NY 10314

SCHILLER, WILLIAM JOSEPH, psychology educator; b. Pitts., June 25, 1946; s. William John and Irene (Molnar) S.; m. Linda Kling, Sept. 21, 1970 (div. 1982); m. Denise LaGrand, Mar. 10, 1990; 1 child, Emilie; 1 stepchild, Michele Schmidt. BA, U. Miami, 1969; MA, N.Mex. State U., 1973; EdD, Idaho State U., 1981. Lic. profl. counselor, marriage and family counselor. Mgmt. trainee Sears, Roebuck & Co., Atlanta, 1968-70; counselor Northeastern Ohio Coun. on Drug Abuse, Warren, Ohio, 1973-74; exec. dir. Contact Ashtabula County (Ohio) Crisis Ctr., 1974-77; ednl. rep. Grolier Ednl. Corp., Danbury, Conn., 1977-78; from counselor to dir. Idaho State U. Family Edn. Ctr., Pocatello, 1979-80; prin. Consol. Counseling and Devel., Pocatello, 1981-83; from asst. to assoc. prof. Northeastern State U. Dept. Psychology, Tahlequah, Okla., 1983-89; dept. chair, prof. dept. psychology Northeastern State U., Tahlequah, 1989—; evaluator, grant writer several sch. dists. and mental health agys., 1983—. Author: (personality inventory) Personal Style Inventory, 1983; producer: (syndicated radio series) Another Way, 1981-85. Named Counselor of Yr. N.E. region Okla. Assn. Counseling and Devel., 1991; recipient merit award Idaho Soc. Tng. and Devel., 1982. Mem. AACD, Okla. Assn. Counseling and Devel. (bd. dirs. 1990—, Counselor Yr. 1991), Am. Assn. for Counselor Edn. and Supervision, Okla. Assn. for Counselor Edn. and Supervision (pres. 1990-91). Office: Northeastern State U Dept Psychology and Counseling Tahlequah OK 74464

SCHILLING, JANET NAOMI, nutritionist, consultant; b. North Platte, Neb., Mar. 1, 1939; d. Jens Harold and Naomi Frances (Meyer) Hansen; children: Allan Edward III, Karl Jens. BS, U. Neb., 1961; MS, Ohio State U., 1965; MPH, U. Calif., Berkeley, 1991. Registered dietitian. Tchr. home econs. Peace Corps., Dimbokro, Ivory Coast, 1962-64; cons. nutrition Wis. Divsn. Health, La Crosse, 1966-67, 69; dietary cons. Cozad (Neb.) Community Hosp., 1968; instr. Viterbo Coll., La Crosse, 1974-81; lectr. U. Wis., La Crosse, 1982-84; teaching asst. ESL Sch. Dist. La Crosse, 1984-87; nutrition educator Women, Infant, and Children Program, 1988-89; nutrition cons. Vis. Nurses, LaCrosse, 1987-89; dietitian Merrithew Meml. Hosp., Martinez, Calif., 1992; pub. health nutrition cons. Women Infant & Childrens Program Policy and Compliance Unit, Sacramento, 1995; nutrition cons. Wis. Winnebago Nation, 1991; pediatric dietitian in Romanian Orphanges thru World Vision, 1993; nutritionist Contra Costa Head Start & Child Devel., 1994; pub. health nutrition cons. Women, Infant and Childrens Program Policy and Compliance unit, Sacramento, 1995—. Author: Life in the Nutrition Community, 1980, Life in the Nutrition Cycle II, 1980; co-author: Nutrition Activities, 1984, Recipe Book of Nutritious Snacks, 1985. Mem. LaCrosse Sch. Dist. Nutrition Task Force, 1976-88; Sunday sch. tchr., supr. Our Savior's Luth. Ch., 1975-86, chmn. Mobile Meals, 1982-86; v.p. membership booster club Ctrl. H.S. LaCrosse, 1985-87, pres., 1987-88; bd. dirs. YMCA, LaCrosse, 1982-88; mem. No. Calif. Returned Peace Corps vols., 1990—; mem. Glide Ch. Housing Task Force, 1995—; trustee East Bay Habitat for Humanity, 1995—. Mem. AAUW (pres. 1978-80, Named Grant scholar 1981), APHA, LaCrosse Area Dietetic Assn. (1st pres. 1968-69, Outstanding Dietitian Yr. 1985), Wis. Dietetic Assn. (chmn. educators 1983-85), No. Wis. Dietetic Assn. (pres. 1982), Am. Dietetic Assn. (educators practice group 1978-90), LaCrosse Jaycees (Carol award 1973), Calif. Dietetic Assn. (pediat. practice group chair-elect 1986-87). Democrat. Home: 1604 Roger Ct El Cerrito CA 94530-2028

SCHILSKY, RICHARD LEWIS, oncologist, researcher; b. N.Y.C., June 6, 1950; s. Murray and Shirley (Cohen) S.; m. Cynthia Schum, Sept. 24, 1977; children: Allison, Meredith. BA cum laude, U. Pa., Phila., 1971; MD with honors, U. Chgo., 1975. Diplomate Nat. Bd. Med. Examiners, Am. Bd. Internal Medicine (subspecialty med. oncology); lic. physician, Mo., Ill. Intern, resident medicine Parkland Meml. Hosp., Southwestern Med. Sch., Dallas, 1975-77; clin. assoc. medicine br. and clin. pharmacology br. Div. Cancer Treatment, Nat. Cancer Inst., Bethesda, Md., 1977-80, cancer expert clin. pharmacology br., 1980-81; asst. prof. dept. internal medicine U. Mo.-Columbia Sch. Medicine, 1981-84; asst. prof. dept. medicine U. Chgo. Pritzker Sch. Medicine and Michael Reese Med. Ctrs., 1984-86, assoc. prof. dept. medicine, 1986-89; assoc. dir. joint sect. hematology and med. oncology U. Chgo. and Michael Reese Med. Ctrs., 1986-89; assoc. prof. dept. medicine, assoc. dir. sect. U. Chgo. Pritzker Sch. Medicine, 1989-91, prof. dept. medicine sect. hematology-oncology, 1991—; dir. U. Chgo. Cancer Rsch. Ctr., 1991—; chmn. Cancer and Leukemia Group B, Chgo., 1995—; Vivian Saykaly vis. prof. oncology McGill U., 1962; mem. sci. com. 5th Internat. Congress on Anti-Cancer Chemotherapy, 1995; mem. adv. panel on hematologic and neoplastic disease U.S. Pharmacopeial Conv., 1991-95; bd. dirs. Assn. Am. Cancer Insts., 1995—; mem. cancer ctr. support grant rev. com. Nat. Cancer Inst., NIH, 1992-95; mem. expert panel on advances in cancer treatment, 1992-93; mem. Cancer Ctrs. Working Group, 1996—. Mem. editl. bd. Investigational New Drugs, 1988-95, Jour. Clin. Oncology, 1990-93, Contemporary Oncology, 1991-95, Jour. Cancer Rsch. and Clin. Oncology, 1991—; assoc. editor Clin. Cancer Rsch., 1994—; contbr. articles to profl. jours., chpts. to books. With USPHS, 1977-80. Recipient Spl. Advancement for Performance award VA, 1983, Fletcher Scholar award Cancer Rsch. Found., 1989; grantee VA, 1981-87, Am. Cancer Soc., 1983-86, 92-95, Ill. Cancer Coun., 1985-86, Michael Reese Inst. Coun., 1985-86, Nat. Cancer Inst., 1987, 88-90, Burroughs-Wellcome Co., 1987-88, NIH/Nat. Cancer Inst., 1988—. Fellow ACP; mem. AAAS, Am. Soc. Clin. Oncology (chmn. pub. rels. com. 1994—), Am. Assn. Cancer Rsch. (chmn. Ill. state legis. com. 1992—), Am. Fedn. Clin. Rsch. (senator Midwest sect. 1983-84, councilor 1983-86, chmn.-elect 1987-88, chmn. 1988-89), Am. Assn. Cancer Edn., Am. Soc. Clin. Pharmacology and Therapeutics, Ctrl. Soc. Clin. Rsch., N.Y. Acad. Scis., Assn. Am. Cancer Insts. (bd. dirs. 1995—), Chgo. Soc. Internal Medicine, Sigma Xi, Alpha Epsilon Delta, Alpha Omega Alpha. Office: U Chgo Cancer Rsch Ctr 5841 S Maryland Ave Chicago IL 60637-1470

SCHILTZ, KAREN LORAINE, neuropsychologist, educator, consultant; b. Marshfield, Wis., May 12, 1957; d. Fred and Loraine (Kath) S.; m. Scott Monroe Mellor, Oct. 7, 1995. BA in Psychology and Sociology, St. Olaf Coll., Northfield, Minn., 1979; MA in Psychology, Calif. Sch. Profl. Psychology, 1982, PhD in Psychology, 1984. Lic. psychologist, Calif.; registered Nat. Register Health Svc. Providers in Psychology. Psychol. asst. St. John's Hosp. Child Study Ctr., L.A., Calif., 1981-82; cons. Xavier Mental Health Clinic, L.A., 1984-87; pvt. practice, L.A., 1984-87, Thousand Oaks, Calif., 1988—; asst. clin. prof. dept. psychiatry and biobehavioral scis. UCLA Sch. Medicine, 1989—, clin. supr. psychophysiol. program dept. neurology Brain Rsch. Inst., 1990-91, clin. supr. neuropsychology dept. Neuropsychiat. Inst., 1993—, clin. neuropsychologist, 1986-91; staff privileges UCLA Sch. Medicine, L.A., St. John's Pleasant Valley Hosp., St. John's Regional Med. Ctr.; mem. courtesy staff Los Robles Regional Med. Ctr.; presenter in field. Contbr. articles to profl. jours. Vol. Head Start, Ventura County, Califl; mem. Ventura County Panel Experts for Diagnosis and Treatment Head Injured Children. Fellow Stanford U., 1978; postdoctoral fellow UCLA, 1985-87. Mem. APA, Internat. Neuropsychol. Soc., Nat. Acad. Neuropsychologists, Nat. Head Injury Found. (mild head injury task force 1990), Undersea and Hyperbaric Med. Soc., Am. Coll. Forensic Examiners, Calif. Neuropsychol. Soc., Calif. Psychol. Assn., Ventura County Psychol. Assn., Psi Chi. Office: 516 Pennsfield Pl Ste 106 Thousand Oaks CA 91360

SCHILTZ, STEPHEN J., social work administrator, educator; b. Des Moines, Dec. 4, 1948; s. John Michael and Jane (Heflen) S.; m. Mary Conroy Terry, May 4, 1974 (div. Jan. 1996); children: Stephen J.M., Marian C.T. BS, Ariz. State U., 1971, MSW, 1973. Cert. ind. social worker. Clin. social worker Cath. Social Svc., Tucson, 1973-75, dir. clin. svcs., 1975-80, assoc. adminstr., 1980-89, dep. dir., 1989—; psychiat. cons. Diocese of Tucson, 1975—; field instr. Ariz. State U., Tempe, 1975—. Mem. NASW (v.p. Tucson chpt. 1977, treas. 1976), Acad. Cert. Social Workers, Registry of Social Workers. Democrat. Roman Catholic. Office: Cath Community Svcs PO Box 5746 155 W Helen Tucson AZ 85703-0746

SCHIMKE, KAREN, public health officer. BA in Social Welfare, U. Nebr., 1963; MSW, Western Res. U., Cleve., 1967; student, Juran Inst., Washington, 1993; student program for sr. execs., Harvard U., 1994. Cert. social worker, N.Y. Child welfare worker Rosebud Indian Reservation S.D. Dept. Welfare, Pierre, 1964-67; supr., caseworker child protection dept. Children's Aid Soc. and SPCC, Buffalo, 1967-68, dir. child protection dept., 1968-70; tchg. asst. SUNY, Buffalo, 1971-72; pvt. counselor, 1972-78, 80-82; tchg. asst., trainer social work program State U. Coll., Buffalo, 1974-75; evaluator Empire State Coll., SUNY, Buffalo, 1976-81; asst. prof. social work program Daemen Coll., Snyder, N.Y., 1977-78; asst. dep. commr. Erie County Dept. Social Svcs., Buffalo, 1978-80; cons. Child and Family Svcs., Buffalo, 1981-82; regional dir. divsn. family & children svcs. N.Y. State Dept. Social Svcs., Buffalo, 1982-88; commr. Erie County Dept. Social Svcs., 1988-93; exec. dep. commr. N.Y. State Dept. Social Svcs., Buffalo, 1993-95, N.Y. State Dept. Health, Albany, 1995—; cons. The Permanent Planning Project, Regional Rsch. Inst. Human Svcs., Portland (Oreg.) State U., 1980, N.Y. State Dept. Social Svcs., Albany, 1981; mem. cmty. adv. com. SUNY-Buffalo Sch. Social Work, 1983-88; mem. Home Energy Assistance Program Block Grant Adv. Coun. N.Y. State, 1991-93; mem. N.Y. State Adv. Com. on Legal Advocacy, 1991-93; mem. adv. com. to N.Y. State Permanent Interagy. Com. on Early Childhood Programs, 1991-93; mem. reorgn. task force on quality N.Y. State Dept. Social Svcs., 1992; mem. child care adv. com. Erie C.C. Bd. dirs. Coordinated Care Mgmt. Corp., 1988-93, Buffalo Urban League, 1988-93, Pvt. Industry Coun., 1988-93; cmty. advisor Jr. League Buffalo, 1984-93; bd. dirs. Parents Anonymous State Resource Office, Rochester, N.Y., 1982-84; bd. dirs. Parents Anonymous of Buffalo and Erie County, 1979-86, pres., 1981-84; bd. trustees Buffalo Gen. Hosp., 1979-80; mem. Erie County Child Abuse Task Force, 1978-80; bd. dirs. Ctrl Erie Cmty. Mental Health Ctr., Inc., 1977-80, pres., 1977-80; bd. dirs. Child and Adolescent Psychiat. Clinic, Inc., 1977-78, Buffalo Gen. Hosp. Cmty. Mental Health Ctr., 1974-80, Citizens Com. for Children of Western N.Y., 1972-78. Recipient Cmty. U. Citation, State U. Buffalo, Cmty. Adv. Coun., 1986, Cmty. Svc. award Coordinated Care Mgmt. Corp., 1989, Leadership and Support award Employees of the Erie County Home & Infirmary, 1989, Civic Leadership award Benedict House, 1989, Cmty. Mental Health award Cmty. Bd. of Buffalo Gen. Hosp. and Cmty. Mental Health Ctr., 1990, award of excellence Everywoman Opportunity Ctr., Inc., 1990, Friend award Ednl. Opportunity Ctr., Divsn. Student Affairs, 1990, Friend of Children award Gateway Children's Home, 1991, Cmty. Recognition award Parents Anonymous, 1991, Disting. Svc. award SUNY-Albany, Rockefeller Coll. Sch. Social Work, 1992, Cmty. Recognition award Ctrl. Referral Svc., 1992, Brotherhood/Sisterhood award in social svcs. NCCJ, 1993, William B. Hoyt Advocacy award Child & Family Svcs., 1993, Humanitarian award Luth. Ch. Home, 1994. Mem. NASW (mem. western divsn. bd. 1982-84, 86-88, Social Worker of Yr. 1979, Nat. Child Labor Com. Lewis Hine award 1985), Acad. Cert. Social Workers, N.Y. Pub. Welfare Assn. (bd. dirs. 1988—), Am. Pub. Welfare Assn., Nat. Assn. Pub. Child Welfare Adminstrs. Home: 230 Oakgrove Dr Buffalo NY 14221 Office: NY Health Dept Corning Tower Empire State Plz Albany NY 12237-0001

SCHIMMER, BARRY MICHAEL, rheumatologist; b. Newark, Jan. 7, 1945; s. Emanuel and Florence Pearl (Haflich) S.;m. Naomi Ann Raicer, May 24, 1970; children: Alexandra Tamar, Rebecca Tal. BA, Rutgers U., 1966; MD, Albert Einstein Coll. Medicine, Bronx, N.Y., 1970. Diplomate Am. Bd. Internal Medicine, subspecialty rheumatology. Intern Hosp. U. Pa., Phila., 1970-71, med. resident, 1971-73; clin. rsch. assoc. Harvard Med. Sch., Boston, 1973-75; clin. assoc. prof. medicine U. Pa. Sch. Medicine, Phila., 1978-95, Thomas Jefferson U., Phila., 1995—; chief rheumatology sect. Pa. Hosp., Phila., 1978—; chmn. grants and scholarship com. Arthritis Found., Ea. Ga. chpt., Phila., 1988-96; med. sec. Rheumatology Subspecialty Bd. Am. Bd. Internal Medicine, Phila., 1990-96; chmn. grants and scholarship com. Harry R. Kellman Acad., Cherry Hill, N.J., 1984-91. Fellow ACP, Am. Coll. Rheumatology; mem. Phila. Rheumatism Soc., Alpha Omega Alpha. Office: Pa Rheumatology Assoc 822 Pine St 1-C Philadelphia PA 19107

SCHINDLER, ADOLF EDUARD, obstetrics, gynecology educator; b. Asch, June 7, 1936; s. Adolf and Barbara (Truka) S. Dr.Med., Johann-Wolfgang-Goethe-U., Frankfurt, West Germany, 1962; PD Dr.Med., Eberhard-Karls-U., Tübingen, West Germany, 1971, apl-Professor, 1974, Prof., 1979. Intern Univ.-Hosp., Frankfurt, 1962; rotating intern U.S. Army Hosp., Landstuhl, West Germany, 1963; resident Universitäts-Frauenklinik, Frankfurt, 1964; sr. research fellow Ford Found., U. Wash., Seattle, 1964-66; resident in obstetrics and gynecology South Western Med. Sch., Dallas, 1966-69; resident in obstetrics and gynecology Univ. Women Clinic, Tuebingen, West Germany, 1969-71, oberarzt, privatdozent, 1971-74; apl. Prof., oberarzt, 1974-76, geschäftsführender apl-Prof., 1976-79, prof. geschaftsfuhrender oberarzt, 1979-86; dir. U. Frauenklinik Essen, 1986—; guest prof.

German-Acad. Exchange Service, Greece, 1971, Roumania, 1974, Rep. of China, 1981. Editor Endometriose, 1983—, Fertilitat, 1987—. Contbr. to profl. jours. Recipient Lynch Meml. award Pacific Coast Obstetric and Gynecology Soc., 1965, Vesalius Medal of Augsburg, 1978; Honorable Mention Student award AMA, 1968. Fellow Am. Fertility Soc., Am. Coll. Obstetricians and Gynecologists (affiliate, Frederic Purdue award 1967, 3d place award Jr. Fellow div. 1968); mem. Deutsche Gesellschaft f. Gynä kologie Geburtschilfe, Oberrheinische Gesellschaft f. Gynä kologie & Geburtshilfe, Deutsche Gesellschaft für Endokrinologie, Deutsche Gesellschaft zum Studium der Fertilitä t und Sterilität, Endocrine Soc., Internat. Menopause Soc., Internat. Soc. of Psychoneuroendocrinology, others. Home: Kupferdreher StraBe, D 45257 Essen 15, Germany

SCHIPITSCH, DOUGLAS ANTHONY, physician; b. Evergreen Park, Ill., Apr. 2, 1950; s. Julius J. and Mary L. (Jurenka) S.; m. Marilyn L. Maas, Mar. 1, 1981. BS, Ill. Benedictine Coll., 1972; MD, Loyola U., Maywood, Ill., 1975. Cert. Am. Bd. Surgery. Intern St. Francis Hosp., Evanston, Ill., 1975-76, resident, 1976-78; resident Loyola U. Med. Ctr., Maywood, Ill., 1978-80; staff surgeon Cumberland (Wis.) Med. Clinic, 1980-82, Redington-Fairview Hosp., Skowhegan, Maine, 1982—. Fellow ACS. Office: 21 Fairview Ave # 629 Skowhegan ME 04976-1403

SCHIRBER, ANNAMARIE RIDDERING, speech and language pathologist, educator; b. Somerset County, N.J., Dec. 18, 1941; d. Pieter C. and Marie Louise (Kerk) Riddering; m. Eric R. Schirber, Aug. 25, 1960; children: Stefan Rene, Ashley Brooke. BA in Speech and Hearing Therapy, Rutgers U., 1964; MA in Edn. of Deaf and Hard of Hearing, Smith Coll., 1968; postgrad., Rutgers U., 1987-93. Cert. tchr. of deaf, hard of hearing, spl. edn., speech correctionist, speech-lang pathologist, N.J. Speech therapist Manatee County Bd. Edn., Bradenton, Fla., 1968-69; speech-lang. specialist Lawrence Twp. Pub. Schs., Lawrenceville, N.J., 1969—; adj. instr. comm. dept. Trenton (N.J.) State Coll., 1983-87; vis. lectr. Rutgers U., New Brunswick, 1993. Author: Teaching Auditory Processing Skills to Children, 1994; co-author: (with Erica Winebrenner) Speech Activities for Children, 1994, Language Activities to Teach Children at Home, 1994. Mem. exec. com. Women's Coll. Symposium, Princeton, N.J., 1982-84; mem. nat. alumnae admissions com. Smith Coll., Northampton, Mass., 1984-86. Grantee Lawrence Twpw. Bd. Edn., 1973, 89, 90. Mem. N.J. Speech-Lang. and Hearing Assn. (legis. com. 1996), Ctrl. Jersey Speech-Lang. and Hearing Assn. (exec. com. 1984, v.p. 1985, pres. 1986-87). Home: 10 Sycamore Ln Skillman NJ 08558-2013 Office: Lawrence Twp Pub Schs Princeton Pike Trenton NJ 08648

SCHIRMACHER, PETER, molecular pathologist, educator; b. Saarbücken, Fed. Republic Germany, Nov. 4, 1961; s. Wolfgang H.E. and Sigrid A.H.E. (Brokate) S.; m. Roya Kamiar-Gilani, Aug. 21, 1991; 1 child, Daniel. MD, Gutenberg U., Mainz, Fed. Republic Germany, 1987; postgrad., Albert Einstein Coll., 1989-90. Postdoctoral rsch. fellow Inst. Pathology U. Mainz, 1987-89, asst. prof., 1991—; Belfer rsch. fellow Albert Einstein Coll. Medicine, Bronx, N.Y., 1989-90, cons., 1991—. Mem. Fed. Republic Germany Army, 1980-81. Mem. AAAS, Internat. Acad. Pathology. Lutheran. Office: Inst Pathology, Langenbeckstr 1, 55101 Mainz Germany

SCHIRMER, ROLF HEINER, biochemist, educator; b. Bremen, Germany, Feb. 1, 1942; s. Walter Christian and Anna Berta (Kleemeyer) S.; m. Ilse E. Eichler, Dec. 8, 1967; children: Markus C., Andreas B., Dominik M. MD, Heidelberg (Germany) U., 1966, Privatdozent, 1975. Postdoctoral fellow Dartmouth Med. Sch., Hanover, N.H., 1967-69; intern, resident various clinics, Germany, 1969-71; asst. Max-Planck-Inst., Heidelberg, 1971-80; prof. dept. biochemistry U. Heidelberg, 1980—; cons. WHO, Geneva, Switzerland, 1990-93; dean med. faculty, Heidelberg, 1992-93; cons. Muscle Disease Soc., Ulm, Germany, 1972-84. Author: (with G.E. Schulz) Principles of Protein Structure, 1979, Japanese edit., 1980, Russian edit., 1982. Named Bicentennial Lectr. U. Pa., Phila., Hanover, N.H., Boston, 1976. Mem. Tropical Medicine Rsch. (steering com. 1986—). Office: Heidelberg U, Dept Biochemistry INF 328, 69120 Heidelberg Germany

SCHIRO-GEIST, CHRISANN, rehabilitation counselor; b. Chgo., Dec. 31, 1946; d. Joseph Frank and Ethel (Fortunato) Schiro; m. John J. Conway Sr., Oct. 26, 1985; children: Jennifer, Daniel; stepchildren: Patricia, Nicole, John Jr., Denise, Christine. BS, Loyola U., Chgo., 1967, MEd, 1970; PhD, Northwestern U., 1974. Registered psychologist, Ill.; cert. sex edn. cons. Tchr. sci. Northbrook (Ill.) Jr. High Sch., 1967-70; dir. career counseling and placement Mundelein Coll., Chgo., 1972-74; counselor human devel. Regional Service Agy., Skokie, Ill., 1975-87; assoc. prof. psychology, rehab. counselor Ill. Inst. Tech., Chgo., 1975-87; full prof. rehab. U. Ill., Champagne-Urbana, 1987—. Co-author: Placement Handbook for Counseling Disabled Persons, 1982; author, editor: Vocational Counseling with Special Populations, 1990. Rsch. grantee Northwestern U., 1974; Region V Short-Term Tng. grantee Rehab. Svcs. Adminstrn., 1978-79, Long-Term Tng. grantee, 1983—; Mary E. Switzer fellow NIDRR, 1989-90, VA, 1991-92, World Rehab. Fund fellow, 1993. Mem. APA, ACA, Nat. Rehab. Assn., Nat. Coun. Rehab. Edn. (named Educator of Yr. 1987), Ill. Rehab. Counseling Assn. (pres. 1979-80), Coun. on Rehab. Edn. (pres. 1982-85, editor jour. 1986-92), Ill. Rehab. Assn. (pres.-elect), Kappa Beta Gamma Alumni Assn. (nat. officer). Office: U Ill Divsn Rehab Edn 1207 S Oak St Champaign IL 61820-6901

SCHLAGER, MAYNARD MORTON, psychologist, consultant; b. Winthrop, Mass., Apr. 3, 1928; s. Saul and Rose Schlager; m. Nathalie Lewin; children: Mason, Diane, David, Michael. BA, L.I. U., 1949; student, Yeshiva Ohr Yisroel, 1956, Mesivta Chaim Berlin, Jewish Theol. Sem., Hebrew Union Coll.; MA, Assumption Coll., 1976; D Ministry, Andover Newton Theol. Sch., 1978. Ordained rabbi, 1956; lic. psychologist, Mass.; accredited Coun. Nat. Register Health svc. and Providers in Psychology. Intern in clin. psychology U. Denver, 1952-54, Danvers State Hosp.-Tewksbury State Hosp.-Melrose-Wakefield, Mass., 1974-75; dir. Am. Counseling Ctrs., Peabody and Melrose, Mass., 1954—; dir. diet workshop div. Am. Counseling Ctrs., Peabody and Melrose, 1985—; supr. Worcester (Mass.) Pastoral Counseling Ctr., 1976-77. Author: Mixed Marriage, 1984; playwright (with Nathalie Schlager) Manhattan Mama, 1995. Acting chaplain USAF, 1950-54. Fellow Internat. Coun. Sex Edn. and Parenthood, Am. U., 1982. Mem. APA, Am. Assn. Marriage and Family Therapy (clin.), Mass. Assn. Marriage and Family Therapy, Mass. Psychol. Assn., Mixed Marriage Soc. U.S.A. (founder, bd. dirs. 1964—), Am. Legion (chaplain Malden 1978-83, Middlesex County 1983-85), Jewish War Vets. (vice comdr. 1965-66, Sugarman trophy 1966), B'nai B'rith (pres. Swampscott-Marblehead chpt. 1961-62, cert. of honor 1962), Masons. Home: 363 Lowell St Peabody MA 01960-2728 Office: Am Counseling Ctrs PO Box 3633 Peabody MA 01961-3633

SCHLAGER, SEYMOUR IRVING, physician; b. Hannover, Germany, Apr. 20, 1949; came to U.S., 1956; s. Conrad and Helen (Topol) S. BS, U. Ill., Chgo., 1969, MS, 1973, PhD, 1975; MD, U. Miami, Fla., 1985; JD, William H. Taft U., Santa Ana, Calif., 1996. Diplomate Nat. Bd. Med. Examiners, Am. Bd. Forensic Medicine. Rsch. scientist Nat. Cancer Inst., Bethesda, Md., 1975-80; assoc. prof. U. Notre Dame, Ind., 1980-83; resident in internal medicine U. Chgo., 1985-88; practicing physician Med. Care Group, Ltd., Skokie, Ill., 1988-89; head antiviral venture Abbott Labs., Abbott Park, Ill., 1989-91; v.p. R&D Acad. Pharms., Inc., Lake Bluff, Ill., 1996—; dir. clin. studies divsn. pharmacology dept. medicine Chgo. Med. Sch., North Chicago, Ill., 1996—; mem. expert adv. bd. WHO, Geneva, 1981-83; physician cons. Ill. Dept. Rehab. Svcs., Springfield, Ill., 1988-89; bd. govs. Midwest Immunology Assn., Chgo., 1983-85. Author: Environmental Science and Technology, 1977; contbr. 187 articles to sci. and med. jours. Bd. dirs. Am. Cancer Soc., Indpls., 1980-83; mem. AMA-Physicians Against Domestic Violence, Chgo., 1992—. Recipient Honored Scientist award Chgo. Assn. Immunology, 1983. Mem. ACP, Am. Coll. Legal Medicine (physician assoc.), Am. Coll. Forensic Examiners (adv. bd. profl. stads. 1995—), Am. Soc. Law, Medicine and Ethics, Crescent Counties Found. for Med. Care. Republican. Jewish. Office: Chgo Med Sch Dept Medicine Divsn Clin Pharmacology 3333 Green Bay Rd North Chicago IL 60064 also: Acad Pharms 21 N Skokie Valley Hwy Lake Bluff IL 60044

SCHLAMOWITZ, SAMUEL THEODORE, cardiologist; b. N.Y.C., Dec. 23, 1917; s. Albert and Rose (Kirchenbaum) S.; m. Elaine Phyllis Bernstein, July 11, 1943; children: Robert Alan, Kevan Eric, Barbara Irene Gilman, Carol Susan Armon. BS, CCYN, 1938; MD, NYU, 1942. Diplomate Am. Bd. Internal Medicine. Fellow, dept. therapeutics NYU Coll. Medicine, 1946-50; instr., pharmacology N.Y. State U., Syracuse, 1946-57, instr., internal medicine, 1962-80, assoc. prof., internal medicine, 1980-86; attending physician St. Joseph's Hosp. Health Ctr., Syracuse, 1960-86; cardiac cons. N.Y. State Dept. Health, 1948-52. With Army Air Force Med. Corps, 1942-47. Recipient Helen Hayes Whitney Found. fellowship in Rheumatic Fever NYU Sch. Medicine, 1947-49. Fellow ACP, Am. Coll. Cardiology, Am. Coll. Chest Physicians, Am. Coll. Geriat., Am. Coll. Angiology, Cardiology Sect.-Pan Am. Soc., Am. Thoracic Soc., N.Y. Trudeau Soc., N.Y. Acad. Medicine; mem. Am. Heart Assn. (past pres. Indian River chpt.). Sigma Xi. Home and Office: 4211 6th Ln SW Vero Beach FL 32968

SCHLANT, ROBERT CARL, cardiologist, educator; b. El Paso, Tex., Apr. 16, 1929; s. Edward Bernard and Elaine Almstaedt (Acker) S; m. Maria Honnef Ellingsen, Apr. 4, 1980; 1 child, Ernestine Stephanie. B.A., Vanderbilt U., 1948, M.D., 1951. Diplomate: Am. Bd. Internal Medicine, Am. Bd. Cardiovascular Disease (bd. dirs. 1977-78). Intern Peter Bent Brigham Hosp., Boston, 1951-53; jr. asst. resident Peter Bent Brigham Hosp., 1952-53, sr. asst. resident, 1955-66, asst. med., 1956-58; research fellow medicine Harvard U., 1956-58; asst. prof. medicine Sch. Medicine Emory U., Atlanta, 1958-62; asso. prof. Sch. Medicine Emory U., 1962-66, prof. medicine (cardiology), 1967-87, dir div. of cardiology, 1958-88. Co-editor: (textbook) The Heart, 1974, 6th edit., 1994, contbr., 1966, 70, editor, 1994; author, editor, co-editor, contbr. books, sci. and med. articles in field; editorial bds. ten sci. jours. Served with U.S. Army, 1953-55. Fellow ACP, Am. Coll. Cardiology (asst. treas., long-range planning com., norms com., trustee); mem. AMA, Am. Heart Assn. (fellow coun. on clin. cardiology, exec. com., mem. sci. adv. com., James B. Herrick award 1994), Ga. Heart Assn. (bd. dirs. 1970-76), Assn. U. Cardiologists (pres. 1982-83), So. Soc. Clin. Investigation, Am. Fedn. Clin. Rsch., Am. Physiol. Soc., Am. Acad. Sports Physicians (bd. govs. 1984-92), Internat. Atherosclerosis Soc., Internat. Soc. Cardiovascular Pharmacotherapy, Phi Beta Kappa, Alpha Omega Alpha, Omicron Delta Kappa, Phi Delta Theta, Phi Chi. Home: 3340 E Wood Valley Rd NW Atlanta GA 30327-1524 Office: 69 Butler St SE Atlanta GA 30303-3033

SCHLASTA, SUSAN GRANCEY, social worker; b. Peckville, Pa., Aug. 25, 1959; d. Thomas A. and Helen (Myshak) Grancey; m. David Schlasta, Aug. 31, 1985; children: David, Daniel, Mary Elizabeth. AA, Keystone Jr. Coll., 1979; BS, Marywood Coll., 1981, MSW, 1986. Lic. social worker. Social worker Lackawanna County Children & Youth Svcs., Scranton, Pa., 1983-87; social worker I Clarks Summit (Pa.) State Hosp., 1987-88, Farview Hosp., Waymart, Pa., 1987-88; social work supr., contract social worker Vis. Nurse Assn., Scranton, Pa., 1988-95; contract lic. med. social worker Interim Health Care, 1995—; asst. with the develop. new programs Fairview State Hosp., Lackawanna County Children and Youth Svcs. Home: RR 2 Box 233 Jermyn PA 18433-9766

SCHLAUCH, ROBERT WILLIAM, psychiatrist; b. N.Y.C., May 15, 1946; s. John A. and Katherine (Sillenbeck) S.; m. Phyllis Jen; children: Michael, Daniel, Amy. BA, Colgate U., 1968; MD, SUNY, Bklyn., 1972. Diplomate Am. Bd. Psychiatry and Neurology. Intern Med. Coll. Va., Richmond, 1972; resident Kings County Hosp., Bklyn., 1973-75; chief resident Peter Bent Brigham Hosp., Boston, 1975-76; asst. dir. Lindemann Mental Health, Boston, 1976-79; attending physician Westwood (Mass.) Lodge Hosp., 1976—; clin. instr. Harvard U. Med. Sch., Boston, 1975-79. Mem. Mass. Med. Soc., Norfolk Med. Soc., Am. Psychiat. Assn., Mass. Psychiat. Assn. Home: 134 Edgewater Dr Needham MA 02192-2776 Office: Westwood Lodge Hosp 45 Clapboardtree St Westwood MA 02090-2930

SCHLEE, MICHELLE RAE, nursing administrator; b. St. Louis Park, Minn., Apr. 16, 1964; d. George Gary and Ellen Rae (Maier) Anderson; m. Ricky Aaron Schlee, Dec. 26, 1988; 1 child, Tara Ann. BSN, U. N.D., 1986. RN, Minn. Staff nurse, charge nurse North County Regional Hosp., Bemidji, Minn., 1987-88, coord., 1988-92; coord. quality care sys. North County Regional Hosp., Bemidji, 1992—. Office: North County Regional Hosp 1100 W 38th St Bemidji MN 56601

SCHLEIFER, STEVEN JAY, psychiatrist; b. N.Y.C., Mar. 10, 1950; s. Jack and Caroline (Rapps) S.; m. Sarah L. Rosenberg, Dec. 1971; children: Jonathan, Jason, Justin, Tara. BA, Columbia Coll., N.Y.C., 1971; MD, Mt. Sinai Sch. Medicine, 1975. Diplomate Nat. Bd. Med. Examiners, Am. Bd. Psychiatry and Neurology. Resident psychiatry (categorical intern) U. So. Calif.-L.A. County Hosp., L.A., 1975-76; resident psychiatry Mt. Sinai Sch. Medicine, N.Y.C., 1976-79; instr. psychiatry Mt. Sinai Sch. Medicine, 1978-81, asst. prof. psychiatry, 1982-87; assoc. prof. psychiatry, dir. divsn. consultation-liasion U. Medicine and Dentistry N.J., N.J. Med. Sch., Newark, 1987-91; acting chmn. dept. psychiatry U. Medicine and Dentistry N.J.-N.J. Med. Sch., Newark, 1991-92, chair Dept. of Psychiatry, 1992—, prof. psychiatry, 1992—. Contbr. articles to profl. jours. Grantee NIMH, 1982, Chernow Found., N.Y.C., 1983, Upjohn Co., Kalamazoo, 1989, NIAAA, 1990. Fellow Am. Psychiat. Assn.; mem. N.J. Psychiat. Assn., Soc. Biol. Psychiatry, Internat. Soc. Psychoendocrinology, Am. Soc. Psychiat. Oncology/AIDS, Am. Psychosomatic Soc., Psychoimmunology Rsch. Soc., Acad. Psychosomatic Medicine, Rsch. Soc. on Alcoholism. Office: U Medicine and Dentistry NJ NJ Med Sch Dept Psychiatry 185 S Orange Ave Newark NJ 07103-2714

SCHLEIFFER, THOMAS, diabetologist, nephrologist, consultant; b. Bremen, Germany, Aug. 31, 1953; s. Gerd and (Miss Chairsell) Schleiffer; m. Miss Canis, Oct. 5, 1979; children: Lisa, Laura. Med. exam, U. Heidelberg, Germany, 1979; MD, U. Heidelberg, 1981. Cert. nephrology cons. Intern surgery Hosp. of Speyer, Germany, 1979-81; resident internal medicine Grünstadt Hosp., Germany, 1981-84; resident internal medicine and nephrology Hosp. Ludwigshafen, Germany. 1984-87, cons., 1987—. Author: (with others) Manual of Nephrology, 1994; contbr. numerous articles to profl. jours. Mem. adv. bd. Germany Hypertension League Ambulatory Blood Pressure Monitoring, 1991—. Mem. Internat. Soc. Nephrology, Am. Kidney Found., N.Y. Acad. Sci., German Soc. Nephrology, German Soc. Diabetes, European Assn. Study Diabetes,. Office: Hosp Ludwigshafen Med Clinic A, Bremserstr 79, 67063 Ludwigshafen Germany

SCHLEMAN, MARGO MAZUR, pediatric cardiologist, researcher; b. N.Y.C., Mar. 20, 1945; d. Samuel and Rita (Halpern) Mazur; m. Samuel Schleman; children: Kimberly, Ilana, Joshua. BA, NYU, 1966, MD, 1970. Intern pediat., 1970-71, resident, 1971-72, fellow pediatric cardiology, 1972-75; pediat. cardiologist Albert Einstein Coll., N.Y.C., 1975-76; pediatric cardiologist St. Christopher's Hosp. for Children, Phila., 1976-81, Jefferson Med. Coll., Phila., 1981-82; asst. dir. rsch Squibb & Son, Princeton, N.J., 1982-83; dir. rsch. Smith Kline Beckman, Phila., 1984-89, Marion Merrell Dow Inc., Kansas City, Mo., 1989-94; vol. staff pediat. Children's Med. Ctr., Cin., 1991-93; exec. dir. clin. rsch. Astra Merck Inc., Wayne, Pa., 1994—. Fellow Am. Acad. Pediat., Am. Coll. Cardiology, Am. Coll. Chest Physicians. Office: Astra Merck Inc 725 Chesterbrook Blvd Wayne PA 19087

SCHLENK, EDWARD FREDERICK, pathologist, nuclear medicine physician; b. Houston, Nov. 23, 1946; s. Fritz and Tilde (Eberle) S. MD, U. Chgo., 1972. Diplomate Am. Bd. Pathology, Am. Bd. Nuclear Medicine. Intern, resident in pathology and nuclear medicine U. Wash., Seattle, 1972-77; pathologist, nuclear medicine physician Scripps Meml. Hosp., La Jolla and Encinitas, Calif., 1977-90; pathologist Marshalltown (Iowa) Med. Surg. Ctr., 1990—. Fellow Coll. Am. Pathology. Office: Marshalltown Med Surg Ctr 3 S 4th Ave Marshalltown IA 50158-2924

SCHLENKER, BARRY RICHARD, psychologist, researcher, educator; b. Passaic, N.J., Feb. 21, 1947; s. Henry Walter Schlenker and Ruth Stephanie (Gammelin) Allis; m. Patricia Anne O'Rorke, July 22, 1972; children: David Richard, Kristine Anne. BA summa cum laude, U. Miami, Fla., 1969; MA, U.S. Internat. U., 1970; PhD, SUNY-Albany, 1972. Asst. prof. U. Fla., Gainesville, 1972-76, assoc. prof., 1976-80, prof. psychology, 1980—, dir. social-personality program, 1984—, prof. mktg., prof. clin. psychology, 1976—. Cons. editor 5 psychology jours.; author 4 books including: A Contemporary Introduction to Social Psychology, 1976; Impression Management, 1980; editor: Self and Social Life, 1985. NSF rsch. grantee, 1977-80, predoctoral fellow, 1970-72; recipient Research Scientist Devel. award NIMH, 1979-83. Fellow Am. Psychol. Assn., Am. Psychol. Soc., Soc. for Psychol. Study of Social Issues; mem. Southeastern Psychol. Assn., Phi Kappa Phi, Phi Eta Sigma. Avocation: Baseball. Home: 8817 NW 6th Pl Gainesville FL 32607-1405 Office: U Fla Dept Psychology Gainesville FL 32611

SCHLESINGER, EDWARD BRUCE, neurological surgeon; b. Pitts., Sept. 6, 1913; s. Samuel B. and Sara Marie (Schlesinger) S.; m. Mary Eddy, Nov. 1941; children—Jane, Mary, Ralph, Prudence. B.A., U. Pa., 1934, M.D., 1938. Diplomate Am. Bd. Neurosurgery. Mem. faculty Columbia Coll. Phys. and Surg., N.Y.C., 1946—; prof. clin. neurol. surgery Columbia Coll. Phys. and Surg., 1964—, Byron Stookey prof., chmn. dept. neurol. surgery, 1973-80, Byron Stookey prof. emeritus, 1980—; dir. neurol. surgery Columbia Presbyn. Hosp., 1973-80, pres. med. bd., 1976-79; cons. in neurosurgery Presbyn. Hosp., 1980-87, cons. emeritus, 1987—. Author rsch. publs. on uses, effects of curare in disease, lesions of central nervous system, localization of brain tumors using radioactive tagged isotopes, genetic problems in neurosurgery and spinal disorders. Trustee Matheson Found., chmn. Elsberg fellowship com.; trustee Sharon (Conn.) Hosp. Recipient emeritus rsch. award Presbyn. Hosp. Fellow N.Y. Acad. Scis., N.Y. Acad. Medicine; mem. AAAS, AMA, Am. Assn. Neurol. Surgeons, Harvey Soc., Neurosurg Soc. Am. (pres. 1970-71), Soc. Neurol. Surgeons, Am. Assn. Surgery of Trauma, Am. Rheumatism Soc., Am. Coll. Clin. Pharmacology and Chemotherapy, Ea. Assn. Electroencephalographers, Sigma Xi. Home: PO Box 3239 Fort Lee NJ 07024-9239 Office: 710 W 168th St New York NY 10032-2603

SCHLESINGER, JAY LAWRENCE, clinical psychologist; b. Oceanside, N.Y., Feb. 12, 1954. BA in Psychology, SUNY, Binghamton, 1976; MA in Counseling Psychology, NYU, 1980; PhD in Clin. Psychology, Adelphi U., 1984. Lic. clin. psychologist, N.Y. Sr. psychologist Westchester County Med. ctr., Valhalla, N.Y., 1984—; pvt. practice White Plains, N.Y., 1987—. Mem. APA. Office: 5 Old Mamaroneck Rd Apt 1L White Plains NY 10605-1711

SCHLESINGER, MILTON J., virology educator, researcher; b. Wheeling, W.Va., Nov. 26, 1927; s. Milton J. and Caroline (Oppenheimer) S.; m. Sondra Orenstein, Jan. 30, 1955. BS, Yale U., 1951; MS, U. Rochester, 1953; PhD, U. Mich., 1959. Rsch. assoc. U. Mich., Ann Arbor, 1953-56, 59-60; guest rsch. investigator Inst. Superiore di Sanita, Rome, 1960-61; rsch. assoc. MIT, Cambridge, 1961-64; asst. prof. virology Washington U. Sch. Medicine, St. Louis, 1964-67, assoc. prof., 1967-72, prof., 1972—; chmn. exec. coun. divsn. biol. and biomed. scis., 1992-94; vis. scientist Imperial Cancer Rsch. Fund, London, 1974-75; vis. scholar Harvard U., Cambridge, 1989-90, 95-96; mem. adv. panels Am. Heart Assn., Dallas, 1975-78, NSF, Washington, 1978-82; mem. sci. adv. bd. Friedrich Miescher Inst., Basel, Switzerland, 1988—, chmn., 1992—; nat. lectr. Sigma Xi, 1991-93. Editor: Heat Shock, 1982, Togaviridae of Flaviviridae, 1986, Lipid Modification of Proteins, 1992, (monographs) The Ubiquitin System, 1988, Stress Proteins, 1990; mem. editl. bd. virology, 1975-92, Jour. Biol. Chemistry, 1982-87, Molecular and Cellular Biology, 1983-92. Bd. dirs. ACLU, St. Louis, 1966-72, Coalition for Environ., St. Louis, 1989-92. Mem. AAAS, Am. Biol. Chemistry and Molecular Biology, Am. Soc. Microbiology, Am. Soc. Virologists, Am. Chem. Soc., Protein Soc. Office: Dept Molecular Micro 8230 Washington U Med Sch 660 S Euclid Ave Saint Louis MO 63110-1010

SCHLESS, GUY LACY, endocrinologist; b. Phila., May 22, 1929; s. Robert A. (M.D.) and Bena S.; BA, Stanford U., 1951; MD, Jefferson Med. Coll., Phila., 1955; m. Nancy Esther Halverson, July 19, 1952; children: Karina Halverson, Laurits Halverson. Intern, Meth. Hosp., Phila., 1955-56; resident and rsch. fellow in metabolism Pa. Hosp., Phila., 1956-53, asst. physician, 1959-68, assoc. physician, 1968-71, physician, 1971—, chief med. clinics, 1965-67, sr. Mellon fellow in medicine, 1962-63; vis. fellow, hon. sr. registrar medicine Guy's Hosp., U. London, 1958-59, vis. rsch. fellow in medicine Med. Sch., 1962-70, hon. cons. in medicine, 1971-90, hon. vis. cons. in metabolic medicine, 1990—; instr. medicine U. Pa., 1962-64, assoc., 1964-68, asst. prof. medicine, 1968-80, clin. assoc. prof. medicine, 1980-95; clin. assoc. prof. medicine Jefferson Med. Coll., Phila., 1995—; fellow in medicine Am. Philos. Soc.; cons. in medicine 5th naval dist. U.S. Navy, 1965—; cons. in medicine U.S. Naval Regional Med. Ctr., Portsmouth, Va., 1965—; participant White House Conf. Food, Nutrition and Health, 1969. Bd. dirs. Brit. Cathedrals and Hist. Chs. Found., Inc. Served as lt. comdr. M.C., USNR, 1960-62. Fellow Royal Soc. Medicine (London), Phila. Coll. Physicians, Royal Soc. Health (London), Royal Soc. Arts (London) (Benjamin Franklin fellow), Am. Coll. Endocrinology; mem. ACP, Am. Diabetes Assn., Athenaeum of Phila., Victorian Soc. in Am. (dir., v.p. 1977, pres. 1984-90, pres. emeritus 1990—), Soc. Archtl. Historians. Republican. Contbr. articles on metabolism to profl. jours. Home: 3926 Henry Ave Philadelphia PA 19129-1008 Office: 2A St Regis Ct PA Hosp 822 Pine St Philadelphia PA 19107-6124

SCHLESSINGER, DAVID ALLEN, ophthalmologist; b. Charleston, S.C., Feb. 22, 1962; m. Donna Beth Goldberg; 1 child, Jake. BA, Franklin and Marshall Coll., Lancaster, Pa., 1984; MD, U. Pitts., 1988. Resident in ophthalmology Interfaith Med. Ctr., Bklyn., 1988-92; postdoctoral fellow U. Minn., 1993; pvt. practice Hauppauge, N.Y., 1995—; dir. neuro-ophthalmology Interfaith Med. Ctr., Bklyn., 1995—. Fellow Am. Acad. Ophthalmology, Nat. Bd. Med. Examiners; mem. AMA, Med. Soc. of State of N.Y. Office: 1377 Motor Pkwy Hauppauge NY 11788

SCHLESSINGER, JOSEPH, pharmacology educator. BSc in Chemistry/Physics magna cum laude, The Hebrew U., Jerusalem, 1968, MSC in Chemistry magna cum laude, 1969; PhD, The Weizmann Inst. Sci., Rehovot, Israel, 1974. Postdoctoral assoc. dept. chemistry Sch. Applied Physics, Cornell U., 1974-76; vis. scientist immunology br. Nat. Cancer Inst., NIH, Bethesda, Md., 1977-78; sr. scientist dept. chem. immunology The Weizmann Inst. Sci., Rehovot, 1978-80, assoc. prof. dept. chem. immunology, 1980-84, prof. dept. chem. immunology, Ruth & Leonard Simon prof., 1984-91; dir. div. molecular biology Biotech. Rsch. Ctr. Meloy Labs., Inc., Rockville, Md., 1985-86, dir. Biotech. Rsch. Ctr., 1986-88; rsch. dir. Rorer Biotech., Inc., King of Prussia, Pa., 1988-90; prof., chmn. dept. pharmcology NYU Med. Ctr., N.Y.C., 1990—. Mem. editorial bds. European Molecular Biology Orgn. Jour., Jour. Cell Biology, Cell Regulation, Cancer Rsch., Receptors, Growth Factors, Cell Growth & Differentiation, Protein Engineering, Oncogenes and Growth Factor Abstracts; contbr. articles to profl. jours. Recipient Sara Leedy Prize, Weizmann Inst. Sci., 1980, Levinson Prize, 1984; Hestrin Prize, Biochem. Soc. Israel, 1983. Mem. European Molecular Biology Orgn. Office: NYU Med Ctr Dept Pharmacology 550 1st Ave New York NY 10016-6481*

SCHLEUNING, ALEXANDER J., II, otolaryngologist; b. Portland, Oreg., 1934. MD, U. Oreg., 1960. Intern Oreg. Hosps., Portland, 1960-61, resident in otolaryngology 1961-65; mem. staff Oreg. Health Sci. U., Portland; prof. otolaryngology Oreg. Health Sci. U. Fellow AAOHNS; mem. AMA, ABO, AADO-HNS. Office: 3181 SW Sam Jackson Park Rd Portland OR 97201-3011

SCHLEUSING, MICHAEL, anesthesiologist; b. Chemnitz, Saxony, Germany, Apr. 1, 1934; s. Adalbert and Sabine (Böhme) S.; m. Rosemary Müller, Oct. 6, 1965; children: Eva, Bettina. MD, Düsseldorf (Germany) U., 1962; PhD, Leipzig (Germany) U., 1991. SHO Inst. Pathology, Chemnitz, 1958-60, Dist. Hosps. in Ludwigsburg, Hall and Rottweil, Germany, 1962-64, Clin. for Thoracical Surgery, Zschadrass, Germany, 1965-66, Univ. Tchg. Hosp., Berlin-Buch, Germany, 1967; cons. Dist. Hosp., Pasewalk, Germany, 1968-69, Altenburg, Germany, 1970-91; cons. Altenburg, Germany, 1992—; dir. Emergency Ambulance Svc., Altenburg, 1979-91. Contbr. articles to profl. publs. Mem. East German Parliament, 1990. Mem. NAW Arztebund, German Acad. Acupuncture. Mem. Christian Democratic Party. Evangelical Lutheran. Home: Riegenstr 7, D-04600 Altenburg Germany Office: Joh Seb Bach Str 2, D-04600 Altenburg Germany

SCHLEY, WILLIAM SHAIN, otorhinolaryngologist; b. Columbus, Ga., Sept. 21, 1940; s. Frances Brooking Schley and Susie (Smith) Mathews. BA, Emory U., 1962, MD, 1966. Intern mixed surg. The Roosevelt Hosp.,

N.Y.C., 1966-67, resident in surgery, 1967-68; resident in otorhinolaryngology N.Y. Hosp.-Cornell Med. Ctr., N.Y.C., 1970-73; clin. instr. otorhinolaryngology Cornell U. Med. Coll., 1972-75, clin. asst. prof., 1975-81, assoc. prof., 1982—, acting chmn. dept. otorhinolaryngology, 1988-94, chmn. dept. otorhinolarygology, 1994—; Otorhinolaryngologist to putpatients with pvt. patient privileges N.Y. Hosp., 1973-75, asst. attending otorhinolaryngologist with pvt. patient privileges, 1975-81, assoc. attending, 1992—, acting otorhinolaryngologist-in-chief, 1988-94, otorhinolaryngologist-in-chief, 1994—; assoc. asst. surgeon otolaryngology Manhattan Eye, Ear, Nose and Throat Hosp., 1988—; sec. med. bd. N.Y. Hosp., 1994—; mem. co-chmn. vis. day com. The N.Y. Hosp.-Cornell Med. Ctr., 1996—. Author: (with others) Pulmonary Diseases of the Fetus Newborn and Child, 1978; contbr. numerous articles to profl. publs. Vestry St. James Ch., N.Y.C., 1994—; mem. ad hoc bd. visitors Emory U., 1994-95. Lt. comdr. USNR. Recipient Eagle Scout Boy Scouts Am., 1954. Fellow ACS (Manhattan dist. #2 com. on applicants 1991—); mem. Am. Acad. Otolaryngology-Head and Neck Surgery, Med. Soc. State of N.Y., N.Y. State Soc. Otolaryngology-Head and Neck Surgery (exec. coun. 1974-80, dist. dir. 1980), County Med. Soc. N.Y., N.Y. Laryngol. Soc. (sec.-treas. 1981-84, v.p. 1984-85, pres. 1985-86), N.Y. Bronchoscopic Soc. (v.p. 1986-94, pres. 1994—), Assn. Emory Alumni (bd. govs. 1990—, pres.-elect 1993-94, pres. 1994-95), Omicron Delta Kappa. Episcopalian. Home: 320 E 72nd St New York NY 10021-4769 Office: NY Hosp Starr 541 525 E 68th St New York NY 10021-4873

SCHLICKE, CARL PAUL, retired surgeon; b. Bklyn., Mar. 16, 1910; s. Carl Paul and Eunice Gertrude (Hope) S.; m. Hilda Meek Hinckley, Aug. 30, 1937; children: Paul Van Waters, Suzanne Parker. AB, UCLA, 1931; MD, Johns Hopkins Med. Sch., 1935; MS in Surgery, U. Minn., 1940. Diplomate Am. Bd. Surgery. Intern John Hopkins Hosp., Balt., 1935; asst. resident in surgery L.I. (N.Y.) Coll. Hosp., 1936-37; fellow in surgery Mayo Clinic, Rochester, Minn., 1937-42; surgeon Rockwood Clinic, 1946-79, sr. surgeon, 1951-75; clin. assoc. prof. surgery U. Wash., Seattle, 1969-75, clin. prof., 1975-82; retired Rockwood Clinic, 1979; clin. prof. emeritus U. Wash., Seattle, 1982—; staff St. Lukes Hosp., 1946-51, Sacred Heart Hosp., 1950-79, chmn. surg. dept., 1958-75; cons Spokane (Wash.) Vets. Hosp., Fairchild AFB Hosp. Author: Working Together: A History of a Medical Group Practice, 1980, General George Wright, Guardian of the Pacific Coast, 1988, Spokane and Inland Empire Blood Bank, 1990; contbr. over 70 articles to profl. jours., 16 articles to hist. jours. Fellow ACS (gov., regent, 1st v.p.), mem. AMA, Spokane County Med. Soc., Washington State Med. Assn. (pres. 1965-66), Am. Surg. Assn. (2d v.p. 1976), Spokane Surg. Soc. (pres. 1960), North Pacific Surg. Assn. (pres. 1964), Western Surg. Assn. (pres. 1972), Pacific Coast Surg. Assn. (pres. 1972), Pacific Coast Surg. Assn. (pres. 1976-77), Internat. Soc. Surgery, Soc. Surgery Alimentary Tract, Surgeon's Travel Club, Mayo Clinic Alumni Assn. (pres. 1968), Barber Surgeons Pacific NW, Alpha Omega Alpha, Sigma Pi. Republican. Home: E 826 Overbluff Rd Spokane WA 99203

SCHLOSE, WILLIAM TIMOTHY, health care executive; b. West Lafayette, Ind., May 16, 1948; s. William Fredrick and Dora Irene (Chitwood) S.; m. Linda Lee Fletcher, June 29, 1968 (div. 1978); children: Vanessa Janine Schlose Hubert, Stephanie Lynn; m. Kelly Marie Martin, June 6, 1987; 1 child, Taylor Jean Martin-Schlose. Student, Bowling Green State U., 1966-68, Long Beach City Coll., 1972-75; teaching credential, UCLA, 1975. Staff respiratory therapist St. Vincent's Med. Ctr., L.A., 1972-75; cardio-pulmonary chief Temple Community Hosp., L.A., 1975-76; adminstrv. dir. spl. svcs. Santa Fe Meml. Hosp., L.A., 1976-79; mem. mktg. and pub. rels. staff Nat. Med. Homecare Corp., Orange, Calif., 1979-81, Medtech of Calif., Inc., Burbank, Calif., 1981-84; regional mgr. Mediq Health Care Group Svcs., Inc., Chatsworth, Calif., 1984-88; pres. Baby Watch Homecare, Whittier, Calif., 1988-90, Tim Schlose and Assocs., Orange, Calif., 1990—; staff instr., Montebello (Calif.) Adult Schs. Author: Fundamental Respiratory Therapy Equipment, 1977. With USN, 1968-72. Mem. Am. Assn. Respiratory Care, Calif. Soc. Respiratory Care (past officer), Nat. Bd. Respiratory Care, Nat. Assn. Apnea Profls., Am. Assn. Physicians Assts., L.A. Pediatric Soc., Calif. Perinatal Assn., Porsche Owners Club L.A., Porsche Club Am. Republican. Methodist. Office: Tim Schlose and Assocs 910 E Chapman Ave Orange CA 92666

SCHLOSSER, DAVID WAYNE, dentist; b. Mpls., Oct. 11, 1958; s. Wayne Henry and Delores Jean (Ludvigson) S.; m. Kathryn Pantelakis, May 25, 1986; children: Renae, Alexis. AS, U. Wis., Rice Lake, 1978; BA, Coll. St. Thomas, St. Paul, Minn., 1980; DDS, Creighton U., 1985. Resident St. Elizabeth's Med. Ctr., Youngstown, Ohio, 1985-86; dentist Dr. William Anderson, Mankato, Minn., 1986-87; ptnr. Stow (Ohio) Dental Group, Stow, 1987—. Fellow Acad. Gen. Dentistry; mem. ADA, Akron Dental Soc. Republican. Greek Orthodox. Home: 3035 Kingston Cir Silver Lake OH 44224 Office: Stow Dental Group Ltd 3506 Darrow Rd Stow OH 44224-4009

SCHLOSSMAN, HOWARD HARVEY, psychoanalysis educator; b. Bklyn., Nov. 8, 1915; s. Joseph and Sadie (Kosakofsky) S.; m. Sylvia Simkin, Apr. 14, 1920; children: Doralynn Pines, Paul. MD, St. Louis U., 1939. Diplomate Am. Bd. Psychiatry and Neurology; cert. Am. Psychoanalytical Assn. Assoc. clin. prof. NYU Sch. Medicine, N.Y.C., 1947—, Albert Einstein Coll. Med., N.Y.C., 1961-74, N.J. Coll. Medicine and Dentistry, Newark, 1961—. Contbr. articles to profl. jours. Capt. U.S. Army, 1941-45, ETO. Fellow Am. Psychiat. Assn.; mem. Am. Psychoanalytic Assn., N.Y. Psychoanalytic Inst. (treas. 1976-80), Internat. Psychoanalytic Assn. (treas. 1985-91). Democrat. Office: 39 Park Pl Englewood NJ 07631-2918

SCHLOSSMAN, STUART FRANKLIN, physician, educator, researcher; b. N.Y.C., Apr. 18, 1935; s. Abe and Pearl (Susser) S.; m. Judith Seryl Rubin, May 25, 1958; children: Robert, Peter. BA magna cum laude, NYU, 1955, MD, 1958; MA, Harvard U., 1975. Intern in medicine med. divsn. III Bellevue Hosp., N.Y.C., 1958-59, asst. resident in medicine med. divsn. III, 1959-60; Nat. Found. fellow dept. microbiology Coll. Physicians Columbia U., N.Y.C., 1960-62; asst. physician med. svc. Vanderbilt Clinic, Coll. Physician USPHS, Washington, 1960-62; Ward hematology fellow dept. internal medicine Sch. Washington U., St. Louis, 1962-63; rsch. assoc. lab. biochemistry Nat. Cancer Inst. USPHS, Washington, 1963-65; clin. instr. in medicine Sch. of Medicine George Washington U., 1964-65; assoc. in medicine, dir. blood bank Beth Israel Hosp., Boston, 1965-66; instr. Med. Sch. Harvard U., Boston, 1966-68, asst. physician, 1967-68, chief clin. immunology, 1971-73; physician Beth Israel Hosp., Boston, 1968—; from asst. to assoc. prof. medicine Harvard Med. Sch., Boston, 1968-77, prof., 1977—, Baruj Benacerraf prof. medicine, 1990—, chief divsn. tumor immunology and immunotherapy, 1973—; sr. physician Brigham and Women's Hosp., Boston, 1976—. Mem. editorial bd. Jour. of Immunology, 1969-74, Cellular Immunology, 1970—, Human Immunology, 1979-84, Clin. Immunology and Immunopathology, 1979—, Hybridoma, 1980—, Cancer Investigation, 1981, Stem Cells, 1981, Cancer Revs., 1984—, Internat. Jour. of Cell Cloning, 1983-86; mem. adv. bd. Cancer Treatment Reports, 1976-80; assoc. editor Human Lymphocyte Differentation, 1980-82; contbr. numerous articles to profl. jours. Recipient Solomon Berson Achievement award, 1984, Robert Koch prize and medal, 1984. Fellow AAAS; mem. NAS, Am. Soc. Hematology, Am. Soc. Immunologists, Am. Soc. Clin. Investigation, Assn. Am. Physicians, Inst. of Medicine, Alpha Omega Alpha. Office: Dana-Farber Cancer Inst 44 Binney St Boston MA 02215-9999

SCHLOTFELDT, ROZELLA MAY, nursing educator; b. DeWitt, Iowa, June 29, 1914; d. John W. and Clara C. (Doering) S. BS, State U. Iowa, 1935; MS, U. Chgo., 1947, PhD, 1956; DSc (hon.), Georgetown U., 1972, Adelphi U., 1979, Wayne State U., 1983, U. Ill., Chgo., 1985, Kent State U., 1987, U. Cin., 1989, Case Western Res. U., 1996; LHD (hon.), Med. U. S.C., 1976. Staff nurse State U. Iowa, VA Hosp., 1935-39; instr., supr. maternity nursing (State U. Iowa), 1939-44; asst. prof. U. Colo. Sch. Nursing, 1947-48; asst., then asso. prof. Wayne State U. Coll. Nursing, 1948-55; prof., asso. dean Wayne State U. Coll. Nursing (Coll. Nursing), 1957-60; dean Frances Payne Bolton Sch. Nursing, Case Western Res. U., 1960-72, prof., 1960-82, prof., dean emeritus, 1982—; vis. prof. Rutgers U., 1984-89, 90—, U. Pa., 1985-86; spl. cons. Surgeon Gen.'s Adv. Group on Nursing, 1961-63; mem. nursing research study sect. USPHS, 1962-66; mem. Nat. League for Nursing-USPHS Com. on Nursing Edn. Facilities, 1962-64; mem. com. on health goals Cleve. Health Council, 1961-66; mem. Cleve. Health Planning and Devel. Commn., 1969-72; adv. com. div. nursing W.K. Kellog Found., 1959-67; v.p. Ohio Bd. Nursing Edn. and Nurse Registration, 1970-71, pres., 1971-72; mem. Nat. Health Services Research Tng. Com., 1970-71; mem. supply and edn. panel Health Manpower Com., 1966-67; rev. com. Nurse Tng. Act, 1967-68; bd. visitors Duke U. Med. Center, 1968-70; mem. council, exec. com. Inst. Medicine of Nat. Acad. Scis., 1971-75; mem. nat. adv. health services council Health Services and Mental Health Adminstrn., 1971-75; mem. def. adv. com. on women in services Dept. Def., 1972-75; bd. mem., treas. Nursing Home Adv. and Research Council, 1975—; mem. adv. panel Health Services Research Commn. on Human Resources, Nat. Acad. Sci., 1977-85; cons. Walter Reed Army Inst.; adv. council on nursing, U.S. VA, 1965-69, chmn., 1966-69; mem. Yale U.; Council Com. on Med. Affairs, 1981-86; mem. adv. bd. Scholarly Inquiry for Nursing Practice, 1987—. Mem. editorial bd.: Advances in Nursing Sci, Inquiry, 1982-85, Jour. Nursing Edn., 1982-91; contbr. numerous articles to profl. jours. Bd. vis. Syracuse U., 1990—. Served to 1st lt. Army Nurse Corps, 1944-46. Recipient Disting. Svc. award U. Iowa, 1973, Case Western Res. U., 1991, N. Watts Lifetime Achievement award, 1995; named Living Legend, Am. Acad. Nursing, 1995. Fellow Am. Acad. Nursing (v.p. 1975-77, Living Legend award 1995), Nat. League Nursing; mem. ANA (chmn. commn. on nurse edn. 1967-70, mem. com. for studying credentialling 1976-79, adv. com. W.K. Kellogg Nat. Fellowship program 1981-85), Pi Lambda Theta, Sigma Theta Tau (nat. v.p. 1948-50, selection com., disting. lectr. program 1986-87, Founders award for creativity 1985). Home: 1111 Carver Rd Cleveland OH 44112-3635 Office: 2121 Abington Rd Cleveland OH 44106-2333

SCHLOTT, D. WILLIAM, physician, medical educator; b. Warren, Ohio, June 10, 1936; m. Pamela Johnson; hcildren: Amy Downing, Ann, Rebecca Redett, Amanda Lietman. BS, Ohio U., 1958; MD, Johns Hopkins U., 1962. Diplomate Am. Bd. Internal Medicine. Intern Johns Hopkins Hosp., Balt., 1962-63, asst. resident, 1965-66, chief resident, 1966-67; clin. assoc. NIH, Bethesda, Md., 1963-65; asst. prof. U. Conn., Farmington, 1967-69; ast. prof. Johns Hopkins Med. Sch., Balt., 1969-93, Phillip Tumulty assoc. prof. medicine, 1993—. Sr. surgeon USPHS, 1963-65. Mem. ACP, Am. Soc. Internal Medicine. Home: 6503 Darnall Rd Baltimore MD 21204 Office: Ste 360 10755 Falls Rd Lutherville MD 21093-4589

SCHLUSSEL, ALAN BARRY, optometrist; b. Hempstead, L.I., Feb. 9, 1958; s. Louis and Annabel (Tannenbaum) S.; m. Susan Ellen Rosenbluth, Sept. 2, 1984; children: Lyle, Amanda. BA, SUNY, 1980, OD, 1984. Assoc. optometrist Dr. Farkas & Kassalow, N.Y.C., 1984-85, Dr. Seligman Rosenberg, Ft. Lee, N.J., 1984-87; pvt. practice N.Y.C., West Orange, N.J., 1985—; bd. dirs. N.J. Eye Care Coun., South Orange, N.J., 1990—. Fellow Am. Acad. Optometry. Office: 520 Pleasant Valley Way West Orange NJ 07052

SCHLUTTER, LOIS COCHRANE, psychologist; b. Indpls., Oct. 18, 1953; d. Roy and Mavis (Wolfe) Cochrane; m. Dennis James Schlutter, Oct. 30, 1976; 1 child, Nathan Paul. BS, U. S.D., 1974, MA, 1975, PhD, 1978. Lic. psychologist, Minn. Psychologist, asst. Neurol. Inst. and Pain Ctr., Sioux City, Iowa, 1975-77; staff Mpls. Psychotherapy Inst., St. Louis Park, Minn., 1978-80; with strategic planning Vail Place, Mpls. and Hopkins (Minn.), 1988-90; owner Schlutter & Assocs., St. Louis Park, Minn., 1994—; bd. dirs. Vail Pl.; allied health staff, disability cons. Meth. Hosp., St. Louis Park, 1978—, mem. hospice adv. com., 1984—, mem. child abuse consortium, 1985-89; staff psychologist Sister Kenny Inst., Mpls., 1980-81; cons. Dept. Vocat. Rehab., St. Paul, 1984-93; supr. pastoral care AAPC, St. Louis Park, 1984—; lectr. St. Mary's Hosp. and Coll., Mpls., 1984-90; psychologist, dir. Family Dynamics, St. Louis Park, 1980-94; owner Employee Assistance Programs; presenter in field. Co-author: (play) The Extrapolator, 1968; contbr. articles to profl. jours. Mem. task force Vinland Nat. Ctr.; chmn. adult edn., Hopkins United Meth. Ch., 1988-91. Recipient rsch. grant Lederle Pharms., 1979. Mem. APA, Am. Coll. Forensic Examiners, Mental Health Assn. Minn., Minn. Psychol. Assn., Am. Assn. Pastoral Counselors (profl. affiliate), Brookside Condominium Assn., Blvd. Condominium Assn., Internat. Platform Assn., Rotary, Twin West C. of C., Phi Beta Kappa, Kappa Alpha Theta, Alpha Lambda Delta, Psi Chi. Office: Schlutter & Assocs 6200 Excelsior Blvd Ste 202 Saint Louis Park MN 55416-2730

SCHMACKE, NORBERT, internist, public health administrator; b. Buende, Germany, Sept. 3, 1948. 1st degree, U. Marburg, Germany, 1973, MD, 1974. Intern Red Cross Hosp., Bremen, Germany, 1977-80; resident Ctrl. Hosp., Bremen-Ost, Germany, 1980-83; dept. leader Pub. Health Office, Bremen, 1983-94; dir. Acad. Pub. Health, Düsseldorf, Germany, 1994—; lectr. pub. health U. Bremen. Author: Psychiatry Between Bourgeois Revolution and Fascism (in German), 1976, Welfare State, Public Health Services and Municipal Self-Governing Body, 1995. Mem. N.Y. Acad. Scis., Assoc. Schs. Pub. Health European Region. Office: Academy of Public Health, PB 250251, 40093 Düuesseldorf Germany

SCHMEER, ARLINE CATHERINE, cancer research development chemotherapy scientist; b. Rochester, N.Y., Nov. 14, 1929; d. Edward Jacob and Madeline Margaret (Haines) S. BA, Coll. St. Mary of the Springs, Columbus, Ohio, 1951; MS in Biology, Notre Dame U., 1961; PhD in Biomedicine, U. Colo., 1969; DSc (hon.), Albertus Magnus Coll., New Haven, Conn., 1974, SUNY, Potsdam, 1990. Chmn. sci. dept. Watterson High Sch./Diocese of Columbus, 1954-59, St. Vincent Ferrer High Sch./Archdiocese of N.Y., N.Y.C., 1959-62; chmn. dept. biology Ohio Dominican Coll., Columbus, 1963-72; chmn. dept. anti-cancer agents of marine origin Am. Cancer Rsch. Ctr., Denver, 1972-82; dir. Mercenene Cancer Rsch. Inst., New Haven, 1982-93; dir. Mercenene Cancer Rsch. Inst. U. Cin. Med. Sch., 1996—; sr. prin. investigator Marine Biol. Lab., Woods Hole, Mass., 1962-72, corp. mem., mem. libr. com., 1964—; rsch. prof. Med. Sch., U. Wüzburg, Germany, 1969-70; pres., chief exec. officer Med. Rsch. Found., 1972—; participant, contbr. Internat. Cancer Congress, 1966—. Contbr. articles to biol. publs. Grantee Am. Cancer Soc., 1965; NSF fellow, 1957-62, NIH fellow, 1966-69; recipient numerous teaching awards, Ohi Acad. Scis. and others. Fellow Royal Microscopical Soc. Eng. (life); mem. N.Y. Acad. Sci. (life), Am. Soc. Cell Biology, Internat. Cancer Congresses. Roman Catholic. Office: Mercenene Cancer Rsch Inst U Cin Med Sch 3130 Highland Ave Cincinnati OH 45202

SCHMELTZLE, TIMOTHY C., physician; b. Allentown, Pa., Oct. 30, 1963; s. Richard W. and Joan Lenore (Blackwell) S.; m. Tina M. Miller, Oct. 10, 1992; children: Shelby Lynn, Colby Jared. BS in Pharmacy cum laude, Phila. Coll. Pharmacy & Sci., 1986; DO, Phila. Coll. Osteo. Medicine, 1990. Diplomate Nat. Bd. Osteo. Med. Examiners; bd. cert. family practice Am. Osteo. Bd. Family Practice. Intern Allentown (Pa.) Osteo. Med. Ctr., 1990-91, family practice resident, 1991-93; pvt. practice family practice Emmaus, Pa., 1993—. Life mem. Macungie (Pa.) Ambulance Corps, 1980—, med. dir., 1994-95. Mem. AMA, Am. Osteo. Assn., Am. Coll. Osteo. Family Physicians, Pa. Med. Soc., Lehigh County Med. Soc. Office: 730 Harrison St Emmaus PA 18049

SCHMEROLD, WILFRIED LOTHAR, dermatologist; b. Munich, Germany, Dec. 30, 1919; came to U.S., 1956; s. Wilhelm and Frieda (Hinterwinkler) S.; m. Perlette J. Joers, 1962 (div. Apr. 1974); children: Klaus, John, Will, James, Susan, Paul, Carl, Mike, Tom, Marianne. Abiturient, Altes Realgymnasium, 1938; MD, U. Munich, 1945. Bd. cert. dermatologist, dermatopathologist. Intern U Munich Med. Faculty, 1945-46; asst. UN Hosp., Munich, 1946-50, Max Plank Inst., Munich, 1951-52, U. Erlangen, Germany, 1952-53, U. Munich, 1953-56; intern Fairview Park Hosp., Cleve., 1956-57; asst. U. Ill., Chgo., 1957-60, instr., 1960-75, clin. asst. prof., 1975—; dermatologist pvt. practice, Carol Stream, Ill., 1959—, dermatopathologist, 1978—. Contbr. articles to profl. jours. Charter mem. founders club Ctrl. DuPage Hosp., Winfield, Ill., 1963. Fellow AMA, Am. Acad. Dermatology (life), German Dermatological Soc. (life), Am. Soc. Dermatopathology, Ill. Dermatological Soc., Ill. State Med. Soc., Chgo. Dermatological Soc. Roman Catholic. Office: Mona Kea Med Park 507 Thornhill Dr # B Carol Stream IL 60188-2703

SCHMETZER, ALAN DAVID, psychiatrist; b. Louisville, Sept. 3, 1946; s. Clarence Fredrick and Catherine Louise (Wootan) S.; m. Janet Lynn Royce, Aug. 25, 1968; children: Angela Beth, Jennifer Lorraine. BA, Ind. U., 1968, MD, 1972. Diplomate Am. Bd. Psychiatry and Neurology with added qualifications in addictions psychiatry. Intern, Ind. U. Hosps., Indpls., 1972-73, resident, 1972-75; dir. clinics PCI, Inc., Anderson, Beech Grove and Kokomo, Ind., 1975-79; psychiat. cons. Community Addiction Svcs. Agy., Indpls., 1975-80; instr. psychiatry in primary care Family Practice Residency Programs, St. Francis Hosp., St. Vincent's Hosp. and Ind. U. Hosps., Indpls., 1975-91; med. dir. Child Guidance Clinic of Marion County, Indpls., 1980-81; chmn. psychiatry dept. St. Francis Hosp., Beech Grove, 1980-82; med. dir. Crisis Intervention Unit, Midtown Mental Health Ctr., 1980-90; dir. Midtown Mental Health Ctr., 1990-96, med. dir. 1996—; coord. emergency psychiat. svcs. Ind. U. Med. Ctr., Indpls., 1980-90; asst. prof. psychiatry, 1975-94, assoc. prof. psychiatry, 1994—, coord. psychiat. edn. of med. students, 1989-95, asst. chmn. dept. psychiatry, 1993-96, dir. psychiatric edn., 1995—; chief psychiatry Wishard Meml. Hosp., 1990—; primary psychiat. cons. Ind. Dept. of Mental Health, 1988-89. Maj. Ind. N.G., 1972-79. Decorated Army Commendation medal; recipient Residents award for outstanding teaching 1985, 90, Roeske Excellence in Teaching award 1992. Fellow Am. Psychiat. Assn., Am. Ortho-psychiat. Assn.; mem. AMA (Physicians Recognition award 1978—), Ind. Med. Assn., Indpls. Med. Soc., Am. Psychiat. Assn., Ind. Psychiat. Soc. (pres. 1989-90), Am. Orthopsychiat. Assn., Am. Acad. Clin. Psychiatry, Alpha Phi Omega, Phi Beta Pi, Psi Chi, Alpha Epsilon Delta. Presbyterian. Clubs: Athenaeum Turnverein, Columbia. Contbr. articles to profl. jours. Office: Midtown CMHC 1001 W 10th St Indianapolis IN 46202-2859

SCHMID, LYNETTE SUE, child and adolescent psychiatrist; b. Tecumseh, Nebr., May 28, 1958; d. Mel Vern John and Janice Wilda (Bohling) S.; m. Vijendra Sundar, June 13, 1987; children: Jesse Christopher Mikaéle, Eric Lynn Kalani, Christina Elizabeth Ululani. BS, U. Nebr., 1979; MD, U. Nebr., Omaha, 1984; postgrad., U. Mo., 1984-89. Diplomate Am. Bd. Med. Examiners, Am. Bd. Psychiatry and Neurology. Child and adolescent psychiatrist Fulton (Mo.) State Hosp., 1990-91, Mid-Mo. Mental Health Ctr., Columbia, Mo., 1991—; clin. asst. prof. psychiatry U. Mo., Columbia, 1990—. Contbr. articles to profl. jours. Mem. Am. Psychiat. Assn., Am. Acad. Child and Adolescent Psychiatry, Ctrl. Mo. Psychiat. Assn. (sec.-treas. 1992-93, pres.- elect 1993-94, pres. 1994-95), U. Nebr. Alumni Assn., Phi Beta Kappa, Alpha Omega Alpha. Republican. Baptist.

SCHMID, RUDI (RUDOLF SCHMID), internist, educator, university official; b. Switzerland, May 2, 1922; came to U.S., 1948, naturalized, 1954; s. Rudolf and Bertha (Schiesser) S.; m. Sonja D. Wild, Sept. 17, 1949; children: Isabelle S., Peter R. BS, Gymnasium Zurich, 1941; MD, U. Zurich, 1947; PhD, U. Minn., 1954. Intern U. Calif. Med. Center, San Francisco, 1948-49; resident medicine U. Minn., 1949-52, instr., 1952-54; research fellow biochemistry Columbia U., 1954-55; investigator NIH, Bethesda, Md., 1955-57; assoc. medicine Harvard U., 1957-59, asst. prof., 1959-62; prof. medicine U. Chgo., 1962-66; prof. medicine U. Calif., San Francisco, 1966-91, prof. emeritus, 1991—, dean Sch. Medicine, 1983-89, assoc. dean internat. rels., 1989-95; Cons. U.S. Army Surgeon Gen., USPHS, VA. Mem. editorial bd. Jour. Clin. Investigation, 1965-70, Blood, 1962-75, Gastroenterology, 1965-70, Jour. Investigative Dermatology, 1968-72, Annals Internal Medicine, 1975-79, Proceedings Soc. Exptl. Biology and Medicine, 1974-84, Chinese Jour. Clin. Scis., Jour. Lab. Clin. Medicine, 1991—, Hepatology Comm. Internat. (Japan), 1993—; cons. editor Gastroenterology, 1981-86. Served with Swiss Army, 1943-48. Master ACP; fellow AAAS, N.Y. Acad. Scis., Royal Coll. Physicians; mem. NAS, Am. Acad. Arts and Scis., Assn. Am. Physicians (pres. 1986), Am. Soc. Clin. Investigation, Am. Soc. Biol. Chemistry and Molecular Biology, Am. Soc. Hematology, Am. Gastroenterol. Assn., Am. Assn. Study Liver Disease (pres. 1965), Internat. Assn. Study Liver (pres. 1980), Swiss Acad. Med. Scis. (mem. senate), Leopoldina, German-Am. Acad. Coun. Home: 211 Woodland Rd Kentfield CA 94904-2631 Office: U Calif Med Sch Office of Dean PO Box 0410 San Francisco CA 94143-0410

SCHMIDT, BRUCE, nursing administrator, consultant; b. Milw., June 19, 1949; s. Roger Lee and Jo Ann (Brunker) S.; m. Kathleen S. Schmidt, Aug. 8, 1987; 1 child, Heather. BSN, U. Wis., Milw., 1976, MS in Nursing, 1984; PhD, U. Mich., 1991. Crisis intervention specialist Milwaukee County Mental Health Complex, Milw.; clin. nurse specialist Mental Health Mgmt., Milw., St. Charles Hosp., Toledo; mental health specialist Catherine McAuley Health Ctr., Ann Arbor, Mich.; project mgr. work redesign U. Mich. Hosps., Ann Arbor, until 1991; adminstrv. dir. ctr. psychiatry and behavioral scis. Akron Gen. Med. Ctr., 1991-95; v.p. nursing Lewistown (Pa.) Hosp., 1995—. With U.S. Army, 1969-71. Nat. Rsrch. Svc. award, 1987, 88-91. Mem. Am. Orgn. Nurse Execs., Am. Coll. Healthcare Execs. (diplomate), Sigma Theta Tau. Home: 115 Laurel Rd Lewistown PA 17044

SCHMIDT, CAROL SUZANNE, hospital administrator; b. River Rouge, Mich., Aug. 8, 1936; d. J. T. Grant Vaden and Virginia Jean (Senker) Vaden Webster; m. Ronald Lee Schmidt, Aug. 18, 1957; children: Karen Suzanne Author, Linda Martin, Ronald Lee. RN diploma Hinsdale Hosp. Sch. Nursing, Ill., 1958; BS in Nursing cum laude, Met. State Coll., Denver, 1981; M.A. cum laude, Webster U.-Denver, 1984. RN, Colo. Operating room nurse Porter Meml. Hosp., Denver, 1961-69, charge relief nurse, 1975-76, adminstrv. supr., 1976-77, head nurse ortho/neuro unit, 1977-82; disease control nurse Vis. Nurse Assn., Denver, 1961-63; nurse Denver Gen. Hosp., 1966-67; office mgr., bookkeeper Timber Ridge Constrn., Evergreen, Colo., 1967-79; asst. dir. nursing Boulder Meml. Hosp., Colo., 1982-83, dir. nursing, 1984-89; v.p., chief clin. officer Avista Hosp., 1989-96, v.p. ops., 1996—. Tchr. Seventh Day Adventist Ch., Boulder and Denver, 1958-85; vol. Colo. Health Fair, Denver, 1979, 80; tchr. basic life support Am. Heart Assn., Denver, 1980-82; mem. Colo. Women's Forum Health Adminstrn., 1990—. Recipient Dist. Nurse of Yr. award Colo. Nurse Assn., 1975. Mem. Am. Coll. Hosp. Execs. of Am. Hosp. Assn., Am. Orgn. Nurse Execs., Assn. Seventh Day Adventist Nurses (bd. dirs. 1984-86), Colo. Soc. Nurse Execs. (active image of nursing 1985, Cir. of Excellence award 1996), Bus. and Profl. Women (legis. com. 1985), Colo. Fedn. Nursing Orgns. Avocations: needlework; travel. Office: Avista Hosp 100 Health Park Dr Louisville CO 80027-9583

SCHMIDT, CHARLES EDWIN, dermatologist; b. Alexandria, Va., Nov. 6, 1943; s. Louis John and Jennie Josephine (D'Alba) S.; m. Diane Lee Schieberl, Aug. 17, 1968; children: Mary Jo, Diane Marie. MD, Georgetown U., 1969. Diplomate Am. Bd. Dermatology. Intern D.C. Gen. Hosp., Washington, 1969-70; gen. med. officer USAF, Yakota AFB, Japan, 1970-73; resident in dermatology U. Miami Sch. of Med., Fla., 1973-76; pvt. practice dermatology Ft. Lauderdale, Fla., 1976—; clin. instr. dermatology U. Miami Sch. Medicine, 1976-81, clin. asst. prof., 1981-88, clin. assoc. prof., 1988—, clinical prof., 1993—. Capt. USAF, 1970-73. Fellow Am. Acad. Dermatology; mem. AMA, Fla. Soc. Dermatology, Broward County Dermatology Soc. (v.p. 1991, pres. 1992), U.S. Navy League. Roman Catholic. Office: Charles E Schmidt MD PA 1122 Bayview Dr Fort Lauderdale FL 33304-2505

SCHMIDT, GUNTER, dentist; b. Nuremberg, Germany, Aug. 22, 1913; s. Willy and Irma (Treumann) S.; m. Corinne Mitchell, May 26, 1944; children: Carol, Linda. Student, U. Munich, 1932-33, U. Wurzburg, 1933; DDS, Washington U., St. Louis, 1937. Gen. practice dentistry, St. Louis, 1937-59, Clayton, Mo., 1959-86; dentist Shriner's Hosp. for Crippled Children, 1938-43; staff dentist Jewish Hosp., 1938-78, sr. dentist, 1978—. Past editor Newsletter of Am. Acad. of Oral Medicine, Greater St. Louis Dental Soc. Bull.; contbr. articles to profl. jours. Past chmn. United Fund Dental Div., Arts and Edn. Fund Dental Div.; mem. adv. com. on dental techs. St. Louis C.C.; trustee Temple Emanuel, 1993-96. Maj. AUS, 1943-46. Recipient Diamond Pin award Am. Acad. Oral Medicine, 1976, Gold medal Greater St. Louis Dental Soc., 1985, Herschfus Meml. award Am. Acad. Oral Medicine, 1986; Am. Acad. Oral Medicine fellow, 1964, Am. Coll. Dentists fellow, 1980. Mem. AARP (pres. chpt. 4048 1992-94, cmty. coord. dist. 8 1994-96). Mem. ADA, Am. Acad. Oral Medicine (sec., trustee, pres. 1962-63), Am. Soc. Geriatric Dentistry (past pres.), Pierre Fauchard Acad., Acad. Gen. Dentistry, Fedn. Dentaire Internat., St. Louis Dental Soc. (chmn. 1989-93, mem. coun. on legis. 1988-91, parliamentarian 1989-96), Mo. Dental Assn. (chmn. coun. on legis. 1970-84, mem. coun. on Constn. 1988-92, Disting. Svc. award 1985), Temple Emanuel Men's Club (founder, bd. trustees 1993—), Temple Israel Men's Club (past pres.). Home: 15 Princeton Ave Saint Louis MO 63130-3158 Office: 7777 Bonhomme Ave Ste 1400 Saint Louis MO 63105-1911

SCHMIDT, JEAN MARIE, microbiology educator; b. Waterloo, Iowa, June 5, 1938; d. John Frederick and Opal Marie (Lowe) S. BA, U. Iowa, 1959, MS, 1961; PhD, U. Calif., Berkeley, 1965. NIH postdoctoral fellow U. Edinburgh, Scotland, 1965-66; asst. prof. Ariz. State U., Tempe, 1966-71, assoc. prof., 1971-79, prof. microbiology, 1979—, assoc. dir. for biology Cancer Rsch. Inst., 1982—, acting chair dept. microbiology, 1988-89. Author: (with others) Bergey's Manual of Systematic Bacteriology, 1989; contbr. articles to jours. NSF grantee, 1981. Fellow AAAS; mem. Am. Soc. Microbiology (divsn. chmn. 1979-80), Phi Beta Kappa, Sigma Xi. Democrat. Methodist.

SCHMIDT, JOSEPH DAVID, urologist; b. Chgo., July 29, 1937; s. Louis and Marian (Fleigel) S.; m. Andrea Maxine Herman, Oct. 28, 1962. BS in Medicine, U. Ill., 1959, MD, 1961. Diplomate Am. Bd. Urology. Rotating intern Presbyn. St. Luke's Hosp., Chgo., 1961-62, resident in surgery, 1962-63; resident in urology The Johns Hopkins Hosp., Balt., 1963-67; faculty U. Iowa Coll. Medicine, Iowa City, 1969-76; faculty U. Calif., San Diego, 1976—, prof., head div. urology, 1976—, vice-chmn. dept. surgery, 1985—; cons. U.S. Dept. Navy, San Diego, 1976—; attending urologist Vets. Affairs Dept., San Diego, 1976—. Author, editor: Gynecological and Obstetric Urology, 1978, 82, 93. Capt. USAF, 1967-69. Recipient Francis Senear award. U. Ill., 1961. Fellow Am. Coll. of Surgeons; mem. AMA, Am. Urol. Assn. Inc., Alpha Omega Alpha. Office: U Calif Med Ctr Divsn Urology 200 W Arbor Dr San Diego CA 92103-8897

SCHMIDT, MARK JAMES, state public health official; b. Milw., July 16, 1955; s. Warren J. and Carolyn Juel (Gissing) S.; m. Janet M. Schmidt, Oct. 5, 1991; 1 child, Andrew T.; stepchildren: Nathan A. and Aaron M. Stotts. BA, U. Wis., Eau Claire, 1977; MSc., Ill. State U., 1978. Dir. debate U. No. Iowa, Cedar Falls, 1978-79; dir. communication Ill. Rep. Party, Springfield, 1979-83; asst. adminstr. driver svc. dept. Office of the Sec. State, Springfield, Ill., 1983-87, asst. dir. driver svc. dept., 1987-91; dir. pub. affairs Ill. Dept. Cen. Mgmt. Svcs., 1991-95; asst. dir. Ill. Dept. Pub. Health, Springfield, 1995—; guest lectr. polit. comm. Ill. State U., Normal, 1980; cons. 6th Congl. Dist. Rep. Com., Lombard, Ill., 1985-90; rep. Ill. Drivers Lic. Compact Com., Falls Church, Va., 1987-91; mem. Ill. Rural Health Assn.; bd. dirs. Ill. Rural Ptnrs., Inc. Editor: Driver's Handbook (annual) Rules of the Road, 1984-91; editor Driver Svcs. Dept. newsletter, 1988-91; contbr. articles to profl. jours. Debate strategist Fahner for Atty. Gen. Ill., 1982, Bertini for Congress, Chgo., 1982; advisor Richard Austin for Congress, Springfield, Ill., 1984; coord. Citizens for Jim Edgar, Springfield, 1985-91; chmn. pub. info. subcom. Ill. Comml. Drivers License Program, 1989-91. Fellow Ill. Pub. Health Leadership Inst.; mem. Masons, Order Eastern Star. Republic. Methodist. Home: 513 W Locust St Chatham IL 62629-1201 Office: Ill Dept Pub Health 535 W Jefferson Springfield IL 62761

SCHMIDT, PATRICIA FAIN, nurse educator; b. Chgo., June 17, 1941; d. Lawrence D. and Catherine B. (Schira) Fain; m. Donald W. Schmidt, July 16, 1966; children: Kathryn, Kristine, Michael. BSN, Coll. of St. Teresa, 1963; MSN, Marquette U., 1965; EdD, U.S. Internat. U., 1981. Instr. Coll. of St. Teresa, Winona, Minn.; asst. prof. San Diego State U.; interim dean for mathematics and natural and health scis. Palomar Coll., San Marcos, Calif. Mem. Sigma Theta Tau. Home: 12573 Utopia Way San Diego CA 92128-2229

SCHMIDT, PATRICIA JEAN, medical lab technician; b. Cleve., June 15, 1941. Cert. applied lab. tech., Cuyahoga C.C., Cleve., 1967. Lic. student driver instr. Lab. sect. supr. Meridia Euclid (Ohio) Hosp., 1968-74; gen. lab. technician, 1974-94; student driving instr. Cleve., 1994—; tutor deaf students in coll. math.; designer including vet.'s memls. Author: A Manual of Disciplines for Interpreters of the Deaf; composer, vocal and stage presentation coach; sculptor and designer. Active voter registration Rep. Party. Recipient Acad. award Math. Assn. Am., Washington, 1959. Mem. Nat. Assn. of the Deaf, Nat. Head Injury Found., Sweet Adeline Internat. Home: PO Box 43123 Cleveland OH 44143-0123

SCHMIDT, ROBERT MILTON, physician, scientist, educator; b. Milw., May 7, 1944; s. Milton W. and Edith J. (Martinek) S.; children Eric Whitney, Edward Huntington. AB, Northwestern U., 1966; MD, Columbia U., 1970; MPH, Harvard U., 1975; PhD in Law, Medicine and Pub. Policy, Emory U., 1982. Diplomate Am. Bd. Preventive Medicine. Resident in internal medicine Univ. Hosp. U. Calif.-San Diego, 1970-71; resident in preventive medicine Ctrs. Disease Control, Atlanta, 1971-74; commd. med. officer USPHS, 1971; advanced through grades to comdr., 1973; dir. hematology div. Nat. Ctr. for Disease Control, Atlanta, 1971-78, spl. asst. to dir., 1978-79, inactive res., 1979—; clin. asst. prof. pediatrics Tufts U. Med. Sch., 1974-86; clin. asst. prof. medicine Emory U. Med. Sch., 1971-81, clin. asst. prof. community health, 1976-86; clin. assoc. prof. humanities in medicine Morehouse Med. Sch., 1977-79; attending physician dept. medicine Wilcox Meml. Hosp., Lihue, Hawaii, 1979-82, Calif. Pacific Med. Ctr., San Francisco, 1983—; dir. Ctr. Preventive Medicine and Health Research, 1983—, dir. Health Watch, 1983—; sr. scientist Inst. Epidemiology and Behavioral Medicine, Inst. Cancer Research, Calif. Pacific Med. Ctr., San Francisco, 1983-88; prof. hematology and gerontology, dir. Ctr. Preventive Medicine and Health Rsch., chair health professions program San Francisco State U., 1983—; cons. WHO, FDA, Washington, NIH, Bethesda, Md., Govt. of China, Mayo Clinic, Rochester, Minn., Northwestern U., Evanston, Ill., U. R.I., Kingston, Pan Am. Health Orgn., Inst. Pub. Health, Italy, Nat. Inst. Aging Rsch. Ctr., Balt., U. Calif., San Diego, U. Ill., Chgo., Columbia U., N.Y.C., Brown U., Providence, U. Calif., L.A., Harvard U., Boston, U. Chgo., Emory U., Atlanta, Duke U., N.C., U. Tex., Houston, Ariz. State U., U. Hawaii, Honolulu, U. Paris, U. Geneva, U. Munich, Heidelberg U., U. Frankfurt, U. Berlin, Cambridge (Eng.) U., U. Singapore, others; vis. rsch. prof. gerontology Ariz. State U., 1989-90; mem. numerous sci. and profl. adv. bds., panels, coms. Mem. editorial bd. Am. Jour. Clin. Pathology, 1976-82, The Advisor, 1988—, Generations, 1989—, Alternative Therapies in Health and Medicine; book and film reviewer Sci. Books and Films, 1988—; author: 17 books and manuals including Hematology Laboratory Series, 4 vols., 1979-86, CRC Handbook Series in Clinical Laboratory Science, 1976—; assoc. editor: Contemporary Gerontology, 1993—; contbr. over 270 articles to sci. jours. Alumni regent Columbia U. Coll. Physicians and Surgeons, 1980—. Northwestern U. scholar, 1964-66; NSF fellow, 1964-66; Health Professions scholar, 1966-70; USPHS fellow, 1967-70; Microbiology, Urology, Upjohn Achievement, Borden Rsch. and Virginia Kneeland Frantz scholar awards Columbia U., 1970; recipient Am. Soc. Pharmacol. and Exptl. Therapy award in pharmacology, 1970, Commendation medal USPHS, 1973, Leadership Recognition awards San Francisco State U., 1984-89, 91-94, Meritorious Performance and Profl. Promise award, 1989, Meritorious Svc. award, San Francisco State U., 1992, Student Disting. Teaching and Svc. award Pre-Health Professions Student Alliance, 1992. Fellow ACP (commentator ACP Jour. Club/Annals of Internal Medicine 1993—), AAAS (med. scis. sect.), Royal Soc. Medicine (London), Gerontol. Soc. Am., Am. Geriatrics Soc., Am. Coll. Preventive Medicine (sci. com.), Am. Soc. Clin. Pathology, Internat. Soc. Hematology; mem. AMA, APHA, Am. Med. Informatics, Internat. Commn. for Standardization in Hematology, Am. Soc. Hematology, Internat. Soc. Thrombosis and Hemostasis, Acad. Clin. Lab. Physicians and Scientists, Am. Assn. Blood Banks, Nat. Assn. Advisors for Health Professions (bd. dirs.), Am. Assn. Med. Informatics (chair prevention and health evaluation informatics WG), Calif. Coun. Gerontology and Geriatrics, Am. Coll. Occupl. and Environ. Medicine, Assn. Tchrs. Preventive Medicine (edn. com., rsch. com.), Am. Soc. Microbiology, Am. Soc. Aging (editl. bd. 1990—, Dychtwald Pub. Spng award 1991), N.Y. Acad. Scis., Internat. Health Evaluation Assn. (v.p. for Ams. 1992—, bd. dirs., pres. 1994—), Cosmos Club, Golden Key (hon. faculty mem.), Army and Navy Club (Washington), Harvard Club (N.Y.), Sigma Xi, others. Home: 25 Hinckley Walk San Francisco CA 94111-2303 Office: Health Watch Ctr 2100 Webster St Ste 508 San Francisco CA 94115-2381

SCHMIDT, SHARON ADAMCZAK, medical librarian; b. Buffalo, Apr. 24, 1961; d. Arthur Stanley and Jacqueline Arlene (Poczkalski) Adamczak; m. Mark Gerard Schmidt, Oct. 20, 1984; 1 child, Alexis Claire. BA in History, SUNY, Buffalo, 1983; MLS, SUNY, 1984. Learning resources libr. Villa Maria Coll., Buffalo, 1984-85; libr. Syracuse (N.Y.) Newspapers, 1985; asst. libr. Ruth M. Lilly Med. Libr., Indpls., 1986-87, serials coord., 1987-89; head libr. Harcourt Brace & Co., Orlando, 1989-95; learning resources coord. Ctrl. Fla. Area Health Edn. Ctr., Apopka, Fla., 1995—; bd. dirs. Ctrl. Fla. Libr. Consortium, 1991-93. Roman Catholic. Home: 4042 Evander Dr Orlando FL 32802 Office: Ctrl Fla Area Health Ctr 328 S Ctrl Ave Apopka FL 32703

SCHMIDT, TERRY LANE, health care executive; b. Chgo., Nov. 28, 1943; s. LeRoy C. and Eunic P. S.; children: Christie Anne, Terry Lane II. B.S., Bowling Green State U., 1965; M.B.A. in Health Care Adminstrn, George Washington U., 1971. Resident in hosp. adminstrn. U. Pitts. Med. Center, VA Hosp., Pitts., 1968-69; adminstrv. asst. Mt. Sinai Med. Center, N.Y.C., 1969-70; asst. dir. Health Facilities Planning Council of Met. Washington, 1970-71; asst. dir. dept. govtl. relations A.M.A., Washington, 1971-74; pres. Terry L. Schmidt Inc. Physician Svcs. Group, San Diego, 1974—; exec. dir., chief operating officer Emergency Health Assocs. P.C., Phoenix, 1989-91, Charleston Emergency Physicians, S.C., S.C., 1990-95, Joplin Emergency Physican Assocs., 1991-92, Big Valley Med. Group, 1991-92, Blue Ridge Emergency Physicians, P.C., 1992-93, Berkeley Emergency Physicians, P.C., 1992-93; pres. Med. Cons. Inc., 1983-84; v.p. Crisis Communications Corp. Ltd., 1982-90; pres. Washington Actions on Health, 1975-78; partner Washington counsel Medicine and Health, 1979-81; pres. Ambulance Corp. Am., La Jolla, Calif., 1984-87; chmn., pres. Univ. Inst., 1992—; lectr., part-time faculty dept. health care adminstrn. George Washington U., 1969-84, preceptor, 1971-84; adj. prof. grad. sch. Pub. Health San Diego State U., 1989—, preceptor, 1989—, clin. prof., 1995—; asst. prof Nat. Naval Sch. Health Care Adminstrn., 1971-73; faculty CSC Legis. Insts., 1972-76, Am. Assn. State Colls. and U. Health Tng. Insts.; mem. adv. com. ambulatory care standards Joint Commn. Accreditation of Hosps., 1971-72; guest lectr. health care adminstrn. Nat. U., San Diego, 1992—; adj. prof. Bus. Adminstrn. U.S. Internat. U., San Diego, 1994-95. Author: Congress and Health: An Introduction to the Legislative Process and the Key Participants, 1976, A Directory of Federal Health Resources and Services for the Disadvantaged, 1976, Health Care Reimbursement: A Glossary, 1983; mem. editl. adv. bd. Nation's Health, 1971-73; contbr. articles to profl. jours. Bd. dirs. Nat. Eye Found., 1976-78. Mem. Am. Hosp. Assn., Med. Group Mgmt. Assn., Hosp. Fin. Mgmt. Assn., Med. Group Mgrs., Assn. Venture Capital Groups (bd. dirs. 1984-89), Med. Adminstrs. of Calif., San Diego Venture Group (chair 1984-87), U. Calif. San Diego Venture Group (chair 1984-87), U. Calif. San Diego Faculty Club, University Club (life), Nat. Dem. Club (life), Nat. Rep. Club (life), Capitol Hill Club (life), Alpha Phi Omega (pres. Bowling Green alumni chpt. 1967-70, sec.-treas. alumni assn. 1968-71). Office: 9191 Towne Center Dr Ste 360 San Diego CA 92122

SCHMIDT, THOMAS MITCHELL, microbiologist; b. Elyria, Ohio, Jan. 16, 1956; s. Eddie Merle and Phyllis Alta (Yunker) S.; m. Susan Kay Ward, Apr. 9, 1983; children: Alexander Ward, Erik Mitchell. BS, U. Mich., 1978; MS, Ohio State U., 1981, PhD, 1985. Postdoctoral researcher Scripps Inst. Oceanography, LaJolla, Calif., 1985, Ctr. Great Lakes Studies, Milw., 1986-87; rsch. scientist Ind. U., Bloomington, 1988-90; asst. prof. dept. microbiology Miami U., Oxford, Ohio, 1991-93, Mich. State U., East Lansing, 1993—. Contbr. articles to New England Jour. Medicine, Jour. Bacteriology, Jour. Molecular Evolution. Mem. AAAS, Am. Soc. Microbiology, Sigma Xi. Office: Mich State U Dept Microbiology East Lansing MI 48824-1101

SCHMIDT, WALDEMAR ADRIAN, pathologist, educator; b. L.A., Aug. 22, 1941; s. Waldemar Adrian and Mary Charlotte (Parker) S.; m. Karmen LaVer Bingham, Feb. 1, 1963; children: Rebecca, Sarah, Waldemar, Diedrich. BS, Oreg. State U., 1965; PhD, U. Oreg., 1969, MD, 1969. Intern U. Oreg. Hosps. and Clinics, Portland, 1969-70, resident, 1970-73; pathologist LDS Hosp., Salt Lake City, 1973-77; prof. pathology U. Tex. Med. Sch., Houston, 1977-91, Oreg. Health Sci. U. and VA Med. Ctr., Portland, 1991—. Author: Principles and Techniques of Surgical Pathology, 1982; editor Cytopathology Annual, 1991—. Asst. scoutmaster Boy Scouts Am., Houston, 1982-91. Maj. U.S. Army, 1970-76. Mem. Coll. Am. Pathologists (program com.), Sigma Xi, Alpha Omega Alpha. Office: VA Med Ctr 3710 SW US Veterans Hosp Rd Portland OR 97207

SCHMIDT, WILLIAM ALEXANDER, physician, lawyer; b. Mpls., Sept. 23, 1947; s. Herbert William and Kathleen (Campbell) S.; 1 child, Alexander Edward. BS in Medicine, U. Minn., 1975, MD, 1976; JD, William Mitchell Coll. Law, 1981. Bar: Minn. 1982, U.S. Dist. Ct. Minn. 1982, U.S. Ct. Appeals (8th cir.) 1982. Intern Northwestern Hosp., Mpls., resident 1976-78; practice medicine specializing in internal medicine, Mpls.; mem. staff Fairview Southdale, Mpls.; former gen. counsel, med. dir. Corview Inc., Mpls., now CEO, 1995—. With U.S. Army, 1967-70; S.E. Asia, 5th Field Hosp., Med. Corps. Fellow Am. Coll. Legal Medicine; mem. Rho Chi Soc. Republican. Home: 2600 179th Ave Andover MN 55436-2231 Office: Profl Bldg 822 Marquette Ave Ste 208 Minneapolis MN 55402-2820 also: Ste 500 3300 County Rd 10 Minneapolis MN 55429

SCHMITT, EARL PHILLIP, optometrist, educator; b. Berkeley, Calif., Oct. 2, 1930; m. Dicksie S. Schmitt, June 17, 1957; children: Gregory Ernest, Carol Joyce, Barbara Elizabeth. BA, Stanford U., 1952, MA in Secondary Edn., 1956; OD, Pacific U., Forrest Grove, Oreg., 1961, MS in Physiol. Optics, 1968; EdD in Higher Ednl. Adminstrn., Memphis State U., 1977; D of Ocular Sci., So. Coll. Optometry, Memphis, 1985. Cert in optometry, Okla. Sci. tchr. Menlo Park (Calif.) H.S., 1956-58; pvt. practice optometry LaGrande, Oreg., 1961-65; mem. faculty So. Coll. Optometry, Memphis, 1967-82, dir. clinics, 1969-74, dean of students, 1974-78; mem. faculty Northeastern State U. Coll. Optometry, Tahlequah, Okla., 1982—, dir. clinics, 1984-89, prof. optometry, 1982—; mem. Nat. Bd. Examiners in Optometry, Washington, 1981-91, sec.-treas., 1982-89, v.p., 1989-91. Author: The Interpretation and Significance of the Embedded and Nonembedded Syndromes in Behavioral Case Analysis, 1993, Guidelines for Clinical Testing Lens Prescribing and Vision Care, 1996. Bd. dris., v.p., pres. Arts Coun., Tahlequah, 1990-95; bd. dirs. Thompson House Preservation Assn., Tahlequah, 1991—. Northeastern State U. faculty rsch. grantee, 1992. Fellow Am. Acad. Optometry; mem. Am. Optometric Assn., C. of C. (bd. dirs., svc. coms. 1990—), Kiwanis Internat. (pres. Tahlequah Kiwanis Club 1995-96, pres. 1996—). Office: Northeastern State U Coll Optometry 1001 Grand Ave Tahlequah OK 74464

SCHMITT, HEINZ-JOSEF, physician, educator; b. Wiesbaden, Germany, May 19, 1954; s. Alois and Elisabeth (Weil) S.; m. Barbara Josephine Zell, Aug. 13, 1982. MD, Gutenberg U., 1980. Cert. Bd. Pediatrics, Bd. Microbiology, Germany. Asst. physician Rodenwaldt Microbiology Lab., Koblenz, 1980-82; asst. psysician Childrens Hosp Gutenberg U., 1983-85; fellow in infectious diseases Meml. Sloan Kettering Cancer Ctr., N.Y.C., 1986-88, asst. physician, 1989-90, attending physician, 1990-95; habilitation J. Gutenberg U., Mainz., Germany, 1993; assoc. prof. clin. microbiology and pediatric infections Christian-Albrechts-U. Kiel (Germany), Germany, 1995—; mem. German Vaccination Adv. Bd., 1995—. Mem. Am. Soc. Microbiology, Deutsche Gesellschaft für Kinderheilkunde, Deutsche Gesellschaft für Pädiatrische Infektiologie, Am. Soc. Infectious Diseases. Roman Catholic. Office: Childrens Hosp, Schwanenweg 20, 24105 Kiel Germany

SCHMITT, VICTOR WARREN, healthcare executive; b. Long Branch, N.J., Oct. 13, 1948; s. Robert J. and Helen (Vroom) S.; m. Pamela Drews, Aug. 21, 1971; children: Christine, Andrew. BS in Bommerce, U. Va., 1971; MBA, U. Md., 1973. Adminstr. Nashville region Am. Nat. Red Cross, Washington, 1976-81, dir. plasma ops., 1981-84, v.p. blood svcs., 1984-89; v.p. bus. devel. Baxter Healthcare, Deerfield, Ill., 1989-92, pres biotech Europe, 1992-94, pres. venture mgmt., 1994—; bd. dirs. First Med. Inc., Mountain View, Calif., Neocrin, Inc., Irvine, Calif.; bd. advisor United Biols., Inc., L.I., N.Y. Office: Baxter Healthcare 1425 Lake Cook Rd Deerfield IL 60015

SCHMUCKER, RUBY ELVY LADRACH, nurse, educator; b. Sugarcreek, Ohio, Nov. 17, 1923; d. Walter F. and Carrie M. (Mizer) Ladrach; R.N., Aultman Hosp., Canton, Ohio, 1945; B.S. in Nursing, U. Akron, 1970, M.S. in Edn., 1973; children: Gary, David, Barbara, Steven. Cert. psychiat. nurse. Gen. duty nurse, head nurse Aultman Hosp., 1945-47, part-time, 1950-62, instr. nursing, 1962-64, 69-74, part-time psychiat. nurse, 1991—; instr. nursing Coll. Nursing, U. Akron (Ohio), 1974-76; instr. div. nursing edn. Children's Hosp., Akron, 1976-78; psychiat. nurse and supr. Massillon (Ohio) State Hosp., 1978-80, cons. to nursing dept., 1980-81, dir. nursing edn., 1981-84; supr. Molly Stark Hosp., 1984-88; charge nurse, individual and group therapist Cuyahoga Falls Gen. Hosp., 1984-90, part-time psychiat. nurse; cons. Stark-Tuscarawas Counties Student Nurses Assn., 1973-74. Health chmn. Avondale Sch. PTA, Canton, 1956, mem. coms., 1954-70; vol. instr. home nursing courses ARC, 1959-62, instr. CPR, 1979-83. Cert. psychiat. nurse. Mem. Aultman Hosp. Sch. Nursing Alumni Assn., Am. Nurses' Assn., Nat. League Nursing, Am. Personnel and Guidance Assn., Am. Coll. Personnel Assn., U. Akron Alumni Assn., Alpha Sigma Lambda, Pi Lambda Theta. Mem. Ch. of Christ. Office: 4214 Bellwood Dr NW Canton OH 44708-1656

SCHMUDE, JUDY GAIL, health care administrator; b. Kenosha, Wis., Mar. 2, 1939; d. Howard D. and Joycelyn V. (Correll) Ohlgart; divorced; children: Frederick E., Randall H. BS, U. Wis., Whitewater, 1962, MS, 1971; MT, Kenosha Mem. Hosp., 1971; PhD, Marquette U., 1983. Cert. tchr. Tchr. gen. sch. Kenosha Unified Schs., 1962-67; instr. sci. Gateway Tech. Inst., Kenosha, 1967-75; edn. coordinator Kenosha Mem. Hosp., 1975-80, dir., 1980-86; v.p. women's care St. Joseph's Hosp. and Med. Ctr., Phoenix, 1986—, v.p. maternal and child health, 1989-90, v.p. ambulatory svcs., 1990—, v.p. patient svcs., 1994-95; exec. dir., CEO Children's Health Network, San Diego, 1995—; adj. faculty U. Phoenix, 1986—; faculty Cardinal Stritch Coll., Milw., 1985-86; cons. Kenosha Mem. Hosp., 1983-86. Author: Quality Assurance Nursing Schools, 1985, Politics in Health Care Administration, 1988; contbr. articles to profl. jours. Pres. Wish. Health Edn., 1986, Am. Cancer Soc., Kenosha, 1985; elected mem. Ariz. Women's Town Hall, 1987, 88, 89, panel chair, 1989, 91, 92; state chair Airz. Prenatal Care Coaliition, 1988-89, 93, 94. Fellow Am. Coll. Hosp. Execs.; mem. Ariz. Hosp. Assn., Squaw Peak Hiking Club, Phi Delta Kappa. Democrat. Lutheran. Office: Childrens Health Network 3702 Ruffen Rd San Diego CA 92123

SCHNABLY, MICHAEL B., marketing executive; b. Lewistown, Pa., July 8, 1964; s. Robert and Patricia (McKee) S.; m. LorieAnn Schnably, Nov. 11, 1989. BS, West Chester U., 1986, MBA, 1990. Cert. systems profl. Programmer, analyst Pfizer, Inc., West Chester, Pa., 1985-88; sr. mktg. rsch. analyst SmithKline Beecham, West Chester, Pa., 1989, sr. forecast analyst, 1989-90; sr. forecast analyst Pfizer, Inc., West Chester, Pa., 1990-92, group product mgr., 1992-95; market mgr. Pfizer, Inc., West Chester, 1995—. Contbr. articles to profl. pubs. Mem. Am. Mktg. Assn. Republican. Office: Pzifer Inc 812 Springdale Ave Exton PA 19341-2803

SCHNAKE, BETTY BERNIECE, nursing educator; b. Marion County, Ill., Nov. 30, 1930; d. Charles E. and Gladys O. (Myers) Talbott; m. Eugene R. Schnake, Apr. 1, 1949; children: Pamela Sue Schnake Devine, Robert, Jeffrey. ADN, Kaskaskia Coll., Centralia, Ill., 1976. RN, Ill.; cert. Alzheimer's instr. ICU/CCU nurse Good Samaritan Hosp., Mt. Vernon, Ill., 1976-77; pvt. duty nurse Nashville, Ill., 1976-77; med.-surg.-oncological floor nurse St. Mary's Hosp., Centralia, 1977—; nursing and bus. edn. instr. Kaskaskia Coll., 1979—, instr. phys. therapy program, 1994—. Active ARC, Am. Cancer Soc. Home: 13215 Plum Tree Rd Hoyleton IL 62803-2705

SCHNALL, EDITH LEA (MRS. HERBERT SCHNALL), microbiologist, educator; b. N.Y.C., Apr. 11, 1922; d. Irving and Sadie (Raab) Spitzer; AB, Hunter Coll., 1942; AM, Columbia U., 1947, PhD, 1967; m. Herbert Schnall, Aug. 21, 1949; children: Neil David, Carolyn Beth. Clin. pathologist Roosevelt Hosp., N.Y.C., 1942-44; instr. Adelphi Coll., Garden City, N.Y., 1944-46; asst. med. mycologist Columbia Coll. Physicians and Surgeons, N.Y.C., 1946-47, 49-50; instr. Bklyn. Coll., 1947; mem. faculty Sarah Lawrence Coll., Bronxville, N.Y., 1947-48; lectr. Hunter Coll., N.Y.C., 1947-67; adj. assoc. prof. Lehman Coll., City U. N.Y., 1968; asst. prof. Queensborough Community Coll., City U. N.Y., 1967, assoc. prof. microbiology, 1968-75, prof., 1975—, adminstr. Med. Lab. Tech. Program, 1985—; vis. prof. Coll. Physicians and Surgeons, Columbia U., N.Y.C., 1974; advanced biology examiner U. London, 1970—. Mem. Alley Restoration Com., N.Y.C., 1971—; mem. legis. adv. com. Assembly of the State of N.Y., 1972. Mem. Community Bd. 11, Queens, N.Y., 1974—, 3d vice-chmn., 1987-92, 2nd vice chmn., 1992—; public dir. of bd. dirs. Inst. Continuing Dental Edn. Queens County, Dental Soc. N.Y. State and ADA, 1973—. Rsch. fellow NIH, 1948-49; faculty rsch. fellow, grantee-in-aid Rsch. Found. of SUNY, 1968-70; faculty rsch. grant Rsch. Found. City U. N.Y., 1971-74. Mem. Internat. Soc. Human and Animal Mycology, AAAS, Am. Soc. Microbiology (coun., N.Y.C. br. 1981—, co-chairperson ann. meeting com. 1981-82, chair program com. 1982-83, v.p. 1984-86, pres. 1986-88), Med. Mycology Soc. N.Y. (sec.-treas. 1967-68, v.p. 1968-69, 78-79, archivist 1974—, fin. advisor 1983—, pres. 1969-70, 79-80, 81-82), Bot. Soc. Am., Med. Mycology Soc. Americas, Mycology Soc. Am., N.Y. Acad. Scis., Sigma Xi, Phi Sigma. Clubs: Torrey Botanical (N.Y. State); Queensborough Community Coll. Women's (pres. 1971-73) (N.Y.C.). Editor: Newsletter of Med. Mycology Soc. N.Y., 1969-85; founder, editor Female Perspective newsletter of Queensborough Community Coll. Women's Club, 1971-73. Home: 21406 29th Ave Flushing NY 11360-2622

SCHNECK, JEROME M., psychiatrist, medical historian, educator; b. N.Y.C., Jan. 2, 1920; s. Maurice and Rose (Weiss) S.; m. Shirley R. Kaufman, July 24, 1943. AB, Cornell U., 1939, MD, SUNY-Bklyn., 1943. Diplomate Am. Bd. Psychiatry and Neurology. Intern Interfaith Med. Ctr., 1943; mem. psychiat. staff Menninger Clinic, Topeka, 1944-45; chief psychiatry and sociology dept. Fort Missoula, Mont., 1946, Camp Cooke, Calif., 1947; mem. psychiat. staff L.I. Coll. Hosp., 1947-48, Kings County Hosp., 1948-70, SUNY Hosp., Bklyn., 1955-70; assoc. vis. psychiatrist Kings County Hosp., 1949-70; mem. psychiat. staff State U. Hosp., Bklyn., 1955-70; pvt. practice N.Y.C., 1947—; attending psychiatrist St. Vincent's Hosp. and Med. Ctr. N.Y., 1970—, hon. sr. psychiatrist, 1990—; psychiat. cons. VA Regional Office, 1947-48, N.Y. State Dept. Social Svcs., 1977-83, N.Y. State Dept. Civil Svc., 1978-84, N.Y. State Office Ct. Adminstrn., 1978-85, N.Y. State Dept. Edn., 1981-83; dir. Mt. Vernon Mental Hygiene Clinic, 1947-52; assoc. chief psychiatrist Westchester County Dept. Health, 1949-50, cons., 1951-52; clin. instr. L.I. Coll. Medicine, 1947-50; clin. assoc. SUNY Coll. Medicine, Bklyn., 1950-53, asst. prof., 1955-58, assoc. prof., 1958-70; supervising psychiatrist Community Guidance Svcs., 1955-70; cons. coun. on mental health AMA, 1956-58; cons. NBC, 1962, Ctr. Rsch. in Hypnotherapy, 1964-70; vis. lectr. N.Y. Med. Coll.-Met. Hosp., 1965; faculty Am. Inst. Psychotherapy and Psychoanalysis, 1970-85. Author: Hypnosis in Modern Medicine, 1953, 2d edit., 1959, Spanish lang. edit., 1962, 3rd edit., 1963, Studies in Scientific Hypnosis, 1954, A History of Psychiatry, 1960, The Principles and Practice of Hypnoanalysis, 1965 (Best Book award Soc. For Clin. and Exptl. Hypnosis 1965); editor: Hypnotherapy, Hypnosis and Personality, 1951; author over 400 med. and sci. publs., book chpts., articles; mem. bd. editors: Personality: Symposia on Topical Issues, 1960-61, Jour. Integrative and Eclectic Psychotherapy, 1986-89; contbg. editor Psychosomatics, 1961-75; mem. editorial bd. Voices—The Art and Science of Psychotherapy, 1965; features editor The Interne, 1942, co-editor, 1943. Capt. AUS, 1945-47. Recipient Clarence B. Farrar award Clarke Inst. of Psychiatry, U. Toronto, 1976. Fellow AAAS, APA, Am. Med. Authors, Acad. Psychosomatic Medicine, Am. Psychiat. Assn. (life), Soc. for Clin. and Exptl. Hypnosis (life, founder, founding pres. 1949-56, exec. coun. 1949—, assoc. editor jour. 1953—, Award of Merit 1955, Gold medal 1958, Bernard B. Raginsky award 1966, Shirley Schneck award 1970, Roy M. Dorcus award 1980, Spl. Presdl. award 1986), Am. Acad. Psychotherapists (co-founder, v.p. 1956-58), Am. Med. Writers Assn., Am. Soc. Psychoanalytic Physicians (founding fellow, bd. dirs. 1958-62), Am. Soc. Clin. Hypnosis (life mem.), Internat. Soc. Clin. and Exptl. Hypnosis (co-founder, bd. dirs. 1958-68, founding fellow), Internat. Acad. Eclectic Psychotherapists (charter fellow); mem. AMA, Soc. Acad. Achievement (charter), Soc. Apothecaries London, Inst. Practicing Psychotherapists, Pan Am. Med. Assn. (v.p. sect. clin. hypnosis 1960-65, N.Am. v.p. 1966), N.Y. Soc. Med. History (exec. com. 1956-62), Am. Bd. Med. Hypnosis (founder, pres. 1958-60, life bd. dirs.), Inst. Rsch. in Hypnosis Inc. (bd. dirs., bd. editors 1957-70), Am. Assn. History Medicine, History of Sci. Soc., Assn. Advancement Psychotherapy (charter) Can. Med. History Assn., N.Y. Soc. for Clin. Psychiatry (chmn. com. on history of psychiatry), Charles F. Menninger Soc., Sigma Xi. Address: 26 W 9th St New York NY 10011-8971

SCHNEE, AMANDA MERYL MACNAB, physician; b. North Berwick, Scotland, Dec. 3, 1945; came to U.S., 1975; d. Hamish Stuart Duncan and Marjorie Daphne Croal (McDonald) M.; M.B., Ch.B., St. Andrews U.,

Scotland, 1968; m. Mark Schnee, Oct. 21, 1967; children—Samantha Joanne, Jicky Miranda, Pippa Meryl, Briony Amanda. Intern, Ballochmyle Hosp., Mauchline, Ayrshire, Scotland, 1968-69; resident in family practice Ayrshire Central Hosp., Irvine, Ayrshire, 1969-71; gen. practice medicine, Glasgow, Scotland, 1971-75; physician USAF, Omaha, 1975-77; mem. faculty U. Tex. Med. Sch., Houston, 1977-81. asst. prof. dept. family practice, 1979-81; dir. Student Health Center, Rice U., Houston, 1981—. Diplomate Am. Bd. Family Practice. Mem. Am. Acad. Family Practice, Am. Med. Women's Assn. Home: 2318 Underwood Blvd Houston TX 77030-3622 Office: Rice U Student Health Ctr PO Box 1892 Houston TX 77251-1892

SCHNEEWIND, ELIZABETH HUGHES, social worker; b. Chgo., May 11, 1940; d. Everett Cherrington and Helen (MacGill) Hughes; m. Jerome Borges Schneewind, Feb. 23, 1963; children: Sarah Katherine, Rachel Miriam, Hannah Elizabeth. BA in Philosophy, U. Chgo., 1959; MA in Philosophy, Brown U., 1962; MSW, U. Md., 1985; postgrad., Yale U., 1962-63. ACSW, LCSW-C; cert. German translator. Program evaluator Coll. Human Svcs., N.Y.C., 1976-77; rsch. asst. Fordham U. Gerontology Ctr., N.Y., 1977-80; field supr. N.Y.C. Dept. Aging Foster Grandparent Program, 1980-82; social worker Levindale Geriatric Ctr., Balt., 1985-88, Johns Hopkins Hosp., Balt., 1988; asst. dir. older adult svcs. Jewish Family Svcs., Balt., 1988—; presentor in field. Pres. Balt. Washington Soc. Psychogeriatrics, 1987-89; exec. bd. Alzheimer's Assn., Balt. chpt. 1985-92; v.p. Women in Urban Crisis, Pitts., 1972-73. Mem. NASW, Md. Soc. Clin. Social Work. Democrat. Home: 325 Woodlawn Rd Baltimore MD 21210-2308 Office: Jewish Family Svcs 5750 Park Heights Ave Baltimore MD 21215-3930

SCHNEIDER, CALVIN, physician; b. N.Y.C., Oct. 23, 1924; s. Harry and Bertha (Green) S.; A.B., U. So. Calif., 1951, M.D., 1955; J.D., LaVerne (Calif.) Coll., 1973; m. Elizabeth Gayle Thomas, Dec. 27, 1967. Intern Los Angeles County Gen. Hosp., 1955-56, staff physician, 1956-57; practice medicine West Covina, Calif., 1957—; staff Inter-Community Med. Ctr., Covina, Calif. Cons. physician Charter Oak Hosp., Covina, 1960—. With USNR, 1943-47. Mem. AMA, Calif., L.A. County med. assns. Republican. Lutheran. Office: 224 W College St Covina CA 91723-1902

SCHNEIDER, CHESTER LOUIS, psychiatrist; b. Phila., July 22, 1922; s. Louis and Clara Bella (Green) S.; m. Dorothy Stam, June 21, 1947; children: Barbara Schneider Smith, Judy Schneider Arvidson, Jeff, John. BA, Wheaton (Ill.) Coll., 1943; MD, Thomas Jefferson U., 1947. Diplomate, Am. Bd. Psychiatry and Neurology. Intern Phila. Gen. Hosp., 1947-49; pvt. practice Glennallen, Alaska, 1950-69, med. missionary, 1950-69; resident in psychiatry Temple U. Hosp., Phila., 1970-73; staff psychiatrist Penn Found., Phila., 1973-74; pvt. practice Erdenheim, Pa., 1974-95; part-time psychiatric cons. outpatient svcs. Philhaven Hosp., Mt. Gretna, Pa., 1996—; vol. faculty family practice residency Lancaster (Pa.) Gen. Hosp., 1996—; clin. asst. prof. dept. psychiatry, Temple U., Phila., 1978-90, dept. family medicine, 1982-89; faculty cons., Northeastern Hosp. Family Practice Residency, Phila., 1978-90, Temple Family Practice Residency, Elkins Park, Pa., 1982-89. With U.S. Army, 1944-46. Mem. AMA, Am. Psychiatric Assn., Christian Med.-Dental Soc. (bd. trustees, 1989-90). Republican. Presbyterian. Home: 660 Willow Valley Sq M-108 Lancaster PA 17602-4874

SCHNEIDER, DANIEL SCOTT, pediatric cardiologist; b. Mitchell, S.D., July 17, 1953; s. Robert George and Lois Irene (Theis) S.; m. Lisa Anne Magri, Oct. 22, 1988; children: Elizabeth, Emily, Luisa. BS, Creighton U., 1975, MD, 1979. Diplomate Am. Bd. Pediat., Am. Bd. Pediat. Cardiology. Commd. ensign USN, 1979, advanced through grades to comdr., 1992; pediat. cardiologist Childrens Hosp. of the Kings Daus., Norfolk, Va., 1992—. Named Tchr. of Yr. Portsmouth Naval Hosp. Pediat. Residents, 1992. Mem. tidewater Down Syndrome Assn. (profl. adv. 1993—), Alpha Sigma Na, Alpha Omega Alpha. Roman Catholic. Office: Childrens Hosp the Kings Daus 601 Childrens Ln Norfolk VA 23507-1910

SCHNEIDER, EDWARD LEWIS, medicine educator, research administrator; b. N.Y.C., June 22, 1940; s. Samuel and Ann (Soskin) S. BS, Rensselaer Poly. Inst., 1961; MD, Boston U., 1966. Intern and resident N.Y. Hosp.-Cornell U., N.Y.C., 1966-68; staff fellow Nat. Inst. Allergy and Infectious Diseases, Bethesda, Md., 1968-70; research fellow U. Calif., San Francisco, 1970-73; chief, sect. on cell aging Nat. Inst. Aging, Balt., 1973-79, assoc. dir., 1980-84, dep. dir., 1984-87; prof. medicine, dir. Davis Inst. on Aging U. Colo., Denver, 1979-80; dean Leonard Davis Sch. Gerontology U. So. Calif., L.A., 1986—, exec. dir. Ethel Percy Andrus Gerontology Ctr., 1986—, prof. medicine, 1987—, William and Sylvia Kugel prof. gerontology, 1989—; sci. dir. Buck Ctr. for Rsch. in Aging, 1989—; cons. MacArthur Found., Chgo., 1985-93, R.W. Johnson Found., Princeton, N.J., 1982-87, Brookdale Found., N.Y.C., 1985-89. Editor: The Genetics of Aging, 1978, The Aging Reproductive System, 1978, Biological Markers of Aging, 1982, Handbook of the Biology of Aging, 1985, 95, Interrelationship Among Aging Cancer and Differentiation, 1985, Teaching Nursing Home, 1985, Modern Biological Theories of Aging, 1987, The Black American Elderly, 1988, Elder Care and the Work Force, 1990. Med. dir. USPHS, 1968—. Recipient Roche award, 1964. Fellow Gerontology Soc., Am. Soc. Clin. Investigation; mem. Am. Assn. Retired Persons, U.S. Naval Acad. Sailing Squadron (coach 1980-86). Office: U So Calif Andrus Gerontology Ctr Los Angeles CA 90089-0191

SCHNEIDER, EDWARD MARTIN, retired physician; b. Cleve., May 12, 1922; s. Sol S. and Beatrice Hilda (Sicherman) S.; m. Jane H. Einstein, June 18, 1950; children: Douglas A., Robert S. Student, Northwestern U., 1940-43; MD, U. Cin., 1946. Diplomate Am. Bd. Internal Medicine. Intern Mt. Sinai Hosp., Cleve., 1946-47, asst. resident medicine, 1947-48, sr. asst. resident medicine, 1950-51; fellow in medicine Cin. Gen. Hosp., 1951-52; asst. prof. of medicine U. Okla. Sch. Medicine, Oklahoma City, 1952-57; sr. physician gastroenterology Miner's Meml. Hosp. Assn., McDowell, Ky., Beckley, W.Va., 1957-61; chief of medicine Cameron Meml. Hosp., Bryan, Ohio, 1961-62; chief medical rsch. sect. Upjohn Co., Kalamazoo, Mich., 1962-67; pvt. practice Woodland Hills, Calif., 1968-81. Author 17 rsch. papers. Capt. M.C., AUS, 1948-50. Fellow Am. Coll. Physicians, Am. Coll. Gastroenterologists; mem. Assn. Mil. Surgeons (life), Am. Assn. Study Liver Disease (emeritus), Soc. of Sigma Xi. Home: 20676 Fairmount Blvd Apt 205 Cleveland OH 44118-4850

SCHNEIDER, ELEONORA FREY, physician; b. Basel, Switzerland, Jan. 17, 1921; came to U.S., 1952; d. Friedrich Ernst and Clara Melanie (Heiz) Frey; m. Jurg Adolf Schneider, Aug. 22, 1946; children: Andreas George, Daphne Eleanor, Diana Veronica, Claudia Elizabeth. MD, U. Basel, 1945. Lic. MD. Pharmacologist Sandoz Pharms., Basel, 1946-47; resident in anesthesiology U. Hosp., Basel, 1950-51; resident Pediatric Dept. Del. Div., Wilmington, 1971-73; physician Wilmington Pub Schs., 1973-79, Pub. Health, Wilmington, 1975-80; staff physician student health svc. U. Del., Newark, 1979—; v.p. Pharmacon, Inc., Wilmington, 1985—. Contbr. articles to profl. jours. V.p. del. Citizens for Clean Air, 1969-71; mem. com. Gov.'s Adv. Coun. for Exceptional Children, Dover, Del.; mem. adv. panel YWCA; vol. Girl Scouts U.S.A., ARC. Mem. AAUW (study group leader 1966-67, area chmn. community problems 1967-69, edn. com. 1968-69, new mems. advisor 1969-70, bd. dirs. 1967-70), AMA, Am. Acad. Pediatrics, Med. Soc. Del., New Castle County Med. Soc. Republican.

SCHNEIDER, ELLEN CAROL, ophthalmologist; b. New Orleans, Aug. 28, 1960; d. Coleman S. and Elsa P. (Lastick) S.; m. Samuel M. Alexander, Feb. 11, 1990; children: Hillary, Benjamin Alexander. BS, Vanderbilt U., 1982; MD, La. State U., 1986. Intern in internal medicine Baylor U. Med. Ctr., 1986-87; resident in ophthalmology La. State U. Eye Ctr., New Orleans, 1987-91, clin. asst. prof., 1991—; pvt. practice Metairie and Slidell, La., 1991—. Office: 3409 N Hullen St Metairie LA 70002 Also: 2250 Gause Blvd Ste 200 Slidell LA 70461

SCHNEIDER, GEORGE, internist, endocrinoligist; b. Boston, Oct. 29, 1939; s. Morris and Doris (Saslovsky) S.; m. Patricia Marian Seymour, aug. 2, 1964; children: Andrew Gordon, Pamela Robin. AB, Harvard U., 1961; MD, Tufts U., Boston, 1965. Diplomate Am. Bd. Internal Medicine, Am. Bd. Internal Medicine in Endocrinology and Metabolism. Intern Bellevue Hosp., N.Y.C., 1965-66, asst. resident, 1966-67; assoc. resident Strong Meml. Hosp., Rochester, N.Y., 1969-70; fellow Yale U. Sch. of Medicine, New Haven, Conn., 1970-72; chief of endocrinology VA Hosp., East Orange, N.J., 1972-80, Beth Israel Med. Ctr., Newark, 1980—; pvt. practice in internal medicine Beth Israel Med. Ctr., Roseland, N.J., 1980—; med. dir. diabetes treatement ctr. Beth Israel Hosp., Newark, 1980—. Contbr. over 36 articles to profl. jours., 1970-90. Lt. cmmdr. USPHS, 1967-69. Fellow ACP, Am. Coll. Endocrinology; mem. AMA, Acad. Medicine of N.J., Am. Diabetes Assn., Endocrine Soc., Alpha Omega Alpha. Office: 204 Eagle Rock Ave Roseland NJ 07068

SCHNEIDER, HORACE LEE, JR., osteopath, gastroenterologist; b. Jefferson City, Mo., Sept. 14, 1953; s. Horace Lee and Stella Lucille (Jackson) S.; m. Brenda Lee Chancellor, May 26, 1979; children: Thomas Michael, Aaaron Lee. BA in Chemistry, U. Mo., Kansas City, 1975; DO, Coll. Osteopathic Medicine, Kirksville, Mo., 1979. Diplomate Am. Osteopathic Bd. Intermal Medicine & Gastroenterology. Intern Doctors' Hosp., Columbus, Ohio, 1979-80; resident Doctors' Hosp., Columbus, 1980-82; fellow Chgo. Coll. Osteopathic Medicine, 1982-84; group practice Metroplex Gastroenterology, Grand Prarie, Tex., 1984-85; pvt. practice in gastroenterology Dallas, 1985-91; pvt. practice Gastroenterology Assocs., Cape Girardeau, Mo., 1991—; physician advisor Tex. Med. Found., Dallas, 1989-91; cons. on practice guidelines Blue Cross of Mo., St. Louis, 1995—. U. Mo. scholar, 1974. Fellow Am. Coll. Gastroenerology; mem. Am. Osteopathic Assn., Am. Gastroenterology Assn., Am. Soc. Gastrointestinal Endoscopy, Mo. State Med. Assn., Sigma Sigma Phi. Office: Gastroenterology Assocs 21 Doctors Park Cape Girardeau MO 63703

SCHNEIDER, HOWARD RAYMOND, ophthalmologist; b. Bklyn., Mar. 14, 1938. MD, SUNY, Bklyn., 1962. Diplomate Am. Bd. Ophthalmology. Resident in ophthalmology Boston U., 1965-68; pvt. practice Wantagh, N.Y., 1968—; ophthalmologist Brunswick Gen. Hosp., 1968—, Mid-Island Hosp., 1968—, Massapequa Gen. Hosp., 1968—; attending physician Brunswick Gen. Hosp., Amityville, N.Y., Mid-Island Hosp., Bathpage, N.Y., Massapequa Gen. Hosp., Seaford, N.Y. Capt. U.S. Army, 1963-65. Mem. Am. Acad. Ophthalmology, N.Y. State Ophthal. Assn., Long Island Ophthal. Assn., Nassau County Med. Assn., N.Y. State Med. Assn. Office: 2185 Wantagh Ave Wantagh NY 11793

SCHNEIDER, JAMES JOSEPH, surgeon; b. Kentfield, Calif., Aug. 19, 1956; s. Richard J. and Patricia M. Schneider; m. Diane Spellberg, Jan. 30, 1993; 1 child, Catherine M. BA in Biology, U. Calif., 1978; MS in Biology, U. San Francisco, 1981; MD, St. Louis U., 1985. Diplomate Am. Bd. Med. Examiners. Intern in internal medicine Naval Hosp., Oakland, Calif., 1985-86; flight surgeon Carrier Air Wing Five, Atsugi, Japan, 1987-90; resident in surgery U. Calif., Davis, 1990-95; ship's surgeon USS Independence, Yokosuka, Japan, 1995—. Contbr. articles to profl. jours. Comdr. USN, 1995—. Recipient Resident Laparoscopic Surgeon award Soc. of Laparoendoscopic Surgeons, 1995. Mem. ACS. Office: USS Independence CV-62 FPO AP 96618

SCHNEIDER, JESSE ALAN, nuclear medicine physician; b. Freeport, N.Y., July 9, 1957; s. Victor Martin and June Susan (Weinberg) S.; m. Nancy Kathleen Deshler, June 23, 1979; 1 child, David Martin. BS, Cornell U., 1982; DO, U. Osteo. Medicine and Health Scis., Des Moines, 1986. Diplomate Am. Bd. Nuclear Medicine, Am. Osteo. Bd. Family Practice. Resident, then chief resident in family practice Long Beach (N.Y.) Meml. Hosp., 1986-89; pvt. practice specializing in family practice Ithaca, N.Y., 1989-90; staff Tompkins Cmty. Hosp., Ithaca, N.Y., 1989-92; resident in nuc. medicine Meml. Sloan-Kettering Cancer Ctr., N.Y.C., 1992-93; fellow in nuc. medicine U. Wash. Sch. Med., Seattle, 1994-95; staff St. John Hosp. and Med. Ctr., Detroit, 1995—; editl. reviewer Jour. Nuc. Medicine, N.Y.C., 1994—. Contbr. articles to profl. jours. Mem. Soc. Nuc. Medicine, Am. Coll. Nuc. Physicians, Am. Osteo. Assn., Am. Coll. Family Practitioners in Osteo. Medicine and Surgery. Office: St John Hosp & Med Ctr 22101 Moross Rd Detroit MI 48236

SCHNEIDER, JOEL ALAN, physician; b. N.Y.C., Mar. 16, 1938; s. Abraham and Etta (Abrams) S.; m. J. Merle Millman, Feb. 24, 1962; children: Alan B., Karen S. BS, CUNY, 1959; MD, Albert Einstein Coll. Medicine, N.Y.C., 1963. Diplomate Am. Bd. Radiology. Chief radiology USAF-Tyndall Air Force Base, Panama City, Fla., 1967-69; pres. Radiology Consultants, Hollywood, Fla., 1969—; clin. asst. prof. radiology U. Miami, Fla., 1978—; radiologist Transitional Hosp. Corp., Hollywood. Contbr. articles to profl. jours. Bd. dirs. Jewish Fedn. South Broward, Hollywood, 1973-89; pres. Jewish Community Ctr. South Broward, 1988-90. Capt. USAF, 1967-69. Jonas Salk scholar City of N.Y., 1959. Fellow Am. Coll. Radiology (fellowship 1988), Am. Coll. Nuclear Medicine; mem. S. Fla. Radiol. Soc. (pres. 1978), Fla. Radiology Soc. (pres. 1986), AMA, Broward County Med. Assn., Radiology Soc. N. Am. Republican. Home: 3851 N 31st Ter Hollywood FL 33021-2610 Office: Radiology Cons Ste 200 210 S Federal Hwy Hollywood FL 33020

SCHNEIDER, OWEN BENNET, psychiatrist; b. N.Y.C., May 19, 1943; m. Marion Block, June 23, 1968; 1 child, Jeremy. AB, Columbia Coll., 1964; MD, SUNY, Syracuse, 1968. Cert. Am. Bd. Psychiatry and Neurology. Clinic dir. W.J.C.S., White Plains, N.Y., 1975-78; chief of med. student tng. Albert Einstein Coll. Medicine, Bronx, N.Y., 1978-85; chief adolescent psychiatry Holliswood (N.Y.) Hosp., 1986-91. Bd. dirs. Soc. for Adolescent Psychiatry, N.Y.C., 1989-93; sect. chief of Child and Adolescent Psychiatry, Bridgeport Hosp., 1992—.

SCHNEIDER, ROBERT JAY, oncologist; b. Miami, Fla., May 31, 1949; s. Irving and Ethel (Pack) S.; m. Barbara Cunningham, June 1, 1974; children: Matthew, Kirsten. Student, Washington U., 1967-69; BA cum laude, Boston U., 1971; MD, Albert Einstein Coll. Medicine, N.Y.C., 1975. Diplomate Am. Bd. Internal Medicine, Am. Bd. Oncology; lic. physician, N.Y. Intern, jr. and sr. resident internal medicine Bronx Mcpl. Hosp., N.Y.C., 1975-78; fellow med. oncology Meml. Sloan-Kettering Cancer Ctr., N.Y.C., 1978-80, adj. attending physician/cons. dept. medicine, 1981—; asst. prof. medicine N.Y. Med. Coll., Valhalla, 1980-81; clin. instr. medicine Cornell U. Med. Coll., 1978-80; jr. clin. faculty fellow Am. Cancer Soc., 1980-81; mem. N.Y. Met. Breast Cancer Group, 1990—; cons. cancer program No. Westchester Hosp. Ctr., Mt. Kisco, N.Y., 1981-82; mem. staff Westchester County Med. Ctr., Valhalla, N.Y., No. Westchester Hosp. Ctr., Mt. Kisco, Meml. Sloan-Kettering Cancer Ctr., N.Y.C. Contbr. articles to profl. jours. Recipient Clin. Fellowship award Am. Cancer Soc., 1978-79. Mem. Am. Soc. Clin. Oncology, Westchester County Med. Soc., N.Y. State Med. Soc., Woodway Country Club. Republican. Presbyterian. Office: 439 E Main St Mount Kisco NY 10549-3404

SCHNEIDER, SHARON KAY, neuropsychologist, educator; b. St. Paul, Oct. 12, 1950; d. Lawrence Emil and Victoria (Roske) Mortenson; m. John Arthur Schneider Jr. (div. Mar. 1980); children: Jennifer Anne, John Arthur III; m. William Joseph Eiswirth, Dec. 31, 1984. BA, U. Minn., 1984; MS, Fla. Inst. Tech., Melbourne, 1986; D of Psychology, Fla. Inst. Tech., 1988. Diplomate in clin. neuropsychology Am. Bd. Profl. Psychology; lic. clin. psychologist. Dir. behavioral med. rehab. div. Mobile (Ala.) Infirmary, 1988-90; asst. prof. neurology U. South Ala., Mobile, 1990-95; pvt. practice, Mobile, 1995—. Asst. dean Leadership Mobile, 1993-94; fellow Am. Stroke Coun. Recipient Rsch. award Isabel Myers Briggs Found., 1987. Mem. APA, Internat. Neuropsychol. Soc., Nat. Neuropsychol. Soc., Nat. Acad. Neuropsychologists, Mobile Assn. Psychologists (pres. 1990), Sigma Xi, Psi Chi. Lutheran. Office: Three Office Park Ste 306 Mobile AL 36609

SCHNEIDER, STANLEY E., psychologist; b. Bangor, Maine, Dec. 6, 1939; s. Samuel and Molly (Chesner) S.; m. Cory R. Friedman, June 27, 1965; children: Steven, David, Scott. BA, U. Maine, 1962; MA, Boston U., 1965; EdD, U. Md., 1969. Lic. psychologist, Pa.; diplomate Am. Bd. Profl. Disability Cons., Am. Bd. Med. Psychotherapists; cert. sch. psychologist, N.J., Pa.; cert. addiction counselor, Pa. Dir. Occupational Evaluation and Tng. Workshop, Milford, Mass., 1965-67; dir. profl. svcs. to coord. rehab. svcs. Phila. Assn. Retarded Children, 1969-71; prog. assoc. Southeastern Region of Pa., Social Sys. Analysis Project, 1970-71; mental retardation coord. Med. Coll. Pa., 1971-72; dep. commr. mental retardation Pa. Dept. Welfare, Harrisburg, 1972-74; dir. of psychol. svcs. Harrisburg State Hosp., 1974-80, chief psychologist, 1980-84; med. advisor/expert cons. Social Security Adminstrn., Office Hearings and Appeals, Harrisburg, 1985—; provisional staff Edgewater Psychiatric Ctr., Harrisburg, 1988-94; dir. Guidance Assocs. of Pa., Camp Hill, 1973—; mem. adj. faculty Nat. Jud. Coll., U. Nev., Reno, 1988-90; mem. faculty Profl. Edn. Sys., Inc., Eau Claire, Wis., 1988—; hearing officer Pa. Right to Edn., Pa. Dept. Edn., 1975-83; cons. in field. Contbr. articles to profl. jours. HEW grantee, 1963-65, 67-69. Mem. Am. Coll. Forensic Psychology, Assn. Family and Conciliation Cts., Am. Psychol. Assn., Pa. Psychol. Assn., Acad. Family Mediators, Harrisburg Area Psychol. Assn., Family and Divorce Mediation Coun. Cen. Pa. (exec. com.), Nat. Coun. for Children's Rights. Office: Guidance Assocs 412 Erford Rd Camp Hill PA 17011-1117

SCHNEIDER, WILLIAM JAMES, plastic and reconstructive surgeon; b. Miami, Fla., Dec. 19, 1943; s. James William and Reva (Gross) S.; m. Rebecca Jo Phillips, June 10, 1967; children: James Carter, Jason Christopher, Brian Phillips. BS, Stetson U., 1966; MD, Vanderbilt U., 1970. Cert. Am. Bd. Plastic Surgery. Intern surgery U. Fla., Gainesville, 1970-71, resident surgery, 1971-72, 1970-72; resident surgery Emory U., Atlanta, 1972-75, rsident plastic surgery, 1975-77; pvt. practice Aesthetic Plastic Surgery Assocs., Knoxville, Tenn., 1977—; chief dept. surgery East Tenn. Children's Hosp., Knoxville, 1982, Ft. Sanders Regional Med. Ctr., Knoxville, 1986. Author chpts. in several books; contbr. articles to profl. jours. Pres. Westbrough Neighborhood Assn., Knoxville, 1986; coach, commr. West Knoxville Youth Baseball, 1978-85. Fellow Am. Coll. Surgeons; mem. Southeastern Soc. Plastic & Reconstructive Surgeons, Tenn. Soc. Plastic & Reconstructive Surgeons (pres. 1988-90), Am. Soc. Plastic & Reconstructive Surgeons, Am. Soc. for Aesthetic Plastic Surgery, Knoxville Surg. Soc. (pres. 1985), Knoxville Acad. Medicine. Methodist. Home: 8101 Osler Ln Knoxville TN 37909-2130 Office: Aesthetic Plastic Surgery 801 Weisgarber Rd NW Knoxville TN 37909-2780

SCHNEIDMAN, BARBARA SUE, psychiatrist; b. Mpls., Jan. 18, 1944; d. Norman Reuben and MIldred (Roberts) S.; m. William McAllister. BA, U. Minn., Mpls., 1966, MD, 1970; MPH, U. Wash., 1974. Diplomate Am. Bd. Psychiatry and Neurology. Resident ob-gyn. U. Wash., Seattle, 1972-74, dir. gynecology, 1974-78, resident in psychiatry, 1978-81, cons. primary care, 1981-88; pvt. practice Seattle, 1981-93; cons. Sexual Assault Ctr., Seattle, 1981-93, Cen. Area Mental Health, Seattle, 1990-92; assoc. v.p. Am. Bd. Med. Specialties, Evanston, Ill., 1993—; mem., chair Wash. State Bd. Med. Examiners, 1982-93; pres. Fedn. State Med. Bds., 1991-92. Mem. AMA, Am. Psychiat. Assn., Ill. State Med. Assn., Ill. Psychiat. Soc., Chgo. Med. Soc. Office: ABMS 1007 Church St Ste 404 Evanston IL 60201-5913

SCHNEIER, HARVEY ALLEN, physician, pharmaceutical researcher; b. Rochester, N.Y., Jan. 5, 1942; s. Jacob G. and Rose (Ergort) S.; m. Lynn C. Teitelbaum, Aug. 9, 1964 (div. Dec. 1981); m. Barrie Mandel; children: Matthew, Margo, Jonathan. AB, Columbia U., 1963, MD, 1967. Diplomate Am. Bd. Internal Medicine. Asst. chief gen. med. svc. Walter Reed Army Med. Ctr., Washington, 1971-72; assoc. in medicine Columbia-Presbyn. Med. Ctr., N.Y.C., 1973-75, asst. attending physician, 1975-89, assoc. attending physician, 1989—; assoc. med. dir. Forest Labs., Inc., N.Y.C., 1993—; asst. prof. clin. medicine Columbia P&S, 1975-89, assoc. clin. prof., 1989—; corp. med. cons. United Brands Co., N.Y.C., 1980-92; cons. Am. Bd. Internal Medicine, Phila., 1991—; assoc. med. dir. Forest Labs., Inc., 1993—. Served to maj. M.C. U.S. Army, 1969-73. Decorated Meritorious Svc. medal. Mem. ACP, AMA, Alpha Omega Alpha. Home: 25 Harrison St New York NY 10013-2705 Office: Forest Labs Inc 909 3rd Ave New York NY 10022-4731

SCHNELLER, EUGENE S., sociology educator; b. Cornwall, N.Y., Apr. 9, 1943; s. Michael Nicholas and Anne Ruth (Gruner) S.; m. Ellen Stauber, Mar. 24, 1968; children: Andrew Jon, Lee Stauber. BA, L.I. U., 1967; AA, SUNY, Buffalo, 1965; PhD, NYU, 1973. Rsch. asst. dept. sociology NYU, N.Y.C., 1968-70; project dir. Montefiore Hosp. and Med. Ctr., Bronx, N.Y., 1970-72; asst. prof. Med. Ctr. and sociology Duke U., Durham, N.C., 1973-75; assoc. prof., chmn. dept. Union Coll., Schenectady, 1975-79, assoc. prof., dir. Health Studies Ctr., 1979-85; prof., dir. Sch. Health Adminstrn. and Policy, Ariz. State U., Tempe, 1985-91, assoc. dean rsch. and adminstrn. Coll. Bus., 1992-94; dir. L. William Seidman Rsch. Ctr., Tempe, 1992-94, counselor to pres. for health profl. edn., 1994-96; clin. prof. cmty. and family medicine U. Ariz., 1995—; prof., dir. Sch. Health Adminstrn. and Policy Ariz. State U., 1996—; vis. rsch. scholar Columbia U., N.Y.C., 1983-84; chmn. Western Network for Edn. in Health Adminstrn., Berkeley, Calif., 1987-92; mem. Ariz. Medicaid Adv. Bd., 1990-92, Ariz. Data Adv. Bd., 1989-91, Ariz. Health Care Group Adv. Bd., 1989; mem. health rsch. coun. N.Y. State Dept. Health, 1977-85; fellow Accrediting Commn. on Edn. for Health Svcs. Adminstrn., 1983-84. Author: The Physician's Assistant, 1980; mem. editorial bd. Work and Occupations, 1975-93, Hosps. and Health Svcs. Adminstrn., 1989-92, Health Adminstrn. Press, 1991-95; contbr. articles to profl. jours., chpt. to book. Trustee Barrow Neurol. Inst., Phoenix, 1989-95; chair nat. adv. com. Nat. Adv. Com. of the Investigator Awards in Health Svcs. Rsch. Robert Wood Johnson Found., 1993-96. Mem. APHA, Am. Sociol. Assn., Assn. Univ. Health Programs Health Adminstrn. (bd. dirs. 1990-96, chmn. bd. dirs. 1994-95). Home: 11843 N 114th Way Scottsdale AZ 85259 Office: Ariz State U Sch Health Admin & Policy Tempe AZ 85287

SCHNETZLER, PATRICIA LEE, nurse educator, rehabilitation nurse; b. San Diego, Jan. 27, 1952; d. Leo R. and Leonora (Rosa) Schwabe; m. Jean G. Schnetzler, Apr. 20, 1985; children: Shawn Michael, Kailee. AA, Bellevue (Wash.) State Coll., 1976; BSN, Mesa State Coll., Grand Junction, Colo., 1988. RN, Colo.; cert. ACLS. Charge nurse Aspen Valley Hosp., Aspen, Colo., 1976-80; case mgr. Aspen Vis. Nurses, 1982-87; staff nurse Clagett Meml. Hosp., Rifle, Colo., 1987; hospice nurse, case mgr. Grand River Home Health, Glenwood Springs, Colo., 1988; staff nurse acute care unit Valley View Hosp., Glenwood Springs, 1988—, staff nurse youth recovery ctr., 1989, staff nurse day surgery unit, 1993; patient educator. Author: From Murmur to Heart Attack (Chelation) in Alternative Medicine: A Definitive Guide, 1993, Ten Little Dinosaurs, 1996. Instr. CPR and tot saver. Pres.'s scholar, 1988. Mem. Mesa State BSN Honor Soc.. Home: 2056 Odin Dr Silt CO 81652-9555

SCHNITZER, BERTRAM, hematopathologist; b. Frankfurt, Germany, June 21, 1929; arrived in Can., 1940; s. Robert Julius and Eva (Rosen) S.; m. Anna-Ercoli, June 2, 1959; children: Bret, Robert, Stefan. BS, NYU, 1952; MD, U. Basle, Switzerland, 1958. Lic. physician, Conn., Va., Mich.; diplomate in anatomic pathology and clin. pathology Am. Bd. Pathology. Intern Balt. City Hosps., 1958-59; resident pathology Georgetown U. Hosp., Washington, 1959-63; pathologist, hematopathologist Armed Forces Inst. Pathology, Washington, 1963-66; instr. pathology U. Mich., Ann Arbor, 1966-67, asst. prof., 1967-69, assoc. prof., 1969-73, prof. pathology, dir. hematopathology, 1973—; cons. VA Hosp., Ann Arbor, 1966—; mem. hematology test com. Am. bd. Pathology, 1980-85. Co-author: Monocytes, Monocytosis and Monocytic Leukemia, 1973, Refractory Anemia, 1975; contbr. articles to profl. jours., chpts. to books; cover photograph Sci., 1972. Recipient First DiGuglielmo Prize in Hematology Italian Nat. Soc., Rome, 1976, S.W. Oncology Group grantee U.S. Govt., Washington. Mem. Soc. Hematopathology (pres. 1988-90), Am. Soc. Clin. Pathologists (expert panel hematology com. 1986—, com. on continuing edn. spl. topics 1989—), Am. Soc. Hematology, Internat. Inflammation Club. Office: U Mich Dept Pathology Ann Arbor MI 48109-0602

SCHNITZLEIN, HAROLD NORMAN, anatomy educator; b. Hannibal, Mo., Aug. 29, 1927; s. Harold Daniel and Martha Anna (Wilhelm) S.; m. Harriett Elizabeth Scheidker, June 2, 1949; children: Jan Elizabeth, Paul Norman, Daniel Richard, Thomas Harry. AB, Westminster Coll., Fulton, Mo., 1950; MS, St. Louis U., 1952, PhD, 1954. USPHS fellow Dept. Anatomy St. Louis U., 1951-54; instr. anatomy U. Ala., Birmingham, 1954-57, asst. prof., 1957-62, assoc. prof., 1962-70, prof., 1970-73; chmn., prof. anatomy U. S. Fla. Coll. Medicine, Tampa, 1973-78, prof., 1978-85, prof. anatomy and radiology, 1985-93, prof. anatomy, radiology, neurology, 1985-93; clin. prof. radiology U. Diagnostic Inst., Tampa, 1993-94, prof. emeritus anatomy, 1995—. Coeditor: Correlative Comparative Anatomy Vertebrate Tel., 1982, Imaging Anatomy: Head and Spine, 2d edit., 1990. Sgt. USAAF, 1946-47. Office: U Diagnostic Inst Dept Anatomy Tampa FL 33612

SCHNOLL, SIDNEY HOWARD, neurologist, addiction treatment specialist; b. Newark, June 14, 1942; married; 2 children. MD, N.J. Coll. Medicine, 1967; PhD in Pharmacology, Thomas Jefferson U., 1976. Intern in medicine Thomas Jefferson U. Hosp., Phila., 1967-68, resident in neurology, 1968-71, NIMH fellow, 1971-73; Nat. Inst. Alcohol Abuse and Alcoholism teaching fellowship U. Pa. Sch. Medicine, Phila., 1973-76; med. dir. HELP Free Clinic, Inc., Phila., 1969-80; physician Pennhurst Ctr., Spring City, Pa., 1970-80; staff neurologist Wilmington (Del.) VA Hosp., 1971-74; asst. prof. pharmacology in psychiatry U. Pa., Phila., 1973-76; asst. attending physician Phila. Gen. Hosp., 1973-77; physician Ctrl. Med. Intake for Drug Users, Phila., 1974-79, West Phila. Mental Health Consortium, 1975-77; med. dir. Eagleville (Pa.) Hosp. and Rehab. Ctr., 1976-80; asst. prof. pharmacology, psychiatry and human behavior Thomas Jefferson U. Hosp., Phila., 1976-80; assoc. prof. psychiatry and behavioral sci. Med. Sch. Northwestern U., Chgo., 1980-86, assoc. prof. pharmacology Med. Sch., 1982-86; mem. grad. faculty Northwestern U., Evanston, Ill., 1982-86; chief chem. dependence program Inst. Psychiatry, assoc. attending staff Northwestern Meml. Hosp., Chgo., 1982-86; dir. divsn. substance abuse medicine Med. Coll. Va. Hosps., Richmond, 1986—; prof. internal medicine and psychiatry Med. Coll. Va. Va. Commonwealth U., Richmond, 1986—, rsch. prof. psychology, 1988—, affiliate prof. pharmacology and toxicology, 1993—; mem. psychiatry adv. com. dept. psychiatry Med. Coll. Va. Hosps., Va. Commonwealth U., Richmond, 1988—, univ. policy com. on substance abuse, 1987—, impaired physicians exec. com., 1987—, 4 yr. subject matter com. Sch. Medicine, 1987—; mem. adv. com. on infectious diseases Va. Commonwealth U., 1987-89; mem. rsch. com. Inst Psychiatry Northwestern Meml. Hosp., Chgo., 1983-86, clin. subcom., 1982-85, curriculum com., 1980-83; mem. med. rsch. com. Northwestern U. Med. Sch., Chgo., 1980-83; mem. adj. clin. faculty Pa. Coll. Podiatric Medicine, Phila., 1978-80; mem. adj. staff Northwestern Meml. Hosp., Chgo., 1980-82, co-chief chem. dependence program Inst. Psychiatry, 1980-82; cons. VA Lakeside Med. Ctr., Chgo., 1980-86; dir. substance abuse program Chgo. Nat. League Baseball Franchise, Chgo., 1982-86; cons. drug abuse Del. Bd. Pub. Instruction, 1970-73, U.S. Army, 1983-90; cons. drug edn. and tng. ctr. Ea. Pa. Psychiatric Inst., 1971-73; lectr. Am. Law Inst. ABA, 1971-72; participant Can./U.S. Exchange Program in Drug Abuse, 1972; cons. alcohol and narcotic subcom. Phila County Med. Soc., 1973-80; chmn. Career Tchr. Steering Com., 1975-76; sr. tech. cons. Nat. Drug Abuse Ctr. for Tng. and Resource Devel., Arlington, Va., 1975-77; physician's cons. N.Y. State Office Drug Abuse Svcs. and Divsn. Med. Svcs., 1977-80; cons. Nat. Ctr. Alcohol Edn., Arlington, 1979-81; chmn. spl. review com. Nat. Inst. Drug Abuse, Rockville, Md., 1981; chmn. ad. hoc adv. panel mgmt. chronic pain Coun. Sci. Affairs AMA, Chgo., 1982-85; cons. Calif. Soc. Treatment Alcoholism and Other Drug Dependencies, San Francisco, 1983-86; co-chmn. tech. adv. group Nat. Perinatal Resource Ctr., 1992-95. Editor Addiction Medicine Edn. Series, 1989—, Nat. Inst. Drug Abuse Series, 1975-78; mem. editorial bd. Jour. Addictive Diseases, 1989—, Substance Abuse, 1979—; mem. editorial review bd. Jour. Psychoactive Drugs, 1981—; mem. editorial adv. bd. Contemporary Drug Problems, 1971-89; contbr. over 95 articles to profl. jours. Mem. Mayor's Working Group on Drug Policy Reform, City of Balt., 1993-95; mem. Metro Richmond Coalition Against Drugs Treatment Rehab. Task Force, 1991-96; med. coord. numerous concerts and festivals, 1970-78. With USAF Med. Corps Reserve, 1968-73. Recipient 6th Ann. Gerald M. Grumet Meml. Lecture award St. Catherine's Hosp., 1987, Disting. Svc. award Ill. Alcoholism and Drug Dependence Assn., 1985, Recognition Cert. St. Joseph Hosp., 1983; grant Ctr. for Substance Abuse T93—, grants Nat. Inst. Alcoholism and Alcohol Abuse, 1987-93, Va. Dept. Health, 1987-88, 91—, Spinal Cord Rsch. Found., 1986-89. Mem. AAAS, Am. Acad. Neurology, Am. Soc. Addiction Medicine (chmn. exam. com. 1988—), Assn. Med. Educators and Rsch. in Substance Abuse (chmn. task force on fellowship 1989-92), pres. 1987-89, 77-79, v.p. 1985-87, exec. bd. 1983-91, chmn. publs. com. 1991-95, Mc Govern award 1992), N.Y. Acad. Scis., Rsch. Soc. on Alcoholism, Coll. on Problems of Drug Dependence, Sigma Xi. Home: 3003 Brook Rd Richmond VA 23227-4802 Office: Substance Abuse Medicine Box 109 MCV 1200 E Broad St Richmond VA 23298-5025

SCHOBER, CHARLES COLEMAN, III, psychiatrist, psychoanalyst; b. Shreveport, La., Nov. 30, 1924; s. Charles Coleman and Mabel Lee (Welsh) S.; B.S., La. State U., 1946, M.D., 1949; m. Martha Elizabeth Welsh, Dec. 27, 1947 (dec.); children—Irene Lee, Ann Welsh; m. 2d, Argeree Maburl Stiles, Feb. 4, 1972; 1 son, Charles Coleman. Intern, Phila. Gen. Hosp., 1949-51; resident in psychiatry Norristown (Pa.) State Hosp., 1953-57; practice medicine specializing in psychiatry and psychoanalysis, Phila., 1957-71; asso. clin. dir. Inst. Pa. Hosp., Phila., 1957-60, clin. dir., 1960-64, attending psychiatrist, 1960-68, sr. attending psychiatrist, 1968-71; mem. faculty Phila. Psychoanalytic Inst., 1966-71; clin. instr. U. Pa. Sch. Medicine, 1957-62, clin. asso., 1962-68, clin. asst. prof., 1968-71; prof., chmn. dept. psychiatry La. State U. Med. Center, Shreveport, 1971-73, chief psychiatry service, 1971-73; chief psychiatry service VA Hosp., Shreveport, 1971-73; faculty New Orleans Psychoanalytic Inst., 1972-73; mem. faculty St. Louis Psychoanalytic Inst., 1973-78; clin. prof. psychiatry St. Louis U. Med. Sch., 1973-78; clin. prof. psychiatry St. Louis U. Med. Sch., 1973-78; active med. staff psychiatry St. Louis U. Hosp., 1973-78; cons. psychiatry Jefferson Barracks VA Hosp., St. Louis, 1973-78; pvt. practice medicine, specializing in psychiatry and psychoanalysis, Shreveport, 1978-93; clin. prof. psychiatry, mem. med. staff psychiatry La. State U. Med. Center Hosp., Shreveport, 1978—; chief psychiatry service Schumpert Med. Center, 1982-84; med. and clin. dir. psychiatry Willis Knighton Med. Ctr., 1986-89; dir. adult psychiatric treatment program Charter Forest Hosp., Shreveport, 1989—, prof. psychiat. La. State U. Med. Ctr., Shreveport, 1992—; dir. in-patient svc. psychiat., psychoanalysis out patient clinic, 1992—. Served to capt. M.C., USAF, 1951-53. Diplomate Am. Bd. Psychiatry and Neurology (examiner). Fellow Am. Coll. Psychiatrists, Am. Psychiat. Assn.; mem. Am. Psychoanalytic Assn., AMA, La. Psychiat. Soc., La. Med. Soc., New Orleans Psychoanalytic Soc., Phila. Psychoanalytic Soc. Club: Rotary. Contbr. articles to profl. and med. jours. Home: 626 Wilder Pl Shreveport LA 71104-4326

SCHOBERT, CAROL MARIE, internist; b. Chgo., July 21, 1953; d. Rudolph C. and Rita J. (Galliers) S.; m. Mark Ballard, Sept. 17, 1977 (div. Jan. 1984); m. Tim L. Carlson, May 11, 1991. BA in Biology, Hanover Coll., 1974; MD, Ind. U., Indpls., 1979. Diplomate Am. Bd. Internal Medicine. Resident in internal medicine Mich. State U., East Lansing, 1979-82; mem. staff LaPorte (Ind.) Hosp., 1982—. Mem. Am. Coll. Physicians; mem. Ind. State Med. Soc., LaPorte Med. Soc. Presbyterian. Office: La Porte Clinic 900 I St La Porte IN 46350

SCHOBORG, THOMAS WILLIAM, urologist; b. Covington, Ky., Oct. 14, 1949; s. William Henry and Adelma Barbara (Timmerman) S.; m. Josephine Ann Valenti, oct. 6, 1973; children: Thomas William, Christopher J. BA in Zoology, U. Cin., 1969; MD, Emory U., 1973. Diplomate Am. Bd. Urology. Resident Univ. Hosp., Jacksonville, Fla., 1973-78, chief resident in urology, 1978-79; chief urology Ga. Bapt. Med. Ctr., Atlanta, 1981; assoc. prof. urology Med. Coll. Ga., Augusta, 1985—; bd. dirs. Nat. Kidney Found. Ga., Atlanta, 1986—. Contbr. articles to profl. jours. Coach youth baseball East Side Baseball, Marietta, Ga., 1993—. Recipient Upjohn Achievement award, 1979. Mem. AMA, Am. Urol. Assn., Atlanta Urol. Assn., Soc. Laparoscopic Surgeons, Endourol. Soc. Roman Catholic. Office: Atlanta Urol Group PC 285 Blvd Ste 215 Atlanta GA 30312

SCHOCH, EUGENE PAUL, JR., dermatologist; b. Austin, Tex., Sept. 24, 1923; s. Eugene Paul and Clara (Gerhard) S.; m. Eugenia Worley, May 12, 1944; children: Eugene Paul III, Gary Wayne. BS, U. Tex., Austin, 1943; MD, U. Tex., Galveston, 1946; MS in Dermatology, U. Minn., Mpls., 1952. Diplomate Am. Bd. Dermatology and Sypyilology. Intern Mpls. Gen. Hosp., 1946-47, resident, 1947-48; resident U. Mpls. Hosp., 1950-52; tchr. fellow U. Minn., Mpls., 1947-48, 50-52; clin. instr. to clin. assoc. prof. dermatology Southwestern U. Med. Sch., Dallas, 1953—; mem. adv. bd. Nat. Program Dermatology, 1974, FDA liaison subcom. 1973, editl. bd. 1973-75. Contbr. articles to profl. jours. Capt. AUS, 1948-50. Fellow ACP, Am. Acad. Dermatology (bd. dirs. 1983-87, exec. com. 1987-95, mem. svcs. com. 1993-95, mem. state issues task force 1993—), Am. Dermatol. Assn. (v.p. 1989-90, membership com. 1987-92), Tex. Dermatol. Soc. (hon., sec. 1971-73, pres. 1974-75), Austin Dermatol. Soc. (pres. 1983), Tex. Med. Soc., Travis County Med. Soc., Soc. Investigative Dermatology, Tex. Med. Assn. (cancer com. 1980-81). Home: 2212 Nueces St Austin TX 78705 Office: 2911 Medical Arts St Austin TX 78705

SCHOCK, CARL D., hospital administrator, mental health nurse; b. Odessa, Tex., Jan. 28, 1957; s. William R. and Martha Jeanne (Scholl) S. BSN, U. Tex., 1983, BA in Psychology, 1980; MSHP, Southwest Tex. State U., 1996. RN, Tex.; cert. psychiat.-mental health nurse. Supr. mental health workers Austin (Tex.) State Hosp., charge nurse; unit dir., dir. clin. svcs. Healthcare Rehab. Ctr., Austin; adminstr. Lakeview NeuroReh Ctr., Waterford, Wis.; v.p. ops. Lakeview Mgmt., Inc. Recipient Leadership award and Outstanding Employee award Healthcare Rehab. Ctr., 1986. Mem. ANA, Am. Coll. Healthcare Execs., Tex. Nurses Assn., Tex. Orgn. Nurse Execs., U. Tex. Ex-Students Assn.

SCHOCK, JACQUI VIRGINIA, counselor, data operations specialist; b. Atlanta, Nov. 24, 1938; d. Herman Lee and Martha Jane (Hunsecker) Turner; m. Raymond J. Torres, Oct. 20, 1990. AA in Human Svcs., Bucks County Community Coll., 1986; BA in Human Svcs., Antioch U., 1987; MS in Addictions, Chestnut Hill Coll., 1983; MA in Applied Psychology, U. Santa Monica, Calif., 1990. Counselor Bucks County Rehab. Ctr., Doylestown, Pa., 1983-88; addictions counselor Clearbrook Friendship Ctr., Phila., 1988-89; in-patient counselor Penn Found., Sellersville, Pa., 1988-89; pvt. practice Willow Grove, Pa., 1989—; outpatient therapist Westmeade Med. Ctr., 1992—; instr. self-esteem Upper Moreland Adult Eveing Sch., 1991—; founder, dir. Crossroads Counseling Svc., Willow Grove, 1990—; data entry operator SPS Techs., Jenkintown, Pa., 1963-65, data engry supr., 1965-70, data mgr., 1970-94; pvt. instr. in computer concepts, 1991—. Mem. exec. bd. Counseling Assn. Greater Phila., 1988—, pres., 1994-95; exec. bd. West Phila. Fund for Human Devel., 1989-92. Mem. NAFE, APA, Am. Counseling Assn., Counseling Assn. Greater Ga. (pres. 1994-95), Pa. Counselors Assn., Data Entry Mgrs. Assn., Nat. Coun. on Self-Esteem, Fraternal Order of Police, Phi Theta Kappa Alumni Assn. Office: Cross Roads Counseling Svc 7600 Stenton Ave 1-G Philadelphia PA 19119

SCHOCK, WILLIAM WALLACE, pediatrician; b. Huntingdon, Pa., Aug. 15, 1923; s. Clarence and Mabel (Decker) S.; m. Doris Ann Wilson, July 1, 1944; 1 child, William Wallace. Student, Juniata Coll., 1941-43; MD, Temple U., 1947. Intern Conemaugh Valley Meml. Hosp., Johnstown, Pa., 1946-48; resident Women AFB, Cheyene, Wyo., 1951-52; pvt. practive medicine Huntingdon, 1948-50; pediatrician Warren AFB Hosp., 1951-52; chief outpatient svc. USAF, Cheyenne, Wyo., 951-52; pvt. practice medicine specializing in pediatrics Huntingdon, 1952—; pediatrician J. C. Blair Meml. Hosp.; local pub. health pediatrician. Pres. Huntingdon chpt. Am. Cancer Soc., 1955-57; bd. dirs. local chpt. Am. Heart Assn., 1955-62; mem. Am. Security Coun., Rep. Nat. Com., 2d Amendment Found. With AUS, 1942-45, USAF, 1950-52. Recipient Wisdom award Leon Gutterman, Wisdom Hall of Fame, 1970. Fellow Royal Soc. Health; mem. AMA, Pa. Med. Soc., Huntingdon County Med. Soc. (past pres.), Med. Alumni Assn. Temple U., Am. Assn. Mil. Surgeons U.S., Am. Acad. Pediatrics (assoc.), Internat. Platform Assn., Phi Rho Sigma, Huntingdon Country Club, Heidelburg Country Club (Altoona, Pa.), U.S. Senatorial Club, Rotary. Republican. Presbyterian. Home and Office: RR 2 Box 69 Huntingdon PA 16652-9115

SCHOEFS, BENOIT, plant physiologist; b. Liege, Belgium, July 28, 1965; s. Joseph and Mariette (Marnette) S. BS, U. Liége, 1989, M in Plant Sci., 1990; PhD, U. Liège, 1994. Prof. French Adminstrn. of Liége City, 1987-95; researcher U. Que., Montreal, Can., 1990, U. Lille, France, 1991-93, U. Liège, Belgium, 1993—. Contbr. chpts. to books, articles to profl. jours. Recipient D. Clos prize Academie des Sciences, Inscriptions et Belles-Lettres of Toulouse, France. Mem. French Soc. Biochemistry and Molecular Biology, Inst. for Sea and Air-Water Interaction, Nat. Geog. Soc., N.Y. Acad. Scis. Office: U Liège Lab Photobiology, Dept Botany (B22), 4000 Liège Belgium

SCHOEN, REGINA NEIMAN, psychotherapist; b. Bronx, N.Y., Feb. 21, 1949; d. Louis and Bertha (Hoffman) Neiman; m. Dennis Leo Schoen, Dec. 2, 1979; 1 child, Leah F. B, Hunter Coll. N.Y.C., 1969; M, Columbia U., N.Y.C., 1971; M (social work), Hunter Coll., N.Y.C., 1977. Cert. Psychoanalytic Psychotherapist, Wash. Square Inst. N.Y.C., 1983, Family Therapist, Postgrad. Ctr. for Mental Health N.Y.C., 1986. Tchr., advisor Brandeis High Sch., N.Y.C., 1972-75; family service counselor N.Y. Assn. for New Am., N.Y.C., 1978-82; psychiatric social worker Lutheran Med. Ctr., Bklyn., 1982-84; mental health practitioner Montefiore Med. Ctr., Riker's Island, N.Y., 1984-86; moderator, spkr. Nat. Assn. Social Workers Alcoholism Inst. N.Y.C., 1989, 91; presenter YWCA, N.Y.C., 1987—; spkr. Greater N.Y. Hosp. Assn., 1983; commentator WNYC Radio Women and Rape N.Y.C., 1982; mem. faculty Postgrad. Ctr. Mental Health, 1990—; spkr. Empire Blue Cross/Blue Shield, N.Y., 1990-95, Fashion Inst. Employee Assistance Program, 1994—. Mem. Nat. Assn. Social Workers. Office: Regina Schoen CSW 488 7th Ave Apt 9A New York NY 10018-6808

SCHOEN, ROY MILES, physician; b. Staten Island, N.Y., Sept. 24, 1940; s. Herbert Edvane and Mary Ann (Levenstein) S. AB, Dartmouth Coll., 1962; DDS, NYU, 1966; MD, Hadassan Med. Sch., Jerusalem, 1971. Diplomate Am. Bd. Psychiatry and Neurology, Am. Bd. Ob-Gyn. Intern Booth Meml. Med. Ctr., Flushing, N.Y., 1969-71; resident in psychiatry Payne Whitney clinic N.Y. Hosp., N.Y.C., 1971-73; resident in child psychiatry N.Y. Psychiatric Inst., N.Y.C., 1973-75; dir. child, adolescent psychiatry North Shore Hosp., Manhasset, N.Y., 1975-79; resident in ob-gyn. Lenox Hill Hosp., N.Y.C., 1979-82; physician Orlando & Schoen, MD, PC, N.Y.C., 1982—. Maj. Army Res. N.G., 1971-81. Fellow Am. Coll. Ob-Gyn., N.Y. Gynecologic Soc. Office: Orlando and Schoen MD PC 17 E 82nd St New York NY 10028-0346

SCHOENDORF, JUDSON RAYMOND, allergist; b. New Orleans, Jan. 13, 1942; s. John Adam and Thelma Elizabeth (Verges) S. BA, Tulane U., 1962; MD, La. State U., 1966; MBA, Pepperdine U., 1992. Lic. physician, La., Calif.; cert. Am. Bd. Med. Mgmt. Intern Charity Hosp. of La., New Orleans, 1966-67; resident in pediatrics L.A. County/U. So. Calif. Med. Ctr., 1969-70; fellow UCLA/Harbor Gen. Hosp., 1970-72; allergist Russell T. Spears, M.D., Long Beach, 1972-76, The Harriman Jones Med. Group, Long Beach, 1976—; chief exec. officer The Harriman Jones Med. Group, 1989-91; pres., CEO, The Harriman Jones Med. Found., 1992-94; staff Kaiser Hosp, Bellflower, 1970-72, Children's Hosp., Long Beach, 1972—, Bauer/St. Mary's Hosp., Long Beach, 1972—, UCLA Hosp., 1972—, Community Hosp., Long Beach, 1977—; faculty UCLA, 1972—, Harbor Gen. Hosp., 1972—, others. Contbr. articles to profl. jours. Bd. dirs. Long Beach Children's Clinic, 1976-81, pres., 1978-81; bd. dirs. Long Beach Symphony Orch., 1985-89; bd. dirs. Am. Lung Assn. Calif., 1985—, exec. com., 1988—; adv. coun. phys. edn. dept. Calif. State U., Long Beach, 1985—; mem. Civil Svc. Commn., City of Long Beach, 1981-89, pres., 1982-83, 85-86; bd. dirs. Long Beach Civic Light Opera, 1986-88; mem. Redevel. Agy., City of Long Beach, 1989—; chair, RDA, 1993—; mem. cultural steering com. Pub. Corp. Arts, Long Beach; bd dirs. Adv. Com. Pub. Art, 1992—; mem. Mayor's Econ. Coun., 1994—, Joint Powers Authority Spring St. Corridor-Long Beach/Singal Hill, 1994—. Lt. USN, 1967-69, capt. USNR, 1985—. Decorated Navy Commendation medal, also others; recipient Katherine White Humanitarian award Long Beach Kiwanis Club, 1995. Mem. Calif. Med. Assn., L.A. County Med. Assn., Long Beach Med. Assn., Acad. Allergy, L.A. Soc. Allergy and Immunology, Am. Acad. Physician Execs. Office: Harriman Jones Med Group 2600 Redondo Ave Long Beach CA 90806-2325

SCHOENFELD, ELINOR RANDI, epidemiologist; b. Manhattan, N.Y., Apr. 9, 1956; d. Samuel and Helen (Goldstein) S. BS, SUNY, Stony Brook, 1977; MS, SUNY, Buffalo, 1980, PhD, 1988. Clin. assoc. Columbia U. Sch. Pub. Health, N.Y.C., 1980-82; data mgr. community oncology program Hackensack (N.J.) Med. Ctr., 1982-83; rsch affiliate Roswell Park Cancer Inst., Buffalo, 1984-85, cancer rsch. scientist, 1985-88; epidemiology cons. Joel Bernstein, MD Otolaryngology, Buffalo, 1984-89; rsch. scientist SUNY Sch. Medicine, Stony Brook, 1988-93, rsch. instr., 1989-90, asst. prof., 1990—, dir. ops., 1992—, sr. rsch. scientist, 1993—; epidemiology cons. Univ. Hosp., Stony Brook, 1990-92; dir. Suffolk County Diabetes Study, 1992—; mem. admissions com. SUNY, Buffalo, 1985-87; presenter, invited speaker in field. Author: Applications of Diffusion Theory to Cancer Care in the United States: 1972-81, 1990, (with others) On Diabetes, Breast Cancer, Cataracts, Otitis Media, 1988-95; contbr. articles to profl. jours. Bd. dirs. Essential Needs for Srs. Efforts, Inc., N.Y.C., 1995—. Predoctoral fellow NYU, 1977-78, Epidemiology Program fellow U. Minn., 1980, fellow in cancer epidemiology Columbia U., 1980-82; Nat. Cancer Inst. grantee NIH, 1987-88, 95—; Nat. Eye Inst. grantee, NIH, 1992—. Mem. APHA, Am. Assn. Diabetes Edn., Am. Diabetes Assn., Soc. Clin. Trials, Soc. Behavioral Medicine, Assn. for Rsch. in Vision & Ophthalmology, N.Y. Acad. Sci., N.Y. State Pub. Health Assn., Soc. for Epidemiologic Rsch., Assn. for Health Svcs. Rsch. Jewish. Office: SUNY Stony Brook Sch Med Dept Prev Med Stony Brook NY 11794

SCHOENFELD, LAWRENCE STEVEN, psychology educator; b. N.Y.C., Dec. 22, 1941; s. Irving and Muriel (Levy) S.; m. Heide Ellen Buchbinder, Aug. 19, 1967; children—Jennifer Dawn, Jessica Leah. BA, Ohio Wesleyan U., 1963; MA, U. Fla., 1965, PhD, 1967. Diplomate Am. Bd. Profl. Psychology. Dir. resident tng. U. Tex. Health Sci. Ctr., San Antonio, 1976-81, chmn.-IRB, 1977-78, prof. anesthesiology, 1980—, prof. psychiatry, 1979—; adj. prof. Trinity U., San Antonio, 1979—; cons. psychology Audie Murphy VA Hosp., San Antonio, 1975—; ethics chmn. Tex. Psychol. Assn., Austin, 1980-86; cons. City of San Antonio, 1973-89, S.W. Rsch. Inst., San Antonio, 1978-90; vice chmn. Tex. State Bd. Examiners of Psychologists, 1988-94. Contbr. articles to profl. jours. Trustee Planned Parenthood, San Antonio, 1979-85, Julie Jordan Free Clinic, San Antonio, 1978-80; bd dirs. Alamo chpt. Big Bros./Big Sisters, 1983-92; exec. dir., founder Crisis Ctr. for San Antonio, 1972-79; bd. dirs. Hidden Forest, 1984-87. Mem. Am. Psychol. Assn., Tex. Psychol. Assn. Home: 16002 Wolf Creek St San Antonio TX 78232-2749 Office: U Tex Health Sci Ctr Dept Psychiatry 7703 Floyd Curl Dr San Antonio TX 78284-6200

SCHOENFELD, MYRON ROYAL, cardiologist; b. N.Y.C., Nov. 10, 1928; s. George M. and Rhoda (Kahn) S.; m. Gloria T. Edis; children: Bradley Jon, Glenn Murray, Dawn Rhoda, Melody Lynn. BA, NYU, 1948; MA, Columbia U., 1949; MD, Chgo. Med. Sch., 1953; postgrad., U. Ill., Chgo., 1950-53. Intern King's County Hosp., Bklyn., 1953-54; asst. resident in internal medicine Bronx VA Hosp., 1954-55, resident in internal medicine, 1958-59; rsch. fellow in cardiology Mt. Sinai Hosp., N.Y.C., 1959-60; founder, pres. Life-Line Spl. Med. Svcs., Scarsdale, 1978-92, Royal Artcrafts, Scarsdale, 1970-92. Editor-in-chief, founder Jour. Cardiovascular Tech., Scarsdale, 1982-92; author: Strictly Confidential How Doctors Make Decisions, 1990; inventor infusion monitor, 1959; contbr. articles to profl. jours. Pres. Deer Hill Civic Assn., Scarsdale, 1970-88; mem. Coun. on Handicapped, Village of Scarsdale, 1990-92; founding dir. Scarsdale Japan Festival, 1992-93; candidate for the Dem. Party nomination N.Y.C. for pres. of the U.S., 1996. Named Disting. Alumnus Chgo. Med. Sch., 1974; recipient First prize, Connie Bellin Meml. Essay Prize, N.Y.C., 1982. Fellow ACP, Am. Coll. Cardiology, Am. Coll. Chest Physicians; mem. AMA, Am. Soc. Clin. Rsch., Poly Math. Soc. (pres., founder), Scarsdale C. of C. (bd. dirs. 1985-89, v.p. 1989—, pres. 1991), Town Club, Phi Beta Kappa (pres. Scarsdale/Westchester 1992—). Democrat. Jewish. Office: 2 Overhill Rd Scarsdale NY 10583-5316

SCHOENFELD, ROBERT LOUIS, biomedical engineer; b. N.Y.C., Apr. 1, 1920; s. Bernard and Mae (Kizelstein) S.; m. Helene Martens, Jan. 22, 1944 (div. 1965); children: David, Joseph, Paul; m. Florence Moskowitz, Dec. 11, 1965 (dec. 1989); children: Nedda, Bethany; m. Shulamith Stechel, July 8, 1990. BA, Washington Square Coll., 1942; BSEE, Columbia U., 1944; MEE, Poly. Inst. Bklyn., 1949, DEE, 1956. Rsch. assoc. Columbia U. Med. Sch., N.Y.C., 1947-51; rsch. fellow Sloan Kettering Cancer Rsch. Inst., N.Y.C., 1951-56; assoc. prof. Poly. Inst. Bklyn., 1947-54; assoc. prof. Rockefeller U., N.Y.C., 1957-90, prof. emeritus, 1990—. Contbr. articles to profl. jours. Lt. Signal Corps, U.S. Army, 1944-46, ETO. Fellow IEEE (mem. editl. bd. 1965-75, Centennial medal 1985), Am. Inst. for Med. and Biol. Engring. Democrat. Jewish. Office: Rockefeller U 1230 York Ave New York NY 10021-6307

SCHOENHARD, WILLIAM CHARLES, JR., health care executive; b. Kansas City, Mo., Sept. 26, 1949; s. William Charles S. and Joyce Evans (Thornsberry) Bell; m. Kathleen Ann Klosterman, June 3, 1972; children: Sarah Elizabeth, Thomas William. BS in Pub. Adminstrn., U. Mo., 1971; M of Health Adminstrn. with honors, Washington U., St. Louis, 1975. V.p., dir. gen. svcs. Deaconess Hosp., St. Louis, 1975-78; assoc. exec. dir. St. Mary's Health Ctr., St. Louis, 1978-81; exec. dir. Arcadia Valley Hosp., Pilot Knob, Mo., 1981-82, St. Joseph Health Ctr., St. Charles, Mo., 1982-86; exec. v.p., COO SSM Health Care Sys., St. Louis, 1986—; bd. dirs. Mark Twain Bank, 1986—. Contbr. articles to profl. jours. Pres. Shaw Neighborhood Improvement Assn., St. Louis, 1979-80; mem. adv. bd. St. Louis chpt. Lifeseekers, 1985-94; mem. bd. mgrs. Kirkwood-Webster (Mo.) YMCA, 1990—, sec., 1996—; mem. bd. mgrs. Nat. Affairs Round Table Sen. Christopher Bond, St. Louis, 1990; mem. nat. adv. coun. Healthcare Forum, 1992—; mem. healthcare adv. bd. Sanford Brown Colls. 1992-94; mem. leadership excellence com. Cath. Health Assn. U.S., 1993—; mem. steering com. Greater St. Louis Healthcare Alliance, 1994-95; bd. dirs. St. Andrews Mgmt. Svcs., Inc., 1994—. With USN, 1971-72, Vietnam. Fellow Am. Coll. Health Care Execs.; mem. Mid-Am. Transplant Assn. (bd. dirs. 1995—), Am. Legion, Navy League U.S., Univ. Club St. Louis, Phi Eta Sigma, Pi Omicron Sigma, Delta Upsilon, Delta Sigma Pi. Roman Catholic. Home: 420 Fairwood Ln Saint Louis MO 63122-4429 Office: SSM Health Care System 477 N Lindbergh Blvd Saint Louis MO 63141-7813

SCHOENHEIT, EDWARD WILLIAM, JR., internist, hospital administrator, lawyer; b. Asheville, N.C., Mar. 10, 1926; s. Edward William and Elizabeth (Kimberly) S.; m. Carol Straehley, Sept. 23, 1950 (div. 1966): children: John William, Thomas Edward, Susan, Ruth; m. Marian Ruth Zintek, Dec. 30, 1976. MD, Harvard U., 1950; JD, Syracuse U., 1984. Diplomate Am. Bd. Internal Medicine. Intern Pa. Hosp., Phila., 1950-52; resident internal medicine Columbia div. Bellevue Hosp., N.Y.C., 1955; resident in chest svc. Columbia div. Bellevue Hosp., 1956; resident in cardiology Columbia Presbyn. Hosp., N.Y.C., 1957; pvt. practice Syracuse, N.Y., 1957-81; med. dir. Oswego (N.Y.) Hosp., 1987-89, Lee Meml. Hosp., Fulton, N.Y., 1987-89; ret., 1989; past pres. med. staff Community Hosp., Syracuse; mem. N.Y. State Bd. Profl. Med. Conduct, 1986—. Lt. M.C., USNR, 1592-54. Fellow ACP, Am. Coll. Legal Medicine; mem. Am. Coll. Physician Execs., Oswego County Med. Soc. Republican. Episcopalian. Home and Office: 74 W 5th St Oswego NY 13126-1528

SCHOEPPE, WILHELM EBERHARD, physician, educator; b. Regensburg, Bavaria, Germany, Feb. 22, 1930; s. Wilhelm and Elisabeth (Doerfler) S.; m. Brigitte Baumgarten, July 25, 1958; children: Thomas, Hans-Jörg. Ärztliche Staatsprüfung, U. Freiburg, Germany, 1955; Priv. Doz., U. Frankfurt a. M., 1966, Prof., 1972. Jr. asst. internal medicine U. Hosp. Freiburg U., Germany, 1956-58, asst. internal medicine U. Hosp., 1959-60; postdoct. fellow Max Planck Ges., Göttingen, Germany, 1958-59; counseling physician dept. internal medicine U. Hosp., Frankfurt a. M., Germany, 1961-66, head renal divsn. dept. internal medicine, 1967-72, full prof. chief neperology, internal medicine, 1972-95, full prof., chief dept. internal medicine, 1981-95; Founder, v.p. Kuratorium Dialyse und Nierentransplantation, 1969—. Pres. German Found. Kidney Rsch., 1978—. Recipient Medaille Louis Pasteur U. Strassbourg, France, 1991. Mem. German Soc. Nephrology, Gesellschaft Nephrology (pres. 1985-86). Office: KFH Kuratorium Dialyse und Nierentransplantation, Emil von Behring Passage, D 63263 Isenburg Germany

SCHOETZ, DAVID JOHN, JR., colon and rectal surgeon; b. Milw., Oct. 29, 1948; s. David John and Beverly (Rogers) S.; m. Ruthanne Brennan, Mar. 25, 1972; children: Elizabeth Anne, David John III. BA, Coll. of Holy Cross, 1970; MD, Med. Coll. Wis., Milw., 1974. Resident in surgery Boston U. Med. Ctr., 1974-81; resident in colon/rectal surgery Lahey Clinic Med. Ctr., Burlington, Mass., 1981-82, staff colon-rectal surgeon, 1982—, chmn. dept. colon-rectal surgery, 1987—. Fellow ACS, Am. Soc. Colon and Rectal Surgeons; mem. Am. Bd. Colon-Rectal Surgery (pres. 1994-95). Office: Lahey Clinic Med Ctr 41 Mall Rd Burlington MA 01803-4136

SCHOFIELD, JANET WARD, psychologist. BA magna cum laude, Radcliffe Coll., 1968; MA, Harvard U., 1969, PhD, 1972. Instr. psychology and sociology Spelman Coll., Atlanta, 1969-70; rsch. psychologist Office Econ. Opportunity, Washington, 1972-73, Nat. Inst. Edn., Washington, 1973-74; asst. prof. U. Pitts., 1974-80, assoc. prof., 1980-86, sr. scientist Learning Rsch. and Devel. Ctr., 1981—, prof. social-personality prog., 1986—; speaker, cons. in field. Reviewer major jours. in field; mem. editl. bd. Sociology of Edn., 1986-89, Social Psychology Quar., 1982-85, Interactive Learning Environments, 1990-93, Peace and Conflict, 1995—, others; author:

Black and White in School: Trust Tension or Tolerance?, 1982, rev. edit., 1989, Computers in the Classroom, 1995; co-author: Strategies for Effective Desegregation: Lessons from Research, 1983. Recipient grants and fellowships in field including Warren Fund Fellowship, Harvard U., 1968-69, Buhl Faculty Fellowship,, U. Pitts., 1978-79. Fellow Am. Psychol. Soc., Am. Psychol. Assn.; mem. Am. Sociol. Assn., Am. Ednl. Rsch. Assn., Soc. for Exptl. Social Psychology, Phi Beta Kappa, others. Home: 319 Nottingham Cir Pittsburgh PA 15215-1535 Office: Univ Pitts Learning Rsch Devel Ctr Pittsburgh PA 15260

SCHOLTEN, PAUL, obstetrician, gynecologist, educator; b. San Francisco, Oct. 14, 1921; s. Henry Francis and Gladys (Lamborn) S.; m. Marion Lucy O'Neil, Feb. 7, 1948; children: Catherine Mary (dec.), Anne Marie, Pauline Marie, Joseph, Stephen, John. AB, San Francisco State U., 1943; postgrad., Stanford U., 1946-47; MD, U. Calif., San Francisco, 1951. Diplomate Am. Bd. Ob-Gyn. Intern San Francisco Gen. Hosp., 1951-52; resident in ob-gyn U. Calif., San Francisco, 1952-55; pvt. practice specializing in ob-gyn San Francisco, 1955-80; coll. physician Student Health Svc. San Francisco State U., 1956-80, dir. women's svcs. Student Health Svc., 1980-91; pvt. practice San Francisco, 1991—; part-time ship's surgeon Delta Lines, 1980-84; assoc. clin. prof. Med. Sch., U. Calif., San Francisco, 1955—, assoc. clin. prof. Nursing Sch., 1987—; preceptor Med. Sch., Stanford U., 1989-91; lectr. on health and wine at numerous univs., profl. groups. Contbr. articles to profl. publs., chpts. to books. Cons. U.S. Wine Inst.; sci. advisor Calif. State Adv. Bd. on Alcohol-Related Problems, 1980-86; bd. dirs. A.W.A.R.E., Century Coun. Sgt. U.S. Army, 1944-46. Mem. AMA, Calif. Med. Assn., Pan Am. Med. Assn., San Francisco Med. Soc. (editor 1971—, historian, past pres.), San Francisco Gynecol. Soc., Am. Coll. Ob-Gyn., Soc. Med. Friends of Wine (bd. dirs. 1955—, past pres.), San Francisco Wine and Food Soc. (bd. dirs. 1960—, past pres.), Internat. Wine and Food Soc. (gov. 1989—, Bronze medal 1989), San Francisco State U. Alumni Assn. (bd. dirs. 1962—), German Wine Soc., Sierra Club. Republican. Roman Catholic. Home and Office: 121 Granville Way San Francisco CA 94127-1133

SCHOLTZ, EVELYN, medical technologist, educator; b. Paterson, N.J., Aug. 17, 1943; d. Frank and Stephanie (Malinkiewicz) S.; A.S. in Chem. Tech., Fairleigh Dickinson U., 1963, B.S. in Med. Tech., 1965; M.A. in Biology, St. Joseph Coll., 1970; M.S. in Health Care Mgmt., Hartford Grad. Center, 1983; M.B.A., Rensselaer Poly. Inst., 1984. Med. technologist bacteriology lab. Hartford (Conn.) Hosp., 1965-67, supr. serology-microscopy lab., 1967-68; edn. coordinator med. lab. asst. program, 1968-71, program dir. lab. edn. Sch. Allied Health, 1979-86; mgr. microbiology lab. Hartford Hosp., 1986—; adj. faculty mem. U. Conn., Storrs, West Conn. State Coll., Danbury, U. Bridgeport (Conn.), St. Joseph Coll., West Hartford, Conn. Bd. dirs. Cromwell Hills Assn., 1974-77. T. Stewart Hamilton fellow, 1976. Mem. Conn. Soc. Clin. Lab. Sci., Am. Soc. Clin. Lab. Sci., AAUW. Contbr. articles to profl. publs. Home: 29 Margo Ct Cromwell CT 06416-1729 Office: 80 Seymour St Hartford CT 06102-5037

SCHOMMER, JON CLIFFORD, pharmaceutical administration educator; b. Fond du Lac, Wis., June 8, 1962; s. Elwyn G. and Janet E. (Gunderson) S.; m. Lisa R. Bath, Aug. 20, 1988. BS in Pharmacy, U. Wis., 1985, MS in Pharmacy, 1989, PhD in Pharmacy, 1992. Pharmacist Kremer Pharmacy, Fond du Lac, 1985-87; cons. Konsult Data Systems, Oshkosh, Wis., 1986-88; fellow U. Wis., Madison, 1987-88, 89-92, teaching asst., 1988-89; asst. prof. Ohio State U., Columbus, 1993—, The Ohio State U., Columbus, 1993—; adv. com. Pharmacy Examining Bd., Madison, 1990—. Ad hoc mem. Wis. Pharmacy Internship Bd., Madison, 1986; coord. Inter Varsity Christian Fellowship Married Couples Group, Madison, 1990—. Recipient Eli Lilly Co. Achievement award, Madison, 1985; named fellow Wis. Alumni Rsch. Found., 1987-88, Am. Found. Pharm. Edn., 1989—, Robert W. Hammel fellow, 1992, Springboard to Teaching fellow Am. Found. Pharm. Edn., 1993-94. Fellow Am. Coll. Apothecaries (assoc.); mem. Am. Pharm. Assn., Am. Assn. Colls. Pharmacy, Am. Assn. Pharm. Scientists, Am. Soc. Con. Pharmacists, Christian Pharmacists Felowship Internat., Rho Chi (v.p. Wis. chpt. 1989-90). Home: 3220 Needham Dr Dublin OH 43017-1767 Office: Ohio State U Coll Pharmacy 500 W 12th Ave Columbus OH 43210-1214

SCHONBERGER, RACHEL ANN POMERANTZ, physician, educator; b. Phila., Nov. 20, 1941; d. Jacob Isaac and Mollie Esther (Orloff) Pomerantz; m. Lawrence Bert Schonberger, May 30, 1968; children: David, Robert. BA, Antioch Coll., 1964; MD, Temple U., 1968; postgrad., U. Besancon, France, 1960-61. Intern Cleve. Clinic, 1968-69; resident Michael Reese Hosp., Chgo., 1969, Ga. Bapt. Hosp., Atlanta, 1971-73; fellow dept. medicine Johns Hopkins U., Balt., 1974-76; dir. satellite clinics, dir. div. primary care Grady Hosp., Emory U., Atlanta, 1990-93, asst. prof. dept. community and preventive medicine, 1976—; interim chair dept cmty. and preventive medicine Emory U. Med. Sch., Atlanta, 1993-94; chief svc. family and preventive medicine Grady Hosp. Emory U., Atlanta, 1995—; asst. prof. dept. family and preventive medicine Emory U., Atlanta, 1994—. Area coord. Northlake Civic Assn., Atlanta, 1980—; pres., v.p. Henderson Hill PTA, Atlanta, 1976-88; sec. Lakeside PTA, Atlanta, 1985-92, Southeastern Region Hadassah, 1988-90, area v.p. 1990-91, orgn. v.p. 1993—. Mem. Am. Coll. Physicians, Am. Women's Med. Assn. (br. 29 pres. 1994—), Physicians for Social Responsibility. Jewish. Office: Emory U Sch Medicine 69 Butler St SE Atlanta GA 30303-3033

SCHÖNBERGER, WINFRIED JOSEF, pediatrics educator; b. Wiesbaden, Hessen, Germany, Apr. 2, 1940; s. Josef Adam and Thea (Brechmann) S.; m. Gisela Schönig, Apr. 8, 1971. MD, Gutenberg U., Mainz, Germany, 1966. Asst. prof. U. Mainz, 1972-75, pvt. docent, 1975-77, prof. pediatrics, 1977—. Author 2 books, 100 papers. Recipient Ann. award German Soc. Dentistry, 1977, Prize, Boehringer Preis, Ingelheim, 1980. Mem. German Soc. Pediatrics, South German Soc. Pediatrics, German Soc. Endocrinology. Home: Pfahlerstr 43, D-65193 Wiesbaden-Sonnenberg Hessen, Germany Office: Johannes Gutenberg U, Langenbeckstr 1, D-55131 Mainz Germany

SCHONFELD, IRVIN SAM, psychologist, educator; b. N.Y.C.; s. George and Ruth (Berson) S.; children: Emily Aviva, Daniel Reuben; m. July 12, 1981. BS, Bklyn. Coll., 1969; MA, New Sch. for Social Rsch., 1974; PhD, CUNY, 1980; MPH, Columbia U., 1987. Cert. psychologist, N.Y. Math. tchr. N.Y.C. Bd. Edn., 1969-75; rsch. assoc. Columbia U., N.Y.C., 1981-85; prof. CUNY, 1985—. Contbr. articles on stress and psychopathology rsch., child, adolescent rsch. to profl. jours. Office: EDFN City Coll NY Dept Rsch New York NY 10031

SCHONHOLTZ, GEORGE JEROME, orthopaedic surgeon; b. Bklyn., June 9, 1930; s. Morris and Rose (Stofsky) S.; m. Joan S. Hirsch, Aug. 21, 1951; children: Margot, Steven, Barbara. BA, NYU, 1950; MD, N.Y. State U., 1954. Diplomate Am. Bd. Orthopaedic Surgery, Nat. Bd. Med. Examination; lic. physician, Md. Intern, resident gen. surgery and orthopaedic surgery Walter Reed Gen. Hosp., Washington, 1954-59; asst. chief orthopaedic surgery Martin Army Hosp., Ft. Benning, Ga., 1960-63, asst. dir., dir. med. edn., 1962, 63; instr. human biology Am. U. Undergrad. Sch., Ft. Benning, 1962, 63; asst. clin. prof. orthopaedic surgery Howard U., Washington, 1964-66, Georgetown U., Washington, 1966-67, George Washington U., Washington, 1968—; pvt. practice Silver Spring, Md., 1964-95; orthopaedic cons. VA Hosp., Martinsburg, W.Va., 1964-68; civilian cons. orthopaedic surgery Walter Reed Army Hosp., Washington, 1968—; chief orthopaedic surgery Holy Cross Hosp., Silver Spring, 1971-74, chmn. infection control com., 1975-76; v.p. med. and dental staff Washington Adventist Hosp., 1988-89, mem. fin. com., 1988-94; rep. Coun. of Musculoskeletal Soc., 1987-90. Author: Arthroscopy of the Shoulder, Elbow and Ankle, 1986, An Atlas of Arthroscopic Surgery of the Knee, 1988. Maj. U.S. Army, 1960-64. Mem. AMA, ACS, Am. Acad. Orthop. Surgery (mem. resolutions com. 1989-95), Am. Coll. Physician Educators, Soc. Mil. Orthop. Surgeons, Internat. Arthroscopy Assn., Ea. Orthop. Assn. (bd. incorporators, bd. dirs. 1970-79), Arthroscopy Assn. N.Am. (pres. 1988-89, bd. dirs. 1983-90), Montgomery County Med. Soc., Med. and Chirurgical Faculty Md., Washington Orthop. Soc., Internat. Soc. Knee, Am. Coll. Physician Execs. Republican.

SCHOOLAR, JOSEPH CLAYTON, psychiatrist, pharmacologist, educator; b. Marks, Miss., Feb. 28, 1928; s. Adrian Taylor and Leah (Covington) S.; m. Betty Jane Peck, Nov. 2, 1960; children—Jonathan Covington, Cynthia Jane, Geoffrey Michael, Catherine Elizabeth, Adrian Carson. A.B., U. Tenn., Memphis, 1950, M.S., 1952; Ph.D., U. Chgo., 1957, M.D., 1960. Diplomate Am. Bd. Psychiatry and Neurology. Chief drug abuse research TRIMS, Houston, 1966-72; assoc. prof. U. Tex. Grad. Sch. Biomed. Scis., Houston, 1968—; prof. psychiatry Baylor Coll. Medicine, Houston, 1975—, prof. pharmacology, 1974—, chief div. psychopharmacology, 1973—; dir. Tex. Research Inst. Mental Scis., Houston, 1972-85; mem. Nat. Bd. Med. Examiners' Task Force on Drug Abuse and Alcoholism, 1982—; mem. Drug Abuse Adv. Com., FDA, Washington, 1983-85, chmn., 1984; chmn. profl. needs planning task force Nat. Inst. Drug Abuse, Washington, 1977—. Editor: Current Issues in Adolescent Psychiatry, 1973, Research and the Psychiatric Patient, 1975, The Kinetics of Psychiatric Drugs, 1979, Serotonin in Biological Psychiatry - Advanced in Biochemical Psychopharmacology, 1982. Cons. Parents' League Houston, 1972-74; mem. coordinating com. Citizens Mental Health Service, Houston, 1976; mem. acad. com. for study of violence Houston Police Dept., 1979; bd. dirs. Can-Do-It, Houston, 1982—. Served to 1st lt. U.S. Army, 1945-47. Recipient Eugen Kahn award Baylor Coll. Medicine, Houston, 1964. Fellow Am. Psychiat. Assn., Am. Coll. Psychiatrists; mem. Am. Coll. Neuropsychopharmacology, Collegium Internationale NeuroPsychopharmacologicum, Am. Soc. Pharmacology and Exptl. Therapeutics. Episcopalian. Home: 2222 Sunset Blvd Houston TX 77005-1530 Office: Baylor Coll Medicine One Baylor Pla Houston TX 77030*

SCHOOLEY, ROBERT T., medical educator; b. Denver, Nov. 10, 1949; s. Robert Enoch and Lelia Francis (Barnhill) S.; m. Pamela Owen Cook, Mar. 29, 1972; children: Kimberly Dana, Elizabeth Kendall. BS, Washington & Lee U., 1970; MD, Johns Hopkins U., 1974. Diplomate Am. Bd. Internal Medicine. Intern Johns Hopkins Hosp., Balt., 1974-75, resident, 1975-76; clin. assoc. lab. clin. investigation Nat. Inst. Allergy & Infectious Disease, NIH, Bethesda, Md., 1976-77, chief clin. assoc. lab. clin. investigation, 1977-78, men. officer lab. clin. investigation, 1978-79; from instr. to assoc. prof. medicine Harvard Med. Sch., Boston, 1979-90; prof. medicine U. Colo., Denver, 1990—; cons. internal medicine Mass. Eye and Ear Infirmary, Boston, 1980-85, cons. infectious diseases Harvard U. Health Svcs., Cambridge, Mass., 1982-90. mem. editorial bd. Anrimicrobial Agts. and Chemotherapy, 1987—, Biotherapy, 1987—, Jour. Acquired Immune Deficiency Syndromes, 1988—, Clin. and Diagnostic Lab. Immunology, 1992; contbr. articles to profl. jours. Clin. and rsch. fellow Infectious Disease Unit, Mass. Gen. Hosp., Boston, 1979-81; rsch. fellow Medicine Harvard Med. Sch., 1979-81. Fellow Infectious Disease Soc. Am.; mem. AAAS, Am. Assn. Immunologists, Am. Soc. Clin. Investigation, Assn. Am. Physicians, Omicron Delta Kappa. Office: U Colo Health Sci Ctr 4200 E 9th Ave B-168 Denver CO 80262

SCHOOLMAN, ARNOLD, neurological surgeon; b. Worcester, Mass., Oct. 31, 1927; s. Samuel and Sarah (Koffman) Schulman; m. Gloria June Feder, Nov. 10, 1963; children: Hugh Sinclair, (Jill) Annette. Student, U. Mass., 1945-46; BA, Emory U., 1950; PhD, Yale U., 1954, MD, 1957. Diplomate Am Bd Neurol. Surgery, Nat. Bd. Med. Examiners. Intern U. Calif. Hosp., San Francisco, 1957-58; resident in neurol. surgery Columbia-Presbyn. Med. Ctr., Neurol. Inst. N.Y., N.Y.C., 1958-62; instr. neurol. surgery U. Kans. Sch. Medicine, Kansas City, 1962, asst. prof. surgery, 1964; assoc. prof. U. Mo. Sch. Medicine, Kansas City, 1976; chief sect. neurosurgery Research Med. Ctr., Kansas City, 1982; dir. Midwest Neurol. Inst., 1982-83. Patentee in field. Served with USN, 1946-48. Fellow ACS (mem. Mo. chpt.); mem. AMA, Mo. State Med. Assn., Kansas City Med. Soc., Kansas City Neurosurg. Soc. (pres. 1984-85), Kansas City Neurol. Soc., Rocky Mountain Neurosurg. Soc., Am. Assn. Neurol. Surgeons, AAAS, Mo. Neurol. Soc., Internat. Coll. Surgeons, Congress Neurol. Surgeons, Brit. Royal Soc. Medicine, Phi Beta Kappa, Sigma Xi. Home: 8705 Catalina St Shawnee Mission KS 66207-2351 Office: 1000 E 50th St Ste 310 Kansas City MO 64110-2215

SCHOON, DORIS VIVIEN, ophthalmologist; b. Luverne, Minn., Dec. 31, 1928; d. Jacob and Esther Viola (Hansen) S. B.A., U. Minn., 1950, M.D., 1954, MS in Elec. Engring. Calif. State U., 1991. Intern, Kings County Hosp., Bklyn., 1954-55; physician Embudo Presbyterian Hosp. (N. Mex.), 1955-57; resident in clin. pathology U. Colo. Med. Ctr., Denver, 1957-58; gen. practice medicine, Anaheim, Calif., 1958-61; resident in ophthalmology Los Angeles Eye and Ear Hosp. at Hollywood Presbyn. Hosp., 1961-64; practice medicine specializing in ophthalmology, Anaheim, 1965-75; dir. Electrophysiology Lab. of Ophthalmology Dept. U. Calif., Irvine, 1978—. Research in field of using fast random stimuli to obtain electroretinograms and visually evoked potentials. Diplomat Am. Bd. Ophthalmology. Fellow Am. Acad. Ophthalmology and Otolaryngology; mem. IEEE, Am. Women's Med. Assn., Internat. Soc. Clin. Electrophysiology in Vision. Republican. Presbyterian. Lodge: Order Eastern Star. Office: 1826 S Eileen Dr Anaheim CA 92802-3104

SCHOR, JOSEPH MARTIN, pharmaceutical executive, biochemist; b. Bklyn., Jan. 10, 1929; s. Aaron Jacob and Rhea Iress (Kay) S.; children: Esther Helen, Joshua David, Gideon Alexander; m. Laura Sharon Strumingher, June 14, 1992. B.S. magna cum laude, CCNY, 1951; Ph.D., Fla. State U., 1957. Sr. research chemist Armour Pharm. Co., Kankakee, Ill., 1957-59, Lederle Labs., Pearl River, N.Y., 1959-64; dir. biochemistry Endo Labs., Garden City, N.Y., 1964-76; v.p. sci. affairs Forest Labs., N.Y.C., 1977-94; sr. v.p. scientific affairs emeritus, Forest Labs, 1995—. Editor, contbr.: Chemical Control of Fibrinolysis-Thrombolysis, 1970. Contbr. articles to profl. jours. Patentee in field. USNR, 1955-57. Fellow Am. Inst. Chemists (cert. profl. chemist); mem. Am. Chem. Soc. (chmn. Nassau County subsect. 1971-72), Internat. Soc. on Thrombosis and Hemostasis, N.Y. Acad. Scis., AAAS, Phi Beta Kappa, Sigma Xi. Home: 28 Meleny Rd Locust Valley NY 11560-1221

SCHOR, OLGA SEEMANN, mental health counselor, real estate broker; b. Havana, Cuba, Mar. 2, 1951; came to U.S., 1961; d. Olga del Carmen (Hernandez) S.; m. David Michael Schor, Apr. 22, 1979; 1 child, Andrew. A.A., Miami Dade Community Coll., 1971; B.A., U. Fla.-Gainesville, 1973; M.Edn., U. Miami, Fla., 1976; Psy.D., Nova U., 1981; cert. Bert Rodgers Sch. Real Estate, Miami, 1981, Gold Coast Sch. Real Estate, 1988; lic. real estate broker. Teaching asst. U. Fla., Gainesville, 1972-73; counselor U. Miami, Fla., 1974-79; assoc. psychotherapist Linda H. Jamrozy & Assocs., Miami, 1976-78, Interactive Systems, Miami, 1978-79; psychometrist Jackson Meml. Hosp., Miami, 1978-79; assoc. psychotherapist Behavioral Medicine Inst., Miami, 1979-85, Tony Ciminero & Assocs., Miami, 1985-86; lectr. U. Miami, 1976-78, Jackson Meml. Hosp. Sch. Nursing, Miami, 1976; real estate broker The Keyes Co. Realtor, Coral Gables, 1981-88, Keyes Asset Mgmt., Miami, 1988—; sec./treas. bd. dirs. BODS Inc., Miami. Chmn. creative writing Jr. Orange Bowl competition. Recipient Assoc. of Quarter award Keyes Co. Realtors, 1986. Mem. Am. Psychol. and Guidance Assn., Keyes Comml. Roundtable, Keyes Inner Circle, Coral Gables Bd. Realtors, Gulliver Acad.'s Parents Bd., Dade County Mental Health Assn., Million Dollar Sales Club. Club: South Fla. Sailing Assn. (Miami). Avocations: sailing; diving; reading; running; theater; acting; tennis. Office: Keyes Asset Mgmt Inc 1 SE 3rd Ave Fl 11 Miami FL 33131-1704

SCHORE, ROBERT, social worker, educator; b. N.Y.C., July 29, 1934; s. David and Helen S.; married, three children. Student, Mesivta Tifereth Jerusalem, N.Y.C., 1947-48; BA, CCNY, 1955; MS, Columbia U., 1959; cert. advanced study, SUNY, New Paltz, 1985; postgrad., Postgrad. Ctr. for Mental, Health, 1967, Inst. for Rational-Emotive, Therapy, Bank St. Coll., 1984, Rockland Conservatory Music, 1992—. Diplomate Clin. Social Work, NASW; cert. social worker, impartial hearing officer, sch. dist. adminstr., supr. sch. social workers, N.Y. Social worker Dept. Social Svcs./Child Placement Svcs., N.Y.C., 1956-58, Edwin Gould Found., N.Y.C., 1959-63; supr. with NIMH dem. project Shield Inst., Bronx, N.Y., 1963-65; sch. social worker N.Y.C. Bd. Edn. Bur. Child Guidance, Bronx, 1965-80; sch. social worker Com. on Spl. Edn., Bronx, 1980-85, High Sch. Clin. Svcs., Bronx, 1986-91; pvt. practice West Nyack, N.Y., 1992-95; psychotherapist Ind. Consultation Ctr., Bronx, 1967, Rockland County Mental Health Ctr., Monsey, N.Y., 1968-69; rsch. assoc., editor/NIMH demo project Nathan Kline Inst., Orangeburg, N.Y., 1968-85; instr. CCNY, 1966; field instr. NYU, 1970-73; adj. prof. Rockland C.C., Suffern, N.Y., 1993—; fair hearing officer N.Y. State Edn. Dept., 1992—; adminstrv. intern Clarkstown Sch. Dist., West Nyack, 1984-85; workshop leader in field. Editor: Orb Mag., 1950-51; contb. chpts. to books, articles to profl. jours. Supr., cons. Vol. Counseling Svc., New City, N.Y., 1992-94; bd. dirs. Rockland Hebrew Day Sch., 1986; violinist Riverdale Orchestra, Suburban Symphony of Rockland, Ramapo Orchestral Soc., N.Y. With USAR, 1957-63. Mem. Am. Fedn. Tchrs., N.Y. State United Tchrs., United Fedn. Tchrs., Acad. Cert. Social Workers. Jewish. Office: PO Box 276 Monsey NY 10952-0276

SCHORN, LARRY W., cardiothoracic surgeon; b. San Antonio, Dec. 27, 1946; s. Milton Ben and Mildred Emillee (Harris) S.; m. Linda Christine Reed, June 12, 1970; children: Deborah, Scott, Ashley. BS in Biology, U. Tex., Arlington, 1969; MD, U. Tex., Dallas, 1973. Diplomate Am. Bd. Surgery, Am. Bd. Thoracic Surgery. Pres. Cardio Thoracic Surgery Assocs. of North Tex., P.A., Irving. Fellow ACS, Am. Coll. Chest Physicians. Home: 1203 Travis Cir N Irving TX 75061 Office: Cardio-Thoracic Surgery 1302 Lane St Ste 400 Irving TX 75061-2201

SCHORR, JANICE LEE, nursing consultant; b. West Mifflin, Pa., June 16, 1956; d. Theodore Mathias and Mary Jane (Dougherty) S.; m. Robert W. Booth, June 21, 1974 (div. July 1978); children: Mary Jeanne Booth, Kelly Ann Booth; m. Lewis Richards Garrett; 1 child, Lewis Mathias Garrett. BSN, Duquesne U., 1984. Stff nurse Millcreek Cmty. Hosp., Erie, Pa., 1984-85; staff and charge nurse Hamot Hosp., Erie, Pa., 1985, Jefferson (Pa.) Hosp., 1985-86; dir. quality assurance S.W. Gen. Hosp., San Antonio, 1988; cons. Superior Care Pharamacy, Salk Lake City, 1988-91; dir. quality assurance Heritage Mgmt. Inc., Salk Lake City, 1991-96; dist. dir. clin. ops. Vencor Inc., Salk Lake City, 1996—; cons. Health Insight, Salt Lake City, 1994—; mem. TB Elimination Adv. Com., Salt Lake City, 1992—, Sub-Com. Long Term Care on Quality Improvement, Salt Lake City, 1994—. Author: Skin Care For The elderly, 1992. Lt. USAF, 1986-88. Mem. Utah Nurses Assn. (2d v.p. dist. 1992-94), Utah Health Care Assn., Utah Assn. Healthcare Quality. Home and Office: 8024 S Old Coventry Cir Sandy UT 84043

SCHORR, LISBETH BAMBERGER, child and family policy analyst, author, educator; b. Munich, Jan. 20, 1931; d. Fred S. and Lotte (Krafft) Bamberger; m. Daniel L. Schorr, Jan. 8, 1967; children—Jonathan, Lisa. BA with highest honors, U. Calif., Berkeley, 1952; LHD (hon.), Wilkes U., 1991, U. Md., 1994. Med. care cons. U.A.W. and Community Health Assn., Detroit, 1956-58; asst. dir. Dept. Social Security AFL-CIO, Washington, 1958-65; acting chief CAP Health Svcs., OEO, 1965-66; chief program planning Office for Health Affairs, OEO, Washington, 1967; cons. Children's Def. Fund, Washington, 1973-79; scholar-in-residence Inst. of Medicine, 1979-80; chmn. Select Panel on Promotion Child Health, 1979-80; adj. prof. maternal and child health U. N.C., Chapel Hill, 1981-85; lectr. social medicine Harvard U. Med. Sch., 1984—; dir. project on effective interventions Harvard U., 1988—; nat. coun. Alan Gutmacher Inst., 1974-79, 82-85; pub. mem. Am. Bd. Pediatrics, 1978-84; vice chmn. Found. for Child Devel., 1978-84, bd. dirs., 1976-84, 86-94; mem. coun. Nat. Ctr. for Children in Poverty, 1987-96; mem. children's program adv. com. Edna McConnell Clark Found., 1987—; bd. dirs. Pub. Edn. Fund Network, 1991-93; co-chair Roundtable on Comprehensive Cmty. Inititatives Aspen Inst., 1992—, chair roundtable steering com. on evaluation, 1994—; mem. bd. on children and families NAS, 1993-95; mem. nat. Commn. State and Local Pub. Svcs., 1992-94; mem. task force on young children Carnegie Corp., 19-94; mem. sec.'s adv. com. Head Start quality and expansion, 1993-94; trustee City Yr., 1994—; mem. exec. com. Harvard Project on Schooling and Children. Author: Within Our Reach: Breaking the Cycle of Disadvantage, 1988. Recipient Dale Richmond Meml. award Am. Acad. Pediatrics, 1977, 9th Ann. Robert F. Kennedy Book award, 1989, Nelson Cruikshank award nat. Coun. Sr. Citizens, 1990, Porter prize, 1993. Mem. Inst. Medicine, NAS, Nat. Acad. on Social Ins., Phi Beta Kappa. Home: 3113 Woodley Rd NW Washington DC 20008-3449

SCHORR, MARTIN MARK, forensic psychologist, educator, writer; b. Sept. 16, 1923; m. Dolores Gene Tyson, June 14, 1952; 1 child, Jeanne Ann. Student Balliol Coll., Oxford (Eng.) U., 1945-46; AB cum laude, Adelphi U., 1949; postgrad., U. Tex., 1949-50; MS, Purdue U., 1953; PhD, U. Denver, 1960; postgrad., U. Tex. Diplomate in psychology; diplomate Am. Bd. Profl. Disability Cons., Am. Bd. Forensic Examiners, Am. Bd. Forensic Medicine; lic. clin. psychologist. Chief clin. psychol. svcs. San Diego County Mental Hosp., 1963-67; clin. dir. human services San Diego County, 1963-76; pvt. practice, forensic specialist San Diego, 1962—; forensic examiner superior, fed. and mil. cts., San Diego, 1962—; prof. abnormal psychology San Diego State U., 1965-68; chief dept. psychology Center City (Calif.) Hosp., 1976-79; cons. Dept. Corrections State of Calif., Minnewawa, 1970-73, Disability Evaluation Dept. Health, 1972-75, Calif. State Indsl. Accident Commn., 1972-78, Calif. Criminal Justice Adminstrn., 1975-77, Vista Hill Found., Mercy Hosp. Mental Health, Foodmaker Corp., Convent Sacred Heart, El Cajon, FAA Examiner. Author: Death by Prescription, 1988; dir.: Alpha Centauri Prodns. Recipient award for aid in developing Whistle Blower Law Calif. Assembly, 1986. Fellow Internat. Assn. Social Psychiatry, Internat. Biog. Assn. (life: Great Britain), Am. Coll. Forensic Examiners (life), Am. Bd. Forensic Med.; mem. AAAS, PEN, APA, Am. Acad. Forensic Scis. (qualified med. evaluator), Internat. Platform Assn., World Mental Health Assn., Mystery Writers Am., Nat. Writers Club, Mensa. Home: University City 2970 Arnoldson Ave San Diego CA 92122-2114 Office: 275 F St Chula Vista CA 91910-2820

SCHOTTLAND, EDWARD MORROW, hospital administrator; b. N.Y.C., Aug. 5, 1946; s. Leo Edward and Harriet (Morrow) S.; m. Nancy Resnick, June 25, 1977; 1 child, David. BA, Queens Coll., CUNY, 1968; MPS, Cornell U., 1973. Asst. adminstr. Mercy Hosp., Rockville Centre, N.Y., 1973-75, asst. adminstr. and dir. planning, 1975-79; pres. Kosair Crippled Children's Hosp., Louisville, 1979-81, sr. v.p., chief adminstrv. officer Kosair Children's Hosp., Louisville, 1983-89; v.p. NKC, Inc., Louisville, 1981-83, sr. v.p., 1983-89; exec. v.p. The Miriam Hosp., Providence, R.I., 1989—; sr. v.p. Lifespan, Providence, R.I., 1995—; mem. Gov.'s Adv. Council on Med. Assistance. Chmn. Jefferson County Child Abuse Authority, Louisville, 1981-83, dir., 1979-86; bd. dirs. Suicide Prevention and Edn. Ctr., Louisville, 1982-86, HARI, 1990—, Interfaith Health Coun., v.p., 1994—, RIMRI, Inc., 1994—; bd. trustee Barrington (R.I.) Pub. Libr.; chmn. bd. Beavertail Prodns., 1995—; Fellow Am. Coll. Health Execs. (regent 1994—); mem. Nat. Assn. Children's Hosps. and Related Institutions (bd. dirs.). Home: 3 Stratford Rd Barrington RI 02806-3617 Office: The Miriam Hosp 164 Summit Ave Providence RI 02906-2800

SCHOWALTER, JOHN ERWIN, child and adolescent psychiatry educator; b. Milw., Mar. 15, 1936; s. Raymond Phillip and Martha (Kowalke) S.; m. Ellen Virginia Leffers, June 11, 1960; children: Jay, Bethany. BS, U. Wis.-Madison, 1957, MD, 1960. Diplomate Am. Bd. Psychiatry and Neurology (com. on cert. in child psychiatry 1983-85, chmn. 1986-87, bd. dirs. 1993—, chmn. com. added qualifications forensic psychiatry 1993—); cert. in adult and child psychiatry also psychoanalysis. Intern in pediatrics Yale-New Haven Hosp., 1960-61; asst. resident in psychiatry Cin. Gen. Hosp., 1961-63; fellow in child psychiatry Yale Child Study Ctr., 1963-65; psychiatrist Mental Hygiene Clinic U.S. Army, Ft. Ord, Calif., 1965-67; asst. prof. Yale U. Child Study Ctr., New Haven, 1967-70, assoc. prof. Sch. Medicine, 1970-75, dir. tng., 1971-96, prof. pediatrics and psychiatry, 1975—, chief child psychiatry, 1982-90, dir. child psychiatry clin. svcs., 1990—, Albert J. Solnit prof. child psychiatry and pediatrics, 1989—; mem. publ. com. Yale U. Press, 1992—; mem. sci. adv. bd. Sophia Found. Med. Rsch., Rotterdam, The Netherlands, 1984-89; dir. mental health and substance abuse Yale Preferred Health Plan, 1995—. Co-author: The Family Handbook of Adolescence, 1979; contbr. numerous articles, book revs.; mem. editorial bd. Pediatrics, 1976-81, Children's Health Care, 1977—, Jour. Am. Psychoanalytic Assn., 1978, Pediatrics in Rev., 1978-85; asst. editor Jour. Am. Acad. Child and Adolescent Psychiatry, 1988—; co-editor Yearbook Psychiatry and Applied Mental Health, 1988—. Capt. U.S. Army, 1965-67. Fellow Am. Acad. Child and Adolescent Psychiatry (sec. 1985-87, pres. 1989-91, Simon Wile award 1996), Am. Coll. Psychiatrists, Am. Acad. Pediatrics (affiliate); mem. Am. Pediatric Soc., Am. Psychoanalytic Assn. (cert. adult and child), Group for Advancement Psychiatry (com. on child psychiatry 1981, bd. dirs. 1989-91, pres. 1993-95), Assn. for Care of Children's Health (pres. 1984-86), AMA (residency rev. com. for psychiatry 1983-87, 89-94), Soc. Profs. Child Psychiatry (pres. 1984-86), We. New Eng. Inst. Psychoanalysis (mem. faculty in child psychoanalysis 1980—, supervisor child psychoanalysis 1984—, pres. 1986-88), Conn. and New Haven med. socs., Conn. Coun. Child Psychiatrists (pres. 1979-81), Benjamin

Rush Soc., DARE Am. (mem. sci. adv. panel), others, Sigma Xi. Lutheran. Home: 606 Ellsworth Ave New Haven CT 06511-1636 Office: Yale U Child Study Ctr PO Box 207900 230 S Frontage Rd New Haven CT 06520-7900

SCHREIBER, ANDREW, psychotherapist; b. Budapest, Hungary, Aug. 1, 1918; s. Alexander and Bella (Gruen) S.; m. Mona Schreiber, Aug. 6, 1950; children: Julie, Brad, Robin. BA, CCNY, 1941, MEd, 1943; MSW, Columbia U., 1949; PhD, Heed U., 1972. Diplomate Am. Bd. Sexology; lic. psychotherapist, Calif. Pvt. practice Belmont, Calif., 1970—; sales mgr. vibro ceramics dir. Gulton Industries, Metuchen, N.J., 1949-57; mktg. mgr. Weldotron Corp., Newark, 1957-63; head dept. spl. edn. San Mateo (Calif.) High Sch. Dist., 1964-70; mem. faculty Heed U., 1970-71, advisor to doctoral candidates on West Coast, 1971; lectr. spl. edn. U. Calif.-Berkeley, 1973; cons. on hypnotherapy Psoriasis Rsch. Inst., Palo Alto, Calif., 1993—. Art Students League of N.Y. scholar, 1933-35, San Francisco State U. grantee. Fellow Am. Acad. Clin. Sexology; mem. NEA, AACD, Learning Disabilities Assn., Am. Assn. Sex Educators, Counselors and Therapists, Calif. Assn. Marriage and Family Therapists, Calif. Tchrs. Assn. Home: 2817 San Ardo Way Belmont CA 94002-1341

SCHREIBER, ELLIOTT HAROLD, psychologist, educator; b. Newark, N.J., Apr. 28, 1933; s. Harry and Sylvia (Schwartz) Schreiber; m. Louise F. Bossio, June 18, 1961; chidlren: Andrea, Pamela, David, Karen. BA, Upsala Coll., 1956; Ma, Bradley U., 1959; EdD, W.Va. U., 1967. Diplomate Am. Bd. Profl. Psychology; lic. clin. psychologist, N.J., Pa. Clin. psychologist admissions svc. Wernersville (Pa.) State Psychiat. Hosp., 1960-63; sch. psychologist Burlington (N.J.) City Schs., 1965-67; prin. psychologist Bordentown (N.J.) Reformatory, 1967, 68; assoc. prof. psychology Rowan Coll. of N.J., Glassboro, 1967—; pvt. clin. psychologist, Moorestown, N.J., 1965—. Author: Violence and Aggression in Human Behavior, 3d edit., 1988, Abnormal Behavior, 5th edit., 1991; contbr. articles to profl. jours. Pres. S. Jersey chpt. United Nations Assn., USA, N.Y.C., 1975—. Fellow Acad. Clin. Psychology; mem. APA, N.J. Psychol. Assn., Pa. Psychol. Assn., N.J. Edn. Assn., Men of Achievement (Hon. award 1968), Kappa Delta Pi. Home: 708 Camden Ave Moorestown NJ 08057-2228 Office: Rowan Coll of N.J. Rte 322 Glassboro NJ 08028

SCHREIBER, JAMES RALPH, obstetrics, gynecology researcher; b. Rosebud, Tex., May 29, 1946; m. Lester B. and Jane Elinore (Hodges) S.; m. Mary Celia Schmitt, Aug. 16, 1968; children: Lisa, Joseph, Laura, Cynthia. BA, Rice U., 1968; MD, Johns Hopkins U., 1972. Cert. Am. Coll. Ob-Gyn, Am. Bd. Reproductive Endocrinology. Intern. ob-gyn. U. So. Calif. Los Angeles County Hosp., 1972-73, resident ob-gyn., 1973-74, 76-78; fellow reproductive endocrinology NIH, Bethesda, Md., 1974-76; asst. prof. ob-gyn U. Calif., San Diego, 1978-82; assoc. prof. U. Chgo., 1982-87, prof., 1988-91; prof., chmn. dept. Washington U., St. Louis, 1991—. Contbr. articles to profl. jours. Grantee NIH, 1978—. Mem. Endocrine Soc., Soc. Gynecologic Investigation. Home: 22 Frontenac Estates Saint Louis MO 63131-2600 Office: Washington U Sch Medicine Dept Ob-Gyn 4911 Barnes Hospital Plz Saint Louis MO 63110-1003

SCHREIBER, MELVYN HIRSH, radiologist; b. Galveston, Tex., May 28, 1931; s. Edward and Sue Schreiber; m. Laurentina; children—William, Diane, Karen, Lori. M.D., U. Tex. Med. Br., Galveston, 1955. Diplomate: Am. Bd. Radiology (trustee 1987—). Intern U. Tex. Med. Br., Galveston, 1955-56; resident U. Tex. Med. Br., 1956-59, asst. prof. radiology, 1961-64, asso. prof., 1964-67, prof., 1967—, chmn. dept. radiology, 1976-91. Author: Old Dog, New Tricks, A Collection of Essays, 1995. Served as capt. M.C. U.S. Army, 1959-61. Markle Found. scholar, 1963-68. Fellow Am. Coll. Radiology; mem. Assn. Univ. Radiologists (pres. 1974-75). Office: U Tex Med Br Dept Radiology Galveston TX 77555

SCHREIBER, RONALD, nephrologist; b. N.Y.C., July 5, 1938; s. Mac M. and Ruth (Abramowitz) S.; m. Leslie S. Schuman, May 30, 1968; children: Deborah, Lisa, Bonnie. AB, Columbia Coll., 1960, MD, 1964. Diplomate Am. Bd. Internal Medicine, Am. Bd. Nephrology. Nephrologist pvt. practice Hollywood, Fla., 1970-82; chief of nephrology Kaiser-Permanente, Va., 1984—; clin. asst. prof. medicine Uniformed Svcs. U. Health Scis., Bethesda, Md., 1995—. Lt. USPHS, 1966-68. Lt. col. USAR, 1984—. Office: Kaiser Permanente 201 N Washington St Falls Church VA 22046-4518

SCHREIER, HAROLD JACOB, molecular biologist; b. Pitts., Oct. 7, 1956; s. Sigmund and Edith (Weingarten) S.; m. Susan Cooperstein; children: Roger, Jeremy, Arianne. BS in Biochemistry, Calif. Poly. State U., San Luis Obispo, 1978; PhD in Biochemistry, Pa. State U., 1983. Teaching asst. Pa. State U., University Park, 1978-83; research fellow Tufts U., Boston, 1983-86; asst. prof. dept. microbiology, Ariz. State U., Tempe, 1986-89; asst. prof. Biotech. Inst. U. Md., 1989-95, assoc. prof., 1995—; asst. prof. dept. biol. sci. U. Md. Balt. County, 1995—; cons. Dynamac Corp., 1995—. Assoc. editor Jour. Bacteriology, 1994—; contbr. articles to profl. jours. Am. Heart Assn. student research fellow, 1977; NIH postdoctoral fellow, 1983-86; recipient NIH First Award, 1988; grantee NSF 1993, 96. Mem. AAAS, Am. Soc. Microbiology, Sigma Xi. Democrat. Achievements include elucidation of mechanisms in nitrogen metabolism in gram-positive bacteria. Home: 6530 Copperfield Rd Baltimore MD 21209-2546 Office: Ctr of Marine Biotech Columbus Ctr 701 E Pratt St Baltimore MD 21202-4031

SCHREINER, BEVERLY ETHEL, medical transcriptionist; b. Spokane, Wash., Dec. 7, 1931; d. Charlie P. and M. Jerrine (Cannon) Nolasco; m. George J. Schreiner, Feb. 4, 1951 (div. Feb. 1961); children: Michael, David, Judy. Student, Franklin Hosp. Sch. Nursing, 1951, San Francisco City Coll., 1953, Am. Inst. Banking, San Francisco. Certified med. transcriptionist. Sec. Darrell Kammer, M.D., Nampa, Idaho, 1967-73; supr. med. records Idaho State Sch. and Hosp., Nampa, 1966-75; pvt. med. transcriptionist, Nampa, 1984—; med. transcriptionist Caldwell Internal Medicine, Idaho, 1976—; supr. evening shift med. records office Mercy Med. Ctr., Nampa, 1967-87. Mem. Nat. Assn. Med. Transcriptionists, Idaho Assn. Med. Transcriptionists. Avocations: reading, sewing, crafts. Home: 102 W Willowbrook Dr Meridian ID 83642-3200 Other: Caldwell Internal Medicine 1818 S 10th Ave Caldwell ID 83605-4815

SCHREINER, MARY ANN, health quality and risk management administrator; b. Buffalo, N.Y., Nov. 30, 1956; d. Anthony Joseph and Shirley Isabel (Kohel) S. BS in Nursing, Niagara U., 1978; MBA, SUNY, Buffalo, 1988. RN, N.Y., Tex. RN coronary care unit Erie County Med. Ctr., Buffalo, 1978-79, St. Luke's Episcopal Hosp., Houston, 1979-82; cardiac rehab. specialist St. Joseph's Hosp., Houston, 1982-85; dir. cardiac rehab. Tri-County Meml. Hosp., Gowanda, N.Y., 1985-87, asst. adminstr. clin. svcs., 1987-89; quality/risk mgmt. dir. Buffalo (N.Y.) Med. Group, P.C., 1989—. Author, editor: Scale Down, 1987. Mem. parish coun. St. Cecilia's Ch., Sheldon, N.Y., 1995—, accompanist, ch. choir, 1987—. Recipient Tchr. of Yr. award St. Cecilia's Ch., 1993. Mem. Western N.Y. Assn. Health Care Quality. Office: Buffalo Medical Group PC 85 High St Buffalo NY 14203

SCHRETER, CAROL ANN, social worker, gerontologist, writer; b. Balt., Nov. 1, 1947; d. A. Harvey and Phyllis (Kolker) S.; m. Jonas J. Fendell, Aug. 12, 1984 (dec. 1994). BA, U. Pa., 1969; MSW, Temple U., 1973; PhD in Social Work, Bryn Mawr (Pa.) Coll., 1983. Caseworker Md. Dept. Welfare, Balt., 1969-70; therapist psychiatry dept. Temple Hosp., Phila., 1970-71; sr. social worker Waxter Ctr. for Sr. Citizens, Balt., 1973-79; freelance writer and researcher, 1976—; coord. found. funds Assoc. Jewish Charities, Balt., 1983-86; cons. Balt. City Area on Aging, 1982, Shared Housing Resource Ctr., Phila., 1981-84, Elvirita Lewis Found., Calif., 1986-91, Grantmakers in Aging, Flint, Mich., 1986-91, Retirement Rsch. Found., Park Ridge, Ill., 1990-91. Co-editor: Allies and Adversaries: the Impact of Managed Care on Mental Health Services, 1994, Managing Care, Not Dollars: the Continuum of Mental Health Services, 1996; contbr. articles to profl. jours. and consumer mags. Home and Office: 1905 Dixon Rd Baltimore MD 21209-3507

SCHREYER, NANCY KRAFT, medical science researcher; b. Chelsea, Mass., Apr. 18, 1952; d. Meyer Louis and Eileen Marguerite (McCauley) Kraft; m. Raymond Scott Schreyer, Aug. 22, 1976; children: Kraftin Ellice, Evan Kraft. BS, Simmons Coll., 1974; PhD, Hahnemann Med. Coll., 1979. Instr. Hahnemann Med. Coll., Coll. Allied Health Professions, Phila., 1977-79, sr. instr., 1979-80; asst. instr. Hahnemann Med. Coll., Phila., 1977-79, instr., 1979-80, sr. instr., 1980-81; asst. prof. Hahnemann U., Sch. Allied Health Professions, Phila., 1980-88, Hahnemann U. Sch. Medicine, Phila., 1981-88, Hahnemann U. Grad. Sch., Phila., 1983—; non-affiliated mem. animal care and use com. Bristol Myers-Squibb Co. N.J., 1988—. Contbr. articles to profl. jours. Rsch. grantee Hahnemann U., 1983, Am. Heart Assn., 1986. Mem. Am. Soc. Hypertension, N.Y. Acad. Scis., Am. Soc. Primatologists, Physiol. Soc. Phila., Am. Assn. Lab. Animal Sci., Am. Physiol. Soc.

SCHRICKER, J. LOUIS, JR., neurosurgeon; b. Salt Lake City; m. Anna Lou Chinn; three children. AB, U. Utah, 1939; MD, Washington U. Sch. Medicine, 1943. Diplomate Am. Bd. Neurol. Surgery. Intern, resident gen. surgery Latter Day Saints Hosp., Salt Lake City, 1944-46; intern neurosurgery Letterman Army Hosp., San Francisco, 1948-49; intern neurosurgery Barnes Hosp., St. Louis, 1948-49, fellow in neurology, 1951-52; assoc. clin. prof. neurology U. Utah Coll. Medicine, Salt Lake City, 1952—. Fellow Am. Coll. Surgeons; mem. AMA, Am. Med. Peer Review Assn., Utah State Med. Assn., Salt Lake County Med. Soc., Salt Lake Surgical Soc., Am. Assn. Neurol. Surgeons, Neurosurg. Soc. Am., Utah Neurosurg. Soc., Congress Neurol. Surgeons. Mormon. Office: 324 10th Ave Ste 189 Salt Lake City UT 84103-2853

SCHRIEBER, LESLIE, rheumatologist; b. Brighton, Sussex, England, Oct. 21, 1948; arrived in Australia, 1958; s. Abraham Michael and Helen (Katz) S.; m. Paula Lysbeth Platt, Sept. 21, 1980; children: Michelle Ellen, Adam Charles. MB, BS with honors, U. Sydney, New South Wales, Australia, 1972; MD, U. New South Wales, 1982. Resident Royal Prince Alfred Hosp., Sydney, 1972-75, med. registrar, 1975-76; immunology registrar St. Vincent's Hosp., Sydney, 1976-77; postgrad. rsch. scholar St. Vincent's Hosp., 1975-81; rsch. fellow Kennedy Inst. Rheumatology, London, 1981-82; rsch. assoc. NIH, Bethesda, Md., 1982-84; sr. lectr. U. Sydney, 1984-91, assoc. prof., 1991—; dir. Sutton Rheumatism Rsch. Lab. Royal North Shore Hosp., Sydney, 1990—; head dept. rheumatology Royal North Shore Hosp., 1993-95; bd. dirs. Arthritis Found. Australia; mem. exec. com. Australian and New Zealand Microcirculation Soc., 1991-95, pres. 1995—; mem. scientific adv. com. Bone & Joint Rsch. Found., U. Sydney, 1990, dep. dir., 1995—. Author (with others): Disease and Society, 1989, Current Opinion in Rheumatology, 1989, 91, 94, Rheumatology, 1994. Convenor New South Wales Med. Rsch. Week, Sydney, 1987; mem. exec. com. United Israel Appeal, Sydney, 1988—. Rheumatology fellow St. Vincent's Hosp., 1977-78, rsch. fellow Kennedy Inst. Rheumatology, London, 1981-82; postgrad. rsch. scholar U. New South Wales, 1978-81, Commonwealth scholar, Australia, 1965, Michael Mason scholar, 1981. Fellow Royal Australian Coll. Physicians; mem. Australian Rheumatology Assn., Australian Soc. Immunology, Australian Soc. Med. Rsch. (dir. 1987-88), Australian Med. Assn., Am. Coll. Rheumatology, New South Wales Fellowship of Jewish Doctors (v.p. 1994—). Jewish. Home: 20 Chelmsford Ave, Lindfield 2070, Australia Office: Royal North Shore Hosp, Dept Rheumatology, Saint Leonards 2065 NSW, Australia

SCHRIER, ROBERT WILLIAM, physician, educator; b. Indpls., Feb. 19, 1936; s. Arthur E. and Helen M. Schrier; m. Barbara Lindley, June 14, 1959; children: David, Debbie, Douglas, Derek, Denise. BA, Depauw U., 1957; MD, Ind. U., 1962. Intern Marion County (Ind.) Hosp., 1962; resident U. Wash., Seattle, 1963-65; pvt. practice specializing in nephrology Denver, 1972—; asst. prof. U. Calif. Med. Ctr., San Francisco, 1969-72, assoc. mem., 1970-72, assoc. dir. renal div., 1971-72, assoc. prof., 1972; prof., head renal disease U. Colo. Sch. Med., Denver, 1972—, prof., chmn. Dept. of Medicine, 1976—. Pres. Nat. Kidney Found., 1984-86. With U.S. Army, 1966-69. Mem. ACP (master), Am. Soc. Nephrology (treas. 1979-81, pres. 1983), Internat. Soc. Nephrology (treas. 1981-90, v.p. 1990-95, pres. 1995—), Am. Clin. and Climatol. Assn. (v.p. 1986), Assn. Am. Physicians (pres. 1994-95), Western Assn. Physicians (pres. 1982), Alpha Omega Alpha. Office: U Colo Health Scis Ctr Dept Medicine 4200 E 9th Ave Denver CO 80220-3706

SCHRIER, STANLEY LEONARD, physician, educator; b. N.Y.C., Jan. 2, 1929; s. Harry and Nettie (Schwartz) S.; m. Peggy Helen Pepper, June 6, 1953; children: Rachel, Leslie, David. A.B., U. Colo., 1949; M.D., Johns Hopkins U., 1954. Diplomate Am. Bd. Internal Medicine (chmn. subsplty. bd. hematology). Intern Oster Med. Service, Johns Hopkins Hosp., 1954-55; resident U. Mich., Ann Arbor, 1955-56, U. Chgo. Hosp., 1958-59; sr. asst. surgeon USPHS, 1956-58; instr. medicine Stanford Sch. Medicine, Calif., 1959-60, asst. prof. medicine Stanford Sch. Medicine, 1960-63, assoc. prof., 1963-72, prof. medicine, 1972-95, chief divsn. hematology, 1968-94; vis. scientist Weizmann Inst., Rehovot, Israel, 1967-68; vis. prof. Oxford U., Eng., 1975-76, Hebrew U., Jerusalem, 1982-83. John and Mary Markle scholar, 1961; recipient Kaiser award Stanford U., 1972, Kaiser award Stanford U., 1974, 75, David Rytand award, 1982, Eleanor Roosevelt Union Internationale Contre le Cancer award, 1975-76. Mem. Am. Soc. Hematology (exec. com.), Am. Physiol. Soc., Soc. Exptl. Biology and Medicine, Am. Soc. Clin. Investigation, Western Assn. Physicians. Democrat. Jewish. Office: Stanford U Sch Medicine 300 Pasteur Dr Palo Alto CA 94304-2203

SCHROCK, RITA EILEEN, optometrist; b. Canton, Ohio, May 16, 1968; d. Joseph L. and Ruby F. (Nisly) S.; m. Von M. Schrock, June 30, 1990; 1 child, Aubrey Kaylin. BA, Goshen Coll., 1989; OD, Ohio State U., 1993. Pvt. practice Orrville, Ohio, 1993—. Mem. Am. Optometric Assn., Ohio Optometric Assn., Ohio State U. Alumni Assn. Mennonite. Office: 252 Cherry St Orrville OH 44667

SCHRODT, JOSEPH, orthopaedic surgeon; b. Canton, Ill., Aug. 15, 1937; s. Ivan Verle and Frances Veronica (Sizek) S.; m. Martha Marie Highland, Sept. 5, 1959; children: Keith, David, Teresa. BA in Liberal Arts, U. Ill., 1959, MD, 1963. Diplomate Am. Bd. Orthopaedic Surgeons. Intern St. Louis County Hosp., 1964; orthopaedic surgery resident U. Ill., 1966-70; surg. staff Decatur Meml. Hosp. and St. Mary's Hosp., 1970—; bd. trustees Decatur Meml. Hosp., 1995—. Capt. USAF, 1964-66. Mem. Macon County Med. Soc. (pres. 1980-82), Am. Acad. of Orthopaedic Surgeons (bd. counselors 1994—). Office: Ste 140 102 W Kenwood Ave Decatur IL 62526

SCHROEDER, DAVID HAROLD, health care facility executive; b. Chgo., Oct. 22, 1940; s. Harry T. and Clara D. (Dexter) S.; m. Clara Doorn, Dec. 27, 1964; children: Gregory D., Elizabeth M. BBA, Kans. State Coll., 1965; MBA, Wichita State U., 1968; postgrad., U. Ill., 1968-69. CPA, Ill. Supt. cost acctg. Boeing Co., Wichita, Kans., 1965-68; sr. v.p., treas. Riverside Med. Ctr., Kankakee, Ill., 1971—; treas. Riverside Health System, 1982—, Kankakee Valley Health Inc., 1985—, Health Info. Systems Coop., 1991—; v.p., treas. Oakside Corp., Kankakee, 1982—; bd. dirs. Harmony Home Health Svc., Inc., Naperville, Ill.; mem. faculty various profl. orgns.; adj. prof. econs. divsn. health adminstrn. Gov.'s State U., University Park, Ill., 1990-95; trustee Riverside Found. Trust, 1989—, RMC Found., 1989—, Sr. Living Ctr., 1989—. Contbg. author: Cost Containment in Hospitals, 1980; contbr. articles to profl. jours. Trustee Riverside Found. Trust, 1989—, RMC Found., 1989—, Sr. Living Ctr., 1989—; pres. Riverside Employees Credit Union, 1976-79; founder Kankakee Trinity Acad., 1980, Riverview Hist. Dist., Kankakee, 1982; pres. Kankakee County Mental Health Ctr., 1982-84, United Way Kankakee County, 1984-85; chmn. Ill. Provider Trust, Naperville, 1983-85; mem. adv. bd. Students in Free Enterprise, Olivet Nazarene U., Kankakee, 1989—; pres. adv. coun. divsn. health adminstrn., preceptor Gov.'s State U., 1987—; trustee, treas. Am. Luth. Ch.; wish granter Make a Wish Found., 1994—; dir. Kankakee County Hist. Soc., 1995. Capt. U.S. Army, 1969-71. Fellow Am. Coll. Healthcare Execs., Healthcare Fin. Mgmt. Assn. (pres. 1975-76, cert. mgr. patient accounts 1981), Fin. Analysts Fedn.; mem. AICPA, Ill. Hosp. Assn. (chmn. coun. health fin. 1982-85), Inst. Chartered Fin. Analysts, Nat. Assn. Accts., Fin. Exec. Inst., Ill. CPA Soc., Healthcare Fin. Mgmt. Assn. (William G. Follmer award 1977, Robert H. Reeves award 1981, Muncie Gold award 1987, Founders medal of honor 1990), Investment Analysts Soc. Chgo., Inc., Kankakee County Hist. Soc. (dir. 1995—), Classic Car Club Am. Packard Club, Kiwanis (pres.), Masons, Alpha Kappa Psi, Sigma Chi. Home: 901 S Chicago Ave Kankakee IL 60901-5236 Office: Riverside Med Ctr 350 N Wall St Kankakee IL 60901-2901

SCHROEDER, DAVID J. DEAN, psychologist; b. Hutchinson, Kans., Mar. 21, 1942; s. D. J. W. and Louise (Wedel) S.; m. Nevonna Joyce Thomas, May 24, 1964; children: Taryn Dee Schroeder Dye, Anita Joy. BA, Tabor Coll., 1964; MS, Kans. State Tchrs. Coll., 1967; PhD, U. Okla., 1971. Lic. psychologist, Kans. Rsch. psychologist FAA Civil Aeromed. Inst., Okla. City, 1970-72, clin. rsch. psychologist, 1980-89, supr., 1989-90, mgr. human factors rsch. lab., 1990-91, mgr. human resources rsch. div., 1991—; postdoctoral intern Norfolk (Nebr.) Regional Ctr., 1972-73; clin. psychologist VA Hosp., Murfreesboro, Tenn., 1973-75, Topeka, 1975-80. Co-author: FAA Employee Survey: National Report, 1984, 86, FAA Employee Survey: Regional/Center Reports, 1984, 86, FAA Job Satisfaction Survey National Report, 1988, FAA Job Satisfaction Survey: Regional/Center/Work Group Reports, 1988; adv. editl. bd. Aviation Space and Environ. Medicine, 1993-95. Senate adv. com. Tabor Coll., Hillsboro, Kans., 1987-89; Christian edn. com. chmn. So. Dist. Conf. Mennonite Brethern Ch., Hillsboro, 1989; Sunday Sch. tchr. Western Oaks Christian Ch., Oklahoma City, 1990—. Fellow APA, Aerospace Med. Assn. (chmn. sci. program com. 1990-91, mem. coun. 1992-95, v.p. 1996—), Aerospace Human Factors Assn. (pres. 1994-95); mem. Okla. Psychol. Assn. (bd. dirs. 1988-89, pres.-elect 1991, pres. 1992). Democrat. Home: 2601 NW 23rd St Oklahoma City OK 73107 Office: PO Box 25082 Oklahoma City OK 73125

SCHROEDER, DONALD J., orthopedic surgeon; b. Omaha, Nebr., Nov. 5, 1938; s. Francis A. and Maire L. (Schleuta) S.; m. Patricia A. Speer, Feb. 11, 1962 (div. June 1980); children: Cynthia, Douglas; m. Carol E. Schaan, Aug. 20, 1983. BS, Creighton U., 1960, MD, 1964. Diplomate Am. Bd. Orthopedic Surgery. Intern Detroit Receiving Hosp., 1964-65; resident gen. surgery & pathology Wayne State U. Affiliated Hosps., Detroit, 1965-67, resident orth. surgery, 1967-69; resident Shriners Hosp./ St. Louis U., 1969-70; resident orth. surgery Wayne State U.; attending surgeon Sacred Heart Gen. Hosp., Eugene, Oreg., 1971—. Pres. Marist Found., Eugene, 1993. Smith Kline fellow, 1964. Fellow Am. Acad. Orthopedic Surgeons; mem. AMA (alt. del. 1993—), Oreg. Med. Assn. (pres. 1993-94), Lane County Med. Soc. (pres. 1987-88), Western Orthopedic Assn. Republican. Roman Catholic. Office: 1180 Paterson Eugene OR 97401

SCHROEDER, GARY WILLIAM, psychologist; b. Buffalo, Jan. 31, 1958; s. Curtis and Alice (Moede) S. BA summa cum laude, SUNY, Buffalo, 1980; MA, U. Iowa, 1983, PhD, 1986. Lic. psychologist, Ark. Psychotherapist Ark. Psychiat. Clinic, North Little Rock, 1986, 1986-94; psychotherapy svcs. mgr. Bridge Way Hosp., North Little Rock, 1990-93; clin. instr. U. Ark. for Med. Scis., Little Rock, 1994—; coord. substance dependence treatment program Bridge Way Hosp., 1986-94. Recipient Grace Capen Meml. Fund award SUNY, Buffalo, 1979, N.Y. State Regents scholarship, 1976. Mem. APA, Ark. Psychol. Assn., Am. Soc. Clin. Hypnosis, Ark. Soc. Clin. Hypnosis, Am. Group Psychotherapy Assn., Psychotherapy Soc. (Ark. group, pres.-elect 1996), Amnesty Internat. (chmn. Little Rock unit 1987-88), Zero Population Growth, Sierra Club (overpopulation subcom. chmn. 1990—), Phi Beta Kappa, Phi Eta Sigma, Alpha Lambda Delta. Office: U Ark Med Scis Dept Psychiatry Slot 554 4301 W Markham St Little Rock AR 72205-9514

SCHROEDER, STEVEN ALFRED, medical educator, researcher, foundation executive; b. N.Y.C., July 26, 1939; s. Arthur Edward and Norma (Scheinberg) S.; m. Sally B. Ross, Oct. 21, 1967; children: David Arthur, Alan Ross. BA, Stanford U., 1960; MD, Harvard U., 1964; LHD (hon.), Rush U., 1994; DSc (hon.), Boston U., 1996. Am. Bd. Internal Medicine. Intern and resident in internal medicine Harvard Med. Service, Boston City Hosp., 1964-66, 68-70; asst. prof., then assoc. prof. George Washington Med. Ctr., Washington, 1971-76; vis. prof. St. Thomas' Hosp. Med. Sch., London, 1982-83; prof. medicine, chief div. gen. internal medicine, mem. Inst. Health Policy Studies U. Calif., San Francisco, 1976-90; pres. Robert Wood Johnson Found., Princeton, N.J., 1990—; cons. various govtl. and philanthropic health orgns.; chair internat. adv. com. faculty medicine Ben Gurion U., Israel. Sr. editor Current Medical Diagnosis and Treatment, 1987-93; mem. editorial bd. New Eng. Mag.; contbr. numerous articles to profl. jours. Mem. U.S. Prospective Payment Assessment Commn., 1983-88. With USPHS, 1966-68. Master ACP; mem. Physicians for Social Responsibility, Am. Pub. Health Assn., Assn. Am. Physicians, Inst. Medicine, Soc. Gen. Internal Medicine (past pres.), Phi Beta Kappa, Alpha Omega Alpha. Home: 49 W Shore Dr Pennington NJ 08534-2006 Office: Robert Wood Johnson Found PO Box 2316 Princeton NJ 08543-2316

SCHROEDL, BRIAN L., optometry; b. Jefferson, Wis., June 11, 1960; s. Donald L. and Germaine L. Schroedl. BS in Bacteriology, U. Wis., 1982; OD, Ill. Coll. Optometry, 1987. Clin. fellow Ill. Eye Inst., Chgo., 1987-88, asst. prof., 1988-90; staff optometrist Lenscrafters, Madison, Wis., 1990-96; pvt. practice Monona, Wis., 1994—. Fellow Ill. Coll. Optometry, Chgo., 1988. Republican. Roman Catholic. Office: 4503 Monona Dr Monona WI 53716

SCHROER, RICHARD ALLEN, biochemist; b. Celina, Ohio, July 10, 1944; s. Clarence Eldo and Esther W. (Tostrick) S.; m. Patricia Ann Trippet, Feb. 26, 1972 (div. Mar. 1990); children: Michael Allen, Arthur Warren. BS, Kent (Ohio) State U., 1966, PhD, 1970. Postdoctoral fellow U. Calif., Irvine, 1970-73; dir. biology dept. Nelson R&D, Irvine, 1973-74; sr. rsch. scientist Am. Cyanamid Co., Pearl River, N.Y., 1975-76, group leader clin. pathology, 1976-88, mgr. clin. pathology, 1989-94; sr. clin. rsch. orgn. monitor Wyeth-Ayerst Rsch., Pearl River, 1995—. Patentee in field; contbr. articles to profl. jours. Kent State U. fellow, 1969, NIH fellow, 1971-73. Mem. Assn. for Clin. Chemistry (chmn. div. animal clin. chemistry 1990-91). Office: Wyeth-Ayerst Rsch N Middletown Rd Pearl River NY 10965

SCHRUMPF, ROBYN LYNN, dentist; b. San Francisco, July 15, 1959; d. Walter Fred and Donna De Ella (Rogelstad) S. BS, U. Calif., Davis, 1981; DDS, Creighton U., 1985; cert. gen. practice residency, VA Med. Ctr., Palo Alto, Calif., 1986. With dental staff VA Med. Ctr., Palo Alto, 1985-86; with dental staff VA Med. Ctr., Menlo Park, Calif., 1985-86, respite team cons. dentist, 1986; assoc. Milpitas (Calif.) Dental Ctr., 1987—, Sunnyvale (Calif.) Dental Group, 1987-89; pvt. practice Sunnyvale, 1989—; dir. dentistry Idylwood Care Ctr., Sunnyvale, Calif., 1991—; dentist Macy (Nebr.) Indian Reservation, 1984, Spinal Cord Injury Ctr., Palo Alto, 1985-86, Blind Rehab. Ctr., Palo Alto, 1985-86; instr. preventive dental care Girl Scouts U.S., Sunnyvale, 1987. Regents scholar U. Calif., Davis, 1977-78, Albert Bijou Meml. scholar U. Calif., Davis, 1978-79; Lonney White scholar Creighton U., 1984. Mem. ADA, Am. Soc. Dentistry for Children (pres. Creighton U. chpt. 1982-85, merit award 1985), Calif. Dental Assn., Calif. Soc. Dentistry for Children, Calif. Scholarship Fedn. (pres. 1977), U.S. Gymnastics Fedn., Omicron Kappa Upsilon. Lutheran

SCHTEINGART, DAVID EDUARDO, internist; b. Buenos Aires, Oct. 17, 1930; came to U.S., 1957; s. Mario and Flora (Garfunkel) S.; m. Monica Naomi Starkman, July 3, 1960; children: Miriam, Judith, M. Daniel. MD, U. Buenos Aires, 1955. Diplomate Am. Bd. Internal Medicine. Fellow Mt. Sinai Hosp., N.Y.C., 1957-58, Maimonides Hosp., Bklyn., 1958-59; fellow U. Mich., Ann Arbor, 1959-62, instr., 1962-63, asst. prof., 1963-68, assoc. prof., 1968-72, prof., 1972—. Contbr. articles to profl. jours., books. Pres. Beth Israel Congregation, Ann Arbor, 1974-79, Hebrew Day Sch., Ann Arbor, 1984-86, Jewish Fedn. Washtenaw County, Ann Arbor. Recipient rsch. grants NIH, Bethesda, Md., 1985—. Fellow Am. Coll. Physicians; mem. Endocrine Soc., N.Y. Acad. Scis., Am. Soc. Clin. Nutrition, Cen. Soc. Clin. Rsch., Am. Fedn. Clin. Rsch. Jewish. Office: U Mich Med Sch 1150 W Medical Center Dr Ann Arbor MI 48109-0726

SCHUBERT, ESTHER VIRGINIA, psychiatrist, physician; b. Glendale, Calif., Mar. 29, 1945; d. William Everett and Katherine (McCoy) S.; m. David A. Chambers, Jan. 15, 1971; children: Daniel, John, Tony, Jeff. AB, Asbury Coll., 1966; MD, Ind. U., 1970; FACEP, Am. Coll. Emergency Physicians, Dallas, 1981; FAAFP, Am. Acad. Family Practice, Kansas City, Mo., 1990; postgrad., Ind. U., 1992-95. Diplomate Am. Bd. Emergency Medicine, Am. Bd. Family Practice, Am. Bd. Psychiatry and Neurology. Family practice Indpls., 1972-73; pvt. practice emergency medicine Ind., Republic of China, 1973-92; pvt. practice psychiatry, cons. for missions Anderson, Ind., Republic of China, 1989—; resident in psychiatry, 1992-95; clin. asst. prof. psychiatry Ind. U., 1995—; cons. physician Ctr. for Mental Health, Anderson, 1989-92. Mem. Youth Task Force, New Castle, Ind.,

1977, Rape Crisis Coun., New Castle, 1975, Child Abuse Panel, New Castle, 1977; bd. dirs. Christian & Missionary Alliance Ch., New Castle, 1988-92. Named one of Outstanding Young Women of Am., 1975, Mother of Yr., Jaycees, Middletown, Ind., 1977. Fellow Am. Psychiat. Assn., Am. Acad. Family Practice, Am. Coll. Emergency Physicians (bd. dirs. Ind. chpt. 1976-82), Christian Med. and Dental Soc. Home and Office: 2239 N Cadiz Pike New Castle IN 47362-9743

SCHUBERT, GUENTHER ERICH, pathologist; b. Mosul, Iraq, Aug. 17, 1930; s. Erich Waldemar and Martha Camilla (Zschitzschmann) S.; m. Gisela Schultz, June 13, 1959; children: Frank, Marion, Dirk. MD, University, Heidelberg, Germany, 1957; pvt. docent in pathology, University, Tuebingen, Germany, 1966. Asst. med. dir. University Tuebingen, Fed. Republic of Germany, 1966-76; head Inst. Pathology, Wuppertal, Fed. Republic of Germany, 1976—; chair of pathology U. Witten-Herdecke, Fed. Republic of Germany, 1985—. Co-author: Coloratlas of Cytodiagnosis of the Prostate, 1975, Endoscopy of the Urinary Bladder, 1989; author: Textbook of Pathology, 1981, 87. Mem. Wissenschaftlicher Beirat, Bundesarztekammer, Bonn, Germany, 1976-85; pres. Medizinisch Naturwissenschaftliche Gesellschaft, Wuppertal, 1984-85, Onkologischer Schwerpunkt, Wuppertal, 1985-93, OSP Bergisch-Land, 1992-95, Bergische Arbeitsgemeinschaft fur Gastroenterologie, Wuppertal, 1987-88, 90-91, 94-95. Mem. Deutsche Gesellschaft fur Pathologie, Deutsche Gesellschaft fur Nephrologie, Deutsche Gesellschaft fur Urologie, Internat. Acad. of Pathology, Lions. Home: Am Anschlag 71, D-42113 Wuppertal 1, Germany Office: Inst of Pathology, Heusner Strasse 40, 42 283 Wuppertal 2, Germany

SCHUBERT, LEO GILBERT, clinical psychologist, educator; b. Morgantown, W.Va., July 30, 1954; s. Oscar Edmund and Phoebe Cary (Ryan) S. BA in Psychology, W.Va. U., 1976, MA in Speech Communication, 1978; PhD in Psychology, U.S. Internat. U., 1985. Cert. clin. psychologist Bd. Medicine, Va. Clin. intern Univ. Counseling Ctr. U. Va., Charlottesville, 1986-87, postdoctoral clin. resident, 1987-88; asst. prof. Va. Poly. Inst. and State U., Blacksburg, 1988-95; pre-profl. advisor Pre-Med. Com., Blacksburg, 1990-91. Bd. dirs. Profl. Singles, Blacksburg, 1990-94. Mem. Internat. Platform Assn., Nat. Space Soc., Phi Beta Kappa, Phi Kappa Phi. *Died Jan. 4, 1995.*

SCHUBERT, WILLIAM KUENNETH, hospital medical center executive; b. Cin., July 12, 1926; s. Wilfred Schubert and Amanda Kuenneth; m. Mary Jane Pamperin, June 5, 1948; children: Carol, Joanne, Barbara, Nancy. BS, U. Cin., 1949, MD, 1952. Diplomate Am. Bd. Pediatrics. Pvt. practice specializing in pediatrics Cin., 1956-63; dir. clin. research ctr. Children's Hosp. Med. Ctr., Cin., 1963-76; dir. div. gastroenterology Children's Hosp., Cin., 1968-79; prof. pediatrics U. Cin., 1969—, assoc. sr. v.p. for children's hosp. affairs Coll. Medicine, 1993—; chief of staff Children's Hosp. Med. Ctr., Cin., 1972-88; chmn. dept. pediatrics U. Cin., 1979-93; dir. Children's Hosp. Rsch. Found., Cin., 1979-93; pres., CEO Children's Hosp. Med. Ctr., Cin., 1983—; v.p. Ohio Solid Organ Transplant Consortium, Columbus, 1986-87, pres., 1987-88, alt. trustee, 1988—; regional bd. dirs. Ameritrust Corp., 1988-91; trustee med. rsch. James N. Gamble Inst., Cin., 1989-95. Contbr. over 100 articles to profl. jours. Trustee Greater Cin. Hosp. Coun., 1986—, Assn. of Ohio Children's Hosp., Columbus, 1986—, The Springer Sch., Cin., 1994—; chmn. Greater Cin. Hosp. Coun., 1989; co-chmn. Citizen's Com. for Med. Ctr., Cin., 1980-81; chmn. Hosp. Divsn. 1988 Fine Arts Fund, Cin., 1987; hon. trustee Babies' Milk Fund, Children's and Prenatal Clinics, Cin., 1994—. Fellow Am. Acad. Pediatrics; mem. Am. Pediatric Soc. (councillor 1986-93), Soc. Pediatric Research, Assn. Med. Sch. Pediatric Dept. Chmn., Cin. Acad. Medicine, AMA, Midwestern Soc. for Pediatric Research, Am. Assn. for Study of Liver Diseases, Central Soc. Clin. Research, Am. Gastroenterological Assn., N.Am. Soc. Pediatric Gastroenterology, Nat. Reye's Syndrome Found. (med. dir. 1976-87), Internat. Assn. Study Liver Diseases. Club: Queen City (Cin.). Office: Children's Hosp Med Ctr 3333 Burnet Ave Cincinnati OH 45229-3026

SCHUCH, CYNTHIA SILLECK, nurse; b. Oceanside, N.Y., Oct. 31, 1956. AAS, SUNY, Morrisville, 1976; cert. in Cardiovascular Nursing, Meth. Hosp., Houston, 1978; BS in Nursing, U. Ala., 1984, MS in Nursing, 1985. RN, N.Y., Va., Ala., Calif. Staff nurse, relief charge nurse, postoperative surgical nurse Meth. Hosp., Houston, 1976-77, staff nurse ICU, 1977-78, cardiovascular nurse specialist, 1978-79; staff nurse ICU U. Va. Hosp., Charlottesville, 1979; staff nurse, relief charge nurse U. Ala. Hosp., Birmingham, 1979-80, scrub nurse, circulating nurse, 1980-83, staff nurse CICU, 1983-84, charge nurse CICU, 1984-86; staff nurse CICU Sutter Meml. Hosp., Sacramento, 1986-89; clin. specialist cardiac surgery unit Sutter Meml. Hosp., 1989—. Vol. instr. cardiac maintenance YMCA Shades Valley Br., Birmingham, 1984; instr. family night CPR, Sacramento, 1987—, BCLS instr., 1986—, ACLS instr., 1988—. Mem. Am. Assn. Critical Care Nurses (Houston-Gulf chpt. 1976-79, Greater Birmingham chpt. 1985-86, Sacramento chpt. 1986—), Phi Theta Kappa, Phi Kappa Phi, Sigma Theta Tau.

SCHUELLEIN, ROBERT JOSEPH, health science administrator, consultant; b. N.Y.C., Feb. 22, 1920; s. Jacob John and Wilma (Metzner) S.; m. Wilma Linkins, June 12, 1970. BS, U. Dayton, 1944; MS, U. Pitts., 1946, PhD, 1956; postdoctoral, Columbia U., 1956-57. Assoc. prof. Univ. Dayton, Ohio, 1953-64; health scientist adminstr. Nat. Heart and Lung Inst., Bethesda, Md., 1964-66; dir. grants assoc. program NIH, Bethesda, 1966-67; chief periodontal and soft tissues diseases program Nat. Inst. Dental Rsch., Bethesda, 1967-73, spl. asst. for man power rsch., 1973-83, rsch. cons., 1983—; dir. McTye Inc., Fairfax, Va., 1964-66. Author: Genetics, 1955, Radiation Lab Manual, 1960, Genetics Lab Manual, 1963. Mem. Am. Genetics Soc., Human Genetics Soc., Sigma Xi, Phi Sigma (v.p. 1965). Democrat. Roman Catholic. Home: 5626 Lamar Rd Bethesda MD 20816-1350 Office: NIDR/DER/PO Natcher Bldg Rm 43AN33A 45 Center Dr MSC 6402 Bethesda MD 20892-6402

SCHUELLER, WILLIAM ALAN, dermatologist; b. Xenia, Ohio, Apr. 14, 1939; s. John Waldo and Jeanne Evelyn (Tipton) S.; m. Joyce Anne Smith, June 22, 1963; children: Robert Alan, Thomas Alan. BA, Ohio State U., 1961; MD, Case Western Reserve U., 1966. Diplomate Am. Bd. Dermatology. Intern Charleston (S.C.) Naval Hosp., 1966-67; resident in dermatology San Diego Regional Med. Ctr., 1969-72; commd. ensign U.S. Navy, 1965; advanced through grades to comdr. U.S. Navy, various, U.S., 1975; resigned U.S. Navy, 1975; pvt. practice in dermatology Johnson City, Tenn., 1976—; active staff Johnson City Med. Ctr., 1976—; cons. staff North Side Hosp., Johnson, City, Tenn. Fellow Am. Acad. Dermatology; mem. AMA, So. Med. Assn., Tenn. Med. Assn., Soc. Investigative Dermatology. Mem. Unitarian Ch. Office: 1611 W Market St Johnson City TN 37604

SCHUH, FREDRIC DEGRAW, plastic surgeon; b. Hackensack, N.J., Sept. 9, 1934; s. Frederick C. and Edna May Schuh; m. Sara Elizabeth Daley, June 14, 1958; children: Alex, Jonathan, Kate, Daniel, Elizabeth. BS, Trinity Coll., Hartford, Conn., 1956; MD, Columbia U., 1960. Lic. physician, S.C. Intern St. Luke's Hosp., N.Y.C., 1960-61, gen. surgery resident, 1961-65; plastic surgery resident Presbyn. Hosp., N.Y.C., 1967-69; asst. in surgery Columbia U., N.Y.C., 1964-65, asst. in plastic surgery, 1967-68, instr. plastic surgery, 1968-69; pvt. practice plastic surgery Charleston, S.C., 1974—; asst. prof. plastic surgery Med. U. S.C., Charleston, 1969-74, asst. clin. prof. surgery, 1974—. Contbr. articles to profl. jours. Elder Presbyn. Ch., Charleston, 1989—. Capt. U.S. Army, 1965-67. Decorated Army Commendation medal. Mem. ACS, Am. Soc. Plastic and Reconstructive Surgeons, Southeastern Soc. Plastic and Reconstructive Surgeons, Lipoplasty Soc. N.Am., Med. Soc. S.C., Charleston County Med. Soc. Republican. Home: 945 Shetland Ct Mount Pleasant SC 29464 Office: 65 Gadsden St Charleston SC 29401

SCHUHMACHER, JOHN FRANKLIN, physician; b. Muskogee, Okla., Feb. 5, 1941; s. Franklin Jacob and Zipporsab Elizabeth (Buh) S.; m. Lesley Carol Creel, Mar. 6, 1973; children: John Collins, John Blake. BS, Northwestern Okla. State U., 1962; MD, U. Okla., 1966. Diplomate Am. Bd. Neurol. Surgery. Intern Sch. Medicine U. Okla., 1966-67, resident, 1967-68; pvt. practice, 1974—. Lt. col. USN, 1968-70. Fellow ACS; mem. Am. Assn. Neurol. Surgeons, Congress Neurol. Surgeons. Republican. Presbyterian.

SCHUKER, ELEANOR SHEILA, psychiatrist, educator; b. N.Y.C., Jan. 3, 1941; d. Louis Aaron and Millicent (Milchman) S.; m. Alan Melowsky, Dec. 26, 1974; 1 child, Julie Millicent. BA, Swarthmore Coll., 1961; MD, Columbia U., 1965; cert. in psychoanalytic medicine, Columbia U. Ctr. for Psychoanalytic Training and Rsch., 1975. Diplomate Am. Bd. Psychiatry and Neurology. Intern Mt. Sinai Hosp., N.Y.C., 1965-66; resident in psychiatry N.Y. State Psychiat. Inst., Columbia U., N.Y.C., 1966-69; attending psychiatrist Columbia U. Health Svc., N.Y.C., 1969-90; co-dir. psychiat. emergency svcs. St. Luke's Hosp., N.Y.C., 1970-72, founder, dir. rape intervention program, 1977-80, assoc. attending psychiatrist, 1978—; collaborating psychoanalyst Columbia U. Psychoanalytic Ctr., N.Y.C., 1975-85, training and supervising analyst, 1985—; asst. clin. prof. psychiatry Columbia U., 1980-90, assoc. clin. prof. psychiatry, 1990—; cons. Women's Counseling Project, N.Y.C., 1974-89. Editor: (with Nadine Levinson) Female Psychology: An Annotated Psychoanalytic Bibliography, 1991; contbr. articles to profl. jours. Fellow Am. Psychiat. Assn.; mem. Am. Psychoanalytic Assn. (cert., alt. del. to exec. coun. 1986-93), Assn. for Psychoanalytic Medicine (pres. 1995—), Alumni Assn. Columbia Psychoanalytic Ctr. (pres. 1978-80). Office: 150 W End Ave Apt 26A New York NY 10023-5743

SCHUL, BILL DEAN, psychological administrator, author; b. Winfield, Kans., Mar. 16, 1928; s. Fred M. and Martha Mildred (Miles) S.; B.A., Southwestern Coll., 1952; M.A., U. Denver, 1954; Ph.D., Am. Internat. U., 1977; m. Virginia Louise Duboise, Aug. 3, 1952; children—Robert Dean, Deva Elizabeth. Reporter and columnist Augusta (Kans.) Daily Gazette, 1954-58, Wichita (Kans.) Eagle-Beacon, 1958-61; Kans. youth dir. under auspices of Kans. Atty. Gen., 1961-65; Kans. state dir. Seventh Step Found., Topeka, 1965-66; mem. staff Dept. Preventive Psychiatry, Menninger Found., Topeka, Kans., 1966-71; dir. cons. Ctr. Improvement Human Functioning, Wichita, 1975—; psychologist Ctr. for Human Devel., Wichita, Kans. Mng. editor: The Register, Oxford, Kans., 1988—; author: (with Edward Greenwood) Mental Health in Kansas Schools, 1965; Let Me Do This Thing, 1969; (with Bill Larson) Hear Me, Barabbas, 1969; How to Be An Effective Group Leader, 1975; The Secret Power of Pyramids, 1975; (with Ed Pettit) The Psychic Power of Pyramids, 1976, Pyramids: The Second Reality, 1979; The Psychic Power of Animals, 1977; Psychic Frontiers of Medicine, 1977, Animal Immortality, 1990, Life Song, 1995. Bd. dirs. Recreation Commn., Topeka, United Funds, Topeka, Adamic Inst., Trees for Life; v.p. Pegasus Way; pres. Intraface Corp., 1989—; mem. adv. bd. Clayton U. Served with USN, 1945-46. Recipient John H. McGinnis Meml. award for Nonfiction, 1972, Am. Freedom Found. award, 1966, Spl. Appreciation award Kans. State Penitentiary, 1967. Mem. Acad. of Parapsychology and Medicine, Kans. Council for Children and Youth (pres. 1965-66), Assn. for Strenghtening the Higher Realities and Aspirations of Man (pres. 1970-71), Smithsonian Inst., Lions (pres. 1957). Address: RR 3 Winfield KS 67156-9803

SCHULBERG, HERBERT CHARLES, psychologist; b. N.Y.C., Feb. 10, 1934; s. Philip and Sarah (Bookin) S.; m. Phyllis Gitelman, June 23, 1957; children: Mark Ira, Michelle Tobi. BA, Yeshiva Coll., 1955; PhD, Columbia U., 1960; MS, Harvard U., 1963. Prof. of psychiatry, psychology and medicine Sch. Medicine U. Pitts., 1976—; vis. scientist NIMH, Rockville, Md., 1986. Office: U Pitts 3811 Ohara St Pittsburgh PA 15213-2593

SCHULDER, MICHAEL, neurosurgery educator; b. Bklyn., Jan. 10, 1957; s. Paul and Shirley (Kestenbaum) S.; m. Lu Steinberg, Nov. 1, 1984; children: Ilana, Talia. BA, Columbia U., 1978, MD, 1982. Diplomate Am. Bd. Neurosurgery. Resident in neurosurgery Yeshiva U. Albert Einstein Coll. Medicine, Bronx, N.Y., 1982-88; asst. prof. neurosurgery N.J. Med. Sch., Newark, 1988—. Contbg. author: Principles of Spinal Surgery, 1995; contbr. articles to med. jours. Mem. Am. Assn. Neurol. Surgeons, Congress Neurol. Surgeons, N.Am. Skull Base Soc., Am. Spinal Injury Assn., N.J. Neurosurg. Soc. (ednl. chmn. 1995—), Med. History Soc. N.J. Office: NJ Med Sch 90 Bergen St Newark NJ 07103

SCHULER, BURTON SILVERMAN, podiatrist; b. N.Y.C., Aug. 4, 1950; s. Irving and Sylvia (Silverman) S.; m. Caroline Davis, Oct. 1989. D Podiatric Medicine, N.Y. Coll. Podiatric Medicine, 1975. Diplomate Nat. Bd. Podiatry Examiners. Pvt. practice Alamogordo, N.Mex., 1975-84, Panama City, Fla., 1984—; dir. Podiatric Pain Mgmt. Ctr.; expert in podiatric malpractice cases. Author: Podiatric Malpractice, 1981, The Agony of De-Feet, A Podiatrist Guide to Foot Care, 1982; contbr. to Collier's Ency., also numerous articles to profl. publs. Active March of Dimes, 1971—; mem. exec. com. Dems. Bay County, Fla.; chmn. 1st congl. dist. com. Fla. Dem. Com. Fellow Acad. Ambulatory Foot Surgery, Am. Acad. Pain Mgmt. (diplomate), Am. Podiatric Circulatory Soc. Office: The Schuler Profl Bldg 2401 W 15th St Panama City FL 32401-1567

SCHULER, JOHN LOUIS, orthodontist; b. Evergreen Park, Ill., Jan. 20, 1957; m. Kathleen Ann Henson, Aug. 23, 1986; children: Ryan, Lauren. BS, No. Ill. U., 1979; DDS, Loyola U., Chgo., 1983; MS, U. Louisville, 1993. Cert. specialist in orthodontics, Ill. Resident in orthodontics U. Louisville, 1991-93; pvt. practice orthodontics Peoria, Ill., 1993—; asst. prof. orthodontics U. Louisville, 1993—. Contbr. articles to profl. jours. Served to maj. USAF, 1983-90. Decorated Air Force Commendation medal. Mem. Peoria Dist. Dental Soc. (dir. pub. rels. 1995-96, bd. govs. 1996—, program chair 1996—), Peoria Rotary North. Republican. Roman Catholic. Office: Orthodontics Ltd 7227 N University Peoria IL 61614

SCHULLER, DAVID EDWARD, cancer center administrator, otolaryngology; b. Cleve., Oct. 20, 1944; m. Carole Ann Hauss, June 24, 1967; children: Rebecca, Michael. BA, Rutgers U., 1966; MD cum laude, Ohio State U., 1970. Diplomate Am. Bd. Otolaryngology 1975. Intern dept. surgery U. Hosps. Cleve., 1970-71; resident dept. otolaryngology Ohio State U., Columbus, 1971-72; resident dept. surgery U. Hosps. Cleve., 1972-73; fellow head and neck surgery Pack Med. Found. with John Conley, N.Y.C., 1973; resident dept. otolaryngology Ohio State U. Hosps., Columbus, 1973-75; fellow head and neck oncology and facial plastic and reconstructive surgery U. Iowa, Iowa City, 1975-76; from clin. instr. to prof. and chmn. dept. otolaryngology The Ohio State U., Columbus, 1971—; dir. Compehensive Cancer Ctr. & Arthur G. James Cancer Hosp. and Rsch. Inst., Columbus, 1988—; prof. Sch. Allied Med. Professions The Ohio State U., 1990—; mem., chmn. various coms. Ohio State U. Hosps. and Coll. Medicine, 1976—; dir. CCC head and neck oncology program Ohio State U., 1977—, hosps. physician flr. coord. 10th flr., 1977-82, dir. laser-microsurgery teaching and rsch. lab., 1987-88; mem. various coms. Grant Hosp., 1980-84; mem. Accreditation Coun. for the Grad. Med. Edn. Residency Review Com. for Otolaryngology, 1985—, chmn., 1988—; vis. prof., lectr. numerous instns. Author: (books) (with others) Otolaryngology-Head and Neck Surgery-4 Vols., 1986, Textbook of Otolaryngology-7th Edit., 1988, Otolaryngology-Head and Neck Surgery-Update I, 1988, Musculocutaneous Flaps in Head and Neck Reconstructive Surgery, 1989, Otolaryngology-Head and Neck Surgery Update II, 1990, Otorinolaringologia-Cirugia de Cabeza y Culleo, 1991, Otolaryngology-Head and Neck Surgery-4 Vols., 1992; contbr. chpts. to books and articles to profl. jours.; mem. editorial bd. New Horizons in Otolaryngology/Head and Neck Surgery, 1982-87, The Laryngoscope, 1986—, Am. Jour. Otolaryngology, 1988—, Facial Plastic Surgery Internat. Quar. Monographs, 1992—; mem. rev. bd. Jour. Head and Neck Surgery, 1985—; mem. editorial rev. bd. Otolaryngology-Head and Neck Surgery, 1990—; reviewer New Eng. Jour Medicine, 1992—. Trustee Ohio Cancer Found., 1988—; dir. Am. Bd. Otolaryngology, 1988—. Recipient Cert. of Appreciation, Scioto Meml. Hosp., 1982, Edmund Prince Fowler award Triological Soc., 1984; Henry Rutgers scholar Rutgers U., 1965-66; grantee Nat. Cancer Inst., 1980-88, 90—, Bremer Found., 1982-83, 87-88, Photomedica Inc., 1986-89, Upjohn Co., 1986-90, others. Mem. AMA (mem. rev. panel Archives of Otolaryngology-Head and Neck Surgery 1984—), Am. Cancer Soc. (mem. instl. grant rev. com. 1980—, chmn. rehab. com. Franklin County unit 1981-82, mem. profl. edn. com. 1981—, chmn. 1982-85, v.p. 1982-83, pres. 1986, 87, trustee Ohio divsn. 1988—), Am. Assn. Cosmetic Surgeons, Am. Acad. Facial Plastic and Reconstructive Surgery (mem. rsch. com. 1977-82, chmn. residency rels. com. 1982-85, mem. program com. 1982-85, v.p. mid. sect. 1983-87, chmn. by-laws com. 1988—, treas. 1988—, Honor award 1989), Am. Coll. Surgeons, Am. Cleft Palate Assn., Assn. Am. Cancer Insts., Am. Soc. Head and Neck Injury, Am. Acad. Otolaryngology Head and Neck Surgery (mem. editorial bd. self-instructional package program 1982—, del. bd. govs. 1982-87, Honor award 1983), Am. Soc. Laser Medicine and Surgery, Am. Laryngological, Rhinological, Otological Soc., Inc., Am. Laryngological Assn., Am. Soc. Clin. Oncology (mem. program com. 1989—), Am. Assn. Cancer Researchers, Am. Soc. Head and Neck Surgery (mem. coun. 1983-86, chmn. scholastic and fellowship award com. 1984-86, mem. profl. rels. and pub. edn. com. 1989—), Southwest Oncology Group (chmn. head and neck com. 1983—), Collegium ORLAS, Ohio State Med. Assn. (pres. sect. otolaryngology 1987—), Ohio Soc. Otolaryngology (pres. 1985, 86, 87), Acad. Medicine of Columbus and Franklin County, Columbus E.E.N.T. Soc., Franklin County Acad. Medicine (mem. profl. rels. com. 1982—), Head an. 1984-86, chmn. 1986-89), Assn. Rsch. Otolaryngology, Ohio State U. Med. Alumni Soc. (class rep. 1980—, v.p. 1987-88, pres. 1989-90), Med. Forum, Med. Review Club, Order of Hippocrates (charter), Alpha Omega Alpha. Office: 456 W 10th Ave Columbus OH 43210-1240 also: Ohio State Univ Comp Cancer Ctr 300 W 10th Ave Columbus OH 43210-1240

SCHULLER, EDWIN ARTHUR, osteopathic physician; b. Darby, Pa., Nov. 12, 1950; s. Edwin Arthur and Rita Mary (McCully) S.; m. Elizabeth Anne Hellmig, Apr. 3, 1971 (div. Jan. 1985); children: Elizabeth Adrienne, Alexandra Lynn, Jamie Christine; m. Peggy L. Smythe; stepchildren: Barry V. Krewson, Daniel L. Krewson. BS in Biology, Villanova U., 1972; DO, Phila. Coll. Osteo. Medicine, 1976. Diplomate Nat. Bd. Examiners in Osteo. Medicine and Surgery, Am. Bd. Emergency Medicine, Am. Bd. Family Practice, Am. Bd. Addiction Medicine; cert. sr. examiner in disability and in vocat. rehab., Pa. Rotating intern Zieger-Botsford Osteo. Hosps., Farmington Hills, Mich., 1976-77, staff physician, emergency medicine physician, 1977-80; resident in ob-gyn. BiCounty Gen. Hosp., Warren, Mich., 1976-77, St. Joseph Mercy Hosp., Pontiac, Mich., 1976-77; staff physician, adminstr. Women's and Crisis Clinic, Common Ground, Inc., Birmingham, Mich., 1978-79; dir. emergency svcs. Zieger Osteo. Hosp., Detroit, 1979; pvt. practice family practice, emergency, addiction medicine Phila., 1980—; cons. in emergency medicine, family practice and mgmt., Detroit, 1977-81; mem. med. bd. for family practice, spinal injuries and substance abuse Radnor Twp. Sch. Dist., 1995—; prin. investigator rsch. study Pfizer, Inc., 1993-94, Glaxo, Inc., 1993; asst. clin. prof. emergency medicine Mich. State U., 1979-80; instr. Widener U. Sch. Law, 1993—; chief med. cons. for addiction medicine Pa. Dental Assn., 1989-90. Author: (poetry) Beyond the Wind...Ahead of the Storm, 1979. Bd. dirs. Common Ground, Inc., Mich., 1979. With M.C., USAF, 1973-80. Recipient T. J. Liljestrand Tchg. award Met. Hosp., 1981, Clin. Rsch. award Boehringer-Ingelheim Co., 1984. Mem. AMA, Pa. Med. Soc., Pa. Osteo. Med. Assn., Phila. County Med. Soc., Am. Osteo. Coll. of Family Practitioners, Am. Soc. Addiction Medicine, Am. Coll. Profl. Execs., Phi Sigma Gamma. Office: Brookhaven Med Ctr 4000 Edgmont Ave Brookhaven PA 19015

SCHULMAN, BRIAN MARTIN, psychiatrist; b. N.Y.C., Aug. 15, 1946; s. Leon and Gertrude (Elkin) S.; m. Cookie Schulman; children: Beth, Lisa, Eric. BA with distinction, George Washington U., 1968, MD, 1971. Intern N.Y. Med. Coll./Met. Hosp., N.Y.C., 1971-72; resident Payne Whitney Clinic/N.Y. Hosp./Cornell Med. Ctr., N.Y.C., 1972-75; pres. Occupational Psychiatry, Inc., Bethesda, Md., 1983—; asst. clin. prof. psychiatry, Georgetown U., Washington, 1975-92. Author: Pain Control, 1982. Lt. comdr. USN, 1975-77. Mem. Am. Coll. Occupl. Medicine, Acad. Orgnl. Occupl. Psychiatry, Montgomery County Med. Soc. Office: 4400 E West Hwy Bethesda MD 20814-4524

SCHULMAN, CHARLES IRWIN, osteopath; b. S.I., N.Y., Feb. 2, 1932; s. Samuel H. and Pauline (Tulipin) S.; m. Norma Janeau, June, 1954 (div. 1979); children: Sharan Levine, David. BS in Pharmacy, Bklyn. Coll. Pharmacy, 1953; DO, Chgo. Coll. Osteo., 1957. Diplomate Am. Osteopathic Bd. Int. Medicine, 1964. Intern Detroit Osteopath Hosp., 1957-58, resident in internal medicine, 1958-61; pvt. practice internal medicine Detroit, 1961-75, West Palm Beach, Fla., 1975—. Fellow Am. Coll. Osteo. Internists. Office: 2151 45th St #109 West Palm Beach FL 33407

SCHULMAN, JOSEPH DANIEL, physician, medical geneticist, executive, reproductive biologist, educator; b. Bklyn., Dec. 20, 1941; s. Max and Miriam (Grossman) S.; m. Dixie A. King; children: Erica N., Julie K. B.A., Bklyn. Coll., 1961; M.D., Harvard U., 1966. Diplomate Am. Bd. Pediatrics, Am. Bd. Ob-Gyn, Am. Bd. Med. Genetics. Intern, resident in pediatrics Mass. Gen. Hosp., Boston, 1966-68; clin. assoc. Nat. Inst. Arthritis and Metabolic Diseases, 1968-70; resident in obstetrics and gynecology and fellow in pediatrics N.Y. Hosp.-Cornell Med. Center, 1970-73; Gilbert and Nat. Found. fellow Cambridge (Eng.) U., 1973-74; head sect. human biochem. genetics Nat. Inst. Child Health and Human Devel., NIH, Bethesda, Md., 1974-83; dir. med. genetics program NIH, Bethesda, Md., 1979-1983; prof. ob/gyn, pediatrics, and genetics George Washington U., 1983-84; dir., CEO Genetics & IVF Inst., Fairfax, Va., 1984—; chmn. Genetics & IVF, Inc., Bethesda, Md., 1988—; prof. human genetics, pediatrics, obstetrics and gynecology Med. Coll. Va., 1984—; with dept. ob-gyn Fairfax Hosp., 1984—; advisor to numerous govt. and private agys. Author 3 books; contbr. numerous articles to med. jours.; editorial bd. Molecular Human Reproduction, 1995—. Served with USPHS, 1968-70, 74-83. Fellow Am. Coll. Obstetricians and Gynecologists; mem. Soc. Pediatric Research, Soc. Gynecologic Investigation, Am. Soc. Clin. Investigation, Am. Soc. Human Genetics, Am. Fertility Soc., Phi Beta Kappa, Sigma Xi. Clubs: Harvard, Cosmos. Office: 3020 Javier Rd Fairfax VA 22031-4627

SCHULMAN, LAWRENCE, orthopaedic surgeon; b. N.Y.C., July 1, 1937; s. Louis and Anna (Kabotsky) S.; m. Susan Brody, Aug. 29, 1965; children: Deborah Lynn, Stephanie Faye, Robert Marc. BS, CCNY, 1959; MD, SUNY, Bklyn., 1963. Diplomate Am. Bd. Orthopaedic Surgery. Intern Maimonides Hosp., Bklyn., 1963-64; resident orthopedics Hosp. for Joint Diseases, N.Y.C., 1966-70; sr. attending orthopedics, chief of orthopedics St. John's Riverside Hosp., Yonkers, N.Y., 1970—; pres. Schulman & Carton, M.D., P.C., Yonkers, 1972—. Capt. Med. Corps-U.S. Army, 1964-66, Korea. Fellow ACS, Am. Acad. Orthopedic Surgeons; mem. Am. Fracture Assn., Ea. Orthopedic Assn. Jewish. Office: Schulman & Carton MD, PC 984 N Broadway Yonkers NY 10701

SCHULMAN, MARTIN FRED, ophthalmologist; b. N.Y.C., Dec. 23, 1943; s. Samuel and Sylvia (Schwartz) S.; m. Susan Brotman, July 15, 1967; children: Robin, Andrew, Aimee. BA, NYU, 1964; PhD in Chemistry, Rutgers U., 1968; MD, George Washington U., 1976. Diplomate Am. Bd. Ophthalmology. Sr. applications chemist Varian Assocs., Springfield, N.J., 1969-72; postdoctoral rsch. fellow Fla. State U., Tallahassee, 1968-69; resident in medicine George Washington U., Washington, 1976-77; resident and chief resident in ophthalmology Mt. Sinai Sch. Medicine, N.Y.C., 1977-80; pvt. practice ophthalmology Hackensack, N.J., 1980—. Contbr. articles to profl. jours. Trustee Gimbel Multiple Sclerosis Clin. Care Ctr., Teaneck, N.J., 1985. Fellow ACS; mem. William Beaumont Med. Rsch. Hon. Soc., Sigma Xi. Office: 75 Essex St Hackensack NJ 07601-4036 also: 333 Old Hook Rd Westwood NJ 07675

SCHULMAN, MARTIN LEWIS, surgeon; b. Bklyn., July 16, 1933; s. Harold Schulman and Gertrude Feinstein Kantor; m. Malkah Baldinger, 1960 (div. 1987); children: Lee Gordon, Julie Sue, David Baldinger; m. Suzanne Margaret Schulman, July 22, 1987. BS, Union Coll., Schenectady, N.Y., 1954; MD, Albany (N.Y.) Med. Coll., 1957. Diplomate Am. Bd. Surgery, Am. Bd. Vasc. Surgery; lic. physician, N.Y., Fla., Calif. Intern Bronx Mcpl. Hosp. Ctr., 1957-58; asst. resident in gen. surgery L.I. Jewish Med. Ctr., New Hyde Park, N.Y., 1958-60, resident in gen. surgery, 1960-61; fellow in cardiovascular surgery Baylor Med. Coll., Houston, 1963-64; clin. asst. prof. surgery SUNY, Stony Brook, 1977, asst. attending in vascular surgery; cons. in vascular surgery VA Hosp., Northport, N.Y.; staff surgeon Little Neck (N.Y.) Cmty. Hosp.; exec. dir. The Deep Vein Found. Contbr. numerous articles to profl. jours.; presenter papers various assns., convs. With U.S. Army, 1961-63. Mem. Internat. Soc. Cardiovascular Surgery (N.Am. chpt.), Michael E. DeBakey Internat. Cardiovascular Soc., N.Y. State Med. Soc., Nassau County Med. Soc., Denton A. Cooley Cardiovascular Surg. Soc., Soc. for Clin. Vascular Surgery, N.Y. Soc. for Cardiovascular Surgery, Phlebology Soc. Am., European Soc. Cardiovascular Surgery, Internat. Union of Angiology, Ea. Vascular Soc., Am. Coll. Angiology, N.Am. Phlebology Soc. Office: 29 Barstow Rd Great Neck NY 11021

SCHULMAN, PAUL STUART, radiologist; b. Buffalo, Mar. 1, 1943; s. Nathan Charles and Beatrice Estelle (Steinberg) S.; m. Suzanne Karen Cherry, Aug. 15, 1965; children: Jennifer Amy, Todd William. BA, SUNY, 1964, MD, 1968. Diplomate Am. Bd. Radiology, Am. Bd. Nuclear Medicine. Intern Rochester (N.Y.) Gen. Hosp., 1968-69; resident in radiology U. Colo., Denver, 1971-74; med. officer Brooke Army Med. Ctr., San Antonio, 1969-71; radiologist Scripps Clinic, La Jolla, Calif., 1974-75; pvt. practice radiology Chula Vista, Calif., 1975-94, San Diego, 1995—; v.p. San Diego Diagnostic Radiology Med. Group Inc. Fellow Am. Coll. Radiology; mem. Calif. Radiol. Soc., Alpha Omega Alpha. Office: San Diego Radiology Group 7930 Frost St Ste 301 San Diego CA 92123

SCHULTES, LORAIN MEDBURY, microbiologist, consultant; b. Bainbridge, N.Y., July 15, 1936; s. Dwight King and Cynthia Aurelia (Medbury) S.; m. Carole Jean Dolesh, Dec. 31, 1958 (dec. July 27, 1989); children: Stanley, Kurt, Eve, Joel, Katrina. BS, Cornell U., 1963; MS, N.C. State U., 1968, PhD, 1969. Rsch. lab. technician Eaton Labs., Norwich, N.Y., 1955-59; sanitary chemist Tompkins County Health Dept., Ithaca, N.Y., 1963-65; sci. assoc. St. Luke's Pathology Assocs., Milw., 1969-75; prin. L.M. Schultes, PhD, Columbus, Ind., 1975—; asst. clin. prof. Med. Coll. of Wis., Milw., 1970-75; lectr. in microbiology Ind. U. Purdue U. Ind. Columbus Campus, 1982-87. Mem. Am. Soc. for Microbiology, South Ctrl. Assn. for Clin. Microbiology (dir. 1983-85), Elks Lodge, Moose Lodge (jr. gov. 1991-92, trustee 1993-96). Home: 213 Newsom Ave Columbus IN 47201-5171 Office: L M Schultes PhD 213 Newsom Ave Columbus IN 47201-5171

SCHULTZ, DONALD G., JR., nursing administrator, nursing educator; b. Peoria, Ill., Mar. 5, 1959; s. Donald G. and Louann (Logan) S.; m. Mary Draeger, May 25, 1991; 1 child, Elizabeth Anne. AA, Ill. Ctrl. Coll., 1982, AAS, 1984; BSN, Bradley U., 1993. Cert. trauma nurse specialist, emergency nurse, CPR instructor, ACLS instructor. Orderly Morton (Ill.) Healthcare, 1981-83; orderly Pekin (Ill.) Hosp., 1983-84, staff nurse, 1984-86, charge nurse, 1986—; clin. instr. in nursing Ill. Ctrl. Coll., East Peoria, 1993—. Mem. Emergency Nurses Assn., Bradley U. Hilltop Nursing Alumni Assn., Sigma Theta Tau Internat. Roman Catholic. Home: 105 Country Lade Dr Pekin IL 61554

SCHULTZ, GREGORY PAUL, health center official; b. Two Rivers, Wis., Nov. 16, 1961; s. Paul Gerald and Carol Jean (Steffel) S. BS in Health Info. Adminstrn., U. Wis., Milw., 1991; M Health Care Adminstrn., Cardinal Stritch Coll., Milw., 1996. Dir. med. records St. Camillus Health Ctr., Wauwatosa, Wis., 1990-96; with W. Tropicana Med. Ctr., Las Vegas, 1996—. Mem. Am. Health Info. Mgmt. Assn. (registered record administr.), Wis. Health Info. Mgmt. Assn. (long term care publs. team 1993—). Democrat. Roman Catholic. Office: W Tropicana Med Ctr 4845 S Rainbow Blvd Ste 401 Las Vegas NV 89103

SCHULTZ, JANE SCHWARTZ, health facility administrator; b. N.Y.C., July 28, 1932; d. Jacob and Helene (Rosenthal) Schwartz; m. Jerome Samson Schultz, Sept. 1, 1955; children: Daniel S., Judith Schultz Nyquist, Kathryn Schultz Hubbard. BA in Chemistry cum laude, CUNY, 1953; MSChemE, Columbia U., 1955; MS in Human Genetics, U. Mich., 1968, PhD, 1970. Rsch. scientist USDA Forest Products Lab., Madison, Wis., 1955-58; sci. tchr. Pearl River (N.Y.) High Sch., 1958-64; sr. rsch. investigator dept. immunohaematology U. Leiden, Holland, 1971-72; geneticist, prin. investigator VA Med. Ctr., Ann Arbor, Mich., 1972-83; asst. prof., then assoc. prof. dept. human genetics U. Mich., Ann Arbor, 1975-83; asst. dean curriculum, then asst. dean student affairs U. Mich. Med. Sch., Ann Arbor, 1979-83; chief genetics and transplantation biology br. Nat. Inst. Allergy and Infectious Diseases/NIH, Bethesda, Md., 1983-88; dir. rsch. adminstrn. health scis., assoc. prof. pathology U. Pitts., 1988-93, rsch. integrity officer, 1991-92; dir., CEO Biomation Ltd., Pitts., 1993—; rsch. assoc. chem engr. U. Pitts., 1993-94, regulatory affairs adminstr. Ctr. Biotech and Bioengring., 1994—; rsch. dir./exec. dir. Nat. Disease Rsch. Interchange, Phila., 1994—; chief divsn. program devel. and rev. VA, Washington, 1977-79; VA liaison rep. genetics study sect. NIH, Bethesda, 1973-77; com. mem. Fed. Interagy. Com. on Recombinant DNA Rsch., Bethesda, 1977-83; VA rep. nat. Insts. Gen. Med. Scis. Coun. /NIH, Bethesda, 1979-83; mem. Organ Tranplantation task force Med. Scis. Coun., NIH, Bethesda, 1985-86. Contbr. over 30 rsch. papers to peer-reviewed jours.; contbr. book revs. to profl. jours. Grantee NIH/Nat. Cancer Inst., 1975-78; recipient Pub. Health Svc. Spl. Achievement award NIAID, 1988. Mem. Am. Soc. Human Genetics, Genetics Soc. Am., Am. Assn. Immunologists, Am. Soc. Histocompatibility and Immunogenetics, Soc. Rsch. Adminstrs., Phi Beta Kappa. Office: Nat Disease Rsch Interch 1880 JFK Blvd Philadelphia PA 19103

SCHULTZ, KAREN ROSE, clinical social worker, author, publisher, speaker; b. Huntington, N.Y., June 16, 1958; d. Eugene Alfred and Laura Rose (Palazzolo) Squeri; m. Richard S. Schultz, Apr. 8, 1989. BA with honors, SUNY, Binghamton, 1980; MA, U. Chgo., 1982. Lic. clin. social worker, Ill. Unit dir., adminstr. Camp Algonquin, Ill., 1981; clin. social worker United Charities Chgo., 1982-86; social worker Hartgrove Hosp., Chgo., 1986-87; pvt. practice, Oak Brook, Ill., 1987—; trainer, speaker various groups, schs. and orgns., DuPage County, Ill., 1988-89; group leader Optifast Program, Oak Park and Aurora, Ill., 1989-90; instr. social work Morraine Valley C.C., Palos Hills, Ill., 1989-90; instr. eating disorders Coll. of Dupage, Glen Ellyn, Ill., 1990-92, mem. eating disorder com., 1989—, tchr. intuition and counseling, 1995—. Editor, contbg. author The River Within newsletter, 1989—. Com. mem. DuPage Consortium, 1987-89. Mem. NASW (registerd, diplomate), acad. Cert. Social Workers, Nat. Speakers Assn., Profl. Speakers Ill., Toastmasters Internat., Women Entrepreneurs DuPage. Office: 900 Jorie Blvd Ste 234 Oak Brook IL 60521-2230

SCHULTZ, K(ENNETH) DAVID, clinical psychologist; b. Mt. Pleasant, Iowa, June 19, 1949; s. Kenneth Darrell and Virginia (Rosa) S.; m. Deborah Boettger, Jan. 6, 1980; children: Sarah, Leah. BA, U. Mich., 1971; MS, Yale U., 1973, PhD, 1976. Lic. clin. psychologist, Conn. Psychotherapist Highland Heights, New Haven, 1971-73; psychologist assoc. VA Med. Ctr., West Haven, Conn., 1973-76; staff psychologist Waterbury (Conn.) Hosp. Health Ctr., 1976-85; dir. psychology Grand View Psychiat. Resource Ctr., Waterbury, 1985-90; psychologist Dept. Children and Youth Svcs., Newtown, Conn., 1990-93; pvt. practice Woodbury, Conn., 1979—; cons. psychologist Waterbury Hosp. Health Ctr., 1994—; asst. clin. prof. Yale U. Sch. Medicine, 1977—; cons. psychologist, Grandview Psychiat. Resource Ctr., Waterbury, 1990-93. Contbr. articles to profl. jours., chpts. to books. Deacon 1st Congl. Ch., Woodbury, 1980-81; personnel com. North Congl. Ch., Woodbury, 1988—, usher ministry, 1990—. Mem. Am. Psychol. Assn., Conn. Psychol. Assn. (key psychologist 1985—), Nat. Acad. Neuropsychology, Am. Bd. Profl. Psychology. Home: 15 Laurel Woods Rd Woodbury CT 06798-2516 Office: Waterbury Hosp Health Ctr Dept Psychiatry 64 Robbins St Waterbury CT 06721

SCHULTZ, MARK ALLAN, emergency medicine physician; b. Waukesha, Wis., Sept. 26, 1964; s. Harold Emil and Audrae Clare (Schlicht) S.; m. Elizabeth Ann Glaser, June 18, 1988; children: Daniel, Lara. BS, U. Wis., 1986; DO, U. Osteo. Medicine, Des Moines, 1990. Intern Garden City (Mich.) Hosp., 1990-91; resident Grace Hosp., Detroit, 1991-94; emergency medicine physician Waukesha Meml. Hosp., 1994—; emergency med. svcs. med. dir. Wales (Wis.) Fire Dept., Big Bend (Wis.) Vernon Fire Dept., 1995—; mem. med. adv. bd. Am. Power Boat Assn. and Unlimited Hydroplane Racing Assn., 1996—. Firefighter, emergency med. tech. Town of Waukesha Fire Dept., 1982-86, Town of Madison (Wis.) Fire Dept., 1984-86, Windsor Heights (Iowa) Fire Dept., 1986-90, Merton (Wis.) Fire Dept., 1995—. Mem. AMA, Am. Osteo. Assn., Am. Coll. Emergency Physicians. Office: Waukesha Meml Hosp 725 American Ave Waukesha WI 53188

SCHULTZ, RICHARD DONALD, thoracic, cardiovascular surgeon; b. Schleswig, Iowa, Oct. 7, 1931; s. Shirley V. and Eileen Rosario (Houston) S.; m. Elizabeth Marie Carlin, Aug. 28, 1954; children: Michael John, Sheryl Lee Schultz Whitehouse. BS, Creighton U., 1954, MD, 1958. Diplomate Am. Bd. Surgeons, added qualifications Am. Bd. Thoracic Surgeons. Resident gen. and thoracic surgery U. Wash. Affiliated Hosps., Seattle, 1966; asst. prof. surgery Creighton U. Sch. Medicine, Omaha, Nebr., 1966-74; assoc. prof. surgery Creighton U. Sch. Medicine, Omaha, 1974-85, prof., 1985-90, chief thoracic and cardiovascular surgery; col., chief thoracic, cardiovascular surgery Landstuhl (Germany) Regional Med. Ctr. (U.S. Mil.), 1991-94; cons. U.S. FDA on Duromedic Heart Valve Prostheses, Washington, 1985, on thoracic and cardiovasc. surgery, Mutual of Omaha Ins., 1988-91. Contbr. 71 articles to med. jours., 7 chpts. to med. texts, 1967-87. Mem. 18 nat. and 6 state med. orgns. Col. U.S. mil., 1991-94. Mem. Omaha Happy Hollow Club, Lincoln Univ. Club, Alpha Omega Alpha. Republican. Roman Catholic. Home: 1629 N 102 St Omaha NE 68114 Office: Creighton Univ Sch Medicine Dept Cardiovascular Surgery Omaha NE 68114

SCHULTZ, RICHARD LANG, otolaryngologist; b. Grenada, Miss., Nov. 27, 1948; s. Neil Barnhardt and Kathleen (Peery) S.; m. Kerry Deniece Hemphill, Nov. 6, 1968 (div. Nov. 1979); children: Kristina Deanne, Bethney Lang; m. Barbara Ann Nabors, Feb. 16, 1980; 1 child, Jeremy. BS, Tenn. Tech. U., 1971; MD, U. Tenn., 1973. Diplomate Am. Bd. Otolaryngology. Intern Meth. Hosp., Memphis, 1973-74, resident in gen. surgery, 1976-77; resident in otolaryngology U. Tenn. Ctr. for Health Scis., Memphis, 1977-80; otolaryngologist USAF Regional Hosp., March AFB, Calif., 1980-83, East Tenn. Otolaryngology-Head and Neck Surgery Ctr., Oak Ridge, 1983—. Maj. USAF, 1974-83. Fellow ACS, Am. Acad. Otolaryngology-Head and Neck Surgery; mem. AMA, Tenn. Med. Assn., Roane-Anderson Med. Soc. Office: East Tenn Otolaryngology Head and Neck Surgery 988 Turnpike # L-10 Oak Ridge TN 37830

SCHULTZ, RICHARD MICHAEL, biochemistry educator, researcher; b. Phila., Oct. 28, 1942; s. William and Beatrice (Levine) S.; m. Rima M. Lunin, Mar. 7, 1965; children: Carl M., Eli J. BA, SUNY, Binghamton, 1964; PhD, Brandeis U., 1969. Rsch. fellow Harvard U. Med. Sch., Boston, 1969-71; asst. prof. Loyola U. Stritch Sch. of Medicine, Maywood, Ill., 1971-78, assoc. prof., 1978-84, prof., 1984—, chmn. dept. molecular and cellular biochemistry, 1984—; mem. adv. med. bd. Leukemia Rsch. Found., Chgo., 1987-91. Contbr. articles to profl. jours. and chpts. to books. Recipient Rsch. grants NIH. Office: Dept Molecular & Cellular Biochemistry Loyola U Sch Medicine Maywood IL 60153

SCHULTZ, SCOTT HERBERT, obstetrician/gynecologist; b. Mpls., May 31, 1962; s. Herbert G. and Kay E. (Bucy) S.; m. Cheeryl L. Paddock, June 12, 1980; children: Gregory, Eric. BS, U. Fla., 1984, MD, 1987. Diplomate Am. Bd. Obstetrics and Gynecology. Ob-gyn. resident U. Ala., Birmingham, 1991; physician USAF, Tampa, Fla., 1991-94; pvt. practice Key West, Fla., 1994—; v.p. Keys Physician Hosp. Alliance, Key West, 1995—. Mem. bd. Healthy Start Coalition, Key West, 1995—. Major, USAF, 1989-93. Fellow Am. Coll. Obstetrics and Gynecology. Republican. Lutheran. Home: 9 Azalea Dr Key West FL 33040 Office: 1501 Government Rd Key West FL 33040

SCHULTZ, STANLEY GEORGE, physiologist, educator; b. Bayonne, N.J., Oct. 26, 1931; s. Aaron and Sylvia (Kaplan) S.; m. Harriet Taran, Dec. 25, 1960; children: Jeffrey, Kenneth. A.B. summa cum laude, Columbia U., 1952; M.D., N.Y. U., 1956. Intern Bellevue Hosp., N.Y.C., 1956-57; resident Bellevue Hosp., 1957-59; research assoc. in biophysics Harvard U., 1959-62, instr. biophysics, 1964-67; assoc. prof. physiology U. Pitts., 1967-70, prof. physiology, 1970-79; prof., chmn. dept. physiology U. Tex. Med. Sch., Houston, 1979—, prof. dept. internal medicine, 1979—; cons. USPHS, NIH, 1970—; mem. physiology test com. Nat. Bd. Med. Examiners, 1974-79, chmn., 1976-79. Editor Am. Jour. Physiology, Jour. Applied Physiology, 1971-75, Physiol. Revs., 1979-85, Handbook of Physiology: The Gastrointestinal Tract, 1989-91—; mem. editl. bd. Jour. Gen. Physiology, 1969-88, Ann. Revs. Physiology, 1974-81, Current Topics in Membranes and Transport, 1975-81, Jour. Membrane Biology, 1977—, Biochim. Biophys. Acta, 1987-89; assoc. editor Ann. Revs. Physiology, 1977-81; assoc. editor News in Physiol. Scis., 1989-94, editor, 1994—; contbr. articles to profl. jours. Served to capt. M.C. USAF, 1962-64. Recipient Research Career award NIH, 1969-74; overseas fellow Churchill Coll., Cambridge U., 1975-76. Mem. AAAS, Am. Heart Assn. (estab. investigator 1964-68), Am. Physiol. Soc. (councillor 1989-91, pres.-elect 1991-92, pres. 1992-93, past pres. 1993-94), Fed. Am. Soc. Exptl. Biology (exec. bd. 1992-95), Biophys. Soc., Soc. Gen. Physiologists, Internat. Cell Rsch. Orgn., Internat. Union Physiol. Scis. (chmn. internat. com. gastrointestinal physiology 1977-80, chmn. U.S. nat. com. 1992—), Assn. Am. Physicians, Am. Assn. Ob-Gyn. (hon. fellow), Assn. Chmn. Depts. Physiology (pres. 1985-86), Sigma Xi, Phi Beta Kappa. Home: 4955 Heatherglen Dr Houston TX 77096-4213

SCHULTZ, THOMAS S., neurosurgeon; b. Cambridge, Mass., Jan. 2, 1944; s. Henry C. and Leocadia A. S. AB in Chemistry, Cornell U., 1965; MS in Biophys. Chemistry, Purdue U., 1967; MD, St. Louis U., 1970. Diplomate Am. Bd. Neurol. & Orthopaedic Surgery, Am. Bd. Disability Evaluating Physicians. NIH rsch. fellow St. Louis U. Med. Sch., 1970-72; intern, then asst. resident Harvard Surg. Svc., Boston, 1972-74; resident in neurol. surgery Neurol. Inst. Columbia Presbyn. Med. Ctr., N.Y.C., 1974-78; pvt. practice West Roxbury, Mass., 1978-84; cons. in neurosurgery N.Y.C., 1984—. Assoc. editor Jour. Disability, 1990-94. David B. Goodstein shcolar Cornell U. Fellow Am. Trauma Soc., Am. Acad. Sports Medicine; mem. Am. Acad. Disability Evaluating Physicians (bd. dirs., sec., v.p. 1987-92), Am. Coll. Emergency Medicine, Am. Med. Writers Assn. Wilderness Med. Soc., Pewter Collecting Club Am., Cornell Club N.Y., Harvard Club Boston, Internat. Wine and Food Soc., U.S. Amateur Ballroom Dancers Assn. (bd. dirs. 1992). Office: PO Box 220419 Great Neck NY 11021

SCHULTZ, TIMOTHY K., orthopedic surgeon; b. Racine, Wis., Apr. 8, 1958; m. Kim Schultz; children: Andrew, Karly, Conner. BS in Psychology, U. Wis., 1980, MD, 1985. Diplomate Am. Bd. Orthopaedic Surgery. Intern Med. Coll. Wis., Milw., 1986, resident in orthopedic surgery, 1986-90; assoc. Orthopaedic Assocs. of Waukesha (Wis.), S.C., 1990—; Otto Aufranc grad. med. tng. fellow New Eng. Bapt. Hosp., Boston, 1993. Mem. AMA, Am. Acad. Orthopaedic Surgeons, Wis. State Med. Soc., Waukesha County Med. Soc., Phi Beta Kappa, Alpha Omega Alpha. Office: Orthopaedic Assocs Waukesha 1111 Delafield St Waukesha WI 53188

SCHULTZ, VICTOR M., physician; b. Pitts., Aug. 14, 1932; s. Irvin and Rose (Reiss) S. BS, Kent (Ohio) State U., 1955; MD, Ohio State U., Columbus, 1958. Diplomate Am. Bd. Dermatology. Pvt. practice Santa Monica, Calif., 1965—. Fellow Am. Acad. Dermatology, Pacific Dermatologic Assn.; mem. AMA, Am. Coll. Physicians, Calif. Med. Assn., L.A. County Med. Assn. Office: 2336 Santa Monica Blvd # 304 Santa Monica CA 90404

SCHULTZ, WILLIAM HERBERT, physician assistant; b. Vicksburg, Miss., Jan. 1, 1946; s. Edward August and Genevieve (Herbert) S.; m. Ann Sciaroni, May 22, 1971; children: Christopher David, Eric James. BA, San Francisco State U., 1981, Duke U., 1981; MHS, Duke U., 1991 Physician asst. pediat. hematology/oncology Duke U. Med. Ctr., Durham, N.C., 1981—; clin. assoc. Duke U. Med. Ctr., 1985—, physician asst. credentials subcom., 1995—; med. cons. Lollipop Power Books, 1991—. Sch. merger task force, Durham, 1991. Served in U.S. Army, 1969-72, Germany. Fellow Am. Acad. Physician Assts., N.C. Acad. Physician Assts.; mem. Internat. Assn. Sickle Cell Nurses and Physician Assts. (founding sec. 1990—), Duke U. Physian Asst. Soc., Assn. Physician Assts. in Oncology. Democrat. Roman Catholic. Office: Duke U Med Ctr Box 2916 Durham NC 27710

SCHULTZE, CHARLES LOUIS, economist, educator; b. Alexandria, Va., Dec. 12, 1924; s. Richard Lee and Nora Woolls (Baggett) S.; m. Rita Irene Hertzog, Sept. 6, 1947; children: Karen M., Kevin C., Helen L., Kathleen, Carol, Mary. A.B., Georgetown U., 1948, M.A., 1950; Ph.D., U. Md., 1960. Mem. staff Pres.'s Council Econ. Advisers, 1952, 54-58; chmn. Pres.'s Council Econ. Advisors, 1977-81; assoc. prof. econs. Ind. U., 1959-61; prof. econs. U. Md., 1961-87; asst. dir. U.S. Bur. of Budget, 1962-64, dir., 1965-67; sr. fellow Brookings Instn., Washington, 1968-76, 81—. Author: (with others) Setting National Priorities, 6 vols., 1970, 71, 72, 73, 83, 90, The Public Use of Private Interest, 1977, Other Times, Other Places, 1986, (with others) Barriers to European Growth, 1987, (with others) An American Trade Strategy, 1990, Memos to the President, 1992. Served with AUS, 1943-46. Decorated Purple Heart, Bronze Star. Mem. Am. Econ. Assn. (pres. 1984). Office: Brookings Instn 1775 Massachusetts Ave NW Washington DC 20036-2188

SCHULZ, RICHARD KENNETH, physician. BS, Tex. A&M U., 1988; MBA, U. Houston, 1990; postgrad., KCOM, Kirksville, Mo. Contbr. articles to profl. jours. Mem. Am. Coll. Emergency Physicians, Am. Coll. Family Physicians, Am. Med. Student Assn., Sigma Sigma Phi. Home: 1734 N New England Chicago IL 60635

SCHULZE, ARTHUR EDWARD, biomedical engineer, researcher; b. Richmond, Tex., Nov. 22, 1938; s. Arthur Dorwin and Ida (Bockhorn) S.; m. Sharon Kay Havemann, Sept. 2, 1962; children: Keith E., Mark A. BSEE, U. Tex., 1962, MSEE, 1963; MS Biomed. Sci., U. Tex., Houston, 1968. Registered profl. engr., Tex. Sr. aerosystems engr. Gen. Dynamics, Ft. Worth, 1963-67; rsch. assoc. U. Tex. Grad. Sch. Biomed. Scis., Houston, 1967-68; mgr., biomed. engr. SCI Systems, Inc., Houston, 1968-74; v.p. Telecare, Inc., Houston, 1974-79; gen. mgr. Tex. Sci. Corp., Houston, 1979-81; dir. R & D Narco Bio-Systems, Houston, 1981-84; pres. Narco Bio-Systems, 1984-86; v.p. Lovelace Sci. Resources, Inc., Houston, 1986-92; pres. Healthcare Tech. Group, 1993—. Contbr. articles to sci. publs. Mem. IEEE, Aerospace Med. Assn., Assn. Advancement Med. Instrumentation, AAAS, Biomed. Technology Club. Home: 8807 Mobud Dr Houston TX 77036-5321 Office: Healthcare Tech Group 6901 Corporate Dr Ste 111 Houston TX 77036-5119

SCHUMACHER, ERVIN, retired social services administrator; b. Eureka, S.D., Apr. 16, 1926; s. Christ and Christina (Klooz) S.; m. Gertrude H. Klipfel, Nov. 2, 1946; children: Candace Schumacher Hilmoe, Randall Ervin. BS in Edn., Bus. and Social Sci., U. N.D., 1961. Lic. cert. social worker, S.D. Farmer, Eureka, 1945-57; counselor McIntosh (S.D.) High Sch., 1961-63; social worker S.D. Dept. Social Svcs., Mobridge, 1963-64; coord. med. svcs. S.D. Dept. Social Svcs., Pierre, 1964-67, dir. medicaid, 1967-90; mem. S.D. Nursing Home Licensing Bd., Pierre, 1971-90. Recipient svc. award S.D. Med. Assn., 1990, S.D. Found. for Med. Care, 1990, S.D. Health Care Assn., 1990. Mem. State Medicaid Dirs. Assn. (Disting. Svc. award 1990), Rotary. Republican. Lutheran. Home: 20375 Cendok Rd Pierre SD 57501

SCHUMACHER, HAROLD ROBERT, laboratory administrator; b. Cin., Dec. 8, 1928; m. Marilyn Schumacher; m. Robert H. Jr., Gail C., Steven M., Mary E., Karen A. BS, U. Cin., 1951, MD, 1955. Commd. lt. (j.g.) USN, 1955, advanced through grades to capt., 1975; intern U.S. Naval Hosp., Portsmouth, Va., 1955-56; resident U.S. Naval Hosp., Phila., 1956-59; dir. hematology USN, Portsmouth, 1959-62; fellow hematology Jefferson Med. Coll., Phila., 1962-64; dir. hematology labs. York (Pa.) Hosp., 1962-70; co-dir. hematology labs. Harrisburg (Pa.) Hosp., 1970-75; dir. lab. hematology UNS Loyola, Chgo., 1975-86, 86-92, U. Cin., 1992—; dir. hematopathology fellowship USN, Bethesda, Md., 1978-86, Loyola, Chgo., 1986-92, U. Cin., 1992—. Author: Introduction to Lab Hematology and Hematopathology, 1984, Acute Leukemia Approach to Diagnosis, 1990, Chronic Leukemia Approach to Diagnosis, 1993, Myelodysplastic Syndrome: Approach to Diagnosis and Treatment, 1995; contbr. articles to profl. jours. Recipient meritorious svc. award Pres. Ronald Reagan, 1986. Fellow ACP, Am. Soc. Clin. Pathology, Am. Coll. Pathologists, Am. Soc. Hematology. Roman Catholic. Home: 623 Balbriggan Ct Cincinnati OH 45255 Office: U Cin Hosp 234 Goodman St Cincinnati OH 45267-0714

SCHUMACHER, H(ARRY) RALPH, internist, researcher, medical educator; b. Montreal, Feb. 14, 1933; s. H. Ralph and Dorothy (Shreiner) S.; m. Elizabeth Jean Swisher, July 13, 1963; children: Heidi Ruth, Kaethe Beth. B.S., Ursinus Coll., 1955; M.D., U. Pa., 1959. Intern Denver Gen. Hosp., 1959-60; resident in medicine Wadsworth VA Hosp., L.A., 1960-62, fellow in rheumatology, 1962-63; fellow in rheumatology Robert B. Brigham Hosp. and Harvard U. Med. Sch., Boston, 1965-67; chief arthritis-immunology ctr. VA Med. Ctr., Phila., 1967—; faculty mem. U. Pa. Sch. Medicine, Phila., 1967—, prof. medicine, 1979—, acting arthritis div. chief, 1978-80, 91-95; vis. scholar NIH, 1994—. Author: Gout and Pseudogout, 1978, Essentials of a Differential Diagnosis of Rhematoid Arthritis, 1981, Rheumatoid Arthritis, 1988, Case Studies in Rheumatology for the House Officer, 1989, Atlas of Synovial Fluid and Crystal Identification, 1991, A Practical Guide to Synovial Fluid Analysis, 1991; editor: Primer on Rheumatic Diseases, 1981—, Jour. Clin. Rheumatology, 1994—; mem. editorial bd. Jour. Rheumatology, 1973—, Arthritis and Rheumatism, 1981-88, Revue du Rhumatisme, 1992—, Brit. Jour. Clin. Practice, 1992—, New European Rheumatology, 1993—, Japanese Jour. Rheumatology, 1993—; contbr. articles to profl. jours.; lectr., author gardening. Pres. Eastern Pa. chpt. Arthritis Found., 1980-82; chmn., founder Phila. Garden Tours, 1987—; bd. dirs. Hemochromatosis Research Found., 1984—, Am. Bd. Med. Advancement China, 1983—. Served with M.C. USAF, 1963-65. Recipient Van-Breeman award The Netherland Rheumatism Soc., 1938; Deposition VA grantee, 1967—, NIH grantee, 1981. Fellow ACP; mem. Am. Coll. Rheumatology (pres. Southeastern region 1981-82), Phila. Rheumatism Soc. (pres. 1980), Phila. Electron Microscopy Soc. (chmn. 1975-76), Rheumatism Soc. Mex., Rheumatism Soc. Australia, Rheumatism Soc. Colombia, Rheumatism Soc. Chile, Rheumatism Soc. Republic of China, Rheumatism Soc. Argentina, Med. Soc. Argentina, Assn. Mil. Surgeons (Philip Hench award 1986), Fedn. Clin. Rsch., AAAS. Office: Hosp U Pa Ste G, 3d fl Ravdin Bldg 3400 Spruce St Philadelphia PA 19104

SCHUMACHER, LARRY P., health facility administrator; b. Waseca, Minn., Apr. 26, 1959; s. James H. and Judith A. (Voight) S.; m. Casey A. Hager, June 26, 1982; children: Matthew, Nicholas, Nathan, Mark. Diploma, Burge Sch. Nursing, 1980; BSN, S.W. Mo. State U., 1983; MS in Nursing, Ind. U., 1985. RN, Iowa; cert. nursing adminstr. advanced, 1989. Dir. critical care and med. nursing Rsch. Med. Ctr., Kansas City, Mo.; v.p. nursing and anesthesia St. Joseph Mercy Hosp., Mason City, Iowa; v.p. patient care svcs. Mercy Hosp., Mason City, Iowa; v.p. patient svcs., chief nursing officer North Iowa Mercy Health Ctr., Mason City; sr. vp. clin. integration, chief nursing officer North Iowa Mercy Health Network. Mem. ACHE, ANA, Nat. League Nursing, Am. Orgn. Nurse Execs. Home: 115 10th St NW Mason City IA 50401-2016

SCHUMAN, DANIEL C., psychiatrist, educator; b. N.Y.C., Aug. 13, 1941. BS, CUNY, 1962; MD, Tufts U., 1966. Diplomate Am. Bd. Psychiatry and Neurology. Med. intern Mt. Zion Hosp. and Med. Ctr., San Francisco, 1966-67; resident in psychiatry New Eng. Med. Ctr. Tufts U., Boston, 1967-68, 70-72; asst. clin. prof. psychiatry Tufts U. Sch. Medicine, Boston, 1973—; pvt. practice Weston, Mass., 1972—; dir. psychiatry Norfolk County Probate and Family Ct., Dedham, Mass., 1972-89; psychiat. cons. Blue Cross Nat. Benefits Mgmt. Co., Boston, 1986-88; psychiatrist specialist IV, Mass. Dept. Mental Health, 1989-92; dep. med. dir. Bridgewater State Hosp., 1994-95. Contbr. articles on family psychodynamics, custody and child abuse to med. jours. Lt. comdr. M.C., USNR, 1968-75. Mem. Am. Psychiat. Assn., Mass. Psychiat. Soc., Am. Acad. Psychiatry and Law, New Eng. Coun. for Child Psychiatry. Home and Office: 23 Summer St Weston MA 02193-2441

SCHUMAN, EARL STANLEY, surgeon; b. L.A., July 9, 1944; s. George and Theresa (Henschel) S.; m. Tamara Aimeé Lanning, June 26, 1971; children: Heidi, Jason. BA, U. So. Calif., 1965; MD, U. Calif., Irvine, 1969. Resident in surgery Good Samaritan Hosp., Portland, Oreg., 1969-71, 74-78; pvt. practice Oreg. Surg. Cons., Portland, 1978—; chair med. staff quality coun. Legacy Portland Hosp., 1994—; mem. adv. bd. Legacy VNA, Portland, 1994—; mem. quality improvement com. Blue Cross Oreg., Portland, 1989—; assoc. prof. clin. surgery Oreg. Health Scis. U., Portland, 1985—. Contbr. articles to profl. jours. Chair bd. dirs. Lake Oswego (Oreg.) Teen Ctr., 1991-93. Major USAF, 1972-74. Fellow ACS; mem. Pacific Coast Surg. Assn., Soc. Laparendoscopic Surgeons, N.W. Soc. Colorectal Surgery, North Pacific Surg. Assn., Portland Surg. Soc. Office: Oreg Surg Cons 1130 NW 22d Ste 300 Portland OR 97210

SCHUMAN, ELLIOTT PAUL, psychologist, educator, psychoanalyst, mediator, arbitrator. BS, U.S. Naval Acad., 1949; MA, Columbia U., 1955, PhD, 1958, profl. diploma in counseling psychology, 1958. Diplomate Am. Bd. Psychotherapy, Am. Bd. Profl. Psychology, Am. Acad. Pain Mgmt., Am. Bd. Med. Psychotherapists; lic. psychologist, N.Y., N.J. From lectr. to asst. to Dean and counselor, Columbia Coll. Columbia U., N.Y.C., 1955-58; lectr., counselor Bklyn. Coll., 1958-60; adj. asst. prof., dir. testing and counseling L.I. U., 1960-62, asst. prof. to prof. psychology, 1962—; coord. grad.

programs in psychology Long Island U., N.Y.C., 1984—; faculty Mid-Manhattan Inst. Modern Psychoanalysis, N.Y.C., 1992—; psychologist Morningside Mental Hygiene Clinic, 1960-66; psychotherapist Community Guidance Svc., N.Y.C., 1962-69, supr., 1969-87; psychoanalyst Theodore Reik Consultation Ctr., 1966-69, tng. analyst, 1969—; mem. faculty Am. Inst. for Psychotherapy and Psychoanalysis, 1972-73, Ctr. for Modern Psychoanalytic Studies, 1973—, Nat. Psychol. Assn. for Psychoanalysis, 1974, Inst. for Expressive Analysis, 1980-81, Inst. for Modern Psychoanalysis, 1981-86; supervisor dept. psychiatry Mt. Sinai Hosp., 1979—. Author: Guide for Evaluation of Instruction, Navy Dept., 1958; contbr. numerous articles to profl. jours. Recipient fellowship Found. for Econ. Edn. Mem. AAAS, APA, AAUP, N.Y. State Psychol. Assn., N.Y. Acad. Scis., N.Y. Soc. Clin. Psychologists, Ea. Psychol. Assn., Soc. Projective Techniques, Nat. Assn. for Advancement Psychoanalysis, Coun. for Nat. Register Health Svc. Providers in Psychology, Am. Group Psychotherapy Assn., Am. Acad. Psychotherapists, N.Y. Soc. for Ericksonian Psychotherapy and Hypnosis, Assn. Family and Conciliation Cts., Sigma Xi, Phi Delta Kappa, Kappa Delta Pi. Home and Office: 116 Prospect Park W Brooklyn NY 11215-3710

SCHUMAN, LEONARD M., medical educator; b. Cleve., Mar. 4, 1913. AB, Oberlin Coll., 1934; MSc, Western Reserve U., 1939, MD, 1940. Diplomate Am. Bd. Preventive Medicine. Teaching and rsch. fellow in hygiene and bacteriology Sch. Medicine Western Reserve U., 1937-39; intern U.S. Marine Hosp., Chgo., 1940-41; asst. epidemiologist Ill. Dept. Pub. Health, 1941-42, dist. health supt. dist. # 2, 1943, asst. chief divsn. local health adminstrn., 1943-45, chief divsn. venereal disease control, 1947-50, acting chief divsn. communicable disease, 1949-50, dep. dir. divsn. preventive medicine, 1950-51, 53-54; assoc. prof. Sch. of Pub. Health U. Minn., 1954-58, prof. epidemiology, 1958-83, Mayo prof., 1983—; epidemiologist U.S. Dept. of Def., 1951-53; vis. lectr. U. Ill. Sch. of Medicine, Chgo., 1947-54; lectr. communicable diseases Springfield Meml. Hosp., Sch. of Nursing, 1947-54; cons. Communicable Disease Ctr., USPHS, 1955-83, Air Pollution Med. Program, 1958—, Nat. Cancer Inst., 1958-79, Divsn. Radiol. Health, 1961-69, Chronic Disease Divsn., 1964-72, mem. Adv. Com. Bio-Effects of Radiation, 1966-69, Grant Rev. Com. for Prevention Ctrs., Ctrs. for Disease Control, 1986-93; cons. Minn. State Health Dept., 1955-90, mem. adv. com. cancer surveillance, 1981—, tech. adv. com. non-smoking and health, 1983—; cons. Hennepin County (Minn.) Gen. Hosp., 1955—. Contbr. articles to profl. jours. With USPHS, 1941-47. Rockefeller Found. fellow, 1946; recipient Samuel Harvey award Am. Assn. Cancer Edn., 1983, Wyeth award Pacific Coast Fertility Soc., 1983, Pioneer award Minn. Dept. of Health, 1991, Recognition award Hennepin County (Minn.) Cmty. Prevention Coalition, 1994, citation from Surgeon Gen. Jocelyn Elders, 1994, Recognition award Assn. Schs. Pub. Health, 1995. Fellow APHA (chmn. infectious disease monograph subcom. 1961-68, mem. com. evaluations and standards 1962-66, governing coun. 1964-70, resolutions com. 1964-65, chmn. subcom. on drugs 1964-65, vice chmn. epidemiology sect. 1966, chmn. epidemiology sect. 1967, program area com. communicable diseases 1966-70, mem. tech. devel. bd. 1966-70, v.p. 1993-94, John Snow award 1983, Sedwick Meml. medal 1996), Am. Coll. Epidemiology (bd. dirs. 1979-89, chmn. edn. com. 1985-92, Abraham H. Lilienfeld award 1989, cert. Appreciation 1991), Am. Heart Assn. (coun. epidemiology 1965); mem. AAAS, AAUP, Am. Assn. Pub. Health Physicians, Am. Coll. Preventive Medicine (sec. coun. rsch. 1956-59, chmn. 1959-64), Am. Epidemiol. Soc. (v.p. 1978), Am. Thoracic Soc. Am. Venereal Disease Assn., Am. Cancer Soc. (Minn. divsn.), Assn. Mil. Surgeons U.S., Assn. Tchrs. Preventive Medicine, Internat. Epidemiol. Soc., Internat. Soc. Cardiology, Internat. Soc. Thrombosis and Hemostasis, Mid. States Pub. Health Assn., Minn. Pub. Health Assn. (Pub. Health Achievement award 1987), N.Y. Acad. Scis., Pub. Health Cancer Assn., Soc. Epidemiol. Rsch. (exec. bd. 1980, award for Outstanding Contbns. to Field of Epidemiology 1992), Phi Beta Kappa, Alpha Omega Alpha, Phi Zeta, Sigma Xi, Phi Kappa Phi, Delta Omega (award selection com. 1985, pres. Pi chpt. 1985—, nat. pres.-elect 1990-92, pres. 1993-95). Home and Office: 200 First St SW Rochester MN 55902

SCHUMAN, ROBERT JAMES, psychiatrist; b. Manhasset, N.Y., Jan. 10, 1956; s. David L. and Harriet Elizabeth (Klein) S.; m. Sheri Lynn Katz, Aug. 21, 1983; children: Michael Leigh, Elisha Rebecca. BA in Psychology summa cum laude, Adelphi U., 1978; MD, Jefferson Med. Coll., 1984. Diplomate Am. Bd. Psychiatry and Neurology. Resident in psychiatry Westchester Med. Ctr., Valhalla, N.Y., 1984-88; attendant on staff Riverview Med. Ctr., Red Bank, N.J., 1988-90; cons. Children's Psychiat. Ctr., Monmouth County, 1988—; pvt. practice Red Bank, 1988—. Mem. Monmouth Med. Soc., Delta Tau Alpha. Jewish. Office: 225 Highway 35 Red Bank NJ 07701-5919

SCHUMANN, ALICE MELCHER, medical technologist, educator, sheep farmer; b. Cleve., Sept. 1, 1931; d. John Henry and Marian Louise (Clark) M.; m. Stuart McKee Struever, Aug. 21, 1956 (div. June 1983); children: Nathan Chester, Hanna Russell; m. John Otto Schumann, July 3, 1985. BS, Colby Coll., New London, N.H., 1953. Cert. tchr.; cert. med. technologist. Rschr. Lakeside Hosp., Cleve., 1953-54, Bambridge (Ohio) Schs., 1954-55, Shalersville (Ohio) Schs., 1955-56, Richtnior Sch., Overland, Mo., 1956-57; sci. tchr. Tonica (Ill.) High Sch., 1956-58, Morton Grove (Ill.) High Sch., 1958-60, Univ. Chgo. Lab Sch., 1960-65; co-founder Ctr. for Am. Archeology, dir. flotation rsch. U. Chgo. Campus, Kampsville, Ill., 1957-71, head of supplies distbn., dir. food svcs. dept.; head mailing dept. Found. for Ill. Archeology, Evanston and Kampsville, Ill., 1971-83; sheep farmer, wool processor Gravel Hill Farm, Kampsville, 1983—. Vol. Mt. Sinai Hosp., Cleve., 1948-49; tchr. Title I Dist. 40, Kampsville, 1970-71. Recipient Beverly Booth award Colby Coll., 1953, 1st prize for hand spun yarn DeKalb County Fair, Sandwich, Ill., 1987, 88. Mem. Precious Fibers Found., Natural Colored Wool Growers Assn., Farm Bur. of Calhoun County. Home and Office: Gravel Hill Farm RR 1 Box 121A Kampsville IL 62053-9720

SCHUPBACK, LOWELL LEON, physician, surgeon, ophthalmologist; b. Kansas City, Mo., Apr. 1, 1929; s. Lot and Helen Lucile (Dameron) S.; m. Edna Madrienne Herlocker, June 21, 1953 (div. Jan. 1985); children: Darla Larkin, Tanya Jacobson, Kevan. BA, Kansas City U., 1951; DO, Kansas City Coll. Osteopathy, 1955. Intern Cmty. Hosp., Jacinton City, Tex., 1956; pvt. practice Houston, 1955—. Minister Jehovah's Witnesses. Mem. Mo. Assn. Osteo. Physicians and Surgeons. Home: 14623 La Quinta Grandview MO 64030 Office: 400 NW Barry #114B Kansas City MO 64030

SCHUR, PETER HENRY, internist; b. Vienna, Austria, May 9, 1933; came to U.S., 1939; s. Max and Helen (Kraus) S.; m. Susan Dorfman, Sept. 3, 1963 (div. 1984); children: Diana, Erica. BS, Yale U., 1955; MD, Harvard U., 1958. Diplomate Am. bd. Internal Medicine, Am. Bd. Allergy and Clin. Immunology and Lab. Clin. Immunology. Intern, then resident Bronx (N.Y.) Mcpl. Hosp., 1958-62; postdoctoral fellow Rockefeller U., N.Y.C., 1964-67; instr., then assoc. prof. Harvard Med. Sch., Boston, 1967-81, prof. medicine, 1981—; sr. physician Robert B. Brigham Hosp., Boston, 1967-81, dir. clin. labs., 1970-81; dir. Clin. Immunology Lab. Brigham and Women's Hosp., Boston, 1981—; sr. physician, dir lupus clinic & rsch. Brigham & Women's Hosp., Boston, 1981—; bd. dirs. Lupus Found. Am., Washington, 1979-89, pres. Mass. unit, 1989-93; bd. dirs. Arthritis Found., Atlanta, 1980-85. Editor: Clinical Management of Systemic Lupus Erythematosus, 1983; co-author: In Search of the Sun, 1989; editor Arthritis and Rheumatism, 1990-95; contbr. over 180 articles to med. and sci. jours. Capt. U.S. Army, 1962-64. Grantee NIH, 1967—, Lupus Found., 1975—. Fellow ACP; mem. Am. Soc. Clin. Investigation, Assn. Am. Physicians, Am. Coll. Rheumatology, N.Y. Acad. Sci. Office: Brigham and Womens Hosp 75 Francis St Boston MA 02115-6110

SCHUR, WALTER ROBERT, physician; b. Webster, Mass., June 17, 1914; s. Robert O. and Alma L. (Gatzke) S.; student Valparaiso U., 1931-34; M.D., Middlesex U., Waltham, Mass., 1940; m. Delta Jean Newman, June 17, 1944; children—Paul, David, Jonathan, Ruth, Timothy, Peter, Stephen, Mary, Joel, Daniel, Rhoda. Resident, Milford (Del.) Meml. Hosp., 1940-41, Grace Hosp. Cleve., 1942-43; intern Lutheran Hosp., Cleve., 1941-42; pvt. practice, Oxford, Mass., 1944—; bd. dirs., pres. Doctors Hosp., Worcester, Mass., chmn. bd., 1978-87; bd. dirs. AdCare Hosp., 1987—, chmn. bd. dirs., 1987-91, Atlantic dist. Luth Ch.-Mo. Synod, 1978-87, mem., sec. edn. com., missions com., 1960-77, mem. stewardship com., youth com., edn. com., 1951-57, chmn. edn. com. Atlantic dist., 1954-57, mem. commn. on mission and ministry in ch., named Dist. Layman of Year, 1966, chmn. com. on ministry Atlantic dist., 1970; , bd. dirs. Luth. Assn. Works of Mercy, Assn. Evang. Luth. Chs.; bd. dirs. Valparaiso U., 1969—, sec., 1984—; pres., scholarship chmn. N.E. dist. Luth. Laymen's League, 1946-57; nat. bd. govs. Nat. Luth. Laymen's League, 1957; vice chmn. Luth. Hour Oper. Com., 1958, chmn. 1959-61; New Eng. bd. dirs. Assn. Evang. Luth. Chs., 1977-87, trustee East Coast Synod, 1977-87, mem. nat. bd. dirs., 1979-88; mem. council New Eng. Synod Evangelical Lutheran Ch. Am. 1988-94; bd. dirs., vice chmn. French River Edn. Ctr., 1985—; mem. Oxford Sch. Com., 1961-86, Mass. Commn. on Christian Unity; assoc. charter mem. Park Ridge Ctr., 1986. Recipient award of Merit, Internat. Luth. Laymen's League, 1963. Recipient Soli Deo Gloria award New Eng. Synod, Evang. Luth Ch. Am., 1994. Fellow Am. Acad. Gen. Practice, Am. Acad. Family Physicians (charter); mem. AMA, Mass. Med. Soc., Worcester Dist. Med. Soc., Am. Geriatrics Assn., New Eng. Ob-Gyn. Soc., Valparaiso U. Alumni Assn. (past pres.), Luth. Acad. for Scholarship (bd. dirs. 1977-86), Concordia Hist. Inst., New Eng. Luth. Hist. Soc. (charter), Internat. Platform Assn., New Eng. Huguenot Soc., Rotary (past pres.). Home: Charlton Rd Oxford MA 01540 Office: 367 Main St Oxford MA 01540-1746

SCHURICHT, ALAN L., surgeon; b. Newark, Jan. 1, 1959; s. Richard R. and Mona D. (Zucker) S.; m. Lori S. Schulman, Aug. 16, 1981; children: Ted, Kyle. BS, Cornell U., 1981; MD, U. S.C., 1985. Diplomate Am. Bd. Surgery. Intern, resident Thomas Jefferson U. Hosp., Phila., 1985-90, staff surgeon, 1990—; staff surgeon Pa. Hosp., Phila., 1993—, dir. residency program dept. surgery Pa. Hosp., Phila., 1993—, dir. surg. critical care, 1993—, dir. videoscopic surgery ctr., 1994—. Fellow ACS; mem. AMA, Soc. of Laparoendoscopic Surgeons, Assn. for Acad. Surgery, Am. Soc. Gen. Surgeons, Alpha Omega Alpha. Office: Pa Surg Assocs 301 S 8th St Philadelphia PA 19106

SCHUSSEL, ALAN LEWIS, rehabilitation counselor; b. Bklyn., Oct. 27, 1963; s. Erwin Marvin and Suellen (Kleppel) S.; m. Clarice Ann West, June 9, 1991; children: Zachary Terence, Marni Amber. BA, Gallaudet U., 1989; MA, U. Ariz., 1994. Cert. rehab. counselor, cmty. coll. tchr., Ariz. Resident advisor Rochester (N.Y.) Inst. Tech., 1983-87; resident advisor Gallaudet U., Washington, 1987-89, tutor, 1987-92; residential counselor Family Svcs. Found., Landover, Md., 1989; case mgr. People Encouraging People, Balt., 1990-92; rehab. counselor dept. econ. security State of Ariz., Tucson, 1993-96; project assoc. Pima Prevention Partnership, Tucson, 1996—; adj. faculty Am. sign lang. Pima C.C., Tucson, 1995—; bd. dirs. Cmty. Outreach Program for Deaf, Rehab. Counselor Dir. Search, Ariz. Coun. for Hearing Impaired, 1994—; mem. preconf. com. Am. Deafness and Rehab. Assn., San Francisco, 1992-93; mem. Statewide Interpreter Planning Com., Phoenix, 1993—, chair subcom. interpreter preparation planning, 1994—; mem. Com. on Real Time Captioning Project, 1995—; dir. New Agy. Planning Project, 1995—; rep. to bd. Ariz. Assn. of the Deaf, 1995-96, v.p., 1996—; panelist on deaf culture, 1992—. Active Silent Protest, U. Ariz., 1993, Deaf Pres. Now, Gallaudet U., Washington, 1988, Empowerment for the Deaf, Phoenix, 1994, Project Pride Cmty. Outreach, Tucson, 1992-93; com. mem. Christopher City Elections, Tucson, 1992. Recipient Pres. Recognition award Ariz. Assn. of Deaf, 1996, Proclamation Pima County Bd. Suprs., 1996. Mem. ACA, Nat. Rehab. Assn., Ariz. Rehab. Assn., Am. Sign Lang. Club (treas. 1992-93), Ariz. Assn. of the Dear (v.p. 1996—), Kappa Sigma. Democrat. Jewish. Home: 16960 W Falcon Ln Marana AZ 85653-9199 Office: Pima Prevention Partnership 345 E Toole Ave Tucson AZ 85701

SCHUSSLER, IRWIN, psychiatrist, educator; b. Bklyn., Nov. 14, 1943; s. Jack and Fannie Yetta (Blank) S.; m. Myra Yvette Paget, June 26, 1966; children: Jeffrey Mitchell, Doreen Robyn, Kimberly Beth, Howard, Brian. BS, Bklyn. Coll., 1964; DO, Chgo. Coll. Osteopathic Medicine, 1968. Diplomate Am. Bd. Psychiatry and Neurology, Am. Bd. Gen. Psychiatry and Child Psychiatry, Am. Osteopathic Bd. Neurology and Psychiatry, Am. Bd. Sexology. Intern Interboro Gen. Hosp., Bklyn., 1968-69; resident in gen. psychiatry U. Fla. Coll. Medicine, Gainesville, 1972-74, asst. prof. psychiatry and pediatrics, 1976-77, dir. in-patient psychotherapy, 1976-77, fellow in child and adolescent psychiatry, 1974-76; fellow in human sexual medicine U. Pa., Phila., 1975; practice medicine specializing in psychiatry Ft. Worth, 1977-79; clin. assoc. prof., vice chmn. dept. psychiatry North Tex. State U. Health Scis. Ctr., Tex. Coll. Osteo. Medicine, Ft. Worth, 1979—; bd. dirs. Osteo. Med. Ctr. Tex., med. dir. psychiatry dept.; bd. dirs. Health Care Tex., Mental Health Assn. Contbr. articles to profl. jours. Bd. dirs. Mental Health Assn. Fellow Am. Coll. Neuropsychiatry, Am. Coll. Sexology; mem. Am. Psychiat. Assn., Am. Acad. Child Psychiatrists, Am. Acad. Clin. Psychiatrists, Am. Assn. Sex Educators, Counselors and Therapists, Tex. Soc. Psychiat. Physicians (pres. Tarrant County chpt.), Am. Osteo. Assn., Tex. Osteo. Med. Assn., Fla. Osteo. Med. Assn., Masters and Johnson Found. Jewish. Home: 3712 Myrtle Springs Rd Fort Worth TX 76116-9213 Office: Psychiat Cons Ft Worth 3704 Mattison Ave Fort Worth TX 76107-2619

SCHUSTER, CARLOTTA LIEF, psychiatrist; b. N.Y.C., Sept. 16, 1936; d. Victor Filler and Nina Lincoln (Rayevsky) Lief; m. David Israel Schuster, Sept. 2, 1962; 1 child, Amanda. BA, Barnard Coll., 1957; MD, NYU, 1964. Cert. Am. Bd. Psychiatry and Neurology; cert. addiction psychiatry. Intern Lenox Hill Hosp., N.Y.C., 1964-65; resident St. Luke's Hosp., N.Y.C., 1965-68; fellow Inst. Sex Edn., U. Pa., Phila., 1968-69; instr. N.Y. Med. Coll., N.Y.C., 1969-72; asst. attending Met. Hosp., N.Y.C., 1969-72; assoc. attending St. Luke's-Roosevelt Hosp. Ctr., N.Y.C., 1972—; staff psychiatrist Silver Hill Found., New Canaan, Conn., 1972-95; clin. assoc. instr. Columbia U., N.Y.C., 1990—; chief substance abuse svc. Silver Hill Found., New Canaan, 1976-95; clin. faculty dept. psychiatry Sch. Medicine NYU, 1995—; dir. recovery clinic Bellevue Hosp., N.Y.C., 1995—. Author: Alcohol and Sexuality, 1988; co-author: Chapter in Advances in Alcohol and Substance Abuse, 1987; contbr. chpt. Mental Health in the Workplace, 1993. Mem. Am. Psychiat. Assn., Am. Med. Soc. on Addictions, Am. Acad. Psychiatrists in Alcohol and Addictions. Democrat. Jewish. Office: 207 E 30th St New York NY 10016

SCHUSTER, CHARLES ROBERTS, federal government scientist; b. Woodbury, N.J., Jan. 24, 1930; s. Charles Roberts and Ruth E. S.; m. Chris-Ellyn Johanson, Nov. 1972. AB, Gettysburg Coll., 1951; MS, U. N.Mex., 1953; PhD, U. Md., 1962. Prof. psychiatry and behavioral scis. U. Chgo., 1972—, dir. rsch ctr. drug abuse, 1973-86, acting chmn. dept. psychiatry, 1985-86; dir. Nat. Inst. on Drug Abuse, Rockville, Md., 1986-92; sr. rsch. scientist, 1992—; mem. Dept. Health Human Svcs. Commn. on Orphan Diseases, 1987-89, Com. on Problems Drug Dependence, Inc., 1978—; chmn. expert com. WHO, 1975, expert adv. panel on drug dependence. Author: Behavioral Pharmacology, 1968, Drug Dependence, 1970; contbr. over 150 articles to profl. jours. Fellow AAAS, Am. Psychol. Assn. (pres. div. 28 1977-78), Am. Coll. Neuropsychopharmacology; mem. Behavioral Pharmacology Soc. (pres. 1976-78), Inst. Medicine. •

SCHUSTER, JACK CLAYTON, biology educator; b. Dearborn, Mich., Feb. 29, 1944; s. Merle Clayton and Virginia (Burton) S.; m. Laura Helen Berkeley, June 4, 1966; 1 child, Kalara Jean. BS, U. Mich., 1966, MS, 1968; PhD, U. Fla., 1975. Cert. jr. coll. tchr., Fla. Instr. Santa Fe Jr. Coll., Gainesville, Fla., 1968-69; vis. prof. Nat. U. Agraria de la Selva, Tingo Maria, Peru, 1969-72; instr. U. Fla., Gainesville, 1972-75; prof. biology U. del Valle de Guatemala, Guatemala City, 1975—, dir. dept. Ecotourism, 1992—, dir. life scis. divsn., 1993—. Contbr. numerous articles to profl. jours.; rec. artist with Guatemalan rock group Alux Nahual, 1979-89. Cons. Defenders of Nature, Guatemala, 1985—. Mem. Soc. Les Voyageurs, Mex. Soc. Entomology, Assn. for Tropical Biology, Coleopterists Soc., Am. Entomol. Soc., Fla. Entomol. Soc., Sigma Xi, Phi Kappa Phi. Home and Office: U del Valle de Guatemala, Apartado 82, Guatemala City Guatemala

SCHUSTER, JAMES MORTON, psychiatrist; b. Louisville, Aug. 31, 1958. BA, Wash. U., St. Louis, 1980; MD, U. Louisville, 1985; MBA, U. Pitts., 1989. Resident U. Pitts., 1985-89; psychiatrist Allegheny Gen. Hosp., Pitts., 1989—, dir. emergency psychiatry, 1991—; asst. prof. psychiatry Med. Coll. Pa., Allegheny, 1991-95; assoc. prof. psychiatry Med. Coll. Pa./ Hahnemann U., Allegheny, 1995—. Recipient S. Spafford Ackerly award U. Louisville, 1985. Mem. AMA, Am. Psychiat. Assn., Pa. Med. Soc., Phi Beta Kappa, Beta Gamma Sigma. Office: Allegheny Gen Hosp 320 E North Ave Pittsburgh PA 15212-4772

SCHUSTER, MARVIN MEIER, physician, educator; b. Danville, Va., Aug. 30, 1929; s. Isaac and Rosel (Katzenstein) S.; m. Lois R. Bernstein, Feb. 19, 1961; children: Roberta, Nancy, Cathy. BA, BS, U. Chgo., 1951; MD, 1955. Diplomate Am. Bd. Internal Medicine. Intern Kings County Hosp., Bklyn., 1955-56; resident Balt. City Hosp., 1956-58; resident Johns Hopkins Bayview Med. Ctr., 1961—; Johns Hopkins Hosp., Balt., 1958-61; prof. medicine and psychiatry Johns Hopkins U. Sch. Medicine, Balt., 1976—, chief digestive disease divsn. Author: Gastrointestinal Disorders: Behavioral and Physiological Basis for Treatment; Keeping Control: Understanding and Managing Fecal Incontinence; editor: Gastrointestinal Motility Disorders, 1981, Atlas of Gastrointestinal Motility, 1994; contbr. chpts. to textbooks, articles to profl. jours.; mem. editorial bd.: Gastroenterology, 1978-81, Gastrointestinal Endoscopy, 1979-81, Psychosomatics, 1979—. Bd. dirs. Am. Cancer Soc., 1975—, pres., 1984-86; chmn. med. adv. bd. Balt. Ostomy Assn., 1966—. Recipient St. George Disting. Service award Am. Cancer Soc., 1979. Fellow ACP, Am. Psychiat. Assn.; mem. Am. Gastroent. Assn. (chmn. audiovisual com. 1975-78), Am. Soc. Gastrointestinal Endoscopy (governing bd. 1975-78), Am. Coll. Gastroenterology (pres. 1996) Am. Physiol. Soc., AAUP. Democrat. Jewish. Research on gastroenterology and application of biofeedback to gastrointestinal control. Home: 10 Red Cedar Ct Baltimore MD 21208-6305 Office: Johns Hopkins Bayview Med Ctr 4940 Eastern Ave Baltimore MD 21224-2735

SCHUSTER, WILLY GOTTFRIED, plant physiologist, virologist, educator; b. Meissen, Saxony, Germany, Apr. 21, 1923; s. Reinhold Willy and Martha Elisabeth (Schmieder) S.; m. Gertraud Geissler, Dec. 11, 1954; children: Reinhard, Michael. Diploma, U. Leipzig, Fed. Republic of Germany, 1951; Dr.'s diploma, U. Leipzig, 1954, Dr. rer. nat. habilitation, 1960. Asst. Inst. Phytopathology, U. Leipzig, 1951-54, head asst., 1954-55; head asst. Div. Agrl. Botany, U. Leipzig, 1955-60, lectr., 1960-62, prof. mit Lehrauftrag, 1962-64, prof. mit vollem Lehrauftrag, 1964-68; prof. dept. bioscis., plant physiology, microbiology U. Leipzig, 1969-89, rsch. prof. dept. bioscis., plant physiology, microbiology, 1989—; vice dean Agrl. faculty of U. Leipzig, 1964-68, vice dir. Dept. Bioscis., 1972-78, dir. Dept. Bioscis., 1978-83. Author: Virus and Virus Diseases, 1957, 4th rev. edit., 1988, Methods and Approaches for the Physiological-Chemical Virus Diagnostic, 1962, (manuals) Plant Cytology and Morphology, 1963, Plant Morphology, 1963, Plant Physiology Part I, 1963, Plant Physiology Part II, 1964, Instructions for Bot. Exercises, 1964, Viruses in the Environment, 1996; editor: Antiphytoviral Compounds, 1982, New Results and Trends of the Plant Physiology, 1987. Office: U Leipzig Div Plant Physiology Microbiology, Talstrasse 33, D-04103 Leipzig Germany

SCHUTTA, HENRY SZCZESNY, neurologist, educator; b. Gdansk, Poland, Sept. 15, 1928; came to U.S., 1962, naturalized, 1967; s. Jakub and Janina (Zerbst) S.; m. Henryka Kosmal, Apr. 29, 1950; children—Katharine, Mark, Caroline. M.B., B.S., U. Sydney, Australia, 1955, M.D., 1968. Jr. resident, then sr. resident St. Vincent's Hosp., Sydney, 1956-58; acad. registrar, house physician Nat. Hosp. Nervous Diseases, London, 1958-62; neurologist Pa. Hosp., Phila., 1962-73; asso. prof. neurology U. Pa. Med. Sch., 1963-73; prof. neurology, chmn. dept. SUNY Downstate Med. Center, Bklyn., 1973-80; prof. U. Wis. Med. Sch., 1980-95, chmn. dept. neurology, 1980-95. Home: 3510 Blackhawk Dr Madison WI 53705-1406 Office: U Hosp 600 Highland Ave Madison WI 53792-0001

SCHUTZ, DONALD FRANK, geochemist, healthcare corporate executive; b. Orange, Tex., Sept. 22, 1934; s. Theodore J. and Mildred Irene (Chandler) S.; m. Beatriz Valera, May 18, 1958; children: Delfino, Celita. BS in Geology cum laude, Yale U., 1956, PhD in Geology, 1964; MA in Geology, Rice U., 1958. Research staff geologist Yale U., New Haven, 1963-64; mgr. nuclear geochemistry dept. Teledyne Isotopes, Westwood, N.J., 1968-70, v.p., 1970-75, pres., 1975-93; engring. group exec. Teledyne, Inc., Westwood, 1989-92; chief scientist Teledyne Environ. Systems, 1992-93; gen. mgr. Teledyne Brown Engring. Environ. Svcs., 1993—; v.p. Teledyne Environ., Inc.; mem. low level waste adv. com. N.J. Dept. Environ. Protection, Trenton, 1988-90; chmn. com. on radioactive materials N.J. BIA, Trenton, 1980-88. Pres. Children's Aid and Adoption Soc. N.J. Inc., Bogota, 1976-95, Am. Amateur Judo Found., River Vale, N.J., 1979-89; bd. dirs. Yale U. Alumni Fund, 1989-94; co-chmn. Children's Aid and Family Svcs. Inc., 1995-96. Recipient Antarctic Service medal U.S. Congress, 1964. Mem. Geochem. Soc., Am. Nuclear Soc. (chmn. no. N.J. sect. 1988-89, environ. scis. divsn., bd. dirs., chair 1995-96, pub. policy com. 1991—), Am. Assn. Engring. Soc. Internat. Affairs (standing com. sustainable devel. 1995—), Geol. Soc. Am., Soc. Petroleum Engrs., Am. Assn. Radon Sci. and Tech. (pres. 1986-89, treas. 1990-95), Am. Assn. Petroleum Geologists, Yale Alumni Assn. (bd. dirs. Bergen County and vicinity chpt. 1989—), Sigma Xi. Office: Teledyne Brown Engring Environ Svcs 50 Van Buren Ave Westwood NJ 07675-3242

SCHUYLER, DEAN, psychiatrist; b. N.Y.C., Sept. 15, 1942; s. Samuel and Ethel (Hershkowitz) S.; m. Theresa Herman; children: Rachel, Amy. AB, NYU, 1963, MD, 1967. Diplomate Am. Bd. Psychiatry and Neurology. Intern Greenwich (Conn.) Hosp., 1967-68; resident in psychiatry U. Pa., Phila., 1968-71; staff psychiatrist NIMH, Rockville, Md., 1971-72; coord. depression research program NIMH, Rockville, 1972-74; clin. asst. prof. psychiatry Georgetown U., Washington, 1976-83; cons. Sheppard Pratt Hosp., Balt., 1983-86; psychiatrist pvt. practice, Rockville, 1971—, cognitive therapist, 1971—; nat. pres. Assn. for Mental Health Affiliation with Israel, Chgo., 1985-87. Author: The Depressive Spectrum, 1974, A Practical Guide to Cognitive Therapy, 1991; contbr. numerous articles to profl. jours. Fellow Am. Psychiat. Assn.; mem. Soc. for Psychotherapy Research, Am. Assn. Suicidology, Assn. for Mental Health Affiliation with Israel. Democrat. Jewish. Office: 6280 Montrose Rd Rockville MD 20852-4119

SCHWAB, H. LAURENCE, family therapist; b. Schenectady, N.Y., Apr. 29, 1952; s. Henry B. and Augusta (Achilles) S.; m. Anna D. Witney (div. 1985); m. Linda J. McMeniman, Apr. 16, 1988; children: Emily, Jeremy, Laurel. BA with hons., Open U., Milton Keynes, Eng., 1976; Cert. Edn., Milton Keynes Coll. Edn., 1975; M.Family Therapy, Hahnemann U., Phila., 1987. Staff producer WMHT, Schenectady, 1980-81; ind. cons. and producer, 1981-85; dir. communication svcs. Hampshire Coll., Amherst, Mass., 1981-85; family therapist intern Fairmount Inst. Adolescent Unit, Phila., 1985-86; family therapist Children's Bur. of Delaware, Wilmington, Del., 1987-89; marriage and family therapist in pvt. practice Wilmington and Media, Pa., 1989—; family therapist Children's Outpatient Svc., Chester and Media, Pa., 1989-92; clin. supr. Hahnemann U., 1989—; clin. preceptor U. Pa., 1990—; coord. family therapy Rockford Ctr., Newark, Del., 1992—. Pres. ch., 1995—. Mem. Am. Assn. Marital and Family Therapy (clin. mem.). Unitarian. Office: Ste 7A 1701 Augustine Cutoff Wilmington DE 19803-3421

SCHWAB, LARRY, ophthalmologist; b. W.Va., Sept. 12, 1940; s. J. Wayne and Helen Ruth (Tidd) S.; m. Martha Harris, June 4, 1966; children: Eric, Mark, Angela. BA, W.Va. U., 1962, MD, 1966. Internship Charity Hosp. of La., New Orleans, 1966-67; residency in ophthalmology W. Va. U., 1969-72; ophthalmologist Internat. Eye Found., Ethiopia, 1972-74; asst. prof. ophthalmology W.Va. U., Morgantown, 1975, 80-82; assoc. dir. Internat. Eye Found., Kenya, 1976-80; project dir. Internat. Eye Found., Malawi, 1982-85, Internat. Eye Found., Royal Commonwealth Soc. for Blind, Zimbabwe, 1986-89; med. dir. Internat. Eye Found., Bethesda, Md., 1993—; adj. clin. prof. dept. ophthalmology W.Va. U., 1994—; adj. assoc. prof. Tulane U. Sch. Tropical Medicine and Pub. Health, New Orleans, 1992—. Author: Eye Care of Developing Nations, 1987, 2d edit., 1990, Pratique de l'Ophtalmologie avev Ressources Limitées, 1993; contbr. numerous sci. articles to profl. jours. Capt. U.S. Army, 1967-69. Named to Acad. of Disting. Alumni W. Va. U., 1993; decorated Bronze Star for Valor and Heroism Rep. of Vietnam, 1968. Fellow Am. Acad. Ophthalmology (Outstanding Humanitarian award 1995), W.Va. Acad. Ophthalmology. Home: 3333 Collins Ferry Rd Morgantown WV 26505-2301 Office: Internat Eye Found 7801 Norfolk Ave Bethesda MD 20814-6015

SCHWAB, MARTIN ERNST, neuroscientist, biology and medicine educator; b. Basle, Switzerland, Apr. 11, 1949; m. Ruth Handschin. PhD in Biology, U. Basle, Switzerland, 1973. Postdoctorate fellow Bioctr. U. Basle, 1974-78; vis. scientist Harvard Med. Sch., Boston, 1978-79; asst. prof. Max Planck Inst. for Psychiatry, Munich, Germany, 1980-85; prof. brain rsch.

Med. Faculty U. Zürich, Switzerland, 1985—. Office: Univ of Zurich, Brain Rsch Inst, Brain Rsch Inst, 8029 Zurich Switzerland

SCHWAB, PAUL JOSIAH, psychiatrist, educator; b. Waxahachie, Tex., Jan. 14, 1932; s. Paul Josiah and Anna Marie (Baeuerle) S.; m. Martha Anne Beed, June 8, 1953; children: Paul Josiah III, John Conrad, Mark Whitney. BA, N. Cen. Coll., 1953; MD, Baylor U., 1957. Diplomate Am. Bd. Psychiatry and Neurology. Intern Phila. Gen. Hosp., 1957-58; clin. assoc. Nat. Cancer Inst., Bethesda, Md., 1958-60; resident in internal medicine U. Chgo., 1960-62, resident psychiatry, 1962-65, chief resident and instr. psychiatry, 1965; pvt. practice Naperville, Ill., 1965—; lectr. psychiatry U. Chgo., 1968-74, assoc. prof., 1974-79; clin. assoc., 1979-86, clin. assoc. prof., 1986—; dir. residency tng. U. Chgo., 1976-79, dir. in-patient unit and day treatment program, 1975-79. Contbr. articles to profl. jours. Bd. trustees North Ctrl. Coll., chair liaison com., 1983—, vice-chmn. acad. and student affairs com., 1983-92, vice chair admissions, fin. aid and student devel., 1992-95. Fellow Am. Psychiat. Assn. (Nancy C.A. Roeske award 1991); mem. AMA, Am. Soc. Clin. Psychopharmacology, Acad. Clin. Psychiatrists, Alpha Omega Alpha. Republican. Methodist. Office: 1200 Tall Oaks Ct Naperville IL 60540-9494

SCHWAB, THOMAS CHARLES, physician; b. Darby, Pa., Aug. 12, 1953; s. Julius Charles and Margaret (Ernst) S.; m. Anne Tyson, May 19, 1978; children: Edward, Laura. BS, Ursinus Coll., 1975; MD, Hahnemann U., 1979. Diplomate Am. Bd. Internal Medicine. Intern, resident Hahnemann Univ., Phila., 1979-82; pvt. practice internal medicine Parkesburg, Pa., 1982—. Mem. AOA Med. Honor Soc. Office: 351 W 1st Ave Parkesburg PA 19365-1201

SCHWABER, MITCHELL KEITH, otolaryngologist; b. Macon, Ga., July 29, 1951; s. Solomon Jack and Emma S.; m. Donna Kay Glover, Oct. 12, 1980; children: Sara Ashley, Anna Rebecca. BS in Medicine, Mercer U., 1972; MD, Baylor U., 1975. Diplomate Am. Bd. Otolaryngology. Intern Johns Hopkins Hosp., Baltimore, 1975-77; resident Baylor Affiliates, Houston, 1977-81; fellow Ear Foundation, Nashville, 1981-82; attending physician St. Vincent's Hosp., Jacksonville, Fla., 1982-86; asst. prof. Vanderbilt U., Nashville, 1987-93, assoc. prof., 1993-96; pres., founder Southeastern Ear Nose & Throat Specialists, Nashville; bd. dirs. Bill Wilkerson Hearing and Speech Ctr. Mem. Am. acad. of Otolaryngology Head-Neck Surgery, Tenn. Acad. Otolaryngology (legis. liason 1988-90), Nashville Acad. Medicine (media and pubs. com. 1986-89), Prosper Meniere Soc., Am. Soc. Evoked Potential Monitoring, Soc. Univ. Otolaryngologists, Centurions of Deafness Rsch. Found., N.Am. Skull Base Soc., Assn for Rsch. in Otolaryngology, Johns Hopkins Med. Alumni Assn., Baylor Alumni Assn., Triological Soc., Am. Neurotology Soc., Soc. for Neurosci., Sigma Xi. Jewish. Office: Southeastern Ear Nose & Throat Specialists 250 25th Ave N Nashville TN 37203

SCHWACH, PAUL P., orthopedic surgeon; b. Buffalo, Aug. 9, 1945; s. Robert J. and Grace C. (Marthia) S.; m. Barbara Frank, Apr. 18, 1976; children: Rebecca C., Catherine M., David I. AB, Boston Coll., 1969; MD, SUNY, Buffalo, 1976. Diplomate Am. Bd. Orthopedic Surgery. Surg. intern Buffalo Gen. Hosp., 1976-77; resident in orthopedics Erie County Med. Ctr., Buffalo, 1977-78, Children's Hosp. Ctr., Buffalo, 1978-79, VA Hosp., Buffalo, 1979-80, Buffalo Gen. Hosp., 1980-81; attending in orthopedics Olean (N.Y.) Gen. Hosp., 1981—, chmn. phys. therapy dept., 1987-89, dir. emergency svcs., 1985-93; exec. dir. Olean Med. Group, 1989-93. Bd. dirs. Civic Music Soc., Olean, 1983-89, YMCA, Olean, 1987-93; active Boy Scouts Am. Fellow Am. Acad. Orthopedic Surgeons; mem. Cattaraugus County Med. Soc. (sec.-treas. 1989-93). Republican. Roman Catholic. Home: 1805 Stardust Ln Olean NY 14760 Office: Olean Med Group 535 Main St Olean NY 14760

SCHWADE, JACK LESTER, cardiologist; b. Chgo., Nov. 12, 1940; s. Raymond J. and Ruth belle (Robinson) S.; m. Goldie Ruth Silverman, Aug. 27, 1963; children: Nathan, Arianne, George. BA, Rice U., 1962; MD, U. Tex. Southwestern, 1966. Resident in internal medicine Dallas VA Hosp., 1970-72, cardiology fellow, 1972-74; pvt. practice Dallas, 1974—; cardiologist Med. City Dallas Hosp., 1974—, med. dir. cardiology, 1980—; instr. in cardiology Dallas VA Hosp., 1974; chief of staff Med. City Dallas Hosp., 1979-80. Contbr. articles to profl. jours. Bd. dirs. Am. Heart Assn., Dallas, 1984-91, pres. Dallas chpt., 1987, fellow clin. coun. Major M.C. U.S. Army, 1967-70. Fellow AMA, ACP, Am. Coll. Cardiology; mem. Dallas County Med. Soc., Tex. Med. Assn., Landmark Club (bd. govs. 1980-91). Jewish. Office: 11617 N Central Expy Ste 240 Dallas TX 75243-3810

SCHWADE, JAMES GARY, radiation oncologist; b. Milw., Dec. 14, 1946; s. Leonard and Esther S.; m. Karyn Karl, July 4, 1982; children: Loryn, David, Jonathan. AB cum laude, Washington U., St. Louis, 1969; Md, Med. Coll. Wis., Milw., 1973. Diplomate Am. Bd. Med. Examiners, therapeutic radiology Am. Bd. Radiologists. From intern to resident in radiaton oncology U. Calif., San Francisco, 1973-77, chief resident radiaiton oncology, 1976-77, instr., 1977-78; acting head radiology sect. radiation oncology br. divsn. cancer treatment, Nat. Cancer Inst., Bethesda, Md., 1978-81; assoc. clin. prof therapeutic radiology U. Miami (Fla.) Sch. Medicine, 1981-87, prof., chmn. dept radiation oncology, 1987-94; assoc. dir. clin. rsch. program Sylvester Cancer Ctr., Miami, 1989-94; med. dir. radiation oncology AMI Palmetto Gen. Hosp., Oncology Treatment Ctr., 1994—; dir. radiation oncology, Gamma Knife unit Miami Neuro Sci. Ctr., Health South Doctor's Hosp., Coral Gables, 1994—; sr. v.p. for medicine and sci. Proton Therapy Corp. of Am., 1995—; spl. asst. for radiation oncology, cancer therapy evaluation program, Divsn. Cancer Treatment, Nat., Cancer Inst., Bethesda, 1977-78; cons. Nat. Naval Med. Ctr., Bethesda, 1978-81; chief dept. radiation oncology, med. dir. regional cancer treatment ctr., Baptist Hosp. Miami, 1981-87; chief radiation oncology svc. Jackson Meml. Hosp., VA Hosp., UMHC/SCCC, Miami, 1981-87; lectr. numerous profl. groups, instns., presenter at nat. and internat. meetings of many profl. groups. Contbr. numerous articles and abstracts to profl. jours., many chpts. to books; assoc editor Internat. Jour. of Radiation Oncology, Biology, Physics, 1991—; revewer ASTRO, Sci. Program 1989-92, Internat. Jour. Oncology. Mem. Am. Cancer Soc., chmn. task force on prostate cancer, Fla. Divsn, mem. rsch. peer rev. subcom; chmn. spl. com. and Fla. com. for Health Care Reform, 1991—; mem. adv. coun. on radiation protection, Fla., HRS, 1985-94, vice chmn. 1988-90, chmn. subcom. on emergency preparedness; chmn. Nat. Assn. for Proton Therapy, 1992. Recipient Order of Red Sword, Am. Cancer Soc., Dade County Unit, Fla., 1988—; grantee Alpha Therapeutic Corp., Inter Am. Pharms. Ltd., Radiation Therapy Oncology Group, Nat. Cancer Inst. Fellow Am. Coll. Radiology; mem. AMA, Fla. Med. Assn., Dade County Med. Assn., Fla. Radiol. Soc. (legis. com. 1984), Am. Radium Soc., Coun. of Affiliated Regional Radiation Therpy Socs. (counselor-at-large Am. Coll. of Radiology ann. mtg. 1988), Am. Soc. for Therapeutic Radiology and Oncology, Am. Endocrinotherapy Soc., Fla. Soc. Clin. Oncology (bd. dirs. 1988-91, legis., legal and ethics com. 1989-90), others. Home: 3501 Anchorage Way Coconut Grove FL 33133-5923 Office: Proton Therapy Corp Am Ste 780 2601 S Bayshore Dr Coconut Grove FL 33133

SCHWAITZBERG, STEVEN DAVID, surgeon; b. Boston, Feb. 13, 1956; s. Carl and Sorra-Lee (Raven) S.; m. Lisa Jane Jacobsen; children: Scott, Andrew, Corey. BA, Johns Hopkins U., 1977; MD, Baylor Coll., 1980. Diplomate Am. Bd. Surgery, Am. Bd. Surgery Critical Care. Chief surgery Lemuel Shattuck, Boston, 1986-89; dir. Surg. ICU New Eng. Med. Ctr., Boston, 1989-96, dir. Ctr. for Minmally Invisive Surgery, 1993—. Maj. U.S. Army, 1990-91. Deocrated Army Commendation medal. Fellow ACS. Office: NEMC # 1047 750 Washington St Boston MA 02111

SCHWANZ, DEBORAH ANN, psychiatric nurse; b. South Bend, Ind., Jan. 1, 1952; d. Ned Christian and Rita Jane (Witucki) S. Diploma in nursing, Meml. Hosp. Sch. Nursing, South Bend, 1973; BS in Health Arts, Coll. of St. Francis, Joliet, Ill., 1991. RN, Fla.; cert. psychiat. and mental health nurse ANCC. House float nurse Meml. Hosp., 1973; psychiat. team leader St. Anthony's Hosp., St. Petersburg, Fla., 1974-81, asst. head nurse, 1981-84, clin. mgr. psychiatry, instr. aggression control techniques, 1984-89; weekend nursing supr. Boley, Inc., St. Petersburg, 1989-92; nurse therapist various nursing homes, St. Petersburg, 1992-93, Physicians' Cmty. Hosp., St. Petersburg, 1993-94; contract psychiat. nurse St. Anthony's Home Health Care, St. Petersburg, 1986-94; psychiat. home health nurse Shands Home Care, Largo, Fla., 1995—; presenter on psychiat. nursing at seminars and workshops, St. Petersburg and Clearwater, Fla., 1984-88. Mem. St. Petersburg Dem. Club. Mem. NOW (past sec. Pinellas chpt.), Mental Health Assn., Meml. Hosp. Sch. Nursing Alumni Assn. Office: 7249 Bryan Dairy Rd Largo FL 33777

SCHWARTZ, ARTHUR ALAN, surgeon; b. N.Y.C., Sept. 16, 1945; s. Philip and Selma (Galen) S.; m. Ann Mass, June 14, 1969 (div. Mar. 1986); 1 child, Chelsea Lara; m. Lorie Jane Lybeck, Mar. 26, 1988; 1 child, Spencer Loren. BA, Columbia Coll., 1965; MD, NYU, 1969. Diplomate Am. Bd. Surgery. Surg. intern N.Y. Hosp.-Cornell Med. Ctr., N.Y.C., 1969-70; surg. resident Peter Bent Brigham Hosp., Children's Hosp., Harvard Med. Sch., Boston, 1970-73; surg. chief resident UCLA Harbor Gen. Hosp., Torrance, Calif., 1973-75, asst. prof. surgery, 1975-78; pvt. practice surgery Aspen (Colo.) Valley Hosp., 1978-92; surgeon No. Calif. Trauma Group, San Jose, Calif., 1992-93; pvt. practice surgery Mid-County Surg. Group, Capitola, Calif., 1993—. Fellow ACS; mem. Santa Cruz Med. Soc. Home: 2520 N Rodeo Gulch Rd Soquel CA 95073 Office: Mid County Surg Group 603 Capitola Ave Capitola CA 95010

SCHWARTZ, BRADLEY FIELDS, urologist; b. Fargo, N.D., July 1, 1964; s. Donald and Lois (Fields) S. BA, Hamline U., St. Paul, 1986; DO, U. North Tex., 1990. Resident in urology Madigan Army Med. Ctr., Tacoma, 1990-96; urologist Fort Benning, Ga., 1996—. Contbr. articles to profl. jours. Maj. U.S. Army, 1990—. Mem. Am. AMA, Am. Urol. Assn., Am. Osteo. Assn. Home: 21 Sanford Rd Colorado Springs CO 80906

SCHWARTZ, CHARLES ELIAS, psychiatrist; b. Mt. Vernon, N.Y., May 4, 1952; s. Marvin Lawrence and Muriel Judith (Schwartz) S.; m. Hope Rebecca Dellon, Apr. 26, 1952; children: Rebecca Elizabeth, Emma Catherine. BA in Psychology, Yale U., 1974; MD, U. Conn., 1978. Diplomate Am. Bd. Internal Medicine, Am. Bd. Psychiatry and Neurology with added qualification in geriatric psychiatry and addiction psychiatry. Resident in internal medicine St. Vincent's Hosp., N.Y.C., 1978-81; resident in psychiatry Columbia Presbyn. Hosp./N.Y. State Psychiat. Inst., 1981-84; fellow in consultation-liaison psychiatry Montfiore Hosp./Albert Einstein Coll. Medicine, Bronx, N.Y., 1984-85; assoc. dir. dept. psychiatry Einstein Coll. Hosp., Bronx, N.Y., 1985-90; dir. med. student tng. in psychiatry Montefiore Hosp., Bronx, N.Y., 1985—; assoc. dir. residency tng. in Psychiatry Albert Einstein Coll. of Medicine, 1988-90; co-chmn. bioethics com. Einstein Coll. Hosp., Bronx, 1989-90; dir. consultation liaison psychiatry North Cen. Bronx Hosp., 1990—; chmn. bioethics com. North Ctrl. Bronx Hosp., 1995—. Mem. ACP, Acad. of Psychosomatic Medicine, Am. Psychiat. Assn., Assn. of Medicine and Psychiatry (bd. dirs. 1991—, pres.-elect 1995—), Soc. Gen. Internal Medicine. Office: North Ctrl Bronx Hosp Dept Psychiatry 11C08 3424 Kossuth Ave Bronx NY 10467-2410

SCHWARTZ, CHARLES JOEL, gastroenterologist; b. N.Y.C., July 31, 1944. BS, Tufts Coll., 1966; MD, SUNY, Bklyn., 1970. Diplomate Am. Bd. Internal Medicine. Intern U. Oreg. Med. Ctr., Portland, 1970-71, jr. med. resident in medicine, 1971-72; GI fellow Beth Israel Hosp., Boston, 1972-73, 74-75, sr. resident, 1973-74; dir. endoscopy Univ. Hosp., Boston U. Med. Ctr., 1975-77; pvt. practice various hosps., Quincy, Mass., 1977-92; dir. gastroenterology Quincy Hosp., 1992—. Contbr. articles to profl. jours. Mem., bd. dirs. Temple Beth David, Westwood, Mass. Capt. USAR, 1971-77. Mem. Am. Coll. Gastroenterology, ACP, AMA, Am. Soc. Gastrointestinal Endoscopy. Office: 500 Congress St Ste 3C Quincy MA 02169-0908

SCHWARTZ, DORIS RUHBEL, nursing educator, consultant; b. Bklyn., May 30, 1915; d. Henry and Florence Marie (Shuttleworth) S. BS, NYU, 1953, MS, 1958. RN, N.Y. Staff nurse Meth. Hosp., Bklyn., 1942-43; pub. health nurse Vis. Nurse Assn., Bklyn., 1947-51; pub. health nurse Cornell U. Med. Coll., Cornell-N.Y. Hosp. Sch. Nursing, N.Y.C., 1951-61, tchr. pub. health nursing, geriatric nursing, 1961-80; ret., 1990; sr. fellow U. Pa. Sch. Nursing, Phila., 1981-90; mem. bd. dirs. Elders With Adult Dependants. Author: Give Us to Go Blithely, 1990 (Book of Yr. award Am. Jour. Nursing 1991); sr. author: The Elderly Chronically Ill Patient: Nursing and Psychosocial Needs, 1963; co-author: Geriatrics and Geriatric Nursing, 1983 (Book of Yr. award Am. Jour. Nursing 1984); contbr. articles to profl. jours. Mem. adv. com. nursing WHO, Geneva, 1971-79; adv. com. Robert Wood Johnson Found., Teaching Nursing Home Project, Princeton, N.J., U. Pa. Wharton Sch. Study of Continuing Care Retirement Communities, 1981-83; vol. Foulkeways Continuing Care Retirement Cmty., Gwynedd, Pa. Served to capt. N.C., U.S. Army, 1943-47, PTO. Rockefeller fellow U. Toronto, 1950-51, Mary Roberts fellow Am. Jour. Nursing, 1955, Fogarty fellow NIH, 1975-76; recipient Diamond Jubilee Nursing award N.Y. County RNs Assn., 1979. Fellow Inst. Medicine of NAS, APHA (Disting. Career award nursing sect. 1979), Am. Acad. Nursing (charter, coun. 1973-74); mem. ANA (Pearl McIver award 1979), Soroptimist (v.p. N.Y.C. club 1974-75), Sigma Theta Tau (Founders award 1979, Mentor award Alpha Upsilon chpt. 1992). Democrat. Mem. Soc. of Friends.

SCHWARTZ, GEORGE R., physician; b. Caribou, Maine; m. Kathleen Schwartz; children: Ruth, Rebekah, Rachel, Moses, Abigail, John Gabriel. BS in Chemistry with honors, Hobart Coll., 1963; MD magna cum laude, SUNY, Bklyn., 1967. Diplomate Am. Bd. Family Practice, Am. Bd. Emergency Medicine; cert. CPR instr. Intern King County Hosp., Seattle, 1967-68; instr. dept. medicine U. Wash., Seattle, 1967-68; resident in psychiatry Hillside Hosp., Glen Oaks, N.Y., 1968-69; resident in surgery Ind. U. Med. Ctr., Indpls., 1971-72; instr. emergency medicine Med. Coll. Pa., Phila., 1972-76, dir. emergency svcs., asst. dir. emergency medicine program, 1972-74; dir. emergency medicine West Jersey Hosp., 1974-76; pvt. practice, 1977; assoc. prof., dir. divsn. emergency medicine U. N.Mex., Albuquerque, 1978-83; staff mem. emergency medicine Heights Gen. Hosp., Albuquerque, 1983-85; with Los Alamos (N.Mex.) Med. Ctr., 1985-90; vis. assoc. prof. Med. Coll. Pa., 1991—. Author: Geriatric Emergencies, 1984; Co-author: (with Tandberg) Emergency Medicine Continuing Edn. Rev., 1981, 2d edit. 1984, (with Bosker) Geriatric Emergency Medicine, 1990; editor: Principles and Practice Emergency Medicine, 1978, 3d edit., 1992; co-editor Trauma Rounds, 1973-75; editorial bd. Annals Emergency Medicine, 1972-81, Resident and Staff Physician, 1978—, Emergency Med. Abstracts, 1978-85, Med. Exam. Publ. Co., 1981-87; contbr. articles to profl. jours., chpts. to textbooks. Med. dir. The Bridge Counselling Ctrs., Los Alamos, N.Mex., 1988-91; dir. planning com. disaster exercise Phila. Internat. Airport, 1974, Camden County Poison Ctr., 1974-76. Recipient Gallup award, 1973, Giraffe award, 1990. Mem. AAAS, AMA, Am. Coll. Emergency Physicians (pres. N.Mex. chpt. 1980-81), N.Mex. Med. Soc., Univ. Assn. Emergency Physicians (chmn. socio-econ. com. 1976-77), Internat. Emergency Care Assn., Am. Trauma Soc. (founding mem.), Am. Acad. Clin. Toxicology, Am. Acad. Emergency Medicine (founding mem., sec. 1994), Internat. Assn. for Study of MSG and Food Additives (pres. 1988). Address: 257 Hyde Park Est Santa Fe NM 87501-8727

SCHWARTZ, GORDON FRANCIS, surgeon, educator; b. Plainfield, N.J., Apr. 29, 1935; s. Samuel H. and Mary (Adelman) S.; m. Rochelle DeG. Krantz, Sept. 5, 1959; children—Amory Blair, Susan Leslie. A.B., Princeton U., 1956; M.D., Harvard U., 1960; MBA, U. Pa., 1990. Intern N.Y. Hosp.-Cornell Med. Ctr., N.Y.C., 1960-61; resident in surgery Columbia-Presbyterian Med. Ctr., N.Y.C., 1963-68; instr. surgery Columbia U., N.Y.C., 1966-68; assoc. in surgery U. Pa., Phila., 1968-70; dir. clin. services Breast Diagnostic Ctr. Jefferson Med. Coll., 1973-78, asst. prof. surgery, 1970-71, assoc. prof., 1971-78, prof., 1978—; practice medicine specializing in surgery and diseases of breast, Phila., 1968—; founder, chmn. acad. com. Breast Health Inst., 1990—; edtl. bd. The Breast Jour., 1994—. Author: (with R.H. Guthrie, Jr.) Reconstructive and Aesthetic Mammoplasty, 1980, (with Douglas Marchant) Breast Disease: Diagnosis and Treatment, 1981, Atlas of Breast Surgery, 1997; contbr. more than 150 articles to profl. jours. Mem. Pa. Gov.'s Task Force on Cancer, 1976-82; mem. breast cancer task force Phila. chpt. Am. Cancer Soc.; mem. clin. investigation rev. com. Nat. Cancer Inst., 1992-95. Served to capt. AUS, 1961-63. NIH Cancer Control fellow, 1968-69. Mem. ACS, AMA, AAUP, Assn. for Acad. Surgery, Allen O. Whipple Surg. Assn., Soc. Surg. Oncology, Internat. Cardiovasc. Soc., Soc. for Surgery Alimentary Tract, Am. Soc. Clin. Oncology, Soc. for Study Breast Diseases (pres. 1981-83), Soc. Internat. Senologie (treas. 1982-90, v.p. 1990-92, sci. com. 1992—), Pa. Med. Soc., Am. Soc. Transplant Surgeons, N.Y. Acad. Scis., Am. Soc. Artificial Internal Organs, Am. Radium Soc., Philadelphia County Med. Soc., Italian Soc. Senology (hon.), Greek Surg. Soc. (hon.), Union League, Locust Club, Princeton Club (pres. Phila. 1989-91), Princeton Club (N.Y.C.), Princeton Terrace Club, Nassau Club, Phi Beta Kappa, Sigma Xi, Alpha Omega Alpha, Nu Sigma Nu. Republican. Jewish. Home: 1805 Delancey Pl Philadelphia PA 19103-6606 Office: 1015 Chestnut St Fl 510 Philadelphia PA 19107-4305

SCHWARTZ, HENRY GERARD, surgeon, educator; b. N.Y.C., Mar. 11, 1909; s. Nathan Theodore and Marie (Zagat) S.; m. Edith Courtenay Robinson, Sept. 13, 1934; children: Henry G., Michael R., Richard H. A.B., Princeton, 1928; M.D., Johns Hopkins, 1932. Diplomate: Am. Bd. Neurol. Surgery (chmn. 1968-70). Denison fellow with Prof. O. Foerster, Breslau, Germany, 1931; surg. house officer Johns Hopkins Hosp., 1932-33; NRC fellow Harvard Med. Sch., 1933-35, instr. anatomy, 1935-36; fellow neurol. surgery Washington U. Med. Sch., St. Louis, 1936-37; instr., asst. prof., assoc. prof. neurol. surgery Washington U. Med. Sch., 1937-46, prof., 1946-88, August Busch prof. emeritus, 1988—; acting surgeon-in-chief Barnes and Allied hosps., 1965-67; chief neurosurgeon Barnes, St. Louis Children's hosps., 1946-74; cons. neurosurgeon St. Louis City, Jewish, Los Alamos (N.M.) hosps.; cons. to surgeon gen. USPHS. to surgeon gen. U.S. Army.; Mem. subcom. neurosurgery NRC; del. World Fedn. Neurosurgery. Mem. editorial bd. Jour. Neurosurgery, chmn. 1967-69, editor, 1975-84. Served with AUS, 1942-45. Decorated Legion of Merit; recipient ofcl. citation and commendation Brit. Army, Harvey Cushing medal, 1979. Fellow ACS (adv. council on neurosurgery 1950, 60, v.p. 1972-73); mem. Soc. Neurol. Surgeons (pres. 1968-69), Am. Acad. Neurol. Surgery (pres. 1951-52), Harvey Cushing Soc. (pres. 1967-68), Am. Neurol. Assn. (hon.), Assn. Research Nervous and Mental Disease, Central Neuropsychiat. Assn. Am., Assn. Anatomists, So. Neurosurg. Soc. (pres. 1953-54), Soc. Med. Cons. to Armed Forces, Am. Surg. Assn. (v.p. 1975-76), Soc. de Neuro-Chirurgie de Langue Francaise, Excelsior Surg. Soc., Johns Hopkins Soc. Scholars, Soc. Internat. de Chirugie (Alpha Omega Alpha leader Am. medicine 1978), World Fedn. Neurosurg. Socs. (hon. pres.), Sigma Xi, Alpha Omega Alpha. Home: 2 Briar Oak Saint Louis MO 63132-4204 Office: Barnes Hosp Pl Saint Louis MO 63110

SCHWARTZ, HOWARD ALAN, periodontist; b. Paterson, N.J., Dec. 27, 1944; s. Samuel and Ruth (Dimond) S.; m. Rita Blumenthal, Dec. 29, 1968; children: Andrew David Schwartz, Steven Austin Schwartz. BS, Fairleigh Dickinson U., 1967, DDS, 1970; cert. in periodontology, Georgetown U., 1972. State Dental Lic. N.J., N.Y., Mass., Pa., Md., Washington. Clin. instr. in periodontics Georgetown U., 1970-72; chief resident Periodontal Section Dept. Dentistry Veteran's Adminstrn. Hosp., Washington, 1972; asst. prof. Periodontics and Oral Medicine Fairleigh Dickinson U. Sch. Dentistry, Hackensack, N.J., 1972-73, part time clin. asst. prof. Periodontics and Oral Medicine, 1973-79, part time clin. assoc. prof. Periodontics and Oral Medicine, 1979-87, part time clin. prof. Periodontics and Oral Medicine, 1987-89; pvt. practice Periodontics and Oral Medicine, 1972—. Author: (with W.A. Gibson) Immunofluorescent Demonstration of IgG, IgM, and IgA in Human Dental Plaque, (with others) Histochemical Localization of Selected Dehydrogenases in Frozen Sections of Human Dental Plaque, (with others) Salvary Composition as related to Dental Calculus Formation in Humans. Mem. Dentist's Div. Com., Hon. Cabinet, United Jewish Community of Bergen County, 1984-85. Fellow Am. Coll. Dentists, Internat. Coll. Dentists. Mem. Am. Dental Assn., Am. Acad. Periodontology, N.J. Dental Assn. (trustee, treas. 1994-96, v.p. 1996—), Internat. Assn. Dental Rsch., Northeastern Soc. Periodontists, Am. Acad. Oral Medicine, N.J. Soc. Periodontology, Bergen County Dental Soc. (pres. 1989-90), Am. Coll. Dentists, Internat. Coll. Dentists. Jewish. Home: 10 Wood Hollow Trl Saddle River NJ 07458-1346 Office: 97 N Dean St Englewood NJ 07631-2806

SCHWARTZ, HOWARD I., gastroenterologist; b. Phila., Aug. 8, 1959; s. Martin and Elaine Schwartz; m. Jill J. Schwartz, Dec. 21, 1985; children: Jennifer, Marissa, Jason. BS, U. Miami, Fla., 1980, MD, 1984. Gastroenterologist Rice & Goldberg, MD, PA, Miami, 1990-93; gastroenterology and rsch. dir. South Fla. Ctr. Digestive Disease, Miami, 1993—; prin. investigator Glaxo Protocol RAN-445, H2B-301, Portocol B5Q-MC-NBBY, Glaxo H2B-304, Abbott M93-100, Glaxo Protocol H2B-306, H2B-312, Abbott 56268 Protocol No. M94-176, Eli Lilly and Pharmaco LSR Protocol H4M-MC-HRRD (A), Astra/Merck Protocol No. 37. Mem. ACP, Am. Coll. Gastroenterology, Am. Gastroent. Assn., Fla. Gastroenterology Soc. Office: South Fla Ctr Digestive Diseases 8950 Newhall #508 Miami FL 33176

SCHWARTZ, HOWARD JULIUS, allergy educator; b. N.Y.C., Nov. 24, 1936; s. Henry and Edna Betty (Herman) S.; m. Gertrude H. Blody, July 1, 1962; children: Adam David, Kaila Jessica, Michael Jonathan. BA, Bklyn. Coll., 1956; MD, Albert Einstein Coll. Medicine, 1960. Diplomate Am. Bd. Allergy and Immunology, Am. Bd. Internal Medicine; lic. allergist Mass., N.Y., Ohio, Nat. Bd. Med. Examiners. Intern, then asst. resident NYU. Med. Services, Bellevue Hosp., N.Y.C., 1960-63, chief resident medicine, psycho-med. div., 1963-64; teaching asst. dept. medicine NYU, N.Y.C., 1961-66; clin. and research fellow in allergy and immunology Mass. Gen. Hosp., Boston, 1966-68; USPHS trainee in medicine Case Western Res. U., Cleve., 1967-71, asst. prof. medicine, 1971-74, mem. Phase II respiratory com., 1971—, mem. hosp. utilization and rev. com., 1975-77, assoc. clin. prof. medicine, 1977-87, clin. prof. medicine, 1987—; asst. physician Univ. Hosps. Cleve., 1968-71, assoc. physician, 1971—, chief allergy clinic, 1972—; staff physician pulmonary sect. Cleve. VA Med. Ctr., 1974-80, cons. in allergy, 1980—; attending physician and cons. in allergy Hillcrest Hosp., Cleve.; cons. staff medicine Mt. Sinai Hosp., Cleve. Author: Hospital Management of the Adult with Status Asthmaticus in Current Therapy of Allergy, 1974, Acute Asthma, Hospital Management-Adult in Current Therapy of Allergy, 1978, Allergic Reactions to Insect Stings in Current Therapy, 1983, also book chpts. and abstracts; contbr. several articles to profl. jours. Served to capt. U.S. M.C., 1964-69. Fellow Am. Acad. Allergy (cutaneous allergy com. 1972-73, penicillin allergy study group 1972—, insect allergy com. 1974—, com. on alternate forms of therapy 1977—, audiovisual com. 1979-81, edn. council 1979-81, chmn. sci. and workshop com. 1982-83, chmn. com. on Am. insects 1980—), Am. Coll. Chest Physicians (com. on allergy 1976—), Am. Coll. Allergy; mem. AMA, Am. Assn. Immunology, Am. Thoracic Soc. (ad hoc com. on definition asthma, allergy, clin. immunology assembly 1979—, program com. 1979-80), Am. Acad. Allergy and Immunology (research council 1980—, sci. and workshop com. 1982—, com. on allergen standardization 1983—, com. on awards, meml. and commemorative lectureships 1984, chmn. com. on anephybis 1992—), Am. Coll. Allergists (com. on insect reactions 1984), Am. Soc. Internal Medicine (com. on internal medicine subspltys. socs. 1984), Asthma and Allergy Found. Am. (med. sci. council 1985), Cen. Soc. Clin. Research, Cleve. Acad. Medicine (health ins. rev. com. splty. panel 1979—), Cleve. Allergy Soc. (sec. treas. 1971, v.p. 1971-72, pres. 1972-74), Cleve. Chest Soc., Cleve. Course in Pulmonary Disease (planning com. 1971-77), Med. Advances Inst. Ohio (allergy com. 1972-73), Midwest Allergy Forum (chmn. 1974, exec. com. 1973-77), Ohio Soc. Allergy and Immunology (program com. 1973-75, sec., treas. 1990, 91, pres.-elect 1991, 92, pres. 1992, 93). Office: Univ Suburban Health Ctr 1611 S Green Rd Cleveland OH 44121-4128

SCHWARTZ, HOWARD WYN, health facility administrator; b. Mpls., June 12, 1951; s. Jerry Schwartz and Geraldine (Berg) Brooks; m. Jeannie Marie Holtzmann, Aug. 2, 1975; children: Abigail Jorene, Rachel Elizabeth. BA cum laude, U. Minn., 1973, MBA, 1982. Acct. Med. Sch., U. Minn., 1973-77, bus. mgr. dept. neurology, 1977-79, adminstr. found. edn. dept., 1979-82, sr. adminstrv. dir., instr. dept. radiology, 1982—; pres. Bus. Mgmt. Svcs., Golden Valley, Minn., 1979—; lectr., author Topics in Radiology Adminstrn., 1984—. Editor-in-chief: RADWORKS Workload Measurement Manual, 1985-87; editor: Radiology Management, 1985-87, Purchasing the Radiology Information System, 1991, Current Concepts in Radiology Management, 1991; contbr. articles to profl. jours. Mem. Cystic Fibrosis Found., Minn., 1980—; chmn. Human Rights Commn., Robbinsdale, 1982-84; sec. Coord. Coun. Minority Concerns, 1984-85; chmn. imaging tech. adv. com. Univ. Hosp. Consortium, 1989-92; dir. Univ. Hosp. Consortium Svcs. Corp., 1990-92, Nat. Summit on Manpower, 1989-92; treas. Tech. Learning Campus Site Coun., Dist. 281, 1990-91, chmn. Bond Referendum campaign, 1995; pres. Armstrong H.S. Parent Assn., Dist. 281, 1991-92. Fellow Am. Healthcare Radiology Adminstrn. (regional pres. 1986-87, nat. pres. 1988-89, sec. edn. found. 1990-91, bd. dirs. edn. found. 1993-95, Outstanding Author award 1990, 93, 96, Midwest Region Disting.

Mem. award 1991, Gold award 1991); mem. Radiologists Bus. Mgrs. Assn., Delta Kappa Epsilon. Home: 7400 Winnetka Heights Dr Golden Valley MN 55427-3549 Office: U Minn Hosp 420 Delaware St SE Minneapolis MN 55455-0374

SCHWARTZ, ILENE, psychotherapist, educator; b. Phila., June 19, 1942; d. Israel Gerson and Susan (Soloway) Schiffman. BS, Temple U., 1970; MEd, Antioch U., 1990. Counselor pvt. practice, Phila., 1978—; cons., crisis counselor in the field. Mem. AAUW, Am. Counseling Assn., Freud Friends.

SCHWARTZ, JEFFREY STEPHEN, physician, educator; b. Paterson, N.J., May 27, 1943; s. Herbert Joseph and Anne (Fabian) S.; m. Susan Hellmann, May 7, 1967; children: Rachel, Jonathan. BA, Rutgers U., 1964; MD, Albert Einstein Coll. Medicine, 1968. Diplomate Am. Bd. Internal Medicine, Am. Bd. Cardiovascular Disease. Resident Lincoln Hosp. Albert Einstein Coll. Medicine, Bronx, N.Y., 1968-71; cardiology fellow Univ. Chgo., 1971-72, 74-75; asst. prof. medicine U. Minn., Mpls., 1977-83, assoc. prof. medicine, 1983-87; prof. medicine SUNY, Buffalo, 1987—; also head div. cardiology, 1991—. Contbr. articles to profl. jours. Maj. U.S. Army, 1972-74. Recipient Henry Rutgers scholarship Rutgers U., 1963-64, Young Investigator Rsch. award NIH, 1977-83, Rsch. grant NIH, 1984-87, 88-92. Mem. Am. Heart Assn., Am. Fedn. for Clin. Rsch., Phi Beta Kappa, Alpha Omega Alpha. Office: Buffalo Gen Hosp 100 High St Buffalo NY 14203-1126

SCHWARTZ, JOHN NORMAN, health care executive; b. Watertown, Minn., Dec. 13, 1945; s. Norman O. and Marion G. (Tesch) S. BA, Augsburg Coll., Mpls., 1967; MHA, U. Minn., 1969. Adminstrv. resident Luth. Hosp. and Med. Ctr., Wheat Ridge, Colo., 1968-69; asst. adminstr. St. Luke's Hosp., Milw., 1969-73, med. adminstr., 1973-75, v.p., 1975-84; sr. v.p. and chief oper. officer Good Samaritan Med. Ctr., Milw., 1984-85, pres. and chief exec. officer, 1985-88; exec. v.p. Aurora Health Care Inc., Milw., 1988-89; gen. mgr. SmithKline Beecham Clin. Labs., Schaumburg, Ill., 1989-90; chief exec. Trinity Hosp. of Advocate Health Care, Chgo., 1991—; bd. dirs. Samaritan Health Plan, Milw., 1984-89. Bd. dirs. Gt. Lakes Hemophilia Found., Milw., 1975-89, Gov.'s appointee to Coun. on Hemophilia and Related Blood Disorders, Madison, 1978, Sullivan Chamber Ensemble, Milw., 1975-84, South Chgo. YMCA, 1993—; bd. dirs. S.E. Chgo. Devel. Commn., 1996—. Recipient Bd. Mem. of Yr. award Great Lake's Hemophilia Found., 1986, Outstanding Cmty. Leadership award Stony Island C. of C., 1996. Fellow Am. Coll. Healthcare Execs. (regent 1993—). Lutheran. Office: Trinity Hosp 2320 E 93rd St Chicago IL 60617-3909

SCHWARTZ, JONATHAN RALPH, psychiatrist; b. N.Y.C., Oct. 4, 1947; s. Jack and Elinor (Landau) S.; m. R. Lisa Sheiman, Dec. 23, 1984; children: Nicholas, Molly. BA, Cornell U., 1968; MD, U. Pitts., 1972. Diplomate Am. Bd. Psychiatry. Intern U. Wis., Madison, 1972-73; physician Curtis Boyd Clinic, Santa Fe, 1976-77; resident Mt. Sinai Hosp., N.Y.C., 1977-80, attending physician, 1980-92, asst. clin. prof. psychiatry, 1982-92; pvt. practice N.Y.C., 1980-92; comm. pvt. practice, 1985-92. Contbr. chpts. to books. With USPHS, 1973-76. Mem. Am. Psychiat. Assn. (com. pvt. practice 1985—), Soc. Sex Therapy and Rsch., Am. Assn. Geriatric Psychiatry. Office: 43 Birch St Derry NH 03038

SCHWARTZ, JOSEPH CHRISTOPHER, ophthalmologist; b. Columbia, Mo., Aug. 15, 1962; s. John T. and Dolores P. Schwartz. BS, U. Md., 1984; MD, U. Md. Sch. Medicine, Balt., 1988. Diplomate Am. Bd. Ophthalmology. Intern internal medicine Mercy Med. Ctr., Balt., 1988-89; resident ophthalmology Washington Hosp. Ctr., 1989-92, fellow vitreoretinal diseases and surgery, 1992-93; attending physician Charles Retina Inst., Memphis, 1993—. Editl. bd. mem. Today's Health Care, 1994-96; contbr. articles to profl. jours. Fellow ACS, Am. Acad. Ophthalmology; mem. AMA, Vitreous Soc., Tenn. Acad. Ophthalmology, Ark. Med. Soc., Memphis Ophthalmol. Soc. Home: 709 College Ln Apt 7 Salisbury MD 21804 Office: Delmagua Vitreoretinal Ctr 105 Pine Bluff Rd Ste 3 Salisbury MD 21801

SCHWARTZ, JOYCE GENSBERG, pathologist; b. San Antonio, July 24, 1950; d. Frank and Sara Gensberg; B.A., U. Tex.-Austin, 1971, M.A., 1972; M.D., U. Tex.-San Antonio, 1980; m. Alan R. Schwartz, July 17, 1977. Speech pathologist Northeast Ind. Sch. Dist., San Antonio, 1971-73; vet. asst., 1973-74; resident in pathology U. Tex. Health Sci. Ctr. at San Antonio, 1980-84, mem. faculty pathology 1984-96; med. dir. Corning Clin. Labs., 1996—. Pres. P.I. Nixon Hist. Libr., 1991-92. Recipient Presdl. Teaching award, 1991, Piper Prof. award, 1992. Mem. AMA, Coll. Am. Pathologists (regional commr.), Tex. Soc. Pathologists (sec. 1994-96), Bexar County Med. Assn., Women's Faculty Assn. (pres. 1988-89), San Antonio Soc. Pathologists (pres. 1988-89), Phi Kappa Phi, Alpha Omega Alpha. Jewish. Office: Corning Clin Labs 4771 Regent Blvd Irving TX 75063

SCHWARTZ, JUDY ELLEN, cardiothoracic surgeon; b. Mason City, Iowa, Oct. 5, 1946; d. Walter Carl and Alice Nevada (Moore) Schwartz. B.S., U. Iowa, 1968, M.P.H. Johns Hopkins U., 1996, M.D., 1971 Diplomate Am. Bd. Surgery, Am. Bd. Thoracic Surgery. Intern, Nat. Naval Med. Center, Bethesda, Md., 1971-72, gen. surgery resident, 1972-76, thoracic surgery resident, 1976-78, staff cardiothoracic surgeon, 1979-82, chief cardiothoracic surgeon, 1982-83; chmn. cardiothoracic surg. dept. Naval Hosp., San Diego, 1983-85, quality assurance program dir., 1985-88, exec. officer Rapidly Deployable Med. Facility Four, 1986-88; asst. prof. surgery Uniformed Services Univ. Health Scis., Bethesda, 1983—; sr. policy analyst quality assurance Profl. Affairs and Quality Assurance, 1988-90, dep. dir. quality assurance, 1990; dir. clin. policy Health Svcs. Ops., Washington, 1990-94; head performance evaluation and improvement Nat. Naval Med. Ctr., 1994—; cardiothoracic speciality cons. to naval med. command U.S. Navy, Washington, 1983-84; Dept. Defense rep. to Joint Commn. Accreditation Health Care Orgn. task force on info. mgmt., 1990-93, chmn. 1991-93, task force on .IMS Tech., 1993-94; chmn. info. mgmt. workshop Fed. Health Care Study Commn.'s Corrd. Fed. Health Care, 1993. Contbr. articles to various publs. Fellow Am. Coll. Cardiology, Am. Coll. Surgeons (com. allied health pers. 1985-91, exec com. 1987-91, accreditation review com. edn. physician asst. 1988-94, treas. accreditation review com. 1991-93, sr. mem. com. allied health pers. 1991-94); mem. AMA, Am. Thoracic Soc., Am. Med. Women's Assn., Am. Mgmt. Assn., Am. Coll. Physician Execs. Lutheran. Office: Nat Naval Med Ctr 8901 Wisconsin Ave Bethesda MD 20889

SCHWARTZ, KENNETH STUART, surgeon; b. N.Y.C., Apr. 3, 1948. BS in Engring. Scis., SUNY, Stony Brook, 1970; MS in Biomed. Engring., U. Fla., Gainesville, 1972; MD, Albert Einstein Coll. Medicine, 1977. Diplomate Am. Bd. Surgery; lic. MD, Calif., N.Y. Resident in surgery Montefiore Hosp., Bronx, N.Y., 1977-81; fellow U. So. Calif., 1981-82; pvt. practice N.Y.C., 1982—; adj. asst. prof. N.Y. Coll. Podiatric Medicine, 1993; assoc. prof. surgery N.Y. Coll. Osteopathic Medicine, 1992; clin. asst. prof. surgery N.Y. Med. Coll., 1982—; chief surgery St. Barnabas Hosp., Bronx, 1987, pres. med. staff, 1990-92; chief vascular surgery sect. White Plains Hosp. Med. Ctr., 1995. Fellow ACS; mem. Am. Med. Soc., N.Y. Cardiovascular Soc., Ea. Vascular Soc., Westchester County Med. Soc., Sigma Xi, Tau Beta Pi. Office: Vascular Surg Assocs 14 Harwood Ct Ste 326 Scarsdale NY 10583-4120

SCHWARTZ, LEONARD, psychiatrist; b. Pitts., July 10, 1925; s. Harry Morris and Jeannette (Harris) S.; m. Mildred Bernstein, Sept. 8, 1946; children: Debra Lynn Schwartz Bailey, Jodi Sue Schwartz Lindner. BS, U. Pitts., 1948, MD, 1952, cert. in psychiatry, 1956, cert. in psychoanalysis, 1968. Diplomate Am. Bd. Psychiatry and Neurology. Intern Montefiore Hosp., 1952-53; resident Western Psychiat. Inst., U. Pitts., 1953-56; pvt. practice Pitts., 1956-87; chmn. dept. psychiatry Montefiore Hosp., Pitts., 1963-87; adj. clin. prof. Dept. Health and Edn., U. Pitts. Author: heavyhands, the Ultimate Exercise, 1982, heavyhands Walking, 1987, The heavyhands Walking Book, 1989; inventor hand weights for exercise. With USN, 1943-46. Mem. Am. Psychiat. Assn., AMA, Allegheny County Med. Soc., Am. Coll. Sports Medicine, Alpha Omega Alpha. Home: PO Box 81867 Pittsburgh PA 15217-0867

SCHWARTZ, LITA LINZER, psychologist, educator; b. N.Y.C., Jan. 14, 1930; d. Aaron Jerome and Dorothy Claire (Linzer) Linzer; m. Melvin Jay Schwartz, June 18, 1950 (div. 1983); children: Arthur Lee, Joshua David, Frederic Seth. AB, Vassar Coll., 1950; EdM, Temple U., 1956; PhD, Bryn Mawr Coll., 1964. Diplomate Am. Bd. Forensic Psychology, Am. Bd. Profl. Psychology; lic. psychologist, Pa. Part-time instr., counselor Pa. State U., Ogontz, Campus, Abington, 1961-66, asst. prof. ednl. psychology, 1966-71, assoc. prof., 1971-76, prof., 1976-93, disting. prof., 1993-95, prof. women's studies, 1993-95, disting. prof. emerita, 1995—; pvt. practice, 1964—; cons. in field. Recipient Humanitarian Award N.Y. Philanthropic League, 1973, Christian R. and Mary F. Lindback award, 1982, Outstanding Tchr. award Pa. State U. Coll. Edn. Alumni, 1982. Fellow APA, Am. Orthopsychiatric Assn.; mem. Am. Bd. Forensic Psychology, Am. Fertility Soc., Internat. Council of Psychologists (bd. dirs. 1995—), Assn. Tchr. Educators (Tchr. Laureate 1993-94), Coun. for Exceptional Children, Assn. Family and Conciliation Cts., Nat. Assn. for Gifted Children, Pa. Assn. Gifted Children, Soc. for Advancement of Field Theory (exec. bd. 1991-93), Acad. Family Mediators (Pa. and Del. Valley chpts., evaluation com. child custody mediation project Del. Valley), Ethnic Studies Assn. Del. Valley (co-chair program com. 1986-88), Psi Chi. Author: American Education, 1969, 74, 78; Educational Psychology, 1972, 77; The Exceptional Child: A Primer, 1975, 79; Exceptional Students in the Mainstream, 1984; (with Natalie Isser) The American School and The Melting Pot, 1985, 89, (with Florence W. Kaslow) The Dynamics of Divorce, 1987; (with Natalie Isser) The History of Conversion and Contemporary Cults, 1988; Alternatives to Infertility: Is Surrogacy the Answer?, 1991, Why Give Gifts to the Gifted?: Investing in a National Resource, 1994; editor: Mid-Life Divorce Counseling, 1994; contbr. over 60 articles to profl. jours., numerous chapters to books. Office: Pa State U Ogontz Campus Abington PA 19001

SCHWARTZ, LOUIS WINN, ophthalmologist; b. Pa., Apr. 19, 1942; s. Edward and Sylvia Beatrice (Winn) S.; m. Linda Weinberg, June 14, 1964; children: Joanne Karen, Geoffrey Paul. AB, Bowdoin Coll., 1963; MD, Jefferson Med. Coll., 1967. Diplomate Am. Bd. Ophthalmology. Intern Phila. Gen. Hosp.-U. Pa., 1967-68; resident in ophthalmology Wills Eye Hosp., Phila., 1970-73; ophthalmologist Ophthalmic Assocs., Lansdale, Pa., 1973—; attending surgeon Wills Eye Hosp. Glaucoma Svc., Phila., 1984—; clin. assoc. prof. ophthalmology Jefferson Med. Coll., Phila., 1984—; chief ophthalmology North Penn Hosp., 1995—. Co-author: Laser Therapy of Anterior Segment, 1988, 7 other books; assoc. editor Contact Lens Assn. Ophthalmology Jour., 1988; contbr. numerous articles to profl. jours. Recipient Honor award Am. Acad. Ophthalmology, 1988. Mem. AMA, Am. Glaucoma Soc., Pa. Acad. Ophthalmology, InterCounty Ophthalmol. Soc. (pres. 1985-86), Ophthalmic Club Phila. (pres. 1985-86). Office: Ophthalmic Assocs 1000 N Broad St Lansdale PA 19446-1138

SCHWARTZ, MARSHALL ZANE, pediatric surgeon; b. Mpls., Sept. 1, 1945; s. Sidney Shay and Peggy Belle (Lieberman) S.; m. Michele Carroll Walker, Oct. 16, 1971; children: Lisa, Jeffrey. BS, U. Minn., 1968, MD, 1970. Diplomate Am. Bd. Surgery, Am. Bd. Pediatric Surgery,. Intern N.Y. Hosp., N.Y.C., 1970-71; resident in gen. surgery U. Minn., Mpls., 1971-73, 75-76, rsch. fellow, 1974-75; jr. resident in pediatric surgery Children's Hosp. Med. Ctr., Harvard Med. Sch., 1973-74, sr. resident in pediatric surgery, 1976-77, chief resident in pediatric surgery, 1977-78; instr. Med. Sch. Harvard U., Boston, 1978-79; asst. in surgery Childrens Hosp. Med. Ctr., Boston, 1978-79; asst. prof. Med. Br. U. Tex., Galveston, 1979-81, assoc. prof. Med. Br., 1981-83, chief. pediatric surgery Med. Br., 1980-83; assoc. prof. U. Calif., Davis, 1983-86, prof., 1986-92, chief pediatric surgery, 1983-92, programmatic subcom., 1984-86, vice chmn. faculty Sch. Medicine, 1990-91, chmn. faculty Sch. Medicine, 1991-92; prof. surgery and pediatrics George Washington Sch. Medicine, 1992—, Thomas Jefferson Sch. Medicine, 1992-96; surgeon-in-chief, chmn. dept. pediatric surgery Children's Nat. Med. Ctr., Washington, 1992-96; assoc. med. dir., assoc. chmn. dept. surgery Alfred I. Dupont Inst. Children's Hosp., Wilmington, Del., 1996—. Editorial bd. Journal of Pediatric Surgery, 1988—. Pres. bd. dirs. Sacramento Children's Hosp. Found., 1990-92; vice chmn. Bd. of Childrens Faculty Assocs., Childrens Nat. Med. Ctr. Recipient Basil O'Connor Rsch. award March of Dimes Found., 1981, Young Investigator award NIH, 1982, Found. for Children Rsch. award, 1982, James W. McLaughlin award U. Tex., 1983. Fellow ACS; mem. Am. Surg. Assn., Soc. Univ. Surgeons, Am. Pediatric Surg. Assn., Soc. Surgery of the Alimentary Tract, Pacific Assn. of Pediatric Surgeons (pres.). Jewish. Office: Alfred I Dupont Inst Childrens Hosp 1600 Rockland Rd Wilmington DE 19899

SCHWARTZ, MARTIN LERNER, physician; b. Newport News, Va., 1945. PhD in Biochemistry, Duke U., 1972, MD, 1973. Resident U. N.C., Chapel Hill, 1973-77; mem. staff Bess Kaiser Hosp., Portland, Oreg., 1977—. Home: 4347 SW Donner Way Portland OR 97201-1598 Office: 3325 N Interstate Ave Portland OR 97227-1020

SCHWARTZ, MARY REBECCA, pathologist; b. Bremen, Germany, Oct. 7, 1953; parents Am. citizens; d. M.E. and Molly (Rosoff) Schwartz; m. David Allen Cech, Apr. 12, 1981; children: Jacqueline Michelle, Daniel Michael. BA with honors, Stanford (Calif.) U., 1974; MD, Washington U., 1978. Diplomate in ant. and clin. pathology with subsplty. in cytopathology Am. Bd. Pathology. Intern, resident Baylor Coll. Medicine, 1978-82; asst. prof. Baylor Coll. Medicine, Houston, 1978-92, assoc. prof. pathology and dermatology, 1992—; clin. assoc. prof. So. Ill. U., Springfield, Ill., 1989-90; attending pathologist St. John's Hosp., Springfield, 1989-90, The Meth. Hosp., Houston, 1978—; residency program dir. Baylor Coll. Medicine, 1990—. Contbr. articles to profl. jours., chpts. to books. Recipient Merck award Washington U. Sch. Medicine, 1978. Fellow Coll. Am. Pathologists, Am. Soc. Clin. Pathologists; mem. U.S. and Can. Acad. Pathology, Papanicolaou Soc. Cytology, Am. Soc. Cytopathology (chmn. edn. devel. com. 1992-95, chmn. lab. accreditation com. 1995—), Phi Beta Kappa, Alpha Omega Alpha. Office: The Methodist Hospital 6565 Fannin MS 205 Houston TX 77030

SCHWARTZ, MELVIN, psychiatry educator; b. N.Y.C., Jan. 30, 1934; s. Meyer and Lillian Dorothy (Nisselson) S.; m. Myrna Joyce Melman, June 15, 1961; children: Steven, Stephanie. BS, Columbia U., 1955; MD, Northwestern U., 1961; postgrad., UCLA, 1962-65. Diplomate Am. Bd. Psychiatry and Neurology. Pvt. practice Santa Ana, Calif., 1967—; assoc. clin. Med. Sch. U. Calif., Irvine, 1980-94; chief of psychiatry St. Joseph Hosp., Orange, Calif., 1970-80, sec., treas. 1975-76; chief of psychiatry Western Med. Ctr., Santa Ana, 1969-75; ind. med. examiner Worker's Compensation Sys., Calif., 19866. Capt. U.S. Army, 1965-67, ETO. Fellow Am. Psychiat. Assn. Republican. Office: 1125 E 17th St Ste 211E Santa Ana CA 92701-2201

SCHWARTZ, MICHAEL ALAN, physician; b. N.Y.C., Dec. 13, 1944; s. David Henry and Ray Schwartz; m. Joan Kay Clayton, Jan. 12, 1979; children: Dana, David, Elizabeth. AB, Princeton, 1965; MD, Cornell U., 1969. Intern, medicine N.Y. Hosp., Cornell, 1969-70; resident, psychiatry N.Y. Hosp., Cornell, Westchester, 1970-74; clin. assoc. NIMH, Washington, 1972-74; asst. prof. psychiatry Cornell Med. Coll., N.Y.C., 1974-76; assoc. to prof. of psychiatry N.Y. Med. Coll., 1976-92; prof. and vice chmn. dept. psychiatry Case Western Res. U., Cleve., 1992—. Editor: (with Manfred Spitzer, Christoph Mundt, Friedrick Uehlein) Phenomenology, Language, and Schizophrenia, 1992, (with John Sadler and Osborn Wiggins) Psychiatric Diagnostic Classification, 1994; asst. editor Integrative Psychiatry, 1990—; mem. editl. bd. Comprehensive Psychiatry, 1991—, Jour. of Personality Disorders, 1992—; assoc. editor Philosophy, Psychiatry, Psychology, 1993—; contbr. articles to numerous sci. jours. Fellow Am. Psychiat. Assn., Assn. for Advancement of Philosophy and Psychiatry (pres. 1991-94, founding pres. 1994—).

SCHWARTZ, MICHAEL ALLEN, cardiologist; b. Kansas City, Mo., Jan. 27, 1946; s. Harry and Esther (Braigan) S.; m. Diane Decher, Nov. 27, 1970; children: David, Kaben. BA, U. Mo., 1968; MD, U. So. Calif., L.A., 1972. Intern Georgetown U. med. div., D.C. Gen. Hosp., 1972-73; Resident medicine Georgetown U. Med. div. D.C. Gen. Hosp., Washington, 1973-75; fellow in cardiology U. Vt., Burlington, 1975-77; pvt. practice Cardiology Specialists, Greenbelt, Md., 1978—; clin. assoc. prof. medicine George Washington U., Washington, 1995—; med. advisor Assn. Am. RRs, Washington, 1985—. Fellow ACP, Am. Coll. Cardiology, Am. Heart Assn.; mem. AMA (physician recognition award 1984—). Office: 7500 Hanover Pkwy Ste 204 Greenbelt MD 20770-2011

SCHWARTZ, MILES JOSEPH, cardiologist; b. Richmond, Va., Aug. 7, 1925; s. Hugo and Ella (Kramer) S.; m. Margery Baer Irish, June 7, 1956 (div. 1972); children: Elizabeth, James, Margaret; m. Katherine Rush, May 26, 1980. BS, Queens Coll., 1947; MD, N.Y.U., 1951. Diplomate Am. Bd. Internal Medicine, Am. Bd. Cardiovascular Disease. Intern Mt. Sinai Hosp., N.Y.C., 1951-52, resident, 1953-54; resident Bronx (N.Y.) VA Hosp., 1952-53, fellow, 1954-55, asst. med. sect. chief, 1956-58; resident, then chief resident St. Luke's Hosp., 1955-56; asst. attending physician St. Luke's Hosp. Ctr., N.Y.C., 1959-64, assoc. attending physician, asst. cardiologist, 1959-69, assoc. cardiologist, 1969, chief hypertension clinic, 1959-81, attending physician, dir. cardiography, 1970—, clin. dir. pvt. med. svc., 1974-78; assoc. dir. medicine St. Luke's/Roosevelt Hosp. Ctr., N.Y.C., 1978-84, dir. clin. cardiology tng. program, 1966—, assoc. dir. divsn. cardiology, 1989-95, acting dir. divsn. cardiology, 1995—; cons. Sharon (Conn.) Hosp., 1976-91; prof. clin. med., Columbia U. Coll. of P & S. With USNR, 1944-46. Fellow ACP, Am. Coll. Cardiology, Alpha Omega Alpha. Jewish. Office: St Luke's/Roosevelt Hosp 1111 Amsterdam Ave New York NY 10025

SCHWARTZ, MORTIMER LEONARD, internist, educator; b. Newark, Jan. 12, 1915; s. Herman and Rose (Nusbaum) S.; m. Rene Kanengiser, Mar. 25, 1941; children—Gary, Jessica Schwartz Auerbach, Alison. M.D., Eclectic Med. Coll., Cin., 1938. Diplomate Am. Bd. Internal Medicine, Am. Bd. Cardiovascular Disease. Intern Alexian Bros. Hosp., Elizabeth, N.J., 1938-39; resident Jersey City Hosp., 1947-48; practiced medicine specializing in internal medicine and cardiovascular disease, N.J., 1940-42, 46-47, 47—; mem. faculty N.J. Med. Sch., Newark, 1958-72; prof. medicine Albert Einstein Coll. Medicine, Bronx, N.Y., 1973-77; chief cardiovascular sect. Bronx Lebanon Hosp., 1972-77; dir. medicine Mountainside Hosp., Montclair, N.J., 1977-80; prof. medicine U. Medicine and Dentistry/N.J. Med. Sch., Newark, 1966-72, 79—; dir. dept. medicine Bergen Pines County Hosp., Paramus, N.J., 1981-84. Served to maj. U.S. Army, 1942-46. Recipient Harry Gold award, 1974. Fellow ACP Am. Coll. Cardiology, Am. Coll. Chest Physicians, Council on Clin. Cardiology of Am. Heart Assn., Am. Coll. Clin. Pharmacology. Research on pharmacology. Home: 321 N Wyoming Ave Apt 4A South Orange NJ 07079-1671

SCHWARTZ, PATRICIA LYNN CREAMER, nurse practitioner; b. Tampa, Fla., Aug. 16, 1955; d. Albert Ed and Mary Lou (Vaughan) Creamer; m. David Wayne Schwartz. ASN, Hillsborough Community Coll., 1981; BS, U. South Fla., 1987, MS, 1989. Cert. family and pediatric nurse practitioner. Emergency rm. nurse Tampa (Fla.) Gen. Hosp., 1975-77, 77-89; nurse cons. Crikiton, Tampa, 1989; advanced nurse practitioner Dr. Wijetilleke, Vero Beach, Fla., 1989—. Mem. ANA, Fla. Nurses Assn. (dist. 17 sec. 1991), Golden Key Honor Soc., Phi Kappa Phi, Sigma Theta Tau. Democrat. Baptist. Home: 1057 6th Ave # 9B Vero Beach FL 32960-5929

SCHWARTZ, PETER ALAN, obstetrician, gynecologist, educator; b. Boston, Jan. 10, 1941; s. Louis Nathaniel and Shirley (Ruby) S.; m. Lynne Ellen Johnson, Nov. 27, 1971; children: Seth Alan, Lael Benjamin, Lee Andrew. BA, Harvard U., 1962; MD, Boston U., 1966. Diploamte Am. Bd. Ob-Gyn. Intern U. Utah, Salt Lake City, 1966-67; resident in ob-gyn. Yale U., New Haven, 1969-73; attending obstetrician and gynecologist Cooley Dickinson Hosp., Northampton, Mass., 1973-86; dir. dept. ob-gyn. The Reading (Pa.) Hosp. and Med. Ctr., 1987—; assoc. clin. prof. U. Pa., Phila., 1987—; oral examiner Am. Bd. Ob-Gyn., Dallas, 1989—. Contbr. chpt. to book, articles to profl. jours. Coach youth soccer Wyomissing (Pa.) Area Soccer Club, 1993-95, bd. dirs., 1994-95. With USPHS, 1967-69. Recipient Nat. Faculty award Coun. for Resident Edn., 1995. Mem. Obstet. Soc. Phila. (coun., treas., v.p., pres.), Am. Coll. Ob-Gyn. (vice chair 1996—). Home: 2009 Regency Dr Wyomissing PA 19610 Office: Reading Hosp and Med Ctr 300 S 6th Ave PO Box 16052 Reading PA 19612-6052

SCHWARTZ, RICHARD HARVEY, pediatrician; b. Bklyn., July 6, 1938; s. Hy and Ruth (Marshak) S.; m. Rose Lynne Hass, May 29, 1960; children: Lisa, Keith, Keira. BA, George Washington U., 1960; MD, Georgetown U., 1965. Diplomate Am. Acad. Pediatrics, Am. Soc. Addiction Medicine. Intern U.S. Army, 1965-66, resident, 1969-71; pediatrician Vienna (Va.) Pediatric Assn., 1972—. Contbr. articles to profl. jours. Maj. U.S. Army, 1965-69. Mem. AMA (Outstanding Contbn. in Adolescent Medicine award 1990), Am. Acad. Pediatrics (rsch. award 1989). Jewish. Office: Vienna Pediatric Assn 410 Maple Ave W Vienna VA 22180-4224

SCHWARTZ, RICHARD STANTON, psychiatrist; b. N.Y.C., Mar. 30, 1948; s. M. Stephen and Doris (Jones) S.; m. Jacqueline Olds, Aug. 26, 1978; children: Nathaniel, Sarah Elizabeth. AB magna cum laude, Harvard Coll., Cambridge, Mass., 1970; MD, Harvard Coll., Boston, 1974; grad., Boston Psychoanalytic Inst., 1989. Diplomate Am. Bd. Psychiatry and Neurology. Intern Mt. Auburn Hosp., Cambridge, 1974-75; resident in psychiatry McLean Hosp., Belmont, Mass., 1975-78; asst. med. dir. Bridgewater (Mass.) State Hosp., 1978-79; psychiatrist-in-charge, Codman II McLean Hosp., Belmont, Mass., 1978-86; instr. psychiatry Harvard Med. Sch., Boston, 1979-91; asst. clin. prof. psychiatry Harvard Med. Sch., 1991—; faculty Boston Psychoanalytic Inst., 1991—; assoc. dir., dir. psychotherapy adult outpatient clinic McLean Hosp., Belmont, Mass., 1986-89; acting dir. Adult Outpatient Clinic McLean Hosp., Belmont, 1989; dir. Adult Outpatient Clinic McLean Hosp., Belmont, Mass., 1990-95, dir. tng. in ambulatory svcs., 1995—. Contbr. articles to profl. jours. Mem. Am. Psychiat. Assn., Mass. Psychiat. Soc., Boston Psychoanalytic Soc., Am. Psychoanalytic Assn. also Office: 30 Hillside Ave Cambridge MA 02140 Office: McLean Hosp 115 Mill St Belmont MA 02178-1041

SCHWARTZ, ROBERT HENRY, pediatrician, allergist; b. Bklyn., Apr. 20, 1936; s. Emanuel and Rose (Mantel) S.; m. Carol Susan Lauretz, May 18, 1938; children: Rhonda Lynn Schwartz Slovic, Lisa Meredith Schwartz Weiss. AB, Dartmouth Coll., 1957; MD with honors, U. Rochester, N.Y., 1962. Diplomate Am. Bd. Pediatrics in pediatric allergy, Am. Bd. Allergy and Immunology. Intern medicine Strong Meml. Hosp., Rochester, 1962-63, resident pediatrics, 1963-64; clin. assoc. NIH, Bethesda, Md., 1964-66; sr. resident Babies Hosp., Columbia-Presbyn. Med. Ctr., N.Y.C., 1966-67; fellow allergy U. Rochester, 1967-69, asst. prof. pediatrics, 1969-73, assoc. prof., 1973-78, prof., 1978—; dir. Cystic Fibrosis Ctr., Strong Meml. Hosp., Rochester, 1967-85, dir. allergy tng. program, 1970-85, dir. pediatric allergy clinic, 1970-85, dir. pediatric clin. allergy, 1991—; dir. Allergy Asthma Immunology of Rochester, 1985—; dir. Am. Bd. Allergy and Immunology, 1978-83, pres., 1983. Sr. editor Pediatric Asthma Allergy and Immunology, 1992—. Pres. Allergy and Asthma Rochester Resource Ctr., 1995—. Lt. comdr. USPHS, 1964-66. Recipient McCurdy-Stornont award Monroe County Med. Soc. Fellow Am. Acad. Allergy Asthma and Immunology, Am. Assn. Cert. Allergists; mem. Soc. Pediatric Rsch., Am. Pediatric Soc., Phi Beta Kappa. Republican. Jewish. Office: Allergy Asthma Immunology 360 Perinton Hills Office Park Fairport NY 14450

SCHWARTZ, ROSELIND SHIRLEY GRANT, podiatrist; b. N.Y.C., Apr. 23, 1922; d. Joseph and Amy (Jacobs) Grant; m. Herman Schwartz, Dec. 19, 1943 (dec. Sept., 1980); children: Arthur Zachary, Raymond Dana. BA, NYU, 1943; D Podiatry cum laude, L.I. U., 1947, DPM, 1970; postgrad., L.A. Trade Tech. Coll., 1973-75. Notary pub., Calif. Pvt. practice Podiatry N.Y.C., 1947-73; cons. L.A., 1973-76, travel cons., 1974—; owner, mgr. Ros Travel, N.Y.C., 1995—. Bd. dirs. Welfare League for Retarded Children, 1955-73, chmn. Annual Souvenir Jour., 1955-65, Annual Luncheon, 25th anniversary, 1968, pres., 1969-70; pres. Sisterhood of Community Ctr. of Israel, N.Y., 1966-67; Cub den mother Boy Scouts Am., N.Y., 1960-63; class mother Pub. Schs., N.Y., 1960-66, pres. Parents' Assn. Jr. High Sch., N.Y., 1966-69; bd. dirs., pres. Barrington-Terryhill Condominium Assn., 1981—; vol. UCLA, 1981—; mem. Adv. Coms., Nurse Anesthesists, Infant & Child Care, 1981—. Recipient testimonial Community Ctr. Israel, Bronx, N.Y., 1971, award for devoted leadership Welfare League, 1963, 65. Mem. ARC, IATA, Assn. Wives of Physicians, Podiatry Soc. N.Y. State, Bus. and Profl. Women. Home and Office: Ros Travel 269 W 11th St Ste 3C New York NY 10014-2493

SCHWARTZ, SEYMOUR IRA, surgeon, educator; b. N.Y.C., Jan. 22, 1928; s. Samuel and Martha (Paul) S.; m. Ruth Elaine Wainer, June 18,

1949; children: Richard, Kenneth, David. BA, U. Wis., 1947; MD, NYU, 1950; PhD (hon.), U. Lund, Sweden, 1989; FRCS (hon.), y. Intern Strong Meml. Hosp., Rochester, N.Y., 1950-51, resident, 1951-52, 54-57; asst. prof. surgery U. Rochester, N.Y., 1959-63, assoc. prof, 1963-67, prof., 1967—, chmn. dept., 1987—, dir. surg. rsch., 1962-82; nat. cons. USAF, 1968-77; mem. surgery study sect. A, NIH, 1974-78. Co-author: Mapping of America, 1980, Surgical Reflections, 1991, Mapping of the French and Indian War, 1994; co-editor: Maingot's Abdominal Operations, 2 edits.; editor-in-chief: Year Book of Surgery, 6 edits., 1969—. Bd. mgrs. Strong Meml. Hosp., Rochester. Lt. (j.g.) USN, 1952-54. Recipient Sesquicentennial medal U. S.C., 1974, Acrel medal Swedish Surg. Assn., 1974, Yandell medal U. Louisville (Ky.), 1978, Roswell Park medal, 1989, Albert Kaiser medal, 1992; John and Mary R. Markle scholar in acad. medicine, 1960. Fellow ACS (regent 1988, chmn. bd. regents 1994—, programs and ethics com. 1989—, Disting. Svc. award 1986), Royal Coll. Surgeons Edinburgh (hon.), Ctrl. Surg. Soc. (pres. 1981-82), So. Surg. Soc., Soc. Univ. Surgeons, Soc. Clin. Surgery (pres. 1985), Am. Surg. Assn. (pres. 1993-94), Am. Antiquarian Soc., Grolier Club (N.Y.C.), Cosmos Club (Washington), Genesee Valley Club, Phi Beta Kappa, Alpha Omega Alpha. Office: U Rochester Med Ctr 601 Elmwood Ave Rochester NY 14642-0001

SCHWARTZ, SORELL LEE, pharmacologist, toxicologist, educator; b. Buffalo, Sept. 13, 1937; s. Jacob M. and Rosalind (Greenberg) S.; m. Marsha Kohlenstein, June 9, 1963; children: Joanne Beth, Rebecca Lynn. B.S., U. Md., 1959; Ph.D., Med. Coll. Va., 1963. Pharmacologist, U.S. Naval Med. Research Inst., Bethesda, Md., 1963-66, head pharmacology div., 1966-68; prof. pharmacology, dir. toxicology and applied pharmacokinetics program Georgetown U. Sch. Medicine, 1968—; sci. dir. Ctr. for Environ. Health and Human Toxicology, Washington, 1983-96; prin. Internat. Ctr. for Toxicology and Medicine, Rockville, Md., 1996—; prin. Internat. Ctr. for Toxicology and Medicine, 1996—. Contbr. numerous articles to sci. jours. Served with USNR, 1963-66. Mem. Am. Soc. Pharmacology and Exptl. Therapeutics, Soc. Toxicology, Am. Coll. Toxicology, Am. Acad. Clin. Toxicology, Soc. Risk Analysis, Soc. for Law, Medicine and Ethics. Jewish. Achievements include research in mathematical modeling of biological systems, risk assessment, risk management, methods for causality assessment and uncertainty judgments. Address: Georgetown U Dept Pharmacology Sch Medicine Washington DC 20007

SCHWARTZ, STANLEY E., surgeon; b. Bklyn., Jan. 14, 1917; s. Robert Lazarus and Rose (Gilman) S.; m. Rosalind W. Wohlstadter, June 21, 1941 (dec. Oct. 1992); children: Wendie-Ann Schwartz Rosenbaum, Teri Lynn Schwartz Zobel, Rob, Wolf, Skai W. BS, U. Md., 1937; MD, U. Md., Balt., 1941; postgrad., N.Y. Med. Coll., 1948-49. Diplomate Am. Bd. Surgery. Rotating intern Queens Gen. Hosp., Jamaica, N.Y., 1941-42, sr. intern in surgery, 1946-47, fellow in surgery, 1947-48, resident, 1949-51, chief resident, 1951-52; pvt. practice, Miami Beach, Fla., 1952-62; sect. chief gen. surgery VA Med. Ctr., Bronx, N.Y., 1962-86, asst. to chief staff, 1973-86; ret., 1986; pvt. practice, Merritt Island, Fla., 1986—; clin. instr. surgery Albert Einstein Coll. Medicine, Bronz, 1963-64, clin. assoc. prof., 1964-66, asst. clin. prof., 1966-73; asst. prof. clin. surgery Mt. Sinai Sch. Medicine, N.Y.C., 1973-86; civilian contract surgeon Patrick AFB (Fla.) Hosp., 1988-92. Contbr. articles to med. jours. Capt. M.C., USAAF, 1942045; col. USAR, ret., 1977. Fellow ACS, Internat. Coll. Surgeons; mem. Southeastern Surg. Congress, Brevard County Med. Soc. (courtesty), Soc. Gen. Surgeons, Res. Officers Assn., Ret. Officers Assn., Assn. VA Surgeons (sec. profl. stds. bd., chmn. med. records com.), Patrick AFB Officers Club,. Republican. Jewish. Home and Office: 15 Tropical Island Ln Merritt Island FL 32952-6801

SCHWARTZ, STEPHEN WAYNE, critical care, emergency and recovery room nurse; b. Alva, Okla., July 4, 1957; s. Arthur Gregory and Fern Marie (Burns) S. Cert. EMT, Phoenix Community Coll., 1982; LPN, Maricopa Tech. Community Coll., 1986, ADN, 1987; AAS in Electro-neuro Diagnostics, Phoenix Coll., 1992. RN, Ariz. EMT Ariz. Ambulance & Rescue, Mesa; LPN orthopedic and psychiatry Maricopa Med. Ctr., Phoenix; RN John C. Lincoln Hosp., Phoenix, Med Pro, Inc., Phoenix, Phoenix Bapt. Hosp., Health Temp, Inc., Phoenix. Mem. The Cousteau Soc.

SCHWARTZ, STEVEN, psychologist, educator; b. N.Y.C., Nov. 5, 1946; arrived in Australia, 1978; s. Robert and Frances (Raiten) S.; m. Carolyn Susan Greenberg, June 23, 1968; children—Seth, Tricia, Gregory. B.A., Bklyn. Coll., 1967; M.S., Syracuse U., 1970, Ph.D., 1971. Asst. prof. No. Ill. U., Dekalb, 1971-75; research psychologist U. Tex., Galveston, 1975-78; sr. lectr. U. Western Australia, Nedlands, 1978-80; prof. dept. psychology U. Queensland, Brisbane, Australia, 1980—; pres. Academic Bd., 1991-93; dean medicine and dentistry U. Western Australia, 1994-95; vice chancellor Murdoch (Australia) U., 1996—; fellow Acad. Social Scis., Australia. Author: Psychopathology of Childhood, 1985, Classic Studies in Abnormal Psychology, 1993; Measuring Reading Competence, 1984; Medical Thinking, 1985; Classic Experiments in Psychology, 1985. NIMH fellow, 1967-71; research grantee NIMH, 1975-78, Ednl. Research Devel. Com., 1979-82, Australian Research Grants Com., 1981—. Mem. Psychonomic Soc., Am. Psychol. Assn., Sigma Xi. Mem. Ch. of England. Home: 66 Kintail Rd, Applecross WA 6153, Australia

SCHWARTZ, STEVEN SCOTT, orthodontist; b. Bklyn., Sept. 11, 1959; s. Jack W. and Harriet (Abramson) S.; m. Amy L. Zuker, Mar. 24, 1990; children: Aaron M., Nathaniel P., Eli S. BA magna cum laude, SUNY, Buffalo, 1981; DDS, SUNY, Stony Brook, 1985; MMSc, Harvard U., 1989. Rsch. assoc. Forsyth Dental Ctr., Boston, 1989-90; clin. asst. prof. SUNY, Stony Brook, 1990—; orthodontist pvt. practice, Wantagh, N.Y., 1990—. Contbr. articles to profl. jours. Regents scholar SUNY, 1977-81, 81-85. Mem. ADA, Am. Assn. Dental Rsch., Am. Assn. Orthodontists, Nassau County Dental Soc. (pub. and profls. rels. com. 1996—), Internat. Assn. Dental Rsch., Phi Beta Kappa. Office: 3341-B Park Ave Wantagh NY 11793

SCHWARTZ, SUSAN JEAN, physician assistant; b. New York, N.J., May 5, 1946; m. Marvin Schwartz, Sept. 4, 1967; children: Jennifer, Brian. BA, NYU, 1968; BS, Rutgers U., 1981; cert. physician asst., U. Medicine and Dentistry N.J., 1981. Asst. scientist Schering-Plough, Kenilworth, N.J., 1968-70; physician asst. St. Barnabus Hosp., Bronx, N.Y., 1981-82, Lyons (N.J.) VA Med. Ctr., 1982—; physician asst. Union (N.J.) Hosp., 1993—; clin. instr. U. Medicine and Dentistry N.J., Newark, 1982—, St. Francis Coll., Laretto, Pa., 1982—. Fellow Am. Acad. Physician Assts. (pub. edn. com. 1985-87, election com. 1985-86), N.J. State Soc. Physician Assts. (treas. 1982-89). Home: 45 Condit Ct Roseland NJ 07068 Office: Lyons VA Med Ctr 101 Knollcroft Rd Lyons NJ 07939

SCHWARTZ, WILLIAM BENJAMIN, educator, physician; b. Montgomery, Ala., May 16, 1922; s. William Benjamin and Molly (Vendruff) S.; children: Eric A., Kenneth B., Laurie A. M.D., Duke U., 1945. Diplomate: Am. Bd. Internal Medicine (mem. test com. nephrology). Intern, then asst. resident medicine U. Chgo. Clinics, 1945-46; asst. medicine Peter Bent Brigham Hosp., Boston; also research fellow medicine Harvard Med. Sch., 1948-50; fellow medicine Children's Hosp., Boston, 1949-50; mem. faculty Tufts U. Sch. Medicine, 1950-96, prof. medicine, 1958-96, Endicott prof., 1975-76, Vannevar Bush Univ. prof., 1976-96, chmn. dept. medicine, 1971-76; mem. staff New Eng. Center Hosps., 1950—, sr. physician, chief renal service, 1959-71, physician-in-chief, 1971-76; prof. medicine U. So. Calif., L.A., 1996—; Established investigator Am. Heart Assn., 1956-61; chmn. gen. medicine study sect. NIH, 1965-69; mem. sci. adv. bd. USAF, 1965-68, Nat. Kidney Found., 1968—, chmn., 1970—; mem. tng. com. Nat. Heart Inst., 1969-70; prin. adviser health scis. program, Rand Corp., 1977-88. Author numerous articles in field. Markle scholar med. scis., 1950-55. Mem. Inst. Medicine NAS, Am. Soc. Nephrology (pres. 1974-75), Acad. Arts and Scis., ACP, Am. Fedn. Clin. Research, Am. Physiol. Soc., Am. Soc. Clin. Investigation, Assn. Am. Physicians, Phi Beta Kappa, Sigma Xi, Alpha Omega Alpha. Office: U So Calif 1355 San Pablo St Ste 143 Los Angeles CA 90033

SCHWARTZ, WILLIAM LEWIS, veterinary pathologist; b. Columbus, Ohio, Dec. 11, 1931; s. Lewis Glenn and Mildred Opal (Basinger) S.; m. Barbara Ann Custer, June 21, 1953; children: Kimberly Ann Schwartz Barbour, Kay Annette Schwartz Carrabba. BSc, Ohio State U., 1953; DVM, Ohi State U., 1957; MS, Tex. A&M U., 1970. Vet. practitioner in pvt. practice Lancaster, Ohio, 1957-60; regulatory veterinarian Ohio Dept. Agr., Lancaster, Ohio, 1960-63; lab. diagnostician Ohio Dept. Agr., Reynoldsburg, Ohio, 1963-64; asst. prof. Ga. Coastal Plain Expt. Sta., Tifton, 1964-67; asst. prof. vet. pathology Coll. of Vet. Med., Tex. A&M U., College Station, 1967-70; vet. pathologist Tex. Vet. Med. Diagnostic Lab., College Station, 1970—. Contbr. over 90 articles to profl. jours. Mem. AVMA, Tex. Vet. Med. Assn., Am. Assn. Vet. Lab. Diagnosticians, Ohio State Vet. Alumni Assn., Lions (pres. 1989-90), Phi Zeta, Sigma Xi. Lutheran. Office: Tex Vet Med Diagnostic Lab PO Box 3040 College Station TX 77841-3040

SCHWARTZBERG, ALLAN ZELIG, psychiatrist, educator; b. Cleve., Dec. 5, 1930; s. Joseph and Jeanette (Eisenman) S.; m. Katherine Weiss, June 19, 1955; children: Shana, Robert. BS cum laude, Case Western Res. U., 1951; MD, Ohio State U., 1955. Diplomate Am. Bd. Psychiatry and Neurology. Intern, resident in psychiatry Johns Hopkins Hosp., Balt., 1955-59; pvt. practice, Gaithersburg, Md.; asst. prof. psychiatry Georgetown U. Sch. Medicine, Washington, 1964-66, asst. clin. prof., 1966-79, assoc. clin. prof., 1979-89, clin. prof., 1989—; vis. prof. faculty seminar in community psychiatry Harvard U. Med. Sch., Boston, 1965-67; cons. Walt Whitman High Sch., Bethesda, Md., 1980—, Passage Crisis Ctr., Montgomery County Health Dept., 1974-82, psychiat. tng. br. NIMH, 1971-74. Editor-in-chief Internat. Annals Adolescent Psychiatry, 1988—; co-editor Adolescent Psychiatry, Vols. 8-19; contbr. articles to med. jours. Recipient Vicennial medal Georgetown U., 1984. Fellow Am. Psychiat. Assn., Am. Soc. for Adolescent Psychiatry, Am. Soc. Psychoanalytic Physicians (pres. 1986-87); mem. AMA, Am. Group Psychotherapy Assn., Am. Coll. Psychiatrists, B'nai B'rith, Phi Beta Kappa. Republican. Jewish. Home: 6616 Kenhill Rd Bethesda MD 20817-6014 Office: Suburban Psychiat Assocs 8943 Shady Grove Ct Gaithersburg MD 20877-1308

SCHWARTZBERG, JOANNE GILBERT, physician; b. Boston, Nov. 30, 1933; d. Richard Vincent and Emma (Cohen) Gilbert; m. Hugh Joel Schwartzberg, July 7, 1956; children: Steven Jonathan, Susan Jennifer. BA magna cum laude, Radcliffe Coll., 1955; MD, Northwestern U., 1960. Diplomate Am. Bd. Quality Assurance and Utilization Rev. Physicians. Founder, med. dir. Chgo. Home Health Svc., 1972-95; founder, bd. dirs., v.p., med. dir. Suburban Home Health Service, Chgo. area, 1975-87; clin. asst. prof. preventive medicine and community health U. Ill. Coll. Medicine, 1985—; dir. Dept. of Geriatric Health AMA, 1990—. Mem. Community Adv. Bd. Joint Youth Devel. Commn. and Health Planning Com., Chgo., 1963-67; pres. Near North Montessori Sch., Chgo., 1972-75, bd. dirs., 1970-83; del. White House Conf. Aging, 1995. Recipient Mayor's Citation City of Chgo., 1963, Physician of Yr. award Nat. Assn. Home Care, 1988. Mem. Inst. Medicine of Chgo. (bd. dirs. 1990—, pres. 1994-95), Am. Acad. of Home Care Physicians (pres. 1992-94, Physician of Yr. award 1992), Am. Coll. Utilization Rev. Physicians, Ill. Geriatrics Soc. (pres. 1990-92), Ill. Med. Soc., Chgo. Med. Soc., Am. Geriatrics Soc., Alexander Graham Bell Assn. for Deaf (bd. dirs. 1984-90; chmn. internat. parents orgn. 1988-90, gen. chmn. internat. conv. 1986). Jewish. Contbr. articles to profl. jours. Home: 853 W Fullerton Ave Chicago IL 60614-2412 Office: 515 N State St Chicago IL 60610-4320

SCHWARTZBERG, ROGER KERRY, osteopath, internist; b. Bklyn., Mar. 30, 1948; s. Erwin and Edna (Kuchlik) S.; m. Linda Lurie, July 1, 1972 (div. Nov. 1974); m. Vicki Ann Davis, Nov. 28, 1976; children: Jeremy Dylan, Joshua Ryan. BA in Psychology, Syracuse U., 1970; DO, Mich. State U., 1973. Diplomate Am. Acad. Osteopathic Internists. Intern, sr. asst. surgeon USPHS Hosp., S.I., N.Y., 1973-74; med. resident Southeastern Med. Ctr., North Miami Beach, Fla., 1974-77, chief resident, 1975-77; pvt. practice Seminole, Fla., 1977—; active staff Univ. Gen. Hosp., Seminole 1978—, chmn. dept. internal medicine, 1981-82, governing bd. 1981-86, 88—, vice chmn. 1986, 88—, Pinellas Community Hosp., Pinellas Park, Fla., 1980—, chief of staff, 1985-86, Seminole Hosp. and Women's Ctr., Seminole, 1989—; adj. clin. faculty U. New Eng. Coll. Osteo. Medicine, Biddeford, Maine, 1985—; clin. asst. prof. internal medicine, 1987—, Nova Southeastern Univ. Coll. of Osteopathic Medicine, 1987—; clin. asst. prof. internal medicine Kirksville (Mo.) Coll. Osteo. Medicine, 1989—; mem. active staff Suncoast Osteo. Hosp., Largo, Fla., 1982—, Largo Med. Ctr. Hosp., 1990—, St. Petersburg Gen. Hosp., 1991—; clin. assoc. prof. coll. osteo. medicine U. Health Scis., 1992—. Named Educator of Yr. Met. Gen. Hosp., Pinellas Park, Fla., 1985. Fellow Am. Acad. Osteo. Internists (certification bd. 1990); mem. Am. Osteo. Assn., Am. Assn. Physician Specialties, Am. Coll. Osteo. Internists, Fla. Osteo. Med. Assn. (trustee 1985-89), Pinellas County Osteo. Med. Soc. (trustee 1985-89, gov. 1989-90, v.p. 1991—). Jewish. Office: Oakhurst Med Clinic 13020 Park Blvd Seminole FL 33776-3639

SCHWARTZENTRUBER, DOUGLAS JAY, oncologist, surgeon, oncology researcher; b. Goshen, Ind., Jan. 10, 1957; s. Earl David and Genivieve Marie (Leichty) S.; children: Alicia, Jared. BA, Goshen Coll., 1974-78; MD, Ind. U., 1978-82. Diplomate Am. Bd. Surgery. Surgery resident Ind. U. Sch. Medicine, Indpls., 1982-87; surg. oncology/immunology fellow Nat. Cancer Inst., Bethesda, Md., 1987-90, sr. investigator, 1990—. Fellow ACS; mem. Am. Soc. Clin. Oncology, Am. Assn. Cancer Rsch., Soc. Surg. Oncology, Soc. Univ. Surgeons. Mennonite. Office: National Cancer Inst Bldg 10 Rm 2B04 Bethesda MD 20892

SCHWARZ, BERTHOLD ERIC, psychiatrist; b. Jersey City, N.Y., Oct. 20, 1924; s. Berthold Theodore D. and Thyra I.W. (Ericson) S.; m. Ardis Marilyn Peterson, Jan. 22, 1955; children: Lisa Thyra, Eric Rolf. AB, Dartmouth Coll., 1945; MD, NYU, 1950; MS, Mayo Grad. Sch. Medicine, 1957. Psychiatrist, researcher pvt. practice, Montclair, N.J., 1955-82, Vero Beach, Fla., 1982—; cons. Essex County Hosp. Ctr., Cedar Grove, N.J., 1965-82, Med. Correctional Assn., Casining, N.Y., 1960-72; exec. dir. Internat. Psychosomatics Inst., Mountain Lakes, N.J., 1995—. Contbr. articles to profl. jours. With USNR, 1943-45. Fellow AAAS, Am. Psychiat. Assn., Am. Soc. Physical Rsch., Am. Geriatric Soc. Republican. Home: 1070 Reef Rd #305 Vero Beach FL 32963 Office: 642 Azelea Ln Bero Beach FL 32963

SCHWARZ, FERDINAND (FRED SCHWARZ), ophthalmologist, ophthalmic plastic surgeon; b. Trenton, N.J., Dec. 13, 1939; s. Ferdinand and Laura Francis Schwarz; m. Carol Ann Snyder, Feb. 26, 1966; children: Lesley Ann, Jeffrey Ryan, Jason Bradley, Allyson Larner. BSEE, Lafayette Coll., 1961; MD, N.J. Coll. Medicine and Dentistry, 1970; MBA, Winthrop Coll., 1991. Diplomate Nat. Bd. Med. Examiners. Project engr. Astro div. RCA, Princeton, N.J., 1961-66; intern Robert Packer Hosp., Sayre, Pa., 1970-71; resident Guthrie Clinic Ophthalmology/Robert Packer Hosp., Sayre, Pa., 1971-74; Heed fellowship in ophthalmic plastic and reconstructive surgery U. Pa. Med. Sch./Temple Med. Sch./Hahnemann Med. Sch., Phila., 1974-75; pvt. practice Columbia, S.C., 1975—; vice chief med. staff Providence Hosp., Columbia, 1984, chief med. staff, 1985; cons Dorn VA Hosp., Columbia, 1975—, Moncrief Hosp., Columbia, 1975-89. Contbr. numerous articles to sci. engring. and med. publs., 1962—. Heed (Found.) Ophthalmic fellow, Chgo., 1975. Mem. AMA, S.C. Med. Soc., S.C. Ophthalmology Soc., Cen. S.C. Ophthalmology Soc. (pres. 1983), Soc. Heed Fellows, Palmetto Club, Spring Valley Country Club. Roman Catholic. Home: PO Box 23038 Columbia SC 29224-3038 Office: Drs Schwarz and Milne PA 1655 Brabham Ave Ste 100 Columbia SC 29204-2039

SCHWARZ, KARL OTTO, physician; b. Arad, Romania, Feb. 12, 1949; came to U.S., 1980; s. Andreas and Juliana (Hönig) S.; m. Susan Chi-Ching Shen, Dec. 21, 1982; 1 child, Charlotte Maria. MD, Tel-Aviv U., 1975. Resident Mt. Sinai Med. Ctr., N.Y.C., 1980-83, Albert Einstein Coll. Medicine, Bronx, 1983-84, U. Health Ctr., Pitts., 1984-85, Allegheny County Coroner's Office, Pitts., 1985-86; chief lab. svc. Highland Dr. VA Med. Ctr., Pitts., 1988; chief, sect. of neuropathology Robert Wood Johnson Med. Sch., New Brunswick, N.J., 1988—. Home: 327 N 8th Ave Edison NJ 08817-2914 Office: Dept Pathology Robert Wood Johnson Med Sch One Robert Wood Johnson Pl New Brunswick NJ 08903-0019

SCHWARZ, RAY PAUL, biomedical engineer; b. Dayton, Ohio, Aug. 24, 1948; s. Ray Paul and Lillian Mary (Fornes) S.; m. Pamela Ann Smith Dec. 19, 1970 (div. 1986); 1 child, Jill Ellen; m. Marion Aguino, Oct. 24, 1992. BS in Engring., Case Western Res. U., 1970. Product engr. Becton-Dickinson Co., Coshocton, Ohio, 1973-77; chief engr. Freund Precision, Inc., Dayton, 1977-79; owner Precision Machine Svcs., Dayton, 1979-81; project engr. GE Govt. Svcs., Houston, 1981-85, Krug Internat., Inc., Houston, 1985-91; co-founder, chief engr. Synthecon, Inc., Houston, 1991—. Patentee in field. Recipient 6 certs. of recognition NASA, 1986-90, named Inventor of Yr., 1991. Mem. Am. Astron. Soc. (Melbourne W. Boynton award 1988). Republican. Home: 1710 White Wing Cir Friendswood TX 77546-5444

SCHWARZ, RICHARD HOWARD, obstetrician, gynecologist, educator; b. Easton, Pa., Jan. 10, 1931; s. Howard Eugene and Blanche Elizabeth (Smith) S.; m. Patricia Marie Lewis, Mar. 11, 1978; children by previous marriage: Martha L., Nancy Schwarz Tedesco, Paul H., Mary Katherine Schwarz Murray. MD, Jefferson Med. Coll., 1955; MA (hon.), U. Pa., Phila., 1971. Diplomate Am. Bd. Ob-Gyn. (examiner 1977—). Intern, then resident Phila. Gen. Hosp., 1955-59; prof. U. Pa., Phila., 1963-78; prof., chmn. Downstate Med. Ctr., Bklyn., 1978-90, dean, v.p. acad. affairs, 1983-89, provost, v.p. clin. affairs, 1988-93, interim pres., 1993-94, prof. ob.-gyn., 1990-96, Disting. Svc. prof. ob.-gyn., 1996; chmn. ob.-gyn. N.Y. Meth. Hosp., Bklyn., 1996—; prof. ob.-gyn. Cornell U. Med. Coll., 1996—; obstetrical cons. March of Dimes Birth Defects Found., 1995—. Author: Septic Abortion, 1968. Editor: Handbook of Obstetric Emergencies, 1984, mem. editorial bd. jour. Ob-Gyn., Milw., 1983-87; contbr. articles to profl. jours. Bd. dirs. March of Dimes, N.Y.C., 1985-95. Capt. USAF, 1959-63. Mem. Am. Coll. Obstetricians and Gynecologists (chmn. dist. 2 1984-87, v.p. 1989-90, pres. elect 1990-91, pres. 1991-92). Republican. Presbyterian. Office: NY Meth Hosp 506 6th St Brooklyn NY 11215-9008

SCHWARZ, WOLFGANG, psychologist; b. Stuttgart, Ger., Oct. 30, 1926; s. Mole and Edith (Gutstein) S.; brought to U.S., 1934, naturalized, 1940; A.B., N.Y. U., 1948, A.M., 1949, Ph.D., 1956; m. Cynthia Mae Johnson, Sept. 12, 1949 (div.); children—Amy Maria, Casey Andrew, Darcy Lynn, Priscilla Anne, Lydia Beth, Emily Jane; m. Susan Decker, 1976; children—Jaime Bartholomew, Noah. Intern, Bellevue Med. Center, N.Y., 1949-51; chief psychology Rip Van Winkle Med. Found., Hudson, N.Y., 1951-53; dir. psychology Hillcrest Med. Center, Tulsa, 1953-56, Hollywood Presbyn. Hosp., Los Angeles, 1956-58; cons. psychology Cedars Lebanon Hosp., Los Angeles, 1956-58; spl. cons. to D.C. Govt., 1959-61, NIH, Bethesda, Md., 1962-64; dir. psychol. research Mass. Dept. Mental Health, Boston and Malden, 1965-68; individual practice clin. psychology, Tulsa, 1953-56, Beverly Hills, Calif., 1956-59, Washington, 1959-63, Concord and Malden, Mass., 1963-73, Mt. Kisco, N.Y., 1973—; lectr. U. Tulsa, 1953-54, Hillcrest Med. Center, Tulsa, 1953-56, Los Angeles State Coll., 1956-57; asst. prof. Howard U., 1961; asso. prof. George Washington U., 1961-62; vis. research asst. Harvard Psychiatry, Lab., 1966-68; prof. Malden Hosp., 1968-71; cons. No. Westchester Hosp., 1974—, United Hosp., 1975—, Four Winds Hosp., 1975-80; cons. psychology Peace Corps, Mass., 1969—. Mem. exec. com. Mayor's Model City Program, Malden, 1967-68. Served with USNR, 1945-46. Recipient Founder's Day award N.Y. U., 1956, Individual award USPHS/NIH, 1960-64. Diplomate Am. Bd. Profl. Psychology. Mem. Am., N.Y., Mass. psychol. assns., Washington Soc. History of Medicine (exec. com. 1963-64), N.Y. Acad. Scis., Psi Chi, Beta Lambda Sigma. Author: A Survey of the Mental Health Facilities in the District of Columbia, 1961; also articles. Home: 81 Paulding Dr Chappaqua NY 10514-2818 Office: 121 Smith Ave Mount Kisco NY 10549-2815

SCHWARZBART, GÜNTER, retired surgeon; b. Berlin, Feb. 3, 1932; came to U.S., 1946; s. Sam and Harriet (Bernstein) S.; m. Rita Sonderegger-Wenzl, Dec. 15, 1954; children: Vivienne Borkan, Sheila Barcelle. BS cum laude, Syracuse U., 1953; MD, Basel (Switzerland) U., 1959. Diplomate Am. Bd. Surgery. Intern Mount Sinai Med. Ctr. of Greater Miami, Miami, Fla., 1959-60; resident in surgery Mount Sinai Med. Ctr. of Greater Miami, Miami, 1960-61; surgical residency VA Hosp., Coral Gables, Fla., 1961-64; pvt. practice of surgery Miami Beach, Fla., 1964-75; staff surgeon VA Hosp., Clarksburg, W.Va., 1975-78; retired, 1979; clin. assoc. prof. surgery, U. W.Va., Morgantown; staff surgeon, VA Med. Ctr., Clarksburg, W.Va. Contbr. articles to numerous profl. jours.; sculptor, shown in group exhbns. Fellow ACS, Internat. Coll. Surgeons, Royal soc. Medicine; mem. AMA, W.Va. Med. Soc., Amnesty Internat., Common Cause, Renew Am., Union Concerned Scientists.

SCHWARZE, ROBERT FRANCIS, osteopath, dermatologist; b. St. Louis, Aug. 13, 1949; s. William Casper and Mary Constance (Glaser) S.; m. Donna Lea Jakubiak, Nov. 3, 1990; children: William, Michael. BS, Maryville Coll., 1971; DO, U. Health Sciences, Kansas City, 1980; Cert. in Dermatology, 1990. Intern Normandy Osteo. Hosp., St. Louis, 1980-81; resident in surgery Deaconess West Hosp., St. Louis County, 1982-83, resident in dermatology, 1986-89; emergency physician St. Louis Regional, Dexter Meml., Met. and other hosps., 1981-89; dir. emergency dept. Lincoln County Meml. Hosp., 1985-87; preceptor in dermatology Met. Hosp., St. Louis, 1986-89; dermatologist St. Louis, 1989—; trainer dermatology residency program, lectr. in dermatology Deaconess West Hosp., St. Louis. Contbr. articles to profl. jours. Vol. Variety Club, St. Louis, 1989—; lectr. Jr. League, St. Louis, 1989; bd. dirs. Maryville Coll., St. Louis, 1971-74; fundraiser Incarnate Word Hosp., 1973-74, Chaminade Coll. Prep. Mem. Am. Osteo. Assn., Am. Coll. Osteo. Dermatology (trustee), St. Louis Met. Med. Soc., Am. Acad. Dermatology, Mo. Med. Soc., Mo. Osteo. Soc., St. Louis Osteo. Assn. Roman Catholic. Home: 17 Godwin Ln Saint Louis MO 63124-1591 Office: North County Dermatology 1120 Graham Rd Florissant MO 63031-8013 also: 11245 St Charles Rock Rd Saint Louis MO 63141

SCHWARZMAN, PHILIP S., emergency physician; b. Passaic, N.J., Jan. 11, 1948; s. Morris and Selma (Naeman) S.; m. Madeline Blank, June 20, 1970; children: Elana, Alexa. AB, Cornell U., 1970; MD, Mt. Sinai Sch. of Medicine, N.Y.C., 1974. Diplomate Am. Bd. Emergency Medicine. Emergency physician St. Joseph Med. Ctr., Burbank, Calif., 1977—, dir. emergency dept., 1992—. Vol. Venice (Calif.) Family Clinic, 1990-95. Fellow ACEP. Office: St. Joseph Med Ctr 501 S Buena Vista Burbank CA 91505

SCHWEBEL, MILTON, psychologist, educator; b. Troy, N.Y., May 11, 1914; s. Frank and Sarah (Oxenhandler) S.; m. Bernice Lois Davison, Sept. 3, 1939; children: Andrew I., Robert S. AB, Union Coll., 1934; MA, SUNY, Albany, 1936; PhD, Columbia U., 1949; Cert. in Psychotherapy, Postgrad. Ctr. Mental Health, N.Y.C., 1958. Lic. psychologist, N.Y., N.J.; diplomate Am. Bd. Examiners Profl. Psychology. Asst. prof. psychology Mohawk Champlain Coll., 1946-49; asst. to prof. edn., dept. chmn., assoc. dean NYU, 1949-67; dean, prof. Grad. Sch. Edn., Rutgers U., New Brunswick, N.J., 1967-77; prof. Grad. Sch. Applied and Profl. Psychology, 1977-85, prof. emeritus, 1985—; vis. prof. U. So. Calif., U. Hawaii; postdoctoral fellow Postgrad. Ctr. Mental Health, 1954-58, lectr. psychology, 1958-66; cons. NIMH, U.S., state and city depts. edn., ednl. ministries in Europe, Asia, univs. and pub. schs.; pvt. cons. psychologist and psychotherapist, 1953—. Author: A Guide to a Happier Family, 1989, Personal Adjustment and Growth, 1990, Student Teachers Handbook, 3d edit., 1996, Interests of Pharmacists, 1951, Health Counseling, 1953, Who Can Be Educated?, 1968; editor: Mental Health Implications of Life in the Nuclear Age, 1986, Facilitating Cognitive Development, 1986, Promoting Cognitive Growth Over the Life Span, 1990, Behavioral Science and Human Survival, 1965, The Impact of Ideology on the I.Q. Controversy, 1975; editor Peace & Conflict: Jour. Peace Psychology, 1993—; co-editor Bull. Peace Psychology, 1991-94; mem. editl. bd. Am. Jour. Orthopsychiatry, Readings in Mental Health, Jour. Contemporary Psychotherapy, Jour. Counseling Psychology, Jour. Social Issues, others. Mem. sci. adv. bd. Internat. Ctr. for Enhancement of Learning Potential, 1988—; trustee Edn. Law Ctr., 1973-81, Nat. Com. Employment Youth, Nat. Child Labor Com., 1967-75, Union Exptl. Colls. and Univs., 1976-78; pres. Nat. Orgn. for Migrant Children, 1980-85; pres. Inst. of Arts and Humanities, 1984-95. Served with AUS, 1943-46, ETO. Met. Applied Rsch. Coun. fellow, 1970-71. Fellow APA, Am. Psychol. Soc., Am. Orthopsychiatry Assn., Soc. Psychol. Study Social Issues, Jean Piaget Soc. (trustee), Am. Ednl. Rsch. Assn., N.Y. Acad. Scis., Psychologists for Social Responsibility (pres.), Inst. Arts and Humanities Edn. (pres.), Sigma Xi. Home: 1050 George St Apt 17L New Brunswick NJ 08901-1025 Office: Rutgers U Grad Sch Applied and Profl Psychology Piscataway NJ 08854

SCHWEBER, SAUL J., oral surgery, educator; b. Fall River, Mass., Nov. 25, 1936; s. Irving Lewis and Freda (Shogel) S.; m. Diane Lafferman, Oct. 13, 1980. BS, U. Conn., 1958; DDS, Northwestern U., 1963; cert. advanced study in oral surgery, Boston U., 1966. Diplomate Am. Bd. Oral and Maxillofacial Surgery, 1972; cert. ACLS, Am. Heart Assn. Jr. and sr.

resident Phila. Gen. Hosp., 1966-68; pvt. practice oral and maxillofacial surgery Silver Spring, Md., 1968—; asst. clin. prof. in oral and maxillofacial surgery U. Md., Sch. Dentistry, 1995—; past oral surgery cons. Montgomery County Health Dept.; attending staff, former chief oral and maxillofacial surgery Holy Cross Hosp.; sub-sect. chmn. oral and maxillofacial surgery Washington Adventist Hosp.; courtesy staff Washington Hosp. Ctr. Contbr. articles to profl. jours. Capt. USAR, 1963-65. Fellow Am. Soc. Oral and Maxillofacial Surgeons; mem. ADA, Md. State Dental Assn., So. Md. Dental Soc., Progressive Dental Study Club (past pres.), Montgomery County Dental Study Club, Oral Surgery Residents of Greater Phila. Study Club (Best Presentatin award 1968), Am. Radio Relay League (advanced class license), Med. Amateur Radio Coun.

SCHWECHTER, LEON ELIOT, osteopath; b. Bklyn., Mar. 20, 1953; s. Israel and Rachelle (Flescher) S.; m. Donna Faithe Tulkoff, Feb. 26, 1984; c hildren: Daniel Robert, Cary Alexander, Serena Lynne. BS, N.Y.U., 1974; DO, Coll. Osteopathic Medicine, Des Moines, 1978. Diplomate Am. Bd. Internal Medicine, Am. Bd. Geriatric Medicine. Intern Interboro Hosp., Brklyn., 1978-79; resident in internal medicine Nassau Hosp., Mineda, N.Y., 1979-82; emergency room physician S. Nassau Comty. Hosp., Oceanside, N.Y., 1982-84; private practice in internal medicine Williston Park, N.Y., 1984—. Republican. Jewish. Office: 80 E Jericho Turnpike Mineola NY 11501

SCHWEICHLER, RICHARD, physical therapist; b. Lackawanna, N.Y.; s. Stanley and Stephanie (Kacasmuka) S.; children: Michele, Richard Jr., Maria, David, Beth. BS in Health and Phys. Edn., SUNY, Brockport, 1950; Cert. Phys. Therapy, U. Buffalo, 1953; MS in Sci. and Edn., Canisius Coll., Buffalo, 1964; Dr. Mechanotherapy Phys. Therapy, Great Lakes Coll., 1966. Lic. phys. therapist N.Y., Fla. Cons. to nursing homes on phys. therapy Erie County Health Dept., 1955-56; staff phys. therapist Wayne County (Mich.) Hosp., 1953-55; supervising phys. therapist Buffalo Mercy Hosp., 1955-59; tchr. health sci., phys. edn. pub. schs., 1959-66; phys. therapy cons. King Manor Nursing Home, Cheektowaga, N.Y., 1966-70; cons., phys. therapist Abbott Manor Nursing Home, Buffalo, 1970-76; clin. coord. phys. therapy Daemen Coll., Amherst, 1975-77, dir. phys. therapy program, 1975—, assoc. prof. phys. therapy, 1986—; cons. in phys. therapy Seneca Manor Nursing Home, West Seneca, N.Y., 1976-83, Garden Gate Nursing Home, Buffalo, 1980-83; lectr. in field; condr. seminars in field; mem. N.Y. State Phys. Therapy Grievance Bd., 1964-68, chmn., 1965; apptd. to 1st Bd. of Phys. Therapy Edn. Dept., 1968, chmn., 1968, chmn. com. on legis. Contbr. articles to profl. jours. Chmn. Cmty. Theater, Lackawanna. With USN WW II. Recipient Cert. of Recognition, Seneca Manor, 1978. Mem. Western N.Y. Phys. Therapy Mgmt. Forum, Am. Phys. Therapy Assn. (mem. edn. sect., past vice chmn. Niagara Frontier dist., past dist. dir., past state dir., past legis. chmn., many others), Coun. of Lic. Physiotherapists of N.Y. State (bd. dirs.), United Socs. of Physiotherapists. Home: 950 Ridge Rd Lackawanna NY 14218 Office: Daemen College Dept Phys Therapy 4380 Main St Amherst NY 14226

SCHWEIKERT, EDGAR OSKAR, dentist; b. Heidelberg, Germany, Aug. 30, 1938; came to U.S., 1972; s. Oskar and Priska (Zehr) S.; m. Mary Lou Como, Apr. 7, 1969; 1 child, Marisa. Degree, Hamburg Dental Sch., 1966; Dr. Med. Dentistry, U. Munich, 1969. Lic. dentist, Calif., N.Y. Dentist, U.S. Army, Frankfurt, Fed. Republic Germany, 1969-72; gen. practice dentistry, L.A., 1972-73, Bklyn., 1973—; lectr. in field. Author Multiple Cantilevers in Fixed Prosthesis, 1988, Spanish edit., 1990; contbr. articles to profl. jours. Served as capt. German Air Force, 1967-69. Mem. ADA, German Dental Assn., Second Dist. Dental Assn., Bay Ridge Dental Soc., Guild Dental Craftsmen. Home and Office: 429 77th St Brooklyn NY 11209-3205

SCHWEIKHART, DOUGLAS PAUL, hospital administrator; b. Dayton, Ohio, July 14, 1963; s. Howard Paul and Rita Ann (Rensing) S. BSBA magna cum laude, Xavier U., 1985; MHA, Duke U., 1987. Cons. Arthur Andersen & Co., Tampa, Fla., 1987-89; asst. adminstr. Shriners Hosp. Internat. Hdqs., Tampa, 1989-92; adminstr. Shriners Hosp. Intermountain, Salt Lake City, 1992—. Mem. Salt Lake C. of C. Healthcare Adv. Coun., Am. Coll. Healthcare Execs. (diplomate). Home: 6965 S Twin Aspen Cove Salt Lake City UT 84121 Office: Shriners Hosp Fairfax Rd at Virginia St Salt Lake City UT 84103

SCHWEITZER, MARK G., pharmaceutical research scientist; b. McKeesport, Pa., July 12, 1957; s. Glenn Carl and Mary Viola (Yeaney) S.; m. Karen Elizabeth Leonard, Aug. 31, 1984 (div. Feb. 1990); m. Sarah Marsh, Oct. 19, 1991; children: Christopher Mark, Lindsay Campbell. BA, Thiel Coll., 1979, 1979; PhD, Ohio State U., 1984. Prin. rsch. chemist Lever Rsch., Edgewater, N.J., 1984-85; rsch. product mgr. Rohm & Haas, Springhouse, Pa., 1985-89; product line mgr. Battelle, Columbus, Ohio, 1989-94; rsch. scientist II GD Searle, Skokie, Ill., 1994—; pres. Analytical Scientists, Inc., Granville, Ohio, 1994. Sec. Easton (Pa.) Chorale, 1985-86. Mem. Am. Chem. Soc. Republican. Lutheran. Home: 1460 Margate Ln Green Oaks IL 60048 Office: GD Searle 4901 Searle Pkwy Skokie IL 60077

SCHWENN, LEE WILLIAM, retired medical center executive; b. Morrisonville, Wis., Dec. 23, 1925; s. LeRoy William and Vivian Mae (Kramer) S.; m. Glenna Edith Mehne, Jan. 16, 1947; 1 son, William Lee. B.S., U. Wis., 1948; M.P.H., U. N.C., 1956. Tchr. pub. schs. Appleton, Wis., 1948-52; teaching cons. Wis. Health Dept., 1952-53; adminstrv. asst. Madison (Wis.) Health Dept., 1953-57; adminstrv. cons. U.S. Children's Bur., Atlanta Regional Office, 1957-58; adminstr. USPHS, Washington, 1958-66; assoc. dir. D.C. Dept. Health, 1966-70, D.C. Dept. Human Resources, 1970-71; exec. v.p. Maimonides Med. Center, Bklyn., 1971-88, pres., 1988-89, spl. cons. Bd. Trustees, 1989-96. Recipient Distinguished Pub. Service award D.C. Govt., 1970. Mem. Am. Pub. Health Assn., Am. Acad. Health Adminstrs., Delta Omega. Home: 1007 Westminster Dr Greensboro NC 27410-4551

SCHWERDTFEGER, WALTER KURT, public health official, researcher; b. Karlsruhe, Fed. Republic of Germany, Apr. 17, 1949; s. Walter Georg Hermann and Anna (Jooss) S.; m. Renate Schenk, May 4, 1984; children: Wolfgang, Cristina, Ines. Diploma in biology, U. Frankfurt, Fed. Republic of Germany, 1973, Dr.Sc., 1977, Privatdozent, 1983. Biol. diplomate. Sci. employee biol. faculty U. Frankfurt, 1974-77; scientist with tenure Max Planck Inst. for Brain Rsch., Frankfurt, 1977-88; head morphology and pathology div. Paul Ehrlich Inst., Langen, Fed. Republic of Germany, 1988-92; head rsch. coordination unit Fed. Ministry Health, Bonn, 1992-95; head drinking water and environ. medicine divsn. Fed. Min. Health, 1995—; lectr. med. faculty U. Frankfurt, 1978—; vis. prof. U. Valencia (Spain), 1985-87; sci. symposia organizer; referee for sci. jours. and founds. Author: Structure and Fiber Connections of the Hippocampus, 1984; co-author: The Brain of the Common Marmoset, 1980; editor: The Forebrain in Reptiles, 1988, The Forebrain in Nonmammals, 1990; co-editor: Current Topics in Biomedical Research, 1992; translator/editor: Histologie, 1990; translator: Farbatlas der Histologie, 1987; contbr. numerous articles to internat. sci. jours. and handbooks. Mem. Working Party on Waste Mgmt. and Environ., Frankfurt, 1991-92. Recipient Dr. Paul and Cilli Weill prize Dr. Paul and Cilli Weill Found., Frankfurt, 1985; grantee Deutsche Forschungsgemeinschaft, Bonn, 1984-88, Comisión Asesora de Investigación Científica y Técnica, Madrid, 1985-86, Ministry of Sci. and Arts, Wiesbaden, Fed. Republic of Germany, 1987. Mem. Deutsche Zoologische Ges., Anatomische Ges., European Neurosci. Assn., Internat. Brain Rsch. Orgn. Office: Fed Ministry Health, Am Propsthof 78a, 53121 Bonn Germany

SCIARRA, JOHN J., pharmaceutical scientist, researcher, consultant; b. Bklyn., Dec. 28, 1927; s. Anthony and Jennie (Ferreri) S.; m. Barbara Kurek, July 4, 1964; children: Christopher, John Jay, Gregory, Brian. BS in Pharmacy, St. John's U., 1951; MS in Pharmacy, Duquesne U., 1953; PhD in Pharmacy, U. Md., 1957. Registered pharmacist, N.Y., Md., Pa. Grad. asst. Sch. Pharmacy Duquesne U., Pitts., 1951-53; tchg. fellow Sch. Pharmacy U. Mich., 1953-54; instr. pharmacy Sch. Pharmacy U. Md., Balt., 1954-57; asst. prof. pharm. chemistry St. John's U., Coll. Pharmacy and Allied Health Professions, Jamaica, N.Y., 1957-59, assoc. prof. pharm. chemistry, 1959-62, chmn. dept. pharm. scis., prof. pharm. chemistry, 1962-66, dir. grad. divsn., prof. pharm. chemistry, 1966-72, asst. dean, chmn. dept. allied health and indsl. scis., prof. pharm. chemistry, 1972-75; dean, prof. indsl. pharmacy Bklyn. Coll. Pharmacy, 1975-76; exec. dean, prof. indsl. pharmacy, Arnold and Marie Schwartz Coll. pharmacy and Health Scis. L.I. Univ., Bkyn., 1976-84, pres. Retail Drug Inst., prof. indsl. pharmacy, Arnold and Marie Scwartz Col. pharmacy and Health Scis., 1984-90, prof. emeritus indsl. pharmacy, Arnold and Marie Schwartz Coll. of pharmacy and Health Scis., 1990—; pres. Sciarra Labs., Hicksville, N.Y., 1986—; mem. U.S. Pharmacopoeia Com. on Pharmaceutics, 1979-80; mem. Nat. Formulary Adv. Panel, 1961-75; vice chmn. aerosol com. Packaging Inst., 1964-65, chmn., 1965-66; chmn. N.Y. State Pharmacy Conf., 1976-78; spkr. in field. Author 2 textbooks, numerous chpts. in textbooks; editor Jour. Soc. Cosmetic Chemists, 1974-78; contbr. over 200 articles to profl. jours. Cpl. U.S. Army, 1946-47. Recipient award Lundsford Richardson Pharmacy, 1955, 56, award Chem. Spltys. Mfr.'s Assn., 1961, Indsl. Pharmacy Achievement award, 1977, L.I. U. Trustee award for scholarly achievement, 1983, Am. Coll. Apothecaries' Deans award for outstanding contbns. to retail pharmacy, 1991. Fellow AAAS, Acad. Pharm. Scientists, Soc. Cosmetic Chemists (edn. com. 1973-74, pres.-elect, pres., chmn. bd. 1978-80, medal), Am. Assn. Pharm. Scientists; mem. Am. Pharm. Assn. (life, chmn. tech. sect. 1972-78, mem. com. 1970—, N.Y. chpt. v.p. 1975-76, pres. 1976-77), Am. Bd. Diplomats in Pharmacy, Am. Assn. Colls. of Pharmacy (com. internatl. pharmacy 1975—), Pharm. Soc. State of N.Y. (sec. 1980-96, regional dir. 1989-92), Rho Chi, Sigma Xi. Home: 8 Allen Dr Locust Valley NY 11560 Office: Sciarra Labs Inc 484-09 S Broadway Hicksville NY 11801

SCIARRA, JOHN J., physician, educator; b. West Haven, Conn., Mar. 4, 1932; s. John and Mary Grace (Sanzone) S.; m. Barbara Crafts Patton, Jan. 9, 1960; children: Vanessa Patton, John Crafts, Leonard Chapman. BS, Yale U., 1953; MD, Columbia U., N.Y.C., 1957, PhD, 1963. Asst. prof. Columbia U., N.Y.C., 1964-68; prof., dept. head U. Minn. Med. Sch., Mpls., 1968-74; prof. Northwestern U. Med. Sch., Chgo., 1974—; chmn. ob-gyn Northwestern Meml. Hosp., Chgo., 1974—. Editor Gyn-Ob Reference Series, 1973—, Internat. Jour. Gyn-Ob, 1985—. V.p. med. affairs Chgo. Maternity Ctr., Chgo., 1974—. Fellow Am. Coll. Ob-Gyn. (chmn. internal affairs com. 1985-89); mem. Internat. Fedn. Ob-Gyn. (pres. elect 1988-91), Assn. Profs. Ob-Gyn. (sec. 1976-79, pres. 1980), Am. Assn. Maternal and Neonatal Health (pres. 1980-89, coun. resident edn. in ob-gyn. 1988—), Gyn-Ob. Found., Am. Fertility Soc. (Hartman award 1965, bd. dirs. 1971-73), Assn. Profs. Ob-Gyn. (sec.-treas. 1987—), Cen. Assn. Ob-Gyn. (trustees 1986—), Yale Club N.Y.C., Carleton Club Chgo. Club: Yale (N.Y.C.); Carleton (Chgo.). Office: Northwestern U Med Sch 333 E Superior St Chicago IL 60611-3015*

SCIBA, JOANN, social worker; b. Manistee, Mich., Oct. 19, 1946; d. Raymond Peter and Bernardine Alice (Wroblewski) Sciba. Student, Muskegon Bus. Coll., 1964-66; BS, Ferris State U., 1969; MSW, Western Mich. U., 1982. Cert. AIDS educator. Tchr. North Muskegon (Mich.) High Sch., 1969-70; caseworker Muskegon County Dept. Social Svcs., Muskegon, 1970-76, child welfare specialist, 1976-88; med. social work cons. Mich. Dept. Social Svcs., 1988—. Vol. United Way, Muskegon, 1985-86; H-PAC mem. March of Dimes, Grand Rapids, Mich., 1988-92; program chmn. Friends of Norton Shores Libr., Muskegon, 1990-94, Muskegon Area AIDS Resource Svcs., 1993—, West Mich. AIDS Forum, Grand Rapids; bd. dirs. Cmty. AIDS Coun. West Ctrl. Mich., chmn. pub. policy com., 1994-96. Recipient Cert. of Recognition Nat. Assn. Social Workers, 1986. Mem. Mich. Coun. Social Svcs. Workers. Democrat. Roman Catholic. Home: 665 Lake Forest Ln R-12 Muskegon MI 49441-4785

SCILEPPI, JOHN A., psychologist, educator; b. Bklyn., Aug. 30, 1946; s. Adolph G. and Marie Theresa (Saccaro) S.; m. Lynn A. Ruggiero, Nov. 27, 1982; 1 child, Luke M.R. BA magna cum laude in Psychology, Marist Coll. (Poughkeepsie), 1967; MA, Loyola U., Chgo., 1969, Ph.D. in Social Psychology, 1973. Lic. psychologist, N.Y. NDEA research and teaching fellow Loyola U., Chgo., 1969-71, lectr., 1970-71; asst. prof. St. Xavier Coll., Chgo., 1971-73; v.p. acad. affairs Oglala Sioux C.C., Pine Ridge, S.D., 1975-76; assoc. prof. psychology Marist Coll., Poughkeepsie, N.Y., 1973-75, 76-88, prof., 1988—, dir. MA Psychology program, 1990—; psychol. cons. for program evaluation, survey research and interpersonal communication. Chmn. bd. Sch. of the New Community of Chgo., 1970-72; bd. dirs. Rehab. Programs Inc., Poughkeepsie, 1981—; mem. planning com. United Way of Dutchess County (N.Y.), 1979-80. Mem. Am. Psychol. Assn., Soc. for Psychol. Study of Social Issues, Eastern Psychol. Assn., Psi Chi, Alpha Sigma Nu. Democrat. Roman Catholic. Abstractor: Psychological Abstracts, 1977-81; author: A Systems View of Education: A Model for Change, 1984, rev. edit., 1988. Home: 1 River Rd Hyde Park NY 12538-1323 Office: Marist Coll Psychology Dept Poughkeepsie NY 12601

SCIME, SAMUEL GENE, ophthalmologist; b. Buffalo, Feb. 26, 1937; s. Joseph and Ida Scime. BS, Canisius Coll., 1958; MD, Med. Coll. of Wis., 1962. Diplomate Am. lBd. Ophthalmology. Clin. instr. in internal medicine Med. Sch. SUNY, Buffalo, 1965-66, clin. instr. Med. Sch., 1967-70; clin. instr. Buffalo Gen. Hosp., 1970; pvt. practice Ft. Lauderdale, Fla., 1970—; airman med. examiner FAA, Tamarac and Ft. Lauderdale, Fla., 1976—. Capt. U.S. Army, 1963-65, Korea. Fellow Am. Acad. Ophthalmology; mem. AMA, Fla. Med. Assn., Fla. Soc. Ophthalmology. Office: 7301 N University Dr Ste 208 Fort Lauderdale FL 33321-2935

SCITOVSKY, ANNE AICKELIN, economist; b. Ludwigshafen, Germany, Apr. 17, 1915; came to U.S., 1931, naturalized, 1938; d. Hans W. and Gertrude Margarete Aickelin; 1 dau., Catherine Margaret. Student, Smith Coll., 1933-35; B.A., Barnard Coll., 1937; postgrad., London Sch. Econs., 1937-39; M.A. in Econs., Columbia U., 1941. Mem. staff legis. reference svc. Libr. of Congress, 1941-44; mem. staff Social Security Bd., 1944-46; with Palo Alto (Calif.) Med. Rsch. Found., 1963—, chief health econs. div., 1973-91, sr. staff scientist, 1992—; lectr. Inst. Health Policy Studies, U. Calif., San Francisco, 1975—; mem. Inst. Medicine of NAS, Nat. Acad. Social Ins., Pres.'s Commn. for Study of Ethical Problems in Medicine and Biomed. and Behavioral Rsch., 1979-82, U.S. Nat. Com. on Vital and Health Stats., 1975-78, Health Resources and Svcs. Adminstrn., AIDS adv. com., 1990-94; cons. HHS, Inst. Medicine Coun. on Health Care Tech. Assessment, 1986-90. Mem. Am. Assn. for Health Svc. Rsch., Am. Pub. Health Assn. Home: 161 Erica Way Menlo Park CA 94028-7459 Office: Palo Alto Med Found Rsch Inst 860 Bryant St Palo Alto CA 94301-2707

SCOLA, GAETANO SALVATORE, clinical laboratory scientist; b. Gloucester, Mass., July 2, 1944; s. Sebastian and Frances T. (Filetto) S. Med. Technologist, Carnegie Inst., Boston, 1966; BA, U. Mass., 1983; MS, Lesley Coll., Cambridge, Mass., 1986. Cert. med. technologist, Ill.; clin. lab. scientist, D.C. Med. technologist Chelsea (Mass.) Soldier's Home, 1966-76, head hematology, 1978-92; lab. cons. MDC Assocs., Beverly Farms, Mass., 1994—; mem. faculty Boston U. Sch. Medicine, 1980-90. Mem. Am. Soc. Clin. Lab. Sci., Elks (esquire 1996), Moose (gov. 1993). Roman Catholic. Home: 49 Centennial Ave Gloucester MA 01930-2541

SCOLLARD, PATRICK JOHN, hospital executive; b. Chgo., Apr. 20, 1937; s. Patrick J. and Kathleen (Cooney) S.; m. Gloria Ann Carroll, July 1, 1961; children: Kevin, Maureen, Daniel, Thomas, Brian. B.S. in Econs., Marquette U., 1959; grad. sr. exec. devel. program, MIT, 1976. With Equitable Life Assurance Soc. U.S., N.Y.C., 1962-79, asst. v.p., 1969-71, v.p., personnel dir., 1971-75, v.p. corp. adminstrv. svcs., 1975-79; sr. v.p. Chem. Bank, N.Y.C., 1979-80, exec. v.p., 1980-87, chief adminstrv. officer, 1987-92; pres., CEO St. Francis Hosp., Roslyn, N.Y., 1992—; bd. dirs. Work in Am.; met. regional adv. bd. Chase Manhattan Corp. Bd. dirs. Cath. Charities, St. Francis Hosp.; mem. Woodstock Theol. Ctr. Office: St Francis Hosp 100 Port Washington Blvd Roslyn NY 11576-1353

SCOLNICK, EDWARD MARK, science administrator; b. Boston, Aug. 9, 1940; s. Barbara (Chasen) Scolnick; m. Barbara Bachrach; children: Laura, Jason, Daniel. AB, Harvard U., 1961; MD, Harvard U. Med. Sch., 1965. Intern Mass. Gen. Hosp., 1965-66, asst. resident internal medicine, 1966-67; research assoc. USPHS, 1967-69; sr. staff fellow lab. biochem. genetics NIH, 1969-70; instr. NIH Sem., 1970; sr. staff fellow viral leukemia and lymphoma br. Nat. Cancer Inst., 1970-71, spl. advisor to spl. virus cancer program, 1973-78, mem. coordinating com. for virus cancer program, 1975-78, chief. lab. tumor virus genetics, head. molecular virology sect., 1975-82; exec. dir. basic research virus and cell biology research Merck Sharp & Dohme Rsch. Labs., West Point, Pa., 1982-83, v.p. virus and cell biology research, 1983-84, sr. v.p., 1984, pres., 1985-93; sr. v.p. Merck & Co., Inc., 1991-93, exec. v.p., pres. rsch., 1993—; adj. prof. microbiology Sch. Medicine U. Pa., 1983-86. Editor-in-chief Jour. Virology; mem. editorial bd. Virology; contbr. numerous articles to profl. jours.;. Served with USPHS, 1965-67. Recipient Arthur S. Fleming award, 1976, PHS Superior Svc. award, 1978, Eli Lilly award, 1980, Indsl. Rsch. Inst. medal, 1990. Mem. NAS, Am. Soc. Biol. Chemists, Am. Soc. Microbiologists. Home: 811 Wickfield Rd Wynnewood PA 19096-1610 Office: Merck Rsch Labs PO Box 2000 Rahway NJ 07065-0900

SCOMMEGNA, ANTONIO, physician, educator; b. Barletta, Italy, Aug. 26, 1931; came to U.S., 1954, naturalized, 1960; s. Francesco Paola and Antonietta (Maresca) S.; m. Lillian F. Sinkiewicz, May 3, 1958; children: Paola, Frank, Roger. B.A., State Lyceum A. Casardi, Barletta, 1947; M.D., U. Bari (Italy), 1953. Diplomate: Am. Bd. Obstetrics and Gynecology, also sub-bd. endocrinology and reprodn. Rotating intern New Eng. Hosp., Boston, 1954-55; resident obstetrics and gynecology Michael Reese Hosp. and Med. Center, Chgo., 1956-59; fellow dept. research human reprodn. Michael Reese Hosp. and Med. Center, 1960-61, research asso., 1961; fellow steroid tng. program Worcester Found. Exptl. Biology, also Clark U., Shrewsbury, Mass., 1964-65; asso. prof. obstetrics and gynecology Chgo. Med. Sch., 1965-69; mem. staff Michael Reese Hosp. and Med. Center, 1961—, attending physician obstetrics and gynecology, 1961—, dir. sect. gynecologic endocrinology, 1965-81; dir. ambulatory care obstetrics and gynecology Mandel Clinic, 1968-69, chmn. dept., 1969—, trustee, 1977-80; prof. dept. obstetrics and gynecology Pritzker Sch. Medicine, U. Chgo., 1969—. Author numerous articles in field. Fulbright fellow, 1954-55. Fellow Am. Coll. Obstetricians and Gynecologists, Endocrine Soc., Chgo. Inst. Medicine, Am. Gynecol. and Obstet. Soc.; mem. AMA, Ill., Chgo. med. socs., Am. Fertility Soc., Chgo. Gynecol. Soc. (sec. 1976-79, pres. 1981-82), Soc. Study Reprodn., AAAS, Soc. for Gynecologic Investigation. Home: 1023E W Vernon Park Pl Chicago IL 60607-3400

SCOPP, IRWIN WALTER, periodontist, educator; b. N.Y.C., Dec. 8, 1909; s. Leon and Anne S.; B.S., CCNY, 1930; DDS, Columbia U., 1934; m. Edith Halprin, Dec. 25, 1941; 1 son, Alfred. Pvt. practice periodontics, N.Y.C., 1934-42; chief dental service VA Med. Center, N.Y.C., 1945-80; prof. periodontics N.Y.U. Coll. Dentistry, 1945-80, dir. continuing dental edn., 1980-85, dir. course in medicine Coll. Dentistry, 1982-90, clin. prof. periodontics, 1990—. Bd. govs. div. oral hygiene N.Y.C. Tech. Coll., 1960-79, chmn., 1979. Served to capt. Dental Corps, AUS, 1942-45. Recipient Disting. Profs. award N.Y.U., 1981. Mem. Northeastern Soc. Periodontics (sec.-treas. 1955-90), ADA (chmn. research 1978), Am. Acad. Periodontology, Am. Acad. Oral Medicine, Am. Coll. Dentists, Am. Acad. Sci., Internat. Assn. Dental Research, Am. Pub. Health Assn., Assn. Mil. Surgeons, Research Soc. Am., Hosp. Dental Chiefs Assn., Am. Acad. Sci. Author: Oral Medicine - A Clinical Approach with Basic Science Correlation, 1969, 2d edit., 1973. Contbr. chpts. to books.

SCORZELLI, JAMES FRANCIS, counseling psychology educator; b. Detroit, June 19, 1943; s. Joseph Ernest and Loretta Barbara (Wolynski) S.; m. Mary Margaret Reinke, Nov. 27, 1970; children: Christopher, Miriam, Caroline, Jonathan. BS, Mich. State U., 1965, MA, 1967; PhD, U. Wis., 1973. Lic. psychologist, Mass.; cert. rehab. counselor. Counselor for deaf Mich. Assn. for Better Hearing, East Lansing, 1965-66; vocat. evaluator, counselor Nev. Rehab. Svcs., Las Vegas, 1967-68; program coord. Ighamn County Jail Rehab. Program, Mason, Mich., 1969-70; rsch. assoc. U. Wis., Madison, 1972-73; prof. dept. counseling psychology, rehab. and spl. edn. Northeastern U., Boston, 1973—; cons. psychologist, Newton, 1976—. Author: Drug Abuse: Prevention and Rehabilitation in Malaysia, 1987; contbr. articles to profl. jours. Sgt. U.S. Army, 1968-69. Fulbright scholar Coun. Internat. Exch. of Scholars, Malaysia, 1984-85; WHO fellow, Malaysia, 1987, 90. Mem. AACD (ad hoc editor 1990—), AAAS, APA, Am. Rehab. Counselors Assn. (newsletter editor, rsch. award 1974), Nat. Rehab. Assn., Nat. Rehab. Counseling Assn., Mass. Psychol. Assn., Fulbright Alumni Assn. Lutheran. Home: 19 Adella Ave Newton MA 02165-1901 Office: Northeastern U 207 Lake Hall Boston MA 02115

SCOTCH, DAVID SOLOMON, physician, educator; b. Boston, Dec. 7, 1938; s. Theodore S. and Frances (Gauchman); m. Barbara C. Brown; children: Jonathan, Peter. AB, Boston U., 1960; MD, NYU, 1964; MS, MIT, 1977—. Intern, Bellevue Hosp., N.Y.C., 1964-65, resident in internal medicine, 1965-68; instr. medicine NYU, N.Y.C., 1968-71, asst. prof., 1971—, asst. dean, 1971-72, asso. dean, 1972—. Maj., USAF, 1969-71. Sloan fellow Mass. Inst. Tech., 1976-77. Mem. Assn. Am. Med. Colls. (chmn. NE reg. on 1974-76), Sigma Xi. Home: 300 E 51st St New York NY 10022 Office: NYU Sch Medicine 550 1st Ave New York NY 10016-6481

SCOTT, ADRIENNE, social worker, psychotherapist; b. N.Y.C.; d. William and Anne Scott; m. Ross F. Grumet, Nov. 10, 1957 (div. Aug. 1969). BA, Finch Coll., 1957; postgrad., NYU, 1958-62, MA in English, 1958; MSW, Adelphi U., 1988. Mem. English faculty Fordham U., N.Y.C., 1966-68; editor Blueboy Mag., Miami, Fla., 1974, "M" Mag., N.Y.C., 1976; freelance writer N.Y.C., 1958—; mem. English faculty NYU, 1958-65; pres. Googolplex Video, N.Y.C., 1981-86; clin. social worker Mt. Sinai Hosp., N.Y.C., 1988-93, Stuyvesant Polyclinic, N.Y.C., 1993—; presenter Nat. Methadone Conf., 1992. Author: Film as Film, 1970; contbg. editor Menstyle Mag., 1995; contbr. articles to numerous mags., including Vogue, Interview, N.Y. mag.; pioneer in fashion video; videographer documentaries; performance artist in Robert Wilson's King of Spain, 1973. Mem. exec. com. Adopt-An-AIDS Rschr. Program Rockefeller U.; nat. co-chairperson Gay Rights Nat. Lobby, 1976. Mem. NASW (cert.), AAUW, Assn. for Psychoanalytic Self Psychology. Home: 165 E 66th St New York NY 10021-6132 Office: 7 Patchin Pl New York NY 10011-8341

SCOTT, AMY ANNETTE HOLLOWAY, nursing educator; b. St. Albans, W.Va., Apr. 10, 1916; d. Oliver and Mary (Lee) Holloway; m. William M. Jefferson, June 22, 1932, (div. Oct. 1933); 1 child, William M. Jefferson, m. Vann Hyland Scott, Mar. 15, 1952, (dec. Dec. 1972). BS in Nursing Edn., Cath. U., Washington, 1948; cert. in psychiat. nursing, U. Paris, Paris, 1959. Indsl. nurse Curtiss Wright Air Plane Co., Lambert Field, St. Louis, 1941-44; faculty St. Thomas U., Manila, Philippines Island, 1948-50; pub. health nurse St. Louis Health Dept., 1951-56; capt. USAF Nursing Corps, Paris, 1956-60; resigned as maj. USAF (Nurse Corps), 1960, 1960; faculty St. Louis State Hosp., 1960-67; dept. head St. Vincents Hosp., St. Louis, 1967-68; faculty RN, creator psychiat. program Sch. of Nursing Jewish Hosp., 1968-72; adminstrv. nurse St. Louis State Hosp., 1972-84; initiated first psychiatric program sch. nursing, Jewish Hosp. Author: (short story) Two Letters, 1962, (novel) Storms, 1987, Life's Journey, 1993. Past bd. dirs. county bd. Mo. U., 1984-88; hon. citizen Colonial Williamsburg, Va.; mem. Rep. Presdl. Task Force; mem. Women in the Arts '94. Recipient Key to Colonial Williamsburg, Va., Medal of Merit, Rep. Presdl. Task Force, 1992; named to Rep. Presdl. Task Force Honor Roll, 1993, Nat. Women's Hall of Fame, 1995, Women's Hall of Fame, 1996. Mem. AAUW, NAFE, Internat. Fedn. Univ. Women, Internat. Soc. Quality Assurance in Health Care, N.Y. Acad. Scis., Am. Biog. Inst. (life, governing bd.), Women in the Arts, Cambridge Centre Engring., Internat. Platform Assn. Roman Catholic.

SCOTT, ANNE, nursing educator; b. Columbus, Ohio, Aug. 15, 1949; d. Raymond and Elizabeth (Isaly) Latham; children: Heather, Jeremy. BSN, Ohio State U., 1971; MSN, Oral Roberts U., 1986; PhD, Tex. Woman's U., 1990; postgrad., U. Ariz., 1992-94. Assoc. prof., dir. rsch. Ga. So. U., 1994—; faculty Kaplan Ednl. Ctr., Ltd., 1995—; perdiem staff nurse Bulloch Meml. Hosp., 1995—. Contbr. articles to profl. jours. Postdoctoral fellow U. Ariz., 1992-94; grantee March of Dimes, 1996. Mem. ANA, Ga. Nurses Assn., Sigma Theta Tau.

SCOTT, C. PAUL, psychiatrist, educator; b. Pitts., June 2, 1943; m. Nancy Ipp, Aug. 17, 1969; children: Rebecca, John. AB, U. Pa., 1964; MD, Case Western Res. U., 1968; postgrad., Pitts. Psychoanalytic Inst., 1984. Diplomate Am. Bd. Psychiatry and Neurology. Intern Mt. Sinai Hosp., Cleve., 1968-69; resident in gen. medicine Univ. Hosp., Cleve., 1969-70; resident in psychiatry Western Psychiat. Inst., Pitts., 1972-75, pres. med. staff, 1985-87; v.p. med. staff U. Pitts. Med. Ctr., 1995—, clin. prof. Sch. Medicine; dir. psychiat. edn. St. Margaret Meml. Hosp. Family Practice Residency, Pitts.; clin. assoc. prof. psychiatry M.C.P. Hahnemann U.; mem. faculty Pitts. Psychoanalytic Inst. Trustee Rodef Shalom Congregation, Pitts., 1986-92;

v.p., treas. Am. Jewish Com., Pitts., 1985-91. With USPHS, 1970-72. Mem. Am. Psychiat. Assn. (Falk fellow 1972-75), Pa. Psychiat. Assn., Pitts. Psychiat. Assn., Pitts. Psychoanalytic Assn., Soc. Tchrs. Family Medicine. Office: 401 Shady Ave Apt 202C Pittsburgh PA 15206-4409

SCOTT, C. RONALD, pediatrics and genetics educator; b. San Diego, Calif., Jan. 25, 1935; s. Clifford Walter and Hattie Mary (Quintrell) S.; m. Susan J. Berg, May 6, 1984; children: Lauren, John, Joseph. MD, U. Wash., 1959. Diplomate Am. Bd. Pediatrics, Am. Bd. Med. Genetics. Resident in pediatrics U. Minn., Mnpls., 1959-61; postdoctoral fellow in genetics Calif. Inst. Tech., Pasadena, Calif., 1961-62; postdoctoral fellow in genetics U. Wash., Seattle, 1964-65, asst. prof., assoc. prof. pediatrics, 1966-76, prof., 1976—, head div. pediatric genetics, 1976—; mem. study sect. NIH, 1985-89. Contr. numerous articles to med. jours., chpts. to books. Capt. M.C., USAF, 1962-64. Numerous research grants. Mem. Soc. Pediatric Rsch., Am. Pediatric Soc., Am. Soc. Human Genetics (bd. dirs. 1991-94), Am. Bd. Med. Genetics (pres. 1988), Soc. Inherited Metabolic Disease (bd. dirs. 1985-92, pres. 1988), Western Soc. Pediatric Rsch. (coun. 1974-77). Office: U Wash Dept Pediatrics # Rd-20 Seattle WA 98195

SCOTT, FRED DACON, surgeon; b. Folsom, Calif., Mar. 12, 1962; s. Winfield Morrill and LaRee (Taggart) S.; m. Deborah Lynn Weese, May 16, 1986; children: Emily Diane, Dacon Spencer, Andrew Tucker, Peter Allen. BS in Biology, Phillips U., Enid, Okla., 1986; DO, Okla. State U., Tulsa, 1990. Diplomate Nat. Bd. Osteo. Med. Examiners. Intern Mt. Clemens (Mich.) Gen. Hosp., 1990-91, resident in gen. surgery, 1991-95, chief resident in gen. surgery, 1994; mem. gen. surgery staff Passavant Area Hosp., Jacksonville, Ill., 1995—. Stake missionary Ch. of Jesus Christ of Latterday Saints, 1992-96, Sunday Sch. tchr., 1991-96, deacon, tchrs. quorums instr., 1986-89, elders quorum/1st counselor, sec., 1989-90, 92-95; mem. U.S. rifle team U.S. Olympic Com., 1980-81. Named to Outstanding Young Men of Am., 1988; named All-Am. Coll. Rifle, NRA, 1981. Mem. AMA, Am. Osteo. Assn., Ill. Med. Assn., Ill. Assn. Osteo. Physicians and Surgeons, Morgan-Scott County Med. Soc., Atlas Frat. Republican. Home: 2 Collins Pl Jacksonville IL 62650 Office: Passavant Area Hosp 800 W State St Jacksonville IL 62650

SCOTT, GENEVA LEE SMITH, nursing educator; b. Codell, Kans., Nov. 2, 1943; d. Lester Lee and Lennicejean Leota (Lynch) Smith; m. Dennis G. Scott, Feb. 20, 1965; children: J.D., Shane, Deminy. BS, Fort Hays Kans. State Coll., 1965; BS in Nursing, Fort Hays State U., 1979; MS in Nursing, West Tex. State U., 1986. Charge nurse Hadley Regional Med. Ctr., Hays, Kans.; sch. nurse Borger (Tex.) Ind. Sch. Dist.; clin. and classroom instr. NCKAVTS, Hays; nursing instr. St. Philip's Coll., San Antonio; sch. nurse Bryan Ind. Sch. Dist., 1993—. Scholarship grant, 1983. Mem. Am. Nurses Assn., Phi Delta Kappa, Beta Sigma Phi (membership chairperson, Girl of Yr. 1978). Home: 2524 Arbor Dr Bryan TX 77802-2127

SCOTT, JAMES LOUIS, health care administrator; b. Glendale, Calif., May 14, 1947; s. Harold Lee and Avis Veola (Parsons) S.; m. S. Jane Mays, May 20, 1972; children: Allison Lee, Matthew John. BS, Kans. State U., 1971; postgrad U. Tex.-Arlington, 1975-76, U. Kans., 1976-78. Vice pres. Kans. Hosp. Assn., Topeka, 1974-81; dir. intergovtl. affairs Health Care Fin. Adminstrn., Balt., 1981; dep. asst. sec. HHS, Washington, 1981-83; assoc. adminstr. Health Care Financing Adminstrn., Balt., 1983-84, Washington, dep. adminstr., 1984-85; pres. Premier Inst. Served with U.S. Army, 1967-69, Vietnam. Decorated Bronze Star with V. Republican. Methodist. Office: Premier Inst 400 N Capitol St NW # 590 Washington DC 20001-1511

SCOTT, JOHN D., pharmacologist; b. Edinburgh, Scotland, Apr. 13, 1958; married; 2 children. BSc in Biochemistry with honors, Herriot-Watt U., Edinburgh, 1980; PhD in Biochemistry, U. Aberdeen, 1983. NIH postdoctoral fellow dept. pharmacology U. Wash., Seattle, 1983-86, rsch. asst. prof. dept. biochemistry, 1986-88; asst. prof. dept. physiology & biophysics, dept. biol. chemistry U. Calif., Irvine, 1988-89; asst. scientist Ctr. Rsch. Occupl. & Environ. Toxicology Oreg. Health Scis. U., 1989-90, asst. scientist Vollum Inst. Advanced Biomed. Rsch., dept. biochemistry & molecular biology, 1990-92, scientist, 1993—; spkr. in field. Editl. bd. Jour. Biol. Chemistry; contbr. articles to profl. jours. Recipient John J. Abel award Am. Soc. Pharmacology & Exptl. Therapeutics, 1996; Med. Endowments Honorary scholar U. Aberdeen, 1980-83. Mem. ASBMB, Biochem. Soc., Protein Soc. Office: Vollum Inst Advanced Biomed Rsch Oreg Health Scis Univ 3181 SW Sam Jackson Park Rd Portland OR 97201*

SCOTT, KAREN ANN, dentist; b. Gary, Ind., Jan. 7, 1957; d. Jay R. and Bernadette (Hogan) S. BS, U. Notre Dame, 1979; BSD, U. Ill., Chgo., 1983, DDS, 1985. Pvt. practice dentistry Chgo., 1985—. Active Grant Park Concert Soc.; mem. adv. bd. Chgo. Archtl. Found.; mem. Chgo. Cares, Habitat for Humanity. Notre Dame scholar, 1975-79; recipient Achievement award Internat coll. Dentists, 1985. Mem. ADA, Ill. Dental Soc. (sci. presenter 1987), Chgo. Dental Soc., Internat. Vis. Ctr., Chgo. Architecture Found. (mem. adv. bd. Cathedral High Sch.), Notre Dame Club Chgo., Alpha Epsilon Delta, Omicron Kappa Upsilon. Clubs: Young Variety (Chgo.), Young Internat. Home: 1400 N State Pky #5B Chicago IL 60610 Office: 55 E Washington St Ste 3102 Chicago IL 60602-2206

SCOTT, KEVIN WINDFIELD, family physician; b. Cheyenne, Wyo., Apr. 13, 1958; s. Norris Mural and Gertrude Loraine (Tennefus) S.; m. Theresa Marie Lopez, May 20, 1989; children: Michael Ryan, Katie Marie. BS in Zoology, U. Wyo., 1989; DO, U. Health Scis., 1993. Diplomate Am. Osteo. Bd. Family Practice, Colo. State Bd. Medicine. Resident Columbia/Health One Family Medicine, Denver, 1993—; internship residency selection com. Health One/Columbia Family Medicine, Denver, 1994-95, 95-96. Alumni Sigma Nu Fraternity, Laramie, Wyo., 1984; past pres. alumni Alpha Epsilon Delta Premed. Honorary, U. Wyo., Laramie, 1986-87. Recipient Hosp. Adminstrs. Discretionary award Ivinson Meml. Hosp., Laramie, 1985, Outstanding EMT Student award Wyo. Ambulance and Emergency Med. Svcs. Assn., Cheyenne, Wyo., 1986, Outstanding Svc. to Children, Big Bros./Big Sisters, Laramie, 1987. Fellow Am. Bd. Osteo. Family Physicians; mem. Am. Acad. Family Physicians, Am. Osteo. Assn., Colo. State Med. Soc., Colo. State Osteo. Med. Soc., Denver Med. Soc., Denver Osteo. Found.

SCOTT, KIRBY JOSEPH, physician, military medical officer; b. Darby, Pa., Aug. 14, 1968; s. Kirby Joseph III and Patricia (McCreesh) S.; m. Colleen Mulqueen, June 11, 1994; 1 child, Keeley Patricia. BS in Chemistry cum laude, U.S. Naval Acad., Annapolis, 1990; DO, Phila. Coll. Osteo. Medicine, 1994. Diplomate Am. Bd. Osteo. Medicine. Lt. USN, 1990—; intern U.S. Naval Hosp. USN, Oakland, Calif., 1994-95; resident Naval Undersea Med. Inst. USN, Groton, Conn., 1995; med. dept. head U.S.S. Emory S. Land USN, Norfolk, Va., 1995—. Mem. AMA, Am. Osteo. Assn., Assn. Mil. Surgeons U.S., Am. Coll. Gen. Practitioners in Osteo. Medicine and Surgery. Home: 1012 Marlbank Ct Chesapeake VA 23320

SCOTT, MARK ALDEN, hospital network executive; b. Chattanooga, Dec. 4, 1959; s. Dewey Alden and Rowena (Lowery) S.; m. Donna Ruth Kibble, Sept. 11, 1982; 1 child, Matthew. Student, Tenn. Tech. U., Cookeville, 1978-80, Chattanooga State U., 1981, 93—. Cert. network engr. Programmer Jerry Bell Constrn., Chattanooga, 1986-88; PC specialist Siskin Steel & Supply, Chattanooga, 1988-89; support and network mgr. Tiger Data Systems, Chattanooga, 1989-90, programmer, 1990; system cons. Data Concepts, Chattanooga, 1990—; microcomputer specialist Meml. Hosp., Chattanooga, 1991-93, network mgr., 1993-96, mgr. network svcs., 1996—; programmer Candlelighters, Chattanooga. Mem. Netware Users Internat., Chattanooga Area Netware Users Group (pres.). Republican. Baptist. Home: 6218 Melton Dr Chattanooga TN 37416-3223 Office: Meml Hosp 2525 Desales Ave Chattanooga TN 37404-1161

SCOTT, MARTHA ANN, clinical social worker; b. Cin., July 19, 1952; d. Richard Arthur and Dorothy (Hewitt) S.; m. Douglas Stephenson Magee, May 3, 1975. BA in Sociology, Denison U., 1973; MSW, Ohio State U., 1977; postgrad., U.Cin., 1981-82. Lic. ind. social worker, Ohio; cert. Nat. Bd. Examiners in Clin. Social Work; cert. fellow in managed care. Med. social worker Bethesda North Hosp., Cin., 1977-78; clin. social worker Cancer Family Care, Cin., 1978-85, casework supr., 1985-91, interim dir., 1988, 90; clin. social worker Edward J. Fisher, Jr., MD Inc., Cin., 1991—. Mem. NASW, Acad. Cert. Social Workers, Nat Assn. Oncology Social Workers (chmn. registration com. nat. conf. 1988), Ohio Soc. for Clin. Social Workers, Social Work Oncology Group Greater Cin. (v.p. 1987, pres. 1988-90). Office: Edward J Fisher Jr MD Inc 7438 Jaeger Ct Cincinnati OH 45230

SCOTT, MARY CELINE, pharmacologist; b. Los Angeles, July 14, 1957; d. Walter Edward and Shirley Jean (Elvin) S. BS in Biol. Sci., U. Calif., Irvine, 1978; MS in Biology, Calif. State U., Long Beach, 1980; PhD in Pharmacology, Purdue U., 1985; MBA in Pharm.-Chem. Studies, Fairleigh Dickinson U., 1995. Teaching asst. Calif. State U., Long Beach, 1979-80; teaching asst. Purdue U., West Lafayette, Ind., 1980-82, grad. instr., 1982-83, rsch. fellow, 1983-85, 1988-89; rsch. fellow Mayo Found. Rochester, Minn., 1985-87; sr. scientist Schering-Plough, Bloomfield, N.J., 1989-92; assoc. prin. scientist Schering-Plough, Kenilworth, N.J., 1993—. Contbr. articles to profl. jours. Mem.-at-large, bd. dirs. Washington Rock Girl Scout Coun. Mem. AAAS, Am. Chem. Soc., Am. Soc. Pharm. and Exptl. Therapeutics, Internat. Soc. for Study Xenobiot, Soc. Electroanalytical Chemistry, Soc. Neurosci., Sigma Xi, Delta Mu Delta. Democrat. Office: Schering-Plough Rsch Inst Dept Drug Metabolism & PK 2015 Galloping Hill Rd Kenilworth NJ 07033-0539

SCOTT, MARY JEAN, medical physicist; b. Bklyn., Nov. 8, 1931; d. Charles Pruitt and Mildred Pamela Scott; m. Edward Cyril Humphrey Silk, Oct. 4, 1959; children: John Carl Vincent, Roland Henry Luke, Carol Anne Marie. BSc in Math., St. Lawrence U., Canton, N.Y., 1952; PhD in Physics, Johns Hopkins U., 1958; diploma in Theology with distinction, Joint Bd. Diploma in Theology, Southern Africa, 1990. Registered med. physicist, radiation South African Med. and Dental Coun. Rsch asst. Brookhaven (N.Y.) Nat. Lab., 1952-58; asst. prof. Bryn Mawr (Md.) Coll., 1958; mem. Film Prodn. Phys. Scis. Study Com., Mass., 1958; rsch. assoc. Atomic Energy Rsch. Establishment, Harwell, Eng., 1958-60; lectr. rsch. U. Witwatersrand, Johannesburg, South Africa, 1960-66; med. physicist Johannesburg/Hillbrow Hosps., 1967—. Author: The Holy Spirit Yesterday and Today, 1976, Bible Studies: Women in Christ's Church, 1989. Editor newspaper Johannesburg Diocese Ch. of Province of So. Africa, 1993—, ch. warden, parish councillor, mem. diocesan coun., diocesan synod, provincial synod. Mem. AAAS, South African Soc. Nuclear Medicine (sec.-treas. 1974-78), South African Inst. Physics, Alister Hardy Rsch. Centre, Am. Phys. Soc., Am. Assn. Physicsts in Medicine, South African Assn. Physicists in Medicine and Biology (council mem. 1981-84), Am. Assn. Physics Tchrs. Anglican. Home and Office: 15 Meyer St Oaklands, Johannesburg 2192, South Africa Office: Hillbrow Hosp Dept Med Phys, Private Bag 23140, Joubert Park 2044, South Africa

SCOTT, MILDRED HOPE, nurse; b. Miami, Fla., July 5, 1926; d. Enos R. and Ruth (Sommers) Eby; m. Thomas Wayne Scott, Dec. 19, 1958; children: Linda Joy Scott Day, Daniel Dean. ThB in Bible Theology, Internat. Bible Inst. and Sem., Plymouth, Fla., 1982. Lic. practical nurse, Fla. Lic. practical nurse various hosps. and nursing homes, Fla. and Mo., 1969-86; sch. nurse Orange County Sch. Bd., Orlando, Fla., 1974-78; pvt. duty nurse Upjohn Healthcare Services, Kansas City, Mo., 1985-89; allergy nurse Aggarwal Allergy Clinic, Raytown, Mo., 1987-89, 92—; sec. to Dr. Lottie McWherter Mission, Kans., 1989-92; staff writer Majestic Records-Countrywine Pub., Linden, Tex., 1987—. Served as cpl. USMC, 1957-59. Mem. ASCAP, Assn. Internat. Gospel Assemblies Ind. (ordained minister). Democrat. Home: PO Box 183 43 Aspen St Belton MO 64012-2091

SCOTT, MIMI KOBLENZ, psychotherapist, actress, publicist. journalist; b. Albany, N.Y., Dec. 15, 1940; d. Edmund Akiba and Tillie (Paul) Koblenz; m. Barry Stuart Scott, Aug. 13, 1961 (dec. Nov. 1991); children: Karen Scott Zantay, Jeffrey B. BA in Speech, English Edn., Russell Sage Coll., 1962; MA in Speech Edn., SUNY, Albany, 1968; M in Social Welfare, SUNY, 1985; PhD in Psychology, Pacific Western U., Encino, Calif., 1985. Cert. tchr., social worker. Tchr. English, speech Albany Pub. Schs., 1961-63; hostess, producer talkshow Sta. WAST-TV 13, Albany, 1973-75; freelance actress N.Y.C., 1975-77; producer, actress Four Seasons Dinner Theater, Albany, 1978-82; instr. of theatre Albany Jr. Coll., 1981-83; pvt. practice psychotherapy Albany, N.Y., 1985-92; exec. producer City of Albany Park Playhouse, 1989-92; actor self-employed N.Y.C., 1992—; actor Off Broadway show Grandma Sylvia's Funeral, 1996; guest psychotherapist Sally Jessy Raphael Show, 1992, 93, Jane Whitney Show, 1994, A Current Affair, 1995, News Talk TV, 1995. Scriptwriter, dir., actress TV movie, 1995; feature writer Backstage, 1995-96; (off-Broadway) Grandma Sylvia's Funeral. Event organizer AmFar, 1985; co-chmn. March of Dimes Telethon, 1985-86; fundraiser Leukemia Found., 1987, Aids Benefit, N. Miami Beach, Fla., 1988; elected to SUNY Albany U. Found., 1990. Recipient FDR Nat. Achievement award March of Dimes, 1985, Recognition Cert. Capital Dist. Psychiat. Ctr., 1983, 84, 85; named Woman of Yr. YWCA, 1986, Commr. Albany Tricentennial Celebration, 1986; Mimi Scott Day proclaimed by Mayor of Albany, 1989. Mem. AEA, SAG, AFTRA, NASW. Jewish. Home and Office: 211 West 71st # 6C New York NY 10023

SCOTT, NANCY ELLEN, psychologist; b. El Paso, Tex., Nov. 1, 1960; d. Robert Churchill and Annie Jo (Schmidt) S. BS, U. Tex., El Paso, 1982; MS, Springfield Coll., 1985; MA, Columbia U., 1987, EdM, 1989; PhD, Fordham U., 1996. Cert. tchr., Tex., cert. clin. hypnotherapy. Assoc. Occupl. Health Consulting Inc., West Nyack, N.Y., 1985-88; psychiat. rehab. counselor Met. Hosp., N.Y.C., 1988-91; psychotherapist Met. Ctr. for Mental Health, N.Y.C., 1991-96; psychology intern Albert Einstein Coll. of Medicine, Bronx, N.Y., 1991-92; psychologist Albert Einstein Coll. Medicine, Bronx, N.Y., 1992-94, Bronx Psychiat. Ctr., Bronx, N.Y., 1994-95; assessor Assessment Sys., Inc., N.Y.C., 1995; pvt. practice N.Y.C., 1995—; neuropsychologist Burke Med. Rsch. Inst., White Plains, N.Y., 1996—. Contbr. articles to profl. jours. Mem. APA. Office: Burke Med Rsch Inst 785 Mamaroneck Ave White Plains NY 10605

SCOTT, NINA OGLE, nurse; b. Pulaski, Va., Feb. 4, 1954; d. Willie James and Oletha (Horton) Ogle; m. Willard Mcntie Newman, Aug. 29, 1981 (div. 1983); 1 child, Travis Willard Newman; m. Jerry Wayne Scott. Nov. 23, 1995. LPN magna cum laude, New River C.C., 1977; AA, Wytheville C.C., 1985. RN, Va. Charge nurse Pulaski Cmty. Hosp., 1977-85; case mgr. Home Link Home Health Agy., Radford, Va., 1985-86; personal care coord. Carroll County Health Dept., Hillsville, Va., 1986-87; performance improvement coord. Twin County Regional Home Health, Galax, Va., 1987—; total quality mgmt. facilitator Twin County Regional Hosp., 1995—. Mem. Nat. Assn. Healthcare Quality, Va. Assn. Healthcare Quality, S.W. Va. Assn. Healthcare Quality, Gold Wing Road Riders Assn. Democrat. Methodist. Home: Rt 1 Box 433-A Austinville VA 24312 Office: Twin County Regional Hosp 200 Hospital Dr Galax VA 24333

SCOTT, PAMELA MOYERS, physician assistant; b. Clarksburg, W.Va., Jan. 5, 1961; d. James Edward and Norma Lee (Holbert) Moyers; m. Troy Allen Scott, July 19, 1986. BS summa cum laude, Alderson-Broaddus Coll., 1983. Cert. physician asst. Physician asst. Weston (W.Va.) State Hosp., 1983-84, Rainelle (W.Va.) Med. Ctr., 1984—; support faculty physician asst. program Coll. W.Va., 1994—, mem. physician asst. adv. coun. 1993—, physician asst. program admission selection com., 1994—; keynote spkr. Alderson-Broadous Coll. Ann. Physician Assn. Banquet, 1992; presenter civa. Task Force on Adolescent Pregnancy and Parenting State Meeting, Charleston, 1992, W.Va. Primary Care Assn. Ann. Conf., Beckley, W.Va., 1994, W.Va. State Rural Health Conf., Morgantown, 1992, Chinese Med. Soc., Beijing, 1992; guest Lifetime TV med. program Physician Jour. Update, 1993; adv. coun. W.Va. Rural Health Networking, 1994—, W.Va. Rural Networking Managed Care Policy Group, 1996. Mem. edtl. bd. Jour. Am. Acad. Physician Assts., dept. editor Procedures in Family Practice Dept., 1996; contbr. articles to profl. jours. Mem. W.Va. State Task Force on Adolescent Pregnancy and Parenting, 1992—; W.Va. Rural Networking Managed Care Study Group, 1995. Named Young Career Woman of Yr. Rainelle chpt. and Dist. V of W. Va., Citation of Honor at State Level of Competition, Bus. and Profl. Women's Club, 1986, Nominee for W. Va. Women's Commn. Celebrate Women award, 1996. Fellow Am. Acad. Physician Assts. (del. to People's Republic China 1992, W.Va. chief del. Ho. of Dels. Nat. Conv. 1992, 94, 95, 96, W.Va. del. 1993, mem. rural health caucus 1991—, chair pub. edn. com. 1996—, presenter ann. CME conf. San Antonio 1994, Las Vegas 1995), W.Va. Assn. Physician Assts. (chair membership com. 1989-91, nominations and elections com. 1990-91, pres. 1991-94, immediate past pres. 1994-95, presenter Continued Med. Edn. Conf. 1993). Republican. Baptist. Home: PO Box 43 Williamsburg WV 24991-0043 Office: Rainelle Med Ctr 645 Kanawha Ave Rainelle WV 25962-1013

SCOTT, PATRICIA (DIANE) WATKINS, psychologist; b. Logan, Utah, Mar. 29, 1952; d. Bruce Omar and Vera Kristine (Jeppesen) Watkins; m. George Martin Scott, July 3, 1974; children: Karen Nicole, Thomas Michael. BA magna cum laude, Utah State U., 1974; MA, U. Tex., Arlington, 1978; spl. student, St. Cloud State U., 1984-87; cert., Ctr. for Cognitive Therapy, Atlanta, 1994. Diplomate Minn. Bd. Psychologists. Intern Veda Knox Sch., Arlington, Tex., 1976; intern, rschr. Trinity Valley Mental Health/Mental Retardation, Fort Worth, 1976-77; vocat. counselor Cheyenne Village, Manitou Springs, Colo., 1978-79; enmerator R.L. Polk, Denver, 1980; human devel. counselor Suburban Cmty. Tng. and Svcs. Ctr., Englewood, Colo., 1980-81; behavior analyst III Regional Treatment Ctr., 1981-88; behavioral psychologist Brainerd (Minn.) RTC, 1988-94, psychologist II, 1994—. Monitor crisis line Help Line Utah State U., Logan, 1972; pres. Students for McGovern, Logan, 1972; summer organizer All Souls Unitarian Ch., Colorado Springs, Colo.; chair precinct Dem. Farmer Labor Party, Brainerd, Minn., 1990, 94; program dir. Northwoods Unitarian Universalist Fellowship, Pine River, Minn., 1992-94, treas., 1993—; vol. Pikes Peak Mental Health Ctr., Colorado Springs, 1979-80, Sexual Assault Ctr., Brainerd, 1993—. Grantee: (Chalice Lighters' grant) Prairie Star Dist. Unitarian Universalist Assn., Pine River, 1992. Mem. AAUW, Minn. Psychol. Assn., Nat. Assn for Behavior Analysis, Phi Kappa Phi, Alpha Lamba Delta. Democrat. Office: Brainerd RTC 1777 E Hwy 18 Brainerd MN 56401

SCOTT, PHILIP JOHN, medical educator, general physician; b. Auckland, New Zealand, June 26, 1931; s. Horace MacDonald and Doris Annie (Ruddock) S.; m. Elizabeth Jane MacMillan, Oct. 3, 1956; children: Janet Elizabeth, Michael John, Jennifer Margaret, Philippa Anne. B of Med. Sci., U. Otago, 1952, MB, BChir, 1955; MD, U. Birmingham, England, 1962. Internship Auckland, Green Lane and Middlemore Hosps., Auckland, New Zealand, 1956-57; royal postgrad. Med. Sch. of London, 1959-60; residency Auckland Hosp., 1958, Queen Elizabeth Hosp., Birmingham, Eng., 1960-62; jr. med. officer Auckland Hosp. Bd., 1956-58; house physician Royal Postgrad. Med. Sch., London, 1959; med. registrar, jr. rsch. fellow Nat. Health Svc. and Med. Rsch. Coun. Gt. Britain, Birmingham, England, 1960-62; from assoc. prof. to head dept. medicine U. Auckland, 1973-87; head acad. unit Middlemore Hosp., Auckland, 1988—; chmn. allocation and orgn. com. New Zealand Bd. Health, Wellington, 1985-87. Contbr. articles to profl. jours. Com. mem. Hosp. and Related Svcs. Task Force, Wellington, 1987-88. Decorated knight comdr. Her Majesty the Queen, 1987. Fellow Royal Australasian Coll. Physicians, Royal Coll. Physicians London, Royal Soc. New Zealand (lead in environment report 1986, pres.-elect 1995-96). Home: 64 Temple St Meadowbank, Auckland 1105, New Zealand Office: Middlemore Hosp Acad Unit, Otahuhu, Auckland New Zealand

SCOTT, RANDOLPH FRITZ, physician, educator; b. Phoenix, May 26, 1957; s. Walter Gibson and Renate Margerate (Hoffman) S.; children: Colin Peter, Jared Michael. AA, Maricopa Tech. Cmty. Coll., 1978, Maricopa Tech. Cmty. Coll., 1978; BS, U. Ariz., 1980; DO, Kirksville Coll. Osteopathic, Mo., 1984. Diplomate Am. Osteopathic Bd. of Family Practice. Family practice Pima Osteopathic Assn., Tucson, Ariz., 1985—; bd. dirs. Tucson Osteopathic Found., Tucson, 1994—; assoc. faculty various osteopathic schs., 1985—; med. dir. Pima Co. Health Choice, 1995—, Manor Care N.H., Tucson, 1995—. Mem. Am. Coll. Osteopathic Family Physicians, Am. Osteopathic Assn., Ariz. Osteopathic Assn. Office: Pima Osteopathic Assn. 2222 N Craycroft No 104 Tucson AZ 85712

SCOTT, RICHARD L., health and medical products company executive; b. Kansas City, Mo., 1953. BSBA, U. Mo.; JD, So. Meth. U. Bar: Tex. Pvt. practice, until 1987; pres., CEO, Columbia/HCA Healthcare Corp., Nashville, 1987—; bd. dirs. Banc One Corp. Recipient silver award as CEO of Yr. Fin. World mag.; named One of Top 25 Performers, U.S. News & World Report, 1995. Mem. Healthcare Leadership Coun., Bus. Roundtable, Bus. Coun. Office: Basic Am Med Inc 201 W Main St Louisville KY 40202-1366*

SCOTT, RONALD WILLIAM, educator, physical therapist, lawyer, writer; b. Pitts., Dec. 19, 1951; s. Richard Jack and Leone Florence (Gore) S.; m. Maria Josefa Barba-Garces, Aug. 5, 1973; children: Ronald William Jr., Paul Steven. BS in Phys. Therapy summa cum laude, U. Pitts., 1977; JD magna cum laude, U. San Diego, 1983; MBA, Boston U., 1986; LLM, Judge Adv. Gen. Sch., Charlottesville, Va., 1988; postgrad., Samuel Merritt Coll., Oakland, Calif. Bar: Calif. 1983, Tex. 1994; cert. orthopaedic phys. therapist. Commd. 1st lt. U.S. Army, 1978, advanced through grades to maj.; atty.-advisor U.S. Army, Frankfurt, Germany, 1983-87; malpractice claims atty. U.S. Army, Ft. Meade, Md., 1988-89; chief phys. therapist U.S. Army, Ft. Polk, La., 1989-92; phys. therapist, clin. instr. Brooke Army Med. Ctr., San Antonio, 1992-94; assoc. prof. dept. phys. therapy Sch. of Allied Health Scis., U. Tex. Health Sci. Ctr., San Antonio, 1994—; presenter numerous profl. seminars on health law, ethics, and quality and risk mgmt.; guest lectr. phys. therapy program Hahnemann U., Phila., 1991—, Southwest Tex. State U., Tex. Woman's U., U.S. Army-Baylor U. Author: Healthcare Malpractice, 1990, Legal Aspects of Documenting Patient Care, 1994, Promoting Legal Awareness, 1996; editor: Law Rev., U. San Diego, 1982-83; also articles; mem. editl. adv. bd. PT: The Mag. of Phys. Therapy, 1991—. Merit badge counselor Boy Scouts Am. Mem. ABA, Am. Phys. Therapy Assn. (chair, jud. com., McMillan scholar 1976), Nat. Health Lawyers Assn., Tex. Phys. Therapy Assn., Soc. for Human Resource Mgmt. (presenter Geriatric Rehab. Conf. Cambridge U. 1995, Trinity Coll., Dublin 1996). Democrat. Methodist. Home: 5815 Spring Crown San Antonio TX 78247-5409 Office: U Tex Health Sci Ctr 7703 Floyd Curl Dr San Antonio TX 78284-6200

SCOTT, STANLEY, physician; b. Poland, May 1, 1948; came to U.S., 1967; s. Moshe and Miriam (Jakobowicz) Skoczylas; m. Joan Keisman, Apr. 13, 1980; children: Matthew, Joseph, Jeffrey. BS, Hunter Coll., 1973; MD, Albert Einstein Sch. Medicine, 1976. Diplomate Am. Bd. Internal Medicine. Pvt. practice internal medicine Queens, N.Y., 1980—. Office: 101-12 78th St Ozone Park NY 11416

SCOTT, TINA LOUISE, physician assistant, paramedic; b. Burgaw, N.C., Aug. 1, 1966; d. George Tilmond Scott and Hazel Mae Rivenbark. BS, U. Okla., 1995; postgrad., Alderson-Broaddus Coll. Commd. U.S. Army, 1984, advanced through grades to 2nd lt., 1995; med. combat specialist U.S. Army, Germany, 1984-87, N.C. Nat. Guard, Goldsboro, 1987—; EMT paramedic Durham (N.C.) County Hosp. Corp., 1988—; physician asst. Betsy Johnson Meml. Hosp., Dunn, N.C., 1995—. Mem. Am. Acad. Physician Assts., N.C. Assn. Physician Assts., Soc. Army Physician Assts., N.C. Assn. EMTs, Army Nat. Guard Assn., N.C. Nat. Guard Assn. Republican. Baptist. Home: 109 Cheshire Dr Hillsborough NC 27278 Office: Betsy Johnson Meml Hosp 800 Tilghman Dr Dunn NC 28334

SCOTT, TODD SYRINGTON, podiatrist; b. Royal Oak, Mich., Apr. 26, 1960; s. Robert H. and Nancy M. (Shile) S. BS, Mich. State Univ., 1985; DPM, Scholl Coll. Podiatric Med., 1989. Resident Thorek Hosp., Chgo., 1989-90; pvt. practice Chgo., 1990—; v.p. podiatric surgery facilty Northwest Ambucare, Chgo., 1995—; assoc. faculty dept. surgery Scholl Coll. Podiatric Medicine, Chgo., 1991-93; podiatric surgeon staff Water Tower Surgi-Ctr., Chgo., 1991-93. Contbr. article to profl. jours. Trainer h.s. football Admusen H.S., Chgo., 1990-93. Recipient Mich. Competetive scholarship, State of Mich., 1979-80. Office: Todd S Scott DPM 1008 W Foster Chicago IL 60640

SCOTT, WALTER NEIL, physiologist, educator; b. Evansville, Ind., Mar. 2, 1935; s. Paul Kruger and Pauline Virginia (Kimbley) S.; children: Walter David Kimbley, Benjamin Bray. B.S., Western Ky. State Coll., 1956; M.D., U. Louisville, 1960. Intern New Eng. Ctr. Hosp., Boston, 1960-61; resident New Eng. Ctr. Hosp., 1961-62; NIH fellow medicine Mass. Meml. Hosps., Boston, 1962-63; USPHS fellow biophys. lab. Harvard Med. Sch., Brookline, Mass., 1963-65; spl. NIH fellow biochemistry MIT, Cambridge, 1965-66; biochemist Sch. Aerospace Medicine, San Antonio, 1966-68; acting chief biochem. pharmacology div. Sch. Aerospace Medicine, 1967-68; asst. prof.

Mt. Sinai Grad. Sch., N.Y.C., 1968-71; mem. grad. faculty CUNY, N.Y.C., 1968-82; asst. prof. ophthalmology Mt. Sinai Med. Sch., N.Y.C., 1971-74; assoc. prof. ophthalmology Mt. Sinai Med. Sch., 1974-79, research prof. ophthalmology, 1979-82, asst. dean research, 1976-81, assoc. dean, 1981-82; chmn. dept. biology NYU, N.Y.C., 1982-87, prof., 1982—; Lancaster vis. prof. Western Ky. U., 1980; mem. cornea task force Nat. Eye Inst., 1972, vision research program com., 1975-79; cons. metabolic biology program NSF, 1976-91; established investigator Am. Heart Assn., 1971-76; Molly Berns sr. investigator N.Y. Heart Assn., 1976-80; chmn. Gordon Conf. Biology and Chemistry of Peptides, 1978; mem. organizing com. 3d Gordon Conf. on Peptides, 6th Am. Peptide Symposium. Contbr. articles to sci. publs. Served to capt. USAF, 1966-68. Fellow N.Y. Acad. Scis. (gov. 1978-82, pres. 1983, chmn. conf. organizing com. 1980-81, 87-88); mem. Am. Physiol. Soc., Am. Soc. Biol. Chemists, Biophys. Soc., Soc. Exptl. Biology and Medicine (editorial bd. procs.), Am. Heart Assn., AAAS, Am. Chem. Soc., Am. Soc. Nephrology, N.Y. Acad. Medicine (com. pub. health 1986—), Endocrine Soc., Soc. Cell Biology, Sigma Xi, Alpha Omega Alpha. Office: NYU Dept Biology 1009 Main Bldg Washington Sq E New York NY 10003

SCOTT, WILLIAM CORYELL, medical executive; b. Sterling, Colo., Nov. 22, 1920; s. James Franklin and Edna Ann (Schillig) S.; m. Jean Marie English, Dec. 23, 1944 (div. 1975); children: Kathryn, James, Margaret; m. Carolyn Florence Hill, June 21, 1975; children: Scott, Amy Jo, Robert. AB, Dartmouth Coll., 1942; MD, U. Colo., 1944, MS in OB/GYN, 1951. Cert. Am. Bd. Ob-Gyn., 1956, 79, Am. Bd. Med. Mgmt., 1991. Intern USN Hosp., Great Lakes, Ill., 1945-46, Denver Gen. Hosp., 1946-47; resident Ob-Gyn St. Joseph's Hosp., Colo. Gen. Hosp., Denver, 1946-51; practice medicine specializing in Ob-Gyn Tucson, 1951-71; assoc. prof. emeritus U. Ariz. Med. Sch., Tucson, 1971-94, 1994; v.p. med. affairs U. Med. Ctr., Tucson, 1984-94. Contbr. articles to med. jours. and chpt. to book. Pres. United Way, Tucson, 1979-80, HSA of Southeastern Ariz., Tucson, 1985-87; chmn. Ariz. Health Facilities Authority, Phoenix, 1974-83. Served to capt. USNR, 1956-58. Recipient Man of Yr. award, Tucson, 1975. Fellow ACS, Am. Coll. Ob-Gyn, Pacific Coast Ob-Gyn Soc., Ctrl. Assn. of Ob-Gyn; mem. AMA (coun. on sci. affairs 1984-93, chmn. 1989-91), Am. Coll. Physician Execs., Am. Coll. Health Care Execs., Ariz. Med. Assn., La Paloma Country Club. Republican. Episcopalian. Home: PO Box 805 Sonoita AZ 85637-0805

SCOTT, W(ILLIAM) RICHARD, sociology educator; b. Parsons, Kan., Dec. 18, 1932; s. Charles Hogue and Hildegarde (Hewit) S.; m. Joy Lee Whitney, Aug. 14, 1955; children: Jennifer Ann, Elliot Whitney, Sydney Brooke. AA, Parsons Jr. Coll., 1952; AB, U. Kans., 1954, MA, 1955; PhD, U. Chgo., 1961. Asst. prof. to assoc. prof. sociology Stanford (Calif.) U., 1960-69, prof., 1969—, chair dept. sociology, 1972-75; courtesy prof. Sch. Medicine, Stanford U., 1972—, Sch. Edn., Grad. Sch. Bus., 1977—; fellow Ctr. for Advanced Study in Behavioral Scis., 1989-90; dir. Orgns. Rsch. Tng. Program, Stanford U., 1972-89, Ctr. for Orgns. Rsch., 1988-96; mem. adv. panel Sociology Program NSF, Washington, 1982-84; mem. epidemiol. and svc. rsch. rev. panel NIMH, Washington, 1984-88; mem. Commn. on Behavioral and Social Scis. and Edn., NAS, 1990—. Author: (with O.D. Duncan et al) Metropolis and Region, 1960, (with P.M. Blau) Formal Organizations, 1962, Social Processes and Social Structures, 1970, (with S.M. Dornbusch) Evaluation and the Exercise of Authority, 1975, Organizations: Rational, Natural and Open Systems, 1981, rev. edit., 1992, (with J.W. Meyer) Organizational Environments: Ritual and Rationality, 1983, edit., 1992, (with A.B. Flood) Hospital Structure and Performance, 1987, (with J.W. Meyer), Institutional Environments and Organizations: Structural Complexity and Individualism, 1994, Institutions and Organizations, 1995, (with S. Christinsen) The Institutional Construction of Organization, 1995; editor Ann. Rev. of Sociology, 1986-91. Fellow Woodrow Wilson, 1954-55; mem. Nat. Commn. Nursing, 1980-83; chair Consortium Orgns. Rsch. Ctrs., 1989-91; elder First Presby. Ch., Palo Alto, Calif., 1977-80, 83-86. Social Sci. Rsch. Coun. fellow, U. Chgo., 1959; named Edmund P. Learned Disting. Prof., Sch. Bus. Adminstrn., U. Kans, 1970-71; recipient Cardinal Citation for Disting. Svc. Labette C.C., Parsons, 1981, Disting. Scholar award Mgmt. and Orgn. Theory divsn. Acad. Mgmt., 1988, Richard D. Irwin award for Scholarly Contbn. to Mgmt., 1996. Mem. Inst. Medicine, Am. Sociol. Assn. (chmn. sect. on orgns. 1970-71, mem. coun. 1989-92), Acad. Mgmt., Sociol. Rsch. Assn., Macro-Organizational Behavior Soc., Phi Beta Kappa. Democrat. Presbyterian. Home: 940 Lathrop Pl Stanford CA 94305-1060 Office: Stanford U Dept Sociology Bldg 120 Stanford CA 94305

SCOTT-CONNER, CAROL ELIZABETH HOFFMAN, surgeon, educator; b. Towanda, Pa., June 24, 1946; d. Charles Wesley and Mary Elizabeth (Lord) Hoffman; m. Christopher Scott, Jan. 29, 1967 (dec. May 1971); m. Harry Faulkner Conner, Aug. 24, 1974. BS, MIT, 1969; MD, NYU, 1976; PhD, U. Ky., 1988. Cert. Nat. Bd. Med. Examiners, 1977, Am. Bd. Surgery, 1982, 90; cert. surg. critical care Am. Bd. Surgery, 1990. Asst. prof. surgery Marshall U., Huntington, W.Va., 1981-85, assoc. prof. surgery, 1985-86; assoc. prof. surgery U. Miss., Jackson, 1986-91, prof. surgery, 1991-95; prof., head surgery U. Iowa, Iowa City, 1995—; W.Va. State Councillor, Am. Coll. Surgery, 1985-86; USMLE testing com., 1994—, mem. Halsted Soc., 1995—. Mem. editl. bd. Clin. Anatomy mag., 1987—, Am. Jour. Surgery, 1996—; contbr. over 90 articles to profl. jours. Bd. dirs. Am. Cancer Soc., 1988-90. Fellow ACS (young surgeon rep. 1984), Am. Coll. Gastroenterology; mem. Am. Surg. Assn., Soc. for Surgery Alimentary Tract, Soc. Univ. Surgeons, So. Surg. Assn., Internat. Soc. Surgery. Office: U Iowa Coll Medicine Dept Surgery 1516 JCP 200 Hawkins Dr Iowa City IA 52242-1086

SCOTTI, ANGELO THOMAS, physician; b. New Brunswick, N.J.; s. Louis A. and Mary (DiMura) S.; m. Geraldine Marie Cinelli, June 5, 1965; children: David, Daniel, Michael. BA in Psychology, Harvard U., 1961; MD, U. Penn., 1965. Diplomate Am. Bd. Internal Medicine. Resident Mayo Clinic, Rochester, Minn., 1971; with IJI Corp., Pittsfield, Mass., 1971-76; emergency medicine dir. Bayshore Emergency Physicians, Holmdel, N.J., 1976-92; med. dir. PruPac, Holmdel, 1977-94; internist Little Silver, N.J., 1991—; cons. Bayshore Hosp., Holmdel, 1976—, Riverview Med. Ctr., Red Bank, N.J., 1977—. Author: (books) Travlers Medical Manual, 1986, Safe Sex, 1990. Lt. comdr. USPHS, 1966-68. Home: 2 Shadowbrook Rd Colts Neck NJ 07722

SCRABECK, JON GILMEN, dental eductor; b. Rochester, Minn., Dec. 6, 1938; s. Clarence and Nancy Alma (Brown) S.; m. DeAnn Louise Jacks, June 16, 1962; children: Joan Louise, Erik Jon. Student, Contra Costa Coll., San Pablo, Calif., 1964-66, U. Calif., Berkeley, 1966-67; DDS, UCLA, 1971; MA in Edn., U. Colo., 1985. Pvt. practice, Santa Rosa, Calif., 1971-78; sr. instr. U. Colo. Sch. Dentistry, Denver, 1978-79, asst. prof., 1980-86, dir. patient care, 1979-80, acting dir. clin. affairs, 1980-81; acting assoc. dean U. Colo. Sch. Dentistry, Denver, 1983-84; acting div. chmn. U. Colo. Sch. Dentistry, Denver, 1984-85; dept. chmn. Marquette U. Sch. Dentistry, Milw., 1986-90, assoc. prof., 1986—, assoc. prof. tenure, 1989, curricular head, 1990—; cons. Dental Student mag.,1983-86, Colo. Bd. Dentistry, Denver, 1985-86, Dentist mag., 1986-90, VA, Milw., 1987-90. Editor Jour. Colo. Dental Assn., 1980-86; contbr. articles and abstracts to dental jours. mem. vol. staff Morey Dental Clinic, Denver, 1982-85, Health Fair, Denver, 1983-85; ofcl. judge S.E. Wis. Sci. Fair, Milw., 1988—. Fellow Internat. Coll. Dentists, Acad. Dental Materials, Am. Coll. Dentists, Pierre Fauchard Acad.; mem. ADA (coun. on journalism 1984-86, coun. on dental rsch. 1986-88, manuscript reviewer 1988—), Acad. Operative Dentistry, Wis. Dental Assn. (assoc. editor Jour. 1987—), Omicron Kappa Upsilon, Alpha Gamma Sigma. Roman Catholic. Home: W349s10140 Bittersweet Ct Eagle WI 53119-1851 Office: Marquette U Sch Dentistry 604 N 16th St Milwaukee WI 53233-2117

SCRAFFORD, DONALD B., ophthalmologist; b. Buffalo, June 4, 1954; s. Robert Lee and Harriet Mae (Smith) S.; m. Cecilia Cruz, July 9, 1977; children: Michael, Deborah, Laura, Jonathan, Cecilia, Sarah. BS magna cum laude, U. South Calif., 1976; MD, U. Calif., San Francisco, 1980. Diplomate Am. Bd. Ophthalmology, Nat. Bd. Med. Examiners. Pvt. practice, Halstead, Kans., 1985—. Trustee Hertzler Rsch. Found., Halstead, 1985-89. Mem. AMA (physician recognition award 1983), Am. Acad. Ophthalmology, Contact Lens Assn. Ophthalmologists, Kans. Med. Soc., Harvey County Med. Soc., Phi Beta Kappa, Phi Kappa Phi. Office: Hertzler Clinic PA 327 Chestnut Halstead KS 67056

SCRIABINE, ALEXANDER, pharmacologist; b. Yelgava, Latvia, Oct. 26, 1926; came to U.S., 1950; s. Constantine and Helene (Gorstkine) S.; m. Kira Kosbun, Jan. 10, 1949 (div. 1963); 1 child, Raisa; m. Christine Brendel, Oct. 24, 1964; 1 child, Nicholas. MD, U. Mainz, 1958; MS in Pharmacology, Cornell U., 1954. Rsch. mgr. Pfizer & Co., Groton, Conn., 1954-56, 59-66; chief pharmacologist Phila. Gen. Hosp., 1966-67; exec. dir. pharmacology Merck Inst., West Point, Pa., 1967-78; assoc. dir. Wyeth Labs., Radnor, Pa., 1978-79; dir. Inst. for Preclin. Pharmacology, Miles Inc., West Haven, Conn., 1979-93; acting dir. Inst. Bone and Joint Diseases, 1993-94; cons. Bayer Corp., West Haven, 1995—; adj. assoc. prof. pharmacology U. Pa., Phila., 1967-84; lectr. Yale U., 1992—. Editl. bd. Jour. Cardiovascular Pharmacology, 1978—; editor: New Drugs Annual: Cardiovascular Drugs, 1983-84, Cardiovascular Drug Revs., 1989—, Ctrl. Nervous Sys. Drug Revs., 1995—; editor 14 books; contbr. over 200 articles to profl. jours., chpts. to books; patentee in field. Mem. German Pharmacol. Soc., Am. Soc. for Pharmacology and Exptl. Therapeutics, Physiol. Soc. Phila. (pres. 1972-73), Am. Soc. for Clin. Pharmacology and Therapeutics, Sigma Xi. Russian Orthodox.

SCRIBNER, CURTIS LEE, physician; b. Sioux City, Iowa, Oct. 17, 1951; s. Charles Lyman and Dorothy June S. AB, Grinnell Coll., 1973; MD, U. Colo., 1977; MBA, U. Md., 1995. Diplomate Am. Coll. Physicians. Comdr. USPHS, 1980-93; intern U. Nebr. Med. Ctr., Omaha, 1977-78, resident in internal medicine, 1978-80, fellow, 1983-84, chief resident, 1984-85; med. officer Ctrs. Disease Control, Atlanta, 1980-81; dir. lassa fever rsch. lab. Ctrs. Disease Control, Segbwema, Sierra Leone, 1981-83; fellow in rheumatology NIH, Bethesda, Md., 1985-87; med. officer FDA, Rockville, Md., 1987-89; br. chief FDA, Rockville, 1989-93; dep. dir. Ctr. for Biologies Evaluation and Rsch. Office of Blood Rsch. and Rev., Rockville, 1995—; vol. physician Whitman-Walker Clin., Washington, 1987—. Contbr. chpts. to books. Office: HFM-300 FDA/CBER/OBRR 1401 Rockville Pike Rockville MD 20852-1443

SCRIBNER, RONALD KENT, microbiologist; b. Denison, Tex., June 22, 1948; s. Theodore Roosevelt and Annabelle (Ellis) S. BS, Okla. State U., 1972; MS, L.I. U., 1980. Research supr. Okla. U. Health Sci. Ctr., Oklahoma City, 1980-87; cons. microbiologist N.W. Labs., Oklahoma City, 1989—; prof. biology Oklahoma City C.C., 1986—; cons. The Med. Letter, Phila., 1985—. Author: Nalidixic Acid, Quinolones and Novobiocin in Antimicrobial Therapy in Infants and Children, 1988; contbr. articles to profl. jours. Mem. AAAS, Am. Soc. Microbiology, Am. Soc. Clin. Pathology, S.W. Assn. Clin. Microbiology, Mensa, Nat. Assn. Biology Tchrs., Nat. Sci. Tchrs. Assn. Democrat. Home: 1836 NW 14th St Oklahoma City OK 73106-2016 Office: Oklahoma City CC 7777 S May Ave Oklahoma City OK 73159-4419

SCRIGGINS, ALAN LEE, developmental pediatrician; b. Englewood, N.J., Jan. 16, 1940; s. Thomas Dalby and Patricia (Fowler) S.; m. Geneva M. Brown, June 5, 1965; children: Jennifer A., Elizabeth B. AB, Middlebury Coll., 1961; MD, McGill U., Montreal, Que., Can., 1965. Diplomate Am. Bd. Pediatrics. Resident in pediats. U. Vt. Hosp., 1968-70; pvt. practice St. Albans, Vt., 1970-79; pediatrician USAF Hosp., Plattsburg AFB, N.Y., 1979-86, USAF Med. Ctr., Andrews AFB, Md., 1986-89; pediat. devel. USAF Hosp./RAF, Lakenheath, U.K., 1989-91; fellow devel. pediats. Georgetown U. Hosp., Washington, 1991-93; devel. pediatrician USAF Med. Ctr., Wright-Patterson AFB, Ohio, 1993—. Fellow Am. Acad. Pediats., Soc. Devel. Pediats.; mem. Am. Assn. Mental Retardation, Learning Disabilities Assn. Office: Wright-Patterson USAF Med Ctr SGOCS, WPMC Wright Patterson AFB OH 45433

SCRIMSHAW, NEVIN STEWART, physician, nutrition and health educator; b. Milw., Jan. 20, 1918; m. Mary Ware Goodrich, 1941; 5 children. B.A. with honors, Ohio Wesleyan U., 1938; M.A. in Biology, Harvard U., 1939, Ph.D. in Physiology, 1941; M.D. with honors, U. Rochester, 1945; M.P.H. with honors, Harvard U., 1959. Diplomate Am. Bd. Med. Examiners. Intern Gorgas Hosp., C.Z., 1945-46; Rockefeller postdoctoral fellow U. Rochester, N.Y., 1946-47, Merck NRC fellow, 1947-49; asst. resident in ob-gyn Strong Meml. Hosp., Genesee Hosp., N.Y., 1948-49; cons. nutrition Pan-Am. San. Bur. WHO, 1948-49, regional advisor on nutrition, 1949-53; dir. Inst. Nutrition C.Am. and Panama, Guatemala, 1949-61, cons. dir., 1961-65, cons. 1965—; dir. Clin. Research Ctr., MIT, 1962-66, 79-85, dir. internat. food and nutrition program, 1976-88, prof. human nutrition, 1961-76, head dept. nutrition and food sci., 1961-79, inst. prof. emeritus, 1988—; vis. prof. Columbia U., N.Y., 1976-88; vis. lectr. 1961-66; vis. lectr. Harvard U., 1968-85; vis. prof. Tufts U; mem. govt. adv. com. NIH; chmn. internat. com. NRC; dir. devel. studies div. U.N. U., 1985-86, food nutrition program 1975—. mem. adv. com. WHO, Nutrition Found., others. Contbr. articles to profl. jours.; editor: (with others) Amino Acid Fortification of Protein Foods, 1971, Nutrition, National Development and Planning, 1973, The Economics, Marketing and Technology of Fish Protein Concentrate, 1974, Nutrition and Agricultural Development: Significance and Potential for the Tropics, 1976, Single-Cell Protein: Safety for Animal and Human Feeding, 1979, Nutrition Policy Implementation: Issues and Experience, 1983, Diarrhea and Malnutrition: Interactions, Mechanisms and Interventions, 1983, Chronic Energy Deficiency, 1987, Acceptability of Milk and Milk Products in Populations With Lactose Intolerance, 1988, Nutrition in the Elderly, 1989, Activity, Energy Expenditure and Energy Requirements of Infants and Children, 1990, RAP: Rapid Assessment Procedures: Qualitative Methodologies for Planning and Evaluation of Health Related Programs, 1992, Protein-energy Interactions, 1992, Community-based Longitudinal Nutrition and Health Studies: Classical Examples from Guatemala, Haiti, and Mexico, 1995, The Effects of Improved Nutrition in Early Childhood: The Institute of Nutrition of Central America and Panama Follow-up Study, 1995, The Nutrition and Health Transition of Democratic Costa Rica, 1995. Recipient Osborne and Mendal award, 1960, Internat. award Inst. Food Technologists, 1969, medal of honor Fundacion F. Cuenca Villoro, Spain, 1978, Bristol-Myers prize, 1988, Alan Shawn Feinstein award, 1991, World Food prize, 1991, also others. Trustee Rockefeller Found., 1971-83, Pan-Am. Health and Edn. Found., 1986-92; pres. Internat. Nutrition Found. for Developing Countries, 1982—. Fellow Am. Inst. Nutrition, Royal Soc. Health, AAAS, Am. Soc. Clin. Nutrition, Am. Pub. Health Assn. (v.p. 1978 award of excellence in promoting and protecting health of people 1974); mem. Am. Coll. Nutrition, NAS (ch. applied biol. section, 1973-76, 88-91), Inst. of Medicine, Am. Acad. Arts Scis., Am. Coll. Preventive Medicine, Am. Bd. Nutrition, Mass. Pub. Health Assn., New Eng. Pub. Health Assn., Mass. Med. Soc., Am. Physiol. Soc., Am. Epidemol. Soc., Internat. Union Nutritional Scis. (pres. 1978-81), Internat. Epidemol. Assn., also others. Home: Sandwich Mountain Farm PO Box 330 Campton NH 03223-0330 Office: Charles St Sta PO Box 500 Boston MA 02114-0500

SCRIMSHAW, SUSAN, dean. PhD in Anthropology, Columbia U., 1974. Dean U. Ill. Sch. Pub. Health, Chgo., 1995—. Recipient Margaret Mead award, 1985. Fellow AAAS; mem. Inst. Medicine-Nat. Acad. Sci., Am. Anthropology Assn., Soc. Applied Anthropology, Nat. Soc. Med. Anthropology (pres. 1985). Office: UCLA School of Public Health 405 Hilgard Ave Los Angeles CA 90024*

SCRUBY, DAVID JOSEPH, physician; b. Kansas City, Mo., May 20, 1952. BA, Ind. U., 1974; MD, Ind. U., Indpls., 1977. Diplomate Am. Bd. Family Practice, Am. Bd. Preventive Medicine. Intern, resident in family practice St. Vincent Hosp. and Health Care Ctr., Indpls., 1977-80; asst. dir. family practice residency program St. Vincent Hosp., Indpls., 1982-83; corp. health svcs. physician Eli Lilly & Co., Indpls., 1983—. Fellow Am. Coll. Preventive Medicine, Am. Coll. Occupl. and Environ. Medicine; mem. Indpls. Med. Soc. (commn. on health and med. affairs 1993—). Office: Eli Lilly and Co Lilly Corporate Ctr Indianapolis IN 46285

SCUDDER, CAROL ANN, speech and language educator; b. Bayonne, N.J., July 6, 1949; d. James Anthony and Rose (Maiello) S. BA, Jersey City State Coll., 1971; Med. Office Specialist, Hudson County C.C., 1996. Cert. elem. edn. tchr., handicapped edn., speech correctionist, N.J.; med. office specialist. Substitute tchr. Bayonne Bd. of Edn., 1972-73, 75-77, Our Lady Star of Sea Sch., Bayonne, 1973-74; tchrs. asst. Bayonne Bd. Edn., 1977-79; libr. asst. Jersey City State Libr., 1980; clk.-typist Hudson County, Jersey City, 1983-84, jud. sec., 1984-85; speech-lang. therapist Ind. Child Study Teams, Jersey City, 1985-94, Weehawken (N.J.) Bd. Edn., 1994—; temp. adminstrv. asst. Ready Personnel, Jersey City, N.J., 1995-96; speech lang. therapist Weehawken Bd. of Edn., 1996-97. Mem. Amici Musicorum, 1983-91, Jersey City State Coll. Collegiate Cantorum, 1993-94;chmn. outreach com. Friends of the Loew's, 1995—; vol. Labor Day telethon Muscular Dystrophy Assn., 1987-94, Am. Diabetes Assn., 1994. Mem. N.J. Edn. Assn., Hudson Reading Coun., Bayonne Bus. and Profl. Women, Cath. Tchrs. Sodality (rec. sec. 1990-91). Home: 119 W 12th St Bayonne NJ 07002-1340

SCUDDER, HARVEY ISRAEL, microbiologist, medical entomologist, educator, consultant; b. Elmira, N.Y., Jan. 2, 1919; s. Henry Spaulding and Charlotte Evelyn (Draper) S.; m. Florence Viola Graff, June 16, 1945; children: Paul Harvey, Barbara Carol. BS, Cornell U., 1939, PhD, 1953; post-grad., NYU, 1939-42. Commd. scientist officer USPHS, 1943, advanced through grades to capt., scientist dir., 1963, exec. sec. NIH rsch. grant study sections, 1957-59; chief/founder viruses and cancer program Nat. Cancer Inst. USPHS, Bethesda, Md., 1959-62; chief/founder health manpower office Bur. State Svcs. USPHS, Washington, 1965-66; ret. USPHS, 1966; prof. microbiology, founder Baccalaureat nursing program Calif. State U., Hayward, 1967-80, head div. biol. and health scis., 1967-70, prof. emeritus, 1980—; malaria cons. AID, Washington, 1979-83, 84-85; coord. Stewart Valley (Nev.) Paleontol. Inventory, U.S. Bur. Land Mgmt., Reno, 1982-86. Contbr. articles on med. entomology and environ. scis. to profl. jours.; pub. numerous reports on pub. health, disease control and natural hist. Mem. air conservation com. Alameda County Lung Assn., Oakland, Calif., 1970-80; mem. Alameda County Comprehensive Health Planning Coun., 1973-76; mem. Alameda County Mosquito Abatement Dist. Bd., 1982—; bd. dirs. Marine Sci. Inst., Redwood City, Calif., 1971—, chmn. bd. dirs., 1974-80, 82—; bd. dirs. St. Rose Hosp., Hayward, Calif., 1969-83, chmn. bd. dirs., 1973-74, mem. instnl. rev. com. Mem. Am. Mosquito Control Assn., AAAS, Am. Pub. Health Assn., Am. Soc. Microbiology, Am. Soc. Tropical Medicine and Hygiene, Western Regional Assn. Advisors for the Health Profession of Am. Assn. Med. Colls., Entomol. Soc. Am., Calif. Mosquito and Vector Control Assn. (sec. 1988, vice-chair 1989 chair 1990, sec. of trustee corp. bd. 1990—), Soc. for Vector Ecology (chmn. adhoc manpower com. 1988-90), Calif. Acad. Scis. (hon. fellow 1987—), Sigma Xi, Phi Kappa Phi. Democrat. Mem. Disciples of Christ. Club: Pub. Health Svc. (Bethesda)(pres. 1962). Home: 7409 Hansen Dr Dublin CA 94568-2742

SCUDERI, ANTHONY JOSEPH, psychotherapist/addictions counselor; b. Phila., Aug. 25, 1958. AA, Bucks County (Pa.) Community, 1978; BS, East Stroudsburg U., 1981; MDiv, Cath. Theol. Union, 1987; MA, Liberty U., 1993; postgrad., Ea. Bapt. Theol. Sem. Cert. addictions counselor; cert. hypnotherapist; registered behavioral therapist. Judo/self-def. instr. Bucks Community Coll., Bucks County, 1977-78; Roman Cath. priest Franciscan Friars of Pulaski (Wis.), 1981-90; quality assurance chmn. Phila. Ctr. for Human Devel., 1989-91, outpatient coord., 1989-90, addictions svc. coord., 1989-90, partial hosp. coord., 1989-92; substance abuse counselor intensive outpatient dept. Mt. Sinai Hosp., 1993-94; exec. dir. The Wedge Med. Ctr., PC, 1994—; in-svc. lectr. Phila. Ctr. for Human Devel., 1989-92. Notary pub., Phila., 1990—. Mem. Am. Assn. Profl. Hypnotherapists, Nat. Bd. Hypnotherapist Examiners, Am. Assn. Behavioral Therapists, Pa. Chem. Abuse Certification Bd. Democrat. Home and Office: 21 Norman St Aston PA 19014-2107 Office: The Wedge Med Ctr PC 2011 S Broad St Philadelphia PA 19148

SCULLY, CRISPIAN MICHAEL, physician, educator; b. Hove, Sussex, Eng., May 24, 1945; m. Zoitsa Boucoumani, Oct. 5, 1977; 1 child, Frances. BDS, U. London, 1968, BSc, 1971, MB BS, 1974; MD, U. Bristol, Eng., 1979. Lectr. U. Glasgow, Scotland, 1978-81, sr. lectr., 1981-82; prof. Ctr. Study Oral Disease U. Bristol, England, 1982-93; dean, dir. studies Eastman Dental Inst., London, 1993—; cons., advisor to chief med. officer UK Dept. Health, 1988—, mem. Medicines Control Agy., 1989—, mem. Cen. Rsch. and Devel. Com., 1991—; chmn. Cen. Examining Bd. Hygienists, 1989—. Author 15 books; contbr. over 300 articles to profl. jours.; editor: Oral Oncology, 1992-93, Oral Diseases, 1993—; mem. editorial bd. Jour. Oral PAthology and Medicine, 1988-93, Current Opinion in Dentistry, 1990-93. Recipient Colgate prize for dental rsch., 1979. Fellow Royal Coll. Surgeons (Glasgow), Royal Soc.. Surgeons (Ireland), Royal Coll. Pathologists. Office: Eastman Dental Inst, 256 Gray's Inn Rd, London WC1X 8LD, England

SCULLY, JOHN ROBERT, oral and maxillofacial surgeon; b. N.Y.C., Mar. 2, 1949; s. Frank Edward and Helen Veronica (Sawyer) S.; m. Bonnie Diane Baron, Aug. 28, 1971; children: AmandaRose, John Robert Jr. BS in Chemistry, Spring Hill Coll., 1970; DDS, Med. Coll. Va., 1974; MS, U. Iowa, 1980. Diplomate Am. bd. Oral and Maxillofacial Surgery. Resident in oral and maxillofacial surgery U. Iowa, 1977-1980; pvt. practice oral and maxillofacial surgery, Asheville, 1980—; chief oral and maxillofacial surgery St. Josephs Hosp., Asheville, 1984—, Meml. Mission Hosp., 1984—; cons. Pardee Hosp., Hendersonville, N.C., 1983—; bd. trustees St. Joseph's Hosp. Found.; adv. bd. Sleep Medicine Ctr. Contbr. chpt. to book; also articles to profl. jours. Capt. USAF, 1974-77. USAF Merit scholar, 1972-74. Fellow Am. Coll. Oral and Maxillofacial Surgeons, Am. Assn. Oral and Maxillofacial Surgery, Internat. Assn. Oral and Maxillofacial Surgeons; mem. ADA, N.C. Dental Soc., Southeastern Soc. Oral and Maxillofacial Surgeons, N.C. Soc. Oral and Maxillofacial Surgeons, Am. Trauma Soc., Internat., Buncombe County Dental Soc., Asheville C. of C., Zebulon Vance Debating Soc., Internat. Platform Assn., Asheville Country Club, Delta Sigma Delta. Avocations: music, rock and folk guitar, dance, tennis, auto racing. Home: 17 Bluebriar Rd Asheville NC 28804-3704 Office: 5 Rockcliff Pl Asheville NC 28801-4510

SCULLY, MARTHA SEEBACH, speech-language pathologist; b. S.I., Nov. 1, 1951; d. Henry F. and Rose Anne (Callahan) Seebach; m. Roger Tehan Scully, Dec. 29, 1979; 1 child, Roger Tehan. BA, Trinity Coll., 1972; MS, George Washington U., 1974; postgrad., Syracuse (N.Y.) U., 1976-79. Lic. speech-lang. pathologist, Md. Clin. supr. Syracuse U., 1976-79; speech-lang. pathologist Fairfax (Va.) County Pub. Schs., 1979—. Bd. dirs. Trinity Coll., Washington, Nat. Children's Choir, 1987-91; trustee Davis Meml. Goodwill Industries, 1994-96, bd. dirs. Goodwill Guild, 1990—, chair ball; docent Folger Shakespearean Libr.; chmn. Nat. Challenge Com. of Disabled, 1985; mem. Ear Ball, 1988, 89; mem. Salvation Army garden party, 1992, mem. internat. children's festival, 1990, 91; co-chmn. Jr. League of Washington Capital Collection, 1990. Recipient First Order Affiliation Order of Franciscans mirror, 1985; named Outstanding Woman in Am., 1987, 88. Mem. Am. Biog. Inst., Am. Speech-Lang.-Hearing Assn., Coun. for Exceptional Children, Montgomery County Assn. for Hearing Impaired Children. Home: 10923 Wickshire Way Rockville MD 20852-3220

SCULLY, STEPHEN J., plastic surgeon; b. Lawrence, Mass., Jan. 29, 1937; s. Joseph A. and Frances M. (Hart) S.; m. Diane Loretta Lizotte, Apr. 22, 1967; children: Stephen, Christopher, Caroline, Jacqueline. AB summa cum laude, Merrimack Coll., 1958; MD cum laude, Georgetown U., 1962. Surg. resident Tufts New Eng. Med. Ctr., Boston, 1962-67; plastic surg. resident NYU, N.Y.C., 1969-72. Trustee Holy Family Hosp., Methuen, Mass., 1993, Merrimack Coll., North Andover, Mass., 1993. Lt. comdr. USNR, 1967-69. Fellow ACS; mem. Am. Soc. Reconstructive Surgeons, Am. Soc. Aesthetic Plastic Surgery. Roman Catholic. Office: Plastic Cosmetic Reconstr Surgery Inc 451 Andover St North Andover MA 01845-5044

SCURR, JOHN HENRY, surgeon; b. Slough, Eng., Mar. 25, 1947; s. Henry Frederick and Joyce (Standerwick) S.; m. Gilian Margaret Mason, July 16, 1969 (div. Jan. 1986); children: Ruth, Ingrid, James; m. Nicola Mary Alexandra Vincent, Apr. 5, 1986; children: Edward, Victoria, Thomas. BSc, U. London, 1969; MB BS, Middlesex Hosp., London, 1972. Lectr. in surgery and physiology Middlesex Hosp., 1974-76, cons. surgeon, 1984—; registrar Westminster Hosp., 1976-78, sr. registrar, 1978-84; cons. surgeon St. Luke's Hosp. for Clergy, 1984—; sr. lectr. U. London, 1984—. Editor: Medical Applications of Microcomputation. Fellow Royal Soc. Medicine (chmn. forum 1993-96), Royal Coll. Surgeons. Home: 5 Balniel Gate, London SW1 V3SD, England Office: Lister House Lister Hosp, Chelsea Bridge Rd, London SW1 W8RH, England

SCUTCHFIELD, F. DOUGLAS, academic administrator; b. Wheelwright, Ky., Apr. 23, 1942; m. Phyllis Scutchfield; 1 child, Alex L. BS magna cum laude, Ea. Ky. U., 1962; MD, U. Ky., 1966; postgrad., Morehead State U., U. Minn., U. Mich. Diplomate Am. Bd. of Family Practice, Am. Bd. of Preventive Medicine. Rotating intern Chgo. Wesley Meml. Hosp. (now Northwestrn Univ. Med. Ctr.), 1967; resident preventive medicine U. Ky. Med. Ctr., Lexington, 1969; dir. continuing profl. edn. St. Claire Med. Ctr., Morehead, Ky., 1969-74; chmn. Dept. of Family and Community Medicine, Coll. of Community Health Scis. U. Ala., 1974-78, assoc. dean acad. affairs Coll. of Community Health Scis., 1975-79; dir. Grad. Sch. of Pub. Health San Diego State U., 1979—; clin. instr. gynecology and obstetrics Sch., Medicine Emory U., Atlanta, 1967-69; vis. lectr. Morehead State U., 1969-74; asst. clin. prof. comprehensive medicie Coll. Medicine, U. Louisville, 1971-74; asst. prof. Dept. of Community Medicine Med. Sch., U. Ky., 1969-72, assoc. prof., 1972-74; prof. Dept. of Family and Community Medicine Coll. of Community Health Scis., U. Ala., 1974-79; vis. prof. Coll. of Medicine U. Calif., Irvine, 1985—; clin. prof. Dept. of Family & Community Medicine U. Calif., San Diego, 1979—; prof. pub. health San Diego State U., 1979—; cons. in field. Assoc. editor: Appalachia Medicine, 1969-71, editor-in-chief, 1971-73; editorial adv. bd. Last, Maxy-Roseneau Preventive Medicine and Public Health, 1977—, assoc. editor, 1988; bd. editors San Diego Physicians, 1982—, Jour. of Community Health, 1974-77, 83-85; sect. editor Western Jour. of Medicine, 1985. Bd. dir. Western Consortium for Pub. Health, 1986—; vice chair edn. com. Assn. of Schs. of Pub. Health, exec. com., 1987-89; sec. coun. on health promotion and disease prevention HHS, 1988—; founding mem. Grand Canyon Group. Traineeship schs. of pub. health; basic rsch. support grantee, others; recipient Meredith J. Cox Premed. award, 1960, Mosby Book award, 1965, Key to the City of Selma, Ala., 1979; named to Honorable Order of Ky. Colonels, 1969. Fellow Am. Acad. of Family Practice, Am. Coll. Preventive Medicine (com. on manpower 1977-81, co-chairperson task force on manpower requirements and supply 1979), Am. Acad. of Polit. and Social Sci., Royal Soc. for Health; mem. AMA (rep. for program 1975-77, alt. del. 1976-80, chair com. on med. licensure, com. on AIDS & med. edn., William Beaumont award 1985), San Diego County Med. Soc., Calif. Med. Assn. (sec. sect. coun. on pub. health and preventive medicine 1981-82, chmn. 1982-83, program chmn., 1981-82, alt. del. 1985—) , Nat. Med. Vets. Soc., Assn. of Tchrs. of Preventive Medicine (bd. dirs. 1974-77, exec. com. 1975-76, chmn. policy com. 1975, chmn. program com. 1976), U.S./Mex. Border Health Assn. Home: 8775 Joeve Ct San Diego CA 92119-2112 Office: San Diego State U Grad Sch Pub Health San Diego CA 92182-4162

SEAGER, FLOYD WILLIAMS, medical educator; b. Ogden, Utah, July 1, 1921; s. Roy Alfred and Florence (Williams) S.; m. Beth Anne Seager, Feb. 6, 1943 (div. June 1965); m. Dauna Gayle Olson, July 7, 1973; children: Stephen, Nancy, Candice, Pamela, Kevin, Karen; stepchildren: Jeff Stokes, John Stokes, Jeannettes Memmott. AS, Weber State U., 1941; BS in Chemistry, U. Utah, 1943; MD, Hahnemann U., 1947. Diplomate Nat. Bd. Med. Examiners. Pvt. practice Ogden, 1949-51; founder Ogden Clinic, 1951; chief of staff McKay Hosp., Ogden, 1979-81, trustee, 1989—; clin. prof. medicine U. Utah Med. Sch., Salt Lake City, 1990—. Editor: (med. jours.) Sub Q, 1980—, Ad Libitum, 1989. Capt. USMC, 1951-53, Korea. Decorated 6 Battle Stars, Bronze Star; Dr. Seager Day named in his honor Mayor of Ogden, 1991; named Dr. of Yr., Utah State Med. Soc., 1993, Quiet Pioneer, Gov. Utah, 1991; recipient Point of Light award Pres. Bush, 1992. Mem. Am. Legion, Dixieland Jazz Soc. (chmn. bd. dirs.), Rotary Club Ogden, Elks. Republican. Mormon. Home and Office: 4046 S 895 E Ogden UT 84403-2416

SEAGLE, EDGAR FRANKLIN, environmental engineer, consultant; b. Lincolnton, N.C., June 27, 1924; s. Franklin Craig and Lillie Mae (James) S.; m. Doris Elaine Long, Mar. 23, 1958; children: Rebecca Jane, Mary Elaine, James Craig, William Franklin. AB in Chemistry, U. N.C., 1949, MS in Pub. Health, 1954; BCE, U. Fla., 1961; DPH, U. Tex., 1974. Registered profl. engr., Ala. Sr. sanitarian Health Dept., City of Charlotte, N.C., 1950-52, chief indsl. hygiene sect., 1956-59; sanitation cons. N.C. State Bd. Health, Raleigh, 1954-56; engr. dir. USPHS, Rockville, Md., 1961-78; asst. dir. Fellowship Office Nat. Acad. Scis., Washington, 1978-83; pub. health engr. Dept. of Environ., State of Md., Balt., 1985-88; ind. engring. cons. Rockville, 1984-85, 88—. Contbr. articles to profl. publs. With USN, 1943-46, PTO. Mem. ASCE, APHA, Am. Acad. Environ. Engrs. (diplomate). Methodist. Home and Office: 14108 Heathfield Ct Rockville MD 20853-2760

SEAGRAVE, MARTHA PARNELL, physician assistant; b. Stamford, Conn., Feb. 16, 1958; d. Norman Parnell and Mary Webb (Ryan) S.; m. Kurt Joseph Kaffenberger, Sept. 11, 1987; children: Samuel, Parnell. BSEd, U. Vt., 1980, BSN, 1987. Bd. cert. physician asst. Cert. physician asst. Given Health Care Ctr., Burlington, Vt., 1986-91; cert. physician asst., clin. instr. Univ. Assocs. in Family Practice/Fletcher Allen Health Care, Colchester, Vt., 1991—; cons. IDX, Med. Software Co., So. Burlington, 1994—, PKC, 1994—. Mem. Burlington Bd. of Health, 1994. Fellow Am. Acad. Physician Assts.; mem. Physician Asst. Acad. of Vt., Sigma Theta Tau. Office: CFHC PO Box 35 170 Blakely Rd Colchester VT 05446

SEAGREN, STEPHEN LINNER, oncologist; b. Mpls., Mar. 13, 1941; s. Morley Raymond and Carol Christine (Linner) S.; m. Jill Garrie; 1 child, Sean Garrie. AB, Harvard U., 1963; MD, Northwestern U., 1967. Diplomate Am. Bd. Internal Medicine, Am. Bd. Med. Oncology, Am. Bd. Radiology. From asst. prof. to assoc. prof. radiology and medicine U. Calif., San Diego, 1977-88, prof., 1988—. Contbr. over 80 articles to profl. jours. Bd. dirs. Wellness Cmty., San Diego, 1988—, chair profl. adv. com., 1988—; chair radiol. oncology com. Cancer and Acute Leukemia Group, Chgo., 1986—. Lt. comdr. USNR, 1971-73. Fellow ACP. Office: U Calif San Diego Med Ctr 200 W Arbor Dr San Diego CA 92103

SEARLES, LYNN MARIE, nurse; b. Cherryvale, Kans., Oct. 29, 1949; d. Darrell Eugene and Beva Caroline (Waller) Stringer; m. Martin Dale Searles, Aug. 23, 1970; children: Jeremy Dale, Michelle Le Anne. Assoc. in Fine Arts, Labette Cmty. Jr. Coll., Parsons, Kans., 1969, ADN, 1970. RN, Kans., Calif. Evening med.-surg. charge nurse Coffeyville (Kans.) Meml. Hosp., 1970-72, med.-surg. head nurse, 1972-73, relief evening house supr. and emergency rm. nurse, 1974, head nurse recovery rm., 1974-81; head nurse recovery rm., ambulatory care unit Coffeyville Meml. Med. Ctr., 1981-83, head nurse recovery rm., ambulatory care unit and surgery, 1983-84; dir. family planning, rural home health aide and multi phasic screening clinics, AIDS edn. and counseling Jefferson County Health Dept., Oskaloosa, Kansas, 1984-87; nurse III, health facility surveyor Lawrence dist. Kans. Dept. Health and Environ., Lawrence, Kans., 1988—. Mem. Nazarene Healthcare Fellowship, Kans. Pub. Health Assn., Am. Soc. Post Anesthesia Nurses (charter mem.). Republican. Nazarene Ch. Office: Kans Dept Health and Environment 808 W 24th St Lawrence KS 66046-4417

SEARLS, LESLIE ROBERT, osteopath; b. Highland Park, Mich., Aug. 9, 1948; s. Robert Jasper and Thelma Florence (Larsen) S.; m. Mary Lou Ozbun; children: Jessica, Cait, Benjamin, Emma. BA, Oakland U., 1970; DO, Mich. State U., 1985. Diplomate Am. Bd. Osteo. Emergency Physicians, Nat. Bd. Med. Examiners. Staff physician Osteo. Physicians Emergency Svcs., Lansing, Mich., 1988-95; dir. of emergency svc. Lansing Gen. Hosp., 1991-95; staff physician Physician Assocs., Lansing, 1995—; chair dept. of emergency medicine Lansing Gen. Hosp., 1991-93, Mich. Capital med. Ctr., Lansing, 1993-95, co-pres. elect, med. staff, 1996—; physicians adv. bd. Capital Area Health Alliance, Lansing, 1995-96; faculty Mich. State U. Affiliated Emergency Med. Residency, Lansing, 1995—. Author: (with others) Emergency Neurology, 1996. Mem. Tri-County Emergency Med. Control Authority, Lansing, 1989—. Mem. Am. Osteo. Assn., Ingham County Osteo. Assn., Mich. State Med. Soc., Ingham County Med. Soc., Am. Coll. of Emergency Physicians, Soc. for Acad. Emergency Medicine. Office: Mich Capital Med Ctr Dept Emergency Medicine 401 W Greenlawn Lansing MI 48910

SEARS, MARVIN, ophthalmologist, educator; b. N.Y.C., Sept. 16, 1928; s. Louis and Blanche Sears; children: Anne, David, Jonathan, Edward, Benjamin. AB, Princeton U., 1949; MD, Columbia U., 1953. Intern Bellevue Hosp., N.Y.C., 1954; resident in ophthalmology Johns Hopkins Hosp., 1954-61; fellow NIH, 1959-60; chmn. sect. ophthalmology Yale-New Haven (Conn.) Hosp., 1961-71; asst. prof. dept. ophthalmology and visual sci. Yale U. Sch. Medicine, 1961-64, assoc. prof., 1964-69, prof., 1969—, chmn., 1971-93; cons. Vets. Meml. Med. Ctr., Meriden, Conn., 1986—, Princess Margaret Hosp., Nassau, 1982—, Waterbury (Conn.) Hosp., 1975—, William W. Backus Hosp., Norwich, Conn., 1974—, Hosp. Albert Schweitzer, Des Chapelles, Haiti, 1968-83, Jenkins (Ky.) Clinic Hosp., 1963, Hosp. St. Raphael, New Haven, New Britain (Conn.) Gen. Hosp.; chief cons. VA Med. Ctr., West Haven, Conn., 1961—; instr. Johns Hopkins Hosp., 1959-61; vis. prof. dept. ophthalmology U. Puerto Rico; mem. numerous adv. coms. Editorial bd.: Am. Jour. Ophthalmology, 1967-82, Investigative Ophthalmology, 1968-78, Jour. Ocular Pharmacology, 1985—; contbr. articles to profl. jours. Recipient McKosh prize/Epistemology, Princeton U., 1949, Schwentker medal Johns Hopkins Hosp., 1958, Alcon Rsch. Inst. award, 1985, Method to Extend Rsch. in Time award Nat. Eye Inst., 1990—; named Gifford lectr. Chgo. Ophthal. Soc., 1985; endowed professorship established in Sears' name Yale U., 1993. Fellow ACS, Pierson Coll. Yale U.; mem. Am. Acad. Ophthalmology, Am. Ophthal. Soc., Assn. for Rsch. in Vision and Ophthalmology (Jonas S. Friedenwald award 1977), Assn. Univ. Profs. Ophthalmology, Conn. State Med. Soc., Internat. Agy. for Prevention Blindness, Internat. Soc. for Eye Rsch., New England Ophthal. Soc. (award 1969), Pan Am. Assn. Ophthalmology, Soc. Eye Surgeons, Wilmer Residents Assn., Appalachian Mountain Club, Audubon Soc., Lions (Melvin Jones fellow). Jewish. Office: Yale Eye Ctr PO Box 208061 330 Cedar St New Haven CT 06520-8061

SEATON, DAVID DEAN, psychologist; b. Peoria, Ill., Oct. 13, 1951; s. Thomas Werner and Mary Elizabeth (Battles) S.; m. Terri Jo Struebing, Aug. 16, 1980; 1 child, Laura Diane. BA, U. Ark., 1974; MA, St. Mary's U., 1977; D of Psychology, Ill. Sch. Profl. Psychology, 1986. Lic. clin. psychologist, Fla. Dir. biofeedback svcs. Incentives Inst., Des Plaines, Ill., 1977-80; mem. psychology staff Children's Med. Ctr., Tulsa, 1982-86, treatment team leader, 1986-89, unit mgr., 1989-90, dir. diagnostic testing, 1990-93, dir. internship tng., 1991-93; dir. psychology/neuropsychology HealthSouth Rehab., Tallahassee, 1993—, dir. pain mgmt. program, 1993—; adj. instr. Fla. State U., Tallahassee, 1994—; clin. cons. Janus Clinic, Tallahassee, 1994—. Mem. bd. editors Micropsych Network Jour., 1985-90. Mem. Am. Psychol. Assn., Okla. Neuropsychol. Soc. (treas. 1991-93). Office: HealthSouth Rehab Hosp 1675 Riggins Rd Tallahassee FL 32308

SEATON, VAUGHN ALLEN, veterinary pathology educator; b. Abilene, Kans., Oct. 11, 1928; m. Clara I. Bertelrud; children: Gregory S., Jeffrey T. BS, Kans. State U., 1954, DVM, 1954; MS, Iowa State U., 1957. Pvt. practice Janesville, Wis., 1954; instr. pathology Vet. Diagnostic Lab. Iowa State U., Ames, 1954-57, from asst. to assoc. prof. pathology Vet. Diagnostic Lab., 1957-64, prof., head Vet. Diagnostic Lab., 1964—; lab. coord. regional emergency animal disease eradication orgn. Animal and Plant Health Inspection Svc. USDA, 1974—; mem. rsch. com. Iowa Beef Industry Coun., 1972-85; mem. adv. bd. Iowa State Water Resources Rsch. Inst., 1973-80; cons. several orgns. Co-author: (monographs) Feasibility Study of College of Veterinary Medicine, 1972, Veterinary Diagnostic Laboratory Facilities-State of New York, 1970; bd. dirs. Iowa State U. Press, 1985-88, mem. manuscript com., 1982-85; contbr. articles to profl. jours. Trustee Ames Pub. Libr., 1979-85; mem. Iowa State Bd. Health, 1971-77, v.p., 1976-77. Mem. AVMA, Am. Assn. Vet. Lab. Diagnosticians (bd. govs. 1973-88, pres. 1968, E.P. Pope award 1980), Am. Coll. Vet. Toxicologists, U.S. Animal Health Assn., Iowa Vet. Med. Assn. (pres. 1971), North Cen. Assn. Vet. Lab. Diagnosticians, Western Vet. Conf. (exec. bd. 1986-90, v.p. 1994, pres.-elect 1995, pres. 1996), World Assn. Vet. Lab. Diagnosticians (pres. 1980-86), masons (bd. dirs. 1985-88), Ames C. of C. (bd. dirs. 1970-73), Phi Kappa Phi, Phi Zeta (pres. 1964), Alpha Zeta, Gamma Sigma Delta. Office: Iowa State U Coll Vet Medicine Vet Diagnostic Lab Ames IA 50011

SEBASTIAN, JAMES ALBERT, obstetrician, gynecologist, educator; b. Milw., Feb. 20, 1945; s. Milton Arthur and Bernice Marian (Friske) S.; m. Jacqulin Victoria Johnson, June 14, 1969; children: Mila, Joel, Jon, Marnie. BS, U. Wis., 1966, MD, 1969. Diplomate Am. Bd. Ob-Gyn. Commd. officer USN, 1965, advanced through grades to lt. comdr., 1972; intern U.S. Naval Hosp., St. Albans, N.Y., 1969-70; resident in ob-gyn Naval Regional Med. Ctr., Portsmouth, Va., 1970-72, mem. staff, 1975-77; mem. staff Naval Hosp., Taipei, Republic of Taiwan, 1972-76; resigned, 1977; pvt. practice Duluth, Minn., 1977—; assoc. clin. prof. ob-gyn U. Minn. Med. Sch., Duluth, 1977—. Fellow Am. Coll. Ob-Gyn. (best rsch. paper award Armed Forces dist. 1976); mem. Am. Fertility Soc., Minn. Perinatal Assn. (bd. dirs. 1978-87, pres. 1985-86), Kiwanis (pres. 1989-90). Office: Duluth Ob-Gyn Assocs 1000 E 1st St Duluth MN 55805

SEBASTIANELLI, CARL THOMAS, clinical psychologist; b. Jessup, Pa., Dec. 12, 1943; s. Carlo and Antonia (Antonelli) S.; B.S. magna cum laude in Psychology, U. Scranton, 1965; M.A. in Psychology, Temple U., Phila., 1967; postgrad. in clin. psychology L.I.U., 1968-70; Ph.D. in Psychopathology/Psychotherapy, Clayton U., 1983. Psychologist, Farview State Hosp., Waymart, Pa., 1967-68; clin. psychology doctoral intern N. Dauphin Mental Health/Mental Retardation Ctr., 1970-71; clin. psychology doctoral intern family therapy center and psychology lab. Harrisburg (Pa.) State Hosp., 1970-71, clin. psychologist, 1971-77, chmn. psychology forum, 1974-76, clin. psychologist, psychiat. treatment center, 1977-79; pvt. practice clin. psychology Comprehensive Health Svcs. Ctr., Dunmore, Pa., 1979-90; ind. pvt. practice clin. psychology, Dunmore, 1990—; mem. adj. faculty U. Scranton, 1979-86, Pa. State U., 1973-86; mem. state bd. Pa. Social Services Union, 1974-75; media commentator psychopathology topics, 1979—. Pa. Profl. Edn. Program scholar L.I.U.; recipient award N.E. Pa. chpt. Am. Diabetes Assn., 1980. Lic. psychologist, Pa. Mem. Am. Psychol. Assn., Internat. Acad. Behavioral Medicine Counseling and Psychotherapy, Anxiety Disorders Assn. Am., Acad. Psychologists Marital, Sex and Family Therapy, Pa. Psychol. Assn. (chmn. public info. com. 1981-83), Northeastern Pa. Psychol. Assn. (sec. 1981, exec. council 1982-83), Nat. Register Health Service Providers in Psychology. Contbr. articles to profl. jours. UPI; interviewed for articles in newspapers and nat. mags.; featured in Pa. Dept. Welfare publ. on subject of family therapy tng. Home: 1224 Monroe Ave Scranton PA 18509-2808

SECCAFICO, JOHN, clinical social worker; b. Jersey City, Oct. 2, 1948; s. James Anthony and Lucille (Mastronardi) S.; m. Alice O'Neill, June 10, 1989; stepchildren: Robert, Sarah. BA, Seton Hall U., 1971, MA, 1974; MSW, Rutgers U., 1983. Diplomate Am. Bd. Med. Psychotherapists, Am. Bd. Med. Examiners in Clin. Social Work; lic. clin. social worker; lic. marriage and family therapist, N.J.; cert. sch. social worker, N.J. Income maintenance specialist Ocean County Bd. Social Svcs., Toms River, N.J., 1974-81; clin. social worker Shore Mental Health Ctr., Lakewood, N.J., 1978-87, Ocean Inst., Manahawkin, N.J., 1983-84; pvt. practice Brick, N.J., 1983—; chief ops. officer Personamax Internat. Ltd.; dir. gerontology Georgian Ct. Coll., Lakewood, 1987-94; field instr. Rutgers U., 1993—, Stockton State Coll., 1993—; adj. instr. Robert Wood Johnson Med. Ctr., 1990-95; ops. officer Ultimate Achievement, 1994—; dir. home psychotherapy program Medex Home Health Care, Inc., Toms River, 1988—. Weekly mental health columnist, 1987. Dir. Toms River Jaycees, 1978. Mem. Acad. Cert. Social Workers, Nat. Assn. Social Workers. Baptist. Home: 821 Bay Ave Toms River NJ 08753-3501 Office: 35 Beaverson Blvd Ste 1D Brick NJ 08723-7854

SEDGWICK, RAE, psychologist, lawyer; b. Kansas City, Kans., Apr. 7, 1944; d. Charles and Helen (Timmons) Sedgwick. RN, Bethany Sch. Nursing, 1965; BS, U. Iowa, 1967; MA, U. Kans., 1970, PhD, 1972, JD, 1986; postgrad. Menninger Sch. Psychiatry & Mental Helath, 1992. Lic. psychologist, Kans.; bar: Kans. 1986. Med./surg., orthopedic and obstet. nurse, Iowa City, Iowa, 1965-67; with Community Mental Health Nursing, Kansas City, Kans., 1967-68; specialist Lab. Edn., Washington, 1971-72; adj. clin. staff community psychiatry, 1975-76; coordinator Health C.A.R.E. Clinic, Pa. State U., 1974-76; head grad. program in community mental health nursing and family therapy, Pa. State U., 1974-76, asst. prof. 1972-76; pvt. practice clin. psychology, Bonner Springs, Kans., 1976—, adj prof. St. Mary Coll., 1992—; cons. in field.; staff Bethany Med. Ctr., Kansas City, Kans., Shawnee Mission Med. Ctr., Providence Med. Ctr. ; del. Internat. Council Nurses, Frankfurt, Germany, People for People, People's Republic of China, 1982, Internat. Congress Psychology, Sydney, Australia, 1988, Monet Art Tour, Paris, 1991, Flying Jayhawk's KU-Switzerland, 1994, Amsterdam, 1995. Active Am. Heart Assn.; city councilwoman Bonner Springs, 1981-89, pres. pro tem, 1983-87, mayoral candidate, 1989; mem. Kans. Internat. Women's Yr. Commn.; psychol. cons. United Meth. Ch., 1995-96. Recipient Outstanding Young Woman award, U. Kans., Bus. and Profl. Women's Club scholar; elected to Kans. U. Women's Hall of Fame, 1987; named clin. psychology fellow Menninger Clinic, 1990-92. Fellow Am. Orthopsychiat. Assn.; mem. AAAS, ABA, Kansas Bar Assn., Am. Assn. Psychiatric Services for Children, Am. Group Psychotherapy Assn. (dir.), Am. Nurses Assn., Am. Psychol. Assn., Anthrop. Assn. for Study of Play, Council of Advanced Practitioners in Psychiat. Mental Health Nursing, Kans. Psychol. Assn., Council Nurse Researchers, Sigma Theta Tau. Republican. Methodist. Club: Pilot. Author: Family Mental Health, 1980; The White Frame House, 1980; contbr. articles to profl. jours.

SEDLACEK, KEITH WAYNE, psychiatrist, educator; b. Grand Island, Nebr., Oct. 24, 1944; s. John J. and Vivian M. (Barney) S.; m. Diane K. Roth, Sept. 3, 1987; children: John Daniel, Heather Jean. BA, Harvard Coll., 1966; MD, Columbia U., 1972. Intern, then psychiat. resident St. Lukes Hosp., N.Y.C., 1972-75, attending physician, 1972-83; instr. clin. psychiatry Columbia Coll. Physicians and Surgeons, N.Y.C., 1972—; attending physician St. Lukes-Roosevelt Hosp. Ctr., N.Y.C., 1983—; med. dir. Stress Regulation Inst., N.Y.C., 1981—; dir. biofeedback psychiat. S.I. U.; bd. dirs. Biofeedback Soc. Am., Denver, 1982-85, Biofeedback Certification Inst. Am., Denver, 1983-87. Author: The Sedlacek Technique, 1989; co-author: How to Avoid Stress Before it Kills You; asst. editor Biofeedback & Self Regulation, 1985—. Rockefeller fellow Rockefellow Fund, Harvard U., 1966-68, Noble fellow in fgn. affairs Noble Found., Columbia U., 1972-73. Mem. AMA, Am. Psychiat. Assn., Am. Psychiat. Assn. (chmn. behavioral therapy N.Y.C. area 1984—), Behavioral Medicine Soc. Office: Stress Regulation Inst 239 E 79th St Ste 1 New York NY 10021-0810

SEDLAK, RICHARD, naturopath, physical therapist; b. Berwyn, Ill., July 7, 1944; s. Richard and Alice H. (Tejcek) S. D in Naprapathy, Nat. Coll. Naprapathy, Chgo., 1966; D in Chiropractic Medicine, Palmer Coll. Chiropractic Medicine, 1970; BS in Phys. Therapy, Wheatfield Coll., 1975, MS in Phys. Therapy, 1978, PhD, 1979; D in Nutrimedicine, John F. Kennedy Ctr. Acad., 1989; PhD in Psychology and Clin. Nutrition, Notre Dame De Lafayette U., 1989; postgrad., Mazinic Ctr., Berwyn, Ill., 1993-94. Diplomate Nat. Bd. Chiropractic and Phys. Therapy, Am. Bd. Phys. Therapy Examiners; cert. naprapath, myotherapist. Phys. therapist West Suburban Hosp., Oak Park, Ill., 1964-66; pvt. practice naprapath, phys. therapist Berwyn, Ill., 1970—; cons. phys. therapist Pershing Convalescent Home, Stickney, Ill., 1985-87; assoc. dean Nat. Coll. Naprapathy, 1966-69, prof. endocrinology and diagnosis, 1968-71, prof. naprapathy, 1973; founder United Health Assn., 1976; counselor holistic health Bernadine U., 1989. Spl. police officer City of Cicero, 1968-90. Recipient Cert. of Merit, Am. Massage Therapy Assn., 1969, Cert. of Achievement Palmer Coll. of Chiropractic Medicine, 1970, Cert. Achievement AMA, 1980. Fellow Soc. for Nutrition and Preventive Medicine, Ill. Naprapathic Assn., Am. Back Soc.; mem. Acad. Holistic Practitioners, Am. Assn. Nutritional Cons., Internat. Assn. Counselors and Therapists. Democrat. Presbyterian. Home: 5537 W 24th Pl Cicero IL 60650-2733 Office: 3223 Harlem Ave Berwyn IL 60402-2807

SEDLOCK, JOY, psychiatric social worker; b. Memphis, Jan. 23, 1958; d. George Rudolph Sedlock and Mary Robson; m. Thomas Robert Jones, Aug. 8, 1983. AA, Ventura (Calif.) Jr. Coll., 1978; BS in Psychology, Calif. Luth. U., 1980; MS in Counseling and Psychology, U. LaVerne, 1983; MSW, Calif. State U., Sacramento, 1986. Research asst. Camarillo (Calif.) State Hosp., 1981, tchr.'s aide, 1982; sub. tchr. asst. Vertura County Sch. Dist., 1981; teaching asst. Ventura Jr. Coll., 1980-82, tchr. adult edn., 1980-84; psychiatric social worker Yolo County Day Treatment Ctr., Broderick, Calif., 1986, Napa (Calif.) State Hosp., 1986—. Bd. dirs. Napa County Humane Soc. Home: PO Box 1095 Yountville CA 94599-1095 Office: Napa State Hosp Napa/Vallejo Hgwy Napa CA 49558

SEDOR, JOHN REID, nephrologist, educator; b. Cleve., Apr. 23, 1952; m. Geralyn M. Presti; children: Jonathon, Jeffrey. BA with distinction, U. Va., 1974, MD, 1978. Diplomate Am. Bd. Internal Medicine, Am. Bd. Nephrology, Nat. Bd. Med. Examiners. Intern Case Western U./Univ. Hosps. of Cleve., 1978-79, resident, 1979-81, fellow in nephrology, 1981-84; asst. physician Univ. Hosps. of Cleve., 1984-90, assoc. physician, 1990—; asst. prof. medicine Case Western Res. U., 1984-90, assoc. prof. medicine, 1990—, assoc. prof. physiology and biophysics, 1992-96, prof. medicine, 1996—; dir. divsn. nephrology MetroHealth Med. Ctr., Cleve., 1991—, assoc. chair for rsch., 1994—; trustee Minority Organ Tissue Transplant Edn. Program, 1994—; mem. pathology study sect. NIH DRG, 1993—, mem. nat. reviewers res. com., 1991-93; mem. spl. study sects. NIDDK, 1989—; mem. merit rev. bd. nephrology Vets. Health Svcs. and Rsch. Adminstrn., Dept. Vets. Affairs, 1992—, chair, 1994-95. Mem. editl. bd. Kidney Internat., 1994—, Jour. Am. Soc. Nephrology, 1990—; contbr. articles to profl. jours. Trustee Kidney Found. of Ohio, 1993—, mem. med. adv. bd. 1987—, chair med. adv. bd., 1992-94, mem. rsch. grants com., 1986—, chmn. rsch. grants com., 1992-94; mem. young investgator grant rev. com. Nat. Kidney Found., 1991-94. Fellow ACP; mem. Am. Soc. Nephrology (mem. abstract rev. com. 1988, 95), Am. Fedn. Clin. Rsch., Internat. Soc. Nephrology, Am. Heart Assn. Coun. on Kidney in Cardiovascular Disease, Am. Assn. Pathologists, Am. Soc. Renal Biochemistry and Metabolism. Office: MetroHealth Med Ctr Divsn Nephrology 2500 MetroHealth Dr Cleveland OH 44109-1998

SEE, WILLIAM MITCHEL (W. MIKE SEE), cardiovascular and thoracic surgeon; b. Columbia, Mo., Jan. 10, 1952; s. William Bernard and Maribeth (Sapp) S. BA in Zoology, U. Mo., 1974, MD, 1980. Diplomate Am. Bd. Surgery, Am. Bd. Thoracic Surgery. Resident in gen. surgery Mayo Grad. Sch. Medicine, Rochester, Minn., 1980-85; chief resident in gen. surgery Mayo Clinic, Rochester, 1984-85; chief resident in cardiothoracic surgery Med. Coll. of Wis., Milw., 1985-87; chief resident and instr. cardiothoracic surgery U. Colo., Denver, 1987-89; with Mo. Cardiovascular and Thoracic Surgeons, Columbia, 1989—. Mem. AMA (mem. governing coun. resident physician's sect. 1984-87, vice-chmn. 1985-87), ACS, Am. Coll. of Chest Physicians. Home: 3100 Woodbine Dr Columbia MO 65203-0932 Office: Mo Cardiovascular and Thoracic Surgeons 1701 E Broadway Columbia MO 65201-8018

SEEBACH, ELIZABETH EMILY, psychology educator, psychologist; b. Springfield, Mass., Dec. 28, 1960; d. Willard Ervin and Suzanne Roberta (Bowman) Jones; m. Bradley Scott Seebach, Aug. 8, 1987; 1 child, Rachel Emily. AB cum laude, Washington U., St. Louis, 1982; MS in Psychology, Vanderbilt U., 1985, PhD in Clin. Psychology, 1988. Lic. psychologist. Psychol. examiner Columbia (Tenn.) Comprehensive Mental Health, 1984-85, Psychiat. Cons., Nashville, 1985-86; intern in psychology Brown U., Providence, 1986-87, postdoctoral fellow Med. Sch., 1987-89; asst. prof. Lawrence U., Appleton, Wis., 1989-91; psychologist Psychology Ctr., Madison, Wis., 1991-94, Cath. Learning Ctr., N.Y.C., 1994-95, Brick Kiln, Bohemia, N.Y., 1995—; adv. Psychology Student Assn., Appleton, 1990-92; lectr. U. Wis., Madison. Contbr. numerous articles to profl. jours. Member steering com. Sabin Alliance, Lawrence U., 1989-91. Mem. APA (teaching psychology div. 2. clin. psychology div. 12, neuropsychology div. 40), Fox Valley Psychol. Assn. Home: 43 Winside Ln Coram NY 11727-1134 Office: Brick Kiln Psychol and Counseling Svcs 3340 Vets Meml Hwy Bohemia NY 11716

SEEBACH, LYDIA MARIE, physician; b. Red Wing, Minn., Nov. 9, 1920; d. John Henry and Marie (Gleusen) S.; m. Keith Edward Wentz, Oct. 16, 1959; children: Brooke Marie, Scott. BS, U. Minn., 1942, MB, 1943, MD, 1944, MS in Medicine, 1951. Diplomate Am. Bd. Internal Medicine. Intern Kings County Hosp., Bklyn., 1944; fellow Mayo Found., Rochester, Minn., 1945-51; pvt. practice Oakland, Calif., 1952-60, San Francisco, 1961—; asst. clin. prof. U. Calif., San Francisco, 1981—; mem., vice chmn. Arthritis Clinic, Presbyn. Hosp., San Francisco, 1961-88, pharmacy com., 1963-78; chief St. Mary's Hosp. Arthritis Clinic, San Francisco, 1968-72; exec. bd. Pacific Med. Ctr., San Francisco, 1974-76. Contbr. articles to med. jours. Fellow ACP; mem. AMA, Am. Med. Womens Assn. (pres. Calif. chpt. 1968-70), Am. Rheumatism Assn., Am. Soc. Internal Medicine, Pan Am. Med. Womens Assn. (treas.), Calif. Acad. Medicine, Calif. Soc. Internal Medicine, Calif. Med. Assn., San Francisco Med. Soc., San Francisco Med. Assn., San Francisco Soc. Internal Medicine, No. Calif. Rheumatism Assn., Internat. Med. Women's Assn., Mayo Alumni (bd. dirs. 1983-89), Iota Sigma Pi. Republican. Lutheran. Office: 490 Post St Ste 939 San Francisco CA 94102-1410

SEEDMAN, SUSAN ANN, surgeon; b. Miami Beach, Fla., Feb. 25, 1952; d. Philip and Dorothy S.; 1 child, Ian Bjorn Greenfield. BS, U. Fla., 1973, MD, 1978. Diplomate Am. Bd. Surgery. Resident in gen. surgery U. Okla., Oklahoma City, 1978-83; pvt. practice gen. surgery Santa Fe, N.Mex., 1983—; chmn. gen., vascular and thoracic sect. dept. of surgery St. Vincent Hosp., Santa Fe, 1988-96, med. dir. surg., women & children's svcs. Mem. vol. bd. N.Mex. divsn. Am. Cancer Soc., Santa Fe, 1992—. Fellow ACS (career lisiaon physician 1992—); mem. AMA, Southwestern Surg. Congress, Assn. Women Surgeons, Am. Med. Women's Assn. Office: Santa Fe Surg Assocs 435 St Michaels Dr Ste B-202 Santa Fe NM 87505

SEEGMILLER, JARVIS EDWIN, biochemist, educator; b. St. George, Utah, June 22, 1920; m. Roberta Eads, 1950; children: Dale S. Maudlin, Robert E., Lisa S. Taylor, Richard L. AB, U. Utah, 1942; MD, U. Chgo., 1948. Asst. U.S. Bur. Mines, Utah, 1941; asst. nat. def. rsch. com. Northwestern Tech. Inst., 1942-44; asst. medicine U. Chgo., 1947-48; intern John Hopkins Hosp., 1948-49; biochemist Nat. Inst. Arthritis and Metabolic Diseases, 1949-51; rsch. assoc. Thorndike Meml. Lab. Harvard Med. Sch., 1952-53; vis. investigator Pub. Health Rsch. Inst., N.Y.C., 1953-54; chief sect. human biochemistry, genetics, asst. sci. dir. Nat. Inst. Arthritis and Metabolic Diseases, 1954-69; prof. dept. medicine, dir. divsn. rheumatology U. Calif., San Diego, 1969-90, prof. emeritus dept. medicine, assoc. dir. Stein Inst. Rsch., 1990—; vis. scientist U. Coll. Hosp. Sch. Medicine, London, 1964-65; Harvey Soc. lectr., 1970. Contbr. numerous articles to profl. jours. Macy scholar Basel Inst. Immunology; Guggenheim fellow Swiss Inst. Exptl. Cancer Rsch., Lausanne, 1982-83, John Simon Guggenheim Meml. Found. fellow, 1982, Fogarty Internat. fellow Oxford U., 1989. Mem. Nat. Acad. Sci., Harvey Soc. (hon.), Am. Soc. Biol. Chemists, Am. Rheumatism Assn., Am. Fedn. Clin. Rsch., Am. Soc. Human Genetics, Am. Soc. Clin. Investigation, AAAS, Assn. Am. Physicians, Am. Acad. Arts and Sci. Office: U Calif at San Diego Stein Inst Rsch on Aging 0664 5094 ESB La Jolla CA 92093*

SEELE, SHIRLEY ANN, healthcare administrator; b. St. Louis, Nov. 26, 1947; d. Edward M. and Delores V. (Gruska) Gorman; divorced. AAS, St. Louis C.C., 1972; B Nursing, St. Louis U., 1977; MHA, Washington U., St. Louis, 1981. RN, Mo. Head nurse Bethesda Gen. Hosp., St. Louis, 1973-75, insvc. coord. infection control coord., 1975-76, day supr., 1976-79; adminstrv. coord. home care Jewish Hosp. St. Louis, 1982-83, adminstrv. asst. in obstetrics, psychiatry, rehab., 1983-84, asst. v.p., 1985-93; v.p. ops. Incarnate Word Hosp., St. Louis, 1994-95; v.p. home health Vis. Nurse Assn., St. Louis, 1995—. Bd. mem., chair rehab. com. Mo. Goodwill Industries, St. Louis, 1988—; mem. Women's Polit. Action, St. Louis, 1992—; mem. Jewish Hosp. Aux., St. Louis, 1985-93. Mem. Am. Coll. Healthcare Execs., Med. Group Mgmt. Assn. Home: 8716 Washington Saint Louis MO 63124 Office: Vis Nurse Assn 1260 Andes Saint Louis MO 63132

SEELEN, MICHAEL COONEY, urologist; b. Orange, N.J., July 28, 1944; s. Harry Read and Helen Marie (Cooney) S.; m. Mary Jean Milbauer, Sept. 19, 1970; children: Christopher, Patrick, Michael, Margaret. AB in Biology, Coll. of Holy Cross, 1966; MD, Georgetown U., 1970. Diplomate Am. Bd. Urology. Intern in surgery N.Y. Hosp., Meml. Hosp., North Shore U. Hosp., N.Y.C., 1970-71, resident in surgery, 1971-72; resident in urology Columbia U., N.Y.C., 1974-78; staff urologist Marshfield (Wis.) Clinic, 1978-84, chief dept., 1984—; chief dept. St. Joseph's Hosp., Marshfield, 1984—. Lt. comdr. M.C., USN, 1972-74. Fellow ACS. Republican. Roman Catholic. Office: Marshfield Clinic 1000 N Oak St Marshfield WI 54449

SEELY, DONA MARLENE, orthodontist; b. Vancouver, Wash., Dec. 13, 1953; d. William Stanley and Marlys Elaine (Spicer) S.; m. Curtis Eugene Carlson, Feb. 14, 1982; children: Gina Christine Carlson, Erik Alan Carlson. DDS, U. Wash., 1978, MSD, 1980. Dentist Bellevue, Wash., 1978-80; orthodontist Bellevue, Seattle, 1980—. Mem. Am. Assn. Orthodontists, Pacific Coast Soc. Orthodontists, Wash. State Soc. Orthodontists, Wash. State Soc. Dentists, Seattle King County Dental Soc., Omicron Kappa Upsilon. Home: 16730 Shore Dr NE Seattle WA 98155

SEELY, ELLEN WELLS, endocrinologist; b. N.Y.C., Sept. 25, 1955; d. Robert Daniel and Marcia (Wells) S.; m. Jonathan David Strongin, June 11, 1983; children: Jessica, Matthew. BA magna cum laude, Brown U., 1977; MD, Columbia U., 1981. Diplomate Am. Bd. Internal Medicine, Endocrinology and Metabolism. Residency internal medicine Brigham & Women Hosp., Boston, 1981-84, fellow in endocrinology, 1984-87; rsch. fellow medicine Harvard U., Boston, 1984-87; dir. clin. rsch. endocrine hypertension divsn. Brigham & Women's Hosp., Boston, 1987—, dir. and assoc. program dir. ambulatory clin. rsch. ctr., 1995—; instr. medicine Harvard Medical Sch., Boston, 1987-91; asst. prof. medicine Harvard Med. Sch., Boston, 1991-95; assoc. physician Brigham & Women's Hosp., 1987-95, physician, 1996—; assoc. physician Beth Israel Hosp., Boston, 1988—; med. internship selection com. Brigham and Women's Hosp., 1983-94, co-dir. endocrinology fellowship tng. program, 1993-95, dir. Pregnancy-Related Endocrine and Hypertensive Disorders Clinic, 1988—; coord. Diabetes and Pregnancy Clinic and Osteoporosis Program, Harvard Com. Health Plan, Boston, 1988—. Contbr. articles to profl. jours. Capps scholar in diabetes Harvard Med. Sch., 1994-96. Mem. ADA, Endocrine Soc., Am. Fedn. Clin. Rsch., Internat. Soc. Study of Hypertension in Pregnancy, Coun. for High Blood Pressure Rsch., Am. Heart Assn., Sigma Si. Office: Brigham & Women's Hosp 221 Longwood Ave Boston MA 02115-5817

SEELY, JOHN F., dean. Dean faculty medicine U. Ottawa, Ont., Can. Office: U Ottawa Faculty Medicine, 451 Smyth Rd, Ottawa, ON Canada K1H 8M5*

SEELY, ROBERT DANIEL, physician, medical educator; b. Woodmere, N.Y., Nov. 4, 1923; s. Harry and Ethel (Weil) S.; m. Marcia Ann Wells, June 19, 1953; children: Ellen Wells, Anne Wells. B.S., NYU, 1943; M.D., Columbia U., 1946. Intern Mt. Sinai Hosp., N.Y.C., 1946-47, asst. resident in medicine, 1950-51, resident in pathology, 1951-52, chief resident in medicine, 1952-53; Sara Welt fellow in cardiovascular research Presbyn. Hosp., N.Y.C., 1953-54; instr. dept. physiology, cardiovascular research Western Res. U., Cleve., 1947-48; chief rheumatic heart disease clinic Mt. Sinai Hosp., N.Y.C., 1961-70, attending physician medicine and cardiology, 1978—, chief of service dept. medicine, 1979—, clin. prof. medicine, cardiology Sch. Medicine, 1970—; practice medicine specializing in cardiovascular disease N.Y.C., 1953—. Contbr. articles to profl. jours. Served to capt. M.C. AUS, 1948-50. Recipient Solomon Berson Meml. award Mt. Sinai Hosp., 1977. Fellow Am. Coll. Cardiology, ACP; mem. N.Y. Heart Assn., AMA, N.Y. County Med. Soc., Soc. Cert. Internists N.Y., Phi Beta Kappa, Alpha Omega Alpha, Beta Lambda Sigma. Office: 994 Fifth Ave New York NY 10028-0100

SEELYE, ROGER RALPH, optometrist; b. Carson City, Mich., Dec. 3, 1941; s. Ralph Adelbert and Margaret E. (Davis) S.; m. Phyllis Marie Goetz, July 27, 1963; children: Rod Jason, Soo-Jin. BS, Adrian Coll., 1963, Ind. U., 1964; M in Optometry, Ind. U., 1966, OD, 1966. OD, Mich., Ind. Pvt. practice Owosso, Mich., 1972—; low vision cons. State of Mich. Sch. for the Blind, Lansing, 1969-95, Commn. for the Blind, 1971—; bd. mem. Mich. Health Coun., Lansing, 1988-90, Mich. Health Occupations Coun., 1991-93. Contbr. articles to profl. jours. Bd. mem. Acko Svcs. Sheltered Workshop for Mentally Handicapped, Owosso, 1980-85. Capt. U.S. Army, 1966-68. Mem. Am. Optometric Assn. (state health care legislation com. 1991—), Mich. Optometric Assn. (pres. 1968—, Optometrist of Yr. 1992-93, Keyperson award 1984, Extra Mile award 1992, Legis. Achievement award 1995), Ctrl. Mich. Optometric Soc. (pres. 1968—), North Ctrl. States Optometric Coun. (cabinet mem. 1980—). Lutheran. Office: Drs Ball & Seelye Optometri 307 N Ball St Owosso MI 48867

SEEMANN, JEFFREY RANDALL, plant physiologist, biochemistry educator, researcher; b. Ithaca, N.Y., Apr. 13, 1955; s. Karl William Seemann and Jacqueline Rose (Cantor) Skolnik; m. Charlotte Eileen Borgeson, July 14, 1985; children: Jocelyn Rose, Gwendolyn May. BA, Oberlin Coll., 1977; PhD, Stanford U., 1982. Postdoctoral fellow Australian Nat. U., Canberra, 1982-83; postdoctoral fellow in plant biology Carnegie Instn., Stanford, Calif., 1983-84; asst. prof. plant physiology Desert Research Inst., Reno, 1984-87; assoc. prof. U. Nev., Reno, 1987-92, prof., 1992—, chmn. dept. Biochemistry, 1990—. Mem. editorial bd. Plant Physiology; contbr. articles to profl. jours. McKnight fellow, Stanford U., 1982; grantee USDA, 1985, 87, 89, 91, 93, NSF, 1986, 88, 92, 94, Dept. of Energy, 1994, U.S. Geol. Survey, 1985, 86. Mem. AAAS, Am. Soc. Plant Physiologists, Australian Soc. Plant Physiologists, Sigma Xi. Office: U Nev Dept Of Biochemistry Reno NV 89557

SEESE, WILLIAM SHOBER, chemistry educator; b. Meyersdale, Pa., June 13, 1932; s. Carmon Doyle and Florence Evelyn (Shober) S.; m. Ann Reeves, July 25, 1958; children: David Scott, John Steven. BS in Pharmacy, U. N.Mex., 1954, MS in Chemistry, 1959; PhD in Chemistry, Wash. State U., 1965. Instr. Ft. Lewis Coll., Durango, Colo., 1958-61; research chemist Internat. Minerals and Chem. Corp., Wasco, Calif., 1965-66; instr. Casper (Wyo.) Coll., 1966-87, emeritus; instr. U. Petroleum and Minerals, Dhahran, Saudi Arabia, 1973-76, U. N.Mex., Gallup, 1976-77; Fulbright lectr., Sudan, 1987-88, Oman, 1993-94; prof. chemistry alice Lloyd Coll., Pippa Passes, Ky., 1989-91. Author: (with G. William Daub) Basic Chemistry, 1972, 7th edit., 1996, In Preparation for College Chemistry, 1974, 5th edit., 1994. Recipient Regional award Chem. Mfrs. Assn. for Outstanding Teaching, 1981. Mem. Am. Chem. Soc. Democrat. Presbyterian. Lodge: Masons. Home: 2915 Ridgecrest Dr Casper WY 82604-4619

SEFCHECK, MARCIA ENGLEMAN, orthodontist; b. Joliet, Ill., Mar. 5, 1952; d. Richard Herbert and Clarice Anita (Blatchley) Engleman; m. Mark Michael Sefcheck, July 30, 1977. AA, Joliet Jr. Coll., 1972; BS with honors, Ea. Ill. U., Charleston, 1974; DDS, Loyola U., Maywood, Ill., 1980, cert. in orthodontics, 1982. Diplomate Am. Bd. Orthodontics. Pvt. practice, Mt. Prospect, Ill., 1982-83, Naperville, Ill., 1983—; clin. instr. orthodontics Loyola U. Sch. Dentistry, 1982, asst. clin. prof., 1983-90. Mem. Am. Assn. Orthodontists, Midwestern Assn. Orthodontists, Ill. Assn. Orthodontists (trustee 1996—), Christian Dental Soc., DAR, Philanthropic Edn. Orgn. Lutheran. Office: 6 W 6th Ave Naperville IL 60563

SEGAL, ALLAN, surgeon; b. Phila., Aug. 2, 1948; s. Maxwell and Jeanette (Snyder) S.; m. B.J. Dozor, June 27, 1976; children: Blake H., James D. BS cum laude, St. Joseph's U., 1970; MD, Temple U., 1974. Diplomate Am. Bd. Surgery. Asst. instr. surgery U. Pa., Phila., 1974-77; chief resident surgery Temple U., Phila., 191978-79; chief of surgery The Med. Ctr., Beaver, Pa., 1990—, past chmn. dept. surgery; active staff The Med. Ctr., Beaver, Pa., U. Pitts. Med. Ctr., Beaver Valley, 1979—. Fellow ACS.

SEGAL, ARLENE ESTA, radiologist; b. N.Y.C., Nov. 12, 1937; d. Moe and Fanny (Schlussel) S. BA, Duke U., 1958; MD, Albert Einstein Coll. Medicine, 1962. Diplomate Am. Bd. Radiology, Am. Bd. Nuclear Medicine. Intern Bronx Mcpl. Hosp. Ctr., N.Y.C., 1962-63, resident in radiology, 1963-66; instr. radiology Albert Einstein Coll. Medicine, N.Y.C., 1966-68, asst. prof., 1968-71; practice medicine specializing in gen. diagnostic radiology Rye, Nanuet and Hornell, N.Y., 1971-82; assoc. prof. U. Mo. Sch. Medicine, Kansas City, 1982—; staff radiologist Children's Mercy Hosp., Kansas City, 1982-83, radiologist-in-chief, 1983-90; staff radiologist Truman Med. Ctr., Kansas City, 1992—. Mem. Soc. for Pediat. Radiology, Radiol. Soc. N.Am., Am. Coll. Radiology, Am. Assn. Women Radiologists, Midwest Soc. for Pediat. Radiology (pres. 1991), Mo. Radiol. Soc. (bd. dirs. 1990-93, pres.-elect 1995, pres. 1996—). Office: Truman Med Ctr 2301 Holmes Kansas City MO 64108

SEGAL, BERNARD, psychology educator; b. N.Y.C., May 9, 1936; s. Jacob L. and Bessie (Melofsky) S.; m. Marjorie Hope Wightman, May 3, 1964; children—Ellen Rise, Neil Jonathan. B.B.A., CUNY, 1960, M.S.E., 1963; Ph.D., U. Okla., 1967. Lic. psychologist, Alaska. Asst. prof. U. R.I., Kingston, 1967-70; prof. Murray State U., Ky., 1970-77; prof. psychology and health scis, U. Alaska, Anchorage, 1977—. Author: (with others) Drugs, Daydreaming and Personality, 1980; Drugs and Behavior, 1988. Editor Drugs and Society: A Jour. of Contemporary Issues, 1985. Contbr. numerous articles to profl. jours. Vice-chmn. Anchorage Mcpl. Health Commn., 1982-83; chmn. adv. bd. Clithroe Ctr., Anchorage, 1982-83. Served with USN, 1956-58. Grantee NIH, Nat. Inst. Drug Abuse, Alaska Dept. Health and Social Services. Mem. Am. Pub. Health Assn. Home: 1841 E 56th Ave Anchorage AK 99507-1606 Office: U Alaska Alaska 3211 Providence Dr # U Anchorage AK 99508

SEGAL, NANCY LEE, psychology educator, twin researcher; b. Boston, Mar. 2, 1951; d. Alfred Maurice and Esther (Rubenstein) S. BA in Psychology and English, Boston U., 1973; MA in Social Sci., U. Chgo., 1974, PhD in Human Devel., 1982. Asst. dir., rsch. assoc. Minn. Ctr. for Twin and Adoption Rsch., Mpls., 1985-91; prof. dept. psychology Calif. State U., Fullerton, 1991—; cons. on twin loss, Mpls., 1984, 87. Contbg. editor Twins Mag., 1984—, mem. editorial bd., 1985—; contbr. articles to profl. jours. Recipient Disting. Alumni award Boston U., 1990. Fellow Am. Psychol. Soc., APA (divsn. 7); mem. Twins Found., Internat. Soc. for Twin Studies, Internat. Soc. for Human Ethology (membership chair), N.Y. Road Runners Club, Sigma Delta Epsilon (rsch. award 1989), Sigma Xi. Office: Calif State U Dept Psychology 800 N State College Blvd Fullerton CA 92834

SEGALL, HERVEY D., neuroradiologist, educator; b. Moose Jaw, Sask, Can., Aug. 11, 1937; s. Ben and Anna Helen (Belovich) S.; m. Doris Muriel Zwirn, July 14, 1962; children: Julie Lynne, Aviva Esther, Penina Louise. BA, U. B.C., 1957, MD, 1961. Dir. neuroradiology U. So. Calif. Med. Sch., L.A., 1976—, prof. radiology, 1979—. Assoc. editor Radiology, 1982-93; mem. edtl. bd. Jour. of Computer Assisted Tomography, 1983-96, Jour. Child Neurology, 1986-94, founding mem.; contbr. numerous articles to profl. jours. Lt. comdr. USNR, 1966-68. Mem. LARS, CRS, RSNA (chmn. neuroradiology meeting notes com. 1989-92), Am. Soc. Neuroradiology (chmn. membership com. 1976-77, chmn. audit com. 1981-82, chmn. sci. exhibits com. 1992-95), Am. Soc. Pediatric Neuroradiology, Western Neuroradiol. Soc. (chmn. awards com. 1990, pres. 1978), Am. Coll. Radiology (assoc. editor Neuroradiology tchg. file 1990—), U. So. Calif. Neuroradiology Alumni Assn. (founder 1993). Home: San Marino CA 91108 Office: U So Calif Med Sch 1200 N State St Los Angeles CA 90033-4525

SEGALL, KEITH EDWARD, physician; b. St. Louis, Jan. 9, 1964; s. Norman and Marcella (Routman) S.; m. Denorah Lee, Apr. 17, 1993; 1 child, Chad Brown. BS in Biology, St. Louis U., 1986; DO cum laude, U. Helath Sci., 1991. Intern Capital Region Med. Ctr., Jefferson City, Mo., 1992-94, resident, 1991-92; physician Vienna (Mo.) Family Practice Clinic, 1994—. Scoutmaster Boy Scouts Am., St. Louis, 1976—. Recipient Ner Tanid award Boy Scouts Am., 1980, Shofar award, 1987, Eagle Scout, 1980. Mem. Am. Osteo. Assn., Am. Coll. Surgeons & Family Practitioners, Masons, Shriners, Scottish Rite, Alpha Phi Omega. Home: 1631 W Main Apt B Jefferson City MO 65109 Office: Vienna Family Practice Clinic HCR 60 Box 5 Vienna MO 65582

SEGALL, SETH ROBERT, psychologist; b. Bklyn., Mar. 5, 1948; s. Edward and Muriel (Goldman) S.; m. Mary Trefethen, Oct. 11, 1969; children: Joshua, Jessica. BA, Harpur Coll., 1969; MA, So. Ill. U., Carbondale, 1975, PhD, 1977. Instr. Southeast Mo. State U., Cape Girardeau, 1977-78; visiting asst. prof. So. Ill. U., Carbondale, 1978-80; staff psychologist Waterbury (Conn.) Hosp. Health Ctr., 1980-86; asst. clin. prof. Yale U. Sch. Medicine, New Haven, Conn., 1980—; program dir. Whitewood Rehab. Ctr., Waterbury, 1986-89; sr. cons. The Consultation Ctr., New Haven, 1989—; clin. psychologist Robert Behrends MD and Assocs., Waterbury, 1989-90; pvt. practice Waterbury, 1990—; adj. profl. staff Waterbury Hosp. Health Ctr., 1981—; med. practice assoc. St. Mary's Hosp., 1994—. Bd. dirs. Partial Hospitalization Assn. of Conn., 1985-86; cubmaster, com. chmn. Cub Scouts, Cheshire, Conn., 1986-88. Mem. APA, Am. Soc. Clin. Hypnosis, Internat. Soc. for Study of Dissociation, Internat. Soc. Traumatic Stress Studies, New Eng. Soc. for Study of Dissociation (bd. dirs. 1996—), Conn. Psychol. Assn. Office: 60 Westwood Ave Waterbury CT 06708

SEGAR, DOUGLAS SCOTT, cardiologist, researcher, medical educator; b. Indpls., Apr. 27, 1958; s. William Elias and Julie Anne (Feld) Segar; m. Doris Nicki Bagios, May 16, 1987; children: Matthew, Nicholas, Rachel. BA, Oberlin Coll., 1980; MD, Ind. U., 1984. Bd. cert. in cardiovasc. diseases, internal medicine. Resident Ind. U., Indpls., 1984-87, cardiology fellow, 1987-90, chief fellow in cardiology, 1989-90, asst. prof. medicine, 1990-96, assoc. prof. medicine, 1996—; chief cardiology Wishard Meml. Hosp., Indpls., 1995—. Assoc. editor Jour. Am. Soc. Echocardiography, 1995—; contbr. chpt. to book. Fellow Am. Coll. Cardiology, Coun. on Clin. Cardiology; mem. Am. Heart Assn. Office: Krannert Inst Cardiology 1111 W Tenth Indianapolis IN 46202

SEGARS, KELLY SCOTT, physician, banker; b. Red Bay, Ala., Mar. 11, 1930; s. Dock and Ora (Sims) S.; m. Martha Ann Thompson, Oct. 3, 1952; children—Kelly, Mark Thompson, Leigh Ann. B.S. in Pharmacy, Auburn U., 1952; M.D., U. Miss.-Jackson, 1959. Diplomate Am. Bd. Family Practice. Intern USPHS Hosp., Norfolk, Va., 1959-60; physician Segars Clinic, Iuka, Miss., 1960—; pres. First Am. Nat. Bank, Iuka, 1964—, Segars Communications, Iuka, 1970—, S & G Cablevision, Iuka, 1978—; pres. Tri-State Savs. & Loan, 1963-64; chief med. staff Tishomingo County Hosp., Iuka, 1968, 76, 82, dir. coronary care unit, 1970—. Chmn. constrn. com. Iuka Airport, 1964, Iuka Mcpl. Library, 1971; exec. council Boy Scouts Am., Tupelo, Miss., 1971—. Served to 1st lt. U.S. Army, 1953-55. Decorated Army Commendation medal. Fellow Am. Acad. Family Physicians; mem. AMA, Miss. Med. Assn., Flying Physicians Assn., Ole Miss Med. Alumni. Republican. Methodist. Club: Rotary. Address: Segars Clinic 1507 W Quitman St Iuka MS 38852-1132

SEGEL, ARNOLD LESTER, surgeon; b. Cambridge, Mass., May 6, 1911; s. Sydney and Celia (Kramer) S.; m. Ruth Cohn, 1948; children: William, Margaret, James, Arthur, Anne. AB, Harvard U., 1932, MD, 1936. Diplomate Am. Bd. Surgery. Intern Beth Israel Hosp., Boston, 1936-38; asst. resident and resident Beth Israel Hosp., 1938-40; surgery asst. to instr. Harvard Med. Sch., 1946-74; asst. prof. Tufts Univ. Med. Sch., Boston, 1983—; pvt. practice Beth Israel Hosp., 1946-74; asst. surgeon to surgeon Beth Israel Hosp., 1946-74; assoc. chief of staff Boston VA Hosp., 1974-88. Contbr. articles to profl. pubs. Decorated Bronze Star, 7 Battle Stars, Presidential citation, Croix de Guerre with Palm (France). Mem. AMA, Mass. Med. Soc., ACS, Mass. chpt. ACS, Boston Surg. Soc.

SEGEL, HAROLD JEROME, psychologist; b. Pitts., Mar. 12; s. Dave and Minnie (Tyrnauer) S.; children—Beth Segel, Kim Sydney. B.S., U. Pitts., 1949, M.S., 1951; Ph.D., Pa. State U., 1955. Diplomate Am. Bd. Profl. Psychology, Am. Bd. Examiners in Clin. Hypnosis. Chief counseling psychology service VA Hosp., Danville, Ill., 1955-56, chief psychology service, Butler, Pa., 1956-59, unit psychology coordinator, Sepulveda, Calif., 1959-80; dir. Psychology Ctr., Sepulveda, 1960-94 ; assoc. clin. prof. psychology U. So. Calif., 1972-80 , UCLA, 1973-80 . Bd. dirs. Calif. Sch. Profl. Psychology, 1976-79. Served with U.S. Army, 1942-46. Mem. Am. Psychol. Assn., Calif. Psychol. Assn., San Fernando Valley Psychol. Assn. (pres. 1968, 75, 85). Club: VA Retirees (pres.). Home: 16059 Ludlow St Granada Hills CA 91344-5330

SEGELMAN, ALLYN EVAN, dentist, researcher; b. Boston, July 25, 1947; s. Edward David John and Harriett Sylvia (Shuman) S.; m. Sandra Ruth Steiman, June 17, 1973 (div. Aug. 1995); children: Tovah Chanah, Rayna Devorah. AB in Biology, Boston U., 1969; DMD, Tufts U., 1973. Diplomate Am. Bd. Oral and Maxillofacial Surgery, Am. Bd. Oral Medicine. Intern Tufts-New Eng. Med. Ctr., 1973-74, fellow in oral cancer, 1974-75; resident Boston City Hosp., 1975-77, chief resident, 1976-77; pvt. practice oral and maxillofacial surgery Mass., 1977-95; asst. clin. prof. oral and maxillofacial surgery Tufts U. Sch. of Dental Medicine, Boston, 1980—; rsch. fellow in dental care adminstrn. Harvard Sch. of Dental Medicine, Harvard Sch. Pub. Health, Boston, 1996—; dir. dental consultative svcs. New Eng. Area Comprehensive Hemophilia Care Ctr., Worcester, Mass., 1977-78; cons. managed care benefit sys. Blue Cross Blue Shield of Mass., Boston, 1984—; cons. Ctrl. Mass. Healthcare Inc., Worcester, 1992, Mass Pro Inc. and Nat. Quality Health Coun., Waltham, 1995. Editor: Procedural Terminology for Oral and Maxillofacial Surgery, 1985, Procedural Terminology with Glossary, 1985; contbr. articles to profl. jours. Gov.'s appointee Legis. Spl. Commn. on Sch. Bus Safety, Boston, 1985-88; bd. registration in dentistry appointee Mass. Dept. Pub. Health Prescription Monitoring Program, Boston, 1994—; chmn. sch. com. Congregation Mishkan Tefila, Newton, Mass., 1993-95, bd. trustees, 1983-95. Recipient Brotherhood award Mass. Com. of Catholics., Protestants and Jews, 1965. Fellow Am. Acad. Oral Medicine (pres. 1996—), Am. Assn. Oral and Maxillofacial Surgeons (chmn. spl. com. coding and nomenclature 1991-94), Mass. Dental Soc. Anesthesiology (pres. 1987-88); mem. Tufts U. Dental Alumni Assn. (exec. coun., pres. 1985-86), Omicron Kappa Upsilon. Democrat. Jewish. Home: 19 Westgate Rd # 4 Chestnut Hill MA 02167 Office: Harvard Sch Dental Medicine Dept Oral Health Policy and Epidemiology 188 Longwood Ave Boston MA 02115

SEGGEV, MEIR, radiologist, educator; b. Burgas, Bulgaria, Jan. 23, 1939; came to U.S., 1969, naturalized, 1976; s. Bouco and Helen (Bejerano) S.; m. Ruth Lerner, Dec. 30, 1964 (div. Apr. 1978); 1 child, Yael.; m. Sandra Lee Slarsky, Apr. 7, 1979. MD, Hebrew U. Hadassah, Jerusalem, 1966. Diplomate Am. Bd. Radiology. Radiology resident Harvard Med. Sch., Beth Israel Hosp., Boston, 1970-73; radiologist Peter Bent Brigham Hosp., Boston, 1973-74, Hale Hosp., Haverhill, Mass., 1974—; assoc. radiologist Beth Israel Hosp., Boston, 1974—; clin. instr. radiology Harvard Med. Sch., Boston, 1973—. Mem. AMA, Am. Inst. Ultrasound in Medicine, Am. Roentgen Ray Soc., Radiol. Soc. N.Am., Am. Coll. Radiology, Mass. Med. Soc., Harvard Club. Home: 35 Morton St Andover MA 01810-2037

SEGRE, EUGENE JOSEPH, drug development consultant, physician; b. Torino, Italy, Sept. 12, 1932; came to U.S., 1943; s. Ernesto and Anna (Jona) S.; m. Zina Cecilia Camarda, June 8, 1956; children: David, Paul, Lisa. BA, Cornell U., 1953, MD, 1956. Diplomate Am. Bd. Internal Medicine, Nat. Bd. Med. Examiners. Staff scientist Worcester Found., Shrewsbury, Mass., 1962-64; assoc. med. dir. Syntex Corp., Palo Alto, Calif., 1964-66; dir. clin. pharmacology Syntex Corp., Palo Alto, 1966-67; assoc. dir. Inst. of Medicine Syntex Corp., Palo Alto, 5, 1967-77, v.p., dir. Inst. of Medicine, 1977-80, sr. v.p. devel. rsch., mem. corp. mgmt. com., 1980-90; cons. Palo Alto, 1990—; mem., chair sci. adv. bds. Hana Biologics, Berkeley, Calif., 1990-92, Pharmagenesis, 1991-95, Acea Pharms., 1991—, Calydon, 1991—; asst. clin. prof. Stanford U. Med. Sch., Palo Alto, 1965-84, emeritus, 1993—. Author: Androgens, Virilization and the Hirsute Female, 1967; contbr. chpts. to books, more than 50 articles to profl. jours.; patentee in field. Capt. USAF, 1957-59, 61-62. Fellow ACP; mem. Am. Soc. for Clin. Pharmacology and Therapeutics, Phi Beta Kappa, Alpha Omega Alpha. Home and Office: 470 Santa Rita Ave Palo Alto CA 94301-3943

SEHNERT, WALTER, physician; b. Schwelm, Germany, July 20, 1946; s. Adolf Robert and Elsbeth (Koester) S. Med. Exam., Freie U., Berlin, 1974; MD, U. Bochum (Germany), 1986. Med. specialist internal medicine. Med. asst. Katholisches Marien Hosp., Essen, Germany, 1975-80; sr. physician Evangelisches Krankenhaus, Herne, Germany, 1980—. Author: Hypertension, 1989; contbr. articles on cardiology and intensive care to profl. jours. Mem. Berufsverband Deutscher Internisten, Deutsche Gesellschaft Intensiv Medizin, Deutsche Gesellschaft fuer Herz und Kreislauf Forschung. Office: Evangelisches Krankenhaus, Wiescherstr 24, 44623 Herne 1, Germany

SEIBEL, HUGO RUDOLF, anatomist, university dean; b. Radautz, Rumania, Nov. 9, 1937; came to U.S. 1952; s. Hugo Josef and Berta (Gertel) S.; m. Edith Edeltrud Kramer, June 14, 1964. BS, Bklyn. Coll., 1960; PhD, U. Rochester, 1967. Coll. sci. asst. Bklyn. Coll., 1960-62; asst. prof. anatomy Med. Coll. Va., Richmond, 1967-70, assoc. prof. anatomy, 1970-75, prof. anatomy, 1975—, curriculum coord., 1976-87, asst. dean medicine, 1984-87, assoc. dean medicine, 1987—. Author: Barron's How to Prepare for the MCAT's, 1976, Essentials of Histology, 1972; contbr. over 130 articles to profl. jours. Recipient Disting. Univ. Tchg. award Va. Commonwealth U., 1988. Mem. AAUP, Am. Assn. Anatomists, Soc. Exptl. Biology and Medicine, Va. Acad. Sci. (co-chair and chair), Sigma Xi (pres.). Office: Med Coll Va Box 565 1101 E Marshall St Richmond VA 23298-5007

SEIBERT, DONALD ALAN, optometrist; b. Feb. 23, 1960; married; 2 children. BS in Microbiology, Pa. State U., 1982; OD, Pa. Coll. Optometry, Phila., 1986. Lic. optometrist Pa., Ill., W.Va., N.C. Resident in hosp.-based optometry Huntington VA Med. Ctr.; teaching asst. Pa. State U., 1982; rsch. asst. in physiologic optics Pa. Coll. Optometry, Phila., 1983; electrodiagnostitan Huntington Autistic Tng. Ctr. of Marshall U., 1986-87; ocular florescein angiographic photographer Huntington VA Med. Ctr., 1986-87, staff optometrist, 1991—, dir. Electrodiagnostic Clinic, 1991—; chief optometry svc. Olympia Fields (Ill.) Osteo. Med. Ctr., 1989-90; prin. electrodiagnostic investigator Ill. Coll. Optometry, 1987-90; adj. prof. clin. optometry Ill. Coll. Optometry, Ind. U. Sch. Optometry, Pa. Coll. Optometry, all 1991—; lectr. in field. Contbr. articles to profl. jours. Recipient William Feinbloom Award for Excellence in Low Vision, 1986. Mem. Pa. Coll. Optometry Alumni Assn., Pa. State U. Alumni Assn., Assn. for Rsch. and Vision in Ophthalmology. Office: Huntington VA Med Ctr 1540 Spring Valley Dr Huntington WV 25704

SEIBERT, STEVEN WAYNE, periodontist; b. Belleville, Ill., Jan. 2, 1955; s. Cletus Francis and Elizabeth Jean (Meyers) S.; m. Cheryl Ellen Mellinger, Aug. 18, 1979; children: Matthew Aaron, Christina Renee. BS in Biomed. Sci. and Biology, So. Ill. U., Edwardsville, 1977, MS in Biology, 1982; D of Dental Medicine, So. Ill. U., Alton, 1982; Cert. in Periodontics, U. Nebr., 1984. Practice dentistry specializing in periodontics Champaign, Ill., 1984; instr. dentistry Parkland Jr. Coll., Champaign, 1984—. Contbr. articles to profl. jours. Mem. ADA, Am. Acad. Periodontology, Sigma Xi (assoc.). Republican. Roman Catholic. Home: 1804 Bentbrook Dr Champaign IL 61821-9218 Office: 303 W Springfield Ave Champaign IL 61820-4833

SEIDEL, GEOFFREY KARL, rehabilitation physician, medical educator; b. Hudson, N.Y., Feb. 5, 1963; m. Paola Marie Piccillo, Mar. 22, 1986; two children. BS, Cornell U., Ithaca, N.Y., 1985; MD, SUNY, Buffalo, 1989. Diplomate Am. Bd Physical Medicine and Rehabilitation. Asst. prof. physical medicine and rehabilitation Wayne State U., 1993—. Contbr. articles to profl. jours. including Jour. of Biomechanics, Archives of Pathology, Archives of Physical Medicine and Rehabilitation. Mem. Am. Assn. Electrodiagnostic Medicine, Assn. Acad. Physiatrists, Am. Acad. Physical Medicine and Rehabilitation, Mich. State Med. Soc., McComb Med. Soc. Office: 43555 Dalloma Dr Ste 4 Clinton Township MI 48038

SEIDEL, JAMES STEPHEN, pediatrician, educator; b. N.Y.C., June 24, 1943; s. Leo and Esther (Mellman) S. BS, Mich. State U., 1964; MSPH, U. N.C., 1967; MD, UCLA, 1973, PhD, 1976. Diplomate Am. Bd. Pediatrics. Chief gen. and emergency pediatrics Harbor/UCLA Med. Ctr., Torrance, Calif., 1977—; asst. prof. UCLA Sch. of Medicine, L.A., 1977-82, assoc. prof., 1982-91, prof. pediatrics, 1994—. Contbr. articles to profl. jours. Recipient Emil Bogen Rsch. prize, 1973. Mem. Am. Acad. Pediatrics (mem. com. on pediatric emergency medicine 1985-92, cons. 1992—), Am. Heart Assn. (chmn. various coms.), Am. Coll. Emergency Physicnas and Am. Acad. Pediatrics, Ambulatory Pediatric Assn., Nat. Acad. Scis., L.A. Pediatric Soc. (exec. bd. 1990—, pres. 1993-94, Joseph W. St. Geme Meml. award 1987), Western Soc. Pediatric Rsch., Am. Soc. Tropical Medicine and Hygiene, Am. Soc. Parasitologists, So. Calif. Parasitologists (pres. 1987), Soc. for Pediatric Emergency Medicine (bd. dirs. 1990—), Brazilian Soc. of Tropical Medicine, Hawaiian Pediatric Soc. (hon.), AAAS, others.

SEIDEL, JOAN CLARE, critical care nurse, educator, consultant; b. Auburn, Wash., June 24, 1938; d. Alexander Jacob and Kathryn Clare (O'Brien) Yambra; m. Verlin Joseph Seidel, June 1, 1963. Diploma in nursing, Providence Hosp. Sch. Nursing, 1959; student, Sacred Heart Dominican Coll., 1965-67; BS, Tex. Woman's U., 1971, MS, 1975. RN, Tex.; cert. ACLS provider and instr.; cert. CPR instr.-trainer. Staff nurse, asst. supr. cardiovascular ICU The Meth. Hosp., Houston, 1961-67, inservice instr. cardiovascular ICU, 1971-74, clin. pratitioner tchr. II critical care, 1979-87, coord. in-patient cardiac rehab. program, 1987-88, educator critical care residency program, 1988-94; supr. coronary care unit, med. ICU, others Houston (Tex.) VA Med. Ctr., 1975-79; clin. nurse specialist coronary care unit, 1979-94; lectr., presenter in field; clin. specialist in diabetes edn., 1994—. Contbr. articles to profl. jours. Mem. AACN (CCRN, treas. Houston-Gulf Coast chpt. 1974-75, pres. 1976-77, chmn. cmty. projects com. 1981-84, rsch. com. 1985-88, sec. 1987-89, treas.-elect 1992-93, treas. 1993-95, rep. to Houston Coun. Nursing Orgns. 1988-92, others), Am. Heart Assn., Cardiovasc. Nurses Soc. (sec. 1984-85, rsch. seminar com. 1988), Houston Coun. Nursing Orgns. (pres.-elect 1991-92, pres. 1992-93), Am. Assn. Diabetes Educators, Am. Diabetes Assn. (cert. diabetes educator), Tex. Nurses Assn. (cert. diabetes educator, bd. dirs. 1994-96). Democrat. Roman Catholic. Home: 4314 Woodvalley Dr Houston TX 77096-3530 Office: The Methodist Hosp 6565 Fannin St Houston TX 77030-2704

SEIDEMAN, BRUCE ANDREW, orthopaedic surgeon; b. N.Y.C., Mar. 17, 1957; s. Thomas and Francine (Tenner) S.; m. Abby Meryl Harris, June 9, 1985; children: Lauren, Blair, Harrison. BS in Biology summa cum laude, Rennsselaer Poly. Inst., 1979; MD, Albany Med. Coll., 1981. Diplomate Am. Bd. Orthopaedic surgery, Nat. Bd. Med. Examiners. Intern gen. surgery The Beth Israel Hosp., Boston, 1981-82; pediat. surgery house officer The Children's Hosp. Med. Ctr., Boston, 1982; resident gen. surgery The Beth Israel Hosp., Boston, 1982-83; resident in orthopaedic surgery The N.Y. Orthopaedic Hosp./Columbia Presbyn. Med. Ctr., N.Y.C., 1983-86; fellow in adult reconstructive surgery The Mayo Clinic, Rochester, Minn., 1986-87; spl. fellow in orthopaedic surgery The Mayo Clinic, Rochester, 1986-87; clin. instr. surgery Cornell U. Med. Coll., 1990—; assoc. attending physician dept. surgery North Shore Univ. Hosp., Manhasset, N.Y.; asst. attending physician dept. orthopaedic surgery Hosp. for Spl. Surgery, N.Y.C.; exec. com. L.I. Orthopaedic Network, 1994—; bd. dirs. NextStage Healthcare Mgmt., L.I. Physicians Holding Corp./MCLI Healthcare. Contbr. articles to profl. jours. Fellow Am. Acad. Orthopaedic Surgeons; mem. Am. Assn. Arthritic Hip and Knee Surgeons, Med. Soc. State N.Y., N.Y. State Soc. Orthopaedic Surgeons, Nassau County Med. Soc., Nassau Acad. Medicine, Mayo Grad. Sch. Medicine Alumni Assn., N.Y. Orthopaedic Hosp. Alumni Assn., Alpha Omega Alpha (pres. Albany Med. Coll. chpt. 1980-81). Office: Orthopaedic Assocs Manhasset 800 Community Dr Manhasset NY 11030

SEIDEMAN, RUTH EVELYN YOUNG, nurse educator; b. Okeene, Okla., July 7, 1934; d. Ewald Julius and Alma Alexandra (Smith) Kramer; m. Jack Lee Young, Nov. 27, 1954 (div. Mar. 1986); children: Stanley Daryl, Steven Glenn, Roger Neil; m. Walter Elmer Seidman, May 21, 1988. BS, Tex. Woman's U., 1958; MA, U. Okla., 1970, MS, 1975, PhD, 1987. RN, Okla. Staff nurse, supr. U. Hosp., Oklahoma City, Okla., 1955-57; sch. nurse Dallas Pub. Schs., 1958-60; staff nurse St. Francis Hosp., Tulsa, 1963-65, Cen. State Hosp., Norman, Okla., 1966-68; supr. Cen. State Hosp., Norman, 1970-71; instr. Oklahoma City U., 1971-72, Sch. Nursing St. Anthony Hosp., Oklahoma City, 1972-75; asst. prof. Coll. Nursing U. Okla., 1975-82, assoc. prof., 1982—. Author: Community Nursing Workbook:Family as Client, 1983; contbr. articles to profl. jours. Mem. Am. Nurses Assn. (del. 1985—), Midwest Nursing Research Soc., Sigma Theta Tau, Sigma Xi. Home: 3104 Canyon Rd Oklahoma City OK 73120-5615 Office: Coll Nursing PO Box 26901 Oklahoma City OK 73126

SEIDERMAN, ARTHUR STANLEY, optometrist, consultant, author; b. Phila., Nov. 28, 1936; s. Morris and Anne (Roseman) S.; m. Susan Levin, Aug. 19, 1965; children: David, Leeann, Scott. Student, U. Vienna (Austria) Med. Sch., 1965; OD, Pa. Coll. of Optometry, 1963; AB, W.Va. Wesleyan Coll., 1959; MA, Fairleigh Dickinson U., 1973. Pvt. practice Elkins Park, Pa., 1971-94, Plymouth Meeting, Pa., 1994—; vision cons. U.S. Olympic Teams, Phila. Flyers Hockey Team. Co-author: The Athletic Eye, 1983, 20/20 Is Not Enough, 1990; mem. editoral adv. bd. Jour. of Learning Disabilities, 1979—. Vice pres. Jewish Nat. Fund, Phila., 1988—. Capt. U.S. Army, 1963-68. Fellow Am. Acad. Optometry, Coll. of Optometrists in Vision Devel.; mem. Multidisciplinary Acad. of Clin. Edn. (pres.), Internat. Reading Assn. (pres. disabled group 1987-89). Home: 155 Sawgrass Dr Blue Bell PA 19422 Office: 919 E Germantown Pike Ste 4 Norristown PA 19401-2442

SEIDES, STUART FLOYD, cardiologist; b. N.Y.C., Mar. 20, 1947; s. Arthur Daniel and Clarie (Bernstein) S.; m. Marjorie Anne Robinson, June 7, 1970; children: Alison Beth, Benjamin Jason. BS, Pa. State U., 1967; MD, Cornell U., 1970. Diplomate Am. Bd. Internal Medicine, Am. Bd. Cardiovascular Disease. Resident in medicine Beth Israel Hosp./Harvard Med. Sch., Boston, 1970-72; rsch. fellow USPHS Hosp., S.I., N.Y., 1972-74; Washington Heart Assn. fellow Georgetown U. Hosp., Washington, 1974-76, chief resident, 1976; sr. investigator cardiology br. NHLBI, NIH, Bethesda, Md., 1976-78; pres. Cardiology Assocs., P.C., Washington, 1978—; vice chair cardiology Washington Hosp. Ctr.; clin. prof. medicine George Washington U., Washington; bd. dirs. Capital Physicians Network, Washington; founder, bd. dirs. Capital Cardiology Network, Washington. Author: Clinical Cardiac Electrophysics, 1979; contbr. articles to profl. jours. Comdr. USPHS, 1972-78. Fellow ACP, Am. Coll. Cardiology, Soc. Cardiac Angiography and Intervention, Coun. on Clin. Cardiology/Am. Heart Assn. (Heart of Gold award 1993), Med. Soc. D.C. (chmn. med. ethics and grievance coms. 1986—). Office: Cardiology Assocs PC 106 Irving St NW # 101 Washington DC 20010

SEIDMAN, MICHAEL DAVID, surgeon, educator; b. Detroit, Oct. 14, 1960; s. Melvin and Rita Seidman; m. Lynn Ann Gaberman; children: Jake, Marlee, Kevin. BS in Human Nutrition, U. Mich., 1981, MD, 1986. Resident in Otolaryngology, Head and Neck Surgery Henry Ford Hosp., Detroit, 1986-91, attending physician, surgeon, 1992—; divsn. head dept. oto-HNS Henry Ford Hosp. W. Bloomfield Satellite, 1996—; fellow in Otology, Neurotology, Skull Base Surgery Ear Rsch. Found., Sarasota, Fla., 1991-92; staff physician Sarasota Mem. Hosp., 1991-92; assoc. staff physician Doctors Hosp., Sarasota, 1991-92; asst. clin. prof. Wayne State U., Detroit, 1993—; med. advisor Self Help Hard of Hearing People Inc., Bethesda, 1988—, mem. healthcare com., 1990-93; bd. dirs. Ear Rsch. Found., 1992—. Contbr. chpts. to books including Common Problems of the Ear, 1996, others; contbr. articles to profl. jours.; mem. editl. bd. Oto-HNS Jour., Hearing Rsch. Recipient Clin. Investigator Devel. award NIH, 1994-99. Fellow ACS; mem. AAAS, Am. Neurotology Soc., Am. Tinnitus Assn., Assn. Rsch. Otolaryngology (edn. com. 1992—), Sir Charles Bell Soc., Am. Acad. Oto-HNS. Office: Henry Ford Hosp 6777 W Maple Rd West Bloomfield MI 48323

SEIFER, RONALD LESLIE, psychologist; b. Liberty, N.Y., Oct. 23, 1942; s. Leon and Pearl (Treibitz) S.; m. Gail Sandra Eagerman, May 29, 1967; children—David Marc, Robert Eric. BA, Queens Coll., 1964; MA, Northeastern U., 1967; PhD, U. Maine, 1971. Lic. psychologist, Fla., N.Y. Intern psychologist Albert Einstein Coll. Medicine, Bronx, N.Y., 1968-69; psychologist St. Vincent's Hosp., Harrison, N.Y., 1969-71; supervising psychologist Saratoga County Mental Health Ctr., Saratoga Springs, N.Y., 1971-76; psychologist Brevard County Mental Health Ctr., Melbourne, Fla., 1976-79; pvt. practice clin. psychology, Melbourne, 1978—; assoc. med. staff Holmes Regional Med. Ctr., Melbourne, 1979—; coord. TOP Soccer, Fla. Youth Soccer Assn., 1990—. Research fellow Northeastern U., 1964-66. Mem. Am. Psychol. Assn., Am. Soc. Clin. Hypnosis, Fla. Soc. Clin. Hypnosis (treas. 1985-88), N.Am. Soc. Psychology of Sport and Phys. Activity, Biofeedback Soc. Am., Brevard County Psychol. Assn. (pres. 1979-80). Avocations: gardening, fishing. Office: Melbourne Psychiatry 109 Silver Palm Ave Melbourne FL 32901-3125

SEIGEL, ARTHUR MICHAEL, neurologist, educator; b. Rochester, N.Y., Oct. 9, 1944; s. Hyman and Judith (Hyman) S.; B.A. in Biology with distinction, SUNY, Buffalo, 1966, M.D, 1970; MBA U. New Haven, 1989; m. Ellen May Streitfeld, June 1, 1969; children—Daniel Aaron, Mark Louis. Cert. instrument pilot, 1994. Intern, SUNY Affiliated Hosps., Buffalo, 1970-71; resident Yale-New Haven Hosp., 1973-76; asst. prof. pediatrics and neurology Yale U. Sch. Medicine, New Haven, 1976-77, clin. instr., 1977-81, clin. asst. prof., 1981—; cons. in neurology Gaylord Rehab. Hosp., Wallingford, Conn., 1976-86; practice medicine specializing in neurology, New Haven, 1977—; attending physician Hosp. St. Raphael, New Haven, Yale-New Haven Hosp. Served with USPHS, 1971-73. Diplomate Am. Bd. Psychiatry and Neurology. Fellow Royal Soc. Medicine; mem. Conn. Neurol. Soc. (v.p. 1987-96), Am. Acad. Neurology, Conn. Med. Soc., New Haven County Med. Soc., Yale Neurology Alumni (pres.(1994-96). Home: 38 Vineyard Ave Guilford CT 06437-3235 Office: 60 Temple St New Haven CT 06510-2716

SEIL, FREDRICK JOHN, neuroscientist, neurologist; b. Nove Sove, Yugoslavia, Nov. 9, 1933; s. Joseph and Theresa (Krieger) S.; m. Daryle Faith Wolfers, July 2, 1955; children: Jonathan Fredrick, Joel Philip Timothy. BA, Oberlin Coll., 1956; MD, Stanford U., 1960. Intern Kaiser Found. Hosp., San Francisco, 1960-61; resident in neurology Stanford (Calif.) U., 1961-64, fellow in neurology, 1964-66; staff neurologist VA Med. Ctr., Palo Alto, Calif., 1969-76; clin. investigator VA Med. Ctr., Portland, Oreg., 1976-79, staff neurologist, 1979-81, dir. VA office regeneration research programs, 1981—; asst. prof. neurology Stanford U., 1969-75, assoc. prof. neurology Oreg. Health Sci. U., Portland, 1976-78, prof. neurology, 1978—, prof. cell biology and anatomy, 1990—. Editor: Nerve, Organ and Tissue Regeneration: Research Perspectives, 1983, Neural Regeneration, 1987, 94, Current Issues in Neural Regeneration and Transplantation, 1989, Advances in Neural Regeneration Research, 1990, Neural Injury and Regeneration: 1993, Multiple Sclerosis: Current Status of Research and Treatment, 1994; contbr. articles to profl. jours. Served to capt. U.S. Army, 1966-68. Grantee VA, 1970—, NIH, 1986—. Mem. Internat. Brain Rsch. Orgn., Internat. Soc. Develop. Neurosci., Am. Neurol. Assn., Am. Assn. Neuropathologists, Soc. Neurosci., Soc. Exptl. Neuropathology. Democrat. Home: 10306 SW Radcliffe Rd Portland OR 97219-7956 Office: VA Med Ctr Office Regeneration Rs Portland OR 97201

SEILER, FRITZ ARNOLD, physicist; b. Basel, Switzerland, Dec. 20, 1931; came to U.S., 1980; s. Friedrich and Marie (Maibach) S.; m. Mary Catherine Coster, Dec. 22, 1964; children: Monica, Simone, Daniel. BA in Econs., Basel Sch. of Econs., 1951; PhD in Physics, U. Basel, 1962. Rsch. assoc. U. Wis., Madison, 1962-63; scientific assoc. U. Basel, 1963-69, privat dozent, 1969-75, dozent, 1975-80; sr. scientist Lovelace Inhalation Toxicology Inst., Albuquerque, 1980-90; sr. tech. assoc. IT Corp., Albuquerque, 1990-92, disting. tech. assoc., 1992—; cons. Swiss Dept. Def., 1968-74; vis. scientist Lawrence Berkeley Labs., 1974-75. Contbr. numerous articles to profl. jours. With Swiss Army staff, 1964-75. Fellow Am. Phys. Soc., Health Physics Soc., Soc. for Risk Analysis, Fachverband fuer Strahlenschutz, Am. Stats. Assn., Am. Nat. Stds. Inst. (mgmt. coun. 1987—, com. N14 1986—). Office: Internat Tech Corp 5301 Central Ave NE Ste 700 Albuquerque NM 87108-1515

SEILER, STEVEN LAWRENCE, health facility administrator; b. Chgo., Dec. 30, 1941; married. B, U. Ariz., 1963; M, U. Iowa, 1965. Adminstrv. resident Rush-Presbyn.-St. Luke's Med. Ctr., Chgo., 1965, adminstrv. asst., 1965-68; asst. adminstr. Lake Forest (Ill.) Hosp., 1968-71, adminstr., 1971-73, pres., 1973-86; exec. v.p Voluntary Hosps. Am., Park Ridge, Ill., 1987-89, sr. v.p., 1986-92; CEO Good Samaritan Regional Med. Ctr. Phoenix, 1992—; adj. prof. Contbr. articles to profl. jours. Mem. AHA (svc. com.), Ill. Hosp. Assn. (chair 1980-81). Home: 3930 E Rancho Dr Paradise Valley AZ 85253-5025 Office: Good Samaritan Regional Med Ctr 1111 E Mcdowell Rd Phoenix AZ 85006-2612*

SEIPEL, JOHN HOWARD, lawyer, neurologist, consultant, medical executive; b. Pitts., Nov. 9, 1925; s. John Howard and Marie Elizabeth (Schaser) S.; m. Janice Lois Duffney, July 4, 1959; children: Janice Marie, John Howard III, Tabitha Ann, William Joseph. BS in Chemistry, Carnegie-Mellon U., 1946, MS in Chemistry, 1947; PhD in Chemistry, Northwestern U., 1958; MD, Harvard U., 1954; JD, George Mason U., 1990. Diplomate in neurology, aviation, aerospace medicine, penologic medicine and clin. pharmacology Am. Bd. Forensic Examiners, Am. Bd. Forensic Medicine. Rotating intern Pa. Hosp., 1954-55, surg. resident, 1955-56; residency program in neurology Georgetown U. Med. Ctr., Washington, 1958-61, asst. resident, then chief resident Med. Ctr., 1959; chief resident D.C. Gen. Hosp., 1960; rsch. fellow in neurology Georgetown U., Washington, 1960-61, chief neurology lab. Georgetown Clin. Rsch. Inst. 1961-66, clin. instr. dept. neurology Georgetown Hosp., 1959-78, asst. prof. dept. neurology, 1978-79; chief electrodiagnostic sect. U.S. VA Hosp., Washington, 1967-69; dir. neurol. rsch. Md. Psychiat. Rsch. Ctr., Balt., 1969-78; chief med. officer D.C. Dept. Corrections, Lorton, Va., 1979—; sr. cons. in neurology Aviation Med. Svc., FAA, Washington, 1972—; cons. various orgns. in field, 1961—. Author: (monograph) The Biophysical Basis and Clinical Applications of Rheoencephalography, 1966 (S. Wier Mitchell award 1966); also book chpts., articles. Master Hunter Edn. instr. Va. Dept. Game and Wildlife, Richmond, 1976—. Capt. USPHS, 1956-58, maj. Res., 1965-81. Greenwalt fellow NYU, 1961. Fellow Brit. Royal Soc. Medicine, Am. Coll. Legal Medicine, Am. Coll. Clin. Pharmacology, Am. Coll. Forensic Examiners (life, bd. advisors for profl. stds. 1995); mem. So. Med. Assn., Va. State Bar Assn., D.C. Bar Assn., Izaac Walton League Am. (chpt. pres., state 1st v.p., other offices 1972—), Sigma Xi (sr.), Phi Lambda Upsilon, Phi Delta Phi. Home: 5335 Summit Dr Fairfax VA 22030-6523 Office: Central Facility PO Box 25 Lorton VA 22199-0025

SEITZ, RÜDIGER JÜRGEN, neurologist, medical educator; b. Hamburg, Germany, May 9, 1956; s. Dieter Rudolf and Elisabeth (Ziese) S.; m. Inès Louise Freiin von Uslar-Gleichen, Aug. 29, 1981; children: Richard, Bernhard, Christiane, Friedrich. Dr med, U. Hamburg, Germany, 1981; PhD, U. Düsseldorf, Germany, 1991. Cert. MD. Residency U. Düsseldorf, Germany, 1982-87; rsch. fellow Karolinska Inst., Stockholm, Sweden, 1987-89; cons. U. Düsseldorf, Germany, 1990—; head Neuro-PET Rsch. Lab., U. Düsseldorf, 1990—. Contbr. to profl jours. Recipient Hugo Spatz prize German Soc. Neurology, 1992. Mem. German Soc. Clin. Neurophysiology, Internat. Soc. Cereb. Blood Flow Metabolism, Soc. Neuroscience, German Soc. Neuropathology, German Soc. Neurology. Office: U Düsseldorf, MoorenstraBe 5, D-40225 Düsseldorf Germany

SEITZ, WALTER STANLEY, cardiovascular research consultant; b. L.A., May 10, 1937; s. Walter and Frances Janette (Schleef) S. BS in Physics and Math., U. Calif., Berkeley, 1959; PhD in Biophysics, U. Vienna, 1981, MD, 1982. Health physicist U. Calif. Radiation Lab., 1959-61; rsch. assoc. NIH at Pacific Union Coll., 1961-63; physicist Lockheed Rsch. Labs., Palo Alto, Calif., 1961-63; staff scientist Xerox Corp., Pasadena, Calif., 1963-66; sr, scientist Applied Physics Cons., Palo Alto, 1966-75; instr. clin. sci. U. Ill Coll. Medicine, Urbana, 1983-84; cons. cardiology Cardiovascular Rsch. Inst. U. Calif. Sch. Medicine, San Francisco, 1987—; sr. scientist Inst. Med. Analysis and Rsch., Berkeley, 1987—. Contbr. articles to profl. jours. Postdoctoral Rsch. fellow, U. Calif. San Francisco, 1984. Fellow Am. Coll. Angiography; mem. AAAS, Royal Soc. Medicine London, N.Y. Acad. Scis., Physicians for Social Responsibility. Office: IMAR Cons Inc 38 Panoramic Way Berkeley CA 94704-1828

SEITZ, WILLIAM HENRY, JR., orthopedic surgeon; b. N.Y.C., Jan. 12, 1950; s. William Henry and Catherine (Kehoe) S.; m. Susan Andrea Versenyi, June 4, 1972; children: David William, Eric Alexander, William Henry III, Elizabeth Andrea. BS, Fairfield U., 1971; grad. cert. phys. therapy, Columbia U., 1972, MD, 1979. Diplomate Am. Bd. Med. Examiners. Resident in gen. surgery St. Vincent's Med. Ctr., N.Y.C., 1979-81; resident in orthopaedic surgery Columbia Presbyn. Med. Ctr., N.Y.C., 1981-83, chief resident, 1983-84, Annie C. Kane fellow in hand surgery, 1984-85; clin. instr. Case Western Res. U., Cleve., 1985-87, asst. clin. prof., 1987-94, assoc. clin. prof., 1995—; head of hand and upper extremity surgery, orthop. rehab. Mr. Sinai Med. Ctr., Cleve., 1985—; cons. Nisonger Ctr. for Child Devel., Columbus, 1985—, Cuyahoga County Md. Mental Retardation, Cleve., 1986—. Editor Current Opinion in Orthops.-Hand and Wrist, 1994, 95; assoc. editor Jour. Hand Surgery, 1994—; reviewer JBJS, 1993—; contbr. articles to profl. jours. Pres. Shaker Heights (Ohio)ú Youth Soccer Assn., 1990-91, 91-92. Fellow Am. Acad. Orthopedic Surgeons; mem. Am. Soc. for Surgery of Hand (internat. traveling fellow 1992-93, Sterling Bunnell fellow 1992, Summer L. Koch award 1990), Am. Orthopedic Assn., Am. Shoulder and Elbow Surgeons Soc., Orthopedic Rsch. Soc., Orthopedic Trauma Assn. Roman Catholic. Home: 3398 Kenmore Rd Shaker Heights OH 44122 Office: Mount Sinai Med Ctr Dept Orthopedic Surgery 1 Mount Sinai Dr Cleveland OH 44106-4191

SEITZ-LUCIANO, JOANNE, women's health nurse, nurse practitioner; b. San Leandro, Calif., Oct. 23, 1963. BSN, U. San Francisco, 1985. RN, Calif.; cert. pub. health nurse; cert. ob-gyn. nurse; cert. as women's healthcare nurse practitioner and in reproductive endocrinology/infertility, ANCC. Staff nurse ob.-gyn. St. Rose Hosp., Hayward, Calif., 1985; pvt. practice Castro Valley, Calif., 1985-87; ob-gyn. nurse practitioner Miles E. Nuddleman, M.D., Castro Valley, 1987-95; clin. nurse coord., ob-gyn. nurse practitioner Biex Clin. Trials UCSF, San Francisco, 1995—. Mem. Pets are Wonderful Support, San Francisco, ARC, Oakland, Calif. Mem. Assn. Women's Health, Obstet. and Neonatal Nursing, Am. Assn. Nurse Practitioners, Calif. Coalition Nurse Practitioners, Am. Assn. Colposcopy and Cervical Pathology, Assn. Clin. Rsch. Nurses. Home: 17847 Kingston Way Castro Valley CA 94546-1128 Office: UCSF Dept Ob-Gyn/Reproductive Scis 505 Parnassus M1496-A San Francisco CA 94143-0132

SEIZINGER, BERND ROBERT, molecular geneticist, physician, researcher; b. Munich, Germany, Dec. 27, 1956; came to U.S., 1984; s. August and Mathilde (Haselbeck) S. MD, Ludwig-Maximilians U. Med. Sch, Munich, Germany, 1983; PhD summa cum laude, Max-Planck Inst., Munich, Germany, 1984. Postdoctoral rsch. assoc. Max Planck Inst. for Psychiatry, Munich, Germany, 1984; postdoctoral rsch. assoc. Harvard Med. Sch., Boston, 1984-86, instr. neurology, 1986-88, asst. prof., 1988-90, assoc. prof. neuroscience, 1990-95; dir. molecular neuro-oncology lab. Mass. Gen. Hosp., Boston, 1989-92, assoc. geneticist, 1990-95; v.p. oncology Bristol-Myers Squibb Pharm. Rsch. Inst., Princeton, N.J., 1992—, v.p. corp. and acad. alliances, 1995—; co-chmn. Internat. Consortium on Neurofibromatosis, N.Y.C., 1988—; chmn. Comm. on Gene Loss in Human Cancers Intern Human Gene Mapping Conf., Oxford, 1991, Rsch. Adv. Bd. Nat. Neurofibromatosis Found., N.Y.C., 1991—, co-chmn. 1993—; vis. rsch. scientist, assoc. mem. faculty Princeton (N.J.) U., 1993—. Recipient Otto Hahn Medal Max Planck Soc., Munich, 1983, Wilson S. Stone Meml. award Cancer Rsch., 1987, Rsch. Faculty Scholar award Am. Cancer Soc., 1989. Mem. Nat. Neurofibromatosis Found. (Von Recklinghausen award 1992, Jr. Investigators award 1985), Am. Soc. Human Genetics, Am. Assn. Cancer Rsch. Office: Bristol-Myers Squibb Pharm Rsch Inst PO Box 4000 Princeton NJ 08543-4000

SEKIGUCHI, JUNE, retired army officer, health professional; b. L.A., Aug. 31, 1941; d. Edgar Y. and Hayami (Ogimachi) S.; m. Roger Hopkins, May 20, 1983. Diploma, Queen of Angels Sch. Nursing, L.A., 1962; BSN and Pub. Health Nurse, Calif. State U., L.A., 1969; MS in Nursing, U. Tex., San Antonio, 1983. RN, Tex.; advanced cert. nurse adminstr. Chief med.-surg. nursing Ft. Carson, Colo., 1983; commd. capt. U.S. Army, 1970, advanced through grades to col., 1989; chief nursing edn. and staff devel. Evans U.S. Army Community Hosp., 1984-86; asst. chief nurse Walson Army Community Hosp., Ft. Dix, N.J., 1986-88; chief med.-surg. nursing, chief ambulatory nursing svc. Walter Reed Army Med. Ctr., Washington, 1988-93; ret., 1995; clin. instr. The Health Inst., San Antonio, 1995; program dir. traumatic brain injury unit Henry M. Jackson Found., San Antonio, 1995—. Mem. ANA (coun. nurse adminstrs.), Md. Nurses Assn., Sigma Theta Tau, Alpha Tau Delta. Office: Henry M Jackson Found The Health Inst San Antonio TX 78239

SEKITANI, TORU, otolaryngologist, educator; b. Kochi, Japan, May 5, 1932; s. Fusaharu and Miyoko (Tokushige) S.; m. Miyoko Uejo, Dec. 26, 1960; children: Miwako, Yoshiko, Tetsuko. MD, Yamaguchi Med. Sch., 1957. Intern Yamaguchi Med. Sch. Hosp., Ube, Japan, 1957-58, asst. prof., 1962, assoc. prof., 1971, prof., chmn. dept. otolaryngology, 1976-93; resident USAF Hosp., Fukuoka, 1959; emeritus prof. Yamaguchi U., Japan, 1993—; dir. Nat Shimonoseki Hosp, Japan; rsch. assoc. Univ. Iowa, Iowa City, 1969-71. Author: (with others) Vertigo: Basic and Clinic, 1976, Vestibular Mechanism in Health and Disease, 1978; editor: Vestibular Ganglia and Vestibular Neuronitis, 1988, Fundamentals of Galvanic Body Sway Test for Dizziness, 1995. Mem. Barany Soc. (Sweden), Prosper Meniere Soc. (U.S.A.), Otorhinolaryngological Soc. Japan, Japan Soc. Equilibrium and Rsch.

SEKOVSKI, BLAZE, physician; b. Macedonia, Sept. 12, 1954; came to U.S., 1969; s. Risto and Tonka (Surgunova) S.; m. Jasna Gojkovic, Apr. 22, 1977; children: Katerina, Lauren, Jessica. BS, Yale U., 1977; MD, Stanford U., 1981. Diplomate Am. Bd. Internal Medicine, Am. Bd. Cardiovascular Diseases. Intern, resident, then fellow in cardiology SUNY-Buffalo Affiliated Hosps., 1981-86; chief cardiology Sisters of Charity Hosp., 1992—; clin. assoc. prof. SUNY/Buffalo Sch. Medicine, 1992—. Fellow Am. Coll. Cardiology; mem. AMA, Am. Coll. Physicians. Democrat. Macedonian Orthodox. Home: 7 Hummingbird Ct Orchard Park NY 14127-2033 Office: Buffalo Med Group 85 High St Buffalo NY 14203-1149

SEKOWSKI, CYNTHIA JEAN, corporate executive, contact lens specialist; b. Chgo., Feb. 14, 1953; d. John L. and Celia L. (Matusiak) S. PhD in Health Svcs. Adminstrn., Columbia Pacific U., 1984, PhD in Health Scis.,

1984. Chief contact lens dept. Lieberman & Kraff, Chgo., 1974-87; pres., CEO Seko Eye Care, Inc., Chgo., 1988—; realtor-assoc. Country Club Realty Group, Naples, Fla., 1995—; researcher, technologist U. Ill., Chgo., 1976-78. Mem. Chgo. Zool. Soc., 1984—, Little City Inner Circle, 1991—; sponsor Save the Children Orgn., 1983—; asst. to campaign mgr. Rep. state senatorial candidate, Chgo., 1972; pres. Compass Point Condo Assn., Naples, Fla., 1996—; mem. budget com. Windstar Masters Assn., Naples. Fellow Contact Lens Soc. Am.; mem. Ill. Soc. Opticianry, Opticians Assn. Am., Better Vision Inst., Nat. Contact Lens Examiners, Fla. Assn. Realtors, Nat. Assn. Realtors, Naples Area Bd. of Realtors, Women's Coun. of Realtors, Nat. Geographic Soc., Columbia Pacific U. Alumnae Assn., Nat. Wildlife Fedn. Roman Catholic. Office: Country Club Realty Ste 105 2640 Golden Gate Pkwy Naples FL 34105

SEKULER, ROBERT WILLIAM, psychology educator, scientist; b. Elizabeth, N.J., May 7, 1939; s. Sidney and Mary (Siegel) S.; m. Susan Pamela Nemser, June 25, 1961; children: Stacia, Allison, Erica. A.B., Brandeis U., 1960; Sc.M., Brown U., 1963, Ph.D., 1964; postgrad. (NIH postdoctoral fellow), M.I.T., 1964-65. Prof. psychology Northwestern U., Evanston, Ill., 1973-89, chmn. dept., 1975-79, prof. ophthalmology Med. Sch., 1978-89, prof. neurobiology and physiology, 1982-89, assoc. dean Coll. Arts and Scis., 1985-89, John Evans prof. neurosci., 1986-89; v.p. Optronix, Inc., 1980-82; provost, dean of faculty Brandeis U., Waltham, Mass., 1989-91, Louis and Frances Salvage prof. psychology, 1989—; mem. Ctr. for Complex Systems, 1990—; rsch. prof. biomed. engring. Boston U., 1992—; adj. prof. cognitive and neural systems Boston U., 1994—; cons. NSF, NIH, AAAS, USAF, U. Calif, Am. Psychol. Assn.; chmn. NRC-Nat. Acad. Sci. Vision Com.; chmn. NRC working Group on Visual Function and Aging; chmn. NRC Working Group on Aging Workers and Visual Impairment. Author: (with D. Kline and K. Dismukes) Aging and Human Visual Function, 1981, (with R. Blake) Perception, 1985, 2d edit., 1990, 3d edit., 1994; editor: Perception & Psychophysics, 1971-86, Jour. Exptl. Psychology, 1973-74, Vision Rsch. Jour., 1974-79, 80-92, Optics Letters, 1977-79, Am. Jour. Psychology, Ophthalmic and Physiol. Optics, 1986—, Intelligent Systems, 1986-92, Psychology and Aging, 1987-92; contbr. Handbook of Geriatric Medicine, 1992; contbr. articles to profl. jours. Grantee Nat. Inst. Neurol. Diseases and Stroke, USAF, NSF, Nat. Eye Inst., Nat. Inst. Aging, USN, James McDonnell Found. Fellow AAAS, Optical Soc. Am., Am. Psychol. Soc.; mem. Assn. Rsch. in Vision and Ophthalmology, Neurosci. Soc., Internat. Neural Network Soc., Psychonomic Soc., Knowles Inst. for Hearing Rsch. (bd. dirs. 1988-90), Sigma Xi. Home: 64 Strawberry Hill Rd Concord MA 01742-5502 Office: Brandeis U Ctr for Complex Systems Waltham MA 02254

SELA, BEN-AMI, biochemist; b. Tel Aviv, June 5, 1944; s. Haim and Eva (Vrubel) S.; m. Etziona-Yoselson, Oct. 26, 1971; children: Karni, Yaron. MS, Tel Aviv U., 1969; PhD, Weitzmann Inst. Sci., Rehovot, Israel, 1973. Postdoctoral fellow The Rockefeller U., 1974-77; rsch. fellow Weitzmann Inst. Sci., Rehovot, 1977-79, sr. scientist, 1979-83; assoc. prof. Tel Aviv U., 1983-89; vis. scientist The Wistar Inst., Phila., 1987-89; dir. Inst. Chem. Pathology, Sheba Med. Ctr., Tel-Hashomer, Israel, 1989—. Lt. Israeli Med. Corps, 1962-94. Recipient award Israel Cancer Rsch. Fund, 1977; named incumbent of Bertram Blank chair German Cancer Rsch. Assn., 1979. Mem. Israel Biochem. Soc., Israel Clin. Chemistry Soc., Am. Assn. Clin. Chemistry. Home: 17 Kakal St, 76345 Rehovot Israel Office: Sheba Med Ctr, 52621 Tel Hashomer Israel

SELBY, COLIN DEREK, respiratory and critical care physician; b. Birmingham, Eng., Jan. 13, 1959; s. Derek and Joyce (Hammant) S.; m. Jacqueline Radbourne, 1985; children: Fiona Joy, Laura Helen. B Med. Sci. with honors, U. Nottingham, Eng., 1979, B Med., 1982, BS, 1982; DM, U. Nottingham, 1992. Registrar medicine Univ. Hosp., Nottingham, 1983-87; lectr. med. unit Hong Kong U., 1987; respiratory registrar Edinburgh (Scotland) Hosps., 1987-92; lectr. gen. and respiratory medicine U. Edinburgh, 1992-96; ALS instr. Rescusitation Coun., 1993—; mem. Scottish Intercollegiate Guidelines Network Asthma Working Party, 1994—. Contbr. articles to profl. jours. Life mem. John Muir Trust, Edinburgh, 1992—. Recipient Traveling fellowships Nottingham Med.-Surg. Soc., Hong Kong, 1987, BTS/Fisons, Miami, 1992. Mem. Brit. Thoracic Soc., Scottish Intensive Care Soc., Royal Coll. Physicians. Office: Dept Medicine, Queen Margaret Hosp, Dunfermline KY12 OSU, Scotland

SELBY, JOHN HORACE, surgeon; b. Springfield, Mass., Nov. 11, 1919; s. Howard Williams and Ethel (Wagg) S.; AB, Dartmouth Coll., 1941; MD, Boston U., 1944; postgrad. U. Pa., 1948; children by previous marriage: John H., Susan, Sherrill, Lucinda; m. 2d, Carolyn Symes, Feb. 14, 1970. Intern Mary Hitchcock Meml. Hosp., Hanover, N.H., 1944-45; resident New Eng. Deaconess Hosp., 1945-46, Portsmouth Naval Hosp., 1946-48, Mass. Meml. Hosp., 1949-50, Boston City Hosp., 1950-51 (all Boston), practice medicine, specializing in thoracic surgery, Lubbock, Tex., 1952—; chief thoracic surgery Meth. Hosp., Lubbock, 1964-73, 77-79, chief surgery, 1954-56, 64-65; chief of staff St. Mary's Hosp., Lubbock, 1973, chief surgery, 1970; chief surgery Univ. Hosp., 1973; active staff Meth. Hosp., St. Mary's, Health Scis. Center; dir. med. staff affairs Highland Hosp., 1986-92; hon. staff West Tex. Hosp.; cons. staff South Park Hosp., Meml., Seminole, Mercy, Slaton, Cook Meml., Levelland Hosps.; regional med. dir. Tex. Med. Found. Peer Rev. Orgn., 1986-94; med. dir. HMI, Inc, 1986-93; mem. med. care adv. com. Tex. Dept. Human Svcs., 1990-94, chmn. physician payment adv. com., 1991-94; chmn. bd. South Plains Health Systems, 1975-81; mem. Statewide Health Coordinating Coun., 1977-85, exec. com., 1979; clin. prof. surgery Tex. Tech. Med. Sch., 1975—; mem. adv. com. Lubbock County Hosp. Dist. Bd., 1979; trustee, med. dir. All Am. Security Life Ins. Co., 1954-55. Bd. dirs. Tex. Tb Assn., pres., 1967-68; bd. dirs. Lubbock Community Planning Council, 1954-56; chmn. adv. bd. Salvation Army, 1956-57; bd. dirs. Inst. for Internat. Rsch. and Devel.; bd. dirs. Lubbock Area Found., 1983—, treas., 1985. Diplomate Am. Bd. Thoracic Surgery, Am. Bd. Surgery. Fellow A.C.S., Am. Coll. Chest Physicians, Internat. Coll. Surgeons, Internat. Acad. Medicine, Southwestern Surg. Coll.; mem. So. Thoracic Surgery Assn., S.W. Surg. Conf., Am. Thoracic Soc., Tex. Trudeau Soc. (pres. 1959-60), Lubbock-Crosby-Garza County Med. Soc. (pres. 1984), Panhandle S-Plains Med. Soc., Tex. Med. Assn. (ho. of dels. 1979—, com. on health planning 1979-83, coun. on socioecons. 1983-90, chmn. 1985-90), AMA, Am. Cancer Soc. (dir. Tex. div. 1961-63), South Plains Heart Assn. (pres. 1957), Lubbock County Tb Assn. (pres. 1959-60, pres. South Plains Kidney Found. 1989—), Sigma Chi (Order Constantine 1994—). Club: Rotary Internat. (pres. Lubbock 1980-81, dist. gov.'s rep. 1981-82, gov. nominee 1982-83, gov. 1983-84, instr. nat. assembly 1985). Home: Park Tower 1617 27th St Lubbock TX 79405-1451 Office: 1500 Broadway Ste 1207 Lubbock TX 79401-3107

SELDIN, DONALD WAYNE, physician, educator; b. N.Y.C., Oct. 24, 1920; s. Abraham L. and Laura (Ueberal) S.; m. Muriel Goldberg, Apr. 1, 1943; children: Leslie Lynn, Donald Craig, Donna Leigh. BA, NYU, 1940; MD, Yale U., 1943; DHL (hon.), So. Meth. U., 1977; DSc (hon.), Med. Coll. Wis., 1980, Yale U., 1988; D honoris causa, Univ. de Paris VI, Pierre et Marie Curie, 1983. Diplomate Am. Bd. Internal Medicine (test com. on nephrology 1970-73). Intern New Haven Hosp., Yale U., 1943-44, resident, 1944-46, instr. medicine, 1948-50, asst. prof. internal medicine, 1950-51; mem. faculty U. Tex. Southwestern Med. Sch., Dallas, 1951—, William Buchanan prof. internal medicine, 1969—, Univ. Tex. System prof., 1988—, chmn. dept. internal medicine, 1952-88; chief med. service Parkland Meml. Hosp., Dallas, 1952—; chmn. dept. medicine Lisbon VA Hosp., Dallas; pres. Southwestern Med. Found., 1988—; cons. Baylor Hosp., St. Paul's Hosp., Presbyn. Hosp., Dallas, Brooke Army Hosp., Ft. Sam Houston, Walter Reed Army Hosp., Washington, also to Surgeon Gen. U.S., Surgeon Gen. USAF, and Eli Lilly Co., 1972—; mem. Bur. Budget, Exec. Office of Pres., 1966-67; chmn. dialysis and transplantation com. of sci. adv. bd. Nat. Kidney Found.; mem. bd. sci. councillors Nat. Inst. Arthritis and Metabolic Diseases, NIH, 1968-71; trustee Rand Corp., 1975-93, adv. trustee, 1993—. Editorial bd.: Jour. Lab. and Clin. Medicine, 1958-60, Nephron, The Clinician, Medicine, Mineral and Electrolyte Metabolism, 1977-79; cons. editor: Am. Jour. Medicine; assoc. editor: Kidney Internat., 1973-79; contbr. articles to profl. jours. Served as capt. U.S. Army, 1946-48. Recipient Disting. Achievement award Modern Medicine, 1977, John P. Peters award Am. Soc. Nephrology, 1983, Disting. U.S. Scientist award Alexander von Humboldt Found., 1989, John K. Lattimer award Am. Urol. Assn., 1989; Friedrich Von Muller hon. lectr. U. Munich, 1968. Master ACP (Disting. Teaching award 1980); Fellow Royal Soc. Medicine, Am. Acad. Arts and Sci.; mem. AMA, Dallas County Med. Soc., Tex. Med. Assn., Dallas Diabetes Assn., So. Soc. Clin. Investigation (pres. 1964, Founders medal 1975), Central Soc. Clin. Research (pres. 1963), Am. Fedn. Clin. Research, Am. Soc. Clin. Investigation (pres. 1966), Assn. Profs. Medicine (pres. 1971, Robert H. Williams Disting. Chmn. Medicine award 1977), Assn. Am. Physicians (pres. 1980, Kober medal 1985), Am. Physiol. Soc., Am. Soc. Nephrology (pres. 1968), Nat. Kidney Found. (David Hume award 1981), Am. Heart Assn., Am. Clin. and Climatol. Assn., Soc. Med. Cons. to Armed Forces, Internat. Soc. Nephrology (councillor 1973-78, pres. 1984-87), Southwestern Med. Found. (pres. 1988-93, vice chmn. 1993—), Australian Soc. Nephrology (hon.), Gesellschaft für Nephrologie, (Volhard medal 1986), Alpha Omega Alpha. Office: 5323 Harry Hines Blvd Dallas TX 75235-7200*

SELF, DANNY LEE, cardiac care nurse; b. Abingdon, Va., Aug. 11, 1969; s. Ralph Lee and Janice Gail (Bryant) S.; m. Selena Gail Artrip, Nov. 29, 1993. AD, Va. Appalachian Tricoll. Prog., Abingdon, 1993. RN, Va., Tenn. Nursing asst. Bristol (Va.-Tenn.) Regional Med. Ctr., 1989-93, cardiac care nurse, 1993—.

SELF, SHARON LYNN, nurse administrator, consultant; b. Cheverly, Md., Oct. 24, 1955; d. Herman Henry and Garnet Marie (Hines) S.; children: Jamin Nichole Stump, Leah Kesiah Stump. AS in Nursing, Shepherd Coll., 1977; BSN, W.Va. U., 1990; MS in Health Care Adminstrn., Med. Coll. Va., 1993. RN, W.Va.; cert. in infection control ANCC. Dir. svcs. Shanandoah Health Svcs., Martinsburg, W.Va., 1990-92; staff nurse City Hosp., Inc., Martinsburg, 1977-85, nursing mgr., 1985-90, dir. infection control, 1992—; mem. Region VIII Task Force for Adolescent Health, Franklin, W.Va., 1994-96. Bd. dirs. ARC, Martinsburg, 1994-96, AIDS Network, Hedgesville, W.Va., 1996—. Mem. Assn. Profls. in Infection Control, Martinsburg C. of C. (Goals 2000 com. 1992-94). Mem. LDS Ch. Office: City Hosp Inc Tavern and Dry Run Rds Martinsburg WV 25401

SELIB, STANLEY ZALMEN, psychotherapist, psychoneuroimmunologist; b. Boston, Mar. 20, 1929; s. Mitchell Samuel and Anna Selib; children: Steven, David. BS, Boston U., 1951; MEd, Harvard U., 1978. Lic. mental health counselor, Mass. Pres. Nat. Supply Assn. Am., Boston, 1956-77; pvt. practice Whole Health Assn., Watertown, Mass., 1980-86, Ctr. for Health, Newton, Mass., 1986-89, Newton, Mass., 1989—; cons. Am. Holistic Med. Assn., LaCrosse, Wis., 1981; bd. dirs. Interface Found., Boston, 1982-83; treas., dir. Vt. Healing Tools Project; dir. Mind, Body, Spirit Inst.; practitioner "Psychology of Mind", 1994—. Contbr. articles to profl. jours. Cpl. U.S. Army, 1951-53. Recipient Key to City, Louisville, 1975. Fellow Internat. Assn. Cancer Counselors (cert. clin. mental health counselor); mem. Am. Acad. Med. Psychotherapists (assoc.), Assn. Humanistic Psychology (assoc.). Office: 9 Beacon Pl # 1 Newton MA 02159-1550

SELIBER-KLEIN, JUNE, physician; b. Chgo., Apr. 13, 1960. MD, Rush Med. Coll., 1986. Diplomate Am. Bd. Psychiatry and Neurology. Med. dir. Sleep Disorder Ctr., Salinas, Calif. Mem. Am. Acad. Neurology, Alpha Omega Alpha. Office: Klein Med Group Inc 335 Katherine Salinas CA 93901

SELIGMANN, MAXIME GÉRARD, medical educator; b. Paris, Mar. 14, 1927; s. Armand Pierre and Antoinette (Baer) S.; m. Francoise Henriette Brolliet, MAr. 11, 1953; children: Christophe, Virginie, Francois. MD, Med. Sch., Paris, 1955. Researcher Inst. Pasteur, Paris, 1953-61; assoc. prof. Med. Sch., Paris, 1961-71; head rsch. unit INSERM Hosp. St. Louis, Paris, 1965-87; prof. immunology Med. Sch. U., Paris, 1971—; head dept. immunology, hematology Hosp. St. Louis, Paris, 1963-93; chmn. scientific coms. INSERM, Paris. Contbr. articles to profl. jours. Fellow Royal Coll. Physicians (U.K.); mem. Am. Assn. Physicians (hon.). Home: 80 rue d'Assas, 75006 Paris France Office: Hosp St Louis, 1 Ave Cl Vellefaux, 75475 Paris 10, France

SELIGSON, FREDERIC LEE, physician, cardiothoracic surgeon; b. Erie, Pa., July 12, 1956. BA, Dartmouth Coll., 1978; MD, U. Pitts., 1982. Diplomate Am. Bd. Thoracic Surgery, Am. Bd. Surgery. Intern, resident in surgery Beth Israel Hosp., Boston, 1982-87; resident in cardiothoracic surgery U. Ill., Chgo., 1987-89; cardiothoracic surgeon Thoracic and Vascular Surgeons, P.C., Prairie Village, Kans., 1989—. Office: Thoracic/Vascular Surgeons 4121 W 83d St # 132 Prairie Village KS 66208

SELIGSON, M. ROSS, psychologist; b. Balt., May 18, 1949; s. Joseph Jerome and Dorothy G. (Greenfeld) S. B.A., U. Md., 1971; Ed.M., Loyola Coll., Balt., 1975; Ph.D., Calif. Sch. Profl. Psychology, 1979. Lic. psychologist, Fla. Clin. psychology intern Long Beach (Calif.) Neuropsychiat. Inst. and Hosp., 1975-76, Orange Coast Coll. Student Health Ctr., Costa Mesa, Calif., 1976-77; psychology field trainee sect. on legal psychiatry UCLA, 1977-78; clin. psychologist Logansport (Ind.) State Hosp. (Isaac Ray Unit), 1978-80, South Fla. State Hosp., Hollywood, 1980-83, Counseling Affiliates, Inc., Ft. Lauderdale, 1981—; chmn. exec. com. Av-Med. Health Plan, Miami, 82 clin. dir. North Miami Community Mental Health Ctr.; AIDS educator to gen. pub.; staff writer Women's Issues, Ft. Lauderdale, 1982; mem. adj. faculty Barry U., 1982, Nova U., 1982-83; cons. N. Broward Hosp. Dist. Urgent Care Ctr., HIV partial hospitalization program CPC Ft. Lauderdale Hosp., 1993—, Fla. Lighthouse for HIV, 1994—; guest appearances include Factline, Selkirk TV Cable Sta., also radio programs. Editor: (with Dr. Karen Peterson) AIDS Prevention and Treatment: Hope Humor and Healing, 1992; contbr. articles to profl. jours. Mem. North Area Adv. Bd. of Regional Mental Health Team of Newport Beach, Costa Mesa and Irvine, Calif., 1976; chairperson edn. subcom. AIDS counseling and edn. project Hospice Care of Broward County, 1988—; chairperson mental health subcom. Broward County AIDS Task Force, 1989. Calif. Sch. Profl. Psychology scholar, 1976; recipient cert. of appreciation Am. Bus. Women's Assn., 1982. Mem. Wash. Area Counsel on Alcohol and Drug Abuse, Calif. Psychol. Assn., Am. Psychol. Assn., Fla. Psychol. Assn. (founder, chairperson AIDS network, Broward County rep., Early Career Contbns. award 1990), Fla. Assn. Practicing Psychologists, Broward County Psychol. Assn. (mem exec. com., pres., founder). Democrat. Jewish. Rsch. on psychol. adjustment, social history factors and tng. performance measures as predictors of suicide prevention. Office: Galleria Profl Bldg 915 Middle River Dr Ste 212 Fort Lauderdale FL 33304-3560

SELINGER, SAMUEL LEE, cardiothoracic surgeon; b. N.J., Oct. 16, 1943; s. Samuel and Stella Selinger; m. Rosemary S. Shone, June 1, 1969; children: Roanne, Matthew. AB, Princeton U., 1965; MD, Johns Hopkins U., 1969. Diplomate Am. Bd. Surgery, Am. Bd. Thoracic Surgery. Intern Mass. Gen. Hosp., Boston, 1969-70, resident in gen. surgery, 1970-72, 74-76, chief resident, 1971-77; pvt. practice Spokane, Wash., 1978—; bd. dirs., past pres. Heart Inst. Spokane. Fellow ACS, Am. Coll. Cardiology, Am. Coll. Chest Physicians; mem. Soc. Thoracic Surgeons, Western Thoracic Surgery Assn., Rotary. Office: 122 W 7th Ave Ste 330 Spokane WA 99204-2329

SELKER, ROBERT GEORGE, neurophysician, researcher; b. Pitts., July 25, 1930; s. Manuel and Bessie (Miller) S.; m. Ellen Ruth Goldenberg, July 5, 1959; children: Adam Paul, Mark David. BS, U. Pitts., 1953, MD, 1957. Diplomate Am. Bd. Neurological Surgery; lic. Conn., Pa., Ga., Ill. Rotating intern Med. Ctr. Hosps. U. Pitts., 1957-58; asst. resident in gen. surgery Hosps. U. Pa., 1958-59, asst. resident in neurosurgery, 1959-61, chief resident, 1961-63; Harrison fellow dept. surgical rsch. U. Pa., 1958-59; vice chmn. dept. neurosurgery U. Pitts., 1973-83, prof. neurosurgery, 1971-90, clin. prof., 1990-93; dir. Ctr. Neuro-Oncology West Pa. Cancer Inst., Pitts., 1990—; chief divsn. neurosurgery West Pa. Hosp., Pitts., 1990—, chmn. dept. surgery, 1992—; protocol devel. com. Pitts. Cancer Inst., 1987-90; profl. adv. com. Keystone Peer Rev. Orgn., 1985—; presenter in field. Contbr. numerous articles to profl. pubs. including Jour. Neuro-Oncology, Neurosurgery, Surgical Neurology, others; patentee in field. Sgt. FC U.S. Army, 1951-52, Korea. Schering-Plough Rsch. grantee, 1995-97, NIH grantee, 1994-96, Nat. Cancer Inst. grantee, 1994-96, others. Fellow ACS (pres. southwestern chpt. 1984-85, coun. mem. 1980-87); mem. AAAS, Am. Assn. Neurological Surgeons (mem. various coms.), Am. Assn. Neurological Surgeons Pediat. Section, Assn. Acad. Surgery, Congress Neurological Surgeons (mem. various coms.), Internat. Clin. Hyperthermia Soc., Internat. Soc. Pediat. Neurosurgery, Mid-Atlantic Neurosurgical Soc. (v.p. 1977-78, pres. 1978-79),. Home: 27 Glen Rdige Ln Pittsburgh PA 15243 Office: West Pa Neurosurgery care 4800 Friendship Ave Pittsburgh PA 15224

SELL, KENNETH WALTER, pathologist, educator; b. Valley City, N.D., Apr. 29, 1931; s. Walter Robert and Patricia Haldora (Gottskalkson) S.; Dec. 20, 1950; children—Gregory, Thomas, Barbette, Susan. B.A., U. N.D., 1953, B.S., 1954; M.D., Harvard U., 1956; Ph.D., Cambridge (Eng.) U., 1968. Diplomate Am. Bd. Pediatrics, Am. Bd. Pathology. Commd. capt. M.C. U.S. Navy, 1956; intern Nat. Naval Med. Center, Bethesda, Md., 1956-57; resident, pediatrician Nat. Naval Med. Center, 1956-65, dir. Navy tissue bank, 1965-70, chmn. dept. clin. and exptl. immunology, 1970-74, inst. comdg. officer, 1974-77; ret., 1977; sci. dir. Nat. Inst. Allergy and Infectious Diseases, Bethesda, 1977-85; prof. and chmn. dept. pathology Emory U., Atlanta, 1985—; dir. Emory Cancer Ctr., 1985-92. Editor: Tissue Banking for Transplantation, 1976. Decorated Legion of Merit. Fellow Am. Acad. Pediatrics, Am. Acad. Pathology; mem. AMA, Soc. Cryobiology, Transplantation Soc., Am. Assn. Immunologists, Soc. Exptl. Hematology, Am. Assn. Tissue Banks (pres.), Am. Coll. Pathology, Am. Soc. Microbiology, Phi Beta Kappa, Sigma Xi, Phi Beta Pi. Home: 2860 Greystone Ln Atlanta GA 30341-5860 Office: Dept Pathology 703 WMB Emory U Sch Medicine Atlanta GA 30322

SELL, LARRY JOHN, health facility administrator; b. Cleve., Mar. 17, 1940; s. Harold Henry and Frances (Winberg) S.; m. Nancy L. Newton, Nov. 21, 1967; children: Jeff, Shelly. BA, No. Mich. U., 1962; MD, U. Mich., 1966. Bd. cert. family medicine Am. Acad. Family Physicians. Intern, resident St. Joe's Mercy, Ann Arbor, Mich., 1966-68; dir. emergency rm. and indsl. medicine Redford Med. Ctr., Detroit, 1967-68; pvt. practice family practitioner Manistique (Mich.) Med. Dental Ctr., 1968-79; dir. primary care ctr. Detroit Receiving Hosp./Univ. Health Ctr., 1980, v.p. ambulatory care, 1980-83; v.p., med. dir. Blue Cross Blue Shield of Mich., Detroit, 1983-85, sr. v.p., med. dir., 1985-89; pres. Med. Mgmt. Assn., Inc., Madison Heights, Mich., 1989—; med. dir. Lakefield Nursing Home, McMillan, Mich., 1967-79; founder, past pres. Manistique (Mich.) Med.-Dental Ctr., 1967-79; dir. edn. Satellite Clinics and Med. Student Programs, Schoolcraft Meml. Hosp., Manistique, 1967-79; med. examiner Schoolcraft County, Mich., 196-69; clin. instr. U. Mich., Manistique, 1968-79; mem. liaison coun. Am. Acad. Med. Dirs., 1979-89; mem. Blue Cross and Blue Shield Assn. Adv. Bd., 1983-89; past bd. mem. Diversified Technologies, 1983-85; mem. Med. Ethics Resource Coun., 1983-91, Health Tech. Assocs. Adv. Panel, 1989—; bd. mem. Mich. Health Edn. and Rsch. Found., Inc., 1983-89, Greater Detroit Area Health Coun., 1984-85, exec. com., 1984-85; bd. mem. UNI/CARE Sys., Inc., 1985-90, Health Svc. Co., 1985. Mem., past chmn., past vice-chmn., bd. control No. Mich. U., Marquette, 1975-83; past mem. nat. bd. dirs. Boy Scouts Am., 1980-86; mem. Gov.'s Task Force on Health Care Costs, Mich., 1983-89; chmn. Gov.'s Blue Ribbon Commn. on AIDS, Mich., 1983-84. Named Man of Yr., Snow-Goer Mag., 1973-74. Mem. Am. Acad. Family Physicians, Am. Assn. Automotive Medicine, Am. Acad. Emergency Physicians (charter), Mich. State Med. Soc. (med. licensure and discipline com. 1983-89), Wayne County Med. Soc., Coll. Physician Execs. Home: 37508 Legends Trail Farmington Hills MI 48331 Office: Med Mgmt Assocs Inc 25179 Dequindre Madison Heights MI 48071

SELLER, ROBERT HERMAN, cardiologist, family physician; b. Phila., Mar. 21, 1931; s. David and Elsie (Straussman) S.; m. Maxine Schwartz, June 3, 1956; children: Michael, Douglas, Stuart. A.B., U. Pa., 1952, M.D., 1956. Intern. Grad. Hosp. of U. Pa., Phila., 1956-57; research asst. dept. pharmacology U. Pa., 1953-55; resident in cardiology, research fellow Am. Heart Assn., Phila. Gen. Hosp., 1957-58; resident in internal medicine Albert Einstein Med. Ctr., Phila., 1958-59; chief resident Albert Einstein Med. Ctr., 1959-60; instr. medicine Hahnemann Med. Coll. and Hosp., Phila., 1960-64; asst. prof. Hahnemann Med. Coll. and Hosp., 1964-69, assoc. prof., 1969-72, dir. Service F, 1962-67, asst. coordinator mil. edn. for nat. def., 1961-64, dir. div. family medicine, 1967-72, acting chmn. dept. family medicine and community health, 1972-74, prof. medicine, family medicine and community health, 1973-74; practice medicine, specializing in cardiology Buffalo, 1974—; prof., chmn. dept. family medicine, prof. medicine SUNY-Buffalo, Deaconess Hosp., 1974-82, chmn. dept. family practice and dir. family practice residency program, 1974-82; prof. medicine and family medicine SUNY-Buffalo, 1974—. Author: Differential Diagnosis of Common Complaints, 1986, 3d edit., 1996; contbr. articles to profl. jours. NIH grantee, 1972-75; Deaconess Hosp. family practice resident tng. grantee, 1975—; health professions spl. projects grantee, 1975—. Fellow ACP, Am. Coll. Cardiology, Am. Acad. Family Physicians, Phila. Coll. Physicians; mem. AMA, N.Y. Med. Soc., Erie County Med. Soc., Am. Fedn. Clin. Research, Am. Heart Assn., Soc. of Tchrs. of Family Medicine, N.Y. Acad. Sci., N.Y. Acad. Family Physicians. Home: 125 Crestwood Ln Buffalo NY 14221-1462 Office: 1542 Maple Rd Buffalo NY 14221-3625

SELLER, STEVEN MARK, pharmacist; b. Buffalo, June 2, 1952; s. Marvin Philip Seller and Molly (Kramer) Lettman. BS in Natural Sci., Niagara U., 1974; BS in Pharmacy, Mass. Coll. Pharmacy, 1976. Clin. rotation Beth Israel Hosp., Boston, 1976; pharmacist CVS Pharmacy, Braintree, Mass., 1977-78; pharmacy mgr. Mall Drugs, Boston, 1978; store and pharmacy mgr. Wagner Leader Drugs, Buffalo, 1978-80; pharmacy mgr. James Super Drug, Buffalo, 1980-83; pharmacist Buffalo RX Ctr., 1983-85; clin. instr. Sch. Pharmacy SUNY, Buffalo, 1984-87; pharmacist Health Care Plan, Buffalo, 1985-94; clin. pharmacy dir. Brookside Park Pharmacy, East Aurora, N.Y., 1994—; cons. pharmacist to nursing homes, pharm. cos. and PBM's, 1983—. Bd. rev. Jour. Cons. Pharmacist, 1990-93. Mem. Mason, Albright-Knox Art Gallery. Fellow Am. Soc. Cons. Pharmacists (upstate dir. N.Y. state chpt. 1985-95, orgnl. affairs coun. 1990-91), Alumni Assn. Mass. Coll. Pharmacy, Nat. Alumni Assn. Niagara U. Democrat. Jewish. Home: 75 Groton Dr # B Buffalo NY 14228-2545 Office: Brookside Park Pharmacy 268 Main St East Aurora NY 14052

SELLERS, SCOTT EUGENE, physician; b. Hutchinson, Kans., Aug. 15, 1958; s. Harold E. and Elanor M. (Frederick) S.; m. Michelle G. Knight, July 31, 1982; children: Tiffany N., Tyler S. BS in Cell Biology, U. Kans., 1980; DO, Kirksville Coll. Osteo. Med., 1985. Diplomate Am. Osteo. Bd. Family Practice. Pvt. practice Med. Ctr., Hutchinson, 1986-93; dir. emergency svcs. Hutchinson Hosp., 1994—; med. dir. Buhler (Kans.) EMS, 1995—. Mem. Am. Osteo. Assn., Am. Osteo. Coll. Family Practice, Kans. Med. Soc., Kans. Assn. Osteo. Medicine (2d v.p.).

SELLEVOLD, OLAV FREDRIK MÜNTER, anesthesiologist; b. Oslo, July 31, 1947; s. Ragnar and Astrid (Münter) S.; m. Anne Brit Misund; children: Fredrik Ragnar, Kristin Liv, Jorgen Tormod. MD, U. Bergen, Norway, 1974; specialist in anesthesiology, U. Trondheim, Norway, 1981, PhD, 1988. Gen. practice medicine, 1976; trainee in pediatrics Haukeland Hosp., Bergen, 1976; trainee in anesthesiology U. Hosp., Trondheim, 1977, 80—, trainee in cardiology, 1979-80, prof. anesthesiology, 1996—; rsch. fellow, 1982-85; cons. Univ. Hosp., Trondheim, 1986—, dir. cardiac anesthesia/intensive care, 1993—, prof. anaesthesiology, 1996—. Author: Glucocorticoids in Myocardial Protection. Bd. dirs. several nat. and internat. orgns. Mem. European Assn. Cardiothoracic Anesthesiology (dep. chmn. 1993-95, chmn. 1995—), Norwegian Soc. Anesthesiology (chmn. 1991-93). Home: Heimstadvn 16, N 7040 Trondheim Norway

SELLIG, ROBERT GEORGE, orthopedist; b. Webster, Mass., May 14, 1941; s. George A. and Marion G. (Melican) S.; m. Sara Grafton; children: Thomas, Elizabeth, Kathryn. BA, Harvard U., 1962; MD, U. Vt., 1966. Cert. Am. Bd. Orthopedic Surgery, 1975. Resident in orthopedic surgery U. Pitts., 1971-73; active staff Glens Falls (N.Y.) Hosp., 1974—. Fellow Am. Acad. Orthopedic Surgeons, ACS, AMA. Office: 88 Broad St Glens Falls NY 12801-4382

SELLITTO, LARRY AUDENO, psychotherapist; b. Greensburg, Pa., Aug. 24, 1955; s. Francesco and Colomba (Stile) S.; m. Karen A. Jackson, Mar. 4, 1989. AS, Salem Coll., 1975; BS, U. Pitts., 1978, MEd, 1984, PhD, 1987. Cert. addiction counselor, Pa.; nat. cert. counselor; internat. cert. alcohol and drug counselor. Detox coord. Monsour Med. Ctr., Jeannette, Pa., 1978-80; psychotherapist Mon-Yough Drug and Alcohol Services, Greensburg, Pa., 1980-82; project coord. St. Francis Med. Ctr., Pitts., 1982-93; program dir. Profls. Edn. Network, Monroeville, Pa., 1987—; cons. physician's health programs Pa. Med. Soc., Harrisburg, 1987—, profls. health monitoring program Pa. Nurses Assn., Harrisburg, 1988—. Psychol. cons. Monroeville (Pa.) Drug and Alcohol Task Force, 1982-86, Penn Hills (Pa.) Family Support Group, 1986-89; chmn. Health and Welfare Coun., Monroeville, 1988-

89; sec., bd. dirs. Jeanette Midget Athletic Assn., 1989—; bus. mgr. Keystone Bantam League, 1995—. Named Outstanding Young Educator Monroeville Jaycees, 1985, Outstanding Young Phys. Leader Jeannette Jaycees, 1986. Mem. Pa. Psychol. Assn., Nat. Assn. Alcoholism and Drug Abuse Counselors, Pa. Assn. Alcohol and Drug Abuse Counselors (cert. bd. dirs. 1995—), Pa. Coalition Addictive Diseases, Pitt Golden Panthers, Laural Valley Corvette Club, Westmoreland County Coaches Assn. Republican. Roman Catholic. Office: Profls Education Network 2550 Mosside Blvd Ste 101 Monroeville PA 15146-3531

SELLKE, FRANK WILLIAM, cardiothoracic surgeon, researcher; b. Ft. Wayne, Ind., Feb. 5, 1956; s. Erwin A. and Anna Luise (Schumacher) S.; m. Amy Marie Brill, Jan. 31, 1987; children: Michelle, Eric, Nicholas. AB summa cum laude, Wabash Coll., 1978; MD, Ind. U., Indpls., 1981. Diplomate Am. Bd. Thoracic Surgery, Am. Bd. Surgery. Intern Ind. U. Hosp., Indpls., 1981-82; emergency physician Culver Union Hosp., Crawfordsville, Ind., 1982-83; resident in surgery Akron (Ohio) City Hosp., 1983-87; postdoctoral fellow cardiac surgery U. Iowa, Iowa City, 1987-90; from instr. to asst. prof. surgery Harvard Med. Sch., Boston, 1990-95, assoc. prof. surgery, 1995—; cardiothoracic surgeon Beth Israel Hosp., Boston, 1990—. Contbr. rsch. articles to profl. jours. Fellow Am. Coll. Cardiology, Am. Coll. Surgeons; mem. AMA, Am. Heart Assn., Am. Physiol. Soc., Am. Coll. Chest Physicians, Soc. Univ. Surgeons, Assn. Acad. Surgeons, Am. Assn. for Thoracic Surgery, Soc. Thoracic Surgeons, Phi Beta Kappa. Lutheran. Home: 121 Monadnock Rd Chestnut Hill MA 02167-1136 Office: Beth Israel Hosp 330 Brookline Ave Boston MA 02215-5400

SELLS, ROBERT ANTHONY, surgeon; b. Leamington, England, Apr. 13, 1938; s. William Blyth and Eleanor Mary S.; m. Paula Gilchrist, Nov. 5, 1977; children: Rupert, Henry, Catherine, Edward, Patrick. MB, BS, U. London, Guy's Hosp., 1962, MRCS, LRCP, 1962. House officer Guy's Hosp., London, 1961-62; rsch. asst. Guy's Hosp., Dept. Medicine, London, 1962-63; asst. lectr. Guy's Hosp., Dept. Anatomy, London, 1963-65; lectr., surgery Guy's Hosp., London, 1967-68; asst. dir. rsch. U. Cambridge, Dept. Surgery, 1968-69; sr. lectr. U. Liverpool, Dept. Surgery, 1971-74; dir. Mersey Regional Transplant Unit, cons. gen. surgeon Royal Liverpool Hosp., 1972—; v.p. Transplantation Soc., chmn. ethical com. Editor: Transplantation Today, 1983, Organ Transplantation-Current Clinical and Immunoloogical Concepts, 1989. Conductor Crosby Symphony Orch., Liverpool, 1985—. Travelling scholar Harvard Med. Sch., Dept. Surgery, Boston, 1970-71. Mem. British Transplantation Soc., Surg. Rsch. Soc., Am. Soc. Transplant Surgeons, Moynihan Chirurgical Travelling Club, XX Club. Office: Royal Liverpool Hosp, Prescot St, L7 8XP Liverpool England

SELMAN, HAROLD W., psychiatrist; b. N.Y.C., Feb. 13, 1949. MD, Chgo. Med. Sch., 1976. Diplomate in psychiatry Am. Bd. Psychiatry and Neurology. Pvt. practice psychiatry N.Y.C. and Manhasset, N.Y. Mem. AMA, Am. Psychiat. Assn. Office: 37 Orchard St Manhasset NY 11030

SELTSER, RAYMOND, epidemiologist, educator; b. Boston, Dec. 17, 1923; s. Israel and Hannah (Littman) S.; m. Charlotte Frances Gale, Nov. 16, 1946; children: Barry Jay, Andrew David. MD, Boston U., 1947; MPH, Johns Hopkins U., 1957. Diplomate Am. Bd. Preventive Medicine (trustee, sec.-treas. 1974-77), Am. Bd. Med. Specialties (mem. exec. com. 1976-77). Asst. chief med. info. and intelligence br. U.S. Dept. Army, 1953-56; epidemiologist div. internal health USPHS, 1956-57; from asst. prof. to prof. epidemiology Johns Hopkins U. Sch. Hygiene and Pub. Health, 1957-81, assoc. dean, 1967-77, dep. dir. Oncology Ctr., 1977-81; dean U. Pitts. Grad. Sch. Pub. Health, 1981-87, prof. epidemiology, 1981-88, emeritus dean, prof. epidemiology, 1988—; assoc. dir. USPHS Ctrs. for Disease Control, Rockville, Md., 1988-90; assoc. dir. Ctr. for Gen. Health Svcs. Extramural Rsch. Agy. for Health Care Policy and Rsch., Rockville, 1990—; cons. NIMH, 1958-70, also various govtl. health agys., 1958-79; expert cons. Pres.'s Commn. on Three Mile Island, 1979-80; mem. Three Mile Island Adv. Panel Health, Nat. Cancer Inst. Cancer Control Grant Rev. Com., Pa. Dept. Health Preventive Health Service Block Grant Adv. Task Force, Gov.'s VietNam Herbicide Info. Commn. Pa.; chmn. Toxic/Health Effects Adv. Com., 1985-87. Trustee, mem. exec. com., chmn. profl. adv. com. Harmarville Rehab. Ctr., Pitts., 1982-87; bd. dirs. Health Edn. Ctr., Media Info. Service. Served to capt. AUS, 1951-53, Korea. Decorated Bronze Star; recipient Centennial Alumni citation Boston U. Sch. Medicine, 1973; elected to Johns Hopkins Soc. of Scholars, 1986. Fellow AAAS, APHA (mem. governing coun. 1975-77, chmn. EPI sect. coun. 1979-80), Pa. Pub. Health Assn. (bd. dirs. 1985-88, pres.-elect 1986-88), Am. Coll. Preventive Medicine, Am. Heart Assn.; mem. Am. Epidemiol. Assn., Internat. Epidemiol. Assn., Am. Soc. Preventive Oncology, Am. Cancer Soc. (bd. dirs. Pa. divsn. 1985-87, mem. exec. com. 1986-87), Assn. Schs. Pub. Health (sec. 1969-71, mem. exec. com., chmn. edn. com. 1983-87), Soc. Med. Cons. Armed Forces, Soc. Epidemiologic Rsch., Nat. Coun. Radiation Protection and Measurements (consociate), Johns Hopkins Alumni Coun. (mem. exec. com. 1994—), Am. Disability Prevention and Wellness Assn. (bd. dirs. 1996—), Sigma Xi, Delta Omega. Office: Agy Health Care Policy Rsch 2101 E Jefferson St Rockville MD 20852

SELTZER, RONALD ANTHONY, radiologist, educator; b. Washington, Mar. 7, 1935; s. Lawrence H. and Sarah (Levin)S.; m. Adele Wishnow, June 25, 1961; children: Jeffrey David, Lauren Jill. AB with distinction, U. Mich., 1956; MD with high distinction, Wayne State U., 1960. Diplomate Am. Bd. Radiology. Resident in radiology Mass. Gen. Hosp., Boston, 1961-62, 64-66; asst. prof. radiology Stanford (Calif.) U. Med. Sch., 1966-67, asst. clin. prof., 1967-73, assoc. clin. prof., 1974-89; pvt. practice San Mateo, Redwood City,, Calif., 1967; mem. med. staff Mills Meml. Hosp., San Mateo, Calif., 1967-69; mem. med. staff Sequoia Hosp., Redwood City, 1969—, pres., 1986-88; cons. on radiation exposure divsn. radiol. health USPHS, 1964-67; cons. on nuclear medicine Palo Alto VA Hosp., 1967-75; cons. on computerized reporting in radiology GE, 1975-78; cons. advanced imaging divsn. Xerox Corp., 1978-82; cons. on electronic imaging Stanford Rsch. Internat., 1980-84; bd. dirs. Hosp. Consortium San Mateo County, 1986-88. Contbr. articles on biol. behavior and radiation dosimaty of radioactive materials, diagnostic radiology and uses of computers in medicine to med. jours. Sr. asst. surgeon USPHS, 1962-64. Fellow Inst. Cardiology Gt. Britain; mem. AMA, Calif. Med. Assn., Radiol. Soc. N.Am., Am. Roentgen Ray Soc., Western Angiography Soc. (pres. 1976-78), San Mateo County Ind. Practice Assn. (bd. dirs. Bay Pacific Health Plan 1979-84), Alpha Omega Alpha. Home: 140 Degas Rd Portola Valley CA 94028-7709 Office: Sequoia Hosp Med Staff Redwood City CA 94062

SELTZER, VICKI LYNN, obstetrician-gynecologist; b. N.Y.C., June 2, 1949; d. Herbert Melvin and Marian Elaine (Willinger) S.; m. Richard Stephen Brach, Sept. 2, 1973; children: Jessica Lillian, Eric Robert. BS, Rensselaer Poly. Inst., 1969; MD, NYU, 1973. Diplomate Am. Bd. Ob-Gyn. Intern Bellevue Hosp., N.Y.C., 1973-74, resident in ob-gyn, 1974-77; fellow gynecol. cancer Am. Cancer Soc., N.Y.C., 1977-78, Meml. Sloan Kettering Cancer Ctr., N.Y.C., 1978-79; assoc. dir. gynecol. cancer Albert Einstein Coll. Medicine, N.Y.C., 1979-83; assoc. prof. ob-gyn., SUNY, Stony Brook, N.Y.C., 1983-89; prof. ob-gyn. Albert Einstein Coll. Medicine, 1989—; chmn. ob-gyn. L.I. Jewish Med. Ctr., 1993—; dir. ob-gyn., Queens Hosp. Ctr., Jamaica, N.Y., 1983-93, pres. med. bd., 1986-89. Author: Every Woman's Guide to Breast Cancer, 1987; editor-in-chief: Primary Care Update for the Ob-Gyn, 1993—; editor: Women's Primary Health Care, 1995; mem. editorial bd. Women's Life mag., 1980-82, Jour. of the Jacobs Inst. Women's Health, 1990—; contbr. over 75 articles to profl. jours.; host Weekly Ob-Gyn. TV Program, Lifetime Med. TV. Chmn. health com. Nat. Coun. Women, N.Y.C., 1979-84; mem. Mayor Beame's Task Force on Rape, N.Y.C., 1974-76; bd. govs. Regional Coun. Women in Medicine, 1985—; chmn. Coun. on Resident Edn. in Ob-Gyn., 1987-93. Galloway Fund fellow 1975; recipient citation Am. Med. Women's Assn., 1973, Nat. Safety Coun., 1978, Achiever award Nat. coun. Women, 1985, Achiever award L.I. Ctr. Bus. and Profl. Women, 1987. Fellow N.Y. Obstet. Soc., Am. Coll. Ob-Gyn (v.p. 1993-94, pres.-elect 1996—, gynecol. practice com. 1981, examener Am. Bd. Obstetrics and Gynecology 1988—); mem. Women's Med. Assn. (v.p. N.Y. 1974-79, editorial bd. jour. 1985—, resident review com. for obstetrics and gynecology 1993—), Am. Med. Women's Assn. (com. chmn. 1975-77, 78-79, editorial bd. jour. 1986—), N.Y. Cancer Soc., NYU Sch. Med. Alumni Assn. (bd. govs. 1979—, v.p. 1987-91, pres. 1992-93), Alpha Omega Alpha. Office: LI Jewish Med Ctr New Hyde Park NY 11040

SEMLEAR, ROBERT DWIGHT, family practice physician; b. Lansing, Mich., Feb. 29, 1952; s. Robert Harry and Thelma Alice (Monaco) S.; m. Diana Lynn Peate, June 19, 1982; children: Sarah Victoria, Chloe Nissa. BA, Amherst Coll., 1974; MD, NYU Med. Sch., 1978. Diplomate Am. Bd. Family Practice. Intern U. Miami Affiliated Hosps., 1978-79; intern, resident in family practice Southside Hosp., Bayshore, N.Y., 1979-81; emergency room physician Southampton (N.Y.) Hosp., 1981-83; pvt. practice Sag Harbor, N.Y., 1983-95; family practice physician Edward W. Sparrow Hosp., Lansing, 1995—. Mem. Am. Acad. Family Practice. Democrat. Presbyn. Office: Sparrow Family Practice 13191 Schavey Rd Ste 3 DeWitt MI 48820

SENAY, LEO CHARLES, JR., retired physiology educator, researcher; b. Fall River, Mass., Jan. 18, 1927; s. Leo Charles and Louise Cecilia (Sullivan) S.; m. Mary Charleen Fowler, May 26, 1951 (dec. Jan. 1989); children: James, Matthew, David, John, Daniel, Mark, Mary; m. Jeanne Marie Albert, June 9, 1990. AB, Harvard U., 1949; PhD, U. Iowa, 1957. Instr. physiology St. Louis U. Med. Sch., 1957-59, asst. prof., 1959-62, assoc. prof., 1962-68, prof., 1968-94; vis. prof. U. Witwatersrand, Johannesburg, Republic South Africa, 1970-82; mem. study sect. NIH, Bethesda, Md., 1976-80. Contbr. articles to profl. jours. Sgt. U.S. Army, 1950-52. Grantee NIH, 1962-84. Fellow Am. Coll. Sports Medicine; mem. AAAS, Am. Physiol. Soc. (editorial bd. 1974-78), Sigma Xi. Office: St Louis U Med Sch 1402 S Grand Blvd Saint Louis MO 63104-1004

SENCER, WALTER, medical educator; b. N.Y.C., June 9, 1921; s. Edward and Bertha (Fleschler) S.; m. Helene Galanty; children: Philip, Nicholas, Claudia. MD, NYU, 1946; Cert. in Psychoanalysis, Columbia U., 1958. Diplomate Am. Bd. Psychiatry and Neurology. From asst. to clin. prof. Neurology Mt. Sinai Hosp. Sch. Medicine, N.Y.C., 1958—; clin. prof. Psychiatry Mt. Sinai Hosp. Sch. Medicine, 1988—. Capt. USAF, 1946-49. Office: 1185 Park Ave New York NY 10128-1308

SENDROWSKI, DAVID PETER, optometrist; b. Worcester, Mass., Jan. 8, 1959; s. Frank Stephen and Geneive Sophia (Watjkon) S.; m. Lori L. Floyd, June 6, 1993. BS, U. Mass., Amherst, 1981; D in Optometry, New Eng. Coll. of Optometry, 1985. Resident VA Hosp., L.A., 1986; asst. prof. So. Calif. Coll. Optometry, Fullerton, 1986—; dir. optometric svcs. North Orange County C.C., Anaheim, Calif., 1989—; chief ocular disease svc. So. Calif. Coll. Optometry, Fullerton, 1991—; ptnr. in pvt. practice Floyd/Sendrowski, Mission Viejo, Calif., 1993—; cons. Calif. State Bd. Optometry, Sacramento, 1990—. Author (book chpts. in) Emergency Medicine, 1994, Hyperthyroid Dysfunction, 1994, Thyroid Eye Disease, 1995. Am. Acad. Optometrist fellow, 1987. Mem. Am. Optometric Assn. (Continuing Edn. award 1987-88), Calif. Optometric Assn. (cons., bd. dirs. pathology edn. com. 1991—), Assn. Optometric Educators, Am. Diabetes Assn., Orange County Optometric Soc. (membership chair 1988-91, trustee 1988—), Beta Sigma Kappa. Republican. Roman Catholic. Office: Floyd/Sendrowski 24000 Alicia Pkwy Ste 11 Mission Viejo CA 92691

SENGBUSCH, HOWARD GEORGE, biology, parasitology educator; b. Buffalo, Dec. 14, 1917; s. Howard Clarence and Blanche Anita (Foreman) S.; m. Beatrice Ardell Ebling, July 2, 1942; children: Craig Howard, Lee Ardell. BS in Edn., Buffalo State Tchrs. Coll., 1939; EdM, U. Buffalo, 1947; MS in Zoology, NYU, 1951, PhD in Parasitology, 1951. Tchr. Lockport (N.Y.) Sch. Dist., 1939-41; mem. faculty SUNY, Buffalo, 1951-81, prof. biology, 1957-81, prof. emeritus biology, 1981—, dean arts and scis., 1965-70; dir. Gt. Lakes Lab., Buffalo, 1965-66; vis. scientist Max Planck Inst. Meeresbiologie, Wilhelmshaven, Germany, 1957-58; Fulbright prof. Cen. Philippine U., Iloilo, 1962-63; vis. prof. parasitology U. Mysore, India, 1969-70; cons. in parasitology Roswell Park Meml. Inst., Buffalo, 1963—; adj. prof. biology Inst. Arthropodology and Parasitology, Ga. So. U., Statesboro, 1982—; courtesy prof. biology Fla. State U., Tallahassee, 1986—. Bd. dirs. Buffalo Zool. Soc., Buffalo Mus. Natural Sci. 1st lt. AUS, 1941-46, scientist dir. USPHS inactive res., 1956—. Fellow AAAS, Indian Acad. Zoology; mem. Acarological Soc. Am. (charter), Entomol. Soc. Am., Ga. Entomol. Soc., Hawaiian Entomol. Soc., Izaak Walton League (bd. dirs.), Rotary, Sigma Xi, Phi Delta Kappa, Kappa Delta Pi. Presbyterian. Home: 2112 Skyland Dr Tallahassee FL 32303-4324

SENIOR, JOHN ROBERT, internist, gastroenterologist, consultant; b. Phila., July 17, 1927; s. John Henry and Catherine (Cumming) S.; m. Sara Elizabeth Spedden, Dec. 27, 1952; children: John Ormond, Laura Bruns Council, Lisa Ann. BS in Physics, Pa. State U., 1950; MD, U. Pa., 1954. Diplomate Am. Bd. Internal Medicine, Am. Bd. Gastroenterology. Intern Hosp. U. Pa., Phila., 1954-55, resident in medicine, 1955-57, clin. fellow in gastroenterology, 1957-59; rsch. fellow in gastroenterology Mass. Gen. Hosp.-Harvard U., Boston, 1959-62; rsch. fellow Harvard U., Cambridge, Mass., 1959-62; dir. gastrointestinal rsch. lab. Phila. Gen. Hosp.-U. Pa., 1962-70; clin. prof. of medicine U. Pa., 1970-79, adj. prof. medicine, 1980—; dir. regulatory affairs E.R. Squibb & Sons, Princeton, N.J., 1979-81; v.p. clin. affairs Sterling-Winthrop Rsch. Inst.-Sterling Drug Corp. Worldwide, N.Y.C. and Rensselear, N.Y., 1981-84; pres. pers. cons. corp. Merion, Pa., 1984—; prin. cons. med. editor for internat. pharm. R&D G. H. Besselaar Assocs., Princeton, N.J., 1986-93; prin. med. cons. for internat. pharm. R&D Therakos, Inc., West Chester, Pa., 1994-95; med. rev. officer divsn. gastrointestinal/coagulation drugs FDA, Rockville, Md., 1995—; mem. gastrointestinal rsch. staff (without compensation) VA Med. Ctr., Phila., 1991—; mem. adv. coun. Nat. Inst. Diabetes and Kidney and Digestive Diseases, Bethesda, Md., 1981-85; senatorial liaison Nat. Commn. Digestive Diseases, Washington, 1978-80. Author: Towards Evaluation of Competence in Medicine, 1976; author, editor: Medium Chain Triglycerides, 1968; contbr. articles to profl. jours. With USNR, 1945-84; rear adm. 1977-84. Fellow ACP; mem. Am. Assn. Study of Liver Diseases (pres. 1973-74), Am. Soc. Clin. Investigation, Am. Gastroenterol. Soc., Cosmos Club, Phi Beta Kappa, Phi Kappa Phi, Sigma Pi Sigma, Alpha Omega Alpha. Republican. Episcopalian. Home: 54 Merbrook Ln Merion Station PA 19066-1613 Office: 6B45 Parklawn HFD-180 5600 Fishers Ln Rockville MD 20857

SENKOWSKY, JON, vascular surgeon; b. Mexico City, Oct. 8, 1957; s. Frank Joseph and Florence (Pasinko) S.; m. Donna Gauntt, May 7, 1983; children: Molly Elizabeth, Emily Ann, Frances Marie. BS, Tulane U., 1979; MD, U. Tex., Dallas, 1983. Diplomate Am. Bd. Surgery, Vascular, Critical Care. Acting clin. dir. Charity Hosp. of La., New Orleans, 1987; program dir. weekly vascular conf. Tulane U. Affiliated Hosp., Dallas, 1988-89; interpreter of studies in non-invasive vascular lab. Tulane Med. Ctr. Hosp. and Clinic, Dallas, 1988-89; ptnr. in pvt. practice Brantigan and Senkowsky, Denver, 1989-96; mem. gen. surgery teaching staff St. Joseph Hosp., Denver, 1989-96; dir. Denver Vascular Diagnostic Ctr., 1989-96; pvt. practice vascular surgery CSANT, Arlington, Tex., 1996 staff physician Denver Wound Care Ctr., staff physician All Saints Wound Care Ctr., Ft. Worth, Tex. Fellow ACS; mem. Rocky Mountain Traumatological Soc. (sec.-treas. 1993—), mem. ISCVS, 1995. Office: Brantigan and Senkowsky 2253 Downing St Denver CO 80205

SENNING, ÅKE, physician, educator emeritus; b. Rättvik, Sweden, Dec. 14, 1915; arrived in Switzerland, 1961; s. Eric David and Elly Mathilda (SäfstrÖm) S.; m. Ulla Britt Ronge, Aug 19, 1942; children: Anne-Charlotte, Johan, Michael, Bjoern. MD, Karolinska Inst., Stockholm, 1952. Internship and residency in surg. clinics Stockholm; assoc. prof. Karolinska Inst., Stockholm, 1953-61, prof. surgery; head of univ. surg. clinic Zürich, 1961-85; ret., 1985—. Contbr. over 400 articles to profl. jours. Home: Belsitstr 14, CH-8044 Zurich Switzerland

SENSABAUGH, GEORGE FRANK, JR., forensic sciences educator; b. Palo Alto, Calif., June 8, 1941; s. George Frank and Elizabeth Katherine (Ake) S.; m. Linda Sallander, Aug. 30, 1963; children: Jeffrey, Laura. BA, Princeton U., 1963; D of Criminology, U. Calif., Berkeley, 1969. Researcher U. Calif., San Diego, 1969-71, Nat. Inst. Med. Rsch., London, 1971-72; from asst. prof. to prof. U. Calif., Berkeley, 1972—. Contbr. articles to profl. jours. Fulbright scholar, 1993. Fellow Am. Acad. Forensic Scis. (Paul L. Kirk award 1987); mem. Am. Chem. Soc., Am. Soc. Human Genetics, Calif. Assn. Criminalists, N.Y. Acad. Scis. Office: U Calif Sch Pub Health Berkeley CA 94720

SENZEL, ALAN JOSEPH, analytical chemistry consultant, music critic; b. Los Angeles, May 26, 1945; s. Bernard and Esther Mildred (Shykin) S.; m. Phyllis Sharon Abt, June 22, 1969; children—Richard Steven, Lisa Beth. B.S. in Chemistry, Calif. State U.-Long Beach, 1967; M.S., UCLA, 1969, Ph.D., 1970. Assoc. editor Am. Chem. Soc., Washington, 1970-74; methods editor Assn. Ofcl. Analytical Chemists, Washington, 1974-78; info. dir. Chem. Industry Inst. Toxicology, Research Triangle Park, N.C., 1978-79; pvt. cons., Raleigh, N.C., 1978—; cons. Engring.-Sci., Cary, N.C. and Fairfax, Va., 1978—, Corning Glass Works, Raleigh, 1979-85, Research Triangle Inst., Research Triangle Park, 1983—, Combustion Engring., Chapel Hill, N.C., 1984-89, KilKelly Environ. Assocs., Raleigh, 1985—, Integrated Lab. Systems, Durham, 1987—, Technical Resources, Inc., Rockville, Md., 1987—, Am. Petroleum Inst., Washington, 1990—, Sanford Cohen & Assocs., Inc., McLean, Va., 1993—, Glaxo Pharmaceuticals, 1993—, Stewart Pesticide Registration Assocs., Inc., 1993—, Spray Drift Task Force, 1993—, Am. Agrl. Svcs., Inc., Cary, N.C., 1994—, Entropy, Inc., 1995—; music critic Raleigh News & Observer, 1982-90, Spectator Mag., 1990—; dep. mgr. Environ. Systems Group, Environ. Resources Mgmt. Inc., Exton, Pa., 1988; project sci. Agrl. Div. Residue Chem. dept. CIBA-GEIGY Corp., Greensboro, N.C., 1989-93. Editor: Instrumentation in Analytical Chemistry, 1973, Newburger's Manual of Cosmetic Analysis, 1977 (FDA award 1978), Safety in the Laboratory, 1984 (STC award 1985); assoc. editor: Official Methods of Analysis, 1975; editor Inclusions Quar., 1993-94. Pres. Congregation Sha'arei Israel, 1981-83. Mem. Soc. Tech. Communication (treas. 1983-85, v.p. 1985-87, achievement award 1985), Am. Chem. Soc., Assn. Official Analytical Chemists. Republican. Jewish. Club: Bridge-Raleigh, Capitol, Vanderbilt. Lodge: B'nai Brith. Avocations: music; tennis; basketball; bridge. Home and Office: 7704 Audubon Dr Raleigh NC 27615-3403

SEOW-CHOEN, FRANCIS, colorectal surgeon; b. Singapore, May 6, 1957; s. Hong-Teng and Lay-Keng (Kong) Seow; m. Ching-Peng Siow, May 28, 1983; children: Isaac, Samuel, Olivia. M.B.B.S., Nat. U. Singapore, 1981. House surgeon Ministry of Health, Singapore, 1981-82, orthopaedic resident, 1984-87; med. officer Ministry of Def., Singapore, 1982-84; registrar in surgery Singapore Gen. Hosp., 1987-89, registrar in colorectal surgery, 1989, sr. registrar coloproctology, 1989-92, cons. surgeon, 1992-95, head, sr. cons., 1996—; rsch. fellow St. Mark's Hosp., London, 1989-90; head and sr. cons. surgeon Singapore Gen. Hosp., 1995—; instr. advanced trauma life support ACS, 1992-94; officer in charge operating theatre Singapore Navy, 1990-94; dir. Endoscopy Ctr., Singapore, 1994—; officer-in-charge med. flight Rep. of Singapore Air Force, 1982-83; chmn. 1st Clin. Nutrition Meeting, 1994; treas. 25th Combined Surg. Meeting, 1992, vice chmn. 26th, 1992, chmn. 28th, 1994; sci. chmn. 28th Malaysia-Singapore Congress, 1994. Mem. editl. bd. Techniques in Coloproctology, Brit. Jour. Surgery; reviewer Internat. Jour. Colorectal Diseases, 1990—; contbr. articles to med. jours. Vol. after-care officer Singapore Anti-Narcotics Assn., 1977-79; organizing com. Steering Com. on Trauma Mgmt., Singapore, 1992, Practice Guidelines of Endoscopists, Singapore, 1992. Capt. Singapore Navy, 1982-94. Beecham scholar Nat. U. Singapore, 1980-81; Manpower Devel. Plan fellow Ministry of Health, Singapore, 1989-90, Overseas Fund fellow Royal Coll. surgeons, Edinburgh, 1989, Internat. Travel fellow Am. Soc. Colon and Rectal Surgeons, 1993. Fellow Acad. Medicine Singapore (sec. 1992-94). Ch. of Eng. Home: 54 Mimosa Walk, Singapore 2880, Singapore Office: Singapore Gen Hosp, Dept Colorectal Surgery, Singapore 0316, Singapore

SEPPÄLÄ, MATTI TAPIO, neurosurgeon; b. Kotka, Finland, Dec. 14, 1958; s. Olavi Viljam and Terttu Johanna (Tuomela) S.; m. Mervi Elina Penttilä, June 8, 1984; children: Tapio Markus, Tuulikki Elina, Terho Olavi. MD, Helsinki (Finland) U., 1983, degree in neurosurgery, 1990. Gen. practitioner Primary Health Care, Hanko, Finland, 1984; registrar neurology Helsinki City Hosp., 1985; registrar neurosurgery Helsinki U. Hosp., 1985-90, cons. neurosurgery, 1990—. Contbr. articles to profl. jours. Mem. Finnish Neurosurgical Assn. (cashier 1993-95), Scandinavian Neurosurgical Assn. Office: Helsinki Univ Hosp, Dept Neurosurgery, Topeliuksenkatu 5, 00260 Helsinki Finland

SEPPALA, PENTTI OLAVI, medical director, physician; b. Uskela, Finland, May 16, 1933; s. Toivo Johannes and Elli Vilhelmiina (Takala) S.; m. Anneli Helena Haroma, June 6, 1958; children: Olli-Pekka, Anna-Leena. MD, U. Turku, Finland, 1958, D Med. Scis., 1964. Instr. in med. chemistry U. Turku, 1955-61, asst. physician dept. medicine, 1961-64, acting assoc. prof., 1964-65, chief physician Student Health Svc., 1965-69, docent internal medicine, 1970—; assoc. chief physician dept. medicine U. Ctrl. Hosp., Turku, 1970-92, med. dir., 1993—; chief physician Cancer Soc. Southwest Finland, 1986—; sr. rsch. fellow Dept. Connective Tissue Rsch. Inst. Biology and Med. Scis., Boston, 1966-67. Contbr. articles to profl. jours. Chmn. bd. Student Health Svc. of Turku, 1970-75, Collegium for Med. Edn./U. Turku, 1975-77, Diabetes Bd. for Dist. of Univ. Ctrl. Hosp. of Turku, 1983-93; bd. dirs. med. faculty U. Turku, 1975-78, Diabetes League in Finland, 1982-90, Cancer Soc. for South-West Finland, 1982—. Recipient Silver medal Student Health Svc., 1976, Golden medal Diabetes League of Finland, 1990, Bronze medal Soc. Ins. of Finland. Mem. AAAS, IDF, Finnish Soc. Internal Medicine (sec. 1969-71), Finnish Soc. Rheumatology, Finnish Soc. Encodrinology, Finnish Soc. Clin. Chemistry, Finnish Med. Soc. Duodecim, Finnish Soc. Gastroenterology, European Assn. Study of Diabetes. Home: Saunakatu 1, 20720 Turku Finland Office: Univ Ctrl Hosp, Kiinamyllynkatu 4-8, 20520 Turku Finland

SERAFETINIDES, EUSTACE AGAPIOS, physician, researcher; b. Athens, June 4, 1930; came to U.S., 1965; s. Agapios E. and Erasmia (Theotokou) S.; m. Jean Mary Rawlinson, May 24, 1965. MD, Nat. U. Greece, Athens, 1953; PhD, U. London, 1964. Rsch. fellow Guy & Maudsley Hosp., London, 1957-64; assoc. prof. Okla. U. Med. Ctr., Oklahoma City, 1965-71; prof. psychiatry UCLA Med. Ctr., 1972-94, prof. emeritus, 1994—; chief rsch. VA Med. Ctr., L.A., 1972-95, emeritus chief rsch., 1995—. Editor: Methods of Biobehavioral Research, 1979, Psychiatric Research in Practice, 1981; editor Psychiat. Annals: Psychiat. Rehab., 1983, Brain and Behavioral Relationships, 1985. 2d lt. Med. Greek Mil., 1953-56. Grantee Med. Rsch. Coun. Gt. Britain (London), 1959-62; fellow Guy & Maudsley Hosp., 1962-63; recipient Career Devel. award NIMH, 1967-72. Mem. Hellenic Univ. Club, U. Calif. Emeriti Assn. Office: UCLA/NPI 760 Westwood Plz Los Angeles CA 90029

SERAFIN, DONALD, plastic surgeon; b. N.Y.C., Jan. 18, 1938; s. Stephen Michael and Julia (Sopko) S.; A.B., Duke U., 1960, M.D., 1964; m. Patricia Serafin; children: Allison Elizabeth, Christina Julia, Donald Stephen, Lara Leigh. Surg. intern Grady Meml. Hosp., Atlanta, 1964-65; resident in surgery Emory U. Hosp., Atlanta, 1965-69; asst. resident in plastic and reconstructive surgery Duke U. Med. Center, Durham, N.C., 1971-73, chief resident, 1973-74; Christine Kleinert fellow in hand surgery U. Louisville Hosp., 1972-73; practice medicine specializing in plastic surgery, Durham; mem. staff Durham County Gen. Hosp.; asst. prof. plastic, reconstructive and maxillofacial surgery Duke U., 1974-77, assoc. prof., 1977-81, prof., 1981-95, chmn. Plastic Surgery Rsch. Council, 1983. Assoc. editor Jour. Reconstructive Microsurgery. Contbr. articles to profl. jours. Served to maj. M.C., USAF, 1969-71, col. M.C., USAR. Diplomate Am. Bd. Surgery, Am. Bd. Plastic Surgery. Recipient Air Force commedation medal, 1971, U.S. Army commendation medal, 1990. Fellow ACS; mem. Internat. Soc. Reconstructive Microsurgery, Am. Soc. Plastic and Reconstructive Surgeons, Am. Assn. Plastic Surgeons, Am. Burn Assn., AMA, Plastic Surgery Research Council, N.C. Soc. Plastic, Maxillofacial and Reconstructive Surgeons, Southeastern Soc. Plastic and Reconstructive Surgeons, Southeastern Med. Dental Soc., Sigma Xi. Office: Duke U Med Ctr PO Box 3708 Durham NC 27710

SERAFINE, MARY LOUISE, psychologist, educator, lawyer; b. Rochester, N.Y., July 2, 1948. B.A. with honors in music, Rutgers U., 1970; Ph.D., U. Fla., 1975; JD, Yale U., 1991. Bar: Calif., D.C.; U.S. Tax Ct. Teaching and research fellow U. Fla., Gainesville, 1970-76; vis. asst. prof. U. Tex.-San Antonio, 1976-77; asst. prof. U. Tex.-Austin, 1977-79; postdoctoral fellow dept psychology Yale U., New Haven, 1979-83, lectr., 1981-83; asst. prof. dept. psychology Vassar Coll. Poughkeepsie, N.Y., 1983-88; with O'Melveny & Myers, L.A., 1988-96, Chadbourne & Parke, L.A. Author: Music as Cognition: The Development of Thought in Sound, 1988. Contbr. articles to profl. jours. Editorial reviewer Child Devel., Devel. Psychology, Am. Scientist, Jour. Experimental Child Psychology, Jour. Applied Developmental

Psychology, Yale Law Jour. Grantee State of Fla., 1974-75, U. Tex.-Austin, 1977, Spencer Found., 1979-85. Office: Chadbourne & Parke Ste 1600 601 South Figueroa St Los Angeles CA 90017

SERBAN, GEORGE, physician; b. Adjud, Vrancea, Rumania, Sept. 12, 1927; came to U.S., 1957; m. Theodora Serban, Dec. 20, 1953; 1 child, Andrew. MD, Bucharest (Rumania) U., 1952. Diplomate Am. Bd. Psychiatry and Neurology. Asst. prof. West U., Timisoara, Rumania, 1953-56; intern Lebanon Hosp., N.Y.C., 1957; resident Mt. Sinai-Queens Hosp., Elmhurst, N.Y., 1958-60; asst. prof. NYU, 1970-75, assoc. clin. prof., 1975—; cons., I.F. Fragrances, N.Y.C., 1988—, Amivest, N.Y.C., 1984—, Hill and Knowlton, N.Y.C., 1987—; med. dir. Inst. Drug Abuse, N.Y.C., 1980-87, Kittay Sci. Found., N.Y.C., 1970-77. Author: Adjustment of Schizophrenics in the Community, 1980, The Tyranny of Magical Thinking, 1982; editor numerous books; contbr. (with others) over 70 articles to med. and sci. publs. Recipient award Environ. and Population Problems of Adaptation, Washington, 1983. Mem. Am. Psychiat. Assn., Internat. Cybernetic Assn. (rschr. 1987—). Office: 103 E 86th St # 1A New York NY 10028-1058

SERGI, ANTHONY ROBERT, physician, surgeon; b. Elizabeth, N.J., May 1, 1963; s. Martin and Agnes (Kraus) S. BS in Biology, Fairleigh Dickinson U., 1985; DPM, Pa. Coll. Medicine, 1989. Surg. resident Kennedy Meml. Hosp., Saddle Brook, N.J., 1989-91, chief surg. resident, 1990-91; pvt. practice Foot and Ankle Surg. Assocs., P.C., Edison, N.J., 1991—. Contbr. articles to profl. jours. Roman Catholic. Office: Foot and Ankle Surg Assocs 5 Summit Ave Hackensack NJ 07601-1271 also: Edison Foot and Ankle Care 1628 Oak Tree Rd Edison NJ 08820-2841

SEROTE, WILLIAM MORRIS, physician; b. L.A., Oct. 3, 1950; s. Paul and Marion (Katz) S.; m. Teresa Ann Thomas, May 24, 1975; children: Nicholas, Alexis. BS, U. Mich., 1972; DO, Coll. Osteopathic Medicine, Des Moines, 1975. Diplomate Am. Bd. Emergency Medicine. Emergency physician Pontiac (Mich.) Gen. Hosp., 1981-85; emergency physician Crittenton Hosp., Rochester, Mich., 1985-92, dir. emergency medicine, 1990-92; emergency physician North Oak Med. Ctr., Pontiac, 1992—; med. dir. Am. Air Ambulance, Dallas, 1993—. Maj. U.S. Army, 1976-80. Fellow Am. Coll. Emergency Physicians; mem. Am. Osteopathic Assn., Mich. Assn. Osteopathic Physicians. Mem. LDS Ch. Office: North Oakland Med Ctr 461 W Huron Pontiac MI 48341

SERPELL, MICHAEL GRAHAM, anesthesiologist; b. Douglas, Isle of Man, U.K., Dec. 5, 1959; s. Barry William Serpell and Esme Ann (Moffett) Forster; m. Lesley Serpell, Dec. 30, 1991. MB ChB, U. Dundee, Scotland, 1983. Resident in medicine/surgery Ninewells Hosp., Dundee, 1983-84; redie resident in anesthesiology, Dundee, 1984-91; fellow in pain mgmt. Dartmouth-Hitchcock Med. Ctr., Lebanon, N.H., 1992; cons. in anesthesia and pain mgmt. West Glasgow (Scotland) U./Nat. Health Svc. Trust, 1993—, coord. audit in anesthesia, 1995—, mem. com. for kings fund accreditation, 1995—. Contbr. articles to profl. jours. Lawrence Bequest & Scottish Hosp. Endowment Rsch. Trust fellow, Örebro, Sweden, 1990. Fellow Royal Coll. Anesthesiologists; mem. North Brit. Pain Soc. (sec. 1996—, mem. coun.), West of Scotland Pain Group (sec. 1996—, mem. coun.). Home: Kelvinside, 3 Lancaster Crescent, Glasgow G12 0RR, Scotland Office: Western Infirmary, Dept Anesthesia, Glasgow G11 6NT, Scotland

SERPICK, ARTHUR ALLEN, health facility administrator, physician; b. Balt., Md., Feb. 21, 1935; s. Jacob and Dorothy (Tapper) S.; married, Sept. 13, 1979. BS, Univ. Md., 1957, MD, 1959. Staff assoc. Nat. Cancer Inst., Bethesda, Md., 1963-65; head med. svc. Balt. Cancer Soc., Balt., 1965-70; head oncology Md. Gen. Hosp., Balt., 1970-87; head dept. medicine St. Joseph Med. Ctr., Towson, Md., 1983—; adv. bd. Corom Health Care, 1995. Active Am. Cancer Soc., 1968-76. Fellow Am. Coll. Physicians, Inst. Soc. Nemtology; mem. Am. Coll. Physicians Execs., Am. Soc. Clinical Oncology. Office: St Joseph Med Ctr 7620 York Rd Towson MD 21204

SERRA, RAMON FERNANDEZ, physician; b. Manresa, Barcelona, Spain, Nov. 29, 1956; s. Josep Malet Serra and Maria Mora Fernandez; m. Conxita Sole Morera, Sept. 25, 1982; children: Serra, Imma, Morera. Cert. orthopaedics surgery and traumatologist. Mem. staff Univ. Hosp., Barcelona, 1989-93, St. Josep Hosp., Manresa, 1986-94; univ. intern supr. U. Ill., Champaign, 1994-95; mem. staff Spanish Basket Fedn., 1994—; dir. TDK Basket Manresa, Manresa, 1982—; mem. staff Hosp. Ctr., Manresa, 1995—. Home: Sequia 38 2on 3a, 08240 Barcelona Spain

SERRANO, ALBERTO C., psychiatrist; b. Buenos Aires, Argentina, Apr. 7, 1931; m. Reina Pages, June 15, 1957; children: Marcos Alberto, Henry John, Claudia Ingrid, Christopher William. BA, Colegio Nacional Mariano Moreno, 1948; MD, U. Buenos Aires, 1956. Intern Clinica Cordoba, Buenos Aires, 1955-57; resident in psychiatry U. Tex. Med. Br., Galveston, 1957-60; resident in child psychiatry U. Tex. Med. Br., 1962-64; chief psychiatrist, exec. dir. Community Guidance Ctr. of Bexas County, San Antonio, 1966-86; clin. prof. psychiatry and pediatrics U. Tex. Health Sci. Ctr., San Antonio, 1968-86; med. dir. Phila. Child Guidance Clinic, 1986—; prof., dir. div. child and adolescent psychiatry Dept. Psychiatry and Pediatrics, U. Pa., 1986—; psychiatrist-in-chief and dir. psychiatry div. Childrens Hosp. of Phila., 1986—; assoc. chmn. dept. psychiatry U. Pa., 1990—; cons. in field; lectr. in field. Contbr. articles to profl. jours.; editorial adv. bd. Family Process, 1972-84, Jour. Marital and Family Therapy, 1979-86, Child Psychiatry and Human Devel., 1970—, Revista Argentina de Psiquiatria y Psicologia de la adolescencia, 1973—, Terapia Familiar, 1978—, Sistemas Familiares, 1985—, Hospital and Community Psychiatry, 1987—, Clin. Pediatrics, 1987—, others. Fellow Am. Psychiatric Assn., Am. Group Psychotherapy Assn. (bd. dirs. 1973-76, 81-84, 89—); mem. AMA, Group Psychotherapy Found (bd. dirs. 1982-84), Am. Acad. Child Psychiatry (fellow), Internat. Assn. Group Psychotherapy (bd. dirs. 1980-81, 83-86, 1st v.p. 1986-89, pres. 1992-95), Am. Family Therapy Assn., Soc. Profs. of Child Psychiatry, Assn. for Hispanic Psychiatrists, Am. Acad. Pediatrics, Am. Assn. Psychiatric Svcs. for Children, Titus Harris Soc., Pa. Med. Soc., Pa. County Med. Soc., many others. Home: 2301 Cherry St Philadelphia PA 19103-1029 Office: 34th St and Civic Ctr Blvd Philadelphia PA 19104

SERRATTO, MARIA E., pediatric cardiologist, educator; b. Genoa, Italy, Mar. 30; came to U.S., 1962; d. Tito and Gemma (Macaluso) S.; m. Riccardo Benvenuto. MD summa cum laude, U. Genoa, 1955. Diplomate Am. Bd. Pediatrics, Am. Bd. Pediatric Cardiology. Intern U. Genova (Italy) Hosp., 1955-56; resident Northwestern U., Chgo., 1957-63; mem. attending staff Cook County Children's Hosp., Chgo., 1971—; prof. pediat. (cardiology) U. Ill., Chgo., 1981—, Rush Med. Sch., Chgo., 1994-96; coord. pediatric cardiology Nat. Ctr. for Advanced Med. Edn., Chgo., 1975—, trustee, 1994—; cons. cardiologist Cardiothoracic Ctr. Monaco, Monte Carlo, 1988—; sr. scientist Rush-Presbyn.-St. Luke's Med. Ctr., Chgo., 1994—; trustee Hektoen Inst. for Med. Rsch., Chgo., 1995—; attending staff U. Ill. Hosps. Chgo., 1981—, Michael Reese Hosp., Chgo., 1995—. Contbr. over 150 articles to med. jours., chpts. to books. Recipient cert. of meitorious svc. Am. Heart Assn., 1965, 84. Fellow Am. Coll. Cardiology, Am. Acad. Pediat., Am. Coll. Chest Physicians; mem. Am. Pediatric Soc., Am. Fedn. for Clin. Rsch., N.Y. Acad. Scis., Italian Soc. Pediatric Cardiology (hon.), Mario Negri Rsch. Inst. (Milan). Roman Catholic. Office: Cook County Children's Hosp 700 S Wood St Chicago IL 60612

SER VAAS, CORY, health sciences association administrator. Pres., CEO Benjamin Franklin Literary Soc., Indpls. Office: BFLMS PO Box 567 Indianapolis IN 46206-0567

SESSIONS, ROGER CARL, emergency physician; b. Stamps, Ark., Oct. 4, 1944; s. Darrell Inman and Linda Evelyn (Rogers) S.; m. Sherri Lorene Steward, June 12, 1971 (div. Oct. 1981); 1 child, David Steward. BSE, So. Ark. U., 1966; MS, Henderson State U., 1971; DO, Tex. Coll. Osteo. Medicine, 1981. Diplomate Am. Bd. Emergency Medicine. Asst. coach Tex. H.S., Texarkana, 1966-67; track coach Atlanta H.S., Tex., 1967-72; football coach, athletic dir. N.W. H.S., Justin, Tex., 1972-77; intern Dallas-Ft. Worth Med. Ctr., Grand Prairie, Tex., 1981-82, practice emergency medicine, 1987-96; pvt. practice emergency medicine, 1982—; with EmCare, Dallas, 1989-96; dir. emergency dept. New Boston Gen. Hosp., Tex., 1984-87, Mesquite (Tex.) Physician's Hosp., 1987-88, North Tex. Med. Ctr., 1991-93; with Baylor Med. Ctr., Grapevine, Tex., 1996—; rsch. dir. Ferris, Inc., Burr Ridge, Ill. Fellow Am. Coll. Emergency Physicians; mem. AMA, Am. Coll. Sports Medicine, Tex. Coll. Emergency Physicians. Avocation: running.

SESSIONS, ROY BRUMBY, otolaryngologist, educator; b. Houston, July 28, 1937; s. Roy Brumby and Elizabeth (Compton) S.; m. Mary Cousart, Aug. 28, 1976: children: Kate, Elizabeth, Abigail, Matthew. BS, La. State U., Baton Rouge, 1958; MD, La. State U., New Orleans, 1962. Resident gen. surgery and otolaryngology Washington U. Sch. Medicine, St. Louis, 1965-69; asst. prof. Baylor Coll. Medicine, Houston, 1969-73, assoc. prof., 1973-83; prof. head and neck surgery Meml. Sloan Kettering Cancer Ctr., N.Y.C., 1983-89; prof., chmn. dept. otolaryngology, head and neck surgery Gerogetown U. Med. Sch., Washington, 1989—. Contbr. articles to profl. jours., chpts. to books. Lt. comdr. USN, 1962-65. Roman Catholic. Georgetown Univ: 3800 Reservoir Rd NW Washington DC 20007

SETARO, RAYMOND ANTHONY, JR., medical technologist, laboratory administrator; b. North Charleroi, Pa., Jan. 30, 1966; m. Kelly Lynn Forman, Jan. 21, 1989; children: Raymond A. III, Kelly Jo. BA in Health Care Adminstrn., Waynesburg Coll., 1987; MS in Psychology, California (Pa.) U., 1988. X-ray lic. Pa. Bd. Medicine. Tchr., coach Allegheny Acad., Pitts., 1988-89; coord. health care svcs. Mon Valley Cmty. Health Ctr., Monessen, Pa., 1989-91; technologist, ops. mgr. Image Radiology MRI, Bentleyville, Pa., 1991—. Active Rep. Nat. Com., 1994—. Recipient Images of Excellence award Toshiba Am. Med. Sys., 1992. Mem. Am. Soc. Radiol. Technologists (cert.), Chiropratic Inst. Thermography (cert.), NRA, FOP (assoc.), Washington County Hist. Soc. Roman Catholic. Home: 613 Crest Ave Charleroi PA 15022

SETHI, SURENDRA KUMAR, cardiologist; b. Indore, India, Feb. 25, 1939; s. Gulabchand and Hem Kunwar (Patni) S.; m. Hira Bai Badjatya; children—Atul Sethi, Namrita Sethi, Alok Sethi. M.B.B.S., M.G.M. Med. Coll., 1962, M.D., 1965. Diplomate Am. Bd. Internal Medicine. Practice medicine specializing in cardiology, Butler, Pa.; active med. staff cardiology W. Pa. Hosp., Pitts., Bultler Meml. Hosp., Armstrong Meml. Hosp. Fellow Am. Coll. Cardiology, Council Clin. Cardiology Am. Heart Assn.; mem. AMA, Pa. Med. Soc., Butler Med. Soc. Home: 114 Grosvenor Dr Butler PA 16001-1652 Office: Sethi Cardiology Ltd 230 S Washington St Butler PA 16001-5754

SETLIFFE, CHARLES DAVID, hospital administrator; b. Chattanooga, Aug. 11, 1931; s. David Bert and Willie Mae (Fussell) S.; m. Eva Gertrude Holladay, Nov. 17, 1951; children: Charles Vaden, David Scott, Susan Lynn. BS, U. Chattanooga, 1956; MHA, Washington U., St. Louis, 1965. Sales rep. Chemetron Corp., Chattanooga, 1956-60; hosp. purchasing agt. Meml. Hosp., Chattanooga, 1960-63; asst. adminstr. Ft. Sanders Presbyn. Hosp., Knoxville, Tenn., 1965-67, Sts. Mary and Elizabeth Hosp., Louisville, 1968-81, adminstr., 1975-81; pres., chief exec. officer Wilson Meml. Hosp., N.C., 1981-91, pres. emeritus, 1992—; health care cons., 1992—; mem. bd. dirs. Meml. Hosp., Chattanooga, 1996—; adminstr. Univ. Surg. Assocs., Inc., Chattanooga, 1995; dir. Statewide Health Coordinating Council, Ky., 1982-83, Ky. Health Systems Agy.-West, Louisville, 1978-81. Bd. dirs. Health Edn. Found. Eastern N.C., 1981-91, treas. 1982-91, exec. com. 1985-91, chmn. bldg. study com. 1984-85, N.C. Constituent of Nat. League Nursing, 1986-91, chmn. fin. com. 1987, Wilson Concerts, Inc., 1982-85, Hospice of Wilson, Inc., 1983-91, Wilson, ARC; sec., treas. Hosp. Adminstrs. Eastern N.C., 1983, vice chmn., chmn. 1984; bd. dirs. United Way Wilson County, 1982-86, 88-91; mem. adv. com. Wilson County Tech. Coll., Blue Cross-Blue Shield N.C. Served to sgt. USAF, 1951-55. Recipient Cross Mil. Svc., John W. Dunham chpt. United Daus. Confederacy, 1989; named Ky. Col., 1977. Mem. Ky. Hosp. Assn. (life, bd. dirs. 1976-81), N.C. Hosp. Assn. (life, mem. coun. fin.), Tenn. Hosp. Assn., Wilson County C. of C. (bd. dirs. 1984-86, chmn. accreditations com. 1986, health care cost containment com. 1983-91). Republican. Presbyterian. Avocations: tennis, travel. Home: 1109 Woodbine Way Signal Mountain TN 37377-2526 Office: Wilson Meml Hosp 1705 Tarboro St SW Wilson NC 27893-3428

SETTLE, GEORGE WARREN, orthopaedic surgeon; b. Balt., Oct. 4, 1926; s. Norman Charles and Charolett (Sanger) S.; m. Geraldine Ann Waybright, May 31, 1953; children: George, Anne, Beth, Thomas. BA, Johns Hopkins U., 1950, MD, 1953. Diplomate Am. Bd. Orthopaedic Surgery. Intern King County Hosp., Seattle, 1953-54; jr. asst. resident in orthopaedic surgery Johns Hopkins U., Seattle, 1954-55, asst. resident in orthopaedic surgery, 1956-57; chief resident in orthosurgery N000, 1957-58, mem. staff, 1958-59; pvt. practice Annapolis, Md., 1959-77, 79—; med. dir. Potomac Electric Power Co., Washington, 1977-78; chief orthopaedic surgery Anne Arundel Gen. Hosp., 1962-67, 81-82, chmn. med. bd., 1965-66, pres. med. staff, 1975-77. Contbr. articles to profl. jours. Mem. jud. nominating commn. Appellate Div., State of Md.; mem. com. and health planning Med & Chi Faculty of Md.; mem. med. rev. bd. City of Annapolis. With USN, 1944-46, PTO, World War II. Fellow Am. Acad. Orthopaedic Surgeons; mem. AMA, Md. Orthopaedic Soc., Anne Arundel County Med. Soc. Office: 195 Duke Of Gloucester St Annapolis MD 21401-2520

SEUERANCE, HARRY WELLS, emergency medicine educator; b. Wilson, N.C.; s. Harry Wells Sr. and Harriet Lucille (Pripps) S. BA in Sociology, Duke U., 1970; BA in Biology, East Carolina U., 1976; MD, Duke U., 1981. Resident East Carolina U., Greenville, N.C., 1982-86; asst. prof. emergency medicine U. Miss. Sch. Medicine, Jackson, 1986-91, Duke U. Med. Ctr., Durham, N.C., 1991—. Contbr. articles to profl. jours. Cardiology rsch. fellow Duke U. Med. Ctr., 1981-82. Fellow Am. Coll. Emergency Physicians (chmn. sect. short term obs. svcs. 1994). Home: 404 Livingstone Dr Cary NC 27513-2919 Office: Duke U Med Ctr Divsn Emergency Medicine Box 3096 Durham NC 27710

SEUNG, HONG IL, physician, educator; b. Seoul, Korea, Aug. 3, 1937; came to U.S., 1963; s. Kwang Kyun and Kwang Sil (Sohn) S.; m. Ran Jo Yu, Oct. 9, 1965; children—Lisa, Sharon, Shauna, Mary, Emily. M.D., Seoul Nat. U., 1962. Diplomate Am. Bd. Otolaryngology. Intern, Hosp. of St. Raphael, New Haven, 1963-64; resident in gen. surgery St. Louis U. Group of Hosps., 1964-65, resident in otolaryngology, 1965-68; fellow in otolaryngology Mt. Sinai Hosp. 1968-69; practice medicine specializing in otolaryngology and head and neck surgery and allergy, Wheeling, W.Va., 1969—; vice-chmn. dept. ophthalmology and otolaryngology Wheeling Hosp., 1975—; clin. assoc. prof. W.Va. U. Sch. Medicine, Morgantown, 1989. Fellow ACS; mem. AMA, Am. Acad. Ophthalmology and Otolaryngology, Am. Soc. Ophthalmologic and Otolaryngologic Allergy, So. Med. Assn., W.Va. Med. Assn., W.Va. Acad. Ophthalmology and Otolaryngology, Ohio County Med. Soc. Republican. Presbyterian. Club: Country (Wheeling). Home: 18 Hawthorne Ct Wheeling WV 26003-6661 Office: Profl Bldg 1300 Market St Wheeling WV 26003-3331

SEVER, JOHN LOUIS, medical researcher and educator; b. Chgo., Apr. 11, 1932; s. John Louis and Harriet (Link) S.; m. Gerane Werle, Mar. 3, 1956; children: Kimberly, Beverly, Valerie. BA, U. Chgo., 1952; MD, Northwestern U., 1955, BS, MS, PhD, 1957. Head sect. infectious diseases NINDS, NIH, Bethesda, Md., 1960-71, chief infectious diseases, 1971-88; chmn. pediatrics Children's Nat. Med. Ctr., Washington, 1988-90, prof. pediatrics, ob-gyn. and microbiology/immunology, 1988—; bd. dirs. Bio Whitaker, Walkersville, Md.; pres. Pan Am. Soc. Rapid Viral Diseases, Western Hemisphere, 1992-94. Editor 10 med. books; contbr. more than 500 articles to profl. jours. Cons. NIH Bethesda, 1988—, Rotary Internat., Evanston, Ill., 1989—, WHO, Geneva, Switzerland, 1991—. Capt. USPHS, 1960-88. Recipient Wellcome Diagnostics award Pan Am. Med. Virology, 1989, Meritorious Alumni award Northwestern U., 1989, Pasteur award Microbiology Soc., 1987, Kimbel award Am. Soc. for Microbiology, 1979, Abbott award, 1996. Mem. Infectious Disease Soc. of Ob-Gyn. (pres. 1992-94), Assn. Med. Clin. and Lab. Immunologists (pres. 1992-94), Teratology Soc. (pres. 1976-77), Price Club, Country Glen Club.

SEVER, MARKO, surgeon; b. Ljubljana, Slovenia, Oct. 12, 1946; s. Bozo and Marija (Golob) S.; m. Marjeta Novosel, Sept. 5, 1975; children: Matjaz, Primoz. MD, U. Ljubljana, 1972, MS, 1987, PhD in Exptl. Acute Pancreatitis, 1991. Intern U. Clin. Ctr., Ljubljana, 1973, resident, 1974; cons. U. Clin. Ctr., Ljubljana, 1988, chief endoscopy, 1989. Co-author: Textbook of Surgery, 1995. Mem. Internat. Gastroenterol. Surg. Club Athens, European Assn. for Endoscopic Surgery. Office: U Clin Ctr, Dept Gastroenterol Surgery, Zaloska 7, 1000 Ljubljana Slovenia

SEVERINGHAUS, CHARLES WILLIAM, wildlife biologist; b. Ithaca, N.Y., Sept. 3, 1916; s. Wilbur Clinton and Jane Margaret (Barden) S.; m. Ethel Long, Dec. 12, 1941 (div. 1971); children: Jane Raena, William Daniel, Charles Long; m. Jacqueline Degraff, Aug. 13, 1971; 1 child, Mark R. BS in Agr., Cornell U., 1939. Conservation laborer N.Y. State Conservation Dept., 1935-41; asst. game rsch. investigator N.Y. State Conservation Dept., Delmar, 1941, game rsch. investigator, 1941-61; dist. game mgr. N.Y. State Conservation Dept., Albany, 1941-44; leader deer mgmt. rsch., leader big game mgmt. rsch. N.Y. State Conservation Dept., Delmar, 1944-61, sr. wildlife biologist, 1961-62, supervising wildlife biologist, 1962-74, prin. wildlife biologist, 1974-77; cons. wildlife biologist Cornell U., Ithaca, N.Y., 1977-86; cons. wildlife biologist in pvt. practice Voorheesville, N.Y., 1986—; discussion leader Big Game session No. Am. Wildlife Conf., 1950; chmn. big game session N.E. Wildlife Conf., 1953, others; co-chmn. N.E. Deer Study Group, 1968. Editorial bd. Jour. Wildlife Mgmt., 1960-67, reviewer, 1972. Active in past numerous civic orgns. including Boy Scouts Am., Meth. Ch. Recipient Conservation award Am. Motors Corp., The Wildlife Soc., 1962, Wildlife Conservationist award Nat. Wildlife Fedn. and Sears Roebuck Found., 1965, Conservation award Sullivan County Sportsmen's Fedn., N.Y., 1966, Outstanding Svc. award Adirondack Deer Forum, 1973, Disting. Svc. award N.Y. State Conservation Coun., 1974, others. Mem. The Wildlife soc. (founding orgn. mem. 1936, co-chmn. N.E. sect. 1959, awards com. 1962, chmn. 1963, N.Y. state rep. 1962-71, N.Y. chpt. v.p. 1972, pres. 1973-74), Am. Soc. Mammalogists, Alumni Assn. of N.Y. State Coll. of Agr. and Life Scis., Cornell U. (Outstanding Alumni award 1987), Gamma Sigma Delta. Home and Office: 19 Lakeside Ave Edinburg NY 12134-5611

SEVERSON, WAYNE LARSON, retired physician; b. Slater, Iowa, Mar. 7, 1921; s. George James and Minnie Christina (Larson) S.; m. Dorothy Weeks, Dec. 1943 (div. 1974); children: Allan, Richard, Brenda, Kelli; m. Eyleen Bond, Aug. 1975 (dec. 1987); m. Maxine Sturdivant, Feb. 14, 1990. BS, Iowa State U., 1943; MD, U. Iowa, 1946. Intern Broadlawns Gen. Hosp., Des Moines, 1946-47; resident St. Joseph's Hosp., Flint, Mich., 1948; pvt. practice, Slater, Iowa, 1948-68; med. dir. Iowa Blue Cross Blue Shield, Des Moines, 1968-83; med. cons. Iowa Found. Med. Care, Des Moines, 1983-86; mem. med. adv. bd. Nat. Blue Cross-Blue Shield, Chgo., 1976-81, pres. bd., 1980-81. Capt. M.C., USAF, 1955-56. Mem. AMA, Am. Acad. Family Practice, Iowa Acad. Family Practice, Iowa Med. Assn., Polk County Med. Assn. Home: 1652 Rio Valley Dr Des Moines IA 50325-6541

SEVERY, LAWRENCE JAMES, psychologist, educator; b. Detroit, Mar. 30, 1943; m. Linda Andrea Anstensen, Aug. 20, 1966; children: Beth Andrea, Lisa Ellen. BS in Psychology, Wayne State U., 1965; MA in Psychology, U. Colo., 1970, PhD in Psychology, 1970. Rsch. asst. Inst. Behavioral Sci., U. Colo., Denver, 1968-69; predoctoral trainee Inst. Genetics and Behavior for Psychologists, U. Colo., Denver, 1969; asst. prof. psychology, sr. rsch. scientist Ark. Rehab. Rsch. and Tng. Ctr., U. Ark., 1970-71; various positions to prof., dept. psychology U. Fla., Gainesville, 1971—, R. David Thomas Endowed Legis. prof. psychology, 1988, assoc. dean for student affairs Coll. Liberal Arts and Scis., 1990—; rsch. fellow Inst. Population Studies, U. Exeter, Devon, Eng., 1982, sr. rsch. assoc. Behavioral Rsch. Inst., 1976-77, postdoctoral trainee, U. N.C. Population Ctr.'s summer inst., 1973 and others; cons. in field. Author: A Contemporary Introduction to Social Psychology, 1976, Advances in Population: Psychosocial Perspectives, Vol. 1 1993, Vol. 2, 1994; contbr. articles, book chpts. and monographs to profl. publs. Recipient numerous grants in population and health fields. Fellow APA (numerous coms.); mem. Southeastern Psychol. Assn., Population Assn. Am. (psycho-social workshop program chmn. 1982, 92), Assn. Consumer Rsch., Internat. Assn. Applied Psychology. Home: 4242 SW 94th Dr Gainesville FL 32608-4164 Office: Coll Liberal Arts & Scis U Fla Gainesville FL 32611

SEVIN, BRADLEY HARVEY, psychiatrist; b. New Haven, Nov. 11, 1943; s. Jack and Sylvia (Ginsberg) S.; m. Elizabeth Guttman, May 30, 1968; children: Jennifer Lynn, Joshua S. BS, Trinity Coll., Hartford, Conn., 1965; MD, Temple U., 1969. Cert. in adult psychiatry Am. Bd. Psychiatry and Neurology, in adult psychoanalysis Am. Psychoanalytic Assn. Dir., consultation-liaison psychiatry Hahnemann U., Phila., 1975-78; pvt. practice psychiatry Phila.; assoc. dir. adult profl. sch. Inst. Phila. Assn. for Psychoanalysis, Phila., 1989-90, dir. adult profl. sch., 1990-93. Co-author: Clinical Therapeutics, 1977, Psychiatric Clinics of North America, 1987. Fellow Am. Psychiat. Assn.; mem. ACP, Consultation-Liaison Assn. Phila. (founder, pres. 1978-90), Phila. Psychiat. Soc. (treas. 1987-88, v.p. 1988-89, exec. coun., pres. elect 1989-90, pres. 1990-91), Am. Psychoanalytic Assn., Am. Psychosomatic Soc., Men's Club Germantown Jewish Ctr. (bd. dirs. Phila. chpt. 1982-85). Democrat. Jewish. Home: 335 Aubrey Rd Wynnewood PA 19096-1812 Office: Pennsylvania Hosp 822 Pine St Ste 4B Philadelphia PA 19107-6124

SEVY, ROGER WARREN, retired pharmacology educator; b. Richfield, Utah, Nov. 6, 1923; s. Carl Spencer and Maude (Malmquist) S.; m. Barbara Florence Snetsinger, Aug. 16, 1948; children—Pamela Jane, Jonathan Carl. Student, Utah State U., 1941-43, Harvard, 1943-45; M.S., U. Vt., 1948; Ph.D., U. Ill., 1951, M.D., 1954. Asst. physiology U. Ill., 1948-51, instr., 1951-54; asst. prof. pharmacology Temple U., Phila., 1954-56, prof., 1956-89, chmn. dept., 1957-73, dean Sch. Medicine, 1973-79, prof. emeritus, 1989—. Served with AUS, 1943-45. Mem. Am. Soc. Pharmacology and Exptl. Therapeutics, Am. Physiol. Soc., Endocrine Soc., AAAS, Sigma Xi, Alpha Omega Alpha. Home: 242 Mather Rd Jenkintown PA 19046-3129 Office: Temple U 3420 N Broad St Philadelphia PA 19140-5104

SEWALL, WARREN, radiologist; b. Hartford, Conn., July 10, 1941; s. Joseph L. and Edna (Shakin) S.; m. Phyllis Nan Vogelhut, Apr. 29, 1970. BS, MIT, 1963; B in Med. Sci., Dartmouth U., 1965; MD, Harvard U., 1967. Diplomate Am. Bd. Radiology. Intern Mt. Auburn Hosp., Cambridge, MA, 1967-68; resident Mass. Gen. Hosp., Boston, 1970-73; radiologist Polyclinic Med. Ctr., Harrisburg, Pa., 1993—. Served to capt. U.S. Army, 1968-70. Named to Legion Membership Chapel of Four Chaplains. Mem. Am. Soc. Therapeutic Radiology and Oncology, Keystone Area Soc. for Radiation Oncology, Am. Coll. Radiology, Pa. Radiologic Soc., Am. Soc. Clin. Oncology, MIT Ednl. Coun. (regional vice-chmn. 1989-92), Dartmouth Med. Sch. Alumni Coun. (chmn. resource com. 1989-91).

SEWARD, JAMES PICKETT, internist, educator; b. N.Y.C., Oct. 14, 1949; s. George C. and Carroll Frances (McKay) S. AB, Harvard U., 1971; M of Pub. Policy, U. Calif., Berkeley, 1977; MD, U. Calif., San Francisco, 1977. Diplomate Am. Bd. Internal Medicine, Am. Bd. Occupational Medicine. Resident U. Calif. Hosps., San Francisco, 1977-80; Robert Woods Johnson postdoctoral fellow U. Calif., San Francisco, 1980-82; med. dir. health svcs. Lawrence Livermore Nat. Lab., 1994—; dir. preventive medicine residency U. Calif., Berkeley, 1991—; assoc. clin. prof. U. Calif., San Francisco, 1983—; asst. clin. prof. Sch. Pub. Health U. Calif., Berkeley, 1986—. Fulbright scholar, 1972-73. Fellow APHA, Am. Coll. Preventive Medicine, Am. Coll. Occupl. and Environ. Medicine. Office: HSD L723 LLNL PO Box 808 Livermore CA 94551-9900

SEWARD, TROILEN GAINEY, psychologist; b. Petersburg, Va., Nov. 26, 1941; d. Troy L. and Mary (Nester) Gainey; m. William E. Seward III, June 29, 1963; children: Susan Blair, William E. IV. BA, Coll. William and Mary, 1963, MEd, 1980, EdS, 1980; MEd, Va. Commonwealth U., 1977. Elem. tchr. Petersburg, 1963-67; secondary tchr. Surry (Va.) Acad., 1967-76, guidance counselor, 1976-77; headmistress Tidewater Acad., Wakefield, Va., 1977-79; psychologist Peninsula Child Devel. Clinic, Newport News, Va., 1980-82; sch. psychologist Dinwiddie (Va.) Pub. Sch., 1982-89, dir. pupil pers. svcs., spl. edn., 1990-93, dir. student svcs., 1993-95, supt., 1996—; mem. human rights com. Southside Tng. Ctr., Petersburg, 1986—. Trustee Ritchie Meml. ch., Claremont, Va., 1971—; mem. Town Coun., Claremont, 1984-90, mem. fin. com., 1984-90. Mem. Nat. Assn. Sch. Psychologists (del. 1992-94), Va. Assn. Sch. Psychologists (chair cert. and licensure com. 1985-87, legis. chair 1987—, pres. 1989-91), Delta Kappa Gamma, Phi Kappa Phi. Episcopalian. Home: PO Box 266 Claremont VA 23899-0266

SEWELL, LINDA MAY, home health nurse; b. Scotland, May 3, 1952; came to U.S., 1972; d. Thomas Wilson and Violet (Nicol) Fisher; m. Elliott Sewell, Jan. 14, 1972; children: Ariel, Jamil, Lilia. ADN, Western Ky. U., 1993, BSN summa cum laude, 1995. Cert. home health nursing ANCC, 1995. Staff nurse TJ Samson Cmty. Hosp., Glasgow, Ky., 1993; home health nurse Family Home Health Care, Burkesville, Ky., 1993—. Mem. ANA, Sigma Theta Tau, Phi Kappa Phi.

SEWELL, ROBERT DALTON, pediatrician; b. Newman, Calif., Apr. 28, 1950; s. James Dalton and Mary Louise (Hartwell) S.; m. Esther Madiedo, Oct. 26, 1975; children: Kevin, David. BA magna cum laude, Pacific Union Coll., 1972; MD, Loma Linda U., 1975. Diplomate Am. Bd. Pediatrics. Pediatric intern and resident White Meml. Med. Ctr., L.A., 1975-77; pediatric resident, chief resident Milton S. Hershey Med. Ctr., Pa. State U., Hershey, 1977-80; pediatrician Children's Med. Ctr. Asheville, N.C., 1980-81, Lincoln City Med. Ctr. P.C., Lincoln City, Oreg., 1982-95; examining physician C.A.R.E.S. Ctr. Emanuel Hosp. & Health Ctr., Portland, Oreg., 1988-90; asst. prof. Loma Linda (Calif.) U. Sch. Medicine, 1995—; chmn. child protection team North Lincoln Hosp., Lincoln City, 1983-89, sec. med. staff, 1990-92, pres. med. staff, 1992-94; mem. Citizens' Rev. Bd. Lincoln County, Newport, Oreg., 1986-92, Early Intervention adv. com., Newport, 1986-90. Mem. North Lincoln Local Sch. Com., Lincoln City, 1983-94, chmn., 1986-90; bd. dirs. Lincoln Shelter and Svcs., Inc., Lincoln City, 1983-89, chmn., 1987-89; mem. North Lincoln divsn. Am. Heart Assn., Lincoln City, 1986-89, v.p., 1987-89; mem. Drug and Alcohol Task Force, Lincoln City, 1988; mem., 2d vice-chmn. Yr. 2000 Plan housing com. Lincoln City Planning Commn., 1987-88; mem. AIDS task force Lincoln County Sch. Dist., 1987-89; mem. Lincoln County Children's Agenda Taskforce, 1988; mem. med. rev. com. Oreg. Med. Assn., 1990-95, mem.-at-large med. staff sect. gov. bd., 1993-95. Named Citizen of Yr. child protection com. Lincoln County, 1984, Man of Yr. Lincoln City C. of C., 1988. Mem. Am. Acad. Pediatrics (sect. on child abuse), Am. Profl. Soc. of Abuse of Children (charter mem.), Nat. Assn. Counsel for Children, Internat. Soc. for Prevention Child Abuse and Neglect, N.Am. Oreg. Profl. Soc. on Abuse of Children (founding pres. 1992-94), Calif. Profl. Soc. on Abuse of Children. Democrat. Seventh-day Adventist. Office: Loma Linda U Med Ctr Dept of Pediatrics 11262 Campus St West Hall Loma Linda CA 92354

SEWELL, WINIFRED, pharmaceutical librarian; b. Newport, Wash., Aug. 12, 1917; d. Harold Arthur and Grace (Vickerman) S. BA, State Coll. Wash., Pullman, 1938; BS in LS, Columbia U., 1940; DSc (hon.), Phila. Coll. Pharmacy and Sci., 1979. Asst. Columbia U. Library, N.Y.C., 1938-42; asst. librarian Wellcome Research Labs., Tuckahoe, N.Y., 1942-43; librarian Wellcome Research Labs., 1943-46, Squibb Inst. Med. Research, 1946-61; subject heading specialist Nat. Library of Medicine, 1961-62, dep. chief bibliog. services div., 1962-65, head drug literature program, 1965-70; adj. asst. prof. U. Md. Sch. Pharmacy, 1970-85; adj. lectr. U. Md. Coll. Libr. and Info. Svcs., 1969-92; cons. Nat. Health Planning Info. Ctr., 1975-81; instr. pharm. lit. and librarianship Columbia U., summer 1959; mem. com on modern methods for handling chem. info. Nat. Acad. Scis.-NRC; mem. Martindale Databank Adv. Panel, 1981-82. Editor: Unlisted Drugs, 1949-59, 62-64; author: Guide to Drug Information, 1976 (Ida and George Eliot award Med. Library Assn. 1977), (with Merle Harrison) Using MeSH for Effective Searching: a Programmed Guide, 1976, (with Sandra D. Teitelbaum) Micromanual for Casual Users of National Library of Medicine Databases, 1986, Reader in Medical Librarianship, 1973; editor: Health Affairs Series, Gale Info. Guides, 1971-80; mem. editorial bd.: Drug Info. Jour. Active Excerpta Medica adv. com., 1985-88. Fellow AAAS; mem. ALA, Am. Soc. for Info. Sci. (chmn. spl. interest group/classification rsch. 1974-75), Med. Libr. Assn. (chmn. Rittenhouse award com. 1975-76, chmn. recert. com. 1979-80, chmn. pub. health and health adminstrn. sect. 1979-80, chmn. med. librs. edn. sect. 1981-82), Spl. Librs. Assn. (chmn. pharm. sect., sci.-tech. divsn. 1952-53, pres. 1960-61, publs. award sci. and tech. divsn. 1966), Drug Info. Assn. (v.p. 1966-67, pres. 1970-71), Am. Assn. Colls. Pharmacy (chmn. librs./ednl. resources sect. 1979-80, del. coun. on sects. adv. bd. 1980-83). Home and Office: 6513 76th Pl Cabin John MD 20818-1413

SEXAUER, BRADLEY LESTER, healthcare administrator; b. Evansville, Ind., Aug. 13, 1951; s. Adolph L. and Edna L. (Ernst) S. BA, DePauw U., 1973; MHA, Tulane U., 1976; MBA, U. S.D., Vermillion, 1980. Adminstrv. asst. Tulane Med. Ctr. Hosp., New Orleans, 1976-77; assoc. dir. S.D. Health Systems Agy., Vermillion, 1977-81; mgr. regional planning Humana Inc., Orange Park, Fla., 1981-84; field v.p. Nat. Med. Enterprises, Atlanta, 1984-87; corp. v.p. planning Ingalls Health System, Harvey, Ill., 1987-92; v.p. planning and mktg. Danville (Va.) Regional Med. Ctr., 1992—. Fellow Am. Coll. Healthcare Execs., Soc. for Healthcare Planning and Mktg., Va. Inst. Polit. Leadership. Home: 228 Oak Creek Dr Danville VA 24541-6269 Office: Danville Regional Med Ctr 142 S Main St Danville VA 24541-2922

SEYFERT, HOWARD BENTLEY, JR., podiatrist; b. Clifton Heights, Pa., July 10, 1918; s. Howard Bentley and Mabel (Ashenbach) S.; m. Anna Mary van Roden, June 26, 1942; 1 child, Joanna Mary Irwin. D of Podiatric Medicine, Temple U., 1940. Cert. Nat. Bd. Podiatry Examiners (past pres.), Ariz. State Bd. Podiatry Examiners (past pres.). Pvt. practice podiatry Phoenix, 1950-82, Sedona, Ariz., 1982—; mem. med. staff Marcus J. Lawrence Meml. Hosp., Cottonwood, Ariz. Served to capt. USAAF, 1942-46, ETO, lt. col. Res. ret. Decorated Bronze Star. Fellow Acad. Ambulatory Foot Surgery, Am. Coll. Foot Surgeons; mem. Ariz. Podiatric Med. Assn. (past pres.), Am. Podiatric Med. Assn. Republican. Presbyterian. Clubs: OakCreek Country (Sedona); Fairfield Flagstaff Country (Flagstaff, Ariz.). Home: Air Force Village W 21364 Westover Circle Riverside CA 92518

SEYKORA, MARGARET S., psychotherapist; b. N.Y.C., June 18, 1947; d. Stanley Sneider and Janet Pick (Sneider) Smith; m. Sern A. Seykora, Jan. 19, 1968 (div. 1984); m. H. Lester Mower, Jr., Nov. 19, 1993. BS in Journalism, U. Fla., 1970; MA in Edn. and Human Devel. Counseling, Rollins Coll., 1991. Lic. mental health counselor, Fla.; lic. mortgage broker, Fla., lic. real estate broker, Fla. Advt. profl. Gainesville (Fla.) Sun, 1968-75, TV mag. editor, 1968-75, Sunday/lesiure/book editor, 1970; stoneware potter, owner Old Town (Fla.) Pottery, 1975-82; real estate salesperson Jack McCormick Realty, Chiefland, Fla., 1982-85, Coldwell Banker, Orlando, Fla., 1985-90; real estate broker The Hood Group, Inc., Orlando, 1990-92; psychotherapist, facilitator, pres. Personal Dynamics Inst., Altamonte Springs, Fla., 1989—; career instr. The Knowledge Shop, Winter Park, Fla., 1992—; outpatient clin. svcs. supr. Lakeside Alternatives, Winter Park, Fla., 1992—; adj. instr. Seminole C.C., Sanford, Fla., 1992—, Valencia C.C., Winter Park, 1992—. Author/facilitator workshops in field. Mem. Nat. Bd. Counselors, Am. Counseling Assn., Assn. for Specialists in Group Work, Nat. Bd. Realtors. Mem. Ch. of Religious Sci. Office: Personal Dynamics Inst 421 Montgomery Rd Ste 105 Altamonte Springs FL 32714-3140

SEYMOUR, HARLAN FRANCIS, healthcare industry executive; b. East Saint Louis, Mo., Jan. 25, 1950; s. Harlan Edward and Agnes Wilhelmina (Noakes) S.; m. Ellen Katheleen Schmitt, Aug. 17, 1973; children: Melissa Ann, Harlan Francis Jr. BA in Math., U. Mo., 1973; MBA, Keller Grad. Sch. Mgmt., 1980. Corp. v.p. Statis. Tabulating Corp., Chgo., 1973-80; dist. mgr. Datacorp, Chgo., 1980-83; exec. v.p. 1st Fin. Mgmt. Corp., Atlanta, 1983-94; pres., CEO 1st Health Svcs. Corp., Richmond, Va., 1989-94; exec. v.p., COO Trigon Blue Cross/Blue Shield, Richmond, 1994—; mem. mgmt. info. systems adv. bd. U. Ga., Athens, 1986-89, Va. Commonwealth U., 1991-93; bd. dirs. J. Sargeant Reynoldds C.C., 1991—. V.p. St. Joseph's Home and Sch., Marietta, Ga., 1987-88. Mem. Nat. Assn. Bank Servicers, Bank Mktg. Assn., Richmond Metro C. of C. (former bd. dirs.), Soc. Internat. Bus. Fellows, Assn. for Corp. Growth (bd. dirs. 1996—). Roman Catholic. Home: 12106 Country Hills Ct Glen Allen VA 23060-5347 Office: Trigon Blue Cross/Blue Shield 7130 Glen Forest Dr Richmond VA 23226-3757

SEYMOUR, JANET MARTHA, psychologist; b. Mineola, N.Y., June 13, 1957; d. John Andrews and Eileen (Brudie) S.; children: Heide Lynn Adams, Hartley Ann Adams, John Kyle Bergerson; m. John Douglas Bergerson, Mar. 26, 1995. BA in Psychology and Music, Wheaton Coll., 1979; MA in Clin. Psychology, Rosemead Sch. Psychology, La Mirada, Calif., 1981, PsyD in Clin. Psychology, 1988. Lic. psychologist, Calif. Psychology intern Colmery Oneil VA Med. Ctr., Topeka, 1985-86; psychotherapist Concord (N.H.) Psychol. Assocs., 1987-88; psychologist Jolliffe & Assocs., Long Beach, Calif., 1989—. Sunday sch. tchr. 1st Evang. Free Ch. Fullerton, Calif., 1990-91, orch. flutist, 1980—; coach Pony Baseball, Whittier, Calif., 1989; mem. Flutes Fantastiques Trio, 1993—; instr. flute tones course Whittier Cmty. Ctr., 1994—. Mem. Calif. Assn. Marriage and Family Therapists, Christian Assn. for Psychol. Studies. Republican. Office: Jolliffe & Assocs 3740 Atlantic Ave Ste 200 Long Beach CA 90807-3440

SEYMOUR, JOHN FRANCIS, medical oncologist; b. Melbourne, Australia, Aug. 25, 1963; s. James Patrick and Wendy Marie (Hankin) S.; m. Helen Symeopoulos, Apr. 28, 1991. MB, U. Melbourne, 1987, B Surgery, 1987. FRACP. Med. trainee St. Vincent's Hosp., Melbourne, 1988-91; fellow MD Anderson Cancer Ctr., Houston, Tex., 1992-93; oncology registrar Royal Melbourne Hosp., 1994, med. oncologist, 1995—. Contbr. articles to profl. jours. Rsch. fellow Australian Coll. of Physicians; recipient clin. rsch. award MD Anderson Cancer Ctr., 1993-94, Med. Postgrad. Rsch. scholar Australian Nat. Health and Med. Rsch. Coun., 1995-96. Mem. Am. Assn. Cancer Rsch., Am. Soc. Clin. Oncology, Am. Soc. Hematology. Office: Royal Melbourne Hosp, Grattan St Parkville, Victoria 3050 Melbourne Australia

SEYMOUR, RICHARD BURT, health educator; b. San Francisco, Aug. 1, 1937; s. Arnold Burt-Oakley and Florence Marguerite (Burt) S.; m. Michelle Driscoll, Sept. 15, 1963 (div. 1972); children: Brian Geoffrey, Kyra Daleth; m. Sharon Harkless, Jan. 5, 1973. BA, Sonoma State U., 1969, MA, 1970. Freelance writer Sausalito, Calif., 1960—; coord., adminstr. Coll. of Mendocino, Boonville, Calif., 1971-73; bus. mgr. Haight Ashbury Free Clinics, San Francisco, 1973-77; exec. adminstr., dir. tng. and edn. projects Height Ashbury Free Clinics, San Francisco, 1977-87; instr. John F. Kennedy U., Orinda, Calif., 1986—; asst. prof. Sonoma State U., Rohnert Park, Calif., 1985—; pres., chief exec. officer Westwind Assocs., Sausalito, Calif., 1988—; cons. Haight Ashbury Free Clinics, San Francisco, 1987—, treas., bd. dirs.; chmn. World Drug Abuse Treatment Network, San Francisco, 1988—; bd. dirs. Slide Ranch. Author: Physician's Guide to Psychoactive Drugs, 1987, Drug Free, 1987, The New Drugs, 1989, The Psychedelic Resurgence, 1993; editor-in-chief Internat. Addictions Infoline, 1995; mng. editor Jour. of Psychoactive Drugs, 1996; contbr. articles to profl. jours. Mem. Calif. Health Profls. for New Health Policy, Washington, 1976-80; chmn. Marin Drug Abuse Adv. Bd., San Rafael, Calif., 1979-81, CalDrug Abuse Svcs. Assn., Sacramento, 1975-79; mem. Alcohol and Drug Counselors Edn. Project, 1985—, San Francisco Delinquency Prevention Commn., 1981—, Calif. Primary Prevention Network, 1980—. Grantee NIMH, 1974—, Nat. Inst. on Drug Abuse, 1974—. Mem. Internat. Platform Assn., Commonwealth Club of Calif. Democrat. Episcopalian. Office: Westwind Assocs 90 Harrison Ave Apt C Sausalito CA 94965-2240

SFEZ, MICHEL VICTOR, anesthesiologist; b. Tunis, Tunisia, Nov. 7, 1955; s. Roland and Claudine (Hayat) S.; m. Brigitte Yvonne Audouin, Nov. 21, 1987; children: Samuel, Pauline. MD, U. Paris VI, 1982; cert. in anesthesiology, U. Paris V, 1984; MS in Biology, U. Paris VII, 1988. Intern pediatrics Service d'Aide Mobile Urgente, Montfermeil, France, 1979-81; resident dept. anesthesiology Hosp. avicenne, Bobigny, Francež, 1981-82; staff pediatric intensivist Service d'Aide Mobile Urgente, Montreuil, France, 1980-82; anesthesiologist, intensivist Mil. Hosp., Cherbourg, France, 1983; anesthesiologist Hopital J. Verdier, Bondy, France, 1983-86; anesthesiologist Hopital St. Vincent de Paul, Paris, 1986-87, pediatric intensivist, 1987-89; pediatric anesthesiologist Clinique Chirurgicale Boulogne, France, 1989—; assoc. dir. Pediat. Service d'Aide Mobile Urgente 93, 1982; cons. Association Franñaise contre les Myopathies, Evry, France, 1993—. Contbr. articles to profl. jours. and chpts. to books. Lt. French Health Svc., 1983. Mem. Société Franñaise d'Anesthésie et de Réanimation, Association des Anesthésistes-Réanimateurs Pédiatriques d'Expression Fran ú318aise, Assn. Paediatric Anaesthetists of Gt. Britain and Ireland, Syndicat Nat. des Anesthesistes Reanimateurs Franñais (regional del. 1995). Office: Clin Chirurg, 105 Ave Victor Hugo, 92100 Boulogne France

SGROI, DONALD ANGELO, obstetrician, gynecologist; b. Newark, Aug. 20, 1943; s. Joseph and Mary (Desimone) S.; m. Phyllis Ann Intorelli, Nov. 19, 1967; children: Donna, Felisa, Chela, Gabriela, Alexandria. BS, Fairleigh Dickinson U., 1970; MD, Autonomous U. Guadalajara, Mex., 1974. Diplomate Am. Bd. Ob-Gyn. Sr. tech. aide Bell Labs., Berkley Heights, N.J., 1967-70; intern St. Michael's Med. Ctr., Newark, 1974-76; resident in ob-gyn. St. Joseph's Med. Ctr., Paterson, N.J., 1976-78, chief resident, 1978-79; assoc. attending physician Wayne (N.J.) Gen. Hosp., 1980-84, co-chmn. dept. ob-gyn., 1980-84, attending physician, 1984—, chmn. tissue rev. com., 1984-88, mem. tissue rev. com., 1988-94, chmn. dept. ob-gyn., 1988-91, co-chmn. dept. ob-gyn., 1991—; sec., treas. med. exec. com., 1988-91, mem. peer assessment com., 1988-91, quality assurance com., 1988, credentials com., 1988—; mem. Peer Rev. Orgn. of N.J., 1991—. Fellow Am. Coll. Ob-Gyn., Am. Fertility Soc. (jr.); mem. Internat. Assn. Gynelogic Laparoscopist, Internat. Corr. Soc. Obstetricians and Gynecolgists. Roman Catholic. Home: 27 Shinnecock Trl Franklin Lakes NJ 07417-1033 Office: 401 Hamburg Tpke Ste 104 Wayne NJ 07470-2139

SHABLOSKI, REGAN PETER, osteopath; b. Wellsboro, Mass., July 23, 1965; s. Michael Anthony and Roberta Ann (Amacher) S. BA, Mansfield (Mass.) U., 1987, Edn. Cert., Specialist, 1988, MS, 1988; DO, Kirksville Coll. Osteo. Med., Mo., 1992; cert. advanced study, Gannon U., Erie, Pa., 1994. Diplomate Nat. Bd. Osto. Med. Examiners. Intern Metro Health Ctr., Erie, 1992, resident, attending staff physician, 1993—; staff physician Prompt Care Clinics, Erie, 1993—; attending staff physician Carry (Pa.) Meml. Hosp., 1993—; dep. med. dir. Erie County Emergency Physicians Assn., 1993—; vol. physician. Mem. AMA, Am. Osteo. Assn., Am. Acad. Osteopathy, Am. Coll. Family Physicians, Am. Coll. Preventive Medicine, Am. Gen. Acad. Republican. Roman Catholic. Office: Metro Health Ctr 252 W 11th St Erie PA 16501 Address: 10526 Pebble Creek Dr Mc Kean PA 16426-1948

SHACKELFORD, MARTIN ROBERT, social worker; b. Boonville, Mo., May 22, 1947; s. Hugh and Carol Lois (Schoene) S. BA in History, U. Mich., 1969. Driver Yellow Cab, Saginaw, Mich., 1969-70; sales clk. Waldenbooks, Saginaw, Mich., 1972; eligibility worker Saginaw County Dept. Social Svcs., 1972-73, employment worker, 1973-77, delinquency svcs. worker, 1977—; charter mem. social work adv. com. Saginaw Valley State U., 1981—. Contbr. articles on JFK assassination to profl. jours. Bd. dirs. Valley Film Soc., Saginaw, 1978—, ACLU, Cen. Mich. Br., 1978—; vice chmn. Lone Tree Coun. Home: 216 N Webster St # 2 Saginaw MI 48602-4243

SHACKLETON, JOY LINDA, prosthodontist researcher; b. Durban, South Africa, June 18, 1961; d. Eric Edward and Rosemary Josephine (Chater) S. B of Dental Sci., U. Witwatersrand, Johannesburg, South Africa, 1984, MS in Dentistry, 1988, M of Dentistry, 1992. Registered with South African Med. and Dental Coun. as dentist and prosthodontist. Dentist, jr. lectr. U. Witwatersrand, Johannesburg, South Africa, 1985-87, registrar, jr. lectr., 1988-90, part time sr. dentist, lectr., 1991-92, specialist lectr., 1992—; part time gen. dentist pvt. practice Johannesburg, South Africa, 1991-92, prosthodontist pvt. practice, 1992—. Contbr. articles to profl. dentistry jours. Mem. Johannesburg Chamber Choir, 1995; com. mem. Transvaal Horse Soc. Driving Discipline, 1993-97. Recipient Frank Reynolds scholarship Durban Girls' Coll., 1974-78, Reeve Shapiro Meml. bursary U. Witwatersrand, 1981, Emma Smith bursary Natal U., 1980-84. Mem. Dental Assn. South Africa, Prosthodontic Soc. South Africa. Office: U Witwatersrand Dept Dentistry, 1 Jan Smuts Ave, 2051 Johannesburg South Africa

SHACKLETT, DAVID EDWARDS, ophthalmologist; b. Atlanta, Ga., Nov. 12, 1935; s. Henry Lamar and Martha (Edwards) S.; m. Anntonia Gail Sapp, Apr. 20, 1963; children: Dena Marie Shacklett Nunn, David Edwards Jr. BA, Emory U., 1961; MD, Emory U. Sch. Medicine, 1967. Diplomate Am. Bd. Ophthalmology. Flight surgeon, resident/fellow ophthalmology USAF/Emory U., Atlanta, 1967-71; chief clin. ophthalmology Sch. Aerospace Medicine, San Antonio, 1971-76; chmn. dept. ophthalmology Wilford Hall USAF Med. Ctr., San Antonio, 1976-82; vice chmn., prof. ophthalmology U. Tex. Health Sci. Ctr., San Antonio, 1982-85; pvt. practice ophthalmology Village Oaks Med. Ctr., San Antonio, 1985—. Trustee Northeast Ind. Sch. Dist., San Antonio, 1984-90; bd. dirs. Boysville, Converse, Tex., 1987-90, Village Oaks Med. Ctr., San Antonio, 1985-87; pres. Baylor Parents League, San Antonio, 1989-91. Col. USAF, 1961-82. Fellow Am. Acad. Ophthalmology; mem. Tex. Med. Assn., Tex. Ophthalmol. Assn., Soc. Mil. Ophthalmologists (pres. 1979-80), San Antonio Soc. Ophthalmology (v.p. 1980-81), Bexar County Med. Soc. Baptist. Home: 13815 Bluff Top San Antonio TX 78216 Office: Northeast Eye Physicians 12709 Toepperwein San Antonio TX 78233

SHACKLETT, LYLE KENT, orthodontist; b. Mountain View, Okla., Oct. 21, 1938; s. Joseph Lyle and Inez Evaline (Kent) S.; m. Jan Kay Wiesenmayer, May 22, 1970; children: Scott, Amy, Laura, Andrew, Karin. DDS, U. Mo. Kansas City, 1963; MS in Dentistry, St. Louis U., 1965. Diplomate Am. Bd. Orthodontics. Capt. USAF, Japan, 1965-68; orthodontist pvt. practice Tulsa, 1968—; teaching staff Charles Tweed Cource, Tuscon, 1989—. Editor Dental Newsletter, 1970-83. Mem. Rotary Internat., Tulsa, 1990—; bd. dirs. Metro Christian Acad., Tulsa, 1990—; tchr. Tulsa Bible Ch., 1968—. Mem. Am. Dental Assn., Am. Assn. Orthodontists, Okla. Dental Assn., Charles H. Tweed Found., Okla. Orthodontic Soc., St. Louis U. Orthodontic Rsch. Found. Republican. Office: Kent Shacklett DDS 3305 East 45th St Tulsa OK 74135

SHADER, RICHARD IRWIN, psychiatrist, educator; b. Mt. Vernon, N.Y., May 27, 1935; s. Myer and Beatrice (Epstein) S.; m. Aline Brown, Sept. 21, 1958; children: Laurel Beth, Jennifer Robin, Robert Andrew. Student, Harvard U., 1952-56; M.D., NYU, 1960; grad., Boston Psychoanalytic Inst., 1970. Diplomate Am. Bd. Psychiatry and Neurology (dir. 1977-84, treas. 1982-83, pres. 1984). Intern Greenwich Hosp., Conn., 1960-61; resident in psychiatry Mass. Mental Health Ctr., Boston, 1961-62, 64-65, NIMH, Bethesda, Md., 1962-64; asso. prof. psychiatry Harvard Med. Sch., 1970-79; prof. dept. psychiatry Tufts U. Med. Sch., Boston, 1979—, chmn. dept., 1979-91; psychiatrist in chief New Eng. Med. Ctr. Hosp., Boston, 1979-91; prof. pharmacology Tufts U. Med. Sch., Boston, 1983—, chmn. dept. pharmacology and exptl. therapeutics, 1991-93. Author: (with A. DiMascio) Psychotropic Drug Side Effects, 1970, (with D.J. Greenblatt) Benzodiazepines in Clinical Practice, 1974, Manual of Psychiatric Therapeutics, 1975, 2d edit., 1994; editor: Psychiatric Complications of Medical Drugs, 1972, (with A. DiMascio) Clinical Handbook of Psychopharmacology, 1970, (with D.J. Greenblatt) Pharmacokinetics in Clinical Practice, 1985, (with A. DiMascio) Butyrophenones in Psychiatry, 1972; MAOI Therapy, 1988, (with J.P. Tupin and D.S. Harnett) Handbook of Clinical Psychopharmacology, 1988, (with others) Drug Interactions in Psychiatry, 1989, 2d edit., 1995, Clinical Manual of Chemical Dependence, 1991; editor-in-chief Jour. Clin. Psychopharmacology, 1980—. Bd. dirs. Med. Found., Inc., 1980-87. Served with USPHS, 1962-64. Joseph J. Michaels merit scholar, 1968-69; fellow Ctr. for Advanced Study in Behavioral Scis., Stanford, Calif., 1990-91; recipient Seymour Vestermark award Am. Psychiat. Assn., 1988, 90. Mem. AMA, Mass. Med. Soc., Am. coll. Neuropsychopharmacology (v.p. 1984, pres. 1990), Am. Soc. Clin. Pharmacology & Therapeutics, Am. Soc. Pharmacology and Exptl. Therapeutics. Democrat. Jewish. Office: Tufts U Sch Medicine 136 Harrison Ave Boston MA 02111-1800

SHADER, SUZAN LYNDA, health and nutritional consultant; b. Orlando, Fla., June 11, 1954; d. Charles Abraham and Reva Ethel (Youdelman) Shader; m. Gary Francis Nassoiy, Feb. 22, 1981 (div. 1985); children: Samantha-Lyn, Dara-Michelle. AAS in Vet. Lab. Tech., Biscayne Paramed. Inst., Miami, Fla, 1975; AS in Nursing, Valencia C.C., Orlando, Fla., 1979, postgrad.; cert. in risk mgmt., U. Cen. Fla., 1989. RN, Fla.; lic. real estate sales and pre-paid legal ins. sales, Fla., lic. in healthcare risk mgmt., Fla. Staff nurse Orlando Regional Med. Ctr., 1979-81, Humana Hosp.-Lucerne, Orlando, 1981-85; with Profl. Found. for Health Care, Inc., 1985-87; utilization rev. mgr. Humana Hosp.-Lucerne, 1987-88; utilization rev. cons., owner Utilization Rev. Cons., Inc., Orlando, 1988-91; nurse reviewer workers compensation claims auditing and utilization rev. Am. Internat. Health and Rehab. Svcs., Inc., Orlando, 1991-93; cons. Body Wise Internat., Inc., 1995—. Mem. Ohev Shalom Synagogue; vol. Orlando Humane Soc., Neighborhood Watch. Mem. Am. Coll. Utilization Rev. Physicians (affiliate mem.), Am. Bd. Quality Assurance and Utilization Rev. (cert., diplomate 1988), Jewish Cmty. Ctr., World Wildlife Fund, Nat. Humane Edn. Soc., Physician's Com. Responsible Medicine, Doris Day Animal League, People for Ethical Treatment Animals, Greenpeace, Swarovski Collectors Soc. (charter 1987), Humane Soc. U.S., Internat. Fund Animal Welfare. Republican. Home: 3416 Neptune Dr Orlando FL 32804-3519

SHADID, EDWARD A., plastic surgeon; b. Oklahoma City, July 22, 1936; s. Albert S. Shadid; m. Ellen Darlene Shadid; children: Edward Jr., Christopher, Gregory, Derek, Nicole. BS, Okla. U., 1957; MD, Okla. U., Oklahoma City, 1960. Diplomate Am. Bd. Plastic Surgery. Gen. surg. resident U. Okla. Health Scis. Ctr., 1961-62, 64-66; plastic surg. resident U. Pitts., 1966-68; plastic surgeon Plastic & Reconstructive Surgery Clinic, Oklahoma City. With USN. Fellow ACS; mem. AMA, Am. Soc. Plastic and Reconstructive Surgeons, Am. Soc. Aesthetic Plastic Surgery, Internat. Soc. Hair Restoration, Lipoplasty Soc. N.Am., Okla. State Med. Assn. Office: Plastic & Reconstructive Surg Cli 13313 N Meridian Ste #A Oklahoma City OK 73120

SHAFER, JAMES ALBERT, health care administrator; b. Chgo., Aug. 26, 1924; s. James Earl and Kathleen (Sutterland) S.; m. Irene Jeanne Yurcega, June 20, 1948; children: Kathleen Mary, Patricia Ann. Technician Zenith Radio Corp., Chgo., 1946-47; owner, operator Eastgate Electronics, Chgo., 1947-61; applications engr. Perfection Mica Co., Bensenville, Ill., 1961-71; pres. Electronics Unltd., Northbrook, Ill., 1972-73, Ariz. Geriatric Enterprises Inc., Safford, 1974-86; sec.-treas. Saguaro Care Inc., 1988—; bd. dirs. Mt. Graham Community Hosp., Safford. Republican. Roman Catholic. Home: Skyline Ranch 10729 W Cottonwood Rd Pima AZ 85543-0630 Office: Saguaro Care Inc PO Drawer H Pima AZ 85543

SHAFF, ALAN MARTIN, chiropractic sports physician; b. Ithaca, N.Y., Mar. 21, 1958; s. Steve I. Shaff and Joan (Cohen) Gilbert; m. Susan Lee Siegel, July 3, 1954. D in Chiropractic, Palmer Coll. Chiropractic, 1983. Diplomate Am. Chiropractic Bd. of Sports Physicians; cert. in manipulation under anesthesia. Assoc. chiropractic Burak Chiropractic Clinic, Miami, Fla., 1983-84; dir. chiropractic dept. Instituto Nazionale Satic, Trieste, Italy, 1984-85; dir. Boca-Delray Chiropractic Ctr., Del Ray Beach, Fla., 1985—. Sports medicine staff U.S. Olympic Tng. Ctr., Colorado Springs, 1996. Mem. Am. Chiropractic Assn. (coun. on sports injuries and phys. fitness), Fla. Chiropractic Assn. (chair ethics com.), Delray Beach Jaycees (v.p. 1987-88), Lions, Toastmasters. Office: Boca Delray Chiropractic 4801 Linton Blvd Ste 9A Delray Beach FL 33445-6501

SHAFFER, DANA C., family medicine physician; b. Sunbury, Pa., June 2, 1955; s. Cameron R. and Joan Irene (Felix) S.; m. Joan Ellen Jacobsen, July 24, 1976; children: Royce, Kirsten. BS, Wilkes Coll., 1981; DO, Phila. Coll. Osteo. Medicine, 1985. Diplomate Am. Bd. Osteopathic Family Practice. Intern Des Moines Gen. Hosp., 1986; pvt. practice Exira, Elk Horn, Iowa, 1986—; faculty U. Osteopathic Medicine & Health Scis., Des Moines, 1991—; staff Audubon County Meml. Hosp., 1986—, Cass County Meml. Hosp., Atlantic, Iowa, 1986—, Myrtue Meml. Hosp., Harlan, Iowa, 1994—. Served in U.S. Navy, 1973-79. Mem. Am. Osteopathic Assn., Am. Coll. Osteopathic Family Physicians, Iowa Assn. Long-Term Care Dirs., Iowa Osteopathic Med. Assn., Am. Coll. Gen. Practitioners, Iowa Found. for Med. Care, Am. Heart Assn., Phila. Coll. Osteopathic Medicine Alumni Assn., Audubon County Med. Soc., Audubon County Lincoln Club. Republican. Lutheran. Office: Exira Family Medicine Clin 207 E Main Box 87 Exira IA 50076

SHAFFER, DEBORAH, nurse; b. Tampa, Fla., Jan. 20, 1954; d. Frank Solomon and Mary Louise (Swann) Shaffer; children: Danny, Dionne. LPN, Suwanee-Hamilton Nursing Sch., Live Oak, Fla., 1984; student, Hillsborough CC, 1992—. LPN, Fla. Nursing experience various hosps. and nursing homes, 10 yrs. Author poems, songs and short stories. Active Neighborhood Crime Watch, Parents Without Ptnrs., The Spring, Literacy Vols. Am.; ESL tutor First Bapt. Ch.; activities instr. A.D.C. Osborne Ctr.

SHAFFER, HOWARD JEFFREY, clinical psychologist, consultant, researcher, educator; b. Boston, Sept. 1, 1948; s. Milton and Ruth Ann (Weiner) S.; m. Linda Marie Andrews; children: David Andrew, Paige

Meredith. BA, U. N.H., 1970; MS, U. Miami, Coral Gables, Fla., 1972, PhD, 1974. Lic. psychologist, Mass., N.H.; registered psychologist Nat. Register Health Service Providers in Psychology, 1982. Research dir. Psycho-Social Rehab. Ctr. Dade County (Fla.), Inc., 1974-75; clin. dir. Project Turnabout, Inc., Hingham, Mass., 1975-78, East Boston (Mass.) Drug Rehab. Clinic, 1976-77; dir. spl. consultation and treatment program for women Judge Gould Inst. Human Resources, Inc., Worcester, Mass., 1977-78; dir. narcotics treatment program Drug Problems Resource Center, dept. psychiatry Harvard Med. Sch. at Cambridge (Mass.) Hosp. and North Charles Found. for Tng. and Research, 1978-82, Ctr. for Addition Studies Harvard Med. Sch. and The Cambridge Hosp., 1986—; chief psychologist N. Charles. Inst. for the Additions, 1983-94; mem. adj. faculty U. Miami, 1974; mem. clin. faculty Barry Coll., 1974-75; mem. field faculty Lone Mountain Coll., 1974-75; teaching cons. U. Lowell, 1975-76; clin. assoc. prof. counseling psychology Boston U., 1976-78; instr. psychology dept. psychiatry Harvard Med. Sch. at Cambridge Hosp., 1978-81, asst. prof. psychology, 1982-93, assoc. prof. psychology, 1994—; mem. faculty Mass. Psychol. Center, Boston, 1980; mem. council on marijuana and health 1981-85; mem. adv. bd. and faculty Northeastern Comprehensive Service Inst., Danvers, Mass., 1983-85; mem. field faculty Grad. Sch. Psychology and Counseling, Lesley Coll., 1983—; chief psychologist North Charles Inst. for Addictions, 1982-94; mem. spl. study sect. NIH and Nat. Cancer Inst., 1984—; dir. Ctr. for Addiction Studies, Harvard Med. Sch., 1986-96, dir. divsn. on addictions, 1995—. Contbr. articles, revs., abstracts to profl. publs., presentations in field; editor: a book about drug issues Myths and Realities, 1977, (with M. E. Burglass) Classic Contributions in the Addictions, 1981 (alt. main selection Behavioral Sci. Book Club 1981); The Addictive Behaviors, 1985; (with H. Milkman) Addictions: Multidisciplinary Perspectives and Treatments, 1984; (with S. Jones) Quitting Cocaine: The Struggle Against Impulse, 1988; (with others) Compulsive Gambling: Theory, Research and Practice, 1989; assoc. editor Jour. of Substance Abuse Treatment, 1983—; assoc. editor: Psychology of Addictive Behavior, 1982—; guest editor: spl. issue Advances in Alcohol and Substance Abuse, 1983; mem. editorial rev. bd.: Jour. Psychoactive Drugs, 1981—, Advances in Alcohol and Substance Abuse, 1982—. Mem. Andover (Mass.) Substance Abuse Com., 1982. Recipient 1st place award U. N.H. Undergrad. Conf. for Psychol. Research, 1969. Mem. AAAS, Am. Psychol. Assn., Soc. Psychologists in Addictive Behavior, Boston Computer Soc., Psi Chi, Phi Kappa Phi. Jewish. Research on cognitive, behavioral, and psychodynamic factors associated with substance use and abuse, social psychology of psychotherapy; philosophy of sci.; psychopathology of adolescent gambling; natural history of addictive disorders. Home: 27 Algonquin Ave Andover MA 01810-5527 Office: Harvard U Med Sch Div Addictions 220 Longwood Ave Boston MA 02115

SHAFFER, JILL, clinical psychologist; b. Columbus, Ohio, May 18, 1958; d. Melvin Warren and Emily (White) S.; m. Robert K. Yost, Jan. 9, 1991; children: Melanie Jill Yost, Robison Kimber Yost. BS in Psychology with honors, Wright State U., 1984, PsyD, 1988. Lic. psychologist, Ohio. Psychology talk show producer/participant Sta. WHIO-AM, Dayton, Ohio, 1981-83; psychology asst. and organizer Terrap S.W. Ohio, Dayton, 1981-83; psychology trainee Oakwood Forensic Ctr., Lima, Ohio, 1984-85, Wright State U., Dayton, 1984-87; predoctoral resident South Community Mental Health Ctr., Dayton, 1987-88; postdoctoral trainee Fulero and Assoc., Dayton, 1988-89; pvt. practice Dayton, 1989—; supervising psychologist GERI-Tech of Dayton, 1990-92; cons. psychologist disability evaluations for worker's compensation and social security disability, 1989-94; state examiner Indsl. Commn. of Ohio, 1989—; owner, mgr. rental properties, 1988—. Author: (article) Strategic Intervention with Transvestism, 1989. Recipient scholarship Sch. of Profl. Psychology, 1985. Mem. APA, NOW, Ohio Psychol. Assn., Dayton Area Psychol. Assn. Office: 2705 Far Hills Ave Ste 4 Dayton OH 45419-1606

SHAFFER, SUSAN E., nutrition specialist; b. Nashville, Apr. 14, 1947; d. James G. and Esther W. Shaffer. B.A. in English, Elmhurst (Ill.) Coll., 1969; MS in Nutrition, Rutgers U., 1991, postgrad., 1991—. Mem. claim dept. Allstate Ins. Co., 1971-76, unit mgr., Springfield, Pa., 1976-77, regional life claim mgr., Basking Ridge, N.J., 1977-79, dist. claim mgr., Latham, N.Y., 1979-87; rsch. asst. food sensory lab. Rutgers U., New Brunswick, N.J., 1991-94, asst. to dir. mkgt. Rescar Inc., Downers Grove, Ill, 1994—. Mem. Ins. Inst. Am. (assoc. in mgmt.). Office: Rescar Inc 1101 31st St Downers Grove IL 60515

SHAFIR, MICHAIL KLEYNER, medical educator; b. Shanghai, China, July 16, 1943; came to U.S., 1974; s. George and Isabella (Kleyner) S.; m. Adela Fruhling, May 6, 1967; children: Alan, Daniela. MD, U. Chile, 1967. Resident Gustave Roussy Cancer Inst., Villejuif, France, 1967-70; surgeon Lopez Perez Cancer Inst., Santiago, Chile, 1970-74; resident Mt. Sinai Hosp., N.Y.C., 1974-79, attending surgeon, 1979—; assoc. prof. surgery, neoplastic diseases Mt. Sinai Sch. Medicine, N.Y.C., 1985—; cons. in field. Jr. Faculty fellow Am. Cancer Soc., N.Y.C., 1982. Fellow Am. Coll. Surgeons; mem. Am. Soc. Clin. Oncology, N.Y. Surg. Soc., Soc. Surg. Oncology. Jewish. Office: 1021 Park Ave New York NY 10028-0959

SHAFRITZ, DAVID ANDREW, physician, research scientist; b. Phila., Oct. 5, 1940; s. Saul and Ethel (Kohn) S.; m. Sharon C. Klemow, Aug. 16, 1964; children: Gregory S., Adam B., Keith M. AB in Chemistry with honors, U. Pa., 1962, MD, 1966. Diplomate Nat. Bd. Med. Examiners, Am. Bd. Internal Medicine. Intern, then asst. resident U. Md. Hosp., Balt., 1966-68; rsch. assoc. NIH, Bethesda, Md., 1968-71; clin. and rsch. fellow Mass. Gen. Hosp., Boston, 1971-73; instr. Harvard Med. Sch., Boston, 1971-73, asst. prof. medicine, 1973; asst. prof. medicine and cell biology Albert Einstein Coll. Medicine, Yeshiva U., Bronx, N.Y., 1973-76, assoc. prof., 1976-81, prof. medicine and cell biology, 1981—, dir. Marion Bessin Liver Rsch. Ctr., 1985—, Herman Lapota prof. liver disease rsch., 1992—; cons. integrated Genetics, Inc., Framingham, Mass., 1981-86, Immuno, Vienna, Austria, 1986-91, Innovir, Inc., N.Y.C., 1991—, Eugenetech Internat., Inc., Ramsey, N.J., 1991-93; temp. advisor WHO, Geneva, 1983; mem. Nat. Com. for Clin. Lab. Stds., Villanova Pa., 1983—, sci. adv. bd. com. liver cancer program Inst. for Cancer Rsch., Fox Chase and Phila., 1987—, mem. rev. panel C. study sect. Nat. Inst. Diabetes and Digestive Kidney Diseases, 1988-92; mem. cen. coord. com. Liver Tissue Procurement and Distbn. Sys., 1986, Nat. Inst. Health Metabolic Pathology Study sect., 1995—; mem. Nat. Bd. Med. Examiners and U.S. Med. Exam. Com., 1996—. Co-author: The Liver: Biology and Pathobiology, 1982, 3rd edit., 1993, Hepatobiliary Diseases, 1991; assoc. editor Hepatology, 1981-86; mem. editl. bd. Jour. Med. Virology, 1982-93, Hepatology, 1990—, Jour. Virology, 1992—; contbr. numerous rsch. articles and revs. to profl. publs.; contbr. chpts. to books; patentee in field. Trustee Westchester Jewish Ctr., Mamaroneck, N.Y., 1980-86. Lt. comdr. USPHS, 1968-71. Recipient Merck award U. Pa., 1962, Morton McCutcheon Meml. Rsch. prize Sch. Medicine, 1966, Career Scientist award Irma T. Hirschl Trust, N.Y.C., 1974-79, NIH Merit award, 1994; European Molecular Biology Orgn. fellow, 1978; recipient Rsch. Career Devel. award NIH, 1975-80, spl. rsch. fellow, 1971-73, rsch. grantee, 1974—. Mem. Am. Assn. for Study of Liver Diseases, Internat. Assn. for Study of Liver, Am. Gastroenterol. Assn., Am. soc. Biochemistry and Molecular Biology, Am. Soc. Investigative Pathology, Am. Soc. Clin. Investigation, Assn. Am. Physicians, N.Y. Acad. Scis., Harvey Soc., Interurban Clin. Club. Democrat. Jewish. Home: 4 Pheasant Run Larchmont NY 10538-3423 Office: Yeshiva U Albert Einstein Coll Med Marion Bessin Liver Rsch Ctr 1300 Morris Park Ave Bronx NY 10461-1926

SHAFRITZ, RANDY, physician, surgeon; b. Phila., Nov. 9, 1962; s. Marlyn Pillet Shafritz; m. Suzanne Mackin, Apr. 6, 1991. BA, Pa. State U., 1984; MA, Hahnemann U., Phila., 1986; MD, Jefferson Med. Coll., 1990. Surg. intern Albert Einstein Med. Ctr., Phila., 1990-91, surg. resident, 1991-95, chief surg. resident, 1995-96; vascular fellow U. Medicine and Dentistry N.J.-Robert Wood Johnson, New Brunswick, 1996—. Mem. Soc. Laparoendoscopic Surgeons.

SHAH, MUBARIK AHMAD, surgeon; b. Lahore, Punjab, Pakistan, Dec. 19, 1949; came to U.S., 1976; s. Tufail Mohammad and Amna (Bibi)) S.; m. Mansoora Nazli, Nov. 10, 1974; children: Rizwan, Maliha, Numaan. FSc, T.I. Coll., Rabwah, Pakistan, 1966; MBBS, Punjab U., Multan, Pakistan, 1971. Diplomate Am. Bd. Surgery. Instr. King Edward Med. Coll., Paskistan, 1975-76; house surgeon N.Y. Polyclinic Hosp., N.Y.C., 1976-77; resident surgery St. Mary Hosp., Waterbury, Conn., 1977-78, New Rochelle (N.Y.) Hosp., 1978-79; resident surgery Presbyn.-U. Pa. Med. Ctr., Phila., 1979-82, fellow vascular surgery, 1982-83; clin. instr. U. Pa. Sch. Medicine, Phila., 1979-83; attending physician, surgeon St. Mary Hosp., Langhorne, Pa., 1990—; dir. trauma svcs. Med. Coll. Hosps., Bucks County Campus, Warminster, Pa., 1988-90. Med. advisor Trevose (Pa.) Rescue, 1988-90; pres. Ahmadiyya Youth Orgn., Phila., 1989-90. Capt. Pakistan Army, 1971-75. Fellow ACS, Internat. Coll. Surgeons, Am. Soc. Abdominal Surgeons; mem. Am. Trauma Soc. Office: St Mary Med Office Bldg Ste 302 1205 Langhorne Newtown Rd Langhorne PA 19047-1222

SHAH, NAREN NATWARLAL, cardiologist; b. Ahmedabad, India, Jan. 12, 1934; came to U.S., 1959; s. Natwarlal G. and Kanta M. Shah; m. Mary Ann Iafolla; children: Jennifer, Jeffrey, Jason. Student, M.G. Sci. Inst., Ahmedabad, 1951; MD, B.J. Med. Coll., Ahmedabad, 1957. Intern Elgin Gen. Hosp., St. Thomas, Ontario, Can., 1959-60; resident in medicine Union Meml. Hosp., Balt., 1960-62; resident in cardiology Phila. Gen. Hosp., 1962-63, fellow in cardiology, 1965-66; resident in cardiology Hahnemann Med. Ctr., Phila., 1963-64, fellow in kidney disease, 1964-65; fellow in medicine Hamilton (Ontario) Gen. Hosp., 1966-67; fellow in cardiology St. Michael's Hosp., Toronto, 1967-68; with Group Health Assn., Washington, 1968-72; chief medicine VA Med. Ctr., Montrose, N.Y., 1980—; attending cardiologist Lincoln Hosp., Bronx, N.Y., 1972-73, Met. Hosp., Manhattan, N.Y., 1973-80; clin. assoc. N.Y. Med. Coll., Valhalla, 1980—. Contbr. articles to profl. jours.; rsch. panel: Sports Medicine, The Medical News. Lt. col. USAR, 1980—. Recipient Physician's Recognition Award AMA, 1979—. Fellow Am. Coll. Physicians, Am. Coll. Angiology; mem. Am. Coll. Cardiology, Am. Soc. Echocardiography, Am. Heart Assn., N.Y. Med. Soc. Home: 67 Tarryhill Rd Tarrytown NY 10591-6511

SHAH, NATVERLAL JAGJIVANDAS, cardiologist; b. Godhra, Gujarat, India, Aug. 3, 1926; s. Jagjivandas Purshottamdas and Mahalaxmi (Jagjivandas) S.; m. Sundri Choitram Malkaney, Mar. 15, 1956; children: Sailesh N., Sarina N. M.D., U. Bombay, 1954. Med. registrar, sr. med. tutor Cardiology King Edward Meml. Hosp., Bombay, 1954-56; hon. assoc. physician Gokuldas Tejpal Hosp., also hon prof. medicine Grant Med. Coll., Bombay, 1959-74; hon. physician and cardiologist, head ICC unit, mobile coronary CCU, exercise stress test Bombay Hosp., 1960—; patron 2d Internat. Conf. on Hypertension, 1985. Author: A Handbook of Endocrine Disorders, 1960, Prevent a Heart Attack, 2d edit., 1977, An Approach to Electrocardiography, 3d edit., 1978, Heart-Before, During, After, 1984, Advanced Electrocardiography, 1986, Clinical Electrocardiography, 1988; contbr. articles to profl. jours. Hon. spl. exec. magistrate Govt. of Maharashtra, 1980—. Mem. Internat. Congress Hypertension (pres. 1977), Cardiol. Soc. Indian (chmn. Bombay br. 1977-78), Internat. Conf. Advances Internat. Medicine (v.p.), Internat. Conf. Prevention Heart Disease and Cardiac Rehab. (v.p. 1978), Nat. Coun. Hypertension (pres., founder 1978-81), Nat. Soc. Prevention Heart Disease and Rehab. (pres. 1988—), Internat. Congress Directions in Cardiovascular Advances (chmn. 1989, Bombay), Wellington Sports Club, Nat. Sports Club (Bombay). Home: 4/D Ananta, Rajaballi Patel Rd, Bombay 400026, India Office: Med Rsch Centre, New Marine Lines, Bombay 400020, India

SHAHBAZI, MICHAEL FARZIN, ophthalmologist; b. Richmond, Va., Sept. 14, 1959. BA, U. Tenn., Knoxville, 1981; MD, U. Tenn., Memphis, 1985. Diplomate Am. Bd. Ophthalmology. Rsdient in ophthalmomogy Vanderbilt U., Nashville, 1986-89; fellow in glaucoma U. Ill., Chgo., 1989-90; staff physician Johnson City (Tenn.) Eye Clinic, 1991—; asst. prof. dept. surgery East Tenn. State U. Med. Sch., Johnson City, 1991—. Mem. Alpha Omega Alpha. Office: Johnson City Eye Clinic 222 E Uraka Ave NE Johnson City TN 37601-4698

SHAIN, RICHARD ARTHUR, psychologist, educational agency administrator; b. Miami Beach, Fla., Mar. 18, 1948; s. Arthur M. and Betty Jane (Hess) S.; m. Debra Kontaxes, Aug. 21, 1990. BA, Queens Coll., Flushing, N.Y., 1969; MA, Temple U., 1972, Ph.D., 1976. Cert. sch. psychologist. Dir. work study div. Lymelight, Inc., South Fallsburg, N.Y., 1969-70; tchr.-coord. spl. edn. Mt. Vernon (N.Y.) Public Schs., 1970; rsch. asst. Temple U., 1971-73, lectr. psychology, 1973-75; mem. early childhood consortium Edn. Commn. States, 1975-76; dir. grants mgmt., rsch. and evaluation Millville (N.J.) Bd. Edn., 1977-81; dir. Title I programs and gifted/talented svcs. Millville Schs., 1978-81, dir. spl. svcs./gifted and talented programs, 1981—; project dir. Cumberland County (N.J.) Presch. Handicapped Program, 1981-84, Tri-County Presch. Handicapped Resource System, N.J. Dept. Edn., 1984-89; mem. faculty dept. psychology Temple U., 1976-77; field reader U.S. Office of Edn., 1980-81; lectr. Grad. Sch. Edn., U. Pa., 1976; cons. in field. Chmn. youth svcs. comn. Citizens Adv. Coun., Cumberland County Family Ct., 1984-90; mem. NJASA Spl. Edn. Com., 1988—. NSF fellow, 1974; Temple U. summer fellow, 1973; recipient Boulton Fund award, 1975, Magna Cum Laude World Poet award, 1970, Ednl. Leadership award Phi Delta Tau, 1990; cert. sch. psychologist, supr. and prin. N.J.; lic. psychologist, Pa. Mem. N.J. Assn. Fed. Program Adminstrs. (conf. evaluation chmn. 1979-84), N.J. Urban Spl. Edn. Adminstrs. Assn. (v.p. 1982-83, exec. bd. 1982-91 , pres. 1983-84), Am. Psychol. Assn., Am. Assn. Sch. Adminstrs., N.J. Assn. Sch. Psychologists, N.J. Assn. Sch. Adminstrs. (spl. edn. com. 1988—), Coun. Exceptional Children, Am. Ednl. Rsch. Assn., Tng. Assn. Phila. Sch. Psychoanalysis, Phi Delta Kappa (treas.). Psi Chi. Contbr. articles to profl. jours. Home: 13 Hardwood Dr Voorhees NJ 08043 Office: Millville Bd Edn Millville NJ 08332

SHAIN-ALVARO, JUDITH CAROL, physician assistant; b. Bronx, N.Y., Aug. 13, 1953; d. Frank and Pearl (Crausman) Shain; m. Virgilio S. Alvaro, May 13, 1990; 1 child, Jessica Blaire. BS in Biology, Fairleigh Dickinson U., 1975; BS in Physician Assistant, Baylor Coll. Medicine, 1978. Cert. physician asst. Nat. Commn. Cert. Physician Assts.; lic. physician asst., N.Y., N.J.; BLS, ACLS, Am. Heart Assn. Resident surg. Montefiore Hosp. and Med. Ctr., Albert Einstein Coll., Bronx, 1979-81; physician asst. dept. cardiothoracic surgery N. Shore U. Hosp., Manhasset, N.Y., 1981-84; lic. med. officer Passenger Cruise Ships, Miami, Fla., 1984-88; med. cons. The Floating Hosp. Bankers Trust Co., N.Y.C., 1988-89; sr. physician asst. Pers. Health Svcs. St. Vincent's Hosp. and Med. Ctr., N.Y.C., 1990-93; sr. physician asst. U. Med. and Dentistry N.J., Newark, 1993—; physician asst. rep. N.J. AIDS Edn. Tng. Ctr., Newark, 1995—; lectr. in field. Fellow Am. Acad. Physician Assts., N.J. State Soc. Physician Assts., N.Y. State Soc. Physician Assts; mem. Sisterhood Cong. Bnai Israel, Filipino Am. Assn. Fair Lawn. Democrat. Jewish. Home: Eighty 27th St Fair Lawn NJ 07410 Office: Univ Medicine Dentistry NJ 65 Bergen St Newark NJ 07107

SHAINESS, NATALIE, psychiatrist, educator; b. N.Y.C., Dec. 2, 1915; d. Jack and Clara (Levy-Hart) S.; div.; children: David Spiegel, Ann Spiegel. BA in Chemistry, NYU, 1936; MD, Va. Commonwealth U., 1939. Diplomate in psychiatry; cert. in psychoanalysis. Pvt. practice N.Y.C., 1955—; faculty William Alanson White Inst. Psychiatry, Psychoanalysis, N.Y.C., 1961-81; asst. clin. prof. psychiatry N.Y. Sch. Psychiatry, N.Y.C., 1964-67; faculty med. edn. div. N.Y. Acad. Medicine, 1966-67; lectr. psychiatry Columbia U. Coll. Physicians and Surgeons, N.Y.C., 1966-80; faculty, supervising analyst L.I. Inst. Psychoanalysis, N.Y., 1980—; invited participant 1st and 2nd Internat. Conf. on Abortion, 1967, 68; research project on menstruation. Editorial bd. Jour. of the Am. Women's Med. Assn., 1985—; author: Sweet Suffering: Woman as Victim, 1984; contbr. over 100 articles to profl. jours. and over 90 profl. book revs. Mem. Physicians for Social Responsibility, Nuclear Freeze, several other anti-nuclear orgns. Fellow Am. Acad. Psychoanalysis (past trustee, organizer several panels), Am. Psychiat. Assn. (life mem., organizer several panels), N.Y. Acad. Medicine (hon.), Soc. Med. Psychoanalyst (councillor, honored for keen erudition, lively imagination and professionalism 1993); mem. Assn. for Advancement Psychotherapy, Women's Med. Assn. N.Y.C. (fin. assistance com., 1st President's award 1990). Home and Office: 140 E 83rd St New York NY 10028-1931

SHAIVITZ, STEPHEN A., neurologist; b. Balt., May 4, 1939; s. Sylvan and Rita (Adler) S.; m. Patricia Miller, June 16, 1966; children: Eli, Adam. AB cum laude, Columbia U., 1961; MD, U. Mich., 1965. Diplomate Am. Bd. Psychiatry and Neurology. Intern Phila. Gen. Hosp., 1965-66; neurologist USPHS, Washington, 1969-71; resident Albert Einstein Coll. Medicine, Bronx, N.Y., 1966-69; adj. prof. Fla. Atlantic U., Boca Raton, Fla., 1983—. Trustee Nat. Multiple Sclerosis Soc., Ft. Lauderdale, Fla., 1975—, mem. med. adv. bd., N.Y.C., 1992—; bd. dirs. Fla. Easter Seal Soc., West Palm Beach, 1990—. Mem. Am. Acad. Neurology, Am. Assn. for Study of Headache, Fla. Soc. Neurology, Bockley Med. Soc. Office: Ste 305 2161 Palm Beach Lakes Blvd West Palm Beach FL 33409-6607

SHALACK, JOAN HELEN, psychiatrist; b. Jersery City, Mar. 6, 1932; d. Edward William and Adele Helen S.; m. Jerome Abraham Sheill (dec. June 1996). Student, Farleigh Dickinson U., 1950-51; BA cum laude, NYU, 1954; MD, Women's Med. Coll. Pa., 1958. Intern Akron (Ohio) Gen. Hosp., 1958-59; resident in psychiatry Camarillo (Calif.) State Hosp., 1959-62; resident in physchiatry UCLA Neuropsychiat. Inst., 1962, U. So. Calif., L.A., 1963; pvt. practice Beverly Hills, Calif., 1963-83, Century City L.A., Calif., 1983-86, Pasadena, Calif., 1986—; pres., chair bd. dirs. Totizo Inc., Beverly Hills, 1969-71; mem. staff Westwood Hosp., 1970-75. Mem. AMA, Calif. Med. Assn., L.A. County Med. Assn., Physicians for Social Responsibility, Union of Concerned Scientists, Phi Beta Kappa, Mu Chi Sigma. Home and Office: 1405 Afton St Pasadena CA 91103-2702

SHALALA, DONNA EDNA, federal official, political scientist, educator, university chancellor; b. Cleve., Feb. 14, 1941; d. James Abraham and Edna (Smith) S. AB, Western Coll., 1962; MSSC, Syracuse U., 1968, PhD, 1970; 16 hon degrees, 1981-91. Vol. Peace Corps, Iran, 1962-64; asst. to dir. met. studies program Syracuse U., 1965-69; instr. asst. to dean Syracuse U. (Maxwell Grad. Sch.), 1969-70; asst. prof. polit. sci. CUNY, 1970-72; assoc. prof. politics and edn. Tchrs. Coll. Columbia U., 1972-79; asst. sec. for policy devel. and research HUD, Washington, 1977-80; prof. polit. sci., pres. Hunter Coll., CUNY, 1980-88; prof. polit. sci., chancellor U. Wis., Madison, 1988-93; sec. Dept. HHS, Washington, 1993—. Author: Neighborhood Governance, 1971, The City and the Constitution, 1972, The Property Tax and the Voters, 1973, The Decentralization Approach, 1974. Bd. govs. Am. Stock Exch., 1981-87; trustee TIAA, 1985-89, Com. Econ. Devel., 1981-93; bd. dirs. Inst. Internat. Econs., 1981-93, Children's Def. Fund, 1980-93, Am. Ditchley Found., 1981-93, Spencer Found., 1988-93, M&I Bank of Madison, 1991-93, NCAA Found., 1991; mem. Trilateral Commn., 1988-93, Knight Commn. on Intercollegiate Sports, 1990-93; trustee Brookings Inst., 1989-93. Ohio Newspaper Women's scholar, 1958, Western Coll. Trustee scholar, 1958-62; Carnegie fellow, 1966-68; Nat. Acad. Edn. Spencer fellow, 1972-73; Guggenheim fellow, 1975-76; recipient Disting. Svc. medal Columbia U. Tchrs. Coll., 1989. Mem. ASPA, Am. Polit. Sci. Assn., Nat. Acad. Arts & Scis., Nat. Acad. Pub. Adminstrn., Coun. Fgn. Rels., Nat. Acad. Edn., Nat. Acad. Arts and Scis. Office: Dept Health and Human Svcs Office of Sec 200 Independence Ave SW Rm 615F Washington DC 20201-0004*

SHALITA, ALAN REMI, dermatologist; b. Bklyn., Mar. 22, 1936; s. Harry and Celia; m. Simone Lea Baum, Sept. 4, 1960; children: Judith and Deborah (twins). AB, Brown U., 1957; BS, U. Brussels, 1960; MD, Bowman Gray Sch. Medicine, 1964; DSc (hon.), L.I. U., 1990. Intern Beth Israel Hosp., N.Y.C., 1964-65; resident dept. dermatology NYU Med. Ctr., 1967-68, NIH tng. grant fellow dept. dermatology, 1968-70, instr. dermatology, 1970-71; asst. prof. NYU, 1971-73, Columbia U., N.Y.C., 1973-75; assoc. prof. medicine, head divsn. dermatology SUNY Downstate Med. Ctr., Bklyn., 1975-79, prof., 1979—, head divsn. dermatology, 1979-80, chmn. dept. dermatology, 1980—, asst. dean, 1977-83; acting dean Queens campus SUNY Downstate Med. Ctr., 1983-84; assoc. dean clin. affairs SUNY Health Sci. Ctr., Bklyn., 1989-92, assoc. provost for clin. affairs, 1992-93, assoc. v.p. clin. affairs, 1993—; disting. tchg. prof. SUNY Health Sci. Ctr., Bklyn., 1996—; asst. attending in dermatology Univ. Hosp., N.Y.C., 1970-73, Bellevue Hosp. Ctr., 1970-73, Manhattan VA Hosp., 1971-73, Presbyn. Hosp., 1973-75; mem. med. bd. Kings County Hosp. Ctr.; cons. dermatology Bklyn. VA Hosp., 1975—; chief dermatology Brookdale Med. Ctr., 1977-90; chief dermatology Univ. Hosp. of Bklyn., 1975—; chief dermatology Kings County Hosp. Ctr., Bklyn., 1975—, acting med. dir., 1989-92; med. dir. Univ. Hosp. Bklyn., 1992-96. Pres. Temple Shaaray Tefila, N.Y.C., 1982-86, chmn. bd. trustees, 1987-95. Lt. M.C. USNR, 1965-67. Recipient Torch of Liberty award Anti-Defamation League, 1987, Surg. and Pediatric awards Beth Israel Hosp., N.Y.C., 1965; spl. fellow NIH, 1970-73. Dem. AMA, AAAS, Am. Acad. Dermatology (bd. dirs. 1983-87, v.p. 1995-96), Soc. Investigative Dermatology, Dermatology Found. (past trustee), Am. Dermatol. Assn. (asst. sec.-treas. 1995-96, sec.-treas. 1996—), Am. Soc. Dermatol. Surgery (past bd. dirs.), Soc. Cosmetic Chemists, Assn. Profs. of Dermatology (sec.-treas. 1988-94, pres.-elect 1994-96), Internat. Soc. Tropical Dermatology, N.Y. Acad. Scis., N.Y. State Med. Soc., N.Y. Acad. Medicine, N.Y. State Dermatol. Soc., Dermatol. Soc. Greater N.Y. (pres. 1980-81), N.Y. Dermatol. Soc. (pres. 1989-90). Republican. Home: 70 E 77th St New York NY 10021-1811 Office: 450 Clarkson Ave Brooklyn NY 11203-2012

SHALLAT, RONALD FREDRICK, physician; b. Chgo., May 22, 1941; s. Charles O. and Minnie A. (Kort) S.; m. Judith M. McHugh, Aug. 24, 1968; children: Ryan, Erin, Kevin. Student, U. Ill., Urbana, 1959-62; MD with honors, U. Ill., Chgo., 1966. Surg. intern Presbyn. St. Lukes, Chgo., 1966-67; resident U. Ill., Chgo., 1966-73; assoc. clin. prof. U. Calif., San Francisco, 1973—; pres. med. staff Childrens Hosp., Oakland, 1994. Contbr. articles to profl. jours. Capt. USAF, 1968-70. Mem. Am. Assn. Neurol. Surgeons. Office: East Bay Med Group 3000 Colby St Ste 101 Berkeley CA 94705

SHALLOWAY, DAVID IRWIN, molecular biologist; b. Miami, Fla., Apr. 6, 1948; s. Charles Leon and Bette (Sir) S.; m. Carolyn Renee Fink, Dec. 24, 1977 (div. Aug. 1983); m. Kelly Lynn Morris, June 30, 1985. S.B., MIT, 1969; M.S., Stanford U., 1970; Ph.D., MIT, 1975. Research assoc. Lab. for Nuclear Studies, Cornell U., Ithaca, N.Y., 1975-77; NIH research fellow in microbiology and molecular genetics Sidney Farber Cancer Inst., Harvard Med. Sch., Boston, 1977-81; asst. prof. molecular biology Pa. State U.-State College, 1982-87, assoc. prof., 1987-90; Greater Phila. Prof. biol scis. Cornell U., Ithaca, N.Y., 1990—. Contbr. articles to profl. jours. Mem. Union Concerned Scientists. Fellow Danforth Found., 1969, Woodrow Wilson Found., 1969, NSF, 1969, Am. Cancer Soc., 1977; recipient Jr. Faculty Research award Am. Cancer Soc., 1983, Research Career Devel. award NIH, 1987; grantee: Nat. Cancer Inst., 1982, Am. Cancer Soc., 1982, March of Dimes, 1983, IBM, 1985, Nat. Cancer Inst., 1985, 88, 91, 92, 93, Alzheimer's Assn., 1991. Mem. AAAS, Am. Soc. Microbiologists. Democrat. Jewish. Office: Cornell U Biotech Bldg Ithaca NY 14853

SHAMBERG, BARBARA A(NN), psychologist; b. Atlantic City, July 22, 1953; d. Martin and Margaret (Fox) S.; m. Allan Weisberg, Aug. 29, 1987; children: Lauren Margaret, Alana Miriam. BA, New Coll., 1975; MA, Hofstra U., 1979, PhD, 1984. Lic. psychologist, N.Y.; diplomate Bd. Cert. Forensic Examiner. Mem. faculty Fairleigh Dickinson U., Madison, N.Y., 1977; psychologist Hofstra U., Hempstead, N.Y., 1978-84, SUNY, Farmingdale, 1981-82, Bd. of Coop. Ednl. Svcs., Yorktown, N.Y., 1982-83, N.Y.C. (N.Y.) Bd. Edn., 1983-88; supervising psychologist Childrens' Village, Dobbs Ferry, N.Y., 1989-91; pvt. practice clin. psychology N.Y.C. and Scarsdale, N.Y., 1984—; dir. psychol. svcs. Midtown Med. and Health Svcs., N.Y.C., 1994—; sr. clin. cons. psychologist Ctr. for Behavior Therapy, Scarsdale, 1989—; lectr., workshop leader in field; expert interviewee ABC News, N.Y.C., Sta. WMID, Atlantic City. Author: Wives' Marital Satisfaction, 1984. Bd. dirs. 218 E. 29th St. Owners' Corp., 1984-89. Mem. Am. Psychol. Assn., N.Y. State Psychol. Assn., Westchester County Psychol. Assn., Am. Assn. Behavioral Therapists, Am. Coll. Forensic Examiners. Home: 4 Hidden Glen Rd Scarsdale NY 10583-1229 Office: Midtown Med Corp 235 E 49th St New York NY 10017

SHAMES, JORDAN NELSON, health care executive, consultant health services; b. Malden, Mass., June 27, 1949; s. Abraham and Annette (Harris) S.; m. Joni Schechter, Apr. 15, 1984; children: Robert Zachary, Rebecca Naomi. BS in Polit. Sci., Allegheny Coll., 1971; postgrad., U. Ky., 1973-74, New Sch. for Social Rsch., N.Y.C., 1983-85. Real estate and nursing home property mgr. H.R.F. Co., Triplex Ltd., Bethpage, N.Y., 1974-77; L.I., N.Y.C. area mgr. Quality Care, Rockville Centre, N.Y., 1977-80; exec. dir. Health Force, East Meadow, N.Y., 1980-82; adminstr. Med. Personnel Pool, White Plains, N.Y., 1982-83; exec. dir. Continental Health Affiliates, White Plains, 1983-85, Community Home Care, Bronx, N.Y., 1985-88; pres., CEO Neighbors Home Care, N.Y., 1989—; mem. profl. adv. bd. Beth Abraham Hosp. Home Health Agy., Bronx, 1986—; bd. dirs. Home Health Mgmt., Inc.; chmn. bd. Bronx Cmty. Home Care, Inc., 1989—; interviewee Nat. Pub. Radio, 1989; bd. dirs. Bedford Park Multi-Svc. Ctr., Bronx, 1991—, St.

Marys Children and Family Svcs., 1996—; chmn. bd. trustees N.Y. State Health Care Providers, Self Ins. Trust for DBL, 1995—. Co-author: Home Health Services Quarterly, 1985, Caring Mag., 1987. Bd. dirs. Bedford Park Multi-Svc. Ctr., Bronx, 1991—; mem. lobby renovation com. Gerard Owners Corp. Coop., Forest Hills, 1986-87, chmn. fin. com., 1991-92; mem. community affairs com. Forest Hills Jewish Ctr., 1990—. Recipient Army Commendation medal, 1974, Cert. Appreciation, Am. Heart Assn., 1976. Mem. Nat. Assn. Home Care (presenter ann. meeting 1985, 89), N.Y. State Home Care Assn. (ann. meeting com. 1990, presenter ann. meeting 1990, 91, svcs. com. 1991, nominating com. 1992), Hospice Assn. Am., Masons. Republican. Jewish. Office: Neighbors Home Care 2532 Boston Rd Bronx NY 10467-9004

SHAMLAYE, CONRAD FRANCOIS, health facility administrator, epidemiologist; b. Victoria, Seychelles, Nov. 10, 1952; s. Francois and Marthe (Ponwaye) S.; m. Heather Elizabeth Thompson, Sept. 19, 1981; children: Catriona Michelle, Julie Anne. B Medicine and B Surgery, U. Glasgow, Scotland, 1978; MSc in Epidemiology, U. London, 1984; MSc in Health Econs., U. York, Eng., 1996. Medical officer Ministry Health, Victoria, Seychelles, 1979-84, epidemiologist, 1984-86, prin. sec., 1986-93, spl. advisor to min., 1993—; exec. bd. dirs. WHO, 1990-93, task force health devel., 1994—; adv. com. Commonwealth Regional Health Cmty., 1990-93. Founder, nat. com. mem. Red Cross Soc. Seychelles, 1990. Home: Danzil, Bel Ombre Mahe, Seychelles Office: Ministry of Health, PO Box 52, Victoria Mahe, Seychelles

SHAMOIAN, CHARLES ANTHONY, psychiatrist, educator; b. Worcester, Mass., Oct. 5, 1931; s. Garabed Sarkis and Anna (Varjabedian) S.; m. Paula Baker, Oct. 8, 1961; children—Paula Ann, Charles Raymond. A.B., Clark U., 1954, M.A., 1956; Ph.D., Tufts U., 1960, M.D., 1966. Diplomate Am. Bd. Psychiatry and Neurology. Intern Bellevue Hosp., N.Y.C., 1966-67; resident Payne Whitney Psychiat. Clinic-N.Y. Hosp., N.Y.C., 1967-70, chief resident, 1970-71, unit chief, 1975-79; asst. prof. psychiatry Cornell U. Med. Coll., N.Y.C., 1970-75, assoc. prof., 1975-84, prof. clin. psychiatry, 1984—; practice medicine specializing in psychiatry, White Plains, N.Y., 1979—; dir. geriatric services N.Y. Hosp.-Cornell U. Med. Ctr., White Plains, 1979-89, dir. partial hospitalization program, 1995—. USPHS postdoctoral fellow, 1960-61. Fellow Gerontol. Soc. Am. (vice chmn. clin. medicine sect. 1984-85), Am. Psychiat. Assn. (chmn. council on aging 1985—); mem. Am. Assn. Geriatric Psychiatry (bd. dirs. 1983-84, sec. 1984-85, pres.-elect 1985). Office: New York Hosp-Cornell Med Ctr 21 Bloomingdale Rd White Plains NY 10605-1504

SHAN, ROBERT KUOCHENG, biology educator; b. Gaoan, Jiangxi, China, Nov. 9, 1927; came to U.S., 1963; m. Lily Yikhwei Chenshan, Sept. 7, 1963; 1 child, Tony Donguang. BS, Taiwan Normal U., 1956; MS, U. B.C., Vancouver, Can., 1962; PhD, Ind. U., 1967. Instr. Taiwan U., Taipei, 1956-59; teaching fellow, rsch. fellow U. B.C., 1959-62; teaching fellow Dalhousie U., Halifax, N.S., Can., 1962-63; rsch. fellow Ind. U., Bloomington, 1963-67, rsch. assoc., 1967-69; asst. prof. biology Fairmont (W.Va.) State Coll., 1969-72, assoc. prof., 1972-75, prof., 1975—. Mem. Am. Inst. Biol. Scis., Ecol. Soc. Am., Am. Soc. Limnology and Oceanography, Sigma Xi. Office: Fairmont State Coll Dept Bio Fairmont WV 26554

SHANABROOK, JED ALEC, occupational health nurse, consultant; b. Hanover, Pa., Apr. 5, 1953; s. Albert Henry and Ardice Barbara (Forscht) S.; m. Linda Jean Jensen, June 17, 1978; children: Erik, Denise. AAS, Middlesex County Coll., 1978; BS in Profl. Occupl. Edn., Rutgers U., 1994. RN, N.J.; cert. CPR, occupl. health nurse specialist; cert. in hearing conservation. Staff nurse J F Kennedy Med. Ctr., Edison, N.J., 1979-89, Bristol-Myers Squibb Co., New Brunswick, N.J., 1989—; RN cons. live for life program Johnson & Johnson Health Mgmt. Inc., New Brunswick, 1990—; relief sch. nurse. Mem. Milltown (N.J.) Rescue Squad, 1972-84, life mem., 1984—, past treas.; adult mem. Boy Scouts Am., South River, N.J., 1991—; bd. dirs. St. Paul's United Ch. Christ, Milltown, 1984—. Mem. Am. Assn. Occupl. Health Nurses, N.J. State Assn. Occupl. Health Nurses, N.E. Assn. Occupl. Health Nurses, Ctrl. N.J. Assn. Occupl. Health Nurses (sec.), Oncology Nursing Soc. Home and Office: 76 1st St Milltown NJ 08850-1835

SHANAFELT, NANCY SUE, organizational development specialist, career counselor; b. Northampton, Mass., Nov. 21, 1947; m. John D. Shanafelt; children: Amy, Nicholas. BS, U. Mass., 1969; MA in Human Resources/Orgnl. Devel., U. San Francisco, 1991. Tchr. Southwick (Mass.) Pub. Schs., 1969-70; acctg. asst. Maricopa County Schs., Phoenix, Ariz., 1973-74; tax auditor to br. chief IRS, San Jose, 1974-89; enrolled agt., 1984-85; OD specialist IRS, San Jose, 1991-93; creator IRS Women's Network, San Francisco, 1981—. Leader Girl Scouts U.S., Santa Clara, 1980-96, Golden Valley, 1996—, cons., 1981-82, svc. mgr., 1982-84, trainer, 1982-84; leader Boy Scouts Am., 1992-96; facilitator Unwed Parents Anonymous, 1992—; master catechist Diocese of San Jose, 1992-96. Recipient Disting. Performance award IRS, 1993. Mem. AAUW, NAFE, ASTD, Calif. Assn. for Counseling and Devel., Federally Employed Women, Commonwealth Club Am., Italian Cath. Fedn. (sec. 1991—), Bay Area Orgnl. Devel. Network, Medugorje PGL. Office: Mail Stop FR4300 821 M St Fresno CA 93721

SHANAHAN, SHEILA ANN, pediatrician, educator; b. N.Y.C., July 1, 1943; d. James Patrick and Eleanor Margaret (Breslin) S.; m. Justin Laurence Cashman Jr., Sept. 14, 1968; children: Justin III, Gillis. BA, Trinity Coll., 1963; MD cum laude, Med. Coll. Pa., 1969. Diplomate Nat. Bd. Med. Examiners, Am. Bd. Pediats. Intern Presbyn. Hosp., N.Y.C., 1969-70, resident in pediats., 1970-72, asst. in clin. pediats., 1972-75, assoc. clin. pediats., 1975-78; pvt. practice specializing in pediats. Greenwich, Conn., 1972-78; asst. attending Greenwich Hosp., 1972-73, assoc. attending, 1973-78; from instr. to assoc. Columbia Coll. Physicians and Surgeons, N.Y.C., 1972-78; asst. prof. pediats. George Washington U. Sch. Medicine, Washington, 1980—, Georgetown U. Sch. Medicine, Washington, 1984—; pvt. practice specializing in pediats. Washington, 1984—; attending dept. ambulatory medicine Children's Hosp. Nat. Med. Ctr., Washington, 1980-84; courtesy staff Georgetown U. Hosp., Washington, 1984—, George Washington U. Hosp., 1984—, Sibley Meml. Hosp., Washington, 1984—, Columbia Hosp. for Women, 1984—, Children's Hosp. Nat. Med. Ctr., 1984—. Fellow Am. Acad. Pediats.; mem. Am. Women's Med. Assn. Office: Drs Ong, Stroud et al 4900 Massachusetts Ave NW Washington DC 20016

SHANAHAN, THOMAS CORNELIUS, immunologist, immunogeneticist; b. Buffalo, Dec. 21, 1952; s. Thomas F. and Eileen T. (Guerin) S.; m. Kathleen McDonald, Oct. 20, 1978; 1 child, Niall Thomas. MS, SUNY, Buffalo, 1979; PhD, Temple U., 1985. Diplomate Am. Bd. Med. Lab. Immunologists. Rsch. assoc. Temple U., Phila., 1983-85; postdoctoral fellow in clin. immunology Royal Victoria Hosp./McGill U., Montreal, Quebec, Canada, 1985-86; dir. histocompatibility and immunogenetics Erie County Med. Ctr., Buffalo, 1986—; dir. Ctr. for Paternity and Immunogenetics ImmCo Diagnostics, 1996—. Author: (with others) Complement Deficiencies and Diseases, 1990, Histocompatibility Antigens and Hearing Disorders, 1988; contbr. articles to profl. jours. Bd. dirs. Upstate N.Y. Transplantation Svcs., Buffalo, 1987-93, regional commr. 1991—, dep. chmn. accreditation com. 1993—; mem. N.Y. State Transplant Coun., 1992—. Mem. Am. Soc. for Histocompatibility and Immunogenetics (regional commr. 1991), Assn. Med. Lab. Immunologists. Roman Catholic. Office: Erie County Med Ctr 462 Grider St Buffalo NY 14215-3075

SHANDLES, IRA DAVID, podiatrist; b. Phila., Feb. 27, 1949; s. Samuel Aaron and Sara (Brooks) S.; divorced; children: Martine, Neil; m. Elizabeth Jacobs, Aug. 1, 1993; 1 child, Aleah. BA, Temple U., 1971; DPM, Pa. Coll. Podiatric Medicine, 1977; postgrad., U. Pa. Sports Medicine Ctr., 1977-79. Diplomate Am. Bd. Podiatric Surgery, Am. Bd. Podiatric Orthopedics and Primary Podiatric Medicine; lic. podiatrist, N.Y., Fla., Pa. Resident in podiatric surgery Oxford Hosp., Phila., 1977-79; asst. instr. pediatric orthopedics Pa. Coll. Podiatric Medicine, Phila., 1977-78; cons. Binghamton (N.Y.) Gen. Hosp. Sports Medicine Ctr., 1979-83; pvt. practice podiatric medicine Binghamton, 1979-83, Tampa, Fla., 1983—; podiatric cons. Tampa Gen. Hosp. Sports Medicine Ctr., 1985—; clin. faculty podiatric residency program Tampa Vets. Hosp., 1985—; staff privileges United Health Svcs., Inc. Binghamton, 1980-83; Tampa Outpatient Surgical Facility, Tampa Gen. Hosp., Centurion Community Hosp., Univ. Community Hosp., Tampa; Humana Hosp., Brandon, Fla. 1986—; cons. Bull Run, U. South Fla., 1986, Fla.'s Sunshine State Games, 1986, Dow Corning Corp. 1987—, Diapulse Corp. Am., 1988—, Edward T. White Hosp., 1992—, Bayfront Med. Ctr., 1992—, St. Petersburg, Chmn. Dept. Podiatric Surgery Univ. Hosp., Tampa, 1992—; speaker to Binghamton Civic Orgns., TV, newspaper interviewee, Binghamton, 1979-83; mem. faculty John H. Weed Meml. Seminars, 1995—, Ontario Soc. Chiropodists, 1993; cons., lectr. U.S. Army Rsch. Inst. Envrion. Medicine, Natick, Mass., 1991-94; cons., clin. faculty mem. locomotor biomechanics program Edward White Hosp., St. Petersburg, 1985—; mem. clin. faculty podiatric residency program Tampa VA Hosp., 1985—; cons. Sports Medicine Ctr. Tampa Gen. Hosp., 1983—; pvt. practice, Tampa. Contbr. articles to profl. jours. Lectr. Hillsborough County Pub. Schs. Sch. Enrichment Resource Vols. Edn. series, 1987—, Edward T. White Hosp., 1992—. Fellow Am. Coll. Foot Surgeons (Outstanding Paper award 1977), Am. Coll. Foot and Ankle Surgery; mem. Hillsborough County Podiatric Med. Assn., Am. Podiatric Med. Assn. Jewish.

SHANE, DORIS JEAN, respiratory therapist, administrator; b. Granite City, Ill., June 30, 1949; d. Elbert Paul and Arline Marie (Zitt) S. AS with clin. honors in respiratory therapy, Presbyn.-St. Luke's Hosp., Chgo., 1973. Registered respiratory therapist. Chief therapist Michael Reese Med. Ctr., Chgo., 1973-78; dir. respiratory therapy Edgewater Hosp., Chgo., 1978-81; dir. respiratory care svcs. Mt. Sinai Med. Ctr., Miami Beach, Fla., 1981-87; chmn. adv. council Respiratory Therapy Miami-Dade Community, 1984-87; bd. dirs. Dade-Monroe Am. Lung Assn., 1982—, Sunny Shores Sea Camp, Miami, 1983-87; healthcare cons. Shane and Assoc., 1987—; coord. rep. Care-Green Briar Nursing Ctr., South Miami Hosp., 1987-88; adminstrv. program dir. of vent and TBI programs West Gables Rehab. Hosp., 1988-89, v.p . health care planning & devel. Intergrated Health Svcs., 1989—. Bd. dirs. Frank M. Rodde Community Ctr., Chgo., 1980; chmn. credit com. Mt. Sinai Fed. Credit Union, 1986. Mem. Fla. Soc. Respiratory Therapy (v.p. 1984-85), Am. Assn. Respiratory Therapy, Internat. Assn. Quality Circles, Am. Soc. Respiratory Care Adminstrs., Am. Bus. Women Assn., Nat. Assn. Female Execs. Democrat. Avocation: racquetball. Home: 1085 Scarlet Oak St Hollywood FL 33019

SHANE, JOHN MARDER, endocrinologist; b. Kansas City, Mo., Oct. 5, 1942; s. Henry Kamsler and Ruth (Marder) S.; m. Eileen Goodart, June 18, 1967; children: Robert M., Edward G. BS, U. Okla., 1964, MD, 1967. Diplomate Am. Bd. Ob-Gyn., Am. Bd. Reproductive Endocrinology. Resident Harvard Med. Sch., Boston, 1970-73, fellowship, 1973-75, instr., 1970-75, asst. prof., 1975-78; pvt. practice Tulsa, 1978—; lectr., cons. Tutorial Svcs. Internat., England, 1984—; bd. dirs. St. Francies G.I.F.T. Lab., Tulsa; cons. to preimplantation genetics project Chapman Genetics Inst. Children's Med. Ctr., Tulsa. Author: CIBA Symposium Infertility: Diagnosis and Treatment; contbr. articles to profl. jours. and publs. Mem. Tulsa Garden Ctr., 1988—; bd. dirs. Temple Israel, Tulsa, 1985-86, cited in The Best Doctor's in Am.:Ctrl. Region. Captain USAF, 1967-69. Recipient Annual award Boston Obstet. Soc., 1977. Mem. ACS, Tulsa Gynecol. Soc. (past pres. 1986-87), Soc. Reproductive Endocrinologists, Tulsa bonsai Soc. (bd. dirs. 1988—), Am. Coll. Ob-Gyn. (v.p. 1971-92, pres. New England Jr. divsn. 1972-73), Am. Bonsai Soc. (nat. bd. dirs.), Chanie des Rotisseurs (l'Ordre Mondial, Tulsa v.p.), Southside Rotary of Tulsa (bd. dirs., pres. elect), Nat. Arboretum (nat. bd. dirs.). Republican. Jewish. Office: 1705 E 19th St Ste 703 Tulsa OK 74104-5418

SHANK, FRED ROSS, federal agency administrator; b. Harrisonburg, Va., Oct. 11, 1940; m. Peggy Anne Westbrook, June 1967; children: Virginia Anne, Fred Ross III. BS in Agriculture, U. Ky., 1962, MS in Nutrition, 1964; PhD, U. Md., 1969. Dep. dir. Office Nutrition and Food Sci. FDA, Washington, 1979-86, dir. Office Phys. Sci., 1986-87, dep. dir. Ctr. for Food SAfety and Applied Nutrition, 1987-89, dir., 1989—. Fellow Inst. Food Technologists; mem. Am. Assn. Cereal Chemists, Am. Inst. Nutrition, Am. Soc. for Clin. Nutrition, Assn. Food and Drug Ofcls. Home: 2621 Steeplechase Dr Reston VA 22091-2130 Office: FDA Ctr Food Safety & Applied Nutrition 200 C St SW Washington DC 20204-0001

SHANK, ROBERT ELY, physician, preventive medicine educator emeritus; b. Louisville, Sept. 2, 1914; s. Oliver Orlando and Isabel Thompson (Ely) S.; m. Eleanor Caswell, July 29, 1942; children: Jane, Robert Oliver, Bruce. A.B., Westminster Coll., 1935; M.D., Washington U., 1939. Diplomate: Am. Bd. Nutrition. Intern, house physician Barnes Hosp., 1939-41; asst. resident physician, asst. in research Hosp. Rockefeller Inst. Med. Research, 1941-46; research asso. div. nutrition and physiology Pub. Health Research Inst. City N.Y., 1946-48; prof. preventive medicine Washington U. Sch. Medicine, 1948-55, Danforth prof. preventive medicine, 1955-83, prof. emeritus preventive medicine, 1983—; Cutter lectr. preventive medicine Harvard, 1964; Mem. food and nutrition bd. NRC, 1949-69; spl. cons. nutrition USPHS, 1949-53; chmn. adv. bd. health and hosps., St. Louis County, 1949-54; med. adv. bd. St. Louis Vis. Nurses Assn., 1950-86; mem. com. food and nutrition nat. adv. bd. health services A.R.C., 1950-53; mem. adv. com. metabolism Office Surgeon Gen., 1956-60, mem. adv. com. on nutrition, 1964-72; mem. Am. Bd. Nutrition, 1955-64, sec., treas., 1958-64; mem. Nat. Bd. Med. Examiners, 1957-58; co-dir. nutrition survey NIH, Peru, 1959, N.E. Brazil, 1963; mem. sci. adv. bd. Nat. Vitamin Found., 1958-61; mem. nutrition study sect. NIH, 1964-68, chmn. sect., 1966-68; mem. gastroenterology and nutrition tng. com., 1968-69, mem. nat. adv. child health and human devel. council, 1969-73; mem. clin. application and prevention adv. com. Nat. Heart, Lung and Blood Inst., 1976-80. Author sects. in med. textbooks, sci. papers relating to nutritional, metabolic disorders.; Asso. editor: Nutrition Revs, 1948-58; editorial adv. bd. Nutrition Today, 1966-76, Hepatology, 1980-85. Served as lt. comdr. M.C. USNR, 1942-46. Recipient Alumni Achievement award Westminster Coll., 1970, Alumni Faculty award Washington U., 1989. Fellow Am. Pub. Health Assn. (governing council 1955-56), Am. Inst. Nutrition; mem. N.Y. Acad. Scis., Harvey Soc., Am. Soc. Biol. Chemists, Soc. Exptl. Biology and Medicine (council 1952-54), Central Soc. Clin. Research, Am. Soc. Clin. Investigation, Assn. Tchrs. Preventive Medicine (v.p. 1955-57, pres. 1957-58), A.M.A. (council on foods and nutrition 1960-69, chmn. 1963-66), Gerontological Soc., Assn. Am. Physicians, Am. Soc. Clin. Nutrition (council 1963-65, pres. 1967-68), Am. Dietetic Assn. (hon.), Am. Soc. for Study Liver Diseases (council 1963-66, pres. 1966), Am. Heart Assn. (chmn. nutrition com. 1973-76, award of merit 1981), Sigma Xi, Alpha Omega Alpha. Presbyterian. Home: 1325 Wilton Ln Saint Louis MO 63122-6940 Office: Wash U Sch Medicine 4566 Scott Ave Saint Louis MO 63110-1031

SHANKLIN, DOUGLAS RADFORD, physician; b. Camden, N.J., Nov. 25, 1930; s. John Ferguson and Muriel (Morgan) S.; student Wilson Tchrs. Coll., 1949; A.B. in Chemistry, Syracuse U., 1952; M.D., SUNY, Syracuse, 1955; m. Virginia McClure, Apr. 7, 1956; children—Elizabeth, Leigh, Lois Virginia, John Carter, Eleanor. Intern in pathology Duke U., 1955-56, resident, 1958; resident in pathology SUNY, Syracuse, 1958-60; practice medicine specializing in pathology, Gainesville, Fla., 1960-67, 78-83; mem. faculty U. Fla., 1960-67; prof. pathology, ob-gyn U. Chgo., 1967-78; pathologist-in-chief Chgo. Lying-In Hosp., 1967-78; prof. dept. pathology U. Tenn.-Memphis, 1983—, prof. obstetrics, 1986—, vice chmn. dept. pathology, 1983-90; vis. prof. U. Okla., 1967, Duke U., Mich. State U., 1969, Leeds U., Dundee U., Karolinska, 1974, Leeds U., 1978, 85, Emory U., 1980, London U., Edinburgh U., 1981, 85, U. Brit. Coll., 1987; jr. investigator Marine Biol. Lab., Woods Hole, Mass., 1951-54, sr. investigator, 1966—, mem. corp., 1970—; parliamentarian, 1990-94; mem. Marine Resources Adv. Com., 1988-90, mem. election com., 1994—; chmn. nat. adv. com. W-I-C evaluation U.S. Dept. Agr., 1979-86; lectr. Coll. Law U. Fla., 1963-67, 77-83; cons. Pan Am. Health Orgn., 1973-89; sr. cons. Santa Fe Found., 1976-79, exec. dir., 1979-83; course dir. Center Continuing Edn., U. Chgo., 1980-82. Trustee Coll. Light Opera Co., Falmouth, Mass., 1970—, Hippodrome Theatre, Gainesville, 1975-83, Opera Memphis, 1989-92. With M.C., USNR, 1956-58. Recipient Best Basic Sci. Teaching award U. Fla., 1967; named freeman citizen of Glasgow, 1981. Fellow Royal Soc Medicine (London); mem. AAAS, Am. Soc. Exptl. Pathology, Am. Soc. Molecular Marine Biology and Biotech., Astronom. Soc. Pacific Am. Hosp. Assn., Am. Coll. Rheumatology (spl. study com. 1995-96), Soc. Pediat. Rsch., Internat. Acad. Pathologists, So. Soc. Pediatric Research, So. Med. Assn., N.Y. Acad. Scis., Am. Coll. Ob-Gyn, Physicians Social Responsibility, Internat. Physicians for Prevention Nuclear War, Coll. Physicians and Surgeons Costa Rica, Pediatric Pathology Club (sec.-treas. 1970-75, pres. 1981-82), Navy League, Cosmos Club, Phi Beta Kappa. Sigma Xi. Author: Syllabus for Study of Gynecologic-Obstetric-Pediatric Disease, 1961, Diseases of Woman, Pregnancy, Child, 1964, Maternal Nutrition and Child Health, 1979, 2nd edit., 1996, Tumors of Placenta and Umbilical Cord, 1990; editor: Interscience Devel. Disorders, 1971-80; assoc. editor Jour. Reproductive Medicine, 1968-70, 79-85, editor in chief, 1970-75; contbr. articles to profl. jours. Home: 1238 NW 18th Ter Gainesville FL 32605-5370 Office: 134 Grove Park Cir Memphis TN 38117-3115

SHANKS, KATHRYN MARY, health care administrator; b. Glens Falls, N.Y., Aug. 4, 1950; d. John Anthony and Lenita (Combs) S. BS summa cum laude, Spring Hill Coll., 1972; MPA, Auburn U., 1976. Program evaluator Mobile Mental Health, Ala., 1972-73; dir. spl. projects Ala. Dept. Mental Health, Montgomery, 1973-76; dir. adminstrn. S.W. Ala. Mental Health/Mental Retardation, Andulusia, Ala., 1976-78; adminstr. Mobile County Health Dept., 1978-82; exec. dir. Coastal Family Health Ctr., Biloxi, Miss., 1982-95; cons. med. group practice, 1995—; ptnr. Shanks & Allen, Mobile, 1979—; healthcare consulting pvt. practice, 1995—; cons. S.W. Health Agy., Tylertown, Miss., 1984-86; preceptor Sch. Nursing, U. So. Miss., Hattiesburg, 1983, 84; advisor Headstart Program, Gulfport, Miss., 1984-95; LPN Program, Gulf Coast C.C., 1984-95; lectr. Auburn U., Montgomery, 1977-78. Bd. dirs. Mobile Cmty. Action Agy., 1979-81, Moore Cmty. House; mem. S.W. Ala. Regional Goals Forum, Mobile, 1971-72, Cardiac Rehab. Study Com., Biloxi, Miss., 1983-84, Mothers and Babies Coalition, Jackson, Miss., 1983-95, Gulf Coast Coalition Human Svcs., Biloxi, Miss., 1983-95; exec. dir. Year for Miss., 1993-94. Spring Hill Coll. Pres.'s scholar, 1972. Mem. Miss. Primary Health Care Assn. (pres.), Med. Group Mgmt. Assn., Biloxi C. of C., ACLU, Soc. for Advancement of Ambulatory Care, Spring Hills Alumni Assn. Avocations: tennis, home restoration, golf.

SHANN, FRANK ATHOL, pediatrician; b. Melbourne, Victoria, Australia, Oct. 25, 1944; s. Frank and Enid Isabell (Wilson) S.; m. Angela Helen Mackenzie, June 30, 1980; children: Helen Mackenzie, Alice Mackenzie, Frank Mackenzie. MB, BS, U. Melbourne, 1968, MD, 1985. Jr. resident Wangaratta Hosp., Victoria, 1969; sr. resident Royal Melbourne Hosp., Victoria, 1970, med. registrar, 1971-72; house officer Nairobi (Kenya) Hosp., 1973; med. registrar Royal Children's Hosp., Victoria, 1974-76, staff specialist, 1982-84, dir. intensive care, 1986—; prof. critical care medicine U. Melbourne, 1995—; specialist pediatrician Goroka Hosp., Papua New Guinea, 1977-81; sr. lectr. U. Melbourne, 1985-86; mem. internat. adv. bd. The Lancet; mem. expert adv. panel on acute respiratory infections WHO. Fellow Royal Australasian Coll. Physicians (Susman prize for med. rsch. 1986), Royal Soc. Tropical Medicine and Hygiene; mem. Australian Coll. Paediatrics (Howard Williams medal 1989), Australian and New Zealand Intensive Care Soc., Australian Med. Assn., Australasian Soc. Infectious Diseases. Office: Royal Children's Hosp, Intensive Care Unit, Parkville Victoria 3052, Australia

SHANNAHAN, J. MICHAEL, surgeon; b. Indpls., Sept. 1, 1942; s. J.J. and Olive (Hinds) S.; m. Glenna Kay Thorpe, Sept. 5, 1964; children: Sean, Jon Paul, Patrick. AB in Zoology, U. Mo., 1964, MD, 1969. Diplomate Am. Bd. Surgery. Surgeon Dean Clinic, Madison, Wis., 1976—; surg. patient rev. chmn. St. Mary's Hosp., Madison, 1977-95. Sponsor com. Duck Unltd., 1990—. Mem. ACS, AMA, Soc. of Thoracic Surgeons, Wis. Surg. Soc., Madison Surg. Soc. Roman Catholic.

SHANNON, MARGARET T., nursing administrator, educator; b. New Haven, June 23, 1939; d. Michael Joseph and Ellen (McNamara) S. MS in Chemistry, St. Louis U., 1967; BSN, Northwestern State U. of La., Nachitoches, 1978; MN, La. State U., New Orleans, 1981; PhD, U. New Orleans, 1987. Staff nurse Touro Infirmary, New Orleans, 1978-80; instr. nursing Touro Infirmary Sch. Nursing, New Orleans, 1980-85; asst. prof. nursing La. State U. Med. Ctr., New Orleans, 1985-87; dean divsn. nursing Our Lady of Holy Cross Coll., New Orleans, 1988—. Author: Giovani & Hayes Drugs and Nursing Implications, 8th edit., 1995, (with B.A. Wilson and C. Stang) Nurses' Drug Guide, 1993, 94, 95, 96. Mem. ANA, NLN, La. League for Nursing, La. State Nurses Assn., Sigma Theta Tau, Phi Kappa Phi, Phi Delta Kappa.

SHANNON, MARY LOU, adult health nursing educator; b. Memphis, Apr. 4, 1938; d. Sidney Richmond Shannon and Lucille (Gwaltney) Cloud. BSN, U. Tenn., 1959; MA, Columbia U., 1963, MEd, 1964, EdD, 1972. Staff nurse City of Memphis Hosps., 1959-60, instr. Sch. Nursing, 1960-62; asst. prof. U. Tenn., Memphis, 1964-70, assoc. prof., 1970-73, prof., 1973-89; prof., chair adult health dept. Sch. Nursing U. Tex., Galveston, 1989—; bd. dirs. Nat. Pressure Ulcer Adv. Panel, Buffalo, 1987-96; vis. prof. U. Alta., Edmonton, Can., 1982; mem. project adv. bd. RAND, Santa Monica, Calif., 1994. Contbr. chpts. to books in field and to periodicals; mem. editl. bd. Advances in Wound Care, 1987—. Trustee Nurses Edn. Funds, N.Y.C., 1972-86. Mem. ANA, Nat. League Nursing (bd. of rev. 1983-86), Orthopedic Nurses Assn., So. Nursing Rsch. Soc., Am. Assn. for History of Nursing. Office: U Tex Sch Nursing 301 University Blvd Galveston TX 77550-2708

SHANNON, WILLIAM GARY, anesthesiologist; b. Charlotte, N.C., Apr. 4, 1946; s. Charles Eugene and Mary (Walters) S.; m. Cynthia Streifel, Dec. 29, 1967 (div. Feb. 1977); m. Gayle C. Shannon, June 15, 1978; 1 child, W. Scott. BS in Chemistry, Lenoir Rhyne Coll., Hickory, N.C., 1968; MD, Bowman Gray Sch. Medicine, 1972. Diplomate Am. Bd. Anesthesiologists. Intern, then resident N.C. Bapt. Hosp., Winston-Salem, 1972-76; anesthesiologist Rowan Meml. Hosp., Salisbury, N.C., 1978—. Maj. U.S. Army, 1976-81. Mem. Am. Acad. Med. Acupuncture (v.p. 1994). Office: Rowan Regional Med Ctr 612 Mocksville Ave Salisbury NC 28144

SHAPERO, HARRIS JOEL, pediatrician; b. Winona, Minn., Nov. 22, 1930; s. Charles and Minnie Sara (Ehrlichman) S.; m. Byong Soon Yu, Nov. 6, 1983; children by previous marriage: Laura, Bradley, James, Charles. AA, UCLA, 1953; BS, Northwestern U., 1954, MD, 1957. Diplomate and cert. specialist occupational medicine Am. Bd. Preventive Medicine; cert. aviation medicine FAA. Intern, L.A. County Harbor Gen. Hosp., 1957-58, resident in pediatrics, 1958-60, staff physician, 1960-64; attending physician Perceptually Handicapped Children's Clinic, 1960-63; disease control officer for tuberculosis, L.A. County Health Dept., 1962-64; pvt. practice medicine specializing in pediatrics and occupational medicine, Cypress, Calif., 1965-85; pediatric cons. L.A. Health Dept., 1963-85, disease control officer sexually transmitted diseases, 1984-85; emergency room dir. AMI, Anaheim, Calif., 1968-78; mem. med. staff Anaheim Gen. Hosp., Beach Cmty. Hosp., Norwalk Cmty. Hosp.; courtesy staff Palm Harbor Gen. Hosp., Bellflower City Hosp.; pediatric staff Hosp. de General, Ensenada, Mex., 1978—; primary care clinician Sacramento County Health, 1987-88; pvt. practice medico-legal evaluation, 1986-92; founder Calif. Legal Evaluation Med. Group; apptd. med. examiner in preventive and occupational medicine State of Calif. Dept. of Indsl. Rels., 1989; health care provider, advisor City of Anaheim, City of Buena Park, City of Cypress, City of Garden Grove, Cypress Sch. Dist., Magnolia Sch. Dist., Savanna Sch. Dist., Anaheim Unified Sch. Dist., Orange County Dept. Edn.; pediatric and tuberculosis cons. numerous other orgns.; FAA med. examiner, founder Pan Am. Childrens Mission. Author: The Silent Epidemic, 1979. Named Headliner in Medicine Orange County Press Club, 1978. Fellow Am. Coll. Preventive Medicine; mem. L.A. County Med. Assn., L.A. County Indsl. Med. Assn., Am. Pub. Health Assn., Mex.-Am. Border Health Assn. Republican. Jewish. Avocations: antique books and manuscripts, photography, graphics, beekeeper. Home: PO Box 228 Wilton CA 95693-0228

SHAPIRO, ALVIN PHILIP, physician, educator; b. Nashville, Dec. 28, 1920; s. Samuel and Mollie (Levine) S.; m. Ruth Thomson, 1951; children: Debra, David. A.B., Cornell U., 1941; M.D., L.I. Coll. Medicine, Bklyn., 1944. Diplomate Nat. Bd. Med. Examiners; cert. Am. Bd. Internal Medicine. Intern L.I. Coll. Hosp., Bklyn., 1944-45; asst. resident internal medicine Goldwater Meml. Hosp., N.Y.C., 1945-46; asst. resident psychiatry L.I. Coll. Hosp. and Kings County Hosp., 1947-48; practice acad. medicine specializing in internal medicine Cin., 1948-51, Dallas, 1951-56, Pitts., 1956—; research fellow Cin. Gen. Hosp., 1948-49; med. teaching fellow Commonwealth Fund Psychosomatic Program, 1949-51, attending physician, 1949-51; attending physician Parkland, VA hosps., Dallas, 1951-56, Presbyn.-Univ. Hosp., Pitts., 1957-61; sr. staff Presbyn.-Univ. Hosp., 1962—;

attending physician VA Hosp., Pitts., 1960-66; cons. VA Hosp., 1967—; attending physician Shadyside Hosp., 1986—; co-dir. hypertension-renal clinic Falk Clinic U. Pitts., 1956-65, dir. hypertension clinic, 1965-86; instr. dept. internal medicine U. Cin. Coll. Medicine, 1949-51; asst. prof. Southwestern Med. Sch., U. Tex., 1951-56; asst. prof. depts. clin. sci. and medicine U. Pitts. Sch. Medicine, 1956-60, assoc. prof. dept. medicine, 1960-67, prof., 1967-93, prof. emeritus, 1993—, dir. psychosomatic program dept. medicine, 1960-71, interim chief renal sect., 1962-65, chief clin. pharmacology-hypertension sect., 1960-71, assoc. dean acad. affairs, 1971-75, vice-chmn. dept. medicine, 1975-79, interim chmn. dept. medicine, 1977-79; dir. Internal Medicine Residency program, Shadyside Hosp., 1986-93; cons. AMA Council on Drugs, 1959, Med. Letter of Drugs and Therapy, 1960; Fulbright vis. prof. U. Utrecht, The Netherlands, 1968; chmn. spl. projects study com. Nat. Heart Inst., 1970, chmn. policy adv. bd. nat. hypertension study, 1972-82. Author: (with S.O. Waife) Clinical Evalution of New Drugs, 1959, Hypertension-Current Management, 1963, 77, Hypertension in Renal Disease, 1969, Pharmacologic Mechanisms in Control of Hypertension, 1971; assoc. editor: Psychosomatic Medicine, 1963-92; assoc. editor Integrative Physiol. and Behavioral Sci., 1990; contbr. articles to profl. jours. Served as capt. M.C. AUS, 1946-47. Co-recipient Albert Lasker spl. pub. health award, 1980. Fellow ACP (Laureate award for teaching excellence Pa. chpt. 1988), AAAS (elected 1989); mem. Am. Fedn. Clin. Rsch., Am. Psychosomatic Soc. (sec.-treas. 1969-73, pres. 1975), AMA, Am. Heart Assn. (med. adv. bd. coun. high blood pressure, coun. on circulation, coun. on epidemiology), Pa. County Med. Soc., Allegheny County Med. Soc., N.Y. Acad. Sci., Am. Diabetes Assn., Am. Soc. Clin. Investigation, Soc. for Exptl. Biology and Medicine, Am. Soc. for Pharmacology and Exptl. Therapeutics, Cen. Soc. Clin. Rsch., Internat. Soc. Hypertension, Acad. Behavioral Medicine (coun. 1986, pres. 1987), Alpha Omega Alpha. Office: Shadyside Hosp Pittsburgh PA 15232

SHAPIRO, BURTON LEONARD, oral pathologist, geneticist, educator; b. N.Y.C., Mar. 29, 1934; s. Nat Lazarus and Fay Rebecca (Gartenhouse) S.; m. Eileen Roman, Aug. 11, 1958; children—Norah Leah, Anne Rachael, Carla Faye. Student, Tufts U., 1951-54; D.D.S., NYU, 1958; M.S., U. Minn., 1962, Ph.D., 1966. Faculty U. Minn. Sch. Dentistry, Mpls., 1962—; assoc. prof. div. oral pathology U. Minn. Sch. Dentistry, 1966-70, prof., chmn. div. oral biology, 1970-79, prof., chmn. dept. oral biology, 1979-88, prof. dept. oral pathology and genetics, 1979-88, dir. grad. studies, mem. grad. faculty genetics, 1966—, prof. dept. oral sci., 1988—, mem. grad. faculty pathobiology, 1979; prof. dept. lab. medicine and pathology U. Minn. Sch. Medicine, 1985—, mem. Human Genetics Inst., 1988—, univ. senator, 1968-72, 88-93; also mem. med. staff U. Minn. Health Scis. Center; exec. com. Grad. Sch. U. Minn., chmn. health scis. policy rev. council, chmn. univ. faculty consultative com., 1988-92; chmn. univ. fin. and planning com. Grad. Sch. U. Minn., 1988; hon. research fellow Galton Lab. dept. human genetics Univ. Coll., London, 1974; spl. vis. prof. Japanese Ministry Edn., Sci. and Culture, 1983. Mem. adv. editorial bd.: Jour. Dental Research, 1971—; Contbr. articles to profl. jours. Served to lt. USNR, 1958-60. Am. Cancer Soc. postdoctoral fellow, 1960-62; advanced fellow, 1965-68; named Century Club Prof. of Yr., 1988. Fellow Am. Acad. Oral Pathology, AAAS; mem. Internat. Assn. Dental Research (councilor 1969), Am. Soc. Human Genetics, Craniofacial Biology Soc. (pres. 1972), Sigma Xi, Omicron Kappa Upsilon. Home: 148 Nina St # 2 Saint Paul MN 55102-2160 Office: U Minn Sch Dentistry Dept Oral Sci Minneapolis MN 55455

SHAPIRO, CAROL SADIE, plastic and reconstructive surgeon; b. Pitts., Sept. 24, 1939; d. Leo I. and Charlotte H. (Heller) S.; m. Donald E. Morgan, May 19, 1974; children: Donald E., Leslie Marie. BS, U. Pitts., 1961; MD, Med. Coll. Pa., 1965. Diplomate Am. Soc. Plastic and Reconstructive Surgery. Intern Phila. Gen. Hosp., 1965-66; resident gen. surgery Georgetown U. Hosp., Washington, 1966-69; practice medicine specalizing in plastic surgery Woodbridge, Manassas, Va., 1972—. Trustee Potomac Hosp., Woodbridge, 1983, 84, 86. Recipient Outstanding Achievement award, Prince Willian County Com. for Disabled, 1988. Mem. AMA (physician's recognition award 1972, 76, 80, 85), Med. Soc. Va. (vice councilor, physician's health and effectiveness com. 1989—), Am. Soc. Plastic and Reconstructive Surgery, Am. Soc. Aesthethic Plastic Surgery, Nat. Capital Soc. Plastic Surgeons, So. Med. Assn., Prince William County Med. Soc., Prince William County C. of C. Home: 7822 Gingerbread Ln Fairfax VA 22039-2201 Office: 1940 Opitz Blvd Woodbridge VA 22191-3304

SHAPIRO, DAVID HOWARD, surgeon; b. Newark, Apr. 20, 1939; s. Nathan and Theresa Marie (Brown) S.; m. Jean R. Vetter, Aug. 16, 1979; children: Seth, Adam, Corey. AB, Williams Coll., 1961; MD, Tufts U., 1965. Diplomate Am. Bd. Surgery, Am. Bd. Med. Examiners. Intern in surgery Boston City Hosp., 1965-66, resident in surgery, 1966-67; resident in ob/gyn Yale-New Haven Hosp., 1967-68, resident, chief resident, 1968-71; from asst. clin. prof. surgery to clin. prof. surgery Univ. South Fla. Coll. Medicine, Tampa, 1973—; pvt. practice surgery Clearwater, Fla., 1973—. Cons. editor Jour. Fla. Med. Assn., 1988-81. Pres. bd. dirs. Pasco County subdiv. West Coast Regional Health Planning Commn., 1973; v.p. bd. trustees Fla. West Coast Regional Health Planning Commn., 1973; bd. dirs. Family Svcs. Pinellas County, 1984, Suncoast Internat. Adoptions, 1982-84; trustee St. Paul's Sch., chmn. strategic long-range planning com.; bd. dirs. Pinellas Regional Health Planning Commn., 1973-76; apptd. Fla. Cancer Control Rsch. Adv. Bd., 1988—; found. trustee Hospice Care, Inc., 1991; trustee, exec. com., quality assurance com., mktg. com. Morton Plant Hosp.; bd. dirs., med. adv. Pasco County div. Am. Cancer Soc., 1973, edn. com. Fla. div., 1978, colo-rectal task force, 1978, bd. dirs. Pinellas div., 1973-86, chmn. profl. edn. com., Fla. profl. edn. com., 1979, com. on rsch., 1978-80, bd. dirs., 1979-80. Maj. USAMC, 1971-73. Fellow Am. Coll. Surgeons (sec.-treas. Fla. chpt. 1980-82, pres.-elect 1982-84, pres. 1984-86, mem. various coms.), Southeastern Surg. Conf.; mem. AMA, Soc. for Laser Medicine and Surgery, Am. Soc. Bariatric Surgery, Soc. Clin. Vascular Surgery, Fla. Vascular Soc., Fla. Soc. Clin. Oncology, Fla. Surg. Assn., Fla. Med. Assn., Tampa Bay Med. Soc. (steering com., sec. 1993), Pinellas County Med. Soc. (bd. govs. 1983, chmn. coms.), Pinellas County Med. Assn., Tampa Bay Surg. Soc. (founding sec.), U South Fla. Soc. Clin. Profs. (founding pres.), Sigma Xi. Office: 1260 S Greenwood Ave Clearwater FL 34616-4172

SHAPIRO, DAVID P., recreational therapist; b. Phila., Dec. 31, 1949; s. Jack and Virginia (James) S. BS in Outdoor Recreation, U. Oreg., 1978. Volleyball coach Eugene (Oreg.) Sch. Dist., 1987-89; camp dir. Lane County 4-H, Eugene, 1989; group worker detention Lane County Youth Svcs., Eugene, 1988-89; dept. head recreational therapy St. Mary Med. Ctr., Walla Walla, Wash., 1990-95; dept. head therapy Nev. Mental Health Inst., Reno, 1995—; cons. in field. Adv. com. Eugene Parks and Recreation, 1982-83, Salem (Oreg.) Parks and Recreation, 1985; mem. Walla Walla Parks Bd., 1992-95. With USAF, 9196-71. Mem. Nat. Therapeutic Recreation Assn., Am. Therapeutic Recreation Assn. Office: Nevada Metnal Health Inst 480 Galletti Way Sparks NV 89431-5564

SHAPIRO, JOAN ISABELLE, laboratory administrator, nurse; b. Fulton, Ill., Aug. 26, 1943; d. Macy James and Frieda Lockhart; m. Ivan Lee Shapiro, Dec. 28, 1968; children: Audrey, Michael. RN, Peoria Methodist Sch. Nursing, Ill., 1964. Nurse, Grant Hosp., Columbus, Ohio, 1975-76; nurse Cardiac Thoracic and Vascular Surgeons Ltd., Geneva, Ill., 1977—, mgr. non-invasive lab., 1979—; owner, operator Shapiro's Mastiff's 1976-82; sec.-treas. Sounds Svcs., 1976—, Mainstream Sounds Inc., 1980-84; co-founder Cardio-Phone Inc., 1982—, Edgewater Vascular Inst., 1987-89, Associated Profls., 1989-92; v.p., bd. dir. Computer Specialists Inc., 1986-89; founder, pres. Vein Ctr., Edema Ctr. Ltd. Mem. Soc. Non-invasive Technologists, Soc. Peripheral Vascular Nursing (community awareness com. 1984—), Oncology Nursing Soc., Internat. Soc. Lymphology, Kane County Med. Soc. Aux. (pres. 1983-84, adviser, 1984-85). Lutheran. Office: Cardiac Thoracic and Vascular Surgeons Ltd PO Box 564 Geneva IL 60134-0564

SHAPIRO, LARRY JAY, pediatrician, scientist, educator; b. Chgo., July 6, 1946; s. Philip and Phyllis (Krause) S.; m. Carol-Ann Uetake; children: Jennifer, Jessica, Brian. A.B., Washington U., St. Louis, 1968, M.D., 1971. Diplomate Am. Bd. Pediatrics, Am. Bd. Med. Examiners, Am. Bd. Med. Genetics. Intern St. Louis Children's Hosp., 1971-72, resident, 1971-73; research assoc. NIH, Bethesda, Md., 1973-75; asst. prof. Sch. Medicine, UCLA, 1975-79, assoc. prof., 1979-83, prof. pediatrics and biol. chemistry, 1983-91; investigator Howard Hughes Med. Inst., 1987-91; prof., chmn. dept. pediat. U. Calif.-San Francisco Sch. Medicine, 1991—, chief pediat. svcs. U. Calif. San Francisco Med. Ctr., 1991—. Contbr. numerous articles to profl. publs. Served to lt. comdr. USPHS, 1973-75. Fellow AAAS, Am. Acad. Pediatrics (E. Mead Johnson award in rsch. 1982); mem. Inst. Medicine-NAS, Soc. Pediatric Rsch. (coun. 1984-87, pres. 1991-92), Western Soc. for Pediatric Rsch. (coun. 1983-87, Ross award in rsch. 1981, pres. 1989-90), Soc. for Inherited Metabolic Disease (coun. 1983-88, pres. 1986-87), Assn. Am. Physicians, Am. Soc. Human Genetics (council 1985-88, pres. elect 1995), Am. Soc. Clin. Investigation, Am. Pediatric Soc., Am. Acad. Arts & Scis. Office: U Calif Third Ave & Parnassus San Francisco CA 94143*

SHAPIRO, LEONARD, immunologist; b. Phila., Apr. 11, 1941; s. Nathan and Lottie (Ginsberg) S.; m. Linda Carol Adelman, June, 1964 (div. 1986); children: Lauren, Jonathan, Brett; m. Janet Susan Rubenstein, Nov. 7, 1987; 1 child, Eliana. AB, Temple U., 1963, MD, 1967. Diplomate Am. Bd. Allergy and Immunology, Am. Bd. Pediat. Intern Pa. Hosp., Phila., 1967-68; resident Children's Hosp., Phila., 1968-70; pvt. practice Reno, 1974—; fellow Nat. Jewish Hosp./Univ. Colo. Med. Sch., 1972-74; assoc. clin. prof. pediat. U. Nev. Med. Sch., 1974-96; cons. VA Hosp., Reno, 1974—. Pres. Temple Emanu El, Reno, 1980, 81, 93, Jewish Cmty. Coun. No. Nev., 1982, 83. Major USAF, 1970-72. Recipient Maimonides award State of Israel, 1982. Fellow Am. Acad. Pediat., Am. Coll. Allergy Asthma Immunology; mem. Alpha Omega Alpha. Republican. Jewish. Office: Allergy Asthma Assocs 2005 Silverada Blvd # 250 Reno NV 89512

SHAPIRO, LESLIE ALAN, ophthalmic surgeon; b. Bklyn., Aug. 21, 1945; s. Sidney Joseph and Betty (Miller) S.; m. Carolyn Bresnick, June 23, 1968; children: Jordan David, Jennifer Elaine. BA, NYU, 1967; MD, George Washington U., 1971. Surg. resident Beth Israel Med. Ctr., N.Y.C., 1971-73, ophthalmology resident, 1973-76; pvt. practice Bayside, N.Y., 1976—; attending surgeon North Shore U. Hosp., Manhasset, N.Y., 1986—, St. Joseph's Hosp., Flushing, N.Y., 1985—, Beth Israel Med. Ctr., N.Y.C., 1976—. Dep. mayor Village of Kensington, Great Neck, N.Y., 1984-88. Fellow ACS, Am. Acad. Ophthalmology, Am. Soc. Cataract and Refractive Surgeons. Office: 200-14 44th Ave Bayside NY 11361-2537

SHAPIRO, LUCILLE, molecular biology educator; b. N.Y.C., July 16, 1940; d. Philip and Yetta (Stein) Cohen; m. Roy Shapiro, Jan. 23, 1960 (div. 1977); 1 child, Peter; m. Harley H. McAdams, July 28, 1978; stepchildren: Paul, Heather. BA, Bklyn. Coll., 1961; PhD, Albert Einstein Coll. Medicine, 1966. Asst. prof. Albert Einstein Coll. Medicine, N.Y.C., 1967-72, assoc. prof., 1972-77, Kramer prof., chmn. dept. molecular biology, 1977-86, dir. biol. scis. div., 1981-86; Eugene Higgins prof., chmn. dept. microbiology, Coll. Physicians and Surgeons Columbia U., N.Y.C., 1986-89; Joseph D. Grant prof., chmn. dept. devel. biology Sch. Medicine, Stanford U., 1989—; bd. dirs. Silicon Graphics; bd. sci. counselors NIH, Washington, 1980-84, DeWitt Stetten disting. lectr., 1989; bd. sci. advisors G.D. Searle Co., Skokie, Ill., 1984-86; sci. adv. bd. Mass. Gen. Hosp., 1990-93, SmithKline Beecham, 1993—, PathoGenesis, 1995—; bd. trustees Scientists Inst. for Pub. Info., 1990-94; lectr. Harvey Soc., 1993; commencement address U. Calif., Berkeley, 1994. Editor: Microbiol. Devel., 1984; mem. editorial bd. Jour. Bacteriology, 1978-86, Trends in Genetics, 1987—, Genes and Development, 1987-91, Cell Regulation, 1990-92, Molecular Biology of the Cell, 1992—, Molecular Microbiology, 1991—, Current Opinion on Genetics and Devel., 1991—; contbr. articles to profl. jours. Mem. sci. bd. Helen Hay Witney Found., N.Y.C., 1986-94; co-chmn. adv. bd. NSF Biology Directorate, 1988-89; vis. com., bd. overseers Harvard U., Cambridge, Mass., 1987-90; mem. sci. bd. Whitehead Inst., MIT, Boston, 1988-93; mem. sci. rev. bd. Howard Hughes Med. Inst., 1990-94, Cancer Ctr. of Mass. Gen. Hosp., Boston, 1994; mem. Presidio Coun. City of San Francisco, 1991-94; mem. Pres. Coun. U. Calif., 1991—. Recipient Hirschl Career Scientist award, 1976, Spirit of Achievement award, 1978, Alumna award of honor Bklyn. Coll., 1983, Excellence in Sci. award Fedn. Am. Soc. Exptl. Biology, 1994; Jane Coffin Child fellow, 1966. Fellow AAAS, Am. Acad. Arts and Scis., Am. Acad. Microbiology; mem. NAS, Inst. Medicine of NAS, Am. Soc. Biochemistry and Molecular Biology (nominating com. 1982, 87, coun. 1990-93), Am. Heart Assn. (sci. adv. bd. 1984-87). Office: Stanford U Sch Medicine Beckman Ctr Dept Devel Biology Stanford CA 94305

SHAPIRO, MARCIA HASKEL, speech and language pathologist; b. N.Y.C., Nov. 6, 1949; d. Ben and Edna Haskel; m. Louis Shapiro, Aug. 1, 1981. BA, Hunter Coll., 1982; MA, NYU, 1983; MA in Speech Pathology, U. Cen. Fla., 1991. Cert. deaf educator, Fla. Tchr. deaf Pub. Sch. 47, N.Y.C., 1983-84; speech pathologist St. Francis Sch. for the Deaf, Bklyn., 1984-86, Seminole County Schs., 1986-87, Lake County Schs., 1987-89, Orange County Schs., Orlando, Fla., 1989-91, West Volusia Meml. Hosp., Deland, Fla., 1991-93, Orlando Regional Med. Ctr., 1993, Sand Lake Hosp., 1993—; staff head swallowing dept. Leesburg Regional Med. Ctr., 1994; dir. speech pathology Fla. Hosp., Waterman, 1994—. Mem. ASHA, AFTRA, EQITY, Annals of Deaf, CAID, Alexander Graham Bell Assn. for Deaf.

SHAPIRO, MARIAN KAPLUN, psychologist; b. N.Y., July 13, 1939; d. David and Bertha Rebecca (Pearlman) Kaplun; m. Irwin Ira Shapiro, Dec. 20, 1959; children: Steven, Nancy. BA, Queens Coll., 1959; MA in Teaching, Harvard U., 1961, EdD, 1978. Cert. psychologist. Tchr. North Quincy High Sch., Quincy, Mass., 1962-64; instr. Carnegie Inst., Boston, 1968-74; staff psychologist South Shore Counselling Assn., Hanover, Mass., 1978-80; pvt. practice psychologist Lexington, Mass., 1980—; adj. instr. Mass. Sch. Profl. Psychology, Dedham, 1985—. Author: 2nd Childhood: Hypnoplay Therapy with Age--Regressed Adults, 1989; contbr. articles on teaching reading, hypnotherapy, multiple personality and other clin. issues to profl. jours. Fellow Am. Orthopsychiat. Assn.; mem. APA, Mass. Psychol. Assn., N.E. Soc. Group Psychotherapy, Am. Soc. Group Psychotherapy (clin.), Am. Soc. Clin. Hypnosis (cert. cons.), New Eng. Soc. for the Study of Multiple Personality Disorders, Internat. Soc. for the Study of Multiple Personality Disorders, New Eng. Soc. Clin. Hypnosis, Sigma Alpha, Pi Lambda Theta. Jewish. Home and Office: 17 Lantern Ln Lexington MA 02173-6029

SHAPIRO, MIKHAIL, osteopath; b. Bobruisk, Russia, May 22, 1953; arrived in U.S., 1989; s. Zyama and Faina (Vayner) S.; m. Anna Kazimirovna Karman, Apr. 26, 1989. MD, Med. Sch. Mil. Med. Acad., Leningrad, USSR, 1977. Physician, charge of aviation & space clin. physiology rsch. Mil. Air Force, Vozdvizenka Base, USSR, 1977-82; dir. of city diagnostic ctr. Bobruisk City Pub. Health Dept., 1982-89; intern Lutheran Med. Ctr., Bklyn., 1996—. Mem. Am. Acupuncture Assn., Am. Osteo. Assn., Am. Coll. of Osteo. Family Physicians. Office: Lutheran Med Ctr 150 55th St Brooklyn NY 11220-2574

SHAPIRO, NELLA IRENE, surgeon; b. N.Y.C., Nov. 13, 1947; d. Eugene and Ethel (Pearl) S.; m. Jack Schwartz, Oct. 16, 1977; children: Max, Molly. BA, Barnard Coll., 1968; MD, Albert Einstein Coll., 1972. Resident in gen. surgery Montefiore Hosp., N.Y.C., 1972-76; mem. staff North Cen. Hosp., Bronx, N.Y., 1976-77, Bronx Mcpl. Hosp., 1977-87; chief gen. surgery Bronx Mcpl. Hosp. Ctr., 1983-87; mem. staff in gen. surgery Albert Einstein Coll. Hosp., Bronx, 1977-93, chief gen. surgery, 1991-93; atty. Lear Surg. Assocs., 1993-94; pvt. solo practive Bronx, 1994—; asst. prof. surgery Albert Einstein Coll., Bronx, 1980—; assoc. dir. gen. surgery Weller Hosp., Bronx, 1991-93; co-founder Whaecom Breast Ctr., Bronx, 1991—. Fellow Am. Coll. Surgeons. Office: 1695 Eastchester Rd Ste 304 Bronx NY 10461-2335

SHAPIRO, RICHARD STANLEY, physician; b. Moline, Ill., June 11, 1925; s. Herbert and Esther Dian (Grant) S.; BS, St. Ambrose Coll., 1947; BS in Pharmacy, U. Iowa, 1951, MS in Preventive Medicine and Environ. Health, 1951, M.D., 1957; m. Arlene Blum, June 12, 1949; children: Michele Pamela, Bruce Grant, Gary Lawrence; m. Merry Lou Cook, Oct. 11, 1971. Pharmacist, Rock Island, Ill., 1951-53; research asst. U. Iowa Coll. Medicine, Iowa City, 1950-51, 53-57; practice medicine specializing in allergy, Beverly Hills, Calif., 1958-62, Lynwood, Calif., 1962—; attending physician Good Hope Found. Allergy Clinic, Los Angeles, 1958-62, Cedars of Lebanon Hosp., Hollywood, Calif., 1959-68, U. So. Calif.-Los Angeles County Med. Center, 1962—; physician St. Francis Hosp., Lynwood, 1962—; assoc. clin. prof. medicine U. So. Calif., 1978-84, emeritus, 1984—. Bd. dirs. Westside Jewish Community Center, 1961-65, Camp JCA, 1964-65. Served with USNR, 1943-45; PTO. Diplomate Am. Bd. Allergy and Immunology. Fellow Am. Geriatric Soc., Am. Coll. Allergy, Am. Assn. Clin. Immunology and Allergy; mem. Am. Soc. Tropical Medicine and Hygiene, Am. Acad. Allergy, Los Angeles Allergy Soc., AMA, Calif., Los Angeles County med. assns., West Coast Allergy Soc., AAAS, Am., Calif. socs. internal medicine, Calif. Soc. Allergy, Am. Heart Assn., Sierra Club, Sigma Xi. Jewish. Mason; mem. B'nai B'rith. Contbr. articles to profl. jours. Office: 8301 Florence Ave Ste 104 Downey CA 90240-3946

SHAPIRO, ROBERT, orthopedist; b. Boston, Mar. 2, 1913; s. Nathan and Rebecca (Korolick) S.; m. Sylvia C. Cohen, July 5, 1935 (dec. Jan. 1996); children: Roberta S., Richard. AB, Harvard U., 1933; MD, Tufts U., 1937. Diplomate Am. Bd. Orthop. Surgery. Intern in medicine Carney Hosp., Boston, 1937-38; intern in surgery Cambridge (Mass.) Hosp., 1939-40; resident in orthop. surgery Lakeville (Mass.) State Hosp., 1946-47, Hosp. for Joint Disease, N.Y.C., 1947-50; pvt. practice Brookline, Mass., 1950—. Maj. U.S. Army, 1940-46. Fellow ACS. Jewish. Home and Office: 155 Seaver St Brookline MA 02146

SHAPIRO, ROBERT FRANCIS, pathologist; b. Omaha, Nebr., Aug. 1, 1940; s. Stanley and Betty (Robinson) S.; m. Dorothy Ann Saylan, Aug. 18, 1963; children: Stephanie Michelle, Jackie Rae. BS, U. Nebr., 1962, MD, 1965; MSHA, U. Colo., 1992. Diplomate Am. Bd. Pathology, Am. Bd. Med. Mgmt. Pathologist Physicians Pathology Lab., Lincoln, Nebr., 1970-73, Pathology Med. Svcs. PC, Lincoln, 1973—. Bd. dirs. South Street Temple, Lincoln, 1982-83. Recipient Leadership award, 1995. Fellow Coll. of Am. Pathologists, Am. Soc. of Clin. Pathology; mem. AMA, Nebr. Med. Assn. (pres. 1993-94, sec., treas. 1984-90), Nebr. Assn. Pathologists (pres. 1982), Am. Pathology Found. (bd. dirs. 1984-90, 94—), Alpha Omega Alpha. Republican. Jewish. Home: 7410 Old Post Rd 8 Lincoln NE 68106

SHAPIRO, ROBERT S., ophthalmologist; b. Trenton, N.J., Mar. 15, 1935; s. Alfred and Mollie (Wolfer) S.; m. Lis Kunzman; children: Michael, Jeffrey, Andrew. BS, Franklin and Marshall Coll., Lancaster, Pa., 1956, MD, 1960. Diplomate Am. Bd. Ophthalmology. Intern Muhlenberg Regional Med. Ctr., resident; pvt. practice, 1963—. Capt. USAF, 1960-63. Mem. AMA, Am. Acad. Ophthalomology. Office: The Eye Ctr 65 Mountain Blvd Warren NJ 07054

SHAPIRO, ROBERTA F., physician; b. N.Y.C., Sept. 22, 1960; d. Jerome and Evelyn (Schloss) S. BA, George Washington U., 1982; DO, Nova-Southeastern U., 1987. Diplomate Am. Bd. Phys. Medicine and Rehab., Am. Bd. Osteo. Medicine. Resident N.Y. Med. Coll., Valhalla, 1989-90, Albert Einstein Coll. Medicine/Montefiore Med. Ctr., Bronx, N.Y., 1990-92; fellow Albert Einstein Coll. Medicine/Kennedy Ctr., Bronx, N.Y., 1992-93, attending physician, 1993—; attending physician Danbury (Conn.) Hosp., 1994-95; pvt. practice N.Y.C., 1996—; cons. Conn. Children with Spl. Needs, Danbury, 1994—, Flushing (N.Y.) Hosp. Med. Ctr., 1996—; lectr. in field. Lectr. Fascioscapulohemeral-Muscular Dystrophy Soc., N.Y.C., 1996. Recipient Excellence in Osteo. Practice and Principle award Merck, Sharpe and Dohme, 1987. Fellow Am. Acad. Phys. Medicine and Rehab.; mem. AMA, Am. Osteo. Assn., Am. Med. Women's Assn. Office: 580 Park Ave New York NY 10021

SHAPIRO, SAM, health care analyst, biostatistician; b. N.Y.C., Feb. 12, 1914; married, 1938; 2 children. BS, Bklyn. Coll., 1933. Chief natality analysis br. Nat. Office Vital Stats., USPHS, 1947-54; sr. study dir. Nat. Opinion Rsch. Ctr., 1954-55; assoc. dir. div. rsch. and stats. Health Ins. Plan Greater N.Y., 1955-59, v.p., dir., 1959-73; dir. Health Svc. R & D Ctr., Balt., 1973-83; prof. health policy and mgmt. Johns Hopkins Sch. Hygiene and Pub. Health, Balt., 1973-85; emeritus prof. Johns Hopkins Sch. Hygiene and Pub. Health, 1985—; lectr. in pub. health Columbia U. Sch. Pub. Health and Adminstrv. Medicine, 1961-80; adj. prof. medicine Mt. Sinai Sch. Medicine, N.Y.C., 1972-78. Recipient prize GM Cancer Rsch. Found., 1988, Disting. Achievement award Am. Soc. Preventive Oncology, 1985. Fellow AAAS, APHA (award for excellence 1977), Am. Statis. Assn., Am. Coll. Radiology (hon.); mem. Inst. Medicine, Assn. for Health Svcs. Rsch. (Disting. Career in Health Svcs. Rsch. award 1985). Office: Johns Hopkins U Sch Hygiene and Pub Health 624 N Broadway Baltimore MD 21205-1901

SHAPIRO, SANDOR SOLOMON, hematologist; b. Bklyn., July 26, 1933. BA, Harvard U., 1954, MD, 1957. Intern Harvard med. svc. Boston City Hosp., 1957-58, asst. resident, 1960-61; asst. surgeon divsn. biol. std. NIH, USPHS, 1958-60; NIH spl. fellow MIT, 1961-64; from instr. to assoc. prof. Cardeza found. Jefferson Med. Coll., Phila., 1964-72, prof. medicine, 1972—, assoc. dir., 1978-85, dir., 1985—; mem. hematology study sect. NIH, 1972-76, 78-79; mem. med. adv. coun. Nat. Hemophilia Found., 1973-75; chmn. Pa. State Hemophilia Adv. Com., 1974-76. Mem. Am. Soc. Clin. Investigation, Am. Soc. Hematology, Am. Assn. Immunologists, Assn. Am. Physicians, Internat. Soc. Thrombosis and Hemostasis. Office: Thomas Jefferson U Cardeza Found Hematologic Rsch 1015 Walnut St Philadelphia PA 19107

SHAPIRO, STEVEN DAVID, dermatologist; b. Oakhurst, N.J., Oct. 15, 1961; s. Alfred J. and Marilyn G. S.; m. Lynn A. Shapiro Feb. 6, 1993. BA cum laude, Vanderbilt U., 1984; MD, N.J. Med. Sch., 1988. Diplomate Nat. Bd. Med. Examiners, Am. Bd. Dermatology; lic. MD N.J., Fla. Intern internal medicine Hahnemann Univ. Hosp., Phila., 1988-89; resident in dermatology Mt. Sinai Med. Ctr. Greater Miami, Miami Beach, Fla., 1989-90; chief resident in dermatology U. Miami Sch. of Medicine, VA Med. Ctr., Mt. Sinai Med. Ctr., Miami, Fla., 1991-92; dermatologist pvt. practice Long Branch, N.J., 1992-95; dermatologist Dermatology Specialists of Palm Beach County P.A., Boca Raton, Fla., 1995—, Steven B. Rosenberg MD P.A., W. Palm Beach, Fla., 1995—; affiliate St. Mary's Hosp, Good Samaritan Hosp., W. Palm Beach; clin. instr. dept. dermatology and cutaneous surgery, U. Miami Sch. of Medicine. Contbr. articles to profl. jours. including Internat. Jour. Dermatology, Cutaneous Pathology and others. Chmn. profl. edn. com. Monmouth County chpt. Am. Cancer Soc., 1992-94, vol. coord. skin cancer screenings, 1992-95, chmn. task force on skin cancer, 1994-95, v.p. 1995; presenter workshops to Am. Acad. Dermatology, San Francisco, 1989, Dermatology Nurses Assn., Atlanta, 1990, Skin Signs of Internal Disease Conf., Neptune, N.J., 1991. Finalist Marion Merrel Dow Pharm. Clin. Cases in Dermatology, 1991; named Physician of Yr. Monmouth County Chpt. Am. Cancer Soc., 1994. Fellow Am. Acad. Dermatology; mem. AMA (Physician's Recognition award 1991), Am. Soc. Dermatologic Surgery, Am. Soc. Dermatology, Am. Soc. Moh's Surgery, Phi Eta Sigma, Alpha Lambda Delta. Home: 11 Via Verona Palm Beach Gardens FL 33418

SHAPIRO, SUE ANNE, psychologist; b. N.Y., May 7, 1947; d. Paul Henry Shapiro and Elaine Rita Brody; m. Clark Sugg (div. 1985). BA, Brandeis U., 1968; MA in clin. psychology, Yeshiva U., 1976, PhD in clin. psychology, 1978; postgrad., NYU, 1983. Devel. examiner Foster Care Project, N.Y., 1972-73; psychologist, asst. unit head, dir. tng. Kingsboro Psychiat. Ctr., N.Y., 1974-79; pvt. practice N.Y.C., 1978—; adj. instr. Bklyn. Coll., CUNY, 1972-73, New Sch. Social Rsch., N.Y.C., 1983-84; mem. faculty, supr. Manhattan Inst. for Psychoanalysis, N.Y.C., 1987—, dir. Ctr. for Study and Treatment Abuse and Incest, 1990—; clin. instr. NYU, 1981—, clin. supr., 1984—, supr. postdoctoral program in psychoanalysis, 1992—; staff psychologist Inst. Contemporary Psychotherapy, 1975-78. Author: Contemporary Theories of Schizophrenia, 1981; contbr. articles to profl. jours. Mem. APA, Psychoanalytic Soc. Office: 14 E 4th St Apt 402 New York NY 10012-1141

SHARFMAN, MARC IRWIN, neurologist; b. Chgo., May 1, 1961; s. Sheldon Marvin Sharfman and Frances June (Harris) Fisher; m. Cindy Joy Karlin, June 12, 1988; 1 child, David Scott. BS in Biology, U. Ill., 1983; MD, U. Health Sci./Chgo. Med. Sch., 1987. Diplomate Nat. Bd. Med. Examiners; cert. Am. Bd. Psychiatry and Neurology. Intern Northwestern Meml. Hosp., Chgo., 1987-88, resident neurology, 1988-89; resident neurology U. Mass. Med. Ctr., Worcester, 1989-91; pvt. practice headache specialist Fla., 1991—; clin. asst. prof. dept. neurology U. South Fla. Coll. Medicine, Tampa, 1991-92; courtesy clin. instr. dept. medicine U. Fla. Coll. Medicine, Gainesville, 1994-96; staff mem. Orlando (Fla.) Regional Med. Ctr., 1992—, Fla. Hosp., Orlando, 1992—, Winter Park (Fla.) Meml. Hosp., 1992—, Morton Plant Hosp., Clearwater, Fla., 1992-93; assoc. dir. Headache

Mgmt. Ctr., Inc., Winter Park, 1992-93; dir. Headache and Neurol. Treatment Inst., Winter Park, 1993—; presenter and lectr. in field. Mem. AMA, Am. Assn. Study Headache, Nat. Headache Found., Internat. Headache Soc., Alpha Omega Alpha. Office: 1936 Lee Rd Ste 137 Winter Park FL 32789

SHARMA, ARJUN DUTTA, cardiologist; b. Bombay, June 2, 1953; came to U.S., 1981; s. Hari D. and Gudrun (Axelsson) S.; m. Carolyn D. Burleigh, May 9, 1981; chldren: Allira, Eric, Harisson. BSc, U. Waterloo, Ont., Can., 1972; MD, U. Toronto, Ont., 1976. Intern Toronto Gen. Hosp., 1976-77, resident in medicine, 1978-80; resident in medicine St. Michael's Hosp., Toronto, 1980-81; residency medicine Toronto Gen. Hosp., 1977-78; Rsch. assoc. Washington U., St. Louis, 1981-83; asst. prof. pharmacy and toxicology U. Western Ont., London, 1985-89, asst. prof. medicine, 1983-89, assoc. prof. medicine, 1989-90; dir. interventional electrophysiology Sutter Meml. Hosp., Sacramento, 1990-95; abstract reviewer, faculty of ann. sci. sessions N.Am. Soc. for Pacing and Electrophysiology, 1993-94; assoc. clin. prof. U. Calif., Davis, 1988—; cons. Medtronic Inc., Mpls., 1985—, Telectronics Pacing Sys., Inc., 1990-94; mem. rsch. com. Sutter Inst. Med. Rsch., 1991—; mem. exec. com. Sutter Heart Inst., 1992. Reviewer profl. jours., including Circulation, Am. Jour. Cardiology; contbr. articles to profl. publs. Mem. coun. for basic sci. Am. Heart Assn., chmn. ann. sci. session, 1989. Recipient John Melady award, 1972, Dr. C.S. Wainwright award, 1973-75, Rsch. prize Toronto Gen. Hosp., 1979, 80, Ont. Career Scientist award Ont. Ministry of Health, 1983-89; Med. Rsch. Coun. Can. fellow, 1981-83. Fellow ACP, Am. Coll. Cardiology; mem. Am. Fedn. Clin. Rsch., Canadian Cardiovasc. Soc., N.Y. Acad. Scis., Sacramento Med. Soc., Eldorado Med. Soc. Office: 3941 J St Ste 260 Sacramento CA 95819-3633

SHARMA, HARI SHANKER, neurophysiologist, researcher; b. Dalmianagar, Bihar, India, Jan. 15, 1955; arrived in Sweden, 1988; s. Ram Rup and Doeraj Kumari S.; m. Aruna Misra, Apr. 14, 1979; children: Prashant Misra, Suraj Misra. BSc (hons), Bihar U., Muzaffarpur, India, 1973, MSc, 1976; PhD, Banaras Hindu U., Varanasi, India, 1982. Rsch. scientist A Banaras Hindu U., Varanasi, India, 1983-86; rsch. scientist B Banaras Hindu U., Varanasi, 1986-88; visiting scientist Uppsala (Sweden) U., 1988-89, 1991—; Group leader Banaras Hindu U., Varanasi, India, 1983-88, Uppsala (Sweden) U., 1991—; Humboldt fellow Free Univ., Berlin, 1989-91. Editor: Progress in Brain Research Series.; contbr. articles, rsch. to profl. jours. Recipient Siri Rsch. prize Indian Assn., Biomed. Scientists, 1986, Shakuntala Amir Chand prize Indian Coun. Med. Rsch., 1988, Carrier award Univ. Grants Com., Varanasi, India, 1987; named Gustafson fellow Gustafson Found., Uppsala, Sweden, 1994-96. Fellow Am. Inst. Stress; mem. AAAS, Internat. Brain Rsch. Orgn., Internat. Brain Edema Rsch. Soc., N.Y. Acad. Scis. Home: Ap 1228 Frödingsgatan 12, S-754 21 Uppsala Sweden Office: Uppsala Univ Hosp, Inst Pathology, S-751 85 Uppsala Sweden

SHARMA, SANTOSH DEVRAJ, obstetrician, gynecologist, educator; b. Kenya, Feb. 24, 1934; came to U.S., Jan. 1972; d. Devraj Chananram and Lakshmi (Devi) S. BS, MB, B.J. Medical Sch., Pune, India, 1960. House surgeon Sasson Hosp., Poona, India, 1960-61; resident in ob-gyn. various hospitals, England, 1961-67; house officer Maelor Gen. Hosp., Wrexham, U.K., 1961-62; asst. prof. ob-gyn. Howard U. Med. Sch., Washington, 1972-74; assoc. prof. John A. Burns Sch. Med., Honolulu, 1974-78, prof., 1978 --. Fellow Royal Coll. Ob-Gyn., Am. Coll. Ob-Gyn. Office: 1319 Punahou St Rm 824 Honolulu HI 96826-1032

SHARMA, VIJAI PRAKASH, clinical psychologist; b. Ahmedabad, Gujrat, India, June 30, 1941; came to U.S., 1980; s. Piarey Lal and Janki Devi (Parashar) S.; m. Sudha Nagrath, Aug. 19, 1967; children: Vaishali, Suvi. PhD in Clin. Psychology, Lund (Sweden) U., 1977. Diplomate Am. Acad. Pain Mgmt. Psychologist B.M. Inst. Mental Health, Ahmedabad, India, 1967-68, dir. psychology, 1973-80; sr. psychologist U. Coll. Hosp., London, 1970-73; clin. psychologist Lakeshore Inst. Mental Health, Knoxville, Tenn., 1981-83; clin. dir. Hiwassee Mental Health Ctr., Cleveland, Tenn., 1983-90; dir. Behavioral Medicine Ctr., Cleveland, 1991—; clin. psychologist, cons. Cleveland, 1991—; cons. Cleveland Community Hosp., 1988—, Bradley Rehab. Ctr., Cleveland, 1990—. Author: Insane Jealousy, 1991. Trainer Bradley U. Hospice Vols., 1986—. Mem. APA, Tenn. Psychol. Assn. (grass roots coord. 1989—). Home: 3250 Blueberry Hill Pl NW Cleveland TN 37312-4401

SHARON, NATHAN, biochemist; b. Brisk, Poland, Nov. 4, 1925; arrived in Israel, 1934; m. Rachel Itzikson, 1948; children: Esther, Osnat. MS, Hebrew U., Jerusalem, 1950, PhD, 1953; Dr. (hon.), U. Rene Descartes, Paris, 1990. Rsch. asst. Agrl. Rsch. Sta., Rehovot, Israel, 1949-53; rsch. asst. dept. biophysics Weizmann Inst. Sci., Rehovot, Israel, 1954-57, rsch. assoc. dept. biophysics, 1957-60, sr. scientist dept. biophysics, 1960-65, assoc. prof. dept. biophysics, 1965-68, prof. dept. biophysics, 1968—; vis. scientist numerous univs. and colls. Author: Complex Carbohydrates: Their Chemistry, Biosynthesis and Functions, 1975; co-editor: Biotechnological Applications of Proteins and Enzymes, 1977, The Lectins: Properties, Functions and Applications in Biology and Medicine, 1986; co-author: Lectins, 1989; contbr. over 400 articles to profl. jours. Recipient Laundau prize Mifal Hapyis, Israel, 1973, Weizmann prize in exact scis. City of Tel Aviv, 1977, Olitzki prize Israel Soc. Microbiology, 1989, Datta lectureship award Fedn. European Biochem. Socs., 1987, Bijvoet medal Utrecht U., 1989, Israel Prize in Biomedical and Medical Research, 1994. Mem. Am. Chem. Soc., Biochem. Soc. Eng., Am. Soc. Biol. Chemists (hon.), European Molecular Biology Orgn., Israel Acad. Scis. and Humanities, Internat. Sci. Writers Assn., Israel Biochem. Soc. (pres. 1969-70), Soc. for Complex Carbohydrates, Fedn. European Biochem. Socs. (chmn. 1980-81), Internat. Glycoconjugate Orgn. (pres. 1989-91). Home: 77 Mishmeret, Afeka Tel Aviv 69012, Israel Office: Weizmann Inst Sci, Dept Membrane Rsch, & Biophysics, Rehovot 76100, Israel

SHARP, DAVID GORDON, internist; b. Utica, N.Y., Nov. 12, 1964; s. Gordon Craig and Sally Joann (Edmunds) S.; m. Rhonda Sue Joekel, June 20, 1992; 1 child, Spencer Edmunds. BA, DePauw U., 1987; MS, N.E. Mo. State U., 1992; DO, Kirksville Coll. Osteo. Med., 1992. Diplomate Am. Osteo. Bd. Internal Medicine. Intern Mich. State U., Grand Rapids, 1992-93; resident in internal medicine U. Nebr. Med. Ctr., Omaha, 1993-95; internist Specialists of Internal Medicine, St. Joseph, Mo., 1995—. Capt. U.S. Army, 1990-93. Mem. ACP (assoc.), Am. Osteo. Assn., Am. Coll. Osteo. Internists. Republican. Home: 2308 Buckingham St Saint Joseph MO 64506 Office: Specialists of Internal Med 711 N 36th St Saint Joseph MO 64506

SHARP, ELAINE CECILE, obstetrician, gynecologist; b. Hoven, S.D., Feb. 19, 1952; d. Lewis Ralph and Bernadette Teresa (Bastien) Arbach; m. Walton H. Sharp, Oct. 26, 1979 (div.); m. Shane Daigle, Nov. 1991; 1 child, Sean Patrick Daigle. BA, No. State U., 1974, BS, 1976; MD, U. Tex., Houston, 1985. Diplomate Am. Bd. Ob-Gyn. Pvt. practice Pensacola, Fla., 1989—; speaker, chmn. Body Talk, Milton, Fla., 1989—. Mem. Am. Med. Womens' Assn., Am. Diabetes Assn., Am. Bus. Womens' Assn., Am. Coll. Ob-Gyn, Soc. Laparoendoscopic Surgeons, Fla. Ob-Gyn Soc., Exec. Club (asst. chmn. cancer com.). Republic. Roman Catholic. Office: PO Box 17062 Pensacola FL 32522-7062 also: Elaine Sharp MD PA 1717 N E St # 436 Pensacola FL 32501-6339

SHARP, JERRILYN SUE, medical technologist; b. Kalamazoo, Mich., July 15, 1957; d. James Cleveland and Jacqueline Jean (Corradini) (Van Atta) Rohlfs; m. Larry Lee Sharp, Apr. 25, 1981 (div. 1989); 1 child, Courtney Maline. Cert. in med. technology, Lakeland Med. Acad., Mpls., 1976. Intern VA Hosp., Sturgis, S.D., 1976; med. technologist Pinal Gen. Hosp., Florence, Ariz., 1976-79, Bronson Vicksburg (Mich.) Hosp., 1979-88, Family Health Ctr., Kalamazoo, 1989-90; med. technologist War Meml. Hosp., Sault Ste. Marie, Mich., 1990—, resident, 1990-91; resident Sheridan (Mich.) Community Hosp., 1991—. Mem. Internat. Soc. Clin. Lab. Technologists. Home: 821 Washington St Greenville MI 48838-2162 Office: Sheridan Community Hosp 301 N Main St Sheridan MI 48884-9220

SHARP, JOHN GRAHAM, cell biologist, anatomist, educator; b. Halifax, England, Feb. 10, 1946; came to the U.S., 1971; s. Granville and Martha (Schofield) S.; m. Sheila Ellen Jamison, June 2, 1973; children: John Andrew, Matthew Edward. BS in Physics, U. Birmingham, England, 1967, MS in Radiobiology, 1968; PhD in Medicine, Med. Sch., Birmingham, 1971. Rsch. fellow in anatomy Med. Sch., 1970-71; asst. instr., instr. anatomy and radiology U. Iowa, Iowa City, 1973; asst. prof. anatomy U. Nebr. Med. Ctr., Omaha, 1973-75, assoc. prof. anatomy, 1975-78, prof. cell biology, anatomy and radiology, 1978—; vis. prof. histopathology Royal Postgrad. Med. Sch., London, 1981-82; Paul Grange Vis. Cancer fellow Monash U., Melbourne, Australia, 1984; advisor MRd Diagnostics, Radiation Health Ctr., Omaha, 1987—. Contbr. over 200 articles to profl. jours. and chpts. to books. Soccer coach Elkhorn (Nebr.) Recreation Assn., 1978-89. Damon Runyon fellow, 1971-73, Yamigawa-Yoshida fellow, 1982; named lectr. Mid Am. U. Consortium, 1984. Mem. Inst. Physics, Inst. Biology. Anglican. Office: U Nebr Med Ctr 600 S 42nd St Omaha NE 68105-6395

SHARP, PHILLIP ALLEN, academic administrator, biologist, educator; b. Ky., June 6, 1944; s. Joseph Walter and Katherin (Colvin) S.; m. Ann Christine Holcombe, Aug. 29, 1964; children: Christine Alynn, Sarah Katherin, Helena Holcombe. BA, Union Coll., Barbourville, Ky., 1966, LHD (hon.), 1991; PhD, U. Ill., 1969; DSc (hon.), U. Tel Aviv, Israel, 1996, Albright Coll., 1996. NIH postdoctoral fellow Calif. Inst. Tech., 1969-71; sr. research investigator Cold Spring Harbor (N.Y.) Lab., 1972-74; assoc. prof. MIT, Cambridge, 1974-79, prof. biology, 1979—, head dept. biology, 1991—, dir. Ctr. Cancer Rsch., 1985-91; co-founder, mem. sci. bd., dir. BIOGEN, 1978—; chmn. sci. bd., 1987—; mem. Pres.' Adv. Coun. on Sci. and Tech., 1991—; mem. bd. trustees Alfred P. Sloan Found., 1995—. Mem. editl. bd. Cell, 1974-95, Jour. Virology, 1974-86, Molecular and Cellular Biology, 1974-85. Co-recipient Nobel Prize in Physiology or Medicine, 1993; recipient awards Am. Cancer Soc., 1974-79, awards Eli Lilly, 1980, awards Nat Acad. Sci./U.S. Steel Found., 1980, Howard Ricketts award U. Chgo., 1985, Alfred P. Sloan Jr. prize Gen. Motors Research Found., 1986, award Gairdner Found. Internat., 1986, award N.Y. Acad. Scis., 1986, Louisa Horwitz prize, 1988, Albert Lasker Basic Med. Rsch. award, 1988, Dickson prize U. Pitts., 1990; awarded Class of '41 chair, 1986-87, John D. MacArthur chair, 1987-92, Salvador E. Luria chair, 1992—. Fellow AAAS; mem. Am. Chem. Soc., Am. Soc. Microbiology, NAS (councilor 1986), Am. Acad. Arts and Scis, European Molecular Biology Orgn. (assoc.), Am. Soc. Biochemistry and Molecular Biology (elected mem. coun.), Am. Philos. Soc. (elected mem.), Inst. of Medicine of NAS (elected mem.). Home: 36 Fairmont Ave Newton MA 02158-2506 Office: MIT Ctr for Cancer Rsch 40 Ames St Rm E17 529B Cambridge MA 02139-4307

SHARP, SHARON LEE, gerontology nurse; b. Beatrice, Nebr., Jan. 14, 1939; d. Clarence Alfred and Edna Clara (Grosshuesch) Wolters; m. Philip Butler, June 27, 1959 (div. 1964); m. Ted C. Sharp, Sept. 21, 1966 (div. 1988); children: Sheryl Butler, Philip Butler. Diploma, Lincoln Gen. Hosp., 1959. RN Nebr. Charge nurse Mary Lanning Meml. Hosp., Hastings, Nebr., 1960-61; asst. head nurse Ingleside State Hosp., Hastings, Nebr., 1961-62; charge nurse Rio Hondo Meml. Hosp., Downey, Calif., 1969-71, Santa Barbara (Calif.) Cottage Hosp., 1974-78; supr. Marlora Manor Convalescent Hosp., Long Beach, Calif., 1979-80; supr. Marlinda Nursing Home, Lynwood, Calif., 1982-84, dir. nursing, 1984-89; dir. nursing Ramona Care Ctr., El Monte, Calif., 1989-90, Oakview Convalescent Hosp., Tujunga, Calif., 1990-91, North Valley Nursing Ctr., Tujunga, Calif., 1992—; asst. dir. nursing Skyline Health Care Ctr. (Gran Care), L.A., 1993-94; resident assessment coord. Country Villa Rehab. Ctr., L.A., 1994-95; case mgr. Vitas Innovative Hospice Care, West Covina, Calif., 1995—; mem. adv. bd. Regional Occupational Program, Downey, 1985-86. Home: 2875 E Del Mar Blvd Pasadena CA 91107-4314

SHARP, THOMAS G., physician, researcher; b. Kittery, Maine, Apr. 12, 1952; s. John T. and Marjorie Sue (Glinn) S.; m. Teresa L. VanSlyke, May 15, 1982; children: Melissa Ann, Thomas Justin, Ryan Andrew. AB, Harvard U., 1974; MD, Columbia U., 1978. Diplomate Am. Bd. Surgery, Am. Bd. Thoracic Surgery. Resident in gen. surgery U. Mich., Ann Arbor, 1978-80, 83-86; clin. assoc. NIH, Bethesda, Md., 1980-83; resident in thoracic surgery Ind. U., Indpls., 1986-88, asst. prof., 1988—; abstract reviewer Am. Coll. Chest Physicians, Chgo., 1995-96. Contbr. articles to profl. jours. Lt. comdr. USPHS, 1980-83. Fellow Am. Coll. Surgeons, Am. Coll. Cardiology; mem. AMA, Soc. Thoracic Surgeons, N.Y. Acad. Sci. Office: Ind Univ 545 Barnhill Dr # 215 Indianapolis IN 46202

SHARP, VERNON HIBBETT, psychiatrist; b. Nashville, Apr. 6, 1932; s. Vernon Hibbett Sr. and Sarah McDonald (Robinson) S.; m. Valeria Nell Parker Storms, Aug. 17, 1956 (div. July 1975); children: Mark, Christopher, Daniel; m. Alix Ingrid Weiss, Nov. 17, 1979; 1 child, Monica Elena. BA, Vanderbilt U., 1953, MD, 1957. Diplomate Am. Bd. Psychiatry and Neurology. Intern internal medicine Washington U., St. Louis, 1957-58; resident psychiatry Yale U., New Haven, 1958-61; asst. prof. dept. psychiatry Cornell U. Med. Ctr., N.Y.C., 1963-66, SUNY, Downstate Med. Ctr., Bklyn., 1966-69; pvt. practice adults, adolescents and families Scarsdale, N.Y., 1969-83; pvt. practice Nashville, 1983-93; clin. asst. prof. psychiatry Vanderbilt U. Sch. Medicine, Nashville, 1983-86, clin. assoc. prof., 1986—; chief dept. psychiatry St. Thomas Hosp., Nashville, 1985-87; dir. family treatment tng. program Vanderbilt Med. Sch., Nashville, 1990—; founding mem. bd. dirs. Ctr. for Family, Nashville, 1985-93; vis. lectr. adolescent psychiatry Columbia U. Sch. Social Work, 1979-81; asst. attending psychiatrist Cornell U. Med. Coll., 1982-83; adj. assoc. prof. human resources Peabody Coll., Vanderbilt U., 1994-95; mem. attending staff various hosps. Contbr. articles to profl. jours. Lt. comdr. USN, 1961-63. Recipient Career Tchr. award NIMH, Downstate Med. Ctr., Bklyn., 1967-69. Mem. Am. Psychiat. Assn., Soc. for Adolescent Psychiatry, Am. Assn. Marriage and Family Therapy, Am. Family Therapy Acad., Coffee House Club (pres. 1985). Democrat. Episcopalian. Home and Office: 215 Leonard Ave Nashville TN 37205-2425

SHARPE, KATHRYN MOYE, psychologist; b. Barnesville, Ga., Nov. 27, 1922; d. Herbert Johnston and Henri Lucile (Winter) Moye; m. William Herschel Sharpe, Mar. 2, 1946; children: William Herschel Jr., Mark Stephens. AB, Piedmont Coll., Demorest, Ga., 1942; MA, U. N.C., 1947; PhD, U. S.C., 1975. Tchr., guidance counselor Charleston (S.C.) Pub. Schs., 1947-66; prof. sociology, chmn. dept. Bapt. Coll. at Charleston, 1966-88, prof. emeritus, 1988—; pvt. practice psychology, Charleston, 1975—. Kathryn Moye Sharpe scholarship given in her honor Bapt. Coll. at Charleston, 1988. Fellow Am. Assn. for Marriage and Family Therapy (approved supr., pres. S.C. div. 1975-77). Congregationalist. Home and Office: 6 Cavalier Ave Charleston SC 29407-7702

SHARRATT, BRENDA RUTH, family practice physician; b. Alexandria, Va., Feb. 6, 1962; d. Edward Elbert and Mabel Payne (Hughes) S. BA in Biology and Psychology cum laude, U. Md., 1985; DO, Phila. Coll. Osteo. Medicine, 1991. Orderly shock trauma unit U. Md., Balt., 1985-86; environ. aide Balt. County Health Dept., 1986-87; intern Mich. Health Care Ctr., Detroit, 1991-92; resident U. Cin., 1992-95; family practice physician missionary Irian Jaya, Indonesia. Summer missionary Child Evang. Fellowship, Balt., 1986. Mem. Christian Med. and Dental Soc., Am. Osteo. Assn., Christian Cmty. Health Fellowship, Am. Acad. Family Practice, Phi Kappa Phi, Omicron Delta Kappa, Psi Chi.

SHARTRAN, ALICE MARIE, medical and surgical nurse, educator; b. Simla, Colo., Oct. 8, 1949; d. Agustus Sherley Garriott and Helen Marie Morris; m. Ricky Lee Cross, May 30, 1981 (dec.); children: Sheila Renee Lee, Lance Edward Lee; m. Donald L. Shartran, Apr. 22, 1989. ADN, Pikes Peak Community Coll., 1978; BSN with distinction, U. So. Colo., 1985. RN, Colo.; cert. BCLS instr.; cert. nursing staff devel. and continuing edn. Staff nurse Penrose Hosp., 1978-88; nurse Med. Pers. Pool, Colorado Springs, Colo., 1978; camp nurse Luth. Valley Retreat, Florissant, Colo., 1978; coord. ednl. resources Penrose-St. Francis Healthcare, 1988-93; nurse mgr., nursing edn. Pikes Peak Hospice, Colorado Springs, 1993—; mem. test devel. com. cert. nursing continuing edn. & staff devel. Am. Nurses Credential Ctr., 1996—. Mem. ANA, Colo. Nurses Assn. (state edn. com. 1988-92), Dist. Nurses Assn. (co-pres. 1986-87, CE chair 1996—), Nat. Nursing Staff Devel. Orgn., Nat. Hospice Orgn., Coun. Hospice Profls. in Nursing, Hospice Nurses Assn., Sigma Theta Tau. Home: 2428 N Meade Ave Colorado Springs CO 80907-6534 Office: Pikes Peak Hospice 3630 Sinton Rd Ste 302 Colorado Springs CO 80907

SHASHY, PAUL MOSES, urologist; b. Ocala, Fla., Nov. 25, 1925; m. Nancy Scott (dec. Nov. 1990); children: Paul Jr., William, Peter, Ann, James, Hugh. MD, U. Ala., Birmingham, 1949. Cert. Am. Bd. Urology. Intern St. Louis City Hosp., 1949-50; resident Grady Meml. Hosp., Emory U., Atlanta, 1950-53; fellow Ochsner Clinic, New Orleans, 1954-57; clin. assoc. prof. urology U. Ala. Sch. Medicine, Birmingham. Office: Drs Shashy and Shashy PA 1722 Pine St Ste 204 Montgomery AL 36106-1158

SHASTRY, BARKUR SRINIVASA, biomedical sciences educator; b. Udipi, Mysore, India, Feb. 6, 1943; came to U.S., 1974; s. Barkur Neelakanta and Indira (Adiga) S.; m. Premalatha Upadhyaya, Aug. 25, 1974; children: Savitha, Rohit. MS, U. Mysore (India), 1969, PhD, 1974. Postdoctoral fellow U. Ill., Urbana, 1974-78; rsch. assoc. Washington U. Med. Sch., St. Louis, 1978-82; sr. rsch. assoc. Rockefeller U., N.Y.C., 1982-85; assoc. prof. biomed. scis. Oakland U., Rochester, Mich., 1986—. Grantee BRSG Oakland U., 1986, 89, Mich. Eye Bank, 1986, 87, NIH, 1988-91, Retinopathy of Prematurity Found., 1994-96, Beaumont Hosp. Rsch. Inst., 1995-97, Fight for Sight, 1995. Mem. Am. Assn. Cancer Rsch., Assn. for Rsch. in Vision & Ophthalmology, Am. Soc. for Biochemistry & Molecular Biology, Internat. Soc. for Eye Rsch., Am. Soc. for Cell Biology, AAAS, Genetic Soc. Am. Office: Oakland U Eye Rsch Institute Rochester MI 48309

SHATIN, HARRY, medical educator, dermatologist; b. N.Y.C., July 7, 1910; s. Samuel and Hannah (Papish) Shatinsky; m. Vera Brusilowsky, Oct. 30, 1943; 1 dau., Beth. B.S., Coll. City N.Y., 1930; M.D., Strasbourg U., France, 1936; postgrad., N.Y. U., 1949-50. Intern Unity Hosp., N.Y.C., 1937-38; pvt. practice medicine, 1938-41; staff physician VA Hosp., Bronx, N.Y., 1946-51; chief sect. dermatology VA Hosp., 1951-74, sr. cons. dermatology, 1974—; prof. clin. medicine Mt. Sinai Sch. Medicine, City U. N.Y., 1969-74, prof. dermatology, chmn. dept., 1974-79, prof. emeritus, 1979—; dir. dermatology Mt. Sinai Hosp., N.Y.C., 1974-79, cons. dermatology, 1979—. Served from lt. to maj. AUS, 1942-46. Fellow Am. Acad. Dermatology, A.C.P. (asso.), N.Y. Acad. Medicine; mem. AMA, Soc. Investigative Dermatology, Manhattan Dermatol. Soc. (pres. 1967-68), Dermatol. Soc. Greater N.Y., Internat. Soc. Tropical Dermatology. Home: 3720 Independence Ave Bronx NY 10463-1429

SHATKIN, BENNETT JAY, cardiologist; b. N.Y.C., Feb. 18, 1955; s. Lawrence and Anita Rosalyn (Zimmerman) S.; children: Julie, Arielle. BA, Columbia U., 1976; MD, U. Chgo., 1981. Bd. cert. Am. Bd. Internal Medicine, Am. Bd. Internal Medicine-Cardiovascular Disease. Reisdent internal medicine U. Miami (Fla.)-Jackson Meml., 1981-82, Montefiore Med. Ctr., Bronx, N.Y., 1982-84; fellow cardiology SUNY, Stony Brook, 1984-87; attending cardiologist Fla. Med. Ctr., Landervale Lakes, 1987-88, Newcomb Med. Ctr., Vineland, N.J., 1988—. Fellow Am. Coll. Cardiology, Am. Coll. Chest Physicians; mem. ACP, N.J. Med. Soc., Cumberland County Med. Soc., Am. Heart Assn. Office: 1076 E Chestnut Ave Vineland NJ 08360

SHATNEY, CLAYTON HENRY, surgeon; b. Bangor, Maine, Nov. 4, 1943; s. Clayton Lewis and Regina (Cossette) S.; m. Deborah Gaye Hansen, Apr. 5, 1977; children: Tony, Andy. BA, Bowdoin Coll., 1965; MD, Tufts U., 1969. Asst. prof. surgery U. Md. Hosp., Balt., 1979-82; assoc. prof. U. Fla. Sch. Medicine, 1982-87; clin. assoc. prof. Stanford (Calif.) U. Sch. Medicine, 1987—; dir. traumatology Md. Inst. Emergency Med. Svcs., Balt., 1979-82; dir. trauma U. Hosp., Jacksonville, 1982-85; assoc. dir. trauma Santa Clara Valley Med. Ctr., 1992—; cons. VA Coop. Studies Program, Washington, 1980—. Mem. editl. bd. Circulatory Shock, 1989-94, Panam Jour. Trauma, 1995—. Maj. U.S. Army, 1977-79. State of Maine scholar Bowdoin Coll., 1961-65. Fellow ACS, Southeastern Surg. Congress, Southwestern Surg. Congress, Soc. Surg. Alimentary Tract, Am. Assn. Surg. Trauma, Soc. Critical Care Medicine, Soc. Internat. de Chirurgie, Western Surg. Assn., Pacific Coast Surg. Assn., Phi Kappa Phi. Home: 900 Larsen Rd Aptos CA 95003-2640 Office: Valley Med Ctr Dept Surgery 751 S Bascom Ave San Jose CA 95128-2604

SHATZ, CARLA J., biology educator. Prof. neurobiology U. Calif., Berkeley. Recipient Charles A. Dana award for pioneering achievements in health Inst. Medicine/NAS, 1995. Office: Univ California Dept Molec & Cell Bio Berkeley CA 94720

SHATZ, DAVID VERNON, surgeon, surgical intensivist; b. Glendale, Calif., July 20, 1954; s. Vernon Peter and Marilyn (Boles) S.; m. Janice Coleman, June 17, 1989. BA in Bacteriology, UCLA, 1977; MD, Loyola U., Maywood, Ill., 1983. Diplomate Am. Bd. Surgery. Resident in gen. surgery U. Hawaii, Honolulu, 1983-86; commd. capt. U.S. Army, 1986, advanced through ranks to major, 1989; resident in gen. surgery Tripler Army Med. Ctr., Honolulu, 1986-89; gen. surgeon Reynolds Army Hosp. U.S. Army, Ft. Sill, Okla., 1989-91; gen. surgeon 47th Field Hosp., Operation Desert Shield, Operation Desert Storm, Operation Desert Storm, 1990-91; fellow in surg. critical care U. Miami (Fla.)-Jackson Meml. Hosp., 1991-92, trauma surgeon, surg. intensivist, 1992—; asst. prof. surgery U. Miami, 1992—; trauma surgeon, surg. intensivist Jackson Meml. Hosp., 1992—; trauma advisor Metro-Dade Fire-Rescue; gen. surgeon VA Hosp., Miami, 1993—. Med. dir. Fed. Emergency Mgmt. Agy. Urban Search and Fescue Fla. Task Force-1; trauma advisor Metro-Dade Fire-Rescue Emergency Med. Svcs., 1996—. Recipient Outstanding Svc. to Humanity award South Dade C. of C., 1995. Fellow ACS.

SHATZ, MARILYN JOYCE, psychologist; b. N.Y.C., Mar. 4, 1939; d. Morris and Freida Reva (Levinthal) Karpman; m. Stephen Sidney Shatz, Dec. 21, 1958 (div. July 1977); children: Geoffrey Ian, Adria Beth; m. Richard Feingold, Jan. 1, 1995. BA, U. Pa., 1971, MA, 1973, PhD, 1975. Asst. prof. Grad. Ctr. NYU, 1975-77; asst. prof. to prof. U. Mich., Ann Arbor, 1977—, dir. linguistics program, 1995—; assoc. editor Lang. Jour. Linguistic Soc. Am., Washington, 1991-93; vis. scholar Inst. Human Devel., Berkeley, Calif., 1991-92. Author: A Toddler's Life: Becoming a Person, 1994; contbr. articles to profl. jours. Fellow Guggenheim, Harvard U., 1980, Nat. Inst. Edn., U. Wis., 1981; Fulbright scholar Cambridge U., 1985; named First Alternate James McKean Cattell, 1991. Home: 2730 Maitland Dr Ann Arbor MI 48105-1565 Office: 525 E University Ave Ann Arbor MI 48109-1109

SHAUGHNESSY, ELIZABETH ANN, surgeon; b. Evanston, Ill., Jan. 4, 1959; d. Terrence Joseph and Mary Ann (Nugent) S.; m. James Dennis Stapleton, Oct. 3, 1987. BS, U. Ill., 1981; MD, U. Ill., Chgo., 1985, PhD, 1990. Intern, resident U. Ill., Chgo., 1985-87, 90-93; fellow in surg. oncology divsn. gen. and oncological surgery City of Hope Nat. Med. Ctr., Duarte, Calif., 1993—. Contbr. articles to profl. jours. Chair speakers bur. Susan G. Komen Breast Cancer Found. L.A. County, 1995—. Fellow ACS (assoc.); mem. Am. Assn. for Cancer Rsch., AAAS, Am. Med. Women's Assn., Soc. for Surg. Oncology, Am. Soc. Clin. Oncology (Young Investigator award 1995). Office: City of Hope Nat Med Ctr 1500 E Duarte Rd Duarte CA 91010

SHAUGHNESSY, MICHAEL FRANCIS, psychology educator; b. N.Y.C., May 1, 1951; s. Daniel and Agnes (Antol) S.; m. Virginia Anne Shaughnessy, July 3, 1984; children: Lauri, Kaaren, Kurt, Travis. BA, Mercy Coll., Dobbs Ferry, N.Y.C., 1973; MEd, PhD, Bank State Coll. Edn., 1976; MS, Coll. New Rochelle, 1981; DEd, U. Nebr., 1983. Cert. sch. psychologist. Counselor Children's Village, Dobbs Ferry, 1971-74; tchr. Sch. Sts. Peter and Paul, Bronx, N.Y., 1974-76; social worker Crystal Run Sch., Fallsburg, N.Y., 1976-80; instr. S.E. Community Coll., Lincoln, Nebr., 1980-83; prof. psychology Eastern N.Mex. U., Portales, 1983—. Editor Creative Child and Adult Quar.; contbr. articles to profl. jours. Recipient Cooper Found. award Nebr. State Dept. Edn., 1982. Mem. Nat. Assn. Creative Children and Adults (pres. 1985-86), Rocky Mountain Psychol. Assn., Inst. Logotherapy. Lodge: Lions. Office: Ea NMex U Dept Psychology Station 35 Portales NM 88130

SHAUL, ROGER LOUIS, JR., health care executive, researcher; b. Hartford, Conn., Jan. 12, 1948; s. Roger Louis Shaul Sr. and Margot (Bradley) Vinson; m. Michele Marie Morland, Dec. 21, 1974; children: Lisa Marie, John Benjamin, Robert Louis. AA, Palm Beach Jr. Coll., Lake Worth, Fla., 1968; BS, U. Fla., 1970, MBA, 1974; cert., Yale U. and U. N.C., 1981, 1984. Adminstrv. resident Univ. Hosp. of Jacksonville, Fla.,

1974-79; dir. rev. svcs. Capital Health Systems Agy., Durham, N.C., 1979; dir. Sun Alliance, Charlotte, N.C., 1979-83; v.p. Sun Health, Inc., Charlotte, 1983-87; pres. Preferred Med. Mktg. Corp., Charlotte, 1987—; mem. adj. faculty, lectr. Duke U., Durham, 1974-78, U. N.C., Chapel Hill, 1974-78; cons. health seminars U. Tex., Am. Hosp. Assn., Am. Coll. Healthcare Execs., N.C. Hosp. Assn., Ga. Hosp. Assn., Fla. Hosp. Assn., Pa. Hosp. Assn. Mem. com. Mecklenburg County chpt. ARC, Charlotte, 1985, bd. dirs. Durham County chpt., 1976-79, chmn. fin. com., 1979; mem. missions com. Myers Pk. United Meth. Ch., Charlotte, 1989—. Mem. Am. Hosp. Assn., Am. Coll. Healthcare Execs., Am. Assn. Preferred Provider Orgn., Mecklenburg Entrepreneurial Coun., Civitan (pres., v.p., sec. Durham chpt. 1976-79). Republican. Methodist. Office: Preferred Med Mktg Corp 7301 Carmel Park Charlotte NC 28226-3662

SHAW, ANTHONY, physician, pediatric surgeon; b. Shanghai, China, Oct. 31, 1929; s. Bruno and Regina (Hyman) S.; m. Iris Violet Azian, Mar. 12, 1955; children: Brian Anthony, Diana Shaw Clark, Daniel Aram. BA cum laude, Harvard Coll., 1950; MD, NYU, 1954. Diplomate Am. Bd. Surgery, Am. Bd. Pediat. Surgery. Intern and resident in surgery Columbia-Presbyn. Med. Ctr., N.Y.C., 1954-56, 58-62; resident in pediat. surgery Babies Hosp., N.Y.C., 1962; asst. prof. surgery Columbia U. Coll. Physicians and Surgeons, N.Y.C., 1965-70; chief pediat. surgery St. Vincent's Hosp., N.Y.C., 1963-70, Harlem Hosp. Ctr., N.Y.C., 1965-70; prof. surgery U. Va., Charlottesville, 1970-81, chief pediat. surgery Med. Ctr., 1970-81; prof. surgery UCLA, 1981—; chief pediat. surgery Olive View-UCLA Med. Ctr., Sylmar, 1986—; expert witness on child abuse L.A. Dependency Ct., 1986—; chmn. gov.'s adv. com. child abuse and neglect Commonwealth of Va., 1975-80; vis. prof. pediat. surgery People's Republic of China, 1985. Contbr. more than 220 articles to profl. jours. Mem. Gov.'s Task Force on Child Abuse Va., 1973-74; bd. dirs. Nat. Burn Victim Found., Orange, N.J., 1996—. Capt. U.S. Army, 1956-58. Recipient Commrs. award Va. Dept. Social Svcs., 1980, award Gov.'s Adv. Bd., Cert. of Recognition HEW, 1978. Fellow Am. Pediat. Surg. Assn. (sec. 1982-85), ACS (v.p. 1987-89); mem. AMA, Pacific Coast Surg. Assn. (v.p. 1989-90), Am. Soc. Law, Medicine, and Ethics, Am. Profl. Soc. on Abuse of Children, Alpha Omega Alpha. Home: One S Orange Grove Blvd # 9 Pasadena CA 91105 Office: Olive View-UCLA Med Ctr 14445 Olive View Dr Sylmar CA 91342

SHAW, DANTE SANDLIN, clinical psychologist; b. Dolthan, Ala., Feb. 17, 1959; s. Jamison Thomas and Sara Frances (Clark) S.; m. Hilary Ann Cummings, Apr. 2, 1992; 1 child, Haley Frances. BA in Psychology, Vanderbilt U., 1981; MS, PhD in Psychology, Auburn (Ala.) U., 1988. Lic. psychologist, Ga. Psychology intern VA Med. Ctr., Decatur, Ga., 1986-87; psychologist Inner Harbor Hosp., Douglasville, Ga., 1988-89; pvt. practice Atlanta, 1989-93, North Gwinnett Ctr, Lawrenceville, Ga., 1993—; psychotherapy, cons. psychol. assessment outpatient and inpatient settings. Mem. APA, Ga. Psychol. Assn. Methodist. Office: North Gwinnett Ctr 415 Scenic Hwy Lawrenceville GA 30245

SHAW, DAVID LEE, neurologist; b. Fort Smith, Ark., May 14, 1947; s. David C. and Margaret Lee (Carolan) S.; m. Jeanne Louise Rand, June 13, 1970; children: Carolan Elizabeth, Todd Richard, Matthew David. BA with honors, Mich. State U., 1969; MD, U. Ark., 1973. Intern U. Fla. Dept. of Med., Gainseville, 1973-74, resident, 1974-75; resident U. Fla. Dept. of Neurology, Gainseville, 1975-78; group practice Med. Ctr. Clinic Dep. of Neurology, Pensacola, Fla., 1978—; dir. West Fla. Regional Med. Ctr. Sleep Lab., Pensacola, 1987—. Contbr. articles to profl. jours. Mem. Am. Acad. Neurology, Am. Sleep Disorder Assn., Fla. Med. Assn., Nat. Kidney Found. (bd. dirs. N.W. chpt. 1987-92), Alpha Omega Alpha. Methodist. Office: Med Ctr Clinic 8333 N Davis Hwy Pensacola FL 32514-6048

SHAW, DWAIN STEVEN, health facility administrator; b. Austin, Tex., Aug. 30, 1962; s. Walter C. and Nora H. (Hearn) Reed; m. Pamela Shaw; children: Brandon Nash, Randall Nash, Grant Shaw. Cert. in vocat. nursing, Austin C.C., 1982; BS in Healthcare Adminstrn., S.W. Tex. State U., 1985; MPH, U. Tex. Health Sci. Ctr., Houston, 1987. Cert. interpreter for deaf. Mem. staff Austin (Tex.) State Hosp., 1981-84, Healthcare Rehab. Ctr., Austin, 1984-89; authorizations supr. Tex. Dept. Health, Austin, 1988-89; dir. admissions, dir. managed care Cypress Creek Hosp., Houston, 1989-91; dir. managed care devel. Charter Kingwood, Houston, 1991-92, Charter Hosps., Houston, 1992-94; asst. v.p. mktg., asst. v.p. payor rels. Vendell Healthcare Inc., Nashville, 1994; assoc. adminstr., asst. v.p. payor rels. Gulf Pines Hosp., Vendell and Houston, 1994—. Mem. Am. Coll. Healthcare Execs., Nat. Assn. Health Svc. Execs. (v.p. 1990-91). Democrat. Baptist. Home: 21319 Deerhaven Spring TX 77388 Office: Gulf Pines Behavioral Hlth Svcs 205 Hollow Tree Ln Houston TX 77090

SHAW, HERBERT WELLER, psychotherapist, educator; b. N.Y.C., Feb. 8, 1935; s. Herbert W. and Mary Edna (Smith) S.; m. Judith Sniscak (div.); children: Suzanne Dengler, Christopher Weller; m. Moira Buxton, Sept. 19, 1974. BA in Chemistry, Haverford (Pa.) Coll., 1956. Assoc. creative dir. Marsteller, Inc., N.Y.C., 1961-65; v.p., creative dir. Muller, Jordan, Herrick, Inc., N.Y.C., 1965-67; pres. Shaw Elliott Inc., N.Y.C., 1967-78; trustee and exec. dir. The Pathwork Inc., N.Y., 1972-83; psychotherapist Lake Hill, N.Y., 1978-94; bus. cons.; trainer and tchr. Pathwork, Inc.; workshop leader for couples and successful men. Contbr. articles to profl. jours. Chez Aimee Found. grantee, 1991. Home: PO Box 221 Lake Hill NY 12448-0221

SHAW, JANINE ANN, psychologist; b. Lamar, Mo., Feb. 21, 1955; d. Gerald Joseph and Lena (Caldwell) S. BA, Centenary Coll., Shreveport, La., 1977; PhD, Tex. Tech. U., Lubbock, 1984. Lic. psychologist. Psychologist Houston Police Dept., 1984-87, VA Med. Ctr., Houston, 1987—; mem. faculty Baylor Coll. Medicine, Houston, 1987—; cons. depts. ob-gyn. and dermatology Baylor Coll. Medicine, 1987—; pvt. practice, Houston, 1984—; mem. appeals bd. Civil Svc. Commn., City of Houston. Contbr. articles to profl. jours. Recipient Superior Performance award VA med. Ctr., Houston, 1989, 90, 92, 93, 94. Mem. APA, Tex. Psychol. Assn. (publicity chair 1989-90, trustee 1988-94, sec.-treas. 1988-89, pres. 1991-92). Democrat. Office: VA Med Ctr Psychology Svc 2002 Holcombe Blvd Houston TX 77030-4211

SHAW, JUDY KELLY, nurse; b. Milford, Del., Sept. 15, 1950; d. Charles and Lorraine Barbara (Applegate) Kelly; m. Daniel B. Shaw, Mar. 15, 1969; children: Meghan K., Aubrey D., Bradford D. BS, Russell Sage Coll., 1993, postgrad., 1993—. RN, N.Y. Rsch. asst. Russell Sage Coll., Troy, N.Y., 1992—; staff nurse S.S. VA Med Ctr., Albany, N.Y., 1993—; cons. hist. rsch., Albany. Co-editor DNA Newsletter, The Nine Times, 1994. Mem. N.Y. State Nurses Assn., N.E. Nursing Rsch. Soc., Dist. 9 Nurses' Assn. (LENS coun. com. mem. 1993—), Sigma Theta Tau. Home: 4189 Windy Hill Rd Greenwich NY 12834

SHAW, KENNETH STEVEN, optometrist; b. Cleve., June 24, 1966; s. James Harvey and Elizabeth Lee (Potter) S.; m. Mary Jane Barbee, Dec. 26, 1992. BS in Biology, The Citadel, 1988; OD, BS, Pa. Coll. Optometry, 1992. Registered optometrist, Tenn. Optometrist 3d infantry divsn. U.S. Army Inf. Divsn. (Mech.), Ft. Stewart, Ga, 1996—; triage officer 903d MSB Med. Co., U.S. Army, Ft. Stewart, 1996—; mem. adj. faculty Pacific Coll. Optometry, Forest Grove, Oreg., 1994—, So. Calif. Coll. Optometry, Fullerton, 1994—, U. Calif.-Berkeley Coll. Optometry, 1994—. Mem. 1st Pres. U.S. Army Hawaii Cycling Team. Capt. U.S. Army, 1992—. Mem. Tri-Svc. Optometric Soc., Armed Forces Optometric Soc., Assn. Mil. Surgeons U.S., Gold Key. Republican. Baptist. Home: 503 Waverly Ct Hinesville GA 31313 Office: C Co 703d MSB 3d Inf Division (Mech) Fort Stewart GA 31314-5300

SHAW, MARTIN ANDREW, clinical and research psychologist; b. N.Y.C., Jan. 27, 1944; s. Aaron S. and Betty Shaw; m. Dorothy Korot, Nov. 7, 1971; 1 child, Anatole Bernard. BS, NYU, 1966; MA, Dalhousie U., 1972; PhD, U. Wis., 1977; postgrad. Advanced Inst. Analytic Psychotherapy, 1977-82. Art tchr. N.Y.C. Schs., 1966-69; art therapist Kingsbridge VA Hosp., Bronx, N.Y., 1969-71; grad. teaching asst. Dalhousie U., 1971-72, Killam Children's Hosp., Halifax Sch. for Blind, N.S., Can., 1971-72; psychometrician, cons. N.Y.C. Bd. Edn., 1977-80; staff therapist, staff psychologist Advanced Ctr. for Psychotherapy, Jamaica, N.Y., 1977-82; clin./child psychologist Health Ins. Plan, Mental Health Service, N.Y.C., 1980-84; pvt. practice clin. and clin. child psychology, N.Y.C., 1981-83, Gt. Neck, N.Y., 1981—; cons. psychologist Hearing and Speech Ctr. of L.I. Jewish-Hillside Med. Ctr., New Hyde Park, N.Y., 1986-87, Trinity-Pawling (N.Y.) Sch., 1986—; exec. dir. ORT Inst., Inc.; trustee Signal Hill Edn. Ctr., Inc., 1983-87. Recipient Founders Day award, N.Y.U., 1966, VA commendation, 1970; lic. psychologist, N.Y. State. Fellow Soc. for Personality Assessment, Brit. Soc. for Projective Psychology (hon.); mem. APA, AAAS, N.Y. State Psychol. Assn., N.Y. Soc. Clin. Psychologists, Nassau County Psychol. Assn., N.Y. Acad. Scis., Internat. Rorschach Soc., Soc. Psychoanalytic Rsch., Internat. Platform Assn., N.AM. Adv. Com. to the World Court of the Environ., Pi Lambda Theta. Author: Object Relations Technique: Objectified Assessment/Basic Rationale, 1993; contbr. papers to profl. jours. and confs. Office: 333 E Shore Rd Ste 206 Manhasset NY 11030

SHAW, MARY ANN, psychologist; b. Dallas, July 5, 1937; d. Leon V. and Mabel (Bartlett) S.; B.S., U. Tex., 1959; M.Ed., U. Houston, 1966, Ed.D., 1973. Diplomate Profl. Acad. Custody Evaluators. Tchr. educable mentally retarded Spring Branch, Tex., 1959-64; vocat. counselor, Houston, 1964-66; psychometrist pvt. psychol. clinic, Houston, 1966-70; coord. rsch. Tex. Edn. Agency grant project, 1970-72; dir. psychol. svcs. Tex. Scottish Rite Hosp. for Crippled Children, Dallas, 1972-82; dir. Dean Evaluation Ctr., Dallas, 1982-84; pvt. practice, 1982—; mem. clin. staff U. Tex. Health Sci. Ctr.; mem. Allied Health Profl. Staff, Green Oaks; cons. Children's Med. Ctr., Dallas, pvt. and pub. schs. Mem. APA, Am. Profl. Soc. on Abuse of Children (diplomate), Am. Coll. Forensic Examiners, Tex. Psychol. Assn., Mental Health Assn. Greater Dallas, Dallas Psychol. Assn., Soc. Pediat. Psychology, Soc. Personality Assessment Assn. Author: What Do I Do When, Because I Said So, Your Anxious Child; contbr. article to profl. jour.; research in field.

SHAW, RANDY LEE, human services administrator; b. Revenna, Ohio, Oct. 18, 1945; s. Robert and Dorothy Mae (Turner) S.; m. Terri Marie Richardson, July 4, 1988; 1 child, Garrett Samuel. BTh, Ridgedale Sem., 1975, ThM, 1977. Cert. social worker. Exec. dir. Boy's Recovery Home, Detroit, 1979; clin. dir. Boniface, Detroit, 1979-83; unit dir. Problem Daily Living, Detroit, 1983-84; clin. dir. Calvin Wells, Detroit, 1984-86; exec. dir. Children Youth Equal Rights Adv. House, Pontiac, Mich., 1986-87, Touch of Hope, Hartford, Mich., 1988-89; program supr. New Ctr. Community Mental Health, Detroit, 1989-91; exec. dir. Nat. Inst. Hypertension Studies, Detroit, 1979-88. Local rep., magician for Make-A-Wish Found.; exec. dir. Magicians Against Gangs, Ignorance, and Crime Intervention Program, M.A.G.I.C., 1991—. Mem. Soc. Am. Magicians (local pres. 1993-94), Magic Circle, Internat. Brotherhood of Magicians (local pres. 1993-94), Supreme Magic Club of U.K. Home and Office: 249 Lolly Pop St Westland MI 48186-6849

SHAW, RICHARD EUGENE, cardiovascular researcher; b. Springfield, Ohio, Jan. 20, 1950; s. Eugene Russell and Marjorie Catherine (Lewe) S.; m. Christine Elizabeth Costa, Nov. 26, 1976; children: Matthew, Brian. BA, Duquesne U., 1972; MA, U.S. Internat. U., San Diego, 1977; PhD, U. Calif., San Francisco, 1984. Cert. nuclear med. technologist. Staff nuclear med. technologist Scripps Meml. Hosp., La Jolla, Calif., 1975-79; rsch. asst. U. Calif. San Francisco Sch. Medicine, 1980-85; mgr. rsch. programs San Francisco Heart Inst., Daly City, Calif., 1985-87, dir. rsch., 1988-90, dir. rsch. and ops., 1991—; sr. advisor steering com. for databases Daus. of Charity Nat. Health Systems, St. Louis, 1993—; cons. HealthLink SmartPhone comms. informatics project, San Francisco, 1992—. Editor-in-chief Jour. Invasive Cardiology, King of Prussia, Pa., 1989—; contbr. more than 200 articles and book chpts. to med. lit. Coach Am. Youth Soccer Orgn., Burlingame, Calif., 1990—. Fellow Am. Coll. Cardiology; mem. Am. Heart Assn., Soc. for Clin. Trials, N.Y. Acad. Scis., Am. Statis. Assn., Am. Med. Informatics Assn., Soc. Behavioral Medicine. Office: San Francisco Heart Inst Seton Med Ctr 1900 Sullivan Ave Daly City CA 94015-2200

SHAW, ROBERT SAMUEL, psychologist; b. Pitts., Jan. 29, 1952; s. Matthew J. and Margaret R. (Greathouse) S.; m. Karen Trimble, Aug. 5, 1972; children: Matthew R., James J. AA, Northeastern Christian Coll., Villanova, Pa., 1971; BA, Abilene Christian U., 1974, MA, 1981; MA, Marywood Coll., Scranton, Pa., 1986. Ordained to ministry Ch. of Christ, 1978. Minister Harding Ch. of Christ, Pittston, Pa., 1978—; dir. pastoral care The Wesley Village, Pittston, 1988-91; psychologist, pvt. practice Dallas, Pa., 1990—. Recipient Eugene Raymond scholarship Marywood Coll., 1984, 85, Immaculate Heart of Mary scholarship, 1982. Mem. APA (assoc.), Pa. Psychol. Assn., Northeastern Pa. Psychol. Assn. (pres. 1994), Rotary (past pres. Pittston club, Paul Harris fellow), Wyoming Valley Coun. of Chs. (chmn. pastoral care com.), Wyo. Conf. United Meth. Ch. (assoc.). Office: Back Mountain Profl Bldg Route 309 Dallas PA 18612-1295

SHAW, RONALD AHREND, physician, educator; b. Toledo, July 20, 1946; s. Harold Michael and Eve Helen (Ganch) S.; m. Carol Ann Rapp, June 13, 1970; children: Robert, Benjamin, Daniel. BS, U. Toledo, 1968; MD, Washington U., 1972. Diplomate Am. Bd. Emergency Medicine. Intern, then resident in surgery St. Luke's Hosp., St. Louis, 1972-73, resident in surgery, 1973; mem. staff Bapt. Med. Ctr.-Montclair, Birmingham, Ala., 1976-81, chief emergency svc., 1979-81; assoc. dir. lifesaver flight ops. Caraway Meth. Med. Ctr., Birmingham, 1981-85; dir. emergency svc. sch. medicine U. Ala., 1985-89; asst. dir. emergency svc. R.I. Hosp., Providence, 1989-95; cons. U. Tex., Houston, 1986, Bell Helicopter, Ft. Worth, 1986, Mut. Assurance, Birmingham, 1986-89, NYU, 1988-89, R.I. State Med. Examiners Office, 1991—, Fla. Dept. Health, EMS Office, 1991—, Joint Underwriters Assocs. of R.I., 1991—; chmn. adv. bd. emergency svc. Ala. Dept. Pub. Health, 1986-89; med. dir. Emergency Med. Svcs. div. R.I. Dept. Health, 1990-95; med. dir. Health Care Rev., Inc., 1995—. Bd. dirs. MADD, Ala., 1986, Univ. Emergency Medicine Found., 1995—; mem. planning com. Youth Baseball, Vestavia Hills, ala., 1986, 87; mem. disaster com. City of Birmingham, 1984-89; mem. 911 Commn., State of R.I., 1991—. Recipient Disting. Achievement award Birmingham Emergency Med. Svc., 1988. Fellow Am. Coll. Emergency Physicians (bd. dirs. Ala. chpt. 1984-89, steering com. EMS sect. 1991-94, sec.-treas. R.I. chpt. 1995—); mem. AAAS, ACS (state com. on trauma R.I. chpt. 1990—), N.Y. Acad. Sci., Med. Assn. Ala. (mem. coun. med. svc. 1985-86). Republican. Office: RI Hosp Dept Emergency Medicine 593 Eddy St Providence RI 02903-4923

SHAW, STANLEY MINER, nuclear pharmacy scientist; b. Parkston, S.D., July 4, 1935; s. George Henry and Jensina (Thompson) S.; m. Excellda J. Watke, Aug. 13, 1961; children: Kimberly Kay, Renee Denise, Elena Aimee. BS, S.D. State U., 1957, MS, 1959; PhD, Purdue U., 1962. Instr. S.D. State U., 1960-62; asst. prof. bionucleonics Purdue U., West Lafayette, Ind., 1962-66; assoc. prof. Purdue U., 1966-71, prof. nuclear pharmacy, 1971—, head. Div. Nuclear Pharmacy, 1990—, acting head Sch. Health Scis., 1990-93; Mem. Bd. Pharm. Spltys., Splty. Council Nuclear Pharmacy, 1978-82. Contbr. sci. articles to profl. jours. Recipient Lederle Pharmacy faculty awards, 1962, 65, Parenteral Drug Assn. rsch. award, 1970, Henry Heine Outstanding Tchr. award Sch. Pharmacy Purdue U., 1989, 93, Disting. Alumnus award S.D. State U., 1991, Disting. Pharmacy Educator award AACP, 1994. Fellow Acad. Pharmacy Practice (chmn. sect. nuclear pharmacy 1979-80, historian 1981-85, mem.-at-large 1993-95, chair-elect 1995-96, chair 1996—), Am. Soc. Hosp. Pharmacy; mem. Health Physics Soc., Am. Pharm. Assn. (ho. of dels. 1977, 79, 86, 92, Founder's award nuclear pharmacy sect.), Sigma Xi, Phi Lambda Upsilon, Phi Lambda Sigma, Rho Chi. Assembly of God. Home: 7208 W Greenview Dr Battleground IN 47920 Office: Purdue U Sch Pharmacy West Lafayette IN 47907-1333

SHAW, VIRGINIA RUTH, clinical psychologist; b. Salina, Kans., Dec. 10, 1952; d. Lawrence Eugene and Gladys (Wilbur) S.; m. Joseph Eugene Scuro Jr., July 14, 1990. BA magna cum laude, Kans. Wesleyan U., 1973; MA, Wichita State U., 1975; PhD, U. Southern Miss., 1984. Diplomate Am. Bd. Med. Psychotherapists (fellow). Rsch. fellow Wichita (Kans.) State U., 1973-75; rsch. fellow, teaching fellow U. So. Miss., 1978-79, 80-81; staff psychologist Big Spring (Tex.) State Hosp., 1976-78; predoctoral clin. psychology intern U. Okla. Health Scis. Ctr., Oklahoma City, 1981-82; postdoctoral fellow in neuropsychology Neuropsychiat. Inst., UCLA, 1982-83; rsch. psychologist, neuropsychologist L.A. VA Med. Ctr. Wadsworth Div., 1983-84; clin. neuropsychologist Patton (Calif.) State Hosp., 1984-85; clin. neuropsychologist Brentwood div. LA VA Med. Ctr., 1985; clinical, neuropsychologist Timberlawn Psychiatric Hosp., Dallas, 1985-87, Dallas Rehab. Inst., 1987-93; cons. clin. neuropsychology Dallas area hosps., Willowbrook Hosp., Waxahachie, Tex., Cedars Hosp., Waxahachie, 1988-96; clin. psychologist Maui child and adolescent mental health team State of Hawaii Dept. Health, 1996—; presenter profl. meetings, 1975—. Contbr. articles to profl. jours. Mem. Dallas Mayor's Com. for Employment of the Disabled (cert. appreciation), 1987, 500 Inc., Dallas, 1988-96. Remiatte Meml. scholar Kans. Wesleyan U., 1970-73; recipient Nat. Disting. Svc. Registry award in rehab., 1989, Early Career Contbns. to Clin. Neuropsychology award candidate Nat. Acad. Neuropsychology, 1993, 94. Mem. APA Divsn. 35/ Psychology of Women (student rsch. prize com. 1996), Internat. Neuropsychol. Soc., Nat. Head Injury Found., Assn. for Women in Psychology, Tex. Head Injury Found., Dallas Head Injury Found. (Vol. award, cert. appreciation 1991), Am. Congress Rehab. Medicine, Nat. Rehab. Assn., Nat. Acad. Neuropsychology (membership com. 1991-94, rsch. consortium 1991—, co-chair poster program com. 1994, 95). Office: 444 Hana Hwy # 202 Kahului HI 96732

SHAW, WILLIAM H., urologist; b. Bklyn., Mar. 15, 1940; m. Ellen Shaw, Aug. 11, 1942; children: Randy, Cathi. BS in Psychology, U. Fla., Miami, 1961; MD, U. Miami, 1965. Diplomate Am. Bd. Urology. Resident in urology Jackson/VA Hosp., N.Y., Fla., 1966-70; pvt. practice urology Midtown Med., Miami Beach, 1970-73, 76-81, Profl. Towers, Miami Beach, 1981-86, Sheridan, Miami Beach, 1986-94, Miami Heart, Miami Beach, 1994—; coord. urology resident program U. Miami/Mit. Sinai, 1972-91, moderator pediat./adult urology, 1972-91, clin. assoc. prof., 1982—; chief urology Miami Heart Inst., 1991—. Chmn. Miami Beach Health Adv., 1994—. Fellow Am. Coll. Surgeons. Office: Miami Heart Inst 2999 NE 191st Ste 250 North Miami Beach FL 33180 also: Miami Heart Inst Main Bldg 1st Fl 4701 N Meridian Ave Miami FL 33140-2910

SHAWL, S. NICOLE, hypnobehavioral scientist; b. South Amboy, N.J., July 26, 1940; d. Michael Joseph and Kathleen Shawl; life ptnr. Donna J. Talcott. BA, Georgian Court Coll., 1971; MA, Kean Coll. of N.J., Union, 1975; PhD, Calif. Coast U., Santa Ana, 1992; postgrad., Saybrook Inst., San Francisco; postgrad. studies in hypno-behavioral psychology, The Union Inst., Cin. Joined Sisters of Mercy, 1958, left, 1966; cert. student pers. svcs. adminstr., prin., supr., dir. student pers. svcs., substance awareness coord. Georgian Ct. Coll., substance awareness coord. State of N.J.; cert. hypnobehavioral therapist. Tchr. pub. and parochial schs., Monmouth & Ocean Counties, N.J., 1960-79; interviewer, pub. rels. mgr. ARC, Toms River, N.J., 1980; editor, writer Prentice-Hall, Englewood Cliffs, N.J., 1980; counselor, asst. dir. coll. program Georgian Court Coll., Lakewood, N.J., 1980—; adj. instr. UCLA, 1975-76; owner, pres. Auntie Nuke Enterprises. Active NOW. Mem. AAUW, ACLU, ACA, NOW, So. Poverty Law Ctr., Mercy Higher Edn. Colloquium Assn., Nat. Guild Hypnotists, Am. Soc. Clin. Hypnosis, Nat. Psychology Adv. Assn., Nat. Bd. for Cert. Clin. Hypnotherapists, Ednl. Opportunity Assn. (nat. coun.), Assn., Union Inst. Ctr. for Women, Internat. Platform Assn., Am. Biog. Inst. (rsch. fellow). Democrat. Office: Georgian Court Coll 900 Lakewood Ave Lakewood NJ 08701-2600

SHAYMAN, JAMES ALAN, nephrologist, educator; b. Chgo., June 14, 1954; s. Benjamin and Chernie (Abrams) S.; children: Rebecca Lynn, David Aaron. AB, Cornell U., 1976; MD, Washington U., St. Louis, 1980. Intern and resident Barnes Hosp., St. Louis, 1980-83; instr. Washington U., St. Louis, 1985-86; asst. prof. U. Mich., Ann Arbor, 1986-92, assoc. prof., 1992—. Mem. Am. Soc. Nephrology, Internat. Soc. Nephrology, Am. Diabetes Assn., Am. Soc. Clin. Investigation, Am. Physiol. Soc., Phi Beta Kappa, Phi Kappa Phi, Alpha Omega Alpha. Office: U Mich Med Ctr 1500 E Med Ctr Dr Ann Arbor MI 48109

SHEA, JOHN JOSEPH, surgeon; b. Memphis, Sept. 4, 1924; s. John Joseph and Catherine (Flanagan) S.; m. Gwyne Cooke Rainer, Mar. 12, 1949 (div. Sept. 1956); children: John Joseph III, Gwyn Rainer; m. Lynda Lee Mead, Dec. 26, 1964; children: Paul Flanagan, Susanna Mead, Peter Ryan. B.S., U. Notre Dame, 1945; M.D., Harvard U., 1947; grad. student, U. Vienna, Austria, 1954; Ph.D. (hon.), Christian Bros. Coll., 1979, Rhodes Coll., 1984. Diplomate: Am. Bd. Otolaryngology. Intern Bellevue Hosp., N.Y.C., 1947-48; resident Mass. Eye and Ear Hosp., 1949-50; founder, since pres. Shea Clinic, 1952; founder Memphis Eye and Ear Hosp., 1967; clin. prof., dept. otolaryngology and maxillofacial surgery U. Tenn., U. N.C., Tulane U.; cons. to surgeon gen. USN; cons. Kennedy VA Hosp., Memphis. Served with USNR, 1943-45; to lt. (j.g.), M.C. 1950-52; now lt. comdr. Res. Decorated Order So. Cross, Brazil, 1962; recipient honors award Tenn. Speech and Hearing Assn., 1974. Mem. AMA, Pan Am., So., Tenn. med. assns., Am. Acad. Ophthalmology and Otolaryngology (1st Gold medal 1960), Acoustical Soc. Am., Am. Auditory Soc., Neuro-Otol. and Equilibriometric Soc., Am. Hearing Assn., Am. Assn. Mental Deficiency, Am. Triological Soc., Royal Soc. Medicine, French, Danish and Buenos Aires socs. otolaryngology, Australian Soc. Medicine (hon.), Memphis and Shelby County Med. Soc., Assn. Am. Physicians and Surgeons, Miss.-La. Soc. Ophthalmology and Otolaryngology, Otosclerosis Study Club (pres. 1979), Am. Council Otolaryngology, Pan Am. Assn. Oto-Rhino-Laryngology and Broncho-Esophagology (pres. 1982-84), Australian, South African socs. otolaryngology, Am. Otol. Soc. (Gold medal Award of Merit 1986), Nat. Hearing Assn. (pres. 1982, 83). Club: Centurian. Office: Shea Clinic 6133 Poplar Pike at Ridgeway PO Box 17987 Memphis TN 38187-0987

SHEA, MARTIN COYLE, JR., otolaryngologist; b. Memphis, Dec. 24, 1929; m. Trina Shea. BS, U. Tenn., 1952, MD, 1952. Resident gen. surgery U.S. Naval Hosp., Bethesda, Md., 1956-57; resident otolaryngology U.S. Naval Hosp., Bethesda, 1957-59; physician Memphis Otologic Clinic, 1962-67, Shea, Hubbard & Futrell, 1967—; assoc. clin. prof. dept. otolaryngology and maxillofacial surgery U. Tenn. Ctr. for Health Scis., 1962—; presenter and lectr. in field. Contbr. articles to profl. jours. Lt. comdr. Med. Corps USN, 1952-62. Recipient Humanitarian award Am. Acad. Otolaryngology, 1993. Fellow ACS; mem. Am. Bd. Otolaryngology, Alpha Omega Alpha. Office: Shea Hubbard & Futrell Ste 411 6027 Walnut Grove Memphis TN 38120

SHEARD, CHARLES, III, dermatologist; b. Toronto, Ontario, Can., Nov. 22, 1914; came to U.S., 1945; s. Charles Jr. and Alice Elizabeth (Ramsay) S.; m. Katherine Patricia Murphy, Nov. 19, 1937; children: Joan Virginia Sheard Cumming, Pamela Carol Sheard McGuiness, Wendy Alice Sheard Geyer. Sr. matriculation, Upper Can. Coll., Toronto, 1933; MD, U. Toronto, 1939. Diplomate Am. Bd. Dermatology. Intern Toronto Gen. Hosp., 1939-40; instr. physiology, anatomy U. Toronto Med. Faculty, 1940-41; surgical asst. resident Hosp. for Sick Children, Toronto, 1945; from resident to chief resident dermatologist Columbia Presbyn. Hosp., N.Y.C., 1945-49; assoc. prof. medicine Cornell U. Med. Coll., N.Y.C., 1950-94, assoc. prof. emeritus, 1994—. Author: (textbook) Treatment in Dermatology, 1978; contbr. articles to profl. jours. Flight lt. RCAF, 1941-45. Fellow ACP, Royal Coll. Physicians (Can.); mem. Metro-Manhattan Dermatol. Soc. N.Y.C. (sec. 1970-80), Can. Club of N.Y., Royal Can. Yacht Club, Wee Burn Golf and Country Club Darien. Republican. Episcopalian.

SHEARER, JAMES NEIL, plastic surgeon; b. Bklyn., Apr. 2, 1951; s. Bernard and Claire (Novograd) S. BS, Union Coll., 1972; MD, N.Y. Med. Coll., 1975. Intern in surgery Med. Coll. Va., Richmond, 1975-77, Mary I. Bassett Hosp., Cooperstown, N.Y., 1977-80; resident in plastic surgery U. N.C., Chapel Hill, 1980-82; pvt. practice plastic surgery Charlotte, N.C., 1982—; clin. instr. surgery Bowman Gray Sch. Medicine, Winston-Salem, N.C., 1986—. Fellow Am. Coll. Surgeons; mem. Am. Soc. Plastic & Reconstructive Surgeons, N.C. Soc. Plastic and Reconstructive Surgeons, Mecklenburg County Med. Soc. Office: 2711 Randolph Rd Ste 502 Charlotte NC 28207

SHEARER, WILLIAM THOMAS, pediatrician, educator; b. Detroit, Aug. 23, 1937. BS, U. Detroit, 1960; PhD, Wayne State U., 1966; MD, Washington U., St. Louis, 1970. Diplomate Am. Bd. Pediatrics, Am. Bd. Allergy and Immunology (chmn. 1994-95, dir. 1990-95), Nat. Bd. Med. Examiners; cert. in diagnostic lab. immunology. Post-doctoral fellow in biochemistry dept. chem. Indiana U., Bloomington, 1966-67; intern in pediatrics St. Louis Children's Hosp., 1970-71, resident in immunology in pediatrics, 1971-72, dir. divsn. allergy and immunology, 1974-78; fellow in immunology in pediatrics Barnes Hosp., Washington U., St. Louis, 1972-74; spl. USPHA sci. rsch. fellow in medicine dept. medicine Washington U., 1972-74, assoc. prof.,

1978, prof., 1978; prof. pediat., microbiology, immunology Baylor Coll. Medicine, Houston, 1978—, dir. AIDS rsch. ctr., 1991—; head sect. allergy & immunology Tex. Children's Hosp., Houston, 1978—; mem. ACTU Cmty. Adv. Bd., Tex. Children's Hosp., Houston, 1991—; chmn. pediat. core com. pediat. AIDS clin. trial group Nat. Inst. Allergy and Infectious Diseases NIH, Bethesda, Md., 1989—, ad hoc reviewer, 1991, mem. therapeutics subcom. AIDS rsch. adv. com., 1993—, chmn. pediat. AIDS clin. trial group immunology com., 1994—, mem. pediat. AIDS clin. trials group exec. com., 1991-95, mem. spl. rev. com. persons affected by chronic granulomatous disease, 1992; site visitor Gen. Clin. rsch. Ctr., NIH, Bethesda, 1993, vice chmn. pediat. AIDS clin. trials group exec. com., 1996—; chmn. study population/patient mgmt. com. Clin. Ctrs. for the Study of Pediat. Lung and Heart Complications of HIV Infection Nat. Heart, Lung and Blood Inst. NIH, Bethesda, 1989—, mem. AIDS ad hoc work group, 1991; dir. pediat. HIV/AIDS Clin. Rsch. Ctr., Houston, 1988—; chmn. exec. com. clin. trial intravenous gammaglobulin in HIV infected children Nat. Inst. Child and Health and Human Devel., Bethesda, 1989—; dir. Am. Bd. Allergy and Immunology, 1990-95, chair, 1994-95. Editor: Pediatric Asthma, Allergy, and Immunology, 1989; editl. bd. Jour. of Allergy and Clin. Immunology, 1993—, Clin. and Diagnostic Lab. Immunology, 1994—; editor Pediatric Allergy and Immunology, 1995—, Allergy and Immunology Tng. Program Dir.; guest editor Seminar Pediatric Infectious Disease, 1990; contbr. intro.: Allergy: Principles and Practice, 1992; contbr. articles to profl. jours. including New Eng. Jour. Medicine. AIDS cons. Houston Ind. Sch. Dist., 1986—; med. adv. Spring Branch Ind. Sch. Dist., Houston, 1987—; chmn. community HIV/AIDS adv. group Tex. Med. Ctr., 1991—. Recipient faculty rsch. award Am. Cancer Soc., 1977-79, Myrtle Wreath award Hadassah, 1985, spl. recognition award Am. Acad. Allergy and Immunology, 1994; rsch. scholar Cystic Fibrosis Found., 1974-77; grantee NIH, 1988—. Mem. Am. Soc. Clin. Investigation, Am. Acad. Pediats. (mem. exec. com. sect. allergy and immunology 1991—), Tex. Allergy Soc. (exec. com. 1990—, Tex. Allergy and Immunology Soc. (chmn. nat. issues com. 1992-96, pres. 1994-96), Am. Acad. allergy and Immunology (chmn. clin. and lab. immunology com. 1994-96, chmn. tng. program dirs. nat. issues subcom. 1994-96), Am. Acad. Allergy, Asthma and Immunology (assoc. chmn. for planning of 1997-98 internat. meetings, profl. ednl. coun.). Office: Tex Childrens Hosp A/I Svc 6621 Fannin St MC 1-3291 Houston TX 77030-2303

SHEAVLY, ROBERT BRUCE, social worker; b. Detroit, Sept. 13, 1952; s. George Brown and Mary Jane (Hoover) S. BA, Georgetown U., 1974; MSW, U. Md., 1981. Lic. ind. clin. social worker; bd. cert. diplomate; ACSW. Bookkeeper, accounts payable mgr. Capitol Area Ins. Assocs., Silver Spring, Md., 1974-77; asst. cons. The Wyatt Co., Washington, 1977-79; counselor Whitman-Walker Clinic, Washington, 1977-79; social worker Dept. Social Svcs. City Balt., 1980; social worker Alcohol and Drug Abuse Program, U. Md. Sch. Medicine, Balt., 1980-81, instr. Sch. Medicine, asst. dir. Family Violence Unit, 1981-82; pvt. practice Balt., 1982-83; social worker alcohol/drug abuse prevention/control program U.S. Army, Giessen (Germany) Cmty. Counseling Ctr., 1983-84; clin. supr. alcohol/drug abuse prevention/control program U.S. Army, Giessen Milcom, Community Counseling Ctr., 1984-85; instr. drug and alcohol abuse divsn. 7th Army Tng. Ctr., Munich, Germany, 1985-91; dir. family program specialized treatment addiction recovery Walter Reed Army Med. Ctr., Washington, 1991-93, cons. dept. clin. pastoral edn., 1993—; assoc. dir. Bill Austin Day Treatment Ctr. for Persons with AIDS Whitman-Walker Clinic, Washington, 1993-94; pvt. practice, 1994—; presenter, guest lectr. in field. Ch. organist, dir. music Ch. of the Nativity, Washington, St. James Episcopal Ch., Washington, 1970-79; mem. diocesan commn. on liturgy and music Episcopal Diocese of Washington. Mem. NASW, AACD (European br.), Acad. Cert. Social Workers, Soc. Neuro-Linguistic Programming, Washington Soc. Jungian Psychology, Phi Kappa Phi. Episcopalian. Home: 2039 New Hampshire Ave NW Washington DC 20009-3479 Office: 1633 Q St Ste 200 Washington DC 20009

SHECTER, FELICE NADINE, clinical psychologist, art therapist, consultant; b. Phila., Oct. 31, 1935; d. David and Rose (Fein) Sandrow; m. Harry Shecter, Sept. 11, 1955; children: Mark J., Jacqueline Stephanie, Pamela Iva. Cert. nursing, Albert Einstein Med. Ctr., 1956; BFA, Ctr. for Creative Studies, 1974; MA, Wayne State U., 1982; postgrad., Psychology Ctr. for Humanistic Studies, 1989; PhD, Union Inst., Cin., 1993. RN, Pa. Art therapist Orchard Hills Psychiat. Ctr., Novi, Mich., 1983—, Providence Hosp., Southfield, Mich., 1989—; pvt. practice Farmington Hills, 1983-90, Novi, Mich., 1990-95, Bigham Farms, Mich., 1995—; mem. Inst. for Study of Eating Disorders, Novi, 1984—, Gabariel Richard Ctr., U. Mich., Dearborn, 1986, Ea. Univ., Ypsilanti, Mich., 1987-88, U. Windsor, Ont., Can., 1987—. Exhibited in group shows at Detroit Inst. Art, 1977 (1st Prize), Mich. Artist 1980-81, 1981, Flint (Mich.) Mid-Western Show, 1962; one woman shows include Xochipilli Gallery, Birmingham, Mich., 1981. Bd. dirs. Anti-Defamation League, Detroit, 1978, Southeastern Hospice, Southfield, 1986-87, found. bd.; mem. ARC, Detroit, 1982. Mem. APA, Mich. Art Therapy (pub. rels. com. 1983—), Mich. Water Color Soc. (hon. Mention), N.Y. Acad. Scis., Am. Humanistic Assn. Home: 31416 W Stonewood Ct Farmington MI 48334-2546 Office: 30400 Telegraph Rd Bingham Farms MI 48025

SHEDD, DONALD POMROY, surgeon; b. New Haven, Aug. 4, 1922; s. Gale and Marion (Young) S.; m. Charlotte Newsom, Mar. 17, 1946; children: Carolyn, David, Ann, Laura. B.S., Yale U., 1944, M.D., 1946. Diplomate Am. Bd. Surgery. Intern Yale New Haven Hosp., 1946-47, asst. resident, resident, 1949-53; instr. surgery Yale U. Med Sch., New Haven, 1953-54, asst. prof., 1954-56, assoc. prof., 1956-67; chief dept. head and neck surgery Roswell Park Cancer Inst., Buffalo, 1967-96, prof. emeritus, 1996—. Co-editor: Surgical and Prosthetic Speech Rehabilitation, 1980, Head and Neck Cancer, 1985; contbr. numerous articles to profl. jours. Founding bd. dirs. Hospice Buffalo, Inc., 1973-83. Served to capt. U.S. Army, 1947-49. Mem. Soc. Univ. Surgeons, Soc. Surg. Oncology, New Eng. Surg. Soc., Soc. Head and Neck Surgeons (pres. 1976-77). Home: 671 Lafayette Ave Buffalo NY 14222-1435 Office: Roswell Park Cancer Inst Elm & Carlton Sts Buffalo NY 14263-0001

SHEDLOCK, KATHLEEN JOAN PETROUSKIE, community health/research nurse; b. Victorville, Calif., Jan. 22, 1952; d. Frank A. and Joan O. (Bird) Petrouskie; m. Ronald Francis Shedlock, Dec. 1, 1973; children: Pamela, Alison. Diploma, York Hosp. Sch. Nursing, 1973; BS in Nursing, SUNY, Utica, 1978; MS in Community Health Nursing, Syracuse U., 1991; MPA in Health Care, Maxwell Sch., 1991. Cert. adult practitioner ANCC, Am. Acad. Nurse Practitioners. Staff nurse, charge nurse emergency rm. Doctors' Hosp., Freeport, N.Y., 1973; staff nurse ICU SUNY Health Sci. Ctr., Syracuse, 1974-76; primary care nurse with pvt. practice ob.-gyn. physician Liverpool, N.Y., 1977-79; staff nurse post anesthesia care unit, diabetes educator Community Gen. Hosp., Syracuse, 1978-87; trainer, supr. home health aides Upjohn Health Care Svcs., Liverpool, 1986; staff nurse, health educator Syracuse U. Health Svcs., 1986-88; mem. faculty Crouse Irving Meml. Hosp. Sch. Nursing, Syracuse, 1987-93; rsch. coord. Hematology-Oncology Assocs. of Cen. N.Y., Syracuse, 1993—; Syracuse coord. Breast Cancer Prevention Trial; psycho-oncology core com. CALGB; cons., planner Oneida (N.Y.) Nation Healthcare Program, 1990; reviewer Mosby Year Book Med. Pub., St. Louis, 1991; presenter at profl. confs. workshops; cons. Ctrl. N.Y. Coun. Occupl. Safety and Health, Syracuse, 1987-90; childbirth educator Childbirth Edn. Assn., Greater Syracuse, 1976-81, consumer rep., 1977; bd. dirs. Onondaga County chpt. Am. Cancer Soc. Mem. ANA, Am. Cancer Soc. (bd. dirs. Onondaga County chpt. 1993—), Oncology Nursing Soc. (chair health policy contact person 1994-96, ethics regional cons.), N.Y. State Nurses Assn. (chair coun. on ethical practice 1990-94, dist. treas. 1990-94, chair nominating com. 1996—, Excellence in Nursing award 1991), Internat. Soc. Nurses in Genetics, Syracuse U. Nursing Alumni Assn. (pres.-elect), York Hosp. Sch. Nursing Alumni Assn., SUNY Coll. Nursing Honors Soc. (nominating com.), Sigma Theta Tau, Omicron and Iota Delta. Home: 8544 E Seneca Tpke Manlius NY 13104-9763 Office: Hematology-Oncology Assocs Ctrl NY 1000 E Genesee St Ste 400 Syracuse NY 13210-1853

SHEEHAN, JOHN FRANCIS, cytopathologist, educator; b. Portsmouth, N.H., July 28, 1906; s. John Thomas and Ellen Agnes (Lynes) S.; m. Grace Anne O'Neil, Aug. 3, 1935; 1 child, John Thomas. B.S., U. N.H., 1928, M.S., 1930; Ph.D., State U. Iowa, 1945; postgrad., McGill U., 1949. Grad. asst. U. N.H., 1928-30; instr. biology Creighton U., 1930-38, asst. prof., 1938-44, assoc. prof., 1944-49, chmn. biology dept., 1949-58, prof. biology, 1949-67, prof. pathology Sch. Medicine, 1967-88, prof. ob-gyn, 1975-88, prof. emeritus pathology and gynecology, 1988—; attending staff AMI St. Joseph Hosp.; dir. cytopathology St. Joseph Hosp., Omaha, 1978-82; dir. cytopathology emeritus St. Joseph Hosp., 1982—; prof. emeritus biology and pathology Creighton U., 1989. Recipient Golden Jubilee Svc. award Creighton U., 1981, Certificate award AAUP, 1988; Dept. Biology Creighton U. lecture hall named in his honor, 1984. Fellow Am. Soc. Colposcopy and Cervical Pathology; mem. AAUP, Am. Soc. Cytopathology, Internat. Coll. Surgeons (vice regent for Nebr. 1984), Am. Inst. Biol. Scis., Am. Micros Soc., Am. Men and Women of Sci., Am. Soc. Clin. Pathologists, Nebr. Heart Assn., Nebr. Acad. Scis., Smithsonian Nat. Assocs., Sigma Xi, Alpha Omega Alpha, Alpha Sigma Nu, Phi Rho Sigma. Home: 7300 Graceland Dr Apt 307A Omaha NE 68134-4341 Office: St Joseph Hosp 601 N 30th St Omaha NE 68131

SHEEN, PORTIA YUNN-LING, retired physician; b. Republic of China, Jan. 13, 1919; came to U.S., 1988; d. Y. C. and A. Y. (Chow) Sheen; m. Kuo, 1944 (dec. 1970); children: William, Ida, Alexander, David, Mimi. MD, Nat. Med. Coll. Shanghai, 1943. Intern, then resident Cen. Hosp., Chungking, Szechuan, China, 1943; with Hong Kong Govt. Med. and Health Dept., 1948-76; med. supt. Kowloon (Hong Kong) Hosp., 1948-63, Queen Elizabeth Hosp., Kowloon, 1963-73, Med. and Health Hdqrs. and Health Ctr., Kowloon, 1973-76, Yan Chai Hosp., New Territories, Hong Kong, 1976-87. Fellow Hong Kong Coll. Gen. Practitioners; mem. AAAS, British Med. Assn., Hong Kong Med. Assn., Hong Kong Pediatric Soc., N.Y. Acad. Sci. Methodist. Home: 1315 Walnut St Berkeley CA 94709-1408

SHEETZ, MICHAEL PATRICK, cell biology educator; b. Hershey, Pa., Dec. 11, 1946; s. David Patrick and Mary Patricia (Blumer) S.; m. Katherine Elliott, Jan. 25, 1968; children: Jonathon Patrick, Jennifer Mikaere, Courtney Elizabeth. BA, Albion Coll., 1968; PhD in Chemistry, Calif. Inst. Tech., 1972. Postdoctoral rsch. fellow U. Calif., San Diego, 1972-74; asst. prof. cell biology dept. physiology U. Conn. Health Ctr., Farmington, 1974-79, assoc. prof., 1980-85; prof. dept. cell biology and physiology Sch. Medicine, Washington U., St. Louis, 1985-90; prof., chmn. dept. cell biology Med. Sch., Duke U., Durham, N.C., 1990—; presenter profl. confs. Contbr. chpt. to Erythrocyte Mechanics and Blood Flow, 1980; co-contbr. chpt. to The Red Cell, 1978, Motility in Cell Function, 1979, White Blood Cell Mechanics, 1984, The Cytoskeleton, 1985, Protein-Membrane Interactions, Current Topics in Membranes and Transport, Vol. 36, 1989; co-contbr. chpts. to Cell Movement, Vol. 2, 1988; contbr. articles to sci. jours. Established investigator Am. Heart Assn., 1981-86. NIH trainee, 1969-72; Dernham jr. fellow Calif. div. Am. Cancer Soc., 1973-74. Office: Duke U Med Ctr Dept Cell Bi PO Box 3011 Durham NC 27715-3011

SHEFTELL, FRED DAVID, psychiatrist; b. N.Y.C., Jan. 4, 1941; s. Joseph and Wilma Elizabeth (Schwartz) S.; m. Karen Ruth Rosenthal, June 13, 1942; children: Lauren Gale, Jason Howard. AB, NYU, 1962, MD, 1966. Diplomate Am. Bd. Psychiatry and Neurology. Resident N.Y. Med. Coll., N.Y.C., 1967-69; chief resident Met. Hosp., N.Y.C., 1969-70; med. dir. Drug Liberation Program, Stamford, Conn., 1972-79; clin. asst. prof. N.Y. Med. Coll., Valhalla, N.Y., 1972—; founder New Eng. Ctr. for Headache, Stamford, 1979—; clin. chief CMHC, Stamford, 1972-79; spkr. in field. Author 5 books on headache; contbr. articles on headache to profl. jours. Maj. U.S. Army, 1970-72. Decorated Army Commendation medal recipient United Way Silver award, 1989; named on of Best Doctors in Am., Woodward & White, 1993. Mem. Am. Psychiat. Assn., Am. Assn. Study of Headache (program dir. 1988, bd. dirs.), Am. Pain Soc., Am. Coun. Headache Edn. (nat. pres. 1994—), Conn. State Med. Soc., Fairfield County Med. Soc. Office: New Eng Ctr for Headache 9778 Longridge Ridge Rd Stamford CT 06902-1251

SHEHADI, SAMEER IBRAHIM, plastic surgeon; b. Zahle, Lebanon, Mar. 3, 1931; came to U.S., 1984; s. Ibrahim A. and Mounira D. (Dumit) S.; m. Leila A. Nassif, June 18, 1960; children: Ramzi Richard, Kamal Sameer, Imad Edward. BA, Am. U. Beirut, 1952, MD, 1956. Diplomate Am. Bd. Surgery, Am. Bd. Plastic Surgery. Intern. Am. U. Hosp., Beirut, resident gen. surgery, 1956-59, chief resident gen. surgery, 1959-60; resident plastic surgery St. Louis U. Hosps., 1960-62; fellow hand surgery Pitts. U. Hosps., 1962; resident head and neck surgery Roswell Park Meml. Inst., Buffalo, N.Y., 1963; clin. asst. prof. Am. U. Beirut, 1963-79, clin. prof. surgery, 1979-84, chmn. dept. surgery, 1976-79, 81-84; prof., dir. div. plastic surgery St. Louis U., 1984—. Contbr. articles to profl. jours. Recipient Chevaliers award Order of the Cedars, Govt. Lebanon, 1968. Fellow ACS (gov. at large Lebanon chpt. 1981-84); mem. AMA, St. Louis Met. Med. Soc., St. Louis Surg. Soc., Mo. Med. Assn., Lebanese Order of Physicians, Am. U. Beirut Med. Alumni Assn., Am. Soc. Plastic and Reconstructive Surgeons, Am. Soc. Maxillofacial Surgeons, Am. Assn. Chmn. Plastic Surgery, Am. Assn. Plastic Surgeons, Am. Assn. Hand Surgeons, Lebanese Soc. Plastic and Reconstructive Surgeons (pres. 1974-84), Internat. Soc. Burn Injuries (Lebanon rep. 1968-84). Home: 12256 Ladue Woods Dr Saint Louis MO 63141-8159 Office: St Louis U Med Ctr PO Box 15250 Saint Louis MO 63110-0250

SHEILL, DONALD ALFRED, occupational clinic medical director; b. Detroit, Jan. 18, 1955; s. Richard Warren and Gladys (Nuffer) S.; m. Joanne Marie Patterson, Dec. 23, 1982; 1 child, Timothy Jung. BS, Wayne State U., 1979, MD, 1983; MPH, Med. Coll. Wis., Milw., 1993. Diplomate Am. Bd. Preventive Medicine, Am. Bd. Family Practice. Intern family medicine St. Marys Hosp., Grand Rapids, Mich., 1983-84; resident family medicine St. Marys Hosp., Grand Rapids, 1984-86; family physician Wyoming (Mich.) Family Medicine, 1986-88; occupational physician Hackley Occupational Health Clinic, Muskegon, Mich., 1988-94, med. dir., 1994—. V.p. Sheldon Dunes Neighborhood Assn., West Olive, Mich., 1992-95. Mem. AMA, Am. Coll. Occupational and Environ. Medicine. Office: Hackley Occupational Health Cli 1675 Leahy Ste 103 Muskegon MI 49417

SHEINART, KARA FAE, neurologist; b. Queens, N.Y., July 11, 1963; d. Henry Jules and Toby (Kwitel) S.; m. Daniel Joseph Alpert, Mar. 4, 1990. BA, Johns Hopkins U., 1985; MD, SUNY Downstate, 1989. Diplomate Am. Nat. Bd. Med. Examiners, Am. Bd. Psychiatry & Neurology. Intern, resident in neurology Mt. Sinai Med. Ctr., N.Y.C., 1989-93, fellow in cerebrovascular disease/stroke, 1993-95, asst. prof. neurology, 1995—; asst. attending physician Mt. Sinai Med. Ctr., 1995—. Fellow Am. Heart Assn. Stroke Coun.; mem. Am. Acad. Neurology. Office: Mt Sinai Med Ctr Dept Neur 1 Gustave Levy Pl Box 1137 New York NY 10029

SHEINBEIN, MARC L., psychologist, marriage and family therapist; b. Oklahoma City, Dec. 11, 1945; s. Isadore and Gloria G. (Davis) S.; m. Andrea Riff, Nov. 30, 1980; children: Amy Michelle, David Benjamin, Andrew Lee, Julia Rose. BA, Vanderbilt U., 1967; MA, U. Tenn., 1969, PhD, 1972. Lic. psychologist, Tex. Intern U. Okla. Med. Sch., Oklahoma City, 1971-72; chief psychologist Children's Med. Ctr., Dallas, 1972-75; asst. prof. U. Tex. Health Sci. Ctr., Dallas, 1972-75; pvt. practice psychology, Dallas, 1973—; cons., Dallas, 1985—. Contbr. articles to profl. jours., also chpts. to books in field. Bd. dirs. Temple Emanuel Brotherhood, Dallas, 1973-75. Recipient Southwest Psychol. Assn. Pubs. prize, 1973. Mem. Am. Psychol. Assn., Dallas Psychol. Assn., Am. Assn. Marriage and Family Therapists, Dallas Assn. Marriage and Family Therapists (past sec., treas., v.p.), Mensa. Avocations: sailing, bicycling, photography, stamp collecting, cooking. Office: 13800 Montfort Dr Ste 200 Dallas TX 75240-4347

SHEINKOPF, DAVID EPHRAIM, oral and maxillofacial surgeon; b. Bklyn., Mar. 27, 1947; s. Leo and Pearl S.; m. Shelley Nan Weiner, Aug. 31, 1975. BA, NYU, 1967; DDS, W.Va. U. Med. Ctr., 1972. Diplomate Am. Bd. Oral and Maxillofacial Surgery. Resident Sydenham Hosp., N.Y.C., 1972-74, Bronx-Mcpl. Hosp. Ctr., N.Y.C., 1974-77; pvt. practice oral surgery N.Y.C., 1977—. Fellow Am. Assn. Oral & Maxillofacial, Am. Dental Soc. Anesthesiology, Internat. Assn. Oral & Maxillofacial Surgeons, Am. Acad. Pain Mgmt., Acad. Osseointegration; mem. Am. Dental Assn., First Dist. Dental Soc. (bd. dirs. 1990-94, 96—). Office: 140 W 58th St Ste A New York NY 10019-2182

SHELBURNE, JOHN DANIEL, pathologist; b. Washington, Aug. 27, 1943; s. Clarence Daniel and Edith (McDanel) S.; m. Katherine Howard Parrish, June 17, 1966; children: Mark, Kerri. BA, U. N.C., 1966; PhD, Duke U., 1971, MD, 1972. Intern, then resident Duke U. Med. Ctr., Durham, N.C., 1973-76; asst. prof. Duke U., Durham, 1973-78, assoc. prof., 1978-85, prof. pathology, 1985—; dir. electron microscopy lab. VA Med. Ctr., Durham, 1976—, chief lab. svc., 1983—; adv. WHO, Manila, 1990; panel mem. VA Program, Washington, 1987—; participant Nordrhein/Westfalen Exchange, Germany, 1988. Editor: Basic Methods in Biological X-Ray Microprobe, 1983; author, editor: Microprobe Analysis in Medicine, 1989. Mem. Appalachian Trail Conf., Harpers Ferry, West, Va., 1970—; bd. dirs. Cen. Carolina Youth Soccer, Durham, 1987-90; founding mem. N.C. Soc. for Electron Microscopy and Microprobe, Research Triangle Park, N.C., 1980—. Recipient Morehead scholarship, 1961-66, AOA Med. Honorary Duke Med. Sch., 1970; named Med. Scientist Tng. Program participant NIH, 1966-72, Shelley Meml. lectr., 1985, Florey Meml. lectr., 1988. Fellow Coll. Am. Pathologists; mem. Am. Assn. Pathologists, Microscopy Soc. Am., Microbeam Analysis Soc. Democrat. Episcopalian. Home: 4302 Malvern Rd Durham NC 27707-5451 Office: Duke U Dept of Pathology PO Box 3712 Durham NC 27710

SHELBY, JAMES STANFORD, cardiovascular surgeon; b. Ringgold, La., June 15, 1934; s. Jesse Audrey and Mable (Martin) S.; BS in Liberal Arts La. Tech. U., 1956; MD, La. State U., 1958; m. Susan Rainey, July 15, 1967; children: Bryan Christian, Christopher Linden. Intern, Charity Hosp. La., New Orleans, 1958-59, resident surgery and thoracic surgery, 1959-65; fellow cardiovascular surgery Baylor U. Coll. Medicine, Houston, 1965-66; practice medicine specializing in cardiovascular surgery, Shreveport, La., 1967—; mem. staff Schumpert Med. Ctr., Highland Hosp., Willis-Knighton Med. Ctr.; assoc. prof. surgery La. State U. Sch. Medicine, Shreveport, 1967—. With M.C., AUS, 1961-62. Diplomate Am. Bd. Surgery, Am. Bd. Thoracic Surgery. Recipient Tower of Medallion award La. Tech. U., 1982. Mem. Am. Coll. Cardiology, AMA, Soc. Thoracic Surgeons, Am. Heart Assn., Southeastern Surg. Congress, So. Thoracic Surg. Assn. Home: 6003 E Ridge Dr Shreveport LA 71106-2425 Office: 3300 Virginia Ave Ste 7B Shreveport LA 71103-3941

SHELDAHL, LOIS MARIE, medical program administrator, researcher; b. Radcliffe, Iowa, Jan. 29, 1943; d. Oswald L. and LaVonne (Varland) S. BA magna cum laude, Concordia Coll., 1966; MEd, U. Ariz., 1968; PhD, Pa. State U., 1978. Instr. Anoka (Minn.)-Hennepin Sch. Dist., 1966-67; instr., women's basketball coach U. Ariz., Tucson, 1968-74; fellowship Pa. State U., State College, 1974-78; physiologist VA Med. Ctr., Milw., 1978—; asst. prof. Med. Coll. Wis., Milw., 1979-90, assoc. prof., 1990—; program dir., cardiopulmonary prevention and rehab. svcs. VA Med. Ctr., Milw., 1995—. Reviewer Cardiopulmonary Rehab.-Nat. Jour., 1980—; contbr. chpts. to books, articles to profl. jours. Mem. cardiac rehab. com. Wis. Heart Assn., Milw., 1980-90. Fellow Am. Coll. Cardiology; mem. Am. Coll. Sports Medicine, Am. Assn. Cardiovascular and Pulmonary Rehab., Am. Heart Assn. (Profl. Practice award 1988), Phi Kappa Phi. Office: VA Med Ctr 111R 5000 W National Ave Milwaukee WI 53295

SHELDON, ELEANOR HARRIET BERNERT, sociologist; b. Hartford, Conn., Mar. 19, 1920; d. M.G. and Fannie (Myers) Bernert; m. James Sheldon, Mar. 19, 1950 (div. 1960); children: James, John Anthony. AA, Colby Jr. Coll., 1940; AB, U. N.C., 1942; PhD, U. Chgo., 1949. Asst. demographer Office Population Rsch., Washington, 1942-43; social scientist USDA, Washington, 1943-45; assoc. dir. Chgo. Community Inventory, U. Chgo., 1947-50; social scientist Social Sci. Rsch. Coun., N.Y.C., 1950-51, rsch. grantee, 1953-55, pres., 1972-79; rsch. assoc. Bur. Applied Social Rsch. Columbia U., 1950-51, lectr. sociology, 1951-52, vis. prof., 1969-71; social scientist UN, N.Y.C., 1951-52; rsch. assoc., lectr. sociology UCLA, 1955-61; assoc. rsch. sociologist, lectr. Sch. Nursing U. Calif., 1957-61; sociologist, exec. assoc. Russell Sage Found., N.Y.C., 1961-72; vis. prof. U. Calif., Santa Barbara, 1971; dir. Equitable Life Assurance Soc., Mobil Corp., H.J. Heinz Co. Author: (with L. Wirth) Chicago Community Fact Book, 1949, America's Children, 1958, (with R.A. Glazier) Pupils and Schools in N.Y.C, 1965; editor: (with W.E. Moore) Indicators of Social Change, Concepts and Measurements, 1968, Family Economic Behavior, 1973; contbr. (with W.E. Moore) articles to profl. jours. Bd. dirs. Colby-Sawyer Coll., 1979-85, UN Rsch. Inst. for Social Devel., 1973-79; trustee Rockefeller Found., 1978-85, Nat. Opinion Rsch. Ctr., 1980-87, Inst. East-West Security Studies, 1984-88, Am. assembly, 1976-95. William Rainey Harper fellow U. Chgo., 1945-47. Fellow Am. Acad. Arts and Scis., Am. Sociol. Assn., Am. Statis. Assn.; mem. AAAS, U. Chgo. Alumni Assn. (Profl. Achievement award), Sociol. Rsch. Assn. (pres. 1971-72), Coun. on Fgn. Rels., Am. Assn. Pub. Opinion Rsch., Ea. Sociol. Soc., Internat. Sociol. Assn., Internat. Union Sci. Study of Population, Population Assn. Am. (2d v.p. 1970-71), Inst. of Medicine (chmn. program com. 1976-77), Cosmopolitan Club. Home and Office: 630 Park Ave New York NY 10021-6544

SHELDON, GEORGE F., medical educator; b. Dec. 20, 1934; s. Richard Robert and Helen Irene (Zerzan) S.; m. Ruth Guy, Aug. 28, 1959; children: Anne Anderson, Elizabeth, Julia. BA, U. Kans., 1957, MD, 1961; postgrad., Mayo Clinic Grad. Sch., 1965. Intern Kans. U. Med. Ctr.; resident in surgery U. Calif., San Francisco, 1965-69; fellow in surg. biology Harvard Med. Sch. of Peter Bent Brigham Hosp., 1969-71; from asst. to full prof. U. Calif., 1971-82; Dr. Zack D. Owens Disting. prof. surgery, dept. chmn. U. N.C., Chapel Hill, 1984—; chmn. residency rev. com. accreditation Coun. for Grad. Med. Edn.; mem. Coun. Grad. Med. Edn. of Health and Human Svcs., 1986; mem. adminstrv. bd. Coun. Acad. Socs. Author: (with J.B. Runnell) Pictorial History of Kansas Medicine, 1961, (with Jill Ridky) Managing in Academics, 1993; editor: (with J.B. Davis) Clinical Surgery, 1995. With USPHS, 1962-64. Recipient Surgeon's awrd for Svc. to Safety, Nat. Safety Coun., 1993, Douglass Stubbs award Nat. Med. Assn., 1991. Hon. fellow Royal Coll. Surgeons of Edinburgh, European Surg. Assn., Assn. of Surgeons of Gt. Britain and Ireland; mem. ACS (regent 1983-92), Am. Bd. Surgery (chmn. 1989-90), Nat. Bd. Med. Examiners (test com. 1981-84), Am. Assn. Surgery of Trauma (pres. 1984), Am. Surg. Assn. (sec. 1989-94, pres. 1994-95), Assn. Am. Med. Colls., Inst. Medicine (sec. com. on employer based health ins. and tech. assessment edn. bds.), Merit Rev. Bd. for Surgery Va. (chmn.). Office: U NC at Chapel Hill 136 Burnett-Womack Bldg 229 Chapel Hill NC 27599

SHELDON, LEE NELSON, periodontist; b. Springfield, Mass., July 7, 1950; s. Julian William and Sonnee (Goldart) S.; m. Eleanor Sue Pritzker, Apr. 14, 1973; children: Daniel, Stephanie, Matthew. BA in Biology, Clark U., 1972; DMD, Tufts U., 1975; cert. in periodontics, U. Conn., 1980; also postgrad. courses in pain therapeutics and dental implants. Resident gen. dentistry Reynolds Army Hosp., Ft. Sill, Okla., 1975-76; staff periodontist U.S. Army War Coll., Carlisle Barracks, Pa., 1976-78; practice dentistry specializing in periodontics, Melbourne, Fla., 1980—; mem. dental staff Holmes Regional Med. Ctr., 1981—, dept. chmn., mem. exec. bd., 1983-84. V.p. Temple Beth Sholom, Satellite Beach, Fla., 1984-89, exec. bd., 1984-95; bd. dirs. S.E. region United Synagogue Conservative Judaism, 1990—, v.p. 1996—. Host Check Up, Time Warner Cable. Served as capt. U.S. Army, 1975-78. Mem. Am. Acad. Periodontology, Fla. Soc. Periodontists, ADA, Fla. Dental Assn., Brevard County Dental Soc., Am. Acad. Implant Dentistry (assoc.). Lodge: B'nai Brith. Avocations: tennis, golf, music. Home: 610 Loggerhead Island Dr Satellite Beach FL 32937-3849 Office: 2223 Sarno Rd Melbourne FL 32935-3003

SHELEY, KATHY ANN, clinical psychologist; b. Marshall, Tex., Mar. 31, 1951; d. William Arthur and Kathlyn Sunshine (Randle) S.; m. Thomas Ray Urbanek, Dec. 16, 1972 (div. Feb. 1988). BA, U. Tex., 1972; MA, U. Fla., 1975, PhD, 1978. Asst. prof. dept. psychiatry, dept. ob-gyn. U. Tex. Health Sci. Ctr. Med. Sch., San Antonio, 1978-80; coord. psychology svc. Robert B. Green Hosp., San Antonio, 1978-80; coord. inpatient psychiat. unit psychology svc. Bexar County Hosp., San Antonio, 1978-80; co-dir. psychosocial clinic Robert B. Green Hosp., San Antonio, 1978-80; dir. program div. of psychology svcs. Clear Lake Ctr., Austin (Tex.) State Hosp., 1980-82; dir. Austin Counseling Ctr. of Galveston (Tex.) Family Inst., 1982-87; clin. faculty Galveston Family Inst., 1983-87; adj. asst. prof. dept. psychology Trinity U., San Antonio, 1978-80; adj. faculty Galveston Family Inst., 1980-81; cons. Tex. Dept. Parks & Wildlife, 1984-90, Lago Vista Police Dept., Tex., 1987-91, Georgetown Police Dept., Tex., 1986-92. Mem. Am.

Assn. for Marriage and Family Therapy, Am. Psychol. Assn., Internat. Platform Assn. Home: 1111 Quail Park Dr Austin TX 78758-6618 Office: Austin Family Ctr 1011 W 31st St Austin TX 78705

SHELLHASE, LESLIE JOHN, social work educator; b. Hardy, Nebr., Jan. 12, 1924; s. John Clayton and Sanna Belle (Muth) S.; m. Fern Eleanor Kleckner, June 8, 1948; children: Jeremy Clayton, Joel Kleckner. Student, U. Calif.-Berkeley, 1943-44; A.B., Midland Coll., 1947; M.S.W., U. Nebr., 1950; D.Social Work, Catholic U. Am., 1961. Lic. social worker, Ala. Parole supr. Child Welfare, Omaha, 1948-49; psychiat. social work intern Letterman Gen. Hosp. San Francisco, 1950-51; commd. 2d lt. U.S. Army, 1949, advanced through grades to lt. col., 1966; chief social worker (6th Inf. Div.), Ft. Ord, Calif., 1952-55; chief med. social worker Walter Reed Gen. Hosp. Washington, 1955-57, research investigator Walter Reed Inst. Research, 1957-63; head social work faculty Med. Field Service Sch., Ft. Sam Houston, Tex., 1963-66; chief sociologist U.S. Army, Washington, 1966-68; prof. Sch. Social Work, U. Ala., Tuscaloosa, 1968-89; prof. emeritus Sch. Social Work, U. Ala., 1989—; pvt. practice social work, 1968—; dir. tour, interpreter to surgeon gen. Belgium Armed Forces, 1961; lectr. Cath. U. Am., 1961-63, 66-68; rsch. dir. Jewish Social Svc. Fedn., San Antonio, 1963-66; rep. to internat. social and behavioral scis. cmty. Dept. Army, 1966-68; cons. Family Svc. Assn. Am., 1969—, Ala. Mental Health Dept., 1989—; mem. expert group on social welfare UN, 1975—; mem. Internat. Rels. Forum, 1981—; rsch. fellow U. Exeter, 1981-82; mem. social work tng. com. NIMH, 1983—; mem. Interfaith Com. on AIDS, 1993; newscaster Radio Reading Svc., Ala. Pub. Broadcast, 1989—; condr. workshops; cons. on group psychotherapy Ala. Dept. Mental Health, 1989—. Author: The Group Life of the Schizophrenic Patient, 1961, Bibliography of Army Social Work, 1962; book rev. editor Social Perspectives, 1979-83; editorial reviewer Social Work Papers, mem. editorial bd., 1986—; editorial reviewer Mac Millan Press, 1990—, Families in Society, 1992—, Oxford U. Press, 1994; internat. editorial bd. Internat. Abstracts Social Sci.; contbr. articles on social and behavioral sci. to nat. and internat. profl. jours., chpts. to books. Bd. dirs. Crisis Intervention Ctr.; bd. dirs., chmn. Soc. for Crippled Children and Adults. Served with inf. U.S. Army, 1942-46. Decorated Legion of Merit, Bronze Star, Purple Heart; recipient letter of commendation from Pres. of U.S., 1968, letter of commendation from Surgeon Gen., 1961. Fellow Am. Sociol. Assn.; mem. NASW (mem. nat. task force on ethics 1976-79, chmn. 1976-77, dir. 1963-66), Coun. social Work Edn., Acad. Cert. Social Workers, Brit. Sociol. Assn., Brit. Assn. Social Workers, Ret. Officers Assn., So. Sociol. Soc. Democrat. Home: 3823 Somerset Pl Tuscaloosa AL 35405-5436 Office: PO Box 870314 Tuscaloosa AL 35487-0314

SHELLY, WALTER MYERS, surgeon; b. East Greenville, Pa., Aug. 27, 1933; s. Howard L. and Emma (Myers) S.; m. Elizabeth Bauman; children: Mark Alan, Lois Anita Shelly Hillegas, Arthur David, Robert Jon. AB, Bluffton Coll., 1955; MD, Jefferson Med. Coll., 1959. Resident in surgery St. Luke's Hosp., Bethlehem, Pa., 1959-61, 63-65; resident in thoracic surgery Alameda County Hosp., Oakland, Calif., 1965-68; med. missionary to Zaire, Africa Africa Intermennonite Mission, Elkhart, Ind., 1961-63, 68-77; pvt. practice thoracic surgery Bethlehem, Pa., 1977-86, Hazard, Ky., 1986—. Fellow ACS; mem. AMA. Office: 200 Medical Center Dr Hazard KY 41701-9422

SHELTON, JAMES H., cardiologist; b. Tex., Oct. 24, 1944; s. Joseph H. and Jean J. (Jones) S.; m. Nancy Breard, June 6, 1970; children: Joseph, David, Kathleen. AB, Harvard U., 1966; MD, Harvard U., Boston, 1970. Diplomate Am. Bd. Internal Medicine with subspecialty in cardiovascular disease. Cardiologist Dallas Cardiology Assocs., Dallas, 1977-95, North Tex. Cardiology, Dallas, 1995—. Bd. dirs. Cistercian Prep Sch., Dallas, 1983-96. Maj. U.S. Army, 1975-77. Fellow Am. Coll. Cardiology, Am. Heart Assn. (clin. coun. 1978, bd. dirs. 1988-96); mem. Tex. Club of Internists, Dallas Country Cub. Office: 3600 Gaston #851 Dallas TX 75246

SHELTON, JANA HARRELL, optometrist; b. Marshall, Tex., Apr. 4, 1966; d. V.P. Harrell and Lanice Harrell Morton; m. Jeffrey T. Shelton, Aug. 4, 1990. BS, Tex. A & M, 1989; OD, So. Coll., Memphis, 1993. Cert. optometrist, Tex., Ark. Clin. instr. U. Ark., Little Rock, 1993-95, Ark. Children's Hosp., Little Rock, 1993-95; optometrist Ben Israel Optical, Little Rock, 1995—. Mem. Am. Optometric Assn., Tex. Optometric Assn., Ark. Optometric Assn. Republican. Baptist. Home: 30 Glendale Dr Cabot AR 72023

SHELTON, JOEL EDWARD, clinical psychologist; b. Havre, Mont., Feb. 7, 1928; s. John Granvil and Roselma Fahy (Ervin) S.; m. Maybelle Platzek, Dec. 17, 1949; 1 child, Sophia. AB, Chico (Calif.) State Coll., 1951; MA, Ohio State U., 1958, PhD, 1960. Psychologist Sutter County Schs., Yuba City, Calif., 1952-53; tchr., vice prin. Lassen View Sch., Los Molinos, Calif., 1953-55; tchr. S.W. Licking Schs., Pataskala, Ohio, 1955-56; child psychologist Franklin Village, Grove City, Ohio, 1957; clin. psychologist Marion (Ohio) Health Clinic, 1958; intern Children's Mental Health Ctr., Columbus, Ohio, 1958-59; acting chief research psychologist Children's Psychiat. Hosp., Columbus, 1959-60; cons. to supt. schs. Sacramento County, Calif., 1960-63; mem. faculty Sacramento State Coll., 1961-69; clin. psychologist DeWitt State Hosp., Auburn, Calif., 1965; exec. dir. Children's Ctr. Sacramento, Citrus Heights, Calif., 1963-64, Gold Bar Ranch, Garden Valley, Calif., 1964-72; clin. psychologist El Dorado County Mental Health Ctr., Placerville, Calif., 1968-70, Butte County Mental Health Dept., Oroville, Calif., 1970-94; dir. dept. consultation, edn. and community services Butte County Mental Health Ctr., Chico, 1974-85, outpatient supr., 1986-94; mgmt. cons., 1972-94; advisor to pres. Protaca Industries, Chico, 1974-80; exec. sec. Protaca Agrl. Rsch., 1974-80; small bus. cons., 1983—; cons. on coll. scholarships and funding, 1991-92, computer cons., 1994—. Mem. APA, Western Psychol. Assn. Home: 1845 Veatch St Oroville CA 95965-4787

SHELTON, STEVEN ROBERT, health services administrator, physician assistant; b. Eagle Pass, Tex., Apr. 25, 1951; s. George Edward and Marilynn May (Davenport) S.; m. Kellie Ann Pickering, July 14, 1990. BS, Angelo State U., San Angelo, Tex., 1973; BS in Health Care Sci., U. Tex., Galveston, 1975; MBA, U. Houston-Clear Lake, 1983. Cert. physician asst. Physician asst. Winnnie, Tex., 1975-77, Uvalde, Tex., 1977-78; from instr. to assoc. prof., physician asst. studies U. Tex. Med. Br., Galveston, 1978—, assoc. chmn. physician asst. studies, 1985-89, clin. asst. prof. dept. family medicine, 1990—, dir. Coastal Bend HETC, 1990—, assoc. dir. East Tex. Area Health Edn. Ctr., 1991—; on-site evaluator accreditation Rev. Com. on Physician Asst. Edn., 1989—. Contbr. articles to profl. jours. Coach Youth Soccer Assn., League City, Tex., 1994—; chair bldg. com., christian nurture com. League City United Meth. Ch., 1994—. Recipient Pres.'s award The Upjohn Co., 1990; Kellogg Leadership Program fellow Am. Soc. Allied Health Professions, 1989. Fellow Am. Acad. Physician Assts.; mem. APHA, Assn. Physician Asst. Programs (pres. 1989-90), Tex. Acad. Physician Assts., Nat. Orgn. AHEC Program Dirs. (sec. 1995—, sec. legis. affairs com. 1994—). Methodist. Office: East Tex AHEC 301 University Blvd Galveston TX 77555-1056

SHEMO, JOHN PALMER DAVID, psychiatrist, educator; b. Waterford, N.Y., Oct. 20, 1948; s. Dominick James and Alice Anne (Morrissey) S.; m. Mary Carroll, May 20, 1972; children: Bryna Carroll, Cordelia Palmer. BS, Wheeling (W.Va.) Jesuit Coll., 1970; MD, W.Va. U., 1975. Asst. prof. behavioral med. and psychiatry W.Va. U., Morgantown, 1978-79, asst. prof. internal med., 1978-79; asst. prof. behavioral med. and phychiatry U. Va., Charlottesville, 1979-82, asst. prof. internal med., 1979-83, assoc. prof. behavioral med. and psychiatry, 1982—, assoc. prof. internal med., 1983—; dir. inpatient psychiatry svc. W.Va. U., 1978-79; dir. psychiat. emergency svc. adn psychiat. cons. svc. U. Va., 1982-86; dir. psychiat. svcs. Charter Hosp., Charlottesville, 1988—; med. dir. Psychiat. Alliance of the Blue Ridge. Co-author: Psychiatry and the Mental Health Professions, 1988; contbr. articles to profl. jours. Fellow Am. Psychiat. Assn.; mem. Psychiat. Soc. Va. (pres.-elect), Group for Advancement Psychiatry (govt. policy com.). Home: 1440 Pinedale Rd Charlottesville VA 22901-9418 Office: 1023 Millmont St Charlottesville VA 22903-4866

SHEMONSKY, NATALIE KAPLIN, physician, lawyer, army officer; b. Bridgeport, Conn., June 5, 1934; d. Harry C. and Clara (Dronkow) Kaplin; m. Sidney Shemonsky, Aug. 26, 1954 (div. 1974); children—Kim R. Shemonsky Fischel, Sherri E. Shemonksy Paulsen, Caryn L. Shemonsky Bart. B.A., Western Conn. State Coll., 1967; M.D., Med. Coll. Pa., 1971; J.D., U. S.D., 1984. Intern, Med. Coll. Pa. Hosp., Phila., 1971-72, resident, 1972-75; clin. dir. USPHS Hosp., Rosebud, S.D., 1975-76; practice medicine specializing in internal medicine, Vermillion, S.D., 1977-81; legal-med. lectr. U. S.D. Sch. Law, Vermillion, 1981-84; commd. maj. U.S. Army, 1984; lt. col. 1986; col. 1992; staff physician-lawyer, Armed Forces Inst. Pathology, Washington, 1984-86; cons. dept. legal medicine, Armed Forces Inst. Pathology, 1986—; pathology resident, Walter Reed Army Med. Ctr., Washington, 1986-90; forensic pathology fellow, Armed Forces Inst. of Pathology, 1990-91; assoc. med. examiner, Office of the Armed Forces Med. Examiner Armed Forces Inst. of Pathology (AFIP), 1991-92; chief deputy med. examiner, 1993—. Assoc. editor Legal Aspects of Med. Practice, 1985—; contbr. articles to med.-legal profl. jours. and chpts. in med. legal textbooks. Fellow ACP, Am. Coll. Legal Medicine; mem. Am. Soc. Law and Medicine, Pitts. Soc. Legal Medicine, Health Lawyers Am., Trial Lawyers Assn. Am. Home: 2704 Herradura Rd Santa Fe NM 87505-5695

SHEMS, ESTHERINA, psychiatrist; b. Tel Aviv, Israel, Apr. 15, 1932; came to U.S., 1950; d. Aaron and Rachel (Yehuda) S.; m. Donald L. Scotland, Jan. 11, 1976. BS cum laude, Lynchburg Coll., 1954; MD, Woman's Med. Coll. Pa., 1958. Rotating intern Lankenau Hosp., Phila., 1958-59; fellow in adult psychiatry U. Pa., Phila., 1960-63; child psychiatry affiliate Child Study Ctr. Phila., 1961-63, Irving Schwartz Inst. for Children and Youth, 1964-66; various staff, adminstrv. positions Phila. Psychiat. Ctr. Irving Schwartz Inst. for Children and Youth, Phila., 1964-80; asst. instr., dept. psychiatry U. Pa. Sch. Medicine, Phila., 1962-63, clin. assoc. in psychiatry, 1979-82; cons. early intervention programs Community Coun. for Mental Health/Mental Retardation, Inc., Phila., 1980—; numerous cons. and teaching positions in field including invited lectr., Inst. of Pediatrics Chinese Acad. of Med. Scis., Beijing, People's Republic of China. Named one of Outstanding Young Women of Am., 1967, one of Outstanding Young Women of Pa., 1967; recipient T. Gibson Hobbs Outstanding Alumni award Lynchburg Coll., 1969, Disting. Alumni award, 1990, Richard H. Thornton award for Excellence, 1995. Fellow Am. Orthopsychiat. Assn., Coll. Physicians Phila.; mem. Med. Women's Internat. Assn. (U.S. del. and session co-chmn. XIX Internat. Congress 1984, XX Internat. Congress 1987, XXII Congress 1995, mem. sci. rsch. com. 1990—, nat. coord. for U.S.A. 1992—), Am. Psychiat. Assn. (life), Am. Med. Women's Assn. (life, mem. exec. com., bd. dirs. 1986-88, 92—, councilor of orgn. 1986-88, mem. various coms. and task forces 1970—), Psychiat. Physicians Pa., Phi Kappa Phi, Chi Beta Phi (various offices), others. Home: 1310 Wyngate Rd Wynnewood PA 19096-2455 Office: Cmty Coun MH/MR Inc 4900 Wyalusing Ave Philadelphia PA 19131-5127

SHEN, EDWARD NIN-DA, cardiologist, educator; b. Hong Kong, July 3, 1950; came to U.S., 1979; s. Han-Ting and Yay-Wen (Tsu) S.; m. MaryRose Yung-Yung Wong, June 19, 1983; 1 child, Erin Pey-Juan. BS in Chemistry with 1st class honors, McGill U., Montreal, Que., Can., 1972, MD, CM, 1976. Diplomate Am. Bd. Internal Medicine, Am. Bd. Cardiovascular Disease, Am. Bd. Electrophysiology; cert. cardiologist Royal Coll. Physicians & Surgeons Can. Resident in internal medicine McGill U., 1976-79; cardiology fellow U. Calif., San Francisco, 1979-81, electrophysiology fellow Cardiovascular Rsch. Inst., 1981-82, instr. in medicine Moffitt Hosp., 1982-83; assoc. chief cardiology Santa Clara Valley Med. Ctr., San Jose, Calif., 1983-85; clin. assoc. prof. U. Calif., San Francisco, Stanford, 1983-85; clin. asst. prof. medicine Straub Clinic, Honolulu, 1986-93, chief of medicine, 1991-93; assoc. prof. medicine U. Hawaii, Honolulu, 1988-93, chief cardiology, 1993—, prof. medicine, 1994—; attending physician Moffit-Long Hosps., 1982-83; dir. electrocqrdiography, co-dir. noninvasive cardiac lab. Santa Clara Valley Med. Ctr., 1983-85; attending cardiologist Queen's Heart Inst., Straub Clinic & Hosp., St. Francis Hosp., Kuakini Hosp., 1993—; fellow Med. Rsch. Coun. Can., 1981-83; presenter in field. Contbr. over 90 articles to profl. jours. Bd. dirs. Am. Heart Assn., 1987-89, mem. peer rev. bd. for grant-in-aid applicants, 1987-89. Univ. scholar, 1968-75; recipient Charles E. Frosst prize and medal, Cushing Meml. prize Montreal Children's Hosp., John C. Milnor Profl. and Grey Champion Activities award Straub Found., 1990; Edward N. Shen scholar award in his honor U. Hawaii. Fellow ACP, Royal Coll. Physicians of Can., Am. Coll. Cardiology (gov. 1989-92), Am. Coll. Chest Physicians, Am. Heart Assn. Coun. Clin. Cardiology (Hawaii rep. 1991-96); mem. N.Am. Soc. Pacing and Electrophysiology, Assn. Profs. of Cardiology, Mensa. Roman Catholic. Office: 1380 Lusitana St # 701 Honolulu HI 96813

SHEN, MASON MING-SUN, medical center administrator; b. Shanghai, Jiang Su, China, Mar. 30, 1945; came to U.S., 1969; s. John Kaung-Hao and Mai-Chu (Sun) S.; m. Nancy Hsia-Hsian Shieh, Aug. 7, 1976; children: Teresa Tao-Yee, Darren Tao-Ru. BS in Chemistry, Taiwan Normal U., 1963-67; MS in Chemistry, S.D. State U., 1971; PhD in Biochemistry, Cornell U., 1977; MS in Chinese Medicine, China Acad., Taipei, Taiwan, 1982; OMD, San Francisco Coll Acupuncture, 1984; AMD (hon.), Asian Am. Acupuncture Coll., San Diego, 1985; MD (Medicina Alternativa), Internat. U., Colombo, Sri Lanka, 1988. Diplomate Nat. Commn. for Cert. of Acupuncturists; lic. acupuncturist. Rsch. assoc. Lawrence Livermore (Calif.) Lab., 1979-80; assoc. prof. Nat. Def. Med. Coll., Taipei, 1980-82; prof. Inst. of Chinese Medicine China Acad., Taipei, 1981-82, San Francisco Coll. Acupuncture, 1983-85; chief acupuncturist Acupuncture Ctr. of Livermore, 1982-93; prof. Acad. Chinese Culture & Health Scis., Oakland, Calif., 1985-86; dir. Pain & Stress Mgmt. Ctr., Danville, Calif., 1989-90; adminstr. Ea. Med. Ctr., Pleasanton, Calif.; chief acupuncturist Acupuncture Ctr. Pleasanton, 1993—, Acupuncture Ctr. Tracy, Calif., 1995-96; pres. Florescent Inst. Traditional Chinese Medicine, Oakland, 1995—; adminstr. Am. Ea. Med. Inst., Pleasanton, 1993—; chmn. adminstrn. subcom., 1991-92, acupuncture com. State of Calif., 1988-92; dir. United Calif. Practitioners of Chinese Medicine, San Francisco, 1995—; bd. dirs. Five Branches Inst., Coll. of Traditional Chinese Medicine, Santa Cruz, Calif., 1996—. Contbr. articles to profl. jours. Rep. Republican Party, Danville, 1988-93; bd. dirs. Asian Rep. Assembly, 1989—; mem. presdnl. adv. com. Republican Presdl. Task Force, 1992; mem. chmn's. adv. bd. Republican Nat. Com., 1993. Recipient Nat. Rsch. Svc. award NIH, 1977, Presdl. Order of Merit, Pres. of the U.S., 1991. Mem. AAAOM, N.Y. Acad. Sci., Calif. Cert. Acupuncturists Assn. (bd. dirs. 1984-88, pres. 1984-85, mem. polit. action com. 1995—), Acupuncture Assn. Am. (bd. dirs. 1986-90, v.p. 1987-89), Am. Assn. Acupuncture and Oriental Medicine (bd. dirs. 1987-92, pres. 1989-90), Nat. Acupuncture Detoxification Assn. (cons. 1987—), Presdl. Round Table (presdl. adv. com.), Hong Kong and Kowloon Chinese Med. Assn. (hon. life pres. 1985). Republican. Home: 3240 Touriga Dr Pleasanton CA 94566-6966 Office: Eastern Med Ctr 3510 Old Santa Rita Rd Ste D Pleasanton CA 94588-3466 also Office: 400 El Cerro Blvd Ste 105 Danville CA 94526

SHEN, STEVE YU-LIANG, physician, researcher; b. Taiwan, Republic of China, Feb. 14, 1946; s. Shui-Yun and Chih-Yu (Hsu) S.; m. Mei-Jung Lee, Aug. 31, 1975; children: Elaine Joan, Jonathan Michael. MD, Taipei (Taiwan) Med. Coll., 1971. Diplomate Am. Bd. Internal Medicine, Am. Bd. Medicine in Subsplty. of Nephrology. Intern St. Francis Hosp., Pitts., 1973-74; resident Wayne State U.-Harper Hosp., Detroit, 1974-76; clin. and rsch. fellow in nephrology U. Md. Hosp., Balt., 1976-79; dir. transplant clinic U. Md. Med. System., Balt., 1983-89; med. dir. trans. svc. U. Md. Med. System, 1982-89; assoc. prof. medicine U. Md., Balt., 1988—; med. dir. acute hemodialysis svc. and therapeutic apheresis Ch. Hosp., Balt., 1990—, chief of nephrology, 1991—; mem. Md. State Commn. on Kidney Disease, 1992—; mem. med. adv. bd. Md. Organ Procurement Ctr., 1982-89; mem. med. rev. bd. Mid-Atlantic Renal Coalition, Richmond, Va., 1988—. Author: (booklet) Kidney Transplantation: An Information Booklet for Patients and their Family, 1984; contbr. articles to profl. jours. Rep. United Network for Organ Sharing, Richmond, Va., 1988—. Fellow ACP; mem. Am. Soc. Transplant Physicians, Internat. Soc. Nephrology, Internat. Transplantation Soc. Home: 307 Meadowcroft Ln Lutherville MD 21093-6422

SHEN, THOMAS TO, environmental engineer; b. Chia-Shing, Chekiang, China, Aug. 14, 1926; m. Cynthia Shen; children: Grace, Joyce. BS in Civil Engring., St. John's U., Shanghai, People's Rep. China, 1948; MS in Sanitary Engring., Northwestern U., 1960; PhD in Environ. Engring., Rensselaer Poly. Inst., 1971. Registered profl. engr., Wash., N.Y. Assoc. engr. Boeing Co., Renton, Wash., 1961-63; sanitary engr. Wash. State Health Dept., Seattle, 1963-66; sr. sanitary engr. N.Y. State Health Dept., Albany, 1966-70; sr. rsch. scientist N.Y. State Dept. Environ. Conservation, Albany, 1970-93; adj. prof. Columbia U., N.Y.C., 1981-93; mem. EPA Sci. Adv. Bd., 1987-90; cons. UN's Environ. Protection Program, various Asian cities, 1983—; lectr. various U.S. and fgn. univs., 1978—; cons. World Bank, 1990; tech. reviewer Annual Pres. Bush's Environ. and Conservation Challenge awards, 1991, 92. Author: Air Pollution and Its Control, 1985, Hazardous Waste Incineration, 1982, Assessment and Control of VOC Emissions from Waste Treatment and Disposal Facilities, 1993, Industrial Pollution Prevention, 1995; author: (with others) Electrostatic Precipitator, 1979, Air Quality Assessment, 1989; contbr. articles to profl. jours. Bd. dirs. Internat. Ctr. of the Capital Region, Albany, 1984-88, Am. Bur. Med. Advancement ot China, N.Y.C., 1985—. Recipient Svc. award Phi Tau Phi, 1986, Nat. award Indsl. Wast. Minimization Taiwan Environ. Protection Adminstrn., Ministry Fgn. Affairs, 1993, Man of Yr. award N.Y. State Capital Region Chinese Am. Alliance, 1995; Named for Outstanding Editorial Contbn. on Pollution Engring., Chgo., 1978, 81. Fellow ASCE (chmn. N.Y. State Coun. 1979-80); mem. Am. Acad. Environ. Engrs. (diplomate 1973), Air and Waste Mgmt. Assn. (com. chmn. 1985—, Frank Chamber award for Outstanding Achievement in Sci. of Air 1993), Delmar Club (pres. 1979-80), Rotary. Home: 146 Fernbank Ave Delmar NY 12054-4215

SHENEFELT, PHILIP DAVID, dermatologist; b. Colfax, Wash., July 31, 1943; s. Roy David and Florence Vanita (Cagle) S.; m. Debrah Ann Levenson; children: Elizabeth, Sara, Shaina. BS with honors, U. Wis.-Madison, 1966, MD, 1970, MS in Adminstrv. Medicine, 1984. Intern U.S. Naval Hosp., Bethesda, Md., 1970-71; general practice Oregon (Wis.) Clinic, 1975; resident in dermatology U. Wis. Hosp., Madison, 1975-78, staff, 1978-87; asst. prof. dermatology sect. Dept. Internal Medicine U. South Fla., 1987—; chief dermatology sect. VA Hosp., Bay Pines, Fla., 1987-89, asst. chief, Tampa, 1988—; dermatologist Univ. Health Svc., U. Wis.-Madison, 1978-87, VA Hosp., Madison, 1982-85. Served to lt. comdr. USN, 1969-74; capt. USNR (ret.). Kellogg fellow, 1980-82. Mem. AMA, Am. Acad. Dermatology, Fla. Dermatol. Soc., Fla. West Coast Dermatol. Soc., Am. Coll. Physician Execs. Episcopalian. Home: 15919 Notting Hill Dr Lutz FL 33549-6147 Office: U South Fla Internal Medicine / Dermatology 12901 Bruce B Downs Blvd # 19 Tampa FL 33612-4742

SHENKER, IRA RONALD, physician; b. N.Y.C., July 8, 1934; s. Morris and Rose (Wilner) S.; m. Caroline Cabin, June 22, 1958; children: Diane Amy, Mitchell Steven. B.S., U. Wis., 1955, M.D., 1958. Diplomate Am. Bd. Pediatrics. Intern, L.I. Jewish Med. Ctr., New Hyde Park, N.Y., 1958-59; resident pediat., 1959-61; resident pub. health Nassau County Health Dept., N.Y., 1961-62; coll. health physician Mt. Holyoke Coll., 1962-64; chief adolescent medicine L.I. Jewish Med. Ctr., 1965—; assoc. prof. pediat. SUNY-Stony Brook, 1979—; prof. pediat. Albert Einstein Coll. Medicine, 1989—. Author: Human Figure Drawings in Adolescence, 1972. Editor: Adolescent Medicine, 1981, Clinical Monographs in Pediatrics: Adolescent Medicine, 1994. Contbr. articles to profl. jours. Bd. dirs. Roslyn Sr. Citizens, N.Y., 1975-78. USPHS grantee, 1965-82. Fellow Am. Acad. Pediat.; mem. Queens Pediat. Soc. (pres. 1981-82), N.Y. Pediat. Soc., Nassau Pediat. Soc., Soc. for Adolescent Medicine (pres. 1986). Home: 5 Fairway Rd Roslyn NY 11576-1099 Address: 270-05 76th Ave New Hyde Park NY 11040-1433 Office: Schneider Children's Hosp of LI Jewish Med Ctr New Hyde Park NY 11042

SHENKIN, HENRY ARNOLD, retired neurosurgeon; b. Phila., June 25, 1915; s. Julius and Rose (Rosenbaum) S.; m. Renee Friedenberg, Jan. 12, 1940 (dec. Nov. 1989); children: Budd, Robert, Katherine Shenkin Seal, Emily Shenkin Simon. AB, U. Pa., 1935; MD, Jefferson Med. Coll., 1939. Diplomate Am. Bd. Neurol. Surgery. Pvt. practice, 1946-88; internship Phila. Gen. Hosp., 1939-41; fellow dept. of Physiology Yale U. Sch. Medicine, 1941-42; residency Hosp. Univ. of Pa., 1942-45; instr., asst. prof. neurosurgery U. Pa. Sch. Medicine, Phila., 1945-60, assoc. prof., 1960-67; clin. prof. Temple U. Sch. Medicine, Phila., 1967-74; prof. Med. Coll. Pa., Phila., 1974-82; ret., 1982; dir. neurosurgery and ind. residency program in neurosurgery Episcopal Hosp., Phila., 1960-82. Author: Clinical Practice and Cost Containment, 1986, Medical Ethics: Evolution, Rights and the Physician, 1991, Medical Care Reform: A Guide to Issues and Choices, 1994, Current Dilemmas in Medical-Care Rationing: A Pragmatic Approach, 1996; contbr. articles to profl. jours. Home: 3300 Darby Rd Apt 3101 Haverford PA 19041-1069

SHEPARD, KIRK VAN, SR., physician, researcher; b. Columbus, Ohio, Aug. 17, 1951; s. Ivan Albert and Miriam Adele (Murray) S.; m. Nadine Joyce Martello, Aug. 27, 1983; children: Kirk Van II, Devin, Austin. BA, Cornell U., 1973; MD, U. Cin., 1978. Diplomate Am. Bd. Internal Medicine, Am. Bd. Med. Oncology, Am. Bd. Hematology. Intern in medicine Case Western Res. U , Cleve., 1978-79, resident in medicine, 1980-81; fellow in hematology and oncology U. Chgo., 1981-84; staff physician Cleve. Clinic Found., 1984-87; med. dir. Roxane Labs., Inc., Columbus, 1987-88, v.p. med. affairs, 1989—; asst. clin. prof. Ohio State U. Med. Ctr., 1988—; mem. publ. com. Hospice Update, 1989—. Author: (with others) Gastroinestinal Malignancies, 1984, Tumors of Upper GI Tract, 1987, Review of Controlled Release Morphine, 1990; editor Palliative Care Letter, 1989—; contbr. over 65 articles to profl. jours. Cornell U. nat. scholar, 1970-73; recipient Disting. Alumni award BVH, 1996. Mem. Northeastern Ohio Soc. Oncologists (mem. at large 1987), Ohio Cancer Pain Inst. (bd. dirs. 1990-91). Office: Roxane Labs Inc PO Box 16532 Columbus OH 43216-6532

SHEPARD, RICHARD BLOUNT, surgeon, educator; b. Birmingham, Ala., May 9, 1926; m. Winyss Renee Acton, Mar. 26, 1955; children: Winyss Elizabeth, Richard Kesniel, Kathryn Bouchelle, Karen Acton. BS in Physics, Pa. State U., 1949; MD, U. Pa., 1953. Intern, resident in surgery U. Pa. Hosp., Phila., 1953-59; instr., rsch. assoc. in physiology U. Pa., Phila., 1954-56; chief resident Fitkin Hosp. Hahnemann Med. Coll., Neptune, N.J., 1959-60; from instr. to prof. surgery U. Ala., Birmingham, 1960—; engr. Victoreen Instrument Co., Cleve., 1946; part-time engr. Haller, Raymond & Brown, State College, Pa., 1948; cons. for device implant mfrs. and electronics mfr., 1960-90; chmn. USRA-NASA biomed. com. for studies selection, shuttle orbital flight tests, 1981-83. Contbr. articles to profl. jours. and chpts. to books. With U.S. Army, 1943-46. Grantee Heart Assn. S.E. Pa., NIH. Fellow ACS, Am. Coll. Cardiology; mem. Soc. Thoracic Surgeons, Soc. for Vascular Surgery.

SHEPARD, ROBERT STANLEY, physiology educator; b. Washington, June 19, 1927; s. Azro Rodgers and Blanche Pearl (Jones) S.; m. Constance Helen Little, Aug. 19, 1950; children: Karen, Mark, Stephen, Garry. BS, George Washington U., 1950, MS, 1951; PhD, State U. Iowa, 1955. Park naturalist U.S. Dept. Interior, Washington, 1948-50; rsch. asst. State U. Iowa, Iowa City, 1952-54; instr., prof. Wayne State U. Sch. Medicine, Detroit, 1955-87; lectr. Mercy Coll., Detroit, 1959-65, Grace Hosp., Detroit, 1966-80; vis. prof. Meharry Med. Coll., Nashville, 1976-82. Author: Human Physiology, 1971, Human Physiology Examination Rev, 1975, 2d edit., 1981, 3d edit., 1985; contbr. articles to profl. jours. With USN, 1945-47. Rsch. grantee NIH, 1961-87, Mich. Heart Assn., 1967-71. Mem. Am. Physiological Soc. (edn. panel 1973-74), Detroit Physiological Soc. (pres. 1967-68, sec. 1960-66). Home: 27130 Sylvan Warren MI 48093-1753

SHEPARD, THOMAS AKERS, physician assistant; b. Buffalo, N.Y., Oct. 4, 1948; s. Richard Marvin and Mabel Elizabeth (McVicker) S.; m. Ruth Virginia Heffleger Zebarth, June 5, 1971 (div. Nov. 1980); 1 child, Jared Nathaniel; m. Denise Hazel Donaldson, Sept. 25, 1993. BA, Franklin & Marshall Coll., 1971; AS in sci., Arapahoe Cmty. Coll., Littleton, Colo., 1977. RN, Colo., Pa. Physician asst. Buffalo Park Medical Assn., Evergreen, Colo., 1975-82, ClearCreek Medical Ctr., Idaho Springs, Colo., 1982-85; occupational health dir. AMAX Inc. Henderson Mine, Empire, Colo., 1985-93; physician asst. urgent care Kaiser Permanente, Denver, 1988-96; mgr. med. svcs. Colo. Compensation Ins. Authority, Denver, 1993—. Co-author (book chpt.): Pain Treatment Centers At a Crossroads, 1996. Rule making testimony Colo. Dept. Labor, Denver, 1993, 94, 95; managed care task force Colo. Div. Workers Comp. Colo. Dept. Labor, 1993-94; apportionment working group, 1994. With Army, 1966-68, Vietnam. Fellow Am. Acad. Physicans Assts., Colo. Acad. Physicians Assts. Office: Colo Compensation Authority Ins 720 S Colorado Blvd Denver CO 80222

SHEPELL, WARREN EDWARD JAMES, industrial psychologist; b. Winnipeg, Man., Can.; s. Stanley and Anne (Schreyer) S.; B.A., U. Man. United Coll., 1965; M.A.Sc., U. Waterloo (Ont., Can.), 1968; Ph.D., U. Pa., 1974. Staff psychologist Man. Penitentiary, Stony Mountain, 1965-66; personnel researcher Ont. Hydro, Toronto, 1967; staff psychologist Canadian Imperial Bank of Commerce, 1968-71, 74-75; lectr. psychol. services U. Pa., 1971-74; human resources lectr. U. Toronto, 1974—; cons. psychologist Stevenson & Kellogg, Ltd., Toronto, 1975-77; cons. psychologist, founding partner Beech Shepell & Partners Ltd., Toronto, 1977-79; indsl. psychologist Ennis Shepell Indsl. Psychologists, Toronto, 1979-80, indsl. psychologist, pres. Warren Shepell & Assocs., Inc., 1980—, chmn. and CEO pres., Warren Shepell Cons. Corp., 1986—. vol. cons. CUSO, Frontier Coll.; speaker in field. Recipient Wesley award United Coll. U. Man., 1965. Mem. Am. Psychol. Assn., Canadian Psychol. Assn., Ont. Soc. in Tng. and Devel., Employee Assistance Program Assn. Toronto, Pres.'s Assn., Ont. Psychol. Assn. (council Bd. Edn. and Tng.), Ont. Amateur Softball Assn., Toronto Bd. of Trade. Club: Bloor Park. Home: 12 Playter Blvd, Toronto, ON Canada M4K 2V9 Office: 170 Bloor St W, Toronto, ON Canada M5S 1T9

SHEPHARD, BRUCE DENNIS, obstetrician, educator, medical writer; b. San Francisco, Apr. 21, 1944; s. Richard G. and Madelyn (Rogers) S.; m. Carroll Anne Swanson; children: Christopher, Carleton, Elizabeth. BA in History, U. Calif., Berkeley, 1966; MD, U. Calif., San Francisco, 1970. Diplomate Am. Bd. Obstetrics and Gynecology. Intern Jackson Meml. Hosp.-U. Miami (Fla.), 1970-71, resident in ob-gyn., 1971-74; obstetrician Tampa (Fla.) Ob-Gyn Assocs., 1976-94; clin. assoc. prof. obstetrics U. So. Fla. Sch. Medicine, Tampa, 1976—; bd. dirs. Ctr. of Excellence, 1983-90, Humana Women's Hosp., Tampa, Fla., 1983-90, Gulf Coast Health Systems Agy., 1980-83; mem. midwifery adv. com. Fla. Dept. Health and Human Resources, Tallahassee, 1982-86. Author: (with Carroll Shephard) The Complete Guide to Women's Health, 1982; prin., writer, spokesperson (series of TV commls.) The Healthy Woman (Gold Link award 1987); mem. med. adv. bd. Baby Talk mag., 1995—; contbr. articles to profl. jours. and women's mags. Served as maj. USAF, 1974-76. Mem. AMA, Am. Coll. Obstetricians and Gynecologists (patient edn. com. 1984-86, John McCain fellow 1981), Am. Med. Writers Assn., Acad. Radio and TV Health Communicators, Phi Beta Kappa. Democrat. Lutheran. Home: 4201 Carrollwood Village Dr Tampa FL 33624-4609 Office: 4302 N Habana Ave Ste 300 Tampa FL 33607-6316

SHEPHERD, GILLIAN MARY, physician; b. Belfast, U.K., Mar. 12, 1948; came to U.S., 1957; d. John Thompson and Helen (Johnston) S.; m. Eduardo Goar Mestre, Aug. 4, 1973; children: Laura Elena, Cristina Alicia., Eduardo Goar. BA, Wheaton Coll., Norton, Mass., 1970, postgrad. Tufts U., 1970-73; MD, N.Y. Med. Coll., 1976. Diplomate Am. Bd. Internal Medicine, Am. Bd. Allergy and Immunology. Intern, resident Lenox Hill Hosp., N.Y.C., 1976-79; fellow in allergy and immunology N.Y. Hosp./Cornell Med. Sch., N.Y.C., 1979-81; assoc. prof. medicine Cornell U. Med. Coll., N.Y.C., 1988—, clin. assoc. prof. medicine, 1995—; assoc. attending physician N.Y. Hosp., N.Y.C.; cons. allergy and immunology dept. medicine Meml. Sloan-Kettering Cancer Ctr., N.Y.C., 1982—. Contbr. articles in field to profl. jours. Fellow ACP, Am. Acad. Asthma, Allergy and Immunology; mem. AAAS, Am. Fedn. for Clin. Research, Joint Coun. Allergy and Immunology, N.Y. Allergy Soc. (exec. com. 1982-94, pres. 1991-92), N.Y. County Med. Soc. Office: 235 E 67th St Ste 203 New York NY 10021

SHEPHERD, LEANNE MARGARET, healthcare administrator; quality manager; b. Mpls., May 15, 1952; d. Albert S. and Muriel L. (Smith) Ganje. Cert. profl. in healthcare quality. Med. record technician Darnall Army Hosp., Ft. Hood, Tex., 1973-74; med. record technician Blanchfield Army Hosp., Ft. Campbell, Ky., 1975-83, med. records supr., 1983-86, quality assurance technician, 1986-91, asst. quality improvement facilitator, 1991—. Mem. Nat. Assn. for Healthcare Quality, Middle Tenn. Assn. for Healthcare Quality. Home: PO Box 2546 Clarksville TN 37042 Office: Blanchfield Army Cmty Hosp 650 Joel Dr Fort Campbell KY 42223

SHEPHERD, TEREASA DIANNE, physical therapist; b. Birmingham, Feb. 12, 1959; d. Charles Henry Sr. and Celia Elizabeth (Bowen) Martin; m. James Michael Duncan Sr., Nov. 1, 1974 (div. June 1978); children: Mike Duncan, Angel Martin; m. Thomas Ralph Shepherd, Aug. 27, 1983. AA, Brevard C.C., Cocoa, Fla., 1990; BS in Molecular Biology and Microbiology, U. Ctrl. Fla., 1992, BS in Phys. Therapy, 1994, MS in Health Svc. Adminstrn., 1996. Returns dept. Am. South Bank, Birmingham, 1978-82; acct. Crystal Petroleum Oil Co., Birmingham, 1982-83; head teller Barnett Bank Ctrl. Fla., Cocoa, 1983-88; driver license examiner State of Fla., Merritt Island, 1988-91; student lab. asst. U. Ctrl. Fla., Orlando, 1991-94; phys. therapist Health South Sea Pines Rehab. Hosp., Melbourne, Fla., 1994-95; sr. phys. therapist Health South Sea Pines Rehab. Hosp., Merritt Island, 1995-96, Coastal Rehab. Inc., Indian Harbor Beach, Fla., 1996—. Tchr., coord., cons. First Bapt. Merritt Island, 1992—. Mem. Am. Phys. Therapy Assn., Fla. Phys. Therapy Assn., Nevro Devel. treatment Assn. Democrat. Southern Baptist. Home: 785 Larkview St Merritt Island FL 32953 Office: Coastal Rehab Inc 2020 Hwy A1A Ste 110 Indian Harbor Beach FL 32937

SHEPHERD, WILLIAM C., pharmaceutical company executive; b. 1939. With Allergan Inc, Irvine, Calif., 1964—, pres., COO, 1984—, pres., CEO, 1992—, bd. dirs. Office: Allergan Inc PO Box 19534 2525 Dupont Dr Irvine CA 92713-9534*

SHEPMAN, BERNARD HAROLD, optometrist; b. Pitts., Apr. 16, 1928; s. Max and Bessie (Greenberg) S.; m. Shirley Cohen, Jan. 28, 1951; children: Ilene, Maxine, Bruce. OD, Pa. Coll. Optometry, Phila., 1954. Cert. optometrist, Pa. Pvt. practice optometry Braddock, Pa., 1954-56, Pitts., 1956-72, Monroeville, Pa., 1972-93, New Eagle, Pa., 1991—. With U.S. Navy, 1946-48. Democrat. Jewish. Home: 2088 New Ramsey Rd Monroeville PA 15146

SHEPPARD, BRETT C., surgeon; b. Harvey, Ill., Feb. 21, 1956; s. Nerl N. and Rosyln C. (Constantine) S.; m. Julie Ann Schultz, May 26, 1987; children: Paige Constance, Scott Charles. BS, U. Wis., 1978; MS, Loyola U., Chgo., 1980; MD, Chgo. Med. Sch., 1984. Diplomate Am. Bd. Surgery. Fellow surgery br. NIH/Nat. Cancer Inst., Bethesda, Md., 1987-89; sr. resident Oreg. Health Scis. U., Portland, Oreg., 1989-90, chief resident, 1990-91; instr. surgery Oreg. Health Scis. U., Portland, 1991-92, asst. prof. surgery, 1992—. Contbr. articles to profl. jours., chpts. to books. Fellow ACS; mem. North Pacific Surg. Assn., Am. Assn. Cancer Rsch., Am. Gastroenterological Assn., Soc. Surgery of Alimentary Tract, Soc. Am. Gastrointestinal Endoscopic Surgeons, Soc. Surg. Oncology. Office: Oreg Health Scis Univ 3181 SW Sam Jackson Portland OR 97201

SHEPPARD, MARY NOELLE, physician, pathologist, researcher, consultant; b. Cork, Ireland, Dec. 24, 1953; d. John and Mary (Walsh) Sheppard; m. James Anthony Long, June 30, 1984; children: Mary Louise, James, Francesca. MB BCh, Univ. Coll., Cork, 1977, BSc, 1979, MD, 1984. Jr. house officer Cork Regional Hosp., Ireland, 1977-78, sr. house officer, 1978-80; rsch. fellow Royal Postgrad. Med. Sch., London, 1980-83; sr. registrar, lectr. Univ. Coll. Hosp., London, 1983-86; sr. lectr., cons. Royal London Hosp., 1987-88, Royal Brompton Hosp., London, 1988—; med. rschr. Royal Brompton Hosp., St. George Hosp., London. Author: Pulmonary Pathology, 1994; author med. articles. Brit. Heart Found. rsch. grantee. Mem. Royal Coll. Pathologsits, Pathol. Soc. Gt. Britain, Assn. Clin. Pathologists, Brit. Thoracic Soc., Brit. Cardiac Soc., European Thoracic Soc. Office: Royal Brompton Hosp Dept Pathology, Sydney St, London SW3 6NP, England

SHEPPERSON, JACQUELINE RUTH, biology educator, researcher; b. Hopewell, Va., Feb. 10, 1935; d. Weaver Augustus and Ruth (Jones) S. BS in Biology, Va. State U., 1954; MS in Biology, N.C. Central U., Durham, 1956; PhD in Zoology, Howard U., Washington, 1964. Cert. tchr., N.C., Va., Washington, Ga. Instr. biology Fort Valley (Ga.) State U., 1955-59; asst. prof. zoology Howard U., 1964-65; prof. biology Winston-Salem (N.C.) State U., 1965—. Author: Parasitology-Lab Exercises, 1985; contbr. articles to sci. rsch. jours. Mem. N.C. Acad. Sci., Helminthological Soc. Washington. Office: Winston-Salem State U PO Box 13145 Winston Salem NC 27110

SHER, JAY ALLAN, endocrinologist; b. Bklyn., Oct. 21, 1953; s. Melvin and Bernice (Karasik) S.; m. Elaine Schwartz, Apr. 14, 1985; children: Heather, Erin, Samantha, Alex. BS, U. Pitts., 1974; MD, Downstate Med. Sch., 1978. Diplomate Am. Bd. Internal Medicine, Endocrine and Metabolism. Asst. program dir. dept. medicine Jersey Shore Med. Ctr., Neptune, N.J., 1988—; clin. asst. prof. Robert Wood Johnson Med. Sch., New Brunswick, N.J., 1988—. Fellow ACP, Am. Assn. Clin. Endocrinologists. Home: 24 Mahoras Dr Wayside NJ 07712 Office: Jersey Shore Med Ctr 1945 Rt 33 Neptune NJ 07754

SHER, PHYLLIS KAMMERMAN, pediatric neurology educator; b. N.Y.C., Aug. 13, 1944; d. Seymour K. and Shirley (Parmit) Kammerman; m. Kenneth Swaiman, Oct. 6, 1985. BA, Brandeis U., 1966; MD, U. Miami, 1970. Diplomate Am. Bd. Psychiatry and Neurology. Pediatric intern Montefiore Hosp., Bronx, N.Y., 1970-71; resident in neurology U. Miami (Fla.) Med. Sch., 1971-73, fellow in pediatric neurology, 1973-75, asst. prof. neurology, 1975-80; rsch. assoc. NIH, Bethesda, Md., 1980-83; asst. prof. neurology and pediatrics U. Minn. Med. Sch., Mpls., 1983-86, assoc. prof., 1986—; dir. Ripple program United Cerebral Palsy Found., Miami, 1972-75; chmn. med. svcs. com. 5-yr. action plan State of Fla., 1975; cons. Minn. Epilepsy Program for Children, 1983-85; vis. prof. Japanese Soc. Child Neurology, 1985, Chinese Child Neurology Ctr., 1989, Hong Kong Soc. Child Neurology & Devel. Pediat., 1995. Mem. editl. bd Pediatric Neurology, 1991—, Brain and Devel., 1994—; contbr. articles and abstracts to med. jours., chpts. to books. Comdr. USPHS, 1980-83. Fellow United Cerebral Palsy Found., 1972-73; rsch. grantee Gillette Children's Hosp., U. Minn. Grad. Sch., Viking Children's Fund, Minn. Med. Found. Fellow Am. Neurol. Assn., Am. Acad. Neurology; mem. Child Neurology Soc. (exec. com., councillor 1993-95), Upper Midwest Child Neurology Soc., So. Clin. Neurology Soc. Home: 420 Delaware St SE PO Box 486 Minneapolis MN 55455 Office: U Minn Med Sch Div Pediatric Neur Box 486 Mayo Minneapolis MN 55455

SHERBINSKI, LINDA ANNE, nurse anesthetist, nursing educator; b. Rochester, N.Y., Jan. 17, 1956; d. Edward Marion and Helen Marie (Kindzera) S. Student, Genesee Hosp. Sch. Nursing, Rochester, N.Y., 1977; BSN, Alfred U., 1978; grad. in anesthesia, Univ. Health Ctr. Pitts., 1987; MSN, Duquesne U., 1991. RN, Pa. Leader day team CCU The Genesee Hosp., 1978-84, staff nurse operating rm., 1984-85; staff nurse ICU Forbes Met. Hosp., Pitts., 1985-87; staff anesthetist Presbyn. Univ. Hosp., Pitts., 1987-92, preceptor anesthetist, 1991-92; instr. Univ. Health Ctr. Pitts. Sch. Anesthesia, 1987-90, U. Pitts. Grad. Anesthesia Program, 1990-92; staff anesthetist Meml. Med. Ctr., Springfield, Ill., 1992-94; anesthetist Rochester (N.Y.) Gen. Hosp., Highland Hosp., Genesee Hosp., N.Y., 1994—; item writer Acad. Item Writers AANA, Chgo., 1991—. Contbr. articles to profl. jours., chpt. to book. Med. vol. Pitts. Marathon, 1990, 91. Mem. Am. Assn. Nurse Anesthetists (cert. nurse anesthetist, program dir. internship grant 1990), Nat. League Nursing, Sigma Theta Tau (sec. Delta Sigma chpt. 1978-80, Rsch. scholar Epsilon Phi chpt. 1991). Roman Catholic. Home: 27 Bella Dr Penfield NY 14526 Office: Rochester Gen Hosp Portland Ave Rochester NY 14621

SHERBLOM, JAMES PETER, biopharmaceutical executive; b. Fall River, Mass., Oct. 6, 1955; s. Edward R. and Ruth P. (Howard) S.; m. Loretta Ho, Mar. 11, 1979; children: Sarah, Robert. MBA, Harvard U., 1980. Cons. Bain & Co., Boston, 1980-81, London, 1981-82; sr. cons. Bain & Co., Munich, 1982-83; dir. fin. Genzyme Corp., Boston, 1984-85; chief fin. officer Genzyme Corp., 1985-89; chmn., chief exec. officer TSI Corp., 1989-93; pres. Seaflowers Assn., Inc., 1993—. Democrat. Mem. Unitarin Universalist Ch. Home: 199 Park Ln Concord MA 01742-1621

SHEREDOS, CAROL ANN, rehabilitation services director; b. N.Y.C., Jan. 29, 1944; d. Robert J. and Margaret M. (Adams) Ross; m. Saleem J. Sheredos, July 14, 1973; children: Emily Joy, Douglas Joseph. BS, Ithaca Coll., 1967; MA in Adulthood and Aging, Coll. of Notre Dame, Balt., 1994. Lic. phys. therapist, N.Y., Md., Fla., N.J. Staff phys. therapist Glen Cove (N.Y.) Community Hosp., 1967-68, Nassau County Health Dept., Mineola, N.Y., 1968-70; rsch. phys. therapist VA, N.Y.C., 1970-71, prosthetics rsch. and edn. specialist, 1971-73; chief phys. therapist Medicus, Wappingers Falls, N.Y., 1983-88; dir. Meridian Rehab. Svcs., Towson, Md., 1989-92; rehab. svcs. dir. Mariner Rehab. Svcs., Balt., 1992-95; dist. mgr. Mariner Rehab. Svcs., 1995—; pvt. practice phys. therapy, N.Y., 1967-83; cons. in disability and aging Alliance, Inc., Balt., 1990-93; co-instr. course The Challenge of Geriatric Rehab., 1994—. Contbr. articles to profl. jours. Host minister St. Joseph's Ch., Tex., Md., 1990—; mem. Gov's. Adv. Coun. Individuals with Disabilities, 1996—. Named One of Ten Most Outstanding Handicapped Americans, Pres.' Com. on Employment of Handicapped, 1971. Mem. Am. Phys. Therapy Assn., Md. Coalition for Assistive Tech., Assn. Christian Therapists, Am. Soc. Aging, Resna. Republican. Roman Catholic. Office: Mariner Rehab Svcs 2700 N Charles St Baltimore MD 21218-4318

SHERIDAN, ANDREW JAMES, III, ophthalmologist; b. Washington, Aug. 19, 1944; s. Andrew J. and Mildred (Stohlman) S.; m. Carol Dinkelacker, Oct. 23, 1971; children: Elizabeth, Margaret. AB, Villanova U., 1966; MD, Georgetown U., 1970. Diplomate Am. Bd. Ophthalmology. Intern Nassau County Med. Ctr., N.Y., 1970-71, resident in ophthalmology, 1973-76; practice medicine specializing in ophthalmology Eye Assocs., Arlington, Va., 1976—; chief of ophthalmology Arlington Hosp., 1980-84, 90-95; clin. instr. ophthalmology Georgetown U., 1982—. Bd. dirs. Va. Med. Polit. Action Com., 1985-89, Polit. Action Com. for Ophthalmology in Va., 1985—, chmn, 1991-94. Lt. comdr. USPHS, 1971-73; pres. Georgetown Clin. Soc., 1987-88. Fellow ACS, Am. Acad. Ophthalmology; mem. AMA, Med. Soc. Va., Arlington County Med. Soc. (exec. bd., sec. 1994, v.p. 1995, pres.-elect 1996), No. Va. Acad. Ophthalmology (v.p. 1988-90, pres. 1990-92, bd. dirs.), Brent Soc. Republican. Roman Catholic. Office: Eye Assocs 1715 N George Mason Dr Ste 206 Arlington VA 22205-3609

SHERIDAN, JOSEPH LEE, psychiatrist, consultant; b. Amboy, Ind., Oct. 28, 1918; s. Abner L. and Kathryn L. (King) S.; m. Janet B. Sawyer; children: Anne Clark, Kathryn Elizabeth. BA, Ind. U., Bloomington, 1939; MD, Ind. U., Indpls., 1943; grad., Washington Psychoanalytic Inst., 1954. Diplomate Am. Bd. Psychiatry. Intern and resident Indpls. City Hosp., 1943-45; med. officer Saint Elizabeth Hosp., Washington, 1947-53; pvt. practice Washington, 1950-88; consulting psychiatrist disability determination div. RHS, Human Svcs., Govt. of D.C., Washington, 1983-90; cons. psychiatrist disabilitaty determination svc. Human Svcs., State of Maine, Augusta, 1993—; asst. clin. prof. psychiatry George Washington U. Med. Ctr., Washington, 1964-80, assoc. clin. prof., 1980-88. Capt. U.S. Army, 1945-47. Fellow AAAS, Am. Psychiat. Assn. (life); mem. AMA, Am. Psychoanalytic Assn. (life), Internat. Psychoanalytic Assn., Washington Psychoanalytic Soc. Democrat. Home: Rackliff Island PO Box 346 Spruce Head ME 04859

SHERIDAN, PHILIP HENRY, pediatrician, neurologist; b. Washington, June 29, 1950; s. Andrew James and Mildred Adele (Stohlman) S.; m. Margaret Mary Williams, Oct. 3, 1987; children: Gerard Andrew, Philip Henry, Kathleen Mary, Patrick Gerard, Mary Margaret Gerard, Mary Anne Gerard. BS magna cum laude, Yale U., 1972; MD cum laude, Georgetown U., 1976. Diplomate Am. Bd. Pediatrics, Am. Bd. Psychiatry and Neurology, Am. Bd. Qualification in Electroencephalography. Resident in pediatrics Children's Hosp. Phila., 1976-79; fellow in pediatric neurology Hosp. of U. Pa., Phila., 1979-82; med. staff fellow NIH, Bethesda, Md., 1982-84, neurologist, epilepsy br. Nat. Inst. Neurol. Disorders and Stroke, 1984—, health scientist adminstr., guest worker researcher, 1984-89, chief Devel. Neurology Br., 1989—, acting chief Epilepsy Br. NIH, 1995—; cons., lectr. Nat. Naval Med. Ctr., Bethesda, 1984—; med. dir. U.S. Pub. Health Svc. Contbr. articles on clin. and rsch. neurology to med. jours. Neurologist Div. Children's Splty. Svcs., Fairfax, Va., 1984—. Mem. Am. Acad. Neurology, Child Neurology Soc. (invited reviewer), Soc. for Neurosci., Alpha Omega Alpha. Roman Catholic. Current work: Planning and administering a comprehensive research program concerning epilepsy, pediatric neurology, developmental neurobiology, and neuromuscular disorders. Subspecialties: Neurology, Pediatrics. Office: NIH Fed Bldg Rm 516 Bethesda MD 20892

SHERMAN, ALAN ROBERT, psychologist, educator; b. N.Y.C., Nov. 18, 1942; s. David R. and Goldie (Wax) S.; m. Llana Helene Tobias, Aug. 14, 1966 (div. 1989); children: Jonathan Colbert, Relissa Anne. BA, Columbia U., 1964; MS, Yale U., 1966, PhD, 1969. Lic. psychologist, Calif. Faculty psychology U. Calif., Santa Barbara, 1969—; clin. psychologist in pvt. practice Santa Barbara, 1981—; cons. in field. Author: Behavior Modification, 1973; contbr. articles to profl. jours. and chpts. in books. Pres. Santa Barbara Mental Health Assn., 1978, 84-85, 91, Mountain View Sch. Site Coun., Santa Barbara, 1978-84. Recipient Vol. of Yr. award Santa Barbara Mental Health Assn., 1979, Tchg. Excellence awards Delta Delta Delta, Alpha Chi Omega, Gamma Phi Beta, Santa Barbara; NIMH predoctoral rsch. fellow, 1964-69; grantee in field. Fellow Behavior Therapy and Rsch. Soc.; mem. APA, AAUP (chpt. pres. 1978-79), Calif. Psychol. Assn., Assn. for Advancement of Behavior Therapy, Santa Barbara County Psychol. Assn. (pres. 1985), Phi Beta Kappa (chpt. pres. 1977-78), Sigma Xi, Psi Chi (chpt. faculty advisor, 1979—). Office: Univ of Calif Dept Psychology Santa Barbara CA 93106-9660

SHERMAN, CHARLES DANIEL, JR., surgeon; b. Avon Park, Fla., Oct. 5, 1920; s. Charles Daniel and Mary Alice (Oliver) S.; m. Jean Riebling, Aug. 13, 1943; children: Rachel, Charles Daniel, Edward. B.S., U. Fla., 1942; M.D., Johns Hopkins U., 1945. Diplomate: Am. Bd. Surgery. Intern Duke U. Hosp., Durham, N.C., 1945-46; resident U. Rochester Med. Center, 1948-52, instr., 1952-56, asst. prof., 1956-64, clin. assoc. prof. surgery, 1964-70, clin. prof., 1970—; fellow Meml. Center for Cancer, 1951; practice medicine specializing in cancer surgery Rochester, 1953—; mem. staff Highland Hosp., Rochester, N.Y.; v.p. Redd Labs., Clearwater, Fla., 1961-70; advisor N.Y. State Bur. Cancer Control, 1964-75; sec.-treas. Monroe County Health Planning Coun., 1967-69; mem. Monroe County Bd. Health, 1966-79; advisor to WHO, 1971, dir. Internat. Network of WHO Collaborating Ctrs. for Cancer Edn., 1996—; mem. advisory com. Nat. Cancer Insts.; dir. Internat. Union Against Cancer Project to Survey Cancer Edn. in L.Am., 1976, Asia, 1977; mem. hosp. adv. com. to Joint Com. on Accreditation of Hosps., 1980-88; organizer WHO/Internat. Union Against Cancer European Congress on Cancer Edn., 1981; mem. Accreditation Coun. for Continuing Med. Edn., 1983-89, vice-chmn., 1988, chmn., 1989; organizer Coordinating Coun. on Cancer Edn. in L.Am., 1986, in Asian-Pacific region, 1987; chmn. Coordinating Coun. for Cancer Edn. in Europe, 1987-88; bd. dirs. Nat. Resident Matching Plan, 1988-92, treas., 1989-90; mem. organizing com. Internat. Med. Scholar Program, 1987-89; keynote spkr. Internat. Cancer Congress, 1992; co-dir. WHO Internat. Network of Cancer Edn. Ctrs., 1996—; lectr. in field. Author: Clinical Concepts in Cancer Management, 1976; co-author: Clinical Oncology, 1974; editor, pub.: Directory of U.S. Oncologists, 1983—; editor: (with others) Programmed Instruction in Medical Education; Newsletter in Cancer, 1968-80; chmn. editorial bd. for 2d, 3d and 4th edits. Clinical Oncology (monograph): (with others) Internat. Union against Cancer, 1978-86; mem. editorial bd. Jour. Cancer Edn., 1984—, Greek Jour. Continuing Med. Edn., 1986—; participant movie on esophogeal reconstrn., 1957; producer exhibits on cancer treatment and cancer edn.; co-contbr. articles to profl. jours. Mem. adv. com. on Continuing Edn. in Oncology of the European Community, 1993; advisor European Sch. Oncology, European Med. Student Assn.; mem. internat. adv. com. Asian Pacific Cancer Congress, Beijing, 1991, Bangkok, 1993, Singapore, 1995, Malaysia, 1996. Fulbright fellow Mendoza, Argentina, 1963; recipient Health Edn. award N.Y. State Pub. Health Assn., 1973; cert. of merit. Rochester Acad. Medicine, 1982. Mem. ACS, AMA (N.Y. state del. to Ho. of Dels., coun. on med. edn. 1983-92, com. on med. liability 1984-85, com. on fgn. grads. 1984, com. on cancer 1970-74, exec. com. 1989-90), Am. Radium Soc., Soc. Head and Neck Surgeons, Royal Soc. Medicine, Am. Assn. Cancer Edn. (pres. 1975-76), Am. Fedn. Clin. Oncologic Socs. (bd. govs. 1974-77), N.Y. State Med. Soc. (councillor 1973-79, asst. treas. 1980-83, treas. 1983-85, v.p. 1986, pres.-elect 1987, pres. 1988-89, trustee 1990—, chair trustees 1994-95, liaison com. on med. edn. 1992-94), N.Y. Acad. Sci., N.Y. State Cancer Programs Assn. (pres. 1970-71, chmn. UICC prof. edn. program 1986-94, exec. coun. 1986-94), Monroe County Med. Soc. (pres. 1965, Edward Mott Moore award 1978), Monroe County Cancer and Leukemia Assn. (pres. 1962-66), European Assn. Cancer Edn. (bd. dirs. 1987-92), Soc. Surg. Oncology (chmn. residents award com. 1963-66), Am. Soc. Preventive Oncology, U.S. Squash Rackets Assn. (dir. 1963-65), Argentine Anti-Smoking Union (hon.), Blue Key Soc., Phi Beta Kappa, Alpha Phi Omega. Home: 127 Southern Pky Rochester NY 14618-1052

SHERMAN, CRAIG HARVEY, radiologist, nuclear medicine physician; b. Bklyn., May 4, 1960; s. Arthur Mitchell and Elaine (Snow) S.; m. Farah Nikravesh, Nov. 23, 1989; children: Joshua, Alexandra, Jonah. BA, Pa. State U., 1980; MD, Jefferson Med. Coll., 1982. Diplomate Am. Bd. Radiology, Am. Bd. Nuclear Medicine. Intern Mt. Sinai Med. Ctr., N.Y.C., 1982-83; resident Meml. Sloan-Kettering, N.Y.C., 1983-84; resident N.Y. Hosp.-Cornell Med. Ctr., N.Y.C., 1984-88, fellow, 1988-90; attending radiologist Beranbaum, Khilnani, Neistadt, Jacobs, Hertz, Sherman, N.Y.C., 1990—; clin. asst. prof. radiology Cornell U. Med. Coll., N.Y.C., 1990—; asst. attending radiologist New York Hosp., N.Y.C., 1990—; attending radiologist Manhattan Eye Ear Throat Hosp., N.Y.C., 1993—. Mem. Am. Soc. Neuroradiology (sr. mem.), Radiol. Soc. N.Am., Soc. Breast Imaging, Alpha Omega Alpha. Office: 340 E 64th St # 85 New York NY 10021-7503*

SHERMAN, FRED, biochemist, educator; b. Mpls., May 21, 1932; s. Harry and Ann (Kaufman) S.; m. Revina Freeman, July 25, 1958 (div.); children: Aaron, Mark, Rhea. B.A., U. Minn., Mpls., 1953; Ph.D., U. Calif., Berkeley, 1958. Postdoctoral fellow U. Wash., Seattle, 1959-60; postdoctoral fellow Lab. Genetique Physiol., Gif-sur-Yvette, France, 1960-61; sr. instr. U. Rochester, N.Y., 1961-62, asst. prof., 1962-66, assoc. prof., 1966-71, prof. dept. biochemistry Sch. Medicine & Dentistry, 1971—, chmn. dept. biochemistry, 1982—; instr. Cold Spring Harbor Lab., N.Y., 1970-87; Wander Meml. lectr., 1975; Wilson prof. U. Rochester, 1982. Co-author: Cold Spring Harbor Manual on Yeast Genetics and Molecular Biology, 1970-87; assoc. editor Genetics, 1975-82, Molecular Cell Biology, 1979-88. Fellow NIH, 1959-61, grantee, 1963—. Mem. NAS, Genetic Soc. Am. (bd. dirs. 1983-85), AAAS, Am. Soc. Microbiology. Home: 69 Westminster Rd Rochester NY 14607-2223 Office: U Rochester Med Sch Dept Biochemistry 601 Elmwood Ave Rochester NY 14642

SHERMAN, FREDERICK SCOTT, pediatric cardiologist; b. Cambridge, Mass., Feb. 7, 1949; s. Henry Sherman and Doris Gimpelson; m. Kathryn Rich; children: Alexis, Nathaniel. AB, Harvard U., 1971; MD, Yale U., 1975. Resident in pediatrics U. Va., Charlottesville, 1975-78; asst. surgeon U.S. Pub. Health Svc., New Canton, Va., 1978-80; fellow in cardiology Children's Hosp., Boston, 1981-84; asst. prof. in pediatrics U. Calif., San Diego, Calif., 1984-88; assoc. prof. of pediatrics U. Pitts., 1988—; dir. perinatal cardiology Magee Women's Hosp., Pitts., 1988—. Bd. dirs. Children's Home, Pitts., 1990—, Opera Theater of Pitts., 1995—. Fellow Am. Coll. Cardiology, Am. Acad. Pediatrics; mem. The Pitts. Golf Club, Am. Heart Assn., Am. Soc. Echocardiography. Office: Magee Womens Hosp 300 Halket St Pittsburgh PA 15213

SHERMAN, GEOFFREY KIMMETT, psychologist; b. Allentown, Pa., June 24, 1961. Mt. St. Mary's Coll., Mt. St. Mary's Coll., Emmitsburg, Md., 1984; MA magna cum laude, Kutztown U. of Pa., 1989. Bd. cert. med. psychotherapist, cert. counselor. Adminstr. Allentown Osteopathic Med. Ctr., 1985-87; psychologist intern Counseling Assocs., Allentown, 1988; psychotherapist Springhaven Counseling Ctr., Allentown, 1989—; med. psychotherapist Orefield (Pa.) Med. Ctr., 1990—, Maulfair Med. Ctr., Mertztown, Pa., 1990—; clin. assoc. Am. Bd. Med. Psychotherapists. Mem. APA, AACD, Pa Psychol. Assn., Am. Mental Health Counselors Assn., Pa. Counseling Assn., Christian Assn. for Psychol. Studies, Pa. Assn. Counselor Educators and Suprs., Pa. Career Devel. Assn., Pa. Mental Health Counselors Assn., Pa. Assn. for Counselors Specializing in Couples and Families, Pa. Assn. for Adult Devel. and Aging. Office: Cedar Crest Psychol Svcs Roma Corp Cepter Ste 520 1605 N Cedar Crest Blvd Allentown PA 18104

SHERMAN, INGRID, spiritual psychologist and healer; b. Cologne, Germany, June 25, 1919; came to U.S., 1940; d. Abraham Kugelmann and Gertrude (Schloss) Koppel; m. Morris Sherman, May 22, 1943 (dec. Aug. 1995); children: Robert A., Gordon L. ND (Naturopathy), Anglo-Am. Inst. Drugless Therapy, Eng., 1961; D in Spiritual Psychology, Sci. of Truth Inst., Cin., 1962; PTh (Poetry Therapy Founder), United Poets Laureate Internat., The Philippines, 1967; PhD (hon.), DPTh (hon.), Internat. U. India, 1969,

70; DLitt (hon.), Internat. Acad. English, 1970; ScD (hon.), U. Danzig, Brazil, 1977; DPE (hon.), Psychoembriology Coll. Brazil. 1978. Pvt. sec. famous film stars and opera singers, N.Y.C., 1959-63; substitute tchr. Yonkers (N.Y.) pub. schs., 1956-62; counselor and healer, founder, pres. Peace of Mind Studio, Yonkers, 1958-84, Oliverea, N.Y., 1960-92, Treasure Island, Fla., 1975—. Author: Natural Remedies for Better Health, 1970, rev. edit., 1993, To Uplift Your Spirits, 1982; author 10 poetry booklets. United Poets Laureate Internat., Hon. Poet Laureate, named First Lady of Poetry Therapy, First Lady of Poetry Therapy, Philippines, 1967; recipient Golden Laurel Wreath, 1967, Cert. of Merit, Acad. Internat. Leonardo da Vinci, Italy, 1968, Gold medal, 1970, Silver medal Centro Studi Italy, 1970, Disting. Svc. to Humanity award Greater N.Y. Citizen's Soc., 1971, Cert. of Distinction, Common Leaders of Am., 1971, Disting. Svc. citation World Poetry Soc. India, 1972, Cert. of Merit, Laurel Publ. Internat., Tampa, Fla., 1974, Cert. of Appreciation, City of Yonkers, 1981, Recognition award Tampa Day Poetry Coun., 1993, Editor's Choice award Nat. Libr. of Poetry, 1994, Royal award Hutt River Province Principality, 1995, Spl. Merit Cert., Family Poets Soc., 1995, Internat. Poet of Merit, Internat. Soc. Poets, 1995, Editor's Choice award Nat. Libr. Poets, Md., 1995, Grand Cross Mil. and Chivalric Order of St. Oswald the Martyr, Eng., 1995; named Dame Grande Cross, Sovereign Order of Alfred the Great of Eng., 1970, Lady of Grace and Devotion, Sovereign and Royal Order of Piasti, Poland, 1970, Baroness, Chancery of Miensk and all Byelorussia, 1973, others. Mem. Nat. Health Fedn., Internat. Soc. Naturopathic Physicians, Acad. Am. Poets (co-founder), Am. Assn. Ret. Persons, Ceylon Fedn. Natural Medicine (hon.). Home and Office: 108-121st Ave Treasure Island FL 33706

SHERMAN, JOHN FOORD, biomedical consultant; b. Oneonta, N.Y., Sept. 4, 1919; s. Henry C. and Ruth (Foord) S.; m. Betsy Deane Murray, Feb. 8, 1944; children: Betsy Deane, Mary Ann. B.S., Albany Coll. Pharmacy of Union U., 1949, D.Sc., 1970; Ph.D., Yale U., 1953. With NIH, 1953-74; assoc. dir. extramural programs Nat. Inst. Neurol. Diseases and Blindness, 1961-62, Nat. Inst. Arthritis and Metabolic Disease, 1962-63; assoc. dir. for extramural programs Office Dir. NIH, 1964-68, dep. dir., 1968-74; v.p. Assn. Am. Med. Colls., Washington, 1974-91, exec. v.p., 1987-91, spl. cons., 1991-94; mem. bd. advisors Am. Bd. Internal Medicine, 1991—; sr. advisor Rsch!Am., 1994—. Asst. surgeon gen. USPHS, 1964-68; spl. rsch. chemotherapy and neuropharmacology; mem. panel on data and studies NRC, 1976-87; mem. biomed. libr. rev. com. NIH; bd. dirs. Spinal Cord Injury Edn. and Tng. Found., 1986-92, Musculoskeletal Transplant Found., 1987—. With U.S. Army, 1941-46. Decorated Bronze Star; recipient Meritorious Svc. award USPHS, 1965, Disting. Svc. award HEW, 1971, Sec.'s Spl. Citation award, 1973, award Nat. Civil Svc. League, 1973, Disting. Alumnus award Union U.-Pharmacy Coll. Coun., 1974, Lifetime Achievement award Nat. Assn. for Biomed. Rsch., 1990. Fellow AAAS; mem. Inst. Medicine NAS, Cosmos Club, Sigma Xi. Congregationalist.

SHERMAN, JOHN WILLIAM, biology educator; b. Buffalo, Apr. 26, 1942; s. Charles Snyder and Mary (Adair) S.; m. Sally Breitenbach, July 31, 1965; children: Jonathan, Julie, Daniel. BA, SUNY, Buffalo, 1964, MEd, 1965. Cert. biology. Tchr. Clarence (N.Y.) Sr. High Sch., 1965-69; prof., chmn. dept. Erie Community Coll. N., Williamsville, N.Y., 1969—. Pres. Bd. Edn. City of Tonawanda, 1971—, Bd. Coop. Svcs., Lancaster, N.Y., 1981—; exec. dir. Youth Bd., Tonawanda, 1982—; bd. dir. DeGraff Hosp. North Tonawanda, 1985—. Recipient Leadership awards, Erie Community Coll., 1987, 88, 92, Tonawanda Boys Club, 1988, Tonawanda Red Cross, 1987. Mem. Masons, Phi Delta Kappa. Office: Erie Community Coll North Main St & Youngs Rd Buffalo NY 14221-7051

SHERMAN, JOSEPH OWEN, pediatric surgeon; b. Chgo., Aug. 15, 1936; s. Joseph Owen and Mary Elizabeth (Kelly) S.; m. June Marie Martin, Mar. 16, 1963; children: Brian William, Lee Ann. Student, U. Ill., 1955-58; BS, Northwestern U., 1959, MD, 1962. Diplomate Am. Bd. Surgery, Am. Bd. Pediatric Surgery; lic. physician, Ill. Rotating intern Passavant Meml. Hosp., Chgo., 1963-64; resident in gen. surgery VA Rsch. Hosp., Chgo., 1964-65, 67-68; Am. Cancer Soc. clin. fellow Northwestern U. Med. Sch., Chgo., 1965-66; resident in pediatric surgery Children's Meml. Hosp., Chgo., 1966, 68-69; resident in thoracic surgery Mcpl. Tb San., Chgo., 1967; from instr. to assoc. prof. surgery Northwestern U. Med. Sch., 1967-86, prof. clin. surgery, 1986—; emeritus staff dept. surgery Children's Meml. Hosp., 1995—, Evanston (Ill.) Hosp., 1995—. Contbr. articles to profl. jours. Served with Ill. Army N.G., 1953-69, Ill. Air N.G., 1966-67. Fellow ACS, Inst. Medicine Chgo.; mem. AMA, Am. Pediat. Surg. Assn., Assn. for Acad. Surgery, Chgo. Med. Soc., Chgo. Surg. Soc., Ill. Pediat. Surg. Assn., Ill. State Med. Soc.

SHERMAN, NEAL, obstetrician, gynecologist; b. N.Y.C., Apr. 13, 1947; s. Joseph and Ruth (Kohn) S.; m. Debora Ann Witt, Nov. 8, 1975; children: Benjamin, Rachael, Joseph. AB, NYU, 1968; DO, Phila. Coll. Osteo. Medicine, 1972. Diplomate Am. Bd. Ob-Gyn. Intern Zieger-Botford Hosps., Detroit, 1972-73; resident Beth Israel Med. Ctr., N.Y.C., 1973-77; pres., physician Florida (N.Y.) Ob-Gyn., P.C., 1977—; chmn. infection control com. Ander Hill Hosp., Goshen, N.Y., 1984—. Fellow Am. Coll. Ob-Gyn.; mem. AMA, Am. Osteo. Soc., Am. Fertility Soc., N.Y. Med. Soc., N.Y. Osteo. Soc. Office: Florida Ob-Gyn PC 158 N Main St Florida NY 10921

SHERMAN, ROBERT DEWAYNE, radiologic technologist, entrepreneur; b. Concord, Calif., May 31, 1949; s. Chester Josiah and Bette Louise (Elrod) S.; m. Cora Sue Donahue, June 15, 1968 (div. 1973); 1 child, Eric James; m. Virginia Marie Mayer, July 27, 1975 (div. 1988); 1 child, Jana Marie. AA, Foothill Coll., Los Altos, Calif., 1970. Cert. radiol. technologist, Calif. Staff technologist Palo Alto (Calif.) Med. Found., 1971-74, CT technologist, 1974-76, CT supr., 1976—, angiography team, 1982—, MRI staff, 1989-93; business exec. Complete Med. Solutions, Newark, Calif., 1996—. Office: 37037 Magnolia St Apt 124 Newark CA 94560-3662

SHERMAN, ROGER TALBOT, surgeon, educator; b. Chgo., Sept. 30, 1923; s. Joseph Bright and Alice Elizabeth (Baur) S.; m. Ruth Kathryn Thieman, Aug. 23, 1952; children: Nann, Alice, Nina, John, Julie. A.B., Kenyon Coll., 1946; M.D., U. Cin., 1948. Diplomate Am. Bd. Surgery (mem.). Intern, fellow in pathology St. Luke's Hosp., Chgo., 1948-50; resident in surgery Cin. Gen. Hosp., 1950-56; chief dept. exptl. surgery Walter Reed Army Med. Center, 1956-59; asst. prof. to prof. surgery U. Tenn., Memphis, 1959-72; prof., chmn. dept. surgery U. South Fla., Tampa, 1972-82; prof. surgery Emory U. Sch. Medicine, Atlanta, 1983-93; chief surgery Grady Meml. Hosp., Atlanta, 1983-92; Whitaker prof. surgery Emory U. Sch. Medicine, Atlanta, 1993—; dir. surg. edn. Piedmont Hosp., Atlanta, 1993—; cons. Walter Reed Army Med. Center. Mem. editorial bd. Am. Surgeon, 1970-91, Jour. Trauma, 1970-93; contbr. articles to profl. jours., chpts. to books. Served to maj. M.C. AUS, 1956-59. Recipient Golden Apple Tchr. of the Yr. award, 1972, Williams Disting. Teaching award Emory U., 1984, Curtis P. Artz award, 1988. Fellow ACS (gov.); mem. Am. Assn. Surgery of Trauma (pres. 1979), Am. Surg. Assn., So. Surg. Assn., Southeastern Surg. Congress (pres. 1985), Internat. Surg. Soc., Soc. Surgery of Alimentary Tract, Am. Burn Assn., Shock Soc., Am. Trauma Soc., Sigma Xi, Psi Upsilon, Alpha Omega Alpha. Home: 1170 Woods Cir NE Atlanta GA 30324-2736 Office: Piedmont Hospital Department of Surgery 1984 Peachtree Rd NW Atlanta GA 30309-1231

SHERMAN, SAMUEL, retired physiatrist; b. July 15, 1910; s. Markus and Pepi Sherman. BS, U. Pitts., 1932; MD, St. Louis U., 1936. Intern St. Francis Hosp., Pitts., 1936-37; gen. and speciality phys. medicine Carnegie, Pa., 1937-39; gen. practice venerealoty and phys. medicine Homestead, Pa., 1939-42; pvt. practice in phys. medicine and rehab. Pitts., 1946—; lectr. rehab. dept. Montefiore Hosp., Phys. Medicine and Rehab. for Pa. State Med. Soc., 1955-56; chief phys. medicine and rehab. Montefiore Hosp. and North Hills Passavant Hosp.; vis. staff Homestead Hosp. and St. John's Hosp.; cons. phys. medicine and rehab. Vets. Hosp., Western Pa. and Regional Office, Pitts.; cons. Penn Ctrl. Railroad, Jones & Laughlin Steel Corp., Alliquippa Works, Bethlehem Mines Corp., Washington County. Contbr. articles to profl. jours. Maj. Med. Corps-USAAF, 1942-46. Recipient Physician Yr. award Pitts. Com. on Employment of the Handicapped, 1978. Mem. Am. Acad. Phys. Medicine and Rehab. (bd. cert.), Am. Congress Rehab. Medicine, Am. Soc. Legal and Indsl. Medicine, Shriners, Alpha Omega Alpha. Home: 6582 Beacon St Pittsburgh PA 15217

SHERMAN, SPENCER ERWIN, ophthalmologist; b. Jersey City, Apr. 8, 1936. AB, Princeton U., 1958; MD, Columbia U. Diplomate Am. Bd. Ophthalmology. Intern Mt. Sinai Hosp., N.Y.C., 1962-63, attending ophthalmologist, 1968—, resident in ophthalmology, 1965-68; attending ophthalmologist Manhattan Eye & Ear Hosp., N.Y.C., 1968—, Lenox Hill Hosp., N.Y.C., 1968—. Capt. USAMC, 1963-65. Mem. Sigma Xi. Office: 166 E 63d St New York NY 10021-7636

SHERRILL, SABRINA RAWLINSON, healthcare administrator; b. Montgomery, Ala., June 3, 1957. BSN, U. Ala., 1979, MS in Nursing, 1981; MBA, La. State U., 1991. RN, Miss.; cert. advanced nursing adminstrn. Staff nurse intermediate coronary care unit Westgate Hosp., Denton, Tex., 1979; staff nurse ICU South Highlands Hosp., Birmingham, Ala., 1980; staff critical care units and emergency rm. Sacred Heart Hosp., Pensacola, Fla., 1981-82, cardiac rehab. clin. nurse specialist, 1982-83; dept. head intensive coronary care unit Bapt. Hosp., Pensacola, 1983-86; nursing adminstrv. supr. Baton Rouge Gen. Hosp., 1986-87; instr. Sch. of Nursing Our Lady of the Lake Regional Med. Ctr., Baton Rouge, 1987-91; dir. clin. svcs. Vol. Hosps. Am., Baton Rouge, 1991-95; dir. Health Choice & Integrity HMO, Jackson, Miss., 1995—. Contbr. articles to profl. publs. Profl. advisor Mended Hearts, Pensacola, 1983. Mem. Am. Soc. Risk Mgrs., Am. Coll. Healthcare, Sigma Theta Tau, Omicron Delta Kappa. Home: 5893 Kristen Dr Jackson MS 39211-2831

SHERROD, LLOYD B., nutritionist; b. Goodland, Kans., Mar. 5, 1931; s. Charles and Helen S.; m. Judith Harms Sherrod, Dec. 21, 1963; children: Donna J., Barbara E. BS, S.D. State U., Brookings, 1958; MS, U. Ark., Fayetteville, 1960; PhD, Okla. State U., Stillwater, 1964. Rsch. assoc. Okla. State U., Stillwater, 1963; asst. prof. U. Hawaii, Hilo, 1964-67; from assoc. prof to prof. Tex. Tech. U. Ctr., Pantex, 1967-79; nutrition-chemistry instr. Frank Phillips Coll., Borger, Tex., 1979-88; part-time nutrition instr. Amarillo (Tex.) Coll., 1989-95; ret., 1995; rschr. in field. Contbr. articles to sci. jours. Served with U.S. Army, 1951-53. Mem. AAAS, Am. Soc. Animal Science, Am. Dairy Science Assn., Am. Soc. Agronomy, Am. Inst. Biol. Scis., Tex. Jr. Coll. Tchrs. Assn., Plains Nutrition Coun., Sigma Xi., Phi Kappa Phi, Gamma Sigma Delta. Home: Box 1017 Panhandle TX 79068

SHERRY, ALFRED R., chiropractor, registered nurse; b. Buffalo, N.Y., Jan. 14, 1951; s. Alfred R. and Joyce Loretta (Huffman) S.; m. Mary M. Engler, June 2, 1978; children: Kaitlyn, Evelyn, Laura. RN, Olympic Coll., 1978; DC, Western States Chiropractic, Portland, Oreg., 1984. Bd. dirs. Liberty Cmty. Corp., Randallstown, Md., 1988—. Fellow Acad. Chiropractic Orthopedists; mem. Md. Chiropractic Assn. (bd. dirs. 1989-93, v.p. 1992-95), Lions (bd. dirs. Pikesville club 1988-90, sec. 1990-93). Office: 8007 Liberty Rd Baltimore MD 21244

SHERRY, RICHARD LESLIE, ophthalmologist; b. St. Louis, May 23, 1955; s. Sol and Dorothy (Sitzman) S.; m. Marna Janice Blank, Nov. 20, 1983; children: Stuart Lawrence, Jacob Stephen. BA in Biology, U. Rochester, 1977; MD, Case Western Res. U., 1981. Diplomate Nat. Bd. Med. Examiners, Am. Bd. Ophthalmologist. Intern internal medicine Georgetown Univ. Hosp., Washington, 1981-82; resident in ophthalmology Pa. State U., Hershey (Pa.) Med. Ctr., 1983-85, Temple U. Hosp., Phila., 1985-86; fellowship ant. segment ophthalmology Med. Ctr. Del., Wilmington, 1986-87; pvt. practice opthalmology Wilmington, 1987—; assoc. med. dir. Blue Cross/Blue Shield of Del., Wilmington, 1995—. Fellow ACS, Am. Acad. Ophthalmology (councillor 1992—); mem. Am. Soc. Cataract/Refracture Surgery, Contact Lens Assn. Ophthalmologists, Med. Soc. Del. (alt. del. 1995). Jewish. Office: Brandywine Eye Ctr 2500 Grubb Rd Ste 234 Wilmington DE 19810

SHERSON, DAVID LEE, internist; b. Phila., June 10, 1948; arrived in Denmark, 1978; s. Jacob S. and Roslyn (Manuson) S.; m. Else Wohlert, May 3, 1977; children: Jacob, Eva, Rosa. BA, U. Pa., 1970; MD, Temple U., 1974. Intern, resident Med. Coll. Pa., Phila., 1974-78; resident OSHA, Copenhagen, 1979-83; fellow in pulmonary medicine Bispebjerg Hosp., Copenhagen, 1983-86; fellow in occupational medicine Vejle (Denmark) Hosp., 1986-91, co-dir. occupational medicine, 1992—; cons. OSHA, Herning, Denmark, 1991-94. Mem. ACP, Am. Coll. Occupational and Environ. Medicine, Danish Soc. for Occupational Medicine (chmn. edn. com. 1996—), Danish Pulmonary Med. Soc., Danish Soc. for Internal Medicine. Home: Omkulevej 31, 7100 Vejle Denmark Office: Vejle Hosp, Dept Occupational Medicine, 7100 Vejle Denmark

SHERTZER, HOWARD GRANT, health educator; b. N.Y.C., Oct. 9, 1945; s. Sidney Maurice and Terry June (Rosenbaum) S.; m. Ellen Lea Shertzer, June 22, 1968; children: Kyle William, Kevin Maurice. BS in Physiology, U. Mich., 1967; PhD in Cell Biology, UCLA, 1973. Postdoctoral fellow Cornell U., Ithaca, N.Y., 1973-75; asst. prof. environ. health Tex. A&M U., College Station, 1975-79; assoc. prof. environ. health U. Cin., 1979—; vis. prof. Karolinska Inst., Stockholm, 1989; cons. in field. Contbr. articles to profl. jours., chpts. to books. NIH grantee, 1976—. Mem. Am. Bd. Master Educators (bd. dirs. 1980—), Am. Soc. Pharmacology and Exptl. Therapeutics, Soc. Toxicology. Office: U Cin Med Ctr 3223 Eden Ave Cincinnati OH 45267-0056

SHERWIN, JOHN MARTIN, orthopaedic surgeon; b. White Plains, N.Y., July 2, 1929; s. Martin Hutchinson and Barbara (Laimbeer) S.; m. Marjorie Richardson, Feb. 23, 1952; children: Elizabeth, James, Jane. BA, Colgate U., 1951; student, Union Theol. Sem., 1951; MD, Albany Med. Coll., 1960. Intern Hartford (Conn.) Hosp., 1960-61, 1960-61, resident in surgery, 1961-62; resident in orthopaedic surgery Newington Children's Hosp., 1963, Yale-New Haven Med. Ctr., 1963-65; resident Yale U., New Haven, 1965; pvt. practice orthopaedic surgery Manchester, N.H., 1965—; pres. med. staff Elliot Hosp., Manchester, 1975; del. to AMA, Chgo., 1984-95. Inventor Sherwin knee retractor, 1971. Capt. USMCR, 1951-56. Fellow ACS, Am. Acad. Orthopaedic Surgeons; mem. AMA, N.H. Med. Soc. (pres. exec. com. 1982), Hillsborough County Med. Soc. Republican. Presbyterian. Home: 246 N Gate Rd Manchester NH 03104-1825 Office: NH Orthopaedic Surgery PA 700 Lake Ave Ste 1 Manchester NH 03103-2776

SHERWINTER, JULIUS, pediatrician; b. Tel Aviv, Israel, Feb. 16, 1947; came to U.S. 1956; s. Gerald and Sarah (Dauber) S.; m. Carol Hoffman, Nov. 14, 1982; children: Daniel Jonah, David Benjamin. BA, U. Pa., 1969, MD, 1973. Diplomate Am. Bd. Pediatrics. Intern Columbia Presbyn. Hosp., N.Y.C., 1973-74; resident Columbia Presbyn. Hosp., 1974-76; rsch. fellow Albert Einstein Coll. Medicine, Bronx, 1976-78; chief renal & hypertension clinic Scottish Rite Clinic, Atlanta, 1978—; dir. dept. pediatric nephrology Scottish Rite Children's Med. Ctr., 1978—; dir. dialysis ctr. Scottish Rite Children's Hosp.; cons. staff Egleston Hosp., Emory U., 1978—; clin. instr. Med. Coll. Ga., 1980-86, Emory U., 1990—. Contbr. articles to profl. jours. Bd. dirs. Parent to Parent, Atlanta, 1977—, Jewish Family Svcs. NIH grantee, 1976-78. Fellow Am. Acad. Pediatrics; mem. AMA, Am. Soc. Nephrology, N.Y. Acad. Scis., Internat. Soc. Nephrology, Am. Soc. Pediatric Nephrology, AAAS, So. Med. Assn. Jewish. Home: 1054 Trailridge Ln Atlanta GA 30338-3924 Office: Julius Sherwinter 5501 Chamblee Dunwoody Rd Atlanta GA 30338-4207

SHERWOOD, JAMES ALAN, physician, scientist, educator; b. Oneida County, N.Y., Jan. 4, 1953; s. Robert Merriam and Sally (Trevett-Edgett) S. AB, Hamilton Coll., 1974; MD, Columbia U., 1978. Diplomate Nat. Bd. Med. Examiners, Am. Bd. Internal Medicine. Intern Duke U. Med. Ctr., Durham, N.C., 1978-79; resident physician Strong Meml. Hosp., Rochester, N.Y., 1979-81; fellow U. Rochester Sch. Medicine and Dentistry, 1981-83, NIH, Bethesda, Md., 1983-86; rsch. investigator Walter Reed Army Inst. Rsch., Washington, 1986-92; vis. scientist Clin. Rsch. Ctr. Kenya Med. Rsch. Inst., Nairobi, 1987-92; physician Saradidi Rural Health Programme, Nyilima, Kenya, 1987-92; rsch. cons. Rockville, Md., 1992-93; physician St. Mary's Hosp., Waterbury, Conn., 1993—; clin. instr. Sch. Medicine Yale U., 1994—. Contbr. chpt. to book, articles to profl. jours. Comty. svc. vol. The Door, N.Y.C., 1976-77; vol. physician Washington Free Clinic, 1985-87; charity Sisters of St. Joseph of Chambery. Lt. col. Med. Corps, USAR, 1986-92. Recipient Norton prize in chemistry, 1974, Underwood prize in chemistry, 1974. Fellow Am. Coll. Physicians; mem. Med. Soc. D.C., Am. Fedn. Clin. Rsch., Am. Soc. Tropical Medicine and Hygiene, Muthaiga Club, Phi Beta Kappa, Sigma Xi. Office: PO Box 112 Waterbury CT 06720

SHERWOOD, LOUIS MAIER, physician, scientist, pharmaceutical company executive; b. N.Y.C., Mar. 1, 1937; s. Arthur Joseph and Blanche (Burger) S.; m. Judith Brimberg, Mar. 27, 1966; children: Jennifer Beth, Arieh David. AB with honors, Johns Hopkins U., 1957; MD with honors, Columbia U., 1961. Diplomate Am. Bd. Internal Medicine, Subsplty. Bd. in Endocrinology and Metabolism. Intern Presbyn. Hosp., N.Y.C., 1961-62, asst. resident in medicine, 1962-63; clin. assoc. research fellow Nat. Heart Inst., NIH, Bethesda, Md., 1963-66; NIH trainee endocrinology and metabolism Coll. Physicians and Surgeons, Columbia U., N.Y.C., 1966-68; assoc. medicine Beth Israel Hosp. and Harvard Med. Sch., Boston, 1968-69; chief endocrinology Beth Israel Hosp., 1968-72; asst. prof. medicine Harvard U., 1969-71, assoc. prof., 1971-72; physician-in-chief, chmn. dept. medicine Michael Reese Hosp. and Med. Ctr., Chgo., 1972-80; prof. medicine, div. biol. scis. Pritzker Sch. Medicine, U. Chgo., 1972-80; Ted and Florence Baumritter prof. medicine and biochemistry Albert Einstein Coll. Medicine, 1980-88, vis. prof. medicine, 1989—, chmn. dept. medicine, 1980-87; physician-in-chief Montefiore Hosp. and Med. Ctr., N.Y.C., 1980-87; adj. prof. medicine U. Pa., 1993—; sr. v.p. med. and sci. affairs Merck, Sharp & Dohme Internat., 1987-89; exec. v.p. worldwide devel. Merck, Sharp & Dohme Rsch. Labs., 1989-92, sr. v.p. U.S. Med. and Sci. Affairs Merck Human Health, 1992—; bd. dirs. Physicians and Surgeons Corp., Michael Reese Med. Ctr., 1973-80, Barren Found., 1974-80; Josiah Macy Jr. Found. fellow and vis. scientist Weizmann Inst., Israel, 1978-79; assoc. mem. bd. on subcom. endocrinology and metabolism Am. Bd. Internal Medicine, 1977-83. Editor: Beth Israel seminars New Eng. Jour. Medicine, 1968-71; mem. editorial bd. Endocrinology, 1969-73; assoc. editor Metabolism, 1970-85, Gen. Medicine B Study Sect., NIH, 1975-79; mem. editorial bd. Yr. in Endocrinology, 1976-86, Calcified Tissue Internat., 1978-80, Internal Medicine Alert, 1979-89; contbr. numerous articles on endocrinology, protein hormones, calcium metabolism and ectopic proteins to jours. Trustee Michael Reese Med. Ctr., 1974-77; mem. vis. council CUNY Med. Sch., 1986—; mem. alumni council Columbia Coll. Physicians and Surgeons, 1986—. Served as surgeon USPHS, 1963-66. Recipient Joseph Mather Smith prize for outstanding alumni research Coll. Physicians and Surgeons, Columbia U., 1972, Sr. Class Teaching award U. Chgo., 1976, 77; grantee USPHS, 1968-88. Fellow ACP (Outstanding Contbn. to Internal Medicine award 1987); mem. AAAS, Am. Fedn. Clin. Rsch. (bd. dirs. Found. 1989-92, Spl. Recognition award 1992), Am. Inst. Chemists, Am. Soc. Biol. Chemists, Am. Soc. Clin. Investigation (pres. 1982-83), Assn. Am. Physicians, Endocrine Soc., Am. Physicians Fellowship for Medicine in Israel (pres. 1993—), N.Y. Acad. Medicine (bd. dirs. 1991-95), Am. Soc. Hypertension (bd. dirs. 1992—), Mass. Med. Soc., Ctrl. Soc. Clin. Rsch., Assn. Program Dirs. Internal Medicine (coun. 1979-85, pres. 1983-84), Assn. Profs. Medicine, Chgo. Soc. Internal Medicine, Assn. Prof. Med. Industry Roundtable, Interurban Clin. Club, Phi Beta Kappa, Alpha Omega Alpha. Office: Merck & Co US Human Health West Point PA 19486

SHERWOOD, RICHARD C., surgeon; b. L.A., Mar. 31, 1950; m. Roberta Weisberg; children: Emily, Mark. BS, Stanford U., 1972; MD, Loyola U., 1976. Diplomate Am. Bd. Plastic Surgery. Pvt. practice, 1983—. Fellow Am. Coll. Surgeons; mem. Am. Soc. Surgery of the Hand, Am. Assn. Hand Surgery. Office: Richard C Sherwood MD 9033 Wilshire Blvd #300 Beverly Hills CA 90211

SHESTACK, DONALD H., optometrist; b. Phila., Mar. 12, 1942; s. Martin M. and Hilda (Vereta) S.; m. Cheryl Bastecki. OD, Pa. Coll. Optometry, 1966. Capt. USAR, 1967-69. Republican. Roman Catholic. Office: 300 South Hills Village Pittsburgh PA 15241

SHETLAR, JAMES FRANCIS, physician; b. Wichita, Dec. 26, 1944. MD, U. Kans., 1970. Resident in family practice Saginaw County Hosp., 1970-72; staff St. Luke's Gen. Hosp.; asst. clin. prof. Mich. State U. Mem. AMA, Am. Assn. Family Practioners, Mich. Assn. Family Practioners. Office: 163 Churchgrove Saginaw MI 48734-1025*

SHETTY, ASHOK KOLKEBAIL, physician; b. Nov. 19, 1945; s. Sheenappa M. and Rajeevi Shetty; m. Rajani Shetty, May 5, 1974; 1 child, Amit. MB, Govt. Med. Coll., Mysore, India, 1970, MD, 1971. Diplomate Am. Bd. Internal Medicine, Am. Geriatric Bd. Sr. house officer infectious disease Castle Hill Hosp., Hull, Eng., 1972-74, sr. house officer respiratory medicine, 1974-75; registrar respiratory medicine Monsall Hosp., Manchester, Eng., 1975-76; resident Shadyside Hosp., Pitts., 1976-78, chief resident internal medicine, 1978-79; pvt. practice Monroeville, Murrysville, Pa., 1979—. Fellow ACP, Am. Geriatric Soc. (mem. med. dir. long term care). Home: 3125 Treeline Dr Murrysville PA 15668-1569 Office: 4212 Old William Penn Hwy Murrysville PA 15668-1901

SHETTY, MULKI RADHAKRISHNA, oncologist, consultant; b. Hiriadka, Karnataka, India, July 10, 1940; came to U.S., 1974; s. Mulki Sunderram and Kusumavati Shetty. MBBS, Stanley Med. Coll., Madras, 1964; DTM, U. Liverpool, Eng., 1968; LMCC, Med. Coun., Can., 1975. House surgeon and physician Bombay Hosp., 1965-66; sr. house officer Manor Pk. Hosp., Bristol, Eng., 1966-67, Torbay Hosp., 1967-68, St. Lukes Hosp., Huddersfield, 1969-70; sr. resident Gen. Hosp. Meml. U., New Foundland, 1971-72; intern Ottawa Gen. Hosp., 1972-73; fellow in chemotherapy Ont. Cancer Found., Ottawa, Can., 1973-74; fellow in clin. oncology U. Fla., Gainesville, 1974-75; attending oncologist N.W. Community Hosp., Arlington Heights, Ill., 1975—; cons. N.W. Community Hosp., 1975—. Author: Lung Cancer, 1980, Redent Advances in Chemotherapy, 1985; contbr. numerous articles to profl. jours.; coined new word calcifectomy; writer lyrics Love Can Make a Grown Up Cry. Recipient Cert. for Outstanding Svc., Am Cancer Soc., 1982. Fellow Royal Soc. Medicine; mem. Internat. Assn. for Study of Lung Cancer, Chgo. Med. Soc. Hindu. Office: NW Community Hosp 800 W Central Rd Arlington Heights IL 60005-2349

SHETTY, TARANATH, neurologist, educator; b. Mangalore, India, Apr. 29, 1938; s. Shankar and Bhavani S.; m. Urmila Shetty, Dec. 1972; children—Neeta, Teena, Geema. M.B.B.S, Madras U., 1962; M.D., Lucknow U., 1965. Diplomate Am. Bd. Pediatrics, Am. Bd. Neurology with Spl. Competence in Child Neurology, Added Qualifications in Clin. Neurophysiology, Am. Bd. Electroencephalography. Resident in pediatrics Children's Hosp. Med. Ctr., Boston, 1967-68, fellow in neurology, 1968-69; research fellow in neurology Harvard U., 1968-69, teaching fellow, 1971-72; resident in neurology Boston City, Hosp., 1969-72; instr. Brown U., Providence, 1973-74, asst. prof., 1974-79, clin. assoc. prof., 1979—; dir. pediatric neurology R.I. Hosp., Providence, 1976—. Fellow Am. Acad. Neurology, Royal Coll. Physicians Can., Royal Soc. Medicine London; mem. Child Neurology Soc. Hindu. Club: University (Providence). Home: 80 Clarendon Ave Providence RI 02906-5826 Office: 120 Dudley St Providence RI 02905-2436

SHEVIN, FREDERICK FRANKLIN, psychoanalyst, psychiatrist; b. Detroit, Nov. 15, 1921; s. William and Rose (Ruberman) S.; m. Helen Dante, Dec. 22, 1945; children: William Elliot, David Mark, Eileen Carol. BS in Chemistry, U. Mich., 1943; MD, Wayne State U., 1946. Diplomate Am. Bd. Psychiatry and Neurology. Pvt. practice N.Y.C., 1953-60, Detroit, 1960—; tng. & supervising analyst Mich. Psychoanalytic Inst., 1980; assoc. prof. Sch. Medicine Wayne State U., Sch. Medicine Mich. State U.; lectr. Univ. Mich. Dept Psychiatry 1992—. Author: (with others) Psychopharmacology and Psychotherapy, Synthesis or Antithesis. Capt. AUS, 1947-50. Recipient Ira Miller Essay prize Mich. Psychoanalytic Soc. and Inst., 1987. Fellow Am. Psychiatric Assn., Am. Psychoanalytic Assn. (life, cert.); mem. Mich. Assn. for Psychoanalysis (pres. 1970-71). Office: 30100 Telegraph Bingham Farms MI 48025

SHEW, ROSE JEAN, nurse; b. Clinton, Ind., June 21, 1952; d. Paul James and Norma Jean (Bonomo) Duchene; m. Robert Morgan Roberts, Aug. 26, 1972 (div. May 1979); children: Joy Lynn, Robert John; m. Howard Edward Shew II, May 4, 1987 (div. Mar. 1994); 1 child, Sara Rose. Student, Ind. Vocat. Tech. Coll., Terre Haute, 1982-83. Float nurse Union Hosp., Terre Haute, 1983-88, ob.-gyn. nurse, 1988—; intensive coronary care Vermillion Country Hosp., Clinton, 1984-88; sec. Shew Excavating, Universal, Ind., 1987-93; ob nurse Union Hosp., 1990—. Chmn. Boy Scouts Am., 1985; troop leader Girl Scouts U.S.A., 1991-92. Mem. Daus. of Nile, Kappa Delta Phi. Roman Catholic. Home: 1440 S 4th St Clinton IN 47842-2232

SHEWAN, DAVID MICHAEL, anesthesiologist, consultant; b. Edinburgh, Dec. 16, 1938; s. Henry Alexander and Ann Fraser (Thomson) S.; m. Margaret Morrison; children: Michael, Jane. BA, Cambridge U., 1960; MBChB, Edinburgh, 1963. House physician We. Gen. Hosp., Edinburgh, 1963-64, sr. house officer anesthetics, 1964-65; house surgeon Royal Infirmary, Edinburgh, 1964, registrar anesthetics, 1965-70, sr. registrar, 1970-73; cons. anesthetics County Hosp., Lincoln, 1973—; Mem. Lincolnshire Area Health Auth., N. Lincolnshire Health Auth. Fellow Royal Coll. Anesthesiologists. Home: 5 Saint Botolph's Close, Lincoln LN2 5QY, England Office: Lincoln County Hosp anesthetics, Greetwell Rd, Lincoln LN2 5QY, England

SHI, WENYUAN, microbiologist; b. Hangzhou, Zhejiang, China, June 26, 1962; came to U.S., 1985; s. Zhuxian Shi; m. Hanjing Yang, Sept. 3, 1987; 1 child, Jamie Young. BS in Genetics, Fudan U., Shanghai, China, 1984; PhD in Genetics, U. Wis., 1992. Rsch. asst. U. Wis., Madison, 1985-92; rsch. scientist U. Calif., Berkeley, 1992-95; prof. UCLA, 1995—. Author: Methods in Molecular Microbiology, 1994; contbr. articles to profl. jours. Pres. SOS China Edn. Fund, Calif., 1992-93, gen. sec., 1994; pres. Smargen Hitechland, Calif., 1994—. Mem. Am. Soc. Microbiology. Home: 7011 Kentwood Ave Los Angeles CA 90045 Office: Sch Medicine and Dentistry Ctr for Health Scis 10833 Le Conte Ave Los Angeles CA 90095-1668

SHIBATA, SHOJI, pharmacology educator, researcher; b. Kyoto, Japan, Nov. 12, 1927; came to U.S., 1963; s. Shuzo and Tetsu Shibata; m. May 1958; children: Toshiyuki, Eri. MD, Nara (Japan) Med. Coll., 1952; PhD, Kyoto U., 1957. Instr. pharmacology Kyoto U. Med. Sch., 1957-60, U. So. Calif., Los Angeles, 1960-62; assoc. prof. Kyoto Coll. Pharmacy, 1962-63; instr. U. Miss., Jackson, 1963-64, asst. prof., 1964-66; assoc. prof. U. Hawaii, Honolulu, 1967-69, prof., 1970—. Author: Recent Developments in Cardiac Muscle Pharmacology, 1982, Factors Influencing Vascular Reactivity, 1977, Basic Methods of Pharmacology, 1981, Vascular Neuroeffector Mechanisms; 4th Internat. Symposium, 1983, recent advances in Ca Channels and Ca antagonist, 1990; editor Jour. Cardiovascular Pharmacology, Cardiovascular Drug Rev., Meeting Reports Cardiovascular. Fellow Japanese Dept. of Edn., 1954-57, Can. Heart Assn., 1978; sr. fellow Japanese Acad. Scis. Assn. Mem. Am. Physiology Soc., Am. Soc. Pharmacology and Exptl. Therapy, Microcirculatory Soc., Internat. Soc. Heart Rsch. Home: 3338 Keahi St Honolulu HI 96822-1206 Office: U Hawaii Sch Medicine 1960 E West Rd Honolulu HI 96822-2319

SHIELD, PAUL HAROLD, psychiatrist, educator; b. N.Y.C., Oct. 1, 1942; m. Renee R. Shield; children: Sonja, Aaron, David, Lily. BA, Swarthmore Coll., 1963; Dr.med., U. Pa., 1967; grad., Boston Psychoanalytic Inst. Diplomate Am. Bd. Psychiatry. Intern Harbor Gen. Hosp., Torrance, Calif., 1967-68; resident Yale U. Dept. Psychiatry, New Haven, Conn., 1968-71; asst. prof. psychiatry U. Pitts., 1973-74; asst. clin. prof. psychiatry Brown U., Providence, R.I., 1975—. Contbr. articles to profl. jours. Maj. USAF, 1971-73. Mem. Am. Psychoanalytic Assn. Office: 172 Cushing St Providence RI 02906-2255

SHIELDS, JAMES RICHARD, alcohol and drug counselor, consultant; b. Milw., Mar. 1, 1935; s. Edmund and Louise S.; m. Marlene Brietkreutz, Nov. 20, 1957. Grad. high sch., Hartford, Wis. Cert. alcohol and drug counselor, Wis.; nat. cert. addiction counselor, alcohol and drug counselor; cert. employee asst. profl.; cert. addictions specialist. Cons. Wis. Energy Corp., Milw., 1979—. With U.S. Army, 1959-66. Mem. Occupational Programing Cons. Assn., Employee Assistance Soc. N.Am., Employee Assistance Program Assn. (cert.). Home: 7230 Maple Ln Hartford WI 53027-9703 Office: Wis Energy Corp A-149 333 W Everett St Milwaukee WI 53203

SHIELDS, LAWRENCE THORNTON, orthopedic surgeon, educator; b. Boston, Oct. 2, 1935; s. George Leo and Catherine Elizabeth (Thornton) S.; AB, Harvard U., 1957; MD, Johns Hopkins U., 1961; m. Karen S. Kraus, Sept. 21, 1968; children: Elizabeth Coulter, Laura Thornton, Sarah Daly, Michael Lawrence. Intern, Barnes Hosp., Washington U., St. Louis, 1961-62, resident, 1962-63; resident orthopedic surgeon Children's Hosp. Med. Ctr., Boston, 1966-67, Mass. Gen. Hosp., Boston, 1967-68, Peter Bent Brigham, Robert Breck Brigham hosps., Boston, 1968-69; resident orthopedic surgeon Harvard Med. Sch., Boston, 1965-69, instr., 1969—; orthopedic surgeon Peter Bent Brigham & Women's Hosp., Children's hosps., 1969—; orthopedic surgeon Waltham (Mass.) -Weston Hosp. and Med. Ctr., 1969—, also chief orthopedic surgery, pres. med. staff; mem. Waltham-Weston Orthopedic Assos.; proprietor Boston Athenaeum; mem. staffs Hahnemann Hosp., Boston, Newton-Wellesley (Mass.) hosps.; cons. orthopedic surgeon VA Hosp., Boston; mem. faculty Harvard Med. Sch.; vis. scholar Cambridge U., 1987; hon. prof. New Eng. Coll, Henniker, N.H. and Sussex, Eng., 1995; bd. dirs. Wal-West Health Systems, 1986—; pres. Massachusetts Bay Investment Trust; dir. Waltham Investment Group. Bd. dirs. Mass. Acad. Emergency Med. Technicians, Waltham Boys' Club; bd. of overseers Boston Lyric Opera, 1993—; trustee, exec. com. Waltham-Weston Hosp. and Med. Ctr. Lt. M.C., USNR, 1963-65. Diplomate Am. Bd. Orthopedic Surgery. Fellow ACS, Am. Acad. Orthopedic Surgeons, Mass. Hist. Soc. Libr., Mass. Hist. Soc.; mem. N.Y. Acad. Scis., Royal Soc. Medicine, Mass. Orthopaedic Assn. (bd. dirs., sec. 1986—), New Eng. Orthopaedic Club, Boston Orthopedic Club, Charles River Dist. (treas., exec. com., pres. 1982-83) Mass. (councillor; v.p. 1982-83) med. socs., R. Austen Freeman Soc. (v.p.), Thomas B. Quigley Sports Medicine Soc., Titanic Hist. Soc., Boston Opera Assns. (bd. dirs.), Harvard Mus. Assn., Thoreau Soc., Emerson Soc., Trollope Soc. (founding mem., bd. dirs., London), Handel and Hayden Soc. (bd. overseers), Waltham Hist. Soc., St. Botolph Club (Boston), Les Amis d'Escoffier Soc., Confrerie de La Chaine des Rotisseurs (elected 1996), Harvard Club, Algonquin Club of Boston (bd. dirs., pres. 1990—), St. Crispin's Soc. Boston (founding mem., pres. 1991—), English Speaking Union (bd. dirs.), Union Club of Boston, St. Botolph Club of Boston, Boston Lyric Opera (bd. overseers 1993), Rotary, Pi Eta (Harvard). Contbr. articles to med. jours. Home: 9 Beverly Rd Newton MA 02161-1112 Office: 721 Huntington Ave Boston MA 02115-6010 Also: 20 Hope Ave Ste 314 Waltham MA 02154-2717

SHIELDS, RICHARD OWEN, JR., emergency physician; b. Toledo, Sept. 26, 1949; s. Richard Owen and Doris Ann (Chambers) S.; m. Leslie Ann Sjogren, Sept. 8, 1971; children: Brent Alan, Erin Christine. BS, Mich. State U., 1974; MD, Wayne State U., 1979. Diplomate Nat. Bd. Med. Examiners. Intern in internal medicine Detroit Gen. Hosp., 1979-80; resident in emergency medicine Detroit Receiving Hosp., 1981-83, emergency physician, 1983-84; emergency physician Meml. Med. Ctr., Savannah, Ga., 1984—, dir. med. edn., 1986—, chmn. dept. emergency medicine, med. dir. Emergency Ctr., 1989-92; dir. Regional Poison Control Ctr., Savannah, 1985-90; oral examiner Am. Bd. Emergency Medicine, 1987—. Served with U.S. Army, 1971-72. Fellow Am. Coll. Emergency Physicians (bd. dirs. Ga. chpt. 1987—, pres. Ga. chpt. 1992-94); mem. Alpha Omega Alpha. Office: Meml Med Ctr Emergency Dept 4700 Waters Ave Savannah GA 31404-6220

SHIELDS, THOMAS FORD, orthopaedic surgeon; b. Paragould, Ark., Nov. 22, 1930; s. James Thomas and Ollie Belle (Jones) S.; m. Bethel Bragdon, Oct. 12, 1957; children: Leslie Elizabeth, Dana Alison, Thomas Bragdon, Ford Davies, James Bryant. BA, Westminster Coll., 1952; MD, St. Louis U., 1956. Diplomate Am. Bd. Orthopedic Surgery. Commd. capt. USAF, 1958, advanced through grades to Maj., 1964, resigned, 1966; intern Milwaukee County Gen. Hosp., Milw., 1956; resident in gen. surgery Passavant Meml. Hosp., Chgo., 1957-58; resident in orthopedic surgery Wilford Hall USAF Hosp., San Antonio, 1959-62; chief orthopaedic surgery St. Mary's Regional Med. Ctr., Lewiston, Maine, 1984-91; chmn. dept. surgery St. Marys Regional Med. Ctr., Lewiston, Maine, 1994-95. Fellow Am. Acad. Orthopaedic Surgrons; mem. AMA, Maine Med. Assn. (speaker ho. of dels. 1985-91, pres.-elect 1991-92, pres. 1992-93), New Eng. Orthopaedic Assn., Ea. Orthopaedic Assn. Presbyterian. Home: 375 Maple Hill Rd Auburn ME 04210-8728 Office: 137 East Ave Lewiston ME 04240-5627

SHIELDS, THOMAS WILLIAM, surgeon, educator; b. Ambridge, Pa., Aug. 17, 1922; s. John Jr. and Elizabeth (Flanagan) S.; m. Dorothea Ann Thomas, June 12, 1948; children: Thomas William, John Leland, Carol Ann. BA, Kenyon Coll., 1943, DSc (hon.), 1978; MD, Temple U., 1947. Resident surgery Northwestern U. Med. Sch., Chgo., 1949-55; prof. surgery Northwestern U. Med. Sch., 1968-92, prof. Emeritus of surgery, 1992—; practice medicine specializing in surgery Chgo., 1956—; chief of surgery VA Lakeside Hosp., Chgo., 1968-87; chief thoracic surgery VA Lakeside Med. Ctr., Chgo., 1987-90. Editor: General Thoracic Surgery, 1972, 4th edit., 1994, Bronchial Carcinoma, 1974, Mediastinal Surgery, 1991; assoc. editor Surgery, Gynecology and Obstetrics, Annals of Thoracic Surgery, 1993—; mem. editorial bd. Annals of Thoracic Surgery, Lung Cancer; contbr. articles to profl. jours. Served with U.S. Army, 1951-53. Mem. ACS, AMA, Am. Assn. for Thoracic Surgery, Soc. Thoracic Surgery, Central, Western Surg. Assns., Société Internationale de Chirurgie, Soc. for Surgery of Alimentary Tract, Internat. Assn. for Study Lung Cancer, Pan Pacific Surg. Assn., Phi Beta Kappa, Sigma Xi, Alpha Omega Alpha. Home: 1721 Jenks St Evanston IL 60201-1528 Office: 250 E Superior St Ste 201 Chicago IL 60611-2914

SHIFFMAN, MELVIN ARTHUR, surgeon, oncologist; b. Bklyn., Aug. 23, 1931; s. Albert and Eva (Krieger) S.; m. Pearl Asher, Aug. 28, 1955; children: Scott, Karen, Denise. BS in Biochemistry, Union Coll., 1949; student dental medicine, Harvard U., 1953-54; MD, Northwestern U., 1957; JD, Western State U., 1976. Diplomate Am. Bd. Surgery; cert. Am. Bd. Cosmetic Surgery, Am. Bd. Forensic Medicine. Intern Los Angeles County Hosp., 1957-58; resident VA Hosp., Long Beach, Calif., 1960-64; pvt. practice oncologic surgery, cosmetic and reconstructive surgery Anaheim, Calif., 1964; chief of surgery Anaheim Gen. Hosp., 1969; chief of surgery Tustin (Calif.) Community Hosp., 1973, also chief of staff, bd. dirs., 1974; asst. clin. prof. surgery U. Calif., Irvine, 1968-83; pvt. practice med.-legal cons. Tustin, 1976; prof. surgery and oncology, St. Lucia (West Indies) Health Scis. U., 1982-84; past chmn. bd. dirs. Monte Park Hosp., El Monte, Calif., 1975. Editor-in-chief Am. Jour. Cosmetic Surgery, 1993—; contbr. articles to med. jours. With USPHS, 1958-60. Fellow Internat. Biog. Assn., Internat. Coll. Surgeons, Am. Coll. Legal Medicine, Am. Soc. Cosmetic Breast Surgery; mem. Soc. Head and Neck Surgeons, Am. Soc. Clin. Oncology, Soc. Abdominal Surgeons, Am. Acad. Cosmetic Surgery, Am. Soc. Liposuction surgery, Am. Soc. Law, Medicine and Ethics, Orange County Oncologic Soc. (founder, pres. 1970), Am. Cancer Soc. (founder, pres. 1970), Am. Cancer Soc. (pres. Orange County chpt. 1971-73) Union Am. Physicians and Dentists (pres. 1982-88, bd. dirs. Calif. Fedn. 1982-88, bd. dirs. Orange County chpt. 1988), Safari Club. Office: 1101 Bryan Ave Ste G Tustin CA 92680-4401

SHIGA, TAKESHI, physiology educator; b. Nishinomiya, Hyogo, Japan, Nov. 29, 1931; s. Isamu and Yasuko (Noguchi) S.; m. Sanae Tanaka, June 15, 1963; children: Jun, Akira. MD, Osaka (Japan) U., 1957, D Med. Sci., 1962. Rsch. assoc. dept. physiology Osaka U., 1962-63, 65-70, assoc. prof., 1970-74, prof., 1989-95; emeritus prof. Osaka U., Palo Alto, Calif., 1995—; postdoctoral fellow instrument div. Varian Assocs., Palo Alto, Calif., 1963-64; postdoctoral fellow dept. biochemistry U. Oreg., Portland, 1964-65; prof. dept. physiology Ehime (Japan) U., 1974-89; vis. fellow Inst. Biol. Phys. Chemistry, Paris, 1966-67. Author: Physiological Chemistry, 1980, Human Physiology, 1991; author, editor: Biological Effect of Magnetic Field, 1991. Mem. Internat. Soc. Biorheology, Internat. Electron Spin Resonance Soc., Japanese Soc. Physiology, Japanese Soc. Biochemistry and Biophysics. Office: Kinran Coll, Dept Physiology, 5-25-1 Fujishirodai Suita, Osaka, Osaka 565, Japan

SHIH, JASON CHIA-HSING, biotechnology educator; b. Chien-Chen, Hunan, China, Oct. 8, 1939; came to U.S., 1969; m. Jane Chu-Huei Chien, Aug. 31, 1966; children: Giles C., Tim C. BS, Nat. Taiwan U., Taipei, 1963; MS, Nat. Taiwan U., 1966; PhD, Cornell U., 1973. Lectr. Tunghai U., Taichung, Taiwan, 1966-69; rsch. asst. Cornell U., Ithaca, N.Y., 1969-73; sr. rsch. assoc. Cornell U., Ithica, N.Y., 1975-76; rshc. assoc. U. Ill., Urbana, 1973-75; asst. prof. N.C. State U., Raleigh, 1976-80; assoc. prof. N.C. State U., Raleigh, N.C., 1980-88, prof., 1988—; vis. fellow U. Coll. Cardiff, Wales, 1983; sci. advisor Shenyang Agrl. U., China, 1985—; vis. prof. Nat. Taiwan U., 1986, spl. advisor to the pres., 1994; vis. specialist UNDP, China, 1987-93; vis. prof. Bowman Gray Sch. Medicine, 1991. Patentee in field. Exec. com. mem. Triangle Area Chinese Am. Soc., Raleigh, 1979-82, pres., 1982-83, chmn. bd., 1992-93; coord. N.C. State U. exch. programs with China and Taiwan, 1985—; sci. exch. fellow to Spelderholt Poultry Rsch. Ctr., The Netherlands, USDA-Office of Internat. Coop. and Devel., 1994, 95. Recipient numerous rsch. grants, 1977—; Pew Nat. fellow faculty scholar, 1990-91. Fellow Am. Heart Assn., Arteriosclerosis Rsch. Coun.; mem. Am. Instn. Nutrition (Travel award 1981, 89), Am. Soc. for Microbiology, Poultry Sci. Assn., Soc. Chinese Bioscientists in Am. (sec. and treas. 1985-86), Phi Kappa Phi, Sigma Iota Rho (J. Rigney award for Internat. Svc. 1994). Office: N C State U Dept Poultry Sci Raleigh NC 27695-7608

SHIH, TING-FANG TIFFANY, radiologist; b. Taipei, Taiwan, China, Jan. 2, 1959; d. Shen-Mou and Rosita (Chen) Shih; m. Tseng-Wu Liu, Jan. 6, 1986; 1 child, Huei-Tien. MB, Nat. Taiwan U., 1980, MD, 1984. Lic. physician, Taiwan; diplomate as Diagnostic Radiologist, Taiwan. Chief resident dept. radiology Nat. Taiwan U. Hosp., Taipei, 1987-88, vis. staff, 1988—, asst. prof., 1989-96, dir. sect. of musculoskeletal image dept. med. image, 1995—; assoc. prof. medicine Nat. Taiwan U., Taipei, 1996—; clin. instr. dept. radiol. sci. UCLA Med. Ctr., 1989-90; organizer, cons. Nat. Inst. Health, Taiwan, 1994—; organizer, cons. An-Drukon Buddhist Hosp., Taipei, 1994—; sr. cons. Sun Yat-Sen Cancer Ctr., Taipei, 1990—. Inventor in field; contbr. articles to profl. jours. Recipient award for best rsch. project China Med. Bd., 1992. Mem. Am. Roentgen Ray Soc., Radiol. Soc. N.Am., Radiol. Soc. Republic of China. Office: National Taiwan Univ Hosp, 7 Chung-Shan S Rd, Taipei Taiwan

SHIKATA, JUN-ICHI, surgery educator; b. Tokyo, Japan, Jan. 28, 1926; s. Keiichi and Masago (Suminokura) S.; m. Sakiko Mita, May 12, 1960. MD, U. Tokyo, 1950, PhD, 1960. Intern and surg. resident U. Tokyo Hosp., 1950-56; rsch. fellow faculty medicine U. Tokyo, 1956-58; rsch. fellow Ind. U. Med. Ctr., Indpls., 1958-59; asst. surgeon U. Tokyo Hosp., 1959-62; chief surgeon Tokyo Met. Bokuto Hosp., 1962-71; clin. assoc. prof. U. Tokyo, 1962-71; prof., chmn. First Dept. Surgery Teikyo U. Sch. Medicine, Tokyo, 1971-92, prof. emeritus, 1992—; cons. Aisei Hosp., Tokyo, 1980-95, Icho (Gastrointestinal) Hosp., Tokyo, 1986-95/. Author: Diagnosis of the Acute Abdomen, 1968, Abdominal Trauma, 1971, Intestinal Obstruction 1990. Sponsor World Ecol. Rsch. Found., Tokyo, 1989—. Mem. ACS, Japan Surg. Soc., Japan Soc. Gastrointestinal Surgery, Soc. for Surgery of the Alimentary Tract, Soc. Internat. de Chirurgie. Home: 1432 Bramwell Rd, West Vancouver, BC Canada V7S 2N9 Office: Teikyo U Sch Medicine, 2-11-1 Kaga, Itabashi-ku Tokyo 173, Japan

SHILLING, KAY MARLENE, psychiatrist; b. Scottsbluff, Nebr., July 1, 1952; d. Harrison Gene and Rose Marie (Allen) Herber; m. Mark Randall Shilling, July 2, 1977. B.S., U. Nebr.-Lincoln, 1976; M.D., U. Nebr.-Omaha, 1980. Diplomate Nat. Bd. Med. Examiners. Resident in psychiatry U. Nebr. Med. Ctr., Omaha, 1981-84; practice medicine specializing in psychiatry, Omaha, 1984—; bd. dirs. La Plaza Cmty. Health Ctr. Mem. AMA, Royal Soc. Medicine, Ctrl. Neuro Psychiat. Assn. (bd. dirs., pres. 1996-97), Am. Med. Women's Assn. (pres. Omaha br. 1986-88, dir. Nebr. State chpt. 1988-94, regional gov. 1993-95, bd. dirs. 1993-95, book reviewer for JAMWA, Outstanding Physician award 1989, 90-93, nat. community svc. award 1990), Am. Psychiat. Assn., Met. Omaha Med. Soc., Nebr. Med. Assn., Alpha Xi Delta. Avocations: gourmet cooking, interior decorating, house renovation. Home: 1103 S 80th St Omaha NE 68124-1419 Office: 7602 Pacific St Ste 302 Omaha NE 68114-5405

SHILLINGBURG, HERBERT THOMPSON, JR., dental educator; b. Ganado, Ariz., Mar. 21, 1938; s. Herbert Thompson and Stefi Marie (Schuster) S.; m. Constance Joanne Murphy, June 11, 1960; children: Lisa Grace, Leslie Susan, Lara Stephanie. Student U. N.Mex., 1955-58, 65-66; DDS, U. So. Calif., 1962. Gen. practice dentistry, Albuquerque, 1964-67; asst. prof. fixed prosthodontics sect. UCLA Sch. Dentistry, 1967-70, chmn. 1970-72; chmn. dept. fixed prosthodontics U. Okla. Coll. Dentistry, Oklahoma City, 1972—, David Ross Boyd Disting. prof., 1983; cons. VA Hosp., Muskogee, Okla., 1975-84, Oklahoma City, 1977-93, U.S. Army Dental Activity, Ft. Knox, Ky., 1980-94. Author: (also in Japanese, German, Greek, Spanish, Italian, French, Portuguese and Polish) Preparations for Cast Gold Restorations, 1974; Fundamentals of Fixed Prosthodontics, 1976, 2d edit., 1981; Guide to Occlusal Waxing, 1979, 2d edit., 1984; Restoration of the Endodontically Treated Tooth, 1984, Fundamentals of Tooth Preparations for Cast Metal and Porcelain Restorations, 1987; co-editor Quintessence of Dental Technology, 1984-88; sect. editor Quintessence Internat., 1988—; mem. editl. coun. Jour. Prosthetic Dentistry. Served to capt. U.S. Army, 1962-64. Recipient award for Teaching Excellence, UCLA Sch. Dentistry, 1969, 72, 73, U. Okla. Coll. Dentistry, 1976, 78, 82, 87, 93, 94, 1st prize Am. Med. Writers Assn., 1988, La Médaille de la Ville de Paris (échelon Argent), 1990; named O U Assocs. Disting. Lectr., 1989. Fellow Am. Coll. Dentists; mem. ADA, Acad. Operative Dentistry, Am. Acad. Fixed Prosthodontics, Am. Acad. Restorative Dentistry, Am. Coll. Prosthodontists (hon.), Okla. State Dental Assn., Internat. Assn. Dental Rsch., Omicron Kappa Upsilon. Republican. Episcopalian. Avocations: travel, photography. Home: 1312 Brixton Rd Edmond OK 73034-3314 Office: U Okla Coll Dentistry PO Box 26901 # U Oklahoma City OK 73190

SHIMADA, KAZUHITO, health facility administrator; b. Asahi, Chiba, Japan, Feb. 18, 1959; s. Tsutomu and Natsumi (Nomura) S.; m. Fumi Matsuyama, Sept. 30, 1990; children: Yumi, Eiji, Mina. MD, U. Tsukuba, Japan, 1983, PhD, 1987; MS in Aerospace Medicine, Wright State Univ., 1995. Otorhinolaryngologist Saku Sogo Hosp., Nagano, Japan, 1987-88; chief otolaryngology Ibaraki (Japan) Kenritsu Chuo Hosp., 1989-93; med. officer Space Sta. Dept., Nat. Space Devel. Agy. of Japan, Ibaraki, 1993; founding dir. Kenritsu Rehab. Ctr., Ibaraki, 1989-90; instr. Wright State U., Ohio, 1993-95; resident NASA Johnson Space Ctr., 1995-96. Author: Sailplane Aerobatics, Japanese edit., 1990, Practical Wave Flying (transl.), 1992. Recipient Cert., Ednl. Commn. for Fgn. Med. Grads., 1983. Mem. AMA, Acoustical Soc. Am., Aerospace Med. Assn. of U.S. and Japan, Civil Aviation Med. Assn. (U.S.), Oto-Rhino-Laryngological Soc. of Japan (delegate). also: Nat Space Devel Agency, Tsukuba Space Ctr, Ibaraki 305, Japan

SHIMAHARA, KENZO, applied microbiology educator; b. Tokyo, Mar. 22, 1928; s. Itsuzo and Mikie (Miyagawa) S.; m. Yoko Tsujii; 1 child, Taku. B. Engring., Keio U., Tokyo, 1950, PhD, 1974. Chem. engr. Nitto-Kagaku Co. Ltd., Yokohama, Japan, 1950-54; tchr. Musashi-Kogyo U. High Sch., Tokyo, 1955-62; lectr. Seikei U., Tokyo, 1962-64, assoc. prof., 1964-74, prof., 1974-93, prof. emeritus, 1993—; guest prof. Liaoning Normal U., Dalian, 1990—. Editor: Lecture Demonstrations in Chemistry, 1982; author: Biochemistry, 1991, (with others) Chitin, Chitosan and Related Enzymes, 1984; editor, author (with others): Erroneous Descriptions in the History of Chemistry, 1988. Mem. Japanese Soc. for the History of Chemistry (bd. dirs. 1982—), Japanese Soc. for Chitin and Chitosan (v.p. 1989-92, pres. 1994-95). Home: 6-27-43 Higashi-Koigakubo, Kokubunji 185, Japan

SHIMAZAKI, YASUHISA, cardiac surgeon; b. Kagoshima, Japan, Feb. 19, 1946; s. Hisashi and Sumiko (Tsukada) S.; m. Yuko Inomata, Oct. 10, 1982; children: Taisuke John, Kyosuke, Yasuro, Mariko. MD, Osaka U., 1970, DMS, 1982. Resident in surgery Osaka U. Hosp., 1970-77; asst. Med. Sch. Osaka U., 1977-82, sr. assoc., 1986—; Graham Traveling Fellow Am. Assn. for Thoracic Surgery, Birmingham, Ala., 1982-83; cardiovascular surgery fellow U. Ala., Birmingham, 1983-84; staff surgeon Osaka Boshi Ctr. Hosp., Sakai, 1984-86; cardiovascular surgery fellow U. Ala., 1988-89; asst. prof. surgery Osaka U., 1991-95, assoc. prof. surgery, 1995-95; prof. surgery Sch. Medicine Yamagata U., 1995—. Mem. Internat. Soc. Cardiovascular Surgery, Interat. Soc. Heart & Lung Transplantation, Japan Assn. Thoracic Surgery, Japan Assn. Pediat. Surgery. Home: 3-4-1-303 Iidanishi, Yamagata 990-23, Japan Office: Yamagata U Sch Medicine, 2-2-2 Iidanishi, Yamagata 990-23, Japan

SHIMMIN, MARGARET ANN, women's health nurse; b. Forbes, N.D., Oct. 26, 1941; d. George Robert and Reba Aleda (Strain) S. Diploma in Nursing, St. Luke's Hosp. Sch. Nursing, Fargo, N.D., 1962; BSW, U. West Fla., 1978; cert. ob-gyn nurse practitioner, U. Ala., Birmingham, 1983, MPH, 1986. Lic. nurse, Fla., N.D., Ala. Head nurse, emergency room St. Luke's Hosps., Fargo, 1962-67; charge nurse, labor and delivery, perinatal nurse educator Sacred Heart Hosp., Pensacola, Fla., 1970-82; ARNP Escambia County Pub. Health Unit, Pensacola, 1983-89; cmty. health nursing cons. Dist. 1 Health and Rehab. Svcs., Pensacola, 1989—. Capt. nurse corps U.S. Army, 1967-70, Japan. Mem. NAACOG (cert. maternal-gynecol.-neonatal nursing 1978, ob-gyn nurse practitioner 1983), Fla. Nurses' Assn., ANA, N.W. Fla. ARNP (past sec./treas.), Fla. Perinatal Assn., Nat. Perinatal Assn., Healthy Mothers/Healthy Babies Coalition, Fla. Pub. Health Assn., U. West Fla. Alumni Assn., U. Ala. at Birmingham Sch. of Public Health Alumni Assn., Phi Alpha. Republican. Presbyterian. Home: 8570 Olympia Rd Pensacola FL 32514-8029 Office: Dist 1 HRS 160 Governmental Ctr Pensacola FL 32501

SHINDELL, SIDNEY, medical educator, physician; b. New Haven, May 31, 1923; s. Benjamin Abraham and Freda (Mann) S.; m. Gloria Emhoff, June 17, 1945; children: Barbara, Roger, Lawrence, Judith. BS, Yale U., 1944; MD, L.I. Coll. Medicine, 1946; postgrad., Emory U., 1948-49; LLB, George Washington U., 1951. Diplomate Am. Bd. Preventive Medicine, Am. Bd. Occupl. Medicine. With USPHS, 1947-52; med. dir. Conn. Commn. on Chronically Ill and Aged, 1952-57, Am. Joint Distbn. Com., 1957-59; asst. prof. preventive medicine U. Pitts., 1960-65; dir. Hosp. Utilization project Western Pa., 1965-66; prof. dept. preventive medicine Med. Coll. Wis., Milw., 1966-93, chmn. dept., 1966-89, dir. office internat. affairs, 1989-93, prof. emeritus, 1993—; exec. dir. Health Svc. Data of Wis., 1967-73; mem. bd. sci. advisers Am. Coun. on Sci. and Health, 1978-87, 92—; mem. Nat. Adv. Com. on Occupl. Safety and Health, U.S. Dept. Labor, 1982-84; cons. Caribbean Epidemiology Ctr. Pan. Am. Health Orgn./WHO, 1988, field epidemiology tng. program, Thailand, 1989, Nat. Office Occupl. and Environ. Medicine Royal Thai Ministry of Pub. Health, 1990—; mem. gov's white paper com. on health care reform, Wis., 1993; acad. cons. Faculties of Medicine, Padjadjaran U., Bandung, Airlangga U., Surabaya, Indonesia, 1993, 94; bd. dirs. Am. Coun. of Sci. and Health, 1987-89, chmn. 1989-92. Author: Statistics, Science and Sense, 1964, A Method of Hospital Utilization Review, 1966, The Law in Medical Practice, 1966, A Coursebook on Health Care Delivery, 1976; contbr. 120 articles to profl. jours. Gubernatorial appointee to bd. trustees Med. Coll. Wis., 1996—; mem. Sch. Bd. Fox Point-Bayside (Wis.), Sch. Dist., 1970-71; vice-chmn. Citizens' Adv. Com. Met. Problems, 1971-72; bd. dirs. Med. Care Evaluation S.E. Wis., 1973-76. With AUS, 1943-46. Recipient Frank L. Babbott Meml. award SUNY Health Sci. Ctr., Bklyn., 1996. Fellow Am. Coll. Preventive Medicine (mem. bd. regents 1982-85), APHA, Am. Coll. Occupl. and Environ. Medicine, Am. Coll. Legal Medicine; mem. Am. Assn. Health Data Sys. (sec. 1972-73), Assn. Tchrs. Preventive Medicine (dir. 1973-74, pres. 1976-77, Spl. Recognition award 1992), Assn. Occupl. Health Profls. (pres. 1980-90), Wis. State Med. Soc. (mem. coun. on health care financing and delivery, mem. coun. on govt. affairs, mem. ho. of dels., 50 Yr. Recognition award 1996), Am. Coll. Physician Execs., Internat. Commn. on Occupl. Health, Aircraft Owners and Pilots Assn., Masons, CAP. Home: 929 N Astor St # 2507 Milwaukee WI 53202-3490 Office: PO Box 26509 Milwaukee WI 53226-0509

SHINE, KENNETH IRWIN, cardiologist, educator; b. Worcester, Mass., 1935. Grad., Harvard Coll., 1957; MD, Harvard U., 1961. Diplomate Am. Bd. Internal Medicine. Intern Mass. Gen. Hosp., 1961-62, resident, 1962-63, 65-66, fellow in cardiology, 1966-68; surgeon USPHS, 1963-65; assoc. in medicine Beth Israel Hosp., Resont, Va., from 1969; instr. Harvard Med. Sch., from 1968; asst. prof. medicine UCLA Sch. Medicine, 1971-73, assoc. prof., 1973-77, prof., 1977-92, prof. emeritus, 1993—, dir. CCU, 1971-75, chief div. cardiology, 1975-79, vice chmn. dept. medicine, 1979-81, exec. chmn., 1981-86, dean, 1986-92; clin. prof. medicine Georgetown U. Med. Ctr., Washington, 1993—; provost for med. scis. UCLA Sch. Medicine, 1991-92; pres. Inst. Medicine, Washington, 1992—. Mem. Am. Heart Assn. (pres. 1986-87), Assn. Am. Med. Colls. (adminstrv. bd. coun. deans 1989-92, exec. bd. 1990-92, chmn. coun. deans 1991-92). Office: Institute of Medicine 2101 Constitution Ave NW Washington DC 20418-0007*

SHINEFIELD, HENRY ROBERT, pediatrician; b. Paterson, N.J., Oct. 11, 1925; s. Louis and Sarah (Kaplan) S.; m. Jacqueline Marilyn Walker; children: Jill, Michael, Kimberley Strome, Melissa Strome. B.A., Columbia U., 1945, M.D., 1948. Diplomate: Am. Bd. Pediatrics (examiner, 1975—, bd. dirs., 1979-84, v.p., 1981-84). Rotating intern Mt. Sinai Hosp., N.Y.C., 1948-49; pediatric intern Duke Hosp., Durham, N.C., 1949-50; asst. resident pediatrician N.Y. Hosp. (Cornell), 1950-51, pediatrician to outpatients, 1953-59, instr. in pediatrics, 1959-60, asst. prof., 1960-64, asso. prof., 1964-65, asst. attending pediatrician, 1959-63, asso. attending pediatrician, 1963-65; pediatrician to outpatients Children's Hosp., Oakland, Calif., 1951-53; chief of pediatrics Kaiser-Permanente Med. Center, San Francisco, 1965-89, chief emeritus, 1989—; co-dir. Kaiser-Permanente Pediat4ric Vaccine Study Ctr., San Francisco, 1984—; asso. clin. prof. pediatrics Sch. Medicine U. Calif., 1966-68, clin. prof. pediatrics, 1968—, clin. prof. dermatology, 1970—; asso. attending pediatrician Paterson (N.J.) Gen. Hosp., 1955-59; chief of pediatrics Kaiser Found. Hosp., San Francisco, 1965—; attending Moffitt Hosp., San Francisco, 1967—; practice medicine specializing in pediatrics Paterson, 1953-59; cons. San Francisco Gen. Hosp., 1967—, Childrens Hosp., San Francisco, 1970—, Mt. Zion Hosp., San Francisco, 1970—; mem. research grants rev. br. NIH, HEW, 1970-74; med. dir. USPHSR, 1969—; bd. dirs. San Francisco Peer Rev. Orgn., 1975-81, sec., exec. com., 1976-81; chmn. Calif. State Child Health Disability Bd., 1973-82; mem. Inst. of Medicine, Nat. Acad. Scis., 1980—; cons. Bur. Drugs FDA, 1970, NIH, HEW, 1974—. Editorial bds. Western Jour. of Medicine, 1968-80, American Jour. of Diseases of Children, 1970-82; contbr. writings to profl. publs. Chmn. San Francisco Med. Adv. Com. Nat. Found. March of Dimes, 1969-80. Served with USPHS, 1951-53. Fellow Am. Acad. Pediatrics (com. of fetus and newborn 1969-76, mem. com. on drugs 1978-82); mem. AMA, Soc. Pediatric Research, Infectious Diseases Soc. Am., Western Pediatric Soc., Western Soc. Clin. Research, Am. Pediatric Soc., Phi Beta Kappa. Home: 2705 Larkin St San Francisco CA 94109-1117 Office: 2200 Ofarrell St San Francisco CA 94115-3357

SHINN, ARTHUR FREDERICK, clinical pharmacologist, business executive, educator; b. N.Y.C., May 23, 1945; s. A. Frederick and Eleanor (McDonald) S.; children: Jeffrey, Kara Nicole, Caitlin Jennifer. BS, L.I. U. Bklyn. Coll. Pharmacy, 1968; PharmD, U. Mich., 1972. Lic. pharmacist, Tenn., Mo., Mich. Supr., dir. drug info. ctr. William Beaumont Hosp., Royal Oak, Mich., 1972-76; asst. prof. clin. pharmacy Wayne State U., Detroit, 1972-76; asst. prof., dir. drug info. ctr. St. Louis Coll. Pharmacy, 1976-78; mgr. profl. relations med. dept. Beecham Labs., Bristol, Tenn., 1978-82; med. dir., exec. v.p. Profl. Drug Systems, St. Louis, 1982-89, also bd. dirs.; v.p. clin. svcs., gen. mgr. Managed Prescription Svcs., Inc., St. Louis, 1989-96; pres. Prescription-Mgmt. Consultants, Inc., Chesterfield, Mo., 1996—; adj. assoc. prof. family practice Quillen Dishner Sch. Medicine, Johnson City, Tenn., 1979-82; staff cons. clin. pharmacology Faith Hosp., Creve Coeur, Mo., 1983-90; adj. clin. instr. pharmacy St. Louis Coll. Pharmacy, 1989-96; pres. Med. Drug Info. Consultants, 1989-96. Editor: Evaluations of Drug Interactions, 1985-89; cons. clin. editor: Mosby's Pharmacology in Nursing, 1986; mem. editorial bd. Jour. of Pharmacy Practice, 1989—, P&T Jour., 1992—; contbr. numerous articles to profl. jours. Fellow NIH, 1968. Fellow Am. Soc. Cons. Pharmacists; mem. Am. Coll. Clin. Pharmacy, Acad. Managed Care Pharmacy, Am. Soc. Hosp. Pharmacists, Drug Info. Assn., Rho Chi, Iota Mu Pi. Office: Prescription Mgmt Consultants Inc 515 N Sixth St Ste # 1100 630 Clovertrail Dr Chesterfield MO 63017

SHINNAR, SHLOMO, child neurologist, educator; b. Haifa, Israel, Nov. 11, 1950; s. Reuel and Miryam (Halpern) S.; m. Shoshana Ellen Cohen, Aug. 11, 1974; children: Ora Rivka, Aviva Batya, Avraham Ever. BA in Physics summa cum laude, Columbia Coll., 1971; PhD, Albert Einstein Coll. Medicine, 1977, MD, 1978. Diplomate Am. Bd. Pediat., Am. Bd. Psychiatry and Neurology, with spl. competence in child neurology. Intern, asst. resident in pediatrics, fellow Johns Hopkins Hosp., Balt., 1978-80, asst. resident, resident in neurology, fellow, 1980-83; from asst. prof. neurology and pediatrics to prof. neurology and pediatrics Albert Einstein Coll. Medicine, Bronx, 1983—; from asst. attending to attending neurology and pediatrics Montefiore Med. Ctr., Bronx Mcpl. & North Ctrl. Bronx Hosps., 1983—; dir. CERC Seizure Clinic R.K. Kennedy Ctr., Bronx, 1983—; co-dir. Epilepsy Mgmt. Ctr. Montefiore Med. Ctr. Albert Einstein Coll. Medicine, Bronx, 1983-86, dir., 1986—; mem. adv. bd. Epilepsy Inst., N.Y.C., 1984—, instnl. rev. bd. protection of human subjects Montefiore Med. Ctr., Bronx, 1985—, vice-chmn., 1989—; adj. sch. scientist Gertrude Sergievsky Ctr. Columbia Coll. Physicians and Surgeons, N.Y.C., 1985—, Sergievsky Scholar, 1986—; cons. in field. Field editor Epilepsy Advances, 1987-93; editl. bd. The Neurologist, 1993—, Epilepsia, 1994—, Pediatric Neurology, 1996—; contbr. articles to profl. jours. N.Y. State Regents scholar, 1967-71; Martin and Emily L. Fisher fellow, 1991—. Fellow Am. Acad. Pediats.; mem. Am. Epilepsy Soc. (profl. adv. bd. chmn. childhood onset epilepsy com. 1993-95, councillor 1992-95, Rsch. Recognition award 1989), Am. Acad. Neurology, Child Neurology Soc., Eastern EEG Soc., Internat. Child Neurology soc., Nat. Assn. Epilepsy Ctrs., Soc. for Pediat. Rsch., Am. Neurol. Assn. Office: Montefiore Med Ctr 111 E 210th St Bronx NY 10467-2490

SHIOIRI, TAKAYUKI, pharmaceutical science educator; b. Yokohama, Kanagawa, Japan, Aug. 15, 1935; s. Hideji and Hisako (Iyoda) S.; m. Haruko Terashima, Mar. 13, 1966; children: Azusa, Akane. BSc, U. Tokyo, 1959, MSc, 1961, PhD, 1967; Diploma, Imperial Coll., London, 1970. Lic. pharmacist. Instr. U. Tokyo, 1962-64, rsch. assoc., 1964-77, assoc. prof., 1977; vis. academics Imperial Coll., London, 1968-70; prof. Sch. Pharm. Scis. Nagoya (Japan) City U., 1977—. Regional editor Tetrahedron, 1990—. Recipient Young Scientists award Pharm. Soc. Japan, 1974, PSJ award, 1993, Abbott award, 1978, Aichi Pharm. award Aichi Pharmacist Soc., 1981. Home: 1-18-12 Minamigaoka, Nisshin Aichi-Ken 470-01, Japan Office: Nagoya City U Sch Pharm Sci, 3-1 Tanabe-Dori, Mizuho-Ku, Nagoya 467, Japan

SHIOMOTO, GAIL MICHIKO, medical oncologist, hematologist; b. Chgo., Mar. 23, 1946; d. Tokumi Shiomoto and Sakae Sako. BS, U. Ill., Chgo., 1968, MD, 1972, M in Health Professions Edn., 1989, MPH, 1989. Diplomate Am. Bd. Internal Medicine, Am. Bd. Hematology, Am. Bd. Med. Oncology. Intern in internal medicine L.A. County Hosp., 1972-73; resident in radiology U. Chgo., 1973-74; resident in internal medicine Hines VA Hosp., Maywood, Ill., 1974-75, Northwestern Ill. Hosp., Chgo., 1975-76; fellow in med. oncology Prebyn. St. Luke's Hosp., Chgo., 1976-78; fellow in hematology Michael Reese Hosp., Chgo., 1978-79; attending physician in hematology and oncology Cook County Hosp., Chgo., 1979-81; chmn. dept. med. oncology Cook County Hosp., 1981—. Home: 5600 N Francisco Chicago IL 60659 Office: Cook County Hosp 1835 W Harrison Chicago IL 60612

SHIOYA, NOBUYUKI, plastic and reconstructive surgery educator; b. Tokyo, Dec. 14, 1931; s. Nobuo and Matsue Shioya; m. Setsuko Ohkubo, July 8, 1957; 1 child, Nobukazu. MD, Tokyo U., 1955. Asst. instr. surgery Albany (N.Y.) Med. Ctr. Hosp., 1957-61, instr. surgery, 1961-62, asst. instr. plastic surgery, 1962-64; instr. plastic surgery Tokyo U. Faculty of Medicine, 1964-68; lectr. plastic surgery Yokohama (Japan) City U. Sch. of Medicine, 1968-73; prof. plastic surgery Kitasato U. Sch. of Medicine, Sagamihara, Kanagawa, Japan, 1973—; mem. staff Washinzaka Hosp., Yokohama, Tokyo Med. Clinic. Author: Plastic Surgery, 1978, The Primer of Plastic Surgery, 1980, Aesthetic Plastic Surgery, 1987; editor: Plastic Surgery Operation, 1982. Recipient prize Japanese Soc. Biomaterials, 1991. Mem. Internat. Confedn. of Plastic and Reconstructive Surgeons (asst. gen. sec.), Japan Soc. Plastic and Reconstructive Surgery (mem. exec. com.). Office: Kitsasato U Sch Medicine, 1-15-1 Kitasato Sagamihara, Kanagawa 228, Japan

SHIPLEY, NANCY LOUISE, health science association executive; b. Wilkinsburg, Pa., June 26, 1950; d. Oran G. and Catherine P. (Soisson) S. BS, Slippery Rock (Pa.) State Coll., 1972, MEd, 1974. Tchr. phys. edn. Monroeville (Pa.) Jr. High Sch., 1972-77; rep. sales Knoll Pharms., Whippany, N.J., 1978-80; N.Y. regional rep. med. sales Surgidev Corp., Morristown, N.J., 1980-82; regional rep. med. sales Ioptex, Morristown, 1982-84; pres. surg. custom trays Surg. Services and Supplies, Inc., Montvale, N.J., 1984-85; sales med. instruments Allergan Humphrey Corp., New Eng., 1985-87; exec. adminstr. Eye Inst. Essex, Belleville, N.J., 1987-89; sr. sales exec. Allergan Med. Optics, Detroit, 1989-90; N.Y. regional sales mgr. Allergan Med. Optics, Scotch Plains, N.J., 1990-91; mgr. med. bus. mgmt. group programs Allergan Med. Optics, Irvine, Calif., 1991-93; v.p. BSM Consulting Group, Incline Village, Nev., 1993-95; sole gen. ptnr. and pres. Nat. Healthcare Bus. Solutions L.P., Laguna Hills, Calif., 1996—. Contbr. articles to profl. jours. Republican. Home: 25402 Shadywood Laguna Niguel CA 92677-1970 Office: Nat Healthcare Business Solutions LP 27071 Cabot Rd Ste 103 Laguna Hills CA 92653

SHIREMAN, JOAN FOSTER, social work educator; b. Cleve., Oct. 28, 1933; d. Louis Omar and Genevieve (Duguid) Foster; m. Charles Howard Shireman, Mar. 18, 1967; 1 child, David Louis. BA, Radcliffe Coll., 1956; MA, U. Chgo., 1959, PhD, 1968. Caseworker N.H. Children's Aid Soc., Manchester, 1959-61; dir. research Chgo. Child Care Soc., 1968-72; assoc. prof. U. Ill., Chgo., 1972-85; prof. Portland (Oreg.) State U., 1985—, dir. PhD program, 1992—; interim exec. dir. Partnership for Rsch., Tng. and Grad. Edn. in Child Welfare, 1994; research cons. child welfare orgns., Ill., 1968-85, Oreg. 1985—; lectr. U. Chgo., 1968-72. Co-author: Care and Commitment: Foster Parent Adoption Decisions, 1985; mem. editl. bd. Jour. Sch. Social Work, 1978-81, Social Work Rsch. and Abstracts, 1990-93, Children and Youth Svcs. Rev., 1990-95, Jour. Social Work Edn., 1990-95; contbr. articles to profl. jours., chpts. to books. Bd. dirs. Oreg. chpt. Nat. Assn. for Prevention Child Abuse, 1985-87; bd. dirs. Friendly House, Portland, 1991—, pres., 1995-96; mem. adv. com. children's svcs. divsn. State of Oreg., 1985-95. Grantee HEW, 1980-82, Chgo. Community Trust, 1982-86, Oreg. Children's Trust Fund, 1991-96. Mem. NASW, AAUP, Am. Profl. Soc. Abuse of Children, Children First Oreg., Acad. Cert. Social Workers, Coun. on Social Work Edn., Phi Beta Kappa. Home: 2535 SW Sherwood Dr Portland OR 97201-1679 Office: Portland State U Grad Sch Social Work PO Box 751 Portland OR 97207-0751

SHIRES, GEORGE THOMAS, surgeon, educator; b. Waco, Tex., Nov. 22, 1925; s. George Thomas and Donna Mae (Smith) S.; m. Robbie Jo Martin, Nov. 27, 1948; children: Donna Blain, George Thomas III, Jo Ellen. MD, U. Tex., Dallas, 1948. Diplomate Am. Bd. Surgery (dir. 1968-74, chmn. 1972-74). Intern Mass. Meml. Hosp., Boston, 1948-49; resident Parkland Meml. Hosp., Dallas, 1950-53; mem. faculty U. Tex. Southwestern Med. Sch. at Dallas, 1953-74, assoc. prof. surgery, acting chmn. dept., 1960-61, prof., chmn. dept., 1961-74; surgeon in chief surg. services Parkland Meml. Hosp., 1960-74; prof., chmn. dept. surgery U. Wash. Sch. Medicine, Seattle, 1974-75; chief of service Harborview Med. Center, Seattle, Univ. Hosp., Seattle, 1974-75; chmn. dept. surgery N.Y. Hosp.-Cornell Univ. Med. Coll., 1975-91; dean and provost for med. affairs Cornell U. Med. Coll., 1987-91; prof., chmn. surgery Tex. Tech. U., Lubbock, 1991-95, Canizaro Disting. prof. surgery, 1995—; Surgeon Gen., U.S. Army, 1965-75, Jamaica Hosp., 1978-91, Inst. Medicine Nat. Acad. Scis., 1975—; mem. com. metabolism and truama Nat. Acad. Scis.-NRC, 1964-71, com. trauma, 1964-71; mem. rsch. program evaluation com., reviewer clin. investigation applications career devel. program VA, 1972-76; mem. gen. med. rsch. program projects com. NIH, 1965-69; mem. Surgery A study sect., 1970-74, chmn., 1976-78; mem. Nat. Adv. Gen. Med. Scis. Coun., 1980-84; cons. editl. bd. Jour. Trauma, 1968—. Mem. editl. bd. Year Book Med. Publs., 1970-92, Annals of Surgery, 1972—, Surg. Techniques Illustrated: An International Comparative Text, 1974-75, Am. Jour. Surgery, 1968—, Contemporary Surgery, 1973-89; assoc. editor-in-chief Infections in Surgery, 1981; mem. editl. coun. Jour. Clin. Surgery, 1980-82; editor Surgery, Gynecology and Obstetrics, 1982-93. Lt. M.C. USNR, 1949-50, 53-55. Life Ins. Med. Rsch. fellow, 1947. Mem. ACS (bd. regents 1971-82, chmn. bd. regents 1978-80, pres. 1981-82), AMA, Dallas Soc. Gen. Surgeons (pres.-elect, pres. 1972-74), Am. Assn. Surgery Trauma, Am. Surg. Assn. (sec. 1969-74, pres. 1980), Digestive Disease Found. (founding mem.), Halsted Soc., Internat. Soc. Burn Injuries, Internat. Surg. Soc. (sec. 1978-81, v.p. 1982-83, pres. U.S. chpt. 1984-85), Pan-Am. Med. Assn. (surgery council 1971—), Pan Pacific Surg. Assn., Soc. Clin. Surgery, Soc. Surgery Alimentary Tract, Soc. Surg. Chairmen (pres. 1972-74), Soc. Univ. Surgeons (chmn. publs. com. 1969-71), So. Surg. Assn., Surg. Biology Club (sec. 1968-70), Western Surg. Assn., Allen O. Whipple Surg. Soc., James IV Assn. Surgeons (bd. dirs. 1980-81, sec. 1981-87, pres. 1987-91), Alpha Omega Alpha, Alpha Pi Alpha, Phi Beta Pi. Office: Tex Tech U Med Coll Lubbock TX 79430

SHIRLEY, AARON, pediatrician; b. Gluckstadt, Miss., Jan. 3, 1933; married; 4 children. BS, Tougaloo Coll., 1955; MD, McHarry Med. Coll., 1959, U. Miss., 1968. Intern Herbert Hosp., Tenn., 1959-60; gen. practice Vicksburg, 1960-65; project dir. Jackson-Hinds Comprehensive Health Ctr., Jackson, Miss., 1980—; mem. faculty medicine Tufts U. Medicine, Mass., 1968-73, U. Miss. Med. Sch., 1970—; head start cons. Am. Acad. Pediats., 1969-74; adv. bd. rural practice project Robert Wood Johnson Found., 1974-78; mem. Select Panel Prom. Child Health, Washington, 1979-81. Mem. Inst. Medicine-NAS (mem. coun. 1988—). Office: Jackson-Hinds Comp Hlth Ctr 4433 Medgar Evers Blvd Jackson MS 39213*

SHIVELY, EUGENE HERMAN, surgeon; b. LEbanon, Ky., June 12, 1944; s. Eugene Bryant and Virginia (Graves) S.; m. Susan Ashley Shaw, Dec. 30, 1977; children: Victoria Ashley, Alexander Gordon. BA, U. Louisville, 1966, MD, 1970. Intern U. Cin. Hosps., 1970-71; resident U. Louisville, 1973-77; with Univ. Surg. Assocs., Campbellsville, Ky.; asst. clin. prof. dept. surgery U. Ky., 1991; clin. prof. surgery U. Louisville, 1994; presenter in field. Contbr. articles to profl. jours. With USAF, 1971-73. Mem. AMA, Am. Coll. Surgeons (faculty 1981), Am. Soc. Gen. Surgeons, Soc. Am. Gastrointestinal Endoscopic Surgeons, So. Med. Assn., So. Surg. Assn., Southeast Surg. Congress, Ky. Med. Soc., Ky. Surg. Soc., Ky. Soc. Gastrointestinal Endoscopy, Jefferson County Med. Soc., Taylor County Med. Soc., Christian Med. Soc., Alpha Omega Alpha. Home: 803 Lebanon Ave Campbellsville KY 42718 Office: Univ Surg Assocs 105B Greenbriar Dr Campbellsville KY 42718

SHIVELY, HAROLD HASTINGS, JR., cardiologist; b. Newton, Mass., Mar. 13, 1937; s. Harold H. and Louise (Van Camp) S.;m. Carol Ann Steele, June 17, 1961; children: David, Debra, Karen. BA, Wesleyan U., 1959, U. Hartford, 1960; MD, George Washington U., 1965. Intern, resident Walter Reed Gen. Hosp., Washington, 1965-69; fellow in cardiology Letterman Army Hosp., San Francisco, 1969-71; interventional cardiologist Specialty Med. Clinic, La Jolla, Calif., 1974-94; pvt. practice interventional cardiology La Jolla, 1994—; from asst. prof. to assoc. prof. medicine U. Calif., San Diego, 1974—; cardiologist Scripps Meml. Hosp., La Jolla, 1974—, chief medicine, 1993-95, chief of staff, 1995—; aviation med. examiner FAA, Washington, 1979—. With U.S. Army, 1959-95, brig. gen. ret. Decorated Legion of Merit award U.S. Army, 1995. Fellow Am. Coll. Cardiology, Am. Coll. Physicians, Am. Heart Assn. Coun. Clin. Cardiology; mem. AMA, Calif. Med. Assn., San Diego Med. Assn., Res. Officers Assn., Sr. Army Res. Cmdr. Assn., Assn. Mil. Surgeons U.S., Soc. Cons. Mil. Surgeon. Republican. Home: 8596 Nottingham Pl La Jolla CA 92037 Office: 9850 Genesee Ave S780 La Jolla CA 92037

SHIVELY, JOHN ADRIAN, pathologist; b. Rossville, Ind., Oct. 29, 1922; s. Henry Adam and Lucy (Gascho) S.; m. Lois Lorene Faris, Aug. 26, 1945; children—David A., Ann M., Theodore J., Janet S. B.A., Ind. U., 1944, M.D., 1946. Intern Phila. Gen. Hosp., 1946-47; resident internal medicine Clinic Hosp., Bluffton, Ind., 1949-50; resident pathology South Bend Med. Found., 1950-52; asst. prof. clin. pathology Ind. U. Sch. Medicine, 1954-57; assoc. prof. pathology U. Ky. Med. Sch., 1962-63; prof. pathology, chief clin. pathology U. Tex. M.D. Anderson Hosp., 1963-68; prof. pathology U. Mo. Med. Sch., 1968-71; prof. pathology, chmn. dept. U. Tenn. Coll. Medicine, 1971-76; vice chancellor for acad. affairs U. Tenn. Ctr. for Health Scis., 1976-82; med. dir. SmithKline Clin. Labs., Tampa, Fla., 1983-88; prof. pathology U.S. Fla. Coll. Medicine, 1988-93, assoc. dean, 1990-93, interim chmn. pathology, 1993-94; prof. emeritus, 1993—; pathologist-in-chief City of Memphis Hosps., 1971-76. Served with AUS, 1947-49. Mem. Am. Soc. Clin. Pathologists, Coll. Am. Pathologists, ACP, Am. Soc. Hematology, Am. Assn. Blood Banks (pres. 1967-68), Phi Beta Kappa, Sigma Xi, Alpha Omega Alpha. Office: 12901 N 30th St # 11 Tampa FL 33612-4742

SHKURKIN, EKATERINA VLADIMIROVNA (KATIA SHKURKIN), social worker; b. Berkeley, Calif., Nov. 20, 1955; d. Vladimir Vladimirovich and Olga Ivanovna (Lisenko) S. Student, U. San Francisco, 1972-73; BA, U. Calif., Berkeley, 1974-77; MSW, Columbia U., 1977-79; postgrad., Union Grad. Sch., 1986. Cert. police instr. domestic violence, Alaska. Social worker Tolstoy Found., N.Y.C., 1978-79, adminstr., 1979-80; program supr. Rehab. Mental Health Ctr., San Jose, Calif., 1980-81; dir. svc. counselor Kodiak (Alaska) Crisis Ctr., 1981-82; domestic violence counselor Abused Women's Aid in Crisis, Anchorage, 1982-85; pvt. practice social work specializing in feminist therapy Susitna Therapy Ctr., Anchorage, 1985—; pvt. practice, 1985-89; field instr. Abused Women's Aid in Crisis, Anchorage, 1983-88, Divsn. Family and Youth Svcs., State of Alaska, 1989-91, South Ctrl. Found.-Dena A. Coy Prematernal Alcohol Treatment Ctr., 1991-92; expert witness Anchorage Mcpl. Ctrs., 1982-96; interim faculty mem. U. Alaska, Anchorage, summer 1985, fall 1988-95, LaVerne U., Anchorage, 1986—; family therapist Anchorage Ctr. for Families, 1994-96. Coordinator Orthodox Christian Fellowship, San Francisco, 1972-76; pub. speaker Abused Women's Aid in Crisis, Anchorage, 1982—; active nat. and local election campaigns, 1968—. Mem. NASW (cert.). Democrat. Russian Orthodox. Home and Office: 1136 Summerfield Dr SE Olympia WA 98513

SHLASKO, EDWARD, pediatric surgeon; b. Bklyn., Aug. 30, 1957; s. Robert and Roberta Shlasko; m. Neonita Ballon, Aug. 29, 1993; children: Gabrielle, Sara. BA in History, Oberlin Coll., 1979; MD, Columbia U., 1985. Diplomate Am. Bd. Surgery, Am. Bd. Pediatric Surgery. Assoc. surgery Mt. Sinai Med. Ctr., N.Y.C., 1990-91, asst. prof. pediatric surgery, 1995—; instr. pediatric surgery SUNY, Bklyn., 1991-93, asst. prof. pediatric surgery, 1993-94. Fellow ACS (assoc.), Am. Acad. Pediat.; mem. AAAS. Office: Mt Sinai Med Ctr 1 Gustave L Levy Pl New York NY 10029

SHMUNES, EDWARD, dermatologist; b. Jacksonville, Fla., July 24, 1940; s. Nathan and Anne Lillian (Berg) S.; m. Barbara Sue Mayson Hagen, Apr. 17, 1996; children: Stephanie, Marjorie, Jennifer. MD, U. Fla., 1965. Diplomate Am. Bd. Dermatology. Intern U.S. Pub. Health Hosp., New Orleans, 1965-66; epidemic intelligence officer svc. Ctr. for Disease Control, Atlanta, 1966-68; resident in dermatology U. Pa., Phila., 1968-71; ptnr. Columbia (S.C.) Skin Clinic, 1973—, pres., 1991—. Grantee: NIH (2 Yr. grant) U. S.C., 1985. Mem. Greek Orthodox Ch. Office: Columbia Skin Clinic 3 Medical Park Ste 500 Columbia SC 29203

SHOCHAT, STEPHEN JAY, pediatric surgeon; b. Balt., Dec. 17, 1938; s. Albert J. and Rose (Blechman) S.; m. Sheila Floam, July 1960 (div. July 1979); children: Francine Lynne, Alisa Joy; m. Carla Ann Centi, Jan. 26, 1980; children: David Robert, Sarah Elizabeth. BS, Randolph Mason Coll., 1959; MD, Med. Coll. Va., 1963. Surg. resident Washington U. Med. Ctr., St. Louis, 1963-68; pediatric surg. resident Boston Children's Hosp., 1968-70; thoracic surg. resident Queen Elizabeth Hosp., Birmingham, Eng., 1970, George Washington Hosp., Washington, 1972; chief pediatric surgery Hershey (Pa.) Med. Ctr., 1973-77, Stanford (Calif.) Med. Ctr., 1977-94; sr. surgeon Children's Hosp. Phila., 1994—. Lt. col. USAF, 1970-72. Office: Children's Hosp Phila 34th & Civic Ctr Blvd Philadelphia PA 19104

SHOCK, JOHN PAUL, physician, medical administrator; b. Webster Springs, W.Va., Mar. 14, 1935; s. John P. Sr. and Beulah (Allman) S.; m. Nancy Carol Hall, June 5, 1959; children: Jeffrey Hall, John Bradford. BS, U.S. Mil. Acad., 1959; MD, Duke U., 1966; postgrad., U. Miami, 1971. Diplomate Am. Bd. Ophthalmology. Commd. 2d lt. U.S. Army, 1959, advanced through grades to col., 1979; intern Walter Reed Army Med. Ctr., 1966-67, ophthalmology resident, 1967-70; asst. chief ophthalmology Letterman Army Med. Ctr., San Francisco, 1971-76; chief ophthalmology Brooke Army Med. Ctr., San Antonio, 1976-79; prof., chair dept. ophthalmology U. Ark. for Med. Scis., Little Rock, 1979—, dir. Jones Eye Inst., 1992—, chief of staff Med. Ctr., 1994—; mem. dean's exec. com. U. Ark. for Med. Scis., 1993—, chancellor's cabinet, 1992—; mem. residency review com. Accreditation Coun. Grad. Med. Edn., Chgo., 1989-95, chmn. residency review com., 1993-95. Author: (chpt.) Lange's General Ophthalmology; patentee in field of cataract removal devices; contbr. articles to profl. jours. Mem. Founders Lion Club, Little Rock, 1993—, Second Presbyn. Ch., Little Rock, 1980—. Decorated Legion of Merit; recipient Alumnus of Yr. award Glenville State Coll., 1982. Office: Univ Ark for Med Scis Dept Ophthalmology Slot 523 4301 W Markham Little Rock AR 72205-7199

SHOCKLEY, CAROL FRANCES, psychologist, psychotherapist; b. Atlanta, Nov. 24, 1948; d. Robert Thomas and Frances Lavada (Scrivner) S. BA, Ga. State U., 1974, MEd, 1976; PhD, U. Ga., 1990. Cert. in gerontology; Diplomate Am. Bd. Forensic Examiners. Counselor Rape Crisis Ctr., Atlanta, 1979-80; emergency mental health clinician Gwinnett Med. Ctr., Lawrenceville, Ga., 1980-86; psychotherapist Fla. Mental Health Inst., Tampa, 1987-89, Tampa Bay Acad., Riverview, Fla., 1990-91; sr. psychologist State of Fla. Dept. of Corrections, Bushnell, 1991-92; ind. practice psychology Brunswick, Ga., 1992—; mem. Adv. Bd. for Mental Health/Mental Retardation, 1992-94. Author: (with others) Relapse Prevention with Sex Offenders, 1989. Vol. Ga. Mental Health Inst., Atlanta, 1972; leader Alzheimer's Disease Support Group, Athens, Ga., 1984; vol. therapist Reminiscence Group for Elderly, Athens, 1984-85. Recipient Meritorious Svc. award Beta Gamma Sigma, 1975. Mem. Am. Psychol. Assn., Ga. Psychol. Assn., Sigma Phi Omega, Psi Chi. Office: 14 Saint Andrews Ct Brunswick GA 31520-6764

SHOCKMAN, GERALD DAVID, microbiologist, educator; b. Mt. Clemens, Mich., Dec. 22, 1925; s. Solomon and Jennie (Madorsky) S.; m. Arlyne Taub, June 2, 1949; children—Joel, Deborah. B.S., Cornell U., 1947; Ph.D., Rutgers U., 1950; Docteur (hon.), U. Liege, 1991. Predoctoral fellow Rutgers U., 1947-50; research asso. U. Pa., 1950-51; research fellow, research asso. Inst. Cancer Research, Phila., 1951-60; asso. prof. Temple U. Sch. Medicine, Phila., 1960-66; prof. dept. microbiology and immunology Temple U. Sch. Medicine, 1966—, chmn. dept., 1974-90. Contbr. articles in field to profl. jours. Served with U.S. Army 1942-44. Recipient Research Career Devel. award NIH, 1965-70, Titular de la Chaire d'Actualité Scientifique U. Liège, Belgium, 1971-72; NRC fellow, 1954-55. Mem. Am. Soc. Biol. Chemists, Am. Acad. Microbiology, Am. Soc. Microbiology, AAAS, Sigma Xi. Home: 901 Rodman St Philadelphia PA 19147-1247 Office: Temple U Sch Medicine 3400 N Broad St Philadelphia PA 19140-5196

SHOGAN, MAUREEN GORDON, clinical nurse specialist, nursing consultant; b. Spokane, Wash., Mar. 4, 1950; d. Alvin E. and Marian K. (Wyatt) Gordon; m. Alexander Joseph Shogan, May 27, 1978. Diploma, Sacred Heart Sch. Nursing, 1971; BS in Nursing, Gonzaga U., 1985; MSN, Intercollegiate Ctr. Nursing, 1992. Cert. infant devel. instr. Staff nurse St. Joseph Hosp., Denver, 1971-75; neonatal transport nurse Deaconess Med. Ctr., Spokane, 1976-78, nurse mgr. neonatal ICU, 1977-78, clin. instr., 1978-94; nursing cons. to law firms. Named Student Nurse of Yr. Wash. State. Mem. AWHONN (cert.), Nat. Assn. Neonatal Nurses, Sigma Theta Tau. Home: 5726 N Sutherlin St Spokane WA 99205-7553 Office: Empire Health Svcs 800 W 5th Ave Spokane WA 99210-0248

SHOHIEB, MOUSTAFA MOHAMED, orthopedic surgeon, researcher; b. Alexandria, Egypt, Apr. 28, 1967; s. Mohamed Sabry S. and B. Anwar Rizk. MBChB, Alexandria U., 1990, MD, 1994. Orthopedic surgeon Alexandria (Egypt) U. Hosp., 1990—; resident ortho. traumatology El-Hadra Univ. Hosp., 1991-93; exec. mgr. ICON Co. Home: PO Box 130 El-Saray, Alexandria 21411, Egypt Office: ICON Co, 197 Abd El-Salam Aaref St, Alexandria Egypt

SHOJI, HIROMU, orthopedic surgeon, educator; b. Chiba-Ken, Japan; grad. Coll. Gen. Edn., 1959, U. Tokyo, grad. Faculty of Medicine, 1964. Intern, U. Tokyo Hosp., 1964-65, resident in orthopedic surgery, 1965-67; resident in surgery Bklyn. Cumberland Med. Ctr., 1967-68, N.Y. U. Med. Center, 1968-69; bone tumor clinic fellow Meml. Sloan-Kettering Med. Ctr., N.Y.C., 1969-70; orthopedic fellow Hosp. for Spl. Surgery, N.Y.C., 1971-72; resident orthopedic surgery Bowman Gray Med. Sch., Winston-Salem, N.C., 1973-74; practice medicine specializing in orthopedic surgery, Sacramento, 1974-76, New Orleans, 1976-90, Riverside, Calif., 1990—; mem. staff Parkview Hosp., Riverside Comty. Hosp., Corona Regional Hosp., St. Bernadine Hosp.; assoc. prof. dept. orthopedic surgery La. State U. Med. Ctr., 1976-80, prof., 1980-90; clin. prof. Loma Linda U., 1990—; asst. prof. dept. orthopedic surgery U. Calif., Davis, 1974-76. Diplomate Am. Bd. Orthopedic Surgery (examiner). Mem. AMA, NAS, Am. Acad. Orthopedic Surgeons, Am. Assn. Hip and Knee Surgeons, Japanese Orthopedic Assn., Orthopedic Rsch. Soc., Japanese Soc. for Connective Tissue Rsch., Japanese Rehab. Assn., Am. Orthopedic Assn., So. Med. Assn., Am. Rheumatism Assn., Calif. Orthopaedic Assn., Internat. Soc. for Orthopedics and Traumatology, Knee Soc., Internat. Soc. Knee Surgery. Contbr. numerous articles on orthopedic surgery to med. jours.; patentee orthopedic devices. Office: 3838 Sherman Dr Riverside CA 92503

SHONICK, WILLIAM, health services educator; b. Poland, Oct. 3, 1919; s. Hyman and Esther (Kubashky) S.; widowed, Mar. 1987; 1 child, Jeremy I. PhD in Bio Statistics, UCLA, 1967. From asst. prof. to prof. Sch. of

Pub. Health, UCLA, 1969-90, emeritus prof., 1991—. Author: (book) Elements of Planning for Health Services, 1976, Government & Health Services, 1995; contbr. numerous articles to profl. jours. Home: 1244 Beverly Green Dr Los Angeles CA 90035

SHONS, ALAN RANCE, plastic surgeon, educator; b. Freeport, Ill., Jan. 10, 1938; s. Ferral Caldwell and Margaret (Zimmerman) S.; AB, Dartmouth Coll., 1960; MD, Case Western Res. U., 1965; PhD in Surgery, U. Minn., 1976; m. Mary Ella Misamore, Aug. 5, 1961; children: Lesley, Susan. Intern, U. Hosp., Cleve., 1965-66, resident in surgery, 1966-67; research fellow transplantation immunology U. Minn., 1969-72; resident in surgery U. Minn. Hosp., 1972-74; resident in plastic surgery NYU, 1974-76; asst. prof. plastic surgery U. Minn., Mpls., 1976-79, assoc. prof., 1979-84, prof., 1984; dir. div. plastic and reconstructive surgery U. Minn. Hosp., St. Paul Ramsey Hosp., Mpls. VA Hosp., 1976-84; cons. plastic surgery St. Louis Park Med. Center, 1980-84; prof. surgery Case Western Res. U., Cleve., 1984-93; dir. div. plastic and reconstructive surgery Univ. Hosps. Cleve., 1984-92; prof. surgery U. South Fla., H. Lee. Moffitt Cancer Ctr. and Rsch. Inst., Tampa, 1993—. Author: (with G.L. Adams and G.A. Brocone) Head and Neck Cancer, 1986; (with R. Jensen) Plastic Surgery Review, 1993. Served to capt. USAF, 1967-69. Diplomate Am. Bd. Surgery, Am. Bd. Plastic Surgery. Fellow ACS (chmn. Minn. com. on trauma 1978-84); mem. Am. Soc. Plastic and Reconstructive Surgeons, Am. Assn. Plastic Surgeons, Minn. Acad. Plastic Surgeons (pres. 1981-82), AMA, Soc. Head and Neck Surgeons, Am. Assn. Surgery Trauma, Transplantation Soc., Plastic Surgery Research Council, Am. Soc. Aesthetic Plastic Surgery, Am. Soc. Maxillofacial Surgeons, Am. Assn. Immunologists, Soc. Exptl. Pathology, Am. Burn Assn., Am. Cleft Palate Assn., Am. Soc. Craniofacial Surgery, Assn. Acad. Surgery, Central Surg. Assn., Fla. Soc. Plastic & Reconstructive Surgeons, Tampa Bay Soc. Plastic & Reconstructive Surgeons, Sigma Xi. Office: H Lee Moffitt Cancer Ctr & Rsch Inst 12902 Magnolia Dr Tampa FL 33612-9497

SHOOTER, ERIC MANVERS, neurobiology educator, consultant; b. Mansfield, Eng., Apr. 18, 1924; came to U.S., 1964; s. Fred and Pattie (Johnson) S.; m. Elaine Staley Arnold, May 28, 1949; 1 child, Annette Elizabeth. BA, Cambridge (Eng.) U., 1945, MA, 1949, PhD, 1950, ScD, 1986; DSc, U. London, 1964. Sr. scientist biochemistry Brewing Industry Rsch. Fedn., 1950-53; biochemistry lectr. Univ. Coll., London, 1953-63; assoc. prof. genetics Stanford U., 1963-68, prof. genetics and biochemistry, 1968-75, prof., chmn. neurobiology dept., 1975-87, prof. neurobiology, 1987—, chmn. Neurosci. PhD Program, 1972-82; assoc. Neurosci. Rsch. Program, N.Y.C., 1979-89; teaching staff Internat. Sch. Neurosci., Praglia, Italy, 1987-93; sr. cons. Markey Charitable Trust, Miami, Fla., 1985—; chair sci. adv. bd., and dir. Regeneron Pharm., Inc., Tarrytown, N.Y., 1988—. Assoc. editor: (book series) Ann. Rev. Neurosci., 1984—; contbr. numerous articles to profl. jours. Recipient Wakeman award Duke U., 1988; Faculty scholar Josiah Macy Jr. Found., N.Y.C., 1974-75. Fellow AAAS, Royal Soc. (London), Am. Acad. Arts and Scis.; mem. Inst. Medicine of NAS (fgn. assoc.), Biochem. Soc., Am. Assn. Biol. Chemists, Soc. for Neurosci. (Ralph W. Gerard prize 1995), Am. Soc. Neurochemistry, Internat. Soc. Neurochemistry, Internat. Brain Rsch. Orgn. Home: 370 Golden Oak Dr Portola Valley CA 94028-7757 Office: Stanford U Sch Medicine Dept Neurobiology Stanford CA 94305

SHOPE, ROBERT ELLIS, epidemiology educator; b. Princeton, N.J., Feb. 21, 1929; s. Richard Edwin Shope and Helen Madden (Ellis) Flemer; m. Virginia Elizabeth Barbour, Dec. 27, 1958; children—Peter, Steven, Deborah, Bonnie. BA, Cornell U., 1951, MD, 1954. Intern then resident Grace-New Haven Hosp., 1954-58; mem. staff Rockefeller Found., Belem, Brazil, 1959-65; dir. Belem Virus Lab., Brazil, 1963-65; from asst. to assoc. prof. epidemiology Yale Sch. Medicine, New Haven, 1965-75, prof., 1975-95; prof. pathology U. Tex. Med. Br., Galveston, 1995—; adv. bd. Gorgas Inst., Panema City, 1972-90; mem. WHO Expert Panel Arboviruses, Geneva, Switzerland, 1974—, U.S. del. U.S.-Japan Coop. Med. Scis. Program, Washington, 1977—, Pan Am. Health Orgn. Commn. for Dengue, Washington, 1980—. Served to capt. U.S. Army, 1955-57, Southeast Asia. Fellow Am. Acad. Microbiology; mem. Am. Soc. Tropical Medicine and Hygiene (pres. 1980, Bailey K. Ashford award 1974, Walter Reed award 1993), Am. Soc. Virology, Am. Soc. Epidemiology, Infectious Diseases Soc. Am. Democrat. Office: U Tex Med Br Dept Pathology 301 University Blvd Galveston TX 77555-0609

SHORE, CAROLE JEAN, nutritionist; b. Dayton, Ohio, Dec. 7, 1948; d. Erroll Victor and Mabell B. (Pallanch) Black; m. Michael J. Shore, June 5, 1976; 1 child, Victoria Jean. BS, Ohio State U., 1971, MS, 1975. Intern Harvard U. Med. Ctr., Boston, 1971-72; pub. health nutritionist Polk County (Fla.) Health Dept., Winter Haven, 1972-73; asst. prof., program dir. Hood Coll., Frederick, Md., 1975-76; nutrition analyst USDA Consumer and Food Econs. Inst., Hyattsville, Md., 1976-79, USDA Human Nutrition Info. Service, Hyattsville, 1979-82; tech. info. specialist USDA Nat. Agrl. Library, Beltsville, Md., 1982-90; coord. Nat. Food Irradiation Info. Ctr.; chief of quality mgmt. for clin. nutrition-computer programs Dept. Vets. Affairs, Washington, 1990—. Author: (with others) Promoting Nutrition Through Education, 1985, Practice Guidelines for VA Dietetic Services, 1994, 95, Nutrition Status Classification Scheme, 1995; contbr. articles to profl. jours. Mem. ASTD, Am. Dietetic Assn. (Recognized Young Dietitian 1979, treas. Comty. Nutrition Rsch. Group 1981-83, chair 1984-85), Clin. Nutrition Mgmt., D.C. Met. Area Dietetic Assn. (chair coun. on practice 1980-82, 87-88, treas. 1982-84, pres. elect 1988-89, pres. 1989-90, chair state adv. com. Am. Dietetic Assn. conv. 1991), Soc. for Nutrition Edn., Inst. Food Technologists, Omicron Nu, Phi Upsilon Omicron. Republican. Roman Catholic. Home: 6356 Crosswoods Dr Falls Church VA 22044-1210 Office: Health Adminstrn Affairs Dept Vets 810 Vermont Ave VHA 14 Washington DC 20420

SHORE, MILES FREDERICK, psychiatrist, educator; b. Chgo., May 26, 1929; s. Miles Victor and Margaret Elizabeth S.; m. Eleanor M. Gossard, July 4, 1953; children: Miles Paul, Rebecca Margaret, Susanna Gladys. BA, U. Chgo., 1948; AB, Harvard U., 1950, MD, 1954. Intern U. Ill. Research and Edn. Hosp., Chgo., 1954-55; resident in psychiatry Mass. Mental Health Center, Beth Israel Hosp., Boston, 1956-61; asst. prof. psychiatry Tufts U. Sch. Medicine, Medford, Mass., 1964-68; assoc. prof. Tufts U. Sch. Medicine, 1968-71, prof., 1971-75, prof. community health, 1972-75; founder, dir. Tufts Community Mental Health Center, 1968-74, assoc. dean community affairs, 1972-75; mem. faculty Boston Psychoanalytic Inst., 1973—; Bullard prof. psychiatry Harvard Med. Sch., Boston, 1975—, dir. div. mental health systems, 1993—; supt. Mass. Mental Health Ctr., 1975-93; vis. scholar John F. Kennedy Sch. Govt. Harvard U., 1993—; dir. program for chronic mental illness Robert Wood Johnson Found., 1985-92. Editl. bd. Psychat. Svcs. Jour., 1990; bd. editors Jour. Interdisciplinary History, 1975, Psycho History Rev., 1978; column editor Harvard Rev. Psychiatry, 1993; contbr. articles to profl. jours. Bd. dirs. Federated Dorchester Neighborhood Houses, Boston, 1975-78, Med. Found., Bosotn, 1987—, Ctr. House, Boston, 1995—; mem. Blue Ribbon Commn., Mass. Dept. Mental Health, 1979-80. Capt. U.S. Army, 1956-58. Community Mental Health Center grantee, 1964-75. Fellow Am. Psychiat. Assn. (life, joint commn. on pub. affairs, adminstrv. psychiatry award 1987), Am. Coll. Psychiatrists (chmn. fin. com. 1983-89, bd. regents 1988-90, 1st v.p. 1994, pres. 1996-97, Bowis award for svc. 1990, Arthur P. Noyes award 1994); mem. Boston Psychoanalytic Soc. and Inst. (chmn. bd. trustees 1970-73), Mass. Psychiat. Soc. (pres. 1970-71), Mass. Hosp. Assn. (trustee 1980-85), Am. Hosp. Assn. (governing coun. mental health and psychiat. svcs. 1985-87, chmn. governing coun. for psychiat. and substance abuse svcs. 1992-93), Roxbury Clinic Record Club, Aesculapian Club, Mass. Hist. Soc. Office: JFK Sch Govt 79 JFK St Cambridge MA 02138-5801

SHORES, CYNTHIA LUCIA, pharmacist; b. Tyler, Tex., Apr. 19, 1961; d. Harold Gene and Lucia Gertrude (Clark) Smith; m. Daniel S. McChesney, Apr. 23, 1982 (div.); children: Rebecca Carol, Patrick Tyler; m. Bruce F. Shores, June 27, 1992; 1 child, Carrie Lillian. BS in Botany, Miss. State U., 1982; BS in Pharmacy, U. Miss., 1990. Pharmacist in-charge Wal-Mart Pharmacy, Pecos, Tex., 1990—; pharmacist-in-charge Planned Parenthood of West Tex., Pecos, 1990-94. Mem. Merry Wives Pecos C. of C. Episcopalian.

SHORES, PEARL MARIE, health care company executive; b. Warsaw, N.Y., Aug. 29, 1946; d. Lawrence Dean and Mary Ellen (Sly) Arnold; m. Bruce Reid Dedrick, May 9, 1964 (div. 1966); 1 child, Dawn Aileen; m. James Lee Shores, Sept. 13, 1981. BBA cum laude, Nat. U. San Diego, 1979; MBA, Nat. U., 1981. Chief lab. technician Schoenfield Clin. Lab., Albuquerque, 1970-76, Allergy Med. Group, San Diego, 1976-78; chemstrip specialist BioDynamics/BMC, San Diego, 1978-80; sr. ter. mgr. Hollister, Inc., San Diego, 1980-84; dist. mgr. Hollister, Inc., New Eng. dist., 1984-86; sales rep. E.R. Squibb/CONVATEC, San Diego, 1986-87; br. mgr. HOMEDCO, San Diego, 1987-89; dir. infusion therapy Spl. Solutions, 1989-90; territory mgt. Sween Corp., 1990-93; dir. Mercy Infusion Therapy, Escondido, Calif., 1993-96; regional sales cons. Dezinc Healthcare Solutions, 1996—.

SHORT, EARL DE GREY, JR., psychiatrist, consultant; b. Talladega, Ala., Jan. 11, 1933; s. Earl de Grey and Adeline Eugenia (McWilliams) S.; m. Martha Burt Rossiter, Oct. 12, 1963; children: Earl D III, Philip A., Catherine E., William R. BS, The Citadel, 1956; MD, Med. U. S.C., Charleston, 1959. Commd. 2d lt. USAR, 1956; entered active duty U.S. Army, 1961, advanced through grades to col., 1976; battalion surgeon 4th Armored BN, 8th Inf. div., Germany, 1961-62; resident psychiatry Walter Reed Army Med. Ctr., Washington, 1962-65; chief dept. psychiatry U.S. Army Hosp., Ft. Polk, La., 1965-68, U.S. Walson Army Hosp., Ft. Dix, N.J., 1968-70; student Command and Gen. Staff Coll., Ft. Leavenworth, Kans., 1970-71; divsn. surgeon, comdr. 2d Med. Bn., 2d Infantry divsn., Korea, 1971-72; chief psychiatry svc. Brooke Army Med. Ctr., Ft. Sam Houston, Tex., 1972-80; ret. U.S. Army, 1980; psychiatrist Mecklenburg County Mental Health Ctr., Charlotte, N.C., 1980-86; ret. Mecklenburg County, 1993; psychiatrist Carolinas Medical Ctr. Ctr. for Mental Health, Charlotte, N.C., 1986—; pvt. practice Carolinas Med. Group, Psychiat. and Psychol. Assocs., 1992—; psychiat. cons. Mecklenburg County, Charlotte, 1987—, Amethyst, Charlotte, 1993-95. Founder Philip Alexander Short Meml. Scholarship Fund, Wingate (N.C.) Coll., 1988, Short Endowment Fund, Wingate Coll., 1991, Philip Alexander Short Meml. Fund, Elon Homes for Children, Elon Coll., N.C., 1989. Decorated Meritorious Svc. medal with 1 oak leaf cluster, U.S. Army, 1972, 80, Army Commendation medal with 1 oak leaf cluster, U.S. Army, 1968, 70; recipient All Am. award The Citadel, 1956. Mem. AMA, Am. Psychiat. Assn., N.C. Med. Soc., N.C. Psychiat. Assn., Charlotte Psychiat. Soc., Assn. Mil. Surgeons, Mecklenburg County Med. Soc., Ret. Officers Assn., Am. Legion, VFW, Sons Am. Revolution, Nat. Assn. for Uniformed Svcs. Republican. Presbyterian. Office: PO Box 18773 Charlotte NC 28218-0773

SHORT, ELIZABETH M., physician, educator, federal agency administrator; b. Boston, June 2, 1942; d. James Edward and Arlene Elizabeth (Mitchell) Meehan; m. Herbert M. Short, Sept. 2, 1963 (div. 1969); 1 child, Timothy Owen; m. Michael Allen Friedman, June 21, 1976; children: Lia Gabrielle, Hannah Ariel, Eleanor Elana. BA Philosophy magna cum laude, Mt. Holyoke Coll., 1963; MD cum laude, Yale U., 1968. Diplomate Am. Bd. Internal Medicine, Am. Bd. Med. Genetics. Intern, jr. resident internal medicine Yale New Haven Hosp., 1968-70; postdoctoral fellow in human genetics Yale Med. Sch., 1970-72; postdoctoral fellow in renal metabolism U. Calif., San Francisco, 1972-73; sr. resident in internal medicine Stanford (Calif.) Med. Sch., 1973-74, chief resident in internal medicine, 1974-75; staff physician Palo Alto Veterans Med. Ctr., Stanford, Calif., 1975-80; asst. prof. of medicine Stanford Med. Sch., 1975-83, asst. dean Student Affairs, 1978-80, assoc. dean Students Affairs/Medical Education, 1980-83; dir. biomed. rsch. and faculty devel. Assn. Am. Med. Colls., Washington, 1983-87, dep. dir. dept. acad. affairs, 1983-87, dep. dir. biomedical rsch., 1987-88; dep. assoc. chief med. dir. for acad. affairs VA, Washington, 1988-92, assoc. chief medical dir. for acad. affairs, 1992—; vis. prof. Human Biology, Stanford U., 1983-86; resource allocation com. Veteran's Health Adminstrn., 1989-91; budget planning and policy review coun. 1991—: planning review com. Veterans Health Adminstrn., 1991—; chair resident work limit task force 1991—; managed care task force, 1993-94; co-chair com. status women Am. Fedn. Clin. Rsch., 1975-77; mem. numerous adminstrv. coms., Yale Med. Sch., Stanford U.; accreditation coun. grad. med. edn., 1988—; mem. public policy com. Am. Soc. Human Genetics, 1984—, chair, 1986-94; mem. White House Task Force on Health Care Reform, 1993-94. assoc. editor Clin. Rsch. Jour., 1976-79, editor elect, 1979-80, editor 1980-84; contbr. articles to profl. jours. Mem. nat. child health adv. coun. NIH, 1991—; mem. com. edn. and training Office Sci. and Tech. Policy, 1991—. Recipient Maclean Zoology award Mt. Holyoke Coll.; Munger scholar, Markle scholar, Sara Williston scholar Mt. Holyoke Coll., 1959-63, Yale Men in Medicine scholar, 1964-68; Bardwell Meml. Med. fellow, 1963. Mem. AAAS, Am. Soc. Human Genetics, Am. Fedn. Clin. Rsch. (bd. dirs. 1973-83, editor 1978-83, nat. coun., exec. com., pub. policy com. 1977-87), Am. Assn. Women in Scis., Western Soc. Clin. Investigation, Calif. Acad. Medicine, Phi Beta Kappa, Alpha Omega Alpha. Home: 6807 Bradley Blvd Bethesda MD 20817-3004 Office: Health Adminstrn Acad Affairs Dept Veterans 810 Vermont Ave VHA 14 Washington DC 20420

SHORT, MARSHALL HILLERY, pathologist; b. St. Paul, July 17, 1930; s. Jacob Short and Elizabeth Ruth (Koppe) Abrahamson; m. Rose Betty Kaufman, Aug. 15, 1954; children: Pamela Healy, Jackie Lee, Stacey Short-Livesey, Daniel. BA, U. Minn., 1952, BS, 1953, MD, 1955. Diplomate Am. Bd. Pathology. Pathologist Midway & Mounds Park Hosps., St. Paul, 1964-69, West Suburban Hosp., Oak Park, Ill., 1970-73, St. George Hosp., Chgo., 1970-71, Loretto Hosp., Chgo., 1971-91; med. dir. Loretto Hosp., 1989-91; pathologist Herrin (Ill.) Hosp., 1991—; bd. dirs. So. Ill. Healthcare Enterprises, Carbondale, 1993—; ho. dels. Coll. Am. Pathologists, Chgo., 1976-82. Capt. U.S. Army, 1958-60. Fellow Coll. Am. Pathologists, Am. Soc. Clin. Pathologists; mem. AMA, Ill. State Med. Soc., Williamson County Med. Soc., Am. Coll. Physician Execs., Ill. Soc. Pathologists (pres. 1979-80), U.S. & Can. Acad. Pathology, Am. Soc. Cytology. Office: Herrin Hosp 201 S 14th St Herrin IL 62948

SHORT, SYDNEY G., cardiologist; b. Richwood, W.Va., Oct. 27, 1958; s. Spencer G. and Beulah E. (Dorsey) S.; m. Teresa N. Anderson, Nov 9, 1991; children: Jacob M., Sydney Adam, Sarah Beth. BA, W.Va. U., 1980, MD, 1983. Diplomate Am. Bd. Internal Medicine, Am. Bd. Cardiology. Cardiology fellow N.C. Bapt. Hosp./Wake Forest U., Winston-Salem, 1986-89; cardiologist Guilford Cardiology Assocs., Greensboro, N.C., 1989-90; pvt. practice cardiology Dalton, Ga., 1990-93, Sanford, N.C., 1993—; cons. assoc. divsn. cardiology Duke U. Med. Ctr., Durham, 1993—. Contbr. articles to profl. publs. Baptist. Office: 1301 B Carthage St Sanford NC 27330

SHORTELL, STEPHEN M., medical educator; b. New London, Wis., Nov. 9, 1944. BBA, U. Notre Dame, 1966; MPH, UCLA, 1968; MBA, U. Chgo., 1970, PhD in Behavioral Sci., 1972. Rsch. asst. Nat. Opinion Rsch. Ctr., 1969; instr., rsch. assoc. Ctr. Health Adminstrv. Studies, 1970-72; acting dir. grad. program hosp. adminstrn. U. Chgo., 1973-74, from asst. prof. to assoc. prof., 1974-79; prof. Sch. Pub. Health & Comty. Medicine, Dept. Health Svc. U. Wash., 1979-82; A. C. Buehler Disting. prof. health svc. mgmt. Northwestern U., Evanston, Ill., 1982—; cons. VA, Robert Wood Found., Henry Keiser found.; asst. prof. Health Svcs. Orgn., U. Chgo., 1972-74; adj. asst. prof. dept. sociology U. Wash., 1975-76, dir. doctoral program dept. health svcs. Sch. Pub. Health & Comty. Medicine, 1976-78; prof. sociology dept. sociology Northwestern U., 1982, prof. comty. medicine dept comty. health & preventive medicine Sch. Medicine. Contbr. numerous publs. to profl. jours. Mem. APHA, Inst. Med.-NAS. Office: Northwestern U J L Kellogg Grad Sch Mgmt Leverone Hall Evanston IL 60208-2007*

SHORTER, DANIEL ALBERT, retired biology educator; b. Goltry, Okla., May 20, 1927; s. Wily Brink and Edna Isabella (Mason) S.; m. Margery Jean Peck, Jan. 13, 1946; children: Cynthia, Edana, Terry, Sherry. BS in Biology Edn., N.W. Okla. State U., 1949; MS in Natural Sci., Okla. State U., 1960, PhD in Entomology, 1965. Cert. secondary tchr., Okla., Kans. Instr. in math. Anthony (Kans.) Pub. Schs., 1949-58; from asst. prof. to prof. biology N.W. Okla. State U., Alva, 1960-87, dir. admissions, 1972-75, prof. emeritus, 1987—; v.p. Okla. Ornithol. Soc., 1967. Mem. Local Vocat. Tech. Bd. Edn., Alva, 1974—; chmn. Alva Hosp. Authority, 1991-95, mem., 1995—. Named Outstanding Conservation Educator, Okla. Soc. Soil Conservation Dists., 1985. Mem. Am. Legion, Ducks Unltd. (zone chmn. 1984—, Outstanding Zone Chmn. award 1989, 90), Kiwanis (pres. 1956, 82, Kiwanian of Yr. 1992, lt. gov. Divsn. 16 1994-95, 95-96), Masons. Democrat. Methodist. Home: 610 14th St Alva OK 73717-2010

SHORTER, NICHOLAS ANDREW, pediatric surgeon; b. London, Oct. 14, 1953; came to the U.S., 1961; s. Roy Gerrard and Rhiannon (Morris) S.; m. Sally Jo Trued, Aug. 28, 1982; children: Timothy Anders, Brittain David, Jaime Elizabeth Rhiannon. AB, AM, Harvard U., 1975; MD, Johns Hopkins U., 1979. Bd. cert. in surgery and pediatric surgery. Intern in surgery The Johns Hopkins Hosp., Balt., 1979-80, jr. asst. resident in surgery, 1980-81, sr. asst. resident in surgery, 1981-82, 83-84, chief resident in surgery, 1984-85; rsch. fellow in surgery The Children's Hosp. Med. Ctr., Boston, 1982-83; asst. chief resident in pediatric surgery The Children's Hosp., Phila., 1985-86, chief resident in pediatric surgery, 1986-87; hosp. staff Duke U. Med. Ctr., Durham, N.C., 1987-91; dir. pediatric surg. svcs. Children's Hosp. at Dartmouth, Dartmouth-Hitchcock Med. Ctr., 1991—, exec. com., 1991—; teaching fellow biology Harvard U., Cambridge, Mass., 1974-75; asst. instr. pediatric surgery U. Pa., Phila., 1985-87, Duke U., Durham, 1987-91, asst. prof. pediatric surgery and pediatrics, 1987-91; asst. prof. pediatrics Dartmouth Med. Sch., Hanover, N.H., 1991-94, asst. prof. surgery, 1991-94, assoc. prof. pediatrics, 1994—, assoc. prof. surgery, 1994—; hosp. staff The Children's Hosp., Phila., 1986-87, Dartmouth-Hitchcock Med. Ctr., Lebanon, N.H., 1991—, Duke U. Med. Ctr., Durham, 1987-91; dir. Kiwanis Affiliated Pediatric Trauma Ctr., Children's Hosp. at Dartmouth, Lebanon, 1993—; others. Referee Jour. Pediatric Surgery; contbr. chpts. to books and articles to profl. jours. Recipient Regular Clin. fellowship Am. Cancer Soc., 1985-86. Fellow ACS, Am. Acad. Pediatrics, Southeastern Surg. Congress, Soc. Surg. Oncology; mem. Am. Pediatric Surg. Assn., Brit. Assn. Pediatric Surgeons, Internat. Soc. Pediatric Oncology, Internat. Pediatric Surg. Oncology, Pediatric Oncology Group (assoc.), Am. Assn. for Cancer Rsch., Assn. for Acad. Surgery, N.H. Med. Soc. (del. Grafton County), N.Y. Acad. Scis., N.H. Pediatric Soc., Kiwanis Club Lebanon, Cum Laude Soc., Phi Beta Kappa, Alpha Omega Alpha. Republican. Episcopalian. Office: Dartmouth-Hitchcock Med Ctr Sect Gen Surgery One Med Ctr Dr Lebanon NH 03756

SHORTLIFFE, EDWARD HANCE, internist, medical informatics educator; b. Edmonton, Alta., Can., Aug. 28, 1947; s. Ernest Carl and Elizabeth Joan (Rankin) S.; m. Linda Marie Dairiki, June 21, 1970; children: Lindsay Ann, Lauren Leigh. AB, Harvard U., 1970; PhD, Stanford U., 1975, MD, 1976. Diplomate Am. Bd. Internal Medicine. Trainee NIH, 1971-76; intern Mass. Gen. Hosp., Boston, 1976-77; resident Stanford Hosp., Palo Alto, Calif., 1977-79; asst. prof. medicine Stanford U. Sch. Medicine, Palo Alto, 1979-85, assoc. prof., 1985-90, prof., 1990—, chief div. gen. internal medicine, 1988-95; assoc. dean info. resources and tech. Stanford U. Sch. Medicine, 1995—; pres. SCAMC, Inc. (Symposium on Computer Applications in Med. Care), Washington, 1988-89; assoc. chair medicine Primary Care, 1993-95; bd. dirs. Smart Valley, Inc.; advisor Nat. Bd. Med. Examiners, Phila., 1987-93; mem. Nat. Fed. Networking Adv. Coun., NSF, 1991-93; mem. computer sci. and telecomm. bd. NRC, 1991-96; bd. regents ACP, 1996—. Editor: Rule-Based Expert Systems, 1984, Readings in Medical Artificial Intelligence, 1984, Medical Informatics: Computer Applications in Health Care, 1990; developer several medical computer programs including MYCIN, 1976 (Grace M. Hopper award Assn. Computing Machinery). Recipient Young Investigator award Western Soc. Clin. Investigation, 1987, rsch. career award Nat. Libr. of Medicine. 1979-84; scholar Kaiser Family Found., 1983-88. Fellow Am. Assn. Artificial Intelligence, Am. Coll. Med. Informatics (pres. 1992-94); mem. Soc. for Med. Decisionmaking (pres. 1989-90), Inst. Medicine, Am. Soc. for Clin. Investigation, Am. Med. Informatics Assn., Assn. Am. Physicians, Am. Clin. and Climatol. Assn. Office: Stanford U Sch Medicine Sect on Med Informatics 300 Pasteur Dr Stanford CA 94305-5479

SHORTLIFFE, LINDA MARIE DAIRIKI, urology educator, researcher; b. Boston, Feb. 28, 1949; d. Setsuo and Norma Masako (Yoshida) Dairiki; m. Edward Hance Shortliffe, June 21, 1980; children: Lindsay Ann, Lauren Leigh. AB, Harvard U.-Radcliffe Coll., 1971; MD, Stanford U., 1975. Resident in gen. surgery Tufts-New Eng. Med. Ctr., Boston, 1976-77; intern in gen. surgery Stanford (Calif.) U. Med. Ctr., 1975-76, resident in urology, 1977-81, chief pediatric urology, 1991—, chair dept. urology, 1995—; asst. prof. surgery (urology) Stanford U., 1981-88, assoc. prof., 1988-93, prof., 1993—; com. mem. spl. grants Nat. Inst. Diabetes, Digestive and Kidney Diseases, Bethesda, Md., 1990-94; spl. site visitor residency rev. com. Accreditation Coun. for Grad. Med. Edn., 1993—; com. mem. bladder health cou. Am. Found. Urol. Disease, Balt., 1991—; m. task force B joint exam. com. Am. Bd. Urology-Am. Urol. Assn., 1991-95, chmn., 1994-95. Contbg. author: Campbell's Urology, 5th edit., 1985, 6th edit., 1992, 7th edit.,1992; mem. editl. bd. Urology, 1993-97; contbr. articles to med. jours. Fellow ACS (program chmn. No. Calif. chpt. 1992), Am. Acad. Pediatrics (exec. com. 1995-97); mem. Am. Urol. Assn. (coun. on edn. 1993-97), Soc. for Pediatric Urology. Office: Stanford U Med Ctr S-287 Dept Urology 300 Pasteur Dr Stanford CA 94305-5118

SHOSKES, DANIEL ARTHUR, transplant surgeon, researcher; b. N.Y.C., Mar. 20, 1961; s. Lew and Maria (Drezner) S.; m. Ruth Morger, Oct. 23, 1987; children: Valerie, Aaron, Jennifer. MD, U. Toronto, Can., 1985; MSc, U. Alberta, Can., 1989. Diplomate Royal Coll. Physicians and Surgeons, Can. Intern Wellesley Hosp., Toronto, 1986-87; resident in urology Toronto Gen. Hosp.; clin. lectr. U. Oxford, Eng., 1991-93; asst. prof. urology UCLA, 1994—; dir. renal transplant programs Harbor-UCLA, Torrance, —, St. Mary's, Long Beach, Calif., —. Mem. exec. bd. L'Chaim Soc., Oxford, 1991—. Recipient Young Investigator award Am. Soc. Transplant Physicians, 1989. Mem. Am. Soc. Transplant Surgeons, Transplantation Soc., Am. Urol. Soc., Western Assn. Transplant Surgeons. Office: Harbor UCLA Med Ctr Box 5 1000 W Carson 51 Torrance CA 90275

SHOTWELL, ALAN JAMES, optometrist; b. Washington, July 28, 1943; s. James Henry Shotwell and Alice Peyton (Taylor) Schaefer; m. Adele Virginia Goss, July 25, 1970; children: Franklin Minor, Lee Stephen, Suzanne Elizabeth, Sara Kristin. BA, U. Va., 1970; BS, OD, Pa. Coll. Optometry, 1975; MS, Pacific Univ., 1984. Lic. optometrist, Va. Commd. ensign USN, 1964, advanced through grades to lt. comdr., mil. practice of optometry, 1975-91, ret., 1991; pvt. practice Orange and Stafford, Va., 1991-93, Culpepper, Spotsylvania, Va., 1993-95; adj. prof. optometry U. Houston Optometric Preceptorship Program, 1989-91. EMT Radian Vol. Fire Dept., swift water and vertical rescue cert.; mem. Culpeper Mid Day Lions Club, 1994—. Fellow Am. Acad. of Optometry; mem. Am. Optometric Assn., Va. Optometric Assn. Home: Box 36 Rapidan VA 22733 Office: 123 W Davis St Culpeper VA 22701

SHOTZ, LINDA FLEISCHMAN, marriage and family therapist, artist; b. Asbury Park, N.J., Aug. 16, 1949; d. Erwin Lewis and Ruth (Koegel) Fleischman; m. Frederick A. Shotz, Sept. 18, 1973. AA Miami Dade Jr. Coll., 1969; BA cum laude U. Fla., 1971; MS summa cum laude Nova U., 1975. Cert. sex therapist, expressive therapist, addictions counselor; licensed marriage and family therapist, lic. mental health counselor. Social worker Divsn. Family Svcs., Miami, 1971-73; clin. psychotherapist Counseling Assocs., Ft. Lauderdale, Fla., 1974—; family therapist, Spectrum Programs, Inc.; fellow in sex therapy, fellow in med. psychotherapy; life drawing, painting, wheel thrown pottery, sculptor, Ft. Lauderdale, Fla.; artist in field. Author: (with others) Training Crisis Counselors; (book of erotic art & poetry) Breathmarks in the Wind, 1988. Mem. AACD, Nat. Assn. Drug Abuse and Alcohol Counselor, Soc. for Sci. Study of Sex. Avocations: reading, video art, travel. Office: Counseling Assocs 2699 Stirling Rd Ste C306D Fort Lauderdale FL 33312-6517

SHOUGH, H. RICHARD, medicinal chemistry educator; b. Springfield, Ohio, Jan. 7, 1942; s. Herbert B. and Dorothy L. (Kennedy) S.; m. Kay Segerson, Sept. 7, 1963; children: Richard Jr., Laura Kay, Evan. BS in pharmacy, U. Tenn., 1964, PhD in pharmaceutical scis., 1968. Registered pharmacist, 1964. Asst. prof. U. Utah Coll. Pharmacy, Salt Lake City, 1968-72, assoc. prof., 1973-78; assoc. prof., asst. dean U. Okla. Coll. Pharmacy, Oklahoma City, 1978-80, prof., asst. dean, 1980-83, prof., acting dean, 1982, prof., interim dean, 1983-84, prof., assoc. dean, 1983—; cons. Palmer Chem. & Equipment Co., Douglasville, Ga., 1965-68. Author (book chpt.) Remington's Pharmaceutical Sciences, 1980-95; contbr. articles to profl. jours. Recipient rsch. grant U. Utah Rsch. Com., 1968-72, Am. Cancer Soc., 1973-74, Smith-Kline Pharm., 1981-83. Mem. Am. Pharm. Assn., Am. Assn. Coll. Pharmacy, Am. Soc. Pharmacognasy, Am. Assn. Pharm. Scientists,

Okla. Pharm. Assn. Office: U Okla Coll Pharmacy 1110 N Stonewall Oklahoma City OK 73190

SHOUSHA, ANNETTE GENTRY, critical care nurse; b. Nashville, May 25, 1936; d. Thurman and Laura (Pugh) Gentry; m. Alfred Shousha, May 29, 1959; children: Mark André, Anne, Mary, Melanie. Diploma, St. Thomas Hosp., Nashville, 1957; student, Belmont Coll., Nashville, 1958, No. State U., Aberdeen, S.D., 1973; BSN, S.D. State U., 1985. Cert. coronary care. Instr. med. nursing Nashville Gen. Hosp., 1958-59, ob-gyn. nurse, 1959-60; insvc. educator Tri County Hosp., Ft. Oglethorpe, Ga., 1960-61; clin. mgr., office nurse Britton, S.D., 1962-90; med. nursing Nashville VA Hosp., 1990-92, gastrointestinal nurse, 1992-94, critical care nurse ICU, 1994-95. Contbr. essays to S.D. Jour. Medicine. Del., S.D. Dem. Conv. Recipient Gov.'s Recognition award for outstanding vol. svc. Mem. ANA, AMA Aux. (state pres.), Nat. Hospice Assn., Nurses Orgn. VA, Donelson/Hermitage C. of C. Home: 2809 Lealto Ct Nashville TN 37214-1813

SHOVLIN, JOSEPH PATRICK, optometrist. BA in Psychology, Gettysburg Coll., 1974; BS in Physiol. Optics, Pa. Coll. of Optometry, 1978, D of Optometry, 1980. Cert. optometrist Pa., N.Y., Va., Md. Assoc. Morrison Assocs., Harrisburg Pa., N.Y.C., 1980-85; clin. assoc. Northeastern Eye Inst., Scranton, Pa., 1985—; cons. Lancaster County Blind Assn., Lancaster, Pa., 1980-85, State Bd. of Optometry, Commonwealth of Pa., 1988-90, Ophthalmic Devices' Adv. Panel, Ctr. for Devices and Radiological Health, Food and Drug Adminstrn., 1987-88, 1992-93; adj. faculty Pa. Coll. of Optometry, 1981—; cons. and expert witness Bur. of Profl. and Occupational Affairs, Commonwealth of Pa., 1983-85; voting mem. Ophthalmic Devices Adv. Panel, Ctr. for Devices and Radiological Health, Food and Drugs Administrn., 1988-92; presenter over 175 formal lectures to major internat., nat., regional and state ophthalmic groups. Author: (with others) Problems in Optometry, 1990, Clinical Contact Lens Practice, 1991, Optometric Pharmacology, 1992, Anterior Segment Complications of Contact Lens Wear, 1994; contbr. numerous articles to profl. jours. including: Review of Optometry (contbg. editor 1984-88, assoc. clin. editor 1988—), Metabolic, Pediatric and Systemic Ophthalmology, Contact Lens Forum, Focus on Product News, International Contact Lens Clinic (contbg. editor 1988-93), Primary Care Optometry News, (cons. editor, 1995—), Contemporary Optometry, Contact Lens Spectrum (consulting editor 1988—), Optometric Management (contbg. editor 1992-95), Practical Optometry, Review of Ophthalmology, American Acad. of Optometry Newsletter; assoc. editor Making Contact, 1982-88, 94—; editl. bd. Contacto; mem. jour. rev. bd. Optometry Clinics, 1991—; cons. editor Primary Care Optometry News, 1995—; referee Jour. Am. Optometric Assn. and Optometry and Vision Sci. Mem. sci. adv. com. Pa. Lions' Sight Conservation and Eye Rsch. Found., nat. adv. eye coun. Nat. Eye Inst. Nat. Insts. Health, 1992-96. Fellow Am. Acad. Optometry (diplomate cornea and contact lens sect. 1985, mem. exec. bd., spkrs. bur., bd. dirs. Pa. chpt. past mem., numerous other coms.); mem. APHA, Internat. Soc. Refractive Surgery (assoc.), Am. Optometric Assn. (sec. contact lens sect. 1988-89, vice chair 1989-90, chair elect 1990-91, chair 1991-92, immediate past chair 1992-93, mem. jour. rev. bd., numerous other coms. and offices, Am. Optometric Recognition award 1980—), Pa. Optometric Assn. (chmn. continuing edn. com. 1993, Keystone contact lens conf. 1987—, com. on contact lenses 1986-94, others), The Assn. for Rsch. in Vision and Ophthalmology, Nat. Eye Rsch. Found., Am. Optometric Found. (bd. dirs. 1988-90), The Prentice Soc., Adv. Bd. Eye Vision Assocs., The Optometric Coun. of the State of N.Y. (Disting. Svc. award 1984). Home: 1308 Oakmont Rd Clark's Summit PA 18411 Office: Northeastern Eye Inst 200 Mifflin Ave Scranton PA 18503

SHOWELL, GINA ROMAYNE, health services administrator; b. Dayton, Ohio, Nov. 7, 1951; d. Russell Lewis Jr. and Clarice Romayne (Douthitt) Austin; m. Charles H. Showell, June 16, 1984; 1 child, Otha Tillman Lewis III. BA, Capitol U., 1982; MSA, Ctrl. Mich. U., 1984. Phlebotomist St. Elizabeth's Med. Ctr., Dayton, 1971-78, cytology technician, 1978-83, administrv. resident, 1983-84, admistrv. asst. to sr. v.p. ops., 1984-85, admnstr. outpatient svcs., 1985-88, v.p. ops., 1988-92; corp. v.p. legis. and internal affairs Franciscan Health Sys., Dayton, 1992—; mem. Ohio Commn. Minority Health Care, Columbus, 1992—. Bd. dirs., pres. YWCA, United Health Svc. Named One of Top 10 Women Dayton Daily News, 1991; recipient Up and Comer award Price Waterhouse, 1990, Cmty. Svc. award Gem City Med. Dental and Pharm. Assn., 1995, also commendations Ohio Ho. of Reps. Fellow Am. Coll. Healthcare Execs., mem. S.W. Ohio Health Execs. Office: Franciscan Health System 601 Edwin C Moses Blvd Dayton OH 45408

SHRAGOWITZ, JACOB, obstetrician, gynecologist, medical educator; b. Kletsk, Poland, Mar. 5, 1923; came to U.S., 1923; s. Rabbi Moses Joshua and Hinde Shragowitz; m. Joyce Rachel Medwed, Nov. 4, 1993; children: Laura Grace Ruth, Michael, Alice Miriam Finer. AB, U. Pa., Phila., 1943, MD, 1947. Diplomate Am. Bd. Ob-Gyn. Instr. Albert Einstein Coll. Med., Bronx, N.Y., 1956-58, asst. prof., 1958-72, assoc. prof. ob-gyn, 1972—. Co-prodr. (teaching film) Surgical Correction of Vaginal Agenesis, 1960. Trustee Port Chester (N.Y.) Pub. Libr., 1990—, treas. 1992—; bd. dirs., pres., sec., treas., v.p. Westchester Obs-Gyn Soc., N.Y., 1945-80. Capt., USAF, 1953-55, Alaska. Fellow ACS (life), ACOG (sr.), N.Y. Acad. Medicine (life), N.Y. Gynecol. Soc.; mem. Westchester County Obs-Gyn Soc., Bronx Ob-Gyn Soc. Democrat. Jewish. Home: 9 Bobbie Lane Rye Brook NY 10573-1205 Office: 709 Jacobi Medical Ctr. Pelham Pkwy Bronx NY 10461

SHRIER, DIANE KESLER, psychiatrist; b. N.Y.C., Mar. 23, 1941; d. Benjamin Arthur and Mollie (Wortman) Kesler; BS magna cum laude in Chemistry and Biology (Regents scholar 1957-61), Queen's Coll., CUNY, 1961; student Washington U. Sch. Medicine, St. Louis, 1960-61; M.D., Yale U., 1964; m. Adam Louis Shrier, June 10, 1961; children: Jonathan Laurence, Lydia Anne, Catherine Jane, David Leopold. Pediatric intern Bellevue Hosp., N.Y.C., 1964-65; psychiat. resident Albert Einstein Coll. Medicine-Bronx (N.Y.) Mcpl. Municipal Hosp. Center, 1966-68, child psychiatry fellow, 1968-70; staff cons. Family Service and Child Guidance Center of the Oranges, Maplewood, Milburn-Orange, N.J., 1970-73, cons., 1973-79; pvt. practice, Montclair, N.J., 1970-92, Washington, 1994—; cons. Community Day Nursery, E. Orange, 1970-79, Montclair State Coll., 1976-78; psychiat. cons. Bloomfield (N.J.) public schs., 1974-75; clin. instr. Albert Einstein Coll. Medicine, 1970-73; clin. asst. prof. psychiatry U. Medicine and Dentistry N.J., 1978-82, clin. assoc. prof., 1982-89, prof. clin. psychiatry, 1989-92; vice chmn., dir. clin. psychiat. svcs. Dept. Psychiatry Children's Nat. Med. Ctr., 1992-94, attending staff, 1994—; prof. psychiatry and pediatrics George Washington U. Med. Ctr., 1992-94, clin. prof. psychairty and pediatrics, 1994—. cons. Walter Reed Med. Ctr., 1994—. Trustee, Montessori Learning Center, Montclair, 1973-75. Diplomate Am. Bd. Psychiatry and Neurology. Fellow Am. Psychiat. Assn., Acad. Child Psychiatry; mem. Tri-County Psychiat. Assn. (exec. com., rec. sec. 1977-78, 2d v.p. 1978-79, 1st v.p. 1979-80, pres. 1977-81), N.J. Psychiat. Assn. (councillor 1981-84), Am. Acad. Child and Adolescent Psychiatry (councillor at large 1992-95), Phi Beta Kappa. Contbr. articles to med. jours. Home: Apt 317B 4000 Cathedral Ave NW Washington DC 20016-5249 Office: 1616 18th St NW Ste 104 Washington DC 20009-2530

SHRIFTER, HAROLD BUDDY, physician; b. Chgo., Apr. 22, 1929; s. Samuel and Rebecca (Mednick) S.; m. Marion Katz, June 11, 1932; children: Karen L. Shrifter Poter, Susan A. Shrifter Fialkow, Robert A. BS, U. Ill., 1949, MD, 1953. Diplomate Am. Bd. Internal Medicine. Rotating intern Cook County Hosp., Chgo., 1953-54, resident in internal medicine, 1954-56, fellow in hematology, 1956-57. Capt. U.S. Army, 1957-59. Fellow Am. Coll. Physicians. Office: 6374 N Lincoln Ave Chicago IL 60659

SHROPSHIRE, DONALD GRAY, hospital executive; b. Winston-Salem, N.C., Aug. 6, 1927; s. John Lee and Bess L. (Shouse) S.; m. Mary Ruth Bodenheimer, Aug. 19, 1950; children: Melanie Shropshire David, John Devin. B.S., U. N.C., 1950; Erickson fellow hosp. adminstrn., U. Chgo., 1958-59; LLD (hon.), U. Ariz., 1992; EdD (hon.), Tucson U., 1994. Personnel asst. Nat. Biscuit Co., Atlanta, 1950-52; asst. personnel mgr. Nat. Biscuit Co., Chgo., 1952-54; adminstr. Eastern State Hosp., Lexington, Ky., 1954-62; assoc. dir. U. Md. Hosp., Balt., 1962-67; adminstr. Tucson Med. Ctr., 1967-82, pres., 1982-92, pres. emeritus, 1992—, bd. dirs., 1995; pres. Tucson Hosps. Med. Edn. Program, 1970-71, sec., 1971-86; pres. So. Ariz. Hosp. Council, 1968-69; bd. dirs. Ariz. Blue Cross, 1967-76, chmn. provider standards com., 1972-76; chmn. Healthways Inc., 1985-92; Bd. dirs. Tucson Med. Found., Tucson Electric Power Co.; adv. bd. Steele Meml. Pediatric Rsch. Ctr., U. of Ariz. Coll. of Medicine, 1996—. Bd. dirs. Health Planning Coun. Tucson, 1992, mem. exec. com., 1969-74; chmn. profl. divsn. United Way, Tucson, 1969-70, vice chmn. campaign, 1988, Ariz. Health Faciltities Authority, bd. dirs., 1992—; chmn. dietary svcs. com., vice chmn., 1988, Md. Hosp. Coun., 1966-67; bd. dirs. Ky. Hosp. Assn., 1961-62, chmn. coun. profl. practice, 1960-61; past pres. Blue Grass Hosp. Coun.; trustee Assn. Western Hosps., 1974-81, pres., 1979-80; mem. accreditation Coun. for Continuing Med. Edn., 1982-87, chair, 1986; bd. govs. Piima C.C., 1970-76, sec., 1973-74, chmn., 1975-76, bd. dirs. Found., 1978-82, Ariz. Bd. Regents, 1982-90, sec., 1983-86, pres., 1987-88; mem. Tucson Airport Authority, 1987-95, bd. dirs., 1990-95, pres., 1995; v.p. Tucson Econ. Devel. Corp., 1977-82; bd. dirs. Vol. Hosps. Am., 1977-88, treas., 1979-82; mem. Ariz. Adv. Health Coun. Dirs., 1976-78; bd. dirs. Tucson Tomorrow, 1983-87, Tucons Downtown Devel. Corp., 1988-95, Rincon Inst., 1992—, Sonoran Inst., 1992—; dir. Mus. No. Ariz., 1988—; nat. bd. advisors Coll. Bus. U. Ariz., 1992—, chmn. Dean's Bd. Fine Arts, 1992-96, pres. Ariz. Coun. Econ. Edn., 1993-95; vis. panel Sch. Health Adminstrn. and Policy Ariz. State U., 1990-92; bd. dirs. Tuscon Cmty. Found., 1996—. Named to Hon. Order Ky. Cols.; named Tucson Man of Yr. 1987; recipient Disting. Svc. award Anti-Defamation League B'nai B'rith, 1989. Mem. Am. Hosp. Assn. (nominating com. 1983-86, trustee 1975-78, ho. dels. 1972-78, chmn. coun. profl. svc. 1973-74, regional adv. bd. 1969-78, chmn. joint com. with NASW 1963-64, Disting. Svc. award 1989), Ariz. Hosp. Assn. (Salisbury award 1982, bd. dirs. 1967-72, pres. 1970-71), Ariz. C. of C. (bd. dirs. 1988-93), Assn. Am. Med. Colls. (mem. assembly 1974-77), Tucson C. of C. (bd. dirs. 1968-69), United Comml. Travelers, Nat. League for Nursing, Ariz. Town Hall (bd. dirs. 1982-92, chmn. 1990-92, treas. 1985), Pima County Acad. Decathlon Assn. (dir. 1983-85), The Rotary Ctr. of Tucson (pres. 1993-94). Baptist (ch. moderator, chmn. finance com., deacon, ch. sch. supt., trustee, bd. dirs. ch. found.). Home: 6734 N Chapultepec Circle Tucson AZ 85750 Office: Tucson Med Ctr 2195 E River Rd Ste 202 Tucson AZ 85718-6586

SHUCART, WILLIAM ARTHUR, neurosurgeon; b. St. Louis, Oct. 23, 1935; s. Frank M. and Beatrice S.; m. Laura Huber, Dec. 16, 1971. AB, Washington U., 1957; MD, U. Mo., 1961. Diplomate Am. Bd. Neurol. Surgery. Intern U. Utah Hosp., Salt Lake City, 1961-62; resident in surgery Peter Bent Brigham Hosp., Boston, 1963-64; resident in neurosurgery Columbia-Presbyn. Hosp., N.Y.C., 1967-70, Hosp. for Sick Children, Toronto, Ont., Can., 1976-71; mem. faculty dept. neurosurgery Med. Sch. Tufts U., Boston, 1971-76, assoc. prof., 1976; prof., chmn. dept. neurosurgery SUNY, Downstate Med. Ctr., Bklyn., 1976-81; neurosurgeon Tufts-New England Med. Ctr., Boston, 1972-76, prof., chmn. dept. neurosurgery, 1981—; chief neurosurgery Beth Israel Hosp., Boston; vis. prof. surgery Harvard Med. Sch. With U.S. Army, 1964-67. Mem. ACS, Am. Assn. Neurol. Surgeons, Soc. Neurol. Surgeons. Home: 100 Meadowbrook Rd Weston MA 02193-2406 Office: New England Med Ctr PO Box 178 750 Washington St Boston MA 02111

SHUCK, JERRY MARK, surgeon, educator; b. Bucyrus, Ohio, Apr. 23, 1934; s. James Edwin and Pearl (Mark) S.; m. Linda Wayne, May 28, 1974; children: Jay Steven, Gail Ellen, Kimberly Ann, Lynn Meredith, Steven James. BS in Pharmacy, U. Cin., 1955, MD, 1959, DSc, 1966. Intern Colo. Gen. Hosp., Denver, 1959-60; resident in surgery U. Cin. Integrated Program, 1960-66; mem. faculty dept. surgery U. N.Mex., Albuquerque, 1968-80; prof. U. N.Mex., 1974-80; founder burn and trauma unit; Oliver H. Payne prof. dept. surgery, chmn. dept. Case-Western Res. U., Cleve., 1980—; interim v.p. for med. affairs, 1993-95; dir. surgery Univ. Hosps. Cleve., 1980—; cons. FDA, 1972-77. Contbr. articles to profl. jours. Served to capt. U.S. Army, 1966-68. Mem. ACS, Am. Surg. Assn., Am. Bd. Surgery (bd. dirs., chmn. 1993-94), Soc. Univ. Surgeons, Am. Assn. Surgery Trauma, Am. Trauma Soc. (founding mem.), Univ. Assn. Emergency Medicine (founding mem.), Am. Burn Assn. (founding mem.), We. Surg. Assn., Ctrl. Surg. Assn. (pres. 1996—), Assn. Acad. Surgery, S.W. Surg. Assn., Cleve. Surg. Soc., Ohio Med. Assn., Acad. Medicine Cleve., Halsted Soc., Surg. Infection Soc. (founding mem.), B'nai B'rith, Jewish Cmty. Ctr. Club, The Temple Club. Democrat. Jewish. Office: Case Western Reserve U Dept Surgery 2074 Abington Rd Cleveland OH 44106-2602

SHUE, TERESA MCGUIRT, maternal women's health nurse; b. Charlotte, N.C., Sept. 17, 1961; d. David Leon and Patricia (Williams) McGuirt; m. Bobby David Shue, Jr., Mar. 21, 1981; 1 child, Jennifer Nicole. ADN with honors., Cabarrus Meml. Sch. Nursing, Concord, N.C., 1991. RN, N.C. Staff nurse high risk labor and delivery Carolinas Med. Ctr., Charlotte, 1991-93, asst. nurse mgr. labor and delivery, 1993—. Mem. AWHONN. Republican. Mem. Full Gospel Ch. Home: 461 Countrywood Rd Concord NC 28025 Office: Carolinas Med Ctr 1000 Blythe Blvd Charlotte NC 28225

SHUER, LAWRENCE MENDEL, neurosurgery educator; b. Toledo, Apr. 12, 1954; s. Bernard Benjamin and Estelle Rose (Drukker) S.; m. Paula Ann Elliott, Sept. 4, 1976; children: Jenna, Tammy, Nichole. BA with high distinction, U. Mich., 1975, MD cum laude, 1978. Diplomate Am. Bd. Neurol. Surgery, Nat. Bd. Med. Examiners. Fellow in neurology Inst. Neurology, London, 1979; intern in surgery Stanford (Calif.) U. Sch. Medicine, 1978-79, resident in neuropathology, 1980, resident in neurosurgery, 1980-84, clin. asst. prof. surgery and neurosurgery, 1984-90, assoc. prof., 1990—, acting chmn. dept. neurosurgery, 1992-95, assoc. dean, 1996—, chief of staff Stanford Health Sys., 1996—; numerous presentations in field. Contbr. articles and abstracts to med. jours., chpts. to books. Recipient Kaiser tchr. award Stanford U., 1993; James B. Angell scholar. Mem. AMA, Am. Assn. Neurol. Surgeons, Congress Neurol. Surgeons, Western Neurosurg. Soc., Calif. Assn. Neurol. Surgeons (bd. dirs., treas. 1995—), Calif. Med. Assn., Am. Heart Assn. (fellow stroke coun.), Santa Clara County Med. Assn., San Francisco Neurol. Soc., Alpha Omega Alpha. Office: R155 Stanford U Med Ctr 300 Pasteur Dr Palo Alto CA 94304-2203

SHUGAR, GARY LEE, pathologist; b. Reading, Pa., Feb. 22, 1948; s. Kenneth R. and Evelyn R. (Meinholz) S.; m. Lisbeth A. Fox, June 9, 1973; children: Daniel L., Rebecca A. BS in Biology, Albright Coll., 1970; MD, Jefferson Med. Coll., 1974. Diplomate Am. Bd. Pathology. Intern Conemaugh Valley Meml. Hosp., Johnstown, Pa., 1974-75; naval flight surgeon tng. Naval Aerospace Med. Inst., Pensacola, Fla., 1975; naval flight surgeon Patrol Squadron 23 USN, Brunswick, Maine, 1976-78; resident pathology, instr. Hershey Med. Ctr. Pa. State U., Hershey, 1978-82; pathologist Clearfield (Pa.) Hosp., 1982-84; med. dir. MDS Labs., Reading, Lemoyne, Pa., 1984-91; pathologist Ephrata (Pa.) Cmty. Hosp., 1991—; staff indsl. medicine East Penn Mfg. Co., Lyons Station, Pa., 1989-90; anatomic pathology fellow Hershey Med. Ctr. Penn State U., 1990-91; med. dir. Corning Clin. Labs., Lemoyne, 1992—; lectr. biology dept. Albright Coll., Reading, 1988-90, Alvernia Coll., Reading, 1990. Contbr. articles to profl. jours. Chmn. Troop 312 com. Boy Scouts Am., Reading; leader trumpet sect. Reading H.S. Alumni Band. Fellow Coll. Am. Pathologists, Am. Soc. Clin. Pathologists. Home: 1508 Bern St Reading PA 19604 Office: Ephrata Cmty Hosp 169 Martin Ave PO Box 1002 Ephrata PA 17522

SHUGARMAN, RICHARD GERALD, ophthalmologist, educator; b. Balt., Feb. 6, 1940; m. Rhona Merle Blank, June 10, 1961; children: Keith David, Marcy Pam, Todd Mitchell. BA, Johns Hopkins U., 1960; MD, U. Md., 1964. Diplomate Am. Bd. Ophthalmology. Intern Sinai Hosp., Balt., 1964-65; resident Balt. Eye and Ear Charity Hosp., 1965-68; fellow U. Fla., Gainesville, 1968-69; pvt. practice West Palm Beach, Fla., 1971—; instr. U. Tex. Med. Sch., San Antonio, 1969-70; assoc. clin. prof. Bascom Palmer Eye Inst., U. Miami (Fla.) Sch. Medicine, 1972—; mem. 4th Dist. Ct. Appeals Nominating Commn., 1995—. Pres. Temple Israel, West Palm Beach, 1980-82; chmn. Israel Bonds, Palm Beach County, 1979-82; treas. Alcohol and Drug Abuse Coun., West Palm Beach, 1973; bd. dirs. Jewish Fedn. Palm Beach County, 1972-94, v.p., 1978-82, Jewish Cmty. Ctr., 1979; active Nat. Young Leadership Cabinet USA, 1978-80; bd. dirs. Jewish Cmty. Day Sch., 1978-92; co-chair Fla. U.S. Meml. Holocaust Mus., 1990; mem. nat. bd. Union Am. Hebrew Congregations, 1988—, mem. exec. com., 1993—. With U.S. Army, 1969-70. Fellow ACS, Internat. Coll. Surgeons, Am. Acad. Ophthalmology; mem. AMA, Fla. Med. Assn., Fla. Ophthal. Soc. (v.p. 1993—), Palm Beach County Ophthalmology Soc. (pres. 1984), South Fla. Redn. Reform Congregations (pres. 1992—), Palm Beach Liturgical Culture Soc. (v.p. 19845-94). Democrat. Jewish. Home: 5407 S Flagler Dr West Palm Beach FL 33405-3311 Office: Palm Beach Eye Assocs 140 John F Kennedy Dr Ste 140 Lake Worth FL 33462-6608

SHULDINER, ALAN RODNEY, physician, endocrinologist, educator; b. Irumagawa, Japan, Feb. 5, 1957; parents Am. citizens; s. Julius and Janet (Gursky) S.; m. Jill Francie Bresman, June 27, 1984; children: Seth David, Scott Ross. AB in Chemistry magna cum laude, Lafayette coll., 1979; MD with honors, Harvard U., 1984. Diplomate Am. Bd. Internal Medicine, Am. Bd. Endocrinology and Metabolism. Intern in medicine Columbia-Presbyn. Hosp., N.Y.C., 1984-85, resident in medicine, 1985-86; med. staff fellow Diabetes Br. Nat. Inst. Diabetes and Digestive and Kidney Diseases NIH, Bethesda, Md., 1986-88, sr. staff fellow, 1988-90; asst. prof. div. geriatric medicine and gerontology Sch. Medicine Johns Hopkins U., Balt., 1990-91, assoc. prof. div. geriatric medicine and gerontology; guest rschr. Nat. Insts. on Aging NIH, Balt., 1991—, lectr. Living with Diabetes Series, 1986-90, lectr. course on diabetes mellitus, 1988-90; dir. summer sch. program Juvenile Diabetes Found. Co-author: Current Therapy in Endocrinology and Metabolism, 3d edit., 1988, 4th edit., 1991; contbr. articles to profl. jours. including Archives Biochem. Biophysics, Jour. Biol. Chemistry, New Eng. Jour. Medicine, Analytical Biochemistry, Endocrinology, Gene, Nucleic Acids Rsch., Procs. NAS, Biotechniques. Mem. AAAS, AMA, ACP, Am. Diabetes Assn. (Rsch. award 1996). Office: Johns Hopkins U 5501 Bayview Blvd Rm 5a42 Baltimore MD 21224

SHULER, GEORGE NIXON, JR., social worker, writer; b. Houston, Apr. 17, 1952; s. George Sr. and Anna Isabel (Huebner) S.; m. Lois Laverne Byram, June 16, 1979. BA, U. Tex., 1977; MSW, U. Houston, 1992. Lic. Master Social Worker, Tex. Mgr. Law Book Co. of Tex., San Antonio, 1973-74; mgr. store Elliot Garner Enterprises, San Antonio, 1974-77; child protective services specialist Karnes County (Tex.) Child Welfare, Karnes City, 1978-80, Atascosa County Child Welfare, Jourdanton, Tex., 1980, Bexar County Child Welfare, San Antonio, 1980-84; supr. child protective services Brazoria County Child Welfare, Angleton, Tex., 1984-86; child protective services specialist Harris County Child Welfare, Houston, 1986-92; respite specialist Galveston County Children's Protective Svcs., Texas City, 1993-95; clin. social worker Social Work Dept./Army Family Advocacy Program, Ft. Hood, Tex., 1995—. Columnist Leon Valley Leader newspaper, San Antonio, 1981-87; contbr. articles to profl. pubs. Dir. state exec. com. Tex. State Employees Union, Austin, 1983-84; del. ctrl. labor coun. AFL-CIO, San Antonio, 1981-84, Tex. Dem. Conf., 1974, 76, 78, 82, 84, 86, 90, 92, 96; campaign aide Dem. Com. Bexar County, San Antonio, 1974; campaign mgr. Jon Roland for U.S. Congress, San Antonio, 1974; chmn. resolutions com. Brazoria County Dem. Conf., Angleton, 1986; mem. rules com. Galveston County Dem. Conv., 1994; mem. exec. bd. North Galveston County Dems., 1994-95; lay min. Ch. of Subgenius of Gulf Coast, 1986—, hierarchy candidate, 1990, initiate, 1993; min. Universal Life Ch., 1994—. Recipient Service award Tex. State Employees Union, 1984. Mem. Masons (Master Mason Tex. City Lodge #1118), AF & AM, Scottish Rite, Galveston Scottish Rite Bodies, Shriners (Noble, El Mina Shrine Temple, AAONMS, Galveston 1995—). Home: 2501 Bacon Ranch Rd #903 Killeen TX 76542 Office: Social Work Dept Bldg 307-A Fort Hood TX 76544

SHULMAN, GERALD, pathologist, medical facility administrator; b. Johannesburg, South Africa, July 13, 1937; came to U.S., 1976; s. Isaac and Lily (Harte) S.; m. Cynthia Cohen, June 20, 1965; 1 child, Leigh. MB, ChB, Witwatersrand Med. Sch., Johannesburg, South Africa, 1960; MRC Pathology, Royal Coll. Pathologists, London, 1970. Registrar, postgrad. Med. Sch., London, 1968-70; sr. pathologist South African Med. Rsch., Johannesburg, 1971-75; asst. prof. Hershey (Pa.) Med. Coll., 1976-82; blood svcs. dir. ARC, Atlanta, 1983-90, Columbia, S.C., 1990-93; blood svcs. dir. U. Tex. Med. Br., Galveston, 1993—; cons., lectr. Medtronic Blood Mgmt., Parker, Colo., 1995—. Contbr. articles to profl. jours. Fellow Royal Soc. Pathologists; mem. Am. Assn. Blood Banks, Am. Soc. Clin. Pathologists, Tex. Med. Assn. Office: Univ Texas Medical Branch 301 University Blvd Galveston TX 77555-0717 Home: 6201 Seawall # 368 Galveston TX 77550

SHULMAN, GERALD I., clinical investigator; b. Detroit, Feb. 8, 1953; s. Herschel A. and Doris (Miller) S. BS with high honors and distinction, U. Mich., 1974; MD, PhD, Wayne State U., 1979. Intern Duke U., Durham, N.C., 1979-80, residency, 1980-81; fellowship in endocrinology and metabolism Mass. Gen. Hosp., Boston, 1981-84; asst. prof. medicine Harvard U., Boston, 1985-87; assoc. prof. Sch. Medicine Yale U., New Haven, 1989—; assoc. dir. Yale MD-PhD Program Sch. Medicine Yale U., New Haven, 1993—; assoc. dir. Yale Diabetes Endocrine Rsch. Ctr. Contbr. articles to med. jours. Fellow ACP; mem. Am. Soc. Clin. Investigation, Am. Diabetes Assn. (clin. rsch. grantee 1996), Am. Physiol. Soc. Office: Sch Medicine Yale Univ Dept Internal Medicine 333 Cedar St # 3333 New Haven CT 06510-3206

SHULMAN, LAWRENCE EDWARD, biomedical research administrator, rheumatologist; b. Boston, July 25, 1919; s. David Herman and Belle (Tishler) S.; m. Pauline K. Flint, July 19, 1946; 1 son, Lawrence E.; m. Reni Trudinger, Mar. 20, 1959; children: Kathryn Verena, Barbara Corina. AB, Harvard U., 1941, postgrad., 1941-42; PhD, Yale U., 1945, MD, 1949. Nat. Bd. Med. Examiners. Intern Johns Hopkins Hosp., 1949-50, resident and fellow in internal medicine, 1950-53; dir. connective tissue div. Johns Hopkins U., 1955-75, assoc. prof. medicine, 1964—; assoc. dir. div. arthritis, musculoskeletal and skin diseases NIH, Bethesda, Md., 1976-82, dir., 1982—; dir. Nat. Inst. Arthritis & Musculoskeletal & Skin Diseases NIH, 1986-94, dir. emeritus, 1994—, emissary for clin. rsch., 1995—; chmn. med. adminstrn. com. Arthritis Found., Atlanta, 1974-75, exec. com., 1972-77; dir. Lupus Found. Am.; med. adv. bd. United. Scleroderma Found., Watsonville, Calif., 1977-88; chair sci. group rheumatic diseases WHO, 1989. Discoverer: Eosinophilic Fasciitis, 1974, new med. sign friction rubs in scleroderma, 1961. Recipient Sr. Investigator award Arthritis Found., 1957-62, Disting. Svc. award, 1979, Heberdeen medal for rsch., London, 1975, Superior Svc. award USPHS, 1985, Spl. Recognition award Nat. Osteoprosis Found., 1991, Spl. award Am. Acad. Orthop. Surgeons, 1992, Presdl. citation for leadership Am. Acad. Dermatology, 1993, Leadership award Lupus Found. Am., 1994, Career Achievement award Am. Coll. Rheumatology, 1994, Outstanding Support Rsch. award Am. Soc. Bone Mineral Rsch., 1994, Gold medal Am. Coll. Rheumatology; named W.R. Graham Meml. lectr., 1973, Cochrane Disting. lectr., 1993. Master Am. Rheumatism Assn. (pres. 1974-75); fellow ACP; mem. Soc. Clin. Trials, Pan-Am. League Against Rheumatism (pres. 1982-86)., Soc. Investigative Dermatology. Home: 6302 Swords Way Bethesda MD 20817-3350

SHULMAN, YALE, urologist; b. Fort Dix, N.J., Dec. 19, 1953; m. Vivian Shulman, June 20, 1976. BA, Yeshiva U., 1973; MD, Albert Einstein Coll. Medicine, 1976. Diplomate Am. Bd. Urology. Pvt. practice urology Jersey City, 1982—; clin. assoc. prof. urology NYU Sch. Medicine; clin. asst. prof. surgery & urology Univ. Medicine & Dentistry of N.J. Office: 2255 Kennedy Blvd Jersey City NJ 07304

SHUMAN, TODD A., cardiothoracic surgeon; b. Lawton, Okla., July 16, 1956; s. Billy Joe and Jeane (Keating) S.; m. Debra Ann Rose, May 9, 1986. BA, U. Colo., 1978; MD, Vanderbilt U., 1983. Diplomate Am. Bd. Surgery, Am. Bd. Thoracic Surgery. Cardiothoracic surgeon Nashville, 1992—. Mem. AMA, Soc. Acad. Surgeons, Nashville Acad. Medicine, Tenn. Med. Assn., H. William Scott Soc., So. Thoracic Surg. Assn., Nashville Surgical Soc., Alpha Omega Alpha, Phi Beta Kappa, Sigma Pi Sigma. Office: 4230 Harding Rd Ste 501 Nashville TN 37205

SHUMATE, CHARLES RAYMOND, oncology and general surgeon; b. Tuscaloosa, Ala., Apr. 14, 1958; s. Frank Allen and Mary Jane (Tennant) S.; m. Mary Pamela Sims, Dec. 17, 1983; children: Clayton Addison, Allyson Blair. BS, U. Ala., Tuscaloosa, 1980; MD, U. Ala., Birmingham, 1984. Diplomate Nat. Bd. Med. Examiners, Am. Bd. Surgery. Intern U. Louisville, 1984-85, resident, 1985-89; fellow M.D. Anderson Cancer Ctr., Houston, 1989-91; asst. prof. surgery U. Ala., Birmingham, 1991-95; sr. scientist Comprehensive Cancer Ctr., Birmingham, 1991-95. Fellow ACS (Best Paper award Ky. chpt. 1988); mem. AMA, So. Med. Assn., Birmingham Surg. Soc., Southeastern Surg. Congress, Soc. Surg. Oncology, Hiram C. Polk Jr. Surg. Soc., Ala. Breast and Cervical Cancer Detection Com., Phi Beta Kappa. Office: Surg Assocs Ste G-2 2018 Brookwood Med Ctr Birmingham AL 35209

SHUMATE, DOROTHY LEE, pharmacist; b. Oak Hill, W.Va., Feb. 4, 1956; d. Garland Lee and Betty Alice (Perry) Pugh; m. David Keith Shumate, Mar. 14, 1981; 1 child, John David. Student Concord Coll., 1974-76; B.S. in Pharmacy, W.Va. U., 1979. Registered pharmacist. Pharmacist, Rural Acres Pharmacy, Beckley, W.Va., 1979-81, Beckley Hosp., 1979, Fairway Drug, Addison, Ill., 1981-82, Martin Ave. Pharmacy, Naperville, Ill., 1982-85, Pulaski (Va.) Drugs, 1985-87, SuperX Drugs, Pulaski, 1987-89, Revco Drugstore, 1989—; Mem. Am. Pharm. Assn., Va. Pharm. Assn., AAUW, Rho Chi, Gamma Beta Phi, Alpha Chi, Lambda Kappa Sigma. Republican. Mem. Ch. of the Brethren. Avocations: ping pong, piano, organ, racquetball. Home: 5650 Meadowcrest St Roanoke VA 24019-4816

SHURLEY, JAY TALMADGE, psychiatrist, medical educator, administrator, behavioral sciences researcher, polar explorer, author, genealogist; b. Sonora, Tex., Dec. 20, 1917; s. Ira L. and Jewell L. (Choate) S.; m. Erwina Bode Cornelison, Dec. 20, 1986. BA in Zoology, U. Tex.-Austin, 1940; MD, U. Tex. Med. Br., Galveston, 1942. Diplomate Am. Bd. Psychiatry and Neurology. Intern. Ind. U.-Indpls. Med. Ctr., 1943; Rockefeller fellow in neuropsychiatry dept. mental and nervous disease Inst. for Mental Hygiene Pa. Hosp., Phila., 1944-47; dir. Markle Meml. Unit for Insulin Therapy dept. for mental and nervous disease Pa. Hosp., Phila., 1945-50; pvt. practice medicine specializing in psychiatry and psychoanalysis Phila., 1947-51, Austin, 1951-52; pvt. practice medicine specializing in psychiatry San Antonio, 1952-54, Chevy Chase, Md., 1955-57; pvt. practice medicine specializing in psychiatry, psychoanalysis and sleep disorders medicine Oklahoma City, 1978-90; acting chief lab. adult psychiat. investigation, clin. investigations NIMH, NIH, Bethesda, 1955-57; chief psychiatry service and mental hygiene clinic VA Hosp., Oklahoma City, 1957-62; sr. med. investigator in psychiatry, research service, dept. medicine and surgery VA, 1962-76; founder and dir. behavioral scis. labs VA Med. Ctr., Oklahoma City, 1962-78; med. dir. outpatient psychiatry clinics Okla. Meml. Hosp. and Clinics, Okla Health Scis. Ctr., Oklahoma City, 1978-81; sci. dir. Oklahoma Mental Health Research Inst., Oklahoma Dept. Mental Health, 1988-89; cons.-liaison in geropsychiatry O'Donoghue Rehab. Inst., Okla. Med. Ctr., 1990-91; med. dir. emeritus Willow View Mental Health Ctr., Oklahoma City, 1985-87; prof. psychiatry U. Okla., Oklahoma City, 1957-62, career research prof. psychiatry and behavioral scis., 1962-77, prof. psychiatry and behavioral scis. Coll. of Medicine and Grad. Coll., 1977-81; prof. emeritus psychiatry and behavioral scis. U. Okla. Coll. Medicine, Oklahoma City, 1981—; adj. prof. human ecology Coll. Health, U. Okla., 1967-81; mem. com. on polar rsch., chmn. panel on biology and medicine NAS/NRC, 1970-74; U.S. rep. Working Group on Biology XII Sci. Com. on Antarctic Rsch., Canberra and Melbourne, Australia, 1972; U.S. rep. Working Group on Human Biology and Medicine XIII Sci. Com. on Antarctic Rsch., Jackson Hole, Wyo., 1974; disting. vis. scientist Acad. Scis. USSR, Moscow and Leningrad, 1972; Centennial Yr. vis. prof. dept. psychol. medicine U. Otago, Dunedin, N.Z., 1975; mem. Health Rsch. Com., Okla. Ctr. for Sci. and Tech., 1986-91, Okla. Alzheimer Rsch. Adv. Coun., 1990-92. Editor: Relating Environment to Mental Health and Illness: The Eco-psychiatric Data Base, 1979, Symposium on Man on the South Polar Plateau, 1970; mem. editorial bd. Jour. Clin. Psychology, 1970-80; contbr. more than 100 articles to sci. publs. Served as capt. M.C. U.S. Army, 1952-54. Recipient Antarctic Svc. medal NSF/NAS, 1970, Disting. Profl. Svc. award Okla. Psychol. Assn., 1972, Sustained Superior Achievement cert. VA, 1974, Disting. Psychiatrist award Mid-Continent Psychiat. Assn., 1986, Okla. Psychiat. Assn., 1990, Sealy Inc. prize Assn. Profl. Sleep Socs., 1991; Shurley Ridge, Pensacola Mountains Antarctica named in his honor. Fellow Am. Psychiat. Assn. (life), Am. Coll. Psychiatrists (life); mem. AMA,Oklahoma County Med. Assn., Okla. State Med. Assn. (life), Okla. Psychiat. Assn. (pres. 1968, chair ethics com. 1989-91), Faculty House Club, Sigma Xi, Alpha Omega Alpha, Alpha Epsilon Delta. Democrat. Address: PO Box 1277 Bastrop TX 78602

SHURTLIFF, SHAUN CARL, physician; b. Logan, Utah, July 16, 1967; s. Larry Richard and Leona (Brooks) S.; m. Lisa Christine Beckstrand, Aug. 15, 1989; children: Carl, Stephanie, Brittany. BS in Chemistry, So. Utah U., 1991; DO, Kirksville Coll. Osteo. Medicine, 1996. Mem. LDS Ch. Home: 2620 E Jerome Mesa AZ 85204

SHUSTER, FREDERICK, internist; b. Newark, Sept. 12, 1933; s. Ralph and Anne (Weinstein) S.; m. Jane B. Block, June 11, 1958; children: Alan R., Robert G. BS, Rutgers U., 1955; MD, U. Chgo., 1959. Diplomate Am. Bd. Internal Medicine, Am. Bd. Gastroenterology. Intern U. Mich. Hosp., Ann Arbor, 1959-60, resident internal medicine, 1960-62; resident gastroenterology VA Hosp. U. Miami, Fla., 1962-63; pvt. practice N. Miami Beach, Fla., 1963—; from clin. instr. to assoc. prof. medicine U. Miami, Fla., 1963—; chmn. dept. medicine Parkway Regional Med. Ctr., N. Miami Beach, 1967, 70, chief of staff, 1974-75, chief divsn. gastroenterology, 1976-77, chmn. pharmacy and therapeutics com., 1978—. Chmn. med. advisory com. Crohn's and Colitis Found., S. Fla. chpt., Miami, 1979—. Major U.S. Army, 1967-69. Recipient Physician's Recognition award in Continung Edn., AMA, Chgo., 1970—. Fellow Am. Coll. Physicians, Am. Coll. Gastroenterology, Alpha Omega Alpha. Jewish. Office: Drs Shuster & Reichbach PA Ste 204 16800 NW Second Ave North Miami Beach FL 33169

SHUTTLEWORTH, ANNE MARGARET, psychiatrist; b. Detroit, Jan. 17, 1931; d. Cornelius Joseph and Alice Catherine (Rice) S.; A.B., Cornell U., 1953, M.D., 1956; m. Joel R. Siegel, Apr. 19, 1959; children: Erika, Peter. Intern, Lenox Hill Hosp., N.Y.C., 1956-57; resident Payne Whitney Clinic-N.Y. Hosp., 1957-60; practice medicine, specializing in psychiatry, Maplewood, N.J., 1960—; cons. Maplewood Sch. System, 1960-62; instr. psychiatry Cornell U. Med. Sch., 1960; mem. Com. to Organize New Sch. Psychology, 1970. Mem. AMA (Physicians Recognition award 1975, 78, 81, 84, 87, 90, 93, 96), Am. Psychiat. Assn., Am. Med. Women's Assn., N.Y. Acad. Scis., Acad. Medicine N.J., Phi Beta Kappa, Phi Kappa Phi. Home: 46 Farbrook Dr Short Hills NJ 07078-3007 Office: 2066 Millburn Ave Maplewood NJ 07040-3715

SHWED, MELANIE SCHLITTLER, medical and surgical nurse, air force officer; b. Monroe, Wis., Oct. 27, 1955; d. Melvin Leroy and Mary Margaret (Hunt) Schlittler; m. John A. Shwed. BSN, Marquette U., 1978; M in Nursing, UCLA, 1993. Cert. clin. nurse specialist. Staff nurse Columbia Hosp., Milw., 1978; commd. USAF, 1978, advanced through grades to lt. col., staff nurse, charge nurse, nurse coord., comdr., 1978—. Mem. Am. Assn. Diabetes Educators, Sigma Theta Tau. Home: 4711 Woodland Point Valdosta GA 31602

SHYBUT, GEORGE THEODORE, orthopedic surgeon, educator; b. Pueblo, Colo.; s. Theodore and Olga (Adarich) S.; m. Rebecca Richards Schuster, Nov. 14, 1977; children: Theodore Benjamin, Alexandrea Ruth, Christopher George, Alexander Charles. BA, Grinnell Coll., 1972; MD, U. Chgo., 1976. Diplomate Am. Bd. Orthopaedic Surgery. Resident in orthopedics U. Chgo., 1977-81; fellow in orthopedics Harvard U., Boston, 1981-82; asst. prof. Northwestern Faculty Found., Chgo., 1982-89, Ctr. Orthopaedic Care, Cin., 1990—; assoc. prof. orthopedics U. Cin., 1995—; team physician U.S. Weightlifting Fedn., Colorado Springs, Colo., 1982-88; co-dir. Ctr. Performing Arts, Cin., 1990—; mem. med. com. U.S. Weightlifting Fedn., 1988—. Patentee knee orthosis. Mem. Com. on Phys. Fitness, Chgo.; med. vol. Ams. Marathon, Chgo., 1986-89; vol. coach AYSO Soccer, Glenview, Ill., 1988; bd. dirs. Cin. Ballet, 1993. Recipient 1st prize for trauma paper ACS, 1979, Berkheiser award Chgo. Inst. Medicine, 1980, Frank Stinchfield award The Hip Soc., 1980; N.Am. travel fellow Am. Orthopedic Assn., 1981. Fellow Am. Acad. Orthopedic Surgeons (knee com.); mem. AMA, Am. Coll. Sports Medicine, Am. Orthopedic Fellowship Group, Assn. Study of Methods of Ilizarov, Performing Arts Med. Assn. (membership com., bd. dirs 1988—). Home: 5069 Signal Hill Ln Cincinnati OH 45244-3822 Office: Ctr Orthopedic Care 2123 Auburn Ave Apt 235 Cincinnati OH 45219-2968

SHYERS, LARRY EDWARD, mental health counselor, educator; b. Middletown, Ohio, Aug. 16, 1948; s. Edward and Ruth Evelyn (Davis) S.; m. Linda Faye Shearon, July 31, 1970; children: Jami Lynn, Karen Lindsey. BA, David Lipscomb Coll., Nashville, 1970; MA, Stetson U., DeLand, Fla., 1973; MEd, U. Cen. Fla., 1981; PhD U. Fla., 1992. Lic. mental health counselor, Fla.; nat. cert. counselor; ordained to ministry non-denominational Ch. of Christ, 1969. Minister Ch. of Christ, Ocala, Fla., 1970-75, Mt. Dora, Fla., 1975-80; tchr. Christian Home and Bible Sch., Mt. Dora, 1970-77, dir. guidance, 1977-86; pvt. practice individual and family counseling, Mount Dora, Fla., 1980—; appointed to state regulatory bd. for clin. social work, marriage, family therapy, mental health counseling, 1987-95, vice-chmn., 1987-88, chmn., 1989-95, legis. liaison, 1988-95; adj. prof. Nova U., 1986—, U. Cen. Fla., 1988—, psychology St. Leo Coll., 1985—, Rollins Coll., 1991—, Reformed Theol. Sem., 1995—; adj. instr. Lake Sumter C.C., 1989—, Stetson U., 1990—, Rollins Coll., 1991—; mem. individual manpower tng. system bd. Vocat.-Tech. Sch., Eustis, 1984-87; mem. adv. bd. U.S. Achievement Bd., 1983—; cons. in field. Dir. edn. Mt. Dora Ch. of Christ, 1983-86. Mem. Fla. Mental Health Counselors Assn. (chmn. award and profl. devel. coms. 1985, chmn. govt. relations com., pres. 1986-87), ACA (govt. rels. com. 1990-95, publs. rev. com. 1991—), Am. Mental Health Counselors Assn. (govt. rels. com. 1987-90, chmn. 1988-90, publs. com. 1991—, PP&L com. 1992-95), Am. Orthopsychiat. Assn., Am. Assn. Christian Counselors, Internat. Assn. Marriage and Family Counselors, Assn. of Assessment in Counseling, Am. Assn. Profl. Hypnotherapists, Lake Sumter Assn. for Counseling and Devel. (Pres. 1987-88), Mount Dora C. of C. (mem. youth com. 1984), Kappa Delta Pi, Pi Lambda Theta, Chi Sigma Iota. Republican. Lodge: Kiwanis. Avocations: amateur radio, target shooting. Office: 3900 Lake Center Dr Ste 5 Mount Dora FL 32757-2203

SIANTZ, MARY LOU DELEON, nursing educator; b. L.A.; d. Santiago and Teresa (Farfan) deLeon; m. James Edward Siantz, Dec. 22, 1973; children: Elena Victoria, Elizabeth Julia. BS, Mt. St. Mary's Coll., L.A., 1969; M in Nursing, UCLA, 1971; PhD, U. Md., 1984. Dir. tng. in nursing. U. So. Calif., L.A., 1971-73; asst. prof. dept. psychat. nursing U. Mich., Ann Arbor, 1974-75; dir. tng. in nursing Georgetown U., Washington, 1975-78; nat. mental health coord. Migrant Headstart Program, Washington, 1978-82; assoc. prof. dept. psychiat. mental health nursing U. Indpls., Bloomington, 199184—; adj. faculty UCLA, Georgetown U., Washington, D.C., sch. of nursing Children's Hosp., L.A.; with program for child devel. U. of Am. Sch. of Nursing; mem. nat. adv. com. Hispanic Health Care Utilization Rsch. Project, 1990-91, infant mortality tech. rev. group office for minority health HHS, 1990; prin. investigator Succesful Adaptation of Migrant Head Start Children. Contbr. articles to various med. jours. Mem. Boys Club Aux., Bloomington, 1985—. Joseph P. Kennedy fellow, 1977-79; recipient Disting. Citizen award Ind. U. Latin-Am. Family Edn. Program, 1989. Fellow Am. Acad. Nursing; mem. Nat. Assn. Hispanic Nurses (chair awards com. 1980—, Ildaura Murrillo Rohde award for Ednl. Excellence 1986), Soc. for Rsch. in Child Devel. (mem. social policy com. 1989—), Advocates for Child Psychiat. Nursing (nat. co-chair, chair advocacy com. 1985-89), Am. Nurses Assn., Soc. for Rsch. and Edn. in Psychiat. Nursing (chair advocacy com. 1989—), Coalition of Spanish Speaking Mental Health and Human Svcs. Orgn. (sr. rsch. fellow 1987-90), Sigma Theta Tau (award in rsch. 1988). Office: Ind U Sch Nursing 1100 W Michigan St Indianapolis IN 46202-2880

SICARD, GUILLERMO RAFAEL, dermatologist; b. LaVega, Dominican Republic, Oct. 25, 1937; came to U.S., 1963; s. Fausto A. and Margarita (Moya) S.; m. Emilia Cordova, Jan. 11, 1963; children: Fausto Antonio, Julia Margarita. BS, Norman Sch., La Vega, Dominican Republic, 1954; MD, U. St. Domingo, Dominican Republic, 1960. Diplomate Am. Bd. Dermatology, Am. Bd. Dermatopathology. Chief of health Health Dept., La Vega, 1960-63; intern Franklin Sq. Hosp., Balt., 1963-64; resident Cleve. Metro Gen. Hosp., 1966-69; ptnr. Gardner, Sicard DMD, Inc., Canton, Ohio, 1969-82; practice medicine specializing in dermatology Canton, 1982—; cons. Aultman Hosp., Canton, 1969—, Timken Mercy Hosp., Canton, 1969—, Massillow Community Hosp., 1982—; asst. prof. Northeastern Ohio U. Coll. Medicine, Rootswoen, 1984—, sect. chief dermatology, 1985—. Investigator medication evaluation, 1984-85. Mem. Stark County Historical Soc., 1972—; sustaining mem. Republican Nat. Com., 1986—. Served to capt. U.S. Army, 1964-66. Fellow Am. Acad. Dermatology; mem. Canton Acad. Medicine (pres. 1981-82, Tennis Champion 1991), Stark County Med. Soc. (sec. 1979-80, pres. 1980-81), Smithsonian Inst., Ohio Dermatol. Assn., Cleve. Dermatol. Soc., Dermatology Found., Leaders Soc. Roman Catholic. Club: Hall of Fame Fitness (Canton). Home: 10695 Kent Ave NE Hartville OH 44632-8756 Office: 4825 Munson St NW Canton OH 44718-3614

SICOLI, MARY LOUISE CORBIN, psychologist, educator; b. Delaware County, Pa., Nov. 15, 1944; d. C.M. Lewis and Lucille (Weber) Corbin; m. Thomas Sicoli, Aug. 27, 1967; children: Michael, Kathryn Francesca. BS (Hannah Kent Schoff scholar), West Chester U., 1966, MS, 1974; MS (grad. fellow), U. Wis., Madison, 1967; Ph.D., Bryn Mawr Coll., 1977. Music tchr. supr. Unionville-Chadds Ford Sch. Dist., 1967-70; supr. student tchrs. Rosemont (Pa.) Coll., 1976-78; prof. psychology, campus psychologist Cabrini Coll., Radnor, Pa., 1974—, also coord. psychol. svcs.; cons. Children's Svcs. Southeastern Pa., 1974-80; supr. doctoral interns in psychology Bryn Mawr Coll., 1979-86; pvt. practice psychol. assessment children & adolescents. Contbr. articles to profl. jours. Founding mem. bd. dirs. Maternal Support System Chester County, 1981—; mem. Citizens Action for Better TV, 1981—; founder, chair Psychol. Aspects Popular Culture, Popular Culture Assn. Recipient Legion of Honor, Chapel for Four Chaplains, 1980, Christian and Mary Lindback award for disting. coll. teaching, 1984. Fellow Pa. Psychol. Assn. (founder campus psychologist network); mem. AAUP, Am. Psychol. Assn., Eastern Psychol. Assn., Jean Piaget Soc., Assn. for Moral Devel., Kappa Delta Pi, Psi Chi, Delta Epsilon Sigma. Home: 404 Darlington Dr West Chester PA 19382-2139 Office: Cabrini Coll Dept Psychology Radnor PA 19087

SIDARWECK, WILLIAM JOHN, educational psychologist; b. Bridgeport, Conn., Oct. 15, 1950; s. John and Mary (DeNigris) S.; m. Corinne Sidarweck; children: William Jr., Christopher, Sarah. BA, Sacred Heart U., 1972; MS, U. Bridgeport, 1975. Cert. sch. psychologist, Conn. Instr. Found. Sch., Orange, Conn., 1972-75, sch. psychologist, 1975-77; assoc. dir., co-founder Elizabeth O'Hara Walsh Sch., Stratford, Conn., 1977—; co-founder, assoc. dir., sch. psychologist Quaezar, Inc., Bridgeport, 1977-83, pres., exec. dir., 1983—. Coach North End Little League, Bridgeport, 1985-94. Mem. Coun. Assn. Pvt. Ednl. Facilities (sec.-treas. 1986-90), Ct. Assn. Residential facilities, Conn. Assn. Autistic Children. Democrat. Roman Catholic. Office: Quaezar Inc Two Research Dr Stratford CT 06604-2730

SIDDENS, JOHN DELMAR, osteopath, ophthalmologist; b. Clearwater, Fla., Jan. 30, 1957; s. Delma and Freda Ellison (Unthank) S.; m. Leslie Ann Sproles, Aug. 7, 1982; children: Jodi Lea, Lindsey Ellison, Mollie Ann. BS in Psychology, Fla. State U., 1980, BS in Biology, 1982; DO, Southeastern Coll. Osteo. Medicine, North Miami Beach, Fla., 1986. Diplomate Am. Osteo. Bd. Ophthalmology. Resident in ophthalmology Botsford Gen. Hosp., Farmington Hills, Mich., 1987-90; fellow in ophthalmic plastic surgery Kresgee Eye Inst., Wayne State U. Sch. Medicine, Detroit, 1990-91; pvt. practice, Greenville, S.C., 1991—; dir. oculoplastics S.C. Eye. Inst., U. S.C. Sch. Medicine, Columbia, 1991—; cons. in oculoplastics Dorn VA Med. Ctr., Columbia, 1991—. Author: Clinical Ophthalmology, 1993, Practical Techniques in Ophthalmic Plastic Surgery, 1993, Mastery of Plastic Surgery, 1993. Mem. AMA, Am. Osteo. Assn., Am. Acad. Ophthalmology, Osteo. Coll. Ophthalmology, S.C. Soc. Ophthalmology, Greenville County Med. Soc. (membership com. 1992—). Methodist. Office: Jervey Eye Group PA 50 Bear Dr Greenville SC 29605

SIDERIS, GEORGE NICHOLAS, biology educator; b. N.Y.C., May 8, 1949; s. Nicholas and Athanasia (LaFazani) S.; 1 child, Meredith Sideris Hopkins. BS in Psychology, CUNY, 1972; MS, L.I. U., 1978; postgrad., NYU, 1984-91. Instr. NYU, N.Y.C., 1977—, N.Y. Inst. Tech., N.Y.C., 1978-84, Coll. of S.I., N.Y.C., 1978—. Mem. AAAS, Am. Lit. Soc., Am. Mus. Natural History, Hellenic Zool. Soc., Soc. Systematic Zoology. Office: NYU Dept Biology 1009 Main Bldg New York NY 10003

SIDMAN, RICHARD LEON, neuroscientist; b. Boston, Sept. 19, 1928; s. Manuel and Annabelle (Seltzer) S.; m. Ljiljana Lekic, 1974. A.B., Harvard U., 1949, M.D. (Jeffries Wyman scholar), 1953. Intern in medicine Boston City Hosp., 1953-54; asst. resident in neurology Mass. Gen. Hosp., Boston, 1955-56; staff scientist NIH, Bethesda, Md., 1956-58; instr. to prof. neuropathology Harvard U. Med. Sch., 1959—, Bullard prof., 1969—; chief div. neurogenetics New Eng. Regional Primate Rsch. Ctr. Harvard Med. Sch., 1991—; chief dept. neurosci. Children's Hosp., Boston, 1972-88; 1st Richard Stearns Meml. lectr. Albert Einstein Coll. Medicine, 1958; Bailey Meml. lectr. U. Sask., Can., 1978; Waisman Meml. lectr. U. Wis. Author: (with M. Sidman) Neuroanatomy - A Programmed Text. vol. 1, 1965, (with others) Catalog of the Neurological Mutants of the Mouse, 1965, (with R.D. Adams) Introduction to Neuropathology, 1968, (with others) Atlas of the Mouse Brain and Spinal Cord, 1971; contbr. numerous articles, book chpts., revs. on neuroembryology, pathology, and genetics to profl. publs. Mem. sci. adv. com. Retinitis Pigmentosa Found.; bd. sci. overseers Jackson Lab., Bar Harbor, Maine. Served with USPHS, 1956-58. Recipient Soma Weiss student research prizes Harvard U. Med. Sch., 1951-53, Boylston Soc. Essay prize, 1953; Harvard U. Mosley Travelling fellow, 1954-55; Neuroscis. Research Program fellow, 1971-79. Fellow Am. Acad. Arts and Scis., Nat. Acad. Sci.; mem. Am. Acad. Neurology, AAAS, Am. Assn. Anatomists, Am. Assn. Neuropathologists, Am. Soc. Cell Biology, Histochem. Soc., Internat. Brain Research Orgn., Soc. Devel. Biology, Internat. Soc. Devel. Neurobiology, Soc. Devel. Neurosci., Soc. Neurosci., Tissue Culture Assn. Office: New England Regional Primat Rsch Ctr Harvard Med Sch 1 Pine Hill Dr Southborough MA 01772

SIDON, CLAUDIA MARIE, psychiatry and mental health nursing educator; b. Bellaire, Ohio, Feb. 6, 1946; d. Paul and Nell (Bernas) DePaulis; m. Michael Sidon; children: Michael II, Babe. Diploma, Wheeling (W.Va.) Hosp. Sch., 1966; BS in Nursing summa cum laude, Ohio U., Athens, 1979; MS in Nursing, W.Va. U., Morgantown, 1982. Cert. social worker. Various staff positions Bellaire City Hosp., 1966-67, 72-77; adj. nursing faculty W.Va. No. Community Coll., Wheeling, 1977-82; nurse clinician, psychotherapist Valley Psychol. and Psychiat. Svcs., Moundsville, W.Va., 1984; psychotherapist, nurse clinician, case mgr. No. Panhandle Behavioral Health Ctr., Wheeling, 1984-88; assoc. prof. ADN program Belmont Tech. Coll., St. Clairsville, Ohio, 1988—; presenter in field. Mem. Tri-State Psychiat. Nursing Assn. (pres., v.p., program chmn.), Nat. League for Nursing (presenter), Phi Kappa Phi, Sigma Theta Tau. Home: 52295 Sidon Rd Dillonvale OH 43917-9538 Office: Belmont Tech Coll 120 Fox Shannon Pl Saint Clairsville OH 43950-8751

SIDRANSKY, HERSCHEL, pathologist; b. Pensacola, Fla., Oct. 17, 1925; s. Ely and Touba (Bear) S.; m. Evelyn Lipsitz, Aug. 18, 1952; children: Ellen, David Ira. B.S., Tulane U., 1948, M.D., 1953, M.S., 1958. Diplomate: Am. Bd. Pathology. Intern Charity Hosp. La., New Orleans, 1953-54; vis. asst. pathologist Charity Hosp. La., 1954-58; practice medicine, specializing in pathology Washington, 1977—; pathologist Nat. Cancer Inst., NIH, Bethesda, Md., 1958-61; instr. pathology Tulane U., 1954-58; prof. pathology U. Pitts., 1961-72; prof., chmn. dept. pathology U. South Fla., Tampa, 1972-77, George Washington U., 1977—; cons. VA Hosp. and Children's Hosp., Washington. Mem. editl. bd. Jour. Nutrition, 1973-77, Cancer Rsch., 1974-77, Human Pathology, 1979-91, Am. Jour. Clin. Nutrition, 1979-82, Am. Jour. Pathology, 1980-85, Jour. Exptl. Pathology, 1982-92, Exptl. Molecular Pathology Jour., 1987—; contbr. articles to profl. jours. Served with AUS, 1944-46. Life Ins. Med. Research fellow, 1956-57; USPHS fellow, 1957-58, 67-68; NIH research grantee, 1961—. Mem. Am. Soc. for Investigative Pathology, Soc. Exptl. Biology and Medicine, Am. Assn. Cancer Rsch., Am. Inst. Nutrition, Am. Soc. Clin. Nutrition, U.S.-Can. Acad. Pathologists, Med. Mycology Soc. Ams., Reticuloendothelial Soc., N.Y. Acad. Scis., AAAS, Washington Acad. Medicine (pres. 1986—), Washington Soc. Pathologists, Assn. Pathology Chmn., Intersoc. Com. on Pathology Info., Sigma Xi. Home: 5144 Macomb St NW Washington DC 20016-2612 Office: 2300 I St NW Washington DC 20037-2337

SIDUN, NANCY MARIE, clinical psychologist, art therapist; b. Newark, July 9, 1955; d. Albert and Mae (Clement) S. BA, Colo. Womens Coll., 1976; MS, Emporia State U., 1978; PsyD, Ill. Sch. Profl. Psychology, 1986. Art therapy intern The Menninger Found., Topeka, 1978-79; art psychotherapist Childrens Med. Ctr., Tulsa, 1979-82; clin. psychologist, pvt. practice Chgo., 1983—; chief psychologist, adminstr. Ill. State Psych. Inst., Chgo., 1987-91; dir. practicum tng. Chgo. Sch. Profl. Psychology, 1991-95, dir. clin. tng., 1995—; adj. asst. prof. U. Ill., Chgo., 1982-84, 91-93; adj. asst. prof. Sch. Art Inst. Chgo., 1985-96, adj. assoc. prof., 1996—; clin. dir. Young Expressions, Chgo., 1985-87; psychologist Henry Horner Children's Ctr., Chgo., 1986-87; cons. Weight Mgmt. Svcs., Chgo., 1988-89, Touchstone Group, Chgo., 1987, Creative Devel. Ctr., Chgo., 1985-88. Contbr. articles to profl. jours. Mem. APA, Am. Art Therapy Assn., Ill. Psychol. Assn., Ill. Art Therapy Assn., Nat. Coalition Art Therapies Assn. Office: 3170 N Sheridan Rd Apt 210 Chicago IL 60657-4825

SIEBERTH, HEINZ-GÜNTER, nephrologist educator; b. Wasungen, Germany, May 6, 1934; s. Alfred and Johanna (Frank) S.; m. Gudrun Hildegard Richter, Sept. 18, 1960; children: Veit, Uta. Dr.Med., Humboldt Univ., Berlin, Germany, 1958. Wiss. asst. Akademie d. Wissenschaften, Berlin, Germany, 1958-59, Univ. Rostock, Germany, 1959-61; asst. Tuberkulosesanatorium, Marburg, Germany, 1961-62; wiss asst. Med. Univ. Poliklinik, Freiburg, Germany, 1962-64; wiss. asst. Med. Univ. Klinik Köln, Germany, 1964-69, habilitation oberarzt, 1969-80; prof. U. Klinik Koln, 1972; dir. mediziniske Klinik II, Tech. U. Aachen, Germany, 1981—; pres. Med. Soc., Nortrheine, 1988-89. Editor: Nieren u. Hochdruckkrankheiten, 1972—, Med. Notfall, 1990; author: Internal Medicine, 1992. Mem. Internat. Soc. Nephrology, European Soc. Dialysis a. Transplant, German Soc. Nephrology, German Soc. Intensive Care (pres. 1985-86), European Soc. Organ Transplants, German Soc. Internal Medicine, Internal Soc. Artificial Internal Organs. Office: Med Klinik II Klinkum, Pauwelsstrasse, 52057 Aachen Germany

SIEDLECKI, ANDREW JOSEPH, ophthalmologist; b. Medina, N.Y., Feb. 10, 1959; s. Richard Joseph and Mary Louise (Ottaviano) S.; m. Rose Maria Trapasso, Sept. 7, 1985; children: Alexander, Andrew, Adam. BA, Dartmouth Coll., 1981; MD, Cornell U., 1985. Diplomate Am. Bd. Ophthalmology. Ptnr. Eye Health Assocs. of Western N.Y., Buffalo, 1989-94, med. dir., 1994—. Fellow Am. Acad. Ophthalmology; mem. AMA, Am. Coll. Phys. Execs. Office: Eye Health Assocs WNY 170 Maple Rd Williamsville NY 14221

SIEGEL, GEORGE LEWIS, endocrinologist; b. Bklyn., June 2, 1934; s. Harry and Bertha (Safier) S.; m. Jean Gellis, May 29, 1964; children: Robert, Steven, Laura. AB, Colgate U., 1955; MD, Union U., 1959. Diplomate Am. Bd. Internal Medicine, Am. Bd. Endocrinology and Metabolism. Asst. clin. prof. Hahneman Sch. of Medicine, Phila., 1968-71, Mt. Sinai Sch. Medicine, N.Y.C., 1971—; attending physician of endocrinology Beth Israel Med. Ctr., N.Y.C., 1971—; chief endocrinology sect. Beth Israel North, N.Y.C., 1989—. Contbr. articles to profl. jours. Capt. M.C., US. Army, 1966-68. Mem. ACP, Am. Assn. Clin. Endocrinologists, Endocrine Soc., Am. Diabetes Assn., N.Y. Acad. Scis., Clin. Diabetes Soc. N.Y., N.Y. County Med. Soc. Home: 40 E 80th St New York NY 10021-0237 Office: 240 E 82nd St New York NY 10028-2703

SIEGEL, JOHN PUTNAM, surgeon, consultant; b. Newark, Oct. 15, 1955; s. Robert Irving and Iris Marie (Griswold) S.; m. Megan O'Reilly, July 8, 1988; (div. Oct. 1990); m. Alice S.Y. Chi, Jan. 16, 1993; 1 child, Kathryn Iris Chi Siegel. AB in Chemistry, Lafayette Coll., 1977; MD, UMDNJ N.J. Med. Sch., 1981. Diplomate Am. Bd. Surgery, Nat. Bd. Med. Examiners. Resident gen. surgery St. Vincent's Hosp. and Med. Ctr., N.Y.C., 1981-86; attending surgeon O'Connor Hosp., San Jose, Calif., 1986-88, 89—; prof. invitado U. Cayetano Heredia, Lima, Peru, 1988-89; cons. Dept. of Justice Drug Enforcement Adminstrn., Lima, Peru, 1988-89. Fellow ACS; mem. Soc. for Critical Care Medicine, San Jose Surgical Soc., Alpha Omega Alpha. Office: John P. Siegel MD FACS 2101 Forest Ave San Jose CA 95128

SIEGEL, MICHAEL ELLIOT, nuclear medicine physician, educator; b. N.Y.C., May 13, 1942; s. Benjamin and Rose (Gilbert) S.; m. Marsha Rose Snower, Mar. 20, 1966; children: Herrick Jove, Meridith Ann. AB, Cornell U., 1964; MD, Chgo. Med. Sch., 1968. Diplomate Nat. Bd. Med. Examiners. Intern Cedars-Sinai Med. Ctr., L.A., 1968-69; resident in radiology, 1969-70; NIH fellow in radiology Temple U. Med. Ctr., Phila., 1970-71; NIH fellow in nuclear medicine Johns Hopkins U. Sch. Medicine, Balt., 1971-73, asst. prof. radiology, 1972-76; assoc. prof. radiology, medicine U. So. Calif., L.A., 1976—; prof. radiology, 1989—, dir. divsn. nuclear medicine, 1982—; dir. Sch. Nuclear Medicine, L.A. County-U. So. Calif. Med. Ctr., 1976—; dir. divsn. nuclear medicine Kenneth Norris Cancer Hosp. and Rsch. Ctr., L.A., 1983—; dir. dept. nuclear medicine Orthopaedic Hosp., L.A., 1981—, Intercommunity Hosp., Covina, Calif., 1981—, U. So. Calif. Univ. Hosp., L.A., 1993—; cons. dept. nuclear medicine Rancho Los Amigos Hosp., Downey, Calif., 1976—. Author: Textbook of Nuclear Medicine, 1978, Vascular Surgery, 1983, 88, and numerous others textbooks; editor: Nuclear Cardiology, 1981, Vascular Disease: Nuclear Medicine, 1983. Mem. Maple Ctr., Beverly Hills. Served as maj. USAF, 1974-76. Recipient Outstanding Alumnus award Chgo. Med. Sch., 1991. Fellow Am. Coll. Nuclear Medicine (sci. investigator 1974, 76, nominations com. 1980, program com. 1983, bd. trustees 1993, disting. fellow, 1993, bd. reps., 1993—, bd. dirs. 1994—, treas. 1996—); mem. Soc. Nuclear Medicine (sci. exhbn. com. 1978-79, program com. 1979-80, Silver medal 1975), Calif. Med. Assn. (sci. adv. bd. 1987—), Radiol. Soc. N.Am., Soc. Nuclear Magnetic Resonance Imaging, Alpha Omega Alpha. Lodge: Friars So. Calif. Research on devel. of nuclear medicine techniques to: evaluate cardiovascular disease and diagnose and treat cancer, clinical utilization of video digital displays in nuclear medicine development; inventor pneumatic radiologic pressure system. Office: U So Calif Med Ctr PO Box 693 1200 N State St Los Angeles CA 90033

SIEGEL, NORMAN JOSEPH, pediatrician, educator; b. Houston, Mar. 8, 1943; m. Rise Joan Ross, Dec. 24, 1967; children: Andrew, Karen. BA, Tulane U., 1964; MA, U. Tex. Med. Br., Galveston, 1968, MD, 1968. Intern, then resident Yale-New Haven Hosp., 1968-70; fellow Sch. Medicine, Yale U., New Haven, 1970-72, asst. prof. pediatrics and medicine, 1972-76, assoc. prof., 1976-82, prof., 1982—, vice chmn. pediatrics, 1979—; acting chmn. pediatrics Yale U., 1995—. Contbr. articles to profl. jours., chpts. to books. Grantee NIH, Am. Heart Assn., Hood Found. Mem. Am. Pediatric Soc. (sec.-treas. 1993—), Am. Soc. Pediatric Nephrology (pres. 1988-89), Nat. Kidney Found. (chmn. com. on pediatric nephrology and urology 1987-91, grantee, scientific adv. com. 1988-91), Soc. Pediatric Rsch. (membership sec. 1979-85), Nat. Bd. Med. Examiners (pediatric test com. 1993-95), Phi Beta Kappa, Mu Delta. Office: Yale U Sch Medicine Dept Pediatrics 333 Cedar St PO Box 208064 New Haven CT 06520-8064

SIEGENTHALER, WALTER ERNST, internal medicine educator; b. Davos, Switzerland, Dec. 14, 1923; s. Walter and Anna S.; m. Gertrud Siegenthaler, Dec. 31, 1957. MD, U. Zurich (Switzerland), 1948; Dr.h.c., Martin Luther U., Halle, Germany, 1991. Chief resident in internal medicine St. Gallen, Switzerland, 1954-58; prof. internal medicine, chmn. dept. U. Bonn (Fed. Republic Germany), 1969-71; asst. in pathology U. Zurich, 1949-50, asst. in internal medicine, 1950-54, chief resident, 1958-61, lectr., 1961-67, asst. prof., 1967-69, assoc. prof., 1971-91, chmn. dept., dean Med. Sch., 1978-80; pres. Conf. Clinic Dirs., Zurich, 1980-91; pres. 10th Internat. Congress Chemotherapy, 1977; pres. Swiss Rsch. Inst. for Climate and Medicine, 1992—. Author textbooks on differential diagnosis, 17th edit., 1993, on clin. pathophysiology, 7th edit., 1994, on internal medicine, 3d edit., 1992; bd. dirs. numerous nat. and internat. sci. jours.; contbr. articles to profl. jours. Bd. dirs. EMDO Found. Zurich, 1974—, Jung Found., Hamburg, 1982-95, Opo Found., Zurich, 1994—, Swiss Found. for the promotion of young people, 1995—. Col. Swiss Army, 1941-88. Recipient Ernst von Bergmann plaque, 1972, Ludwig Heilmeyer gold medal, 1984. Fellow Infectious Diseases Soc. Am. (corr. 1983); mem. German Soc. Internal Medicine (pres. 1983-84, bd. dirs., hon. mem. 1992), Swiss Soc. Internal Medicine (bd. dirs., hon. mem. 1993), Acad. Naturforscher Leopoldina, Soc. for Progress in Internal Medicine (Cologne; bd. dirs., pres. 1992—), Paul Ehrlich Soc. (pres. 1969-71, 73-75, 75-77, hon. 1994), Rotary. Home: Forsterstrasse 6l, CH-8044 Zurich Switzerland Office: Univ Hosp, Rämistrasse 100, CH-8091 Zurich Switzerland

SIEGERT, BARBARA (MARIE), health care administrator; b. Boston, May 22, 1935; d. Salvatore Mario and Mary Kathleen (Wagner) Tartaglia; m. Herbert C. Siegert (dec. Apr. 1974); children: Carolyn Marie, Herbert Christian Jr. Diploma, Newton-Wellesley (Mass.) Hosp. Sch. Nursing, 1956; MEd, Antioch U., 1980. Diplomate Am. Bd. Med. Psychotherapists. Supr. nursing Hogan Regional Ctr., Hathorne, Mass., 1974-78; community mental health nursing advisor Cape Ann area office Dept. Mental Health, Beverly, Mass., 1978-79; dir. case mgmt. Dept. Mental Health, Beverly, 1979-87, dir. case mgmt. north shore area office, 1988-91; dir. case mgmt. Dept. Mental Health-north shore area-Lynn (Mass.) site, Lynn, Mass., 1991-92; mem. interdisciplinary faculty, profl. cons. com., lecture staff clin. pastoral counseling program Danvers State Hosp./Hogan/Berry Regional Ctrs., Hathorne, Mass., 1982-86; nursing edn. adv. com. North Shore Community Coll., Beverly, 1983-91; tng. staff Balter Inst., Ipswich, Mass., 1987-88. Mem. Internat. Cultural Diploma Honor, 1989—. Recipient Spl. Recognition award Lexington (Mass.) Pub. Schs., 1973, Peter Torci award Lexington Friends of Children in Spl. Edn., 1974; named Internat. Biog. Roll. of Honor, 1989—. Fellow Am. Biog. Inst. (life, Woman of Yr. 1990); mem. World Inst. Achievement. Home: 63 Willow Rd # B Boxford MA 01921-1218

SIEGESMUND, KENNETH AUGUST, forensic anatomist, consultant, educator; b. Milw., Nov. 28, 1932; s. August Emil and Martha Laura (Schwarz) S.; m. Patricia Diane Dreyer, Apr. 15, 1959; children: Mark, Sandra, Carolyn, John. BS, U. Wis., 1954, PhD, 1960. Rsch. assoc. Marquette U., Milw., 1960-62; asst. prof. anatomy Med. Coll. Wis., Milw., 1962-69, assoc. prof., 1969—; cons. Milwaukee County Hosp., 1962-67, VA Hosp., Milw., 1963-78, Trinity Hosp., Milw., 1977-86, St. Lukes Hosp., Milw., 1982-85. Contbr. numerous articles to profl. jours.; patentee in field. NIH grantee, 1985, 86-88, 89. Mem. Electron Microscope Soc. Am., Midwest Microscope Soc. Am. (pres. 1970-71), Am. Assn. Anatomy, Am. Acad. Forensic Sci., Neuroelectric Soc. Am., Casal Club. Home: 17825 Primrose Ln Brookfield WI 53045-1231 Office: Med Coll Wis 8701 W Watertown Plank Rd Milwaukee WI 53226-3548

SIEGLER, MARK, internist, educator; b. N.Y.C., June 20, 1941; s. Abraham J. and Florence (Sternlieb) S.; m. Anna Elizabeth Hollinger, June 4, 1967; children:Dillan, Alison, Richard, Jessica. AB with honors, Princeton U., 1963; MD, U. Chgo., 1967. Diplomate Am. Bd. Internal Medicine. Resident, chief resident internal medicine U. Chgo., 1967-71; hon. sr. registrar in medicine Royal Postgrad. Med. Sch., London, 1971-72; asst. prof. medicine U. Chgo., 1972-78, assoc. prof. medicine, 1979-85, acting dir. div. gen. internal medicine, 1983-85, dir. Ctr. Clin. Med. Ethics, 1984—, prof. medicine, 1985—, dir. nat. leadership tng. program in clin. med. ethics, 1986—; vis. asst. prof. medicine U. Wis., Madison, 1977; vis. assoc. prof. medicine U. Va., Charlottesville, 1981-82. Co-author: Clinical Ethics, 1981, 2d edit., 1986, 3d edit., 1992, An Annotated Bibliography of Medical Ethics, 1988, Institutional Protocols for Decisions About Life-Sustaining Treatment, 1988; co-editor: Changing Values in Medicine, 1985, Medical Innovations and Bad Outcomes, 1987; editl. bd. Am. Jour. Medicine. 1979-94, Archives Internal Medicine, 1979-90, Bibliography of Bioethics, Jour. Med. Philosophy, 1978-89, Jour. Clin. Ethics; contbr. articles to profl. jours. Bd. govs. Josephson Inst. for Advancement of Ethics, L.A., 1986-92. Grantee Andrew W. Mellon Found., Henry J. Kaiser Family Found., Pew Charitable Trusts, Field Found. Ill., Ira De Camp Found.; Phi Beta Kappa vis. scholar, 1991-92, others. Fellow ACP (human rights com., ethics com. 1985-90), Hastings Ctr.; mem. Chgo. Clin. Ethics Program (pres. 1989-90). Office: Univ Chgo MC 6098 MacLean Ctr Clin Med Ethics 5841 S Maryland Ave Chicago IL 60637-1470

SIEKIERSKI, KAMILLA MALGORZATA, dental laboratory technician; b. Warsaw, Poland, Aug. 4, 1938; came to U.S., 1963, naturalized, 1970; d. Tomasz and Janina W. (Sendzimir) Piotrowski; cert. dental technician Sch. Dental Technicians, Krakow, Poland, 1957; m. Kazimierz Siekierski, Nov. 25, 1959; children—Marzanna, Eva. Owner, operator Kama's Dental Lab., Krakow, 1963; dental technician Dan's Dental Lab., Waterbury, Conn., 1963-65, Wilcox Dental Lab., Wethersfield, Conn., 1965-68; pres. Dentek, Inc., Milford, Conn., 1980—; nat.-internat. lectr. in field. Mem. Conn. Dental Lab. Assn. (pres. 1977-79), Nat. Assn. Dental Labs., Conf. Dental Labs. Home: 350 Gulf St Milford CT 06460-6534 Office: PO Box 3649 233 Research Dr Milford CT 06460-8526

SIEMAN, ROBERT STANLEY, obstetrician, gynecologist; b. Chgo., Feb. 5, 1944; s. Stanley J. and Viola (Grella) S.; m. Loretta J. Tursi, Aug. 19, 1967; children: Brian, Kevin. BS in Pharmacy, Drake U., 1966; DO, Coll. Osteo. Medicine & Surg., 1973. Resident St. Joseph Hosp. Health Ctr., Syracuse, N.Y., 1973-75, SUNY, Upstate Med. Ctr., Syracuse, N.Y., 1975-78; ob-gyn. James J. Kelso MD, Des Moines, 1978—. Fellow Am. Coll. Ob-gyn.; mem. AMA, Am. Soc. Reproductive Medicine, Iowa Med. Soc., Des Moines Ob-Gyn. Soc., Polk County Med. Soc. Office: 1410 Woodland Des Moines IA 50309

SIEPERMAN, KATHLEEN LOUISE, nurse; b. Morristown, N.J., June 21, 1962; d. Raymond Joseph and Doris Marie Louise (Scheppard) S.; m. William Grimm, May 11, 1991 (div. Oct. 1995). ADN, Scottsdale Cmty., Scottsdale, Ariz., 1984; BSN, Univ. Phoenix, 1996—. RN; cert. registered nurse intravenous. Staff RN burn unit ICU Maricopa County Hosp., Phoenix, 1984-86, staff RN dialysis unit, 1986; staff charge RN intensive care Humana Hosp., Phoenix, 1987-88; clinical specialist IV therapy Infusion Care, Phoenix, 1988; dischange planner Humana Hosp., Phoenix, 1989-90; area mgr. infusion Kimberly Quality Care, Phoenix, 1990-91, regional mgr. infusion, 1991-92, divsn. mgr. infusion, 1993-95, western U.S. mgr. infusion, 1995—. Mem. Young Dem. Soc., Phoenix, 1995—. Recipient Nursing Excellence award Humana Hosp., 1988. Mem. Intravenous Nurses Soc., Soc. Pain Mgmt. Nursing, Nat. Assn. Vascular Acess Networks, Am.-Soc. Parenteral & Enteral Nutrition. Methodist. Office: Olsten Kimberly Quality Care 711 E Missouri Ste 300 Phoenix AZ 85014

SIEPSER, STUART LEWIS, internist, cardiologist; s. Jesse and Miriam (Spector) S.; m. Lynn Perkel, Mar. 15, 1969; children: Gabrielle, Craig, Amy. BA, Columbia Coll., 1964; MD, NYU, 1968. Diplomate Am. Bd. Internal Medicine, Am. Bd. Cardiology. Intern Bellevue Hosp., 1968-69, resident in medicine, 1969-70; fellow in cardiology NYU Med. Ctr., 1970-72; ptnr. Cardiology Assocs. North Jersey, PA, Wayne, N.J., 1974—; clin. asst. prof. N.J. Med. Sch. Coll. Medicine and Dentistry N.J., 1976—; pres. med. dental staff Chilton Meml. Hosp.; cardiology liaison Morristown (N.J.) Meml. Hosp., 1993—; mem. med. care appraisal com. Chilton Meml. Hosp., 1980—, hosp. pharmacy and therapeutics com., 1980-84, 93—, chmn. sect. cardiology, 1993—. Maj. U.S. Army, 1972-74. Fellow Am. Coll. Cardiology, Am. Coll. Physicians; mem. AMA, Soc. Internal Medicine, Passaic County Med. Soc., Alpha Omega Alpha. Home: 44 Littlewood Ct Wayne NJ 07470-5013 Office: Cardiology Assocs North Jersey PA 1777 Hamburg Tpke Wayne NJ 07470-5200

SIEVER, LARRY JOSEPH, psychiatrist; b. Chgo., Sept. 2, 1947; s. Raymond and Doris (Fisher) S.; m. Lissa Weinstein, Oct. 14, 1989; children: David William, Daniel Robert. BA, Harvard U., 1969; MD, Stanford U., 1975. Diplomate Am. Bd. Psychiatry and Neurology. Med. intern Mary's Help Hosp., Daly City, Calif., 1975; resident and fellow in psychiatry McLean Hosp./Harvard Med. Sch., Belmont, Mass., 1975-78; staff fellow NIMH, Clin. Neuropharmacology Br., Bethesda, Md., 1978-80, chief unit on biol. correlated behavior, 1980-82; prof. Mt. Sinai Sch. Medicine, N.Y.C., 1990—; dir. psychiatry out-patient clinic Bronx VA Med. Ctr., 1982-87; dir. out-patient div. Mt. Sinai Sch. Medicine and Bronx Med. Ctr., 1987—; mem. NIMH Psychopharmacology and Clin. Biology Rev. Com., 1988-92. Contbr. numerous articles to profl. jours.; assoc. editor jour. Personality Disorders, 1987—, Depression, 1991—. NIMH Merit awardee, 1988, VA Merit awardee, 1989. Mem. AAAS, Am. Coll. Neuropsychopharmacology, Soc. of Biologic Psychiatry, Am. Psychiat. Assn., N.Y. Psychiat. Assn., Phi Beta Kappa, Sigma Xi. Office: Bronx VA Med Ctr Dept Psychiatry 130 W Kingsbridge Rd Bronx NY 10468-3992

SIEVERTS, FRANK ARNE, association executive; b. Frankfurt, Fed. Republic Germany, June 19, 1933; s. Helmut J. and Cecile M. (Behrendt) S.; m. Jane Woodbridge, Dec. 31, 1957 (div.); children: Lisa, Michael; m. Sue Hubbell, Feb. 13, 1988; 1 stepchild, Brian. BA, Swarthmore Coll., 1955; M in Philosophy (Rhodes Scholar), Balliol Coll. Oxford U., 1957; postgrad., Nuffield Coll., 1957-59. News corr. Time mag., London and Washington, 1959-60; legis. asst. U.S. Senator Washington, 1960-62; with Dept. of State, Washington, 1962-86, spl. asst. to ambassador at large Averell Harriman, 1966-68, adviser on prisoner of war matters to U.S. delegation to Vietnam peace talks, spl. asst. to dep. sec. of state for prisoner of war matters, 1969-75, dep. asst. sec. for prisoner of war and missing in action matters, 1976—, dep. asst. sec. for refugee and migration affairs, 1978—; minister-counselor for humanitarian affairs U.S. Mission, Geneva, 1980-95; spl. asst. for refugee programs, 1982-86; spokesman for Com. on Fgn. Relations U.S. Senate, 1987-95; asst. to head of delegation for U.S., Can. Internat. Com. Red Cross, Washington, 1995—; mem. advance team for release Am. prisoners of war, Hanoi, 1973. Editorial bd.: The Am. Oxonian. Mem. U.S. delegation to 20th Internat. Conf. Red Cross, Vienna, 1965, 21st Conf., Istanbul, 1969, 22d Conf., Tehran, 1973; chmn. 23d Conf., Bucharest, 1977, 24th Conf., Manila, 1981, 25th Conf., Geneva, 1986; U.S. del. Diplomatic Conf. on Humanitarian Law in Armed Conflicts, Geneva, 1974-77, to exec. com. of UN High Commn. for Refugees, 1978, 79, 80; staff dir. Indochinese Refugee panel, 1986. Mem. Am. Assn. Rhodes Scholars (bd. dirs.). Office: Internat Com Red Cross Ste 545 2100 Pennsylvania Ave NW Washington DC 20037

SIFFERT, ROBERT SPENCER, orthopedic surgeon; b. N.Y.C., June 16, 1918; s. Oscar and Sadye (Rusoff) S.; m. Miriam Sand, June 29, 1941; children: Joan, John. AB in Biology with honors, NYU, 1939, MD, 1943. Diplomate Am. Bd. Orthop. Surgery, Nat. Bd. Med. Examiners. Intern Kings County Hosp., Bklyn., 1943; resident in orthop. surgery Mt. Sinai Hosp., N.Y.C., 1946-49, fellow in pathology, 1949-52, mem. staff, 1949—, dir. orthor. surgery, orthop. surgeon in chief, 1960-86, Lasker/Siffert Disting. Svc. prof., 1986—; pvt. practice N.Y.C., 1949—; dir. dept. orthops. City Hosp., Elmhurst, 1965-86; sr. orthop. cons. N.Y.C. Dept. Health, 1952-60; attending orthop. surgeon Blythedale Children's Hosp., Valhalla, N.Y., 1960-86, cons., 1986-90; prof., chmn. dept. orthops. Mt. Sinai Sch. Medicine, 1966-86, Dr. Robert K. Lippman prof., 1983-86, acting chmn., 1993-94. Author: See How They Grow, 1985; co-author: (with J.F. Katz) Management of Hip Disorders in Children, 1983; contbr. over 100 articles to profl. jours. Mem. adv. bd. CARE-MEDICO, 1972-83, bd. dirs., 1981-83, chmn., 1981-83; bd. dirs. CARE, 1983-90; adv. bd. Orthopaedics Overseas, 1981-93; bd. dirs., mem. profl. adv. com. Easter Seal Soc. for Crippled Children and Adults, 1st v.p., 1977-79. Capt. USAAF, 1944-46, CBI. Decorated 4 Battle Stars; recipient annual award medicine N.Y. Pub. Health Assn., 1958, annual award medicine N.Y. Philanthropic League, 1959, Richman award for humanism in medicine Mt. Sinai Sch. Medicine, 1989. Fellow ACS, APHA; mem. Am. Orthop. Assn., Am. Acad. Orthop. Surgery (chmn. com. on care of handicapped child), Assn. Bone and Joint Surgeons, Internat. Soc. Orthop. Surgery and Traumatology, Internat. Skeletal Soc., Orthop. Rsch. Soc., N.Y. Acad. Medicine (fellow orthop. sect. 1952, sec. 1962-63, chmn. 1963-64), N.Y. State Med. Soc. (chmn. orthop. sect. 1967-68), Century Assn. (N.Y.C.), Phi Beta Kappa, Alpha Omega Alpha. Office: 955 Fifth Ave New York NY 10021-1738

SIFONTES, JOSE E., pediatrics educator; b. Arecibo, P.R.; s. Jose E. and Josefa M. (Fontan) S.; m. Iris J. Sotomayor, Dec. 20, 1952; children: J. Jaime, Mariat, Iris, J. Roberto, Myrta, J. Ricardo, Beatriz. MD, Syracuse U., 1948. Diplomate Am. Bd. Pediatrics. Dir. USPHS TB Rsch., San Juan, Puerto Rico, 1958-66; dean U. Puerto Rico Sch. of Medicine, San Juan, 1966-71; chief of pediatrics U. Puerto Rico Sch. Medicine, San Juan, 1974-77, chief pediatric pulmonary program, 1960-66, prof. pediatrics, 1966—; pvt. practice specializing in pulmonary pediatrics, San Juan, 1982—; cons. to many nat. and internat. health orgns. including WHO, UN, PAHTO, 1954-82. Author: (Spanish textbook) Neumologia Pediatrica, 1974; contbr. over 100 articles to profl. jours. Vol. Am. Thoracic Soc. ATS, AZA, 1953—. Surgeon USPHS, 1957-59. Grantee: USPHS, NIH, 1954-82. Mem. Am. Acad. Pediatrics (fellow chest sect., nat. chmn. 1964-65), Am. Pediatric Soc. Roman Catholic.

SIGALL, HAROLD FRED, psychology educator; b. N.Y.C., June 29, 1943; s. Walter and Regine (Goldenberg) S.; m. Brenda Ann Alpert, Aug. 8, 1965; children: Elana, Jennifer, Emily. BS, CUNY, 1964; PhD, U. Tex., 1968. Asst. prof. psychology U. Rochester, N.Y., 1968-72; assoc. prof. U. Md., College Park, 1972-78, prof., 1978—, dir. grad. program in social psychology; consulting editor Journal of Applied Social psychology, 1992—; cons. social research and decision making to numerous orgns., lectr. Smithsonian Inst., Washington, 1984, 85. Editor Personality and Social Psychology Bull., 1977-81; contbr. numerous articles to profl. jours. Bd. dirs. Columbia (Md.) Jewish Congregation, 1985-87, Howard County (Md.) Jewish Cmty. Sch., Columbia, 1986-87; mem. Human Rights Commn., Howard County, 1994—. NDEA fellow, 1967-68, Danforth Found. fellow, 1970-71. Fellow Am. Psychol. Assn., Am. Psychol. Soc.; mem. Soc. Exptl. Social Psychology. Home: 5060 Castlemoor Dr Columbia MD 21044-1454 Office: U of Md Dept Psychology College Park MD 20742

SIGELL, LEONARD T., pharmacologist, educator; b. Portland, Oreg., Dec. 28, 1938; s. Edward Trilluck and Rose (Lichtgarn) S. BS (RPh) Pharmacy, Oregon State U., 1961; PhD in Pharmacology, U. Oreg., 1964. Reg. pharmacist, Oreg.; cert. prevention specialist. Registered pharmacist Fred Meyer Pharmacy, Portland, 1962-64; staff Oregon Poison Ctr., Portland, 1962-64; mem. faculty dept. pharmacology dept medicine U. Cin., 1964—; dir. Drug and Poison Info. Ctr., Portland, 1966—; former evaluator Law Enforcement Assistance Adminstrn., Open House Counseling Svc., Inc., Charlotte, N.C.; former mem. Nat. Adv. Panel to HEW Model Health Care Tech. Ctr. U. Mo., student rsch. awards com. Am. Assn. Poison Control Ctrs.; mem. profl. effectiveness program com. U. Cin., adv. com. Med. Ctr. Librs., past mem. admissions com. U. Coll. Medicine, Univ. Hosp.; mem. Cin. Health Dept. Pharmacy and Therapeutics com., Hamilton County Drug Abuse Coordinating Com.; past mem. steering com. Hamilton County Comty. Mental Health Bd.; former cons. multi-purpose Arthritis Ctr. for Tri-State area. Contbr. articles to numerous profl. jours; mem. edtl. bd. Poisindex, former mem. editors cons. panel Jour. Am. Med. Assn.; past book reviewer Archives Internal Medicine, past reviewer Am. Jour. Diseases of Children; reviewer Drug Intelligence and Clin. Pharmacy; past referee Am. Jour. Hosp. Pharmacy. Mem. Alcohol and Drug Abuse Prevention Assn. of Ohio, Assn. of Ohio Substance Abuse Programs; past mem. Citizens Against Substance Abuse; bd. dirs. Adolescent Clinic of Children's Hosp. Med. Ctr., U.S. Pharmacopoeia Conv. Recipient Oscar Schmidt Pub. Svc. award, U. Cin., 1990-91; grantee, Nat. Inst. Occupational Safety and Health, Marion Merrell Dow, McNeil Consumer Products Co. Mem. Am. Assn. Poison Control Ctrs., Drug Info. Assn., Am. Soc. Hosp. Pharmacists (assoc.), Ohio Assn. Poison Control Ctrs. (pres.), Cin. Bar Assn./ Acad. Medicine Substance Abuse Task Force, Rho Chi, Kappa Psi. Office: U Cin Coll Medicine PO Box 670144 Cincinnati OH 45267

SIGETY, CHARLES BIRGE, health care supply manufacturing company executive; b. N.Y.C., Sept. 30, 1952; s. Charles Edward and Katharine Kinne (Snell) S.; m. Elizabeth Ross Pennington, Nov. 27, 1976; children: Austin Douglas, Katharine Colyer, Alexander Birge. BA in English Lit., Bates Coll., 1975. Lic. nursing home adminstr. Adminstr. in tng. Florence Nightingale Nursing Home, N.Y.C., 1972, asst. dir. facility ops., 1975, dir. facility ops., 1975-78, assoc. adminstr., 1978-81, exec. dir., 1981-82; pres., CEO Profl. Med. Products, Inc., Greenwood, S.C., 1982-96; dir. Upper Savannah Internat. Trade Assn., Greenwood, S.C., 1993-94; pres. Upper Savannah Internat. Trade Assn., Greenwood, 1993; prin. Bison Investments, Inc., Tampa, Fla., 1996—; mem. Liberty Mutual Ins. Cos. S.C. Adv. Bd., 1986-96; mem. Nations Bank's S.C. Adv. Bd., 1984-96; bd. dirs. Profl. Med. Products, Inc.; mem. County Bank Adv. Bd., Greenwood, 1981; vice chmn. Upper Savannah Bus. Group on Health Care, Greenwood, 1982-87; mem. S.C. Bus. Roundtable for The Initiative for Work Force Excellence, Columbia, 1988-92; dir., mem. exec. com. OSTEO Am., Inc., 1993—; bd. dir. Help for Incontinent People, 1993-96. Bd. visitors Med. U. S.C., 1988. Mem. Young Pres. Orgn., Am. Coll. of Health Care Adminstrs., Health Industry Mfrs. Assn. (official rep. 1982-96), Upper Savannah Internat. Trade Assn. (pres. 1993). Republican. Presbyterian. Office: Bison Investments Inc Box 236 3225 S MacDill Ave Tampa FL 33629

SIGETY, CHARLES EDWARD, lawyer, family business consultant; b. N.Y.C., Oct. 10, 1922; s. Charles and Anna (Toth) S.; m. Katharine K. Snell, July 17, 1948; children: Charles, Katharine, Robert, Cornelius, Elizabeth. BS, Columbia U., 1944; MBA, Harvard U., 1947; LLB, Yale U., 1951; LHD (hon.), Cazenovia Coll., 1994. Bar: N.Y. 1952, D.C. 1958. With Bankers Trust Co., 1939-42; instr. adminstrv. engring. Pratt Inst., 1948; instr. econs. Yale U., 1948-50; vis. lectr. acctg. Sch. Gen. Studies Columbia U., N.Y.C., 1948-50, 52; rapporteur com. fed. taxation for U.S. coun. Internat. C. of C., 1952-53; asst. to com. fed. taxation Am. Inst. Accts., 1950-53; with Compton Advt. Agy., N.Y.C., 1954; vis. lectr. law Yale U., 1952; pvt. practice law N.Y.C., 1952-67; pres., dir. Video Vittles, Inc., N.Y.C., 1953-67; dep. commr. FHA, 1955-57; of counsel Javits and Javits, 1959-60; 1st asst. atty. gen. N.Y., 1958-59; dir., mem. exec. com. Gotham Bank, N.Y.C., 1961-63; dir. N.Y. State Housing Fin. Agy., 1962-63; chmn. Met. Ski Slopes, Inc., N.Y.C., 1962-65; pres., exec. adminstr. Florence Nightingale Health Ctr., N.Y.C., 1965-85; chmn. bd. Profl. Med. Products, Inc., Greenwood, S.C., 1982-96; dir. Schaerer AG, Wabern, Switzerland, 1982-88; professorial lectr. Sch. Architecture, Pratt Inst., N.Y.C., 1962-66; mem. Sigety Assocs., cons. in housing mortgage financing and urban renewal, 1957-67; ho. cons. Govt. of Peru, 1956; mem. missions to Hungary, Poland, Fed. Republic Germany, Malta, Czechoslovakia, Russia, Israel, Overseas Pvt. Investment Corp., 1990-92; owner, operator Peppermill Farms, Pipersville, Pa., 1956—. Bd. dirs., sec., v.p., treas. Nat. Coun. Health Ctrs., 1969-85; bd. dirs. Am.-Hungarian Found., 1974-76, Pritikin Rsch. Found., 1991—, Stratford Arms Condo Assn., 1992-93, Global LEadership Inst., 1993—; trustee Cazenovia (N.Y.) Coll., 1981-95; del. White House Conf. on Aging, 1971, White House Conf. on Mgmt. Tng. and Market Econs. Edn. in Ctrl. and Ea. Europe, 1991; bd. visitors Lander Coll., U. S.C., Greenwood, 1982-84; mem. fin. com. World Games, Santa Clara, 1981, London, 1985, Karlsruhe, 1989, The Hague, 1993, Confrerie des Chevaliers du Tastevin, Confrerie de la Chaine des Rotisseurs, Wine and Food Soc., Wednesday 10. Recipient President's medal Cazenovia Coll., 1990; Baker scholar Harvard U., 1947. Mem. Harvard Bus. Sch. Assn. (exec. coun. 1966-69, area chmn. 1967-69), Townsend Harris Alumni Assn. (bd. dirs. 1993—), Yale Club (N.Y.C.), Harvard Bus. Sch. Club (N.Y.C., pres. 1964-65, chmn. 1965-66, bd. dirs. 1964-70), Harvard Club (N.Y.C.), Met. Club (Washington), Alpha Kappa Psi, Phi Delta Phi. Presbyterian. Home: 3600 S Ocean Blvd Boca Raton FL 33432 Office: 1760 3d Ave New York NY 10029

SIGMAN, MELVIN MONROE, psychiatrist; b. N.Y.C., Dec. 15, 1935; s. Irving and Lillian (Pearlman) S. BA, Columbia U., 1956; MD, SUNY, N.Y.C., 1960; postgrad., William Alanson White Analytic Inst., N.Y.C., 1969. Staff psychiatrist Hawthorne (N.Y.) Cedar Knolls Sch., 1966-68; pvt. practice psychiatry N.Y.C., 1966-72, Fresno, Calif., 1974-87; staff psychiatrist Fresno County Dept. of Health, 1974-87, Psychol. Svcs. for Adults, L.A., 1987-93; psychiatrist pvt. practice, L.A., 1993—; attending staff psychiatry Bellevue Hosp., N.Y.C., 1966-68; cons. N.Y. Foundling Hosp., N.Y.C., 1966-72; assoc. attending staff Roosevelt Hosp., N.Y.C., 1967-72; asst. clin. prof U. Calif. San Francisco, Fresno, 1977; chmn. cen. Calif. com. Columbia Coll. Nat. Alumni Secondary Schs. Served to capt. USAF, 1961-63. Fellow Royal Soc. Health, Am. Orthopsychiat. Assn.; mem. Holiday Spa Clif., Fresno Racquet Club. Presbyterian. Office: 10780 Santa Monica Blvd Ste 250 Los Angeles CA 90025-4749

SIGMON, CHARLES LARRY, medical technologist; b. Crestview, Fla., Nov. 27, 1946; s. Charles Vernon and Dora Elizabeth (Wells) S.; m. Nga Tran, Nov. 26, 1982; 1 child, Jonathan. Cert. med. lab. technician, High Forest Acad., 1970; postgrad., Okaloosa-Walton C.C., 1971-72, Pensacola Jr. Coll., 1972-74. cert. clin. lab. technologist. Med. lab. technician Okaloosa County Hosp. Sys., Crestview, 1972-73, Med. Ctr. Clinic, Pensacola, Fla., 1973-74; med. technologist W. Fla. Regl. Med. Ctr., Pensacola, Fla., 1975—; instr. W. Fla. Regl. Med. Ctr., 1990—. Mem. Good Govt. Group W. Fla. Hosp., Pensacola, 1985—, Friends of Pensacola Pub. Libr., 1990—, Fla. Coalition Profl. Lab. Orgns., Orlando, 1994—. With U.S. Mcht. Marines, Saigon, 1968 (recipient Vietnam Svc. Bar). Mem. Am. Med. Technologists, Fla. State Soc. Am. Med. Technologists, N.W. Fla. Lab. Assn. Democrat. Home: 226 Boiling Brook Cir Pensacola FL 32503 Office: W Fla Regl Med Ctr 8383 N Davis Hwy Pensacola FL 32514

SIGMON, SCOTT B., psychologist; b. Newark, Dec. 30, 1946; s. Henry and Shirley (Juffe) S. BA, Bloomfield Coll., 1973; MA, Montclair State Coll., 1975; profl. diploma in sch. psychology, Kean Coll., 1977; EdD, Rutgers U., 1985. Sch. psychologist Middlesex Borough Pub. Schs., N.J., 1976-77, Milton Sch., Millburn, N.J., 1977-78; sch. psychologist, chair child study team Irvington Pub. Schs., N.J., 1978-87; psychotherapist Family Svc. Bureau of Newark, 1987; supr. child study East Orange (N.J.) Sch. Dist. 1987-88; sch. psychologist Elizabeth (N.J.) Pub. Schs., 1988-89; sch. psychologist, child study team chairperson Carlstadt-East Rutherford Regional High Sch. Dist., N.J., 1989—; pvt. practice psychologist, Union, N.J., 1991—; adj. prof. grad. psychology, Kean Coll. N.J., 1986, adj. prof. grad. psychology and spl. edn. Seton Hall U. (N.J.), 1988-90; asst. prof. coun.

svcs. program William Paterson Coll. of N.J., 1992-95. Author: Radical Socioeducational Analysis, 1985, Radical Analysis of Special Education: Focus on Historical Development and Learning Disabilities, 1987; author/editor Critical Voices on Special Education: Problems and Progress Concerning the Mildly Handicapped, 1990; editor The N.J. Sch. Psychologist newsletter, 1986-88; contbr. articles to profl. jours. Served with USMC, 1966-69. Mem. ACA, N.Am. Soc. Psychology of Sport and Phys. Activity, N.J. Assn. Sch. Psychologists, N.J. Psychol Assn. Home: 678 Winchester Ave Union NJ 07083-7630 Office: 1961 Morris Ave Union NJ 07083-3519

SIGURDSON, JON FREDERICK PAGE, orthopedic surgeon; b. Winnipeg, Manitoba, Can., July 2, 1933; came to U.S., 1960; s. Larus Arthur and Helen (Page) S.; m. Margaret Jean Watson, July 19, 1958; 1 child, Helen Sigurdson Hayes. BA, U. Manitoba, 1955, MD, BSc in Medicine, 1959. Diplomate Am. Bd. Orthopedics. Ptnr. orthopedic dept. Permanente Med. Group, Oakland, Calif., 1964-70; pvt. practice Oakland, 1970—; chief orthopedics Providence Hosp., Oakland, 1983-87. Fellow Am. Acad. Orthopedics Surgeons (councillor 1983-89), Internat. Coll. Surgeons (sec., treas. 1979-87), Royal Coll. Surgeons (Can.), Royal Soc. Medicine; mem. Western Orthopaedic Assn. (bd. dirs.), Canadian Orthopaedic Assn. Office: 2838 Summit St Oakland CA 94609-3605

SIGWART, ULRICH, cardiologist; b. Mar. 9, 1941; s. Christine Sartorius, Sept. 2, 1967; children: Anne, Philip, Jan, Catherine. MD, U. Münster, 1967; Dr. med. magna cum laude, U. Freiburg, 1967; Dr.med.habil., U. Düsseldorf, 1978, Prof. Dr. Med. Habil., 1985. Intern Community Hosp. Loerrach, 1967-68; resident Framingham Union Hosp., Boston VA Hosp., 1968-71; fellowship in cardiology Baylor Coll. of Medicine, 1971-72; chief of cath lab. Gollwitzer Meier Inst., Bad Oeynhausen, 1973-79; chief of invasive cardiology U. Hosp., Lausanne, 1979-89; dir. dept. invasive cardiology Royal Brompton Hosp., 1990—; cons. Royal Brompton Hosp., London, Harley St. Clinic, London, Humana Wellington Hosp., London, Cromwell Hosp., London, London Bridge Hosp., Clinique de Genolier, Switzerland, Clinique Cecile, Lausanne, Switzerland, Centre Cardiothoracique de Monaco; prof. medicine U. Düsseldorf; assoc. prof. cariology U. Lausanne; lectr. in field. Editl. bd. Clin. Cardiology, Herz & Gefässe, Cardiac Imagin, Interventional Cardiology, Frontiers in Cardiology, Latinamer Jour. Hemodyn., Angiogr. & Therap. Cath.; co-editor Handbook on Cardiovascular Interventions; contbr. over 400 articles to profl. jours. Fellow Am. Coll. Cardiology, European Soc. of Cardiology (founding fellow, past chmn. working group myocardial function), Am. Coll. Angiology, Royal Coll. Physicians; mem. Swiss Soc. of Cardiology (founding chmn. working group PTCA & Lysis, Internat. Stent Investigators Group, British Cardiac Soc., Soc. Vandoise de Mèdicine, German Soc. of Cardiology, Am. Soc. of Cardiac Interventionists, Internat. Andreas Grüntzig Soc., Internat. Soc. for Endovascular Surgery, Am. Coll. of Angiol., Am. Heart Assn., N.Y. Acad. Scis., British Cardiac Interventionist Soc., Royal Soc. of Medicine, Med. Pilots Assn. Office: Royal Brompton Hosp, Dept Invasive Cardiology, Sydney St, London SW3 6NP, England

SIIVOLA, JOUKO REINO, clinical neurophysiologist, researcher; b. Hameenlinna, Finland, Jan. 13, 1944; s. Reino Valdemar and Helmi Elina (Raisanen) S.; m. Seija Anneli Jarvi, May 23, 1969; children: Ari-Juhani, Johanna. MD, U. Helsinki, 1973; postgrad., U. Oulu, Finland, 1979, PhD, 1982. Cert. specialist in clin. neurophysiology, in medicine. Gen. practitioner Health Care Ctr., Kuusamo, Finland, 1973-76; asst. physician dept. clin. neurophysiology Univ. Hosp., Oulu, 1976-78; asst., asst. tchr. dept. physiology Oulu U., 1979-81; specialist in neurophysiology Tammiharjo Hosp., Tammisaari, Finland, 1982-90; chief dept. neurophysiology Kainuu Ctrl. Hosp., Kajaani, Finland, 1990—; chmn. exec. com. JEEMED Ltd., Kajaani, 1994—; mem. rsch. com. Biohit Ltd., Kajaani, 1989-91. Contbr. articles to profl. jours.; patentee infield. Recipient award Invention Found. Finland, 1994. Mem. Kainuu Invention Soc. (vice chmn. 1993), Finnish Med. Assn. (chmn. Kainuu sect. 1993-94), Internat. Brain Rsch. Orgn., N.Y. Acad. Scis. Lutheran. Office: Kainuu Ctrl Hosp, 87140 Kajaani Finland

SIKER, EPHRAIM S., anesthesiologist; b. Port Chester, N.Y., Mar. 24, 1926; s. Samuel S. and Adele (Weiser) S.; m. m . Eileen Mary Bohnel, Aug. 5, 1951; children—Kathleen Ellen, Jeffrey Stephen, David Alan, Paul William, Richard Francis. Student, Duke U., 1943-45; M.D., N.Y.U., 1949. Diplomate: Am. Bd. Anesthesiology (dir. 1971—, sec.-treas. 1974-82, pres. 1982-83) Nat. Bd. Med. Examiners. Intern Grasslands Hosp., Valhalla, N.Y., 1949-50, resident in anesthesia, 1950; resident dept. anesthesiology Mercy Hosp., Pitts., 1952-53; assoc. dir. dept. Mercy Hosp., 1955-62, chmn., 1962-92; practice medicine, specializing in anesthesiology Pitts., 1954—; pres. Pitts. Anesthesia Assocs., Ltd., 1967-89; dir. anesthesia services Central Med. Ctr., Pitts., 1973-89; courtesy staff St. Clair Meml. Hosp., Pitts., 1954-89, St. Margaret Meml. Hosp., 1962—; clin. prof. dept. anesthesiology U. Pitts. Sch. Medicine, 1968—; mem. exec. com. Am. Bd. Med. Spltys., 1978-81; Exch. cons. Welsh Nat. Sch. Medicine, Cardiff, 1955-56; mem. Pa. Gov.'s Commn. on Profl. Liability Ins., 1968-70; mem. adv. panel U.S. Pharmacopeia, 1970-76; mem. Am. acupuncture anesthesia study group of Nat. Acad. Scis. to Peoples Republic China, 1974; mem. adv. com. on splty. and geog. distbn. of physicians Inst. Medicine, Nat. Acad. Scis., 1974-76; trustee Ednl. Coun. for Fgn. Med. Grads., 1980-82, Mercy Hosp. Found., 1983-95; bd. dirs., sec. Anesthesia Patient Safety Foun., 1985-89, mem. exec. com., 1985-92, exec. dir., 1992—. Author: (with F.F. Foldes) Narcotics and Narcotic Antagonists, 1964; sect. on narcotic: (with F.F. Foldes) numerous other publs. in med. lit. Ency. Brittanica. Served to lt. M.C. USNR, 1950-52. USPHS postdoctoral research fellow, 1954; hon. fellow faculty anaesthetists Royal Coll. Surgeons, Eng., 1974; hon. fellow faculty anesthetists Coll. Medicine South Africa, 1983; recipient Hippocratic award Mercy Hosp., 1982. Fellow Royal Coll. Surgeons Ireland, Faculty Anaesthetists (hon. 1988); mem. Am. Soc. Anesthesiologists (pres. 1973—, bd. dirs. Disting. Svc. award 1984), AMA (alt. del. 1962), Pa. Med. Soc., Allegheny County Med. Soc., Pa. Soc. Anesthesiologists (pres. 1965, Disting. Svc. award 1986), Royal Soc. Medicine (Eng.), Pitts. Acad. Medicine, Am. Coll. Anesthesiologists (bd. govs. 1969-7l), World Fedn. Anesthesiologists (chmn. exec. com. 1980-84, v.p. 1984-88), Assn. Anesthesia Program Dirs. (pres. 1987-89). Home: 185 Crestvue Manor Dr Pittsburgh PA 15228-1814 Office: 1400 Locust St Pittsburgh PA 15219-5166

SIKES, JAN LEA, family practice physician; b. Dallas, Feb. 7, 1951; d. A.Q. and Hazel Belle (Hern) Roberts. AAS, Dallas County CC, 1975; BA, U. North Tex., 1977, MS, 1979; DO, Tex. Coll. Osteo. Medicine, 1985. Diplomate Am. Acad. Family Practice. Intern Botsford Gen. Hosp., Detroit, 1985-86, resident in ob-gyn., 1986-87; locum tenens Jackson Coker, Pitts., 1994; pvt. practice East Tex. Profl. Group, Palestine, Tex., 1995—. Lt. comdr. USN, 1988-94. Baptist.

SIKORA, SUZANNE MARIE, dentist; b. Kenosha, Wis., Dec. 4, 1952; d. Leo F. and Ida A. (Dupuis) S. BS, U. Wis., Parkside, 1975; DDS, Marquette U., 1981. Assoc. Paul G. Hagemann, DDS, Racine, Wis., 1981-84; pvt. practice dentistry Racine, 1984—; cons. Westview Health Care Ctr., Racine, 1981-89, Lincoln Luth. Home, Racine, 1981—, Becker-Shoop Ctr., Racine, 1981—, Lincoln Village Convalescent Ctr., Racine, 1986—, Racine Community Care Ctr., 1989—. Mem. ad hoc study com. County Health Dept., Racine, 1982-83. Mem. ADA, Wis. Dental Assn. (coun. on access prevention and wellness com. 1984-86, impaired provider program intervenor 1990—, del. 1993—). Office: 1900 Lathrop Ave Racine WI 53405-3707

SILA, CATHY A., neurologist; b. Cleve., Apr. 21, 1955; d. Andrew Lee and Mary Florence (Patrick) S.; m. Gene H. Barnett, Dec. 9, 1990; children: Austin Andrew, Addison Edgar. BA Chemistry, Zoology, Miami U., 1977; MD, Case Western Res. Sch. Med., 1981. Intern, resident in neurology Cleve. Clinic, 1981-83; resident in neurology Mayo Clinic, Rochester, Minn., 1983-85; rsch. fellow in cerebrovascular rsch. studies Cleve. Clinic, 1985-86; assoc. med. dir. cerebrovascular ctr. Cleve. Clin. Found., 1987—. Fellow Am. Heart Assn., Am. Acad. Neurology; mem. AMA, Nat. Stroke Assn., Internat. Stroke Soc. Office: Cleve Clinic Found S91 9500 Euclid Ave Cleveland OH 44195

SILANE, MICHAEL FRANCIS, vascular surgeon, surgery educator; b. N.Y.C., May 9, 1943; s. Roy and Louise (Murano) S.; m. Margaret Welles Barber, June 11, 1977; children: Jennifer, Carolyn. B.S., Georgetown U., 1965, M.D., 1969. Diplomate Am. Bd. Surgery; Cert. Spl. Competence in Gen. Vascular Surgery. Intern, Cornell-N.Y. Hosp., N.Y.C., 1969-70, resident, 1970-72, 74-76; instr. in surgery Cornell Med. Sch., N.Y.C., 1975-76; clin. instr. U. Calif., San Francisco, 1977-78; fellow Harvard Med. Sch., Boston, 1978-79; asst. prof. surgery Cornell Med. Sch., N.Y.C., 1976-84, assoc. prof., 1984-91, clin. assoc. prof. surgery, 1991—; co-chief div. vascular surgery Cornell-N.Y. Hosp., N.Y.C., 1989-90; chief divsn. vascular surgery Beth Israel Med. Ctr., N.Y.C., 1994—; cons. Meml. Hosp., N.Y.C., 1984-85, assoc. attending surgeon, 1985—; attending surgeon Beth Israel North Hosp., 1991—. Contbr. articles to profl. jours. and chpts. to books. Served to lt. commdr. USNR, 1972-74. N.Y. State Engring. scholar, 1961; NIH fellow, 1978. Fellow Am. Coll. Surgeons; mem. Internat. Cardiovascular Soc., Assn. Acad. Surgeons, N.Y. Regional Vascular Soc., Eastern Regional Vascular Soc., N.Y. Cardiovascular Soc., N.Y. Surg. Soc., Alpha Omega Alpha. Roman Catholic. Club: Pelham Country (N.Y.). Avocations: skiing, computers, golf, tennis. Office: 170 East End Ave Ste 400 New York NY 10128

SILBER, AUSTIN, psychiatrist; b. N.Y.C., Jan. 3, 1923; s. Samuel and Sophie (Levitsky) S.; m. Diana Feder, June 19, 1949; children: Michael Adam, Elizabeth Ann, Madeline Eve. BA in Sci., NYU, 1946; MD, SUNY, Bklyn., 1951. Diplomate Am. Bd. Psychiatry and Neurology. Intern, resident Kings County Hosp. Ctr., Bklyn., 1951-55; pvt. practice N.Y.C., 1956—; faculty div. psychoanalytic edn. SUNY Downstate Med. Ctr., N.Y.C., 1960-79; from clin. instr. to assoc. prof. psychiatry SUNY Downstate Med. Ctr., 1955-79; clin. prof. dept. psychiatry NYU Med. Ctr., N.Y.C., 1979—; tng. and supr. analyst Psan edn. div. SUNY Downstate Med. Ctr., 1970-79; past dir., tng. and supervising analyst Psychoanalytic Inst., NYU Med. Ctr., 1979—; dir. Psan Inst. NYU Med. Ctr., 1984-88. Contbr. articles to profl. jours. Pfc. AUS, 1943-45, PTO. Fellow Am. Psychoanalytic Assn. (bd. profl. stds., sec. 1984-88, mem. coms., editl. bd. jour. 1982-85); mem. Internat. Jour. Psychoanalysts (mem. N.Am. editl. bd.), Ctr. Advanced Psychoanalytic Studies, Alpha Omega Alpha. Office: 1199 Park Ave New York NY 10128-1711

SILBER, JUDY G., dermatologist; b. Newark, July 26, 1953. MD, SUNY, Bklyn., 1978. Intern Brookdale Med. Ctr., Bklyn., 1978-79; resident in dermatology Kings County Hosp., Bklyn., 1979-82; pvt. practice dermatology; affiliated with Meadowlands Med. Ctr., Secaucus, N.J. Fellow Am. Acad. Dermatology; mem. AMA, N.J. Med. Soc. Office: 992 Clifton Ave Clifton NJ 07013-3502

SILBERBERG, DONALD H., neurologist; b. Washington, Mar. 2, 1934; s. William Aaron and Leslie Frances (Stone) S.; m. Marilyn Alice Damsky, June 7, 1959; children: Mark, Alan. MD, U. Mich., 1958; MA (hon.), U. Pa., 1971. Intern Mt. Sinai Hosp., N.Y.C., 1958-59; clin. assoc. in neurology NIH, Bethesda, Md., 1959-61; Fulbright scholar Nat. Hosp., London, 1961-62; NINDB spl. fellow in neuro-ophthalmology Washington U., St. Louis, 1962-63; assoc. neurology U. Pa., 1963-65, asst. prof., 1965-67, assoc. prof., 1967-71, prof., 1971-73, acting chmn. dept., 1973-74, prof., vice chmn. neurology, 1974-82, chmn., 1982-94, assoc. dean internat. programs, 1994—; active staff U. Pa. Med. Ctr., Phila.; cons. Children's Hosp., Phila.; pres., CEO Betasteron Found., Inc., 1994—. Contbr. articles to profl. jours., abstracts, chpts. in books. Recipient grants in study of multiple sclerosis. Mem. Am. Acad. Neurology, Am. Assn. Neuropathologists, Am. Neurol. Assn., Am. Soc. Neurochemistry, Assn. Rsch. in Nervous and Mental Diseases, Coll. Physicians Phila., Internat. Brain Rsch. Orgn., Internat. Soc. Devel. Neurosci., Internat. Soc. Neurochemistry, John Morgan Soc. U. Pa. (pres. 1974-75), N.Y. Acad. Scis., Nat. Multiple Sclerosis Soc. (rsch. programs adv. bd.), Assn. Univ. Profs. Neurology (pres.-elect 1993), Phila. Neurol. Soc. (pres. 1978-79), Soc. Neurosci., World Fedn. Neurology (co-chair rsch. group on organziation & delivery of neurol. care, pres. rsch. group assn., Inc.), Alpha Omega Alpha. Office: U Pa Med Ctr Dept Neurology 3400 Spruce St Philadelphia PA 19104

SILBERFARB, PETER MICHAEL, psychiatrist, educator; b. Jersey City, Oct. 28, 1938; m. Anne Wagner, 1962; children: Benjamin, Leah S. BS, Bucknell U., 1960; postgrad., NYU, 1960-61; MD, Hahnemann Coll., 1965; MA (hon.), Dartmouth Coll., 1986. Diplomate Nat. Bd. Med. Examiners, Am. Bd. Psychiatry and Neurology (sr. examiner 1985-90, bd. dirs. 1991—). Intern Hahnemann Med. Coll. Hosp., Phila., 1965-66; resident in internal medicine Dartmouth Affiliated Hosps., Hanover, N.H., 1966-68, resident in internal medicine and psychiatry, 1968-69, psychiatry resident, 1971-72, chief resident in psychiatry, 1972-73; instr. in psychiatry Med. Sch., Dartmouth Coll., Hanover, 1972-73, asst. prof. of psychiatry, 1973-77, assoc. prof. clin. psychiatry, assoc. prof. clin. medicine, 1977-80, dir. grad. edn. and residency tng., 1978-86, assoc. prof. psychiatry, assoc. prof. medicine, 1980-82, prof. psychiatry, assoc. prof. medicine, 1982-85, dir. tng. and edn., 1984—, prof. psychiatry, prof. medicine, 1986—, chmn. dept. psychiatry, 1986—, Raymond Sobel prof. psychiatry, 1993; cons. psychiatrist Mary Hitchcock Meml. Hosp., Hanover, 1973—; dir. psychiat. in-patient svc. Dartmouth-Hitchcock Med. Ctr., 1973-75, dir. cancer psychiatry program Norris Cotton Cancer Ctr., 1975—, acting dir. psychiatry consultation svc., 1977-79, assoc. dir. cancer control Norris Ctr., 1981-86; sec. psychiatry com. Cancer and Leukemia Group B, 1976-79, vice chmn., 1979—; mem. grant rev. com. for cancer control Nat. Cancer Inst., 1979, 80, mem. spl. grant rev. com., 1981, 82, 85, cons. to bd. sci. counselors, 1982, mem. cancer control grant rev. com., 1986-90; vice chmn. adv. com. for psychosocial and behavioral rsch. Am. Cancer Soc., 1982-88, chmn., 1988-89; cons. collaborative ctr. for cancer pain relief WHO, Milan, 1985; mem. accreditation coun. for grad. med. edn. Appeals Bd. for Psychiatry, Chgo., 1983, specialist site visitor, 1985-90, mem. residency rev. com. for psychiatry, 1991—; prin. investigator in field. Author chpts. to books; mem. editl. bd. Jour. Psychosocial Oncology, 1983—, Internat. Jour. Psychiatry in Medicine, 1986-90, Contemporary Psychiatry, 1987-91, Psychooncology, 1991—; referee numerous manuscripts; contbr. articles to profl. jours. Surgeon USPHS, 1969-71. Fellow Am. Psychiat. Assn. (cons. to task force on treatment if psychiat. disorders 1989), Am. Coll. Psychiatrists; mem. AMA, Am. Soc. Psychiat. Oncology/AIDS, Am. Soc. Clin. Oncology, Am. Assn. Dirs. Psychiat. Residency Tng. (mem. curriculum com. 1979-88, mem. task force on med. students and residents, chmn. com. regional dirs. 1984-88, mem. exec. com. 1984-88), Am. Psychosomatic Soc., N.H. Psychiat. Soc. (chmn. membership com. 1974-76, chmn. continuing edn. com. 1977-79), N.H. Med. Soc., Assn. Rsch. in Nervous and Mental Disease, Assn. Acad. Psychiatry, Benjamin Rush Soc. Home: Bragg Hill Norwich VT 05055 Office: Dartmouth Coll Med Sch Dept Psychiatry Lebanon NH 03756-0001

SILBERGELD, ELLEN KOVNER, environmental epidemiologist and toxicologist; b. Washington, July 29, 1945; d. Joseph and Mary (Gion) Kovner; m. Alan Mark Silbergeld, 1969; children: Sophia, Nicholas. AB, Vassar Coll., 1967; PhD, Johns Hopkins U., 1972. Kennedy fellow Johns Hopkins Med. Sch., Balt., 1974-75; scientist NIH, Bethesda, Md., 1975-81; chief toxics scientist Environ. Def. Fund, Washington, 1982-90; prof. epidemiology, toxicology and pharmacology U.Md., Balt., 1990—, affil. prof. environ. law, 1990—; adj. prof. Johns Hopkins Med. Insts., 1990—; guest scientist NIH, 1982-84; mem. sci. adv. bd. EPA, 1983-89, 94—, Dept. Energy, 1994-95; mem. bd. on environ. sci. and toxicology NAS-NRC, 1983-89; mem. com. geosci. environment and resources, 1994—; mem. bd. sci. counselors Nat. Inst. Environ. Health Scis., 1987-93; cons. Oil and CHem. Atomic Workers, 1970, NSF, 1974-75, OECD, 1987—. Mem. editl. bd. Neurotoxicology, 1981-86, Neurobehavioral Toxicology, 1979-87, Am. Jour. Indsl. Medicine, 1980—, Hazardous Waste, 1985—, Archives Environ. Health, 1986—; mem. editl. bd. Environ. Rsch., 1983—, editor-in-chief, 1994—; contbr. articles to profl. jours. Mem. Homewood Friends Meeting. Recipient Wolman award Md. Pub. Health Assn., 1991, Barsky award APHA, 1992, Md. Gov. Excellence citation, 1990, 93; Fulbright fellow, London, 1967, Woodrow Wilson and Danforth fellow, 1967; NAS exch. fellow, Yugoslavia, 1976; MacArthur Found. fellow, 1993; Baldwin scholar Coll. Notre Dame. Mem. AAAS, Am. Soc. Pharmacology and Exptl. Therapeutics, Soc. for Occupational and Environ. Health (sec.-treas. 1983-85, pres. 1987-89), Soc. Toxicology, Soc. for Neurosci., Am. Pub. Health Assn., Collegium Ramazzini, Phi Beta Kappa. Office: U Md Med Sch Dept Epid Prev Medicine Howard Hall 104 Baltimore MD 21201

SILBERGELD, SAM, psychiatrist; b. Wengrov, Poland, Mar. 1, 1918; came to U.S., 1923; s. Hyman and Frieda (Orenstein) S.; m. Mae Ann Driscoll, June 22, 1952; children: Sandra Sue, Daniel Lance, Janet Joy, Nancy Ann. AA, Blackburn Coll., 1938; BS, U. Chgo., 1939; PhD in Chemistry, U. Ill., 1943; MD, Duke U., 1955. Cert. specialist in psychiatry, Md. Instr. biochemistry Mayo Found., Rochester, Minn., 1942-44; instr., asst. prof. chemistry U. Ill., Chgo., 1945-46, 46-52; med. officer U.S. Pub. Health Svcs., Bethesda, Md., 1956-88; staff asst. to dir. Div. Biologic Standards, NIH, Bethesda, 1956-59; rsch. grants specialist Div. Gen. Med. Sci., NIH, Bethesda, 1959-60; chief gen. clin. rsch. NIH, Bethesda, 1960-64; various rsch. positions NIMH, Md., 1964-81; staff psychiatrist, adminstr. geriatric program St. Elizabeth Hosp., Washington, 1981-87; staff psychiatrist Sheppard & Enoch Pratt Hosp., Balt., 1988-89; clin. prof. dept. psychiatry Uniformed Svcs. of the Health Scis. Sch. of Medicine, Bethesda, 1982—; adj. prof. U. Md., College Park, 1979-87, part-time instr., 1992—. Contbr. numerous articles to profl. jours. Mem. vis. com. in scis. Blackburn Coll., Carlinville, Ill., 1986, trustee, 1987—; ad hoc mem. Eagle Scout Review Bd., Bethesda, 1987—; chmn. Boy Scout Troop Com., Kensington, Md., 1973-80. Rsch. grantee Dept. Psychiatry Stanford Sch. Medicine, 1966-67; recipient Leadership Citation Blackburn U., 1989, Editors Choice award for Outstanding Achievement in Poetry, 1996. Mem. AMA, AAAS, Am. Chem. Soc., Am. Psychiat. Assn., Am. Psychosomatic Soc., N.Y. Acad. Scis., Md. Psychiat. Soc. (mem. quality revue com., peer revue com. 1991—). Home: Box 377 10704 Clermont Ave Garrett Park MD 20896

SILBERMAN, ALLAN WALTER, surgical oncologist; b. Phila., Oct. 22, 1946. BA, Pa. State U., 1968; PhD in Biochemistry, Boston U., 1973, MD, 1975. Diplomate Am. Bd. Surgery. Intern and resident Tufts-New Eng. Med. Ctr., Boston, 1975-80; asst. prof. surgery UCLA, 1980-86; assoc. prof. U. So. Calif. Sch. Medicine, L.A., 1990—; attending surgeon Cedars Sinai Med. Ctr., L.A., 1985—. Fellow ACS; mem. Am. Soc. Clin. Oncology, Soc. Surg. Oncology, Am. Radium Soc., Soc. Surgery Alimentary Tract, Pacific Coast Surg. Assn. Office: Cedars Sinai Comprehensive Cancer Ctr 8700 Beverly Blvd Los Angeles CA 90048

SILBERMAN, ARLIN JOEL, psychiatrist; b. Phila., Nov. 2, 1947; s. Paris and Eleanor (Sacks) S.; m. Marilyn J. Heine, Mar. 10, 1991. BA, Pa. State U., University Park, 1969; DO, U. Osteopathic Medicine, Des Moines, 1973. Diplomate Am. Bd. Psychiatry and Neurology, Am. Osteopathic Bd. Neurology and Psychiatry. Intern Tri-County Hosp., Springfield, Pa., 1973-74; resident Hahnemann Hosp., Phila. State Hosp., 1974-77; psychiatric fellow Phila. Mental Health Clinic, 1974-77; coord. detoxification unit Thomas Jefferson U. Hosp., Phila., 1980-81; psychiatrist Eagleville (Pa.) Hosp., 1975-90, dir. psychiatry, 1990—; psychiatrist, dir. emergency psychiatry North Central Community Mental Health/Mental Retardation Ctr, Phila., 1977-80; clin. instr. psychiatry dept. psychiatry Temple U., Phila., 1979—; clin. asst. prof. psychiatry dept. psychiatry and human behavior Thomas Jefferson U., Phila., 1980—. Recipient Legion of Honor, Chapel of Four Chaplains, Phila., 1981. Mem. Am. Coll. Neuropsychiatrists, Am. Psychiat. Assn., Am. Osteo. Assn., Am. Osteo. Acad. of Addiction Medicine (sec.-treas. 1995—). Republican. Office: Eagleville Hosp 100 Eagleville Rd Norristown PA 19403-1829

SILBERMAN, IRWIN ALAN, public health physician; b. Newport News, Va., Sept. 1, 1932; s. Henry and Toby (Weiss) S.; m. Lynne Sussman, Feb. 1954 (div. 1961); children: Denise, Donn; m. Mitsue Fukuyama, May 1964 (div. 1984); children: Daniel, Dean, Dana; m. Andrea Z. George, Nov. 1993. BA, U. Calif., Berkeley, 1953; MD, U. Calif., San Francisco, 1956; MS, U. No. Colo., 1980. Intern L.A. County Harbor Gen. Hosp., Torrance, Calif., 1956-57; resident ob-gyn. Harbor/UCLA Med. Ctr., Torrance, 1957-61; commd. USAF, 1961, advanced through grades to col., 1973; staff obstetrician-gynecologist Tachikawa (Japan) Air Base, 1963-65; chief ob-gyn. Mather Air Force Base, Sacramento, 1965-66; chief aeromed. services Yokota Air Base, Tokyo, 1966-68; dir. base med. services Itazuke Air Base, Fukuoka, Japan, 1968-70, Kirtland Air Force Base, Albuquerque, 1970-72; chief hosp. services USAF Hosp. Davis-Monthan, Tucson, 1972-81; ret. USAF, 1981; med. dir. CIGNA Healthplan of Fla., Tampa, 1981-83; chief women's clinic H.C. Hudson Comprehensive Health Ctr., L.A., 1983-85; dir. maternal health and family planning programs Los Angeles County Dept. Health Svcs., L.A., 1985-91, dir. family health programs, maternal and child health, 1991—; mil. cons. to surgeon-gen. USAF, 1980-81; bd. dirs. L.A. Regional Family Planning Coun.; pres. Perinatal Adv. Coun. of L.A. Comtys., 1993-94. Chmn. health profls. adv. com. March of Dimes, Los Angeles, 1988; camp physician Boy Scouts Nat. Jamboree, Fort Hill, Va., 1985. Recipient Meritorious Service medal, USAF, 1972, 81, Air Force Commendation medal, 1980, Air medal, 1969. Fellow Am. Coll. Obstetricians and Gynecologists, Am. Coll. Physician Execs., Am. Coll. Preventive Medicine; mem. APHA, Am. Acad. Med. Dirs., So. Calif. Pub. Health Assn. Home: 3716 Beverly Ridge Dr Sherman Oaks CA 91423-4509 Office: LA County Dept Health Svcs 241 N Figueroa St Los Angeles CA 90012-2693

SILBERSTEIN, EDWARD BERNARD, nuclear medicine educator, researcher; b. Cin., Sept. 3, 1936; s. Bernard Gympert and Harriet Louise (Kahn) S.; m. Jacqueline Rose Mervis, Oct. 2, 1988; children: Scott, Lisa. BS, Yale U., 1958; MD, Harvard U., 1962. Intern Cin. Gen. Hosp., 1962-63, resident in internal medicine, 1963-64; resident Univ. Hosps. Cleve., 1966-67; NIH fellow in hematology New Eng. Med. Ctr., Boston, 1967-68; asst. prof. radiol. medicine U. Cin. Med. Ctr., 1968-72, assoc. prof. radiol. medicine, 1972-76, prof. radiol. medicine, 1976—; assoc. dir. E.L. Saenger Radioisotope Lab., 1980—; chmn. Environ. Safety Health Com. Dept. Energy Fernald Facility, 1986-91; cons. Nuclear Regulatory Commn., 1988—; dir. divsn. nuclear medicine Jewish Hosp., 1976-95; cancer pain panel Agy. for Health Care Planning and Rsch., 1992-93. Author: Differential Diagnosis in Nuclear Medicine, 1984, Bone Scintigraphy, 1984; contbr. articles to profl. jours. Bd. dirs. Talbert House, 1969—, Air Pollution Control League, Cin., 1980-95; active Race Rels. Commn. Greater Cin., 1995—, Jewish Cmty. Rels. Coun., 1992—; bd. trustees Cin. Opera Assn., 1993—, Isaac M. Wise, 1993—. Capt. U.S. Army, 1964-66. Mem. Soc. Nuclear Medicine (sec. 1989-92, pres. S.E. chpt. 1990-91, chair sci. program 1992—). Jewish. Home: 3530 Verger Ln Cincinnati OH 45237-2512 Office: U Cin Med Ctr ML 577 PO Box 670577 Cincinnati OH 45267

SILBIGER, MARTIN L., radiologist, medical educator, college dean; b. Ravenna, Ohio, Mar. 17, 1938; s. Alfred James and Evelyn Norma (Cheswick) S.; m. Ruth Hope Steele, June 4, 1957; children: Martin, Eve, Jonathan, Holly, Wendy. BA, U. Pa., 1958; MD, Western Reserve U., 1962; MBA, U. South Fla., 1989. Diplomate Am. Bd. Radiology, Am. Bd. Nuclear Medicine. Intern Univ. Hosps. Cleve., 1962-63; resident Johns Hopkins Hosp., 1963-66; with NIH, 1966-68; radiologist Tampa (Fla.) Gen. Hosp., 1968—; prof. U. South Fla., Tampa, 1982—; chief of staff Tampa Gen. Hosp., 1978-80; chmn. dept. radiology U. South Fla. Coll. Medicine, 1982-95; dean coll. medicine U. South Fla., 1995—, v.p. health scis., 1995—. Founder Hillsborough County Med. assn. Found., Tampa, 1992; treas. Cmty. Found. Tampa, 1993-95; bd. dirs. Moffitt Cancer Ctr., Tampa, 1985—, Moffitt Cancer Ctr. Found., 1994—. Home: 1827 Bayshore Blvd Tampa FL 33606 Office: 3301 Alumni Dr Tampa FL 33612-9413 also: Univ South Fl Coll of Med Box 66 1209 Bruce B Downs Blvd Tampa FL 33612-4799

SILEN, WILLIAM, physician, surgery educator; b. San Francisco, Sept. 13, 1927; s. Dave and Rose (Miller) S.; m. Ruth Heppner, July 13, 1947; children: Stephen, Deborah, Mark. BA, U. Calif., Berkeley, 1946; MD, U. Calif., San Francisco, 1949; MA (hon.), Harvard U., 1966. Diplomate Am. Bd. Surgery. Intern U. Calif., San Francisco, 1949-50, asst. resident gen. surgery, 1950-56, chief resident gen. surgery, 1956-57; asst. chief surgery Denver VA Hosp., 1957-59, chief surgery, 1959-60; asst. chief surgery San Francisco Gen. Hosp., 1960-61, chief surgery, 1961-66; surgeon-in-chief Beth Israel Hosp., Boston, 1966-94; instr. surgery, asst. prof. surgery U. Colo. Med. Sch., Denver, 1957-60; asst. prof. then assoc. prof. surgery U. Calif. Sch. Medicine, San Francisco, 1960-66; prof. surgery Harvard Med. Sch., Boston, 1966—, Johnson and Johnson prof. surgery, 1966-94; dir. Harvard Digestive Diseases Ctr. NIH, Bethesda, Md., 1984-94. Author: Cope's Early Diagnosis of the Acute Abdomen, 1995, Conservative Management of Breast Cancer, 1983, Atlas of Techniques in Breast Surgery, 1995. With USAF, 1950-52. Mem. AMA, ACS, Soc. Univ. Surgeons, H.C. Naffziger Surg. Soc., Phi Beta Kappa. Office: Beth Israel Hosp 330 Brookline Ave Boston MA 02215-5400

SILKISS, RONA ZEL, ophthalmic plastic, reconstructive surgeon; b. N.Y.C., Oct. 19, 1957; d. Emanuel and Rose Silkiss. BS, Northwestern U., Evanston, Ill., 1974-76; MD, Northwestern U., Chgo., 1980. Diplomate Am. Bd. Ophthalmology, Am. Bd. Ophthalmic Plastic Surgery, Am. Bd. Pediats. Resident pediat. Children's Hosp., L.A., 1980-82, N.Y. Hosp., N.Y.C., 1982-83; resident in ophthalmology Jules Stein Eye Inst., L.A., 1983-86; fellow oculoplastic surgery Jules Stein Eye Inst. UCLA, L.A., 1986-87; cons. Sunrise Tech. Fremont, Calif., 1991—, Landec Corp., Fremont, 1992, Prizm Pharms., 1995—; cons. surgeon Orbis Internat., N.Y.C., 1993; asst. clin. prof. U. Calif., Berkeley, asst. clin. prof. ophthalmology, U. Calif., San Francisco. Contbr. articles to profl. jours. Recipient Jules Stein Rsch. Prize UCLA, 1986. Fellow ACS, Am. Soc. Ophthalmic Plastic and Reconstructive Surgery, Am. Acad. Ophthalmology; mem. East Bay Ophthalmology Soc. (pres. 1993-95), Alpha Omega Alpha. Office: 491 30th St Ste 103 Oakland CA 94609-3209 also: 122 La Casa Vie Ste 221 Walnut Creek CA 94598 also: 2675 Stevenson Rd Fremont CA 94538 also: 22 Battery St Ste 905 San Francisco CA 94111

SILL, WILLIAM FRAZIER, physician; b. Grand Rapids, Mich., June 13, 1944; s. William Hervey and Emogene Margaret (Perschbacher) S.; m. Bette Louise Armentrout, Aug. 25, 1968; children: Jonathan Bagshaw, Tara Louise. Grad., Millikin U., 1966; DO, Kirksville (Mo.) Coll. Osteopathic Medicine, 1970; chief family practice, St. Peters Hosp., 1983, chief dept. medicine, 1985. Diplomate Am. Bd. Family Practice. Intern Normandy Osteopathic Hosp., St. Louis, 1970-71; resident in family practice USAF Med. Ctr., Scott AFB, Ill., 1973-75; physician St. Charles (Mo.) Clinic, 1976-81; physician family practice St. Peters, Mo., 1982—; chief family practice St. Peters Hosp., 1988, chief dept. medicine, 1985; chief family practice dept. St. Joseph Health Ctr., St. Charles, 1986, 89; chief of staff Barnes St. Peter's Hosp., 1996; instr. aviation physiology and mem. hyperboric treatment team Sch. Aerospace Medicine USAF, Brooks AFB, Tex., 1971-73; assoc. clin. instr. family practice residency program, Scott AFB, Ill., 1975-76. Served to maj. USAF, 1971-76. Fellow Am. Acad. Family Phyicians; mem. Mo. Acad. Family Physicians, St. Louis Acat. Family Physicians, Mo. State Med. Assn. Presbyterian. Home: 12 Berkshire Saint Charles MO 63301-4516 Office: 6 Jungermann Cir Saint Peters MO 63376-1621

SILLANPÄÄ, MATTI LAURI, pediatric neurology educator; b. Noormarkku, Finland, Aug. 4, 1936; s. Lauri Herman and Elma Sylvia (Wahlroos) S.; m. Pirjo Kaarina Huida, Oct. 30, 1964; 1 child, Jukka. MB, U. Turku, Turku, Finland, 1958; Licentiate of Medicine, U. Turku, 1962, MD, 1973. Licenced physician, 1962, pediatrician, 1967, pediatric neurologist, 1969. Community health officer Town of Loimaa, Loimaa, Finland, 1962-64; house officer dept. of pediatrics U. Turku, Turku, 1964-67; house officer dept. of neurology U. Turku, 1967-68; house officer sect. of child neurology, dept. of pediatrics U. Uppsala, Uppsala, Sweden, 1968-69; chief physician Inst. for Mentally Retarded, Turku, 1969; hosp. specialist, sr. cons. dept. pediatrics U. Turku, 1970-88, assoc. prof. dept. of pub. health, 1976—, prof. pediatric neurology, 1990—; acting prof. Dept. of Pub. Health, U. Turku, 1981-88; sr. cons. Dept. of Pediatrics, Univ. of Tampere, Finland, 1971-76, Dept. of Pediatrics, Satakunta Cen. Hosp., Pori, Finland, 1976—. Author: Carbamazepine, 1981; Ambulatory Child Neurology (Finnish), 1987, Social Function of Chronically Ill Children, 1987; editor Medical Application of Cyclotrons, 1977, (with others) Epilepsy: Progress in Treatment, 1987, (with others) Pediatric Epilepsy, 1990; mem. editl. bd. Current Topics in Neurology, Recent Research Developments in Neurology. Mem. com. epidemiology and prognosis of epilepsy Internat. League Against Epilepsy, 1991—. Lt. Sanitary Svc., 1967-73. Named hon. mem. Academia Medicorum Litteratorum, Vicenza, Italy, 1980, Paul Harris fellow Rotary Found., Rotary Internat., Chgo., 1985, comdr. Order of St. Constantine the Great, Athens, 1986, mem. Order of St. Constantine the Great, Athens, 1986, mem. Order of Amarantine, Stockholm, 1989; recipient gold medal of merit Nat. Epilepsy Assn. Finland, 1993, Amb. award, Epilepsy Internat. Mem. Finnish Assn. Physicians, Scandinavian Pediatric Assn., Internat. Child Neurology Assn., PEDEKOS: Internat. Acad. for Children with Spl. Needs (sec. 1977—, silver badge of merit 1986), Acta Neurol Scand (mem. editorial bd. 1990), Pediatr Neurol (mem. editorial bd. 1991), Nat. Epilepsy Assn. Finland, Rotary (pres. Sampaalinna chpt. 1981-82), Fraternitas 68 Lodge. Home: Honkatie 32 B 1, 20540 Turku Finland Office: Dept Pediatric Neurology, 20520 Turku Finland

SILLIGAM, KEITH H., assistant hospital administrator; b. Seattle, Sept. 25, 1967; s. Robert E. and Marilyn E. (Bice) S.; m. Nancy L. DiGruttilla, June 13, 1992. BS in Bus. Adminstrn., Mktg., Wilkes U., 1990; M in Health Adminstrn., Duke U., 1992. Adminstrv. intern Nash Gen. Hosp., Rocky Mount, N.C., 1991; adminstrv. resident Ochsner Clinic of Baton Rouge, La., 1992-93; adminstrv. assoc. Med. Ctr. of Baton Rouge, 1993-94, asst. adminstr., 1994—. Vol. Ramsey (N.J.) Rescue Squad, 1984-90, vol. EMT Ramsey Ambulance Corps, 1986-90; chmn. Med. Ctr. of Baton Rouge United Way Campaign, 1995. Mem. Am. Hosp. Assn. Soc. for Healthcare Planning and Mktg., Am. Coll. Healthcare Execs. (diplomate). Office: Med Ctr of Baton Rouge 17000 Medical Center Dr Baton Rouge LA 70816

SILLIVIS SMITT, PETER, neurologist; b. Haarlem, The Netherlands, Nov. 31, 1958. MD, U. Amsterdam, The Netherlands, 1985, PhD, 1992; Neurologist, Acad. Med. Ctr., Amsterdam, 1992. Bd. cert. neurologist. Resident Acad. Med. Ctr., Amsterdam, 1987-92; fellow Meml. Sloan-Kettering Cancer Ctr., N.Y.C., 1992-94; mem. faculty Daniel Den Hoed Cancer Ctr., Rotterdam, The Netherlands, 1995—. Mem. Am. Assn. Neurologists, Nederlandse Vereniging Neurologie. Office: Daniel Den Hoed Cancer Ctr, PO Box 5201, 3008AE Rotterdam The Netherlands

SILLMAN, EMMANUEL, zoologist, educator; b. Phila., Dec. 7, 1915; s. Maxwell and Esther K. Sillman. BS, Bucknell U., 1937; MA in Zoology, U. Mich., 1948, PhD in Zoology, 1954. Teaching fellow U. Mich., Ann Arbor, 1951-53; from isntr. to asst. prof. U. Guelph, Guelph, Ont., Can., 1953-58; asst. prof. U. Manitoba, Winnipeg, Can., 1958-60; asst. prof., prof. Duquesne U., Pitts., 1960-80; liaison Pa. Coun. Sci. Edn., Pitts., 1981—. Contbr. articles to profl. jours. Bd. dirs. Group Against Smog and Pollution, Pitts., 1971-89; v.p. Pitts. Secular Humanists, 1990—. Capt. U.S. Army, 1943-47. Rsch. grantee Nat. Rsch. Coun. Can., 1954-60; recipient Commendation medal U.S. Army. Mem. AAAS, Ams. United for Separation of Ch. and State, Ams. for Religious Liberty, Nat. Ctr. Sci. Edn., Natural Resources Def. Coun., People for the Am. Way, Environ. Def. Fund. Home: 4700 Fifth Ave Pittsburgh PA 15213-2942

SILLS, LAUREL ANNE, psychologist; b. Detroit, Apr. 30, 1960; d. Richard D. and Geraldine Barbara (Zlatkin) S. BA, Mich. State U., 1982; D Psychology, Wright State U., 1987. Lic. clin. psychologist. Psychology intern Henry Ford Hosp., Detroit, 1986-87; postdoctoral intern Heritage Hosp., Taylor, Mich., 1987-88; pvt. practice, Ann Arbor, 1988-89; staff psychologist St. Joseph Mercy Hosp., Pontiac, Mich., 1989-92; assoc. psychologist Northpoint Mental Health Assocs., Farmington Hills, Mich., 1988-94; pvt. practice psychology Southfield, Mich., 1992-94, Franklin Village, Mich., 1993—; chmn. quality assurance com. St. Joseph Mercy Hosp., Pontiac, 1991-92; community speaker, 1993—. Bd. dirs. Lowwer SE Region Mich. Heart Assn. Mem. APA, Am. Arthritis Found., Mich. Psychol. Assn., Mich. Women Psychologists Assn., Jewish Welfare Fedn., Phi Kappa Phi.

SILLS, STEPHEN JOEL, ophthalmologist; b. N.Y.C., Mar. 1, 1939; s. Reuben and Edna Henrietta (Epstein) S.; m. Nancy Mintz, Apr. 17, 1966; children: Eric Howard, Ronnie Lynne. BS, Rensselaer Poly. Inst., Troy, N.Y., 1972; MD cum laude, Albany Med. Coll., 1962. Lic. physician, N.Y.; diplomate Am. Bd. Ophthalmology. Surg. intern Columbia-Presbyn. Med. Ctr., N.Y.C., 1962-63, resident Inst. Ophthalmology, 1965-69; pvt. practice ophthalmology Albany, 1969—. Mem. hwy. safety med. com. N.Y. State Dept. Health, Albany, 1976; mem. med. adv. bd. N.Y. State Athletic Commn., N.Y.C., 1980-93. Capt. M.C. USAF, 1963-65. Fellow Am. Acad. Ophthalmology; mem. AMA, N.Y. State Ophthal. Soc. (dir. 1975-78), Eastern N.Y. Eye, Ear, Nose and Throat Assn. (pres. 1987), Med. Soc. State N.Y. (chmn. sect. on ophthalmology 1976), Albany County Med. Soc., Lake George Club. Home: 16 Hiawatha Dr Guilderland NY 12084 Office: 632 New Scotland Ave Albany NY 12208

SILTANEN, PENTTI KUSTAA PIETARI, cardiologist; b. Tampere, Finland, June 6, 1926; s. Lauri A. and Saimi E. (Silventoinen) S.; m. 1950 (div. 1975); children: Marjukka, Riitta, Juha P.; m. Pirkko H. Parviainen, Oct. 4, 1975; children: Helena, Juha K. and Timo Saarelainen. MB, Helsinki U., 1949, lic. of Medicine, 1954, MD, 1968, prof. (hon.), 1983. Diplomate in Medicine, 1954, Internal Medicine, 1961, Cardiology, 1965, Ins. Medicine, 1994. Med. officer of health various rural communities, Finland, 1950-57; asst. physician Salus Hosp. of the Wihuri Rsch. Inst., Helsinki, 1959; asst. physician, 3d dept. medicine Helsinki U., 1960-62, sr. cardiologist, dept. thoracic surgery, 1963-72, sr. lectr. in cardiology, 1970—, dir. cardiovascular lab., 1st dept. medicine, 1972-89, dir., lectr. postgrad. course in cardiology for gen. practitioners, 1979-90; cons. cardiologist The Finnish Nat. Bd. Health, Helsinki, 1981-91, Ministry Health, 1991—, The Finnish Heart Assn., Helsinki, 1961-68, The Dist. Hosp. Kiljava, 1960-76, The North Carelia Cen. Hosp., Joensuu, 1974-86; mem. med. expert coms. Red Cross of Finland, The Finnish Heart Assn., Valio Co. of Dairy Products, 1960—; cons. physician Life Ins. Co. Suomi-Salama, Helsinki, 1962-72; dir. rsch. dept. Finnish Heart Assn., 1969-78; dir. Helsinki Coronary Register, 1969-78; med. advisor World Health Orgn., 1970-76; lectr. med. tech. Helsinki U. Tech., 1985. Editor various books; contbr. articles to profl. jours., textbooks on clin. cardiology, pathology, biochemistry, epidemiology, psychosomatics, electrocardiography. Chmn. exec. com. Coun. Med. Tech. on the Helsiki Dist., 1982-89; mem. expert coms. Finnish Red Cross Orgn., Helsinki, 1970—; mem. planning and sci. coms. The Norh Carelia Project, 1972-76; vice chmn. bd. Finnish Heart Assn., 1991-94. Grantee Acad. Finland, various pvt. founds. Fellow European Soc. Cardiology; mem. Finnish Soc. Clin. Physiology (founding mem., hon.), Finnish Soc. Ins. Medicine, Finnish Soc. Angiology (bd. dirs. 1985-90), Finnish Cardiac Soc. (founding mem., treas. 1968-70, pres. 1988-90, hon. mem. 1991), Lions. Evangelic-Lutheran. Home: Leppakertuntie 4C, 02120 Espoo Finland Office: Helsinki U Cen Hosp, Meilahti Med Ctr, 00290 Helsinki 29, Finland

SILVA, BENEDICTO ALVES DE CASTRO, surgeon, educator; b. Salvador, Bahia, Brazil, June 26, 1927; s. Octacílio Alves de Castro and Nathercia Crusoé Silva; m. Maria Guanaes, Dec. 20, 1958; children: Catia Maria, Marta Maria, Gloria Maria. Degree, Bahia U., Salvador, 1952. Asst. prof. faculty odontology Bahia U., 1962-72, adj. prof. faculty odontology, 1972—, maxillar buco surgeon, 1962—; maxillar buco surgeon Santa Izabel Hosp., Salvador, 1953-72, Hosp. Martagão Gesteira, Salvador, 1958-60; coord. Bahia Oral Cancer Ctr., Salvador, 1988—; coord. Oncology Ctr.-Mouth-Bahia, Salvador, 1988—. Author: Patients of High Risk, 1988; contbr. chpt. to book: Phamacology, 1980. Pres. Bahia Dental Coun., Salvador, 1981-85. Officer Brazilian Army, 1944-45. Mem. Brit. Assn. Oral Maxillar Surgery (assoc.), Bahia Dental Acad., Pierre Fuchard Acad. (medal 1990), Minas Gerais Dental Acad. (medal 1990), Brazilian Soc. Cancer, European Sch. Oncology, Bahia Acad. Odontology (pres. 1985—). Home: Padre Daniel Lisboa # 5-A, 40 285-560 Salvador Brazil Office: Med Ctr Graça, Humberton de Campos St # 11, 40150 Salvador Brazil

SILVA, LINCOLN BRASIL E, neurologist; b. Paraguaçu, Sao Paulo, Brazil, Mar. 30, 1934; s. José Bonifacio and Evangelina Rodrigues Silva; m. Luiza Leonor Cavazotti, Apr. 15, 1966; children: André, Ana Luiza, Fabio, Suzana. Degree, Coll. Bandeiras, Sao Paulo, 1954; MD, Escola Paulista Medicina, Sao Paulo, 1960. 1st neurologist Hinterland of Parana State, 1962; past chief neurologist Hosp. Evangelico, Santacasa Hosp.; pvt. practice Londrina, Parana, Brazil; past cons. Metrix Inc., Colo.; lectr., presenter confs. in field of brain mapping. Mem. Brazilian Med. Assn., Parana Med. Assn., Londrina Med. Assn., Brazilian Acad. Neurology, Brazilian League Against Epilepsy, Brazilian Soc. Clin. Neurophysics (founding mem.), Londrina Acad. Arts and Scis., Internat. Soc. Brain Topography and Electromagnetism (first Brazilian mem.), Assn. of the Friends of Londrina Mus. (counselor, treas. music festival). Roman Catholic. Office: 790 Ave Bandeirantes, 86010010 Londrina Parana, Brazil

SILVA, PATRICIO, medicine educator, hospital administrator; b. Santiago, Chile, July 7, 1939; came to U.S., 1969; s. Mario Julio and Luisa Emma (MacIver) S.; m. Vjera Maritza Bakovic, Nov. 21, 1964; children: Patricio, Jose Pablo, Marcela Cecilia. MD, U. Chile, Santiago, 1964; LM, Cath. U. Chile, Santiago, 1964. Instr. Med. Sch., Harvard U., Boston, 1972-74, asst. prof., 1974-78, assoc. prof., 1978; staff physician Beth Israel Hosp., Boston, 1973—, assoc. dir. renal div., 1981-90; staff physician Joslin Diabetes Ctr., Boston, 1990; staff physician Joslin Diabetes Ctr. New Eng. Deaconess Hosp., Boston, 1990—; trustee Mt. Desert Island Biol. Lab., Salisbury Cove, Maine, 1978-84. Contbr. numerous articles to profl. jours. Mem. Am. Soc. Nephrology, Am. Soc. Renal Biochemistry and Metabolism (pres. 1991-93), Am. Physiol. Soc., Am. Soc. for Clin. Investigation, Am. Soc. for Exptl. Biology and Medicine, Internat. Soc. Nephrology. Office: Joslin Diabetes Ctr 1 Joslin Pl Boston MA 02215-5306

SILVA, PAUL DOUGLAS, reproductive endocrinologist; b. Durban, Natal, Republic South Africa, Oct. 29, 1956; came to U.S., 1968; s. George Douglas and Georgette Marie (Schedivetz) S.; m. Diane Elisabeth Deterville, June 28, 1980; children: Julie Renee, Jennifer Marie, Dawn Elisabeth. BA in Biology, UCLA, 1976; MD, U. Calif., Davis, 1981. Diplomate Am. Bd. Ob-Gyn, Am. Bd. Reproductive Endocrinology. Resident in ob-gyn U. Calif., Irvine, 1981-85; fellow in reproductive endocrinology U. So. Calif., L.A., 1985-87; reproductive endocrinologist Gundersen/Luth. Med. Ctr., La Crosse, Wis., 1987—; med. researcher Gundersen Med. Found., La Crosse, 1987—; cons. St. Francis Med. Ctr., La Crosse, 1988—. Coontbr. articles to Jour. Am. Acad. Dermatology, Am. Jour. Ob-Gyn, Jour. Clin. Endocrinology and Metabolism, Acta Endocrinology, also others. Lectr. to community orgns. Recipient Geog. Acad. award U. Calif., Irvine, 1984, rsch. award Soc. for Gynecologic Investigation, 1987, svc. award Pacific Coast Fertility Soc., 1987; Gundersen Med. Found. grantee, 1989-93. Fellow Am. Coll. Ob-Gyn., Am. Fertility Soc.; mem. Am. Assn. Gynecologic Laparoscopists, Soc. Reproductive Endocrinologists. Roman Catholic. Office: Gundersen Clinic 1836 South Ave La Crosse WI 54601-5429

SILVER, GEORGE ALBERT, physician, educator; b. Phila., Dec. 23, 1913; s. Morris M. and Sara (Tutelman) S.; m. Mitzi Blieden, June 5, 1937; children—James David, Jane, Judith Ellen. B.A., U. Pa., Phila., 1934; M.D., Jefferson Med. Coll., Phila., 1938; M.P.H., Johns Hopkins U., Balt., 1948; M.A. (hon.), Yale U., New Haven, 1969. Diplomate Am. Bd. Preventive Medicine. Asst. demonstrator Jefferson Med. Coll., Phila., 1939-42; health officer Balt. City Health Dept., 1948-51; asst. prof. Johns Hopkins U., Balt., 1948-51; chief div. social medicine Montefiore Hosp., N.Y.C., 1951-65; assoc. prof. health adminstrn. Columbia U., N.Y.C., 1952-59; prof. social medicine Albert Einstein Coll. Medicine, N.Y.C., 1959-65; dep. asst. sec. health and sci. affairs HEW, Washington, 1965-68; health exec. Nat. Urban Coalition, Washington, 1968-71; prof. pub. health Yale U., New Haven, 1969-84, emeritus prof. pub. health, 1984—; chair com. on health policy Fedn. Am. Scientists. Author: Family Medical Care, 1963, Spy in the House of Medicine, 1974, Child Health: America's Future, 1978; contbg. editor Am. Jour. Pub. Health. Served to maj. M.C., U.S. Army, 1942-46. Recipient Superior Svc. award HEW, 1966; named to Soc. of Scholars, Johns Hopkins U., 1993; fellow Branford Coll., Yale U. Fellow APHA (assoc. editor jour. 1993—), Nat. Acad. Social Ins., N.Y. Acad. Medicine, Inst. Medicine; mem. NAS (sr.), Elizabethan Club, Sigma Xi. Democrat. Jewish. Home: 590 Ellsworth Ave New Haven CT 06511-1636 Office: Yale U 89 Trumbull St New Haven CT 06511-3723

SILVER, MARC A., physician; b. Chgo., Oct. 14, 1949; s. Samuel and Ida (Reiter) S.; m. Laureen Dunne, Aug. 5, 1983. AB, U. Ill., Chgo., 1971; MD, Rush Med. Coll., Chgo., 1979. Instr. Rush Med. Coll., Chgo., 1979-82, instr. medicine and pathology, 1984-86; fellow NIH, Bethesda, Md., 1982-84; asst. prof. Loyola U. Med. Ctr., Maywood, Ill., 1986-88; assoc. prof. medicine and pathology Michael Reese Hosp. Med. Ctr., Chgo., 1988—, med. dir. cardiac surveillance unit, 1988—, chief div. cardiology and cardiovascular inst., 1988—, dir. heart failure programs, 1988—; prof. medicine Stritch Sch. Medicine, dir. Outpatient Heart Failure Ctr., assoc. dir. heart transplant program Loyola U., 1994—; lectr. cardiac pathology Stritch Sch. Medicine, Loyola U. Med. Ctr.; dir. Midwest Ctr. for Heart Failure, 1992—. Contbr. articles to profl. jours.; mem. editl. bd. of several jours. Manuscript Review Several Profl. Jours. Fellow ACP, Am. Coll. Cardiology, Am. Coll. Chest Physicians; mem. Internat. Soc. Heart Transplantation, Am. Heart Assn., soc. for Cardiovascular Pathology, Alpha Omega Alpha.

SILVER, PAUL ANDREW, internist, psychiatrist; b. Phila., July 14, 1953; s. William Aaron and Barbara Ethel (Sharlach) S.; m. Rochelle Rosenblatt, Aug. 21, 1977; children: Aryeh Nathan, Sarah Shoshana, Malka Tziporah. AB, Kenyon Coll., 1975; MD, Hahnemann U., 1979. Diplomate Am. Bd. Psychiatry and Neurology. Resident in family medicine Hahnemann U., Phila., 1979-80, resident in psychiatry, 1980-83, sr. instr., 1984-85, asst. prof., 1985-89; research fellow Med. Coll. Pa., Phila., 1987-88, asst. prof., 1989-90; asst. prof. Georgetown U., Washington, 1990-94; resident in internal medicine Johns Hopkins U./Sinai Hosp., Balt., 1994-96; pvt. practice, Silver Spring, Md., 1996—; reviewer Psychosomatics, Washington, 1987—. Author: (with others) Current Therapy in Neurology, 1987, Current Concepts in MAOI Therapy, 1989. Author: (with others) Current Therapyin Internal Medicine, 1987. Mem. ACP, Am. Psychiat. Assn., Washington Psychiat. Soc., Acad. Psychosomatic Medicine. Jewish. Office: 13975 Connecticut Ave Silver Spring MD 20906

SILVER, RICHARD TOBIAS, physician, educator; b. Jan. 18, 1929; m. Barbara Silver; 1 son, Adam Bennett. Diploma, A.B., Cornell U., 1950, M.D., 1953. Diplomate: Nat. Bd. Med. Examiners, Am. Bd. Internal Medicine, Am. Bd. Clin. Oncology. Intern N.Y. Hosp.-Cornell Med. Ctr., N.Y.C., 1953-54, asst. resident in medicine, 1956-57, resident in hematology, 1957-58; clin. assoc. gen. medicine br. Nat. Cancer Inst., NIH, Bethesda, Md., 1954-56; asst. in medicine Cornell U. Med. Coll., N.Y.C., 1956-58, instr. medicine, 1958-62, clin. asst. prof., 1962-67, clin. assoc. prof., 1967-73, clin. prof., 1973—; pres. N.Y. State Soc. Med. Oncologists and Hematologists, 1991—; asst. attending physician N.Y. Hosp., 1964-67, assoc. attending physician, 1967-73, attending physician, 1973—; asst. vis. physician 2d Cornell Med. div. Bellevue Hosp., N.Y.C., 1963-66; vis. Fulbright prof. U. Bahia Sch. Medicine, Brazil, 1958-59; vis. prof. Hershey Hosp.-Pa. State Hosp., 1976, Mayo Clinic, 1977, Upstate Med. Ctr., Binghamton, N.Y., 1977, Med. Coll. Va., 1979, Med. Sch. Colubia U., 1982, N.J. Coll. Medicine, New Brunswick, 1983, Meml. Med. Ctr. U. Ga., 1984, 86; invited lectr. Med. Coll. Shanghai and Chengchow, 1979, VIII Brazilian Hematology Congress, Salvador, 1981, 14th Internat. Congress Chemotherapy, Kyoto, Japan, 1985, XI Brazilian Congress of Cancerology, Florianopolis, Santa Catarina, 1987, 2d Internat. Conf. CML, Bologna, Italy, 1992; mem. rev. bd. NIH, Nat. Cancer Inst.; cons. Cancer Chemotherapy Investigative Rev. Bd., 1980, clin. trials com., 1979-81; mem. Cornell U. COuncil, 1987—. Author: Morphology of the Blood and Marrow in Clinical Practice, 1970; co-author: (with R.D. Lauper, C.I. Jarowski) A Synopsis of Cancer Chemotherapy, 1977, ed edit., 1987; editor, contbr.: Topics in Cancer, 1982; contbr. chpts. to books and articles to profl. jours., to nat. and internat. profl. confs., seminars and workshops in medicine. Fellow ACP; mem. N.Y. State Soc. Med. Hematologists and Oncologists (pres. 1991—), Cornell U. Med. Coll. Alumni Assn. (pres. 1973-76, sr. advisor 1976—), Am. Soc. Clin. Oncology, Internat. Soc. Hematology, Am. Soc. Hematology, N.Y. Soc. Study of Blood, N.Y. County Med. Soc., N.Y. State Med. Soc. Oncologists and Hematologists (pres. 1991-93), Harvey Soc., Am. Fedn. Clin. Rsch., Am. Assn. Cancer Rsch., Explorers Club (bd. dirs., chmn. sci. adv. com. 1987), Sigma Xi. Office: NY Hosp Cornell Med Ctr 525 E 68th St New York NY 10021-4873 also: 1440 York Ave New York NY 10021-2577

SILVER, SAMUEL MICHAEL, hematologist, oncologist; b. Paterson, N.J., May 13, 1950; s. Elihu A. and Carol Ann (Salzberg) S.; m. Nancy Beth Straussberg, Jan. 1982; children: Aaron E., Emily R. AB, Brandeis U., Waltham, Mass., 1972; PhD, Rockefeller U., N.Y.C., 1978; MD, Cornell U., N.Y.C., 1979. Diplomate Am. Bd. Internal Medicine. Intern, resident in internal medicine U. Calif. H.C. Moffitt Hosp., San Francisco, 1979-82; fellow hematology/oncology U. Pa., Phila., 1982-86; asst. prof. internal medicine U. Mich., Ann Arbor, 1986-96, clin. assoc. prof. internal medicine, 1996—, dir. adult bone marrow transplantation, 1990—; med. cons. Aastrom Bioscis., Inc.; mem. funding bd. Huron Valley (Mich.) Vis. Nurse Assn., 1995—; med. advisor K.P. McCarthy Found. Grantee NIH, 1985, Am. Heart Assn. Mich., 1987, Am. Cancer Soc. Mich., 1989. Fellow ACP; mem. AMA, Am. Heart Assn., Southwestern Oncology Group, Mich. Soc. Hematology and Oncology (bd. dirs.), N.Am. Bone Marrow Transplant Registry, Nat. Bone Marrow Transplant Link (bd. dirs.), Med. Ombudsman Program, Am. Soc. Clin. Oncology (mem. clin. practice com.), Am. Soc. Hematology (vice chair clin. practice com., chair medicaid reimbursement com.), Phi Beta Kappa, Sigma Xi. Home: 3272 Bluett Rd Ann Arbor MI 48105-1528 Office: U Mich 1500 E Med Ctr Dr Ann Arbor MI 48109-0247

SILVER, STEPHEN CHAITT, colon and rectal surgeon, educator; b. Harrisburg, Pa., July 1, 1946; s. Morris A. and Mollie (Chaitt) S.; m. Susan C. Silver; children: Chuck, Beth, Aaron, Alan. BS, Dickinson Coll., 1967; MD, Jefferson Med. Coll., 1971. Diplomate Am. Bd. Surgery, Am. Bd. Colon and Rectal Surgery. Surg. resident Cleve. Clinic Edn. Found., 1972-73, 75-77, colon and rectal surgery fellow, 1977-78; chief colon and rectal surgery Del. County Meml. Hosp., Drexel HIll, Pa., 1978—; asst. prof. surgery Jefferson Med. Coll., Phila., 1978—. Contbr. articles to profl. jours. Maj. USAF, 1973-75. Fellow ACS, Am. Soc. Colon and Rectal Surgeons, Pa. Soc. Colon and Rectal Surgery (pres.), Phila. Acad. Surgery. Office: 1010 W Chester Pike Ste 201 Havertown PA 19083-3442

SILVERBERG, STUART OWEN, obstetrician, gynecologist; b. Denver, Oct. 14, 1931; s. Edward M. and Sara (Morris) S.; BA, U. Colo., 1952, MD, 1955; m. Joan E. Snyderman, June 19, 1954 (div. Apr. 1970); children: Debra Sue Owen, Eric Owen, Alan Kent; m. 2d, Kay Ellen Conklin, Oct. 18, 1970 (div. Apr. 1982); 1 son, Cris S.; m. 3d, Sandra Kay Miller, Jan., 1983. Intern Women's Hosp. Phila., 1955-56; resident Kings County Hosp., Bklyn., 1958-62; practice medicine specializing in obstetrics and gynecology, Denver, 1962—; mem. staff Rose Med. Ctr., N. Suburban Med. Ctr., U. Hosp., St. Anthony Hosp.; med. exec. bd., chmn. dept. obstetrics and gynecology, 1976-77, 86-87, dir. Laser Ctr., 1994-95; clin. instr. U. Colo. Sch. Medicine, Denver, 1962-72, asst. clin. prof., 1972-88, assoc. clin. prof., 1989—, dir. gynecol. endoscopy and laser surgery, 1988-90; v.p. Productos Alimenticos, La Ponderosa, S.A.; dir., chmn. bd. Wicker Works Video Prodns., Inc., 1983-91; cons. Ft. Logan Mental Health Ctr., Denver, 1964-70; mem. Gov.'s Panel Mental Retardation, 1966; med. adv. bd. Colo. Planned Parenthood, 1966-68, Am. Med. Ctr., Spivak, Colo., 1967-70. Mem. Colo. Emergency Resources Bd., Denver, 1965—. Served to maj. AUS, 1956-58; Germany. Diplomate Am. Bd. Obstetrics and Gynecology, Am. Bd. Laser Surgery. Fellow Am. Coll. Obstetricians and Gynecologists, Am. Soc. Laser Medicine and Surgery, ACS; mem. Am. Internat. fertility socs., Colo. Gynecologists and Obstetricians Soc., Hellman Obstet. and Gynecol. Soc., Colo. Med. Soc. (bd. dirs. 1987-95, speaker of the house 1989-95), Clear Creek Valley Med. Soc. (trustee 1978, 80, 87, 93—, pres. 1995), Phi Sigma Delta, Flying Physicians Assn., Aircraft Owners and Pilots Assn., Nu Sigma Nu, Alpha Epsilon Delta. Jewish. Mem. editorial rev. bd. Colo. Women's Mag.; editor in chief First Image, Physicians Video Jour., 1984-86. Office: 8300 N Alcott St Ste 301 Westminster CO 80030

SILVERGLEID, ARTHUR JAY, medical educator, health science facility executive; b. N.Y.C., June 17, 1942; s. David and Dorothy (Hoffman) S.; m. Naomi Gail Schwartzman, June 20, 1964 (div. June 1982); children: Courtenay Sheridan, Jordan Evan; m. Margaret Anderson, Sept. 10, 1983. AB magna cum laude, U. Rochester, 1963; MD, NYU, 1967. Diplomate Am. Bd. Internal Medicine; cert. blood banking, hematology subspecialty. Intern Stanford (Calif.) U. Hosp., 1967-68, asst. resident, 1968-69, sr. asst. resident, 1971-72, fellow in hematology, 1972-74; clin. assoc. hematology NIH, Bethesda, Md., 1969-71; physician specialist in medicine and hematology, clin. asst. prof. Stanford U. Sch. Medicine, 1974-77; assoc. med. dir., sci. dir. ARC-Stanford U. Blood Ctr. and Stanford U. Hosp. Transfusion Service, 1974-77; med., exec. dir. Blood Bank of San Bernardino and Riverside Counties, Calif., 1977—; assoc. clin. prof. lab. medicine Loma Linda (Calif.) U., 1980—; assoc. clin. prof. UCLA Sch. Medicine, 1980—. Contbr. articles to profl. med. jours. Vice chmn. Aids Adv. Task Force, San Bernardino, 1985-86. Served to lt. comdr. USPHS, 1969-71. Mem. AMA, Am. Assn. Blood Banks (mem. various coms. 1979—, mem. bd. dirs. 1986—, pres. 1992-93), Am. Fedn. Clin. Rsch., Am. Soc. Hematology (chmn. transfusion sect. 1978, 81), Calif. Blood Bank System (mem. various coms., bd. dirs. 1980-86, pres. 1983-84), Calif. Med. Assn. (com. blood banks), Inland Soc. Internal Medicine, San Bernardino County Med. Soc. (publ. com. 1978-79), Blood Ctrs. Calif., Inc (pres. 1988-89), Nat. Blood Found. (chmn. bd. trustees 1994—). Democrat. Jewish. Home: 13063 Helen Dr Redlands CA 92373-7434 Office: Blood Bank San Bernardino PO Box 5729 San Bernardino CA 92412-5729

SILVERMAN, ALBERT JACK, psychiatrist, educator; b. Montreal, Que., Can., Jan. 27, 1925; came to U.S., 1950, naturalized, 1955; s. Norman and Molly (Cohen) S.; m. Halina Weinthal, June 22, 1947; children: Barry Evan, Marcy Lynn. B.Sc., McGill U., 1947, M.D., C.M., 1949; grad., Washington Psychoanalytic Inst., 1964. Diplomate: Am. Bd. Psychiatry and Neurology. Intern Jewish Gen. Hosp., Montreal, 1949-50; resident psychiatry Colo. U. Med. Center, 1950-53, instr., 1953; from assoc. to assoc. prof. psychiatry Duke Med. Center, 1953-63; prof. psychiatry, chmn. dept. Rutgers U. Med. Sch., 1964-70; prof. psychiatry U. Mich. Med. Sch., Ann Arbor, 1970-90, prof. emeritus, 1990—; chmn. dept. U. Mich. Med. Sch., 1970-81; cons. Dept. of Def., 1974—; mem. biol. scis. tng. rev. com. NIMH, 1964-69, chmn., 1968-69, mem. rsch. scientist devel. award com., 1970-75, chmn., 1973-75, mem. merit rev. bd. in behavioral scis. VA, 1975-78, chmn., 1976-78, mem. small grants awards com., 1985-89; bd. mgrs. N.J. Neuropsychiat. Inst., 1965-69; trustee N.J. Fund Rsch. and Devel. Nervous and Mental Diseases, 1965-67; bd. dirs. N.J. Mental Health Assn., 1964-69; mem. behavioral sci. com. Nat. Bd. Med. Examiners, 1978-82, chmn., 1984-87, mem. comprehensive com., 1986-93, task force for nervous system, 1989-91; chmn. task force on Cons. Liaison Psychiat., 1991-92. Cons. editor: Psychophysiology, 1970-74, Psychosomatic Medicine, 1972-87; Contbr. articles in field. Served as capt. M.C. USAF, 1955-57. Fellow Am. Coll. Psychiatry (charter), Am. Psychiat. Assn. (chmn. coun. on med. edn. 1970-75, chair task force on DSM III ednl. materials 1979-81), Am. Acad. Psychoanalysis, Am. Coll. Neuropsychopharmacology; mem. Am. Psychosomatic Soc. (coun. 1964-68, 70-74, pres. 1976-77, vis. scholar com. 1992-96, co-chair program com. 1992-93), N.J. Psychoanalytic Soc. (trustee 1968-70), Assn. Rsch. Nervous and Mental Diseases, N.J. Neuropsychiat. Assn. (coun. 1966-69), Group Advancement Psychiatry (chmn. com. psychopathology 1968-74), Soc. Psychophys. Rsch., Soc. Biol. Psychiatry, Mich. Psychiat. Soc. (coun. 1975-77). Home: 19 Regent Dr Ann Arbor MI 48104-1738 Office: Mental Health Rsch Inst 205 Zina Pitcher Pl Ann Arbor MI 48109-0720

SILVERMAN, ANNA MAE, nurse; b. Phila., July 5, 1928; d. Charles Girth and Maude Yoast; m. Edward Silverman, Sept. 1, 1955 (div. Oct. 1978); children: Gail, Debra, Jeffrey. Diploma, Meth. Hosp., 1953. RN; cert. psychiatric nurse. Mem. RN staff Meth. Hosp., Phila., 1953-55, Wernesville (Pa.) State Hosp., 1968-70, St. Joseph Hosp., Reading, Pa., 1974-91; ret., 1991—; counselor, nurse Callowhill Family Therapy Ctr., Reading, Pa., 1992—; part time counselor Progressions of Berks County, 1994. Contbr. article to Nursing World Jour., 1986. Home: RR 3 Box 3786 Mohnton PA 19540-9231

SILVERMAN, CHARLOTTE, federal agency administrator, medical epidemiologist; b. N.Y.C., May 21, 1913; d. Harry and Gussie (Goldman) S. BA, Bklyn. Coll., 1933; MD, Med. Coll. Pa., 1938; MPH, Johns Hopkins U., 1942, DrPH, 1948. Diplomate Am. Bd. Preventive Medicine. Intern Beekman Hosp., N.Y.C., 1939-40; resident Sea View Hosp., Staten Island, N.Y., 1940-41; asst. dir., dir. Bur. Tuberculosis Balt. City Health Dept., 1946-56; chief epidemiology, planning and rsch. Md. State Dept. Health, Balt., 1956-62; med. officer in various programs NIMH, Bethesda, Md., 1962-68; dep. dir. div. biol. effects and other positions Bur. Radiol. Health USPHS, Rockville, Md., 1968-83; assoc. dir. for human studies FDA, Rockville, 1983-92; mem. faculty dept. epidemiology Johns Hopkins U. Sch. Hygiene and Pub. Health, Balt., 1950—. Author: Epidemiology of Depression, 1968; contbr. articles to profl. jours. Sr. Surg. USPHS, 1944-45. Recipient Mary Pemberton Nourse Meml. award AAUW, 1941-42, Alumni Life Achievement award Bklyn. Coll., 1994. Fellow APHA, Am. Coll. Preventive Medicine, Am. Orthopsychiat. Assn., Am. Coll. Epidemiology; mem. Delta Omega. Home: 4977 Battery Ln Bethesda MD 20814-4927

SILVERMAN, ELLEN-MARIE, speech and language pathologist; b. Milw., Oct. 12, 1942; d. Roy and Bettie (Schlaeger) Loebel; m. Feb. 5, 1967 (div.); 1 child, Catherine Bette. BS, U. Wis., Milw., 1964; MA, U. Iowa, 1967, PhD, 1970. Rsch. assoc. U. Ill., Urbana, 1969-71; asst. prof. speech pathology Marquette U., Milw., 1973-79; assoc. prof. speech pathology Marquette U., 1979-85; pvt. practice speech and lang. pathology, Milw., 1985—; owner, pres. The Speech Source, Inc. Contbr. articles to profl. jours., chpts. to books. Marquette U. grantee, 1982. Fellow Am. Speech, Hearing, Lang. Assn.; mem. Wis. Speech, Hearing, Lang. Assn., Sigma Xi.

SILVERMAN, FRANKLIN HAROLD, speech pathologist, educator; b. Providence, Aug. 16, 1933; s. Meyer and Reba (Sack) S.; m. Ellen-Marie Loebel, Feb., 1967 (div. Feb. 1981); 1 child, Catherine; m. Evelyn Ellen Chanda, Nov. 13, 1983. BS in Speech, Emerson Coll., 1960; MA, Northwestern U., 1961; PhD, U. Iowa, 1966. Lic. speech-lang. pathologist, Wis. Rsch. assoc. U. Iowa, Iowa City, 1965-67; asst. prof. U. Ill., Champaign, 1968-71; assoc. prof. Marquette U., Milw., 1971-77, prof., 1978—; clin. prof. Med. Coll. Wis., Wauwatosa, 1978—; mem. adv. bd. Wis. Telecomm. Relay Svcs., Madison, 1991—; cons. USAID Palestinian Speech Pathology Tng. Program, Gaza City, Gaza Strip, 1993—. Author: Speech, Language, and Hearing Disorders, 1995, Communication for the Speechless, 3d edit., 1995, Stuttering and Other Fluency Disorders, 2d edit., 1996; contbr. numerous rsch. papers to profl. jours. Fellow Am. Speech-Lang.-Hearing Assn.; mem. Text and Acad. Authors Assn. (sec. 1993-94, pres.-elect 1996). Jewish. Home: 5918 Currant Ln Greendale WI 53129 Office: Marquette U Dept Speech Pathology Milwaukee WI 53233

SILVERMAN, GARY JAY, physician; b. Phila., July 24, 1957; s. Tom and Hilaa (Schlam) S.; m. Joan Ellen Levy, Nov. 28, 1987; children: Michael, Avery. DO, UMDNJ, 1983. Clin. assoc. Emory U., Atlanta, 1989; pvt. practice rheumatology Scottsdale, Ariz., 1989—; pres. Motivational Medicine, Scottsdale, 1994—. Author (audio tape) Fatt is a 4 Letter Word, 1994, Stresspoints, 1995. Named one of Top 10 Alumni, UMDNJ, 1994. Fellow Am. Coll. Rheumatology. Republican. Jewish. Office: 3126 Civic Center Plz Scottsdale AZ 85251

SILVERMAN, HAROLD IRVING, pharmaceutical executive; b. Lawrence, Mass., Apr. 27, 1928; s. Jack David and Norma (Illman) S.; m. Arlene Jacobowitz, Nov. 25, 1951; children: Robert L., Richard L. BSc, Phila. Coll. of Pharmacy, 1951, MSc, 1952, DSc, 1956. Instr. Phila. Coll. of Pharmacy, 1952-56; prof. pharmaceutics L.I. U., Bklyn., 1956-64; sr. scientist Warner Lambert Rsch. Inst., Morris Plains, N.J., 1958-60; v.p. sci. dir. Knoll Pharm. Co., West Orange, N.J., 1964-68; prof., assoc. dean Mass. Coll. of Pharmacy, Boston, 1968-85; sr. v.p. Thompson Med. Co., N.Y.C., 1985-92, Bascomb Found. for Med. Rsch., N.Y.C., 1992—; lectr. Boston U. Sch. Medicine, 1971-73, New Eng. Coll. of Optometry, Boston, 1971-80. Contbr. numerous articles to sci. jours. Mem. human subcom. Peter Bent Brigham, Boston, 1980-85, Boston U., 1983-85; cons. Mass. Bd. Optometry, Boston, 1974-80, WHO, Washington, 1985. Named Man of the Yr., Boston Assn. Druggists, 1977; recipient Disting. Svc. award Am. Optometric Assn., 1974. Fellow Soc. Cosmetic Chemists; mem. AAAS, Am. Pharm. Assn. (Phytochemistry award 1956), Am. Chem. Soc., Am. Soc. Hosp. Pharmacists, Am. Oil Chemists Soc., Am. Assn. Pharm. Scientists. Home and Office: 45 Crest Rd Framingham MA 01702

SILVERMAN, HIRSCH LAZAAR, psychologist, educator, administrator; b. N.Y.C., June 19, 1915; s. Herman Bear and Ida (Mackta) S.; m. Mildred Friedlander, Mar. 1, 1942; children: Hyla Susan, Morton Maier, Stuart Edward. BS, CCNY, 1936; MS, CUNY, 1938; MA, NYU, 1947; PhD, Yeshiva U., 1951; MA, Seton Hall U., 1957; DSC, Lane Coll., Jackson, Tenn., 1962; LLD (hon.), Fla. Memorial Coll., 1965; D of Humane Letters, Ohio Coll. of Podiatric Med., 1972. Diplomate Clin. Psychology, Forensic Psychology, Neuropsychology, Behavioral Med., Psychotherapy, Am. Bd. Profl. Psychologists, Am. Bd. Forensic Psychologists, Am. Bd. Behavioral Med. Asst. prof. Mohawk Coll., Utica, N.Y., 1946-48; ednl., vocat. cons. Stevens Inst. Tech., Hoboken, N.J., 1948-49; asst. prof., psychology Rutgers U., New Brunswick, N.J., 1948-53; asst. supt. Nutley (N.J.) Bd. Edn., 1953-59; prof., chmn. ednl. psychology Yeshiva U., N.Y.C., 1959-65; prof., chmn. ednl. administrn. Seton Hall U., South Orange, N.J., 1965-80; pvt. practice psychologist Newark, West Orange, N.J., 1951—; expert witness, cons. Superior Ct. of N.J.; prof. emeritus Seton Hall U., 1980—; research clin. psychologist Columbus Hosp., St. Vincent's Hosp., N.Y. Med. Coll.; vis. prof. Lane Coll. and Fla. Meml. Coll. Author 20 pub. books; mem. bd. editors several profl. jours., including Jour. of Divorce, Social Scis., Contemporary Psychology, Psychotherapy in Pvt. Practice; contbr. over 190 articles to profl. jours. Mem. White House Conf. on Families, Washington, 1978-80; cons. N.J. Rehab. Commn., Trenton, 1951—, Essex County Mental Health Commn., Newark, 1985-87. Capt. U.S. Army, 1942-46, PTO. Recipient Townsend Harris medal CCNY, 1976; named Disting. Practitioner in Psychology Nat. Academies of Practice. Fellow APHA, Coll. of Preceptors, Assn. for Advancement of Psychotherapy, Soc. for Adolescent Medicine, Royal Soc. Medicine, Royal Soc. Health, World Acad. Arts and Scis.; mem. APA, Am. Assn. Clin. Counselors, Acad. Psychologists in Marital Therapy, Philos. Soc. Eng. (v.p.), N.J. Assn. Marriage and Family Therapists (pres. 1964-67), Phi Beta Kappa, Sigma Xi, Psi Chi, Phi Sigma Tau, Kappa Delta Pi. Home: 123 Gregory Ave West Orange NJ 07052-4740 Office: NW Corner of Northfield and Gregory Aves West Orange NJ 07052

SILVERMAN, JEFFREY MICHAEL, radiologist; b. Columbus, Ohio, Mar. 28, 1960. BA, U. Calif. San Diego, 1981, MD, 1985. Diplomate Am. Bd. Radiology, Am. Bd. Med. Examiners. Intern Cedars-Sinai Med. Ctr., L.A., 1985-86, resident, 1986-90; vis. fellow UCLA, Stanford (Calif.) U., U. Calif./Irvine, San Francisco, 1991; radiologist Tower Imaging, L.A., 1991-92, Cedars-Sinai Med. Ctr., L.A., 1992—; active numerous coms. in field; assoc. editor Cedars-Sinai Med. Ctr. Rsch. Editl. Adv. Com., 1989; prsenter in field. Reviewer Jour. of Magnetic Resonance Imaging, 1994, Am. Jour. Roentgenology, 1995, Chest, 1993, others; contbr. articles to profl. jours. and publs. Grantee in field. Mem. AMA, Am. Coll. Radiology, Radiol. Soc. N.Am., Am. Roentgen Ray Soc., Soc. Magnetic Resonance in Medicine, Soc. for Magnetic Resonance Imaging, Calif. Radiol. Soc., L.A. County Med. Assn., L.A. Radiol. Soc., Am. Coll. Chest Physicians, N.Am. Soc. Cardiac Imaging, Am. Heart Assn. Cardiovascular Radiology Coun. Office: Cedars Sinai Med Ctr 8700 Beverly Blvd Los Angeles CA 90048-1804

SILVERMAN, MERVYN F., health science association administrator, consultant. BS cum laude, Washington and Lee U., 1960; MD, Tulane U., 1964; MPH, Harvard U., 1969. Diplomate Am. Bd. Preventive Medicine. Physician Peace Corps, Thailand, 1965-67; regional med. dir. East Asia and the Pacific Peace Corps, Washington, 1967-68; spl. asst. to commr. FDA, Washington, 1969-70, dir. Office of Consumer Affairs, 1970-72; dir. health Wichita (Kans.)-Sedgwick County Dept. Cmty. Health, 1972-77; med. dir. Planned Parenthood Kans., Wichita, 1976-77; dir. health Dept. Health, San Francisco, 1977-85; health care cons. Mervyn F. Silverman & Assocs., Inc., 1985—; dir. AIDS health svcs. program Robert Wood Johnson Found., 1986-92; nat. spokesperson Am. Found. for AIDS Rsch., 1986-96, pres., also bd. dirs.; resident physician Sta. KPIX-TV, San Francisco, 1979-85; dir., prodr., host weekly health program Sta. KMPX Radio, 1980-82; sr. tech. advisor Acad. Ednl. Devel.-AIDSCOM, 1990-92; advisor to pres. Pan Am. AIDS Found., 1991-93, advisor to mayor of San Juan, Puerto Rico, 1991-93; former med. advisor to bd. dirs. Golden Gate chpt. ARC, San Francisco; past vice chmn. Adv. Health Coun., State of Calif.; former assoc. clin. prof. Wichita State U.; assoc. clin. prof. U. Hawaii; adj. assoc. prof. Sch. Pub. Health and Tropical Medicine Tulane U.; adj. prof. Inst. Health Policy Studies, Sch. Medicine, U. Calif., San Francisco; mem. nat. adv. coun. Harvard AIDS Inst.; spkr., presenter in field. Author: (with others) Humanistic Perspectives in Medical Ethics, 1972, What to Do About AIDS, 1986, AIDS and Patient Management: Legal, Ethical and Social Issues, 1986, AIDS: Facts and Issues, 1986, AIDS in Children, Adolescents and Heterosexual Adults: An Interdisciplinary Approach to Prevention, 1988, others; contbg. and consulting editor Modern Medicine Publs., Mpls., 1970-75; contbg. editor Healthline, 1983-85; contbr. articles to profl. jours. Bd. dirs., vice-chmn. U.S.-China Ednl. Inst. Recipient Award for Courageous Leadership, San Francisco Found., Award of Excellence, KAIROS Support for Care Givers, Civic Achievement award Bay Area Non-Partisan Alliance; Wear Found. fellow Wichita State U.; adj. scholar Kans. Newman Coll. Mem. APHA, AMA, Calif. Med. Assn., San Francisco Med. Soc., Omicron Delta Kappa, Delta Omega. Address: 119 Frederick St San Francisco CA 94117

SILVERMAN, NORMAN A., cardiac surgeon; b. Boston, Dec. 19, 1946. BA, Dartmouth Coll., 1968; MD, Boston U., 1971. Prof. surgery U. Ill., Chgo., 1980-89; divsn. head Henry Ford Hosp., Detroit, 1989—; prof. surgery Case-Western Res. U., Cleve., 1992—. Contbr. 200 scientific articles to profl. jours. Lt. comdr. USPHS, 1973-75. Fellow Am. Coll. Surgeons, Am. coll. Cardiology, Am. Coll. Chest Physicians. Office: Henry Ford Hosp 2799 W Grand Blvd Detroit MI 48202

SILVERMAN, PAUL LEONARD, clinical psychologist; b. Newark, Apr. 29, 1937; s. Samuel and Ann (Schwam) S.; m. Judith Shapiro, June 18, 1961; children: Michael, Noah. BA, Rutgers U., 1959; MA, U. Md., 1962, PhD, 1964. Clin. psychologist Bur. Mental Health, Washington, 1964-67, dir. psychology tng., 1967-68; chief psychologist Youth Svcs. Adminstrn., Washington, 1968-87, chief office program svcs., 1987-88; pvt. practice clin. psychology Kensington, Md., 1988—; bd. appeals Nat. Register Health Svc. Providers, Washington, 1985-87; vis. assoc. psychologist Taylor Manor Hosp., Ellicott City, Md., 1989—; cons. Cooksville (Md.) Acad. for Boys, 1989-90; ind. examiner St. Elizabeth Hosp., Washington, 1989-91; provider Blue Cross/Blue Shield Md., Blue Cross/Blue Shield Nat. Capital Area, Medicare. Contbr. articles to profl. jours. Chmn. ACLU, Montgomery County, Md., 1971-72. Fellow Md. Psychol. Assn.; mem. APA, D.C. Psychol. Assn. (cert. recognition 1982), Nat. Capital Area Cello Club (bd. dirs. 1985—). Democrat. Jewish. Home: 14315 Bauer Dr Rockville MD 20853-2345 Office: Kensington Mental Health 10400 Connecticut Ave Kensington MD 20895-3910

SILVERMAN, PAUL M., physician, researcher; b. Boston, Feb. 26, 1952; s. Allyn Morris and Molly (Natzer) S.; m. Amy Susan Winthrop, Apr. 17, 1979; children: Zachary, Rebecca. BA, Brandeis U., 1973; MD, U. Mass., 1977. Diplomate Am. Bd. Radiology, Nat. Bd. Med. Examiners. Intern in medicine/surgery Hartford (Conn.) Hosp., 1977-78; resident in radiology Stanford U., Palo Alto, Calif., 1978-81; fellow computed tomography, ultrasound Duke U. Med. Ctr., Durham, N.C., 1981-82, asst. prof. radiology, 1982-86; staff radiologist Alexandria (Va.) Hosp., 1986-87; prof. radiology Georgetown U., Washington, 1987—; mem. med. adv. bd. GE Med. Sys., Milw., 1989—; cons. Med. Inc., Pitts., 1996—; cons. med. edn. program Time Life Med., N.Y.C., 1995—. Author 4 books; contbr. chpts. to books and over 125 articles to profl. jours. Bd. dirs. Beth el Hebrew Congregation, Alexandria, 1992-94. Recipient Rsch. grant GE Med. Sys., 1992-96. Fellow Am. Cancer Soc.; mem. Soc. Computed Body Tomography and Magnetic Resonance, Soc. Gastrointestinal Radiologists, Radiol. Soc. N.Am., Assn. U. Radiologists, Radiology Centennial Com. Office: Georgetown Univ Med Ctr 3800 Reservoir Rd NW Washington DC 20007

SILVERMAN, ROBERT NEIL, optometrist; b. N.Y.C., Mar. 2, 1949; s. Fred and Toby (Soroka) S.; m. Madeline Ruth Shapiro, June 13, 1971; children: Ethan, Leslie. BS, Hofstra U., 1970; OD, Penn. Coll. Optometry, 1974. Optometrist Greenbush Eye Ctr., East Greenbush, N.Y., 1975—. Pres. Congregation Ohav Shalom, Albany, N.Y., 1992-94. Fellow Am. Acad. Optometry; mem. N.Y. State Optometric Assn. (trea. 1994, Comms. award), Ea. N.Y. Optometric Soc. (pres. 1988-90). Home: 9 Edge of Woods Latham NY 12110 Office: Greenbush Eye Ctr PO Box 459 1528 Columbia Tpke East Greenbush NY 12061

SILVERMAN, SAMUEL, psychiatrist; b. Boston, Aug. 29, 1912; s. Harry and Fannie (Messing) S.; m. Edith R. Levine, 1942 (div. 1970); children: Harry J., Neil M. BA, Harvard U., 1933, MD, 1938. Diplomate Am. Bd. Psychiatry and Neurology. Med. intern Boston City Hosp., 1939-40; jr. and sr. physician in psychiatry Boston State Hosp., 1940-42; asst. chief neuropsychiat. svc. Cushing VA Hosp., Framingham, Mass., 1946-52; chief psychosomatic sect. VA Hosp., Boston, 1952-59; attending psychiatrist McLean Hosp., Belmont, Mass., 1959-63, dir. clin. psychiatry, 1963-65 pvt. practice Boston and Brookline, Mass., 1946—; asst. prof. psychiatry Tufts U. and Boston U. Med. Schs., 1952-60; asst. clin. prof. psychiatry Harvard U. Med. Sch., Boston, 1961-73, assoc. clin. prof. psychiatry, 1973-79; hon. psychiatrist Mass. Gen. Hosp., 1980—; tng. analyst Boston Psychoanalytic Soc.-Inst., Psychoanalytic Inst. New England East. Author: Psychological Aspects of Physical Symptoms, 1968, Psychological Cues in Forecasting Physical Symptoms, 1970, How Will You Feel Tomorrow?, 1973; frequent-contbr. articles to profl. jours. Lt. to maj. U.S. Army, 1942-46. Fellow Am. Psychoanalytic Assn., Am. Psychiat. Assn., Internat. Psycho-Analytic Assn., Mass. Med. Soc.

SILVERS, MICHAEL JULIUS, physician; b. N.Y.C., Mar. 5, 1960; s. Julius Silvers and Mildred Catherine (Ormston) Jorgensen. AS, Crafton Hills Jr. Coll., Yucuipa, Calif., 1980; BS in Biology, U. Calif., Irvine, 1982; DO, Chgo. Coll. Osteo. Medicine, 1990; MPH, U. S.C., 1992. Resident in family and preventive medicine Richland Meml. Hosp., Columbia, S.C., 1990-92; chief resident in preventive medicine U. S.C., Columbia, 1991-92; internat. health fellow Ctr. for Disease Control, Atlanta, 1992-93; med. dir. Serologicals Corp., Columbia, Atlanta, 1991-93; chief med. advisor U.S. Peace Corps, Washington, 1993-95, regional med. officer for So. Africa, 1995—. Inventor remote rack, 1994. Pres. Assn. de Salude Rural, Chgo., Columbia, 1990-94. Recipient Excellence in Rsch. award U. Calif. at Irvine, 1982. Home and Office: US Peace Corps, PO Box 93, Gaborone Botswana

SILVERSTEIN, BURTON VICTOR, cardiologist; b. Durham, N.C., May 7, 1945; s. Jacob Morris and Beatrice Deborah (Grodner) S.; m. Janet H. Fisher, Aug. 18, 1968; children: Craig Daryl, Todd Alan. AB in Chemistry, U. Rochester, 1966; MD, U. Pa., 1970. Diplomate Am. Bd. Internal Medicine, Am. Bd. Cardiovascular Disease, Nat. Bd. Med. Examiners. Intern Hosp. of U. Pa., Phila., 1970-71, jr. asst. resident medicine, 1971-72, sr. asst. resident medicine, 1974-75; cardiology fellow Duke U. Med. Ctr., Durham, N.C., 1975-77; clin. asst. prof. medicine U. Fla., Gainesville, 1978—; assoc. dir. cardiovascular lab. Alachua Gen. Hosp., Gainesville, 1978—, attending physician, 1979—; pvt. practice Cardiology Assocs. of Gainesville, 1978—; assoc. in medicine Duke U. Med. Ctr., 1977-78; dir. non-invasive lab. Vet.'s Hosp., Durham, 1977-78; clin. asst. prof. medicine U. Fla., Gainesville, 1979—; clin. instr. medicine Duke U. Med. Ctr., 1975-77. Mem. edn. com. Fla. Heart Assn., 1979-82. Maj. USAF, 1972-74. Fellow Am. Coll. Cardiology, Soc. Cardiac Angiography and Interventions, Am. Soc. Cardiovascular Interventionalists; mem. Am. Heart Assn., Fla. Heart Assn., Fla. Med. Soc., Alachua County Med. Soc. Office: Cardiology Assocs 1026 SW 2d Ave Gainesville FL 32601

SILVERSTEIN, ELLIOT M., psychologist, lawyer; b. Syracuse, N.Y., Oct. 12, 1947; s. Harry Joseph and Shirley Jane (Weisberg) S.; m. Carol Kauffman, June 10, 1973; children: Scott, Alan. BS in Econ., U. Pa., 1969; JD, Harvard U., 1973; PhD in Clin. Psychology, U. N.C., 1977. Diplomate Am. Bd. Forensic Psychology. Staff psychologist Dorothea Dix Hosp., Raleigh, N.C., 1977-81; dir. psychol. svcs., adolescent svcs. Dorothea Dix Hosp., Raleigh, 1981-83, co-dir. psychol. svcs., 1983-95, dir. psychol. svcs., 1996—; pvt. practice Cary, N.C., 1982—; clin. assoc. prof. psychiatry U. N.C. Med. Sch., Chapel Hill, 1988—; adj. lectr. U. N.C. Law Sch., Chapel Hill, 1985—. Contbr. articles to profl. jours. Mem. APA, N.C. Psychol. Assn., Assn. for the Advancement of Psychology. Jewish. Office: Dorothea Dix Hosp Raleigh NC 27603

SILVERSTEIN, EMANUEL, medical educator, biochemist and molecular biologist, internist; b. N.Y.C., Feb. 14, 1930; s. Israel Isidore Suris and Raize Rose (Rubock) S.; m. Shoshana Sham'e Tubi, Mar. 25, 1975; children: Roselle Rama, Daniel Doron. BS magna cum laude, CUNY, 1950; MD, SUNY Health Sci. Ctr., Bklyn., 1954; PhD in Biochemistry, U. Minn., 1963. Diplomate Nat. Bd. Med. Examiners. Intern in medicine U. Minn. Hosps., Mpls., 1954-55, resident, NIH fellow in medicine, 1958-59, postdoctoral fellow in biochemistry, 1959-63; intern in pathology Sch. of Medicine Yale U., New Haven, 1955-56; sr. asst. surg. lab. pathology and histochemistry Nat. Inst. Arthritis & Metabolic Disease USPHS, Bethesda, Md., 1956-58; postdoctoral fellow dept. biology MIT, Cambridge, 1963-64; asst. prof. medicine SUNY Health Sci. Ctr., Bklyn., 1964-69, assoc. prof. medicine, 1970-72, assoc. prof. medicine and grad. program in physiology, 1972-77, assoc. prof. grad. program in biochemistry, 1975-77, prof. medicine and grad. program in biochemistry, 1977—; vis. scientist Weizmann Inst. Sci., Rehovoth, Israel, 1971, 81. Contbr. articles to profl. jours. Sr. asst. surgeon USPHS, 1956-58. N.Y. State Regents scholar, 1947-50, 50-54. Fellow N.Y. Acad. Sci.; mem. AAAA, Am. Soc. Biochemistry and Molecular Biology, Am. Soc. for Investigative Pathology, Am. Chem. Soc. (divsn. biol. chemistry), Biophys. Soc., The Harvey Soc., Am. Soc. Microbiology, Genetics Soc. Am., Am. Soc. Human Genetics, Am. Fedn. Clin. Rsch., Am. Thoracic Soc., Am. Heart Assn., N.Y. Heart Assn., Soc. Exptl. Biology of Medicine, Enzyme Club, Phi Beta Kappa, Sigma Xi. Office: SUNY Health Sci Ctr 450 Clarkson Ave Brooklyn NY 11203-2012

SILVERSTEIN, MARTIN ELLIOT, surgeon, author, consultant; b. N.Y.C., Sept. 6, 1922; s. Louis and Ethel (Statman) S.; m. Mabelle A. Cremer, Dec. 10, 1962. AB cum laude, Collumbia U., 1945; MD, N.Y. Med. Coll., 1948. Instr. bacteriology N.Y. Med. Coll., 1953-57, asst. to dean for clin. scis., 1953-58, instr. surgery, 1953-55, asst. dean, 1958; asst. vis. surgeon Bird S. Coler Hosp., N.Y.C., 1953-57, assoc. vis. surgeon, 1957-60; asst. vis. surgeon Met. Hosp., N.Y.C., 1953-57, assoc. vis. surgeon, 1957-60; asst. attending surgeon Flower and 5th Ave. Hosps., N.Y.C., 1953-57; asst. attending surgeon Monorah Med. Ctr. U. Kans. Sch. Medicine, N.Y.C., 1963-65; exec. dir. Monorah Med. Ctr. U. Kans. Sch. Medicine, Kansas City, 1963-65; exec. dir. Danciger Inst. for Health Scis. U. Kans. Sch. Medicine, Kansas City, Mo., 1963-66; chmn. dept. exptl. surgery Danciger Inst. for Health Scis. U. Kans. Sch. Medicine, Kansas City, 1963-66; chmn. dept. Surgery Menorah Med. Ctr. U. Kans. Sch. Medicine Affiliate, Kansas City, 1963-66; assoc. clin. prof. surgery U. Kans. Sch. Medicine, Kansas City, 1966-67; surgeon courtesy staff N.Y. Infirmary, 1969; surgeon Grand Canyon Med. Group and Hosp., 1979-70; chief sect. on surgery of trauma, dept. surgery U. Ariz. Coll. Med., Tucson, 1974-80, adj. assoc. prof. optical scis., 1979-83, assoc. prof. surgery, 1974-83, dir. quality assurance Univ. Hosp., 1983-84, rsch. prof. family and community medicine, internat. medicine, 1984-85, rsch. prof. surgical biology, 1984-85; sr. fellow in sci. and tch. Ctr. for Strategic and Internat. Studies Georgetown U., Washington, 1983-87; pres. Claude Gips Found. Inc., N.Y.C., 1967-93; disting. vis. prof. Uniformed Svcs. U. Health Scis., 1984, clin. prof. surgery F. Edward Hepert Sch. Medicine, 1984—; disting. vis. prof. Tulane U. Med. Sch., 1984; mem. internat. adv. bd. Univ. Microfilms Internat. Collections on Terrorism, 1987—; internat. cons. Disaster Mgmt. and Disaster Medicine, Australia, India, others, 1983—; gov. emeritus Internat. Coun. for Computer Comm., 1996—, exec. com., v.p., 1972-92. Author: Disaster: Your Right to Survive, 1991; mem. editorial bd. Terrorism, 1976—, Jour. Prehosp. Care, 1984-85, Prehosp. and Disaster Medicine, 1989—; contbr. articles to profl. jours. With U.S. Army, 1943-45; lt. (j.g.) USNR, 1946-53. Fgn. fellow NSF, 1974. Fellow ACS (chmn. Ariz. State com. of trauma 1979-84), Am. Assn. for Surgery of Trauma, Am. Coll. Emergency Physicians, Am. Coll. Gastroenterology, Am. Coll. Nuc. Medicine; mem. World Assn. for Emergency and Disaster Medicine (exec. com. 1987-92). Republican.

SILVERSTEIN, SAMUEL CHARLES, cellular biology and physiology educator, researcher; b. N.Y.C., Feb. 11, 1937; s. Paul Robert and Jeanette (Kamen) S.; m. Jo Ann Kleinman, Apr. 2, 1967; children: David Paul, Jennifer Kate. A.B., Dartmouth Coll., 1958; M.D., Albert Einstein Coll. Medicine, 1963. Intern in medicine U. Colo. Med. Center, 1963-64; postdoctoral fellow dept. cell biology Rockefeller U., 1964-67, asst. prof. cellular physiology and immunology, 1968-71, assoc. prof., physician, 1972—; John Dalton prof. physiology Columbia U. Coll. Physicians and Surgeons, N.Y.C., 1983—, chmn. dept., 1983—; asst. resident in medicine Mass. Gen. Hosp., Boston, 1967-68; established investigator Am. Heart Assn., 1972-77; mem. sci. adv. com. Cancer Rsch. Fund of Damon Runyon-Walter Winchell Found., 1975-79, bd. dirs., 1990—; mem. sci. adv. com. N.Y. Blood Ctr.; cons. Nat. Inst. Gen. Med. Scis., 1985-89, Am. Heart Assn., 1986-89; mem. coun. Am. Soc. Cell Biology, 1988-92; chmn. Gordon Conf. Lysosomes, 1982; founder, dir. Columbia U. Summer Rsch. Program for Sci. Tchrs.; bd. dirs. Rsch. Am.; cons. Nat. Inst. Allergy and Infectious Diseases, 1977-78, mem. adv. coun., dir., 1995—; mem. sci. adv. com. Keystone Symposia, 1993—, mgmt. com., 1996—. Editor: Transport of Macromolecules in Cellular Systems, 1979; chmn. editl. bd. Jour. Cell Biology, 1979-82, editor, 1978-89. Helen Hay Whitney fellow, 1964-67, John Simon Guggenheim fellow, 1995; recipient John Oliver LaGorce medal Nat. Geog. Soc., 1967, Marie Bonazinga Rsch. award Soc. Leukocyte Biology, 1984, Disting. Alumnus award Albert Einstein Coll. Medicine, 1987. Fellow AAAS, Am. Soc. Microbiology; mem. Am. Soc. Cell Biology, Am. Soc. Clin. Investigation, Am. Assn. Immunologists, Infectious Diseases Soc. Am., Sm. Soc. Biol. Chemists, Am. Physiol. Soc., Assn. Am. Physicians, Practitioners Soc. N.Y., Fedn. Am. Socs. for Exptl. Biology (bd. dirs. 1991—, v.p. 1993-94, pres. 1994-95, chmn. Pub. Affairs adv. coun. 1995-96). Clubs: Am. Alpine (dir. 1963-64, 69-74), Explorers. Home: 110 Riverside Dr New York

NY 10024-3715 Office: Columbia U Coll Physicians & Surgeons 630 W 168th St New York NY 10032-3702

SILVERSTEIN, SETH, physician; b. N.Y.C., May 20, 1939; s. Reuben B. and Mollie (Silver) S. BS, L.I. U., 1963; MS, Hofstra U., 1967; MD, U. Cen. Del Este, Dominican Republic, 1980. Lic. physician N.Y., Pa., La. Diagnostic radiology resident Queens Hosp. Ctr., Jamaica, N.Y., 1983-84, Newark (N.J.) Beth Israel Med. Ctr., 1984-85; resident nuclear medicine VA Med. Ctr., Northport, N.Y., 1985-86, SUNY U. Hosp., Stony Brook, 1986-87; diagnostic radiologist La. State U., New Orleans, 1987-89; pvt. practice in diagnostic radiology nuclear medicine, 1990—; parole officer N.Y.C.; tchr. N.Y. City Bd. Edn. Mem. AMA, Radiol. Soc. N.Am., Radiol. Soc. La., New Orleans Radiol. Soc., N.Y. Med. Soc., N.Y. Roentgen Soc., King's County Med. Soc., Soc. Nuclear Medicine. Jewish. Home: 4629 Southshore Dr Metairie LA 70002-1430

SILVERSTEIN, STEVEN MARC, ophthalmologist; b. Phila., Jan. 8, 1961; m. Elisa S. Silverstein; three children. BA, Emory U., 1982; MD, U. Okla., 1986. Diplomate Am. Bd. Ophthalmology. Intern St. Elizabeth's Hosp., Boston, 1986-87; resident Tufts New Eng. Med. Ctr., Boston, 1987-90; fellow Kellogg Eye Ctr., U. Mich., Ann Arbor, 1990-91; attending surgeon VA Hosp., Ann Arbor, Mich., 1990-91; clin. prof. dept. ophthalmology City Med. Sch., Kansas City, Mo., 1992—; vis. lectr. Midwest Physician's Winter Seminar, Denver, 1988. Contbr. articles to profl. jours. City councilman Lake Winnebago, Mo., 1994-96, chmn. planning and zoning, 1994-95, police commr., 1995—. Harris scholar dept. physiology and biophysics U. Okla. Coll. Medicine, 1983. Fellow ACS; mem. AMA, Acad. Ophthalmology, Midwest Cornea Soc., Castroviejo Internat. Cornea Soc., Mo. Med. Soc., Kansas City Soc. Ophthalmology and Otolaryngology, Alpha Epsilon Delta, Rotary Internat. Office: 4240 Blue Ridge Blvd #610 Kansas City MO 64133

SILVESTRI, JAMES JOSEPH, psychotherapist; b. N.Y.C., Oct. 27, 1938; s. Philip and Helen (Bartoli) S.; m. Bonnie Marsteller, Feb. 25, 1961; children: Peter, Timothy. BA, Lafayette Coll., 1960; MSW, NYU, 1963; PhD, Columbia Pacific U., 1981. Lic. social worker, N.J. Pvt. practice Nutley, N.J. Mem. Citizens League of Elizabeth, N.J., past pres. With USAR, 1963-69. Mem. Am. Bd. Med. Psychotherapy, Nat. Register Clin. Social Workers, Orthopsychiat. Assn. Home: 363 Centre St Nutley NJ 07110

SILVIO, JOSEPH ROCCO, psychiatrist, psychoanalyst; b. Elizabeth, N.J., Apr. 14, 1943; s. Benjamin Joseph and Faye Ann (Paternoster) S.; m. Nancy Schaap, Apr. 15, 1964; children: Teri Jayne, Jay Benjamin. BA, Cornell U., 1965; MD, Harvard U., 1969. Diplomate Am. Bd. Psychiatry and Neurology; cert. bd. profl. standards Am. Psychoanalytic Assn. Project officer Nat. Inst. on Drug Abuse, Rockville, Md., 1973-75; pvt. practice Bethesda, Md., 1975—; staff psychiatrist Community Psychiat. Clinic, Wheaton, Md., 1975-80, Georgetown U. Student Health Svc., Washington, 1981-82; pvt. practice psychoanalysis, Bethesda, Md., 1979—. Bd. dirs. Audubon Nature Soc. of Cen. Atlantic States, Chevy Chase, Md., 1985—. With USPHS, 1973-75. Mem. Am. Psychiat. Assn., Am. Psychoanalytic Assn., Am. Acad. Psychoanalysis, Wash. Psychoanalytic Assn., Wash. Psychiat. Soc., Phi Beta Kappa. Office: 4400 E West Hwy Apt 725 Bethesda MD 20814-4508

SIME, JAMES THOMSON, psychologist, consultant; b. Elgin, Moray, Scotland, Aug. 9, 1927; s. James Alexander and Jessie Ann (Scott) S.; divorced; children: James A., Julie-Ann; m. Jaya Rani Sinha, June 3, 1992. MA, U. Edinburgh, Scotland, 1954, diploma in edn., 1955; cert. in teaching, Moray House, Edinburgh, 1955; MEd, U. Glasgow, Scotland, 1957. Chartered psychologist. Psychologist in charge various psychol. svcs., 1960-64, 67-80, pvt. practice as psychotherapist, 1960-84; cons. psychologist brain damage, pain, post-traumatic stress U.K., 1984—; lectr., 1964-67. Served with Royal Air Force, 1945-48. Fellow Brit. Psychol. Soc. (assoc.); mem. Internat. Auster Pilot Club (founder 1973, hon. v.p.). Home and Office: 19 Cedric Rise, Livingston EH54 6JR, England Office: 8 Lindley St, Rotherham S65 1RT, England

ŠIMEČEK, CYRIL METHODEJ, physician, educator; b. Brno, Morava, Czech Republic, May 13, 1920; s. Cyril Š. and Marie (Korínková) Šmečková; m. Blanka Hnátková, May 26, 1951; 1 child, Blanka. M in Pharmacology, Charles U., Prague, 1946, MD, 1950, DSc, 1983; MS, Palacky U., Olomuc, Czechoslovakia, 1963. Physician U. Hosp., Olomuc, Czechoslovakia, 1950-55; lectr., asst. prof. Palacky U., Olomuc, Czechoslovakia, 1956-67; dir. dept. pneumology U. Hosp., Plzeň, Czechoslovakia, 1967-85, researcher, 1986-92; cons. St. George Hosp., Plzeň, Czechoslovakia, 1993—; lectr. Inst. Postgrad. Edn., Bratislava, Czechoslovakia, 1962-82; v.p. Symposium Cancerology, Brussels, 1971. Author: Nemoci prudučnice a prudužek Bronchology, 1978 (Czech Literary Grant Agy. award 1978), (in Czech) Differential Diagnosis in Pneumology, 1984 (Czech Literary Grant Agy. award 1984), Citologická vyčsetřní v pneumologii Cytologica examinations, 1963; inventor apparatus for distribn. evaln. regional lung ventilation. Decorated Chévalier d'Honneur Chavalerie du Fourquet, 1971, Medal Pro Merito Assn. Internat. Bronchopneumologic, 1976. Mem. Czech Med. Assn. (hon.), Cz. Pneumo-ptisiologic Soc., Soc. Europeen Patho-physiol. Respir. Home: V koutê 152, 330 08 Zru č-Senec Plze ň, Czech Republic Office: St George Hosp, Staniční 74, 312 17 Plzeň Czech Republic

SIMERVILLE, JAMES JASPER, occupational and environmental physician; b. Bend, Oreg., Sept. 15, 1939; s. George Melvin and Clara Louise (Jasper) S.; m. Carol Marie Smith, Dec. 26, 1961; children: Pamela Marie, Steven James, Jeffrey Alan. BS, Oreg. State U., 1961; MD, U. Oreg., 1965. Diplomate Am. Bd. Pediatrics; diplomate in occupational medicine Am. Bd. Preventive Medicine. Commd. 2d lt. USAF, 1964, advanced through grades to col., 1979; intern USAF Hosp. Travis, Travis AFB, Calif., 1965-66; resident USAF Hosp. Wilford Hall, Lackland AFB, Tex., 1966-68; chief pediatric svc. USAF, Westover AFB, Mass., Lakenheath, Eng., and Scott AFB, Ill., Eng., 1968-75; dir. med. edn. USAF Hosp. Scott, Scott AFB, 1975-84; cons. in pediatrics, then dep. comdr. U.S. Air Force Acad. Hosp., Colorado Springs, Colo., 1976-84; retired USAF, 1984; dir. Colorado Springs Sports Medicine Clinic, 1984-87, Colo. Ctr. Occupational Medicine, Colorado Springs, 1985-92; med. dir. Colorado Springs Health Ptnrs., 1992-96, FHP, 1996—; med. cons. sports medicine program, Chapman Coll., Colorado Springs, 1983-88. Fellow Am. Acad. Pediatrics, Am. Coll. Preventive Medicine; mem. Am. Coll. Occupational Medicine, Colo. Med. Soc., El Daso County Med. Soc. Roman Catholic. Office: FHP 5725 Mark Dabling Blvd Colorado Springs CO 80919

SIMMERT, JOSEPH BRADLEY, pediatrician; b. Missoula, Mont., Oct. 11, 1963; s. Albert Leroy and Darlene Joyce (Hamilton) S.; m. Beth Ann Reed, Aug. 22, 1987; children: Andrew Robert, Alyssa Carolene, Colleen Joy. BA in Biology, Moorhead State U., 1987; DO, Kirksville Coll. Osteo. Med., 1992. Intern Flint (Mich.) Osteo. Hosp., 1992-93; resident Hurley Med. Ctr., Flint, Mich., 1993-96; pediatrician Pediat. Assocs., Flint, Mich., 1996—. Mem. Salvation Army Med. Fellowship, 1996—. Fellow Am. Acad. Pediats. (resident rep. 1994-96); mem. Mich. State Med. Soc., Genessee County Med. Soc., Christian Med. Dental Soc.

SIMMONDS, DORIS, clinical diabetes nurse specialist; b. Peekskill, N.Y., Feb. 27, 1935; d. George Leo and Sarah Jane (Bremner) Conley; m. Arthur W. Simmonds, Dec. 8, 1956; children: Scott Willia, David Paul, Susan Ann. Diploma in Nursing, Vassar Sch. Nursing, 1956; BSN, U. Hartford, 1978, MS, 1989. RN, Conn. Nurse mgr. Wesley Hosp., Wichita, Kans., 1956-61; ICU nurse Manchester (Conn.) Meml. Hosp., 1966-69, discharge coord., 1985-93, mgr. diabetes self-mgmt. program, 1993—; vis. nurse South Windsor (Conn.) Vis. Nurse Assn., 1978-80; clin. supr. St. Francis Hosp. and Med. Ctr., Hartford, 1980-85; adv. bd. Diabetes Self Mgmt., Manchester, 1993—. Deacon Vernon (Conn.) Congl. Ch. Mem. Am. Diabetes Assn. (Recognition award 1995, Program Svc. award 1994), Conn. Assn. Diabetes Edn. (bd. dirs. 1996—), Am. Assn. Diabetes Edn., Juvenile Diabetes Fedn., Iowa Upsilon (sec. 1994—). Home: 145 Irene Dr Vernon CT 06066 Office: Manchester Meml Hosp 71 Haynes St Manchester CT 06040

SIMMONS, BARRY PUTNAM, orthopaedic physician, educator; b. Boston, Dec. 18, 1939; s. Arthur Maxwell and Kathleen Matheson, Oct. 9, 1968; children: Quincey Rebecca, Sara Putnam, Molly MacMhathin. BA, Harvard U., 1961; MD, Columbia U., 1965. Cert. Am. Bd. of Orthopaedic Surgery. Resident Combined Harvard Orthopaedic Program, Boston, 1969-73; fellow hand surgery Group de l'Etude de la Main, Paris, 1973; fellow trauma Swiss Assn. for Internat. Fixator, Basel, 1974; orthopaedic surgeon Children's Hosp., Boston, 1974—; assoc. orthopaedic surgeon Brigham and Women's Hosp., Boston, 1974—, Harvard U. Health Svc., 1974—; asst. prof. Med. Sch. Harvard U., Cambridge, Mass., 1982-87; assoc. prof. orthopaedic surgery Med. Sch. Harvard U., Cambridge, 1988—; orthopedic surgeon Brigham Orthopedic Assocs. Inc., Boston, 1974—; chief hand surgery svc. Children's Hosp. Boston, 1981—, Brigham and Women's Hosp., Boston, 1981—. Assoc. editor Jour. hand Surgery, 1985-91, Chirurgie de la Main, Paris, 1985; editor: Yearbook of Orthopedics, 1993-94; contbr. numerous articles to profl. jours. Marshall Harvard 25th reunion, 1986; vis. prof. many univs., co-chmn. residency selecton Combined Harvard Orthopaedic Residency Program . Lt. comdr. USN 1967-69 (Vietnam). Fellow Am. Acad. Orthopaedic; mem. Am. Orthopaedic Assn., Am. Soc. for Surgery of the Hand, Am. Acad. orthopaedic Surgery (bd. dirs. 1993-94, sec. coun. muscule skeltal specialties 1992-93, chmn. elect 1993-94, chmn. musculoskeletal specialties 1994-95), Brit Soc. for Surgery of the Hand, French Soc. for Surgery of Hand, Academic Orthopaedic Soc., Hand Study Soc. Minn., Harvard Club. Jewish. Office: Brigham and Womens Hosp 75 Francis St Boston MA 02115-6110

SIMMONS, CECELIA E., quality improvement, infection control and employee health nurse; b. Norfolk, Va., Aug. 20, 1949; d. Oscar Y. Jr. and Evelyn C. (Hermann) McClannan; m. Richard P. Simmons Jr., June 28, 1970; children: Robin Lea, Paul David. Diploma in nursing, Norfolk Gen. Hosp., 1970; degree in nursing, St. Phillips Coll., San Antonio, 1986, San Antonio Coll., 1988; postgrad., U. Tex. Health Sci. Ctr., San Antonio. Cert. in infection control. Home health specialist Luth. Gen. Hosp., San Antonio; oncology nurse San Antonio Tumor and Blood Clinic, San Antonio; dir. medicare dept. Personal Touch Home Care, San Antonio; infection control-employee health nurse, outpatient coord. Warm Springs Rehab. Hosp., San Antonio; quality improvement coord., infection control coord. Cancer Therapy and Rsch. Ctr., San Antonio, occupational health nurse. Mem. Oncology Nurses Soc., Assn. Practitioners Infection Control (chpt. treas.), Assn. of Occupational Health Nurses, Tex. Soc. of Infection Control Practitioners, Tex. Hosp. Assn., Assn. Profls. in Healthcare Quality. Home: 6315 Willow Hill St San Antonio TX 78247-1116

SIMMONS, DONNA MARIE, neuroscientist, neurobiology researcher, histotechnologist; b. Hartford, Conn., Oct. 13, 1943; d. John Henry and Ellen Louise (Meehl) Strayer; m. Corvin Gale Simmons, Sept. 17, 1964. Student, U. Wash., Western Wash. State U.; postgrad. U. Southern Calif., 1994—. Histologic technician, instr. Tacoma Gen. Hosp. Sch. Med. Tech., Tacoma, Wash., 1963; lab. technician Med. Sch. U. Wash., 1964; histologic technician Northgate Med. Lab., Seattle, 1964-67; rsch. technologist in neuroanatomy Regional Primate Rsch. Ctr., U. Wash., 1967-82; rsch. asst. Devel. Neurobiology Lab. Salk Inst., La Jolla, Calif., 1982-85; sr. technician, lab. mgr. Neural Systems Lab. Howard Hughes Med. Inst. at Salk Inst., 1985-90; vis. fac. dept Neurosciences, Baylor U. Med. Sch., 1990; Rsrch assoc. dept. of biol. scis.-neurobiology, U. So. Calif., L.A., 1990—; cons., lectr. in field.; judge Greater San Diego Sci. and Engring. Fair, 1987-89, Calif. Sci. Fair, 1992, 95; leader sci. del. to People's Rep. of China, 1986; chair China Scientist Exchange Fund, 1986-87; mem. Swiss Histology Meeting Exch., 1990. Author tech. articles, revs. in field; mem. editl. bd. Jour. histotech. Recipient Diamond Cover award Jour. of Histotech., 1990; various svc. awards; best non-clin. pub. in field, 1985; Hudson Hoagland USA-Australia Exch. Med. Rsch. fellow Prince Henry's Rsch. Inst. Monash U., 1996. Mem. AAAS, Am. Soc. Clin. Pathologists (affiliate), Wash. State Histology Soc. (past pres., histology liaison Am. Soc. Med. Tech.), Nat. Soc. Histotech. (charter mem., regional dir. 1980-82, jud. chair 1983-86), Calif. Soc. Histotech. (San Diego dir. protem 1985-86), Assn. Women in Sci. (San Diego charter mem., bd. dir. 1985-90), Soc. for Neurosci., Swiss Soc. for Histotech., Women in Neurosci., N.Y. Acad. Sci., NOW, Am. Alpine Club, J.B. Johnston Club. Office: U So Calif Hedco Neurosci Bldg MC 2520 Los Angeles CA 90089

SIMMONS, FREDERICK HARRISON, retired otolaryngologist; b. Chgo., Feb. 14, 1915; s. Lloyd H. and Rose (Patterson) S.; wife dec.; children: Fred Jr., Richard, David. BS, Ind. U., 1938; MD, Ind. U., Inpls., 1940. Diplomate Am. Bd. Otolaryngology. Intern St. Vincent's Hosp., Indpls., 1940-41; resident Ind. U. Med. Ctr., Indpls., 1945-48; pvt. practice otolaryngologist Marion, Ind., 1948-90; ret., 1990—; cons. VA Hosp., Marion, 1948-96. Capt. U.S. Army, 1941-46. Home: 11638 N Sunrise Dr Syracuse IN 46567

SIMMONS, GEOFFREY STUART, physician; b. Camp Gordon, Ga., July 28, 1943; s. Ted R. and Jane A. (Lavander) S.; m. Sherry Simmons, Sept. 7, 1985; children: Bradley, Anais. BS, U. Ill., 1965, MD, 1969. Intern U. So. Calif., L.A., 1969-70, resident, 1971-74; pvt. practice Astoria, Oreg., 1974-77, Eugene, Oreg., 1977—; bd. dirs. Lane County Med. Soc. Author: The Z Papers, 1977, The Adam Experiment, 1978, Pandemic, 1980, Murdock, 1982, The Glue Factory, 1995. Office: 1200 Hilyard St Ste 200 S Eugene OR 97401-8133

SIMMONS, JEANNE COLLINS, medical technologist, physician assistant; b. Boissevain, Va., May 19, 1936; d. Daniel Frank, Sr. and Effie Greaver (Dillon) Collins; m. Charles Wesley Gilmore Jr., Dec. 26, 1954 (div.); 1 child, Lynn Porter Gilmore Harman; m. James Lawrence Simmons Sr., May 25, 1993; children: James L. Jr., Susan Simmons Briley, Michael Simmons. Cert. med. technologist, AMT, 1962. Med. sec., med. asst. Dr. H.A. Porter, Pocahontas, Va., 1953-60, St. Lukes Hosp., Bluefield, W. Va., 1963; lab. dir. Fowlkes, King Ob-Gyn Clinic, Bluefield, W. Va., 1964; lab. dir., physician nurse various Drs. of surgery and gen. practice, Pocahontas, 1964—; mem. adv. bd. Nat. Bus. Coll., Bluefield, 1994—; owner, operator Laurel Inn Bed & Breakfast, Pocahontas. Active officer Princess Pocahontas, 1965-69; pres., other offices Pocahontas Womans Club, 1958-65; choir dir., youth councilor United Meth. Ch., 1964—; v.p., pres. PTAs, Pocahontas, 1965-69; founder Hist. Pocanontas Inc. Named Outstanding Young Women of America, Jr. C. of C., 1965, Outstanding Technologist of Yr., Va. State Soc. Med. Technologists, 1965. Democrat. Methodist. Home: 386 87 West Water Pocahontas VA 24635

SIMMONS, MARGUERITE SAFFOLD, pharmaceutical sales professional; b. Montgomery, Ala., Oct. 21, 1954; d. Arthur Edward and Gwendolyn Jane (Saffold) S. BS in Communications, U. Tenn., 1976. Press sec. Met. Mayor's Office, Nashville, 1976-77; advt. copywriter United Meth. Pub. House, Nashville, 1977-78; sales rep. No Nonsense Pantyhose, Houston, 1978-81, Breon Labs., Houston, 1981-82; profl. sales rep. Janssen Pharmaceutica, Inc., Houston, 1982-88, sr. sales rep., 1988—. Vol. Dem. Nat. Conv., Atlanta, 1988. Named to Outstanding Young Women in Am., 1981, 87. Mem. NAFE, U. Tenn. Alumni Assn. (bd. dirs. Atlanta chpt. 1989-90), U. Tenn. Black Alumni Assn. (bd. dirs. Atlanta chpt. 1989—, pres.- elect bd. dirs. 1995), Ga. Trust Hist. Soc., Ala. Geneal. Soc., Ga. Geneal. Soc., Nat. Trust Hist. Preservation, Delta Sigma Theta. Baptist. Office: PO Box 16934 Atlanta GA 30321-0934

SIMMONS, MICHAEL ANTHONY, dean; m. Margaret Clare Martindale; children: Kristen Ann, Jeffrey Michael, Jennifer Clare Roe, Jason Davis. AB cum laude, Harvard Coll., 1963, MD, 1967. Diplomate Am. Bd. Pediatrics, Am. Bd. Neonatal-Perinatal Medicine. Intern Harriet Lane Svc., Johns Hopkins Hosp., Balt., 1967-68, asst. resident, 1968-69, sr. asst. resident, 1969; chief resident Dept. Pediatrics, U. Colo. Med. Ctr., Denver, 1971-72, rsch. fellow in perinatal medicine, 1972-74, clin. instr. in pediatrics, 1974-77, assoc. prof. pediatrics, 1977; assoc. prof. pediatrics and obstetrics Johns Hopkins U. Sch. Medicine, Balt., 1977-83; prof., chmn. dept. pediatrics U. Utah Sch. of Medicine, Salt Lake City, 1983-94; prof. pediatrics, dean U. N.C. at Chapel Hill Sch. Medicine, 1994—; adj. prof. dept. obstetrics and gynecology U. Utah Sch. of Medicine, Salt Lake City, 1984-94; co-dir. newborn svcs. U. Colo. Med. Ctr., Denver, 1974-77, Johns Hopkins Hosp., 1977-83; mem. staff Denver Gen. Hosp., 1976-77, Denver Children's Hosp., 1976-77; vice chmn. clin. affairs dept. pediatrics Johns Hopkins Hosp., 1981-83; chief of pediatrics U. Utah Med. Ctr., Salt Lake, City, 1983-94; med. dir. Primary Children's Med. Ctr., 1983-94; bd. dirs. Triangle Univs. Licensing Consortium, U. N.C. Hosps. Contbr. numerous articles to profl. jours. Fellow Am. Acad. of Pediatrics (excellence in pediatric rsch. com. 1991—, coun. on govt. affairs 1992—); mem. Perinatal Rsch. Soc. (coun. 1982-84, pres.-elect 1985-87, pres. 1989), Western Soc. for Pediatric Rsch. (coun. 1985-86, pres.-elect 1987, pres. 1988), Soc. for Pediatric Rsch., Am. Bd. Pediatrics (sub-bd. of neonatal-perinatal medicine 1983-89, chmn. 1984-88). Office: U NC Sch of Medicine Chapel Hill NC 27599-7000*

SIMMONS, RICHARD L., surgeon; b. Boston, Feb. 23, 1934; s. Nathanial J. and Anne Dorothy (Levenson) S.; widowed (Feb. 1993); children: Nicole, Janine. AB in Biochem. Scis. magna cum laude, Harvard U., 1955; MD summa cum laude, Boston U., 1959. Diplomate Am. Bd. Surgery. Intern, resident in surgery Columbia Presbyn. Med. Ctr., N.Y.C., 1959-66; clin. and rsch. fellow Mass. Gen. Hosp., Boston, 1965; rsch. fellow in surgery Harvard Med. Sch., Boston, 1965; instr. surgery Columbia U. Coll. P&S, N.Y.C., 1965-68; from asst. prof. to assoc. prof. surgery U. Minn., Mpls., 1968-72, prof. surgery and microbiology, 1972-87; George V. Foster prof. surgery, chair dept. surgery U. Pitts., 1987—, assoc. dean for clin. affairs Sch. Medicine, 1989—, prof. molecular genetics and biochemistry, 1992—; assoc. v.p. for clin. affairs U. Pitts. Med. Ctr., 1989—, med. dir., 1996; chief of surgery Presbyn.-Univ. Hosp., Pitts., 1987—; staff Children's Hosp. of Pitts.; cons. staff VA Med. Ctr. Author/co-author 11 books; contbr. more than 1200 articles to profl. jours. Recipient awards and grants. Mem. AMA, AAAS, ACS (pres. Southwestern Pa. chpt. 1992), NAS Inst. Medicine, Am. Soc. for Microbiology, Am. Soc. Transplant Physicians (pres. 1980-81), Am. Assn. Immunologists, Am. Assn. Pathologists, Am. Surg. Assn. (chmn. program com. 1990), Assn. for Acad. Surgery, Ctrl. Surg. Assn., Cell Transplant Soc., Halsted Soc., Infectious Diseases Soc. Am., Midwest Surg. Soc. (hon.), Reticuloendothelial Soc., Soc. for Leukocyte Biology, Soc. for Microbiology, Soc. Clin. Oncologists, Surg. Infection Soc. (pres. 1988), Soc. Surg. Chmn., Soc. Univ. Surgeons (exec. coun. 1973-81, pres. 1977-78), Allegheny County Med. Soc., Transplantation Soc. (councillor 1974-80), others. Office: U Pitts Sch Medicine Dept Surgery 3500 Terrace St 497 Scaife Pittsburgh PA 15261

SIMMS, MARIA ESTER, health services administrator; b. Bahia Blanca, Argentina; came to U.S., 1963; d. Jose and Esther (Guays) Barberio Esandi; m. Michael Simms, July 15, 1973 (Aug. 1993); children: Michelle Bonnie Lee Carla, Michael London Valentine, Matthew Brandon. Degree medicine, Facultad del Centenario, Rosario, Argentina, 1962; Physician Asst. Cert. (hon.), U. So. Calif., 1977. Medical diplomate. Pres. Midtown Svcs. Inc., L.A., 1973—. Chmn. bd. Am.'s Film Inst., Washington; chmn. bd. trustees World Film Inst. Nominated chairwoman of bd. trustees World Film Inst. Fellow Am. Acad. Physicians' Assts.; mem. Bus. for Law Enforcement (northeast divsn.), Physicians for Social Responsibility, Mercy Crusade Inc., Internat. Found. for Survival Rsch., Noetic Scis. Soc., Inst. Noetic Scis., So. Calif. Alliance for Survival, Supreme Emblem Club of U.S., Order Eastern Star, Flying Samaritans, Shriners.

SIMON, ANITA, psychologist; b. Phila., May 20, 1936; d. Harry and Bertha (Rosenberg) Mongin. BS summa cum laude, UCLA, 1962; MEd, Temple U., Phila., 1964, EdD with honors, 1966. Lic. psychologist, Pa. Program dir. Rsch. for Better Schs., Phila., 1966-73; dir. edn. The Restaurant Sch., Phila., 1973-80; psychologist in pvt. practice Phila., 1979—; developer/trainer SAVI-System for Analyzing Verbal Behavior, Phila., 1965—. Author: The Parents Solution Book, 1983; editor: (anthology) Mirrors for Behavior, 1970; editor The Classroom Interaction Newsletter, 1964-68. Mem. APA, Systems Centered Therapy Network, Delaware Valley Gr. Psychotherapy Assn., Phi Beta Kappa. Office: 1831 Chestnut St #801 Philadelphia PA 19103

SIMON, CHARLOTTE TULCHIN, psychology educator; b. N.Y.C., Dec. 10, 1925; d. Sam and Celia (Kamin) Tulchin; m. Ralph Simon, Sept. 5, 1946; children: Ellen,. Randy (dec.), Lisa, Russell. BA, Bklyn. Coll., 1945; PhD, Syracuse U., 1953. Instr. psychology Syracuse (N.Y.) U., 1947-50; social psychologist VA Hosp., Perry Point, Md., 1958-59; asst. prof. psychology U. Md., College Park, 1959-60; cons. NIMH, Rockville, Md., 1964, Montgomery County Dept. Health, Rockville, 1966-69; prof. Montgomery Coll., Rockville, 1969—. Mem. Am. Psychol. Assn., Psychology of Women Div. 35, AAUP. Home: 6213 Hollins Dr Bethesda MD 20817-2348 Office: Montgomery Coll Dept Psychology Rockville MD 20850

SIMON, EDWARD HARVEY, virologist, biology educator; b. Elizabeth, N.J., June 25, 1934; s. David and Esther (Saferstein) S.; m. Cyrelle Ovsiew, Dec. 22, 1956; children: Shira, Rashi, Hillel, Ronit. BS, Rutgers U., 1956; PhD, Calif. Inst. Tech., Pasadena, 1960. Prof. biology Purdue U., Lafayette, Ind., 1960—; vis. prof. Weiztmann Inst., Rehovoth, Israel, 1966-67, 79-80, 85-86, 91, Hebrew U., Jerusalem, 1972-73. Author: (book) Challenge of Genetics, 1971; contbr. articles to profl. jours. Pres. B'nai B'rith, Lafayette, 1987-90, Sons of Abraham Synagogue, 1976-79, Fed. Charity, 1980-81. Recipient fellowships and/or rsch. grants NIH, NSF, Nat. Cancer Soc. Mem. AAAS, AAUP, Am. Soc. Microbiology, Internat. Soc. Interferon Rsch., Phi Beta Kappa. Jewish. Office: Purdue U Dept Biology West Lafayette IN 47907

SIMON, GARY LEONARD, internist, educator; b. Bklyn., Dec. 18, 1946; s. Bernard and Dorothy (Ligeti) S.; m. Vicki Thiessen, Aug. 29, 1970; children: Jason, Jessica. BS, U. Md., 1968; PhD, U. Wis., 1972; MD, U. Md., 1975. Diplomate Am. Bd. Internal Medicine, Am. Bd. Infectious Diseases. Asst. prof. dept. medicine George Washington U., Washington, 1980-84, assoc. prof., 1984-89, assoc. chmn. medicine, 1984—, prof., 1989—, dir. divsn. infectious diseases, 1993—; cons. on AIDS Assn. Am. Med. Coll., Washington, 1990—. Contbr. articles to profl. jours. on AIDS and infectious diseases. Fellow Am. Coll. Physicians, Infectious Disease Soc. Am.; mem. Am. Soc. Microbiology, Assn. Program Dirs. in Internal Medicine. Office: George Washington U 2150 Pennsylvania Ave NW Washington DC 20037-2396

SIMON, HOWARD, physician; b. N.Y.C., Jan. 13, 1947; s. Solomon and Claire (Hornstein) S.; m. Lorraine Kaloski, Oct. 22, 1971; children: Sarah, Lindsay. BA, Adelphi U., 1968; MD, U. Autonoma of Guadalajara, Mexico, 1975. Intern Regina Gen. Hosp., Sask., Can., 1975-76; family practice resident Southside Hosp./SUNY Stony Brook, Bayshore, N.Y., 1976-77; resident ob-gyn L.I. Jewish Hosp., New Hyde Park, N.Y., 1977-80; ob-gyn practitioner County Ob-Gyn, P.C., New Haven, Conn., 1980—; attending physician Yale-New Haven Hosp., New Haven, 1980—; assoc. prof. Yale U. Sch. Medicine, New Haven, 1982—; residency program coord., 1993—; mem. med. adv. bd. Women's Surg. Ctr., New Haven, 1989—, credentials com. Yale-Hew Haven Hosp., 1991-93, perinatal mortality and morbidity rev. com., 1989-92; quality assurance bd., New Haven Ind. Practitioners Assn., 1989-93. Pub. speaker vol. ambulance assns. and women's groups. Mem. New Haven Obstet. Soc. (pres. 1995-96), Conn. State Med. Soc., AMA, Am. Coll. Ob-Gyn. Office: County Ob-Gyn 687 Main St Branford CT 06405

SIMON, JAMES NEAL, anesthesiologist; b. Phila., June 10, 1955; s. R. Morton and Joann (Myers) S.; m. Oct. 13, 1990; 1 child, Zachary. BA in Zoology, Drew U., Madison, N.J., 1977; DO, Pa. Coll. Medicine, 1981. Diplomate Am. Bd. Anesthesiology, Am. Bd. Pain Medicine. Intern and resident Cleve. Clinic, 1981-85, fellow, 1985-86; asst. prof. U. Md. Sch. Med., 1986-88; pvt. practice Calif., 1988-90, Phila., 1991-93; chmn. anesthesiology Atlantic City (N.J.) Med. Ctr., 1990-91, Union Hosp., Elkton, Md., 1993—; med. dir. Pain Mgmt. Ctr., U. Md., 1986-88, Pain Mgmt. Ctr., Elkton, 1993—. Mem. Am. Pain Soc., Am. Acad. Med. Acupuncture, Am. Soc. Anesthesiologists, Am. Soc. Regional Anesthesiology. Home: PO Box 707 Elkton MD 21922 Office: Dept Anesthesiology 106 Bow St Elkton MD 21922

SIMON, JIMMY LOUIS, pediatrician, educator; b. San Francisco, Dec. 27, 1930; s. Sylvain L. and Hilda H. (Netter) S.; m. Marilyn S. Wachter, June 21, 1953; children: Kent, Nancy. A.B., U. Calif.-Berkeley, 1952; M.D., U. Calif.-Berkeley, San Francisco, 1955. Diplomate Am. Bd. Pediatrics. Intern U. Calif., San Francisco, 1955-56; resident Grace-New Haven Hosp., 1956-57; sr. asst. resident Boston Children's Hosp., 1957-58; instr., asst. prof. pediatrics U. Okla., Oklahoma City, 1960-64; asso. prof. U. Tex. Med. Br., Galveston, 1966-72; prof. pediatrics U. Tex. Med. Br., 1972-74; prof., chmn. pediatrics Bowman Gray Sch. Medicine, Wake Forest U., Winston-Salem,

N.C., 1974-96; prof., chmn. emeritus pediatric Bowman Gray Sch. Medicine Wake Forest U., Winston-Salem, N.C., 1996—. Served with USAF, 1958-60. Mem. Am. Pediatric Soc., Am. Acad. Pediatrics, So. Soc. Pediatric Rsch., Am. Bd. Pediatrics, Ambulatory Pediatric Assn., Alpha Omega Alpha. Office: Bowman Gray Sch Med Dept Pediatrics Medical Center Blvd Winston Salem NC 27157

SIMON, JOHN CLARK, physician; b. New Orleans, May 9, 1961; s. H. Paul and Carolyn (Perkins) S.; m. Heather Jaet. BA in Biochemistry, Columbia Coll., 1983; MD, Tulane U., 1990. Diplomate Am. Bd. Internal Medicine. Intern Emory U., Atlanta, 1990-91; resident in internal medicine Tulane U., New Orleans, 1991-93, chief resident, 1993-94, fellowship in nephrology/critical care, 1994-96. Mem. Am. Coll. Physicians. Home: 113 Brewster Rd Madisonville LA 70447 Office: 210 Greenbriar Blvd Covington LA 70433

SIMON, JONATHAN EDWARD, physician; b. Watford, Eng., Oct. 19, 1949; arrived in New Zealand, 1982; s. Derrick and Valerie Estelle (Jacobs) S.; m. Josephine Susan Aschan, Jan. 2, 1976; childen: Daniel Eliot, Rachel Louise, Joshua Derrick. BSc, Bristol (Eng.) U., 1970; B in Medicine and Surgery, Magdalen Coll., Oxford, Eng., 1973. Intern Radcliffe U., Oxford, 1973-74; demonstrator in anatomy U. Bristol, 1975; mem. tng. group Bath (Eng.) Hosps., 1975-78; family physician Beaumont St. Oxford, 1979-82, Otuemoetal Health Ctr., Tauranga, New Zealand, 1982—; chmn. Prime Network Lab, 1993—. Ben Gurion U. fellow, 1987. Fellow Royal New Zealand Coll. Gen. Practitioners (hon. sec. 1991—), Royal Coll. Gen. Practitioners (London). Jewish. Home: 107 Manuwai Dr, Tauranga New Zealand Office: Otumoetal Health Ctr, 506 Otumoetal Rd, Tauranga New Zealand Office: Royal NZ Coll of Gen Pratitioner, 23 Palmer ST, Wellington New Zealand

SIMON, MARK WILLIAM, ophthalmologist; b. Cin., June 10, 1965. BA, Thomas More Coll., 1985; MD, U. Ky., 1989. Diplomate Am. Bd. Ophthalmology. Ophthalmologist Ky. Eye Inst., Lexington, 1993—. Office: Ky Eye Inst 1401 Harrodsburg Rd B-75 Lexington KY 40504

SIMON, NORMA PLAVNICK, psychologist; b. Washington, Sept. 20, 1930; d. Mark and Mary Plavnick; m. Robert G. Simon, Dec. 18, 1949; children: Mark Allan, Susan. BA, NYU, 1952, cert. in psychoanalysis, 1977; MA, Columbia U., 1953, EdD, 1968. Diplomate Am. Bd. Profl. Psychology, 1988. Psychologist Queens Coll. Counseling Ctr., Flushing, N.Y., 1968-70, asst. dir., 1970-76, dir., 1976; gen. practice psychology N.Y.C., 1976—; faculty, supr. New Hope Guild, Bklyn., 1976—, dir. child and adolescent tng. prog., 1988—; adj. prof. clin. psychology Columbia U., N.Y.C., 1986—; supr. NYU Postdoctoral Prog. in Psychoanalysis, 1988—. Author: (with Robert G. Simon): Choosing a College Major: Social Science, 1981; mem. editorial bd. The Counseling Psychologist jour., 1986-89. Vice chairperson N.Y. State Bd. for Psychology State Edn. Dept., Albany, 1978-82, chairperson, 1982-88; bd. dirs. Pelham (N.Y.) Guidance Coun., 1980-83; pres.-elect Assn. State and Provincial Psychology Bds., 1990, pres., 1991. Recipient Karl Heiser award, 1993. Fellow APA (mem. bd. profl. affairs 1987-89, chair bd. profl. affairs 1989-90, policy and planning bd. 1991-93, mem. ethics com. 1995-98, vice chair ethics com. 1996—, John Black award 1994), Nat. Acads. of Practice (elected disting. practitioner). Office: 500A E 87th St # 5A New York NY 10128-7626

SIMON, NORMAN M., nephrologist, medical educator; b. Chgo., Mar. 30, 1929; m. Harriet Devorkin, May 19, 1957; children: Judith, Daniel, Amy. BA, Harvard U., 1950; MS in Psychology, Yale U., 1951; MD, Northwestern U., 1955. Diplomate Am. Bd. Internal Medicine, Am. Bd. Nephrology. Instr. Northwestern U. Med. Sch., Chgo., 1963-64; assoc. Northwestern U. Med. Sch., 1964-66, asst. prof. medicine, 1966-70, assoc. prof. medicine, 1970-82, prof. medicine, 1982—; head divsn. nephrology Evanston (Ill.) Hosp., 1988—. Contbr. over 70 articles to profl. jours. Chmn. hypertension com. Chgo. Heart Assn., 1977-80, med. adv. bd. Nat. Kidney Found. Ill., Chgo., 1982-85; mem. exec. com. Renal Physicians Assn., Washington, 1987-90; pres. Anshe Emet Synagogue, Chgo., 1974-78. Capt. U.S. Army, 1957-59. Fellow ACP; mem. Am. Soc. Nephrology, Internat. Soc. Nephrology, Ctrl. Soc. Clin. Rsch., Chgo. Soc. Internal Medicine (pres. 1990-91), Alpha Omega Alpha. Jewish. Office: Evanston Hosp 2650 Ridge Ave Evanston IL 60201

SIMON, RICHARD DELOE, JR., internist; b. Toledo, Ohio, May 25, 1950; s. Richard DeLoe Sr. and Perla Lifsey (Hill) S.; m. Deborah Marie Simon, June 23, 1973; children: Michael Taylor, Anna DeLoe. AB in Chemistry, Whitman Coll., 1972; MD, U. Chgo., 1976; cert. in med. ethics, U. Wash., 1991. Diplomate Am. Bd. Internal Medicine, Am. Bd. Sleep Disorders Medicine. Intern internal medicine U. Chgo. Hosps. & Clinics, 1976-77, resident internal medicine, 1977-79, chief resident internal medicine, 1980; instr. in medicine U. Chgo., 1980; internist Walla Walla (Wash.) Clinic, 1981—; med. dir. Kathryn Severyns Dement Sleep Disorders Ctr. St. Mary Med. Ctr., Walla Walla, 1994—. Contbr. articles to profl. publs., chpt. to book. Saxophone soloist Walla Walla Symphony, 1994; mem. adv. bd. Walla Walla YMCA, 1982-94; mem. cmty. vision task force Walla Walla C. of C., 1995. Recipient Recognition cert. Wash. State Assn. Supervision & Curriculum Devel., 1996. Mem. ACP, Am. Soc. Law, Medicine and Ethics, Am. Sleep Disorders Assn., Walla Walla Valley Med. Soc. (pres. 1985, Physician Recognition award 1994), Wash. State Med. Soc., Walla Walla Jazz Soc. (founder, bd. dirs. 1992—). Democrat. Home: 733 Bryant Ave Walla Walla WA 99362 Office: Walla Walla Clinic 301 W Poplar Walla Walla WA 99362

SIMON, STEVEN MICHEL, rehabilitation physician; b. Kansas City, Mo., Aug. 17, 1947; s. Melvin and Toby (Divine) S.;m. Ileene Joyce, Oct. 28, 1973; children: Jennifer, Stacey. BA in Psychology, Mo. U., Columbia, 1969; BS in Pharmacy, U. Mo., Kansas City, 1972; MD, Ross U., Portsmouth, Dominica, 1983; DSc (hon.), Coll. Audiometry & Rehab., Kansas City, Mo., 1975, PhD (hon.), 1975. Asst. med. dir. phys. med. rehab. Bellay Hosp., Kansas City, 1986-89; med. dir. Mid Am. Rehab. Hosp., Overland Park, Kans., 1989-94; med. dir. clin. affairs Overland Park Regional Med. Ctr., 1994—; med. dir. rehab. svcs. Shawnee Mission Med. Ctr., Overland Park, 1987—; advisor Orme Becter Products, Calif., 1992-95. Rev. editor: Stroke Rehabilitation, 1995; reviewer Archives Phys. Med. Rehab., 1985—, Found. Med. Care, 1992—. Reviewer Medicare, Topeka, 1994—. Mem. AMA, Met. Psychiat.Soc. (sec. 1992—), Kans. Med. Soc., Johnson County Med. Soc. Home: 12008 Pawnee Leawood KS 66209 Office: Mid Am Rehab Hosp 5701 W 110th Overland Park KS 66210

SIMON, THEODORE RONALD, physician, medical educator; b. Hartford, Conn., Feb. 2, 1949; s. Theologos Lingos and Lillian (Faix) S.; m. Marcia Anyzeski, Apr. 5, 1974; children: Jacob T., Theodore H., Mark G. BA cum laude, Trinity Coll., Hartford, 1970; MD, Yale U., 1975. Diplomate Am. Bd. Nuclear Medicine, Diplomate Nat. Bd. Med. Examiners; lic. Calif., Tex. Intern in surgery Strong Meml. Hosp., Rochester, N.Y., 1975-76; resident in diagnostic radiology U. Calif.. San Francisco, 1976-78; resident in nuclear medicine Yale-New Haven Hosp., Conn., 1978-80, chief resident, 1979-80; asst. prof. nuclear medicine U. Tex. Southwestern Med. Ctr., Dallas, 1980-88, assoc. prof., 1990—; cons. nuclear medicine St. Paul's Hosp., Dallas, 1981-88; cons. internal medicine Presbyn. Hosp., Dallas, 1981-88, 90, Med. City Hosp., Dallas, 1989—; cons. nuclear medicine VA Med. Ctr., Dallas, 1981-82, chief nuclear medicine svc., 1982-88; nat. dep. dir. nuclear medicine VA, 1985-88; dep. chief nuclear medicine NIH, Bethesda, Md., 1988-90; mem. del. Taiwan Atomic Energy, U.S. State Dept., 1990. Mem. editorial bd. Jour. History of Med. and Allied Scis., 1974-75; contbr. articles to Internat. Jour. Radiol. Applications, Jour. Nuclear Medicine, Am. Jour. Cardiology, Clin. Nuclear Medicine, Circulation, Yale Jour. Biol. Medicine, Radiology, Surg. Radiology, and others. Pres. Christ Lutheran Ch., University Park, Tex. Mem. Soc. Nuclear Medicine (treas. correlative imaging coun. 1988-90, mem. exec. com 1988—). Home and Office: 4429 Southern Ave Dallas TX 75205-2622

SIMONDS, CARY BRENT, surgeon, consultant; b. Al Hambra, Calif., June 3, 1948; s. Robert L. Simonds and Dawn (Gustin) Albarian; m. Alex Mahealani Sucher, Mar. 23, 1975; children: Victoria, Elizabeth. AA, Orange Coast Coll., 1968; DDS, Loma Linda U., 1973, MS, 1976. Diplomate Am. Bd. Oral and Maxillofacial Surgeons. Surg. resident U. Calif., Irvine, 1973-76; fellow Am. Assn. of Oral and Maxillofacial Surgeons. Co-author: (book) Management of the Disorders: a Multi-Disciplinary Approach. Treas. Nat. PAC, Spokane, Wash., 1995-96. Recipient Pinicle of Achievement award in bowhunting, Safari Club Internat., Ruscon, Ariz., 1990. Mem. Regional Dental Soc. (pres. Calif. chpt.), The Acad. of Med. Econs. (chmn. San Francisco chpt.). Home: 5705 S Willamette Spokane WA 99223

SIMONE, REGINA, family practice physician; b. Trenton, N.J., Mar. 20, 1961; d. Michael Simone and Amelia Ann Mastrogiovanni. BS in Microbiology, Gannon U., 1983, MS in Microbiology, 1986; DO, U. New Eng. Coll. Medicine, 1993. Bd. eligible family practice DO; cert. BCLS Level C, ACLS. Instr. microbiology/asst. rschr. Gannon U., Erie, Pa., 1984-86; rschr. microbiology Temple U. Sch. Medicine, Phila., 1986-87; supr. quality control Wissahickon Spring Water Co., Phila., 1987-89; instr./asst. microbiology U. New Eng. Coll. Medicine, Biddeford, Maine, 1989-91; student physician U. New Eng. Coll. Medicine, 1989-93; resident in internal medicine St. Vincent's Hosp., Worcester, Mass., 1993-94; chief resident in family practice Garden City (Mich.) Hosp., 1994-96; mem. house staff tng. com. Garden City Hosp., 1995-96. Mem. AMA, Am. Med. Women's Assn., Am. Osteo. Assn., Am. Coll. Osteo. Physicians, Am. Coll. Gen. Practitioners. Roman Catholic.

SIMONELLI, ANTHONY PETER, medical education administrator; b. Bridgeport, Conn., June 28, 1924; s. Nicholas and Lucy (Del Vecchio) s.; m. Joan Ann La Storia, Aug. 25, 1956; children: David Anthony, Gloria Joan, Peter Nicholas. BS, BA, U. Conn., 1955; MS, U. Wis., 1958, PhD, 1960. Registered pharmacist, Conn. From asst. to assoc. prof. Med. Coll. Va., Richmond, 1960-64, U. Mich., Ann Arbor, 1964-72; prof., chmn. U. Conn., Storrs, 1972-93; prof., dir. PhD program L.I. Univ., Bklyn., 1993—; cons. in field, 1972—; vis. prof. Upjohn Pharms., Kalamazoo, Mich., 1965, U. Wis., U. Iowa, U. Minn.; scientific bd. mem. Menley James Pharms., Phila., 1984-86. Chmn. United Fund, Ann Arbor, 1970. Served in U.S. Army, 1943-46. Grantee NIH, 1978-80, Nat. Cancer Inst., 1968-72, numerous drug cos. Fellow AAAS, Am. Assn. Pharm. Sci., Am. Colls. Pharmacy, Acad. Pharm. Sci. Roman Catholic. Home: 20 Baybury Ct East Hanover NJ 07936 Office: LI Univ University Plz Brooklyn NY 11201

SIMONETTI, FRANCESCO, radiologist, Italian navy officer; b. Taranto, Italy, Feb. 7, 1949; s. Giuseppe and Chiara (Leogrande) S.; m. Donatella Failla, Dec. 23, 1989. MD, Pisa Med. Sch., 1975, specialist radiology, 1979; tng. ultrasonography, Med. Sch. Ancona, 1983; hosp. mgmt. cert., Advanced Sch. Med. Studies, Rome, 1988. Cert. radiologist. Commd. officer Italian Navy, advanced through grades to rear adm., chief med. officer, 1976-77; from asst. x-ray dept. to dir. Main Naval Hosp., La Spezia, Italy, 1977-91; dir. Naval Med. Sch., Leghorn, Italy, 1991-93; head studies and planning office Naval Med. Svc., Rome, 1993-94; asst. surgeon gen. Surgeon Gen. Office, Rome, 1994-96; med. advisor Allied Command Europe, SHAPE, Brussels, 1996—; chmn. working group emergency medicine NATO, 1992-96; coord. healthcare projects Ministry of Health, Rome, 1995-96. Contbr. chpts. in books and articles to profl. jours. Mem. Italian Soc. Radiology and Nuclear Medicine, Assn. Mil. Surgeons U.S. (hon.), Rotary Club Rome. Office: SHAPE, OPS/LOG Divsn, B 7010 Brussels Belgium

SIMONIAN, SIMON JOHN, surgeon, scientist, educator; b. Antioch, French Ter., Apr. 20, 1932; came to U.S., 1965, naturalized, 1976.; s. John Simon and Marie Cecile (Tomboulian) S.; m. Arpi Ani Yeghiayan, July 11, 1965; children: Leonard Armen, Charles Haig, Andrew Hovig. MD, U. London, 1957; BA in Animal Physiology, St. Edmund Hall U. Oxford, Eng., 1964; MA in Animal Physiology, U. Oxford, Eng., 1969; MSc in nutrition, immunology & genetics, Harvard U., 1967, ScD in nutrition, immunology & genetics, 1969. Diplomate Am. Bd. Surgery. Rsch. asst. immunology unit Lister Inst. Preventive Medicine, Elstree, Essex, U.K., 1952; intern in medicine Univ. Coll. Hosp., London, 1957; intern in surgery Edinburgh (Scotland) Royal Infirmary, 1957-58, resident in surgery, 1961-62; clin. clk. Nat. Hosp. & Inst. of Neurology, 1958; resident Edinburgh Western Gen. Hosp., 1958-59, City Hosp., Edinburgh, Birmingham Accident and Burns Hosp., U. Birmingham, Eng., 1959-60; demonstrator dept. anatomy Edinburgh U., 1960-61; rsch. fellow in pathology Lab. Chem. Pathology Harvard U., Boston, 1965-68; trainee NIH Harvard U., 1967; instr. immunology Harvard Med. Sch., Boston, 1966-70; instr., assoc in surgery Harvard Med. Sch., 1968-70, surg. dir. course on transplantation, biology and medicine, 1968-70; vis. prof. Harvard Med. Sch., Mass. Gen. Hosp., Brigham and Womens Hosp., New Eng. Deaconess Hosp., 1982; dir. transplantation immunology unit, asst. in surgery Brigham and Womens Hosp., Boston, 1968-70; resident in surgery Boston City Hosp., 1970-74; attending surgeon in transplantation and gen. surgery services U. Chgo. Med. Ctr., 1974-77; asst. prof. surgery, mem. com. immunology U. Chgo., 1974-77; head div. renal transplantation Hahnemann U. Sch. Medicine and Hosp., 1978-87, prof. surgery, 1978-88, chmn. Transplantation Com., 1983-88, chmn. quality assurance of surgery com., 1986-88; dept. surgery coord. with joint commn. for accreditation of hosps. Hahnemann U. Sch. Medicine, 1986; chief and chmn. dept. surgery St. John Hosp. and Med. Ctr., Detroit, 1988-89, chmn. credentials com. of surgery and oper. rm. com., 1988-89, assoc. v.p. for med. affairs, 1989-90; pres., CEO Vein Inst. of Met. Washington, Inc., 1990—; assoc. Fairfax Hosp., Falls Church, Va., 1990-92, active faculty, 1992—; guest lectr., 1994; clin. assoc. prof. surgery Georgetown U. Sch. Medicine, Washington, 1992—; lectr. in field; vis. prof. Vanderbilt U., 1968, Cedars-Sinai Med. Ctr. UCLA, 1977, Addenbroke's Hosp., Cambridge U., 1977, Karolinska Inst., 1977, Huddinge Hosp. U. Stockholm, 1977, Med. Coll. Pa. and Hosp., 1980, 81, 85, Grad. Hosp. U. Pa., 1981, 85, U. Athens, 1981, U. Coll. Hosp., U. London, 1981, VA Hosp., Tufts U., 1982, Nat. Acad. Scis., Yerevan, Republic Armenia, 1995; cons. Michael Reese Hosp., Chgo., 1976-77, cons. in gen. surgery City of Phila., 1986-88, cons. in vascular surgery Coll. Podiatry, Phila., 1986-88, chief med. team support for U.S. Presdl. visits to Detroit, 1988, 89; vis. surgeon Inst. Vein Disease, Mich., 1989-90; vis. scientist Argonne (Ill.) Nat. Lab., 1969, 74-77; guest lectr., panelist 8th Internat. Congress of Nephrology, Athens, Greece, 1981, 1st Congress Internat. Soc. Edn. and Rsch. in Vascular Disease, San Diego, bd. dirs. 1992, 4th Internat. Dialogue Transition to Global Soc., U. Md., College Park, 1995; chmn. session 5th Armenian Med. World Congress, Paris, 1992, 11th World Congress Internat. Union of Phlebology, Montreal, 1992, 22d World Congress Inernat. Soc. for Cardiovasc. Surgery, Kyoto, Japan, 1995, 6th Annual Congress N. Am. Soc. of Phlebology, Lake Buena Vista, Fla., 1993, sec., bd. dirs. Woodstock, Inc., 1992-93; eminent scholar, external assessor U. Zambia, Lusaka, 1994; chmn. panel, session chmn., panel co-chmn., guest lectr., panelist 17th World Congress Internat. Union Angiology, London, 1995; chmn. panel, adv. bd. 12th World Congress Union Internat. Phlebologie, London, 1995; chmn. panel 1996 N. Am. Soc. Phlebology Ann. Congress, San Diego. Cuthor: Manual of Vascular Access Procedures, 1987; cons. to editorial bd. dateline: Issues in Transplantation, 1985-87; mem. editorial bd. Phila. Medicine, 1988, Transplantation Proc., 1987—, Jour. Transplantation Abstracts, 1968-70; reviewer New England Jour. Medicine, 1993—, Jour. Am. Med. Assn., 1993, Jour. Oncology and Dermatologic Surgery, 1993; contbr. articles to profl. jours. and books; appeared in med. movie Giving. Co-founder Armenian Youth Soc., Eng., 1953, pres. 1953-54; Armenian Studies Program U. Chgo., 1975; bd. govs. Friends Sch., London, 1964-65; Mass. del., co-founder Armenian Assembly, Washington, 1970-74; trustee, fellow co-founder Entry into Manhood of Armenian Youth at Age 13, 1981; co-founder Armenian Am. Health Assn. of Greater Washington, 1992, mem. pharms. com. 1992—, chmn. nominating com., 1993; mem. Am. Friends of St. Edmund Hall, U. Oxford, 1992—, U.S. Campaign for St. Edmund Hall, 1995—, Rep. Presdl. Task Force; mem. St. Mary's Armenian Apostolic Ch., Washington, guest preacher, 1994, 95, 96; mem. Am. Friends Am. U. Armenia, Yerevan, 1994; bd. dirs. Arlington (Va.) Symphony Orch., 1992; mem. regional com. U.S. Campaign for Univ. Oxford, 1993; bd. dirs. First Western Found., Inc., 1994; active amphitheatre endowment fund Boston City Hosp., 1994. Nairn scholar, 1949-52; Middlesex scholar, 1952-57; recipient Suckling prize, 1956, Brit. Med. Research Council award, 1962-64, Alt prize, 1973, Thompson award, 1974-77, Johnson award, 1975-77, Presdl. Medal of Merit, 1982, Kabakjian award Armenian Student Assn. Am., 1986; named outstanding new citizen of Citizenship Coun. of Met. Chgo. and Dept. Justice, Washington, 1976-77, Jonathan E. Rhoads ann. orator, 1984; co-endowed The John and Marie J. Simonian Award, St. Nerces Sem., 1981, John R. Pfeifer, MD, Rsch. Award, Providence Hosp., Southfield, Mich., 1992; endowed the Dennis Knight prize Royal Acad. Music, London, 1991; endowed The Marie J. Simonian Prize, Georgetown U. Med. Sch., 1991 (prize com. 1991—); established The John N.D. Kelly Prize in Med. Studies St. Edmund Hall, U. Oxford, 1992, The Simon J. and Arpi A. Simonian Prize for scholastic excellence for doctoral candidates, Harvard U., 1992; recognized for philanthropy to Hahnemann U. by placques in med. sch. and hosp. lobbies., Simon and Arpi Simonian room Sch. of Humanities and Scis. U. Yerevan, Armenia, 1994, plaque in Cyrus Vesuna Auditorium and Conf. Ctr., Fairfax Hosp., Falls Church, Va., 1995; grantee U.S. Govt., industry cos., founds. Fellow Royal Coll. Surgeons Edinburgh, ACS (Phila., Mich. and Washington chpts.), Phila. Acad. Surgery (Jonathan E. Rhoads ann. orator 1984—, Samuel D. Gross prize com. 1988, councillor 1988); mem. AAAS, AMA (mem. jour. rev. 1993), AAUP, Royal Coll. Surgeons of Eng., Royal Coll. Physicians of London Licentiates, Nat. Assn. Armenian Studies and Rsch. (rep. Midatlantic region 1994—), Armenian Gen. Benevolent Union (pres.' club 1990—), Knights of Vartan, Am. Armenian Med. Assn. (co-founder 1972, treas. 1972-74), Brit. Med. Assn., Immunology Club Boston, Cancer Rsch. Assn. Boston, Physicians for Social Responsibility, Am. Pub. Health Assn., Assn. for Study of Med. Edn., Armenian Med. and Dental Assn. Greater Phila. (co-founder 1983, pres. 1983-85, Outreach award 1986), Assn. Acad. Surgery, Transplantation Soc. (mem. membership com. 1980-82), Am. Fedn. Clin. Rsch., N.Y. Acad. Scis., Am. Soc. Transplant Surgeons (co-founding mem. 1974, chmn. immunosuppression study com. 1974-77, membership com. 1985-87), Am. Venous Forum, Assn. of Ill. Transplant Surgeons, Chgo. Assn. Immunologists, Chgo. Soc. Gastroenterology, Phila. Acad. Scis. (co-chmn. membership com. 1980-88, guest lectr. 1982), Greater Delaware Valley Soc. Transplant Surgeons (councillor 1978-80, 85-88, pres. elect 1980-82, pres. 1982-85), Phila. County Med. Soc. (rep. City Ctr. br. 1981-83, pres. 1984, bd. dirs. 1985-87, chmn. long range planning com. 1986-88), Pa. Med. Soc., Samuel Hahnemann SurAm. Technion Soc., Am. Soc. Artificial Internal Organs, European Soc. Organ Transplant, Oxford and Cambridge Soc. of Phila. and Washington, Internat. Cardiovascular Soc. (N.Am. chpt.), N. Am. Soc. Phlebology (curriculum devel. projects com. 1992—, faculty 1993-95), End Stage Renal Disease Network 24 (mem. med. rev. bd. 1980-82, 86-87), Am. Coll. Physician Execs., Detroit Acad. Surgery, Detroit Surgical Assn., Transplantation Soc. Mich., Organ Procurement Agy. Mich. (adv. bd. 1988-89), Wayne County Med. Soc., Mich. State Med. Soc., Fairfax County Med. Soc., Med. Soc. Va., Met. Vascular Conf., Soc. Brigham Surg. Alumni, Greater Washington Telecomm. Assn. (pres.'s club 1994), Chesapeake Vascular Soc., Oxford Soc. Washington, Harvard Club (Phila. and Washington), Med. Club (Phila.), U. Chgo. Club (Washington), Langley Hill Freinds Meeting, Sigma Xi. Mem. Soc. of Friends. Office: 3301 Woodburn Rd Annandale VA 22003-1229

SIMONOWITZ, DAVID ALAN, surgeon; b. New London, Conn., Dec. 4, 1946; s. George and Mary (Gilman) S.; m. Jean Weaver, Sept. 1967 (div. 1977); m. Barbara A. Joiner Lewandowski, Apr. 22, 1978; 1 child, Ethan Walter. BS, U. Conn., 1966; MD, U. Chgo., 1970. Lic. physician, Wash., Ill.; diplomate Am. Bd. Surgery. Intern dept. surgery straight surg. U. Chgo. Hosps., 1970-71, jr. asst. resident gen. surgery, 1971-72, asst. resident, 1974-75, sr. resident, 1975-76, chief resident, 1976-77; asst. prof. surgery U. Wash., 1977-82, clin. asst. prof., 1982-94; clin. assoc. prof. U. Chgo. Hosps., 1994—; clin. asst. prof. surgery Coll. Osteo. Medicine of Pacific, 1985-86; pvt. practice, 1982—; dir. Nutrition Support Svc., 1978-82, Out-Patient Surgery Clinics, 1978-82; sec.-treas. Overlake Hosp., 1984, chief surgery, 1986-88, chief quality assurance/utilization rev., 1988—; presenter various orgns. Contbr. articles to profl. jours. Maj. U.S. Army, 1972-74, Korea. Univ. scholar U. Conn., 1964-66; recipient Hilgar Perry Jenkins award for excellence in performance of acad. and patient oriented svc., 1972-77. Fellow ACS (program com. state chpt. 1981-82); mem. Am. Soc. Gen. Surgeons, Assn. Acad. Surgery, King County Med. Soc., Henry Harkins Surg. Soc., Am. Soc. Parenteral and Enteral Nutrition, Soc. for Surgery of Alimentary Tract, Seattle Surg. Soc., Collegium Internat. Chirurgiae Digestivae, North Pacific Surg. Assn., Pacific Coast Surg. Office: 1700 116th St NE Bellevue WA 98004

SIMONS, HELEN, school psychologist, psychotherapist; b. Chgo., Feb. 13, 1930; d. Leo and Sarah (Shrayer) Pomper; m. Broudy Simons, May 20, 1956 (May 1972); children: Larry, Sheri. BA in Biol., Lake Forest Coll., 1951; MA in Clin. Psychology, Roosevelt U., 1972; D of Psychology, Ill. Sch. Profl. Psychology, 1980. Intern Cook County Hosp., Chgo., 1979-80; pvt. practice psychotherapist Chgo., 1980—; sch. psychologist Chgo. Bd. Edn., 1974-79, 80—. Contbr. articles on psychotherapy of A.D.D. and P.T.S.D. children to profl. jours. Mem. APA, Nat. Sch. Psychologists Assn., Midwestern Psychol. Assn., Mental Health Assn. Ill., Ill. Psychol. Assn., Ill. Sch. Psychologists Assn., Chgo. Psychol. Assn., Internat. Coun. of Psychologists, Chgo. Sch. Psychol. Assn. Home: 6145 N Sheridan Rd Apt 29D Chicago IL 60660-2883 Office: Brennemann Sch 4251 N Clarendon Ave Chicago IL 60613-1523

SIMONS, JOSEPH BERNARD, psychologist, psychology educator; b. Janesville, Wis., Feb. 3, 1933; s. Joseph Bernard and Helen Elizabeth (Farrington) S.; m. Jeanne Reidy, May 22, 1969. Student, U. Mich., 1957-59; M.S., Notre Dame U., 1963, Ph.D., 1967; postgrad. Yale U., 1964. Lic. psychologist, Calif. Asst. dean students Notre Dame, South Bend, Ind., 1964-65, dean of students, 1965-67, clin. psychologist, 1967-69; tchr. Santa Rosa Jr. Coll., Calif., 1969—; prof. Santa Rosa Coll., 1969—; clin. mem. Erikson Inst., Santa Rosa, 1979-83; clin. dir. Santa Rosa Counseling Ctr., 1983—; cons. St. Rose Alcohol Recovery, Santa Rosa, 1983—. Author: Risk of Loving, 1968, Wisdom's Child, 1969, Risk of Freedom, 1970, Human Art of Counseling, 1971, Living Together, 1978, Search For Self, 1980. Med. adv. com., vol. Psychologist Home Hospice of Sonoma, Santa Rosa, 1980—; vol. psychologist Ptnrs. for Adoption, Santa Rosa, 1983—, St. Rose Alcohol Recovery Program, Santa Rosa, 1983—. Mem. Am. Psychol. Assn., Calif. Psychol. Assn., Am. Humanistic Psychol. Assn. Democrat. Home: 2057 Rolling Hill Dr Santa Rosa CA 95404-2349 Office: Santa Rose Counseling Ctr 1212 College Ave #B Santa Rosa CA 95404-3908

SIMONS, RICHARD KEITH, medical educator; b. Leicester, U.K., Apr. 29, 1952; s. Robert William and Audry Joyce (Robinson) S.; m. Christine Mary Willick, May 12, 1984; children: Jonathan Robert, Mark Alexander, Philip Arthur. BA, Cambridge U., London, 1973, MA, 1976, MB, BCh, 1976. Diplomate Am. Bd. Surgery, U.K. Gen. Med. Coun.; MD Calif. Med. Bd. Clin. instr. U. Wash., Seattle, 1990-91; asst. prof. U. Calif., San Diego, 1991-96, U. B.C., Vancouver, 1996—; attending physician U. Calif. San Diego Med. Ctr., 1991-96, ethics com., 1993-96, infection control com., 1993-96; chair ATLS subcom. San Diego County ACS/COT, 1991-96. Contbr. articles to profl. jours. Grantee U. Calif. San Diego Acad. Senate, 1992-94. Fellow ACS, Royal Coll. Surgeons Eng., Royal Coll. Surgeons Can.; mem. Am. Assn. Surgery Trauma, Surg. Infection Soc. (fellow 1985-86), Shock Soc. Office: Univ BC Dept Surgery, 855 W 10th St, Vancouver, BC Canada V5Z 4E3

SIMONS, SAMUEL STONEY, JR., medical researcher; b. Phila., Sept. 13, 1945; s. S. Stoney and Virginia Laurie S.; m. Cyrena Scott; children: C. Torrey, Caroline S. AB, Princeton U., 1963-67; PhD, Harvard U., 1972. Postdoctoral fellow U. Calif., San Francisco, 1972-75; from staff fellow to chief steroid hormones sect. NIH, Bethesda, Md., 1975—. Edtl. bd. Jour. Biol. Chemistry, 1992—, Receptors, 1989—; contbr. articles to profl. jours. Class of 1967 regional co-chmn. Princeton U. Ann. Giving, Bethesda, 1982—. Mem. Am. Chem. Soc., Am. Soc. Biochemistry & Molecular Biology. Office: NIH Bldg 8 Rm B2A-07 Bethesda MD 20892

SIMONS, SHIRLEY ANN, director quality and risk management; b. Wichita Falls, Tex., Dec. 13, 1951; d. Henry Anthony and Gertrude Margaret (Martini) S.; m. Robert Leo May, May 4, 1991. BS in nursing, Tex. Woman's Univ., 1973; MS in nursing, Univ. Tex., 1978; MA in mgmt., Bellevue Univ., 1995. RN, Nebr. Head nurse Wichita Gen. Hosp., Wichita Falls, 1973-75; asst. prof. Midwestern State Univ., Wichita Falls, 1975-78, Creighton Univ., Omaha, Nebr., 1978-85; asst. v.p. St. Joseph Hosp., Omaha, 1985-94; dir. quality and risk mgmt. Dept. Vet. Affairs, Omaha, 1994—; cons. Jennie Melhom Meml. Medical Ctr., Broken Bow, Nebr., 1994; adj. faculty Creighton Univ., 1985-93. Contbr. articles to profl. jours. Adv. bd. St. Joseph Villa Home Care, Omaha, 1994—. Mem. Nebr. Assn. Healthcare Quality (pres. 1995-96), Federal Execs. Assn., Nat. Assn. Healthcare Quality (team mem. 1995-96), Sigma Theta Tau. Office: Dept Veterans Affairs Med Ctr (0QA) 4101 Woolworth Ave Omaha NE 68105

SIMONSON, LLOYD GRANT, microbiologist; b. San Jose, Calif., Dec. 1, 1943; s. Rolfe Lau and Dorothy Fay (Scully) S.; m. Katherine Lenora Peck,

Aug. 24, 1968. PhD, Ill. State U., 1974; MBA with honors, Roosevelt U., 1984. Prin. investigator Naval Dental Rsch. Inst., Great Lakes, Ill., 1968-88, chief scientist, 1988—; adj. prof. Dental Sch., Northwestern U., Chgo., 1990—; cons. Chgo. Med. Sch., North Chicago, 1977-80; reviewer grant applications Med. Rsch. Coun. of Can. Contbr. articles to profl. jours. Mem. Internat. Assn. Dental Rsch. (pres. microbiology-immunology group 1988-89), Am. Assn. Dental Rsch. (pres. Chgo. chpt. 1988-89, Young Investigator 1979), Am. Soc. Microbiology, Sigma Xi. Office: Naval Dental Rsch Inst Bldg 1-H Great Lakes IL 60088-5259

SIMONSON, SUSAN KAY, hospital administrator; b. La Porte, Ind., Dec. 5, 1946; d. George Randolph and Myrtle Lucille (Opfel) Menkes; m. Richard Bruce Simonson, Aug. 25, 1973. BA with honors, Ind. U., 1969; MA, Washington U., St. Louis, 1972. Perinatal social worker Yakima Valley Meml. Hosp., Yakima, Wash., 1979-81, dir. patient support and hospice program, 1981—, dir. social svc., 1982—; instr. Spanish, ethnic studies, sociology Yakima Valley Coll., Yakima, Wash., 1981—; pres. Yakima Child Abuse Council, 1983-85; developer nat. patient support program, 1981. Contbr. articles to profl. jours. Mem. Jr. League, Yakima; mem. adv. council Robert Wood Johnson Found. Rural Infant Health Care Project, Yakima, 1980, Pregnancy Loss and Compassionate Friends Support Groups, Yakima, 1982—, Teen Outreach Program, Yakima, 1984—. Recipient NSF award, 1967, discharge planning program of yr. regional award Nat. Glasrock Home Health Care Discharge Planning Program, 1987; research grantee Ind. U., 1968, Fulbright grantee U.S. Dept. State, 1969-70; Nat. Def. Edn. Act fellowship, 1970-73. Mem. AAUW, Soc. Med. Anthropology, Soc. Hosp. Social Work Dirs. of Am. Hosp. Assn. (regional award 1989), Nat. Assn. Social Workers, Phi Beta Kappa. Office: Yakima Valley Meml Hosp 2811 Tieton Dr Yakima WA 98902-3761

SIMONTACCHI, CAROL NADINE, nutritionist, retail store executive; b. Bellingham, Wash., July 6, 1947; d. Ralph Eugene and Sylvia Arleta (Tyler) Walmer; m. Bob Simontacchi, Oct. 3, 1981; children: Caryl Anne, Bobbie Anne, Melissa Anne, Laurie Anne. BS in Health and Human Svcs., Columbia Pacific U., 1996, postgrad., 1996—. Cert. nutritionist, Wash. CEO The Health Haus, Inc., Vancouver, Wash., 1985—; host radio program Back to the Beginning, Vancouver, 1990—; CEO The Natural Physician Ctr., Beaverton, Oreg., 1995—. Author: Your Fat is Not Your Fault, 1994, The Sun Rise Book: Living Beyond Depression, 1996, The Attention! Book, Living Beyond ADHD, 1996. Mem. Soc. Cert. Nutritionists (pres. bd. 1992-93), Nat. Nutritional Foods Assn. (chair edn. com., N.W. region legis. chair 1991—). Republican. Christian Ch. Office: The Health Haus Inc 101 E 8th St Ste 250 Vancouver WA 98660-3294

SIMONTON, DEAN KEITH, psychology educator; b. Glendale, Calif., Jan. 27, 1948; s. Dean Clarence Simonton and Laverne (Merkobrad) Williams; m. Susan Youel, June 21, 1971 (div. 1982); m. Melody Boyer, Dec. 29, 1984. BA magna cum laude in Psychology, Occidental Coll., 1970; MA in Social Psychology, Harvard U., 1973, PhD with distinction, 1975. Asst. prof. psychology, U. Ark., Fayetteville, 1974-76; asst. prof. U. Calif., Davis, 1976-81, assoc. prof. 1981-85, prof., 1985—; cons. Wissenschaftzentrun, Berlin, 1979, Ctr. for Creative Leadership, Greensboro, N.C., 1983, NATO, Brussels, Belgium, 1980-81, Dept. Def., Washington, 1983, Creative Problem Solving Inst., 1984, Arvin Perlmutter, Inc., 1992, Milken Family Found., 1994. Author: Genius, Creativity and Leadership, 1984, Why Presidents Succeed, 1987, Scientific Genius, 1988, Psychology, Science, and History, 1990, Greatness, 1994; author of selected papers on genius and creativity, 1996; editor Jour. Creative Behavior, 1993—; contbr. numerous articles to profl. jours. Recipient Excellence award Mensa Edn. and Research Found., 1986. Fellow Am. Psychol. Soc., Am. Assn. Applied and Preventive Psychology, Am. Psychol. Assn. (mem-at-large 1979-82, pres. psychology and the arts div. 1985-86, Rudolf Arnheim award Outstnding Contbn. fo Psychology and the Arts 1996); Mem. Phi Beta Kappa, Sigma Xi. Home: 2903 Solito St Davis CA 95616-0274 Office: U Calif Dept Psychology Davis CA 95616

SIMPKINS, HENRY, medical educator. BS in Chemistry, U. London, 1964, PhD in Biophys. and Molecular Biology, 1967; MD, U. Miami, 1975. Rsch. biologist U. Calif., San Deigo, 1967-69; head lab. molecular biology and biophys. Lady Davis Inst. Med. Rsch. of Jewish Gen. Hosp., Montreal, Can., 1969-75; asst. prof. dept. biochemistry U. Montreal, 1970-73, assoc. prof., 1973-75; resident U. Colo. Med. Ctr., Denver, 1975-78, instr. dept. pathology, 1976-78, asst. prof. dept. pathology, 1976-77, assoc. prof. dept. pathology, 1977-78; assoc. prof. dept. pathology U. Calif., Irvine, 1978-81, prof. dept. pathology, 1981-85; prof. pathology SUNY, N.Y.C., 1985-91; prof., chmn. dept. pathology and lab. medicine Temple U. Med. Sch., Phila., 1991—; head divsns. chem. pathology and hematopathology U. Calif., Irvine, 1978-81, head disvn. hematopathology, 1981-83, head divsn. hematopathology.blood bank, 1983-85, acting chmn. dept. pathology, 1984; cons. hematopathology Long Beach VA Hosp., 1979-85; dir. dept. pathology and lab. medicine U. Hosp. S.I., N.Y., 1985-91; presenter in field. Contbr. articles to profl. jours. Postdoctoral fellow King's Coll., London, 1964-67, U. Calif., San Diego, 1967-69; Ministry Edn. State scholar, Gt. Britain, 1961-64, Sci. Rsch. Coun. scholar, Gt. Britain, 1964-67; Can. MEd. Rsch. Coun. scholar, 1970-75. Mem. Am. Soc. Clin. Pathologists, Am. Assn. Blood Banks, Am. Soc. Hematology, Coll. Am. Pathologists, Internat. Acad. Pathology, The Pluto Club. Office: Temple U Sch Medicine Dept Pathology and Lab Med Philadelphia PA 19140*

SIMPSON, CHARLES EUGENE, physician, military officer; b. Cheboygan, Mich., Aug. 21, 1950; s. Elmon Eugene and Helen Rose (McLaughlin) S.; m. Lou Ann Prinzo, Feb. 10, 1983; children: Dana Anne Cates, Charles Jr., Richard Lee II. BA, U. Mich., 1972; postgrad., Ea. Mich. U., 1976-78; DO, Mich. State U., 1981; MS, U. Cin., 1990. Commd. ensign U.S. Navy, 1972, advanced through grades to capt., 1994, line officer USS J.F. Kennedy, 1972-75; sr. med. officer U.S. Navy Seabee Constrn. Ctr., Gulfport, Miss., 1982-85, U.S. Navy Br. Med. Clinic, Jacksonville, Fla., 1990-92; sr. flight surgeon USMC Air Sta. Cherry Point, Havelock, N.C., 1987-88; sr. med. officer occupational med. divsn. Naval Air Sta., Jacksonville, Fla., 1992—; head occupl. med. dept. U.S. Naval Hosp., Jacksonville, 1991-92, dir. ind. duty corpsman program, 1990-96; flight surgeon HSI/HS Wing/USN, Jacksonville, 1990-93; dir. Br. Med. Clinic, NAS Cecil Field, 1995—; cmdr. Fleet Hosp. 4, 1995—. Navy ROTC scholar U.S. Navy, 1968; Health Scis. Edn. and Tng. Command scholar U.S. Navy, 1978. Fellow Am. Coll. Preventive Medicine (bd. cert. occupational medicine); mem. Assn. Mil. Surgeons of U.S., Aerospace Med. Assn., Soc. U.S. Naval Flight Surgeons, Am. Osteo. Assn., Assn. Mil. Osteo. Physicians and Surgeons, Fla. Osteo. Med. Assn. Episcopalian. Home: 3557 Sheldon Rd Orange Park FL 32065-6938 Office: Naval Air Sta Occupl Med Clinic Jacksonville FL 32212-5000

SIMPSON, ELIZABETH ANN, pharmacist, educator; b. Steubenville, Ohio, Nov. 11, 1941; d. Robert Thompson and Elizabeth Ann (Rogers) Lucas; m. James Lewis Simpson, Nov. 8, 1963; children: James L., Mary Elizabeth. BS in Pharmacy, W.Va. U., 1963; postgrad., U. Tex., 1986. Staff pharmacist, Mich., Pa., N.J.; staff pharmacist Mass., W.Va., 1964-80; staff pharmacist St. John Hosp. and Med. Ctr., Detroit, 1980-83, dir. pharmacy svcs. St. John Outpatient Corp., 1983-93; asst. dir. div. pharmacy svcs. St. John Health System, 1993—; adj. clin. instr. dept. pharmacy practice Coll. Pharmacy and Allied Health Professions, Wayne State U., Detroit, 1982—; presenter in field, 1986—; mem. pharmacy and therapeutics com. Georgian East Nursing Home, 1987-89. Contbr. articles to profl. jours. Pres. bd. dirs. Meml. Co-Op Nursery Sch., 1973-75; mem. various PTO coms. and bds. Grosse Pointe (Mich.) Sch. System, 1975-89; chmn. pub. affairs com. Jr. League Detroit, 1975-76, mem. exec. com., 1978-80; chmn. pub. affairs com. Jr. Leagues Mich., 1976-78; mem. adv. bd. Chesterfield Twp. Police, 1992-93; mem. zoning bd. appeals Chesterfield Twp., 1993—, chmn., 1996—; chmn. fin. com. Grace United Meth. Ch., Chesterfield, Mich., 1996—. Recipient Vol. of Yr. award Jr. League Detroit, 1976, Torch Drive Communication award United Found., 1985. Fellow Am. Coll. Cons. Pharmacists, Acad. Pharmacy Practice and Mgmt. (policy com. 1987, chmn. instnl. practice sect. 1990—, mem. edn. com. 1988-89); mem. Am. Soc. Hosp. Pharmacists, Am. Pharm. Assn. (ho. of dels. 1987—, William S. Apple program fellow 1986), Mich. Pharmacists Assn. (physician dispensing adv. com. 1988-91, chmn. profl. and pub. affairs com. 1987-90, chmn. pharm. care task force), Mich. Soc. Hosp. Pharmacists (profl. and legal affairs com. 1987-90), Southeastern Mich. Soc. Hosp. Pharmacists, Lambda Kappa Sigma. Republican. Home: 46978 Jans Dr Chesterfield MI 48047-5128 Office: St John Hosp and Med Ctr 22101 Moross Rd Grosse Pointe MI 48236-2148

SIMPSON, GARY LAVERN, public health medical director; b. St. Louis, Jan. 3, 1947; m. Sandra Cheryl Lapham; children: Cassandra Alyn, Courtney Meredith. BS, U. Ill., 1969, MS, 1970, PhD, 1973; MD, Rush Med. Coll., Chgo., 1974; MSc in Clin. Medicine, U. Oxford, Eng., 1977; MPH in Tropical Pub. Health, Harvard U., 1978. Diplomate Mass. Bd. Med. Examiners, Am. Bd. Internal Medicine, Calif. Bd. Med. Examiners, N.Mex. Bd. Med. Examiners. Intern Peter Bent Brigham Hosp., Boston, 1974-75, resident, 1975-76; sr. registrar in internal medicine/infectious diseases U. Oxford, Clin. Med. Sch., Radcliffe Infirmary, Eng., 1976-77; fellow infectious diseases divsn. infectious diseases Stanford (Calif.) U., 1978-79; asst. prof. medicine divsn. infectious diseases U. N.Mex., Albuquerque, 1979-83, clin. assoc. prof. medicine, 1983-88; attending physician Presbyn. Healthcare Svcs., Albuquerque, 1987-89; med. dir. infectious diseases Pub. Health divsn. Dept. Health, State of N.Mex., Santa Fe, 1992—; teaching asst. U. Ill., Champaign-Urbana, 1969-70, rsch. assoc., 1970-72; rsch. cons. U. N.Mex., Albuquerque, 1973-74, adj. assoc. prof. dept. biology, 1986-87; rsch. scientist Rush Med. Sch., 1973-74; clin. fellow Harvard Med. Sch., Boston, 1974-76; dir., chief medicine Raymond Hosp., Wrentham, Mass., 1976; staff physician Children's Hosp. Med. Ctr., Boston, 1976; vis. prof. Instituto Nacional de Salud, Bogota, Colombia, 1979-80; attending physician U. N.Mex. Hosp., 1979-87, VA Med. Ctr., Albuquerque, 1980-87; assoc. scientist Lovelace Med. Found., Albuquerque, 1983-86; med. dir. Cottonwood de Albuquerque, Residential Treatment Ctr., Los Lunas, N.Mex., 1983-84, Jim Kelly Counseling Assocs., Albuquerque, 1984-86, Presbyn. Alcohol and Drug Treatment Ctr., Northside Presbyn. Hosp., Albuquerque, 1987-89; sr. cons. bur. communicable diseases AID, Dept. State, Washington, 1984—; cons. Am. Inst. Biol. Scis., Washington, 1984—; Eagleson lectr. Am. Biol. Safety Assn. 36th Annual Conf., Albuquerque, lectr. in field; vis. prof. dept. med. microbiology and sec. of infectious diseases Faculty of Medicine U. Manitoba, Winnipeg, Can. Contbr. articles to profl. jours. Recipient Cert. award U.S. Indian Health Svc., 1995; Robert Wood Johnson fellow, 1977, Agy. for Internat. Devel. Edn. fellow, 1978, Palo Alto Med. Rsch. Found. fellow, 1979; hon. I award U. Ill. Fellow ACP; mem. AAAS, Oxford Med. Soc., Royal Soc. Tropical Medicine and Hygiene, Am. Soc. Microbiology, Am. Soc. Tropical Medicine and Hygiene, Am. Fedn. Clin. Rsch., Infectious Diseases Soc. Am., Am. Soc. Addiction Medicine (cert.). Home: 18 Senda Aliento Placitas NM 87043

SIMPSON, GEORGE MEGAHY, psychiatrist; b. Phila., Sept. 28, 1926; m. Inger M. Lilja. BS in Biochemistry, Glasgow U., 1948; MB, ChB in Medicine, Liverpool (Eng.) U., 1955; Degree in Medicine (hon.), U. Goteborg, Sweden, 1994. Intern Royal So. Hosp., Liverpool, Eng., 1955-56; asst. resident Dept. Psychiary, Allen Meml. Inst., Royal Victoria Hosp., 1956-57; resident in psychiatry Rockland State Hosp. Rsch. Ctr., Orangeburg, N.Y., 1957-59; assoc. dir. Rockland County Mental Health Assn., Monsey, N.Y., 1958-62; asst. in psychiatry Columbia U., N.Y.C., 1959-77; sr. psychiatrist rsch. ctr. Rockland State Hosp., Orangeburg, 1959-61, supervising psychiatrist rsch. ctr., 1961-68; Assoc. dir. Bergen Pines County Hosp., Paramus, N.J., 1968-75; prin. research psychiatrist Rockland Psychiat. Ctr., Orangeburg, N.Y., 1968-77; unit chief Rockland Psychiat. Ctr., 1971-75; assoc. clin. prof. N.Y. Med. Coll., N.Y.C., 1974-77; research cons. Bergen Pines County Hosp., Paramus, 1975-77; dir. U. So. Calif./Metro Psychopharm Svcs., Norwalk, Calif., 1977-80; prof. psychiatry U. So. Calif., L.A., 1977-83; dir. adult psychiat. ctr. Dept. Mental Health, L.A., 1980-83; prof. psychiatry and pharmacology, dir. clin. psychopharmacology Med. Coll. Pa., Phila., 1983-94; prof. rsch. psychiatry, dept. psychiatry/behavioral scis. U. So. Calif. Sch. Medicine, L.A., 1994—; mem. com. on A.E. Bennet Awards, Soc. Biol. Psychiatry, 1989—; vis. prof. Menninger Clinic, Topeka, Kans., 1968; mem. N.Y. State Dept. of Mental Hygiene Com. on Therapeutics, 1976-78, APA Task Force on Tardive Dyskinesia, 1977-78, chmn. task force on sudden death in psychiatry, 1982-88; mem. com. for protection of human subjects cons., HEW and FDA on areas related to psychotropic agts. and side effects State of Calif., 1978-81; chmn. search com. for dir. psychiatry and law U. So. Calif., 1982-83; chmn. young investigators travel award coms. 5th World Congress Biol. Psychiatry, 1989—; mem. adv. bd. Schizophrenia Diagnostic & Cons. Ctr. Med. Coll. Pa./EPPI, chmn. mental health and neuroscis. planning com., 1990; active numerous other career related positions. Contbr. articles to profl. jours. Member Mayor's Task Force on Homeless Mentally Ill, Phila., 1986-88; mem. adv. bd. Schizophrenia Diagnostic & Consultation Ctr., MCP/EPPI, 1989-91, chmn. mental health and neuroscis. planning com., 1990. Recipient Arthur P. Noyes award, 1991. Mem. Biol. Psychiatry (adv. editor), Brit. Med. Assn., Am. Coll. Clin. Pharmacology, Pa. Med. Soc., Nat. Alliance for Mentally Ill, Am. Coll. Neuropsychopharmacology (chmn. nominating com. 1986, task force to revise guidelines for clin. trials of psychotropic drugs 1990-91, mental health leadership forum liaison 1990-91, honorifics com. 1990-91, pres. 1991). Office: U So Calif Sch Medicine Dept Psych/Behavioral Scis 1937 Hospital Pl Rm 239 Los Angeles CA 90033

SIMPSON, IAN JAMES, medical educator; b. Waihi, New Zealand, May 3, 1942; s. Arthur John and Miriel Annie (Takle) S.; m. Judith Lois, Jan. 16, 1965; children: Mark Ian, Jane Katherine. MB ChB, Otago Med. Sch., Dunedin, 1966; MD, Auckland U., 1985. Nephrologist Auckland Hosp., 1975-78; sr. lectr. medicine Auckland Med. Sch., 1978-89, assoc. prof., 1989—, sub dean (acad.), 1989-95, prof. medicine, 1995—. Rsch. fellow Royal Postgrad. Med. Sch., London, 1972-75. Fellow Royal Australian Coll. Physicians (sr. censor 1983-86, chmn. com. physician tng., councillor 1983-86); mem. Internat. Soc. Nephrology, Australian New Zealand Soc. Nephrology, Australian New Zealand Transplantation Soc., Australian Soc. Immunology. Office: Gilgit Rd Specialist Ctr, 15 Gilgit Rd Epsom, Auckland 5, New Zealand

SIMPSON, JOE LEIGH, obstetrics and gynecology educator; b. Birmingham, Ala., Apr. 4, 1943; s. Robert S. and Winnie (Leigh) S.; m. Sandra A. Carson, May 6, 1978; children: Scott, Reid. MD, Duke U., 1968. Diplomate Am. Bd. Ob-Gyn, Am. Bd. Med. Genetics. Fellow in ob-gyn Cornell Med. Coll., N.Y.C., 1968-73; clin. assoc. N.Y. Blood Ctr., N.Y.C., 1969-73; asst. clin. prof. ob-gyn U. Tex., San Antonio, 1973-75; assoc. prof., head ob-gyn Northwestern U. Med. Sch., Chgo., 1975-79, prof. ob-gyn, 1979-86; Faculty prof. chmn. dept. ob-gyn U. Tenn., Memphis, 1986-94; Ernst W. Bertner chmn. and prof. dept. ob-gyn., prof. dept. molecular and human genetics Baylor Coll. of Medicine, Houston, 1994—; mem. genetics grant rev. and adv. bd. HHS, 1979-82; mem. clin. rsch. panel March of Dimes, 1986-94, chmn. adv. panel reproductive hazards, 1988-92; mem. accreditation coun. grad. med. edn. Residency Rev. Com. Med. Genetics, 1993—. Author: Disorders of Sexual Development, 1976; author: (with others) Genetics in Obstetrics and Gynecology, 1982, 2d edit., 1992, Obstetrics: Normal and Problem Pregnancies, 1986, 2d edit., 1991; co-editor: Genetic Diseases in Pregnancy, 1981, Material Serum Screening for Fetal Genetic Disorders, 1992, Essentials of Prenatal Diagnosis, 1993; contbr. numerous articles to profl. jours. and chpts. to books. Maj. U.S. Army, 1973-75. Recipient numerous awards Nat. Insts. Child Health and Devel., March of Dimes, Wyeth-Ayerest pub. recognition award Assn. Profs. Ob-Gyn, 1992. Fellow Am. Coll. Obstetricians and Gynecologists (chmn. genetics subcom. 1981-84); mem. Am. Gynecol. and Obstet. Soc., Am. Fertility Soc. (bd. dirs. 1984-87, pres. 1993-94), Soc. Gynecologic Investigation (mem. coun., Pres.'s Achievement award 1986), Soc. Advancement Contraception (bd. dirs. 1988—, treas. 1992—), Am. Soc. Human Genetics (mem. program com. 1988-91). Office: Baylor Coll of Medicine Dept Ob/Gyn 6650 Fannin St Ste 701 Houston TX 77030-2311*

SIMPSON, JOHN NOEL, health care administrator; b. Durham, N.C., Feb. 27, 1936; s. William Hays and Lucile (McNab) S.; A.B., Duke U., 1957; M.H.A., Med. Coll. Va., 1959; m. Virginia Marshall, June 27, 1959; children: John Noel, William M. Asst. adminstr. Riverside Health Sys., Newport News, Va., 1962-65, assoc. adminstr., 1965-70; assoc. adminstr. Richmond (Va.) Meml. Hosp., 1970-74, sr. v.p., adminstr., 1974-77, exec. v.p., 1977-80, pres., 1980-85; pres. Health Corp. Va., 1985—; preceptor Sch. Health Adminstrn., Duke U. and Med. Coll. Va., Washington U., St. Louis; bd. dirs. Sun Health, Inc./Sun Alliance, 1979-92, vice chmn., 1984, chmn., 1985-87; vice-chmn. Med./Bus. Coalition, 1981-83; participant Leadership Met. Richmond; bd. dirs. Ctrl. Va. Health Sys. Agy., 1980-84, Richmond chpt. ARC, 1980-83; mem. Va. Bd. Med. Assistance, 1980-84; mem. joint subcom. studying Va.'s med. malpractice laws divsn. legal svcs. Gen. Assembly of Comm. of Va., 1984; chmn. Va. Health Network, 1989-91; chmn. Hanover Bus. Coun., 1994-95; mem. Gov.'s Regional Econ. Devel. Adv. Coun., 1994-95. Served with Med. Service Corps, U.S. Army, 1959-62. Fellow Am. Coll. Healthcare Execs. (Council of Regents 1976-82, Edgar C. Hayhow award 1976, bd. govs. 1990-94, regents award sr. exec. level 1995); mem. Am. Hosp. Assn. (chmn. RPBIII 1994—, del. 1989-93, mem. bd. trustees 1994—, Va. Hosp. Assn. (dir. 1974—, chmn.-elect, chmn. 1984-85), Va. Ins. Reciprocal (chmn. 1977-79), Met. Richmond C. of C. (bd. dirs.). Republican. Presbyterian. Home: 9127 Carterham Rd Richmond VA 23229-7752 Office: Health Corp of Va 1300 Westwood Ave Richmond VA 23227-4612

SIMPSON, LISA A., government agency administrator, physician; b. Lagos, Nigeria, Feb. 9, 1958; d. Howard Russell and Mary Alice (Turner) S. MB, B of Surgery, Trinity Coll., Dublin, Ireland, 1981; MPH, U. Hawaii, 1986. Diplomate Am. Bd. Pediat. Resident in pediat. U. Hawaii, Honolulu, 1982-85; resident in preventive medicine U. N.C., Chapel Hill, 1987-88; dir. Maternal and Child Health Bur. State Dept. Health, Honolulu, 1988-90; policy advisor Office of Asst. Sec. for Health HHS, Washington, 1993-94; sr. advisor Agy. for Health Care Policy and Rsch. HHS, Rockville, Md., 1994-95, acting dep. adminstr. Agy. for Health Care Policy and Rsch., 1995-96, dep. adminstr. Agy. for Health Care Policy and Rsch., 1996—; mid-career fellow Inst. Health Policy Studies, San Francisco, 1991-93; adj. faculty dept. health policy and mgmt. Johns Hopkins U., Balt., 1995—. Contbr. articles to profl. jours. Recipient Preventive Medicine traineeship Pub. Health Svc., 1986. Fellow Am. Acad. Pediat.; mem. APHA (governing coun. 1995—), Assn. for Health Svcs. Rsch. Home: 4507 Middleton Ln Bethesda MD 20814 Office: Agy for Health Care Policy and Rsch 2101 E Jefferson Rockville MD 20852

SIMPSON, MADELINE LOUISA, psychologist; b. Norfolk, Va., June 22, 1923; d. David Edward and Zenobia Eleanor (Ross) S. BA, Fisk U., 1944; MS, Boston U., 1951; MA, The New Sch., 1967; PhD, U. Md., 1981; MPA, Va. Commonwealth U., 1985. Psychologist, N.Y. Practitioner Norfolk County Dept. Pub. Welfare, Portsmouth, Va., 1946-51, N.Y.C. Dept. Hosps. and the Hosp. for Joint Diseases, 1951-56; founder, dir. Centre d'Etudes Sociales, Port-au-Prince, Haiti, 1959-61; social work practitioner and supr. Child Welfare Agy., N.Y.C., 1961-68; asst. prof. pscychol. Del. State Coll., Dover, 1969-71; assoc. prof. psychol. Cheyney (Pa.) State Coll., 1972-75, 78; asst. prof. psychol. Longwood Coll., Farmville, Va., 1979-85; assoc prof. St. Paul's Coll., Lawrenceville, Va., 1985-90. Mem. local human rights com. Va. Dept. Mental Health, Mental Retardation and Substance Abuse Svcs., Piedmont Geriatric Hosp., Burkeville, Va., 1983-89, recipient Cert. of Recognition, 1988. Mem. Gold Circle Club of Am. Psychol. Assn., Delta Sigma Theta (life).

SIMPSON, MARY ANN JORDAN, nursing educator; b. Charlotte, N.C., Nov. 10, 1938; d. Ralph Biggers and Sarah Helen (Abee) Jordan; m. Melvyn C. Simpson, Apr. 19, 1964; children: Bryan Todd, Pamela Ann. Diploma, Charlotte Meml. Hosp. Sch. Nursing, 1960; student, Advanced Studies Inst. for Diabetes Edn., 1989; BS in Profl. Arts, St. Joseph's Coll., Windham, Maine, 1990. Cert. diabetes educator, BCLS instr. Am. Heart Assn. Clin. instr. Sch. Nursing Rex Hosp., Raleigh, N.C., 1964-66, in-svc. edn. dept. instr., 1966-70; clin. instr.LPN program Forsyth Tech. Inst., Winston-Salem, N.C., 1971-76; instr. edn. svc. dept. Rex Hosp., Raleigh, N.C., 1976-87, diabetes educator, 1987—. Mem. adv. bd. Diabetes Prevention Project Wake County, 1991-94; bd. dirs. Triangle chpt. Am. Diabetes Assn., 1984-87, N.C. affiliate bd. dirs., 1985-88, 90-95, chair patient edn. com., 1986-91, pres., 1992-93. Recipient Outstanding Diabetes Educator award, 1991, the Great 100-RN Excellence in N.C., 1991. Mem. Am. Assn. Diabetes Educators, Am. Diabetes Assn. (N.C. Affiliate Vol. of Yr. 1994), Rsch. Triangle Assn. Diabetes Educators. Methodist. Home: 6601 Brookhollow Dr Raleigh NC 27615-6610 Office: Rex Hosp 4420 Lake Boone Trl Raleigh NC 27607-7505

SIMPSON, MARY SAUNDERS, physician assistant; b. High Point, N.C., Jan. 19, 1954; d. Stanley Steward and Anne Callaway (Zipplies) Saunders; m. John Wimberley; children: Benjamin, Anne, Richard Thomas. BS, King Coll., 1976, The Med. Coll. Ga., 1978. Physician asst. in ob/gyn Atlanta, 1978-85; physician asst. in intensive care Columbus, Ga., 1985-86; instr. Hughston Sports Medicine Clinic, Columbus, 1986-87; physician asst. in family practice Columbus, 1987—. Mem. Am. Acad. Physician Assts. Home: Rt 1 Box 37 Talbotton GA 31827

SIMPSON, MICHAEL HOMER, dermatologist; b. Hamilton, Tex., Mar. 8, 1938; s. Edgar Randell and Lucille (Patterson) S.; m. Bertha Delia Meraz. BA, N. Tex. U., 1959; MD, U. Tex. S.W. Med. Sch., 1963. Diplomate Am. Bd. Dermatology. Resident in dermatology U. Tex. Med. Br., Galveston, 1966-69; pvt. practice dermatology El Paso, Tex., 1970—. Capt. USAF., 1964-66. Office: 1501 Arizona Ave Ste 1A El Paso TX 79902

SIMPSON, MICHAEL THOMAS, cardiologist; b. Gainesville, Ga., May 4, 1947; s. Fred Baker and Helen Morine (Stringer) S.; m. Dorothy Faye Altman, June 8, 1968; children: Matthew Curtis, Natalie Elaine. AB, Ga. So. Coll., 1969; MD, Med. Coll. Ga., 1974. Cert. Nat. Bd. Med. Examiners, Am. Bd. Internal Medicine, Am. Bd. Internal Medicine-Subspeciality Bd. Cardiovascular Diseases. Intern in medicine U. Ala. Med. Ctr., Birmingham, 1974-75, resident in medicine, 1975-77, fellow in cardiology, 1977-79; pvt. practice in cardiology West Ga. Med. Ctr., LaGrange, 1979-86, Carraway Meth. Med. Ctr., Birmingham, 1986-94, Med. Ctr. East, Birmingham, 1988—; nat. faculty ACLS Am. Heart Assn., Ga., 1982-86; assoc. clin. prof. medicine U. Ala. Med. Ctr., Birmingham, 1985—; preceptor in cardiology Med. Ctr. East Family Practice Program, Birmingham, 1988—. Contbr. articles to profl. jours. Fellow Am. Coll. Cardiology, Coun. on Clin. Cardiology-Am. Heart Assn.; mem. ACP, Rotary Club (LaGrange). Republican. Home: 2668 Altadena Rd Birmingham AL 35243 Office: Ste 215 52 Medical Park East Dr Birmingham AL 35235

SIMPSON, RICHARD KENDALL, JR., surgeon, physician, researcher; b. Atlanta, Sept. 10, 1953; s. Richard Kendall and Juliet Hodges (Rowsey) S.; m. Martha Anne Baucom, Sept. 22, 1984. BA, Coker Coll., 1975; PhD, Med. U. S.C., 1980, MD, 1982; postgrad. Warnborough Coll., Oxford, Eng., 1974. Diplomate Nat. Bd. Med. Examiners, Am. Bd. Neurosurgery. Teaching asst. dept. physiology Med. U. S.C., Charleston, 1976-80, research assoc., 1980-83, intern neurology, 1982-83; resident neurosurgery dept. neurosurgery Baylor Coll. Medicine, Houston, 1983-89, asst. prof., 1989-94, assoc. prof. dept. neurosurgery, anesthesiology and physical medicine and rehab., 1994—; chief neurosurgery sect. VA Med. Ctr., 1991—. Author: Peripheral Nerve Fiber Group and Spinal Corp Pathway Contributions to the Somatosensory Evoked Potential, 1980. Recipient Clin. Neurology Rsch. award, 1983, Mayfield award, 1989, Minora Suzuki award, 1989, Young Alumni award, 1990, William H. Sweet award, 1994; ACS scholar, 1986; ACS Faculty fellow, 1994, Watson fellow Coker Coll., 1974, Baylor Coll. of Medicine Master Tchr. fellowship, 1995. Mem. AMA, Am. Pain Soc., Am. Acad. Clin. Neurophysiology, Am. Acad. Pain Med., Tex. Med. Found., Soc. Neurosci., Houston Neurol. Soc., Sigma Xi, Alpha Omega Alpha. Soc. Episcopalian. Home: 14314 River Forest Dr Houston TX 77079-7417 Office: Baylor Coll Med Dept Neurosurgery 1 Baylor Plz Houston TX 77030-3411

SIMPSON, STEPHEN PHILIP, orthodontist; b. Kokomo, Ind., Aug. 12, 1954; s. Irving Gelet and Margaret Irene (Hammill) S.; m. Gail Marie Towey, Nov. 30, 1985; children: Patrick, Margaret, Timothy, Joseph. BS, U. Notre Dame, South Bend, Ind., 1976; DDS, U. Tenn., 1981; MS, St. Louis U., 1983. Diplomate Am. Bd. Orthodontics. Pvt. practice orthodontist Springfield, Ill., 1983-86, Hudson, Ohio, 1986—; clin. instr. So. Ill. U. Sch. Medicine, Springfield, 1983-86, Case Western Res. U., Cleve., 1988—; cons. Matheny Pub. Health Clinic, Springfield, 1983-86, Akron (Ohio) Children's Hosp., 1987—; mem. courtesy staff Springfield Meml. Hosp., 1984-86; dental chmn. United Way Campaign, Springfield, 1985; cons. County Sch. Health Bd., Ravenna, Ohio, 1987-91, Akron Craniofacial Clinic, 1987—. Swimming instr. Hudson Sch. Vols., 1987-92; co-chief YMCA Indian Guides, Hudson, 1992; mem. parish coun. St. Mary's Ch., Hudson, 1994. Recipient fellowships Honor Soc., Coll. Dentistry, U. Tenn., 1983, Pierre Fauchard Acad., 1993, Internat. Coll. Dentists, 1996. Mem. Ohio Assn. Orthodontists (bd. trustees 1986—), Ohio Dental Assn. (coun. chmn. 1986—), Cleve. Soc. Orthodontists (bd. dirs. 1986—), Cleve. Dental Soc. (coun. chmn. 1986—), St. Mary's Men's Club, Hudson C. of C. (awards banquet chmn. 1986),

Dean-Doggett Honor Soc., Psi Omega. Office: 33 Milford Dr Ste 4 Hudson OH 44236

SIMPSON, TERI RUTH, flight care nurse; b. South Bend, Ind., June 28, 1962; d. Kenneth E. and Joellen A. (Gring) S. AAS, Southwestern Mich. Coll., 1983, ADN, 1985; BSN, Ferris State U., 1989; postgrad., Grand Valley State U. RN, Mich., Ind.; cert. ACLS instr., BCLS instr., pediatric life support, emergency nurse. Nurse's aide, then critical care technician Berrien Gen. Hosp., Berrien Center, Mich., 1985-86; charge nurse ICU/CCU, staff nurse emergency rm. Pawating Hosp., Niles, Mich., 1986-93, staff nurse outpatient pacemaker clinic, 1987-88; charge nurse trauma care unit Bronson Meth. Hosp., Kalamazoo, 1988-91, charge nurse Trauma and Emergency Ctr., 1991—, trauma and emergency nursing course coord., 1994—; staff nurse emergency rm. Three Rivers (Mich.) Hosp., 1990; ACLS instr. Lakeland Regional Health Ctr., Niles, 1988—; BLS instr. Bronson Meth. Hosp., 1989—; on call fixed wing flight nurse West Mich. Air Care, 1995—. Mem. Emergency Nurse Assn., Nat. Flight Nurse Assn. Office: W Mich Air Care 252 E Lovell St 1535 Gull Rd Ste 100 Kalamazoo MI 49001-1628

SIMS, FRED WILLIAM, SR., orthodontist; b. Weatherford, Okla., Feb. 4, 1915; s. Fred E. and Lodine H. (Strong) S.; m. Helen L. Abbe; children: Fred W. Jr., Sandra Jean Sims Reeve. BS, Kans. State U., 1939; DDS, Baylor U., 1955; MS, U. Tenn., 1956. Pvt. practice orthodontics Tulsa, 1956-89; ret., 1989; mem. Found. Orthodontic Research; v.p. Okla. Dental Found. Research and Edn., 1971-72, pres., 1973-74, bd. dirs., 1961—. Served as maj. USAF, 1941-46, ETO. Fellow Internat. Coll. Dentists, Am. Coll. Dentists; mem. ADA (life), Okla. Dental Assn. (life, Okla. Man in Dentistry award 1974), Am. Assn. Orthodontists, Southwestern Soc. Orthodontists (life), Oaks Country Club (Tulsa), Rotary (charter mem. Southside club Tulsa), Masons (32 degrees), Blue Key, Beta Theta Pi, Psi Omega. Republican. Home: 2927 E 75th St Tulsa OK 74136-5642

SIMS, JOHN LEROY, gastroenterology and internal medicine educator, physician; b. Houston, Sept. 21, 1912; s. Frank Jacob and Jennie Elizabeth (Ramsey) S.; m. Anne M. Schurch, May 30, 1942; children: John Ernest, Elizabeth Anne, Thomas LeRoy. AB, Rice U., 1933; MD, U. Tex., Galveston, 1937. Diplomate Am. Bd. Internal Medicine. Intern Wis. Gen. Hosp., Madison, 1937-38, resident in medicine, 1939-42; resident Midway Hosp, St. Paul, 1938-39; mem. faculty Sch. Medicine U. Wis., Madison, 1946—, prof. Sch. Medicine, 1959-83, prof. emeritus, 1983—; coord. outreach continuing med. edn. U. Wis. Med. Sch. and Hosps., 1983—. With AUS, 1942-46, col. ret. USAR. Fellow ACP (gov. Wis. 1963-69); mem. AAAS, AMA, Am. Fedn. Clin. Rsch., Cen. Soc. Clin. Rsch., Cen. Clin. Rsch. Club, Wis. Soc. Internal Medicine (pres. 1959-60), Phi Beta Kappa, Sigma Xi, Alpha Omega Alpha. Presbyterian. Home: 942 S Midvale Blvd Madison WI 53711-2832 Office: U Wis Hosps H6/516 Madison WI 53792

SIMS, KONSTANZE OLEVIA, social worker; b. Dallas, Dec. 20, 1944; d. Kenneth Winn and Odie Lee (Wells) S. Student, U. Dallas, 1963-64; BA, U. Tex., Arlington, 1968; MEd, U. North Tex., 1972. Sec. Stillman Coll. Regional Campaign Fund, Dallas, 1969; employment interviewer Zale Corp., Dallas, 1969-71; sch. counselor Bishop Dunne High Sch, Dallas, 1973-78; dir. guidance Notre Dame High Sch., Wichita Falls, Tex., 1978-81; taxpayer svc. rep. IRS, Dallas, 1981-83, acct. analyst, 1983-88; freelance Dallas, 1989-90; social worker Tex. Dept. Human Svcs., Dallas, 1991-96, Tex. Workforce Commn., 1996—. Reader, North Tex. Taping & Radio for the Blind, Dallas, 1991—; mem. choir St. Peter the Apostle Cath. Ch.; mem. Whale Adoption Project; mem. Union Chorale. Mem. AAUW, Am. Counseling Assn., Nat. Specialty Merchandising Assn., Am. Multicultural Counseling Assn., Am. Bible Tchrs. Assn., Tex. Counseling Assn., Tex. Multicultural Counseling Assn., Assn. Rsch. and Enlightenment, Inc., Assn. for Spiritual, Ethical, and Religious Values in Counseling, U. Tex Arlington Alumni Assn., U. North Tex. Alumni Assn. Office: Tex Workforce Commn 4533 Ross Ave Dallas TX 75204-8417

SIMSON, JO ANNE, anatomy and cell biology educator; b. Chgo., Nov. 19, 1936; d. Kenneth Brown and Helen Marjorie (Pascoe) Valentine; m. Arnold Simson, June 1961 (div.); 1 child, Maria; m. Michael Smith, Nov. 10, 1971 (div.); children: Elizabeth Smith, Briana Smith. BA, Kalamazoo Coll., 1959; MS, U. Mich., 1961; PhD, SUNY, Syracuse, 1969. Postdoctoral fellow Temple U. Health Sci. Ctr., Phila., 1968-70; asst. prof. Med. U. S.C., Charleston, 1970-76, assoc. prof., 1976-83, prof. anatomy and cell biology, 1983—; featured in Smithsonian exhibit, Sci. in Am. Life, 1994—. Contbr. articles to profl. jours.; author short stories and poems. Active adult edn. Unitarian Ch., Charleston, 1973-75, social action, 1990-92. Grantee NSF, 1959-60, NIH, 1966-67, 72-87, 91-95. Mem. Am. Assn. Anatomists, Am. Soc. Cell Biology, Histochem. Soc. (sec. 1979-82, exec. com. 1985-89), Fogarty Internat. Fellowship Bioctr. (Basel, Switzerland, 1987-88), Amnesty Internat. (newsletter editor Group 168 1982-86), Phi Beta Kappa. Home: 1760 Pittsford Cir Charleston SC 29412-4110 Office: Med U SC Anatomy 171 Ashley Ave Charleston SC 29425-0001

SINATRA, THOMAS J., medical center administrator; b. Bklyn., June 21, 1928. BA, Columbia U., 1948; MD, NYU, 1952. Diplomate Am. Bd. Urology, Am. Bd. Quality Assurance and Utilization Rev. Physicians; lic. physician, N.Y., Fla. Intern Kings County Hosp., Bklyn., 1952-53, resident, 1953-56; med. dir. N.Y. Shipping Assn.-Internat. Longshoremen's Assn. Med. Ctr. N.Y., Inc., N.Y.C., 1965—; clin. asst. prof. urology SUNY, Bklyn.; clin. assoc. prof. N.Y. Med. Coll., Valhalla. Mem. bd. profl. med. conduct N.Y. State Dep. Health, 1980—; mem. N.Y. State Hosp. Rev. and Planning Coun., 1990—. Reicpient Cert. of Merit, N.Y. State Senate, 1988; named Man of Yr., Nuova Identita Italo, 1988. Fellow ACS, N.Y. Acad. Medicine; mem. AMA, Am. Urol. Assn., Am. Assn. Clin. Urologists, Assn. Am. Med. Colls., Med. Soc. N.Y., Kings County Med. Soc. (past del. and trustee), N.Y. County Med. Soc. (assoc.), Bay Ridge Med. Soc., Morgagni Med. Soc. (trustee), Pan Am. Med. Assn. (diplomate), Sovereign Mil. Order of malta (master knight). Office: NYSA-ILA Med Ctr NY 600 Ave of The Americas New York NY 10011

SINCLAIR, DUNCAN GORDON, physiology educator, university administrator; b. Rochester, N.Y., Nov. 2, 1933; arrived in Canada, 1937; s. Robert Gordon and Elizabeth Winter Marquick (Broadbridge) S.; m. Leona Mae Payne, 1958; children: Robert Gordon, Colin Edward (dec.). DVM, DVS, U. Toronto, Guelph, Ont., 1958, MS in Agriculture, 1960; PhD, Queens U., 1963. Asst. prof. physiology Queens U., Kingston, Ont., 1966-68, assoc. prof., 1968-72, prof., 1972—, dean arts and sci., 1974-83, vice prin. instl. rels., 1984-86, vice prin. svcs., 1986-88, vice prin. health scis., dean medicine, 1988—; dir. gen. programs Med. Rsch. Coun., Ottawa, Ont., 1983-84; chmn. bd. dirs. Ptnrs. in Tech. Rsch. and Innovation, Kingston, 1986-91. Markle scholar U. Kingston, 1966-71,. Fellow Royal Coll. Physicians & Surgeons Can. (hon.); mem. Can. Physiol. Soc. Anglican.

SINCLAIR, JAMES WALTER, lawyer; b. Twin Falls, Idaho, June 17, 1953; s. James A. and Orriette (Coiner) S.; m. Jeanne L. Williams, Mar. 18, 1983. BA, Stanford U., 1975; JD, U. Idaho, 1978. Bar: Idaho 1978, U.S. Dist. Ct. Idaho 1978. Assoc. Benoit & Alexander, Twin Falls, 1978-81; ptnr. Benoit, Alexander & Sinclair, Twin Falls, 1981-85, Benoit, Alexander, Sinclair, Harwood & High, Twin Falls, 1985—. Pres. Magic Valley Regional Med. Ctr. Found., Inc., Twin Falls, 1987-89; chair ind. affiliates Am. Heart Assn., 1992-93, chair-elect Rocky Mountain com., 1993-94; chmn. profl. com. United Way, 1980, bd. dirs., 1981-83, assoc. campaign chmn., 1982, v.p., campaign chmn., 1983, loaned exec., 1989-90; mem. guidance adv. bd. Twin Falls Sch. Dist., 1989-91, incorporator and legal counsel, 1991, sec., bd. dirs. Ednl. Found., Inc., 1991—; bd. dirs. Magic Valley Regional Med. Ctr. Found., Inc., 1987-90, pres., 1989; mem. profl. adv. com. Coll. So. Idaho Estate Planning Coun., 1991—. Mem. ABA (young lawyers divsn. 1978-83, chmn. membership Idaho young lawyer divsn. 1978-80, arson project com. 1982-83, law & media com. 1982-83), Am. Heart Assn. (bd. dirs. Idaho 1987—, chmn. 1992-93, divsn. pres. 1993—, co-chair divsn. heart ball 1993—, chair North West Rocky Mountain Region heart com. 1994, chair Idaho long range/ strategic planning com. 1994—, bd. dirs. 1996—, nominating issues task force 1996, co-chair structure task force 1996, Meritorious Achievement award 1996), Internat. Assn. Def. Coun., Def. Rsch. Inst., Idaho Bar Assn. (profl. conduct review com. 1982-84, civil rules adv. bd. 1984-88, fee arbitration com. 1996, sec./treas. Ffith Jud. Dist. 1980-81, v.p. Fifth Dist. 1981), Idaho Def. Counsel Assn., Young Family Christian Assn. (bd. dirs. 1981-83, membership com. 1982-83, first v.p. 1983), Stanford Club Idaho (co-pres. 1982-83). Office: Benoit Alexander Sinclair Harwood & High PO Box 366 126 2d Ave N Twin Falls ID 83303-0366*

SINCLAIR, JOHN DAVID, psychologist; b. Bluefield, W.Va., Mar. 28, 1943; s. John Thornton and Carolyn June (Biddle) S.; m. Kirsti Kaarina Laine, May 18, 1973; children: Stephanie, Joanna, Pamela, Annette. BA, U. Cin., 1965, MA, 1967; PhD, U. Oreg., 1972. Teaching asst. U. Cin., 1963-67, rsch. asst., 1964-67; NDEA fellow U. Oreg., Eugene, 1967-70; NSF trainee U. Oreg., 1970-71; coord. psychol. rsch. Alko Group Ltd., Helsinki, Finland, 1972-96; coord. psychol. rsch. dept. alcohol rsch. Nat. Pub. Health Inst., Helsinki, 1996—; docent U. Helsinki, 1994—, lectr., 1978; vis. scientist Ctr. for Advanced Study in Theoreticl Psychology, Edmonton, 1979, U. N.C., Chapel Hill, 1980, Ind. Univ. Sch. Medicine, Indpls., 1988, 90; chmn. bd. ContrAl Clinics, Helsinki, 1996—. Co-author: Analyzing Data, 1970; editor: Animal Models in Alcohol Resarch, 1980; author: The Rest Principle, 1981; patentee extinction treatment with naltrexone and nalmefene for alcoholism; permanent exhibit designer Finnish Sci. Ctr., Vantaa, 1984-92, Løten, Norway, 1994—. Mem. AAAS, Internat. Soc. for Biomed. Rsch. on Alcoholism, Internat. Behavioral Neurosci. Soc., Rsch. Soc. on Alcoholism. Home: Nokkalanniemi 7, FIN-02230 Espoo Finland Office: Nat Pub Health Inst, Dept Alcohol Rsch POBox 719, FIN-00101 Helsinki Finland

SINCLAIR, JOHN STEPHEN, audiologist, educator; b. Pasadena, Calif., Dec. 1, 1947; s. Gilbert Emerson and Clara Mae (Strubinger) S.; m. Joan Michele Mahon, Dec. 29, 1972; children: Betsy, Laura. Andrew. AB, U. Redlands, 1969, MS, 1974; PhD, Vanderbilt U., 1980. Prof. audiology, chair dept. comm. disorders and scis. Calif. State U., Northridge, 1980—; forensic audiologist Associated Specialists in Hearing, Los Angeles, 1983-89; cons. in audiology and hearing conservation St. Joseph's Med. Ctr., Burbank, Calif., 1985-93, Med. Rsch. Consultation Assocs., Tarzana, Calif., 1990—; co-investigator Use of Hearing Aids in Schs., Siemens Corp., 1978, Auditory Trainers in Schs., U.S. Office of Edn., 1979, multi-channel cochlear implant, Humana Hosp.-West Hills, 1985; prin. investigator Auditory Trainers, U.S. Office of Edn., 1979; mem. instnl. rev. com. Humana Hosp.-West Hills, Canoga Park, Calif., 1985—; cons. in hearing conservation Vector Hearing Mgmt., Inc., Newport Beach, Calif., 1982-89; mem. profl. adv. bd. Tripod Sch. for Deaf, Burbank, Calif., 1990—; mem. speech pathology and audiology examining com. Calif. Dept. of Consumer Affairs, 1994—, chair, 1995—. Co-editor: Amplification in Education, 1981; contbr. articles to profl. jours. Served to capt. U.S. Army, 1974-76, lt. col. USAR, 1976—. Recipient Outstanding Faculty award Nat. Ctr. Deafness, 1993. Fellow Am. Acad. Audiology; mem. Am. Nat. Standards Inst. (chmn. working group auditory trainers 1981-87), Am. Speech and Hearing Assn., Am. Auditory Soc., Acoustical Soc. Am., Mil. Audiology Assn., Calif. Speech and Hearing Assn. Republican. Mem. Christian Ch. Club: Magic Castle (Hollywood, Calif.). Office: Calif State U Dept Communicative Dis Northridge CA 91330

SINCLAIR, ROBERT EWALD, physician, educator; b. Columbus, Ohio, Jan. 19, 1924; s. George Albert and Bertha Florence (Ewald) S.; m. Mary Almira Underwood, Mar. 31, 1945; children: Marcia Ann, Bonnie Sue. BA, Ohio State U., 1948, MD, 1952. Licensed physician, Ohio, Colo. Ala., Kans. Intern, Mt. Carmel Hosp., Columbus, 1952-53; resident in neurology and psychiatry Columbus State Hosp., 1964-66, chief psychiatric resident adolescent unit, 1965-66; pvt. practice medicine, Columbus, 1953-57, Granville, Ohio, 1957-64; dir. student health service, prof. health edn., team physician Denison U., 1957-64; dir. student health service, prof. health edn., team physician U. Cin., 1966-70; dir. Lafene Student Health Ctr. and U. Hosp., team physician Kans. State U., Manhattan, 1970-80; dir. Russell Student Health Ctr. and Hosp., and prof. medicine U. Ala., University, 1980-92, ret.; physician Westinghouse Electric Corp., Columbus, 1953-57; asst. zone chief Civilian Def., Columbus, 1954-57; mem. Licking County Bd. Health, Ohio, 1958-59. Bd. dirs. social health com. Cin. and Hamilton County, Ohio, 1967-70, drug abuse and edn. com., 1968-70. Served with USNR, 1943-46. Mem. AMA, Ohio Med. Soc., Kans. Med. Soc., Ala. Med. Soc., Columbus Acad. Medicine, Licking County Med. Soc. (Ohio), Riley County Med. Soc. (Kans.), Tuscaloosa County Med. Soc., Nat. Athletic Trainers Assn., Ohio Coll. Health Assn. (editor Newsletter 1968-70, pres. 1970-71), Central Coll. Health Assn. (pres. 1972-73), So. Coll. Health Assn. (pres. 1986), St. Andrews Soc., Delta Tau Delta (faculty advisor), Nu Sigma Nu, Nu Sigma Nu Alumni Assn. (pres. 1953-54). Lodges: Kiwanis, Rotary. Home: 1 Rollingwood Tuscaloosa AL 35406-2261 Office: U Ala Russell Student Health Ctr Tuscaloosa AL 35487

SINCLAIR, SARA VORIS, health facility administrator, nurse; b. Kansas City, Mo., Apr. 13, 1942; d. Franklin Defenbaugh and Inez Estelle (Figenbaum) Voris; m. James W. Sinclair, June 13, 1964; children: Thomas James, Elizabeth Kathleen, Joan Sara. BSN, UCLA, 1965. RN, Utah; lic. health care facility adminstr.; cert. health care adminstr. Staff nurse UCLA Med. Ctr. Hosp., 1964-65; charge nurse Boulder (Colo.) Meml. Hosp., 1966, Boulder (Colo.) Manor Nursing Home, 1974-75, Four Seasons Nursing Home, Joliet, Ill., 1975-76; dir. nursing Home Health Agy of Olympia Fields, Joliet, Ill., 1977-79; dir. nursing Sunshine Terr. Found., Inc., Logan, Utah, 1980-81, assoc. adminstr., 1980-81, adminstr., 1981-93; dir. divsn. health systems improvement Utah Dept. Health, Salt Lake City, 1993—; mem. long term care profl. and tech. adv. com. Joint Commn. on Accreditation Healthcare Orgns., Chgo., 1987-91, chmn., 1990-91; adj. lectr. Utah State U., 1991-93; mem. adj. clin. faculty Weber State U., Ogden, Utah; moderator radio program Healthwise Sta. KUSU-FM, 1985-93; spkr. Nat. Coun. Aging, 1993, Alzheimer's Disease Assn. Ann. Conf., 1993; del. White House Conf. on Aging, 1995; chmn. Utah Dept. of Health's Ethics, Instnl. Rev. Bd. Com., 1995—, Utah Dept. Health Risk Mgmt. Com., 1995—; exec. com. Utah Long Term Care Coalition, 1995; presenter in field. Contbg. author: Associate Degree Nursing and The Nursing Home, 1988. Mem. dean's adv. coun. Coll. Bus. Utah State U., Logan, 1989-91, mem. presdl. search com., 1991-92; chmn., co-founder Cache Cmty. Health Coun., Logan, 1985; chmn. bd. Hospice of Cache Valley, Logan, 1986; mem. Utah State Adv. Coun. on Aging, 1986-93; apptd. chmn. Utah Health Facilities Com., 1989-91; chmn. Bear River Dist. Adv. Coun. on Aging, 1989-91; chmn health and human svcs. subcom. Cache 2010, 1992-93. Recipient Disting. Svc. award Utah State U., 1989. Fellow Am. Coll. Health Care Adminstrs. (presenter 1992-93, 95, presenter 1996 ann. convocation New Orleans, v.p. Utah chpt. 1992-94, convocation and edn. coms. 1992-93, region IX vice gov. 1994-96); mem. Am. Healthcare Assn. (non-proprietary v.p. 1986-87, region v.p. 1987-89, presenter workshop conv. 1990-93, presenter ann. convocation 1995, exec. com. 1993), Utah Health Care Assn. (pres. 1983-85, treas. 1991-93, Disting. Svc. award 1991), Utah Gerontol. Soc. (bd. dirs. 1992-93, 95—, chmn. nominating com. 1993-94, chmn. ann. conf. 1996, pres.-elect 1996), Cache C. of C. (pres. 1991), Logan Bus. and Profl. Women's Club (pres. 1989, Woman of Achievement award 1982, Woman of Yr. 1982), Rotary (Logan chpt., chair comty. svc. com. 1989-90). Office: Utah Dept Health Div Health Sys Improvement 288 N 1460 W Salt Lake City UT 84114-2851 also: PO Box 142851 Salt Lake City UT 84114-2851

SING, ROBERT FONG, physician; b. Camden, N.J., May 29, 1953; s. William Fong and Elizabeth (Maxwell) S.; m. Lauren McNamee, May 11, 1991. BS in Biology, Ursinus Coll., 1975; DO, Coll. Osteo. Medicine, Surgery, 1978. Intern, then resident Met. Hosp., Phila., 1978-80; dir. Emergency Dept. Springfield (Pa.) Hosp., 1984—; dir. sports medicine Sports Sci. Ctr., 1987—; med. dir. Emergency Ambulance Svcs., Inc., 1994-95; owner J. Enright Jewelers, Inc., Swarthmore, Pa., 1995—; owner, pres. Finish Line Sports, Inc., Phila., 1988-94; owner J. Enright Jewelers, Inc. Swarthmore, Pa.; sch. and team physician Springfield Sch. Dist., 1989, Rose Tree-Media (Pa.) Sch. Dist., 1987; chief med. officer Kent Profl. Bicyling Tour of China, 1995, U.S. Olympic Cycling Trials, 1996. Author Dynamics of the Javelin Throw, 1984. Med. dir. Springfield Ambulance Corp., 1988—. Named to Athletic Hall of Fame, 1985. Fellow Am. Coll. Emergency Physicians, Am. Coll. Sports Medicine, Am. Coll. Osteo. Emergency Physicians. Home: 1274 Gradyville Rd Glen Mills PA 19342-9614 Office: Springfield Hosp 700 S Chester Rd Swarthmore PA 19081

SINGER, JEFFREY ALAN, surgeon; b. Bklyn., Feb. 2, 1952; s. Harold and Hilda (Ginsburg) S.; m. Margaret Sue Gordon, May 23, 1976; children: Deborah Suzanne, Pamela Michelle. BA cum laude, Bklyn. Coll., 1973; MD, N.Y. Med. Coll., 1976. Diplomate Am. Bd. Surgery. Intern Maricopa County Gen. Hosp., Phoenix, 1976-77, resident, 1977-81, mem. teaching faculty, 1981—; trauma cons. John C. Lincoln Hosp., Phoenix, 1981-83; pvt. practice Phoenix, 1981-87; group pvt. practice Valley Surg. Clinics, Ltd., Phoenix, 1987-96, S.W. Surg. Clinics, P.C., Phoenix, 1996—; sec.-treas. med. staff Humana Desert Valley Hosp., Phoenix, 1987-89, chief surgery, 1985-87, 91-93, exec. com., 1993-95. Assoc. editor Ariz. Medicine. Rep. precinct committeeman, Phoenix, 1986—. Fellow ACS, Internat. Coll. Surgeons, Southwestern Surg. Congress, Am. Soc. Abdominal Surgeons; mem. AMA, Ariz. Med. Assn. (bd. dirs. polit. com. 1985, chmn. bd. dirs. polit. com. 1991-93, legis. com. 1986—), Alpha Omega Alpha. Office: Valley Surg Clinics Ltd 16601 N 40th St Ste 105 Phoenix AZ 85032-3353

SINGER, JERRY H., urologist; b. N.Y.C., June 2, 1954; s. Gyula and Sari (Soiffer) S.; m. Lauretta Caryn Harmon, Nov. 28, 1981; children: Jordana, Howard, Gregory. BA, Columbia Coll., 1976; MD, NYU, 1980. Bd. cert. Am. Bd. Urology. Physician Urologic Specialists, Lake Worth, Fla., 1985—; chmn. bd. dirs. Wellington (Fla.) Regional Med. Ctr., 1990—. Contbr. articles to profl. jours. Pulitzer scholar Columbia U., 1972. Fellow Am. Bd. Urology; mem. Am. Urol. Assn., Fla. Med. Soc., Palm Beach County Med. Soc. Office: Urologic Specialists 3230 Lake Worth Rd Lake Worth FL 33461 also: 10131 Forest Hill Blvd Wellington FL 33414

SINGER, LINDIA LEE, family nurse practitioner, health care coordinator; b. Adena, Ohio, July 31, 1939; d. Wilmer Townsend and Alma Agnes (Gow) Hawthorne; m. Rodney Leland Singer, Sept. 1, 1962; 1 child, Rodney Lee. RN, Ruth Brant Sch. Nursing, Martins Ferry, Ohio, 1960; FNP, Ohio State U., 1978; BSN, Ohio U., 1980. RN, Ohio, W.Va.; cert. AFNP, W.Va., Ohio. Oper. rm. staff nurse East Ohio Regional Hosp., Martins Ferry, Ohio, 1960-63, head nurse, 1963-67; RN Harrisville Health Ctr., Adena, Ohio, 1967-70; charge nurse Reynolds Nursing Home, Adena, 1968-70; DON Bellaire, Harrisville & Powhatan Health Ctrs., 1970-77; FNP A FNP Bellaire and Harrisville Health Ctrs., 1977-92; charge nurse Sunset Health Care Inc., Adena, 1991—; FNP A FNP Wheeling (W.Va.) Health Right Inc., 1992—. Office: Wheeling Health Right Inc 88 14th St Wheeling WV 26003

SINGER, MAXINE FRANK, biochemist, think tank executive; b. N.Y.C., Feb. 15, 1931; d. Hyman S. and Henrietta (Perlowitz) Frank; m. Daniel Morris Singer, June 15, 1952; children: Amy Elizabeth, Ellen Ruth, David Byrd, Stephanie Frank. AB, Swarthmore Coll., 1952, DSc (hon.), 1978; PhD, Yale U., 1957; DSc (hon.), Wesleyan U., 1977, Swarthmore Coll., 1978, U. Md.-Baltimore County, 1985, Cedar Crest Coll., 1986, CUNY, 1988, Brandeis U., 1988, Radcliffe Coll., 1990, Williams Coll., 1990, Franklin and Marshall Coll., 1991, George Washington U., 1991, NYU, 1992, Lehigh U., 1992, Dartmouth Coll., 1993, Yale U., 1994, Harvard U., 1994; PhD honoris causa, Weizmann Inst. Sci., 1995. USPHS postdoctoral fellow NIH, Bethesda, Md., 1956-58; rsch. chemist biochemistry NIH, 1958-74; head sect. on nucleic acid enzymology Nat. Cancer Inst., 1974-79; chief Lab. of Biochemistry, Nat. Cancer Inst., 1979-87, rsch. chemist, 1987-88; pres. Carnegie Inst. Washington, 1988—; Regents vis. lectr. U. Calif., Berkeley, 1981; bd. dirs. Johnson & Johnson; mem. sci. coun. Internat. Inst. Genetics and Biophysics, Naples, Italy, 1982-86; mem. adv. bd. Chulabhorn Rsch. Inst., 1990—. Mem. editorial bd. Jour. Biol. Chemistry, 1968-74, Sci. mag., 1972-82; chmn. editorial bd. Procs. of NAS, 1985-88; author (with Paul Berg) 2 books on molecular biology; contbr. articles to scholarly jours. Trustee Wesleyan U., Middletown, Conn., 1972-75, Yale Corp., New Haven, 1975-90; bd. govs. Weizmann Inst. Sci., Rehovot, Israel, 1978—; bd. dirs. Whitehead Inst., 1985-94; chmn. Smithsonian Coun., 1992-93. Recipient award for achievement in biol. scis. Washington Acad. Scis., 1969, award for rsch. in biol. scis. Yale Sci. and Engring. Assn., 1974, Superior Svc. Honor award HEW, 1975, Dirs. award NIH, 1977, Disting. Svc medal HHS, 1983, Presdl. Disting. Exec. Rank award, 1987, U.S. Disting. Exec. Rank award, 1987, Mory's Cup Bd. Govs. Mory's Assn., 1991, Wilbur Lucius Cross Medal for Honor Yale Grad. Sch. Assn., 1991, Nat. Medal Sci. NSF, 1992, Pub. Svc. award NIH Alumni Assn., 1995. Fellow Am. Acad. Arts and Scis.; mem. NAS (coun. 1982-85, com. sci., engring and pub. policy 1989-91), AAAS (Sci. Freedom and Responsibility award 1982), Am. Soc. Biol. Chemists, Am. Soc. Microbiologists, Am. Chem. Soc., Am. Philos. Soc., Inst. Medicine of NAS, Pontifical Acad. of Scis, Human Genome Orgn., N.Y. Acad. Scis. Home: 5410 39th St NW Washington DC 20015-2902 Office: Carnegie Inst Washington 1530 P St NW Washington DC 20005-1910

SINGER, MERRILL CHARLES, health researcher; b. McKeesport, Pa., Oct. 6, 1950; s. Herman and Hannah (Acker) S.; m. Cheryl Gorn, June 1977 (div. 1982); m. Lani Hillis Davison, Dec. 15, 1983; children: Jacob, Elyse. BA, Calif. State U., 1972, MA, 1975; PhD, U. Utah, 1979. Postdoctoral fellow George Washington U., Washington, 1979-80; asst. prof. Am. U., Washington, 1980-82; postdoctoral fellow U. Conn., Hartford, 1982-83; project dir. Hispanic Health Coun., Hartford, 1983-87, dir. rsch., 1988—, dep. dir., 1990—, acting exec. dir., 1993-94; cons., Hartford, 1990—. Author: African American Religion, 1992, Critical Medical Anthropology, 1995; author, editor: New Approached to AIDS Prevention, 1993. Mem. Nat. Assn. Profl. Anthropologists (exec. com., bd. dirs. 1993-95), AIDS and Anthropology Rsch. Group (steering com. 1991-94, Paper prize 1993), Am. Anthropol. Assn., Am. Anthropol. Assn. AIDS Commn., Soc. Med. Anthropology (Rudolph Virchow prize 1991), Soc. Applied Anthropology. Office: Hispanic Health Coun 175 Main St Hartford CT 06106

SINGER, PAUL RICHARD, ophthalmologist; b. N.Y.C., Feb. 1, 1947; m. Katherine W. Singer, June 13, 1970; children: Amy E., Evan P. BA with honors, U. Rochester, N.Y., 1969, MD, 1973. Diplomate Am. Bd. Ophthalmology. Internal medicine intern U. N.C., Chapel Hill, 1973-74, resident in neurology, 1974-75; resident in ophthalmology Washington U. Sch. Medicine, St. Louis, 1975-78, Fight for Sight postdoctoral rsch. fellow dept ophthalmology, 1978-79; pres. Hartford (Conn.) Eye Physicians, 1980—; sr. staff dept. ophthalmology Hartford Hosp., 1980—. Chmn. bd. dirs. Prevent Blindness Conn., Middletown, 1990-92, Combined Health Appeal, Hartford, 1993-95. Recipient Cmty. Svc. award Hartford County Med. Assn., 1993, Robert Polk award for outstanding vol. svc. Prevent Blindness Conn., 1993. Office: Hartford Eye Physicians 100 Retreat Ave Hartford CT 06106

SINGER, SAUL, retired surgeon; b. N.Y.C, June 9, 1937; s. Jack and Renee (LeViloff) S.; m. Susan Green Hauff; children: Sharon Lynn, Sara Jean, Steven Mitchell. BA, Princeton U., 1959; MD, SUNY, Bklyn., 1963. Diplomate Am. Bd. Surgery. Intern Presbyn. Hosp., N.Y.C., 1963-64, resident, 1964-69; surgeon in chief Humana Biscayne Hosp., North Miami, Fla., 1984-85; vice chief surgery Meml. Hosp., Hollywood, Fla., 1985-86, surgeon in chief, 2987—. Mem. schs. com. Princeton U., 1980-87; pres. Jewish Fedn. of South Broward, Hollywood, 1986-87, Am. Friends Hebrew U., Hollywood, 1987; nat. vice chmn. United Jewish Appeal, N.Y.C., 1987. Fellow ACS; mem. Alpha Omega Alpha. Home: 922 S South Lake Dr Hollywood FL 33019-1930

SINGER, STEPHANIE MARIE, obstetrician, gynecologist; b. Bklyn., July 22, 1967; d. Jerome Singer and Florence (Limandri) Brent. DO, N.Y. Coll. Osteopath. Medicine, 1993. Resident ob/gyn L.I. Coll. Hosp., Bklyn., 1993—. Fellow Am. Coll. Obstetrics and Gynecology; mem. AMA, Osteopath. Physicians & Surgeons Calif. Office: Long Island Coll Hosp 340 Henry St Brooklyn NY 11201

SINGH, BHRIGU NATH, physician, surgeon; b. Koirauly Hathwa, Bihar, India, Oct. 28, 1945; s. Kanahi and Muneshwari S.; m. Bhagyawati Singh, Sept. 26, 1971; children: Rajiv Ranjan, Rajani. BSc, D.A.V., Siwan, India, 1964; MBBS, Darbhanga, India, 1969. Family planning doctor Bihar State Health Svcs., India, 1971-72; asst. C.O. DO, India, 1972-74, BMO, 1974-83; surgeon Ministry of Health, Saudi Arabia, 1983—; dir. Ministry of Health, Faidah-Al-Mofas, Saudi Arabia, 1988—. Pres. of Sch., India, 1956. Mem. Am. Med. Soc. in Vienna (life). Home: Khajasarai PO Laheriasarai, Bihar Darbhanga India Office: Ministry of Health, Faidah Al-Mofas, Riyadh 11911 Daloadmi Saudi Arabia

SINGH, MANMOHAN, orthopedic surgeon, educator; b. Patiala, Punjab, India, Oct. 5, 1940; came to U.S., 1969; s. Ajmer and Kartar (Kaur) S.; m. Manjit Anand, Jan. 1, 1974; children: Kirpal, Gurmeet. MB, BS, Govt. Med. Coll., Patiala, 1964; MSurgery, Panjab U., Chandigarh, India, 1968. Diplomate Am. Bd. Orthopaedic Surgery. Rsch. fellow Inst. Internat. Edn.,

Chgo., 1969-74; resident in orthopedic surgery Michael Reese Hosp. and Med. Ctr., Chgo., 1974-78, mem. attending staff, dir. orthopedic rsch., 1979-94; fellow in orthopedic oncology Mayo Clinic and Mayo Found., Rochester, Minn., 1979; assoc. prof. U. Ill., Chgo., 1996—; pvt. practice, Chgo., 1979—; mem. vis. faculty Mayo Grad. Sch., Rochester, 1969. Developer x-ray method (Singh Index) and bone density method (Radius Index) for diagnosis of osteoporosis. Fulbright travel grantee, 1968. Fellow Am. Acad. Orthop. Surgeons, Am. Orthop. Foot and Ankle Soc.; mem. Orthop. Rsch. Soc., Am. Soc. for Bone and Mineral Rsch., Internat. Bone and Mineral Soc. Democrat. Sikh. Office: 443 E 31st St Chicago IL 60616-4051

SINGH, MAYA PRAKASH, medical research scientist, microbiologist; b. Bhagalpur, Bihar, India, Jan. 3, 1954; came to U.S., 1992; s. Indrajit and Manilal Singh; m. Madhulika Singh, Mar. 5, 1984; children: Mila, Manindra, Mridul. BPharm, Birla Inst. Tech., Ranchi, India, 1977; MPharm, Jadavpur U., Calcutta, 1980, PhD, 1983. Asst. prof. Birla Inst. Tech. and Sci., Pilani, India, 1983-84; postdoctoral fellow U. Alta., Edmonton, Can., 1984-86; sr. rsch. scientist SynPhar Labs., Inc., Edmonton, 1987-91, Am. Cyanamid Co., Pearl River, N.Y., 1992-94; sr. rsch. microbiologist Wyeth-Ayerst Rsch., Pearl River, 1995—; mem. Biotech. Adv. Com., Edmonton, 1990-92. Contbr. articles to profl. jours.; patentee in field; med. rschr. Alta. Heritage Found. for Med. Rsch. postdoctoral fellow, 1986; Univ. Grants Commn. India scholar, 1973-80. Mem. Am. Soc. for Microbiology, Indian Pharmacy Grad. Assn. (life), Instn. of Chemists Caluctta (assoc.). Office: Wyeth-Ayerst Rsch 401 N Middletown Rd Pearl River NY 10965

SINGH, NIRBHAY NAND, psychology educator, researcher; b. Suva, Fiji, Jan. 27, 1952; arrived in New Zealand, 1970; s. Shiri Ram and Janki Kumari (Singh) S.; m. Judy Daya, May 17, 1973; children: Ashvind Nand, Subhashi Devi. Ph.D., U. Auckland, New Zealand, 1979. Sr. clin. psychologist, head psychology dept. Mangere Hosp. and Tng. Sch., Auckland, 1976-81; assoc. in clin. psychology U. Auckland, 1977-80; lectr. psychology U. Canterbury, Christchurch, New Zealand, 1981-82, sr. lectr. psychology, 1983-87; sr. rsch. scientist Ednl. Rsch. and Svcs. Ctr., De Kalb, Ill., 1987-89; prof. psychiatry and pediatrics Med. Coll. of Va., Richmond, 1989—; dir. Commonwealth Inst. for Child and Family Studies, Richmond, 1989—; clin. prof. of psychology Va. Commonwealth U., 1994—; cons. Project MESH, U. Otago, Dunedin, New Zealand, 1982-87, external examiner, diploma in edn., 1982-87; cons. Kimberley Hosp. and Tng. Sch., Levin, N.Z., 1984-87; cons. adv. com. tng. officers Dept. Health, Wellington, 1984-87; cons. curriculum adv. com. Vol. Welfare Agy. Tng. Bd., Wellington, 1984-87; cons. spl. edn. adv. com. Christchurch Tchrs.' Coll., 1986-87; expert cons. Dept. Justice, Washington, 1988—. Co-author: I Can Cook. Editor: Mental Retardation in New Zealand: Research and Policy Issues, 1983; Mental Retardation in New Zealand: Provisions, Services and Research, 1985; Exceptional Children in New Zealand, 1987, Psychopharmacology of the Developmental Disabilities, 1988, Perspective on the Use of Non-aversive and Aversive Interventions for Persons With Developmental Disabilities, 1990, The Regular Education Initiative, 1991, Learning Disabilities: Nature Theory and Treatment, 1992, Self-Injury: Analysis, Assessment and Treatment, 1992; editor-in-chief Jour. of Behavioral Edn., Jour. of Child and Family Studies, SED Quar.; contbr. chpts. to books; editorial bd. numerous jours. Winifred Gimblett scholar 1974; Med. Rsch. Coun. postgrad. scholar, 1975-76; Erskine fellow U. Canterbury, 1984. Fellow APA, APS, Behavior Therapy and Research Soc.; mem. Am. Assn. Mental Deficiency, Assn. Severely Handicapped, Assn. Child Psychology and Psychiatry, Assn. Advancement Behavior Therapy, Soc. Advancement Behavior Analysis, Psychonomic Soc., N.Y. Acad. Scis. Avocations: squash, racquetball. Office: Med Coll Va Dept Psychiatry PO Box 980489 Richmond VA 23298-0489

SINGH, SANT PARKASH, endocrinologist, educator, physician, researcher; b. Anokhsinghwala, Punjab, India, Oct. 2, 1936; came to U.S., 1961; s. Jarnail and Harbans (Kaur) S.; m. Satinder Kaur, Apr. 20, 1968; 1 child, Kiran. MB, BS, Punjab U., 1959; MS in Exptl. Medicine, McGill U., Montreal, Que., 1973. Diplomate Am. Bd. Internal Medicine, Am. Bd. Endocrinology Metabolism, Am. Bd. Nuclear Medicine. Intern in medicine Bergen Pines County Hosp., Paramus, N.Y., 1961-63, resident in medicine, 1964-65; fellow in endocrinology Phila. Gen. Hosp., 1963-64, SUNY Downstate Med. Ctr., Bklyn., 1965-66, McGill U., 1966-70; assoc. and chief endocrinology and metabolism depts. Bklyn.-Cumberland Med. Ctr., Bklyn., 1971-73; assoc. chief of staff VA Med. Ctr., North Chicago, Ill., 1973—; chief endocrinology and metabolism, prof. medicine and physiology Chgo. Med. Sch., North Chicago, 1974—. Contbr. over 150 articles to profl. jours. Med. Rsch. Coun. of Can. fellow, 1968-70; grantee U.S. Vets. Affairs Dept., Nat. Inst. on Alcoholism. Fellow ACP; mem. Am. Diabetes Assn., Am. Fedn. Clin. Rsch., Endocrine Soc., Rsch. Soc. of Alcoholism, Alpha Omega Alpha. Home: 111 N Ridge Rd Lake Forest IL 60045-2049 Office: Chgo Med Sch 3333 Green Bay Rd North Chicago IL 60064-3037

SINGH, UPINDER, medical researcher. BS in Biochemistry cum laude, Ohio State U., 1987, MD summa cum laude, 1992. Diplomate Am. Bd. Internal Medicine. Internal medicine resident Health Scis. Ctr. U. Va., Charlottesville, 1992-95, infectious diseases fellow, 1995—. Contbr. articles to profl. jours. Post Sophomore Pathology fellow Ohio State U., 1989-90; Roessler Found. fellow, 1990, Summer Rsch. Opportunities fellow, 1986, Nat. Found. Infectious Diseases fellow, 1996; Glenna joyce scholar Ohio State U., 1983-87. Mem. ACP (Clinical Vignette award Nat. sect. 1994, Clin. Vignette award Regional sect. 1995), Alpha Omega Alpha. Office: U Va Health Scis Ctr Charlottesville VA 22903*

SINGHAL, PRAVIN C., nephrologist, educator; b. Jewar, India, June 20, 1947; arrived in U.S., 1981; s. Mahesh C. Singhal and Shanti Govil; married. MD, PBM Medical Coll., Bikoner, India, 1968. Diplomate Am. Bd. Internal Medicine. Chief, nephrology Long Island Jewish Medical Ctr., New Hyde Park, N.Y., 1994—. Fellow Am. Coll. Physicians. Home: 410 Old Courthouse Rd New Hyde Park NY 11040 Office: Nephrology Divsn Long Island Jewish Med Ctr New Hyde Park NY 11040

SINGHVI, SAMPAT MANAKCHAND, pharmaceutical scientist; b. Jodhpur, India, Oct. 14, 1947; came to U.S., 1968; s. Manakchand R. and Jethi (Balai) S.; m. Usha Lalchand Mutha, July 17, 1971; children: Nikhil, Nilima. B Pharm, Birla Inst. Tech. and Sci., Pilani, India, 1967; MS, Phila. Coll. Pharmacy, 1970; PhD, SUNY, Buffalo, 1974; MBA, Rider Coll., 1979. Rsch. investigator E.R. Squibb & Sons, Princeton, N.J., 1974-78, sr. rsch. investigator, 1978-79, rsch. group leader, 1979-88, sr. rsch. group leader, 1988; assoc. dir. Bristol-Myers Squibb Co., Princeton, 1988-94; dir. Bristol-Myers Squibb Co., Princeton, 1995—. Contbr. articles, abstracts and book chpts. to profl. publs. Mem. Am. Soc. Pharmacology and Exptl. Therapeutics, Am. Assn. Pharm. Scientists, Am. Pharm. Assn., Drug Info. Assn., Regulatory Affairs Profl. Soc., Rho Chi. Office: Bristol Myers Squibb Co PO Box 4000 Princeton NJ 08543-4000

SINGLETON, ALBERT OLIN, III, physician; b. Galesburg, Ill., Feb. 16, 1946; s. Albert Olin Jr. and Eliz Joan (Anderson) S.; m. Ann Terrell, Mar. 30, 1975; children: Terrell Albert Olin IV, Caroline, Sidney Elizabeth. BA in English, U. Tex., 1969; MD, U. Tex., Galveston, 1973. bd. cert. Gen. Psychiatry, 1981, Geriatric Psychiatry, 1994. Gen. psychiatry intern, resident U. Tex. Med. Branch, 1973-76, child and adolescent psychiatry fellow, 1976-78; instr. U. Tex. Med. Br., Galveston, 1978—, Colo. Health Sci. Ctr., Denver, 1993—; pres. Titus Harris Clinic, Galveston, 1982-93; asst. chief psychiatry, asst. chief med. staff Colo. Mental Health Inst., Pueblo, 1994-95, chief med. staff, chief psychiatry, 1995—, med. dir., 1996—, dir. med. student edn., 1996—; bd. dirs. Gulf Health Network, Galveston, 1991-93. Chmn. bd. Ctr. for Transp. and Commerce, Galveston, 1990-92; S.W. region dir. AAPRCO, Washington, 1992—. Mem. Galveston County Med. Soc. (pres. 1993). Episcopalian. Office: 2989 Broadmoor Valley Rd Colorado Springs CO 80906-4467

SINGLETON, JOHN WEIR, gastroenterology educator, consultant; b. Denver, May 29, 1931; s. John Henry and Isabelle Douglas (Weir) S.; m. Louise Randolph Robinson, Oct. 3, 1959; children: John Robinson, Martha Weir Pennell, David Randolph, William Reynolds. BA, Yale U., 1953; MD, Harvard U., 1957. Cert. in internal medicine & gastroenterology. Intern medicine Mass. Gen. Hosp., Boston, 1957-58, resident medicine, 1958-59, 61-62; clin. assoc. NIH, NIAMDD, Bethesda, Md., 1959-61; fellow gastroenterology Health Sci. Ctr. U. Colo., Denver, 1962-65, asst. clin. prof., 1965-68, asst. prof. medicine, 1968-74, assoc. prof. medicine, 1974-83, prof., 1983—; mem. rsch. tng. awards com. CCFA, N.Y.C., 1984-90; mem. subspecialty bd. Gastroenterology Am. Bd. Internal Medicine; bd. dirs. Rocky Mountain chpt. Crohn's & Colitis Found. Am. Mem. editl. bd. Inflamatory Bowel Diseases, 1995—; contbr. articles to profl. jours. Bd. dirs. Vis. Nurse Assn., Denver, 1980-82, Kent-Denver Country Day Sch., Denver, 1980-86. With USPHS, 1969-71. Fellow ACP; mem. Am. Gastroent. Assn., Inflammatory Bowel Disease Forum (pres. 1981-84, 88-93). Democrat. Presbyterian. Office: B-158 4200 E 9th Ave Denver CO 80262

SINKFORD, JEANNE CRAIG, dentist, educator; b. Washington, Jan. 30, 1933; d. Richard E. and Geneva (Jefferson) Craig; m. Stanley M. Sinkford, Dec. 8, 1951; children: Dianne Sylvia, Janet Lynn, Stanley M. III. BS, Howard U., 1953, MS, 1962, DDS, 1958, PhD, 1963; DSc (hon.), Georgetown U., 1978; DSc (Hon.), U. Med. and Dentistry of N.J., 1992. Instr. prosthodontics Sch. Dentistry Howard U., Washington, 1958-60, mem. faculty dentistry, 1964—, rsch. coord., co-chmn. dept. restorative dentistry, assoc. dean, 1968-75, dean, 1975-91, prof. Prosthodontics Grad. Sch., 1977-91; dean emeritus, prof. Sch. Dentistry Howard U.; spl. asst. Am. Assn. Dental Schs., 1991-93, dir. office women and minority affairs, 1993—; instr. rsch. and crown and bridge Northwestern U. Sch. Dentistry, 1963-64; cons. prosthodontics and rsch. VA Hosp., Washington, 1965—; resident Children's Hosp. Nat. Med. Ctr., 1974-75; cons. St. Elizabeth's Hosp.; mem. attending staff Freedman's Hosp., Washington, 1964—; adv. bd. D.C. Gen. Hosp., 1975—; mem. Nat. Adv. Dental Rsch. Coun., Nat. Bd. Dental Examiners; mem. ad hoc adv. panel Tuskegee Syphilis Study for HEW; sponsor D.C. Pub. Health Apprentice Program; mem. adv. coun. to dir. NIH; adv. com. NIH/NIDR/NIA Aging Rsch. Coun.; mem. dental devices classification panel FDA; mem. select panel for promotion child health, 1979-80; mem. spl. med. adv. group VA; bd. overseers U. Pa. Dental Sch., Boston U. Dental Sch.; bd. advs. U. Pitts. Dental Sch.; mem. anat. rev. bd. for D.C. NRC Gov. Bd.; cons. Food and Drug Adminstrn.; Nat. Adv. Rsch. Coun., 1993—; active Nat. Rsch. Coun. Governing Bd. Mem. editorial rev. bd. Jour. Am. Coll. Dentists, 1988—. Adv. bd. United Negro Coll. Fund, Robert Wood Johnson Health Policy Fellowships; mem. Mayor's Block Grant Adv. Com., 1982; mem. parents' coun. Sidwell Friends, 1983; mem. adv. bd. D.C., mem. Women's Health Task Force, NIH; bd. dirs. Girl Scouts U.S.A., 1993—. Louise C. Ball fellow grad. tng., 1960-63. Fellow Am. Coll. Dentists (sec.-treas. Wash. met. sect.), Internat. Coll. Dentists (award of merit); mem. ADA (chmn. appeal bd. coun. on dental edn. 1975-82), Am. Soc. for Geriatric Dentistry (bd. dirs.), Internat. Assn. Dental Research, Dist. Dental Soc., Am. Inst. Oral Biology, North Portal Civic League, Inst. Grad. Dentists (trustee), So. Conf. Dental Deans (chmn.), Wash. Coun. Adminstrv. Women, Assn. Am. Women Dentists, Am. Pedodontic Soc., Am. Prosthodontic Soc., Fed. Prosthodontic Orgn., Nat. Dental Assn., Inst. Medicine (coun.), Am. Soc. Dentistry for Children, N.Y. Acad. Scis., Smithsonian Assocs., Dean's Coun., Proctor and Gamble, Golden Key Honor Soc., Links Inc., Sigma Xi (pres.), Phi Beta Kappa, Omicron Kappa Upsilon, Psi Chi, Beta Kappa Chi. Address: 1765 Verbena St NW Washington DC 20012-1048

SINKMAN, ARTHUR M., psychiatrist, educator; b. Bklyn., Feb. 24, 1946. AB, Columbia U., 1966; MD, U. Pitts., 1970. Diplomate Am. Bd. Psychiatry and Neurology. Intern Maimonides Hosp., Bklyn., 1970-71; resident Kings County Hosp.-Downstate Med. Ctr., SUNY, Bklyn., 1971-74, clin. instr., 1974-84, asst. prof., 1984-93; clin. assoc. prof. SUNY, Bklyn., 1993—; psychiatrist Phelps Meml. Hosp., North Tarrytown, N.Y., 1984-88; dir. group therapy St. Luke's Hosp., N.Y.C., 1986-88; asst. prof. Columbia U. Med. Ctr., N.Y.C., 1987—; chmn. psychiatry svc. Bklyn. VA Hosp., Bklyn., 1988—. Contbr. articles to profl. jours. Mem. Am. Psychiat. Assn. Office: 295 Central Park W New York NY 10024-3008

SINKO, PATRICK J., pharmacist, educator; b. Passaic, N.J., Jan. 7, 1959; s. Patrick and Patricia (Anderson) S.; m. Noreen Marie Seccia, Apr. 29, 1989; children: Patrick, Kathryn. BS in Pharmacy, Rutgers U., 1982; PhD in Pharmaceutics, U. Mich., 1988. Rsch. scientist U. Mich./TSRL, Inc., Ann Arbor, 1988-91; asst. prof. pharmaceutics Rutgers U., Piscataway, N.J., 1991—. Contbr. articles to profl. publs. Grantee NIH, 1992, Unigene Labs., Inc., 1992, Assn. Insts. Material Scis., 1994; recipient Young Investigator award Eli Lilly and Co., 1992, AAPS, 1993, Innovative Rsch. award Hoechst-Celanese, 1995; named Outstanding Tchr. of Yr., Rutgers Coll. Parent Assn., 1994. Mem. Am. Assn. Pharm. Scis. (elected sec.-treas. pharmaceutics and drug delivery sect. 1995), N.Y. Acad. Sci., Nat. Eagle Scout Assn., Sigma Xi. Office: Rutgers U Coll Pharmacy PO Box 789 Piscataway NJ 08855

SINKOVICS, JOSEPH GEZA, physician, virologist, oncologist; b. Budapest, Hungary, June 17, 1924; came to U.S., 1956; s. Joseph Sinkovics and Maria Rajnocha; divorced; children: Geza S., Eszter S. Matriculation, Zrinyi Miklos Gymnasium, Budapest, 1934-42; MD, Peter Pazmany U., Budapest, 1942-48. Intern, then resident Cook County Hosp., Chgo., 1958-61; chief sect. clin. tumor virology & immunology, melanoma sarcoma svc. MD Anderson Hosp., Houston, 1964-79; prof. medicine U. Tex. Anderson Hosp., Houston, 1972-79; vis. prof. virology/epidemiology Baylor Coll. Medicine, Houston, 1979-89; prof. medicine/med. microbiology U. South Fla. Coll. Medicine, Tampa, 1983—; med. dir. Cancer Inst. St. Joseph's Hosp., Tampa, 1983-96, dir., 1996—; pvt. practice Tampa; adj. prof. microbiology Inst. Microbiology Peter Pazmany U. Eotvos L. U., Budapest, 1948-50; virologist State Inst. Pub. Health, 1954-56; cons. prof. oncology M.D. Anderson Cancer Ctr., Houston, 1979—. Author: Die Grundlagen der Virus-Forschung, 1956, Medical Oncology, 1979, 86; co-author: The Immunology of Malignant Disease, 1972, 76; contbr. articles to profl. jours. Rockefeller fellow Inst. Microbiology Rutgers, New Brunswick, N.J., 1957; Am. Cancer Soc. fellow MD Anderson Hosp., Houston, 1959; recipient Rsch. Career award NCI/NIH MD Anderson Hosp., Houston, 1962-68, Wadsworth award Rush-Presbyn. U. Med. Sch., Chgo., 1978, Semmelweis award Georgetown U. Jefferson Hosp., Washington, 1978, Grace Faillace award Goodwin Inst. Cancer Rsch., Ft. Lauderdale, Fla., 1980, Original Rsch. award So. Med. Assn., 1992. Mem. Hungarian Soc. Microbiology (hon.), Hungarian Scientific Acad. Office: St Joseph's Hosp Cancer Inst 3001 W Dr ML King Blvd Tampa FL 33677-4227 also: 4600 N Habana Ave Tampa FL 33614-7123

SINNETT, PETER FRANK, geriatrician, educator; b. Sydney, Australia, Dec. 16, 1934; s. Sydney Thomas and Minty (Pottinger) S. MB, BChir, U. Sydney, 1960, D of Medicine, 1973. Resident med. officer Sydney Hosp., 1960-62, cardiology fellow, 1964, clin. rsch. registrar, 1965; tng. fellow U. Sydney, 1962-64; Nat. Heart Found. rsch. fellow Australian Nat. U./U. Papua New Guinea, 1965-71; coun. mem., prof. rep. U. Papua New Guinea, 1971-73, found. prof. human biology, 1971-76, mem. working party on future of univ., 1973, mem. acad. planning and rsch. coms.; found. prof. geriatrics U. NSW, Woden, Australia, 1979-94; emeritus prof. geriatrics, 1994—; clin. dir. rehab. and aged care svc. Woden Valley Hosp., Canberra; cons. to auditor-gen. on med. adminstrv. aspects of nursing home programs, 1980; chmn. bd. censors, mem. coun. Australian Coll. Rehab., 1980-82; mem. Consultative Com. on Social Welfare, 1980-81; dir. rehab. and aged care svc. Australian Capital Ter. Authority, 1984—; vis. fellow Australian Nat. U., 1987—; coun. mem. Papua New Guinea Inst. for Med. Rsch., 1973-75; chair of sci. and rsch. com. Continence Found. of Australia, 1993. Author: The People of Murapin, 1978; contbr. articles to profl. publs. Mem. med. rsch. adv. com., mem. food and nutrition adv. com. Govt. of Papua New Guinea, 1974-75. Fellow Royal Australian Coll. Physicians, Royal Australian Coll. Rehab. Medicine; mem. Am. Acad. Phys. Medicine and Rehab., Australian Epidemiol. Assn. (mem. found. 1987).

SINNI-MCKEEHEN, BARBARA JANE, nurse; b. Bklyn., Aug. 22, 1943; d. Francis Xavier and Jane Leverich (VanSchaick) Keller; m. Eugene Francis Farabaugh, Apr. 21, 1965 (div. 1972); 1 son, Robert Matthew Farabaugh; m. Paul John Sinni, Dec. 15, 1973 (div. 1991); 1 dau., Kristina Joy; m. Michael Robert McKeehen, Feb. 14, 1993. B.S.N., Syracuse U., 1964; cert. Nursing Edn., SUNY-Stony Brook, 1968; M.S.N., Hunter Coll., CUNY, 1979. R.N., N.Y., Fla.; advanced registered nurse practitioner, Fla. Asst. head nurse outpatient clinics East Orange (N.J.) Gen. Hosp., 1965; charge nurse medicine and surgery Clara Maas Gen. Hosp., Belleville, N.J., 1966; instr. nursing L.A. Wilson Tech. Inst., Lindenhurst, N.Y., 1966-68; sch. nurse, tchr. West Babylon (N.Y.) Sch. Dist., 1968-71; clin. instr. med.-surg. nursing Southampton Hosp., Riverhead, N.Y., 1971; nurse unit adminstr. psychiatry Northport VA Med. Ctr. (N.Y.), 1971-72, community health nurse satellite clinics, 1973, clin. inservice coordinator, nurse, 1973-74, instr. phys. assessment, 1971-79, clin. preceptor, 1971-79, cons. to assoc. chief of staff/dean clin. campus SUNY, 1974-78; nurse practitioner Brookhaven Meml. Hosp., East Patchogue, N.Y., 1976-77; dir. nursing services Patchogue Nursing Ctr., 1979-80; assoc. dir. nursing services Bayonet Point-Hudson Regional Med. Ctr., Hudson, Fla., 1981; instr. Pasco-Hernando Community Coll., New Port Richey, Fla., 1981-83; nurse practitioner, clin. research coordinator, Med. Service VA Med. Ctr., Bay Pines, Fla., 1983-90, nurse practitioner substance abuse treatment program, 1990-92, dermatology nurse practitioner, 1993—; adj. prof. C.W. Post U., Greenvale, N.Y., 1973-76; adj. mem. faculty St. Petersburg (Fla.) Jr. Coll., 1995—; clin. instr. divsn. dermatology & cutaneous surgery U. So. Fla. Coll. of Medicine, Tampa, 1995—; cons. Community Hosp., New Port Richey, Fla. Contbr. articles to profl. jours.; contbr. chpt. to Guide to Patient Evaluation. Vol. Am. Cancer Soc., L.I. div.; pres. Bellport Beach Property Owners Assn., 1977-80. Served to lt. Nurse Corps, U.S. Army, 1963-65. Scholar, Syracuse U., Hunter Coll. Mem. Fla. Nurses Assn., Am. Fedn. Bus. and Profl. Women, Mensa, Delta Gamma, Sigma Theta Tau. Republican. Roman Catholic. Lodge: Ladies of Elks.

SINNING, MARK ALAN, thoracic and vascular surgeon; b. Holton, Kans., Apr. 24, 1953; s. Henry Harold andf Valere Madelene (Davey) S.; m. Kathy Diann Pugh, Sept. 25, 1982; children: Sarah, Emily, Mark, Rachel, Walter. BA, U. Kans., 1975; MD, U. Kans., Kansas City, 1978. Diplomate Am. Bd. Surgery, Am. Bd. Thoracic Surgery. Gen. surgery resident St. Luke's Hosp., Kansas City, Mo., 1978-83, thoracic surgery resident, 1983-85; pvt. practice Coastal Surg. Specialists, PA, New Bern, N.C., 1986—; attending staff Danbury (Conn.) Hosp., 1985-86, Craven Regional Med. Ctr., New Bern, 1986—; asst. clin. prof. East Carolina U., Greenville, 1992—. Fellow ACS, Am. Coll. Chest Physicians; mem. AMA, Soc. Thoracic Surgeons, So. Assn. Thoracic Surgery, N.C. Med. Soc., Phi Beta Kappa, Alpha Omega Alpha. Office: Coastal Surgical Specialists 800 Hospital Dr New Bern NC 28560

SINTON, CHRISTOPHER MICHAEL, neurophysiologist, educator; b. Beckenham, Kent, Eng., Sept. 10, 1946; came to U.S., 1983; s. Leslie George and Evelyn Mabel (Burn) S. BA, Cambridge U., Eng., 1968, MA, 1977; BSc, London U., 1978; PhD, U. Lyon, France, 1981. Rsch. fellow U. Lyon, 1980-83; rsch. assoc. Princeton (N.J.) U., 1983-84; sr. scientist Ciba-Geigy Corp., Summit, N.J., 1984-88; dir. electrophysiology Neurogen Corp., Branford, Conn., 1988-94; asst. prof. U. Tex. Southwestern Med. Ctr., Dallas, 1994—; rsch. asst. prof. medicine NYU, N.y.C., 1986-94. Contbr. 40 articles to profl. jours. Med. Rsch. Coun. vis. scholar, France, 1983. Mem. N.Y. Acad. Scis., Soc. Neurosci., European Neurosci. Assn., European Sleep Rsch. Soc., Sleep Rsch. Soc. Office: U Tex SW Med Ctr Dept Psychiatry 5323 Harry Hines Blvd Dallas TX 75235-9070

SIOMA, JAMES E., osteopath; b. Cheltenham, Pa., Feb. 26, 1956; s. Edward Michael and Phyllis Eileen (Perry) S.; m. Nancy Bell Hopkins, Jan. 21, 1989; children: John Hopkins, David Bell. BS, Eastern Coll., 1978; MS, Drexel U., 1980; DO, Phila. Coll. Osteo. Medicine, 1985. Diplomate Am. Osteo. Bd. Family Physicians. Pvt. practice Mt. Joy, Pa., 1987-91; physician East Pa. Family Practice, Allentown, 1991-93, Meml. Health Svcs., York, Pa., 1993—; chmn. infectious disease com. Cmty. Hosp. Lancaster, Pa., 1987-91, Meml. Health Sys., York. Contbr. articles to profl. jours. Named Outstanding Young Man Am., 1985-86. Mem. Am. Osteopathic Assn., Pa. Osteopathic Med. Assn., York County Osteopathic Med. Assn., Christian Med. Soc. Office: Meml Health Sys 3198 E Market St York PA 17402

SIPES, IVAN GLENN, toxicologist; b. Tarentum, Pa., July 26, 1942; s. Ivan I. and Marjorie (Yough) S. BS, U. Cin., 1965; PhD, U. Pitts., 1969. Registered pharmacist. Staff fellow Nat. Heart Lung and Blood Inst. div. NIH, Bethesda, Md., 1969-71, sr. staff fellow, 1971-73; asst. prof. coll. of medicine U. Ariz., Tucson, 1973-78, assoc. prof. coll. of pharmacy, 1978-82, prof., head dept. pharmacology and toxicology (pharmacy), 1982—, head dept. pharmacology (medicine), 1993—. Burroughs-Wellcome toxicology scholar, 1985-90. Fellow AAAS; mem. NAS (com. on toxicology 1988-90), NAS/NRC (bd. on environ. scis. and toxicology 1988—), NIH (chair toxicology study sect. 1988—), Am. Assn. Study Liver Disease, Am. Assn. Cancer Rsch., Soc. Toxicology (sec.-councilor 1985-89, editor Toxicology and Applied Pharmacology 1986—, pres. 1993), Internat. Soc. for Study Xenobiotics (charter, councilor). Home: 2713 E Prince Rd Tucson AZ 85716-1161 Office: U Ariz Dept Pharmacol/Toxicology PO Box 210207 Toxicology Tucson AZ 85721-0207

SIPICZKI, MATTHIAS, geneticist; b. Bekescsaba, Hungary, Oct. 31, 1948; s. Matthias and Dorota (Lepeny) S.; m. Esther Sos, July 24, 1970; children: Bojana, Martin Csaba. MSc, U. Szeged, Hungary, 1973, PhD, 1976. Asst. prof. U. Szeged, 1976-82, assoc. prof., 1982-84; prof. U. Debrecen, Hungary, 1984—; head dept. genetics U. Debrecen, 1984—, dir. Inst. of Biology, 1993—. Contbr. over 100 articles to profl. jours. Chmn. Associated Slovaks in Hungary, Budapest, 1988-92. 1st Lt. armoured corps. Hungary Armed Forces Res., 1967-68. Mem. German Soc. Biology, Chech and Slovak Soc. Microbiology, Hungarian Sco. for Microbiology, Genetics, Biochemistry and Biology, Acta Biologica Hungarica (editorial bd.). Lutheran. Office: Univ Debrecen Dept Genetics, PO Box 56, H-4010 Debrecen Hungary

SIPINEN, SEPPO ANTERO, obstetrician, gynecologist; b. Helsinki, Finland, Aug. 11, 1946; s. Uno Emil Rafael and Martta Liisa (Knuuttila) S.; m. Taru Katriina, Oct. 19, 1968; children: Samuel, Susanne. MD, U. Freiburg, Fed. Republic Germany, 1971, U. Helsinki, 1972; cert. specialist ob.-gyn., U. Helsinki, 1979, D in Med. Sci., 1981, specialist in diving medicine, 1994; completed Nat. Defense Course, 1994. Cert. diving medicine and hyperbaric oxygen treatment specialist. Resident in Ob-Gyn. and Surgery U. Helsinki, State Maternity Hosp., Helsinki, 1973-80; sr. physician Ob-Gyn. State Maternity Hosp., Helsinki, 1981-83; commd. comdr. Finnish Navy Med. Corps., 1990; surgeon gen. Finnish Navy Med. Corps., Helsinki, 1983—; head. naval dept. Rsch. Inst. Mil. Medicine, Helsinki, 1983—; cons. ob-gyn. Finnish Def. Forces, 1983—, Subway in Helsinki, 1976-77; rsch. group Dept. Med. Chemistry, U. Helsinki, 1977-86; lectr. diving and hyperbaric physiology and medicine, 1977-82; cons. devel. group State Dept. Finland, 1984-86; head diving and hyperbaric med. treatment of State Salv. Edn. Inst., Finland, 1985-86; cons. devel. group of Profl. Diving Nat. Bd. Labor Protection, Finland, 1989-90, Compressed Air Work of Subway, 1976-77; mem., rep. for Finland European Diving Tech. Com., 1986—; mem. sci. bd. Diving Alert Network Europe, 1991; mem. European Commn. Hyperbaric Medicine, 1991—; cons. Ministry Social Affairs and Health, Nat. Rsch. and Devel. Ctr. for Welfare and Health in Finland, 1994—; pres. Ist ann. meeting European Underwater and Baromic Soc., Helsinki, 1995. Contbr. over 90 articles in endocrinoly, bacteriology, serology, diving and hyperbaric medicine to profl. jours. Recipient medal for Mil. Merits, 1988; decorated Knight 1st class, Order of White Rose of Finland, 1995. Mem. AAAS, Finnish Soc. Ob-Gyn., European Underwater and Baromed. Soc. (at-large exec. com., pres. XXIst ann. meeting, Helsinki 1995), Finnish Med. Assn., Finnish Soc. Perinatal Medicine, Finnish Soc. Diving and Hyperbaric Medicine (pres. 1977—), Undersea and Hyperbaric Med. Soc., Finnish Sport Divers Fedn. (safety com. 1976-79, pres. 1977-79, exec. bd. 1977-79, med. com. pres. 1980, Silver medal 1988, Diver of Yr. 1989), Espoo Gymnastics Team (v.p.), Finnish Gymnastics Fedn. (v.p. 1993, Silver medal 1993). Office: Finnish Naval Hdqrs, Pohjoiskaari 36, FIN00201 Helsinki Finland

SIPPO, ARTHUR CARMINE, occupational medicine physician; b. Jan. 30, 1953; s. Carmine Constantine and Mildred Angela (Musto) S.; m. Katherine Velma Sager, Jan. 87, 1987; children: Sean, Tiffany, Courtney. BS in Chemistry magna cum laude, St. Peter's Coll., Jersey City, 1974; MD, Vanderbilt U., 1978; MPH, Johns Hopkins U., 1983. Diplomate Am. Bd. Preventive Medicine. Commd. 2d lt. U.S. Army, 1978, advanced through grades to lt. col., 1992; intern in ob-gyn. Walter Reed Army Med. Ctr., 1978-79; 1st brigade surgeon 101st Airborne Div., Ft. Campbell, Ky., 1979-81; resident in aerospace medicine USAF Sch. Aerospace Medicine, Brooks AFB, Tex., 1981-83; dir. biodynamics rsch. div. U.S. Army Aeromed. Rsch. Lab., Ft. Rucker, Ala., 1983-86; exch. officer RAF Inst. Aviation Medicine, Farnborough, Hants., Eng., 1986-90; ret., 1990; occupational medicine physicians Occupational Care Cons., Holland, Ohio, 1990-92; comdr. 145th M.A.S.H., Camp Perry, Ohio, 1992-94; dep. comdr. for clin. svcs. 112th

Med. Brigade Ohio Army Nat. Guard, Columbus, 1994-95; asst. state surgeon Ohio Army N.G., Columbus, 1995—; med. dir. Libbey Glass, Inc., Toledo, 1990—, Clyde (Ohio) divsn. Whirlpool Corp., 1990—; mem. aerospace cons. adv. panel U.S. Army Surgeon Gen.'s Office. Author: Arthropometic Considerations of the U.S. Army, 1988. Mem. Ohio N.G., 1990—. Master Am. Coll. Occup. and Environ. Medicine; fellow Am. Coll. Preventive Medicine, Aerospace Med. Assn.; mem. Soc. U.S. Army Flight Surgeons, Am. Coll. Emergency Physicians, Fellowship Cath. Scholars. Roman Catholic. Office: Occupational Care Cons 6855 Spring Valley Dr Ste 160 Holland OH 43528-9374

SIRICA, ALPHONSE EUGENE, pathology educator; b. Waterbury, Conn., Jan. 16, 1944; s. Alphonse Eugene and Elena Virginia (Mascolo) S.; m. Annette Marie Murray, June 9, 1984; children: Gabrielle Theresa, Nicholas Steven. MS, Fordham U., 1968; PhD in Biomed. Sci., U. Conn., 1977. Asst. prof. U. Wis., Madison, 1979-84; assoc. prof. Med. Coll. Va., Va. Commonwealth U., Richmond, 1984-90, prof. of pathology, 1990—, divsn. chair exptl. pathology, 1992—; regular mem. sci. adv. com. on carcinogenesis and nutrition Am. Cancer Soc., Atlanta, 1989-92, metabolic pathology study sect., NIH, Bethesda, 1991-95. Editor, author: The Pathobiology of Neoplasia, 1989, The Role of Cell Types in Hepatocarcinogenesis, 1992, Cellular and Molecular Pathogenesis, 1996; co-editor, author: Biliary and Pancreatic Ductal Epithelia: Pathobiology and Pathophysiology, 1996; mem. editl. bd. Pathobiology, 1990—, Hepatology, 1991-94; rev. bd. In Vitro Cellular and Devel. Biology, 1987—; contbr. rsch. papers to Am. Jour. Pathology, Cancer Rsch., others. Mem. AAAS, Am. Soc. Cell Biology, Am. Assn. Cancer Rsch. (chmn. Va. state legis. com. 1992-95), Soc. for In Vitro Biology, Assn.Clin. Scientist, Am. Soc. Investigative Pathology (chair program com. 1994-96), Am. Assn. Study Liver Diseases, N.Y. Acad. Scis., Soc. Exptl. Biology and Medicine, Hans Popper Hepatopathology Soc., Soc. Toxicology. Democrat. Roman Catholic. Office: Med Coll Va Va Commonwealth U PO Box 980297 Richmond VA 23298-0297

SIRIPOONYA, PRAPUTT, neonatologist, educator; b. Bangkok, Thailand, Jan. 1, 1938; s. Ruthai and Ngo S.; M.D., U. Med. Scis., Bangkok, 1962; m. Sunisa Chompumivet, Apr. 25, 1969; children—Christ, Pavena, Vasinee. Asst. instr. pediatrics SUNY, Bklyn., 1965-66; asst. in pediatrics Jefferson Med. Coll., Phila., 1966-68; assoc. prof. pediatrics Ramathibodi Hosp., Mahidol U., Bangkok, 1968-82, prof. pediatrics, 1983—. Diplomate Am. Bd. Pediatrics. Fellow Am. Acad. Pediatrics; mem. Thai Med. Assn., Thai Pediatrics Soc., Neonatal Soc. Thailand (sec.). Author: Baby and Child Care (1st class award Thai Social Service Acad. 1980), 1970; editor: Advances in Pediatrics, 1979; Newborn Manual, 1979; Neonatology, 1982; contbr. articles to periodicals, newspapers. Office: Ramathibodi Hosp, Rama VI Rd, Bangkok Thailand

SIRKEN, DAVID H., neurologist; b. Phila., May 22, 1961. BA, Rutgers Coll., 1983; DO, N.Y. Coll. Osteo. Medicine, 1987. Diplomate Am. Bd. Psychiatry and Neurology. Intern Methodist Hosp. of Bklyn., N.Y., 1987-88; resident in internal medicine Mercy Catholic Med. Ctr., Darby, Pa., 1988-89; resident in neurology Med. Coll. Pa., Phila., 1989-92, fellow in clin. neurophysiology, 1992-93; neurologist Neurocare Diagnostics, Inc., Huntingdon Valley, Pa., 1993—. Mem. Am. Acad. Neurology. Office: Neurocare Diagnostics, Inc 727 Welsh Rd Ste 202 Huntingdon Valley PA 19006

SIRKEN, MONROE GILBERT, statistician; b. N.Y.C., Jan. 11, 1921; s. Irving and Henrietta (Oram) S.; m. Blanche Skalak Horvitz (div. 1960); children: Robert, Philip. BA, UCLA, 1946, MA, 1947; PhD, U. Wash., 1950. Lectr. Med. Sch. U. Wash., Seattle, 1949; fellow Stats. Lab. U. Calif., Berkeley, 1950; statistician Census Bur., Suitland, Md., 1951-54, Pub. Health Svc., Washington, 1954-60, Nat. Ctr. Health Stats., Hyattsville, Md., 1961—; cons. NIH, 1980-85, Nat. Inst. Drug Addiction, 1976-80, NSF, 1986—, Health Care Fin. Adminstrn., 1989-90. Contbr. articles to Jour. Am. Statis. Assn., Biometrics, Demography, Jour. APHA, Pub. Health Reports, also others. Home: 3309 Claridge Ct Silver Spring MD 20902-2201

SIROTY, ROBERT RAYMOND, internist; b. Bklyn., Aug. 1, 1935; s. Irving Benjamin and Rose (Domash) S.; m. Margo Marilyn Arens, June 21, 1959; children: David Mark, Beth Michelle, Hedy Gayle. AB, Columbia U., 1956; MD, SUNY, Syracuse, 1960. Diplomate Am. Bd. Internal Medicine. Intern internal medicine Kings County Hosp. Ctr., Bklyn., 1960-61, resident, 1961-62; sr. asst. surgeon USPHS Hosp., Balt., 1962-63; surgeon, chief outpatient svcs. USPHS Svc. Hosp., Balt., 1963-64; resident internal medicine Montefiore Hosp. & Med. Ctr., Bronx, N.Y., 1964-65, resident hematology, 1965-66; pvt. practice Dover, N.J., 1966—. Trustee Dover (N.J.) Gen. Hosp. and Med. Ctr., 1973-74, North Jersey Blood Ctr., East Orange, 1976-79, Hospice of Morris County, Morristown, N.J., 1984-94, N.W. Covenant Med. Ctr., 1994—; mem. Bd. Health, Randolph Twp., N.J., 1989—. Lt. comdr. USPHS, 1962-64. Fellow Internat. Soc. Hematology; mem. Am. Soc. Hematology. Office: 375 E McFarlan St Dover NJ 07801

SISCO, RALPH O., health services management executive; b. Pineville, La., Nov. 19, 1948; s. Elbert J. and Florene Ila (Turner) Sands; m. Evelyn Elaine Kees, June 27, 1970; children: Claire Nicole, Kirk David. BA, La. Coll., Pineville, 1970; MEd, Northwestern State U., Natchitoches, La., 1973. Cert. nursing facility adminstr. Tchr. Rapides Parish Schs., Alexandria, La., 1970-76; adminstr. Dept. Corrections, State of La., Ball, 1976-82; pres. Rapides Mgmt. Corp., Alexandria, 1982—; cons. Grant Manor Nursing Home, Colfax, La., 1979; mgr., bd. dirs. Gerricare Inc. Nursing Homes, Joneville, Ferriday, La., 1986-89. Mem. La. Nursing Home Assn., Alexandria C. of C., Rotary. Democrat. Baptist. Office: Rapides Mgmt Corp 4310 Heyman Ln Alexandria LA 71303

SISKIND, GREGORY WILLIAM, medical educator, academic administrator; b. N.Y.C., Mar. 3, 1934; s. Jesse and Zenaida (Drabkin) S. BA, Cornell U., 1955; MD, NYU, 1959. Intern in medicine 3d med. divsn. Bellevue Hosp./NYU Sch. of Medicine, 1959-60, asst. resident in medicine 3d med. divsn., 1960-61; rsch. fellow dept. microbiology Sch. of Medicine Washington U., 1961-62; rsch. fellow in biology Harvard U., 1962-64; rsch. fellow dept. medicine Sch. of Medicine, NYU, 1964-65, instr., 1965-66, asst. prof., 1966-68; asst. attending physician Bellevue Hosp., 1964-68; assoc. prof. Med. Coll., Cornell U., N.Y.C., 1969-76, head divsn. allergy and immunology dept. medicine, prof., 1970-93, assoc. dean rsch. and sponsored programs, 1983-84, 85—; attending physician dept. of medicine N.Y. Hosp., 1976—; mem. AIDS rsch. rev. com. NIH, Bethesda, Md., 1989-91. Editor: Immune Depression and Cancer, 1975, Clinical Evaluation of Immune Function in Man, 1976, Immune Effector Mechanisms in Disease, 1977, Developmental Immunobiology, 1979; editor, chief Proceedings of Soc. Exptl. Biology and Medicine, 1989—; contbr. numerous articles to profl. jours. Fellow Am. Acad. Allergy; mem. Am. Assn. Immunologists, Am. Soc. Clin. Investigation, N.Y. Allergy Soc. (pres. 1979). Office: Cornell U Med Coll 1300 York Ave New York NY 10021-4805

SISSON, GEORGE MAYNARD, scientific services administrator; b. Boston, Feb. 3, 1922; s. David and Bessie Sisson; m. Frances Ann Sisson, June 29, 1952 (div. Sept. 1968); children: Barbara Carol, Brenda Harriet, Richard Lewis. BS, Tufts Coll., 1947; PhD, U. Rochester, 1952. Jr. scientist Brookhaven Nat. Lab., Upton, N.Y., 1952; vis. fellow Columbia U. Coll. Phys. and Surg., N.Y.C., 1952-54; group leader Lederle Labs., Pearl Rvr, N.Y., Stamford, Conn., 1954-59; asst. dir. pharmacology U.S. Vitamin and Pharm. Corp., Yonkers, N.Y., 1959-61; dir. pharm. product info. Mead Johnson Rsch. Ctr., Evansville, Ind., 1961-66; dir. sci. and regulatory affairs Mead Johnson & Co., Evansville, 1966-77, dir. dept. regulatory affairs, 1979—; cons. Adria Labs., Dublin, Ohio, 1988-91. Co-author: Pharmacological and Biochemical Profiles of Drug Substances, 1979; contbr. articles to profl. jours. Lt. (j.g.) USNR, 1942-47, PTO. Mem. AAAS.

SITA, MICHAEL JOHN, pharmacist, educator; b. St. Louis, Apr. 28, 1953; s. Julianne Gail Sita; children: Michael John, Paul Thomas, Julianne Joyce. BS, St. Louis Coll. Pharmacy, 1976; MBA, So. Ill. U., 1983. Registered pharmacist, Mo., Ill. Staff pharmacist Luth. Med. Ctr., St. Louis, 1976-78, asst. chief pharmacist, 1978-81, adminstrv. coord. pharmacy svcs., 1981-85; dir. pharmacy svcs. Jefferson Meml. Hosp., 1985—; instr. St. Louis Coll. Health Careers, 1983-86; adj. instr. pharmacy practice St. Louis Coll. Pharmacy, 1980—; relief pharmacist Dolgins Apothecary, St. Louis, 1976-86, Best Pharmacy, 1986-88, Carraige Drugs, 1989-93, Medicine Shoppe, Festus, Mo., 1990—. Author/editor Pharmacy Capsule quar., 1977-85. Mem. St. Louis Soc. Hosp. Pharmacists (treas. 1985-87, pres. 1988-89, sec. 1990-92, Pharmacist of Yr. 1994-95), Mo. Soc. Hosp. Pharmacists, Am. Soc. Hosp. Pharmacists, Am. Pharm. Assn., Hosp. Assn. Met. St. Louis (chmn. pharmacy tech. adv. com. 1985-86). Avocations: carpentry, rehabbing. Home: 111 Ward Ter Crystal City MO 63019-1707 Office: PO Box 350 Crystal City MO 63019-0350

SIVAK, ANDREW, toxicologist; b. New Brunswick, N.J., May 31, 1931; s. Andrew and Isabelle (Paragh) S.; children: Thomas, Gustav; m. Joyce L. Spears, 1995. BS, Rutgers U., 1952, MS, 1957, PhD, 1960. Rsch. scientist Arthur D. Little Inc., Cambridge, Mass., 1961-63, v.p., 1975-89; v.p. BioDynamics, East Millstone, N.J., 1963-64; assoc. prof. NYU Med. Ctr., N.Y.C., 1964-74; pres. Health Effects Inst., Cambridge, 1989-92, exec. dir. asbestos rsch., 1990-92. Editor: Mechanisms of Tumor Promotion, 1978; contbr. over 150 articles to profl. jours. State of N.J. scholar, 1948-52; USPHS postdoctoral fellow, 1960-61. Fellow Am. Coll. Toxicology; mem. AAAS, Am. Assn. Cancer Rsch., Environ. Mutagen Soc., Soc. for Risk Analysis, Soc. of Toxicology. Office: PO Box 2128 Saint Augustine FL 32085-2128

SIVASUBRAMANIAN, KOLINJAVADI NAGARAJAN, neonatologist, educator; b. Coimbatore, Madras, India, May 9, 1945; came to U.S., 1971; s. Kolinjavadi Ramaswamy and Sukanthi (Subramanian) Nagarajan; m. Kalyani Hariharier, Feb. 5, 1975; children: Ramya, Rajeev, Ranjan. BSc, Madras U., 1964, MD, 1969. Diplomate Am. Bd. Pediatrics and Neonatal-Perinatal Medicine. Intern in pediatrics Jewish Hosp. and Med. Ctr., Bklyn., 1971-72; resident in pediatrics U. Md. Hosp., Balt., 1972-74; fellow in neonatology Georgetown U. Hosp., Washington, 1974-76, attending neonatologist, 1976—, dir. nurseries, chief neonatology, 1981—, vice chair pediatrics, 1988—, prof. pediatrics and ob-gyn. Editor: Trace Elements/Mineral Metablolism During Development, 1993; editor pub. SIDS Series, 1985; editor jour. Current Concepts in Neonatology, India, 1990—; internat. editor Indian Jour. Pediatrics, India, 1988—. Chmn. Siva Vishnu Temple, Lanham, Md., 1981-91; mem. Fetus and New Born com., Washington, 1988; founder, bd. dirs. Coun. of Hindu Temples U.S.A.; founder, coord. United Hindu Temples of Met. Washington; 1st v.p. Interfaith Conf., Washington. Recipient "Preemies" cover article Newsweek, 1988. Fellow Am. Coll. Nutrition, Am. Acad. Pediatrics; mem. AAAS, N.Y. Acad. Sci., Internat. Soc. for Trace Element Rsch. in Humans, Soc. for Bioethics Consultation, Am. Soc. Law, Medicine and Ethics. Hindu. Office: Georgetown U Hosp 3 South Hospital 3800 Reservoir Rd NW Washington DC 20007-2196

SIZEMORE, CAROLYN LEE, nuclear medicine technologist; b. Indpls., July 22, 1945; d. Alonzo Chester and Elsie Louise Marie (Osterman) Armstrong; m. Jessie S. Sizemore Sr., June 9, 1966; 1 child, Jessie S. Jr. AA in Nuclear Medicine, Prince George's Community Coll, Largo, Md., 1981; BA in Bus. Adminstrn., Trinity Coll., 1988. Registered technologist (nuclear medicine); cert. nuclear medicine technologist, Md.; lic. nuclear med. technologist. Nuclear med. technologist Washington Hosp. Ctr., 1981-88; chief technologist, mem. com. Capitol Hill Hosp., Washington, 1988-91; chief technologist, asst. radiation safety officer Nat. Hosp. Med. Ctr., Arlington, Va., 1991—; mem. Am. Registry of Radiologic Technologists Nuclear Medicine Exam. Com., 1990-93. Contbr. articles to profl. jours. Mem. com. Medlantic Rsch. Found., Washington, 1989-93; sec. Crestview Area Citizens Assn., 1994-95. Mem. Va. Soc. Radiol. Technologists, Potomac Dist. Soc. Radiol. Technologists, Med. Soc. Radiol. Technologists, Med. Soc. Nuclear Medicine Technologists, Soc. Nuclear Medicine (chmn. membership 1983-85, sec. 1985-87, 88-89, co-editor Isotopics 1991, editor Isotopics 1992-96, nominating com. 1995-96), Nuclear Medicine Adv. Bd., Am. Legion Aux. (exec. com. 1975-76), Internat. Platform Assn., Crestview Area Citizens Assn. (sec. 1994-95). Republican. Lutheran. Home: 6700 Danford Dr Clinton MD 20735-4019

SIZEMORE, JOYCE LYNN BAILEY, parent education specialist; b. Phila., Apr. 24, 1957; d. James J. Sr. and Joan Marie (Weaver) Bailey; m. R. Scott Sizemore; children: Elizabeth Lynn, Natalie Marie, Audrey Lorraine. Diploma, Germantown Hosp. Sch. Nursing, Phila., 1980; BSN, LaSalle U., 1984; MS, Tex. Women's U., 1987. Cert. chem. dependency nurse. Staff nurse Germantown Hosp. and Med. Ctr., Phila., 1980-84; with dept. head obstetrics Burdette Tomlin Meml. Hosp., Cape May Court House, N.J., 1985-89; nurse educator, risk reduction specialist So. N.J. Perinatal Coop., Camden, N.J., 1989-90; rsch. nurse Pharmacology Rsch. Inst., Irvine, Calif., 1991-92, parent edn. specialist, 1993—; clin. instr. Collin County C.C., McKinney, Tex., 1996. Mem. NAACOG, Nat. League for Nursing, Nat. Consortium Chem. Dependency Nurses, ASPO, Lamaze.

SIZEMORE, ROBERT CARLEN, immunologist, educator; b. Lexington, Ky., Sept. 30, 1951; s. Dewey and Juanita (Peel) S.; m. Katherine Killelea, Sept. 29, 1990; children: Katherine Peel, Robert Carlen Jr. BS, U. Ky., 1973, MS, 1975; PhD, U. Louisville, 1982. Postdoctoral rsch. assoc. U. Miss. Med. Ctr., Jackson, 1982-84; dir. immunology IMREG. Inc., New Orleans, 1984-94; adj. asst. prof. Tulane U. Sch. Medicine, New Orleans, 1985-94, asst. prof., 1994—. Patentee in field; contbr. articles and poems to profl. jours. Recipient Project award U. Louisville, 1978, Grad. Dean's Citation U. Louisville, 1983; named Outstanding Young Men of Am., 1984. Mem. Am. Assn. Immunologists, Internat. AIDS Soc., Am. Soc. Tropical Medicine & Hygiene, Internat. Soc. Devel. & Comparative Immunology, Fedn. Am. Scientists, AAAS. Home: 4401 Copernicus St New Orleans LA 70131-3615

SIZONENKO, PIERRE CLAUDE, pediatric endocrinology educator; b. Paris, Apr. 19, 1932; s. Vladimir and Sarah Lea (Prigogine) S.; m. Marie-Thérèse Magnin, Apr. 30, 1960; children: Ivan, Stephane, Alexandre. Med. diplomate, Sch. Medicine, Paris, 1957; BSc, Sch. Scis., Paris, 1964; MD, Sch. Medicine, Paris, 1965; MSc, Sch. Scis., Paris, 1970. Diplomate Bd. Pediatrics, Bd. Pediatric Endocrinology. Intern Paris U. Hosp., 1957-59, resident, 1961-65, fellow, 1965-67; fellow dept. pediatrics U. Calif., San Francisco, 1967-68; sr. rsch. fellow Paris U. Hosp., 1968-69; rsch. assoc. Geneva Med. Sch., 1969-72, asst. prof., 1972-79, assoc. prof., 1979-82, prof. pediatrics, 1982—; head Div. Biology Growth and Reproduction, Geneva, 1982—; cons. WHO, Geneva, 1975—. Editor, co-author: Pediatric Endocrinology, 1993, Control of the Onset of Puberty II, 1990, Developmental Endocrinology, 1994. 1st lt. French Air Force, 1959-61. Recipient Bernard Dreyfuss prize Acad. Medicine, Paris, 1965, Nessim Habif World prize U. Geneva, 1981. Mem. Endocrine Soc. USA, Swiss Endocrine Soc. (pres. 1983-85), Swiss Assn. Diabetology (coun. mem. 1984-90), European Soc. for Pediatric Endocrinology (treas. 1977-83, pres. 1980-81, Andrea Prader prize 1995), European Soc. for Pediatric Rsch., Lawson Wilkins Pediatric Endocrine Soc. (corr.). Russian Orthodox. Home: 17 rue Toepffer, 1206 Geneva Switzerland Office: Hopital des Enfants HCUG, 6 Rue Willy Donze, 1211 Geneva 14, Switzerland

SJÖBERG, LENNART, psychology educator; b. Stockholm, Sweden, Mar. 23, 1939; s. Hans and Signe (Carlsson) S.; m. Britt Marie Drottz, June 24, 1988. BA, U. Stockholm, 1959, PhD, 1965. Lic. psychologist. Asst. prof. U. Stockholm, 1965-66; acting prof. U. Lund, Sweden, 1966, U. Uppsala, Sweden, 1967-68; vis. assoc. prof. U. Calif., Berkeley, 1968-69; prof. U. Göteborg, Sweden, 1970-88, Stockholm Sch. Econs., 1988—; head dept. econ. psychol., 1992—; mem. Swedish Social Sci. Rsch. Coun., 1983-88; head Ctr. for Risk Rsch., Stockholm, 1988—. Author: Decision Making, 1978; contbr. articles to profl. jours. Fellow Soc. Risk Analysis; mem. Royal Swedish Acad. Engring. Scis., N.Y. Acad. Scis. Home: Odengatan 50, 11351 Stockholm Sweden Office: Stockholm Sch Econs, Box 6501, 11383 Stockholm Sweden

SJOGREN, ROBERT WILLIAM, internist; b. Ft. Collins, Colo., Aug. 4, 1919; s. John William and Flora Anne (Anderson) S.; m. Amenta Margaret Robeson, June 18, 1942; children: Robert Jr., Jane Durbin Fitch, Margaret Leigh. BS in Biology, Va. Poly. U., 1940; MD, U. Va., 1943. Diplomate Am. Bd. Internal Medicine. Home: HC 73 Box 856B Locust Grove VA 22508-9572

SKADELAND, DEAN RAY, neuropsychologist, minister; b. Bismarck, N.D., June 4, 1957; s. Donald G. and Harolyn (Kimball) S.; m. Linda Johnson, Aug. 19, 1978; 1 child, Glori Lyn. BA, U. Nebr., 1979; MA, Abilene (Tex.) Christian U., 1984; D in Clin. Psychology, Fla. Inst. Tech., 1987. Lic. psychologist; lic. minister. Clin. adminstr., psychologist N.E. Kans. Mental Health Ctr., Leavenworth, 1987-88; clin. dir., minister Tiffany Counseling Ctr., Kansas City, Mo., 1987—; dir. neuropsychology clinic VA Med. Ctr., Kansas City, 1988—; adj. asst. prof. psychiatry Kans. U. Med. Ctr., Kansas City, 1990—, U. Mo., Kansas City, 1991—, U. Kans., Lawrence, 1992. Mem. APA, Internat. Neuropsychol. Soc., Nat. Acad. Neuropsychology, Soc. for Personality Assessment, Soc. for Pentecostal Studies. Republican. Office: Tiffany Fellowship 7315 NW Barry Rd Kansas City MO 64153-1723

SKAFF, KAREN O., dental hygiene educator; b. Rochester, Pa., Mar. 22, 1948; d. Robert Eugene and Margaret (Nitsche) Onuska; m. David M. Skaff, May 29, 1972; children: Erin, Brandon, Megan, Katrin, Stefan. Dental hygiene cert., U. Pitts., 1968; BS in Edn., Calif. (Pa.) U., 1970; MS, Columbia U., 1971; PhD in Edn. Policy Studies, U. Ky., 1995. Lic. dental hygienist, Ky., Va., Pa. Instr. dental hygiene W.Va. U. Sch. Dentistry, Morgantown, 1971-72; instr. dept. arts and scis. Old Dominion U., Norfolk, Va., 1972-74, Loyola of New Orleans, 1974-76; assoc. prof. dept. heatlh svcs. U. Ky., Lexington, 1977—. Contbr. articles to profl. jours. Mem. Am. Assn. Dental Schs., Am. Dental Hygienists Assn., Am. Assn. for Higher Edn., Assn. for Practical and Profl. Ethics. Eastern Orthodox Christian. Home: 118 Paddock Dr Nicholasville KY 40356 Office: Univ Ky Med Ctr Lexington KY 40536

SKALKA, HAROLD WALTER, ophthalmologist, educator; b. N.Y.C., Aug. 22, 1941; s. Jack and Sylvia Skalka; m. Barbara Jean Herbert, Oct. 2, 1965; children: Jennifer, Gretchen, Kirsten. AB with distinction, Cornell U., 1962; MD, NYU, 1966. Intern Greenwich (Conn.) Hosp., 1966-67; resident in ophthalmology Bellevue Hosp., Univ. Hosp., Manhattan VA Hosp., 1967-70; fellow in retinal physiology and ultrasonography, 1970-71; cons. in ophthalmology St. Jude's Hosp., Montgomery, Ala., 1971-73; asst. prof. ophthalmology U. Ala., Birmingham, 1973-75, assoc. prof., 1975-80, prof., 1980-81, assoc. prof. dept. medicine, 1980—, chmn. combined program in ophthalmology, 1981—, Nathan E. Miles prof., 1986—; acting chmn. combined program ophthalmology U. Ala., 1974-76; ophthalmologist Lowndes County Bd. Health Community Health Project, 1972. Contbr. articles to Am. Jour. Ophthalmology, Eye, Ear, Nose and Throat Monthly, Annals of Ophthalmology, Ophthalmic Surgery, Jour. Clin. Ultrasound, Jour. Pediatric Ophthalmology and Strabismus, The Lancet, AMA Archives of Ophthalmology, Jour. So. Med. Assn., Acta Ophthalmologica, Metabolic and Pediatric Ophthalmology, Applied Radiology, British Jour. Ophthalmology, Blood, Neuro-Ophthalmology; editorial bd.: Ala. Jour. Med. Sci. Major USAFMC, 1971-73. Mem. AAAS, AMA, ACS, SIDUO, Ala. Sight Conservation Assn., Ala. Conservancy, Ala. Wildlife Fedn., Eye Bank Bd., Am. Acad. Ophthalmology, Am. Inst. Ultrasound in Medicine, Internat. Soc. for Clin. Electrophysiology of Vision, Internat. Soc. on Metabolic Eye Disease, Assn. for Rsch. in Vision and Ophthalmology, AAUP, Am. Intraocular Implant Soc., Am. Assn. Ophthalmology, Pan Am. Assn. Ophthalmology, So. Med. Assn., Rsch. to Prevent Blindness, Ala. Acad. Ophthalmology, Ala. Med. Assn., Jefferson County Med. Soc., Contact Lens Assn. Ophthalmologists, Ala. Ultrasound Soc., Royal Soc. Medicine, N.Y. Acad. Scis., Am. Soc. Standardized Ophthalmic Echography (charter exec. bd. mem.), Am. Coll. Nutrition. Office: Eye Found Hosp U Ala 700 18th St S Ste 300 Birmingham AL 35233-1856

SKARDA, RICHARD JOSEPH, clinical social worker; b. Santa Monica, Calif., Jan. 2, 1952; s. Robert Ralph and Cathryn Marie (Tourek) S. AA, Los Angeles Valley Coll., Van Nuys, Calif., 1976; BA, U. Calif., Berkeley, 1978; MSW, UCLA, 1980. Lic. clin. social worker, Calif.; Diplomate Am. Bd. Clin. Social Workers. Children's svcs. worker L.A. County Dept. Children's Svcs., Panorama City, Calif., 1980-82; police svc. rep. L.A. Police Dept., 1982; psychiatric social worker Penny Lane, Sepulveda, Calif., 1983; children's services worker Ventura (Calif.) County Pub. Social Svcs. Agy., 1983-85; head social work dept. Naval Med. Clinic, Port Hueneme, Calif., 1985-94; pvt. practice, 1996—. Mem. dean's coun. UCLA Sch. Social Welfare. With USN, 1970-74. Fellow Calif. Soc. Clin. Social Work; mem. Nat. Assn. Social Workers (diplomate), Acad. Cert. Social Workers.

SKARF, BARRY, neuro-ophthalmologist, vision researcher; b. Montreal, Quebec, Can., Mar. 22, 1947; came to U.S., 1987; s. Nathan and Jean S.; m. Barbara Sheila Kerkofsky, Mar. 7, 1971; children: Lara, Shayna, Joshua, Alissa. BSc, McGill U., Montreal, Can., 1968; MD, CM, McGill U., 1977; MA, Johns Hopkins U., 1971, PhD, 1973. Diplomate Am. Bd. Ophthalmology. Asst. prof. U. Toronto, Ontario, Can., 1983-87; staff ophthalmologist Hosp. for Sick Children, Toronto, 1983-88, Henry Ford Hosp., Detroit, 1987—; assoc. clin. prof. U. Mich., Ann Arbor, 1988-94. Fellow N. Am. Neuro-Ophthalmology Soc., Am. Acad. Ophthalmology; mem. AMA, Assn. for Rsch. in Vision and Ophthalmology. Office: Henry Ford Hosp 2799 W Grand Blvd Detroit MI 48202

SKARPATHIOTIS, GEORGE IOANNOU, pediatrician; b. Istanbul, Turkey, Dec. 11, 1949; came to U.S., 1981; s. Yianni Demos and Anna S. Maroulakis, June 4, 1980; children: Yianni, Stratos, Andreas. MD, U. Athens, Greece, 1976. Diplomate Am. Bd. Pediatrics. Resident surgery Gen. Hosp. Piraeus, Greece, 1979-80; resident pediatrics Rush Presbyn.-St. Luke's Med. Ctr., Chgo., 1986; dir. health sys. Dept. Health Cyclades Island, Santorini, Greece, 1977-79; med. and surg. asst. South Chgo. Cmty. Hosp., 1982-83; primary care physician Humana Medfirst, Chgo., 1985-89; pediatric physician Oak Lawn & Palos Heights, Ill., 1986—. Pres. Paideia Found., 1995. Mem. AMA, Ill. State Med. Assn., Chgo. Med. Soc. Greek Orthodox. Office: 7110 W 127th St Palos Heights IL 60463

SKAUEN, DONALD MATTHEW, retired pharmaceutical educator; b. Newton, Mass., May 14, 1916; s. Marcus and Mary A. (Duncan) S.; m. Rachel M. Burns, Oct. 25, 1942; children: Deborah Skauen Hinchcliffe, Bruce. BS, Mass. Coll. Pharmacy, 1938, MS, 1942; PhD, Purdue U., 1949. Dir. pharm. svc. Children's Hosp. Med. Ctr., Boston, 1940-46; teaching asst. Purdue U., West Lafayette, Ind., 1946-48; asst. prof. pharmaceutics U. Conn., Storrs, 1948-53, assoc. prof., 1953-59, prof., 1959-79, prof. emeritus, 1979—; mem. del. of med. scientists to discuss biol. and pharm. uses of ultrasound Nat. Coun. U.S.-China Trade, People's Republic China, 1979. Co-author: American Pharmacy, 4th edit., 1955, 5th edit., 1961, 6th edit., 1966, Husa's Pharmaceutical Dispensing, 1959, 2d edit., 1966, Radioecology, 1963; contbr. numerous articles to Sci., Nature, Jour. Am. Pharm. Assn. Mem. Am. Pharm. Assn., Am. Soc. Hosp. Pharmacists, Sigma Xi. Home: 16 Storrs Heights Rd Storrs Mansfield CT 06268-2322

SKEF, ZAFER, surgeon; b. Aleppo, Syria, Aug. 29, 1948; came to U.S., 1973; s. Muhamad Saleh and Khadija Skef; m. Lina Kamal; children: Suzan, Wasseem. MD, Damascus U., 1972. Diplomate Am. Bd. Gen. Surgery, Am. Bd. Pediatric Surgery, Am. Bd. Plastic Surgery. Intern, resident Hamot Med. Ctr., Erie, Pa.; with Children's Meml. Hosp., Chgo., The Milton S. Hershey Med. Coll., Erie; attending pediatric/plastic surgeon Med. Coll. U. Ill., Chgo., coord. Micro-Surg. Lab.; attending pediatrician/plastic surgeon Cook County Hosp., Chgo.; chief plastic surgeon, plastic surgery svc. Kalmiate Hosp., Aleppo, Syria, 1985-87; attending pediatric surgeon Red Crescent Hosp. for Children, Aleppo; chief div. pediatrics and plastic surgery Security Forces Hosp., Riyadh, Saudi Arabia. Recipient Physician Recognition award AMA, 1988. Mem. Am. Acad. Pediatrics, Am. Assn. Hand Surgery, Am. Soc. Plastic and Reconstructive Surgeons, Inc., Warren H. Cole Soc., Am. Pediatric Surg. Assn., Ill. Pediatric Surg. Assn., Hershey Surg. Soc. Office: Security Forces Hosp, PO Box 3643, Riyadh 11481, Saudi Arabia

SKELTON, JOHN GOSS, JR., psychologist; b. Columbus, Ga.; s. John Goss and Willie Mae (Langford) S.; B.A., Emory U., 1950; M.Ed., Our Lady of Lake U., 1964; Ph.D., Tex. Tech. U., 1967. Positions with advt. agy., newspaper, trade assn., 1950-63; staff psychologist San Antonio State Hosp., 1963-65; resident in clin. psychology U. Tex. Med. Br., Galveston, 1966-67; dir., clin. psychologist Psychol. Services Clinic, Harlingen, Tex., 1967-68; clin. psychologist Santa Rosa Med. Center, San Antonio, 1968-71; pvt. practice clin. psychology San Antonio, 1971—; chmn. dept. psychology Park North Gen. Hosp., San Antonio, 1971-83; clin. asst. prof. U. Tex. Health Sci. Center, San Antonio, 1971-78; cons. S.W. Ind. Sch. Dist. San Antonio,

1974—, Parkside Lodge Ctr., San Antonio; instr. Our Lady of Lake U., San Antonio, summers 1968-71, Tex. Tech U., summer 1967. Pres., Vis. Nurses Assn. Bexar County, 1976-77; bd. dirs. Halfway House San Antonio, 1964-65, Mental Health Assn. Bexar County, 1969-75; dir. steering com. San Antonio Area Crisis Center, 1971-74. Served with USN, 1945-46. Vocat. Rehab. fellow, 1965-67. Mem. Am. Psychol. Assn., Bexar County Psychol. Assn. (pres. 1970-71), Biofeedback Soc. Tex., Tex. Psychol. Assn., Soc. Behavioral Medicine, San Antonio Mus. Assn. Episcopalian. Office: Ste 100 4402 Vance Jackson Rd San Antonio TX 78230

SKELTON, W. DOUGLAS, dean. Dean Mercer U. Sch. Med., Macon, Ga., 1995—. Office: Mercer Univ Sch of Medicine Office of the Provost 1400 Coleman Ave Macon GA 31207-1000 Office: Mercer Univ Sch Medicine 1550 College St Macon GA 31207*

SKIDMORE, JUNE E., histologist; b. Charleston, W.Va., June 1, 1945; d. William Harold and Inez Dennie (Thurston) Simmons; m. Ronald Wade SKidmore, Feb. 19, 1965; children: Justin Wade, Ashley Bryant. Cert., Thomas Hosp. Lab. Sch., 1965, AMT cert., 1968, ASCPHT cert., 1994. Gen. lab. Kanawha Valley Meml. Hosp., Charleston, 1965-68, Morehead Meml. Hosp., Eden, N.C., 1968-70, Princeton Cmty. Hosp., Princeton, W.Va., 1971-72; analyser Craven County Hosp., New Bern, N.C., 1972-74; chemistry, hematology Bluefield (W.Va.) Santarioum Clinic, 1974-75; receptionist J. Elliott Blaydes M.D., Bluefield, W.Va., 1977-78; urinalysis, serology, hematology Keith T. Edwards M.D., Bluefield, 1978-79; gen. lab. procedures James E. McGee M.D., Bluefield, 1980; staff tech. St. Lukes Hosp., Bluefield, 1987; rotating staff tech. Waynesboro (Pa.) Hosp., 1988—. Contbr. articles to profl. jours. Children's Ch. dir. Edgemont Bapt. Ch., Bluefield, 1974-88, jr. choir dir., 1974-88, adult choir dir. Dublin Mills (Pa.) Cmty. Ch., 1989-94, music and choir dir. Central Bapt. Ch., Mont Alto, Pa., 1994—. Mem. Am. Medical Tech., Am. Soc. Histology. Baptist. Home: 57 N Franklin St Chambersburg PA 17201

SKIENS, WILLIAM EUGENE, electrical interconnect systems scientist, polymer engineer; b. Burns, Oreg., Feb. 21, 1928; s. William Poleman and Eugenia Glenn (Hibbard) S.; m. Vesta Lorraine Franz, Nov. 4, 1955; children: Rebecca, Beverly, Michael. Student, N.W. Nazarene Coll., 1946-48; BS in Chemistry, Oreg. State U., 1951; PhD in Phys. Chemistry, U. Wash., 1957. Chemist Dow Chem. Co., Pittsburg, Calif., 1951-53; research chemist Dow Chem. Co., Midland, Mich. and Walnut Creek, Calif., 1957-58, 1958-73, E.I DuPont de Nemours, Wilmington, Del., 1955; sr. research chemist Battelle Meml. Inst., Richland, Wash., 1973-84, also cons., 1984—; mgr. media system devel. Optical Data, Inc., Beaverton, Oreg., 1984-89; chief scientist Precision Interconnect, Portland, Oreg., 1989—; cons. WHO, Geneva, 1978-85, PI Med., Portland, 1991—. Contbr. chpts. to books, articles to profl. jours.; patentee in field. Com. chmn. Concord, Calif. council Boy Scouts Am., 1969-72; sec. Tri-Cities Nuclear Council, Richland, Wash., 1984. Named Alumni of Yr. N.W. Nazarene Coll., 1982. Mem. Am. Chem. Soc. (chmn. Richland sect. 1982), Sigma Xi. Republican. Mem. Ch. Nazarene. Home: 31179 SW Country View Ln Wilsonville OR 97070-7479 Office: Precision Interconnect 16640 SW 72nd Ave Portland OR 97224-7756

SKILLING, VINCENT, anesthesiologist; b. Miami Beach, Dec. 8, 1947; s. Francis Curie and Leona Marie (Mazzoni) S.; m. Nancy Ellen Piesco, Feb. 24, 1973; children: Matthew David, Melissa Ellen, Amanda Grace. BA, St. Leo Coll., 1969; BS, Fla. Internat. U., 1974; MD, Am. U. Caribbean, 1981. Diplomate Am. Coll. Forensic Examiners. Police officer Miami Police Dept., 1969-74; adminstr. Miami Dade C.C., 1974-76; anesthesiology Med. Ctr. Ctrl. Ga., Macon, 1985—; dir. obstetric anesthesiology Mercer U. Sch. Medicine, 1995—, asst. prof. anesthesiology, 1991—; ceo Provider Healthcare Svcs., Macon, 1994—. Mem. Internat. Assn. Chiefs of Police, Am. Soc. Anesthesiologists, Soc. Critical Care Anesthesiologists, Ga. Soc. Anesthesiologists, Am. Coll. Physician Execs. Office: Ctrl Ga Anesthesia Svcs 840 Pine St #700 Macon GA 31201

SKINNER, DAVID BERNT, surgeon, educator; b. Joliet, Ill., Apr. 28, 1935; s. James Madden and Bertha Elinor (Tapper) S.; m. May Elinor Tischer, Aug. 25, 1956; children: Linda Elinor, Kristin Anne, Carise Berntine, Margaret Leigh. B.A. with high honors, U. Rochester, N.Y., 1958, Sc.D. (hon.), 1980; M.D. cum laude, Yale U., 1959; MD (hon.), U. Lund, 1994, Technishe U. Munich, 1995. Diplomate: Am. Bd. Surgery (dir. 1974-80), Am. Bd. Thoracic Surgery. Intern, then resident in surgery Mass. Gen. Hosp., Boston, 1959-65; sr. registrar in thoracic surgery Frenchay Hosp., Bristol, Eng., 1963-64; teaching fellow Harvard U. Med. Sch., 1965; from asst. prof. surgery to prof. Johns Hopkins U. Med. Sch., also surgeon Johns Hopkins Hosp., 1968-72; Dallas B. Phemister prof. surgery, chmn. dept. U. Chgo. Hosps. and Clinics, 1972-87; prof. surgery Cornell U., 1987—; pres., CEO N.Y. Hosp., 1987—; dir. Omnis Surg. Inc., 1984-85, Churchill Livingston, 1990-93, Lab. Corp. Am.; mem. Pres.' Biomed. Rsch. Panel, 1975-76. Author: Atlas of Esophageal Surgery, 1991; author: (with others) Gastroesophageal Reflux and Hiatal Hernia, 1972, Management of Esophageal Diseases, 1988; editor: Surgical Practice Illustrated, 1988-95; editor Current Topics in Surg. Rsch., 1969-71, Jour. Surg. Rsch., 1972-83; co-editor: Surg. Treatment of Digestive Disease, 1985, Esophageal Disorders, 1985, Reconstructive Surgery of the Gastrointestinal Tract, 1985, Primary Motility Disorders of the Esophagus, 1991; mem. editl. bd. Jour. Thoracic and Cardiovascular Surgery, Annals of Surgery; contbr. profl. jours., chpts. in books. Elder Fourth Presbyn. Ch., Chgo., 1976-87, clk. of session, 1978-82, 84-87; bd. visitors Cornell U. Med. Coll., 1980-87. Served to maj. M.C. USAF, 1966-68. Decorated Chevalier Nat. Order of Merit (France); John and Mary Markle scholar acad. medicine, 1969-74. Fellow ACS; mem. AMA, Internat. Surg. Group, Am., Western, So. Surg. Assns., Soc. Univ. Surgeons (pres. 1978-79), Am. Soc. Artificial Internal Organs (pres. 1977), Soc. Surg. Chmn. (pres. 1980-82), Am. Assn. Thoracic Surgery (pres. 1996—), Soc. Vascular Surgery, Soc. Thoracic Surgery, Soc. Pelvic Surgeons, Soc. Surgery Alimentary Tract, Soc. Internat. de Chirurgie, Collegium Internat. de Chirurgie Digestivae, Am. Coll. Chest Physicians, Ctrl. Surg. Soc., Internat. Soc. Diseases Esophagus (pres. 1992-95), Assn. Acad. Surgery, Halsted Soc., Soc. Clin. Surgery (pres. 1986-88), Phi Beta Kappa, Alpha Omega Alpha. Clubs: Quadrangle (Chgo.); Cosmos (Washington); University (N.Y.C.); River (N.Y.C.). Home: 79 E 79th St New York NY 10021-0202 Office: New York Hosp Cornell Univ Office Pres 525 E 68th St New York NY 10021-4873

SKINNER, EDWARD FOLLAND, retired thoracic surgeon; b. Hamilton, Ont., Can., Sept. 26, 1909; s. Edward Blake and Addie Maude (Large) S.; m. Helen Love Draper, Nov. 27, 1935 (dec. 1980); children: Wendy Skinner Templeton, Terri Skinner Chadwick, Edward D.; m. Lois Ellis Walker, May 29, 1984; children: James H. Kelley Jr., Anne W. Strand, William C. Walker Jr., Frances Walker McCampbell. BS, Detroit City Coll., now Wayne State U., 1931; B Medicine, Detroit Coll. Medicine, now Wayne State U., 1935; MD, Detroit Coll. Medicine, 1936. Diplomate Am. Bd. Thoracic Surgery. Intern St. Mary's Hosp., Detroit, 1935-36; chief resident St. Mary's Hosp., Saginaw, Mich., 1936-37; resident Herman Kiefer Hosp., Detroit, 1937-39, 42-45; resident in thoracic surgery No. Mich. Tuberculosis Sanatorium, Gaylord, 1939-41; pvt. practice Memphis, 1945-72; ret., 1972; asst. prof. surgery, U. Tenn. Med. Sch., Memphis, 1951-72; instr., Bapt. Meml. Hosp. Sch. Nursing, 1945-72, St. Joseph's Hosp. Sch. Nursing, 1945-72; cons., USPHS, Memphis, 1946-72. Author: Your Health, Wealth, and Happiness; contbr. numerous articles to med. jours. Fellow Am. Coll. Chest Physicians, AMA; mem. Am. Assn. Thoracic Surgery, Soc. Thoracic Surgeons, Memphis Surg. Assn., Mid-South Writers Assn. (pres. 1986-89), Writers Guild (founder Memphis sect.), Memphis Thoracic Soc., Forrest City Country Club. Presbyterian. Home: 165 Picardy St Memphis TN 38111-1925

SKINNER, HARRY BRYANT, orthopaedic surgery educator; b. Cleve., Oct. 13, 1943; s. Harry Bryant and Marion (Eastlick) S. BS, Alfred U., 1965; MS, PhD, U. Calif., Berkeley, 1970; MD, Med. U. S.C., 1975. Asst. prof. Youngstown (Ohio) State U., 1970-71; postdoctoral research assoc. Clemson (S.C.) U., 1971-72; lectr. Calif. State U., Sacramento, 1977-79; asst./assoc. prof. Tulane U., New Orleans, 1979-82; assoc. prof. orthopaedic surgery U. Calif., San Francisco, 1983-86, prof., 1986-94; prof. mech. engring. U. Calif., Berkeley, 1993—; chair grad. group U. Calif., Berkeley and San Francisco; prof., chmn. dept. orthopedic surgery U. Calif., Irvine, 1994—, prof. mech. and aerospace engring. Engring. Sch., 1995—; adj. asst./assoc. prof. Sch. Engring., Tulane U., New Orleans, 1979-82; dir. rehab. research and devel. VA Med. Ctr., San Francisco, 1983—. Mem. editorial bd. Orthopaedics jour., 1984-88, guest editor, 1985, Jour. Biomed. Materials Research, 1983—; contbr. articles to profl. jours. Grantee NIH, 1978-84, Nat. Inst. Dental Rsch., 1978-84, VA, 1978—, Schleider Found., 1980-82, Am. Fedn. Aging Rsch., 1986-89. Fellow ACS, Am. Acad, Orthopaedic Surgeons; mem. Orthopaedic Rsch. Soc., Soc. for Biomaterials (charter), Am. Orthopaedic Assn., The Hip Soc., Sigma Xi. Office: U Calif Dept Orthopaedic Surgery 29A 101 City Dr S Orange CA 92668

SKIVER, EDNA, medical laboratory technologist; b. Pittsford, Mich., Dec. 10, 1936; d. Lester Lavern La Mee and Jean Ceabell (Church) Doolittle; m. Leo V. Skiver, Feb. 28, 1959 (div. Nov. 1985); 1 child, Leona. Tech., Elkhart Bus. Univ., 1956. Medical lab, x-ray tech. Rogers City (Mich.) Hosp., 1956-59, Hillsdale (Mich.) Cmty. Health Ctr., 1960—. Bd. dirs. ISCLT; cub scout leader Boy Scouts Am., 1960-63; asst. camp fire girls leader, 1971-72; 4H leader 4-H of Hillsdale Co., 1975-80. Mem. AMT, ARRT. Office: Hillsdale Cmty Health Ctr 168S Nowell St Hillsdale MI 49242

SKLANSKY, MORRIS AARON, psychiatrist, psychoanalyst; b. Poland, Dec. 7, 1919; came to U.S., 1922; s. Eli and Eska (Chernin) S.; m. Alice V. Reizen, June 12, 1946; children: Laura, Paul, Andrew. AB, Drew U., 1941; MD, U. Louisville, 1945. Diplomate Am. Bd. Psychiatry. Intern Michael Reese Hosp., Chgo., 1945-46, resident, 1948-51, psychiatrist, 1951-90; lectr. Sch. Social Work, U. Chgo., 1953-83, clin. prof. dept. psychiatry, 1960-93; lectr. Sch. Medicine, Northwestern U., Chgo., 1970, 90; cons. Scholarship and Guidance Assn., Chgo., 1953—; tng. and supervising analyst Inst. Psychoanalysis, 1960—; pvt. cons. and supr. in psychoanalysis and psychotherapy. Author: Drop Outs, 1970, Creative Counseling, 1975. Mem. Am. Psychoanalytic Assn. Home: 800 Roslyn Ter Evanston IL 60201-1724 Office: Inst for Psychoanalysis 180 N Michigan Ave Chicago IL 60601-7401

SKLAREW, ROBERT JAY, biomedical research educator, consultant; b. N.Y.C., Nov. 25, 1941; s. Arthur and Jeanette (Laven) S.; m. Toby Willner, July 15, 1970; children: David Michael, Gary Richard. BA in Zoology, Cornell U., 1963; MS, NYU, 1965, PhD in Biology, 1970. Assoc. rsch. scientist Sch. of Medicine NYU, N.Y.C., 1965-70, rsch. scientist Sch. of Medicine, 1971-73, sr. rsch. scientist Sch. of Medicine, 1973-79; rsch. asst. prof. pathology Sch. of Medicine Goldwater Meml. Hosp., N.Y.C., 1979-87, rsch. assoc. prof. pathology Sch. of Medicine, 1987-88, dir. cytokinetics and imaging lab. NYU Rsch. Svc., 1980-88; prof. cell biology, anatomy and medicine N.Y. Med. Coll., Valhalla, 1988—; rsch. assoc. dept. pathology Lenox Hill Hosp., N.Y.C., 1981-88; pres., CEO R.J. Sklarew Imaging Assoc., Inc., Larchmont, N.Y., 1990—; chmn. consensus panel for diagnostic cancer imaging Nat. Cancer Inst., 1994. Author: Microscopic Imaging of Steroid Receptors, 1990; sr. author: Cytometry, Jour. Histochem. Cytochem., Cancer, Exptl. Cell Rsch. Mem. Beth Emeth Synagogue, Larchmont, 1974—; group leader Boy Scouts Am., Larchmont, 1978-80. Grantee Am. Cancer Soc., Nat. Cancer Inst./NIH Conc. for Tobacco Rsch., R.J. Reynolds Industries Found., NYU; recipient Shannon award Nat. Cancer Inst., 1991. Mem. AAAS, Cell Kinetics Soc. (sec. 1983-85, 85-87, v.p. 1987-88, pres. 1988-89, chmn. nominations 1991, 93), N.Y. Acad. Sci., Soc. for Analytic Cytology, Soc. for Cell Biology, Tissue Culture Assn., Union Concerned Scientists, Kappa Delta Rho. Democrat. Home: 8 Vine Rd Larchmont NY 10538-1247 Office: NY Med Coll Cancer Rsch Inst 100 Grasslands Rd Elmsford NY 10523-1110

SKLARIN, BURTON S., endocrinologist; b. N.Y.C., Feb. 28, 1932; s. Louis and Molla (Beiser) S.; m. Ann Hirsch, June 29, 1960; children: Laurie, Richard, Peter. A.B., NYU, 1953, M.D., 1957. Diplomate: Am. Bd. Internal Medicine, Am. Bd. Endocrinology and Metabolism. Intern Bellevue Hosp., N.Y.C., 1957-58, resident, 1958-61, asst. vis. clin. physician, 1961—; practice medicine specializing in endocrinology Lawrence, N.Y., 1961—; chief endocrinology St. John's Episcopal Hosp., 1961—, pres. med. staff, 1978-80, also chmn. med. exec. com.; asst. prof. clin. medicine NYU, 1961—, asst. in medicine Univ. Hosp., 1961; endocrinologist, staff physician L.I. Jewish Hosp.; cons. Franklin Gen Hosp. Contbr. articles on endocrinology to profl. publs. Vice pres. bd. trustees Woodmere Acad. Fellow ACP, Am. Coll. Endocrinology, N.Y. Acad. Medicine, Soc. Nuclear Medicine; mem. Nassau County Med. Soc., N.Y. Diabetes Assn., Endocrine Soc., Rockaway Med. Soc. (past pres.), Am. Assn. Clin. Endocrinologists. Home and Office: 501 Broadway Lawrence NY 11559-2501

SKLAVER, ALLEN ROBERT, infectious diseases physician, educator; b. Waterbury, Conn., Mar. 31, 1946; s. Joseph and Viola Sklaver; m. Jane Feigenbaum, June 23, 1968; children: Alissa, Jennifer. BA cum laude, Williams Coll., 1968; MD, George Washington U., 1972. Diplomate Am. Bd. Internal Medicine, Infectious Diseases, Nat. Bd. Med. Examiners; lic. Conn., Fla. Intern Hartford (Conn.) Hosp., 1972-73, resident, 1973-75; fellow infectious diseases Jackson Meml. Hosp., Miami, Fla., 1975-77; clin. asst. prof. medicine U. Miami, 1977-94, clin. assoc. prof. medicine, 1994—; staff physician Plantation Gen. Hosp., Fla. Med. Ctr., Westside Regional Med. Ctr., Fla. Med. Ctr. South. Fellow ACP; mem. AMA, Am. Soc. Microbiology, Soc. Internal Medicine, Infectious Diseases Soc. Am., Assn. Practitioners in Infection Control, Am. Bd. Advanced Achievement in Internal Medicine. Office: Sachs Morris & Sklaver Inc 7353 NW 4th St Plantation FL 33317

SKLOOT, BETSY A(NN), health care administrator; b. Batesville, Ind., Mar. 29, 1942; d. James Robert and Cynthia Hahn (Stocker) Lee; children: Matthew Lee, Rebecca Lee. B.A. with high honors, So. Ill. U., 1966, M.A., 1970. Instr. in English, Carbondale High Sch. and So. Ill. U., 1966-72; budget analyst and mgr. State of Ill., Springfield, 1973-76, assoc. Medicaid adminstr., 1978-81, Medicaid adminstr., 1981-84; budget analyst and mgr. State of Wash., Olympia, 1976-78; dir. Multnomah County Dept. Human Services, Portland, Oreg., 1984-87; planning and mktg. adminstr. Providence Med. Ctr., Portland, 1988-90; area svcs. mgr. Kaiser Permanente, Portland, 1990—. Office: Kaiser Permanente 3600 N Intrstate Ave Portland OR 97227-1191

SKLOVSKY, ROBERT JOEL, pharmacology educator; b. Bronx, N.Y., Nov. 19, 1952; s. Nathan and Esther (Steinberg) S. BS, Bklyn. Coll., 1975; MA in Sci. Edn., Columbia U., 1976; PharmD, U. of Pacific, 1977; D in Naturopathic Medicine, Nat. Coll. Naturopathic Medicine, 1983. Intern Tripler Army Med. Ctr., Honolulu, 1977; prof. pharmacology Nat. Coll. Naturopathic Medicine, Portland, Oreg., 1982-85; pvt. practice specializing in naturopathic medicine Milwaukie, Oreg., 1983—; cons. State Bd. Naturopathic Examiners, Oreg., Hawaii, Clackamas County Sherriff's Dept.; cons. Internat. Drug Info. Ctr., N.Y.C., 1983—; cons. Albert Roy Davis Scientific Research Lab, Orange Park, Fla. 1986. Recipient Bristol Labs. award, 1983. Fellow Am. Coll. Apothecaries; mem. Am. Assn. Naturopathic Physicians, Oreg. Assn. Naturopathic Physicians, N.Y. Acad. Sci. Office: 6910 SE Lake Rd Portland OR 97267-2196

SKOFF, HILLEL DAVID, orthopedist, hand surgeon; b. Duluth, Minn., Apr. 22, 1954; s. Benson and Rosalind (Cohen) S.; m. Roberta Sue Murachver, Aug. 12, 1990; 1 child, Molly. AB, Washington U., 1976; MD, Yale U., 1980. Resident Wash. U., 1980-82, Yale U., 1983-85; fellow Europe/Duke/MGH, 1985-87; Instr. orthopedics and plastic surgery Harvard U. Med. Sch., Boston, 1987—. Mem. AMA, Am. Acad. Orthopedic Surgeons, Am. Soc. for Surgery of the Hand, Phi Beta Kappa, Sigma Xi. Office: 1269 Beacon St Brookline MA 02146 also: 330 Brookline Ave Boston MA 02215

SKOGLUND, ELIZABETH RUTH, marriage, child and family counselor; b. Chgo., June 17, 1937; d. Ragnar Emmanuel and Elizabeth Alvera (Benson) S. BA, UCLA, 1959; MA, Pasadena Coll., 1969. Cert. tchr., Calif.; cert. marriage, family and child counselor, Calif. Tchr. Marlborough Sch., Los Angeles, 1959-61; tchr., counselor Glendale (Calif.) High Sch., 1961-72; pvt. practice family counseling Burbank, Calif., 1972—. Author: over 20 books including It's OK to Be a Woman Again, 1988, Making Bad Times Good, 1991, Safety Zones, 1991, Harold's Dog Horace is Scared of the Dark, 1992, Life on the Line, 1992, The Welcoming Hearth, 1993, Amma: The Life and Words of Amy Carmichael, 1994. Mem. Calif. Assn. Marriage and Family Therapists, Simon Wiesenthal Ctr. Republican.

SKOLNICK, PHIL, pharmacologist, psychiatry educator; b. N.Y.C., Feb. 26, 1947; s. David Louis and Gertrude (Gewirtzman) S.; m. Nancy Louise Ostrowski, July 17, 1985; children: Michael, Stephen. BS summa cum laude, L.I. U., 1968; PhD, George Washington U., 1972; DSc (hon.), L.I. U., 1993, U. Wis., Milw., 1995. Staff fellow NIH, Bethesda, Md., 1972-75, sr. staff fellow, 1975-77, sr. investigator, 1977-83, chief neurobiology sect., 1983-86, chief Lab. of Neurosci., 1986—; Wellcome prof. Burroughs-Wellcome Trust, 1988, 92; prof. dept. psychiatry Uniformed Svcs., U. of health Scis., Bethesda, 1989—; adj. prof. anesthesiology Johns Hopkins U., Balt., 1994—. Recipient A.E. Bennett award Soc. Biol. Psychiatry, 1981, Mathilde Solowey award, 1983, Sci. Achievement award Washington Acad. Sci., 1984, Superior Svc. award USPHS, 1993. Fellow Am. Coll. Neuropsychopharmacology; mem. Am. Soc. Pharmacology and Exptl. Therapeutics, Soc. Neurosci., Internat. Soc. Neurochemistry. Office: NIH/NIDDK/LN Nih Niddk Ln Rm 111 Bethesda MD 20892

SKOLNIK, RICHARD ALAN, plastic surgeon; b. N.Y.C., Jan. 7, 1951. BA in Biology summa cum laude, C.W. Post Coll., 1972; MD, Cornell U., 1976. Cert. Am. Bd. Plastic and Reconstructive Surgery. Resident gen. surgery Mt. Sinai Med. Ctr., N.Y.C., 1976-79, resident plastic surgery, 1979-82; clin. instr. Mt. Sinai Sch. Medicine, N.Y.C., 1982-84, asst. clin. prof., 1985—; assoc. attending Mt. Sinai Med. Ctr., N.Y.C., 1982—, Beth Israel Med. Ctr., N.Y.C., 1984—; courtesy staff Beth Israel North (Doctor's Hosp.), N.Y.C., 1987—; fellow cleft lip and palate Children's Hosp., Lima, Peru, 1982; vis. prof. Reconstructive Surgery Found., Maceo, Brazil, 1990. Fellow ACS; mem. Am. Soc. of Plastic and Reconstructive Surgeons, N.Y. Regional Soc. Plastic and Reconstructive Surgeons, AMA, Barsky Soc., N.Y. State Med. Soc. Office: 21 E 87th St New York NY 10128-0506

SKOOG, WILLIAM ARTHUR, former oncologist; b. Culver City, Calif., Apr. 10, 1925; s. John Lundeen and Allis Rose (Gatz) S.; m. Ann Douglas, Sept. 17, 1949; children: Karen, William Arthur, James Douglas, Allison. AA, UCLA, 1944; BA with gt. distinction, Stanford U., 1946, MD, 1949. Intern in medicine Stanford Hosp., San Francisco, 1948-49, asst. resident medicine, 1949-50; asst. resident medicine N.Y. Hosp., N.Y.C., 1950-51; sr. resident medicine Wadsworth VA Hosp., Los Angeles, 1951, attending specialist internal medicine, 1962-68; practice medicine specializing in internal medicine, Los Altos, Calif., 1959-61; pvt. practice hematology and oncology Calif. Oncologic and Surg. Med. Group, Inc., Santa Monica, Calif., 1971-72; pvt. practice med. oncology, San Bernardino, Calif., 1972-94; assoc. staff Palo Alto-Stanford (Calif.) Hosp. Center, 1959-61, U. Calif. Med. Center, San Francisco, 1959-61; asso. attending physician U. Calif. at Los Angeles Hosp. and Clinics, 1961-78; vis. physician internal medicine Harbor Gen. Hosp., Torrance, Calif., 1962-65, attending physician, 1965-71; cons. chemistry Clin. Lab., UCLA Hosp., 1963-68; affiliate cons. staff St. John's Hosp., Santa Monica, Calif., 1967-71, courtesy staff, 1971-72; courtesy attending med. staff Santa Monica Hosp., 1967-72; staff physician St. Bernardine (Calif.) Hosp., 1972-94, hon. staff, 1994—; staff physician San Bernardino Cmty. Hosp., 1972-90, courtesy staff, 1990-94; chief sect. oncology San Bernardino County Hosp., 1972-76; cons. staff Redlands (Calif.) Cmty. Hosp., 1972-83, courtesy staff, 1983-94, hon. staff, 1994—; asst. in medicine Cornell Med. Coll., N.Y.C., 1950-51; jr. rsch. physician UCLA Atomic Energy Project, 1954-55; instr. medicine, asst. rsch. physician dept. medicine UCLA Med. Center, 1955-56, asst. prof. medicine, asst. rsch. physician, 1956-59; clin. asso. hematology VA Center, Los Angeles, 1956-59; co-dir. metabolic rsch. unit UCLA Center for Health Scis., 1955-59, 61-65; co-dir. Health Scis. Clin. Rsch. Ctr., 1965-68, dir., 1968-72; clin. instr. medicine Stanford, 1959-61; asst. clin. prof. medicine, assoc. rsch. physician U. Calif. Med. Center, San Francisco, 1959-61; lectr. medicine UCLA Sch. Medicine, 1961-62, assoc. prof. medicine, 1962-73, assoc. clin. prof. medicine, 1973—. Served with USNR, 1943-46, lt. M.C., 1951-53. Fellow ACP; mem. Am., Calif. med. assns., So. Calif. Acad. Clin. Oncology, Western Soc. Clin. Research, Am. Fedn. Clin. Research, Los Angeles Acad. Medicine, San Bernardino County Med. Soc., Am. Soc. Clin. Oncology, Am. Soc. Internal Medicine, Calif. Soc. Internal Medicine, Inland Soc. Internal Medicine, Phi Beta Kappa, Alpha Omega Alpha, Sigma Xi, Alpha Kappa Kappa. Episcopalian (vestryman 1965-70). Club: Redlands Country. Contbr. articles to profl. jours. Home: 1119 Kimberly Pl Redlands CA 92373-6786

SKOTTE, DANIEL MARK, physician, flight surgeon; b. Jackson, Minn., May 20, 1949; s. Reynold John B. and Virginia Mae (Sperry) S.; m. Nancy Irene, June 7, 1975; children: Daniel Mark Jr., Sarah Elizabeth, Joel Matthew. BS, USAF Acad., 1972; DO, Chgo. Coll. Osteo. Med., 1982. Cert. Am. Osteo. Acad. of Family Practice of Sports Medicine. Lt. col. USAF, 1967—; pres. High Desert Family Medicine, Sun River, Oreg., 1983-95; chief physician 3 Rivers Med. Care, Sun River, 1995—; flight surgeon 173 Fighter Wing, Kingsley AFB, Oreg., 1975—; team physician Lapine (Oreg.) H.S., Gilchrest (Oreg.) H.S., 1983—; vol. physician Lapine Rodeo, Special Olympics, Sunriver, 1984—; bd. trustees Osteo. Physicians Surgeons Oreg., 1986—, pres., 1993-95; med. examiner Deschutes County, Oreg., 1991—. Bd. trustee ARC, Deschutes County, 1993—. Mem. Osteo. Physicians and Surgeons of Oreg. (pres. 1993-95). Republican. Home & Office: PO Box 3572 Sunriver OR 97707

SKOUSE, DOUGLAS, cardiologist; b. Milan, Italy, Dec. 30, 1953; s. William and Ebe Skouse; m. Liana Spechenhauser, Sept. 17, 1983; children: Barbara, Alan. MD, U. Milan, 1980; postgrad. in cardiology, U. Pavia, 1986; Specialization in Anaesthesiology, U. Modena, 1990. Internship S. Carlo Hosp., Milan, Italy, 1980-81; vice dir. dept. cardiology Ospedale Bormio-Sondalo, Italy, 1988—. Mem. Assn. Nat. Medici Cardiologi Ospedalieri. Home: Via Guicciardi 8, 23032 Bormio Italy Office: Ospedale Bormio Sondalo, Via Zubian 33, 23030 Sondalo Italy

SKOWRON, TADEUSZ ADAM, physician; b. Czestochowa, Poland, Dec. 17, 1950; came to U.S., 1976; s. Stanislaw and Genowefa (Widera) S.; m. Elizabeth Sliwowska, Feb. 17, 1990; children: Sebastian Adam, Annette Kira. MD, Med. Acad., Lodz, Poland, 1975. House physician Bklyn.-Cumberland Med. Ctr., 1979-80, fellow in neurology, 1981-83; resident in medicine Marshall U. Sch. Medicine, Huntington, W.Va., 1983-86, instr., 1986-87; pvt. practice, Bridgeport, Conn., 1987—; clin. specialist II, State Sch., Newark, 1981; advisor Congress Med. Polonia, Czestochowa, 1990—. Mem. Polish cultural events com. Sacred Heart U., Fairfield, Conn., 1990—. Mem. ACP, AMA, AAAS, N.Y. Acad. Scis. Home: 47 Mcquillan Ave Stratford CT 06497-4626 Office: 50 Ridgefield Ave Ste 317 Bridgeport CT 06610-3106

SKRIP, LINDA JEAN, nursing administrator; b. Neenah, Wis., Apr. 16, 1963; d. Donald Charles and Kathryn Amelia Patrikus; m. Stephen Michael, May 21, 1988. BSN, U. Wis., 1986. Staff nurse U. Hosp. Ill., Chgo., 1986-87; asst. clin. nurse mgr. Northwestern Meml. Hosp., Chgo., 1987-88; nursing coord. Pitt County Meml. Hosp., Greenville, N.C., 1988-91; nursing supr. Chesapeake (Va.) Gen. Hosp., 1991-92, case mgmt. coord., 1992—, cert. case mgr., 1993—. Mem. ANA. Roman Catholic. Home: 1253 Smokey Mountain Trl Chesapeake VA 23320-8187

SKROCKI, EDMUND STANLEY, II, health fair promoter, executive; b. Schenectady, N.Y., Sept. 6, 1953; s. Edmund Stanley I and Lorraine (Nocian) S.; m. Diane Carolyn Sittig, Sept. 6, 1976 (div. 1992); children: Carolyn, Michelle, Edmund III; life ptnr. Leslee Erickson; 1 child, Johnathon Edmund. AA, LaValley Coll., 1981; BA, Sonoma State U., 1982, MA, 1987; postgrad., Am. Inst. Hypnotherapy. Pres. Skrocki's Philos. Svc., Lakeview Terrace, Calif., 1971-81, Redding, Calif., 1982—; pres., CEO Skrocki's Superior Svc., Lakeview Terrace, 1971-76, Redding, Calif., 1976—; pres., CEO, promoter, prodr. Redding (Calif.) Health Faire, 1991—. Bd. govs., deacon Ch. of Universal Knowledge, 1991—. Named one of Outstanding Young Men Am., 1980. Mem. Shasta Submarine Soc. (pres. 1984—). Home and Office: 755 Quartz Hill Rd Redding CA 96003-2118

SKROKOV, ROBERT A., physician, dermatologist; b. N.Y.C., Nov. 2, 1955; s. M. Robert and Olga (Grib) S.; m. Patricia, June 9, 1984. AB, Rutgers U., New Brunswick, N.J., 1978; MD Downstate Med. Ctr., SUNY, Bklyn., 1982. Diplomate Am. Bd. Dermatology. Intern in internal medicine Albert Einstein Coll. Medicine, Bronx, N.Y., 1982-83; resident in dermatology SUNY Downstate Med. Ctr., Bklyn., 1983-85, chief resident dermatology, 1985-86; attending dermatologist Dermatology Group P.C.,

Bay Shore, L.I., 1986—; clin. asst. prof. SUNY Downstate Med. Ctr., 1986-89, SUNY Health Scis. Ctr., Stony Brook, N.Y., 1991—. skin care screening vol. Am. Cancer Soc. and Am. Acad. Dermatology, 1986—; vol. instr. Dept. Dermatology SUNY. Fellow Am. Acad. Dermatology; mem. AMA, N.Y. Acad. Medicine, N.Y. State Med. Soc., N.Y. State Dermatology Soc., L.I. Dermatology Soc., Suffolk Dermatology Soc. (pres. 1992-94). Office: Dermatology Group PC 332 E Main St Bay Shore NY 11706

SKUBITZ, KEITH, oncologist, educator; b. Cooperstown, N.Y.; s. Mitchell G. and Irene Skubitz. AB, Cornell U., 1972; MD, Johns Hopkins U., 1976. Diplomate Am. Internal Medicine, Am. Bd. Med. Oncology. Intern, resident in medicine U. Minn., Mpls., 1976-79, fellow med. oncology, 1982-83, asst. prof., 1983-88, assoc. prof., 1988—; fellow clin. pharmacology Johns Hopkins U., Balt., 1979-82; cons. Tel-Tech., Mpls., 1988—. Contbr. over 60 articles to profl. jours., 12 chpts. to books; patentee glutamine for stomatitis. Grantee Am. Heart Assn., NIH, others. Mem. ACP, AAAS, Am. Assn. Cancer Rsch., Am. Soc. Hematology, Am. Soc. Clin. Oncology, Am. Soc. Cell Biology, Internat. Soc. Hematology, Soc. for Leukacyte Biology, N.Y. Acad. Scis., Ctrl. Soc. for Clin. Rsch., Am. Fedn. Clin. Rsch. Office: Univ Hosp 424 Harvard St SE Box 325 Minneapolis MN 55455

SKUDDER, PAUL ALBERT, vascular surgeon; b. N.Y.C., Oct. 15, 1953; s. Paul Albert and Margaret Ann (Youmans) S.; m. Joanne Carol Moruzzi, May 31, 1980; children: Paul, Carolyn, Rebecca. BA, Williams Coll., 1975; MD, Cornell U. Med. Coll., 1979. Diplomate Am. Bd. Surgery, also bd. certified in gen. vasc. surgery and surg. critical care; MD, Mass., Vt., D.C., N.Y. Intern, resident, chief resident in surgery U. Rochester, N.Y., 1979-84; fellow in vascular surgery Lahey Clinic, Burlington, Mass., 1984-85; asst. prof. surgery George Washington U. Sch. of Medicine, Washington, 1985-86; vascular and gen. surgeon, dir. vascular lab. Williamstown, Mass., 1986-91; clin. asst. prof. surgery Uniformed Svcs. U. of Health Scis., Bethesda, Md., 1991—; vascular, gen. surgeon Schenectady, N.Y., 1991—. Editor: (book) Visceral Vascular Surgery, 1987; contbr. numerous articles to profl. jours. Med. v.p. No. Berkshire Unit of Am. Cancer Soc., 1987-89; exec. bd. Mt. Greylock Ski club, 1988-89; nat. ski patrol, Jiminy Peak, Hancock, Mass., 1988—; med. advisor Williams Coll. Ski Patrol, 1990—; quality assurance com. Ellis Hosp., 1991—; chairperson Ellis-St. Clare's Vascular Surgery Clin. Pathway Task Force, 1993—; med. advisor Western Mass. Region, Nat. Ski Patrol, 1993—, Stephentown N.Y. Fire Dept., 1994—; bd. dirs. Inter-County Home Care, Albany, N.Y., 1995—; tech. assessment com. Ellis Hosp., 1995—. Recipient Benedict prize for Excellence in Biology, Williams Coll., 1975, Resident Prize paper Upstate N.Y. Vascular Surgery Soc., 1983, Outstanding Sci. Paper-Fourth prize for Hemodynamics, 1987; nominee for Golden Apple Clin. Teaching award Georgetown U. Med. Sch., 1986. Fellow ACS; mem. Soc. Critical Care Medicine, Internat. Soc. for Cardiovascular Surgery, Soc. for Vascular Technology, New Eng. Soc. for Vascular Surgery, Eastern Vascular Soc., Peripheral Vascular Surgery Soc., Upstate N.Y. Soc. for Vascular Surgery, Mass. Med. Soc., Chesapeake Vascular Soc. Roman Catholic. Office: 1201 Nott St Ste 202 Schenectady NY 12308

SKYLV, GRETHE KROGH, rheumatologist, anthropologist; b. Copenhagen, Denmark, May 31, 1938; d. Aage Krogh and Herdis Fischer (Lindeskov) Christoffersen; m. Axel Skylv, Jan. 12, 1962 (div. Feb. 1994); children: Lise, Kirsten, Mikael; m. Klaus Bruhn Jensen, Oct. 15, 1994. MD, U. Copenhagen, 1967, MA in Anthropology, 1990. Resident various hosps., Copenhagen, 1967-79; pvt. practice Hillerod, Denmark, 1979-84; dept. head Rehab. Ctr. for Torture Victims, Copenhagen, 1985-92; cons. Danish Red Cross, 1993—; rsch. scholar on cross-cultural interpersonal comm. Faculty of Humanities, U. Copenhagen, 1994—; cons. Orgn. for Manual Therapy, Denmark, 1985—, Internat. Rehab. Medicine Assn., 1991—, various Danish treatment ctrs. for torture victims & refugees, 1993—; com. mem. North-South issues Univ.-wide rsch.; mem. interdisciplinary rsch. groups comm. med. contexts, 1994—; bd. dirs. Network for Interdisciplinary Qualitative Rsch., Denmark, 1989—. Guest editor: Danish Soc. for Anthropology Soc. Jour., 1988-89; contbr. articles to profl. jours. Recipient Honorary award Cranio-Facial Pain Ctr. 1990. Fellow European Assn. Social Anthropologists, Danish Med. Assn. (bd. for ethnic minorities 1996—), Danish Manual Therapy Orgn., Danish Assn. for Rheumatology, Danish Assn. Internal Medicine, Danish Soc. for Social Anthropology, Physicians for Human Rights. Home: Mosesvinget 54, DK-2400 Copenhagen Denmark

SLABY, ANDREW EDMUND, psychiatrist, epidemiologist; b. Milw., July 14, 1942; s. Andrew and Evelyn (Herde) S. BS, U. Wis., 1964; MD, Columbia U., 1968; MPH, Yale U., 1974, PhD, 1977. Intern medicine Boston City Hosp., 1968-69; resident psychiatry Yale U., 1969-72; aast. prof. psychiatry Yale Univ., New Haven, 1974-77; dir. emergency psychiat. svcs. Yale-New Haven (Conn.) Hosp., 1975-77; psychiatrist-in-chief Dept. Psychiatry-R.I. Hosp., Providence, 1978-87; prof. psychiatry Brown Univ., Providence, 1979-87; psychiatrist-in-chief Women & Infants Hosp., Providence, 1981-87; clin. prof. psychiatry NYU, N.Y.C., 1987—, N.Y. Med. Coll., 1987—; med. dir. Fair Oaks Hosp., Summit, N.J., 1987-92; psychiatrist-in-chief The Regent Hosp., N.Y.C., 1988-93; mem. Am. Assn. Suicidology, 1990-91; chmn. bd. dirs. Am. Wine Alliance for Rsch. and Edn., San Francisco, 1990-94; dir. CONTACT, USA, 1991-94; mem. adv. bd. Men's Fitness mag., 1993-95. Author: The Handbook of Emergency Psychiatry, 1993, Adapting to Life Threatening Illness, 1985, Sixty Ways to Make Stress Work for You, 1989, Aftershock, 1990, No One Saw My Pain, 1994. Bd. mem. The Samaritians of R.I., Providence, 1980-86; trustee Thomas Bechet Found., Providence, 1984-86; bd. mem. Summit (N.J.) Jr. League, 1987-90. Lt. comdr. USPHS, 1972-74. Elected Top 20 Lectrs. in psychiatry The Psychiat. Times, 1988. Fellow Am. Psychiat. Assn., Am. Coll. Psychiatrists, N.Y. Acad. Medicine; mem. Am. Assn. Gen. Hosp. Psychiatrists (coun. mem. 1984-92), Am. Assn. Emergency Psychiatrists (trustee 1985—), Internat. Soc. Law and Mental Health, Am. Suicide Found. (pres. Ea. divsn. 1989-94, nat. v.p. 1989-93, No. N.J. chpt. pres. 1996—, N.Y.C. chpt. pres. 1995—), N.J. Assn. Suicidology, N.J. Psychiat. Soc., Tri-County Psychiat. Soc. (pres. 1991-92). Roman Catholic. Home: 50 E New England Ave Summit NJ 07901-1818 Office: 129B E 71st St New York NY 10021-4201

SLACHTA, GREGORY ANDREW, urologist; b. Paterson, N.J., Mar. 17, 1946; s. Andrew Gregory and Mary Catherine (Shimko) S.; children: Gregory Andrew, Lara Ann, Andrea; m. Patricia A. Albano, Nov. 7, 1981. BS, Pa. State U., 1966; MD, Jefferson Med. Coll., 1968. Diplomate Am. Bd. Urology. Intern Lankenan Hosp., Phila., 1968-69; resident in urology Temple U. Hosp., Phila., 1969-70, 1973-75; pvt. practice, Springfield, Mass., 1975—; owner Puppy Ctr. & Aquarium, Springfield, 1982—. Author: Inflammatory Diseases of the Male Genital Tract, 1982. Mem. City Council Com. for Health Ins., Springfield, 1984, Springfield Planning Bd., 1991. Maj. U.S. Army, 1971-73. Fellow ACS; mem. AMA, Am. Urol. Assn. (chmn. socioecon. com. 1986-91, del. to AMA 1991—), Mass. Med. Soc. (alt. del. to AMA 1986-91, vice chmn. legis. and nat. legis. affairs com. 1987-89), Hampden Dist. Med. Soc. (pres. 1986-88), Mass. Assn. Practicing Urologists (pres. 1985-87). Democrat. Roman Catholic. Office: Urology Group of Western New Eng 222 Carew St Springfield MA 01104-4103

SLADE, HARRY WARREN, neurological surgeon; b. Highland Park, Mich., Nov. 29, 1922; s. Leon Harrison and Clara A. (Nestrom) S.; m. Betty Arlene Hummer, Jan. 28, 1950; children: Theodore Leigh, Cynthia Ann Slade Bennetzen; Steven Lawrence, Christina Louise. BS, Wayne U., 1944; MD, Baylor U., 1946. Diplomate Am. Bd. Neurol. Surgeons. Intern Grace Hosp., Detroit, 1946-47; resident in gen. surgery Meth. Hosp., Houston, 1949; resident in neurosurgery Hosp. U. Pa., Phila., 1949-52; resident in neurology Grad. Hosp. U. Pa., Phila., 1950-51; resident in pediatric neurosurgery Childrens' Hosp. Phila., 1951; pvt. practice neurosurgery Cleve., 1953-57, Waco, Tex., 1957—; instr. neurosurgery, U. Pa. Sch. Medicine, Phila., 1949-53; sr. instr. neurosurgery, Western Res. U., Cleve., 1953-57; med. adviser Waco March of Dimes, 1959-87. Co-editor audio cassettes on neurology, neurosurgery. Fellow ACS; mem. AMA, Tex. Med. Assn., McLennan County Med. Soc., Am. Assn. Neurol. Surgeons, Cong. Neurol. Surgeons, Tex. Assn. Neurol. Surgeons, Rocky Mt. Neurosurg. Soc., So. Clin.-Neurol. Assn., Pan Pacific Surg. Soc., Lions, Masons, Shriners. Baptist. Office: Waco Neurol Assn 3500 Hillcrest Dr Waco TX 76708-3157

SLADEN, BERNARD JACOB, psychologist; b. Chgo., Mar. 30, 1952; s. Mayer and Anne S. BA, U. Ill., 1974; PhD, Washington U., St. Louis, 1979. Intern U. Minn., Mpls., 1976-77; psychologist Mental Health Ctr., Inc., Ft. Wayne, Ind., 1978-80, Hines (Ill.) VA Hosp., 1980—; pvt. practice psychology Chgo., 1982—; asst. prof. Northwestern U. Med. Sch., Chgo., 1983-92; cons. Assocs. in Adolescent Psychiatry Mental Health Resources, Forest Park, Ill., 1985—, Assoc. in Clin. Psychology, Westchester, Ill., 1985-87. VA traineeship, 1974-76; NIMH fellow, 1977-78. Mem. APA, Am. Orthopsychiat. Assn. Home: 421 W Melrose St Apt 12 D Chicago IL 60657-3806 Office: 421 W Melrose St Apt 12 B Chicago IL 60657-3809

SLAFF, BERTRAM ALLEN, psychiatrist, educator; b. Passaic, N.J., Oct. 19, 1921; s. Max and Dora (Levy) S. AB, Harvard U., 1942; MD, L.I. Coll. Medicine, 1945. Diplomate Am. Bd. Psychiatry and Neurology, Am. Bd. Child Psychiatry. Intern St. Louis City Hosp., 1945-46; resident in psychiatry VA Hosp., Lexington, Ky., 1946-48, Bronx, N.Y., 1948-49; pvt. practice N.Y.C., 1949—; affiliate div. child and adolescent psychiatry Mt. Sinai Hosp., N.Y.C., 1949—; lectr. N.Y. Sch. Psychiatry, N.Y.C., 1959-64; assoc. clin. prof. psychiatry Mt. Sinai Med. Ctr., N.Y.C., 1966—; co-pres. Pan-Am. Forum for Study Adolescence, 1973-75; lit. executor Estate Coleman Dowell. Contbr. articles to med. jours., chpts. to books. Del. White House Conf. on Children, Washington, 1970, White House Conf. on Youth, Estes Park, Colo., 1971. Capt. M.C., AUS, 1946-48. Fellow Am. Soc. Adolescent Psychiatry (pres. 1970-71), Am. Psychiat. Assn., Internat. Soc. for Adolescent Psychiatry (v.p. 1988-92, treas. 1994-95), Pan-Am. Congress on Adolescent Psychiatry (hon. co-pres. 1971), Harvard Club. Office: 1100 Madison Ave New York NY 10028-0310

SLAGER, MICHAEL, internist; b. N.Y.C., July 2, 1950; s. Harold and Esther (Goldfarb) S.; AB, Boston U., 1972, MD, 1974; diplomate Am. Bd. Internal Medicine, Am. Bd. Emergency Medicine; m. Pamela T. Jarvi, Sept. 11, 1976; 2 sons, Jeremy Mark, Jonathan Daniel. Intern, then resident in internal medicine St. Elizabeth's Hosp., Boston, 1974-77; emergency medicine physician Melrose (Mass.)-Wakefield Hosp., 1977-79, dir. emergency services, 1979-85; emergency medicine physician Milton (Mass.) Med. Ctr. 1986-91; emergency med. physician North Shore Med. Ctr., 1991—. Fellow Am. Coll. Emergency Physicians, Am. Acad. Emergency Medicine; mem. Am. Coll. Forensic Examiners, Mass. Med. Soc.

SLAGLE, MARJORIE WITMAN, occupational health program manager, educator; b. Bellefonte, Pa., July 13, 1950; d. Harold Francis and Carole Elizabeth Witman; children, Karl David Slagle, Michael Allen Slagle. BS, Gustavus Adolphus Coll., 1972; M in Nursing, U. Washington. 1993; FNP, Seattle Pacific U., 1996. RN, Wash. Commd. ensign USN, 1971, advanced through grades to capt., 1993, resigned, 1993; charge nurse, evening supr. U.S. Naval Hosp., Portsmouth, Va., 1972-77; staff nurse, ICU Gen. Hosp., Portsmouth, Va., 1978, staff nurse, maternal-child care dept, 1979-84; relief charge nurse Primacare Urgent Care Ctr., Carrolton, Tex., 1984; asst. charge nurse, pub. rels., maternal child-care dept. Adventist Hosp., Simi Valley, Calif., 1985-87; staff nurse emergency room, med. surg., maternal-child depts Nursefinders, Seattle, 1987-90; asst. dir. nursing svcs. U.S. Naval Hosp., Bremerton, Wash., 1989; tng. coord., headquarters, combat zone field hosp. USN, Seattle, 1987-90; relief dept. head maternal-child, and other duties U.S. Naval Hosp., Oakland, Calif., 1990-91; head, inpatient nursing svcs., combat zone field hosp. USN, Seattle, 1991-93; regional mgr., employee assistance program coord. USPHS Fed. Occupl. Health, Seattle, 1993—, regional mgr. clin. ops., 1996—. Health and fitness speaker, Mt. Bachelor Acad., Prineville, Oreg., 1993-94. Mem. Assn. Mil. Assns. U.S. (com. chair, Navy Nurse Corps program of annual conf. 1989-91, speaker 1988-89), Res. Officers Assn., USN Meml. Found., Women in Mil. Svc. for Am. Meml. Found., Inc., Uniformed Svcs. Nurse Practitioner Assn., Am. Assn. Occupl. Health Nurses, USPHS Commd. Officers Assn., Wash. State Assn. Occupl. Health Nurses, Sigma Theta Tau Internat. Honor Soc. Nursing. Christian. Home: 5736 S 238th Ct No E5 Kent WA 98032

SLAHTA, MARY JO, nursing home administrator; b. Louisville, Nov. 9, 1952; d. James Joseph and Dorothy Mae (Stilger) D.; m. Steven D. Slahta, Aug. 5, 1972; 1 child, Jennifer Leigh. BSBA, U. Louisville, 1983; MA in Health Svcs., Webster U., 1991. Sch. sec. State Govt. Jefferson State Voc., Louisville, 1972-76, St. Govt. Ctrl. Ky. Vocat. Sch., Louisville, 1976-84; adminstrv. asst. State Govt. Ctr. State Hosp., Louisville, 1976-84; dir. mem. svc. Ky. Assn. of Health Care Facility, Frankfort, Ky., 1985-86; account exec. IntraCorp, Louisville, 1986-87; adminstr. SeniorCare, Klondike Manor, Louisville, 1987-92, SeniorCare, Regency Health, Louisville, 1993—. Allocation com. Metro United Way, Louisville, 1992-94; co-chair annual jail n-bond Am. Cancer Soc., Louisville, 1996; bd. dirs. ElderServe, Inc., Louisville, 1992-94. Mem. Am. Coll. of Health Care Adminstrs. (treas. 1995-96), Ky. Assn. of Health Care Facilities (legis. com. 1988-92, facility stds. 1988-96, chmn. mktg. comm. com., 1993-95, convention com. 1993-96). Office: Regency Health Care Ctr 1550 Raydale Dr Louisville KY 40219

SLÁMA, KAREL, biologist, zoologist; b. Tichá, Czechoslovakia, Czech Republic, Dec. 17, 1934; s. Vladimír Sláma and Marie (Michlová) Slámová; m. Věra Ležatková, June 25, 1960; children: Pavla, Martina, Tereza. MSc, Masaryk U., Brno, Czechoslovakia, 1957; PhD, Czechoslovakian Acad. Scis., Prague, 1961. Rsch. asst. Czechoslovakian Acad Scis., Prague, 1961-64, rschr. Entomology Inst., 1965-85, rschr. Inst. Organic Chemistry, 1985-90; rsch. fellow Harvard U., Cambridge, Mass., 1964-65; dir. rsch. Lab. Ecol. Pharm. Intereco, Prague, 1990-92; dir Entomology Inst. Czech Acad Scis., 1993-95. Co-author: Insect Hormones and Bioanalogues, 1974; mng. dir. European Jour. Entomology; contbr. over 150 sci. papers on insect hormones, chpt. to book. Home: Evropska 674, 160 00 Prague Czech Republic Office: Czech Acad Scis, Drnovská 507, 16100 Prague 6 Czech Republic

SLAP, JOSEPH WILLIAM, psychiatrist; b. N.Y.C., Aug. 27, 1927; s. Leonard and Elizabeth (Goodman) S.; m. Elizabeth Draper Sagle, Oct. 23, 1954; children: Laura, Robert, Leonard, Edward. BS, CCNY, 1948; MD, Hahnemann Med. Coll., 1952. Diplomate Am. Bd. Psychiatry and Neurology. Intern Phila. Gen. Hosp., 1952-53, resident in psychiatry, 1953-54; resident in psychiatry Hillside Hosp., Glen Oaks, N.Y., 1954-56; pvt. practice Phila., 1956—; tng. analyst Inst. of Phila. Assn. for Psyehoanalysis, Bala Cynwyd, Pa., 1976—; clin. prof. psychiatry Hahnemann Med. Coll., Phila., 1974-90, Jefferson Med. Coll., Phila., 1990—. Author: (with L. Slap-Shelton) The Schema in Clinical Psychoanalysis, 1991; contbr. articles to profl. jours. With U.S. Army, 1946-47. Mem. AMA, Am. Psychiatric Assn., Am. Psychoanalytic Assn., Phila. Assn. for Psychoanalysis, Phi Beta Kappa, Alpha Omega Alpha. Home: 553 Heath Rd Merion Station PA 19066-1422 Office: Psychiatric Assocs 1601 Walnut St Ste 1312 Philadelphia PA 19102-2913

SLATE, JOE HUTSON, psychologist, educator; b. Hartselle, Ala., Sept. 21, 1930; s. Murphy Edmund and Marie (Hutson) S.; m. Rachel Holladay, July 1, 1950; children: Marc Allan, John David, James Daryl. B.S., Athens Coll., 1960; M.A., U. Ala., 1965, Ph.D., 1970. Mem. faculty Athens (Ala.) State Coll., 1965-92, prof. psychology, 1974-92, chmn. behavioral scis., 1974-92; pvt. practice psychology Athens, 1970-92, Hartselle, 1992—; v.p. Slate Security Systems, Hartselle, Ala., 1984—. Author: Psychic Phenomena, 1988, Self-Empowerment, 1991, Psychic Empowerment, 1995, Psychic Empowerment for Health and Fitness, 1996. Named hon. prof. Montevallo U., 1973, prof. emeritus Athens State, Coll., 1992. Mem. APA, Am Soc. Clin. Hypnosis, Inst. Parapsychol. Rsch. (founder), Coun. for Nat. Register Health Svc. Providers in Psychology, NEA, Ala. Edn. Assn., Delta Tau Delta, Phi Delta Kappa, Kappa Delta Pi. Home and Office: 1807 Highway 31 NW Hartselle AL 35640-4442

SLATE, JOHN R., psychologist, educator; b. Dyer, Tenn., Oct. 13, 1955; s. John William and Virginia Lee (Gowers) Richelderfer; m. Gina C. Viglietti, July 27, 1985. BA, Eastern Ill. U., 1977; MA, U. Tenn., 1982, PhD, 1984. Lic. psychologist, Ark, sch. psychology specialist. Teaching asst. Treatment & Learning Ctr., Mattoon, Ill., 1978-79; psychologist intern profl. svcs. Knox County Schs., Knoxville, Tenn., 1980-81, Knoxville City Schs., 1982-83; sch. psychologist Sevier County Schs., Sevierville, Tenn., 1983-84; instr. evening sch. U. Tenn., Knoxville, 1984; asst. prof. dept. psychology Western Carolina U., Cullowhee, N.C., 1984-87; assoc. prof. Ark. State U., State University, 1987-93, prof., 1993-95; prof. edtl. leadership Valdosta State U., 1996—; cons. gifted program The Cullowhee Experience, 1986; cons. tchr. incentive program Haywood County Schs., Waynesville, N.C., 1985-87; cons. WAIS III revision The Psychol. Corp.; rsch. psychologist Transition Info. and Demonstration Evaluation Project. Contbr. numerous articles to profl. jours. Grantee Head Start, 1992; recipient Ark. Sch. Psychologists of Yr. award, 1994. Mem. Nat. Assn. Sch. Psychology, Ark. Sch. Psychology Assn. (pres. 1990-91), Mid-South Ednl. Rsch. Assn. Office: Valdosta State U Dept Edn Leadership Valdosta GA 31698-0090

SLATE, ROBERT WESLEY, general surgeon; b. Atlanta, Jan. 9, 1938; s. Geoge Washington and Hazel Corene (Freeman) S.; m. Mary Elizabeth Hampton, Nov. 23, 1960; children: Robert Wesley Jr., Elizabeth Ann Cook, George Brian, Benjamin Wade. Student, Emory U., 1956-58, MD, 1962. Diplomate Am. Bd. Surgery. Intern surgery Grady Meml. Hosp., Atlanta, 1962-63; gen. med. officer USN, Oxnard, Calif., 1963-65; resident in gen. surgery Balboa Naval Hosp., San Diego, 1965-69; asst. chief surgery Orlando (Fla.) Naval Hosp., 1969-71; gen. surgeon Stephens County Hosp., Toccoa, Ga., 1971—; pvt. practice Toccoa, Ga., 19716; cons. gen. surgery Rabon County Hosp., Clayton, Ga., 1985-91. With USN, 1969-70, Viet Nam. Fellow Am. Coll. Surgeons, Southeastern Surgical Soc., Surgical Assn. Gastrointestinal Endoscopy. Republican. Baptist. Office: Falls Rd Profl Park PO Box 609 Toccoa GA 30577-0609

SLATER, ANDREA, biomechanical engineer; b. Troy, N.Y., Nov. 10, 1958; d. Andrew Albert and Theresa Mary (Giuliano) Inco; m. Jeffrey Clark Slater, Sept. 26, 1982 (div. Jan. 1989); 1 child, Mark Andrew. BSME, Union Coll., 1981, BS in Biology, 1981. Mech. engr. Instrumentation Lab., Inc., Lexington, Mass., 1981-82; product devel. engr. USCI divsn. C.R. Bard, Inc., Billerica, Mass., 1982-83; project engr. U.S. Catheters and Instruments div. C.R. Bard, Inc., Billerica, Mass., 1983-85, sr. project engr., 1985-87, engring. sect. head, 1987-90; mgr. product engring. and diagnostics Cordis Corp., Miami, Fla., 1990-93; program mgr. applied devel. Meadox Meds., Inc., Oakland, N.J., 1993-95; staff engrin., project mgr. New Products Devel. Cordis a Johnson and Johnson Co., Warren, N.J., 1995—. Patentee soft tip guiding catheter and mfg. method, med. instrument valve with foam partition member having vapor permeable skin, check valve manifold assembly for use in angioplasty, one piece vessel dilator/catheter sheath introducer, pumping apparatus for perfusion and other fluid catheterization procedures. Mem. ASME, AAAS, Am. Soc. Plastics Engrs., Am. Mgmt. Assn., NAFE, Internat. Soc. for Endovascular Surgery. Roman Catholic. Office: New Product Devel. Johnson and Johnson Co. 40 Technology Dr Warren NJ 07059

SLATON, CHARLES R., hospital administrator; b. Quanah, Tex., Nov. 28, 1956; s. Charles L. and Margaret E. (Graham) S.; m. Lori Renee Downs, Oct. 11, 1979; children: Charles M., Preston H., McKinsay L. BBA in Mgmt., Tex. Tech. U., 1979, MBA in Health Orgn. Mgmt., 1988. Exec. dir. physe ventures St. Mary Hosp., Lubbock, 1986-89; v.p. strategic devel. Santa Rosa (Calif.) Meml. Hosp., 1989-94; v.p. physician rels. St. Francis Hosp., Memphis, 1994—. Office: St Francis Hospital 5959 Park Ave Memphis TN 38119

SLATON, JOSEPH GUILFORD, social worker; b. N.Y.C., Sept. 29, 1951; s. Joseph Slachta and Hilda Elizabeth (Sims) S.; 1 child, Nicholas Michael. BS, E. Carolina U., 1974; MSW, U. N.C., 1977. Cert. pub. mgr. Cottage parent supr. N.C. Div. Youth Svcs., Rocky Mount, 1974-75; juvenile evaluation counselor N.C. Div. Youth Svcs., Rocky Mount and Butner, N.C., 1975-77; social worker Murdoch Ctr., N.C. Dept. Human Resources, Butner, 1977-78; facility survey cons., mental retardation profl. N.C. Div. Facility Svcs., Raleigh, 1978-81, facility survey cons. long-term care programs, 1981-83, program mgr. health care facilities br., 1983-87, human svcs. planner cert. of need program, 1987-94; sr. analyst, 1994—; asst. Scoutmaster BSA Troop 300, speaker in field. Mem. N.C. Rehab. Task Force, Raleigh, 1988-90; chmn. subcom. N.C. Mental Retardation Task Force, Raleigh, 1982-83; active N.C. Regional Strategic Planning Task Force, Raleigh, 1982-83; active N.C. Regional Strategic Planning Task Force on Mental Retardation, 1982; mem. allocations panel Wake County United Way, Raleigh, 1984-95; mem. planning com. Wake County Ptnrs. Program—Sta. WRAL-TV, Raleigh, 1980, coord. Auction Day, 1981, mem. exec. planning com., 1982; campaign mgr., vol. coord., treas. rep. for N.C. Ho. Reps. Mem. NASW (legis. policy com.), Acad. Cert. Social Workers, Triangle Health Execs.' Forum. Episcopalian. Office: NC Div Facility Svcs PO Box 29530 Raleigh NC 27626-0530

SLATTERY, CHARLES WILBUR, biochemistry educator; b. La Junta, Colo., Nov. 18, 1937; s. Robert Ernest Slattery and Virgie Belle (Chamberlain) Tobin; m. Arline Sylvia Reile, June 15, 1958; children: Scott Charles, Coleen Kay. BA, Union Coll., 1959; MS, U. Nebr., 1961, PhD, 1965. Instr. chemistry Union Coll., Lincoln, Nebr., 1961-63; asst. prof., assoc. prof. chemistry Atlantic Union Coll., South Lancaster, Mass., 1963-68; rsch. assoc. biophysics MIT, Cambridge, 1967-70; asst. prof., then prof. biochemistry Loma Linda U., Calif., 1970-80, prof. biochemistry-pediatrics, 1980—, chmn. dept., 1983—; vis. prof. U. So. Calif., L.A., 1978-79. Contbr. articles to profl. jours. NIH grantee, 1979-82, 86-89, Am. Heart Assn. (Calif.), 1981-83, 83-84. Mem. AAAS, Am. Chem. Soc. (biochemistry div.), Am. Dairy Sci. Assn., Am. Heart Assn. Thrombosis Coun., N.Y. Acad. Scis., The Protein Soc., Am. Soc. Biochemistry and Molecular Biology. Internat. Soc. for Rsch. on Human Milk and Lactation, Sigma Xi. Office: Loma Linda U Sch of Medicine Dept of Biochemistry Loma Linda CA 92350

SLAUGHTER, FREEMAN CLUFF, dentist; b. Estes, Miss., Dec. 30, 1926; s. William Cluff and Vay (Fox) S.; student Wake Forest Coll., 1944; student Emory U., 1946-47, DDS, 1951; m. Genevieve Anne Parks, July 30, 1948; children: Mary Anne, Thomas Freeman, James Hugh. Practice gen. dentistry, Kannapolis, N.C., 1951-89; ret.; mem. N.C. Bd. Dental Examiners, 1966-75, pres., 1968-69, sec.-treas., 1971-74; chief dental staff Cabarrus Meml. Hosp., Concord, N.C., 1965-66, 75; mem. N.C. Adv. Com. for Edn. Dental Aux. Personnel-N.C. State Bd. Edn., 1967-70; adviser dental asst. program Rowan Tech. Inst., 1974-76; Duke Med. Ctr. Davison Century Club. Trustee N.C. Symphony Soc., 1962-68, pres. Kannapolis chpt., 1961; mem. Cabarrus County Bd. Health, 1977-83, chmn., 1981-83, acting health dir., 1981; vice chmn. Kannapolis Charter Commn., 1983-84; mem. City Council Kannapolis, 1984-85; Mayor protem, Kannapolis, 1984-85; active Boy Scouts Am., Eagle scout with silver palm. Served with USN, 1944-46, WW II. ETO, MTO. Recipient Kannapolis Citizen of Yr. award, 1982; lic. real estate broker. Fellow Am. Coll. Dentists; mem. Am. Legion, Kannapolis Jr. C. of C. (v.p. 1952), Toastmasters Internat. (pres. Kannapolis 1963-64), ADA (life), Am. Assn. Dental Examiners (Dentist Citizen of Year 1975; v.p. 1977-79), So. Conf. Dental Deans and Examiners (v.p. 1969), N.C. Dental Soc. (resolution of commendation 1975), N.C. Dental Soc. Anesthesiology (pres. 1964), Southeastern Acad. Prosthodontics, So. Acad. Oral Surgery, Am. Soc. Dentistry for Children (pres. N.C. unit 1957), Internat. Assn. Dental Research, Cabarrus County Dental Soc. (pres. 1953-54, 63-64, 69), N.C. Assn. Professions (dir. 1976-80), Omicron Kappa Upsilon, Alpha Epsilon Upsilon. Clubs: Masons, Shriners, Kannapolis Music (pres. 1962-63), Rotary (dir. 1977-80).

SLAVEN, BETTYE DEJON, psychotherapist; b. New Orleans, Sept. 27, 1946; d. Edward William and Bettye (Ray) DeJ.; m. Richard W. Slaven, Nov. 28, 1968; children: Kelly DeJon Slaven, Richard Daniel. BA, Tex. Tech U., 1969; MA, U. Houston, 1974; postgrad. N. Tex. State U., 1974-76. Lic. counselor, Tex., marriage and family therapist, Tex. Tchr. Richardson Ind. Sch. Dist., Tex., 1970-71, 73-74, Somerville Pub. Schs., Mass., 1971-72, Trinity Episcopal Sch., New Orleans, 1972-73; with Goals for Dallas-Devel., 1975—; pvt. practice psychotherapy, Dallas, 1979—; therapist family crisis intervention Dallas Ind. Sch. Dist., 1986-94. Bd. dirs. Way Back House-Vol. Psychol. Assistance, 1979—, Freedom Rides Found, bylaws com., 1987—, Foster Child Advocate Services, 1987—, sec. 1989-90, v.p., pers. chmn., 1990—; founder, project chmn. Women's Way Back House, 1979; project chairman, bd. dirs. Interfaith Housing Coalition, 1987-88; pres. living bible class Highland Park Meth. Ch., Dallas, 1982, 90-91, mem. adminstrv. bd., 1986, also bd. dirs.; adv. bd.; bd. dirs. Dallas County Mental Health Assn., 1989, Dallas Coun. Alcoholism, 1989-90; mem. Communities Found. Tex. Networking, 1986—, Letot task force, 1986, nominating com. Camp Fire Girls Inc., 1987-90; city chmn. Dallas Area Rapid Transit, 1983; pub. affairs chmn. Jr. League Dallas, 1984, resch. and devel. chmn., 1985-86, cmty. v.p., 1986-87, exec. and pub. rels. coms., 1986-87, grantee sr. mentor program at

N. Dallas H.S., 1995-96; chmn. Camp Task Force for Chronically Ill Children, 1986-87, Spl. Camps for Spl. Kids, 1987-88, bd. dirs. 1988-89, adv. bd., 1989-92; pres. McCulloch Middle Sch. PTA, 1987—; chmn. Career Day Highland High Sch. PTA, 1990, coll. night chair, 1991; assoc. Pathways to Prevention, 1989-91; pers. chmn. bd. dirs. Foster Child Advocates Svcs., 1989-93; bd. dirs. Dallas Mental Health Assn., 1990-95; co-chmn. Jr. Symphony Ball, 1993; bldg. coord. Safe Haven grant, 1995-96. Recipient Lenz award cmty. agy. liaison Susan G. Komen luncheon com., 1996; named one of Outstanding Young Women in Am., 1980. Avocations: sailing, swimming, reading.

SLAVIN, RAYMOND GRANAM, allergist, immunologist; b. Cleve., June 29, 1930; s. Philip and Dinah (Baskind) S.; m. Alberta Cohrt, June 10, 1953; children: Philip, Stuart, David, Linda. A.B., U. Mich., 1952; M.D., St. Louis U., 1956; M.S., Northwestern U., 1963. Diplomate: Am. Bd. Internal Medicine, Am. Bd. Allergy and Immunology (treas.). Intern U. Mich. Hosp., Ann Arbor, 1956-57; resident St. Louis U. Hosp., 1959-61; fellow in allergy and immunology Northwestern U. Med. Sch., 1961-64; asst. prof. internal medicine and microbiology St. Louis U., 1965-70, assoc., 1970-73, prof., 1973—, dir. div. allergy and immunology, 1965—; mem. NIH study sect., 1985-89; cons. U.S. Army M.C. Contbr. numerous articles to med. publs.; editorial bd.: Jour. Allergy and Clin. Immunology, 1975-81, Tice Practice Medicine, 1973-84, Jour. Club of Allergy, 1978-80. Chmn. bd. Asthma and Allergy Found. Am., 1985-88. With M.C., U.S. Army, 1957-59. Grantee NIH, 1967-70, 84—, Nat. Inst. Occpl. Safety and Health, 1974-80. Fellow ACP, Am. Acad. Allergy and Immunology (exec. bd., historian, pres. 1983-84); mem. Am. Assn. Immunologists, Central Soc. Clin. Research, AAAS. Democrat. Jewish. Home: 631 E Polo Dr Saint Louis MO 63105-2629 Office: 1402 S Grand Blvd Saint Louis MO 63104-1004

SLAVINSKA, NONNA, psychoanalyst, psychotherapist; b. Warsaw, Poland; came to U.S., 1953, naturalized, 1958; d. Paul and Nadezda (von Vetter) Slawinski; m. Vaclav L. de P. Holy, Feb. 22, 1970; 1 child, Alexander Levitsky. MS cum laude, L.I. U., 1957; PhD, NYU, 1967; cert. psychoanalysis and psychotheraphy, Postgrad. Ctr. Mental Health, 1971, cert. group psychotherapy, 1974, cert. supervision psychoanalytic process, 1975. Pvt. practice clin. psychology, 1957—; clin. psychologist N.J. Dept. Instns. and Agencies, Trenton, 1957-64; cons. spl. edn. Howell Twp. Bd. Edn., N.J., 1964-66, Monmouth County High Sch., N.J., 1966-68; cons. in psychology Dept. Labor and Industry, Newark, 1970-75; supr. Inst. Mental Health Edn., Engelwood, N.J., 1976-80; supr. faculty Payne-Whitney Clinic, N.Y. Hosp., Cornell Med. Ctr., N.Y.C., 1978-82; supr. Psychol. Ctr. CCNY, 1981-82; supr. Psychoanalytic Inst. Postgrad. Ctr. for Mental Health, N.Y.C., 1983—, sr. supr. group therapy dept., 1982—, faculty, 1972—, asst. supr. faculty group therapy dept., 1976—; supr. group and family studies div. Albert Einstein Coll. Medicine, Yeshiva U., N.Y.C., 1987—; founder, chairperson com. on mental health Kosciuszko Found., N.Y.C., 1982-88; founder, chairperson interdisciplinary psychology and mental health sect. Polish Inst. Arts and Scis., N.Y.C., 1984—; vis. prof. dept. psychiatry Jagiellonian U., Poland. Internat. editor GROUP Jour., 1983-86; internat. coord., cons. editor Internat. Jour. Group Psychotherapy, 1984-87. Recipient Five Yr. Service to N.J. award, 1963, Founder's Day award NYU, 1968, Cert., Am. Group Psychotherapy Assn., 1981. Fellow APA (internat. rels. com., Am. Group Psychotherapy Assn. (internat. aspects com.); mem. Internat. Assn. Group Psychotherapy (bd. dirs. 193-386, founder, chairperson adv. com. on inquiry and rsch. 1984—), N.J. Psychol. Assn., Internat. Assn. Applied Psychology, Internat Div. 29 Am. Psychol. Assn. (chmn. com. on rsch. 1985—). Office: 9 E 96th St # 9B New York NY 10128-0778

SLAWIATYNSKY, MARION MICHAEL, biomedical electronics engineer, software consultant; b. Phila., Nov. 21, 1958; s. Walter Wasyl and Maria Margaret (Sauer) S. BA in Biology, LaSalle U., 1980; MS in Biomed. Engring., Drexel U., 1984, BS in Electronics Engring. (hon.), 1982. Sr. systems engr. Innovative Med. Systems, Ivyland, Pa., 1983-95; sr. software engr. Advanced Tech. Labs., Bothell, Wash., 1995—. Soloist Male Chorus Prometheus, 1976-95; mem. Steuben Soc. Am., Phila., 1990-95. Mem. IEEE, Assn. for Advancement of Med. Instrumentation. Republican. Roman Catholic. Home: 20129 Holly Hills Dr NE Bothell WA 98011-7603 Office: ATL 22100 Bothell Everett Hwy PO Box 3003 MS265 Bothell WA 98041-3003

SLAY, DAVID KENNETH, psychologist, educator; b. Oskaloosa, Iowa, Nov. 28, 1943; s. Kenneth P. and Beatrice M. (White) S.; m. Madeline Woo, Aug. 28, 1976; children: Dana Lee, Lindsay Lee. BA, Calif. State U., Long Beach, 1966, MA, 1969; PhD, Calif. Sch. Profl. Psychology, 1975. Diplomate Am. Bd. Profl. Psychology; lic. psychologist, Calif. Clin. psychologist Child Guidance Ctr., Fullerton, Calif., 1975-80; dir. psychol. tng. Child Guidance Ctr., Fullerton, 1980-85, clin. dir., 1985-91; Greater Long Beach Child Guidance Ctr., 1991—; adj. prof. Pepperdine U., Irvine, Calif., 1978-80, Chapman Coll., Orange Calif., 1989-91; oral exam. commr. Calif. Bd. of Psychology, 1989—. Contbr. articles to profl. jours. With U.S. Army, 1969-71. Mem. APA, Nat. Acad. Neuropsychology. Office: Greater Long Beach Child Guidance Ctr Inc 2801 Atlantic Ave Long Beach CA 90801-1428

SLAYMAN, CAROLYN WALCH, geneticist, educator; b. Portland, Maine, Mar. 11, 1937; d. John Weston and Ruth Dyer (Sanborn) Walch; m. Clifford L. Slayman; children—Andrew, Rachel. B.A. with highest honors, Swarthmore Coll., 1958; Ph.D., Rockefeller U., 1963; D.Sc. (hon.), Bowdoin Coll., 1985. Instr., then asst. prof. Case Western Res. U., Cleve., 1967; from asst. prof. to prof. genetics Yale U. Sch. Medicine, New Haven, 1967—, Sterling prof. genetics, 1991—, chmn. dept. genetics, 1984-95, dep. dean for acad. and sci. affairs, 1995—; chmn. genetic basis of disease rev. commn. NIH, 1981-85, nat. adv. gen. med. scis. coun., 1989-93; bd. dirs. J. Weston Walch Pub., Portland, Maine, The Perkin-Elmer Corp.; mem. sci. rev. bd. Howard Hughes Med. Inst., 1992—. Mem. editorial bd. Jour. Biol. Chemistry, 1989-94; contbr. articles to sci. jours. Trustee Foote Sch., New Haven, Conn., 1983-89, Hopkins Sch., New Haven, 1988-93; bd. overseers Bowdoin Coll., Brunswick, Maine, 1976-88, trustee, 1988—. Recipient Deborah Morton award Westbrook Coll., 1986. Mem. Am. Soc. Biol. Chemists, Genetics Soc. Am., Soc. Gen. Physiologists, Am. Soc. Microbiology, Phi Beta Kappa. Office: Yale U Sch Medicine Dept Genetics 333 Cedar St New Haven CT 06510-3206

SLEDGE, CLEMENT BLOUNT, orthopedic surgeon, educator; b. Ada, Okla., Nov. 1, 1930; s. John B. and Mollie D. (Blount) S.; m. Georgia Kurrus, Apr. 13, 1957; children—Margaret, John, Matthew, Claire. M.D., Yale U., 1955; M.A. (hon.), Harvard U., 1970; ScD (hon.), U. The South, 1987. Diplomate: Am. Bd. Orthopedic Surgery. Intern Barnes Hosp., St. Louis, 1955-56; resident in orthopedic surgery Harvard U., 1960-63; fellow in orthopedic pathology Armed Forces Inst. Pathology, 1963; vis. scientist Strangeways Research Lab., Cambridge (Eng.) U., 1963-66; asst. prof. orthopedic surgery Harvard U., 1963-67, assoc. prof., 1967-70, prof., 1970—, chmn. dept., 1970-96; chmn. Brigham and Women's Physician Hosp. Orgn., 1995—; chmn. dept. orthopedic surgery Brigham and Women's Hosp. Editor: Textbook of Rheumatology, 1981, 85, 89, 93; contbr. more than 100 articles to sci. jours. Active Arthritis Found.; chmn. Nat. Arthritis Adv. Bd., 1978-80. Served with M.C. USNR, 1956-58. Fellow Med. Found. Boston, 1963-66; Gebbie research fellow, 1968; NIH grantee, 1967—. Mem. Am. Acad. Orthopedic Surgeons (pres. 1985-86), Orthopedic Rsch. Soc. (pres. 1978-80), Am. Rheumatism Assn., Inst. of Medicine, Nat. Acad. Sci., Interurban Orthopedic Club, The Hip Soc. (pres. 1985). Episcopalian. Office: Brigham and Women's Hosp 75 Francis St Boston MA 02115

SLEETER, JOHN WILLIAM HIGGS, physician, health service administrator; b. Toledo, Iowa, Feb. 16, 1917; s. Charles Elmer and Meta DeLad (Higgs) S.; m. Betti Deming, Aug. 28, 1943 (div. Mar. 1963); m. Patricia Catherine Parrillo, July 8, 1989; children: John William, Marilee Ann, Thomas David. BA, Cornell Coll., Mt. Vernon, Iowa, 1942; MD, U. Iowa, 1945. Pres. San Gabriel Primary Care, Arcadia, Calif., 1952-62, L.A. County Acad. GP, Calif., 1965-66; inst. paramedic care St. Terisita Hosp., Duarte, Calif., 1970-75; pres., chief operating officer Profsnl. Rev. Area 21, 1970-75; 1st pres. L.A. County Paramedic Commn., 1974-75; pres., CEO, dir. pvt. practice assn., Arcadia, 1984—. Capt, AUS, 1945-49. Mem. Balboa Bay Club, San Gabriel Country Club, Masons (32d degree). Republican. Office: 1041 W Huntington Dr Arcadia CA 91007

SLEMROVA, MIRIAM, physician; b. Prague, Czech Republic, Jan. 27, 1957; came to U.S., 1984; d. Joseph and Ludmila (Cermakova) S. DMD, Charles U., Prague, 1981; DO, Coll. Osteo. Medicine, Des Moines, 1995. Dentist Dental Clin., Tanvald, No. Bohemia, 1981-82; dental asst. Carney Hosp., Boston, 1984-86; sr. rsch. asst. Oreg. Health Scis. Univ., Portland, 1986-88, radiology tech., 1990-91; resident Tucson Hosp. Med. Edn. Program, 1995-96. Mem. Christian Med. Dental Soc., Phi Theta Kappa. Roman Catholic.

SLICK, GARY L., medical educator; b. Balt., Apr. 13, 1941; s. Roy M. Slick and Mildred F. (Nelson) Ward; m. Marylyn Maxwell, July 6, 1968; children: Jacquelyn, Christopher. BA, Eastern Nazarene Coll., Quincy, Mass., 1963; MA, U. Kansas, 1969; DO, Kansas City (Mo.) Coll. Osteopathy and Surgery, 1969; cert. in internal medicine and nephrology, Am. Osteopathic Bd. Internal Medicine. Attending nephrologist Detroit Osteopathic Hosp., 1974-82; assoc. clin. prof. medicine coll. osteopathic medicine Mich. State U., East Lansing, Mich, 1975-82; dir. clerkship tng. MSU/Detroit Osteopathic Hosp., 1977-82; prof., chmn. dept. medicine Okla. Coll. Osteopathic Medicine, Tulsa, 1982-83; prof., chmn. dept. internal medicine Chgo. Coll. Osteopathic Medicine, 1983—; exec. dir. Am. Osteopathic Bd. Internal Medicine, Chgo., 1988—; vice chmn. Am. Osteopathic Bd. Internal Medicine, 1982-83, chmn., Chgo., 1983-88; pres. Am. Osteopathic Found. Internal Medicine, Washington, 1990-94. Contbr. articles to profl. jours. Mem. sci. adv. bd. Mich. Kidney Found., Ann Arbor, 1979-82; chmn. high blood pressure com. Mich. Heart Assn., Detroit, 1980-82; mem. editorial adv. bd. Jour. Am. Osteopathic Assn., Chgo., 1988—. Recipient Mosby Book award Mosby Pub. Co., 1969; named Outstanding Tchr. of Yr. Med. Residents Detroit Osteopathic Hosp., 1980. Fellow Am. Coll. Osteo. Internists (Disting. Svc. award 1986, chmn. nephrology sect. 1979-82, bd. dirs. 1987-95, pres. 1993-94); mem. Am. Fedn. for Clin. Rsch., Am. Soc. Nephrology, Am. Physiol. Soc., Am. Soc. Artificial Internal Organs, Internat. Soc. Nephrology, Nat. Kidney Found. Methodist. Office: Chgo Coll Osteo Medicine 5200 S Ellis Ave Chicago IL 60615-4314

SLICK, RUTH JUANITA, health facility administrator, retired; b. Anton, Colo., Aug. 28, 1921; d. Charles Oliver and Flora (Elliott) Krauth; m. Eugene Laurns Slick, June 29, 1947; children: Janvier, Evan, Mardi, Kahlei. RN, Beth-El Sch. Nursing, 1943; postgrad., U. Colo., 1946. Office nurse Dr. Howard Kurtz, Salem, Oreg., 1947-49; charge nurse, dir. nursing, adminstr. Willamette Meth. Convalescent Ctr., Milwaukie, Oreg., 1959-87; ret., 1987. Lt. (j.g.) USN, 1944-45. Fellow Am. Coll. Health Care Assn. (emeritus, life), Am. Coll. Nursing Home Adminstrs. Home: 12705 SE River Rd Apt 505 E Milwaukie OR 97222

SLIFKIN, MALCOLM, clinical microbiologist, educator; b. Newark, Nov. 9, 1933; s. William and Raye (Nalebuff) S.; B.S., Furman U., 1955; M.S. in Pub. Health, U. N.C., 1956, M.S., 1959; Ph.D., Rutgers U., 1964; Diplomate Am. Bd. Med. Microbiology in Pub. Health and Med. Lab. Microbiology; m. Janet E. Saperstein, July 31, 1966; children—Joshua Michael, Robert Seth. Instr., Yale U. Sch. Medicine, New Haven, 1962-64; head. microbiology sect. Allegheny Gen. Hosp., Pitts., 1964—; adj. assoc. prof. microbiology Pa. State U., 1965—; clin. asst. pathology U. Pitts., 1955-71; cons. Coll. Am. Pathologists, Chgo. 1978-80; sr. scientist Allegheny Gen. Hosp., 1980—; prof. lab. medicine and pathology Allegheny U., 1990—, prof. microbiology and immunology, 1991—. Mem. Pitts. Savoyard Orch., 1965—, Pitts. Woodwind Quintet, 1964—. Am. Cancer Soc. grantee, 1969-70, NIH grantee, 1971-72. Fellow Am. Acad. Microbiology (com. on postdoctoral ednl. programs 1974-79); mem. Western Pa. Soc. Clin. Microbiologists (pres. 1971—), Am. Soc. Microbiology (ethical practices com.), AAAS, N.Y. Acad. Scis., Sigma Xi. Jewish. Contbr. numerous sci. articles to profl. publs. Home: 1230 Wightman St Pittsburgh PA 15217-1221 Office: 320 E North Ave Pittsburgh PA 15212

SLIFKIN, ROBERT FELDMAN, nephrologist; b. Phila., Jan. 5, 1940; s. Leon and Carrie (Feldman) S.; m. Margaret Moran, May 3, 1989; children: Michelle, Joseph, Bonnie, Denise, David, Michael. BSc, Dickinson Coll., 1960; MD, Hahnemann U., 1964. Diplomate Nat. Bd. Med. Examiners, Am. Bd. Internal Medicine. Rotating intern Phila. Gen. Hosp., 1964-65; gen. med. officer U.S. Army, Europe, 1965-68; resident in internal medicine Hahnemann Hosp., Phila., 1968-69, chief med. resident, 1969-70, NIH rsch. fellow in nephrology, 1970-72; clin. assoc. Dept. Medicine Mount Sinai Sch. of Medicine CUNY, 1972-73; asst. attending physician-Mount Sinai Svcs. City Hosp. Ctr. at Elmhurst, 1972-73, assoc. attending physician-Mount Sinai Svcs., 1974-86; asst. clin. prof. Dept. of Medicine Mount Sinai Sch. of Medicine CCNY, 1974-78, assoc. clin. prof. Dept. of Medicine, 1979—; med. dir. Queens (N.Y.) Artificial Kidney Ctr., 1974—; attending Mount Sinai Svcs. City Hosp. Ctr. at Elmhurst, 1986—; med. dir. South Queens Dialysis Ctr., 1986—; Contbr. numerous articles to profl. jours. Capt. U.S. Army, 1965-68. Recipient R.S. Raue Pediatrics prize Hahnemann Med. Coll., 1964. Mem. AMA, Internat. Soc. Nephrology, Am. Soc. Nephrology, N.Y. State Med. Soc., Med. Soc. County of Queens, Am. Heart Assn.-Coun. on Kidney in Cardiovascular Disease, Nat. Kidney Found.-Coun. of Clin. Nephrology Dialysis and Transplantation, Am. Soc. Transplant Physicians, Am. Soc. Law and Medicine, Am. Coun. on Transplantation, Internat. Soc. for Peritoneal Dialysis, Am. Soc. Internal Medicine, N.Y. State Soc. Internal Medicine, Queens Soc. Internal Medicine, Am. Soc. Artificial Internal Organs, Alpha Omega Alpha. Office: Queens Artificial Kidney Ctr 3435 70th St Jackson Heights NY 11372

SLINGLUFF, CRAIG LEE, JR., surgeon; b. Norfolk, Va., June 29, 1958; s. Craig Lee and Emily (Hunter) S. BA, U. Va., 1980, MD, 1984. Intern and resident dept. surgery Duke U., Durham, N.C., 1984-91; rsch. fellow Melanoma Immunobiology Lab., Duke U., Durham, N.C., 1986-88; asst. prof. surgery U. Va., Charlottesville, 1991-95, assoc. prof. surgery, 1995—, chief divsn. surg. oncology, 1994—. Contbr. articles to profl. jours. Mem. Soc. Surg. Oncology, Soc. Biol. Therapy, Soc. Univ. Surgeons. Office: Univ of Va Dept Surgery Charlottesville VA 22908 Address: 256 Woodlands Rd Charlottesville VA 22901-8936

SLIPMAN, (SAMUEL) RONALD, hospital administrator; b. New Orleans, Aug. 24, 1939; s. Jake and Esther (Steinman) S.; m. Carole Marie Green, July 1, 1961 (div. Feb. 1982); children: Susan Rachel, Lawrence Jay; m. Marilyn Morais, Feb. 5, 1983 (dec. June 1985); m. Lelia Ruth Foster, Jan. 12, 1986; children: Ronald Andrew, Brian Edward. BS, Tulane U., 1961; cert. in supervision techniques, La. State U., 1984; postgrad., NE La. U., 1978-79, 80-81. Design progress estimator Boeing Co., New Orleans, 1964-66; interviewer Tex. Employment Commn., Tyler and Lufkin, 1977-78; pers. technician State of La., Baton Rouge, 1961-62, 63-64, 73-75, 81; rsch. statistician La. Ins. Commn., Baton Rouge, 1967-68; labor market analyst La. Dept. Labor, Baton Rouge, 1969-70, 77; pers. dir. Royal Orleans Hotel, New Orleans, 1966-67; mgmt. analyst for quality assurance Earl K. Long Hosp., Baton Rouge, 1981-84, dir. ancillary svcs., 1984-86; mgmt. analyst, spl. asst. to dir. for total quality mgmt. Dept. Vets. Affairs Med. Ctr., Alexandria, La., 1987-88, 89-90; mgmt. cons., 1990—. Mem. adminstrv. bd. 1st United Ch., chmn. presch. bd.; cubmaster pack 10 Boy Scouts Am., 1993-94, 96—, asst. cubmaster, 1994-96. Mem. La. Soc. Hosp. Pharmacists, Ctrl. La. Soc. for Human Resource Mgmt., S.W. La. Bridge Assn. (pres., bd. dirs.). Republican. Methodist. Home and Office: Rt 2 105 Fox Fire Ln Alexandria LA 71302-8638

SLIPP, SAMUEL, psychiatrist, psychoanalyst, family therapist; b. Newark, Oct. 12, 1924; s. William and Ida (Dubin) S.; m. Jean Hershon (dec.); m. Sandra Rodetsky; 1 child, Elena Willa. Student, Rutgers U., 1941-43, NYU, 1945-46; BS, MD, Ind. U., 1950; postgrad., NYU, 1950-51, Ohio State U., 1951-52, U. Calif., Langley Porter, 1952-57; BS, MD, Ind. U., 1950. Pvt. practice San Francisco and N.Y.C., 1957—; dir. psychiatry Los Guillocos Sch. for Girls Calif. Youth Authority, Santa Rosa, Calif., 1957-58; assoc. prof. psychology San Francisco State Coll., 1957-65; assoc. attending psychiatrist Sch. Medicine Stanford U., San Francisco, 1957-65; assoc. prof. psychiatry N.Y. Med Coll., N.Y.C., 1965-68; clin. prof. psychiatry Sch. Medicine NYU, N.Y.C., 1968—; adj. psychiatrist Mt. Zion Hosp., San Francisco, 1957-65; vis. lectr. U. London Inst. Psychiatry, Maudsley Hosp., 1965; med. dir. Postgrad. Ctr. for Mental Health, 1979-83; tng. and supervising analyst psychoanalytic inst. N.Y. Med. Coll., 1984—. Author: Curative Factors in Dynamic Psychotherapy, 1982, Object Relations: A Dynamic Bridge Between Individual and Family Treatment, 1984, The Technique and Practice of Object Relations Family Therapy, 1988, The Freudian Mystique: Freud, Women and Feminism, 1994, Healing the Gender Wars, 1996; (with Edward Pinney Jr.) Glossary of Group and Family Therapy, 1982. Sgt. U.S. Inf., 1943-45, World War II. Fellow Am. Psychiat. Assn. (life), Am. Acad. Psychoanalysis (trustee 1984-89), Am. Coll. Psychoanalysts; mem. Am. Family Therapy Assn. (charter), Soc. Med. Psychoanalysts (pres. 1984-85), Assn. Med. Group Psychoanalysts (pres. 1971-72). Home: 220 Chestnut St Englewood NJ 07631-3134 Office: 262 Central Park W New York NY 10024-3512

SLIPPEN, MICHAEL, otolaryngologist; b. N.Y.C., Feb. 2, 1942; s. Morton and Eleanor (Weinstock) S.; m. Carol Susan Goldman; children: Jeffrey, Mark, Daniel. MD, Cath. U. Louvain (Belgium), 1969. Chief otolaryngology Parker Jewish Geriatric Inst., New Hyde Park, N.Y., 1978-93. Pres. L.I. Soc. of Otolaryngology, 1986. Maj. USAF, 1975-77. Fellow ACS, Am. Acad. Otolaryngology.

SLOAN, FRANK ALLEN, economics educator; b. Greensboro, N.C., Aug. 15, 1942; s. Harry Benjamin and Edith (Vortrefflich) S.; m. Paula Jane Rackoff, June 22, 1969; children: Elyse Valerie, Richard Matthew. A.B., Oberlin Coll., 1964; Ph.D., Harvard U., 1969. Research economist Rand Corp., Santa Monica, Calif., 1968-71; asst. prof. econs. U. Fla., Gainesville, 1971-73, assoc. prof., 1973-76; prof. econs. Vanderbilt U., Nashville, 1976-84; Centennial prof. econs. Vanderbilt U., 1984-93, chmn. dept., 1986-89; J. Alexander McMahon Prof. econs. Duke University, Durham, NC, 1993—; dir. Health Policy Ctr. Vanderbilt U. Inst. Pub. Policy Studies, 1976—; mem. Inst. Medicine, Washington, 1982—, dist. medicine coun., 1990—; mem. Nat. Coun. Health Care Tech., Washington, 1979-81, Nat. Allergy and Infectious Disease Council, Washington, 1971-74; cons. adv. coun. Social Security, Washington, 1983. Co-author: Private Physicians and Public Programs, 1978, Hospital Labor Markets, 1980, Insurance, Regulation and Hospital Costs, 1980, Uncompensated Hospital Care: Rights and Responsibilities, 1986, Insuring Medical Malpractice, 1991. Mem. Am. Econ. Assn., So. Econ. Assn., Western Econ. Assn. Home: 109 Millbrae Ln Chapel Hill NC 27514 Office: Duke University Ctr for Health Policy PO Box 90253 Durham NC 27708

SLOAN, HERBERT ELIAS, physician, surgeon; b. Clarksburg, W.Va., Oct. 10, 1914; s. Herbert Elias and Luella (Dye) S.; m. Doris Edwards, May 3, 1943; children: Herbert, Ann, Elizabeth, John, Robert. A.B., Washington and Lee U., 1936; M.D., Johns Hopkins U., 1940. Diplomate Am. Bd. Surgery, Am. Bd. Thoracic Surgery (bd. dirs. 1966-86, v.p. 1971-73, sec.-treas. 1973-86). Resident in surgery Johns Hopkins Hosp., 1941-44; instr. dept. surgery Johns Hopkins U., 1943-44; resident in thoracic surgery U. Mich. Hosp., Ann Arbor, 1947-49, instr. thoracic surgery, 1949-50; asst. prof. U. Mich., Ann Arbor, 1950-53, assoc. prof., 1953-62, prof. surgery, 1962-87, head sect. thoracic surgery, 1970-85; chief clin. affairs U. Mich. Hosps., Ann Arbor, 1982-86, med. dir. operating room, 1986-87, prof. emeritus surgery, 1987—; med. dir. managed health care U. Mich., Ann Arbor, 1989-96; mem. staff VA Hosp., Ann Arbor, 1953—, cons., 1968—. Author: (with Marvin M. Kirsh) Blunt Chest Trauma, General Principles of Management, 1977; editor Annals of Thoracic Surgery, 1969-85; contbr. (with Marvin M. Kirsh) chpts. to books, articles to profl. jours. Served to maj. M.C. U.S. Army, 1944-47. Recipient Bruce Douglas award in thoracic diseases, 1974, Med. Alumni Svc. award Johns Hopkins Sch. Medicine, 1973, Disting. Svc. award Johns Hopkins U. Sch. Medicine, 1983, Disting. Svc. award Mich. Med. Ctr. Alumni Soc., 1988. Mem. ACS, Am. Surg. Assn., Am. Heart Assn., Am. Assn. Thoracic Surgery (pres. 1979-80), Soc. Thoracic Surgeons (pres. 1974-75, Disting. Svc. award 1981), Central Surg. Assn., Soc. Univ. Surgeons, So. Thoracic Surgery Assn. (hon.), Thoracic Soc. Gt. Britain (hon.), John Alexander Soc., Western Thoracic Surg. Assn. (hon.), Cardiovascular Surgeons Club, Detroit Heart Club, Am. Trudeau Soc., Mich. Heart Assn., Mich. Trudeau Soc., Am. Acad. Pediatrics, Soc. Vascular Surgery, Frederick A. Coller Surg. Soc., U. Mich. Med. Alumni Soc. (Disting. Svc. award 1988), Rsch. Club, Phi Beta Kappa, Alpha Omega Alpha, Omicron Delta Kappa, Sigma Xi. Club: Ann Arbor Figure Skating (pres. 1965-66). Home: 471 N Barton Dr Ann Arbor MI 48105-1017 Office: Taubman Health Care Ctr Sect Thoracic Surgery PO Box 344 100 Rm 2120 Ann Arbor MI 48109

SLOAN, REBA FAYE, dietitian, consultant; b. South Bend, Ind., Feb. 5, 1955; d. Kenneth and Ruby Faye (Long) Lewis; m. Gilbert Kevin Sloan, May 22, 1976. BS, Harding U., 1976; MPH, Loma Linda U., 1989; Cert. Tng. in Child/Adolescent Obesity, U. Calif., San Francisco. Registered dietitian; lic. dietitian and nutritionist; cert. advanced clin. tng. adolescent obesity. Dietetic intern Vanderbilt U. Med. Ctr., Nashville, 1978, rsch. dietitian, 1979-80; therapeutic dietitian Bapt. Hosp., Nashville, 1981-85; staff dietitian Nautilus Total Fitness Ctrs., Nashville, 1983-86; cons. dietitian Nashville Met. Govt., 1986-95, Bapt. Hosp. Ctr. for Health Promotion, Nashville, 1987-91, Parkwest Eating Disorder Clinic, Nashville, 1989-91; nutrition therapist, pvt. practice Nashville, Tenn., 1992—; adj. prof. Vanderbilt U., 1995; nutrition cons. The Nashville Striders, 1979-81; cons. nutritionist; mem. Vanderbilt U. Eating Disorder Com. Vol. Belmont Ch. Ministries, Nashville, 1981—; speaker Am. Heart Assn., Nashville, 1990—. Recipient cert. of appreciation Am. Heart Assn., 1990; Leaders fellow YMCA. Mem. Am. Dietetic Assn., Sports and Cardiovascular Nutritionists, Cons. Nutritionists, Am. Coll. Sports Medicine, Am. Running and Fitness Assn., Nashville Dist. Dietetic Assn. (contbr. diet manual 1984), Nat. Assn. for Chrisian Recovery, Alpha Chi. Home: 1817 Shackleford Rd Nashville TN 37215-3525 Office: 121 21st Ave N Ste 208 Nashville TN 37203-5213

SLOAN, ROSALIND, nurse, military officer; b. New Haven, Apr. 22, 1953; d. Paul and Blanche (Kopp) S. BSN, U. Conn., 1976; M of Ednl. Adminstrn., San Diego State U., 1993. Staff nurse Peter Bent Brigham Hosp., Boston, 1976-79; commd. officer USN, 1979, advanced through grades to comdr., 1988; staff nurse Portsmouth (Va.) Naval Hosp., 1979-83, Charleston (S.C.) Naval Hosp., 1983-85; charge nurse labor and delivery U.S. Naval Hosp., Subic Bay, Philippines, 1985-88; instr. Basic Hosp. Corps Sch.-Naval Sch. Health Scis., San Diego, 1988-90, asst. dir., 1990-91; asst. officer-in-charge, acad. officer Naval Sch. Dental Assisting and Tech., San Diego, 1991-92; dept. head command edn. and tng. Naval Med. Ctr., Oakland, Calif., 1993-96; mgr. rsch. and evaluation studies Bur. of Medicine & Surgery, Washington, 1996—. Recipient Naval Commendation medal USN, Subic Day, 1988, Naval Commendation medal Naval Sch. Health Scis., San Diego, 1991. Mem. Nat. Nursing Staff Devel. Orgn., Nat. Holistic Nursing Assn., Bay Area Soc. Health Edn. and Tng. (treas.), Coun. Coll. and Mil. Educators, Phi Kappa Phi.

SLOAN, SANDRA LYNN, health care administrator; b. Oak Park, Ill., July 2, 1958; d. David John and Donna Marie (Theis) S.; m. Glenn Eric Hahn, Oct. 5, 1985; children: Cody, Haley. BA, U. Ill., 1981; MS, Rush U., 1991. Realtor C-21 Sloan, Bensenville, Ill., 1981-89; asst. product mgr. Am. Hosp. Assn., Chgo., 1991-92; mgr. contract svcs. Rush Med. Assn., Chgo., 1992-94; dir. contract svcs. SNI Mgmt. Assn., Hinsdale, Ill., 1994—. Republican. Office: SNI Mgmt Assn Ste 128 911 N Elm Hinsdale IL 60521

SLOAND, JAMES ANTHONY, physician; b. Rochester, N.Y., Mar. 3, 1954; s. Anthony Sylvester and Muriel Ann (Kieffer) S.; m. Mary Ann Liebman, May 15, 1982; children: David, Colin, Meaghan. BA summa cum laude, Canisius Coll., Bufflo, 1976; MD, St. Louis U., 1980. Diplomate in internal medicine and nephrology Am. Bd. Internal Medicine. Intern, resident in internal medicine St. Luke's/St. Louis City (Washington U.), St. Louis, 1980-83; sr. instr. medicine U. Rochester, 1985-86, asst. prof., 1986-92, assoc. prof., 1992—; mem. staff Highland Hosp., Rochester; mem. med. adv. bd. Lupus Found. Am., Rochester, 1994—. Mem. editorial rev. bd. Archives of Internal Medicine, 1991—; contbr. articles to profl. jours. Fellow ACP; mem. Am. Soc. Nephrology, Internat. Soc. Nephrology, Nat. Kidney Found., Am. Soc. Hypertension, Internat. Assn. Hypertension in Blacks, Beta Beta Beta. Office: Highland Hosp 1000 South Ave Rochester NY 14620

SLOANE, ALEC MAURICE, retired physician, consultant; b. Pietermaritzburg, Natal, South Africa, Jan. 19, 1915; s. Jacob and Sarah (Pruss) Slom; m. Hetty Bertha Myerson Shirley; 1 child, Margot Isa. BS in Chemistry Physics, U. South Africa, 1939; MBCLB, U. Witwatersrand, South Africa, 1947; postgrad., Hammersmith Postgrad. Hosp., London.

Diplomate Am. Bd. Internal Medicine. Resident Johannesburg Hosp., 1948; pvt. practice Pretoria, South Africa, 1950-53, South Africa, 1955-63; resident U. Minn., Mpls., 1963-64; staff physician Vets. Hosp., Mpls., 1965-67; chief oncology Vets. Hosp., Houston, 1967-70; med. adv. U.S. Embassy, Pretoria, South Africa, 1971-75; lectr., tchr. Med. Sch., Pretoria, South Africa, 1972-77; sr. resident Baragwanerth Hosp., Johannesburg, 1990—; rsch. assoc. S.W. Cancer Chemotherapy Group, Houston, 1968-70. Contbr. articles to profl. jours. With No. Rhodesian Holding Unit, 1940-43. Mem. South African Med. Assn., South African Cardiac Soc., Pretoria Country Club, Wingate Park Country Golf Club. Home: 4 Greenoak Mews 243 Schroder, Pretoria 0181, South Africa

SLOANE, HARVEY I., public health officer. BA, Yale U., 1958; MD, Case Western Res. U., 1963. Intern Cleve. Clinic, 1964; physician Appalachian Health Program USPHS, Ky., 1964-66; founder, project dir. Park Du Valle Neighborhood Health Ctr., Louisville, 1967-72; mayor Louisville, 1973-77, 81-85; county judge exec. County of Jefferson, Louisville, 1986-90; pres., co-founder Health Care for Am. and Health Care for Am. Policy Inst., Washington, 1991-93; pres. Leukemia Soc. Am. Rsch. Found., Washington, 1993-94; project dir. health professions tng. and devel. Nat. Assn. Cmty. Health Ctrs., Washington, 1994-95; acting commr. D.C. Commn. Pub. Health, 1995—; dir. Rural Ky. Housing Found., 1979-81; vis. scholar health care policy rsch. George Washington U., 1990-91, adj. assoc. prof. health care scis., 1993—; vol. physician AMA's Physician Exch. Program, Vietnam, 1966. Chair Easter Seal Campaign, Ky., 1982, 83; active Action for Clean Air, Louisville, 1968-73, Louisville/Jefferson County Pollution Control Bd., 1969-73. Mem. AMA, 20th Century Fund (bd. dirs.), NAACP, Leukemia Soc. Am. (bd. dirs.), Partnership for Prevention (bd. dirs.). Office: DC Commn Public Health 1660 G St NW Washington DC 20001*

SLOANE, ROBERT MALCOLM, healthcare consultant; b. Boston, Feb. 11, 1933; s. Alvin and Florence (Goldberg) S.; m. Beverly LeBov, Sept. 27, 1959; 1 dau., Alison. A.B., Brown U., 1954; M.S., Columbia U., 1958. Adminstrv. resident Mt. Auburn Hosp., Cambridge, Mass., 1957-58; med. adminstr. AT&T, N.Y.C., 1959-60; asst. dir. Yale New Haven Hosp., 1961-67; assoc. adminstr. Monmouth Med. Center, Long Branch, N.J., 1967-69; adminstr. City of Hope Nat. Med. Center, Duarte, Calif., 1969-80; pres. Los Angeles Orthopedic Hosp., Los Angeles Orthopedic Found., 1980-86; pres., CEO Anaheim (Calif.) Meml. Hosp., 1986-94; pres. Vol. Hosp. Am. West, Inc., L.A., 1990-95; healthcare cons. Arcadia, Calif., 1996—; mem. faculty Columbia U. Sch. Medicine, 1958-59, Yale U. Sch. Medicine, 1963-67, Quinnipac Coll., 1963-67, Pasadena City Coll., 1972-73, Calif. Inst. Tech., 1973-85, U. So. Calif., 1976-79, clin. prof. 1987—, UCLA, 1985-87; chmn. bd. Health Data Net, 1971-73; bd. dirs. Intervalley Health Plan, 1995—; pres. Anaheim (Calif.) Meml. Hosp., 1986-94, Anaheim Meml. Devel. Found., 1986-94. Author: (with B. L. Sloane) A Guide to Health Facilities: Personnel and Management, 1971, 3d edit., 1992; mem. editorial and adv. bd. Health Devices, 1972-90; contbr. articles to hosp. jours. Bd. dirs. Health Systems Agy. Los Angeles County, 1977-78; bd. dirs. Calif. Hosp. Polit. Action Com., 1979-87, vice chmn., 1980-83, chmn., 1983-85. Served to lt. (j.g.) USNR, 1954-56. Fellow Am. Coll. Hosp. Adminstrs. (regent 1989-93, nominations com. 1994—); mem. Am. Hosp. Assn., Hosp Coun. So. Calif. (bd. dirs. , sec. 1982, treas. 1983, chmn. elect 1984, chmn. 1985, past chmn. 1986, 89), Calif. Hosp. Assn. (bd. dirs. exec. com. 1984-86, 89), Anaheim C. of C. (bd. dirs. 1994). Home: 1301 N Santa Anita Ave Arcadia CA 91006-2419 Office: 150 N Santa Anita Ste 300 Arcadia CA 91006

SLOAS, HAROLD ANDREW, JR., ophthalmologist, physician; b. Cape Girardeau, Mo., Apr. 6, 1942; s. Harold Andrew Sr. and Mildred Lee (Coffee) S.; m. Jean Rae Sloas, June 24, 1972; children: Harold, Elliott, Susan. BS, U. Miss., 1966; MS, U. Fla., 1973; DO, Kansas City Coll. Osteopathy, 1977. Diplomate Am. Bd. Ophthalmology. Enlisted USN, advanced through grades to capt.; head ophthalmology dept. U.S. Naval Hosp., Camp Lejeune, N.C., 1981-83, Orlando, Fla., 1983-95. Contbr. articles to profl. jours. Fellow Am. Acad. Ophthalmology; mem. Cen. Fla. Soc. Ophthalmology, AMA, Osteo. Coll. of Ophthalmology and Otorhinology. Republican. Presbyterian. Home: 729 Bear Creek Cir Winter Spgs FL 32708-3892 Office: VA Hosp Ophthalmology Dept Orlando FL 32803

SLOBIN, DAN ISAAC, psychology educator; b. Detroit, May 7, 1939; s. Norval L. and Judith (Liepah) S.; divorced; children: Shem Alexander, Heida Quisno Shoemaker. BA, U. Mich., 1960; PhD, Harvard U., 1964. From asst. prof. to assoc. prof. U. Calif., Berkeley, 1964-72, prof., 1972—; chair adv. bd. Max-Planck-Inst. for Psycholinguistics, Nijmegen, Netherlands; mem. steering com. European Sci. Found. Rsch. Project, 1981-88. Mem. editorial bd. Cognition, Discourse Processes, Jour. Narrative and Life History, Pragmatics; contbr. articles to profl. jours., chpts. to books; writer, editor books. Named Behavioral Scientist of Yr., N.Y. Acad. Scis., 1986; rsch. grantee NSF, NIH, NIMH, Ford Found., The Grant Found., 1968—; Guggenheim fellow, 1984. Mem. Internat. Assn. for Study Child Lang. (v.p. 1984-87), Internat. Assn. Cross-Cultural Psychology, Linguistics Soc. Am., Internat. Assn. Cognitive Linguistics (adv. bd. 1989—), Assn. Linguistic Typology, Internat. Pragmatics Assn., Soc. Rsch. Child Devel., Turkish Studies Assn. Democrat. Jewish. Home: 2323 Rose St Berkeley CA 94708-1807

SLOBODIEN, HOWARD DAVID, surgeon; b. Perth Amboy, N.J., July 25, 1923; s. Albert Leo and Anna Frances (Sontag) S.; B.S., Rutgers Coll., 1943; M.D., N.Y.U., 1947; m. Sally Doris Yerkes, May 9, 1950; children—David, Donald, Daniel, Douglas. Intern, Morrisania City Hosp., N.Y.C., 1947-48, resident, 1948-52; practice medicine specializing in surgery, Perth Amboy, 1955—; pres. John F. Kennedy Med. Center, Edison, N.J., 1967-70, dir. surgery, 1975-79; attending surgeon Gen. Hosp., Perth Amboy, dir. surgery, 1970-74; chief gen. surgery, past pres. med. staff Roosevelt Hosp., Edison; cons. surgery Meml. Hosp., South Amboy; clin. asst. prof. surgery Rutgers U. Med. Sch., 1971-84, mem. adv. council Office Consumer Health Edn., 1973-81; mem. adv. council Middlesex County Coll., 1968-78; v.p. Regional Health Facilities Planning Council, 1970-73. Editor N.J. Medicine, 1988—. Pack committeeman Cub Scouts, 1960-64; active steering com. Metuchen YMCA, 1962. Served with USNR, 1943-45, USAF, 1952-54. Diplomate Am. Bd. Surgery. Fellow ACS; mem. AMA, World, Pan-Am. med. assns., N.J. (trustee 1972-84, chmn. pub. relations council 1973-76, pres. 1982-83), Middlesex County (pres. 1970-71) med. socs., Pan-Pacific Surg. Assn., Am. Geriatric Soc., Royal Soc. Health, Am. Acad. Med. Adminstrs., Royal Soc. Medicine, N.J. Acad. Medicine (trustee 1974-78), Middlesex County Med. Assts. Assn. (county med. adviser 1973-80), N.J. Soc. Surgeons, Phi Beta Kappa. Clubs: Metuchen Country. Home: 34 Linden Ave Metuchen NJ 08840-1418 Office: 500 Lawrie St Perth Amboy NJ 08861-3046

SLOCHOWER, JOYCE ANNE, psychologist, psychoanalyst, educator; b. N.Y.C., May 6, 1950; d. Harry and Muriel (Zimmerman) S.; m. Bruce Rodin, July 20, 1975; children: Jesse, Alison, Avi. Student, Clark U., 1968-70; BA, NYU, 1970-72; PhD, Columbia U., 1975. Cert. psychoanalyst, N.Y. Asst. prof. psychology Hunter Coll., CUNY, 1975-82, assoc. prof., 1982—; prof. Hunter Coll., CUNY, N.Y.C., 1982-94; supr. Nat. Inst. for Psychotherapies, 1994—; pvt. practice, N.Y.C., 1976—; mem. faculty NYU postdoctoral program in psychoanalysis, 1994—. Author: Excessive Eating, 1983, Holding and Psychoanalysis: A Relational Perspective, 1996; contbr. numerous articles to profl. jours. NIMH grantee, 1980-82, CUNY grantee, 1981-83. Mem. APA, Eastern Psychol. Assn., N.Y. Psychol. Assn., NYU Postdoctoral Soc., Phi Beta Kappa. Jewish. Home and Office: 15 W 75th St New York NY 10023-2014

SLOCUM, DONALD HILLMAN, product development executive; b. Flushing, N.Y., Jan. 6, 1930; s. John G. and Frances H. S.; m. June Manning, Sept. 22, 1952 (dec. 1976); children: Richard, Mark, Carol; m. Barbara M. Ruane, Nov. 1, 1986. BS, Davis and Elkins Coll., 1951; MS, U. Vt., 1956; PhD, Ohio State U., 1958; LLD, Fla. Tech. Inst., 1968; MBA, Rider Coll., 1971; ScD, Norton U., 1972; Dr. Profl. Studies, Pace U., 1974. Rsch. chem. Charles Pfizer, Inc., Bklyn., 1954; rsch. scientist Procter & Gamble, Cin., 1958-68; mgr. product devel. E.I. DuPont de Nemours & Co., Wilmington, Del., 1960-68; dir. new ventures N.L. Industries, N.Y.C., 1968-71; dir. fin. planning Hoffmann LaRoche, Nutley, N.J., 1971-74; v.p. Curtiss-Wright Corp., Woodridge, N.J., 1974-78; sr. v.p. Masonite-USG, Chgo., 1978-85; pres. Doner-Viking Corp., Madison, N.J., 1985-87, Woodtec, Inc. subs. Masco, Taylor, Mich., 1987-96, Versitec Industries, 1996—. Author: New Venture Methodology, 1974; contbr. articles to tech. and bus. publs.; patentee in field. Lt. U.S. Army, 1951-54, Korea, Col. Res., ret. Home: 61 Chimney Ridge Dr Morristown NJ 07960-4722 Office: SRA 3400 Bee Ridge Rd Sarasota FL 34239-7223

SLOCUM, HAROLD ELWYN, health facility administrator; b. Syracuse, N.Y., Nov. 16, 1944; s. Harold Rouse and Louise C. (Scull) S.; m. Linda M. Rader, Aug. 20, 1972; children: Christopher L., Laura E., Julia L. BA in Biology, Ea. Bapt. Coll., 1967; MD, SUNY, Syracuse, 1971; postgrad., Scranton U., Bucknell U. Diplomate Am. Bd. Family Practice, Geriatrics; lic. Ohio, Pa., N.Y. Intern, resident St. Joseph's Hosp. Health Ctr., Syracuse, 1971-74; assoc. Geisinger Med. Ctr., Danville, Pa., 1976-91; clin. assoc. Blue Cross HMO, Cleve., 1992—; regional med. dir. Cleve. West Region Blue Cross Health Ohio, 1993—; physicians' assistance com. mem. Fairview Gen. Hosp., 1993—; clin. instr. Case-We. Res. Med. Sch., 1993—; clin. asst. prof. Jefferson Med. Coll., 1988-91, Pa. State U., 1976-88, U. Va., 1974-75. Contbr. articles to profl. jours. Maj. U.S. Army, 1974-76. Mem. AMA, Am. Acad. Physician Execs., Am. Acad. Family Practice, Ohio Med. Assn., Ohio Acad. Family Practice, Lorain County Med. Assn. Republican. Mem. Ch. of Christ. Home: 13280 Clark Ln Oberlin OH 44074-9701 Office: Blue Cross Ohio HMO 4330 W 150th St Cleveland OH 44135-1365

SLOGOFF, STEPHEN, anesthesiologist, educator; b. Phila., PA, July 7, 1942; s. Israel and Lillian (Rittenberg) S.; m. Barbara Anita Gershman, June 2, 1963; children: Michele, Deborah. AB in Biology, Franklin and Marshall Coll., 1964; MD, Jefferson Med. Coll., 1967. Diplomate Am. Bd. Med. Examiners, Am. Bd. Anesthesiology (jr. assoc. examiner 1977-80, sr. assoc. examiner 1980-81, bd. dirs. 1981-93, pres. 1989-90, joint coun. on in-tng. exams, vice chmn. 1983-86, chmn. 1986-92). Intern Harrisburg (Pa.) Hosp., 1967-68; resident in anesthesiology Jefferson Med. Coll. Hosp., 1968-71; chief anesthesia sect. U.S. Army, Brooke Army Med. Ctr., Fort Sam Houston, Tex., 1971-74; staff anesthesiologist Baylor Coll. Medicne, Houston, 1974-75; attending cardiovascular anesthesiologist U. Tex. Health Sci. Ctr., Houston, 1974-93, clin. asst. prof., 1977-81, clin. assoc. prof., 1981-85, clin. prof., 1985-93; prof., chmn. dept. anesthesiology Loyola U., Chgo., 1993—; chmn. rsch com., co-dir. rsch. labs Tex. Heart Inst., Houston, 1990-93. Contbr. articles to profl. jours. Mem. Am. Soc. Anesthesiologists, Alpha Omega Alpha. Office: Loyola U Med Ctr Dept Anesthesia 2160 S 1st Ave Maywood IL 60153-3304

SLONIM, ARNOLD ROBERT, biochemist, physiologist; b. Springfield, Mass., Feb. 15, 1926; s. Sam and Esther (Kantor) S.; married, 1951; 3 children; m. 1984. BS, Tufts Coll., 1947; AM, Boston U., 1948; PhD, Johns Hopkins U., 1953. Rsch. asst. nutrition Sterling-Winthrop Rsch. Inst., Rensselaer, N.Y., 1948-49; rsch. asst. pharmacology George Washington U. Med. Sch., Washington, 1949-50; rsch. asst., jr. instr. biology Johns Hopkins U., Balt., 1950-53; rsch. assoc. chemotherapy Children's Cancer Rsch. Found. Harvard U., Boston, 1953-54; head chem. lab. Lynn (Mass.) Hosp., 1955-56; various positions including chief applied ecology, supervisory rsch. biologist, physiologist & biochemist, phys. sci. adminstr., biotech. mgr. Aerospace Med. Rsch. Lab., Wright-Patterson AFB, Ohio, 1956-86; cons., pres. ARSLO Assocs., Columbus, Ohio, 1987—; lectr. Mass. Sch. Physiotherapy, Boston, 1955-56, Antioch U., 1984-85; mem. internat. bioastronautics com. Internat. Astronautical Fedn., 1966—; mem. environ. carcinogens program Internat. Agy. for Rsch. on Cancer/WHO, Paris, 1981—. Mem. com. on biol. handbooks Fedn. Am. Socs. for Exptl. Biology, 1966-71; mem. editorial bd. Aerospace Medicine, 1967-71; contbr. articles to profl. jours. Served with USN, 1944-46. Mem. Aerospace Med. Assn., Am. Soc. Biochemistry and Molecular Biology, Am. Physiol. Soc., N.Y. Acad. Sci., Internat. Acad. Aviation and Space Medicine, Sigma Xi, Masons, Scottish Rite, Shriners. Office: 630 Cranfield Pl Columbus OH 43213-3407

SLOSAR, JAY R., clinical psychologist; b. Gary, Ind., Aug. 29, 1952; s. Joseph and Ann Slusar (Pipas) S. BS in Psychology, Jacksonville U., 1974; MA in Psychology, Wichita State U., 1976; PhD in Counseling Psychology, U. So. Calif., 1981. Lic. clin. psychologist, Calif. Cons. Brakthin Cons., Long Beach, Calif., 1978-80; psychologist Dawson Ednl. Ctr., La Mirada, Calif., 1981-87, Family Solutions, Orange, Calif., 1987-90; pvt. practice Santa Ana, Calif., 1990—; bd. dirs. Calif. Coalitioin of Ethical Mental Healthcare, San Francisco, 1995—. Author: (manual) Staff Training Manual for Residential Treatment of Children and Adolescents, 1995. Mem. Am. Psychiat. Assn., Orange County Psychiat. Assn. (chair care of ins. task force 1996—). Democrat. Office: JR Slosar 505 N Tustin Ave Ste 195 Santa Ana CA 92705

SLOT, LARRY LEE, molecular biologist; b. Grand Rapids, Mich., Nov. 8, 1947; s. Russell Lee and Vivian June (Wolfert) S.; m. Pamela Chronis, Nov. 25, 1948; children: Franchot, Jason, Lara. AS, Grand Rapids Jr. Coll., 1971; BS, Mich. State U., 1982. Pub. Grand Rapids Interpreter, Mich., 1975-78; bush pilot Palacios, Honduras, 1978-80; pres. Genemsco Corp., Kingston, Mass., 1984—. Sculptures include The Pontibus, 1986; creator, copywriter (cell cloning and gene splicing module) The Dr. Cloner's Genetic Engineering Home Clothing Kit, 1984, Business Plan for the Planet, 1994. With USMC, 1966-69. NSF fellow, 1982. Mem. AAAS, Am. Soc. Microbiology, Airplane Owners and Pilots Assn., Pontibus Soc. (founder 1986, pres. 1986-87), Golden Key Soc., Phi Kappa Phi. Home: 10 Braintree Ave Kingston MA 02364-1714 Office: Genemsco Corp Genemsco Beach Kingston MA 02364-1714

SLOWINSKI, JULIAN WALTER, clinical psychologist; b. Newark, Apr. 19, 1942; s. Julius W. and Nora H. (Majeski) S.; m. Betty Jeannine Armbruster, Aug. 10, 1971; 1 child, Stefan Julien. BA, St. Benedict's Coll., Kans., 1965; MS, Hahnemann Med. Coll., Phila., 1974; PsyD, Rutgers U., 1977. Mem. Order of St. Benedict, 1960-68; chief psychologist Corinthian Guidance Ctr., Hahnemann Hosp., Phila., 1974-77; supr. child and family services Hall-Mercer Ctr., Pa. Hosp., Phila., 1977-80, dir. child and family outpatient services, 1980-85; clin. assoc. dept. psychiatry U. Pa. Sch. Medicine, 1978-85, clin. asst. prof., 1985-95, clin. asst. prof. Hahnemann Med. Coll., 1974-85. Contbr. articles to profl. jours. and books. Lic. clin. psychologist, Pa.; diplomate Am. Bd. Family Psychology, Am. Bd. Psychology. Fellow Phila. Soc. Clin. Psychologists; mem. Am. Psychol. Assn., Pa. Psychol. Assn., Am. Assn. Sex Educators, Counselors and Therapists, (cert.) nd Family Therapy, Soc. Sci. Study of Sex, Soc. Sex Therapy and Research. Home: 239C S Hutchinson St Philadelphia PA 19107-5722 Office: Pa Hosp 700 Spruce Pa Hospital Ste 501 Philadelphia PA 19106

SLUGG, PETER HILL, clinical pharmacologist; b. Oak Park, Ill., Oct. 2, 1941; s. Peter Lythm and Hope Slugg; children: Amy, Jennifer. MD, U. Ill., Chgo., 1966. Diplomate Am. Bd. Internal Medicine, also cert. clin. pharmacology. Resident in internal medicine Cleve. Clinic Found., 1966-70, resident in nephrology, 1972-73, mem. profl. staff, 1973-92, head sect. clin. pharmacology, 1986-92; dir. clin. pharmacology Bristol-Myers Squibb Pharm. Rsch. Inst., Princeton, N.J.; clin. assoc. prof. U. Medicine and Dentistry N.J., 1994—. Maj. USAF, 1970-72. Fellow ACP; mem. Am. Soc. Clin. Pharmacology and Therapeutics, Omega Beta Pi. Office: Bristol Myers Squibb Human Pharmacology PO Box 4000 Princeton NJ 03543-4000

SLUSHER, M. MADISON, ophthalmology educator; b. Pineville, Ky., July 19, 1938. BA, Harvard U., 1960; MD, U. Ky., 1964. Diplomate Am. Bd. Ophthalmology. Clin. instr. Albany Med. Ctr., Dept. Ophthalmology, 1970-73; asst. prof. ophthalmology Wake Forest U., Bowman Gray Sch. Medicine, Winston-Salem, N.C., 1973-77, assoc. prof., 1977-81; cons. dept. ophthalmology U. Wash., Seattle, 1981-82; prof., chmn. dept. ophthalmology Wake Forest U., Bowman Gray Sch. Medicine, 1986—; dir. Wake Forest U. Eye Ctr., Winston-Salem, 1988—. Recipient Honor award Am. Acad. Ophthalmology. Office: Wake Forest Eye Ctr Med Ctr Blvd Winston Salem NC 27157

SLUSSER, TODD GORDON, optometrist; b. St. Joseph, Mich., Apr. 24, 1968; s. Thomas Slusser and Linda (Binkley) Ramge; m. Corinne Busby, July 25, 1992; 1 child, Anna Lauree. OD, Ohio State U., 1992; MS, U. Ala. Birmingham, 1994. Resident contact lens U. Ala. Birmingham, 1992-93; ptnr. Rupert, Idaho, 1994—. Contbr. articles to profl. jours. Mem. Am. Optometric Assn., Fellowship Christian Optometrists, Optometric Ext. Program, Idaho Optometric Assn. Office: 714 G St Rupert ID 83350

SLUTSKY, MORTON, plastic surgeon; b. Chattanooga, Apr. 19, 1937; s. Morris Joe and Anetha (Pavlow) S.; m. Ina Elaine Turner, Mar. 17, 1963; children: Bradley, David. BS, Vanderbilt U., 1958; MD, Tulane Sch. Medicine, 1962. Diplomate Am. Bd. Plastic Surgery. Intern Michael Reese Hosp., 1962-63; resident Grad. Hosp. U. Pa., Phila., 1965-68, Episc. Hosp., 1968-69, R.I. Hosp., 1969-71; pvt. practice Atlanta, 1971—; asst. instr. U. Pa., Phila., 1965-68; clin. instr. Emory Sch. Medicine, 1971; hosp. staff Atlanta Outpatient Surgery Ctr., Outpatient Surgery Ctr., Healthsouth Outpatient Surgery Ctr., Northside Hosp., St. Joseph's Hosp., Scottish Rite Hosp., Dunwoody Med. Hosp. Contbr. articles to profl. jours.; presenter in field. Capt. USAF, 1963-65. Mem. AMA, Am. Soc. Plastic and Reconstructive Surgeons, Am. Acad. Cosmetic Surgeons, Ga. Soc. Plastic Surgeons, Med. Assn. Ga., Med. Assn. Atlanta. Jewish. Office: 993C Johnson Ferry Rd #215 Atlanta GA 30342

SLY, RIDGE MICHAEL, physician, educator; b. Seattle, Nov. 3, 1933; s. Ridge Joseph and Eva Jean (Ruddell) S.; m. Ann Turner Jennings, June 12, 1957; children: Teresa Ann Perper, Cynthia Marie Schattenfield. A.B., Kenyon Coll., 1956; M.D., Washington U., St. Louis, 1960. Diplomate Am. Bd. Pediatrics, Am. Sub-Bd. Pediatric Allergy, Am. Bd. Allergy and Immunology. Intern, resident in pediatrics St. Louis Children's Hosp, 1960-62; chief resident in pediatrics U. Ky. Med. Ctr., Lexington, 1962-63; fellow in allergy and immunology UCLA Med. Ctr., 1965-67; asst. prof., assoc. prof., prof. pediatrics La. State U. Med. Ctr., New Orleans, 1967-78; dir. allergy and immunology Children's Nat. Med. Ctr., Washington, 1978—; prof. pediatrics George Washington U., Washington, 1978—. Author: Textbook of Pediatric Allergy, 1985; mem. editl. bd. Annals of Allergy, Asthma, & Immunology, 1982—, Jour. Asthma, 1982-93, Clin. Revs. in Allergy, 1982—, Pediat. Asthma, Allergy, & Immunology, 1987—; assoc. editor Annals of Allergy, Asthma, & Immunology, 1989-90, editor, 1990—; contbr. articles to profl. jours. Served to capt. USAF, 1963-65. Recipient La. plaque Am. Lung Assn. of La., 1978. Fellow Am. Acad. Allergy, Asthma & Immunology (chmn. com. on drugs 1981-87), Am. Acad. Pediats. (sect. on allergy com. 1972-75), Am. Coll. Allergy, Asthma, and Immunology (Disting. Fellow award 1993); mem. Am. Thoracic Soc., Assn. for Care of Asthma (pres. 1980-81, dir. postgrad. courses 1980—, Peshkin Meml. award 1983), Am. Med. Writer's Assn., Coun. Biology Editors, Phi Beta Kappa. Republican. Baptist. Office: Children's Nat Med Ctr 111 Michigan Ave NW Washington DC 20010-2970

SLY, WILLIAM S., biochemist, educator; b. East St. Louis, Ill., Oct. 19, 1932. MD, St. Louis U., 1957. Intern, asst. resident Ward Med Barnes Hosp., St. Louis, 1957-59; clin. assoc. nat. heart inst. NIH, Bethesda, Md., 1959-63, rsch. biochemist, 1959-63; dir. divsn. med. genetics, dept. medicine and pediatrics, sch. medicine Washington U., 1964-84, from asst. prof. to prof. medicine, 1964-78, from asst. prof. to prof. pediatrics, 1967-78, prof. pediatrics, medicine and genetics, 1978-84; prof. biochemistry, chmn. E. A. Doisy dept. biochemistry, prof. pediatrics sch. med. St. Louis U., 1984—; vis. physician Nat. Heart Inst., 1961-63, pediatric genetics clinic U. Wis., Madison, 1963-64; Am. Cancer Soc. fellow lab. enzymol Nat. Ctr. Sci. Rsch., Gif-sur-Yvette, France, 1963, dept. biochemistry and genetics U. Wis., 1963-64; attending physician St. Louis County Hosp., Mo., 1964-84; asst. physician Barnes Hosp., St. Louis, 1964-84, St. Louis Children's Hosp., 1967-84; genetics cons. Homer G. Philips Hosp., St. Louis, 1969-81; mem. genetics study sect. divsn. rsch. grants NIH, 1971-75; mem. active staff Cardinal Glennon Children's Hosp., St. Louis, 1984—; mem. med. adv. bd. Howard Hughes Med. Inst., 1989-92. Recipient Merit award NIH, 1988; named Passano Found. laureate, 1991; Travelling fellow Royal Soc. Medicine, 1973. Mem. NAS, AMA, AAAS, Am. Soc. Human Genetics (mem. steering com. human cell biology program 1971-73, com. genetic counseling 1972-76), Am. Soc. Clin. Investigation, Am. Chem. Soc., Genetics Soc. Am., Am. Soc. Microbiology, Soc. Pediatric Rsch., Sigma Xi. Office: St Louis U Med Sch Dept Biochemistry 1402 S Grand Blvd Saint Louis MO 63104-1004

SLYTER, LEONARD LEROY, microbiologist; b. Fontana, Kans., Nov. 13, 1933; s. Elmer Jess and Anna Dorothea (Rodewald) S.; m. Dolores Jean Reifel, Sept. 6, 1958; children: Susan Lynn, Sandra Jean. BS in Dairy Prodn. Agr., Kans. State U., 1955; MS in Agr., U. Mo., 1958; PhD in Nutrition, N.C. State U., 1963. Rsch. asst. U. Mo., Columbia, 1957-58, N.C. State U., Raleigh, 1959-62; rsch. assoc. U. Ill., Urbana, 1963-64; rsch. chemist Agrl. Rsch. Svc., USDA, Beltsville, Md., 1965-78, microbiologist, 1979-96, retired, 1996—; coop. scientist Office Internat. Coop. and Devel., New Delhi, 1986-91, dept. animal sci. and agrl. biochemistry U. Del., Newark, 1988-90, Colo. State U., Ft. Collins, 1974-76. Contbr. articles to profl. publs. 1st lt. U.S. Army, 1955-57. Flood fellow, 1951-52. Mem. Am. Soc. Microbiology, Am. Soc. Animal Sci. Republican. Lutheran.

SMAISTRLA, JEAN ANN, family therapist; b. South Gate, Calif., Oct. 12, 1936; d. Benjamin J. and Janet (Pollock) Craig; m. Charles J. Smaistrla, July 12, 1958; children: Amy Jean, Ben, John. BBA in Mktg., Lamar U., 1958; elec. edn. cert. Tex. Wesleyan Coll., 1963; MEd in Counseling, Tex. Christian U., 1975. Lic. profl. counselor. Tchr. Houston Ind. Schs., 1958-61, Arlington Ind. Schs., Tex., 1961-72; counselor, therapist Arlington Counseling and Cons. Ctr., 1983-85; family therapist Willow Creek Adolescent Ctr., Arlington, 1985-86, dir. edn., 1986-90; therapist, Bob Caprenter PhD and Assoc., 1987-89; pvt. practice Triage Therapist Kaiser Permanente, Ft. Worth, 1989—; owner, founder, chmn. bd. Adolescent Svcs. Arlington, 1981—, founder, owner Mindtime, 1988-90; triage counselor Kaiser Permanente, Ft. Worth, 1991—; cons. Charles J. Smaistrla, D.D.S., Arlington, 1978-85. Vice chmn. bd. Arlington Cmty. Hosp., 1981-85, Willow Creek Adolescent Ctr., 1984-90. Life mem. PTA; bd. dirs. Arlington Art Assn., 1981-85, S. Arlington Med. Ctr., 1987, Ctr. for Well-Being, 1985; chmn. clin. svcs. Parenting Ctr. for Tarrant County, Ft. Worth, 1992—, v.p., 1994-95, pres.-elect, 1994-96, pres. bd., 1996—. Mem. Am. Assn. Marriage and Family Therapy (assoc.), Tarrant County Assn. Marriage and Family Therapy, North Central Tex. Assn. Counseling and Devel., Am. Assn. Counseling and Devel., Alpha Delta Pi. Republican. Roman Catholic. Clubs: Jr. League Arlington, Arlington Women's. Avocations: Sailing; sewing; doll collecting.

SMALDONE, GERALD CHRISTOPHER, physiologist; b. N.Y.C., Sept. 1, 1947; s. Gerald J. and Theresa (Petrolino) S.; m. Arlene Merne, July 29, 1972; children: Marc, Lauren. BSChE, NYU, 1969, MD, PhD, 1975. Intern, resident Strong Meml. Hosp. U. Rochester, N.Y., 1975-77; fellow in medicine Johns Hopkins U., Balt., 1977-80, fellow in environ. health sci., 1977-80; asst. prof. medicine, physiology and biophysics SUNY, Stony Brook, 1980-86, assoc. prof., 1986—; cons. to pvt. industry and govt., 1988—. Contbr. articles to profl. jours.: editor: Jour. Aerosol Medicine, 1987—. Mem. Internat. Soc. for Aerosols in Medicine (bd. dirs. 1991—). Office: SUNY Pulmonary Critical Care Div HSC T-17040 Stony Brook NY 11794-8172

SMALHEISER, NEIL RAYMOND, neurobiologist; b. N.Y.C., Dec. 10, 1954. BA with honors, U. Iowa, 1974; MD, Phd, Yeshiva U., 1982. Asst. prof. U. Chgo., 1988—. Office: U Chgo MC 5058 5841 S Maryland Ave Chicago IL 60637-1463

SMALL, ALVAN, health services administrator; b. Boston, Dec. 31, 1953; s. Leonard and Ruth (Weiner) S.; m. Lori Small, Aug. 25, 1990. BA, Yeshiva U., 1976; MBA, Adelphi U., 1981. Lic. nursing home adminstr., Conn., N.Y., N.J., Mass. Adminstr., CEO Freeport (N.Y.) Hosp., 1980-85; v.p. ops. Jewish Home for the Elderly of Fairfield (Conn.) County, 1985—. Named Young Exec. of Yr. N.Am. Assn. Jewish Homes and Housing for the Aged, 1996. Mem. Am. Coll. Healthcare Medicine. Home: 40 Boxwood Dr Stamford CT 06906 Office: Jewish Home for the Elderly Fairfield County 175 Jefferson St Fairfield CT 06432

SMALL, DONALD MACFARLAND, biophysics educator, gastroenterologist; b. Newton, Mass., Sept. 15, 1931; s. Grace (MacFarland) S.; m. Elisabeth Chan, July 8, 1957 (div. 1979); children: Geoffrey, Philip; m. Kathryn Ross, July 26, 1986; 1 child, Samuel. BA, Occidental Coll., 1954; MA (hon.), Oxford (Eng.) U., 1964; MD, UCLA, 1960. Intern, asst. resident in medicine Mass. Meml. Hosps., Boston, 1960-62; sr. resident Boston City Hosp., 1962-63, vis. physician med. svcs., 1965—; asst. prof. medicine Boston U. Sch. Medicine, 1968-69, assoc. prof. medicine and biochemistry,

1969-73, prof., 1973—, prof. biophysics, chmn. dept., 1989—, dir. Biophysics Inst., 1972—; spl. tng. in phys. chemistry of lipids Inst. Pasteur, Paris, 1963-65; mem. adv. bd. Gladstone Found Labs., San Francisco, 1980—, Liver Ctr., U. Colo., Denver, 1985—; George Lyman Duff Meml. lectr. Coun. Arteriosclerosis, Am. Heart Assn., 1986; cons. Nat. Inst. Arthritis and Metabolic Diseases, NIH, 1968-72, mem. task force Nat. Heart, Lung and Blood Inst., 1990; also others. Author, editor: Physical Chemistry of Lipids, 1986; mem. editl. bd. Gastroenterology, 1967-74, Arteriosclerosis, 1980—, Jour. Biol. Chemistry, Current Opinions in Structural Biology, 1990; sub-editor: Jour. Lipid Rsch., 1974-78, editor, 1979-83; editor: (with R. Havel) Advances in Lipid Rsch., 1989—; mem. internat. bd. editors Jour. Nutritional Biochemistry, 1989—; contbr. articles and revs. to profl. jours.; author: (with A. Adams) The Healthy Meateaters Cookbook, 1991. Bd. dirs. Franconia (N.H.) Ski Racing Club, 1974-77. Recipient Eppinger prize IV Internat. Congress on Liver Disease, 1976, Disting. Achievment award Modern Medicine, 1978, UCLA Sch. Medicine Alumni Assn., 1988; Marshall scholar Magdalen Coll., Oxford, 1956-58, Aesculapian scholar UCLA, 1958-60, Markle scholar, 1966-70; also others. Mem. AAAS, Am. Heart Assn. (fellow coun. arteriosclerosis, chmn. program com. 1988-90, chmn. coun. 1992-94), Am. Assn. Physicians, Am. Soc. Biol. Chemists, Biophys. Soc., Am. Soc. Clin. Investigation, Am. Gastroent. Assn. (Ann. Disting. Achievement award 1972), Am. Oil Chemists Soc., Am. Fedn. Clin. Rsch., Am. Chem. Soc., Mass. Med. Soc., Suffolk Dist. Med. Soc., Phi Beta Kappa, Alpha Omega Alpha, Sigma Xi. Office: Boston U Sch Medicine Dept Biophysics 80 E Concord St Roxbury MA 02118-2307

SMALL, JAMES WILLIAM, occupational medicine physician; b. Lincoln, Nebr., Jan. 23, 1951; s. LaVerne D. and Nora C. Small; m. Susan E. Koch; children: James J., Nicole E. BA, U. Nebr., Lincoln, 1973; MD, U. Nebr., Omaha, 1982; MPH, Johns Hopkins U., 1984. Commd. 2nd lt. U.S. Army, 1973, advanced through grades to lt. col., 1996; intern in neurology Walter Reed Army Med. Ctr., Washington, 1982-83; resident in preventive medicine Walter Reed Army Inst. Rsch., Washington, 1984-85; epidemiologist U.S. Army, Washington, 1985-86; chief preventive medicine III Corps U.S. Army, Ft. Hood, Tex., 1986-89; retired U.S. Army, 1989; resident in occupl. medicine U. Okla., 1989-91; exec. med. dir. Workmed Occupl. Health Network, Tulsa, 1989—. Fellow Am. Coll. Occupl. and Environ. Medicine, Am. Coll. Preventive Medicine; mem. Am. Coll. Physician Execs. Home: 10617 E 99th St S Tulsa OK 74133

SMALL, JOYCE GRAHAM, psychiatrist, educator; b. Edmonton, Alberta, Can., June 12, 1931; came to U.S., 1956; d. John Earl and Rachel C. (Redmond) Graham; m. Iver Francis Small, May 26, 1954; children: Michael, Jeffrey. BA, U. Saskatchewan, Can., 1951; MD, U. Manitoba, Can., 1956; MS, U. Mich., 1959. Diplomat Am. Bd. Psychiatry and Neurology, Am. Bd. Electroencephalography. Instr. in psychiatry Neuropsychiat. Inst. U. Mich., Ann Arbor, 1959-60; instr. in psychiatry med. sch. U. Oreg., Portland, 1960-61, asst. prof. in psychiatry med. sch., 1961-62; asst. prof. in psychiatry sch. of medicine Washington U., St. Louis, 1962-65; assoc. prof. in psychiatry sch. of medicine Ind. U., Indpls., 1965-69, prof. psychiatry sch. of medicine, 1969—; mem. initial rev. groups NIMH, Washington, 1972-76, 79-82, 87-91; assoc. mem. Inst. Psychiat. Rsch., Indpls., 1974—. Editorial bd.: Quar. Jour. of Convulsive Theravp, 1984, Clin. Electroencephalography, 1990, and more than 150 publs. in field; contbr. articles to profl. jours. Rsch. grantee NIMH, Portland, Oreg., 1961-62, St. Louis, 1962-64, Indpls., 1967—, Epilepsy Found., Dreyfus Found., Indpls., 1965; recipient Merit award NIMH, Indpls., 1990. Fellow Am. Psychiat. Assn., Am. Electroencephalographic Soc. (councillor 1972-75, 1982); mem. Soc. Biol. Psychiatry, Cen. Assn. Electroencephalographers (sec., treas. 1967-68, pres. 1970, councillor 1971-72), Sigma Xi. Office: Larue D Carter Meml Hosp 1315 W 10th St Indianapolis IN 46202-2802

SMALL, MAX S., radiology edicator; b. Chgo., Sept. 12, 1924; s. Joseph and Rebecca (Rusenwald) S.; m. Gertrude Axelrod, Sept. 12, 1945; children: Melinda Gandin, Gary, Rena Wilson. BA, U. Ill., 1944, BS, 1945, MD, 1947. Lic. radiologist Calif., Md., ; bd. cert. radiology and nuclear medicine. Dir. radiology Sherman Oaks (Calif.) Hosp., 1958-83; clin. asst. prof. radiology Olive View-UCLA Med. Ctr., Sylmar, Calif., 1984—; cons. in field. Capt. USAF, 1951-53. Mem. Am. Coll. Radiology, Phi Kappa Phi, Alpha Omega Alpha. Office: Olive View-UCLA Med Ctr 14445 Olive View Dr Sylmar CA 91342

SMALL, MELVIN D., physician, educator; b. Somerville, Mass., May 22, 1925; s. Sidney J. and Ida (Gelbsman) S.; m. Judith Nogee, Dec. 23, 1962; children: Michael Dorian, Michele. AB, U. Wis., 1953; MD, Duke U. Sch. Medicine, 1959; studied under Dr. Gregory Pincus, Worcester Found. Exptl. Biol. and Medicine, 1950-53; studied under Prof. Brian Abel-Smith, London Sch. Econs, 1986-90. Lic. physician, Fla., Md., D.C., Va. Intern Georgetown U. Med. Ctr., Washington, 1959-60, resident, 1960-61; chief gastrointestinal rsch. Georgetown U. Med. Ctr., 1961-64, instr. medicine, 1961-66, asst. prof. medicine, 1966-67, asst. clin. prof. medicine, 1967-81, 93—; chief gastroenterology sect. Georgetown divsn. D.C. Gen. Hosp., 1964-68; cons. Children's Hosp., Washington, 1962-66; active staff Fairfax (Va.) Hosp., 1961-73, Commonwealth Drs. Hosp., Fairfax, 1969-74, Arlington (Va.) Hosp., 1961-85, Circle Terr. Hosp., Alexandria, 1965-85, Mt. Vernon Hosp., Alexandria, 1976-85; hon. staff mem. Alexandria Hosp., 1985-89, 92—; attending physician D.C. Gen. Hosp., 1961-68, Georgetown U. Hosp., 1961-81, 93—, Mt. Sinai Hosp., Miami Beach, Fla., 1992—; chief animal experimentation Cancer rsch. under Dr. Sidney Farber Children's Med. Ctr., Boston, 1948-50; rsch. asst. Boston U. Sch. Medicine, 1956-57; chmn. dept. medicine Alexandria Hosp., 1964-85; founder, chmn., No. Va. Consortium for Continuing Med. Edn., 1974-86, chmn. emeritus, 1986; lectr. in field. Author publs. in field. Trustee Jefferson Meml. Hosp., 1965-74, mem. founding group, 1965, chmn. pharmacy com., 1965-76, co-chmn. tissue com., 1965-74; nominated candidate for Palm Beach (Fla.) Town Coun. Rsch. fellow under Norman Zamcheck Mallory Inst. Pathology, Boston, 1953-59, Gastroenterology rsch. under Franz Ingelfinger, Evans Meml. Hosp., Boston, AEC, 1951-53. Mem. AMA, Am. Coll. Gastroenterology, ACP, Am. Gastroent. Assn., Am. Inst. Nutrition, Am. Physiol. Soc., Am. Soc. Gastrointestinal Endoscopy, D.C. Med. Soc., Med. Soc. Va. (chmn. commn. on continuing med. edn. 1978-81), Alexandria Med. Soc. (v.p. 1979-80), Royal Soc. Medicine. Home: 47 Saint George Pl Palm Beach Gardens FL 33418

SMALL, MICHAEL L., surgeon, educator; b. Phila., Nov. 7, 1935; m. Minika L. Zachaebitz, Sep. 26, 1974; children: Linn, Maria. BS, Cornell U., 1957; MD, Jefferson Med. Coll., 1961. Fellow experimental surgery Royal Port Grad. Med. Sch., London, 1965-66; fellow in thoracic surgery Mem. Sloan Kettering Med. Ctr., N.Y.C., 1969-70; chief thoracic surgery Shanta Bhawan & Bir. Hosps., Kathmanou, Nepal, 1970-73; staff surgeon Calif. Pacific Med. Ctr., San Fransisco, 1975—, chief, divsn. thoracic surgery, 1994—; clin. assoc. prof. surgery U. Calif., San Fransisco, 1992—. Capt. U.S. Army, 1961-64. Office: 2100 Webster Ste 200 San Fransisco CA 94115

SMALL, NATALIE SETTIMELLI, pediatric mental health counselor; b. Quincy, Mass., June 2, 1933; d. Joseph Peter and Edmea Natalie (Bagnaschi) Settimelli; m. Parker Adams Small, Jr., Aug. 26, 1956; children: Parker Adams III, Peter McMichael, Carla Edmea. BA, Tufts U., 1955; MA, EdS, U. Fla., 1976; PhD, 1987. Cert. child life specialist. Pediatric counselor U. Fla. Coll. Medicine, Gainesville, 1976-80; pediatric counselor Shands Hosp.-U. Fla., Gainesville, 1980-87, supr. child life dept. patient and family resources, 1987—; adminstrv. liaison for self-dir. work teams, mem. faculty Ctr. for Coop. Learning for Health and Sci. Edn., Gainesville, 1988—, assoc. dir., 1996; cons. and lectr. in field. Author: Parents Know Best, 1991; co-author team packs series for teaching at risk adolescent health edn. and coop. learning. Bd. dirs. Ronald McDonald House, Gainesville, 1980—, mem. exec. com., 1991—; bd. dirs. Gainesville Assn. Creative Arts, 1994—; mem. health profl. adv. com. March of Dimes, Gainesville, 1986—, HIV prevention planning partnership, 1995. Boston Stewart Club scholar, Florence, Italy, 1955; grantee Jessie Ball Du Pont Fund, 1978, Children's Miracle Network, 1990, 92, 93, 94, 95; recipient Caring and Sharing award Ronald McDonald House, 1995. Mem. ACA, Nat. Bd. Cert. Counselors, Am. Assn. Mental Health Counselors, Assn. for the Care of Children's Health, Fla. Assn. Child Life Profls., Child Life Coun. Roman Catholic. Home: 3454 NW 12th Ave Gainesville FL 32605-4811 Office: Shands Hosp Patient and Family Resources PO Box 100306 Gainesville FL 32610

SMALL, PARKER ADAMS, JR., pediatrician, educator; b. Cin., July 5, 1932; s. Parker Adams and Grace (McMichael) S.; m. Natalie Settimelli, Aug. 26, 1956; children: Parker Adams, Peter McMichael, Carla Edmea. Student, Tufts U., 1950-53; MD, U. Cin., 1957. Med. intern Pa. Hosp., Phila., 1957-58; research assoc. Nat. Heart Inst. NIH, Washington, 1958-60; research fellow St. Mary's Hosp., London, Eng., 1960-61; sr. surgeon NIMH, Washington, 1961-66; prof. immunology and med. microbiology U. Fla., 1966-95, chmn. dept., 1966-75, prof. pediatrics, 1979—, prof. pathology, 1995—; dir. Ctr. for Coop. Learning for Health Sci. Edn., U. Fla., 1988—; vis. prof. U. Lausanne, Switzerland, 1972, U. Lagos, Nigeria, 1982, Al Hada Hosp., Saudi Arabia, 1983; vis. scholar Assn. Am. Med. Colls., Washington, 1973; assoc. life scis. panel Nat. Acad. Scis., 1981-88, co-chmn., 1982-83; bd. dirs. biol. scis. curriculum study Biol. Sci. Curriculum Study, 1984-90, exec. bd., 1987-90; mem. adv. com. Nat. Fund Med. Edn., 1984-87; mem. study com. Nat. Bd. Med. Examiners, 1983-85, mem. nat. vaccine adv. com., 1987-91, chmn. subcom. on new vaccines, 1987-91; cons. in field. Creator patient oriented problem solving system/POPS, for teaching immunology and coop. learning to med. students and Team Packs for teaching K-12 & college students health edn. and coop. learning; editor: The Secretory Immunologic System, 1971; mem. editorial bd. Infection and Immunity, 1974-76, Jour. Med. Edn., 1978-80; cons. editor Microbios, Cytobios; contbr. articles to profl. jours. Sec., treas. Oakmont, Md., 1964-65, mayor, 1965-66; chmn. Citizens for Pub. Schs. Gainesville, Fla., 1969-70. With USPHS, 1958-60, 61-66. Named Tchr. of Yr. U. Fla. Coll. Medicine, 1978-79, Disting. Lectr. AMA, 1986; recipient Presdl. medallion U. Fla., 1987, Nat. Basic Sci. Disting. Teaching award Alpha Omega Alpha, 1993, Jacob Ehrenzeller award, 1995; NIH spl. fellow, 1960-61, rsch. grantee, 1966—, U. Fla. Tchr./Scholar and commencement spkr., 1987; invited lectr. Assn. Am. Med. Colls., 1992. Mem. AAAS, Am. Assn. Immunologists (edn. com. 1983-86), Physicians for Social Responsibility, Fla. Med. Assn., Phi Beta Kappa, Sigma Xi, Theta Delta Chi. Home: 3454 NW 12th Ave Gainesville FL 32605-4811 Office: U Fla Coll Med PO Box 100275 Gainesville FL 32610-0275

SMALL, RALPH EDWARD, pharmacy educator, consultant; b. Welland, Ont., Can., Apr. 30, 1950; s. George Edward and Margaret Emma Verna (Young) S.; m. Sharon McRae Stevens, Sept. 21, 1985. BS in Pharmacy, U. Toronto, Ont., Can., 1973; PharmD, Duquesne U., 1975. Prof. pharmacy and medicine Med. Coll. of Va. Va. Commonwealth U., Richmond, 1975—. Mem. med. adv. bd. Cen. Va. chpt. Lupus Found., Richmond, 1983—; pharmacy capt. United Way Greater Richmond, 1988; pres. West End Manor Civic Assn., Richmond, 1984, J.R. Tucker High Sch. Community Coun., Richmond, 1986; bd. dirs. Va. chpt. Arthritis Found., Richmond, 1986—. Recipient Pub. Svc. award and Lifetime Achievement award Arthritis Found., 1986, Dist. Vol. of Yr., 1992, Excellence award United Way, 1988, NARD Leadership award, 1990, Va. Commonwealth Univ. Disting. Svc. award, 1994. Fellow Am. Coll. Clin. Pharmacy, Am. Soc. Health System Pharmacists; mem. Am. Assn. Colls. Pharmacy, Am. Soc. Health System Pharmacists, Va. Pharm. Assn. (pres. 1990-91, Bowl of Hygeia 1988, Svc. award 1994), Am. Pharm. Assn. (trustee 1996—), Richmond Pharm. Assn. (pres. 1986, Dist. Pres. award 1987). Home: 1800 Locust Hill Rd Richmond VA 23233-4148 Office: Va Commonwealth U Med Coll Va PO Box 980533 Richmond VA 23298-0533

SMALL, SALLY CHRISTINE (CHRIS), registered nurse; b. Science Hill, Ky., Feb. 10, 1951; d. William Roland Van Hoosier and Georgia (Mayfield) Miller; m. Larry W. Small, May 24, 1968; children: Jeanette L., Larry W., Charlotte A., Daniel J. AS in Nursing, Seward County C.C., Liberal, Kans., 1983; BSN, Fort Hays State U., 1992. RN, Kans.; cert. BLS, Am. Heart Assn.; cert. ACLS, Am. Heart Assn., trauma nurse core course; cert. EMT, Kans.; cert. nurse aide. Nurse aide Satanta (Kans.) Dist. Hosp., 1981-82, LPN, 1982-83, RN, 1983—, infection control RN, 1984-93, labor and delivery supr. RN, 1985-93, asst. dir. RN, 1988-93; contract RN Bob Wilson Meml. Hosp., Ulysses, Kans., 1984, Stevens County Hosp., Hugoton, Kans., 1984-85, St. Catherine's Hosp., Garden City, Kans., 1986; child-birth class instr., Haskell County, 1985-93. EMT Satanta Emergency Med. Svc., 1984—, tech. tng. officer, 1986—; CPR instr. Haskell County schs. and bus., 1988—, ACLS instr.; dir. communicable disease prevention program Satanta H.S., 1991. Republican. Home: Box 505 Satanta KS 67870 Office: Satanta Dist Hosp Box 159 Satanta KS 67870

SMALL, S(AUL) MOUCHLY, psychiatrist, educator; b. N.Y.C., Oct. 11, 1913; s. Joseph and Esther (Mouchly) S.; m. Sophie Scholl, June 13, 1937; children: Susan Steinhart, Laurie Block, Jonathan, Cynthia McDonald. BS, CCNY, 1933; MD cum laude, Cornell U., 1937. Diplomate Am. Bd. Psychiatry and Neurology. Instr. psychiatry Cornell Med. Coll., N.Y.C., 1940-43; lectr. psychiatry Columbia U., N.Y.C., 1948-51; adj. and assoc. attending psychiatrist Mt. Sinai Hosp., N.Y.C., 1946-51; prof., chmn. dept. psychiatry SUNY, Buffalo, 1951-78; prof. emeritus dept. psychiatry SUNY, 1978—; dir. psychiatry Meyer Meml. Hosp., Buffalo, 1951-78; attending psychiatrist Erie County Med. Ctr., Buffalo, 1951—, Buffalo Gen. Hosp., 1963—; chief psychiatric cons. VA Hosp., Buffalo, 1952—; neuropsychiat. cons. Surgeon Gen. U.S. Army, 1947-70; cons. U.S. DOD, Washington, 1966—; mem. N.Y. State Bd. Profl. Med. Conduct, Albany, 1985—; emeritus dir. Am. Bd. Psychiatry and Neurology, 1986—. Co-author textbook: Handbook of Psychiatry, 1943; contbr. articles to profl. jours., chpts. to books. Acting dir. Erie County Mental Health Bd., Buffalo, then mem. bd. dirs.; pres. Muscular Dystrophy Assn., N.Y.C., 1980-89, bd. dirs., chmn. exec. com., 1989—, pres. emeritus, 1989—. Fellow Am. Psychiat. Assn. (Disting. Svc. citation 1978, Psychiatrist of Yr. award 1975), Am. Coll. Psychiatrists (Bowis gold medal 1975), Am. Coll. Psychoanalysts, Am. Assn. Social Psychiatry; mem. AMA, N.Y. Acad. Medicine. Home: 75 Oakbrook Dr # G Buffalo NY 14221-3560 Office: Erie County Med Ctr K-Annex Bldg 462 Grider St Buffalo NY 14215-3075

SMALL, WILFRED THOMAS, surgeon, educator; b. Boston, June 13, 1920; s. Fred Wentworth and Isabelle (Scott) S.; BS, Bowdoin Coll., 1943; MD, Tufts U., 1946; m. Muriel Yoe Gratton, Sept. 25, 1948; children: Wilfred Thomas, Richard Gratton, James Stewart, John Wentworth. Diplomate Am. Bd. Surgery. Intern surg. svc. The Boston Children's Hosp., 1946-47, then research fellow; assoc. in surgery Peter Bent Brigham Hosp., Harvard U., 1949-50; resident, chief resident in surgery New Eng. Med. Ctr., Tufts U., 1950-53; practice medicine specializing in surgery, Worcester, Mass., 1953-88; assoc. prof. surgery U. Mass., from 1973, now prof. surgery; mem. staff Meml. Hosp., 1953-88, chief div. surgery, 1973-81; instr. Harvard U., 1949-50, Tufts U., 1952-60. Active Worcester Art Mus., Worcester County Music Assn.; sec. bd. dirs. Indian River UN Assn. Served to lt. (j.g.) USN, 1947-49. Fellow ACS (pres. Mass. chpt. 1979); mem. AMA, New Eng. Surg. Soc., New Eng. Cancer Soc., Soc. Surgery Alimentary Tract, Mass., Pan Am. Med. Socs., Am. Trauma Soc., Indian River Hosp. Assn. (bd. dirs.), Vis. Nurses Assn. (bd. dirs.), Worcester Econs. Club (past pres.), Worcester Council on Fgn. Rels., Tatnuck Country Club, Sakonnet Golf Club, Riomar Golf Club (Vero Beach, Fla.). Episcopalian. Contbr. articles to profl. jours. Home: 16 Warrens Point Rd Little Compton RI 02837-1433

SMALLEY, BRIAN WADE, surgeon, military officer; b. West Union, Ohio, Sept. 24, 1966; s. William Joseph and Linda Carol (Johnson) S.; m. Teresa Lee Jones, June 20, 1992 (div. June 1995). BS in Zoology, Ohio U., 1989, DO, 1993. Commd. U.S. Army, 1994—, advanced through grades to capt.; emergency rm. physician U.S. Army, Ft. Knox, Ky., 1994-95, flight surgeon, 1995—, chief aviation medicine, aviation safety, 1995—. Mem. Am. Osteo. Assn., Army Aviation Assn. Am., Army Flight Surgeons Soc. Home: 1658 Preston St Radcliff KY 40160-9102

SMALLEY, PENNY JUDITH, laser nursing consultant; b. Chgo., Feb. 20, 1947; d. Ernest Rich and Muriel L. (Touff) Brown; m. Ivan H. Smalley, Jan. 11, 1972; children: Cherie Ann, Michael John, Geoffry Paul. Grad., Evanston Hosp. Sch. Nursing, Ill., 1980. Cert. Am. Bd. Laser Surgery, 1989. Staff nurse Evanston Hosp., 1979-81, laser coord., 1981-83; office mgr. Women's Health Group, 1981; laser nurse specialist Cooper Lasersonics, various, 1983-86; pres., CEO Technology Concepts Internat., Inc., Chgo., 1986—; lectr., writer Sino Fgn. Laser Conf., People's Republic of China, 1987; bd. dirs. Laser Inst. Am. Contbg. author: Nursing Clinics of North America, 1990; editorial bd. Clin. Laser Monthly, Laser Nursing mag., 1989—, Minimally Invasive Surg. Nursing; contbr. articles to profl. jours. Mem. Am. Soc. Laser Medicine and Surgery (chmn. edn. com. 1987-90, standards of practice com. 1990, quality assurance com., nursing sect. chmn. 1992-94), award for Excellence in Laser Nursing 1993), Laser Inst. Am. (bd. dirs.), Am. Nat. Standards Com., Inst. Com. Lasers in Health Care (exec. com., nurse rep.), Brit. Med. Laser Assn. (course dir. first laser nursing conf. in U.K., 1990), Assn. Oper. Rm. Nurses (tchr. nat. seminars, spl. com. on internat. issues), Internat. Soc. Laser Surgery and Medicine (chmn. nursing 1988—). Democrat. Home and Office: 1444 W Farwell Ave Chicago IL 60626-3410

SMART, ELNORA SUE, psychologist; b. Kansas City, Mo., Nov. 20, 1953; d. Carl J. and Bernice (Benner) Smart. BS in Edn., Cen. Mo. State U., 1974, MS in Psychology, 1976; EdS, Pittsburg (Kans.) State U., 1985. Lic. psychologist, Mo. Psychology intern Fulton (Mo.) State Hosp., 1975-76; clin. psychologist I and II Nevada (Mo.) State Hosp., 1976-81; sch. psychologist Shawnee Mission (Kans.) Sch. Dist., 1981—; family and individual psychologist Shawnee Mission Schs. Clinic, 1983-90. Named Young Career Woman of Yr., Bus. and Profl. Women's Assn., Nevada, Mo., 1978. Mem. Kans. Assn. Sch. Psychologists, Nat. Assn. Sch. Psychologists. Office: DO Old Mission 4901 Reinhardt Shawnee Mission KS 66205

SMATRESK, NEAL JOSEPH, biology educator, science education consultant; b. Worcester, Mass., July 9, 1951; s. Edwin C. and Dorothy (Lincoln) S.; m. Deborah Hoddick, Aug. 12, 1978; children: Erik Neal, Kristen Elise. BA, Gettysburg Coll., 1973; MA, SUNY, Buffalo, 1978; PhD, U. Tex., 1980. Rsch. expedition NSF, Alpha Helix, Micronesia, 1979; NIH trainee U. Pa. Med. Sch., Phila., 1980-82; asst. prof. biology U. Tex., Arlington, 1982-88; assoc. prof. biology U. Tex., 1988-94; prof., chmn. biology, 1994—; sci. edn. cons. local schs., Fielder Mus., Arlington, 1984—. Ad hoc reviewer numerous profl. jours.; contbr. articles, revs., and book chpt. to profl. publs. V.p. Fielder Mus. Sch., Arlington, 1989—; coach Little League Baseball, Arlington, 1989—. Recipient Outstanding Tchr. award, U. Tex. Chancellor, 1988; grantee NSF (3), 1989—, NIH, 1991—. Mem. Am. Physiol. Soc., Am. Zool. Soc., Can. Zool. Soc., Optimist. Office: U Tex Dept Biology PO Box 19498 Arlington TX 76019

SMAYLING, LYDA MOZELLA, speech pathologist; b. Britton, Okla., Apr. 19, 1923; d. Miles and Evelyn (King) Maxwell; m. George F. Smayling, Sept. 12, 1944 (dec. 1985); children: Sally, Michael, Miles. BA magna cum laude, U. Wichita, Wichita, Kans., 1944; MA summa cum laude, U. Wichita, 1947. Dir., cons., assoc. U. Kans. Med. Ctr., Kans. City, 1947-56; cons. Westchester County Cerebral Palsy Assn., Bedford Village, N.Y., 1947-54; asst. dir. Inst. Logopedics, Wichita, 1957-68; instr. Wichita (Kans.) State U., 1957-68; cons. Wichita, 1957-68; pvt. practice Mpls., 1968—. Contbr. articles to profl. jours. V.p. PTA, Wichita, 1957-64, tchr. Unitarian Ch., Wichita, 1959-64;. Mem. Am. Speech-Lang. Hearing Assn., Kans. Speech-Lang. Hearing Assn. (v.p., bd. dirs., treas.). Unitarian Universalist. Home and Office: 3145 Dean Ct # 903 Minneapolis MN 55416-4390

SMEDH, ROLF KENNET, surgeon, educator; b. Solna, Sweden, June 3, 1951; s. Gosta Sixten and Ragnhild (Holmquist) S.; m. Eva Marie Carlsson, July 14, 1984; children: Anna, Carl Linus, Hedvig. MD, U. Karolinska Inst., 1978; PhD of Surgery, U. Linkoping, 1994. Intern Hosp. Enkoping, Sweden, 1978-80; resident in surgery Hosp. Enkoping, Kalmar, 1980-83; sr. resident in surgery Hosp. Kalmar, Sweden, 1983-87, U. Hosp. Linkoping, Sweden, 1987-95; assoc. prof. Hosp. Vasteras, Sweden, 1996—. Contbr. articles to profl. jours. Mem. Swedish Med. Assn., Swedish Soc. Medicine, Swedish Surg. Soc., Scandinavian Surg. Soc., Swedish Soc. Gastroenteral and Endoscopy, Swedish Soc. Colon and Rectal Surgery. Home: Via Bergsgatan 6H, S-72460 Vasteras Sweden Office: Dept Surgery, Ctrl Hosp Vasteras, S-72981 Vasteras Sweden

SMELTER, KATHERINE VAFAKAS, psychologist, educator; b. Detroit, Dec. 30, 1941; d. Nicholas A. and Fannie D. (Pappas) Vafakas; m. Bernard Smelter, June 21, 1975; 1 dau., Christine Katherine. BS, Ea. Mich. U., 1965; MEd, Wayne State U., 1967, EdD, 1972. Dept. chairperson counseling Oakland C.C., Mich., 1967-72; asst. prof. dept. psychology Northwestern State U., La., 1972-73; asst. prof. dept. counseling edn. U. Bridgeport (Conn.), 1973-75; adj. prof. L.I. U., 1975—, Mt. St. Mary Coll., 1990—; sch. psychologist Wappingers Falls (N.Y.) Central Schs., 1982—; chairperson, com. spl. edn. Wappingers Cen. Sch. Dist.; keynote speaker, guest speaker profl. confs.; co-founder Garrison Taxpayers Assn. Bd. dirs. Putnam County Community Svcs., N.Y., also sec. Mem. APA, Nat. Assn. Sch. Psychologists (nat. cert.). Editor profl. jours.; contbr. articles to profl. jours. Home: PO Box 231 Garrison NY 10524-0231

SMETANA, GERALD WILLIAM, internist; b. Evanston, Ill., Oct. 29, 1958; s. Frank Gerald Smetana and Carol Ann (Breyer) McCully. BS in Biochemistry, UCLA, 1980; MD, U. Calif., San Francisco, 1984. Diplomate Am. Bd. Internal Medicine; lic. physician, Mass. Intern Beth Israel Hosp., Boston, 1984-85, resident in internal medicine, 1985-87, assoc. physician, 1987—; internist Healthcare Assocs./Beth Israel Hosp., Boston, 1987—, assoc. firm chief dept. medicine, 1992—; instr. medicine Harvard Med. Sch., Boston, 1987—. Mem. ACP, Soc. Gen. Internal Medicine, Phi Beta Kappa, Alpha Omega Alpha. Office: Beth Israel Hosp 330 Brookline Ave Boston MA 02215

SMIDT, CARSTEN RAINER, nutritionist; b. Hilden, Germany, Apr. 29, 1961; came to U.S., 1985; m. JoAnn Stedman, July 15, 1989; children: Kevin Alexander, Alexander Carsten. Diploma, U. Bonn, Germany, 1985; BS in Nutrition, U. Calif., Davis, 1987, MS in Nutrition, 1988, PhD in Nutrition, 1990. Rsch. scientist Mead Johnson Nutritional Group, Evansville, Ind., 1991-93; sr. rsch. scientist Mead Johnson Nutritional Group, Evansville, 1993-95; tech. specialist NuSkin Internat., Provo, Utah, 1996—. Mem. Am. Inst. Nutrition (predoctoral fellowship 1989), Am. Soc. for Parenteral and Enteral Nutrition, Am. Soc. Clin. Nutrition. Home: 4556 N Northgate Dr Provo UT 84604 Office: Mead Johnson Nutritional Group 75 W Center St Provo UT 84601

SMILEY, DANIEL RAY, emergency medical services director, educator; b. San Jose, Calif., Sept. 5, 1956; s. Wayne Austin and Esther Ella (Weichert) S.; m. Beverly Ann Scheeler,. AS, Merced Coll., 1981; BS, Calif. State U., Fresno, 1983; MPA, U. San Francisco, 1987; DPA, U. So. Calif., 1992. Paramedic, emergency med. technician Riggs Ambulance, Merced, Calif., 1974-81; paramedic Jones Ambulance, Fresno, Calif., 1979-83; emergency med. services instr. Fresno County Dept. of Health, Fresno, 1981-83, dir. of emergency med. services, 1983-89; chief dep. dir. Calif. Emergency Med. Svcs. Authority, Sacramento, 1989—, acting dir., 1989-93; lectr., faculty Fresno City Coll., 1982-83, Calif. State U., Fresno, 1987-88. Mem. Emergency Med. Svcs. Adminstrn. Assn. of Calif. (pres. 1988-89), Am. Soc. Public Adminstrn., Am. Public Health Assn. Republican. Mormon. Office: State of Calif 1930 9th St Ste 100 Sacramento CA 95814-7044

SMILOWITZ, HENRY MARTIN, pharmacology educator; b. Bklyn., Sept. 25, 1946; s. Benjamin and Doris (Prager) S.; m. Connie Dollin, June 17, 1979; children: Benjamin, Talya, Joshua. AB, Reed Coll., 1968; PhD, MIT, 1972. Postdoctoral fellow Tufts U. Med. Sch., Boston, 1972-73, Harvard Med. Sch., Boston, 1973-76; asst. prof. U. Conn. Health Ctr., Farmington, 1976-82, assoc. prof., 1982—. Contbr. over 50 articles and abstracts to profl. publs. Mem. Ad Hoc Adv. Com. on Electric and Magnetic Fields, State of Conn. Dept. Environ. Protection, Hartford, 1991—. NIH rsch. grantee, 1977-94; fellow Woodrow Wilson Found., 1968, Muscular Dystrophy Found., 1973-75. Office: U Conn Health Ctr 263 Farmington Ave Farmington CT 06030-0001

SMITH, ALBERT CARL, physician, pathologist, marine biologist; b. L.A., Sept. 13, 1934; s. Salmon and Sadie (Lewis) S.; m. Deborah Joan Townsend, Feb. 24, 1967; children: Shana Lynn, Chelsea Frances. PhD, U. Calif., Irvine, 1967; MD, U. Hawaii, 1975. Diplomate Am. Bd. Pathology. Program dir. pathology Aquatic Scis., Inc., Boca Raton, Fla., 1969; researcher Calif. Dept. Fish and Game, Long Beach, 1961-63, 1965-66, 1970; assoc. prof. biology U. Hawaii, 1970-73; pathology rsch. fellow John A. Burns Sch. Medicine, U. Hawaii, 1975-76; resident in pathology St. Francis Hosp./U. Hawaii, 1976-77, Queen's Med. Ctr./U. Hawaii, 1978-79; chief clin. lab. VA Med. Ctr., Gainesville, Fla., 1980-85; chief clin. pathology VA Med. Ctr.,

Bay Pines, Fla., 1985-89, dir. pathology spl. studies, chief chemistry sect., 1989-91; med. dir. Trenton (Fla.) Med. Ctr., 1991-93; dir. Bay County Pub. Health Unit., 1993-94; physician Bay Walk-In Clinic, 1994-95; dir. lab. svcs. Gulf Pines Hosp., Port St. Joe, Fla., 1994—, Emerald Coast Hosp., Apalachicola, Fla., 1994—; chief cons. Hawaii Biomarine, Honolulu, 1973-80; sr. scientist Oceanic Inst., Waimanalo, Hawaii, 1977-79; dir. Med. Labs. Hawaii, Honolulu, 1979-80; clin. pathology cons. Sunland Ctr., Gainesville, Fla., 1980-83; adj. asst. prof. Vet. Coll., U. Fla., Gainesville, 1987—; courtesy prof. dept. marine sci. U. South Fla., St. Petersburgh, 1987—. Contbr. over 80 articles to profl. jours. Fellow Coll. Am. Pathologists; mem. Internat. Soc. Aquatic Medicine (hon.), Soc. for Invertebrate Pathology (charter), Am. Longevity Soc. (hon.), AAAS, Internat. Soc. Devel. and Comparative Immunology, Am. Soc. Zoologists, N.Y. Acad. Scis., Fla. Med. Assn., Bays Med. Soc.

SMITH, ALLAN, psychologist; b. Bklyn., May 13, 1949; s. Philip and Stella (Silverstein) S.; m. Robin Gail Tivoli, July 26, 1980; children: Stephen, Adam. BA, Queens Coll., 1971, MA, 1974; PhD, Hofstra U., 1988. Lic. psychologist, N.Y. Psychology asst. III Pilgrim Psychiat. Ctr., West Brentwood, N.Y., 1976-79; psychologist I Sagtikos Intermediate Care Facility/Mental Retardation, Melville, N.Y., 1979-86; psychologist II Kings Park (N.Y.) Psychiat. Ctr., 1986-93, assoc. psychologist, 1993—, dir. tng. psychology intern program, 1992—; pvt. practice Levittown, N.Y., 1990—, Wantagh, N.Y., 1993—; ind. contractor Cath. Psychoednl. Svcs., Williston Park, N.Y., 1990-91, South Manor Sch. Dist., Manorville, N.Y., 1991; supervising psychologist Adults and Children With Learning Disabilities, 1993-94. Coach Levittown-South Wantagh Baseball, Levittown, 1991. Mem. Nassau County Psychol. Assn. Democrat. Jewish. Home and Office: 162 Tardy Ln Wantagh NY 11793-1931

SMITH, ALLEN ANDERSON, biology and chemistry educator; b. Boston, Apr. 27, 1939; s. Caleb Allen and Jeannette Anderson (Poole) S.; m. Irit Irena Urman, Apr. 28, 1974; children: Amalia May, Rebekah Felicia. AB, Brown U., 1961; PhD, U. Oreg., 1969; BSc, Widener U., 1986; MA, Temple U., 1991. Predoctoral fellow Oreg. Primate Rsch. Ctr., Beaverton, 1963-69; sr. instr. Hahnemann Med. Coll., Phila., 1969-70; guest instr. Tel-Aviv (Israel) U., 1970-71; rsch. assoc. Temple U., Phila., 1971-74; asst. prof. Widener Coll., Chester, Pa., 1974-78; assoc. prof. Widener U., Chester, Pa., 1978-89; assoc. prof. Sch. Podiatric Medicine Barry U., Miami Shores, Fla., 1989—. Author: Manual of Mink Anatomy, 1979; contbr. articles to profl. jours. Mountaineering chair Delaware Valley chpt. Appalachian Mountain Club, Springfield, Pa., 1972-75, 78-80, 83-84. Mem. AAAS, Histochem. Soc., Am. Chem. Soc., Delaware County Sci. Tchrs. Assn. (pres. 1984-85), Fla. Acad. Sci. (chair med. sci. sect. 1996—), Nat. Soc. Histotechnology. Democrat. Jewish. Office: Sch Podiatric Medicine Barry U Miami FL 33135

SMITH, ANDREW JEPTHA KINCANNON, neurosurgeon; b. Houston, Sept. 28, 1942; s. A.J. Kincannon and Helen (Townes) S.; m. Mary Ethlyn Hill, July 10, 1965; children: Emily, Andrew, Bradley. BA, U. Tex., Austin, 1964; MA, U. Tex. Southwestern Med. Sch., Dallas, 1968, MD, 1969; PhD, U. Minn., 1977. Diplomate Am. Bd. Neurol. Surgeons. Intern U. Minn. Hosp., Mpls., 1969-70, resident in neurol. surgery, 1972-77; staff assoc. NIH, Bethesda, Md., 1970-72; clin. instr. U. Minn., Mpls., 1977—; practice medicine specializing in neurosurgery Mpls. Neurol. Surgeons Ltd., 1977—; chmn. laser and critical care com. Meth. Hosp., Mpls., 1986-88, sec., treas. med. staff, 1987, pres. elect med. staff, 1988, pres., 1989; bd. govs., 1988—; bd. dirs. West Metro. Ind. Physicians Assocs., Mpls., pres., 1988-89; mem. Council of State Neurosurg. Socs. (Minn. rep. 1982-84, 87, mem. negotiation and reimbursement methodologies com. 1983-86); bd. dirs. Midwest Med. Ins. Co., 1993—, vice-chair, 1995, chair-elect, 1996; alt. com. Minn. Health Care Commn., 1993—; bd. dirs. Criterion Health Care Network, 1993—, chair, 1993-96. Mem. Gov.'s Task Force on Violoence, 1995—. Served to lt. comdr. USPHS, 1970-72. Mem. AMA (alt. del. 1994-95, del. 1996—), Minn. Med. Assn. (chmn. communications com. 1986-88, del. 1984-88, ad hoc com. on worker's compensation 1983, chmn. task force on risk mgmt. 1985, mem. task force on rural health 1986, profl. liability com. 1987, policy implementation com. 1987-88, bd. trustees 1988-96, bd. chair 1990-93, pres. 1994), Minn. Neurosurg. Soc. (pres. 1987), Am. Assn. Neurol. Surgeons, Minn. Physicians Found. (bd. dirs. 1987-92), Hennepin County Med. Soc. (bd. dirs. 1987-95), Congress of Neurol. Surgeons, Allina Found. (bd. dirs. 1994—). Republican. Episcopalian. Home: 515 Ferndale Rd N Wayzata MN 55391-1008 Office: Mpls Neurol Surgeons Ltd 911 Medical Arts Bldg 505 N Highway 169 Plymouth MN 55441

SMITH, ANDREW JOHN, dental surgeon, microbiologist; b. Rhondda, Wales, Jan. 22, 1965; s. Raymond and Beryl Smith; m. Lisa Murphy. B of Dental Sci., U. Wales, 1987, PhD, 1993. Gen. practitioner NHS, Bristol, Eng., 1987-88; sr. house officer Cardiff (Wales) Dental Sch., 1988-90, rsch. asst., 1990-93, comty. dental officer, 1993-94; lectr. periodontology Glasgow Dental Sch., 1994-95, lectr. oral microbiology, 1995—; hon. registrar bacteriology Glasgow Royal Infirmary, 1995—; chmn. sci. seminar series Glasgow Dental Sch., 1995-96. Editor: (jour.) Procs. Univ. of Wales Postgrad. Meeting, 1993; contbr. papers to profl. jours. Asst. diving instr. Brit. Sub-Aqua Club. Recipient Colgate Rsch. award Brit. Soc. Dental Rsch., 1993. Fellow Royal Coll. Surgeons Edinburgh; mem. Brit. and Internat. Soc. for Dental Rsch., Brit. Soc. Periodontology, Brit. Assn. Inflammation Rsch. Office: Glasgow Dental Sch, 378 Sauchiehall St, Glasgow G2 3J2, Scotland

SMITH, ANTHONY YOUNGER, urologist, surgeon; b. Rochester, Minn., June 11, 1955; s. William George and Georgia Lee (Carter) S.; m. Sheila Jean Pym, July 4, 1982; children: Cameron Younger, Sheldon Laverick. BSChemE, N.Mex. State U., 1977; MD, U. Tex., Dallas, 1981. Diplomate Am. Bd. Urology. Intern then resident in gen. surgery U. Louisville, 1981-83; resident in urology U. N.Mex., Albuquerque, 1983-86, assoc. prof. surgery, 1987—; fellow in transplantation U. Tex., Houston, 1986-87; dir. urologic oncology U. N.Mex. Sch. Medicine, Albuquerque, 1987—. Author several chpts. in books; contbr. articles to profl. jours. Fellow Am. Coll. Surgeons; mem. Am. Soc. Transplant Surgery, Am. Soc. Transplant Physicians, Am. Urologic Assn., Urologic Soc. Transplantation & Vascular Surgery, S.W. Oncology Group (com. mem.), Western Assn. Transplant Surgeons. Republican. Methodist. Office: Univ N Mex Med Sch Div Urology Lomas Blvd # 2211 Albuquerque NM 87101

SMITH, BARBARA DAIL, school nurse; b. Oklahoma City, July 15, 1949; d. James E. and Juanita E. (Butler) Berryhill; m. William Ben Smith, May 23, 1975; children: Rebecca Sue and James Ben. BS in Biology, Oklahoma City U., 1975, BS in Health Edn., 1984; RN diploma St. Anthony Hosp., 1979; MPH, U. Okla., 1990. Mgmt. nurse St. Anthony Hosp., Oklahoma City, 1979-83; cons. family help group cancer patients, 1981-83; nurse Oklahoma City Bd. Edn., 1983—, EPSDT CASE mgr., 1994-96, supr. health svcs., 1996—; nurse Baptist Hosp., 1991—; Author: (with others) Chemotherapy Cert. Program, 1981-82. Leader Camp Fire Orgn. Am., Oklahoma City, 1982-84; mem. Cen. Okla. Task Force Com. for children with spl. needs; mem. Oklahoma County Task Force Com. on Child Abuse; mem. spl. edn. task force com. Oklahoma City Pub. Schs., 1986-87; mem. gov.'s task force Child Abuse, 1985-86; mem. Okla. County Task Force on Children with Spl. Needs; mem. Okla. County Immunization Coalition, Okla. City Eye Care Task Force; mem. spl. edn. task force com. Oklahoma City Bd. Edn.; mem. exec. bd. Oklahoma City Fedn. of Tchrs. Local 2309 of the Am. Fedn. of Tchrs.; sec., co-coord. Children with Attention Deficit Disorder of Ctrl. Okla., 1992. Mem. Nat. Oncol. Nursing Soc., Okla. Oncol. Nursing Soc., Okla. City Sch. Nurses Soc. (pres. 1985-87), Oklahoma City Pub. Sch. Nurses (procedures com., sec. 1986-87), Sch. Nurse Orgn. Okla. (chair continuing edn./workshop com. 1985—, legis. lobby com. 1988-90, bd. dirs. 1985—, pres.-elect 1990, pres. 1992-94), Children with Attention Deficit Disorder (sec. Okla. chpt. 1992, assoc. chair 1993-95), YWCA, Nat. Assn. Sch. Nurses, Beta Beta Beta. Democrat. Lodge: Fraternal Order of Police Aux.

SMITH, BARRY DAVID, obstetrician-gynecologist, educator; b. Suffern, N.Y., July 3, 1938; s. Alexander N. and Beatrice (Morris) S.; m. Maryann Blair, Oct. 11, 1963; children: Gillian, Adam. AB, Dartmouth Coll., 1959; MD, Cornell U., 1962. Diplomate Am. Bd. Ob-Gyn. Resident in ob-gyn N.Y. Hosp. Cornell U. Med. Ctr., N.Y.C., 1963-67, chief resident, instr., 1967-68; staff obstetrician/gynecologist Mary Hitchcock Meml. Hosp., Hanover, N.H., 1970—; asst. prof. Dartmouth Coll., Hanover, 1970-78, assoc. prof., 1979—; chief sect. ob-gyn. Hitchcock Clinic, 1977-95, bd. govs., 1975-85, bd. dirs., 1980-86; chief sect. ob-gyn. Dartmouth Med. Ctr., 1977—, chmn. dept. ob-gyn., 1992-95, vice chair dept., 1995—. Treas., pres. Norwich (Vt.) Recreation and Conservation Council, 1975-77. Served to comdr. USNR. Fellow Am. Coll. Ob-gyn. (v.p. N.H. sect. 1991-94, pres. 1994—, chair N.H. sect. 1994—), Am. Fertility Soc., Am. Soc. Colposcopy. Office: Dartmouth Hitchcock Clinic 1 Medical Center Dr Lebanon NH 03756-0001

SMITH, BERT KRUGER, mental health services professional, consultant; b. Wichita Falls, Tex., Nov. 18, 1915; d. Sam and Fania (Feldman) Kruger; m. Sidney Stewart Smith, Jan. 19, 1936; children: Sheldon Stuart, Jared Burt (dec.), Randy Smith Huke. BJ, U. Mo., 1936; MA, U. Tex., 1949; DHL (hon.), U. Mo., 1985. Soc. and entertainment editor Wichita Falls Post, 1936-37; freelance writer Juneau, Alaska, 1937; assoc. pub. Coleman Daily Dem. Voice, 1950-51; assoc. editor Jr. Coll. Jour., Austin, Tex., 1952-55; spl. cons., exec. Hogg Found. for Mental Health, Austin, 1952—; chmn. bd. Austin Groups for the Elderly, 1985—. Author: No Language But A Cry, 1964, Your Non-Learning Child, 1968, A Teaspoon of Honey, 1970, Insights for Uptights, 1970, Aging in America, 1973, The Pursuit of Dignity, 1977, Looking Forward, 1983; contbr. numerous articles to profl. jours. Bert Kruger Smith professorship Sch. Social Work U. Tex., 1982; recipient Disting. Svc. award City of Austin, 1988, Cert. of Appreciation, Tex. Dept. Human Svcs., 1989, Ann Bert Smith award Sr.'s Respite Svc., 1989, S.W. Found. Founders' Spirit award, 1990, Tex. Leadership award Ann. Tex. Joint Conf. on Aging, 1992, Tex. Leadership award Tex. Dept. on Aging, 1992; named to Tex. Women's Hall of Fame, 1988. Mem. Women in Comm. (Lifetime Achievement award 1994), Am. Fedn. for Aging Rsch., Adult Svc. Coun. (bd. dirs. 1970—, Family Elder Care Guardian Angel award 1996), Family Eldercare (bd. dirs. 1979—), Authors Guild, Nat. Assn. Sci. Writers, Hadassah, B'nai B'rith Women, Delta Kappa Gamma (hon). Jewish. Home: 5818 Westslope Dr Austin TX 78731-3633 Office: Hogg Found Mental Health PO Box 7998 Austin TX 78713-7998 also: U Tex Austin Austin TX 78713

SMITH, BERTRAM LEON, vascular surgeon; b. Dallas, May 16, 1948; s. Bertram Leon Smith and Dora June (Fain) Day; m. Robin Arnold, June 20, 1980; children: Zan, Andrew, Alyson. BA, Tulane U., 1970; MD, U. Tex. Southwestern, 1974. Intern U. Tex. Health Sci. Ctr., San Antonio, 1974, resident, 1975-79; fellow in peripheral vascular surgery Vanderbilt-St. Thomas Hosp., 1979-80; attending physician Baylor Univ. Med. Ctr., Dallas, 1982—. Fellow Am. Coll. Surgeons; mem. Internat. Soc. Cardiovascular Surgeons, So. Assn. Vascular Surgeons, Tex. Surg. Soc., Dallas Soc. Gen. Surgery, Tex. Med. Assn. Episcopalian. Office: Thompson Talkington et al 712 N Washington #509 Dallas TX 75246

SMITH, BRIAN RICHARD, hematologist, oncologist, immunologist; b. Glen Cove, N.Y., May 7, 1952; s. Frank C. and Gloria R. S.; m. Keiren Donovan, April 17, 1993. A.B. in Chemistry summa cum laude, Princeton U., 1972; M.D., Harvard U., 1976. Clin. fellow in medicine Harvard U., also med. house officer Peter Bent Brigham Hosp., Boston, 1976-77, asst. resident physician, 1977-78, clin. fellow in hematology-oncology, 1978-81; instr. medicine Harvard Med. Sch. and asso. Brigham and Women's Hosp., Children's Hosp., Dana-Farber Cancer Inst., Boston, 1981-88; asst. prof. medicine Harvard Med. Sch., 1985-88; assoc. prof. medicine, lab. medicine and pediatrics Sch. of Medicine Yale U., New Haven, 1988-96, prof. medicine, lab. medicine and pediatrics, 1996—; dir. rsch. Yale Bone Marrow Transplant Unit, dir. clin. immunohematology; DeCamp lectr. biomed. ethics, 1992. Recipient George A. Howe prize Princeton U., 1976; Am. Cancer Soc. fellow, 1981-84; Leukemia Soc. fellow, 1982-88, scholar Leukemia Soc. Am., 1989, Stohlman scholar Leukemia Soc. Am., 1993. Diplomate Am. Bd. Internal Medicine. Fellow ACP; mem. NIH (recombinant DNA adv. com., 1992-96), Phi Beta Kappa, Sigma Xi, Alpha Omega Alpha. Roman Catholic. Office: Yale U Med Sch PO Box 208035 New Haven CT 06520-8035

SMITH, BRUCE STEWART, oral and maxillofacial surgeon; b. Houston, June 5, 1954; s. John Duncan and Lois Virginia (Derry) S.; m. Nancy Marie Mohrman, Aug. 16, 1982; children: Scott M., Brian A. BS with merit, U.S. Naval Acad., 1977; DDS, Baylor Coll. Dentistry, 1986. Lic. dentist, Tex. Pvt. practice oral and maxillofacial surgery Houston, 1990—; clin. asst. prof. U. Tex. Dental Br., Houston, 1990—; presenter in field. Lt. USN, 1977-82. Fellow Am. Assn. Oral and Maxillofacial Surgeons; mem. ADA, Tex. Soc. Oral and Maxillofacial Surgeons, Houston Soc. Oral and Maxillofacial Surgeons, Tex. Dental Assn., Greater Houston Dental Soc. Republican. Methodist. Office: 1213 Hermann Dr Ste 250 Houston TX 77004-7009

SMITH, CASON CONRAD, dermatologist; b. Augusta, Ga., Feb. 3, 1920; s. Walter Cason and Violet Marie (Knapp) S.; m. Jean Celeste Rae, June 29, 1942; children: C. Conrad Jr., Gail, Stephen, Barry, Joel. BS, U. Ga., 1940; MD, Med. Coll. of Ga., 1943; MSc in Dermatology, NYU, 1953. Diplomate Am. Bd. Dermatology. Intern Univ. Hosp., Augusta, Ga., 1943-44; resident and fellow skin and cancer unit NYU and Bellevue Med. Ctr., N.Y.C., 1950-53; gen. practice medicine, Chester, S.C., 1946-50; practice medicine specializing in dermatology, Augusta, 1953—; cons. dermatologist Univ. Hosp., St. Joseph Hosp., Humana Hosp., Augusta; clin. prof. dermatology Med. Coll. Ga., Augusta. Contbr. articles to profl. jours., chpts. to books. Served to capt. M.C., U.S. Army, 1944-46. Fellow Am. Acad. Dermatology; mem. N.Y. Acad. Scis., Ga. Soc. Dermatologists (pres. 1964, 67), Southeastern Dermatol. Assn. (v.p. 1981, bd. dirs. 1982-85), AMA, So. Med. Assn., Ga. Med. Assn., Richmond County Med. Soc. Presbyterian. Clubs: Augusta Country; Savannah River Hunting (Jackson, S.C.). Lodge: Elks. Avocations: hunting; fishing; antique weapons collecting. Home: 1 7th St Apt 1402 Augusta GA 30901-1343

SMITH, CLYDE GAYLON, obstetrician, gynecologist; b. Caraway, Ark., Nov. 9, 1945; s. William Harry and Thelma Lee (Johnson) S.; m. Deanna Sue Holland, July 22, 1967; children—Craig, Keith. B.S., Harding U., 1967; M.D., U. Tenn., 1971. Diplomate Am. Bd. Ob-Gyn. Intern, Meth. Hosp., Memphis, 1972; resident in ob-gyn. City of Memphis Hosp., 1973, Meth. Hosp., Memphis, 1974-75; practice medicine, specializing in obstetrics and gynecology, Memphis, 1976—; lectr. dept. nursing Meth. Hosp., 1976-82, Bapt. Meml. Hosp., 1983-86; staff Methodis Hosp., 1976—, Bapt. East Hosp., Memphis, 1981—, St. Francis Hosp., 1981—; clin. instr. dept. ob-gyn U. Tenn. Ctr. Health Scis., Memphis, 1977-88, 95—. Mem. devel. council Harding U., Searcy, Ark., 1975—; sec. Cherry Rd. Found., 1994—; pres. Harding Acad. Found., Memphis, 1994—, Fla. Christian Found., 1995—; adv. bd. Heartbeat, 1982, campaign div. chmn., 1981; sponsoring com., rev. editor Upreach, 1982-90; deacon Ch. of Christ. Fellow ACS, Am. Coll. Obstetricians and Gynecologists (AMA Physician Recognition award 1976, 79, 82, 85, 88, 91, 94); mem. AMA, Tenn. Med. Soc., Memphis Shelby County Med. Soc., Soc. Obstetrical Anesthesia and Perinatology, Am. Fertility Soc., Am. Assn. Region Anesthesia, Am. Inst. of Ultrasound in Medicine, Nat. Perinatology Soc., So. Perinatal Soc., Memphis Obstetrical and Gynecol. Soc., Tenn. Obstetrical and Gynecol. Soc., Am. Assn Gynecol. Laparoscopists, Am. Inst. UltraSound in Medicine, Mem. Gynecol. Laser Soc. Contbr. articles to profl. jours.; rev. editor Practical Gastroenterology, 1979-84, Upreach, 1981-82. Home: 174 Grove Park Cir Memphis TN 38117-3134 Office: 6266 Poplar St Memphis TN 38119

SMITH, DAVID BERYL DEAN, psychology educator; b. Willows, Calif., Apr. 13, 1933; s. Jack Townsend and Gladys Mae (Clevenger) S.; m. Faith Victoria Smith, June 11, 1960; children: Deborah, Lawrence. BA, UCLA, 1958, PhD, 1964. Instr. psychology UCLA, 1964; research psychologist NASA, Mountain View, Calif., 1965-68; prof. U. So. Calif., L.A., 1969—, chmn. dept. human factors, 1976-87, rsch. assoc. Gerontology Ctr., 1976—, emeritus prof., 1995—. Author: Man and Systems Mgmt., 1974; contbr. articles to profl. jours. Mem. Am. Psychol. Assn., Human Factors Soc., Internat. Ergonomics Assn., Sigma Xi. Home: 1311 Brass Lantern Dr La Habra CA 90631-6333 Office: U So Calif Los Angeles CA 90089

SMITH, DAVID ELVIN, physician; b. Bakersfield, Calif., Feb. 7, 1939; s. Elvin W. and Dorothy (McGinnis) S.; m. Millicent Buxton; children: Julia, Suzanne, Christopher Buxton-Smith, Sabree Hill. Intern San Francisco Gen. Hosp., 1965; fellow pharmacology and toxicology U. Calif., San Francisco, 1965-67, assoc. clin. prof. occupational medicine, clin. toxicology, 1967—, dir. psychopharmacology study group, 1966-70; practice specializing in toxicology/addiction medicine San Francisco, 1965—; physician Presbyn. Alcoholic Clinic, 1965-67, Contra Cost Alcoholic Clinic, 1965-67; dir. alcohol and drug abuse screening unit San Francisco Gen. Hosp., 1967-68; co-dir. Calif. drug abuse info. project U. Calif. Med. Ctr., 1967-72; founder, med. dir. Haight-Ashbury Free Med. Clinic, San Francisco, 1967—; rsch. dir. Merritt Peralta Chem. Dependency Hosp., Oakland, Calif., 1984—; chmn. Nat. Drug Abuse Conf., 1977; mem. Calif. Gov.'s Commn. on Narcotics and Drug Abuse, 1977—; nat. health adviser to former U.S. Pres. Jimmy Carter; mem. Pres. Clinton's Health Care Task Force on Addiction and Nat. Health Reform, 1993; with Office Drug Abuse Policy, White House Task Force Physicians for Drug Abuse Prevention; dir. Benzodiazepine Rsch. and Tng. Project, Substance Abuse and Sexual Concerns Project, PCP Rsch. and Tng. Project; cons. numerous fed. drug abuse agys. Author: Love Needs Care, 1970, The New Social Drug: Cultural, Medical and Legal Perspectives on Marijuana, 1971, The Free Clnic: Community Approaches to Health Care and Drug Abuse, 1971, Treating the Cocaine Abuser, 1985, The Benzodiazepines: Current Standard Medical Practice, 1986, Physicians' Guide to Drug Abuse, 1987; co-author: It's So Good, Don't Even Try it Once: Heroin in Perspective, 1972, Uppers and Downers, 1973, Drugs in the Classroom, 1973, Barbiturate Use and Abuse, 1977, A Multicultural View of Drug Abuse, 1978, Amphetamine Use, Misuse and Abuse, 1979, PCP: Problems and Prevention, 1981, Sexological Aspects of Substance Use and Abuse, Treatment of the Cocaine Abuser, 1985, The Haight Ashbury Free Medical Clinic: Still Free After All These Years, Drug Free: Alternatives to Drug Abuse, 1987, Treatment of Opiate Dependence, Designer Drugs, 1988, Treatment of Cocaine Dependence, 1988, Treatment of Opiate Dependence, 1988, The New Drugs, 1989, Crack and Ice in the Era of Smokeable Drugs, 1992, others; also drug edn. films; founder, editor Jour. Psychedelic Drugs (now Jour. Psychoactive Drugs), 1967—; contbr. over 300 articles to profl. jours. Mem. Physicians for Prevention White House Office Drug Abuse Policy, 1995; pres. Youth Projects, Inc.; founder, chmn. bd., pres. Nat. Free Clin. Coun., 1968-72. Recipient Rsch. award Borden Found., 1964, AMA Rsch. award, 1977, Cmty. Svc. award U. Calif.-San Francisco, 1974, Calif. State Drug Abuse Treatment award, 1984, Vernelle Fox Drug Abuse Treatment award, 1985, UCLA Sidney Cohen Addiction Medicine award, 1989, U. Calif. San Francisco medal of honor, 1995; named one of Best Doctors in U.S., 1995. Mem. AMA (alt. del.), CMA (alt. del.), Am. Soc. on Addiction Medicine (bd. dirs., pres. 1995), San Francisco Med. Soc., Am. Pub. Health Assn., Calif. Soc. on Addiction Medicine (pres., bd. dirs.), Am. Soc. Addiction Medicine, Sigma Xi, Phi Beta Kappa. Methodist. Home: 289 Frederick St San Francisco CA 94117-4051 Office: Haight Asbury Free Clinics 612 Clayton St San Francisco CA 94117-1911

SMITH, DAVID ENGLISH, physician, educator; b. San Francisco, June 9, 1920; s. David English and Myrtle (Goodin) S.; m. Margaret Elizabeth Bronson, June 9, 1948; children: Ann English Smith Elbert, David Bronson, Mary Margaret. A.B., Central Coll. Mo., 1941; M.D. cum laude, Washington U., St. Louis, 1944. Intern, resident pathology Barnes Hosp., St. Louis, 1944-46; instr. pathology Washington U. Med. Sch., 1948-51, asst. prof., 1951-54, asst. head dept., 1953-54, assoc. prof., 1954-55; prof. pathology U. Va. Sch. Medicine, 1955-73, chmn. dept., 1958-73; dir. div. U. Va. Sch. Medicine (Cancer Studies), 1972-73; prof. pathology Northwestern U. Sch. Medicine, 1974-75, U. Pa. Sch. Medicine, 1976-80; prof. pathology Tulane U. Sch. Medicine, 1980-85, assoc. dean, 1980-85; prof. pathology U. Tex. Med. Br., 1986—; assoc. dir. Am. Bd. Med. Spltys., 1974-75; v.p., sec., dir. undergrad. evaluation Nat. Bd. Med. Examiners, 1975-80; trustee Am. Bd. Pathology, 1966-73, v.p., 1973; mem. Nat. Bd. Med. Examiners, chmn. pathology test com., 1966-72; chmn. test com. Ednl. Commn. for Fgn. Med. Grads., 1979-91. Editor: Survey of Pathology in Medicine and Surgery, 1966-70; contbr. articles to profl. publs. Pres. Va. div. Am. Cancer Soc., 1967-69. Served from 1st lt. to capt. M.C. AUS, 1946-48. Mem. Va. Soc. Pathology (pres. 1960), Am. Assn. Pathologists, Internat. Acad. Pathology (council 1956-59, pres. 1964-65), Am. Soc. Clin. Pathologists (co-dir. self assessment program 1970-75), AMA, Am. Assn. Neuropathologists, AAAS, Sigma Xi, Alpha Omega Alpha, Phi Beta Pi, Alpha Epsilon Delta. Home: 59 Colony Park Cir Galveston TX 77551-1737

SMITH, DAVID HELMAR, plastic surgeon; b. Columbia, Mo., Mar. 18, 1940; s. Dwight David and Grace (Latimer) S.; m. Roberta M. Smith, June 12, 1965; 4 children. AB, Dartmouth Coll., 1962; MD, Duke U., 1966. Diplomate Am. Bd. Plastic Surgery, Am. Bd. Surgery. Intern and resident in surgery Med. Coll. Va., Richmond, 1966-72; plastic and maxillofacial resident Duke U. Med. Ctr., Durham, N.C., 1974-77; hand fellow U. Louisville, 1975-76; pvt. practice Savannah, Ga., 1977—. Contbr. articles to profl. jours. Lt. comdr. USNR, 1972-74. Fellow ACS; mem. AMA, Am. Cleft Palate Assn., Am. Soc. Plastic and Reconstructive Surgeons, Am. Soc. Aesthetic Plastic Surgery, Ga. Med. Soc., Ga. Soc. Plastic Surgeons, Med. Assn. Ga., Southeastern Soc. Plastic and Reconstructive Surgeons, Humera Soc. Office: Plastic Surgery Ctr 5361 Reynolds St Savannah GA 31405

SMITH, DAVID JOHN, JR., plastic surgeon; b. Indpls., Feb. 20, 1947; s. David John and Carolyn (Culp) S.; m. Nancy Loonsten, June 7, 1975; children: Matthew, Peter, Hadley. BA, Wesleyan U., 1969; MD, Ind. U., 1973. Diplomate Am. Bd. Plastic Surgery. Resident Emory U.-Grady Hosp., Atlanta, 1973-78; resident Ind. U. Med. Ctr., Indpls., 1978-80; Christine Kleinert fellow in hand surgery, 1979; asst. prof. surgery Ind. U. Sch. Medicine, 1980-84; assoc. prof. of surgery Wayne State U. Sch. Medicine, 1984-87; assoc. prof. plastic surgery, surgery sect. head U. Mich. Med. Ctr., Ann Arbor, 1987-92, prof. surgery sect. head, 1992—; mem. Residency Rev. Com. for Plastic Surgery, 1992, vice chmn., 1994, chmn. 1996—. Mem. editl. bd. Jour. of Surg. Rsch., 1989-95, Annals of Plastic Surgery, 1992—, assoc. editor, 1994, Yearbook of Hand Surgery, 1989—; guest reviewer Surgery, 1988—, Plastic and Reconstructive Surgery, 1988—; contbr. articles to profl. jours. Recipient numerous grants. Fellow ACS (many coms.), Soc. Univ. Surgeons, Am. Assn. Plastic Surgeons, Am. Surg. Assn., Am. Bd. Plastic Surgeons, Assn. for Acad. Surgery, Western Surg. Assn., Ctrl. Surg. Assn., Am. Soc. for Surgery of the Hand. Am. Soc. Plastic and Reconstructive Surgeons, Plastic Surgery Ednl. Found. (bd. dirs. 1988—, treas. 1994, v.p., pres.-elec., other coms.), Plastic Surgery Rsch. Coun., Am. Burn Assn., Am. Burn Life Support Nat. Faculty, Am. Assn. for Hand Surgeons (pres. 1994). Home: 769 Heatherway St Ann Arbor MI 48104-2731 Office: U Mich Med Ctr 2130 Taubman Health Ctr 1500 E Medical Center Dr Ann Arbor MI 48109-0340

SMITH, DAVID LAWRENCE, surgeon, educator, air force officer; b. Berkeley, Calif., Oct. 10, 1961; s. Earl Eugene and Dona Mae (Sterner) S.; m. Rita Diaz, July 16, 1983; children: Erika Lynne, Amanda Lee. BS in Chemistry and Biology, U. Pacific, 1983; MD, Uniformed Svcs. U., 1988. Diplomate Am. Bd. Surgery. Commd. 2d. lt. USAF, 1984, advanced through grades to maj., 1994; resident in surgery U. N.C., Chapel Hill, 1988-93, fellow in critical care, 1993-94; mem. gen. and trauma surgery staff Wilford Hall USAF Med. Ctr., San Antonio, 1994—, advanced trauma life support trainer, 1995—, dir. nutrition support svc., dir. surg. ICU, 1995—; asst. prof. surgery Uniformed Svcs. U., Bethesda, Md., 1995—. Contbr. articles to med. jours., chpt. to book. Named Surg. Resident of Yr., U.N.C., 1993; named to Manteca H.S. Hall of Fame, 1994. Fellow ACS (assoc.); mem. AMA, Soc. Critical Care Medicine, Am. Burn Assn., Womack Surg. Soc., Assn. Parenteral and Enteral Nutrition, Alamo Chpt. Assn. Parenteral and Enteral Nutrition, Am. Trauma Soc., DeMolay (master councilor), Phi Kappa Phi. Republican.

SMITH, DAVID WALDO EDWARD, pathology and gerontology educator, physician; b. Fargo, N.D., Apr. 3, 1934; s. Waldo Edward and Martha (Althaus) S.; m. Diane Leigh Walker, June 18, 1960. BA, Swarthmore Coll., 1956; MD, Yale U., 1960. Intern, asst. resident, research fellow pathology Yale U. Med. Sch., 1960-62; research assoc. lab. molecular biology Nat. Inst. Arthritis and Metabolic Diseases, 1962-64, investigator lab. exptl. pathology, 1964-67; assoc. prof. pathology and microbiology Ind. U. Med. Sch., 1967-69; prof. pathology Northwestern U. Med. Sch., 1969—, dir. Ctr. on Aging, 1988—; Guest investigator Internat. Lab. Genetics and Biophysics, Naples, Italy, 1969; mem. ad hoc biochemistry study sect. NIH, 1974-75, mem. pathobiol. chemistry study sect., 1975-79, cons., 1982; sabbatical leave NIH, 1986-87; chmn. NIH Conf. on Gender and Longevity: Why Do Women Live Longer Than Men?, 1987. Author: Human Longevity, 1993, also research papers, chpts. in books.; editorial bd. Yale Jour. Biology and Medicine, 1957-60. Sr. surgeon USPHS, 1958-67. Recipient Career Devel. award NIH,

1968-69. Mem. AAAS, Am. Soc.for Investigative Pathology, Am. Soc. for Biochem. and Molecular Biology, Gerontol. Soc. Am., Sigma Xi, Alpha Omega Alpha. Home: Apt 33 1212 N Lake Shore Dr Chicago IL 60610-2362 Office: Northwestern U Med Sch Dept Pathology 303 E Chicago Ave Chicago IL 60611-3008

SMITH, DENNIS LEE, pharmacist; b. Memphis, Dec. 22, 1945; s. Carl Lynn and Frances Lee (Partlow) S.; m. Patsee Jane Zagers, Mar. 31, 1973 (div. 1994); children: Matthew Carl, Michael David; m. Cindy R. Freeman, Feb. 9, 1996. Student, Westminster Coll., 1976-78; BS in Pharmacy, U. Utah, 1981. Registered pharmacist. Pharmacist Skaggs Drugs, Elko, Nev., 1981-82; dir. of pharmacy Bolt Drugs, Gatlinburg, Tenn., 1982-84, Eckerd Drugs, Jefferson City, Tenn., 1984-85; dir. of pharmacy Rite Aid Corp., Newport, Tenn., 1985-87, Athens, Tenn., 1987, Oliver Springs, Tenn., 1987-88; dir. of pharmacy Super X Drugs, Sevierville, 1988-89; pres. TET 68 Inc., 1989-92; pharmacist in charge Revco DS, Knoxville, Tenn., 1992-95; pres. M.S. & G., Inc., Gatlinburg, 1984-95, TET-68 Mil. Surplus, Sevierville, Tenn. Vol. capt. Pittman Ctr. (Tenn.) Fire Dept., 1985; field dep. Sevier County (Tenn.) Sheriff Dept., 1986-90; bd. dirs. Sevierville Little League Football, 1987-89. With U.S. Army, 1967-69, Vietnam, USANG. Charter mem. Sons of Confederate Vets. (Col. Richard Saffel Camp, Sevierville). Lodge: Rotary (sec. Gatlinburg club 1985). Office: TET 68 Inc 611 Park Way Box 5 Sevierville TN 37862

SMITH, DENNIS LYNN, optometrist, educator, researcher; b. Coronado, Calif., Nov. 2, 1953; s. Jimmie Lee and Joan F. (Holcombe) S.; m. Nada Jo Lingel, May 27, 1990. BS, Towson State U., 1976; OD, So. Coll. Optometry, 1981; MS in Physiol. Optics, Pacific U., 1987, MS in Clin. Optometry, 1987. Lic. optometrist, Tex., Oreg. Commd. capt. USAF, 1981, advanced through grades to maj.; staff optometrist Carswell USAF Regional Hosp., Ft. Worth, 1981-85; chief optometry svcs. Sheppard USAF Regional Hosp., Wichita Falls, Tex., 1987-91; assoc. prof. Pacific U. Coll. Optometry, Forest Grove, Oreg., 1991—; dir. Forest Grove Area Satellite Clinics, 1996—; advisor curriculum com. Pacific U. Coll. Optometry, 1995—, advisor faculty devel. com., 1994-95, chmn. stds. and appeals com., 1992-94, mem./advisor coll. coordinating coun., 1992-94. Author: (chpt.) Clinical Decision Making, 1994; contbr. articles to profl. jours. 2d lt., USAFR. Mem. Assn. Optometric Educators, Res. Officer Assn., Air Force Assn., Armed Forces Optometric Soc., Am. Acad. Optometry. Episcopalian. Office: Pacific Univ Coll Optometry 2043 College Way Forest Grove OR 97116

SMITH, DENNIS P., molecular biologist; b. Trenton, N.J., June 25, 1953. BS, Murray State U., 1975; MS, So. Ill. U., 1980. Rsch. technician U.S. Steel Corp., Morrisville, Pa., 1975; rsch. asst. Murray (Ky.) State U., 1975-76; teaching asst., then rsch. asst. So. Ill. U., Carbondale, 1976-80; med. researcher Washington U., St. Louis, 1980-82; assoc. biologist Eli Lilly & Co., Indpls., 1982-83, biologist, 1983-91, asst. sr. biologist, 1991—. Author: Antiobesity Action of Leptin, 1995; contbr. to profl. publs.

SMITH, DONALD CAMERON, physician, educator; b. Peterborough, Ont., Can., Feb. 2, 1922; came to U.S., 1952, naturalized, 1960; s. James Cameron and Clarice (Leighton) S.; m. Jean Ida Morningstar, Sept. 11, 1946; children: Douglas Frazer, Scot Earle, Donald Ian. MD, Queen's U., 1945; MSc in Medicine, U. Toronto, 1948, DPH, 1949. Diplomate Am. Bd. Preventive Medicine (ofcl. examiner 1966-76), Am. Bd. Pediatrics. Intern Victoria Hosp., London, Ont., 1945-46; fellow in physiology U. Toronto, 1947-48; asst. med. officer health East York-Leaside (Ont.) Health Unit, 1949-50; lectr. pub. health adminstrn. U. Toronto, 1949-50; med. officer health Kent County (Ont.) Health Unit, 1950-51; Commonwealth Fund fellow in pediatrics U. Mich. Hosp., 1952-55; asst. prof. maternal and child health, clin. instr. pediatrics U. Mich., Ann Arbor, 1956-57; asso. prof. maternal and child health, research asso. pediatrics U. Mich., 1957-61; prof. maternal and child health U. Mich. (Sch. Pub. Health); prof. pediatrics U. Mich. (Med. Sch.), 1961-79, chmn. dept. health and human devel., 1961-79; prof. psychiatry and behavioral scis. Northwestern U. Med. Sch., Chgo., 1979-85; pres. Barton Hills Corp., 1970-72, 90—; mem. adv. coun. on health protection and disease prevention Dept. Health, Edn. and Welfare, 1969-72, chmn. med. assistance adv. coun., 1969-72; prin. advisor on health and med. affairs to gov. Mich., 1972-78; dir. Mich. Dept. Mental Health, 1974-78; chmn. health care policy bd. Mich. Dept. Corrections, 1986-91; chmn. State Pub. Health Adv. Coun., 1982-90; chmn. Expert Com. on AIDS, 1985-88; sr. v.p. Joint Commn. on Accreditation Hosps., Chgo., 1979-81; sr. med. adviser Sisters of Mercy Health Corp., 1978-86; dir. Office Behavioral Medicine, Cmty. Hosp. Authority Mich., 1986-91; pres. Mental Health Assn. Mich., 1992—; spl. cons. on maternal and child health and family planning programs South Korean Ministry Social Affairs, 1969; chmn., cross-nat. study of health care svcs. HEW, 1971; vis. prof. maternal and child health Harvard U., 1969-72; med. dir. Physician's Rev. Orgn. Mich., 1992—. Author: Contbr. to: Manual on Standards of Child Health Care, 1971, Barnett's Pediatrics, 1971, Pediatric Clinics of North America; also articles in med. and pub. health jours. Med. dir. Mich. Crippled Children Commn., 1962-64, Mich. United Fund, 1964-67. Served to Surgeon lt. Royal Canadian Navy, 1946-47. Fellow Am. Pub. Health Assn. (chmn. com. pub. med. care for children 1967-70, chmn. sect. maternal and child health 1968-70), Am. Acad. Pediatrics (chmn. com. on legis. 1966-73, chmn. council pediatric practice 1966-73), Royal Coll. of Physician and Surgeons of Canada; mem. AMA, Internat. Epidemiol. Assn., Delta Omega (pres. 1967-68). Home: 1000 Country Club Rd Ann Arbor MI 48105-1039

SMITH, DORIS CORINNE KEMP, retired nurse; b. Bogalusa, La., Nov. 22, 1919; d. Milton Jones and Maude Maria (Fortenberry) Kemp; m. Joseph William Smith, Oct. 13, 1940 (dec.). BS in Nursing, U. Colo., 1957, MS in Nursing Adminstrn., 1958. RN, Colo. Head nurse Chgo. Bridge & Iron Co., Morgan City, La., 1941-45, Shannon Hosp., San Angelo, Tex., 1945-50; dir. nursing Yoakum County Hosp., Denver City, Tex., 1951-52; hosp. supr. Med. Arts Hosp., Odessa, Tex., 1952-55; dir. insvc. edn. St. Anthony Hosp., Denver, 1961-66; coord. Sch. Vocat. Nursing, Kiamichi Area Vocat.-Tech. Nursing Sch., Wilburton, Okla., 1969-77; supr. non-ambulatory unit Lubbock (Tex.) State Sch., 1978-85, ret., 1985; mem. steering com. Western Interstate Commn. on Higher Edn. for Nurses, Denver, 1963-65; mem. curriculum and materials com. Okla. Bd. Vocat.-Tech. Edn., Stillwater, 1971-76; mem. Invitational Conf. To Plan Nursing for Future, Oklahoma City, 1976-77; mem. survey team to appraise Sch. of Vocat.-Tech. Edn. Schs. for Okla. Dept. Vocat.-Tech. Edn., 1975-76. Author, editor: Survey of Functions Expected of the General Duty Nurse, State of Colorado, 1958; co-editor: Curriculum Guides; contbr. numerous articles to profl. jours. Recipient citation of merit Okla. State U., 1976; named Woman of Yr. Sunrise chpt. Am. Bus. Women's Assn., 1994-95. Mem. AAAS, ANA, AAUW (life), Nat. League for Nursing, Tex. League for Nursing, Tex. Nurses Assn., Dist. 18 Nurses Assn., Tex. Employees Assn. (v.p. 1984-85), U. Colo. Alumni Assn., Am. Bus. Women's Assn. (pres. Lubbock chpt. 1986-87, rec. sec. 1989-90, edn. chair 1994-95, hospitality chair 1995-96), Bus. and Profl. Women's Assn. (sec. 1992-95), Chancellor's Club U. Colo., Pi Lambda Theta (sec. local chpt. 1957-58). Republican. Home: 2103 55th St Lubbock TX 79412-2612

SMITH, DOROTHY LOUISE, pharmacy consultant, author; b. Regina, Sask., Can., Apr. 29, 1946; d. William Edward and Edna Irene (Libby) S. BS in Pharmacy, U. Saskatchewan, 1968; PharmD, U. Cin., 1972. Asst. prof. pharmacy U. B.C., Can., 1972-74; assoc. prof. clin. pharmacy U. Toronto, Ont., Can., 1974-80; coord. ambulatory pharmacy care Sunnybrook Med. Ctr., Toronto, 1974-79; dir. clin. affairs Am. Pharm. Assn., Washington, 1980-83; pres. Consumer Health Info. Corp., McLean, Va., 1983—; assoc. clin. prof. Sch. Pharmacy, Med. Coll. Va., 1991—; adj. assoc. prof. community and family medicine Georgetown U., Washington, 1983—. Author several books in field; contbr. articles to profl. jours. Mem. nat. bd. advisors Coll. Pharmacy, Ariz., 1987—. Fellow Am. Coll. Clin. Pharmacy, Am. Coll. Apothecaries; mem. Am. Soc. Hosp. Pharmacists, Am. Pharm. Assn. (chmn. policy com. on pub. affairs), Internat. Order Job's Daughters, Rotary. Presbyterian. Office: Consumer Health Info Corp 8300 Greensboro Dr Ste 1220 Mc Lean VA 22102-3604

SMITH, DOUGLAS B., physician; b. Caribou, Maine, Oct. 9, 1956. BS, Houghton (N.Y.) Coll., 1978; MD, Tufts U., 1982. Resident in internal medicine St. Elizabeth's Hosp., Boston, 1982-85; staff physician USPHS, Fremont, Ohio, 1985-89; fellow in rheumatology Ind. U. Med. Ctr., Indpls., 1989-91; physician in pvt. practice Iowa Med. Clinic, Cedar Rapids, 1991-92, Rheumatology Assocs., Indpls., 1992—; speaker in field. Contbr. articles to profl. jours. Fellow Am. Coll. Rheumatology; mem. ACP, Soc. for Clin. Densitometry. Office: Rheumatology Assocs PC 8802 N Meridian St # 108 Indianapolis IN 46260

SMITH, DOUGLAS GERALD, health care consultant; b. Passaic, N.J., Feb. 21, 1947; s. Frederick Gerald and Yvonne Virginia (d'Ablemont) S.; m. Martha Engquist, May 23, 1970; children: Matthew Cary, Nicholas Sinclair. BSC, Ohio U., 1969; grad., Crosby Quality Coll., Orlando, Fla., 1985. Mgr. ops. Concord Comm., Chgo., 1969-70; dir. comm. A.B. Dick Co., Chgo., 1970-72; dir. bus. devel. Martin Marietta Corp., Orlando, Fla., 1972-87; v.p. bus. devel. ROI, Barrington, Ill., 1987-93; cons., pres. FERS Health Care Group, Chgo., 1993—; mem. adv. bd. Imaging Svcs., Inc., Chgo., 1995—; cons. various health systems, hosps., physician orgns., health plans, 1993—; faculty guest, spkr. lectr. N.C. State Med. Soc., 1995, Conn. State Med. Soc., 1995, AMA Fn. & Practice Mgmt., 1995, Nat. Ctr. Advanced Med. Edn., 1995, 96. Mem. Med. Group Mgmt. Assn., Healthcare Fin. Mgmt. Assn., Assn. U.S. Army (pres. 1985-87). Republican. Office: FERS Health Care Group Continental Towers III 1701 Golf Rd Ste 1200 Rolling Meadows IL 60008

SMITH, DUNBAR WALLACE, retired physician, clergyman; b. Dunbar, Nebr., Oct. 17, 1910; s. Clarence Dunbar and Marie Christine (Eden) S.; m. Kathryn Avis Johnson, May 2, 1935; children: Dunbar Wesley, John Wallace. BSc, La Sierra Coll., Riverside, Calif., 1949; MD, Loma Linda U., 1950; DTM and Hygiene, Sch. of Tropical Med. London U., 1951; MPH, Columbia U., 1967. Diplomate Nat. Bd. Med. Examiners. Pastor 7th-day Adventist Chs., San Diego, Omaha, N.Y., India, Ceylon, 1935-44; med. dir. 7th-Day Adventist Mission Hosps., India, 1951-056; adminstr. Battle Creek (Mich.) Sanitarium, 1957-62; med. dir. Bates Meml. Hosp., Yonkers, N.Y., 1962-67; dep. commr. health Nassau County, N.Y., 1967-69; dir. dept. health for Africa, 7th-day Adventist Ch., 1969-76; dir. dept. health for Far East, 7th-day Adventist Ch., Singapore, 1976-80; adj. asst. prof. internat. health Loma Linda (Calif.) U., 1980-90; pres. Emerald Health and Edn. Found., Loma Linda, 1986-91. Author: Report of CME (now Loma Linda U. Sch. Medicine) Rsch. to Date, 1946, (textbook) Home Health Aide, 1960, Autobiography of Dunbar W. Smith, 1994, (booklet) The Cold Turkey Way to Stop Smoking; contbr. numerous articles to various publs. V.p. Emerald Health and Edn. Found., 1991—. Recipient Honored Alumnus award Loma Linda U. Sch. Medicine, 1975, Golden award La Sierra U. Alumni Soc., 1992. Fellow AMA, SAR, Am. Coll. Nutrition, Royal Soc. Tropical Medicine, Royal Soc. Health, Internat. Med. Assn. (bd. dirs. 1987—); mem. N.Y. Acad. Scis. Republican. Home: 1414 Bella Vista Crest Redlands CA 92320-1507 Office: Emerald Health and Edn Found PO Box 8877 Redlands CA 92375-2077

SMITH, ELDON, dean. Dean U. Calgary, Alberta, Can. Office: U Calgary Faculty of Medicine, 3300 Hosp Dr, Calgary, AB Canada T2N 4N1*

SMITH, ERIC MORGAN, virology educator; b. Lafayette, Ind., Feb. 13, 1953; s. James E. and Betty Carolyn (Hanlin) S.; m. Janice Marie Kelly, May 26, 1979; children: David Kendall, Ben Pham. BS cum laude, Syracuse U., 1975; PhD, Baylor Coll. of Medicine, 1980. Postdoctoral fellow Dept. Microbiology, U. Tex. Med. Br., Galveston, Tex., 1979-81, asst. prof., 1982-85, assoc. prof., 1985-90, prof., 1990—; editl. bd. Progress in Neuro-Endocrin Immunology, Washington, 1988-92, Behavior and Immunity, 1993—, Cellular and Molecular Neurobiology, 1994—; mem. mental health AIDS and immunity rev. com. NIMH, 1992—. Founding co-editor Advances in Neuroimmunmology, 1991; contbr. over 100 articles to profl. jours. Mem. Galveston Hist. Found., 1980—. Mem. AAAS, Am. Soc. for Microbiology, Am. Assn. Immunologists, Internat. Soc. Immunopharmacology, Internat. Working Group on Neuroimmunomodulation, Assn. Immuno-Neurobiologists (co-founding pres.), Galveston Yacht Club, Syracuse Scuba Soc. (v.p. 1975). Office: U Tex Med Br Dept Psychiatry Galveston TX 77550

SMITH, EVA JOYCE, nurse; b. New Eagle, Pa., Mar. 16, 1932; d. Harold Elwood John and Vera Lena (Herd) Schlosser; m. Lyell G. Smith (div. 1980); children: Stephen Mark, Stephanie Anne, Shari Linne. Student, Marshall Coll., 1949-50; diploma, Wheeling Hosp. Sch. Nursing, W.Va., 1953; BS, Coll. St. Francis, Joliet, Ill., 1982, MS, 1986. R.N., Ill. Staff nurse Didsbury (Alta.) Hosp., Can., 1957-60, Annapolis Hosp., Wayne, Mich., 1963-64, Stagg Clinic, Hartford, Mich., 1969-72, Hinsdale (Ill.) Sanitorium and Hosp., 1972-76; staff nurse, instr., then clin. edn. coord. St. Luke's Med. Ctr., Phoenix, Ill., 1977-85; asst. dir. health arts program Coll. St. Francis, Joliet, 1985-87; clinic dir. Memory Assessment Clinics, Inc., Scottsdale, Ariz., 1988-96; clin. rsch. adminstr. Phoenix Ctr. for Clin. Rsch., 1996—. Mem. NAFE, Profl. Assn. Gerontology Educators and Svcs. (sec. 1985), Drug Info. Assn. (assoc. in clin. pharmacology 1995—). Republican. Baptist. Home: 19060 N 91st St Scottsdale AZ 85255-5318

SMITH, FRANCIS XAVIER, nurse; b. Towanda, Pa., Nov. 22, 1936; s. Theodore Franklin and Lillian Caroline (Goldbruch) S. Nursing diploma, Essex Vocat. Tech. Inst., Practical Nursing Sch., 1968. Surg. nurse Salem (Mass.) Gen. Hosp., 1969; nurse emergency rm. Cable Meml. Hosp., Ipswich, Mass., 1969-71; med. nurse Greenwood Convalescent Home, Hartford, Conn., 1971-72; supr. 11-7 shift St. Martin de Porres Infirmary, Hartford, 1972-78; pvt. duty nurse Nashua, N.H., 1979-88; nursing staff Hartford (Conn.) Dispensary Methadone Treatment Program, 1988-91; nursing staff AIDS unit Project Mercy, Hartford, 1991-96; clin. instr. CNA's E.C. Goodwin RVTS, New Britain, Conn., 1996—. Bd. dirs. Nashua (N.H.) Symphony, 1986-88; mem. adv. bd. for religious Archdiocese of Hartford, 1995-97. Recipient Bronze Pelican award Boy Scouts Am., Hartford, 1980, Dist. award of merit, 1983, St. George award Boy Scouts Am., Nashua, 1985, Dist. award of merit, 1986, Cath. Youth Orgn. award St. Benedict the Moor Soc., Washington, 1983. Mem. Nat. Cath. AIDS Network, Assn. Nurses in AIDS Care (sec. 1995-96), Conn. League of Nurses, So. New Eng. AIDS Assn. (treas. 1991-93), Conn. LPN Assn. Inc. (1st v.p. 1991-93, pres. 1993-97). Republican. Home: Missionaries La Salette 85 New Park Ave Hartford CT 06106-2184

SMITH, FREDRICA EMRICH, rheumatologist, internist; b. Princeton, N.J., Apr. 28, 1945; d. Raymond Jay and Carolyn Sarah (Schleicher) Emrich; m. Paul David Smith, June 10, 1967. AB, Bryn Mawr Coll., 1967; MD, Duke U., 1971. Intern, resident U. N.Mex. Affiliated Hosps., 1971-73; fellow U. Va. Hosp., Charlottesville, 1974-75; pvt. practice, Los Alamos, N.Mex., 1975—; chmn. credentials com. Los Alamos Med. Ctr., 1983—, chief staff, 1990; bd. dirs. N.Mex. Physicians Mut. Liability Ins. Co., Albuquerque. Contbr. articles to med. jours. Mem. bass sect. Los Alamos Symphony, 1975—; mem. Los Alamos County Parks and Recreation Bd., 1984-88, 92—, Los Alamos County Med. Indigent Health Care Task Force, 1989—; mem. ops. subcom. Aquatic Ctr., Los Alamos County, 1988—. Fellow ACP, Am. Coll. Rheumatology; mem. N.Mex. Soc. Internal Medicine (pres. 1993—), Friends of Bandelier. Democrat. Office: Los Alamos Med Ctr 3917 West Rd Los Alamos NM 87544-2222

SMITH, GEORGE F., health association administrator, physician; b. Nacogdoches, Tex., Nov. 25, 1948; s. Leoanrd L. and Gladys M. (Nichols) S.; m. Kelly M. Reynolds, Aug. 4, 1979; children: Megan Alexsis, Garrett Malone. BA, U. Tex., Austin, 1971; MS, U. Tex. Sch. Pub. Health, Houston, 1973; MD, U. Tex. Med. Br., Galveston, 1977. Diplomate Am. Bd. Family Practice. Resident Ctr. Tex. Med. Found., Austin, 1977-80; pvt. practice Family Practice Assn. South Austin, Austin, 1980-90; v.p. med. affairs PCA Health Plans of Tex., Austin, 1990-95; pres. PLA Med. Group of Tex., P.A., Austin, 1993-95; exec. dir. PLA Health Plans of Tex., Inc., Austin, 1996—; pres. med. staff HCA-South Austin Med. Ctr., 1987-88, trustee 1988-90, chmn. bd. trustees 1990; HMO adv. bd. Tex. Dept. Health, Austin, 1990—. Developer, author case mgmt. program Physician Executive, 1994. Fellow Am. Acad. Family Practice Physicians; mem. Am. Coll. Physician Execs. (Merck award for Quality Innovation 1994), Tex. Acad. Family Physicians, Tex. Med. Assn. (pres. resident physicians 1979-80, del. 1988—), Alpha Omega Alpha. Home: 8 Rob Roy Rd Austin TX 78746 Office: PLA Health Plans of Tex Inc 8303 Mopac Ste 450 Austin TX 78759

SMITH, GEORGE ROBERT, surgeon; b. Shreveport, La., Dec. 7, 1936; s. James Monroe and Elizabeth (Mahon) S.; m. Ethel Mae Stackhouse, Sept. 11, 1962; children: Michael Kevin, Margaret Elizabeth. BS, Baylor U., 1957; MD, La. State U., 1961; MBA, Tulane U., 1995. Intern Confederate Meml. Med. Ctr., Shreveport, 1961-62; resident in surgery Grad. Sch. Medicine Mayo Clinic, Rochester, Minn., 1962-66; pvt. practice Lafayette, La., 1968—. Bd. dirs., pres. S.W. La. Ednl. and Referral Ctr., Lafayette, 1987-89. Capt. USAF, 1966-68, Vietnam. Mem. Lafayette Parish Med. Soc. (pres. 1977). Methodist. Office: George R Smith MD AMC 155 Hospital Dr Ste 400 Lafayette LA 70503-2852

SMITH, GERARD PETER, neuroscientist; b. Phila., Mar. 24, 1935; s. Stanley Alward and Agnes Marie (McLarney) S.; m. Barbara McInnis, May 12, 1962; children: Christopher, Mark, Hilary, Maura. BS, St. Joseph's U., Phila., 1956; MD, U. Pa., 1960. Intern, resident N.Y. Hosp., 1960-62; asst. prof. physiology U. Pa. Sch. Medicine, Phila., 1964-68; from asst. to assoc. prof. Cornell U., N.Y.C., 1968—, prof. psychiatry (behavioral neurosci.), 1973—; vis. prof. MIT, 1973-74, Rockefeller U., 1979-80; adj. prof., 1982-86; cons. NIH; Curt Richter lectr. Johns Hopkins U., 1976; Leon lectr. U. Pa., 1990, Stellar lectr. U. Pa., 1993; Rushton lectr. Fla. State U., 1992, Merck, Sharpe, and Dohm prof. neurosci. U. Flinder, Australia, 1992; dir. Eating Disorders Inst., N.Y. Hosp.-Cornell Med. Ctr., 1984-88. Recipient Rsch. Scientist USPHS, 1982; NIH grantee. Mem. AAAS, Am. Physiol. Soc., Soc. for Neurosci., Ea. Psychol. Assn., Am. Assn. for Rsch. in Nervous and Mental Disease, Endocrine Soc., Soc. Biol. Psychiatry, Soc. for Study Ingestive Behavior (pres.), Internat. Behavioral Neurosci. Soc. (pres.), Alpha Omega Alpha, Alpha Sigma Nu. Office: NY Hosp Cornell Med Ctr EW Bourne Behavioral Rsch Lab 21 Bloomingdale Rd White Plains NY 10605-1504

SMITH, H. BRET, health services administrator; b. Corpus Christi, Tex., June 20, 1959; s. Herschel Basil Smith and Erma Louise (Crawford) Calhoun; m. Angela Gay Glover, Sept. 23, 1981 (div. Sept. 1991); children: Dustin, Cameron, Carlyse; m. Lynne Brooks, July 10, 1993; 1 child, Brandon. BS, Tex. A&M U., 1981; BBS, Abilene Christian U., 1983; MEd, U. North Tex., 1989. Nat. cert. counselor; master addictions counselor. Campus minister Ctrl. Ch. Christ, Valdosta, Ga., 1983-84; singles minister Saturn Rd. Ch. Christ, Garland, Tex., 1984-89, North Atlanta Ch. Christ, 1989-90; therapist Scott & Assocs., P.C., Atlanta, 1990-91; mgr. Relationship enrichment Ctr., Marietta, Ga., 1991—; v.p. REC Mgmt., Inc., Marietta, 1995—; pres. Assistance Plus, Inc., Marietta, 1994—. Mem. ACA, Lic. Profl. Counselors Assn. (vendor chmn. 1994—, cert.), Am. Mental Health Counselors Assn., Employee Assistance Profl. Assn. (cert.), Nat. Assn. Drug and Alcohol Counselors. Office: REC Management Inc Bldg 28 Ste 350 1640 Powers Ferry Rd Marietta GA 30067

SMITH, HAMILTON OTHANEL, molecular biologist, educator; b. N.Y.C., N.Y., Aug. 23, 1931; s. Bunnie Othanel and Tommie Harkey S.; m. Elizabeth Anne Bolton, May 25, 1957; children: Joel, Barry, Dirk, Bryan, Kirsten. Student, U. Ill., 1948-50; A.B. in Math, U. Calif., Berkeley, 1952; M.D., Johns Hopkins U., 1956. Intern Barnes Hosp., St. Louis, 1956-57; resident in medicine Henry Ford Hosp., Detroit, 1959-62; USPHS fellow dept. human genetics U. Mich., Ann Arbor, 1962-64; rsch. assoc. U. Mich., 1964-67; asst. prof. molecular biology and genetics Sch. Medicine Johns Hopkins U., Balt., 1967-69; assoc. prof. Johns Hopkins U., 1969-73, prof., 1973—; assoc. Inst. für Molekularbologie der U. Zurich, Switzerland, 1975-76; assoc. Rsch. Inst. Molecular Pathology, Vienna, 1990-91. Contbr. articles to profl. jours. Served to lt. M.C. USNR, 1957-59. Recipient Nobel Prize in medicine, 1978; Guggenheim fellow, 1975-76. Mem. Am. Soc. Microbiology, AAAS, Am. Soc. Biol. Chemists, Nat. Acad. Sci. Office: Johns Hopkins U Sch Med Dept Molecular Genetics 725 N Wolfe St Baltimore MD 21205-2105

SMITH, HARRY ALCIDE, pharmacy educator; b. Casey County, Ky., July 8, 1925; m. Norma Florence Gabhart, Apr. 8, 1951; children: Elizabeth Ann, Harry Alcide III. BS in Pharmacy, U. Ky., 1949; MS in Pharmacy Adminstrn., Purdue U., 1956, PhD in Pharmacy Adminstrn. and Pharmacy, 1959. Lic. pharmacist, Ky. Pharmacist, Liberty, Ky., 1949-50, Campbellsville, Ky., 1952-53, Springfield, Ky., 1953-54; teaching asst. Purdue U., West Lafayette, Ind., 1955-56; part-time community and hosp. pharmacist Ky., 1959-64; asst. prof. U. Ky., Lexington, 1957-61, assoc. prof., 1961-65, prof. pharmacy adminstrn., 1970-94; assoc. prof., asst. dir. Bur. Pharm. Svcs., U. Miss., Oxford, 1965-70; prof. pharmacy adminstrn. U. Ky., Lexington, 1970-94, asst. dir. div. pharmacy adminstrn. and practice, 1980-82, mem. senate, 1979-84; cons. to various community pharmacists, 1970—, Ky. Med. Assistance Program, 1976-77, Ky. Legis. Rsch. Commn., 1979, Effective Pharmacy Mgmt. Found., 1980—, Patti Clay Hosp., 1986, also others; speaker in field; manuscript reviewer Am. Jour. Pharm. Edn., Jour. Pharm. Mktg. and Mktg., Jour. Social and Adminstrv. Pharmacy, Jour. Pharm. Teaching, Jour. Pharmacoepidemiology. Author: Principles and Methods of Pharmacy Management, 1975, 3d edit., 1986; mem. editorial bd. Jour. Pharm. Mktg. and Mgmt.; contbr. editor Am. Pharmacy, 1978-81; contbr. over 150 articles to profl. jours., monographs, proc. Bd. dirs. Southeastern Christian Coll., Winchester, Ky., 1973-83, chmn. acad. affairs com., 1976-79, mem. exec. and fin. coms., 1975-79, vice chmn. bd. dirs., 1977-78, 79-82, chmn., 1982-83; bd. dirs. Southeastern Christian Edn. Corp., Winchester, 1983-87, chmn. grants and scholarship com., 1983-84; bd. dirs. Christian Pharmacists Fellowship Internat., Inc., 1984-94; coll. coord. United Way, 1978, 82. With U.S. Army, 1950-52. Recipient spl. recognition award Miss. Soc. Hosp. Pharmacists, Warren Weaver award for outstanding svc. and leadership, 1994, Outstanding Alumnus award U. Ky. Coll. Pharmacy, 1996. Fellow Am. Found. for Pharm. Edn., Acad. Pharm. Rsch. and Scis., Am. Coll. Apothecaries (assoc.); mem. AAUP, Am. Pharm. Assn., Acad. Gen. Pharmacy Practice, Acad. Pharm. Scis., Am. Assn. Colls. Pharmacy (chmn. sect. tchrs. pharmacy adminstrn. 1970-71, 87-88), Ky. Pharmacists Assn. (econ. affairs com. 1987-93), Blue Grass Pharmacists Assn. (bd. dirs. 1971-75), Nat. Assn. Retail Druggists (assoc.; Reed Peterson award 1986), Sigma Xi, Rho Chi. Home: 2216 Markham Ct Lexington KY 40504-3219 Office: U Ky Coll Pharmacy Pharmacy Bldg 214 Lexington KY 40536-0082

SMITH, HARWELL FITZHUGH, III, clinical psychologist; b. Heidelberg, Germany, Nov. 1, 1951; came to U.S., 1952; s. Harwell Fitzhugh Jr. and Louise Mae (Hocking) S.; m. Marthanne Olivia Manion, June 11, 1977; 1 child, Hayley Manion. B.S., U. Tenn., 1973, M.A., 1976, Ph.D., 1978. Lic. psychologist, Ky; diplomate in clin. psychology Am. Bd. Profl. Psychology. Clin. psychologist Foothills Mental Health Program, Lenoir, N.C., 1978-81; program dir. Eastern State Hosp., Lexington, Ky., 1982-85; pvt. practice clin. psychology, Lexington, 1985—. Mem. Am. Psychol. Assn., Southeastern Psychol. Assn., Ky. Psychol. Assn. Democrat. Home: 1639 Duntreath Dr Lexington KY 40504-2352 Office: 1401 Harrodsburg Rd # C-425 Lexington KY 40504-3751

SMITH, HENRY LEWIS, medical products company executive; b. Wilson, N.C., June 13, 1945; s. Henry Tyson and Cleo (Lewis) S.; m. Tracey Fodor, Feb. 16, 1986; 1 child, Hannah Lilly. BS in Chemistry, Campbell U., 1967; BS in Pharmacy, U. N.C., 1972. Instr. U. N.C. Sch. Pharmacy, Chapel Hill, 1972-82; v.p., co-owner Carolina Med. Products Co., Farmville, N.C., 1982—. Recipient Disting. Alumni award Campbell U., 1990. Mem. N.C. Pharm. Assn. (pres.-elect 1991), Farmville C. of C. (chmn. 1988). Republican. Mem. Christian Ch. (Disciples of Christ). Office: Carolina Med Products Co PO Box 147 Farmville NC 27828-0147

SMITH, HUBBARD WRIGHT, internist; b. Paris, Ky., Sept. 17, 1926; s. James Kiser and Lena (Tebbs) S.; m. Pearl Yvonne Davey, May 23, 1953; children: Chris, Carrie, Gregory, Holly, Stephen. BS, U. Ky., 1948; MD, Northwestern U., Chgo., 1952, MS, 1954. Diplomate Am. Bd. Internal Medicine. Pvt. practice Med. Group of Greeley, Colo., 1957-85, Greeley Med. Clinic, 1985-92; dir. med. staff affairs North Colo. Med. Ctr., Greeley, 1993—; assoc. clin. prof. medicine U. Colo. Health Sci. Ctr., Denver, 1961-92. With USN, 1945-46. Mem. AMA, ACP, Am. Soc. Internal Medicine, Colo. Med. Soc. Roman Catholic. Office: North Colorado Medical Ctr 1801 16th St Greeley CO 80631

SMITH, IRA AUSTIN, psychologist, consultant; b. Wakefield, R.I., Jan. 28, 1945; s. Percy Austin and Ruth (Eastwood) S.; m. Kathryn Rigney Kelley, Aug. 13, 1977; children: Heather, Andrew, Rebecca. BA, U. R.I., 1966, MA, 1969. Lic. psychologist, R.I. Clin. psychologist Dr. Joseph Ladd Sch., Exeter, R.I., 1968-72; chief clin. psychologist Dr. Joseph Ladd Ctr., Exeter, R.I., 1972-87; sr. clin. psychologist divsn. devel. disabilities State of

R.I., Cranston, 1987—; cons. Regional Diagnostic Team, Newport, R.I., 1970-71, Cranston Regional Ctr., Cranston, 1972-90, AVATAR, Residential Svc. Provider, Warwick, 1990—; mem. adv. bd. U. Affiliated Program R.I. Coll., Providence, 1995—; workshop presenter in field. Contbr. articles to profl. jours. Coach Little League, Narragansett, R.I., 1981-86, Naragansett Recreation Program, 1981-87; treas. Assn. Betterment Billington Sea, Plymouth, Mass., 1993—; water monitor Billington Sea Assn., Plymouth, 1993—. Recipient Govtl. Svc. award Ocean State Assn. Residential Resources, 1989. Mem. APA, Am. Assn. Mental Retardation (bd. dirs. region 10, 1985-92,94—, Membership award, 1986, R.I. chpt. pres. 1985-92, 94—, treas., sec. 1993-94), Assn. Persons with Severe Handicaps. Office: State Operated Facilities Simpson Hall DDD/MHRH PO Box 20523 Cranston RI 02920

SMITH, J. ALEXANDER, oral maxillofacial surgeon; b. Balt., Sept. 30, 1954; s. John Walter Jr. and Joan Ann (Boswell) S.; m. Jerri Lee Muskopf, Aug. 6, 1977; children: Elizabeth Ann, Charles Alexander. BA, U. Mo., 1976; D in Dental Medicine, Washington U., 1981. Diplomate Am. Bd. Oral and Maxillofacial Surgery. Gen. practice resident Scott AFB (Ill.) Med. Ctr., 1981-82; pvt. practice gen. dentist Kirkwood, Mo., 1984-87; resident oral maxillofacial surgery U. Md., Balt., 1987-91; pvt. practice oral maxillofacial surgeon Tampa, Fla., 1991-94, Bel Air, Md., 1994—. Capt. USAF, 1981-84. Fellow Am. Assn. Oral and Maxillofacial Surgeons; mem. ADA, Harford-Cecil Dental Soc. (sec.-treas. 1994-96). Office: 136 E Broadway Bel Air MD 21014-2904

SMITH, JAMES WARREN, pathologist, microbiologist, parasitologist; b. Logan, Utah, July 5, 1934; s. Kenneth Warren and Nina Lou (Sykes) S.; m. Nancy Chesterman, July 19, 1958; children: Warren, Scott. BS, U. Iowa, 1956, MD, 1959. Diplomate Am. Bd. Pathology. Intern, Colo. Gen. Hosp., Denver, 1959-60; resident U. Iowa Hosps., Iowa City, 1960-65; asst. prof. pathology U. Vt., Burlington, 1967-70; prof. pathology Ind. U., Indpls., 1970—, chmn. dept. pathology and lab. med., 1992—. Contbr. articles to profl. jours. Served to lt. comdr. USN, 1965-67. Recipient Oustanding Contbrn. to Clin. Microbiology award South Central Assn. Clin. Microbiology, 1977. Fellow Coll. Am. Pathologists (chmn. microbiology resource com. 1981-85), Infectious Disease Soc. Am., Am. Soc. Investigative Pathology, Royal Soc. Tropical Medicine and Hygiene, AMA, Am. Soc. Clin. Pathology, Am. Soc. Microbiology, Am. Soc. Tropical Medicine and Hygiene, U.S.-Can. Acad. Pathology, Assn. Pathology Chairs, Binford Dammin Soc. Infectious Disease Pathologists. Soc. Protozoologists Office: Ind Univ Med Ctr 635 Barnhill Dr Rm 128A Indianapolis IN 46202-5120

SMITH, JEFFRY ALAN, health administrator, physician, consultant; b. L.A., Dec. 8, 1943; s. Stanley W. and Marjorie E. S.; m. Jo Anne Hague. BA in Philosophy, UCLA, 1967, MPH, 1972; BA in Biology, Calif. State U., Northridge, 1971; MD, UACJ, 1977. Diplomate Am. Bd. Family Practice. Resident in family practice WAH, Takoma Park, Md., NIH, Bethesda, Md., Walter Reed Army Hosp., Washington, Children's Hosp. Nat. Med. Ctr., Washington, 1977-80; occupational physician Nev. Test Site, U.S. Dept. Energy, Las Vegas, 1981-82; dir. occupational medicine and environ. health Pacific Missile Test Ctr., Point Mugu, Calif., 1982-84; dist. health officer State Hawaii Dept. Health, Kauai, 1984-86; asst. dir. health County of Riverside (Calif.) Dept. Health, 1986-87; regional med. dir. Calif. Forensic Med. Group, Monterey, Calif., 1987-94; med. dir. Cmty. Human Svcs., Monterey, Calif., 1987-94, Colstrip (Mont.) Med. Ctr., 1994—. Fellow Am. Acad. Family Physicians; mem. AMA, Am. Occupational Medicine Assn., Flying Physicians, Am. Pub. Health Assn. Office: PO Box 1907 Colstrip MT 59323

SMITH, JEROME HAZEN, pathologist; b. Omaha, Oct. 9, 1936; s. Hazen Dow and Helen Kellogg (Hewitt) S.; m. Marilyn Kay Stauber, 1961; children: Nathaniel, Kathryn Hewitt, Andrew Kellogg. B.S. in Medicine, U. Nebr., 1960, M.D., 1963, M.S. in Anatomy, 1962; M.Sc. Hygiene in Tropical Pub. Health, Harvard U., 1969. Diplomate: Am. Bd. Pathology. Rotating intern Mpls.-Hennepin County Gen. Hosp., 1963-64; from jr. asst. resident in pathology to chief resident in clin. pathology Peter Bent Brigham Hosp., Boston, 1964-72, assoc. pathologist, 1973; from rsch. fellow in pathology to instr. Harvard U. Med. Sch., Boston, 1964-73; pathologist, head dept. Inst. Med. Evangelique, Kimpese, Congo, 1968; chief autopsy svcs. Inst.Tropical Medicine, Hosp. Mama Yemo, Fomeco, Kinshasa, Zaire, 1973-74; med. dir. anatomic pathology Inst. Tropical Medicine, Hosp. Mama Yemo, Fomeco, Kinshasa, Zaire, 1974; asst. prof. anatomic pathology U. Ariz. Med. Sch., Tucson; dir. anatomic pathology and microbiology Tucson VA Hosp., 1975-76; mem. faculty U. Tex. Med. Br., Galveston, 1976-84, 90—, prof. pathology, 1979-84, 90—, dir. autopsy service, 1977-84, dir. clin. parasitology lab., 1977-81, 90-94, dir. pathology edn., 1993-95, prof. grad. sch., 1980-84, 90—, adj. prof. pathology, 1989-90; cons. Shriners Burn Inst., Galveston, 1980-84, 90-91; prof pathology and lab. medicine Tex. A&M U. Coll. Medicine, College Station, 1984-88; pres. Birch Tree, Inc., 1995—. Contbr. numerous articles to med. jours. Comdr. M.C. USNR, 1969-71. Recipient Avalon tuition award, 1961; NSF fellow, 1959; Poynter fellow, 1960; USPHS trainee, 1961, 68-69. Mem. NRA (life), Am. Soc. Clin. Pathologists, U.S.-Can. Acad. Pathologists, Am. Soc. Parasitologists, N.Y. Acad. Scis., Tex. Med. Assn., Tex. Soc. Pathologists, Tex. Soc. Infectious Diseases, Galveston County Med. Soc., Am. Soc. Tropical Medicine and Hygiene, Houston Soc. Clin. Pathologists (Harlan Spjut award 1995), Houston Safari Club (bd. dirs. 1994-96), Sigma Xi. Republican. Home: 2706 Wilmington Dr Dickinson TX 77539-4664 Office: U Tex Med Br Dept Pathology Galveston TX 77550

SMITH, JERRY WAYNE, physician assistant; b. Blair, Nebr., Aug. 13, 1943; s. Wayne Harrison and Margaret Lillian (Hemmingsen) S.; m. Pamela Luise Haltner, Dec. 19, 1970; children: Jason and Joshua (twins), Jarrod. B Health Sci., Duke U., 1973; BS, U. Wis., 1970. Cert. Physician Asst., Wis. Physician asst. dept. pediatrics Milw. Med. Clinic, 1973—; bd. dirs.,v.p. Wis. Camp for Kids with Asthma, Camp Wikidas, Madison, 1982-88; guest lectr. physician asst. program U. Wis.-Madison, 1979-82. Co-pres. PTO Golda Meir Sch. for Gifted and Talented, Milw., 1985; baseball and basketball coach AAU/USA Jr. Olympics. With Spl. Forces U.S. Army, 1964-67, Vietnam. Fellow Am. Acad. Physician Assts., Internat. Coll. Pediatrics, Wis. Acad. Physician Assts. (founding fellow), Soc. Ear, Nose, Throat Advances in Children (assoc.), Soc. Physician Assts. in Pediatrics); mem. Spl. Forces Assn., Duke Alumni Assn. Methodist. Home: N106 W7320 Chatham St Cedarburg WI 53012 Office: Milw Med Clinic 3003 W Good Hope Rd Milwaukee WI 53217

SMITH, JESSE GRAHAM, JR., dermatologist, educator; b. Winston-Salem, N.C., Nov. 22, 1928; s. Jesse Graham and Pauline Field (Griffith) S.; m. Dorothy Jean Butler, Dec. 28, 1950; children: Jesse Graham, Cynthia Lynn, Grant Butler. B.S., Duke U., 1962, M.D., 1951. Diplomate: Am. Bd. Dermatology (dir. 1974-83, pres. 1980-81). Intern VA Hosp., Chamblee, Ga., 1951-52; resident in dermatology Duke U., 1954-56, assoc. prof. dermatology, 1960-62, prof., 1962-67; resident U. Miami, 1956-57, asst. prof., 1957-60; prof. dermatology Med. Coll. Ga., 1967-91, chmn. dept. dermatology, 1967-91, acting chmn. dept. pathology, 1973-75, acting v.p. devel., 1984-85; chief staff Talmadge Meml. Hosp., Augusta, Ga., 1970-72; prof. dermatology, chief div. of dermatology U. South Ala., Mobile, 1991—; mem. advisory council Nat. Inst. Arthritis, 1975-79. Editorial bd. Archives of Dermatology, 1963-72, Jour. Investigative Dermatology, 1966-67, Jour. AMA, 1974-80; editorial bd. So. Med. Jour., 1976—, assoc. editor, 1991-92, editor, 1992—; editor Jour. Am. Acad. Dermatology, 1978-88; contbr. chpts. to books, articles to profl. jours. Served with USPHS, 1952-54. Recipient Disting. Alumnus award Duke U. 1981. Fellow ACP, Royal Soc. Medicine; mem. Am. Acad. Dermatology (hon., dir. 1971-74, 78-88, pres.-elect 1988-89, pres. 1989-90), Can. Dermatol. Assn. (hon.), Am. Dermatol. Assn. (hon. sec. 1976-81, pres. 1981-82), Soc. Investigative Dermatology (dir. 1964-69, pres. 1979-80), S.E. Dermatol. Assn. (sec. 1970-71, pres. 1975-76), Ga. Soc. Dermatology (pres. 1979-80), So. Med. Assn. (chmn. sect. dermatology 1981-84), Assn. Profs. Dermatology (dir. 1976-77, 80-82, pres. 1984-86), Med. Rsch. Found. Ga. (bd. dirs. 1967-91, pres. 1974-75), Alpha Omega Alpha. Home: 4272 Bitand Spur # 4 Mobile AL 36608 Office: USAMC 3401 Medical Park Dr Ste 103 Mobile AL 36693-3318

SMITH, JESSE GRAHAM, III, hospital executive; b. Durham, N.C., Oct. 16, 1954; s. Jesse Graham Jr. and Dorothy Jean (Butler) S.; m. Susan Kathleen Allen, June 5, 1976; children: Christin Kimberly, Amy Rebecca. BS, Ga. Tech. U., 1976; MBA, MSPH, U. Mo., 1978. Asst. adminstr. Bluefield (W.Va.) Community Hosp., 1978-80, Parkway Regional Hosp., Lithia Springs, Ga., 1980-83; adminstr. Peach County Hosp., Ft. Valley, Ga., 1983-86; div. dir. HCA Physician Svcs. Co., Atlanta, 1986-87; CEO Aiken (S.C.) Regional Med. Ctrs., 1987-94; Augusta (Ga.) Regional Med. Ctr., 1994-96; pres. Health Caer Advisors, Inc., Augusta, 1996—; mem. faculty Ctr. Health Studies, Nashville, 1979-93; chmn. Augusta Area Hosp. Coun., 1990-92. Chmn. Commn. on Future Aiken County, 1992; div. mgr. United Way, 1990; bd. dirs. Jr. Achievement. Named Man of Yr., Peach County C. of C., 1986, Vol. of Yr., United Way, 1994. Mem. Am. Coll. Healthcare Execs., Healthcare Fin. Mgmt. Assn., Med. Group Mgmt. Assn., Greater Aiken C. of C. (chmn. 1991), Rotary (Rookie of Yr. award 1988). Home: 4119 Hammonds Ferry Evans GA 30809-9426 Office: PO Box 2206 Augusta GA 30903-2206

SMITH, JOAN H., women's health nurse, educator; b. Akron, Ohio; d. Joseph A. and Troynette M. (Lower) McDonald; m. William G. Smith; children: Sue Ann, Priscilla, Timothy. Diploma, Akron City Hosp., 1948; BSN in Edn., U. Akron, 1972, MA in Family Devel., 1980. Cert. in inpatient obstetric nursing. Mem. faculty Akron Gen. Med. Ctr. Sch. Nursing, 1964; former dir. obstet. spl. procedures Speakers Bur., Women's Health Ctrs. Akron Gen. Med. Ctr., 1988;, 1990; cons., speaker women's health care. Mem. Assn. Women's Health, Obstet. and Neonatal Nursing (charter, past sec.-treas., past vice chmn. Ohio sect., chmn. program various confs.). Home: 873 Kirkwall Dr Copley OH 44321-1751

SMITH, JOEL FRANKLIN, surgeon; b. Yonkers, N.Y., May 29, 1937; s. William and Mollie (Masoff) S.; children: Chelsea Bridgette, Benjamin Jules. BA, NYU, 1959; MD, N.Y. Med. Coll., 1963. Diplomate Am. Bd. Surgery, Am. Bd. Surgeons. Intern Good Samaritan Hosp., West Palm Beach, Fla., 1963-64; resident Albany Med. Ctr., 1964-65, N.Y. Med. Coll.-Met. Med. Ctr., N.Y.C., 1965-69; surgeon pvt. practice, Palm Beach County, Fla., 1971—; staff mem. Jupiter Med. Ctr., Plam Beach Gardens Med. Ctr., Good Samaritan Med. Ctr., Everglades Meml. Hosp.; chief surgery Jupiter Med. Ctr., 1991-92, 93-94, 95-96. Contbr. articles to profl. jours. Maj. USAF, 1969-71. Exptl. and clin. renal and hepatic transplantation fellow N.Y. Med. Coll.-Met. Med. Ctr., 1968-69. Fellow Am. Coll. Surgeons, Southeast Surg. Soc., Internat. Coll. Surgeons; mem.. Am. Soc. Abdominal Surgeons, Southeastern Surg. Soc., Fla. Assn. Gen. Surgeons, Palm Beach County Med. Soc. Home: 4225 Magnolia St Palm Beach Gardens FL 33418 Office: 12300 Alternate AIA Ste 120 Palm Beach Gardens FL 33410

SMITH, JOHN ANTHONY, exercise and sports physiologist; b. Cootamundra, N.S.W., Australia, Mar. 4, 1961; s. Frederick Anthony and Annette Margaret (Morton) S. BS with honors, Australian Nat. U., Canberra, 1988, PhD in Biochemistry/Molecular Biology, 1994. Rsch. scientist Nat. Quality of Life Found., Canberra, 1994-95; cons. physiologist Australian Inst. of Sport, Canberra, 1995—; rsch. scientist Australian Sports Performance Inst., Canberra, 1995-96; cons. physiologist Australian Olympic Track & Field Team; mem. nat. consultative com. for wellness and survival programme Nat. Ctr. for HIV Social Rsch., Brisbane, Australia, 1992—; cons. Australian Sports Commn., 1995; lectr. in field. Contbr. articles to profl. jours. Recipient Commendation, Australian Sports Medicine Fedn., 1993, 95, Commonwealth Postgrad. Rsch. award, 1988-92, Australian Nat. U. Postgrad. Travel award, 1990; grantee Australian Nat. U., 1993, Nat. Quality of Life Found., 1994, Australian Sports Commn., 1995. Mem. Internat. Soc. for Free Radical Rsch. (Young Investigator award 1990), Am. Coll. Sports Medicine, Internat. Soc. for Exercise and Immunology (program com. 1996—). Office: Australian Inst Sport, Leverrier Crescent, Belconnen 2616 ACT, Australia

SMITH, JOHN MORTON, internist; b. Atlanta; s. John Morton and Camilla (Adams) S.; m. Anne Plourde, Dec. 28, 1967; children: John III, Elaine, Cynthia, Christina, Mark. AB, U. Notre Dame, 1961; MD, Med. Coll. Va., 1966. Intern Med. Coll. Hosp., Richmond, Va., 1966-67; resident Med. Coll. Hosp., Richmond, 1967-68; chief med. resident Oakland (Calif.) Naval Hosp., 1968-69; asst. chief of medicine Charleston (S.C.) Naval Hosp., 1969-72; staff internist Brunswick (Ga.) Hosp., 1972—. Lt. comdr. USNR, 1968-72. Mem. AMA, Am. Coll. Physicians, Ga. Med. Soc., Glynn County Med. Soc., Alpha Omega Alpha. Office: 1 Retreat Pl Saint Simons Island GA 31522

SMITH, JOHN WALLACE, surgeon, educator; b. Hutchinson, Kans., Feb. 18, 1931; s. W. Donald and Claramary (Smith) S.; m. Margaret Lee, Dec. 26, 1959; children: John Wallace Jr., Frances, George MacDonell. AB, Harvard U., 1952; MD, U. Nebr., 1956. Diplomate Am. Bd. Surgery, Am. Bd. Gen. Vascular Surgery. Intern San Francisco Hosp., 1956-57; resident Stanford U. Hosps., San Francisco, 1957-60, U. Calif. Hosps., San Francisco, 1960-62; pvt. practice in gen. surgery Omaha, 1964-70; practice specializing in vascular surgery, pres. Vascular Surgery, P.C., Omaha, 1970-96; clin. assoc. prof. surgery Coll. Medicine U. Nebr., Omaha, 1966—; pres. med. staff Meth. Hosp., Omaha, 1986-87. Contbr. articles to profl. jours. Bd. dirs. Omaha Symphony Assn., 1974-96. Served to capt. Med. Corps U.S. Army, 1962-64. Fellow ACS (gov. 1987-92); mem. Midwestern Vascular Surg. Soc. (chmn. membership com. 1982), Internat. Soc. Cardiovascular Surgery, Western Surg. Assn. (chmn. membership com. 1995), Alpha Omega Alpha (pres. 1982-83). Office: 8111 Dodge St Omaha NE 68114

SMITH, JOHN WAYNE, internist, nephrologist; b. Pine Bluff, Ark., Aug. 13, 1955; s. Henry J. and Catherine Ann (Ashcraft) S.; m. Laura Lee Parker, June 4, 1977; children: Melanie, Melissa, Andrew. BS, Northeastern La. U., 1977; MD, U. Ark., Little Rock, 1981. Resident in internal medicine U. Ark. for Med. Scis., 1981-84, fellow in nephrology, 1985-86; pvt. practice, Hot Springs, Ark., 1986—; trustee Bapt. Health Sys., Little Rock, 1990—; vice chmn. Ark. Kidney Disease Commn., Little Rock, 1990—. Deacon 1st Bapt. Ch., Hot Springs, 1991—. Fellow ACP; mem. AMA, Nat. Kidney Found., Ark. Med. Soc., Renal Physicians Assn. Home: 206 Whispering Hills Hot Springs AR 71901 Office: Ark Nephrology Svcs 1900 Malvern Ave Ste 102 Hot Springs AR 71901-7776

SMITH, JONATHAN DAVID, medical educator; b. Cleve., Jan. 10, 1955. BS, U. Calif., Santa Cruz, 1978; PhD, Harvard U., 1984. Postdoctoral Lab. Biochem. Genetics and Metabolism The Rockefeller U., N.Y.C., 1984-89, asst. prof., 1989—. Contbr. articles to profl. jours. Recipient Nat. Rsch. Svc. award NIH, 1985-87, Program Project award, 1995—. Mem. AAAS, Am. Heart Assn. (Investigatorship award N.Y.C. affiliate 1989-92, Grant-in-Aid 1989-92, 92-95, Established Investigator 1994—). *

SMITH, JOSEPH LORENZO, physician; b. Green River, Wyo., Oct. 15, 1946; s. Joseph F. and Vera (Robinson) S.; m. Judy Peterson, Aug. 8, 1969; children: Joseph L. II, A. Theodore, Brett L., Heather, Megan, Jason Jon. BS magna cum laude, U. Utah, 1970; MD, Cornell U., 1972. Diplomate Am. Bd. Med. Examiners, E.I.S. Ctr. for Disease Control, Am. Bd. Internal Medicine, Infectious Diseases, Pulmonary Diseases, Advanced Achievment in Internal Medicine, Critical Care Medicine. Intern Hershey Med. Ctr. Pa. State U., Hershey, 1972-73, resident, 1973-74; surgeon Ctrs. for Disease Control, Pub. Health Svc., Phoenix, 1974-76; fellow Div. Infectious Diseases Stanford U. Sch. Medicine. Stanford, Calif., 1976-78; pvt. practice specializing in infectious diseases Ogden, Utah, 1979-81; fellow Pulmonary Medicine, Div. Respiratory Care U. Utah Coll. of Medicine and LDS Hosp., Salt Lake City, 1981-82; fellow critical care medicine div. respiratory care U. Utah Coll. Medicine and LDS Hosp., Salt Lake City, 1982-83; physician University Internists Wayne State U. faculty practice plan, Detroit, 1983-84, Geisinger Clinic Critical Care Medicine, Danville, Pa., 1984—; clin. instr. Dept. Medicine Divsn. Infectious Diseases U. Utah, Salt Lake City, 1979-81; asst. prof. medicine Wayne State U., Detroit, 1983-84; asst. clin. prof. medicine Pa. State. U., Hershey, 1985-86, assoc. clin. prof., 1986-87; assoc. clin. prof. Jefferson Med. Coll., 1989-93, clin. prof., 1993—; cons. ADA, 1975, Am. Hosp. Assn. Com. on Hosp. Infections, 1976, Utah State Dept. of Health, 1979-83, McKay Dee Hosp., Ogden, Utah, 1981-83; assoc. dir. Intensive Care Harper Hosp., Detroit, 1983-84, dir. critical care rsch. and edn. program Geisinger Med. Ctr., 1985-93. Contbr. many abstracts and articles to profl. jours. Active youth soccer orgns., Boy Scouts Am., Ch. of Latter Day Saints youth orgns.; mem. Union Pacific R.R. Hist. Soc.; mem. sch. bd. Lewisburg (Pa.) Sch. Dist.; nominating com., sch. bd. acad. adv. task force Pa. Sch. Bd. Assn. Recipient Cert. of Appreciation Interagency Task Force Indochina Refugees, 1975, AMA Physician's Recognition award, 1985-88, 88-91, 91-94, 94-97; named one of Best Tchrs. by graduating medicine residents Geisinger Med. Ctr., 1987. Fellow Am. Coll. Physicians, Am. Coll. Chest Physicians, Am. Coll. Critical Care Medicine; mem. AMA, Am. Thoracic Soc., Pa. Med. Soc., Pa. Thoracic Soc., Mountour County Med. Soc., Infectious Disease Soc. Am., Soc. Critical Care Medicine, Alpha Epsilon Delta, Phi Kappa Phi. Republican. Office: Geisinger Med Ctr N Acadeny Ave N Academy Ave Danville PA 17822

SMITH, JOSEPH R., neurosurgeon, educator; b. Seattle, Sept. 20, 1940; m. Peach Smith; 1 child, Jordan. BS in Psychology, U. Wash., 1963, MD, 1967. Diplomate Am. Bd. Neurosurgery. Straight surg. intern Kans. U. Med. Ctr., 1967-68; resident in neurosurgery U. Wash. Med. Sch., Seattle, 1968-73; fellow in physiol. neurosurgery Med. Coll. Ga., Augusta, 1985, instr. neurosurgery, 1985-86, assoc. prof. surgery (neurosurgery), 1986-91; attending neurosurgeon VA Med. Ctr., Augusta, 1986-92, cons. neurosurgeon, 1992—; presenter in field. Contbr. numerous articles to profl. jours. Fellow ACS; mem. Congress of Neurol. Surgeons, Am. Soc. Stereotaxic Neurosurgery, World Soc. Stereotaxic Neurosurgery, Am. Acad. Clin. Neurophysiology, Internat. Assn. Study of Pain, Am. Assn. Neurol. Surgeons, Am. Epilepsy Soc., Ga. Neurosurg. Soc. Office: Med Coll Ga Sect Neurosurg Rm BIW-350 1120 15th St Augusta GA 20912

SMITH, JULIA JO-ANN, health facility director; b. West Palm Beach, Fla., July 23, 1942; m. Wellington H. Smith Jr., Jan. 2, 1988; children: Hope, Alan. AA, Palm Beach Jr. Coll., 1978; BPS, Barry U., 1984; MBA, Nova U., 1987. Cert. patient accts. mgr. Asst. supr. Good Samaritan Hosp., West Palm Beach, 1974-76; mgr. Doctor Hosp., Lake Worth, Fla., 1976-79, Jupiter (Fla.) Hosp., 1979-81; dir. fin. svcs. Southeastern Med. Ctr., N. Miami Beach, 1981-86; dir. clin. ops. SECOM, N. Miami Beach, 1986-87; dir. patient acctg. Mercy Hosps., Charlotte, N.C., 1988—; cons. in field, 1981—. Contbr. articles to profl. jours. Mem. Ch. Christ, West Palm Beach, Monroe, N.C., 1942—. Mem. Healthcare Fin. Mgmt. Assocs. Office: Mercy Hosps 2001 Vail Ave Charlotte NC 28207

SMITH, JULIAN ANDERSON, cardiothoracic surgeon; b. Melbourne, Victoria, Australia, July 5, 1958; ss. Hubert Reynolds and Beryl Hilda (Anderson) S.; m. Sally Ann Leslie, Jan. 7, 1994; 1 child, Madeleine Jane. B Medicine B Surgery, U. Melbourne, Australia, 1981, M Surgery, 1986. l. Resident med. officer Royal Melbourne Hosp., 1982-84, gen. surg. registrar, 1985-88; cardiothoracic surgery registrar Royal Melbourne Hosp. Alfred Healthcare Group, 1989-91; chief resident in cardiothoracic surgery and transplantation Stanford (Calif.) U. Sch. Medicine, 1992-93; hon. cardiothoracic surgery registrar, sr. transplant fellow Papworth Hosp., Cambridge, Eng., 1994; cons. cardiothoracic surgeon Alfred Healthcare Group, Melbourne, 1995—, dep. head heart and lung transplant unit, 1995—; sr. lectr. dept. surgery Monash U., Melbourne, 1995—; sr. rsch. assoc. Baker Med. Rsch. Inst., Melbourne, 1995—; cons. Heartport, Ind., Redwood, Calif., 1993—, Baxter Novacor, Inc., Oakland, Calif., 1994—. Editor: The Stanford Manual of Cardiopulmonary Transplantation, 1996; assoc. editor Asia Pacific Jour. Thoracic and Cardiovascular Surgery, 1995—; contbr. numerous articles to profl. jours.; implanted first permanent left ventricular assist device. D.W. Keir fellow in med. rsch. Royal Melbourne Hosp., 1985. Fellow Royal Australasian Coll. Surgeons (sec. divsn. cardiothoracic surgery 1995—); mem. Australian Med. Assn. (award 1981), Internat. Soc. for Heart and Lung Transplantation. Mem. Ch. of England. Office: Alfred Healthcare Group, Heart/Lung Transplant Unit, Commercial Rd, Pahran Victoria 3181, Australia

SMITH, KATHLEEN ANN, medical technologist; b. Buffalo, Mar. 13, 1935; d. Joseph John and Rose Ann (Starke) S.; B.A., Mercyhurst Coll., 1956. From chemist to supr. hemostasis lab. Hamot Hosp., Erie, Pa., 1956-69; with Warner Lambert Co., 1969-85, supr. hemostasis ednl. services, 1972-85; system specialist Hemostasis Organon Teknika Co., 1985-87, mgr. quality control release and inspection, 1987-96, mgr. quality control inspection and lab. support, 1996—; adv. bd. Morris County Coll., 1980-86; presentor seminars in field. Named Med. Technologist of Yr. in N.J., 1982. Mem. Am. Soc. Med. Tech. (chmn. hemotology-hemostasis sect. 1982-84), N.C. Soc. Med. Tech., Am. Soc. Quality Control, Am. Soc. Clin. Pathology, N.J. Soc. Med. Tech. (pres. 1975), Alpha Mu Tau. Republican. Roman Catholic. Club: Morristown (N.J.) Woman's. Co-author Hemostasis Manual. Assoc. editor Clotters Corner, 1980-87. Office: 100 Akzo Ave Durham NC 27712-9402

SMITH, KEITH DAVIS, endocrinologist; b. Portsmouth, Ohio, Dec. 14, 1930; s. Millard Brown and Susan Irene (Davis) S.; m. Connie L. Beahan, June 14, 1958; children: Karen Lynne Smith Dodd, Brian Lawrence, Valerie Suzanne Smith Yake. BS in Premed., Pa. State U., 1952; MD, U. Pitts., 1959. Diplomate Am. Bd. Internal Medicine. Chief endocrinology Mercy Hosp., Pitts., 1964-68; clin. instr. U. Pitts. Med. Sch., 1968; mem. divsn. endocrinology and human reprodn. A. Einstein Med. Ctr., Phila., 1969-71; assoc. prof. U. Tex. Med. Sch., Houston, 1971-74, prof., 1975-83; v.p., sec. Tex. Inst. Reproductive Medicine & Endocrinology, Houston, 1983—; clin. prof. U. Tex. Med. Sch., Houston, 1983—; mem., chmn. various med. schs., hosps. or nat. orgn. coms., 1968—; prin. investigator NIH, Bethesda, 1972-79; co-investigator Ford Found. Grant, 1974-78, NIH, Bethesda, 1974-83. Contbr. articles to profl. jours., chpts. to books. Lt. USNR, 1952-58. Fellow Am. Coll. Endocrinology; mem. Am. Assn. Clin. Endocrinology, Endocrine Soc., Am. Assn. Andrology (dir. 1986-88), Am. Soc. for Reproductive Medicine. Office: Tex Inst Reprodn Medicine & Endocrinology 7400 Fannin # 850 Houston TX 77054

SMITH, KURT ALLEN, physician; b. Charles City, Iowa, Nov. 26, 1965; s. Jeffrey Allen and Rose Elizabeth (Rekow) S. BA, Wartburg Coll., 1988; DO, U. Osteo. Medicine and Health Scis., 1992. Intern Muskegon (Mich.) Gen. Hosp., 1992-93; resident in phys. medicine and rehab. U. Minn., Mpls., 1993-96; staff phys. medicine and rehab. Iowa Orthopedic Ctr., P.C., Des Moines, 1996—; chief intern Muskegon Gen. Hosp., 1992-93; chief resident U. Minn., Mpls., 1995-96. Fellow Am. Acad. Phys. Medicine and Rehab.; mem. AMA, Am. Osteo. Assn., Am. Acad. Phys. Medicine and Rehab. (assoc.).

SMITH, LARRY DALE, psychologist; b. Uniontown, Pa., Aug. 9, 1938; s. Dale and Opal (Adams) S. Student, Wake Forest U., 1956-58; BA, W.Va. U., 1960; MEd, Indiana U. Pa., 1964; PhD, U. Pitts., 1975. Lic. psychologist, pub. sch. psychologist, Pa. Psychologist Torrance (Pa.) State Hosp., 1962-65, 86-89, Washington (Pa.) County Schs., 1965-66, Woodville State Hosp., Carnegie, Pa., 1967-86, Forbes Health System, Monroeville, Pa., 1979-86, Braddock (Pa.) Gen. Hosp., 1977—; pvt. practice Pitts., 1976—; instr., Allegheny County C.C., Pitts., 1983-85. Fellow Am. Bd. Med. Psychotherapists; mem. APA, Nat. Acad. Neuropsychologists, Am. Soc. Clin. Hypnosis, Pa. Psychol. Assn., Phi Delta Kappa. Home: 16 Pocono Dr Pittsburgh PA 15220-3231 Office: 990 Greentree Rd Pittsburgh PA 15220-3239

SMITH, LARRY DEAN, ostoeopath, medical association administrator; b. Flint, Mich., Oct. 4, 1962; s. Floyd Edgar and Betty Jean (Meyer) S.; m. Dawn Marie Harris, June 27, 1987; children: Mackenzee Dawn, Summer Marie. BS in Biology, Ea. Wash. U., 1984; DO, Coll. Osteo. Medicine Pacific, Pomona, Calif., 1988. Intern Flint (Mich.) Osteo. Hosp., 1988-89, resident in internal medicine, 1989-90; resident in internal medicine Tucson (Ariz.) Osteo. Hosp., 1990-92; emergency room physician Davis-Matham AFB, Tucson, 1990-92; clin. practice Newport (Wash.) Cmty. Hosp., 1992—; med. dir. Pend Oreille Nursing Home, Newport, Wash., 1992—; asst. prof. internal medicine Coll. Osteo. Medicine Pacific, 1993—; chief med. staff Newport Cmty. Hosp., 1994, dir. med. edn., 1996—; manuscript rev. bd. Jour. Clin. Outcomes Mgmt., Wayne, Pa., 1995—; adj. prof. clin. medicine Saba (The Netherlands-Antilles) U. Sch. Medicine, 1996—. Soccer coach Youth Soccer League, Newport, 1995. Mem. Am. Osteo. Assn., Am. Soc. Barratric Physicians, Am. Coll. Osteo. Family Practitioners, Am. Coll. Osteo. Pain Mgmt. and Sclerotherapists, Wash. Oste. Med. Assn., Ducks Unlimited, Eagles. Office: Newport Cmty Hosp Clinic 231 S Washington Newport WA 99156

SMITH, LARRY WAYNE, medical/surgical nurse; b. Washington, N.C., Jan. 2, 1962; s. Larry Grey and Norma D. Wilson. Grad. lic. practical nurse, Craven Community Coll., 1984, AAS, 1989. RN; cert. BCLS, ACLS, PALS. Patient care asst. Craven Regional Med. Ctr., New Bern, N.C., 1980-84, lic. practical nurse surg. unit, 1984-89, nurse in surg. unit, 1989, nurse in hosp. homecare, 1989, neurology nurse, 1989-90, staff nurse ICU, 1990-94; staff nurse ICU Naval Hosp., Camp Lejeune, N.C., 1991—. Home: PO Box 4004 Emerald Isle NC 28594-4004 Office: Craven Regional Med Ctr 2000 Neuse Blvd New Bern NC 28560-3449

SMITH, LEE ELTON, surgery educator, retired military officer; b. Ventura, Calif., July 19, 1937; s. Raymond Elroy and Edith Irene (Jordan) S.; m. Carole Sue Smith; children: Justine Diane, Alexander Loren. BS, U. Calif., Berkeley, 1959; MD, U. Calif., San Francisco, 1962. Diplomate Am. Bd. Surgery, Am. Bd. Colon and Rectal Surgery (pres. 1992-93). Commd. ens. USN, 1960, advanced through grades to capt., 1977; intern U. Utah, Salt Lake City, 1962-63; resident USN, San Diego, Calif., 1966-70; staff surgeon USN, Bremerton, Wash., 1970-72; resident colorectal surgery U. Minn., Mpls., 1972-73; dir. colorectal surgery Nat. Naval Med. Ctr. USN, Bethesda, Md., 1973-82; ret. USN, 1983, Seattle, 1982; prof. surgery George Washington U., Washington, 1983-96, clin. prof. surgery, 1996—; clin. prof. surgery Uniformed Svcs. U., Bethesda, 1994—; dir. sect. of colon and rectal surgery Washington Hosp. Ctr., 1996—; pres. Am. Bd. Colon and Rectal Surgery, 1993-94. Editor: Practical Guide to Anorectal Physiology, 1990, 2d edit., 1995; assoc. editor Diseases of the Colon & Rectum, 1984—, Perspectives in Colon and Rectal Surgery, 1989—. Mem. ACS (pres. Met. Washington chpt. 1993-94), Soc. Am. Gastrointestinal Endoscopic Surgeons (pres. 1989-90), Am. Cancer Soc. (v.p. D.C. chpt. 1985—). Home: 1200 N Nash St Apt 518 Arlington VA 22209-3614 Office: Washington Hosp Ctr 110 Irving St Washington DC 20010

SMITH, LESLIE ROPER, hospital and healthcare administrator; b. Stockton, Calif., June 20, 1928; s. Austin J. and Helen (Roper) S.; m. Edith Sue Fincher, June 22, 1952; children: Melinda Sue, Leslie Erin, Timothy Brian. A.B., U. Pacific, 1951; M.S. in Pub. Adminstrn, U. So. Calif., 1956. Adminstrv. asst. Ranchos Los Amigos Hosp., Downey, Calif., 1953-57; asst. adminstr. Harbor Gen. Hosp., Torrance, Calif., 1957-65; adminstr. Harbor Gen. Hosp., 1966-71; acting regional dir. Los Angeles County Coastal Health Services Region, 1973; pres. San Pedro Peninsula Hosp., San Pedro, Cal., 1974-86; exec. dir. Los Angeles County/U. So. Calif. Med. Center, 1971-73; adminstr. Long Beach (Calif.) Hosp., 1965-66; asso. clin. prof. community medicine and pub. health, also emergency medicine U. So. Calif., 1968-78; instr. U. So. Calif. (Sch. Pub. Adminstrn.), 1968; preceptor hosp. adminstrn. UCLA Sch. Pub. Health, 1964—; chief exec. officer French Hosp. Med. Ctr. and Health Plan, 1986-87; dir. health care services McCormack & Farrow, 1987—; lectr. in field, 1963—; cons. emergency health services HEW, 1970-73; chmn. com. diaster preparedness Hosp. Council So. Calif., 1966-72, sec., 1971—, pres., 1973; mem. Calif. Assembly Com. on Emergency Med. Services, 1970, Calif. Emergency Med. Adv. Com., 1972-75, Los Angeles County Commn. on Emergency Med. Services, 1975-83, Los Angeles Health Planning and Devel. Agy. Commn., 1980-83; bd. dirs. Blue Cross of So. Calif.; mem. hosp. relations com. Blue Cross of Calif.; mem. adv. com. on emergency health services Calif. Dept. Health, 1974-75; bd. dirs., mem. exec. com. Truck Ins. Exchange of Farmers Ins. Group, 1977-82; bd. dirs. Hosp. Council of So. Calif., 1966-76, 81-86, Health Resources Inst., 1985-86; chmn. Preferred Health Network, 1983-86. Mem. goals com., Torrance, 1968—; pres. Silver Spur Little League, Palos Verdes, 1969-70. Served with AUS, 1946-48. Recipient Silver Knight and Gold Knight award Nat. Mgmt. Assn., 1970, 85, Walker Fellowship award, 1976. Fellow Am. Coll. Health Care Execs. (life); mem. Am., Nat. mgmt. assns., Am. Hosp. Assn. (chmn. com. on community emergency health services 1973), Calif. Hosp. Assn. (chmn. com. emergency services 1965-70, trustee 1973-76, bd. dirs. Calif. Ins. Service Group 1980-82), County Suprs. Assn. Calif. (chmn. joint subcom. on emergency care 1970). Presbyn. (elder, trustee). Home: 27 Marseille Laguna Niguel CA 92677

SMITH, LEWIS ALAN, surgeon, educator; b. Atlanta, Aug. 9, 1946; s. Laurin G. and Mary Alice (Boggs) S.; m. Lavonne Elaine Brown, Apr. 3, 1979; children: Allison, Derek, Alana, Trevor. BS, U. Fla., 1968; MD, U. Miami, 1972. Diplomate Am. Bd. Surgery. Intern, Univ. Hosp., Jacksonville, Fla., 1972-73; resident in surgery Jacksonville Health Edn. Program, Jacksonville, 1974-78; practice medicine specializing in gen. surgery, Jacksonville, 1978—; clin. asst. prof. surgery U. Fla., Jacksonville, 1978—. Served to lt. USNR, 1971-73. Mem. ACS, S.E. Surg. Congress, Fla. Surg. Soc. Office: 3636 University Blvd S Suite C-1 Jacksonville FL 32216

SMITH, LEY S., pharmaceutical company executive; b. 1934. BA, U. Western Ont., Can., 1958. With Upjohn Co., Kalamazoo, Mich., 1958—, now pres. & COO. Office: Pharmacia and Upjohn Inc 7000 Portage Rd Kalamazoo MI 49001-0102*

SMITH, LINDA SUE, nurse, educator; b. Racine, Wis., July 8, 1950; d. Eugene Walter and Betty Ruth (Peters) Jenista; m. Jeffrey J. Smith, July 12, 1969; children: Angela Marie, Ryan James. AAS in Nursing, Milw. Area Tech. Coll., 1971; BSN, Alverno Coll., 1979; MSN, U. Wis., Milw., 1982; postgrad., U. Ala. RN, Wis. Ward clk., then staff nurse, charge nurse St. Luke's Hosp., Racine, 1965-72; critical care charge nurse, staff nurse St. Mary's Med. Ctr., Racine, 1972-79; shift supr. High Ridge Health Care Ctr., Racine, 1979-80; staff nurse St. Mary's Med. Ctr., Racine, 1982, 89-92; mem. nursing faculty Gateway Tech. Coll., Kenosha, Wis., 1980-96; asst. prof. State U. of West Ga., 1996—; cons. FDA/HHS Med. Devices Adv. Com., 1995—; v.p. Data Design, Inc., Mableton, Ga.; reviewer nursing materials Saunders-Psychiatric Nursing, 1986—, Mosby-Psychiatric Nursing, 1992—; presenter at profl. confs., workshops; presenter women's health issues program on local pub. radio, 1977-79; spkr. at career day and similar functions at area H.S.'s and svc. clubs. Co-founder, pub., editl. dir. Advancing Clin. Care Jour., 1985-91; contbr. chpts. to books, articles to profl. jours. Mem. Strategic Planning Com. Racine County; mem. adv. bd. U. Wis. Extension. Recipient Humanitarin award U.S./USSR Friendship Soc.; inducted into S.E. Wis. Educator's Hall of Fame; named Disting. Alumnus of Yr. Milw. Area Tech. Coll. Mem. All Russian Nurses Assn. (hon.), U.S.-Russian Nurse Exch. Consortium (charter, founder), Phi Kappa Phi (life), Sigma Theta Tau Internat. Roman Catholic. Home: 5339 St Martins Ct Mableton GA 30059

SMITH, LLOYD HOLLINGSWORTH, physician; b. Easley, S.C., Mar. 27, 1924; s. Lloyd H. and Phyllis (Page) S.; m. Margaret Constance Avery, Feb. 27, 1954; children—Virginia Constance, Christopher Avery, Rebecca Anne, Charlotte Page, Elizabeth Hollingsworth, Jeffrey Hollingsworth. A.B., Washington and Lee U., 1944, D.Sc., 1969; M.D., Harvard, 1948. Intern, then resident Mass. Gen. Hosp., Boston, 1948-50; chief resident physician Mass. Gen. Hosp., 1955-56; mem. Harvard Soc. Fellows, 1952-54; asst. prof. Harvard Soc. Fellows (Med. Sch.), 1956-63; vis. investigator Karolinska Inst., Stockholm, 1954-55, Oxford (Eng.) U., 1963-64; prof. medicine, chmn. dept. U. Calif. Med. Sch., San Francisco, 1964-85, assoc dean, 1985—; Mem. Pres.'s Sci. Adv. Com., 1970-73. Bd. overseers Harvard, 1974-80. Served to capt., M.C. AUS, 1950-52. Mem. Am. Acad. Arts and Scis., Am. Soc. Clin. Investigation (pres. 1969-70), Western Soc. Clin. Rsch. (pres. 1969-70), Assn. Am. Physicians (pres. 1974-75), Am. Fedn. Clin. Rsch. Home: 309 Evergreen Dr Kentfield CA 94904-2709 Office: U Calif San Francisco Med Ctr San Francisco CA 94143

SMITH, LYMAN LEE, JR., dentist; b. Atlanta, July 16, 1933; s. Lyman Lee and Evelyn (Freeman) S.; m. Melda Twisdale, June 1957 (div. June 1970); m. Doris Palm, Dec. 1970 (div. Aug. 1977); children: Lee, Frank, Byron, Donna, Evelyn, Robyn; m. Jean Edwards, Feb. 1992. Student, Emory U., 1951-57, DDS, 1957. Dentist, capt. U.S. Army, Ft. Benning, Ga., 1957-60; dentist pvt. practice Atlanta, 1960—. Mem. Ga. Dental Assn., Am. Dental Assn., Hinman Dental Soc., Masons Shrine. Methodist. Home: 725 Glen Forrest Rd NE Atlanta GA 30328-5211 Office: 1150 Hammond Dr NE Ste A-1145 Atlanta GA 30328-5334

SMITH, LYMAN SCOTT-WILLIAM, physician; b. Portland, Oreg., Sept. 24, 1956; s. William Walter and Hertha Gail (Lohse) S.; m. Patricia W. Smith, June 14, 1985; children: Stephanie, Julianne, Ned. BS, Duke Univ., 1978, MD, 1984. Diplomate Am. Bd. Orthopaedic Surgeon. Professional football player Miami Dolphins, Miami, 1978, Minn. Vikings, Minnesota, 1978-79; phlebotomy team Duke Univ. Medical Ctr., Durham, N.C., 1981-84, CORE lab. tech., 1982, 83; orthopaedic surgeon Raleigh Orthopaedic Clinic, Raleigh, N.C., 1991—; adv. bd. N.C. Youth Fitness Com., 1995—, Wake County Coun. Physical Fitness & Health, 1995—. Contbr. articles to profl. jours. Mem. Am. Acad. Orthopaedic Surgeons, Wake County Medical Soc., N.C. Medical Soc. (sports com. 1993—). Office: Raleigh Orthopaedic Clinic 3515 Glenwood Ave Raleigh NC 27612

SMITH, MARTIN JAY, physician, biomedical research scientist; b. Bklyn., May 21, 1934; s. I. Richard and Marilyn (Bernard) S.; m. Joyce Ellen Gleason, June 26, 1960 (div. Nov. 1968); children: Danielle, Robert, Alexander; m. Ruby Helen Rhodes, Apr. 7, 1972. BA, Hofstra Coll., 1955; MD, Columbia U., 1959. Diplomate Am. Bd. Internal Medicine, Am. Bd. Internal Medicine in Hematology, Am. Bd. Pathology in Clin. Pathology, Am. Bd. Pathology in Immunopathology. Intern in medicine Meth. Hosp., N.Y.C., 1959-60, resident in medicine, 1960-61; resident in medicine Montefiore Hosp., N.Y.C., 1963-64; rsch. fellow in medicine Harvard Coll., Cambridge, Mass., 1964-66; clin. and rsch. fellow in medicine Mass. Gen. Hosp., Boston, 1964-66; physician Gundersen Clinic and Luth. Hosp., La Crosse, Wis., 1966—, chmn. dept. internal medicine, 1971-73; dir. spl. hematology lab. Gundersen Clinic, 1967—, chmn. dept. lab. medicine, 1973—; dir. lab. medicine Luth. Hosp., La Crosse, 1973—; dir. rsch. Gundersen Med. Found., 1975-88; med. dir. Med. Lab. Tech. Program Western Wis. Tech. Inst., 1978—. Contbr. articles to New Eng. Jour Medicine, Jour. Lab. Clin. Medicine, Blood, Ann. Internal Medicine, Am. Jour. Hematology, Clin. Chemistry, others. Capt. USNR, ret. Fellow ACP, Coll. Am. Pathologists (inspector labs. 1983—); mem. Am. Assn. for Cancer Rsch., Am. Soc. Hematology, Internat. Soc. Hematology, Assn. Med. Lab. Immunologists, Phi Beta Kappa. Home: 1428 Main St La Crosse WI 54601-4225 Office: Gundersen Clinic Ltd 1836 South Ave La Crosse WI 54601-5429

SMITH, MARY FRAN, ophthalmologist; b. Roanoke, Va., June 30, 1961; d. Sam Frank Jr. and Jacqueline (Via) S.; m. James William Doyle. BA, U. Va., 1983; MD, Northwestern U., Chgo., 1987. Intern Mercy Hosp., Pitts., 1987-88; residency in ophthalmology U. Fla., Gainesville, 1988-91, fellow in glaucoma, 1991-92, asst. prof. dept. ophthalmology, 1992—; chief ophthalmology sect. VA Med. Ctr., Gainesville, 1992—; program dir. dept. ophthalmology U. Fla., Gainesville, 1995—. Contbr. articles to profl. jours. Regional coord. Glaucoma 2001, 1996. Mem. Am. Acad. Ophthalmology (course instr. 1994—), Am. Univ. Profs. Ophthalmology (assoc.), Assn. Rsch. in Vision and Ophthalmology, Fla. Soc. Ophthalmology (lectr., instr. 1995). Republican. Baptist. Office: Dept Ophthalmology U Fla 1600 Archer Gainesville FL 32610

SMITH, MARY FRANCES, social worker, educator; b. Albany, N.Y., Aug. 24, 1943; d. Egon and Hildegard (Weyrauch) Plager; m. Francis N. Smith, June 24, 1967; 1 child, Christopher Francis. BS in Biology, Nazareth Coll., Rochester, N.Y., 1965; MSW, Syracuse U., 1967; PhD, SUNY, Albany, 1990. Cert. social worker. Psychiat. social worker St. Anne Inst., Albany, 1967-71; supervising social worker Albany County Mental Health Clinic, 1971-74; assoc. prof. dept. family practice Albany Med. Coll., 1979—. Grantee N.Y. State Acad. Family Physicians Rsch. and Edn. Found., 1990-91. Mem. NASW, Soc. Tchrs. Family Medicine, Gerontol. Soc. Am., Acad. Cert. Social Workers. Roman Catholic. Home: 3 Westlyn Ct Albany NY 12203 Office: Albany Med Coll Dept Family Practice 1 Clara Barton Dr Albany NY 12208-3401

SMITH, MICHAEL JAMES, industrial engineering educator; b. Madison, Wis., May 12, 1945; s. James William and Ruth Gladys (Murphy) S.; m. Patricia Ann Bentley, June 22, 1968; children: Megan Colleen, Melissa Maureen. BA, U. Wis., 1968, MA, 1970, PhD, 1973. Rsch. analyst Wis. Dept. Industry Labor, Madison, 1971-74; rsch. psychologist Nat. Inst. for Occupational Safety and Health, USPHS, Cin., 1974-84; prof. U. Wis., Madison, 1984—; owner, prin. M.J. Smith Assocs. Inc., Madison, 1991—. Contbr. articles to profl. jours. Mem. APA, Inst. Indsl. Engrs. (sr.), Human Factors Soc., Assn. Computer Machinery, Am. Soc. Testing and Measurement. Home: 6719 Shamrock Glen Cir Middleton WI 53562-1144 Office: U Wis Dept Indsl Enging Human Factors Rsch Lab 1513 University Ave Madison WI 53706-1539

SMITH, MICHAEL JOSEPH, orthopaedic surgeon, educator; b. Mpls., May 4, 1960; m. Cara J. Smith; 3 children. BS in Biology magna cum laude, Cath. U. Am., 1978-82; MD, U. Minn., 1986. Diplomate Am. Bd. Orthopaedic Surgery Med. Examiners; lic. physician, Ohio. Intern Akron (Ohio) Gen. Med. Ctr., 1986-87, resident in orthopaedic surgery, 1987-91; fellow in spine surgery Thomas Jefferson Med. Ctr.-Pa. Hosp., Rothmann Inst., 1991-92; hosp. staff Akron Gen. Med. Ctr., Summa Health Sys., clin. instr. in orthopaedic surgery Coll. Medicine, Northeastern Ohio Univ., Rootstown; mem. curriculum com. orthopaedic residency program daily conf. Akron Gen. Med. Ctr.; presenter and lectr. in field. Contbr. rsch. articles to profl. publs. Full acad. scholar Cath. U. Am., 1978-82. Mem. Ohio Orthopaedic Soc., Summit County Med. Soc., SRS, NASS. Office: NE Ohio Orthopaedic Assocs Ste 440 224 W Exchange St Akron OH 44302-1707

SMITH, MICHAEL OGLESBY, physician assistant, writer; b. Columbus, Ga., May 30, 1947; s. Charles Ray and Myrtle (Oglesby) S.; m. Sue Mary Dear, Aug. 20, 1978; children: Barbara Nicole Klasky, Sarah Elizabeth. BS in Pre-Med and Geology, Emory U., 1970; BS, Med. Coll. Ga., 1975. LPN, Pa.; cert. physician asst. Nurse Augusta, Ga., 1973-75; psychiat. nurse Grady Hosp., Atlanta, 1973; physician asst. Family Practice/Bowdon, Ga., 1975-76, Family Practice, Columbus, Ga., 1976-77; med. dir. Dept. Corrections, Columbus, 1977-89; med. dir., physician asst. Dept. Human Resources, Savannah, 1989-90; chief clinician, physician asst. NIU Clinic Bur. of Prisons, Jesup, Ga., 1990—; writer on treasure hunting. Author: Relic Hunters Manual, 1996; contbr. articles to profl. jours. V.p. Wayne county Hist. Soc., Jesup, 1993—; surgeon SCV, Columbus, Ga., 1985-88. Served to comdr. USPHS, 1990—. Recipient awards and commendations. Fellow Am. Acad. Physician Assts., Ga. Assn. Physician Assts. (bd. dirs.), Soc. Army Physician Assts., Pub. Health Svc. Assn. Physician Assts. (bd. dirs. 1995—); mem. Optimist Club (bd. dirs. 1993-95). Republican. Methodist. Home: 1435 Bennett Crossing Jesup GA 31545 Office: Bur of Prisons HW 3015 Jesup GA 31545

SMITH, MICHAEL SPINNER, neurologist, medical administrator; b. Berkeley, Calif., Dec. 5, 1948; s. Paul Edward and Ruth Frances (O'Grady) S.; m. Janice Rae Littleton, Aug. 29, 1971. AB, Dartmouth Coll., 1970; MD, U. Colo., 1974. Diplomate Am. Bd. Psychiatry and Neurology, Am. Bd. Med. Mgmt. Resident in neurology U. Ariz., Tucson, 1977-80, asst. prof. neurology, 1979-81; neurologist Neurologic Assocs. of Tucson, 1981-92; med. dir. St. Mary's Hosp., Tucson, 1992—; bd. dirs. Ariz. Med. Assn. Contbr. articles to profl. jours.; astronomy columnist Ariz. Daily Star, Tucson, 1984—. Vol. Superior Nat. Forest, Ely, Minn., 1992. Lt. USNR, 1975-77. Mem. Ariz. Med. Assn. (bd. dirs. 1995—), Phi Beta Kappa, Alpha Omega Alpha. Office: St Marys Hosp 1601 W St Marys Rd Tucson AZ 85745

SMITH, MICHAEL VINCENT, surgeon; b. Athens, Ga., Mar. 30, 1957; s. Thomas Allen and Lucile Vivian (Jackson) S.; m. Jeralyn Demetria Scott, July 28, 1979; 1 child, Demetria Joy. BS in Agr., U. Ga., 1979; MD, Med. Coll. of Ga., 1983. Diplomate Nat. Bd. Med. Examiners, Diplomate Am. Bd. Surgery, Am. Bd. Thoracic Surgery. Intern in surgery U. Ky. Med. Ctr., Lexington, 1983-84, resident in surgery, 1984-89, chief resident in gen. surgery, 1988-89; clin. asst. prof. surgery Sch. Medicine Morehouse Coll., Atlanta, 1989-90; assoc. vascular surgeon Midtown Vascular Surgery, Atlanta, 1989-90; attending surgeon Ga. Bapt. Med. Ctr., Atlanta, 1989-90, 96, Crawford Long Hosp. of Emory U., Atlanta, 1989-90, Northlake Regional Med. Ctr./S.W. Cmty. Hosp. and Med., Atlanta, 1989-90; assoc. cardiothoracic surgeon Atlanta Cardiac and Thoracic Surgery Assocs., 1995—; fellow in cardiothoracic surgery Coll. of Medicine Mt. Sinai Med. Ctr., N.Y.C., 1990-91; fellow cardiovascular rsch. U. Mass. Med. Ctr., Worcester, 1991-92, resident cardiothoracic, 1992-95; attending surgeon St. Joseph Hosp., Atlanta, 1996, cardiothoracic surgery chief resident, 1994-95; attending surgeon Piedmont Hosp., Atlanta, 1996, Dunwoody Med. Ctr., Atlanta, 1996, South Fulton Med. Ctr., Atlanta, 1989-90, 96, Southern Regional Med. Ctr., Riverdale, 1996; mem. ICU S.W. Community Hosp., Atlanta, 1989-90; mem. clin. pathway coms. St. Joseph Hosp., 1996, Ga. Bapt. Med. Ctr., 1996. Sunday sch. tchr. 1st African Meth. Episcopal Ch., Athens, Ga., 1975-79, Bethel African Meth. Episcopal Ch., Augusta, Ga., 1980-83, St. Paul African Meth. Episcopal Ch., Lexington, Ky., 1985-89. Sunday sch. tchr. First A.M.E. Ch., Athens, Ga., 1975-79, Bethel African Meth. Episcopal Ch., Augusta, Ga., 1980-83, St. Paul A.M.E. Ch., Lexington, Ky., 1985-89, St. Philip A.M.E. Ch., 1996. Nat. Achievement scholar, 1974; named one of Outstanding Young Men of the Yr., Jaycees, 1983. Mem. ACS (mem. candidate group), AMA, Atlanta Med. Assn., Southeastern Surg. Congres (assoc.), Assn. Acad. Surgery, Soc. Black Acad. Surgeons, Nat. Med. Assn., Mass. Med. Soc., Am. Heart Assn. (affiliate in tng.), Am. Coll. Cardiology, NAACP (Worchester chpt.), Alpha Phi Alpha. Office: St Joseph Med Ctr Ste 350 5671 Peachtree Dunwoody Rd NE Atlanta GA 30342

SMITH, MICHAEL WILLIAM, biomedical engineer, consultant; b. Hancock, Mich., Mar. 14, 1957; s. Jackson B. and Vivian Elizabeth (Pier) S. AAS in Biomed. Engring., Western Wis. Tech. Coll., 1977; B of Biomed. Engring. Tech., Milw. Sch. Engring., 1983. Registered profl. engr., Wis. Quality engr. GE Med. Sys., Waukesha, Wis., 1984-85, supr., 1985-87, project leader, 1987-91; dir. engring. Miller Med. Sys., Indpls., 1991-93; med. sys. engr. Comdisco Med. Exch., Wood Dale, Ill., 1993—. Pres. Madison Home Owners Assn., Waukesha, 1989-91. Mem. IEEE, NSPE. Office: Comdisco Med Exch 1421 N Wood Dale Rd Wood Dale IL 60191-1078

SMITH, MIKEL DWAINE, physician, educator, researcher; b. Eugene, Oreg., Jan. 3, 1952; s. Charles G. and Helen Jean (Giles) S.; m. Barbara Anne Phillips, June 27, 1980 (div. April 1993); children: Ellen Anne, Benjamin Hatfield; m. Annette Louise Cater, Nov. 19, 1993. BS, Murray (Ky.) State U., 1973; MD Coll. Medicine, U. Ky., Lexington, 1977. Diplomate Nat. Bd. Med. Examiners, Am. Bd. Internal Medicine. Intern in internal medicine Med. Coll. Va., Richmond, 1977-78, resident in internal medicine, 1978-80, fellow in cardiology, 1980-82; instr. in medicine Coll. Medicine U. Ky., Lexington, 1982-83, asst. prof. medicine/cardiology, 1983-87, assoc. prof. medicine/cardiology, 1987-92, prof. medicine/cardiology, 1992—; dir. cardiovascular fellow Coll. Medicine U. Ky., Lexington, 1987—, dir. adult echocardiography, 1989—. Contbg. author 11 books in field; contbr. numerous articles to sci. jours. Recipient Outstanding Tchr. award Am. Coll. Physicians, U. Ky., 1996. Fellow Am. Coll. Cardiology, Am. Heart Assn. (com. on echo 1992-94); mem. Am. Soc. Echocardiography (bd. dirs. 1994—, com. on tng. 1993-95). Methodist. Office: U Ky Coll Medicine L-548 Kentucky Clinic Lexington KY 40536

SMITH, MITCHELL REED, physician, researcher; b. Glen Cove, N.Y., May 7, 1952; s. Lester I. and Meta (Moskowitz) S. BS, Stanford U., 1973; MD, PhD, Case Western Res., 1979. Intern L.I. Jewish Hosp., New Hyde Park, N.Y., 1979-80; resident in pathology Wash. U., St. Louis, 1980-83; resident in medicine Jewish Hosp., St. Louis, 1983-84; fellow med. oncology Meml. Sloan Kettering, N.Y.C., 1984-88; asst. prof. medicine Wayne State U., Harper Hosp., Detroit, 1988-93; mem. dir. lymphoma svc. Fox Chase Cancer Ctr., Phila., 1993—. Mem. AAAS, Am. Soc. of Clin. Oncology (program com.), Am. Soc. Hematology, Am. Assn. of Cancer Rsch. Office: Fox Chase Cancer Ctr 7701 Burholme Ave Philadelphia PA 19111

SMITH, MORTON EDWARD, ophthalmology educator, dean; b. Balt., Oct. 17, 1934. BS, U. Md., 1956, MD, 1960. Bd. cert. Ophthalmology Bd.; lic. physician Mo., Md., Wis. Rotating intern Denver Gen. Hosp., 1960-61; resident, nat. inst. of neurol. diseases and blindness fellow in opthalmology Washington U. Sch. Medicine-Barnes Hosp., 1961-63; NIH spl. fellow in ophthalmic pathology Armed Forces Inst. of Pathology, Washington, 1964; chief resident, instr. ophthalmology Washington U. Sch. Medicine, St. Louis, 1965-66, instr. ophthalmology, 1966-67, asst. prof. ophthalmology and pathology, 1967-69, assoc. prof. ophthalmology and pathology, 1969-75, prof. ophthalmology and pathology, 1975—, asst. dean, 1978-91, assoc. dean, 1991-96, prof. emeritus, assoc. dean emeritus, 1996—; prof. ophthalmology U. Wis., Madison, 1995—; vis. scholar Eye Inst., Columbia Presbyn. Med. Ctr., N.Y.C., 1966; prof./lectr. Montefiore Hosp., Pitts., 1969, U. Ark., 1970, 77, 80, 82, 84, 86, 88, U. Fla., 1972, 81, U. Tex. and Lackland AFB, San Antonio, 1973, U. Colo., 1974, 82, U. Mo., 1974, 79, 80, 88, So. Ill. U., Springfield, 1974, U. Md., 1975, Montreal (Can.) Gen. Hosp., 1975, U. Wis., 1976, 87, 93, U. Pitts., 1977, 83, 87, U. Iowa, 1977, 87, Cleve. Clinic, 1978, Colo. Ophthalmol. Soc., 1978, Brooke Army Hosp., San Antonio, 1979, Wills Eye Hosp., Phila., 1980, USPHS Hosp., San Francisco, 1981, U. Calif., Davis, 1981, Sinai Hosp., Balt., 1985, 89, 94, U. Calif., San Diego, 1985, Tufts U., Boston, 1985, Cornell U., Ithaca, N.Y., 1988, U. Wash., Seattle, 1990, Brown U., Providence, 1990, Vanderbilt U., Nashville, 1991, Duke U., Durham, N.C., 1992; Chandler lectr. Harvard U., 1988; The Lois A. Young-Thomas Meml. lectr. U. Md., 1991; Braley lectr. U. Iowa, 1993; Havener Meml. lectr. Ohio State, 1994. Editor pathology sect.: Perspectives in Ophthalmology, 1977; mem. editl. bd. Ophthalmic Plastic & Reconstructive Surgery, 1986-90; contbr. articles to profl. jours. With USAR M.C., 1958-66. Scholar U. Md., 1958, 59. Fellow Am. Acad. Ophthalmology (ophthalmic pathology com. 1977-83, chmn. ophthalmic com. 1979-83, Honor award for svc. 1981, Sr. Honor award 1992); mem. AMA, Am. Bd. Ophthalmology (diplomate, bd. dirs. 1992—), Assn. for Rsch. in Vision and Ophthalmology (chmn. sect. pathology ann. meeting 1971), Am. Assn. Ophthalmic Pathologists (pres. 1977-80), Assn. Am. Med. Colls. (group med. edn. 1985—), Mo. Med. Assn., Mo. Ophthalmol. Soc., Verhoeff Soc., Theobald Soc., St. Louis Med. Soc., St. Louis Ophthalmol. Soc., Soc. Med. Coll. Dirs. for Continuing Med. Edn., Alpha Omega Alpha (sec.-treas. Wash. U. chpt. 1993—). Office: U Wis Dept Ophthalmology F4/336 CSC 600 Highland Madison WI 53792-3220

SMITH, NELSON F., psychology educator, behavioral consultant; b. Leominster, Mass., Feb. 15, 1937; s. A. Fay and Katherine M. (Sheehan) S.; m. Virginia A. Kotowski, Jan. 27, 1966; children: Kevin J., Beverly A. BA in Psychology, Colgate U., 1959; MA in Psychology, Coll. William and Mary, 1961; PhD in Psychology, Princeton U., 1963. Rsch. assoc. Princeton (N.J.) U., 1964-65; from asst. prof. to assoc. prof. psychology U. R.I., Kingston, 1965-75, prof. psychology, 1975—, chair psychology dept., 1984-90; cons. in field. Contbr. articles to profl. jours. Home: 13 Rose Cir Peace Dale RI 02883-2416 Office: Univ R I 303 Chafee Ctr Kingston RI 02881

SMITH, NOEL WILSON, psychology educator; b. Marion, Ind., Nov. 2, 1933; s. Anthony and Mary Louise (Wilson) S.; m. Marilyn C. Coleman, June 17, 1954; children: Thor and Lance (twins). AB, Ind. U., 1955, PhD, 1962; MA, U. Colo., 1958; 1971-95. Asst. prof. psychology Wis. State U., Platteville, 1962-63; asst. prof. psychology SUNY, Plattsburgh, 1963-66, assoc. prof., 1966-71, prof., 1971-95, prof. emeritus, 1995—. Author: Greek and Interbehavioral Psychology, 1990, rev. edit., 1993, An Analysis of Ice Age Art: Its Psychology and Belief, 1992; co-author: The Science of Psychology: Interbehavioral Survey, 1975; sr. editor: Reassessment in Psychology, 1983; editor: Interbehavioral Psychology newsletter, 1970-77; contbr. articles to profl. jours. Fellow APA; mem. AAUP (pres. SUNY coun. 1980-82), Am. Psychol. Soc., Cheiron Internat. Soc. History of Behavior Sci., Sigma Xi. Home: 7 W Court St Plattsburgh NY 12901-2301 Office: SUNY Dept Psychology Beaumont Hall Plattsburgh NY 12901

SMITH, PAUL HARVEY, pathology educator, researcher; b. Wallasey, Eng., May 27, 1944; s. Arthur James and Vera (Moore) S.; m. Christine Jane Jesson, Jan. 10, 1970; children: David, Suzannah, Tamara, Jeremy. BSc, U. Liverpool, Eng., 1967, BSc in Zoology with honors, 1968, PhD, 1972. Asst. lectr. U. Liverpool, 1968-69, lectr., 1969-74; rsch. fellow Can. Heart Found., London, 1974-75; sr. lectr. in pathology Royal Liverpool Univ. Hosp., 1976—. Co-author: Pathology of the Carotid Body, 1985, Pathology of the Lung, 1988, Diseases of the Human Cartid Body, 1992, Spencer's Pathology of the Lung, 1996. Rsch. grantee N.W. Cancer Rsch. Fund, 1983, Wellcome Trust, 1987, Brit. Heart Found. Mem. Pathol. Soc. Gt. Britain and Ireland. Office: U Liverpool Dept Pathology, PO Box 147, Liverpool L69 3BX, England

SMITH, PAUL JOHN, plastic and reconstructive surgeon, consultant; b. Bangor, Ireland, July 25, 1945; s. John Joseph and Mary Patricia (Maher) S.; m. Anne Westmoreland Snowdon, July 14, 1972; children: Mark, Jaime,

Victoria, Francesca. MB BS, Newcastle (Eng.) U., 1968. Lectr. in anatomy Glasgow (Scotland) U., 1969-71; surgical trainee Western Infirmary, Glasgow, 1971-76; rsch. asst. Dept. of Microsurgery, U. Louisville, 1978; Christine Kleinert Fellow in hand surgery U. Louisville, 1978-79; resident and clin. instr. in plastic surgery Duke U., Durham, N.C., 1979-80; sr. registrar in plastic surgery Mt. Vernon Hosp., London, 1980-82, cons. plastic surgeon, 1982—; cons. plastic surgeon The Hosp. for Sick Children, Great Ormond St., London, 1988—; sec. Royal Soc. of Medicine, London, 1988; editorial com. Jour. of Hand Surgery (British volume), London, 1987-91. Author: Principles of Hand Surgery, 1989; contbr. articles to profl. jours. Mem. rsch. com. Restoration of Appearance and Function Trust Found. Recipient 1st prize resident competition, Am. Assn. of Hand Surgery, Toronto, 1979. Fellow Royal Coll. Surgeons; mem. British Assn. Plastic Surgeons (organizing com. advanced courses plastic surgery, Hayward found. scholarship 1978), British Soc. for Surgery of the Hand (Pulvertaft prize, 1986), British Assn. of Aesthetic Plastic Surgeons. Office: Mt Vernon Hosp, Rickmansworth Rd, Northwood HA6 2RN, England

SMITH, PAULA MARION, urology and medical/surgical nurse; b. Provincetown, Mass., Apr. 2, 1930; d. Manuel V. and Marion V. (Cabral) Raymond; m. George A. Smith, July 2, 1952; children: Steven, Michael, Elizabeth. Diploma in nursing, Quincy (Mass.) City Hosp., 1951; student, Boston Coll., U. S.C. RN, Tex., Kans., Mass. Operating room nurse Richland County Hosp., El Paso, Tex., 1958-62, Hotel Dieu, El Paso, 1962-64, U.S. Army Hosp., Ft. Riley, Kans., 1967-68; splty. head nurse urology unit Cape Cod Hosp., Hyannis, Mass., 1972-1994, Health Ctrl., Orlando, Fla., 1995—; cons. Urologic Nursing Jour. Past editor Uro-Gram. Recipient H. Harrison Hartwell award. Mem. ANA, Assn. Operating Rm. Nurses, Internat. Acad. Nurse Editors, Am. Urologic Assn. Allied (editor Uro-Gram, award New Eng. chpt. 1988).

SMITH, PETER KENELM, psychology educator; b. Chichester, Sussex, Eng., Sept. 23, 1943; s. Kenelm B.S. Smith and Ruth E.B. (Warner) Smith Farrance; m. Christine Clark; children: James, Samuel Robert; m. Helen Alexander Cowie; 1 child, Benjamin Thomas Finlayson. B.A., Oxford U., Eng., 1964; Ph.D., Sheffield U., Eng., 1970. Lectr. dept. psychology U. Sheffield, 1974-83, sr. lectr., 1983-85, reader, 1985-91, prof. 1991-95; prof. dept. psychology Goldsmith's Coll., U. London, 1995—; vis. lectr. Inst. Child Devel., U. Minn., Mpls., 1981, vis. rsch. fellow Sch. Edn. Flinders U., Australia, 1994, Sch. Edn. Chuo U., Tokyo, 1995. Author: The Ecology of Preschool Behaviour, 1980, The Psychology of Grandparenthood, 1991, Practical Approaches to Bullying, 1991, School Bullying: Insights and Perspectives, 1994; also numerous articles in profl. jours., chpts. in books. Editor: Play in Animals and Humans, 1984, Children's Play, 1986, Theories of Theories of Mind, 1996; mem. editorial bd. Brit. Jour. Psychology, 1986-90, Social Devel., 1991—; assoc. editor Internat. Jour. of Behavioral Devel., 1990-95; European editor Ethology and Sociobiology, 1992—. Fellow Brit. Psychol. Soc.; mem. Assn. Child Psychologists and Psychiatrists, Assn. for Study Animal Behavior, Soc. for Research in Child Devel., Soc. for Reproductive and Infant Psychology. Avocations: walking; chess; photography. Office: Goldmiths Coll Dept Psychology, U London, New Cross London SE14 6NW, England

SMITH, QUENTIN TED, child and adolescent psychiatrist; b. Seaford, Del., May 1, 1937; s. Carlton Leo and Elizabeth Mary (Holland) S.; m. Marjorie Patricia McCoy; children: Candace, Jason, Michael. AB, Fisk U., 1961; MD, Howard U., 1967. Diplomate Am. Bd. Psychiatry and Neurology. Caseworker Cook County Dept. Welfare, Chgo., 1962-63; dir. day hosp. Fairhill Mental Health Ctr., Cleve., 1971; asst. prof. psychiatry Case Western Res. U., Cleve., 1973-74; dir. out patient child and adolescent psychiatry Grady Meml. Hosp., Atlanta, 1976-82; assoc. prof. psychiatry Emory U., Atlanta, 1974—; prof. clin. psychiatry Morehouse U. Sch. Medicine, Atlanta, 1978—, dir. 3d and 4th yr. psychiatry clerkships com. biomed. scis., 1990—; assoc. dir. child and adolescent svcs. Ridgeview Inst., Smyrna, Ga., 1982-90, dir. adolescent chem. dependence svcs., 1990-95; dir. child and adolescent svcs. Ridgeview Inst., Smyrna, 1995—; mem. clin. adv. com. Ridgeview Inst., 1990—; mem. residency tng. com. in psychiatry Morehouse Sch. Medicine, bd. dirs. child abuse and prevention; bd. dirs. Cork Inst. for Alcohol Studies. Contbr.: (book) Psychiatric Aspects of Adolescent Chemical Dependence, 1987. Mem. spkrs. bur., comty. involvement com. 100 Black Men of Atlanta, 1987—, read to succeed com., 1994—, anti-violence com.1994—; mem. Ga. Gov.'s Children's Trust Fund Commn., 1990—. Recipient fellowship, Woodrow Wilson, U. Chgo., 1961, Nat. Med. Fellowships, Inc., Howard U., 1963-67. Fellow Am. Psychiat. Assn; mem. Am. Acad. Child and Adolescent Psychiatry, Ga. Psychiatry Physicians Assn., Am. Orthopsychiat. Assn., Am. Assn. Adolescent Psychiatry, Am. Acad. of Psychiatrists in Alcoholism and Addiction, Black Psychiatrists of Am. (pres. Atlanta chpt., mem.-at-large, mem. exec. com.), Nat. Med. Assn., Dirs. of Med. Student Edn. in Psychiatry, Phi Beta Kappa. Democrat. Roman Catholic. Office: Ridgeview Inst 3995 S Cobb Dr Smyrna GA 30080-6342

SMITH, R. STEPHEN, surgeon; b. Russellville, Ark., Nov. 26, 1955; s. Robert Harold and Audra Mae (Hardcastle) S.; m. Nellie Shinmon, Feb. 18, 1989; children: Ryan Michael, Nicole Rieko. BS in Biology, Ark. Tech. U., 1977; MD, U. Ark., 1981. Diplomate gen. surgery and critical care Am. Bd. Surgery. Comdr. USN, 1987-94. Fellow ACS, Southwestern Surg. Congress; mem. Am. Assn. for the Surgery of Trauma, Midwestern Surg. Assn. Office: UKSM-Wichita Dept Surgery 929 N St Francis St Wichita KS 67214

SMITH, RALPH EARL, virologist; b. Yuma, Colo., May 10, 1940; s. Robert C. and Esther C. (Schwarz) S.; m. Sheila L. Kondy, Aug. 29, 1961 (div. 1986); 1 child, Andrea Denise; m. Janet M. Keller, 1988. BS, Colo. State U., 1961; PhD, U. Colo., 1968. Registered microbiologist Am. Soc. Clin. Pathologists. Postdoctoral fellow Duke U. Med. Ctr., Durham, N.C., 1968-70, asst. prof., 1970-74, assoc. prof., 1974-80, prof. virology, 1980-82; prof., head dept. microbiology Colo. State U., Ft. Collins, 1983-88, prof. microbiology, assoc. v.p. rsch., 1989—, interim v.p. rsch., 1990-91, prof. microbiology, assoc. v.p. rsch., 1991—; cons. Bellco Glass Co., Vineland, N.J., 1976-80, Proctor & Gamble Co., Cin., 1985-86, Schering Plough Corp., Bloomfield, N.J., 1987-89. Contbr. articles to profl. jours.; patentee in field. Bd. dirs. Colo. Ctr. for Environ. Mgmt., v.p. for rsch.; mem. pollution prevention adv. bd. Colo. Dept. Pub. Health and Environment; mem. Rocky Mountain U. Consortium on Environ. Restoration, Environ. Inst. Rocky Flats; asst. scoutmaster Boy Scouts Am., Durham, 1972-82, com. mem., Ft. Collins, 1986-91; mem. adminstrv. bd. 1st United Meth. Ch., Ft. Collins. Eleanor Roosevelt fellow Internat. Union Against Cancer 1978-79. Mem. AAAS, Am. Soc. Microbiology, N.Y. Acad. Scis., Am. Soc. Virology, Am. Assn. Immunologists, Am. Assn. Avian Pathologists, Am. Assn. Cancer Rsch., Gamma Sigma Delta. Democrat. Methodist. Home: 2406 Creekwood Dr Fort Collins CO 80525-2034 Office: Colo State U VP Rsch Fort Collins CO 80523

SMITH, RALPH EDWARD, psychology assistant; b. Bellfountaine, Ohio, May 19, 1953; s. Ralph Raymond and Virginia (Picklesimer) S.; m. Melody Lee Welbaum Smith, Sept. 3, 1988. B of Gen. Studies, Ohio U., 1980; MS in Edn., U. Dayton, 1987. Houseparent Roweton Boys Ranch, Chillicothe, Ohio, 1974-86, social worker, 1981-82; employment counselor Ross County Community Action, Chillicothe, 1980-81, 83; social worker Roweton Residential Ctr., Chillicothe, 1986-87; psychology asst. Ross Correctional Inst., Chillicothe, 1988-89, Chillicothe Correctional Inst., State of Ohio, 1989—; pres. H.Y.S. Fed. Credit Union, Chillicothe, 1981-86. Vol. Ross County Community Action, Inc., Chillicothe, 1983-87, commodity distbn. vol. Office: Chillicothe Correctional Inst PO Box 5500 Chillicothe OH 45601-0990

SMITH, RANDALL L., optometry educator; b. Des Moines, Feb. 26, 1954; s. Lowell W. and Lorain E. (Bell) S.; m. Barbara Jean Hajek, June 10, 1986; children: Ellen Marie, Erin Elizabeth, Benjamin Lee. BS in Indsl. Adminstrn., Iowa State U., 1976; AAS in Ophthalmic Dispensing, Ferris State U., 1983, MS in Career and Tech. Edn., 1995. Dispensing optician Soderberg, Inc., St. Paul, 1983-85, customer svc./officer mgr., 1985-87; mgr. The Glasses Pl., Mpls., 1987-89; optical dir. Vision Care Assocs., Aberdeen, S.D., 1989-91; asst. prof. Coll. Optometry Ferris State U., Big Rapids, Mich., 1991—; lectr. in field.; staff trainer Lapeer County Vision Ctrs., Lapeer, Mich., 1994. Recipient cert. of recogiotion Nat. Acad. Opticianry. Home: 15877 Belmont Dr Big Rapids MI 49307 Office: 401 Pennock Hall 410 Pennock Hall 1310 Cramer Cir Big Rapids MI 49307

SMITH, RANDALL NORMAN, orthopedist; b. Hicksville, N.Y., Mar. 1, 1948; s. Lester I. and Meta (Moskowitz) S.; m. Marcia Hope Bluestein, Jan. 23, 1949; children: Todd Adam, Taryn Leigh. BS, Ohio U. 1969; MD, Temple U., 1973. Diplomate Am. Bd. Orthopedics. Intern Einstein Med. Ctr., Phila., 1973-74, orthopedic resident, 1974-78, chief resident, 1976-78, staff physician, 1978—; pvt. practice Phila., 1978—; dir. emergency rm. JFK Hosp., Phila., 1975-79; spkr. in field. Contbr. articles to profl. jours. Bd. dirs. Plymouth Soccer League, Plymouth Twp.hi , Pa., 1986-90; coach Plymouth Baseball and Basketball League, Plymouth Twp., 1982-89; referee Whitemarsh Soccer and Basketball, Lafayette Hill, Pa., 1985-91; mem. golf com. Meadowlands Country Club, Blue Bell, Pa., 1986-93. Recipient Pharmacy Family of Yr., Nat. Assn. Retail Druggists, 1972. Fellow Am. Acad. Orthopedics; mem. Am. Coll. Sports Medicine, Am. Coll. Occupl. Medicine, Ea. Orthopedic Assn., Am. Running and Fitness Assn., Brotherhood of Ami. Jewish. Office: Palmaccio Smith Assoc 12000 Bustleton Ave Philadelphia PA 19116

SMITH, RANDOLPH RELIHAN, plastic surgeon; b. Augusta, Ga., Apr. 13, 1944; s. Lester Vernon and Maxine (Relihan) S.; m. Becky Jo Hardy; children: Katherine, Randolph, Rececca, Michael. BS, Clemson U., 1966; M.D., Coll. Ga., 1970. Intern Bowman Gray Sch. Medicine, Winston-Salem, N.C., 1970-71; resident in surgery and otolaryngology Duke U., Durham, N.C., 1971-75; resident in plastic and reconstructive surgery Med. Coll. Ga., 1975-77; Christine Kleinert fellow in hand surgery U. Louisville, 1977; attending physician Univ. Hosp., Augusta, Ga., 1977—; asst. clin. prof. plastic surgery Med. Coll. Ga., 1978—; pres. med. staff Univ. Hosp., Augusta. Bd. dirs. Ga. Bank and Trust Co. of Augusta, Richmond County Hosp. Authority; vestryman St. Paul's Ch.; trustee Univ. Health, Inc. Served to maj. M.C., U.S. Army, 1971-77. Diplomate Am. Bd. Otolaryngology, Am. Bd. Plastic Surgery. Fellow ACS, Am. Acad. Otolaryngology; mem. Am. Soc. Plastic and Reconstructive Surgeons, Am. Soc. Aesthetic Plastic Surgery, Ga. Soc. Plastic and Reconstructive Surgeons, Southeastern Soc. Plastic and Reconstructive Surgeons. Episcopalian. Clubs: Exchange (bd. dirs.), Augusta Symphony League. Contbr. articles in field to profl. jours. Office: Univ Hosp Med Ctr 811 13th St Bldg # 3 Ste 28 Augusta GA 30901

SMITH, RAYMOND EDWARD, health care administrator; b. Freeport, N.Y., June 17, 1932; s. Jerry Edward and Madelyn Holman (Jones) S.; BS in Edn., Temple U., 1953; MHA, Baylor U., 1966; m. Lena Kathryn Jernigan Hughes, Oct. 28, 1983; children: Douglas, Ronald, Kevin, Doris Jean, Raymond. Commd. 2d lt. U.S. Army, 1953, advanced through grades to lt. col., 1973; helicopter ambulance pilot, 1953-63; comdr. helicopter ambulance units, Korea, 1955, Fed. Republic of Germany, 1961; various hosp. adminstrv. assignments, 1963-73; pers. dir. Valley Forge (Pa.) Gen. Hosp., 1966; adminstr. evacuation hosp., Vietnam, 1967; dep. insp. Walter Reed Gen. Hosp., Washington, 1970; dir. personnel divsn. Office of Army Surgeon Gen., Washington, 1971-73, ret., 1973; adminstr. Health Care Ctrs., Phila. Coll. Osteo. Medicine, 1974-76; dir. bur. hosps. Pa. Dept. Health, Harrisburg, 1976-79; contract mgr. Blue Cross of Calif., San Diego, 1979-88, Cmty. Care Network, San Diego, 1989-95, ret. Decorated Bronze Star, Legion of Merit. Mem. Am. Hosp. Assn., Am. Legion, Ret. Officers Assn., Kappa Alpha Psi. Episcopalian. Club: Masons. Home: 7630 Lake Adlon Dr San Diego CA 92119-2518

SMITH, RAYMOND LEIGH, plastic surgeon; b. Norristown, Pa., Sept. 27, 1940; s. Walter Joseph and Pauline C. (Wolfskill) S.; m. Coralynn Elder, Jan. 8, 1966; children: Susan, Elizabeth, Christine. BS, Ursinus Coll., 1962; MD, Temple U., 1966. Diplomate Nat. Bd. Med. Examiners, Am. Bd. Plastic Surgery. Active staff Reading Hosp., Pa., 1976—, chief sect. of plastic surgery, 1994—, St. Joseph Hosp., Reading, 1976—, Cmty. Gen. Hosp., Reading, 1976—. Mem. ACS, Republican Majority Found., Washington Legal Found. Mem. Am. Soc. Plastic and Reconstructive Surgery, Robert H. Ivy Soc., Am. Assn. Hand Surgery, Northeastern Soc. Plastic Surgeons, Pa. Med. Soc., Lipoplasty Soc. N.Am., Berks County Med. Soc. Lutheran. Office: 926 Penn Ave Wyomissing PA 19610-3017

SMITH, REGINALD BRIAN FURNESS, anesthesiologist, educator; b. Warrington, Eng., Feb. 7, 1931; s. Reginald and Betty (Bell) S.; m. Margarete Groppe, July 18, 1963; children: Corinne, Malcolm. MB, BS, U. London, 1955; DTM and H, Liverpool Sch. Tropical Medicine, 1959. Intern Poole Gen. Hosp., Dorset, Eng., 1955-56, Wilson Meml. Hosp., Johnson City, N.Y., 1962-63; resident in anesthesiology Med. Coll. Va., Richmond, 1963-64; resident in anesthesiology U. Pitts., 1964-65, clin. instr., 1965-66; asst. prof., 1969-71, asso. clin. prof., 1971-74, prof., 1974-78, acting chmn. dept. anesthesiology, 1977-78; prof., chmn. dept. U. Tex. Health Sci. Center, San Antonio, 1978—; anesthesiologist in chief hosps. U. Tex. Health Sci. Ctr., 1978—, med. dir. hyperbaric medicine unit Univ. Hosp., 1993—; dir. anesthesiology Eye and Ear Hosp., Pitts., 1971-76; Univ. Hosp.; anesthesiologist in chief Presbyn. Univ. Hosp., Pitts., 1976-78. Contbg. editor: Internat. Ophthalmology Clinics, 1973, Internat. Anesthesiology Clinics, 1983; contbr. articles to profl. jours. Served to capt. Brit. Army, 1957-59. Fellow ACP, Am. Coll. Anesthesiologists, Am. Coll. Chest Physicians, Am. Coll. Hyperbaric Physicians; mem. AMA, Internat. Anesthesia Rsch. Soc., Am. Soc. Anesthesiologists (pres. Western Pa. 1974-75), Tex. Soc. Anesthesiologists, San Antonio Soc. Anesthesiologists (pres. 1990), Tex. Med. Assn., Bexar County Med. Soc. Home: 213 Canada Verde St San Antonio TX 78232-1104 Office: 7703 Floyd Curl Dr San Antonio TX 78284-6200

SMITH, RICHARD A., physician, educator; b. Norwalk, Conn., Oct. 13, 1932. BS, Howard U., 1953, MD, 1957; MPH, Columbia U., 1960. Diplomat Am. Bd. Preventive Medicine. Intern USPHS Hosp., Seattle, 1957-58; resident L.A. City Health Dept., 1958-59; epidemiologist Wash. State Health Dept., 1960-61; sr. physician Peace Corps, Lagos, Nigeria, 1961-63; asst. prof. dept. preventive medicine Howard U., Washington, 1963-68; assoc. prof., dir. Medex program Sch. Pub. Health and Cmty. Medicine U. Wash., 1968-72; dir. Medex group John A. Burns Sch. Medicine, U. Hawaii, Honolulu, 1972—; Africa regional med. officer med. program divsn. Peace Corps., 1963-64, dep. dir., 1964-65; exec. mgmt. trainee Office Surgeon Gen., 1965-66, spl. asst. dir. Office Internat. Health, 1966, chief Office Planning, 1967, dep. dir. Office Internat. Health, 1967-68; clin. asst. prof. dept. cmty. and internat. health Sch. Medicine Georgetown U., Washington, 1967-68; advisor, U.S. del. WHO, 1967, 70; mem. Internat. Task Force World Health Manpower, 1970, cons., 1977—; adj. prof. family practice and cmty. health U. Hawaii, Honolulu, 1972—; mem. Nat. Adv. Allied Health Profl. Coun., NIH, 1971; bd. dirs. Am. Inst. Rsch. Fellow Am. Coll. Preventive Medicine; mem. Inst. Medicine-NAS, APHA, Am. Soc. Tropical Medicine and Hygiene. *

SMITH, ROBERT FRANK, microscopist, photographer, educator; b. N.Y.C., Mar. 30, 1917; s. William and Barbara Elizabeth (Boesch) S.; m. Jacqueline Louise Brennan, June 20, 1936; children: Gail Smith Miller, Robert Frank (dec.), Wendy Smith Meehan, Gregory J. Student Columbia U., 1936-39; diploma Royal Microscopical Soc., Oxford, Eng., 1977. Registered biol. photographer in medicine and natural sci. Dir. microscopy and biol. photography Brookhaven Nat. Lab., Upton, N.Y., 1947-73; dir. biomed. communication, prof. microscopy, N.Y. State Coll. Vet. Medicine, Cornell U., Ithaca, N.Y., 1973-82, ret., 1982; prof. microscopy and photomicrography, Miner Inst. and SUNY, Plattsburgh, N.Y., 1983—; bd. dirs. for in-vitro cell biology and biotech Plattsburgh U.; cons. C. Zeiss, Thornwood, N.Y., 1953-73, Nikon, Garden City, N.Y., 1975—, Smith Kline and French, Phila., 1955—, Am. Optical Co., Buffalo, 1980—; invited U.S. rep. in microscopy and photomicrography USSR, 1977; mem. Joint Task Force 7, organizer, dir. biol. photography Brookhaven Nat. Lab. med. survey of Marshallese people exposed to Hydrogen Bomb fallout, 1959-69; guest lectr. various univs. U.S. and Europe; Examined microscopically and photographed first moon rocks brought back by Apollo 11, 1969-70; author, condr. course in microscopy Med. Sch., U. Berne, Switzerland, 1970; author: A Practical Guide, 1982, Microscopy and Photomicrography: A Working Manual, 1991, revised 2d edit., 1994; contbr. chpt. to book, articles to profl. jours. including Jour. Biol. Photographic Assn., Am. Lab., Visual Sonic Medicine, Natural History, Functional Photography, Am. Forests, Photographie und Forschung, African Violet Jour., AMA Archives of Ophthalmology; tech. editor Functional Photography, 1976—, (bi-monthly column) Indsl. Photography, 1989—, contbr. bi-monthly column, 1976. With USMC, 1943-45, PTO. Recipient cert. participation in USSR, USIA 1977. Fellow Biol. Photographic Assn. (bd. govs. 1968-70, 4 Charles Foster Meml. Citations, 2 First awards, emeritus status), Royal Microscopial Soc.; mem. Rochester Acad. Sci. (hon.). Roman Catholic. Achievements include development of a microscopical technique for differential color optical staining of living tissue using microfiber optics. Home: 11 Hunter Ln Ithaca NY 14850-9662 Office: Indsl Photography PTN Pub Co 445 Broadhollow Rd Melville NY 11747-3601

SMITH, ROSE ANN, family nurse practitioner, deacon; b. Santa Fe, June 4, 1938; d. William Edward and Rosamond (Koury) McAtee; m. Jon George Fraser, Sept. 28, 1957 (div. Aug. 1965); m. William Burnham Smith, Nov. 18, 1968; children: William Thomas, Jon Sidney, Michael Burns. Diploma in Nursing, Northwest Tex. Sch. Nursing, 1973; BSN, West Tex. State U., 1983; MSN, West Tex. A & M U., 1993. cert. gerontological nursing, family nurse practitioner. Nurses aid, LVN. lab. technician Deaf Smith Gen. Hosp., Hereford, Tex., 1965-75; staff nurse, supr. ICU, WIC, FNP S. Plains Health Providers Orgn., Dimmit and Hereford, Tex., 1975-80; RN team leader St. Anthony's Hosp., Amarillo, Tex., 1981-83; vocat. nursing instr. Amarillo Coll., Hereford, 1983-85; quality assurance coord. Deaf Smith Gen. Hosp., Hereford, 1984-85; clinic mgr., med. provider South Plains Health Providers Orgn., Hereford and Amarillo, 1985—; mem. divsn. of nursing leaders adv. bd. West Tex. A&M, Canyon, Tex., 1992—. Mem. bd. dirs. Panhandle AIDS Support Orgn., 1988-90, United Way, 1990-91, Amarillo Area HIV/AIDS Consortium, 1993—; chair Episcopal AIDS Task Force-Diocese of Northwest, 1988-90. Mem. ANA, Tex. Nurses Assn., Am. Acad. Nurse Practitioners, Tex. Nurse Practitioners, Sigma Theta Tau (Delta Delta chpt.). Episcopalian. Home: 3500 Barclay Amarillo TX 79109 Office: South Plains Health Providers Orgn Inc 200 S Tyler Amarillo TX 79101

SMITH, ROY EUGENE, oncologist; b. Warren, Ohio, July 8, 1946; s. Paul Eugene and Helen Louise (Sillitoe) S.; m. Loretta Marie DiVecchia, Sept. 11, 1981; children: Jesse, Jonathan. BS, Ohio State U., 1969, MD, 1973. Diplomate Am. Bd. Internal Medicine, Am. Bd. Med. Oncology, Am. Bd. Hematology. Intern in med. Ohio State U., Columbus, 1973-74, resident in med., 1974-76, fellowship hematology and oncology, 1976-78, clin. instr. dept. of medicine, 1973-76, asst. prof. medicine, 1978-80, dir. spl. hematology coagulation lab., 1978-80; asst. prof. medicine U. Va. Sch. Medicine, Charlottesville, 1980-81; dir. adult med. oncology clinic U. Va., Charlottesville, 1981-83; investigator Nat. Cancer Inst., 1980—; pvt. practice Zanesville, Ohio, 1983-86; asst. prof. medicine Med. Coll. of Wis., Milw., 1986-87, med. dir. clin. coagulation svc., 1987-90; assoc. prof. clin. internal medicine Ohio State U. Coll. of Medicine, Columbus, 1990-94, dir. hematology tng. program, 1990-94; coord. oncology svcs., divsn. chief hematology and oncology Shadyside Hosp., Pitts., 1994—; admissions com. Med. Coll. of Wis., 1988, exec. com. 1988; mem. head and neck com. S.W. Oncology Group; mem. cancer adv. com. Ohio State U. Comprehensive Cancer Ctr.; cancer com. Shadyside Hosp., autologous bone marrow transplant and peer rev. com., clin. care com., edn. and rsch. com., continuing med. edn. com., utilization rev. com.; presenter in field. Contbr. articles to profl. jours.; reviewer Archives of Internal Medicine, Ob-Gyn. Recipient Rsch. award Ctrl. Ohio Heart Assn., 1979, numerous rsch. grants. Fellow ACP; mem. Am. Soc. of Hematology, Am. Soc. of Clin. Oncology, Am. Heart Assn. (thrombosis coun.), Am. Cancer Soc. (bd. dirs.), Internal Soc. for Preventive Oncology, Inc., Eastern Coop. Oncology Group, Southwestern Oncology Group, Am. Soc. for Apheresis, Va. Leukemia Soc. (bd. dirs.), Muskingum County Cancer Soc. (bd. dirs., Am. Soc. of Clin. Oncology (constitution and by laws com. 1985-86). Home: 105 Deer Run Ln Cheswick PA 15024 Office: Shadyside Hosp 5230 Centre Ave Rm 205 Pittsburgh PA 15232

SMITH, ROY LEONARD, psychology educator, psychotherapist; b. Santa Cruz, Calif.; s. Raymond Woodrow and Nola May (Walker) S.; m. Geraldine Marie Moran; children: Stacy Raeleen, Rebecca Louise, Bruce Edward, Michelle Kathleen. BA, Seattle Pacific U., 1958; postgrad, Fuller Theol. Sem., 1959-60; MEd, Wash. U., St. Louis, 1970, PhD, 1970. Lic. psychologist, N.Y. Asst. min. Fairview Heights Bapt. Ch., Inglewood, Calif., 1959-60; tchr. elem. North Monterey County S.D., Moss Landing, Calif., 1959-60; tchr. Watsonville (Calif.) Union, 1962-63; tchr., counselor Ramey (P.R.) Base Schs., (Dept. of Def.), 1963-64; counselor Tacoma Pub. Schs., 1964-67; instr. psychology Wash. U., 1969-70; asst. prof. Smith Coll., Northampton, Mass., 1970-72; prof. psychology L.I.U., Brookville, N.Y., 1972—; cons. in field; pvt. practice, 1986—. Co-author: Educational Psychology, 1972; contbr. articles to profl. mags. Mem. APA (div. neuropsychology), APA-Psychologists Interested in Religious Issues. Mem. Church of Christ. Home: 1979 Revere Ct Vista CA 92083-9070 Office: CW Post Campus Northern Blvd Brookville NY 11718

SMITH, SAM CORRY, retired foundation executive, consultant; b. Enid, Okla., July 3, 1922; s. Chester Hubbert and Nelle Kate (Corry) S.; m. Dorothy Jean Bank, Sept. 21, 1945; children: Linda Jean, Nancy Kay, Susan Diane. Student, Phillips U., 1940-43; BS in Chemistry, U. Okla., 1947, MS in Chemistry, 1948; PhD in Biochemistry, U. Wis., 1951. Asst. and assoc. prof. U. Okla., Oklahoma City, 1951-55; assoc. dir. grants Research Corp., N.Y.C., 1957-65, dir., 1965-68, v.p. grants, 1968-75; exec. dir. M.J. Murdock Charitable Trust, Vancouver, Wash., 1975-88; foundation cons., 1988—; pres. Pacific Northwest Grantmakers Forum, 1983-84. Contbr. sci. articles to profl. jours. Trustee Nutrition Found., Washington, 1976-84, Internat. Life Scis. Inst., Washington, 1984-86; bd. councilors U. So. Calif. Med. Sch., L.A., 1977-82; mem. adv. com. Coll. Natural Scis. Colo. State U., 1977-80; pres. Cardiopulmonary Rehab. Programs Oreg., 1990-91; bd. dirs. Clark Coll. Found., 1993—. Named Boss of Yr., Am. Bus. Women's Assn., 1982, Bus. Assoc. of Yr., 1983. Fellow AAAS; mem. Am. Chem. Soc. Home: 5204 Dubois Dr Vancouver WA 98661-6617

SMITH, SCOTT PAUL, physician, administrator; b. Tulsa, Jan. 2, 1952; s. William P. and Peggy O. (Taylor) S.; m. Janis Kay Dexter, July 7, 1973; children: Joshua W.D., Joel M.T, Jonathan F.D. BA, U. Calif., San Diego, 1973; MD, U. Calif., Davis, 1977; MPH, U. Ill., 1989. Diplomate Am. Bd. Internal Medicine, Am. Bd. Med. Mgmt., Am. Bd. Preventive Medicine. Med. dir. Maricopa County Health Dept., Phoenix, 1981-85, Health Am. of Ga., Atlanta, 1985-87; assoc. med. dir. Michael Reese Health Plan, Chgo., 1987-89; regional med. dir. Lincoln Nat. Gt. Lakes, Chgo., 1989-91; asst. v.p. Healthcare Compare, Downer's Grove, Ill., 1991—; cons. Joint Commn. on Accreditation of Healthcare Orgns., Chgo., 1987—, Nat. Com. on Quality Assurance, 1991—; v.p., nat. med. dir. Healthcare COMPARE. Mem. Dem. Party, 1980—, Physicians for Social Responsibility, 1985—, Wilderness Soc., 1985—, World Wildlife Fund. With USPHS, 1980-81. Fellow ACP, Am. Coll. Preventive Medicine; mem. Am. Coll. Preventive Medicine, Am. Coll. Physician Execs., Am. Pub. Health Assn., Alpha Omega Alpha, Delta Omega. Evangelical. Office: Healthcare Compare 3200 Highland Ave 747 E 22D St Downer's Grove IL 60515

SMITH, SHELAGH ALISON, public health educator; b. Oak Ridge, Tenn., June 3, 1949; d. Nicholas Monroe and Elizabeth (Kimbrough) S.; m. Milton John Axley, 1991; 1 child, Elizabeth Claire. BS in Edn., U. Tenn., 1971, AS in Dental Hygiene, 1974; MPH in Health Svcs. Adminstrn., Johns Hopkins, 1979. Lic., cert. health edn. specialist, 1989. Social sci. rsch. analyst Dept. Health and Human Svcs., Health Care Fin. Adminstrn., Balt., 1980-85; pub. health educator, evaluator Nat. Cancer Inst.-NIH, Bethesda, Md., 1985-90; sr. policy analyst NIMH, Rockville, Md., 1990-92; pub. health advisor Ctr. Mental Health Svcs., Rockville, Md., 1992—. Recipient adminstr.'s citation Health Care Fin. Adminstrn., 1981, dir.'s award Nat. Cancer Inst., 1989; Gen. Alumni scholar U. Tenn., 1973. Mem. APHA (pub. health edn. sect., chmn. fin. and reimbursement for prevention svcs. com. 1987-89, 96), Md. Pub. health Assn. (governing coun. 1996—, membership chmn. 1980, treas. 1981), Md. Women's Health Coalition, Planned Parenthood Md., Soc. Pub. Health Edn. (governing bd. and ho. of dels. 1993-95, legis. co-chmn. 1990-91, nat. capital area exec. bd., profl. devel. chair 1996, chpt. pres. 1996-97), Phi Kappa Phi. Democrat. Home: 14106 Heathfield Ct Rockville MD 20853-2760 Office: SAMHSA Ctr Mental Health Svc 5600 Fishers Ln Rockville MD 20857-0001

SMITH, SHELDON LEROY, health care executive; b. Ithaca, N.Y., Nov. 25, 1942; s. Charles Leroy and Doris Irene (Milliken) S.; 1 child, Laura Lee. BA, Princeton U., 1964; MBA, Cornell U., 1966. V.p., dir. Vari-Care,

Inc., Rochester, N.Y., 1969-85; founder, pres. Sr. Living Svcs., Austin, Tex., 1985—; Lectr. Cornell Hotel Sch., Ithaca Coll., Hilton Coll. of Hotel and Restaurant Mgmt., Houston, SUNY, Utica; panelist Sch. of Arch., Auburn, Ala. 1st lt. U.S. Army, 1966-69. Mem. Am. Assn. of Homes for the Aging, Am. Health Care Assn., Nat. Multi Housing Assn. Home and Office: 1103 Challenger Austin TX 78734-3801

SMITH, STAFFORD MICHAEL, cardiologist; b. Wilkes-Barre, Pa., Nov. 1, 1956; s. Joseph Hyman and Libby (Leibman) S.; m. Mary Rose Anne Salerno, Mar. 26, 1988; children: Noah Meyer, Tiffany Tiana. BA, U. S. Fla., 1981; MD, St. George's U., 1985. Diplomate Am. Bd. Internal Medicine, Cardiovascular Disease. Intern NE Pa. Affiliated Hosp., Wilkes-Barre, 1986-87; resident Presbyn./U. Pa. Med. Ctr., Phila., 1987-89; fellow Phila. Heart Inst., 1989-91, Med. Coll. Va., Richmond, 1991-92; cardiologist Blair Med. Assocs., Altoona, Pa., 1992-93, Giamber, Dale & Smith, Bethlehem, Pa., 1993—; clin. instr. U. Pa., Phila., 1987-91, Med. Coll. Va., Richmond, 1991-92; clin. asst. prof. Temple U., Phila., 1994; attending physician Albert Einstein Med. Ctr., Phila., 1989-91, Presbyn. Med. Ctr., Phila., 1987-91, Med. Coll. Va. Hosp., Richmond, 1991-92, Altoona Hosp. Ctr. for Medicine, 1992-93, Allegheny Family Physicians Residency Program, 1992-93, St. Luke's Hosp. Internal Medicine Residency Program, 1993—, Muhlenberg Hosp. Ctr., Bethlehem, 1993—. Contbr. articles to profl. jours. Fellow ACP, Am. Coll. Cardiology, Am. Coll. Chest Physicians, Am. Coll. Angiology, Am. Heart Assn. (sci. coun. clin. cardiology); mem. Am. Soc. Cardiovascular Interventionists, Soc. Cardiac Angiography and Interventions. Home: 504 Eagle Dr Emmaus PA 18049-1929 Office: Giamber Dale & Smith 618 Delaware Ave Bethlehem PA 18015-1134

SMITH, STEPHEN BRENT, surgeon; b. Madison, Wis., Nov. 29, 1950; s. Vearl Robert and Ramona Irene (Yearsley) S.; m. Jan Christiansen, Feb. 15, 1974; children: Elliot Christiansen, Alexander Judson, Audrey Elizabeth, Mitchell Stephen, Quentin Christiansen. BA, U. Utah, 1974; MD, George Washington U., 1978. Diplomate Am. Bd. Surgery, Am. Bd. Colon and Rectal Surgery. Surgeon U.S. Army M.C., 1978-90, Salt Lake Clinic, Sandy, Utah, 1990—. Lt. col. U.S. Army, 1978-90. Fellow ACS; mem. Am. Soc. Colon and Rectal Surgeons. Mormon. Office: Salt Lake Clinic-Sandy 9500 S 1300 E Sandy UT 84094

SMITH, STEPHEN ROSS, physician; b. Iowa City, Iowa, Mar. 5, 1938; s. Wendell Ross and Ruth Anne (Frudenfeld) S.; m. Elaine Cashman Frazier, July 4, 1964 (div. Dec. 1990); children: Julia Helene, Stuart Ross; m. Regina Alilada Clarito, Dec. 26, 1990; 1 child, Alexander Ross. AB, Princeton U., 1959; MD, Harvard Med. Sch., 1963. Instr. medicine Johns Hopkins U. Sch. Medicine, Balt., 1970-72, asst. prof. medicine, 1972-73, 82—; chief endocrinology Kern County Hosp., Bakersfield, Calif., 1973-76; assoc. prof. medicine Tex. Tech. U. Sch. Medicine, El Paso, 1977-80; chief medicine Thomason Gen. Hosp., El Paso, 1977-80, Bon Secours Hosp., Balt., 1980-83, Security Forces Hosp., Riyadh, Saudi Arabia, 1984-88; physician internal medicine, endocrinology pvt. practice, Balt., 1988—; med. dir. Nat. Clin. Rsch. Ctrs., Bethesda, 1988-93; rsch. assoc. Johns Hopkins Ctr. Med. Rsch. and Tng., Calcutta, India, 1970-72; bd. dirs. El Paso Diabetes Assn., 1978-80; cons. Liberty Med. Ctr. Diabetes Mgmt. Ctr., Balt., 1991—, pharm. industry, 1993—; pres. med. staff Deaton Hosp., Balt., 1996. Contbr. articles to profl. jours. Capt. USAF, 1965-67. Fellow Am. Coll. Physicians; mem. Am. Diabetes Assn., Am. Fedn. Clin. Rsch., Princeton Club Md., Hampton Swim Club. Republican. Home: 1104 Temfield Rd Baltimore MD 21286-1648 Office: 8709 Harford Rd Baltimore MD 21234-4607

SMITH, STEVEN SIDNEY, molecular biologist; b. Idaho Falls, Idaho, Feb. 11, 1946; s. Sidney Ervin and Hermie Phyllis (Robertson) S.; m. Nancy Louise Turner, Dec. 20, 1974. BS, U. Idaho, 1968; PhD, UCLA, 1974. Asst. research scientist Beckman Research Inst. City of Hope Nat. Med. Ctr., Duarte, Calif., 1982-84, staff Cancer Ctr., 1983—, asst. research scientist depts. Thoracic Surgery and Molecular Biology, 1985-87, assoc. research scientist, 1987-95; rsch. sci. Beckman Research Inst. City of Hope Nat. Med. Ctr., Duarte, 1995—; rsch. scientist City of Hope Nat. Med. Ctr., 1995—; dir. dept. cell and tumor biology Beckman Research Inst. City of Hope Nat. Med. Ctr., Duarte, Calif., 1990—; Wellcome vis. prof. medicine Okla. State U., 1995-96; cons. Molecular Biosystems Inc., San Diego, 1981-84, Am. Inst. Biol. Scis., Washington, 1994. Contbr. articles to profl. jours. Grantee NIH, 1983-93, Coun. for Tobacco Rsch., 1983-92, March of Dimes, 1988-91, Smokeless Tobacco Rsch. Coun., 1992—, Office of Naval Rsch., 1994—; Swiss Nat. Sci. Found. fellow U. Bern, 1974-77, Scripps Clinic and Rsch. Found., La Jolla, Calif., 1978-82, NIH fellow Scripps Clinic, 1979-81. Mem. Am. Soc. Cell Biology, Am. Assn. Cancer Rsch., Am. Crystallographic Assn., Am. Chem. Soc., Am. Weightlifting Assn., Phi Beta Kappa. Office: City of Hope Nat Med Ctr 1500 Duarte Rd Duarte CA 91010-3012

SMITH, STEVEN SPENCER, osteopath, health facility administrator; b. Phila., Oct. 13, 1947; s. Selden Emerson and Marjorie Louise (Pittman) S.; m. Nicolette Joy Dukes, July 14, 1972; 1 child, Brandon Christopher. BA in Biology, Austin Coll., 1969; DO, U. Health Scis., 1973. Diplomate Am. Bd. Osteopathic Internal Medicine. Intern Detroit Osteopathic Hosp., Highland Park, Mich., 1973-74; resident Univ. Health Scis., Kansas City, Mo., 1974-77, assoc. prof. internal medicine, 1977-85; from chief medicine to internist Group Health Plan, St. Louis, 1986-95; med. dir. Horizon Health Systems, Taylor, Mich., 1995—. Mem. Am. Osteo. Assn., Am Coll. Osteo. Internists. Democrat. Office: Horizon Family Health Ctr 8790 S Telegraph Rd Taylor MI 48180

SMITH, S(TEWART) GREGORY, ophthalmologist, inventor, product developer, consultant, author; b. Wyandotte, Mich., Jan. 24, 1953; s. Stewart Gene and Veronica (Latta) S. BA in Econs. with distinction, U. Mich., 1974; MD, Wayne State U., 1978. Diplomate Am. Bd. Ophthalmology, Nat. Bd. Med. Examiners. Intern, Sacred Heart Med. Ctr., Spokane, Wash.,1978; resident in ophthalmology U. Minn., Mpls., 1979-82, fellow cornea and anterior segment surgery, 1982-83; practice medicine specializing in cornea and anterior segment surgery, and ophthalmology Wilmington, Del., 1983—; clin. prof. ophthalmology U. Pa., Hershey Med. Ctr., 1984—; clin. asst. prof. Thomas JeffersonU.; attending surgeon Wills Eye Hosp., Phila., 1984—; mem. sr. faculty 3M Vision Care Dept., Mpls., 1984-90, rsch. cons., 1984, lectr., 1983—, cons. Am. Cyanamid Opthalmic Divsn., 1990-94, Am. Home Product, 1995—; lectr. in field, Korea, Hong Kong, Thailand, Malaysia, Phillipines, France, Spain, Ireland, Portugal, Holland, Denmark, England; cons. Am. Home Products, 1995—. Author: Complications ofIntraocular Lenses and Their Management, 1988; co-author: Vision Without Glasses, 1990, Sight for Life, 1990, Can You Really See Clearly Without Glasses, 1996; contbr. articles to Fly Fisherman Mag. and other profl. publs. Patentee investigational devices and pharmaceutical, tilt control for automotive vehicles. Recipient award for Best Sci. Poster, Contact Lens Assn. of Ophthalmologists, 1980; Best Film award Internat. Congress of Cataract Surgeons, 1985; Grand Prize Am. Soc. Cataract and Refractive Surgeons Film Festival, 1986. Fellow Am. Intraocular Implant Soc., Castroviejo Soc. (Best Paper award 1984), AMA, Eye Bank Assn. Am., Am. Soc. Cataract and Refractive Surgery Internat. Soc. Refractive Surgery, Am. Acad. Ophthalmology, Assn. for Rsch. and Vision in Ophthalmology, Internat. Intraocular Implant Club, Wills Eye Hosp. Alumni Soc., European Soc. Cataract & Refracture Soc. Avocations: fly fishing, hunting, saxophone, tennis, skiing. Home: Nine Gates Rd Yorklyn DE 19736 Office: 1100 N Grant Ave Wilmington DE 19805-2670

SMITH, SUSAN ANN, nursing educator; b. Newport, Ark., Mar. 24, 1953; d. Thomas Vernon and Helen (Huie) Wise; m. David Bruce Smith; children: Bryan, Chad. BS in Nursing, U. Central Ark., 1975; MS in Nursing U. Cen. Ark., 1987. Registered nurse practitioner, JArk. Office nurse Smith Clinic, Bradford, Ark., 1975-76; team leader psychiatry Bapt. Med. Ctr., Little Rock, 1976-78, instr. Sch. Practical Nursing, 1978-79; infection control nurse Central Ark. Gen. Hosp., Searcy, 1979-81, tng. and devel. coordinator, 1981-86; instr. nursing Harding U., 1985-89; instr. nursing med. scis. U. Ark., 1989-90; dept. chair, assoc. prof. Ark. State U., Beebe, 1990-94, asst. prof. Ark. State U., Jonesboro; mem. governing bd. Am. Med. Internat. Ctrl. Ark. Hosp.; bd. dirs. Rape Crisis White County, ArLeague for Nursing, 1993—; bd. trustees Ctrl. Bapt. Coll.; mem. adv. coun. for drug free schs. and coms. Wilbur Mills Edn. Svc. Coop. Recipient Acad. Excellence award Dept. Nursing U. Cen. Ark., 1987, Outstanding Rsch. award Sigma Theta Tau Epsilon Omicron, 1989. Mem. Gamma Beta Phi, Sigma Theta Tau. Baptist. Avocations: crocheting, counted cross stitching, water sports, family activities. Home: PO Box 116 Searcy AR 72145-0116

SMITH, TERRI BURDO, quality improvement administrator; b. Carbondale, Pa., Oct. 13, 1956; d. Michael R. and Mary T. (Voinski) Burdo; m. Thomas P. Smith, May 19, 1984; 1 child, Sydney. BSN, Wilkes U., 1978; MS, Coll. Misericordia, 1984. RN, Pa. Surg. and office nurse Chest & Cardiovascular Assoc., Scranton, Pa.; house supr., charge nurse VA Med. Ctr., Wilkes-Barre, Pa.; mgr. adult psychiatry 1st Hosp. Wyoming Valley, Wilkes-Barre, Pa., dir continuous quality improvement, risk mgr.; dir. quality improvement cmty. counseling svcs. Behavioral Healthcare Integrated Delivery Sys., 1995—; cons. in field. Contbr. articles to profl. jours. Bd. dirs. Victim's Resource Ctr., Wilkes-Barre; alt. mem. Com. to Improve Women's Health in the Wyoming Valley. Mem. NAFE, Nat. League for Nursing, N.E. Pa. Quality Assurance Profls., Am. Bus. Women's Assn. (Community Woman of Yr. award 1989), Nat. Assn. Med. Staff Svcs., Nat. Assn. Quality Assurance Profls., Jr. League of Wilkes-Barre. Home: 268 Reynolds St Wilkes Barre PA 18704-5244

SMITH, THEODORE ROOSEVELT, JR., psychologist; b. Wheeler County, Ga., Apr. 20, 1943; s. Theodore Roosevelt Sr. and Nedora (Williams) S.; m. Bernice Swiggett, Aug. 19, 1966; children: Theodore R. III, Michael A., Samuel W., Tamela M., Christopher I. BS in Bus. Mgmt., Hampton U., 1971; MS in Guidance and Counseling, Ea. Ill. U., 1975; EdS, Ball State U., 1978; D in Psychology, Wright State U., 1982; postgrad., Iowa U. Lic. psychologist, Fla., Ill.; cert. hypnotist Nat. Bd. Hypnosis, 1994. Aircraft mechanic, maintenance officer USAF, 1963-78; social action/drug counselor USAF, Hahn, Germany, 1978; clin. psychologist USAF, 1980-84; pvt. practice Macon, Jay, Ga., Fla., 1984—. Mem. APA, Am. Soc. Clin. Hypnosis, Fla. Psychol. Assn., Nat. Registry, Masons (3d degree, 32d degree). Baptist. Home: 1063 Foxmeadow Trl Middleburg FL 32068 Office: Psychol Assessment and Treatment Ctr 5038 San Juan Ave Jacksonville FL 32068

SMITH, THOMAS HUNTER, ophthalmologist, ophthalmic plastic and orbital surgeon; b. Silver Creek, Miss., Aug. 10, 1939; s. Hunter and Wincil (Barr) S.; m. Michele Ann Campbell, Feb. 27, 1982; 1 child, Thomas Hunter IV. BA, U. So. Miss., 1961; MD, Tulane U., 1967; BA in Latin Am. Studies, Tex. Christian U., 1987, MA in Latin Am. History, 1995. Diplomate Am. Bd. Ophthalmology. Intern Charity Hosp., New Orleans, 1967-68; resident in ophthalmology Tulane U., New Orleans, 1968-71; dir., sec. bd. dirs. Ophthalmology Assocs., Ft. Worth, 1971—; clin. prof. Tex. Tech. U. Med. Sch., Lubbock, 1979—; bd. examiners Am. Bd. Ophthalmology, 1983-90; guest lectr., invited speaker numerous schs., confs., symposia throughout N.Am., Ctrl. Am., South Am., Europe and India; hon. mem. ophthalmology dept. Santa Casa de São Paulo Med. Sch. Contbr. articles to profl. jours. Cons. ophthalmologist Helen Keller Internat.; deacon South Hills Christian Ch.; mem. Rocky Mountain Coun. Latin Am. Studies. Recipient Tex. Chpt. award Am. Assn. Workers for the Blind, 1978, Recognition award Lions Club Sight & Tissue Found., Cen. Am., 1977-79; named to Alumni Hall of Fame U. So. Miss., 1989. Fellow ACS, Am. Acad. Ophthalmology (bd. counsellors 1995—), Am. Acad. Facial Plastic and Reconstructive Surgery; mem. Tex. Med. Assn. (com. socio-econs.), Pan-Am. Assn. Ophthalmology (adminstr. 1988-93, bd. dirs. 1993—), Internat. Cos. Cryosurgery, Royal Soc. Medicine (affiliate), Tex. Soc. Ophthalmology and Otolaryngology, Peruvian Ophthalmol. Soc. (hon.), Santa Casa De São Paulo (hon. assoc.), Tex. Ophthalmol. Assn. (past mem. exec. coun., treas.), Tex. Med. Assn., Tarrant County Med. Soc., Byron Smith Ex Fellows Assn., Tarrant County Multiple Sclerosis Soc. (past pres.), Tarrant County Assn. for Blind, Tulane Med. Alumni Assn. (bd. dirs.), S.Am. Explorers Club, Colonial Country Club, Petroleum Club Ft. Worth, Sigma Xi, Omicron Delta Kappa. Mem. Disciples of Christ. Office: Ophthalmology Assocs 1201 Summit Ave Fort Worth TX 76102-4413

SMITH, THOMAS WILLIAM DAVID, orthopedic surgeon; b. Haltemprice, Yorkshire, Eng., Aug. 4, 1939; s. George Ernest and Dora (Staniforth) S.; m. Christina Mary O'Connor, Nov. 25, 1967; children: Nicholas, Gillian, Thomas, Alexandra, Hugh. BA, U. Cambridge, Eng., 1960, MA, 1963, M.B.B.Ch., 1963. Resident St. Mary's Hosp., London, 1963-67; registrar Nuffield Orthopaedic Ctr., Oxford, Eng., 1968-69; sr. registrar United Sheffield Hosps., 1969-73; pvt. practice Sheffield, 1976—; cons. Sheffield Hosp., 1976—. Editor The Foot Jour., 1992—. Fellow Royal Coll. Surgeons Edinburgh, Royal Coll. Surgeons; mem. South Yorkshire Medico-Legal Soc. (pres. 1995-96). Home: 3 Whitworth Rd, Sheffield S10 3HD, England Office: Northern General Hospital, Herries Rd, Sheffield S5 7AU, England

SMITH, THOMAS WOODWARD, cardiologist, educator; b. Akron, Ohio, Mar. 29, 1936; s. Luther David and Beatrice Pearl (Woodward) S.; m. Sherley Louise Goodwin, Sept. 13, 1958; children: Julia Goodwin, Geoffrey Woodward, Allison Lloyd. A.B., Harvard U., 1958, M.D., 1965. Diplomate: Am. Bd. Internal Medicine; Am. Bd. Cardiovascular Diseases. Intern in medicine Mass. Gen. Hosp., Boston, 1965-66, asst. resident in medicine, 1966-67, clin. and research fellow in cardiology, 1967-69, Nat. Heart and Lung Inst. spl. fellow, 1969-71, asst. in medicine, 1969-72, assoc. program dir. myocardial infarction research unit, 1972-74, asst. physician, 1972-77, cons. in medicine, 1977—; asst. prof. medicine Harvard U. Med. Sch., 1971-73, assoc. prof., 1973-79, prof., 1979—; physician Peter Bent Brigham Hosp. (now Brigham and Women's Hosp.), Boston, chief cardiovascular div.; cons. in cardiology Children's Hosp. Med. Ctr. and Sidney Farber Cancer Inst. (now Dana-Farber Cancer Inst.); prof. medicine MIT div. Health Scis. and Tech.; Hall vis. prof., Sydney, Australia, 1977; Sir Henry Hallett Dale vis. prof. Johns Hopkins U. Med. Sch., 1979; Nahum lectr. Yale U. Sch. Medicine, 1979. Reviewer med. jours.; contbr. articles to profl. publs. Mem. Am. Heart Assn. (council clin. cardiology, council basic sci., council on circulation, established investigator 1971-76 Rosenthal award), Am. Fedn. Clin. Research, Paul Dudley White Soc., AAAS, Am. Soc. Pharmacology and Exptl. Therapeutics, Am. Soc. Clin. Investigation, Am. Coll. Cardiology, ACP, Assn. Univ. Cardiologists, Am. Physiol. Soc., Assn. Am. Physicians, Soc. Gen. Physiologists, Alpha Omega Alpha. Home: 128 Wellesley St Weston MA 02193-1555 Office: Brigham and Women's Hosp 75 Francis St Boston MA 02115-6110

SMITH, V. ROY, neurosurgeon; b. N.Y.C., Feb. 12, 1943; s. Leslie Ewart and Vera (Dlosh) S.; m. Elizabeth Kay Bartlett, June 12, 1971; children: Rebecca L., Adam L., Andrew R. BA, Ohio State U., 1964, MD, 1967. Diplomate Am. Bd. Neurol. Surgeons. Ptnr. Fresno Neurol. Med. Group, Calif., 1975—; pres. med. staff St. Agnes Hosp., Fresno, Calif., 1987-89, chief of surgery, 1983-85, chmn. div. neurosurgery, 1993-95. Lt. U.S. Navy, 1969-71, Vietnam. Fellow Am. Bd. Neurol. Surgeons, Am. Coll. Surgeons, Am. Assn. Neurol. Surgeons. Home: 2627 E Birch Ave Clovis CA 93611 Office: Fresno Neurosurg Med Group 6137 N Thesta Ave #103 Fresno CA 93710

SMITH, VIVIAN LOUISE, substance abuse prevention professional, social worker; b. Tampa, Fla., Oct. 4, 1931; d. Oliver and Janie (Peterson) Clark; m. Julius L. Smith Sr., Oct. 4, 1952 (div.); children: Julius L. Jr., Michael E. BA, Ohio State U., 1951; MSW, Cath. U. Am., 1960. Lic. and cert. social worker. Social worker, supr. social svcs. dept. St. Elizabeths Hosp., Washington, 1960-69, dir. cmty. liaison and pub. edn. Area D Cmty. Mental Health Ctr., 1969-73, acting dep. dir., 1973, dep. dir., 1973-74, acting dir., 1974-78, dir., 1978-87; cmty. coord. mental health sys, reorganization office Dept. Human Svcs., Washington, 1984-87; dep. dir. office substance abuse prevention/office adminstr., alcohol, drug abuse and mental health adminstr. PHS, Rockville, Md., 1987-92, acting dir., 1992-94; dep. dir. Ctr. Substance Abuse Prevention, Substance Abuse and Mental Health Svcs. Adminstrn., Washington, 1992—; lectr. nursing St. Elizabeths Hosp., 1963-66, Cath. U. Sch. Nursing, 1964-66; with The Washington Sch. Psychiatry, 1972-75, Met. Mental Health Skills Ctr., 1973-74; chairperson D.C. Bd. Social Work, 1987-94. Bd. dirs. Frederick Douglas Meml. and Hist. Assn., 1973—, also trustee, treas., pres., Frederick Douglas Housing Corp., Washington, 1975-82; active Mt. Moriah Bapt. Ch., Washington, also past asst. supt. Sunday sch., deptl. supt. and tchr., deptl. supt. and tchr. Vacation Bible sch., chair various coms. and programs. With USAF, 1951-53. Recipient Appreciation cert. City of Washington, 1973, Greater Southeast Ctr. for Aging, 1982, Mental Health award Delta Sigma Theta, 1976, Kiwanis Club, 1977, Outstanding Svc. award Washington Area D Coun. on Alcoholism and Drug Abuse, 1977, Frederick Douglas Meml. and Hist. Assn., 1981, Cmty. Svc. award East of River Health Assn., 1980, Good Neighbor award Congress Heights Civic Assn., 1981, Dedicated Svc. award Vols. in Edn., 1981, Disting. Svc. award Nat. Coun. Cmty. Mental Health Ctrs., 1982, Vol. award DHHS, 1982, Outstanding and Dedicated Svc. award Frederick Douglas Housing Corp., 1982, Meritorious Contbn. award Middletown Jaycees, 1988, LeBaron D. Brazier Cmty. Svc. award D.C. Bd. Social Work, 1990, Presdl. Rank awards 1990, 92, 95, Disting. Rank award Sr. Execs. Assn., 1995. Mem. NASW (lifetime achievement award 1996), Am. Coll. Mental Health Adminstrn. (treas. membership com., chair ann. meeting, pres.-elect, pres. 1994), Am. Cancer Soc. (bd. dirs. D.C. divsn. 1977-83, asst. sec. 1979-82, sec. 1982-83, S.E. unit, pres., chairperson income devel. and crusade, Outstanding Leadership award 1981, Disting. Svc. to Cause of Cancer award 1982, Charles E. Qualls award 1985, Edward F. Bartlet award 1986, Appreciation award 1990), Nat. Conf. Social Workers, Med. Soc. St. Elizabeths,. Home: 3523 Carpenter St SE Washington DC 20020-2335 Office: Ctr for Substance Abuse Prevention 5600 Fishers Ln Rockville MD 20857-0001

SMITH, W. JAMES, health facility administrator; b. Shenandoah, Iowa, Mar. 26, 1942; s. Willis C. and Lois M. (Hurst) S.; m. Sharon E. Hogue, May 4, 1940; children: Sharon Wendy, W. James II, Stacey E. BA in Psychology, Nat. Coll. Kansas City, 1960; MA in Psychology, Gerontology, John F. Kennedy U., 1969. Lic. nursing home adminstr., Fla., Iowa, Nebr., Calif. Pres. Retirement Svcs., Oakland, Calif., 1966-77; adminstr. Good Samaritan Soc., Sioux Falls, S.D., 1977-80; pres. Good Shepherd Ctrs., Palm Harbor, Fla., 1980-84; program coord. Hospice of Fla. Suncoast, Inc., Largo, Fla., 1984-91; pres., CEO Alzheimer's Ctrs., Inc., 1991—. Home: 491 Willow Ln Palm Harbor FL 34633

SMITH, WAYNE THOMAS, healthcare company executive; b. 1946. BS, Auburn Univ, 1968, MS, 1969; M in hosp. adminstrn., Trinity U.; postgrad., King's Fund Coll. Hosp. Adminstrn. With Trinity Univ, 1971-73; with Humana Inc, Louisville, 1973—, v.p. ctrl. hosp. region, 1978-80, sr. v.p., 1980-85, exec. v.p., 1985-86, pres., COO group health divsn., 1986—, also bd. dirs.; exec. v.p. Humana Health Care Ops., Louisville, 1991—; exec. v.p. health plan ops., bd. dirs. Humana Health Plan, Inc., Louisville; pres. Humana Health Ins. Nev., Inc., Humana Health Plan Fla., Inc., Humana Health Plan Ohio, Inc., Humana Health Chgo. Ins. Co., Humana Kansas City, Inc.; pres., COO Humana Health Plan Tex., Prime Health Mgmt. Svcs.; pres., bd. dirs. HMPK, Inc. Bd. dirs. Gov.'s Scholars Program, Ky., Actors Theatre of Louisville, Ky. Ctr. for the Arts, The Louisville Orchestra; bd. overseers U. Louisville; mem. exec. com. Greater Louisville Fund for the Arts; past chair bd. dirs. Louisville Collegiate Sch. With U.S. Army, 1969-73, capt., 1973. Mem. Group Health Assn. Am. (bd. dirs.), Health Ins. Assn. Am. (bd. dirs.). Office: Humana Inc 500 W Main St Ste 1438 Louisville KY 40202-2946

SMITH, WILBUR LAZEAR, radiologist, educator; b. Warwick, N.Y., Oct. 11, 1943; s. Wilbur and Betty (Norris) S.; m. Rebecca Rowlands, June 19, 1965; children: Jason, Daniel, Joanna, Noah, Ethan, Jacob. BA, SUNY-Buffalo, 1965, MD, 1969. Diplomate Am. Bd. Radiology, Am. Bd. Pediatrics. Intern, then resident Buffalo Children's Hosp., 1969-71; resident in pediatric radiology Cin. Gen. and Children Hosp., 1971-74; asst. prof. pediatrics and radiology Ind. U., Indpls., 1975-78, assoc. prof., 1978-80, acting dir. pediatric radiology, 1979-80; assoc. prof. U. Iowa, Iowa City, 1980-82, prof., 1982—, dir. med. edn. radiology, 1980-86, vice chmn. dept. radiology, 1986-94, interim head, 1994-96, dir. pediatric radiology, 1980-92. Contbr. articles to profl. jours. Served with USAR, 1969-77. Assoc. editor Gastrointestinal Imaging in Pediatrics, Acad. Radiology, 1992—. Soccer coach Iowa City Kickers, 1980—; mem. equity adv. com. Iowa City Sch. Bd., 1983-87. Recipient Merke Prize Medicine award SUNY, 1968, Wurlitzer Prize Medicine SUNY, 1968. Fellow Am. Acad. Pediatrics, Am. Coll. Radiology; mem. AMA, Iowa Radiol. Soc. (pres. 1987-88), Assn. Univ. Radiologists (pres. 1995-96), Soc. Pediat. Radiology (treas. 1995—). Mem. Soc. Friends. Avocation: photography. Home: 2271 Cae Dr Iowa City IA 52246-4515 Office: U Iowa Dept Radiology Iowa City IA 52242

SMITHIES, OLIVER, geneticist, educator; b. Halifax, Eng., June 23, 1925; naturalized citizen; PhD in Biochemistry, Oxford U., Eng., 1951. Postdoctoral fellow phys. chemistry U. Wis., Madison, 1951-53, from asst. prof. to prof. genetics and med. genetics, 1960-63, Leon J. Cole prof., 1971-80, Hilldale prof., 1980-88; rsch. asst., assoc. Connaught Med. Rsch. Lab., Toronto, Can., 1953-60; Excellence prof. pathology U. N.C., Chapel Hill, 1988—; mem. nat. adv. med. sci. coun. NIH, 1985. Contbr. articles to profl. jours. Recipient William Allen Meml. award Am. Soc. Human Genetics, 1964, Karl Landsteiner Meml. award Am. Assn. Blood Banks, 1984, Internat. award Gairdner Found., 1990, 93, State of N.C. award, 1994, Alfred P. Sloan Jr. prize, 1994; Markle scholar, 1961. Fellow AAAS; mem. NAS, Am. Acad. Arts & Sci., Genetics Soc. Am. (v.p. 1974, pres. 1975). Office: Univ of N C Dept Pathology Chapel Hill NC 27599-7525

SMITHKEY, JOHN, III, public health nurse, consultant; b. Akron, Ohio, Nov. 14, 1953; s. John C. and Catherine V. (Ennis) S.; m. Kathleen Ann Cuenot, Apr. 9, 1994. BS in Edn., U. Akron, 1977, BS in Nursing, 1988; Med. Lab. Specialist, U.S. Acad. Health Scis., Ft. Sam Houston, Tex., 1983. RN, Ohio; cert. ARC nurse, advanced cardiac life support; cert. instr. , trainerCPR, HIV/AIDS, sch. nurse. Med. asst. instr. So. Ohio Coll., Mogadore, 1984-86; EMT Plain Twp. Fire Dept., 1985-88; commd. 2d lt. USAF, 1988, advanced through grades to lst lt., 1990; staff nurse USAF, Goldsboro, N.C., 1988-91; pub. health nurse Summit County Health Dept., 1991-96, Physicians Indsl. and Instnl. Svcs., 1996—, Carriere Care Svcs., 1996—. Author: Prevention is the Cure for Hearing Loss Caused by Noise in the Lab, 1991, The Use of Narcotics in Controlling Patient Pain, 1993; contbr. articles to profl. jours. Home: 4242 20th St NW Canton OH 44708-2847

SMITH-RISCH, JUDY DIANNE, optometrist; b. Connersville, Ind., Mar. 25, 1965; d. Lawrence Michael and Catherine Ann (Pflum) Risch; m. Randy Lee Smith, Nov. 9, 1991. BS in Optometry, Ind. U., 1988; OD, Ind. U. Sch. Optometry, 1990. Optometrist Richmond (Ind.) Eye Ctr., 1991—; optometrist Dr. Thomas Edwards, Brookville, Batesville, Ind., 1991—. Mem. Am. Optometric Assn., Ind. Optometric Assn. (v.p., pres.), Whitewater Valley Optometric Soc. (pres. 1996—), Beta Sigma Kappa. Roman Catholic. Office: Richmond Eye Ctr 1900 Chester Blvd Richmond IN 47374

SMITH-YOUNG, ANNE VICTORIA, health services coordinator; b. Long Beach, Calif., Aug. 25, 1947; d. James Warren and Jeanne Anne (Cooney) Wright; m. Lynn Walker Smith, Aug. 11, 1968 (div. Feb. 1980); children: Amy Lyanne and Caroline Walker (twins); m. Stephen Nicholas Young, May 29, 1982. AS, Long Beach City Coll., 1967; BS, Marymount Coll., 1984. Diplomate Am. Bd. Urologic Allied Health Profls. Mgr. office Williams-Brinton Med. Corp., Huntington Beach, Calif., 1975-80; adminstr. Westchester Urol. Assocs., White Plains, N.Y., 1980-82; adminstr. Pediatric Urol. Assocs. Westchester County Med. Ctr., Valhalla, N.Y., 1982-86; clin. coord. urodynamics lab. cystoscopy ste. dept. urology Westchester County Med. Ctr., Valhalla, 1986—, chairperson exec. com. employee adv. coun., 1987—; cons. Office Career Svcs., Marymount (N.Y.) Coll., 1984—, Am. Bd. Urologic Allied Health Profls., 1980-87, sec., 1987-93; pres., co-dir. Continence Restored Inc., 1984—; cons. to mfrs., individuals and healthcare providers on urinary incontinence and urodynamics; pres. Y&Y Interactives, 1996—. Mem. editorial bd. Sex Over Forty; contbr. articles to profl. jours. Mem. NAFE, Am. Urol. Assn. Allied (nat. fundraiser 1980-86, bd. dirs. N.Y. chpt. 1988—, Recognition award 1984), Assn. Urinary Continence Control (bd. dirs. 1988—), Am. Assn. Med. Assts., Nat. Trust for Historic Preservation, Mothers of Twins Club (pres. Long Beach 1974-75), Lions (bd. dirs. White Plains 1989, editor Lions Roar newsletter, pres. 1991-93, zone chmn. 1993-94, region chmn. 1994-95, cabinet sec. 1995-96, cabinet treas. 1996—, Lion of Month award 1990, Officer of Yr. award 1991, Melvin Jones fellow 1996). Democrat. Home: 407 Strawberry Hill Ave Stamford CT 06902-2513 Office: Westchester County Med Ctr Dept Urology Macy # 1058 Valhalla NY 10595

SMITS, HELEN LIDA, physician, administrator, educator; b. Long Beach, Calif., Dec. 3, 1936; d. Theodore Richard Smits and Anna Mary Wells; m. Roger LeCompte, Aug. 28, 1976; 1 child, Theodore. BA with honors,

Swarthmore Coll., 1958; MA, Yale U., 1961, MD cum laude, 1967. Intern, asst. resident Hosp. U. Pa., 1967-68; fellow Beth Israel Hosp., Boston, 1969-70; chief resident Hosp. U. Pa., 1970-71; chief med. clinic U. Pa., 1971-75; assoc. adminstr. for patient care svcs. U. Pa. Hosp., 1975-77; v.p. med. affairs Community Health Plan Georgetown U., Washington, 1977; dir. health standards and quality bur. Health Care Financing Adminstrn., HHS, Washington, 1977-80; sr. rsch. assoc. The Urban Inst., Washington, 1980-81; assoc. prof. Yale U. Med. Sch., New Haven, 1981-85; assoc. v.p. for health affairs U. Conn. Health Ctr., Farmington, 1985-87; prof. community medicine U. Conn. Sch. Medicine, Farmington, 1985-93; hosp. dir. John Dempsey Hosp., Farmington, 1987-93; dep. adminstr. Health Care Financing Adminstrn., Washington, 1993-96; pres., med. dir. Health Right, Inc., Meriden, Conn., 1996—; commr. Joint Com. on Accreditation Hosps., Chgo., 1989-93, chair, 1991-92. Contbr. numerous articles to profl. jours. Bd. dirs. The Ivoryton Playhouse Fedn., Inc., 1990-92, The Connecticut River Mus., 1990-93, Hartford Stage, 1990-93; mem. Dem. Town Com., Essex, Conn., 1982-89. Recipient Superior Svc. award HHS, Washington, 1982; Royal Soc. Medicine Found. fellow, London, 1973; Fulbright scholar, 1959-60. Mem. ACP (master, regent 1984-90), Phi Beta Kappa, Alpha Omega Alpha. Episcopalian. Home: 81 Main St Ivoryton CT 06442-1032 Office: Health Right Inc 184 State St Meriden CT 06450

SMOLAR, EDWARD NELSON, physician, consultant; b. Bklyn., Sept. 26, 1943; s. Harry and Diane (Orans) S.; m. Sharon Elaine Wechsler, June 24, 1973; children: Todd Devon, Gregory Fielding. BS in Biol. Scis. with honors, Union Coll., 1964; MD, Albert Einstein Coll. of Medicine, 1968; MBA with honors, Nova U., 1985, MS, 1990. Diplomate Am. Bd. Internal Medicine, Am. Bd. Endocrinology and Metabolism, Am. Bd. Geriatric Medicine, Nat. Bd. Med. Examiners; CLU, ChFC, CFP. Asst. instr. of medicine SUNY, Bklyn., 1973-75; clin. instr. of medicine N.Y. Med. Coll., 1974-79; physician pvt. practice, N.Y., 1975-80; asst. prof. of clin. medicine N.Y. Med. Coll., 1979-80; pvt. practice N.Y.C., 1975-80, Pompano Beach, 1980-84, Ft. Lauderdale, Fla., 1984—; clin. asst. prof. medicine U. Miami, Fla., 1982-89; adj. faculty Friedt Sch. Bus., Nova U., Ft. Lauderdale, Fla., 1987-88;. cons. Profl. Fin. Cons. Palm Beach, Inc., Boca Raton, Fla., 1988—. Contbr. articles to med. jours. Pres. Am. Diabetes Assn., 1980-81, bd. dirs., 1987—; mem. adv. bd. Hospice, Inc., 1985—. Surgeon USPHS, 1968-71, inactive res., 1971—. Fellow ACP, Am. Coll. Angiology, Am. Coll. Endocrinology, N.Y. Acad. Medicine (life), Royal Soc. Health, Royal Soc. Medicine; mem. Am. Acad. Polit. and Social Sci., Endocrine Soc., Am. Acad. Polit. Sci. (life), Assn. Mil. Surgeons U.S. (life), U.S. Naval Inst. (life), Am. Soc. CLUs and ChFCs. Republican. Jewish. Office: 5601 N Dixie Hwy Fort Lauderdale FL 33334-4148

SMOLAR, SCOTT BRIAN, psychiatrist; b. N.Y.C., July 4, 1963: s. Theodore and Terry H. (Edelson) S. BA cum laude, Hobart and William Smith Coll., 1985; DO, U. New Eng. Coll. Osteo., 1991. Intern Oreg. Health Scis. U., Portland, 1991-92, resident in psychiatry, 1992-94, resident in child and adolescent psychiatry, 1994-96; rsch. and clin. fellow in substance abuse psychiatry U. Calif. VA Med. Ctr., San Francisco, 1996—. Psychiat. cons. to homeless youth program Outside In, Portland, 1995-96. Mem. AMA, Am. Acad. Child/Adolescent Psychiatry, Am. Osteo. Assn., Am. Psychiat. Assn., Calif. Osteopathic Med. Assn. Office: San Francisco VA Med Ctr 4150 Clement Ave 116E San Francisco CA 94121

SMOLENSKY, GERALD LEON, orthopaedic surgeon; b. Port Chester, N.Y., Mar. 6, 1940; s. Irving and Blanche Smolensky; m. Rhoda Smolensky, July 11, 1965; children: Nancy, Michael. BS, Tufts U., 1962, MD, 1966. Diplomate Am. Bd. Orthopaedic Surgery. Surg. intern Albert Einstein Coll. Medicine, Bronx, N.Y., 1966-68, surg. resident, 1967-68; orthopaedic resident U. Miami Sch. Medicine/Jackson Meml. Hosp., Miami, 1968-71; orthopaedic surgeon Mease Helath Care, Dunedin, Fla., 1973—. Maj. USAF, 1971-73. Fellow ACS, Am. Acad. Orthopaedic Surgeons, Internat. Coll. Surgeons; mem. Fla. Orthopaedic Soc., Ea. Orthopaedic Soc. Office: Mese Med Arts Bldg PO Box 760 646 Virginia St Ste 202 Dunedin FL 34697-0760

SMOLLER, BRUCE MELVYN, psychiatrist; b. Chgo., Sept. 19, 1944; s. Norman and Beatrice Betty (Janows) S.; m. Cosette Nieporent, Aug. 20, 1967; children: Jamie, Lauren. AB, Cornell U., 1965; MD, Tulane U., 1969. Diplomate Am. Bd. Psychiatry and Neurology. Intern Maimonides Med. Ctr., N.Y.C., 1969-70; resident in orthopedic surgery Einstein Med. Ctr., N.Y.C., 1970-73; resident in psychiatry Cornell Med. Ctr., N.Y.C., 1973-76; pvt. practice medicine specializing in psychiatry with spl. emphasis on clin. and rsch. aspects of pain Bethesda, Md., 1976—; chmn. dept. psychiatry Holy Cross Hosp., Silver Spring, Md., 1980-83; assoc. clin. prof. psychiarty George Washington U., 1977-91, clin. prof. psychiatry, 1991—; cons. NIH. Co-author: Pain Control: The Bethesda Program. Mem. alumni interviewing com. Cornell U. With MC, USAR, 1970-78. Mem. Am. Psychiat. Assn., Am. Psychosomatic Soc., Internat. Soc. for Study Pain, Washington Psychiat. Soc., Am. Acad. of Psychiat. and Law. Office: 5530 Wisconsin Ave Bethesda MD 20815-4404

SMOOT, LESLIE ALLEN, microbiologist; b. Hawthorne, Nev., Feb. 11, 1953; s. Earl Alexander and Mary Maxine (Brown) S.; m. L. Michele Martin, July 16, 1966. BS in Biology, Va. Tech., 1975, MS in Food Sci., 1977, PhD in Food Sci., 1981. Rsch. scientist Fritolay, Inc., Dallas, 1981-84; sr. project leader Ralston Purina Co., St. Louis, 1984-86, mgr. microbiology, 1986-89; dir. spl. microbiology ABC Rsch. Corp., Gainesville, Fla., 1989-90, v.p. microbiology, 1990-94; quality advisor in microbiology quality mgmt. Nestle, Vevey, Switzerland, 1994—. Contbr. articles to scientific jours. Mem. Inst. Food Technologists, Am. Meat Scis. Assn., Am. Soc. Microbiology, Assn. Ofcl. Analytical Chemists, Internat. Assn. Milk, Food and Environ. Sanitarians, Sigma Xi, Sigma Phi Epsilon, Gamma Sigma Delta, Phi Sigma, Phi Tau Sigma. Methodist. Home: Rue des Vaudres 23 Apt 42, CH-1815 Clarens Switzerland Office: Nestec Ltd, Avenue Nestle 55, CH-1800 Vevey Switzerland

SMOWTON, JEFFREY STEPHEN, emergency physician; b. Cedar Rapids, Aug. 8, 1957; s. David Lionel and Betty Lou (Erickson) S.; m. Diane Teresa Ossi, May 21, 1991; children: Ashley, Danielle. BS, Eckerd Coll., 1980; MD, U. Fla., 1986. Diplomate Am. Coll. Physicians. Attending physician, med. dir. Baptist Med. Ctr., Jacksonville Beach, 1992—; clin. faculty U. Fla. Div. Emergency Medicine, Jacksonville, 1992—; med. svcs. med. dir. Fla. Cmty. Coll., Jacksonville, 1992—; asst. flight surgeons NASA, Titusville, Fla., 1992—. Med. dir. ARC, Jacksonville, 1993—. Fellow Am. Coll. Emergency Physicians; mem. AMA, Am. Coll. Physicians, Fla. Coll. Emergency Physicians, Duval County Med. Soc. Home: 12910 Littleton Bend Rd Jacksonville FL 32224 Office: Emergency Physicians Inc 820 Prudential Dr Ste 713 Jacksonville FL 32207

SMUCKER, DAVID TODD, physician; b. Illinois, Ill., Oct. 18, 1952; s. Harvey Glasgow and Harriet Carol (Victor) S.; m. Maxine Claire Tabas, May 18, 1954; children: Zachary, Zoe. BS, Georgetown U., 1974, MD, 1978. Dir. emergency room Jewish Hosp. St. Louis, 1981-83; pvt. practice Florissant, Mo., 1983-87, Orlando, Fla., 1987-88, 1990—, San Jose, Calif., 1989-90; chmn. Utilization Rev., Fla. Hosp., 1995; chmn. dept. internal medicine, 1996—. Mem. ACP, Am. Geriatrics Soc., Fla. Med. Assn., Orange County Med. Soc. Office: 1701 N Mills Ave Orlando FL 32803

SMULDERS, ANTHONY PETER, biology educator; b. Oss, North Brabant, The Netherlands, July 6, 1942; came to U.S., 1963; s. Arnoldus A.P. and Maria A.A. (Horsten) S. T.C. in Edn. and Psychology, St. Stanislaus T.T.C., Tilburg, The Netherlands, 1962; BS in Biology summa cum laude, Loyola U., Los Angeles, 1966; PhD in Physiology with distinction, UCLA, 1970. Joined Bros. of Our Lady Mother of Mercy, Roman Cath. Ch., 1959. Tchr. Loon op Zand (The Netherlands) elem. schs., 1962-63, Santa Clara High Sch., Oxnard, Calif., 1965-67; research physiologist UCLA, 1970—; prof. biology Loyola Marymount U., Los Angeles, 1970—, assoc. dean sci., 1972-94, dir. health professions info. program, 1995—; mem. L.A. County Narcotics and Dangerous Drugs Commn., 1973—, Calif. State Adv. Bd. on Drug Programs, 1982-92. Contbr. articles to profl. jours. Mem. AAUP, AAAS, The Biophys. Soc., Nat. Assn. Advisors for Health Professions (pres. 1978-84), Western Assn. Advisors for Health Professions, Sigma Xi, Sigma Pi Sigma. Democrat. Lodge: KC. Office: Loyola Marymount U 7101 W 80th St Los Angeles CA 90045-2659

SMYE, STEPHEN WILLIAM, medical physicist, researcher; b. Belfast, Northern Ireland, July 13, 1957; s. Frederick William and Sheelagh Mary (Collins) S.; m. Rachael Margaret Sykes, Jan. 3, 1981; children: Peter, Andrew, Shona. BA, Cambridge U., 1979, MA, 1983; MS, London U., 1980; PhD, Leeds U., 1992. Optical physicist Ferranti PLC, Dundee, Scotland, 1980-81; med. physicist Barnsley (Eng.) Hosp., 1981-85; sr. med. physicist St. James's U. Hosp., Leeds, 1985-87; prin. med. physicist St. James's U. Hosp., 1987-90, cons. med. physicist, 1990—. Inventor Smye equation (math. equation to predict dialysis dose), 1992; contbr. articles to profl. jours.; hon. sr. lectr. Leeds U., 1994—. Mem. Inst. Physics and Engring. in Medicine and Biology (coun. mem. 1995—), Ctr. for Biomechanics Leeds U. (sec. 1993—).

SMYTH, JOHN FLETCHER, oncologist; b. Dursley, Gloucester, England, Oct. 26, 1945; s. Henry James Robert and Doreen Stanger (Fletcher) S.; m. Catherine Lindsay Ellis, Sept. 15, 1973; children: Sarah Bethan, Anna Mary. MB, B.Chir., Cambridge U., 1970, MA, 1971, MD, 1976; MSc, London U., 1975. Intern St. Bartholomew's Hosp., London, 1970-71, Royal Berkshire Hosp., 1971; resident Royal Postgrad. Med. Sch. Hammersmith Hosp., London, 1971-72; asst. lectr. St. Bartholomew's Hosp., London, 1972-73; rsch. fellow Inst. Cancer Rsch., London, 1973-75; internat. vis. fellow Nat. Cancer Inst., N.I.H., Bethesda, Md., 1975-76; sr. registrar Royal Marsden Hosp., London, 1976-77; sr. lectr. Inst. Cancer Rsch., London, 1976-79; vis. prof. medicine Cancer Rsch. Ctr., U. Chgo., 1979; prof. med. oncology U. Edinburgh, Scotland, 1979—, head, dept. clin. oncology Lothian Health Bd., 1980-91; hon. dir. Imperial Cancer Rsch. Fund, Med. Oncology Unit, Edinburgh, 1980—; chmn. U.K. Coordinating Com. Cancer Rsch./Sub-com. on lung cancer, London, 1982-92, Scottish Melanoma Group, Edinburg, 1985, EORTC Pharmacokinetics Group, Brussels, 1979-82. Contbr. over 200 articles on med. mgmt. of malignant diseases to med. jours., chpts. to books. Gov. Bryanston Sch., Dorset, Eng., 1979—, Imperial Cancer Rsch. Fund, London, 1988-91; councillor European Orgn. for Rsch. and Treatment of Cancer, Brussells, 1988-95. Fellow Royal Coll. Physicians (Edinburgh and London), Royal Coll. Surgeons (Edinburg), Royal Soc. of Edinburgh, Royal Coll. of Radiologists; mem. European Soc. Med. Oncologists (pres. 1991-93), Am. Assn. Cancer Rsch., Assn. Physicians of Gt. Britain, British Assn. Cancer Rsch., Athenaeum. Office: Univ Dept Clin Oncology, Crewe Rd, Edinburgh EH42XU, Scotland

SMYTH, NICHOLAS PATRICK D., surgeon; b. Dublin, Ireland, Apr. 1, 1924; came to U.S., 1951; s. Patrick Joseph and Nano Elizabeth (Dillon) S.; m. Elizabeth Stavely Long; children: Sheila, Brian, Nicholas, Augustine, Patrick. BSc, Univ. Coll. Dublin, 1946, MSc, 1948, MB BCh, 1949; MS, U. Mich., 1954. Diplomate Am. Bd. Surgery, Am. Bd. Thoracic Surgery. Intern Mater Misericordiae Hosp., Dublin, 1949-50, Norfolk and Norwich Hosp., Eng., 1950-51; resident in gen. surgery Henry Ford Hosp., Detroit, 1951-52, 53-55; resident in thoracic surgery George Washington U. Hosp., Washington, 1957-59; pvt. practice, Washington, 1959-86; clin. prof. surgery emeritus George Washington U. Sch. Medicine, Washington; mem. staff, Washington Hosp. Ctr., George Washington U. Med. Ctr.; consulting surgeon, VA Hosp., Washington, NIH, Bethesda, Md., Walter Reed Army Med. Ctr., Washington; pres. Potomac Fund Cardiovascular Rsch. Contbr. numerous articles to profl. jours.; patentee in field. Capt. M.C., U.S. Army, 1955-57. Fellow ACS, Am. Coll. Chest Physicians, Am. Coll. Cardiology; mem. D.C. Thoracic Soc., Washington Heart Assn., Am. Heart Assn., AMA, Med. Soc. D.C., Am. Assn. Thoracic Surgery, Washington Acad. Surgery, Am. Fedn. Clin. Rsch., Pan Am. Med. Assn., World Med. Assn., Soc. Thoracic Surgery, So. Thoracic Surg. Assn., So. Med. Assn., AAAS, Assn. Advancement Med. Instrumentation, Soc. Vascular Surgery, Internat. Cardiovascular Soc., N.Am. Soc. Pacing and Electrophysiology, Royal Soc. Medicine. Republican. Roman Catholic. Office: 3612 Winfield Ln NW Washington DC 20007-2385

SMYTHE, CHEVES MCCORD, dean, medical educator; b. May 25, 1924. Attended, Yale Coll., 1942-43; MD cum laude, Harvard, 1947. Diplomate Am. Bd. Internal Medicine, Am. Bd. Geriatrics. Lectr. medicine Sch. Medicine Northwestern U., 1966-70; intern, asst. resident Harvard Med. Svc., Boston City Hosp., 1947-49, chief resident, 1954-55; resident chest svc. Bellevue, 1949-50; rsch. fellow Presbyn. Hosp., N.Y.C., 1950-52; with Med. Coll. Hosp., Charleston, S.C., 1955-66; instr. medicine Med. Coll. S.C. Sch. Medicine, 1955-56, assoc. medicine, 1956-58, asst. prof. medicine, 1958-60, assoc. prof. medicine, 1960-66, dean, 1963-65; attending physician Wesley Meml., Cook County North Side VA Hosps., Chgo., 1967-70; with Hermann Hosp., Houston, 1970, Aga Khan U. Hosp., Karachi, Pakistan, 1990-91; dean faculty health scis., prof. medicine Aga Khan U., Karachi, Pakistan, 1982-85, prof., chmn. dept. medicine, 1990-91; with Meml. Southwest Hosp., Houston, 1991, LBJ Hosp., Houston, 1991; chief Med. Svcs. at LBJ Hosp., Houston, 1991-95; prof. divsn. gen. medicine dept. internal medicine U. Tex. Med. Sch., Houston, 1970—, dean, 1970-75, dean pro tem, 1995-96; lectr. U. Va., 1976, U. Guadalajara, 1976, U. So. Calif. Sch. Medicine, 1986-87; adj. prof. dept. family practice and cmty. medicine U. Tex. Med. Sch., Houston, 1991; cons. Regional Med. Libr. Adv. Com., Uniformed Svcs. Health Scis. U., U. S.D., U. Conn., Mercer U. Sch. Medicine, Oral Roberts U. Sch. Medicine, others. Contbr. articles to profl. jours., chpts. to books. Mem. AAAS, AMA, ACP, Am. Fedn. for Clin. Rsch. (chmn. southern sect.), Assn. Am. Med. Colls. (assoc. dir. 1966-70, dir. dept. acad. affairs 1969-70, chmn. med. sch. admissions assessment program 1973, mem. program advancement program steering com. 1973-75, mem. task force health manpower legislation 1974-75, chmn. deans of new and developing med. schs. group 1975, disting. svc. mem. 1979, others), Am. Heart Assn., Am. Clin. and Climatological Assn., Am. Soc. Nephrology, Am. Geriatrics Soc., Soc. for Exptl. Biology and Medicine, Tex. Geriatric Soc. (pres. 1991), Tex. Med. Assn. (cons. coun. on edn. and hosps.), Tex. Med. Found., Harris County Med. Soc. (mem. adv. com. on aging 1991, chmn. subcom. on continuing edn.), Houston Soc. Internal Medicine (v.p. 1976), Houston Geriatric Soc. (pres. 1989), Houston Acad. Medicine (vice-chmn., bd. dirs.), Southern Med. Assn., Southern Soc. for Clin. Rsch., Alpha Omega Alpha. Office: Univ Tex Med Sch 6431 Fannin Houston TX 77030

SNAREY, JOHN ROBERT, psychologist, researcher, educator; b. New Brighton, Pa., Jan. 12, 1948; s. John Herbert and Esther Snarey; m. Carol Dunn Snarey, June 11, 1970; children: Johnny, Elizabeth. BS, Geneva Coll., 1969; MA, Wheaton (Ill.) Coll., 1973; EdD, Harvard U., 1982. Postdoctoral rsch. fellow dept. psychiatry Harvard U., Cambridge, Mass., 1982-84; assoc. rsch. psychologist Wellesley (Mass.) Coll., 1984-85; assoc. prof. human devel. Northwestern U., Evanston, Ill., 1985-87; prof. human devel. Emory U., Atlanta, 1987—. Author: How Fathers Care for the Next Generation, 1993; mem. editl. bd. Harvard Ednl. Rev., 1979-81; mem. editl. adv. bd. Lawrence Erlbaum Assocs., 1988-90; contbr. numerous articles to profl. jours. Recipient Exemplary Dissertation award Nat. Coun. for the Social Studies, 1982, Kuhmerker Dissertation award Assn. for Moral Edn., 1983, Outstanding Human Devel. Rsch. award Am. Ednl. Rsch., 1988, James D. Moran Book award Assn. Family and Consumer Scis., 1994. Mem. APA, Am. Ednl. Rsch. Assn. (div. E exec. bd. 1990—, moral devel. and edn. spl. interest group co-chair 1994—), Assn. for Moral Edn. (exec. bd. 1986—), Soc. for Rsch. in Child Devel., Nat. Coun. on Family Rels. Home: 2165 Pine Forest Dr NE Atlanta GA 30345-4184

SNAVLEY, DOROTHY J., nursing home administrator; b. Icaville, Ind., Apr. 27, 1931; d. George M. and Julia Josephine (Blocher) Young; m. Paul E. Ryan, June 11, 1950 (div. Dec. 1957); 1 child, Beth A. Ryan Mitchell; m. Robert J. Snavley, Oct. 11, 1958; 1 child, Diane C. Snavley Stephens. AAS, Purdue U., Westville, Ind., 1985; Cert. in Nursing Home Adminstrn., Ball State U. Bookkeeper Monticello (Inc.) Healthcare, 1974-79; adminstr. Lakeside Health Ctr., Michigan City, Ind., 1979-89, Tioga Pines Nursing Home, Monticello, 1989-91, Meadows Manor North, Inc., Terre Haute, Ind., 1991—. Bd. dirs. Meadows Home Health Bd., Terre Haute, 1991—, Vigo County Health Careers, Terre Haute, 1991—. Recipient Pres.'s award Am. Coll., Indpls., 1982-83, Fellow award, Terre Hauge, 1995. Mem. Ind. Health Care Assn. (ecn./conv. com. 1980—, sec.-treas. 1993-94). Democrat. Methodist. Home: 1306 N 8th St Terre Haute IN 47807 Office: Meadows Manor North Inc 3150 N 7th St Terre Haute IN 47804

SNEARY, MAX EUGENE, retired physician; b. Zanesfield, Ohio, Oct. 13, 1930; s. Kenneth Douglas and Grace Agnes (Yeiser) S.; m. Joy Ann Preston, Apr. 4, 1950; children: Candice Barbulesco, Jennifer Laur. Student, Wabash Coll., 1949-52; MD, Ind. U., 1956. Pvt. practice Avilla, Ind., 1957-95; retired, 1995; coroner Noble County (Ind.) Coroner's Office, 1960-64, 72-76; pres. bd. dirs. McCray Meml. Hosp., Kendallville, Ind., 1961-64; mem. Noble County Bd. of Health, 1962-65, 76-80, health officer, 1965-67. Bd. dirs. Kendalville Bank & Trust Co., 1980-88, chmn., 1987-88. Named Citizen of the Yr., Town of Avilla, 1988, Indian Family Physician of the Yr., 1990. Fellow Am. Acad. Family Physicians; mem. AMA, Am. Bd. Family Physicians (charter), Ind. Med. Assn., Noble County Med. Soc., Alpha Omega Alpha. Home: 205 Baum St #140 Avilla IN 46710

SNELBECKER, GLENN EUGENE, psychologist, educator; b. Dover, Pa., Sept. 24, 1931; s. William S. and Anna M. Snelbecker; m. Janice C. Fixler, Sept. 23, 1962; children: David M., Karen A., Laura B. BS in Bus. Edn., Elizabethtown Coll., 1957; MS in Guidance and Counseling, Bucknell U., 1958; PhD, Cornell U., 1961; diploma in Acctg., Thompson coll., 1952. Lic. psychologist, Pa. Postdoctoral intern VA Hosp., Brockton, Mass., 1961-62, clin. psychologist, Behavior Rsch. Lab. supr., 1962-67; assoc. prof. psychol. studies Temple U., Phila., 1967-72, prof. psychol. studies, 1972—; cons., author in pvt. practice Mgmt. Assocs. for Tech., Comms. and Health, 1963—; investigator NSF computer project Retraining High Sch. Tchrs. and Elem. Sch. Tchrs. Temple U., Phila., 1985-92. Author: Learning Theory, Instructional Theory, 1985; author: (with others) The ASTD Instructional Technology Handbook, 1993; contbr. articles to profl. jours., chpts. to books. Sgt. U.S. Army, 1952-55. Mem. Am. Edn. Rsch. Assn., Am. Psycholog. Assn., Phila. Area Computer Soc., Phila. Soc. Clin. Psychologists. Office: Temple U Ra217 Tu 004 00 Dept Psychol Studies Philadelphia PA 19122

SNELL, RICHARD SAXON, anatomist; b. Richmond, Surrey, Eng., May 3, 1925; came to U.S., 1963; s. Claude Saxon and Daisy Lilian S.; m. Maureen Cashin, June 4, 1949; children: Georgina Sara, Nicola Ann, Melanie Jane, Richard Robin, Charles Edward. M.B., B.S., Kings Coll., U. London, 1949, Ph.D., 1955, M.D., 1961. House surgeon Sir Cecil P.G. Wakeley, Kings Coll. Hosp. and Belgrave Hosp. for Children, London, 1948-49; lectr. anatomy Kings Coll., U. London, 1949-59, U. Durham, Eng., 1959-63; asst. prof. anatomy and medicine Yale U., 1963-65, assoc. prof., 1965-67, vis. prof. anatomy, 1969; prof., chmn. dept. anatomy N.J. Coll. Medicine and Dentistry, Jersey City, 1967-69; vis. prof. anatomy Harvard U., 1970, 71, 80, 86; prof. anatomy Coll. Medicine, U. Ariz., Tucson, 1970; prof., chmn. dept. anatomy George Washington U. Med. Ctr., Washington, 1972-88, prof. emeritus, 1988—. Author: Clinical Embryology for Medical Students, 1972, 3d edit., 1983, Clinical Anatomy for Medical Students, 1973, 5th edit., 1995, Atlas of Normal Radiographic Anatomy, 1976, Atlas of Clinical Anatomy, 1978, Gross Anatomy Dissector, 1978, Clinical Neuroanatomy for Medical Students, 1980, 3d edit., 1992, Student's Aid to Gross Anatomy, 1986, Clinical Anatomy for Anesthesiologists, 1988, Clinical Anatomy of the Eye, 1989, Gross Anatomy: A Review with Questions and Explanations, 1990, Neuroanatomy: A Review with questions and Explanations, 1992, Clinical Anatomy for Emergency Medicine, 1993, Clinical Anatomy: An Illustrated Review with Questions and Explanations, 2d edit., 1996; contbr. articles to med. jours. Med. Research Council grantee, 1959; NIH grantee, 1963-65. Mem. Anat. Soc. Gt. Britain, Am. Soc. Anatomists, Alpha Omega Alpha. Home: 518 Boston Post Rd Madison CT 06443-2930

SNELL, WILLIAM EDWARD, physician; b. Clinton, Iowa, Dec. 18, 1949; s. Robert H. and Orrel Ann (McGrath) S.; m. Suzette Marie Mohr, Jul 1, 1972; children: Richard Robert, Meredith Ann. BS, Iowa State U., 1972; DO, Chgo. Coll. Osteopathic Medicine, 1980. Intern Chgo. Osteo. Hosp., 1980-81; resident in family practice MacNeal Hosp., Berwyn, Ill., 1981-83; pvt. practice, Marietta, Ga., 1983—; dir. medicine Project ADAPT, Marietta, 1983—; team physician Walton High Sch., Maretta, 1983-86; prof. family practice W.Va. Sch. Osteopathic Medicine, Lewisburg, 1983—, U. Ill., Champaign and Chgo., 1981-83. Fellow Am. Acad. Family Practice; mem. Ga. Osteopathic Medicine Assn., Am. Osteopathic Assn., Cobb County C. of C. Republican. Roman Catholic. Lodges: Optimists, Masons. Home: 1814 Jacksons Creek Blf Marietta GA 30068-1504

SNIDER, GHERI TEREZAS, transpersonal psychological and wholistic healthcare consultant, educator; b. Canton, Ohio, Feb. 23, 1939; d. Sam G. and Mary M. (Kopp) Terezas; m. Delmer Snider, Dec. 24, 1970 (div. Feb. 1980); children: Peter John, Ruth Anne. Registered Nurse, Aultman Hosp. Sch. of Nursing, 1960; BSN, U. San Francisco, 1974; MS in Nursing Edn. and Adminstrn., Univ. Calif. San Francisco, 1975; MA in Transpersonal Psychology, Inst. Transpersonal Psychology, Palo Alto, Calif., 1982, PhD in Transpersonal Psychology, 1995. RN. Staff nurse, charge nurse Timken Mercy Hosp., Canton, 1960-63; supr. St. John's Hosp., St. Vincent Charity Hosp., Cleve., 1963-67; charge nurse Univ. Hosp., Cleve., 1968-69; head nurse Stanford (Calif.) Univ. Hosp., 1969-72; dir., founder Council Post-Anesthesia Nurses, Stanford, 1971-74; assoc. dir. nurses St. Mary's Hosp., Reno, 1975-77; dir. Delphic Assn. Consultation and Counseling, Carson City, Nev., 1978—; dir. nursing edn. svcs. Natividad Med. Ctr., Salinas, Calif., 1984-90; cons., educator Transpersonal Svcs., Monterey, Calif., 1990—; adj. faculty Calif. Inst. Transpersonal Psychology, Palo Alto, 1985; acting asst. adminstr. nursing svcs. Navidad Med. Ctr., Salinas, 1988-89. Mem. Internat. Flying Nurses Assn., Assn. for Transpersonal Psychology, No. Calif. Acad. Hypnosis, alumni assns. Univ. San Francisco, Univ. Calif. San Francisco, Inst. Transpersonal Psychology, Sigma Theta Tau. Office: Pacific Heights 1 Lorraine Ct Seaside CA 93955

SNIDER, GORDON B., medical educator; b. Columbus, Ohio, Dec. 19, 1928; s. James M. and Rose G. (Joyce) S.; m. Mary Louise Graham, July 19, 1952; children: Mary Katherine, Cynthia L., John M., James G., Martha R. BA in Bacteriology, Ohio State U., 1950, MD, 1954. Diplomate Am. Bd. Internal Medicine. Intern Mt. Carmel Hosp., Columbus, 1954-55, resident, 1955-57; Henry Ford Hosp., Detroit, 1957-58; pvt. practice Lancaster, Ohio, 1960-94; dir. med. edn. Fairfield Med. Ctr., Lancaster, 1994—; clin. assoc. prof. medicine Ohio State U. Coll. Med., Columbus, 1981—; bd. dirs. Fairfield Med. Ctr., Lancaster, 1990-96. Founder, dir. paramedic program Lancaster fire Dept., 1985. Capt., M.C., U.S. Army, 1958-60. Fellow ACP, Lancaster Rotary (past pres.); mem. Fairfield Med. Soc. (past pres.), Ohio State Med. Assn., Ohio Soc. Internal Medicine (past pres.). Roman Catholic. Office: Fairfield Med Ctr 401 N Ewing St Lancaster OH 43130

SNIDER, JAMES RHODES, radiologist; b. Pawnee, Okla., May 16, 1931; s. John Henry and Gladys Opal (Rhodes) S.; B.S., U. Okla., 1953, M.D., 1956; m. Lynadell Vivion, Dec. 27, 1954; children—Jon, Jan. Intern, Edward Meyer Meml. Hosp., Buffalo, 1956-57; resident radiology U. Okla. Med. Center, 1959-62; radiologist Holt-Krock Clinic and Sparks Regional Med. Center, Ft. Smith, Ark., 1962—, dir. Fairfield Community Land Co., Little Rock, 1968-87, Fairfield Communities, Inc., 1968-87. Mem. Ark. Bd. Pub. Welfare, 1969-71. Bd. dirs. U. Okla. Assn., 1967-70, U. Okla. Alumni Devel. Fund, 1970-74; bd. visitors U. Okla. Served to lt. comdr. USNR, 1957-62. Mem. Am. Coll. Radiology, Radiol. Soc. N.Am., Am. Roentgen Ray Soc., AMA, Phi Beta Kappa, Beta Theta Pi, Alpha Epsilon Delta. Asso. editor Computerized Tomography, 1976-88. Home: 5814 S Cliff Dr Fort Smith AR 72903-3845 Office: 1500 Dodson Ave Fort Smith AR 72901-5128

SNIDER, STEVEN PAUL, podiatrist; b. Detroit, Nov. 30, 1952; s. Donald David and Geraldine Mae (Silverman) S.; m. Lillian Mae Foreman; children: Bryan Fanick, Daniel Snider. BS in Med. Tech., Mich. State U., 1975; DPM, Calif. Coll. Podiatric Med, 1979. Diplomate Am. Bd. Podiatric Surgery. Pvt. practice San Antonio, 1980—. Jewish. Office: Snider and Assocs. Ste 301 10615 Perrin Beitel San Antonio TX 78217

SNIDERMAN, MARVIN, dentist; b. Pitts., Oct. 23, 1923; s. Abraham and Rebecca (Hecht) S.; BS in Pharmacy, U. Pitts., 1943, DMD, 1947; m. Eleanore Jessie Cohen, Dec. 25, 1947; 1 child, Abby Milstein. Pvt. dental practice Pitts., 1947-50, 53—; chief oral surgery dept. Pitts. Skin and Cancer Found., 1947-67. Mem. dental adv. com. Allegheny County Dept. Health, div. dental health, 1958-70; mem. undergrad. and postgrad. faculty U. Pitts. Sch. Dental Medicine, 1962—, assoc. prof. oral medicine, 1972-89, clin. assoc. prof. diagnostic svcs., 1989—; mem. charter council, 1986—; chief dental service Rehab. Inst. Pitts., 1948—. Mem. health adv. com. Pitts. Bd. Pub. Edn., 1965-70, dental health com. Mayor's Com. on Human Resources, Operation Head Start, 1965, adv. com. on health Mayor's Com. on Human Resources,

1965-70, charter council U. Pitts., 1986—; dental cons. USPHS, 1965-78; bd. dirs. Delta Dental of Pa., 1971-78; health edn. com. Allegheny County Adv. Council, 1972-74, 78—; mem. dental adv. com. Office Med. Programs Pa. Dept. Pub. Welfare, 1976-89; bd. dirs., sec. editorial com. Jewish Chronicle of Pitts., 1987—; vis. lectr. Emory U., U. Pa., Polyclinic and French Med. Sch., N.J. Coll. Medicine Dentistry, Temple Dental Sch. Albert Einstein Coll. Medicine, NYU Dental Sch., N.Y.C.; bd. dirs. Health/Edn. Commn. of Allegheny County, 1978—. Editor Odontological Bull. Western Pa., 1960-70, Pa. Dental Assn., 1970-72; cons. editor Jour. Dental Practice Adminstrn., 1980—; abstractor Jour. Oral Rsch. Abstracts; contbr. articles in field. Served with AUS, 1943-44, to capt., Dental Corps, 1950-53. Recipient Bicentennial Medallion of Distinction, 1987 U. Pitts.; named Alumnus of Yr. U. Pits. Sch. Dental Medicine, 1996. Fellow Am. Coll. Dentists (pres. Pitts. sect. 1972), Acad. Dentistry for Handicapped (charter), Acad. Gen. Dentistry (master), (charter), Soc. Oral Physiology and Occlusion, Internat. Coll. Dentists (dep. regent 1970-76, counselor 1981—), Am. Endodontic Soc. (charter), Internat. Coll. Applied Nutrition, Acad. Oral Medicine (academic, charter), Acad. Dentistry Internat. (charter), Am. Soc. Dentistry for Children, Am. Acad. Craniomandibular Orthopedics (charter), Acad. Stress and Chronic Disease (charter), Am. Equilibration Soc.; mem. AAUP, ADA (councils on journalism and dental rsch. and coun. on dental practice 1989, cons. editor jour.), Pa. Dental Assn. (vis. lectr., editor 1970-92, editor emeritus 1992—), Pierre Fauchard Acad. (Annual award 1992), Am. Soc. Acupuncture, Am. Assn. Functional Orthodontics, Am. Acad. Oral Medicine (charter), Am. Soc. Assn. Execs., N.Y. Acad. Scis., Am. Assn. Dental Editors, Internat. Assn. Study Pain, Am. Pain Soc. (Charter), Odontological Soc. Western Pa. (pres. 1965, Albert R. Pechan award of excellence, 1981), Am. Internat. Acad. Preventive Medicine, Am. Prosthodontic Soc., Internat. Assn. Dental Research, AAAS, Am. Assn. Hosp. Dentists, Am. Assn. Dental Sch., Am. Acad. Implant Dentistry, Fedn. Prosthodontic Assns., Am. Endodontic Soc., Am. Dental Soc. Anesthesiology, Am. Analgesia Soc., Am. Acad. Dental Practice Adminstrn., Internat. Coll. of Oral Implantologists, U. Pitts. Dental Alumni Assn. (pres. 1973-74, Alumnus Distinction 1986), Am. Med. Writers Assn. Jewish. Home: 5633 Callowhill St Pittsburgh PA 15206-1452 Office: 204 5th Ave Pittsburgh PA 15222-2706

SNODGRASS, TIMOTHY JOHN, family practice physician; b. Marshfield, Wis., June 16, 1959. BA, Carthage Coll., 1981; DO, Kirksville Coll., 1986. Diplomate Am. Bd. Family Physicians. Intern Naval Hosp., Pensacola, Fla., 1986-87; staff physician Naval CB Clinic, Gulfport, Miss., 1987-88; med. officer Naval Mobile Constrn. Battalion, Gulfport, 1988-90; resident The Med. Ctr., Columbus, Ga., 1990-92; physician Office of John L. Cossu, DO, P.A., Ft. Myers, Fla., 1992-93, Gulf Coast Family Physicians, Ft. Myers, 1993—; mem. critical care subcom. Gulf Coast Hosp., Ft. Myers, 1994-96, mem. credentials com., 1996—; mem. pharmacy and therapeutics com. S.W. Fla. Regional Med. Ctr., Ft. Myers, 1994-95. Lt. USNR, 1986-90. Mem. Am. Acad. Family Physicians, Am. Osteo. Assn., Fla. Osteo. Med. Assn. Republican. Lutheran. Office: Gulf Coast Family Physician 6140 Winkler Rd Ste D Fort Myers FL 33919

SNODGRASS, WARREN, urologist; b. Galveston, Tex., Nov. 2, 1954; s. Peggy (Jaronitsky) S.; m. Laura Virginia Snodgrass, Aug. 25, 1977; children: Laura Virginia, Will, Phillip. BA, Tex. Tech. U., 1976; MD, U. Tex. Med. Br., Galveston. Intern in gen. surgery Ochsner Med. Found., New Orleans, 1980-82; resident in urology Baylor Coll. of Medicine, Houston, 1982-86; pvt. practice Lubbock, Tex., 1986—. Contbr. articles to profl. jours. Fellow Am. Acad. Pediat.; mem. Sigma Chi (chpt. advisor Epsilon Nu 1987—). Office: Urologic Assocs 3606 21st Ste 207 Lubbock TX 79410

SNOW, JAMES B., health science association administrator. MD cum laude, Harvard U., 1956. Intern surgery Johns Hopkins Hosp., Balt.; resident otolaryngology Mass. Eye and Ear Infirmary, Boston; prof., head dept. otorhinolaryngology U. Okla. Med. Ctr.; prof., chair dept. otorhinolaryngology and human comm. U. Pa. Sch. Medicine, 1972-90; dir. Nat. Inst. Deafness and Other Communication Disorders NIH, Bethesda, Md., 1990—; cons. prof. Shanghai Second U. Med. Scis., China. Author over 175 articles, abstracts and books. Recipient Regent's award U. Okla., 1970, Disting. Achievement award Deafness Rsch. Found., 1993, Presdl. Meritorious Exec. Rank award, 1994; named to Soc. Scholars Johns Hopkins U., 1991. Fellow Japan Broncho-Esophagological Soc.; mem. Am. Broncho-Esophagological Assn., Soc. Univ. Otolaryngologists-Head and Neck Surgeons, Assn. Acad. Depts. Otolaryngology-Head and Neck Surgery, Am. Laryngological Assn., Internat. Fedn. Oto-rhino-laryngological Socs. (Golden award 1989). *

SNOW, JAMES BYRON, JR., physician, research administrator; b. Oklahoma City, Mar. 12, 1932; s. James B. and Charlotte Louise (Andersen) S.; m. Sallie Lee Ricker, July 16, 1954; children: James B., John Andrew, Sallie Lee Louise. BS, U. Okla., 1953; MD cum laude, Harvard U., 1956; MA (hon.), U. Pa., 1973. Diplomate: Am. Bd. Otolaryngology (dir. 1972-90). Intern Johns Hopkins Hosp., Balt., 1956-57; resident Mass. Eye and Ear Infirmary, Boston, 1957-60; prof., head dept. otorhinolaryngology Sch. Medicine U. Okla., Oklahoma City, 1962-72; prof., chmn. dept. otorhinolaryngology and human communication U. Pa. at Phila., 1972-90; dir. Nat. Inst. on Deafness and Other Comm. Disorders/NIH, Bethesda, Md., 1990—; mem. nat. adv. coun. neurol. and communicative disorders and stroke NIH, 1972-76, 82-86; chmn. Nat. Com. Rsch. Neurol. and Communicative Disorders, 1979-80. Editor: Am. Jour. Otolaryngology, 1979-83; Contbr. articles to sci. and profl. jours. Served with M.C. AUS, 1960-62. Recipient Regents award for superior tchg. U. Okla., 1970, Golden award Internat. Fedn. Otorhinolaryngological Socs., 1989, Disting. Achievement award Deafness Rsch. Found., 1993, Presdl. Meritorious Exec. Rank award, 1994; named to Soc. Scholars Johns Hopkins U., 1991. Fellow Japan Broncho-Esophagological Soc. (hon.), Am. Laryngological Assn. (hon.); mem. ACS (regent 1982-90), AMA (coun. on sci. affairs 1975-86), Soc. Univ. Otolaryngologists (pres. 1975), Am. Acad. Otolaryngology-Head and Neck Surgery, Assn. Acad. Depts. Otolaryngology (pres. 1981-82), Am. Laryngol., Rhinol. and Otol. Soc., Am. Otol. Soc., Am. Laryngol. Assn. (editor 1983-89, pres. 1990-91), Am. Broncho-Esophagol. Assn. (editor trans. 1973-77, pres. 1979), Collegium Otorhinolaryngologicum, Phi Beta Kappa, Alpha Omega Alpha. Home: 119 Driscoll Way Gaithersburg MD 20878-5210 Office: Nat Inst Deafness & Other Comm Disorders 9000 Rockville Pike Bldg 31 Bethesda MD 20892-0001

SNOW, LLOYD DALE, biochemistry educator; b. Lake City, Ark., Dec. 3, 1947; s. William Lloyd and Lila Mae (Rittenberry) S.; m. Marcella Joy Moore, Apr. 15, 1978; children: Amanda Camille, Lloyd Joseph. BS, Ark. State U., Jonesboro, 1969; MS, Ark. State U., 1972; PhD, Okla. State U., 1976. Sci. tchr. Bay-Brown Pub. Sch., Bay, Ark., 1969-71; NIH postdoctoral fellow Baylor Coll. Medicine, Houston, 1976-79; asst. prof. biochemistry La. Tech. U., Ruston, 1979-83, assoc. prof., 1983-89, prof., 1989—; adv. com. pre-med. and pre-dentistry La. Tech. U., 1979—; NASA/ASEE summer faculty fellow Johnson Space Ctr., Houston, 1994, 95. Mem. undergrad. rsch. com. Am. Heart Assn., La., 1980-95, bd. dirs. 1982-86, 88-92. Recipient Univ. Senate Chair award La. Tech.U., 1996; Quest for Quality fellow La. Tech. U., 1995. Mem. Am. Chem. soc. (chmn. Quachita Valley sect. 1986), La. Acad. Scis. (chair chemistry sect. 1986-92, dir. phys. scis. divsn. 1992-95), Sigma Xi, Phi Kappa Phi, Phi Lambda Upsilon, Phi Eta Sigma, Beta Beta Beta. Methodist. Home: 151 Camillia Cir Ruston LA 71270 Office: La Tech U Biochemistry Lab PO Box 3159 Tech Sta Ruston LA 71272

SNOW, ROBERT BARTLEY, neurosurgeon; b. Teaneck, N.J., July 28, 1952; s. Howard Robert and Claire Eileen (Barth) S.; m. Margaret Ellis, June 23, 1979; children: Lauren, Caitlin. BS, Syracuse U., 1974; AM, U. Chgo., 1976, PhD, 1980, MD, Stanford U., 1981. Cert. M.D. New York State, 1982. Assoc. prof. neurol. surgery Cornell U. Med. Sch., N.Y.C., 1982—. Contbr. over 30 articles to profl. jours., chpts. to books. Fellow ACS; mem. Congress of Neurol. Surgeons, Am. Assn. Neurologic Surgeons, Internat. Pituitary Soc. Office: 523 E 72d St New York NY 10021

SNUSTAD, DIANE GAIL, medical educator; b. Fargo, N.D., Dec. 14, 1952; d. Nels Owen and Myrtle Iola (Christianson) S.; m. Paul William Humphreys, July 14, 1984; children: Emily Victoria, Alexandra Elizabeth. BA, U. Minn., 1974, MD, 1979. Resident W.Va. U., Morgantown, 1979-82; asst. prof. medicine U. Pitts., 1982-85, Med. Coll. Va., Richmond, 1985-86, U. Va., Charlottesville, 1986—; med. dir. Colonnades Health Care Ctr., Charlottesville, 1991—. Contbr. articles to profl. jours. Mem. AMA, Am. Coll. Physicians, Am. Geriatrics Soc., Am. Soc. Aging, Gerontological Soc. Am., Phi Beta Kappa. Office: Colonnades Med Assocs 2610 Barracks Rd Charlottesville VA 27903

SNYDER, CHERYL ANN, physician; b. Detroit, July 31, 1958; d. Fred Frank Claassen and El Jean Delma (Mattice) Claassen Eggebeen; m. Gregory Michael Snyder, Feb. 14, 1988; children: Faith, Serena. AS, Cypress (Calif.) Coll., 1979; BSN, Calif. State U., Fullerton, 1984; DO, Coll. of The Pacific, Pomona, Calif., 1991. RN, Wash.; cert. family nurse practitioner. Emergency physician Kennewick (Wash.) Gen. Hosp., 1992—; assoc. clin. prof. EMT program CBC Coll., Pasco, Wash., 1993—; occupational health physician Advantage Occupation Health, Kennewick, Wash., 1995—. Rotary scholar, 1988, Steven Dyer Meml. scholar, 1991. Mem. Assn. Emergency Physicians, Christian Missionary Pilots. Home: 4009 S Morain Loop Kennewick WA 99337

SNYDER, DAVID ALLEN, military officer, surgeon; b. Portsmouth, Va., Nov. 8, 1948; s. William Allen and Betty Jane (Coffman) S.; m. Jan Karen Mitchell; children: Robert Patrick, Elizabeth Caroline. BA, U. Calif., Berkeley, 1970; MD, U. So. Calif., L.A., 1974; MPA, Troy State U., 1993. Diplomate Am. Bd. Surgery, Am. Bd. Med. Mgmt., Am. Coll. Healthcare Execs. Commd. ensign USN, 1970, advanced through grades to capt., 1988; intern and resident in surgery Naval Regional Med. Ctr., San Diego, 1974-79; staff surgeon Naval Regional Med. Ctr., Yokosoka, Japan, 1979-82; staff surgeon, quality assurance coord. Naval Hosp., Camp Pendleton, Calif., 1982-85; head dept. surgery Naval Hosp., Long Beach, Calif., 1985-87; staff, surgeon gen. of the Navy Bur. of Medicine & Surgery, Washington, 1987-88; chmn. surgery, dir. surg. svcs. Nat. Naval Med. Ctr., Bethesda, Md., 1988-93; exec. officer, chief med. staff Naval Med. Ctr., Oakland, Calif., 1993-94; commdr. Naval Med. Ctr., Oakland, 1994-96; force surgeon Surface Forces U.S. Pacific Fleet, 1996—; physician adv. bd. mem. Office of Champus, Aurora, Colo., 1989-92; assoc. prof. clin. surgery Uniformed Svcs. U. of the Health Scis., 1989-96. Contbr. articles to profl. jours. Sponsor Navy League, San Francisco, 1993-96, Combined Fed. Campaign, San Francisco, 1993-96; facility sponsor ARC, San Francisco, 1993-96; mem. Base Closure Coord. Com., San Francisco, 1994—. Decorated Navy Achievement medal USN, 1982, Navy Commendation medal USN, 1984, five Meritorious Svc. medals USN, 1987-94, Legion of Merit, 1996. Fellow ACS, Am. Coll. Physician Execs.; mem. San Francisco Surg. Soc., Alpha Omega Alpha, Phi Beta Kappa. Office: US Pacific Fleet Naval Surface Force 2841 Rendova Rd San Diego CA 92155-5490

SNYDER, JOHN JOSEPH, optometrist; b. Wonewoc, Wis., June 30, 1908; s. Burt Frederick and Alta Lavinia (Hearn) S.; A.B., UCLA, 1931, postgrad., 1931-32; postgrad. U. Colo., 1936, 38, 40, 41, U. So. Calif., 1945-46; B.S. in Optometry, Los Angeles Coll. Optometry, 1948, O.D., 1949. Tchr., La Plata County (Colo.) Pub. Schs., 1927-28; supt. Marvel (Colo.) Pub. Schs., 1932-33; tchr. Durango (Colo.) High Sch., 1933-41; pvt. practice optometry, Los Angeles, 1952-72, Torrance, Calif., 1972-78; now retired. Former bd. dirs. Francia Boys' Club, Los Angeles; former pres. Exchange Club South Los Angeles, also sec. Mem. AAAS, Am. Inst. Biol. Scis., Am., Calif., Los Angeles County Optometric Assn., Internat. Biog. Assn. Republican. Home: 25937 Reynolds St Loma Linda CA 92354-3962

SNYDER, MARTIN, podiatrist; b. Phila., Mar. 28, 1920; s. Aaron and Lena (Granick) S.; m. Janet Helen Fabe, Dec. 2, 1945; 1 child, Joel Mark. D of Podiatric Medicine, Calif. Coll. Podiatric Med, 1950. Diplomate Am. Bd. Podiatric Opthopaedics. Podiatrist pvt. practice, Tucson, Ariz., 1951-80; chief podiatry residency program Tuscon VA Med. Ctr., 1980-88; sr. clin. lectr. internal medicine & orthopedic surgery U. Ariz. Sch. Medicine, Tucson, 1988—; cons. in field. Contbg. author: Decision Making in Medicine, 1990. Pres. Temple Emanuel, Tucson, 1960-62. Recipient Arthritis Found. Vol. award, Atlanta, 1989. Fellow Am. Coll. Podaitric Orthopedics. Office: Rheumatology Sect 1501 N Campbell Tucson AZ 85724

SNYDER, PAUL EUGENE, dermatologist; b. Abington, Pa., Nov. 5, 1952; s. Eugene A. and Norma S. (Capri) S.; m. Karen E. Minati, 1976; children: Craig, Owen. Student, L.I. U., 1970-72; BA in Biology, U. pa., 1974; MD, Pa. State U., 1978. Diplomate Am. Bd. Internal Medicine, Am. Bd. Dermatology. Intern in medicine R.I. Hosp., Brown U., Providence, 1978-79, resident in medicine, 1979-81; resident in dermatology Roger Williams Gen. Hosp., Brown U., Providence, 1981-84; pvt. practice dermatology New Bedford, Mass., 1984—; rschr., presenter in field; chmn. divsn. dermatology St. Luke's Hosp., New Bedford; clin. instr. in medicine Brown U. Sch. Medicine, 1990—; mem. clin. tng. program Joint St. Luke's Hosp./Tufts Med. Sch. Contbr. articles to profl. publs. Health fair organizer Children's Mus. Dartmouth. Fellow Am. Acad. Dermatology; mem. Am. Soc. Dermatol. Surgery, Am. Cancer Soc. (area med. chair skin cancer task force), Bristol County Med. Soc., Lloyd Ctr. Environ. Studies, Mass. Acad. Dermatology, Mass. Med. Soc., New Eng. Dermatology Soc., Audubon Soc., Sierra Club. Home: 16 White Alder Way South Dartmouth MA 02748 Office: 334 Union St New Bedford MA 02740

SNYDER, PETER M., medical educator, medical researcher. BA in Biology summa cum laude, Luther Coll., 1984; MD, U. Iowa, 1989. Diplomate Am. Bd. Internal Medicine. Resident in internal medicine U. Tex., Dallas, 1989-92; fellow in cardiovascular diseases Dept. Internal Medicine U. Iowa Hosp. & Clinics, Iowa City, 1992-96, asst. prof. Dept. Internal Medicine, 1996—. Contbr. articles to profl. jours. Student Rsch. fellow U. Iowa, 1985; Student fellow Am. Heart Assn., 1987-88, recipient Clinician Scientist award, 1996. Mem. ACP, Alpha Omega Alpha. Office: U Iowa Coll of Medicine Dept Internal Medicine 200 Hawkins Dr Iowa City IA 52242-1081

SNYDER, ROBERT LEE, anesthesiologist; b. Midland, Mich., Aug. 26, 1952; s. Robert M. and Kathleen M. (Bogan) S.; m. Shelley Ann Marquiss, June 29, 1974; children: Kenneth Robert, Kacie Lee Ann. BS in Zoology, Mich. State U., 1974, D of Osteopathy, 1979. Diplomate Am. Osteopathic Bd. Anesthesiology. Intern Saginaw (Mich.) Osteo. Hosp., 1979-80, cons., 1982—; resident in anesthesia Flint (Mich.) Osteo. Hosp., 1980-82; staff anesthesiologist McPherson Community Health Ctr., Howell, Mich., 1982-88, chief of anesthesia services, 1986-88, chmn. dept. anesthesia, 1986-87; chmn. dept. anesthesia McPherson Cmty. Health Ctr., 1988-89; staff anesthesiologist Mid-Mich. Regional Med. Ctr., Midland, Mich., 1988—; cons. privileges anesthesia Mid-Mich. Regional Med. Ctr., Clare, Mich., 1991—; med. dir., chmn. dept. anesthesia Mid-Mich. Regional Med. Ctr., Midland, Mich., 1994—; examiner Am. Osteo. Bd. Anesthesiologists, 1990—; cons. Herrick Meml. Hosp., Tecumseh, Mich., 1982; assoc. clin. prof. Mich. State U. East Lansing, 1982—; lectr. Mich. Osteo. Med. Ctr., Detroit, 1986; program chmn. Am. Osteo. Coll. Anesthesiologist Ann. Conv. and Sci. Seminar, 1990. Legis. asst. to Thomas Holcomb State Rep., 1974-75; physician liaison United Way, Livingston County, Mich., 1986. Recipient Richard P. Alper Meml. award for Community Service, Mich. State U., 1979. Fellow Am. Osteo. Coll. Anesthesiologists (bd. govs.); mem. Am. Osteo. Assn. (residency inspector 1994—), Mich. Assn. Osteo. Physicians and Surgeons (del. 1985-89, numerous coms.), Livingston County Osteo. Assn. (sec.-treas. 1984-86), Mich. Soc. Osteo. Anesthesiologists (pres. 1988-90, chmn. bd. trustees 1990-92), Mich. Soc. Anesthesiologists, Am. Soc. Anesthesiologists, Mich. State Med. Soc. (del. 1993—), Midland County Med. Soc. (sec.-treas. 1993, v.p. 1994, pres. 1995—), Mich. State U. Alumni Assn., Jaycees, Sigma Sigma Phi (founding chpt. pres. 1977). Methodist. Home and Office: 2367 N Deer Valley Dr Midland MI 48642-8800

SNYDER, ROBERT LEROY, pathology educator; b. Ellwood City, Pa., Apr. 24, 1926; s. Albert R. and Helen M. (Schweinsburg) S.; m. Patricia L. Daugherty, Sept. 10, 1949; children: David L., James R., Mark A., Matthew J. BS, Pa. State U., University Park, 1950, MS, 1952; ScD, Johns Hopkins U., 1960. Rsch. asst. U.S. Fish & Wildlife Svc., Boston, 1951-52; rsch. biologist Pa. Game Commn., Harrisburg, 1952-57; rsch. assoc. Johns Hopkins U., Balt., 1957-59; adj. prof. comparative pathology U. Pa., Phila., 1961—; dir. Penrose Rsch. Lab., Phila., 1959-89. Author: Biology of Population Growth, 1976. Midshipman USN, 1943-47. Lutheran.

SNYDER, SOLOMON HALBERT, psychiatrist, pharmacologist; b. Washington, Dec. 26, 1938; s. Samuel Simon and Patricia (Yakerson) S.; m. Elaine Borko, June 10, 1962; children: Judith Rhea, Deborah Lynn. M.D. cum laude, Georgetown U., 1962, D.Sc. (hon.), 1986; D.Sc. (hon.), Northwestern U., 1981; PhD (hon.), Ben Gurion U., 1990. Intern Kaiser Found. Hosp., San Francisco, 1962-63; rsch. assoc. NIMH, Bethesda, Md., 1963-65; resident psychiatry Johns Hopkins Hosp., Balt., 1965-68; assoc. prof. psychiatry and pharmacology Johns Hopkins Med. Sch., 1968-70, prof., 1970-77, disting. svc. prof. psychiatry and pharmacology, 1977-80, disting. svc. prof. neurosci., psychiatry, and pharmacology, 1980—, dir. dept. neurosci., 1980—; NIH lectr., 1979. Author: Uses of Marijuana, 1971, Madness and the Brain, 1973, Opiate Receptor Mechanisms, 1975, The Troubled Mind, 1976, Biologic Aspects of Mental Disorder, 1980, Drugs and the Brain, 1986, Brainstorming, 1989; editor Perspectives in Neuropharmacology, 1971, Frontiers in Catecholamine Research, 1973, Handbook of Psychopharmacology, 1974; contbr. articles to profl. jours. Served with USPHS, 1963-65. Recipient Outstanding Scientist award Md. Acad. Scis., 1969, John Jacob Abel award Am. Pharmacology Soc., 1970, A.E. Bennett award Soc. Biol. Psychiatry, 1970; Gaddum award Brit. Pharm. Soc., 1974, F.O. Schmitt award in neuroscis. MIT, 1974, Nicholas Giarman lecture award Yale U., 1975, Rennebohm award U. Uis., 1976, Salmon award 1977, Stanley Dean award Am. Coll. Psychiatrists, 1978, Harvey Lecture. award, 1978, Lasker award, 1978, Wolf prize, 1983, Dickson prize, 1983, Sci. Achievement award AMA, 1985, Ciba-Gigy-Drew award, 1985, Strecker prize, 1986, Edward Sachar Meml. award Columbia U., 1986, Paul K. Smith Meml. lecture award George Washington U., 1986; Sense of Smell award Fragrance Rsch. Found., 1987, Julius Axelrod lecture award CUNY. 1988, John Flynn Meml. lecture award, Yale U., 1988, V. Erspamer lecture award Georgetown U., 1990, J. Allyn Taylor prize, 1990, Pasarow Found. award, 1991; Bower award Achievement Sci. Franklin Inst., 1991, Chauncey Leake Lecture award, 1992; William Veatch lecture award Harvard Med. Sch., 1992, Joseph Priestley prize Dickinson Coll., 1992, Konrad Bloch lecture award Harvard U., 1992, Basic Neurochem. lecture award Am. Soc. Neurochem., 1993, Nanine Duke lecture award Duke U., 1993, Salvador Luria lecture award MIT, 1993, Rudin lecture award Columbia U., 1995, Christian Herter lecture award NYU, 1995, Maclean lecture award, Baylor Med. Coll., 1995, Baxter award Am. Assn. Med. Colls., 1995, Bristol-Myers-Squibb Neurosci. prize, 1996. Fellow Am. Coll. Neuropsychopharmacology (Daniel Efron award 1974), Am. Psychiat. Assn. (Hofheimer award 1972, Disting. Svc. award 1989), Am. Acad. Arts and Scis., Am. Philosophical Soc.; mem. Nat. Acad. Scis., Soc. for Neurosci. (pres. 1979-80), Am. Soc. Biol. Chemists, Am. Pharmacology Soc., Inst. Medicine. Home: 3801 Canterbury Rd Apt 1001 Baltimore MD 21218-2315 Office: Johns Hopkins U Med Sch Dept Neurosciences 725 N Wolfe St Baltimore MD 21205-2105

SNYDERMAN, MICHELLE LYNN, physician; b. Bklyn., Oct. 6, 1966; d. Paul Gilbert and Diane Anita (Grant) S.; m. William Sullivan, June 7, 1996. BS in Psychology, Syracuse U., 1988; DO, N.Y. Coll. Osteo. Medicine, 1993. Intern St. Barnabas Hosp., Bronx, 1993-94; resident MacNeal Family Practice, Berwyn, Ill., 1994-96; physician Oak Lawn (Ill.) Med. Ctr., 1996—. Mem. AMA, Am. Osteo. Assn., Am. Acad. Family Practitioners. Home: PO Box 1415 Oak Park IL 60304 Office: Law MEd Office 4301 W 95th St Oak Lawn IL 60453

SNYDERMAN, RALPH, medical educator, physician; b. Bklyn., Mar. 13, 1940; m. Judith Ann Krebs, Nov. 18, 1967; 1 child, Theodore Benjamin. B.S., Washington Coll., Chestertown, Md., 1961; M.D., SUNY-Bklyn., 1965. Diplomate Am. Bd. Internal Medicine, Am. Bd. Allergy and Immunology. Med. intern Duke U. Hosp., Durham, N.C., 1965-66, med. resident, 1966-67, asst. prof. medicine and immunology, 1972-74, assoc. prof., 1974-77, chief, div. rheumatology and immunology, 1975-87, prof. medicine and immunology, 1980-87, Frederic M. Hanes prof. medicine, prof. immunology, 1984-87, adj. prof. medicine, 1987-89; surgeon USPHS, NIH, Bethesda, Md., 1967-69; sr. staff fellow Nat. Inst. Dental Research, NIH, Bethesda, Md., 1969-70, sr. investigator immunology sect. lab. microbiology and immunology, 1970-72; chief, div. rheumatology Durham VA Hosp., Bethesda, Md., 1972-75; v.p. med. rsch. and devel. Genentech, Inc., South San Francisco, Calif., 1987-88, sr. v.p. med. rsch. and devel., 1988-89; chancellor for health affairs, dean Sch. Medicine Duke U., Durham, 1989—, James E. Duke prof. medicine, 1989—; CEO Duke U. Health System; adj. asst. prof. oral biology U. N.C. Sch. Dental Medicine, Chapel Hill, 1974-75; Howard Hughes med. investigator, Durham, 1972-77; dir. Lab Immune Effector Function, Howard Hughes Med. Inst., Durham, 1977-87; adj. prof. medicine U. Calif., San Francisco, 1987-89. Editor: Contemporary Topics in Immunobiology, 1979, Inflammation: Basic Concepts and Clinical Correlates, 1988, 2d edit., 1992; contbr. articles to profl. jours. Recipient McLaughlin award for inflammation rsch., 1978, Alexander von Humboldt award Fed. Republic Germany, 1985, award for lifetime achievements in inflammation rsch. Ciba-Geigy Morris Ziff, 1991, Bonniziang award for excellence in leukocyte biology rsch., 1993, Disting. Alumni Achievement award SUNY Bklyn., 1995, Disting. Alumni citation Washington Coll., 1996, others. Mem. NAS, Inst. Medicine, Assn. Am. Physicians, Am. Assn. Immunologists, Am. Soc. Clin. Investigation, Am. Acad. Allergy, Am. Assn. Cancer Rsch., Soc. for Leukocyte Biology, Am. Fedn. Clin. Rsch., Am. Assn. Pathologists, Am. Soc. for Biochemistry and Molecular Biology, Assn. Acad. Health Ctrs., Am. Coll. Rheumatology, Am. Assn. for Med. Colls., Soc. for Med. Adminstrs., Sigma Xi. Office: Duke U Sch Medicine PO Box 3701 Durham NC 27710

SNYDERS, DIRK JOHAN, electrophysiologist, biophysicist, educator; b. Wilrijk, Antwerpen, Belgium, July 18, 1955; came to U.S., 1984; s. Godlief Stefaan and Mariette L. (Dieu) S. BS in Med. Sci., U. Antwerp, Belgium, 1976; MD with great honor, U. Antwerp, 1980. Lic. physician, cert. cardiologist, Belgium. Resident then fellow in internal medicine and cardiology Univ. Hosp. Antwerp, 1980-84; postdoctoral fellow U. Calif., San Francisco, 1984-85; instr. medicine Vanderbilt U., Nashville, 1986-87, asst. prof., 1987-95, assoc. prof. medicine and pharmacology, 1995—. Co-author: The Heart and the Cardiovascular System, 1991; mem. editorial bd. Circulation Rsch.; reviewer Jour. Gen. Physiology, Cardiovascular Rsch., Jour. Molecular and Cellular Cardiology, Molecular Pharmacology, European Jour. Pharmacology; contbr. articles to profl. jours. Lt. Med. Svc., Belgian Army, 1987-88, Germany. Recipient Specia award Specia NV., Belgium, 1980; hon. fellow Belgian Am. Ednl. Found., NATO rsch. fellow, 1984, med. rsch. fellow Alta. Heritage Found., 1984; rsch. grantee NIH. Mem. AAAS, Biophys. Soc., Soc. Gen. Physiologists, Am. Heart Assn. (Basic Sci. Coun.). Office: Vanderbilt U Med Ctr 554 MRB 2 Nashville TN 37232-6602

SNYDMAN, DAVID RICHARD, infectious diseases specialist, educator; b. Phila., Sept. 23, 1946; s. Leonard and Marie (Perrin) S.; m. Diane Canter, June 26, 1971; children: Laura Kate, Alexander Julian. BA, Williams Coll., 1968; MD, U. Pa., 1972. Diplomate Am Bd. Infectious Disease. Intern New Eng. Med. Ctr., Boston, 1972-73, resident in medicine, 1973-74; asst. prof. Sch. Medicine Tufts U., Boston, 1979-84, assoc. prof., 1984-90, prof. medicine and pathology, 1990—; hosp. epidemiologist New Eng. Med. Ctr., Boston, 1979-89, dir. clin. microbiology, 1987—; Epidemic Intelligence Svc. officer CDC, Atlanta, 1974-76. Assoc. editor: Yearbook of Infectious Diseases, 1986—; contbr. over 140 articles to New Eng. Jour. Medicine, Jour. Infectious Diseases, others. Lt. comdr. USPHS, 1974-76. Grantee NIH, 1982-93. Fellow Infectious Disease Soc. (Bristol fellow 1978-79); mem. ACP (Tchng. and Rsch. scholar 1979-82), Soc. Hosp. Epidemiologists, Am. Soc. Transplant Physicians. Office: New Eng Med Ctr 750 Washington St Boston MA 02111-1533

SOARES, GREGORY LOUIS, social services administrator, consultant; b. Fall River, Mass., Nov. 14, 1951; s. Louis Massa and Hilda (Enos) S.; m. Maria Fatima Fernandes, July 9, 1977 (div. 1982); m. Deborah Ann Smusz, Apr. 28, 1984. AA in Pre-profl. Studies, Bristol Community Coll., Fall River, Mass., 1971; BA in Psychology, Roger Williams Coll., 1973; MEd in Integrated Studies, Cambridge (Mass.) Coll., 1989. Nat. bd. cert. clin. hypnotherapist. Spl. edn. tchr. St. Vincent's Home, Fall River, 1973-80, coord. vocat. edn. programs, 1980-83; family therapist Edgehill Newport, Newport, R.I., 1983-88, supr. family dept., 1988-90, dir. inpatient/outpatient rehab. svcs., 1991—; cons., New Eng. area, 1986—.

SOBCZAK, JUDY MARIE, clinical psychologist; b. Detroit, Dec. 28, 1949; d. Thaddeus Joseph and Bernice Agnes (Sowinski) Gorski; m. John Nicholas

Sobczak, Aug. 17, 1974. BE cum laude, U. Toledo, 1971; postgrad., Ea. Mich. U., 1980-82; PhD, U. Toledo, 1987. Lic. psychologist. Tchr. Ottawa (Ohio)-Glandorf Schs., 1971-73; prin., tchr. St. Mary Sch., Assumption, Ohio, 1973-77; tchr. Our Lady of Perpetual Help Sch., Toledo, 1978-79; staff psychologist Outer Dr. Hosp., Lincoln Park, Mich., 1987-90; psychologist Adult/Youth Devel. Svcs., Farmington, Mich., 1991-95, Davis Counseling Ctr., Farmington Hills, Mich., 1996—; with Northwestern Cmty. Svcs., Livonia, Mich., 1996—, Orchard Hills Psychiat. Ctr., Plymouth, Mich., 1996—; adj. asst. prof. Madonna U., Livonia, Mich., 1987-94. Eucharistic minister St. Anthony Cath. Ch., Belleville, Mich., 1991—, parish coun. 1993-96; Cath. Svc. Appeal co-chmn., 1993—; sec. bd. dirs. Children Are Precious Respite Care Ctr., 1995. Fellow Mich. Women Psychologists (charter; newsletter editor 1987-92, treas 1989-93, Plaque of Appreciation 1992-96, sec. 1993—); mem. Mich. Psychol. Assn., Phi Kappa Phi. Home: 41498 Mckinley St Belleville MI 48111-3439 Office: Davis Counseling Ctr 37923 W Twelve Mile Rd Farmington Hills MI 48331

SOBECKI-RYNIAK, DIANE MARIE, women's health nurse; b. Wyandotte, Mich., Mar. 6, 1960; d. Leonard Francis and Rita Norma (Dziedzic) Sobecki; m. Timothy Gregory Boik, May 3, 1980 (div. Feb. 1990); children: Sarah Ann Boik, Jennifer Marie Boik; m. Gary James Ryniak, Nov. 13, 1993; children: Joseph Leonard Ryniak, Hannah Rose Ryniak. BSN, U. Mich., 1994. RN, Mich.; cert. BLS. Clin. nurse Goddard Clinic, Allen Park, Mich., 1979-87, to family practice physician, Allen Park, 1987-92, to obstetrician/gynecologist, Trenton, Mich., 1987—; neonatal, labor and delivery nurse Riverside Osteo. Hosp., Trenton, 1994—. Catechism instr. St. Cyprian Sch./Parish, Riverview, Mich., 1994. Mem. AWOHNN, Sigma Theta Tau. Republican. Roman Catholic. Home: 26733 Park Ln Woodhaven MI 48183-4383 Office: Riverside Osteo Hosp Truax St Trenton MI 48183

SOBEL, MARK ESAR, physician, researcher; b. N.Y.C., Apr. 14, 1949; s. Abraham David and Selma Etta (Spitzer) S. BA, Brandeis U., 1970; MD, Mt. Sinai Sch. Medicine, N.Y.C., 1975; PhD in Biomed. Scis., CUNY, 1975. Diplomate Nat. Bd. Med. Examiners. Med. intern, clin. fellow in pediatrics Children's Hosp. Med. Ctr./Harvard U. Med. Sch., Boston, 1975-76; rsch. assoc. NIH, Bethesda, Md., 1976-79, 80-83; sr. investigator Nat. Cancer Inst., Bethesda, 1983-92, chief molecular pathology sect., 1992—; vis. scientist Max Planck Inst. for Biochemistry, Martinsried bei Munchen, Germany, 1979-80; dir. Concepts in Molecular Biology course Am. Soc. Investigative Pathology, Rockville, Md., 1987-95. Contbr. more than 80 articles to profl. jours.; patentee in field. Capt. USPHS, 1975—. Recipient Commendation medal USPHS, 1989, other awards. Mem. Am. Soc. for Biochemistry and Molecular Biology, Am. Soc. Investigative Pathology (councilor 1995—), Am. Soc. for Cell Biology, Am. Soc. Microbiology, Am. Assn. for Cancer Rsch., Assn. for Molecular Pathology (sec.-treas. 1995—), Phi Beta Kappa, Alpha Omega Alpha. Jewish. Office: Nat Cancer Inst Bldg 10 Rm 2A33 NIH Bethesda MD 20892-1500

SOBEL, NANCY B., obstetrician, gynecologist, educator; b. Chgo., June 15, 1954; d. Walter Howard and Betty Jane (Debs) S. BA in Chemistry-Biology, Skidmore Coll., 1976; PhD in Pharmacological and Physiol. Scis., U. Chgo., 1982, MD, 1984. Diplomate Am. Bd. Ob-Gyn. Intern, resident in gen. surgery U. Chgo. Hosp. and Clinics, 1984-86; resident in ob-gyn. Yale New Haven (Conn.) Hosp., 1986-89; assoc. Arborway Group St. Margaret's Hosp. for Women, Boston, 1989-91, med. dir. Nurse Midwifery Svc., 1991-92; assoc. staff dept. gynecology Lahey Clinic Med. Ctr., Burlington, Mass., 1992—; asst. prof. ob-gyn. Tufts U. Sch. Medicine, 1989-93; clin. instr. obgyn., reproductive biology Harvard Med. Sch., 1992—. Contbr. articles to profl. jours. Active Bus. and Profl. Assn. Chgo. Symphony Orch., 1982—; alumni liaison Boston chpt. Achievement Rewards for Coll. Scientists Found., 1991-92, bd. dirs., 1992—, pres., 1994—; mem. CLiff Swellers, Chgo., 1991—; bd. adv. Nat. Youth Leadership Forum Boston, 1994, Metropolitans Wang Ctr., Boston, 1995—. NIH Gen. Med. Scis. fellow Pharmacological Scis. Rsch. Tng. Program, 1977-81, William Scott Bond fellow Ben May Lab. for Cancer Rsch., 1981; Achievement Rewards for Coll. Scientists scholar, 1983-84. Fellow ACOG (dist. 1 quality assurance com. 1990—, practice com. 1993—), Am. Coll. Surgeons (assoc.); mem. AMA, Mass. Med. Soc., Am. Med. Women's Assn., Am. Soc. Law and Medicine, Assn. Women Surgeons, N. Am. Menopause Soc. Office: Lahey Hitchcock Clinic 41 Mall Rd Burlington MA 01805-0001

SOBEL, RICHARD STEPHEN, pediatric dentist; b. Cleve., Apr. 10, 1943; s. Murray and Matty (Mostoff) S.; married, 1994. BA, Queens Coll., 1965; DDS, SUNY, 1967. Resident in pediatric dentistry Childrens' Hosp. Med. Ctr., Boston, 1967-70; fellow in pediatric dentistry Harvard U., Boston, 1967-70; faculty clinic U. Pacific Sch. Dentistry, San Francisco, 1971-73, practice dentistry specializing in pediatrics, 1973-76, asst. prof., 1970-74, assoc. prof., 1974—; dir. pediatric dentistry residency program Childrens' Hosp. Med. Ctr., Oakland, Calif., 1974-82; practice dentistry specializing in pediatrics San Leandro, Calif., 1982-84; chief sect. pediatric dentistry Mt. Zion Hosp., San Francisco, 1982-87; practice dentistry specializing in pediatrics Antioch (Calif.) Pediatric Dentistry, 1984—; lectr., asst. prof. U. Calif. Sch. Dentistry, San Francisco, 1972-75, 1979—; cons. VA Hosp., Highland Hosp., Travis AFB, 1978-87; cons. craniofacial team Children's Hosp., Oakland, 1987—. Founder Bay Area Guidance Coun. for the Disabled, San Francisco; chairperson Childrens Health Week, San Francisco, 1974, 75. Mem. ADA, Am. Acad. Pediatric Dentistry (trustee 1994—), Calif. Dental Assn., Am. Soc. Dentistry Children, Calif. Soc. Dentistry Children (treas. 1976-82, pres. 1984-85), Am. Soc. Human Genetics, Internat. Assn. Dental Rsch., Calif. Soc. Pediatric Dentists (exec. bd. 1980-82, treas. 1987, sec. 1988, v.p. 1989, pres.-elect 1990, pres. 1991), Soc. Cranio Facial Genetics, Fedn. Dentaire Internat., Dental Assn. for Persons With Disabilities, Pierre Fauchand Hon. Dental Acad., Am. Assn. Hosp. Dentistry, Harvard U. Alumni Assn., SUNY at Buffalo Alumni Assn. Office: Antioch Pediatric Dentistry 2901 Lone Tree Way Antioch CA 94509-4963

SOBIN, LESLIE HOWARD, pathologist, educator; b. N.Y.C., Feb. 10, 1934; s. Martin L. and Kitty N. Sobin; m. Margareta E.D. Ahlstrom, Dec. 21, 1962; 1 child, Annika D. BS, Union Coll., 1955; MD, SUNY, N.Y.C., 1959. Diplomate Am. Bd. Pathology. Instr. pathology Cornell U. Med. Coll., N.Y.C., 1962-65, asst. prof. pathology, 1965; WHO visiting prof. pathology Univ. Kabul, Afghanistan, 1965-68; assoc. prof. pathology Cornell U. Med. Coll., 1968-70; pathologist WHO, Geneva, 1970-81; prof. pathology Uniformed Svcs. Univ. Health Scis., Bethesda, Md., 1984—; head WHO collaborating ctr. tumor classification Armed Forces Inst. Pathology, Washington, 1983—, assoc. dir. sci. publs., 1987—, chief gastrointestinal pathology, 1991—; adj. prof. pathology Cornell U. Med. Coll., 1980—, Georgetown U. Med. Coll., 1992—; expert, panel on cancer WHO, Geneva, 1981—. Author: Pathology Primer in Verse, 1978, Tales of the Ampulla of Vater, 1994, The Last Examination: The Prosecutor's Guide to the Autopsy—In Verse, 1996; editor: International Histological Classification of Tumors, 1970—, TNM Classification of Tumors, 1987, 92. Recipient Sr. Exec. Svc. award Dept. of Army, 1990, Meritorious Presdl. Rank award, 1991. Fellow Royal Coll. Pathologists; mem. Internat. Acad. Pathology (sec. 1982-88). Office: Armed Forces Inst Pathology Washington DC 20306

SOBKOW, ROSEANNE, nurse; b. N.Y.C., Mar. 4, 1938; d. John and Mary (Heryla) S. Diploma in nursing, St. Agnes Hosp., 1965; BA, U. Redlands, Calif., 1978. RN. Hosp. corps WAVE USN, 1957-61, commd. ensign, 1967, advanced through grades to capt., 1989; from staff nurse to asst. dir. nursing, oper. rm. specialist USN Nurse Corps, 1967-92; ret.; tech. cons. Mil. Field Med. Systems Standards, Ft. Detrick, Md., 1982; tech. asst. U.S. Dept. Navy, Hosp. Ship Mercy, San Diego, 1986. Mem., support Humane Soc. U.S., Washington, 1991-95; mem., friend Nat. Parks & Conservation Assn., Washington, 1991-95, Zool. Soc. San Diego, 1991-95. Mem. Assn. Oper. Rm. Nurses, Assn. Mil. Surgeons of U.S., Assn. for Advancement Med. Instrumentation, Navy Nurse Corps Assn., Nature Conservancy.

SOBKOWICZ, HANNA MARIA, neurology researcher; b. Warsaw, Poland, Jan. 1, 1931; came to U.S., 1963; d. Stanislaw and Jadwiga (Ignaczak) S.; m. Jerzy E. Rose, Mar. 12, 1972. B.A., Girls State Lyceum, Gilwice, Poland, 1949; M.D, Med. Acad., Warsaw, 1954, Ph.D., 1962. Intern. 1st Internal Med. Clinic Med. Acad., Warsaw, 1954-55; resident 1st Internal Med. Clinic, Med. Acad., Warsaw, 1955-59; resident Neurol. Clinic, Med. Acad., 1959, jr. asst., 1959-61, sr. asst., 1961-63; research fellow neurology Mt. Sinai Hosp., N.Y.C., 1963-65; Nat. Multiple Sclerosis Soc. fellow Columbia U., N.Y.C., 1965-66; asst. prof. neurology U. Wis., Madison, 1966-72, assoc. prof., 1972-79, prof., 1979—. Contbr. articles to profl. jours. NIH research grantee, 1968—. Mem. Internat. Brain Rsch. Orgn., Assn. Rsch. in Otolaryngology, Soc. Neurosci., Internat. Soc. Devel. Neurosci. (editorial bd. 1984—), Electron Microscopy Soc. Am. Office: U Wis Dept Neurology 1300 University Ave Madison WI 53706-1510

SOBOL, BRUCE J., internist, educator, researcher; b. N.Y.C., June 10, 1923; s. Ira J. and Ida S. (Gelula) S.; B.A., Swarthmore Coll., 1947; M.D., N.Y.U., 1950; m. Barbara Sue Gordon, Apr. 30, 1951; children: Peter Gordon, Scott David. Intern, Bellevue Hosp., N.Y.C., 1950-51, resident, 1951-52, N.Y. Heart Assn. fellow, 1953-55; resident VA Hosp., Boston, 1952-53; practice medicine specializing in internal medicine, White Plains, N.Y., 1955-59; dir. cardio-pulmonary lab. Westchester County (N.Y.) Med. Ctr., Valhalla, 1959-78; rsch. prof. medicine N.Y. Med. Coll., 1970-78; dir. med. rsch. Boehringer Ingelheim, Ltd., Ridgefield, Conn., 1978-83. Bd. dirs. Westchester Community Svcs. Coun., 1977-79; pres. Westchester Heart Assn., 1976-79. Served with inf. AUS, World War II; ETO. Diplomate Am. Bd. Internal Medicine. Fellow ACP, Am. Coll. Allergy, Am. Coll. Chest Physicians, N.Y. Acad. Scis.; mem. Am. Physiol. Soc., Am. Heart Assn., N.Y. Trudea Soc., Am. Thoracic Soc., Am. Fedn. Clin. Rsch. Contbr. numerous articles to profl. publs. Office: 275 Ridgebury Rd Ridgefield CT 06877-1410

SOBRERO, MARIA-INES ADELA, physician, consultant; b Santa Fe, Argentina, Nov. 5, 1955; came to U.S., 1958; d. Aquiles José and Adela Hortensia Sobrero; m. Osvaldo Enrique Sobrero, Oct. 5, 1984; children: Ana Cristina, Gabriela Paula, Carlos Andrés. MD, Universidad Nac. de Rosario, Argentina, 983. Intern, resident Lincoln Hosp., N.Y.C., 1983-86; fellow Northwestern U., Chgo., 1987-91; physician Neomedica, Inc., Chgo., 1991—; ABIM, 1986, ABIM Nephrology, 1994. Office: Neomedica 450 E Ohio St Chicago IL 60611

SOCHET, MARY ALLEN, psychotherapist, community organizer, writer; b. Plattsburgh, N.Y., Feb. 10, 1938; d. Edwin Elisha and Mary Elizabeth (Thomson) Allen; m. Marvin J. Sochet, 1963; children: Melorra, David. BS in Childhood Edn., SUNY, Plattsburgh, 1958; MA in Human Rels., NYU, 1961, PhD in Human Devel., 1963. Tchr. kindergarten L.I. Pub. Schs., 1958-62; tchr. N.Y.C. Pub. Schs., 1962-64; prof. early childhood edn., child devel. and psychology Bklyn. Coll., 1964-71; program dir., acting exec. dir. Newark Pre-Sch. Coun., 1965-66; psychotherapist N.Y.C. Community Guidance Svc., 1966-78; staff cons. Human Resources Inst., 1966—; pvt. practice psychotherapy N.Y.C., 1966—; writer, lectr., ednl. cons. and editorial cons. in field. Author: (with Robert Allen) Toward a Caring Community, 1980; contbr. articles on edn., community orgns., peace and mental health to various jours. Founding mem. Community Loft, 1971-74, Neighbor's Network, 1979—; organizing mem. Children's Free Sch., 1969-81; co-chair Kids Meeting Kids Can Make a Difference, 1982—. NCCJ fellow, 1961-62; recipient Founder's Day award NYU, 1963. Mem. Am. Psychol. Assn., Soc. Psychol. Study Social Issues, Psychologists for Social Responsibility. Home and Office: 380 Riverside Dr New York NY 10025-1858

SOCOLOW, EDWARD LLOYD, physician; b. N.Y.C., Mar. 30, 1934; s. Albert and Florence (Creamer) S.; m. Roxanne Miller, Mar. 19, 1960; children: John, Brian. BS, Yale Coll., 1955, MD, 1958. Diplomate Am. Bd. Internal Medicine, Am. Bd. Endocrinology and Metabolism, Nat. Bd. Med. Examiners. Intern New Haven (Conn.) Hosp., 1958-59; asst. resident U. Calif. Hosp., L.A., 1959-60; rsch. staff Atomic Bomb Casualty Commn., Hiroshima, 1960-62; clin., rsch. fellow Mass. Gen. Hosp. and Harvard Med. Sch., 1962-63; chief resident New England Ctr. Hosp., Boston, 1963-64; clin., rsch. fellow endocrine divsn. Thorndike Meml. Lab. Boston City Hosp. and Harvard Med. Sch., 1964-66; asst. physician Boston City Hosp., 1966-68; attending physician med. svc. and endocrine clinic Jacobi Med. Ctr., N.Y., 1969—; asst. clin. prof. of medicine Albert Einstein Coll. of Medicine; instr. Harvard Med. Sch., 1966-67, assoc. in medicine, 1967-68; endocrine cons. Boston Hosp. for Women, 1966-68, Putnam Hsop. Ctr., Carmel, N.Y., 1969—; attending physician in endocrinology, No. Westchester Hosp., Mount Kisco, N.Y., 1969—. Contbr. articles to profl. pubs. With USPHS, 1960-62. Mem. Endocrine Soc., Am. Thyroid Assn., Am. Fertility Soc., N.Y. State Med. Soc., Westchester County Med. Soc., Putnam County Med. Soc., Mass. Med. Soc., Clin. Soc. N.Y. Diabetes Assn., Am. Diabetes Assn., Sigma Xi. Home: 21 Brevoort Pl Chappaqua NY 10514 Office: 359 Main St Mount Kisco NY 10549-3028

SODARO, EDWARD RICHARD, psychiatrist; b. Glen Cove, N.Y., Oct. 3, 1947; s. Edward Richard and Mae Florence (Culp) S.; m. Denise Roberta Stetch; 2 children. BS, Siena Coll., Loudonville, N.Y., 1969; MD, Georgetown U., 1973; MA, Grad. Faculty of New Sch., N.Y.C., 1976. Diplomate Am. Bd. Psychiatry and Neurology, Am. Bd. Adolescent Psychiatry, Am. Bd. Quality Assurance and Utilization Rev. Physicians, Am. Soc. Addiction Medicine, Am. Forensic Psychiatry, Am. Bd. Geriatric Psychiatry, Am. Bd. Addiction Psychiatry; cert. geriatric psychiatry specialist; cert. forensic psychiatrist; cert. med. rev. officer. Resident in psychiatry L.I. Jewish Hosp., New Hyde Park, N.Y., 1973-76; staff psychiatrist N.Y. Hosp./Cornell Med. Ctr., White Plains, N.Y., 1979-81; faculty N.Y. Hosp./Cornell Med. Ctr., 1979-81; sr. psychiatrist South Oaks Hosp., Amityville, N.Y., 1981—; clin. asst. prof. SUNY Stony Brook Sch. Medicine. Mem. Am. Psychiat. Assn., Med. Soc. State of N.Y. (com. for physicians, health), Am. Soc. Addiction Medicine, Am. Coll. Physician Execs., Sons Am. Revolution. Roman Catholic. Office: South Oaks Hosp 400 Sunrise Hwy Amityville NY 11701-2508

SODER, DEE A., psychologist; b. Oklahoma City, June 20, 1947; d. Keats Endymion Soder. BS with distinction, U. Okla., 1969, PhD in Psychology, 1976. Sr. rsch. psychologist U.S. Office Pers. Mgmt., Washington, 1974-77, Exec. Office Pres. U.S., Washington, 1978; staffing dir. for D.C., 1979; v.p. human resources devel. Prudential Ins. Co. Am., 1980-84; founder Endymion Co., N.Y.C., 1986—, CEO Perspective Group, 1996—. Author: Job Analysis, An Effective Management Tool, 1983, Breaking Through the Glass Ceiling, Corporate Board, 1993; profiled in Fortune Mag. and numerous other mags. and profl. jours. Founder Pers. Testing Coun. Met. Washington; prin. Ctr. for Excellence in Govt.; bd. dirs. Women's Campaign Fund, Women's Econ. Roundtable. Office: US Endymion Co Inc 50 Rockefeller Plz 2nd Flr New York NY 10020

SODER-ALDERFER, KAY CHRISTIE, counseling administrator; b. Evanston, Ill., Oct. 25, 1949; d. Earl Eugene and Alice Kathryn (Lien) Soder; m. David Luther Alderfer, May 15, 1976. BSE, No. Ill. U., 1972; postgrad., Luth. Sch. Theology, Phila., 1973; MA, Gov.'s State U., University Park, Ill., 1978; PhD, Walden U., 1985. Consecrated deaconess Luth. Ch., 1974. News reporter Suburban Life Newspaper, La Grange Park, Ill., 1972; counselor various orgns. Ill. & Pa., 1973—; parish worker Luth. Ch., De Kalb, Ill., 1973-74; pub. rels. asst. Luth. Ch. Women, Phila., 1974-76; editor Luth. Ch., Chgo., 1979—; spiritual dir. Gentle Pathways, Downers Grove, Ill., 1988—, counseling psychologist, 1990—, also bd. dirs.; cons. Evang. Luth. Ch. in Am., Chgo., 1988—, Lehigh Valley Hosp. Assn., Allentown, Pa., 1986. Author: Gentle Journeys, 1993, With Those Who Grieve, 1995, Help! There's a Monster in My Head, 1996; editor Entree, 1988-93, Multicultural Jour., 1992—; graphic designs exhbn. Franklin Mus., Phila., 1981. Spokeswoman Progressive Epilepsy Network, Phila., 1980-85; chair spiritual life com. Luth. Deaconess Cmty., Gladwyne, Pa., 1990-92; founder Teens with Epilepsy and Motivation, 1995; vol. March of Dimes, Ill., 1991-93; amb. of goodwill Good Bears of the World, 1993-94; spiritual dir. Evang. Luth. Ch. in Am. Recipient Silver award Delaware Valley Neographics Soc., 1981; 50th anniversary scholar Luth. Deaconess Community, 1983. Mem. AAUW, APA (div. women and psychology, div. psychology and the arts, div. psychology and religion). Office: Gentle Pathways 1207 55th St Downers Grove IL 60515-4810

SODERLAND, CARL ALBERT, physician; b. Falmouth, Mass., Oct. 24, 1948; s. Albert and Eloise (McDowell) S.; m. Diane Palmer, Aug. 7, 1971; children: Peter, Callie. AB, Dartmouth Coll., 1971; MD with honor. U. Rochester, 1975; MPH, Harvard Sch. Pub. Health, 1988. Diplomate Am. Bd. Internal Medicine. Physician Family Practice Assocs., Ipswich, Mass., 1979-85; med. dir. GTE Electric Products Group, Danvers, Mass., 1985-89, North Shore Comprehensive Care, Ipswich, Danvers, Beverly, Mass., 1989-93; med. dir. cmty. group practice Lahey Health Network, Burlington, Mass., 1993-94; exec. med. dir. Lahey HCHP Partnership, Lynnfield, Mass., 1994—; med. dir. North Shore Rehab., Danvers, 1992—; mem. Lahey-Hitchcock bd. govs., Concord, N.H., 1995—. Trustee Coburn Charitable Soc., Ipswich, 1983—, Caldwell Convalescent Home, Ipswich, 1988—, Beverly (Mass.) Hosp. N.E./Cape Ann Health Sys., 1988—; chmn. bd. dirs. Bay Area Vis. Nurse Assn., Beverly, 1985-93. Mem. Boston Flycasters. Episcopalian. Home: 2 Green St Ipswich MA 01958 Office: Lahey Ipswich 130 County Rd Ipswich MA 01938

SODERSTROM, GERALD DOUGLAS, psychologist, educator; b. Junction City, Kans., July 21, 1941; s. Victor Herbert and Marjorie Elaine (Brouddus) S.; m. Virginia Ann Phelps, Oct. 15, 1966; 1 child, Michael Douglas. BSBA, Kans. State U., 1964; MA in Psychology and Counseling, Colo. State Coll., 1966; MS in Clin. Psychology, Ctrl. Mo. State Coll., 1970; PhD in Psychology, Utah State U., 1976. Dir. counseling Thief River Falls (Minn.) State Jr. Coll., 1966-68; instr. psychology Edison Jr. Coll., Ft. Myers, Fla., 1969-70; instr. sociology Ctrl. Oreg. C.C., Bend, 1972-73; counselor Ft. Scott (Kans.) C.C., 1973-76, Kilgore (Tex.) Coll., 1976-78; instr. psychology Wharton (Tex.) County Jr. Coll., 1978—; pvt. practice counseling Wharton, 1985-91; textbook cons. for various pub. cos., 1980-95; bd. dirs. Ft. Scott Mental Health Assn., 1974-76. Author: The Truth Less Told: Understanding Ourselves As We Really Are, 1995; contbr. articles, poems to profl. publs. Mem. Tex. Jr. Coll. Tchrs. Assn., Viktor Frankl Inst. of Logotherapy (Edn. for Social Conscience award 1989). Democrat. Christian Humanist. Home: 1212 Briar Ln Wharton TX 77488 Office: Wharton County Jr Coll 911 E Boling Hwy Wharton TX 77488

SODERSTROM, ROBERT MERRINER, dermatologist; b. Streator, Ill., Sept. 9, 1947; s. Carl William and Virginia Rose (Merriner) S.; m. Susan Joy Nichols, Jan. 23, 1971; children: Sara, Paul, Lance. BS, U. Ill., 1969; MD, U. Mich., 1972. Dir. dermatology Hurley Med. Ctr., Flint, Mich., 1980—, Genesys Med. Ctr., Flint, Mich., 1993—; clin. prof. Mich. State U. Sch. Medicine, East Lansing, 1994—. Fellow Am. Coll. Physicians, Am. Acad. Dermatology; mem. Genesee County Med. Soc. (pres. 1993-94). Office: G-5131 W Bristol Flint MI 48507

SOECHTIG, CARL EUGENE, pathologist, laboratory director; b. Jamaica, N.Y., Oct. 9, 1934; s. Charles Bertholdt and Alice Eugenie (Bomhard) S.; m. Margaret Alice Wilkens, Aug. 20, 1956 (div. Aug. 1983); 1 child, Curt Eugene; m. Patricia Ann McNeely, Dec. 29, 1984. AB, Colgate U., Hamilton, N.Y., 1956; DO, Phila. Coll. Osteo. Medicine, 1960. Diplomate Am. Bd. Pathology. Intern Riverside Osteo. Hosp., Trenton, Mich., 1960-61; resident in internal medicine Detroit Osteo. Hosp., 1961-62; gen. practice medicine Harrington Park, N.J., 1962-69; intern pathology Holy Name Hosp., Teaneck, N.J., 1969-70, resident in pathology, 1970-71; resident in pathology Albert Einstein Coll. Medicine, Bronx, 1971-74; dir. labs. Met. Hosp., Grand Rapids, Mich., 1974—, chief of staff, 1993—; cons. Sheridan (Mich.) Cmty. Hosp., 1990—; mem. Mich. State Cervical Cytology Task Force, 1989-90. Contbr. articles to profl. jours. Pres., bd. dirs. Grand Valley Bldg. Program, Grand Rapids, 1993-95; chmn. bd. govs. Grand Valley Blood Ctr., 1993. Fellow Coll. Am. Pathologists, Am. Soc. Clin. Pathology; mem. Mich. Soc. Pathologists (trustee and current pres.), U.S./Can. Acad. Pathologists, Am. Osteo. Assn., Mich. Assn. Osteo. Physicians and Surgeons (del. 1980—), Kent County Osteo. Physicians and Surgeons (pres. 1988-90), Am. Assn. Blood Banks, Am. Soc. Cytologists. Office: Metropolitan Hospital 1919 Boston St SE Grand Rapids MI 49506

SOETANTO, KAWAN, biomedical-electrical engineering educator, researcher, scientist, inventor; b. Surabaya, Jawa, Indonesia, Mar. 10, 1951; came to U.S., 1987; s. Khelim and Suin S.; m. Jennie Herman, Aug. 31, 1976; children: Nerrie, Jun, Ainie. M Engring., Tokyo U. of A&T, 1982; DEng, Tokyo Inst. Tech., 1984; D in Medicine, Tohoku U., Sendai, Japan, 1987. Mgr. fgn. div. R&D Pacific Electronic Co., Surabaya and Tokyo, 1972-80; rsch. asst. surgery dept. Nissei Hosp., Osaka, Japan, 1979-82; rsch. engr./cons. Tokin, Ricoh, Aloka, Tokyo, 1979-88; rsch. fellow diagnostic imaging dept. Kanto Cen. Hosp., Tokyo, 1982-87; sr. rsch. scientist Med. Engring. Lab. Toshiba Corp., Nasu, Japan, 1985-87; rsch. scholar Inst. Chest Diseases & Cancer, Tohoku U., Sendai, Japan, 1984-88; vis. prof. Univ. Sci. and Tech. of China, Beijing, 1987, Indonesia U., 1988, Tokyo Inst. Tech., 1989, 90, Calif. Inst. Tech., 1990, Duke U., 1991, U. Calif., 1992; assoc. prof. biomed. engring. Drexel U., Phila., 1987-93; prof. dept. control and system engring. Toin Univ. Yokohama, Japan, 1993—; core prof., dir. med. engring. program Toin Univ., Yokohama, Japan, 1995—, mem. steering com. Human Sci. & Tech. Ctr., 1993—; assoc. dir. Toin Univ., Yokohama, 1996—; adj. assoc. prof. radiology dept. Thomas Jefferson U., Phila., 1989—; mem. US-Japan Collaborating on Sci. Project, Sendai, 1984-86; liaison, exec. mem. AFSUMB, Tokyo, Bali, 1985-88; cons. advanced tech. lab. ATL, Inc., Seattle, 1988; exec. com. Toin Human Sci. and Tech. Ctr. (HUSTEC), 1993—; adj. fellow and tech. cons. Electronic Industries Assn. of Japan, 1994—. Author: (with others) Medical Ultrasonic Measurement Technique, 1984, Invasive/Noninvasive Technique, 1988, Ultrasound Imaging & Signal Processing, 1986, Ultrasound Speckle Analysis; contbr. articles to EMCJ, Elec. Engring. Jpn., Inst. Electronic Com. Jpn. US, Bull. PME, Japan Jour. Med. Ultra., Japanese Jour. Apply Phys., Jour. Acoustics Japan, Jour. Acoustic Soc. Am., Jour. Ultrasound in Medicine and Biology, IEEE Transaction on Ultrasonics, Ferroelectrics and Frequency Control. Adv. mem. Pan Asian Assn. of Greater Phila., 1989-91, bd. dirs. 1991—; observer Internat. Electrotechnical Commn., 1988, Mayor's Asian Adv. Bd., Phila., 1990; v.p. Indonesian Communities of Delaware Valley, 1990—; sch. affair mem. Japanese Assn. Greater Phila., 1989—; mem. Pa. Heritage Affairs Commn., 1993—; guest speaker radio Japan Edn. in Japan, 1994, TVK Talk Show With State Eminent Person, 1996. Recipient Best Educator of the Yr. 1994, 95, The Favorite Educator, 1993, Toin U. of Yokohama, Outstanding Achievement awards Pan Asian Assn., 1990, medals Asian Fedn. Socs. of Ultrasound in Medicine and Biology, 1987, 89, rsch. awards Toshiba Corp. Med. Engring. Lab., Japan, 1986-88, Outstanding Rsch. award Tokyu Found., 1985-88, Best Rsch. award Computer and Comm. Found. NEC, 1986-87, Cert. of Honor, Japan and Indonesian Soc. Ultrasound in Medicine, 1985, 87; Tokyu Found. fellow, 1985-88, Japan Ministry Edn. predoctoral fellow, 1980-82, doctoral fellow, 1982-85; Japan Ministry Edn. Undergrad. scholar, 1978-80; Nat. Cancer Inst. grantee NIH, 1990-93, Japanese Ministry Edn. grantee, 1993, 94; Pvt. U. Grad. Sch. Priority Funding grantee, 1995. Fellow Am. Inst. Ultrasound in Medicine (ethics and profl. standards com. 1993—); mem. IEEE/EMBS (co-chmn. Phila. chpt. 1990-92, chmn. 1992—, internat. program com. 1991—), IEEE (sr.), Acoustical Soc. Japan, Acoustical Soc. Am., N.Y. Acad. Sci., Japan Soc. Med. Electronics and Biol. Engring., Japan Soc. Ultrasound in Medicine (exec. sec. basic tech. rsch. sect. 1994—, mem. Internet com. 1995, ultrasonics and microbubles sect. 1996—, councilor 1996—). Office: Toin U Yokohama Human Sci & Tech Ctr, Toin Human Sci & Tech, 1614 Kurogane-Cho, Aoba-ku Yokohama 225, Japan

SOFFER, ROSEMARY S., community health nurse, consultant, educator; b. N.Y.C., June 29, 1953; d. E.F. Harvey and Paula L. Show. Diploma, Hosp. U. Pa. Sch. Nursing, 1975; BSN, Neumann Coll., 1980; postgrad., Temple U./Beh Sci, 1983—, Neumann Coll., 1994—. RN, Pa., Del.; cert. CPR instr. Educator nursing sch., consulting nurse practitioner, educator Ambilikkai Village Health Clinic, India; program devel., nurse cons. Anglican Ch. India, 1995; charge nurse Hosp. of U. Pa., Phila., audit ventricular tachycardia, 1980; community nurse Community Nursing Svc., Chester, Pa.; program devel. nurse cons. Anglican Ch. India, Phila./Delaware County, Pa., 1995; ind. nurse contractor, 1994, 95; spkr. in field at Neumann Coll., chs. and orgns.; presenter numerous seminars on internat. nursing issues; exec. dir. Christian Ministry Internat. Author: The Real Rambo, 1989, Coping Mechanism of the Chronically Ill During Separation, 1983, Opened Eyes, 1990. Exec. com. Rambo Co., Inc. Sight for Curable Blind; bd. dirs. Ecumenical Caring Coalition-Chester Food Cupboard; elder Yeadon Presbyn. Ch., 1990-93; pres., dir. Ministry Internat., 1995—. Named one of Outstanding Young Women of Am., nominated by Dept. Atty. Gen. Harrisburg, 1991-92, Professionalism award Yeaden High Sch., 1971. Mem. Internat. Nursing Soc., Pa. Med. Missionary Soc. (bd. dirs. 1990-95), Sigma Theta Tau.

SOFFRONOFF, PIERCE, physician; b. Phila., Jan. 14, 1949; s. Ernest Carl Gustave and Jane Kynett (Coggeshall) S.; m. Strachelle Barry, Jan. 1, 1976; children: Strachelle B., Alexandra J. Cesny P. BA in Biology, Baylor U., 1970; MD, U. Tex., 1974. Diplomate Am. Bd. Ob-Gyn. Resident in ob-gyn. U. Pitts., 1974-77; pvt. practice, attending physician Magee Women's Hosp., Pitts., 1978—; asst. clin. prof. dept. ob-gyn. Sch. Medicine U. Pitts., 1978-90, assoc. clin. prof., 1990—. Fellow ACOG; mem. AMA, Am. Fertility Soc., Pitts. Ob-Gyn. Soc., Allegheny County Med. Soc., Pa. Med. Soc. Office: Magee Womens Hosp 300 Halket St Pittsburgh PA 15213-3108

SOFIA, R. D., pharmacologist; b. Ellwood City, Pa., Oct. 8, 1942. BS, Geneva Coll., 1964; MS, Fairleigh-Dickenson U., 1969; PhD in Pharmacology, U. Pitts., 1971. Rsch. biologist Lederle Labs., N.Y., 1964-67; rsch. assoc. pharmacology Union Carbide Corp., 1967-69; sr. pharmacologist Pharmakon Labs., Pa., 1969; sr. rsch. pharmacologist Pharmakon Labs., 1971-73, dir. dept. Pharmacology and Toxicology, 1973-76, v.p. biology rsch., 1976-80, v.p. R&D, 1980-82; v.p. pre-clin. rsch. Wallace Labs., Cranbury, 1982—; cons. Pharmakon Labs., 1969-71. Mem. Am. Soc. Pharmacology and Experimental Therapeutics, Soc. Toxicology, SOc. Neuroscience, Internat. Soc. Study Pain, Am. Rheumatism Assn. Office: Carter-Wallace Inc Half-acre Rd # 1001 Cranbury NJ 08512

SOGANDARES-BERNAL, FRANKLIN, biology educator, researcher, consultant; b. Ancon, C.A., Panama, May 12, 1931; came to U.S., 1951; s. Anastasio and Blanca Helena Bernal-Almillategui; m. Lucy Ann McAlister, 1960 (div. 1982); children: Franklin McAlister, Maria Helena, John Francis Marion. BS, Tulane U., 1954; MS, U. Nebr., Lincoln, 1955, PhD, 1958. Instr., asst. prof., prof. Tulane U., New Orleans, 1959-71, coordinator sci. planning, 1965-68; prof., chmn. zoology U. Mont., Missoula, 1971-72, prof. microbiology, 1972-74; prof. biology So. Meth. U., Dallas, 1974-96, prof. emeritus, 1996—, chmn. biology, 1974-76; pres. Custom Antibodies Tex., 1993—; cons. in pathology Baylor U. Med. Center, Dallas, 1974-89, med. staff affiliate, 1978—, dir. Ctr. for Infectious Disease Research, Baylor Research Found., 1985-94; research affiliate Nebr. State Mus., Lincoln, 1972—; pvt. practice cons. immunologist, Dallas, 1978—; cons. engr. Sputtertex Corp., Dallas, 1985; sci. adv. bd. EPA, Washington, 1980-82. Contbr. articles to profl. jours. Mem. Am. Soc. Parasitologists (council 1970-73, editorial bd 1964-67, H.B. Ward medal 1969), Am. Assn. Pathologists, Nat. Rifle Assn. (life). Democrat. Office: So Meth U Dept Biol Scis Dallas TX 75275

SOHN, BYUNG-WHA, orthodontist, researcher; b. Seoul, Nov. 14, 1941; s. Chang-Su and Chun-Kyung (Kim) S.; m. Hae-Ja Cha, June 2, 1972; children: Sang-Hee, Ju-Young. Bachelor, Seoul Nat. U., 1967; Master, Yonsei U., Seoul, 1974; PhD, Koryu U., Seoul, 1981. Resident orthodontic dept. Dental Hosp. Yonsei U., Seoul, 1971-74, clin. prof. orthodontic dept. Dental Coll., 1974-78, instr. orthodontic dept. Dental Coll., 1978-79, chmn. orthodontic dept. Dental Coll., 1985-87, prof. orthodontic dept. Dental Coll., 1985—; pvt. practice Seoul, 1974-78; vis. prof. orthodontic dept. Dental Coll. U. Ill., 1982-83; pres. Craniofacial Deformity Rsch. Ctr., Seoul, 1992—. Author: Removable Orthodontic Appliance, 1983, Cephalometrics, 1983, Crowding, 1988, Bimaxillary Protrusion, 1988. Capt. Non-San Mil. Hosp., 1967-70. Mem. Korean Assn. Orthodontics (v.p. 1988-90, pres. 1990-92, pres. (hon.) 1993-95), Internat. Assn. Dental Rsch., Japan Orthontic Soc., Japanese Cleft Palate Assn. Office: Yonsei U Coll Dentistry Dept Orhtodontics, 134 Shinchon-Dong, Sudaemoon-Gu Seoul 120-749, Republic of Korea

SOIKE, KENNETH FIEROE, virologist; b. Mpls., July 8, 1927; s. Kenneth Fieroe and Viola Mabel (Marquardt) S.; m. Marian Elaine Laursen, June 11, 1950 (div. 1975); children: David, Kevin, Kathryn; m. Mary Eleanor Morris, Feb. 14, 1978. BA, U. Minn., 1949; PhD, Oreg. State U., 1955. Lab. technician U. Minn., Austin, 1949-50; rsch. asst. Oreg. State U., Corvallis, 1950-55; rsch. mem. Sterling Drug, Rensselaer, N.Y., 1955-61; assoc. prof. Albany (N.Y.) Med. Coll., 1961-73; assoc. dir. Inst. Environ. Safety, Alamogordo, N.Mex., 1973-75; sr. rsch. scientist emeritus Tulane Regional Primate Rsch. Ctr., Covington, La., 1975-93, 1993—; cons. Primate Rsch. Inst., Alamogordo, 1980-91, Triton Biocscis., Alameda, Calif., 1985-90. With USN, 1945-47. Mem. Am. Soc. Microbiology, Am. Soc. Virology, Soc. Antiviral Rsch., Internat. Soc. Interferon Rsch., Interam. Soc. Chemotherapy, Sigma Xi. Home: 17 Beth Dr Covington LA 70433-1121 Office: Tulane Regional Primate Rsch Ctr 18703 Three Rivers Rd Covington LA 70433-8915

SOJKA, GARY ALLAN, biologist, educator, university official; b. Cedar Rapids, Iowa, July 15, 1940; s. Marvin F. and Ruth Ann (Waddington) Sojka Green; m. Sandra Kay Smith, Aug 5, 1962; children: Lisa Kay, Dirk Allan. BS, Coe Coll., 1962; MS, Purdue U., 1965, PhD, 1967; LLD, Lycoming Coll., 1995. Rsch. assoc. Ind. U., Bloomington, 1967-69, asst. prof., 1969-73, assoc. prof., 1973-79, prof., 1979-84, assoc. chmn. biology, 1977-79, chmn. biology, 1979-81, dean arts and scis., 1981-84; pres. Bucknell U., Lewisburg, Pa., 1984-95; prof. biology, 1995—; mem. higher edn. commn. Mid. States Assn. Colls. and Schs., 1992—; chmn. tax policy subcom. Nat. Assn. Ind. Colls. and Univs., 1991-93; mem. study group on internat. edn. Am. Coun. Edn., 1992-94. Chmn. bd. dirs. Stone Belt Coun. Ret. Citizens, Bloomington, 1977-78; mem. nominating com. Ind. Assn. Ret. Citizens, Indpls., 1979; mem. So. Ind. Health Sys. Agy., Bedford; bd. dirs. Geisinger Med. Found., Danville, Pa., Inst. European Studies; trustee St. Mary-of-the-Woods Coll., Ind., 1988-94; chmn. Pa. Commn. Ind. Colls. and Univs., 1989-90; dir. Suncom Industries, Northcumberland, Pa., 1991-93; mem. Pres.'s Commn. NCAA, 1993-95; bd. dirs. Bethesda Found., Lewisburg, 1996—. Recipient Ind. U. Sr. Class Tchg. award, 1975, Frederick B. Lieber award, 1977, Coe Coll. Alumni award of merit, 1982, Gary A. Sojka award Bucknell U., 1992, Cmty. Leadership award Susquahanna Valley Boy Scouts, 1994; named to Coe Coll. Athletic Hall of Fame, 1988. Mem. Am. Assn. Microbiology, Am. Acad. Microbiology, Am. Soc. Biol. Chemists, Soc. Gen. Microbiology, Nat. Assn. Independent Colls. and Univs. (subcom. chmn. 1991-93), Am. Coun. Edn. (mem. study group on internat. edn. 1992-94), Sigma Xi, Sigma Nu, Omicron Delta Kappa. Baptist. Home: Bend-in-the-Creek Farm 141 Creek Rd Middleburg PA 17842 Office: Bucknell U Dept Biology Lewisburg PA 17842

SOKAS, ROSEMARY KELLY, physician, educator; b. Cleve., Jan. 17, 1951; d. Peter Paul and Jeanne Kathleen (O'Toole) S.; m. Ahmed Achrati, June 13, 1980; children: Nora Achrati, Sara Achrati, Adam Achrati. BA, Boston U., 1972, MD, 1974; M in Occupl. Health, Harvard U., 1980, MS, 1981. Diplomate Am. Bd. Internal Medicine, Am. Bd. Preventive Medicine. Intern, resident in internal medicine Boston City Hosp., 1974-77; med. dir. Las Marias (P.R.) Migrant Health Ctr., 1977-78; instr. in medicine U. P.R., Mayaguez, 1977-78; internist Rev. Martin Luther King Health Ctr., Bronx, N.Y., 1978-79; asst. prof. medicine U. Pa., Phila., 1982-88; asst. prof. medicine George Washington U., Washington, 1988-90, assoc. prof. medicine, 1990-96, prof. medicine, 1996—, dir. occupl. medicine residency, 1993—, dir. Inst. for Environ., 1995—; vis. assoc. prof. cmty. medicine Faculty of Medicine and Health Scis., Al Ain, United Arab Emirates, 1992-93; cons. Internat. Ladies' Garment Workers Union, 1981-86, Social Security Disability Rev., Phila., 1981-88, ARC Disability Rev., Washington, 1989-95. Contbr. articles to profl. jours. Bd. dirs. Friends of Farmworkers, Inc., Phila., 1984-88; mem. adv. bd. Delaware Valley Regional Poison Control, Phila., 1986-88; mem. program adv. com. AFL-CIO HIV/AIDS Edn., Washington, 1989-91; mem. task force Inst. Medicine, Washington, 1994-95. Lt. comdr. USPHS, 1977-79. Recipient Spl. Emphasis Rsch. Career award Nat. Inst. Occupl. Safety and Health, 1984, Acad. award in environ. medicine Nat. Inst. Environ. Health Scis., 1991. Fellow ACP, Am. Coll. Occupl. and environ. Medicine (regional chpt. bd. dirs.); mem. APHA, Am. Coll. Preventive Medicine, Assn. Tchrs. Preventive Medicine, Soc. Gen. Internal Medicine, Alpha Omega Alpha, BEGG Med. Honor Soc. Roman Catholic. Office: George Washington U 2300 K St NW # 201 Washington DC 20037

SOKOL, ARNOLD, physician; b. Phila., July 16, 1934; s. Max and Fannie Sokol; m. Phyllis Goldman; children: Leslie, Marc, Jodi. BA, U. Pa., 1957; DO, Phila. Coll. Osteopathy, 1962. Intern Riverview Osteo. Hosp., Norristown, Pa., 1962-63; physician in gen. practice Norristown, Pa., 1963—; attending staff Suburban Gen. Hosp., Norristown, chmn. dept. gen. practice, 1975—, chmn. staff, 1971-72, chmn. interns and residents com., 1974—, mem. exec. com., 1968—, bd. dirs., 1980-89, 91-95, trainor for gen. practice residency, 1976—, trainor for externs, 1972—; preceptor Phila. Coll. Osteo. Medicine in Gen. Practice, 1978—, clin. asst. prof. in gen. practice; trustee Am. Osteo. Bd. Gen. Practice, 1988—, mem. examiners in gen. practice, 1987—; dir. Am. Osteo. Bd. Family Physicians, 1990—; del. Am. Coll. Gen. Practitioners. Bd. trustees Montgomery/Bucks Profl. Standards Rev. Orgn.; mem., bd. dirs. Or Ami Synagogue, 1979-81. Recipient Mary J. Lindbach Scholarship award for outstanding student, 1961, Physician of Yr. award Pa. Osteo. Family Physicians, 1987, Frederick Solomon award Pa. Osteo. Family Physicians, 1988, Standing Cmty. Svc. award to New Hope Batp. Ch., Norristown, 1990. Fellow Am. Coll. Gen. Practitioners in Osteo. Medicine and Surgery (del., com. on edn. and evaluation 1989—); mem. Am. Osteo. Assn., Pa. Osteo. Med. Assn. (chmn. Dist. 10 1977-87, del. 1979—, trustee 1979-85, 87—, v.p. 1988-89, bd. dirs. 1990—, pres. 1995-96), Pa. Osteo. General Practitioners Soc. (past pres.). Office: 1548 DeKalb St Norristown PA 19401

SOKOL, DENNIS ALLEN, hospital administrator; b. Chgo., May 3, 1945; s. Stanley John and Mildred Veronica (Krenslake) S.; m. Gwen Noble, Dec. 19, 1971 (div.); children: Anne, Ellen; m. Jolene K. Buehrer, Jan, 28, 1989. BS in Bus., No. Ill. U., 1968; MBA, U. Nebr., Omaha, 1974; M of Hosp. Adminstrn., U. Minn., 1976. Radio personality various stas., Ill., Iowa and Nebr., 1968-72; pub. relations officer Children's Meml. Hosp., Omaha, 1972-73, Meth. Hosp., Omaha, 1973-74; v.p. adminstrn. Golden Valley (Minn.) Health Ctr., 1976-82; pres. Sacred Heart Health Svcs., Yankton, S.D., 1982—; regional pres. Presentation Health Sys., 1996; instr. health care mgmt. Mt. Marty Coll., 1986-87, U. Minn., 1986-88. Pres. Valley Health Svcs., Inc., 1984—, Health Mgmt. Svcs., 1987—. Fellow Am. Coll. Health Care Execs. (regent 1991-95); mem. S.D. Hosp. Assn. (trustee 1990—), Missouri Valley Health Network (v.p. 1986—), Yankton Area C. of C. (pres. 1989-90), Rotary. Republican. Roman Catholic. Office: Sacred Heart Hosp 501 Summit St Yankton SD 57078-3855

SOKOL, HAROLD MARC, internist; b. Bronx, Feb. 9, 1956; s. David Harris and Estelle Lenore (Rossman) S.; m. Gail Deitcher, July 11, 1981; children: Rebekah, Drue. BS in Biology, SUNY, Stony Brook, 1975; MD, Albany Med. Coll., 1979. Diplolmate Am. Bd. Internal Medicine. Intern Met. Hosp., N.Y.C., 1979-80; med. resident CHC at Elmhurst, N.Y., 1980-82; pulmonary fellow Albany Med. Coll., 1982-84; ptnr., physician Capital Pulmonary and Critical Care Svcs., Albany, 1984—; med. dir. respiratory therapy and PFT lab. Meml. Hosp., Albany, 1990—, head dept. internal medicine, 1994—. Fellow ACP, Am. Coll. Chest Physicians; mem. Med. Soc. Albany County (treas. 1994-96, sec. 1996—, bd. censors 1990-95). Office: Capital Pulmonary/CC Svcs 63 Shaker Rd Albany NY 12204

SOKOL, MICHAEL STUART, internist, endocrinologist; b. Akron, Ohio, Oct. 18, 1959; m. Shari Baron, Sept. 1, 1986; 2 children. BS summa cum laude, Kent State U., 1983; MD, Northeastern Ohio Univs. Coll. of Medicine, 1983. Diplomate Am. Bd. Internal Medicine, Am. Bd. Endocrinology, Diabetes and Metabolism, Am. Bd. Psychiatry and Neurology, Nat. Bd. Med. Examiners; cert. Nat. Cert. Bd. for Diabetes Educators. AMA Joseph Goldberger scholar in clin. nutrition Columbia U. Coll. Physicians and Surgeons, N.Y.C., 1982; intern in medicine St. Thomas Hosp. Med. Ctr., Akron, 1983-84; resident in medicine Miriam Hosp.-Brown U., Providence, 1984-86; resident in psychiatry Brown U., 1985-89; fellow dept. endocrinology and metabolism Walter Reed Army Med. Ctr., Washington, 1989-91; pvt. practice, Kansas City, Mo., 1994—; tchg. fellow dept. molecular pathology Northeastern Ohio Univs. Coll. Medicine, Rootstown, 1980-83; clin. asst. prof. dept. medicine Med. Coll. Ga., Augusta, 1993-94. Contbr. articles to med. jours. Maj. M.C., U.S. Army, 1989-93. Fellow ACP, Am. Coll. Endocrinologists; mem. Am. Assn. Clin. Endocrinologists, Mo. Med. Assn., Jackson County Med. Soc., Met. Med. Soc. Home: 8119 W 96th Ter Overland Park KS 66212 Office: Statland Clinic 6724 Troost Ave Rm 710 Kansas City MO 64131-1501

SOKOL, ROBERT JAMES, obstetrician, gynecologist, educator; b. Rochester, N.Y., Nov. 18, 1941; s. Eli and Mildred (Levine) S.; m. Roberta Sue Kahn, July 26, 1964; children: Melissa Anne, Eric Russell, Andrew Ian. BA with highest distinction in Philosophy, U. Rochester, 1963, MD with honors, 1966. Diplomate Am. Bd. Ob-Gyn (assoc. examiner 1984-86), Sub-Bd. Maternal-Fetal Medicine. Intern Barnes Hosp., Washington U., St. Louis, 1966-67, resident in ob-gyn., 1967-70, asst. in ob-gyn., 1966-70, rsch. asst., 1967-68, instr. clin. ob-gyn., 1970; Buswell fellow in maternal fetal medicine Strong Meml. Hosp.-U. Rochester, 1972-73; fellow in maternal-fetal medicine Cleve. Met. Gen. Hosp.-Case Western Res. U., Cleve., 1974-75, assoc. obstetrician and gynecologist, 1973-83, asst. prof. ob-gyn., 1973-77; asst. program dir. Perinatal Clin. Rsch. Ctr., 1973-78, co-program dir., 1978-82, program dir., 1982-83, acting dir. obstetrics, 1974-75, co-dir., 1977-83, assoc. prof., 1977-81, prof., 1981-83, assoc. dir. dept. ob-gyn., 1981-83; prof. ob-gyn. Wayne State U., Detroit, 1983—, chmn. dept. ob-gyn., 1983-89, mem. grad. faculty dept. physiology, 1984—, interim dean Med. Sch., 1988-89, dean, 1989—, pres. Fund for Med. Rsch. and Edn., 1988—; chief ob-gyn. Hutzel Hosp. Detroit, 1983-89; dir. C.S. Mott Ctr. for Human Growth and Devel., 1983-89; interim chmn. med. bd. Detroit Med. Ctr., 1988-89, chmn. med. bd., 1989—, sr. v.p. med. affairs, 1992—, trustee, 1990—; past pres. med. staff Cuyahoga County Hosps.; mem. profl. adv. bd. Educated Childbirth Inc., 1976-80; sr. Ob cons. Symposia Medicus; cons. Nat. Inst. Child Health and Human Devel., Nat. Inst. Alcohol Abuse and Alcoholism, Ctr. for Disease Control, NIH, Health Resources and Services Adminstrn., Nat. Clearinghouse for Alcohol Info., Am. Psychol. Assn.; mem. alcohol psychosocial research rev. com. Nat. Inst. Alcohol Abuse and Alcoholism, 1982-86; mem. ob/gyn adv. panel U.S. Pharmacopeial Conv., 1985-90. Mem. internat. editorial bd. Israel Jour. Obstetrics and Gynecology; reviewer med. jours.; mem. editorial bd. Jour. Perinatal Medicine; editor-in-chief Interactions: Programs in Clinical Decision-Making, 1987-90; researcher computer applications in perinatal medicine, alcohol-related birth defects, perinatal risk and neurobehavioral devel.; contbr. articles to profl. jours. Mem. Pres.'s leadership council U. Rochester, 1976-80; mem. exec. com. bd. trustees Oakland Health Edn. Program, 1987—; mem. voluntary alumni admissions com. U. Rochester, 1986—. Served to maj. M.C. USAF, 1970-72. Mem. AMA, NAS (Inst. of Medicine), ACOG (chmn. steering com. drug and alcohol abuse contract 1986-87), Am. Med. Informatics Assn., Soc. Gynecologic Investigation, Perinatal Rsch. Soc., Assn. Profs. Gyn.-Ob, Royal Soc. Medicine, Mich. Med. Soc., Wayne County Med. Soc., Detroit Acad. Medicine, Cen. Assn. Obstetricians-Gynecologists, Rsch. Soc. Alcoholism, Soc. Perinatal Obstetricians (v.p., pres.-elect 1987-88, pres. 1988-89, achievement award 1995), Liaison Com. for Ob-Gyn., Am. Gynecol. and Obstetrical Soc., Neurobehavioral Teratology Soc., APHA, Am. Med. Soc. on Alcoholism and Other Drug Dependencies, Soc. for Neuroscis. (Mich. chpt.), Internat. Soc. Computers in Obstetrics, Neonatology, Gynecology (v.p. 1987-89, pres. 1989-92, immediate past pres. 1992—), World Assn. Perinatal Medicine, Soc. Physicians Reproductive Choice and Health, Am. Assn. Med. Colls. (coun. of deans), Detroit Physiol. Soc. (hon.), Polish Gynecologists World Club, Phi Beta Kappa, Sigma Xi, Alpha Omega Alpha. Republican. Jewish. Home: 5200 Rector Ct Bloomfield Hills MI 48302-2654 Office: Wayne State U Sch Medicine 540 E Canfield St Detroit MI 48201-1928

SOKOLOFF, LEON, pathology educator; b. Bklyn., May 9, 1919; s. Barnet and Ray (Cohen) S.; m. Barbara Snow, June 1950 (dec. 1960); children—Michael D., Naomi B. Sokoloff Berry; m. Beverly Beinfeld Trachtenberg, July 18, 1971. BA, NYU, 1938, MD, 1944; postgrad. Columbia U., 1938-39. Diplomate Am. Bd. Pathology. Resident, Bellevue Hosp., N.Y.C., 1945-47; asst. prof. NYU, N.Y.C., 1948-52; chief, sect. on rheumatic diseases Lab. Exptl. Pathology, NIH, Bethesda, Md., 1953-73; prof. pathology SUNY-Stony Brook, 1973-91. emeritus, 1991—; vis. prof. Royal Soc. Medicine, Eng., 1985. Author: Biology of Degenerative Joint Disease, 1969. Editor: The Joints and Synovial Tissue, 1978. Contbr. articles to profl. jours. Served to capt. USPHS, 1953-73. Recipient J. van Breemen medal Dutch Rheumatism Assn., 1967, Disting. Alumnus award NYU, 1975; NIH grantee, 1973-87. Mem. Am. Coll. Rheumatol (Master 1987), Am. Soc. Investigative Pathology, Am. Coll. Veterinary Pathologists, 1992, (hon. mem.); Jewish. Avocation: medical history. Office: SUNY Dept Pathology Health Sci Ctr Stony Brook NY 11794-8691

SOKOLOFF, NORMAN FRED, orthopedic surgeon; b. Phila., May 29, 1946; s. Harry and Evelyn (Feldbine) S.; m. Ilene Edyth Safra, June 25, 1967; children: Bret Robert, Cari Jaye. BS, Pa. State U., 1967; MD, Jefferson Med. Coll., 1969. Diplomate Am. Bd. Orthopedic Surgery. Surg. intern St. Vincent's Hosp. and Med. Ctr., N.Y.C., 1969-70; orthopedic resident Albert Einstein Bronx Mcpl. Med. Ctr., Bronx, N.Y., 1970-71, U. Calif., San Diego, 1971-74; orthopedic surgeon, chmn. of bd., pres. Camelot Med. Group, Inc., Sunnyvale, Calif., 1976—; dir., treas. El Camino IPA, Mountain View, Calif., 1995-96. Maj. U.S. Army, 1974-76. Fellow Am. Acad. Orthopedic Surgeons; mem. Western Occupl. amd Environ. Med. Assn., Calif. Med. Assn., Santa Clara County Med. Assn. Office: Camelot Med Group Inc 500 E Remington Dr # 20 Sunnyvale CA 94087

SOKOLOV, JACQUE JENNING, health care executive, nuclear cardiologist; b. L.A., Sept. 13, 1954; s. Albert I. and Frances (Burgess) S. BA in Medicine magna cum laude, U. So. Calif., 1974, MD with hons., 1978; postgrad., Mayo Clinic, Rochester, Minn., 1978-81, U. Tex., Dallas, 1981-83. Med. diplomate. Cardiologist, nuclear cardiologist Health Sci. Ctr. U. Tex., 1981-84; chief med. officer Baylor Ctr. for Health Promotion Wellness & Lifestyle Corp., Dallas, 1985-87; v.p., dir. health care dept., corp. med. dir. So. Calif. Edison Co., Rosemead, Calif., 1987-92; CEO Advanced Health Plans, Inc./Sokolov Strategic Alliance, L.A., 1992—; chmn. bd. Coastal Physician Group, Inc., 1994—; cons. Health Care Strategic Planning Southwestern Bell, AT&T, Wang, Rosewood Corp., Dallas, 1985-87; bd. dirs. Calif. Health Decisions. Contbr. articles to profl. jours. Tech. advisor Coun. Social Security; bd. dirs. Washington Bus. Group Health. Grantee NIH, Bethesda, Md., 1983. Office: Ste 800 9000 Sunset Blvd Los Angeles CA 90069

SOLAN, HAROLD A., optometrist; b. N.Y.C., Nov. 28, 1921; s. Karl S. and Louise (Klein) S.; m. Shirley Smith, Sept. 20, 1945; children: Lawrence, Debra, Fern. BS, CCNY, 1947; D in Optometry, Columbia U., 1949; MA, Tchr.'s Coll. Columbia U., 1951, 70. Diplomate Am. Acad. Optometry. Pvt. practice optometry Teaneck, N.J., 1949-81; prof. SUNY Coll. Optometry, N.Y.C., 1981-94, disting. svc. prof., 1994—; lectr. Columbia U., 1950-56; dir. orthoptic clinic Harlem Eye & Ear Hosp., N.Y.C., 1956-59; adj. prof. Fairleigh Dickinson U., 1963-82. Co-author: Visual Training with the Prism Reader, 1955, Tests & Measurements for the Behavioral Optometrist, 1991, Developmental and Perceptual Assessment of Learning Disabled Children, 1993; editor: Psychology of Learning and Reading Difficulties, 1973, Treatment and Management of Children With Learning Disabilities, 1982; editl. bd. Jour. Behavioral Optometry, 1990—, Jour. Optometric Vision Devel., 1987—; cons. editor. Jour. Learning Disabilities, 1984—; contbr. articles to profl. jours. cons. Bd. Edn., Teaneck, 1968-73; chair med. adv. bd. March of Dimes, 1971-80. Served in USAFR, 1942-46, 46-53, WWII. Named Disting. Practitioner Nat. Acads. Practice, Washington, 1995. Fellow Internat. Acad. Rsch. in Learning, Soc. for Scientific Study of Reading, Coll. Optometrists in Vision Devel., N.Y. Acad. Optometry (pres. 1960-62, disting. svc. award 1962); mem. Am. Acad. Optometry. Office: SUNY Coll Optometry 100 E 24th St New York NY 10010

SOLARO, ROSS JOHN, physiologist, biophysicist; b. Wadsworth, Ohio, Jan. 9, 1942; s. Ross and Lena (Chuppa) S.; m. Kathleen Marie Cole, Sept. 18, 1965; children: Christopher, Elizabeth. BS, U. Cin., 1965; PhD, U. Pitts., 1971. Asst. prof. Med. Coll. Va., Richmond, 1973-77; assoc. prof. pharmacology and physiology U. Cin., 1977-81, prof. pharmacology and cell biophysics, 1981-85, prof. physiology, 1981-88; prof. physiology, head U. Ill., Chgo., 1988—; sec. gen. Internat. Soc. Heart Rsch., 1989-93, sec./treas., chmn. dept. physiology, 1994—; chmn. exptl. cardiovascular study sect. NIH, 1990-92; vice-chmn. physiology U. Cin., 1995—. Editor: Protein Phosphorylation in Heart Muscle, 1986; contbr. articles to profl. jours. including Nature, Jour. Biol. Chemistry, Circulation Rsch. Chmn. rsch. coun. Am. Heart Assn., Met. Chgo., 1990—. Grantee NIH, 1977—, 77-82, 89—, Fogarty fellow, 1986; Brit. Am. Heart fellow Am. Heart Assn., 1974-75; Sr. Internat. fellow U. Coll. London, 1987. Mem. Am. Physiol. Soc. (chmn. subgroup), Am. Soc. Pharm. Exptl. Therapeutics, Biophys. Soc. (chmn. subgroup 1983-84). Office: U Ill at Chgo Dept MC901 Physiology & Biophysics 835 S Wolcott Ave Chicago IL 60612-7340

SOLBERG, JOANNA DEE, cardiology office nurse; b. Billings, Mont., Oct. 20, 1964; d. Marvin Magnus and Benita Ardea (Steel) S. BSN with honors, Mont. State U., 1987. RN, Mont. Office nurse Welch Heart Ctr., 1988—. Mem. Mont. Nurses Assn., ANA, AACN, Sigma Theta Tau. Home: 122 Ave B Billings MT 59101

SOLEY, ROBERT LAWRENCE, plastic surgeon; b. N.Y.C., Feb. 26, 1935; s. Max and Saide (Leader) S.; m. Judy Wasserman, June 16, 1963; children: John, Jill. BS, Yale U., 1956; MD, NYU, 1959. Diplomate Am. Bd. Surgery, Am. Bd. Plastic Surgery. Intern Bellevue Hosp., N.Y.C., 1959-60; resident in gen. surgery Mt. Sinai Hosp., N.Y.C., 1960-65; resident in plastic surgery Hosp. of U. Pa., Phila., 1967-69; practice medicine specializing in plastic surgery, White Plains, N.Y., 1969—; mem. staff, mem. med. bd. White Plains Hosp., 1985-88, chief sect. plastic surgery, 1988-94; mem. staff Westchester County Med. Ctr., St. Agnes Hosp.; clin. asst. prof. plastic surgery N.Y. Med. Coll., Valhalla, 1972—. Contbr. articles to med. jours. Capt. M.C., USAF, 1965-67. USPHS grantee, 1968-69. Fellow ACS; mem. Am. Soc. Plastic and Reconstructive Surgery, Am. Soc. Aesthetic Surgery, N.Y. State Med. Soc., Westchester County Med. Soc. (pres. 1996—, bd. dirs. 1988—, del. state conv. 1989—), Cleft Palate Assn., Am. Burn Assn., Rotary (bd. dirs. White Plains chpt. 1982-85). Home: 30 Griffin Ave Scarsdale NY 10583-7661 Office: 170 Maple Ave White Plains NY 10601-4710

SOLHAUG, JAN HELGE, surgeon; b. Oslo, Mar. 24, 1938; s. Helge and Margit (Nygaard) S.; m. Anna Cecilie Helland-Hansen, Dec. 29, 1962; children: Dag, Rune, Tone, Trine. Med. cand., U. Groningen, The Netherlands, 1962; cand. med., U. Gothenburg, Sweden, 1966, U. Oslo, 1970; PhD, U. Bergen, Norway, 1979. Chief surgeon Torsby Hosp., Sweden, 1956-85, Elverum Hosp., Norway, 1985-89, Diakonhjemmets Hosp., Norway, 1989—; resident Hosp. Karlstad, Sweden, 1966-71, Haukeland Hosp., Norway, 1971-76; dir. Elverum Hosp., 1986-87; sec. gen. United European Gastroenterology Week, Oslo, 1994. Author: Prostheses and Abdominal Wall, 1994, Tratamento Cirurgico Da Obesidade Morbida, 1994; mem. editl. bd. Current Surgery, 1980; contbr. over 100 articles to profl. jours. Mem. Assn. des Socs. Nat. European et Mediterraneennes di Gastroenterologie (v.p. 1995—), Scandinavian Clinics for Ulcer Rsch. (bd. dirs. 1982—). Office: Diakonhemmets Hosp, 0319 Oslo Norway

SOLIMENA, MICHELE, endocrinologist, educator, researcher; b. Milan, Nov. 29, 1960. MD summa cum laude, U. Milan, 1986, PhD in Pharmacology with highest honors, 1992. Postdoctoral fellow Ctr. Cytopharmacology dept. pharmacology Sch. Medicine U. Milan, 1986-88; neurology trainee Clinica Neurologica U. Pavia (Italy) Sch. Medicine, 1986-88; postdoctoral fellow dept. cell biology Sch. Medicine Yale U., New Haven, 1988-93, asst. prof. dept. internal medicine sect. endocrinology, 1994—. Contbr. articles to profl. jours. Recipient Career Devel. award Juvenile Diabetes Found., 1994—; grantee ADA, 1996—, Donaghue Found. New Investigator grantee, 1996—; Trabucchi fellow, 1987, Levi fellow Lincei's Nat. Acad., 1988, Muscular Dystrophy Assn. fellow, 1989, Sydney Blakmer fellow, 1990-91, Juvenile Diabetes Found. fellow, 1992-93. Office: Yale U Med Sch Dept Internal Medicine 333 Cedar St New Haven CT 06520-8020

SOLINSKY, ALAN ETHAN, ophthalmologist; b. N.Y.C., Jan. 20, 1960; s. Norman and Frances (Gladstein) S.; m. Susan Michelle Seltzer, June 14, 1987; children: Lara, Brian, Jason. BA, Brandeis U., 1982; MD, U. Conn. Sch. Medicine, 1986. Diplomate Am. Acad. Ophthalmology. Resident Hartford (Conn.) Hosp., 1986-87, Hahnemann U., Phila., 1987-90; pvt. practice ophthalmology West Hartford, Conn., 1992—. Office: 928 Farmington Ave West Hartford CT 06107

SOLLARS, GARY MICHAEL, emergency physician; b. Detroit, July 8, 1947; s. Paul Joseph and Irene Alexandra (Cecot) S.; m. Halina Josephine Czerniejewski, Oct. 3, 1981; children: Claire Mikhaila, Kendra Elizabeth. AB honors, U. Detroit, 1969; MD, U. Mich., 1974. Diplomate Am. Bd. Emergency Medicine (examiner 1983--). Resident in emergency medicine U. Chgo., 1974-77; attending staff Northwestern Meml. Hosp., Chgo., 1977-85, assoc. chief sec. emergency medicine, 1979-85; pvt. practice Phoenix, 1985—; attending staff Mesa (Ariz.) Luth. Hosp., 1985—, Valley

Luth. Hosp., Mesa, 1985—, Boswell Meml. Hosp., Sun City, Ariz., 1987—, Del Webb Meml. Hosp., Sun City, 1988—; lectr. in field, 1977—; cons. med. dept. People's Energy Corp., 1979-85; med.-legal case reviewer, Chgo., 1983-85. Author: (with others) Quality Assessment in the Emergency Department, 1984; contbr. articles to med. jours. Pub. service appearances various radio and TV stas., Chgo., 1978-83. Fellow Am. Coll. Emergency Physicians (bd. dirs. Ariz. chpt. 1988—); mem. Ariz. Med. Assn. (Physician of Day resource person for Ariz. Ho. of Reps. 1988—), Hastings Ctr.-Inst. Soc., Ethics, and Life Scis. Roman Catholic. Office: Emergency Physicians Inc 1741 E Morten Ave Ste 1C Phoenix AZ 85020-4645

SOLLER, HERBERT ISAAC, internist; b. Hazleton, Pa., Jan. 14, 1937; s. Joseph and Miriam Soller; m. Carol Rudnick, June 17, 1962; children: Jeffrey, Jonathan, Amy. BS, Franklin and Marshall Coll., 1958; MD, Hahnemann U., 1962. Diplomate Am. Bd. Internal Medicine. Resident in internal medicine Allentown (Pa.) Hosp. and Atlantic City Hosp., 1962-65; fellow in vascular disease and hypertension Hahnemann U. Med. Coll., Phila., 1965-66; pvt. practice, Harrisburg, Pa., 1968—; mem. staff Harrisburg Hosp., Holy Spirit Hosp., Hershey Med. Ctr., Pinnacle Health System. Capt. M.C., USAF, 1966-68. Mem. ACP, Am. Soc. Internal Medicine, Am. Soc. Nephrology, Internat. Soc. Nephrology. Office: 100 Chestnut St Harrisburg PA 17101-2518

SOLNIT, ALBERT JAY, physician, commissioner, educator; b. Los Angeles, Aug. 26, 1919; s. Benjamin and Bertha (Pavin) S.; m. Martha Benedict, 1949; children—David, Ruth, Benjamin, Aaron. B.A. in Med. Scis., U. Calif., 1940, M.A. in Anatomy, 1942, M.D., 1943; M.A. (hon.), Yale U., 1964. Rotating intern L.I. Coll. Hosp., 1944, asst. resident in pediatrics, 1944-45; resident in pediatrics and communicable diseases U. Calif. div. San Francisco Hosp., 1947-48; asst. resident dept. psychiatry and mental hygiene Yale U., 1948-49, sr. resident, 1949-50, fellow in child psychiatry, 1950-52, instr. pediatrics and psychiatry, 1952-53, asst. prof., 1953-60, assoc. prof., 1960-64, prof., 1964-70, Sterling prof., 1970—, dir. Child Study Ctr., 1966-83; commr. dept. mental health and addiction svcs. State of Conn., Hartford, 1991—; tng. and supervising analyst Western New Eng. Inst. Psychoanalysis, 1962—, N.Y. Psychoanalytic Inst., 1962—; cons. Childrens Bur., HEW; mem. adv. coun. Erikson Inst. for early Childhood Edn., 1966—; nat. adviser Children, publ. of Children's Bur., 1965—; mem. com. on publs. Yale U. Press, 1971—; adv. bd. Action for Children's TV, Newtonville, Mass., 1973—; mem. div. med. scis. Assembly Life Scis., NRC, 1974—; cons. div. mental health svc. program NIMH, 1974—; Sigmund Freud Meml. prof. U. Coll. London, 1983-84; Sigmund Freud prof., dir. Freud Ctr. Psychoanalytic Studies Hebrew U., Jerusalem, 1985-87. Author: (with M.J.E. Senn) Problems in Child Behavior and Develpment, 1968), (with A. Freud, J. Goldstein) Beyond the Best Interests of the Child, 19732, (with Goldstein) Divorce and Your Child, 1983, (with R. Lord, B. Nordhaus) When Home Is No Haven, 1992; The Many Meanings of Play, 1993; editor: (with S. Provence) Modern Perspectives in Child Development, 1963; mng. editor Psychoanalytic Study of the Child, 1971—; mem. editorial bd. Israel Annals Psychiatry and Related Disciplines, 1969—. WHO prof. psychiatry and human devel. U. Negev, Beer-Sheva, Israel, 1973-74. With USAAF, 1945-47. Recipient Disting. Svc. award Am. Psychiatric Assn., 1992. Mem. AAAS, Inst. Medicine of NAS, Am. Orthopsychiatric. Assn. (editorial bd. jour. 1974-82), Am. Psychoanalytic Assn. (past pres., editorial bd. jour. 1972-74), Am. Acad. Child and Adolescent Psychiatry (past pres., editorial bd. jour. 1975, Simon Wile Award, 1991), Internat. Pediatric Soc., Am. Assn. Child Psychoanalysis (past pres.), Am. Acad. Pediatrics (editorial bd. jour. 1968-76, task force pediatric edn.), Internat. Psychoanalytic Assn., Internat. Assn. Child and Adolescent Psychiatry (pres. 1974-78, hon. pres. 1990—), N.Y. Psychoanalytic Soc., Soc. Profs. Child Psychiatry. Home: 107 Cottage St New Haven CT 06511-2465 Office: 333 Cedar St New Haven CT 06510-3206 also: 410 Capitol Ave Hartford CT 06106

SOLO, ALAN JERE, medicinal chemistry educator, consultant; b. Phila., Nov. 7, 1933; s. David H. and Marion J. (Gottschall) S.; m. Elma Mardirosian, Oct. 5, 1963; children: David Matthew, Julia Ann. SB, MIT, 1955; MA, Columbia U., 1956, PhD, 1959. Rsch. assoc. Rockefeller U., N.Y.C., 1958-62; asst. prof. med. chemistry SUNY, Buffalo, 1962-65, assoc. prof., 1965-70, dir. grad. studies med. chemistry, 1967-69, chmn. med. chemistry, 1969—, prof., chmn., 1970—; cons. Westwood Pharms. Inc., Buffalo, 1971-92. Predoctoral fellow NSF, 1955-56, NIH, 1957-58. Mem. Am. Chem. Soc., N.Y. Acad. Scis., Sigma Xi. Office: SUNY Sch Pharmacy 439 Cooke Hall Buffalo NY 14260

SOLOMON, ARTHUR CHARLES, pharmacist; b. Gary, Ind., May 30, 1947; s. Laurence A. and Dorothy B. (Klippel) S.; m. Janet Evelyn Irak, Aug. 23, 1969; children: Thomas, Michael, Mark, Jill. BS in Pharmacy, Purdue U., 1970, MS in Clin. Pharmacy, 1972; PharmD. Registered pharmacist; cert. nuclear pharmacist. Clin. prof. pharmacy U. Tex., Austin, 1972-75; v.p. Nuclear Pharmacy, Inc., Atlanta, 1975-83; exec. v.p., managed care officer Diagnostek, Inc., Albuquerque, 1983-95; pres. Health Care Svcs., Inc., 1990-95; exec. v.p., COO Value Rx, Albuquerque, 1995—; adj. prof. U. N.Mex., 1992—. Contbr. articles to profl. jours. Mem. Am. Pharm. Assn., Am. Soc. Hosp. Pharmacy, Nat. Assn. Retail Druggists, Nat. Coun. Prescription Drug Programs, Am. Managed Care Pharmacy Assn. (pres., dir.), Am. Soc. Cons. Pharmacists, Rho Chi, Pi Kappa Phi. Republican. Roman Catholic. Home: 1504 Catron Ave SE Albuquerque NM 87123-4218 Office: Value Rx 4500 Alexander Blvd NE Albuquerque NM 87107-6805

SOLOMON, CAREN G., internist; b. N.Y.C., Feb. 20, 1963. MD, Harvard U., 1988. Resident Brigham Womens Hosp., Boston, 1988-90, fellow in endocrinology, 1990-93, assoc. physician, 1993—; instr. medicine Harvard Med. Sch., 1993—. Recipient Clinican Scientist award Am. Heart Assn., 1995-96. Mem .ACP. Office: Brigham Womens Hosp 75 Francis St Boston MA 02215*

SOLOMON, CHARLES STANLEY, endodontist; b. N.Y.C., May 25, 1935; s. Louis William and Sylvia Ruth (Segal) S.; m. Brenda Barnett, Apr. 11, 1965; children: Stephen B., Lawrence W., Laura D. AB, Columbia Coll., 1955, DDS, 1958. Diplomate Am. Bd. Endodontics. Pvt. practice Endodontic Assocs. of Greater N.Y., N.Y.C., 1962—; clin. prof. endodontics Columbia U. Sch. Dental and Oral Surgery, N.Y.C., 1968—; dental cons. Office of Chief Med. Examiner, 1981—, forensic dental cons. Dental Soc. State of N.Y. Task Force, 1990—; cons. examiner North East Regional Bds., Washington, 1986—. Contbr. articles to profl. jours. Named Hon. Police Surgeon N.Y.C. Police Dept., 1980. Fellow N.Y. Acad. of Dentistry (pres. 1990); mem. ADA, N.Y. Soc. of Forensic Dentistry, Am. Assn. of Endodontists, N.Y. State Dental Soc. (first dist.), Omicron Kappa Upsilon (pres. 1988-89), Sigma Xi. Republican. Jewish. Home: 120 E 79th St Apt 6E New York NY 10021 also: 15 Montrose Ct Roslyn Harbor NY 11576 Office: Endodontic Assocs of Greater NY 515 Madison Ave New York NY 10022

SOLOMON, CLIVE, surgeon; b. Johannesburg, Transvaal, South Africa, Oct. 30, 1963; arrived in New Zealand, 1990; s. Mervyn Hirsh Solomon and Sarah (Weinstock) Barr; m. Hayley Ann Swiel, Dec. 28, 1986; children: Raoul, Raphael. BSc in Medicine, U. Cape Town, 1984, MBChB, 1988; postgrad., U. Otago, 1995—. Registered med. practitioner, New Zealand. House surgeon Transvaal Provincial Adminstrn., South Africa, 1989-90; surg. registrar Wanganui Hosp., New Zealand, 1990-92, Health Care Otago, Dunedin, New Zealand, 1992-93, 95; lectr. dept. surgery U. Otago, 1993-94, rsch. supr., 1994-96; rschr. Ultrasonography Vascular Lab., U. Otago, 1993-95. Contbr. articles to profl. jours. Recipient rsch. fellowship Royal Australasian Coll. Surgeons, 1993, tng. fellowship Health Rsch. Coun., New Zealand, 1995, travel award Health Rsch. Coun., New Zealand, 1995. Mem. Otago Med. Rsch. Found., Surg. Rsch. Soc. Home: 7 Northfield Ave, Dunedin Otago, New Zealand Office: U Otago, Dept Surgery, Dunedin New Zealand

SOLOMON, DAVID HARRIS, physician, educator; b. Cambridge, Mass., Mar. 7, 1923; s. Frank and Rose (Roud) S.; m. Ronda L. Markson, June 23, 1946; children: Patti Jean (Mrs. Richard E. Sinaiko), Nancy Ellen (Mrs. Marvin Evans.). A.B., Brown U., 1944; M.D., Harvard U., 1946. Intern Peter Bent Brigham Hosp., Boston, 1946-47, resident, 1947-48, 50-51; fellow endocrinology New Eng. Center Hosp., Boston, 1951-52; faculty UCLA Sch. Medicine, 1952—, prof. medicine, 1966-93, vice chmn. dept. medicine, 1968-71, chmn. dept., 1971-81, assoc. dir. geriatrics, 1982-89; dir. UCLA Ctr. on Aging, 1991—; prof. emeritus UCLA, 1993—; chief med. svc. Harbor Gen. Hosp., Torrance, Calif., 1966-71; cons. Wadsworth VA Hosp., L.A., 1952—, Sepulveda VA Hosp., 1971—; cons. metabolism tng. com. USPHS, 1960-64, endocrinology study sect., 1970-73. Editor: Jour. Am. Geriatric Soc., 1988-93; contbr. numerous articles to profl. jours. Recipient Mayo Soley award, 1986. Master ACP; mem. Assn. Am. Physicians, Am. Soc. Clin. Investigation, Western Soc. Clin. Research (councillor 1963-65), Endocrine Soc. (Robert H. Williams award 1989), Am. Thyroid Assn. (pres. 1973-74, Disting. Service award 1986), Inst. Medicine Nat. Acad. Scis., AAAS, Assn. Profs. Medicine (pres. 1980-81), Western Assn. Physicians (councillor 1972-75, pres. 1983-84), Am. Fedn. Aging Rsch. (Irving S. Wright award), Am. Geriatrics Soc. (bd. dirs. 1985-93, Milo Leavitt award 1992, Disting. Svc. award 1993), Phi Beta Kappa, Sigma Xi, Alpha Omega Alpha. Home: 863 Woodacres Rd Santa Monica CA 90402-2107 Office: UCLA Sch Medicine Dept Medicine Los Angeles CA 90024-1687

SOLOMON, GAIL E., physician; b. Bklyn., May 26, 1938; d. Samuel and Estelle (Suffin) S.; m. Harvey Hecht, Oct. 28, 1962; children: Daniel, Jonathan, Elizabeth. AB, Smith Coll., 1958; MD, Albert Einstein Coll. Medicine, 1962. Diplomate Am. Bd. Pediats., Am. Bd. Psychiatry and Neurology (assoc. examiner), Am. Bd. Electroencephalography, Am. Bd. Electroencephalography and Neurophysiology, Am. Bd. Clin. Neurophysiology. Intern in pediats. Bronx Mcpl. Hosp. Ctr., 1962-63, resident in pediats., 1963-64; resident in pediats. N.Y. Hosp.-Cornell U. Med. Coll., 1964-65; NIH vis. fellow in neurology and child neurology Columbia-Presbyn. Med. Ctr., 1965-68, NIH vis. fellow in clin. neurophysiology/electroenceph.; instr. neurology Columbia U. Coll. of Physicians and Surgeons, 1968-69; instr. in neurology and pediats. Cornell U. Med. Coll., 1969-70, asst. prof. neurology and pediats., 1970-76; asst. attending in neurology and pediats. N.Y. Hosp., 1969-76, dir. electroencephalography, 1969—, assoc. attending in neurology and pediats., 1976—, assoc. attending neurologist in psychiatry, 1983—; mem. joint com. for stroke facilities NIH; mem. FDA Peripheral and CNS Adv. Com., 1979-83, chmn., 1983, cons., 1983-84; mem. med. audit com. N.Y. Hosp., mem. utilization rev. com.; mem. profl. adv. bd. N.Y. State Epilepsy Assn.; adj. attending physician in neurology Meml.-Sloan Kettering Cancer Ctr., 1982-93; neurology cons. Blythedale Children's Hosp., Valhalla, N.Y., 1991—, Meml.-Sloan Kettering Cancer Ctr., 1993—. Contbr. articles to profl. jours. Fellow Am. Acad. Neurology, Am. Acad. Pediats., Am. Electroencephalographic Soc. mem. AMA (Physician's Recognition award in Continuing Med. Edn.), N.Y. State Med. Soc., N.Y. County Med. Soc., Am. Med. Women's Assn., Am. Epilepsy Soc., Am. Acad. Clin. Neurophysiology, Eastern EEG Soc., Am. Med. EEG Assn., Child Neurology Soc., Internat. Child Neurology Assn., Tristate Child Neurology Soc., Assn. for Rsch. in Nervous and Mental Diseases, N.Y. Acad. Sci. Office: NY Hosp-Cornell U Med Coll 525 E 68th St New York NY 10021

SOLOMON, GEORGE FREEMAN, academic psychiatrist; b. Freeport, N.Y., Nov. 25, 1931; s. Joseph C. and Ruth (Freeman) S.; children: Joshua Ben, Jared Freeman. A.B., Stanford U., 1952, M.D., 1955. Intern, Barnes Hosp., St. Louis, 1955-56; resident in psychiatry Langley Porter Neuropsychiat. Inst., U. Calif. Med. Sch., San Francisco, 1956-59; asst. to asso. prof. psychiatry Stanford U. Med. Sch., 1962-73; dir. med. edn. Fresno County (Calif.) Dept. Health, 1973-83; clin. prof. UCLA Med. Sch., 1974-78; clin. prof. psychiatry U. Calif. Med. Sch., San Francisco, 1976-79, prof., 1980-84, vice-chmn. dept., 1978-83; adj. prof. U. Calif., San Francisco, 1984-90; prof. psychiatry and biobehavioral sci. UCLA, 1984-95, prof. emeritus, 1995—; chief chem. dependency treatment ctr. VA Med. Ctr., Sepulveda, Calif., 1984-89; chief psychoneuroimmunology, 1989-94; chief psychiatry Valley Med. Center, Fresno, 1974-83. Co-author: The Psychology of Strength, 1975; contbr. over 150 papers and articles on psychoneuroimmunology, violence, Vietnam and other topics to profl. jours. and various publs. Capt. USAR, 1959-61. Fellow Internat. Coll. Psychosomatic Medicine, Am. Psychiat. Assn., Acad. of Behavioral Med. Research., Royal Coll. Psychiatrists. Home: 19054 Pacific Coast Hwy Malibu CA 90265-5406 Office: UCLA Sch Med Dean's Office N Cousins Prog Psychoneuro 12-138CHS Los Angeles CA 90025

SOLOMON, GLEN DAVID, physician, researcher; b. Jersey City, Mar. 24, 1955; s. Ernest and Shirley (Schlosky)S. BA, Northwestern U., 1976; MD, Rush Med. Coll., 1980. Diplomate Am. Bd. Internal Medicine, Nat. Bd. Med. Examiners. Intern and resident in internal medicine USAF Med. Ctr., Wright-Patterson AFB, Ohio, Wright State U. Affiliated Hosps., Dayton, Ohio, 1980-83; physician Diamond Headache Clinic, Chgo., 1986-88; internist Headache Sect. Cleve. Clinic Found., 1988—; internist, dir. headache sect., 1994—; adj. asst. prof. Chgo. Med. Sch., 1987-88; prof. medicine Pa. State U., 1989—; assoc. prof. medicine Ohio State U., 1992—; attending staff Louis A. Weiss Hosp., Chgo., 1986-88; lectr. sci. and lay orgns. in fields of headaches, pain mgmt., internal medicine, pharmacology; med. educator in internal medicine and headache medicine. Contbr. chpts. to books and articles to profl. jours. Maj. USAF, 1980-86. Named one of Outstanding Young Men of Am., 1986, Best Doctors in Am. Midwest Region, 1996; recipient tchg. award Am. Acad. Family Physicians, 1984, 85, 86. Fellow ACP, Am. Assn. for Study of Headache (bd. dirs. 1990-95); mem. Internat. Headache Soc., Am. Soc. Clin. Pharmacology and Therapeutics (chmn. headache sect. 1993-96), Nat. Headache Found. (bd. dirs. 1995—), Alpha Omega Alpha, Psi Upsilon. Office: Cleve Clinic Found 9500 Euclid Ave Cleveland OH 44195-0001

SOLOMON, HARVEY, surgeon, educator; b. Toledo, Ohio, Apr. 27, 1949; s. Ernest Herbert and Freda Solomon; m. Miriam Schwalb; children: Ruth, Michael, Tamar. Student, Antioch Coll., Yellow Springs, Ohio, 1969, Hebrew U., Jerusalem; postgrad., Hebrew U., Jerusalem, 1977. Intern Hadassah Med. Ctr., Jerusalem, 1978-79; resident in gen. surgery Soroka Med. Ctr., Beer Sheba, Israel, 1979-87; surg. rsch. fellow dept. fellow Baylor Med. Ctr., Dallas, 1987-89, transplantation fellow, 1989-91; instr. surgery Ben Gurion U., 1982-88; asst. prof. surgery St. Louis U., 1988—; mem. HLA oversight com., lab. utilization com., oper. rm. com. St. Louis U. Recipient Distinction award Am. Physicians for Israel, 1981. Mem. ASA, AASLD, ILTS, Am. Soc. Transplant Surgeons. Office: St Louis U Med Ctr 3635 Vista Ave Saint Louis MO 63110

SOLOMON, IRA SETH, ophthalmologist; b. N.Y.C., Mar. 6, 1959; s. Maurice and Loretta (Levine) S.; m. Sherry Kaplan, June 15, 1986; children: Marissa, Taylor, Scott. BS summa cum laude, Pa. State U., 1980; MD, Jefferson Med. Coll., 1982. Intern in internal medicine Lenox Hill Hosp., N.Y.C., 1982-83; resident in ophthalmology Montefiore Med. Ctr.-Albert Einstein Coll. Medicine, Bronx, N.Y., 1983-85, chief resident, 1985-86; fellow in glaucoma N.Y. Eye and Ear Infirmary, N.Y.C., 1986-87; asst. clin. prof. Albert Einstein Coll. Med., 1990—; pvt. practice New Rochelle, N.Y., 1987-88, Bronxville, N.Y., 1988—. Contbr. chpts. to textbooks: Ophthalmic Lasers, 3d edit., 1988, The Glaucomas, 1989, Clinical Foundations in Ophthalmology, 1990. Fellow ACS, Am. Acad. Ophthalmology. Office: 77 Pondfield Rd Bronxville NY 10708

SOLOMON, JULIUS OSCAR LEE, pharmacist, hypnotherapist; b. N.Y.C., Aug. 14, 1917; s. John and Jeannette (Krieger) S.; student Bklyn. Coll., 1935-36, CCNY, 1936-37; BS in Pharmacy, U. So. Calif., 1949; postgrad. Long Beach State U., 1971-72, Southwestern Colls., 1979, 81-82, San Diego State U., 1994—; PhD, Am. Inst. Hypnotherapy, 1988; postgrad. San Diego State U., 1994—. m. Sylvia Smith, June 26, 1941 (div. Jan. 1975); children: Marc Irwin, Evan Scott, Jeri Lee. Cert. hypnotherapist; cert. hypnoanaesthesia therapist. Dye maker Fred Fear & Co., Bklyn., 1935; apprentice interior decorator Dorothy Draper, 1936; various jobs, N.Y. State Police, 1940-45; rsch. asst. Union Oil Co., 1945; lighting cons. Joe Rosenberg & Co., 1946-49; owner Banner Drug, Lomita, 1949-53, Redondo Beach, Calif., 1953-72, El Prado Pharmacy, Redondo Beach, 1961-65; pres. Banner Drug, Inc., Redondo Beach, 1953-72, Thrifty Drugs, 1972-74, also Guild Drug, Longs Drug, Drug King, 1976-83; pres. Socoma, Inc. doing bus. as Lee & Ana Pharmacy, 1983-86, now Two Hearts Help Clinic, 1986—. Charter commr., founder Redondo Beach Youth Baseball Council; sponsor Little League Baseball, basketball, football, bowling; pres. Redondo Beach Boys Club; v.p. South Bay Children's Health Ctr., 1974, Redondo Beach Coordinating Coun., 1975; bd. dirs. So. Bay Assn. Little Theatres, 1972-75; actor in 8 shows; founder Redondo Beach Community Theater, 1975; actor Man of La Mancha Vangard Theatre, San Diego, 1995; active maj. gift drive YMCA, 1975; mem. SCAG Com. on Criminal Justice, 1974, League Calif. Environ. Quality Com., 1975; mem. Dem. State Cen. Com., Los Angeles County Dem. Cen. Com.; del. Dem. Nat. Conv., 1972; chmn. Redondo Beach Recreation and Parks Commn.; mem. San Diego County Parks Adv. Commn., 1982; mem. San Diego Juvenile Justice Commn., 1986-92; mem. San Diego County Adv. Com. Adult Detention, 1987-92; mem. human resource devel. com., pub. improvement com. Nat. League of Cities; v.p. Redondo Beach Coordinating Coun.; councilman, Redondo Beach, 1961-69, 73-77; treas. 46th Assembly Dist. Coun.; candidate 46 Assembly dist. 1966; nat. chmn. Pharmacists for Humphrey, 1968, 72; pres. bd. dirs. South Bay Exceptional Childrens Soc., Chapel Theatre; bd. dirs. sc. div. League Calif. Cities, U.S.-Mex. Sister Cities Assn., Boy's Club Found. San Diego County, Autumn Hills Condominium Assn. (pres.), Calif. Employee Pharmacists Assn. (pres. 1985), Our House, Chula Vista, Calif., 1984-86; mem. South Bay Inter-City Hwy. Com., Redondo Beach Round Table, 1973-77; mem. State Calif. Commn. of Californias (U.S.-Mexico), 1975-78; mem. Chula Vista Safety Commn., 1978, chmn., 1980-81; chmn. San Diego County Juvenile Camp Contract Com., 1982-83; mem. San Diego County Juvenile Delinquency Prevention Commn., 1983-85, 89-91, San Diego County Juvenile Justice Commn., 1986-91, San Diego County Adv. Com. for Adult Detention, 1987-91; spl. participant Calif. Crime and Violence Workshop; mem. Montgomery Planning Commn., 1983-86; mem. Constnl. Observance Com., 1990-93, Troubled Teenagers Hypnosis Treatment Program, 1989—. With USCGR, 1942-45. Recipient Pop Warner Youth award, 1960, 1962, award of merit Calif. Pharm. Assn., 1962, award Am. Assn. Blood Banks, 1982. Diplomate Am. Bd. Diplomates Pharmacy Internat., 1977-81; Fellow Am. Coll. Pharmacists (pres. 1949-57); mem. South Bay Pharm. Assn. (pres.), South Bay Councilman Assn. (founder, pres.), Palos Verdes Peninsula Navy League (charter), Am. Legion, U. So. Calif. Alumni Assn. (life), Assn. Former N.Y. State Troopers (life), AFTRA, Am. Pharm. Assn., Nat. Assn. Retail Druggists, Calif. Pharmacists Assn., Calif. Employee Pharmacist Assn. (bd. dirs. 1980-81), Hon. Dep. Sheriff's Assn., San Ysidro C. of C. (bd. dirs. 1985-87), Fraternal Order of Police, San Diego County Fish and Game Assn., Rho Pi Phi (pres. alumni). Club: Trojan (life). Lodges: Elks (life), Masons (32 deg.; life), Lions (charter mem. North Redondo). Established Lee and Ana Solomon award for varsity athlete witghest scholastic average at 10 L.A. South Bay High Schs. in Los Angeles County and 3 San Diego area South Bay High Schs.

SOLOMON, NEIL, retired physician and scientist; b. Pitts., Feb. 27, 1932; s. Max Maurice and Clara (Eisenstein) S.; m. Frema Sindell, June 26, 1955; children: Ted, Scott, Clifford. AB, Western Res. U., 1954, MD, 1961, MS, 1961; PhD, U. Md., 1965. Diplomate Nat. Bd. Med. Examiners. Fellow in physiology Western Res. U., Cleve., 1955-61; trainee in physiology USPHS, 1955-61; predoctoral fellow Arthritis and Rheumatism Found., 1956-61; intern and asst. resident in medicine Johns Hopkins Hosp., Osler Med. Svc., Balt., 1961-63; asst. sr. surgeon NIH, Child Health and Human Devel., 1963-65; asst. in medicine Johns Hopkins Hosp., Balt., 1963-64; instr. in medicine Johns Hopkins U. Sch. Medicine, Balt., 1964-69; asst. prof. psychiatry and behavioral scis. Johns Hopkins U. Sch. Medicine, 1971-79; assoc. prof. physiology, asst. prof. medicine U. Md. Sch. Medicine, Balt., 1965-69; vis. clin. prof. pharmacology U. Miami (Fla.) Sch. Medicine, 1980; advisor to Pres. Richard Nixon-Transition Com., Health Affairs, 1968, Sec. of Health, Edn. and Welfare, 1969-71; chmn. Comprehensive Planning, 1968-69; sec. of health and mental hygiene State of Md., 1969-79; med. commentator Cable News Network TV; med. editor WBAL-NBC radio; health editor WBAL-TV Hello Balt.; lectr. in field. Syndicated med. columnist for L.A. Times Syndicate, 1975-93; contbr. articles to profl. jours. Trustee Non-Profit Housing for Elderly People, 1965, Homewood Sch., 1968, Balt. Hebrew Congregation, 1972; med. adv. bd. mem. Am. Joint Distbn. Com., 1972; adv. bd. St. Jude Vols., 1973, Md. Acupuncture Found., 1973; active Brotherhood, Blat. Hebrew Congregation, 1969, Nat. Adv. Com. for the State of Md. to the Selective Svc. Sys., 1970, Gov.'s Commn. on Environ. Pollution, 1970, Citizen's Awards Dinner Com., 1972, Environ. Coun. for Md., 1972, Md. Commn. on Aging, 1974, Patuxent River Watershed Adv. Com., 1977, Jewish Nat. Fund Coun., 1979, others. Lt. comdr. USPHS, 1963-64. Mem. AMA, AAUP, Am. Acad. Otolaryngological Allergy, Am. Fedn. for Clin. Rsch., Am. Fedn. TV and Radio Artists, Am. Geriat. Soc., Am. Health Assn., Am. Heart assn., Fedn. Am. Socs. for Exptl. Biology, Am. Physiol. Soc., Balt. City Med. Soc., Authors League, Authors Guild, Inc., Alpha Omega Alpha. Home: 2209 Ken Oak Rd Baltimore MD 21209

SOLOMON, PAUL ROBERT, neuropsychologist, educator; b. Bklyn., Aug. 27, 1948; s. Maynard and Norma Harris (Ruben) S.; m. Suellen Zablow, Aug. 16, 1970; children: Todd, Jessica. BA in Psychology, SUNY, New Paltz, 1970, MA in Psychology, 1972; PhD in Psychology, U. Mass., 1972. lic. Psychologist, Mass. Prof. psychology and neuroscience Williams Coll, Williamstown, Mass., 1976—, neuroscience program chmn., 1990—; dir. memory disorders clinic S.W. Vt. Med. Ctr., Bennington, 1990—; bd. dirs. No. Berkshire Mental Health Assn., North Adams, Mass. Author: Scientific Writings, 1985, Memory, 1989, Psychology 4th edit., 1993; contbr. articles to profl. jours. Bd. dirs. W. Mass. Alzheimers Assn., 1992—. Recipient Distinguished Teaching award U. Mass., Amherst, 1975; Rsch. grantee EPA, NIH, NSF, 1978—; Rsch. fellowships NIH, 1979, NSF, 1980. Fellow APA, AAAS, Am. Psychol. Soc.; mem. Soc. for Neuroscience. Home: 130 Forest Rd Williamstown MA 01267-2029 Office: Williams Coll Dept Psychology Williamstown MA 01262

SOLOMON, PHYLLIS LINDA, social work educator, researcher; b. Hartford, Conn., Dec. 6, 1945; d. Louis Calvin and Annabell Lee (Nitzberg) S. BA in Sociology, Russell Sage Coll., 1968; MA in Sociology, Case Western Res. U., 1970, PhD in Social Welfare, 1978. Lic. social worker, Pa. Rsch. assoc. Inst. Urban Studies Cleve. State U., 1970-71; program evaluator Cleve. State Hosp., 1971-74; project dir. Ohio Mental Health and Mental Retardation Rsch. Ctr., Cleve., 1974-75; rsch. assoc. Psychiat. Rsch. Found. of Cleve., 1975; project dir. Ohio Mental Health and Mental Retardation Rsch. Ctr., 1977-78; rsch. assoc. dirs. rsch. and mental health planning Fedn. for Community Planning, 1978-88; prof. dept. mental health scis., dir. sect. mental health svcs. and systems research Hahnemann U., Phila., 1988-94; prof. Sch. Social Work U. Pa., Phila., 1994—; secondary appointment Prof. Social Work in Psychiatry U. Pa. Sch. Medicine; adj. prof. Med. Coll. Pa., Hahnemann U. Author: (with others) Community Services to Discharged Psychiatric Patients, 1984; co-editor: New Developments in Psychiatric Rehabilitation, 1990, Psychiatric Rehabilitation in Practice, 1993; editorial adv. bd. Community Mental Health Jour., 1988—; contbr. articles to profl. jours. Trustee Cleve. Rape Crisis Ctr., 1981-84, CIT Mental Health Svcs., Cleve., 1985-88; mem. citizen's adv. bd. Sagamore Hills (Ohio) Children's Psychiat. Hosp., 1984-88. Named Evaluator of the Yr., Ohio Program Evaluators Group, 1987; recipient Ann. award Cuyahoga County Community Mental Health Bd., 1988. Mem. Internat. Assn. Psychosocial Rehab. Svcs. Jewish. Home: 220 E Mermaid Ln Apt 186 Philadelphia PA 19118-3215 Office: U Pa Sch Social Work 3701 Locust Walk Philadelphia PA 19104-6214

SOLOMON, RANDALL ADAM, physician; b. Bay Shore, N.Y., Dec. 24, 1957. MD, SUNY, Buffalo, 1984. Diplomate Am. Bd. Psychiatry. Staff psychiatrist VA Med. Ctr., Northport, N.Y., 1988-89; pvt. practice psychiatry VA Med. Ctr., Port Jefferson, N.Y., 1989-92; staff psychiatrist J.T. Mather Hosp., Port Jefferson, N.Y., 1989—; pvt. practice psychiatry J.T. Mather Hosp., South Setauket, N.Y., 1992—; cons. N.Y. State Dept. Social Svcs., DCAP Unit, Hauppage, N.Y., 1989—. Mem. Am. Psychiat. Assn. Office: Randall Solomon MD 3771 Nesconset Hwy # 103 South Setauket NY 11720

SOLOMON, RICHARD J., internist; b. N.Y.C., Oct. 8, 1944; s. Harold I. and Ruth Barbara (Bomhoff) S.; m. Margaret Virginia Johnson, Aug. 27, 1966; children: Garrett, Hadley, Avery, Samuel. BA, Harvard Coll., 1966; MD, Yale U., 1970. Diplomate Am. Bd. Internal Medicine, Am. Bd. Nephrology. Assoc. prof. medicine Brown U., 1975-86, N.Y. Med. Coll., 1986-90, Harvard Med. Sch., 1990—; hypertension faculty Merck, Sharpe & Davis, West Point, Pa., 1980—; med. dir. REN Brookline (Mass.) Dialysis Unit, 1994—. Mem. Am. Soc. Nephrology, Am. Soc. Hypertension. Office: Joslin Diabetes Ctr One Joslin Place Boston MA 02215

SOLOMON, ROBERT DOUGLAS, pathology educator; b. Delavan, Wis., Aug. 28, 1917; s. Lewis Jacob and Sara (Ludgin) S.; m. Helen Fisher, Apr. 4, 1943; children: Susan, Wendy, James, William. Student, MIT, 1934-36; BS in Biochemistry, U. Chgo., 1938; MD, Johns Hopkins U., 1942. Intern John's Hopkins Hosp., 1942-43; resident in pathology Michael Reese Hosp., 1947-49; lectr. U. Ill., Chgo., 1947-50; fellow NIH pathology U. Ill., 1949-50; asst. prof. U. Md., Balt., 1955-60; assoc. prof. U. So. Calif., L.A., 1960-70; chief of staff City of Hope Nat. Med. Ctr., 1966-67; prof. U. Mo., Kansas City, 1977-78, SUNY, Syracuse, 1968-78; chief of staff The Hosp., Sidney, N.Y., 1985-86; adj. prof. U. N.C., Wilmington, 1988—; cons. VA Hosp., Balt., 1955-60, Med. Svc. Lab., Wilmington, 1989-93. Co-author: Progress in Gerontological Research, 1967; contbr. papers and profl. jours. and rsch. in biochemistry, revascular of heart, carcinogenesis, cancer chemotherapy, atherogenesis, discovery of reversibility of atherosclerosis. V.p. Rotary, Duarte, Calif., 1967; v.p. and pres. Force for an Informed Electorate. Capt. Med. Corps, AUS, 1943-46, PTO. Grantee NIH, Fleischmann Found., Am. Heart Assn., Nat. Cancer Inst., 1958-70. Fellow ACP (pres. Md. chpt.); mem. Coll. Am. Pathologists (past pres. Md. chpt.), Am. Soc. Clin. Pathologists, Assn. Clin. Scientists, Am. Chem. Soc., Royal Soc. Medicine (London). Home: 113 S Belvedere Dr Hampstead NC 28443-2504

SOLOMON, SEYMOUR, neurologist, consultant; b. Milw., May 27, 1924; s. Morris and Sylvia (Heifetz) S.; m. Ethel Marion Ross, Mar. 28, 1948; children: Robert, Debora. Student, Marquette U., 1942-44, MD, 1947. Diplomate Am. Bd. Psychiatry and Neurology. Intern Mt. Sinai Hosp., Milw., 1947-48, resident in internal medicine, 1948-50; resident in neurology Montefiore Hosp., N.Y.C., 1950-52; chief neurology Phila. Gen. Hosp., 1952-53; instr. neurology Temple U. Sch. Medicine, Phila., 1952-55, Woman's Med. Coll., Phila., 1952-55; attending neurologist Montefiore Med. Ctr., Bronx, N.Y., 1955—; dir. headache unit Montefiore Med. Ctr., Bronx, 1980—; asst. clin. prof. neurology Columbia U. Coll. Physicians and Surgeons, N.Y.C., 1958-64; assoc. prof. neurology Albert Einstein Coll. Medicine, Bronx, 1980-83, prof. neurology, 1983—. Author: The Headache Book, 1991; author 22 book chpts. and revs.; editor abstracts Jour. Headache, 1987-96; editor Headache Rev., 1988-92; contbr. 150 articles to profl. jours. Capt. USAF, 1953-55. Fellow Am. Acad. Neurology, Am. Assn. for Study of Headache (pres.); mem. AMA, Am. Neurol. Assn., Am. Coun. Headache Edn., Am. Heart Assn., Internat. Assn for Study of Pain, Internat. Headache Soc., Assn. for Rsch. in Nervous and Mental Diseases. Office: Montefiore Med Ctr 111 E 210th St Bronx NY 10467-2490

SOLOMON, SOLOMON SIDNEY, endocrinologist, pharmacologist, scientist; b. N.Y.C., Dec. 2, 1936; s. Nathan and Irene (Oransky) S.; m. Linda M. Shaw, June 17, 1962 (div. 1980); children: Joan Geller, Rebecca Karen. AB in Chemistry, Harvard U., 1958; MD, U. Rochester, 1962. Intern in internal medicine New Eng. Med. Ctr., Tufts U., Boston, 1963; resident in internal medicine Boston City Hosp., 1964, 65; fellow in endocrinology and metabolism U. Wash. Sch. Medicine, Seattle, 1965-67; teaching fellow Tufts U. and Boston City Hosp., Boston, 1964-65; asst. prof., assoc. prof. then prof. medicine U. Tenn. Sch. Medicine, Memphis, 1969—, assoc. dean for rsch., 1983—, prof. pharmacology, 1986—; chief endocrinology and metabolism VA Med. Ctr., Memphis, 1971—; cons. in field; mem. merit rev. bd. VA Rsch. Svc., Washington, 1978-81. Coeditor: The Lab in Clinical Diagnosis, 1981; contbr. numerous articles and abstracts to profl. jours. Capt. MC, USAF, 1967-69. Harvard Coll. scholar, 1954-58; Whipple scholar, 1959-62; VA and NIH grantee, 1965—. recipient career and devel. award VA Ctrl. Office Rsch. Svc., 1969-71, 1st place for excellence in clin. rsch. Memphis Area Health Industry Couns., 1994. Fellow Am. Coll. Endocrinology; mem. Am. Diabetes Assn. (pres. Tenn. chpt. 1975-76, rsch. com., chmn. metabolism sect. 1982), So. Soc. Clin. Investigation (chmn. metabolism sect. 1975, 88, nominating com. 1989), Endocrine Soc., Am. Fedn. for Clin. Rsch. (counselor south sect. 1976-79), Am. Soc. Clin. Investigation, Cen. Soc. for Clin. Rsch., Am. Soc. Pharmacology and Exptl. Therapy, Fedn. Am. Soc. Exptl. Biology. Jewish. Home: 5196 Longmeadow Dr Memphis TN 38134-4316 Office: VA Med Ctr 1030 Jefferson Ave Memphis TN 38104-2127

SOLOMONOW, MOSHE, biomedical engineer, educator; b. Tel Aviv, Oct. 24, 1944; came to U.S., 1965; s. Jonathan and Eva (Efraim) S.; m. Susanne Elisbeth Nickerson, May 31, 1981; children: Deborah Leigh, Esther Monique. BSc, Calif. State U., L.A., 1970, MSc, 1972; PhD, UCLA, 1976. Rsch. engr. UCLA, 1976-80; assoc. prof. La. State Univ. Med. Ctr., 1980-87, prof., 1987—; assoc. prof. Tulane Univ., New Orleans, 1980-83; dir. bioengrng. La. State U. Med. Ctr., New Orleans, 1983—; dir. paraplegic clinic Rehab. Inst. New Orleans, 1991—; cons. NIH, 1978—, NSF, 1985—, Dept. Vets. Affairs, 1978—, others. Editor-in-chief Jour. EMG & Kinesiology, 1991—; reviewer 16 scientific jours., patentee in field; contbr. over 80 articles to profl. jours. Pres. Lakeshore Day Sch., New Orleans, 1990. Recipient Crump award UCLA, 1977, Mayor's medal City of Rennes, France, 1992, Disting. Merit award Delta 7 Assn., Paris, 1991. Office: Dept Orthopedic Surgery 2025 Gravier St # 400 New Orleans LA 70112

SOLON, LEONARD R(AYMOND), physicist, educator, consultant; b. White Plains, N.Y., Sept. 11, 1925; s. Morris and Rebecca (Bobrov) S.; BA, Hamilton Coll., 1947; MSc, Rutgers U., 1949; PhD, NYU, 1960; m. Charlotte Rothman, June 30, 1946; children: Miriam Beth, Matthew Benjamin, Emily Lynn. Physicist, Nuc. Devel. Assos., Inc., White Plains, 1950-52; asst. chief, then chief radiation br. AEC, N.Y.C., 1952-60; dir. applied nuc. tech. Tech. Rsch. Group, Inc., Syosset, N.Y., 1960-62; cons. Burns & Roe, N.Y.C. and Servo Corp. Am., Hicksville, N.Y., 1962-64; mgr. R & D Del Electronics Corp., Mt. Vernon, N.Y., 1964-67; founder, exec. v.p., tech. dir. Hadron, Inc., Yonkers, N.Y., 1967-75; dir. bur. radiation control N.Y.C. Dept. Health, 1975-91; lectr., then adj. assoc. prof. N.Y.U. Inst. Environ. Medicine, 1955-93; environ. & radiol. health cons.; prof. health physics U.S. Mcht. Marine Acad., 1963. Served with inf. U.S. Army, 1944-46; ETO. Cert. Am. Bd. Health Physics. Mem. Am. Nuclear Soc., Health Physics Soc., Am. Phys. Soc., N.Y. Acad. Scis., Conf. Radiation Control Program Dirs., AAAS, Radiol. and Med. Physics Soc. N.Y., Phi Beta Kappa. Contbr. articles to profl. jours. Co-patentee: laser photocoagulator used in treatment of detached retina; powering lasers using nuclear sources. Home and Office: 1756 Lakefront Blvd Fort Pierce FL 34982-8003

SOLOVIEFF, EUGENE NICOLAS, orthopedic surgeon; b. San Francisco, Feb. 15, 1926; s. Nicolas Nicolas and Lydia Alexandra (Lempert) S.; m. Mary Ann Reynolds, June 3, 1950; children: Katherine, Nicolas, Michael, Constance. Student, Carroll Coll., Helena, Mont., 1943-45; MD, Creighton U., 1950. Diplomate Am. Bd. Orthopedic Surgery. Pvt. practice orthopedic surgery San Francisco, 1956-96; asst. prof. anatomy Coll. Phys. and Surgeons/A Dental Sch., San Francisco, 1958-93; asst. clin. prof. dept. orthopedic surgery U. Calif., San Francisco; chmn. dept. orthopedics St. Marys Hosp. and Med. Ctr., San Francisco, 1968-74. Lt. USNR, 1952-54. Mem. Am. Acad. Orthopedic Surgery, Am. Arthritis Found., Western Orthopedic Assn. (bd. dirs.), Calif. Orthopedic Assn. Home: 229 Ricardo Rd Mill Valley CA 94941

SOLOWAY, MARK S., urologist, urologic oncologist; b. Balt., Jan. 24, 1943; s. Louis and Ada (Yoffee) S.; m. Cynthia T. Soloway, May 30, 1966; children: Scott, Deanna. Student, Northwestern U.; MD, Case Western Reserve U., 1968. Diplomate Am. Bd. Urology; lic. MD, Ohio, Tenn., Mo., Fla. Clin. assoc. surgery br. Nat. Cancer Inst., 1970-72; resident in urology Univ. Hosps., Cleve., 1972-75; asst. prof. urology U. Tenn., Memphis, 1975-78; assoc. prof. urology U. Miami (Fla.) Sch. Medicine, 1978-80, prof. urology, 1980-91, prof., chair dept. urology, 1991—; mem. med. staff U. Tenn./William F. Bowld Hosp., Memphis, 1975-91, pres. med. staff, 1979, mem. exec. com., 1979; mem. med. staff Bapt. Meml. Hosp., Memphis, 1975-91, mem. cancer com.; mem. med. staff VA Hosp., Memphis, 1975-91, St. Jude Children's Rsch. Hosp., Memphis, 1975-91, Cedars Med. Ctr., Miami, 1991—, mem. operating room com., 1991—, acad. affairs com., 1991—; mem. med. staff Jackson Meml. Hosp., Miami, 1991—, VA Hosp., Miami, 1991—; vis. prof. various univs. in U.S. and internat.; presenter over 350 confs. and lectures in field. Editor Urology Internat.; mem. editl. bd. Postgrad. Medicine, Urology, Urologists Now, Organo Ufficiale Suicmi (Italy); mem. internat. adv. bd. Progres en Urologie; reviewer Jour. Urology, Investigative Urology, 1978—, Cancer, Jour. Am. Med. Assn.; contbr. over 235 articles to profl. jours., over 35 chpts. to books in field. Bd. dirs. Memphis Am. Cancer Soc.; mem. exec. com. Nat. Bladder Cancer Collaborative Group A, 1979-83, chmn. Protocol 5 com., co-chmn. Protocols 8, 10, 11, 12, 13; mem. cancer edn. com. U. Tenn., 1983—; reviewer Nat. VA Protocols, 1978—; mem. protocol com. Nat. Prostatic Cancer Project, 1985; mem. Organ Systems Program Bladder Cancer Working Group, 1984-88; mem. program com. Ann. Meeting Am. Urol. Assn., 1984—. Lt. comdr. USPHS, 1970-72. Grantee NIH, 1975-87; Clin. fellow Am. Cancer Soc., 1973-74, Jr. Facility Clin. fellow, 1976-79; recipient 1st prize Cleve. Urol. Soc. Essay Contest, 1974. Mem. AMA, ACS, Am. Urol. Assn. (Southeastern sect., Gold Cystoscope award 1984, North Ctrl. Sect. Traveling fellow 1972-73), Am. Soc. Clin. Oncology, Am. Assn. Cancer Rsch., Soc. Surg. Oncology, Urol. Rsch. Soc., Soc. Urol. Oncology, Tenn. Med. Assn., Memphis and Shelby County Med. Assn., Greater Miami Urol. Soc., Dutch Urol. Soc. (hon.), Buffalo Urol. Soc. (hon.), Phi Beta Kappa. Home: 1780 Daytonia Rd Miami Beach FL 33141 Office: PO Box 016960 (M814) Miami FL 33101

SOLOWAY, ROSE ANN GOULD, clinical toxicologist; b. Plainfield, N.J., Apr. 19, 1949; d. George Spencer Jr. and Rose Emma (Frank) Gould; m. Irving H. Soloway, Dec. 13, 1979. BSN, Villanova U., 1971; MS in Edn., U. Pa., 1976. Diplomate Am. Bd. Applied Toxicology. Staff nurse Hosp. of U. Pa., Phila., 1971-73; asst. clin. instr. Hosp. of U. Pa. Sch. Nursing, Phila., 1973-77; staff devel. instr. Hosp. of Med. Coll. Pa., Phila., 1977-78; dir. Emergency Nurse Tng. Program Ctr. for Study of Emergency Health Svcs., U. Pa., Phila., 1979-80; edn./comms. coord. Nat. Capital Poison Ctr. Georgetown U. Hosp., Washington, 1980-94; clin. toxicologist Nat. Capital Poison Ctr. George Washington U. Med. Ctr., Washington, 1994—; adminstr. Am. Assn. Poison Control Ctrs., Washington, 1994—; mem. Clin. Toxicology and Substance Abuse Adv. Panel, U.S. Pharmacopeial Conv., Inc., Washington, 1990-95, 95—; bd. dirs. Am. Bd. Applied Toxicology. Contbr. articles to profl. publs. Mem. APHA, Am. Assn. Poison Control Ctrs. (co-chmn. pub. edn. com. 1985-90), Poison Prevention Week Coun. (vice chmn. 1988-91, chair 1991-93). Office: Am Assn Poison Control Ctrs 3201 New Mexico Ave NW Ste 310 Washington DC 20016-2756

SOLT, ROBERT LEE, JR., surgeon; b. Bucyrus, Ohio, Dec. 28, 1931; s. Robert Lee and Grace Velma (Rinehart) S.; m. Marilyn J. Smith, June 11, 1955; children: Robert L. III, Timothy S. BS, Ohio State U., 1953, MD, 1957. Diplomate Am. Bd. Surgery. Intern White Cross Hosp., Columbus, Ohio, 1957-58; resident White Cross Hosp. (name now Riverside Meth. Hosp.), Columbus, Ohio, 1958-62; pvt. practice Bucyrus, 1962—. Contbr. articles to profl. jours. Fellow ACS; mem. Ohio State Med. Assn., AMA. Home and Office: 1401 Home Circle Bucyrus OH 44820

SOLTANOFF, JACK, nutritionist, chiropractor; b. Newark, Apr. 24, 1915; s. Louis and Rose (Yomteff) S.; m. Esther Katcher, Sept. 29, 1939; children: Howard, Ruth C. Soltanoff Jacobs, Hillory Soltanoff Seaton. N.M.D. Mecca Coll. Chiropractic Medicine, 1938, U.S. Sch. Naturopathy and Allied Scis., 1951; D.Chiropractic, Chiropractic Inst. N.Y., 1956; postgrad. Atlantic States Chiropractic Inst., 1962-63, Nat. Coll. Chiropractic, 1964-65; PhD, diplomate in nutrition Fla. Natural Health Coll., 1982. Gen. practice chiropractic medicine, cons. in nutrition, N.Y.C., 1956-75, West Hurley, N.Y. and Singer Island, Fla., 1975—; lectr., cons. in field. Author: Natural Healing; pub. Warner Books; contbr. articles to profl. jours. Syndicated newspaper columnist. Fellow Internat. Coll. Naturopathic Physicians; mem. Am. Chiropractic Assn., Internat. Chiropractic Assn., Brit. Chiropractic Assn., N.Y. Acad. Scis., Am. Council on Diagnosis and Internal Disorders, Council on Nutrition, Ethical Culture Soc. Unitarian. Instrumental in instituting chiropractic care in union contracts for mems. of Teamsters Union. Home: 25 Holiday Dr West Hurley NY 12491 also: Martinique II 4100 N Ocean Dr West Palm Beach FL 33404-2855 Office: 948 Rt 28 Kingston NY 12401

SOLTERO-HARRINGTON, LUIS RUBÉN, surgeon, educator; b. San Juan, P.R., Sept. 4, 1925; s. Augusto Rafael Soltero and Anna Lila Harrington; m. Alice Joyce Carpenter, Apr. 24, 1958; children: Luis Ruben, Kathleen Ann, Susan Joyce, Robert Richard, Sharon Theresa. BS in Agr., U. P.R., Rio Piedras, 1945; BM, MD, Northwestern U., Chgo., 1949. Diplomate Am. Bd. Surgery, Nat. Be. Med. Examiners, P.R. Rd. Med. Examiners. Intern Michael Reese Hosp., Chgo., 1949-50; resident in gen. surgery Aguadilla (P.R.) Dist. Hosp., 1950-51; resident in gen. surgery, instr. Baylor U. Coll. Medicine and Affiliated Hosps., Houston, 1954-59; resident in gen. surgery Jefferson Davis, VA and M.D. Anderson Hosps., Houston, 1954-57; resident in pediatric, thoracic and cardiovasc. surgery St. Luke's-Tex. Children's Hosp., Houston, 1957-59; asst. prof. surgery U. P.R. Sch. Medicine, 1960-64, assoc. clin. prof., 1972-73, assoc. clin prof., 1973—, in charge devel. heart surgery program, 1960-64, dir. surgery residency tng. program, 1961-64; pvt. practice, San Juan, P.R., 1959—; prof. surgery U. del Caribe Sch. Medicine, Cayey, P.R., 1981—; cons. in cardiovasc. and thoracic surgery Med. Examing Bd. P.R., San Juan, 1989; chief thoracic and cardiovasc. surgery Tchrs. Hosp., San Juan, from 1959; dir. surgery residency tng. program Univ. Hosp., Rio Piedras, from 1961; cons. in thoracic and cardiovasc. surgery San Juan City Hosp., 1962—, cons. in surgery, 1964—; cons. in surgery Presbyn. Hosp., 1972—, Mimiya's Hosp., 1987—; cons. in thoracic and cardiovasc. surgery Indsl. Hosp., San Juan, 1975—, Hosp. Met., 1982—, Clinic Fernández García, 1983—; chief surgery Ruiz Arnau Hosp., Bayamon, P.R., 1978—; asst. dir. ICU, Hosp. del Maestro, 1987—; bd. dirs. Rsch. Found. Cardiovasc. Surgery Tex., 1984—, Am. Cancer Soc., 1974; mem. Nat. Adv. Cun. Mended Hearts, Inc., 1969. Contbr. articles to med. jours.; patentee partial occlusion vascular clamp to be used in small blood vessels; inventor respirator for infants based on electronic equipment. Capt., M.C., USAF, 1953-54. Recipient award for outstanding work in cardiovasc. surgery Lions Club, Hato Rey, 1961. Fellow Am. Acad. Pediat., Am. Coll. Legal Medicine (assoc.); mem. AMA (physician recognition award 1986); mem. Denton A. Cooley Cardiovasc. Surg. Soc., Michael E. De Bakey Internat. Cardiovasc. Soc., Pan Am. Med. Assn. (coun. pediatric surgery), P.R. Soc. Cardiology, Am. Heart Assn., P.R. Hear Assn., Phi Chi. Office: 400 Domenech Ave Ste 502 San Juan PR 00918

SOLURSH, LIONEL PAUL, psychiatrist; b. Toronto, Jan. 14, 1936; came to U.S., 1986, naturalized, 1994; s. Coleman Bernard and Zelma Dorothy (Singer) S.; m. Marcia Persin (div.); children: Fern, Susan, Marc; m. Diane Sue Mullenax; children: Lia, Janine. MD, U. Toronto, 1959; Diploma in Psychiatry, U. Toronto, Can., 1962; CRCPC, Royal Coll. Physicians, 1964, FRCPC, 1965. Diplomate Am. Bd. Sexology; bd. cert. sex educator and clin. supr. Asst. prof. U. Toronto, 1965-73; staff psychiatrist Toronto Western Hosp., 1966-80, assoc. head psychiatry, 1973-79; outpatient psychiatrist Toronto East Gen. and Orthopaedic Hosp., 1980-86; assoc. prof. psychiatry U. Toronto, 1974-86; cons. psychiatrist Augusta (Ga.) Correctional Med. Inst., 1990—, chief psychiat. cons., 1992—; dir. PTSD out-patient psychiatry VA Med. Ctr., Augusta, 1986-95, med. dir. SIPU/PTSD rehab. unit, 1991-95; med. dir. trauma team SIPU/PTSD rehab. unit, 1995—; med. dir. PTSD treatment team VA Med. Ctr., Augusta, 1995—; prof. psychiatry and health behavior Med. Coll. of Ga., Augusta, 1986—; assoc. fellow Am. Coll. Sexology, 1995—; cons. Ga. Regional Hosp. and Richmond County Cmty. Mental Health Ctr., 1995—; spkr. in field. Author: (audiotape) Human Sexuality, 1967, 71, 95, (videotape) Art, Symbolism & Mental Health, 1991; contbr. chpts. to books and book revs. and more than 148 papers to profl. jours. Named R.S. McLaughlin Traveling fellow, 1966, Outstanding Young Canadian, 1974, Minister of Health Gold medalist U. Toronto, 1962. Fellow Am. Orthopsychiat. Assn., Am. Psychiat. Assn., Am. Acad. Clinical Sexologists; mem. Am. Acad. Psychiatrists in Alcoholism & Addictions, AMA, Can. Psychiat. Assn., Internat. Soc. for Traumatic Stress Studies, Am. Assn. Sex Educators, Counselors and Therapists. Jewish. Office: VA Med Ctr 1 Freedom Way Augusta GA 30904-6258

SÖLVEBORN, SVEN-ANDERS, orthopaedic surgeon; b. Ystad, Scania, Sweden, May 24, 1950; s. Per-Hilding and Ruth Cecilia (Svensson) S.; children: Caroline, Sophie, Hanna Christine. MD, U. Lund, Sweden, 1979. Specialist in orthopaedic surgery Nat. Swedish Bd. Health and Welfare, 1984, sports medicine cert. advanced level Swedish Soc. Sports Medicine, 1989. Resident in surgery Ystad and Lund (Sweden) U. Hosp., 1979-85; cons. orthopaedic surgery Acad. Hosp., Uppsala, Sweden, 1985-93, Samaritian Hosp., Uppsala, 1993—; pvt. cons. in sports medicine and orthopaedic surgery Sports Trauma Ctr., Uppsala, 1985—. Author: The Book About Stretching, 1982, 17th edit., 1994 (translated 16 langs.); editor Swedish Sports Medicine mag., 1992-93; contbr. articles to profl. jours. Capt. Swedish Army, 1978, 85—. Fellow North West European Chpt. World Sports Medicine Fedn.; mem. Swedish Med. Assn., Swedish Soc. Medicine, European Fedn. of Sports Medicine (sec.), Swedish Soc. Sports Medicine (chmn. ednl. com. 1991-95, pres. 1995—), Swedish Handball Assn. (team physician 1989—, ednl. leader 1989—, diploma 1986), Sports Medicine Assn. Uppsala Region (chmn. 1986—). Home: Snårestad 8:16, S-271 93 Ystad Scania, Sweden Office: Samaritian Hosp, Box 609, S-751 25 Uppsala Upland, Sweden

SOMANI, PETER, human service administrator; b. Chirawah, India, Oct. 31, 1937; came to U.S., naturalized; m. Kamlesh; children: Anita Somani-Richardson, Jyoti, Alok. MD, Vikram U., Ujjain, India, 1960; PhD, Marquette U., Milw., 1965. Demonstrator pharmacology All India Inst. Med. Scis., New Delhi, 1960-62, external examiner PhD program, 1974, 79, 85, 86; instr. dept. pharmacology Marquette U. Sch. Medicine, Milw., 1965-66, asst. prof. dept. pharmacology, 1966-69; assoc. prof. dept. pharmacology Med. Coll. Wis., Milw., 1969-71, assoc. clin. prof. pharmacology, 1971-74; head cardiovasc. pharmacology Abbott Labs., North Chgo., Ill., 1971-72; attending physician Jackson Meml. Hosp., dir. hypertension clinic, 1978-80; attending physician U. Miami Hosps. and Clinics; dir. clin. pharmacology Med. Coll. Ohio, 1980—; dir. of health Ohio Dept. Health, Columbus, 1992—; cons. Geigy Pharms., Arduously, N.Y., 1969-70, Abbott Labs. North Chgo., 1970-71; vis. prof. Med. U. Szeged, Hungary, 1971, Christian Med. Coll., Vellore, India, 1980; Pfizer vis. prof. clin. pharmacology U. Miss. Sch. Medicine, Jackson, 1982; organizer Symposium on Antiarrhythmic Drugs, 1983; UN vis. prof. TOKTEN program Coun. Scientific and Indsl. Rsch., India, 1987; external examiner U. Western Ontario, Can., 1988. Mem. editl. bd. jour. Pharmacology and Exptl. Therapeutics, 1978, Jour. Cardiovasc. Pharmacology, 1979, Internat. Jour. Clin. Pharmacology and Biopharmacy, 1979; spkr. in field; contbr. articles to profl. jours. Office: Ohio Dept Health PO Box 118 246 N High St Columbus OH 43266-0118

SOMERS, ANNE RAMSAY, medical educator; b. Memphis, Sept. 9, 1913; d. Henry Ashton and Amanda Vick (Woolfolk) Ramsey; m. Herman Miles Somers, Aug. 31, 1946; children: Sara Ramsay, Margaret Ramsay. BA, Vassar Coll., 1935; postgrad., U. N.C., 1939-40; DSc (hon.), Med. Coll. Wis., 1975. Ednl. dir. Internat. Ladies Garment Workers Union, 1937-42; labor economist U.S. Dept. Labor, 1943-46; rsch. assoc. Haverford Coll., 1957-63; rsch. assoc. indsl. rels. sect. Princeton U., 1964-84; prof. U. Medicine and Dentistry of N.J.-R. Wood Johnson Med. Sch. (formerly Rutgers Med. Sch.), 1971-84, adj. prof., 1984—; adj. prof. geriat. medicine U. Pa. Sch. Medicine, 1990—; mem. Nat. Bd. Med. Examiners, 1983-86; cons. in health econs., health edn., geriats., gerontology, realted areas. Author: Hospital Regulation: The Dilemma of Public Policy, 1969, Health Care in Transition: Directions for the Future, 1971, (with H.M. Somers) Workmen's Compensation: The Prevention, Rehabilitation and Financing of Occupational Disability, 1954, Medicare and the Hospitals, 1967, Doctors, Patients and Health Insurance, 1961, Health and Health Care: Policies in Perspective, 1977, (with N.L. Spears) The Continuing Care Retirement Community: A Significant Option for Long Care?, 1992; editor: (with D.R. Fabian) The Geriatric Imperative: An Introduction to Gerontology and Clinical Geriatrics, 1981. Mem. bd. visitors. Duke U. Med. Ctr., 1972-77, U. Tex. Health Scis. Ctr., Houston, 1980-86. Recipient Elizur Wright award Am. Risk and Ins. Assn., 1962; named to Health Care Hall of Fame, 1993. Fellow Am. Coll. Hosp. Adminstrs. (hon.), Coll. Physicians Phila. (hon.); mem. Inst. Medicine of NAS, Soc. Tchrs. of Family Medicine (hon.). Home: Pennswood Vlg # G-205 Newtown PA 18940

SOMERS, HERMAN HENDRIK, psychologist, researcher; b. Antwerp, Belgium, Oct. 3, 1921; s. Adolf Theodore Victor Somers and Angela Wivina (Pauwels) S. D in Philosophy and Arts, U. Leuven, Belgium, 1948, D in Applied Psychology, 1961; ThD, U. Gregoriana, Rome, 1956. Researcher, writer Leuven, Belgium. Author: The Problem of Pilate: The Relationship of Church and State, 1954, Mathematical Analysis of Language, 1959, Statistical Analysis of Style, 1966, The Measurement of Psychomotor Speed, 1974, Noise and Environment, 1974, Jesus the Messiah: Was Christianity a Mistake?, 1986, While God Was Sleeping, Man Wrote the Bible: The Bible Seen by a Psychologist, 1990, Secret and Wisdom of the Jesuits: The Epopee of a Militant Order, 1991, An Other Muhammad, 1993, Jehovah's Witnesses: Towards the End of World Chaos?, 1995; contbr. articles to profl. jours., chpts. to books. Home and Office: Tivolistr 31, B-3001 Leuven Belgium

SOMES, GRANT WILLIAM, statistician, biomedical researcher; b. Bloomington, Ind., Jan. 30, 1947; s. William Henry and Margaret Juanita (Sparks) S.; m. Brenda Sue Weddle, Sept. 2, 1967; children: Anthony William, Joshua Michael, Meghan Elizabeth. AB, Ind. U., 1968; PhD, U. Ky., 1975. Asst. prof. dept. community medicine U. Ky., Lexington, 1975-79; assoc. prof., dir. Biostats./Epidemiology Rsch. Lab. East Carolina U., Greenville, N.C., 1979-84; prof., chmn. dept. biostats. & epidemiology U. Tenn., Memphis, 1984—; cons. Community Health Mgmt. Info. System, Memphis, 1992—, Mid-South Found. for Med. Care, Memphis, 1992—. Contbr. 72 articles to profl. jours.; author 70 presented papers/abstracts. Coach Little League baseball, Lexington, 1976-79, Aydon, N.C., 1979-84. Recipient Outstanding Alumni award U. Ky., 1993. Mem. Am. Statis. Assn. (v.p. West Tenn. chpt. 1985-86), Biometric Soc., Sigma Xi, Pi Mu Epsilon.

SOMLO, GEORGE, oncologist; b. Budapest, Hungary, Mar. 31, 1954; came to U.S., 1981; s. Andor and Magdolna (Propper) S.; m. Vicky Vajda, Dec. 27, 1978; children: Esther, David. MD, U. Semmelweis, 1978. Diplomate Am. Bd. Internal Medicine, Am. Bd. Hematology, Am. Bd. Med. Oncology. Staff physician med. Oncology and Therapeutic Rsch. City of Hope Nat. Med. Ctr., Duarte, Calif., 1988—, staff physician Hematology and Bone Marrow Transplantation, 1988—; Reviewer Jour. Cancer, 1994. Fellow Am. Coll. Physicians; mem. Am. Soc. Clin. Oncology, Hematology & Bone Marrow Transplantation. Office: City of Hope Nat Med Ctr 1500 E Duarte Rd Duarte CA 91010

SOMLYO, ANDREW PAUL, physiology, biophysics and cardiology educator; b. Budapest, Hungary; s. Anton and Clara Maria (Kiss) S.; m. Avril V. Russell, May 25, 1961; 1 child, Andrew Paul. BS, U. Ill., 1954, MS, 1956, MD, 1956; MS, Drexel Inst. Tech., Phila., 1963; MA (hon.), U. Pa., Phila., 1981. Asst. physician Columbia-Presbyn. Med. Ctr., N.Y.C., 1960-61; rsch. assoc. Presbyn. Hosp., Phila., 1961-67; asst. prof. pathology U. Pa., Phila., 1964-67, assoc. prof., 1967-71, prof., 1971-88, prof. physiology and pathology, 1973-88, dir. Pa. Muscle Inst., 1973-88; Charles Slaughter prof. molecular physiology-biol. physics U. Va., Charlottesville, 1988—, chmn. dept., 1988—, prof. cardiology, 1988—; cons. NIH; Brit. Heart Found. vis. prof. Hammersmith Hosp., London, Shanghai (China) Med. U.. Author: (with others) Vascular Neuroeffector Systems, 1971, The Handbook of Physiology, Vascular Smooth Muscle, 1981, Microprobe Analysis of Biological Systems, 1981, Recent Advances in Light and Optical Imaging in Biology and Medicine, 1986; editor: Jour. Muscle Research and Cell Motility; contbr. numerous articles to jours. including Biol. Chemistry, Jour. Physiology, Am. Heart Jour., Jour. Pediatrics, Jour. Cell Biology, Cell Calcium, others; mem. editl. bd. Blood Vessels, Am. Jour. Physiology, 1979-83, Magnesium: Experimental and Clinical Rsch., Jour. Structural Biology. Recipient The Louis and Artur Lucian award for rsch. in circulatory diseases, 1995. Mem. AAAS, Soc. Gen. Physiologists, Am. Physiol. Soc. Biophys. Soc., Electron Microscopy Soc., Microbeam Analysis Soc. (Presdl. Sci. award 1996), Am. Soc. for Cell Biology, Hungarian Physiol. Soc. (hon.), Microscopy Soc. Am. (Disting. Scientist award for biol. scis. 1994), Alpha Omega Alpha Med. Soc. (CIBA-GEIGY award for Hypertension Rsch. 1991). Office: U Va Sch Medicine Dept PO Box 10011 449 Jordan Hall Charlottesville VA 22906-0011

SOMMER, ALFRED, medical educator, scientist, ophthalmologist; b. N.Y.C., Oct. 2, 1942; s. Joseph and Natalie Sommer; m. Jill Abramson, Sept. 1, 1963; children: Charles Andrew, Marni Jane. BS summa cum laude, Union Coll., 1963; MD, Harvard U., 1967; MHS in Epidemiology, Johns Hopkins U., 1973. Diplomate Am. Bd. Ophthalmology, Nat. Bd. Med. Examiners. Teaching fellow in medicine Harvard U. Med. Sch., Boston, 1968-69; dir. Nutritional Blindness Prevention Rsch. Program, Bandung, Indonesia, 1976-79; vis. fellow Inst. Ophthalmology U. London, Eng., 1979-80; founding dir., Dana Ctr. for Preventive Ophthalmology Johns Hopkins Med. Insts., Balt., 1980-90; assoc. prof. Johns Hopkins U., Balt., 1981-85, prof. ophthalmology, epidemiology and internat. health, 1985—, dean Johns Hopkins Sch. Hygiene and Pub. Health, 1990—; vis. prof. ophthalmology U.

Padjadjaran, Indonesia, 1976-79; cons., advisor Helen Keller Internat., N.Y.C., 1973—; cons., chmn. com. NIH, Bethesda, Md., 1981—; bd. dirs. Internat. Agy. for the Prevention of Blindness, Geneva, Switzerland, 1978—; cons., com. mem. Nat. Acad. Scis., Washington, 1989; chmn. program adv. group on blindness prevention WHO, Geneva, 1989-90, com. mem., 1978-90, expert com., 1990—; chmn. steering com. Internat. Vitamin A Cons. Group, Washington, 1975—; pres. Internat. Fedn. of Tissue Banks; chmn. sci. adv. bd. Edna McConnell Clark Found.; mem. adv. com. Internat. Coun. Ophthalmology. Author: Epidemiology and Statistics for the Ophthalmologist, 1980, Nutritional Blindness: Xerophthalmia and Keratomalacia, 1982, Vitamin A Deficiency: Health, Survival and Vision, 1995, Detection and Control of Vitamin A Deficiency and Xerophthalmia, 1978, 82, 95; chmn. bd. overseers Am. Jours. Epidemiology and Epidemiologic Revs., 1990—. Charles A. Dana Found. award for Pioneering Achievement in Health, 1988, Disting. Svc. award for Contbn. to Vision Care AOHA, 1988, E.V. McCollum Internat. Lectureship in Nutrition Am. Inst. Nutrition, 1988, Second Ann. Am. Coll. Advancement in Medicine Achievement award in Preventive Medicine, 1990, Disting. Contbn. to World Ophthalmology award Internat. Fedn. Ophthalmol. Socs., 1990, Smadel award Infectious Diseases Soc. Am., 1990, Doyne Meml. award Oxford. Mem. Inst. Medicine of NAS (Food and Nutrition bd.), Am. Acad. Opthalmology (chmn. pub. health com. 1982-88, chmn. Quality of Care/Clin. Guidelines 1986-90, Hon. award 1986), Nat. Soc. to Prevent Blindness (bd. dirs. 1989) Internat. Assn. to Prevent Blindness (bd. dirs. 1978—). Office: Johns Hopkins Sch Hygiene and Pub Health 615 N Wolfe St Rm 1041 Baltimore MD 21205-2103

SOMMER, SANDRA READING, medical educator; b. Davenport, Iowa, Aug. 20, 1947; d. Gerald Wesley and Mary Evelyn (Johnston) R.; m. Steven Arnold Sommer, Aug. 23, 1969; children: Mark, Valerie. BA, Wartburg Coll., 1969; MS, Va. Commonwealth U., 1974, PhD, 1987. Cert. med. technologist; spl. hematology. Staff technologist Finley Hosp./Mercy Med. Ctr., Dubuque, Iowa, 1969-70; bacteriologist Mercy Hosp., Davenport, Iowa, 1970-71; supr. Quad-Cities Pathologists Group, Davenport, 1971-72; instr. Va. Commonwealth U., Richmond, 1974-77, asst. prof., 1977-91, assoc. prof., 1991—; reviewer Nat. Cert. Agy. for Med. Lab Personnel, Washington, 1981-85, Nat. Accrediting Agy. for Clin. Lab. Scis., 1992—. Editorial bd. Clinical Laboratory Science, Washington, 1989—; co-author: (series of 6 monographs) Blood Cell Morphology; contbg. author: NCA Review for the Clinical Lab Scientist, 1985; contbr. articles to profl. jours. Fin. com. St. Luke Evangel. Ch., Richmond, Va., 1985-91, Christian Edn. tchr., 1982—, chair, 1990-93, treas. Sunday Sch., 1984-93; mem. PTA, Binford Middle Sch., Richmond, 1982-95, Richmond Community High Sch. Named to President's Honor Roll, Am. Soc. for Medical Technology, 1979-81. Mem. Am. Soc. Clin. Pathologists (assoc., exam. com., bd. registry 1986-91, com. 1983-85, com. on continuing edn. 1990—, reviewer Laboratory Medicine expert panel), Am. Soc. Clin. Lab. Sci. (region II coun. sec. 1979-81), Va. Soc. Clin. Lab. Sci. (pres. 1979-80), Am. Soc. Microbiology, Phi Kappa Phi, Alpha Chi, Beta Beta Beta. Lutheran. Office: Va Commonwealth U PO Box 980583 Richmond VA 23205-0583

SOMMER, STEVE S., molecular geneticist; m. Janet L. Sobell. BA, U. Pa., 1972; PhD, Rockefeller U., 1978; MD, Cornell U., 1979. Resident Nat. Cancer Inst., Bethesda, Md., 1979-80; med. staff fellow NIH, Bethesda, 1980-85; fellow in clin. genetics Nat. Inst. Child Health, Childrens Hosp. Nat. Med. Ctr., Washington, 1982-84; asst. prof. molecular biology Mayo Clinic/Found., Rochester, Minn., 1985-90; assoc. prof. molecular biology Mayo Clinic/Found., Rochester, 1990-94, prof. molecular biology, 1994—, joint appointment dept. medicine, 1995—. Office: Mayo Clinic/Found 200 First St SW Rochester MN 55905

SOMMERVILLE, KENNETH WILLIAM, neurologist; b. Bklyn., June 3, 1951; s. James Martin Chalmers and Margaret Cecilia (Foreman) S.; m. Karen Lynette Matheson, Oct. 16, 1976; children: Stephen William, Andrew Kenneth, Timothy Edward. Student, Rutgers U., 1969-72; MD, Jefferson Med. Coll., 1976. Diplomate Am. Bd. Neurology. Intern Wilmington (Del.) Med. Ctr., 1977; resident Jefferson Hosp., Phila., 1980; attending neurologist Good Samaritan Hosp., Lebanon, Pa., 1980-91, Lebanon Valley Hosp., 1980-88; cons. neurologist Philhaven Hosp., Mt. Gretna, Pa., 1986-91; pres. Lebanon Neurologic Assocs., 1985—; clin. rsch. physician Marion Merrell Dow Pharmaceuticals, 1991—, asst. project leader for vigabatrin, 1991—; clin. asst. prof. Hershey (Pa.) Med. Ctr., 1980-91; chmn. med. edn. Good Samaritan Hosp., Lebanon, 1987—, chmn. med. ethics, 1984-91. Del. Diocese of Bethlehem Conv., 1983, 84, 85, 86, 87 and 89; founder St. Luke's Ch. Physicians and Dentists, Lebanon, 1989. Mem. AMA, Am. Acad. Neurology, Christian Med. Soc., Am. Epilepsy Soc., Am. Acad. Med. Ethics. Republican. Episcopalian. Home: 317 Mckinley Ave Libertyville IL 60048-2732 Office: Bldg 31-1 2110 E Galbraith Rd Cincinnati OH 45237-1625

SONDAK, VERNON KEITH, surgeon, educator, researcher; b. N.Y.C., June 3, 1957. BA, Boston U., 1980, MD, 1980. Intern UCLA Sch. Med., 1980-82, fellow surg. oncology, 1982-84, resident gen. surgery, 1984-87; asst. prof. surgery U. Mich., Ann Arbor, 1987-93, assoc. prof. surgery, 1993—, also dir. sarcoma program, 1990—; chmn. Melanoma com. Southwest Oncology Group, 1990—; chmn. surgery com. Southwest Oncology Group, 1995—. Recipient Career Devel. award Am. Cancer Soc. 1989-92, R-29 FIRST award NIH 1991—. Fellow Am. Coll. Surgeons; mem. Soc. Surg. Oncology, Am. Soc. Clin. Oncology, Am. Assn. Cancer Rsch., Soc. U. Surgeons.

SONDEL, PAUL MARK, pediatric oncologist, educator; b. Milw., Aug. 14, 1950; s. Robert F. and Audrey J. (Dworkus) S.; m. Sherie Ann Katz, Jan. 1, 1973; children: Jesse Adam, Beth Leah, Elana Rose, Jodi Zipporah. BS with honors, U. Wis., 1971, PhD in Genetics, 1975; MD magna cum laude, Harvard Med. Sch., Boston, 1977. Diplomate Nat. Bd. Med. Examiners, Am. Bd. Pediatrics; lic. physician, Wis. Postdoctoral rsch. fellow Harvard Med. Sch., Boston, 1975-77; intern in pediatrics U. Minn. Hosp., Mpls., 1977-78; resident in pediatris U. Wis. Hosp. and Clinics, Madison, 1978-80; asst. prof. pediatrics, human oncology and genetics U. Wis., Madison, 1980-84, assoc. prof., 1984-86, prof. pediatrics, human oncology and genetics, 1987—, head divsn. pediatric hematology/oncology, program leader, 1990—; sub-fellow pediatric oncology; Midwest Children's Cancer Ctr., Milw., 1980; vis. scientist dept. cell biology Weizmann Inst. Sci., Rehovot, Israel, 1987. Mem. editorial bd. Jour. Immunology, 1985-87, Jour. Nat. Cancer Inst., 1987—, Jour. Biol. Response Modifiers, 1990—, BLOOD, 1992—, Natural Immunity, 1992—; contbr. articles to Jour. Exptl. Medicine, Jour. Immunology, Cellular Immunology, Immunol. Revs., Med. Pediatric Oncology, Wis. State Med. Jour., Jour. Biol. Response Modifiers, Jour. Pediatrics, Jour. Clin. Oncology, Jour. Clin. Investigation, and others. State of Wis. Regents scholar, 1968; J.A. and G.L. Hartford Found. fellow, 1981-84. Mem. Am. Assn. Immunologists, Am. Assn. Clin. Histocompatibility Typing, Am. Fedn. Clin. Rsch., Am. Soc. Pediatric Hematology/Oncology, Am. Assn. Cancer Rsch., Am. Soc. Transplant Physicians, Am. Soc. Clin. Oncology, Am. Acad. Pediatrics, Leukeima Soc. Am. (bd. dirs. Wis. chpt. 1987—), Disting. Physicians Am., Am. Cancer Soc. (sci. adv. com. immunology 1992—), Midwest Soc. Pediatric Rsch., Soc. Biol. Therapy (bd. dirs. 1989—, sci. adv. bd. 1989—), Transplantation Soc., Phi Beta Kappa, others. Home: 1114 Winston Dr Madison WI 53711-3161 Office: U Wis K4/448 Clin Sci Ctr 600 Highland Ave Madison WI 53792-0001

SONDEREGGER, THEO BROWN, psychology educator; b. Birmingham, Ala., May 31, 1925; d. Ernest T. and Vera M. (Sillox) Brown; children: Richard Paul, Diane Carol, Douglas Robert. BS, Fla. State U., 1946; MA in Chemistry, U. Nebr., 1948, MA in Exptl. Psychology, 1960; PhD in Clin. Psychology, U. Nebr., 1965. Lic. psychologist, Calif; clin. lic., cert. Nebr. Asst. prof. U. Nebr. Med. Ctr., Omaha, 1965-71, Nebr. Wesleyan U., Lincoln, 1965-68; asst. prof. U. Nebr., Lincoln, 1968-71, assoc. prof., 1971-76, prof., 1976-94; ret., 1994, prof. emeritus, 1995—; vol. assoc. prof. U. Nebr. Med. Ctr., 1972-77, courtesy prof. med. psychology, 1977-95. Editor: Nebr. Symposium on Motivation, 1974, 84, 91, Problems of Perinatal Drug Dependence: Research and Clinical Implications, 1986, Neurobehavioral Toxicology and Teratology vol. 8, 1988-89, Problems of Perinatal Drug Dependence, 1979, 82, 84, Feminist Therapy Interchange, 1988-89, 91, Perinatal Substance Abuse: Research and Clinical Implications, 1992, Agendas for Aging, 1994—. Mem. grant rev. coms. Nat. Inst. Drug Abuse, 1983-84, 85, 91-94. Tribute to Women award Lincoln YMCA, 1985, named Outstanding Rsch. Scientist Nebr. Chpt. Sigma Xi, 1991, Outstanding Contbn. to Status of Women, N N-L Chancellors Commn. on Status of Women, 1994, Pound Howard Disting. Career Achievement award, 1996. Fellow AAAS, Am. Psychol. Assn., Am. Psychol. Soc.; mem. Midwestern Psychol. Assn., Internat. Soc. Devel. Psychobiology, Internat. Soc. Psychoneuroendocrinolty, Nebr. Psychol. Assn. (pres. 1972), Soc. Neuroscis., Advanced Feminist Therapy Inst., Region V Adv. Coun. on Drugs, Fetal Alcohol Adv. Coun., Phi Beta Kappa (sec. Nebr. chpt. 1974), Sigma Xi (pres. 1986). Club: Altrusa YWCA.

SONE, PHILIP GEARY, health psychologist; b. Detroit, Jan. 16, 1949; s. Geary Masami and Monica Kazuko (Itoi) S. BA in Psychology and Sociology, Bowling Green U., 1971; MA in Clinical Psychology, W. Ga. Coll., 1974; PhD in Psychology, Ariz. State U., 1981; JD, U. Denver. Lic. psychologist. Family psychologist Family Service Ctr., Canton, Ohio, 1974-77; counselor and trainer Ariz. State U., Tempe, 1977-79; health psychologist Mesa Luth. Hosp., 1979-86, Health Psychology & Counseling Assocs., Phoenix and Mesa, 1983—, Rehab. Medicine Assocs., Ariz. Phys. Medicine, Mesa, 1986—; trainer, med. staff, Phoenix Gen. Hosp., 1984; cons., trainer ITT Courier, Inc., Phoenix, 1985, Garrett Pneumatic Industries, Inc., Phoenix, 1985, Coen Engring., Inc., Phoenix, 1985. Mem. Am. Psychol. Assn. (health psychology divsn.), Ariz. Assn. for Health Psychology, Phoenix Group for Study of Chronic Pain. Office: Ariz Phys Medicine & Rehab 445 W 5th Pl # E Mesa AZ 85201-5618

SONEA, SORIN I., microbiologist; b. Cluj, Romania, Mar. 14, 1920; arrived in Can., 1950; m. Rodica Vlad, Feb. 2, 1946; children: Ioana, Peter, Michael, Alexander. M.D., Faculty of Medicine, Bucharest, Romania, 1944; Diploma of Hygiene, Faculty of Medicine, Paris, 1949; Doctorate (honoris causa), U. Que., 1988. Cert. specialist in med. microbiology. Asst. prof. microbiology U. Montreal, Que., Can., 1950-55, assoc. prof., 1955-60, prof., 1960-93, prof. emeritus, 1993—, head dept., 1964-79. Author: Introduction a la Nouvelle Bacteriologie, 1980, A New Bacteriology, 1983, Le strutture biologiche Batteri, 1993 contbr. numerous articles to profl. jours. Recipient award Can. Soc. Microbiologists, Montreal, 1978. Fellow Acad. Sci., Royal Soc. Can., Royal Coll. Physicians and Surgeons of Can. Home: 4282 Badgley St, Montreal, PQ Canada H4P 1N8 Office: Univ Montreal Microbiology Dept, C P 6128, Montreal, PQ Canada

SONENSHEIN, ABRAHAM LINCOLN, microbiology educator; b. Paterson, N.J., Jan. 13, 1944; s. Israel Louis and Celia (Rabinowitz) S.; m. Gail Entner, Jan. 28, 1967; children: Dina Miriam, Adam Israel. AB, Princeton U., 1965; PhD, MIT, 1970. Postdoctoral fellow U. Paris, Orsay, France, 1970-72; asst. prof. Tufts U., Boston, 1972-78, assoc. prof., 1978-82, prof., 1982—. Rsch. grantee NIH, 1972—; fellow Am. Cancer Soc., 1970-72. Mem. AAAS, Am. Soc. for Microbiology, Am. Acad. Microbiology, Fedn. Am. Scientists, Sigma Xi. Office: Tufts U 136 Harrison Ave Boston MA 02111-1800

SONG, JOSEPH, pathologist, educator; b. Pyong Yang, Korea, May 11, 1927; s. Ha Ju and Hwa Soon (Koh) S.; m. Kumsan Ryu, Apr. 12, 1958; children: Patricia, Michael, Jeff. MD, Seoul (Korea) U. Sch. Medicine, 1950; MS in Pathology, U. Tenn., Memphis, 1956; MD, U. Ark. Med. Sch., Little Rock, 1965. Diplomate Am. Bd. Pathology. Pathologist in charge State Cancer Detection Survey, Providence, R.I., 1956-59; assoc. pathologist Providence Lying-In Hosp., 1959-61; assoc. prof. pathology U. Ark. Med. Ctr., Little Rock, 1961-64; dir. lab. Mercy Hosp., Des Moines, Iowa, 1965-92; cancer rschr. Mercy Hosp., Des Moines, 1993-95; clin. prof. pathology Creighton U. Sch. Medicine, Omaha, Nebr., 1968-95; med. dir. Corning Clin. Labs., Des Moines, 1995—; cons. EPA, Washington, 1975-85; pres. med. staff Mercy Hosp., Des Moines, 1981. Author: (books) The Human Uterus, 1964, Pathology of Sickle Cell Anemia, 1971 (award 1975),. Elder Windsor Presbyn. Ch., Des Moines, 1964; com. mem. Aldersgate Meth Ch., Des Moines, 1995. Major Med. Corps, 1950-52, Korea. Recipient Martin Luther King Med. Achievement award, So. Christian Leadership Conf., Statesmanship award Am. Assn. Med. Adminstrs., Las Vegas, Nev., 1987. Fellow Am. Coll. of Physicians, Coll. of Am. Pathologists, Am. Soc. of Clin. Pathology, Am. Assn. for Cancer Rsch. Methodist. Home: 2345 Park Ave Des Moines IA 50321

SONG, MOON KI, biomedical research scientist; b. Taejon, Korea, May 24, 1931; s. Yong Kuk and Kuy Nam (Min) S.; m. Jong Soon Lee, Feb. 26, 1966; children: Julie Mijin, Albert Moonjin. BA, U. Hawaii, 1964, MS, 1966, PhD, 1972. Rsch. asst. U. Hawaii, Honolulu, 1962-65, jr. researcher, 1965-69; asst. rsch. prof. UCLA Sch. Medicine, 1980-87, assoc. rsch. prof., 1987-93, rsch. prof., 1993—; rsch. chemist Dept. Vet. Affairs Med. Ctr., North Hills, Calif., 1974-83; chief rsch. lab. Dept. Vet. Affairs Med. Ctr., Sepulveda, Calif., 1983—; postdoctoral fellow Ind. U., Indpls., 1974; manuscript reviewer 10 sci. jours., 1980—; ad hoc rsch. application reviewer NIH, Dept. Vets. Affairs Rsch. Svcs., Am. Diabetic Assn., USDA Rsch. Svcs., 1980—. Contbr. numerous articles to profl. jours.; patentee in field. Mem. of Two com. Northridge (Calif.) United Meth. Ch., 1988—. Cancer rsch. grantee Ind. U. Cancer Rsch. Inst., 1974; DVA Med. Rsch. Svc. grantee, 1982—. Fellow Am. Coll. Nutrition; mem. Am. Inst. of Nutrition, Am. Soc. Clin. Nutrition, Am. Diabetes Assn. Democrat. Home: 10922 Yolanda Ave Northridge CA 91326-2724 Office: Dept Vets Affairs Wilshire & Sawtelle Blvds Los Angeles CA 90073

SONGSIRIDEJ, VANEE, physician; b. Bangkok, Thailand, Feb. 21, 1949; Came to US 1977; d. Songsakdi and Mayuree (Wasantachat) S. MD, Siriraj Med. Sch Mahidol U., Bangkok, 1974. Residency in internal medicine St. Joseph Hosp. Affil. with Northwestern U., Chgo., Ill., 1977-80; fellow in allergy and clinical immunology U. Wis., Madison, 1980-82; allergist internist Gundersen Clinic, La Crosse, Wis., 1982—, chief sect. allergy, 1994—; med. dir. Stress Reduction and Relaxation Clinic, 1993—; clin. asst. prof. U. Wis., Madison, 1995—. Fellow Am. Coll. Chest Physicians; mem. AMA, ACP, Am. Lung Assn. Wis. (bd. dirs. 1989-94), Am. Coll. Physician Execs., Am. Acad. Allergy and Clin. Immunology, Wis. Med. Soc., Wis. Allergy Soc., La Crosse County Med. Soc. Office: Gundersen Clinic 1836 South Ave La Crosse WI 54601-5429

SÖNKSEN, PETER HENRI, endocrinology and chemical pathology educator; b. Hamburg, Germany, Mar. 29, 1936; arrived in Eng., 1939; s. Hans Alvin and Hazel Rose (Bond) S.; m. Patricia Mary Egan, June 2, 1960 (div. 1976); children: Camilla Jane, Julian Richard; m. Susan Lesley Hills, May 25, 1979. MB, BS, Middlesex Hosp. Med. Sch., London, 1960; MD, U. London, 1967. Levenhulme fellow Middlesex Hosp., London, 1963-64, registrar, 1965-66, rsch. fellow, 1967, sr. registrar, 1969-70; Harkness fellow Harvard U. Med. Sch., Boston, 1967-69; sr. lectr. medicine St. Thomas Hosp. Med. Sch., London, 1971-75, reader medicine, 1975-79; prof. endocrinology United Med. and Dental Sch. Guy's and St. Thomas Hosps., 1979—; dir. diabetes and endocrinology Guy's and St. Thomas Hosp. Trust, 1989—, vice chmn. divsn. of medicine, 1994—; prof. emeritus Cath. Sch. Medicine, Seoul, 1984; med. advisor ICI, Eng., 1988-91, Bayer, Fed. Republic Germany, 1988—, Wyeth, U.K. and U.S., 1989—, Kabi-Pharmacia, 1994—. Author: Diabetes Reference Book, 1985, Diabetes At Your Fingertips, 1991, 95; contbr. articles to med. jours. Fellow Royal Coll. Physicians, Royal Soc. Medicine (coun. 1972-75); mem. Brit. Diabetic Assn. (hon. sec. 1969-72, R.D. Lawrence lectr. 1974, group rsch. grantee 1979), Brit. Med. Assn., European Assn. for Study Diabetes, Internat. Olympic Med. Commn (mem subcommn. on doping). Office: St Thomas Hosp, London SE1 7EH, England

SONNENBLICK, HARVEY IRWIN, psychiatrist; b. NYC., June 3, 1936; s. Paul and Adele (Newman) S.; children: Lissa, Jordan. BA, U. Va., 1958; MD, NYU, 1962. Diplomate Am. Bd. Psychiatry and Neurology. Intern Kings County Hosp., Bklyn., 1962-63, resident, 1963-65; resident, fellow S.I. (N.Y.) Mental Health Soc., 1965-67; staff psychiatrist Soc. for Seamen's Children, S.I., 1978—, Jewish Bd. Family & Children's Svcs., S.I. and Bklyn., 1981—; vis. psychiatrist Sea View Hosp. Rehab. Ctr. and Home, S.I., 1966—. Maj. U.S. Army, 1968-70. Mem. AMA, Am. Psychiat. Assn., Phi Beta Kappa.

SONNINO, ROBERTA ELENA, pediatric surgeon; b. N.Y.C., Aug. 14, 1952; d. Giorgio Guido and Sandra (Oreffice) S. BS, U. Mich., 1973; MD, U. Padova, Verona, Italy, 1979. Diplomate Am. Bd. Surgery. Surg. resident U. Minn., Mpls., 1980-82, Henry Ford Hosp., Detroit, 1982-86; rsch. assoc. Columbus (Ohio) Children's Hosp., 1986-87; fellow pediatric surgery Montreal (Que.) Children's Hosp., 1987-89; asst. prof. pediatric surgery Case Western Res. U., Cleve., 1989-93; assoc. prof. surgery and pediatrics Med. Coll. Va., Richmond, 1993—; attending pediatric surgeon Rainbow Babies and Children's Hosp., Cleve., 1989—; prin. investigator small bowel transplantation Case Western Res. U., Cleve., 1989-93, Med. Coll. Va., 1993—. Contbr. articles to profl. jours. Rsch. grantee Henry Ford Hosp., 1983, Case Western Res. U., 1989-90, 90-91, Med. Coll. Va., 1993-95. Fellow ACS, Am. Acad. Pediatrics (chmn. surg. com. Ohio chpt. 1990); mem. AMA, AAAS, Assn. Acad. Surgery, Acad. Surg. Rsch., Soc. Surgery Alimentary Tract, Am. Pediatric Surgery Assn. Democrat. Jewish. Home: 13300 Hollyhock Pl Richmond VA 23233-7535 Office: Med Coll Va PO Box 980015 Richmond VA 23298

SONTAG, HARVEY, industrial psychologist; b. N.Y.C., Dec. 27, 1943. BA in Sociology, NYU, 1966, MA in Psychology, 1977, PhD in Psychology, 1985. Internal cons. in human resources Merrill Lynch, N.Y.C., 1980-81; human resources cons. Met. Life, N.Y.C., 1982-84, quality cons., 1984-87, sr. market rsch. and planning cons., 1987—. Co-author: The Right Mix--How to Pick Mutual Funds for Your Portfolio, 1993; author: Corporate Perceptions, 1989, Percezioni Aziendali, 1991. Mem. Am. Soc. for Quality Control. Office: Met Life Corp Mktg 31A 1 Madison Ave New York NY 10010-3603

SOOKNE, HERMAN SOLOMON (HANK SOOKNE), retirement center senior executive; b. Far Rockaway, N.Y., June 30, 1932; s. Harry Martin Sookne and Sarah (Kopolov) Sterenstein; m. Joan Gilman, Apr. 12, 1954 (div. Apr. 9, 1971); children: Charles Michael, David Howard, Susan Frances; m. Polly Henry Johnson, Mar. 1972. Student, Georgetown U., 1949-50; BS in Bus. & Econs., NYU, 1953. Pres., owner Gilclan Bldg. Corp., Merrick, N.Y., 1955-68; divsn. mgr. Boise Cascade Bldg. Corp., Freehold, N.J., 1968-70; dir. property mgmt. and engring. Amprop, Inc., Miami, Fla., 1970-73; pres., CEO Bowman Property Investors, Dallas, 1973-79; gen. mgr. Fidinam, Inc., Houston, 1979-82; mktg. cons. Cooper Communities, Inc., Bella Vista, Ark., 1982-88; dir. mktg. and funds devel. Epworth Villa, Oklahoma City, 1988—. Scoutmaster Boy Scouts Am., L.I., N.Y., 1955-60; bd. dirs., pres. Copperchase Condo's Inc., Oklahoma City, 1991-95; trustee United Meth. Ch. of the Servant. With U.S. Army, 1953-55, Korea. Mem. Ark. Bd. Realtors, Nat. Soc. for Fund Raising Execs., Soc. for Advancement of Mgmt., Nat. Assn. Home Builders, Nat. Soc. Heat, Refrigeration & Air Conditioning Engrs; bd. trustees Methodist Ch. Republican. Methodist. Home: #152 11300 N Pennsylvania Ave Oklahoma City OK 73120-7774 Office: 14901 N Pennsylvania Ave Oklahoma City OK 73134-6071

SOONG, H. KAZ, physician, surgeon; b. Tokyo, Oct. 29, 1949; s. Yueh Lun and Hsia Ching (Hung) S.; m. Barbara Nevins, Nov. 26, 1976; children: Michael Robert, Brian William, Andrea May. BSEE, MIT, 1971; MSEE and Neurobiology, Cornell U., 1974; MD, Columbia U., 1978. Intern internal medicine Mary Imogene Bassett Hosp., Cooperstown, N.Y., 1978-79; resident in ophthalmology Wilmer Eye Inst., Johns Hopkins U. Hosp., Balt., 1979-82; fellow cornea and external disease Mass. Eye and Ear Infirmary, Harvard Med. Sch., Boston, 1982-84; asst. prof. ophthalmology U. Mich. Med. Sch., Ann Arbor, 1984-89, assoc. prof. ophthalmology, 1989—; cons. in ophthalmology VA Hosp., Ann Arbor, 1984—; cons. in orphan drugs FDA, Rockville, Md., 1993—; assoc. examiner Am. Bd. Ophthalmology, Bala Cynwyd, Pa.; publ. rev. com. Nat. Soc. to Prevent Blindness, Chgo., 1992—. Editor: Ophthalmology Clinics in North America, 1990; author: Cornea, 1996; guest editor Refractive and Corneal Surgery, 1989; author: (clin. brochure) Focal Points, Am. Acad. Ophthalmology, 1992. Fellow Am. Acad. Ophthalmology; mem. AMA, Am. Radio Relay League. Office: WK Kellogg Eye Ctr Univ Mich 1000 Wall St Ann Arbor MI 48105

SOOTHILL, PETER WILLIAM, fetal medicine educator; b. Droitwich, Worcester, Eng., Oct. 30, 1957; s. John Farrar and Brenda (Thornton) S.; m. Carline Jane Mackenzie, Aug. 4, 1984; children: Emily, Germander, Bryony. BSc, U. London, 1979, PhD, 1987; MB BS, Guys Hosp., London, 1982. Sr. house officer John Radcliffe Hosp., Oxford, Eng., 1987-88; registrar St. Michael's Hosp., Bristol, Eng., 1988-89; lectr. King's Coll. Hosp., London, 1989-92; sr. lectr., cons. Univ. Coll., London, 1992-95; prof. fetal medicine U. Bristol, Eng., 1995—; hon. cons. Univ. Coll. Hosp., London, 1992-95, Gt. Ormond St. Children's Hosp., 1992-95, St. Michael's Hosp., Bristol, 1995—. Contbr. numerous articles to profl. jours. Mem. genetic approach to human health com. Med. Rsch. Coun., London, 1994—. Rsch. grantee various orgns., 1991—. Mem. Royal Coll. Ob-Gyn. (mem. subspecialty com. 1985—). Office: St Michael's Hosp/U Bristol, Southwest St, Bristol England

SOPER, DAVID EDWARD, obstetrician, gynecologist, educator; b. Orlando, Fla., Nov. 16, 1950; s. Leroy Dilmore and Alma Joyce (Gardner) S.; m. Susan Alvina White, Dec. 29, 1971; children: Joshua Edward, Jason Gardner. BA, Fla. State U., 1972; MD, U. Miami, Fla., 1976. Diplomate Nat. Bd. Med. Examiners, Am. Bd. Ob./Gyn. (mem. preliminary examination com. 1988; examiner 1994—); lic. Calif., Va., S.C. Intern Naval Regional Med. Ctr., San Diego, 1976-77, resident, 1977-80; fellow in infectious diseases Naval Hosp., San Diego, 1982-84; commd. lt. USNR, 1976, advanced through grades to commdr., 1984, resigned, 1986; clin. instr. dept. reproductive medicine U. Calif., San Diego, 1983-84; asst. prof. dept. ob./gyn. Eastern Va. Med. Sch., Norfolk, 1985-86; asst. prof. dept. ob./gyn. and internal medicine divsn. infectious diseases Med. Coll. Va. Commonwealth U., Richmond, 1986-91; assoc. prof. Med. Coll. Va. Commonwealth U., Richmond, 1991-94, prof., 1994-95; prof. depts. ob. and gyn. and internal medicine, divsn. infectious diseases Med. U. S.C., Charleston, 1995—; mem. numerous coms. Med. Coll. Va. Hosps., mem. hosp. infection com., 1987—, chmn. 1991-95; dir. Colposcopy Clinic 1989-95; numerous coms. Med. Coll. Va. Ob/Gyn. Dept. including exec. com. 1992-95, chmn. resident recruitment com. 1992-93, resident edn. com. 1989-90, 93—; residency program dir., 1993-95; reviewer March of Dimes Birth Defects Found; dir. divsn. of begign gynecology, 1995—. Contbr. over 33 articles to profl. jours., chpts. to 14 med. books; reviewer for Obstetrics and Gynecology, Am. Jour. Ob. and Gyn., Jour. Reproduction and Fertility, Archives of Internal Medicine 1988, Am. Jour. Gynecologic Health 1990, Jour. AMA, Jour. Women's Health, Clin. Infectious Diseases; assoc. editor Infectious Diseases in Obstetrics and Gynecology. Recipient CREOG Nat. Faculty award, 1994. Fellow Am. Coll. Obstetricians and Gynecologists, Infectious Disease Soc. Am.; mem. Am. Soc. for Microbiology, Richmond Acad. Medicine, Richmond Ob. and Gyn. Soc. (pres. 1993), Va. Ob. and Gyn. Soc., Infectious Disease Soc. for Obstetrics and Gynecology, S. Atlantic Assn. of Obstetricians and Gynecologists, Assn. Reproductive Health Profls., N. Am. Soc. for Colposcopy and Cervical Pathology, H. Hudnall Ware Jr. Soc. (hon. mem.), Alpha Omega Alpha. Office: Med U SC 171 Ashley St Charleston SC 29425

SORARUF, LOUIS PETER, IV, physician; b. Allentown, Pa., Mar. 2, 1948; s. Louis Peter III and Alma Caroline (Fredericks) S.; m. Susan Louise Bishop, June 13, 1970; children: Rachel Eleanor, Louis Peter V. AB, Lafayette U., 1970; MD, Jefferson Med. Coll., 1974. Diplomate Am. Bd. Family Practice. Resident Wilmington (Del.) Med. Ctr., 1974-77; pvt. practice. Coach little league, Kennett Square, 1991; coach mid. sch. basketball, Kenwett Square, 1992. Fellow Am. Acad. Family Practice, Phila. Coll. Physicians; mem. Rotary (v.p. 1991—). Episcopalian. Office: 687 Unionville Rd Kennett Square PA 19348

SORDAHL, LOUIS A., medical scientist, educator; b. Chgo., Aug. 24, 1936; s. Louis O. and Margaret G. (Froiland) S.; m. Barbara Moore, June 9, 1961 (div. 1970); children: Nancy Lynn, Michael Louis; m. Stephanie H. Fantle, Oct. 8, 1971. AB, Rutgers U., 1958, MS, 1961, PhD, 1964. Rsch. asst. Rutgers U., Newark, 1958-62, instr. biology and physiology, 1962-64; staff fellow enzymology NIH, Bethesda, Md., 1964-66; instr. pharmacology Coll. Medicine, Baylor U., Houston, 1966-68, asst. prof., 1968-72; assoc. prof. biochemistry and pharmacology Med. Br., U. Tex., Galveston, 1972-77, prof., 1977—, dir., 1988—; cons. cardiovasc. diseases NIH, 1974—; vis. prof. myocardial biochemistry Mayo Med. Sch., Rochester, Minn., 1976—; adj. prof. cardiovasc. rsch. Coll. Medicine, Baylor U., 1978—; chmn. cardiovasc. rsch. merit rev. bd. Dept. Vets. Affairs, Washington, 1988-91, mem. career devel. bd., 1992-96. Co-editor: Texas Reports, 1979; contbr. numerous articles to sci. publs., 1960—. Mem. Galveston div. Am. Heart Assn., bd.

dirs., 1974-76, pres., 1991-92. Recipient Hektoen Gold medal AMA, Chgo., 1970, Cert. of Honor, Tex. Med. Assn., 1971, Disting. Achievement award Tex. affiliate Am. Heart Assn., 1975, 76. Fellow Am. Coll. Cardiology; mem. Internat. Soc. Heart Rsch., Am. Physiol. Soc., Am. Soc. Biochemistry and Molecular Biology. Lutheran. Office: Univ Tex Med Br Dept Human Biol Chemistry And Gen Galveston TX 77555

SOREFAN, MOHAMED MOUSTOUFA, cardiologist; b. Phoenix, Mauritius, Feb. 13, 1951; s. Ahmud and Bibi Aissa (Subratty) S.; m. Bibi Shehnaz Beedassy, Aug. 2, 1982; children: Bibi Ayesha, Sanaa, Ismaël Ahmed. M.B.B.S., Guy's Hosp., London, 1975. Intern in gen. surgery Bouingbroke Hosp., London, 1975; intern in gen. medicine Whipps Cross Hosp., London, 1976; sr. house physician Basildon hosp., Essex, Eng., 1977; registrar internal medicine Basildon Hosp., Essex, 1978; specialist Sir Seewoosagur Ramgoolam Hosp., Mauritus, 1978-84; specialist physician/cardiologist Sir Seewoosagur Ramgoolam Hosp., 1991—; cons. cardiologist King Fahad Hosp., Jeddah, Saudi Arabia, 1984-91; specialist physician/cardiologist Seewoosagur Ramgoolan Hosp., 1991—. Contbr. articles to profl. jours. Saudi Heart Centre fellow, 1991. Fellow Royal Coll. Physicians Edinburgh, Royal Coll. Physicians and Surgeons of Glasgow; mem. Royal Coll. Physicians U.K. Muslim. Home: Highlands Branch Rd, Phoenix Mauritius Office: Sir Seewoosagur Ramgoolam, National Hospital, Pamplemousses Mauritius

SOREMARK, RUNE, dentistry educator; b. Goteborg, Sweden, Mar. 14, 1926; s. Arnold and Ester (Magnusson) S.; m. Ulla Lofberg, Feb. 6, 1954; children: Helene, Josefine, Patrik. DDS, Karolinska Inst., Stockholm, 1953; DMD, Harvard U., 1967; PhD, Karolinska Inst., 1960. Asst. prof. Karolinska Inst., Stockholm, 1955-61, assoc. prof., 1961-63; prof. Harvard U., Boston, 1964-67, Umea (Sweden) U., 1968-71, Karolinska Inst., Stockholm, 1971-92; chief exec. officer Ctr. for Dental Tech. and Biomaterials, Karolinska Inst., Stockholm, 1985-92; ret., 1992; cons. Internat. Atomic Energy Agy., Vienna, Austria, 1962-63. Contbr. numerous sci. articles to profl. jours. Chmn. Scandinavian Dental Rsch. Assn., Stockholm, 1976-79, European Assn. for Dental Edn., London, 1982-84, Swedish Dental Soc., Stockholm, 1974-76. Recipient Rsch. award Swedish Dental Soc., 1961, The Miller award, 1974; named Knight of North Star, His Majesty the King of Sweden, 1967. Home: Gravlingsv 26, S 16156 Bromma Sweden

SOREN, STANLEY, orthopaedic surgeon; b. N.Y.C., Dec. 16, 1935; s. Albert David and Rose S.; m. Ruth, Jan. 29, 1961; 1 child, Steven. BA, Columbia Coll., 1956; MD, Chgo. Med. Sch., 1961. Diplomate Am. Bd. Orthopaedic Surgery. Intern King's County Hosp., 1961-62; resident in orthop. surgery VA Hosp. and King's County Hosp., 1962-66; pvt. practice pediat. orthop. surgery St. Charles Hosp., S.I., N.Y., 1966—. Sr. surgeon USPHS, N.Y., 1966-68. Office: 2371 Victory Blvd Staten Island NY 10314

SORENSEN, JERRY, pharmacist; b. Mt. Pleasant, Utah, Mar. 27, 1949; s. Gorden and Ethel Sorensen; m. Suzette C. Sorensen, Sept. 2, 1972; children: Thomas, Rachel, Becky, Debbie. AS, Snow Coll., Ephraim, Utah, 1971; BS cum laude, U. Utah, 1974. Registered pharmacist. Mng. pharmacist Hillyard's Pharmacy, Fallon, Nev., 1974-75, Williams Pharmacy, Provo, Utah, 1975-76; staff pharmacist St. Benedicts Hosp., Ogden, Utah, 1976-78, Utah Valley Regional Med. Ctr., Provo, 1978—. Bd. dirs. Churchill County Sr. Citizens, Fallon, 1974-75; vol. Provo City Libr., 1985-87, 95—. Recipient Outstanding Libr. Vol. award, 1986. Mem. Am. Soc. Hosp. Pharmacists, Utah Soc. Hosp. Pharmacists, Rho Chi. Office: Utah Valley Regional MC 1034 N 500 W Provo UT 84604

SORENSON, JOANNE CAROLE, social worker, psychotherapist; b. Harlan, Iowa, Feb. 23, 1950; d. Russell Howard and Helen Shirley (Tippett) S. BA, Doane Coll., 1972; MSW, U. Iowa, 1977. Sch. social worker Miss. Bend Area Edn. Agy., Davenport, Iowa, 1977-78, Adams County 5 Star Sch. Dist., Northglen, Colo., 1978-91; pvt. practice psychotherapist Denver, 1991—; workshop facilitator Wild Women Weekends, Denver, 1993—. Author: 92 Romantic Things To Do in Denver, 1992. Mem. NASW, People Making of Colo. Office: 1777 S Bellaire St Ste 415 Denver CO 80222-4322

SORKIN, MARC JOEL, dermatologist; b. Omaha, Nov. 23, 1949; s. Albert and Shirley Frances (Belzer) S.;m. Laurie Annette Bragg, June 29, 1980; children: Adam Michael, Alison Claire, Jonathan Andrew. BS, U. Nebr., 1972, MD, 1974. Instr. medicine Creighton U. Sch. Medicine, Omaha, 1976-77; dermatologist pvt. practice, Denver, 1980—. Author: (textbook) Medical Problems in PRegnancy, 1983. Fellow Am. Acad. Dermatology. Office: 2005 Franklin St #690 Denver CO 80205

SORKNESS, RONALD, physiologist, pharmacist; b. Milw., Sept. 16, 1949; s. Delno and Irene (Blanchard) S.; m. Christine A. Sczupak, Jan. 5, 1980. BS, U. Wis., 1972, MS in Hosp. Pharmacy, 1974, PhD in Physiology, 1986. Registered pharmacist, Wis. Asst. prof. pharmacy SUNY, Buffalo, 1974-77; clin. asst. prof. pharmacy U. Wis., Madison, 1977-81, clin. assoc. prof., 1981-94, assoc. scientist in medicine, 1989-94, assoc. prof. pharmacy and medicine, 1994—. Contbr. articles to profl. jours. Mem. Am. Physiol. Soc., Am. Thoracic Soc., Am. Soc. Health Sys. Pharmacists, Soc. Critical Care Medicine. Office: U Wis 425 N Charter St Madison WI 53706

SORKOW, ELI, family practice physician; b. Bklyn., Jan. 10, 1923; s. Jack and Kate Sorkowitz; m. Claire Fannie Kushner, Mar. 5, 1945; children: Louis Charles, William Edward. BS, McNeese State U., Lake Charles, La., 1974; MD, La. State U., New Orleans, 1952. Diplomate Am. Bd. Family Practice. Intern Robert B. Green Hosp., San Antonio, 1952-53; resident Lafayette (La.) Gen. Hosp., 1953-54; pvt. practice, Lake Charles, 1954-83; program dir. Family Practice Residency, Lake Charles, 1972-89; med. dir. W.O. Moss Regional Hosp., Lake Charles, 1976-89; acting chmn. dept. family medicine La. State U. Sch. Medicine, New Orleans, 1986-88; med. dir. S.W. La. Home Health Agy., Lake Charles, 1996-90; cons. Family Medicine Residency Assistance Program, Kansas City, Mo., 1982-89; mem. editl. adv. bd. Postgrad. Medicine, Mpls., 1989-95. Chmn. Lake Charles Dem. Exec. Com., 1960-76; pres. Temple Sinai, Lake Charles, 1968. Sgt. U.S. Army, 1942-46. Fellow Am. Acad. Family Physicians (Presdl. award 1980). Home and Office: 3900 Buccaneer Ln Lake Charles LA 70605-3316

SOROM, TERRY ALLEN, ophthalmic surgeon; b. Lanesboro, Minn., Jan. 9, 1940; s. Martin John and Elvira (Lodahl) S.; m. Suzanne A. Johnson, children: Martin, Jeb, Abraham, Theodore. BS, Luther Coll., 1962; MD, U. Minn.-Mpls., 1966. Diplomate Am. Bd. Ophthalmology. Intern. U. Oreg., Portland, 1967, resident in ophthalmology, 1969-73; ophthalmic surgeon Eye and Ear Clinic, Inc., Wenatchee, Wash., 1973—. Charter trustee Wenatchee Visitor and Conv. Bur., 1980; bd. dirs. Blue Cross Wash., and Alaska, Ctrl. Wash. Health Plan; pres. Wenatchee Valley Coll. Found., 1986-88. Capt. M.C., USAF, 1967-69. Mem. AMA, Am. Acad. Ophthalmology, Contact Lens Assn. Ophthalmology, Am. Intraocular Implant Soc., Wash. State Acad. Ophthalmology (trustee 1978-80), Oregon Ophthalmologic Alumni Assn. (pres. 1988—), Greater Wenatchee Found. (bd. dirs.), Chelan-Douglas County Med. Assn., Wash. State Acad. Eye Physicians and Surgeons (pres. 1996—), Rotary (pres. 1993-94). Republican. Lutheran. Office: Eye & Ear Clinic Wenatchee Inc PS 600 Orondo Ave PO Box 3027 Wenatchee WA 98801

SOROSKY, JOEL I., physician; b. Chgo., Feb. 10, 1952; s. Saul and Nettie 9Gordon) S.; m. Debra R. Sorosky, Oct. 12, 1985; children: Michael, Steven. BS cum laude, Tulane U., 1973; MD, U. Health Scis./Chgo. Med., Sch., 1976. Diplomate Am. Bd. Ob-Gyn., Am. Bd. Gynecol. Oncology. Resident Ob-Gyn Hartford (Conn.) Hosp., 1976-80; clin. instr. U. Conn. Sch. of Medicine, Farmington, 1980-83, clin. asst. prof., 1983-86; asst. prof. Pa. State U. Hosp., Hershey, 1986-88, fellow in gynecol. oncology, 1988-91, asst. prof., 1991-93; assoc. prof. U. Iowa Hosp., Iowa City, 1993—. Lt. col. USAR, 1980-91. Fellow Am. Coll. Ob-Gyn, Am. Coll. Surgeons; mem. Soc. Gynecol. Oncologists, Am. Soc. Clin. Oncology. Office: Univ Iowa Hosps 200 Hawkins Dr Iowa City IA 52242

SOROURI, PARVIZ, gastroenterologist; b. Tehran, Iran, Feb. 14, 1929; s. Mohammad and Malekeh (Edalat) S.; m. Sally Elaine Simounet, June 22, 1957; children: Bijan, Kayvan, Andria. AB, Temple U., 1951; MS, U. Pa., 1953; MD, George Washington U., 1957. Intern Charity Hosp., New Orleans, 1958; resident in internal medicine Henry Ford Hosp., Detroit, 1961; resident in gastroenterology U. Pa. Grad. Hosp., Phila., 1962; prof. medicine Nat. U., Tehran, Iran, 1962-79, chmn. dept. medicine, 1970-79, chief div. gastroenterology, 1972-79, vice chancellor, 1977-79, dean sch. medicine, 1978-79; practice medicine specializing in gastroenterology Newark, Del., 1979—; chmn. research com. Med. Ctr. of Del., Wilmington, 1982-86; chmn. program and library com. St. Francis Hosp., Wilmington, 1987—; adv. to Minister of Health, Tehran, 1970-78, to Prime Minister, 1970-78. Author: (book) Gastrointestinal Cancer, 1983. Felsen fellow, U. Pa., 1952. Fellow Backus Internat. Soc. Gastroenterology; mem. AMA, Hercules Country Club, Wilminton Country, Lions, Rotary. Republican. Moslem. Home: 900 Hillside Rd Wilmington DE 19807-2212 Office: Darwin Profl Ctr 10 Darwin Dr Newark DE 19711-6658

SORREL, WILLIAM EDWIN, psychiatrist, educator, psychoanalyst; b. N.Y.C., May 27, 1913; s. Simon and Lee (Lesenger) S.; m. Rita Marcus, July 1, 1950; children: Ellyn Gail, Joy Shelley, Beth Mara. BS, NYU, 1932; MA, Columbia U., 1934, MD, 1939; PhD, NYU, 1963. Diplomate Am. Bd. Med. Psychotherapists (profl. adv. coun. 1992—); qualified psychiatrist, also cert.examiner N.Y. State Dept. Mental Hygiene. Intern Madison (Tenn.) Sanitarium and Hosp., 1939; resident physician Alexian Bros. Hosp., St. Louis, 1940; officer instrn. St. Louis U. Sch. Medicine, 1940-41; asst. psychiatrist Central State Hosp., Nashville, 1941; assoc. psychiatrist Eastern State Hosp., Knoxville, 1942-44; assoc. attending neuropsychiatrist, chief clin. psychiatry Jewish Meml. Hosp., N.Y.C., 1946-59; assoc. attending neuropsychiatrist, chief clin. child psychiatry Lebanon Hosp., Bronx, N.Y., 1947-65; psychiatrist-in-chief Psychiatry Clinic, Yeshiva U., 1950-66, asst. prof. psychiatry, 1952-54, assoc. prof., 1954-58, prof., 1959-62, psychiatrist-in-chief, assoc. dir. Psychol. Center,, 1957-67; prof. human behavior Touro Coll., 1974—; attending psychiatrist St. Clare's Hosp., N.Y.C., 1983—; asst. prof. clin. psychiatry Albert Einstein Coll. Medicine, 1986—; psychiat. cons. SSS, 1951, N.Y. State Workmens Compensation Bd., 1951—, Bronx-Lebanon Med. Ctr., 1985—; vis. psychiatrist Fordham Hosp., N.Y.C., 1951; attending neuropsychiatrist, chief mental hygiene svc. Beth-David Hosp., 1950-60; attending neuropsychiatrist Grand Central Hosp., 1958-66, Morrisania Hosp., 1959-72; psychiatrist-in-chief Beth Abraham Hosp., 1954-60; psychiat. cons. L.I. U. Guidance Ctr., 1955-60, Daytop Village, 1970-71; assoc. psychiatrist Seton City Hosp., 1955; guest lectr. U. London, 1947; vis. prof. Jerusalem, Israel Acad. Med., 1960, Hebrew U., 1960; mem. psychiat. staff Gracie Sq. Hosp., 1960—; chief psychiatry Trafalgar Hosp., 1962-72; vis. prof. psychiatry Tokyo U. Sch. Medicine, 1964; adj. prof. N.Y. Inst. Tech., 1968; vis. lectr. in psychiatry N.Y. U., 1971-73; Am. del. Internat. Conf. Mental Health, London, 1948; mem. Am. Psychiat. Commn. to USSR, Poland and Finland, 1963, Empire State Med., Sci. and Ednl. Found. Author: (booklets) Neurosis in a Child, 1949, A Psychiatric Viewpoint on Child Adoption, 1954, Shock Therapy in Psychiatric Practice, 1957, The Genesis of Neurosis, 1958, The Prejudiced Personality, 1962, The Schizophrenic Process, 1962, The Prognosis of Electroshock Therapy Success, 1963, Psychodynamic Effects of Abortion, 1967, Violence Towards Self, 1971, Basic Concepts of Transference in Psychoanalysis, 1973, A Study in Suicide, 1972, Masochism, 1973, Emotional Factors Involved in Skeletal Deformities, 1977, Cults & Cult Suicide, 1979, Further Viewpoints on the Genesis of Neurosis, 1996; assoc. editor: Jour. Pan Am. Med. Assn., 1992—; contbr. articles on the psychoses. Vice pres. Golden Years Found.; N.Y.C. chmn. Com. Med. Standards in Psychiatry, 1952-54. Recipient Sir William Osler Internat. Honor Med. Soc. Gold Key; 3d prize oil paintings N.Y. State Med. Art Exhibit, 1954; NYU Founders Day award, 1963; Presdl. Achievement award, 1984; others. Fellow Am. Psychiat. Assn. (life, pres. Bronx dist. 1960-61, other offices, Gold medal 1974, 94), Am. Assn. Psychoanalytic Physicians (pres. 1971-72, bd. govs. 1972—); mem. AMA, Ea. Psychiat. Assn., N.Y. State Soc. Med. Rsch., Am. Med. Writers Assn., N.Y. Med. Soc., N.Y. County Med. Soc., N.Y. Soc. for Clin. Psychiatry, Pan Am. Med. Assn. (various offices including pres. 1989—, assoc. editor jour. 1992—), Assn. for Advancement Psychotherapy, Bronx Soc. Neurology and Psychotherapy (pres. 1960-61, Silver medal 1970), Mensa. Home: 23 Meadow Rd Scarsdale NY 10583-7642 Office: 263 W End Ave New York NY 10023-2612

SORRELLS, JOHN ENNIS, JR., ophthalmologist; b. Lake Charles, La., Sept. 26, 1937; s. John Ennis and Bertha Gwin (Knox) S.; m. Marlene Dorthen Stitzlein, June 17, 1961; children: Cynthia, John III, Teddy Paul. BS, La. Coll., 1959; MD, La. State U., 1965. Intern Ark. Bapt. Hosp., Little Rock, 1966-68; resident Confederate Meml. Hosp., Shreveport, La., 1968-71; pvt. practice Lake Charles, La., 1971—; pres. staff St. Patrick Hosp. Dist. chmn. Boy Scouts Am., Lake Charles. Capt. U.S. Army, 1966-68. Mem. Parish Med. Soc. (pres.), Lake Charles Kiwanis (bd. dirs., exec. officer). Lutheran. Office: Eye Clinic 1717 Oak Park Blvd Lake Charles LA 70601

SORRELLS, LINDA SULLIVAN, nursing administrator; b. Batesville, Miss., May 10, 1949; d. James Watson Sullivan and Geneva Grace (Duvall) Appleton; m. James Robert Sorrells, June 9, 1967; children: Stacy Lynn, Jason Rodric, Robert Andrew. RN, Northwest C.C., Senatobia, Miss., 1984; postgrad., Regeant's Coll. Staff nurse Sardis (Miss.) Cmty. Hosp., 1984-86, Oxford (Miss.) Layfayette Hosp., 1986-87; home health vis. nurse, high risk mothers, neonate support Miss. State Dept. Health, Batesville, Hernando, 1987-89; instr. LPN Northwest C.C., Senatobia, Miss., 1989-91; dir. home health Northwest Miss. Regional Med. Ctr., Clarksdale, 1991—. Bd. dirs. Miss. Hosp. Assn. for Home Care, Jackson, 1992-93. Baptist. Home: RR 3 Box 395 Batesville MS 38606

SORRELLS, VALERIE L., medical and surgical and staff nurse; b. Gary, Ind., May 27, 1961; d. Courtney B. and Loretta M. (Kostka) S. ADN, Ind. State U., Terre Haute, 1981, BSN cum laude, 1983; MS, Ball State U., Muncie, Ind., 1988. Cert. healing touch practitioner. Clin. nurse Whiteriver Indian Hosp., Ariz., 1996—. Mem. Am. Holistic Nurses Assn., Native ANA (assoc.), Sigma Theta Tau. Home: PO Box 297 Whiteriver AZ 85941

SORRELS, JOHN PAUL, psychology educator; b. Dallas, Nov. 11, 1950; s. Thomas T. and Laverna L. (Elam) S.; m. Cherry Marie Reever, Dec. 16, 1972; children: Michele, Julie. BA, Howard Payne U., 1972; MA, Tex. Woman's U., 1975, PhD, 1978. Lic. psychologist, Tex. Grad. teaching asst. Tex. Woman's U., Denton, 1975-77; staff therapist, instr. psychology Dallas Bapt. Coll., 1977-78; asst. prof. psychology Wayland Bapt. U., Plainveiw, Tex., 1979-83; prof. psychology Hardin-Simmons U., Abilene, Tex., 1983—, dir. grad. program in family psychology, 1984-94, dean grad. studies, 1993—; pres. dir. C.H. Love & Co., Abilene, 1985-91. Contbr. articles to profl. jours. Bd. dirs. Mend-A-Child, Abilene; community advisor Jr. League, Abilene. Abilene Community Found. grantee, 1987. Mem. APA, Am. Assn. Marriage and Family Therapy, Nat. Coun. Family Rels., Tex. Assn. Marriage and Family Therapy, So. Bapt. Assn. of Counseling and Family Ministry, Tex. Bapt. Assn. Family Ministry (pres. 1986-88, Presdl. award 1990), Mental Health Assn. (bd. dirs. 1990-91). Office: Hardin-Simmons Univ Box 984 Box 16210 Abilene TX 79698

SORRENTINO, DARIO ROSARIO, medical educator; b. Alghero, Sassari, Italy, July 25, 1957; came to U.S., 1983; s. Antonio and Rosa (Messina) S. BS, Liceo Sci., Alghero, 1976; MD magna cum laude, U. Sassari, 1982. Cert. ECFMG. Vis. scientist King's Coll. Hosp., London, 1978, Royal Free Hosp., London, 1979-80; rsch. fellow U. Calif., San Francisco, 1983-86; asst. prof. medicine Mt. Sinai Sch. Medicine, N.Y.C., 1986-92, clin. fellow medicine, 1992; asst. prof. medicine U. Udine, Italy, 1993—; vis. prof. Cath. U., Louvain, Belgium, 1988, U. Queensland, Brisbane, Australia, 1990-91, McGill U., Montreal, 1992, Universite de Rennes, France, 1993; reviewer Jour. Clin. Investigation, Hepatology, Am. Jour. Physiology, Jour. Hepatology, Gastroenterology, 1988—; cons. NIH, 1993. Mem. editorial bd. Hepatology, 1991—; contbr. articles to Biochem. Biophysics Rsch. Comms., Procs. NAS, Jour. Clin. Investigation, Baillere Clin. Gastroenterology, Am. Jour. Physiology, Progress in Liver Diseases, Jour. of Hepatology, Hepatology, Gut, Gastroenterology, Jour. Biol. Chemistry. Grantee U. Calif. Acad. Senate, 1985, Italian Ministry Edn., 1987-90, Mt. Sinai Sch. Medicine, 1990-91, European Soc. Clin. Investigation/Bayer, 1991-93. Mem. Internat. Assn. Study Liver, Am. Assn. Study Liver Disease, European Assn. Study Liver, N.Y. Acad. Scis., New Italian Endoscopic Club, European Study Group of Hepatobiliary Transport, Societa Italiana Gastroenterologia (mem. foreign commn.). Office: Medicina Interna Policlinico Univ, Pza Santa Maria Misericordia # 1, 33100 Udine Italy

SORRENTINO, MATTHEW JOSEPH, internist, educator; b. Chgo., June 22, 1958; s. Frank and Jeanne (Powers) S.; m. Jeannette B. Martens, June 16, 1984; children: Katrina, Alyssa, Georgina. BS, De Paul U., 1980; MD, U. Chgo., 1984. Intern in internal medicine U. Chgo., 1984-85, resident in internal medicine, 1985-87, fellow in cardiology, 1987-91, chief resident in internal medicine, 1988, asst. prof. medicine, 1991—, dir. clin. programs, 1994—; attending physician in echocardiography U. Chgo. Hosp., 1992—. Fellow Am. Coll. Cardiology; mem. Am. Heart Assn., Am. Soc. Echocardiography, Alpha Omega Alpha. Office: U Chgo 5841 S Maryland Ave Chicago IL 60637

SORRILL, MARCIA ANN, medical services manager; b. Springfield, Ill., Dec. 14, 1957; d. Alvin L. and Margie (Doellman) Deters; m. Jeffrey S. Sorrill, Oct. 4, 1980; children: Melissa, Michelle. Nurse, Blessing Hosp. Sch. Nursing, 1980; BSN, Quincy Coll., 1991; MBA, Quincy U., 1996. Cert. ACLS instr., nephrology nurse. Nurse dialysis, cons., supr. Blessing Hosp., Quincy, Ill., 1980-94; dir. renal dialysis svcs. Blessing Hosp., Quincy, 1994—; loan officer United Way Adams County, Quincy, 1995. Author: (pamphlet) For Patients Only, 1993. Mem. Am. Nephrology Nurses Assn. (cert.), Nat. Kidney Found., Nat. Renal Adminstr. Assn., Renal Network Ill., Ill. Orgn. Nursing Leaders (Kathryn E. Williams Meml. scholarship 1995). Office: Blessing Hosp Broadway at 11th St Quincy IL 62305-7005

SORVINO, ALPHONSE RONALD, psychiatrist; b. Bklyn., June 4, 1933; s. Ford and Marietta (Renzi) S.; m. Barbara Anne Sonowski, June 12, 1958; children: Noel, Ronald, Heidi, Damian, Kerry, Krista. BS in Chemistry magna cum laude, St. John's U., 1954; MD, SUNY, Bklyn., 1958. Lic. psychiatrist, N.J.; diplomate Am. Bd. Psychiatry and Neurology. Resident then intern King County Hosp., Bklyn., 1958-62; cons. DVR Family Svc., Newport, R.I., 1963-64; pvt. practice New Providence, N.J., 1965—; co-founder Odyssey House, N.Y.C., 1966; instr. psychiatry N.Y. Med. Coll., 1964-66; med. staff dept. psychiatry Overlook Hosp., Summit, N.J., 1965—; mem. bioethcis com., 1984—. Lt. comdr. USNR, 1962-64. Mem. AMA, AAAS, Internat. Psychiatric Assn. for Advancement Electrotherapy, Am. Psychiatric Assn., Am. Acad. Psychiatry and Law, Med. Soc. N.J., N.J. Psychiatric Assn., Tri-County Psychiatric Assn., Union County Med. Soc. Roman Catholic. Office: 29 South St New Providence NJ 07974-1996

SORWEIDE, DERRICK JOHN, osteopath; b. Seattle, Jan. 19, 1967; s. Dennis Frank and Billie Jean (Dale) S.; m. Kimberly Ann Woodruff, Jan. 1, 1996. BA, No. Ariz. U., 1990; DO, Kirksville Coll., 1996. Intern in family medicine Columbia Med. Ctr. Dallas S.W.; physical therapy technician Desert Inn Physical Therapy, Las Vegas, 1990-92; occupl. med. instr. Cmty. Rehab. Svcs., Las Vegas, 1992. Mem. Am. Coll. Osteo. Emergency Medicine, Am. Coll. Osteo. Family Practitioners, Am. Osteo. Acad. of Sports Medicine (past pres.), Am. Acad. Family Practitioners, Am. Med. Student Assn. Republican.

SOSNOW, PETER LEWIS, emergency medicine educator; b. N.Y.C., Oct. 15, 1951; m. Jeanne Munson, Apr. 21, 1985; children: Sara, Emily, Molly. BA, Amherst Coll., 1973; MD, Tulane U., 1977. Diplomate Am. Bd. Emergency Medicine, Am. Bd. Internal Medicine. Dir. emergency svcs. Wing Meml Hosp., Palmer, Mass., 1982-90; asst. prof. Medicine U. Mass. Med. Sch., Worcester, 1982—; dir. emergency & outpatient svcs. Albany (N.Y.) Meml. Hosp., 1990—; adj. asst. prof. emergency medicine Albany Med. Coll., Albany, 1990—; pres. Capital Region Emergency Medicine, Albany, 1991—. Author (book chpts.) Electrical Injuries in the Clinical Practice of Emergency Medicine, 1995, The Hypochondriacal Patient, 1992. Fellow Am. Coll. Emergency Physicians (bd. dirs. 1986-90, 91-96). Office: Albany Meml Hosp 600 Northern Blvd Albany NY 12204-1083

SOSS, DANIEL LEE, social work educator; b. Spokane, Wash., May 30, 1931; s. Walter Lee and Ethelyn F. (Daniel) S.; m. Dorine C., June 17, 1955; children: Nancy Lee, Mark Daniel, Leslie Ann, Shari Lee, Allen James, Michael Wayne. BA, Ea. Wash. U., 1955; MSW, U. Wash., 1963. Asst. prof. emeritus Wash. State U., Pullman; adminstr. juvenile ct. Whitman County Superior Ct., Colfax, Wash.; pub. health adminstr. Thurston-Mason Health Dist., Olympia, Wash. Dir. social svcs. Nursing Home and Retirement Ctr. Mem. NASW, Nat. Eagle Scout Assn. Home: 167 Walker Way Sagle ID 83860-9662

SOSSI, NUNZIO PIERGIORGIO, ophthalmologist; b. Milan, Nov. 29, 1948; came to U.S., 1974; s. Cosimo and Maria (Pignatelli) S.; m. Giuseppina Chiarelli, Apr. 27, 1970; 1 child, Lea. PhD in Biochemistry, U. Milan, 1974; MD, U. Miami, 1986. Diplomate Am. Bd. Ophthalmology. Rsch. assoc. Vanderbilt U., Nashville, 1974-75, Nat. Cancer Inst., NIH, Washington, 1976-79, Bascom Palmer Eye Inst., Miami, Fla., 1979-84; intern U. Miami, 1986-87; resident in ophthalmology U. Pitts., 1987-90; fellow in cornea and anterior segment U. Calif., San Diego, 1990-91; pvt. practice, West Palm Beach, Fla., 1991—; cons. in infectious diseases Good Samaritan Hosp., West Palm Beach, 1995—. Contbr. articles to med. jours. Officer Hidden Key Assn., North Palm Beach, Fla., 1996. With arty. Italian Army, 1975-76. Grantee Nat. Eye. Inst., 1982. Fellow ACS. Home: 11700 Landing Pl North Palm Beach FL 33408 Office: Palm Beach Eye Clinic 130 Butler St West Palm Beach FL 33407

SOTELO, JULIO EVERARDO, neurologist, researcher; b. Mexico City, Oct. 20, 1950; s. Fernando and Josefina (Morales) S.; m. Claudia Diaz, Jan. 5, 1991. MD, U. Mexico, Mexico City, 1974; neurology, Nat. Inst. Mex., Mexico City, 1977; neurovirology, NIH, 1981; neuroimmunology, London U., 1989. Med. diplomate; nat. researcher III. Head neuroimmunology dept. Nat. Inst. Neurology Mex., Mexico City, 1981—, dir. rsch., 1983—; prof. postgrad. in neurology, immunology and exptl. medicine Nat. Univ. Mex., Mexico City, 1982—. Contbr. numerous articles to books and profl. jours. Mem. Mexican Soc. Neurology and Psychiatry (pres. 1988-89), Mexican Acad. Medicine, Mexican Acad. Sci. Home: Chilapa 101, 14000 Mexico City Mexico Office: Nat Inst Neurology, Insurgentes Sur 3877, 14269 Mexico City Mexico

SOTHORON, WARREN HADDOX, orthopedic surgeon; b. Balt., Nov. 3, 1936; s. Warren Haddox and Lulah Mae (Bartleson) S.; m. Glenda Carolyn Parks, Sept. 2, 1961; children: Stephen Haddox, Kathy Lynne, Jeffrey Parks, Wendy Lee; m. Jacqueline Grace Hess, May 24, 1996. BS, Juniata Coll., 1958; MD, U. Md., 1962. Diplomate Am. Bd. Orthopedic Surgery. Resident in orthopedic surgery U. Md., Balt., 1971; pvt. practice orthopedics Howard County, Md., 1972-85; orthopedic surgeon Patuxent Med. Group, Columbia, Md., 1985—; asst. prof. U. Md., 1971-72; orthopedic subcontractor Columbia Med. Plan, 1972-85; physician adv. Care Advantage Health Sys., Newark, N.J., 1994-95. Lt. comdr. U.S. Navy, 1963-67. Fellow Am. Coll. Surgeons, Am. Acad. Orthopedic Surgeons, Eastern Orthopedic Assn.; mem. AMA, Md. Orthopedic Soc. (pres. 1985-86), Med. & Chirurgical Faculty Md., Howard County Med. Soc. (pres. 1978-79). Methodist. Office: Patuxent Med Group Inc 2 Knoll North Dr Columbia MD 21045

SOTO, JANINA, optometrist; b. Calexico, Calif., Apr. 14, 1964; d. Raymond G. and Consuelo (Lara) S. AA, Imperial (Calif.) Valley Coll., 1985; B Visual Sci., So. Calif. Coll. Optometry, Fullerton, 1987, OD, 1991. Assoc. Valley Vision, Elcentro, Calif., 1991-93; optometrist F.E. Warren AFB, Cheyenne, Wyo., 1994; owner Family Eye Care, El Centro, Calif., 1995—. Mem. Calif. Optometric Soc. (keyperson 1995), Rotary. Republican. Office: 444 S 8th St El Centro CA 92243

SOTOMORA-VON AHN, RICARDO FEDERICO, pediatrician, educator; b. Guatemala City, Guatemala, Oct. 22, 1947; s. Ricardo and Evelyn (Von Ahn) S.; m. Eileen Marie Holcomb, May 9, 1990. M.D., San Carlos U., 1972; M.S. in Physiology, U. Minn., 1978; m. Victoria Monzon, Nov. 26, 1971; children—Marisol, Clarisa, Ricardo, III, Charlotte Marie. Rotating intern Gen. Hosp. Guatemala, 1971-72; pediatric intern U. Ark., 1972-73, resident, 1973-75; fellow in pediatric cardiology U. Minn., 1975-78; research assoc. in cardiovascular pathology United Hosps., St. Paul, 1976; fellow in neonatal-perinatal medicine St. Paul's Children's Hosp., 1977-78, U. Ark., 1981-82; instr. pediatrics U. Minn., 1978-79; pediatric cardiologist, unit cardiovascular surgery Roosevelt Hosp., Guatemala City, 1979-81; asst. prof. pediatrics (cardiology and neonatology), U. Ark., Little Rock, 1981-83; practice medicine specializing in pediatric cardiology-neonatology, 1983—. Diplomate Am. Bd. Pediatrics, Sub-Bd. Pediatric Cardiology, Neonatal-Perinatal Medicine. Fellow Am. Acad. Pediatrics, Am. Coll. Cardiology, Am. Coll. Chest Physicians, Am. Coll. Angiology; mem. AMA, AAAS, Ark. Med. Soc., N.Y. Acad. Scis., Am. Heart Assn., Soc. Pediatric Echocardiography, Guatemala Coll. Physicians and Surgeons, Central Ark. Pediatric Soc., So. Soc. Pediatric Research, Soc. Critical Care Medicine. Clubs: Pleasant Valley Country (Little Rock). Home: 25 River Ridge Cir Little Rock AR 72227 Office: # 5 Office Park Dr Ste 105 Little Rock AR 72211

SOUDER, ELAINE, geropsychiatric nurse, researcher, educator; b. Phoenixville, Pa.; d. Kraybill and Ethel (Good) S. BSN, U. Pa., 1970, MSN, 1972; PhD, Boston Coll., 1988. RN; cert. clin. specialist in adult psychiat. nursing. Instr. New Eng. Deaconess Sch. Nursing, Boston, 1975-79; sr. instr. Peter Bent Brigham Sch. Nursing, Boston, 1979-84; instr. Mass Gen. Hosp. Inst. Health Professions, Boston, 1985-88; postdoctoral fellow, rsch. assoc. U. Pa., Phila., 1988-91; asst. prof. U. Ark., Little Rock, 1991-95, assoc. prof., 1995—. Contbr. articles to profl. jours. including Nurse Practitioner, Geriatrics, Jour. Nuclear Medicine, Jour. Neurosci. Nursing. Clin. Mental Health Acad. awardee NIMH, 1994—; NINR rsch. grantee, 1994—. Mem. Gerontol. Soc. Am., Internat. Neuropsychol. Assn., Sigma Theta Tau. Home: 11 Lenon Dr Little Rock AR 72207 Office: U Ark for Med Scis 4301 W Markham M/S 529 Little Rock AR 72205

SOUKOP, MICHEL, oncologist, consultant; b. London, Apr. 15, 1947; s. Willi Joseph and Simone (Moser) S.; m. Margaret Tannahill Suttie; children: Deborah, Gillian, Anna. B of Surgery, St. Andrews (Scotland) U., 1971; specialist accreditation med. oncology, Royal Colls., England, 1979, specialist accreditation internal med., 1979. Profl. house officer Dundee (England) Royal Infirmary, 1971-72; sr. house officer Inst. Radiotherapy, Glasgow, Scotland, 1972-73; registrar Western Infirmary, Glasgow, 1973-75; registrar then sr. registrar dept. med. oncology U. Glasgow, 1975-79; cons. physician, hon. sr. lectr. dept. med. oncology U. Glasgow Royal Infirmary, 1980—, head dept. med. oncology, 1980—; vis. lectr. U. Wis., Madison, 1979-80; cons. Ross Hall Hosp., Glasgow, 1984—; mem. Cancer Rsch. Campaign Phase I & II Group, London, 1984—; mem. United Kingdom Lymphoma Group, London, 1992—; mem. Royal Coll. Joint Coun., London, 1992—; mem. Specialist Adv. Com., Royal Coll., London, 1993—; examiner Royal Colls., 1986—. Contbr. articles in cancer field to profl. jours. Rsch. Grantee Cancer Rsch. Campaign, 1984—. Fellow Royal Colls. (Glasgow, Edin, London); mem. Rotary. Home: 15 Cleveden Gardens, Glasgow G12 0PU, Scotland Office: Royal Infirmary, Castle St, Glasgow G4 0SF, Scotland

SOULSBY, MICHEAL EDWARD, physiology, biophysics and toxicology educator, consultant; b. Montgomery, W.Va., Sept. 4, 1941; s. Paul Clarence and Reba Deane (Burnett) S.; m. Ruth Steelman, Nov. 18, 1983; children: Michael Jr., Paul C., Sean P., Kevin T. AB, W.Va. U., 1963, MS, 1968, PhD, 1971. Postdoctoral fellow Appalachian Lab. Respiratory Disease, Morgantown, W.Va., 1971-72; instr. Va. Commonwealth U., Richmond, 1972-74, asst. prof., 1972-76; asst. prof. U. Ark. for Med. Scis., Little Rock, 1977-83, assoc. prof., 1983—; bd. dirs. Am. Heart Assn. Va. affiliate, Am. Heart Assn., 1974, chmn. rsch. coun., Little Rock, 1980-86, so. rsch. coun., 1987—. U.S. Army ROTC, 1957-61. Rsch. grantee Nat. Insts. Health, Bethesda, Md., 1976, Am. Heart Assn., Ark., 1978, 80, 86. Mem. APS, Soc. Exptl. Biology and Medicine (chmn. S.W. sect. 1994—), Shock Soc., Biophys. Soc. Office: Univ Ark Medical Sch 4301 W Markham St Little Rock AR 72205-7101

SOUNEY, PAUL FREDERICK, pharmacist; b. Bristol, Conn., Mar. 29, 1947; s. Frederick Raymond and Julia Yvonne (Weeks) S.; m. Billie Lorraine Petersen, Apr. 7, 1972; children: Jared Paul, Jeremy Christian. BS, Northeastern U., 1971, MS, 1984. Drug info. pharmacist Hartford (Conn.) Hosp., 1971-77; pharmacy supervisor Boston Hosp. for Women, 1977-81; clin. rsch. pharmacist Channing Labs./Harvard Med. Sch., Boston, 1981-92; med. info. scientist Astra Merck Inc., Providence, R.I., 1992—; dir. drug info. Brigham and Women's Hosp., Boston, 1981-90, dir. clin. pharmacy, 1985-92; cons. in field. Editor: Comprehensive Pharmacy Review, 3d edit., 1996; contbr. articles to profl. jours.; editl. adv. panelist Internat. Pharm. Abstracts, Pharmacy Practice News. Treas. men's club First Congl. Ch., 1993—; vol. Mansfield (Mass.) Animal Shelter, 1990-94. Mem. Am. Coll. Clin. Pharmacy, Am. Soc. Health Sys. Pharmacists, Am. Pharmaceutical Assn., Acad. Managed Case Pharmacy, New Eng. Coun. Hosp. Pharmacists, Northeastern Univ. Alumnae Assn. Office: Astra Merck Inc One Citizens Plz Providence RI 02903

SOUSA, ALBERT WILLIAM, health facility administrator; b. Waterbury, Conn., July 29, 1954; s. Albert and Lourdes (Nobrega) S.; m. Melody Jan Nelson, Jan. 19, 1954; children: Kristin Maria, Albert Benjamin, Richard Allen, Kathrine Jan. Assocs. in Respiratory Therapy, St. Petersburg Jr. Coll., Fla. Day shift supr. Bayfront Med. Ctr., St. Petersburg, 1976-78; mktg. rep. Linde Home Care, St. Petersburg, 1978-79; ins. agt. Equitable Life/Mutual Security, Tampa, Fla., 1979-82; mktg. dir., home care mgr. Greene & Kellogg, St. Petersburg, 1982-84; dir. ops., regional mktg. coord. Healthcare Prescription, Fla., 1984-88; dir. ancillery svcs. Medi-Save Pharmacies, Fla., 1988-92; v.p. med. specialty svcs. Horizon/CMS Health Care, Albuquerque, 1992—. Mem. Am. Assn. Respiratory Therapy, Nat. Assn. Hospice, U.S. Soccer Fedn. Office: Horizon/CMS Health Care 6001 Indian Sch Rd Albuquerque NM 87110

SOUSA, CONSUELO MARIA, pediatrician; b. New Bedford, Mass., Aug. 5, 1931; d. Edward Rogers and Candida Helena (Rogers) S.; m. Timothy Leonard Stephens, July 7, 1959; children: Timothy Leonard III, Susan Ellen, Amy Louise. BS, Howard U., Washington, 1953, MD, 1958; MPH, Harvard U., 1962; MBA, Case Western Res. U., Cleve., 1983. Diplomate Am. Bd. Pediatrics. Intern St. Luke's Hosp., New Bedford, 1958; resident pediatrics Freedmen's Hosp., Washington, 1959-61; fellow dept. maternal and child health Harvard Sch. Pub. Health, Boston, 1961-62; instr. preventive medicine Boston U. Sch. Medicine, 1962-63; asst. physician home med. svc. Mass. Meml. Svc. Hosp., 1962-63; pvt. practice, assoc. attending staff St. Luke's Hosp., New Bedford, 1963-66; pediatrician Well Child Conf., Fairhaven, Mass., 1965-66; clin. instr. pediatrics Case Western Res. U., Cleve., 1967-94; mem. pediatric staff Rainbow Babes and Children's Hosp., Cleve., 1967-94; chief pediatrics Hough Norwood Family Health Care Ctr., Cleve., 1967-76; vis. asst. pediatrics Cleve. Met. Gen. Hosp., 1967-91; dir. health svcs. Buckeye Health Plan, Inc., Cleve., 1976-79, acting exec. dir., 1979, med. health svcs. dir., 1979-80; v.p., med. adminstr. Assocs. in Orthopaedics, Inc., Cleve., 1982—, cons., 1980-82; chmn. med. staff Health Hill Hosp., Cleve., 1982-84; mem. Headstart Health Adv. Com., Cleve., 1971-78, chmn., 1977-78. Contbr. articles to profl. jours. Mem. Citizens Adv. Bd. of Juvenile Ct. Cuyahoga County, 1975-90, chmn. bd., 1985-89; appointed commr. Cuyahoga Met. Housing Authority, 1990; mem. bd., founding trustee Harambee Svcs. to Black Families, Cleve., 1979-85; mem. adv. bd. Youth Svcs., Cuyahoga County, 1980-90. Named Outstanding American, Cape Verdean Am. Vets., New Bedford, 1972. Fellow Am. Acad. Pediatrics; mem. AMA, Nat. Med. Assn., No. Ohio Pediatric Soc. Home: 13475 N Park Blvd Cleveland OH 44118-4927 Office: Assocs in Orthopaedics Inc 11201 Shaker Blvd Ste 328 Cleveland OH 44104-3833

SOUSER, ROSLYN COSKERY, plastic and reconstructive surgeon; b. Phila., Mar. 27, 1939; children: Kenneth, Eugene C. AB, Duke U., 1961; MD, Woman's Med. Coll. Pa., 1966; student, U. Munich, 1959-60; MBA, St. Joseph U., 1996. Lic. physician, Pa.; diplomate Nat. Bd. Med. Examiners, Am. Bd. Surgery, Am. Bd. Plastic Surgery. Intern in surgery Bryn Mawr (Pa.) Hosp., 1967-71, VA Hosp., Wilmington, Del., 1969-70; resident in plastic surgery Temple U. Hosp., 1971-72, Hosp. of U. Pa., 1972-73; pvt. practice Ardmore, West Chester, Pa., 1973—; sr. attending in plastic and reconstrv. surgery Bryn Mawr Hosp.; active staff Chester County Hosp., West Chester, Mercy-Haverford Hosp., Havertown, Pa.; instr. surgery U. Pa. Plastic Surgery Div., Phila.; lectr. in field. Contbr. numerous articles to profl. jours. Former bd. trustees Harcum Jr. Coll., Bryn Mawr, 1987-88. Fellow ACS, AMA, Coll. Physicians Phila.; mem. Montgomery County Med. Soc., Pa. Med. Soc., Am. Med. Women's Assn. (past chpt. pres.), Women's Med. Coll. Pa. Alumnae Assn. (sec. to exec. bd. 1975-76), Robert H. Ivy Soc., Am. Soc. Plastic and Reconstructive Surgeons, Am. Assn. for Hand Surgery, AAUW, Northeastern Soc. Plastic Surgeons (founding mem.), Internat. Soc. Clin. Plastic Surgeons. Home and Office: 44 Haverford Rd Ardmore PA 19003-1021 Also: Westtown Bus Ctr 1558 Mcdaniel Dr West Chester PA 19380-7036

SOUSOULAS, JAMES GEORGE, dentist; b. Memphis, May 29, 1928; s. Frank George and Mary (Pappademitriou) S.; m. Sophie Makris, June 20, 1954; children—Stephanie Marie, George James. B.S., Memphis State U., 1950; D.D.S., U. Tenn., 1954. Gen. practice dentistry, Memphis, 1957—; assoc. prof. U. Tenn., 1961-76. Served to capt. USAF, 1955-57. Home: 3047 Central Ave Memphis TN 38111 Office: Dental Clinic 555 Perkins Extd Ste 309 Memphis TN 38117-4477

SOUTAR, DAVID STRANG, plastic surgeon; b. Arbroath, Scotland, Dec. 19, 1947; s. Alexander Anderson and Lisbeth Agnes (Anderson) S.; m. Myra Banks, July 19, 1972; children: Martin, Paul, Claire. MB ChB, Aberdeen (Scotland) U., 1972, ChM, 1986. Lectr. in pathology Aberdeen U., 1973-74; gen. surg. registrar Grampian Region, Aberdeen, 1974-78; registrar, then sr. registrar Canniesburn Hosp., Glasgow, Scotland, 1978-81; cons. plastic surgeon West of Scotland Regional Plastic and Maxillofacial Surgery, Glasgow, 1981—, Western Infirmary, Glasgow, 1981—; clin. lectr. U. Glasgow, 1981—; hon. sec., Scottish Melanoma Group, 1984-88. Co-author: Practical Guide to Free Tissue Transfer, 1986; author video, The Radial Firearm Flam, 1986 (Barron prize 1987); mem. editorial bd., Brit. Jour. Plastic Surgery, 1986-89, European Jour. Plastic Surgery. Fellow Royal Coll. Surgeons Edinburgh, Royal Coll. Surgeons Glasgow; mem. Brit. Assn. Plastic Surgeons (mem. coun. 1988), Brit. Assn. Head and Neck Oncologists (com. mem. 1984—), Brit. Microsurg. Soc. Conservative. Anglican. Home: 7 Chesters Rd, G61 4AF Glasgow Scotland Office: Canniesburn Hosp, Plastic Maxillofacial Surg, G61 1QL Glasgow Scotland

SOUTHAM, CHESTER MILTON, physician; b. Salem, Mass., Oct. 4, 1919; s. Walter Aloysius and Elizabeth Effie (Furbish) S.; m. Anna Lenore Skow, Sept. 24, 1939 (div.); children: Lawrence Albert, Lenore Elizabeth, Arthur Milton; m. Gertrude Elizabeth Lundin, June 9, 1973. BS, U. Idaho, 1941, MS, 1943; MD, Columbia U., 1947. Intern Presbyn. Hosp., N.Y.C., 1947-48; rsch. fellow to full mem., chief divsn. virology/immunology Sloan-Kettering Inst. Cancer Rsch., N.Y.C., 1948-71; from clin. fellow to attending physician Meml. Hosp. for Cancer, N.Y.C., 1948-71; from instr. to assoc. prof. medicine Cornell U. Med. Ctr., N.Y.C., 1951-71; head Div. Med. Oncology Thomas Jefferson U. Med. Coll., Phila., 1971-79, prof. medicine, 1971—; attending physician Dept. Medicine Thomas Jefferson U. Hosp., Phila., 1971—. Contbr. articles to profl. jours. Trustee Leopold Shepp Found., N.Y.C., 1961-67, Strang Clinic and Preventive Medicine Inst., N.Y.C., 1963-68; adv. com. on rsch. and therapy cancer Am. Cancer Soc., N.Y.C., 1961-66; sci. adv. com. Damon Runyon Fund, N.Y.C., 1961-68; com. virology and immunology Internat. Union Against Cancer, Geneva, 1966-90; adv. com. tobacco and health rsch. AMA Edn. and Rsch. Found., Chgo., 1965-66; bd. dirs. Am. Assn. Cancer Rsch., 1966-70, pres., 1968-69. Capt. U.S. Army, 1953-55. Mem. Am. Soc. Clin. Oncologists. Home and Office: 3705 Darby Rd Bryn Mawr PA 19010-2009

SOUTHBY, RICHARD MCKELLAR FAIRFAX, health services administration educator, consultant; b. Melbourne, Victoria, Australia, Feb. 3, 1940; came to U.S. 1979, naturalized 1985; s. Robert and Marie Heywood (Whyte) S.; m. Janet Sue Rexrode, June 9, 1979. B.Com., U. Melbourne, 1965; M.P.A., Cornell U., 1967; Ph.D., Monash U., Clayton, Victoria, Australia, 1973. Research asst. Inst. Applied Econ. Research, U. Melbourne, 1965; Sloan scholar in hosp. and med. care adminstrn. Cornell U., Ithaca, N.Y., 1965-67; teaching fellow Monash U., Victoria, Australia, 1967-70, sr. teaching fellow dept. social and preventive medicine Faculty of Medicine, 1970, lectr. in social and preventive medicine, 1971-75, sr. lectr., 1975-78; commr. Australian Hosps. and Health Services Commn., Canberra, Australian Capital Territory, 1975; dir. pub. health services research and tchg. Sch. Pub. Health and Tropical Medicine, U. Sydney, New South Wales, Australia, 1978-79; chmn. and Friesen prof. internat. health and health policy and prof. health care scis., Dept. Health Svcs. Mgmt. and Policy, The George Washington U., Washington, 1979—; adj. prof. dept. preventive medicine and biometrics Sch. Medicine, Uniformed Services U. Health Scis. Dept. Def., Bethesda, Md., 1979—; dir. Interagy.-Inst. for Fed. Health Care Execs., 1984—; cons. in hosp. adminstrn. Walter Reed Army Med. Ctr., Washington, 1983—. Author: (with E. Chesterman) Australia: Health Facts, 1979; editor: (with others) Health Care Technology Under Financial Constraints, 1987, Health Care Law and Ethics, 1989, AIDS and Long Term Care: A New Dimension, 1989. Fellow Australian Coll. Health Svc. Execs.; mem. Am. Pub. Health Assn., Internat. Epidemiol. Assn., Assn. Mil. Surgeons U.S. Anglican. Clubs: Wallaby, Naval and Mil. (Melbourne); Army and Navy (Washington), Cosmos (Washington). Avocations: tennis, gardening, hiking. Office: George Washington Univ Dept Health Svcs Mgmt & Policy Washington DC 20052

SOUTHERN, PAUL MORRIS, JR., internist, educator, microbiologist; b. Ft. Worth, June 26, 1932; s. Paul Morris and Margaret M. (Moore) S.; BS, Abilene Christian Coll., 1953; MD, U. Tex., 1959; DTM&H London Sch. Hygiene and Tropical Medicine, 1993; children by previous marriage: Sheryl Ann, Mark Lee. Intern, Parkland Meml. Hosp., Dallas, 1959-60, resident, 1960-62; research fellow infectious diseases U. Tex. Southwestern Med. Sch., Dallas, 1962-63, 66-68; practice medicine, specializing in internal medicine, Irving, Tex., 1963-66; asst. prof. internal medicine U. Tex. Southwestern Med. Sch., Dallas, 1968-71, asso. prof. pathology and internal medicine, 1973-81, prof., 1981—; asst. prof. lab. medicine Washington U. Sch. Medicine, St. Louis, 1971-73; dir. clin. microbiology Parkland Meml. Hosp., Dallas, 1973—; vis. prof. dept. microbiology St. Thomas's Hosp. Med. Sch., London, 1980-81, Kuwait U. Faculty Medicine, 1981, 82 Diplomate Am. Bd. Internal Medicine, Am. Bd. Infectious Diseases, Am. Bd. Pathology. Fellow A.C.P.; mem. Tex. Soc. Clin. Microbiology (pres. 1974-76), Acad. Clin. Lab. Physicians and Scientists, Am. Soc. Microbiology, Infectious Diseases Soc. Am., Tex. Infectious Diseases Soc. (pres. 1983-84), Am Soc. Clin. Pathologists, So. Soc. Clin. Investigation, Southwestern Assn. Clin. Microbiology (pres. 1994-95), Royal Soc. Tropical Medicine and Hygiene, Am. Fedn. Clin. Research, Alpha Omega Alpha. Contbr. articles to profl. jours. Home: 3607 Cole Ave #151 Dallas TX 75204 Office: U Tex Southwestern Med Ctr 5323 Harry Hines Blvd Dallas TX 75235-7200

SOUTHWARD, PATRICIA ANN, school psychologist; b. Circleville, Ohio, Jan. 17, 1942; d. Stanley Pearl and Orpha Josephine (Eveland) Frazier; m. Rodger Lee Southward, June 5, 1966; children: Nichol Jocinda, Teratia Jo, Rebecca Leigh-Ann. BS, Ohio State U., 1964, MA, 1967. Cert. tchr. English, speech, Ohio; lic. sch. counselor Ohio; lic. sch. psychologist, Ohio. Tchr. Teays Valley H.S., Ashville, Ohio, 1964-67; sch. psychologist South-Western City Schs., Grove City, Ohio, 1967-71, 78—; sch. psychologist Circleville City Schs., 1972-77, ret., 1995; with Pickaway County Ednl. Svcs., Circleville, 1995—. Named Outstanding Young Educator, Sertoma, 1975. Mem. Ohio Sch. Psychologists Assn. (F. Peter Gross Best Practices award 1995), Sch. Psychologists of Ctrl. Ohio (Best Practices award 1994), Nat. Assn. Sch. Psychologists, Coun. of Exceptional Children, Ohio State U. Alumni Assn. (pres. Pickaway County chpt. 1995—), Kiwanis (v.p. 1994-95, sec. 1992-94), Delta Kappa Gamma (historian Theta chpt.). Methodist. Home: 125 Maple St Ashville OH 43103-1569 Office: Pickaway County Ednl Svcs Ctr Franklin St Circleville OH 43113

SOUTHWICK, CHRISTOPHER LYN, anesthesiologist; b. Salina, Kans., Jan. 12, 1956; s. Forest Arthur II and Carolyn Kay (Kauth) S.; m. Laura Lee Stuck, Nov. 17, 1984; children: Andrew William, Kylie Marie, Caitlin Lee. BS in Chem. Sci., Kans. State U., 1978; MD, U. Kans., 1984. Certified Am. Bd. Anesthesiology. Intern Western Res. Care System, Youngstown, Ohio, 1984-85, resident, 1985-87; anesthesiologist Columbia (Mo.) Regional Hosp., 1987-88, Boone Hosp. Ctr., Columbia, 1988—. Mem. AMA, Am. Soc. Anesthesiologists, Mo. Med. Soc. (sec./treas. 1996—), Theta Xi, Alpha Delta Epsilon (pres. 1976-78). Republican. Home: 1001 Lake Point Ln Columbia MO 65203-2900 Office: Columbia Anesthesia Assoc Inc 1506 E Broadway Ste 302 Columbia MO 65201-8078

SOUTHWICK, HARRY WEBB, surgeon; b. Grand Rapids, Mich., Nov. 21, 1918; s. G. Howard and Jessie (Webb) S.; m. Lorraine Hinsdale, June 27, 1942; children: Harry Webb Jr., Sandra, Charles Howard, Gay. B.S., Harvard U., 1940, M.D., 1943. Intern Presbyn. Hosp., Chgo., 1944-45, resident in surgery, 1945-46; surg. resident U. Ill. Research and Ednl. Hosps., 1948-50; chmn. dept. gen. surgery Rush-Presbyn.-St. Luke's Med. Center, Chgo., 1970-84; pvt. practice surgery Chgo., 1950-84; clin. assoc. prof. surgery U. Ill. Med. Sch., 1957-63, clin. prof., 1963-71; Helen Shedd Keith prof. surgery Rush Med. Coll., 1971-84; bd. dirs. Howard Young Med. Ctr., sec., 1987-89, vice-chmn., 1989-90, chmn., 1990—; bd. dris. Howard Young Health Care, Eagle River Meml. Hosp. Contbr. articles to med. jours. Pres. Chgo. unit Am. Cancer Soc., 1964-66, pres. Ill. div. 1972-73; bd. dirs. Eagle River Meml. Hosp., 1989—. Lt. (j.g.) M.C., USNR, 1946-48. Fellow ACS; mem. Am. Surg. Assn., Pan Am. Surg. Soc., Minn. Surg. Soc. (hon.), Western Surg. Soc., Cen. Surg. Soc., Chgo. Surg. Soc. (pres. 1979-80), Soc. Head and Neck Surgeons (sec.-treas. 1956-63, pres. 1964-65), Soc. Surgery Alimentary Tract, Soc. Surg. Oncology, Plum Lake Golf Club. Home and Office: 8155 N Lost Lake Dr Sayner WI 54560

SOVIE, MARGARET DOE, nursing administrator, college dean, educator; b. Ogdensburg, N.Y., July 7, 1934; d. William Gordon and Mary Rose (Bruyere) Doe; m. Alfred L. Sovie, May 8, 1954; 1 child, Scot Marc. Student, U. Rochester, 1950-51; diploma in nursing, St. Lawrence State Hosp. Sch. Nursing, Ogdensburg, 1954; postgrad., St. Lawrence U., 1956-60; BS in Nursing summa cum laude, Syracuse U., 1964, MS in Edn., 1968, PhD in Edn., 1972; DSc (hon.), Health Sci. Ctr. SUNY, Syracuse, 1989; MSN, U. Pa., 1995. Cert. adult health nurse practitioner. Staff nurse, clin. instr. St. Lawrence State Hosp., Ogdensburg, 1954-55, instr. nursing, 1955-62; staff nurse Good Shepherd Hosp., Syracuse, 1962; nursing supr. SUNY Upstate Med. Ctr., Syracuse, 1963-65, insvc. instr., 1965-66, edn. dir. and coord. nursing svc., 1966-71, asst. dean Coll. Health Related Professions, 1972-84, assoc. prof. nursing, 1973-76, dir. continuing edn. in nursing, 1974-76, assoc. dean and dir. div. continuing edn. Coll. Health Related Professions, 1974-76; spl. assignment in pres.'s office SUNY Upstate Med. Ctr. and Syracuse U., 1972-73; assoc. dean for nursing U. Rochester, N.Y., 1976-88, assoc. prof. nursing, 1976-85, prof., 1985-88; assoc. dir. for nursing Strong Meml. Hosp., U. Rochester Med. Ctr., 1976-88; chief nursing officer Hosp. U. Pa., Phila., 1988-96, assoc. exec. dir., 1988-94, assoc. dean for nursing practice Sch. Nursing, 1988-96, Jane Delano prof. nursing adminstrn. Sch. Nursing, 1988—, chief nursing officer, 1988-96; sr. fellow Leonard Davis Inst. Health Econs. U. Pa., Phila., 1992—; trustee bd. U. Pa. Health Sys., Phila., 1993-96; nursing coord. and project dir. Cen. N.Y. Regional Med. Program, Syracuse, 1968-71; mem. edn. dept. State Bd. Nursing, Albany, N.Y., 1974-84, chmn., 1981-83, chmn. practice com., 1975-80, mem. joint practice com., 1975-80, vice chmn., 1980-81; mem. adv. com. to clin. nurse scholars program Robert Wood Johnson found., Princeton, N.J., 1982-88; adj. assoc. prof. Syracuse U. Sch. Nursing, 1973-76; mem. Gov.'s Health Adv. Panel N.Y. State Health Planning Commn., 1976-82, task force on health manpower policy, 1978, informal support networks sect. steering com., 1980; mem. health manpower tng. and utilization task force State N.Y. Commn. on Health Edn.and Illness Prevention, 1979; mem. task force on nursing personnel N.Y. State Health Adv. Coun., 1980; mem. adv. panel on nursing svcs. U.S. Pharm. Conv. Inc., Washington, 1985-90; cons. Nat. Ctr. for Svcs. Rsch. and Health Care Tech. Assessment, Rockville, Md., 1987; mem. nursing stds. task force Joint Commn. Accreditation Health Care Orgns., 1988-90; mem. various other adv. coms.; lectr. in field. Mem. editl. bd. Health Care Supr., 1982-87, Nursing Econs., 1983—, Best Practices and Benchmarking in Health Care, 1995—; manuscript rev. panel Nursing Outlook, 1987-91; mem. editorial bd. Seminars for Nurse Mgrs., 1994—; contbr. articles to profl. jours., chpts. to books. Mem. bd. visitors Sch. Nursing U. Md., Balt., 1984-89; mem. bd. mgrs. Strong Meml. Hosp., Rochester, 1983-88; bd. dirs. Monroe County Assn. for Hearing, Rochester, 1979-82, Vis. Nurse Svc., Rochester and Monroe County, 1978, Southeastern Pa. chpt. ARC, 1991—. Ann. Margaret D. Sovie lectureship inaugurated Strong Meml. Hosp. U. Rochester, 1989; spl. nurse rsch. fellow NIH, 1971-72; grantee various orgns.; recipient Dean's Outstanding Alumni award Coll. of Nursing, Syracuse U., 1994. Fellow Am. Acad. Nursing (program com. 1980-81, task force on hosp. nursing 1981-83, chair expert panel on quality health 1994—); mem. ANA (nat. rev. com. for expanded role programs 1975-78, site visitor to programs requesting accreditation 1976-78, cabinet on nursing svcs. 1986-90, cert. bd. nursing adminstrn. 1983-86, Ad Hoc com. on advanced practice 1992-95), Am. Orgn. Nurse Execs. (stds. task force 1987), N.Y. State Nurses Assn. (med. surg. nursing group, chmn. edn. com. dist. 4 1974-76, chmn. cmty. planning group for nursing dist. 4 1974-75, couegional planning in nursing 1974-76, del. to conv. 1978, Nursing Svc. Adminstrn. award 1985), Inst. Medicine (com. design strategy for quality rev. and assurance in Medicare 1988-90), Sigma Theta Tau, Pi Lambda Theta. Republican. Roman Catholic. Office: U Pa Sch Nursing 420 Guardian Dr Philadelphia PA 19104-6096

SOWERS, AMELIA BARNET, speech and language pathologist; b. Houston, Mar. 13, 1952; d. Albert Glenn and Helen June (Meador) Barnet; m. George Vernon Sowers Jr., Aug. 23, 1975; children: George Vernon III, Adam Glenn. BA, U. Houston, 1975, MA, 1993. Lic. and cert. speech-lang. pathologist, Tex. Speech-lang. pathologist Aldine Ind. Sch. Dist., Houston, 1976-78, Tomball (Tex.) Ind. Sch. Dist., 1978-83, Conroe (Tex.) Ind. Sch. Dist., 1984-96; pvt. practice, 1996—. Bd. dirs. Crighton Players. Mem. NEA, Am. Speech, Lang. and Hearing Assn., Tex. Speech and Hearing Assn., Tex. Tchrs. Assn., Houston Assn. Comm. Disorders, Montgomery County Performing Arts Soc. (com.). Methodist. Home and Office: 25 Village Hill Dr Conroe TX 77304

SOX, HAROLD CARLETON, JR., physician, educator; b. Palo Alto, Calif., Aug. 18, 1939; s. Harold Carleton and Mary (Griffiths) S.; m. Carol Helen Hill, Aug. 26, 1962; children: Colin Montgomery, Lara Katherine. BS, Stanford U., 1961; MD cum laude, Harvard U., 1966. Diplomate Am. Bd. Internal Medicine (pretest writing com. 1992-94). Intern and resident Mass. Gen. Hosp., Boston, 1966-68; clin. assoc. Nat. Cancer Inst., Bethesda, Md., 1968-70; instr. Dartmouth Med. Sch., Hanover, N.H., 1970-73; asst. prof. medicine to prof. Stanford U. Sch. Medicine, Calif., 1973-88; Joseph Huber prof., chmn. dept. medicine Dartmouth Med. Sch., 1988—; panel mem. Nat. Bd. Med. Examiners, Physicians Assts. Nat. Certifying Exam., 1973-76, chair com. on priority-setting for health tech. assessment Inst. Medicine, 1990-91, chair U.S. preventive svcs. task force, 1990-95, chair Inst. Medicine com. on HIV and U.S. blood supply, 1994-95; chair task force to revise internal medicine residency curriculum Federated Coun. Internal Medicine, 1993—. Author: Medical Decision Making, 1988; editor: Common Diagnostic Tests, 1987, 2d edit., 1990; mem. editorial bd. Med. Decision Making, 1980-87, Jour. Gen. Internal Medicine, 1985-87, New Eng. Jour. Medicine, 1990—; cons. assoc. editor Am. Jour. Medicine, 1988-95; assoc. editor Sci. Am. Medicine, 1995—; contbr. chpts. to books and articles to profl. jours. Fellow ACP (clin. efficacy assessment subcom. 1985-92, bd. regents, 1991—, chmn. ednl. policy com. 1994—); mem. Soc. for Gen. Internal Medicine (coun. 1980-83), Soc. for Med. Decision Making (trustee 1980-83, pres. 1983-84), Am. Fedn. Clin. Rsch., Assn. Am. Physicians, Assn. Profs. Medicine, Inst. Medicine of NAS, Alpha Omega Alpha. Home: Faraway Ln Hanover NH 03755-2312 Office: Darthmouth-Hitchcock Med Ctr Dept Lebanon NH 03756

SOYER, PHILIPPE ALAIN, radiologist, researcher; b. Paris; s. François André and Madeleine Hortensia (Stéphani) S.; m. Emmanuelle Bastide, June 15, 1991; 1 child, Matteo. MD, Bichat U., Paris, 1989, bd. cert., Tours (France) U., 1989; MS, Bicêtre U., 1991. Resident Hosp. Bretonneau, Tours, France, 1985-90; fellow Hops. Bichat, Paris, 1990-92; vis. prof. Johns Hopkins Hosp., Balt., 1993-94; asst. prof. Hosp. Foch, Suresnes, France, 1994—, Johns Hopkins Hosp., Balt., 1995—; assoc. editor Radiology Balt., 1994—; bd. mem. European Jour. Radiology, Rotterdam, Netherlands, 1993—. Editor: Liver Imaging, 1994; contbr. scientific papers in Radiology. Grantee S.F.R., 1993, Kodak, 1991, DuPont de Nemours, 1992. Home: 94 Rue Saint-Dominique, 75007 Paris France Office: Hôpital Foch, 40 Rue Worth BP36, 92151 Suresnes France

SOYKE, JENNIFER MAE, emergency and family physician; b. McKeesport, Pa., Feb. 2, 1952; d. Edgar Arthur and Phyllis Jean (Parks) S.; m. Jeff Willensky, Sept. 25, 1977; 1 child, Jordana Soyke-Willensky. BA in Biology, U. Oreg., 1983; MD, Oreg. Health Scis. U., 1988. Diplomate Am. Bd. Family Practice. Resident Madigan Army Med. Ctr., Tacoma, Wash., 1988-91; staff physician U.S. Army Blanchfield Army Cmty. Hosp., Fort Campbell, Ky., 1991-95; pvt. practice Springfield, Oreg., 1995—; chair family practice quality improvement Blanchfield Army Cmty. Hosp., Fort Campbell, 1992-94; White Primary Care Clinic, 1993-95, patient edn. coord., 1993-95; emergency room part-time, Smith County Meml. Hosp., Carthage, Tenn., 1992-95, Sumner Regional Med. Ctr., Gallatin, Tenn., 1992-95, Trinity Hosp., Erin, Tenn., 1994-95; staff physician Miller Med Group and Edgefield Hosp., Nashville, part time emergency rm., urgent care clinic, 1992. Contbr. articles to profl. jours. Chair, bd. dirs. Amazon Coop. Pre-sch. Amazon U. of Oreg. Housing, Eugene, 1981-82; mem. bd. dirs. and newsletter editor Lake Louise Elem. Sch. Parent Tchr. Student Assn., 1989-90. Major U.S. Army Med. Corps, 1988-95. Recipient Nurses Choice award Dept. Family Practice, Madigan Army Med. Ctr., 1989; Mead Johnson award for excellence in family practice, 1990. Fellow Am. Acad. Family Physicians (many coms., chair com. on spl. constituencies 1996, convenor nat. conf. of women, minority and new physicians, 1996; also active during residency and student period); mem. AMA, (alt. del. to young physician sect. 1993, Army del. to young physician sect. 1993, 94, Am. Acad. Family Physicians del. to young physician sect. 1995. 96), Oreg. Acad. Family Physicians (bd. dirs. student mem. 1985-86), Doctors Ought to Care (founding mem. Oreg. chpt. 1987-88, bd. trustees Wash. chpt. 1989-91), Uniformed Svcs. Acad. Family Physicians (chair membership com. 1993-95).

SPADONE, DONALD PAUL, physician; b. Ithaca, N.Y., Aug. 22, 1955; s. Donald and Joyce Spadone; m. Kathleen Spadone, June 6, 1981; children: Paul Edward, Alan Matthew. BS, St. Lawrence U., 1977; MD, SUNY, Buffalo, 1981. Diplomate in critical care and vascular surgery Am. Bd. Surgery. Fellow in vascular surgery So. Ill. U., Springfield, 1990; asst. prof. surgery U. Mo., Columbia, 1990—. Mem. editorial bd. Jour. Colon Flow Imaging. Fellow ACS; mem. Soc. Critical Care Medicine, St. Louis Vascular Soc. (sec.). Office: Univ Hosp and Clinics Dept Surgery Columbia MO 65212

SPAEDY, TONY J., cardiologist; b. Boonville, Mo., Mar. 8, 1963; s. Darrell Eugene and Marjorie Ann (Schuster) S.; m. Shellie Jeannine Bills, Feb. 14, 1987; children: Emily, Andrew, Abigail. BA in Biology with distinction, U. Mo., Kansas City, 1986, MD, 1987. Diplomate Am. Bd. Internal Medicine, Am. Bd. Cardiovascular Disease. Intern, resident Parkland Meml. Hosp./U. Tex. Southwestern Med. Ctr., Dallas, 1987-90; fellow in cardiology Krannert Inst. Cardiology/Ind. U. Sch. Medicine, 1990-92, chief fellow in cardiology, 1992-93, fellow in interventional cardiology, 1993-94; cardiologist Mo. Cardiovascular Specialists, Columbia, 1994—. Contbr. articles to profl. jours. Grantee Am. Heart Assn. Ind. affiliate, 1992-93. Fellow Am. Coll. Cardiology (co-chmn. study session 43d ann. sci. session 1994); mem. AMA, ACP, Am. Coll. Chest Physicians, Boone Med. Soc. Republican. Roman Catholic. Home: 5005 Cullen Ct Columbia MO 65203 Office: Mo Cardiovascular Specialists 401 Keene St Columbia MO 65201

SPAETH, DONALD GEORGE, physician, researcher, educator; b. Detroit, June 2, 1942; s. Fredrick George and Dorothy (Vossberg) S.; m. Patricia Louise Hodson, Aug. 18, 1973; children: T. Michele, Mary, Mindy, Heidi. BS, Valparaiso U., 1964; MS, W. Va. U., 1966; PhD, SUNY, Buffalo, 1969; DO, Coll. Osteo. Medicine, Kansas City, Mo., 1981. Diplomate Nat. Bd. Examiners for Osteopathic Physicians and Surgeons; cert. in gen./family practice Am. Osteopathic Bd. of Family Physicians. Rsch. scientist Mead Johnson & Co., Evansville, Ind., 1970-77; pvt. practice Sandusky, Ohio, 1983-94; assoc. prof. Coll. Osteo. Medicine Ohio U., Athens, 1994—; med. dir. Huron (Ohio) Health Care, 1984-94, Twin Maples Nursing Home, McArthur, Ohio, 1994—; dep. coroner Erie County, Ohio, 1989-93. Contbr. chpt. to book (Taurine Metabolism), 1975; contbr. articles to profl. jours. Mem. Am. Osteopathic Assn., Ohio Osteopathic Assn. (sec.-treas. dist. IX), Am. Inst. Nutrition, Fed. Am. Soc. Exptl. Biol. Medicine, Christian Med. and Dental Soc. Office: Coll Osteo Medicine Ohio U Athens OH 45701

SPAETH, GEORGE LINK, physician, ophthalmology educator; b. Phila., Mar. 3, 1932; s. Edmund Benjamin and Lena Marie (Link) S.; m. Ann Ward, May 17, 1955; children: Kristin Lea Crowley, George Link Jr., Eric Edmund. BA magna cum laude, Yale U., 1954; MD cum laude, Harvard U., 1959; postgrad., U. Mich., 1960, U. Pa., 1971. Diplomate Am. Bd. Ophthalmology. Resident surgeon Wills Eye Hosp., Phila., 1960-63, attending surgeon, 1970—, dir. glaucoma svc., 1968—; clin. fellow NIH, Bethesda, Md., 1963-65; instr. U. Pa., Phila., 1965-68; pvt. practice Phila., 1965-68; prof. ophthalmology Temple U. Med. Sch., Phila., 1968-75, Jefferson Med. Coll., Phila., 1975—; ophthalmologist Chestnut Hill Hosp., Phila., 1975—; attending surgeon, Graduate Hosp.; cons., Bryn Mawr Hosp. Author: 14 books in ophthalmology and surgery, 1970—; contbr. over 500 articles to profl. jours.; editor: Ophthalmic Surgery jour., 1985-96; patentee differometer, tonometer tip cover. Pres. Chestnut Hill Cmty. Assn., Phila., 1970-72; trustee, treas. Thomas Harrison Found., 1975—; founder, pres. E.B. Spaeth and The Eye Disease Found., 1978—, Profls. for Nuclear Army Control, 1985-88; interviewer Yale Alumni Schs. Com., Phila., 1965—; Yale Class coun., 1968—, Yale Assn. Alumni Reps., 1996—; curriculum com. Jefferson Med. Coll., 1987-90; institutional review bd. Jefferson Med. Coll., 1990—. Lt. comdr. USPHS, 1963-68. Recipient Pub. Svc. award Chestnut Hill Coll., 1972, Sir Stuart Duke Elder Glaucoma award Internat. Glaucoma Soc., 1986, Newberg award Lawyers Alliance for World Security, 1995, Derrick Vail award Ill. Ophthal. Soc., 1996; NIH grantee, 1968—. Fellow Am. Acad. Ophthalmology (chmn. ethics com. San Francisco 1987-95, coun. 1980-93, vice chmn. residency rev. com. Chgo. 1982-88, Sr. honor award 1988), Ind. Assn. Rsch. in Vision and Ophthalmology, Royal Coll. Ophthalmologist, United Kingdom, Danish Ophthalmological Soc.; mem. Am. Glaucoma Soc. (pres. 1983-85), Coll. Physicians Phila. (sec. 1976-84), Phila. County Med. Soc., Pa. Acad. Ophthalmology (pres. coun.), Physicians for Social Responsibility (pres. Phila. chpt.), ACS (bd. govs., chmn. adv. coun., chmn. subcom. monitoring), Phila. Club, Phila. Cricket Club, Franklin Inn Club (Phila.), Moral Values Book Club, Phi Beta Kappa, Alpha Omega Alpha. Democrat. Episcopalian. Office: Wills Eye Hosp 900 Walnut St Philadelphia PA 19107-5509

SPAGNOLO, SAMUEL VINCENT, internist, pulmonary specialist, educator; b. Pitts., Sept. 3, 1939; s. Vincent Anthony and Mary Grace (Culotta) S.; m. Lucy Aleta Weyandt, June 20, 1961 (div. Feb., 1992); children: Samuel, Brad, Gregg. BA, Washington & Jefferson Coll., 1961; MD, Temple U., 1965. Diplomate Am. Bd. Internal Medicine, Bd. of Pulmonary Disease; active lic. physician in Fla., Calif., Md., D.C.; inactive Pa., Mass. Sr. resident in medicine VA Med. Ctr., Boston, 1969-70, chief resident in medicine, 1970-71; Harvard Clin. and Rsch. fellow in pulmonary diseases Mass. Gen. Hosp., Boston, 1971-72; asst. chief med. svc. VA Med. Ctr., Washington, 1972-75, acting chief med. svc., 1975-76, chief pulmonary disease sect., 1976-94; instr. in medicine Boston U. Sch. of Medicine, Tufts u. Sch. Medicine, Boston, 1970-71; clin. and rsch. fellow in pulmonary diseases Harvard U. Sch. of Medicine, Mass. Gen. Hosp., Boston, 1971-72; clin. asst. prof. medicine Georgetown U., Washington, 1975-77; asst. prof. medicine George Washington U. Sch. of Medicine and Health Scis., Washington, 1972-75, assoc. prof., 1975-81, prof. medicine, 1981—, dir. divsn. pulmonary diseases and allergy, 1978-93; assoc. chmn. dept. medicine George Washington U. Med. Ctr., Washington, 1986-89; cons. in pulmonary diseases The Washington Hosp. Ctr., Washington, D.C., 1977—, Will Rogers Inst., White Plains, N.Y., 1980—, U.S. Dept. Labor, Washington, 1980—, Walter Reed Army Med. Ctr., Washington, 1987; rep. Am. Coll. Chest Physicians to Am. Registry Pathology, Washington, 1981-92; numerous radio tv appearances on Health Oriented Programs; invited lectr. in U.S., Russia, Jordan; chmn., mem. many coms. George Washington U. Sch. of Medicine, George Washington Med. Ctr., VA Med. Ctr., Washington; med. chest cons. in attempted assasination of former Pres. Regan. Author: (books): Clinical Assessment of Patients with Pulmonary Disease, 1986; co-author: (with A.E. Medinger) Handbook of Pulmonary Emergencies, 1986, (with others) Handbook of Pulmonary Drug Therapy, 1993, (with Witorsch, P.) Air Pollution and Lung Disease in Adults, 1994; contbr. numerous articles to profl jours. including Med. Clin. N. Am., Chest, So. Med. Jour., Am. Jour. Cardiology, Jour. Am. Med. Assn., Clin. Rsch., Am. Rev. Respiratory Disease, Am. Lung Assn. Bull., Clin. Notes on Respiratory Diseases, Jour. Nuclear Medicine, Drug Therapy; presented abstracts at over 13 profl. meetings; reviewer for Chest, Am. Review Respiratory Diseases. Lt. cmmdr. U.S. Pub. Health Svc., 1966-68. Decorated Cavaliere in Order of Merit, Republic of Italy, 1983; nominated for Golden Apple award by med. students Geo. Washington Sch. of Medicine, Phila., 1977; recipient cert. appreciation D.C. Lung Assn., 1983. Fellow Am. Coll. Physicians (coun. critical care 1983-85), Am. Coll. Chest Physicians (gov. D.C., coun. of govs. 1989-96); mem. Am. Thoracic Soc. (exec. com. D.C. chpt. 1978, 85, 89, mem. adv. com. tuberculosis control, 1978-84, pres. D.C. chpt. 1981-83), Nat. Assn. VA Physicians (sec. 1987-89, v.p. 1989-91, pres. 1992—), Internat. Lung Found. (pres. 1991—). Office: Geo Washington U 2150 Pennsylvania Ave NW Washington DC 20037

SPAGNUOLO, PASQUALINA MARIE, rehabilitation nurse; b. Phila., Jan. 21, 1942; d. Charles and Lena (Damiano) Caruolo; children: Louis, Charles, Jason. Lic. practical nurse diploma, Salem (N.J.) Community Coll., 1985; BSN, Widener U., Chester, Pa., 1989. Lic. practical nurse, Del., N.J., Pa.; RN, Del., N.J., Pa. Practical nurse A.I. Dupont Rehab. Hosp., Wilmington, Del.; med. sec. Underwood Meml. Hosp., Woodbury, N.J., nurse's aide; pvt. duty nurse, Mt. Ephraim, N.J. Merit scholar Widener U., 1985-86, Charlotte Newcomb scholar, 1986-87; recipient Eleanore O. Dower award, 1988.

SPAIDE, RICHARD FREDERICK, ophthalmologist; b. Allentown, Pa., Nov. 19, 1955; s. Frederick and Dorothy Spaide; m. Wai Chang Ho, May 25, 1985; children: Theodore, Christopher, Emily. BS, Muhlenberg U., 1977; MD, Jefferson Med. Coll., 1981. Diplomate Am. Bd. Ophthalmology. Resident in ophthalmology St. Vincent's Hosp., N.Y.C., 1982-85; chief ophthalmologist Landstuhl (Germany) Army Regional Med. Ctr., 1986-89; fellow in retina Manhattan Eye, Ear, Throat Hosp., N.Y.C., 1989-90; pvt. practice ophthalmologist N.Y.C., 1990—; ophthalmologist Vitreous, Retina, Macula Cons. of N.Y., N.Y.C., 1994—; clin. asst. prof. N.Y. Med. Coll., N.Y.C., 1993—. Med. advisor Jour. Ophthalmic Photography; contbr. chpts. to books and articles to profl. jours.; inventor in field. Named one of the best ophthalmologist in N.Y. The Best Doctors N.Y. Metro Area, 1994, 96. Fellow Am. Acad. Ophthalmology; mem. Am. Uveitis Soc., Macula Soc., Vitreous Soc., Nat. Assn. for Visually Handicapped (bd. med. dirs. 1995—), Assn. for Rsch. in Vision and Ophthalmology, N.Y. Soc. Clin. Ophthalmology, N.Y. Med. Soc., N.Y. Ophthalmol. Soc. Home: 1365 York Ave New York NY 10021 Office: Ste 417 36 Seventh Ave New York NY 10011

SPANGLER, LORNA CARRIE, pharmacy technician; b. San Jose, Calif., Feb. 4, 1938; d. Earl Albert and Elsie Carol (Lincoln) LaPorte; children: Kirk Earl, Eric Clair, David Paul, Linda Jean Spangler-Whiting. AA, Monterey Peninsula Coll., 1958; AS in Pharmacy Tech., Santa Ana (Calif.) Coll., 1982; BSBA, Calif. State U., Long Beach, 1986, MS in Vocat. Edn., 1992. Registered pharmacy technician, Calif.; cert. Pharmacy Technician Certification Bd., 1995; cert. C.C. instr., Calif. Pharmacy technician Meml. Med. Ctr., Long Beach, Calif., 1974-77, technician coord., 1979-87; pharmacy technician Hoag Meml. Hosp., Newport Beach, Calif., 1987-92, Sharp Health Care, Murrieta, Calif., 1992—; preceptor Pharmacy Technician Interns, 1992—; accreditation team Am. Bur. Health Edn. Schs., 1987-91; adv. com. Cerritos (Calif.) Coll., 1982-87; speaker in field. Mem. Assn. of Pharmacy Technicians (founder, treas. 1989-91), Valley Computer Soc. (founder 1991), So. Calif. Assn. Pharmacy Technicians (treas. 1990-92, sec. 1992-96, pres. 1996—), Am. Vocat. Assn., Calif. Soc. of Hosp. Pharmacy (task force mem. 1982, nominating com. technician div., 1988), Omicron Tau Theta (Nu chpt. 1988). Office: Sharp Health Care Murrieta 25500 Medical Center Dr Murrieta CA 92562-5965

SPANGLER, MICHAEL D., chemist; b. Lancaster, Pa., Aug. 22, 1961. BS in Chemistry, Juniata Coll., 1983. Rsch. tech. Temple U., Phila., 1984; analyst Warner-Lambert/Parke-Davis, Lititz, Pa., 1984-87; rsch. scientist Purdue Frederick Rsch. Ctr., Yonkers, N.Y., 1987-89, Schering-Plough Rsch. Inst., Kenilworth, N.J., 1989—; presenter poster at Ea. Analytical Symposium, 1992. Mem. N.J. Chromatography Topical Group, The Lab. Robotic Interest Group of N.J., The Chromatography Forum of Delaware Valley (life). Office: Schering-Plough Rsch Inst 2000 Galloping Hill Rd Kenilworth NJ 07033

SPANGOLO, WALTER, oncologist; b. Pollenza, Italy, July 16, 1944; s. Giovanni Spagnolo and Maria La Torre; m. Antonella Romeo, July 28, 1970 (div. 1983); children: Sertio, Stefano; m. Giuliana Composto, Feb. 18, 1985. Degree in biology, U. ME, Italy, 1980; MD, U. CT, Italy, 1993. Diplomate Italian Bd. Medicine. Cons. Boehringer Mannh, Milan, Italy, 1969-83; sci. dir. Sorin Biomedica, Saluggia, Italy, 1983-85, sci. project leader, 1985-93; project leader Sorin Biomedica Cardio, Saluggia, 1993—. Mem. AIMN, EANM. Home: Via Paolo Gaidano 8, 10137 Turin Italy Office: Sorin Biomedica Cardio, Stradda Per Crescentino, 13040 Saluggia Piemonte Italy

SPANN, JAMES FLETCHER, cardiologist, medical educator; b. Dothan, Ala., Nov. 21, 1935; s. James Fletcher Sr. and Elizabeth Daffin (Smith) S.; m. Emory Jo Harris, Dec. 16, 1956 (div. 1975); children: William Steadman, Elizabeth Spann Duggan; m. Constance Suzanne Roussin, June 13, 1976. Student, The Citadel, 1954-56, Emory U., 1956-57; MD, Emory U., 1961. Intern in medicine Mass. Gen. Hosp./Harvard Med. Sch., Boston, 1961-62, asst. resident in medicine, 1962-63; postdoctoral cardiology fellow Nat. Heart Inst., NIH, Bethesda, Md., 1963-65, spl. fellow cardiology br., 1965-66; sr. investigator, attending physician, cons. cardiologist NIH, Bethesda, 1966-68; assoc. prof. medicine and physiology U. Calif., Davis, 1968-70, chief cardiovascular diagnosis, 1968-70, asst. chief sect. cardiovascular medicine, 1968-70; chief cardiology sect., prof. medicine Temple U. Sch. Medicine, Phila., 1970-85; founding dir. Gazes Cardiac Rsch. Inst. Med. U. S.C., Charleston, 1985-94, dir. cardiology divsn., 1985-96, prof. medicine, 1985—, exec. assoc. dean Coll. Medicine, 1996—; cons. lectr. in cardiovascular disease Naval Regional Med. Ctr., Dept. of Navy, Phila., 1976-80; clin. asst. prof. medicine Georgetown U., Washington, 1967-68; asst. coord. Heart, Regional Med. Programs of Area II, Davis, 1969-70. Mem. editl. bd. Am. Jour. Cardiology, 1972-78, editl. cons., 1978—; editl. cons. Chest, 1971, Heart and Lung, 1971-73, Am. Journ. Physiology, 1979—, Circulation Rsch., 1982—, New Eng. Jour. Medicine, 1983—, mem. editl. bd. Heart Failure, 1985—; editor: Modern Concepts of Cardiovascular Disease, 1988-91; contbr. over 175 articles to profl. publs. Bd. govs. Heart Assn. Southeastern Pa., 1971-84, mem. profl. edn. com., 1970-74, chmn. profl. edn. com., 1971-72, v.p., 1979-80, mem. rsch. com., 1970-78, chmn. rsch. com., 1978-80, 83-84, mem. rehab. com., 1976-77, mem. ctrl. program com., 1979-82, pres.-elect 1980-81, exec. com., 1980-84, pres., 1981-82. Sr. asst. surgeon USPHS, 1966-68. Grantee Temple U., 1970-71, NIH, 1970-73, 71-72, 71-76, 76-79, 83-86, 83-87, 70-86, 74-84, Deborah Hosp. Found., 1976-77, W.W. Smith Charitable Trust, 1980-81, Delaware chpt. Am. Heart Assn., 1983-84, MacNeil Pharm., 1981, Hoescht-roussel, 1981, Burroughs Wellcome Co., 1986. Mem. ACP, AAAS, Am. Coll. Cardiology (mem. nat. com. for continuing med. edn. 1971-74, nat. extramural continuing edn. com. 1990—, mem. nat. young investigators' awards com. 1984-90), Am. Fedn. Cin. Rsch., Am. Heart Assn. (mem. nat. com. for sci. sessions 1970-73, coun. rep. for State of Pa. 1980-83), Am. Physiol. Soc., Am. Soc. Pharmacology and Exptl. Therapeutics, Assn. Univ. Cardiologists, Coll. Physicians Phila., Coun. on Circulation of Am. Heart Assn., Coun. on Clin. Cardiology of Am. Heart Assn. (mem. exec. com. 1971-73, mem. nat. com. for clin. sessions program 1970-73, chmn. nat. com. for clin. sessions program 1971-73), N.Y. Acad. Scis., Assn. Profs. of Cardiology, Alpha Omega Alpha. Office: Med U SC Dean's Office Sch Medicine 171 Ashley Ave Charleston SC 29425

SPANN, MILTON GRAHAM, JR., psychology educator; b. Greenville, S.C., Mar. 31, 1942; s. Milton Graham and Sara Margaret (Chalmers) S.; m. Nancy Lee Gray, Aug. 16, 1964; 1 child, Milton Graham III. BA, St. Andrews Presbyn. Coll., Laurinburg, N.C., 1964; MA, Presbyn. Sch. Christian Edn., Richmond, Va., 1966; PhD, U. Tex., 1976. Ordained elder Presbyn. Ch. U.S.A., 1976. Dir. student activities Montreat (N.C.)-Anderson Coll., 1964-69; dir. advancement studies program Southeastern Community Coll., Whiteville, N.C., 1969-74; dir. Nat. Ctr. for Devel. Edn., Appalachian State U., Boone, N.C., 1976-88, prof. higher edn., 1982-88, prof. human devel. and psychol. counseling, 1988—; cons. to over 300 colls. and univs., 1966—. Editor Jour. Devel. Edn., 1978—. Trustee Blowing Rock (N.C.) Stage Co., 1987-89. Recipient Outstanding Svc. award Nat. Assn. Devel. Edn., 1981, Outstanding Contbn. award Assn. for Religious and Value Issues in Counseling, 1992. Democrat. Office: Appalachian State U Dept Human Devel and Psy Counsel Boone NC 28608

SPARACINO, MICHAEL LOVIS, medical program director, osteopath, educator; b. Owatonna, Minn., Apr. 4, 1957; s. Dominic Leonard and Maxine Louise (Parsons) S.; m. Liz Ann Scott, May 20, 1983; 1 child, Christopher Mahlon. BS, North Ctrl. Coll., Naperville, Ill., 1979; DO, Kirksville (Md.) Coll., 1984. Diplomate Am. Bd. Family Practice. Dir. emergency svcs. USAF, Osan, Korea, 1987-88; asst. prof. USAF, Scott AFB, Ill., 1988-91; high-risk obstetrics fellow U. N.C., Asheville, 1991-92; dir. obstetrical fellowship Deaconess Health Sys., St. Louis, 1992-95; dir. family practice residency North Iowa Mercy Health Ctr., Mason City, 1995—; cons. Managed Prescription Svcs., St. Louis, 1972-95, Legis. Affairs Iowa Academy, Des Moines, 1995—. Contbr. chpts. to books. Dir. North Iowa Transition Ctr., Mason City, 1995. To major, USAF, 1984-92. Recipient Meritorious Svc. medal USAF, 1991. Fellow Am. Acad. Family Physicians (Mead-Johnson award 1985); mem. AMA, AAAS, Am. Osteo. Assn., Iowa Acad. Family Physicians, Mo. Acad. Sci., Sigma Sigma Pi, Psi Sigma Alpha. Roman Catholic. Office: North Iowa Mercy Health Ctr 101 South Taylor Mason City IA 50401

SPARBERG, MARSHALL STUART, gastroenterologist, educator; b. Chgo., May 20, 1936; s. Max Shane and Mildred Rose (Haffron) S.; m. Eve Gaymont Enda, Mar. 15, 1987. B.A., Northwestern U., 1957, M.D., 1960. Intern Evanston Hosp., Ill., 1960-61; resident in internal medicine Barnes Hosp., St. Louis, 1961-63; fellow U. Chgo., 1963-65; practice medicine specializing in gastroenterolgy Chgo., 1967—; asst. prof. medicine Northwestern U., 1967-72, assoc. prof., 1972-80, prof. clin. medicine, 1980—; instr. Washington U., St. Louis, 1961-63, U. Chgo., 1963-65. Author: Ileostomy Care, 1969, Primer of Clinical Diagnosis, 1972, Ulcerative Colitis, 1978, Inflammatory Bowel Disease, 1982; contbr. numerous articles to profl. jours. Pres. Fine Arts Music Found., 1974-76, Crohn's Disease and Colitis Found. of Am., pres. Ill. chpt., 1994-97; bd. dirs. Lyric Opera Guild, 1974—, Chamber Music Soc. North Shore Chgo., 1984—; physician to Chgo. Symphony Orch., 1981—. With USAF, 1965-67. Named Outstanding Tchr. Northwestern U. Med. Sch., 1972. Mem. AMA, ACP, Am. Gastroent. Assn., Am. Coll. Gastroent. (bd. govs.), Chgo. Med. Soc., Chgo. Soc. Internal Medicine, Chgo. Soc. Gastroenterology (pres.), Chgo. Soc. Gastrointestinal Endoscopy (pres.). Democrat. Jewish. Office: 676 N Saint Clair St Ste 1525 Chicago IL 60611

SPARGO, BENJAMIN H., educator, renal pathologist; b. Six Mile Run, Pa., Aug. 11, 1919; s. Benjamin H. and Lillian (Rankin) S.; m. Barbara Scollard, Mar. 12, 1942; children—Janet, Patricia. B.S. in Biol. Scis, U. Chgo., 1948, M.S. in Pathology, 1952, M.D. with honors, 1952. Intern Univ. Hosp., Ann Arbor, Mich., 1953-54; resident pathology U. Chgo. Med. Sch., 1954-55, mem. faculty, 1954—, prof. renal pathology, 1964-95; prof. pathology emeritus, 1995—, assoc. chmn. dept., 1974-80; cons. Armed Forces Inst. Pathology, 1975-79, Midwest Regional Organ Bank of Ill., 1989-94. Served with USAAF, 1941-46. Recipient Research Career award Nat. Heart Inst., 1964. Mem. Internat. Acad. Pathology (chmn. edn. com. 1975-77). Home: 5719 S Kenwood Ave Chicago IL 60637-1743

SPARKMAN, MARY M., medical, surgical and rehabilitation nurse; b. Ft. Leavenworth, Kans., Jan. 8, 1949; d. Ancil Woodrow and Margaret Louise (Conners) Hopper; m. Paul Aus Sparkman, Oct. 5, 1989; children: Michelle Marie Bingham, Andrea Marlene Bingham. Student, Cameron U., Lawton, Okla., 1980-82; BSN with distinction, U. Okla., 1984. Cert. in chemotherapy, fetal monitoring, arterial blood gases, coronary care, CPR instr. Mem. crisis intervention team Gt. Plains Hosp., Lawton; charge nurse spinal cord unit O'Donoghue Rehab. Inst., Oklahoma City; clin. nurse Lawton Indian Hosp., USPHS; therapy coord. Infusion Svcs., Lawton, Okla.; clin. nurse, charge nurse Reynold's Army Community Hosp., Ft. Sill, Okla. With U.S. Army, 1970-73. Mem. Nat. League Nursing, Okla. Nurses Assn., Golden Key, Phi Kappa Phi. Office: PO Box 2094 Lawton OK 73502-2094

SPARKS, BEVERLY JEAN, nurse, medical products development executive; b. Bakersfield, Calif., Aug. 4, 1933; d. LeRoy Glen and Dorothy Evelyn (Foust) Sparks. Diploma, San Jose State U., 1954; BSN, Old Dominion U., 1972; MA in Edn., Pepperdine U., 1977; postgrad., Clayton Coll. Natural Medicine, Birmingham, Ala., 1995—. RN, Calif. Oper. rm. supr. U.S. Navy, 1955-60, 64-82; nurse cons. Devon Industries, Inc., Chatsworth, Calif., 1982-84; pres., CEO Sparco, Inc., Vista, Calif., 1984—; lectr. in field. Patentee surg. instrument system sterilization and transport, surg. leg holding device. Capt. USN, 1978-82. Decorated Meritorious Svc. medal, Commendation medal Achievement medal. Mem. Assn. for Advancement of Med. Instrumentation (sterilization guidelines reviewer 1996). Office: Sparco Inc 2141 A&B Industrial Ct Vista CA 92083

SPATZ, BRUCE ANTHONY, physician assistant; b. Wausau, Wis., May 30, 1961; s. John Anthony and Gertrude Dorothy (Lenard) S.; m. Michelle Renee Stiles, Oct. 12, 1985; children: Kelsey Lauren, Tyler John. BS in Health Sci. as Physician Asst., Wichita State U., 1984. Cert. physician asst. Physician asst. Family Physicians S.C., Wausau, 1984; physician asst. cardiology Galichia Cardiovascular, Wichita, 1985-87, FHP Internat., Fountain Valley, Calif., 1987-90; physician asst. orthops. Bone & Joint Clinic, Wausau, 1990-94; physician asst. cardiology Cardiovascular Assocs. of No. Wis. S.C., Wausau, 1994—. Fellow Am. Acad. Physician Assts., Wis. Acad. Physician Assts. Roman Catholic. Home: 1235 Elm St Wausau WI 54401 Office: Cardiovascular Assocs No Wi 520 N 28th Ave Wausau WI 54401

SPEAR, CARL HUBBELL, optometrist, lecturer; b. Glasgow, Ky.; s. Carl H. and Sandra M. (McMurtrey) S.; m. Nadja Ivette Robles; 1 child, Jurgen Carl. BS, Western Ky. U., 1987; OD, U. Ala., 1991. Chief Kelly Hill Optometry Clinic, Ft. Benning, Ga., 1991-93; staff optometrist Martin Army Hosp., Ft. Benning, Ga., 1993-94; primary care residency Northeastern State U., 1994-95; chief liason svcs. Specialty Care Clinic Northeastern State U. Coll. of Optometry, Tahlequah, Okla., 1995—, dir. continuing edn., 1995—; optometric lectr. various locations, 1994—; co-cons. Am. Airlines, 1995—. Co-author, editor Differential Diagnosis of Ocula-Disease, 1996; contbr. articles to profl. jours. Capt. U.S. Army, 1991-94. Mem. Am. Optometric Assn., Am. Acad. Optometry, Armed Forces Optometric Soc., Mason. Home: 416 Joe Carrol St Tahlequah OK 74464 Office: NSU Coll Optometry 1001 N Grand Ave Tahlequah OK 74464

SPEAR, LEONARD, optometrist; b. New Haven, Conn., July 4, 1926; s. David and Lena (Janoff) S.; m. Harriet D. Dolgow, June 20, 1954; children: Robin, Gayle. OD, No. Ill. Coll. Optometry, Chgo., 1949. Optometrist Branford (Conn.) Optometric Assocs., 1951—. Patentee Lensco Meter, 1955. Pres. Branford United Way, 1980-81, Internat. Ctr. of New Haven, 1980-81. With U.S. Army/USAF, 1944-45. Named Citizen of Yr., Branford Review newspaper, 1980. Mem. Rotary (pres. Branford club 1967-68), Elm City Banjo Soc., Conn. Soc. Optometrists (pres. 1967-68), Am. Optometric Assn. Home: 33 Quarry Dock Rd Branford CT 06405 Office: Branford Optometric Assocs 60 Montowese St Branford CT 06405

SPEAR, PAUL WILLIAM, physician, educator; b. Balt., Nov. 3, 1908; s. Sidney Paul and Edna (Lauer) S.; m. Belle Kazan, June 30, 1944 (dec. Dec. 1972); children: Susan, Margaret Ellen, Michael Lauer; m. Belle Kasofsky Ripps, Jan. 11, 1974. BA, Johns Hopkins U., 1930, MD, 1934. Diplomate Am. Bd. Internal Medicine. Intern medicine Sinai Hosp., Balt., 1934-35, asst. resident, 1935-36, chief resident, 1936-37; asst. chief and chief of medicine VA, Bklyn., 1947-63; dir. medicine Morrisania-Montefiore Affiliation, Bronx, N.Y., 1963-76; med. dir. Queens (N.Y) County Profl. Standards Rev. Orgn., 1977-85, Queens County div. Island Peer Rev. Orgn., 1984-86; attending physician Montefiore Hosp., Bronx, 1963—; prof. medicine emeritus Albert Einstein Coll. Medicine, Bronx, 1976—. Contbr. articles to profl. jours. Lt. col. U.S. Army, 1941-45. Fellow ACP; mem. Am. Soc. Hematology, N.Y. Acad. Medicine, Am. Fedn. for Clin. Rsch., N.Y. Soc. for the Study of Blood, Physicians Forum (pres. 1971-72), Phi Beta Kappa. Democrat. Jewish. Home: 55 Manhasset Woods Rd Manhasset NY 11030-2612

SPEARS, CAROLYN SULLIVAN, laboratory director, medical technologist; b. Bainbridge, Ga., June 1, 1952; d. William Kermit and Belle Carroll (Trulock) Sullivan; m. Danny Wayne Spears, Mar. 25, 1974 (div. Sep. 1994); children: Andrew E., Daniel J., David A. BS in Med. Tech., Troy State U., 1974. Cert. med. technologist Am. Soc. Clin. Pathologists. Med. technologist Bapt. Hosp., Pensacola, Fla., 1974-78; med. technologist L.V. Stabler Mem. Hosp., Greenville, Ala., 1978-80, hematology supr., 1980-86, PRN, 1986-92, lab. mgr., dir., 1992—; lectr. cell morphology, various schs., Greenville, 1992—. Sec. Greenville Middle Sch., 1995-96; v.p. Bapt. Hill Sch. PTA, Greenville, 1988. Mem. Clin. Lab. Mgrs. Assn., Ala. Lab. Mgrs. Assn. Baptist. Home: 109 Northgate Rd Greenville AL 36037 Office: L.V. Stabler Mem Hosp Hwy 10 West Greenville AL 36037

SPEARS, MARIAN CADDY, dietetics and institutional management educator; b. East Liverpool, Ohio, Jan. 12, 1921; d. Frederick Louis and Marie (Jerman) Caddy; m. Sholto M. Spears, May 29, 1959. BS, Case Western Res. U., 1942, MS, 1947; PhD, U. Mo., 1971. Chief dietitian Bellefaire Children's Home, Cleve., 1942-53; head dietitian Drs. Hosp., Cleve., 1953-57; assoc. dir. dietetics Barnes Hosp., St. Louis, 1957-59; asst. prof. U. Ark., Fayetteville, 1959-68; assoc. prof. U. Mo., Columbia, 1971-75; prof., head dept. hotel, restaurant, instn. mgmt. and dietetics Kans. State U., Manhattan, 1975-89; cons. dietitian small hosps. and nursing homes; cons. dietetic edn. Author: Foodservice Organizations Textbook, 3d edit., 1995; contbr. articles to profl. jours. Mem. Am. Dietetic Assn. (Copher award 1989), Am. Sch. Foodsvc. Assn., Food Systems Mgmt. Edn. Coun., Soc. Advancement of Foodsvc. Rsch., Nat. Restaurant Assn., Coun. Hotel, Restaurant, Inst. Mgmt. Edn., Manhattan C. of C., Sigma Xi, Gamma Sigma Delta, Omicron Nu, Phi Kappa Phi. Home: 1522 Williamsburg Dr Manhattan KS 66502-0408 Office: Kans State U 105 Justin Hall Manhattan KS 66506-1400

SPEASE, LOREN WILLIAM, chiropractor; b. Luverne, Minn., Sept. 15, 1930; s. Chester Clair and Ethelwyn Mary (Coon) S.; m. Darlene Mae Braa, Apr. 15, 1953; children: Bryce, Craig, Laura, Julie. D of Chiropractic, Northwestern Coll. Chiropractic, 1958. Enlisted USMC, 1948, advanced through grades to staff sgt., discharged, 1952; ptnr. Spease Tire Shop, Luverne, Minn., 1952-55; founder, owner Spease Chiropractic Back Care Ctr., Brookings, S.D., 1958—. Judge advocate Dakota Marine Detachment, USMC League, Sioux Falls, 1992—. 2d lt. Minn. Nat. Guard and USAR. Mem. S.D. Chiropractors Assn. (chmn., resolutions com. 1958—), Sioux Valley Chiropractic Soc. (past pres.), Habitat for Humanity, Elks, Am. Legion, Chi Omega Phi. Republican. Baptist. Home: 404 W Wye Mesa Brookings SD 57006-4533 Office: Spease Chiropractic Back Care Ctr 406 4th St Brookings SD 57006

SPECA, JOHN MICHAEL, orthopaedic surgeon; b. Chicago Heights, Ill., Sept. 22, 1953; s. Angelo William and Frances Mae (Saculla) S.; m. Deborah Stier, Feb. 10, 1979; children: Michael, Matthew, Andrew, Thomas, Kristen. BS in Biology, Loyola U., Chgo., 1975; MD, Loyola U., 1979. Diplomate Am. Bd. Orthopedic Surgery. Orthopedic surgeon St. Mary's Hosp., Kankakee, Ill., 1985-86, Riverside Hosp., Kankakee, 1985-86, Galesburg (Ill.) Cottage Hosp., 1986-94, St. Mary's Med. Ctr., Galesburg, 1986-94, Kewanee (Ill.) Hosp., 1988-94, Mercer County Joint Twp. Cmty. Hosp., Coldwater, Ohio, 1994—; mem. med. staff U.S. Ski Team, Park City, Utah, 1992—. Bd. dirs. YMCA, Galesburg, 1991-94. Fellow Am. Acad. Orthopedic Surgeons; mem. Am. Coll. Sports Medicine, Ohio State Med. Soc., Mercer County Med. Soc., Ohio Orthopaedic Soc., Mid-Am. Orthopaedic Soc. Roman Catholic. Office: Celina Orthopedic & Sports Med Ctr Inc 950 S Main St Celina OH 45822-2417

SPECHT, CARL FREDERICK, hospital chaplain; b. St. Louis, Nov. 25, 1947; s. Charles W. and Jeanette Ann (Beehan) S.; m. Deborah Jane Simonton. BA in Psychology, Fla. Internat. U., Miami, 1973; MDiv in Theology magna cum laude, Denver Bapt. Theol. Sem., 1979; Clin. Pastoral Edn. degree, Washington U. Med. Ctr., 1986; CPE, Prairie View Mental Health Ctr, 1987. Tchr. Adams City Christian Sch., Denver, 1979-81, Mill Rd. Christian Sch., Evansville, Ind., 1981-85; hosp. chaplain intern Washington U. Med. Ctr., St. Louis, 1986, Prairie View Mental Health Ctr., Newton, Kans., 1986-87; hosp. chaplain Charter Hosp., Wichita, Kans., 1987-88, Camarillo (Calif.) State Hosp., 1989—, Charter Hosp., Thousand Oaks, Calif., 1990-91; pastoral counselor Grace Bapt. Ch., Santa Barbara, Calif., 1993—; guest lectr. psychology internships program, Camarillo State Hosp., 1991-92, hosp. chaplain grief counseling Trauma Response Team, 1992-93. Mem. Am. Assn. Christian Counselors. Home: Santa Barbara CA 93110 Office: Camarillo State Hosp PO Box 6022 Camarillo CA 93011

SPECIAN, ROBERT DAVID, cell biology educator; b. Niagara Falls, N.Y., Apr. 25, 1950; s. Robert William and Abbie (Brantingham) S.; m. Janis Gabriel, Oct. 1, 1994; children: Victoria, Robert Jr. BS, So. Meth. U., 1972, MS, 1974; PhD, Tulane U., 1980. Asst. prof. La. State U. Sch. Medicine, Shreveport, 1981-85, assoc. prof., 1985-90, prof., 1990—. Author: (with others) Biology of Bats of the New World Family Phyllostomatidae, 1977, The Biology of Hymenolepis diminuta, 1980; contbr. articles to profl. jours. Grantee NIH, 1988-91, 91-96, Cystic Fibrosis Found., 1982-84, 87-89; Cystic Fibrosis Postdoctoral fellow, 1979-81. Mem. Am. Soc. Cell Biologists, Am. Assn. Anatomists, N.Y. Acad. Scis., Am. Microscopical Soc., Am. Soc. Parasitologists. Office: La State U Sch Medicine 1501 Kings Hwy Shreveport LA 71103-4228

SPECK, DAVID DEAN, ophthalmologist; b. Auburn, N.Y., Mar. 19, 1953; s. Michael Stephen and Anne Margaret (Sopohak) S. AB in Chemistry, Cornell U., 1975, MD, 1979. Diplomate Am. Bd. Ophthalmology. Intern in medicine M. Bassett Hosp., Cooperstown, N.Y., 1979-80; resident ophthalmology St. Luke's-Roosevelt Hosp., N.Y.C., 1980-83; pvt. practice ophthalmology Auburn, N.Y., 1983—; pvt. practice cons. med. computing, Auburn, 1983—; chair utilization rev. com. Auburn Meml. Hosp., 1985—. Vice chair Cmty. Preservation Com., Auburn, 1989—; trustee, auditor St. Nicholas Ch., Auburn, 1989-93. Fellow Am. Acad. Ophthalmology; mem. AMA, Med. Soc. of the State of N.Y., Cayuga County Med. Soc., Golden Glow of Christmas Past, TESLA Coil Builders Assn. Office: 35 Franklin St Auburn NY 13021-2785

SPECK, HILDA, retired social services administrator; b. Stalybridge, Cheshire, Eng., Mar. 2, 1916; came to U.S., 1923; d. John Robert and Rose Ethel (Tymns) Smith; m. Willmot Hilton Speck, Sept. 4, 1937 (dec. Jan 1968); foster children: Barbara Ann Beranek Renfrow, Winifred June Beranek Aguilar. Student, Community Coll., Flint, Mich. Lic. social worker, Mich. Founder of Social Svc. Dept. and dir. social svcs. The Salvation Army, Flint, 1945-86; mem. establishing com. 4C Child Care Agy.; life mem. Salvation Army Adv. Bd., Flint, Mich. Acting founding Safe House for domestic violence victims, Flint, 1976-80; mem. convalescent home com. Ch. Women United; adminstr. clothing distbn.; dir. disaster rehab. program Salvation Army; mem. original planning com. Planned Parenthood Orgn.; mem. aux. McLaren Regional Med. Ctr., Salvation Army, Flint, League of Mercy, Ch. Salvation Army, Centennial Planning Com., Flint; mem. Genesee County CD; mem. organizing com. Big Sisters Agy., Flint, Shelter for Homeless Women. Recipient Hands of Mercy award The Salvation Army, 1967, Centennial Youth award The Salvation Army, 1965, 20 Yr. Svc. award Big. Bros. of Genesee County, award for exceptional svc. The Salvation Army, 1993, Mich. Cmty. Svc. award Ky. Col's. Way, 1996; named Women of Week local radio sta., 1957, Mich. winner Sr. Citizens KFC Colonel's award program for comty. svc., 1996. Mem. Coun. Social Agys., Genesee County Commn. on Aging (v.p. 1971—), GLS Counties Health Planning Coun. Bd., Genesee County Emergency Task Force, Zonta. Salvation Army. Home: 1041 Leisure Dr Flint MI 48507-4058

SPECK, LISA BETH, internist; b. Phila., Jan. 2, 1953; d. Seymour and Ruth Barbara (Festenstein) Marshak; m. John Peyton Speck, Aug. 25, 1974; children: Amanda Renée, Adam Peyton. BS, U. Mich., 1973; MD, Wayne State U., 1977. Diplomate Am. Bd. Internal Medicine, Am. Bd Geriat. Intern, resident William Beaumont Hosp., Royal Oak, Mich., 1977-80; physician Woodland Clinic, Novi, Mich., 1980-85; pvt. practice Farmington Hills, Mich., 1985—; tching faculty staff svc. William Beaumont Hosp., Royal Oak, Mich., 1985—, tching faculty acute care clinic, 1990—; clin. asst. prof. Wayne State U. Sch. Medicine, Detroit, 1995—, preceptor primary care medicine, 1985—; presenter in field. Contbr. articles to profl. jours. Recipient Top Doc award Detroit Monthly Mag., 1996. Fellow ACP; mem. Am. Soc. Internal Medicine, Mich. State Med. Soc., Mich. Soc. Internal Medicine, Oakland County Med. Soc. Office: 32905 12 Mile Rd #400 Farmington Hills MI 48334

SPECK, ROSS VICTOR, retired psychiatrist; b. St. Catharines, Ont., Can., Oct. 22, 1927; s. Victor E. and Evelyn C. (Fritshaw) S.; m. Joan L. Speck. MD, U. Toronto, 1951. Clin. prof. dept. psychiatry Jefferson Med. Coll., Phila., 1980-93. Co-author: The New Families, 1972, Family Networks, 1973; co-editor: Therapeutic Intervention, 1982. Capt. AUS, 1956-58. Fellow Royal Coll. Physicians, Am. Psychiatric Assn., Am. Assn. Marriage and Family Therapists, Am. Soc. Psychoanalytic Physicians. Home: 1350 Janet Dr Mount Joy PA 17552-9027

SPECK, WILLIAM T., physician, health facility administrator. MD. Pres., CEO Presbyn. Hosp. in City of N.Y./Columbia-Presbyn. Med. Ctr., N.Y.C. Office: NY Presbyn Hosp Columbia-Presbyn Med Ctr New York NY 10032-3784

SPECTOR, HARVEY M., osteopathic physician; b. Phila., July 10, 1938; s. Philip and Sylvia (Rischall) S.; m. Rochelle Fleishman, June 16, 1963; children: Jill, Larry. DO, Phila. Coll. Osteo. Medicine, 1963. Osteopathic physician Phila., 1964—; preceptor Hershey (Pa.) Med. Sch., 1987—, Phila. Coll. Osteopathic Medicine, 1989—; assoc. prof. medicine Med. Coll. Pa., 1991—. Recipient Humanitarian award Chapel of Four Chaplains, Phila., 1984. Mem. Am. Osteo. Assn. (del.), Pa. Osteo. Med. Assn. (del.), Am. Acad. Osteo. Gen. Practitioners, Phila. County Osteo Med. Soc. Med. Club Phila., Abington Dolphins Aquatic Club (pres. 1984-86), B'nai B'rith. Jewish. Office: 1220 Cottman Ave Philadelphia PA 19111-3650

SPEICHER, CARL EUGENE, pathologist; b. Carbondale, Pa., Mar. 21, 1933; s. William Joseph and Elizabeth Marcella (Connolly) S.; m. Mary Louise Walsh, June 21, 1958; children: Carl E. Jr., Gregory, Erik. BS in Biology, King's Coll., 1954; MD, U. Pa., 1958; primary course in aeroship medicine, Sch. of Aerospace Medicine, Brooks AFB, Tex., 1969; fellowship in med. chemistry, SUNY, Syracuse, 1970-71. Diplomate Am. Bd. Pathology. Intern U. Pa. Hosp., Phila., 1958-63, resdient, 1959-63; chief lab. svcs. USAF Hosp., London, Eng., 1963-66, USAF Med. Ctr. Wright Patterson, Dayton, Ohio, 1966-79; dir. clin. labs. and chmn. dept. pathology Wilford Hall USAF Med. Ctr., San Antonio, Tex., 1971-77; prof. dept. pathology Ohio State U., Columbus, 1977—; co-dir. James Cancer Club James Hosp. and Rsch. Ctr., Columbus, 1990—; vice chair dept. pathology Ohio State Univ., Columbus, 1992—; dir. clin. svcs. Ohio State U. Med. Ctr., Columbus, 1977—. Co-author: Choosing Effective Laboratory Tests, 1983; author: (book) The Right Test 1st edit., 1990, 2d rev. edit., 1993. Col. USAF, 1963-77. Decorated Legion of Merit, 1977, USAF; fellowship in med. chemistry SUNY, Syracuse, 1970-71. Mem. AMA (Physicians Recognition award), Ohio Soc. Pathologists, Ctrl. Ohio Soc. Pathologists, Royal Soc. of Medicine (Eng.), Coll. of Am. Pathologists, Am. Soc. Clin. Pathologists, Alpha Omega Alpha. Office: Ohio State U Med Ctr Rm N 337 Doan Hall 410 W 10th Ave Columbus OH 43210

SPEIER, KAREN RINARDO, psychologist; b. New Orleans, Aug. 19, 1947; d. William Joseph Rinardo and Shirley Eva (Spreen) Christensen; m. Joe Max Sobotka, Nov. 27, 1970 (div. 1972); m. Anthony Herman Speier, May 29, 1982; children: Anthony Herman III, Austin Clay. Student, Vanderbilt U., 1965-67; BA, La. State U., New Orleans, 1969; MS, U. New Orleans, 1974; PhD, La. State U., 1985. Lic. psychologist, La. Tchr. spl. edn. Huntsville (Ala.) Achievement Sch., 1970-72; instr. neurology La. State U. Med. Ctr., New Orleans, 1972-78; clin. assoc. Dawson Psychol. Assocs., Baton Rouge, 1979-81; tchr. asst. dept. psychology La. State U., Baton Rouge, 1979-81; psychol. examiner La. Sch. for Deaf, Baton Rouge, 1979-80; psychology intern VA Med. Ctr., Martinez, Calif., 1981-82; psychology extern East La. State Hosp., Jackson, 1982-83; clin. assoc. Baton Rouge Psychol. Assocs., 1983-86, pvt. practice clin. psychology, 1986—; sr. neuropsychologist Rehab. Hosp. of Baton Rouge, 1995-96; sec. bd. dirs. Baton Rouge Employment Devel. Svcs., 1987-89; mem. psychology cons. com. Meadow Wood Hosp., Baton Rouge, 1987-89; mem. psychology adv. com. Parkland Hosp., Baton Rouge, 1989-92. Contbr. articles to profl. publs. Mem. steering com. Baton Rouge Stepfamily Support Group, 1983-90; tchr. St. James Episcopal Sunday Sch., Baton Rouge, 1984-86, 90-91, 92—). Mem. Orton Dyslexia Soc. (bd. dirs., pres. La. br.), Nat. Head Injury Found., Agenda For Children, Baton Rouge Area Soc. Psychologists, La. Psychol. Assn., Am. Psychology Assn., Internat. Soc. Child Abuse and Neglect, Mental Health Assn. La. Office: Ctr Psychol Resources 4521 Jamestown Ave Ste 2 Baton Rouge LA 70808-3234

SPEISER, ROBERT DOUGLAS, health care executive; b. Decatur, Ala., June 6, 1953; s. Marvin M. and Laura Dorothy (Green) S. BA, U. Pa., 1974; JD, U. Chgo., 1977, MBA, 1979. Counsel and sec. Goeken Systems, Inc., Chgo., 1979-80; v.p. Capitol Hardware Mfg. Co., Inc., Chgo., 1980; v.p. Health-Chem. Corp., N.Y.C., 1980-86, sr. v.p., 1986-94, exec. v.p., 1994—, also bd. dirs.; gen. mgr. Union Br. Corp., N.Y.C., 1982-83, pres., 1983-91, also bd. dirs.; pres. Hercon Labs. Corp., 1990—, also bd. dirs.; pres., CEO Transderm Labs. Corp., 1995—, also bd. dirs. Mem. ABA, Grand Prix Video Club, Phi Beta Kappa. Home: 205 W 57th St New York NY 10019 Office: Transderm Labs Corp 1212 Avenue Of The Americas New York NY 10036-1602

SPELLACY, WILLIAM NELSON, obstetrician, gynecologist, educator; b. St. Paul, May 10, 1934; s. Jack F. and Elmyra L. (Nelson) S.; m. Lynn Larsen; children: Kathleen Ann, Kimberly Joan, William Nelson. B.A., U. Minn., 1955, B.S., 1956, M.D., 1959. Diplomate: Am. Bd. Ob-Gyn, subsplty. cert. in maternal and fetal medicine. Intern Hennepin County Gen. Hosp., Mpls., 1959-60; resident U. Minn., Mpls., 1960-63; practice medicine specializing in ob-gyn. Mpls., 1963-67, Miami, Fla., 1967-73, Gainesville, Fla., 1973-79, Chgo., 1979-88; prof., head dept. U. Ill. Coll. Medicine, Chgo., 1979-88; prof., chmn. dept. U. So. Fla. Coll. Medicine, Tampa, 1988—; prof. dept. obstetrics and gynecology U. Miami, 1967-73; prof., chmn. dept. U. Fla., 1974-79. Contbr. articles to med. jours. Mem. AMA, Am. Gynecol. Soc., Am. Assn. Obstetricians and Gynecologists, Am. Gynecol. and Obstet. Soc., Soc. Gynecol. Investigation, Am. Coll. Obstetricians and Gynecologists, Endocrine Soc., Am. Fertility Soc., Assn. Profs. Gynecology and Obstetrics, Am. Diabetes Assn., Perinatal Research Soc., South Atlantic Soc. Obstetrics and Gynecology, Central Assn. Obstetrics and Gynecology, Soc. Perinatal Obstetricians, Ill. Med. Soc., Inst. of Medicine. Episcopalian. Club: Rotary. Home: 845 Seddon Cove Way Tampa FL 33602-5704 Office: U South Fla Coll Medicine Dept OBGYN 4 Columbia Dr Ste 514 Tampa FL 33606-3589

SPELLBERG, DAVID MARK, urologist; b. Chgo., Aug. 28, 1960. BS, U. Ill., 1982; MD, Rush Med. Coll., 1986. Diplomate Am. Bd. Urology. Resident urology Rush Presbyn.-St. Luke's Med. Ctr., Chgo., 1986-91; pvt. practice urology Naples, Fla., 1991—. Exec. bd. dirs. Am. Cancer Soc., Naples, 19914—. Fellow Am. Coll. Surgeons; mem. AMA, Am. Urol. Assn., Am. Assn. Clin. Urologists, Fla. Med. Assn., Collier County Med. Assn.

SPELLMAN, GEORGE GENESER, SR., internist; b. Woodward, Iowa, Sept. 11, 1920; s. Martin Edward and Corinne (Geneser) S.; m. Mary Carolyn Dwight, Aug. 26, 1942; children: Carolyn Anne Spellman Rambow, George G. Jr., Mary Alice, Elizabeth Spellman-Chrisinger, John Martin Pile-Spellman, Loretta Suzanne Spellman Hoffman. B.S., St. Ambrose Coll., 1940; M.D., State U. Iowa, 1943. Diplomate Am. Bd. Internal Medicine. Intern Providence Hosp., Detroit, 1944; resident in internal medicine State U. Iowa, Iowa City, 1944-46; practice medicine specializing in internal medicine Mitchell, S.D., 1948-50, Sioux City, Iowa, 1950-91; instr. Coll. Medicine U. Iowa, 1975-77, clin. assoc. Coll. Medicine, 1977-95, ret., 1995; mem. Iowa Bd. Med. Examiners, 1989-95; instr. schs. nursing St. Vincent Hosp. and Luth. Hosp.; bd. dirs. St. Joseph Mercy Hosp. (merged with St. Vincent's Hosp. into Marian Health Ctr. 1977), 1977-80, 87-90, mem. staff, 1950-91, chief of staff, 1963; bd. dirs. St. Vincent's Hosp., 1965-77, also bd. dirs.; clin. assoc. prof. medicine State U. Iowa; bd. dirs. Mid-Step Svcs. Mentally Handicapped, Hospice of Siouxland, Marian Health Ctr., 1974-80, 89-91, also co-founder, 1st pres., chmn. dependency unit, founder renal dialysis unit, 1964, St. Joseph Mercy-St. Vincent's Hosps., 1977-89. Contbr. articles to med. jours. Ordained deacon Cath. Ch., 1988; vol. cons. Siouxland Community Health Ctr., 1993—. Capt. M.C., U.S. Army, 1946-48. Decorated Knight of St. Gregory (Vatican); named Internist of Yr., Iowa Soc. Internal Medicine, 1987; recipient Laureate award Iowa Chpt. ACP, 1991, Humanitarian award Siouxland Community, 1991. Fellow ACP; mem. AMA, Am. Acad. Scis., Iowa State Med. Soc., Woodbury Med. Soc., Am. Soc. Internal Medicine, Iowa Soc. Internal Medicine, Am. Thoracic Soc., Iowa Thoracic Soc., Am. Heart Assn., Iowa Heart Assn., Am. Geriatric Soc., Alpha Omega Alpha. Home: 3849 Jones St Sioux City IA 51104-1447

SPELLMAN, MARTIN ADELBERT, radiologist; b. San Francisco, Jan. 17, 1933; s. Martin C. and Kathleen C. (Dolan) S.; m. Sherrie Joyce Steinman, Dec. 29, 1956; children: Shannon, Patrick, Peter. AB, Stanford U., 1954, MD, 1957. Intern L.A. County Hosp., 1957-58; resident Stanford U., Palo Alto, Calif., 1962-65; radiologist Washington Hosp., Fremont, Calif., 1966—; asst. prof. clin. radiology Stanford U., 1968—; chief radiology U.S. Army Hosp., Bremerhaven, Germany, 1959-62. Capt. U.S. Army, 1958-62. Mem. Alameda County Med. Assn., Calif. Med. Assn., Calif. Radiol. Soc., Radiol. Soc. N.Am., East Bay Radiol. Soc., Soc. Nuclear Medicine. Office: Washington Hosp 2000 Mowry Ave Fremont CA 94538

SPELLMAN, MITCHELL WRIGHT, surgeon, academic administrator; b. Alexandria, La., Dec. 1, 1919; s. Frank Jackson and Altonette Beulah (Mitchell) S.; m. Billie Rita Rhodes, June 27, 1947; children: Frank A., Michael A., Mitchell A., Maria A., Melva A., Mark A., Manly A., Rita A. A.B. magna cum laude, Dillard U., 1940, LL.D. (hon.), 1983; M.D., Howard U., 1944; Ph.D. in Surgery (Commonwealth Fund fellow), U. Minn., Mpls., 1955; D.Sc. (hon.), Georgetown U., 1974, U. Fla., 1977. Intern Cleve. Met. Gen. Hosp., 1944-45, asst. resident in surgery, 1945-46; asst. resident in surgery Howard U. and Freedmen's Hosp., Washington, 1946-47; chief resident in thoracic surgery Howard U. and Freedmen's Hosp., 1947-48, teaching asst. in physiology, 1948-49, chief resident in surgery, 1949-50, teaching asst. in surgery, 1950-51; asst. prof. surgery Howard U., 1954-56, assoc. prof., 1956-60, prof., 1960-68; dir. Howard surgery service at D.C. Gen. Hosp., 1961-68; fellow in surgery U. Minn., 1951-54; sr. resident in surgery U. Minn. Med. Sch. and Hosp., 1953-54; dean Charles R. Drew Postgrad. Med. Sch., Los Angeles, 1969-77; prof. surgery Charles R. Drew Postgrad. Med. Sch., 1969-78; asst. dean, prof. surgery Sch. Medicine, U. Calif. at Los Angeles, 1969-78; clin. prof. surgery Sch. Med., U. So. Calif., 1969-78; dean for med. svcs., prof. surgery Harvard Med. Sch., Boston, 1978-90, dean emeritus for med. svcs., 1990—, dean emeritus for internat. projects, 1990—, prof. surgery emeritus, 1990—; dir. internat. exch. programs Harvard Med. Internat., 1995—; exec. v.p. Harvard Med. Ctr., 1978-90; fellow Ctr. for Advanced Study in Behavioral Scis.; vis. prof. Stanford, 1975-76; bd. dirs. Kaiser Found. Hosps., Kaiser Found. Health Plan, 1971-89; mem. D.C. Bd. Examiners in Medicine and Osteopathy, 1955-68; mem. Nat. Rev. Com. for Regional Med. Programs, 1968-70; mem. spl. med. adv. group, nat. surg. cons. VA, 1969-73; mem. Commn. for Study Accreditation of Selected Health Ednl. Programs, 1970-72; chmn. adv. com. br. med. devices Nat. Heart and Lung Inst., 1972; Am. health del. to visit People's Republic of China, 1973; hon. dir. State Mut. Cos., 1990—; mem. com. mandatory retirement in higher edn. NAS/NRC, 1989-91. Mem. editorial bd.: Jour. Medicine and Philosophy, 1977-90; Contbr. articles on cardiovascular physiology and surgery, measurement of blood volume, and radiation biology to profl. jours. Past bd. dirs. Sun Valley Forum on Nat. Health; mem. ethics adv. bd. HEW, 1977-81; bd. dirs. Harvard Comty. Health Plan, 1979-84; former trustee Occidental Coll.; former bd. overseers com. to visit univ. health svc. Harvard, bd. overseers Harvard Comty. Health Plan, 1984-95; former regent Georgetown U.; former vis. com. U. Mass. Med. Ctr.; mem. bd. visitors UCLA Sch. Medicine; mem. corp. MIT; adv. bd. PEW Scholars Program in Biomed. Scis., 1984-86; bd. dirs. Med. Edn. for South African Blacks, 1985—. Markle scholar in med. scis., 1954-59; recipient Distinguished Alumnus award Dillard U., 1963; Distinguished Postgrad. Achievement award Howard U., 1974; Outstanding Achievement award U. Minn., 1979. Mem. AMA, AAAS, AAUP, ACS, Nat. Med. Assn. (William A. Sinkler Surgery award 1968), Soc. Univ. Surgeons, Am. Coll. Cardiology, Am. Surg. Assn., Inst. of Medicine of Nat. Acad. Scis. (chmn. program com. 1977-79, governing coun. 1978-80), Nat. Acad. Practice in Medicine, Am. Assn. Sovereign Mil. Order of Malta (Knights and Dames of Malta), MIT Corp. (life mem. emeritus), Cosmos Club. Roman Catholic. Office: 138 Harvard St Ste 300 Brookline MA 02146-6418

SPELLMAN, NICHOLAS THOMAS, physiatrist; b. Norwich, Conn., Oct. 20, 1959; s. Nicholas Joseph Jr. and Mary Therese (Donovan) S.; m. Marie Lynn Fishbone, Apr. 20, 1991. AB, Coll. of Holy Cross, 1981; MD, Tufts U., 1985. Intern Faulkner Hosp., Boston, 1985-86; resident in phys. medicine Tufts-New Eng. Med. Ctr., Boston, 1986-89; staff physiatrist Walter Reed Army Med. Ctr., Washington, 1989, dir. inpatient rehab., 1989-91, dir. electromyography lab., 1992-95; fellow in electromyography Boston U., 1991-92; asst. prof. Uniformed Svcs. U. Health Scis. Sch. Medicine, 1991-95, Tufts U. Sch. Medicine, Boston, 1996—; attending physiatrist Baystate Med. Ctr., Springfield, Mass., 1995—; examiner Am. Bd. Phys. Medicine and Rehab., Rochester, Minn., 1995. Contbr. articles to profl. jours. and chpts. to books. Major U.S. Army, 1989-95. Fellow Am. Acad. Phys. Medicine, Am. Assn. Electrodiagnostic Medicine; mem. AMA, Mass. Med. Assn., Frank Lloyd Wright Assn., U.S. Sailing Assn. Office: Baystate Med Ctr 759 Chestnut St Springfield MA 01199

SPENCE, DONALD POND, psychologist, psychoanalyst; b. N.Y.C., Feb. 8, 1926; s. Ralph Beckett and Rita (Pond) S.; m. Mary Newbold Cross, June 2, 1951; children: Keith, Sarah, Laura, Katherine. AB, Harvard U., 1949; PhD, Columbia U., 1955. Lic. psychologist, N.Y., N.J. From rsch. asst. to prof. psychology NYU, 1954-74; prof. psychiatry Robert Wood Johnson Med. Sch., Piscataway, N.J., 1974-95; ret., 1995; vis. prof. psychology Stanford (Calif.) U., 1971-72, Princeton (N.J.) U., 1975-95, Louvain-la-Neuve, Belgium, 1980, William Alanson White Inst., N.Y.C., 1992; mem. personality and cognition rsch. rev. com. NIMH, 1969-73. Author: Narrative Truth and Historical Truth, 1982, The Freudian Metaphor, 1987, The Rhetorical Voice of Psychoanalysis, 1994; mem. editl. bd. Psychoanalysis and Contemporary Thought, Psychol. Inquiry, Theory and Psychology; contbr. articles to profl. jours. With U.S. Army, 1944-46, ETO. Recipient rsch. scientist award NIMH, 1968-74. Mem. APA (pres. theoretical and philos. divsn. 1992-93), Am. Psychoanalytic Assn., N.Y. Acad. Sci., Sigma Xi. Democrat. Home: 9 Haslet Ave Princeton NJ 08540-4913

SPENCE, ROBERT JAMES, plastic surgeon; b. Troy, N.Y., Mar. 9, 1947; s. James Robert and Ruth Elizabeth (Swanker) S.; m. Cressy Ann Starkweather, Aug. 14, 1971; children: Courtney Ann, Erin Elizabeth, Kevin Robert. BA, Johns Hopkins U., 1969, MD, 1972. Diplomate Am. Bd. Plastic Surgery, Am. Bd. Surgery. Asst. prof. plastic surgery U. Md., Balt., 1980-85, Johns Hopkins Med. Sch., Balt., 1985—; assoc. prof. plastic surgery; chief of plastic surgery Johns Hopkins Bayview Medical Ctr., Balt., 1985—; dir. Ctr. for Burn Reconstrn., Balt., 1990—; med. dir. Md. Tissue Bank, Balt., 1984—; co-dir. Balt. Regional Burn Ctr., 1985—. Patentee in field; contbg. author four books; contbr. articles to profl. jours. Bd. dirs., v.p. Transplant Resource Ctr. of Md., Balt., 1991-92; bd. dirs. Balt. Regional Burn Ctr. Found., 1986—, exec. v.p., 1993. Recipient Henry Strong Denison scholarship for med. rsch., 1970. Fellow ACS; mem. Am. Soc. Plastic and Reconstructive Surgeons, Northeastern Soc. Plastic Surgeons (bd. dirs. 1990-92), John Staige Davis Soc. Plastic Surgeons (sec. 1984-86, pres. 1991-92), Am. Assn. Tissue Banks, Am. Burn Assn. (chmn. edn. com. 1996—), Balt. Acad. Surgery (sec. 1993-95, v.p. 1995-96, pres. 1996—). Office: Johns Hopkins Bayview Med Ctr 4940 Eastern Ave Baltimore MD 21224-2735

SPENCER, FRANK COLE, medical educator; b. Haskell, Tex., 1925. MD, Vanderbilt U., 1947. Intern Johns Hopkins U., Balt., 1947-48, fellow in surgery, 1947-48, asst. resident in surgery, 1953-54; resident in surgery Johns Hopkins Sch. Medicine, Balt., 1954-55; surgeon, outpatient dept. Johns Hopkins Hosp., 1955; resident in surgery Wadsworth VA Ctr. Hosp., 1949-50; fellow cardiovascular surgery USPHS, Los Angeles, 1951; asst. prof. surgery Johns Hopkins U., 1955-59, assoc. prof., 1959-61; prof. surgery U. Ky.; now chmn. dept. surgery, George David Steward prof. surgery NYU. Served to lt. M.C., USN, 1951-53. John and Mary R. Markle scholar in med. sci. Johns Hopkins U., 1956. Office: NYU Sch of Medicine Dept of Surgery 550 1st Ave New York NY 10016-6481*

SPENCER, JOHN, surgery educator; b. Bedford, Eng., July 17, 1933; s. Arthur George and Nellie (Housden) S.; m. Gwyneth Ann Griffiths, Dec. 5, 1958; children: Stephen Mark, Joanna Mary, Helen Clare, Timothy Paul, Anthony John. MB, BS, U. London, 1957, MS, 1976. House surgeon Harrow Hosp., London, 1957; house physician Charing Cross Hosp., London, 1958; med. officer Uganda Med. Service, 1958-61; surg. registrar Bath City Hosps., Eng., 1962-64; surg. registrar Hammersmith Hosp.,

London, 1964-66, sr. surg. registrar, 1966-69; sr. lectr. Royal Postgrad. Med. Sch., London, 1970-87, reader in surgery, 1987—. Research fellow UCLA, 1969-70. Fellow Royal Soc. Medicine, Assn. Surgeons U.K.; mem. Brit. Soc. Gastroenterology, Surg. Research Soc. Home: 99 Brunswick Rd, London W5 1AQ, England Office: Royal Postgrad Med Sch, Ducane Rd, London W12 0NN, England

SPENCER, JOHN ANTHONY DAVID, obstetrician and gynecologist; b. London, Oct. 7, 1951; s. Peter John Clement and Ivy May (Peto) S.; m. Athena Giaka, June 24, 1972; children: Katherine, Alexander. BSc with honors, King's Coll., London, 1973; M.B.,B.S., St. Georges Hosp. Med. Sch., London, 1976. Registrar Royal Berkshire Hosp., Reading, U.K., 1981-82; rsch. fellow, clin. lectr. U. Oxford/John Radcliffe Hosp., 1982-86; sr. clin. lectr., hon. cons. Royal Postgrad. Med. Sch., London, 1986-90, Univ. Coll. London Med. Sch., 1990-94; cons., hon. sr. lectr. Northwick Park Hosp., Harrow, Middlesex, U.K., 1994—; hon. tutor St. Mary's Hosp. Med. Sch., London, 1991—; recognized tchr. U. London, 1987—. Editor: Fetal Monitoring, 1991, Fetal Heart Rate Monitoring, 1993, Fetus and Neonate (3 vols.), 1993, 94, 95; editor Brit. Jour. Obstetrics and Gynecology, 1995—; patentee in field. Hon. Rsch. fellow Western Australia Inst. for Child Rsch., 1993; Action Rsch. for Crippled Child grantee, 1992—. Fellow Royal Coll. Obstetricians and Gynecologists (mem. sci. adv. com. 1992-94, working party on role of cons. 1996—), Royal Soc. Medicine; mem. Blair Bell Rsch. Soc. (hon. sec. 1990-94), Brit. Med. Assn., Brit. Assn. Perinatal Medicine (exec. com. 1995—). Home: 83 Abbotsbury Gardens, Harrow HA5 1TB, England Office: Northwick Park Hospital, Watford Rd, Harrow HA1 3UJ, England

SPENCER, LAVAL WING, physician; b. Lehi, Utah, Apr. 12, 1928; s. Lawrence Valdor and Mary Georgia (Wing) S.; m. Betty Jean Robertson, Nov. 10, 1950; children: Scott, Kelly, James, Debra Jean. AS, Weber Coll., 1956; BS, U. Utah, 1959, MD, 1963. Diplomate Am. Bd. Family Practice. Electronic technician Hill AFB, Ogden, Utah, 1950-53, med. officer, 1985-88; resident in gen. practice Dee Hosp., Ogden, 1963-66; pvt. practice Ogden, 1966-85; hon. med. staff McKay-Dee Hosp., 1988—; mem. Utah emergency and comm. com. Utah Med. Assn., Salt Lake City, 1970-77; chmn. med. edn. and rsch. com. McKay-Dee Hosp., Ogden, 1972-73, pres. med. staff, 1973; clin. instr. U. Utah, Salt Lake City, 1978-88. Contbr. articles and essays to profl. publs. Sgt. USAAF, 1946-49, PTO. Recipient award Women's Coun., 1995, Stewart Rehab. Ct., McKay-Dee Found. Fellow Am. Acad. Family Physicians (charter); mem. AMA, Utah Med. Assn., Weber County Med. Soc., Ogden Surg.-Med. Soc. (treas. 1970-75), Old Timers Club (life). Home: 1365 Lark Cir Ogden UT 84403-2141

SPENCER, RICHARD PAUL, biochemist, educator, physician; b. N.Y.C., June 7, 1929; s. David E. and Frances (Fried) S.; m. Gwendolyn Enid Williams, Apr. 7, 1956; children: Carolyn Roberts, Jennifer Holt, Priscilla James. AB, Dartmouth Coll., 1951; MD, U. So. Calif., 1954; MA (NSF fellow, Helen Hay Whitney fellow), Harvard U., 1958, PhD, 1961. Intern Beth Israel Hosp., Boston, 1954-55; practice medicine specializing in nuclear medicine; mem. faculty biophysics U. Buffalo, 1961-63; chief radioisotope service VA Hosp., Buffalo, 1961-63; asso. prof. nuclear medicine Yale Sch. Medicine, 1963-68, prof., 1968-74; prof., chmn. dept. nuclear medicine U. Conn. Health Center, 1974—. Author: The Intestinal Tract, 1960, (with others) Biophysical Principles, 1965, Radionuclide Studies of the Spleen, 1975, Clinical Focus on Nuclear Medicine, 1977, Handbook of Nuclear Medicine, 1977, Therapy in Nuclear Medicine, 1978, Radiopharmaceuticals: Structure-Activity Relationships, 1981, Interventional Nuclear Medicine, 1984, New Procedures In Nuclear Medicine, 1988; contbr. (with others) articles to profl. jours. Mem. Am. Physiol. Soc., AAAS, Soc. Nuclear Medicine, Biophys. Soc. Office: U Conn Health Ctr Farmington CT 06030

SPENCER, RICHARD THOMAS, III, healthcare industry executive; b. Oak Park, Ill., Mar. 18, 1936; s. Richard Thomas Jr. and Lois Anne (Pollock) S.; m. Andrea B. Schlickeiser, June 29, 1962; 1 child, Richard Thomas IV. BA, U. Mich., 1959; postgrad., U. Pa., 1976, Stanford U., 1984, Clemson U., 1985. Mktg. group Mobil Oil Co., Detroit, 1962; internat. trade specialist U.S. Dept. Commerce, Detroit, 1963-64; account exec. J. Walter Thompson Co., Detroit, 1965-66; sales mgr. Sarns Inc., Ann Arbor, Mich., 1967-69; v.p. mktg. Cordis Dow Corp., Miami, Fla., 1970-81; pres. mktg. div. Cordis Corp., Miami, Fla., 1982-87; pres., CEO Uni-Med Internat. Corp., Miami, Fla., 1988—; bd. dirs. World Med. Mfg. Corp., Sunrise, Fla.; cons. in field. Contbr. articles to profl. jours. With U.S. Army, 1959-61. Republican. Office: Uni-Med Internat Corp PO Box 331120 Miami FL 33233-1120

SPENCER, ROGER FELIX, psychiatrist, psychoanalyst, medical educator; b. Vienna, Austria, Apr. 19, 1934; s. Eugene S. Spitzer and Santa (Kurz) Spencer; m. Barbara Ann Houser, Aug. 18, 1958; children—Geoffrey, Jennifer, Rebecca. B.S., Yale Coll., 1956; M.D., Harvard Med. Sch., 1959. Diplomate Am. Bd. Psychiatry. Intern, N.C. Meml. Hosp., Chapel Hill, 1959-60, resident in psychiatry, 1960-63; instr. U. N.C. Sch. Medicine, 1963-66, asst. prof., 1966-69, assoc. prof., 1969-76, prof., 1976—, dir. of liaison and cons., 1967-77, dir. out patient psychiatry, 1977—. Recipient Career Tchr. award NIMH, 1965-67. Fellow Am. Psychiat. Assn., Am. Psychoanalytic Assn.; mem. N.C. Psychoanalytic Soc., N.C. Neuropsychiat. Assn. Club: Chapel Hill Tennis. Contbr. articles to profl. jours. Office: UNC Hosps Psychiatry Dept CB 7160 Chapel Hill NC 27599

SPENCER, SHERWOOD FREDRICK, home healthcare executive; b. N.Y.C., July 14, 1928; s. Abraham and Lillian (Lowenberg) S.; m. Renee Joyce Friedman, Mar. 8, 1958; children: Lauren Gail, Karen Anne. BA, U. Wis., 1948; MBA, Columbia U., 1952. Chief exec. officer A.C. Sears Co., N.Y.C., 1948-86, A Caring Hand Health Care Co., N.Y.C., 1986—; mem. com. Clinton Adv. Coun., N.Y.C., 1986—, Manhattan geriatric com., 1987—. Treas. Westchester Disabled on the Move, 1989—. Office: A Caring Hand Healthcare Co 267 5th Ave New York NY 10016-7503

SPENCER, WILLIAM A., physician, educational administrator; b. Oklahoma City, Feb. 16, 1922. B.S. cum laude, Georgetown U., 1942; M.D., Johns Hopkins U., 1946. Diplomate Am. Bd. Pediatrics. Intern Johns Hopkins Hosp Harriet Lane Home, Balt., 1946-47, resident, 1947-48; med. dir. Southwestern Poliomyelitis Respiratory Ctr., Houston, 1950-59; dir. Tex. Inst. Rehab. and Research, Houston, 1959-77; pres. Inst. for Rehab. and Research, Houston, 1977-88; instr. dept. pediatrics Baylor Coll. Medicine, Houston, 1950-55, asst. prof. dept. pediatrics, 1955-57, asst. prof. dept. physiology, 1954-57, prof., chmn. dept. rehab. medicine, 1957-88; vis. mem. grad. faculty Tex. A&M U., College Station; cons. staff VA Hosp., Houston; cons. spinal injury service and phys. medicine and rehab. VA Hosp., Houston; cons. dept. biomath. and phys. medicine and rehab. M.D. Anderson Hosp. and Tumor Inst., Houston; asst. attending physician Ben Taub Gen. Hosp., Houston; mem. active staff Tex. Children's Hosp., Houston, Inst. for Rehab. and Research, Houston; mem. courtesy staff St. Anthony's Ctr., Houston; Horowitz vis. prof. Inst. Phys. Medicine and Rehab., NYU Med. Ctr., 1964; mem. U. Houston Ctr. for Pub. Policy Adv. Council, 1981—; mem. VA Rehab., Research and Devel., Sci. Merit Rev. Bd., 1981—; mem. sci. adv. bd. Paralyzed Vets. Am. Tech. and Research Found., 1981—; mem. com. on health care of racial/ethnic minorities and handicapped persons Nat. Acad. Sci., 1980-81; mem. panel on testing of handicapped Nat. Acad. Sci., 1980-81; intermittent cons. Nat. Inst. Handicapped Research, Washington, 1979—; mem. Inst. Medicine, Nat. Acad. Scis., 1971—; mem. phys. medicine services adv. com. Joint Commn. on Accreditation of Hosps., 1972—; mem. med. commn. Rehab. Internat., 1977—; ad hoc mem. VA Sci. Rev. and Evaluation Bd. for Rehab. Engring. Research and Devel., 1981—. Cons. editor Jour. Am. Phys. Therapy Assn., 1965-71; mem. editorial bd. Med. Informatics Jour., Health Services Hosp. Research and Ednl. Trust, 1967-73, Computer Programs in Biomedicine, 1968—, Stroke-A Jour. of the Cerebral Circulation, 1969-70, Computers and Human Concern, 1973—, Am. Jour. Phys. Medicine, 1975—, Informatique Medicine, 1975—, Bull. Prosthetics Research, 1982—. Served to capt., M.C., U.S. Army, 1948-50. Recipient Physician's award Pres. Commn. on Employment of Handicapped, 1964, Gold medal 6th Internat. Congress Phys. Medicine, 1972, Disting. Citizens award Goodwill Industries, 1976. Mem. AMA, Am. Physiol. Soc., Am. Congress Rehab. Medicine (Gold Key 1972, Culter award 1978), AAAS, Tex. Med. Assn., Harris County Med. Soc., Houston Pediatric Soc., Nat. Rehab. Assn., N.Y. Acad. Scis., So. Med. Assn., So. Soc. Pediatric Research, Soc. Advanced Med. Systems, Assn. Computing Machinery, Am. Assn. Med. Systems and Informatics, Am. Documentation Inst., Internat. Rehab. Medicine Assn., Am. Acad. Orthopedics (assoc.), Am. Acad. Phys. Medicine (hon.), Am. Coll. Physicians in Computation, Tex. Soc. Profl. Engrs. (hon.), Nat. Assn. Rehab. and Research Ctrs. (exec. com. of bd. 1982—), Houston C. of C., Sigma Xi, Phi Beta Kappa, Alpha Omega Alpha. Office: Tex Inst Rehab & Rsch 1333 Mousund Ave Houston TX 77030

SPENCER, WILLIAM H., ophthalmologist; b. N.Y.C., 1925. MD, U. Calif., San Francisco, 1954. Diplomate Am. Bd. Ophthalmology (exec. dir.). Intern Phila. Gen. Hosp., 1954-55; resident in ophthalmology U. Calif., San Francisco, 1955-58. Office: Calif-Pacific Med Ctr 2340 Clay St 5th Fl San Francisco CA 94115-1932

SPENCER-DAHLEM, ANITA JOYCE, medical, surgical and critical care nurse; b. Weirton, W.Va., Aug. 26, 1961; d. Carlas A. and Evelyn Faye (Miller) Spencer; m. Terry Dahlem. BS, Alderson-Broaddus Coll., Philippi, W.Va., 1984. Staff nurse, orthopedic unit Charleston (W.Va.) Area Med. Ctr., 1984-86; ICU staff nurse Ohio Valley Hosp., Steubenville, Ohio, 1986—; nurse on cardiac catheterization unit Ohio Valley Hosp., Steubenville, 1994—. Mem. Ohio Nurses Assn.

SPENGLER, DAN MICHAEL, orthopedic surgery educator, researcher, surgeon; b. Defiance, Ohio, Feb. 25, 1941; s. Harold A. and Wilhelmina Spengler; m. Cynthia Niswonger; children: Christina, Craig. BS, Baldwin-Wallace Coll., 1962; MD, U. Mich., 1966. Diplomate Am. Bd. Orthopaedic Surgery (bd. dirs. 1988—). Intern in gen. surgery King County Hosp., Seattle, 1967-68; resident in orthopedics U. Mich., Ann Arbor, 1970-73; asst. prof. U. Wash., Seattle, 1974-78, assoc. prof., 1978-83; bd. dirs. Am. Bd. Orthopaedic Surgery. Author: Low Back Pain, 1982. Fellow Am. Acad. Orthopaedic Surgeons; mem. Am. Orthopaedic Assn., ACS, Am. Bd. Orthopaedic Surgeons (pres. 1993-94), Assn. Bone and Joint Surgeons, Internat. Soc. for Study of Lumbar Pain, U. Nashville Club. Office: Vanderbilt U Dept Orthopedic Rehab 1211 21st Ave S # D-4208 Nashville TN 37212-2717

SPENSLEY, JAMES, physician, educator; b. Detroit, May 19, 1938; s. Herbert A. and Ruth H. (Hurford) S.; m. Jeanette A. Mattern, Feb. 17, 1962; children: Patrick, Michelle, Andrea, Chris. Student, U. Mich., 1956-63, MD, 1963. Diplomate Am. Bd. Psychiatry and Neurology. Practice medicine specializing in psychiatry; faculty mem. U. Calif. Sch. Medicine, Davis, 1969—, asst. prof. in residence, 1973-76, assoc. prof., 1976-82, assoc. clin. prof., 1982—; adj. prof. Pacific Grad. Sch. of Psychology, 1981—; cons. Westminster Counseling, 1970—, Marriage Tribunal, 1980—. Contbr. articles to profl. jours. Active Cath. Community Services, Sacramento, 1981—, Physicians for Social Responsibility, 1982—, Bread for the World, 1982—. Served to capt. USAR, 1964-67, lt. USNR, 1967-69. Fellow Am. Psychiat. Assn.; mem. Cen. Calif. Psychiat. Soc., Calif. Med. Assn., Am. Soc. for Clin. Hypnosis, Sigma Xi. Democrat. Home: 4217 Winding Woods Way Fair Oaks CA 95628-6446 Office: 4401 Hazel Ave Ste 205 Fair Oaks CA 95628-6668

SPERA, ANTHONY PETER, cardiologist; b. Queens, N.Y., May 31, 1960; s. Michael and Anna (Gentilini) S.; m. Celia L. Borja, Mar. 10, 1990; 1 child, Andrew. BS in Biology, Adelphi U., 1982; MD, SUNY, Bklyn., 1987. Diplomate Am. Bd. Internal Medicine. Intern/resident in internal medicine L.I. Jewish Med. Ctr., New Hyde Park, N.Y., 1987-90; fellow in cardiology Nassau County Med. Ctr., East Meadow, N.Y., 1990-93; cardiologist Queens-L.I. Med. Group, Hempstead, N.Y., 1993—; assoc. attending dept. medicine divsn. cardiology Syosset (N.Y.) Hosp., 1993—. Fellow Am. Coll. Cardiology (assoc.), Am. Coll. Chest Physicians (assoc.); mem. AMA, ACP, Am. Heart Assn. Roman Catholic. Home: 610 Washington Ave Plainview NY 11803 Office: Queens-Long Island Medical Group 226 Clinton St Hempstead NY 11550

SPERANDIO, GLEN JOSEPH, pharmacy educator; b. Glen Carbon, Ill., May 8, 1918; s. Henry A. and Marjorie (Dunstedter) A.; m. Dorys Bell, June 21, 1946; 1 child, James Glen. B.S., St. Louis Coll. Pharmacy, 1940; M.S., Purdue U., 1947, Ph.D., 1950. Pharmacist, 1936-41; analytical chemist Grove Labs., St. Louis, 1941-43, 45; mfg. pharmacist William R. Warner Co., St. Louis, 1944; instr. Purdue U., 1946-50, asst. prof. pharmacy, 1950-53, assoc. prof., 1953-62, prof., 1962—, head dept., 1966-78, assoc. dean, 1978-83, assoc. dean emeritus, 1984—; exec. dir. Ind. Soc. Hosp. Pharmacists, 1984—; indsl. cons., 1955-81; pharm. cons. VA Hosp., Indpls., 1963-69; mem. blue ribbon com. on standardized bd. exams. Nat. Assn. Bds. Pharmacy, 1969; cons. on clin. pharmacy Surgeon Gen., U.S. Army, 1973-80. Author: Laboratory Manual of Cosmetics, 1956, (with others) Scoville's Art of Compounding, 1959, (with others) Clinical Pharmacy, 1966; author, editor: (with others) Hosp. Pharmacy Notes, 1959-74. Served with USCGR, 1944. Named 1st prof. clin. pharmacy in U.S., Distinguished Alumnus St. Louis Coll. Pharmacy, 1969. Mem. AMA, Am. Soc. Hosp. Pharmacists, Parenteral Drug Assn. (regional v.p. 1965-67), Nat. Formulary, Ind. Soc. Hosp. Pharmacists (pres. 1955-57, hon. mem., disting. educator 1980), Am. Pharm. Assn. (sec.-treas. sect. practical pharmacy 1956), Ind. Pharm. Assn., Tipp County Pharm. Assn., Internat. Fedn. Pharmacists, Soc. Cosmetic Shemists, Am. Legion, Masons (32 deg.), Golden Key, Sigma Xi, Kappa Psi (nat. svc. award 1967, nat. pres. 1963-67), Rho Chi, Phi Lambda Upsilon. Home: PO Box 2509 West Lafayette IN 47906-0509 Office: Purdue U Sch Pharmacy Lafayette IN 47907

SPERANZA, DAVID NICHOLAS, physician; b. Bklyn., June 15, 1953; m. Diane Brady, Sept. 17, 1994. BS, York Coll./CUNY, Jamaica, 1975; MD, Loyola U., Chgo., 1981. Diplomate in internal medicine and gastroenterology Am. Bd. Internal Medicine. Resident in internal medicine Loyola U., Maywood, Ill., 1981-84; attending physician Michael Reese Hosp., Chgo., 1984-86; fellow in gastroenterology Chgo. Med. Sch., North Chicago, Ill., 1986-87, Loyola U., Maywood, 1987-89; assoc. in gastroenterology Geisinger Clinic, Wilkes-Barre, Pa., 1989—. Mem. ACP, Am. Coll. Gastroenterology, Am. Gastroenterol. Assn. Roman Catholic. Office: Geisinger Med Clinic 1010 E Mountain Dr Wilkes Barre PA 18711

SPERELAKIS, NICHOLAS, SR., physiology and biophysics educator, researcher; b. Joliet, Ill., Mar. 3, 1930; s. James and Arestia (Kayadakis) S.; m. Dolores Martinis, Jan. 28, 1960; children: Nicholas Jr., Mark, Christine, Sophia, Thomas, Anthony. BS in Chemistry, U. Ill., 1951; diploma, U.S Navy & Marine Corps Electronics Sch., 1952; MS in Physiology, U. Ill., 1955, PhD in Physiology, 1957. Teaching asst. U. Ill., Urbana, 1954-57; instr. Case Western Res. U., Cleve., 1957-59, asst. prof., 1959-66, assoc. prof., 1966; prof. U. Va., Charlottesville, 1966-83; Joseph Eichberg prof. physiology Coll. Medicine U. Cin., 1983—, chmn. dept., 1983-93; cons. NPS Pharm., Inc., Salt Lake City, 1988-95, Carter Wallace, Inc. Cranbury, N.J., 1988-91; vis. prof. U. St. Andrews, Scotland, 1972-73, U. San Luis Potosi, Mex., 1986, U. Athens, Greece, 1994; Rosenblueth prof. Centro de Investigacion y Avanzades, Mex., 1972; mem. sci. adv. com. several internat. meetings, editorial bd. numerous sci. jours. Co-editor: Handbook of Physiology and Pathophysiology of the Heart, 1984, 2d edit., 1988, 3d edit., 1995, Calcium Antagonists: Mechanisms of Action on Cardiac Muscle and Vascular Smooth Muscle, 1984, Cell Interactions and Gap Junctions, vols. I and II, 1989, Frontiers in Smooth Muscle Research, 1990, Ion Channels in Vascular Smooth Muscle and Endothelial Cells, 1991, Essentials of Physiology, 1992, 2d edit., 1996, Cell Physiology Source Book, 1995, Electrogenesis of Biopotentials, 1995; assoc. editor Circulation Rsch., 1970-75, Molecular Cellular Cardiology; contbr. articles to profl. jours.; author/co-author over 490 rsch. publs. and book chpts. Lectr. Project Hope, Peru, 1962. Sgt. USMC, 1951-53, Res., 1953-59. Recipient Disting. Alumnus award Rockdale (Ill.) Pub. Schs., 1958; U. Cin. Grad. fellow, 1989; NIH grantee, 1959—. Mem. Am. Physiol. Soc. (chair steering com. sect. 1981-82), Biophys. Soc. (coun. 1990-93), Am. Soc. Pharmacology and Exptl. Therapeutics, Internat. Soc. Heart Rsch. (coun. 1980-89, 92—), Am. Heart Assn. (established investigator 1961-66, Rsch. Merit award 1995, Sam Kaplan Rsch. award, 1996), Am. Hellenic Ednl. Progressive Assn. (pres. Charlottesville chpt. 1980-82), Ohio Physiol. Soc. (pres. 1990-91), Phi Kappa Phi. Democrat. Greek Orthodox. Office: U Cin Coll Medicine 231 Bethesda Ave Cincinnati OH 45229-2827

SPERHAC, ARLENE MISKLOW, nursing educator, program administrator; b. Pitts.; d. Lawrence P. and Julia Misklow; m. Robert G. Sperhac; children: Jeanette, Julia. Diploma, Shadyside Hosp., 1963; BSN, Fla. State U., 1966; MN, U. Pitts., 1973; PNP, U. Colo., Denver, 1981; PhD, U. Denver, 1982. Staff nurse Fla. State U. Hosp., Tallahassee, 1965-66; relief charge nurse Grady Meml. Hosp., Atlanta, 1967; head nurse Kinderklink Eduard-Pfieffer Heim, Stuttgart, Fed. Republic Germany, 1967-68; instr. Children's Hosp. Pitts., 1968-69; relief charge nurse Doctor's Hosp., Pitts., 1971-72; nurse pediatric clinic Thurston County Health Dept., Olympia, Wash., 1974-75; asst. prof. Health Scis. Ctr. U. Colo., Denver, 1977-82; assoc. prof. child health Mass. Gen. Hosp. Inst. Health Professions, Boston, 1982-86; assoc. prof. Boston Coll., Chestnut Hill, Mass., 1986-87; dir. nursing edn., rsch. Children's Meml. Hosp., Chgo., 1988-95; coord. pediatric nurse practitioner program Rush U. Coll. Nursing, Chgo., 1995—; mem. adj. faculty U. Ill.; cons. curriculum U. South Fla., Tampa, 1987; cons. pre-admission program Children's Hosp., Boston, 1986; cons. fed. grand Beyond Collaboration, 1989-91. Author: (with others) Nursing Management of Pediatric Emergencies, 1988; co-editor, author: Nursing Care of Children and Families, 2d edit., 1990 (Am. Jour. Nursing Book of Yr. award 1990); reviewer Jour. Pediatric Nursing, 1988, Jour. Am. Acad. Nurse Practitioners. Grantee HEW, 1965-66, 72-78, Boston Coll., 1987; Dean's scholar U. Denver, 1982. Office: Rush Presbyn St Lukes Med Ctr 1653 W Congress Pkwy Chicago IL 60612

SPERING, MARK ANDREW, optometrist; b. Montrose, Pa., Oct. 1, 1969; s. Henry L. and Mary Ann (Sipe) S.; m. Kimberly Ann Scherer, July 9, 1994. BS in Natural Sci., Indiana U. Pa., 1991; BS in Optometry, Pa. Coll. Optometry, 1992, OD, 1994. Pvt. practice, Erie, Pa., 1994-95, Allentown, Pa., 1995—. Mem. Am. Optometric Assn. (specialist in contact lens divsn.), Pa. Optometric Assn., Lehigh Valley Optometric Soc. Office: Allentown Eye Assocs PC 2004 Allen St Allentown PA 18104

SPERLING, ARTHUR LAWRENCE, oral and maxillofacial surgeon; b. Boston, June 23, 1939; s. William B. and Ethyl J. (Berry) S.; m. Harriet L. Feldman, Aug. 6, 1961; children: Bradley, Audrey. DMD, Tufts U., 1964; postgrad., Harvard U., 1964-67. Diplomate Am. Bd. Oral and Maxillofacial Surgery. Tchg. fellow Mass. Gen. Hosp., Boston, 1966-67; rsch. assoc. electrophysiology Tufts U., Boston, 1962-65; instr. oral/maxillofacial surgery Harvard U., Boston, 1966-67; clin. tchg. staff Hartford (Conn.) Hosp., 1969—; assoc. prof. surgery U. Conn. Health Ctr., Farmington, 1971—; pvt. practice oral and maxillofacial surgery Middletown, Glastonbury, Conn., 1969—, Avon, Conn., 1969—; vis. lectr. Boston U. Grad. Sch. Medicine, 1965-67; bd. dirs Connecticare HMO, Farmington, Conn., 1988—. Bd. dirs. Conn. unit Am. Heart Assn., Hartford, 1979-82. Capt. USAF, 1967-69. Fellow Internat. Assn. Oral and Maxillofacial Surgeons, Am. Coll. Oral and Maxillofacial Surgeons, Am. Dental Soc. Anesthesiology, Am. Assn. Oral and Maxillofacial Surgeons, Pierre Fauchard Honor Acad.; mem. ADA, Conn. Soc. Oral and Maxillofacial Surgeons (pres. 1981-83), Hartford Alpha Omega (pres. 1978-79). Office: Oral & Maxillofacial Surgeons PC 80 S Main St Middletown CT 06457

SPERLING, GEORGE, cognitive scientist, educator; s. Otto and Melitta Sperling. BS in Math., U. Mich., 1955; MA in Psychology, Columbia U., 1956; PhD in Psychology, Harvard U., 1959. Rsch. asst. in biophysics Brookhaven Nat. Labs., Upton, N.Y., summer 1955; rsch. asst. in psychology Harvard U., Cambridge, Mass., 1957-59; mem. tech. rsch. staff Acoustical and Behavioral Rsch. Ctr., AT&T Bell Labs., Murray Hill, N.J., 1958-86; prof. psychology and neural sci. NYU, N.Y.C., 1970-92; disting. prof. cognitive scis. and psychobiology U. Calif., Irvine, 1992—; instr. psychology Washington Sq. Coll., NYU, 1962-63; vis. assoc. prof. psychology Duke U., spring 1964; adj. assoc. prof. psychology Columbia U., 1964-65; acting assoc. prof. psychology UCLA, 1967-68; hon. rsch. assoc. Univ. Coll., U. London, 1969-70; vis. prof. psychology U. Western Australia, Perth, 1972, U. Wash., Seattle, 1977; vis. scholar Stanford (Calif.) U., 1984; mem. sci. adv. bd. USAF, 1988-92. Recipient Meritorious Civilian Svc. medal USAF, 1993; Gomberg scholar U. Mich., 1953-54; Guggenheim fellow, 1969-70. Fellow AAAS, APA (Disting. Sci. Contbn. award 1988), Am. Acad. Arts and Sci., Optical Soc. Am.; mem. NAS, Assn. for Rsch. in Vision and Ophthalmology, Ann. Interdisciplinary Conf. (founder, organizer 1975—), Eastern Psychol. Assn. (bd. dirs. 1982-85), Soc. for Computers in Psychology (steering com. 1974-78), Psychonomic Soc., Soc. Exptl. Psychologists (Warren medal 1996), Soc. for Math. Psychology (chmn. 1983-84, exec. bd. 1979-85), Phi Beta Kappa, Sigma Xi. Office: U Calif Dept Cognitive Scis SS Tower Irvine CA 92717

SPERLING, MICHAEL ROBERT, neurologist; b. Phila., May 14, 1953; s. Ralph L. and May (Rosen) S.; m. Janet Fleetwood, Oct. 17, 1982; children: Alissa Rose, Brian Scott. BA, Temple U., 1974, MD, 1978. Diplomate Am. Bd. Psychiatry & Neurology, Am. Bd. Clin. Neurophysiology. Resident in medicine, neurology Mt. Sinai Hosp., N.Y.C., 1978-82; fellow in epilepsy UCLA, 1982-84; from asst. prof. to assoc. prof. neurology U. Pa., Phila., 1985-95; clin. assoc. prof. neurology Temple U., Phila., 1995-96, clin. prof. neurology, 1996—. Author: Atlas of Electroencephalography, 1993; contbr. articles to profl. jours. Fellow Am. Neurophysiol. Soc.; mem. Am. Acad. Neurology, Am. Epilepsy Soc., Easter Assn. Electroencephalographers, Epilepsy Found. S.E. Pa. (bd. dirs. 1989—, chmn. profl. adv. bd. 1989—). Office: Grad Hosp 1 Graduate Pl Philadelphia PA 19146

SPERO, JEANNETTE RABINOWITZ, nursing educator; b. N.Y.C., June 10, 1925; d. Albert and Pauline (Malloy) S.; children: Job, Adam. BS, NYU, 1952, MA, 1959, PhD, 1968; MPH, Johns Hopkins U., 1964. Staff nurse Queens Gen. Hosp., N.Y.C., 1946-51; staff, supr. Vis. Nurse Svc. N.Y., N.Y.C., 1951-59; instr., asst. prof. NYU, N.Y.C., 1959-69; asst. prof., dept. head SUNY, Buffalo, 1969-72, prof., dept. head, 1972-74, prof., dean, 1974-78; prof., dean U. Cin., 1978-90, prof. nursing, 1990—; cons. N.J. Dept. Health Edn., 1985, Ball State U., Muncie, Ind., 1987, U. Nuevo Leon, Mexico, 1987, U. N.D., 1988. Bd. dirs. Vis. Nurse Assn. Greater Cin., 1979-84; bd. trustees Psychoanlaytic Found., Cin., 1981-83; mem. adv. bd. Emerson No. Hosp., Cin., 1988-90; bd. dirs. Llanfair Retirement Community, Cin., 1992—. Recipient Outstanding Svc. award Ohio League Nursing, 1982. Fellow APHA; mem. ANA, Am. Assn. Coll. Nursing (assoc., pres. 1986-88, S.R. Bernadette Arminger award 1991), Nat. League Nursing (Adelaide Nutting award 1991), S.W. Ohio Nurses Assn. (bd. dirs. 1991-93). Office: U Cin Coll Nursing & Health Cincinnati OH 45221

SPERO, MITCHELL E., psychologist; b. Phila., Jan. 9, 1958; s. Jerome B. and Vera O. (Lieberman) S.; divorced; 1 child, Jessica R. BS in Psychology, U. Pitts., 1979; MS in Edn., U. Miami, 1981; Psychology Doctorate in Clin. Psychology Nova U., 1987. Diplomate Am. Bd. Cert. Managed Care Providers; lic. psychologist. Psychometrist Highland Park Gen. Hosp., Miami, Fla., 1981-82; psychology instr. Ft. Lauderdale Coll., 1981, Ft. Lauderdale Adult Edn. Program, 1983-84; youth intervention coord. Ctr. for Counseling and Edn., Miami, 1981-82; assoc. Marvin Fredman, PhD, P.A., Ctr. for Psychol. Services, Lauderhill, Fla., 1983-89; pvt. practice psychologist, 1989—; pres., owner Mitchell E. Spero, Psy.D. & Assocs., P.A., 1989-93; dir. Child & Family Psychologists, Plantation, Fla., 1993—; v.p. CCBT Ctr. for Cognitive Behavior Therapy, Inc.; adj. instr. counseling psychology Nova U., 1987—; staff psychologist Crossroads Sch., 1989-93, supervising psychologist of clin. svcs., 1993—; cons. So. Fla. Psychiat. Assn., Miami, 1983-85; clin. psychology doctoral intern N.W. Dade Community Mental Health Ctr., Hialeah, Fla., 1985-86; ptnr. COR Counseling Ctr., Miami, 1982. Sunday Sch. tchr. Temple Beth Israel, Pitts., 1978-79; vol. Dade County Halfway House for Boys, Miami, 1979; mem. adv. bd. The Club House for Kids, 1987-88. Mem. Am. Psychol. Assn., Mental Health Assn. Broward County (cert. appreciation 1984), Fla. Psychology Assn., Broward County Psychology Assn. (co-chmn. legis. com. 1989-93, pres.-elect 1992, pres. 1993), Broward Counseling Assn. (exec. bd. dirs. 1992-94), U. Pitts. Varsity Letter Club, U. Pitts. Club S. Fla., Nat. Humane Edn. Soc., Phi Kappa Phi. Democrat. Jewish. Lodge: Fraternal Order Police. Avocations: gymnastics, guitar, woodworking, swimming, golf. Office: 7520 NW 5th St Ste 204 Plantation FL 33317-1613

SPERRAZZO, GERALD, psychology educator; b. N.Y.C., Dec. 16, 1931; s. Gretand and Maria (Bordonaro) S.; m. Mary Christine Torcisi, Sept. 30, 1961; children: Mark, Christine, John, Anne. BA, U. Idaho, 1953; MA, St. Louis U., 1956; PhD, U. Ottawa (Ont., Can.), 1961. Diplomate Am. Bd.

Profl. Psychology. Asst. prof. psychology Georgetown U., Washington, 1961-66; dir. Ednl. Devel. Ctr. U. San Diego, 1966-69, chmn. dept. psychology, 1966-73, chmn. dept. behavioral scis., 1973-75, prof. psychology, 1966—; cons. Nat. Security Agy., Ft. Mead, Md., 1963-65, Social Security Adminstrn., Office Hearings and Appeals, San Diego, 1986-87; pvt. practice Psychology Assocs., San Diego, 1968—. Editor: Psychology and International Relations, 1965, Behavior Disorders of Children and Adolescents, 1988. Cons. mayor's Social Sci. Adv. Commn., San Diego, 1970-72, Mayor's Quality of Life Bd., San Diego, 1973-77. Cpl. U.S. Army, 1953-56. Mem. Calif. Psychol. Assn., Acad. San Diego Psychologists (pres. 1970-71), Sigma Xi. Roman Catholic. Office: U San Diego Dept Psychology San Diego CA 92110

SPEZIA, ANTHONY L., medical facility administrator; b. St. Louis, Jan. 2, 1949; m. Sharie Marie Hoffman, Aug. 8, 1970; children: Alicia, Anthony III. MBA, Mich. State U., 1985; BS, St. Louis U., 1971. Diplomate Am. Coll. Healthcare Execs. Audit mgr., cons. Arthur Andersen & Co., 1971-80; v.p. planning and control, chief fin. officer, exec. v.p. Indsl. Fuels Corp., 1980-89; fin. and bus. cons. Louisville, Tenn., 1989-91; exec. v.p. Peninsula Hosp., Louisville, 1991-95; sr. v.p. Fort Sanders Alliance/Peninsula Hosp., Louisville, 1995—. Fellow Healthcare Fin. Mgmt. Assn. (cert. managed care profl.). Office: Peninsula Hosp PO Box 2000 Louisville TN 37777

SPHIRE, RAYMOND DANIEL, anesthesiologist; b. Detroit, Feb. 12, 1927; s. Samuel Raymond and Nora Mae (Allen) S.; m. Joan Lois Baker, Sept. 5, 1953; children—Suzanne M., Raymond Daniel, Catherine J. BS, U. Detroit, 1948; MD, Loyola U., Chgo., 1952. Diplomate Am. Bd. Anesthesiology. Intern Grace Hosp., Detroit, 1952-53; resident Harvard Anesthesia Lab.-Mass. Gen. Hosp., 1953-55; attending anesthesiologist Grace Hosp., Detroit, 1955-72, dir. dept. inhalation therapy, 1968-70; sr. attending anesthesiologist, dir. dept., dir. dept. respiratory therapy Detroit-Macomb Hosps. Assn., 1970—, trustee, 1978—, chief of staff, 1980—; clin. asst. prof. Wayne State U. Sch. Medicine, 1967—; clin. prof. respiratory therapy Macomb Community Coll., Mount Clemens, Mich., 1971—; examiner Am. Registry Respiratory Therapists, 1972—; insp. Joint Rev. Com. Respiratory Therapy Edn., 1972—. Co-author: Operative Neurosurgery, 1970, First Aid Guide for the Small Business or Industry, 1978. With AUS, 1944-45; 1st lt. M.C., USAF, 1952. Fellow Am. Coll. Anesthesiologists, Am. Coll. Chest Physicians; mem. AMA, Am. Soc. Anesthesiologists, Wayne County Soc. Anesthesiologists (pres. 1967-69), Am. Assn. Respiratory Therapists, Soc. Critical Care Medicine, Detroit Athletic Club, Country Club of Detroit, Cumberland Club (Portland, Maine), Severance Lodge. Roman Catholic. Home: 19874 Westchester Dr Clinton Township MI 48038 Office: 119 Kercheval Ave Grosse Pointe MI 48236-3618

SPIEGEL, ALLEN D., medical educator, consultant; b. N.Y.C., June 11, 1927; s. Max and Betty (Silver) S.; m. Lila Spiegel, Apr. 16, 1958; children: Merrill S., Marc B., Andrea M. AB, Bklyn. Coll., 1947; MPH, Columbia U., 1954; PhD, Brandeis U., 1969. Chief radio & TV unit N.Y.C. Health Dept., 1951-61; health edn. assoc. The Med. Found., Inc., Boston, 1961-69; prof. SUNY Health Sci. Ctr. at Bklyn., 1969—; cons. in field. Author, editor of numerous books including Strategic Health Planning, 1991, Home Health Care, 2d rev. edit., 1987; contbr. articles to profl. jours.; mem. editorial adv. bd. The Nation's Health. NEH fellow, 1979, WHO study/travel fellow, 1974, Nat. Ctr. for Health Svcs. Rsch. fellow, 1966-69; recipient of citations from govtl. and pub. agys; seminar leader Profl. Continuing Edn. Programs (overseas), 1988. Mem. Am. Pub. Health Assn. (com. chmn.), Internat. Union for Health Edn., Columbia U. Sch. of Pub. Health Alumni Assn., Community Agy. Pub. Rels. Assn., Coun. on Med. Television, Soc. of Pub. Health Educators, Health Edn. Media Assn., Consumer Commn. on the Accreditation of Health Svcs. Home: 47 Jensen Rd Sayreville NJ 08872-1969 Office: SUNY Health Sci Ctr 450 Clarkson Ave # 43 Brooklyn NY 11203-2012

SPIEGEL, HERBERT, psychiatrist, educator; b. McKeesport, Pa., June 29, 1914; s. Samuel and Lena (Mendlowitz) S.; m. Natalie Shainess, Apr. 24, 1944 (div. Apr. 1965); children: David, Ann; m. Marcia Greenleaf, Jan. 29, 1989. B.S., U. Md., 1936, M.D., 1939. Diplomate: Am. Bd. Psychiatry. Intern St. Francis Hosp., Pitts., 1939-40; resident in psychiatry St. Elizabeth's Hosp., Washington, 1940-42; practice medicine specializing in psychiatry N.Y.C., 1946—; attending psychiatrist Columbia-Presbyn. Hosp., N.Y.C., 1960—; faculty psychiatry Columbia U. Coll. Physicians and Surgeons, 1960—; adj. prof. psychology John Jay Coll. Criminal Justice, CUNY, 1983—; mem. faculty Sch. Mil. Neuropsychiatry, Mason Gen. Hosp., Brentwood, N.Y., 1944-46. Author: (with A. Kardiner) War Stress and Neurotic Illness, 1947, (with D. Spiegel) Trance and Treatment: Clinical Uses of Hypnosis, 1978; subject of book: (by Donald S. Connery) The Inner Source: Exploring Hypnosis with Herbert Spiegel, M.D.; Mem. editorial bd.: Preventive Medicine, 1972; Contbr. articles to profl. jours. Mem. profl. advisory com. Am. Health Found.; mem. pub. edn. com., smoking and health com. N.Y.C. div. Am. Cancer Soc.; mem. adv. com. Nat. Aid to Visually Handicapped. Served with M.C. AUS, 1942-46. Decorated Purple Heart. Fellow Am. Psychiat. Assn., Am. Coll. Psychiatrists, Am. Soc. Clin. Hypnosis, Am. Acad. Psychoanalysis, Internat. Soc. Clin. and Exptl. Hypnosis, William A. White Psychoanalytic Soc., N.Y. Acad. Medicine, N.Y. Acad. Scis.; mem. Am. Orthopsychiat. Assn., Am. Psychosomatic Soc., AAAS, AMA, N.Y. County Med. Soc. Office: 19 E 88th St New York NY 10128-0557

SPIEGEL, RENÉ, psychopharmacologist; b. Zurich, Switzerland, July 10, 1943; s. Ludwig and Klara (Dukas) S.; m. Jeanne-Louise Klibansky, Aug. 7, 1969; children: Ivo, Adrian, Simon. Grad. Kantonsschule, Zurich, 1962; Ph.D. U. Zurich, 1968; Venia legendi, U. Basel, 1979. Clin. researcher Sandoz Ltd., Basel, Switzerland, 1968-72, group leader, 1974-84, dep. head Cen. Nervous System Rsch. Dept. 1985-91; assoc. prof. clin. psychology U. Basel, 1986—; head Dementia Project Unit Sandoz Pharma Ltd., 1992-93, Drug Regulatory and Registration Affairs, 1993—; vis. scientist Stanford U., Calif., 1973. Author/co-author 4 books; contbr. articles to profl. jours. and books. Bd. dirs. Acads. Assn. Sandoz, 1982-86. Bd. Jewish community, Basel, 1993—. Recipient First Prize award Swiss Found. Applied Psychology, 1981, Ednl. Film award German Fed. Chambers of Physicians, 1993. Mem. APA (fgn. affiliate), German Soc. Psychology, Swiss Soc. Gerontology, Arbeitsgemeinschaft Neuro-Psychopharmacology, Swiss Assn. Biol. Psychiatry (bd. dirs. 1981-87), European Coll. Neuro-Psychopharmacology, Internat. Psychogeriatric Assn., Collegium Internationale Neuro-Psychopharmacologicum. Jewish. Avocations: sports, painting, reading. Home: Oberalpstr 55, CH 4054 Basel Switzerland Office: Sandoz Pharma AG, Postfach, CH 4002 Basel Switzerland

SPIEGEL, STANLEY, retired psychologist; b. N.Y.C., Apr. 18, 1925; s. Samuel and Hermina (Manheim) S.; children: Joseph, Laura. BS in Psychology, Adelphi U., 1950; MS, CUNY, 1951; PhD in Psychology, U. Fla., 1957. Diplomate clin. psychology. Psychologist Highland Hosp., Asheville, N.C., 1951-53; researcher Health Ctr./U. Fla., Gainesville, 1956-57; chief psychologist Portsmouth (Va.) Guidance Ctr., 1957-62; pvt. practice N.Y.C. and Nyack, N.Y., 1962—; clin. prof. psychology Adelphi U., Garden City, N.Y., 1980—; supervising analyst W.A. White Inst., N.Y.C., 1986—. Author: An Interpersonal Approach to Child Therapy, 1989, softcover edit., 1996; contbr. articles to profl. jours.; assoc. editor: Contemporary Psychoanalysis, 1991—. Exec. bd. dirs. faculty Adelphi U., 1985-89. With USAAF, 1943-46. Mem. W.A. White Soc. (bd. dirs. 1986-89, sec. 1977), Va. Psychol. Assn. (pres. 1961), Am. Psychol. Assn. (del. 1959). Home: 501 Garcia St Santa Fe NM 87501-2855

SPIEGELBERG, ELDORA HASKELL, retired psychologist, civic worker; b. Philippopolis, Bulgaria, Feb. 6, 1915; d. Edward Bell and Elisabeth (Frohlich) Haskell; m. Herbert Spiegelberg, July 6, 1944 (dec.); children: Gwen Elisabeth (dec.), Lynne Sylvia. BA, Beloit (Wis.) Coll., 1937; MA, Oberlin (Ohio) Coll., 1938; postgrad., U. Pitts., 1940, Pa. State U., 1956. Cert. elem. edn. and tchr. of deaf, Wis., Mo. Tchr., psychologist Western Pa. Sch. for the Deaf, Pitts., 1939-44; psychologist pub. schs. Appleton, Wis., 1949-63; lectr. in clin. psychology Lawrence U., Appleton, 1955-57; sch. and rsch. psychologist pub. schs. University City, Mo., 1964-80, ret., 1980; mem. parents as tchrs. University City Bd., 1984—; vol., storyteller Reading is Fundamental, St. Louis, 1985—. Pres. Women's Internat. League for Peace and Freedom, St. Louis, 1966-68, 74-79, 89-93, bd. dirs., 1993—; mem. program com. Am. Friends Svc. Com., 1977-83, 89-95; facilitator prison workshops Alternatives To Violence Program, 1994—. Named Ethical Humanist of Yr. Ethical Soc., 1981; recipient Disting. Svc. award Mayor of University City, 1981. Mem. APA (dues-exempt com.). Democratic Socialist. Home: 7200 Pershing Ave Saint Louis MO 63130-4244

SPIEGELBERG, HANS LEONHARD, medical educator; b. Basel, Switzerland, Jan. 8, 1933; came to U.S., 1961; s. Hans G. S.; m. Elizabeth von der Crone, May 19, 1962; children: Franzi, Daniel, Markus. MD, U. Basel, Basel, 1958. Med. diplomate, Switzerland. Intern and resident in pediatric allergy and immunology Dept. of Medicine, U. of Basel, Switzerland; intern and resident in allergy and immunology NYU, N.Y.C., 1961-63; with Scripps Rsch. Inst., La Jolla, Calif., 1963-90; prof. U. Calif., San Diego, 1990—; cons. VA Med. Ctr., L.A., 1966-90. Editor (jour.) Seminars in Immunopathology, 1988—. Home: 2234 Paseo Dorado La Jolla CA 92037 Office: U Calif San Diego 9500 Gilman Dr La Jolla CA 92093-0609

SPIEGEL-HOPKINS, PHYLLIS MARIE, psychotherapist; b. Chgo., Oct. 28, 1947; d. Joseph Frank and Marie Ann (Hejhal) Spiegel; m. Daniel Mark Hopkins, Jan. 14, 1984. BSE, Chgo. State U., 1968, MA in History, 1972; MA in Clin. Psychology, Ill. Sch. Profl. Psychology, Chgo., 1983; D in Clin. Hypnotherapy, Am. Inst. Hypnotherapy, Santa Ana, Calif., 1991. Cert. tchr., Ill; cert. clin. hypnotherapist. Tchr. Holy Cross Grammar Sch., Chgo., 1968-69, Chgo. Bd. Edn., 1969-81, Mt. Asissi Acad., Lemont, Ill., 1981-82; police officer Chgo. Police Dept., 1982—; psychotherapist pvt. practice Chgo., 1988—; mem. Am. Bd. Hypnotherapy. Mem. ACA, Nat. Guild Hypnotists, S.W. Hypnosis Soc., Assn. for Study Dreams, Internat. Med. and Dental Hypnotherapy Assn., C.G. Jung Inst. Chgo., Assn. Past-Life Therapy and Rsch. (life), Internat. Assn. Counselors and Therapists (life), Am. Psychotherapy and Med. Hypnosis Assn., Fraternal Order Police. Office: PO Box 185 Bedford Park IL 60499-0185

SPIER, JULIANN RUPPEL, pharmacist; b. Milw., Aug. 27, 1962; d. Teddy T. and Karen Marie (Bell) Ruppelp; m. Derek Dwayne Spier; children: Derek Ryan, Nicholas Cade. BS. Sam Houston State, 1983; BS in Pharmacy, U. Houston, 1986. Registered pharmacist. Lab. instr. Sam Houston State U., Huntsville, Tex., 1982-83; pharmacy technician Eckerd Drugs, Houston, 1983-86; staff pharmacist Randalls Food Market Inc., Houston, 1987-89, pharmacy mgr., 1989-95; pharmacy coord. Randalls Food Market Inc., 1995—; preceptor U. Houston, 1987—, U. Tex., Austin, 1990—. Mem. United Meth. Ch.; mem. exec. bd. U. Houston Pharmacy Golf Tournament Com., pres., 1989—. Named one of Outstanding Young Women of Am., 1983, 86, Preceptor of the Yr. Univ. Houston, 1995. Mem. Harris County Pharm. Assn., Tex. Pharm. Assn., Am. Pharm. Assn. Home: 3024 High Plains Dr Katy TX 77449-6211

SPIERER, ROBERT, physician; b. S.I., N.Y., June 26, 1945; s. Efram and Regina (Stern) S.; m. Marilyn J. Borack, July 7, 1968; children: Sharon, Henry, Eric. BA, Columbia U., 1967; MD, Albert Einstein Coll. Medicine, 1971. Diplomate Am. Bd. Internal Medicine, Am. Bd. Pediatrics, Am. Bd. Family Medicine, Am. Bd. Emergency Medicine, Am. Bd. Geriatric Medicine. Physician Edison (N.J.) Med. Group, 1977—. With USPHS, 1973-75. Office: Edison Med Group 16 Ethel Rd Edison NJ 08817

SPIES, JACOB JOHN, health care executive; b. Sheboygan, Wis., Jan. 27, 1931; s. Jacob Alfred and Julia Effie (Wescott) S.; m. Donna Dolores Jerale, June 17, 1954; children: Gary, Joni, Shari. BBA, U. Wis., 1955. V.p. health care systems Wausau (Wis.) Ins. Cos., 1972-77, v.p. mgmt. systems, 1977-79; dep. dir. Health Policy Inst. Boston U., 1979-85; pres., chief exec. officer Co-Med, Inc., Columbus, Ohio, 1984-85; sr. v.p. PARTNERS Nat. Health Plans, Irving, Tex., 1985-90; chmn. PARTNERS Health Plans of Colo., Denver, 1986-90; prin. The Furst Group, Dallas, 1990—; pres., CEO Dallas/Ft. Worth Health Industry Coun., 1994—; bd. dirs. Integrated Healthcare Corp.; adv. bd. Healthcare Adminstrn.; chmn. Tex. Women's U. Co-author: A Corporations Experience with IPA-HMO, 1981, Health Care Cost Containment, 1983. Sgt. U.S. Army, 1952-54, Korea. Decorated Bronze Star, 1953. Mem. Group Health Assn. Am. (com. mem. 1988, 91), Am. Managed Care and Rev. Assn. (bd. dirs.), Nat. Assn. Employers on Health Care Actions (chmn.), North Tex. Med. Edn. Consortium (bd. trustees 1995—), LaCima Club, Denton Country Club. Episcopalian. Home: 1492 Rockgate Rd S Roanoke TX 76262-7899 Office: The Furst Group 5215 N O Connor Blvd Ste 975 Irving TX 75039-3713

SPIGELMAN, ALAN VICTOR, ophthalmologist; b. Chgo., 1956. BS in Biology summa cum laude, U. Ill., Urbana, 1977; MD, U. Ill., Chgo., 1981. Intern UCLA, 1982; resident ophthalmology Ill. Eye & Ear Infirmary, Chgo., 1986; fellow cornea, refractive surgery U. Minn, Mpls., 1987; cornea and refractive surgery specialist Franklin Eye Cons., Southfield, Mich., 1987—; resident dir. ophthalmology Sinai Hosp., Detroit, 1988—. Fellow Am. Acad. Ophthalmology; mem. AMA, Mich. Acad. Ophthalmology, Mich. Keratorefractice Soc. Office: Franklin Eye Cons Ste 100 29275 Northwestern Hwy Southfield MI 48034-5743

SPILKA, BERNARD, psychology educator; b. Bronx, N.Y., Aug. 12, 1926. BA, NYU, 1949; MS, Purdue U., 1950, PhD, 1952. Grad. teaching asst. Purdue U., Lafayette, Ind., 1950, sr. grad. rsch. asst. voice sci. lab., 1950-52; rsch. psychologist combat crew lab. Human Resources Rsch. Ctr., Randolph Field, Tex., 1952-53; staff psychologist tng. dept. human engring. U.S. Navy Spl. Devices Ctr., Sands Point, N.Y., 1953-55; asst. prof. psychology Washburn U., Topeka, 1955-57; instr. U. Kans. Extension, Topeka, 1956-57; asst. prof. psychology U. Denver, 1957-61, assoc. prof. psychology, 1961-65, prof. psychology, 1965—; cons. Fed. Youth Ctr., Englewood, Colo., Nat. Coun. Chs. of Christ, Community Rels. Commn. of Denver, Civil Rights Commn. of Colo., U.S. Office Edn., Indian Health Svc., Bur. Indian Affairs, Bur. Reclamation, Luth. Ch. Am., Reorganized Ch. LDS, Children's Hosp., Denver, Search Inst., Mpls. Author: Psychology in Literature: A Reader for Introductory Psychology, 1985, (with others) The Psychology of Religion: An Empirical Approach, 1985, Religion in Psychodynamic Perspective, 1996; cons. editor Jour. for the Sci. Study of Religion, 1969-71, editorial reader, 1971—; assoc. editor Rev. of Religious Rsch., 1970—; mem. editorial bd. Omega, 1976—, Internat. Jour. of the Psychology of Religion, 1989—; book rev. editor Religious Studies Rev., 1983-85; contbr. articles to profl. jours. Recipient Commendation award USN, 1955, Cert. Appreciation award Am. Optometric Assn., 1961; NIMH grantee, 1965-68. Fellow APA (divsn. 36, chair fellows com. 1982-83, pres. 1985-86, chair awards com. 1987—, William James award 1982, Cert. Appreciation 1986, 90), Rocky Mountain Psychol. Assn. (chmn. conv. program 1965, pres. 1967-68, chmn. nominations com. 1968-69, chmn. membership and elections com. 1969-70, Disting. Svc. award 1978), Soc. for the Sci. Study of Religion (v.p. 1978-79, chair publs. com. 1977-79), Religious Rsch. Assn.; mem. AAUP (v.p. Washburn U. chpt. 1956-57, pres. U. Denver chpt. 1962-63, sec.-treas., 1966-67), Acad. Religion and Mental Health, Psi Chi, Sigma Xi, Phi Beta Kappa. Home: 1949 S Olive St Denver CO 80224-2255 Office: U Denver Dept Psychology Denver CO 80208-0204

SPILLER, HART, microbiologist; b. Berlin, Dec. 1, 1939; came to U.S., 1979; s. Helmut and Erika (Hurt) S. Degree, Pedagogical Coll. Univ., 1962, FA Univ. Erlangen, 1972; PhD, FA Univ. Erlangen, 1975. Registered primary, secondary tchr., Australia. Head tchr. Evang. Lutheran Ch., Territory Papua, New Guinea, Australia, 1963-65; supr. English schs. New Guinea, 1966; postdoctoral rsch. assoc. U. Konstanz, West Germany, 1975-78; fellow U. Calif., Davis, 1979-80; adj. postdoctoral assoc. U. Fla., Gainesville, 1981-85; postdoctoral assoc. U. Fla., 1986-87; rsch. asst. prof. biology Fisk U., Nashville, 1989-94. Active Amnesty Internat., Konstanz, Davis, 1977-79; founder, referee commr. Gainesville Recreational Soccer, 1981-88; bd. dirs. Clergy & Laity Concerned, Nashville, 1990-94; scoutmaster troop 76 Boy Scouts Am., 1990-94, scout coord.; councillor Corinthian Bapt. Ch., Nashville, 1989-94, ch. councillor 1994—. Mem. Am. Soc. Plant Physiologists, Am. Soc. Microbiology. Office: Corinthian Bapt Ch 819 33rd Ave N Nashville TN 37209

SPINA, HORACIO ANSELMO, physician; b. Buenos Aires, Mar. 19, 1939; came to U.S., 1970; s. Antonio and Rosa Palma S.; m. Patricia Anne Duffy, Apr. 4, 1985; children: Alicia V., Cristina V., Mario A. Nat. U. Cordoba, Universidad Nacional Cordoba, Argentina, 1968; MD in Psychiatry, U. Pitts., 1974. Diplomate Am. Bd. Psychiatry and Neurology. Resident U. Pitts., 1971-74; rotating intern Shadyside Hosp., Pitts., 1970-71; med. dirs. psychiat. svcs. and chem. dependence program St. Clair Mem. Hosp., Pitts., 1980—; clin. asst. prof. psychiatry U. Pitts. Mem. APA, InterAm. Coll. Physicians and Surgeons, Psychiat. Physicians Pa., Cordoba Soc. Pharmacology and Therapeutics, N.Y. Acad. Scis., Am. Soc. Clin. Psychopharmacology, Acad. Psychosomatic Medicine, Nat. Alliance for the Mentally Ill. Office: 1050 Bower Hill Rd Ste 303 Pittsburgh PA 15243-1869

SPINALE, FRANCIS G., medical educator, research cardiologist; b. Beverly, Mass., July 14, 1956; m. Molly R. Thomas, Sept. 11, 1982. BS in Biology, Northeastern U., 1979; MS in Biometry, Med. U. S.C., 1984, PhD in Pathology, 1988, MD, 1993. Diplomate Nat. Bd. Med. Examiners. Rsch. assoc., divsn. cardiothoracic surgery Med. U. S.C., Charleston, 1985-88, asst. prof., divsn. cardiothoracic surgery, 1988-92, assoc. prof. cardiothoracic surgery and physiology, 1992—, assc. prof. pediat., 1994-96, prof. surgery, anesthesiology, physiology and pediatrics, 1996—; adj. prof. dept. bioengring. Clemson U., 1988—. Contbr. over 100 articles to profl. jours.; editl. rev. bd. Am. Jour. Physiology, Jour. Molecular and Cellular Cardiology, Circulation Rsch., Annals of Thoracic Surgery, Cardiovascular Rsch., Basic Rsch. in Cardiology, PACE, Circulation; abstract reviewer Am. Heart Assn. 66th Scientific Sessions, 1993, 94, 95; editor: (book) The Pathophysiology of Tachycardia Induced Heart Failure,, 1995. Recipient Sec.'s Cmty. Health Promotion award for excellence, U.S. Dept. Health and Human Svcs., 1984, grad. rsch. scholarship award Am. Lung Assn. S.C., 1986, Young Investigators award Am. Heart Assn., 1989, 1st prize Young Investigator Award Heart Inst. for Children, Chgo., 1990, 1st Investigator award R29 NIH, Heart Lung and Blood Inst., 1991, Est. Investigator award Am. Heart Assn., 1994-99; invited spkr. various confs. Mem. AMA, Acad. Surg. Rsch., Soc. Exptl. Biology and Medicine, Internat. Soc. Heart Rsch., Am. Physiol. Soc. (fellow cardiovasc. sect. 1994), S.C. Med. Assn. Home: 1528 Newberry St Charleston SC 29412 Office: Med Univ SC Divsn Cardiothoracic Surg 171 Ashley Ave Charleston SC 29425

SPINDELL, ROBERT FREEMAN, osteopath; b. Boston, Nov. 4, 1953; s. Freeman Arthur and Barbara Ethel (Berry) S.; m. Theresa May Michaud (div. 1982); 1 child, Ryan Robert F.; m. Debra Alice Buote, Dec. 24, 1983; children: Robert Richard F., Tyson Freeman, Sarah Tamson, Dustin Emerson. BA, Tulane U., 1975; DO, Kirksville Coll. Osteo. Medicine, 1979. Diplomate Am. Osteo. Bd. Family Physicians; cert. ACLS instr., advanced trauma life support, advanced pediatric life support. Intern Osteo. Hosp. of Maine Inc., 1979-80; pvt. practice Madison, Fla., 1980-88; dir. emergency medicine Suwannee Hosp. Inc., Live Oak, Fla., 1991-96; dir. emergency med. svc. Madison County Emergeny Med. Svcs., Madison, 1992-96, Lafayette County Emergency Med. Svcs., Mayo, Fla., 1993-96, Suwannee County Emergency Med. Svcs., Live Oak, 1994-96; mem. affiliate faculty Fla. affiliate Am. Heart Assn., 1995—. Maj. USAR, 1990-91. Mem. Am. Osteo. Assn., Am. Osteo. Coll. Family Physicians, Assn. Mil. Surgeons U.S., Assn. Osteo. Mil. Surgeons U.S., Soc. U.S Army Flight Surgeons, Fla. Assn. Emergency Med. Svcs. Med. dirs. Republican. Home: Rt 3 Box 1185 Madison FL 32340

SPINDLER, SUZANNE JOAN, psychologist; b. Chgo., Dec. 27, 1946; d. Warner Max and Shirley Rose (Evenstein) Linfield; children: Joe U. Lilienfeld, David Louis. BA in English and French, U. Tex., Arlington, 1969; MA in Psychology, Tex. Woman's U., 1986, PhD in Psychology, 1990. Lic. psychologist, Tex.; lic. marriage and family therapist, Tex. Teaching asst. dept. psychology and philosophy Tex. Woman's U., Denton, 1985-87; psychometrician Devel. Learning Materials, Allen, Tex., 1988, Psychol. Corp., San Antonio, 1989; psychologist Adlerian Counseling Ctr. North Tex., Arlington, 1988-91; psychol. intern Psychol. Svcs. Dallas Ind. Sch. Dist., 1989-90; sch. psychologist Ft. Worth Ind. Sch. Dist., 1990—, internship dir. psychol. svcs., 1993-96; pvt. practice Arlington, 1991—; cons. Dallas County Schs., Dallas County Juvenile Dept. Youth Village, 1990. Author: (manual) Pre-Doctoral Internship, 1991; contbr. articles to profl. jours. Bd. mem. Parents and Children Together, Fed. Correctional Inst., Ft. Worth, 1990—. Scholar Tex. Woman's U., 1985, 86. Mem. APA, NASP, Tex. Psychol. Assn., Alpha Chi, Phi Kappa Phi, Psi Chi, Kappa Delta Pi, Sigma Delta Tau. Jewish. Office: Ft Worth Ind Sch Dist Psychol Svcs 100 N University Dr Fort Worth TX 76107-1360

SPINELLA, JUDY LYNN, healthcare administrator; b. Ft. Worth, Apr. 8, 1948; d. Gettis Breon and Velrea Inez (Webb) Prothro; children: Scott Slater, Jennifer. BS, U. Tex., 1971; MS, Tex. Woman's U., 1973; MBA, Vanderbilt U., 1993. RN, Tex., Calif., Tenn. Asst. prof. U. Tex., Arlington, 1976-81; dir. emergency svcs. San Francisco Gen. Hosp., 1981-84, assoc. adminstr. for clin. svcs., 1984-88; exec. dir. for nursing svcs. Vanderbilt U. Med. Ctr., Nashville, 1988-93, dir. patient care svcs., 1993-94; dir., COO Vanderbilt U. Hosp., Nashville, 1994-96; healthcare cons. APM, Inc., N.Y.C., 1996—. Wharton fellow Johnson & Johnson, 1987. Mem. Am. Orgn. Nurse Execs., Emergency Nurses Assn. (bd. dirs., treas. 1979-86), Tenn. Orgn. Nurse Execs. (bd. dirs. 1989-91), Sigma Theta Tau. Home: 175 E 96th St Apt 27L New York NY 10128

SPINGARN, CLIFFORD LEROY, internist, educator; b. Bklyn., May 8, 1912; s. Alexander and Eleanor (Trinz) S.; m. Eleanor Harrison, June 9, 1937; children: John Harrison, Alexandra. AB, Columbia U., 1933, MD, 1937. Diplomate Am. Bd. Internal Medicine. Intern Mt. Sinai Hosp., N.Y.C., 1937-40, asst. attending physician, 1946-63, assoc. attending physician, 1963—, chief parasitology clinic, 1956-80; attending physician Doctors Hosp., N.Y.C., 1968-85, chmn. com. on continuing med. edn., 1976-85; attending physician Beth Israel Med. Ctr., N.Y.C., 1986—; pvt. practice internal medicine N.Y.C., 1946—; instr. pharmacology Columbia, 1940-42; asst. clin. prof. preventive medicine NYU, 1956-68; assoc. clin. prof. medicine Mt. Sinai Sch. Medicine, 1966-83, lectr. in medicine, 1983—; attending physician north divsn. Beth Israel Hosp., N.Y.C., 1986—. Author numerous papers. Trustee Milton Helpern Libr. Legal Medicine, 1982—; bd. dirs. N.Y. Faculty Continuing Med. Edn., 1982-86. Lt. (j.g.) to lt. comdr. M.C., USNR, 1942-46; lt. comdr. ret. res. Recipient Disting. Svc. award Doctors Hosp., 1987. Fellow ACP, N.Y. Acad. Medicine; mem. AAAS, N.Y. Soc. Tropical Medicine, Am. Soc. Tropical Medicine and Hygiene, Am. Soc. Parasitologists, Am. Soc. Internal Medicine, Med. Soc. County N.Y. (chmn. grievance com. 1969-72, chmn. bd. censors 1978-80, pres. 1981, trustee 1982-87, Disting. Svc. award 1986), Gerontol. Soc. Am., Soc. Internal Medicine County New York (pres. 1965-67), N.Y. State Soc. Internal Medicine, N.Y. Cardiological Soc. (bd. dir. 1971-73), Phi Beta Kappa, Sigma Xi, Alpha Omega Alpha. Home: 201 E 79th St New York NY 10021-0830 Office: 66 E 80th St New York NY 10021-0223

SPINKS, DAVID WAYNE, osteopathic physician; b. Pasadena, Tex., Sept. 20, 1952; s. Victor Eugene and Evelyn Ollie (Lubojasky) S.; m. Andrea Rachelle DelSardo; children: Damon, Dustin, Devin, Collin. BS magna cum laude, Tex. A&M U., 1975; DO, Tex. Coll. Osteo. Medicine-North Tex. State U., 1979. Intern Okla. Osteo. Hosp., Tulsa, 1979-80; practice osteo. family medicine Deer Park Clinic, Tex., 1980-82; ptnr., physician San Augustine Family Medicine Clinic, Deer Park, 1982—; co-owner San Augustine Indsl. Clinic and Mobile Med. Svcs., Deer Park; ptnr. Vista Healthcare, Pasadena, River Oaks Imaging and Diagnostic, Houston, East Side Imaging, Houston, Southwest Widgets, Premier Health Care, McShane Med., Diversified Innovators, Inc.; dir. Physical Change program; bd. dirs. Tex. Coastal IPA; team physician Laporte High Sch.; staff physician Bay Shore Hosp., Humana Hosp. Southmore, Vista Healthcare, Surgicare, Pasadena; affiliate physician St. Lukes Episcopal Hosp., Houston, Kelsey-Seibold Clinic, Houston. Supporting mem. Met. Mus. Art, Houston Mus. Natural Sci., Houston Ballet, George Bush Libr.-Tex. A&M U. Mem. Am. Acad. Family Physicians, Am. Coll. Gen. Practice, Am. Osteo. Assn., Tex. Osteo. Med. Assn., Tex. A&M Aggie Club, Life Extension Internat., Alumni Assn. Tex. Coll. of Osteopathic Medicine, Nat. Acad. Sports Medicine, Am. Preventive Med. Assn., Am. Acad. Anti-aging Medicine, Am. Aging Assn., Century Club Tex. A&M, Former Students Assn. Tex. A&M, Tex. Acad. Family Physicians, Cure Old Age Disease Soc., Atlas Club Tex. Coll. Osteopathic Medicine, Century Club Tex. Coll. Osteopathic Medicine, Baywood Shadows Civic Club, Phi Eta Sigma, Psi Chi, Phi Kappa Phi, Sigma Sigma Phi. Republican. Co-patented anti-snoring device. Avocations: travel, skiing, jogging, weight lifting. Home: 6842 Cedar Lawn Cir Pasadena TX 77505-4304 Office: San Augustine Family Medicine Clinic 321 W San Augustine St Deer Park TX

77536-4027 also: Diversified Innovators Inc 4808 Fairmont Ste 215 Pasadena TX 77505

SPINNER, GARY FREDERICK, physician assistant; b. Newark, N.J., Nov. 8, 1949; s. Harry Spinner and Adele (Spinner) Armm; m. Janet Crocker, July 14, 1974; children: Jacob Adam, Anna Ruth. BA, Rutgers U., 1972; cert. physician asst., Yale Sch. Medicine, 1983; MPH, U. Conn., 1993. Social worker Cath. Social Svcs., Syracuse, N.Y., 1974-78; paramedic, co-dir. Plenty Ambulance Svc., Bronx, N.Y., 1978-81; physician asst. Alex Isant, MD, Newtown, Conn., 1983-84; physician asst., adminstr. managed care Hill Health Corp., New Haven, Conn., 1984—; corp. dir. Columbus House, New Haven, 1987—; chairperson Homeless Healthcare Network, New Haven, 1988-95; co-chair Conn. Dept. Social Svcs. Statewide Adv. Coun., Hartford, 1993-96; bd. dirs. Cmty. Health Network, Meridan, chairperson quality mgmt. and improvement com., 1995—; faculty Yale Univ. Sch. Medicine; presenter and lectr. in field. Recipient Humanitarian Svc. award Jack W. Cole Soc., 1986. Fellow Am. Acad. Physician Assts. (Outstanding Physician Asst. award 1990), Conn. Acad. Physician Assts.; mem. APHA. Office: Hill Health Corp 400 Columbus Ave New Haven CT 06519

SPINNER, ROBERT JAY, orthopedic surgeon; b. N.Y.C., Dec. 8, 1961; s. Morton and Paula (Lerner) S. SB, MIT, 1984; M of Studies, Oxford (Eng.) U., 1985; MD, Mayo Clinic, 1989. Rsch. fellow, Luce scholar Prince of Wales Hosp., Hong Kong, 1989-90; intern in surgery Duke Univ., Durham, N.C., 1990-91, jr. resident in surgery, 1991-92, resident in orthopaedic surgery, 1992-96; resident in neurosurgery Mayo Clinic, Rochester, Minn., 1996—. Recipient Davison Teaching award Duke U. Med. Sch., 1993, Schilling scholar Mayo Found., 1984-86, Goldner Rsch. award in Orthopaedic Surgery Duke U. Med. Ctr., 1996. Mem. Phi Beta Kappa, Sigma Xi, Alpha Chi Sigma. Office: Mayo Clinic Dept Neurosurgery Rochester MN 55905

SPINWEBER, CHERYL LYNN, research psychologist; b. Jersey City, July 26, 1950; d. Stanley A. And Evelyn M. (Pfleger) S.; m. Michael E. Bruich, June 18, 1977; children: Sean Michael Bruich, Gregory Alan Bruich. AB with distinction, Cornell U., 1972; PhD in Exptl. Psychology, Harvard U., 1977. Lic. psychologist, Calif. Asst. prof. psychiatry Tufts U. Sch. Medicine, Medford, Mass., 1977-79; asst. dir. sleep lab. Boston State Hosp., 1973-79; dep. head dept. behavioral psychopharmacology Naval Health Research Ctr., San Diego, 1978-86, head dept. behavioral psychopharmacology, 1986-89; research asst. prof. dept. psychiatry Uniformed Svcs. U. of the Health Scis., Bethesda, Md., 1985—; lectr. workshop instr. U. Calif. San Diego, La Jolla, 1979-81, vis. lectr. 1979-86; assoc. adj. prof. Dept. Psychology, 1989-94, adj. prof., 1994—; courtesy clin. staff appointee dept. psychiatry Naval Hosp., San Diego, 1984-89, clin. dir. Sleep Disorders Ctr. Mercy Hosp., San Diego, 1991—; pediatric sleep specialist Children's Hosp., San Diego, 1992-95. Contbr. articles to profl. jours. Scholar Cornell U., Ithaca, N.Y., 1968-72, West Essex Tuition, 1968-72, Cornell U. Fedn. Women, 1917-72, Harvard U., 1972-73, 74-76, NDEA Title IV, 1973-74; postdoctoral associateship Nat. Research Council, 1978-80, Outstanding Tchg. award U. Calif. San Diego, 1994. Fellow Am. Sleep Disorders Assn., Clin. Sleep Soc., We. Psychol. Assn. (sec.-treas. 1986—); mem. Am. Men and Women of Sci., Sleep Rsch. Soc. (exec. com. 1986-89), Calif. Sleep Soc., Sigma Xi. Office: U Calif San Diego Dept Psychology 0109 La Jolla CA 92093

SPIRA, MELVIN, plastic surgeon; b. Chgo., July 3, 1925; s. Samuel and Jessie (Tivin) S.; m. Rita Silver, Nov. 27, 1952; children—Mary Ann, Joel Bennett, Pamela Beth. Student, Wright Jr. Coll, Chgo., 1942-43, Franklin and Marshall Coll., Lancaster, Pa., 1943-44; DDS, Northwestern U., 1947, MSD, 1951; MD, Med. Coll. of Ga., 1956. Diplomate Am. Bd. Plastic Surgery. Intern Duke U. Hosp., Durham, N.C., 1956-57, jr. asst. resident, 1958-59, asst. resident, 1959-60; resident Jefferson Davis Hosp, Houston, 1960-61, asst. in surgery and plastic surgery; sr. attending physician Ben Taub Gen. Hosp, Houston, chief of plastic surgery; attending physician Tex. Children's Hosp., Houston; chief plastic surgery Meth. Hosp., Houston, St. Lukes Episc. Hosp., Houston, VA Hosp., Houston; prof. Baylor Coll. Medicine, Houston, head div. plastic surgery; chmn. Am. Bd. Plastic Surgery, 1984-85. Served with USN, 1943-45, 48-50. Fellow ACS; mem. Houston Surg. Soc., Am. Soc. Maxillofacial Surgeons (pres. 1974-75), Am. Soc. Plastic and Reconstructive Surgeons, Harris County Med. Soc., Plastic Surgery Research Council, So. Med. Assn., Tex. Med. Assn., Am. Trauma Soc., G.V. Black Soc., Internat. Soc. for Burn Injuries, Am. Burn Assn., Am. Cleft Palate Assn., Am. Assn. Plastic Surgeons (pres. 1992-93), Acad. Plastic Surgery Forum, Internat. Soc. Reconstructive Microsurgery, Tex. Surg. Soc., Michael E. DeBakey Internat. Cardiovascular Soc., Baron Hardy Soc., Am. Soc. for Aesthetic Plastic Surgery, Alpha Omega Alpha, Sigma Xi. Office: Baylor Coll Medicine Div Plastic Surgery 6560 Fannin St Ste 800 Houston TX 77030-2725

SPIRA, ROBERT SIDNEY, gastroenterologist; b. N.Y.C., June 20, 1949; s. Bernhard and Molly (Linchitz) S.; m. Naomi Nutkis, Dec. 29, 1973; children: Daniele, Etan, Benjamin. BA, NYU, 1971, MD, 1975. Diplomate Nat. Bd. Med. Examiners, Am. Bd. Internal Medicine, Am. Bd. Gastroenterology. Resident in medicine NYU and N.Y. VA Med. Ctr., N.Y.C., 1975-79; fellow in gastroenterology N.Y. VA Med. Ctr., N.Y.C., 1979-81; clin. asst. prof. medicine N.J. Sch. Medicine, Newark, 1983—; assoc. prof. medicine Sch. Post Grad. Medicine, Seton Hall U., Newark, 1988—; chief dept. gastrointestinal endoscopy St. Michael's Meml. Med. Ctr., Newark, 1992—; bd. dirs. Advanced Nuclear Magnetic Resonance. Presenter in field, 1981—. Fellow Acad. Medicine N.J.; mem. ACP, N.J. Soc. Gastrointestinal Endoscopy (pres. 1990-91), N.J. Soc. Gastroenterology (exec. bd. 1987—, pres. 1994), Ileitis Colitis Found. (adv. bd. 1991—). Jewish. Office: 743 Northfield Ave West Orange NJ 07052-1107

SPIRE, JEAN-PAUL CHARLES, neurologist, researcher, director laboratory; b. Lyon, Rhone, France, June 16, 1942; came to U.S., 1970; s. Etienne and Loulette (Planque) S.; m. Ikuko Mizuno, Dec. 25, 1984. BSc, McGill U., Mont., Can., 1962; MD, U. Mont., 1966. Instr. U. Calif., San Francisco, 1971-73, asst. prof., 1973-76; asst. prof. U. Chgo., 1976-82, dir. clin. neurophysiology labs., 1976—, assoc. prof., 1982-87, prof., 1987—. Office: U Chgo 5841 S Maryland Ave Chicago IL 60637-1463

SPIRNAK, JOHN PATRICK, urologist, educator; b. Cleve., Mar. 17, 1951; s. John Joseph and Mary Barbara (Mancos) S.; m. Diane Lynne Miller, Sept. 15, 1979; children: Jennifer, Patrick, Christopher. BS in Zoology, Ohio U., 1973; MD, Emory U., 1977; degree in Urology, Case Western Reserve U., 1983. Diplomate Am. Bd. Urology. Intern, gen. surg. resident Univ. Hosp., Cleve., 1977-79, urology resident, 1980-83; nephrology rsch. resident Metro Health Med. Ctr., Cleve., 1979-80, dir. urology, 1987—; sr. instr. divns. urology Case Western Reserve U., Cleve., 1983-85, asst. prof. urology, 1985-91, assoc. prof. urology, 1991—; adv. panel mem. U.S. Pharmacopeia Urology, Washington, 1986—. Editor Urologic Decision Making, 1991, New Diagnostic Tests, 1996; manuscript reviewer Jour. Endourology, 1989—, Urology, 1993—, Jour. Urology, 1994—; contbr. articles to profl. jours. and chpts. to books. Named One of Top Doctors Cleve. Mag., 1996. Fellow ACS; mem. AMA, Am. Assn. Surgery Trauma, Am. Urol. Assn., Cleve. Urol. Soc. (sec./treas. 1986-88, pres. 1988-89). Home: 2178 Silveridge Trail Westlake OH 44145 Office: Metro Health Med Ctr 2500 Metro Health Dr Cleveland OH 44109

SPIRO, MELFORD ELLIOT, anthropology educator; b. Cleve., Apr. 26, 1920; s. Wilbert I. and Sophie (Goodman) S.; m. Audrey Goldman, May 27, 1950; children: Michael, Jonathan. B.A., U. Minn., 1941; Ph.D., Northwestern U., 1950. Mem. faculty Washington U., St. Louis, 1948-52, U. Conn., 1952-57, U. Wash., 1957-64; prof. anthropology U. Chgo., 1964-68; prof., chmn. dept. anthropology U. Calif., San Diego, 1968—; Bd. dirs. Social Sci. Research Council, 1960-62. Author: (with E.G. Burrows) An Atoll Culture, 1953, Kibbutz: Venture in Utopia, 1955, Children of Kibbutz, 1958, Burmese Supernaturalism, 1967, Buddhism and Society: A Great Tradition and Its Burmese Vicissitudes, 1971, Kinship and Marriage in Burma, 1977, Gender and Culture: Kibbutz Women Revisited, 1979, Human Nature and Culture, 1993; editor: Context and Meaning in Culture Anthropology, 1965, Oedipus in the Trobriands, 1982, Burmese Brother or Anthropological Other?, 1992. Fellow Am. Acad. Arts and Scis., Nat. Acad. Scis.; mem. Am. Anthrop. Assn., Am. Ethnol. Soc. (pres. 1967-68), AAAS, Soc. for Psychol. Anthropology (pres. 1979-80). Home: 2500 Torrey Pines Rd La Jolla CA 92037

SPIRO, RONALD HARVEY, surgeon; b. N.Y.C., Aug. 17, 1930; s. Carl and Henrietta (Feinman) S.; m. Nina M. Koshetz, June 21, 1954; children: Jeffrey, Kenneth, Mark, Rebecca. AB, Syracuse U., 1951; MD, SUNY at Syracuse, 1955. Diplomate Am. Bd. Surgery (Gen. Surgery). Internship Mt. Sinai Hosp., 1955-56; residency in gen. surgery Bronx VA Hosp., 1956-60; fellowship in surgical oncology Meml. Sloan Kettering, 1962-65; assoc. attending surgeon Mt. Sinai Hosp., N.Y.C., 1966-72; asst. clin. prof. surgery Mt. Sinai Sch. of Medicine, N.Y.C., 1966-72; attending surgeon Manhattan Eye Ear Throat Hosp., N.Y.C., 1967-89, Meml. Sloan Kettering, N.Y.C., 1972—; prof. clin. surgery Cornell Med. Coll., N.Y.C., 1988—. Editor: Current Concepts in Head & Neck, 1989; contbr. over 150 articles to profl. surg. jours. Capt. USAF, 1960-62. Fellow ACS, Soc. Surg. Oncology, Soc. Head & Neck Surgeons (v.p. 1995-96, pres.- elect 1996—, Hays Martin lectureship 1993), N.Y. Head and Neck Soc. (pres. 1988-89), Alpha Omega Alpha. Office: Meml Sloan Kettering Cancer Ctr 425 E 67th St New York NY 10804

SPITLER, ANTHONY DAVID, optometrist; b. Mar. 28, 1967; s. Lionel Donald and Rita Elizabeth S. BS in Biology, Ferris State U., Big Rapids, Mich., 1989, BS in Vision Sci., 1993, OD with high distinction honors, 1993. Optometrist Detroit Optometric Clinic, Warren, Mich., 1993—. Mem. Am. Optometric Assn., Mich. Optometric Assn. Roman Catholic. Home: 13335 Stonegate Dr Apt 8 Sterling Heights MI 48312 Office: Detroit Optometric Clinic 26768 Deguindre Warren MI 48091

SPITSBERGEN, DOROTHY MAY, children's healthcare specialist; b. Eaton Rapids, Mich., May 13, 1932; d. Herbert Madison and Eva (Bunker) Van Aken; m. Merlin D. Spitsbergen, Dec. 27, 1952; children: Karen Richardson, Jan, Raymond (dec.), John, Claire Cooper. Student, Mich. State U., 1950-53; BS in Sociology, Oakland U., 1973, MA in Teaching Early Childhood Edn., 1980. Cert. child life specialist. Child life specialist Crittenton Hosp., Rochester, Mich., 1980-94; hosp. play cons. Hong Kogn Hosps., 1994-95; instr. Oakland U., 1996—; lectr. Oakland U., 1981—, Wayne State U., Macomb C.C., 1982—, Mott C.C., Flint, Mich., 1992; creator Pediatric Edn. Program, 1981—, Child Body Safety Program, 1985—; state presentor in field. Co-author: Infants and Toddlers in the Hospital, 1993. Bev Erikson Meml. grantee, 1987. Mem. Assn. for Care Children's Health (sec. state chpt. 1984-86, nat. presenter 1984, 87, state presentor 1983, 86), Child Life Coun., Rochester Tuesday Musicale Club (past pres., v.p., sec.), Delta Psi Kappa. Democrat. Home and Office: 3959 Ella Mae St Oakland MI 48363-2854

SPITZ, JORGE RONALD, physician; b. Rio de Janeiro, Brazil, June 25, 1950; s. Tibor and Eugenia (Fruchthandler) S.; m. Lucia Lerner, Oct. 22, 1974; children: Mariana, Lidia. MD, UFRJ, Rio de Janeiro, 1973. Resident Mt. Sinai Med. Svc., N.Y.C., 1974-76; fellow Tufts Med. Ctr. Hosp., Boston, 1976-78; dir. Clinica Spitz, Rio de Janeiro, 1978—. Mem. ACP, ACR. Office: Rm 405, Av Ataulto de Paiva 1251, CEP 22440-031 Rio de Janeiro Brazil

SPITZ, MARK CONRAD, neurologist; b. Phoenix, Oct. 5, 1952; s. Arthur and Heddy (Smilovic) S.; m. Carol Jaye Rivkin, July 25, 1977; children: Joshua, Marilyn. BA in Chemistry, Ariz. State U., 1975; MD, U. Ariz., 1979. Diplomate Am. Bd. Neurophysiology, Am. Bd. Neurology. Med. resident Baylor Affiliated Hosps., Houston, 1979-80, neurology resident, 1980-83; electrophysiology fellow Columbia Presbyn. Hosp., N.Y.C., 1983-85; neurology faculty U. Colo., Denver, 1985—; profl. adv. bd. pres. Epilepsy Found., Colo., 1985—, Denver, 1989-96; profl. adv. bd. Epilepsy Found. of Am., Landover, Md., 1988—, bd. dirs. Contbr. articles to profl. jours. Named Hero of Week Rocky Mountain News, 1993. Mem. EEG Soc. (head membership com. 1990—), Epilepsy Found. of Am., Am. Epilepsy Soc., Am. Acad. Neurology. Office: U Colo Health Scis Ctr Box B150 4200 E 9th Ave Denver CO 80262

SPITZER, JACLYN B. RUBINSON, audiologist; b. Bklyn., July 3, 1951; d. Victor and Elaine (Mendelsohn) Rubinson; m. Jack Spitzer, Aug. 20, 1972; 1 child, Raquel Adina. BA cum laude, Bklyn. Coll., 1972; MS, Tchrs. Coll., 1973, MPhil, 1977; PhD, Columbia U., 1978. Cert. tchr. speech improvement, N.Y.; cert. tchr. speech and hearing handicapped, N.Y; lic. audiologist, Ohio, Conn.; lic. hearing aid dealer, Conn. Substitute tchr. N.Y.C. Bd. Edn., 1973; audiology doctoral stipend trainee Bklyn. VA Hosp., 1973-76; acting dir. audiology dept. Cleve. Hearing and Speech Ctr., 1977-78; instr. dept. speech communication Case Western Res. U., 1977-78, asst. prof. audiology and speech pathology div. otolaryngology and surgery, 1978-79, adj. asst. prof. dept. communication scis., 1980-82; rsch. assoc. Cleve. VA. Med., 1978-79, audiologist, 1980-82; chief audiology and speech pathology svc. West Haven Med. Ctr., 1982—; asst. clin. prof. dept. surgery Yale U., 1982-89, assoc. clin. prof. dept. surgery, 1989—; adj. asst. prof. dept. speech and hearing Cleve. State U., 1980-82; adj. prof. dept. communication disorders So. Conn. State U., 1984-89; vis. prof. dept. communication scis. U. Conn., 1985-89. Editorial cons. to sci. jours.; contbr. articles and book chpts. to profl. jours. Recipient N.Y. State regent's scholarship. Fellow Am. Acad. Audiology, Am. Speech and Hearing Assn. (task force on nat. exam. 1978, state coord. for Ea. Ohio, congl. action contact network 1979-82, com. on disorders ctrl. auditory processing 1980-82, com. on aural rehab. 1986-91, program com. 1986-87, ad hoc com. on advances in audiologic practice 1990—), Ohio Speech and Hearing Assn. (audiologic affairs com. 1979, legis. affairs com. 1980-81), Ohio Coun. on Audiology (task force on early identification of hearing loss in infants 1979-81), Acoustical Soc. Am., Am. Auditory Soc., Conn. Speech and Hearing Assn. Home: 1287 Mt Carmel Ave North Haven CT 06473-1048

SPITZER, ROXANE, executive, educator, consultant; b. N.Y.C., July 5, 1939; d. Irving and Lillian (Gardos) Blumberg; children: Michael, David, Deborah. BS, Adelphi U., Garden City, N.Y., 1960; MA, Columbia U., 1972; MA, MBA, Claremont Coll., 1989, PhD, 1994. Assoc. dean Coll. Nursing U. Ill., Chgo.; assoc. hosp. dir. nursing U. Ill. Hosp. Clinic, Chgo.; v.p. patient care svcs. Cedars-Sinai Med. Ctr., L.A.; corp. v.p. St. Joseph Health Sys., Orange, Calif.; commr. Prospective Payment Assessment Commn., Orange, Calif., 1991—; exec. v.p., COO Hosp. of Good Samaritan, L.A., 1992; v.p. managed care Med. Sys., 1992-95; prof. Owen Sch. Mgmt., prof., assoc. dean practice mgmt. Vanderbilt U. Sch. Nursing, Nashville, 1995—; nursing adv. panel HBO & Co., physician adv. panel; cons. in field; lectr. in field. Author books; contbr. articles to profl. jours.; adv. bd. Nursing Adminstrn. Quar., Nursing Mgmt. Mag.; editl. bd. Nursing Adminstrn. Quar., Quality Rev. Jour. Fellow Am. Acad. Nursing, Wharton Nurse Exec. Fellows Program; mem. Orgn. Nurse Execs. of Calif., Am. Hosp. Assn. (coun. of nursing 1987-89, diplomate), Am. Coll. Health Care Execs., Am. Orgn. Nurse Execs., Am. Nurses Assn., Sigma Theta Tau. Home: 3911 Vailwood Dr Nashville TN 37215

SPITZER, WILLIAM JOHN, healthcare social work administrator; b. Chgo., Jan. 31, 1949; s. William Carl and Violet (Kramer) S.; m. Eugena Ann Spitzer; 1 child, Colin William. BA, BS, U. Ill., 1971, MSW, 1973, PhD in Social Work, Bus. Adminstrn., 1981. Lic. social worker, Oreg., Tex; cert. sch. social worker, Ill. Dir. foster care svcs. Cath. Social Svcs., Grand Rapids, Mich., 1973-76, dir. residential group treatment, 1975-76; dir., founder Human Devel. Cons. Svcs., Urbana, Ill., 1977-89; dir. dept. social svcs. Sarah Bush Lincoln Health Ctr., Mattoon, Ill., 1982-86; dir. dept. social work svc. Oreg. Health Scis. U., Portland, 1986—; adj. asst. prof. social work Portland State U., 1986—; state clin. dir. Oreg. Critical Response Team, 1988—; v.p. Interagy. Coun. Coles County, Ill., 1984-85; chmn. Area Child Abuse Mgmt. Team Coles County, Ill., 1986. Mem. NASW (chair com. continuing edn. Oreg. chpt. 1988—, bd. dirs. Oreg. chpt. 1987-89, com. minority scholarship 1989, adv. com. LCSW bd. 1990—), Soc. Hosp. Social Work Dirs. (nat. chmn. Hy Weiner leadership award com. 1988, v.p. cen. Ill. dist. 1984-86, nat. com. social work edn. practicum 1987—, Oreg. Social Work Dir. of Yr. 1990, Oreg. Social Work Program of Yr. 1989), Oreg. Soc. Hosp. Social Work Dirs. (pres. 1989-90, exec. bd. 1987-91, chair com. grad. edn. 1986—, chair com. profl. edn. 1990—). Home: 12208 Chadsworth Ct Glen Allen VA 23060-6931 Office: Oreg Health Scis U 3181 SW Sam Jackson Park Rd Portland OR 97201-3011

SPITZNAGEL, JOHN KEITH, periodontist, researcher; b. St. Louis, Feb. 22, 1951; s. John Keith and Anne Moulton (Sirch) S.; m. Susan Victoria Lipton, Jan. 2, 1981; children: Matthew, Katya. BS in Biology, U. N.C., 1977, DDS, 1982, cert. in Periodontology, 1992, PhD in Microbiology, 1994. Postdoctoral fellow Forsyth Dental Ctr., Boston, 1983-85; cons. in bioinformatics, 1984—; periodontic resident U. Tex. Health Sci. Ctr., San Antonio, 1985-91, dentist-scientist fellow, 1987-93; asst. prof. periodontology U. Tenn., Memphis, 1993—. Contbr. articles to profl. jours. Scout leader Boy Scouts Am., Chapel Hill, N.C., 1978-81, Memphis, 1995—. With USCG, 1971-75. Recipient Dentist Scientist award Nat. Inst. Dental Rsch., 1987. Mem. ADA, AAAS, Am. Acad. Periodontology, Am. Soc. for Microbiology, Internat. Assn. Dental Rsch., Delta Sigma Delta. Episcopalian. Office: U Tenn Coll of Dentistry 875 Union Ave Memphis TN 38103-3513

SPIVEY, GARY HUGH, epidemiology educator; b. Midland, Tex., Dec. 3, 1943; s. Robert C. and Ruth Spivey; m. Lavinia Anne Constable, Apr. 10, 1965; children: Sarah Ellen, Terrill McClure. BA in Zoology, U. Calif., Davis, 1965; MD, U. Calif., San Francisco, 1969; gen. preventive medicine, MPH, Johns Hopkins U., 1975. Asst. prof. epidemiology UCLA, 1975-80, assoc. prof., 1980-83, adj. assoc. prof., 1983-95; mgr. epidemiology and environ. medicine Unocal Corp., L.A., 1983-91, mgr. epidemiology and indsl. hygiene, 1991-95; prin. clin. coord. Kans. Found. for Med. Care, Topeka, 1995—. Contbr. articles to profl. jours. Served to lt. comdr. USPHS, 1970-72. Postdoctoral fellow Johns Hopkins U., Balt., 1974-75. Fellow Am. Coll. Preventive Medicine, Am. Coll. Epidemiology; mem. Am. Pub. Health Assn., Soc. Epidemiol. Rsch., Soc. Occupational and Environ. Health (governing coun. 1990-92), Am. Coll. Occupational and Environ. Medicine, Sigma Xi, Phi Kappa Phi, Delta Omega. Office: KFMC 2947 SW Wanamaker Dr Topeka KS 66614

SPIZZIRI, JOSEPH, physician assistant; b. Braddock, Pa., Dec. 6, 1949; s. Anthony and Elizabeth (Bombarderi) S. AA, Valley Jr. Coll., 1976; BSBA, U. Redlands, 1982, MHA, 1986. CRTT Behren's Meml. Hosp., Van Nuys, Calif., 1976, '77; RN Valley Presbyn. Hosp., Van Nuys, 1978-80; asst. adminstr. West Lake Med. Ctr., West Lake Village, Calif., 1980-82; dir. ICU, respiratory therapy, emergency room Christian Hosp., Perris, Calif., 1990-94; physician's asst. Pvt. Practice, Beaumont, Calif., 1994—. Foster parent GLASS, West Hollywood, Calif., 1985-93. Mem. Acad. Physicians' Assts. Home: 24895 Baxter Ranch Rd Lake Elsinore CA 92530

SPLAIN, SHEPARD HOWARD, orthopedic surgeon; b. N.Y., June 3, 1947. BA, Queens Coll., 1968; DO, Mich. State Univ., 1973. Diplomate Am. Bd. Orthopedic Surgery. Physician in charge sports medicine Brookdale Hosp., N.Y., 1980—, vice chmn. dept. orthopedic surgery, 1984—; prof. chmn. dept. surgery N.Y. Coll. Orthopedic Medicine, Old Westbury, N.Y., 1990—. Contbr. articles to profl. jours. Home: 145-70 7 Ave Whitestone NY 11387 Office: 1 Brookdale Plaza Brooklyn NY 11212

SPLANE, RICHARD BEVERLEY, social work educator; b. Calgary, Alta., Can., Sept. 25, 1916; s. Alfred William and Clara Jane (Allyn) S.; m. Verna Marie Huffman, Feb. 22, 1971. BA, McMaster U., 1940, LLD (hon.), 1990; cert. social sci. and adminstrn., London Sch. Econs., 1947; MA, U. Toronto, 1948, MSW, 1951, PhD, 1961; LLD (hon.), Wilfrid Laurier U., 1988, U. B.C., Can., 1996. Exec. dir. Children's Aid Soc., Cornwall, Ont., Can., 1948-50; with Health and Welfare Can., Ottawa, 1952-72; exec. asst. to dep. minister nat. welfare Health and Welfare Can., 1959-60, dir. unemployment assistance, 1960-62, dir. gen. welfare assistance and services, 1960-70, asst. dep. minister social allowances and services, 1970-72; vis. prof. U. Alta., Edmonton, 1972-73; prof. social policy Sch. Social Work, U. B.C., Vancouver, 1973—; cons. Govt. Can., Govt. Alta., UNICEF. Author: The Development of Social Welfare in Ontario, 1965; (with Verna Huffman Splane) Chief Nursing Officers in National Ministries of Health, 1994. Served with RCAF, 1942-45. Recipient Centennial medal Govt. Can., 1967, Charles E. Hendry award U. Toronto, 1981, Commemorative medal for 125th anniversary of Confederation of Canada, 1992. Mem. Can. Assn. Social Workers (Outstanding Nat. Svc. award 1985), Can. Inst. Pub. Adminstrn., Can. Hist. Assn., Can. Coun. on Social Devel. (Lifetime Achievement award 1995), Internat. Assn. Schs. Social Work, Internat. Confs. Social Devel. (pres.), World Federalists of Can. (pres. Vancouver br.), Vancouver Club, Order of Can. Mem. United Ch. Can. Office: U BC Sch Social Work, 208 West Mall, Vancouver, BC Canada V6T 1Z2

SPLAVER, SARAH, psychologist; b. N.Y.C.; d. Morris and Rose (Farber) S. BA, Hunter Coll., N.Y.C.; MA, Columbia U; PhD, NYU, 1953. Cert. psychologist, N.Y. Psychologist N.Y.C., 1953—, writer, 1949—; guidance dir. Rhodes Preparatory Sch., N.Y.C., 1946-52; editor, publisher Occu-Press, N.Y.C., 1953-70; editorial cons. Socioguidrama Series, N.Y.C., 1953-73; pres. Cancer Counselor, Breast Diseases Assn. Am., N.Y.C., 1975-80, Cancer Hopefuls United for Mut. Support, 1980-87. Author: Your Career -- If You're Not Going to College, 1971, Your College Education -- How to Pay for It, 1968, Your Handicap -- Don't Let It Handicap You, 1974, Your Personality and You, 1965, You and Today's Troubled World, 1970, Nontraditional Careers for Women, 1973, Your Mind and Breast Diseases, 1978. Co-chmn. Mental Health Profls. Com., N.Y.C., 1976; exec. dir. Com. for Establishment of Breast Splty., 1989-92; bd. dirs. Herzl Hadassah, 1991—. Named Woman of the Yr. CHUMS, 1985, Outstanding Woman Woman's Day Mag. 1987, City Coun. Citation, Coun. of City of N.Y., 1985. Fellow APA, Internat. Coun. Psychologists, Am. Counseling Assn.; mem. Nat. Career Devel. Assn. (life), Am. Rehab. Counseling Assn., Authors Guild, Bermuda Club (pres.), Poetry Club. Jewish. Home and Office: 6350 NW 62nd St Apt 207 Fort Lauderdale FL 33319-6287

SPLENDIANI, GIORGIO, nephrology educator; b. Macerata, Marche, Italy, July 26, 1934; s. Fiorino and Finimola (Pettorossi) S.; m. Maria Sofia Giordano, Mar. 4, 1961; children: Francesco, Alessandra Gemma, Roberto, Nicola. MD, U. Rome, Italy, 1958. Med. asst. Goverative Hosp., Tripoli, Libia, 1960-61, Civil Hosp., L'Aquila, Italy, 1962-65; med. aivto Civil Hosp., L'Aquila, 1965-70, dir. nephrology dept., 1971-86; assoc. prof. nephrology U. Rome, Italy, 1986—. Editor: Artificial Support in Severe Organ Failure, 1984, (symposium procs.) Hemoferfusion Adborbento Immobilist Bioreactants, 1992. Mem. Internat. Soc. Nephrology, Internat. Soc. Artificial Organs, Am. Soc. Artificial Organs, Rotary Club (past pres.). Home: Via P Colagrandel 1-a, 67100 L Aquila Italy Office: Univ Tor Vergata, Via Pineta Sacchetti 506, 00100 Rome Italy

SPLITTSTOESSER, DON FREDERICK, microbiologist, educator; b. Norwalk, Wis., Aug. 17, 1927; s. Frederick Albert and Martha (Rosenwald) S.; m. Clara Mae Quinnell, Mar. 19, 1959. B.S., U. Wis., 1951, M.S., 1952, Ph.D., 1956. Mem. faculty Cornell U., prof. microbiology N.Y. State Agrl. Expt. Sta., Geneva, chmn. dept. food sci. and tech., 1982-89; chmn. food protection com. NRC, 1981-85. Editor: Food Microbiology: Public Health and Spoilage Aspects, 1976. Editor: Compendium of Methods for the Microbiological Examination of Foods, 3rd edit., 1992; contbr. articles to profl. publs. Bd. dirs., treas. Family Counseling Service, Geneva, 1960-63; chmn. Geneva Zoning Bd. Appeals, 1972-83. Served as 1st lt. U.S. Army, 1956-58. Fellow Inst. Food Technologists (chmn. N.Y. sect. 1970); mem. Am. Soc. Microbiology (pres. N.Y. br. 1966), Am. Soc. Enology and Viticulture (chmn. eastern sect. 1979). Democrat. Unitarian. Clubs: Torch (pres. 1970), Geneva Country (Geneva). Avocations: winemaking; golf. Office: Cornell U Ny State Agrl Expt Sta Geneva NY 14456

SPOCK, BENJAMIN MCLANE, physician, educator; b. New Haven, Conn., May 2, 1903; s. Benjamin Ives and Mildred Louise (Stoughton) S.; m. Jane Davenport Cheney, June 25, 1927 (div. 1976); children: Michael, John Cheney; m. Mary Morgan Councille, Oct. 24, 1976. B.A., Yale U., 1925, student Med. Sch., 1925-27; M.D., Columbia U., 1929. Intern in medicine Presbyn. Hosp., N.Y.C., 1929-31; in pediatrics N.Y. Nursery and Child's Hosp., 1931-32; in psychiatry N.Y. Hosp., 1932-33; practice pediatrics N.Y.C., 1933-44, 46-47; instr. pediatrics Cornell Med. Coll., 1933-47; asst. attending pediatrician N.Y. Hosp., 1933-47; cons. in pediatric psychiatry N.Y. City Health Dept., 1942-47; cons. psychiatry Mayo Clinic and Rochester Child Health Project, Rochester, Minn.; asso. prof. psychiatry Mayo Found., U. Minn., 1947-51; prof. child devel. U. Pitts., 1951-55, Western Res. U., 1955-67. Author: Baby and Child Care, 1946, (with J. Reinhart and W. Miller) A Baby's First Year, 1954, (with M. Lowenberg)

Feeding Your Baby and Child, 1955, Dr. Spock Talks with Mothers, 1961, Problems of Parents, 1962, (with M. Lerrigo) Caring for Your Disabled Child, 1965, (with Mitchell Zimmerman) Dr. Spock on Vietnam, 1968, Decent and Indecent, 1970, A Teenagers Guide to Life and Love, 1970, Raising Children in a Difficult Time, 1974, Spock on Parenting, 1988, (with Mary Morgan) Spock on Spock: A Memoir of Growing Up With the Century, 1989, A Better World for Our Children, 1994. Presdl. candidate Peoples Party, 1972, advocator Nat. Com. for a Sane Nuclear Policy (SANE), co-chmn., 1962 . Served to lt. comdr. M.C., USNR, 1944-46. Home: PO Box 1268 Camden ME 04843-1268

SPODAK, MICHAEL KENNETH, forensic psychiatrist; b. Bklyn., Nov. 5, 1944; s. Harry and Betty (Rahn) S.; children: Lisa Beth, Brett David. B.S., Union Coll., 1966; M.D., SUNY-Syracuse, 1970. Diplomate: Nat. Bd. Med. Examiners, Am. Bd. Neurology and Psychiatry. Intern Mary Imogene Bassett Hosp., Cooperstown, N.Y., 1970-71; resident John Hopkins Hosp., Balt., 1974-77; practice medicine specializing in civil and criminal forensic psychiatry Towson, Md., 1977—; chief dept. psychiatry Balt. County Gen. Hosp., Randallstown, 1978-85; mem. staff Clifton T. Perkins Hosp. Ctr., Jessup, Md., 1977-92; clin. asst. prof. psychiatry U. Md. Hosp., Balt., 1983—; psychiat. cons. Bur. Disability Ins., Social Security Adminstrn., Workmen's compensation Commn., Balt., 1981—; dir. community forensic services Mental Hygiene Adminstrn., Md., 1982-92; faculty Nat. Jud. Coll., 1988—; mem. Md. Task Force on Somatic Therapies. Contbr. numerous articles on forensic psychiatry to profl. jours., chpt. to book. Served with M.C. USN, 1972-74. Mem. Am. Acad. Psychiatry and Law, Am. Psychiat. Assn., Md. Psychiat. Soc., Md. Med. Soc. (chmn. occupational health com. 1983-90), Baltimore County Med. Soc. Office: 26 W Pennsylvania Ave Towson MD 21204-5001

SPODICK, PEARL BLEGEN, counselor, medical psychotherapist; b. Mpls., June 4, 1927; d. Harry Cornelius and Vera Maude (Kidder) Blegen; m. Robert Casper Spodick, Nov. 1, 1955; children: Michael, Peter, Russell, Edward, Rebecca. BA, Albertus Magnus Coll., 1978; MA in Psychology and Art Therapy, Goddard Coll., 1980; postgrad., Simmon's Coll., 1977. Cert. med. psychotherapist, clin. mental health counselor; nat. cert. counselor; CHAMPUS (Civilian Health and Med. Program for Uniformed Svcs.) authorized marriage and family therapist, Conn. Cons., art psychotherapist Conn. D.C.Y.S., 1978—, Conn. Sexual Trauma Tratment Program, 1978-79, Arden House Long Term Care Facility, Hamden, Conn., 1979-82, Ctr. for Study of Normative Behavior, Hamden, 1982-85, Curtis Home Children's Residential Treatment Ctr., Meriden, Conn., 1982-93; instr. psychology Albertus Magnus Coll., Hamden, 1988-90; med. psychotherapist, counselor The Psychotherapy Ctr., Woodbridge, Conn., 1980-93, Hamden, Conn., 1993—; med. psychotherapist, counselor Art Psychotherapy and Counseling Ctr., Woodbridge, 1980-93, Hamden, 1993—. Fellow Am. Bd. Med. Psychotherapists (diplomate); mem. ACA (cert.), Nat. Bd. Cert. Clin. Hypnotherapists (cert.), Am. Art Therapy Assn. (ATR, legis. rep. 1983-89), Am. Assn. Study Mental Imagery, Am. Assn. Cert. Clin. Mental Health Counselors (cert.), Am. Bd. Behavioral Therapists (cert.), Am. Mental Health Counselors Assn. Democrat. Jewish. Office: The Psychotherapy Ctr Ste 208 1890 Dixwell Ave Hamden CT 06514

SPOHN, HERBERT EMIL, psychologist; b. Berlin, Germany, June 10, 1923; s. Herbert F. and Bertha S.; m. Billie M. Powell, July 28, 1973; children—Jessica, Madeleine. B.S.S., CCNY, 1949; Ph.D., Columbia U., 1955. Research psychologist VA Hosp., Montrose, N.Y., 1955-60; chief research sect. VA Hosp., 1960-64; sr. research psychologist Menninger Found., Topeka, 1965-80; dir. hosp. research Menninger Found., 1979-94, dir. research dept., 1981-94; ret., prof. emeritus for rsch., 1994—; mem. mental health small grant com. NIMH, 1972-76, mem. treatment assessment rev. com., 1983-86, chmn. 1986-87. Author: (with Gardner Murphy) Encounter with Reality, 1968; assoc. editor: Schizophrenia Bull, 1970-87, 91—; contbr. articles to profl. jours. Served with AUS, World War II. USPHS grantee, 1964—. Fellow Am. Psychopath. Assn.; mem. AAAS, N.Y. Acad. Sci., Soc. Psychopath. Research, Phi Beta Kappa, Sigma Xi. Office: Menninger Found PO Box 829 Topeka KS 66601-0829

SPOKANE, ROBERT BRUCE, biophysical chemist; b. Cleve., Aug. 5, 1952; s. Herbert Norman and Marjorie Ellen (Firsten) S.; m. Linda Carol Wright, June 20, 1976; children: Lea, Hannah, Tara. BS in Chemistry, Ohio U., 1975; MS in Biophys. Chemistry, U. Colo., 1978, PhD in Biophys. Chemistry, 1981. Cert. full cave diver. Teaching asst. Dept. Chemistry, U. Colo., Boulder, 1975-77, rsch. asst., 1977-81; staff scientist Procter & Gamble Co., Cin., 1981-84; rsch. scientist Dept. Neurophysiology, Children's Hosp., Cin., 1984-90, YSI Co., Rsch. Ctr., Yellow Springs, Ohio, 1990—; cons. Synthetic Blood Internat., Yellow Springs, 1992. Contbr. articles to profl. jours. Rescuer, treas. Boulder Emergency Squad, 1980; rescue diver Kitty Hawk Scuba, Dayton, Ohio, 1992. Recipient Merck Index award Ohio U., 1975. Mem. Am. Chem. Soc., N.Y. Acad. Sci., Am. Physiol. Soc., Nat. Speleological Soc. (cave diving sect.), Sigma Xi. Home: 1715 Garry Dr Bellbrook OH 45305-1362 Office: YSI Co 1725 Brannum Ln Yellow Springs OH 45387-1107

SPONSELLER, CRAIG EUGENE, physician assistant; b. Kendallville, Ind., Aug. 2, 1948; s. Harold Eugene and Carolyn Jane (Roy) S.; m. Jacqueline Keyes, Dec. 22, 1973; children: Tarah, Jena, Luke. Assocs., Ind. U., 1968, B in Allied Health, 1970. Cert. physician's asst., Ind. Radiol. technologist Marion County Gen. Hosp., Indpls., 1968-70, St. Joseph Hosp., Ft. Wayne, Ind., 1970; physician asst. Patten (Maine) Health Ctr., 1974-80, State of Mich. Corrections, Jackson, 1980-93, Albion (Mich.) Cmty. Hosp., 1993—; ACLS instr. Am. Heart Assn., Mich., 1985—. Selectman Patten Town Bd., 1977-78; adjunctant Am. Legion, Munith, Mich., 1989-92, vice-comdr., 1993-94. With U.S. Army, 1970-72, Vietnam. Fellow Am. Acad. Physician Assts., Mich. Acad. Physicians Assts. Baptist. Home: 2318 Spring Arbor Rd Jackson MI 49203 Office: Sponseller Health Svcs 2318 Spring Arbor Rd Jackson MI 49203

SPOONER, ERIC W., pediatric cardiologist; b. Ann Arbor, Mich., May 7, 1945; s. Charles W. and Vera (Warbasse) S.; m. Maria A., June 21, 1969; children: Emily, Molly. BS, U. Mich., 1967; MD, Wayne State U., 1971. Instr. pediatrics U. Mich. Sch. Medicine, Ann Arbor, 1976-77; asst. prof. pediatrics Albany Med. Ctr., 1977-81, clin. asst. prof. pediatrics, 1981—; sec., treas. Shaher, Farina, Spooner, Albany, 1980—. Fellow Am. Coll. Cardiology, Am. Acad. Pediatrics, Am. Soc. Echo Cardiology; mem. N.Y. Coll. Cardiology, Upstate N.Y. Cardiac Soc. Office: 319 S Manning Blvd Ste 203 Albany NY 12208

SPOOR, JOHN EDWARD, physician; b. Laurens, N.Y., Nov. 14, 1935; s. Elmer Eugene and Helen Blanche (Stanton) S.; m. Donna Lou Crandall; children: Kevin Chandler, Brian Stephen. MD, U. Buffalo, 1966. Diplomate Nat. Bd. Med. Examiners, Am. Bd. Emergency Medicine. Intern Lakeland (Fla.) Gen. Hosp., 1966-67; pvt. practice Laurens, N.Y., 1967-69; emergency physician Fox Hosp., Oneonta, N.Y., 1969-85; dir. health ctr. State U. Coll. Oneonta, 1977-81; dir. emergency dept. Park Ridge Hosp., Rochester, N.Y., 1978, Fox Hosp., Oneonta, 1981-85; dir. emergency svcs. M.I. Basstt Hosp., Cooperstown, N.Y., 1985-92, chief emergency medicine, 1988-92; dir. emergency svcs. Community Meml. Hosp., Hamilton, N.Y., 1993-95, med. dir., 1993-95; v.p. med. affairs Cortland (N.Y.) Meml. Hosp., 1995—, 1995—; cons. emergency medicine Cortland Meml. Hosp.; cons. Schoharie County Cmty. Hosp., Cobleskill, N.Y., 1985-90; med. dirs. Susquehanna Adirondack EMS Program, Binghamton, N.Y.; mem. adv. com. Otsego County Emergency Health Svcs., 1974-76, 79-92; mem. com. in emergency health svcs. Med. Soc. State N.Y., 1979-94; mem. Adirondack Appalachian Regional EMS Coun., 1984-90; mem. emd. adv. com. N.Y. State EMS Devel. Office, 1987-89; mem. adv. group Office Health Systems Mgmt., Syracuse, N.Y., 1994—. Contbr. articles to profl. jours. Otsego County coroner, 1970-72; mem. bd. edn. Morris Ctrl. Sch., 1971-73; chpt. faculty Am. Heart Assn., Utica, N.Y., 1981-93, bd. dirs., 1986-88; chmn. N.Y. Stte Emergency Med. Svcs. Coun., Albany, 1982; mem. Otsego County Econ. Devel. Coun., Oneonta, 1988. With USN, 1953-57. Recipient svc. award Otsego County Emergency Squad Assn., Cooperstown, 1979, award for outstanding community svc. Fox Hosp., Oneonta, 1981, First Aider of Yr. award Cen. N.Y. Emergency Squad Assn., Norwich, 1974, recognition of svc. award Otsego County CD, Cooperstown, 1982. Mem. Am. Coll. Emergency Physicians (com. emergency resources 1987-91, chair sect. rural emergency medicine 1991-92, editor newsletter sect. rural emergency medicine 1992-93), Am. Coll. Physician Execs., Nat. Rural Health Assn. (mem. spl. task force on rural EMS 1988-90, bd. dirs. 1992), N.Y. State Med. Soc., Ostego County Med. Soc., Am. Acad. Med. Dirs. Home: RR 1 Box 157 Laurens NY 13796-9780 Office: Cortland Meml Hosp 134 Homer Ave Cortland NY 13045

SPORN, ALFRED BERNARD, psychiatrist; b. Frumosu, Roumania, Nov. 29, 1926; came to U.S., 1973; s. Bernard and Ernestine (Pesati) S.; m. Raisa T. Sitkova, Nov. 29, 1955; children: Natalie, Steven. Dr. Med., Med. Sch., Roumania, 1951; PhD, Med. Sch., Leningrad, Russia, 1954. Diplomate Am. Bd. Psychiatry and Neurology. Dir. dept. Inst. Pub. Health, Bucharest, Roumania, 1954-73; resident psychiatry Beth Israel Med. Ctr., N.Y.C., 1974-76; chief resident Beth Israel Med. Ctr., 1976-77, physician in charge, 1977-83; chief psychiatrist Our Lady of Mercy Med. Ctr., Bronx, N.Y., 1983-91, dir. dept. psychiatry, 1991—; asst. prof. clin. psychiatry Mt. Sinai Sch. Medicine, N.Y.C., 1977-91; clin. assoc. prof. psychiatry N.Y. Med. Coll., 1991—. Mem. Am. Psychiatry Assn. Home: 33 Parkway E Mount Vernon NY 10552-1218

SPORN, MICHAEL BENJAMIN, cancer etiologist; b. N.Y.C., Feb. 15, 1933; married; 2 children. MD, U. Rochester, 1959. Intern U. Rochester Sch. Medicine, 1959-60; mem. staff lab. neurochemistry Nat. Inst. Neurol. Diseases and Blindness, 1960-64; mem. staff Nat. Cancer Inst., Bethesda, Md., 1964-70, head lung cancer unit, 1970-73, chief lung cancer br., 1973-78, chief lab. chemoprevention, 1978-95; prof. pharmacology Dartmouth Med. Sch., Hanover, N.H., 1995—. Recipient Am. Cancer Soc. Medal of Honor, 1994. Mem. Am. Assn. Cancer Rsch. (B.F. Cain Meml. award 1991), Am. Assn. Biol. Chemistry. Office: Dept Pharmacology Dartmouth Med Sch Hanover NH 03755-3835

SPOTO, ANGELO PETER, JR., internist, allergist; b. Tampa, Fla., Mar. 25, 1933; s. Angelo Peter and Zillah Marie (Renfroe) S.; m. Carolyn Jeanette Barbee, Aug. 30, 1958; children: Keith Peter, Elizabeth Anne, Jacqueline Marie. AA, U. Fla., 1953; BS in Medicine, Duke U., 1956, MD, 1957. Diplomate Am. Bd. Internal Medicine, Am. Bd. Allergy and Immunology. Intern Duke U. Med. Ctr., Durham, 1957-58, fellow in medicine (allergy), 1958-59; resident in internal medicine USAF Hosp., Lackland AFB, Tex., 1960-62; resident in allergy Walter Reed Army Med. Ctr., Washington, 1962-63; staff allergist Watson Clinic LLP, Lakeland, Fla., 1966—; ptnr., 1968—; med. staff Lakeland Reg. Med. Ctr., 1966—; bd. dirs. Watson Clinic Found., 1984—, pres., 1984-93; clin. assoc. prof. medicine U South Fla., Tampa, 1973-77; chmn. bd. dirs. Polk Internat., Inc., 1986—; bd. dirs. Am. Group Practice Corp., 1991-94, chmn., 1992-94. Contbr. articles to profl. jours. Ruling elder Presbyn. Ch., 1970—. Maj. USAF, 1959-66. Decorated Air Force Commendation medal. Fellow ACP, Am. Acad. Allergy, Am. Coll. Allergy; mem. AMA (alt. del. 1992), Polk County Med. Assn. (exec. com. 1971), Fla. Med. Assn., Fla. Allergy Soc. (pres. 1973-74, exec. com. 1972-78), Southeastern Allergy Assn., So. Med. Assn., Am. Group Practice Assn. (trustee 1985-94, pres. 1991-92), Assn. Cert. Allergists (bd. govs. 1971-75), Lakeland C. of C. (bd. dirs. 1987-89). Republican. Presbyterian. Home: 2515 Hollingsworth Hill Ave Lakeland FL 33803-3236 Office: Watson Clinic LLP 1600 Lakeland Hills Blvd Lakeland FL 33805-3019

SPOTT, MARY ANN, health facility administrator; b. Scranton, Pa., Aug. 21, 1963; d. Frederick Charles and Mary Ann (Maglio) S. BS in Biology, U. Scranton, 1985; BS in Health Records, York Coll. Pa., 1989; MPA, Pa. State U., 1995. RRA, Am. Health Info. Mgmt. Assn.; CPHQ, Nat. Assn. for Healthcare Quality. Clk. Frederick C. Spott & Assoc., Scranton, 1979-84, J.C. Penneys, Scranton, 1986-88; med. record asst. Pa. Dept. Health, Harrisburg, 1988, cancer registry specialist, 1989-92; mgr. quality assurance and trauma registry Pa. Trauma Sys. Fedn., Mechanicsburg, Pa., 1992-95; asst. dir. MIS and trauma registry Pa. Trauma Sys. Fedn., Mechanicsburg, 1995—; cons. Village Vista Nursing Home, Millersville, Pa., 1990—, First Step, Harrisburg, 1990-94, Gaudenzia, Harrisburg, 1994; mem. adv. bd. Delta Devel., Camp Hill, Pa., 1993. Sec. of records West Shore Rotary, Camp Hill, 1992-95; v.p. Am. Bus. Women's Assn., Camp Hill, 1992-95.

SPRABERY, CAROL ANN, health facility administrator; b. North Island, Calif., July 6, 1945; d. Thomas Eugene and Dorothy Frances (Grimes) Forister; div.; children: Scott Ellis, Cynthia Anne. BS, U. Miss. 1967; MEd, Miss. State U., 1986, PhD, 1990. Lic. profl. counselor; cert. psychometrist, nat. counselor. Adolescent counselor Laurelwood Psychiat., Meridian, Miss.; counselor Lamar Sch., Meridian; tchr. counselor edn. Weems Cmty. Mental Health Ctr., Meridian, 1990-95; pvt. practice Glen Burnie, Md., 1995—; mem. adj. faculty Miss. State U., 1990—. Mem. ACA, Miss. Counselors Assn., Assn. Mental Health Counselors, Assn. Sch. Counselors, Lauderdale County Mental Health Bd. Office: Ste 409 1600 S Crain Hwy Glen Burnie MD 21061

SPRAFKIN, ROBERT PETER, psychologist, educator; b. N.Y.C., Dec. 18, 1940; s. Benjamin R. and Dora M. (Berman) S.; m. Barbara Marcus, July 19, 1964; children: Jeffrey P., Neal R., Noah M. AB, Dartmouth Coll., 1962; MA, Columbia U., 1964; PhD, Ohio State U., 1968. Lic. psychologist, N.Y. Asst. prof. psychology Syracuse (N.Y.) U., 1968-71, adj. assoc. prof., 1973-88, adj. prof., 1989—; chief day treatment ctr. VA Med. Ctr., Syracuse, 1971-95, dir. psychology tng. program, 1983—; clin. assoc. prof. dept. psychiatry SUNY Health Sci. Ctr., Syracuse, 1973-95; cons. psychologist Assn. for Retarded Citizens, Syracuse, 1993—, clin. prof. dept. psychiatry, 1995—; chief Behavioral Medicine Sect. Psychology Svc., 1994—; acting. chief psychology svc., 1994-96, chief, 1996—. Co-author: Skilltraining for Community Living, 1976, Skillstreaming the Adolescent, 1980, Social Skills for Mental Health, 1993. Mem. Onondaga County Legis. Coun. on Disabled, Syracuse, 1982-94; mem. cmty. svcs. bd. County Dept. Mental Health, 1987—. Mem. APA, Assn. Advancement of Behavior Therapy, Soc. Behavioral Medicine, Cen. N.Y. Psychol. Assn. (pres.), Dartmouth Club (pres.). Office: VA Med Ctr 800 Irving Ave Syracuse NY 13210-2716

SPRAGUE, CHARLES CAMERON, medical foundation president; b. Dallas, Nov. 14, 1916; s. George Able and Minna (Schwartz) S.; m. Margaret Frederica Dickson, Sept. 7, 1943; 1 dau., Cynthia Cameron. BBA, BS, DSc, So. Meth. U.; MD, U. Tex. Med. Branch, Galveston, 1943; DSc (hon.), U. Dallas, 1983, Tulane U., 1991. Diplomate Am. Bd. Internal Medicine. Intern U.S. Naval Med. Center, Bethesda, Md., 1943-44; resident Charity Hosp., New Orleans, 1947-48, Tulane U. Med. Sch., 1948-50; Commonwealth research fellow in hematology Washington U. Sch. Medicine, St. Louis, also Oxford (Eng.) U., 1950-52; mem. faculty Med. Sch. Tulane U., 1952-67, prof. medicine, 1959-67; dean Med. Sch. Tulane U. (Sch. Medicine), 1963-67; prof., dean U. Tex. Southwestern Med. Sch., Dallas, 1967-72; pres. U. Tex. Health Sci. Center, Dallas, 1972-86; pres. SW Med. Found., 1987-88, chmn. bd., CEO, 1988-95; pres. emeritus U. Tex. SW Med. Ctr., 1988-95; chmn. emeritus SW Med. Found., 1995—; Mem. Nat. Adv. Council, 1966-70; mem. adv. com. to dir. NIH, 1973—; chmn. Gov.'s Task Force Health Manpower, 1981, Gov.'s Med. Edn. Mgmt. Effectiveness Com.; chmn. allied health edn. adv. com., coordinating bd. Tex. Coll. and Univ. System.; mem. coordinating bd., Tex. Higher Edn., 1989—, vice chmn., 1990— Adv. com. Ctr. Sci. and Soc., U. Tex., Dallas, 1991—. With USNR, 1943-47. Recipient Ashbel Smith Disting. Alumnus award U. Tex. Med. Br., 1967; Disting. Alumnus award So. Meth. U., 1965; recipient Sports Illustrated Silver Anniversary award, 1963. Mem. Assn. Am. Med. Colls. (chmn. council deans 1970, chmn. exec. council and assembly 1972-73), Am. Soc. Hematology (pres. 1966), Assn. Acad. Health Ctrs. (bd. dirs. 1982—, chmn. bd. 1985-86). Office: Southwestern Medical Found PO Box 45708 5323 Harry Hines Blvd Dallas TX 75245-0708

SPRAGUE, JAMES B., ophthalmologist, educator; b. Balt., Apr. 8, 1942; s. James Mather and Isabelle (Baird) S. BA, Harvard U., 1965; MD, U. Pa., 1969. Intern Presbyn.-St. Luke's Med. Ctr., Chgo., 1969-70, resident in medicine, 1970-71; epidemiologist Ctrs. for Disease Control, Atlanta, 1971-73; resident in ophthalmology U. Colo., Denver, 1973-76, fellow in pediatric ophthalmology, 1976-77, asst. prof., 1977-83, assoc. prof., 1983-84; pvt. practice pediatric ophthalmology, McLean, Va., 1984—; clin. assoc. prof. Georgetown U., Washington, 1984—. Office: 1515 Chain Bridge Rd Mc Lean VA 22101-4421

SPRAGUE, MARY JANE ANN, nurse; b. Delphas, Ohio, Oct. 10, 1955; d. Richard John and Margaret Emma (Pittner) Burger; m. John Eugene Sprague, Aug. 18, 1979. Diploma, Bowling Green Area Sch. Nurses, 1974. RN, Ohio. Staff nurse Med. Coll. Ohio, Toledo, 1974-76, Cleve. Clinic, 1976-77, St. Rita's Med. Ctr., Lima, Ohio, 1977-79, Ohio State Med. Ctr., Columbus, 1979-93; transplant coord. Ohio State Med. Ctr., 5, 1993—. Sec., treas. Galleon, Inc., Key West, Fla., 1994, 95, 96. Mem. ANA, Nat. Kidney Found., Am. Heart Assn., N.Am. Transplant Coords. Orgn., Internat. Transplant Nurses Soc., Rotary. Roman Catholic. Office: Ohio State U Med Ctr 770 Kinnear Rd Columbus OH 43212

SPRAGUE, RICHARD STANTON, JR., gastroenterologist; b. Bangor, Maine, July 11, 1957; s. Richard Stanton and Jacqueline Mae (Springer) S.; m. Marilyn Elizabeth Evans, May 28, 1983; children: Ross, Kelly, Emily. BA magna cum laude, Bowdoin Coll., 1979; MD, U. Vt., 1983. Diplomate Am. Bd. Internal Medicine, Am. Bd. Gastroenterology, Nat. Bd. Med. Examiners. Internal medicine intern Harvard Med. Sch./New Eng. Deaconess Hosp., Boston, 1983-84, resident in internal medicine, 1984-86; fellow in gasteroenterology Duke U. Med. Ctr., Durham, N.C., 1986-88; gastroenterologist Riverside Clinic, Jacksonville, Fla., 1988—; chmn. dept. medicine Riverside Hosp., Jacksonville, 1992-94, pres. med. staff, 1994-96; bd. dirs. Riverside Clinic, Jacksonville, 1993-95, chief dept. internal medicine, 1994-96. Contbr. articles to profl. jours. State of Maine scholar, 1975, James Bowdoin scholar, 1975-79. Mem. AMA, ACP, Am. Gastroenterology Assn., Am. Coll. Gastroenterologists, Fla. Med. Soc., Fla. Gastroenterology Soc., Alpha Omega Alpha. Office: 2005 Riverside Ave Jacksonville FL 32204

SPRAINGS, VIOLET EVELYN, psychologist; b. Omaha, Aug. 1, 1930; d. Henry Elbert and Straunella (Hunter) S.; A.B., U. Calif., Berkeley, 1948, M.A., 1951, postgrad., 1960-64, Ph.D., San Francisco, 1982. Tchr., Oakland (Calif.) Public Schs., 1951-58; psychologist Med. Edn. Diagnostic Ctr., San Francisco, 1959-62; dir. psychol. edn. and lang. services Calif. Dept. Edn., 1963-71; asst. prof. San Francisco State U., 1964-71; assoc. prof. ednl. psychology Calif. State U., Hayward, 1971-79; dir. Spraings Acad., Orinda, Lafayette and Walnut Creek, 1967—; psychologist in pvt. practice, 1962—; dir. Western Women's Bank; mem. adv. bd. Bay Area Health Systems Agy.; instr. U. Calif., Berkeley extension, 1964—; mem. oral bd. for Ednl. Psychologists, 1972—; mem. Calif. Dept. Task Force on Psychol. Assessment, 1987—. Mem. adv. com. Foothill Jr. Coll. Dist.; cons. Psychol. Casey Family Program, 1986—. Recipient Phoebe Apperson Heart award San Francisco Examiner, 1968. Mem. Am. Psychol. Assn., Internat. Neurospychol. Assn. (charter), Calif. Psychol. Assn., Calif. Assn. Sch. Psychologists and Psychometrists, Western Psychol. Assn., Nat. Council Negro Women, AAUW, Delta Sigma Theta, Psi Chi, Pi Lambda Theta. Contbr. articles to profl. jours. Home: 170 Glorietta Blvd Orinda CA 94563-3543 Office: 89 Moraga Way Orinda CA 94563-3023

SPRANG, MILTON LEROY, obstetrician, gynecologist, educator; b. Chgo., Jan. 15, 1944; s. Eugene and Carmella (Bruno) S.; m. Sandra Lee Karabelas, July 16, 1966; children: David, Christina, Michael. Student, St. Mary's Coll., 1962-65; MD, Loyola U., 1969. Diplomate Am. Bd. Ob-gyn; Nat. Bd. Med. Examiners; CME accreditation. Intern St. Francis Hosp., Evanston, Ill., 1969-70, resident, 1972-75, sr. attending physician, 1985—; assoc. attending phsycian Evanston Hosp., 1975-79, attending physician, 1980-84, sr. attending physician, 1985—, v.p. med. staff, 1990-91, pres.-elect, 1991-92, pres., 1992-93; also bd. dirs., 1991-94; sec. exec. com. Evanston Hosp., 1993-94; chmn. ob-gyn Cook County Grad. Sch. Medicine,, Chgo., 1983-91; instr. Northwestern U. Med. Sch., Chgo., 1975-78, asst. prof., 1984-85, assoc. prof., 1995—; pres. Northwestern Healthcare Network Physician Leadership, 1994; lectr. acad. and civic groups OB-Gyn. Nat. Ctr. Advanced Med. Edn., 1991—; bd. dirs. Ill. Found. Med. Rev.; bd. trustees Ill. State Ins. Svcs., 1992-96; bd. govs. Ill. State Med. Inter-Inst. Exch., 1987-92. Editor: Profl. Staff News, 1992-93; chmn. editorial bd. Jour. Chgo. Medicine, 1986-91; contbr. articles to profl. jours. Bd. dirs. Am. Cancer Sooc., chmn. profl. edn. com. North Shoore unit, 1982-85; bd. dirs. Chgo. Community Info. Network, 1994-95; mem. Nat. Rep. Congrl. Com., 1981—, Ill. Med. Polit. Action Com. With USN, 1970-72. Fellow ACS, Am. Coll.Ob-Gyn. (chmn. Ill. sect. 1975-76), Am. Soc. Colposcopy and Cervical Pathology; mem. AMA (Physician Recognition award 1977, 80, 83), Ill. Med. Soc. (del. to AMA 1987, 91—, ho. dels., govt. affairs com. 1988-96, chmn. reference com. 1989, chmn. bd. trustees 1996—, chmn. fin. com. 1992-94, sec.-treas. 1994-96), Chgo. Med. Soc. (v.p. 1984-85, adv. com. advt. stds. 1978-84, counselor, physician's rev. com. 1980-85, chmn. 1985 , sec. 1989—, exec. coun. north suburban br. 1981-82, 86, chmn. 1985, trustee ins. bd. 1982—, nominating com. 1985-96, trustee 1986-92, treas. 1986-89, sec. 1989-90, pres.-elect 1990-91, pres. 1991-92, chmn. fin. com. 1985-89, pres. 1991-93, chmn. ethical rels. com. 1994-96, chmn. bd. trustees 1990-91), Chgo. Found. Med. Care (nominating com. 1980-84, med. care evaluation and edn. com. 1980-83, practice guidelines com. 1984), Physician Benefit Trust (chmn. fin. com. 1993-96). Roman Catholic. Home: 4442 Concord Ln Skokie IL 60076-2606 Office: AGSO 1000 Central St Evanston IL 60201-1777

SPRATT, JOHN ARTHUR, surgery educator, researcher; b. Orange, Tex., Jan. 9, 1954; s. John Stricklin and Beverly Winfele (Satcher) S.; m. Linda Sue Simonson, Jan. 6, 1984; children: John Robert, Madeline Susanne, Abigail Louisa, Thomas Edward. BA in Maths., U. Colo., 1975; MS in Maths., U. Mo., 1976; MD, Washington U., St. Louis, 1980. Diplomate Am. Bd. Surgery, Am. Bd. Thoracic Surgery. Resident in surgery Duke U. Med. Ctr., Durham, N.C., 1980-87, fellow in cardio-thoracic surgery, 1988-90; asst. prof. Med. Coll. Va., Richmond, 1990—. Contbr. articles to profl. jours. Fellow ACS (assoc.), Soc. Thoracic Surgeons, Va. Surg. Soc., So. Thoracic Surg. Assn.; mem. Southeastern Surg. Congress. Cell Kinetics Soc., Am. Med. Informatics Assn., Rotary. Baptist. Office: Med Coll Va PO Box 68 Richmond VA 23201-0068

SPRATT, JOHN STRICKLIN, surgeon, educator, researcher; b. San Angelo, Tex., Jan. 3, 1929; s. John Stricklin and Nannie Lee (Morgan) S.; m. Beverly Jane Winfiele, Dec. 27, 1951; children: John Arthur, Shelley Winfiele, Robert Stricklin. AS, U. Tex.-Arlington, 1947; BS with high honors, So. Methodist U., 1949; MD, U. Tex.-Dallas, 1952; MSPH, U. Mo., 1970; postgrad. Washington U., St. Louis, 1961. Asst. in physiology Southwestern Med. Sch., U. Tex., Dallas, 1952; intern, Barnes Hosp., Washington U., St. Louis, 1952-53, asst. resident in surgery, 1955-57, resident, Am. Cancer Soc. fellow in surgery, 1958-59; USPHS Cancer Research fellow in radiotherapy and surgery Mallinckrodt Inst. Radiology, St. Louis, 1957-58, chief resident, 1958-59; mem. surg. faculty Washington U., 1952-76; chief surgeon Ellis Fischel State Cancer Hosp., Columbia, Mo., 1961-76; practice medicine specializing in surgery, Louisville, 1976—; mem. staffs U. Louisville Hosp., Norton-Kosair Children's Hosp., VA Hosp., Bapt. Hosp. East, Jewish Hosp.; prof. surgery U. Mo.-Columbia, 1961-76; prof. surgery U. Louisville, 1976—, prof. health systems, 1980—; clin. prof. surgery F. Edward Hebert Sch. Medicine Uniformed Svcs. U. Health Scis., Bethesda, Md., 1988. Contbr. numerous articles in cancer, surgery and med. edn. fields to sci. publs. Mem. editorial bd. Cancer mag., 1964-91, Am. Jour. Surgery, Jour. Surg. Oncology. Editor, editor-in-chief Louisville Medicine mag., 1979-82, Jour. Pelvic Surgery, 1995—, served to capt. USNR, 1952-93, (ret.). Grantee Nat. Cancer Inst., Am. Cancer Soc. Fellow ACS, Royal Soc. Health; mem. AMA, Am. Surg. Assn., Soc. Surg. Oncology, Res. Officers Assn., Naval Res. Assn., Assn. Mil. Surgeons U.S., Soc. Med. Cons. Armed Forces, Soc. Pelvic Surgeons, Ctrl. Surg. Assn., Soc. Surgery Alimentary Tract, Cell Proliferation Soc., Am. Assn. Cancer Edn., Soc. Univ. Surgeons, Am. Coll. Physician Execs., Alpha Omega Alpha. Democrat. Baptist. Club: Cosmos (Washington). Lodge: Rotary. Home: 2206 Bell Tavern Ct Louisville KY 40207-1215 Office: 529 S Jackson St Louisville KY 40202

SPRAUER, CYNTHIA CAROL, optometrist; b. Bridgeton, N.J., Apr. 11, 1962; d. Frederick Henry and Edna Catherine (Hepner) S. BS in Biology, Va. Tech., 1984; BS in Visual Sci., Pa. Coll. Optometry, 1988, OD, 1991. Tech. rep. Vineland (N.J.) Chem., 1984-87; optometrist Office of Drs. Klein & Schwab, Mays Landing, N.J., 1991-93, Nu Vision, Northfield, N.J., 1993—. Mem. Am. Optometric Assn., N.J. Optometric Assn., South Jersey Optometric Soc., Beta Sigma Kappa. Home: 3627 Whitehall Ct Mays Landing NJ 08330-3244

SPRAY, PAUL, surgeon; b. Wilkinsburg, Pa., Apr. 9, 1921; s. Lester E. and Phoebe Gertrude (Hull) S.; m. Mary Louise Conover, Nov. 28, 1943; children: David C., Thomas L., Mary Lynn (Mrs. Thomas Branham). BS, U. Pitts., 1942; MD, George Washington U., 1944; MS, U. Minn., 1950. Diplomate Am. Bd. Orthopedic Surgery. Intern U.S. Marine Hosp., S.I., 1944-45; resident Mayo Found., Rochester, Minn., 1945-46, 48-50; practice medicine specializing in orthopedic surgery Oak Ridge, Tenn., 1950—; mem. staff Oak Ridge Hosp., Park West Hosp., Knoxville, Harriman Hosp., Tenn.; vol. vis. cons. CARE Medico, Jordan, 1959, Nigeria, 1962, 65, Algeria, 1963, Afghanistan, 1970, Bangladesh, 1975, 77, 79, Peru, 1980, U. Ghana, 1982; AMA vol. physician, Vietnam, 1967, 72; vis. assoc. prof. U. Nairobi, 1973; mem. tchg. team Internat. Coll. Surgeons to Khartoum; vis. prof. orthop. surgery U. Khartoum, 1976; hon. prof. San Luis Gonzaga U., Ica, Peru; AmDoc vol. cons. U. Biafra Tchg. Hosp., 1969; vis. prof. Mayo Clinic, 1988; sec. orthops. overseas divsn. CARE Medico, 1971-76, sec. Medico adv. bd., 1974-76, vice chmn., 1976, chmn., 1977-79, v.p. CARE, Inc., 1977-79, pub. mem. CARE bd. dirs., 1980-90, mem. bd. overseers, 1991—; chmn. Orthops. Overseas, Inc., 1982-86, treas., 1986-88, emeritus mem., 1994; mem. U.S. organizing com. 1st Internat. Acad. Symposium on Orthops., Tianjin, China, 1983; mem. CUPP Internat. Adv. Coun., 1986—; invited guest spkr. Japan Orthop. Assn., 1994. Mem. editorial bd. Contemporary Orthopedics, 1984-96. V.p. Anderson County Health Coun., 1975, pres., 1976-77, hon. bd. dirs., 1991; pres. health commn. Coun. So. Mountains, 1958-65, sec., bd. dirs., 1965-66; Tenn. pres. UN Assn., 1966-67; vice-chmn. bd. Camelot Care Ctr., Tenn., 1979-82, chmn., 1982-86; chmn. bd. dirs. Camelot Found., 1986-87; hon. mem. World Orthopedic Concern, 1990; with del. to Vietnam People to People, 1993, citizen amb. to Vietnam, 1993; del. to Oak Ridge's Sister City, Obinsk, Russia, 1993; trustee Vietnam Am. Scholarship Fund, 1992-95. Recipient Svc. to Mankind award Sertoma, 1967, Humanitarian award Lions Club, 1968, Freedom Citation Sertoma, 1978, Amb. Goodwill Lions Club, award 1979, Medico Disting. Svc. award, 1990, 1st Ann. Vocat. Svc. award Oak Ridge Rotary, 1979, Tech. Communication award East Tenn. chpt. Soc. for Tech. Communication, 1983, Individual Achievement award Meth. Med. Ctr. of Oak Ridge, 1991, Humanitarian award Orthopaedics Overseas, 1992; Melvin Jones fellow Lions Club, 1993. Fellow ACS, Internat. Coll. Surgeons (Tenn. regent 1976-80, bd. councillors 1980-84, hon. chmn. bd. turstees 1981-83, trustee 1983-84, v.p. U.S. sect. 1982-83, mem. surg. teams com. 1983-90, Humanitarian award 1992); mem. AMA (Humanitarian Svc. award 1967, 72), Sociètè International Chirugie Orthopèdique et de Traumuatologie, So. Orthopedic Assn., Western Pacific Orthopedic Assn., Am. Fracture Assn., Am. Acad. Orthopedic Surgeons (mem. com. on injuries 1980-86), Tenn. Med. Assn. (com. on emergency med. svcs. 1978-88), Peru Acad. Surgery (corr.), Peruvian Soc. Orthopedic Surgery and Traumatology (corr.), Clin. Orthopedic Soc., Mid-Am. Orthopaedic Soc., Rotary Club (Oak Ridge chpt.). Home: 507 Delaware Ave Oak Ridge TN 37830-3902 Office: Ste C 160 W Tennessee Ave Oak Ridge TN 37830

SPRECHER, GUSTAV EWALD, pharmacy educator; b. Kupferzell, Germany, Nov. 17, 1922; s. Emil and Emma (Küstner) S.; m. Helga Mohr, Aug. 28, 1955; 1 child, Wolfram. BS in Pharmacy, Tech. U. Karlsruhe, 1953, Dr. rer. nat., 1956, Dr. Habil., 1960. Asst. prof. Tech. U. Karlsruhe, Fed. Republic Germany, 1955-64; assoc. prof. Tech. U. Karlsruhe, 1964-69; prof. U. Hamburg, Fed. Republic Germany, from 1969; now prof. emeritus U. Hamburg. Author: Arzneistoffproduktion, 1983, (with F. Deutschmann and B. Hohmann) Drogenaualyse I: Morph. Anatomie, 1992; contbr. articles to sci. publs. Mem. German Pharm. Soc. (Hermann-Thoms medal), Soc. Medicinal Plant Rsch. (hon. mem., pres. 1988-89). Home: Sandmoorweg 31, D 22559 Hamburg Germany

SPRENGER, CRAIG, physician assistant; b. Hackensack, N.J., Apr. 6, 1953; s. Walter Vernon and Madeline (Denardo) S.; m. Heather Murray, July 29, 1994; children: James Walter, Laiken Alexa. BS in Biology, Yale Coll., 1976; degree in physician asst., Cornell Med. Coll., 1982. Cert. physician asst. Physician asst. in cardiothoracic surgery St. Francis Hosp., Roslyn, N.Y., 1983-85; physician asst. in gen. orthopaedics R.M. Thorne, MD, Lake Worth, Fla., 1985-88; physician asst. in joint replacement Robert Zann, MD, Boca Raton, Fla., 1988—; clin. investigator med. rsch., 1994—. Fellow Am. Acad. Physician Assts. (teaching asst. 1988—), Fla. Acad. Physician Assts. Home: 1398 SW 18th St Boca Raton FL 33486 Office: Orthopaedic Surgery Assocs 1590 NW 10th Ave # 202 Boca Raton FL 33486

SPRENGER, THOMAS ROBERT, orthopedic surgeon; b. Seymour, Ind., Aug. 22, 1931; s. Robert D. and Margaret Sprenger; m. Justine Gambill Stinson, June 24, 1956; children: Rebecca Lee, Michael Thomas. BS, Marshall U., 1976; MD, Ind. U., 1956; grad. U.S. Army War Coll., 1975, U.S. Army Command and Gen. Staff Coll., 1970. Diplomate Am. Bd. Orthopedic Surgery. Intern St. Vincent's Hosp., Indpls., 1956-57; resident in orthopedic surgery Indpls. Gen. Hosp., 1957-58, Riley Children's Hosp. Ind. U., 1958-59, VA Hosp., New Orleans, 1959-60, Tampa Gen. Hosp., 1960; practice medicine specializing in orthopedic surgery, Bradenton, Fla., 1961—; orthopedic surgeon Pitts. Pirates, Bradenton, 1969-87; sr. attending orthopedic surgeon Manatee Meml. Hosp., Bradenton, 1961—, chief of staff, 1967; sr. attending orthopedic surgeon L.W. Blake Meml. Hosp., Bradenton, 1973—, trustee, 1971-83, sec. bd., 1970-80, vice chmn. bd., 1980-81, chmn. bd., 1982-84. Pres., Gulfcoast chpt. Nat. Arthritis Found., 1965, 82—; mem. Bd. Pub. Instrn. Manatee County, 1966-71, chmn., 1967-69; mem. exec. com. Bishop Mus. and Planetarium, 1967-69; founding mem. Health Systems Agy. Manatee County, 1968, mem., 1968-79. With BG Army NG, 1956-91, ret. Contbr. articles to profl. jours. Mem. Pres.'s Council, U. South Fla., 1981. Mem. Am. Acad. Orthopedic Surgeons, ACS, Internat. Coll. Surgeons, Assn. Mil. Surgeons U.S., Am. Fracture Assn., Orthopedics Letters Club, Fla. Orthopedics Letters Club, Fla. Orthopedic Soc. (chmn. membership 1982-86, pres. 1989-90), Fla. Med. Soc., So. Orthopedic Assn., AMA, So. Med. Assn., Manatee County Med. Soc., Eastern Orthopedic Assn., Soc. Med. Cons. to Armed Forces, N.G. Officers Assn. Fla. (pres. 1980-81), Army Res. Forces (policy com. 1989-91), Phi Eta Sigma, Alpha Epsilon Delta. Presbyterian. Home: 8221 Desoto Memorial Hwy Bradenton FL 34209-9790 Office: 2101 61st St W Bradenton FL 34209-5528

SPRINGER, J. KENT, toxicologist; b. Flint, Mich., Feb. 11, 1956; s. John Edward and Betty Lu (Wenger) S.; m. Joan Diane Hild, May 23, 1981; children: David Kent, J. Paul, Kayla Michelle. BA, U. Colo., 1979; MS, Ill. Inst. Tech., 1987. Diplomate Am. Bd. Toxicology. Rsch. assoc. Am. Critical Care, Waukegan, Ill., 1980-88; rsch. scientist DuPont Merck, Wilmington, Del., 1988-92; sr. toxicologist Somatogen, Inc., Boulder, Colo., 1992-94; mgr. toxicology Caphalon, Inc., West Chester, Pa., 1994—. Mem. Am. Coll. Toxicology. Office: Cephalon Inc 145 Brandywine Pky West Chester PA 19380

SPRINGER, WAYNE RICHARD, medical center safety director; b. Milw., Nov. 16, 1946; s. Richard Andrew and Irma Edna (Richter) S.; m. Jane Bradley, Aug. 19, 1972; chldren: Matthew Bradley, Katherine Jane. BA, Northwestern U., 1968; PhD, U. Calif., Berkeley, 1977. Vol. Peace Corps, Washington, 1969-72; postdoctoral fellow U. Calif., San Diego, 1977-79, rsch. biochemist, 1979-92; assoc. project biochemist, 1992—; rsch. biochemist VA Med. Ctr., San Diego, 1979—, chem. hygiene officer, 1992-94, dir. environ., health and safety, 1994—. Coach Little League, Bobby Sox. Mem. Am. Soc. Biochem. Molecular Biology, Am. Soc. Cell Biology. Office: VA Med Ctr (138S) 3350 La Jolla Village Dr San Diego CA 92161

SPROAT, THOMAS TODD, pharmacotherapy specialist; b. Fort Wayne, Ind., June 14, 1963; s. Donald Gene and Marjorie Louise (Arnett) S. BS, U. Fla., 1985, D in Pharmacy, 1989. Lic. pharmacist, Fla.; bd. cert. pharmacotherapy specialist. Resident adult internal medicine/cardiology VA Med. Ctr., Gainesville, Fla., 1989-90; fellow, vis. instr. Dept. Pharmacy Practice, U. Fla., Gainesville, 1990-91; pharmacotherapy specialist adult internal medicine Fla. Hosp. Med. Ctr., Orlando, 1991-94, pharmacotherapy specialist cardiology/critical care, 1991-94; asst. prof. Auburn (Ala.) U. Sch. Pharmacy, 1994-95; cons., lectr. Informed, Inc., Orlando, 1995—; peer rev. process Annals of Pharmacotherapy, Cin., 1989—. Contbr. chpt. to book and articles to profl. jours. Alachua County Cmty. Resource vol. Alachua County Bd. Edn., Gainesville, 1990-91. Mem. Am. Coll. Clin. Pharmacology (mem. cardiology practice and rsch. network), Am. Soc. Health Sys. Pharmacists, Fla. Soc. Health Sys. Pharmacists (clin. coun., edn. coun.), Rho Chi, Golden Key, Phi Sigma Kappa. Republican. Home: 14506 Amaca Ct Orlando FL 32837

SPROLE, FRANK ARNOTT, retired pharmaceutical company executive, lawyer; b. Bklyn., Sept. 13, 1918; s. Frank Newland and Eleanor Arnott (Greenberg) S.; m. Sarah Louise Knapp, Sept. 23, 1944; children—Wendy Sprole Bangs, Frank J., Anne Sprole Mauk, Jonathan K., Sarah Sprole Obregon. B.A., Yale U., 1942; LL.B., Columbia U., 1949. Bar: N.Y. 1949. Assoc. firm Winthrop Stimson, Putnam & Roberts, N.Y.C., 1949-50; atty. Bristol-Myers Co., N.Y.C., 1950-52, asst. sec., 1952-55, sec., 1955-67, v.p., 1965-73, sr. v.p., 1973-77, vice chmn. bd., 1977-84; bd. dirs., officer Proprietary Assn., Washington, 1978-84; dir., officer Knapp Fund, N.Y.C., 1960-93. Pres. bd. trustees Hotchkiss Sch., Lakeville, Conn., 1980-85; trustee Internat. Inst. Rural Reconstrn., N.Y.C., and Manila, 1983-87. Served to lt. comdr. USNR, 1942-45, PTO. Mem. Assn. of Bar of City of N.Y., Yale Club of N.Y.C., Wee Burn Country Club, Bohemian Club, Mid Ocean Club, John's Island Club, Riomar Country Club. Republican. Episcopalian. Home: 394 Mansfield Ave Darien CT 06820-2112

SPROUSE, CYNTHIA JO, infectious disease nurse clinician; b. Augusta, Ga., Jan. 31, 1959; d. Joel Franklin and Mary Louise (Garrett) S. ADN, Augusta Coll., 1981; BSN, Med. Coll. Ga., 1986. RN, Ga. Med.-surg. staff nurse Humana Corp., Augusta, 1981-83; ICU sr. staff nurse Med. Coll. Ga., Augusta, 1983-86; emergency dept. sr. staff nurse Univ. Hosp., Augusta, 1986-88; infectious disease nurse Eisenhower Army Med. Ctr., Ft. Gordon, Ga., 1988-92; HIV clin. coord. Univ. Hosp., Augusta, 1992-94, Prime Care, Augusta, 1994-95; mgr., HIV clinician Progressive Health Alliance, Augusta, 1995—. Author: Hemodynamic Monitoring, 1986. Bd. dirs., officer St. Stephen's AIDS Svc. Orgn., Augusta, 1993-95. Recipient Comdr.'s award for pub. svc. U.S. Army, 1991. Mem. Augusta Area Assn. Nurses in AIDS Care (sec. 1996—), Augusta Area Coun. on AIDS (chmn. 1995—), Ga. Women Preventing AIDS, Internat. AIDS Soc. Office: Progressive Health Alliance 1456-B Walton Way Augusta GA 30901

SPRUIELL, VANN, psychoanalyst, educator, editor, researcher; b. Leeds, Ala., Oct. 16, 1926; s. Vann Lindley and Zada (Morton) S.; m. Iris Taylor, Sept. 20, 1951 (div. Oct. 1966); children: Graham, Fain, Garth; m. Joyce Ellis, Feb. 11, 1967; stepchildren: Sidney Reavey, Catherine Ellis, Matson Ellis. BS, U. Ala., Tuscaloosa, 1948; MD, Harvard U., 1952. Resident Bellevue Hosp., N.Y.C., 1952-53, N.Y. Hosp., N.Y.C., 1953-55; fellow Tulane Sch. Medicine, New Orleans, 1955-57; pvt. practice New Orleans, 1957—; vis. rschr. Anna Freud Ctr., London, 1972-73; co-pub. JOURLIT and BOOKREV; pres. and founding mem. Psychoanalytic Archives CD-ROM Texts (PACT), New Orleans, 1993—; clin. prof. psychiatry La. State U. Sch. Medicine, Tulane U. Sch. Medicine; sec. Ctr. for Advanced Studies in Psychoanalysis, 1989—. Editl. bd. Psychoanalytic Quarterly, 1973—; N.Am. editor Internat. Jour. Psychoanalysis, London, 1988-93; mem. various other editl. bds.; contbr. articles to profl. jours. and books. Sgt. U.S. Army, 1944-46. Mem. Am. Psychoanalytic Assn. (sec. bd. on profl. stds. 1979-92), Wyvern Club. Home: 215 Iona St Metairie LA 70005-4137

SPRUNGL, JANICE MARIE, nurse; b. Brooklyn, Ohio, Mar. 9, 1960; d. Donald Edward and Delores Jane (Slys) S. BS in Nursing, U. Akron, 1982. RN, Ohio, Colo. Commd. 2d lt. U.S. Air Force, 1982, advanced through grades to major, 1994; clin. nurse Med. Ctr. Keesler U.S. Air Force, Biloxi, Miss., 1982-86; charge nurse Med. Ctr. Keesler U.S. Air Force, 1986-88; charge nurse U.S. Air Force Acad. Hosp. U.S. Air Force, Colorado Springs, Colo., 1988-91; charge nurse primary care clinic ambulance svcs. Lowry Clinic U.S. Air Force, 1991-94; clin. nurse, educator Family Practice Clinic, USAF Acad. Hosp., 1994—. Vol., Spl. Olympics, Keesler AFB, 1983-87; fundraiser, Biloxi unit Am. Cancer Soc., 1984. Mem. Ohio Nursing Assn., Air Force Assn., Colo. Nursing Assn., Nat. Nursing Staff Devel. Orgn.

SPUDICH, JAMES A., biology educator; b. Collinsville, Ill., Jan. 7, 1942; married, 1964; 2 children. BS, U. Ill., 1963; PhD in Biochemistry, Stanford U., 1968. USPHS trainee Stanford (Calif.) U., 1968; asst. prof. biochemistry U. Calif., San Francisco, 1971-74, assoc. prof., 1974-76; prof., 1976; prof. biochemistry and devel. biology Beckman Ctr., Stanford U. Sch. Medicine, 1977—. Editor: Annual Rev. Cell Biology, 1994. Recipient Lewis S. Rosentiel award for disting. work in basic med. rsch. Brandeis U., 1996. Mem. Am. Soc. Cell Biologists (pres. 1989). Office: Stanford U Dept Biochemistry Stanford Med Ctr Stanford CA 94305

SPURGAS, PAUL EDWARD, neurosurgeon; b. Niskayuna, N.Y., Aug. 30, 1950; s. Edward Joseph and Florence (Tanski) S.; m. Deborah Lee Scott, Aug. 4, 1975; children: Brooke Liza, Morgan Paul. BS, Union Coll., 1972; MD, Temple U., 1976. Asst. prof. neurol. surgery Geisinger Med. Ctr., Danville, Pa., 1982-84; chief divsn. neurosurgery Ellis Hosp., Schenectady, N.Y., 1984—; trustee Ellis Hosp. Found., 1994-96. Founding mem. Saratoga (N.Y.) Therapeutic Equestrian Program, 1994. Fellow Nat. Bd. Med. Examiners; mem. AMA, Am. Assn. Neurol. Surgeons, N.Y. State Neurosurg. Soc., N.Y. State Med. Soc., Congress Neurol. Surgeons. Republican. Roman Catholic. Office: North East Neurosurgery 1201 Nott St Ste 204 Schenectady NY 12308

SPYROPOULOS, GEORGE NICHOLAS, physician; b. Westwood, N.J., July 24, 1965; s. Nicholas George and Asimina Vasilios (Tassini) S.; m. Maria Evangelia Stavropoulos, May 3, 1968. BA in Biology, Franklin and Marshall, 1987; DO, Phila. Coll. Osteo. Medicine, 1992. Diplomate Am. Acad. Family Practice. Intern Crozer-Chester Med. Ctr., Springfield, Pa., 1992-93; resident family and community medicine Med. Ctr. Delaware, Wilmington, 1993-95; attending family physician Med. Ctr. Delaware, Chadds Ford, Pa., 1995—; active staff Med. Ctr. of Delaware, Wilmington, 1995, So. Chester County Med. Ctr., Jennersville, Pa., 1996; courtesy staff A.I. DuPont Children's Hosp., Wilmington, 1996, The chester County Hosp., West Chester, Pa., 1996. Vice pres. The Peloponnesian Soc. of Greater Delaware Valley, 1996—. Recipient Ahepa Dist. scholarship, 1984-85. Mem. AMA. Am. Osteo. Assn., Pa. Med. Soc., Delaware Med. Soc., Del. State Osteo. Med. Soc., Chester County Med. Soc., Hellenic U. Club of Phila. Home: 756 Hinchley Run West Chester PA 19382 Office: Med Ctr Del Chadds Ford Ctr 602 Chadds Ford Dr Chadds Ford PA 19317

SQUIER, LESLIE HAMILTON, psychology educator; b. San Francisco, Nov. 17, 1917; s. Leslie Hamilton and Alma Ida (Bergmann) S.; m. Anne Frances Wood, Dec. 12, 1959; children—Renata, Leslie III, Stafford, Kurt. B.A., U. Calif.-Berkeley, 1950, Ph.D., 1953. From instr. to prof. psychology Reed Coll., Portland, Oreg. 1953-88, dean of students, 1955-61, prof. emeritus, 1988—; vis. scientist Oceanic Inst., Makapuu, Oahu, Hawaii, 1969-70, 71; vis. prof. Paine Coll., Augusta, Ga., 1984; NSF fellow U. Oreg. Med. Sch., Portland, 1976, U. Hawaii Med. Sch., Honolulu, 1977. Trustee Portland Zool. Soc., 1962-68. Served with USAF, 1942-46. Mem. AAAS, APA, Am. Psychol. Soc., Oreg. Psychol. Assn. (pres. 1965), Western Psychol. Assn., Assn. for the Study of Dreaming, Phi Beta Kappa, Sigma Xi. Home: 5647 SE 38th Ave Portland OR 97202-7501 Office: Reed Coll Dept Psychology Portland OR 97202

SQUIRES, JANET E., pediatrician, educator; b. Evansville, Ind., Nov. 13, 1950; d. Eugene Endress and Mary Loehrlein; m. Robert Hilton Squires Jr.; children: Gregory, Jim, Beth. BS in Math., St. Mary's Coll., South Bend, Ind., 1972; MD, Ind. U., 1976. Fellow in pediatrics Washington U. Sch. Med., St. Louis, 1979, fellow in pediatric infectious disease, 1982; pvt. practice Cook-Ft. Worth Children's Hosp., 1982-87; asst. prof. pediatrics U. Tex. Southwestern Med. Ctr., Dallas, 1987-93, assoc. prof., 1993—; dir. HIV program Children's Med. Ctr., Dallas, 1988—, dir. divsn. gen. pediatrics, 1990—, dir. child abuse program, 1992—, pres. med. staff, 1996; Bd. dirs. Child Advocacy Ctr., Dallas, 1992—, Tex. Med. Assn. Found., Austin, 1995—. Recipient Miracle Maker physician award Lederle Pharm. Co., 1996. Mem. Tex. Pediatric Soc. (bd. dirs.), Am. Acad. Pediatrics, Pediatric Soc. of Greater Dallas (sec.-treas. 1992—), Physicians Violence-Free Soc., Zero Tolerance Violence, Soc. Prevention Child Abuse. Office: Children's Med Ctr 1935 Motor St Dallas TX 75234

SRAMEK, STEPHEN JOHN, ophthalmologist; b. Gary, Ind., Dec. 16, 1950; m. Marlie Myhren Sramek, May 22, 1976. BS, U. Notre Dame, 1972; PhD, Med. Coll. of Wis., 1976; MD, U. Tex. Health Sci. Ctr., 1982. Diplomate Am. Bd. Ophthalmology. Rsch. fellow Nat. Cancer Soc., Baylor Coll. of Medicine, Houston, 1975-78; intern in internal medicine U. Wis., Madison, 1982-83, resident in ophthalmology, 1983-86, retina fellow, 1986-87; pvt. practice, retinal diseases Davis Duehr Eye Assocs., Madison, 1988—; clin. asst. prof. dept. ophthalmology U. Wis. Med. Sch., 1988—; chmn. dept. ophthalmology Meriter Park Hosp., Madison, 1993-96; low vision com. State of Wis., Madison, 1992-94. Contbr. articles to profl. jours. Grantee Nat. Eye Inst., 1986, 90-93, Diabetes Rsch. and Edn. Found., 1988, Am. Diabetes Assn., 1988. Mem. AMA, Assn. for Rsch. in Vision and Ophthalmology, Am. Acad. Ophthalmology, Alpha Omega Alpha. Office: Davis Duehr Dean Dept Ophthalmology 1025 Regent St Madison WI 53715

SREEBNY, LEO M., oral biology and pathology educator; b. N.Y.C., Jan. 8, 1922; s. Morris and Lillie (Bogdanoff) S.; m. Mathilda H. Sternfeld, Mar. 9, 1945; children—Oren, Daniel. B.A., U. Ill., 1942, D.D.S., 1945, M.S., 1950, Ph.D., 1954. With dept. periodontics U. Ill., 1948-57, asso. prof., 1956-57; asso. prof., chmn. dept. oral biology U. Wash., Seattle, 1957-60; prof. U. Wash., 1960-75; dir. U. Wash. (Center for Research Oral Biology), 1967-75; dean Sch. Dental Medicine, SUNY-Stony Brook, 1975-79, prof. dept. oral biology and pathology, 1979—; cons. VA Hosp., Seattle, 1960—; mem. dental study sect. NIH, 1964-68, chmn., 1967-68; mem. com. on sci. policy Nat. Acad. Sci., 1973-74. Author: (with Julia Meyer) Secretory Mechanisms in Salivary Glands, 1963, The Salivary System, 1987; contbr. numerous articles to sci., biol. jours. Served with AUS, 1942-45; with USNR, 1946-48. Recipient Internat. Assn. for Dental Research Sci. award, 1969; Silver medal for contbns. to dental sci. and art City of Paris, 1979; Salivary Research Group Award, 1987. Mem. Fedn. Dentaire Internat. (chmn. sci. assembly com. 1973—, rep. UN Conf. on Youth 1983-84), Internat. Assn. Dental Research (bd. govs. 1981), Fedn. Dentaire Internat. (list of honor 1988), Am. Assn. Dental Research, ADA. Home: 35 Gnarled Hollow Rd East Setauket NY 11733-2929 Office: SUNY Stony Brook Sch Dental Medicine Stony Brook NY 11794

SRINIVASAN, ARUL MALAR, physician; b. Trichirapalli, Madras, India, Mar. 12, 1953; d. Sivan Arul Ramalingam and Ginanadesikan Seturam; m. Michael Srinivasan, Jan. 17, 1977 (div. 1983); 1 child, Veena. MBBS, Stanley Med. Coll., Madras, India, 1977; DGM, Royal Coll. Physicians, London, 1989, MRCP, 1990. Rotating ho. officer Govt. Stanley Hosp., Madras, 1976-77; resident medical officer Govt. Emerie Hosp., Kuwait, 1977-81; sr. ho. officer St. Mary Abbot's Hosp., London, 1982-83, Wythenshawe Hosp., Manchester, 1983-85; registrar Newsham Gen. Hosp., Liverpool, 1985-87; registrar in medicine/geriatrics Stoke Mandeville Hosp., Aylesbury, 1987-90, registrar rheumatology/gen. medicine, 1990-94; sr. registrar rheumatology/rehab. Royal Nat. Orthopaedic Hosp., Stanmore Middlesex Hosp., London, 1994—. Mem. Roayl Coll. Physicians, British Soc. of Rheumatology. Home: 17 Bowmont Dr, Aylesbury, Bucks HP21 9UH, England Office: Royal Nat Orthopaedic Hosp, Mandeville Rd, Stanmore Middlesex HP21, England

SRINIVASAN, MANDYAM VEERAMBUDI, neuroscientist; b. Poona, India, Sept. 15, 1948; s. Mandyam Veerambudi Sundararajan and Mandyam Veerambudi Vedavalliammal; m. Jaishree Parthasarathy, June 12, 1975. BE in Engring., Bangalore U., 1968; ME, Indian Inst. Sci., Bangalore, 1970; MPhil, Yale U., 1972, PhD, 1976; DSc, Australian Nat. U., 1994. Rsch. scientist Yale U., New Haven, 1976-78; rsch. fellow Australian Nat. U., Canberra, 1978-82, prof. visual scis. Rsch. Sch. Biol. Scis., dir. Visual Scis., fellow, 1985—; asst. prof. U. Zurich, Switzerland, 1982-85; vis. fellow Academia Sinica, Beijing, 1987, U. Zurich, 1988, Max-Planck Inst. Biol. Cybernetics, Tubingen, 1991. Fellow Australian Acad. Sci.; mem. European Neurosci. Assn., Computer Soc. IEEE, Australian Neurosci. Soc., Australian Neural Networks Soc., Colour Soc. Australia (treas. 1989), Sigma Xi. Home: 36 Challinor Crescent, Florey 2615, Australia Office: Australian Nat U, Rsch Sch Biol Scis, PO Box 475, Canberra 2601, Australia

SRIVATSA, KADIYALI MADHAVA, paediatrician; b. Udupi, karnatak, India; arrived in U.K., 1984; s. Kadiyali Madhava and Prema (Upadhya. M.B.B.S., Bangalore (India) Med. Coll., 1982. Resident Victoria Hosp., Bangalore, 1982-83; paediatric sr. house officer Ch. of South India Hosp., Bangalore, 1983, Walsgrave Hosp., Coventry, U.K., 1983-84, Princess of Wales Hosp., Brigand, U.K., 1984-85; registrar in paediatrics Staincliffe Hosp., Dewsbury, U.K., 1985-87, Prince of Wales Hosp., Merthyr Tyofil, U.K., 1987-89; staff paediatrician St. Cross Hosp., Rugby, U.K., 1990-5, Stoke Mandivelle Hosp., U.K., 1995; paediatrics locum registrar John Radcliff Hosp., Oxford, U.K., 1995; cons. med. new product devel. Rochford Medicals, High Wycomb, U.K., 1995—. Contbr. articles to profl. jours.; inventor in field. Recipient Innovation award Welsh Devel. Agy., Cardiff, 1992. Fellow N.Y. Acad. Sci. Home: Sunbury on Thames, 137 The Avenue, London TW16 5EP, England

SROUJI, MAURICE NAKHLEH, pediatric surgeon; b. Nazareth, Palestine, June 13, 1928; came to U.S., 1965; s. Nakhleh Y. and Edma S. (Shomar) S.; m. Batishwa Badawi, June 25, 1966; children: Maureen G., Nadeen M. BA, Am. U. Beirut, 1948, MD, 1953; MA (hon.), U. Pa., 1974. Diplomate Am. Bd. Surgery (Gen. and Pediatric). Dir. surgery Holy Family Hosp., Nazareth, Israel, 1960-62; fellow in cardiovascular rsch. Rsch. Inst., Hosp. for Sick Children, Toronto, 1964-65; fellow in pediatric surg. rsch. Children's Hosp., Phila., 1965; rsch. assoc. in pediatric surgery Children's Hosp./U. Pa., Phila., 1966-67; chief pediatric surgery, attending surgeon Phila. Gen. Hosp./U. Pa., 1967-76; asst. surgeon Children's Hosp., Phila., 1967-71, assoc. surgeon, 1972-84; asst. prof. pediatric surgery U. Pa., Phila., 1968-74, assoc. prof., 1974—; vis. prof. surgery Am. U. Hosp., Beirut, 1984-85; vis. cons. in pediatric surgery Hamad Gen. Hosp., Ministry of Health, Doha, Qatar, 1986, King Fahd N.G. Hosp., Riyadh, Saudi Arabia, 1987; vis. pediatric surgeon Nazareth Hosp., 1987. Contbr. articles to profl. jours. Fellow ACS, Am. Acad. Pediatrics (surg. sect.), Am. Pediatric Surg. Assn.; mem. AMA, Pan Am. Med. Assn., Am. U. Beirut Alumni Surg. Soc. N.Am., AAUP. Roman Catholic. Home and Office: 303 Penbree Cir Bala Cynwyd PA 19004-2332

STAAS, WILLIAM E., JR., physiatrist; b. Phila., 1936. MD, Jefferson Med. Coll., 1962. Intern Mercy Hosp., Darby, Pa., 1962-63; resident in phys. medicine and rehab. U. Pa. Hosp., 1965-68; attending physiatrist Magee Rehab. Hosp., Phila.; prof. rehab. medicine Jefferson Med. Coll. Office: Magee Rehab Hosp 6 Franklin Plz Philadelphia PA 19102-1177*

STAAT, ROBERT H., microbiology educator; b. Denver, Apr. 2, 1942; s. Charles H. and Margaret O. (Jesiop) S.; m. Judith H. Ginn, Apr. 7, 1965 (div. Oct. 1979); children: Cynthia H., Barton C.; m. Cynthia R. Alfery, Nov. 20, 1979; 1 child, Sarah C. BS, U. N.Mex., 1965, MS, 1968; PhD, U. Minn., 1975. Rsch. assoc. U. N.Mex./NASA, Albuquerque, 1968-70; asst. prof. microbiology Med. U. S.C., Charleston, 1975-76; asst. prof. microbiology U. Louisville, 1976-79, assoc. prof. microbiology, 1979-84, prof. microbiology, 1984—; pres. R.C. Henry Co., Inc., Louisville, 1985-95, RCH, Inc., Louisville, 1995—. Contbr. rsch. papers to profl. publs., chpts. to textbook; patentee in field. NIH rsch. grantee, 1975, 86, 81. Mem. APHA, Internat. Assn. Dental Rsch., Am. Assn. Microbiology, Am. Assn. Dental Schs. (pres. admissions officers 1980—). Home: 1207 Pebble Pt Goshen KY 40026 Office: U Louisville Sch Dentistry 501 S Preston Louisville KY 40292

STAATS, ARTHUR W., psychology educator; b. Jan. 17, 1924. BA in Psychology, UCLA, 1949, MA in Psychology, 1953, PhD in Gen. Exptl. and Clin. Psychology, 1956. Psychologist UCLA Counseling Ctr., Los Angeles, 1950-53; clin. trainee VA Hosps., Los Angeles, 1953-55; instr. psychology Ariz. State U., Tempe, 1955-56, asst. prof., 1956-58, assoc. prof., 1958-60, prof., 1960-64; NSF faculty fellow U. London, 1961-62; vis. prof. U. Calif., Berkeley, 1964-65; prof. ednl. psychology and research U. Wis. Research and Devel. Ctr. Cognitive Learning, Madison, 1965-67; vis. prof. U. Hawaii, Honolulu, 1966-67, prof. psychology and ednl. psychology, 1967—. Author Complex Human Behavior, 1963, Child Learning, Intelligence, and Personality: A Behavioral Interaction Approach, 1971, Social Behaviorism, 1975, Psychology's Crisis of Disunity: Philosophy and Method for the Revolution to a Unified Science, 1983, Behavior and Personality: Psychological Behaviorism, 1996; editor Human Learning, 1964, Current Issues in Theoretical Psychology, 1987, Annals of Theoretical Psychology, Vol. 5, 1987; contbr. over 70 articles to profl. jours. and 59 chpts. to books; editl. bd. 9 Am. and internat. jours. Fellow AAAS, APA (gen. psychology divsn., exptl. psychology divsn., devel. psychology divsn., personality and social psychology divs., clin. psychology divsn., ednl. psychology divsn., theoretical and philos. psychology divsn., exptl. analysis of behavior divsn.); mem. Sociedad Interamericana de Psicologia, Psychonomic Soc., Assn. Latinoamericana del Analisis y Modificacion del Comportamiento, Soc. for Exptl. Social Psychology. Home: 1460 Kamole St Honolulu HI 96821-1422 Office: U Hawaii Dept Psychology Honolulu HI 96822

STAATS, THOMAS ELWYN, neuropsychologist; b. Marietta, Ohio; s. Percy Anderson and Julia (Bourmorck) S.; m. Debra R.; children: Lauren Malu, Kara Kristyn, Stacy Rhnea, Ronald Derek. B.A. cum laude, Emory U., 1970; M.A., U. Ala., 1972, Ph.D., 1974; postgrad. U. Tex., Tyler, 1992. Diplomate Am. Bd. Profl. Disability Cons.; lic. psychologist. Dir., chief psychologist Caddo Parish Diagnostic Ctr., Shreveport, La., 1974-81; exec. dir. Doctors Psychol. Ctr., Shreveport, 1979-91, Comprehensive Assessments, 1991—; cons. to Charter Forest Hosp., Shreveport Impairment and Disability Evaluation Ctr.; neuropsychol. cons. La. State U. Med. Ctr.; clin. assoc. prof. psychology La. State U., Shreveport, 1977—, clin. assoc. prof. psychiatry Sch. Medicine, 1980—; mem. faculty Am. Acad. Disability Evaluating Physicians. Author: Manual For the Stress Vector Analysis Test Series, 1983, The Doctors Guide to Instant Stress Relief, 1987; Stress Management and Relaxation Training System Handbook. Contbr. articles to profl. jours. and popular mags. Mem. Gov's. Com. of 1000, La., 1979. U. Ala. Grad. Research Council fellow, 1974; recipient AADEP award 1991. Fellow Am. Inst. Stress; mem. APA, Nat. Acad. Neuropsychology. Republican, Nat. Register of Health Svc. Providers in Psychology. Episcopalian. Avocations: scuba diving, gun collecting, camping, boating, stress, malingering and chronic pain research. Home: 10816 Sunrise Pointe Shreveport LA 71106 Office: Comprehensive Assessments Inc 1532 Irving Pl Shreveport LA 71101-4604

STABA, EMIL JOHN, pharmacognosy and medicinal chemistry educator; b. N.Y.C., May 16, 1928; s. Frank and Marianna T. (Mack) P.; m. Joyce Elizabeth Ellert, June 19, 1954; children—Marianna, Joanna, Sarah Jane, John, Mark. B.S. cum laude, St. John's U., 1952; M.S., Duquesne U., 1954; Ph.D., U. Conn., 1957. Asst. prof. U. Nebr., 1957-60, prof., chmn. dept., 1968; prof. dept. pharmacognosy U. Minn., 1968—; cons. econs. plants and plant tissue culture U.S. Army Q.M.C.; cons. on drug plants and plant tissue culture NASA; cons. N.C.I. at NIH on anti-cancer natural product prodn., 1991-92; cons. Govt. of Korea, food and pharm. industry cons. NSF-Egyptian Acad. Sci. Rsch. Tech., 1984—; internat. vis. prof. Dalhousie U., 1983; cons. on Indonesia biotech. devel. World Bank-Midwestern Univs. Consortium for Internat. Activities, 1985-90, Thailand, 1989; mem. natural products revision com. U.S. Pharmacopeia, 1980—, chair subcom. natural products, 1995-2000; mem. adv. coun. on life scis. NASA, 1984-87. Mem. editorial bd.: Jour. Plant Cell, Tissue and Organ Culture, 1980-86, plant cellular and developmental biology sect. of In Vitro, 1988—. Served with USNR, 1945-46, PTO. Sr. fgn. fellow NSF, Poland, 1969; Fulbright fellow, Germany, 1970; Coun. Sci. and Indsl. Rsch.-NSF fellow, India, 1973, Pakistani Coun. Sci. and Indsl. Rsch.-NSF fellow, Pakistan, 1978; fellow U.K. Sci. Engring. Rsch. Coun., 1989. Fellow AAAS; mem. Am. Soc. Pharmacognosy (pres. 1971-72), Am. Assn. Colls. Pharmacy (chmn. tchrs. sect. 1972-73, dir. 1976-77), Tissue Culture Assn. (pres. plant sect. 1972-74), Am. Pharm. Assn. and Acad. (chmn. pharmacognosy and nat. products 1977), Soc. Econ. Botany, Am. Soc. Pharmacognosy. Home: 2840 Stinson Blvd Minneapolis MN 55418-3127 Office: U Minn Coll Pharmacy Unit F-9106 Minneapolis MN 55455

STABILITO, JEAN DOLORES, geriatrics nurse; b. Phila., Feb. 11, 1943; d. Domenico and Maria (Luccianetti) Pietrinferno; children: Jeanine, Donald Joseph, Dana. Student, St. Joseph U., Phila., 1960-63, Gwynedd (Pa.) Mercy Coll., 1963-67; Eastern Montgomery County, Willow Grove, Pa., 1993. LPN, Pa. Charge nurse Dresher Hill Nursing Facility, Dresher, Pa., 1993-94; primary nurse Artman Home, Ambler, Pa., 1994—; aid station nurse Totus Tuus Conf., Phila., 1994. Co-founder, Down Syndrome Interest Group, Montgomery County, Pa., 1981; leader, St. Anthony Prayer cmty., 1986—, Music Ministry, 1986—; founder, tchr., La Scuola Materna, 1989-91; co-founder, steward, Soc. Apostolic Life, 1989—; religious educator, Archdiocese of Phila., 1982-92. Recipient Pius X award, Archdiocese of Phila., 1992; Nightingale scholar, Harrisburg, Pa., 1993. Republican. Roman Catholic. Home: 31 Greystone Rd Ambler PA 19002-5210 Office: Artman Home 250 Bethlehem Pike Ambler PA 19002

STABLEIN, JOHN JOSEPH, III, physician; b. Galesburg, Ill., Nov. 26, 1951; s. John Joseph Jr. and Evelyn May (Haggerty) S.; m. Diane Catherine Jansen, June 6, 1976; children: David James, Kara Marie. Student, Loyola U., Chgo., 1969-72; MD, U. Ill., Chgo., 1976. Diplomate Am. Bd. Allergy and Immunology, Am. Bd. Internal Medicine. Intern, resident U. South Fla. Affiliated Hosps.; asst. prof. medicine U. South Fla., Tampa, 1981-86; pvt. practice Brandon, Fla., 1981—; chief of medicine Humana Hosp. Brandon, 1987-89. Mem. Hillsborough County Med. Assn. (sec. 1989-90), Fla. Allergy Soc. (pres. 1988-89). Office: 500 Vonderburg Dr Ste 103 East Tower Brandon FL 33511-5968

STABLER, JOHN ROBERTS, psychologist, educator; b. New Rochelle, N.Y., Apr. 11, 1932; s. Charles Norman and Elizabeth (Miller) S.; m. Joan Obrist, Oct. 13, 1955; children—Hetty Suzanne, John Michael. B.A., Antioch Coll., 1956; M.A., So. Methodist U., 1958; Ph.D., U. Tex., 1961. Asst. prof. psychology La. State U., Baton Rouge, 1961-68, assoc. prof., 1968-69, dir. Office Child Research, 1963-69; vis. prof. So. U., Baton Rouge, 1964-65; assoc. prof. psychology Ga. State U., Atlanta, 1969—, dir. Office Devel. Research, 1971-76. Bd. dirs. Ga. Youth Advocate Program. Served with U.S. Army, 1955-57. Mem. AAUP, APA, Southeastern Psychol. Assn., So. Gerontol. Soc. (cert. gerontology). Home: 2072 Clairmont Ter NE Atlanta GA 30345-2312 Office: Ga State U Dept Psychology Atlanta GA 30303

STACK, CAROL MARIE, advanced practice ambulatory care nurse; b. Easton, Pa., July 26, 1943; d. Richard H. and Hilda A. (Schwarz) Helwick; children: Eric Stephen, Heidi Reneé. Diploma, Allentown (Pa.) Hosp. Sch. Nursing, 1964; cert. in NP, U. Vt., 1978; BS, New Eng. Coll., 1988; MSN, U. Vt., 1994. RN, Vt. RN Sch. for Internat. Tng., Brattleboro, Vt.; pvt. practice NP Brattleboro; NP Planned Parenthood Fedn., Brattleboro; NP, clinic coord. Brattleboro Retreat. Mem. ANA, Vt. Nurse's Assn. (by-laws com. dist. 3), Vt. Nurse Practitioners Interest Group.

STACK, DIANE VIRGINIA, hospital administrator; b. Schenectady, N.Y., June 14, 1958; d. Albert Ross and Irene Anne (Lajeunesse) Musick; m. Robert Michael Stack, June 27, 1981; children: Kelly Irene, Julie Theresa, Tina Marie. BBA in Acctg., U. Mass., 1980. CPA, Mass. Staff acct. Stavisky, Shapiro & Whyte, Boston, 1980-84; asst. controller Joslin Diabetes Ctr., Boston, 1984-88; dir. fin. Marlborough (Mass.) Hosp., 1988-95, v.p. fin., CFO, 1995—; treas. Marlborough Physician Svc's. Corp., 1992—, The Health Care Mgr. of New Eng., Inc., Marlborough, 1992—; guest lectr. Framingham State Coll. Mem. Am. Hosp. Assn., Mass. Soc. CPA's, Hosp. Fin. Mgmt. Assn. Republican. Home: 106 Cherry St Framingham MA 01701-4499 Office: Marlborough Hosp 57 Union St Marlborough MA 01752-1208

STACK, EDWARD FITZGERALD, physician management executive; b. New Rochelle, N.Y., Jan. 28, 1964; s. Edward Donald and Mary Jane (Meara) S.; m. Laurel Elizabeth Davey, Apr. 15, 1989; children: Scott Patrick, Kelli Elizabeth. BBA in Acctg., James Madison U. CPA, Va. Sr. auditor Ernst & Whinney, Washington, 1986-88; healthcare cons., mgr. Ernst & Young, Washington, 1989-92; dir. practice mgmt. Medaphis Corp., Phila., 1992-93, v.p. client svc., 1993-94; prin. Integrated Med. Mgmt., Malvern, Pa., 1994-95, pres., 1995—, also bd. dirs.; pres. EFS Mgmt., Lansdale, Pa., 1995—. Mem. HFMA, AICPA, PICAA, Internatl Billing Assn.

STACK, SISTER JEANNE MARY, nursing educator, administrator; b. Batavia, N.Y., Mar. 14, 1925; d. Warren Daniel and Alice Jeanne (Elmore) S. Diploma, Mercy Hosp. Sch. Nursing, Buffalo, 1945; BSN magna cum laude, Canisius Coll., 1950, MEd, 1956; PhD, Bowling Green State U., 1976. Diplomate Am. Coll. Healthcare Execs.; RN, N.Y., Ohio. Staff nurse obstetrics and oper. rm. St. Jerome Hosp., Batavia, 1945-50; instr. Providence Hosp. Sch. Nursing, Sandusky, Ohio, 1950-55, dir., 1955-78; adminstr., pres. Providence Hosp., Sandusky, Ohio, 1978-86; dir. edn./mission Franciscan Svcs. Corp., Sylvania, Ohio, 1986—; camp nurse Genesee Region Girl Scout Day Camp, Batavia, 1946, 47, 50; sch. nurse, instr. Lourdes Coll.-St. Clare Acad., Sylvania, summers 1961, 62, 63, 65; part time instr. Mary Manse Coll., Toledo, 1963-67. Author: (bulletin) Assembly of Hospital Schools of Nursing, 1978; contbr. articles to profl. publs. Instr. home nursing ARC, Sandusky, 1950-57, vol. nurse, 1952-60; pres. Erie County Community Coun., Sandusky, 1968-70; sec., bd. dirs. Firelands Audubon Soc., Huron, Ohio, 1977-86; vol. tutor Read for Literacy, Toledo, 1987—. Recipient Outstanding Community Svc. award AMVETS Sad Sacks, Sandusky, 1981; named Nurse of Yr. Erie-Huron Dist. Nurses Assn., Sandusky, 1961; Sr. Jeanne Stack scholarship fund established by Providence Hosp. Sch. Nursing, 1979; Sr. Jeanne Stack Week proclaimed by Erie County Commrs., Sandusky, 1986. Mem. Nat. League for Nursing (accreditation visitor 1958-75, chmn. appeals panel 1977-81), Am. Soc. Healthcare Edn. and Tng., Srs. of St. Francis of Sylvania, Franciscan Properties Inc. (pres. bd. trustees 1983—). Democrat. Home: 6959 Clare Ct Sylvania OH 43560-2845 Office: Franciscan Svcs Corp 6832 Convent Blvd Sylvania OH 43560

STACK, WILLIAM VINCENT, healthcare administrator; b. Pitts., Apr. 21, 1955; s. William G. and Mildred (Schenkel) S.; m. Janice Mary Kordenbrock, Sept. 8, 1979; children: Julie Marie, Thomas, Laura Kelly. BS in Acctg., Pa. State U., 1977; MS in Fin., Loyola Coll., Balt., 1986. CPA, Md. Auditor Ernst and Young, Balt., 1977-79; mgr. corporate reporting Md. Nat. Corp., Balt., 1979-86; v.p., contr. Balt. Fed. Fin., 1986-88; dir. fin. Blue Cross and Blue Shield of Md., Balt., 1988-90, dir. fin. planning and managed care analysis, 1995—; contr. CFS Health Group, Balt., 1990-94; dir. Managed Home Care, Balt., 1993-95; guest spkr. Loyola Coll. Exec. MBA Program, Balt., 1994. Mem. AICPAs, Md. Inst. CPAs, Healthcare Fin. Mgmt. Assn. (CFO forum). Office: Blue Cross & Blue Shield of Md 10455 Mill Run Cir Owings Mills MD 21117

STADNICKI, STANLEY WALTER, JR., health science association administrator; b. Norwich, Conn., Sept. 30, 1943; s. Stanley Walter Sr. and Beatrice Catherine (Dumais) S.; m. Jeanne Marie Couture, Sept. 6, 1965; children: Sandra, Scott, Steven, Robert. BA, Assumption Coll., Worcester, Mass., 1965; MA, Clark U., Worcester, 1970; PhD, Worcester Poly. Inst., 1976. Neurophysiologist Dept. Toxicology and Pharmacology, E.G. & G. Mason Research Inst., Worcester, 1967-70, sect. head, 1970-75, research scientist, 1975-76; toxicologist Drug Safety Evaluation, Pfizer, Inc., Groton, Conn., 1976-79, sr. toxicologist, 1979-81, project leader, 1981-85, mgr., 1985-86, asst. dir., 1986—; Contbr. articles to profl. jours. Leader Cub Scouts, East Lyme, Conn., 1978; mgr. East Lyme Little League Baseball, 1978-83; coach Babe Ruth Baseball, East Lyme, 1984-86; mem. Athletic Booster Club, East Lyme, 1984—. Clark U. grad. fellow, 1965-66. Mem. IEEE, Am. Soc. Pharmacology and Exptl. Therapeutics, Am. Coll. Toxicology, Soc. Toxicology (pres. N.E. chpt. 1990-92), Can. Soc. Toxicology. Roman Catholic. Home: 66 Quailcrest Rd East Lyme CT 06333-1328 Office: Pfizer Inc Drug Safety Evaluation Eastern Point Rd Groton CT 06340-4947

STAEHELI, JOHN WILLIAM, orthopedic surgeon; b. Tacoma, Wash., Aug. 9, 1954; s. George William and Ann (Kneeshaw) S.; m. Marilyn Arline Maier, Nov. 8, 1980; children: Gregory, Joseph, Anne. BS, Gonzaga U., 1976; MD, Creighton U., 1980. Diplomate Am. Bd. Orthop. Surgery., Nat. Bd. Med. Examiners; lic. Wash. Intern Balboa Naval Hosp., San Diego, 1980-81; resident Mayo Clinic, Rochester, Minn., 1981-85; advanced orthop. trauma tng. Balt. Shock Trauma Unit, 1985; orthop. surgeon USN Portsmouth (Va.) Naval Hosp., 1985-89, Rockwood Clinic, Spokane, Wash., 1989-94, Northwest Orthop. Assocs., Richland, Wash., 1994—; team physician Gonzaga U., Spokane, 1990-94; asst. prof. Uniformed Svcs. U., Bethesda, Md., 1985-89; clin. instr. orthop. Ea. Va. Med. Sch., Norfolk, 1986-89. Contbr. chpts. in books and articles to profl. jours. Fellow Am. Acad. Orthop. Surgeons; mem. Orthop. Trauma Assn., Soc. Mil. Orthop. Surgeons, Benton-Franklin County Med. Soc., Gonzaga U. Alumni Assn., Mayo Clin. Alumni Assn. Republican. Roman Catholic. Office: Northwest Orthop Assocs 875 Swift Blvd Richland WA 99352

STAFFA-SUKKAR, LAURA CHRISTINE, physician assistant; b. Houston, Apr. 14, 1968; d. Charles Virgil and Darlene Estelle (Scheffler) Staffa; m. Samir Sukkar, Oct. 22, 1994. BA, Tex. Tech. U., 1989; BS, U. Tex. Med. Br., Galveston, 1992, Physician Asst. Degree, 1992. Physician asst. NICU Hermann Hosp., Houston, 1992—, physician asst. adv. bd., 1992—, adminstrv. dir. physician asst. svcs. Comms. Dept. of Tex. Tech. U. Pendleton scholar, 1989. Fellow Am. Acad. Physician Assts., Tex. Acad. Physician Assts.; mem. Kappa Kappa Gamma (sec.), Omicron Delta Kappa. Republican. Roman Catholic. Home: 2819 Lafayette Houston TX 77005 Office: Hermann Hosp NICU 6411 Fannin Houston TX 77030

STAFFORD, ARTHUR CHARLES, medical association administrator; b. Cleve., May 10, 1947; s. Charles Arthur and Florence Mildred (Hovey) S.; m. Patricia Anne Cz, Dec. 20, 1991. BS, Kent State U., 1977; MBA, Lake Erie Coll., 1984. Med. tech. VA, Cleve., 1977-81, supr. med. tech., 1981—; instr. Lake Erie Coll., Painesville, Ohio, 1980-82, Cuyahoga C.C., Cleve., 1988-91; pres. Kent State U. Veterans Assn., 1974, mem. Kent State U Budget Review Com., 1975. Contbr. articles to profl. jour. Mem. Am. Legion, 1974, VFW, 1973. With USN, 1968-72. Mem. Am. Soc. Clin. Pathologists, Clin. Lab. Mgmt. Assn. (treas. Cleve. chpt. 1990—), Founders Club, Rock and Roll Hall of Fame. Republican. Home: 2193 Chimney Ridge Dr Madison OH 44057-2588 Office: VA Med Ctr 10701 East Blvd Cleveland OH 44106-1702

STAFFORD, JOHN ROGERS, pharmaceutical and household products company executive; b. Harrisburg, Pa., Oct. 24, 1937; s. Paul Henry and Gladys Lee (Sharp) S.; m. Inge Paul, Aug. 22, 1959; children—Carolyn, Jennifer, Christina, Charlotte. AB, Dickinson Coll., 1959; LLB with distinction, George Washington U., 1962, Degree (hon.), 1994. Bar: D.C. 1962. Assoc. Steptoe & Johnson, Washington, 1962-66; gen. atty. Hoffman-LaRoche, Nutley, N.J., 1966-67, group atty., 1967-70; gen. counsel Am. Home Products Corp., N.Y.C., 1970-74, v.p., 1972-77, sr. v.p., 1977-80, exec. v.p., 1980-81, pres., 1981—, chmn., chief exec. officer, 1986—; bd. dirs. The Chase Manhattan Corp., Allied Signal Inc., Grocery Mfrs. Am., Inc., Nynex Corp. Bd. dirs. Ctrl. Park Conservancy, Project Hope, Am.-China Soc., Am. Paralysis Assn. Recipient John Bell Larner 1st Scholar award George Washington U. Law Sch., 1962, Outstanding Achievement Alumnus award, 1981. Mem. ABA, D.C. Bar ASsn., Nat. Assn. Mfrs. (bd. dirs.), Sky Club (N.Y.C.), Essex Fells (N.J.) Country, Links Club (N.Y.C.), Baltusrol (N.J.), Robert Trent Jones (Va.). Office: American Home Products Corp 5 Giralda Farms Madison NJ 07940-1027

STAFFORD, WILLIAM BUTLER, retired psychology educator; b. Pitts., Feb. 6, 1931; s. Lee Elmer and Helen Huston (Butler) S.; student Adrian (Mich.) Coll., 1949-50; AB, Ohio U., 1954, MA, 1955; EdD, Ind. U., 1965; m. Barbara Anne Svoboda, Aug. 11, 1956; children: Mark William, Debra Anne. Residence counselor Ohio U., 1954-55; counselor dean of students' staff DePauw U., 1955-57; instr. Ind. U., 1957-65, asst. prof. edn., 1965-67; counselor Univ. Sch., Bloomington, Ind., 1957-65, dir. pupil pers. svcs., 1965-67; asst. prof. edn. Lehigh U., 1967-72, assoc. prof. counseling psychology, 1972-94, prof. emeritus, 1994—; cons. North Ctrl. Assn. Secondary Schs. and Colls., Ind. Dept. Public Instrn., Pa. Dept. Edn. Patients rights and rev. com. Allentown State Hosp. Cert. tchr., dir. guidance services, Ind., nat. bd. cert. counselor; Jesse Smith Noyes fellow, 1980. Mem. ACA, APA (counseling psychology divsn.), Am. Sch. Counselors Assn., Assn. Counselor Educators and Suprs., Am. Edn. Rsch. Assn., Pa. Counseling Assn., Pa. Sch. Counselors Assn. (Pa. Counselor of Yr. 1994), Internat. Alliance Invitational Edn. (adv. coun., mem. editl. bd., editor Jour. Invitational Theory and Practice), Pa. Alliance Invitational Edn. (editor newsletter), Chi Sigma Iota (chpt. adviser). Episcopalian. Author: Schools Without Counselors: Guidance Practices for the Teacher in the Elementary School, 1975. Home: 168 Lindfield Cir Macungie PA 18062

STAGE, GINGER ROOKS, psychologist; b. Allentown, Pa., Sept. 23, 1946; d. John Myers Rooks and Catherine Estelle (Graser) Rooks Bistritz; m. Robert Roy Stage, Aug. 23, 1969; 1 child, Stephen. BA in Psychology magna cum laude, Moravian Coll., 1968; MA in Psychology, Temple U., 1969. Lic. psychologist, Pa. Instr. Beaver campus Pa. State U., Monaca, 1969-74; staff psychologist St. Francis Community Mental Health Ctr., Pitts., 1974-83; pvt. practice family therapy Coraopolis, Pa., 1977—; mem. Greenstein Family Therapy Consultation Group, Pitts., 1981—; mem., speaker Human Sexuality Alliance, Pitts., 1989-91; speaker on marital, family and parenting issues. Mem. Am. Psychol. Assn., Greater Pitts. Psychol. Assn., Western Pa. Family Ctr. Episcopalian. Home: 112 Wessex Hills Dr Coraopolis PA 15108-1021 Office: 409 Mill St Coraopolis PA 15108-1607

STAGE, KEY HUTCHINSON, urologist; b. Washington, June 12, 1947; s. Anson H. and Lucie T. Stage; m. Jo-Ellen Arpin; children: Jennifer, Amanda. BA, Linfield Coll., 1969; MD, U. Oreg., 1973. Diplomate Am. Bd. Urology. Intern U.S. Naval Regional Med. Ctr., Oakland, Calif., 1973-74; resident in urology U. Tex. Southwestern Med. Sch., Dallas, 1977-81; pvt. practice Dallas, 1981—. Lt. comdr. USNR, 1973-77. Fellow ACS; mem. Am. Urol. Assn. Episcopalian. Office: 3600 Gaston Ave # 907 Dallas TX 75246

STAGER, DAVID R., ophthmalogist; b. Dover, Ohio, Sept. 8, 1935; s. Walter Raymond and Calista S.; m. Phyllis Ann Hugo, Aug. 5, 1961 (div. June 1981); children: James Jeffrey, Thomas Russell, David R., Elizabeth; m. Patricia Ann Tarvin, Nov. 29, 1986. Student, Holy Cross Coll., 1953-55; BS, John Carroll U., 1957; MD, Ohio State U., 1961. Diplomate Am. Bd. Ophthalmology. Intern St. Luke's Hosp., Cleve., 1961-62; resident Univ. Hosp., Columbus, Ohio, 1962-65; fellow Nat. Children's Hosp., Washington, 1967-68; dir. ophthalmology Children's Med. Ctr., Dallas, 1974—, co-dir. pediatric ophthalmology, 1974—, asst. dir. surg. svcs., 1981-84; instr. dept. ophthalmology Southwestern Med. Sch., Dallas, 1968-77, assoc. clin. prof. ophthalmology, 1981-85, clin. prof., 1985—; Herman Burian lectr. U. Houston, 1993. Contbr. more than 50 articles to profl. jours. Bd. dirs. Retina Found. of S.W., Dallas, 1991—, Nat. Children's Eye Care Found., Dallas, 1991—. With M.C., U.S. Army, 1965-67. Mem. AMA, Am. Acad. Pediatrics (dir. ophthalmology sect. 1991-92), Am. Assn. Pediatric Ophthalmology and Strabismus (chmn. socio-econ. com. 1987-91), Tex. Soc. Pediatric Ophthalmology and Strabismus, Am. Acad. Ophthalmology, Dallas Acad. Ophthalmology (bd. dirs., past pres.), Squint Club. Home: 17223 Club Hill Dr Dallas TX 75248 Office: Pediatric Ophthalmology PA 8201 Preston Rd 140-A Dallas TX 75225

STAGNER, JOHN IRVIN, III, physiologist, biochemist, educator; b. Eldorado, Kans., July 10, 1944; s. John Irvin Jr. and Elizabeth Fern (Keen) S.; m. MaryEllen G. Radway, Aug. 30, 1969; children: Laura Anne, Matthew Keen. BA, U. Kans., 1966; MA, Webster U., 1984; PhD, Iowa State U., 1974. Grad. teaching asst. Iowa State U., Ames, 1966-74, instr. zoology, 1967-69; rsch. assoc. VA Med. Ctr., Iowa City, 1974-75; asst. rsch. scientist U. Iowa Hosp. and Clinics, Iowa City, 1975-78; adj. asst. prof. medicine U. Louisville Sch. Medicine, 1978-88, adj. assoc. prof. medicine, 1988—; rsch. chemist VA Med. Ctr., Louisville, 1978—, staff asst. for edn., 1991—, chief sect. of clin. and staff edn., 1995—; cons. Clin. Rsch. Found., Louisville, 1990—. Contbr. chpts. to books, articles to profl. jours. Mayor, City of Coldstream (Ky.), 1982-84. Mem. AAAS, Internat. Pancreas and Islet Transplantation Assn., Sigma Xi. Office: Edn Svc (14A) 800 Zorn Ave Louisville KY 40206-1433

STAHARA, LORI LYNN, physician assistant; b. Homestead, Pa., Aug. 4, 1962; d. C. Charles and Patricia L. Fullard (Mitchell) S. BS in Med. Sci., Alderson Broaddus Coll., 1984. Physician asst. Weston (W.Va.) State Hosp., 1984-86; physician asst. geriatric care W.Va. U., Univ. Health Assn., Morgantown, 1986—; clin. rsch. coord. W.Va. U., Morgantown, 1986-93, lectr. 1986—, student preceptor, 1990—. Vol. Health Rite Free Med. Clinic, Morgantown, 1986—. Mem. Am. Assn. Physician Assts. (cert.), W.Va. Assn. Physician Assts. (com. chair 1988, 96, pres. 1989), Nat. Assn. Girls and Women in Sports (volleyball ofcl. 1993—), W.Va. Secondary Sch. Activities Commn. (volleyball ofcl. 1986—, softball ofcl. 1993—), N.C. Ofcls. Bd. (treas. 1988-96, tng. dir. 1996—). Democrat. Roman Catholic. Home: RR 5 Box 299 Morgantown WV 26505 Office: Physician Office Ctr PO Box 782 Morgantown WV 26507

STAHL, PHILIP DAMIEN, physiology and cell biology educator; b. Wheeling, W.Va., Oct. 4, 1941; married; 3 children. BS, West Liberty State Coll., 1964; PhD in Pharmacology, W.Va. U., 1967. From asst. to assoc. prof. Washington U. Med. Sch., St. Louis, 1971-81, prof. physiology, from 1982—, head dept., 1984—, now Edward Mallinckrodt Jr. prof. cell biology and physiology; fellow Space Sci. Research Ctr., U. Mo., 1967; Arthritis Found. fellow molecular biology, Vanderbilt U., 1968-70. Mem. Brit. Biochem. Soc., Am. Chem. Soc., Am. Physiol. Soc., Am. Soc. Biol. Chemists. Office: Washington Univ Sch Medicine Dept Cell Biology & Physiology 660 S Euclid Ave # 8228 Saint Louis MO 63110-1010*

STAHL, RICHARD SHELDON, surgeon; b. Chattanooga, Tenn., Dec. 8, 1950; s. Paul and Alena S. BA in Physics, Emory U., 1972; MD, Vanderbilt U., 1976; MBA, U. New Haven, 1994. Diplomate Nat. Bd. Med. Examiners, Am. Bd. Surgery, Am. Bd. Plastic Surgery. Intern, asst. resident dept. surgery Yale U. Sch. Medicine, New Haven, Conn., 1976-80, chief resident, 1980-81; resident plastic and reconstructive surgery Emory U. Sch. Medicine, 1981-82, chief resident, 1982-83; instr. surgery Yale U. Sch. Medicine, 1980-81, asst. prof. plastic surgery, 1983-89, assoc. prof. plastic surgery, 1989-90, assoc. clin. prof. plastic surgery, 1991-95, clin. prof. plastic surgery, 1995—; attending physician dept. surgery Yale-New Haven Hosp., 1980-81, 83—, asst. med. dir. surgery emergency svcs., 1983-90, attending physician surg. ICU, 1986-88; assoc. chief dept. surgery Yale-New Haven Hosp., 1994—, dir. internat. ops., 1995—; attending physician Yale Vascular Ctr. Yale U. Sch. Medicine, 1986-90; attending physician Hosp. St. Raphael, 1983—, West Haven VA Hosp., 1983—; founding co-dir. Yale Breast Care Ctr., 1989-90; cons. physicians assoc. surg. residency program Yale U.-Norwalk Hosp., 1978-81; resident surgeon Ho'pital Albert Schweitzer, Deschapelles, Haiti, 1980; spkr. in field. Sports reporter The Chattanooga Times, 1967-69; contbr. over 40 articles to profl. jours. Pres. Kingswood Homeowner's Assn., 1987-93; mem. Charter Oak Bassett Hound Club, 1981—. Recipient Rsch. grant Charles W. Ohse Fund, Rsch. grant Smith Kline and French Labs., Rsch. grant Kendall Co. Fellow Am. Coll. Surgeons (mem. Conn. chpt.); mem. APHA, AMA, Am. Assn. Plastic Surgeons, Am. Soc. Plastic and Reconstructive Surgeons, Am. Coll. Physician Execs., Am. Coll. Med. Quality, Am. Burn Assn., Soc. for Critical Care Medicine, N.Y. Regional Soc. Plastic and Reconstructive Surgery, New Eng. Soc. Plastic and Reconstructive Surgeons, New Haven County Med. Soc., Conn. Soc. Am. Bd. Surgeons, Conn. State Med. Soc., Sigma Xi. Office: Yale New Haven Hosp Dir Internat Ops-Dept Surgery CB228 20 York St New Haven CT 06504

STAHLMAN, MILDRED THORNTON, pediatrics and pathology educator, researcher; b. Nashville, July 31, 1922; d. James Geddes and Mildred (Thornton) S. AB, Vanderbilt U., 1943, MD, 1946; MD (hon.), U. Goteborg, Sweden, 1973, U. Nancy, France, 1982. Diplomate Am. Bd. Pediatrics, Am. Bd. Neonatology. Cardiac resident La Rabida Sanitarium, Chgo., 1951; instr. pediatrics Vanderbilt U., Nashville, 1951-58, instr. physiology, 1954-60, asst. prof. pediatrics, 1959-64, asst. prof. physiology, 1960-62, assoc. prof. pediatrics, 1964-70, prof., 1970—, prof. pathology, 1982—, Harvie Branscomb Disting. prof., 1984, dir. div. neonatology, 1961-89. Editor: Respiratory Distress Syndromes, 1989; contbr. over 140 articles to profl. publs. Recipient Thomas Jefferson award Vanderbilt U., 1980, Apgar award Am. Acad. Pediatrics, 1987; NIH grantee, 1954—. Mem. AAAS, Am. Pediatric Soc. (pres. 1984), Soc. Pediatric Rsch., Am. Physiology Soc., So. Soc. Pediatric Rsch. (pres. 1961-62), Royal Swedish Acad. Scis., Inst. of Medicine of the Nat Acad. of Scis. Episcopalian. Home: 538 Beech Creek Rd S Brentwood TN 37027-3421 Office: Vanderbilt U Med Ctr 21st Ave Nashville TN 37232*

STAIN, STEVEN CHARLES, surgeon, educator; b. San Antonio, Feb. 18, 1958; s. Stanley and Olga (Semee) S.; m. Hyacinth Rowena Catherine Mason, July 10, 1993. BS, U. Calif., Irvine, 1979, MD, 1983. Diplomate in surgery and surg. critical care Am. Bd. Surgery. Clin. instr. U. So. Calif., L.A., 1988-89, asst. prof., 1989-96, assoc. prof., 1996—. Rsch. grantee Am. Cancer Soc., 1994, Norris Cancer Hosp., 1995. Fellow ACS; mem. AMA, Pacific Coast Surg. Assn., Soc. Am. Gastrointestinal Surgeons (co-chair rsch. com. 1993—, rsch. grantee 1994), L.A. Surg. Soc., Southwestern Surg. Congress, Western Surg. Assn., Internat. Soc. Surgery, Pan Pacific Surg. Assn., Internat. Hepatopancreatobiliary Assn., Nat. Med. Assn., Soc. Black Acad. Surgeons, Assn. Acad. Surgery, Soc. Critical Care Medicine, Soc. Surgery

Alimentary Tract. Office: Sch Medicine U So Calif 1510 San Pablo St #430 Los Angeles CA 90033

STAINBROOK, DAVID GRANT, JR., internist; b. Des Moines, Feb. 7, 1966; s. David Grant and Barbara Marie (Timmins) S.; m. Sally Ann McMillan, Oct. 2, 1993; children: Emily Rose, David Grant. BS, Akron (Ohio) U., 1987; DO, Ohio U., 1991. Diplomate Am. Bd. Internal Medicine. Intern Doctors Hosp., Columbus, Ohio, 1991-92, resident, 1992-94, staff physician, 1996—; rheumatology fellow Henry Ford Hosp., Detroit, 1994-96; pvt. practice internal medicine Columbus, 1996—. Author abstracts/posters. Home: 9832 Camden Livonia MI 48150

STAIR, J(OHN) MICHAEL, general, vascular and thoracic surgeon; b. Ft. Smith, Ark., Aug. 13, 1953; s. John Anthony and Inez (Bugg) S.; m. Janis Clare Aulik, Apr. 10, 1982. BS, U. Ark., Fayetteville, 1975; MD, U. Ark., Little Rock, 1979. Diplomate Am. Bd. Surgery. Pvt. practice surgery Pulaski Surgery Clinic, North Little Rock, Ark., 1985—; staff surgeon J.L. McClellan VA Hosp., Little Rock, 1984-85. Contbr. numerous articles to profl. jours. Recipient Carl Moyer Resident award Am. Burn Assn., 1982. Fellow ACS, Southwestern Surg. Congress, Am. Soc. for Gastrointestinal Endoscopy. Office: Pulaski Surgery Clinic 2001 Pershing Cir Ste 1-A North Little Rock AR 72114

STAIR, THOMAS OSBORNE, physician, educator; b. Richmond, Va., Jan. 10, 1950; s. Frederick Rogers Jr. and Martha (Osborne) S.; m. Lucy Caldwell, Dec. 28, 1973; children: Rebecca Caldwell, Peter Caldwell. AB, U. N.C., 1971; MD, Harvard U., 1975. Diplomate Am. Bd. Emergency Medicine (examiner 1982-88). Residency dir. emergency dept. Georgetown U. Hosp., Washington, 1979-85, asst. dir. emergency dept., 1979-89; asst. dean for continuing med. edn. Georgetown U. Sch. Medicine, Washington, 1985-89; chair dept. emergency medicine, 1989-95; prof. U. Md., Balt., 1995—. Co-author: Common Simple Emergencies, 1985. Recipient Excellence in Teaching award Emergency Medicine Residents Assn., 1986. Fellow Am. Coll. Emergency Physicians; mem. Soc. Acad. Emergency Medicine, Am. Med. Informatics Assn. Home: 4822 Quebec St NW Washington DC 20016-3229 Office: Univ Maryland Baltimore MD

STALAND, (JOHAN GUSTAF) BERTIL, retired gynecologist; b. Dalsland, Sweden, May 24, 1913; s. Olof Gustaf and Selma Kristina (Johansson) Magnuson; m. Britt Frick, June 8, 1946; children: Gustaf Peter, John Gunnar. MM, U. Uppsala, Stockholm, 1941. Authorized physician, specialist in gynecology and gen. surgery. Asst. physician various hosps., Sweden, 1942-53; head gynecology Samariterhemmet, Uppsala, Sweden, 1953-79, ret., 1979. Contbr. articles to profl. jours. Physician Red Cross Hosp., Norway, 1945. Capt. Swedish mi., WWII. Mem. Internat. Menopause Soc., Swedish Assn. Ob-Gyn., Scandinavian Assn. Ob-Gyn., Scandinavian Oncologic Soc. Home: Hästeskovägen 22, S 311 37 Falkenberg Sweden

STALLINGS, W(ILLIAM) TERRY, urologist; b. Troy, Ala., July 10, 1956; children: William Ryan, Lauren Ashley. BS, U. Ala., Tuscaloosa, 1978; MD, U. South Ala., 1983. Diplomate Am. Bd. Urology. Pvt. practice, Montgomery, Ala., 1989—. Fellow ACS; mem. AMA, Am. Urol. Assn., Am. Assn. Clin. Urologists, Med. Assn. Ala. Home: 2441 Sedgefield Ln Montgomery AL 36106 Office: Montgomery Urology Assocs 2055 E South Blvd Ste 308 Montgomery AL 36116

STALLONE, THOMAS MICHAEL, clinical psychologist; b. N.Y.C., Dec. 5, 1952; s. Vito Joseph and Mary Ellen (Kearney) S.; m. Bonnie Elizabeth Wenk, May 30, 1982. B in Psychology, N.Y. Inst. Tech., 1987; MA, Spalding U., 1991; D in Clin. Psychology, Pacific U., 1994. Lic. psychologist, Wash.; cert. psychol. assoc. in clin. psychology, rational emotive therapy; diplomate Am. Bd. Forensic Examiners; registered Nat. Register Health Providers in Psychology. Internat. banker Sumitomo Bank, Ltd., N.Y.C., 1980-82; pvt. practice hypnosis cons. LaGrange, Ky. and N.Y.C., 1982—; internat. banker Bank of N.Y., N.Y.C., 1982-87; rehab. specialist Goodwill Industries Ky., Louisville, 1989; psychol. assoc. div. mental health Ky. Corrections Cabinet, La Grange, 1989-91; teaching asst. Pacific U., Forest Grove, Oreg., 1991-93; psychotherapist Portland, Oreg., 1991-95; clin. psychologist Vancouver, Wash., 1995—; Author: The Boke of Taliesyne, 1979, The Effects of Psychodrama on Inmates Within a Structured Residential Behavior Modification Program, 1993, Rational Emotive Therapy and Subpersonalities, 1996. Author: The Boke of Taliesyne, 1979, The Effects of Psychodrama on Inmates Within a Structured Residential Behavior Modification Program, 1993. Cons. Hist. Arms, Ltd., N.Y.C., 1983-87, N.Y. Medieval Festival, 1984-86; dir., cons. Whitestone (N.Y.) Creative Arts Workshop, 1977, Ky. Shakespeare Festival, Louisville, 1987-88; treas., advisor 4H Exec. Coun., La Grange, 1988-91. Decorated Grant of Arms Chief Herald of Ireland; named to Honorable Order of Ky. Col. Mem. Am. Psychol. Assn., Am. Soc. Group Psychotherapy and Psychodrama, Internat. Soc. for Profl. Hypnosis, Western Psychol. Assn., Ancient Order Hibernians, Mensa.

STALLTER, CHRISTOPHER JOHN, family practice physician; b. Hinsdale, Ill., July 5, 1966; s. Donald Edward and Nancy Joan (Timmel) S. BS, Valparaiso U., 1988; DO, Chgo. Coll. Osteo. Medicine, 1992. Diplomate Am. Coll. Family Physicians. Intern Chgo. Osteo. Hosp. and Med. Ctr., 1992-93, resident family practice, 1993-95; pvt. practice family practice Dubuque, Iowa, 1995—. Mem. Am. Osteo. Assn. Lutheran. Office: 3385 Hillcrest Rd Dubuque IA 52002

STALLWORTH, CHARLES DEROTHEA, JR., psychologist; b. Riderwood, Ala., July 4, 1940; s. Charles D. and Annie (Horn) S. B.S., Tenn. State U., Nashville, 1963, M.S., 1966; postgrad, Calif. Sch. Profl. Psychology, 1977-79, U. Ky., 1980, U. South Ala., summer 1967, Tuskegee Inst., summer 1968, Auburn U., summer 1969, Harvard U., summer 1975; Ph.D. in Psychology, Internat. Coll., 1983. Diplomate Am. Bd. Psychotherapy. Psychiat. asst. Hubbard Hosp., Nashville, 1964-66; counselor, math tchr. North Central High Sch., Chatom, Ala., 1966-68; math tchr., Washington County H.S., 1969-70; supr. adult edn. Washington County Bd. Edn., Chatom, 1968-70; dir. counseling ctr. Albany State Coll., Ga., 1970-92; pvt. practice, 1993—; staff assistance Auburn U., 1969; cons. Peace Corps, 1979-82. Bd. dirs. Dougherty County CODAC, Inc., Albany, 1973-77, Albany Area Council V.D. Control, 1975-77. Recipient grants HEW, 1970-77, U.S. Office Edn., 1972, Eagle Scout award, 1955. Mem. Am. Psychol. Assn. (assoc.), Acad. Certified Neurotherapists, Alpha Phi Alpha. Democrat. Baptist. Research on impact of affective domain on learning outcomes and on application of cognitive therapies as a means of controlling negative effects. Home: 805 E 4th Ave Albany GA 31705-1203

STALLWORTH, TERRESA LOUISE, psychiatrist; b. Tuscaloosa, Ala.; d. William Wesley and Louise Clara Catherine (Goodrich) S.; student Va. Intermont Coll., 1954-55; BMus (Elsa Strong piano scholar, 1955-58), U. Tenn., 1959, MD, 1963. Diplomate Am. Bd. Psychiatry and Neurology, Am. Bd. Adminstrv. Psychiatry. Intern U. Tenn. Meml. Hosp. and Rsch. Center, 1963-64; resident in neurology City of Memphis Hosp., 1964-65; resident in psychiatry U. Mo., St. Louis, 1966-68, chief resident, 1968; clin. dir., asst. supt., acting supt. Lakeshore Mental Health Inst., Knoxville, Tenn., 1969-74; dir. cmty. programs and specialty units, San Antonio State Hosp., 1974—; dir. Camino Real State Operated Cmty. Mental Health Ctr., 1993-95; exec. dir. Camino Real Cmty. MH/MR Svcs., 1995—; assoc. clin. prof. psychiatry U. Tex. Health Scis. Center, San Antonio, 1974—; chmn. profl. adv. bd. Bexar County Mental Health/Mental Retardation Center, 1979-81; mem. profl. adv. bd. Horizon House Day Care Center. Concert pianist, various concerts Trinity U., St. Mary's U., Incarnate Word Coll., 1975—, concert appearances with San Antonio Symphony, city grant-sponsored concerts San Antonio State Hosp., U. Tenn, Knoxville, 1989. Winner first prize Memphis and Mid-South piano contest, 1958. Fellow Am. Psychiat. Assn.; mem. Tex. Psychiat. Assn. (com. on women), Bexar County Psychiat. Soc. (pres.-elect 1996—), AMA, Tex. Med. Assn., Bexar County Med. Soc., NOW, Chopin found. U.S.A., Alpha Omega Alpha. Clubs: Tuesday Music, Sigma Kappa Alumnae. Premier performance own Piano Sonata, 1980; contbr. article to profl. med. jour. Office: San Antonio State Hosp Antonio TX 78222

STALNAKER, JOHN HULBERT, physician; b. Portland, Oreg., Aug. 29, 1918; s. William Park II and Helen Caryl (Hulbert) S.; m. Louise Isabel Lucas, Sept. 8, 1946; children: Carol Ann, Janet Lee, Mary Louise, John Park, Laurie Jean, James Mark. Student, Reed Coll., Portland, 1936-38; AB, Willamette U., Salem, Oreg., 1941; MD, Oreg. Health Scis. U., 1945. Diplomate Am. Bd. Internal Medicine. Intern Emanuel Hosp., Portland, 1945-46; resident in internal medicine St. Vincent Hosp., Portland, 1948-51; clin. instr. U. Oreg. Med. Sch., 1951-54, 60-62; staff physician VA Hosp., Vancouver, Wash., 1970-79; cons. in internal medicine, 1951-79. Contbr. articles to profl. jours. Pianist various civic and club meetings, Portland; leader Johnny Stalnaker's Dance Orch., 1936-39. Lt. (j.g.) USNR, 1946-48. Fellow ACP; mem. AMA, Multnomah County Med. Soc., Oreg. State Med. Assn., N.Am. Lily Soc., Am. Rose Soc. Home: 2204 SW Sunset Dr Portland OR 97201-2068

STALTER, RICHARD B., biology educator, researcher; b. Montvale, N.J., Jan. 16, 1942; s. Lester C. and Betty R. Stalter; divorced; 1 child, Laurie. B.S., Rutgers U., 1963; M.S., U. R.I., 1966; Ph.D., U. S.C., 1968. Asst. prof. High Point Coll., N.C., 1968-69, Pfeiffer Coll., Misenheimer, N.C., 1969-70; fish kill expert S.C. Pollution Control Authority, Columbia, 1970-71; prof. biology St. John's U., Jamaica, N.Y., 1971—; cons. So. Engring. Co., Atlanta, 1972-75, Cabot Corp., Boston, 1974-75; trustee N.Y. Ocean Sci. Lab., Montauk, N.Y., 1974-82. Author: Barrier Island Botany, 1992, Barrier Island Botany The Southeastern United States, 1993. Contbr. articles to profl. jours. Mem. Torrey Bot. Club, Assn. S.E. Biologists, So. Appalachian Bot. Club, N.E. Weed Sci. Soc., Sigma Xi, Phi Sigma, Skull and Circle Honor Soc., S.C. Acad. of Sci. Republican. Episcopalian. Home: 36 Glade Ln Levittown NY 11756-3918

STAM, LAWRENCE E., nephrologist; b. Bklyn., Mar. 12, 1953. BA, Columbia Coll., 1974; MD, SUNY, 1978. Diplomate Am. Bd. Nephrology, Am. Bd. Internal Medicine. Intern St. Elizabeth's Hosp., Boston, 1978-79, resident internal medicine, 1979-81; nephrology fellow Bklyn. Jewish Hosp., 1982-84; attending physician N.Y. Meth. Hosp., Bklyn., 1984—; clin. asst. prof. SUNY Downstate, Bklyn., 1986—, Sch. Medicine Cornell U. Office: NY Meth Hosp 506 6th St Brooklyn NY 11215

STAMBAUGH, JOHN EDGAR, oncologist, hematologist, pharmacologist, educator; b. Everett, Pa., Apr. 30, 1940; s. John Edgar and Rhoda Irene (Becker) S.; B.S. cum laude in Chemistry, Dickinson Coll., 1962; M.D., Jefferson Med. Coll., 1966, Ph.D., 1968; m. Shirley Louise Fultz, June 24, 1961; 4 children. Intern, Thomas Jefferson U. Hosp., Phila., 1968-69, resident, 1969-70; oncology fellow Jefferson Med. Coll., 1970-72, instr. pharmacology, 1969-70, asst. prof., 1970-74, assoc. prof., 1974-82, prof., 1982—, asst. prof. medicine, 1976—; pvt. practice medical oncology Hematology and Chronic Pain, Woodbury, N.J.; staff physician Cooper Med. Center, Camden, N.J., 1972—, Underwood Meml. Hosp., Woodbury, 1972—, West Jersey Hosp., 1973—, J.F. Kennedy Hosp., 1978—, Our Lady of Lourdes Hosp., 1990—. Fellow Am. Coll. Clin. Pharmacology, Am. Acad. Pain Mgmt., Am. Soc. Pain Mgmt.; mem. ABA, AMA, Am. Soc. Clin. Pharmacology, N.J. Med. Soc., Gloucester County Med. Soc., Camden County Med. Soc., Am. Soc. for Pharmacology and Exptl. Therapeutics, Am. Soc. Clin. Oncology, Am. Assn. for Cancer Research, Internat. Assn. for Study of Pain, Am. Pain Soc., Am. Assn. Clin. Research, Sigma Xi. Contbr. articles to profl. jours. Office: 17 W Red Bank Ave Ste 101 Woodbury NJ 08096-1630

STAMBAUGH, TERESA THAYER, quality management health facility administrator; b. Belleville, Kans., Nov. 5, 1950; d. Jon Dale and Rhae Elaine (Murphy) Thayer; m. John Charles Stambaugh, June 11, 1994; 1 child from previous marriage: Cora Lee Glisson. BSN, Ft. Hays Kans. State U., 1973; MS in Human Devel. and Family, U. Nebr., Lincoln, 1984. RN, Kans.; cert. profl. in healthcare quality. Discharge planner, charge control analyst, nurse Lincoln Gen. Hosp., 1973-81, coord. discharge planning, 1981-85; dir. quality assurance and utilization rev. Equicor-Equitable HCA Corp., Wichita, Kans., 1985-88; risk mgmt. specialist State of Kans., Topeka, 1988-90; dir. quality mgmt. The Menninger Clinic, Topeka, 1990-95; quality improvement/risk mgr. Cmty. Hosp., Omaga, 1995—; adj. clin. instr. Wichita State U., 1987, 88, 94. Author articles. Vol. The Marion Clinic, Topeka. Mem. Nat. Assn. for Healthcare Quality, Am. Soc. for Healthcare Risk Mgmt., Kans. Assn. Quality and Utilization Profls., Kans. Assn. Risk and Quality Mgmt., Sigma Theta Tau. Methodist. Home: 4608 SE Oak Bend Dr Berryton KS 66409

STAMBONE-SOVA, LISA MARIE, pharmacist; b. Scranton, Pa., June 22, 1964; d. Anthony Dominick and Therese Elaine (Motts) S. BS in Pharmacy, Temple U., 1987. Intern pharmacy Scranton State Gen. Hosp., 1985, Stephen's Pharmacy, Moscow, Pa., 1986, Rite Aid Pharmacy, Peckville, Pa., 1987; pharmacist mgr., computer tng. mgr. Rite Aid Pharmacy, Peckville, 1987—; cons. pharmacist drug therapy, blood pressure and glucose screenings, cholesterol screening, patient counseling and patient compliance follow-up, 1987—. Ch. lectr. St. Mary's Assumption Ch., Jessup, Pa., 1982-84. Mem. Am. Pharm. Assn., Pa. Pharm. Assn., Lackawanna Pharm. Assn., Rho Pi Phi. Democrat. Roman Catholic. Home: 113 Maria Blvd Archbald PA 18403 Office: Rite Aid Pharmacy 1500 Main St Peckville PA 18452-2033

STAMEY, THOMAS ALEXANDER, physician, urology educator; b. Rutherfordton, N.C., Apr. 26, 1928; s. Owen and Virginia (Link) S.; m. Kathryn Simmons Dec. 1, 1973; children: Fred M., Charline, Thomas A. III, Allison, Theron. BA, Vanderbilt U., 1948; MD, Johns Hopkins U., 1952. Diplomate Am. Bd. Urology. Intern, then resident Johns Hopkins Hosp., 1952-56; asst. prof. urology Johns Hopkins U. Sch. Medicine, Balt., 1958-60, assoc. prof., 1960-61; assoc. prof. Stanford (Calif.) U., 1961-64, 1964-90, prof., chmn. dept., 1991-94, chmn. divsn. urology, 1961-90. Author: Renovascular Hypertension, 1967, Pathogenesis and Treatment of Urinary Tract Infections, 1980, Urinalysis and Urinary Sediment: A Practical Guide for the Health Science Professional, 1985; editor: Campbell's Urology, Monographs in Urology, 1980—. Capt. M.C., USAF, 1956-58. Recipient Sheen award ACS, 1990, Ferdinand C. Valentine award N.Y. Acad. Medicine, 1991. Mem. Am. Urol. Assn. (Ramon Guiteras award 1995), Am. Surg. Assn. (sr.), Inst. Medicine of NAS. Office: Stanford U Med Ctr 300 Pasteur Dr Palo Alto CA 94304-2203

STAMM, JOHN WILLIAM RUDOLPH, dentist, educator, academic dean; b. Germany, Nov. 3, 1942; married; 2 children. DDS, U. Alta., Can., 1967; DDPH, U. Toronto, Can., 1969, MScD, 1971. Diplomate Am. Bd. Dental Pub. Health. Dental dir. Baffin region Nat. Health & Welfare, 1967; pvt. dental practice Fort Saskatchewan, Alta., 1968; rsch. asst. & biometrics Sch. Hygiene & Faculty Dentistry U. Toronto, 1968-71; asst. prof. Faculty Dentistry McGill U., 1971-74, assoc. prof., 1974-80, chmn., 1974-84, prof., 1980-84; dir. Dental Rsch. Ctr. U. N.C., 1985-89, prof. Sch. Dentistry, 1985—, asst. dean, 1985-89, dean, 1989—; vis. prof. U. Riyadh, Saudi Arabia, 1980; mem. expert adv. panel oral health WHO, 1984-90; mem. study sect. oral biology & medicine NIH, 1988-90; cons. Quebec Ministry Social Affairs, 1974-76, Alta. Health Unit Assn., 1977-79, Can. Electrolytic Zinc, 1978-82, Can. Dental Assn., 1980, Am. Fund Dental Health, 1980-83, Dental Health St. Regis Indians N.Y. State Dept. Health, 1980. Editl. bd. Jour. Dental Edn., 1980-83, Jour. Cmty. Dentistry & Oral Epidemiology, 1988—, Oral Diseases, 1994—; assoc. editor Caries Rsch., 1995—; contbr. articles to profl. jours. Grantee Ont. Dept. Health, 1969, McGill U., 1973, Quebec Health Sci. Rsch. Coun., 1973, Ministry Social Affairs Quebec, 1972-74, Nat. Inst. Dental Rsch., 1976-78, 85, Med. Rsch. Coun., 1981-84, Nat. Health & Welfare, 1982-85, NIH, 1985—, Robert Wood Johnson Found., 1986-91. Fellow AAAS, Royal Coll. Dentists Can. (chief examiner 1980-82), Internat. Coll. Dentists, Am. Coll. Dentists, Acad. Dentistry Internat.; mem. Am. Assn. Dental Schs., Am. Assn. Pub. Health Dentists, Am. Bd. Dental Pub. Health, Am. Assn. Dental Rsch., Can. Dental Assn., Can. Soc. Pub. Health Dentists (pres. 1979-81), Internat. Assn. Dental Rsch., Omicron Kappa Upsilon. Office: U NC Sch Dentistry CB #7450 Chapel Hill NC 27599-7450

STAMM, WALTER, pharmacology educator; b. St. Goarshausen, Rhineland, Germany, Jan. 19, 1924; s. Josef and Maria (Gross) S.; m. Irmgard Stahl, May 29, 1954; 1 child, Cornelia. MD, U. Frankfurt/Main, Fed. Republic Germany, 1950; prof. pharmacology, U. Basel, Switzerland, 1977. Sci. collaborator Ciba-Geigy AG, Basel, Switzerland, 1960-89; lectr. pharmacology U. Basel, 1959-96; mgr. Ciba-Geiby AG, Basel, 1969-89. Contbr. articles to profl. jours. Mem. Deutsche Gesellschaft für Biologische Chemie, Schweizerischer Pharmakologenverein, Vereinigung Schweizer Aerzte. Home and Office: Fünfeichenweg 2, CH 4126 Bettingen Switzerland

STAMOS, MICHAEL JERRY, colon and rectal surgeon, educator; b. Miami Beach, Fla., Sept. 22, 1959; s. Peter and Carol Sue (Adams) S.; m. Bridget Thompson, Mar. 3, 1990. BA, Case Western Res. U., 1981, MD, 1985; asst. prof. surgery. Fellow in colon and rectal surgery Ochsner Clinic, New Orleans, 1990-91; asst. prof. surgery UCLA, 1991—; chief sect. colon and rectal surgery Harbor UCLA Med. Ctr., Torrance, 1992—. Contbr. articles to med. jours., chpt. to books. Fellow ACS(adv. coun. colon and rectal surgery 1995-97), Am. Soc. Colon and Rectal Surgeons; mem. Soc. Am. Gastrointestinal Endoscopic Surgeons, Internat. Soc. Univ. Colon and Rectal Surgeons, Southwestern Surg. Congress. Office: Harbor UCLA Med. Ctr. 1000 W Carson St Ste 25 Torrance CA 90509

STAMPER, ROBERT LEWIS, ophthalmologist, educator; b. N.Y.C., July 27, 1939; m. Naomi T. Belson, June 23, 1963; children: Juliet, Marjorie, Alison. BA, Cornell U., 1957-61; MD, SUNY-Downstate, 1965. Diplomate Am. Bd. Ophthalmology (assoc. examiner 1976-92, bd. dirs. 1992—, mem. glaucoma panel 1993—); lic. physician, Calif. Intern Mt. Sinai Hosp., N.Y.C., 1965-66; resident in ophthalmology Washington U.-Barnes Hosp., St. Louis, 1968-71; Nat. Eye Inst.-NIH fellow dept. ophthalmology Washington U., St. Louis, 1971-72, from instr. ophthalmology to asst. prof. dept. ophthalmology, 1971-72; asst. prof. dept. ophthalmology Pacific Presbyn. Med. Ctr., San Francisco, 1972-76, assoc. prof. ophthalmology, 1976-87; chmn. dept. ophthalmology Calif. Pacific Med. Ctr. (formerly Pacific Presbyn. Med. Ctr.), San Francisco, 1987-96; asst. opthalmologist Barnes Hosp., St. Louis, 1971-72, Harkness Hosp., San Francisco, 1973-74; dir. ophthalmic photography and fluorescin angiography, dept. ophthalmology Washington U., St. Louis, 1969-72; dir. resident tng. Pacific Presbyn. Med. Ctr., 1972-89, dir. glaucoma svc., vice-chmn. dept. ophthalmology, 1974-87; chief ophthalmology svc. Highland Hosp., Oakland, Calif., 1974-76; clin. instr. dept. ophthalmology U. Calif., San Francisco, 1974-77; clin. asst. prof. ophthalmology U. Calif., Berkeley, 1974-78, asst. clin. prof. ophthalmology, 1978-85; sr. rsch. assoc. Smith-Kettlewell Inst. Visual Scis., San Francisco, 1972-89; project co-dir. ophthalmic curriculum for med. students Nat. Libr. Medicine, 1973-75; commr. Joint Commn. on Allied Health Pers. in Ophthalmology, 1975-87, bd. dirs., 1978-88, sec., 1980, v.p., 1982-83, pres., 1984-85; provisional asst. chief dept. ophthalmology Mt. Zion Hosp., San Francisco, 1976-87, assoc. chief dept. ophthalmology, 1982-86; ophthalmic cons. Ft. Ord, Calif., 1976—, Oakland (Calif.) Naval Hosp., 1978-83; instr. Stanford (Calif.) U., 1977—; glaucoma cons. U. Calif., Davis, 1978-84; vis. lectr. dept. ophthalmology Hadassah Hebrew U. Med. Ctr., Jerusalem, 1978, Oxford (Eng.) U. Eye Hosp., 1986; ind. med. examiner State of Calif., 1979—; mem. appeals hearing panel Accreditation Coun. for Grad. Med. Edn., 1986-93, mem. residency rev. com. for ophthalmology, 1993—; mem. provisional courtesy staff Peralta Hosp., Oakland, 1988-92; mem. ophthalmic devices adv. panel USFDA, 1989-92; presenter, lectr. in field. Editor Ophthalmology Clinics of North Am., 1988—; mem. editl. adv. com. Ophthalmology, 1982-89, mem. editl. bd., 1983-94; contbr. articles to profl. jours. Chmn. bd. Agy. for Jewish Edn., Oakland, 1986-89; bd. dirs. Jewish Fedn. Greater East Bay, Oakland, 1992-94; bd. dirs. Found. for Glaucoma Rsch.; mem. glaucoma adv. com. Nat. Soc. to Prevent Blindness, 1981—; mem. Am. Diabetes Assn. Surgeon USPHS, 1966-68. Recipient Nat. Soc. for Performance and Instrn. award for self-instrnl. material in ophthalmology, 1975, Honor award Am. Acad. Ophthalmology, 1982, Sr. Honor award, 1992, Statesmanship award Joint Commn. on Allied Health Pers. in Ophthalmology, 1989; N.Y. State Regents scholar, 1961, N.Y. State scholar in medicine, 1965; Blalock student fellow UCLA Sch. Medicine, 1961, Fight for Sight student fellow dept. ophthalmology N.Y. Hosp. and Cornell Med. Ctr., 1962, 63, 64. Fellow Am. Acad. Ophthalmology and Otolaryngology (rep. to joint commn. on allied health pers., faculty home study course sect. X, chmn. sect. VIII 1983-85, bd. councilors, editl. adv. com. Opthalmology jour. 1982-89, editl. bd. Ophthalmology jour. 1983-94, and many others), ACS; mem. AMA (Physician's Recognition award 1989), Am. Ophthalmologic Soc., Assn. for Rsch. in Vision and Ophthalmology, Calif. Med. Assn. (asst. sec. sect. ophthalmology, chmn., sci. bd. rep. adv. panel on ophthalmology 1985-91), Nat. Soc. Prevent Blindness (mem. glaucoma adv. com. 1981—, bd. dirs. 1986—), No. Calif. Soc. Prevent Blindness, Calif. Assn. Ophthalmology, Pan Am. Ophthalmological Soc., N.Y. Acad. Scis., Las Vegas Ophthalmologican.). Office: Calif Pacific Med Ctr 2340 Clay St San Francisco CA 94115-1932

STAMPFER, MEIR JONATHAN, epidemiologist, nutritionist, educator; b. Lincoln, Nebr., Mar. 1, 1950; s. Joshua and Goldie Stampfer; m. Claire Diane Blum, Dec. 30, 1975; children: Samuel, Eliane, Orly. AB, Columbia Coll., 1973; Dr.med., NYU, 1977; MPH, Harvard U., 1980, D in Pub. Health, 1985. Diplomate Am. Bd. Med. Examiners. Instr. medicine Harvard Med. Sch., Boston, 1982-85; asst. prof. medicine Harvard Med. Sch., 1985-88; assoc. prof. Harvard Sch. Pub. Health, Boston, 1988-93, prof., 1993—; assoc. physician Brigham & Women's Hosp., Boston, 1982-92; physician Brigham and Women's Hosp., Boston, 1992—; lectr. in field. Contbr. numerous articles to profl. jours. Recipient Nat. Rsch. Svc. award NIH, 1977-82; NIH grantee, 1982—. Fellow Am. Heart Assn., Am. Coll. Nutrition; mem. Internat. Soc. Cardiology, Soc. Epidemiologic Rsch. Democrat. Jewish. Office: Channing Lab 181 Longwood Ave Boston MA 02115-5821

STAMPFLI, WENDELL PHILLIPS, JR., physician, consultant in medical antiquities; b. McDonald, Pa., Oct. 22, 1914; s. Wendell Phillips and laura Louise (Schayes) S.; m. Carol Jean Wolkins; children: Judith Anne, Carol Jean, Martin Scott, Wendell Phillips III, Stephen Michael. BS, U. Tex., Austin, 1936; MD, U. Tex., Galveston, 1940; postgrad., U. Chgo. Diplomate Am. Bd. Radiology. Dir. radiology St. Lukes Hosp., Denver, 1945-70; cons. radiologist Denver Gen. Hosp., 1950-70, U.S. VA Hosp., 1955-70; clin. prof. radiology U. Colo. Sch. Medicine, Denver, 1955-70; cons. in med. antiquities, 1970—; lectr. on med. microscope U. Iowa, Mayo Clinic. Contbr. numerous articles to profl. jours; numerous exhibits in museums of med. history. U.S. Dept. Pub. Health rsch. and teaching grantee, 1966-70. Fellow AAAS, Am. Coll. Radiology (emeritus), Royal Microscopical Soc. (London). Home: 2 Glendale Cir Iowa City IA 52245

STANAITIS, SANDRA LEE, nurse; b. Chester, Pa., Dec. 27, 1958; d. Leon David and Margaret (Sharpless) S. BA in Psychology, Widener U., 1980; BS in Biology, SUNY, Albany, 1983; postgrad., East Carolina U., 1984; BSN, West Chester U., 1993. RN, Del., N.J., Pa.; cert. in venipuncture, perioperative nursing. Instr. biology lab. East Carolina U., Greenville, N.C., 1987-88, tutor math. and sci., 1986-88, technician biol. lab. Sea Grant Program, 1987, adj. lectr. biology, 1987-88; tutor math. and sci. Vocat. Rehab., Greenville, 1987-88; technician environ. lab. Weyerhauser Pulp Mill, New Bern, N.C., 1987-88; insp. pharm. quality control Burroughs-Wellcome, Greenville, 1988; clin. data asst. Wyeth Labs., Radnor, Pa., 1988-89; rep. customer svc. Met. Pers., Wayne, Pa., 1989-92, Bayada Nurses Home Health Care Specialist, 1993—; charge nurse subacute care ctr. Genesis Health Ventures, Suburban Woods, Norristown, Pa., 1994—; instr. med.-surg. clin. nursing Delaware County C.C., 1995. James McDaniel Meml. scholar East Carolina U., 1986-88, Army Nurse Corps scholar, 1991-93, U. N.C. Inst. Nutrition scholar, 1985-87. Mem. Nat. League for Nursing, Assn. Oper. Rm. Nurses, U.S. Figure Skating Assn., Recreation Skating Inst. Am., Skating Club Wilmington, West Chester U. Nursing Honor Soc., Sigma Xi, Sigma Theta Tau. Office: Suburban Woods 2751 DeKalb Pike Norristown PA 19403

STANBURY, JOHN BRUTON, physician, educator; b. Clinton, N.C., May 15, 1915; s. Walter A. and Zula (Bruton) S.; m. Jean F. Cook, Jan. 6, 1945; children: John Bruton, Martha Jean, Sarah Katherine, David McNeill, Pamela Cook. A.B., Duke U., 1935; M.D., Harvard U., 1939; M.D. (hon.), U. Leiden (Netherlands), 1975; postgrad., U. Pisa, Italy, 1994. House officer Mass. Gen. Hosp., 1940-41, asst. resident, 1946, chief med. resident, 1948, mem. med. staff, 1949—; research fellow pharmacology Harvard Med. Sch., 1947; vis. prof. medicine U. Leiden, 1955; prof. exptl. medicine MIT, Cambridge, 1966-80; emeritus MIT, 1980—; cons. Pan Am. Health Orgn., WHO, UNICEF, U.S. AEC. Author: Endemic Goiter: The adaptation of man to iodine deficiency, 1954, Metabolic Basis of Inherited Disease, 5th edit., 1984, The Thyroid and Its Diseases, 5th edit., 1984, Endemic Goiter, 1969, Human Development and the Thyroid, 1972, Endemic Goiter and Endemic Cretinism, 1980, Prevention and Control of Iodine Deficiency Disorders, 1987,

A Constant Ferment, 1991, The Damaged Brain of Iodine Deficiency, 1994, The Inborn Errors of the Thyroid System, 1994. Served from lt. (j.g.) to comdr. USNR, 1941-45. Recipient Delmar S. Fahrney medal Franklin Inst., 1993, Prince Mahidol award, Thailand, 1994. Mem. Am. Assn. Physicians, Soc. Clin. Investigation, Am. Thyroid Assn. (pres. 1969), Am. Acad. Arts and Scis., Endocrine Soc., Endocrine Socs. Finland, Colombia, Peru, Ecuador and Argentina, Internat. Coun. for Control of Iodine Deficiency Disorders. Democrat. Episcopalian. Home: 43 Circuit Rd Chestnut Hill MA 02167-1802

STANCZYK, DENNIS J., urologic surgeon; b. Chgo., Oct. 10, 1941; s. Benjamin and Irene Stanczyk; m. Judy Ann Stoll (dec. Oct. 1994); children: Christopher, Geoffrey, Lara, Jason, Emilie, Ashley. BS in Biology, Ill. Benedictine Coll., 1963; MD, St. Louis U., 1968. Cert. Am. Bd. Urology. Intern Charity Hosp. of La., New Orleans, 1968-69; resident gen. and vascular surgery St. Louis U. Hosps., 1971-73, resident urologic surgery, 1973-76; pvt. practice emergency rm. medicine Victory Meml. Hosp., Waukegan, Ill., 1970-71; pvt. practice Urol. Assocs. of Bellville, Ill., 1977—; surg. staff St. Elizabeth's Hosp., Belleville, The Meml. Hosp., Belleville, Notre Dame Surg. Ctr, Belleville, Stone Treatment Ctr., West County, Mo.; clin. prof. dept. family practice and surgery So. Ill. U.; sec. dept. surgery St. Elizabeth's Hosp., 1979-80, vice chmn. dept. surgery, 1981-82, chmn. dept. surgery, 1983-84, exec. com., 1983-84; exec. com. St. Clair County Med. Soc., 1980-88; vice chmn. dept. surgery The Meml. Hosp., 1989-90, chmn. dept. surgery, 1990-91, exec. com., 1990-91; presenter in field. Sch. bd. mem., bldg. and grounds com., policy com. Signal Hill Dist. 181; sec., exec. bd. Belle-Clair Soccer League, 1980—; steering com. Belleville West Athletic Booster Club; bd. dirs. Kapala Condos Owners Assn., 1986-87. Lt.comdr. USN, 1969-70, USMC, 1970-71. Decorated Nat. Def. medal, 1969, Republic of Viet Nam medal, 1969, Viet Nam Svc. medal, 1969, Navy Commendation medal with combat V, 1970. Mem. AMA, ACS (com. on applicants, also Ill. chpt.), ISMS (sports medicine com., mem. coun. on med. svcs. 1986, past mem. com. on accreditation for CME 1980-85,), Am. Urologic Assn., Ill. Urologic Assn., Ill. State Med. Soc. (alt. del., ho. of dels. 1982-83, 85, del. 1986-96), St. Louis Med. Soc., St. Clair County Med. Soc. (bd. dirs. 1979, 80, 83, 94, entertainment com. 1982, nomination com. 1984, peer rev. com. 1985, v.p. 1985, pres. 1987), Fertility and Sterility Soc., Phi Rho Sigma.

STANGER, ROBERT HENRY, psychiatrist, educator; b. N.Y.C., N.Y., May 19, 1937; s. Sidney and Mary (Strassner) S.; m. Andrea Rogin, Aug. 28, 1960; children: Lee Ann, David Neal. AB, Guilford Coll., 1959; MD, Emory U., 1964. Intern in internal medicine Wake Forest U., 1964-65; resident in gen. psychiatry U. Pitts., 1967-70; resident in psychiatry; pvt. practice Monroeville, Pa., 1970—; med. dir. Allegheny Valley Mental Health-Mental Retardation Ctr., New Kensington, Pa., 1970-76; dir. psychiat. svcs. Allegheny Valley Hosp., Natrona Heights, Pa., 1984—; chmn. dept. psychiatry and behavioral medicine Allegheny Valley Hosp., 1984—; clin. instr. psychiatry U. Pitts. Sch. Medicine, 1970-79, clin. asst. prof., 1980—; cons. Westinghouse Elec. Corp., East Pitts., 1977-87; mem. ethics com. human rsch. Allegheny Valley Hosp., 1976—; chmn. dept. psychiatry Citizens Gen. Hosp., 1978-88. Capt. M.C., U.S. Army, 1965-67, Vietnam. Mem. AMA, Am. Psychiat. Assn. (del. 1986-88), Pa. Psychiat. Soc. (councilor 1976-79, treas. 1979-80, sec. 1980-81, v.p. 1981-82, pres.-elect 1982-83, pres. 1983-84), Pitts. Psychiat. Soc. (councilor 1974-76, sec. 1977-78, pres.-elect 1978-79, pres. 1979-80), Allegheny County Med. Soc. Home and Office: 120 Daugherty Dr Monroeville PA 15146-2710 Office: Allegheny Valley Hosp 1301 Carlisle St Natrona Heights PA 15065

STANISLAO, JOSEPH, consulting engineer, educator; b. Manchester, Conn., Nov. 21, 1928; s. Eduardo and Rose (Zaccaro) S.; m. Bettie Chloe Carter, Sept. 6, 1960. BS, Tex. Tech. U., 1957; MS, Pa. State U., 1959; Eng.ScD, Columbia U., 1970. Registered profl. engr., Mass., Mont. Asst. engr. Naval Ordnance Research, University Park, Pa., 1958-59; asst. prof. N.C. State U., Raleigh, 1959-61; dir. research Darlington Fabrics Corp., Pawtucket, R.I., 1961-62; from asst. prof. to prof. U. R.I., Kingston, 1962-71; prof., chmn. dept. Cleve. State U., 1971-75; prof., dean N.D. State U., Fargo, 1975-94, acting v.p. agrl. affairs, 1983-85, asst. to pres., 1983—; dir. Engring. Computer Ctr. N.D. State U., 1984—; prof. emeritus indsl. engring. and mgmt. N.D. State U., Fargo, 1994—; pres. XOX Corp., 1984-90; chmn. bd., chief exec. officer ATSCO, 1989-94, chief engr., 1993—; prof. emeritus N.D. State U., 1994; adj. prof. Mont. State U., 1994—, dir. indsl. and mgmt. engring. program, 1996—. Contbr. chpts. to books, articles to profl. jours.; patentee pump apparatus, pump fluid housing. Served to sgt. USMC, 1948-51. Recipient Sigma Xi award, 1968; Order of the Iron Ring award N.D. State U., 1972, Econ. Devel. award, 1991; USAF recognition award, 1979, ROTC appreciation award, 1982. Mem. Am. Inst. Indsl. Engrs. (sr.; v.p. 1964-65), ASME, Am. Soc. Engring. Edn. (campus coord. 1979-81), Acad. Indsl. Engrs. Tex. Tech U., Lions, Elks, Am. Legion, Phi Kappa Phi, Tau Beta Pi (advisor 1978-79). Roman Catholic. Home: 8 Park Plaza Dr Bozeman MT 59715-9343

STANKIEWICZ, ANDRZEJ JERZY, physician, biochemistry educator; b. Lidzbark, Poland, Sept. 28, 1948; came to U.S., 1981; s. Wincenty and Zofia (Plawgo) S. MD, Med. Sch., Gdansk, Poland, 1972, PhD, 1976. Asst. prof. Med. Sch., Gdansk, 1972-77; adj. prof., lectr. Med. Sch., 1978-81; rsch. fellow Med. Sch. Harvard U., Boston, 1981-84; resident Sch. of Medicine Brown U., Providence, 1984-87, fellow in oncology Sch. of Medicine, 1987-90; pvt. practice Providence, 1990—. Contbr. over 49 articles to profl. jours. Mem. Physicians for Social Responsibility, Internat. Phys. Rev. Nuclear War, Union Concerned Scientists. Fellow Internat. Union Biochemistry; mem. AAAS, ACP, AMA, Societas Scientiarum Gedanensis. Roman Catholic. Office: St Josephs Hosp 200 High Service Ave North Providence RI 02904

STANNARD, DAPHNE EVON, critical care nurse; b. New Haven, Oct. 12, 1963; d. Jerry Wilmert and Katherine Evon (Moore) S.; m. Bertram C.H. Simon, July 18, 1992. BSN, Vanderbilt U., 1986; MS in Critical Care Nursing, U. Calif., San Francisco, 1991; postgrad., U. Calif. San Francisco, San Francisco, 1991—. CCRN, Calif.; cert. ACLS. Critical care nurse U. Mich. Med. Ctr., Ann Arbor, 1986-87; nurse recovery room UCLA Med. Ctr., 1987; pub. health nurse Home Care Ptnrs., L.A., 1988; surg. ICU critical care nurse Cedars-Sinai Med. Ctr., L.A., 1988-89; critical care nurse med. surg. ICU U. Calif. Med. Ctr., San Francisco, 1989-91, critical care nurse, adult critical care float unit, 1992-95; recovery rm. nurse Mt. Zion Med. Ctr./Calif. at San Francisco Med. Ctr., San Francisco, 1992-96. Contbr. articles to profl. jours. Mem. ANA, AACN (mem. subject matter expert group for the study of practice 1995—, pres. San Francisco chpt. 1995-96, mem. editl. bd. Nursing SCAN' Critical Care 1994—), Soc. Critical Care Medicine (bd. dirs. Calif. chpt. 1995—), Nat. Coun. Family Rels., Sigma Theta Tau, Omicron Delta Kappa. Home: 1265 Washington St Apt 9 San Francisco CA 94108 Office: Dept Psychological Nursing Box 0610 U Calif San Francisco Sch Nursing San Francisco CA 94143

STANNARD, JAMES NEWELL, radiation biologist and toxicologist educator; b. Owego, N.Y., Jan. 2, 1910; s. Jay Ellis and Miriam (Newell) S.; m. Grace L. Kingsley, Aug. 7, 1935; 1 child, Susan L. Stannard Frazier; m. Helena R. WoodRouse, Jan. 24, 1994. AB, Oberlin Coll., 1931; MA, Harvard U., 1934, PhD, 1935. Instr. physiology U. Rochester, N.Y., 1935-39, asst. prof. radiation biology and biophysics, 1947-49, assoc. prof. radiation biology and biophysics, 1949-59, prof., 1959-75, prof. pharmacology and toxicology, 1952-75, emeritus prof., 1975—; assoc. dir. Atomic Energy Project U. Rochester, 1959-69; assoc. dean for grad. studies U. Rochester, N.Y., 1959-75; adj. prof. cmty. med., preventive med., radiology U. Calif.-San Diego, La Jolla, 1977—; asst. prof. pharmacology Emory U., Atlanta, 1939-41; sr. pharmacologist to prin. physiologist NIH, Bethesda, Md., 1941-47; vis. prof. U. Calif. Med. Ctr., San Francisco, 1954; cons., mem. sci. adv. com. Battelle Pacific NW Lab.; cons. to NAS/NRC, others; Parker lectr. Battelle Inst., 1988; mem. task group Internat. Commn. on Radiol. Protection; chmn., mem. sci. coms., life mem. Nat. Coun. on Radiation Protection and Measurements, Taylor lectr., 1990; mem. adv. bd. Hanford Environ. Health Found; J. Newell Stannard lectr. series, 1993-96. Author: Radioactivity and Health-A History, 1988, 94; author, editor; Handbook of Experimental Pharmacology, vol. 36, 1973; editor: Radioisotopes in the Aquatic Environment, 1976; contbr. sci. articles to profl. jours. Sec., bd. dirs. Oaks North Mgmt. Corp. Number 1, San Diego; pres. Rancho Bernardo Stroke Club, 1991-94, Seven Oaks Garden Club, San Diego, 1995-96. Recipient cert. of appreciation HEW, 1970, cert. appreciation AEC, 1975, cert. appreciation EPA, 1977. Mem. Am. Indsl. Hygiene Assn., AAAS, Am. Soc. Pharmacology and Exptl. Therapeutics, Am. Physiol. Soc., Radiation Rsch. Soc. (chair com. on edn.), Health Physics Soc. (dir. 1965-71, pres. 1969-70, editor, mem. editl. bd. 1975-81, Disting. Achievement award 1977, chmn. history com. 1988—, historian 1993—, Morgan lectr. 1995), Biophys. Soc., Soc. Gen. Physiologists, Phi Beta Kappa, Sigma Xi. Home: 17446 Plaza Dolores San Diego CA 92128-2243 Office: U Calif San Diego M-022 La Jolla CA 92093

STANNARD, JEFFREY BRIAN, dentist; b. Cortland, N.Y., Sept. 14, 1953; s. Earl Clifford and Virginia May (Murray) Stannard-Mendoza; m. Cynthia Karen Ulrich, June 30, 1990. BS in Chemistry, St. Lawrence U., Canton, N.Y., 1975; MS in Audiology and Speech Pathology, Ithaca (N.Y.) Coll., 1977; DDS, NYU, 1981; Cert. in Gen. Dentistry, U. Rochester, 1982; Cert. in Prosthodontics, SUNY, Buffalo, 1984; Cert. in Maxillofacial Prosthetics, Roswell Park Meml. Inst., Buffalo, 1985. Diplomate Am. Soc. Osseointegration. Audiologist Govt. of U.S. V.I., St. Croix, 1977-78; asst. instr. SUNY, Buffalo, 1982-84; pvt. practice prosthodontics and maxillofacial prosthetics Syracuse, 1985—; prosthodontist, mem. cleft palate and craniofacial team SUNY Health Sci. Ctr., Syracuse, 1985—; med. staff Crouse Irving Meml. Hosp., Syracuse, 1985—. Fund-raiser St. Lawrence U. Alumni Com., 1985—. Mem. ADA, N.Y. State Dental Soc., 5th Dist. Dental Soc., Onondaga County Dental Soc., Am. Coll. Prosthodontists, Syracuse Dental Seminar (pres. 1993), Upper N.Y. State Dental Study Club (pres. 1995). Home: 5640 Rt 80 Tully NY 13159 Office: 2800 Court St Syracuse NY 13208

STANNERS, CLIFFORD PAUL, molecular and cell biologist, biochemistry educator; b. Sutton, Surrey, Eng., Oct. 19, 1937; married; 3 children. BSc, McMaster U., 1958; MSc, U. Toronto, 1960, PhD, 1963. Fellow molecular biology MIT, Cambridge, Mass., 1962-64; from asst. prof. to prof. med. biophysics U. Toronto, Can., 1964-82; sr. sci. biol. rsch. Ont. (Can.) Cancer Inst., 1964-82; prof. biochemistry McGill U., Montreal, 1982—, dir. McGill Cancer Ctr., 1988—; mem. grants Med. Rsch. Coun. & Nat. Cancer Inst. Can., 1965—, U.S. Nat. Cancer Inst., 1973-79. Assoc. editor Jour. Cell Physiology, 1973-92, Cell, 1975-84. Mem. AAAS, Can. Biochem. Soc., Can. Soc. Cell Biology, Am. Assn. Cancer Rsch. Office: McGill U, 3655 Drummond St, Montreal, PQ Canada H3G 1Y6

STANSELL, JAMES LEWIS, pharmacist, consultant; b. Duncan, Okla., May 24, 1953; s. James Clyde and Mary Louise (Lewis) S.; m. Trena Larue Day, Dec. 20, 1975 (div. Oct. 1984); children: Kristopher Lee, Marie Louise; m. Debra J. Sarchet, June 1, 1991 (div. Feb. 1994). AAA, Cisco (Tex.) Jr. Coll., 1973; BS in Pharmacy, Southwestern Okla. State U., 1976. Lic. pharmacist, Tex. Pharmacist-in-charge Sav-x Drug, Abilene, Tex., 1976-80, Eckerd Drug, Lubbock, Tex., 1980-82; pharmacist Hilley Pharmacy, Midlothian, Tex., 1982-88; pharmacist-in-charge, 1989; pharmacist-in-charge Eckerd Drug, 1989-90; asst. pharmacy mgr. Hypermart 1801 Pharmacy divsn. of Wal-Mart Stores, Inc., Arlington, Tex., 1990-91, pharmacy mgr., 1991; pharmacist-in-charge Wal-Mart Pharmacy 939, Duncanville, Tex., 1991-92; asst. pharmacy mgr. Eckerd Drug 894, Waxahachie, Tex., 1992-96; pharmacist in charge Eckerd Drug 2913, Midlothian, 1996—; mem. Pharmacy Adv. Com., Abilene, 1979-80; cons. Abilene area nursing home's, 1976-80, River Oaks Ranch, Red Oak, Tex., 1982—; speaker Abilene Ind. Sch. Dist., 1977-80, Midlothian Ind. Sch. Dist., 1984, 86, 87, 89; co-organizer Jr./Sr. Discount Program, 1978. Cons. Abilene Youth Council, 1977-80; bd. dirs. Midlothian Coun. on Alcohol and Substance Abuse, 1988, Reach Midlothian, Inc., 1988-89; rsch. bd. advisors Am. Biog. Inst., 1989. Named to Outstanding Young Men of Am., 1988. Democrat. Baptist. Home: PO Box 853 Midlothian TX 76065-0853 Office: Eckerd Drug 2913 301 N 8th Midlothian TX 76065

STANTON, G(ARDNER) KIMMEL, pharmacist, educator; b. Waurika, Okla., July 24, 1942; s. Jake Mack and Syble Emma (Gardner) S.; m. Jymmie Lea Pass, June 29, 1961; children: David Landon, Michael Scott. BS in Pharmacy, Okla. U., 1964, MS, 1968. Lic. pharmacist, Okla., Ark. Dir. pharmacy St. Edwards Mercy Hosp., Fort Smith, Ark., 1964-65, Norman Regional Hosp., Okla., 1965-94; poison control specialist Okla. Poison Ctr., 1996—; instr. pharmacy Okla. U., Oklahoma City, 1975—, pharmacy program cons. Cen. Okla. Vocat.-Tech. Adminstrn., Norman, 1976—; instr. pharmacology Norman area Vocat.-Tech. Nursing Program, 1966-94; mem adv. panel Drug Topics, 1987—. Editor: (jour. column) Okla. Pharmacist, 1973-80, (newsletter) Okla. Soc. Hosp. Pharmacists Lantern, 1965-75; mem. editorial bd. The Jour. of Irreproducible Results, Annals of Improbable Rsch.; columnist The Norman Transcript, 1993—; contbr. articles to profl. jours. and poetry to lit. mags. Mem. Okla. Soc. Hosp. Pharmacists (pres. 1970-71, 1978-79; Squibb Leadership award 1970, 79, Geigy Pharmacist award 1971, 79), Am. Soc. Hosp. Pharmacists, Am. Pharm. Assn., Okla. Pharm. Assn. (dist. dir. 1976, dist. pres. 1989-90), Okla. Pharm. Heritage Found., Okla. Pharmacy Alumni Assn. (pres. 1966-67).

STANTON, JOSEPH ROBERT, physician; b. Boston, Aug. 8, 1920; s. Joseph S. and Mary Elizabeth (Sullivan) S.; m. Mary Frances Gordon, May 10, 1950; children: Michael, Anne Marie, Joseph, John, Mark (dec.), Paul, William, Kathleen, Matthew, Luke, Thomas. AB, Boston Coll., 1942; MD, Yale U., 1945; LLD, St. Anselm Coll., 1973, Our Lady of Elms, 1974. Diplomate Am. Bd. Internal Medicine. Asst. surg. and medicine Boston U. Sch. Medicine, 1946-51; rsch. fellow Evans Meml. Hosp., 1946-51; instr. medicine Tufts Med. Sch., 1951-58, assoc. clin. prof. medicine, 1958-85; mem. attending staff Holy Ghost Hosp., Cambridge, Mass., 1948-55; attending physician Bethany Infirmary, Framingham, Mass., 1948-75; vis. physician St. Elizabeth's Hosp., Boston, 1952-85; del. White House Conf. on Aging, 1981; grant reviewer HHS, 1983; cons. Medico Moral Commn. Mass Cath. Conf., 1978-91. Contbr. or co-contbr. over 30 articles to med. publs. Founding mem., sec.-treas. Americans United for Life, Chgo., 1971-85; founding mem., dir. Value of Life Com., Boston, 1970-91; founding mem., dir., v.p. Mass. Citizens for Life, 1974-91. Recipient Alumni Sci. award Boston Coll., 1980, Poverello award U. STeubenville, Ohio, 1989, Pro Vita award Archdiocese of Boston, 1991, Ignalian award Boston Coll. H.S., 1991, Christendom Coll. medal, 1992. Fellow AMA, ACP, Mass. Med. Soc.; mem. Boston Coll. Alumni Assn. (McKenney award 1992), Yale Med. Alumni Assn. Roman Catholic. Home: 760 Highland Ave Needham MA 02194-1635 Office: Value of Life Com PO Box 35279 Brighton MA 02135

STANTON, ROBERT ALAN, orthopaedic surgeon; b. N.Y.C., June 28, 1946; s. Jay and Shirley (Rader) S.; m. Debby Ellen Beach, June 16, 1973; 1 child, Jim. BA, Williams Coll., 1968; MD, Coll. Physicians and Surgeons, 1972. Intern Columbia-Presbyn. Med. Ctr., N.Y.C., 1972-73, resident in surgery, 1973-74; resident in orthopaedics Yale U., 1974-77; pres., dir. Orthopaedic Specialty Group, P.C., Fairfield, Conn., 1981—. Chmn. Alumni Fund of Williams Coll., Williamstown, Mass., 1993—; bd. dirs. Bridgeport Hosp. Found., 1988-95; bd. assocs. Bridgeport Hosp., 1995—. Edward John Noble Found. fellow Columbia U., 1969-70. Fellow ACS, Am. Acad. Ortho. Surgeons; mem. Am. Ortho. Soc. Sports Medicine, Arthroscopy Assn. N.Am., Am. Acad. Sports Physicians, Williams Club N.Y., Nantucket Yacht Club, Fairfield County Hunt Club (pres.). Office: Orthopaedic Specialty Group PC 325 Reef Rd Fairfield CT 06430-6537

STANTON, RUFUS H., JR., dentist; b. Galveston, Tex., May 27, 1925; s. Rufus H. and Carrie Whitsett (McFadden) S.; m. Janice D. Splane, Apr. 7, 1944; children—Rufus H. III, Deborah Ann Stanton Burke, Robert T. II. B.A., Wiley Coll., 1948; D.D.S., Meharry Med. Coll., 1953. Practice dentistry, Galveston, 1953—; dir. U.S. Nat. Bank, Galveston, Tex. Bd. dirs. Galveston Mcpl. Golf Course, 1963-73; chmn. bd. trustees Reedy Chapel AME Ch., 1979—; mem. integration com. adv. bd. Galveston Ind. Sch. Dist., 1965-70; bd. dirs. St. Vincents House, 1975-80. Served with U.S. Army, 1944-46. Mem. ADA, Nat. Dental Assn., 9th Dist. Dental Soc., Gulf States Dental Assn. (past pres.), Tex. Dental Assn., Charles A. George Dental Soc., Am Legion, Alpha Phi Alpha. Democrat. Avocations: golf; bicycling. Home: 3615 Avenue O Galveston TX 77550

STANTON-HICKS, MICHAEL D'ARCY, anesthesiologist, educator; b. Adelaide, Australia, June 3, 1931; came to U.S., 1972; s. Cedric Stanton-Hicks and Florence (Haggett) Perrin; m. Kristina Litsmark, Aug. 4, 1969 (div. Aug. 1984); children: Erik Michael, Leif Neal; m. Ursula Koch, Aug. 27, 1985. MB, BS, Adelaide U., 1962; Dr. of medicine, U. Dusseldorf, 1984. Bd. equivalent Am. Bd. Anesthesiology; diplomate Am. Bd. Pain Medicine. Intern Queen Elizabeth Hosp., Adelaide, 1961-62, tutor, staff anesthesiologist, 1970-72; resident Royal Postgrad. Med. Sch., London and Lasarettet Köping, 1966-68; asst. dir. anesthesiology intensive care Södersjükhuset, Stockholm, 1968-69; instr. anesthesiology U. Wash. Med. Sch., Seattle, 1969-70, asst. prof., 1972-75; prof., chmn. dept. U. Mass. Med. Sch., Worcester, 1975-83; prof. U. Colo. Health Scis. Ctr., Denver, 1983-86, vice chmn. dept., 1983-85, acting chmn., 1985-86; prof., dir. pain clinic and rsch. Johannes Gutenberg U., Mainz, Fed. Republic Germany, 1986-88, prof., 1986—; dir. pain mgmt. ctr. Cleve. Clinic Found., 1988—. Author, editor: Regional Anesthesia: Advances and Selected Topics, 1978; (with Boas) Chronic Low Back Pain, 1982; author: (with Raj and Nolte) Illustrated Manual of Regional Anesthesia, 1988 (Most Beautiful Book of Yr. award Frankfurt, Fed. Republic Germany Pubs. Book Conv. 1989), Pain and Sympathetic Nervous System, 1989; (with Janig and Boas) Reflex Sympathetic Dystrophy, 1989; (with Janig) Reflex Sympathetic Dystrophy: A Reappraisal, 1996. Squadron leader res. Royal Australian Air Force, 1962-65. Australian Univs. Commn. mature age scholar, 1953-60. Fellow Royal Coll. Surgeons (faculty anesthetists), Royal Coll. Anesthetists, Am. Acad. Pain Medicine; mem. Internat. Assn. Study Pain (chmn. spl. interest group on sympathetically maintained pain 1990—), Am. Soc. Regional Anesthesia (bd. dirs. 1979-91, pres. 1989-90), Am. Soc. Anesthesiologists, Assn. Anesthetists Gt. Britain and Ireland, Ohio State Med. Assn., Cleve. Acad. Medicine, Am. Acad. Med. Infrared Imaging (bd. dirs. 1991—, pres. 1994-95), Am. Pain Soc., Am. Acad. Pain Medicine, Am. Neuromodulation Soc. (pres. 1994—), Army-Navy-Air Force Club. Republican. Anglican. Home: 198 Woodsong Way Chagrin Falls OH 44023-6703 Office: Cleve Clinic Found 9500 Euclid Ave Cleveland OH 44195-0001

STAPLEY, EDWARD OLLEY, retired microbiologist, research administrator; b. Bklyn., Sept. 25, 1927; s. Charles Olley and Helen Beulay (Mirrielees) S.; m. Helen Alberta Strang, July 2, 1949; children: Susan Jean, Robin Lynn, Janice Carol. BS, Rutgers U., 1950, MS, 1954, PhD, 1959. Microbiologist Merck & Co., Inc., Rahway, N.J., 1950-58; sr. rsch. microbiologist Merck Sharp & Dohme Rsch. Labs., Rahway, 1959-64, rsch. fellow in microbiology, 1965-68, asst. dir. microbiology, 1969-74, dir. microbiology, 1974-77, sr. dir. microbiology, 1978-83, exec. dir. microbiology, 1984-92; vis. biologist program speaker Am. Inst. Biol. Scis., 1969-72. Mem. editorial bd. Jour. of Antibiotics, 1974—. Mem. Spotswood (N.J.) Bd. of Edn., 1965, pres., 1967-68. Named to Selman A. Wakeman Lectureship, Theobald Smith Soc., 1990. Fellow Am. Acad. Microbiology, Sigma Xi; mem. Soc. for Indsl. Microbiology (speaker's bur. 1968-71). Republican. Episcopalian. Home: 110 Highland Ave Metuchen NJ 08840-1913

STARCK, PATRICIA LEE, academic dean; b. Americus, Ga., Sept. 15, 1938; d. Ernest W. Lee and Margaret Inez (Pilcher) Rush; m. Edward J. Rice, Feb. 11, 1991; children: Jaime Catherine Schier, Patricia Ann Reitz. AA, Ga. Southwestern Coll., 1959; BSN, Emory U., 1960, M in Nursing, 1963; DSN, U. Ala., Birmingham, 1979. RN; cert. logotherapist. Staff nurse Emory U. Hosp., Atlanta, 1959-60; rehab. nursing cons. Liberty Mut. Ins. Co., Atlanta, 1960-61; instr. Grady Meml. Hosp., Atlanta, 1961-62, Ga. Bapt. Hosp., Atlanta, 1963-64; asst. prof. Ga. Southwestern Coll., Americus, 1966, 70-72, 1974-75; tchr. St. Petersburg (Fla.) Jr. Coll., 1972-74; dept. chair nursing Albany (Ga.) State Coll., 1975-77; dean, prof. Troy (Ala.) State U., 1979-84, U. Tex. Health Sci. Ctr., Houston, 1984—; cons. various univs., 1979—; bd. dirs. CURAFLEX Home Health Svc., Houston, 1985-86. Author: The Invisible Dimension of Illness-Human Suffering, 1992; contbr. articles to profl. jours. Mem. Tex. Med. Assn. Task Force, Austin, 1989-90. Mem. Inst. of Logotherapy (diplomate), Nat. League for Nursing (bd. of revs.), Am. Assn. Colls. of Nursing (bd. dirs., chair pub. rels. and resolutions), Coun. Deans, Dirs. Nursing Execs. (chair), Tex. Med. Ctr. Nursing Exec. (chair-elect, Tex. Nurses Assn. (v.p. dist. 9 1991—), Rotary Club Houston (com. mem.). Baptist. Home: 5001 Beech St Bellaire TX 77401-3407

STARE, FREDRICK JOHN, nutritionist, biochemist, physician; b. Columbus, Wis., Apr. 11, 1910; s. Fredrick Arthur and Susan (Seidell) S.; m. Joyce Allen, Sept. 14, 1935 (dec. May 1957); children: Fredrick Allen, David, Mary; m. Helen Haxton Foreman, June 9, 1959 (dec. Feb. 1974); m. Mary Bartlett Engle, Dec. 30, 1976 (div. 1983); m. Irene Mackey Kinsey, Sept. 15, 1984. B.S., U. Wis., 1931, M.S., 1932, Ph.D., 1934; M.D., U. Chgo., 1941; MA (hon.), Harvard U., 1945; D.Sc., Suffolk, 1963, Trinity Coll., Dublin, 1964, Muskingum Coll., 1977. Asst. biochemist U. Wis., 1931-34; Nat. Research fellow Washington U. Sch. Medicine, St. Louis, 1934-35; Gen. Edn. Bd. fellow Cambridge (Eng.) U., 1935-36, Szeged, Hungary, 1936, Zurich, 1937; research assoc. Bowman Cancer Found., Wis., 1937-39; intern Barnes Hosp., St. Louis, 1941-42; asst. prof. nutrition Harvard Med. Sch. and Sch. Pub. Health; prof. nutrition, chmn. dept. nutrition, 1942-76; prof. nutrition emeritus Harvard Sch. Pub. Health, 1976—; jr. asso. medicine Peter Bent Brigham Hosp., 1942-44, asso. in medicine, 1944-50, sr. asso. medicine, 1950-60, cons. medicine, 1960-70; co-founder syndicated radio program Healthline; dir. Continental Group; former mem. food and nutrition bd. NRC; cons. nutrition Sec. War, USPHS; mem. health adv. com. Fgn. Operations Administrn.; com. health Commn. on Inter-govtl. Relations; mem. Nat. Health Edn. Com. Author: Living Nutrition, Scope Manual on Nutrition, Eat OK-Feel OK, Food for Today's Teens, Food for Fitness After Fifty; The Executive Diet, Panic in the Pantry, Your Basic Guide to Nutrition, Dear Dr. Stare: What Shall I Eat?, The Harvard Square Diet; Nutrition for Good Health, The 100% Natural, Purely Organic, Cholesterol-Free, Megavitamin, Low-carbohydrate Nutrition Hoax, Balanced Nutrition Beyond The Cholesterol Scare, Adventures in Nutrition, Your Guide to Good Nutrition; nat. syndicated columnist: Food and Your Health; former editor: Nutrition Revs. Overseer emeritus New Eng. Conservatory Music; bd. dir. Lown Cardiovascular Found., Pathfinder Internat.; co-founder, bd. dirs. Am. Coun. Sci. and Health. Recipient Pub. Svc. award U. Chgo., 1982, medal of honor Internat. Found. for Nutrition Rsch. and Edn., 1989, Disting. Svc. award U. Chgo. Med. and Biol. Scis. Alumni Assn., 1992, Excellence in Med. Nutrition Edn. award Am. Soc. Clin. Nutrition, 1993, Disting. Emeritus Prof. award Harvard Sch. Pub. Health, 1993, citation for 50 yrs. of svc. Harvard U., 1993, Am. Coun. Sci. and Health award, 1994; Fredrick John Stare professorship of nutrition established by Harvard U., 1991; John Harvard fellow, 1996. Fellow APHA, Royal Irish Coll. Physicians (hon.); mem. AMA (Goldberger award 1961), Am. Acad. Arts and Scis., Mass. Med. Soc., Am. Chem. Soc., Am. Soc. Biol. Chemists, Am. Inst. Nutrition (Elvehjem award 1969), Biochem. Soc. (Eng.), Am. Soc. Clin. Investigation, Am. Soc. Arteriosclerosis, Am. Dietetic Assn. (hon.), Group of European Nutritionists (hon.), Soc. Nutrition Edn., Harvard Club (Boston, N.Y.C.), Cosmos Club, Sigma Xi. Home: 267 Cartwright Rd Box 812085 Wellesley MA 02181-0013 Office: Harvard U Sch Pub Health 665 Huntington Ave Boston MA 02115-6021

STARFIELD, BARBARA HELEN, physician, educator; b. Bklyn., Dec. 18, 1932; d. Martin and Eva (Illions) S.; m. Neil A. Holtzman, June 12, 1955; children: Robert, Jon, Steven, Deborah. AB, Swarthmore Coll., 1954; MD, SUNY, 1959; MPH, Johns Hopkins U., 1963. Teaching asst. in anatomy Downstate Med. Ctr., N.Y.C., 1955-57; intern in pediatrics Johns Hopkins U., 1959-60, resident, 1960-62, dir. pediatric med. care clinic, 1963-66, dir. community staff comprehensive child care project, 1966-67, dir. pediatric clin. scholars program, 1971-76, prof. health policy, joint appointment in pediatrics, 1975—, disting. univ. prof., 1994—; mem. Nat. Com. Vital Stats., 1994—; cons. DHHS; mem. nat. adv. coun. Agy. for Health Care Policy and Rsch., 1990-94; adv. subcom. on Health Systems and Svcs. Rsch. Pan Am. Health Orgn., 1988-92, 1995—; cons. Health Care Fin. Adminstrn., 1980—. Editorial bd. Med. Care, 1977-79, Pediatrics, 1977-82, Internat. Jour. Health Svcs., 1 978—, Med. Care Rev., 1980-84; contbr. articles to profl. jours. Recipient Dave Luckman Meml. award, 1958; HEW Career Devel. award, 1970-75, Am. Pub. Health Assn. Martha May Eliot award, 1995, Disting. Investigator award, Assn. for Health Svcs. Rsch., 1995, 1st Primary Care Achievement award, Pew Charitable Trust Fund, 1994, 1st Annual Rsch. award of Ambulatory Pediatric Assn., 1990. Fellow Am. Acad. Pediat.; mem. APHA (Martha May Eliot award 1995), NAS Inst. Medicine (governing coun. 1981-83), Am. Pediat. Soc., Soc. Pediat. Rsch., Internat. Epidemiologic Assn., Ambulatory Pediat. Assn. (pres. 1980), Sigma Xi, Alpha Omega Alpha. Office: Johns Hopkins Sch Hygiene 624 N Broadway Baltimore MD 21205-1901

STARK, BRUCE IRA, ophthalmologist; b. Bklyn., Mar. 7, 1953. BA cum laude, Brandeis U., 1974; MD, U. Mich., 1978. Resident in ophthalmology Wills Eye Hosp., 1979-82; pvt. practice Chester County Eye Care Assocs., West Chester, Pa., 1982—. Contbr. articles to profl. jours. Fellow Am. Acad. Ophthalmology; mem. Am. Soc. Cataract and Refractive Surgery, Pa. Acad. Ophthalmology, Am. Diabetic Assn. (bd. dirs. 1994—). Office: 606 E Marshall St West Chester PA 19380

STARK, JAROSLAV FRANTISEK, pediatric cardiothoracic surgeon; b. Prague, Czechoslovakia, Jan. 29, 1934; s. Jaroslav Stark and Jirina (Matouskova) Starkova; m. Olga Slugova, Aug. 20, 1934; 1 child, Jaroslav. MD with honors, Charles U., Prague, 1958; PhD, Charles U., 1967. Instr. anatomy Charles U., Praha, 1953-56, surg. asst., rsch. asst., 1962-65; intern Dept. Gen. Surgery, Nova Paka, 1958, resident, 1959; sr. registrar Hosp. for Sick Children, London, 1965-70; rsch. fellow Children's Hosp. (Harvard), Boston, 1970-71; staff surgeon Children's Hosp., Prague, 1967-68; cons. surgeon Hosp. for Sick Children, GOS, London, 1971—. Editor, co-author: Surgery for Cong. Heart Disease, 1983, Reoperations in Cardiac Surgery, 1989; contbr. over 260 articles to profl. jours., chpts. to books. Named Knight of Falcon, Pres. of Iceland. Fellow ACS, Am. Coll. Cardiology; mem. Brit. Assn. Pediatric Surgeons, Soc. Thoracic Surgeons Gt. Britain and Ireland, Brit. Cardiac Soc., Am. Soc. Thoracic Surgeons,Soc. Thoracic and Cardiovasc. Surgery of French Lang. (hon.), Scandinavian Assn. Thoracic and Cardiothoracic Surgery (corr.), Asian Assn. Cardiothoracic Wurgery (hon.), European Assn. Cardiothoracic Surgery (past pres.), Am. Assn. Thoracic Surgery (hon.). Office: Hosp for Sick Children, Great Ormond St, London WC1, England

STARK, JEANNE M., health facility administrator; b. Fort Atkinson, Wis.; d. Ruben A. and Doris M. (Twining) S. Diploma in nursing, Madison Gen. Hosp., 1972; BS in Mgmt., Cardinal Stritch Coll., 1985. RN, Wis. Staff nurse South Miami (Fla.) Hosp., 1972-73, asst. head nurse, 1973-74, PM nursing supr., 1974-77, insvc. instr., 1977-78; med. nursing supr. St. Catherine's Hosp., Kenosha, Wis., 1978-86, dir. chem. dependency, 1982-86; mgr. Optifast program Sinai Hosp., Milw., 1987-89; coord. ancillary svcs. All Saints Healthcare, Racine, Wis., 1989-92, adminstr. gerontol. svcs., 1992—; bd. dirs. Racine Area Geriatric Assessment Ctr., Villa St. Anna, Racine. Mem. Wis. Assn. Homes and Svcs. for Aging, Internat. Subacute Healthcare Assn., Am. Assn. Homes and Svcs. for Aging, NAFE. Home: 1300 Jones Ave Racine WI 53402 Office: All Saints Healthcare 1320 Wisconsin Ave Racine WI 53403

STARK, JOEL, speech pathologist; b. N.Y.C., Nov. 18, 1930; s. Jacob William and Naomi (Peck) S.; m. Muriel Weiner, Dec. 16, 1950 (div. 1967); children: Holly, James; m. Arlene Kraat, Mar. 2, 1992. BA, L.I. U., 1950; MA, Columbia U., 1951; PhD, NYU, 1956. Instr. L.I. U., Bklyn., 1951-54; asst. prof. CCNY, 1954-62; assoc. prof. Stanford (Calif.) U., 1965-68; prof. speech/lang. pathology Queens Coll., Flushing, N.Y., 1968—; cons. Nassau County Med. Ctr., East Meadow, N.Y., 1968—. Contbr. articles to profl. jours. Fellow Am. Speech Lang. Hearing Assn. Office: Queens Coll Speech & Hearing Ctr Flushing NY 11367-1597

STARK, LAWRENCE WENDELL, oral and maxillofacial surgeon; b. Englewood, N.J., July 3, 1931; s. Oscar Clifton and Farilyn Lee (Robbins) S.; m. Solveig Eleanor Sognnaes, Dec. 30, 1961 (div. July 1979); children: Erik Gustafson, Fredrik Reidar, Karen Elizabeth, Walter Lee; m. Catherine Rae Burhenn, Sept. 30, 1994. AB in Econs., Duke U., 1953; DMD, Harvard U., Boston, 1964. Commd. USN, 1953-88, advanced through grades to capt.; oral surgeon US Naval Hosp., Portsmouth, Va., 1967-68, Sta. Hosp., Vietnam, 1968-69, Naval Dental Ctr., San Diego, 1969-70; pvt. practice Long Beach, Calif., 1970-95; oral surgeon North Kern State Prison, Deland, Calif., 1994—. Mem. ADA, Calif. Dental Assn., Harbor Dental Soc. (pres. 1979-80, Man of the Yr.), So. Calif. Soc. Oral and Maxillofacial Surgeons, Calif. Assn. Oral and Maxillofacial Surgeons, Am. Assn. Oral and Maxillofacial Surgeons, Assn. Naval Aviation, Tailhook Assn., Rotary. Republican. Home: 123 Atlantic Ave Long Beach CA 90802 Office: North Kern State Prison Dental Dept 2737 W Cecil Ave Deland CA 93216

STARK, NATHAN J., medical administrator, lawyer; b. Mpls., Nov. 9, 1920; s. Harold and Anna (Berlow) S.; m. Lucile D. Seidler, Nov. 28, 1943; children: Paul S., David H., Robert, Margaret J. AA, Woodrow Wilson Jr. Coll., Chgo., 1940; BS, U.S. Mcht. Marine Acad., 1943; JD, Ill. Inst. Tech., 1948; LLD (hon.), Park Coll., 1969, U. Mo., 1980; DHL, Scholl Coll., Hahnemann U., 1987. Bar: Ill. 1947, Mo. 1952. Plant mgr. Englander Co., Inc., Chgo., 1949-51; partner law firm Downey, Abrams, Stark & Sullivan, Kansas City, Mo., 1952-53; v.p. Rival Mfg. Co., Kansas City, 1954-59; sr. v.p. ops. Hallmark Cards, Inc., Kansas City, 1959-74; dir. Hallmark Cards, Inc., 1960-74; pres., chmn. Crown Center Redevel. Corp., 1971-74; sr. vice chancellor health scis. Schs. Health Professions, U. Pitts., until 1984, sr. vice chancellor emeritus, 1984—, also pres. Univ. Health Center, 1974-79, 81—, also prof. Grad. Sch. Public Health; undersec. HEW, Washington, 1979-81; of counsel Fort & Schlefor, Washington; lawyer, treas., pres., CEO Nat. Acad. of Social Ins., 1992-95; dir. ERC Corp., 1970-79, Hallmark Continental Ltd., Ireland, 1971-73; mem. exec. bd. Nat. Bd. Med. Contbr. articles to profl. and bus. jours. Legal counsel Lyric Opera Theatre, Kansas City, Mo., 1958-72; mem. com. undergrad. med. edn. AMA, 1966-73; vice chmn. health ins. benefits adv. com. NEW, 1965-70; sec. task force on Medicaid, 1960-70, chmn. adv. commn. incentive reimbursement experimentation, 1968-70; chmn. capital investment conf. HEW-HRA, 1976; mem. liaison com. Am. Assn. Med. Colls.-AMA, 1970-74; chmn. task force lifelong learning opportunities Kellogg Found., 1975-77; chmn. cmty. hosp.-med. staff group practice program Robert Wood Johnson Found., 1974-79; mem.-at-large Nat. Bd. Med. Examiners; mem. bd. Blue Cross Western Pa., 1975-79, Am. Nurses Found., 1975-77, Health Sys. Agy. SW Pa., 1976—; v.p. Kansas City Philharm. Assn., 1954; sec. Eddie Jacobson Meml. Found., 1960—; mem. tech. bd. Milbank Meml. Fund, 1976-78; pres., chmn. Kansas City Gen. Hosp. and Med. Ctr., 1962-74; trustee Allegheny Found., 1975—, Pitts. Ballet Theater, 1977-79, Pitts. Chamber Opera Theater, 1978—; mem. VA Scholars Bd. Governance, 1979—; hon. fellow, trustee Hastings Ctr., 1981; v.p. Pitts. Opera; adv. bd. of trustees St. Joseph Coll., trustee, 1994. Recipient Chancellor's medal U. Mo. at Kansas City, 1969; Pro-Meritus award Rockhurst Coll., 1967; Layman award; AMA, 1974. Fellow Am. Acad. Pediatrics (hon.); mem. Inst. Medicine of NAS (coun. 1973-76), Am. Hosp. Assn. (hon. mem., Trustee award 1968), Am. Coll. Hosp. Adminstrs., Nat. Acad. Social Ins. (bd. trustees, pres. 1992-94). Home: 4343 Westover Pl NW Washington DC 20016-5554

STARK, RICHARD BOIES, surgeon, artist; b. Conrad, Iowa, Mar. 31, 1915; s. Eugene and Hazel (Carson) S.; m. Judy Thornton, Oct. 31, 1967. A.B., Stanford U., 1936; postgrad., U. Heidelberg, 1936-37; M.D., Cornell U., 1941. Diplomate Am. Bd. Plastic Surgery (pres. 1967-68). Intern Peter Bent Brigham Hosp., Boston, 1941-42; asst. resident surgery Childrens Hosp., Boston, 1942; plastic surgeon Northington Gen. Hosp., Ala., 1945-46, Percy Jones Gen. Hosp., Mich., 1946; postwar fellow anatomy and embryology Stanford U., 1946-47; from asst. resident to resident in head and neck surgery VA Hosp., Bronx, N.Y., 1947-50; asst. resident, resident surgery, plastic, head and neck and gen. surgery N.Y. Hosp., 1947-50; instr. surgery Cornell U., 1950-52, asst. prof., 1952-55, assoc. prof., 1955; asst. attending surgeon N.Y. Hosp., 1950-55; asst. prof. surgery Columbia U., 1955-58, assoc. prof., 1958-73, prof. clin. surgery, 1973—; assoc. attending surgeon St. Luke's Hosp., N.Y.C., 1955-58, founding attending surgeon dept. plastic surgery, 1958—; founder dept. plastic surgery, 1955; cons. Walter Reed Med. Ctr., 1970-77. Author: Plastic Surgery, 1962, Cleft Palate, 1968, Plastic Surgery at the New York Hospital 100 Years Ago, 1952, Aesthetic Plastic Surgery, 1980, Total Facial Reconstruction, 1985, Plastic Surgery of the Head and Neck, 1986; contbr. numerous chpts. to books, articles to profl. jours.; assoc. editor: Plastic Reconstructive Surgery, 1977-82; founding editor: Annals Plastic Surgery, 1978-81; 20 one-person art shows, 1946—. Chmn. Medico Adv. Bd., 1976-77; mem., v.p. CARE Bd.; v.p. Wellborn Found., N.Y.C. Served with AUS, 1943-46. Decorated Bronze Star (U.S.); Medal of Honor (2) (Vietnam); cavallero Order of San Carlos (Colombia), Dieffenbach medal (Berlin), Gold medal Nat. Inst. Social Scis. Fellow ACS; mem. Am. Assn. Plastic Surgeons, Am. Soc. Plastic and Reconstructive Surgery (pres. 1966, Spl. Achievement award), Found. Am. Soc. Plastic and Reconstructive Surgery (pres. 1961-65), Am. Surg. Assn., Soc. Univ. Surgeons, French Soc. Plastic Surgeons, Brasilian Soc. Plastic Surgeons, Colombian Soc. Plastic Surgeons, Argentina Soc. Plastic Surgeons, Brit. Assn. Plastic Surgery, Peruvian Acad. Surgeons, N.Y. Surg. Soc., N.Y. Acad. Medicine (pres. Friends Rare Book Room), Plastic and Reconstructive Surgery (sec., pres. 1966), N.Y. State Med. Soc. (pres., sec., med. history), N.Y. Regional Soc. Plastic and Reconstructive Surgery (pres. 1064-65), Halsted Soc. (pres. 1973-74), James IV Assn. Surgeons, Am. Soc. Aesthetic Plastic Surgery (pres. 1974-75), Nat. Arts Club (exhibiting mem.), Century Club (profl. artist), Artist Fellowship. Home: 35 E 75th St New York NY 10021-2761

STARK, RICHARD JAMES, neurologist; b. Melbourne, Victoria, Australia, Oct. 6, 1950; s. James Walter and Nola Ellen (Muhlhan) S.; m. Janet Mary Keys-Brown, Dec. 15, 1972; children: Anthony, Catherine. M.B.B.S., Monash U., Melbourne, 1973. RMO/neurology registrar Alfred Hosp., Melbourne, 1974-79; neurology registrar London Hosp., 1979-81, Nat. Hosp. for Nervous Diseases, London, 1981-82; vis. neurologist Alfred Hosp./Caulfield Hosp., Melbourne, 1982—, Peter MacCallum Hosp./Cancer Inst., Melbourne, 1982—; hon. sr. lectr. Monash U., Melbourne, 1993—. Contbr. articles to profl. jours. Mem. coun., dir. Australian Brain Found., 1985-91; v.p. Migraine Found. Australia, 1996—; patron IN Group (Inflammatory Neuropathy Support Group), Melbourne, 1992—; sci. advisor Acoustic Neuroma Soc., Melbourne, 1990—. Recipient Sophie Davis prize for top med. student Monash U., 1973; Bushell fellow, 1980. Fellow Royal Australasian Coll. Physicians (mem. com. for examinations 1992—, specialist adv. com. neurology 1984-87, 92—); mem. Australian Assn. Neurologists (hon. sec. 1984-87, chmn. Victorian State com. 1989-92), Australian Med. Assn. Office: 15 Collins St, Melbourne 3000 VIC, Australia

STARK, ROBIN CARYL, psychotherapist, consultant; b. Yonkers, N.Y., Apr. 16, 1953; d. Louis and Bernice (Cooper) S. BA cum laude Psychology, Hunter Coll., 1979; MSW, NYU, 1982. Diplomate Am. Bd. Clin. Social Work; lic. social worker, N.Y.; cert. psychoanalytic psychotherapy, psychotherapy of eating disorders. Pvt. practice psychotherapy N.Y.C., 1983—; mem. adj. field faculty Grad. Sch. Social Svc., Fordham U., N.Y.C., 1986-87, Grad. Sch. Social Work, Hunter Coll., N.Y.C., 1987-88; coord. patient care svcs. Achievement and Guidance Ctrs. Am., Inc., N.Y.C., 1988-89; staff psychotherapist Ctr. for Study of Anorexia and Bulimia, 1990-94, facilitator wellness support chonic & life-challenging illness, 1993—. Recipient Service award Young Adult Inst., 1987; N.Y.C. Youth Bur. grantee, 1983-85. Mem. NASW, Acad. Cert. Social Workers. Office: 410 E 57th St Ste 1A New York NY 10022-3059

STARK, STEVEN PAUL, surgeon, educator; b. Boone, Iowa, Jan. 10, 1962; s. Paul Henry and Gretchen (Kinter) S.; m. Kelly Lynn Rhodes, May 25, 1991; 1 child, Hillary. BS with distinction, Iowa State U., 1984; MD, U. Iowa, 1987. Diplomate Am. Bd. Surgery. Intern in surgery U. Louisville (Ky.), 1987-88, resident in surgery, 1988-92; attending surgeon Dept. Vets. Affairs Med. Ctr., Kansas City, Mo., 1992—; asst. prof. surgery U. Kans. Med. Ctr., Kansas City, Kans., 1992—; cancer com., med. dir. surg. ICU Dept. Vets. Affairs Med. Ctr., Kansas Citym Mo., 1993—, spl. nutrition adv. com., resource mgmt. bd., 1994-96. Recipient Lange Med. Publs. award, 1987. Fellow ACS; mem. Kansas City Surg. Soc., Alpha Omega Alpha, Phi Beta Kappa. Republican. Methodist. Home: 4909 Belinder Westwood KS 66205 Office: Dept Vets Affairs Med Ctr 4801 Linwood Blvd Kansas City MO 64128

STARKEY, RALPH HERBERT, internist, endocrinologist, educator; b. Summit, N.J., Apr. 19, 1944; s. S. Herbert and Gertrude E. (Schneeweiss) S.; m. Peggy E. Crossland, Aug. 23, 1969; children: Christine, Kathryn, Lauren, Russell. BA, DePauw U., 1966; MD, Temple U., 1970. Diplomate Am. Bd. Internal Medicine, Am. Bd. Endocrinology and Metabolism. Resident in internal medicine Washington U.-Barnes Hosp., St. Louis, 1970-73; fellow in endocrinology Vanderbilt U., Nashville, 1973-75; staff physician Geisinger Med. Ctr., Danville, Pa., 1977—; dir. dept. endocrinology Geisinger Med. Ctr., Danville, 1995—; clin. prof. medicine Jefferson Med. Coll., Phila., 1988—. Elder 1st Presbyn. Ch., Lewisburg, Pa., 1990-93. Lt. comdr. M.C., USN, 1975-77. Fellow ACP, Am. Coll. Endocrinology; mem. Endocrine Soc., Am. Assn. Clin. Endocrinologists. Republican. Office: Geisinger Med Ctr N Academy Ave Danville PA 17822

STARR, DOROTHY ANNE, psychiatrist; b. N.Y.C., July 17, 1922; d. James Edward and Eileen Lillian (Gorman) S.; m. Charles O. Olsen, Aug. 29 1953; children: Margrete, Therese, Sara, Marie. BS, NYU, 1943; MD, SUNY, 1950. Intern St. Johns Episcopal Hosp., Bklyn., 1950-51; resident in ob-gyn St. Albans Naval Hosp., N.Y., 1951-52; resident psychiatrist Bethesda (Md.) Naval Hosp., 1953-54, St. Elizabeth's Hosp., Washington, 1954-56; pvt. practice psychiatry Washington, 1957—; chief adult mental health Dept. Pub. Health, Washington, 1960-64; cons. St. Elizabeth's Hosp., Washington, 1965-73; physician mem. Mental Health Commn., Washington, 1969-73;/ asst. clin. prof. Georgetown U., Washington, 1975-81; assy. rep. Am. Psychiatric Assn., 1981-87, asys. recorder, 1987-88; bd. dirs. Nat. Capital Underwriters, Inc., Washington, 1980—, Legal Resources Fund, Washington, 1982-84. With U.S. Army, 1943-45, USN, 1950-54. Mem. AMA (mem. adv. panel on women in medicine 1989-91, chmn. adv. panel 1991-92), Am. Med. Women's Assn., Washington Psychiatry Soc. (mem. coun. 1965-67, 71-72, asst. del. 1981-87, sec. 1972-73), Med. Soc. D.C. (pres. 1980, mem. exec. bd. 1974-92, chmn. exec. bd. 1981, alt. del. 1983-87, del. 1988-92), Am. Psychiat. Assn. (fellow, recorder assembly 1987-88). Home: 8427 Ramsburg Rd Thurmont MD 21788-2945 Office: 2119 Bancroft Pl NW Washington DC 20008

STARR, GRIER FORSYTHE, retired pathologist; b. Jamestown, N.D., Oct. 6, 1926; s. Earl Grier and Grace (Forsythe) S.; m. Virginia Lucille Heidinger, June 25, 1948; children: William Grier, Joan Elizabeth Starr Barton. BS cum laude, Jamestown (N.D.) Coll., 1947; MD, Northwestern U., 1951; MS in Pathology, U. Minn., 1956. Diplomate Nat. Bd. Med. Examiners, 1952, Minn., Mich., Oreg. and Wash. state bds., Am. Bd. Pathology in Clin. Pathology, 1956, and in Pathol. Anatomy, 1957. Intern Evanston (Ill.) Hosp., 1951-52; sr. resident in pathology Henry Ford Hosp., Detroit, 1955-56; fellow in pathology Mayo Clinic, Rochester, Minn., 1952-55, cons. surgical pathology, 1956-59; cons., pathologist Lab. Pathology and Pathology Cons., Eugene, Oreg., 1959-91, pres., 1973-85; mem. staff McKenzie-Willamette Hosp., Springfield, Oreg., 1959-91—; mem. staff Sacred Heart Gen. Hosp., Eugene, Oreg., 1959-91, chief of staff, 1969-71, dir. labs., 1973-86, emeritus staff, 1992—; chmn. bd., chief ops. officer Oreg. Consol. Labs., Eugene, Oreg., 1986-89; bd. dirs. PeaceHealth (Sisters of St. Joseph of Peace), Bellevue, Wash., Peace Health Oreg.; affiliate in pathology Oreg. Health Scis. Ctr., Portland, 1972-88; assoc. prof. U. Oreg., Eugene, 1986. Contbr. articles to profl. jours. Served with USN, 1944-46. Fellow Am. Coll. Pathologists, Am. Soc. Clin. Pathologists; mem. AMA, Lane County Med. Soc. (pres. 1984-85), Am. Soc. Cytology, Internat. Acad. Pathologists, Pacific NW Soc. Pathologists (pres. 1979-80), Oreg. State Soc. Pathologists, Am. Soc. Dermatopathology (chmn. 1984, peer rev. com. 1976-91). Republican. Presbyterian. Home: 2455 S Louis Ln Eugene OR 97405-1026

STASKIN, DAVID R., urologist; b. Chester, Pa., May 21, 1953; s. Bernard and Irene Staskin. BA, Cornell U., 1975; MD, Hahnemann U., Phila., 1979. Resident U. Pa., Phila., 1984-85; fellow UCLA, Phila., 1985-89; pvt. practice Boston, 1989—; faculty Boston U., 1989—, Harvard U., Boston, 1989—; panel mem. Agy. for Healthcare Policy and Rsch., Washington, 1993-95; chief surgery Malden (Mass.) Hosp., 1995—; urologic dir. Beth Israel Continence Ctr., Boston, 1990—. Mem. Am. Urologic Assn., Am. Urogynecological Soc. (bd. dirs. 1993-95). Office: Beth Israel Hospital 330 Brookline Ave Boston MA 02215

STASZEL, KAREN M., medical records administrator; b. Garden City, Mich., Jan. 13, 1958; d. Walter John and Lois Jean (Sproat) Siembab; m. Michael Anthony Siembab Staszel, Nov. 17, 1984; children: Joseph, James. BS, Mercy Coll., Detroit, 1976-80. Asst. dir. quality assurance Toledo Hosp., 1980-81; asst. dir. med. records Pontiac (Mich.) Osteo. Hosp., 1981-82, St. Joseph Mercy Hosp., Pontiac, 1982-85; sys. cons.records Sisters of Mercy Healthcare, Bloomfield, Mich., 1985; supr. ctrl. transcription Beaumont Hosp., Royal Oak, Mich., 1985-86; instr. med. record programs Mercy Coll., Detroit, 1986-92; dir. data mgmt. Angela Hospice, Livonia, Mich., 1992—; cons. Angela Hospice, Livonia, 1986-92; mem. adv. bd. Angela Home Health Care, Livonia, 1991—; directed practice supr. Mercy Coll., Detroit, Ferris State Coll., Big Rapids, Mich., 1981-85. Mem. Am. Health Info. Mgmt. Assn. (reg. record adminstr.), Mich. Health Info. Mgmt. Assn. Home: 456 Berkley Dearborn MI 48124 Office: Angela Hospice 14100 Newburgh Rd Livonia MI 48154

STATE, DAVID, surgeon, educator; b. London, Ont., Can., Nov. 12, 1914; s. Louis and Sara (Rosenberg) S.; m. Avis Gae Lorberbaum, Nov. 25, 1945; children—Norman, Claudia, Leslie, Rosanne, Mathew. B.A., U. Western Ont., 1936, M.D., 1939; M.S., U. Minn., 1943, Ph.D., 1945. Diplomate Am. Bd. Surgery. Instr. surgery U. Minn. Med. Sch., Mpls., 1946-47, asst. prof., 1947-50, assoc. prof., 1950-52; dir. surgery Cedars of Lebanon Hosp., Los Angeles, 1952-58; prof., chmn. dept. surgery Albert Einstein Coll. Medicine, N.Y.C., 1958-71; prof. surgery Harbor/UCLA Med. Ctr., Los Angeles, 1971—, chmn. dept., 1971-81. Contbr. numerous articles to med. jours. Am. Diabetic Assn. grantee, 1978-83; Nat. Surg. Adjuvant Project grantee, 1979—. Mem. Allen O. Whipple Surg. Soc., AAAS, Am. Assn. History of Medicine, Am. Assn. Thoracic and Cardiovascular Diseases, ACS, Am. Gastroent. Assn., Am. Heart Assn. (sci. council cardiovascular surgery), Am. Soc. Artificial Internal Organs, Am. Surg. Assn., Am. Trudeau Soc., Halsted Soc., Inernat. Soc. Surgery, Los Angeles Surg. Soc., Med. Research Assn. Calif., Pacific Coast Surg. Assn., Transplantation Soc., Soc. Exptl. Biology and Medicine, Soc. Surgery of Alimentary Tract, Soc. Univ. Surgeons, Sigma Xi. Democrat. Jewish. Home: 1 Reata Ln Palos Verdes Peninsula CA 90274-5201 Office: Harbor/UCLA Med Ctr Dept Surgery PO Box 25 Torrance CA 90507-0025

STATES, DAVID JOHNSON, biomedical scientist, physician; b. Boston, July 12, 1953; m. Angel W. Lee, Sept. 1, 1979. BA, Harvard Coll., 1975; MD, PhD, Harvard U., 1983. Diplomate Am. Bd. Internal Medicine. Staff scientist Nat. Magnet Lab. MIT, Cambridge, 1983-84; resident and intern in internal medicine U. Calif., San Diego, 1984-86; staff fellow NIH, Bethesda, Md., 1986-89; sr. staff fellow Nat. Ctr. Biotechnology Info. Nat. Libr. Medicine, Bethesda, 1989-92; dir., assoc. prof. inst. biomedical computing Washington U., St. Louis, 1992—. Lt. Comdr. USPHS, 1990—. Mem. AAAS, Am. Fedn. Clin. Rsch. Office: Washington Univ Inst Biomedical Computing 700 S Euclid Ave Saint Louis MO 63110-1012

STATES, DAVID JOHNSON, orthopaedic surgeon; b. Rochester, N.Y., Sept. 30, 1927; s. Eugene Johnson and Alida Genefried (Dunham) S.; m. Jean Elizabeth Carpenter, Apr. 14, 1952; children: Jeffrey, Alice, Christopher, Sandra, Robert. BA, U. Rochester, 1949; MD, N.Y. Med. Coll., 1953. Intern Rochester Gen. Hosp., 1953-54, resident in gen. surgery, 1954, 57; resident in orthopaedic surgery Strong Meml. Hosp., Rochester, 1957-60; pvt. practice Rochester, 1960-81; orthopaedic cons. Eastman Kodak Co., Rochester, 1981-92; disability evaluation Riverfront Med. Ctr., Rochester, 1989—. Author: (with others) The Medical Disability Advisor, 1991. Capt. U.S. Army, 1954-56. Fellow Am. Acad. of Disability Evaluating Physicians, Am. Acad. of Orthopedic Surgeons. Home: 26 Old Farm Circle Pittsford NY 14534 Office: Riverfront Med Ctr 259 Alexander St Rochester NY 14607

STAUB, JAMES RICHARD, chiropractor; b. Peoria, Ill., Apr. 22, 1938; s. John and Dorothy Christine (Benson) S.; student Bradley U., 1956-60, U. Wis., 1972; D.Chiropractic, Palmer Coll. Chiropractic, 1972; B.A., Columbia Coll., 1977; m. Sandra Lee Herman, Dec. 21, 1958 (div. July 1979); children: Gary James, Gregory Alan; m. Sheryl Ann Vander Velde, Nov. 17, 1979; children: Abigail Joy, Elizabeth Christine, Naomi Loraine, Rebecca Ruth, Anna Rachael. Cert. Am. Acad. Pain Mgmt. Asst. to mgr. A & J Lumber Co., Peoria Hts., Ill., 1956-60; with Cen. Ill. Light Co., Peoria, 1961-69; pvt. practice chiropractic, Valparaiso, Ind., 1972—. Missionary to Haiti, Christian Chiropractic Assn., 1984; min. of music South Haven Ch. of Nazarene, 1985-93, recipient local preachers lic., bd. dirs., 1987-93, assoc. pastor, 1990. Recipient certificate of merit Palmer Coll. Chiropractic Clinic, 1972. Mem. Valpariaso Bus. and Profl. Couples Club (chmn. 1974-75), Ky., Ind., Porter County (v.p. 1975-76), N.W. Dist. Ind. (sec. 1975-76), Christian chiropractic Assns., Internat. Chiropractic Assn. Ind., Palmer Coll. Alumni Assn. (Ind. pres. 1974-79), Porter County Home Educators Assn. (bd. dirs.), N.W. Ind. Comprehensive Health Planning Council, Exchange Club (adv. bd. 1988-89), Gideons Internat., Phi Mu Alpha. Home: 1400 Evans Ave Valparaiso IN 46383-4330 Office: 1402 Evans Ave Valparaiso IN 46383-4330

STAVE, CARL EDWARD, obstetrician, gynecologist; b. Paterson, N.J., Jan. 30, 1942; s. Thomas Lewis and Sadye Marrion (Goldberg) S.; m. Norma Ann Weinberg, Aug. 22, 1964; children: Todd Michael, Nancy Tara. BA, Rutgers U., 1963; MD, Tufts U., 1967. Diplomate Am. Bd. Ob-Gyn, Am. Bd. Sexology. Intern Maimonides Hosp., Bklyn., 1967-68; resident in ob-gyn Pa. Hosp., Phila., 1968-71; pvt. practice, College Park, Md., 1973—; physician, surgeon Harrisburg (Pa.) Reproductive Health Svcs., 1976—, Prince Georges Reproductive Health Svcs., Adelphi, Md., 1975—, Germantown (Md.) Reproductive Health Svcs., 1991—. Maj. M.C., USAF, 1971-73. Mem. AMA, Am. Fertility Soc., Md. Med. Soc., Prince Georges County Med. Soc., Am. Assn. Gynecol. Laparoscopists, Am. Assn. Sex Educators, Councilors and Therapists. Jewish. Office: 4700 Berwyn House Rd College Park MD 20740-2474

STAVE, JONATHAN ALFRED, psychologist; b. St. Petersburg, Fla., Mar. 20, 1948; s. Al Stave and Betty (Tredenick) S. BA, U. So. Fla.; MEd, Temple U., PhD in Ednl. Psychology; PsyD in Clin. Psychology, Fla. Tech. Lic. psychologist, Pa. Clin. psychologist U.S. Army Med. Svc. Corp., 1979-85, Deveraux Found., Malvern, Pa., 1986-89, Pottsdown, Pa., 1989——; adj. faculty Fla. Tech., Melbourne, 1985-86; cons. geriatric and health psychology, Apogee, Inc., Phila., 1990—; cons. clin. psychology Raleigh Hills Hosp., San Antonio, Tex., 1984-85. Contbr. articles to profl. publs. Chmn. edn. com. Congregation Truth and Mercy, Pottstown, 1994. Maj. U.S. Army, 1979-85. Fellow Pa. Psychol. Assn. Democrat. Jewish. Office: Ste 717 Summit Ct 262 King St Pottstown PA 19464

STAW, BARRY MARTIN, business and psychology educator; b. Los Angeles, Sept. 13, 1945; s. Harold Paul and Shirley C. (Posner) S.; m. Adrienne McDonnell; 1 child, Jonah Martin. BS, U. Oreg., 1967; MBA, U. Mich., 1968; PhD, Northwestern U., 1972. Asst. prof. bus. adminstrn. U. Ill., Urbana, 1972-75; assoc. prof. Northwestern U., Evanston, Ill., 1975-77, prof., 1977-80; prof. U. Calif., Berkeley, 1980—, Mitchell prof. Leadership and communication, 1986—; researcher in organizational psychology. Editor: Psychological Dimensions of Organizational Behavior; co-editor: New Directions in Organizational Behavior, (book series) Research in Organizational Behavior; mem. editl. bd. Adminstrv. Sci. Quar., Organizational Behavior and Human Decision Processes, 1974—, Basic and Applied Social Psychology; contbr. numerous articles to profl. jours. Fellow APA, Am. Psychol. Soc., Acad. Mgmt. Soc. for Organizational Behavior. Democrat. Jewish. Office: Univ of Calif Haas Sch Bus Adminstrn Berkeley CA 94720

STAYTON, WILLIAM RALPH, psychologist, educator; b. Kelso, Wash., Dec. 25, 1933; s. Ralph Willard and Marguerite (Hunter) S.; m. Kathleen Boucher, Sept. 4, 1954; children: Mark, John, Cheryl, Paul. BA, U. Redlands, 1956; MDiv, Andover Newton Theol. Sem., 1960; ThD, Boston U., 1967. Ordained to ministry Am. Bapt. Ch., 1959. Assoc. min. 1st Bapt. Ch. in Newton, Mass., 1956-61; min. 1st Bapt. Ch., Gloucester, Mass., 1961-68; chaplain New Eng. Bapt. Hosp., Boston, 1968-71; asst. prof. Sch. Medicine U. Pa., Phila., 1971-78, adj. assoc. prof. Grad. Sch. Edn., lectr., mem. faculty Grad. Sch. Edn., 1982—; marriage and family therapist Wm R. Stayton & Assocs., Ltd., P.C., Phila., 1978—; mem. faculty La Salle U., Phila., 1983—. Editor spl. issue Topics in Clin. Nursing, 1980; contbr. articles to profl. jours., chpts. to books. Pres. Cmty. Svcs. for Human Growth, Paoli, Pa., 1989-91, bd. dirs., 1981—. Named Man of Yr., B'nai B'rith, Gloucester, Mass., 1968; recipient Outstanding Svc. award Community Svcs. for Human Growth, 1990. Mem. APA, Am. Assn. Marriage and Family Therapists, Am. Assn. Sex Educators, Counselors and Therapists (bd. dirs. 1982-86, 88-90, chmn. dist. VI 1982-86, pres. 1996—, Outstanding Svc. award 1978, 87), Sex Info. and Edn. Coun. U.S. (pres. 1985-87, sec. 1990-92), Soc. for Sci. Study Sex (chmn. ann. meeting 1983), Pa. Assn. Marriage and Family Therapists (continuing edn. com. 1985-90). Democrat. Home: 188 Blackberry Ln Malvern PA 19355-9630 Office: 987 Old Eagle School Rd Ste 719 Wayne PA 19087-1708

STEAD, EUGENE ANSON, JR., physician; b. Atlanta, Oct. 6, 1908; s. Eugene Anson and Emily (White) S.; m. Evelyn Selby, June 15, 1940; children: Nancy White, Lucy Ellen, William Wallace. B.S., Emory U., 1928, M.D., 1932. Med. intern Peter Bent Brigham Hosp., Boston, 1932-33; surg. intern Peter Bent Brigham Hosp., 1934-35, assoc. medicine, 1939-42, acting physician-in-chief, 1942; research fellow medicine Harvard, 1933-34; asst. resident medicine Cin. Gen. Hosp., 1935-36, resident, 1936-37; instr. medicine U. Cin., 1935-37; resident phys. Thorndike Meml. Lab.; asst. medicine Harvard and Boston City Hosp., 1937-39; instr. medicine Harvard, 1938-41, assoc., 1941-42; prof. medicine Emory U.; physician-in-chief Grady Hosp., Atlanta, 1942-46; dean Emory U., 1945-46; physician in chief Duke Hosp., 1947-67; prof. medicine Duke U. Sch. Medicine, 1947-78; disting. physician VA, 1978-85. Editor: Circulation, 1973-78, N.C. Med. Jour., 1983-92; Contbr. numerous articles on various aspects of circulation to med. jours. Mem. N.C. Med. Soc., Am. Fedn. Clin. Research, Assn. Am. Physicians, Am. Soc. Clin. Investigation, Alpha Omega Alpha, Sigma Xi, Phi Beta Kappa. Methodist. Home: 5113 Townsville Rd Bullock NC 27507-9438 Office: Duke U Dept Medicine Durham NC 27710

STEADMAN, ROBERT KEMPTON, oral and maxillofacial surgeon; b. Mpls., July 8, 1943; s. Henry Kempton and Helen Vivian (Berg) S.; m. Susan E. Hoffman; children: Andrea Helene, Darcy Joanne, Richard Kempton, Michael Dean. BS, U. Wash., Seattle, 1969, DDS, 1974. Diplomate Am. Bd. Oral and Maxillofacial Surgery. Residency USAF, Elgin AFB, Fla., 1974-75; resident oral and maxillofacial surgery U. Okla., 1977-80, La. State U., Shreveport, 1980-81; pvt. practice Spokane, Wash., 1981—; cons. Group Health Coop., 1989—; mem. adv. bd. Osteoporosis Awareness Resource, 1988—. Select recruiting ptnr. U. Wash. Sch. Dentistry, 1990. Fellow Am. Coll. Oral & Maxillofacial Surgery, Am. Soc. Oral & Maxillofacial Surgery, Acad. Gen. Dentistry; mem. Internat. Soc. Plastic, Aesthetic and Reconstructive Surgery, Delta Sigma Delta (pres. 1987-88). Office: 801 W 5th Ave Ste 212 Spokane WA 99204-2800

STEARNS, FREDERIC WILLIAM, dermatologist; b. Battle Creek, Mich., Feb. 12, 1943; s. William Frank and Leora (Cornell) S.; m. Linda Comfort, Sept. 23, 1978; children: Gillian Lind, Victoria Cornell. AB, Harvard U., 1964; MD, Baylor U., 1968; postgrad., U. Minn., 1964, SUNY, Buffalo, 1976. Diplomate Am. Acad. Dermatology. Intern, 1968-69; resident in internal medicine Rochester (N.Y.) Gen. Hosp., 1972-73; resident in dermatology SUNY, Buffalo, 1973-76; pvt. practice Williamsville, N.Y., 1976-78, Springer Clinic, Tulsa, 1978-87, Tulsa, 1987—. Active Tulsa C. of C., 1978-87. Col. USAF, ret. Fellow Am. Acad. Dermatology; mem. AMA, Okla. Dermatological Soc. (pres., sec., treas. Tulsa chpt.), Tulsa Dermatological Soc. (pres.), Okla. Med. Assn., Cen. States Dermatological Soc. (sec., treas.). Office: 6465 S Yale Ave Ste 320 Tulsa OK 74136-7805

STECKEL, RICHARD J., radiologist, academic administrator; b. Scranton, Pa., Apr. 17, 1936; s. Morris Leo and Lucille (Yellin) S.; m. Julie Raskin, June 16, 1960; children: Jan Marie, David Matthew. BS magna cum laude, Harvard U., 1957, MD cum laude, 1961. Diplomate: Am. Bd. Radiology. Intern UCLA Hosp., 1961-62; resident in radiology Mass. Gen. Hosp., Boston, 1962-65; clin./rsch. assoc. Nat. Cancer Inst., 1965-67; mem. faculty UCLA Med. Sch., 1967—, prof. radiol. scis. and radiation oncology, dir. Jonsson Comprehensive Cancer Ctr., 1974-94; chair dept. radiol. scis. UCLA Med. Ctr., 1994—; pres. Assn. Am. Cancer Insts., 1981. Author/editor 3 books; contbr. over 130 articles on radiology and cancer diagnosis to profl. pubis. Fellow Am. Coll. Radiology; mem. Radiol. Soc. N. Am., Am. Roentgen Ray Soc., Assn. Univ. Radiologists. Office: UCLA Med Ctr Dept Radiol Scis 10833 Le Conte Ave Los Angeles CA 90095-1721

STEED, CONNIE MANTLE, nurse; b. Ft. Riley, Kans., Oct. 6, 1956; d. Ronald James Jr. and Ivey Coene (Jenkins) Mantle; m. Thomas Joseph Steed, Jr., Aug. 27, 1979; children: Christopher Michael, Robert James. ADN, Columbus Coll., 1976; postgrad. RN, S.C.; cert. in infection control. Nurse aide Bradley Ctr. Psychiatric Hosp., Columbus, Ga., 1975-76; staff nurse West Ga. Med. CTr., LaGrange, 1976-78, nurse epidemiologist, 1978-87, nurse edn. coord., 1987-88; employee health coord. Spartanburg Regional Med. Ctr., S.C., 1988-89; nurse epidemiologist Greenville Meml. Hosp., S.C., 1989—; nat. infection control adv. bd. mem. SmithKline and Beecham, Inc., 1991-92; nat. adv. com. mem. Standard Textiles, Inc., Cin., 1993-94; cons. Kimberly Clark Healthcare Divsn., Roswell, Ga., 1992, B. Braun, Inc., Bethlehem, Pa., 1992-93; mem. regulatory affairs com. S.C. Hosp. Assn., 1995, 96; chmn. S.C. TB Task Force, 1993-96. Co-author: Home Health Infection Control Manual, 1988; contbr. articles to profl. jours. Recipient scholarship for abstract devel. Palmetto Hosp. Trust, Inc., 1995. Mem. Am. Heart Assn. (dist. 4 chmn. 1984-87, Ray Johnson award for edn. achievement Ga. affiliate 1987), Assn. for Profls. in Infection Control and Epidemiology, Inc. (Horizon award Palmetto chpt. 1995, nat. govt. affairs com. mem. 1994, 95), Nat. Assn. for Profls. in Infection Control and Epidemiology, Ga. Infection Control Network (mem. of yr. award 1988), Inc. (chmn. bd. 1982-91, award 1988). Republican. Office: Greenville Meml Hosp 701 Grove Rd Greenville SC 29605

STEEDLE, JOSEPH RICHARD, orthodontist; b. Pitts., Dec. 30, 1952; s. Otto Henry Jr. and Rita Mary (Kiefer) S.; m. Holly Shaw Chambers, May 22, 1982; children: Megan Chambers Steedle, Kevin Chambers Steedle. BS, U. Notre Dame, 1974; DMD, U. Pa., 1978, MS in Edn., 1978; MS in Orthodontics, U. N.C., 1981. Diplomate Am. Bd. Orthodontics. Asst. prof. Bowman Gray Sch. Medicine, Wake Forest U., Winston-Salem, N.C., 1980-85; ptnr. Steedle and McLain, Winston-Salem, 1985—; cons. Winston-Salem Dental Care Plan, 1981-84; rostered orthodontist Cleft Lip and Palate Team, Forsyth Meml. Hosp., Winston-Salem, 1981—. Contbr. articles to profl. jours. Fellowship John Motley Morehead Found., Chapel Hill, N.C., 1978, NIH, Bethesda, Md., 1979. Mem. Am. Assn. Orthodontists, Am. Dental Assn., Internat. Assn. Dental Rsch., Am. Cleft Palate Assn. Democrat. Office: 1564 N Peace Haven Rd Winston Salem NC 27104-1328

STEEG, CARL NATHAN, pediatric cardiologist; b. Karlsruhe, Baden, Germany, Nov. 29, 1937; came to U.S., 1939; s. Paul Samuel and Margaret (Kahn) S.; m. Suzanne Kaye, May 24, 1964 (div. Feb. 1987); children: Jennifer, Julie; m. Rhonda Sue Kline, Aug. 7, 1988. AB, Johns Hopkins U., 1958; MD, N.Y. Med. Coll., N.Y.C., 1962. Diplomate Am. Bd. Pediatrics, Am. Sub-bd. Pediatric Cardiology. Intern Mt. Zion Hosp. and Med. Ctr., San Francisco, 1962-63; resident pediatrics L.I. Jewish Med. Ctr., New Hyde Park, N.Y., 1963-64, 66-67; fellow pediatric cardiology Columbia-Presbyn. Med. Ctr., N.Y.C., 1967-69, asst. dir. pediatric cardiovacular lab., 1969-71, dir. pediatric cardiovascular lab., 1971-85, acting (dir.) pediatric cardiology, 1984-85; dir. pediatric cardiology Albert Einstein Coll. Medicine, Montefiore Med. Ctr., Bronx, N.Y., 1985—. Contbr. articles to profl.. jours. Capt. U.S. Army, 1964-66. Fellow Am. Acad. Pediatrics, Am. Coll. Cardiology; mem. Am. Heart Assn. (exec. com. coun. cardiovascular disease in the young 1979-80), N.Y. Cardiol. Inst., Pediatric Cardiology Soc. Greater N.Y. (pres. 1982-83). Jewish. Home: 31 Glenside Rd South Orange NJ 07079-1601 Office: Montefiore Med Ctr 111 E 210th St Bronx NY 10467-2490

STEEL, HOWARD HALDEMAN, pediatric orthopedic surgeon; b. Phila., Apr. 17, 1921; s. Howard Hinchman and Elizabeth (Haldeman) S.; m. Joan Elizabeth Clack, Aug. 16, 1964; children—Michael, Celia, Turner, Kathleen, Patrick, Townsend, Anna, Howard H. III. A.B., Colgate U., 1942; M.D., Temple U., 1945, M.S., 1951; Ph.D. in Anatomy, U. Wash., 1966. Enlisted U.S. Navy, 1941, advanced through grades to lt. comdr. M.C., 1955; ret., 1956; intern Temple U. Med. Center, Phila., 1945-46; resident in orthopaedic surgery Temple U. Med. Center, 1948-51; prof. orthopaedic surgery U. Wash., Seattle, 1965-66, Temple U., 1966—; endowed chair, prof. pediatric orthopaedics Temple U. Hosp., 1989—; clin. prof. orthopaedic surgery Med. Coll. Pa., 1985—; chief surgeon Shriners Hosp. for Crippled Children, Phila., 1966-86, emeritus chief of staff, 1986—; pres. Steel Fudge Shops, Inc., Atlantic City, 1958—; chmn. bd. Steels Fudge, Inc.; Hunterian lectr., London, 1958; med. cons. U.S. Army Med. Corps, USN, 1965-85; clin. prof. emeritus U. Pa., 1985—; prof. emeritus orthopaedic surgery Temple U., 1985—. Contbr. articles to profl. jours. Mem. Pine Barrens Conservation com. N.J. Legislature, Trenton, 1973-75; v.p. Colgate U. Alumni Corp., 1965-78; trustee Colgate U., 1972-78; hon. mem. Nat. Treasure of Japan, 1992. Recipient Apple Tchg. awards Sr. Class U. Wash., 1966, Temple U. Med. Sch., 1976, Disting. Alumnus award Colgate U., 1975, Humanitarian award City of Phila., 1978, Presdl. citation for rsch. in Berrylium, 1942, Humanitarian award Chapel of Four Chaplains, 1981. Fellow A.C.S.; mem. AMA (Billings Gold medal), Am. Orthopaedic Assn., Phila. Orthopaedic Soc. (pres. 1970), Am. Acad. Orthopaedic Surgeons, Pediatric Orthopaedic Soc., Orthopaedic Research Soc., Scoliosis Research Soc., Phila. Acad. Surgeons, Phila. Coll. Medicine, Eastern Orthopaedic Assn. (founder, 1st pres., Disting. Service award 1978), Jefferson Orthopaedic Soc., Phila. Roentgen Ray Soc., Am. Spinal Injury Assn., Hon. Nat. Treasure Japan, Phi Beta Kappa, Alpha Omega Alpha. Clubs: Phila. Country, Phila. Skating & Humane Soc., Merion Cricket, Merion Golf, The Courts Gladwyne, Wissahickon Skating, Wissahickon Ski, Confrerie des Chevalier du Tastevin, Union League Phila., Orpheus Club Phila., Ocean City Yacht, Corinthian Yacht, Masons (columbia 91 award 1981), Shriners. Office: Shriners Hosp for Crippled Children 8400 Roosevelt Blvd Philadelphia PA 19152-1212

STEELE, GLENN DANIEL, JR., surgical oncologist; b. Balt., June 23, 1944; m. Diana; 1 child, Joshua; m. Lisa; children: Kirsten, Lara. AB magna cum laude, Harvard Coll., 1966; MD, NYU, 1970; PhD, Lund U., Sweden, 1975. Intern, then resident Med. Ctr. U. Colo., Denver, 1970-76; fellow NIH in immunology Univ. Lund, Sweden, 1973-75; asst. surgeon Sidney Farber Cancer Inst., Boston, 1976-78; clin. assoc. surgical oncology Sidney Farber Cancer Inst., 1978-79; jr. assoc. in surgery Peter Bent Brigham Hosp., Boston, 1976-82; instr. surgery Med. Sch. Harvard, Boston, 1976-78; asst. prof. surgery Med. Sch. Harvard Coll., 1978-81; asst. physician surgical oncology Sidney Farber Cancer Inst., 1979-82; assoc. prof. surgery Med. Sch. Harvard Coll., 1981-84; surgeon Brigham & Women's Hosp., 1982-84; assoc. physician surgical oncology Dana-Farber Cancer Inst., 1982-84, physician surg. oncology, 1984-95; chmn. dept. surgery, deaconess Harvard Surg. Svc. New England Deaconess Hosp., Boston, 1985-95; William V. McDermott prof. surgery Med. Sch. Harvard Coll., 1985-95; prof. Univ. Chgo.; dean biological scis. divsn. Pritzker Sch. Medicine, v.p. medical affairs; cons. surgeon Boston Hosp. for Women, 1977-80. assoc. editor Jour. of Clin. Oncology, 1986—, Jour. of Hepatobiliary-Pancreatic Surgery, 1993—; mem. editorial bd. Annals of Surgery, Annals of Surg. Oncology, British Jour. of Surgery, Surgery, Surgical Oncology; contbr. numerous articles to profl. jours. Recipient NIH fellow 1973-75, Am. Cancer Soc. fellow 1972-73, 76-79, various other rsch. grants. Fellow Am. Coll. Surgeons (chmn. patient care and rsch. com. commn. on cancer 1989-91, mem. bd. govs. 1991—, chmn. commn. on cancer 1991-93, exec. com. 1993—0); mem. Am. Assn. Immunologists, Am. Bd. Surgery (dir. 1993—), Ill. Surgical Soc., Am. Bd. Med. Specialists, Am. Soc. Clin. Oncology, Am. Surg. Assn., Assn. Program Dirs. in Surgery, Assn. for Surgical Edn., Internat. Fedn. Surg. Colls., Internat. Surg. Group, New England Cancer Soc., and numerous other mems. Office: Univ Chicago MC 1000 5841 S Maryland Ave MC1000 Chicago IL 60637-1470

STEELE, SAMUEL MCDOWELL, urologist; b. Osawatomie, Kans., Mar. 16, 1939; s. Samuel McDowell and Maxine Rose (Meek) S.; m. Olivia Ann Smith, June 4, 1960; 1 child, Rodney Andrew. BS, Pitts. State U., 1961, MS, 1962; MD, U. Kans., 1968. Commd. officer USN, 1964; advanced through grades to capt., 1980; sr. med. officer Armed Forces Exam and Entrance Sta., Kansas City, Mo., 1970-71; urology resident Naval Reginal Med. Ctr., Phila., 1971-75; chmn. dept. urology Naval Hosp., Camp LeJeune, N.C., 1975-78; chmn. dept. urology, dir. urology resident tng. Naval Hosp., Portsmouth, Va., 1978-81; dir. combat casualty care course-task force Ft. Sam, Houston, 1981-84; physician advisor quality assurance, staff urologist Navy Hosp., Bethesda, Md., 1985-86; asst. chief staff plans and ops. Pacific Region Naval Med. Command, Barbers Point, Hawaii, 1986-89; comdr. joint med. readiness tng. ctr. Ft. Sam, 1989-93; ret. USN, 1993; staff mem. Sloop Meml. Hosp., Crossnore, N.C., 1993—, Cannon Meml. Hosp., Banner Elk, N.C., 1993—; staff urologist Tripler Army Med. Ctr., Honolulu, 1987-89, Brooke Army Med. Ctr., Ft Sam, 1990-93. Contbr. articles to profl. publs. Mem. AMA (award of appreciation 1984), Am. Urological Assn., Am. Fertility Soc., Am. Coll. Physician Execs., Assn. Mil. Surgeons of U.S., Soc. Govt. Svcs. Urologists (Col. John F. Patton award 1983), Uniformed Svcs. Univ. Surgical Assocs. Office: Sloop Meml Hosp One Crossnore Dr Crossnore NC 28616 also: Cannon Meml Hosp Banner Elk NC 28604

STEELE, SANDRA ELAINE NOEL, nursing educator; b. Warren, Pa., May 8, 1939; d. Cecil Harry Johnson and Romaine Mae (Goodwin) Hamblin; children: Lynne Cerise, William Leslie. Diploma in nursing, Allegheny Gen. Hosp., 1961; postgrad., City U., Bellevue, Wash., 1988-89, Bus. Computer Tng. Inst., 1994. RN, Wash.; CNOR. Staff nurse oper. rm. Allegheny Gen. Hosp., Pitts., 1961-62, Dr.'s Hosp., Seattle, 1962-66; staff nurse immunization clinic Snohomish County Health Dept., Everett, Wash., 1969-77; staff nurse oper. rm. Gen. Hosp. Med. Ctr., Everett, 1977-82, clin. educator surg. svcs., 1982-93; patient coord. Cascade Regional Eye Ctr., Marysville, 1993-94; nursing educator Cascade Valley Hosp., Arlington, Wash., 1994-96, dir. hosp. edn., 1996—; cons. Reed, McClure, Moceri, Thonn and Moriarty Legal Firm, Seattle, 1989—. Pres. Tulalip Elem. Sch. PTSA, Marysville, Wash., 1974-76, pres. Marysville PTSA Coun., 1976-80; leader Campfire Girls, Marysville, 1972-76; bd. dirs. N.W. Laser Network, Seattle, 1988-90. Recipient Outstanding Svc. award Washington State PTSA, 1974, Goledn Acorn award Marysville PTSA Coun., 1979, People Taking Significant Action award Marysville PTSA, 1978. Mem. Assn. Oper. Rm. Nurses, Nat. Nursing Staff Devel. Lutheran. Home: 418 Priest Point Dr NW Marysville WA 98271-6823

STEELMAN, SUZANNE, surgeon; b. N.Y.C., Aug. 30, 1957. BS, U. Fla., 1979; MD, SUNY, Bklyn., 1987. Diplomate Am. Bd. Surgery. Intern, resident UMDNJ, Newark, 1987-92; assoc. attending physician Med. Ctr. Ocean County, Pt. Pleasant, N.J., 1993—; mem. womens adv. com. and breast tumor adv. bd. Med. Ctr. Ocean County. Fellow ACS (assoc.); mem. Assn. Women Surgeons. Office: Jersey Coast Vasc Assoc 1 River Rd Brielle NJ 08730

STEEN, LOWELL HARRISON, physician; b. Kenosha, Wis., Nov. 27, 1923; s. Joseph Arthur and Camilla Marie (Henriksen) S.; m. Cheryl Ann Rectanus, Nov. 20, 1969; children—Linda C., Laura A., Lowell Harrison Jr., Herbert J., Kirsten M. B.S., Ind. U., 1945, M.D., 1948. Intern Mercy Hosp.-Loyola U. Clinics, Chgo., 1948-49; resident in internal medicine VA Hosp., Hines, Ill., 1950-53; pvt. practice, Highland, Ind., 1953—; pres., chief exec. officer Whiting Clinic, 1960-85; mem sr. staff St. Catherine Hosp., East Chicago, Ind.; staff Community Hosp., Munster, Ind.; bd. commrs. Joint Commn. Accreditation of Hosps. Served with M.C., AUS, 1949-50, 55-56. Recipient Disting. Alumni Service award Ind. U., 1983. Fellow ACP; mem. AMA (trustee 1975, chmn. bd. trustees 1979-81), Ind. Med. Assn. (pres. 1970, chmn. bd. 1968-70), World Med. Assn. (dir. 1978-82, chmn. 1981-82, del. world assembly), Ind. Soc. Internal Medicine (pres. 1963), Am. Soc. Internal Medicine (Disting. Internist award 1981), Lake County Med. Soc., Ind. U. Sch. Medicine Alumni Assn. (pres. 1989-90, Disting. Alumnus award 1981). Presbyterian. Home: 8800 Parkway Dr Hammond IN 46322-1520 also: Gateway 11481 Waterford Village Dr Fort Myers FL 33913-7917 Office: 3641 Ridge Rd Hammond IN 46322-2064

STEENMAN, LINDA CAROL, internist; b. Kokomo, Ind., Mar. 29, 1951; d. Carroll Omer and Mary Ilene (Milholland) Pearson; m. Dennis Alan Steenman, June 3, 1978; 1 child, Caleb. A in Nursing, Ind. U., Kokomo, 1982, B in Gen. Studies, 1983; DO, U. Osteopathic Medicine, 1995. RN. RN St. Joseph Hosp., Kokomo, 1983-86, Oncology-Internal Medicine Office, Kokomo, 1987-91; RN Des Moines Gen. Hosp., 1992-95, internal medicine resident, 1995—. Mem. Am. Osteo. Assn., Am. Acad. Osteopathy, Ind. U. Alumni Assn., Univ. Osteo. Medicine and Health Scis. Alumni Assn. Home: 3419 Rutland Ave Des Moines IA 50311 Office: Des Moines Gen Hosp 603 E 12th St Des Moines IA 50309

STEER, MAX DAVID, speech pathologist, educator; b. N.Y.C., June 14, 1910; s. Charles and Sadie (Hisiger) S.; m. Ruth Pittelman, Aug. 25, 1942. B.S., L.I. U., 1932, LL.D., 1957; A.M., U. Iowa, 1933, Ph.D., 1938. Diplomate: in clin. psychology Am. Bd. Examiners in Profl. Psychology. Student tchr. N.Y.C. Pub. Schs., 1931-32; research asst. psychol. and speech clinic U. Iowa, 1934-35; instr. speech, dir. speech clinic Purdue U., 1935-37, asst. prof., 1938-40, asso. prof., 1940-46, prof. speech, dir. speech and hearing clinic, dir. voice sci. lab., dir. Purdue Naval voice communications research program, supr. pub. sch. hearing t, 1946—, head dept. audiology and speech scis., 1963-70, Hanley disting. prof. audiology and speech scis., 1970-76, disting. prof. emeritus, 1976—; Cons. speech, hearing problems Ind. Bd. Health, 1954-55, chmn. hearing and speech adv. com., 1956; cons. neurol. and sensory diseases service program USPHS; cons. Ind. Sch. for Deaf, Muscatatuck State Sch. for Retarded, Ft. Wayne State Sch. for Retarded, Pan Am. Health Orgn., WHO, 1972—, U. Bogota, 1974—; mem. nat. research adv. com. Bur. Edn. for Handicapped, U.S. Office Edn., HEW, 1972—; cons., vis. lectr. Nat. Rehab. Inst., Panama, 1974—; cons. various govt. agys., 1965—; mem. Ind. Hearing Commn., chmn., 1958-60, 67—. Contbr. research reports to psychol., speech jours. Bd. dirs. Ind. Soc. Crippled Children, 1947-49, v.p., 1950-51; bd. dirs. Purdue Research Found., 1974—; Pres. Am. Speech and Hearing Found. Served as lt. comdr. USNR, 1942-46. Recipient citation as hon. old master Purdue U., 1975; Kephart award for disting. service to handicapped, 1974; Sagamore of Wabash citation Gov. Ind., 1976; M.D. Steer Audiology and Speech-Lang. Ctr. dedicated at Purdue U., 1986. Mem. Am. Speech and Hearing Assn. (pres. 1951), Internat. Assn. Logopedics and Phoniatrics (v.p. 1959-65, 68-80, exec. v.p. 1980—), Speech Assn. Am. (chmn. speech sci. com. 1948), Acoustical Soc. Am., Am. Psychol. Assn., AAAS, Ind. Speech Correction Assn. (pres. 1938, exec. council 1946-49), Ind. Clin. Psychol. Assn., AAUP, Latin Am. Fedn. Logopedics, Phoniatrics and Audiology (cons. 1972—, hon. mem. exec. bd. 1973—, award 1973), Sigma Xi. Home: 342 Westview Cir West Lafayette IN 47906-1662

STEER, PAUL L., internist; b. Bklyn., Oct. 10, 1941; s. Arthur and Esther (Richter) S.; m. Priscille Coughlin, Mar. 4, 1967; children: Zachary, Rebecca, Rachel. AB, Duke U., 1963; MD, U. Colo., 1967. Diplomate Am. Bd. Internal Medicine. Intern U. Cin., 1967-68; resident, fellow in infectious diseases U. Colo. Med. Ctr., Denver, 1968-71; officer USPHS Ctr. for Disease Control, Anchorage, Alaska, 1971-73; chief resident U. Colo. Med. Ctr., 1973-74; pvt. practice Anchorage, 1974—; assoc. clin. prof. U. Alaska, Anchorage, 1978—. Office: 3300 Providence Dr Ste 314 Anchorage AK 99508

STEERE, WILLIAM CAMPBELL, JR., pharmaceutical company executive; b. Ann Arbor, Mich., June 17, 1936; s. William Campbell and Dorothy (Osborne) S.; m. Lynda Gay Powers, Jan. 29, 1957; children: William, Mark, Christopher. BS, Stanford U., 1959. Sales rep. Pfizer & Co., Modesto, Calif., 1970-72; v.p., dir. ops. Pfizer Labs, N.Y.C., 1982-84; sr. v.p., dir. ops. Pfizer Pharms., N.Y.C., 1982-84, exec. v.p., 1984-86, pres., 1986-91; pres., CEO Pfizer Inc., 1991-92, chmn. bd., CEO, 1992—, also bd. dirs.; bd. dirs. Texaco Inc., NYU Med. Ctr., Minerals Techs. Inc., Fed. Res. Bank of N.Y., Sta. WNET-TV. Trustee N.Y. Bot. Garden; bd. overseers Meml. Sloan-Kettering Cancer Ctr. Mem. Pharm. Rsch. and Mfrs. Am. (bd. dirs.), Bus. Coun. (bd. dirs.), Bus. Roundtable, Univ. Club, N.Y. Yacht Club. Office: Pfizer Inc 235 E 42nd St New York NY 10017-5703

STEEVES, RICHARD ALLISON, radiation oncologist; b. Fredericksburg, Va., Feb. 2, 1938; s. William Horace and Doris Calkin (Cole) S.; m. Elyane Monique Brunet, July 17, 1965; children: Pascal William, Colin Richard, Rachel Simonne. MD, U. Western Ont., London, Can., 1961; PhD, U. Toronto, Can., 1966. Diplomate Am. Bd. Radiology. Sr. and assoc. scienitist Roswell Park Meml. Inst., Buffalo, N.Y., 1967-72; assoc. prof. genetics Albert Einstein Coll. of Medicine, Bronx, N.Y., 1972-80; assoc. prof. human oncology U. Wis., Madison, 1980-92, prof., 1992—. Author: A Cancer Patient's Guide to Radiation Therapy, 1992; contbr. articles to profl. jours. Office: U Wis 600 Highland Ave Madison WI 53792

STEFANIAK, DAWN MARIE, medical and surgical nurse; b. Lackawanna, N.Y., July 13, 1970; d. James Paul and Donna Marie (Paul) Stefaniak. ADS, Millard Fillmore Hosp., Buffalo, 1993. RN, N.Y. Med.-surg. nurse Millard Fillmore Hosp., Buffalo, 1993—. Mem Millard Fillmore Hosp. Sch. Nursing Alumni Assn. Episcopalian. Home: 37 Greene St Buffalo NY 14206

STEFANIDES, CHRISTINE MARIE, health facility administrator; b. Pitts., Oct. 20, 1953; d. John Thomas and Dorothy Jean (Cotter) Hensley; m. Gary Alan Stefanides, Aug. 19, 1972; 1 child, Krista Dawn. BSN, W.Va. U., 1978; MS, U. Md., 1992. Cert. in nursing adminstrn. Staff nurse W.Va. Univ. Hosps., Morgantown, 1978-79, Physicians Meml. Hosp., La Plata, Md., 1979-80; patient care mgr. Physicians Meml. Hosp., La Plata, 1980-85, v.p. nursing and patient svcs., 1985-95, sr. v.p. acute care svcs., 1995—. Bd. dirs. United Way of Charles County, 1990—, pres., 1995; bd. dirs. Hospice of Charles County, Charles County Nursing and Rehab. Ctr. Mem. Am. Orgn. Nurse Execs., Am. Coll. Health Execs. (assoc.), Md. Orgn. Nurse Execs., Soc. Ambulatory Care Profls., W.Va. Alumni Assn., U. Md. Nursing Alumni Assn., Sigma Theta Tau. Office: Physicians Meml Hosp PO Box 1070 701 E Charlest St La Plata MD 20646-1070

STEFANO, GEORGE B., neurobiologist, researcher; b. N.Y.C., Sept. 11, 1945; s. George and Agnes (Hendrickson) S.; m. Judith Mary Stefano, Aug. 24, 1968; 1 child, Michelle Laura. Ph.D., Fordham U., 1973. Mem. faculty N.Y.C. C.C., 1972-79, Medgar Evers Coll., CUNY, 1979-82; prof. cell biology, chmn. dept. biol. sci. SUNY, Old Westbury, 1982-86, asst. v.p. rsch., 1985-89, dir. Old Westbury Neurosci. Inst. and Gerontology Ctr., 1986—; pres., dir. East Coast Neurosci. Found., Dix Hills, N.Y., 1977-82; rsch. coord. dept. anesthesiology St. Joseph Hosp. and Med. Ctr., Paterson, N.J., 1979-82; disting. teaching prof. SUNY, 1991; adj. prof. surgery, dir. cardiac rsch. program SUNY, Stony Brook, 1995—; rsch. assoc. dept. psychiatry Harvard Med. Sch., 1995—. cons. NIDA. Co-founder, mem. editl. bd. Molecular Cellular Neurobiology and Prog. Neuro Endcini Immunology; editor Advances in Neuroimmunology; contbr. over 240 papers to sci. jours. Named CASE Prof. N.Y., 1991. Nat. Acad. Scis. grantee, 1978, 80; NIMH grantee, 1979—; NSF grantee, 1989—; Nat. Inst. Drug Abuse grantee 1993—. project dir. NIMH-COR, 1983—. Mem. AAAS, Soc. Neurosci. (pres. Old Westbury chpt.), Assn. Immuno-Neurobiologists (exec. pres. 1991—), N.Y. Acad. Sci., Gerontol. Soc. Am.

STEFANOWICZ, JOHN PAUL, psychologist; b. Newark, Apr. 24, 1943; s. Joseph C. and Helen (Gurdziel) S.; chidlren: Susan Stefanowicz Jensen, Robert, Kathryn. BS, Seton Hall U., 1965; MS, Iowa State U., 1967, PhD, 1969. Diplomate Am. Bd. Profl. Psychology. Intern VA, Des Moines, 1968-69; resident in psychology Norristown (Pa.) State Hosp., 1969-70; psychologist Smith-Glynn-Callaway Clinic, Springfield, Mo., 1970-79; pvt. practice Springfield, Mo., 1979-85; psychologist Burrell Ctr., Inc., Springfield, Mo., 1985—. Mem. Mayor's Human Rights Commn., Springfield, 1971-75. Mem. APA, Am. Bd. Profl. Psychology. Office: Burrell Ctr 1300 Bradford Pkwy Springfield MO 65804

STEFENELLI, GEORGE EDWARD, physician; b. Bklyn., Sept. 27, 1948; s. George Edward and Ann Marie (Mandel) S.; m. Rosemary Elizebeth Stefenelli, June 16, 1973; children: Stephanie, Rory, George, Samantha. BSN, SUNY, Stony Brook, 1975; DO, Phila. Sch. Osteo. Medicine, 1986. Diplomate Am. Bd. Ob-Gyn.; lic. physician, N.J., Pa., Md. Intern Interfaith Med. Ctr., Bklyn., 1986-87; resident U. Medicine and Dentistry of N.J., Stratford, 1987-91; asst. prof. clin. ob-gyn. U. Medicine and Dentistry N.J., Stratford, 1992—; ptnr. Potomac Ob-Gyn., Waynesboro, Pa., 1993—. Capt. U.S. Army, 1976-82. Mem. Am. Osteo. Assn., Am. Coll. Osteo. Ob-Gyn., Am. Coll. Ob-Gyn., Pa. Med. Soc., Franklin County Med. Soc., Pa. Osteo. Med. Soc., Am. Soc. Colposcopy and Cervical Pathology, Am. Assn. Gynecologic Laparoscopists, Am. Soc. for Reproductive Medicine. Home: 11681 Dellwood Dr Waynesboro PA 17268

STEFFENHAGEN, RONALD ALBERT, psychologist, educator; b. Buffalo, Nov. 6, 1923; s. Robert Frederick and Alfreda Lena (Stolzenberg) S.; m. Marie Shirley Steffenhagen, Aug. 11, 1950 (dec. June 1989); children: Eric Ronald, Mark Lee, Lori Ann. BA, U. Buffalo, 1950; MSA, Wayne State U., 1953; PhD, SUNY, Buffalo, 1966. Pub. health educator Louisville TB Assn., 1953-55; assoc. prof. Rochester (N.Y.) Inst. Tech., 1955-65; prof. U. Vt., Burlington, 1966-88; prof. emeritus U. Vt., 1989—; pvt. practice, Durham/Raleigh, N.C. Author: Self-esteem Therapy, 1990; co-author: The Social Dynamics of Self-esteem, 1987; editor: Hypnotic Techniques for Increasing Self Esteem, 1983; contbr. articles profl. jours. With USAAF, 1943-46. Univ. Rochester fellow, 1958; U.S. Pub. Health Svc. grantee, 1968. Mem. Am. Psychol. Assn., Am. Soc. Clin. Hypnosis. Republican. Roman Catholic. Home: 5108 Old Adams Rd Holly Springs NC 27540

STEFFENS, JOHN HOWARD, cytotechnologist; b. Glendale, Calif., Aug. 5, 1941; s. Amzel Emmet Steffens and Wanda Elgain (Haylock) Clark; m. Yvonne Marie Croxen, Sept. 9, 1966; children: Roberta Mae, Deena Marie, Adam Kemp. BS, Warner Pacific Coll., Portland, Oreg., 1970; cert. cytotech., U. Kans., 1973. Cert. cyto-technologist. Messenger, orderly Palo Alto (Calif.) Stanford Hosp., 1957-62; warehouse worker Loma Linda Foods, Riverside, Calif., 1962-64; apiary worker Albert Knoefler Honey Co., Riverside, 1962-65; cyto-technician United Med. Labs., Portland, 1966-70; mgr. Independence (Mo.) Fire & Safety Equipment Co., 1970-72; res. and substitute tchr. Independence Sch. System, 1970-72, 90-95; cyto-technologist, med. technologist U. Health Scis., Kansas City, Mo., 1973-85; cyto-technologist Kansas City VA Hosp., 1973—, Rsch. Med. Ctr., Kansas City, 1984-90, Johnson Med. and Reference Labs., Independence, 1990—; cons. Univ. Diagnostics, Independence, 1991—; quality control supr. United Med. Labs, Portland, 1968-70; lab. safety officer U. Health Scis., Kansas City, 1980-84. Mem. Burroughs Aubudon Soc., Kansas City, Cmty. Assn. for the Arts. Recipient Performance award Kansas City City VA Hosp., 1987, Svc. award, 1988, Outstanding Rating Cert., 1988, 94, 95. Mem. Heart of Am. Assn. Cytotechnologists, Am. Beekeeping Fedn., Mo. Beekeepers Assn., Midwestern Beekeepers Assn. (bd. dirs. 1987-89, pres. 1990, honey plants com., Beekeeper of Yr. award 1990), Nat. Audubon Soc., Pathfinder Club (bd. dirs. 1973-76, dep. dir. 1974-76). Republican. Seventh Day Adventist. Home: 913 Main Rd Independence MO 64056-2417 Office: Kansas City VA Hosp 4801 E Linwood Blvd Kansas City MO 64128-2226

STEGALL, MARK D., surgeon, medical educator; b. Lubbock, Tex., June 24, 1957. BA, Harvard Coll., 1979; postgrad., Trinity Coll., Oxford (Eng.), 1979; MD, Columbia U., 1984. Diplomate Am. Bd. Surgery. Resident in surgery Presbyn. Hosp., N.Y.C., 1984-91; post-doctoral rsch. scientist Columbia U., N.Y.C., 1987-89; fellow in transplantation U. Wis., Madison, 1991-93; asst. prof. surgery divsn. transplantation U. Colo., Denver, 1993—. Post-Doctoral Rsch. fellow N.Y. State Diabetes Fund, 1987-88; recipient NIH-NIAID Individual Nat. Rsch. Svc. award, 1988-89, Upjohn prize N.Y. State Transplantation Soc., 1988. Mem. Am. Soc. Transplant Surgeons (Upjohn award 1989, Ortho Faculty Devel. award 1995), Internat. Liver Transplantation Soc., Assn. Acad. Surgery. Office: U Colo Health Sch Medicine Campus Box C-318 4200 E 9th Ave Denver CO 80262*

STEGEMAN, JAMES R., family practice physician; b. Quincy, Ill., Dec. 23, 1952; s. Floyd Carl and Mildred A. (Van den Boom) S.; m. Susan Strow, July 26, 1986; children: Elizabeth, Michael, Matthew, Joseph. BA, St. Louis U., 1975; MD, So. Ill. U., 1978. Diplomate Am. Bd. Family Practice. Resident So. Ill. U., Springfield, 1978-81; chmn. emergency medicine Carle Clinic, Urbana, Ill., 1981-86; family physician Springfield Clinic, 1987—; chmn. sports medicine Carle Clinic, 1984-85; from assoc. prof. to asst. prof. U. Ill., Urbana, 1984-86; team physician U.S. Olympic Tng. Ctr., Colorado Springs, 1988; assoc. clin. prof. So. Ill. U. Sch. Medicine, 1987—; chmn. family practice St. John's Hosp., Springfield, 1994—; team physician Ill. Express prof. basketball, Springfield, 1990-92. Trustee United Way Sangamon County, 1992—; pres. Am. Heart Assn., Sangamon County, 1988-90; vol. coach YMCA, Springfield, 1991—. Mem. AMA, Am. Acad. Family Physicians, Am. Coll. Sports Medicine. Roman Catholic. Office: Wabash Family Practice 2200 W Wabash Springfield IL 62704

STEGMANN, THOMAS JOSEPH, physician; b. Hannover, Fed. Republic Germany, Nov. 20, 1946; s. Adalbert and Marianne (Grindel) S.; m. Dagmar Reddert, Sept. 7, 1984; 1 child, Christoph-Alexander. Student med. scis., U. Bonn, from 1968; MD, U. Heidelberg, Fed. Republic Germany, 1974. Fellow Med. High Sch., Hannover, 1976-82, docent, 1982, resident, 1982-84; dir., dept. thoracic and cardiovascular surgery Fulda Med. Ctr., 1985—, prof. surgery, 1989—. Author: Heart Hypertrophy, 1974, Coronary and Cerebral Air Embolism, 1983, Surgery for Aortic Dissection, 1987, Heart Transplantation, 1988, Pacemaker-Implant, 1989, Coronary Artery Surger, 1991, Lung Transplantation, 1994; editor Jour. for Heart Medicine, 1985. Mem. German Soc. for Thoracic, Cardiac and Vascular Surgery (chmn. com. for med. acctg. 1995, Rudolf-Nissen Meml. award 1982), German Soc. for Surgery, Internat. Soc. for Heart and Lung Transplantation, European Soc. for Cardiovascular Surgery, European Assn. for Thoracic and Cardiovascular Surgery, Lions (Fulda). Home: Spiegelstr 10, D-36100 Petersberg Germany Office: Fulda Med Ctr, Pacelli Allee 4, D-36043 Fulda Germany

STEHMAN, FREDERICK BATES, gynecologic oncologist, educator; b. Washington, July 20, 1946; s. Vernon Andrew and Elizabeth Coats (Bates) S.; m. Helen Sellinger, July 17, 1971; children—Christine Renee, Eileen Patricia, Andrea Kathleen, Lara Michelle. A.B., U. Mich., 1968, M.D., 1972. Diplomate Am. Bd. Ob-gyn. Resident in ob-gyn. U. Kans. Med. Ctr., Kansas City, 1972-75, resident in surgery, 1975-77; fellow in gynecol. oncology UCLA, 1977-79; asst. prof., attending staff Ind. U. Med. Ctr., Indpls., 1979-83, assoc. prof., 1983-87, prof., 1987—, chief gynecol. oncology, 1984-88, interim chmn., 1992-94, chair 1994—; chief ob-gyn service Wishard Meml. Hosp., Indpls., 1987-95. Author: (with B.J. Masterson and R.P. Carter) Gynecologic Oncology for Medical Students, 1975; also articles. Nat. Cancer Inst. grantee, 1981-89. Fellow Am. Coll. Obstetricians and Gynecologists, ACS (chpt. dir. 1984-92); mem. AMA, Am. Soc. Clin. Oncology, Am. Cancer Soc., Am. Gynecology and Obstetrics Soc., Ind. Med. Assn., Assn. Profs. Gynecology and Obstetrics, Central Assn. Obstetricians and Gynecologists, Gynecol. Oncology Group, K.E. Krantz Soc., Marion County Med. Soc., Soc. Gynecol. Oncologists, Western Assn. Gynecol. Oncologists, Phi Chi. Office: Ind U Med Ctr 550 N University Blvd 2440 UH Indianapolis IN 46202-5274

STEHN, LORRAINE STRELNICK, physician; b. Richmond, Ind., Aug. 27, 1950; d. Daniel H. and Eleanor Gayle (Robertson) Strelnick; m. Thomas Veasey Stehn, June 16, 1973; children—Alexander Veasey, Andrew Thomas. BA, Carleton Coll., 1972; DO, Coll. Osteo. Medicine and Surgery, 1976. Diplomate Am. Bd. Family Practice. Intern, Pontiac Osteo. Hosp., Mich., 1976-77; vol. med. officer U.S. Peace Corps, Swaziland, 1977-79; resident in family practice St. Mary's Hosp., Port Arthur, Tex., 1980-82; family practice osteo. medicine, Aransas Pass, Tex., 1982—; med. adv. Christian Service Ctr., Aransas Pass, 1983—; chief staff Coastal Bend Hosp., Aransas Pass, 1985, 90, 95. Pres. bd. dirs. Corpus Christi (Tex.) Chorale, 1995-96. Recipient Service award Aransas Pass Jr. High 1984. Fellow Am. Acad. Family Practice (pres. bd. dirs. profl. counseling services); mem. Tex. Med. Assn. Democrat. Home: 1613 S Saunders St Aransas Pass TX 78336-3107

STEHSEL, MELVIN LOUIS, biology educator; b. Long Beach, Oct. 3, 1924; s. Louis Joseph Stehsel and Ida Batchelder; m. Beatrice Henrietta Solli, Nov. 30, 1957; children: Dené, Craig. BS in Chemistry, U. Calif., Berkeley, 1945, MS in Plant Physiology, 1947, PhD in Plant Physiology, 1950. Research fellow Calif. Inst. Tech., Pasadena, Calif., 1948-51; chemist Mobil Oil, Los Angeles, 1951-56; sr. engr. Aerojet, Azusa, Calif., 1956-65; prof. biology Pasadena City Coll., 1965—; cons. plant tissue culture LA County Arboretum, Arcadia, Calif., 1975—. Editor: (newsletter) Foothill's Rare Fruit Growers. Rockefellow scholar U. Chgo., 1942; French Govt. fellow, 1951. Mem. AAAS, Am. Chem. Soc., Am. Botanical Soc., Am. Orchid Soc. Republican. Presbyterian. Home: 1049 Rancho Rd Arcadia CA 91006-2225 Office: Pasadena City Coll 1570 E Colorado Blvd Pasadena CA 91106-2003

STEIGBIGEL, ROY THEODORE, infectious disease physician and scientist, educator; b. Bklyn., Nov. 23, 1941; s. Samuel and Lillian I. (Parker) S.; m. Julia Ann Enterline, June 10, 1967 (div. 1983), children: Keith D., Glenn N.; m. Sidonie Ann Morrison, Oct. 15, 1985; 1 child, Andrew M. BA, Carleton Coll., 1962; MD, U. Rochester, 1966. Diplomate Am. Bd. Internal Medicine, Am. Bd. Infectious Disease. Resident U. Rochester, N.Y., 1966-68; resident Stanford U., Palo Alto, Calif., 1970-71, fellow, 1971-73; from asst. to assoc. prof. U. Rochester, N.Y., 1973-83; prof. SUNY, Stony Brook, 1983—; mem. adv. bd. infectious disease U.S. Pharmacopea, Rockville, Md., 1980—; mem. adv. panels NIH, Bethesda, Md., 1985-87. Contbr. over 10 chpts. to books and over 95 articles to profl. jours. Served in USPHS, 1968-70. Fellow NIH, 1971-73, grantee, 1985—. Fellow ACP, Infectious Disease Soc. Am. Office: SUNY Stony Brook School of Medicine HSC-T-15-080 Stony Brook NY 11794-8153

STEILING, SYLVIA ANN, surgeon; b. Washington, May 2, 1944; d. Carl Herman and Lottie Barbara (Schlatter) S. AB, Washington U., 1966; MD, St. Louis U., 1970. Intern, resident St. Louis U. Group Hosps., 1970-76; pvt. practice Kennerly Surg. Group, St. Louis. Mem. AMA, St. Louis Surg. Soc., ACS, Am. Med. Women's Assn., St. Louis Met. Med. Soc., Am. Women in Surgery. Office: Kennerly Surg Group 10007 Kennerly Rd Saint Louis MO 63128

STEIN, ALVIN, surgeon; b. Paterson, N.J., Oct. 16, 1936; s. David and Minnie (Bochner) S.; B.A., N.Y. U., 1957; M.D., Chgo. Med. Sch., 1961; m. Leona L. Greenbaum, June 22, 1958; children—Eileen Gale, Randy Sue, David. DiplomateIntern, Hosp. for Joint Diseases, N.Y.C., 1961-62, resident, 1962-63; resident Met. Hosp. and Flower-Fifth Ave. Hosp., N.Y.C., 1963-64, 65-66, Hosp. for Crippled Children, Newark, 1964-65; practice medicine, specializing in orthopedic surgery, Bronx, N.Y., 1966-73, Ft. Lauderdale area, Fla., 1973—; chief Children's Orthopedic Service and Bronx Lebanon Hosp., 1960-73; chief staff Fla. Med. Center, 1974-75; mem. staff Westside Regional Med. Ctr. Bennett, Plantation, Fla., Plantation Gen. Hosp., Univ. Community Hosp., Tamarac, Fla., Cypress Community Hosp., 1973-77, Pompano Beach, Fla.; expert witness, State Fla. Dept. Profl. Regulations, 1991—; dir. Pointe Fed. Savs. Bank, Boca Raton, Fla. Bd. dirs. Miami Hebrew Acad., 1973-81, mem. exec. com. bd., 1975-81; bd. dirs. Moriah Sch., Englewood, N.J., 1968-75, Yeshiva Torah Vodaath and Mesifta, Bklyn., 1965—; v.p. Hebrew Acad. Greater Miami, 1977-80; bd. trustees Finch U. Health Scis. The Chgo. Med. Sch. 1990—. Diplomate Am. Bd. Orthopedic Surgery. Fellow A.C.S., Am. Acad. Orthopedic Surgeons, Internat. Coll. Surgeons, Am. Bd. Quality Assurance Utilization Review Physicians, 1993; mem. Fla., Eastern Orthopedic assns., Broward County Orthopedic Soc., Internat. Arthroscopy Soc., Chgo. Med. Sch. Alumni Assn. (nat. exec. com. 1975—, 1st v.p. 1981-85, nat. pres. 1985-87, bd. govs., Distinguished Alumnus award 1988), Am. Acad. Neuromuscular Thermography (cert.), Biofeedback Soc. Am. Mason (Shriner). Home: 3650 N 45th Ave Hollywood FL 33021 Office: 8251 W Broward Blvd Fort Lauderdale FL 33324

STEIN, ARTHUR HAROLD, psychiatrist; b. Norfolk, Va., Dec. 1, 1940; s. Jack and Annette (Kleinfeld) S.; m. Carrie MacKillop, Aug. 10, 1969; children: Shana Helen, Juliana Frances, Benjamin Jacob. BA cum laude, Harvard U., 1962; MD, Cornell U., 1966; grad. in Psychoanalysis, Balt.-Washington Inst., 1985, grad. Child & Adolescent Psychoanalysis, 1988. Diplomate Am. Bd. Psychiatry and Neurology in Psychiatry and in Child Psychiatry; cert. in psychoanalysis and in child and adolescent psychoanalysis by Am. Psychoanalytic Assn. Intern, asst. in medicine Washington U. Med. Sch., St. Louis, 1966-67; resident Mass. Mental Health Ctr., Boston, 1967-70; teaching fellow in psychiatry Harvard Med. Sch., Boston, 1967-70; fellow George Washington U. Med. Sch., Washington, 1972-73, asst. in psychiatry, 1972-73, asst. clin. prof. psychiatry and behavioral scis., 1973-86; chief youth svcs. Area B Community Mental Health Ctr., Washington, 1973-81; mem. acad. staff dept. psychiatry Children's Hosp. Nat. Med. Ctr., Washington, 1973—; staff psychiatrist North Community Mental Health Ctr., Washington, 1981-88, Children & Youth Svcs. Adminstrn., Washington, 1988—; pvt. practice Washington, 1973—; assoc. teaching analyst Balt.-Washington Inst. for Psychoanalysis, 1989, teaching analyst, 1990, assoc. supr. child and adolescent analysis, 1990-95, dir. Washington Psychoanalytic Clinic, 1989—; asst. clin. prof. psychology Grad. Sch. Arts and Scis., George Washington U., 1995—. Lt. comdr. USPHS, 1970-72. Mem. Am. Psychiat. Assn., Am. Psychoanalytic Assn. (cert.), Am. Acad. Child and Adolescent Psychiatry, Am. Soc. for Adolescent Psychiatry, Assn. for Child Psychoanalysis, Alpha Omega Alpha. Jewish. Home: 6 Kittery Ct Bethesda MD 20817-2137 Office: 5410 Connecticut Ave NW Ste 108 Washington DC 20015-2819

STEIN, ARTHUR OSCAR, pediatrician; b. Bklyn., Apr. 3, 1932; s. Irving I. and Sadie (Brander) S.; AB, Harvard U., 1953; MD, Tufts U., 1957; postgrad. U. Chgo., 1963-66, San Jose State U., 1995—; m. Judith Lenore Hurwitz, Aug. 27, 1955; children: Susan, Jeffrey, Benjamin. Intern U. Chgo. Hosps., 1957-58, resident, 1958-59; resident N.Y. Hosp.-Cornell U. Med. Center, 1959-61; practice medicine specializing in pediatrics, 1963-95, ret., 1995; instr. pediatrics U. Chgo., 1963-66, asst. prof. pediatrics, 1966-70; mem. Healthguard Med. Group, San Jose, Calif., 1970-72; mem. Permanente Med. Group, San Jose, 1972-95; ret. 1995; asst. chief pediatrics Santa Teresa Med. Center, 1979-87; clin. instr. Santa Clara Valley Med. Center, Stanford U., 1970-72. Served to capt., M.C., AUS, 1961-63. USPHS Postdoctoral fellow, 1963-66. Fellow Am. Acad. Pediatrics. Jewish (v.p. congregation 1969-70, pres. 1972-73), Santa Clara County Med. Assn., Calif. Med. Assn. Clubs: Light and Shadow Camera (pres. 1978-80) (San Jose); Central Coast Counties Camera (v.p. 1980-81, pres. 1981-82), Santa Clara Camera. (pres. 1991). Co-discoverer (with Glyn Dawson) genetic disease Lactosylceramidosis, 1969. Home: 956 Redmond Ave San Jose CA 95120-1831

STEIN, BENNETT MUELLER, neurosurgeon; b. N.Y.C., Feb. 2, 1931; s. Walter Charles and Marjorie Clare (Bennett) S.; m. Doreen Holmes, May 28, 1955 (dec. 1984); children: Susan, Marjorie; m. Bonita Soontit, Sept. 19, 1987; 1 child, Bennett Charles. A.B., Dartmouth Coll., 1952; M.D., C.M., McGill U., Montreal, Que., Can., 1955. Diplomate: Am. Bd. Neurol. Surgery, Nat. Bd. Med. Examiners. Rotating intern U.S. Naval Hosp., St. Albans, N.Y., 1955-56; Fulbright scholar Inst. Neurology, Nat. Hosp., London, 1958-59; asst. resident in surgery Presbyn. Hosp., N.Y.C., 1959-60; asst. resident in neurosurgery Presbyn. Hosp., 1960-63, chief resident, 1963-64; spl. fellow neuroanatomy Nat. Inst. Neurol. Diseases and Blindness, 1964-66; asso. in neurol. Surgery Columbia U. Coll. Phys. and Surgeons, 1964-68, mem. faculty, 1968—, Byron Stookey prof. neurol. surgery, 1980-96; dir. service neurol. surgery Presbyn. Hosp., 1980-96; prof. neurol. surgery, chmn. dept. Tufts-New Eng. Med. Center, Boston, 1971-80; dir. Am. Bd. Neurol. Surgeons, 1988—. Author articles in field; mem. editorial bds. profl. jours. Served as officer M.C. USNR, 1956-58. Fellow A.C.S.; mem. Am. Assn. Anatomists, AMA, Acad. Neurol. Surgeons, Congress Neurol. Surgeons, Am. Assn. Neurol. Surgeons, Am. Acad. Neurol. Surgeons, Soc. Neurol. Surgeons, Cajal Club, Brazilian Neurol. Soc. (corr.), N.Y. State Neurosurg. Soc., New Eng. Neurosurg. Soc., Mass. Med. Soc., Boston Surg. Soc., Boston Soc. Psychiatry and Neurology, Sigma Xi, Alpha Omega Alpha, Alpha Kappa Kappa. Lutheran. Office: Presbyn Hosp Columbia-Presbyn Med Ctr 710 W 168th St New York NY 10032-2603

STEIN, DANIEL P., neurologist; b. Bklyn., May 24, 1960. BS, U. Rochester, 1982; MD, Albany Med. Coll., 1987. Diplomate Am. Bd. Psychiatry & Neurology. Resident in neurology Cleve. Clinic Found., 1988-91; fellow in neuromuscular disease NIH, Bethesda, Md., 1994-93; pvt. practice neurology Sarasota, Fla., 1993—. Office: 1921 Waldenere St Ste 701 Sarasota FL 34239

STEIN, GORDON EDWARD, mental health and chemical dependency nurse; b. Phila., Dec. 14, 1953; s. Maurice and Charlotte Eveloff (Liss) Stein; m. Judy Poletti, June 30, 1982. ADN, Miami Dade Community Coll., 1985; BSW in Social Work, Fla. Internat. U., Miami, 1979. Cert. psychiat. and mental health nurse, chem. dependency, assoc. addiction profl.; cert. correctional health care profl. Substance abuse staff nurse Humana Hosp., Pompano Beach, Fla., 1986-88, Wellington Regional Med. Ctr., West Palm Beach, Fla., 1988-89; psychiat. unit staff nurse Bethesda Hosp., Boynton Beach, Fla., 1989-90; psychiat. nurse Prison Health Svcs., Pompano Beach, Fla., 1990-93; head nurse EMSA Correction Care, Ft. Lauderdale, Fla., 1993—. Mem. Fla. Nurses Assn., Nat. Consortium of Chem. Dependency Nurses, Fla. Internat. U. Alumni Assn.

STEIN, H. DAVID, surgeon; b. N.Y.C., July 25, 1941; s. Joseph Max and Sadie (Spiritos) S.; m. Ruth Elizabeth Klein Stein, June 9, 1963; children: Lynn A. Melnick, Sharon L. Stein, Deborah M. Stein. BS, MIT, 1962; MD, Albert Einstein Coll. Medicine, 1966. Diplomate Am. Bd. Surgery. Resident in surgery Albert Einstein Coll. Medicine/Bronx Mcpl. Hosp. Ctr., 1966-68, 70-73; attending surgeon Lincoln Hosp., Bronx, N.Y., 1973-76; asst. prof. surgery Albert Einstein Coll. of Medicine, Bronx, 1975-80, assoc. prof. surgery, 1980-84, prof. surgery, 1987—; attending surgeon Bronx (N.Y.) Mcpl. Hosp. Ctr., 1976-84; dir. surgery Woodhull Hosp., Bklyn., 1984-87; prof. clin. surgery SUNY, Bklyn., 1984-87; chmn. dept. surgery Flushing Hosp. Med. Ctr., Queens, N.Y., 1987—; bd. mem. Mental Hygiene Med. Rev. Bd., State of N.Y. Commn. on Quality of Care for the Mentally Disabled, N.Y.C., 1988—. Contbr. articles to profl. jours. Lt. comdr. USPHS, 1968-70. Fellow ACS; mem. Soc. for Surgery of Alimentary Tract, N.Y. Surg. Soc., Am. Soc. for Bariatric Surgery, Surg. Infection Soc. Office: Flushing Hosp Med Ctr Dept of Surgery 45th Ave & Parsons Blvd Flushing NY 11355

STEIN, HERBERT I., internist, educator; b. L.A., Dec. 23, 1933; s. Joseph and Cecilia K. Stein; m. Elaine E. Alpert, Dec. 28, 1969; children: Alison Jay, Lauren Denise. AB in Zoology, UCLA, 1955, MA in Zoology, 1957; MD, U. Pitts., 1961. Resident in internal medicine Cedars of Lebanon Hosp., L.A., 1962-64, fellow in cardiovasc. diseases, 1965-66; pvt. practice, L.A., 1965—; co-dir. Regional Med. Program, L.A., 1966-68; asst. clin. prof. medicine UCLA Sch. Medicine, L.A., 1980—. Contbr. articles to med. jours. Fellow ACP, Am. Coll. Cardiology. Office: 2080 Century Park E Los Angeles CA 90067

STEIN, JEFFREY M., orthodontist; b. Cleve., July 13, 1962; s. Samuel L. and Virginia A. (Bauer) S.; m. Kathleen M. Stein, June 24, 1989. BS, Case Western Reserve U., 1986, DDS, 1988; MSD, St. Louis U., 1992. Assoc. orthodontist Daniel J. Endrizal, DDS, PA, Ft. Myers, Fla., 1991-93; pres., orthodontist Orthodontics Exclusively, Clearwater, Fla., 1993—; adv. Clearwater Eagles, 1995—. Pres. Young Republicans Club, Columbus, Ohio, 1984-85, Cleve., 1985-86. Mem. DA, Am. Assn. Orthodontists, Othodontic and Edn. Rsch. Found., Fla. Dental Assn., Fla. Assn. Orthodontists, Delta Sigma Delta. Republican. Jewish. Office: Orthodontics Exclusively 1601 South Highland Ave Clearwater FL 34616

STEIN, MARK, ophthalmologist; b. Munich, W. Germany, July 14, 1946; s. Henry and Hannah (Kesten) S.; came to U.S., 1951, naturalized, 1957; B.A. cum laude, Brooklyn Coll., 1967; M.D., Albert Einstein Coll. of Medicine, 1971; m. Toby Wietschner, June 22, 1968; children—Erika Beth, Scott Howard, Stephanie Dana. Intern, Beth Israel Hosp., N.Y.C., 1971-72, resident in ophthalmology 1972-75; practice medicine specializing in ophthalmology, N.Y.C., 1975—; mem. staff Mt. Sinai Hosp., Brunswick Hosp., Mid-Island Hosp., Nassau County Med. Center; clin. instr. dept. ophthalmology Mt. Sinai Sch. of Medicine, N.Y.C., 1976—. Diplomate Am. Bd. Ophthalmology. Fellow ACS, Am. Acad. of Ophthalmology and Otolaryngology; mem. Am. Assn. of Ophthalmology, Am. Contemporary Soc. of Ophthalmology, N.Y. State, Nassau County med. socs., Nassau Acad. Medicine, AMA, Long Island Ophthalmological Soc., Internat. Glaucoma Congress. Office: 2185 Wantagh Ave Wantagh NY 11793-3917

STEIN, MARK RODGER, allergist; b. Phila., Apr. 24, 1943; s. Eli and Norma Ruth (Berman) S.; m. Phyllis Mary Feinstein, Dec. 27, 1964; children: Amy Lynn, Philip Warren. BA, LaSalle Coll., Phila., 1964; MD, Jefferson Med. Coll., Phila., 1968. Diplomate Nat. Bd. Med. Examiners, Am. Bd. Internal Medicine, Am. Bd. Allergy and Immunology. Intern Abington (Pa.) Meml. Hosp., 1968-69; resident internal medicine Letterman Army Med. Ctr., San Francisco, 1972-75; fellow allergy and clin. immunology Fitzsimons Army Med. Ctr., Denver, 1975-77; pvt. practice West Palm Beach, Fla., 1979—; asst. prof. depts. medicine and pediat. Uniformed Svcs. U. Health Scis., Sch. Medicine, Bethesda, Md., 1978-79; clin. asst. prof. dept. internal medicine U. South Fla. Coll. Medicine, Tampa, 1979-83; clin. care cons. Clin. Ctr., NIH, Bethesda, 1978-79; mem. active staff, chief dept. allergy, Good Samaritan Hosp., West Palm Beach, St. Mary's Hosp., West Palm Beach, 1985—; mem. active staff Palm Beach Gardens Med. Ctr., Jupiter Med. Ctr. Contbr. articles to profl. jours. Trustee Am. Lung Assn., West Palm Beach, 1984-93, 95—. Fellow ACP, Am. Acad. Allergy, Asthma and Immunology, Am. Coll. Allergy, Asthma and Immunology (chmn. geriatric com. 1988-90), Am. Assn. Cert. Allergists; mem. Am. Thoracic Soc., Mil. Allergists, Fla. Med. Assn., Palm Beach County Med. Assn., Asthma and Allergy Found. Am., Fla. Allergy and Immunology Soc. (pres. 1987-88), Southeastern Allergy Assn., B'nai B'rith. Jewish. Office: 840 US Hwy 1 North Palm Beach FL 33408-3830

STEIN, MARK VICTOR, health services administrator; b. Balt., Feb. 3, 1958; s. Leonard Albert and Rona Lee (Weitzman) S.; m. Jane Edith Rubini, Apr. 19, 1991; children: Chloe Rubini, Isabel Judith. BS in Psychology, U. Md., 1980; MA, Johns Hopkins U., 1984. Fire and casualty comml. underwriter Reliance Ins. Co., Columbia, Md., 1982-84; program analyst Johns Hopkins Health Plan, Balt., 1984-85; dir. planning and devel. Sierra health Svcs., Las Vegas, 1985-87, HMO Project mgr., 1987-88; dir., provider rels. Prudential Mid-Atlantic, Balt., 1988-92; CEO Sinai Care, Inc., Balt., 1993-95, v.p., managed care, 1996—; exec. dir. Health Start Med. Svcs., Balt., 1993—, also, sec. bd. dirs. Author: Machine Age to Jet Age, 1995. Mem. Group Health Assn. of Am. Office: SHOB Dept Managed Care 1501 Salgrave Ave # 301 Baltimore MD 21209

STEIN, MARVIN, psychiatrist, educator; b. St. Louis, Dec. 8, 1923; s. Samuel G. and Dora (Kline) S.; m. Ann Hackman, May 5, 1950; children: Leslie, David, Lisa. BS, MD, Washington U., St. Louis, 1949; grad., Phila. Psychoanalytic Inst., 1959. Intern St. Louis City Hosp., 1949-50; asst. resident in psychiatry Barnes Hosp., St. Louis, 1950-51; fellow in psychiatry Hosp. U. Pa., 1953-55; asst. prof., then assoc. prof. psychiatry U. Pa. Med. Sch., 1956-63; prof. psychiatry Cornell U. Med. Sch., N.Y.C., 1963-66; prof., chmn. dept. psychiatry SUNY Downstate Med. Ctr., Bklyn., 1966-71; chmn. dept. psychiatry Mt. Sinai Sch. Medicine, N.Y.C., 1971-87, Esther and Joseph Klingenstein prof., 1971-94, Esther and Joseph Klingenstein prof. emeritus, 1994—; mem. fellowships rev. panel NIMH, 1961-64, chmn. mental health extramural rsch. adv. com., 1968-71, chmn. rev. com. Mental Health Aspects of AIDS, 1988-90; mem. rsch. adv. com. VA, 1965-68, mem. rsch. svc. merit rev. bd. in behavioral sci., 1972-75; chmn. Mental Health Rsch. Career Award Com., 1963-67; chmn. bd. dirs. Founds. Fund for Rsch. in Psychiatry, 1967-70; mem. behavioral medicine study sect. NIH, 1981-83, geriatric rev. com., 1986-88. Contbr. articles on brain and behavior and immune function to med. jours. USPHS postdoctoral fellow, 1951-53; mental health career investigator, 1956-61; sr. fellow grantee, 1961-63. Mem. Am. Psychiat. Assn. (chmn. rsch. coun. 1981-84), N.Y. Acad. Medicine (Salmon com. 1984—). Home: 5700 Arlington Ave Bronx NY 10471-1503 Office: Mt Sinai Sch Medicine 1 Gustave L Levy Pl New York NY 10029-6504

STEIN, MARVIN, urologist; b. Bklyn., Mar. 3, 1948. BS, Bklyn. Coll., 1967; MD, SUNY, Buffalo, 1971. Diplomate Am. Bd. Urology, Am. Bd. Quality Assurance and Utilization Rev. Intern Mt. Sinai Ctr., N.Y.C., 1971-72, resident in surgery, 1972-73, resident, chief resident in urology, 1975-78; vice chief surgery N.W. Regional Hosp., Margate, Fla.; pres. Urology Cons. South Fla., Margate, 1990—. Maj. USAF, 1972-75. Fellow ACS, Internat. Coll. Surgeons; mem. Am. Fertility Soc., Soc. Reproductive Medicine, Am. Urology Assn. Office: South Florida Urology Cons 5800 Colonial Dr Margate FL 33063

STEIN, MITCHELL B., physician; b. Queens, N.Y., Nov. 11, 1954; s. Philip and Doris (Kramer) S.; m. Barbara Ellen Pollard, Mar. 24, 1980; children: Julie, Laura. BA, Columbia Coll., 1975; MD, Albert Einstein Coll. Medicine, 1979. Diplomate Am. Bd. Internal Medicine, Am. Bd. Ophthalmology. Pvt. practice Bedford Hills, N.Y., 1987—; asst. clinical prof. Albert Einstein Coll. Medicine, Bronx, N.Y., 1994—; chief dept. ophthalmology Northern Westchester Hosp. Ctr., Mt. Kisco, N.Y., 1996—. Office: 35 Adams St PO Box 279 Bedford Hills NY 10507

STEIN, PAUL DAVID, cardiologist; b. Cin., Apr. 13, 1934; s. Simon and Sadie (Friedman) S.; m. Janet Louise Tucker, Aug. 14, 1966; children: Simon, Douglas, Rebecca. BS, U. Cin., 1955, MD, 1959. Intern Jewish Hosp., Cin., 1959-60, med. resident, 1961-62; med. resident Gorgas Hosp., C.Z., 1960-61; fellow in cardiology U. Cin., 1962-63, Mt. Sinai Hosp., N.Y.C., 1963-64; rsch. fellow Harvard Med. Sch., Boston, 1964-66; asst. dir. cardiac catheterization lab. Baylor U. Med. Ctr., Dallas, 1966-67; asst. prof. medicine Creighton U., Omaha, 1967-69; assoc. prof. medicine U. Okla., Oklahoma City, 1969-73; prof. rsch. medicine U. Okla. Coll. Medicine, Oklahoma City, 1973-76; dir. cardiovascular rsch. Henry Ford Hosp., Detroit, 1976-94, med. dir. cardiovascular rehab., 1994—; adj. prof. physics Oakland U., Rochester, Mich., 1985—; prof. medicine (Henry Ford) Case Western Res. U., Cleve., 1994—. Author: A Physical and Physiological Basis for the Interpretation of Cardiac Ausculation: Evaluations Based Primarily on Second Sound and Ejection Murmurs, 1981; contbr. articles to profl. jours. Coun. on Clin. Cardiology fellow Am. Heart Assn., 1971, Coun. on Circulation fellow, 1972. Fellow ACP, Am. Coll. Cardiology, Am. Coll. Chest Physicians (pres. 1993), Internat. Acad. Chest Physicians and

Surgeons (pres. 1993); mem. ASME, Am. Physiol. Soc., Ctrl. Soc. Clin. Rsch. Office: Henry Ford Cardiac Wellness Ctr New Center Pavillion 6525 Second Ave Detroit MI 48202-3006

STEIN, PAUL MARC, physiologist; b. Providence, R.I., Nov. 8, 1953; s. Harold and June Marian (Shore) S.; m. Janet Amy Solomon, Oct. 11, 1987; children: Michael Jonathan, David Solomon. BS, Worcester Polytech. Inst., 1975; MS, U. N.D., 1978; PhD, Albany (N.Y.) Med. Coll., 1982. Rsch. assoc. Ind. U. Med. Ctr., Indpls., 1981-83; asst. prof. W.M. Scholl Coll. Podiat. Medicine, Chgo., 1983-85, Med. Coll. of Ohio, Toledo, 1985-86; rsch. asst. prof. U. Kans. Med. Ctr., Kansas City, 1986-87; staff scientist Medtronic, Inc., Mpls., 1988-91, study coord., 1991-93, study dir., 1993—; vis. rsch. prof. Loyola U. Stritch Sch. Medicine, Maywood, Ill., 1983-85; pres. preclin. study dir. Medtronic, Inc., 1993—. Contbr. articles to profl. jours. Biomed. rsch. support grant Med. Coll. of Ohio, 1986. Mem. AAAS, Soc. for Exptl. Biology and Medicine, N.Y. Acad. of Scis., Sigma Xi. Home: 6876 Timber Crest Dr Maple Grove MN 55311 Office: Medtronic Inc 1385 115th Ave NW Minneapolis MN 55448

STEIN, PAUL STUART GREENBAUM, biology educator, neurophysiologist; b. N.Y.C., Apr. 3, 1943. BA, Harvard U., 1964; MA, U. Calif., 1965; PhD, Stanford U., 1970. Postdoctoral fellow U. Calif., San Diego, 1969-71; asst. prof. biology Washington U., St. Louis, 1971-77, assoc. prof., 1977-86, prof., 1986—. Co-editor: (book) Neural Control of Locomotion, 1976, Neurobiology of Vertebrate Locomotion, 1986. Mem. Internat. Soc. for Neuroethology, Soc. for Neurosci. Office: Washington U Dept Biology Saint Louis MO 63130

STEIN, PAULA NANCY, psychologist, educator; b. N.Y.C., Aug. 23, 1963; d. Michael and Evelyn (Graber) S.; m. Andreas Howard Smoller, Sept. 2, 1991; 1 child, Rebecca Leigh Smoller. BA, Skidmore Coll., 1985; MA with distinction, Hofstra U., 1986, PhD, 1989. Lic. clin. psychologist, N.Y.; cert. in sch. psychology, N.Y. Intern NYU Med. Ctr.-Rusk Inst., N.Y.C., 1988-89; instr. Mt. Sinai Med. Ctr., N.Y.C., 1989-93, asst. prof. rehab. medicine, 1993—; chief psychologist Fishkill (N.Y.) Consultation Group, 1991—. Contbr. chpt. to book, articles to profl. jours. Kraewic scholar Skidmore Coll., 1985. Mem. APA, Am. Congress Rehab. Medicine (subcom. on tng.), Assn. for Advancement of Behavior Therapy, Hudson Valley Psychol. Assn., Phi Beta Kappa. Jewish. Office: Fishkill Consultation Group Box 446 90 Main St Fishkill NY 12524

STEIN, THEODORE ANTHONY, biochemist, educator; b. St. Louis, Aug. 30, 1938; s. Leonard A. and Mathilda M. (Ellwangen) S.; m. Virginia M. (Loos) Stein, 1994. BS, St. Louis U., 1960; MS, So. Ill. U., 1970, PhD, CUNY, 1987. Rsch. instr. surgery Washington U. Sch. Medicine, St. Louis, 1972-75; rsch. supr. surgery L.I. Jewish-Hillside Med. Ctr., New Hyde Pk., N.Y., 1975-76, rsch. coord. surgery, 1977-93; asst. prof. surgery SUNY, Stony Brook, 1978-89, Albert Einstein Sch. of Medicine, Bronx, N.Y., 1989—; dir. rsch. L.I. Vascular Ctr., Rosyln, N.Y., 1994—; biostats. cons. NIH grantee, 1962; Am. Liver Found. grantee, 1984. Mem. AAAS, N.Y. Acad. Scis., Am. Fedn. Clin. Rsch., Am. Pub. Health Assn., Am. Gastroenterol. Assn., Sigma Xi. Republican. Roman Catholic. Contbr. articles to profl. jours. Achievements include development of chromatographic methods to determine prostaglandin and leukotriene content in tissues using fluorescent agents to increase sensitivity, elastase activity in the aorta with disease, and active anabolites of 5-fluorouracil in tumors; improvement of regulation of liver growth after surgery by diet; demonstration of diagnostic value of liver function tests, surgery on obese patients interferes with sugar metabolism and intestinal function; research in etiology of pancreatitis and pharmacological modification of pancreatic function; effect of stress on the stomach and colon; investigation of the mediators of inflammatory bowel disease, the long-term reduction of stroke after carotid endarterectomy, the benefit of composite grafts for distal limb salvage, the value of completion angiography for distal bypass, and factors which alter the progression of vascular diseases. Home: 10 Glamford Rd Port Washington NY 11050-2437 Office: LI Vascular Ctr 1050 Northern Blvd Roslyn NY 11576-1503

STEINBERG, AMY WISHNER, dermatologist; b. N.Y.C., Nov. 19, 1959; d. Arnold Blaine and Sylvia Fay (Bernoff) Wishner; m. Alan Lloyd Steinberg, June 15, 1986; children: Joshua Darren, Arielle Dana, Natalie Tara. BS, Northwestern U., Evanston, Ill., 1981; MD, Northwestern U., Chgo., 1983. Clin. instr. Univ. Hosp., Stony Brook, N.Y., 1987—; pvt. practice Stony Brook, 1987—. Fellow Am. Acad. Dermatology; mem. AMA, Suffolk Dermatology Soc. Office: 2500 Rt 347 Bldg 5 Stony Brook NY 11790

STEINBERG, ARNOLD DAVID, dentist; b. Warsaw, Poland, Oct. 25, 1930; s. Morris Arron and Leila Merium (Baum) S.; m. June Bender, June 14, 1953; children: Steven, Barbara, Ruth, Mark. DDS, Northwestern U., 1954; MS, U. Ill., 1964. Assoc. attending dentist Michael Reese Hosp., Chgo., 1958-79; practice gen. dentistry Evergreen Park, Ill., 1956-94; prof. biochemistry and periodontics U. Ill. Med. Ctr., 1976—; dir. Lincoln Dental Caries Study, 1963-71. Contbr. articles to profl. jours. Served to capt. USAF, 1954-56. Grantee Epilepsy Found., 1967, 70, NIH, 1970, Collagen Corp., 1981-83, Calcitek Corp., 1988-92. Fellow Internat. Coll. Dentists, Am. Coll. Dentists, Acad. Gen. Dentistry, Acad. Dentistry Handicapped (pres. 1971-72),; mem. AAAS, Tay Sachs Assn. (med. chmn. 1959-75, med. adv. bd. 1969-73, Man of Yr. 1960). Republican. Jewish. Home: 3724 Arcadia St Skokie IL 60076-1741

STEINBERG, ARTHUR IRWIN, periodontist, educator; b. Pitts., Sept. 16, 1935; s. Ben and Sylvia (Jacobs) S.; B.S. in Microbiology, U. Pitts., 1957, D.M.D. cum laude, 1963, postgrad. in radiobiology, 1957-59; diploma in periodontology-immunology (USPHS fellow), Harvard U., 1966; m. Barbara Fay Ehrenkranz, May 23, 1959; children: Sharon Jill, Mindy Ruth, Michael Eli. Asst. prof. periodontology SUNY, Buffalo, 1966-67; assoc. prof. periodontology Temple U., Phila., 1967-68, assoc. prof. grad. periodontology, 1968-70; attending periodontist Phoenixville (Pa.) Hosp., 1971—, now mem. infections control com., by-laws com., religious affairs com., 1977—, credentials com., 1982—; mem. staff Suburban Gen. Hosp., Norristown, Pa., 1972—, Phoenixville Hosp., 1976—; asst. prof. periodontics U. Pa., 1973-82, clin. assoc. prof., 1982—; lectr. continuing edn., off-campus program U. Pitts., 1973—; Fulbright-Hays lectr. Nat. U. Ireland, Cork, 1970-71; vis. prof. Cork Dental Sch. and Hosp., 1971—; lectr. Periodontology Soc. Madrid, Spain, 1980, 5th region Soc. Periodontology Viña Del Mar, Chile, 1985; dentist in pediatrics Charlestown (Mass.) Boys Club, 1965-66; speaker Periodontists Conv., Chgo., 1966, N.J. Coll. Medicine and Dentistry, Conn. Dental Assn., 1967, U. Ind. Schs. Dentistry and Medicine, Phila. Ann. Dental Sci. Session, 1969, N.J. Dental Assn., 1970, Wilmington chpt. Sigma Epsilon Delta, 1974, Lehigh Valley Dental Soc., 1974, Inst. Medicine, Bucharest, Rumania, 1976, Irish Dental Assn., 1992, other confs. and convs.; participant Project Head Start, Childrens Hosp., Boston, 1966; mem. fund-raising subcom. Harvard U. Sch. Dental Medicine, 1980—; mem. faculty U. Pitts, 1988—; commencement speaker U. Pa. Sch. Dental Medicine, 1988, Harcum Coll. Dental Hygiene Program, 1994-95; presentor Phila. County Dental Soc. Ann. Meeting Liberty Dental Conf., 1988, 90, Acad. Gen. Dentistry Ann. Meeting, 1988. Contbg.-author The Fulbright Experience. Inducted into Phoenixville Hosps. Hall of Honor, 1996; mem. Legion Honor Chapel Four Chaplains, Valley Forge, Pa. Fellow Am. Coll. Dentists, Coll. Physicians Phila., Pierre Fauchard Acad., Acad. Dentistry Internat., Internat. Acad. Dental Studies; mem. AMA, Am. Dental Assn., AAUP, Harvard Dental, Fulbright (dir. 1977-79, mem. fin. resources com. 1983—) alumni assns., Pa. Soc. Periodontists (chmn. ins. com. 1967-69), Harvard Odontological Soc., Fulbright Assn., Nat. Fulbright-Alumni Assn. (a founder 1976, v.p. fin. affairs 1976-79), Am. Acad. Periodontology (ins. com. 1969, hosp. care com. 1973-74, continuing edn. speaker 1976 conv., 1983 conv.; nominating com. chmn. Pa. region to exec. council 1975, nat. clin. affairs com., 1984), Am. Coll. Clin. Pharmacology, Northeastern Soc. Periodontists, Acad. Stomatology Phila., Phila. Acad. Scis., Sigma Xi, Omicron Kappa Upsilon, Psi Omega (dep. councillor Zeta chpt. 1977-79). Clubs: Masons (32 deg., Shriner), Rotary (dir. 1973-76, chmn. found. com., chmn. internat. svc. 1974-76), B'nai B'rith, Harvard of Phila., Pottstown (Pa.) Area Study (pres. 1976-77). Contbg. author: Dentistry and the Allergic Patient, 1973; contbr. numerous articles to profl. jours. Home and Office: 1681 Pheasant Ln Norristown PA 19403-3331

STEINBERG, AVRAHAM, pediatric neurologist; b. Hof, Germany, Aug. 25, 1947; arrived in Israel, 1949; s. Moshe and Gitla (Gleicher) S.; m. Lynne Weinberg, Nov. 29, 1949; children: Yitzchak, Lea, Bat-Sheva. Student, Yeshivat Mercas Harav, Jerusalem, 1966; MD, Hebrew U., Jerusalem, 1972. Ordained rabbi, 1966. Dir. Inst. for Medicine and Halakha, Jerusalem, 1969-82; attending physician Bikur Cholim Hosp., Jerusalem, 1982-88; attending physician Shaare Zedek Med. Ctr., Jerusalem, 1982, clin. assoc. prof. med. ethics dept. pediatrics; dir. Cen. for Medical Ethics, Jerusalem, 1988—. Author: Encyclopedia of Jewish Medical Ethics, 1986; co-author: Neurological Manifestations of Systemic Diseases in Children, 1993; editor Assia, 1979-82; contbr. articles to profl. jours. Major Air Force, 1990. Mem. Israeli Soc. Pediatrics Neurology (sec.), Israeli Soc. Medical Ethics, Internat. Child Neurology Assn., Am. Child Neurology Soc., Israel Soc. Medicine and Law. Jewish. Home: 6 Shalom Aleichem St, Jerusalem Israel Office: Shaare Zedek Med Ctr, PO Box 3235, Jerusalem 91931, Israel

STEINBERG, EUGENE BARRY, optician, researcher, contact lens specialist, ophthalmic technician, writer; b. Bklyn., Sept. 16, 1953; s. Lester and Hannah (Bailowitz) S.; m. Ilene G. Richards, Oct. 22, 1977; children—Jessica Brittany, Melissa Heather, Richard Jeremy. A.A. with honors, U. Hartford, 1973; B.A. with honors in Psychology, SUNY-Binghamton, 1975; A. Applied Sci. in Ophthalmic Dispensing with honors, N.Y.C. Tech. Coll., 1979. Lic. dispensing optician, Ga., Va., N.Y. lic. contact lens specialist, N.Y. Apprentice optician Am. Vision Ctr., Bklyn., 1977-78; mgr. Cohens Fashion Optical, Bklyn., 1978-79; chief contact lens fitter Digby Opticians, Atlanta, 1979-80; clin. research coordinator dept. ophthalmology Emory U. Eye Ctr. Prospective Eval. Radial Keratotomy Study Atlanta, 1980-86, ophthalmic technician Emory Eye Ctr., 1980-87; pres. Eye to Eye Vision Ctr., Inc., Marietta, Ga., 1986—. Contbr. articles to profl. jours. and books. Recipient Disting. Service award Nat. Eye Inst., 1983, Appreciation cert. Binghamton Psychiatric Ctr., 1975. Mem. Opticians Assn. Ga., Atlanta Lawn Tennis Assn., Cobb C. of C., Tau Phi Sigma. Democrat. Jewish. Avocations: guitarist, vocalist, recording artist. Office: Eye to Eye Vision Ctr 2100 Roswell Rd Ste 100D Marietta GA 30062-3879

STEINBERG, JOHN RICHARD, physician, educator; b. Balt., Dec. 22, 1954; s. Marvin Bernard Steinberg and Ilene Sharon (Abel) Heaney; m. Marcy Robin, May 30, 19891 (div. Aug. 1989). BS with high honors, Mich. State U., 1976; MD, U. Md., 1981. Cert. in addiction medicine. Resident in internal medicine Greater Balt. Med. Ctr., 1981-84; pvt. practice internal medicine Balt., 1984—; clin. asst. prof. U. Md. Sch. Medicine, Balt., 1987—; med. dir. drug and alcohol programs Greater Balt. Med. Ctr., 1986-91; lectr., cons. in field.; cons. on drug and alcohol issues Md. Gen. Assembly, 1987—; med. dir. Marylanders for a Drug Free Workplace, Balt., 1987-89; cons. curriculum devel. Howard County Dept. Edn., 1986-90. Expert reviewer, advisor for textbook Alcohol in American Society, 1991; contbr. articles to profl. jours. Chair Baltimore County Substance Abuse Adv. Coun., Balt., 1988-90; mem. Md. State Adv. Coun. on Alcohol and Drug Abuse, 1988—; mem. Md. Gov.'s Alliance Against Drug Abuse, 1988-90. Mem. ACP, Am. Med. Soc., Md. Soc. Addiction Medicine (pres. 1990—), Am. Soc. Internal Medicine, Am. Soc. Addiction Medicine and Chirurgical Faculty of Md., Baltimore County Med. Soc., Phi Beta Kappa. Office: U Md Sch Medicine U Md Profl Bldg Ste 540 419 W Redwood St Baltimore MD 21201-1734

STEINBERG, LAURENCE, psychology educator; b. Long Branch, N.J., July 8, 1952; s. Irwin I. and Mollie (Deutsch) S.; m. Wendy Brodhead, Aug. 27, 1982; 1 child, Benjamin. AB, Vassar Coll., 1974; PhD, Cornell U., 1977. Asst. to assoc. prof. U. Calif., Irvine, 1977-83; prof. U. Wis., Madison, 1983-88; prof. psychology Temple U., Phila., 1988—; cons. Carnegie Corp., N.Y.C., 1987—, W.T. Grant Found., N.Y.C., 1989, MacArthur Found., Chgo., 1993—. Author: When Teenagers Work, 1985, You and Your Adolescent, 1990, Infacy, Childhood and Adolescence, 1991, Adolscence, 1996, Crossing Paths, 1994, Beyond the Classroom, 1996; contbr. articles to profl. jours. Faculty scholar W.T. Grant Found., 1983; recipient faculty excellence award U. Wis., 1988. Mem. Phi Beta Kappa. Office: Dept Psychology Temple U Philadelphia PA 19122

STEINBERG, MARK J., dentist; b. Bklyn., Aug. 24, 1953; s. Samuel and Shirley (Jacobs) S.; m. Trina Lee Alley, June 9, 1991; 1 child, Rachel Ann. BA cum laude, SUNY, Buffalo, 1975; DDS, Northwestern U., 1979; MD, Hahnemann U., 1986. Diplomate Am. Bd. Oral and Maxillofacial Surgery. Asst. program dir. oral and maxillofacial surgery Cook County Hosp., Chgo., 1983-84, Michael Reese Hosp., Chgo., 1987-93; chief sect. of oral and maxillofacial surgery Loyola U., Maywood, Ill. Author chpts. to books and contbr. articles to profl. jours. Vol. surgeon Multiple Med. Missions Abroad, S.Am. Fellow ACS, Am. Assn. Oral and Maxillofacial Surgeons, Internat. Assn. Oral and Maxillofacial Surgeons.

STEINBERG, MARSHALL, toxicologist; b. Pitts., Sept. 18, 1932; s. Harry Lionel and Eva (Goldstein) S.; m. Patricia Louise Zobac, Nov. 3, 1962; children: Leslie Renee, Michael Allan, Maureen Sara. BS, Georgetown U., 1954; MS, U. Pitts., 1956; PhD, U. Tex., 1966. Commd. U.S. Army, 1956, advanced through grades to col., 1957-74, ret., 1976; prin. investigator Tracor Jitco, Rockville, Md., 1977, v.p., chief ops., 1977-78; v.p., dir. life scis. Hazleton Labs. Am., Vienna, Va., 1978-83; v.p., sci. dir. Hazleton Labs. Corp., Vienna, Va., 1983-87, v.p. Asian ops., 1987-90; v.p. health and environment Hercules, Inc., Wilmington, Del., 1990—; chmn. safety panel Fed. Working Group on Pest Mgmt., Washington, 1973-74; cons. Office of Pesticide Programs; EPA, Washington, 1975-77; mem. expert in pharmacology and toxicology French Govt., 1985-90; chmn. safety com. Internat. Pharm. Excipients Coun., 1990—, also bd. dirs.; bd. dirs. Global Environ. Svcs., Inc. Author articles, govt. reports. book chpts. Bd. dirs. Del. chpt. Am. Lung Assn.; trustee Health Environ. Scis. Inst.; mem. sci. adv. bd. Digene, 1986-89. Decorated Legion of Merit. Mem. Soc. Toxicology (sec. 1983, 85), Am. Coll. Toxicology (pres. 1986), Am. Indsl. Hygiene Assn., Toxicology Lab. Accreditation Bd. (sec. 1985-91), Acad. Toxicological Scis. (fellow, councillor 1982-85, v.p. 1990-91), Royal Soc. Medicine, Internat. Soc. Regulatory Toxicology and Pharmacology, Brandywine Valley Assn. (bd. dirs.). Jewish. Office: Hercules Inc Hercules Plz Wilmington DE 19894

STEINBERG, MARVIN EDWARD, orthopaedic surgeon, educator; b. New Brunswick, N.J., Aug. 31, 1933; s. David and Fannie (Karshmer) S.; m. Delores Gusky White, Nov. 22, 1956; children: David, James, Susan, Julie. BA, Princeton U., 1954; MD, U. Pa., 1958; MA, U. Oxford, Eng., 1964. Cert. Am. Bd. Orthopaedic Surgery, re-cert.; lic. Pa., N.J. Asst. prof. orthopaedic surgery dept. orthopaedic surgery U. Pa., Phila., 1968-73, assoc. prof., 1973-80, vice-chmn., 1977—, prof. orthopaedic surgery, 1980—, prof. orthopaedic surgery in medicine, 1988—, interim chmn., 1994-95; dir. Joint Reconstrn. Ctr., Hosp. U. of Pa., Phila., 1987—; examiner Am. Bd. Orthpaedic Surgeons, Chgo., 1977—. Editor, author: The Hip & Its Disorders, 1991; guest editor: Orthopaedic Clinics of N.America, 1932, (jour.) Seminars in Arthroplasty, 1991; editl. cons. Clin. Orthopaedics and Related Rsch., 1987; assoc. editor Jour. Bone & Joint Surgery, 1992—; contbr. numerous articles to jours. and textbooks. Named one of The Best Drs. in Phila., Phila. Mag., 1984, 87, 94; Fulbright scholar, Oxford, 1963-64; fellow Arthritis Found., Oxford, 1963-64. Fellow ACS, Am. Acad. Orthopaedic Surgeons; mem. AMA, Assn. for Acad. Surgery, Ea. Orthopaedic Assn. (pres. 1975-76), Orthopaedic Rsch. Soc., Internat. Soc. for Orthopaedic Surgery and Traumatology (asst. sec., treas. 1993-96), Am. Orthopaedic Assn., The Hip Soc. Jewish. Home: 221 Winding Way Merion PA 19066 Office: Hosp of U of Pa 3400 Spruce St Philadelphia PA 19104

STEINBERG, PAUL, allergist, immunologist; b. N.Y.C., Nov. 5, 1937; s. Harry and Mary Steinberg; m. Vivian Claire Gallo, June 26, 1960; children: David Charles, Douglas Allen. BS, CCNY, 1959; MD, Johns Hopkins U., 1963. Diplomate Am. Bd. Allergy and Immunology. Intern, resident dept. medicine Strong Meml. Hosp., Rochester, N.Y., 1963-65; epidemic intelligence svcs. officer Nat. Communicable Disease Ctr., Atlanta, 1965-67; staff assoc. NIH, Bethesda, Md., 1967-70; spl. fellow div. clin. immunology Johns Hopkins U., Balt., 1970-72; asst. prof. dept medicine U. Mich., Ann Arbor, 1972-76; dir. allergy sect. Park Nicollet Med. Ctr., Mpls., 1980-85; clin. prof. dept. medicine U. Minn., Mpls., 1983—; dir. allergy and immunclogy div. Hennepin County Med. Ctr., Mpls., 1985—. Contbr. numerous articles to profl. jours. and chpt. to book. Exec. bd. dirs. Minn. chpt. Asthma and Allergy Found. of Am., Mpls., 1984-88. Served to surgeon USPHS, 1965-67. Fellow Am. Acad. Allergy and Immunology, Am. Coll. Allergy and Immunology; mem. Minn. Allergy Soc. (pres. 1983-84, 87-89), Minn. Med. Assn. (Interspecialty Coun. rep. 1987—), Sigma Xi, Phi Beta Kappa. Office: Hennepin County Med Ctr 701 Park Ave Minneapolis MN 55415-1623

STEINBERG, PAUL JAY, psychiatrist; b. Norwalk, Conn., Mar. 5, 1948; s. Benjamin and Ethel (Friedman) S.; m. Helen Katz; children: Miritte, Arielle. BA, U. Pa., 1970; MD, SUNY, Bkyln., 1974. Diplomate Am. Bd. Psychiatry and Neurology. Intern U. Rochester, Rochester, N.Y., 1974-75; resident George Washington U., Washington, 1975-78; staff psychiatrist Psychiat. Inst. D.C., Washington, 1978-81; psychiatrist U. Md., College Park, 1981-89; asst. dir. counseling and psychiat. svc. Georgetown U., Washington, 1989—; coord. drug and alcohol treatment U. Md., College Park, 1981-89. Contbr. articles to profl. jours. Mem. Am. Psychiat. Assn., Am. Soc. Adolescent Psychiatry, Am. Coll. Health Assn., D.C. Med. Soc. Jewish. Office: Georgetown U Counseling and Psychiat Svc 37th and O Streets NW Washington DC 20057

STEINBERG, ROBIN FAITH, ophthalmologist; b. Kansas City, Mo., Feb. 23, 1954; d. Milton Stanley and Norma (Cohen) S.; m. Phillip M. Gendelman; children: Alana, Joshua, Ashira, Mirit. BA, Smith Coll., 1976; MD, Columbia U., 1980. Diplomate Am. Bd. Ophthalmology. Intern Lenox Hill Hosp., N.Y.C., 1980-81; resident Barnes Hosp./Washington U. Med. Ctr., St. Louis, 1981-82, Tufts/New Eng. Med. Ctr., Boston, 1982-84; attending ophthalmologist Burlington (Mass.) Eye Assn., 1984—; reviewer Mass. Peer Rev. Orgn., Waltham, Mass., 1994—. Home: 17 Childs Rd Lexington MA 02173

STEINBERG, RUSSELL MAX, behavioral pediatrician, educator; b. Salinas, Calif., Aug. 18, 1941; s. Martin and Eve S. AB in Zoology, UCLA, 1963, MA in Zoology and Endocrinology, 1964, PhD in Zoology and Endocrinology with distinction, 1969; MD, Med. Coll. Ohio, Toledo, 1972. Diplomate Nat. Bd. Med. Examiners. Intern in pediatrics Affiliated Hosps. U. Calif., Irvine, 1972-73, resident in pediatrics Affiliated Hosps., 1973-74; chief resident in pediatrics then mem. staff Childrens Hosp. of Orange County and U. Calif.; fellow in behavioral pediatrics and learning disabilities UCLA, 1975-76; behavioral pediatrician Childrens Med. Group, Anaheim, Calif., 1976-79; physician in child devel. program Fairview Devel. Ctr., Costa Mesa, 1979-81, physician behavior adjustment program, 1981—; asst. clin. prof. pediatrics U. Calif., Irvine, 1990-94; adj. asst. prof. zoology UCLA, 1969, instr. pediatrics, 1976; adj. asst. prof. pharmacy, U. Toledo, 1970-71; vis. lectr. Tchr. Edn. U. Calif., Irvine, 1980-93; lectr. and presenter in field. Contbr. articles to profl. jours. Rsch. fellow Ford Found., 1966, U.S. Pub. Health Svc., 1965-69. Mem. Am. Acad. Pediatrics (assoc.), Soc. for Behavioral Pediatrics, Orange County Pediatric Soc., Sigma Xi. Office: Fairview Devel Ctr Behavior Adjustment Program 2501 Harbor Blvd Costa Mesa CA 92626-6143

STEINBERG, SUSAN, pharmacist, consulting company executive; b. Bklyn., July 7, 1949; d. Rembert Samuel and Elizabeth (Bransford) Kizer; m. Ralf Gunther Steinberg, July 16, 1977; children: Gretel Susanne, Heidi Virginia. BS in Pharmacy with honors, U. S.C., 1972, MS in Pharmacy, 1975. Lic. pharmacist, S.C., Ont., Can. Clin. pharmacist Sunnybrook Health Sci. Ctr., Toronto, Ont., 1975-86; asst. prof. U. Toronto, 1975—; pres. Can. Pharmacy Cons. Inc., Toronto, 1985—. Author: Development of a Palliative Care Manual foe Elderly Patients, 1984 (McNeil award); author articles on geriatric care and pharmacy practice. Fellow Am. Soc. Cons. Pharmacists; mem. Can. Soc. Hosp. Pharmacists, Can. Pharm. Assn., Can. Found. Pharmacy (bd. dirs. 1986-88), Phi Beta Kappa, Rho Chi, Lambda Kappa Sigma, Phi Lambda Sigma. Home: 92 Ruscica Dr, Toronto, ON Canada M4A 1R4 Office: Can Pharmacy Cons Inc, 1315 Lawrence Ave E Ste 210, Don Mills, ON Canada M3A 3R3

STEINBERG, WILLIAM, physician; b. N.Y.C., Apr. 16, 1945; s. Louis and Florence (Weisberger) S.; m. Leah Stern, 1970; 3 children. BA, Columbia Coll., 1966; MD, NYU, 1970. Intern in medicine Kings County/Downstate, N.Y.C., 1970-71; resident in medicine Boston U., 1973-74, U. Conn., Hartford, 1974-75; fellow in gastroenterology U. Fla., Gainesville, 1976-79; asst. prof. gastroenterology George Washington U., Washington, 1979-83, assoc. prof. medicine, 1983-90, prof. gastroenterology, 1990—. Fellow ACP, Am. Coll. Gastroenterology; mem. Am. Pancreatic Assn. (pres. 1995-96), Am. Gastroent. Assn. Office: George Wash U 2150 Pennsylvania Ave NW Washington DC 20037

STEINBOOK, RICHARD MARK, psychiatrist, educator; b. Bklyn., Apr. 16, 1940; s. Sol B. and Mildred (Silverman) S.; m. Suzanne Richard, Dec. 25, 1966; children: Darren, Brett. BS in Psychology, U. Fla., 1961, MD, 1965. Diplomate Am. Bd. Psychiatry and Neurology, Nat. Bd. Med. Examiners. Intern Jackson Meml. Hosp., Miami, Fla., 1965; resident and fellow in psychiatry Henry Phipps Clinic Johns Hopkins Hosp., Balt., 1966-69; asst. prof. U. Miami Sch. Medicine, 1971-75, assoc. prof., 1975-86, dir. psychiat. residency, 1975—, prof., 1986—; vice chmn. grad. med. edn. com. U. Miami Sch. Medicine, 1995—; ednl. leader Soviet/Am. Psychiat. Study Group, Moscow, Tashkent, Leningrad, 1984, Japanese/Am. Psychiat. Study Group, Tokyo, Kyoto, Bangkok, Hong Kong, Singapore, 1986. Contbr. articles to profl. jours. Major USAF, 1969-71. Recipient Exemplary Psychiatrist award Nat. Alliance for Mentally Ill, 1994. Fellow Am. Psychiat. Assn., South Fla. Psychiat. Soc. (v.p. 1995-96, pres.-elect 1996-97); mem. Am. Assn. Dirs. Psychiat. Residency Tng., Am. Soc. Clin. Psychopharmacology. Office: U Miami Sch Medicine Dept Psychiatry D-29 1611 NW 12th Ave Inst 112B Miami FL 33136

STEINER, DANIEL RICHARD, physician; b. Pitts., Apr. 3, 1958; s. Isador and June B. (Kutis) S.; m. Mary E. Colombatto, July 7, 1984; children: Tara, Elyse, Vanessa. BA, Washington & Jefferson Coll., Washington, Pa., 1979; MD, Hahnemann U., 1983. Diplomate Am. Bd. Internal Medicine; cert. added qualification in geriatrics, cert. med. dir. Intern, resident Western Pa. Hosp., 1983-86, chief med. resident, 1985-86; physician Premier Med. Assocs., Pitts., 1986—; med. dir. St. Margaret's Meml. Hosp. Diabetes Ctr., 1993—; med. dir. Presbyn. Sr. Care, Oakmont, Pa., 1988—, Longwood at Oakmont, 1991-95. Alumni exec. com. Washington and Jefferson Coll., 1994—. Mem. ACP, Am. Med. Dirs. Assn., Pa. Med. Dirs. Assn. (bd. dirs. 1993—, pres. 1996—), Pa. W. Va. Geriatrics Soc. (bd. dirs. 1995—). Office: 1215 Hulton Rd Oakmont PA 15139

STEINER, GLORIA LITWIN, psychologist; b. Newark, Oct. 21, 1922; d. David Milton and Minna (Krasner) Litwin; m. Charles Steiner, Aug. 29, 1942; children: Charles Jr., Susan Steiner Sher, Jeanne. BA, U. Pa., 1944; MS, CCNY, 1956; EdD, Columbia U., 1965. Psychologist St. Michael's Hosp. and Mt. Carmel, Newark, 1956-62; chief psychologist Children's Hosp., Newark, 1965-78; prof. psychology, dir. psychol. svc. Child Study Ctr., Kean Coll., Union, N.J., 1971-78; vis. assoc. prof. grad. sch. applied and profl. psychology Rutgers U., Piscataway, N.J., 1976-94; clin. assoc. prof., former dir. psychology tng. U. Medicine and Dentistry N.J.-N.J. Med. Sch., Newark, 1978—; psychology cons. Nat. Pediatric HIV Resource Ctr., 1991-94. Co-author: Traumatic Abuse/Children, 1980; co-editor: Children, Families and HIV/AIDS: Psychosocial and Psychotherapeutic Issues, 1995; contbr. articles to profl. jours.; mem. editl. bd. Jour. Psychotherapy, 1981-96. Mem. N.J. State Task Force on AIDS, 1986-89, N.J. State Bd. Psychol. Exam., 1978-84, Regional Health Planning Coun., N.J., 1984-85, child adv. com. Mental Health Assn., N.J., 1974-80; trustee, founder N.J. Acad. Psychology, 1978-83, bd. trustees, 1994—. Grantee tng. health care workers Regional AIDS Edn. and Tng. Ctr. U. Medicine and Dentistry N.J., Newark, 1990, Nat. Pediat. HIV Resource Ctr., Newark, 1991-94. Fellow Am. Orthopsychiat. Assn.; mem. N.Y. Acad. Scis., N.J. Assn. for the Advancement Family Therapy (vice-chmn. 1979-81), Am. Psychol. Assn. Home and Office: 35 Sequoia Dr Watchung NJ 07060-6113

STEINER, HENRY, surgeon; b. N.Y.C., Aug. 9, 1950; s. Zoltan and Irene (Eisler) S.; m. Irene Neuman, Aug. 27, 1972; children: Ari Michael, Elana Faye, Zachary Ethan, Samuel Theodore. BS, Bklyn. Coll., 1972; MD, SUNY, Bklyn., 1976. Diplomate Am. Bd. Surgery. Resident in gen. surgery Maimonides Med. Ctr., Bklyn., 1976-80, fellow in vascular surgery, 1980-81; surgeon in pvt. practice Bklyn., 1993—. Fellow ACS; mem. AMA, Med. Soc. Kings County, N.Y. Soc. for Cardiovascular Surgery. Office: 8105 Bay Pkwy Brooklyn NY 11214

STEINER, KAREN RUTH, physician's assistant; b. Milw., Nov. 25, 1953; d. Carl Gustav Martin and Lois Pauline Edna (Koch) S.; m. Christian Joseph Nichols, Sept. 15, 1990. AA in Sci., Glendale Community Coll., 1974; cert. of surg. tech., Maricopa County Tech. Coll., 1976; AA physician asst. pgrm., Essex Community Coll., Balt., 1980. Registered physician asst., Ariz.; lic. phys. asst., Mich.; cert. Nat. Commn. Cert. Physician's Assts. and Nat. Bd. Examiners. Operating room technician Maricopa County Gen. Hosp., Phoenix, 1976-77, Greater Balt. Med. Ctr., 1977-78; resident dept. surgery Franklin Square Hosp., Balt., 1980-811; physician's asst. urgent care unit Ariz. Health Plan, Phoenix, 1981-82; physician's asst. family practice unit CIGNA Healthplan, Tempe, Ariz., 1982-83; physician's asst. cardiac-thoracic surgery dept. Henry Ford Hosp., Detroit, 1983-87, Thoracic Surgeon's Assocs., Grand Rapids, Mich., 1987-88; physician's asst. surg. White Mountain Hosp., 1988-89; physicians asst. Grace Hosp., Detroit, 1989-91, St. John Hosp., 1991—, Women's Health Ctr., Clarkston, Mich., 1993, Livonia (Mich.) Family Physicians, 1994-96, Emergency Med. Physician's Group, Ann Arbor, Mich., 1996—. Choral Mem. Ariz. State U., Tempe, 1977, 82, Balt. Choral Arts Soc., 1978, White Mtn. Chorale, 1988. Fellow Am. Acad. Physician's Assts., Assn. Physician Assts. in Cardiovascular Surgery, Mich. Acad. Physician Assts. Democrat. Lutheran.

STEINER, MICHAEL LOUIS, pediatrician; b. Youngstown, Ohio, Jan. 27, 1937; s. Morris Louis and Blanche Evelyn Steiner; m. Diane W. Martin, Dec. 24, 1961; children: Jocelyn, Mindy, Susan. AB, U. Pa., 1958; MD, St. Louis U., 1962. Diplomate Am. Bd. Pediatrics. Intern U. Fla. Teaching Hosp., Gainesville, 1962-63, resident in pediatrics, 1963-65, instr. pediatrics, 1965; practice medicine specializing in pediatrics and pediatric cardiology Palm Beach Gardens, Fla., 1967—; cons. cardiology div. children's med. services State of Fla., 1968—. Contbr. articles to profl. jours. Served to capt. U.S. Army, 1965-67. Recipient Physician Recognition award AMA, 1970-97. Fellow Am. Acad. Pediats.; mem. Am. Heart Assn. (rsch. com. 1970—), Fla. Pediat. Soc., Palm Beach County Med. Soc. Republican. Jewish.

STEINER, NICHOLAS V., internist; b. Stuttgart, Germany, Oct. 11, 1934; came to U.S., 1935; s. Hans L. and Bridget (Marquard) S.; m. 1968 (div. 1988). BA, Yale U., 1956; medical student, U. Basel, Switzerland, 1956-59; MD, Wayne State U., 1962. Diplomate Am. Bd. Internal Medicine. Attending physician St. Luke's Roosvelt Hosp., N.Y.C., 1968-84, attending physician (emeritus), 1984—; assoc. in clin. medicine (part time) Coll. Physicians and Surgeons, Columbia U., N.Y.C., 1984—. Co-author: (book) When Doctors Get Sick, 1987; author: (book) Hope Beyond The Shadow (German), 1990. Home: 30 Engle St Apt 8 Tenafly NJ 07670

STEINER, ROBERT S., psychologist; b. Newark, N.J., Feb. 20, 1952; s. Henry and Hilda (Eisenberg) S.; m. Pamela Nadine Abrams, Oct. 11, 1984; children: Michael, James. BA cum laude, Clark U., 1973, MA, 1974; postgrad., The Merrill-Palmer Inst., Detroit, 1978; PsyD with distinction, Yeshiva U., 1987. Lic. psychologist, N.Y. Staff psychologist Elmcrest Psychiat. Inst., Portland, Conn., 1980-82; sch. psychologist N.Y. City Pub. Schs., Bklyn., 1982-85; instr. and tutor SUNY Empire State Coll., N.Y.C., 1983-86; adj. asst. prof. psychology L.I. U., Bklyn. Ctr., 1983-88; psychotherapist Comprehensive Counseling Ctr., Rego Park, N.Y., 1988—; sch. psychologist The Lowell Sch., Bayside, N.Y., 1985-89, clin. dir., 1989-92; sr. psychologist Luth. Med. Ctr., Bklyn., 1992-95; clinic adminstr. Canarsie Mental Health Clinic, Bklyn., 1995—; pvt. practice psychology Bklyn., 1995—; Reviewer books, Small Press Mag., 1992. Editl. bd. Humanistic Psychology Inst. Rev., 1977. Mem. Am. Psychol. Assn., Psychologists for Social Responsibility, Phi Beta Kappa. Home: 86 Prospect Park West Brooklyn NY 11215

STEINER, TIMOTHY JOHN, medical researcher; b. Hawkhurst, Kent, Eng., Apr. 26, 1946; s. Raymond Eugene and Barbara Ruth (Ward) S.; m. Susan Elizabeth Nee George, 1967. BSc with honors, Chelsea Coll., London, 1969, PhD, 1975; MB, BS, Charing Cross Hosp. Med. Sch., London, 1976; LLM, U. Wales, 1991. Cert. gen. med. council, 1978. Demonstrator in physiology Chelsea Coll., London, 1969-73; house physician, surgeon Charing Cross Hosp., London, 1977, lectr. in exptl. neurology, 1980-86, hon. cons., 1986—; sr. lectr. in clin. physiology Charing Cross and Westminster Med. Sch., London, 1986—; research head The Princess Margaret Migraine Clin., 1987—. Contbr. articles to profl. jours. Trustee, corr. The Way Ahead, London, 1987—, chmn. bd. trustees, 1989—. Research scholar Med. Research Council Gt. Brit. Chelsea Coll., London, 1967-69, research grantee. Fellow Med. Soc. London (coun. 1985-88), Am. Heart Assn. (stroke coun.); mem. European Headache Fedn. (bd. dirs.), Internat. Headache Soc. (gen. sec. 1993—, edn. sub-com., chmn. ethics sub-com., sec. clin. trials sub-com.), Inst. Med. Ethics, Medicolegal Soc., Soc. Pharm. Medicine, Royal Soc. Medicine (angiology forum com.), Assn. Brit. Neurologists. Home: 95 Kingston Hill, Kingston Upon Thames England KT2 7PZ Office: Charing Cross & Westminster Med Sch, St Dunstans Rd, London England W6 8RP

STEINFELD, JESSE LEONARD, physician, medical college president; b. W. Aliquippa, Pa., Jan. 6, 1927; s. Jack and Lena Helen (Klein) S.; m. Mildred Stokes, July 12, 1953; children—Mary Beth, Katherine Jody, Frances Susan. B.S., U. Pitts., 1945; M.D., Western Res. U., 1949; LL.D. (hon.), Gannon Coll., 1972. Sr. investigator Nat. Cancer Inst., Bethesda, Md., 1952-58; dep. dir. Nat. Cancer Inst., 1968-69, cons., 1961-68, 74—; acting chief medicine City of Hope Med. Center, Duarte, Calif., 1958-59; asst. prof. medicine U. So. Calif., Los Angeles, 1959-62; asso. prof. U. So. Calif., 1962-66, prof., 1967-68; Surgeon Gen. of U.S. Washington, 1969-73; dir. Comprehensive Cancer Center Mayo Clinic, Rochester, Minn., 1973-74; prof. medicine U. Calif., Irvine, 1974-76; dean Sch. Medicine, Med. Coll. Va., Richmond, 1976-83; pres. Med. Coll. Ga., Augusta, 1983-87; cons., chmn. ad hoc com. on research and smoking Am. Cancer Soc. Contbr. articles on cancer chemotherapy, metabolic changes in cancer patients, and smoking and pub. health to med. jours. Chmn. YMCA Phys. Fitness and Health Nat. Policy Bd. Served with USPHS, 1952-58, 69-73. Fellow A.C.P., Royal Soc. Health (hon.); mem. Am. Soc. Clin. Oncology (pres. 1970), Am. Assn. Cancer Research, Soc. Nuclear Medicine, Am. Soc. Hematology. Home: 18676 Avenida Cordillera San Diego CA 92128

STEINFELD, PHILIP S., pediatrician; b. Bronx, Mar. 4, 1932; s. Samuel and Sarah (Frishman) S.; m. Ruth L. Hyman, Aug., 1961 (div. June 1977); children: Andrea, Melissa, David; m. Sherry Lynn Rubinroit, Jan. 15, 1978; 1 child, Sara. BS, Queens Coll., 1953; MD, U. Basle, Switzerland, 1960. Diplomate Am. Bd. Pediatrics. Rotating intern Kings County Hosp. Ctr., Bklyn., 1960-61; resident pediatrics Mt. Sinai Hosp., N.Y.C., 1961-63, jr. clin. asst. pediatrics, 1963-65, sr. clin. asst., 1965-68; attending pediatrician L.I. Jewish Hosp., 1968—, North Shore Univ. Hosp., 1970—; clin. instr. pediatrics Cornell U., N.Y.C., 1986-90, clin. asst. prof. pediatrics, 1991—; mem. adv. bd. TEMPO, Woodmere, N.Y., 1975—, Five Town Adolescent Ctr., Woodmere, 1975—. Fellow Am. Acad. Pediatrics. Office: 1573 Broadway Hewlett NY 11557-1428

STEINGARTEN, KAREN ANN, psychologist; b. N.Y.C., Jan. 25, 1948; d. Robert and Susan Lucy (Ruben) Steingarten; m. David Nicholas Russo, Mar., 1989. B.A., Syracuse U., 1968; M.S., U. Ga., 1974, Ph.D., 1977. Diplomate Am. Bd. Profl. Neuropsychology. Lic. psychologist, Fla. Psychologist, U.S. Navy, Yokosuka, Japan, 1977-79, Jacksonville, Fla., 1979-82; pvt. practice psychology, Jacksonville, 1982—; neuropsychologist Alzheimers Clinic, Baptist Med. Ctr., Jacksonville, 1984-88; chief psychol. services St. Johns River Hosp., Jacksonville, 1982-88; examiner Am. Bd. Profl. Neuropsychology, 1991—; sec. exec. bd. Am. Bd. Profl. Neuropsychology, 1995. Served to lt. USN, 1975-82. Mem. APA, Fla. Psychol. Assn. (elected sec. 1990-92, 92-93, pres. 1995-96), Nat. Acad. Neuropsychologists, Internat. Neuropsychol. Soc. Democrat. Jewish. Avocations: gardening; bridge; cooking. Office: 3000 11 Hartley Rd Jacksonville FL 32257

STEINGRUB, JAY STANLEY, critical care physician, educator; b. N.Y.C., Feb. 29, 1952; m. Milagrow C. Rosal, Oct. 17, 1993. BA, SUNY, Buffalo, 1973; MD, SUNY, Syracuse, 1977. Diplomate Am. Bd. Internal Medicine (question provider, relevancy reviewer, critical care medicine test and policy com. 1992—), Am. Bd. Critical Care Medicine. Intern in medicine Rochester (N.Y.) Gen. Hosp.-U. Rochester, 1977-78, resident in medicine, 1978-80; clin. fellow in critical care medicine Univ. Health Ctr. Pitts., 1980-81, rsch. fellow in critical care medicine, 1981-82; asst. prof. medicine Tufts U. Sch. Medicine, Boston, 1982—, asst. prof. surgery, 1995—; assoc. dir. adult critical care ctr. Baystate Med. Ctr., Springfield, Mass., 1982—, dir. med. ICU, 1985—; ICU physician Park Ridge Hosp., Rochester, 1978-80; emergency room physician Allegheny Gen. Hosp., Pitts., 1980-81; lectr. in field, 1982—. Contbr. articles to med. jours. Grantee NIH, Miles, Cortech, Ohmeda PPD, Liposomal Co. Fellow ACP, Am. Coll. Chest Physicians (abstract reviewer 1993—), mem. Critical Care Soc., Shock Soc., Soc. Critical Care Medicine (cert. course instr. for fundamental critical care support, abstract reviewer 1992—, rep. internal medicine sect. to rsch. award selection com. 1995—), N.Y. Acad. Scis., Arista, Phi Beta Kappa. Office: Baystate Med Ctr 759 Chestnut St Springfield MA 01199

STEINHART, LEO, radiologist; b. Prague, Czech Republic, Apr. 13, 1924; s. Bruno and Marie (Caháková) S.; m. Libuše Satynková, Oct. 7, 1950; children: Magdalena, Miloš. MD, Charles U., 1950, PhD, 1960, DrSc, 1966. Radiologist Faculty of Medicine, Charles U., Hradec Králové, 1950-67; cons. radiologist Al Sabah Hosp., Kuwait, 1967-71, prof. radiology, chmn., 1971-81; prof., chmn. radiology Kuwait U., 1981-82; prof., chmn. radiology Charles U., Hradec Králové, 1982-89, chmn. radiology Faculty Medicine, 1982-89; cons. radiologist Univ. Hosp., Hradec Králové, 1989—. Contbr. articles to profl. jours. Lt. col. Czech Army, 1950-58. Recipient Prize of Ministry of Health, 1987, Golden Plaque, Acad. Scis. Czech republic, 1984, Silver medal Charles U., 1984. Mem. Czech Radiol. Soc., Soc. Cardiology, Soc. Ontervent. Radiology, Soc. Neuroradiology, Radiol. Soc. Slovak Republic (hon.), Radiol. Soc. Soviet Union (hon.), Radiol. soc. East Germany (hon.). Home: Fričova 1043, 500 06 Hradec Králové Bohemia, Czech Republic Office: University Hospital, Hradec Králové, 500 36 Hradec Králové Czech Republic

STEINHAUER, BRUCE W., health facility administrator. CEO Lahey Hitchcock Clinic formerly Lahey Clinic, Burlington, Mass., 1992—. Office: Lahey Clinic Medical Ctr 41 Mall Rd Burlington MA 01805-0001*

STEINHEBER, FRANCIS ULRICH, physician; b. N.Y.C., Feb. 26, 1940; s. Ulrich and Hilda S. B.A., NYU, 1961, M.D., 1965. Intern Bellevue Hosp., 1965-66, resident, 1966-69; assoc. chief medicine USPHS, Staten Island, N.Y., 1965-71; chief, assoc. chief medicine Coney Island Hosp., Bklyn., 1971-80; chief gastrointestinal service, 1971—; asst. prof. clin. medicine NYU Sch. Medicine, 1975—. Author: Doctor's Guide to Growing Older, 1980; contbr. articles on aging and gastrointestinal tract to profl. jours. Served to lt. comdr. USPHS, 1969-71. Fellow ACP, Am. Coll. Gastroenterology; mem. Am. Gastroenterol Assn., Am. Soc. for GI Endoscopy. Roman Catholic. Avocations: music; environmental activities. Office: Coney Island Hosp 2601 Ocean Pkwy Brooklyn NY 11238

STEINHERZ, LAUREL JUDITH, pediatric cardiologist; b. N.Y.C., Jan. 5, 1947; d. Bernard and Adeline Weinberger; m. Peter Gustav Steinherz, July 4, 1967; children: Jennifer, Jonathan, Daniel, David. Student, Hebrew U., Jerusalem, 1966; BA with distinction, U. Rochester, 1967; MD, Albert Einstein Coll. Medicine, 1970. Diplomate Am. Bd. Pediatrics, sub-bd. pediatric cardiology. Intern in pediatrics N.Y. Hosp.-Cornell Med. Ctr., N.Y.C., 1970-71; pediatric cardiology fellow N.Y. Hosp. Cornell U. Med. Ctr., N.Y.C., 1973-75, asst. attending pediatrician, 1978-85, assoc. attending pediatrician, 1985—; resident in pediatrics St. Louis Children's Hosp., 1971-72; attending pediatrician State U. Hosp. and King County Med. Ctr., Bklyn., 1975-77; asst. prof. pediatrics Cornell U. Med. Coll., N.Y.C., 1977-85, assoc. prof. pediatrics, 1985—; from asst. to assoc. attending pediatrician Meml. Sloan Kettering Cancer Ctr., N.Y.C., 1977—, dir. pediatric cardiology, 1977—. Contbg. author: Adolescent Medicine II, 1976, Principles and Practice of Oncology, 1992; contbr. articles to profl. jours. Hutzler Found. grantee, 1987. Fellow Am. Acad. Pediatrics, Am. Coll. Cardiology; mem. Am. Heart Assn., N.Y. Acad. Sci., Children's Cancer Group (chair cardiology discipline com.). Office: Meml Sloan Kettering Cancer Ctr 1275 York Ave New York NY 10021-6007

STEINLING, MARC, nuclear medicine physician, researcher; b. Toulouse, France, Dec. 3, 1946. MD, Strasbourg, France, 1973; Specialist in Nuclear Medicine, Lille, France, 1975; PhD, Bordeaux, 1983. Asst. Ctr. Anti Cancereux, Strasbourg, France, 1972, U. Louis Pasteur, Strasbourg, France, 1972-74; asst. U. Lille (France) II, 1974-77, master of conf., 1977-94, prof., 1994—. Office: Centre Hospitalier Regional, 59037 Lille Cedex, France

STEINMAN, GARY DAVID, physician; b. Detroit, June 1, 1941; s. Morris and Mildred Steinman; children: Jessica, Allegra, Ahuvah, Schuyler, Moriah, Jeremiah, Breana. BS, Mich. State U., 1963, MS, 1963; PhD, U. Calif., 1965; MD, U. Miami, 1973. Diplomate Nat. Bd. Med. Examiners, Am. Bd. Ob-Gyn, Am. Bd. Forensic Medicine. Resident in ob-gyn Dept. Ob-Gyn Albert Einstein Affiliated Hosps., N.Y.C., 1974-77; pvt. practice Astoria, N.Y., 1977—; pres. David Diagnostics, Inc., Astoria, 1984—. Scholar Elks Nat. Found., 1959-60, Disting. Alumni scholar, 1959-63, Wheeler Found., 1963-64, NSF, 1964-66. Fellowship NSF, 1964-66, Wheeler Found., 1963-64; Disting. Alumni scholarship 1959-63, Elks Nat. Found. scholarship 1959-60. Office: 4601 Broadway Long Island City NY 11103-1627

STEINMAN, JOHN FRANCIS, psychiatrist; b. N.Y.C., May 5, 1916; s. David Barnard and Irene Stella (Hoffman) S.; m. Helen G. Meyer (div. 1963); children: James, Judith, Jill; m. Roxane Bear (div. 1972); m. Ellen M. Sears, Nov. 16, 1985. AB with hons., Columbia U., 1936, MD, 1940. Diplomate Am. Bd. Psychiatry and Neurology. Intern Strong Meml. Hosp., Rochester, N.Y. and Cin. Gen. Hosp., 1940-43; resident psychiatry Nebr. Psychiat. Inst., 1948, 58, R.I. Med. Ctr., 1961; psychiatrist, dir. Lincoln (Nebr.) and Lancaster County Child Guidance Ctr., 1948-61; instr. pediatrics, psychiatry and neurology U. Nebr., Lincoln, 1951-52; postdoctoral fellow in psychiatry Yale U., New Haven, Conn., 1962-64; psychiatrist U. Conn., Storrs, 1964-69, Community Mental Health Services, San Francisco, 1971-79; pvt. practice psychiatry San Francisco, 1979—. Delgate, chmn. Nebr. health com. White House Conf. Children and Youth, Washington, 1960. Served to capt. M.C., AUS, 1943-46, PTO. Mem. Am. Psychiat. Assn. (life), Am. Orthopsychiat. Assn., N.Y. Acad. Scis., Phi Beta Kappa. Home and Office: 164 Otsego Ave San Francisco CA 94112-2536

STEINMAN, LYNNE ANN, psychologist; b. N.Y.C., June 15, 1953; d. Alfred Maurice and Roslyn (Bennett) S. BS, U. Ill., Champaign, 1974; MA, U. So. Calif., 1978, PhD, 1982; postdoctoral, UCLA, 1986-88. lic. clin. psychologist, Calif. Pvt. practice psychology Los Angeles, 1980—; past clin. dir. adult svcs. Ingleside Hosp., Rosemead, Calif. Mem. Am. Psychol. Assn., Phi Kappa Phi. Office: 23504 Lyons Ave Ste 305 Santa Clarita CA 91321-2534

STEINMETZ, HELMUTH, neurologist; b. Cologne, Germany, Sept. 5, 1955; s. Thilo and Ingeborg (Dunker) S. MD, U. Giessen, 1983; privatdozent, U. Duesseldorf, 1991. Resident U. Tuebingen, 1984-87, U. Duesseldorf, 1987-89; asst. med. dir. neurology U. Duesseldorf, Duesseldorf, 1989—; Hermann and Lilly Schilling prof. neurology U. Duesseldorf, 1994. Author: Cerebral Asymmetry, 1991. With German Army, 1982-84. Office: U Düsseldorf, Moorenstr 5 Neurology Dept, D-40001 Düsseldorf Germany

STEINMETZ, JON DAVID, mental health executive, psychologist; b. N.Y.C., June 4, 1940; s. Lewis I. and Rose (Josefsberg) S.; m. Jane Audrey Hilton, Dec. 24, 1964; children: Jonna Lynn, Jay Daniel. BA, NYU, 1962; MA, Bradley U., 1963. Lic. psychologist, Ill. Intern in psychology Galesburg (Ill.) State Rsch. Hosp., 1963-64; staff psychologist Manteno (Ill.) State Hosp., 1964-68, program dir., 1968-70, asst. dir., 1970-72; dep. dir. Manteno Mental Health Ctr., 1972-80, Tinley Park (Ill.) Mental Health Ctr., 1980-88; dir. Chgo. Read Mental Health Ctr., 1988-91; ret., 1991; clin. dir. Jane Addams Hull House Assn., 1992—. Trustee Village of Park Forest, Cook and Will Counties, Ill.; officer, bd. dirs. various civic orgns., Park Forest. Home: 200 Hickory St Park Forest IL 60466-1016

STEINMETZ, SEYMOUR, pediatrician; b. Czechoslovakia, Oct. 6, 1934; s. Nathan and Gisela (Perl) S.; m. Ronnie P. Simons, June 24, 1973. BA, Yeshiva U., N.Y.C., 1956; MD, Albert Einstein Coll. Medicine, Bronx, N.Y., 1960. Diplomate Am. Bd. Pediatrics. Intern UCLA Hosp., L.A., 1960-61, resident pediatrician, 1961-62; chief resident pediatrician Montefiore Hosp., Bronx, N.Y., 1964-65; fellow in child psychiatry Jacobi Hosp., Bronx, N.Y., 1965-66; pvt. practice, Gt. Neck, N.Y., 1966-74; pvt. practice Fremont (Calif.) Pediatric Med. Group, 1974—, pres., 1984—. With USAF, 1962-64. With M.C., USAF, 1962-64. Fellow Am. Acad. Pediatrics. Office: Fremont Pediatric Med Group 3755 Beacon Ave Fremont CA 94538-1411

STEINWACHS, DONALD MICHAEL, public health educator; b. Boise, Idaho, Sept. 9, 1946; s. Don Peter and Emma Bertha (Weisshaupt) S.; m. Sharon Kay Carlson, Aug. 25, 1972. MS, U. Ariz., 1970; PhD, Johns Hopkins U., 1973. Asst. prof. health svcs. adminstrn. Johns Hopkins U., Balt., 1973-79, assoc. prof. health policy and mgmt., 1979-86, dir. Health Svcs. Rsch. & Devel. Ctr., 1982—, prof. health policy and mgmt., 1986—, chairperson health policy and mgmt., 1994—; sec. adv. com. Dept. Vets. Affairs, Washington, 1991-92; mem. Inst. Medicine, NAS, Washington, 1993—; bd. dirs. Health Outcomes Inst., Inc., Mathematica Policy Rsch., Inc. Contbr. articles to profl. jours. Mem. Gov.'s Commn. on Health Policy Rsch. and Fin., Md., 1988-90. Capt. U.S. Army, 1973. Grantee NIMH, Agy. for Health Care Policy and Rsch., Robert Wood Johnson Found. Mem. Ops. Rsch. Soc. Am., Assn. Health Svc. Rsch. (bd. dirs., pres.), Found. for Health Svc. Rsch. (bd. dirs., pres.). Office: Johns Hopkins U Dept Healthcare Policy & Mgmt 624 N Broadway Rm 482 Baltimore MD 21205-1996*

STEK, ROBERT JOSEPH, psychologist; b. Woodbridge, N.J., Oct. 23, 1948; s. Joseph and Ruth (Purkall) S.; m. Bonnie Eberle, July 27, 1991; children: Christopher, Ben, Ann. BS in Psychology, Rensselaer Poly. Inst., 1970; MS in Psychology, Ind. State U., 1972; PhD, U. Regina, Sask., 1978. Psychologist Wascana Hosp., Regina, 1973-74, Regina Mental Health Clinic, 1975-78; mgr. manpower and tng. Sask. Computer Utility Corp., Regina, 1978-80; psychologist PBS Assocs., Regina, 1980-84, Ctr. for Individual and Group Psychotherapy, Vernon, Conn., 1984-94, Conn. Dept. Corrections, Somers, 1985-87; dir. mental health program devel. Conn. Dept. Corrections, Hartford, 1987-93; dir. quality assurance Conn. Dept. of Mental Health, Middletown, 1993—. Editor: An Electronic Holmes Companion, 1987. Mem. Assn. for Transpersonal Psychology, Am. Soc. Psychical Rsch., Inst. Noetic Scis., Ancient Illuminated Seers of Bavaria. Home: 744 Shenipsit Lake Rd Tolland CT 06084-2020

STELLA, JOSEPH JAMES, physician, pharmacist; b. Pittston, Pa., July 31, 1962; s. Joseph Eugene and Claire (DeGregorio) S.; m. Lisa Ann Begliomini, July 9, 1988; children: Alyssa, Amanda. BS in Pharmacy, Temple U., 1985; DO, Phila. Coll Osteo. Medicine, 1991. Registered pharmacist, Pa. Pharmacist Wilkes-Barre (Pa.) Gen. Hosp., 1985-87; intern Allentown (Pa.) Osteo. Med. Ctr., 1991-92; resident in surgery Kennedy Meml. Hosp., Stratford, N.J., 1992-93; resident in anesthesia Thomas Jefferson Hosp., Phila., 1993-94; resident in surgery Suburban Gen. Hosp., Norristown, Pa., 1994—; mem. exec. com. Luzerne County Pharm. Assn., Wilkes-Barre, 1985-87. Recipient Richard Colarusso scholarship, 1990, Thomas Rowland award PCOM, 1991. Mem. AMA, Am. Osteo. Assn., Am. Coll. Osteo. Surgeons, Pa. Med. Soc., Pa. Osteo. Assn., Kappa Psi. Office: Suburban Gen Hosp 2701 DeKalb Pike Norristown PA 19401

STELLMAN, STEVEN DALE, epidemiologist; b. Toronto, May 7, 1945; s. Samuel David and Lillian (Mandlsohn) S.; m. Jeanne Esther Mager, Sept. 10, 1967; children: Andrew, Emma. BS in Chemistry, Ohio State U., 1966; PhD in Phys. Chemistry, NYU, 1971; MPH in Health Policy and Mgmt., Columbia U., 1992. Rsch. assoc. biochem. sci. Princeton (N.J.) U., 1971-73; lectr. in chemistry U. Colo., Denver, 1973-74; chief div. computing and biostats. Am. Health Found., N.Y.C., 1975-80, chief divsn. epidemiology, 1991—; asst. v.p. epidemiology Am. Cancer Soc., N.Y.C., 1980-88; asst. commr. biostat. and epidemiol. rsch. N.Y.C. Dept. Health, 1988-91; adj. assoc. prof. dept. cmty. medicine Mt. Sinai Sch. Medicine, N.Y.C., 1981—; 1981—; sci. cons. agt. orange vet. payment program U.S. Dist. Ct., Bklyn., 1985—; mem. adv. bd. pub. health grad. program Robert Wood Johnson Sch. Medicine, Piscataway, N.J., 1986—; cons. in epidemiology and biostats. Meml. Sloan-Kettering Cancer Ctr., N.Y.C., 1993—. Author Women and Cancer, 1986; editor Vital Stats. Summaries, N.Y.C., 1988-91; assoc. editor Women and Health, 1991—; contbr. articles to profl. publs.; co-author spl. issue Environ. Rsch., 1988. Condr. DeRossi singers Kane St. Synagogue. Fogarty Sr. Internat. fellow NIH, 1992-93. Mem. APHA, Am. Coll. Epidemiology, Soc. for Epidemiologic Rsch., Am. Chem. Soc. Democrat. Jewish. Home: 117 Saint Johns Pl Brooklyn NY 11217-3401 Office: Am Health Found 320 E 43rd St New York NY 10017-4816

STELLNER, HERBERT MARTIN, JR., health facility administrator; b. Aberdeen, S.D., Oct. 6, 1929; s. Herbert Martin and Maude (Lee) S.; m. Geraldine Edith Morris, June 11, 1960; children: Hilary Morris, Herbert Martin III, Winston Lee. AB, St. Olaf Coll., 1950; postgrad., Harvard U., 1950-51. Adminstr. Mayo Clinic, Rochester, Minn., 1952-58, IBM Corp., Rochester, 1958-69; broker Dain, Kalman & Quail, Rochester, 1969-71; asst. v.p. Marquette Bank, Rochester, 1971-72, v.p., 1972-77, sr. v.p., 1977-86; devel. officer Mayo Found., Rochester, 1986—; instr. Minn. Sch. Banking, Northfield, 1984, 86. Pres. Rochester Art Ctr., 1973-74; treas. Rochester Meth. Hosp. Found., 1977-86; vice chmn. Coll. St. Teresa, Winona, Minn. 1982-85, chmn. 1985-87; chmn. State of Minn. Higher Edn. Facilities Authority, St. Paul, 1983-84, Rochester Area Found., 1983-85; bd. adv. Rochester Ctr. Winona State U., 1988-91; trust com. Minn. Bankers Assn., 1985-86. Mem. Rochester Univ. Club (chmn. 1975-76), Vesterheim, Norwegian-Am. Hist. Assn., Torske Klubben Mpls., Phi Beta Kappa, Pi Gamma Mu. Lutheran. Home: 208 2nd Ave NW Kasson MN 55944-1452 Office: Mayo Found Rochester MN 55905

STELMACH, WALTER JACK, physician, medical education administrator; b. Kansas City, Kans., Mar. 7, 1926; s. Jacob and Stella (Wanchuk) S.; m. Patricia Ann Scherrer, June 19, 1948; children: Christopher Stephen, Cheryl Anne, Jeffrey David. BA, U. Mo.-Kansas City, 1949; MD, Kans. U.-Kansas City, 1953. Diplomate Am. Bd. Family Practice (bd. dirs. 1980-85, exec. com. 1980-82, pres. 1983). Intern St. Mary's Hosp. and Children's Mercy Hosp., Kansas City, Mo., 1953-54; practice family medicine Kansas City, Mo., 1954-74; clin. prof. medicine Sch. Medicine U. Mo., Kansas City, 1974—, asst. dean, chmn. council on evaluation, 1974-75, chmn. dept. community and family medicine Truman Med. Ctr., 1977-78; pres. med. staff Baptist Meml. Hosp., 1967-68, chmn. sect. gen. practice, 1969-71, dir. Family Practice Residency Program, 1974-93, chmn. Residency Assistance Program Project Bd., 1975-80; v.p. med. affairs Bapt. Med. Ctr., 1993-96; preceptor Sch. Medicine, U. Mo., Columbia; chmn. sect. family practice Research Hosp., 1969-71; participant Ditchley Park Conf. on Devel. of Health Services and Med. Care, Brit., Can., U.S., 1972; mem. Grad. Med. Edn. Nat. Adv. Com., 1976-80, chmn., 1976-78; bd. dirs. Council of Med. Splty. Socs., 1979-81, pres., 1980-81; chmn. Council for Med. Affairs, 1981. Contbr. articles to med. jours., presentations to profl. confs. Pres. Family Health Found. Am., 1980-85; trustee U. Mo., Kansas City, 1981. Served with USN, 1943-46. Recipient John G. Walsh award, 1981, Max Cheplove award, 1981, Alumni award U. Mo., Kansas City, 1981. Charter fellow Am. Acad. Family Physicians (del. 1969-74, mem. commn. on edn. 1971-76, chmn. 1974-75, 75-76, bd. dirs. 1974-77, chmn. bd. 1976-77, pres. 1978-79); mem. AMA, Mo. State Med. Assn. (del. 1964-73), Mo. Acad. Family Physicians (bd. dirs. 1966-69, pres. 1973-74), Kansas City Acad. Family Physicians (pres. 1965-66), Jackson County Med. Soc. (sec. 1960-61), Southwest Clin. Soc. (sec. 1967-68, bd. dirs. 1967-69, assoc. dir. clinics 1972-73), dir. clinics 1975), Kansas City Acad. Medicine, Kans. U. Med. Alumni (1st v.p. 1972-73), Alpha Omega Alpha. Mem. Unity Ch. Home: 5252 Sunset Dr Kansas City MO 64112-2356

STELOW, MARIE THERESE, mental health counselor; b. Joliet, Ill., Dec. 9, 1930; d. Frank W. and Marie M. (Stonich) Culik; m. William F. Stelow, Nov. 23, 1950; children: Marla, Melissa, Michelle, Melanie, Maureen, Miriam. AB, Joliet Jr. Coll., 1971; BA in English & Spanish magna cum laude, Coll. St. Francis, Joliet, 1971; MS in Counseling Psychology, George Williams Coll., Downers Grove, Ill., 1982. Nat. cert. counselor; lic. clin. profl. counselor, Ill. Tchr. English Joliet Cath. H.S., 1971-72; tchr. lang. arts St. Mary's Sch., Jr. H.S., Mokena, Ill., 1972-74; tchr. English and reading Plainfield (Ill.) H.S., 1974-79; co-dir. 1st Ch. Cmty. Counseling Ctr., Lombard, Ill., 1982-92; instr. social psychology Joliet Jr. Coll., 1991—; mental health counselor Healy & Assocs., Joliet, 1991—. Mem. ACA, Am. Mental Health Counselors Assn., Lambda Iota Tau. Democrat. Roman

Catholic. Home: 619 Shorewood Dr Shorewood IL 60431 Office: 121 Springfield Ave Joliet IL 60435

STEMMLER, EDWARD JOSEPH, physician, retired association executive, retired academic dean; b. Phila., Feb. 15, 1929; s. Edward C. and Josephine (Heitzmann) S.; m. Joan C. Koster, Dec. 27, 1958; children: Elizabeth, Margaret, Edward C., Catherine, Joan. B.A., La Salle Coll., Phila., 1950, Sc.D. (hon.), 1983; M.D., U. Pa., 1960; Sc.D. (hon.), Ursinus Coll., 1977, Phila. Coll. Pharmacy and Sci., 1989; L.H.D. (hon.), Rush U., 1986, Med. Coll. Pa., 1994; ScD (hon.), SUNY, Syracuse, 1994. Diplomate Am. Bd. Internal Medicine. Intern U. Pa. Hosp., 1960-61, med. resident, 1961-63, fellow in cardiology, 1963-64, chief med. resident, 1964-65, chief med. outpatient dept., 1966-67; chief of medicine U. Pa. Med. Svc., VA Hosp., Phila., 1967-73; mem. deans com. VA Hosp., 1974-88; instr. medicine Grad. Div. Medicine, U. Pa., 1964-66, NIH postdoctoral rsch. trainee, dept. physiology, 1965-67, assoc. in medicine, 1966-67; assoc. in physiology Grad. Div. Medicine, 1967-72, asst. prof. medicine, 1967-70, assoc. prof., 1970-74, prof., 1974—, Robert G. Dunlop prof., 1981-91, prof. emeritus, 1991—; assoc. dean Univ. Hosp. (Sch. Medicine), 1973, assoc. dean student affairs, 1973-75, acting dean, 1974-75, dean, 1975-88, dean emeritus, 1989—; exec. v.p. U. Pa. Med. Ctr., 1986-89; exec. v.p. Assn. Am. Med. Colls., 1990-94, sr. adv. to pres., 1994-95; mem. Nat. Bd. Med. Examiners, 1974-76, nominating and ad hoc governance coms., 1985, vice chmn., 1987-89, treas., 1989-91, chmn., 1991-95; mem. exec. com.; mem. ednl. policy com. Nat. Fund for Med. Edn., 1975-77; mem. deans com. VA Hosp., 1974-89; trustee Dorothy Rider Pool Healthcare Trust, 1991—, Ursinus Coll., 1991—, Wintergreen Nature Found., 1996—. Contbr. articles to profl. jours. Chmn. Pa. Deans Com., 1976-87; bd. govs. Mid-Ea. Regional Med. Libr. Svcs., 1977-81, chmn., 1978-81; bd. visitors U. Pitts. Sch. Medicine, 1980-85, U. Md. Sch. Medicine, 1991-94; mem. bd. overseers Dartmouth Med. Sch. and C. Everett Koop Inst., 1992—; mem. adv. com. dept. medicine U. Ala., Birmingham, 1985-89; mem. vis. com. Tufts U. Sch. Medicine, 1990-94, Med. U. S.C., 1990—, U. Calif., Davis, 1993—. Decorated Commendation medal; recipient Frederick A. Packard award, 1960, Albert Einstein Med. Ctr. staff award, 1960, Roche award, 1960. Master ACP (treas., chmn. investment com. 1975-80, Laureate award Ea. Pa. region 1986); mem. AMA (health policy agenda), Med. Soc. D.C., Inst. Medicine NAS, Assn. Am. Med. Colls. (ad hoc external exam. rev. com. 1980—, exec. coun. 1980—, coun. of deans adminstrv. bd. 1980—, chmn. 1983-84, nat. chmn.-elect 1985-86, chmn. assembly 1986-87), Coll. of Physicians of Phila. (bd. censors 1979-85, coun. 1979-85, 90-92), Am. Clin. and Climatological Soc., Alpha Omega Alpha. Republican. Mem. Christian Ch. Home: Rt #1 Box 676 Roseland VA 22967

STEMPEL, THOMAS K., surgeon; b. Homestead, Pa., Sept. 6, 1947. BA in Chemistry, Thiel Coll., 1969; MD, Temple U., 1973. Resident Baystate Med. Ctr., Springfield, Mass., 1973-77; chief surgery Phoenix Indian Med. Ctr., 1991—; sr. clinician in surgery Indian Health Svc., Rockville, Md., 1992—. Pres. Moon Valley Soccer Club, Phoenix, 1994—. With USPHS, 1977—. Fellow Am. Coll. Surgeons, Southwestern Surg. Congress; mem. USPHS Commd. Officers Assn. Office: Phoenix Med Ctr 4212 N 16th St Phoenix AZ 85016

STENCHEVER, MORTON ALBERT, physician, educator; b. Paterson, N.J., Jan. 25, 1931; s. Harold and Lena (Suresky) S.; m. Diane Bilsky, June 19, 1955; children: Michael A., Marc R., Douglas A. A.B., NYU, 1951; M.D., U. Buffalo, 1956. Intern Mt. Sinai Hosp., 1956-57; resident obstetrics and gynecology Columbia-Presbyn. Med. Center, N.Y.C., 1957-60; asst. prof., Oglebey research fellow Case-Western Res. U., Cleve., 1962-66; asso. prof. dept. reproductive biology Case-Western Res. U., 1967-70, dir. Tissue Culture Lab., 1965-70, coordinator Phase II Med. Sch. program, 1969-70; prof., chmn. dept. obstetrics-gynecology U. Utah Med. Sch., Salt Lake City, 1970-77; prof., chmn. dept. obstetrics-gynecology U. Wash. Sch. Medicine, Seattle, 1977-96, prof., 1977—; test com. chmn. for Ob-Gyn Nat. Bd. Med. Examiners, 1979-82. Author: Labor: Workbook in Obstetrics, 1968, 2d edit., 1993, Human Sexual Behavior: A Workbook in Reproductive Biology, 1970, Human Cytogenics: A Workbook in Reproductive Biology, 1973, Introductory Gynecology: A Workbook in Reproductive Biology, 1974; co-author: Comprehensive Biology, 1974; co-author: Comprehensive Gynecology, 1987, 2d edit., 1992, Caring for the Older Woman, 1991, 2d edit., 1996, Health Care for the Older Woman, 1996, Office Gynecology, 1992, 2d edit., 1996; assoc. editor Ob-Gyn., 1986—, Ob-Gyn. Survey; mem. editorial bd. Western Jour. Medicine; contbr. articles to profl. jours. Served to capt. USAF, 1960-62. Fellow Am. Coll. Obstetricians and Gynecologists (com. on residency edn. 1974-80, learning resource commn. 1980-86, vice chmn. 1982-83, chmn. prolog self-assessment program 1982-86, vice chair com. health care for the underserved women 1995—), Am. Assn. Obstetricians and Gynecologists, Am. Gynecol. Soc., Am. Soc. Ob-Gyn., Pacific Coast Ob-Gyn. Soc.; mem. AAAS, AMA, Assn. Profs. Gynecology and Obstetrics (chmn. steering com. teaching methodis in ob-gyn. 1970-79, v.p. 1975-76, pres. 1983-84, v.p. Found. 1986-87, pres. Found. 1987-91), Pacific N.W. Ob-Gyn. Soc., Wash. State Med. Assn., Seattle Gynec. Soc. (v.p. 1981, pres.-elect 1982, pres. 1982-83), Pacific Coast Ob-Gyn. Soc., Am. Soc. Human Genetics, Ctrl. Assn. Ob-Gyn., Soc. Gynecologic Investigation, Wash. State Obstet. Soc., Tissue Culture Assn., N.Y. Acad. Sci., Utah Ob-Gyn. Soc., Utah State Med. Assn., Teratology Soc., Am. Fertility Soc., Am. Bd. Ob-Gyn. (bd. dirs. 1988—, v.p. 1990-92, treas. 1992-96, chmn. 1996—, mem. resident rev. com. Ob-Gyn. 1993—, chmn. divsn. urogynocology of reconstructive pilvic surgery). Home: 8301 SE 83rd St Mercer Island WA 98040-5644 Office: U Wash Dept Ob-Gyn 1959 NE Pacific St Seattle WA 98195-0004

STENDAHL, ULF HERMAN, gynocologist, oncologist; b. Hammarby, Sweden, July 4, 1936; s. Bjorn and Sigrid Anna Maria (Balckman) S.; children: Måns Joakim, Johanna Maria; m. Kim Ohman, 1994; 1 child, Anna Elin Katarina. M.D., Uppsala U., Sweden, 1970, degree in Gynecol. Oncology, 1975, PhD, 1981. Specialist in Gynecol. Oncology. Clin. Dept. Gynecol. Oncology Univ. Hosp., Uppsala, Lund,, Sweden, 1971-84, head of dept., chmn., 1984-93; prof. gynecol. oncology Univ. Hosp., Umeå, Sweden, 1988—. Contbr. articles to profl. jours. Office: Dept Gynecology Oncology, Univ Hosp, 90185 Umeå Sweden

STENKVIST, BJÖRN GUNNAR, cytologist; b. Årjäng, Sweden, Mar. 27, 1934; s. Gösta C. and Elisabeth S. (Ivarsson) S.; m. Elisabeth C. Olding, June 13, 1959; children: Anna, Dag, Erik. MD, U. Uppsala, Sweden, 1962; PhD, U. Uppsala, 1966. Dir. cytology Univ. Hosp., Uppsala, 1967-85, Karolinska Inst., Stockholm, 1985—; sci. advisor Swedish Med. Bd., Stockholm, 1974—; project mgr. com. on cytology EEC, Brussels, 1984—; co-dir. collaborating ctr. WHO, Geneva, 1987—. Patentee automatic focusing device and cell preparation; contbr. articles to med. jours. Recipient Sairin Mehtari award, Indian Acad. Cytology, 1987. Fellow Internat. Acad. Cytology; mem. Coll. Am. Pathologists, Brit. Soc. Cytology (Ericha Wachtel award 1987). Lutheran. Home: Döbelnsgatan 13, 75237 Uppsala Sweden Office: Karolinska Inst and Hosp, 17176 Stockholm Sweden

STENSON, SUSAN MARY, ophthalmologist; b. Jersey City, Sept. 25, 1947; d. Joseph Neal and Anna Marie (Zimmerman) Stenson; m. Gary David Derish, Aug. 10, 1979. MD, Northwestern U., Chgo., 1970. Diplomate Am. Bd. Ophthalmology. Intern Temple U., Phila., 1970-71; resident in ophthalmology NYU, 1971-74, fellow in cornea/external disease, 1974-75; clin. prof. NYU Sch. Medicine, N.Y.C.; pvt. practice N.Y.C.; attending physician N.Y. Eye and Ear Infirmary, N.Y.C., Tisch Hosp., N.Y.C., Bellevue Hosp., N.Y.C., Cabrini Med. Ctr., N.Y.C. Editor: AIDS and the Eye, 1995, Surgical Management in External Disease of Eye, 1995. Mem. Am. Acad. Ophthalmologists (mem. coun., honor award 1986), Contact Lens Assn. Ophthalmologists (bd. dirs.). Office: 333 E 34th St Apt 1E New York NY 10016-4933

STENWICK, MICHAEL WILLIAM, internist, geriatric medicine consultant; b. Red Wing, Minn., Nov. 12, 1941; s. Vincent Ferdinand and Geraldine Frances (Veith) S.; m. Judith Ann Nelson, June 10, 1961; children: Scott Michael, Gregg William. BS cum laude, Hamline U., 1963; MD, U. Minn., 1969. Diplomate Am. Bd. Internal Medicine. Fellow dept. pharmacology U. Minn., Mpls., 1966-68; intern in internal medicine Northwestern Hosp., Mpls., 1969-70, resident in internal medicine, 1970-73; sr. internist internal medicine sect. Bloomington Lake Clinic, Mpls., 1973—; bd. dirs. Bloomington Lake Clinic, Mpls., pres. 1977, v.p. 1989—, fin. com., 1987—, chmn. properties, 1984—, chmn. trustees profit sharing; med. adviser Kimberly Quality Care, St. Paul, 1990-94; internal medicine cons. Fairview Multiple Sclerosis Ctr. and Rehab. Unit, Mpls., 1986—; informal adviser internal medicine sect. Minn. Relative Value Index, Mpls., 1971; mem. task force Riverside Med. Ctr., Mpls., 1988-91, chmn. critical care com., 1986-91, reviewer quality assurance subcom., 1989-90. Contbr. articles to profl. jours. Mem., co-organizer, 1st pres. Cyrus Barnum Soc., U. Minn. Med. Sch., Mpls.; bd. dirs. Signal Inn Beach and Racquetball Club, Sanibel Island, Fla., 1983-84, 89—, Signal Inn Condominium Assn., Sanibel Island, 1983-84, 89—; co-emcee Nursing Talent Show, Northwestern Hosp., Mpls., 1969; 1st med. dir. Beltrami Health Ctr., Mpls., 1970-72. Recipient scholarship Charles and Alora Allis Found., 1960-63, Walter Kenyon award, 1963, grant U. Minn., 1963. Fellow Am. Coll. Physicians; mem. AMA, Am. Soc. Internal Medicine, Minn. Med. Assn., Hennepin County Med. Assn., Mpls. Soc. Internal Medicine. Republican. Lutheran. Office: Bloomington Lake Clinic 3017 Bloomington Ave Minneapolis MN 55407-1715

STENZEL, KURT HODGSON, physician, nephrologist, educator; b. Stamford, Conn., Nov. 3, 1932; s. Alfred B. and Aurelie C. (Hodgson) S.; m. Carolyn Briggs, Dec. 21, 1957; children—Matthew, Jennifer, Mary. BA magna cum laude, N.Y. U., 1954; M.D., Cornell U., 1958. Intern Bellevue Hosp., N.Y.C., 1958-59; resident, 1959-60, 62-63; asst. in medicine Cornell U. Med. Coll., N.Y.C., 1959-60; asst. prof. medicine Cornell U. Med. Coll., 1965-68, asso. prof. biochemistry and surgery, 1969-75, prof. biochemistry, medicine and surgery, 1976—, chief div. nephrology (medicine), 1979-92, dir. Rogosin Kidney Ctr., 1970—; attending physician, surgeon N.Y. Hosp., N.Y.C., 1976—; Diplomate Am. Bd. Internal Medicine and Nephrology. contbr. articles to profl. publs. Served to lt., M.C. USNR, 1960-62. Recipient Nat. Kidney Found. Hoenig award for excellence in renal medicine. Fellow ACP; mem. Am. Soc. Biol. Chemists, Am. Soc. Nephrology, Transplantation Soc., Am. Fedn. Clin. Research, Am. Assn. Immunologists, Am. Soc. for Artificial Internal Organs, Phi Beta Kappa. Office: The Rogosin Inst 505 E 70th St New York NY 10021

STEPHANI, NANCY JEAN, social worker, journalist; b. Garden City, Mich., Feb. 19, 1955; d. Ernest Helmut Schulz and Margaret Mary Fowler Thompson; m. Edward Jeffrey Stephani, Aug. 29, 1975; children: Edward J., Margaret J., James E. AA, Northwood Inst., Midland, Mich., 1975; student in theology, Boston Coll., 1991; BS summa cum laude, Lourdes Coll., Sylvania, Ohio, 1992; MSW, Ohio State U., 1995. Lic. social worker. Profl. facilitator Parents United, Findlay, Ohio, 1989-94; contbg. writer Cath. Chronicle, Toledo, 1988-95; mem. ministry formation faculty Cath. Diocese of Toledo, 1992-96, mem. accreditation com., ministry formation program, 1996-97; crisis intervention specialist John C. Hutson Ctr., 1994—; social work clinician Family Svc. Hancock County, Blanchard Valley Home Health Social Svc.; trustee, bd. dirs. Hope House for the Homeless, Findlay, 1990—, v.p. 1996-97; adult edn. coord. St. Michael Parish, Findlay, 1986-93, mem. strategic plan core com., 1989-91, v.p., pres. parish coun., 1985-89; program planning com. Family Life Conf., Cath. Diocese, 1994-95, mem. accreditation com. ministry formation dept.; profl. facilitator Hope Plus Program through Hancock County Common Pleas Ct., 1996—. Founder Food Coop., MPBA, Findlay, 1981; founding mem. Chopin Hall, Findlay, 1983; mem. Hancock County AIDS Task Force, 1994—; strategic planning com. mem., co-chair goal setting com. Findlay Pub. Schs., 1994. Nat. Inst. Food Svcs. grantee, 1974; Diocese of Toledo grantee, 1991; Ohio State U. Coll. Social Work grantee, 1994. Mem. NOW, NASW, Am. Assn. on Child Abuse, Transpsychol. Assn., Friends of Creation Spirituality, Cognitive/Behavioral Profl. Soc., Call to Action, Pax Christi. Home: 2615 Goldenrod Ln Findlay OH 45840-1025

STEPHANICK, CAROL ANN, dentist, consultant; b. South Amboy, N.J., Feb. 5, 1952; d. Edward Eugene and Gladys (Pionkowski) S. BS, Rutgers U., 1974; MS, Med. Coll. Pa., 1980; DMD, Temple U., 1984. Lic. dentist, Pa., N.J., Vt. Med. technologist Jersey Shore Med. Ctr., Neptune, N.J., 1975-76, South Amboy Meml. Hosp., 1976-78, Smith-Kline Clin. Labs., King of Prussia, Pa., 1981; instr. dept. biology St. Peter's Coll., Jersey City, 1976-78; instr., edn. coord. Coll. Allied Health, Hahnemann U., Phila., 1978-80; instr. dept. oral radiology Sch. Dentistry, Temple U., Phila., 1984-87; assoc. dentist Personal Choice Dental Assocs., South Amboy, 1985-86, Marcucci and Marcucci, P.C., Phila., 1986-90, Gwynedd Dental Assocs., Springhouse, Pa., 1990-92; spl. events coord. Liberty Dental Conf., Phila., 1990—. Neighbor patrol Sprague St. Neighbors Town Watch, Phila., 1986-93. Named to Legion of Honor, Chapel of Four Chaplains, 1987. Mem. ADA, Pa. Dental Assn., Philadelphia County Dental Soc. (publicity coord. 1990—, pub. info. coord. 1991, semi-finalist judge sr. smile contest 1990—, com. on concerns of women dentists, select com. 1988—), Delaware Valley Assn. Women Dentists, Am. Assn. for Functional Orthodontics, Am. Soc. Clin. Pathologists (med. technologist), Delta Sigma Delta. Roman Catholic. Home: PO Box 386 Haddonfield NJ 08033-0310 Office: 777 White Horse Pike S Hammonton NJ 08037-2029

STEPHEN, RICHARD JOSEPH, oral and maxillofacial surgeon; b. Joliet, Ill., Jan. 2, 1945; s. Joseph E. and Marcella M. (Pearson) S.; children: Anne, Susan, George. Student, Lewis U., Lockport, Ill., 1962-65; DDS, Loyola U., Chgo., 1969; Cert. in Oral and Maxillofacial Surgery, Loyola U., Maywood, Ill., 1972. Practice dentistry specializing in oral and maxillofacial surgery Mt. Vernon, Ill., 1972—; cons. Ill. Cancer Council, Chgo., 1979—; Centralia (Ill.) Correctional Facility, 1980—, Vandalia (Ill.) Correctional Facility, 1980—. Fellow Am. Coll. Stomatologic Surgeons, Am. Coll. Oral and Maxillofacial Surgeons, Am. Soc. Oral and Maxillofacial Surgeons, Am. Dental Soc. of Anesthesiology, Internat. Assn. Oral Surgery, Internat. Assn. Maxillofacial Surgery, Lions, Elks. Home: RR 5 Box 226 Mount Vernon IL 62864-9323 Office: 2413 Broadway St # 582 Mount Vernon IL 62864-2917

STEPHENS, BRYON JOHN, surgeon; b. East Chicago, Ind., Feb. 22, 1961; s. Richard Penn and Sylvia S.; m. Inga Maria Rice, June 16, 1990; children: Rachel Elizabeth, Andrea Nicole. BS, Wabash Coll., 1983; MD, Ind. U., 1987. Diplomate Am. Bd. Surgery. Intern, then resident Saginaw (Mich.) Coop. Hosps., Inc., 1987-92; ptnr. Northeast Ind. Surgeons, Ft. Wayne, 1992-95, Ind. Surg. Specialists, Ft. Wayne, 1995—. Contbr. articles to profl. jours. Fellow Am. Coll. Surgeons; mem. Midwest Surg. Assn., Ind. State Med. Assn., Ft. Wayne Med. Soc. Office: Ind Surg Specialists 7900 W Jefferson Ste 304 Fort Wayne IN 46804

STEPHENS, CALVIN WELDON, pharmacist; b. Birmingham, Ala., Nov. 13, 1948; s. Calvin Coolidge and Dorothy Sue (Burttram) S.; Marilyn Kay Maxwell, Mar. 18, 1972; children: Jon Maxwell, Joseph Weldon. BS in Chemistry, U. Ala., Tuscaloosa, 1971; BS in Pharmacy, Auburn U., 1973. Pharmacy intern Vestavia (Ala.) Drugs, 1973-74; pharmacy intern Reynolds Pharmacy, Homewood, Ala., 1974-75, staff pharmacist, 1975-76; staff pharmacist Miller Drug Co., Oneonta, Ala., 1976-77; staff pharmacist, asst. mgr. Harco Drug Co., Northport, Ala., 1977-80, store mgr., pharmacist, 1980—; com. mem. Sub-Com. on Continuing Edn. State Bd. of Pharmacy, Birmingham, 1985-86. Mem. Ala. Pharm. Assn. (bd. trustees 1993—), Am. Pharm. Assn., Auburn Pharmacy Alumni Assn., Kappa Psi, Rho Chi. Methodist. Office: Harco Drug #205 2300 McFarland Blvd Northport AL 35476

STEPHENS, DEBORAH LYNN, health facility executive; b. Newton, Iowa, May 30, 1952; d. Clarence Harry and Nancy Elizabeth (Gass) Wright; m. David K. Brender, Dec. 18, 1971 (div.); m. Michael E. Stephens, May 21, 1988 (div.). BS, U. Iowa, 1974; postgrad., U. Wis., Milw., 1978-80, U. Calif., Berkeley, 1987. Asst. to dean of fin. U. Iowa Coll. Medicine, Iowa City, 1975-77; contract audit acct. Miller Brewing Co., Milw., 1977-79; asst. controller Unicare Health Facilities, Milw., 1979-81; v.p. fin. Sacred Heart Rehab. Hosp., Milw., 1981-84; exec. v.p., chief operating officer Sacred Heart Rehab. Hosp., Med. Rehab. Inst., Milw., 1984-88; prin. founding mem., pres., chief exec. officer Behavioral Health Systems, Birmingham, Ala., 1989—, also bd. dirs.; cons. on rehab., fin., multi-corp. planning and zero-base budgeting, Birmiingham, 1988; founding mem. Am. Rehab. Network, Inc., Washington, 1986-87; mem. oral exam. bd. City of Milw., 1984-86, Jefferson County, Ala., 1995; mem. prospective payment adv. com. HHS, Washington, 1986; nat. presenter on zero-base budgeting, cor. reorgns., managed care, and planning. Contbr. articles to profl. jours. Mem. healthcare cost containment com. Bus. Coun. Ala., Rotary Club of Birmingham. Named One of Top 5 Thriving Bus. Women in Birmingham, Bus. to Bus., 1995; featured in Healthwatch, Open Minds, Birmingham Post Herald, Birmingham News. Mem. Hosp. Fin. Mgmt. Assn. (governing bd. 1981-88), Nat. Forensic League (life), Nat. Assn. Accts., Nat. Assn. Rehab. Facilities (prospective payment adv. bd. 1986-88, com. on med. oriented facilities 1983-88), Ga. Managed Care Assn. (bd. dirs. 1995), Birmingham C. of C. (Small Bus. Person of Yr. award 1995), Venture Club, Kappa Kappa Gamma. Office: Behavioral Health Systems 2 Metroplex Dr Ste 503 Birmingham AL 35209-6827

STEPHENS, MICHAEL MASSY, orthopaedic surgeon; b. Dublin, Ireland, Feb. 8, 1951; s. Patrick Horace and Audrey (Pim) S.; m. Juliet Kathleen Ensor, June 6, 1977; children: Linda, Wendy, Nigel. Student, St. Columbas Coll., Dublin, Ireland, 1964-69, De La Salle Coll., Waterford, 1969-70; MSc, U. Strathclyde, Glasgow, Scotland, 1984; dipl. obstetrics, Royal Coll. Surgeons, Dublin, 1981. Sr. registrar Dublin Scheme, 1984-87; sr. lectr. Hong Kong U., 1987; fellow foot surgery U. Cin., 1988; cons. Dublin, 1989—; cons., dir. foot clinic Mater Misericordae Hosp., Cappagh Orthopaedic Hosp., Children's Hosp., Ctrl. Remedial Clinic, Dublin, 1989—. Contbg. author: Foot in Diabetes, 1991; author: Foot and Ankle Manual, 1991; mem. editl. bd. The Foot, Foot Diseases, European Jour. Foot and Ankle Surgery. Fellow Robert Jones and Agneshunt Hosp., Shropshire, U.K., 1981-82. Fellow Royal Coll. Surgeons (Ireland), Brit. Assn. Clin. Anatomists, European Soc. Foot and Ankle Surgeons (founder, v.p. 1992—), Brit. Orthopaedic Assn.; mem. Brit. Orthopaedic Foot and Ankle Surg. Soc., Irish Orthopaedic Assn. (sec. 1990—), Am. Orthopaedic Foot and Ankle Soc. (hon.). Office: Mater Pvt Hosp, Eccles St Ste 8, Dublin 7, Ireland

STEPHENS, SHERYL LYNNE, family practice physician; b. Huntington, W.Va., Dec. 11, 1949; d. William Clayton Stephens and Virginia Eleanor (Hatten) Stephens Terry; 1 child, William Earl Hicks III (dec.); m. Lannie Dale Rowe, Jan. 17, 1981; 1 child, Seton Christopher. BA, U. Ky., 1972; MA, Marshall U., 1982, MD, 1988. Tchr. Wayne County Bd. Edn., Ceredo, W.Va., 1973-83; real estate developer Huntington, 1981-88; resident in family practice Grant Med. Ctr., Columbus, Ohio, 1988-91; gen. practice physician Columbus (Ohio) Health Dept., 1991—; med. dir. Billie Brown Jones Family Health Ctr., 1992—; sch. physician Columbus Bd. Edn., 1994—; med. dir. St. Stephens Health Care Ctr., Columbus, 1995—; chairperson Coll. Health Dept. Com. on Pharmacy and Therapeutics, 1994—; rschr., 1976-81. Counselor, instr. Contact of Huntington, 1975-88; polit. activist pro choice movement and ratification of equal rights amemdment, 1976-81. Recipient Leadership award Marshall U., 1985. Mem. Am. Assn. Family Practitioners (pres. 1984-85, Leadership award 1985), Am. Med. Women's Assn. (sec. 1985-86), NOW (pres. 1976-78, 79-81, v.p. Huntington 1978-79, sec. 1981-82), Nat. Abortion Rights Action League. Democrat. Home: 9323 McCord Rd Orient OH 43146 Office: Columbus Health Dept 181 S Washington Ave Columbus OH 43215-5327 Office: St Stephens Health Care Ctr 1824 Cleveland Ave Columbus OH 43211

STEPHENS, SUSAN ELLEN, orthopaedic surgeon; b. Washington, Sept. 14, 1960; d. Timothy Leonard and Consuelo Maria (Sousa) S. BA, Princeton U., 1982; MD, U. Pa., 1986. Diplomate Am. Acad. Orthopaedic Surgery. Intern UCLA, L.A., 1986-87, resident, 1987-91; orthopaedic surgeon assocs. in ORthopaedics, Cleve., 1992—; staff mem., clin. teaching staff St. Luke's Hosp., Cleve., 1992; assoc. staff Meridia Huron Hosp., East Cleveland, Ohio, 1992, courtesy staff St. Vincent Charity Hosp., Cleve., 1992, Mt. Sinai Hosp., Cleve., 1994, Bedford (Ohio) Med. Ctr., 1994; researcher in field. Contbr. articles to profl. jours. Trustee Ctr. Families & Children, Cleve., 1995—, Campbell Court Retirement Ctr., Cleve., 1994—, Stopping AIDS Is My Mission, Cleve., 1993—, Hauken Sch. Alumnae Assn., Cleve., 1993. Spine fellow Cleve. Clinic Found., 1991-92. Mem. AMA, Nat. Med. Assn., N.Am. Spine Soc., Ohio Orthopaedic Soc., Cleve. Orthopaedic Club, Acad. Medicine Cleve., Ruth Jackson Soc., U. Pa. Med. Sch. Alumni Assn., Princeton U. Alumni Assn. Office: Assocs in Orthopaedics 11201 Shaker Bldg #304 Cleveland OH 44104

STEPHENSON, JOSEPH ELMER, surgeon; b. Pikeville, Ky., Oct. 3, 1917; s. Elmer D'Ester and Emabel (Bennett) S.; A.B., U. Ky., 1939; M.D., U. Louisville, 1942; m. Juanita Jeanice (Polly) Floyd, Dec. 30, 1939; children—Joseph Floyd, John Wesley, James Gibbs Rich. Diplomate Am. Bd. Surgery. Intern Charity Hosp. La., New Orleans, 1942-43; practice medicine, Elkhorn City, Ky., 1946-51; resident div. grad. medicine Tulane U. Med. Sch., 1951-54, fellow in gen. surgery Ochsner Found. Hosp. and Clinic, 1951-54; sr. surg. resident Lallie Kemp Charity Hosp., Independence, La., 1954-55; practice medicine specializing in gen. surgery, Ashland, Ky., 1956-83. Served to capt. M.C., USAAF, 1943-46. Fellow ACS; mem. Ky. Med. Soc., AMA, Boyd County Med. Soc., Ochsner Surg. Soc., Ky. Hist. Soc. (life), Sigma Chi (life), Alpha Kappa Kappa, Alpha Omega Alpha. Author 2 books. Home: 2726 Cumberland Ave Ashland KY 41102-4547

STEPHENSON, LINDA SUSAN, medical and surgical nurse, naval officer; b. Olathe, Kans., Sept. 5, 1962; d. Samuel Baker and Barbara Joan (Armstrong) Holt; m. David Maurice Stephenson, Oct. 27, 1985; children: Timothy, Christopher. BA in Psychology, Eastern Nazarene Coll., Quincy, Mass.; BSN, U. Mass., Dartmouth. RN, Mass. Nurse tech. St. Luke's Hosp., New Bedford, Mass., 1993-94; RN U.S. Navy Nurse Corps Naval Hosp., Camp Lejeune, N.C., 1994—; coord. staff edn. med.-surg. ward Naval Hosp., Camp Lejeune, 1994—. Vol. disaster nurse ARC, Jacksonville, N.C., 1995. With USN, 1984—. Mem. Sigma Theta Tau.

STEPHENSON, SAMUEL EDWARD, JR., physician; b. Bristol, Tenn., May 16, 1926; s. Samuel Edward and Hazel Beatrice (Walters) S.; m. Janet Sue Spotts, May 16, 1970; children: Samuel Edward III, William Douglas, Dorothea Louise, Judith Maria. BS, U. S.C., 1946; MD, Vanderbilt U., 1950. Intern Butterworth Hosp., Grand Rapids, Mich., 1950-51; instr. to asso. prof. surgery Vanderbilt U., 1955-67; prof. surgery U. Fla., 1967-95, emeritus prof. clin. surgery, 1995—; chmn. dept. surgery Univ. Hosp., Jacksonville, 1967-78. Asst. editor So. Med. Jour., 1968-88; contbr. articles to profl. jours. Co-chmn. Fla. Burn and Trauma Registry, 1974-77. Served with USNR, 1944-45. Fellow A.C.S.; mem. Am. Coll. Chest Physicians. Mason. Club: University (Jacksonville). Home: 10553 Scott Mill Rd Jacksonville FL 32257-6227 Office: 1501 San Marco Blvd Jacksonville FL 32207-2905

STEPITA, DONALD SCOTT, plastic surgeon, educator; b. Gary, Ind., Sept. 25, 1946; s. Michael and Mary Louise (Darling) S.; m. Helen Smith, Sept. 1, 1971 (div. Dec. 1995); children: Meredith Elizabeth, Ashley Brooke, Michael Scott. AB in Chemistry, Ind. U., Bloomington, 1968; MD, Ind. U., Indpls., 1971. Diplomate Am. Bd. Plastic Surgery. Intern in surgery Ind. U. Hosps., Indpls., 1971-72, resident, 1972-73; resident Ochsner Found. Hosp., New Orleans, 1973-75; resident in plastic surgery Baylor Coll. Medicine, Houston, 1975-77; pvt. practice, Chevy Chase, Md., 1979—; assoc. prof. surgery Uniformed Svcs. U., Bethesda, Md., 1979—. Chmn. camp svcs. com. YMCA Camp Letts, Edgewater, Md., 1994—; vice chmn. Montgomery County (Md.) Commn. on Health 1995—. Maj. M.C., U.S. Army, 1977-79. Recipient gov.'s citation State of Md., 1993. Mem. Am. Soc. Plastic and Reconstructive Surgeons, Nat. Capital Soc. Plastic Surgeons (pres. 1991), Med. and Chirurg. Faculty Md. (counselor 1991-93), Montgomery County Med. Soc. (pres. 1994), Rotary (bd. dirs. Friendship Heights, Md. 1991—). Republican. Office: 5530 Wisconsin Ave Chevy Chase MD 20815

STEPKA, WILLIAM, pharmacologist, educator; b. Veseli, Minn., Apr. 13, 1917; s. John J. and Mary (Jasan) S.; m. Bonnie Gene Thomas, July 15, 1948; 1 child, Donald Thomas. BA, U. Rochester, 1946; PhD, U. Calif., Berkeley, 1951. Grad. teaching asst. U. Rochester, 1946-47; grad. rsch. asst. U. Calif., Berkeley, 1948-49; rsch. assoc. U. Pa., Phila., 1951-54, ass.t prof. botany, 1954-55; sr. scientist The Am. Tobacco Co., Richmond, Va., 1955-68; asst. prof. rsch. physiology Med. Coll. Va., Richmond, Va., 1955-60; assoc. prof. rsch. physiology Med. Coll. Va., Richmond, 1960-67, assoc. prof. rsch. pharmacology, 1967-68; prof. pharmacognosy Va. Commonwealth U., Richmond, 1968-82, prof. emeritus, 1982—; cons. Va. Commonwealth U., 1982—, chmn. Sch. Pharmacy Reaccreditation Com., 1977, 82, 88, radiation safety com., 1955-82. Contbr. articles to profl. jours., chpts. to books. Magisterial rep. Henrico County Dem. Com., 1988-94; lobbyist Faculty Interests and Higher Edn. in Va., 1979—. 1st lt. USAAF, 1943-46. AEC predoctoral fellow, 1949-51. Mem. AAUP (chair com. on pub. affairs 1978, pres. Va. conf. 1991), Sigma Xi, Rho Chi. Democrat. Home and Office: 715 Glendale Dr Richmond VA 23229-6409

STEPTOE, ANDREW PATRICK ARTHUR, psychologist, educator; b. London, Apr. 24, 1951; s. Patrick Christopher and Sheena Macleod Steptoe; m. Jane Furneux Horncastle, 1980 (div. 1984); 1 child, William; m. Jane Wardle, 1991; 1 child, Matthew. BA, Cambridge (Eng.) U., 1972, MA, 1976; DPhil, Oxford (Eng.) U., 1976, DSc, 1995. Rsch. lectr. Christ Ch., Oxford U., 1975-77; lectr. St. George's Hosp. Med. Sch., U. London, 1977-81, sr. lectr., 1981-87, reader, 1987-88, prof. psychology, 1988—. Author: Psychological Factors in Cardiovascular Disorders, 1981, Essential Psychology for Medical Practice, 1988, The Mozart - Da Ponte Operas, 1988; editor: Psychosocial Processes and Health, 1994, Brit. Jour. of Health Psychology, 1995—; assoc. editor Annals of Behavioral Medicine, 1991—, Psychophysiology, 1982-86. Fellow Brit. Psychol. Soc.; mem. Internat. Soc. Behavioral Medicine (pres. 1994-96), Soc. for Psychosomatic Rsch. (pres. 1983-85), Swedish Soc. Behavioral Medicine (hon.). Office: St George's Hosp Med Sch, Cranmer Terr, London SW17 0RE, England

STERIOFF, SYLVESTER, surgeon; b. St. Louis, Jan. 19, 1938; s. Sylvester and Jessie (Gitcho) S.; children: Andrew, Kathleen Gabrielle, Alexander; m. Yvonne Carey, Sept. 14, 1991. AB, Harvard U., 1959; MD, Washington U., 1963. Intern, resident U. Hosps. of Cleve., 1963-68; transplant and gen. surgeon Johns Hopkins Med. Inst., Balt., 1970-76; transplant and gen. surgeon, prof. surgery Mayo Clinic, Rochester, Minn., 1976—, also mem. bd. govs., 1995—; bd. dirs. The Partnership, Boston, LifeSource, St. Paul. Contbr. numerous articles to profl. jours. Vol. physician and surgeon AmeriCares, Croatia, Kenya, Tanzania, 1991—. Major USAF, 1968-70. Mem. Am. Surg. Assn. Office: Mayo Clinic 200 First St SW Rochester MN 55905

STERN, BARNEY JOEL, neurologist; b. N.Y.C., July 11, 1949; s. Leo and Henny (Cohnen) S.; m. Elyce Geller, Jan. 26, 1975; children: Rachel, Melissa, Jamie. BS, CUNY, 1970; MD, U. Rochester, 1974. Diplomate Am. Bd. Neurology. Intern Boston City Hosp., 1974-75, resident in internal medicine, 1975-76; resident neurology Strong Meml. Hosp., Rochester, N.Y., 1976-79; assoc. prof. neurology Johns Hopkins U., Balt., 1988; dir. divsn. neurology Sinai Hosp., Balt., 1990-94; chief clin. svcs. dept. neurology, prof. neurology Emory U., Atlanta, 1994—. Fellow Am. Acad. Neurology; mem. Am. Neurol. Assn. Office: Emory U Hosp Ste C296D 1364 CLifton Rd NE Atlanta GA 30322

STERN, CLAUDIO DANIEL, medical educator, embryological researcher; b. Montevideo, Uruguay, Feb. 9, 1954; came to U.S., 1994; s. Erico and Trude Stern. BSc with honors, U. Sussex, 1975, DPhil, 1978; MA, U. Oxford, 1985, DS, 1994. Asst. prof. anatomy dept. Cambridge (England) U., 1984-85; assoc. prof. dept. human anatomy U. Oxford (England), 1985-93; prof., chmn. dept. genetics and devel. Coll. Physicians and Surgeons Columbia U., N.Y.C., 1994—. Contbr. articles to profl. jours.; mng. editor Mechanisms of Devel.; mem. editorial adv. bd. Devel.; mem. editorial bd. Internat. Jour. Devel. Biology. Rsch. fellow U. Coll. London, 1978-84, fellow Christ Ch. Coll., 1985-93. Office: Columbia U Dept Genetics & Devel 701 W 168th St New York NY 10032

STERN, DARRYL R., psychiatrist; b. Milw., June 6, 1942; s. Jack and Viola (Newman) S.; m. Helen B. Sheps, Jan. 22, 1966; children: Ariann N., Miles B. BS, U. Wis., 1963, MD, 1967. Diplomate Am. Bd. Psychiatry and Neurology. Resident in psychiatry U. Wis. dept. Psychiatry, Madison, 1968-71; dir. Mental Health Clinic, Camelback Hosp. Mental Health Ctr., Scottsdale, Ariz., 1973-75; pvt. practice medicine specializing in psychaitry Tempe, Ariz., 1975—; cons. Camelback Hosp. Day Trtmt. Program, Scottsdale, 1985-87; chmn. dept. psychiatry Desert Samaritan Hosp., Mesa, Ariz., 1987-89; med. dir. geropsychiatry Mesa Luth. Hosp., 1994—; med. dir. adult svcs. Desert Vista Hosp., Mesa, 1987—. Maj. USAF, 1971-73. Mem. AMA, Am. Psychiatric Assn., Am. Assn. Geriatric Psychiatry, Am. Acad. Psychiatrists in Alcoholism and Addictions. Office: 2034 E Southern Ave Tempe AZ 85282-7522

STERN, DONALD R., state commissioner, public health service officer. Commr. Va. Dept. Health, Richmond. Office: State of Va Health Dept 1500 E Main St Richmond VA 23219-3634

STERN, JASON ADAM, hematologist, oncologist; b. Detroit, Jan. 26, 1963; s. Edward L. and Betty (Wiener) S.; m. Patricia L. Bias, June 4, 1993; children: Jonathan, Michael. BS in Biology, Wayne State U., 1985; DO, Kirksville Coll. Osteo. Med., 1989. Diplomate Am. Bd. Internal Medicine. Intern Detroit Osteopathic Hosp., Highland Park, Mich., 1989; resident Cleve. Clinic Found., 1990-93; fellow Henry Ford Hosp., Detroit, 1993—. Home: 10776 Howard Dr Chardon OH 44024 Office: Hillcrest Hosp 6780 Mayfield Rd Mayfield Heights OH 44124

STERN, JOHN ALAN, vascular surgeon; b. Pitts., Oct. 27, 1956; s. George and Marian (bradlin) S.; m. Randal Chalik, Nov. 12, 1983; children: Leslie Ann, Gregory Alan, Thomas Joseph. BA in Natural Sci., Johns Hopkins U., 1978; MD, St. Louis U., 1982. Diplomate in gen. surgery and vascular surgery Am. Bd. Surgery. Intern and resident in gen. surgery St. Louis Univ. Group Hosps., 1982-88; fellow in vascular surgery U. Iowa Hosps., Iowa City, 1988-90; dir. vascular lab. Mercy Hosp., Des Moines, 1990—, chief surg. svc., 1994—; adj. asst. prof. surgery Univ. Osteo. Medicine, Des Moines, 1993—. Recipient scholarship and awards. Fellow ACS, Soc. Clin. Vascular Surgery; mem. AMA, Iowa Med. Soc., Polk County Med. Soc., Iowa Acad. Surgery, Soc. Vascular Tech., Iowa Vascular Surgery Soc. Office: Surg Affiliates PC 411 Laurel Ste 2100 Des Moines IA 50314

STERN, JUDITH S., nutritional researcher, educator; b. Bklyn.; d. Sidney and Lillian (Rosen) Schneider; m. Richard C. Stern; 1 child, Daniel Arthur. BS, Cornell U., 1964; MS, Harvard U. Sch. Pub. Health, 1966, ScD, 1970. Research asst. dept. food sci. and nutrition MIT, Cambridge, 1964-65; research assoc. dept. human behavior and metabolism, The Rockefeller U., N.Y.C., 1969-72, asst. prof. dept. human behavior and metabolism, 1972-74; contbg. editor Vogue Mag., Conde Nast Publs., N.Y.C., 1974; asst. prof. nutrition U. Calif., Davis, 1975-77, assoc. prof. dept. nutrition, 1977-82, dir. food intake lab. group, 1980—, prof. dept. nutrition, 1982—, prof. divsn. clin. nutrition and metabolism dept. internal medicine, 1988—. Mem. editorial bd. Internat. Jour. Obesity, 1976-85, Appetite, 1990, Obesity Rsch., 1993—. Mem. nutrition adv. bd. Avocado Growers Calif., 1975—; bd. sci. advisors Am. Council Sci. and Health, 1980—; mem. U.S. Dept. Agr. Dietary Guidelines Adv. Com., 1983-85; bd. advisors Inst. Behavioral Edn.; mem. obesity task force AAAS, Inst. Nutrition, 1974—. NIH tng. grant, 1979—. Mem. Am. Inst. Nutrition (chair pub. info. com. 1992-94), Am. Soc. Clin. Nutrition (pres. 1995-96), Am. Dietetic Assn., N.Am. Assn. for Study of Obesity (pres. 1992-93), Inst. Medicine NAS, Inst. Food Technologists, Am. Obesity Assn. (v.p. 1995—), Sigma Xi, Delta Omega. Office: Univ California Dept Nutrition Davis CA 95616

STERN, LARRY S., orthopaedic surgeon; b. Chgo., Sept. 28, 1951; s. Gerald Joseph and Sally (Welham) S.; m. Lynda Joy Henning, May 20, 1981; children: Adam, Andrea. BA, Washington U., St. Louis, 1973; MD, Northwestern U., 1977. Surgeon St. Paul Orthopaedic Surgery; surgeon, ptnr. Summit ORthopaedics, St. Paul, 1985—; chief of staff United Hosp., St. Paul, 1996—; mem. Allina Physicians Coun., Mpls., 1995-96. Fellow Am. Acad. Orthopaedic Surgeons. Office: Summit Orthopaedic Surgeons 293 W 7th Ste 100 Saint Paul MN 55102

STERN, LEON, psychiatrist; b. Vilnius, Lithuania, May 5, 1947; came to the U.S., 1976; s. Moisej and Beyle (Fain) S.; m. Cyla Gordon, Mar. 15, 1977. MD, Kaunas Med. Inst., 1971. Diplomate Am. Bd. Psychiatry and Neurology. Resident Rambam Hosp., Haifa, Israel, 1973-74; internt Hosp. Esquirol, Paris, 1975-76; resident in pschiatry Beth Israel Med. Ctr., N.Y.C., 1978-82; pvt. practice Bklyn., 1982—. Mem. Am. Psychiat. Assn. (mem. del. to USSR 1989), Acad. Medicine. Office: 307 Ocean View Ave Brooklyn NY 11235-6826

STERN, MARVIN, psychiatrist, educator; b. N.Y.C., Jan. 6, 1916; s. Jacob and Mary (Kappel) S.; m. Libby Rifkin, Jan. 18, 1942; children: Carol S., Robert M., Theodore A. B.S., CCNY, 1935; M.D., NYU, 1939. Diplomate Am. Bd. Psychiatry and Neurology. Intern in medicine and surgery Bellevue Hosp., N.Y.C., 1939-40, resident in medicine and psychiatry, 1940-42, fellow in psychiatry, 1946-47; practice medicine specializing in psychiatry N.Y.C., 1947—; asst. prof. psychiatry NYU Med. Ctr., N.Y.C., 1948-55, assoc. prof., 1955-62, prof., 1962-79, Menas S. Gregory prof. psychiatry, 1979-86, prof., 1986-95; prof. emeritus, 1995—; prof. emeritus NYU Med. Ctr., N.Y.C., 1995—, exec. chmn. dept. psychiatry, 1976-86; mem. staff NYU Hosp., Bellevue Hosp.; cons. psychiatrist VA Hosp.; cons. psychiatrist emeritus Brookdale Hosp. Served to maj. AUS, 1942-46. Fellow Am. Psychiat. Assn. (sec. dist. br. 1956-63, pres. dist. br. 1964, area chmn. 1962-63); mem. Am. Psychosomatic Assn., N.Y.C. Acad. Medicine, Harvey Soc., NYU Med. Alumni Assn. (pres. 1979-80), Phi Beta Kappa, Sigma Xi, Alpha Omega Alpha. Home: 300 E 33rd St Apt 12C New York NY 10016-9415 Office: NYU Sch Medicine 550 1st Ave New York NY 10016-6481

STERN, MICHAEL DAVID, dentist; b. Cleve., Feb. 26, 1946; s. Milton B. and Harriette (Hoffman) S.; m. Ellen Weiner, June 9, 1968; children: Gregory, Stephanie, Jeffrey. BS, Ohio State U., 1968, DDS, 1972; cert., L.I. U., N.Y.C., 1981. Cert. pain mgmt., Am. Acad. Pain Mgmt., instruction in temporomandibular joint disfunction syndrome, L.I. U. Staff dentist Office of Drs. Rhodes and Rinaldi, Cleve., 1972-73; assoc. dentist Office of William Rothkopf, DDS, Cleve., 1973-75; practice dentistry specializing in temporomandibular joint disorders Wickliffe, Ohio, 1975-93, Willoughby Hills, Ohio, 1993—; resident in cranio facial pain Coll. Dentistry U. Fla., Gainsville, 1989; media spokesperson Morning Exch., WEWS-TV, Cleve., 1981-85; cons. Richmond Hts. (Ohio) Hosp., 1983; adj. grad. lectr. Cleve. State U., 1983-84; preceptorship lectr. Case Western Res. U., Cleve., 1986-95; mem. staff Pain Ctr., Meridia South Pointe Hosp., 1991-96. Fellow Am. Endodontic Soc., Acad. Gen. Dentistry, Internat. Coll. Craniomandibular Orthopedics; mem. ADA, Ohio Dental Assn., N.E. Ohio Dental Soc. (pub. rels. chmn. 1979—). Jewish. Office: 34950 Chardon Rd Ste 209 Willoughby OH 44094-9162

STERN, ROBERT MORRIS, gastrointestinal psychophysiology researcher, psychology educator; b. N.Y.C., June 18, 1937; s. Irving Dan and Nellie (Wachstetter) S.; m. Wilma Olch, June 19, 1960; children—Jessica Leigh, Alison Rachel. A.B., Franklin and Marshall Coll., 1958; M.S., Tufts U., 1960; Ph.D., Ind. U., 1963. Research assoc. dept. psychology Ind. U., 1963-65; asst. prof. psychology Pa. State U., 1965-68, assoc. prof., 1968-73, prof., 1973—, disting. prof., 1992—, head dept., 1978-87. Author: (with W.J. Ray) Biofeedback, 1977, (with W.J. Ray and C.M. Davis) Psychophysiological Recording, 1980, (with K.L. Koch) Electrogastrography, 1985; contbr. articles to profl. jours. Recipient Nat. Media award Am. Psychol. Found., 1978. Mem. Am. Psychol. Soc., Aerospace Med. Assn., Soc. Psychophysiol. Rsch., Am. Gastroent. Assn. Home: 1360 Greenwood Cir State College PA 16803-3232 Office: Pa State U 512 Moore Bldg University Park PA 16802-3105

STERN, STANLEY, psychiatrist; b. N.Y.C., Apr. 5, 1933; s. Frank and Gussie S.; children: Marcus F., David S. BA cum laude, N.Y. U., 1953; MD, SUNY, 1957. Intern Ohio State U. Hosp., Columbus, 1957-58; resident in psychiatry Inst. Living, Hartford, Conn., 1958-60, Austen Riggs Ctr., Stockbridge, Mass., 1960-61; psychoanalytic tng. We. New Eng. Inst. for Psychoanalysis, New Haven, Conn., 1965-73; asst. clin. prof. psychiatry Yale U., New Haven, Conn., 1975-81; assoc. clin. prof. psychiatry U. Calif., San Diego, 1982-84; pvt. practice New Haven, 1965-82, La Jolla, Calif., 1982-84, Phoenix, 1984—; mem. faculty San Diego Psychoanalytic Inst., 1980-84; pres. Ariz. Psychoanalytic Study Group, Phoenix, 1986-88, Phoenix Psychoanalytic Study Group, 1986-88; tng. and supervising analyst So. Calif. Psychoanalytic Inst., 1989; chmn. edn. com. Ariz. Psychoanalytic New Tng. Facility, 1990-91; lectr., presenter, participant seminars and confs. in field. Contbr. article to profl. jours. Trustee, Gesell Inst., New Haven, 1986-88, Ctr. for the Exceptional Patient, New Haven; bd. dirs. ACLU. Capt. USAF, 1961-63. Mem. Am. Coll. Psychoanalysts, Am. Psychoanalytic Assn. (cert.), Am. Psychiatric Assn., Am. Acad. Psychoanalysts, Irene Josselyn Group Advancement of Psychoanalysis, So. Calif. Psychoanalytic Inst. and Soc. (faculty), San Diego Psychoanalytic Inst., Council for the Advancement of Psychoanalysis (treas. 1972-73, pres.-elect 1973-74, pres. 1974-75, councillor 1975-80), Phi Beta Kappa, Beta Lambda Sigma, Psi Chi. Home and Office: 3352 E Camelback Rd Ste D Phoenix AZ 85018-2312

STERN, THEODORE ALLAN, psychiatrist; b. N.Y.C., July 18, 1949; s. Marvin and Libby (Rifkin) S.; m. Kathryn T. Greenthal, Aug. 14, 1974; 1 child, Thomas William. BA, NYU, 1970, MD, 1975. Diplomate Am. Bd. Psychiatry and Neurology. Intern Met. Hosp. Ctr., N.Y.C., 1975-76; resident in Psychiatry Mass. Gen. Hosp., Boston, 1976-79; instr. psychiatry Med. Sch. Harvard U., Boston, 1979-84, asst. prof. psychiatry Med. Sch., 1984-89, assoc. prof. psychiatry Med. Sch., 1989—; dir. resident psychiat. consultation svc. Mass. Gen. Hosp., Boston, 1988—, psychiatrist, 1991—; chief psychiat. cons. svc. Mass. Gen. Hosp., Boston, 1995—. Asst. editor Psychosomatics, 1987—; mem. editorial bd. Jour. Intensive Care Medicine, 1985—, Jour. Geriatric Psychiatry and Neurology, 1987—, Internat. Jour. Psychiatry and Medicine, 1990, Heart & Lung, 1990—, Am. Jour. Critical Care, 1992—; contbr. numerous articles to profl. jours. and chpts. to books. Fellow Am. Psychiat. Assn. (exec. coun.), Acad. Psychomatic Medicine; mem. AMA, Am. Soc. Psychiat. Oncology/AIDS. Democrat. Office: Mass Gen Hosp Warren # 605 Boston MA 02114

STERN, THOMAS LEE, physician, educator, medical association administrator; b. San Francisco, Jan. 14, 1920; s. Bernard Michael and Alice Sarah (Halberstadt) S.; m. Gladys Crawford, June 26, 1944; children: Donnel Bernard, Lee Crawford, Pamela Ann. BS, Willamette U., 1947; MD, U. Oreg., 1950; DSc (hon.), Med. Coll. Ohio, 1982. Rotating intern St. Vincents Hosp., 1950-51, resident in general surgery, 1951-52; tech. advisor Marcus Welby M.D.-TV, Universal City, Calif., 1970-75; residency dir. Santa Monica (Calif.) Hosp., 1969-74; lectr. preventive and social medicine UCLA, L.A., 1970-73; v.p. Am. Acad. Family Physicians, Kansas City, Mo., 1974-83; assoc. prof. family medicine Kans. U. Med. Ctr., Kansas City, 1975-83; pres. Internat. Ctr. for Family Medicine, Buenos Aires, 1982-83; prof. family medicine U. Fla. Med. Ctr., Gainesville, 1983-86; v.p. Am. Acad. Family Physicians Found., Kansas City, 1983-91, audio tape editor, 1991—; cons. U.S. Naval Med. Corps, U.S. Army Med. Corps, Washington, 1975-82. With USN, 1941-45, PTO. Recipient F. Marian Bishop award Soc. Tchrs. Family Medicine, 1991. Fellow Am. Acad. Family Physicians (Thomas Johnson award 1985, Award of Merit 1983, John Walsh award 1991); mem. AMA. Home: 4441 W 124th Ter Shawnee Mission KS 66209-2280 Office: Am Acad Family Physicians Home Study 8800 Ward Pky Kansas City MO 64114-2762

STERN, THOMAS NEUTON, physician, educator; b. Memphis, Apr. 22, 1926; s. Neuton Samuel and Beatrice (Wolf) S.; m. Harriet Wise, June 16, 1957; children—Susan, Carol, David. Student Harvard U., 1943-44; M.D., Washington U., St. Louis, 1948. Diplomate Am. Bd. Internal Medicine, Am. Bd. Cardiovascular Disease. Practice medicine specializing in cardiology, Memphis, 1952—; clin. prof. medicine and cardiology U. Tenn.; dir. cardiovascular tng. Baptist Meml. Hosp., Memphis. Mem. Memphis City Schs. Bd. Edn., 1980—, (pres. 1982, 86); bd. dirs. Council Great City Schs., 1986— bd. dirs Comty Founder Greater Memphis, 1994, bd. dirs. Memphis Books Museum of Arts, 1994—, bd. dir. Memphis Housing Trust, 1994—, (pres. 94-96); pres. Memphis Heart Assn., 1963-64; v.p. Opera Memphis, 1979; v.p. Memphis Arts Council, 1974, 78; mem. nat. exec. com. Am. Jewish Com. Served to capt. USMC, 1953-55. (Fellow) ACP, Am. Coll. Cardiology, Am. Heart Assn. (council on clin. cardiology); mem. Nat. Sch. Bd. Assn. Democrat. Jewish. Author: (with Neuton S. Stern) The Bases of Treatment, 1957; Clinical Examination, 1964; contbr. articles to profl. jours. Office: 930 Madison Ave # 500 Memphis TN 38103-3401

STERN, WALTER EUGENE, neurosurgeon, educator; b. Portland, Oreg., Jan. 1, 1920; s. Walter Eugene and Ida May (McCoy) S.; m. Elizabeth Naffziger, May 24, 1946; children: Geoffrey Alexander, Howard Christian, Eugenia Louise, Walter Eugene III. AB cum laude, U. Calif., 1941; MD, 1943. Diplomate: Am. Bd. Neurol. Surg. (vice chmn. 1975-80). Surg. intern, asst. resident surgery and neurol. surgery U. Calif. Hosp., 1943-46, asst. resident neurol. surgery and neuropathology, 1948; clin. clk. Nat. Hosp. Paralyzed and Epileptic, London, Eng., 1948-49; Nat. Research fellow med. sci. Johns Hopkins, 1949-50; asst. resident, resident U. Calif. Service, 1951; NIH spl. fellow univ. lab. physiology Oxford U., 1961-62; clin. instr. U. Calif., 1951; asst. prof. neurosurgery UCLA, 1952-56, assoc. prof., 1956-59, prof., 1959-87, now emeritus, chief div. neurosurgery, 1952-85, chmn. dept. surgery, 1981-87; cons. neurosurgery, Wadsworth VA Hosp. Former mem., chmn. editorial bd. Jour. Neurosurgery; contbr. articles to sci. jours., chpts. in books. Lt. to capt. M.C. AUS, 1946-48. Fellow ACS (sec.); mem. AMA, Am. Surg. Assn., Pacific Coast Surg. Assn., L.A. Surg. Soc. (pres. 1978), Am. Assn. Neurol. Surgeons (pres. 1979-80, Cushing medalist, 1992), James IV Assn. Surgeons, Western Neurosurg. Soc. (past pres.), Soc. Neurol. Surgeons (past pres.), Neurosurg. Soc. Am., Am. Neurol. Assn., Soc. Univ. Surgeons, Soc. Brit. Neurol. Surgeons (hon.), Phi Beta Kappa, Sigma Xi, Alpha Omega Alpha. Republican. Episcopalian. Home: 435 Georgina Ave Santa Monica CA 90402-1909 Office: U Calif Sch Medicine Los Angeles CA 90024

STERNAL, SANDRA GAUNT, nutrition services administrator; b. Chgo., Oct. 1, 1946; d. George A. and Beatrice Gaunt; m. Joseph F. Sternal; children: Chandra, Karn Ann, John, Joseph. BS in Dietetics and Instl. Mgmt., U. Wis., 1969. Adminstrv. dietitian Luth Hosp., LaCrosse, Wis., 1970-73; cons. State of Wis., Madison, 1973-76, specialist procurement, 1976-81; dir. dietetic svcs. SunHealth, Charlotte, N.C., 1981-85; dist. mgr. ARA, Hunt Valley, Md., 1985-87, Morrison's Health Care Inc., Atlanta, 1987—; adminstr. nutrition svcs. Jackson Meml. Hosp., Miami, Fla., 1994—. Mem. Am. Dietetic Assn., Fla. Dietetic Assn., Dietitians in Bus. and Comm. (sec. 1986-87). Republican. Methodist. Office: Jackson Meml Hosp 1511 NW 12th Ave Miami FL 33136

STERNBERG, DAVID EDWARD, psychiatrist; b. Norfolk, Va., Jan. 18, 1946; s. Theodore and Bella (Rosenblatt) S.; m. Frances Toby Glazer; children: Jonathan Theodore, Daniel Alexander. BA in Biopsychology, U. Chgo., 1967; MD, Tufts U., 1971. Fellow in psychiatry Yale U., New Haven, 1972-75; staff psychiatrist, dir. alcohol rehab. Nat. Naval Med. Ctr., Bethesda, Md., 1975-77; rsch. coord., staff psychiatrist Biol. Psychiatry br. NIMH, Bethesda, 1977-79; asst. prof., chief clin. rsch. unit Yale U., New Haven, 1979-83; med. dir. Falkirk Hosp., Central Valley, N.Y., 1983-88, Kansas Inst., Olathe, 1988-90; dir. Assocs. for Psychiatry and Psychotherapy, Overland Pk., Kans., 1990—; lectr. Karl. Menninger Sch. Psychiatry, Topeka, 1988-91, dept. psychiatry Yale U., New Haven, 1983-92; assoc. clin. prof., U. Kans., Kansas City, 1988—. Author: Evaluation and Treatment of Drug Abuse, 1990, (with others) Dual Diagnosis: Addiction and Psychiatric Disorders, 1988; contbr. 87 articles to profl. jours. Lt. comdr. USN, 1975-77, comdr. USPHS, 1977-79. Mem. Am. Psychiat. Assn., Soc. for Biol. Psychiatry, Soc. Neurosci., Acad. Clin. Psychiatrists, Am. Acad. Psychiatrist in Alcoholism and Addictions. Office: Assocs for Psychiatry 6900 College Blvd Ste 850 Shawnee Mission KS 66211-1536

STERNBERG, RICHARD IRA, psychologist; b. Bklyn.; s. Jay and Rae (Eisenberg) S.; m. Vivian Sternberg; children: Adam Joshua, Jared Scott, Brittany Lauren. B.A., Yeshiva U.; M.S., CCNY; Ph.D., Calif. Sch. Profl. Psychology. Lic. clin. psychologist; cert. forensic examiner; diplomate Am. Bd. Voc. Experts, Social Security Adminstrn. Maine, Vt. Grad. faculty CCNY, 1974-76; pvt. practice clin. psychology, Hartford, 1977—; instr. Eastern Mich. U., Ypsilanti, 1977-78; staff psychologist, then asst. dir. evaluation unit, exec. dir. Ctr. Forensic Psychiatry, Ann Arbor, Mich. 1976-79; chief psychologist, dir. diagnostic unit Whiting Forensic Inst. Middletown, Conn., 1976-79; cons. State Calif., 1977-78; cons. on sexual assaults HEW, 1977; cons. Child Murders Task Force, 1978-79; cons. career services CCNY, 1981-82; cons. youth services, Newington, Conn., 1982-84; vocat. disability expert examiner Social Security Adminstrn., 1982—, liaison Employee Assistance Program, 1986—; indsl. cons., 1985—; pres., clin. dir. Clin. Psychology Assocs. P.C., West Hartford, 1986—, EAP coord., 1985—; mem. probate judges ct. panel, 1983—; adj. prof. St. Joseph Coll., 1984-89; mem. grad. sch. faculty U. Hartford, 1986-87; chief cons. Rocky Hill Fire and Police Depts., 1983-85; mem. adv. bd. Police Athletic League, 1988—; cons. Police Dept., 1988—; acad. screening officer Calif. Sch. Profl. Psychology. Fellow Am. Bd. Vocat. Experts; mem. Am. Psychol. Assn. (editorial rev. bd. 1977), N.J. Psychol. Assn., Conn. Psychol. Assn., Nat. Migraine Found., Menninger Found., Alumni Assn. Yeshiva U., Alumni Assn. CCNY, Calif. Sch. Profl. Psychology Alumni Assn. Contbr. articles to profl. jours. Office: 836 Farmington Ave Ste 201 West Hartford CT 06119-1544

STERNBERG, ROBERT JEFFREY, psychology educator; b. Newark, Dec. 8, 1949; s. Joseph Sternberg and Lilliam Myriam (Politzer) Weingast; children: Seth, Sara; m. Alejandra Campos, 1991. BA summa cum laude, Yale U., 1972; PhD, Stanford U., 1975; D honoris causa, Complutense U., 1994. Mem. faculty dept. psychology Yale U., New Haven, 1975—; prof. psychology Yale U., 1983-86, IBM prof. psychology and edn., 1986—. Editor-in-chief Ency. of Human Intelligence, Psychol. Bull., 1991-95; cons. editor Learning and Individual Differences, 1992—, Intelligence, 1977—, Devel. Rev., 1987-91, Jour. Personality and Social Psychology, 1989-91, Psychol. Rev., 1989-91; author: Intelligence, Information Processing and Analogical Reasoning, 1977, Beyond IQ, 1985, The Triarchic Mind, 1988, Metaphors of Mind, 1990, In Search of the Human Mind, 1995, (with T. Lubart) Defying the Crowd, 1995, Successful Intelligence, 1996, Pathways to Psychology, 1996. Recipient award for Excellence Mensa Edn. and Rsch. Found., 1989; Guggenheim Found. fellow, 1985-86. Fellow APA (past pres. divsns. 1 and 15, McCandless Young Scientist award divsn devel. psychology 1982, Disting. Sci. award for early career contbn. 1981), AAAS, Am. Acad. Arts and Scis.; me. Am. Edni. Rsch. Assn. (Rsch. Rev. award 1986, Outstanding Book award 1987, Sylvia Scribner award 1996), Soc. Multivariate Exptl. Psychology (Cattell award 1982), Nat. Assn. Gifted Children (Disting. Scholar award 1985), Phi Beta Kappa. Home: 105 Spruce Bank Rd Hamden CT 06518-2233 Office: Yale Univ Dept Psychology PO Box 208205 New Haven CT 06520-8205

STERNFELD, LEON, health facility administrator; b. Bklyn., June 15, 1913; s. Solomon and Goldie (Levine) S.; m. Ruth Schwartz Sternfeld, Aug. 25, 1934; children: Kay, Barbara. BS, U. Chgo., 1932, MD, 1936, PhD, 1937; MSPH, Columbia U., 1943. Diplomate Am. Bd. Pediatrics, Am. Bd. Preventive Medicine. Asst. dist. health officer N.Y. State Dept. Health, Buffalo, N.Y., 1943-44; dir. Med. Rehab. N.Y. State Dept. Health, Albany, N.Y., 1944-50; asst. dir. Tuberculosis Control Mass. Dept. Pub. Health, Boston, 1950-52; dir. field training Harvard Sch. Pub. Health, Boston, 1952-53; active military duty U.S. Army Med. Corps., Korea, 1953-55; commr. Pub. Health City Cambridge, Mass., 1955-60; deputy commr. Mass. Dept. Pub. Health, Boston, 1960-70; cons. in med. care Fedn. Jewish Philanthropies, N.Y.C., 1970-71; med. dir. United Cerebral Palsy Assn., N.Y.C., 1971-93; retired, 1993; assoc. prof. Maternal and Child Health, Harvard Sch. Pub. Health, 1960-70; dir. Commn. Accreditation Rehab. Facilities, Tuscon, 1987-93, Accreditation Coun. Disabilities, Landover, Md., 1974-91. Contbr. articles to profl. jours. Col. U.S. Army, 1953-73, Korea. Recipient Disting. Svc. award Am. Acad. for Cerebral Palsy and Developmental Medicine, Louisville, Ky., 1991. Fellow Am. Pub. Health Assn., Am. Acad. Cerebral Palsy and Developmental Medicine. Jewish. Home: 1385 York Ave New York NY 10021-3904

STETLER-STEVENSON, WILLIAM G., pathologist; b. Trenton, N.J., Nov. 27, 1953. BS in Biochemistry cum laude, Albright Coll., 1975; PhD in Biochemistry & Molecular Biology, Northwestern U., 1983, MD, 1984. Diplomate Am. Bd. Pathology. Mem. house staff anatomic pathology McGaw Med. Ctr., 1984-87; sr. staff fellow NIH, 1987-91, med. officer, rschr., 1991—, chief extracellular matrix pathology sect., 1993—. Editl. bd. Diagnostic Molecular Pathology, Am. Jour. Pathology, Invasion & Metastasis; contbr. articles to profl. jours. Recipient Warner Lambert/Parke-Davis award, 1996; Kemper Found. Med. scholar, 1978-79. Mem. ASBMB, Am. Chem. Soc., Am. Soc. Investigative Pathology. Office: Nat Cancer Inst Lab Pathology Extracellular Matrix Pathology Sect Bldg 10 Rm 2A33 700 Rockville Pike Bethesda MD 20892*

STETTER, MIRIAM, gastroenterologist; b. Munich, Germany, Aug. 23, 1961; arrived in Austria, 1968; d. Hans Jorg and Christine (Schmidt) S.; m. Robert Tautner, May 2, 1989; children: Patricia, Claudia. MD, U. Vienna, 1985, degree in internal medicine, 1992, degree in gastroenterology, 1995. Trainee for internal medicine Gen. Hosp., Vienna, 1985-92; sr. dr. Hosp. Amstetter, Austria, 1993—. Home: Unk Mauer, 3362 Mauer-Ohling Austria Office: Gen Hosp Amstetter, Krankenhausstr 21, 3300 Amstetter Austria

STEUBER, GARY LEE, chiropractor; b. Erlanger, Ky., May 23, 1963; s. James Phillip and Virginia Mary (Hoffman) S. AA in Sci., Broward C.C., 1988; D Chiropractic, Life Chiropractic Coll., 1993. Chiropractor Chiro-Care Ctrs., Plantation, Fla., 1993—. Recipient Presdl. Leadership award Phi Theta Kappa, 1988. Mem. Am. Chiropractic Assn., Fla. Chiropractic Assn., Fla. Chiropractic Soc. Office: Chiro-Care Ctrs Broward 6950 Cypress Rd Ste 105 Plantation FL 33317

STEVENS, BRENDA ANITA, psychologist, educator; b. N.Y.C., Oct. 23, 1949; d. Henry Stevens and Frances Marie (Russo) Incorvaia; m. Edwin Randall Trinkle, Feb. 21, 1976 (div. 1987); m. John Alexander Czaja, Sept. 10, 1994; 1 child, Peter A. BS, Boston U., 1971, MEd, 1971, CAGS, 1973; PhD in Edn., U. Tenn., 1991. Nat. cert. sch. psychologist. Sch. adjustment counselor Dedham (Mass.) Pub. Schs., 1972-73; testing specialist Children's Hosp. Med. Ctr., Boston, 1973-74; sch. psychologist North Middlesex Regional Schs., Townsend, Mass., 1974-78; grad. asst. U. Tenn., Knoxville, 1978-79, 89-90, program evaluator, 1983-84, clinic coord., 1989-90; psychology assoc. Cherokee Mental Health Ctr., Morristown, Tenn., 1985; asst. prof. U. Nebr., Kearney, 1990-93, Miami U., Oxford, Ohio, 1993—; psychol. cons. Roane County Pub. Schs., Kingston, Tenn., 1978-89; cons., adminstrv. intern Knox County Pub. Schs., Knoxville, 1984-85; sch. psychologist Jefferson County Pub. Schs., Dandridge, Tenn., 1986-88, Oak Ridge (Tenn.) Pub. Schs., 1989; cons. Psychol. Corp., 1994-96. Commr.'s appointee Mass. State Coun. for Hearing Impaired, Boston, 1976-78; bd. dirs. Luth. Social Ministries Tenn., Knoxville, 1989; exec. bd. Luth. Community Svcs., Knoxville, 1987-89; cons. Mass. State Dept. Edn., Boston, 1974-78. Head Start grantee, 1991-94, Project One to One grantee Dawson County, 1991; Trustee scholar Boston U., 1968-71; recipient Women of Achievement award Commn. Women, 1983. Mem. Am. Psychol. Assn., Nat. Assn. Sch. Psychologists, Phi Kappa Phi, Pi Lambda Theta, Ohio Sch. Psychologists Assn, Phi Delta Kappa. Office: Miami U Dept Ednl Psychology 201 McGuffey Oxford OH 45056

STEVENS, BRUCE RUSSELL, physiology educator, researcher; b. Ogden, Utah, Apr. 1, 1952. BS, Valparaiso U., 1974; MS, Ill. State U., 1977, PhD, 1980; postgrad., UCLA Med. Sch., 1980-84. Asst. rsch. physiologist UCLA Med. Sch., 1983-84; asst. prof. physiology U. Fla. Coll. Medicine, Gainesville, 1984-89, assoc. prof. physiology, 1989-96, prof., 1996—; reviewer for internat. jours. in field; cons. in field. Contbr. articles to books and profl. jours. Recipient NIH nat. rsch. grants and awards. Office: U Fla Coll Medicine Dept Physiology PO Box 100274 Gainesville FL 32610-0274

STEVENS, DAVID JOHN, health facility administrator; b. Rome, N.Y., May 30, 1954; s. Charles Edward and Janet Rose (Berthold) S.; m. Dianne Ellen Farria, Oct. 16, 1976; children: Sharron Marie, Angela Lauren. BS in Biology, Belmont Abbey Coll., 1976. Staff technologist Potomac Hosp. Corp., Woodbridge, Va., 1980-89, asst. mgr. lab. info sys., 1989—; chmn. regional user group Sunquest Info. Sys., 1995—, co-chair regional user group, 1994-95. Ofcl., sec., pres. Skyline Football Ofcls., Woodbridge, 1978—. Office: Potomac Hosp Corp 2300 Opitz Blvd Woodbridge VA 22191

STEVENS, ELAINE THERESA, nursing educator, staff nurse; b. Hutchinson, Minn., Dec. 29, 1964; d. James Alois and Lorraine Lucy (Sobiech) Petron; m. Jay Walter Stevens, Oct. 19, 1991; 1 child, Nicole Elizabeth. BSN, Mankato State U., BS in Psychology; MSN, U. Minn. RN, MSN, CCRN, Minn. Staff nurse surg. floor St. Mary's Hosp., Rochester, Minn., 1988-89; staff nurse critical care Fairview Riverside Med. Ctr., Mpls., 1989-94, edn. specialist critical care, 1994—. Contbr. articles to profl. jours. Mem. bd. dirs. AACN (publ. chair 1995-96), Zeta chpt. Sigma Theta Tau (fundraising chair 1995-96). Office: Fairview Riverside Med Ctr 2450 Riverside Ave Minneapolis MN 55454

STEVENS, ELIZABETH, psychotherapist, consultant; b. Evanston, Ill., Jan. 11, 1950; d. Kenneth M. and C. Jane (Reynolds) S.; m. David W. Handy, Oct. 3, 1986. BA in Psychology, U. Fla., 1973; MA in Clin. Psychology, Kent State U., 1976. Lic. profl. counselor; lic. marriage and family therapist. Exec. dir. Genesis Women's Shelter, Dallas, 1986-87; dir. outpatient svcs. Green Oaks Hosp., Dallas, 1987-88; mgmt. cons. Houston, 1977—, pvt. practice, 1990—; founder Integrated Clin. Resources, Inc., The Stevens Co., healthcare cons., Humble, Tex., 1995—; cons., amb. St. Joseph Hosp., 1977—; co-founder N.E. Hospice, Med. Affiliates, Support N.E. Cancer Workers, Emergency Support Systems for Police, fire Dept. and Ambulance Svc.; founder Stevens Counseling Ctrs., The Psychoimmunology Ctr., Stevens, Lancaster and Assocs.; cons. to devel. utilization rev. Kelsey-Seybold Clinics, 1992—; cons. creating feasibility studies for venture capitalists. Contbr. articles to profl. jours., mags., and newspapers. Vol. Mental Health Assn., Houston and Harris County, bd. dirs., 1988—, chair nominating com., membership com., sec. exec. com.; bd. advisors N.E. Hospice; co-founder Associated Mental Health Group, Inc.; mem. strategic planning team Sisters of Charity; cons. devel. Triage. Named Exceptional Vol. of Yr. Mental Health Assn., Speakers Bur. award. Mem. Walden Country Club. Office: 300 Main St Humble TX 77338

STEVENS, GEORGE M., III, surgeon; b. Knoxville, May 29, 1934; s. George Miller and Helen Margaret (Brown) S.; m. Mary Alberta Campbell, Aug. 25, 1955; children: George IV, Julia Christine Muller, Mac Campbell. MD, U. Tenn., 1959. Diplomate Am. Bd. Orthopedic Surgery. Instr. orthopedics U. N.C., Chapel Hill, 1964-65; orthopedist Meth. Med. Ctr. Oak Ridge, Tenn., 1965—; instr. orthopedics U. Tenn. Meml. Rsch. Ctr., Knoxville, 1967-75. Fellow Internat. Coll. Surgeons, Am. Acad. Orthopedic Surgeons; mem. Am. Fracture Assn., Mid-Am. Orthopedic Assn., Tenn. Orthopedic Soc. Republican. Presbyn. Office: Oak Ridge Ortho Ctr 988 Oak Ridge Tpk Oak Ridge TN 37830

STEVENS, LINDA LOUISE HALBUR, addiction counselor; b. Huron, S.D., Oct. 28, 1960; d. Alvin LeRoy and Esther Louise (Schroeder) Halbur; m. Lowell Eugene Stevens, July 26, 1980 (div. 1995); children: Lowell John, Tracie Lynn. BSW, U. N.D., 1991; MEd, N.D. State U., 1993. Lic. social worker, N.D.; lic. addiction counselor, N.D. Tracker Luth. Soc. Svcs., Hillsboro, N.D., 1990-94; addiction counselor Heartland Med. Ctr., Fargo, N.D., 1993-94, S.E. Human Svc. Ctr., Fargo, 1994—; dual diagnosis Off Main Program, Fargo, 1995. Local/state officer N.D. Women of Today, Hillsboro, 1982-87. Recipient Presdl. award of excellence N.D. women of Today, 1986, 87. Mem. NASW, Am. Counseling Assn. Home: 1717 40th St S Apt 114 Fargo ND 58103-4445 Office: SE Human Svc Ctr Off Main 9 9th St S Fargo ND 58103

STEVENS, LISA LAJUANA, physician assistant; b. Atlanta, Nov. 7, 1965; d. David and Josephine (Dunlap) Williams; m. Eddie Lee Stevens, Dec. 21, 1994. AS in Med. Tech., Atlanta Met. Coll., 1987; BS, Howard U., Washington, 1990. Physician asst. Gerald Family Care Assocs., P.C., Washington, 1990—, office mgr., 1994—. Mem. Am. Acad. Physician Assts., Prince Georges Soc. Health Profls.

STEVENS, LLOYD WEAKLEY, retired surgeon, retired medical educator; b. Phila., Jan. 14, 1914; s. Lloyd Percy and Caroline (Fredrickson) S.; m. Eleanor Van Dyke, June 1971; children: Mary-Ellen, Carol Ann Hovey, Susan Worrell Plaza. BA, U. Pa., 1933; MD, U. Pa., 1937, 1937. Diplomate Am. Bd. Surgery. Intern Hosp. Univ. Pa., Phila., 1937-39, surg. resident and fellow, 1939-44, staff mem., 1944-50; staff mem. Grad. Hosp. U. Pa., Phila., 1944-50, Women's Med. Coll. Hosp., Phila., 1944-50, Phila. (Pa.) Gen. Hosp., 1944-76, Presbyn.-Univ. Pa. Med. Ctr., Phila., 1944—; assoc. prof. surgery Grad. Sch. Medicine, Phila., Med. Coll. Pa., 1945-50; chmn. dept. surgery Phila. (Pa.) Gen. Hosp., 1950-76; dir. surgery Presbyn. U. Pa. Med. Ctr., Phila., 1960-79; emeritus prof. clin. surgery U. Pa. Sch. Medicine, Phila., 1979-95; surgeon Phila. (Pa.) Eagles Profl. Football Team, 1945-50. Contbr. chpt. to book and articles to profl. jours. Speaking staff Exec. Ministry of Campus Crusade for Christ, 1980-91. Fellow ACS, Phila. Acad. Surgery, Coll. Physicians Phila.; mem. Soc. for Surgery of Alimentary Track, Dominican Republic Gastroenterol. Soc. (citation 1975), Alpha Omega Alpha. Republican. Home: 1204 Round Hill Rd Bryn Mawr PA 19010

STEVENS, MARK ALAN, health club official; b. Amarillo, Tex., Oct. 21, 1965; s. Willie Lee and Judith Faye (Hancock) S.; m. Hailey Dee Martin, Apr. 15, 1990; 1 child, Parker Alan. BS in Exercise Sci., Abilene Christian U., 1988. Fitness specialist Big Country Sports Rehab., Abilene, Tex., 1988-90; athletic dir. Club Sports Internat., San Antonio, 1990-91, gen. mgr., 1991-94; dir. fitness and spa Four Seasons Regent Resorts, Dallas, 1994—; cons., Dallas, 1994—. Contbr. articles to profl. publs. Team coach Abilene Recreation Ctrs., 1984-89; team coach, parent vol. YMCA, Arlington, Tex., 1994—. Mem. Am. Coll. Sports Medicine (cert. fitness specialist), Internat. Health and Sportsclub Assn., Club Industry. Office: Four Seasons Resort and Club 4150 N MacArthur Blvd Irving TX 75038

STEVENS, PAUL ACHIEL, pediatrician, neonatologist; b. Lier, Belgium, Dec. 29, 1956; s. Paul J. Stevens and Godelieve Van Obbergen; m. Barbara Schadow; 1 child, Marieke. MD, Cath. U. Leuven, 1981. Pediatric residency Children's Hosp. U. Bochum (Germany), 1981-85; postdoctoral rsch. fellow Cardiovascular Rsch. Inst., U. Calif., San Francisco, 1985-88; attending physician dept. neonatology Free U. Berlin, 1988-93; rsch. scientist Dept. Neonatology, Charité, Humboldt U., Berlin, 1993—. Contbr. chpts. to books, articles on lung surfactant rsch. to profl. jours. Grantee Am. Heart Assn., 1985-87, Am. Lung Assn., 1987-88, Deutsche Forschungs-Gemeinschaft, 1989—, Bundesministerium fur Forschungs und Technologie, 1991—. Mem. AAAS, Am. Thoracic Soc., European Soc. Pediatric Rsch., German Soc. Cell Biology. Home: Elberfelder St 35, 10555 Berlin Germany Office: Charite Humboldt U Dept Neonatology, Schumann Str 20-21, 10098 Berlin Germany

STEVENS, PETER SHELDON, pediatric urologist; b. Boston, Feb. 16, 1942; s. Harry Wellington and Sophia Lillian (White) S.; m. Barbara Glafenhein, June 14, 1964; 1 child, Margaret Sheldon. BS, Emory U., 1964, MD, 1967. Intern in surgery U. Minn. Hosp., 1967-68; resident in surgery Duke U., 1970-71, resident in urology, 1971-75; resident in pediatric surgery Queen Mary's Hosp. for Children, London, 1974-75; staff physician, asst. prof. U. N.C., Chapel Hill, 1975-78; pediatric urologist pvt. practice, Jacksonville, Fla., 1978-85; chief pediatric urology Nemours Childrens Clinic, Jacksonville, Fla., 1986-94. Lt. comdr. USN, 1968-70. Mem. Rotary. Republican. Presbyterian. Office: Nemours Childrens Clinic 807 Nira St Jacksonville FL 32207

STEVENS, ROSEMARY A., academic dean, public health and social history educator; b. Bourne, Eng.; came to U.S., 1961, naturalized, 1968; d. William Edward and Mary Agnes (Tricks) Wallace; m. Robert B. Stevens, Jan. 28, 1961 (div. 1983); children: Carey, Richard; m. Jack D. Barchas, Aug. 9, 1994. BA, Oxford (Eng.) U., 1957; Diploma in Social Adminstrn., Manchester (Eng.) U., 1959; MPH, Yale U., 1963, PhD, 1968. Various hosp. adminstrv. positions Eng., 1959-61; rsch. assoc. Med. Sch. Yale U., 1962-68, asst. prof. Med. Sch., 1968-71, assoc. prof. Med. Sch., 1971-74, prof. pub. health Med. Sch., 1974-76; master Jonathan Edwards Coll., 1974-75; prof. dept. health systems mgmt. and polit. sci. Tulane U., New Orleans, 1976-78; chmn. dept. health systems mgmt. Tulane U., 1977-78; prof. history and sociology of sci. U. Pa., Phila., 1979—, chmn. dept., 1980-83, 86-91, UPS Found. prof., 1990-91, dean Sch. Arts and Scis., Thomas S. Gates prof., 1991—; vis. lectr. Johns Hopkins U., 1967-68; guest scholar Brookings Instn., Washington, 1967-68; acad. visitor London Sch. Econs., 1962-64, 1973-74. Author: Medical Practice in Modern England: The Impact of Specialization and State Medicine, 1966, American Medicine and the Public Interest, 1971, In Sickness and in Wealth: American Hospitals in the Twentieth Century, 1989, (with others) Foreign Trained Physicians and American Medicine, 1972, Welfare Medicine in America, 1974, Alien Doctors: Foreign Medical Graduates in American Hospitals, 1978. Bd. dirs. Milbank Meml. Fund; chmn. bd. dirs. Ctr. for Advancement of Health. Fellow Am. Acad. Arts and Scis.; mem. Inst. Medicine of Nat. Acad. Sci., History of Sci. Soc., Am. Assn. for History of Medicine, Coll. Physicians of Phila., Cosmopolitan Club. Home: 1900 Rittenhouse Sq # 18 A Philadelphia PA 19103-5735 Office: U Pa Office of Dean 116 College Hall Philadelphia PA 19104-6377

STEVENS, ROY WHITE, microbiologist; b. Troy, N.Y., Sept. 4, 1934; s. Edward M. and Bernice B. (White) S.; BS, SUNY, Albany, 1956, MS, 1958; PhD, Albany (N.Y.) Med. Coll., 1965; m. Shirley A. Brehm, Aug. 4, 1956; children: Scott D., Mark G. Rsch. scientist Wadsworth Ctr., N.Y. State Dept. Health, Albany, 1967-70, assoc. rsch. scientist, 1970-73, prin. rsch. scientist, 1973—, dir. labs. for diagnostic immunology, 1979-85, retrovirology and immunology, 1985-91; adj. prof. microbiology and immunology Albany Med. Coll., 1982-92; assoc. prof. sch. pub. health SUNY, Albany, 1988—; pres. Biomed. Resource Group, Albany, 1991—; trustee Bender Hygienic Lab., Albany, 1986—. Served with USAF, 1961-62. Diplomate Am. Bd. Med. Microbiology. Fellow Am. Acad. Microbiology; mem. AAAS, APHA, Am. Soc. Microbiology (pres. Eastern N.Y. br. 1981, chair-elect clin. & diagnostic immunology divsn. 1996), Am. Assn. Clin. Chemistry, Assn. Med. Lab. Immunologists (v.p. 1988, pres. 1989). Mem. editorial bd. Clin. Immunology Newsletter, 1980-86, Jour. Clin. Microbiology, 1981-87, Manual of Clinical Microbiology ASM, 1991. Editor: Diagnostic Devices Manual and Directory, 1986. Home: 507 Acre Dr Schenectady NY 12303-5226 Office: Biomedical Resource Group PO Box 12393 Albany NY 12212-2393

STEVENS, STANLEY EDWARD, JR., microbiology educator; b. Ringgold, Tex., June 25, 1944; s. Stanley Edward and Josephine M. (Fenley) S.; m. Catherine Lee Reifel, Feb. 1, 1969; children: Kathleen Misty, Heather Lee, Nathan Edward. BA, U. Tex., 1966, MA, 1968, PhD, 1971. Research assoc. I U. Tex., Austin, 1970-71, research assoc. II, 1974; mem. vis. staff U. Calif.-Los Alamos Sci. Lab., 1975-77; asst. prof. Pa. State U., University Park, 1975-81, assoc. prof. microbiology, 1981-87, prof., 1987-88, dir. indsl. affiliate program, 1983-88, assoc. dir. Biotechnol. Inst., 1984-88; prof. Memphis State U., 1989—, apptd. W. Harry Feinstone chair of excellence in molecular biology, 1989—, dir. divsn. molecular sci. and microbiology, 1994—, chair dept. biology, 1996, chair dept. microbiology and molecular cell scis., 1996—, dir. The Feinstone Inst. of Molecular Biology, 1996—; program mgr. USDA/Competetive Research Grants Office Biol Nitrogen Fixation Program, 1987; cons. in field. Contbr. chpts. to books, articles to profl. jours; patentee in field. V.p. Corl St. PTO, State College, Pa., 1984-85, pres., 1985-86. Recipient Inventors Incentive award Pa. Research Corp., 1987, Rsch. Achievement award U. Memphis, 1992; USPHS fellow, 1969-70, 71-75; grantee NIH, 1977—, USDA, 1979—, NSF, 1985—; named to Tenn. Sci. & Tech. Adv. Coun. Fellow Am. Acad. for Microbiology; mem. AAAS, Am. Soc. Biochemistry and Molecular Biology, Am. Soc. Microbiology, Am. Soc. Plant Physiologists, Phycol. Soc. Am., Sigma Xi. Democrat. Avocations: history, woodworking. Office: U Memphis 509 Life Science Bldg Memphis TN 38152

STEVENS, STEPHEN EDWARD, psychiatrist; b. Phila.; s. Edward and Antonia S.; BA cum laude, LaSalle Coll., 1950; MD, Temple U., Phila., 1954; LLB, Blackstone Sch. Law, 1973; m. Isabelle Helen Gallacher, Dec. 27, 1953. Intern, Frankford Hosp., Phila., 1954-55; resident in psychiatry Phila. State Hosp., 1955-58; practice medicine specializing in psychiatry Woodland Hills, Calif., 1958-63, Santa Barbara, Calif., 1970-77; asst. supt. Camarillo (Calif.) State Hosp., 1963-70; cons. ct. psychiatrist Santa Barbara County, 1974-77; clin. dir. Kailua Mental Health Ctr., Oahu, Hawaii, 1977—. Author: Treating Mental Illness, 1961. Served with M.C. USAAF. Diplomate Am. Bd. Psychiatry and Neurology. Decorated Purple Heart. Fellow Am. Geriatrics Soc. (founding); mem. Am. Acad. Psychiatry and Law, AMA, Am. Psychiat. Assn., Am. Legion, DAV (Oahu chpt. 1), Caledonia Soc., Am. Hypnosis Soc., Am. Soc. Adolescent Psychiatry, Hawaiian Canoe Club, Honolulu Club, Elks (BPOE 616), Aloha String Band (founder and pres.). Home: PO Box 26413 Honolulu HI 96825-6413

STEVENS, WIM JOZEF, medical educator; b. Antwerp, Belgium, Dec. 19, 1944; m. Frida Swartelé; children: Manuel, Frank. MD, U. Gent, Belgium, 1970; PhD, U. Antwerpen, 1982. Intern U. Gent, 1970-74, head dept. immunology, 1983; resident U. Antwerpen, 1975-76; dean dept. medicine U. Antwerpen, 1991-95. Office: Univ Antwerpen Immunology Dept, Universiteitsplein 1, 2610 Antwerp Antwerp, Belgium

STEVENSON, EDWARD WARD, retired physician, surgeon, otolaryngologist; b. Chester, S.C., Jan. 9, 1926; s. Thomas M. and Annie Lou (Ward) S.; m. Dorothy Giles, Sept. 2, 1947; children: Sally Anne Stevenson Yeilding, Laura Stevenson Healey, Nancy Stevenson Schonberger (dec.), Molly Stevenson Walker. Degree, Duke U., 1945; MD, U. Md., Balt., 1949. Intern Bapt. Meml. Hosp., Memphis, 1949-50; resident Med. Coll. Va. Hosp., Richmond, 1953-55; fellow Ochsner Found. Hosp., New Orleans, 1955-56; staff otolaryngologist Ochsner Clinic, New Orleans, 1956-57; pvt. practice Birmingham, 1957-60, 65-94; instr., clin. asst. prof. surgery U. Ala., Birmingham, 1957-94; pvt. practice Decatur, Ala., 1960-65; ret., 1994; faculty Tulane U. Sch. Medicine, 1956-57; mem. staff Bapt. Med. Ctr.-Montclair, Birmingham. Contbr. articles to profl. jours. Bd. dirs. So. Mus. Flight, Birmingham, 1989-96. Mem. AMA, ACS, Am. Laryngol., Rhinol. and Otol. Soc. (sec.-treas. so. sect. 1990-93, v.p. so. sect. 1993-94), Am. Soc. Head and Neck Surgery, Am. Acad. Otolaryn., Am. Soc. Ophthal. and Otolaryn. Allergy, So. Med. Assn., Jefferson County Med. Soc., Am. Sleep Disorders Assn., Ala. Otolaryn. Soc. (founder, pres. 1971), Med. Assn. State Ala., Morgan County Med. Soc. (pres. 1969), Tri-State Otolaryn. Assembly (co-founder), Birmngham Otolaryn. Soc. (pres. 1984), Birmingham Aero Club (pres. 1996), Birmingham Downtown Rotary Club. Methodist. Home: 4249 Antietam Dr Birmingham AL 35213-3221

STEVENSON, JAMES D(ONALD), JR., psychologist, counselor; b. Ft. Wayne, Ind., July 6, 1943; s. James Donald Sr. and Charlotte Eileen (Starnes) S.; m. Sharon Sue Kearns, Nov. 26, 1965 (div. 1978); 1 child, E. Willow; m. Diane Kulesza, Apr. 13, 1980; 1 child, James Wesley. BA, Whittier (Calif.) Coll., 1965; MA, Calif. State U., Northridge, 1974; PhD, Calif. Coast U., 1986. Lic. counselor, Calif. Auditor State Compensation Ins. Fund, Arcadia, Calif., 1965-66, supervising auditor, 1969-74; dir. social svcs. Buena Vista Acad., Ventura, Calif., 1974-76, benefits counselor, 1976-77; counselor Calif. Dept. of Rehab., Thousand Oaks, 1977-82; vocat. psychologist Calif. Dept. of Rehab., Pleasant Hill, 1982—; prin. James Stevenson Pubs., 1994—, Career Interest Testing Svc., Ventura and Contra Costa Countys, 1980-83; instr. Ventura Coll., 1975; cons. Ctr. for Career Evaluation, Oakland, Calif., 1986-87, St. Vincent De Paul Soc., Pittsburg, Calif., 1986—, Allied Fellowship Svcs., Oakland, 1990. Contbr. articles to profl. jours. With U.S. Army, 1965-67, ETO. Mem. Nat. Rehab. Assn. (exec. bd. San Francisco chpt. 1986-93, pres. San Francisco East Bay div. 1991-92), AACD, Ventura County Mental Health Assn. (bd. dirs. 1978-81), Los Padres Rehab. Assn. (pres. Ventura chpt. 1978-79), Am. Legion. Office: Calif Dept of Rehab 2285 Morello Ave Pleasant Hill CA 94523-1850

STEVENSON, JAMES RALPH, school psychologist, author; b. Kemmerer, Wyo., June 29, 1949; s. Harold Ralph and Dora (Borino) S.; m. Alice M. Paolucci, June 17, 1972; children: Tiffany Jo, Brian Jeffrey. BA, U. No. Colo., 1971, MA, 1974, EdS, 1975. Lic. elem. sch. counselor, sch. psychologist, Colo.; nationally cert. sch. psychologist. Sch. psychologist Jefferson County Pub. Schs., Golden, Colo., 1975-87, 89-91, Weld County Sch. Dist. 6, Greeley, Colo., 1987-89, Weld Bd. Coop. Edn. Svcs., LaSalle, Colo., 1991-95; spl. edn. coord. Weld Bd. Coop. Edn. Svcs., LaSalle, 1995; sch. psychologist Fort Lupton (Colo.) Schs., 1995—; ltd. pvt. practice sch. psychologist Pathways, Greeley, 1994—. Asst. coach Young Am. Baseball, Greeley, 1989, 90, head coach, 1992, 93; asst. basketball coach Recreation League for 6th-7th Grades, 1992, 93. U. No. Colo. scholar, 1974. Mem. NEA, NASP (alt. del. Colo. chpt. 1975-77, dir. Apple II users group Washington chpt. 1989—), Colo. Soc. Sch. Psychologists (chmn. task force on presch. assessment 1991—), Colo. Edn. Assn., Ft. Lupton Edn. Assn., Jefferson County Psychologists Assn. (sec. 1986-87), Colo. Assn. for Play Therapy, Am. Orthopsychiat. Assn. Democrat. Roman Catholic. Home: 1937 24th Ave Greeley CO 80631-5027 Office: Fort Lupton Schs 301 Reynolds St Fort Lupton CO 80621

STEVENSON, JAMES RICHARD, radiologist, lawyer; b. Ft. Dodge, Iowa, May 30, 1937; s. Lester Lawrence and Esther Irene (Johnson) S.; m. Sara Jean Hayman, Sept. 4, 1958; children: Bradford Allen, Tiffany Ann, Jill Renee, Trevor Ashley. BS, U. N.Mex., 1959; MD, U. Colo., 1963; JD, U. N.Mex. 1987. Diplomate Am. Bd. Radiology, Am. Bd. Nuclear Medicine, Am. Bd. Legal Medicine, 1989; Bar: N.Mex. 1987, U.S. Dist. Ct. N.Mex. 1988. Intern U.S. Gen. Hosp., Tripler, Honolulu, 1963-64; resident in radiology U.S. Gen. Hosp., Brook and San Antonio, Tex., 1964-67; radiologist, ptnr. Van Atta Labs., Albuquerque, 1970-88, Radiology Assocs. of Albuquerque, 1988—, pres., 1994—; radiologist, ptnr. Civerolo, Hansen & Wolf, Albuquerque, 1988-89; adj. asst. prof. radiology U. N.Mex., 1970-71; pres. med. staff AT & SF Meml. Hosp., 1979-80, chief of staff, 1980-81, trustee, 1981-83. Author: District Attorney manual, 1987. Participant breast screening, Am. Cancer Soc., Albuquerque, 1987-88; dir. profl. div. United Way, Albuquerque, 1975. Maj. U.S. Army 1963-70, Vietnam; col. M.C. USAR, 1988—. Decorated Bronze Star. Allergy fellow, 1960. Med.-Legal Tort Scholar award, 1987. Fellow Am. Coll. Radiology (councilor 1980-86, mem. med. legal com. 1990—), Am. Coll. Legal Medicine, Am. Coll. Nuclear Medicine, Radiology Assn. of Albuquerque; mem. AMA (Physicians' Recognition award 1969—), Am. Soc. Law & Medicine, Am. Arbitration Assn., Albbuquerque Bar Assn., Am. Coll. Nuclear Physicians (charter), Soc. Nuclear Medicine (v.p. Rocky Mountain chpt. 1975-76), Am. Inst. Ultrasound in Medicine, N.Am. Radiol. Soc. (chmn. med. legal com. 1992-95), N.Mex. Radiol. Soc. (pres. 1978-79), N.Mex. Med. Soc. (chmn. grievance com.), Albuquerque-Bernalillo County Med. Soc. (scholar 1959), Nat. Assn. Health Lawyers, ABA (antitrust sect. 1986—), N. Mex. State Bar, Albuquerque Bar Assn., Sigma Chi. Republican. Methodist. Club: Albuquerque Country. Lodges: Elks, Masons, Shriners. Home: 3333 Santa Clara Ave SE Albuquerque NM 87106-1530 Office: Van Atta Imaging Ctr A-6 Med Arts Sq 801 Encino Pl NE Albuquerque NM 87102-2612

STEVENSON, ROBERT BENJAMIN, III, prosthodontist, writer; b. Topeka, Feb. 13, 1950; s. Robert Benjamin and Martha (McClelland) S.; m. Barbara Jean Sulick, June 6, 1975; children: Jody Ann, Robert Woodrow. BS, U. Miami, Coral Gables, Fla., 1972; DDS, Ohio State U., 1975, MS, MA, 1980, cert. in prosthodontics splty. tng., 1980. Practice dentistry specializing in prosthodontics Columbus, Ohio, 1981—; clin. asst. prof. Ohio State U., Columbus, 1981-87; chmn. oral cancer com. Columbus Dental Soc., 1981-85, Am. Cancer Soc., Columbus, 1985—; vol. dentist Provodencialis Ctr., Turks and Chicos Islands, Brit. West Indies, 1982-87. Editor: Columbus Dental Soc. Bull., 1981-87, 89-92; assoc. editor Ohio State U. Dental Alumni Quar., 1982—, Am. Med. Writer's Assn. Ohio Newsletter, 1983-86, Ohio State Journalism Alumni Assn. Newsletter, 1986-88; assoc. editor Jour. Prosthetic Dentistry, 1987-92; inventor intraoral measuring device. Vol. Am. Cancer Soc., Columbus, 1982—, Gaharına and Reynoldsburg, Ohio, 1983, 84; fundraiser Columbus council Boy Scouts of Am., 1984. Served to capt. USAF, 1975-78. Mem. ADA, Am. Coll. Prosthodontists, Ohio Dental Assn. (alt. del. 1982-89, del. 1990-92, new products editor newsletter 1988—), Carl Boucher Prosthodontic Conf. (editor 1987-92, sec. 1992—), Proscrastinator's Club Am. Home: 1300 Southport Cir Columbus OH 43235-7642 Office: 3600 Olentangy River Rd Columbus OH 43214-3437

STEVENSON, ROBERT NEWTON, cardiologist; b. Sevenoaks, Kent, England, Dec. 11, 1958; s. Arthur James and Marie (Evans) S.; m. Lindsey Jane Yeoman, Mar. 18, 1995; 1 child, Trevor Arthur. BS with honors, London U., 1980, MBBS, 1983, MD, 1993. Registrar in cardiology Univ. Coll. Hosp., London, 1986-87; registrar in cardiology London Chest Hosp., 1987-89, rsch. fellow, 1989-93; cons. cardiologist Huddersfield (England) Royal Infirmary, 1993—; presenter in field. Contbr. articles to profl. jours. Mem. Royal Coll. Physicians, Brit. Cardiac Soc. Home: Kestrel House Green Abbey, Holmfirth HD7 1SH, England Office: Huddersfield Royal Infirmar, Acre St Lindley, Huddersfield HD3 3EA, England

STEVENSON, ROGER E., geneticist; b. Neeses, S.C., 1940. MD, Bowman Gray Sch. of Medicine, Winston Salem, S.C., 1966. Office: 1 Gregor Mendel Cir Greenwood SC 29646-2307*

STEVENSON, SHARON, veterinarian, educator; b. Columbus, Ohio, Aug. 28, 1949; d. John David and Marilyn (Miller) S.; m. Donald R.G. DeOreo, Dec. 15, 1990 dec. Nov., 1994). D in Veterinary Medicine, Ohio State U., 1975, MSc in Veterinary Pathobiology, 1978; PhD in Comparative Pathology, U. Calif., Davis, 1985. Diplomate Am. Coll. Vet. Surgeons; lic. vet., Ohio. Intern in large animal medicine and surgery U. Pa. New Bolton Ctr., Kennett Sq., Pa., 1975-76; postdoctoral NIH trainee dept. vet. pathobiology Ohio State U., Columbus, 1976-77, resident in small animal surgery, 1977-80; vis. surgeon Ctr. Hosp. Animal Il de France, Creteil, France, 1979; rotation in pediatric thoracic surgery Children's Hosp., Columbus, 1980; clin. asst. prof. small animal surgery Coll. Vet. Medicine Ohio State U., Columbus, 1980; adj. clin. asst. prof. dept. vet. clin. scis. Coll.

Vet. Medicine, Ohio State U., Columbus, 1986—; asst. prof. dept surgery Tufts U. Coll. Vet. Medicine, Boston, 1981-82; postgrad. rsch. pathologist dept. pathology Sch. of Vet. Medicine U. Calif., Davis, 1982-85; asst. prof. dept. orthop. Sch. Medicine Case Western Reserve U., Cleve., 1985-93, assoc. dir. rsch. dept. orthop., 1992—, assoc. prof. dept. orthop., 1993—; staff surgeon Crago Vet. Clinic, Youngstown, Ohio, 1987-90, Akron (Ohio) Vet. Surg. Assocs., 1991—; rsch. dir. Musculoskeletal Tansplant Found., Holmdel, N.J., 1990—; sst. Anatomisches Inst., U. Bern, Switzerland, 1981; asst. prof. dept. surgery Coll. Vet. Medicine, Tufts U., 1981-82; cons., reviewer Jour. Bone and Joint Surgery, Jour. Am. Vet. Med. Assn., Jour. Biomed. Materials Rsch., Jour. Orthop. Rsch.; mem. bd. consulting editors for Rsch., Jour. of Bone and Joint Surgery. Contbr. numerous articles and abstracts to profl. jours.; author: (with others) Techniques in Small Animal Surgery, 1983, 89, Textbook of Small Animal Surgery, 1985, rev. 2d edit. 1991, Surgery of the Musculoskeletal System, 2d edit. 1989, Bone and Cartilege Allografts, 1991, Allografts in Orthopaedic Practice, 1992, Seminars in Arthroplasty: Grafts in Arthroplasty Surgery, 1993. Recipient Oscar V. Brumley award, 1975, Angela Knott Butler award, 1979, Outstanding Young Alumnus award, Ohio State U. Vet. Medicine Alumni Assn., 1985, Russell Hibbs award, Scoliosis Rsch. Soc., 1992; grantee: Biomed. Rsch. Support Program, 1983, 84, Morris Animal Found., 1984-85, NIH, 1985-96, 85-96, 85-89, 87-92, 93-98, Rsch. Initiation grant, 1986-87, Orthop. Rsch. and Edn. Found., 1988-90. Mem. Am. Vet. Med. Assn., Orthop. Rsch. Soc., Vet. Orthop. Soc., A-O Vet, Am. Acad. Orthop. Surgeons. Office: Case Western Reserve U Dept Orthops 11100 Euclid Ave Cleveland OH 44106

STEVENSON, THOMAS RAY, plastic surgeon; b. Kansas City, Mo., Jan. 22, 1946; s. John Adolph and Helen Ray (Clarke) S.; m. Judith Ann Hunter, Aug. 17, 1968; children: Anne Hunter, Andrew Thomas. BA, U. Kans., 1968, MD. Diplomate Am. Bd. Plastic and Reconstructive Surgery, Am. Bd. Surgery. Resident in gen. surgery U. Va., Charlottesville, 1972-78; resident in plastic surgery Emory U., Atlanta, 1980-82; asst. prof. surgery U. Mich., 1982-88, assoc. prof. surgery, 1988—; chief plastic surgery Ann Arbor VA Hosp., 1982—. Served to maj. USAR, 1978-80. Fellow ACS; mem. Am. Soc. Plastic and Reconstructive Surgery.

STEWARD, LESTER HOWARD, addictiologist, academic administrator; b. Burt, Iowa, Nov. 6, 1930; m. Patricia Byrness Roach, June 17, 1953; children: Donald Howard, Thomas Eugene, Susan Elaine, Joan Marsha. BS, Ariz. State U., 1958, MA in Sci. Edn., 1969; PhD in Psychology, Calif. Coast U., 1974; postgrad., Escuela Nat. U., Mex., 1971-80; MD, Western U. Hahnemann Coll., 1980. Rscher. drug abuse and alcoholism Western Australia U., Perth, Australia, 1970-71; intern in psychiatry Helix Hosp., San Diego, Calif., 1971-72; rscher. drug addiction North Mountain Behavioral Inst., Phoenix, 1975-77; exec. v.p., chief exec. officer James Tyler Kent Coll., 1977-80; pres., chief exec. officer Western U. Sch. Medicine, 1980-86; instr. psychology USN Westpac, Subic Bay, Philippines, 1988-91; pvt. practice preventive medicine Tecate, Baja California, Mexico, 1971-88; instr. Modern Hypnosis Instrn. Ctr., 1974—, Maricopa Tech. Community Coll., Phoenix, 1975-77; mem. Nt. Ctr. Homeopathy, Washington, Menninger Found., Wichita, Kans. Contbr. numerous papers to profl. confs. Leader Creighton Sch. dist. Boy Scouts Am., Phoenix, 1954-58. Lt. Cmdr. USN, 1949-54, 60-63, Korea. Fellow Am. Acad. Med. Adminstrs., Am. Assn. Clinic Physicians and Surgeons, Internat. Coll. Physicians and Surgeons, Am. Coll. Homeopathic Physicians, Am. Counc. Sex Therapy; mem. numerous orgns. including Nat. Psychol. Assn., Am. Psychotherapy Assn., Royal Soc. Physicians, World Med. Assn., Am. Acad. Preventive Medicine, Am. Bd. Examiners in Psychotherapy, Am. Bd. Examiners in Homeopathy, Western Homeopathic Med. Soc. (exec. dir.), Ariz. Profl. Soc. Hypnosis (founder 1974). Home: 515 W Townley Ave Phoenix AZ 85021-4566

STEWARD, OSWALD, neuroscience educator, researcher; b. Sept. 12, 1948; m. Kathy L. Pyle; children: Jessica, Oswald IV. BA in Psychology magna cum laude, U. Colo., 1970; PhD in Psychobiology, U. Calif., Irvine, 1974. Asst. prof. neurosurgery and physiology U. Va. Sch. Medicine, Charlottesville, 1974-79, assoc. prof., 1979-84, prof., 1984-86, acting chmn. neurosci. dept., 1986-88, chmn., 1988—. Author: Principles of Cellular, Molecular, and Developmental Neuroscience, 1989; contbr. about 125 articles and revs. to profl. publs. Predoctoral fellow NIMH, Bethesda, Md., 1971-74; rsch. career devel. grantee NIH, 1978-83, Jacob Javitts neurosci. grantee NIH, 1987-94. Mem. Soc. for Neurosci. (chmn. chpts. com. 1985-87). Office: U Va Sch Medicine PO Box 5148 Charlottesville VA 22908

STEWART, ALBERT, JR., retired physician; b. Fayetteville, N.C., Sept. 23, 1920; s. Albert and Winnie Davis (Bruton) S.; student U. S.C., 1936-37; A.B., U. N.C., 1941; M.D., Washington U., 1944; m. Mary Inglesby DuBose, Oct. 5, 1951; children—Albert III, David DuBose, Paul Finley, Charles Inglesby, James Bruton. Intern, Barnes Hosp., St. Louis, 1944-45; fellow in medicine Washington U., St. Louis, 1946-47; ships surgeon Grace Line, N.Y.C., 1947; resident physician Meml. Hosp., Charlotte, N.C., 1948; fellow in gastroenterology Lahey Clinic, Boston, 1949; practice medicine specializing in internal medicine, Fayetteville, 1950-94; ret., 1994; physician VA Hosp., Fayetteville, 1950-51, cons., 1955-70; attending physician Cape Fear Valley Hosp., chief of staff, 1959; attending physician Highsmith Hosp., chief staff, 1965; clin. assoc. prof. medicine U. N.C. Sch. Medicine, 1968-89; dir. East Coast Fed. Savs. Bank. Trustee, Highsmith-Rainey Meml. Hosp., 1983-86, N.C. Cancer Inst., 1978-86. Served as lt. (j.g.) M.C., USNR, 1945-46, to lt. M.C., USNR, 1952-54. Diplomate Am. Bd. Internal Medicine. Fellow ACP (councillor N.C. chpt. 1982-85); mem. AMA, N.C. Med. Soc. (1st v.p. 1978-79), Cumberland County Med. Soc. (pres. 1952), Am. Soc. Internal Medicine, N.C. Soc. Internal Medicine (pres. 1981-82), Fayetteville Area C. of C. (dir. 1974-77), St. Andrew's Soc. of N.C. (dir. 1982-88), Cape Fear Assembly (pres. 1971-73). Republican. Episcopalian. Club: Kiwanis (dir. 1980-81). Home: 1507 Morganton Rd Fayetteville NC 28305-4735

STEWART, ALEXANDER CONSTANTINE, medical technologist; b. N.Y.C., Nov. 3, 1957; s. Dudley Constantine and Lillian Eunice (Mills) S.; m. Shirlene Denise Keys, June 22, 1985; children: Shechianh Faith, Akilah Danielle, Omari Joseph Constantine. Student, Herbert H. Lehman Coll., 1975-77; BS in Med. Tech., U. Kans., 1979; BTh, Northgate Bible Coll., 1989. Cert. med. technologist Am. Soc. Clin. Pathologists.$Dert. clin. lab. supr. Nat. Cert. Agy. Med. Lab. Pers. Chemistry technologist White Plains (N.Y.) Med. Ctr., 1979-89, Mt. Vernon (N.Y.) Hosp., 1987-89; chemistry supr. St. Agnes Hosp., White Plains, 1989-92, Westchester Sq. Med. Ctr., Bronx, N.Y., 1992-93; med. technologist Richland Meml. Hosp., Columbia, S.C., 1993—; instr. William Lee Bonner Sch. Bible & Theology, 1995—. Asst. historian Ch. of Our Lord Jesus Christ, 1989—; deacon Refuge Temple, Ch. of Our Lord Jesus Christ, 1993—. Mem. NAACP, Soc. Pentecostal Studies (editl. com. 1992—), Pentecostal Hist. Soc. Democrat. Pentecostal. Home: 801 River Walk Way Irmo SC 29063-9375 also: Refuge Temple 4450 Argent Ct Columbia SC 29203 also: 4159 Grace Ave Bronx NY 10466-2015

STEWART, ANN PARRIS, gerontology nurse, educator; b. Jamaica, W.I., May 26, 1940; d. Ivan Samuel and Gladys May (Barrett) Parris; m. Alvin James Stewart, Nov. 6, 1971; children: Nedra Ann, Alwyn James. Diploma, St. Mary's Hosp., 1970; BS, St. Francis Coll., 1978; MS in Gerontology, Coll. of New Rochelle, N.Y., 1986. Patient care coord. Westchester Sq. Hosp., Bronx, N.Y.; staff nurse VA Hosp., Bronx; pub. health nurse, coord. Bronx VA Hosp., staff devel. coord., nursing educator; patient care coord. Bronx VA Med. Ctr. Mem. N.Y. State Nurse's Assn. Home: 1126 W Laurelton Pky # W Teaneck NJ 07666-2750

STEWART, ARTHUR VAN, dental educator, geriatric health administrator; b. Buffalo, N.Y., July 25, 1938; s. Arthur Sharpe and Doris (Simpson) S.; m. Jacqueline Fischer, June 5, 1965; children: Mark Van, Laura Kristin, Jeffrey Fischer. BS in Chemistry, U. Pitts., 1960, DMD, 1968, PhD, 1973. Clin. lic. Ky., Pa., N.J. USPHS postdoctoral fellow U. Pitts., 1968-70; chair, cmty. dentistry dept.; dean, student affairs Fairleigh Dickinson U., Teaneck, N.J., 1970-75; dean for acad. affairs U. Louisville Dental Sch., 1975-88, asst. provost, 1985-89, prof. dentistry, 1975—; dir., Ctr. on Aging U. Louisville Health Scis. Ctr., 1995—; cons. ADA, Chgo., OVAR: Geriatric Edn. Ctr., Lexington, Ky.; ednl. cons. Baylor U., Dallas; cons. Am. Assn. Dental Schs., Washington. Contbr. over 300 articles to profl. jours., chpts. to books, separately published monographs; presenter in field. Bd. mem. U. of Louisville Student Ctr., 1986-89, YMCA Camp Piomingo, Louisville, 1980-90; leader Cub Scout/Weblos, Boy Scouts of Am., Louisville, 1985-90. Recipient tchg. award Metroversity of Louisville, 1989, 90, 92; recipient over $2,000,000 in rsch. grants and awards. Mem. Ky. Dental Assn. (del. 1988—), Louisville Dental Soc. (chmn. 1994-95, Pres.'s award 1995), Ky. Assn. for Gerontology (pres. 1995-96), Quest for Excellence (dir. 1988-96), OKU Honorary Soc. (pres. 1978-79), Delphi Honorary Soc. (pres. 1980-96). Office: Univ of Louisville Sch of Dentistry 501 S Preston Louisville KY 40292

STEWART, BARBARA LYNNE, geriatrics nursing educator; b. Youngstown, Ohio, May 10, 1953; d. Carl Arvid and Margaret (Ashton) Swanson; m. James G. Stewart, Mar. 17, 1973; children: Trevor J., Troy C. AAS, Youngstown State U., 1973, BS, 1982. Cert. gerontol. nurse, ANCC. Asst. dist. office supr. divsn. quality assurance Bureau of Healthcare Stds. and Quality; supr., dir. nursing svcs. Peaceful Acres Nursing Home, North Lima, Ohio; nurse repondent Health Sci. Ctr. U. Colo., Denver; charge nurse Westwood Rehab. Med. Ctr., Inc., Boardman, Ohio, Park Vista Health Care Ctr., Youngstown, Ohio; dir. nursing Rolling Acres Care Ctr., North Lima, Ohio; primary instr. Alliance (Ohio) Tng. Ctr., Inc.; asst. dist. office supr. divsn. of quality assurance Bureau Healthcare Stds. and Quality, Akron, Ohio. Former instr. CPR, ARC. Mem. Tri County Dir. Nurses Assn., Nat. Gerontol. Nursing Assn. (nomination com.), Youngstown State U. Alumni Assn.

STEWART, BETTY LOUISE, family nurse practitioner; b. Brawley, Calif., Jan. 21, 1952; d. Herman Rainey and Laura Mae Masters Lawrence; m. Charles James Stewart, May 4, 1974 (div. 1986); children: Sikia, Soyini. Studetn, San Diego City Coll., 1971-72; AS, Contra Costa Coll., San Pablo, Calif., 1980, student, 1982-85; student, U. Calif., Davis, 1990-92. RN, Calif., Ga.; cert. family nurse practitioner. Nurse Skilled Nursing Facilities, Richmond/San Diego, 1972-78, Merrithew Meml. Hosp., Martinez, Calif., 1978-79; nurse Kaiser Hosp., Richmond, 1979-87, Sacramento, 1987-93; family nurse practitioner Mercy Med. Clinic, Sacramento, 1993, Dr. Juan Roman Family Practice, Sacramento, 1994, U. Calif. Davis Child Protection Ctr., Sacramento, 1994, West Coast Med. Ctr., Sacramento, 1994; nurse Fulton Correctional Facility, Atlanta, 1995—; vol. St. Claire's Skilled Nursing Facility, Sacramento, 1989-94. Vol. Mt. Calvary Bapt. Ch., Sacramento, 1987—. Sinkler-Miller Med. Assn. scholar, 1990, Sacramento Black Nurses Assn. scholar, 1990. Democrat. Home: PO Box 1351 Smyrna GA 30081-1351

STEWART, BOBBY GENE, laboratory director; b. Jesse, W.Va., Apr. 18, 1940; s. Leonard Mart and Zeta Marie Stewart; m. Linda May Smith, Mar. 17, 1961; children: Barbara Lynn, Ramona Jean Stewart Pinkerman. Cert. in med. tech., Army Med. Svc. Sch., 1960; cert. blood banking specialist, 10th Med. Rsch. Lab., Landstuhl, Germany, 1961. Lic. nursing home adminstr., Mo.; cert. clin. lab. scientist, bioanalytical lab. mgr. Med. and x-ray technologist Oceana (W.Va.) Med. Ctr., 1962-68; clin. mgr., med. technologist Sigourney (Iowa) Med. Clinic, 1968-69; staff med. and x-ray technologist Van Buren County Hosp., Keosauqua, Iowa, 1969; dir. lab. and x-ray svcs. Scotland County Hosp., Memphis, Mo., 1969-71; dir. lab. svcs. Keller Meml. Hosp., Fayette, Mo., 1971-95, Regional Med. Assocs., Fayette, 1995—; clin. lab. mgr. Mem. city coun. City of Fayette, 1977-85, mayor pro-tem, 1980-85, chmn. parks and recreation com., 1977-80, chmn. elec. dist. com., 1981-85. With U.S. Army, 1959-62. Mem. Am. Med. Technologists (dist. councillor 1977-81, 88-93, nat. bd. dirs. 1993—, nat. treas. 1994—, Disting. Achievement award 1976, Exceptional Merit award 1981), Mo. State Soc. of AMT (legis. chmn. 1975-90, v.p. 1973-74, 89-90, pres. 1975-76, Med. Technologist of Yr. 1977). Home: 410 Cooper St Fayette MO 65248 Office: Regional Med Assocs 600 W Morrison Fayette MO 65248

STEWART, BONNIE LOUISE, psychologist; b. Pittsfield, Mass., Nov. 9, 1952; d. Alan Perkins and Suzanne R. (Forster) S.; m. Allen Arthur Meyer, Sept. 13, 1975. BS, Springfield Coll., 1975; MEd, U. Pa., 1983, PhD, 1990. Asst. payroll mgr. G. Fox & Co., Hartford, Conn., 1973-77; territory mgr. Certain Teed Corp., Valley Forge, Pa., 1977-81; rsch. coord. U. Pa. Counseling Ctr., Phila., 1985-88, U. Pa. Ctr. for Cognitive Therapy, Phila., 1988-90; project coord. Dave Garroway Lab., Phila., 1990-92; psychotherapist Psych Resource Assocs., Havertown, Pa., 1990—. Contbr. articles to profl. jours. Mem. APA. Office: Psych Resource Assocs 105 Town Center Rd Ste 1 King of Prussia PA 19406

STEWART, BRUCE EDMUND, SR., retired mechanical designer, writer; b. Mpls., Nov. 9, 1930; s. Milford James and Ivah Delano (Gallant) S.; m. Mary Incornata Christofore Stewart, May 25, 1957; children: Bruce Edmund Stewart Jr., Robert Daniel Stewart. AA, U. Minn., Mpls., 1950. Mem. engrng. dept. St. Paul Divsn. Whirlpool Corp., St. Paul, 1959-85; contractor Possis Tech. Svcs., Mpls., 1986-87; contract designer St. Croix Personnel, Inc., St. Paul, 1987-88; designer Distinction in Design, Mpls., 1988, St. Paul, 1988-91, Distinction in Design, Mpls., 1991; engr. Possis Tech. Svcs., Mpls., 1991, Source Tech., Mpls., 1992. Patentee in field. Sgt. Army Security Agy., 1950-53. Mem. Moose Lodge #963, Inventor's Network, Night Scribes. Home: 771 Belland Ave Saint Paul MN 55127

STEWART, DAVID DICKSON, psychologist; b. Sharon, Pa., Aug. 19, 1949; s. Thomas Dickson and Mary Ella (Rodecker) S.; m. Jodi Anne Martin, Dec. 13, 1970. BA, Mich. State U., 1971; MS, George Williams Coll., Downers Grove, Ill., 1974; PhD, U.S. Internat. U., San Diego, 1981. Lic. psychologist, Minn. Family therapist, team leader Youth in Crisis, Berwyn, Ill., 1974-75, counseling coordinator, 1975-77; program coordinator Harmonium, Inc., Poway, Calif., 1979-80; psychology intern Hennepin County Med. Ctr., Mpls., 1980-81; staff psychologist Dakota Mental Health Ctr., South St. Paul, Minn., 1981-86, dir. psychol. services, 1986, clin. dir., 1987-92; clin. dir. Linden Ctr. Psychol. Health, Eagan, Minn., 1992—. Mem. Am. Psychol. Assn., Minn. Psychol. Assn. Democrat. Office: Linden Ctr Psychological Health 3459 Washington Dr Saint Paul MN 55122-1347

STEWART, DAVID JAMES, cardiologist; b. Midland, Mich., Dec. 27, 1934; s. Leroy Hepburn and Zoa Irene (Hatchet) S.; m. Abbie Gale Pickett, Sept. 7, 1957; children: Kirk, Julia, Laura, Kenneth. BS in Chem. Engring., U. Colo., Boulder, 1957; MD, U. Colo., Denver, 1961. Diplomate Am. Bd. Internal Medicine and Cardiovascular Disease. Rotating intern Cin. Gen. Hosp., 1961-62, resident, 1962-63; resident in cardiology Cleveland Metropolitan Gen. Hosp., 1965-67, chief resident medicine, 1967-68; cardiologist The Everett (Wash.) Clinic, 1968-95; dir. Heart Ctr. Providence Gen. Med. Ctr., Everett, 1995—; bd. dirs. Gen. Hosp. Med. Ctr., Everett, 1975-95; bd. dirs. The Everett Clinic, 1975-79, pres., 1979; mem. med. dir. Heart Ctr. Gen. Hosp. Med. Ctr., Everett, 1984-87; med. dir. Saunders Reg. Heart Ctr., 1987—; med. coord. Cardiac Emergency Network, 1988—. Editor Cardiac Emergency Network (newspaper), 1988-91. Bd. dirs. Am. Heart Assn. Wash., Seattle, 1970-90, pres., 1979-80, pres. Snohomish Divsn., 1995-96; mem. adv. bd. Pros. Attys., Snohomish County, 1985-86. Capt. USAF, 1963-65. Fellow Am. Coll. Cardiology, Am. Coll. Internal Medicine, North Pacific Soc. Internal Medicine. Home: 5028 27th Ave W Everett WA 98203 Office: Providence Gen Med Ctr 13th & Colby Everett WA 98201

STEWART, GORDON THALLON, public health educator; b. Paisley, Scotland, Feb. 5, 1919; s. John and Mary Lang (Thallon) S.; m. Joan Kego, Mar. 27, 1946 (div. Mar. 1975); children: Linda, Ian, Jane, Jonathan; m. Georgina Houston Walker, Mar. 21, 1975. BSc, U. Glasgow, Scotland, 1939, MB, ChB, 1942, MD, 1949; Diploma in Hygiene and Tropical Medicine, U. Liverpool, Eng., 1947. Med. diplomate in internal medicine, pathology and pub. health. Sr. resident City Hosp. Aberdeen, Scotland, 1946; rsch. fellow U. Liverpool, 1946-48; sr. registrar, tutor St. Mary's Hosp., London, 1949-52; vis. prof. WHO, Geneva, 1953-54; cons. microbiology SW Met. Hosp. Bd., London, 1954-63; prof. epidemiology U. N.C., Chapel Hill, 1963-68, Tulane U., New Orleans, 1968-71; prof. pub. health U. Glasgow, 1972-83, prof. emeritus, 1983—; vis. prof. Dow Med. Coll., Karachi, Pakistan, 1953, Cornell U., N.Y.C., 1971-72; cons. WHO, 1952-86, Research Triangle, N.C., 1964-70, N.Y.C. Health Dept., 1970-71. Author: Penicillin Group of Drugs, 1965; editor: Penicillin Allergy, 1971, Trends in Epidemiology, 1972; patentee in field. Dir. Drug Abuse Rsch. Team, New Orleans, 1968-72, inter-univ. Health Rsch. Tng., N.Y.C., 1971; sr. adviser Med. TV 4 Programmes, London, 1980—; commentator radio and TV, Europe and U.S.A., 1964—. Lt. Royal Navy, 1943-46. NSF fellow, 1964, Royal Coll. Physicians fellow, 1972, Royal Coll. Pathology fellow, 1964; NIH grantee, 1964-71. Fellow Med. Soc. London, Royal Soc. Medicine, Infectious Disease Soc. Am. Home: Glenavon Clifton Down, Bristol BS8 3HT, England

STEWART, HAROLD LEROY, pathologist, educator, cancer investigator; b. Houtzdale, Pa., Aug. 6, 1899; s. Alexander and Lillie (Cox) S.; m. Cecelia Eleanor Finn, Sept. 30, 1929; children: Robert Campbell, Janet Eileen. Student, U. Pa., 1919-20, Dickinson Coll., 1921-22; M.D., Jefferson Med. Coll., 1926; grad., Army Med. Sch., Washington, 1929; research fellow, Jefferson Med. Coll., 1929-30, Harvard, 1937-39; Med. Sc.D. (hon.), Jefferson Med. Coll., 1964; D.Medicine and Surgery (hon.), U. Perugia, 1965, U. Turku, Finland, 1970; Doctor (hon.), Kagawa (Japan) Med. Sch., 1992. Diplomate Am. Bd. Pathology, Pan Am. Med. Assn. Intern Fitzimmons Gen. Hosp., Denver, 1926-27; instr. to asst. prof. pathology Jefferson Med. Coll., 1930-37; asst. pathologist Jefferson Med. Coll. Hosp., Phila. Gen. Hosp., 1929-37; pathologist Office Cancer Investigations Harvard, USPHS, 1937-39; chief lab. pathology Nat. Cancer Inst., USPHS, Bethesda, Md., 1939-69; chief pathologic anatomy dept. clin. ctr. NIH, 1954-69; organizer Registry Exptl. Cancers, 1970—, Sci. emeritus, 1976—; prin. investigator, head WHO Collaborating Centre for Rsch. on Tumors Lab. Animals, 1976-96; clin. prof. pathology Georgetown U., 1965—; Cons. FDA, 1969-71, Nat. Cancer Inst., 1970-76, Armed Forces Inst. Pathology, 1950—; cons., mem. study groups WHO, 1957-81, mem. expert adv. panel cancer, 1957-81; Mem. subcom. oncology NRC, 1947-65, mem. com. pathology, 1958-66, com. cancer diagnosis and therapy, 1951-57, mem. com. animal models and genetic stocks, 1972-75, chmn. com. histologic classification Lab. Animal Tumors, 1975-79; chmn. subcom. classification rat liver tumors NRC (Lab. Animal Tumors), 1976-79; chmn. U.S.A. Com. Internat. Coun. Socs. Pathology, 1957-62, 69-75; chmn. U.S. nat. com. Internat. Union Against Cancer, 1953-59, U.S. del., 1952-74; Mem. adv. bd. Leonard Wood Meml., 1961-66; mem. com. to advance world-wide fight against cancer Am. Cancer Soc., 1963-76; mem. med. rsch. coun. Referees, New Zealand, 1987. Mem. editoral bd. Cancer Rsch., 1941-49, A.M.A. Archives of Pathology, 1957-62, Jour. Toxicology Pathology, 1988; editorial adviser Jour. Nat. Cancer Inst, 1947-56; contbr. articles to profl. jours. Trustee Thomas Jefferson U., Phila., 1969-72. Served as pvt. USMC, 1918-19; lt. M.C. U.S. Army, 1926-29; from maj. to lt. col. M.C. AUS, 1942-46. Recipient Lucy Wortham James award James Ewing Soc., 1967, Alumni Achievement award Jefferson Med. Coll., 1966, Disting. Svc. award HEW, 1966, Honors award NIH, The Dirs. award NIH, 1988, Dean's medal Jefferson Med. Coll., 1994; Dedication Jour. Exptl. Pathology, Vol. 1, No. 2, 1987, Harold L. Stewart Fund for Exptl. Pathology and Harold L. Stewart Lectureship established at Uniformed Svcs. U. of Health Scis., Bethesda, Md., 1986; honored by dedication in two books. Mem. Soc. Clin. Pathologists (Ward Burdick award 1957), Am. Assn. Cancer Rsch. (pres. 1958-59), Am. Soc. Exptl. Pathology (hon., pres. 1995), Am. Assn. Pathologists (Gold-headed Cane award 1978), Coll. Am. Pathologists, Md. Soc. Pathologists (pres. 1950-51), Washington Soc. Pathologists (sec.-treas. 1947-51), Internat. Acad. Pathology (pres. 1953-55, F.K. Mostofi award 1976), Internat. Union Against Cancer (exec. com. 1952-70, v.p. 1962), Mass. Med. Soc., Internat. Coun. Socs. Pathology (pres. 1962), Internat. Soc. Geog. Pathology, Colegio Anatomico Brasilerio (hon.), Soc. Italiana di Cancerologia (hon.), Inst. Nat. de Cancerologia Mex. (hon.), Soc. Columbiana de Patologia (hon.), Soc. Belge d' Anatomie Pathologique (hon.), Soc. Peruana Cancerologia (hon.), Soc. Cryobiology, Soc. Toxicologic Pathologists (hon.), Japanese Cancer Soc. (hon.), Basic Found. Internat. Inst of Immanopathology Clin. Ctr. Humablt U., Berlin (hon. sci. dir.), Purdy Stout Surg. Pathology Soc. (hon.), others. Home: 119 S Adams St Rockville MD 20850-2315

STEWART, JAMES RUSSELL, military flight surgeon, physician, air force officer; b. Pasadena, Calif., Apr. 26, 1955; s. Quentin Theodore and Mary Elizabeth (King) S.; m. Margie Stewart, Aug. 10, 1978; children: Cameron, Kylie, Phillip, Ashley, Andrew. BA, Brigham Young U., 1981; DO, Kirksville Coll. Osteo., 1985. Diplomate Am. Bd. Family Practice. Commd. 2d lt. U.S. Army, 1985, advanced through grades to maj., 1995; family practice resident Martin Army Cmty. Hosp., Ft. Benning, Ga., 1985-88; staff flight surgeon, family physician Weed Army Cmty. Hosp., Ft. Irwin, Calif., 1988-89, med. chief staff, 1989-91; staff family physician Evans Army Cmty. Hosp., Ft. Carson, Colo., 1991-92; sr. med. officer, flight surgeon Coast Guard Air Sta., Clearwater, Fla., 1992-94; transferred to USAF, Mountain Home AFB, Idaho, 1994-95; chief family practice 366th Med. Ops. Squadron, Mountain Home AFB, Idaho, 1994-96; sr. flight surgeon, comdr. 366th Aerospace Medicine Squadron, Mountain Home AFB, Idaho, 1995-96; chief resident Martin Army Cmty. Hosp., 1987-88; dep. commdr. clin. svcs. Weed Army Cmty. Hosp., 1989-91. Contbr. articles to profl. jours., chpt. to book. Recipient Gen. Douglas MacArthur Leadership award MacArthur Found., Norfolk, Va., 1989, Positive Medicine Profile award Positive Medicine Project AMA and Am. hosp. Assn., Phila., 1995. Fellow Am. Acad. Family Practice; mem. Uniformed Svcs. Acad. Family Practice, Soc. USAF Flight Surgeons, Assn. Mil. Osteo. Physicians and Surgeons (program dir. 1994). Mem. Ch. LDS. Office: 366th Aerospace Medicine Squadron/CC 90 Hope Dr Mountain Home AFB ID 83648

STEWART, JEAN CATHERINE, critical care and neuroscience trauma nurse, educator; b. Pitts., July 12, 1948; d. Frank E. and Bertha G. (Drawdy) Henry. BSN, Ariz. State U., 1971; MSN, U. Tex., Houston, 1988. Cert. neurosci. RN; cert. emergency nurse; cert. trauma nurse; instr. ACLS. Neurosurg. nursing cons. The Meth. Hosp., Houston, 1981-84; staff devel. instr. M.D. Anderson Hosp. and Tumor Inst., Houston, 1984-85; staff nurse Ben Taub Gen. Hosp., Houston, 1985-87, continuing edn. instr., 1987-91; clin. nurse specialist neurosci./orthopedics/trauma div. U. Calif. Med. Ctr., San Diego, 1991-96; presenter meetings and confs. various profl. orgns.; announcer Dial A Shuttle program Nat. Space Insts. Mem. manuscript rev. bd. Jour. Neuroscis. Nurses.; editorial rev. bd. Dimensions in Oncology Nursing. Recipient Millie Fields Rsch. Assistance award U. Tex., 1987. Mem. AACN (Rsch. award 1987, rsch. grantee Houston Gulf Coast chpt.), Emergency Nurses Assn., Am. Assn. Neurosci. Nurses (founding mem., past treas. S.C. chpt., pres. and program dir. Houston chpt., bd. dirs. div. nursing affairs 1991-93), Am. Assn. Neurol. Surgeons, Harvey Cushing Soc. (assoc.), World Fedn. Neurosci. Nurses, Soc. Trauma Nursing, Nat. Space Inst., Sigma Theta Tau. Home and Office: 1640 10th Ave # 103 San Diego CA 92101

STEWART, JOHN ANTENEN, retired physician; b. Hamilton, Ohio, Sept. 1, 1920; s. James E.B. and Rose Carol (Antenen) S.; m. Marian Louise Vail, June 23, 1945; children: John Vail, Robert Vail, Barbara Vail Stewart Keating. BS, U. Cin., 1942, MD, 1945. Diplomate Am. Bd. Ob-Gyn. Intern Harper Hosp., Detroit, 1945-46; at VA Hosp., 1946-48; resident Chgo. Maternity Ctr., 1948-49, Chgo. Lying-In Hosp., 1949, Ravenswood Hosp., Chgo., 1949-51; practice medicine specializing in ob-gyn Hamilton, Ohio, 1951-93; ret. Mem. Hist. Hamilton; elder Presbyn. Ch. Served to capt. M.C., U.S. Army, 1942-48. Fellow Am. Coll. Ob-Gyn; mem. AMA, Ohio Med. Soc., Butler County Med. Soc., Hamilton Acad. Medicine, Royal Soc. Medicine (Eng.), Am. Inst. Ultrasound Medicine, Am. Assn. Laparoscopists and Colposcopists, Am. Soc. for Colposcopy and Cervical Pathology, Am. Inst. Nuclear Magnetic Resonance, Am. Guild Organists, Am. Theatre Organists Assn., Ohio Genealogy Soc., Butler County Hist. Soc. Republican. Home and Office: 701 Oakwood Dr Hamilton OH 45013-3601

STEWART, JOHN CAMERON, environmental protection specialist; b. Detroit, Oct. 2, 1943; s. Glenn Angus and Florence Ida (Cameron) S.; m. Maxine Helen Bohnet, June 20, 1980; 1 child, Ian Maximilian. BA, U. Miami, 1966; MA, U. Memphis, 1970. Urban planner Harland Bartholomew & Assocs., Memphis, 1968-70; sr. planner Jacksonville (Fla.) Area Planning Bd., 1970-73; prin. environ. planner Md. Nat. Capital Park and Planning Commn., Silver Spring, 1973-80; environ. protection specialist U.S. Dept. of Def., Alexandria, Va., 1980-81; rsch. scientist U.S. Nuclear Regulatory Commn., Washington, 1981-89; sr. envir. protection specialist Dept. Energy, Washington, 1989—. Author: The Application of Low Level Waste Siting Criteria to Geographic Information Systems, 1988, Politics and Planning for the Nuclear State, 1987, Geographic Guidelines for the Siting of Low-Level Disposal Sites, 1987, U.S. Department of Energy Uses GIS to Evaluate Waste Management Alternatives, 1993; contbr. articles to profl. jours. 1st trombonist Rockville (Md.) Concert Band, 1987—. Mem. Am. Inst. Cert. Planners, St. Andrews Soc. of Washington (newsletter bus. mgr.), Clan Stewart Soc. of Am., Audubon Naturalist Soc. Episcopalian. Home:

3705 Dupont Ave Kensington MD 20895-2511 Office: US Dept Energy Washington DC 20585

STEWART, JULIAN MARK, pediatric cardiologist; b. Bklyn., July 24, 1947; s. Edward and Sally (Dinces) S.; m. Ellen L. Stewart, Sept. 12, 1970; children: Allison, Elizabeth, Michael. AB in Physics, Cornell U., 1968; PhD in Physiology, U. Chgo., 1976, MD, 1977. Diplomate Am. Bd. Pediatrics; cert. in pediatric cardiology. Asst. prof. pediat. Cornell Med. Ctr., N.Y.C., 1982-83; asst. prof. pediat. N.Y. Med. Coll., Valhalla, 1983-89, assoc. prof. pediat., 1989-96, prof. pediat. and physiology, 1996—; chmn. rsch. protocol com., Westchester Med. Ctr., Valhalla. Contbr. (book) Progress of Atrially Active Peptides, 1989. Fellow Am. Acad. Pediat., Am. Physiol. Soc., Am. Coll. Cardiology; mem. Am. Heart Assn., Phi Beta Kappa. Home: 75 Taymil Rd New Rochelle NY 10804 Office: NY Medical College Munger Pavilion Valhalla NY 10804

STEWART, KATHY JANE, anesthetist; b. Alexander City, Ala., Mar. 21, 1957; d. James Iverson and Eleanor (Alexander) S.; m. Charles Wade Gillard, June 21, 1981. BS, Emory U., 1983, MS in Anesthesiology with honors, 1991. Physicians asst. neonatal ICU Ga. Bapt. Med. Ctr., Atlanta, 1983-92; anesthetist Pediatric Anesthesia Specialist, Atlanta, 1991-92, Northside Anesthesiology, Atlanta, 1992—. Mem. Am. Acad. Anesthesiologist Asst. (pres. 1993-95), Am. Acad. Physician Assts. (pres. 1993-95). Home: 1462 Shenta Oak Dr Norcross GA 30093

STEWART, KENDALL LEUOMON, psychiatrist; b. Rome, Ga., Sept. 19, 1950; s. Leuomon and Flora Mae (Miller) S.; m. J. Faye Alley, Nov. 16, 1974; children: Jonathan Brock, Timothy Brenton. BS magna cum laude, Berry Coll., 1972; MD, Med. Coll. Ga., 1976. Diplomate Nat. Bd. Med. Examiners, Am. Bd. Psychiatry and Neurology. Resident in psychiatry Med. Coll. Ga., Augusta, 1976-79; pvt. practice medicine specializing in psychiatry Mercy Hosp., Portsmouth, Ohio, 1982-90, Scioto Meml. Hosp., Portsmouth, 1982-90, So. Hills Hosp., Portsmouth, 1982-87, So. Ohio Med. Ctr., Portsmouth, 1990—; cons. psychiatrist Beekman Ctr. for Mental Health Svcs., Greenwood, S.C., 1977-79, Comprehend, Inc., Maysville, Ky., 1982-83, Portsmouth Receiving Hosp., 1983, 91, So. Ohio Correctional Facility, Lucasville, 1982, Pathways, Inc., Greenup, Ky., 1982-87, Shawnee Mental Health Clinic, 1986-88, Sr. Citizen Ctr., 1988, Pastoral Counseling Ctr., 1991; mem. med. staff exec. com. Mercy Hosp., Portsmouth, 1984-87, chief of staff, 1986, Mental Health Bd. of Adams, Lawrence and Scioto Counties, 1982; dir. eating disorders clinic, 1986-93, agoraphobic clinic, 1986-93, St. Francis Pavillion Ctr., 1987-93, chief of psychiatry, 1988-90, 92; chmn. ethics com. So. Ohio Med. Ctr., quality assurance com., 1989, med. dir. 1992—; part-time asst. prof. psychiatry Ohio U. Coll. Osteo. Medicine, Athens, 1985—. Exec. bd. dirs. Scioto Area coun. Boy Scouts Am., 1993. Capt. USAF, 1979-81. Named one of Outstanding Young Men Am.; recipient Outstanding Faculty award Ohio U. Coll. Osteo. Medicine, 1986, Faculty Teaching award, 1991, 92, 93, 94. Mem. AMA, Am. Psychiat. Assn., Ohio Psychiat. Assn. (ethics com. 1988—, chair ethics com. 1991—, treas. 1993—), Ohio State Med. Assn., Scioto County Med. Soc., Portsmouth Rotary Club (bd. dirs. 1993). Republican. Home: 3251 Indian Dr Portsmouth OH 45662-2406 Office: 1671 Grant St Portsmouth OH 45662-3662

STEWART, LARRY R., oral surgeon; b. Memphis, Aug. 23, 1953; m. Deborah Lynn Malone, 1979; children: Todd Elliott, Meagan Ann. BA, Austin Coll., 1975; DDS, Baylor Coll. Dentistry, 1979; MS, U. Tex., 1982. Diplomate Am. Bd. Oral and Maxillofacial Surgeons. Sr. resident in oral and maxillofacial surgery Harris County Hosp. Dist., Ben Taub Hosp., 1982; active staff HCA Med. Ctr., Plano, Tex., 1982—; chief dept. surgery HCA Med. Ctr., Plano, 1988; courtesy staff Richardson Med. Ctr., 1983—; clin. assoc. prof. oral and maxillofacial surgery dept. Baylor Coll. Dentistry, 1993—; presenter in field. Recipient Bernard Gottlieb award in oral pathology and oral medicine, 1978. Fellow Am. Assn. Oral and Maxillofacial Surgeons; mem. ADA, Am. Acad. Implant Dentistry, Tex. Soc. Oral and Maxillofacial Surgeons (chmn. membership and ethics com. 1988-89, treas. 1989-90, v.p. 1990-91, pres.-elect 1991-92), North Tex. Soc. Oral and Maxillofacial Surgeons (pres. 1988), S.W. Soc. Oral and Maxillofacial Surgeons, Tex. Dental Assn. (den pac region IV rep. 1985-89, del. 1995-96), Greater Plano Dental Soc. (pres. 1989-90), Dallas County Dental Soc. (legis. com. mem. 1986, chmn. legis. com. 1990-91). Home: 1928 Carmel Dr Plano TX 75075 Office: Ste 403 3713 W 15th St Plano TX 75075

STEWART, LYN VARN, critical care nurse; b. Charleston, S.C., July 3, 1957; d. Allen Hamilton and Merilyn (Windsor) Varn; m. James Milton Stewart Jr., May 26, 1979; children: Kevin James, Sean Allen. BA in History, Clemson U., 1979; ADN, U. S.C., 1983. Cert. BLS, ACLS. Staff RN med.-surg. units Piedmont Med. Ctr., Rock Hill, S.C., 1983-85, staff nurse progressive care unit, 1985-94, RN, asst. head nurse progressive care unit, 1991-92, preceptor coord., 1991-93, quality improvement rep. progressive care unit, 1991-92; office nurse, cardiac stress testing Carolinas Med. Group-Shiland, Rock Hill, 1995—; preceptor coord., quality improvement rep. progressive care unit Piedmont Med. Ctr., Rock Hill, 1991-92; office RN cardiac stress testing Carolinas Med. Group-Shiland, Rock Hill, 1995—. Bd. dirs. Westminster Christian Sch., Rock Hill., 1991-93, mem. yearbook staff, 1991-93, mem. PTO bd., 1992-93, coach Westminster Little Tigers soccer team, 1992-93, asst. coach Westminster Lions soccer team, 1992-93; bd. trustees Westminster Catawba Christian Sch., Rock Hill, 1993-94, mem. PTO bd., 1993-95, newsletter editor, 1992—, co-coord. sch. soccer program, 1992-95, asst. coach under-10 & under-12 soccer team, 1994—; sec. Westminster Catawba Christian Sch. Athletic Booster Club, 1994—; founding mem. Spirit Soccer League, Rock Hill, 1996—. Mem. S.C. Assn. Nurses Endorsing Transplantation. Home: 603 Greenbriar Ave Rock Hill SC 29730-3301

STEWART, MIRIAM, utilization review professional; b. Afton, Wyo., Apr. 8, 1958; d. Howard William Vos and Carolyn Grace (Walker) Davis; children: Lesley, Vanessa. ADN, Indian Hills Community Coll., Ottumwa, Iowa, 1978. Staff nurse med./surg. St. Joseph Mercy Hosp., Clinton, Iowa, 1978-80; staff nurse surg. floor Wyo. Med. Ctr., Casper, 1980; staff nurse med./surg./ICU Meml. Hosp. Sheridan County, Wyo., 1981-82; with quality assurance/utilization rev. Meml. Hosp. Sheridan County, 1985-92; utilization rev. coord. Meml. Hosp. of Sheridan County, Wyo., 1992—.

STEWART, PAMELA MARY, pediatrics nurse; b. London, Aug. 8, 1927; d. Percy Gordon and Gladys Ann (Mummery) Finlow; m. Mark A. Stewart, Mar. 19, 1955; children: Sarah Gillian, Rosemary Anne, Duncan Robert. PNP cert., Washington U., 1972. CPNP, CNS pediatrics dept. U. Iowa, Iowa City, ret.; rep. caregiver Gov.'s Adv. Bd. on Alzheimers. Bd. dirs. Elderly Svcs., Inc., Hancher Guild. Fellow NAPAP; mem. Iowa Assn. Pediatric Nurse Practitioners. Home: 2012 Kestrel Rdg SW Oxford IA 52322-9111

STEWART, PAUL ARTHUR, pharmaceutical company executive; b. Greensburg, Ind., Sept. 28, 1955; s. John Arthur and Alberta Jeannette (Densford) S.; m. Susan Rhodes, Dec. 20, 1975; children: John Rhodes, Daniel Robbins; BS, Purdue U., 1976; MBA, Harvard Bus. Sch., 1987. Grad. asst. Purdue U., West Lafayette, Ind, 1977; asst. treas. Stewart Seeds, Inc., Greensburg, Ind., 1977-82, sec., treas., 1982-84; cons. The Boston Cons. Group, Inc., Chgo., 1986; founder, owner PASCO Group, mgmt. and computer cons., aircraft leasing, 1979-87; mgr. bus. planning-agrichems. Eli Lilly & Co., Indpls., 1987-88, dist. sales mgr. agrichems., 1989-90, tech. acquisition mgr. med. devices and diagnostics divsn., 1990-92; dir. mktg. info. and bus. devel. IVAC Corp. subs. Eli Lilly & Co., 1992-94, advisor corp., fin. and investment banking, 1994-96, mgr. global bus. devel. (animal health), 1996—. Mem. Greensburg-Decatur County Bd. of Airport Commrs., 1980-85, pres., 1980, 81, 83; mem. Decatur County Data Processing Bd., 1982-85; deacon 2nd Presbyn. Ch. of Indpls., 1991-92, elder, 1996—. Mem. Alpha Gamma Rho. Republican. Presbyterian. Office: Eli Lilly & Co Lilly Corp Ctr Indianapolis IN 46285

STEWART, RALPH EDWARD, ophthalmologist; b. Cleve., Aug. 30, 1962; s. Jack and Tudy (Newman) S.; m. Rachael Ellen Lander, May 29, 1988; 1 child, Adam Gregory. BS in medicine, Northwestern U., 1984, MD, 1986. Diplomate Am. Bd. Ophthalmology. Internal medicine intern Univ. Hosps. of Cleve., 1986-87; resident in ophthalmology L.I. Jewish Med. Ctr., New Hyde Park, N.Y., 1987-90; fellow in med. retina La. State U. Med. Ctr., New Orleans, 1990-91; attending ophthalmologist Western Res. Eye Ctr., Rocky River, Ohio, 1991-92, Kaiser Permanente, Parma, Ohio, 1993—. Bd. dirs., v.p. for publicity Am. Red Magen David for Israel, Cleve., 1994—; bd. dirs., social v.p. New Generation Group, Park Synagogue, Cleveland Heights, Ohio, 1993—; sec. Pepperwood Park Homeowners Assn., Solon, Ohio, 1995—. Fellow Am. Acad. Ophthalmology; mem. AMA, Ohio State Med. Assn., Cleve. Ophthalmol. Soc., Acad. Medicine of Cleve. (mem. med.-surg. peer rev. com. 1994—), Masons. Home: 36500 Pepper Dr Solon OH 44139 Office: Kaiser Permanente 12301 Snow Rd Parma OH 44130

STEWART, ROBERT MALCOLM, neurologist; b. El Paso, Tex., Sept. 22, 1941; s. Raymond Malcolm and Marie Ada (Palm) S.; m. Rege Piroska Szuts, June 24, 1967; children: Charles Eaton, Sharon Marie. BS in Biology, N.Mex. State U., 1963; MD, Northwestern U., Chgo., 1967. Diplomate Am. Bd. Psychiatry and Neurology. Rotating intern Chgo. Wesley Meml., 1967-68; resident neurology Northwestern U., Chgo., 1968-69; chief of neurology Reynolds Army Hosp., Ft. Sill, Okla., 1969-71; resident in neurology Mass. Gen. Hosp., Boston, 1971-74, rsch. fellow in psychiatry, 1974-77; asst. prof. neurology U. Tex. Southwestern Med. Sch., Dallas, 1977-83, clin. assoc. prof. neurology, 1983-95, clin. prof. neurology, 1995—; pres. Neurology Specialists of Dallas, 1993—; med. adv. bd. Dallas Area Parkinsonism Soc., 1977-96; dir. Parkinson Disease Info. and Referral Ctr., Am. Parkinson Disease Assn., N.Y.C., 1993-96; chief of neurology Presbyn. Hosp. Dallas, 1993-96; med. adv. bd. Dallas Epilepsy Soc., Dallas, 1983-96. Contbr. articles to profl. jours. Speaker Parkinson Soc., Multiple Sclerosis Soc., Tex.; advisor Greer Garson Gala of Hope, Dallas, 1993—. Capt. U.S. Army, 1969-71. Rsch. fellow NIH, Harvard, 1974; clin. rsch. pharm. cos., 1971—; honorary citizen, City of Tyler, Tex., 1980. Fellow Am. Acad. Neurology (scientific adv. com. 1977-83); mem. Soc. Neurosci., n.Y. Acad. Sci., AAAS, AMA, Am. Soc. Clin. Hypnosis. Presbyterian. Home: 3939 Hockaday Dallas TX 75229 Office: Neurology Specialists of Dallas 9400 North Central # 1100 Dallas TX 75231

STEWART, THOMAS DAVID, psychiatrist; b. Indpls., Jan. 2, 1942; s. Lynn Nixon and Irene (Boman) S.; m. Carroll Brown, June 7, 1963 (div. 1975); children: Branner N., Marian I.; m. Jeanne M. Ledoux, Apr. 27, 1985; 1 child, Lynne M. BS, Depauw U., 1963; MD, Stanford U., 1968. Intern in pediatrics Stanford U., Palo Alto, Calif., 1968-69; resident in psychiatry Mass. Gen. Hosp., Boston, 1969-73; psychiatrist West Roxbury (Mass.) VA Hosp., 1973-77; dir. psychiat. out-patient dept. Waltham (Mass.) Hosp., 1977-81; dir. consultation psychiatry Beth Israel Hosp., Boston, 1981-90; chmn. dept. psychiatry The Hosp. of St. Raphael, New Haven, 1990—; asst. prof. psychiatry Harvard U., Boston, 1983-90; clin. assoc. prof. psychiatry Yale U., New Haven, 1991—. Contbr. articles to profl. jours. Dupont-Warren fellow, Harvard U., 1973. Fellow Am. Psychiat. Assn.; mem. Phi Beta Kappa. Office: The Hosp of St Raphael 1450 Chapel St New Haven CT 06511-4405

STEWART, WILLIAM CHARLES, ophthalmology educator; b. New Orleans, June 14, 1955; s. Robert Bell and Margaret (Hollifield) S.; m. Jeanette Adams, Aug. 29, 1981. BA, So. Meth. U., 1977; MD, Southwestern Med. Sch., 1981. Diplomate Am. Bd. Ophthalmology. Internship St. Paul's Hosp., Dallas, 1981-82; residency in ophthalmology U. Mo. at Kansas City, 1983-86; fellowship in glaucoma Duke U., Durham, N.C., 1986-87; asst. prof. ophthalmology Med. U. S.C., Charleston, 1987-93; assoc. prof. medicine U. S.C., Charleston, 1993-96, Pharm. Rsch. Corp., James Island, S.C., 1996—; cons., lectr. Pharm. Cos. Author: Clinical Practice of Glaucoma, 1990; contbr. over 160 articles to sci. jours. Fellow Am. Acad. Ophthalmology; mem. Am. Glaucoma Soc., S.C. Ophthalmology Soc., Charleston Ophthalmology Soc., Phi Beta Kappa. Office: Pharm Rsch Corp 1639 Tatum St James Island SC 29412

STEWART, WILLIAM JAMES, cardiologist; b. Cleve., Aug. 17, 1951; s. James B. and Virginia Stewart; m. Denise Elizabeth Balk, Dec. 30, 1972; children: Emily, Travis. AB in Biology cum laude, Harvard U., 1973; MD, U. Cin., 1977. Diplomate Am. Bd. Internal Medicine with subspecialty in cardiovascular disease; lic. physician, Ohio. Intern/resident U. Mich. Affiliated Hosps., Ann Arbor, 1977-80; clin. fellow dept. cardiology Boston U. Hosp., 1980-82; clin./rsch. fellow Cardiac Ultrasound Lab. Mass. Gen. Hosp./Harvard Med. Sch., Boston, 1982-84; staff physician Cleve. Clinic, 1984—, dir. Echo Lab, 1992—; clin. assoc. in medicine Boston U., 1980-82; rsch. fellow in medicine Harvard Med. Sch., 1982-84; asst. prof. medicine Ohio State U., Columbus, 1992-94, assoc. prof., 1995—. Contbr. numerous articles and abstracts to profl. jours., chpts. to books; reviewer Circulation, Jour. Am. Coll. Cardiology, Jour. Am. Soc. Echocardiography, Echocardiography, Am. Heart Jour., Am. Jour. Cardology, Brit. Heart Jour., Annals of Thoracic Surgery, Jour. Thoracic and Cardiovascular Surgery, Am. Jour. Cardiac Imaging; editl. bd. Echocardiography, 1992—, Jour. Am. Soc. Echocardiography, 1991—. Fellow Am. Coll. Cardiology (Ohio chpt. adv. expert team in echocardiography 1995—), chmn. task force tng. in echocardiography 1994, mem. echocardiography com. 1991—); mem. Am. Heart Assn. (mem. edn. com. N.E. Ohio chpt. 1985-88), Am. Soc. Echocardiography (chmn. sci. sessions 1996, abstract chmn. sci. sessions 1994, mem. physicians' edn. and tng. com. 1993—, abstract vice chmn. 1993, bd. dirs. 1989-92), Internat. Soc. Ultrasound in Cardiac Surgery (pres. 1994—), Greater Cleve. Soc. Echocardiography (founder, bd. dirs. 1985—). Episcopalian. Office: Cleveland Clinic Found Dept Cardiology 9500 Euclid Ave Cleveland OH 44195

STEYERBERG, EWOUT WILLEM, biostatistician, researcher; b. Delft, The Netherlands, July 26, 1967; s. Willem R.A. and Anja Aleida (Steenbergen) S.; m. Aleida Wilhelmina Sluijk, May 20, 1995. BS in Medicine, Leiden (The Netherlands) U., 1986, MS in Biomed. Scis., 1991; PhD in Medicine, Erasmus U., Rotterdam, The Netherlands, 1996. Student asst. U. Leiden, 1991; asst. prof. Erasmus U., 1991—. Referee European Jour. Radiology, 1993—. Treas. Symfonic Orch. Bellitoni, The Hague, The Netherlands, 1994—. Mem. Soc. for Med. Decision Making (Student prize 1995). Home: Statensingel 156c, 3039 LW Rotterdam The Netherlands Office: Erasmus Univ, PO Box 1738 EC 2091, Ee 2091 Rotterdam The Netherlands

STIBLER, HELENA E.C., neurologist; b. Stockholm, July 24, 1943; d. Sture G.A. and Karin E. (Blanche) S. MSc, Karolinska Inst., Sweden, 1966, MD, 1971, Specialist Degree in Neurology, 1977, PhD in Neurology, 1978. Cert. ECFMG U.S.A., 1972. Resident Karolinska Hosp., Stockholm, 1971-76, specialist ward physician, 1977-85, dir. Neurochemistry Rsch. Lab., 1982—, asst. chief physician, 1986-91, chief physician, 1991—, neurology dir. neurooncology sect., 1993—; assoc. prof. Karolinska Inst., 1979—, univ. lectr., 1986—; vis. prof., invited lectr. various Universities, Scandinavia, France, Italy, Germany, Belgium, Can. 1977—. Author, editor: Acta Paediatrica Scandinavica, 1991; author, co-author numerous articles in profl. jours. and books. U. Toronto Rsch. fellow, 1980-81, INSERM Rsch. fellow, 1987; grantee Karolinska Inst., 1975—, Swedish Coun. for Planning Coord. of Rsch., 1980-82, 94, Swedish Med. Rsch. Coun., 1983—, Vivian Smith Found., 1984-87, INSERM, 1987, Cornell Found., 1990, others. Mem. Swedish Soc. Medicine (Lennmals award, 1979), Swedish Med. Assn., Swedish Soc. Neurology (auditor), Internat. Soc. Biomedical Rsch. Alcoholism, Internat. Soc. Developmental Neuroscience. Office: Karolinska Hosp, Dept Neurology, 17176 Stockholm Sweden

STICKLER, GUNNAR BRYNOLF, pediatrician; b. Peterskirchen, Germany, June 13, 1925; came to U.S., 1951, naturalized, 1958; s. Fritz and Astrid (Wennerberg) S.; m. Duci M. Kronenbitter, Aug. 30, 1956; children: Katarina Anna, George David. M.D., U. Munich, Germany, 1949; Ph.D., U. Minn., Mpls., 1957. Diplomate Am. Bd. Pediatrics, ofcl. examiner and mem., 1965-95. Resident in clin. pathology Krankenhaus III Orden, Munich, 1950; resident in pathology U. Munich, 1950-51; intern Mountainside Hosp., Montclair, N.J., 1951-52; fellow in pediatrics Mayo Grad. Sch., Rochester, Minn., 1953-56; sr. cancer research scientist Roswell Park Meml. Inst., Buffalo, 1956-57; asst. to staff Mayo Clinic, Rochester, 1957-58; cons. in pediatrics Mayo Clinic, 1959-89, head sect. pediatrics, 1969-74; prof. pediatrics, chmn. dept. pediatrics Mayo Clinic and Mayo Med. Sch., 1974-80; mem. test com. III Nat. Bd. Med. Examiners, 1973-75; vis. prof. at various univs and instns., including U. Dusseldorf (Germany) and U. Munich, 1971, Pahlavi U., Iran, 1975, Olga Hosp., Stuttgart, Germany, 1978, Martin Luther King Hosp., Los Angeles, 1979, U. Man., 1981; mem. emeritus staff Mayo Clinic, 1989. Contbr. numerous articles to med. publs.; editorial bd. Clin. Pediatrics, 1968-76, 79—, European Jour. Pediatrics, 1976-84, Pediatrics, 1983-89. Recipient Humanitarian award Chgo. region chpt. Nat. Found. Ileitis and Colitis, 1978, award for excellence of subject matter and presentation So. Minn. Med. Assn., 1978. Mem. Am. Acad. Pediatrics, Soc. Pediatric Research, Am. Pediatric Soc., Midwest Soc. Pediatric Research (council 1967-69, pres. 1970-71), N.W. Pediatric Soc. (pres. 1973-74).

STIDD, LINDA MARIE, rehabilitation nurse; b. Martins Ferry, Ohio, Mar. 20, 1947; d. Stephen George and Helen Jane (Cupryk) Mularcik; m. William Leroy Stidd, May 4, 1968; 1 child, Christopher Alan. Diploma, Ohio Valley Gen. Hosp., 1968; BSN, Ohio U., 1995. CRRN; RN cert. in gerontology. Staff nurse Ohio Valley Gen. Hosp., Wheeling, W.Va., 1968-69, 73-79; supr. Woodland Acres Nursing Home, St. Clairsville, Ohio, 1971-73; staff nurse Ohio Valley Med. Ctr., Wheeling, 1973-79, head nurse rehab., 1981-91; nurse mgr. OVMC Rehab. at Woodsdale, Wheeling, 1991-92; nurse mgr. for skilled care/rehab. Peterson Rehab. Hosp. and Geriatric Ctr., Wheeling, 1991-95. Mem. Assn. Rehab. Nurses, W.Va. Assn. Rehab. Nurses, W.Va. Orgn. Nurse Execs., Nat. Disting. Svc. Registry Med. and Vocat. Rehab. Democrat. Roman Catholic. Office: Peterson Rehab Hosp and Geriatric Ctr Homestead Ave Wheeling WV 26003-6697

STIEFVATER, PAMELA JEAN, chiropractor; b. Utica, N.Y., Oct. 16, 1956; d. Kenneth Carl and Henriette Ramona (Billick) S. BS cum laude, SUNY, Oswego, 1977; D of Chiropractic cum laude, Palmer Coll., 1984. Lic. chiropractor, N.Y., Mass.; diplomate Nat. Bd. Chiropractic Examiners. Sci. tchr. Altmar, Parish, Williamstown High Sch., Parish, N.Y., 1978-80; chiropractor, owner Bayside Chiropractic, South Dennis, Mass., 1986—. Mem. Am. Chiropractic Soc., Mass. Chiropractic Soc., Cape Code Chiropractic Soc. Office: Bayside Chiropractic 430 Old Bass River Rd South Dennis MA 02660-2724

STIEHL, JACOLYNNE DONAHUE, healthcare executive; b. Green Bay, Wis., Oct. 31, 1939; d. Roy August and Emma Elizabeth (Bruckner) Jorns; children: Terry, John, Thomas, James, David, Judith; m. Charles W. Stiehl, Feb. 15, 1994. Grad. high sch. Sec. von Stiehl Wine Inc., Milw., 1968—; mgr. Med. Dr.'s Emergency Svc., Milw., 1970; sec.-treas. Wis. Collection Corp., Milw., 1972-76; pres., owner Heirloom Collections, Internat., Milw., 1987—; gen. mgr. von Stiehl Corp., Milw., 1981—; owner Watch Designs by Jacolynne, Milw., 1989—; mgr. M.D. Wellness Clinic, St. Helena, Calif., 1989—. Republican. Roman Catholic. Home: 328 Temperance Ave Clovis CA 93611-5452 Office: MD Wellness Clinic 1314 Main St Saint Helena CA 94574-1905

STIEHM, E. RICHARD, pediatrician, educator; b. Milw., Jan. 22, 1933; s. Reuben Harold and Marie Dueno S.; m. Judith Hicks, July 12, 1958; children: Jamie Elizabeth, Carrie Eleanor, Meredith Ellen. B.S., U. Wis., 1954, M.D., 1957. Diplomate: Am. Bd. Pediatrics, Am. Bd. Allergy and Clin. Immunology (bd. dirs. 1977-83), Am. Bd. Diagnostic Lab. Immunology. Intern Phila. Gen. Hosp., 1957-58; fellow in physiol. chemistry U. Wis., 1959-61; med. officer USNR, Johnsville, Pa., 1961-63; resident in pediat. Babies Hosp., N.Y.C., 1963-65; rsch. fellow in pediat. immunology U. Calif., San Francisco, 1965-68; asst. prof. pediat. U. Wis., 1968-69, assoc. prof., 1969-72; assoc. prof. UCLA, 1972-78, prof., 1978-87, chief div. immunology and allergy, 1972—, assoc. dir. Ctr. for Interdisciplinary Rsch. in Immunologic Diseases, 1981-82, co-dir. Cystic Fibrosis Ctr., 1988—, vice chair acad. affairs dept. pediatrics, 1989—; vis. scientist metabolism br. Nat. Cancer Inst., Bethesda, Md., 1982-88; vis. prof. Yale U., Mayo Clinic, U. Cin.; bd. sci. dirs. Immune Deficiency Found., 1981—, Eczema Found., 1988—, Pediat. AIDS Found., 1989—; task force on pediat. allergy NIH, 1977; mem. gen. clin. rsch. ctr. study sect. NIH, 1978-82, 84-88; adv. com. Hartford Fellowship, 1984-88; co-dir. L.A. Pediat. AIDS Consortium, 1988—; commr. HHS adv. commn. on childhood vaccines, 1988-90. Editor: (with V. Fulginiti) Immunologic Disorders in Infants and Children, 1972, 80, 89; Am. editor: Pediatric Research, 1984-89; assoc. editor: Pediatrics Update, 1978-85; mem. editorial bd. Pediatrics, 1972-78, Pediatrics in Rev., 1978-81, Jour. Allergy and Clin. Immunology, 1976-80, Jour. Clin. Immunology, 1985-89, Jour. Asthma Pediatric Allergy and Immunology, 1987-91, Am. Jour. Diseases of Children, 1987—, Contemporary Pediatrics, 1991—, Am. Jour. Clin. Nutrition, 1992—; contbr. articles to profl. jours. Mem. HHS Commn. on Childhood Vaccines, 1988-90; mem. clin. rsch. adv. com. Nat. Found. March of Dimes, 1992—. Recipient Career Devel. award NIAID, 1967-69, E. Mead Johnson award for Pediat. Rsch., 1974, Alumni Citation award U. Wis. Med. Sch., 1988, Lifetime Achievement award Immune Deficiency Found., 1995; Markle scholar, 1967-72. Mem. AAAS, Am. Assn. Immunologists, Western Soc. Pediatric Research (coun. 1977-80, pres. 1983, Ross Rsch. award 1971), Soc. Pediatric Research, Am. Pediatric Soc., Am. Acad. Allergy and Clin. Immunology, Am. Acad. Pediatrics (infectious diseases com. 1971-77), Am. Soc. Clin. Investigation, Clin. Immunology Soc., Alpha Delta Phi, Phi Beta Kappa, Alpha Omega Alpha.

STIENS, SCOTT ROBERT, health policy analyst; b. Cin., Nov. 23, 1965; s. William John and Jean Cathrine (Duffy) S. BSBA, Xavier U., 1987; MBA in Internat. Fin., 1990; MHA, Xavier U., 1991; postgrad., Cambridge (Eng.) U., 1990-92. Cert. internat. trader. Internat. Trade Inst. Adminstr. Children's Hosp. Med. Ctr., Cin., 1987-88; grad. asst. mktg. and acad. computing Xavier U., Cin., 1988-89; grad. intern Internat. Trade Adminstrn. U.S. Dept. of Commerce, Cin., 1989; grad. asst. health policy and planning Xavier U., 1989-90; legis. draftman state health planning policy Miami Valley Health Improvement Coun., Huber Heights, Ohio, 1990; legal clk. internat. taxation and contracts Thompson Hine & Flory, Neuchatel, Switzerland, 1990; lectr. bus. mgmt. Cambridge (Eng.) Bus. Coll., 1990-92; health facility adminstr. Addenbrooke's Hosp., Cambridge, Eng., 1992—; phys. therapy aid Children's Hosp. Med. Ctr., Cin., 1981-84; youth counselor Joslin Diabetes Ctr., Boston, 1984-86; program dir., counselor trainer Diabetic Youth Found., San Francisco, 1987; instr. Presidential Classroom, The White House, Washington. Page City Coun. of Cin., 1983-84; counselor Stepping Stones Ctr. for the Handicapped, Cin., 1983-84; instr. ARC; coord. Big Bros. Am.; vol. Youth Hospice; HIV counselor dept. infectious diseases Georgetown U. Med. Ctr.; advisor Jr. Achievement of Am. Mem. Am. Soc. Law and Medicine, Xavier U. Black Students Assn., Brit. Inst. Health Svcs. Mgmt., Jefferson Island Club, Am. Coll. Health Care Execs., Kappa Sigma. Home: 5706 Macarthur Blvd NW Washington DC 20016-5303 Office: Addenbrooke's Hosp, Hills Rd, Cambridge England CB2 2QQ also: US Dept Vets Affairs Office Asst Sec Washington DC 20420 also: Wht House Off Spl Projects Health Care Reform Office Washington DC 20500

STIENS, STEVEN A., rehabilitation physician, educator; b. Cin., Apr. 13, 1959; s. William Joseph and Jean Catherine Stien; m. Elizabeth Ann Marcelain; children: Hanna, Duffy. BS in Natural Sciences, 1981; MD, U. Cin., 1986; MS, U. Wash., 1990. Diplomate Am. Bd. Physical Medicine and Rehabilitation. Intern in internal medicine Jewish Hosp. Cin., 1986-87, rehab. physician, 1986-87; resident in physical medicine and rehabilitation U. Wash., 1987-90; instr. dept. rehab. Johns Hopkins U., 1990-93; dir. phys. medicine and rehab. cons. svc. Johns Hopkins Hosp. and Kennedy-Krieger Inst., 1990-93; rehab. physician Good Samaritan Hosp., Balt., 1990-93, Childrens Orthopedic Hosp., Balt., 1990-93; staff phys. Veteran Affairs Med. Ctr., Seattle, 1993—; acting asst. prof. dept. rehab. U. Wash., 1993-94, asst. prof., 1994—; lectr. and presenter in field; mem. Spinal Cord Injury Forum. Contbr. chpts. to books: Electrodiagnosis in Spinal Cord Injury, Physical Medicine and Rehabilitation Clinics of North America, 1994, Cardiac Rehabilitation in the Patient With Spinal Cord Injury, 1995, Rehabilitation Of The Shoulder After Repetitive Motion Injury, 1995; contbr. articles to profl. pubs. including Archives of Physical Medicine and Rehabilitation, Stroke Connection Mag., 1995, Paraplegia News, 1994, Patient Care, 1995, others; pub. tapes and interviews. Bd. dirs. HOW (Handicapped is Only a Word) Conf. Com., 1991—; cons. United Cerebral Palsy of King County, 1993—; bd. dirs. United Cerebral Palsy of King and Snohomish Counties, 1995—. Nat. Inst. for Disability and Rehab. Rsch. grantee, 1993-94. Fellow Am. Acad. Phys. Medicine and Rehab.; mem. AMA, Am. Soc. Handicapped Physicians, Nat. Spinal Cord Injury Found., Am. Paraplegia Soc., Am. Cong. Rehab. Medicine, Assn. Academic Physiatrists, Soc. Disability Studies, Internat. Rehab. Med. Assn., Johns Hopkins Med. and Surg. Soc. Home: 18019 3d Ave NW Seattle WA 98177 Office: U Wash VAMC 1660 S Columbian Way Seattle WA 98108-1597

STIFF, ROBERT HENRY, dentist, educator; b. Pitts., Apr. 23, 1923; s. Oliver R. and Ruth A. (Goucher) S.; m. Margaret J. Raley, Oct. 18, 1945; children—Barry, Dwight, Heather. B.S., U. Pitts., 1940. D.D.S., 1945, M.Ed., 1953. Engaged in pvt. practice dentistry Pitts., 1945-59; instr. U. Pitts., 1945-50, asst. prof., 1950-53, asso. prof., 1954-65, prof., head dept. oral medicine and radiology, 1963-76, dir. clinics, 1976—; asst. dean U. Pitts. (Sch. Dental Medicine), 1979-81, assoc. dean, 1981-84; cons. U. Garyounis, Benghazi, Libya, 1978—, Pa. Dept. Health, 1964, 66, Bd. Edn., City of Pitts. (dental asst. program 1983-86). Served to capt. Dental Corps AUS, 1946-48. Fellow Am. Coll. Dentists; mem. Am. Acad. Oral Pathology, ADA (pres. 1979-80), Orgn. Tchrs. Oral Diagnosis, Pa. Dental Assn., Sigma Xi, Omicron Kappa Upsilon. Home: 4601 Doverdell Dr Pittsburgh PA 15236-1824

STILES, GERALD EARL, healthcare company executive; b. Muscatine, Iowa, Apr. 19, 1935; s. Gerald Leroy and Rosa Lee (Everly) S.; BS, U. Mo., 1957, MA in Biology, 1959; PhD in Biol. Scis., N.Y. U., 1971; m. Gail Stevens Young, Aug. 11, 1956; children: Cynthia Gail, Brian Keith, Valerie Jean. With Lederle Labs., Pearl River, N.Y., 1959-77, group leader, 1972-75, head dept., 1975-77; dir. R & D diagnostics Fisher Sci. Co., Orangeburg, N.Y., 1977-79; v.p. rsch., exec. v.p., pres., CEO, Serono Labs., Randolph, Mass., 1980-85, apptd. chmn., 1985; corp. v.p. quality/tech. affairs Ares-Serono, N.V., Boston, 1986-92; founder, pres. Bantam Sci., Dataw Island, S.C., 1993—. Mem. Am. Soc. Microbiology, Am. Fertility Soc., Am. Mgmt. Assn., U.S. Power Squadron. Contbr. articles to profl. jours.; patentee in field. Office: Bantam Sci 147 Dataw Dr Dataw Island SC 29920-9340

STILL, CHARLES NEAL, neurologist, consultant; b. Richmond, Va., Apr. 15, 1929; s. Charles Wright and Ruth (Kemp) S.; m. Dorothy Lee Varn, Dec. 27, 1958; children: Charles Herbert, Carl Nelson, Sara Alice. BS in Chemistry, Clemson U., 1949; MS in Biochemistry, Purdue U., 1951; MD, Med. U. S.C., 1959. Diplomate Am. Bd. Psychiatry and Neurology. Instr. chemistry Clemson (S.C.) U., 1951-52; rotating intern U. Chgo. Clinics, 1959-60; neurology fellow Sch. Medicine Johns Hopkins U., Balt., 1960-63; resident in neurology Johns Hopkins-Balt. City Hosp., 1960-63; NIH rsch. fellow Harvard U.-McLean Hosp., Belmont, Mass., 1963-65; chief neurology svcs. William S. Hall. Psychiat. Inst., Columbia, S.C., 1965-81, assoc. dir. gen. psychiatry and neurology, 1989-92; dir. C. M. Tucker Human Resources Ctr., Columbia, 1981-88; instr. chemistry U.S. Mil. Acad., West Point, N.Y., 1953-55; assoc. clin. prof. neurology Med. U. S.C., Charleston, 1973-92, assoc. prof. neuropsychiatry, 1976-78, prof. neuropsychiatry, 1978—; adj. prof. epidemiology Sch. Pub. Health U. S.C., Columbia, 1988-92. Author: (with others) Handbook of Clinical Neurology, 1976, Neurologic Clinics, 1984, Movement Disorders, 1986; editor The Recorder Columbia Med. Soc., 1991—; mem. editl. bd. S.C. Med. Assn., 1980—, Jour. Applied Gerontology, 1983-88; contbr. articles to profl. jours. Chmn. grants rev. bd. S.C. Dept. Mental Health, Columbia, 1973-78; mem. exec. bd. Alzheimer's Assn. Columbia, 1985-93, pres. Mid-State chpt. Alzheimer's Assn., 1991-92; med. dir. Alzheimer's Disease Registry, Columbia, 1989-92, Alzheimer's Daycare Ctr., Columbia, 1989-92; mem. Gov.'s Adv. Coun. to Alzheimer's Disease and Related Disorders Resource Coordination Ctr., 1995—. 1st lt. U.S. Army, 1952-55. Fellow Am. Acad. Neurology, Am. Geriatrics Soc., Am. Inst. Chemists (life); mem. AMA, World Fedn. Neurology. Baptist. Home: 2 Culpepper Cir Columbia SC 29209-2234 Office: WJB Dorn VA Med Ctr Psychiatry Svc Columbia SC 29209-1639

STILL, EUGENE FONTAINE, II, plastic surgeon, educator; b. Rocky Mount, N.C., Sept. 2, 1937; s. Eugene Fontaine and Eva Ruth (Stevens) S.; m. Frances Davis, Aug. 14, 1965; 1 child, Eugene Fontaine III. BA, Vanderbilt U., 1959; MD, U. Ark., 1966. Diplomate Am. Bd. Comseteic Surgery (examiner, trustee 1994—), Am. Bd. Plastic Surgery, Inc. Intern Univ. Hosp., Little Rock, 1966-67; resident in gen. surgery U. Tenn. Med. Ctr., Memphis, 1967-71; resident in plastic surgery U. Mo. Med. Ctr., Kansas City, 1971-73; instr. surgery U. Mo., Kansas City, 1972-73; sr. surgeon dept. plastic surgery Holt-Krock Clinic, Ft. Smith, Ark., 1973-87; asst. prof. surgery U. Ark., Little Rock, 1974—; chief surgery Sparks Regional Med. Cen., Ft. Smith, 1979; pres. Bd. Cert. Plastic Srugeons, Ft. Smith, 1979—; dir. Ark. Ctr. Plastic Surgery, Van Buren, 1984—; chief of surgery St. Edward Mercy Med. Ctr., Ft. Smith, Ark., 1989-93, Crawford Meml. Hosp., 1993, 94; chief staff St. Edward Mercy Med. Ctr., 1990, 91; bd. trustees Crawford Meml. Hosp., 1985-86, 95—, St. Edwards Mercy Med. Ctr., 1996—, Am. Bd. Cosmetic Surgery, 1994—, examiner, 1990-95;. Served with U.S. Army, 1960-62. Merck Pharm. Co. scholar, 1966. Fellow ACS, Am. Acad. Cosmetic Surgery; mem. Am. Soc. Plastic Surgeons, Southeastern Soc. Plastic Surgeons, Ark. Soc. Plastic Surgeons (sec.-treas. 1983-85, pres.-elect 1986-88, co-founder, pres. 1988-93), Am. Soc. Liposuction Surgery, Am. Coll. Physician Execs., Am. Soc. Maxillofacial Surgeons, Ark. Med. Soc. (chmn. ins. com. 1984-90), Ft. Smith Town, Handscrabble County Club, Alpha Omega Alpha. Home: 10101 Highway 253 Fort Smith AR 72916-4118 Office: Plastic Surgery Specialists 2717 S 74th St Fort Smith AR 72903-5100

STILL, MARGARET MARY, internist; b. Islip, N.Y., Aug. 29, 1965; d. Joseph Charles and Patricia Catherine (Ewald) Schuchman; m. Christopher Doubet Still, Oct. 23, 1993; 1 child, Christopher Joseph. BS in Biology, Fordham U., Bronx, N.Y., 1987; D Osteo. Medicine, Phila. Coll. Osteo. Medicine, 1991. Rsch. asst. Fordham U., Bronx, 1986-87; lab. asst. SUNY, Stony Brook, 1986-87; student libr. Phila. Coll. Osteo. Medicine, 1988, computer technician, 1988; physician for elderly nuns St. Cyril's Acad., Danville, Pa., 1995-96; osteo. rotating intern Lewistown (Pa.) Hosp., 1991-92; resident physician internal medicine/pediatrics Geisinger Med. Ctr., Danville, Pa., 1992—, chief resident internal medicine, resident pediatrics, 1995-96; author, presenter lectrs. N.Y. State Regents scholar, 1983-87. Mem. ACP, AMA, Am. Acad. Pediatrics, Pa. Osteo. Med. Assn., Alpha Epsilon Delta. Democrat. Roman Catholic.

STILLMAN, DIANE, health services administrator; b. Roanoke, Va., Nov. 23, 1944; d. Lawrence Vincent and Melda Jane (Stacy) Gobroski; m. Douglas Erwin Stillman, Sep. 3, 1966; children: Melanie Anne, Colleen Michele. Diploma, St. Cabrini Sch. Nursing, Seattle, 1966. RN, Wash. Staff nurse Harrison Mem. Hosp., Brementon, Wash., 1966-67, St. Cabrini Hosp., Seattle, 1966-67; staff nurse profl. nurses bur. Sharp Hosp., San Diego, 1978-79; asst. nurse mgr. Mason Gen. Hosp., Shelton, Wash., 1979-85, dir. nurses, 1985-88, chief operating officer, 1988—; mem. adv. bd. Sound Home Care, 1984-86, South Puget Sound Cmty. Coll., 1986-92, E. Warsing Asst. State of Wash., 1991-94, all at Olympia, Wash., YMCA, Tacoma; dir. Grapeview (Wash.) Sch. Dist. No. 54, Wash., 1974-77. Mem. Am. Orgn. Nurse Execs., Wash. Orgn. Nurse Execs (coun. chair 1991—). Republican. Roman Catholic. Home: PO Box 2286 581128 Ave NW Gig Harbor WA 98335 Office: Mason Gen Hosp 901 Mt View Bldg 1 Shelton WA 98585

STILLMAN, MICHAEL ALLEN, dermatologist; b. N.Y.C., Apr. 12, 1943; s. Aaron and Anne (Turansky) S.; m. Susan Fuchs, July 10, 1950; children: Julie, Jeremy. BA, Clark U., 1963; MD, SUNY, 1967. Diplomate Am. Acad. Dermatology. Med. intern Marmonides Hosp., Bklyn., 1967-68; dermatology resident NYU Med. Ctr. and Bellevue Hosp., N.Y.C., 1970-73; pvt. practice Mt. Kisco, N.Y., 1973—; cons. in dermatology U.S. Mil. Acad., West Point, N.Y., 1973-75. Contbr. essays and articles to profl. jours. and newspapers. Bd. trustees South Salem (N.Y.) Libr., 1990—; boys varsity tennis coach John Jay H.S., Katmah, N.Y., 1996. Capt. USAF, 1968-70, Vietnam. Decorated Combat Inf. badge. Fellow Am. Soc. Dermatol. Surgeons, Am. Acad. Dermatology; mem. N.Y. State Med. Soc. Office: Box 268 Mount Kisco NY 10549

STILLWAGON, GARY BOULDIN, radiation oncologist; b. Memphis, Dec. 30, 1951; s. Jack Wright and Ida Jean (Bouldin) S.; m. Leta Fern Miller, Jan. 20, 1979. B.S. in Physics, Ga. Inst. Tech., 1974, M.S. in Nuclear Engring. 1975, Ph.D., 1978; M.D., U. Tenn., 1983. Cert. FLEX, 1983; diplomate Nat. Bd. Med. Examiners, 1984, Am. Bd. Radiology in Radiation Oncology. Med. physicist Meth. Hosp., Memphis, 1974; research asst. Ga. Inst. Tech., Atlanta, 1975-78; radiation safety officer, and physicist VA Med. Center, Memphis, 1978-80, cons. radiation safety, 1980-83; fellow in radiation oncology Johns Hopkins U. and Hosp., Balt., 1983-87, asst. prof. oncology and radiology Johns Hopkins U. Sch. Medicine, Balt., 1987— ; Am. Cancer Soc. clin. fellow, 1986-87 ; vis. researcher radiobiology lab. U. Utah, 1978; cons. in radiation safety to various area hosps. Contbr. articles to profl. jours. Active Boy Scouts Am., Bapt. Ch. Sunday Sch. Dept. Energy fellow, 1976-78. Mem. Health Physics Soc., Am. Assn. Physicists in Medicine, Am. Nuclear Soc., Am. Soc. Therapeutic Radiology and Oncology, Am. Coll. Radiology, AAAS, AMA, Am. Soc. Clin. Oncology, Sigma Xi. Republican. Home: 655 River Chase Rdg NW Atlanta GA 30328-3568 Office: Ste # 119 1136 Cleveland Ave Atlanta GA 30344

STILLWELL, KATHLEEN ANN SWANGER, healthcare consultant; b. Glendale, Calif., Aug. 12, 1950; d. Robert Dowayne and Irene Margaret (Sawatzky) Swanger; m. Joseph Wayne Stillwell, Nov. 11, 1971; children: Shannon Kristine, Nathan Joseph. AA, Cypress Coll., 1971; AS & diploma, Golden West Coll., 1981; BA in English Lit., Long Beach State U., 1982; MPA, Health Svcs. Adminstrn., U. San Francisco, 1989. RN Calif. Staff nurse Long Beach (Calif.) Meml. Hosp., 1981-84; sr. claims analyst Caronia Corp., Tustin, Calif., 1984-87; dir. quality assurance & risk mgmt. St. Mary Med. Ctr., Long Beach, 1987-89; cons. quality assurance, risk mgmt. Am. Med. Internat., Costa Mesa, Calif., 1989-91; cons. healthcare, 1991—; adj. faculty U. San Francisco, Woodbury U., 1996; faculty Am. Soc. Healthcare Risk Mgrs. Cert. Program; v.p. Patient Care Assessment Coun., L.A., 1988-89, pres., 1989-90, bd. dirs.; pres. State Bd. Patient Care Coun., 1990-92, past pres., 1992-94; speaker in field. Vol. Calif. Health Decisions, Orange County, 1989—, PTA, Am. Cancer Soc., Patient Care Assessment Coun.; active Constnl. Rights Found.; mem. edn. com. Bus. in Soc., Bus. Leadership, 1995, World Future Soc., 1995. Mem. NLN, Am. Soc. Healthcare Risk Mgmt., Nat. Assn. Healthcare Quality (exec. fin. com. 1993-95), Am. Soc. Quality Control Profls. (sec. healhtcare divsn. 1995—, chair membership 1994-95, chair-elect healthcare divsn. 1996-97), Am. Soc. Healthcare Risk Mgrs., So. Calif. Assn. Healthcare Risk Mgrs. (sec. 1989-90, mem. chmn. 1989-90), Calif. League for Nurses (bd. dirs. 1993-95), Patient Care Assessment Coun. (v.p. So. Calif. 1988, pres. So. Calif. 1989-90, state bd. pres. 1990-92, state bd. dirs. 1992-94). Democrat. Lutheran. Home and Office: 825 Coastline Dr Seal Beach CA 90740-5810

STILSON, WALTER LESLIE, radiologist, educator; b. Sioux Falls, S.D., Dec. 13, 1908; s. George Warren and Elizabeth Margaret (Zager) S.; m. Grace Beall Bramble, Aug. 15, 1933 (dec. June 1984); children: Carolyn G. Palmieri, Walter E., Judith A. Stirling; m. Lula Ann Birchel, June 30, 1985. BA, Columbia Union Coll., 1929; MD, Loma Linda U., 1934. Diplomate Am. Bd. Radiology, Nat. Bd. Med. Examiners. Intern White Meml. Hosp., Los Angeles, 1933-34; resident radiology Los Angeles County Gen. Hosp., 1934-36; instr. radiology Loma Linda (Calif.) U. Sch. Medicine, 1935-41, asst. prof., 1941-49, exec. sec. radiology, 1945-50, assoc. prof., 1949-55, head dept. radiology, 1950-55, prof. radiology, 1955-83, chmn. dept. radiology, 1955-69, emeritus prof., 1983—; chief radiology service White Meml. Hosp., Los Angeles, 1941-65, Loma Linda U. Med. Ctr., 1966-69; chmn. dept. radiologic tech. Sch. Allied Health Professions, 1966-75, med. dir. dept. radiologic tech., 1975-83. Contbr. articles to health jours. Fellow Am. Coll. Radiology; mem. AAAS, Los Angeles Radiol. Soc. (sec. 1960-61, treas. 1961-62, pres. 1963-64), Radiol. Soc. N.Am., Am. Roentgen Ray Soc., N.Y. Acad. Sci., Inland Radiol. Soc. (pres. 1971), Alpha Omega Alpha. Republican. Adventist. Home: 25045 Crestview Dr Loma Linda CA 92354-3414 Office: Loma Linda Radiol Med Group 11234 Anderson St Loma Linda CA 92354-2804

STINE, GORDAN BERNARD, dentist, educator; b. Charleston, S.C., Feb. 10, 1924; s. Abe Jack and Helen (Pinosky) S.; m. Barbara Berlinsky, Jan. 20, 1951; children: Steven Mark, Robert Jay. BS in Chemistry, Coll. of Charleston, 1944; DDS, Emory U., 1950. Lic. dentist, Ga., S.C. pvt. practice gen. dentistry, Charleston, 1953-87; spl. asst. to pres. Med. U., S.C., Charleston, 1983—, clin. assoc. prof. community dentistry, 1983—, dir. Dental Continuing Edn., 1984—, bd. visitors, 1982, 83, chmn., 1982, chmn. Cultural Projects Coun., 1984—, Continuing Edn. Adv. Com., 1986-89; dental coord. Area Health Edn. Ctrs., 1987—; bd. trustees Coll. of Charleston, 1988—, vice-chmn, 1992—; instr. Trident Tech. Coll., 1981; mem. State Coll. bd. trustees, 1987-88; mem. dental adv. com. Div. Dental Health S.C. State Bd. Health, 1967-68; mem. regional adv. group S.C. Regional Med. Program, 1974-75. Chmn. S.C. Dental Polit. Action Com., 1973-74, 76-84, bd. dirs., 1973-85, chmn. 1973-83; bd. dirs. Coastal Carolina Fair Assn., 1957-61, 63-65, pres., 1965, 66; bd. dirs. Charleston Symphony Assn., 1963-68, pres. 1965, mem. pres.' coun. 1983-84; bd. dirs. Charleston Civic Ballet, 1968, S.C. Art Alliance, 1973-74, Charleston Concert Assn., 1967-73, Charleston R.R. Hist. Soc., 1967-68; bd. dirs. Coastal Carolina coun. Boy Scouts Am., 1972, 74, 75, 82, 83, 84, v.p. for Southern Region Coun. Exec. Com. Programs 1985, 86, pres., 1990, 91, adv. com. 1972, 74, 75, 82, 83, 84, 85, chmn. Kiawah Dist. 1982; chmn., Coll. Prep. Sch., 1963-67, vice chmn. 1964-66, mem. regional bd., 1992—; mem. Task Force for Martin Luther King, Jr. Legal Holiday, YMCA of Greater Charleston, 1974-75; founder Charleston Mini Parks, 1969, bd. mem., 1969-71, chmn., 1969, 71; bd. mem. Charleston Pride, 1996, chmn., 1973-74, 74-75, 83-85; chmn. dental div. Trident United Way, 1962, 69, bd. mem. 1970-73, 74-76, 78-80, 81-85, community welfare planning council 1967, 68, chmn. pub. svc. sect., 1993, pres. 1982, chmn. fund drive, 1977, mem. exec. com. 1977-79, 81-84; chmn. fund raising dental div. Cancer Soc., 1956, 61, 66, 70, 71; chmn. Charleston County Dems., 1968-72; Charleston County councilman 1975-84, chmn. 1979-80; alderman Ward 13 City of Charleston 1971-75; active pub. service coms. including S.C. Assembly on Growth, 1981, Trident Devel. Coun. 1972, legis. com. S.C. Assn. Counties 1979, 81, 82, Charleston Waterfront Park Adv. Com. 1982-83, Charleston Neighborhood Housing Services Bd. 1984; state senatorial candidate, 1975; vice chmn. Berkeley-Charleston-Dorchester Coun. of Govts., 1983-90, sec. 1985-90, chmn. 1991-95, mem. & chmn. various coms.; exec. com. Charleston Mus. 1980, bd. mem. 1977-78, steering com. 1978-80; chmn. Charleston Bicentennial Com. 1972-75; bd. mem. Carolina Art Assn. 1978; fund drive chmn. Roper Hosp. 1973; bd. mem. Coastal Fed. Credit Union 1979-80, pres. 1979; exec. com. Greater Charleston Safety Coun., 1976-85, v.p., 1986-88, pres. 1989; bd. mem. Trident Area Found., 1977-80, adv. bd., 1981-82, life mem. bd. dirs., 1995; mem. steering com. Charleston campaign United Negro Coll. Fund, 1972, 73; bd. mem. Robert Shaw Boys Ctr., 1975-77, Mil. Svcs. Ctr., 1979-82, Trident 100, 1980-81; chmn. State Health Fair Adv. Bd. for Nat. Health Screening Coun., 1984-85; mem. Pres.' Adv. Coun. Winthrop Coll., 1984-85; mem. extension adv. bd. Clemson U., 1985, 86, chmn. 1987-89, statewide community devel. adv. com., 1985; bd. mem. Hebrew Benevolent Soc., 1968-71, pres., 1970, 71; mem. Hebrew Orphan Soc., 1972—, v.p., 1988-89, pres., 1990, 91, 92; trustee Congregation Beth Elohim, 1959-64, pres., 1967, 68, Brotherhood pres., 1960; pres. Jewish Welfare Bd., 1970-71, mem. various coms. With USMC, 1942, with USN, 1945-46, 51-53, res. 1953-72, res. ret. 1971-84. Named Coll. of Charleston Alumnus of Yr., 1966, Community Leader Am., 1968-71; recipient Hettie Rickett Community Devel. award, 1979, award adv. dental bd. Carolina Continental Ins. Co., 1983-84, Gov.'s Order of Palmetto award, 1985, 9ellow ACD, Royal Soc. Health; mem. ADA, APHA, Coastal Dist. Dental Soc. (pres. 1954), Charleston Dental Soc. (pres. 1957-58, dentist of the year award 1992), Nat. Assn. Regional Couns. (bd. dirs. 1991-95), Israel Dental Assn., Hebrew Orphan Soc. (pres. 1991, 92, 93), Pierre Fauchard Acad. (state chmn. 1991, 93), S.C. Dental Assn. (pres. 1974-75, edn. com. 1985-90, Cmty. Svc. award 1995), S.C. Downtown Devel. Assn. (bd. dirs. 1983—, pres. 1992-93), S.C. County Gen. Dentistry (newsletter editor 1995-96), Charleston Trident C. of C. (pres. 1972, bd. mem. 1968-74, 80), S.C. Assn. Regional Couns. (pres. 1986-87), Exch. Club of Charleston (pres. 1962), S.C. State Exch. Club (bd. dirs. 1965-68), Alpha Omega (pres. 1949-50, Disting. Svc. award 1976-77, pres. Southeastern group 1960-78, charter mem., emeritus mem. 1993), Tau Epsilon Phi (chpt. pres. 1943). Avocations: gardening, community service. Home: 27 Wraggborough Ln Charleston SC 29403-6362 Office: 171 Ashley Ave Charleston SC 29425-0001

STINE, ROBERT HOWARD, pediatrician; b. Nov. 1, 1929; s. Harry Raymond and Mabel Eva (Newhard) S.; m. Lois Elaine Kihlgren, Oct. 22, 1960; children: Robert E., Karen, Jonathan. BS in Biology, Moravian Coll., 1952. Diplomate Am. Bd. Pediatrics, Am. Subbd. Pediatric Allergy, Am. Allergy and Immunology. Intern St. Luke's Hosp., Bethlehem, Pa., 1960-61, resident in surgery, 1961-62; physician Jefferson Med. Coll., Phila., 1956-60; resident in pediatrics U. N.Y., Syracuse, 1962-64; resident in allergy Robert A. Cooke Inst. Allergy Roosevelt Hosp., N.Y.C., 1964-65; clin. instr. pediatrics U. Ill., Chgo., 1965-71; mem. courtesy staff Proctor Community Hosp., Peoria, Ill., 1966-77, mem. active staff, 1977—, chmn. dept. medicine, 1988—; pres. elect. med. staff, 1990-91, pres. med. staff, 1991-92; mem. teaching staff St. Francis Hosp., Peoria, 1969—; clin. instr. pediatrics Rush-Presbyn. St. Luke's Hosp., Chgo., 1971—. Lt. (j.g.), USN, 1953-56. Fellow Am. Acad. Pediatrics, Am. Acad. Allergy and Immunology, Am. Coll. Allergists, Am. Assn. Cert. Allergists; mem. Ill. Soc. Allergy and Clin. Immunology, Peoria Med. Soc. (pres.-elect 1963, pres. 1964). Home: 105 Hollands Grove Ln Washington IL 61571-9623 Office: 710 E Archer Ave Peoria IL 61603-2636

STINGL, GEORG, dermatologist, scientist; b. Vienna, Austria, Oct. 28, 1948; s. Kurt and Elfriede (Wafek) S.; m. Laura A. Gazze, Dec. 13, 1980. MD, U. Vienna, 1973. Resident dept. dermatology I Univ. Vienna (Austria) Med. Sch., 1973-76; guest rschr. dermatol. br. Nat. Cancer Inst., NIH, Bethesda, Md., 1977-78; mem. staff dept. dermatology Med. Sch., U. Innsbruck, Austria, 1978-81, assoc. prof. dermatology, 1980; mem. staff dept. dermatology Med. Sch., U. Vienna, 1981-85, full prof., head div. cutaneous immunobiology, dept. dermatology I, 1985-91, prof., chmn. div. immunology, allergy and infectious diseases, dept. dermatology, 1991—; vis. scientist lab. immunology Nat. Inst. Allergy and Infectious Diseases, NIH, Bethesda, 1985-86. Section editor: Immunology of Jour. Invest Dermatology, 1987—; European deputy editor Jour. Invest. Dermatology, 1992—; contbr. chpts. to books and articles to profl. jours. Mem. European Soc. Dermatol. Rsch., Soc. Investigative Dermatology, Am. Assn. Immunologists, Austrian Acad. Scis., German Acad. Scis. Roman Catholic. Home: St Ulrichs Platz 2-7, A 1070 Vienna Austria Office: Univ Vienna Med Sch, Dept Dermatology, A 1090 Vienna Austria

STINSON, MARY FLORENCE, nursing educator; b. Wheeling, W.Va., Feb. 11, 1931; d. Rolland Francis and Mary Angela (Voellinger) Kellogg; m. Charles Walter Stinson, Feb. 12, 1955; children: Kenneth Charles, Karen Marie, Kathryn Anne. BSN, Coll. Mt. St. Joseph, 1953, postgrad., 1983; MEd, Xavier U., Cin., 1967; postgrad. U. Cin., 1981. Staff nurse contagious disease ward Cin. Gen. Hosp., 1953-54, asst. head nurse med. and polio wards, 1955, acting head nurse, clin. instr., 1955-56; instr. St. Francis Hosp. Sch. Practical Nursing, Cin., 1956-57; instr. Good Samaritan Hosp. Sch. Nursing, Cin., 1957-65; instr. refresher courses for nurses Cin. Bd. Edn. and Ohio State Nurses Assn. Dist. 8, 1967-70; coord. sch. health office Coll. Mt. St. Joseph (Ohio), 1969-72, instr. dept. nursing, 1974-79, asst. prof., 1979-89; part-time staff nurse St. Francis/St. George Hosp., Cin., 1988-89; RN assessor Passport program Ohio Coun. on Aging, 1989-90, quality assurance coord., 1990-93; quality assurance supr. Passport and Elderly Svcs. Program, 1993-94; quality assurance mgr. Coun. Aging, Cin., 1995—. Charter mem. Adoptive Parents Assn. St. Joseph Infant and Maternity Home; active Women's Com. for Performing Arts Series, Coll. Mt. St. Joseph; mem. St. Antoninus Rosary Altar Rosary and Sch. Soc., St. Antoninus Athletic Club, com. chmn., 1969-70; bd. dirs. Coll. Mt. St. Joseph Alumnae Assn., 1982-84, sec., 1968-69, v.p., 1969-70, pres., 1970-71, chmn. revision of constn., 1976-77; homecoming chmn. Coll. Mt. St. Joseph, 1970, co-chmn., 1977; mem. Gamble Nippert YMCA. Mem. O.K.I. Gerontol. Nursing Assn. Democrat. Roman Catholic. Club: River Squares (v.p. 1967). Home: 5549 Cleander Dr Cincinnati OH 45238-4266 Office: Coun on Aging of Cin Holiday Office Pk 644 Linn St Cincinnati OH 45203-1720

STITNIZKY, JOHN LOUIS, health facilities and hospital services professional; b. Chgo., Oct. 10, 1939; s. John and Laura Lucille (Elzroth) S.; m. Yasuko Terada, June 2, 1961; children: Janet Laura, Diane Lynn, Sherry Jean. BA in Bus., Chaminade U. of Honolulu, 1977, postgrad., 1980-81. Enlisted USN, 1956, advanced through grades to sr. chief, ret., 1977; ins. underwriter Conn. Mut., Honolulu, 1977-80; gen. mgr. Waikiki Grand Hotel, Honolulu, 1980-81; auditor, night mgr. Outrigger Hotel, Honolulu, 1981-86; asst. dir. environ. svcs. St. Mary Med. Ctr. United Health Services, Inc., Long Beach, Calif., 1987-88; dir. environ. svcs. Fairview Devel. Ctr., Costa Mesa, Calif., 1988-89, Marriott Facilities Mgmt., Camarillo State Hosp., 1989-91; mgr., dir. environ. svcs. L.A. Dodgers Stadium, 1991-92; mgr. Gene Autry Western Heritage Mus., 1993-94; ops. mgr. Marriott Mgmt. Svcs./St. Francis Hosp., Evanston, Ill., 1994-96, Rush-Presbyn. Hosp., Chgo., 1996—. Big brother Big Bros. of Hawaii, Honolulu, 1975-76; del. Rep. Conv., Honolulu, 1980. Mem. Navy League U.S. (life, sec., v.p. 1978-79, Sailor of Yr. award 1977), Am. Legion (comdr., dist. vice comdr. Post 56 1979), Fleet Res. (bd. dirs. bd. 46 1978), VFW, NRA (Cert. saftey instructor), Nat. Exec. Housekeepers Assn. (reg. mem.), Elks. Lutheran. Office: Mariott Health Care Svcs 3020 Woodcreek Dr Ste B Downers Grove IL 60515

STITZEL, ROBERT E., health science educator; b. N.Y.C., Feb. 22, 1937; s. Louis H. and Betty (Podell) S.; m. Judith Gold, June 4, 1961; 1 child, David L. BS, Columbia U., 1959, MS, 1961; PhD, U. Minn., 1964. Asst. prof. W.Va. U., Morgantown, 1965-69, assoc. prof., 1969-73, prof., 1973—, acting chmn., 1978, 85, 87, assoc. chmn. dept. pharmacology and toxicology, 1979—, spl. asst. to provost, dir. grad. studies, 1991-94; vis. prof. U. Adelaide, Australia, 1973, U. Innsbruck, Austria, 1977; chmn. study sect. NIH, Bethesda, Md., 1983-84, 84-85. Editor: Modern Pharmacology, 5 edits., 1980—; editor-in-chief jour. Pharmacol. Revs., 1989-95; contbr. articles to profl. jours. Sr. rsch. fellow Swedish Med. Rsch. Coun., Goteborg, 1966-67, hon. rsch. fellow Univ. Coll. London, 1977; vis. rsch. scientist divsn. human nutrition CSIRO, Adelaide, 1987; recipient Rsch. Career Devel. award NIH, 1970-75. Mem. AAAS, Am. Soc. for Pharmacology and Exptl. Therapeutics (sec.-treas. 1993-96). Office: WV U Med Ctr Dept Pharmacology/Toxicoloq Morgantown WV 26506

STIVER, JAMES FREDERICK, pharmacist, health physicist, administrator, scientist; b. Elkhart, Ind., Jan. 27, 1943; s. Melvin Hugh and Pauline Anna (Schrock) S.; m. Joan Louise Trindle, Aug. 14, 1965; children: Gregory James, Richard Frederick, Kristin Louise, Elizabeth Ann. BS in Pharmacy and Pharm. Scis., Purdue U., 1966, MS, 1968, PhD, 1970. Lic. pharmacist, Ind., N.D. Asst. prof. N.D. State U., Fargo, 1969-73, assoc. prof., 1973-76, radiol. safety officer, 1969-76; radiation safety officer KMS Fusion Inc., Ann Arbor, Mich., 1976-80; mgr., pharmacist Kroger Sav-On Pharmacy Co., Elkhart, Ind., 1980-81; pharmacist Elkhart Gen. Hosp., 1981; environ. regulatory affairs adminstr. Upjohn Co., Kalamazoo, Mich., 1981-88; patent liaison scientist, 1988-92; sr. patent liaison scientist, 1992-94; pharmacist, asst. mgr. Judd Drugs, Elkhart, 1994-95; pharmacist Meijer Pharmacy, Goshen, Ind., 1995—; cons., lectr. Mem. Trinity Luth. Ch., Goshen, Ind. Named to Honorable Order Ky. Cols. Fellow Am. Inst. Chemists; mem. AAAS, Am. Pharm. Assn., Ind. Pharmacists Assn., N.D. Pharm. Assn., Am. Chem. Soc., Health Physics Soc., Internat. Radiation Protection Assn., Am. Biol. Safety Assn., N.Y. Acad. Scis., Kappa Psi, Rho Chi, Phi Lambda Upsilon, Sigma Xi. Contbr. articles, abstracts to publs. Home: 505 Skyview Dr Middlebury IN 46540-9427 Office: Meijer Inc Goshen IN 46526

STIVERS, JAMES ROBERT, urologist; b. Augusta, Ga., Sept. 20, 1943; s. Robert Winthrop and Jean Margie (Megerle) S. BS, Western Ky. U., 1965; MD, U. Ky., 1971. Diplomate Am. Bd. Urology. Intern in surgery N.Y. Hosp. Cornell Med. Ctr., 1971-72, resident in urology, 1974-77; pvt. practice Springs Med. Ctr., Louisville, Louisville, 1980—; asst. surgeon in urology N.Y. Hosp., 1974-76, surgeon in urology, 1977; asst. clin. prof. urology U. Louisville, 1983; chief urology Audubon Regional Med. Ctr., Louisville, 1984—, chief surgery, 1989—. Fellow ACS; mem. Am. Urol. Assn., Southeastern Urol. Assn., Ky. Urol. Assn. Office: 6400 Dutchmans Pkwy #155 Louisville KY 40205

STOBO, JOHN DAVID, physician, educator; b. Somerville, Mass., Sept. 1, 1941. BA, Dartmouth Coll., 1963; MD, SUNY, Buffalo, 1968. Intern Osler Med. Services, Johns Hopkins, Balt., 1968-69, asst. med. resident, 1969-70, chief med. resident, 1972-73; research assoc. NIH, Bethesda, 1970-72; asst. prof. Mayo Clinic and Research Found., Rochester, Minn., 1973-76; assoc. prof. Moffitt Hosp., San Francisco, 1976-82, prof., head section rheumatology, clin. immunology, 1982-85; William Osler prof. medicine, chmn. dept. medicine John Hopkins Hosp. and Univ., Balt., 1985-94, vice dean clin. sci., assoc. v.p. medicine, 1994—; v.p. Johns Hopkins Health System, Balt., 1994—; chmn., CEO Johns Hopkins Healthcare LLC, Balt. Mem. editorial bds. Jour. Immunology, 1981-86, Jour. Lab. and Clin. Investigation, 1977-82, Arthritis and Rheumatism 1980-85, Jour. Reticuloendothelial Soc., 1982-84, Jour. Clin. Investigation, 1981-86, Jour. Clin. Immunology, 1982-87, Jour. Molecular and Cellular Immunology, 1984-86, Rheumatology Internat., 1984-86, Jour. Immunology, 1985-87; contbr. numerous articles to profl. jours. Transp. and immunobiology adv. com. NIAID, 1976-81; vice chmn. research com. Arthritis Found., 1982-84, chmn., 1984-86, sr. investigator, 1974-77; bd. scientific counselors Nat. Cancer Inst., 1982—; scientific adv. bd. exec. com. Lupus Research Inst.; research adv. bd. DuPont Co.,

1987-94. Recipient Merck award 1967, Maimonides Med. Soc. award 1968; SUNY fellow, 1965-66. Fellow ACP, Am. Clin. and Climatol. Assn., Balt. City Med. Soc., Interurban Clin. Club, Md. Soc. Internal Medicine; mem. AAAS, Inst. Medicine, Am. Coll. Rheumatology (pres. 1989-90), Am. Rheumatism Assn. (sec., treas., 1st v.p. 1985-89), Am. Assn. Immunologists, Am. Assn. Physicians, Am. Fedn. Clin. Rsch., Am. Soc. Clin. Investigation, Assn. Profs. Medicine (sec.-treas. 1991-92, pres. 1994-95), Alpha Omega Alpha. Office: Johns Hopkins Outpatient Ctr 601 N Caroline St Ste 2080 Baltimore MD 21287-0764*

STOCK, JEFFRY BENTON, molecular biology educator; b. L.A., Dec. 27, 1946; s. Gene and Jane S.; m. Regina Hackenbeck. BA, Johns Hopkins U., 1967, PhD, 1975. Rsch. assoc. Johns Hopkins Univ., Balt., 1975-77; cystic fibrosis fellow Univ. Calif., Berkeley, 1977-79, rsch. assoc., 1979-82; assoc. mem., asst. prof. Princeton (N.J.) Univ., 1982-88, mem. molecular biophysiology, assoc. mem., assoc. prof., 1988-92, prof. molecular biology, 1992—; lectr. Sigma Xi, 1979; vis. scholar Inst. Pasteur, 1995-96. Named Predoctoral fellow NIH, 1967-75; recipient fellowship Cystic Fibrosis, 1977-80, Wilson Coll. Faculty, 1986. Mem. AAAS, Am. Soc. for Biochemistry and Molecular Biology, Am. Soc. for Microbiology, Am. Chem. Soc., N.Y. Acad. Sci., Theabald Smith Soc. Office: Princeton Univ Dept Molecular Biology Princeton NJ 08544

STOCK, JOHN FREDERICK, family practice physician; b. Alexandria, Minn., Feb. 9, 1947; s. Leslie Edward and Evelyn Marie (Larson) S.; m. Victoria Ann Zenk, June 18, 1977 (div. June 1990); children: Jennifer, Jaci. BS, U. Minn., 1969, MD, 1972. Rotating med. intern St. Paul (Minn.) Ramsey Hosp., 1972-73; gen. practice Morris (Minn.) Med. Ctr., 1973-77; internal medicine resident U. Minn. Assn. Hosps., Mpls., 1977-79; internal medicine practice West Ctrl. Internal Medicine, Morris, Minn., 1979—; aviation med. examiner FAA, Morris, Minn., 1975—; bd. dirs. Cmty. First Nat. Bank, Morris, 1987—. Inventor patented Fulga Snare, 1992. Bd. dirs. Barnes-Aasted Soil and Water Conservation Assn., Morris, 1982—. Mem. West Ctrl. Minn. Med. Soc. (pres. 1990—), Aircraft Owners and Pilots Assn. Lutheran. Home: Rte 1 Box 5 Kensington MN 56343 Office: West Ctrl Internal Medicine Montana at 1st St Box 466 Morris MN 56267

STOCK, MARGOT THERESE, nurse, anthropologist, consultant, educator; b. Toronto, Ont., Can., Aug. 10, 1936; Arrived in US 1967.; d. Karl Dwight and Marguerite Anne (Lafitte) K.; m. Philip Anthony, Jan. 11, 1946; children: Dwight, Scott, Kayler, Travis & Anthony (twins) Sean. AAS, Suffolk County Com. Coll., Selden, N.Y., 1981; BS in Nursing, U. S. Fla., Ft. Myers, Fla., 1983; MS in Nursing, U. Tex., 1984; DPhil in Social Anthropology, U. Oxford, England, 1989. Nurse Sarasota Meml. Hosp., Fla., 1981-82, LW Blake Meml. Hosp., Bradenton, Fla., 1982-83, Med. Center Del Oro, Houston, 1983-85, Pitt County Meml. Hosp., Greenville, N.C.; asst. prof. E. Carolina U., Greenville, N.C., 1985-89; Cons. Gerontol. Nursing Network Greensboro N.C. Designer Game and Software (computer), Nursing Math Made Easy, Understanding Mgmt., Teaching Nursing Theory 1984; Author (with others) Book Clinical Pharmacology & Nursing 1987, Poetry Evolution Lycidas Jaso 1980-87. Mem. AAUW, Sigma Theta Tau, Sigma Kappa Found. (Houston Sigma Kappa award), Phi Theta Kappa (pres. 1981). Roman Catholic. Home: 118 Old London Rd Greenville NC 27834-8833 Office: East Carolina U Sch of Nursing Greenville NC 27858-4353

STOCKARD, JOE LEE, public health service officer, consultant; b. Lees Summit, Mo., May 5, 1924; s. Joseph Frederick and Madge Lorraine (Jones) S.; m. Elsie Anne Chamberlain, Dec. 27, 1957. BS, Yale U., 1945; MD, U. Kans., 1948; MPH, Johns Hopkins U., 1961. Med. officer U.S. Army Med. Corps, Korea and Malaya, 1952-55; asst. prof. preventive medicine Sch. Medicine U. Md., Balt., 1955-58; dep. dir. Cholera Rsch. Lab., Dhaka, Bangladesh, 1960-63; advanced through grades to capt., epidemiologist USPHS, Washington, 1960-76, 64-67; chief preventive medicine sect. USAID, Saigon, Vietnam, 1965-68; assoc. dir. Office Internat. Health, Office of Surgeon Gen. USPHS, Washington, 1967-69; epidemiologist, med. officer Agy. for Internat. Devel., Washington, 1969-87; mem. expert adv. com. WHO, Ouagadougou, Burkina, Faso, 1987-92; mem. joint programme com. AID project officer Onchocerciasis Control Program, West Africa, 1975-87; mem. officer AID Africa Bur., Washington, 1976-87; guest speaker prol. seminar on leptospirosis, 1956; organizer plague sect. meeting 8th Internat. Congress Tropical Medicine, 1969. Author: (with others) Communicable and Infectious Diseases, 1964; contbr. articles to U.S. Armed Forces Med. Jour., N.Y. Acad. Scis. Jour. Citizens rep. on regional water quality adv. com. Low County Coun. of Govts., 1996—. Recognized for support of onchocerciasis control in West Africa by Pres. Jerry Rawlings, Rep. of Ghana, 1986. Fellow Royal Soc. Tropical Medicine and Hygiene; mem. APHA, Am. Soc. Tropical Medicine and Hygiene, Retired Officers Assn. Office: 17 Angel Wing Dr Hilton Head Island SC 29926-1903

STOCKER, ROLAND, biomedical scientist; b. Lucerne, Switzerland, Oct. 5, 1956. Diploma, Fed. Inst. Tech., Zurich, Switzerland, 1981; PhD, Australian Nat. U., Canberra, 1985. Postdoctoral fellow U. Calif., Berkeley, 1986-87; asst. prof. U. Berne, Switzerland, 1987-89; unit leader Heart Rsch. Inst., Sydney, Australia, 1989—; rsch. fellow NH&MRC, 1994—; CEO Heart Rsch. Developments, Sydney, 1994—. Asst. nat. coach Swiss Rowing Assn., 1987-89, mem. Swiss Olympic Team, Moscow Olympics, 1980; coach Australia Rowing Team, 1984. Recipient Joy London award Nat. Heart Found., Australia, 1995. Mem. Internat. Soc. Free Radical Rsch. (pres.-elect 1995—, Young Investigator award 1987). Office: Heart Rsch Inst, 145 Missenden Rd, Sydney NSW 2050, Australia

STOCKFORD, STEVEN ALAN, medical technologist; b. Tampa, Fla., Jan. 30, 1963; s. Charles James Stockford and Joyce (Newell) Sundheim; m. Lynn Janet Weilbrenner, July 15, 1989. AA, U. Maine, 1985, BS in Earth Sci., 1987; AAS in Med. Technology, Ea. Maine Tech. Coll., 1990. Cert. med. technologist. Med. technologist I Sebasticook Valley Hosp., Pittsfield, Maine; med. technologist II Mid Coast Hosp., Brunswick, Maine. Sgt. U.S. Army, Desert Shield/Desert Storm. Decorated Army Commendation medal. Mem. Am. Med. Technologists, Soc. Armed Forces Med. Lab. Scientists. Home: 40B Atwood Rd Topsham ME 04086

STOCKHOUSE, BURTON EDWIN, orthodontist; b. Sheridan, Wyo., Aug. 15, 1928; s. Erland Stockhouse and Francis (Gillett) Miller; m. Louise Mary Claar, June 17, 1951; children: Janet, James, L'nette, Bruce, Heidi. DDS, St. Louis U., 1955, MS, 1965. Diplomate Am. Bd. Orthodontists. Pvt. practice dentistry Worland, Wyo., 1955-63; pvt. practice orthodontics Riverton, Wyo., 1965—. Fellow Am. Coll. Dentists; mem. Am. Dental Assn., Am. Assn. Orthodontists, Am. Soc. Dentistry for Children (Wyo. chpt. pres. 1960), Wyo. Ortho. Assn. (pres. 1976-77), Rocky Mountain Soc. Orthodontists (pres. 1987-88), Orthodontic Ed. and Rsch. Found. (pres. 1982-83). Republican. Presbyn. Home: 400 N 1st St Riverton WY 82501-3432

STOCKMAN, JAMES ANTHONY, III, pediatrician; b. Phila., 1943. MD, Jefferson Med. Coll., 1969. Diplomate Am. Bd. Pediatrics. Intern Childrens Hosp. Pa., 1969-70, resident in pediatrics, 1970-72; fellow in pediatric hematology/oncology SUNY, Syracuse, 1972-74; now cons. prof. Duke U.; also with U. N.C., Chapel Hill. Office: Am Bd Pediatrics 111 Silver Cedar Ct Chapel Hill NC 27514-1512

STOCKTON, WILLIAM JAMES, psychiatrist, psychoanalyst; b. Paris, Tex., July 30, 1929; s. William James and Charlotte (Landers) S.; m. Irma Ford, Aug. 21, 1953; children: Rebecca Louise, Charlotte Kathryn, Deborah Lynn. Student, Okla. U., 1948-52; MD, Okla. Med. Sch., Oklahoma City, 1956. Diplomte Am. Bd. Psychiatry and Neurology; cert. in psychoanalysis. Intern Walter Reed Gen. Hosp., Washington, 1956-57; resident Walter Reed Gen. Hosp., 1957-60; pvt. practice psychiatry-psychoanalysis Stockton, Md., 1964—, Washington, 1964—; clin. prof. psychiatry George Washington U., Washington, 1964—; teaching staff Walter Reed Gen. Hosp., Washington, 1964-95; tng. and supervising analyst Balt.-D.C. Inst. for Psychoanalysis, 1973-87. Citizens com. D.C. Bar Assn., Washington, 1972-74. Maj. U.S. Army, 1956-64. Fellow Am. Psychiat. Assn. (chmn. consortium on treatment issues 1996—); mem. Washington Psychiat. Soc. (pres. 1977-78), Balt.-D.C. Psychoanalytic Soc. (pres. 1985-86), AMA, Med. Soc. D.C.. Republican. Presbyterian. Home: 2715 Daniel Rd Bethesda MD 20815-3150 Office: 1601 18th St NW Apt 1004 Washington DC 20009-2519

STOECKER, WILLIAM VAN, physician, computer scientist; b. St. Louis, Mar. 18, 1946; s. William Clayton and Mary Eugenia (Gaunt) S.; m. Ruth Carl, May 21, 1977; children: Charles, Will, John. BS, Calif. Inst. Tech., 1968; MS, UCLA, 1970; MD, U. Mo. Columbia, 1977. adj. asst. prof. computer sci. U. Mo., Rolla, 1985—; v.p. Sulzberger Inst., Schaumburg, Ill., 1994—. Editor: Computer Apple Dermatology, 1993; inventor liquid lance. Cubmaster Cub Scouts Am., Rolla, 1989—. Me. Internat. Soc. Digital Imaging (pres. 1995-97). Office: 1100 W 10th St Rolla MO 65401-2937

STOELTING, ROBERT K., anesthesiologist, medical association executive; b. Indpls., 1939. MD, Ind. U., 1964. Diplomate Am. Bd. Anesthesiology. Intern Blodgett Hosp., Grand Rapids, Mich., 1964-65; resident U. Calif., San Francisco, 1965-68; resident anesthesiologist Ind. U. Med. Sch., Indpls., 1968—; pres. Am. Bd. Anesthesiology. Mem. Am. Surg. Assn., Internat. Anesthesia Rsch. Soc. Office: Ind U Med Sch 1120 South Dr Indianapolis IN 46202-5135

STOHLER, MICHAEL JOE, dentist; b. Anderson, Ind., Mar. 26, 1956; s. Herbert Warren and Mary Jo (Philbert) S.; m. Mary Anne Poinsette, May 16, 1981; children: James Lawrence, Maria Christine, Benjamin Joseph. Student, Lake-Sumter C.C., Leesburg, Fla., 1974-76; BS, Ball State U., 1978; DDS, Ind. U., 1982. Gen. practice dentistry Anderson, 1982—. Mem. ADA, Ind. Dental Assn., East Ctrl. Dental Assn., Madison County Dental Assn., Acad. Gen. Dentistry, Acad. Dentistry for Handicapped, Ind. U. Alumni Assn. (assoc., life), Rotary (sgt.-at-arms Anderson Suburban chpt. 1986), Psi Omega. Home: 2829 W Ridge Ln Anderson IN 46013-9749 Office: 2012 E 53rd St Anderson IN 46013-3102

STOHLMAN, CONNIE SUZANNE, obstetrical gynecological nurse; b. Tucson, Sept. 27, 1960; d. Irvin Wendell and Betty Jo (Stewart) Holmes; m. Bruce R. Stohlman, Sept. 14, 1991. BSN, Bishop Clarkson Coll. Nursing, 1987; BA, U. Nebr., 1982; cert. med. asst., Omaha Coll. Health Careers, 1983. Primary nurse I U. Md. Med. System, Balt., 1987-90; staff nurse St. Joseph Hosp., Omaha, 1990—; mem. quality assurance task force U. Md. Med. System, 1987-90; mem. quality assurance com. St. Joseph Hosp., 1992—. Named to Outstanding Young Women of Am., 1986.

STOJILKOVIC, STANKO STAMEN, biologist; b. Karavukovo, Yugoslavia, Aug. 25, 1950; came to U.S., 1985; s. Stamen and Ana (Radojevic) S.; 1 child, Kosta. BSc in Biology, U. Novi Sad (Yugoslavia), 1974; MSc in Physiology, U. Belgrade (Yugoslavia), 1979; PhD in Endocrinology, U. Novi Sad, 1982. Rsch. asst. U. Novi Sad, 1975-83, asst. prof., 1983-87; vis. scientist NIH, Bethesda, Md., 1988-93; head unit on cellular signaling NICHD, NIH, Bethesda, 1991—; assoc. prof. U. Belgrade, 1991—. Author: General Physiology, 1985, 2d edit., 1989; contbr. chpts. in books, numerous articles to profl. jours. Mem. Am. Soc. Biochemistry and Molecular Biology, Endocrine Soc.

STOKEN, JACQUELINE MARIE, physician; b. Beaver Falls, Pa., Sept. 29, 1948; d. Jack Marc and Lillian Marie Stoken; m. John F. Edge, June 2, 1990; children: Randi Elizabeth; stepchildren: Lisa Adrienne, Alexander Joseph. Nursing diploma, Presbyn.-U. Hosp. Sch. Nursing, Pitts., 1970; BS in Biology with honors, Chatham Coll., Pitts., 1986; DO, U. Osteo. Med. & Health Scis., Des Moines, 1990. RN, Pa., Iowa; cert. ACLS, BCLS. Home care staff nurse South Hills Health System, Pitts., 1976-89; intern internal medicine Des Moines Gen. Hosp., 1990-91; resident physician dept. phys. medicine and rehab. U. Minn., Mpls., 1991-94; lectr. Internat. Rehab. Med. Assn., Des Moines, 1994—; physiatrist Iowa Orthopaedic Ctr., Des Moines, 1994—; guest lectr. dept. phys. therapy U. Minn., Mpls., 1991-94, dept. ocupational therapy, 1991-94, U. Osteo. Medicine and Health Sci., Des Moines, 1990, 95, 96, IOFP, 1996—; chief resident dept. phys. medicine and rehab. U. Minn., Mpls., 1992-93; mem. Iowa Gov.'s Task Force on Rural Health, 1989. Mem. AMA, Am. Acad. Phys. Medicine and Rehab., Am. Osteo. Assn. (sec. coun. student coun. pres. 1988-89), Iowa Osteo Med. Assn. (student del. ho. of dels. 1987-88, student coun. rep. 1987-88), Am. Med. Women's Assn., Am. Holistic Med. Assn., Am. Acad. Osteopathy, Cranial Acad., Sigma Sigma Phi.

STOKES, DAVID KERSHAW, JR., family physician; b. Camden, S.C., Feb. 3, 1927; s. David Kershaw and Annie Bell (Smith) S.; m. Louise W. Stokes (div. 1987); children: Donna, David III, Tina; m. Norma Jean Todd, July 31, 1987. BS, Clemson U., 1948; MS, U. Ga., 1952; PhD, Tex. A&M U., 1956; MD, Med. U. S.C., 1957. Diplomate, Am. Bd. Family Practice. Intern Spartanburg (S.C.) Regional Med. Ctr., 1958; pvt. practice Inman, S.C., 1959-72; dir. family practice residency program Spartanburg Regional Med. Ctr., 1972-78, chief geriatric tng. family practice residency program, 1979-92; med. dir. Camphaven Nursing Home, Inman, 1965-91; ret., 1992; med. dir. attending physician Valley Falls Ter. Nursing Home, 1992—, Tryon Estates Med. Facility, 1994-95. Bd. trustees S.C. Bapt. Ministries on Aging, 1994—. With U.S. Army, 1945-47, ETO. Fellow Am. Acad. Family Physicians, Am. Geriatric Soc. (bd. dirs. 1985-88); mem. Am. Med. Dirs. Assn. (pres. 1983-84), Spartanburg County Med. Soc., Inman Rotary Club. Republican. Baptist. Home and Office: 34 Chestnut Ridge Dr Spartanburg SC 29303-4517

STOKES, DEBORAH CYNTHIA, physician; b. Swainsboro, Ga., June 12, 1957; d. David and Anner (Williams) S. AA in Chemistry, East Ga. Coll., 1977; BA in Chemistry/Biology with honors, Mercer U., 1979; DO, Mich. State U., 1987. Diplomate Am. Bd. Neurology. Biology lab instr. Ga. So. Univ., Statesboro, Ga., 1979-80; biology/phys. sci. tchr. Swainsboro (Ga.) High Sch., 1980-81, Emanuel County Inst., Twin City, Ga., 1981-82; intern Mich. Health Care, 1987-88; resident in internal medicine Providence Hosp., 1988-90; resident in neurology Oakland Gen. Hosp., 1991-94; family practitioner Mich. Health Care, Detroit, 1990—; pvt.practice neurology Ball Meml. Hosp., 1995—. Recipient Bausch and Lomb Hon. Sci. award, 1975; named Disting. Youth in Am., 1979, Outstanding Young Woman of Am., 1979. Mem. Am. Osteo. Assn., Ga. Osteo. Med. Assn., Mich. Lupus Found., Am. Coll. Osteo. Neurologists and Psychiatrists, Assn. Osteo. Physicians and Surgeons, Mich. Assn. Osteo. Physicians and Surgeons, Wayne County Med. Assn. African Methodist Episcopal. Home: 6904 W Saint Andrews Ave Yorktown IN 47396-9693

STOKES, KATHLEEN S., dermatologist; b. Springfield, Mass., Oct. 18, 1954; d. John Fracis and Margaret Cecelia (MacDonnell) S.; m. William Walter Greaves, Sept. 20, 1981; children: Ian R., Spencer W., Malcolm W. BS, U. Utah, 1978, MS, 1980; MD, Med. Coll. Wis., 1987. Diplomate Am. Bd. Dermatology. Resident in dermatology Med. Coll. Wis. Milw., 1988-90, chief resident, 1990-91; pvt. practice, Milw., 1991—. Contbr. articles to med. jours., including Critical Care Medicine, Jour. Pediatric Dermatology. Fellow Am. Acad. Dermatology, Milw. Acad. Medicine; mem. AMA, Wis. Dermatol. Soc., Women's Dermatologic Soc., Alpha Omega Alpha. Office: Affiliated Dermatologists 2300 N Mayfair Rd Milwaukee WI 53223

STOLL, HENRY WAGNER, physician assistant, educator; b. Newport, R.I., Dec. 10, 1949; s. Ralph Foeste and Ruth Esther (Wagner) S.; m. Wendy Fusae Hamai, July 18, 1990; 1 child, Kenji Hamai. AB, Brown U., 1971; AS, Hahnemann U., 1975; postgrad., U. Wash., 1988-90. Cert. physician asst. Instr. physician asst. program Hahnemann Med. Coll. and Hosp. (now Hahnemann U.), Phila., 1975-78; lectr. dept. health svcs. U. Wash., Seattle, 1978-93, asst. dir. MEDEX Northwest, 1981-93, interim dir., 1985, sr. lectr. dept. med. edn., 1994—; mem. physician asst. subcom Wash. State Bd. Med. Examiners, 1982-84. Author chpts. to book. Mem. Am. Acad. Physician Assts (chair pub. award 1984-88, mem. edn. coun. 1990-94, rep. to accreditation rev. com. on edn. for The Physician Asst. 1995—). Assn. Physician Asst. Programs (chmn. faculty and staff devel. com. 1984-85), Wash. Acad. Physician Assts. (sec. and editor newsletter editor 1989-93, chair student/profl. affairs com. 1985-90, mem. scholarship award com. 1986, bd. dirs. 1982-84).

STOLL, JOHN FREDERICK, internist; b. Lincoln, Ill., Nov. 11, 1947; s. George Frederick and Ruth Maybelle (Everman) S.; m. Stephanie Stuckel, June 7, 1969; children: Stephen, Susanne. BS, U. Ill., 1969, MD, 1973. Diplomate Am. Bd. Internal Medicine. Resident in internal medicine Henry Ford Hosp. and Clinic, 1973-76; pvt. practice Fort Collins, Colo., 1976-84; adult medicine Carle Clinic Assn., Urbana, Ill., 1984—; med. dir. quality and resource mgmt. Carle Found. Hosp., Urbana, 1990—; med. dept. head Carle Clinic Assn., Urbana, 1994-96. Recipient cert. Advanced Achievement in Internal Medicine, Am. Bd. Internal Medicine, 1987, Added Qualifications in Geriatrics, 1988. Fellow Am. Coll. Physicians. Office: Carle Clinic Assn 602 W University Urbana IL 61801

STOLLAR, BERNARD DAVID, biochemist, educator; b. Saskatoon, Sask., Can., Aug. 11, 1936; came to U.S., 1960; s. Percival and Rose (Direnfeld) S.; m. Carol A. Singer, Oct. 7, 1956; children: Lawrence, Michael, Suzanne. BA, U. Sask., 1958, MD, 1959. Intern U. Sask. Hosp., Saskatoon, 1959-60; postdoctoral fellow Brandeis U., Waltham, Mass., 1960-62; dep. chief divsn. biol. scis. USAF Office of sci. Rsch., Washington, 1962-64; asst. prof. dept. pharmacology Tufts U. Schs. Medicine and Dental Medicine, Boston, 1964-67, asst. prof. dept. biochemistry, 1967-68, assoc. prof. biochemistry/pharmacology, 1968-74, prof., 1974—, acting chmn. dept. biochemistry and pharmacology, 1984-86, chmn. dept. biochemistry, 1986—; vis. prof. internat. course in immunology and immunochemistry Mexico City, 1971; sr. fellow Weizmann Inst. Sci., Rehovot, Israel, 1971-71; vis. prof. chemistry Wellesley (Mass.) Coll., 1976, U. Tromsö, Norway, 1981; Dozor vis. prof. Ben-Gurion U. Sch. Medicine, Beer Sheva, Israel, 1986; cons. USAF Office Sci. Rsch., 1966-69, Seragen, Inc., 1983-88, Cetus, 1982-85, Gene-Trak, 1986-89, Alkermes, Inc., 1989—, Catalytic Antibodies, Inc., 1993—; mem. allergy/transplantation rsch. com. NIH/NIAID, 1990-94. Contbr. over 200 articles to profl. jours., chpts. to books; exec. editl. bd. Analytical Biochemistry, 1988—; editl. bd. Jour. Immunology, 1981-85, Molecular Immunology, 1980-95, Arthritis and Rheumatism, 1986-89, Jour. Immunological Methods, 1988-95. Mem. adult edn. com. Temple Reyim, Newton, Mass. Capt. USAF, 1962-64. Recipient Copland prize U. Sask. Coll. Arts and Sci., 1958, Gold medalist, Coll. of Medicine, 1959, Medalist in Medicine, Pediatrics, Obstetrics, Gynecology, 1959; decorated Air Force Commendation medal; Weizmann Inst. Sci. sr. fellow, 1971-72; named Third Ann. Alumni Lectr., U. Sask. Coll. Medicine, 1989; rsch. grantee NSF, NIH, 1964—. Mem. AAAS, Am. Assn. Immunologists, Am. Soc. Biochemistry and Molecular Biology, Am. Coll. Rheumatology, Clin. Immunology Soc. Office: Tufts Univ Sch Medicine Dept Biochemistry 136 Harrison Ave Boston MA 02111-1800

STOLLER, STEVEN E., ophthalmologist, eye surgeon; b. Ft. Wayne, Ind., Sept. 19, 1947; s. Norman and Joan Stoller; m. Margie Stoller, Jan. 25, 1975; children: David, Laura, Brian. AB in Zoology, Ind. U., 1969, MD, 1973. Diplomate Am. Bd. Ophthalmology, Am. Bd. Eye Surgery, subsplty. cert. in cataract/IOL surg. Intern Emory U. Affiliated Hosp., Atlanta, 1973-75; resident Ind. U. Med. Ctr., Indpls., 1976-79; emergency room physician Douglas Gen. Hosp., Douglasville, Ga., 1975-76; pvt. practice Richmond (Ind.) Eye Ctr., 1979—; COO Eye Ctr. Group Muncie/Richmond/Marion/Connersville Ind., 1996—; med. dir. Richmond Surgery Ctr., 1994—. Mem. Richmond Symphonic Chorus, 1990—; choral dir. Christ Presbyn. Ch., Richmond, 1986-93. Gave Outstanding CME lectr. of yr. Reid Hosp., Richmond, 1988, 91; Bus. of Yr. AIDS Task Force of Richmond, 1995. Fellow Am. Acad. Ophthalmology, Am. Coll. Eye Surgeons; mem. AMA, Am. Soc. Cataract and Refractive Surgery, Ind. Acad. Ophthalmology, Ind. State Med. Assn. Home: 3430 Lantern Trail Richmond IN 47374 Office: Richmond Eye Center 1900 Chester Blvd Richmond IN 47374

STOLLEY, PAUL DAVID, medical educator, researcher; b. Pawling, N.Y., June 17, 1937; s. Herman and Rosalie (Chertock) S.; m. Jo Ann Goldenberg, June 13, 1959; children: Jonathan, Dorie, Anna. B.A., Lafayette Coll., 1957; M.D., Cornell U., 1962; M.P.H., Johns Hopkins U., 1968; M.A. hon., U. Pa., 1976. Diplomate: Am. Coll. Preventive Medicine, Am. Coll. Epidemiology. Intern U. Wis. Med. Ctr., 1962-63, resident in medicine, 1963-64; med. officer USPHS, Washington, 1964-67; asst. prof. Johns Hopkins Sch. Pub. Health, Balt., 1968-71, assoc. prof., 1971-76; Herbert C. Rorer prof. medicine U. Pa. Sch. Medicine, Phila., 1976-91; prof. and chmn. dept. epidemiology U. Md. Sch. Medicine, Balt., 1991—. Co-author: Foundations of Epidemiology, 3d edit., 1994, Epidemiology: Investigating Disease, 1995; contbg. author: Case-Control Studies, 1982; mem. editl. bd. New Eng. Jour. Medicine, 1989-93, Milbank Quar., Health and Soc., 1986—; assoc. editor Clin. Pharmacology and Therapeutics, 1987-93; contbr. articles to med. jours. Mem. Physicians for Social Responsibility, 1961—. Served to lt. comdr. USPHS, 1964-67. Fellow ACP; mem. Am. Coll. Epidemiology (pres. 1987-89), Inst. Medicine of NAS, Soc. Epidemiol. Rsch. (pres. 1982-84), Am. Epidemiol. Soc. (pres. 1994—), Internat. Epidemiol. Assn. (treas. 1982-84), Johns Hopkins Soc. Scholars. Home: Watermark Pl Apt 106 10001 Windstream Dr Columbia MD 21044 Office: Univ of Md Sch Medicine 660 W Redwood St Baltimore MD 21201-1541

STOLOV, JERRY FRANKLIN, healthcare executive; b. Kansas City, Mo., Jan. 31, 1946; s. I. Paul and Marion R. (Rothberg) Stolov. BA, Washington U., 1968; MPA, Roosevelt U., 1972. Adminstrv. asst. U. Ill. Chgo. Circle & Med. Sch. Campuses, Chgo., 1970-75; exec. dir. Hosp. Hill Health Svcs. Corp., Kansas City, Mo., 1976—; also bd. dirs. Hosp. Hill Health Svcs. Corp., Kansas City, 1976—; bd. dirs. Kansas City Psychoanalytic Found., 1996—; adv. dir. Mchts. Bank Corp., Kansas City, 1985-92. Leadership tng. C. of C., Kansas City, 1977-78. Mem. Assn. Am. Med. Colls. (group on faculty practice), Med. Group Mgmt. Assn., Internat. City Mgrs. Assn., Am. Soc. Pub. Health Adminstrs., Acad. Polit. Sci. (contbg. mem.). Office: Hosp Hill Health Svcs Corp 800 Hospital Hill Ctr 2310 Holmes St Kansas City MO 64108-2634

STOLOV, WALTER CHARLES, physician, rehabilitation educator, psychiatrist; b. N.Y.C., Jan. 6, 1928; s. Arthur and Rose F. (Gordon) S.; m. Anita Carvel Noodelman, Aug. 9, 1953; children: Nancy, Amy, Lynne. BS in Physics, CCNY, 1948; MA in Physics, U. Minn., 1951, MD, 1956. Diplomate Am. Bd. Phys. Med. and Rehab., Am. Bd. Electrodiagnostic Medicine. Physicist U.S. Naval Gun Factory, Nat. Bur. Stds., Washington, 1948-49; teaching and rsch. asst. U. Minn., Mpls., 1950-54; from instr. to assoc. prof. U. Wash., Seattle, 1960-70, prof., 1970—, also chmn., 1987—; editl. bd. Archives Phys. Medicine and Rehab., 1967-78, Muscle and Nerve, 1983-89, 92-95; cons. Social Security Adminstrn., Seattle, 1975—; sec. Am. Bd. Electrodiagnostic Medicine, 1995—. Co-editor: Handbook of Severe Disability, 1981; contbr. articles to profl. jours. Surgeon USPHS, 1956-57. Recipient Townsend Harris medal CCNY, 1990. Fellow AAAS, Am. Heart Assn.; mem. Am. Acad. Phys. Medicine & Rehab. (Disting. Clinician award 1987), Am. Congress Rehab. Medicine (Essay award 1959), Assn. Acad. Physiatrists, Am. Assn. Electrodiagnostic Medicine (pres. 1987-88), Am. Spinal Cord Injury Assn. Office: U Wash Box 356490 1959 NE Pacific St Seattle WA 98195-0004

STOLPE, MARILYN KATHLEEN, nursing administrator; b. Oak Park, Ill., July 14, 1944; d. George and Helen (Cibery) Yurik; m. William J. Stolpe, July 6, 1968; children: William J. Jr., Michael A. Diploma, Little Co. Mary, 1965; BS, Coll. St. Francis, 1987; MA in Psychology, Forest Inst. Profl. Psychology, 1991, postgrad., 1991—. RN, Ill. Asst. head nurse Gottlieb Meml. Hosp., Melrose Park, Ill., 1966-68, staff nurse, 1974-86, nursing supr., coord. utilization & case mgmt., 1986—; psychotherapist William Rainey Harper Coll., Palatine, Ill., 1992—. Recipient Oustanding Student award Coll. St. Francis, 1987. Mem. Psi Chi Honor Soc. Home: 35 Charlemagne Circle Roselle IL 60172-3087

STOLTZE, DAVID A., physician; b. San Francisco, Feb. 13, 1950; s. Albert C. and Marjorie L. (Born) S.; m. Rosemarie Drechsler, Oct. 25, 1980; 1 child, Karl. AB, U. Calif., Berkeley, 1972; MD, U. Calif., San Diego, 1976; MPH, U. Ill., 1983. Intern Cook County Hosp., Chgo., 1977-78; resident in family practice Merced Cmty. Med. Ctr.-U. Calif. Davis, 1979-81; family physician Health Ctrs. No. N.Mex., Las Vegas, 1982—, Northeastern Regional Hosp., Las Vegas, 1982—; asst. clin. prof. U. N.Mex. Med. Sch., Albuquerque, 1983—; Nicaragua tng. exch. vol. U. Nacional Autonoma de Nicaragua, Managua, 1989. Mem. steering com. Com. for Health Rights in the Ams., San Francisco, 1994—. Fellow Am. Acad. Family Physicians; mem. APHA, N.Mex. Med. Soc., Physicians for Social Responsibility. Office: Health Ctrs No NMex PO Box 1928 Las Vegas NM 87701

STOLZBERG, MARK ELLIOTT, psychologist; b. N.Y.C., Apr. 30, 1944; s. Seymour and Ruth (Petesky) S.; B.A., Hofstra U., 1966; M.A. in Exptl. Psychology (Coll. fellow), C. W. Post Coll., 1970; postgrad. in clin.

psychology (N.Y. State War Service scholar), SUNY-Albany, 1973; Ph.D., Hofstra U.; m. Marilyn Goldberg, Mar. 18, 1972; children—Susan Beth, David Jonathan, Daniel Jason. Intern in clin. psychology Maimonides Hosp., Bklyn., 1972-73; pres. Stolzberg Research Inc., Stony Brook, N.Y., 1976—; adj. lectr. Bklyn. Coll., 1973; mem. faculty Coll. Optometry, SUNY, 1985-86. Recipient Disting. Achievement award for Research N.Y. State Optometric Assn., 1983. Mem. N.Y. Acad. Scis. Contbr. articles to profl. jours. Home and Office: 3 Seabrook Ct Stony Brook NY 11790-3305

STONE, ALFRED WARD, educator; b. Meadville, Pa., Aug. 13, 1925; s. Clifford Alsworths and Freda (Bruehl) S.; m. Dolores Stone, Dec. 1, 1951 (div.); children: Clifford, John, Bonalyn, David; m. Mary L. Girardat, June 1, 1968; 1 child, 1 Scott. BA in Econs., Allegheny Coll., 1950, MEd, 1957; PhD in Psychology, U. Pitts., 1978; postgrad., U. So. Calif., L.A., 1979. Phys. boys sec. YMCA, Meadville, 1952-57; state sec. YMCA, Harrisburg, Pa., 1957-62; acting exec. sec. YMCA, Allentown, Pa., 1962-63; exec. dir. War on Poverty, C.A.P., Meadville, 1964-67; prof. emeritus psychology dept., co-dir. gerontology program Edinboro (Pa.) U., 1967—; host TV program Understanding People, 1970—; pres. Regional Cmty. Svcs., Inc., Edinboro U., coord. gerontology programs. Bd. dirs. Westbury Meth. Cmty., West Pa. Health Smart; pres., mem. Profl. Assn. of Specialists of Aging, N.W. Pa., 1978-86. With U.S. Merchant Marine, 1943-46, U.S. Army, 1950-52. Mem. APHA, Gerontol. Soc. Am., Am. Psychol. Assn.,. Home: 220 Meadville St Edinboro PA 16412-2558 Office: Edinboro U Dept Psychology Crompton Hall Edinboro PA 16444

STONE, ANTHONY VAN WEZEL, psychologist; b. London, Apr. 1, 1947; came to U.S., 1948; s. Albert M. Stone and Louisa (Van Wezel) Schwartz; m. Cynthia Maraman, Nov. 15, 1983 (div. Mar. 1989); 1 child, Adam William Maramn Stone; m. Sandra Smith, Aug. 4, 1990. BA, Johns Hopkins U., 1971; PhD, U. South Fla., 1977; MPH, U. N.C., 1980. Lic. psychologist, Ga. Unit dir. Fla. Mental Health Inst., Tampa, 1975-77; postdoctoral fellow U. N.C., Chapel Hill, 1978-80; v.p. Psychol. Resources Inc., Atlanta, 1980-86, Willow Springs Health Assocs., Atlanta, 1989-91; pvt. practice psychologist Atlanta, 1986—; cons. psychologist U.S. Dept. Justice Immigration and Naturalization Svc., Washington, 1990—; police psychologist Ga. Inst. Tech., Kennesaw Coll., Ga. Div. Youth Svcs., 1988—, Cobb County (Ga.), Marrieta (Ga.), Smyrna (Ga.), Conyers, Ga., 1988—; pub. safety psychologist City of Atlanta, 1986-91; cons. U.S. Dept. Justice, Washington, 1990—, many local govts./police depts., 1986—, many state govts., counties, sheriff's depts., 1980—, Ga. Dept. Human Resources, Decatur, 1986—. Contbr. articles to profl. jours. Mem. Coun. Polic Psychol. Svcs. (pres. 1991), Ga. Psychol. Assn., Internat. Assn. Chiefs Police, APA, Nat. Assn. Disability Examiners, Phi Kappa Phi. Home: 2078 Amberwood Way NE Atlanta GA 30345-3904 Office: 4015 S Cobb Dr Ste 280 Smyrna GA 30080-6316

STONE, BARTLETT HENRY, gynecologist, educator; b. St. Johnsbury, Vt., Oct. 26, 1916; s. Edward Enos and Gladys Bennett (Newell) Stone; m. Mable Catherine Larbey, Dec. 22, 1942; children: Bartlett Dimick, Pamela Stone Kennedy. B.S., U. Vt., Burlington, 1938; M.D., 1941. Diplomate Am. Bd. Med. Examiners, Am. Bd. Obstetrics-Gynecology. Intern Springfield Hosp. (Mass.); resident in surgery New Eng. Deaconess Hosp., Boston; resident in obstetrics Boston Lying-In Hosp., resident in gynecology Free Hosp. for Women, Brookline, Mass., also fellow in gynecol. pathology; instr ob-gyn Harvard U. Med. Sch. Boston, 1954-86, emeritus, 1986—; active staff Newton Wellesley Hosp., Newton Lower Falls, Mass., 1952-82, assoc. staff, 1982-84, emeritus, 1986; obstetrician, gynecologist Brigham and Woman's Hosp., Boston, 1953-86, emeritus, 1986—; clin. assoc. gynecol. surgery Mass. Gen. Hosp., Boston, 1954-86, cons. 1986—; active staff gynecology and surgery New Eng. Deaconess Hosp., 1964-86, hon. staff mem. 1986—; cons. ob-gyn Norwood (Mass.) Hosp., 1953-60, Sturdy Meml. Hosp., Attleboro, Mass., 1953-60, Mass. Eye & Ear Infirmary, Boston, 1957-60; trustee Ryder Meml. Hosp., Humacao, P.R., 1964-70, five day vis. gynecol. surgeon, 1963. Contbr. articles in field to publs. Deacon Wellesley Hills Congregational Ch., 1960-63. Served to maj. U.S. Army, 1941-46; ETO, N. Africa. Fellow Am. Coll. Ob-Gyn, ACS, Am. Soc. Colposcopy and Cervical Pathology; mem. AMA (physicians achievement awards 1980-84), Mass. Med. Soc., Gynecol. Laser Soc. (founding) Am. Assn. Gynecol. Laparoscopists, Obstet. Soc. Boston, Am. Soc. Study Sterility, Am. Soc. Study Breast Disease, Phi Delta Theta. Republican. Congregationalist. Clubs: Mill Reef (Antigua, W.I.); Harvard (Boston); Wellesley, Wellesley Coll. Lodges: Masons, Shriners.

STONE, BRENDA HEMPHILL, nurse practitioner; b. Hagerstown, Md., June 27, 1944; d. Harold Bruce and Lillian May (Gelsinger) Hemphill; m. Daniel Stewart Stone, June 11, 1966; children: Laura Stewart, Michael Watson. BS in Nursing, Duke U., 1966; MS in Nursing, U. Md., 1973. Cert. adult nurse practitioner. Clin. nurse Johns Hopkins Hosp., Balt., 1975-76, instr., 1976-78, clin. specialist, 1979-84, nurse practitioner, 1986—. Pres. Parents Assn. Waldorf Sch. Balt., 1985; bd. trustees Waldorf Sch. Balt., 1988-90; vol. Pets on Wheels, Dept. on Aging, Balt., 1985-88. Lt. nurse corp USNR, ret. Mem. Am. Nurses Assn., Md. Nurses Assn. Home: 26998 Bunny Ln Easton MD 21601 Office: Johns Hopkins Bayview Med Ctr 4940 Eastern Ave Baltimore MD 21224-2735

STONE, HERBERT ALLEN, management consultant; b. Washington, Sept. 14, 1934; s. Joseph and Marion (Solomon) S.; m. Marjorie Nelke Sterling, June 14, 1964; children: Joanna, Lisa. BSc, U. Mass., 1955, MSc, 1958; PhD, U. Calif., Davis, 1962. Specialist Exptl. Sta. U. Calif., Davis, 1961-62; food scientist SRI, Menlo Park, Calif., 1962-67, dir. food and plant sci., 1967-74; pres. Tragon Corp., Redwood City, Calif., 1974—. Author: Sensory Evaluation Practices, 1985, 2d edit., 1993; assoc. editor Jour. Food Sci., 1977-80; contbr. sci. and tech. articles to profl. jours.; patentee in field. Fellow Inst. Food Exec. Com. (pres. S.E. divsn. 1977-73, exec. com.); mem. AAAS, Am. Soc. Enology, European Chemoreception Orgn., Ladera Oaks Club (Menlo Park, Calif.). Home: 990 San Mateo Dr Menlo Park CA 94025-5640 Office: Tragon Corp 365 Convention Way Redwood City CA 94063-1402

STONE, JAMES MICHAEL, medical educator; b. Oct. 30, 1952. BS in Psychology magna cum laude, U. Ill., 1974; MD, Northwestern U., Chgo., 1978. Diplomate Nat. Bd. Med. Examiners, Am. Bd. Surgery, Am. Bd. Colon and Rectal Surgery; lic. physician, Calif. Intern surgery Michael Reese Hosp. & Med. Ctr., Chgo., 1978-79, resident, 1979-83, adminstrv. chief resident, 1982-83; trauma rsch. fellow U. Calif.-San Francisco, San Francisco Gen. Hosp., 1980-81; asst. prof. surgery U. Ill., 1983-85; attending surgeon, co-dir. hyperalimentation svc. Cook County Hosp., Chgo., 1983-85; clin. asst. prof. Stanford U. Med. Ctr., 1986-89, asst. prof. surgery, divsn. surg. oncology, 1990—, chief divsn. trauma, 1992—; chief gen. surgery Palo Alto VA Med. Ctr., 1986-89; med. fellow dept. colon and rectal surgery U. Minn., 1989-90; mem. staff U. Ill. Hosp. and Clinics, Cook County Hosp., 1983-85, Stanford U. Med. Ctr., Palo Alto VA Med. Ctr., 1985-89, U. Minn. Med. Ctr., 1989-90, Stanford U. Med. Ctr., 1990—. Contbr. articles to profl. jours., chpts. to books. James scholar U. Ill., Urbana, 1970-74, Paul M. Cheremeta award Paralyzed Vets. Am., 1988, grant Spinal Cord Rsch. Found., 1988-90. Mem. Phi Beta Kappa, Phi Kappa Phi. Home: 40 Willow Park Menlo Park CA 94025*

STONE, JAMES ROBERT, surgeon; b. Greeley, Colo., Jan. 8, 1948; s. Anthony Joseph and Dolores Concetta (Pietrafeso) S.; m. Kaye Janet Friedman, May 16, 1970; children: Jeffrey, Marisa. BA, U. Colo., 1970; MD, U. Guadalajara, Mex., 1976. Diplomate Am. Bd. Surgery, Am. Bd. Surg. Critical Care. Intern Md. Gen. Hosp., Balt., 1978-79; resident in surgery St. Joseph Hosp., Denver, 1979-83; practice medicine specializing in surgery Grand Junction, Colo., 1983-87; staff surgeon. dir. critical care Va. Med. Ctr., Grand Junction, 1987-88; dir. trauma surgery and critical care, chief surgery St. Francis Hosp., Colorado Springs, Colo., 1988-91; pvt. practice Kodiak, Alaska, 1991-92; with South Denver Surg. Cons., Englewood, Colo., 1992-93, Summit Surg. Assocs., 1993—; asst. clin. prof. surgery U. Colo. Health Sci. Ctr., Denver, 1984—; pres. Stone Aire Cons., Grand Junction, 1988—; owner, operator Jjnka Ranch, Flourissant, Colo.; spl. advisor CAP, wing med. officer, 1992—; mem. advisor med. com. unit, 1990-92; advisor Colo. Ground Team Search and Rescue, 1994—. Contbr. articles to profl. jours.; inventor in field. Bd. dirs. Mesa County Cancer Soc., 1988-89, Colo. Trauma Inst., 1988-91. Colo. Speaks out on Health grantee, 1988; recipient Bronze medal of Valor Civil Air Patrol. Fellow Denver Acad. Surgery, Southwestern Surg. Congress, Am. Coll. Chest Physicians, Am. Coll. Surgeons (trauma com. Colo. chpt.), Am. Coll. Critical Care; mem. Am. Coll. Physician Execs., Soc. Critical Care (task force 1988—). Roman Catholic.

STONE, KENNETH SAMUEL, cardiothoracic surgeon; b. Detroit, Sept. 19, 1953; s. Robert M. and Harriett E. (Stober) S.; m. Jane K. Tournell, June 14, 1980 (div. Feb. 1990); 1 child, Kaitlin; m. Nancy Marie Penix, Nov. 29, 1991; children: Ashley Stewart, Candace Stewart, Jeffrey Stone. BA, Kalamazoo Coll., 1975; MD, Mich. State U., 1978. Diplomate Am. Bd. Surgery, Am. Bd. Thoracic Surgery. Surg. intern Butterworth Hosp./Mich. State U., 1979, resident in gen. surgery, 1980-84; resident in thoracic surgery Ind. U., 1984-86; cardiothoracic surgeon Thoracic Surgeons Assoc., Grand Rapids, Mich., 1986-88, Arnett Clinic, Lafayette, Ind., 1988—; presenter in field; mem. dean's adv. coun. Coll. Human Medicine, Mich. State U., 1978-79. Recipient Leo J. Kenney award Dept. Surgery, Butterworth Hosp., 1987-88, Best Designed Clin. Study award GRAMEC, 1980, Craig Booher award for Excellence in Rsch. GRAMEC, 1983, Outstanding Resident Tchr. award GRAMEC, 1982-83, Best Basic Rsch. award GRAMEC, 1982, Best Clin. Study award Midwest Surg. Assn., 1980. Fellow ACS (Frederick Coller award Mich. chpt. 1981), Am. Coll. Cardiology, Am. Coll. Chest Physicians, Am. Coll. Angiology; mem. Soc. Thoracic Surgeons, Alpha Omega Alpha. Office: Arnett Clinic PO Box 5545 Lafayette IN 47903-5545

STONE, LINDA CHAPMAN, family practice physician, consultant; b. Detroit, Apr. 20, 1943; d. Harry Walter and Kathryn Ann (Forshee) Chapman; m. Laurence B. Stone, July 10, 1965; 1 child, Robert Laurence. BA, Mich. State U., 1961-65; MA, Ohio U., 1971; MD, Ohio State U., 1979. Diplomate Am. Bd. Family Practice. Tchr. local high schs., Mich., 1965-69; instr. comms. Ohio U., 1970-71; resident physician Riverside Meth. Hosp., Columbus, Ohio, 1979-82, chief resident, 1981-82; family physician Beechwold Med. Ctr., Columbus, Ohio, 1983-93; family physician, instr. U. Mich., 1993; v.p. physician ednl. comms. U.S. Health Corp., Columbus, 1994, v.p. primary care devel., 1995-96; clin. prof. medicine Ohio State U.; exec. v.p. Med. Group Ohio, 1996; bd. dirs. Elizabeth Blackwell Ctr., Columbus, 1983-89, 94—, chair, 1995—; bd. dirs. Gerlach Ctr. Sr. Health, Columbus, 1995-96. Healthcare adv. various women's orgns., 1983—. Fellow Am. Acad. Family Physicians; mem. Ohio Acad. Family Physicians (bd. dirs. 1992-96); Ctrl. Ohio Acad. Family Physicians, Delta Gamma. Democrat. Methodist. Office: Med Group Ohio 770 Jasonway Columbus OH 43214

STONE, MICHAEL OMARR, family practice physician, medical executive; b. Abilene, Tex., July 30, 1937; s. J. Allyn and W. Myrtle (Waters) S.; children: Pamala A., Allyn O. BS in Chemistry, N.Mex. State U., 1961, MS in Chemistry, 1963; PhD in Biochemistry, Tulane U., 1969; MD, U. N.Mex., 1974. Diplomate Am. Bd. Family Practice. Family practice residency Roanoke (Va.) Meml. Hosp., 1975-77; family practice Dr. Ruidoso, N.Mex., 1977-85; chmn. family practice Cigna Healthplan of Fla., Inc., Clearwater, 1985-90; med. dir. Martin Marietta Specialty Components, Largo, Fla., 1990-94; family practice physician CIGNA Healthcare of Fla., St. Petersburg, 1994—. Recipient postdoctoral fellowship Am. Cancer Soc., 1970. Fellow Am. Acad. Family Practice; mem. Fla. Acad. Family Practice. Office: CIGNA Healthcare Fla 3745 33rd St N Saint Petersburg FL 33713-1556

STONE, NORMAN MICHAEL, psychologist; b. Balt., Mar. 23, 1949; s. Forrest Leon and Beverly Iola (Gendason) S.; m. Susan Foster Hoitt, May 18, 1981; children: Shannon, Caroline, Brittany Rain, Forrest. BA, UCLA, 1971; PhD, U. Iowa, 1976. Lic. psychologist, Tex., Calif. Chief youth and family svcs. Abilene (Tex.) Mental Health-Mental Retardation Regional Ctr., 1976-79; coord. family crisis team San Fernando Valley Guidance Clinic, Northridge, Calif., 1980-88, sr. clin. supr., 1989-95; sr. cmty. psychologist L.A. County Dept. Children's Mental Health, L.A., 1995—; mem. psychiat. panel of experts on dependency and family law Calif. Superior Ct., 1987-96; mem. adj. faculty Hardin-Simmons U., Abilene, 1977-79; vis. prof. UCLA, 1980-81; clin. prof. Fuller Theol. Sem., L.A., 1982-94. Contbr. numerous articles on psychology, psychiatry, law and social welfare to internat. profl. jours., books and film. USPHS fellow, 1972-76; Simon Found. rsch. grantee, 1982, 89. Mem. AAAPP, Am. Psychol. Soc., Sojourners. Office: LA County Dept Childrens Mental Health 505 S Virgil Los Angeles CA 90020

STONE, PETER HOWARD, cardiologist, educator; b. N.Y.C., Mar. 31, 1948; s. Harvey and Ronnie (Eilenberg) S.; m. Lisa Vosburgh, May 6, 1984; children: Emily, Michael, Benjamin. BA, Princeton U., 1970; MD, Cornell U., 1974. Intern in internal medicine San Francisco Gen. Hosp., 1974-75; resident in internal medicine U. Calif., San Francisco, 1975-77; cardiology fellow Pacific Med. Ctr., San Francisco, 1977-79; rsch. fellow in medicine Peter Bent Brigham Hosp., Boston, 1979-80; instr. in medicine Harvard Med. Sch., Boston, 1979-83, asst. prof. medicine, 1983-91; assoc. prof. medicine, 1991—; assoc. dir. Samuel A. Levine cardiac unit Brigham and Women's Hosp., Boston, 1982-93; co-dir. Samuel A. Levine cardiac unit Brigham and Women's Hosp., Boston, 1993—; dir. clin. trials, cardiovascular div. Brigham and Women's Hosp., 1991—; dir. Clin. Trials Ctr. Brigham & Women's Hosp., 1995—. Fellow Am. Coll. Cardiology, Am. Heart Assn. (coun. on clin. cardiology). Office: Brigham & Women's Hosp Cardiovascular Div 75 Francis St Boston MA 02115-6110

STONE, ROBERT EDWARD, JR., speech pathologist; b. Spokane, Wash., Feb. 20, 1937; s. Robert Edward and Merle Lucille (Beals) S.; m. Dee Ann Vick, Aug. 18, 1962; children: Kimberly, Julie, Robert. BS, Whitworth Coll., 1960; MEd, U. Oreg., 1964; PhD, U. Mich., 1971. Tchr. Lake Oswego (Oreg.) Pub. Schs., 1960-63; speech pathologist Portland (Oreg.) Pub. Schs., 1963-69; instr. U. Mich. Med. Sch., Ann Arbor, 1968-71, asst. prof., 1971-78; assoc. prof. Ind. U. Med. Sch. dept. otolaryngology, Indpls., 1978-87, Vanderbilt U. dept. otolaryngology, Nashville, Tenn., 1987—; v.p. Oreg. Speech Hearing Assn., 1964, Mich. Speech Hearing Assn. 1977; mem. sci. adv. bd. Voice Found. N.Y.C., 1973—; dir. Vanderbilt Voice Ctr., Nashville, 1992—. Author: (book) Help Employ Laryngectomized Persons, 1983; assoc. editor Am. Jour. of Speech-Lang. Pathology,, 1993—. Fellow Am. Speech Hearing Assn. (cert. C.C.C.), Sertoma Club (sec. Indpls. 1984, v.p. 1985, pres. 1986, v.p. Nashville downtown, 1996). Office: Nashville Voice Ctr 1500 21st Ave S Ste 2700 Nashville TN 37212

STONE, ROSS GLUCK, physician; b. Pottsville, Pa., May 14, 1951; s. Jerome M. and Alma (Gluck) S.; m. Wendy E. Reiner, March 21, 1987; children: Melissa, Logan. BA in Philosophy, Yale U., 1973, MD, Columbia U., 1977. Diplomate Am. Bd. Orthopaedic Surgery. Intern, resident Harvard U., 1977-79; resident, vis. clin. fellow Columbia U., 1979-83; pvt. practice Atlantis, Fla., 1983—; clin. fellow in surgery Harvard Med. Sch., 1978-79; expert med. advisor Fla. Dept. Labor & Employment, 1995-97; editl. adv. bd. Am. Jour. Pain Mgmt., 1992—; chmn. surg. rev. com. Palm Beach Regional Hosp., 1995, institnl. rev. com. John F. Kennedy Med. Ctr., 1995-96, divsn. ortho. surgery Columbia Hosp., 1994—. Contbr. articles to profl. jours.; invented tension headache reliever device. Recipient Physician's Choice award So. Med. Assn. 88th Assembly, 1994, Scientific Poster recognition So. Med. Assn. 88th Assembly, 1994, 89th Assembly, 1995, Sr. Resident award Eastern Ortho. Assn. 14th ann. meeting, 1983. Mem. Palm Beach County (Fla.) Med. Soc. (bd. dirs. 1995—, del. Fla. Med. Assn. 1995, legis. com. 1995-96, emergency med. svc. and disaster relief plan coms. 1994-95, pub. rels. com. 1995—, health and human svcs. com. 1994-95). Republican. Jewish. Office: Ste 124 120 John F Kennedy Dr Atlantis FL 33462-6606

STONE, STEPHEN PAUL, dermatologist; b. N.Y.C., Aug. 22, 1941; s. C. Sidney and Sylvia (Alpher) S.; m. Lisa Jane Wald, Mar. 1, 1969; children: Jason Harris, Erica Lauren, Charles David. AB cum laude, Tufts U., 1963; MD, NYU, 1967. Diplomate Am. Bd. Dermatology, Nat. Bd. Med. Examiners. Intern Lincoln Hosp., Bronx, N.Y., 1967-68, resident in internal medicine, 1968-69; resident in dermatology Mayo Grad. Sch. Medicine, Rochester, Minn., 1971-74; pres. Dermatology Ctr. Ltd., Springfield, Ill., 1974—; clin. assoc. prof. medicine, former chief dermatology So. Ill. U. Sch. Medicine, Springfield. Editor-in-chief: Dialogs in Dermatology, 1993-97, assoc. editor, 1976-93; contbr. articles to profl. jours. Pres. Springfield Jewish Cmty. Rels. Coun., 1986-88, 90-91; mem. adv. coun. Nat. Jewish Cmty. Rels., vice chair, 1993—, mem. exec. com., 1990-93; bd. dirs. Coun. of Jewish Fedns., 1981-83, 85-95, chmn. small cities nat. com., 1987-88, nat. com. leadership devel., 1981-87, v.p., 1988-91; bd. dirs. Springfield Jewish Fedn., 1976—, v.p., 1977-79, pres., 1980-83; bd. dirs. Springfield Jewish Fedn. Found., 1983-93, pres., 1984-85; bd. dirs. Springfield Zool. Soc., 1983-86, United Way of Greater Sangamon County, 1985-91, Planned Parenthood, Springfield area, 1979-80; trustee, bd. dirs. Temple B'rith Sholom, 1984-90; trustee Lincoln Libr., 1991—, v.p., 1993-94, pres., 1995-96; mem. United Jewish Appeal, Nat. Young Leadership Cabinet, 1977-82, regional chmn., 1980-81, midwest regional cabinet, 1980-94, midwest project renewal cabinet, 1986-88, region II small cmtys. chmn., 1991-93; sec. B'nai Israel Synagogue, Rochester, Minn., 1973-74; bd. dirs. West Ctrl. Ill. Health Sys. Agy., 1978-83, exec. bd., 1978-84, v.p., 1982-84; mem., treas. Springfield Parks Found., 1992-95. Mem. AMA, Chgo. Dermatological Soc. (plans and policy com. 1982-84), Ill. Dermatologic Soc. (sec.-treas. 1978-80, pres. 1981), Ill. State Med. Soc. (alternate del. 1984-85, coun. on govtl. affairs 1983-86), Internat. Soc. Tropical Dermatology, Noah Worcester Dermatological Soc. (trustee 1987-90, continuing med. edn. com. 1982-83), Sangamon County Med. Soc. (chmn. liason com. 1985), Soc. for Investigative Dermatology, N.Y. Bd. Med. examiners (cert.), Minn. Bd. Med. Examiners, Calif. Bd. Med. Examiners, Ill. Bd. Med. Examiners, Am. Acad. Dermatology (coun. on communicaitons 1980-84, chmn. 1987-89). Lodge: Emes, B'nai Brith (v.p. Springfield, 1975-76, pres. 1976-77). Home: 3013 Mill Bank Ln Springfield IL 62704-1020 Office: 630 N 1st St Springfield IL 62702-4934

STONE, SUSAN FOSTER, mental health services professional, psychologist; b. Salem, Mass., Mar. 15, 1954; d. Bruce and Carolyn (Foster) Hoitt; m. Norman Michael Stone, May 18, 1981; children: Brittany, Forrest. Student, U. York, Eng., 1974-75; BA in Psychology, Colby Coll., 1976; MS in Clin. Psychology, Abilene Christian U., 1979; PhD in Clin. Psychology, Calif. Sch. Profl. Psychology, 1985. Lic. psychologist, Calif. Mem. emergency response team Simi (Calif.) Dept. Police, 1980-81; cons. Children's Hosp. L.A., 1984-85; postdoctoral fellow Neuropsychiat. Inst. UCLA, 1985-86; clin. dir. Santa Clarita (Calif.) Child and Family Devel. Ctr., 1987-94, dir. tng., 1995—; cons. L.A. County Adoptions, 1985-88; expert witness L.A. Superior Ct., 1987—, State Funded Early Mental Health Initiatives, 1994; assisted in drafting congl. managed health care proposal, 1995; presenter in field. Mem. adv. coun. L.A. Foster Parent Assn., 1989-91. Office Juvenile Justice Systems grantee Spl. Children's Ctr., 1990, L.A. Regional Ctr. grantee, 1990. Mem. APA, Assn. Family and Conciliation Cts., Sierra Club, Santa Clarita C. of C. Office: 235 Lyons Ave #30 Newhall CA 91321

STONE, WILLIAM COY, surgeon; b. Carlsbad, N.Mex., Sept. 22, 1934; s. Coy Smith and Mattye Marie (Swint) S.; m. Carolyn Vaughn, Nov. 3, 1963; children: Coy Steven, Allison Ann. BA, Baylor U., 1956; MD, Tulane Med. Sch., 1960. Diplomate Am. Bd. Surgery. Rotating intern Parkland Meml. Hosp., Dallas, 1960-61, resident gen. surgery, 1961-65; pvt. practice gen. surgery Hobbs, N.Mex., 1967—. Capt. U.S. Army, 1965-67, Korea. Fellow ACS, Southwestern Surg. Congress; mem. Am. Soc. Gen. Surgeons (founding), Lubbock Surg. Soc., Parkland Surg. Soc. (founding), Alpha Omega Alpha. Baptist. Office: Norte Vista Med Ctr 2410 N Fowler Hobbs NM 88240

STONER, GARY DAVID, pathology educator; b. Bozeman, Mont., Oct. 25, 1942; married; 2 children. BS, Mont. State U., 1964; MS, U. Mich., 1968, PhD in Microbiol., 1970. Asst. rsch. scientist U. Calif., San Diego, 1970-72, assoc. rsch. scientist, 1972-75; cancer expert Nat. Cancer Inst., 1976-79; assoc. prof. pathology Med. Coll. Ohio, 1979-83; prof. pathology, 1983-92; prof. preventive medicine and pathology Ohio State U., Columbus, 1992—, assoc. dir. Ctr. for Molecular and Environ. Health, 1993—, assoc. dir. basic rsch. Comp Cancer Ctr, 1994—, prof., chmn. divsn. environ. health scis. Sch. Pub. Health, 1995—; cons. Nat. Heart Lung & Blood Inst., 1974—, EPA, 1979—, Cancer Inst., 1979—, Nat. Toxicol. Program, 1981—; lectr. W. Alton Jones Cell Sci. Ctr., 1978—; mem. study sect. NIH, 1980-88, Am. Cancer Soc., Ohio, 1982—, Am. Cancer Soc., Nat., 1995—. Grantee Nat. Cancer Inst., EPA, U.S. Army R & D Command. Mem. AAAS, Am. Assn. Cancer Rsch., Am. Tissue Culture Assn., Am. Assn. Pathologists, Am. Soc. Cell Biology. Office: Ohio State U Sch Pub Health 1148 CHRI 300 W 10th Ave Columbus OH 43210-1240

STOOKEY, GEORGE KENNETH, research institute administrator, dental educator; b. Waterloo, Ind., Nov. 6, 1935; s. Emra Gladison and Mary Catherine (Anglin) S.; m. Nola Jean Meek, Jan. 15, 1955; children—Lynda, Lisa, Laura, Kenneth. A.B. in Chemistry, Ind. U., 1957, M.S.D., 1962, Ph.D. in Preventive Dentistry, 1971. Asst. dir. Preventive Dentistry Research Inst., U. Ind., Indpls., 1968-70, assoc. dir. Oral Health Research Inst., U. Ind., 1974-81, dir., 1981—; assoc. prof. preventive dentistry Sch. of Dentistry, Ind. U., 1973-78, prof., 1978—, assoc. dean research, 1987—, acting dean, 1996; cons. USAF, San Antonio, 1973—, ADA, Chgo., 1972—, Nat. Inst. Dental Rsch., Bethesda, Md., 1978-82, 91-95. Author: (with others) Introduction to Oral Biology and Preventive Dentistry, 1971, Preventive Dentistry for the Dental Assistant and Dental Hygienist, 1977, Preventive Dentistry in Action, 1972, 80 (Meritorious award 1973); contbr. articles to profl. jours. Mem. Internat. Assn. for Dental Research, European Orgn. Caries Research, Am. Assn. Lab. Animal Sci. Republican. Office: Oral Health Research Inst 415 Lansing St Indianapolis IN 46202-2855

STOOPLER, MARK BENJAMIN, physician; b. N.Y.C., Sept. 29, 1950; s. Alex and Blanche Sylvia (Kappel) S.; m. Lynn Sara Fruchter, Jan. 10, 1982; children: David Andrew, Emily Rachel, Jesse Bryan. BS, Tulane U., 1971; MD, Cornell U., 1975. Diplomate Am. Bd. Internal Medicine, Am. Bd. Oncology. Intern and resident in internal medicine North Shore U. Hosp., Manhasset, N.Y., 1975-78; intern and resident in internal medicine Meml. Sloan-Kettering Cancer Ctr., N.Y.C., 1975-78, asst. chief resident in medicine, 1978, fellow in med. oncology, 1978-80; asst. attending physician Presbyn. Hosp., N.Y.C., 1980-93, assoc. attending physician, 1993—; asst. clin. prof. medicine Columbia U. Coll. of Physicians and Surgeons, N.Y.C., 1980-93; assoc. clin. prof. medicine, 1993—. Contbr. articles to profl. jours. Recipient U. scholar Tulane U., 1970-71. Fellow ACP; mem. Am. Soc. of Clin. Oncology, Am. Fedn. for Clin. Research, Internat. Assn. for the Study of Lung Cancer, Phi Beta Kappa. Office: Columbia-Presbyn Med Ctr 161 Ft Washington Ave New York NY 10032-3713

STORER, MICHAEL WILLIAM, physician assistant; b. Cin., Feb. 15, 1957; s. Robert William Storer and Mary Carol (Prichard) Moorman; m. Karen L. Storer, Feb. 26, 1992; children: Molly, Michelle. AS in Physician Assisting, Kettering Coll. Med. Arts, 1982; student, U. Cin. Nat. cert. physician asst. Nat. Cert. Coun. Physician Assts.; registered physician asst., Ohio. Nursing asst. Good Samaritan Hosp., Cin., 1979-81; physician asst. Univ. Hosp., Jacksonville, Fla., 1982-84, Mayo Clinic, Rochester, Minn., 1984, MHO & CEC Inc., Cin., 1984-92, QESI, Cin., 1992-94, Jackson Park Family Practice, Seymour, Ind., 1994-95, Premier Health Care, Dayton, Ohio, 1995—; Physician asst., tchr. med. residents Clifton Emergency Cons., Cin., 1984-92, mem. quality assurance com., 1988-92. Sgt. USAF, 1975-79. Mem. Am. Assn. Physician Assts., Golden Key, Phi Alpha Theta. Roman Catholic. Home: 2424 Windsor Village Dr Miamisburg OH 45342

STORM, JACKIE, nutritionist, health education specialist; b. Halifax, N.S., Can., Sept. 20, 1943; d. Jack Charles Stone and Kathleen (Clow) Deviser. BA, NYU, 1979, MA, 1982, PhD, 1995. Nutrition educator N.Y. Health and Racquet Club, N.Y.C., 1973—; tchr. New Sch. for Social Research, N.Y.C., 1980-87; adj. prof. Kingsborough C.C., Bklyn., 1987—, St. Francis Coll., Bklyn., 1987—; cons. Eating Disorders Ctr., N.Y.C., 1983—. Author: There's No Such Thing As A Fattening Food!, 1983. Mem. Am. Coll. Nutrition, Soc. for Pub. Health Edn., Soc. for Nutrition Edn. Avocations: gardening; weight lifting. Office: 110 W 56th St New York NY 10019

STORMEON, BEVERLY MASON, nurse; b. Panama City, Fla., Apr. 12, 1945; d. Arthur Phillip and Lois Helen (Sipr) Mason; m. Robert Ralph Stormeon, Nov. 28, 1964; children: Kimberly, Thomas, Michael. ADN, Prairit State U., 1976; BSN, De Paul U., 1983, MS in Nursing, 1985. Team leader Holy Family Hosp., Des Plaines, Ill., 1976-78, staff nurse critical care, 1978-82, cons. critical care, 1982-86; clin. specialist transplant U. Ill., Chgo., 1986—, clin. instr. Coll. Nursing, 1987—. Mem. 125th Anniversary Com., Wilmette, Ill., 1996. Mem. Nat. Kidney Found., Nat. Am. Transplant Coords. Orgn., Internat. Transplant Nurses Soc., Sigma Theta Tau, Phi Theta Kappa. Home: 1630 Sheridan Rd Wilmette IL 60091

STORMONT, CLYDE JUNIOR, laboratory company executive; b. Viola, Wis., June 25, 1916; s. Clyde James and Lulu Elizabeth (Mathews) S.; m. Marguerite Butzen, Aug. 31, 1940; children: Bonnie Lu, Michael Clyde, Robert Thomas, Charles James, Janet Jean. BA in Zoology, U. Wis., 1938, PhD in Genetics, 1947; DVM (hon.) U. Veterinaria & Pharmaceutica, Brno, Czech Republic, 1994. Instr., lectr. then asst. prof. U. Wis.-Madison, 1946-50; asst. prof. dept. vet. microbiology U. Calif.-Davis, 1950-54, assoc. prof., 1954-59, prof., 1959-73, prof. dept. reprodn., 1973-82, prof. emeritus, 1982—; chmn. Stormont Labs., Inc., Woodland, Calif., 1981—. Contbr. articles to profl. jours. Lt. (j.g.) USNR, 1944-46, PTO. Fulbright fellow, 1949-50, Ellen B. Scripps fellow, 1957-58, 64-65. Mem. Am. Genetic Assn., Genetics Soc. Am., Nat. Bison Assn., N.Y. Acad. Sci., Am. Soc. Human Genetics, Soc. Exptl. Biology and Medicine, Internat. Soc. for Animal Genetics, Sigma Xi. Office: Stormont Labs Inc 1237 E Beamer St Ste D Woodland CA 95776-6000

STORMS, WILLIAM WALLACE, physician; b. Racine, Wis., May 18, 1942; m. Bette Bear, Aug. 14, 1965; children: Cathy, Trisha, Jenny. BA, Northwestern U., 1964; MD, U. Wis., 1968. Diplomate Am. Bd. Internal Medicine, Am. Bd. Allergy and Immunology. Intern San Francisco Gen. Hosp., 1968-69; resident in internal med. U. Wis. Hosps., Madison, 1969-70, 73-73, fellow in allergy/immunology, 1973-75; allergist Allergy Assocs., Colorado Springs, 1975-81; from asst. clin. prof. to prof. medicine Health Scis. Ctr. U. Colo., Denver, 1981—; practice medicine specializing in immunology Allergy Assocs., Colorado Springs, Colo., 1975—; bd. dirs. W.C. Svc. Allergy and Asthma Rsch. Found., Colorado Springs, 1982—; bd. of regents Am. Coll. Allergy and Immunology, 1990-93. Contbr. articles to profl. jours. Vestryman Chapel Our Saviour Episcopal Ch., Colorado Springs, 1978-81. Served with U.S. Army, 1970-72. Fellow ACP, Am. Acad. Allergy, Am. Coll. Allergists, Coll. Chest Physicians; mem. Am. Thoracic Soc., Western Soc. Allergy and Immunology (exec. coun. 1983-88, pres. 1987-88), Colo. Allergy Soc. (pres. 1988-90). Republican. Office: Allergy Assocs. 2709 N Tejon St Colorado Springs CO 80907-6231

STORTS, DOUGLAS RAY, molecular biologist; b. Springfield, Ohio, Sept. 12, 1957; s. Ralph William and Betty Lou (Riley) S.; m. Pamela Sue Shumaker, June 8, 1985; children:Jason Ray, Michael Alan. BS, Manchester Coll., North Manchester, Ind., 1978; MS, Miami U., Oxford, Ohio, 1982, PhD, 1985. Analytical chemist IWD Chem. Disposal, Springfield, 1978-80; process devel. chemist Systech, Xenia, Ohio, 1980; grad. asst. Miami U., 1980-82, teaching fellow, 1982-85; rsch. assoc., instr. U. Chgo., 1985-89; prin. scientist Ambion, Inc., Austin, Tex., 1989-91; sr. scientist Promega Corp., Madison, Wis., 1991—; Contbr. articles to sci. jours. Rsch. grantee Sigma Xi, 1984. Mem. Am. Soc. for Microbiology (travel grantee 1985), Am. Soc. for Biochemistry and Molecular Biology. Home: 2210 Frisch Rd Madison WI 53711-4008 Office: Promega Corp 2800 Woods Hollow Rd Madison WI 53711-5300

STORVICK, CLARA AMANDA, nutrition educator emerita; b. Emmons, Minn., Oct. 31, 1906; d. Ole A. and Elise A. (Opdahl) S. AB, St. Olaf Coll., 1929; MS, Iowa State U., 1933; PhD, Cornell U., 1941. Chemistry instr. Augustana Acad., Canton, S.D., 1930-32; rsch. asst. Iowa State U., Ames, 1932-34; nutiritionist Fed. Emergency Relief Adminstrn., Brainerd, Minn., 1934-36; asst. prof. nutrition Okla. State U., Stillwater, 1936-38; rsch. asst. Cornell U., Ithaca, N.Y., 1938-41; asst. prof. nutrition U. Wash., Seattle, 1941-45; assoc. prof. nutrition to prof. Oreg. State U., Corvallis, 1945-72, prof. nutrition and head home econ. rsch., 1955-72, dir. nutrition rsch. inst., 1965-72; ret., 1972. Contbr. over 70 articles to profl. jours. Recipient Borden award Am. Home Econs. Assn., 1952, Disting. Alumni award St. Olaf Coll., 1955, Alumni Achievement award Iowa State U., Ames, 1966. Fellow AAAS, Am. Pub. Health Assn., Am. Inst. Nutrition; mem. N.Y. Acad. Scis., Am. Chem. Soc., Phi Kappa Phi, Sigma Xi, Iota Sigma Pi (nat. pres.), Omicron Nu. Republican. Lutheran. Home: 124 NW 29th St Corvallis OR 97330-5343

STORY, DAVID FREDERICK, pharmacologist, educator; b. Launceston, Australia, July 27, 1940; s. Frederick Joseph and Gladys Ray (Stone) S.; m. Margot Elizabeth Turner, May 25, 1966; children: Andrew David, Michael Barry. BS, U. Melbourne, 1966, PhD, 1972. Head pharmacology Riker Labs. Australia, Thornleigh, 1966-69; sr. rsch. officer dept. pharmacology U. Melbourne, Australia, 1972, lectr., 1973-75, dept. head, 1986-92, sr. lectr., 1976-86, reader, 1987-89, assoc. prof., 1989-93; prof. pharmacology, head dept. med. lab. sci. Royal Melbourne Inst. Tech., 1993-95, dean faculty biomed. and health scis., 1995—. Contbr. articles to profl. jours. Mem. Australian Physiol. and Pharmacological Soc., High Blood Pressure Rsch. Coun. Australia, Australasian Soc. Clin. and Experimental Pharmacologists (pres. 1992). Office: Royal Melbourne Inst Tech, Faculty Biomed/Health Scis, Melbourne 3000, Australia

STOTZKY, GUENTHER, microbiologist, educator; b. Leipzig, Germany, May 24, 1931; came to U.S., 1939; s. Moritz Stotzky and Erna (Angres) Kester; m. Kayla Baker, Mar. 17, 1958; children: Jay, Martha, Deborah. BS, Calif. Poly. State U., 1952; MS, Ohio State U., 1954, PhD, 1956. Spl. sci. employee Argonne Nat. Lab. USAEC, Lemont, Ill., 1955; rsch. assoc. Dept. Botany U. Mich., Ann Arbor, 1956-58; head soil microbiology Cen. Rsch. Labs. United Fruit Co., Norwood, Mass., 1958-63; chmn., microbiologist Kitchawan Rsch. Labs. Bklyn. Botanic Garden, Ossining, N.Y., 1963-68; assoc. prof. Dept. Biology NYU, 1967-70, prof., 1970—, chmn., 1970-77. Editor: Soil Biochemistry, 1990—; series editor Marcel Dekker, Inc., 1986-92; contbr. over 250 articles to profl. jours. and chpts. to books. With USCG, 1957. Recipient Selman A. Waksman Hon. Lecture award Theobald Smith Soc., 1989, Honored Alumnus of Yr. award Calif. Poly. State U., 1992; named Disting. Vis. Scientist, U.S. EPA, 1986-89. Fellow AAAS, Am. Acad. Microbiology, Am. Soc. Microbiology (Fisher Co. award for applied and environ. microbiology 1990, Excellence in Tchg. award N.Y.C. br. 1994), Am. Soc. Agronomy, Soil Sci. Soc. Am. Jewish. Office: NYU Dept Biology 1009 Main New York NY 10003

STOUDT, HOWARD WEBSTER, biological anthropologist, human factors specialist, consultant; b. Pitts., May 13, 1925; s. Howard Webster and Harriet Catharine (Powers) S.; m. Jean Gorey Henderson, Feb. 14, 1953; children: Katharine Webster, Roberta Henderson. AB, Harvard Coll., 1949; MA, U. Pa., 1953, PhD, 1959; SM in Hygiene, Harvard U., 1963. Rsch. asst. Harvard Sch. Pub. Health, Boston, 1952-55; rsch. specialist Air U., U.S. Air Force, Montgomery, Ala., 1955-57; rsch. assoc. Harvard Sch. Pub. Health, Boston, 1957-66, asst. prof., 1966-73; prof. community medicine Mich. State U., East Lansing, 1973-88, chmn. dept., 1973-78, prof. emeritus, 1988—; cons. Stoudt Assocs., Bath, Maine, 1988—; cons. U.S. Army, USAF, NASA, USPHS, VA, NRC, NAS, pvt. industry, 1952—. Author: Physical Anthropology of Ceylon, 1961; co-author: Human Body in Equipment Design, 1971; contbr. over 40 articles to profl. jours. Sgt. U.S. Army, 1943-46, Europe. Harrison fellow U. Pa., Phila., 1951-52, USPHS fellow, Boston, 1961-62. Fellow Human Biology Coun.; mem. AAAS, Am. Assn. Phys. Anthropologists, Am. Coll. Epidemiology, Human Factors and Ergonomics Soc. Democrat. Home and Office: 4 Schooner Ridge Rd Bath ME 04530-1639

STOUFFER, RICHARD LEE, physiology educator, researcher; b. Hagerstown, Md., July 27, 1949; s. Vernon Leo and Jane Recher (Dubel) S.; m. Gwendolyn Mae Frush, June 10, 1972; children—Erin Elizabeth, Brian Avery. B.Sc., Va. Poly. Inst., 1971; Ph.D., Duke U., 1975. Staff fellow NIH, Bethesda, Md., 1975-77; asst. prof. U. Ariz., Tucson, 1977-83; assoc. prof., 1983-85; scientist Oreg. Regional Primate Research Ctr; grant reviewer NIH, 1983-95; head divsn. reproductive scis., 1996—; assoc. prof. Oreg. Health Scis. U., 1985-95, prof., 1995—. Contbr. articles to profl. jours. Recipient Potomac Edison scholarship, 1967-71, James B. Duke grad. scholarship, 1971-74; NIH Career Devel. award, 1982-87, grantee, 1983-95. Mem. Endocrine Soc., Am. Physiol. Soc., Soc. Study Reproduction (pres. 1995-96), AAAS. Republican. Methodist. Office: Oreg Regional Primate Rsch Ctr 505 NW 185th Ave Beaverton OR 97006-3448

STOUGH, EILEEN SHINN, intensive care nurse; b. Chgo., Mar. 13, 1970; d. Kang H. and Song Y. (Park) Shinn; m. Bryan W. Stough, Apr. 30, 1994. BSN, U. N.C., 1993. RN, N.C. Mem. nursing staff Cape Fear Valley Med. Ctr., Fayetteville, N.C., 1993-94, Presbyn. Health Svcs. Corp., Charlotte, N.C., 1995—. Mem. Nat. Assn. Neonatal Nurses. Republican. Methodist. Home: 8900 Daventry Pl Charlotte NC 28215

STOUGHT, CYNTHIA MARIE, psychiatric nurse; b. Connellsville, Pa., Jan. 24, 1953; d. Matthew J. and Veronica Marie (Hertznell) Kremposky; m. Richard C. Stought, Apr. 26, 1975; children: Adam, Jeffrey. Diploma, Shadyside Hosp., 1973; BSN, Lebanon Valley Coll., 1981, postgrad., 1993—. RN, Pa.; cert. psychiat./mental health nurse. Staff nurse Holy Spirit Hosp. Cmty. Mental Health Ctr., Camp Hill, Pa., 1977-94; case mgr. State Employee Assistance Program, Harrisburg, 1994-95. Bd. dirs. Capital Area Share, 1988; active Jr. League of Harrisburg, 1982-93, bd. dirs., 1991-92, sustaining mem., 1993—.

STOUPEL, ELIJAH, medical educator; b. Kaunas, Lithuania, June 20, 1929; arrived in Israel, 1974; s. Gregory and Ester (Lan) S.; m. Sophia Danguole Nugaraite; children: Jannet, Ylana. MD, Vilnius (Lithuania) U., 1952, PhD in Medicine, 1960, D of Med. Sci., 1967. Dir. Dist. Dept. Health and Dept. Internal Medicine, Nementzine, Lithuania, 1952-55; faculty appointment, family physician Vilnius U. Hosp., 1955-58, cardiologist dept. thoracic surgery, 1958-62, asst. prof. faculty for postgrad. med. studies, 1962-66, assoc. prof., 1966-70, full prof. medicine, 1970-74; chief cons. in cardiology Heart Inst. Beilinson Med. Ctr., Petah-Tiqva, Israel, 1975—; prof. cardiology Tel Aviv U., 1994—. Author: Prognosis in Cardiology, 1971, Mitral Valve Disease After Comissurotomy, 1973, Forecasting in Cardiology, 1976, Studies in Clinical Cosmobiology, 1968-95. Pres. Israeli br. Internat. Physicians for Prevention of Nuclear War, 1984-91. Fellow Internat. Soc. Internal Medicine, European Soc. Cardiology, Israel Heart Soc. Home: 27 Habanim, Hod Hasharon 45268, Israel Office: Rabin Med Ctr Beilinson Campus, Petah Tikva 49100, Israel

STOUT, CHRIS EDWARD, clinical psychologist; b. Dallas, May 8, 1959; s. Carlos Leon and Helen Elizabeth (Simmons) S.; m. Karen Louise Beckstrand, Oct. 20, 1985. AA, Purdue U., 1979, BS, 1981; PsyD, Forest Inst., 1985; MBA, Newport U., 1996. Lic. clin. psychologist, Ill., Wis. Pvt. practice, 1985—; assoc. adminstr., chief of psychology Forest Hosp., Des Plaines, Ill., 1981—, dir. rsch. dept., 1986—, dir. psychodiagnostics div., 1987—, clin. supr., 1987-88; exec. clin. dir. Forest Day Schs., Ill., 1987—; pediatric psychologist, 1988-89; assoc. adminstr., chief psychologist Forest Hosp., Des Plaines, Ill., 1991—; clin. cons. Forest Day Sch., Des Plaines, 1986-87, Mudelein Coll., Chgo., 1986-91, the White House, Washington (D.C.), 1988-90; adv. bd., coord. counsel Lake County (Ill.) Bd Health, 1989—. Editor: Annals of Clinical Psychology, 1988, Parent Handbook, 1990, Handbook of Addictive Disorders, 1992, Current Advances in Inpatient Psychiatric Care, 1993, Handbook of APHD, 1993, Transistions, 1993, The Other Side of the Coins, 1993, Neuropsychology and Mental Disorders, 1994; editor in chief Clin. Rev. Newsletter Des Plaines, 1987—; reviewer jours., 1986—; editorial bds. Micro Psych Jour., Med. Psychotherapist, 1989—; contbr. over 250 articles to profl. jours. Adv. bd. Holy Family Luth. Sch., Chgo., 1989-91. Recipient Forest Found., Des Plaines, 1986, 88; fellow Harvard Med. Sch., Boston, 1987. Mem. AAAS, Am. Psychol. Assn. (travel award 1989), Am. Bd. Med. Psychotherapists, Nat. Acad. Neuropsychology, Union Concerned Scientists, Amnesty Internat., Sigma Phi Alpha. Home: 154 Ironwood Ct Buffalo Grove IL 60089-6626 Office: Forest Hosp 555 Wilson Ln Des Plaines IL 60016-4729

STOUT, DONALD ROY, obstetrician, gynecologist; b. Shattuck, Okla., Aug. 19, 1938; s. Clyde Emory and Velma Irene (Sappington) S.; m. Judith A. Krauth, Nov. 7, 1964; children: Spencer R., Jeffrey S., Kristin L. BS, U. Okla., 1960; MD, Baylor Coll. Medicine, 1964. Diplomate Am. Bd. Ob-Gyn. Rotating intern Ben Taub Gen. Hosp. Houston, 1964-65; resident in ob-gyn. Baylor Affiliated Residency Program, Houston, 1967-70; physician Tulsa Ob-Gyn. Assocs., Inc., 1970—; assoc. clin. prof. Tulsa Med. Coll. U. Okla., 1980-92, clin. prof., 1992—. Capt. USAF, 1965-67. Fellow Am. Coll. Ob-Gyn., Am. Fertility Soc., Cen. Assn. Ob-Gyn.; mem. AMA, Am. Assn. Gynecologic Laparoscopists, Tulsa Ob-Gyn. Soc., Utica Physicians Assn. Ltd. (pres. 1985—), Okla. State Med. Assn. Republican. Methodist. Office: Tulsa Ob-Gyn Assocs Inc 1725 E 19th St Ste 400 Tulsa OK 74104-5421

STOUT, EDWARD IRVIN, medical manufacturing company executive; b. Washington, Iowa, Mar. 2, 1939; s. George L. and M. Gladys (Gorsh) S.; m. Dixie Lee Farris (div.); children: Deborah Lee Stout Poole, Cathy Ann Stout Phillips, Angela Fay; m. Marjorie Soria. BS, Iowa Wesleyan Coll., 1960; MS in Chemistry, Bradley U., 1968; PhD in Organic Chemistry, U. Ariz., 1973. Analytical chemist Lever Bros. Rsch., Edgewater, N.J., 1961-62; rsch. chemist USDA, Peoria, Ill., 1962-78; dir. rsch. Spenco Med. Corp., Waco, Tex., 1978-81; pres. S.W. Techs. Inc., Kansas City, Mo., 1981-96, chmn. bd., 1996—; dir. rsch. Chemstar Product Co., Mpls., 1982-86, cons., 1979-81; cons. Stout Supply Co., Ainsworth, Iowa, 1985—; instr. Bradley U., Peoria, 1970-78. Contbr. articles to profl. jours.; patentee in field. Mem. Am. Chem. Soc., Inst. Food Technologists, Am. Assn. Cereal Chemists, Am. Burn Assn., Soc. Plastic Engrs., Mid-Am. Inventors Assn. (v.p. 1988). Home: 10590 Haskins St Shawnee Mission KS 66215-4306 Office: SW Techs Inc 2018 Baltimore Ave Kansas City MO 64108-1914

STOUTENBEEK, CHRISTIAAN PETER, anesthesiologist, intensivist; b. Utrecht, the Netherlands, Aug. 12, 1947; s. Pieter Willem Cornelis and Alida Catharina (Goedkoop) S.; m. Margot Liesbeth Nijboer, Aug. 4, 1970; children: Astrid Catharina, Robin Christiaan. MD, U. Utrecht, 1973; PhD, U. Groningen (the Netherlands), 1987. House officer surgery, internal medicine, ob-gyn. Bleuland Hosp., Gouda, 1973-74; tropical doctor Albert Schweitzer Hosp., Lambarene, Gabon, 1975-76; resident anesthesiology Univ. Hosp., Groningen, 1976-79, staff mem. intensive care, 1979-87; dir. intensive care Onze Lieve Vrouwe Gasthuis, Amsterdam, the Netherlands, 1987-94, Academisch Medisch Centrum, U. Amsterdam, 1994—; prof. intensive care U. Amsterdam, 1995—. Recipient Hon. Medal, Akademia Medyczna Gdansk, Poland, 1991, Investigators award Arbeitskreis Intensivmedizin München/Münster, Munich, 1988. Mem. European Intensive Care Soc., Dutch Soc. Anesthesiology (chmn. sect. intensive care 1991—, chmn. nat. intensive care com. 1995—). Office: Academisch Medisch Centrum, U Amsterdam, Meibergdreef 9, 1105 AZ Amsterdam The Netherlands

STOWENS, DANIEL, pathologist; b. N.Y.C., Oct. 27, 1919; s. Oscar and Rose Lillian (Galkin) S.; m. Barbara Jean Hagmann, Sept. 28, 1944 (wid. May 1984); children: Daniel W., Christopher D.; m. Lamya Mary Shaheen, Mar. 20, 1985. AB, Columbia Coll., 1941; MD, Coll. Physicians and Surgeons, N.Y.C., 1943. Diplomate Am. Bd. Pediatrics, Pathology. Intern, resident Gorgas Hosp., Ancon, Canal Zone, 1944-45; instr., med. sch. Am. Univ., Beirut, 1947-48; fellow pediatrics Ochsner Clinic and Tulane Univ., New Orleans, 1948-51; resident, pathology Walter Reed Army Hosp., Washington, 1952-53; fellow, pathology Childrens Hosp., Boston, 1953-54; chief, pediatric pathology Armed Forces Inst. Pathology, Washington, 1954-58; dir. labs., assoc. prof. Childrens' Hosp./U. So. Calif. Med. Sch., L.A., 1958-60, Childrens' Hosp./U. Louisville, 1960-65; dir. labs. St. Luke's Meml. Hosp., Utica, N.Y., 1965-85; med. dir. MDS Labs, Rome, N.Y., 1985—. Author: Pediatric Pathology, 1959, 2d edit., 1965; contbr. articles to profl. jours. Maj. U.S. Army, 1945-47. Recipient 2nd prize Am. Soc. Gastroenterology, 1960. Mem. Am. Acad. Pediatrics, Am. Soc. Clin. Pathology (Gold medal 1955), N.Y. Acad. Sci., Am. Assn. Pathology, Internat. Acad. Pathology. Home and Office: 3214 Fountain St Clinton NY 13323-3923

STRACK, J. GARY, hospital administrator; b. Orlando, Fla., Aug. 1, 1945; married. Bachelors degree, U. Fla., 1967, masters degree, 1969. Adminstrv. rschr. Va. Med. Ctr., Gainesville, Fla., 1969; program mgr. Fla. Regional Med. Program, Gainesville, 1969-70; asst. prof. program in hosp. adminstrn. U. Fla., Gainesville, 1970-74; assoc. dir. Holiday Hosp., Orlando, 1974-77; assoc. exec. dir. Orlando Regional Med. Ctr., 1977-80; pres., CEO Orlando Regional Healthcare System, 1980—. Contbr. articles to profl. jours. Mem. AHA, Fla. Hosp. Assn. (bd. dirs. 1979-80). Home: 6305 Gibson Dr Orlando FL 32809-6148 Office: Orlando Regional Healthcare System 1414 Kuhl Ave Orlando FL 32806-2008

STRACK, STEPHEN NAYLOR, psychologist; b. Rome, N.Y., Nov. 13, 1955; s. Ralph and Grace (Naylor) S.; m. Leni Ferrero. BA, U. Calif., Berkeley, 1978; PhD, U. Miami, Fla., 1983. Psychologist L.A. County Dept. Mental Health, 1984-85; staff psychologist VA Outpatient Clinic, L.A., 1985-92, dir. tng., 1992—; clin. assoc. U. So. Calif., L.A., 1986—; adj. assoc. prof. Calif. Sch. Profl. Psychology, L.A., 1989—; clin. prof. Fuller Grad. Sch. Psychology, Pasadena, 1986-95, adj. prof. Author (test): Personality Adjective Check List, 1987; co-author (book): Differentiating Normal and Abnormal Personality, 1994; contbr. articles to profl. jours. U.S. Dept. Vets Affairs grantee, 1986-93, 96—. Fellow Soc. for Personality Assessment; mem. APA, Calif. Psychol. Assn., European Assn. of Psychol. Assessment, Soc. for Rsch. in Psychopathology, Western Psychol. Assn., Sigma Xi. Office: VA Outpatient Clinic 351 E Temple St Los Angeles CA 90012-3328

STRADER, KYLE WOODROW, internist, rheumatologist, educator; b. Clarksburg, W.Va., June 24, 1955; s. Woodrow Wilson and Sally Christine (Criss) S.; m. Deborah Jean Cain, Apr. 11, 1979. BA in Biology, W.Va. U., 1977, MD, 1981. Diplomate Am. Bd. Internal Medicine, Am. Bd. Rheumatology. Resident in internal medicine Hershey (Pa.) Med. Sch., 1981-84; fellow in rheumatology Wake Forest U. Bowman Gray Sch. Medicine, Winston-Salem, N.C., 1984-86; pvt. practice, Raleigh, N.C., 1986—; clin. instr. dept. medicine U. N.C., Chapel Hill, 1987—; prin. investigator or co-investigator numerous drug studies, 1987—. Contbr. articles to med. jours. Recipient Disting. Svc. award Arthritis Found., Raleigh, 1990. Mem. ACP, AMA, Am. Coll. Rheumatology, Am. Assn. for Clin. Immunology and Allergy, Am. Coll. Allergists, Am. Soc. Internal Medicine, Phi Beta Kappa, Alpha Omega Alpha. Methodist. Office: NC Arthritis and Allergy Care Ctr 3831 Merton Dr Raleigh NC 27609

STRAHILEVITZ, MEIR, inventor, researcher, psychiatry educator; b. Beirut, July 13, 1935; s. Jacob and Chana Strahilevitz; m. Aharona Nattiv, 1958; children: Michal, Lior. MD, Hadassah Hebrew U. Med. Sch., 1963. Diplomate Am. Bd. Psychiatry and Neurology, Royal Coll. Physicians and Surgeons Can. Asst. prof. Washington U. Med. Sch., St. Louis, 1971-74; assoc. prof. So. Ill. U., Springfield, 1974-77, U. Chgo., 1977, U. Tex. Med. Br., Galveston, 1978-81; chmn. dept. psychiatry Kaplan Hosp., Rehovot, Israel, 1987-88; clin. assoc. prof. U. Wash., Seattle, 1981-88; prof. U. Tex. Med. Sch., Houston, 1988-92. Contbr. articles to profl. jours. Fellow Am. Psychiat. Assn., Royal Coll. Physicians and Surgeons Can. Office: PO Box 190 Hansville WA 98340-0190

STRAIN, EDWARD RICHARD, psychologist; b. Indpls., Apr. 12, 1925; s. Edward Richard and Ernestine (Kidd) S.; m. Marsha Ellen Beeler, 1972; children: Douglas MacDonald, Elizabeth Stacy, Chadwick Edward, Sarah Abigail, Zachary Richard. AB, Butler U., 1948; PhD, Duke U., 1952. Clin. psychologist Ohio State Med. Ctr., Columbus, 1952-53, Ind. U. Med. Ctr., Indpls., 1953-56; pvt. practice cons. psychology Indpls., 1956—; lectr. dept. psychology Butler U., Indpls., 1958-68; pres. Marion County (Ind.) Mental Health Assn., 1967-69. Mem. 500 Festival Assocs., Indpls., 1961—; pres. Perry Twp. (Ind.) Rep. Club, 1968-69; founder Downtown Sr. Citizens Ctr., 1961; vestryman Episcopal Ch., 1975-77, 86-88, sr. warden, 1976-77. Recipient Disting. Tech. Alumni award Arsenal Tech. H.S., 1993, Hansen H. Anderson Cmty. Svc. Merit medal Arsenal Tech. H.S., 1994. Mem. Masons, Rotary, Indpls. Club, Athletic Club, Indpls. Press Club. Office: 17 W Market St Ste 750 Indianapolis IN 46204-2929

STRAIN, JAMES ELLSWORTH, pediatrician, retired association administrator; b. Lincoln, Nebr., Apr. 23, 1923; s. Elmer Ellsworth and Tessa Elizabeth (Stevens) S.; m. Ruby Lee Shepard; children: James A., John D., Janet M. Strain McKinney, Jeffrey Lee Phillips-Strain. AB, Phillips U., Enid, Okla., 1945; MD, U. Colo., Denver, 1947. Diplomate Am. Bd. Pediatrics (examiner 1984-89, mem. 1989-93, emeritus mem. 1993—). Intern Mpls. Gen. Hosp., 1947-48; resident in pediatrics Denver Children's Hosp., 1948-50, pres. med. staff, 1964, dir. genetic unit, 1982-86; pvt. practice specializing in pediatrics, Denver, 1950-86; exec. dir. Am. Acad. Pediatrics, Elk Grove Village, Ill., 1986-93, ret., 1993; pres. med. bd. Colo. Gen. Hosp., 1969-70; clin. prof. pediatrics U. Colo. Med. Ctr., 1969-86, 93—, U. Chgo., 1987-93; mem. Colo. Med. Adv. Coun. for Title 19, 1968-75, chmn., 1968-71; mem. Task Force on Iowa Health Care Stds. Project, 1984-85; presenter numerous profl. confs. Mem. editorial bd. Pediatrics in Rev.; reviewer Jour. Pediatrics; contbr. articles to profl. publs. Mem. Colo. Commn. on Children and Youth, 1971-75; trustee Phillips U., 1974—. Capt. U.S. Army, 1953-55. Recipient Disting. Alumnus award Phillips U., 1974, Florence Sabin award U. Colo., 1984, Excellence in Pub. Svc. award U.S. Surgeon Gen., 1988, Abraham Jacobi award AMA and Am. Acad. Pediatrics, 1994; James E. Strain Child Advocacy award established in his name Denver Children's Hosp., 1983. Fellow Am. Acad. Pediatrics (numerous offices and com. memberships at chpt., dist. and nat. level, including pres. 1982-83, Clifford Grulee award 1985); mem. APHA, AMA (mem. coun. sect. pediatrics 1971-93, chmn. coun. 1974-79, sect. del. 1978-79), Colo. Med. Soc. (mem. coun. dels. 1964-80), Denver Med. Soc. (mem. coun. dels. 1964-80), Can. Pediatric Soc., Ambulatory Pediatric Assn., Inst. Medicine, Alpha Omega Alpha. Republican. Mem. Disciples of Christ.

STRANDBERG, JOHN DAVID, comparative pathologist; b. Alexandria, Minn., Aug. 28, 1939; s. Winfred Carl and Evelyn Joyce (Studlien) S. AB, Johns Hopkins U., 1960; DVM, Cornell U., 1964, PhD, 1968. Diplomate Am. Coll. Vet. Pathologists. USPHS-NIH postdoctoral fellow Cornell U., Ithaca, N.Y., 1964-67; fellow, resident in pathology Sch. Medicine, Johns Hopkins U., Balt., 1966-67; instr. dept. pathology/divsn. animal medicine Sch. Medicine Johns Hopkins U., Balt., 1967-68, asst. prof. pathology/divsn. lab. animal medicine, 1968-75, dir. comparative pathology tng. program Sch. Medicine, 1973—, asst. prof. pathobiology Sch. Hygiene and Pub. Health, 1974-77, acting dir. divsn. lab. animal medicine Sch. Medicine, 1974-76, assoc. prof. pathology and comparative medicine, 1975—, assoc. prof. pathobiology Sch. Hygiene and Pub. Health, 1977—, dir. divsn. comparative medicine Sch. Medicine, 1983—; vis. scientist Marine Biol. Lab., Woods Hole, Mass., 1993; cons., panelist, presenter in field; mem. peer rev. group Nat. Zool. Park, 1987, 88, 90; chmn. Md. Coun. on Sci. Use of Animals, 1989—; mem. adv. con. Nat. Ctr. for Rsch. Resources NIH, 1991—; mem. adv. bd. Nat. Aquarium in Balt., 1986—, Ctr. for Alternatives to Animal Testing, Balt., 1985—. Mem. editorial rev. bd. The Biomedical Investigator's Handbook, 1987; contbr. articles to profl. publs. V.p. Balt. Zool. Soc., 1978-82, chmn. med. com., 1973-86. Mem. AAAS, AMVA, Am. Coll. Vet. Pathologists (com. on tng. programs 1976-82), U.S. and Can. Acad. Pathology, Am. Assn. Pathologists, Md. State Vet. Med. Assn. (com. on liaison to humane orgns. 1986-88, com. on registration of vet. technicians 1977—), Am. Soc. Microbiology, Electron Microscopy Soc. Am., Med. Zool. Soc., Wildlife Disease Assn., Am. Soc. Lab. Animal Practitioners, Phi Beta Kappa, Phi Kappa Phi, Phi Zeta.

STRANDNESS, DONALD EUGENE, JR., surgeon; b. Bowman, N.D., Sept. 22, 1928; s. Donald Eugene and Merinda Clarine (Peterson) S.; m. Edith V., June 30, 1957; children: Erik Lee, Tracy Lynn, Jill Marie, Sandra Kay. BA, Pacific Lutheran U., 1950; MD, U. Wash., 1954. From instr. to prof. U. Wash., Seattle, 1962—; chief div. vascular surgery U. Wash., 1975-95. Served to capt. USAF, 1957-59. Recipient disting. alumnus award Pacific Lutheran U., 1980. Fellow Soc. for Vascular Surgery (pres. 1988); mem. Am. Coll. Surgeons, Am. Surg. Assn. Republican. Lutheran. Office: U Wash Dept Surgery 1959 Pacific Seattle WA 98195

STRANG, RUTH HANCOCK, pediatric educator, pediatric cardiologist, priest; b. Bridgeport, Conn., Mar. 11, 1923; d. Robert Hallock Wright and Ruth (Hancock) S. BA, Wellesley Coll., 1944, postgrad., 1944-45; MD, N.Y. Med. Coll., 1949; MDiv, Seabury Western Theol. Sem., 1993. Diplomate Am. Bd. Pediat.; ordained deacon Episc. Ch., 1993, priest, 1994. Intern Flower and Fifth Ave. Hosp., N.Y.C., 1949-50, resident in pediatrics, 1950-52; mem. faculty N.Y. Med. Coll., N.Y.C., 1952-57; fellow cardiology Babies Hosp., N.Y.C., 1956-57, Harriet Lane Cardiac Clinic, Johns Hopkins Hosp., Balt., 1957-59, Children's Hosp., Boston, 1959-62; mem. faculty U. Mich., Univ. Hosp., Ann Arbor, 1962-89, prof. pediatrics, 1970-89, prof. emeritus, 1989—; priest-in-charge St. Johns Episcopal Ch., Howell, Mich., 1994—; dir. pediatrics Wayne County Gen. Hosp., Westland, Mich, 1965-85; mem. staff U. Mich. Hosps.; mem. med. adv. com. Wayne County chpt. Nat. Cystic Fibrosis Rsch. Found., 1966-80, chmn. med. adv. com. nat. found., Detroit, 1971-78; cons. cardiology Plymouth (Mich.) State Home and Tng. Sch., 1970-81. Author: Clinical Aspects of Operable Heart Disease, 1968; contbr. numerous articles to profl. jours. Mem. citizen's adv. coun. to Juvenile Ct., Ann Arbor, 1968-76; mem. med. adv. bd. Ann Arbor Continuing Edn. Dept., 1968-77; mem. Diocesan Com. for World Relief, Detroit, 1970-72, Am. Heart Assn. Mich. (v.p. 1989, pres. 1991); trustee Episcopal

Med. Chaplaincy, Ann Arbor, 1971—; mem. bishop's com. St. Aidan's Episc. Ch., 1966-69, sec., 1966-68, vestry, 1973-76, 78-80. 84-86, 90-91, sr. warden, 1975, 76, 78, 80, 86, 90; del. Episc. Diocesan Conv., 1980, 91; bd. dirs. Livingston Cmty. Hospice, 1995—. Mem. AMA, Am. Acad. Pediatrics, Am. Coll. Cardiology, Mich. Med. Soc., Washtenaw County Med. Soc., N.Y. Acad. Medicine, Am. Heart Assn., Women's Rsch. Club (membership sec. 1966-67), Ambulatory Pediatric Assn., Am. Assn. Child Care in Hosps., Am. Assn. Med. Colls., Assn. Faculties of Pediatric Nurse Assn./Practitioners Programs (pres. 1978-81, exec. com. 1981-84), Episc. Clergy Assn. Mich., Northside Assn. Ministries (pres. 1975, 76, 79-80). Home: 4500 E Huron River Dr Ann Arbor MI 48105-9335

STRANGE, DONALD ERNEST, health care company executive; b. Ann Arbor, Mich., Aug. 13, 1944; s. Carl Britton and Donna Ernestine (Tenney) S.; m. Lyn Marie Purdy, Aug. 3, 1968; children: Laurel Lyn, Chadwick Donald. BA, Mich. State U., 1966, MBA, 1968. Asst. dir. Holland (Mich.) City Hosp., 1968-72, assoc. dir., 1972-74; exec. dir. Bascom Palmer Eye Inst./Anne Bates Leach Eye Hosp., U. Miami, Fla., 1974-77; v.p. strategic planning and rsch. Hosp. Corp. Am., Nashville, 1977-80; group v.p. Hosp. Corp. Am., Boston, 1980-82, regional v.p., 1982-87; chmn., chief exec. officer HCA Healthcare Can., 1985-87; exec. v.p. Avon Products, Inc., 1987-89; chmn. Sigecom, Ltd., 1989-94, U.S. HomeCare Corp., 1990-91; exec. v.p., COO, dir. EPIC Healthcare Group, Dallas, 1991-93; chmn, CEO TransCare Corp., Dallas, 1993—; bd. dirs. Access Radiology, Inc., Boston, Bon Secours Health System, Balt. Author: Hospital Corporate Planning, 1981. Mem. Harvard Club (Boston), Nat. Arts Club (N.Y.). Republican. Episcopalian. Office: TransCare 3232 Mckinney Ave Ste 1160 Dallas TX 75204-2470

STRANGE, GARY R., medical educator; b. Mammoth Cave, Ky., Jan. 16, 1947. BS Biology and Chemistry summa cum laude, Western Ky. U., 1966, MA in Secondary Edn., 1968; postgrad. in pharmacology, Vanderbilt U., 1967-68; postgrad. in edn., U. Ky., 1968-69, MD, 1974. Diplomate Am. Bd. Emergency Medicine. Intern in ob-gyn. Letterman Army Med. Ctr., San Francisco, 1974-75; resident in emergency medicine U. So. Calif. Med. Ctr., L.A., 1977-79; attending staff emergency medicine various hosps., Calif., 1978-79, Grayson Cmty. Hosp., Leitchfield, Ky., 1979-81; dir. emergency medicine Ireland Army Cmty. Hosp., Ft. Knox, Ky., 1979-81; attending staff emergency medicine Hardin Meml. Hosp., Elizabethtown, Ky., 1980-81, various hosps., Ill., 1981—; dir. emergency medicine Mercy Hosp. and Med. Ctr., Chgo., 1981-86, assoc. dir. emergency medicine, 1986-90; chief emergency svc. U. Ill. Hosp., Chgo., 1990—; dir. U. Ill. Affiliated Hosps. Emergency Medicine Residency, Chgo., 1986-93; head dept. emergency medicine U. Ill. Coll. Medicine, 1990—, assoc. prof. emergency medicine, 1991—. Contbr. articles to profl. jours. Mem. adv. bd. on emergency med. svcs. for children Ill. Dept. Pub. Health, 1994—; mem. panels Agency for Health Care Policy/Rsch., 1994, 95; regional coord. Yr. of the Child Nat. Campaign, 1990-91; com. on pediatric emergency med. svcs. Nat. Rsch. Coun. Inst. Medicine, 1991-93. Hubbell scholar 1971-72; recipient Lange Med. Publs. award 1971-72. Fellow Am. Coll. Emergency Physicians (councillor 1987-92, coun. steering com. 1991-93, chmn. course devel. task force mktg. and diversification 1986-87, infant and childhood emergencies com. 1983—, chmn. pediatric emergencies com. 1988-90, chmn. sect. pediatric emergency medicine 1990-91, sects. task force 1992—, core content task force, Chgo., 1993); mem. AMA, Am. Bd. Emergency Medicine (bd. examiner panel 1987—), Ill. chpt. Am. Coll. Emergency Physicians (bd. dirs. 1985—, chmn. med. econs. com. 1984-87, edn. com. 1982-84, product devel. com. 1988—, various other coms.), Soc. Tchrs. Emergency Medicine (chmn. ednl. resources com. 1982-86), Soc. Acad. Emergency Medicine (chmn. edn. com. 1989-93, program com. 1989-93, task force on developing residencies in traditional med. schs. 1991-93, injury prevention com. 1991—), Ill. Med. Soc., Chgo. Heart Assn. (ACSL Affiliate Faculty 1986-91, 92—), Chgo. Med. Soc. (diagnostic and therapeutic tech. assessment panel 1991). Office: Univ Illinois Dept Emergency Medicine Univ Illinois Hospital Chicago IL 60612*

STRANGES, STEVEN MICHAEL, neurological surgeon; b. Galveston, Tex., Apr. 29, 1954; s. Anthony Joseph and Margaret Ann (Atkinson) S. BS, U. S.C., 1976, MD, 1981. Diplmate Am. Bd. Neurol. Surgery. Staff neurosurgeon Meml. Miss. Med. Ctr., Asheville, N.C., 1987—, St. Joseph's Hosp., Asheville, 1987—; chmn. neurosurgery Meml. Miss. Med. Ctr. and St. Joseph's Hosp., Asheville, 1988-91, 93-95. Fellow Am. Assn. Neurosurgeons, Congress of Neurosurgeons. Office: Mountain Neurol Ctr 7 McDowell St Asheville NC 28801

STRASNICK, BRIAN J., psychologist; b. Maiden, Mass., Feb. 15, 1953; s. Phillip and Elaine (Bornstein) S.; m. Bonnie Ellen, Sept. 7, 1974; children: Meredith, Jilliam, Craig. BA, Northeastern U., 1974; EDM, Northwestern U., 1976; PhD, C.P.U., 1980. Bd. cert. NCC, CCMHC, MAC. Pres. Primary Care & Mental Health, Inc., Lynn, Mass. Fellow ABMP; mem. AACD, AMHCA. Home: 30 Nason Rd Swampscott MA 01907-2352 Office: Willow St Med Ctr 100 Willow St Lynn MA 01901

STRATFORD, CAROL ANN DEERING, occupational therapist; b. Columbus, Ohio, Dec. 17, 1946; d. Earl Brent and Gladys May (Wade) Deering; A.A., Brevard Jr. Coll., 1966; B.S., U. Fla., 1968; m. Francis A. Stratford, Jr., Aug. 4, 1973. Staff occupational therapist Hosp. Albert Einstein Coll. Medicine, Bronx, N.Y., 1968-74; sr. research therapist Inst. Rehab. Medicine N.Y. U. Med. Center, N.Y.C., 1975-81, mem. developmental team voice recognition, wheel chair and environ. control system; supr. dept. occupational therapy Danbury (Conn.) Hosp., 1982-84; tech. aids cons., 1984—. Registered occupational therapist. Mem. Am. Occupational Therapy Assn., Rehab. Engring. Soc. N. Am. Co-author, editor: (monograph) Environmental Control Systems and Vocational Aids for Persons with High Level Quadriplegia, 1979; contbr. articles to profl. jours. Methodist. Home: 16 N State St Dover DE 19901-3833

STRATOUDAKIS, JAMES PETER, psychologist; b. Stamford, Conn., Feb. 21, 1949; s. James and Rose L. (Rotante) S.; m. Carol Jay Colello, Aug. 14, 1971; 1 child, Alexander Jay. BA, Fairfield U., 1971; MS, DePaul U., 1973; PhD, Mich. State U., 1976. Psychotherapist Battle Creek (Mich.) Sanitarium Hosp., 1975-77; coord. info., asst. prof. internat. rehab. and spl. edn. Mich. State U., East Lansing, 1976-78, asst. prof. urban devel. and met. studies, 1978-80; pvt. practice psychology East Lansing, 1977-80; dir. clin. svcs. Social Ctr. for Psychiat. Rehab., Alexandria, Va., 1980-82; dir. no. region Va. Dept. Mental Health, Richmond, 1982-84, community svcs. bd., facility liaison for mental health, mental retardation, substance abuse, 1984; dir. community planning, program dev. and tng., community support programs Del. div. Alcoholism Drug Abuse & Mental Health, New Castle, 1984-86; regional dir. Greater Wilmington/New Castle County Community Mental Health Program, New Castle, 1986-88, Mass. Dept. Mental Health, Taunton, 1988-90; dir. office mental health svcs. Fairfax Falls Ch. Cmty. Svcs. Bd., Fairfax County, Va., 1990—; adj. prof. Va. Commonwealth U., 1984—, U. Del., 1986-88, 90, Bridgewater State Coll., George Washington U., 1991—, U. Va., 1991-93; cons. psychologist, Washington, 1980—; mem. nat. adv. coun. State Mental Health Planning, 1990-93, Rehab. Rsch. and Tng. Ctr. for Persons with Psychiat. Disabilities/Albert Einstein Coll. Medicine, 1985-90. Sec. D.C. Psychology Polit. Action Com., 1983-84. Mem. APA (past chmn. cmty. and state hosp psychology sect.), World Rehab. Assn. for Psychosocially Disabled (founding mem.), Nat. Assn. County Behavioral Health Care Dirs., Va. Assn. Cmty. Svcs. Bds. (chmn. statewide mental health coun. 1995—), Phi Kappa Theta. Unitarian. Office: Office of Mental Health Svcs Human Svcs Ctr Ste 800 12011 Government Ctr Pkwy Fairfax VA 22035-1105

STRATTON, JULIUS AUGUSTUS, psychologist, consultant; b. Norfolk, Va., July 9, 1924; s. Julius Augustus and Annie (Thornton) S. BS, Hampton U., Va., 1947; MEd, Cornell U., 1957; postgrad., Harvard U., 1966-67, U. Chgo., 1965. Instr., chmn. dept. counseling Roosevelt High Sch., Gary, Ind., 1952-68; assoc. faculty Ind. U. N.W., Gary, 1971-74; research dir. Gary Sch. Corp., 1968-76; v.p. Cornell Urban Cons., Chgo., 1976—. Author: Nonintellectual Factors Associated with Academic Achievement, 1957; contbr. articles to profl. jours. Mem. Nat. Coun. Tchrs. of Math., Assn. for Measurement and Evaluation in Counseling & Devel., Alpha Phi Alpha, Phi Delta Kappa, Sigma Gamma Mu. Democrat. Episcopalian. Office: Cornell Urban Cons PO Box 16651 Chicago IL 60616-0651

STRATTON, MARIANN, retired naval nursing administrator; b. Houston, Apr. 6, 1945; d. Max Millard and Beatrice Agnes (Roemer) S.; m. Lawrence Mallory Stickney, nov. 15, 1977 (dec.). BSN, BA in English, Sacred Heart Dominican Coll., 1966; MA in Mgmt., Webster Coll., 1977; MSN, U. Va., 1981. Cert. adult nurse practitioner. Ensign USN, 1966, advanced through grades to rear adm., 1991; patient care coord. Naval Regional Med. Ctr., Charleston, S.C., 1981-83; nurse corps plans officer Naval Med. Command, Washington, 1983-86; dir. nursing svcs. U.S. Naval Hosp., Naples, Italy, 1986-89, Naval Hosp., San Diego, 1989-91; chief pers. mgmt. Bur. Medicine & Surgery, Washington, 1991-94; dir. USN Nurse Corps, Washington, 1991-94; ret. Oct. 1, 1994 USN, 1994. Decorated Disting. Svc. medal, Meritorious Svc. medal with two stars, Naval Achievement medal. Mem. ANA, Assn. Mil. Surgeons of U.s., Interagy. Inst. of Fed. Health Car Execs.

STRATTON, TIMOTHY PATRICK, pharmacy educator; b. Santa Rosa, Calif., Apr. 5, 1957; s. Robert Arthur and Carol Lee (St. Clair) S.; m. Suzanne Wasilczuk, Apr. 1, 1989. AS in Pre-Pharmacy, Santa Rosa (Calif.) Jr. Coll., 1977; BS in Pharmacy, Idaho State U., 1980; MS in Hosp. Pharmacy, U. Ariz., 1982, PhD in Pharmacy Adminstrn., 1986. Pharmacist lic. Ariz., Calif., Alaska. Tchg. asst. U. Ariz. Coll. Pharmacy, Tucson, 1980-85; staff pharmacist Tucson (Ariz.) Med. Ctr., 1982-84, White's Pharmacy, Sitka, Alaska, 1985-89; dir. pharm. svcs. Sitka (Alaska) Cmty. Hosp., 1985-89; asst. prof. pharm. adminstrn. U. B.C., Vancouver, 1989-93, U. Mont. Sch. Pharm., Missoula, 1993-96; assoc. prof. pharmacy adminstrn. U. Mont. Sch. Pharmacy, Missoula, 1996—; cons. pharmacist Wrangell (Alaska) Hosp., 1987-89; rsch. cons. B.C. Pharmacy Assn., Vancouver, 1989-93, B.C. Coll. Pharmacists, Vancouver, 1989-93. Contbr. articles to profl. jours. United Way campaigner U. B.C., Vancouver, 1992-93, Missoula, 1994. Mem. Am. Assn. Colls. Pharm. (com. mem. 1992—), Am. Pharm. Assn., Mont. Pharm. Assn. (legis. com. mem. 1995), Missoula Model Railroad Club (pres. 1995—). Democrat. Unitarian. Home: 1529 Fox Field Dr Missoula MT 59802 Office: Univ Montana Sch Pharmacy Missoula MT 59812

STRATTON-WHITCRAFT, CATHLEEN SUE, critical care, pediatrics nurse; b. Jackson, Mich., Jan. 14, 1964; d. Ronald Alfred and Shirley Anne (Wickham) Stratton; m. David R. Whitcraft, Aug. 14, 1988. BSN magna cum laude, SUNY, Brockport, 1985. Cert. critical care nurse, ACLS. Student clin. asst. Yale-New Haven Hosp., 1984; charge nurse Walter Reed Army Med. Ctr., Washington, 1990; clin. nurse, critical care med. ICU and pediatric ICU SRT-Med. Staff Agy., Springfield, Va., 1985-88; asst. head nurse Sinai Hosp., Balt., 1988-90; charge nurse surg. SICU ICU VA Med. Ctr., Balt., 1991—. 1st lt. U.S. Army Nurse Corps, 1985-88, Res., 1988-93. Recipient Cert. of Achievement, Elizabeth Dole.

STRAUB, PETER FRANCIS, biologist; b. Rockville, N.Y., Feb. 13, 1958; s. Richard Joseph and Anne Moran (Gibbons) S.; m. Paula Eileen Grey, Jan. 3, 1983; children: Andrew Peter, Alexandra Lorana. BS, Stockton State Coll., 1980; MS, U. Del., 1985, PhD, 1990. Lab. asst. mgr. Atlantic Community Coll., Mays Landing, N.J., 1980-82; postdoctoral rsch. assoc. biology Washington U., St. Louis, 1989-94; asst. prof. biology Richard Stockton Coll. of N.J., Pomona, 1994—. Contbr. articles to Am. Jour. Botany, Plant Cell and Environ. Plant Cell, Tissue and Organ Culture, Plant Molecular Biology, Applied and Environ. Microbiology. Mem. Bot. Soc. Am. Democrat. Roman Catholic.

STRAUCH, BARRY S., physician, educator; b. N.Y.C., Feb. 2, 1941; s. Leo J. and Mildred M. (Meistery) S.; m. Evelyn Marion Springer, Aug. 18, 1963; children: Lara, Eric. BA, Johns Hopkins U., 1962, MD, 1965. Diplmate Am. Bd. Internal Medicien and Nephrology. Asst. prof. Yale U., Balt., 1971-73; clin. assoc. prof. Georgetown U., Washington, 1974-94, clin. prof. medicine, 1994—; chief nephrology sect. Fairfax Hosp., Falls Church, Va., 1974—; cons. Med., Legal and Pub. Policy, Washington, 1978—; ptnr. Washington Nephrology Assocs., Bethesda, Md., 1984—, chmn., 1989—. Contbr. numerous articles to profl. jours. Bd. dirs. Helath Care Adv. Bd., Fairfax County, 1975-77; chmn. Renal Network 23, Washington, 1978-82; exec. com. Nat. Forum Network, Washington, 1978-82; bd. dirs. Mid-Atlantic Renal Coalition, Richmond, Va., 1987—. Lt. comdr. USPHS, 1967-69. Fellow ACP; mem. Am. Soc. Nephrology, Cosmos Club. Office: 8316 Arlington Blvd Fairfax VA 22031

STRAUCH, HAROLD BENJAMIN, orthopaedic surgeon; b. Sacramento, June 15, 1934; s. Harold Rudolph and Dorothy Gertrude (Harrigan) S.; m. Lilla Lou Witharm, June 1, 1962; children: Michael, Kristin, Kimberly, Marc, Matthew. BA, Stanford U., 1956, MD, 1959. Diplomate Am. Bd. Orthopaedic Surgery. Intern Phila. Gen. Hosp., Sacramento, 1959-60; resident U. Calif., San Francisco, 1960-61, Pacific Presbyn. Med. Ctr., San Francisco, 1961-63, Shermans Hosp., L.A., 1963-64; pvt. practice Sacramento, 1964—. Chmn. bd. Sutter Cmty. Hosps., Sacramento, 1993-94. Mem. ACS, AMA, Am. Acad. Orthopedic Surgeons, Western Orthopedic Assn., Calif. Med. Assn., Sacramento Med. Soc. Office: 2801 K St Ste 400 Sacramento CA 95816

STRAUGHN, WILLIAM RINGGOLD, III, pediatrician; b. Salisbury, Md., Sept. 10, 1942; s. William Ringgold Jr. and Mary Constance (Belknap) S.; m. Gloria Gay Giaveno, Apr. 11, 1970; children: Mary Celka Kristine, Ian Blaisdell. AB, U. N.C., 1964, MD, 1970. Pediatrician USN, Camp Lejeune, N.C., 1973-75, Mare Island, Calif., 1975-77; pediatrician Manchester (N.H.) Pediatric Group, 1977-87, Lahay-Hitchcock Clinic, Manchester, 1987—; chief pediatrics Cath. Med. Ctr., Manchester, 1992—; cons. on lead poisoning N.H. Pub. Health Dept., 1982—. Bd. dirs. N.H. Trust Fund for Prevention of Child Abuse, Concord, 1987-94, Pastoral Counseling Svcs., Manchester, 1983-85, Child Health Svcs., Manchester, 1985-87. Fellow Am. Acad. Pediatrics; mem. AMA, Am. Soc. Mil. Surgeons, N.H. Pediatric Soc., Naval Res. Assn. Office: Lahey-Hitchcock Clinic 275 Mammoth Rd Manchester NH 03109-4124

STRAUS, HELEN LORNA PUTTKAMMER, biologist, educator; b. Chgo., Feb. 15, 1933; d. Ernst Wilfred and Helen Louise (Monroe) Puttkammer; m. Francis Howe Straus II, June 11, 1955; children: Francis Howe III, Helen E., Christopher M., Michael W. AB magna cum laude, Radcliffe Coll., 1955; MS in Anatomy, U. Chgo., 1960, PhD in Anatomy, 1962. With U. Chgo., 1964—, asst. prof. anatomy, 1967-73, dean of students, 1971-82, assoc. prof., 1973-87, dean of admissions, 1975-80, prof. anatomy and biol. scis., 1987—; bd. govs. U. Chgo. Internat. House, 1987—. Trustee Radcliffe Coll., Cambridge, Mass., 1973-83. Recipient Quantrell Award for Excellence in teaching, U. Chgo., 1970, 87, Silver medal Case Outstanding Tchr. Program, 1987. Mem. AAAS, NCAA (acad. requirements com. 1986-92, chmn. 1990-92, rsch. com. 1996—), Nat. Sci. Tchrs. Assn., Am. Assn. Anatomists, Harvard U. Alumni Assn. (bd. dirs. 1980-83), Phi Beta Kappa (sec., treas. U. Chgo. chpt. 1984—). Home: 5642 S Kimbark Ave Chicago IL 60637-1606 Office: U Chgo 5845 S Ellis Ave Chicago IL 60637-1404

STRAUS, ROBERT, behavioral sciences educator; b. New Haven, Jan. 9, 1923; s. Samuel Hirsh and Alma (Fleischner) S.; m. Ruth Elisabeth Dawson, Sept. 8, 1945; children: Robert James, Carol Martin, Margaret Dawson, John William. BA, Yale U., 1943, MA, 1945, PhD, 1947. Asst. prof. Yale U., 1948-51, research asso. applied psychology, 1951-53; acting dir. Conn. Child Study and Treatment Home, New Haven, 1952-53; assoc. prof. preventive medicine SUNY Upstate Med. Center, 1953-56; prof. med. sociology U. Ky., Lexington, 1956-59; prof. dept. behavioral sci. Coll. Medicine, also chmn. dept. U. Ky., 1959-87; dir. for sci. devel. Med. Rsch. Inst. San Francisco, 1991-93; vis. fellow Yale U., 1968-69; vis. prof. U. Calif., Berkeley, 1978, 86; sec. Com. Med. Sociology, 1955-57; chmn. Coop. Com. Study Alcoholism, 1961-63; chmn. Nat. Adv. Com. on Alcoholism, 1966-69; mem. Nat. Adv. Coun. on Alcohol Abuse and Alcoholism, 1984-87; trustee Med. Rsch. Inst. San Francisco, 1988-93; mem. Calif. Pacific Med. Ctr. Rsch. Coun., 1993. Author: Medical Care for Seamen, 1950 (with S.D. Bacon), Drinking in College, 1953, Alcohol and Society, 1973, Escape From Custody, 1974; A Medical School is Born, 1996; co-editor: Medicine and Society, 1963; mem. editorial bd.: Jour. Studies on Alcohol. Pres., Bluegrass R.R. Mus., 1980. Mem. Inst. Medicine NAS, Am. Sociol. Assn. (chmn. med. sociology sect. 1967-68), Assn. Behavioral Scis. and Med. Edn. (pres. 1974), Am. Pub. Health Assn. (lifetime achievement award sect. on alcohol, tobacco and other drugs 1993), Acad. Behavioral Medicine Rsch., Phi Beta Kappa, Sigma Xi. Home: 656 Raintree Rd Lexington KY 40502-2874

STRAUSFELD, NICHOLAS JAMES, neurobiology and evolutionary biology researcher, educator; b. Claygate, England, Oct. 22, 1942. BSc in Zoology, U. Coll. London, 1965, PhD in Neurophysiology, 1968; PhD in Neurophysiology, Habilitation, Frankfurt, Germany, 1985. Prof. U. Ariz., Tucson. Author: (books) Atlas of an Insect Brain, 1976, Functional Neuroanatomy, 1983. John Simon Guggenheim fellow, 1984, MacArthur fellow, 1995; recipient award for excellence in environ. health rsch. Lovelance Inst., Albuquerque, 1995. Office: U Arizona Rsch Labs Divsn Neurobiology Tucson AZ 85721

STRAUSS, DOROTHY BRANDFON, marital, family, and sex therapist; b. Bklyn.; d. Marcus and Beatrice (Wilson) Brandfon; widowed; 1 child, Josette E. MacNaughton. BA, Bklyn. Coll., 1932; MA, NYU, 1937, PhD, 1963. Diplomate Am. Bd. Sexology. Instr. Hunter Coll. CUNY, 1960-63; prof. Kean Coll., Union, N.J., 1963-77; pvt. practice and clin. supervision Bklyn. and, N.J., 1970—; clin. assoc. prof. psychiatry Downstate Med. Ctr., SUNY, Bklyn., 1974—; assoc. dir. Ctr. for Human Sexuality, 1974-82; mem. NIMH rsch. team U. Pa., 1973-82. Contbr. articles on gerontology and sexual dysfunctions to profl. jours. Fellow Am. Assn. Clin. Sexologists (founding); mem. Am. Psychol. Assn., Am. Assn. for Marital and Family Therapy (clin. mem. 1971—, supr. 1981—), Am. Assn. Sex Therapists, Counselors and Educators (chairperson task force on supervision 1984-86, chairperson supr. cert. com. 1986-93, chair cert. steering com. 1992—), Kappa Delta Pi. Home and Office: 1401 Ocean Ave Brooklyn NY 11230-3971

STRAUSS, ELTON, orthopaedic surgeon; b. N.Y.C., Apr. 24, 1948; s. Carl and Shirley(Pinchuck) S.; m. Karen Louise Gustin, Jan. 2, 1971; children: Eric, Elisa. BA in Biology, C.W. Post Coll., 1970; MD, U. Autonoma, Guadalajara, Mexico, 1974. Intern Bronx-Lebanon Hosp., 1975-76, resident, 1976-79; pvt. practice N.Y.C., 1979—; chief orthopaedic trauma Mt. Sinai Sch. Medicine, N.Y.C., 1987—; assoc. dir. City Hosp. Ctr. at Elmhurst, Queens, N.Y., 1987—. Trustee Harlem Youth Devel. Found., N.Y. Geriatric scholar Mt. Sinai Sch. Medicine, 1992. Fellow ACS, Am. Bd. Orthopaedic Surgeons; mem. Am. Foot Soc., Am. Fracture Soc., N.Y. Med. Soc., Orthopaedic Trauma Assn. Office: Mt Sinai Sch Medicine 5 E 98th St New York NY 10029-6501

STRAUSS, HAROLD CARL, cardiology educator; b. Montreal, Que., Can.; married; 3 children. BSc, McGill U., Montreal, Can., 1960, MD CM, 1964. Diplomate Am. Bd. Internal Medicine. Summer fellow Univ. Med. Clinic Montreal Gen. Hosp., 1962-63; rotating intern Jewish Gen. Hosp., Montreal, 1964-65, jr. resident, 1965-66; postdoctoral fellow dept. pharmacology Coll. Physicians and Surgeons Columbia U., N.Y.C., 1966-68, assoc. in pharmacology Coll. Physicians and Surgeons, 1971-72; 1st yr. resident dept. medicine Bronx Mcpl. Hosp. Ctr. Albert Einstein Coll. Medicine, N.Y., 1968-69; cardiology resident dept. medicine Presbyn. Hosp. in the City of N.Y., 1969-71; asst. prof. medicine Duke U. Med. Ctr., Durham, N.C., 1972-77, asst. prof. pharmacology, 1975-77, assoc. prof. medicine, 1977-84, assoc. prof. pharmacology, 1979-86; prof. medicine %, Durham, N.C., 1985—, prof. pharmacology, 1986—, Edward S. Orgain prof. cardiology, 1990—; assoc. dir. Specialized Ctr. of Rsch. in Ischemic Heart Disease, 1982-84, dir., 1985-95; dir. Specialized Ctr. Rsch. in Congestive Heart Failure, 1995—; lectr. in field. Assoc. editor: Circulation, 1973-77, mem. editl. bd., 1986-88, 93-94; mem. editl. bd. Circulation Rsch., 1980-85, assoc. editor, 1991—; mem. editl. bd. Jour. Cardiovasc. Electrophysiology, 1990—; contbr. articles to profl. jours. Mem. AAAS, Am. Fedn. Clin. Rsch., Am. Heart Assn. (mem. N.C. affiliate, mem. rsch. program and evaluation com. 1988-90, mem. pharm. round table 1992-94, mem. steering com. for rsch. med. and cmty. programs 1992-94, v.p. rsch. 1992-94, bd. dirs. 1992-94, chmn. rsch. animals issues com. 1992-93, mem. animals in rsch. task force 1993-94, mem. task force on clin. trials 1993-94, sci. coun.'s disting. achievement award coun. on basic sci. 1994, award of meritorious achievement 1996, others), Am. Physiol. Soc., Am. Soc. Clin. Investigation, Assn. Am. Physicians, Assn. Univ. Cardiologists, Biophys. Soc., Cardiac Eletrophysiology Soc. (sec. 1981-82, pres. 1982-84), N.Y. Acad. Scis., Soc. Gen. Physiologists. Office: Duke U Specialised Ctr Ischemic Heart Dis Dept Medicine Divsn Cadiology PO Box 3845 Durham NC 27702-3845*

STRAUSS, JEFFREY LEWIS, healthcare executive; b. Balt., Aug. 16, 1963; s. Ronald Jay and Roberta Maude (Henriques) S.; m. Melissa Marie Nieding, Sept. 2, 1990. AA in Acctg., Purdue U., Westville, Ind., 1984, BA in Acctg., 1985. Staff acct. Bon Secour Hosp., Balt., 1986-88, Helix Health Systems/Franklin Sq. Hosp. Ctr., Balt., 1988-89; budget mgr., dir. provider svcs. Rush Prudential Health Plans, Chgo., 1989-93; dir. managed care fin. ops. West Suburban Hosp. Med. Ctr., Oak Park, Ill., 1993-94; dir. West Suburban Health Providers, Inc., Oak Park, 1995—. Mem. Antique Automobile Club Am. (life). Democrat. Jewish. Home: 497 Grosse Pointe Cir Vernon Hills IL 60061-3045 Office: West Suburban Health Providers Inc 1000 Lake St Oak Park IL 60301

STRAUSS, JEROME FRANK, III, physician, educator; b. Chgo., May 2, 1947; s. Jerome Frank Fr. and Josephine (Newberger) S.; m. Catherine Blumlein, June 20, 1970; children: Jordan L., Elizabeth J. BA, Brown U., 1969; MD, U. Pa., 1974, PhD, 1975. Asst. prof. Sch. of Medicine U. Pa., Phila., 1976-83, assoc. prof. Sch. of Medicine, 1983-85, prof. Sch. of Medicine, 1985—, assoc. chair Sch. of Medicine, 1987—, assoc. dean Sch. of Medicine, 1990—; Luigi Mastroianni jr. prof. and dir. Ctr. Rsch. on Women's Health and Reproduction, Phila., 1990-94; prof. Inst. of Medicine NAS, Phila., 1994—; mem. Biochem. Endocrinology study sect. NIH, 1983-87; mem., chair Population Rsch. Com. Nat. Inst. Child Health and Human Devel., 1989-92. Editor; Lipoprotein and Cholesterol Metabolism in Sterodogenic Tissues, 1985, Current Topics in Membrane Research, vol. 31, 1987, Uterine and Embryonic Factors in Early Pregnancy, 1991; (jour.) Steroid, 1993—; assoc. editor, mem. editorial bd. Jour. Lipid Rsch., 1982-90; mem. editorial bd. Endocrinology, 1986-90, Biology of Reprodn., 1986-90, Jour. of Women's Health, 1991—. Mem. Am. Assn. Pathologists, Am. Physiol. Soc., Soc. Gynecologic Investigation (Pres.'s Achievement award 1990), Endocrine Soc., Soc. for Study of Reprodn. (bd. dirs. 1989-91, Rsch. award 1992). Office: U Pa Dept Ob/Gyn 415 Curie Blvd Philadelphia PA 19104-6140

STRAUSS, JOHN STEAVEN, psychiatrist, educator; b. Cleve., Aug. 18, 1932; s. Walton and Augusta S.; children: Jeffrey, Sarah. BA, Swarthmore Coll., 1954; postgrad., Jean Piaget, Geneva, 1956-57; MD, Yale U., 1959; cert. community psychiatry, Washington Sch. Psychiatry, 1966. Intern New Eng. Ctr. Hosp., Boston, 1959-60; resident in medicine Boston City Hosp., 1960-61; resident in psychiatry McLean/Beth Israel Hosps., Boston, 1961-64; clin. assoc. USPHS, Bethesda, Md., 1964-66; chief psychiat. assessment NIMH, Bethesda, 1968-72; collaborating investigator WHO, Bethesda, 1966-76, U.S. rep. to Program on Internat. Collaboration for Psychiat. Diagnosis, 1980-83; assoc. prof. psychiatry U. Rochester, N.Y., 1972-76, prof., 1976-77; prof. psychiatry Yale U., New Haven, 1977—; bd. dir. dept. psychiatry Ctr. for Studies of Prolonged Psychiat. Disorders Conn. Mental Health Ctr. Yale U. Med. Sch., 1985—; cons. Woodley House, Washington, 1966-72. Co-author: Schizophrenia, 1981; editor: The Psychotherapy of Schizophrenia, 1980. NIMH grantee, 1980—. Fellow Am. Psychiat. Assn. (cons. Task Force on Nomenclature 1974-80, Stanley Dean award 1980, Samuel G. Hibbs award 1983, Van Ameringen award 1988, Armin Loeb award 1990); mem. Assn. Clin. Psychiatry Rsch., Soc. Life History Rsch. in Psychopathology (chmn. 1975-76). Home: 50 Burton St New Haven CT 06515-2116 Office: Yale U Sch Medicine Dept Psychiatry 34 Park St New Haven CT 06519-1109

STRAUSS, JOHN STEINERT, dermatologist, educator; b. New Haven, July 15, 1926; s. Maurice Jacob and Carolyn Mina (Ullman) S.; m. Susan Thalheimer, Aug. 19, 1950; children—Joan Sue, Mary Lynn. B.S., Yale U., 1946; M.D., 1950. Intern U. Chgo., 1950-51; resident in dermatology U. Pa., Phila., 1951-52, 54-55; fellow in dermatology U. Pa., 1955-57, instr., 1956-57; mem. faculty Boston U. Med. Sch., 1958-78, prof., 1966-78; prof., head dept. dermatology U. Iowa, Iowa City, 1978—. Mem. editorial bd. Archives of Dermatology, 1970-79, Jour. Am. Acad. Dermatology, 1979-89, Jour. Investigative Dermatology, 1977-82; contbr. articles to profl. jours. Served with USNR, 1952-54. James H. Brown jr. fellow, 1947-48; USPHS fellow, 1955-57; USPHS grantee. Fellow Am. Acad. Dermatology (pres.); mem. Soc. Investigative Dermatology (sec.-treas., pres.), Dermatology Found. (pres.), Am. Bd. Dermatology (bd. dirs., pres.), Am. Dermatol. Assn. (sec., pres.),

Assn. Am. Physicians, Central Soc. Clin. Rsch., Am. Fedn. Clin. Rsch., Coun. Med. Splty. Socs. (pres.), 18th World Congress Dermatology (pres.), Internat. League Dermatol. Socs. (pres. 1992—), Internat. Com. Dermatology (pres. 1992—), others. Office: U Iowa Hosp & Clinics Dept of Dermatology 200 Hawkins Dr # Bt2045 1 Iowa City IA 52242-1009

STRAUSS, JUDITH FEIGIN, physician; b. N.Y., Mar. 7, 1942; d. Milton M. and Blanche (Tobias) Feigin; m. Harry William Strauss, June 14, 1964; children: Cheryl, Marcy. BS, Cornell U., Ithaca, 1963; MD, SUNY, 1967. Pediatrics. Pediatric resident SUNY, N.Y.C., 1976-68, Sinai Hosp., Balt., 1968-69; fellow pediatrics and psychiatry Johns Hopkins Hosp., Balt., 1969-70; pvt. practice in pediatrics Sacramento; cons. in pediatrics Bur. of Disability Ins. Social Security, Balt., 1973-74; pediatrician East Balt. Med. Plan, 1974-76; dir. pediats. USPHS Hosp., Boston, 1976-80; pvt. practice in pediatrics Boston, 1980-87; dir. med. svcs. Mediqual Systems, 1988-92; pres. Strauss Healthcare Consulting, Skillman, N.J., 1992-94; v.p. med. affairs Sutter Health Bay Region, 1995; chief med. officer Calif. Advantage, Inc., San Francisco, 1995—; chief med. officer Calif. Advantage, Inc., 1995—. Fellow Am. Acad. Pediatrics; mem. Am. Coll. Physicians Execs., Mass. Med. Soc., Calif. Med. Assn., Alpha Lambda Delta. Home: 45 Summit Ridge Pl Redwood City CA 94062

STRAUSS, RAYMOND BERNARD, otolaryngologist; b. N.Y.C., Mar. 25, 1930; s. Victor M. and Fannie (Price) S.; m. Lois Kelly, June 12, 1958; children: Steven Douglas, Keith Andrew. AB, Washington U., St. Louis, 1950; PhD, U. Fla., 1956; MD, Case-Western Res. U., 1958. Diplomate Am. Bd. Otolaryngology, Am. Bd. Cosmetic Plastic Surgery. Intern dept. medicine Univ. Hosps., Cleve., 1958-59, asst. resident surgery, 1959-60; resident otolaryngology Columbia-Presbyn. Med. Center, N.Y.C., 1960-63; practice medicine, specializing in otolaryngology and facial plastic surgery, Englewood, N.J., 1963—; attending otolaryngologist, chief otolaryngology Englewood Hosp.; assoc. attending otolaryngologist Vanderbilt Clinic and Presbyn. Hosp., N.Y.C.; past dir. facial plastic surgery clin.; assoc. prof. clin. otolaryngology Coll. Physicians and Surgeons, Columbia U.; dir., vice-chmn. bd. dirs. NVE Savs. Bank; past trustee Dwight-Englewood Sch.; bd. dirs. No. Valley chpt. ARC. Served to capt. M.C., AUS, 1964-66. Recipient Coakley Meml. prize in otolaryngology Columbia U., 1958; Marie and Henry Heiner fellow in otolaryngology, 1961-62; decorated Army Commendation medal. Fellow ACS, Internat. Coll. Surgeons, Am. Acad. Facial Plastic and Reconstructive Surgery, Am. Acad. Cosmetic Surgery, Am. Acad. Otolaryngology and Head and Neck Surgery; mem. AMA, Am. Speech and Hearing Assn. (cert. clin. competence in speech pathology and audiology), N.J. Med. Soc., Bergen County Med. Soc., N.Y. County Med. Soc., Bergen County Soc. Otolaryngologists, Head and Neck Surgeons (past pres.), N.Y. Laryngol. Soc. (past pres.), N.Y. Bronchoscopic Soc. (past pres.), N.Y. Otol. Soc. (past pres.), N.J. Soc. Cosmetic Surgery (trustee), N.J. Acad. Ophthalmology and Otolaryngology-Head and Neck Surgery (past pres.), Royal Soc. Medicine, First Presbyn. Ch. Mens Assn. (past pres.), Phi Beta Kappa, Alpha Omega Alpha, Nu Sigma Nu. Presbyterian (elder, past clk. of session, past pres. bd. trustees). Clubs: N.Y. Athletic; Englewood (past pres., Disting. Service award 1980), Knickerbocker Country. Lodge: Rotary (past pres.). Home: 436 Lewelen Cir Englewood NJ 07631-2021 Office: 216 Engle St Englewood NJ 07631-2428

STRAUSS, STEVEN, pharmacy educator; b. Dec. 4, 1930. BS in Pharmacy, Bklyn. Coll. Pharmacy, 1955, MS in Pharmacy Adminstrn., 1965; PhD, U. Pitts., 1970. Registered pharmacist, N.Y., Fla., N.J.; cert. EMT, N.Y., advanced first aid, ARC. Asst. prof. Bklyn. Coll. Pharmacy, 1966-72, assoc. prof., 1972-81; prof. Schwartz Coll. Pharmacy, Bklyn., 1981—; notary pub., N.Y., 195—. Editor: U.S. Pharmacist mag., 1976-90; author numerous books, including: Patient Dosage Instructions - A Guide for Pharmacists, 1st edit., 1972, 3d edit., 1975, Patient Dosage Instructions - A Guide for Nurses, 1975, Your Prescription and You - A Pharmacy Handbook for Consumers, 1977, 5th edit. 1982, The Pharmacist and the Law, 1980, The Pharmacist's Answer Book, 1986, Strauss's Pharmacy Law and Examination Review Book, 1988, 3d rev. edit. 1995, Strauss's Pharmacy Law Examination Review Book - New York State, 1989, 5th edit., 1994, Strauss's Pharmacy Law Examination Review Book - New Jersey, 1990, 3d edit., 1993, Strauss's Pharmacy Law Examination Review Book - Florida, 1990, 3d edit. 1995, The Inverted Medical Dictionary, 1991, Medical Terminology for Pharmacists, 1991, Pharmacy Ethics, 1991, Understanding Medical Terms - A Guide for Pharmacy Practice, 1992; contbr. articles to profl. jours.; radio commentator and host "Health and Science News", Valhalla, N.Y., 1981, 82, Greenvale, N.Y., 1982. bd. dirs. Westchester Symphony Orchestra, 1987-95, v.p. 1988-95; coach Ardsley Arrows Soccer Club, 1979-80, Ardsley Little League, 1979; assoc. coach Ardsley Darts Soccer Club, 1979; Ardsley-Secor Vol. Ambulance Corps. 1982—, treas. 1986-88, others. With U.S. Army, 1956-62. Recipient Order of the Double Star, Alpha Zeta Omega Pharm. Fraternity, 1979, Disting. Alumni award U. Pitts., 1980, Alumni Assn., Arnold & Marie Schwartz Coll. of Pharmacy and Health Scis., 1980, 91, others. Mem. Masons (Master 1984-85), others.

STRAWDERMAN, TIMOTHY WAYNE, academic administrator; b. Bethesda, Md., Dec. 17, 1962; s. Larry Richard and Anna Margaret (Bowman) S. BS cum laude, Tex. A&M U., 1985, MPA, 1987. Grad. asst. dept. polit. sci. Tex. A&M U., College Station, 1985-87; analyst higher edn. Legis. Budget Bd., Austin, Tex., 1987-94; asst. dir. Health Policy Inst. U. Tex. Health Sci. Ctr., Houston, 1995—. Vol. Steven's House, Houston, 1995—, AIDS Svcs. of Austin, 1990-94; team mem. Christ the King Luth. AIDS Respite Care Team, Houston, 1995—. Mem. Pi Sigma Alpha, Phi Kappa Phi. Home: PO Box 541534 Houston TX 77254 Office: Health Policy Inst Ste 909 1200 Herman Pressler Houston TX 77030

STRAYER, DAVID S., medical educator; b. N.Y.C., Apr. 25, 1949; s. Robert and Julia B. (Aboulafia) S.; m. Frances, June 27, 1971 (div. June 1989); children: Reuben, Rebecca, Rachel; m. Marlene S., Nov. 23, 1991; children: Michelle, Joshua. AB in Chemistry, Cornell U., 1970; PhD in Pathology, U. Chgo., 1974, MD. Cert. Am. Bd. Pathology. Resident Washington U., St. Louis, 1976-79, instr., 1979-80; asst. prof. U. Calif., LaJolla, 1980-83; assoc. prof. Yale U. Sch. Medicine, New Haven, Conn., 1983-85; assoc. prof., prof. U. Tex. Health Sci. Ctr., Houston, 1986-92; prof. Jefferson Med. Coll., Phila., 1992—. Contbr. articles to profl. jours. Grantee NIH, Am. Cancer Soc., Coun. Tobacco Rsch. Mem. Am. Soc. Investigative Pathology, Am. Assn. Immunologists, Am. Soc. Urology, Am. Soc. Nicrobiology, Am. soc. Cell Biology. Office: Jefferson Med Coll 1020 Locust St Philadelphia PA 19107

STRECKER, E. BRADLEY, nurse, hospital administrator; b. Columbia, Mo., Mar. 1, 1957; s. John E. and Annetta Faye (Osborne) S. BS in Nursing, U. Wyo., 1983; MA in Health Care Adminstrn., Webster U., Kansas City. RN, Mo., Kans. Staff nurse Med. Ctr. Independence (Mo.), 1983-89, house supr., 1987-89; dir. ops. Gold Cross Ambulance, 1986-88; dir. critical care svcs. Heartland Hosps., St. Joseph, Mo., 1988-90; dir. neonatal svcs. Overland Park (Kans.) Regional Med. Ctr., 1990-95; asst. adminstr., COO Vencor Hosp., Kansas City, 1995—. Capt. USAFR, 1985. Mem. Am. Assn. Critical Care Nurses (cert.), Soc. Critical Care Medicine, Res. Officer Assn., Am. Heart Assn., Air Force Assn. Office: Vencor Hosp 8701 Troost Kansas City MO 64131

STREEM, STEVAN BRIAN, urologist, educator; b. Cleve., Nov. 30, 1949; m. Linda Smiley; 2 children. BS, U. Ill., 1971, MD, 1975. Bd. cert. Nat. Bd. Med. Examiners, Am. Bd. Urology. Resident gen. surgery Albany (N.Y.) Med. Ctr. Hosp., 1975-77, resident urology, 1977-80; spl. fellow renal transplantation Cleve. Clinic Found., 1981-82, staff physician dept. urology, head sect. stone diseases, 1983—; asst. prof. surgery Albany (N.Y.) Med. Coll.-Union U., 1980, Ohio State U. Coll. Medicine, Columbus, 1982; manuscript reviewer Jour. Urology, Urology, Jour. Endourology, Jour. Lithotripsy and Stone Disease, Transplantation Procs., Investigative Urology. Editor: Renal Stone Disease, 1985, (with AC Novick and EJ Pontes) Stewart's Operative Urology, 2d edit., 1989; contbr. chpts. to books and articles to profl. jours. Mem. ACS, Am. Soc. Transplant Surgeons, Am. Urol. Assn., Cleve. Urol. Assn. (past sec./treas., past pres.), Endourological Soc., Internat. Soc. Urologic Endoscopy, North Ctrl. Sect. Am. Urol. Assn. (rep. from Ohio Urologic Soc., chmn. bylaws com.), Ohio Urol. Soc., Rock Soc., Soc. Internat. d'Urologie, Soc. Univ. Urologists, Transplantation Soc., Transplantation Soc. Northeastern Ohio (past pres.), Urologic Soc. for Transplantation and Vascular Surgery, Phi Beta Kappa, Alpha Omega Alpha. Office: Cleve Clinic Found 9500 Euclid Ave Cleveland OH 44195

STREETEN, DAVID HENRY PALMER, internist, educator; b Bloemfontein, South Africa, Oct. 3, 1921; came to U.S., 1951; s. Reginald Craufurd and Olive Gladys (Palmer) S.; m. Barbara Anne Wiard, Aug. 2, 1952; children—Robert Duncan, Elizabeth Anne, John Palmer. B.Sc., U. Orange Free State (South Africa), 1941; M.B., B.Ch., U. Witwatersrand (South Africa), 1946; D.Phil., Oxford U., 1951. Diplomate Am. Bd. Internal Medicine (endocrinology). Nuffield Found. fellow, 1948-51; Rockefeller fellow, 1951-52; Howard Hughes fellow, 1959-61. Asst. prof. internal medicine U. Mich., Ann Arbor, 1955-60; assoc. prof. SUNY Upstate Med. Ctr., Syracuse, 1960-64, prof. Health Sci. Ctr., 1964—. Fellow AAAS, Royal Coll. Physicians, Am. Coll. Physicians; mem. Am. Diabetes Assn. (pres. Syracuse chpt. 1981-83), Cen. Soc. Clin. Rsch., Endocrine Soc. Internat. Soc. Hypertension, Am. Soc. Hypertension, Am. Autonomic Soc. (nat. pres. 1995-96). Episcopalian. Home: 334 Berkley Dr Syracuse NY 13210-3000 Office: 750 E Adams St Syracuse NY 13210-2306

STREETER, BERNARD ALBRA, JR., medical facility development and public affairs executive; b. Keene, N.H., Feb. 6, 1935; s. Bernard A. Sr. and Isabella Cameron (Crane) S.; m. Janice Bowman, Aug. 30, 1958; children: Shannon Lea, Christopher Bowman, Stephanie Crane. BS, Boston U., 1957. Dir. pub. rels. Colby Sawyer Coll., New London, N.H., 1959-63, Am. Cancer Soc., Boston, 1963-66; dir. devel. Somerville (Mass.) Hosp., 1966-68; v.p. devel., found. v.p., exec. dir. Saints Meml. Med. Ctr., Lowell, Mass., 1968-94; v.p. pub. affairs So. N.H. Regional Med. Ctr., Nashua, 1994—; exec. councilor State of N.H., Concord, 1969—; bd. dirs. The Plus Co. Bd. dirs. Greater Nashua United Way, 1994—, Marguerite's Pl., Nashua, 1993—. Sgt. USAFR, 1957-63. Dir. Am. Stage Festival, 1991—; bd. dirs. French Hill Neighborhood Housing Svcs., 1996—. Sgt. USAF Res., 1957-63. Recipient Outstanding Hosp. Pub. Rels. award Mass. Hosp. Assn., 1969, 71; named Outstanding Young Man of the Yr., N.H. Jaycees, 1966. Mem. Am. Hosp. Assn., Assn. for Health Care Philanthropy, Am. Hosp. Pub. Rels. and Mktg., Rotary (Nashua West club), Greater Nashua C. of C. Republican. Methodist. Home: 26 Indiana Dr Nashua NH 03060-5132 Office: So NH Regional Med Ctr PO Box 2014 Nashua NH 03061-2014

STRENGER, GEORGE, surgeon; b. N.Y., Sept. 5, 1906; s. Philip and Tillie (Strassman) S.; m. Florence Serxner, June 9, 1931; children: Philip J., Laurence N. BA, Columbia U., 1928, MD, 1931. Diplomate Am. Bd. Surg., 1942. surgeon Bklyn. Jew. Hosp., N.Y., 1934-72, Goldwater Meml. Hosp., N.Y., 1939-53; chief surg. svc. N.Y. regional office VA, 1948-72; surgeon Coney Island Hosp., N.Y., 1953-72; instr. Long Island Med. Coll., N.Y., 1934-36. Mem. Ditmas Pk. Assn. (pres. 1953-54). Comdr. field hosp. U.S. Army, 1942-46, ETO. Recipient commendation Gen. Eisenhower, 1945. Fellow Am. Coll. Surgeons. Home: 31397 E Nine Dr Laguna Niguel CA 92677-2909

STRESING, HARLAND ALBERT, urology educator; b. Dec. 7, 1944; s. Albert A. and Martha (Jourdan) S.; widowed; children: Sam, Jason. BA, Baylor U., 1966; MD, Med. U. S.C., 1970. Intern Med. U. S.C., Charleston, 1970-71; resident in gen. surgery La. State U., New Orleans, 1973-74; resident in urology Med. U. S.C., Charleston, 1974-77; assoc. clin. prof. urology Med. U. S.C., Spartanburg, 1991—; med. dir. Spartanburg Urology Surg. Ctr., 1993—; mem. bd. dirs. Cmty. Clin. Oncology Program Spartanburg Reg. Med. Ctr. Capt. U.S. Army, 1971-73, Vietnam. Decorated Bronze star. Fellow Am. Coll. Surgeons; mem. Am. Urol. Assn., S.C. Med. Assn. (del. 1977—), Spartanburg County Med. Assn., Lions. Lutheran. Office: 391 Serpentine Dr Ste 500 Spartanburg SC 29303

STRICK, SADIE ELAINE, psychologist; b. Masontown, Pa., May 5, 1929; d. Michael and Mary (Oziemblowski) Wierzbicki; m. John Mackovjak, Dec. 31, 1947 (dec. Mar. 1972); children: Deborah, Susan; m. Ellis Strick, Aug. 11, 1974. BSW, U. Pitts., 1975, MEd, 1977, PhD, 1981. Lic. psychologist; fellow, diplomate Am. Bd. Med. Psychotherapists. Psychologist I Mayview State Hosp., Bridgeville, Pa., 1984-87; owner Counseling & Behavior Specialists, P.C., Pitts., 1981—; mem. C.G. Jung Ednl. Ctr., Pitts., 1980—; guest speaker Compassionate Friends, Pitts., 1986—, Womens Career Conv., Pitts., 1982. Bd. dirs. OAR/Allegheny, Pitts., 1981-82. Fellow Pa. Psychol. Assn.; mem. Am. Psychol. Assn., Pitts. Assn. for Theory and Practice of Psychoanalysis. Home: 2160 Greentree Rd Apt 605 Pittsburgh PA 15220-1437 Office: Counseling and Behavior Specialists PC 429 Forbes Ave Ste 1614 Pittsburgh PA 15219-1604

STRICKER, RAPHAEL BECHER, hematologist; b. N.Y.C., Jan. 7, 1950; s. William and Jenny (Becher) S. BA, Columbia U., 1971, MD, 1978. Resident St. Lukes-Roosevelt Hosp., N.Y.C., 1978-81; fellow U. Calif., San Francisco, 1981-84, rsch. scholar, 1984-85, instr., 1985-86, asst. prof., 1986-89; assoc. dir. immunotherapy div. Calif. Pacific Med. Ctr., San Francisco, 1989-93; assoc. med. dir. HemaCare Corp., 1993—; assoc. dir. Bay Area Mobile Apheresis Program, San Francisco, 1990-93. Contbr. articles to profl. jours. and chpts. to books. NIH grantee, 1982-84, 87-89, Am. Heart Assn. grantee, 1985-87, AIDS Task Force grantee, 1987-89, Taylor Found. grantee, 1989—. Mem. So. Med. Assn., AAAS, WWF, Am. Soc. Hematology, Am. Fedn. for Clin. Rsch., Am. Soc. for Apheresis, World Affairs Coun., Smithsonian Assocs., Nat. Geographic Soc. Democrat. Jewish. Office: HemaCare Corp 450 Sutter St Rm 1504 San Francisco CA 94108-4004

STRICKLAND, (CATHERINE) MICHELLE, physician assistant; b. Marietta, Ga., Nov. 2, 1968; d. Michael Richard and Catherine Linda (Folkerts) S. BS in Biology, North Ga. Coll., 1991; BS, Med. Coll. Ga., 1994. Cert. physician asst., Ga. Personnel records specialist Ga. Army Nat. Guard, Atlanta, 1987-91; emergency med. technician Bartow County EMS, Cartersville, Ga., 1992; surg. physician asst. Dr. David Thompson, MD, Rome, Ga., 1994—; physician asst. Rome Emergency Physicians, 1994—. Med. svc. officer Nat. Guard U.S.A., Atlanta, 1991—, 1st lt. Fellow Am. Assn. Physician Assts., Ga. Assn.Physician Assts. (regional coord. liaison 1994—). Baptist. Office: Floyd Emergency Rm Turner McCall Blvd Rome GA 30161

STRICKLAND, SANDRA JEAN HEINRICH, nursing educator; b. Tucson, Sept. 18, 1943; d. Henry and Ada (Schmidt) Heinrich; BS, U. Tex. Sch. Nursing, 1965; MS in Nursing (fellow), U. Md., 1969; DrPH, U. Tex., 1978; m. William C. Strickland, Aug. 18, 1973; children: William Henry, Angela Lee. Clin. instr. U. Tex. Sch. Nursing, Galveston, 1965-66; staff nurse Hidalgo County Health Dept., Edinburg, Tex., 1966-67; supr. nursing Tex. Dept. Health Tb Control, Austin, 1969-70; instr. St. Luke's Hosp. Sch. Nursing, Houston, 1971-72, Tex. Women's U. Sch. Nursing, Houston and Dallas, 1972-73; dir. nursing Dallas City Health Dept., 1974-80; assoc. prof. community health nursing grad. program Tex. Woman's U., Dallas, 1980-87, U. Incarnate Word, 1987—; mem. profl. adv. com. Dallas Vis. Nurse Assn., 1978-83, Santa Rosa Home Health Agy., 1991-94; mem. health adv. bd. Dallas Ind. Sch. Dist., 1976-84; chmn. nursing and health services Dallas chpt. ARC, 1984-86, bd. dirs. San Antonio chpt., 1990; Tex. Lung Assn., 1991—, bd. dirs. San Antonio Chpt., Tex. Public Health Assn. fellow, 1977. Mem. APHA, Tex. Public Health Assn., Sigma Theta Tau. Methodist. Home: 508 US Highway 90 E Castroville TX 78009-5230

STRICKLER, HOWARD MARTIN, physician; b. New Haven, Conn., Oct. 26, 1950; s. Thomas David and Mildred Laing (Martin) S.; m. Susan Hunter, May 2, 1982; children: Hunter Gregory, Howard Martin Jr. BA, Berea Coll., 1975; MD, Univ. Louisville, 1979. Diplomate Am. Bd. Family Practice. Resident Anniston (Ala.) Family Practice Residency, 1979-82; pvt. practice Monteagle, Tenn., 1982-85; fellow in addictive diseases Willingway Hosp., Statesboro, Ga., 1985-86; faculty devel. fellow Univ. N.C., Chapel Hill, 1985-86; pvt. practice Birmingham, Ala., 1986-90; pres. Employers Drug Program Mgmt., Inc., Birmingham, 1990—; med. dir. Am. Health Svcs., Inc., 1993—; med. dir. Bradford Facilities, Birmingham, 1987-90, New Life Clinic, Bessemer, ala., Physicians Smoke Free Clinic, Birmingham, 1988-90, Am. Health Svcs., Inc., 1993—; chmn. dept. family practice and emergency medicine Bessemer Carraway Med. Ctr., 1993-95. With U.S. Army, 1969-72, Vietnam. Decorated Bronze Star, 1971, Vietnam Campaign medal, Vietnam Svc. medal 3 Stars, 1971. Fellow Am. Acad. Family Physicians; mem. Am. Soc. Addiction Medicine (cert.), Am. Coll. Occupl. and Environ. Medicine, Am. Assn. Med. Rev. Officers (cert.), Med. Assn. State of Ala., Am. Bd. Forensic Examiners, Phi Kappa Phi. Methodist. Home: 868 Tulip Poplar Dr Birmingham AL 35244-1633 Office: 616 9th St S Birmingham AL 35233-1113

STRICKLER, JEFFREY HAROLD, pediatrician; b. Mpls., Oct. 14, 1943; s. Jacob Harold and Helen Cecelia (Mitchell) S.; m. Karen Anne Stewart, June 18, 1966; children: Hans Stewart, Liesl Ann. BA, Carleton Coll., 1965; MD, U. Minn., 1969. Diplomate Am. Bd. Pediatrics. Resident in pediatrics Stanford (Calif.) U., 1969-73; pvt. practice Helena, Mont., 1975—; chief staff Shodair Children's Hosp., Helena, 1984-86; dir. maternal-child health Lewis and Clark County, Helena, 1978-88; chief of staff St. Peters Hosp., Helena, 1994-96; bd.dirs. Helena Health Alliance. Mem. Mont. Gov.'s Task Force on Child Abuse, 1978-79; mem. steering com. Region VIII Child Abuse Prevention, Denver, 1979-82; bd. dirs. Helena Dist. 1 Sch. Bd., 1982-88, vice chmn., 1985-87. Maj. M.C., USAF, 1973-75. Fellow Am. Acad. Pediatrics (vice chmn. Mont. chpt. 1981-84, chmn. 1984-87, mem. nat. nominating com. 1987-90, chmn. 1989-90, coun. on govt. affairs 1990-96, Wyeth award 1987); mem. Rotary (youth exchange chmn. dist. 539, 1984-88, pres. Helena 1988-89). Office: Helena Pediatric Clinic 1122 N Montana Ave Helena MT 59601-3513

STRIEFEL, SEBASTIAN, psychologist, educator; b. Orrin, N.D., May 18, 1941; s. Anton and Pauline (Wentz) S.; m. Janet L. Hager, June 19, 1965 (div. 1975); children: Marnie R., Seth R. BS, S.D. State U., 1964; MA, U. S.D., 1966; PhD, U. Kans., 1968. Diplomate Am. Bd. Adminstrv. Psychology; diplomate in neurofeedback. Rsch. assoc., adj. asst. prof. U. Kans., Parsons, 1970-74; pvt. practice psychology Parsons, 1972-74, Logan, Utah, 1974—; asst. prof. psychology Utah State U., Logan, 1974-76; dir. div. svcs. Utah State U., 1975—, assoc. prof. psychology, 1976-80, prof. psychology, 1980—; cons. in field; vis. scientist U. S. Fla. Mental Health Inst., Tampa, 1987-88; vis. prof. U. Tex., 1994-95. Author: (with others): Functional Integration for Success: Preschool Intervention, 1991, (with M.J. Cadez) The program Assessment and Planning Guide for Developmentally Disabled and Preschool Children, 1983; author: How to Teach Through Modeling and Imitation, 1981, others; contbr. numerous articles to profl. jours. Mem. adv. bd. sys. change Utah Office Edn., Salt Lake City, 1989-90; mem. select com. Div. Svcs. for Handicapped, 1990; mem. Legis. Task Force, State of Utah, 1989-90; mem. Cache County Human Resource Com., 1979—, others. Capt. U.S. Army, 1968-70. Recipient Shiela Adler Svc. award, Assn. Applied Psychophysiology/Biofeedback, 1988, Individual Merit award, Mt. Plains Resource Ctr. for Deaf/Blind, 1983; numerous grants, 1970—. Fellow Am. Assn. Mental Deficiency, Am. Bd. Med. Psychotherapists; mem. APA, Utah Bd. Mental Health (chmn. 1989-91), Assn. Applied Psychophysiology and Biofeedback (treas. 1989-95, pres.-elect 1996—, cert. neurotherapist 1995—). Roman catholic. Office: Ctr for Persons Disabilitie UMC 6800 Utah State Univ Logan UT 84322

STRIMEL, WILLIAM HOSKIN, JR., pathologist, health facility administrator; b. Norristown, Pa., Aug. 23, 1924; s. William Hoskin and Emma Mae (Robinson) S.; m. Claudia Ruth Feldner, Apr. 10, 1947 (div. Apr. 1982); children: Kathleen may, Marianne Ruth; m. Nancy Lynn Beighley, Apr. 22, 1982; 1 child, Abigail Cristy. BS, Rutgers U., 1948; MD, Jefferson Med. Coll., 1952. Rotating intern Germantown Hosp., Phila., 1952-53, resident in pathology, 1953-57; resident in pathology New Eng. Deaconess Hosp., Boston, 1958-59; pathologist Germantown Hosp., Phila., 1959-76, chmn. dept. pathology, 1976-81; dir. labs. Champlain Valley/Physician Hosp., Plattsburgh, N.Y., 1981—. Coroners physician Clinton County, N.Y., 1995—. Sgt. U.S. Army, 1943-46. Mem. Clinton County Med. Soc. (pres. 1994-96). Republican. Methodist. Home: 146 Sunrise Dr Plattsburgh NY 12901 Office: Champlain Valley Physicians Hosp 75 Beekman St Plattsburgh NY 12901

STRIMER, ROBERT MERRILL, JR., urologist; b. Parkersburg, W. Va., Feb. 3, 1943; s. Robert Merrill and Jane Rose (Overton) S.; m. Diane Leigh Taylor, July 4, 1970; children: Kirstin Anna, Robert Merrill III, Rebecca Leigh. BA, Amherst Coll., 1965; MD, Case Western Res. U., 1969. Diplomate Am. Bd. Urology. Pvt. practice Greeneville, Tenn., 1976—. Maj. USAF, 1971-73. Republican. Episcopalian. Home: 430 Patricia Ln Greeneville TN 37743 Office: 1410 Tusculean Blvd #1000 Greeneville TN 37745-3816

STRISOWER, SUZANNE, clinical hypnotherapist, counselor; b. San Francisco, Oct. 27, 1956; d. Edward Herman and Beverly Gene (Boutell) S. BFA, JFK U., Orinda, Calif., 1988; MA, Pacifica Grad. Inst., 1994. Cert. clin. hypnotherapist; cert. counselor. Wallcovering installer Orinda, Calif., 1974-82; interior designer Lyons, Hill & Ruga Inc., Pleasant Hill, Calif., 1983-85; project mgr. Wayne Ruga Inc., Martinez, Calif., 1985-88; exec. dir. Nat. Symposium for Healthcare Interior Design, Martinez, 1986-88; treatment counselor Youth Homes Inc., Walnut Creek, Calif., 1988-93; clin. hypnotherapist The Inner Journey, Walnut Creek, Calif., 1991—, marriage, family and child counselor, 1994-95; aide and community liaison to supr. Contra Costa County Dist. II, 1995——; tchr. Acalanes Adult Edn. Ctr., Walnut Creek, 1992—; lectr. in field. Child advisor, vice chairperson Contra Costa County Mental Health Commn., 1991-93; pres. Orgn. of Youth Svcs., 1991-94; mem. Juv. Justice Delinquency Prevention Commn. Contra Costa County, 1988-95, mem. family and children's trust com., mem. juv. sys. planning adv. com. Mem. Am. Coun. Hypnotist Examiners. Home: 4143 Chaucer Dr Concord CA 94521

STROBER, MARK DAVID, physician; b. Rochester, N.Y., Aug. 18, 1962; s. Warren and Susan (Backinoff) S. BA, U. Rochester, 1984; MD, Albert Einstein Coll. Med., 1988. Diplomate Am. Bd. Nuclear Medicine. Attending physician St. Joseph Med. Ctr., Towson, Md., 1992—; attending physician Laurel (Md.) Regional Hosp., 1994—. Mem. Am. Coll. Nuclear Physicians, Soc. Nuclear Medicine. Office: 7620 York Rd Baltimore MD 21204-7508

STROBER, SAMUEL, immunologist, educator; b. N.Y.C., May 8, 1940; s. Julius and Lee (Lander) S.; m. Linda Carol Higgins, July 6, 1991; children: William, Jesse; children from previous marriage: Jason, Elizabeth. AB in Liberal Arts, Columbia U., 1961; MD magna cum laude, Harvard U., 1966. Intern Mass. Gen. Hosp., Boston, 1966-67; resident in internal medicine Stanford U. Hosp., Calif., 1970-71; rsch. fellow Peter Bent Brigham Hosp., Boston, 1962-63, 65-66, Oxford U., Eng., 1963-64; rsch. assoc. Lab. Cell Biology, Nat. Cancer Inst., NIH, Bethesda, Md., 1967-70; instr. medicine Stanford U., 1971-72, asst. prof., 1972-78, assoc. prof. medicine, 1978-82, prof. medicine, 1982—, Diane Goldstone Meml. lectr., John Putnam Merrill Meml. lectr., chief div. immunology and rheumatology, 1978—; investigator Howard Hughes Med. Inst., Miami, Fla., 1976-81. Assoc. editor Jour. Immunology, 1981-84, Transplantation, 1981-85, Internat. Jour. Immunotherapy, 1985—, Transplant Immunology, 1992—; contbr. articles to profl. jours. bd. dirs. La Jolla Inst. for Allergy and Immunology; founder Activated Cell Therapy, Inc. Served with USPHS, 1967-70. Recipient Leon Reznick Meml. Research prize Harvard U., 1966. Mem. Am. Assn. Immunology, Am. Soc. Clin. Investigation, Am. Rheumatism Assn., Transplantation Soc. (councilor 1986-89), Am. Soc. Transplantation Physicians, Western Soc. Medicine, Am. Assn. Physicians, Clin. Immunology Soc. (pres. 1996), Alpha Omega. Home: 435 Golden Oak Dr Menlo Park CA 94028-7734 Office: Stanford U Sch Medicine 300 Pasteur Dr Palo Alto CA 94305

STRODE, GERALD MARVIN, physician assistant; b. Fargo, N.D., Sept. 25, 1946; s. Marvin Lloyd Strode and Ruth Elaine (Holt) Gabert; m. Cheryl Helen Ford, Sept. 25, 1982; children: Gerald John, Nicholas Daniel. Grad., U. Utah, 1975; DHL (hon.), U. Humanatic Studies, 1986. Cert. physician asst. Commd. USNG, 1966, advanced through grades to; dir. rural outreach program Vets. Adminstrn., Salt Lake City, 1983-88; mem. staff physician assts. Valley Children's Hosp., Fresno, Calif., 1990-94; physician asst. Washington Orthop. and Sports Medicine, Kirkland, Wash., 1994-95; owner Physician Asst. Surg. Svcs., Kirkland, 1995—; chmn. Wash. Gov. Com. on Employment of Handicapped, Olympia, 1976-78; advisor Wash. State Bd. Med. Examiners, Olympia, 1978-82. Decorated Navy Cross. Fellow Am. Acad. Physician Assts. (del.), Wash. Acad. Physician Assts. (pres. 1979, 81), Physician Assts. Orthop. Surgery (pres.-elect 1995); mem. Ducks Unltd. (area and zone chmn. 1988—, Disting. Svc. award 1993). Republican.

Lutheran. Home: 15401 206th Ave NE Woodinville WA 98072 Office: Physician Asst Surg Svcs Kirkland WA 98034

STRODE, STEVEN WAYNE, physician; b. Dallas, Jan. 4, 1949; s. Royall Maurice and Maida (Somerville) S.; m. Peggy Lee O'Neill, Sept. 21, 1974; children: Sean Wayne, Colleen Leigh. BS, So. Meth. U., 1969; MD, U. Tex. Southwestern Med. Sch., 1974. Intern U. Ark. for Med. Scis., Little Rock, 1974-75; resident in family practice U. Ark. for Med. Scis., Little Rock, 1974-77, chief resident in family medicine, 1976-77, assoc. prof. dept. family and community medicine, 1978—; med. dir. Rural Hosp. Program; dir. Telemedicine Programs; teaching fellow in family medicine U. Western Ont., London, Can., 1977; pvt. practice family medicine, Jacksonville, Ark., 1977, Sherwood, Ark., 1980-84. Diplomate Am. Bd. Family Practice. Fellow Am. Acad. Family Physicians; mem. Ark. Acad. Family Physicians (v.p., pres.), Soc. Tchrs. Family Medicine, Phi Beta Kappa, Phi Eta Sigma, Beta Beta Beta. Methodist. Home: 104 Charter Ct North Little Rock AR 72120-5049 Office: U Ark Med Scis 4301 W. Market Lane Slot # 599A Little Rock AR 72205

STROEBEL, GEORGE E., anesthesiologist; b. Wheeling, W. Va., Nov. 9, 1936; s. George E. and Loueline (White) S. AB, Harvard Coll., 1958; MD, Harvard U. Anesthesiologist U.S.A.F., 1966-68, U. Pa., 1966-75; anesthesiologist Reading (Pa.) Hosp., 1975-90, pain mgmt. specialist, 1990—. Bd. dirs. Rainbow Home (AIDS Hosp.), Banks County, Pa. Capt. USAF. Office: Pain Mgmt Svcs 14 Philadelphia Ave Shillington PA 19607

STROHECKER, LEON HARRY, JR., orthodontist; b. Schuylkill Haven, Pa., Aug. 14, 1932; s. Leon Harry and Anna (Fabian) S.; m. Juanita Mary Puyoou, Apr. 13, 1957; children: Sandra Lee Strohecker Beckett, Leon Harry III. Student, U. Pa., 1950-53, DDS, 1957, orthodontic cert., 1960. Bd. cert. Am. Bd. Orthodontics. Pres., pvt. practice Lansdale, Pa., 1961—; dir. Face Head & Neck Pain and Trauma Ctr., Lansdale, 1987—; bd. dirs. Artman Home Retirement Ctr., Ambler; treas., bd. dirs. Valley Ctr. Mental Health Clinic, Lansdale, 1984—; guest lectr. in field. Pres. Lansdale Rotary Club, 1967-68; coun. mem. Trinity Luth. Ch., Lansdale, 1977-85, chmn. fin. com., 1980-85. Lt. (j.g.) USN, 1957-59. Mem. ADA, Internat. Acad. Head, Neck and Facial Pain, Internat. Coll. Cranio-Mandibular Orthopedics, Am. Acad. Pain Mgmt. (diplomate), Am. Assn. for Functional Orthodontics, Am. Profl. Practice Assn., Am. Soc. Dentistry for Children, Am. Acad. Oral Medicine, Am. Assn. Orthodontists, Am. Assn. Stomatologists, Am. Acad. Oral Medicine, Middle Atlantic Orthodontic Soc., Pa. Orthodontic Soc., Phila. Orthodontic Soc., Pa. Dental Assn., Second Dist. Dental Assn., Montgomery-Bucks Dental Soc., Alpha Omega, Omicron Kappa Epsilon. Home: 1512 Cedar Hill Rd Ambler PA 19002 Office: 456 E Hancock St Lansdale PA 19446

STROHLEIN, STEPHEN SANTO, physician; b. Bklyn., Apr. 7, 1953; s. James Michael and Carmella (LaSenna) S.; m. Annette Vazquez-Aran, June 8, 1985; children: Lisa Marie, Marissa Lynn. BA in Biology, Lafayete Coll., Easton, Pa., 1976; MD in Surgery, U. Rome (Italy), 1982. Diplomate Am. Bd. Internal Medicine and Gastroenterology. Intern, resident Interfaith Med. Ctr., Bklyn., 1982-84, chief resident in Medicine, 1984-85, fellow in Gastroenterology, 1985-86; sr. fellow in Gastroenterology Tufts U., Boston, 1986-87; mem. staff in Gastroenterology Pocono Med. Ctr., East Stroudsburg, Pa., 1987—, dir. Endoscopy, 1988—. Fellow Am. Coll. Gastroenterology; mem. ACP, NRA, Am. Gastroenterological Assn. Office: PO Box 301 East Stroudsburg PA 18301-0301

STROJNY, NORMAN, analytical chemist; b. Edwardsville, Pa., June 14, 1943; s. John M. and Brunislawa (Stawarz) S. BS in Chemistry, Wilkes Coll., 1966; MS in Chemistry, Montclair State Coll., 1974; PhD in Analyt. Chemistry, Rutgers U., 1980, MBA in Mgmt., 1985. From jr. chemist to sr. chemist Hoffmann LaRoche, Nutley, N.J., 1965-85; from sr. chemist to supr. Danbury Pharmacal, Carmel, N.Y., 1985—. Contbr. articles to profl. jours. Mem. APHA, Am. Chem. Soc., Am. Inst. Chemistry, Soc. Applied Spectroscopy (local chmn. 1983-84, ea. analytical symposium bd. dirs. 1983-84). Office: Danbury Pharmacal PO Box 990 Stoneleigh Ave Carmel NY 10512

STROM, PRISCILLA RUTH, surgeon; b. Darjeeling, India, May 19, 1952; (parents Am. citizens); d. Richard B. and Donna E. (Young) S. BA, Covenant Coll., Lookout Mountain, Ga., 1972; MD, Emory U., 1976. Diplomate Am. Bd. Surgery. Resident in gen. surgery Emory U. Sch. Medicine, Atlanta, 1976-81, fellow in trauma, 1981-82; med. dir., missionary surgeon Lamb Hosp., Parbatipur, Bangladesh, 1984-94; pvt. practice, Gainesville, Ga., 1994—. Contbr. articles to med. jours. Vol. physician Good News Cmty. Health Ctr., Gainesville, 1994—. Named Alumna of Yr., Covenant Coll. Alumni Assn., 1982. Fellow ACS; mem. Assn. Women Surgeons, So. Med. Assn., Hall County Med. Soc., Christian Med. and Dental Soc. Office: Dixon & Dixon 669 Lanier Park Dr NE Gainesville GA 30505

STROM, TERRY BARTON, physician, immunologist; b. Chgo., Nov. 30, 1941; s. David and Sylvia (Abelson) S.; m. Margot Stern, Aug. 2, 1964; children: Adam, Rachel. Student U. Ill.-Chgo./Urbana, 1959-62; M.D., U. Ill. Coll. Medicine, Chgo., 1966; MA (hon.) Harvard U., 1989; DSc (hon.) Hahnemann U., 1990. Diplomate Am. Bd. Internal Medicine. Intern/jr. resident U. Ill. Hosp., Chgo., 1966-68; sr. resident in internal medicine Beth Israel Hosp., Boston, 1970-71; research fellow in medicine Peter Bent Brigham Hosp. and Harvard Med. Sch., Boston, 1971-73; asst. prof. medicine Harvard Med. Sch., 1974-78, assoc. prof. medicine, 1978-88, prof. medicine, 1988—; med. dir. renal transplant svc. Peter Bent Brigham Hosp., 1973-83, assoc. dir. lab. immunogenetics and transplantation; sr. physician Beth Israel Hosp., med. dir. renal transplant service, 1983—, dir. div. clin. immunology, 1983—; Lilly lectr. Royal Coll. Physicians, London, 1991; Clarke lectr. U. Pa., 1995; Billingham vis. prof. Vanderbilt U., 1990; Bernard Pimstone vis. prof. U. Capetown, 1995. Author: 4 books, contbr. 400 articles to profl. jours.; also holder 6 patents. Campaign worker polit. campaigns and peace orgns.; mem. U.S. Congl. Task Force on Transplantation, 1985-87, adv. panel for allergy and transplantation NIAID, 1988-91, NIH; cons. FDA, 1993—. Served to capt. USAF, 1968-70. Ill. State Scholar, 1959-56; recipient Rsch. Career Devel. award NIH, 1976-81; Acad. Honors Day award U. Ill., 1959-61; Ill. State scholar, 1959-66. Fellow Molecular Medicine Soc.; mem. Internat. Soc. Nephrology (councilor), Assn. Am. Immunologists, Internat. Transplant Soc., Am. Soc. Clin. Investigation, Am. Soc. Transplant Physicians (founding past pres. 1981), Assn. Am. Phys., Clin. Immunol. Soc. (pres. 1990), Inter Urban Clin. Club. Democrat. Jewish. Office: Beth Israel Hosp 330 Brookline Ave Boston MA 02215-5400

STROME, MARSHALL, otolaryngologist, educator; b. Lynn, Mass., Apr. 27, 1940; s. David and Rose (Cantor) S.; m. Deena Lazarov, Sept. 23, 1962; children: Scott Eric, Randall Alan. Degree, U. Mich., 1960, MD, 1964, MS, 1970. Resident in otolaryngology U. Mich., Ann Arbor, 1966-70; asst. prof. U. Conn., Hartford, 1971; asst. prof. Beth Israel-Harvard, Boston, 1972-77, chief otolaryngology, 1977-93; prof., chmn. otolaryngology Cleve. Clinic Found., 1993—; sr. surgeon Brigham & Women's Hosp., Boston, 1982-93; assoc. prof. harvard Med. Sch., Boston, 1989-93, Longwood ORL coord., 1982-90; mem. cons. bd. Xomed Treace Corp., Jacksonville, Fla., 1987-90; advisor SLT Laser Corp., Oaks, Pa., 1994—; dir. Great Comebacks, Gresham, Oreg. Mem. editl. bd. Harvard Health News Letter, 1976-85; author: Differential Diagnoses in Pediatric ORL, 1975; editor: Manual of Otolaryngology, 1985, Complications of Laser Surgery of the Head and Neck, 1986. Mem. fund raising com. Belmont Hill (Mass.) Sch., 1984. Capt. U.S. Army, 1965-71. Recipient Medal, City of Paris, 1987, Sword of Saudi Arabia, 1991; named One of Best Doctors in Cleve., Cleve. Mag., 1995. Fellow ACS; mem. Am. Acad. Facial Plastic Reconstructive Surgery (Medallion of Honor 1989), Am. Acad. Otolaryngology (Honor award 1987), Am. Soc. Head and Neck Surgery; mem. Triological Soc. ((v.p. 1990-91), Cartesian Soc. (pres. 1989), U. Mich. Med. Ctr. Alumni Soc. (chair bd. govs. 1992-93, host alumni function 1994, coord. New Eng. Fund Raising 1992). Office: Cleve Clinic Found 9500 Euclid Ave Cleveland OH 44195

STROMINGER, JACK LEONARD, biochemist; b. N.Y.C., Aug. 7, 1925. AB, Harvard U., 1944; MD, Yale U., 1948; DSc (hon.), Trinity Coll., Dublin, 1975, Washington U., 1988. From asst. prof. to prof. pharmacology sch. med. Washington U., St. Louis, 1955-61, prof. pharmacology and microbiology, 1961-64; prof. pharmacology and chem. microbiology med. sch. U. Wis., Madison, 1964-68; prof. biochemistry Harvard U., 1968-83, chmn. dept. biochemistry and molecular biology, 1970-73, Higgins prof. biochemistry, 1983—; head tumor virol. divsn. Dana-Farber Cancer Inst., Boston, 1977—. Recipient John J. Abel award, 1960, Paul-Lewis Lab award, 1962, Rose Payne award Am. Soc. Histocompat. & Immunogen., 1986, Hoechst-Roussel award, 1990, Pasteur medal, 1990, Albert Lasker Award for Basic Med. Rsch., 1995; named Passano Found. laureate, 1993. Mem. NAS (mem. inst. medicine, Microbiology award 1968, Selman Waxman award 1968), AAAS, Am. Soc. Biol. Chemists, Am. Soc. Pharmacology & Exptl. Therapeutics, Am. Assn. Immunologists, Am. Soc. Microbiologists, Am. Chem. Soc., Am. Acad. Arts & Sci., European Molecular Biol. Orgn., Sigma Xi. Office: Dana Farber Cancer Inst Dept of Biochem 44 Binney St Boston MA 02115-6013*

STROMME, LU ANN JOY, nurse, educator; b. Devils Lake, N.D., Aug. 17, 1958; d. James Arthur and Janet Joy (Miller) Ackerman; m. James Robert Stromme, June 1, 1985; children: Trent James, Trevor John, Danielle Leigh. BS, N.D. State U., 1980; postgrad., U. Minn., 1981; diploma, St. Luke's Sch. Nursing, 1984. RN, N.D.; cert. tchr., N.D.; cert. infection control. Instr. domestic sci. Royal Russel Acad., London, Eng., 1980; instr. home econs. Buffalo (Minn.) High Sch., 1981-82; nurse technician St. Luke's Hosp., Fargo, N.D., 1982-84; resident mgr. Coldwell Banker-1st Realty, Fargo, N.D., 1982-83; neuro ICU nurse U. Tex. Med. Ctr., Galveston, 1984-85; critical care nurse Mercy Hosp., Devils Lake, 1985-89; staff devel. coord., dir. edn., infection control practitioner, Medicare coord. Lake Region Luth. Home, Devils Lake, 1989-91, safety chmn., 1990-91, infection control pratitioner, 1991—; nursing asst. manual skills examiner Psychol. Corp., Devils Lake, 1989—. Author newspaper editorial Honoring Our Elderly Residents, 1990, Long Term Care Recognition, 1991. Instr. water safety ARC, N.D., 1977—; instr. CPR, Am. Heart Assn., N.D., 1982—, instr. ACLS, 1988-91; tchr. mem. com. Our Saviors Luth. Ch., Devils Lake, 1985—; mem. Lake Region Job Svc. Employers Com. Bush Found. grantee, 1981; named Outstanding Young Woman in Am., 1988. Mem. AAUW (program v.p. 1992-94, branch pres. 1994-96, state treas. 1995-97), AACN (Devil's Lake Dist. Equity com. rep. 1994-97), Mortar Bd. (officer 1979-80), Phi Upsilon Omicron (officer 1979-80). Home: HC 1 # 164 Crary ND 58327-9801

STRONG, DAVID WARREN, urologist; b. Lansing, Mich., May 30, 1943; s. Warren Murray and Kathleen Louise (Kieppe) S.; m. Jacquelene Sue Wallace, June 15, 1967; children: Kimberly Ann Strong Moss, Vicki Lynn. BA, Yale U., 1965; MD, Wayne State U., 1969. Diplomate Am. Bd. Urology. Intern Cleve. Metro. Gen. Hosp., 1969-70; resident gen. surgery, urology U. Oreg. Med. Sch., Portland, 1970-76; lt. cmdr. U.S. Navy, San Diego, 1976-78; pvt. practice urology Phoenix, 1978—. Fellow Am. Coll. Surgeons; mem. Internat. Soc. Urology, Am. Urol. Assn. Republican. Office: Canyon State Urology 4616 N 51st Ave #206 Phoenix AZ 85031-1716

STRONG, LEROY E., physician; b. Remus, Mich., May 26, 1933; s. Roy F. and Veda Dorothy (Main) S.; m. Marjorie L. Carr (div. Dec. 1980); children: Bruce, Ruth, John, Elizabeth; m. Linda H. Baehr Strong, Feb. 20, 1982; children: Nathan, Benjamin, Katharine, Anna, Samuel. MD, U. Mich., 1957. Intern William Beaumont Gen. Hosp., El Paso, Tex., 1957-58, resident, 1958-60, 1960-63; Diplomate Am. Bd. Ophthalmology. Lt. col. U.S. Army Res., 1993. Fellow Am. Acad. Ophthalmology (alt.), Am. Coll. Surgeons, Mich. Ophthalmol. Soc., Vitreous Soc., Great Lakes Retina Soc., Kent County Med. Soc., Mich. State Med. Soc. Lutheran. Home: 1960 Cascade Farms Dr SE Grand Rapids MI 49546 Office: Assoc Retinal Cons 1000 E Paris SE Grand Rapids MI 49546

STRONG, LINDA RAE, pediatrician; b. Ponca City, Okla., June 9, 1953; d. Robert Sherman and Blanche Selma (Tanner) Mathews; m. John C. Strong, May 28, 1978; children: Whitney Rachel, Erica Nichole. BS, U. Okla. City, 1976; DO, Coll. Osteopathic Medicine, Kirksville, Mo., 1983. Diplomate Am. Bd. Pediatrics. Resident in pediatrics U. Mo., Columbia, 1988-91, fellow in adolescent medicine, 1991-93; pvt. practice Mo., 1983-88; dir. adolescent medicine Children's Hosp. U. Mo., Columbia, 1991-93; assoc. prof. adolescent medicine U. Mo., Columbia, 1991-93; dir. pediatrics Kaiser Permanente Hosp., Wailuku, Hawaii, 1993—. Named Outstanding Tchr., Student Body Med. Sch., U. Mo. Fellow Am. Acad. Pediatrics; mem. AMA, Am. Osteo. Assn. Office: Kaiser Permanente Hosp 80 Mahalani St Maunaloa HI 96770

STRONG, MAYDA NEL, psychologist, educator; b. Albuquerque, May 6, 1942; d. Floyd Samuel and Wanda Christmas (Martin) Strong; 1 child, Robert Allen Willingham. BA in Speech-Theatre cum laude, Tex. Western Coll., 1963; EdM, U. Tex., Austin, 1972, PhD in Counseling Psychology, 1978; lic. clin. psychologist, Colo., 1984; cert. alcohol counselor III, Colo., 1987, nat. addiction counselor II, 1991; diplomate, bd. cert. Forensic Examiner; diplomate Am. Bd. Disability Analysts. Asst. instr. in ednl. psychology U. Tex., Austin, 1974-78; instr. psychology Austin C.C., 1974-78, Otero Jr. Coll., La Junta, Colo., 1979-89; dir. outpatient and emergency svcs. S.E. Colo. Family Guidance and Mental Health Ctr., Inc., La Junta, 1978-81; pvt. practice psychol. therapy, La Junta, 1981—; exec. dir. Pathfinders Chem. Dependency program, 1985-94, clin. cons., 1994—, mem. adv. bd., 1995—; clin. psychologist Inst. Forensic Psychiatry, Colo. Mental Health Inst., Pueblo, 1989-94; adj. faculty Adams State Coll., 1992; dir. Allstrong Enterprises, Inc., 1992-94; sr. disability analyst, diplomate Am. Bd. Disability Analysts, 1995—. Del. to County Dem. Conv., 1988. Appeared in The Good Doctor, 1980, On Golden Pond, 1981, Chase Me Comrade, 1989, Plaza Suite, 1987; co-dir. The Odd Couple, 1995. Bd. dirs. Picketwire Cmty. Theatre, 1995. AAUW fellow, 1974-76. Mem. Am. Coll. Forensic Examiners, Bus. and Profl. People (legis. chairperson 1982-83, chmn. news election svc. 1982-88), Colo. Psychol. Assn. (legis. chmn. for dist.), Am. Contract Bridge League. Contbr. articles in field to profl. publs. Author poems in Chinook: Paths through the Puzzle, Decisions, Passion. Home: 500 Holly Ave PO Box 177 Swink CO 81077-0177 Office: 315 W 3rd St Ste 204 La Junta CO 81050

STRONG, MICHAEL DAVID, cardiothoracic surgeon; b. Raleigh, N.C., July 1, 1941; s. Michael David II and Pearl Jane (Knause) S.; m. Barbara Helen Fullerton, Feb. 20, 1971; children: Michael Davis IV, John Templeton. BA, U. Pa., 1962; MD, Jefferson Med. Coll., 1966. Diplomate Am. Bd. Thoracic Surgery. Asst. prof. surgery Temple U., Phila., 1975-77; attending surgeon Deborah Heart & Lung Ctr., Brown Mills, N.J., 1978-86; asst. prof. cardiothoracic surgery Hahnemann U., Phila., 1986-93, assoc. prof., 1993—; pvt. practice CTS Cardiac & Thoracic Surgeons P.C., Phila. Brig. gen. USAR, 1990-91. Fellow ACS, Am. Coll. Chest Physicians, Am. Coll. Cardiology; mem. AMA, Riverton Country Club (bd. dirs. 1994—). Republican. Episcopalian. Office: Hahnemann U Hosp Mail Stop 111 Broad & Vine Sts Philadelphia PA 19102*

STRONG, SARA DOUGHERTY, psychologist, family and custody mediator; b. Phila., May 30, 1927; d. Augustus Joseph and Orpha Elizabeth (Dock) Dougherty; m. David Mather Strong, Dec. 21, 1954. BA in Psychology, Pa. State U., 1949; MA in Clin. Psychology, Temple U., 1960, postgrad., 1968-72; cert. in Family Therapy, Family Inst. Phila., 1978. Lic. psychologist, Pa. Med. br. psychologist Family Ct. Phila., 1960-85, asst. chief psychologist, 1985-88, chief psychologist, 1988-92; retired, 1992; pvt. practice Phila., 1992—; cons. St. Joseph's Home for Girls, Phila., 1963-84, Daughters of Charity of St. Vincent De Paul, Albany, N.Y., 1965-90. Mem. APA (assoc.), Am. Assn. Marriage and Family Therapists, Pa. Psychol. Assn., Nat. Register of Health Svc. Providers in Psychology, Family Inst. Phila. Democrat.

STROOP, JOHN R., orthodontist; b. Nashville, Dec. 25, 1952; s. John R. and Freedie Mae (Pinckley) S.; m. Kathrine Jeane Nichols, Jan. 18, 1975; children: Jonathan, Nikki. BS, David Lipscomb Univ., Nashville, 1974; DMD, Univ. La., 1979; orthodontic specialist, Medical Coll. Ga., 1981. Contbr. article to profl. jours. Bd. dirs. Ga. Agape Adoption Foster, Atlanta, 1989-91, pres. bd., 1991-93; deacon North Atlanta Ch. of Christ, 1986—. Recipient Am. Cancer Inst. grant, 1974. Mem. Cobb County Dental Soc. (sec. 1989-90, treas. 1991-92, v.p. 1992-93, pres. 1993-94), Ga. Dental Assn., Am. Dental Soc., Am. Assn. Orthodontist, Southern Assn. Orthodontist. Home: 3290 Kingshorse Commons Alpharetta GA 30202

STROTHER, ALLEN, biochemical pharmacologist, researcher; b. Nolan County, Tex., Feb. 20, 1928; s. Henry Allen and Minnie Etta (Taylor) S.; m. Julia Ann Gutch, Feb. 7, 1957; children: Wesley Allen, Lori Ann. BS, Tex. Tech. U., 1955; MS, U. Calif., 1957; PhD, Tex. A&M U., 1963. Rsch. asst. Tex. A&M, Coll. Sta., 1959-63; rsch. biochemist FDA, Washington, 1963-65; asst. prof. pharmacology Loma Linda (Calif.) U., 1965-70, assoc. prof., 1970-75, prof., 1975-95, retired, vol. faculty, 1995—; cons. WHO, Geneva, 1982-86. Contbr. numerous articles to profl. jours.; chpt. to WHO Bull. Pilot CAP/USAF Search and Rescue San Bernardino, Calif., 1967-75; pilot examiner CAP Air Force Aux., Norton AFB, 1970-86. Named Investigator of Yr. Walter E. McPherson Soc., Loma Linda U., 1984, Basic Sci. Fellow of Yr., 1986. Mem. Am. Soc. Pharmacology and Exptl. Therapeutics, Am. Chem. Soc., Xzenobiotic Soc. Home: 74448 Nevada Cir E Palm Desert CA 92260 Office: Loma Lind U Sch Medicine Loma Linda CA 92354

STROUD, DAVID SHELDON, internist; b. Raleigh, N.C., Feb. 3, 1949; s. David and Dorothea Elaine (Sheldon) S.; m. Ashleyn S. Peterson, Aug. 30, 1969; children: Heather, Stephanie, Suzanne, Kaidi. BS in Pharmacy, U. N.C., 1972; MD, Wake Forest U., 1976. Diplomate Am. Bd. Internal Medicine. Intern St. Elizabeth's Hosp., Boston, 1976-77, resident, 1977-79; pvt. practice Wareham, Mass., 1979—; assoc. med. dir. Gateway IRA, Wareham, 1995-96. Mem. Lions. Republican. Congregationalist. Office: 53 Marion Rd Wareham MA 02571

STROUD, ROBERT MALONE, internist, educator; b. St. Louis, Mar. 12, 1931; s. Carliss Malone and Frances Elizabeth (Glasscock) S.; m. Gloria June Flowers, June 19, 1955; children: Robert M. Jr., Katharine Ware. BA in Math. cum laude, Harvard U., 1952, MD, 1956. Diplomate Am. Bd. Internal Medicine, Am. Bd. Rheumatology, Am. Bd. Allergy and Immunology. Intern Cook County Hosp., Chgo., 1956-57; resident Barnes Hosp., St. Louis, 1959-61; instr. dept. microbiology Johns Hopkins Med. Sch., Balt., 1963-65; asst. prof. dept. medicine U. Ala., Birmingham, 1966-70, assoc. prof., 1971-76, prof., 1976-81, asst. prof. dept. microbiology, 1967-71, assoc. prof., 1971-76, prof., 1976-81; clin. prof. dept. medicine U. Fla., Gainesville, 1982—; pvt. practice Ormond Beach, Fla., 1981-92; dir. rheumatology and rheumatology rsch. Ga. Warm Springs Found., 1965-66; mem. affiliated staff Ormond Hosp., Halifax Hosp. Med. Ctr., Humana Hosp.; mem. VA Rsch. Rev. Com., cancer cause and prevention subcom. NIH, Complement Workshop Com., allergy and immunology rev. com. NIH, Am. Bd. Med. Lab. Immunologists, Infectious Disease Course Com., Task Force on Immunology and Disease, allergy and clin. immunology rsch. com. NIH. Assoc. editor Arthritis and Rheumatism; adv. editor Immunochemistry, Jour. Allergy and Clin. Immunology; sect. editor Jour. Immunology, Critical Revs. in Immunology; contbr. numerous articles to profl. jours. Capt. U.S. Army, 1957-59. Postdoctoral rsch. fellow Johns Hopkins U., 1962-63, Helen Hay Whitney Found. fellow, 1962-65. Fellow ACP, Am. Coll. Allergy, Am. Acad. Allergy; mem. AMA, Am. Soc. Clin. Investigation, Am. Assn. Immunologists (award com., edn. com.), Infectious Diseases Soc. Am., Am. Coll. Rheumatology, Fla. Med. Assn., Volusia County Med. Soc., So. Soc. Clin. Investigation.

STROUD, SHERWOOD CLIFTON, JR., physician assistant; b. Greenville, S.C., Mar. 27, 1947; s. Sherwood Clifton and Laura Elizabeth (Dilworth) S.; m. Doris Ann Willis, June 22, 1971; children: Maria Kristina, Melissa Michelle, Alice Eugenia. AA, North Greenville Coll., 1966; BA in Psychology and Sociology, Ga. So. U., 1968; BS, U. Nebr., 1975. Commd. 2d lt. USAF, 1978, advanced through grades to maj., retired, 1990; physician asst. dermatology Dr. Gary Waldman, Charlotte & Monroe, N.C., 1990-92; physician asst. North Hills Med. Ctr., Greenville, S.C., 1992—. Fellow Am. Acad. Physician Assts., Soc. Dermatology Physician Assts., Soc. S.C. Physician Assts. Republican. Baptist. Home: 320 Watson Rd Travelers Rest SC 29690 Office: North Hills Med Ctr 800 Pelham Rd Greenville SC 29615

STRUCK, ROBERT FREDERICK, cancer research scientist; b. Pensacola, Fla., Jan. 9, 1932; s. Carl Herman and Hilda (Ropke) S.; m. Ruby Richardson, June 8, 1963; children: Lesley Dianne, Bert Richardson. BS, Auburn U., 1953, MS, 1957, PhD, 1961. Assoc. scientist So. Rsch. Inst., Brimingham, Ala., 1957-58; rsch. scientist So. Rsch. Inst., Birmingham, Ala., 1961-64, sr. rsch. scientist, 1964-81, head metabolism sect., 1981-88; head biol. chemistry div. So. Rsch. Inst., Brimingham, Ala., 1988-93, dir. biol. chemistry dept., 1994—; mem. exptl. therapeutics study sect. NIH, Bethesda, Md., 1983-86. Contbr. articles on cancer rsch. to profl. jours., chpts. to books. 1st lt. USAF, 1954-56. Grantee NIH, 1979—. Mem. Am. Assn. Cancer Rsch., Am. Soc. Pharmacology and Exptl. Therapeutics. Democrat. Presbyterian. Home: 3533 Laurel View Ln Birmingham AL 35216-3859 Office: So Rsch Inst 2000 9th Ave S Birmingham AL 35205-2708

STRUHL, THEODORE ROOSEVELT, surgeon; b. N.Y.C., Jan. 5, 1917; s. Samuel and Florence (Kossoy) S.; m. Ruth Brand, Oct. 19, 1941; children: Karsten, Wendy. BA, NYU, 1936, MS, 1938; MD, N.Y. Med. Coll., 1942, MS in Surgery, 1947; grad. Julliard Conservatory of Music, 1933. Diplomate Am. Bd. Abdominal Surgery, Am. Bd. Surgery. Intern Queens Gen. Hosp., Jamaica, N.Y., 1942-43; resident VA Hosp. Newington, Conn., 1947-48, Cumberland Med. Ctr., Bklyn., 1948-51; practice medicine specializing in surgery, Miami, Fla., 1951—; mem. staff Mt. Sinai Med. Ctr., Miami Beach, Fla., Jackson Meml. Hosp., Cedars of Lebanon Health Care Ctr. Variety Children's Hosp., South Shore Hosp., Miami Beach, Victoria Hosp.; former instr. in anatomy L.I. Coll. Medicine, N.Y.; instr. in surgery, instr. in anatomy and surg. anatomy U. Miami; instr. in surg. anatomy and surgery Mt. Sinai Med. Ctr.; med. adviser ARC of Dade County, Fla.; chief med. examiner Miami Beach Boxing Commn.; chief med. adviser World Boxing Assn., U.S. Boxing Assn.; med. adviser World Martial Arts, Judo and Karate; mem. Am. Bd. Quality Assurance and Utilization Rev. Physicians; formerly instr. in diving medicine Underwater Demolition Team Sch., U.S. Navy, Key West, Fla.; lectr., instr. in scuba diving, diving medicine; lectr. on medicine and surgery, cancer, artificial respiration, anatomy, hypnosis, boxing, weight lifting, judo, skin and scuba diving, swimming, water skiing, small craft, wrestling, music. Active ARC, 1936—, now bd. dirs., chmn. safety services ARC of Dade County; instr./trainer in CPR, instr. in advanced cardiac life support Am. Heart Assn.; former mem. N.Y. div. Olympic Wrestling Com. Served to maj. M.C., U.S. Army, World War II; ETO. Contbr. articles to profl. and sports publs. Fellow ACS, Internat. Coll. Surgeons (vice-regent Fla.), Am. Coll. Angiology, Internat. Acad. Proctology; mem. AMA, So. Med. Assn., Fla. Med. Assn., Dade County Med. Assn., Israeli Med. Assn., Fla. Assn. Gen. Surgeons (charter), Med. Hypnosis Assn. Dade County (past pres.), Am. Coll. Angiology, Pan Am. Med. Assn., Am. Soc. Abdominal Surgeons, Am. Soc. Contemporary Medicine and Surgery, Med. Aspects of Atomic Explosion, Assn. Mil. Surgeons U.S., Am. Coll. Sports Medicine, Commodore Longfellow Soc., Miami Beach Power Squadron (charter), Am. Canoe Assn., Am. White Water Assn., Underwater Med. Soc., Photog. Soc. Am., Contin Hon. Soc. of N.Y. Med. Coll., Phi Delta Epsilon (past pres. chpt.). Democrat. Jewish. Avocations: judo (3rd degree black belt), karate (black belt, 4th degree). Home: 44 Star Island Dr Miami FL 33139-5146 Office: 1444 Biscayne Blvd Ste 304 Miami FL 33132-1423

STRUNK, ROBERT CHARLES, physician; b. Evanston, Ill., May 29, 1942; s. Norman Wesley and Marion Mildred (Ree) S.; m. Alison Leigh Gans, Apr. 3, 1971; children: Christopher Robert, Alix Elizabeth. BA in Chemistry, Northwestern U., 1964, MS in Biochemistry, 1968, MD, 1968. Lic. MD, Ariz., Colo., Mass., Mo. Resident in pediatrics Cin. Children's Hosp., 1968-70; pediatrician Newport (R.I.) Naval Hosp., 1970-72; rsch. fellow in pediatrics Harvard Med. Sch., Boston, 1972-74; asst. prof. pediatrics U. Ariz. Health Sci. Ctr., Tucson, 1974-78; dir. clin. svcs. Nat. Jewish Ctr. for Immunology and Respiratory Med., Denver, 1978-87; sabbatical leave Boston Children's Hosp., 1984-85; dir. divsn. allergy and pulmonary medicine Children's Hosp., St. Louis, 1987--; pediatrician Barnes and Allied Hosp., St. Louis, 1987--; prof. pediatrics Sch. Medicine Washington U., St. Louis, 1987--. Recipient Allergic Disease Acad. award Nat. Inst. Allergy and Infectious Disease of NIH. Mem. Am. Acad. Allergy and Immunology, Am. Thoracic Soc. Office: Washington U Sch Med Dept Pediatrics 400 S Kingshighway Blvd Saint Louis MO 63110-1014

STRUPP, HANS HERMANN, psychologist, educator; b. Frankfurt am Main, Germany, Aug. 25, 1921; came to U.S., 1939, naturalized, 1945; s. Josef and Anna (Metzger) S.; m. Lottie Metzger, Aug. 19, 1951; children: Karen, Barbara, John. AB with distinction, George Washington U., 1945,

AM, 1947, PhD, 1954; MD (hon.), U. Ulm, Fed. Republic of Germany, 1986. Diplomate in clin. psychology Am. Bd. Profl. Psychology; lic. clin. psychologist, Tenn. Research psychologist Human Factors Ops. Research Labs., Dept. Air Force, Washington, 1949-54; supervisory research psychologist, personnel research br. Adj. Gen.'s Office, Dept. of Army, Washington, 1954-55; dir. psychotherapy research project Sch. Medicine, George Washington U., Washington, 1955-57; dir. psychol. services, dept. psychiatry U. N.C. Sch. Medicine, Chapel Hill, 1957-64; asso. prof. psychology U. N.C. Sch. Medicine, 1957-62, prof., 1962-66; prof. dept. psychology Vanderbilt U., Nashville, 1966-76, dir. clin. tng., dept. psychology, 1967-76, disting. prof., 1976-94, disting. prof. emeritus, Harvie Branscomb disting. prof., 1985-86; disting. prof. emeritus, 1994—. Mem. editorial adv. bd. Psychotherapy: Theory, Research and Practice, 1963—, Jour. Cons. and Clin. Psychology, 1964—, Jour. Nervous and Mental Disease, 1965—, Jour. Am. Acad. Psychoanalysis, 1972—, Jour. Contemporary Psychotherapy, 1972-86, Psychiatry Research, 1979-86, Jour. Profl. Psychology, 1976-89, others; contbr. chpts. to books, articles and revs. to profl. jours. Recipient Helen Sargent meml. prize Menninger Found., 1963; Alumni Achievement award George Washington U., 1972; Disting. Profl. Achievement award Am. Bd. Profl. Psychology, 1976, Disting. Profl. Contbns. to Knowledge award Am. Psychol. Assn., 1987; others. Fellow Am. Psychol. Assn. (mem. exec. council 1964, exec. bd. 1969-72, council of reps. 1970-73, chmn. com. on fellows div. psychotherapy 1970-74, pres. div. clin. psychology 1974-75, recipient Disting. Profl. Psychologist award 1973, Disting. Scientist award 1979), Tenn. Psychol. Assn., AAAS; mem. Eastern Psychol. Assn., Southeastern Psychol. Assn., Am. Psychopathol. Assn., Soc. for Psychotherapy Research (pres. 1972-73, Career Contbr. award 1986), Psychologists Interested in Advancement of Psychoanalysis, Phi Beta Kappa, Sigma Xi. Home: 4117 Dorman Dr Nashville TN 37215-2404 Office: Vanderbilt U Dept Psychology Nashville TN 37240

STUART, MARIE JEAN, physician, hematologist, researcher; b. Bangalore, India, Sept. 11, 1943; came to U.S., 1967; d. Norman and Dorothy (Dias) S. BS, Madras (India) U., MB. Asst. prof. pediatrics SUNY Health Sci. Ctr., Syracuse, 1972-76, assoc. prof., 1976-81, prof. pediatrics, 1981-87; prof. chief hematology and oncology div. St. Christophers Hosp. for Children and Temple U., Phila., 1987—; prof. thrombosis rsch. Temple U., 1987—; mem. nat. child health com. Nat. Inst. Child Health and Human Devel., Bethesda, Md., 1982-86; mem. nat. heart, lung and blood rsch. tng. com., NIH, Bethesda, 1993—. Contbr. articles to profl. jours.; contbr. book chpts. Mem. Am. Fedn. Clin. Research. Am. Pediatric Soc., Soc. for Pediatric Research. Mem. Christian Ch. Home: 10B W Society Hill Towers Philadelphia PA 19106 Office: St Christophers Hosp Children Div Hematolog Philadelphia PA 19134

STUART, PHILIP JOHN, urologist; b. Keith, Banffshire, Scotland, Nov. 16, 1949; came to U.S., 1990; s. John and Winifred May (Smith) S.; m. Lucy Anne Iris Jeffares Uptgrove, Dec. 30, 1972 (div. June 1989); children: Amy Patricia, Holly Anne, Luke Philip; m. Tracy Lynn Brunton, July 15, 1989. BA, U. Gwelph, Can., 1974, BS, 1975; MS, U. Western Ont., London, Can., 1980, MD, 1982. Diplomate Am. Bd. Urology. Intern St. Paul's Hosp., Vancouver, B.C., Canada, 1982-83; resident in gen. surgery U. Ottowa, Canada, 1984-86; resident in urology U. Western Ontario, Canada, 1986-89; urologist Port Arthur Clinic, Thunder Bay, Can., 1989-90, Olean (N.Y.) Med. Group, 1990-94, Elmira (N.Y.) Urol. Assoc., 1994—. Capt. Can. Armed Forces, 1979-86. Fellow ACS, Royal Coll. Physicians and Surgeons Can.; mem. Am. Urol. Assn., Am. Assn. Clin. Urologists, Can. Urol. Assn., Med. Soc. N.Y. Office: Elmira Urol Assocs 301 Hoffman St Elmira NY 14905

STUART, WAYNE CHRISTOPHER, orthopedic surgeon; b. Fontainebleau, France, May 29, 1956; s. Clarence Edgar and Elizabeth Emily (Freeland) S.; m. Michele Ann Sparks, Aug. 16, 1980; children: Christopher James, Emily Adair. BS, Davidson Coll., 1978; MD, Med. U. S.C., 1982. Diplomate Am. Bd. Orthop. Surgery, Med. Examiners; lic. Va., Pa. From gen. med. officer to chief orthop. surgeon, maj. U.S. Army, 1983-94; orthop. surgeon Ortho Surg. Group, Quakertown, Pa., 1994—; mem. oper. rm. com. St. Lukes Quakertown Hosp., 1994—; mem. med. mgmt. com. Ea. Pa. Health Network, Bethlehem, 1996—. Recipient Southwest Asia Svc. medal U.S. Army, 1991, Meritorious Svc. medal, 1994, Kuwait Liberation medal Saudi Arabia, 1991. Fellow ACS (assoc.), Am. Acad. Orthop. Surgeons; mem. AMA, Pa. Med. Soc. Office: Ortho Surg Group 2100 Quaker Pointe Dr #102 Quakertown PA 18951

STUBBLEFIELD, JAMES IRVIN, emergency medicine physician, health facility administrator; b. Phila., Aug. 17, 1953; s. James Irvin Sr. and Geri (Harvey) S.; m. Linda Marie Simms, Aug. 12, 1978; children: Lindsay, Shannon. BSEE, MS in Bioengring., U. Pa., 1977; MD, Hahnemann U., Phila., 1982. Diplomate Am. Bd. Emergency Medicine, 1991. Mgr. energy engring. Norcross, Inc., Bryn Mawr, Pa., 1977-78; commd. 2d lt. U.S. Army, 1977, advanced through grades to lt. col., 1993; intern in gen. surgery Letterman Army Med. Ctr., San Francisco, 1982-83; flight surgeon, brigade surgeon 101st Airborne Div., Ft. Campbell, Ky., 1983-87; resident in emergency medicine Madigan Army Med. Ctr., Ft. Lewis, Wash., 1987-90; chief dep. emergency medicine and primary care Silas B. Hays Army Hosp., Ft. Ord, Calif., 1990-94; flight surgeon attack helicopter battalion Operation Desert Storm, Persian Gulf, 1991. Decorated Bronze Star, Air medal. Fellow Am. Coll. Emergency Physicians; mem. AMA, U.S. Army Flight Surgeon Soc., Assn. Mil. Surgeons U.S., Tau Beta Pi, Eta Kappa Nu, Alpha Epsilon Delta. Roman Catholic. Home: 18506 Candace Ln Watsonville CA 95076

STUBBLEFIELD, TERRY WAYNE, dentist; b. Murray, Ky., Mar. 18, 1952; s. Ewing J. and Youlanda Gray (McClure) S.; m. Deborah Louise Bondurant, Aug. 4, 1973; children: Andrew W., Andrew R., Laura E. AA, Freed-Hardsman U., 1972; BS, Murray State U., 1973; DMD, U. Ala., 1977. Dentist, owner Stubblefield Dental Clinic, Vernon, Ala., 1977—; guest lectr. U. Ala. Sch. Dentistry, 1978-82. Mem. devel. coun. Freed-Hardsmen U., Henderson, Tenn., 1986—; deacon Columbus Ch. of Christ, 1994. Mem. ADA, Ala. Dental Assn., 6th Dist. Dental Soc., Miss. Dental Assn., Vernon Dental Study Club, Columbus Hist. Assn. (v.p. 1994-95, pres. 1995-96).

STUBBLEFIELD, TRAVIS ELTON, retired genetics educator; b. Austin, Tex., May 27, 1935; s. Lloyd Travis and Louise (Yarbrough) S.; m. Jacqueline Gail Ellis, July 26, 1957; children: Michael Scott, Mary Susan. BS in Biology, North Tex. State Coll., 1957; MS in Exptl. Oncology, U. Wis., 1959, PhD in Exptl. Oncology, 1961. Predoctoral fellow McArdle Lab. U. Wis., Madison, 1957-61; postdoctoral fellow Max Planck Inst. Virus Rsch., Tübingen, Fed. Republic Germany, 1962; asst. prof. biology M.D. Anderson Cancer Ctr., Houston, 1963-67, assoc. prof., 1967-77, prof. genetics, 1977-90; ret., 1990—. Contbr. articles to profl. jours. Mem. Am. Soc. Cell Biology, Sigma Xi. Mem. Ch. of Christ.

STUBENHAUS, JAY HACKEL, psychiatrist; b. N.Y.C., Jan. 23, 1923; s. Edward Abraham and Mattie (Hackel) S.; m. Beverly Solorow, June 1, 1924; children: Eric Charles, Neil Hugo, Amy Dorian. MD, N.Y. Med. Coll., 1947. Diplomate Am. Bd. Psychiatry and Neurology. Rotating intern Sydenham Hosp., N.Y.C., 1947-48; resident psychiatry U.S. VA Hosp., Lyons, N.J., 1948-51; ward psychiatrist U.S. Army Hosp., Ft. Dix, N.J., 1951-53; attending psychiatrist Bridgeport Hosp., Bridgeport, Conn., 1953—; pvt. practice psychiatry Fairfield, Bridgeport, Conn., 1953-93; attending psychiatrist Park City Hosp., Bridgeport, 1977-95; med. dir. Bridgeport Partial Hosp. Day Program, 1994—; cons. psychiatrist Family Svc. Soc., Fairfield, 1957-61, U. Bridgeport, 1966-86, Jewish Home for the Elderly, Fairfield, 1975-88, Jewish Family Svc., Bridgeport, 1979-95. Adv. bd. Mental Health Assn., Bridgeport, 1960-70, Vis. Nurses Assn., Bridgeport, 1962-65. Capt. Med. Corps, U.S. Army, 1951-53. Fellow Am. Psychiat. Assn. (life); mem. AMA, Conn. State Med. Soc., Fairfield County Med. Soc., Conn. Psychiat. Soc., Physicians for Social Responsibility. Democrat. Jewish.

STUCKEY, SUSAN JANE, perioperative nurse, consultant. Diploma in nursing, The Polyclinic Med. Ctr., 1971; BBA in Health Care Adminstrn., Pa. State U., 1985; cert., Del. County C.C., Media, Pa., 1988; MBA, Kutztown U., 1996. RN, Pa.; cert. operating rm. nurse; cert. RN first asst. Charge nurse Nightingale Nursing Home, Camp Hill, Pa., 1971-72; clin. educator oper. rm. svcs., staff nurse Harrisburg (Pa.) Hosp., 1972-80; adminstr., nursing coord. Hillcrest Women's Med. Ctr., Harrisburg, 1978-81; office mgr., pvt. scrub nurse Office Dr. Henry Train, Harrisburg, 1979-82; with Kimberly Nurses Med Temps, Cleve., 1982-84; sr. splty. nurse oper. rm. Harrisburg Hosp., Harrisburg, 1984-88, splty. supr. surg. svcs. cept., 1988-90; 1st asst. laser/abdominal endoscopy Women's Med. Assocs. P.C., Harrisburg, 1990-96; 1st asst., cons., owner PeriOperative Care Assocs., Harrisburg, 1996—; proprietor, first asst., cons. C.B. Laser Assocs. Inc., Camp Hill, Pa., 1990-96; faculty mem. Pa. Jr. Coll. Med. Arts. Contbr. articles to profl. jours. Mem. Assn. Oper. Rm. Nurses, Am. Assn. Gyneco. Laparoscopists, Am. Soc. for Laser Medicine and Surgery. Home: 68 Fairfax Vlg Harrisburg PA 17112-9556 Office: Peri Operative Care Assocs 68 Fairfax N Harrisburg PA 17112

STUCKEY, WALTER JACKSON, physician, educator; b. Fairfield, Ala., Mar. 6, 1927; s. Walter Jackson and Lena (Brackin) S.; m. Mildred Creel Roberts, Nov. 27, 1952; children: Walter Jackson, III, John Hamlin, James Allan. B.S., U. Ala., 1947; M.D., Tulane U., 1951. Intern Charity Hosp. La., New Orleans, 1951-52; resident in gen. practice Lafayette (La.) Charity Hosp., 1952; resident in internal medicine Tulane med. service Charity Hosp. La., VA Hosp., New Orleans, 1955-57; fellow, instr. dept. medicine Tulane U. Sch. Medicine, 1958-60, asst. prof., 1960-62, asso. prof., 1962-68, prof., 1968-92, prof. emeritus, 1992—, chief sect. hematology/med. oncology, 1963-92; ret.; cons. Charity Hosp., 1968—; active staff Tulane Med. Center Hosp.; practice medicine specializing in hematology and oncology New Orleans; cons. VA, Mercy; East Jefferson; Highland Park, St. Tammany Hosp., (Covington, La.). Served with USNR, 1952-54. Fellow ACP; mem. AMA, AAAS, Am. Assn. Cancer Edn., Am. Soc. Internal Medicine, La. Parish Med. Soc., Orleans Parish Med. Soc., New Orleans Acad. Internal Medicine, N.Y. Acad. Scis., Internat. Soc. Hematology, Am. Soc. Hematology, Am. Soc. Clin. Oncology. Methodist. Home: 7325 Cameo St New Orleans LA 70124-2510

STULBERG, BERNARD NATHAN, orthopaedic surgeon, research scientist; b. Kalamazoo, Aug. 2, 1948; s. Julius and Esther (Lieberman) S.; m. Carolyn Sue McComish, Oct. 16, 1976; children: Jonah James, Benjamin L., Micah Adam, John Samuel. BA, U. Mich., 1970, MD, 1974. Diplomate Am. Bd. Orthopaedic Surgery. Intern U. Chgo., 1974-75, basic surg. residency, 1974-76; orthopaedic surgery residency Hosp. for Spl. Surgery, N.Y.C., 1979; fellow in orthopaedic rsch. Hosp. for Spl. Surgery, 1980; staff surgeon in orthopaedic surgery Cleve. Clinic Found., 1980-90, staff scientist dept. musculoskeletal rsch., 1985-90; head div. of arthritis surgery Case Western Res. U., Cleve., 1990-92; dir. Cleve. Ctr. for Joint Reconstruction, 1992—; cons. Johnson & Johnson ORthopaedic Divsn., Inc., New Brunswick, N.J., 1983-89, Techmedia Corp., 1986-94, Implex Corp., 1994—, Wright Med., 1994—, Collaborative Clin. Rsch. Scientific Adv. Bd., 1995—. Contbr. orthopaedic articles to profl. jours.; patentee in field. ABC Exch. fellow Am. Orthopaedic Assn., 1987. Mem. AMA, Am. Acad. Orthopaedic Surgeons (chmn. FDA device adv. bd. 1996—), Orthopaedic Rsch. Soc. (bd. dirs. 1988-89), Am. Orthopaedic Assn., Mid-Am. Orthopaedic Assn., The Hip Soc., The Knee Soc., Ohio Orthopaedic Soc., Cleve. ORthopaedic Club, Internat. Soc. Tech. in Arthrhoapksty (pres. 1994-95), Phi Beta Kappa, Phi Kappa Phi, Pi Sigma Alpha. Jewish. Home: 7470 Water Fall Trl Chagrin Falls OH 44022-3967 Office: Cleve Ctr Joint Reconstruction Dept of Orthopaedic Surgery 2322 E 22d St Ste 102 Cleveland OH 44115

STULC, JAROSLAV PETER, surgeon, educator; b. Teplitz, Czechoslovakia, Sept. 14, 1947; came to U.S., 1948; s. Jaroslav Pavel and Emilie Vanca Stulc; m. Diana Susan Minassian, Dec. 27, 189; children: Alexan Christopher, Evan Thomas. BA, Cornell Coll., Mt. Vernon, Iowa 1969; MD, U. Iowa, 1973. Diplomate Am. Bd. Surgery. Intern SUNY, Syracuse, 1973-75; resident in surgery Georgetown U., Washington, 1975-80 instr. surgery, 1979-80; instr. surgery, fellow transplant surgery Loyola U., Chgo., 1980-83; fellow surg. oncology Roswell Park Cancer Inst., Buffalo, 1983-85, attending surgeon, 1985-90; asst. prof. surgery SUNY, Buffalo, 1988-91; chief surgery VA Hosp., Buffalo, 1990-91; attending surgeon Trover Clinic Found., Madisonville, Ky., 1991—; clin. faculty U. Louisville, 1991—; co-dir. Mahr Cancer Ctr., Madisonville, 1992—. Editor Ky. Med. Jour., Physician Focus; contbr. articles and abstracts to publs. Vis. lectr. outreach program Am. Cancer Soc., bd. dirs. Ky. chpt., 1993—. Capt. USNR, 1987—. Fellow ACS (cert. advanced trauma life support), Internat. Coll. Surgeons; mem. AMA, AAAS, Am. Soc. Gastrointestinal Endoscopy, Am. Soc. Abdominal Surgeons, Am. Soc. Clin. Oncology, Soc. Am. Gastrointestinal Surgeons, Nat. Surg. Adjuvant Breast and Bowel Protocl, Ea. Coop. Oncology Group, Iowa Jr. Acad. Sci., Chgo. Assn. Immunologists, Roswell Park Surg. Soc., Buffalo Surg. Soc., Acad. Surg. Rsch., Assn. Acad. Surgery, Adrian Kantrowitz Surg. Rsch. Soc. Phi Beta. Presbyterian. Home: 1200 College Dr Madisonville KY 42431-9182 Office: Trover Clinic Found 435 N Kentucky Ave Madisonville KY 42431-1768

STULTZ, PATRICIA ADKINS, health care risk administrator; b. Wayne, W. Va.; d. John B. and Gladys (Osburn) Adkins; m. Joseph L. Stultz; children: Debra, Tammy. AS, Marshall U., 1978, BS, 1982; MS in Nursing, Bellarmine Coll., Louisville, Ky., 1990. RN, W. Va. Staff nurse Huntington (W.Va.) Hosp., 1978-79; staff nurse St. Mary's Hosp., 1979-82, nursing supr., 1982-89, nursing quality care, 1989-94, dir. risk mgmt., 1994—. Mem. Nat. Assn. Health Care Quality (cert. profl., presenter 1992 conf.), W. Va. Assn. Health Care Quality, Am. Assn. Healthcare Risk Mgmt., W. Va. Assn. Healtcare Risk Mgmt., Sigma Theta Tau (Nu Alpha chpt.). Home: 110 Beuhring St Lavalette WV 25535 Office: St Mary's Hosp 2900 First Ave Huntington WV 25701

STUMACHER, RUSSELL JEAN, infectious disease physician; b. Phila., June 11, 1972; s. Nathan and Paula (Kimmel) S.; m. Sharon Garzfried, June 11, 1972; children: Roger Elias, Alison Olivia. AB in English, U. Pa., 1964; MD, Jefferson Med. Coll., Phila., 1968. Diplomate in internal medicine and infectious diseases Am. Bd. Internal Medicine. Intern internal medicine Cornell U. Cooperation Hosps., Manhasset, N.Y., 1968-69; resident Montreal (Que., Can.) Gen. Hosp., 1969—; fellow infectious disease Boston U. Med. Ctr., 1972-74, Channing Lab. for Infectious Disease, Boston City Hosp., 1974-75; chief infectious disease divsn. Grad. Hosp., Phila., 1975—; clin. asst. prof. medicine U. Pa. Sch. Medicine, Phila., 1975-84; clin. assoc. prof. U. Pa. Sch. Medicine, 1984—; mem. med. adv. bd. WCAU TV, Phila., 1983. Author: Clinical Infectious Diseases, 1987. Fellow ACP; mem. Infectious Disease Soc. Am., Soc. Health Care Epidemiologists Am., Phila. County Med. Soc. (mem. subcom. on infectious diseases 1993). Home: 1400 Hillside Rd Wynnewood PA 19096 Office: Grad Hosp Infectious Disease Unit Philadelphia PA 19146

STUMP, EARL SPENCER, psychologist; b. Parkersburg, W.Va., Dec. 12, 1943; s. Amos Earl Stump and Harriet Gertrude (White) Stiff; m. Ann Chadwick, Sept. 30, 1967 (div. 1985); 1 child, Andrea Renee; m. Joan Irene Croft, Sept. 28, 1985. BA, Ohio State U., 1966; MS in Corrections, Xavier U., 1971. Lic. psychologist, Ohio, profl. clin. counselor. Psychiat. aide Harding Hosp., Worthington, Ohio, 1965-67; psychology trainee Athens (Ohio) State Hosp., 1966-67; psychologist Ohio Dept. Rehab. and Correction, Columbus, 1967—; supr. psychology Chillicothe (Ohio) Correctional Inst., 1977—; pvt. practice psychology Columbus Mental Health Clinic, Columbus, 1976-77; instr. psychology Hocking Tech. Coll., Chillicothe, 1973-78; instr. diagnostics Ohio U., Athens, 1983-84. Mem. Biofeedback Soc. Ohio, Antique Wireless Assn., Nat. Acad. Neuropsychology (affiliate). Home: 15 N May Ave Athens OH 45701-1817 Office: Chillicothe Correctional Inst Box 5500 Chillicothe OH 45601

STUMPF, DAVID ALLEN, pediatrician and neurologist; b. L.A., May 8, 1945; s. Herman A. and Dorothy F. (Davis) S.; children: Jennifer F., Kaitrin E.; m. Elizabeth Dusenbery, Feb. 2, 1989; stepchildren: Todd Coleman, Shilo Walker. BA, Lewis and Clark Coll., 1966; MD cum laude, U. Colo., 1972, PhD, 1972. Pediatric intern Strong Meml. Hosp., Rochester, N.Y., 1972-73, resident, 1973-74; neurology resident Harvard Med. Sch., Boston, 1974-77; dir. pediatric neurology U. Colo. Health Sci. Ctr., Denver, 1977-85; chief neurology Children's Meml. Hosp., Chgo., 1985-89; chmn. neurology, Benjamin and Virginia T. Boshes Prof. Northwestern U., 1989—; mem. sci. adv. co. Muscular Dystrophy Assn., 1981-87. Editorial bd. Neurology, 1982-87; contbr. articles to sci. jours. NIH grantee, 1979-84; Muscular Dystrophy Assn. grantee, 1977-89; March of Dimes grantee, 1983-85; recipient Lewis and Clark Coll. Disting. Alumni award, 1991. Fellow Am. Acad. Neurology; mem. Child Neurology Soc. (counsellor 1982-84, pres. 1985-87), Am. Neurol. Assn., Am. Pediatric Soc., Soc. Pediatric Rsch. Presbyterian. Home: 540 Judson Ave Evanston IL 60202-3084 Office: 645 N Michigan Ave Ste 1058 Chicago IL 60611

STUNDZA, WILLIAM ANTHONY, mental health and retardation nurse; b. Lawrence, Mass., June 1, 1952; s. John A. and Matilda J. (Stanulonis) S. BA, Merrimack Coll., North Andover, Mass., 1974; postgrad., N.E. Broadcasting, Boston, 1977; cert. nursing asst., No. Essex C.C., Haverhill, Mass., 1985; Lic. Practical Nurse, Essex Agr. and Tech. Inst., Hathorne, Mass., 1989; AS in Nurse Edn., Northshore C.C., Danvers, Mass., 1993; student, Salem (Mass.) State Coll., 1993—. Nurse Greater Lynn (Mass.) Mental Health/Mental Retardation Assn., 1989-91; lic. practical nurse community residents' program Walter E. Fernald State Sch., Waltham, Mass., 1991-93; staff nurse geri-psych unit speciality Winthrop Hosp., Winthrop, Mass., 1993-94; charge nurse Correctional Med. Sys. of Mo., Concord, Mass., 1994; staff nurse Ctr. for Behavioral Medicine Holy Family Hosp., Methuen, Mass., 1994-96; psychiat. nurse On-Duty Med. Mass., Inc., Arlington, Mass., 1996—.

STUNKARD, ALBERT JAMES, psychiatrist, educator; b. N.Y.C., Feb. 7, 1922; s. Horace Wesley and Frances (Klank) S. BS, Yale U., 1943; MD, Columbia U., 1945; MD (hon.), U. Edinburgh, 1992. Intern in medicine Mass. Gen. Hosp., Boston, 1945-46; resident physician psychiatry Johns Hopkins Hosp., 1948-51, rsch. fellow psychiatry, 1951-52; rsch. fellow medicine Columbia U. Svc., Goldwater Meml. Hosp., N.Y.C., 1952-53; Commonwealth rsch. fellow, then asst. prof. medicine Cornell U. Med. Coll., 1953-57; mem. faculty U. Pa., 1957-73, 76—, prof. psychiatry, 1962-73, 76—, Kenneth Appel prof. psychiatry, 1968-73, chmn. dept., 1962-73; prof. psychiatry Med. Sch., Stanford U., 1973-76. Contbr. articles on psychol., physiol., sociol. and genetic aspects of obesity to profl. jours. Capt. M.C., AUS, 1946-48. Ctr. for Advanced Study in Behavioral Scis. fellow, 1971-72, Dist. Service award Am. Psychiatric Association, 1994. Mem. Inst. Medicine of NAS, Am. Assn. of Chmn. of Depts. of Psychiatry (past pres.), Acad. Behavioral Medicine Rsch. (past pres.), Am. Psychosomatic Soc. (past pres.), Assn. Rsch. in Nervous and Mental Diseases (past pres.), Soc. Behavioral Medicine (past pres.). Office: U Pa Sch Medicine Dept Psychiatry 3600 Market St Ste 734 Philadelphia PA 19104-2611

STUNZ, JOHN HENRY, JR., physician; b. Freeland, Pa., May 20, 1921; s. John Henry and Anna Amelia (Gross) S.; m. Geraldine Kutz, July 2, 1944; children: Beverly A. Stunz Boyd, Geri Stunz Konstantin. BA, U. Pa., 1943, MD, 1946. Diplomate Am. Bd. Occupational Medicine. Intern U.S. Naval Hosp., Saint Albans, N.Y., 1946-47; pvt. practice Freeland, 1949-50; plant physician Harrison Radiator div. Gen. Motors Corp., Lockport, N.Y., 1950-52, med. dir., 1952-78; med. dir. Cadillac Motor Car div. Gen. Motors Corp., Detroit, 1978-86; occupational medicine cons. Preferred Med. Assocs., Southfield, Mich., 1987—; pres. Niagara County (N.Y.) Bd. Health, 1966; acting commr. health Niagara County, 1972-73. Lt. (j.g.) M.C., USNR, 1946-49. Fellow Am. Coll. Occupl. and Environ. Medicine; mem. Mich. State Med. Soc., Oakland County Med. Soc. (environ. health com. 1988), Mich. Occupl. and Environ. Med. Assn. (bd. dirs. 1985-88), Detroit Occupl. Physicians Assn. Republican. Presbyterian. Home: 735 Ardmoor Dr Bloomfield Hills MI 48301-2417 Office: Preferred Med Assocs 29200 Southfield Rd Southfield MI 48076-1906

STUPPY, ROBERT JOSEPH, cardiologist; b. Perryville, Mo., Apr. 9, 1958; s. Francis Joseph and Edna Gertrude (Mueller) S.; m. Becky Kay Benjamin, Feb. 16, 1984; children: Kathryn, Jacob, August. BA in Biology, U. Mo., Kansas City, 1980, MD, 1982. Diplomate Am. Bd. Med. Examiners; diplomate in internal medicine and cardiovascular diseases Am. Bd. Internal Medicine. Med. intern Barnes Hosp./Washington U., St. Louis, 1982-83, resident in medicine, 1983-85, fellow in clin. cardiology, 1987-89; rsch. fellow div. cardiac biochemistry Washington U., 1985-87; cons. cardiologist St. John's Regional Hosp., Joplin, Mo., 1989—, chmn. dept. medicine, 1994. Author abstracts. NSF summer scholar, 1975; U. Mo. scholar, 1982. Fellow Am. Coll. Cardiology (regional coun. Mo. chpt. 1992-95). Home: 831 Rustic Ridge Joplin MO 64804 Office: Heartcare Assocs Ste 224 2817 McClelland Blvd Joplin MO 64804

STURDEE, DAVID WILLIAM, obstetrician-gynecologist; b. Walmer, Kent, England, May 13, 1945; s. Peter Doveton and Daphne S.; m. Elizabeth Morton Muir, Sept. 4, 1971; children: Simon, Claire. MB, BS, St. Thomas' Hosp. Med. Sch., London, 1969; MD, U. Birmingham, Eng., 1979. Rsch. fellow U. Birmingham, 1975-77, clin. lectr., 1981—; sr. registrar Coventry and Birmingham Hosps., West Midlands, Eng., 1978-81; cons. obstetrician-gynaecologist Solihull Hosp., West Midlands, 1981—, clin. dir., 1991-95. Contbr. articles to profl. jours. and chpts. to med. books. Fellow Royal Coll. Ob-gyn (higher tng. com., subsplty bd. 1988-90, jour. editor 1994—); mem. Internat. Menopause Soc. (founding mem., mem. editl. bd. Menopause Digest), Brit. Menopause Soc. (founding mem., coun. mem. 1989—, hon. treas. 1991-95, chmn. 1996—), Brit. Med. Assn. (chmn. Solihull divsn. 1991-93), Brit. Soc. Colposcopy and Cervical Pathology, Copt Heath Golf Club. Anglican. Office: Solihull Hosp, Dept Ob-Gyn, Solihull B91 2JL, England

STURDIVANT, LINDA LEE, psychotherapist; b. Pitts., Dec. 19, 1949; d. Matthew Lewis and Doris (Richardson) S.; m. James D. Chandler, Dec. 19, 1980. BS in Psychology, U. Pitts., 1981, MEd, 1982. Cert. employee assistance profl. Addictions therapist St. Francis Med. Ctr., Pitts., 1978-80; adolescent therapist U. Pitts., 1980-82; counseling cons. USX Corp., Pitts., 1982-86; employee counselor U. Pitts. Med. Ctr., 1986—; bd. dirs. Allegheny Valley Mental Health/Mental Retardation, New Kensington, Pa.; therapist Turtle Creek Mental Health/Mental Retardation, Pitts., 1986—. Bd. dirs. Pa. Orgn. Women in Early Recovery, Pitts., 1990—, United Way, Pitts., 1991—. Mem. Coalition for Addictive Diseases, Employee Assistance Profls. Assn. (pres. Pitts. chpt. 1989-92, bd. dirs. 1993—, chairperson women's issues com. 1993-94, nat. treas. 1994—). Democrat. Roman Catholic. Home: 620 Milltown Rd Kensington PA 15068-9330 Office: Univ Pitts Med Ctr-EAP 200 Lothrop St Pittsburgh PA 15213

STURGE, KARL, surgeon; b. Bklyn., June 24, 1935; s. Percy and Dora (Leonard) S.; m. Edna Clark, June 10, 1961; children: Karl E., Mark W., Edna Lynn, Clarke S. BS, U. Miami, 1957; MD, Seton Hall U., 1961. Diplomate Am. Bd. Urology. Chief surgery Columbia-Deering Hosp., Miami, Fla., 1989—, chief of staff, chmn. med. bd. Lt. col. USAF, 1962-72. Mem. Am. Lithotrypsy Soc., Fla. Med. Assn., Fla. Urol. Soc., Dade County Med. Assn., Greater Miami Urology Soc. Republican. Episcopalian. Office: 9299 Coral Reef Dr Ste 205 Miami FL 33157

STURGEON, ROBERT STANLEY, clinical psychologist, psychology educator; b. Twin Falls, Idaho, July 4, 1932; s. Stanley Robert and Elizabeth Ethel (Drury) S.; m. Geraldine Ellene Day; children: Russell, Paul, Douglas, Clay. BS, Abilene Christian Coll., 1959; MS, Okla. State U., 1961; PhD, Brigham Young U., 1968; cert., Syracuse U., 1953. Lic. clinical psychologist, Tenn. Staff psychologist Utah State Hosp. and Utah County Mental Health Ctr., Provo, 1966-67; assoc. prof. David Lipscomb Coll., Nashville, Tenn., 1961-73, Mid. Tenn. State U., Murphreesboro, 1973-79; psychologist, Care Unit Hendrick Med. Ctr., Abilene, Tex., 1980-83; clin. psychologist Cunningham & Assocs., Abilene, Tex., 1983-90; prof. psychology Abilene Christian U., 1979-87; pvt. practice Abilene, 1991-94; prof. David Lipscomb U., Nashville, 1994—; cons. disability determination svc. Social Security Ins., Tenn.; cons. psychologist Harriet Cohn Mental Health Ctr., Clarksville, Tenn., 1976-77; pastoral counselor Belmont Ch., Nashville, 1977-79; biofeedback cons. VA. Psychiat. Hosp., Murphreesboro, 1978-79; presenter numerous workshops and seminars on stress, hypnosis, and neurolinguistic programming, 1975—. Contbr. articles to profl. jours. S/Sgt. USAF, 1952-56. Grantee Cullen Found., 1983-87. Mem. APA (mem. psychologists in ind. practice 1982—), Abilene Psychol. Assn. (pres. 1982-83). Office: David Lipscomb U Granny White Pike Nashville TN 37204-3951

STURGEON, WILLIAM HOWARD, medical device engineer; b. Pitts., Apr. 10, 1931; s. William Howard and Blanche (Ziegler) S.; m. Olive Mary Gunther, Jan. 20, 1958 (dec. Feb. 1960); 1 child, Melanie Ann; m. Pamela Evans, Aug. 20, 1993. BSME, U. Calif., 1960. Registered profl. engr. Product design engr. Beckman Industries, Richmond, Calif., 1958-62; assoc.

engr. U. Calif. Lawrence Lab., Berkeley, 1962-64; staff engr. UCLA Dept. Physics, 1964-68; sr. devel. engr. UCLA Brain Rsch. Inst., 1968-71; mktg. mgr. Siliconix Inc., Santa Clara, Calif., 1971-73; pres. Sturgeon Engring. Co., Petrolia, Calif., 1973—. Author: Strobelight Manual, 1970, Triplepoint, 1992. Bd. trustees Mattole Valley Cmty. Ctr., Petrolia, 1975-81. Cpl. U.S. Army, 1952-54.

STURGES, SIDNEY JAMES, pharmacist, educator, investment and development company executive; b. Kansas City, Mo., Sept. 29, 1936; s. Sidney Alexander and Lenore Caroline (Lemley) S.; m. Martha Grace Leonard, Nov. 29, 1957 (div. 1979); 1 child, Grace Caroline; m. Gloria June Kitch, Sept. 17, 1983. BS in Pharmacy, U. Mo., 1957, post grad.; MBA in Pharmacy Adminstrn., U. Kans., 1980; PhD in Bus. Adminstrn., Pacific Western U., 1980; cert. in Gerentology, Avila Coll., 1986. Registered pharmacist, Mo., Kans.; registered nursing home adminstr., Mo.; cert. vocat. tchr., Mo. Pharmacist, mgr. Crown Drugs, Kansas City, Mo., 1957-60; pharmacist, owner Sav-On-Drugs and Pharmacy, Kansas City, 1960-62; ptnr. Sam's Bargain Town Drugs, Raytown, Mo., 1961-62; pharmacist, owner Sturges Drugs DBA Barnard Pharmacy, Independence, Mo., 1962—; pres., owner Sturges Med. Corp., Independence, Mo., 1967-1977, Sturgess Investment Corp., Independence, 1967-1978, Sturwood Investment Corp., Independence, 1968—, Sturges Agri-Bus. Co., Independence, 1977—, Sturges Devel. Co., 1984—; bd. dirs. Comprehensive Mental Health Corp., Truman Med. Ctr., 1992; instr. pharmacology Penn Valley C.C., 1976-92; instr., lectr. various clubs and groups. Contbr. articles to profl. jours. Bd. dirs. Independence House, 1981-83; mem. Criminal Justice Adv. Commn., Independence, 1982—. Recipient Outstanding award Kans. City Alcohol and Drug Abuse Council, 1982. Mem. Mo. Sheriffs Assn., Mo. Pharm. Assn. (pharmacy dr. 1981, Pharmacists Against Drug Abuse award 1989), Mo. Found. Pharm. Care, U. Mo. Alumni Assn. Home and Office: Sturges Co 16805 E Cogan Rd Ste B Independence MO 64055-2815

STURM, MICHEL ROBERT, dentist; b. Parris Isle, S.C., Nov. 2, 1947; s. Robert Joseph and Patricia Ann (Cass) S.; m. Diana Jo Anderson, Dec. 30, 1972; children: Kelly J., Andrew R., Abbey K., Cassie R., Charles M. BS in Biology and Chemistry, Xavier U., 1969; DDS, Ind U., Indpls., 1973. Gen. practice dentistry Ft. Wayne, Ind., 1973—; mem. staff Luth. Hosp., St. Joseph's Hosp., 1977—, mem. community rels. com. Author: How Does Your Gardiner Grow?, 1989; contbg. editor: Ind. Dental Jour., 1991-93. Founder, pres. Pathways Inc. (crisis ctr. for youth), 1991-96; sci. curriculum advisor East Allen Sch. Dist.; bd. dirs. Am. Cancer Soc., Ft. Wayne, 1975; chmn. Harlan (Ind.) Town Fair, 1986; scoutmaster Boy Scouts Am., 1984-93, exec. bd. Anthony Wayne Area coun., 1988—; ofcl. Santa Claus Embassy Found., 1987—, Ft. Wayne Philharm., 1987—; bd. dirs. student affairs com. St. Francis Coll.; bd. dirs. cmty. rels. com. St. Joseph's Med. Ctr. Mem. Acad. Operative Dentistry, ADA, Ind. Dental Assn. (master of ceremonies State Dental Meeting 1991), Isaac Knapp Dental Soc. (bd. dirs. 1981-83, 84—). Republican. Roman Catholic. Lodge: Rotary. Home: 18519 Killian Rd Spencerville IN 46788-9645 Office: 4302 E State Blvd Fort Wayne IN 46815-6915

STURROCK, JOHN R., nurse anesthetist, administrator; b. Hamilton, Ont., Can., Aug. 21, 1945; s. John William and Verna Bernice (Pickard) S.; m. Karen Sue Burch, Aug. 14, 1984; children: Christine, Suzanne, Timothy, Katalin, Erin. Diploma, St. Joseph's Sch. Nursing, Hamilton, 1968; BS in Mgmt. summa cum laude, Golden Gate U., 1982; MBA, Bryant Coll., Smithfield, R.I., 1986; MS in Systems Mgmt., U. So. Calif., 1989. Cert. RN anesthetist. Sr. nurse anesthetist Naval Hosp., Camp Lejeune, N.C., Newport, R.I.; dir. nursing svc. Naval Hosp., Twentynine Palms, Calif.; asst. dir. nursing svc. Naval Hosp., Bremerton, Wash.; teams mgr. Group Health Coop. Puget Sound, Tacoma, Wash.; clinic mgr. Medalia Healthcare, Tacoma. Comdr. USN, 1969—. Mem. ASQC, Am. Assn. Nurse Anesthetists, Wash. Orgn. Nurse Execs., Inst. Safety and Systems Mgmt. Triumvivate, Med. Group Mgmt. Assn., Ret. Officers Assn. Home: PO Box 3467 Silverdale WA 98383-3467

STURTEVANT, RUTHANN PATTERSON, anatomy educator; b. Rockford, Ill., Feb. 7, 1927; d. Joseph Heylman and Virginia (Wharton) P.; m. Frank Milton Sturtevant Jr., Mar. 18, 1950; children: Barbara (dec.), Jill Sturtevant Rovanl, Jan Sturtevant Cassidy. BS, Northwestern U., 1949, MS, 1950; PhD, U. Ark., 1972. Instr. life scis. Ind. State U., Evansville, Ind., 1965-72; asst. prof. Ind. State U., 1972-74; asst. prof. anatomy Ind. U. Sch. Medicine, Evansville, 1972-74, U. Evansville, 1972-74; lectr. anatomy Northwestern U., Chgo., 1974-75; asst. prof. anatomy and surgery Loyola U., Maywood, 1975-81; assoc. prof. Loyola U. Sch. Medicine, Maywood, 1981-88; prof. Loyola U. Sch. Medicine, 1988-90, prof. emerita, 1990—. Contbr. articles to profl. jours.; editorial bd. Chronobiology Internat., 1988-90; reviewer numerous profl. jours. Mem. Mayor's Task Force on High Tech. Devel., Chgo., 1983-85; exec. bd. Anatomical Gifts Assn. Ill., Chgo., 1978-89. Grantee, Pott's Found., NIH, others, 1978-88. Mem. Am. Assn. Anatomists, So. Soc. Anatomists (councillor 1978-80), Internat. Soc. Chronobiologists, Am. Soc. Pharmacology and Exptl. Therapeutics, Soc. for Exptl. Biology and Medicine, Am. Assn. Clin. Anatomists, League of Underwater Photographers, Chgo. Area Camera Assn., Sarasota Scuba Club, Sigma Xi. Address: 5740 Midnight Pass Rd Unit 208-F Sarasota FL 34242

STURTZ, DONALD LEE, physician, naval officer; b. Coshocton, Ohio, Apr. 18, 1933; s. Walter Raymond and Helene Josephine (Kubic) S.; m. Alice Marie McGuire, June 11, 1955; children: Jimalee, Janel. BS, U.S. Navel Acad., Annapolis, Md., 1955; MD, U. Pa., 1965. Diplomate Am. Bd. Surgery. Surg. resident USN, Phila., 1965-70; ship's surgeon USN, 1970-71; staff surgeon Bethesda Naval Hosp., USN, 1971-80; chief of surgery San Diego Naval Hosp., USN, 1980-84; exec. officer Oakland (Calif.) Naval Hosp., USN, 1984-85; prof. clin. surgery USN, Bethesda, Md., 1985-87; commd. Naval Med. Command USN, 1987-88; fleet surgeon USN, Norfolk, Va., 1989-91; surgeon USUHS, Bethesda, Md., 1991—. Contbr. articles to profl. jours. Recipient B.D. Larrey award for Surgical Excellence, Surgical Dept. USUHS, Bethesda, 1988. Fellow ACS (gov. 1985-88); mem. Am. Assn. for Surgery of Trauma, Assn. Mil. Surgeons, USN Inst. Republican. Methodist. Office: USUHS Dept Surgery 4301 Jones Bridge Rd Bethesda MD 20814-4712

STUTES, SUSAN EDITH, physician, educator; b. Springfield, Ill., May 30, 1955; d. Henry Minor and Maude Eva (Ervin) S. BA, U. Colo., Colorado Springs, 1977; MD, U. Colo., Denver, 1981. Diplomate Am. Bd. Family Practice. Commd. 1st lt. U.S. Army, 1981, advanced through grades to capt., 1981; intern Madigan Army Med. Ctr., Tacoma, Wash., 1981-82; resident in family practice Dwight David Eisenhower Army Med. Ctr., Augusta, Ga., 1982-84; staff physician Bayne-Jones Army Cmty. Hosp., Ft. Polk, La., 1984-86, Scott and White Clinic, Gatesville, Tex., 1986-90; asst. prof. dept. family practice Tex. A&M Med. Sch., Temple, 1986-90; faculty St. Mary U. Tex. Med. Br. Family Medicine Residency, Port Arthur, Tex., 1991-96; assoc. dir. St. Mary UTMB Family Med. Residency, Port Arthur, Tex., 1992-96; asst. prof. dept. family medicine U. Tex. Med. Br., Galveston, 1991-96; asst. prof. Meml. Hosp.- East Tenn. State U. Family Practice Residency, Chattanooga, 1996—; chairperson single room maternity care steering com. Coryell Meml. Hosp., Gatesville, 1988-90; lectr. in field. Chairperson Am. Cancer Soc., Gatesville, 1987. Fellow Am. Acad. Family Practice; mem. Am. Acad. Family Practice, Tex. Acad. Family Practice, Uniformed Scis. Acad. Family Practice. Methodist. Home: 2610 Winter Garden Dr Chattanooga TN 37421 Office: Meml Hosp and East Tenn State U Family Medicine Residency 2525 de Sales Ave Chattanooga TN 37404

STUTTS, GARY THOMAS, health facility administrator; b. Dyersburg, Tenn., Feb. 13, 1957; s. Wiley Thomas and Betty Jane (Weeks) S.; m. Amy Ayers, June 19, 1993; children: Andrew Thomas, Emily Lynn, Joseph Wayne. AS, Austin Peay State U., Clarksville, Tenn., 1982; BS, Coll. St. Francis, Joliet, Ill., 1991. RN, Tenn. Organ donor coord. Nashville Regional Organ Procurement Agy., 1984-85; staff nurse emergency unit Jesse Holman Jones Hosp., Springfield, Tenn., 1982-83; mem. nursing staff emergency dept. Jackson-Madison County Gen. Hosp., Jackson, Tenn., 1983-94; nursing instr. Tenn. Tech. Ctr. at Jackson, 1994-95; asst. program dir. sr. care ctr. Bolivar (Tenn.) Gen. Hosp., 1995—; nurse preceptor Genentech, Inc.; mem. nursing practice adv. com. Tenn. Bd. Nursing. Home: 229 Farmington Dr Jackson TN 38305-3818

STUTZ, ROLF S., medical association administrator; b. Boston, May 1, 1949; s. Rolf and Nancy (Sturman) S.; m. Cornelia Green, Juny 17, 1976; 1 child, Cornelia. BA, U. N.C., 1971; MBA, Harvard U., 1978. Various positions Millipore Corp., Bedford, Mass., 1978-83; pres., CEO Zoll Med. Corp., Burlington, Mass., 1983—; bd. dirs. Hemasure Inc., Marlboro, Mass., Cambridge Heart Inc., Burlington. Named Entrepreneur of Yr. Ernst & Young, 1987. Office: Zoll Med Corp 32 2d Ave Burlington MA 01803

STUTZEL, WILLIAM MONROE, orthodontist, educator; b. N.Y.C., Aug. 9, 1931; s. Louis and Esther (Schiller) S.; m. Carole Knopf, Dec. 17, 1961. BA, NYU., 1953; orthodontia cert., NYU, 1970; DMD, Temple U., 1960. Lic. dentist, N.Y. Dental internship N.Y. Womens Infirmary Hosp., N.Y.C., 1960-61; dentist N.Y.C. Dept. Health and Health and Hosps. Corp., 1961-84; orthodonic cons. Empire Blue Cross and Blue Shield, N.Y.C., 1984-91; clin. asst. prof. orthodontics N.Y.U. Coll. Dentistry, 1991—. Component Reporter The New York State Dental Jour., 1992—; reviewer Jour. of Am. Dental Assn. With U.S. Army, 1953-55. Fellow Internat. Coll. Dentists; mem. Am. Dental Assn. (alt. del. to convention 1996), First Dist. Dental Soc. State of N.Y. (chmn. ethics com. 1990, 91), Eastern Dental Soc. (pres. 1993), Am. Assn. Orthodontists. Home: 201 E 17th St New York NY 10003 Office: NYU Coll of Dentistry 345 E 24th St New York NY 10010

STYNE, DENNIS MICHAEL, physician; b. Chgo., July 31, 1947; s. Irving and Bernice (Coopersmith) S.; m. Donna Petre, Sept. 5, 1971; children: Rachel, Jonathan, Juliana, Aaron. BS, Northwestern U., 1969, MD, 1971. Diplomate Am. Bd. Pediats. Intern in pediatrics U. Calif., San Diego, 1971-72, resident in pediatrics, 1972-73; resident in pediatrics Yale U., New Haven, 1973-74; fellow in pediatric endocrinology U. Calif., San Francisco, 1974-77, asst. prof. pediatrics, 1977-83; assoc. prof. U. Calif., Davis, 1983-90; prof., 1990—, chair pediatrics, 1989—. Author numerous book chpts., contbr. articles to profl. jours. Mem. Endocrine Soc., Soc. Pediat. Rsch., Am. Pediat. Soc., Am. Acad. Pediats., Lawson Wilkins Soc. for Pediat. Endocrinology. Office: U Calif Dept Pediatrics Davis CA 95616

STYRT, JEROME, psychiatrist; b. Chgo., Dec. 12, 1919; m. Mary Avery Onken, Feb. 21, 1946; 2 children. BS in Chemistry, U. Chgo., 1940, MD, 1945; Grad., Balt. Psychoanalytic Inst., 1957. Diplomate Am. Bd. Psychiatry and Neurology. Intern U. Chgo. Clinics, 1945-46; resident in psychiatry Sheppard Pratt Hosp., 1946-48; registrar in psychiatry The Retreat, York, Eng., 1948, Belmont Hosp., Surrey, 1949; fellow in preventive medicine, Commonwealth Fund fellow Johns Hopkins U., Balt., 1949-50; sr. surgeon USPHS, 1950-52; instr. psychiatry U. Md., Balt., 1953-54; pvt. practice psychiatry and psychoanalysis Balt., 1953—; clin. assoc. prof. psychiatry U. Md., 1970—; supr. psychotherapy Sheppard Pratt Hosp., Towson, Md., 1971—; mem. tchg. faculty Balt.-Wash. Psychoanalytic Inst., 1963-93; cons. in field. Recipient Disting. Teaching award in psychiatry, Sheppard Pratt Hosp., 1989, Outstanding Vol. Tchg. Faculty award U. Md. Sch. Medicine, 1995. Fellow Am. Psychiatric Assn., Am. Orthopsychiatric Assn.; mem. Am. Psychoanalytic Assn., Med. and Chirurgical Faculty of Md., Balt. Wash. Soc. Psychoanalysis, Meadow Mill Athletic Club, Alpha Omega Alpha. Home: 1615 Burnwood Rd Baltimore MD 21239-3604 Office: The Rotunda 711 W 40th St Ste 404 Baltimore MD 21211-2110

SUAREZ, CARMEN IRENE, pediatrician, medical administrator; b. Rio Piedras, P.R., Feb. 26, 1964; d. Jose Suarez Navas and Carmen Maria (Martinez) Suarez; m. Felix G. Del Rio, June 10, 1989; children: Felix G. Del Rio, Cristina I. Del Rio. BS, Recinto Univ. Mayaguez, P.R., 1985; MD, Univ. Cen. Del Caribe, Bayamon, P.R., 1989; degree in pediats., Maimonides Med. Ctr., Bklyn., 1992. Chief resident Maimonides Med. Ctr., Bklyn., 1992, asst. attending emergency med. pediats., 1992-93, chief inpatient svcs., 1993—; clin. asst. prof. pediats. SUNY, Bklyn., 1995, St. George's Sch. Medicine, Bay Shore, N.Y., 1995; adj. clin. instr. pediats. N.Y. Coll. Osteopathic Medicine, N.Y.C., 1995. Fellow Am. Acad. Pediats.; mem. Am. Coll. Nutrition, Bklyn. Pediat. Soc. Roman Catholic. Office: Maimonides Med Ctr Dept Pediats 977 48th St Brooklyn NY 11219

SUAREZ, LOUIS A., cardiothoracic surgeon; b. Havana, Cuba, Dec. 30, 1947; came to U.S., 1962; s. Louis A. and Irma C. (Abate-Daga) S.; m. Denise Marie Bolano, June 2, 1973; children: Louis A. III, Megan, Michael. BS, Loyola U., Chgo., 1970; MD, U. Ill., Chgo., 1974. Diplomate Am. Bd. Surgery, Am. Bd. Thoracic Surgery, Am. Bd. Surg. Critical Care. Staff surgeon Appleton (Wis.) Med. Ctr., 1983—; chief cardiac surgery Appleton Heart Inst., 1993—; chief surgery Unified Med. Staff, Appleton, 1994&. Lt. comdr. USNR, 1975-77. Fellow ACS, Am. Coll. Cardiology, Am. Coll. Chest Physicians, Soc. for Thoracic Surgery, Wis. Surg. Soc. (coun. 1990-96), Wis. Surg. Travelling Club. Roman Catholic. Home: 2011 N Nicholas St Appleton WI 54914 Office: Appleton Heart Surgeons 820 E Grant St Appleton WI 54911

SUAREZ, SALLY ANN TEVIS, health care administrator, nurse, consultant; b. Jersey City, Jan. 23, 1944; d. Paul John and Gertrude Marie (Clancey) Tevis; 1 child, Maria E. Diploma, St. Mary Hosp. Sch. Nursing, 1965; BA in Health Edn. and Nursing, Jersey City State Coll., 1966, MA in Health Sci., 1977. Staff nurse St. Mary Hosp., Hoboken, N.J., 1965, Bayonne (N.J.) Hosp., 1966, Jersey City Med. Ctr., 1965-66; adminstr. Hoboken Med. Arts Family Health Ctr., 1969-75; adj. faculty Jersey City State Coll., 1976-77; adminstrv. supr. St. Mary Hosp., Hoboken, 1977-80; dir. North Hudson Commn. Action Corp. Clinic, West New York, N.J., 1979-88; nursing clin. dir. St. Mary Hosp., Hoboken, 1988-89; corp. dir. nursing Francisan Health System N.J., 1989-92; dir. maternal child health svcs. St. James Hosp., Newark, 1992-93, dir. Family Care Ctr., Cathedral Healthcare Sys., 1993—, dir. nursing, 1996—; instr. nursing St. Mary Hosp. Sch. Nursing; cons. Creative Concepts in Counseling, Rutherford, N.J., 1979-82, Com. for Cytogenetics, Newark, 1986-88. Active March of Dimes, Hudson County, 1982-88, Hudson County ARC, 1984-88, United Way, 1984-94; mem. Hudson County Perinatal Consortium Bd., 1987-92, Gateway Consortium, 1993—; mem. adv. bd. Health Start, 1995—. Mem. Am. Cancer Soc., Am. Nurses Assn., Am. Nursing Found., Nat. Assn. Women Health Profls., N.J. Family Planning Forum (exec. com. 1980-86), Family Planning Assn. N.J. (exec. com. 1986-88). Democrat. Roman Catholic. Home: 113 Wilson Ave Rutherford NJ 07070-2726 Office: Cathedral Healthcare System St James Hosp 155 Jefferson St Newark NJ 07105-1706

SUBER, ROBIN HALL, former medical, surgical nurse; b. Bethlehem, Pa., Mar. 14, 1952; d. Arthur Albert and Sarah Virginia (Smith) Hall; m. David A. Suber, July 28, 1979; 1 child, Benjamin A. BSN, Ohio State U., 1974. RN, Ariz., Ohio. Formerly staff nurse Desert Samaritan Hosp., Mesa, Ariz. Lt. USN, 1974-80. Mem. ANA, Sigma Theta Tau.

SUBRAHMANYAM, M., surgeon; b. Atreyapuram, India, Dec. 20, 1947; s. Suryanarayana and Bhudevi; m. M. Padmavathi, Aug. 31, 1977; 1 daughter. MBBS, Kurnool Med. Coll., India, 1971; MS, Postgrad. Inst. of Med. Edn., Chandigarh, India, 1976. Lectr. in surgery Mahatma Gandhi Inst., Wardha, India, 1976-77; reader in surgery, surgeon Miraj Med. Coll., India, 1977-87; prof., head surgery, chief surgeon V.M. Med. Coll., Solapur, India, 1987—; rector Ladies hostel V.M. Med. Coll., Solapur, 1988—; chmn. bd. studies Shivaji U., India, 1984-87, mem. acad. coun., 1984-87, bd. studies, Kolhapur, 1984—. Author publs. in field. Recipient award for Best Published Rsch. Work, Indian Med. Assn., Delhi, 1980, Best Paper award Med. Rsch. Coun., Solapur, 1991, Best Paper at Conf., 1992. Mem. N.Y. Acad. of Scis., Assn. of Surgeons of India, Deccan Surg. Soc. (exec. com. 1984). Office: Dept of Surgery, Vaishampayan Meml Med Coll, 413 003 Maharashtra Solapur, India

SUCHER, BENJAMIN MARC, physician; b. Detroit, Feb. 5, 1951; s. Harold M. and Janet M. (Michel) S.; m. Eugenia F. Sucher, Aug. 20, 1972; 1 child, Erin F. BS, U. Mich., 1973; DO, Mich. State U., 1976. Diplomate Am. Bd. Phys. Medicine and Rehab., Am. Bd. Osteo. Rehab. Medicine. Rsch. grad. asst., 1974-76; intern Phoenix Gen. Hosp., 1976-77; resident Northwestern U. Med. Ctr., Chgo., 1978-80; pres., sec., treas. Benjamin M. Sucher D.O., 1989—; v.p. Clin. Solutions, Inc., 1992—; medical dir. Ctr. for Carpal Tunnel Studies, Paradise Valley, 1993—; mem. hosp. staff Good Samaritan Hosp. and Med. Ctr., 1981—, Paradise Valley Hosp., 1983-94, Scottsdale Meml. Hosp., 1988—, St. Joseph's Hosp. and Medical Ctr., 1981-91, Phoenix Gen. Hosp., 1981-89, Cmty. Hosp. Medical Ctr., 1981-90, Mesa Gen. Hosp., 1981-88, Scottsdale Cmty. Hosp., 1981-88, Valley View Cmty. Hosp., 1982-86; presenter and lectr. various confs. throughtout the country; prin. investigator for carpal tunnel syndrome, 1991—; instr. Record-Phoenix Coll., 1995; mem. adv. com. Oregon Health Scis. U., 1993—; preceptor Scottsdale Meml. Health Sys., Inc., 1993—; med. cons. W.L. Gore and Assocs., Inc., 1991—; med.dir. Advanced Ergonomic Sys., Inc., 1991-92; mem. per rev. com. dept. rehab. medicine Good Samaritan Hosp., 1989-92. Contbr. numerous articles to profl. jours; patentee in field. Mem. edn./libr. com. Scottsdale Meml. Hosp., 1990—. Recipient numerous rsch. grants. Mem. Am. Osteo. Assn., Am. Osteo. Coll. Rehab. Medicine, Ariz. Osteo. Med. Assn. (mem. legis. com. 1991-93), Am. Acad. Phys. Medicine and Rehab., Am. Assn. Electrodiagnostic Medicine, Am. Acad. Thermology. Office: Ctr for Carpal Tunnel Studies 10555 N Tatum Ste A 104 Paradise Valley AZ 85253

SUCHINSKY, RICHARD THEODORE, psychiatrist; b. Buffalo, N.Y., May 21, 1930; s. Ralph and Sarah (Bercoon) S.; m. Mindy Sue Garoon, Nov. 29, 1981; children: David, Raquela. Student, Cornell U., 1948-51; MD, U. Buffalo, 1955. Diplomate Am. Bd. Psychiatry and Neurology; cert. addiction psychiatrist. Intern Buffalo Gen. Hosp., 1955-56; chief, sec. on blood and blood derivations DBS-NIH, Bethesda, Md., 1956-60; resident in psychiatry N.Y.C. Hosp., 1960-63; asst. prof. psychiatry Stanford U., Palo Alto, Calif., 1963-67, SUNY, Bklyn., 1967-68; psychiatry Jewish Bd. Guardians, N.Y.C., 1968-70; exec. dir. Bensonhurst Mental Health Clinic, Bklyn., 1970-83; clin. assoc. prof. psychiatry Cornell U., N.Y.C., 1977-83; chief psychiatric svcs. VA Med. Ctr., Lakeside, Chgo., 1983-86; dir., chem. dependence Northwestern Meml. Hosp., Chgo., 1986-87; asst. prof. psychiatry Northwestern U., Chgo., 1986-87; assoc. dir. addictive disorders and psychiat. rehab. Dept Vets. Affairs, Washington, 1987—; clin. assoc. prof. psychiatry Georgetown U., Washington, 1990—; cons. Dept. Mental Hygiene, Calif., 1963-67, Peace Corps, VISTA, Calif., N.Y., 1965-82, Westchester County Mental Health Bd., White Plains, N.Y., 1971-73; assoc. curriculum coord. Inst. for Tng. in Child Mental Health, N.Y.C., 1965-72. Surgeon USPHS, 1956-60. Fellow Am. Psychiatry Assn.; mem. AMA, Washington Psychiatry Soc., Alpha Omega Alpha. Jewish. Office: Dept VA 810 Vermont Ave NW Washington DC 20420-0001

SUCICH, DIANA CATHERINE, school psychologist, counselor; b. N.Y.C., Apr. 23, 1948; d. Nicholas and Mildred (Bobich) S. MEd, Springfield (Mass.) Coll., 1973, cert. counseling, 1974; PhD, U.S. Internat. U., 1975. Cert. trainer, educator and practioner in psychodrama, sociometry and group psychotherapy. Dean of women Anderson Sch., Staatsburg, N.Y., 1971; cons. human devel. dept. YMCA, San Diego, 1975-77; postdoctoral resident Navy Alcohol Rehab. and Tng. Ctr., San Diego, 1975-77; instr. Chapman Coll., Orange, Calif., 1977-79; pvt. practice cons.; cons., instr. Moreno Acad. Psychodrama, Beacon, N.Y., 1982-83; cons. sch. psychologist Hillbrook Ctrl. Sch. Dist., N.Y., 1983-84; sch. psychologist Rhinebeck (N.Y.) Cen. Sch. Dist., 1984-86, Beacon City Sch. Dist., 1986-87, Wappingers Cen. Sch. Dist., Wappingers Falls, N.Y., 1987-92, Orange-Ulsta BOCES, 1992-93, Wallkill Ctrl. Sch. Dist., Wappingers Falls, N.Y., 1993-94; Wappingers Ctrl. Sch. Dist., Wappingers Falls, 1994—; AIDS dist. com. and sexual abuse prevention program trainer.; sch. psychologist, cons. N.Y. State mandated course on child abuse reporting and suicide prevention, devel. of abduction prevention program. Mem. APA, Psychologists in Marital and Family Therapy, Fedn. Trainers and Tng. Programs in Psychodrama, Am. Bd. Examiners Psychodramas, Psi Chi Psychol. Honor Soc. Home: Stony Brook Estate 237 Old Hopewell Rd Wappingers Falls NY 12590-4428 Office: Stony Brook Estate Wappingers Falls NY 12590

SUCKLE, HENRY M., physician; b. Coztesville, Pa., Dec. 26, 1916; s. Albert M. and Dora Suckle; m. Esther Sweet, Mar. 6, 1948; children: Helaine, Sally Ann. BA, U. Pa., 1938, MD, 1941. Diplomate Am. Bd. Neurol. Surgery. Intern U. Wisc., Madison, 1942-43, resident, 1943-48; asst. clin. prof. U. Wis., Madison, 1945-64; cons. VA, Madison, 1948-64; chief of surgery San Jose (Calif.) Hosp., 1982-84, asst. chief of staff, 1984-86. Mem. Am. Assn. Neurol. Surgeons, Congress Neurol. Surgeons (bd. dirs. 1952-54). Office: 25 N 14th St Ste 940 San Jose CA 95112

SUE, ALAN KWAI KEONG, dentist; b. Honolulu, Apr. 26, 1946; s. Henry Tin Yee and Chiyoko (Ohata) S.; m. Ginger Kazue Fukushima, Mar. 19, 1972; 1 child, Dawn Marie. BS in Chemistry with honors, U. Hawaii, 1968; BS, U. Calif., San Francisco, 1972, DDS, 1972. Film editor, photographer Sta. KHVH-TV ABC, Honolulu, 1964-71; staff dentist Strong-Carter Dental Clinic, Honolulu, 1972-73; dentist Waianae Dental Clinic, Honolulu, 1972-73; pvt. practice Pearl City, Hawaii, 1973—; chief exec. officer Dental Image Specialists, Pearl City, 1975—; dental dir. Hawaii Dental Health Plan, Honolulu, 1987—; dental cons. Calif. Dental Health Plan, Tustin, 1987—, Pacific Group Med. Assn., The Queen's Health Care Plan, Honolulu, 1993—; dental cons. Pacific Group Med. Assn., 1994—; cons. Hawaii Mgmt. Alliance Assn., 1996—; bd. dirs. Kula Bay Tropical Clothing Co., Hawaiian Ind. Dental Alliance; mem. exec. bd. St. Francis Hosp., Honolulu, 1976-78, chief dept. dentistry, 1976-78; mem. expert med. panel Am. Internat. Claim Svc., 1995—. Mem. adv. bd. Health Svcs. for Sr. Citizens, 1976—; mem. West Honolulu Sub-Area Health Planning Coun., 1981-84; mem. dental task force Hawaii Statewide Health Coordinating Coun., 1980, mem. plan devel. com., 1981-84; vol. oral cancer screening program Am. Cancer Soc.; v.p. Pearl City Shopping Ctr. Merchants Assn., 1975-84, 92-93, pres., 1994—. Regents' scholar U. Calif., San Francisco, 1968-72. Fellow Pierre Fauchard Acad., Acad. Gen. Dentistry; mem. ADA, Acad. Implants and Transplants, Am. Acad. Implant Dentistry, Hawaii Dental Assn. (trustee 1978-80), Honolulu County Dental Soc. (pres. 1982), Am. Acad. and Bd. Head, Facial, Neck Pain and TMJ Orthopedics, Intertel, Internat. Platform Assn., Mensa, Porsche Club, Pantera Owners Club, Mercedes Benz Club. Democrat. Office: Dental Image Specialists 850 Kam Hwy Ste 116 Pearl City HI 96782-2603

SUEDFELD, PETER, psychologist, educator; b. Budapest, Hungary, Aug. 30, 1935; emigrated to U.S., 1948, naturalized, 1952; s. Leslie John and Jolan (Eichenbaum) Field; m. Gabrielle Debra Guterman, June 11, 1961 (div. 1980); children: Michael Thomas, Joanne Ruth, David Lee; m. Phyllis Jean Johnson, Oct. 19, 1991. Student, U. Philippines, 1956-57; B.A., Queens Coll., 1960; M.A., Princeton U., 1962, Ph.D., 1963. Research assoc. Princeton U.; lectr. Trenton State Coll., 1963-64; vis. asst. prof. psychology U. Ill., 1964-65; asst. prof. psychology Univ. Coll. Rutgers U., 1965-67, assoc. prof., 1967-71, prof., 1971-72, chmn. dept., 1967-72; prof. psychology U. B.C., Vancouver, 1972—; head dept. U. B.C., 1972-84, dean faculty grad. studies, 1984-90; cons. in field; chmn. Can. Antarctic Rsch. Program. Author: Restricted Environmental Stimulation: Research and Clinical Applications, 1980; editor: Attitude Change: The Competing Views, 1971, Personality Theory and Information Processing, 1971, The Behavioral Basis of Design, 1976, Psychology and Torture, 1990, Restricted Environmental Stimulation: Theoretical and Empirical Developments in Flotation REST, 1990, Psychology and Social Policy, 1991; editor Jour. Applied Social Psychology, 1975-82; assoc. editor Environment and Behavior, 1992—; contbr. articles to profl. jours. Served with U.S. Army, 1955-58. Recipient Antarctica svc. medal, 1994, Donald O. Hebb award, 1996; grantee NIMH, 1970-72, Can. Coun., 1973—, Nat. Rsch. Coun. Can., 1973-90, NIH, 1980-84. Fellow Royal Soc. Can., Can. Psychol. Assn., Am. Psychol. Assn., Am. Psychol. Soc., Acad. Behavioral Medicine Research, Soc. Behavioral Medicine, N.Y. Acad. Scis.; mem. AAAS, Psychonomic Soc., Soc. Exptl. Social Psychology, Phi Beta Kappa, Sigma Xi. Office: U BC, Dept Psychology, Vancouver, BC Canada V6T 1Z4

SUENAGA, RONSUKE, immunologist, medical investigator; b. Tokyo, Japan, Nov. 20, 1953; married. MD, Gunma U., Maebashi, Japan, 1979; D of Med. Sci., Nihon U., Tokyo, 1989. Postdoctoral fellow U. Kans. Med. Ctr., Kansas City, 1984-87; clin. fellow Nihon U. Hosp., Tokyo, 1979-88; chief internal medicine Takada Nat. Hosp., Joetsu, Japan, 1988-90; sr. rsch. assoc./med. investigator St. Luke's Hosp., Kansas City, Mo., 1990—. Contbr. articles to Jour. Immunology, Clin. Exptl. Immunology, Jour. Rheumatology, others. Fellow Clin. Immunology Soc., Am. Assn. Immunologists; mem. Am. Coll. Rheumatology. Office: St Luke's Hosp Immunology Rsch Lab 4400 Wornall Rd Kansas City MO 64111

SUESS, JAMES FRANCIS, clinical psychologist; b. Evanston, Ill., Aug. 8, 1950; s. James Francis and Rae Love (Miller) S.; m. Linda Grace Powell, July 31, 1976; 1 child, Misty Lynne. BS, U. So. Miss., 1974, MS, 1978,

PhD, 1982. Lic. psychologist, N.Y., Ala.; diplomate Am. Bd. Profl. Psychology, Am. Bd. Med. Psychotherapists, Profl. Assn. Custody Evaluators, Am. Coll. Forensic Examiners. Assoc. psychologist State of Miss., Ellisville, 1978-80; clin. psychologist SUNY Med. Sch./Erie County Med. Ctr., Buffalo, 1982-84, supervisiong clin. psychologist, 1984-87, assoc. dir., 1987—; dir. practica SUNY Med. Sch., 1982-90, faculty counsel, 1988—; cons. Buffalo Dept. Social Svcs., 1985—; mem. spkrs. bur. Erie Alliance for Mentally Ill, 1986—; vis. prof. U. Guadalajara Sch. Medicine, 1985—; clin. dir. Stickney Adolescent Ctr. Mobile Met. Hosp. Ctr., 1993—. Author: Annotated Bibliography of Sex Roles, 1972, Personality Disorder and Self Psychology, 1991; contbr. articles to refereed jours. including Perceptual and Motor Skills, Jour. Clin. and Consulting Psychology, Am. Annals of Deaf. With USAR, 1969-76. Fellow Am. Orthopsychiat. Assn., Soc. Personality Assessment; mem. Am. Psychol. Assn. Home: 407 Stillwood Ln Mobile AL 36608-5847 Office: Baycare Hosp Stickney Ctr 1504 Springhill Ave Mobile AL 36604

SUESS, JAMES FRANCIS, retired psychiatry educator; b. Rock Island, Ill., Nov. 27, 1919; s. Joseph John and Elizabeth Ida (Dalton) S.; m. Rae Love Miller, Mar. 24, 1946; children: Rae Anne, James Francis, John Randall. B Med. Sci., Northwestern U., 1950, MD, 1952; postgrad., Coll. Physicians and Surgeons, Columbia U. and N.Y. Psychiat. Inst., 1958. Diplomate Am. Bd. Psychiatry and Neurology (examiner various times). Intern USPHS Hosp., New Orleans, 1952-53; resident in psychiatry Warren (Pa.) State Hosp., 1953-56, clin. dir., 1956-62; asst. prof. psychiatry U. Miss. Med. Sch., Jackson, 1962-65, assoc. prof., 1965-69, prof., 1969-82; prof. emeritus, 1982—, chmn. dept., 1967-69, 73-75, asst. dean, 1978-82; assoc. chief staff for edn. VA Med. Ctr., Jackson, 1978-82; vis. prof. Inst. Psychiatry, London, 1977, 83; referee editl. bd. Am. Jour. Psychiatry, Washington. Contbr. articles to med. jours., including Am. Jour. Psychiatry, Jour. Med. Edn., chpts. to books. Capt. U.S. Army, 1941-45. Fellow Am. Psychiat. Assn., So. Psychiat. Assn. (edn. com. 1973-77), Miss. Psychiat. Assn. (pres. 1968-69); mem. Am. Assn. Dirs. Psychiat. Tng. (a founder, exec. bd. 1969-71). Home: 1415 Radcliffe St Jackson MS 39211

SUFFICOOL, WESLEY LLOYD, JR., surgeon; b. Redlands, Calif., Jan. 16, 1959; s. Wesley Lloyd and Barbara (Downes) S.; m. Geralyn Marie Zilla; children: Wesley, Makenzy, Chad, Zachary. BS, Okla. State U., 1983; DO, U. Osteo. Med. & Health Scis., Des Moines, 1987. Diplomate Nat. Bd. Osteo. Physicians and Surgeons, Am. Osteo. Bd. Surgeons. Intern Doctors Hosp., Colorado Springs, Colo., 1987-88; resident surgery Flint (Mich.) Osteo. Hosp., 1988-92; gen. surgeon Fairmont (Minn.) Clinic-Mayo Health Sys., 1992, West River Surgery, Rapid City, S.D., 1992—. Mem. Am. Osteo. Assn., Am. Coll. Osteo. Surgeons, S.D. State Med. Assn., S.D. State Osteo. Med. Assn., Black Hills Med. Soc. Home: 4941 Springtree Ct Rapid City SD 57702 Office: West River Surgery 3615 5th St Rapid City SD 57701

SUFRIN, ERICA MARIE, clinical psychologist; b. Washington, Jan. 17, 1944; d. Sidney Charles and Grace (de Jong) S.; m. Edward Gustav Horn, June 18, 1976; children: Christopher Charles, Matthew Garrett. BS, Russell Sage Coll., 1965; cert. phys. therapy, Albany Med. Coll., 1965; MA, U. So. Calif., L.A., 1970, PhD, 1975. Lic. psychologist, N.Y. Clin. assoc. Suicide Prevention Ctr., L.A., 1970-72; clin. psychology intern L.A. County-U. So. Calif. Med. Ctr., 1971-72; chmn., dir. Sch. Phys. Therapy Russell Sage Coll./Albany (N.Y.) Med. Coll., 1972-77; mem. staff Sexual Function Clinic Albany Med. Coll., 1976-78; dir. Geriatric Day Hosp. Capital Dist. Psychiatric Ctr., Albany, 1977-78, chief Geriatric Svcs., 1978-80; clin. assoc. prof. Albany Med. Coll., 1980—; pvt. practice, 1980—; cons. psychologist St. Anne Inst., Albany, 1981-84; mem. N.Y. State Bd. Psychology, 1985—, vice chmn., 1991-94, chmn., 1994-95, licensure, disciplinary panel mem., 1995—. Author: (with Couture and Edelstein) Behavior Assessment of the Traumatically Brain Damaged, 1984. Mem. budget com. Voorheesville (N.Y.) Ctrl. Schs., 1991-92, sci. club com., 1991-92, trustee, 1992—. Grantee Rehab. Svcs. Adminstrn., Washington, 1964-65, 68-69, 69-71. Mem. APA, Assn. State and Provincial Bds. Psychology (membership svcs. com. 1993-95), N.Y. State Psychol. Assn., Psychol. Assn. Northeastern N.Y. (pres. 1982-83), Psi Chi. Office: Erica M Sufrin PhD 785 Delaware Ave Delmar NY 12054-9797

SUGAI, NAOSUKE, anesthesiologist, researcher; b. Nakatsugawa, Gifu-ken, Japan, Sept. 11, 1936; s. Saikichi and Akiko (Fujita) S.; m. Yuriko Hashimoto, June 1, 1969; children: Etsuko, Satoko, Kyoko. MD, Nagoya (Japan) U., 1962; PhD, U. London, 1974; D of Med. Sci., U. Tokyo, 1978. Diplomate Am. Bd. Anesthesiologists, Japanese Bd. Anesthesiologists; lic. physicican, Japan. Intern Tosei Hosp., Seto, Aichiken, Japan, 1962-63; resident Boston City Hosp., 1963-64; resident New Eng. Med. Ctr., Boston, 1964-65, fellow, 1965-68; asst. U. Tokyo Hosp., 1968-69; dir. dept. anesthesiology Mitsui Meml. Hosp., Tokyo, 1969-72; Wellcome Found. traveling fellow Royal Coll. of Surgeons of Eng., London, 1972-74; lectr. in anesthesiology faculty of medicine U. Tokyo, 1974—; staff, pain relief ctr. U. Tokyo Hosp., 1994—. Contbr. articles to med. jours. Mem. program com. Kamakura (Japan) Symphony Orch., 1991—. Recipient Rsch. award Mass. Heart Assn., 1967; recipient rsch. grant Ministry Edn. Japan, 1975-95. Fellow Am. Coll. Anesthesiologists; mem. Internat. Assn. for Study of Pain (task force on acute pain 1991—), Soc. for Tech. in Anesthesiology (Far East editor 1991—), Am. Soc. Anesthesiologists, Japanese Soc. Anesthesiologists, Internat. Anesthesia Rsch. Soc. Home: 423-16 Shiromeguri, Kamakura Kanagawa-ken 247, Japan Office: U Tokyo Dept Anesthesiology, 7-3-1 Hongo Bunkyoku, Tokyo 113, Japan

SUGARMAN, CHARLES JULES, podiatrist; b. Flint, Mich., July 8, 1949; s. Isadore and Roslyn Sylvia (Rosenfeld) S.; m. Cynthia Ruth Grubbs, Nov. 15, 1956; children: Anna Ruth, Noah Camden, Bren Rose. BS in Biology, U. Cin., 1979; BS in Human Health Sci., Ill. Coll. Podiatric Medicine, 1984, DPM, 1984. Diplomate Am. Coun. Cert. Podiatric Physicians and Surgeons, Nat. Bd. Podiatry Examiners, Am. Bd. Podiatric Orthops. Preceptor Family Foot Clinic, Brookfield, Ill., 1984-85; staff podiatrist No. Ky. Health Ctr., Covington, 1985—; pvt. practice Highland Heights, Ky., 1986—; lectr. No. Ky. Diabetes Assn., Ft. Mitchell, 1987—. Lectr. Ft. Thomas (Ky.) Bd. Edn., 1987—; med. provider March of Dimes Walk-A-Thon, Newport, Ky., 1988; mem. organizing com. Nat. Multiple Sclerosis Soc. MS150 Cycling Event. Named Ky. col. State of Ky., 1987. Fellow Am. Coll. Foot and Ankle Orthopedics and Medicine; mem. Am. Podiatric Med. Assn., Ky. Podiatric Med. Assn., Nat. Podiatric Circulatory Soc. (assoc.), Cin. Cycle Club, Am. Running and Fitness Assn. (profl.), Am. Assn. Podiatric Sports Medicine (assoc.). Republican. Home: 69 Covert Run Pike Fort Thomas KY 41075-1054 Office: 2021 Alexandria Pike Highland Heights KY 41076

SUGAYA, EIICHI, physiology educator; b. Tokyo, Mar. 25, 1929; s. Tsuneshino and Huchi (Yamada) S.; m. Aiko Sugaya, May 3, 1967. MD, Keio U., Tokyo, 1953, PhD, 1958. Asst. dept. physiology Keio U., Tokyo, 1954-58; boursier (French govt.) dept. physiology Sorbonne, Paris, 1956-58, Neurophysiology Lab. Musee Oceanographique, Monaco, 1958; asst. dept. surgery Keiu U., Tokyo, 1958-64; gen. surgeon Ichikawa (Japan) Hosp., Tokyo Dental Coll., 1959-60; surgeon neurosurgery 2d Tokyo Nat. Hosp., 1960-64; rsch. fellow div. neurol. surgery Washington U., St. Louis, 1962-63; prof. physiology dept. physiology Kanagawa Dental Coll., Yokosuka, Japan, 1964-96; prof. divsn. oriental medicine Sch. Medicine Tokai U., Tokyo, 1996—; cons. Tsumura (Pharm.) Co., Tokyo, 1983—; specialist doctor Rappongi Hosp. (Oriental medicine), Tokyo, 1964—; vis. prof. Inst. for Oriental medicine Sch. of Medicine, Keio U., Tokyo, 1992-96; chief rschr. lab. molecular & devel. medicine Inst. Exptl. Animals, Kawasaki, 1996—. Mem. Japan Soc. Oriental Medicine (specialist), Japan Autonomic Nerve Soc. (councilor, editing exec.), Japan Physiol. Soc. (councilor 1964—). Office: Tokyo Hosp Sch Medicine, Divsn Oriental Medicine Yoyogi, Shibuya-ku Tokyo 151, Japan

SUGERMAN, ABRAHAM ARTHUR, psychiatrist; b. Dublin, Ireland, Jan. 20, 1929; came to U.S., 1958, naturalized, 1963; s. Hyman and Anne (Goldstone) S.; m. Ruth Nerissa Alexander, June 5, 1960; children: Jeremy, Michael, Adam, Rebecca. BA, Trinity Coll., Dublin, 1950, MB, BChir, BA in Obstetrics, 1952; DSc, SUNY, Bklyn., 1962. Diplomate Am. Bd. Psychiatry and Neurology. House officer Meath Hosp., Dublin, 1952-53, St. Nicholas Hosp., London, 1953-54; sr. house physician Brook Gen. Hosp., London, 1954; registrar in psychiatry Kingsway Hosp. Derby and Kings Coll. Med. Sch., Newcastle, Eng., 1955-58; clin. psychiatrist Trenton (N.J.) Psychiat. Hosp., 1958-59; cons. psychiatry, 1964-80; rsch. fellow Downstate Med. Ctr., Bklyn., 1959-61; chief investigative psychiatry sect. N.J. Bur. Rsch., Princeton, 1961-73; cons. rsch., assoc. psychiatrist Carrier Clinic, Belle Mead, N.J., 1968-72, 78-90, dir. outpatient svcs., 1972-74, 77-78, med. dir., 1974-77; dir. rsch. Carrier Found., Belle Mead, N.J., 1972-79; med. dir. addiction recovery svcs. Cmty. Mental Health Ctr., U. Medicine and Dentistry of N.J., Piscataway, 1990-93; cons. psychiatry Med. Ctr., Princeton, N.J., 1972—; clin. assoc. prof. psychiatry Rutgers Med. Sch. (now Robert Wood Johnson Med. Sch.), New Brunswick, N.J., 1972-78, clin. prof., 1978—; vis. prof. Rutgers Ctr. for Alcohol Studies, 1977-83, Hahnemann Med. Coll., Phila., 1978-93; contbg. faculty Grad. Sch. Applied and Profl. Psychology, Rutgers U., 1974-78. Editor: (with Ralph E. Tarter) Alcoholism: Interdisciplinary Approaches to an Enduring Problem, 1976, Expanding Dimensions of Consciousness, 1978; contbr. articles to profl. jours. Bd. dirs. N.J. Mental Health R & D Fund, Princeton, 1968-74; v.p. Jewish Family Svc., Trenton, 1972-78; 1st v.p. Trenton Hebrew Acad., 1972-75. Fellow AAAS, Am. Psychiat. Assn., Am. Coll. Neuropsychopharmacology, Am. Coll. Clin. Pharmacology, Am. Coll. Psychiatrists, Royal Coll. Psychiatrists; mem. AMA, Soc. Biol. Psychiatry, Assn. Rsch. Nervous and Mental Diseases, Ea. Psychol. Assn., Am. Med. EEG Assn., Am. Soc. Addiction Medicine. Office: 100 Herrontown Rd Princeton NJ 08540

SUGGS, STEPHEN PATRICK, neurologist; b. Birmingham, Ala., Mar. 20, 1962; s. A. Kenneth and Kay O. (Gamble) S.; m. Dorothy Dansby Bates, June 29, 1985; children: Sarah, Emily, Annie. BS in Psychology, U. Ala., 1984; MD, U. Ala. Birmingham, 1988. Diplomate Am. Bd. Psychiatry and Neurology, Nat. Bd. Med. Examiners. Resident U. Ala. Birmingham, 1988-92; staff physician Decatur (Ala.) Gen. Hosp., 1992—; staff physician Decatur Gen. W, 1992—, Parkway Med. Ctr., Decatur, 1992—; consulting staff Athens-Limestone Hosp., Decatur, 1992—, Hartselle Med. Ctr., Decatur, 1992—, Lurleen B. Wallace Devel. Ctr., Decatur, 1992—. Contbr. articles to profl. jours. Bd. dirs. Kiwanis Club, Decatur. Mem. AMA, Am. Heart Assn. Stroke Coun., Med. Assn. State of Ala., Morgan County Med. Soc. Episcopalian. Home: 2408 Huntington Ln SE Decatur AL 35601 Office: 1215 7th St SE Decatur AL 35601

SUGIHARA, JARED GENJI, physician; b. Honolulu, Dec. 2, 1941; s. Clarence Yoshio and Chieno (Yamane) S.; m. Valerie Hinton, Oct. 10, 1970; children—Robin Emi, Rebecca Mie. B.A., Yale U., 1963; M.D., Harvard U., 1967. Diplomate Am. Bd. Internal Medicine, Am. Bd. Nephrology Intern, Presbyn.-St. Luke's Hosp., Chgo., 1967-68, resident, 1968-69; resident Rush-Presbyn.-St. Luke's Hosp., Chgo., 1971-72; fellow Mass. Gen. Hosp., Boston, 1972-74; physician Straub Clinic, Honolulu, 1974-77, Nephrology Assocs., Honolulu, 1977-85, Wong-Sugihara, Honolulu, 1985-89—, Nephrology cons., 1989— asst. clin. prof. medicine John Burns Sch. Medicine, Honolulu, 1975-76, asst. prof. medicine, 1976—. med dir. St Francis Ints;, . Bd. dirs. Hawaii Lupus Found., 1976-87, Pacific Standards Rev. Orgn., 1977-82. Served to capt. USAR, 1969-71, Korea, U.S. Fellow ACP; mem. Am. Soc. Nephrology, Internat. Soc. Nephrology. Office: Wong-Sugihara 1380 Lusitana St Suite 814 Honolulu HI 96813

SUGIKI, SHIGEMI, ophthalmologist, educator; b. Wailuku, Hawaii, May 12, 1936; s. Sentaro and Kameno (Matoba) S.; AB, Washington U., St. Louis, 1957, M.D., 1961; m. Bernice T. Murakami, Dec. 28, 1958; children: Kevin S., Boyd R. Intern St. Luke's Hosp., St. Louis, 1961-62, resident ophthalmology, Washington U., St. Louis, 1962-65; chmn. dept. ophthalmology Straub Clinic, Honolulu, 1965-70, Queen's Med Ctr., Honolulu, 1970-73, 80-83, 88-90, 93—; assoc. clin. prof. ophthalmology Sch. Medicine, U. Hawaii, 1973—. Served to maj. M.C., AUS, 1968-70. Decorated Hawaiian NG Commendation medal, 1968. Fellow ACS; mem. Am., Hawaii med. assns., Honolulu County Med. Soc., Am. Acad. Ophthalmology, Contact Lens Assn. Opthalmologists, Pacific Coast Oto-Ophthal. Soc., Pan-Pacific Surg. Assn., Am. Soc. Cataract and Refractive Surgery, Am. Glaucoma Soc., Internat. Assn. Ocular Surgeons, Am. Soc. Contemporary Ophthalmology, Washington U. Eye Alumni Assn., Hawaii Ophthal. Soc., Rsch. To Prevent Blindness. Home: 2398 Aina Lani Pl Honolulu HI 96822-2024 Office: 1380 Lusitana St Ste 714 Honolulu HI 96813-2449

SUGINTAS, NORA MARIA, veterinarian, scientist, medical company executive; b. Evergreen Park, Ill., Mar. 12, 1956; d. George and Mary (Navickas) S. BS in Biol. Scis. with highest distinction, U. Ill., Chgo., 1978; DVM, U. Ill., 1982. Lic. veterinarian, Ill. Profl. hosp. specialist Abbott Labs., Detroit, 1983-87; anes./crit. care patient monitoring equipment acct. exec. Shiley, Inc., Detroit, 1987-91; anesthesia and critical care monitoring equipment sales exec. and cons. Ohmeda, Detroit, 1991-94; regional mgr. Criticare Systems, Detroit, 1994-95, nat. acct. dir., 1995—. Journalist The Lithuanian World-Wide Daily Newspaper, 1975; author: The Production S-Adenosylmethionine by Saccharomyces cerevisiae and Candida utilis. Troop leader Girl Scouts Lithuanian, Chgo., 1972-77, camp dir., 1977. Recipient Louis Pasteur award for Academic Excellence in the Biol. Scis. and Ind. Rsch. U. Ill., 1978. Mem. NAFE, Econ. Club Detroit, Phi Beta Kappa. Republican. Office: 6284 Aspen Ridge West Bloomfield MI 48322-4433

SUGITA, EDWIN T., educator; b. Honolulu. Hawaii, Feb. 1, 1937; s. Charles E. and Beatrice H. (Yamane) S.; m. Gail M.R. Matsuno, May 25, 1959; children: Darrell C., Brent E. BS in Pharmacy, Purdue U., 1959, MS in Pharmaceutics, 1962, PhD in Pharmaceutics, 1963. Biochemist U.S. Army Edgewood Arsenal, Edgewood, Md., 1963-64; prof. pharmacy Phila. Coll. Pharm. & Sci., Phila., 1964—; cons. DURC Dept. Health N.J., Trenton, 1980—. Capt. U.S. Army, 1963-64. Mem. Am. Pharmaceutical Assn., Am. Assn. Coll. Pharmacy, Am. Assn. Pharmaceutical Scientists, Rho Chi, Sigma Xi, Kappa Psi. Home: 95 Daylesford Blvd Berwyn PA 19312 Office: Phila Coll Pharm & Sci 600 S 43 St Philadelphia PA 19104

SUGIURA, MASAHIRO, genetics educator; b. Okazaki, Aichi, Japan, Sept. 25, 1936; s. Tokiaki and Kyoko (Watanabe) S.; m. Noriko Toyoshima, Mar. 18, 1972; 1 child, Yoshinori Toyoshima. BS, Nagoya U., Japan, 1960, MS, 1962, DSc, 1967. Rsch. assoc. Ill. U., Urbana, Ill., 1963-65; rsch biologist Calif. U., San Diego, 1965-66; asst. Hiroshima U., Japan, 1966-68, Kyoto U., Japan, 1969-72; lab. head Nat. Inst. Genetics, Mishima, Japan, 1972-82; prof. Nagoya U., Japan, 1982—; dir. Ctr. for Gene Rsch., Nagoya U., Japan, 1986—; prof. Tokyo U., 1993—; bd. dirs. Internat. Soc. for Plant Molecular Biology, Athens, Ga., 1984-89; expert mem. Coun. for Sci. and Technology, 1984—; sci. bd. Inst. Genetic Engring., Kostinbrod, Bulgaria, 1988—; bd. dirs. Kazusa (Japan) DNA Inst., 1991—. Editorial bd.: Plant Sci., 1984—, Plant Molecular Biology, 1985-90, Critical Revs. in Plant Scis., 1990—, Asian-Pacific Jour. Molecular Biology and Biotechnology, 1993—; editor-in-chief: DNA Rsch., 1993—. Recipient Grant-in-Aid for Specially Disting. Rsch., Ministry of Edn., 1984, Genetic Promotion prize Genetics Promotion Found., 1987, Mendel medal Deutsche Acad. der Naturforscher Leopoldina, 1991, Mieschler-Ishida prize Internat. Soc. Endocytobiol. Tübingen, 1992; named Hon. Prof., Fudan U., China, 1992. Home: Town-Kamiyagoto 3-204, Hachimanyama 1101-1, Tenpaku-ku 468, Japan Office: Ctr for Gene Rsch, Nagoya U, Nagoya 464-01, Japan

SUGIYAMA, YUKIMARU, biologist; b. Changchun, China, May 16, 1935; s. Torata and Toshiko (Anazawa) S.; m. Nanako Kobayashi, June 9, 1963; children: Sawa, Miki, Shino. BSc, Tokyo U. Edn., 1958; MSc, Kyoto (Japan) U., 1960, DSc, 1966. Asst. prof. Kyoto U., 1963-70, assoc. prof., 1970-87; prof. Primate Rsch. Inst. Kyoto U., Inuyama, Japan, 1987—, dir. Primate Rsch. Inst., 1996—. Author: (in Japanese) People and Chimpanzees of Bossou Village, 1978, Eco-Ethology of Infanticide, 1981, Studies on Behavior and Society of Wild Chimpanzees, 1981, Human Nature in Non-Human Primates, 1984. Home: Kitabesso 23-3, Inuyama Aichi 484, Japan Office: Kyoto U, Primate Rsch Inst, Inuyama Aichi 484, Japan

SUH, BYUNGSE, internal medicine educator; b. Ansung, Korea, Mar. 6, 1941; came to U.S., 1964; s. Sang Keun and Chong Sang (Lee) S.; m. Youngjoo Lee, Dec. 21, 1974; children: Jason, Jessica, Janice. BS, Chungang U., Seoul, Korea, 1962; MA, U. Kans., 1967, PhD, 1969; MD, U. Miami, 1973. Diplomate Am. Bd. Internal Medicine; diplomate Am. Bd. Infectious Diseases. Asst. prof. medicine Temple U. Sch. Medicine, Phila., 1978-83, assoc. prof. medicine, 1983-90, prof. medicine, 1990—. Contbr. articles to profl. jours. Fellow Infectious Diseases Soc. Am., Am. Coll. Physicians, Coll. Physicians Phila., Am. Coll. Clin. Pharmacology; mem Am. Soc. Microbiology, Alpha Omega Alpha. Office: Temple U Sch Medicine Sect Infectious Diseases Broad and Ontario Sts Philadelphia PA 19140

SUHR, GERALDINE M., medical/surgical nurse; b. Sumner, Iowa, Mar. 16, 1960; d. Marvin Edward and Peggy Marie (Reiser) S. Diploma, Allen Meml. Luth. Sch. Nursing, Waterloo, Iowa, 1982; student, U. No. Iowa, Cedar Falls, 1979, U. Tenn., 1995. Sr. ship's nurse Carnival Cruise Lines, Miami, Fla.; emergency room and ICU/CCU nurse New Hampton (Iowa) Community Hosp.; charge nurse Trav Corps, Malden, Mass., Flying Nurses, Dallas, Hosp. Staffing Inc., Fla.; charge nurse, critical care nurse So. Hills Hosp., Nashville.

SUK, JIN HONG, pathologist; b. Seoul, Sept. 11, 1937; came to U.S., 1965; s. Il Keun and Soon Ae (Lee) S.; m. Soon Ja Lee, June 7, 1967; children: Peter, Mary. MD, Yonsei U., Seoul, 1962. Diplomate Am. Bd. Pathology. Staff pathologist Franklin (Pa.) Hosp., 1970-71; dir. lab. Grove City (Pa.) Hosp., 1971-75; staff pathologist N.W. Med. Ctr., Franklin, Pa., 1975—. Lt. USN, 1962-65. Mem. AMA, Am. Soc. Clin. Pathologist, Am. Soc. Cytology, Pa. Med. Soc., Internat. Acad. Pathology (U.S. and Can. div.). Democrat. Roman Catholic. Office: NW Med Ctr 1 Spruce St Franklin PA 16323-2544

SUKOV, RICHARD JOEL, radiologist; b. Mpls., Nov. 13, 1944; s. Marvin and Annette Sukov; Susan Judith Grossman, Aug. 11, 1968; children: Stacy Faye, Jessica Erin. BA, BS, U. Minn., 1967, MD, 1970; student, U. Calif.-Berkeley, 1962-64. Diplomate Am. Bd. Radiology; lic. physician Minn., Calif. Intern pediatrics U. Minn., Mpls., 1970-71; resident radiology UCLA Ctr. for Health Sci., 1973-76; fellow in ultrasound and computed tomography UCLA, 1976-77; staff radiologist Centinela Hosp. Med. Ctr., Inglewood, Calif., 1977-85; staff radiologist Daniel Freeman Meml. Hosp., Inglewood, Calif., 1977—, dir. radiology, 1988-90; asst. clin. prof. radiology UCLA Ctr. for Health Scis., 1977-83; adv. bd. Aerobics and Fitness Assn. Am., 1983—. Contbr. articles to profl. jours. Vol. Venice Family Clinic, 1985—. Lt. comdr. USPHS, 1970-72. U. Minn. fellow, 1964-65, 66, 70. Mem. AMA, Soc. Radiologists in Ultrasound (charter), Minn. Med. Alumni Assn., L.A. County Med. Assn., Calif. Med. Assn. Radiol. Soc. N.Am., L.A. Radiol. Soc. (continuing edn. com. 1990—, chmn.), L.A. Ultrasound Soc., Am. Coll. Radiology. Office: Ingelwood Radiology Ste 160 323 N Prairie Ave Inglewood CA 90301-4502

SULIK, EDWIN (PETE SULIK), health care administrator; b. Bryan, Tex., Feb. 1, 1957; s. Edwin Peter and Bonny Jo (Robertson) S.; m. Kolleen Marie Stevens, Aug. 8, 1981; 1 child, Laine Sheridan. Student, Blinn Jr. Coll., 1977-78, U. Tex., 1977, Tex. A&M U., 1977-83; BBA, Ky. Western. U., 1990; MBA, Ky. Western U., 1994. Lic. long term care adminstr.; cert. preceptor. Sr. v.p. ops. Sherwood Health Care, Inc., Bryan, 1976-90, pres., 1990—; sec.-treas. Sherwood Health Care, Inc., Lubbock, Tex., 1987-89; pres. Sherwood Health Care, Inc., Bryan, 1990, Lubbock, 1990; pres., owner Brazos Mgmt. Health Care, Inc., Bryan, 1991; owner Sherwood Forest Children's Ctr., 1991; pres. Sherwood Gardens Adult Day Health Care, 1996. Mem. Lt. Gov. Bullock's Nursing Home Work Group, 1991-92; participant state debate with Lt. Gov. Hobby, Austin, Tex., 1987; mem. Legis. Oversight Com.; active St. Joseph Sch. Bd. Fellow Am. Coll. Health Care Adminstrs., Am. Health Care Assn., Tex. Health Care Assn. (bd. dirs. 1987-90, chair, chpt. pres. 1987-88, facility stds. com. 1987—, payment for svcs. com. 1987—, Medicare com. 1989—, Omnibus Budget Reconciliation Act of 1987 com. 1987—, patient admission screening and resident rev. com. 1989—, legis. com. 1987-89, co-chair budget and fin. com. 1990-91, automation com. 1990-91, pilot project site NHIC automation 1990-91, nursing home quality and case mix demonstration pilot project 1995—), Bryan Coll. C. of C. Inner Cir., Am. Assn. Ret. Persons (Medicare/Medicaid steering com.), Tex. A&M U. Century Club, KC, Elks. Republican. Roman Catholic. Home: PO Box 3553 Bryan TX 77805-3553 Office: Sherwood Health Care Inc 1401 Memorial Dr Bryan TX 77802-5218

SULLEBARGER, JOHN THOMPSON, physician, educator; b. Plainfield, N.J., May 2, 1957; s. Franklyn Jackson and Joanne Abbott (Aspinall) S.; m. Lorrie Jeanne Miller, June 14, 1980; children: Jeffrey Franklyn, Melissa Jeanne. Student, U. Mainz, 1977; AB, Dartmouth Coll., 1979; MD, Johns Hopkins U., 1983. Intern in medicine U. Rochester, Rochester, N.Y., 1983-84; resident in medicine U. Rochester, Rochester, 1984-86, fellow in cardiology, 1986-89, sr. instr., 1989-90, asst. prof., 1990-92; asst. prof. U. South Fla., Tampa, 1992—; dir. Cardiac Catheterization Lab., James Haley VA Hosp., Tampa, 1992—; dir. interventional cardiology U. South Fla., 1994—; attending physician Strong Meml. Hosp., Rochester, 1989-92, Tampa Gen. Hosp., 1992—. Author: (with others) book chapters; contrb. articles to profl. jours. Chmn. Bd. Christian Svc., 1st Bapt. Ch., Rochester, 1991-92. Fellow ACP, 1992, Am. Coll. of Cardiology, 1991, Counc. on Clin. Cardiology of Am. Heart Assn., 1991, N.Y. Cardiological Soc., 1992. Fellow Soc. Cardiac Angiography and Interventions. Office: Harborside 4 Columbia Dr Ste 630 Tampa FL 33606-3568

SULLIVAN, BARBARA ANN, attorney, rehabilitation services professional; b. Haverhill, Mass., Mar. 20, 1952; d. Vincent R. and Helen (Lane) S. Diploma in nursing, Lynn Hosp. Sch. Nursing, 1979; MEd in Rehab. Adminstrn. magna cum laude, Northeastern U., 1988; postgrad., Mass. Gen. Hosp., 1987-89; JD, Mass. Law Sch., 1994. RN, Mass.; lic. rehab. counselor; cert. case mgr. Nurse various hosps., 1979-84; liaison, health care mktg. rep. Cambridge (Mass.) Vis. Nurse Assn., 1984-87; med./vocat. rehab. specialist Comprehensive Rehab. Assocs., Inc., North Andover, Mass., 1987-88; rehab. adminstrn. intern Class, Inc., Lawrence, Mass., 1988; rehab. cons., med. claims reviewer Am. Internat. Health and Rehab. Svcs., Boston, 1988-89; ind. contractor, home health care nurse Community Health Network, Cambridge, 1989-90; rehab. mgr. Commonwealth of Mass. Pub. Employee Retirement Adminstrn., Boston, 1990-91; nurse cons. risk mgmt., case mgmt., disability, workers comp, 1991-95; nurse cons. U.S. Dept. Labor, Boston, 1992—. Mem. Am. Assn. Nurse Attys., Nat. Rehab. Assn., Northeastern U. Alumni Assn., Mass. Nurses Assn. (co-chmn. pub. rels. com. 1986-88), Kappa Delta Pi. Home: 30 Emily St Haverhill MA 01832-3031

SULLIVAN, CHRISTOPHER MICHAEL, pediatric orthopaedic surgeon, educator; b. St. Louis, Sept. 18, 1954; s. C. Jerome and Kathleen M. (O'Connor) S.; m. Jannine M. Carrere, Dec. 16, 1991. BS, USAF Acad., Colo. Springs, 1976; MPH, UCLA, 1980, MD, 1980. Diplomate Am. Bd. Orthopaedic Surgery. Resident Northwestern U., 1981-85; chief orthopaedics George AFB, Calif., 1985-88; fellow in pediat. orthopaedics San Diego Children's Hosp., 1988-89; asst. prof. clin. surgery in orthopaedics U. Chgo., 1989—. Maj. USAF, 1976-88. Recipient C.I.B.A. award for cmty. svc., L.A., 1978. Fellow Am. Acad. Orthopaedic Surgeons, Pediat. Orthopaedic Soc. N. Am.; mem. Academic Orthopaedic Soc., Am. Acad. Cerebral Palsy Medicine.

SULLIVAN, COLLEEN ANNE, physician, educator; b. Lucknow, India, Feb. 11, 1937; came to U.S., 1961; d. Douglas George and Nancy Irene (MacLeod) S.; m. Alexander Walter Gotta, July 17, 1965; 1 child, Nancy Colleen. MB ChB, U. St. Andrews, Scotland, 1961. Diplomate Am. Bd. Anesthesiology, Am. Coll. Anesthesiologists. Rotating intern Nassau Hosp., Mineola, N.Y., 1961-62; clin. instr. Cornell U., N.Y.C., 1962-64; resident in anesthesiology N.Y. Hosp./Cornell U., 1962-64; fellow in anesthesiology Meml. Sloan-Kettering Cancer Ctr., N.Y.C., 1964-67, asst. prof. Cornell U. Med. Coll., 1978-79; assoc. dir. anesthesia St. Mary's Hosp.-Cath. Med. Ctr., Bklyn., 1968-78; clin. assoc. prof. SUNY, Bklyn., 1979-90, clin. prof. anesthesiology, 1990—, clin. dir. anesthesia, 1990-93; clin. dir. anesthesia Kings County Hosp., Bklyn., 1983-90, med. dir. ambulatory surg. unit, 1993—. Author numerous chpt. in anesthesiology textbooks; contbr. articles to profl. jours. Mem. N.Y. State Soc. Anesthesiologists (ho. of dels. 1983—, asst. editor Sphere 1990-95, com. sci. program 1990—). Republican. Roman Catholic. Office: Kings County Hosp Dept Anesthesia 450 Clarkson Ave Brooklyn NY 11203-2012

SULLIVAN, DAVID STAFFORD, psychologist, consulting company executive, publishing company executive, real estate developer; b. Oak Park, Ill., Dec. 11, 1943; s. Orville A. and Voris Allene (Stafford) S.; m. Sharon Eenigenburg, May 30, 1964; 1 child, David Jr. BA, No. Ill. U., 1965, MA, 1968, PhD, 1974. Assoc. prof. Wheaton (Ill.) Coll., 1967-73; clin. psychologist North Park Clinic, S.C., Park Ridge, Ill., 1973-82; pres. Brook Clinic, P.C., Oak Brook, Ill., 1982-87; gen. ptnr. Elgin Airport Property, Ltd., Wheaton, 1979—; pvt. practice clin. psychology Wheaton, 1987—; pres. Sullivan Pub. Co., Elmhurst, Ill., 1981—; cons. Redirections, Inc., Chgo., 1988-93, pres., 1993—. Author: Thoroughbred Racing: Predicting the Outcome, 1973, Harness Racing: Predicting the Outcome, 1975, S/A Advanced Method, 1975; contbr. articles to profl. jours. and sports publs. Mem. Am. Psychol. Assn. (chmn. Ill. ethics com. 1985-91).

SULLIVAN, DOROTHY LOUISE, nurse; b. Alton, Ill., July 20, 1938; d. Walter George William and Edna Louise (Poag) Huebner; m. Thomas L. Sullivan, Oct. 10, 1964 (div. 1989); children: Thomas L. Jr., Catherine L., Joseph D., Theresa E. RN, Alton Meml. Hosp., 1959; student, So. Ill. U., 1960, Ind. U., Bloomington, 1961-62, Community Coll. Allegheny Co., 1985, 87, Pa. State U., 1990. RN, Ill., Pa. Surgical nurse, operating room Alton (Ill.) Meml. Hosp., 1959-61; nurse, supr. Bloomington (Ind.) Hosp., 1961-63; surgical nursing, rehab. nursing Meth. Med. Ctr. of Ill., Peoria, 1963-65; operating room nurse St. Francis Med. Ctr., Peoria, 1965-66; staff nurse, inservice utilization Farmington (Ill.) Nursing Home, 1978-82, acting dir. nurses, instr. nurses aide, 1982; devel. and instr. nurses aide cert. program Spoon River Community Coll., Canton, Ill., 1981-82; surgical charge nurse, staff nurse St. Joseph Med. Ctr., Bloomington, Ill., 1982-84; day staff charge nurse, supr. Murray Manor Convalescent Ctr., Murrysville, Pa., 1984—. Med. chairperson Farmington PTA, 1980-81. Mem. Farmington Nurses Club (v.p. 1980-82). Republican. Roman Catholic. Home: 4828 Havana Dr Pittsburgh PA 15239-2420

SULLIVAN, ELEANOR J., dean. Dean Sch. Nursing U. Kans. Med. Ctr., City. Office: U of KS Medical Center 39th Rainbow Blvd Kansas City KS 66160

SULLIVAN, GEORGE ANERSON, orthodontist; b. Bon Aqua, Tenn.; s. Joe Marble and Ruby Christine (Luther) S.; m. Edith Melvina Timmons, May 11, 1957; children: Scott Patrick, Shawn Michael. AS, Henry Ford Community Coll., Dearborn, Mich., 1957; student, Eastern Mich. U., 1958-59; DDS, U. Mich., 1963, MS, 1966. Diplomate Am. Bd. Orthodontics. Pvt. practice specializing in orthodontics Phoenix, 1966—; pres. Ammons Meml. Dental Clinic, Phoenix, 1979-80. Chmn. Phoenix Meml. Hosp., 1977-80. Served with USNR, 1955-63. Mem. Am. Assn. Orthodontics, Cen. Ariz. Dental Soc., Ariz. State Dental Assn., ADA, Ariz. Orthodontic Soc., Pacific Coast Soc. Orthodontics, Optimist Club (pres. Phoenix chpt. 1967-68), Lions (pres. 1972-73), Elks. Republican. Office: 4909 N 44th St Ste E Phoenix AZ 85018-2748 also: 4805 W Thomas Rd Ste D Phoenix AZ 85031-4005 also: 10752 89th St Ste 111 Scottsdale AZ 85260

SULLIVAN, JAY MICHAEL, medical educator; b. Brockton, Mass., Aug. 3, 1936; s. William Dennis and Wanda Nancy (Kelpsh) S.; m. Mary Suzanne Baxter, Dec. 30, 1964; children: Elizabeth, Suzanne, Christopher. B.S. cum laude, Georgetown U., 1958, M.D. magna cum laude, 1962. Diplomate Nat. Bd. Med. Examiners, Am. Bd. Internal Medicine. Med. intern Peter Bent Brigham Hosp., Boston, 1962-63; resident Peter Bent Brigham Hosp., 1963-64, 66-67, chief resident, 1969-70, fellow in cardiology, 1964-66, dir. hypertension unit, 1970-74; Nat. Heart Inst. fellow, 1964, Med. Found. research fellow, 1967; preceptorship in biol. chemistry Harvard U. Med. Sch., Boston, 1967-69; asst. prof. medicine Harvard U. Med. Sch., 1970-74; dir. med. services Boston Hosp. for Women, 1973-74; prof. medicine, chief div. cardiovascular diseases U. Tenn. Coll. Medicine, Memphis, 1974—; vice-chmn. dept. medicine U. Tenn. Coll. Medicine, 1982-85; mem. staff Regional Med. Ctr., Memphis, VA, Bapt. Meml. hosps., U. Tenn. Medical Center-Wm. F. Bowld Hosp., Le Bonheur Children's Hosp., Saint Jude Children's Rsch. Hosp.; fellow Council for High Blood Pressure Research; cons. Nat. Heart, Lung and Blood Inst., 1974—, VA, 1983—. Contbr. articles to sci. jours. Served with M.C., U.S. Army, 1963-70. Fellow ACP, Am. Coll. Cardiology (bd. govs., pres. Tenn. chpt.); mem. AAAS, Am. Heart Assn. (fellow coun. on circulation, chpt. pres. 1982-83, affiliate pres. 1994-95), Assn. Univ. Cardiologists, Assn. Profs. Cardiology, Internat. Soc. Hypertension, Am. Fedn. Clin. Rsch., Racquet Club Memphis, Sigma Xi, Alpha Omega Alpha, Alpha Sigma Nu. Roman Catholic. Home: 6077 Maiden Ln Memphis TN 38120-3104 Office: Univ TN Divsn Cardiovascular Diseases 951 Court Ave Rm 353D Memphis TN 38103-2813

SULLIVAN, JERRY WARNER, educator, physician; b. Madisonville, Ky., Sept. 26, 1942; s. Henry Warner and Elsie (Lutz) S.; m. Judith Allen, June 13, 1964 (div. May 1988); children: Suzanne Robin, John Christopher. BS, Georgetown Coll., 1964; MD, U. Louisville, 1968. Intern San Diego Naval Hosp., 1968-69; resident in surgery Med. Sch. Tulane U., New Orleans, 1971-72, resident in urology Med. Sch., 1972-76; fellow in urology Sloan Kettering Meml. Hosp., N.Y.C., 1976-77; instr. in urology Med. Sch. La. State U., New Orleans, 1977-78, asst. prof., 1978-82, assoc. prof., 1982-87, chmn. dept. urology, 1984—, prof., 1987—; sec. La. Lithotripter, Inc., New Orleans, 1987-91; sec.-treas. med. staff Hotel Dieu Hosp., New Orleans, 1985-90, pres. med. staff, 1991-92, bd. dirs., 1990. Bd. dirs. YMCA, New Orleans, 1980—; bd. dirs. La. State U. Clinic, 1987-92, chmn., 1990-92. Mem. AMA, ACS, Am. Urologic Assn., Soc. Surg. Oncologists, Southeastern Sect. Am. Urologic Assn., Southwest Oncology Group, Am. Soc. Clin. Oncology. Home: 7576 Pearl St New Orleans LA 70118-3836 Office: La State U Med Sch Dept of Urology 1542 Tulane Ave New Orleans LA 70112-2825

SULLIVAN, JOHN GERARD, surgeon; b. Boston, Mar. 2, 1941; s. Francis Gerard and Anna Maria (Maiorana) S.; m. Margaret B. McIntyre; children: Meghan, Erin, Caitlin. BS, Boston Coll., 1962; MD, Tufts U., 1966. Diplomate Am. Bd. Surgery. Intern St. Elizabeth's Hosp., Boston, 1966-67; asst. resident surgery St. Luke's Hosp., N.Y.C., 1969-72; chief surgical resident St. Luke's Med. Ctr., N.Y.C., 1972-73; gen. surgeon Brighton (Mass.) Surg. Assocs.; assoc. dir. surg. ICU, coord. surg. residency St. Elizabeth's Hosp., Boston, 1981-84, chmn. dept. surgery, 1984—; clin. instr. surgery Tufts U., 1973-77, asst. clin. prof. surgery, 1977-79, assoc. clin. prof. surgery, 1980-85, clin. prof. surgery, 1985—. Capt. U.S. Army, 1967-68, Vietnam. Mem. Mass. Med. Assn., Am. Coll. Surgeons (councilor Mass. chpt. 1982-85), Assn. Surg. Edn., Boston Surg. Soc., New Eng. Program Dirs. in Surgery, Assn. Program Dirs. in Surgery, New Eng. Surg. Soc., Boston Coll. Alumni Assn., Fides Club, 4th Inf. Div. Assn. Office: Seton Gen Surgery Assocs 11 Nevins St Ste 201 Brighton MA 02135-3514 also: St Elizabeth's Med Ctr Dept Surgery 736 Cambridge St Boston MA 02135

SULLIVAN, JOHN HARVEY, ophthalmologist, plastic surgeon; b. Charleston, W.Va., Jan. 10, 1939; m. Susan O'Connor, 1975; children: Brian, Patrick, Katerine. BA, U. Notre Dame, 1960; MD, Georgetown U., 1964. Diplomate Nat. Bd. Med. Examiners, Am. Bd. Ophthalmology; lic. physician, Calif. Med. intern Ohio State U., Columbus, 1964-65; resident in ophthalmology U. Calif., San Francisco, 1968-71; fellow St. John's Ophthalmol. Hosp., Jerusalem, 1971-72, Melbourne (Australia) U., 1972-73; ophthalmologist in pvt. practice San Jose, Calif., 1973—; pvt. practice El Segundo, Calif., 1967-68; clin. instr. ophthalmology U. Calif., San Francisco, 1973-75, asst. clin. prof., 1975-83, assoc. clin. prof., 1983-89, clin. prof., 1989—; vol. clin. faculty Stanford (Calif.) U., 1992—. Contbr. articles to profl. jours. Pres. Prevent Blindness No. Calif., 1996; Capt. M.C. U.S. Army, 1965-67. Sr. Fulbright-Hays postdoctoral fellwo, 1972, Oculoplastic Surgery fellow U. Calif., San Francisco, 1994-95. Fellow Am. Acad. Ophthalmology, Am. Soc. Oculoplastic and Reconstructive Surgery; mem. AMA, Calif. Med. Assn., Peninsula Eye Soc. (sec. 1995-96), Fredrick C. Cordes Eye Soc. (exec. sec. 1982-87, pres. 1988-89), Santa Clara Med. Assn. (pub. svc. com.), Calif. Assn. Ophthalmology. Office: Eye Med Clinic 220 Meridian Ave San Jose CA 95126

SULLIVAN, JOHN P., physician; b. Bridgeport, Conn., Nov. 10, 1922; s. John P. and Helen G. (Lyons) S.; m. Muriel Kleinke, Apr. 26, 1952 (dec. Oct. 1995); children: Kathryn S., Rosemary, John P., Jr., Michael V., Mark D. BA, St. Anselm Coll., 1943; MD, Tufts U., 1947. Diplomate Am. Bd. Pathology Anatomical/Clin. Chief of pathology Holy Name Hosp., Teaneck, N.J., 1957-58; attending pathologist Baystate Med. Ctr., Springfield, Mass., 1958-66; chmn. dept. pathology Baystate Med. Ctr., Springfield, 1966-92; med. dir. Greater Springfield (Mass.) Path., 1992—; cons. pathologist Shriner's Hosp., Springfield, 1976—, Springfield Mcpl. Hosp., 1960—. Lt. USNR, 1951-53. Fellow Coll. of Am. Pathologist (chmn. N.E. AAB-BI&A program 1970-75); mem. New Eng. Soc. Pathology (pres. 1976-77), Mass. Soc. Pathologist (pres. 1971-77), Am. Assn. Blood Banks (bd. dirs. 1972-74), Am. Soc. Pathologists, AMA, Mass. Med. Soc., Rotary. Home: 5 Canborne Way Suffield CT 06078 Office: Greater Springfield Path 222 Carew St Springfield MA 01104

SULLIVAN, JOSEPH DEUEL, psychiatrist; b. N.Y.C., Oct. 17, 1913; s. Cornelius F. and Mary R. (Brennan) S.; m. Dorothy S. Schwartz, Jan. 16, 1944; children: Michael, Deborah, Peter. BS, Fordham U., 1935; MD, Cornell U., 1939. Diplomate Am. Bd. Neurology & Psychiatry. Intern Albany (N.Y.) Hosp., 1940-41, resident, 1941-42; pvt. practice N.Y.C., 1946—; assoc. prof. clin. psychiatry med. coll. Cornell U., N.Y.C., 1946-85; assoc. attending psychiatrist N.Y. Hosp., 1946-85; attending psychiatrist St. Vincent's Hosp., N.Y.C., 1946—; emeritus staff psychiatry N.Y. Hosp.-Cornell Med. Ctr., 1985—; dir. Mental Health Clinic Internat. Ctr. for the Disabled, N.Y.C., 1950-56; instr. psychiatry Columbia Med. Coll., 1950-56; adj. attending psychiatrist Montefiore Hosp., Bronx, N.Y., 1951-55; cons. psychiatrist Josephine Baird Home for Elderly, N.Y.C., 1964-74, N.Y. State Crime Victims Bd., 1973—; impartial psychiat. cons. N.Y. State Workers' Compensation Bd., 1974—; ind. psychiat. cons. Fed. Employees' Compensation Program, 1983—; mem. exec. bd. Am. Acad. Legal and Indsl. Medicine, 1974-91; attending psychiatrist Cabrini Med. Ctr., N.Y.C., 1974—; panel psychiatrist N.Y. State Supreme Ct.-Mental Hygiene Legal Svcs., med. malpractice panel appellate divsn., 1990-91. Maj., U.S. Army, 1942-46, Italy, N. Africa. Fellow Am. Psychiat. Assn. (life, N.Y. dist. br.), Med. Soc. N.Y. County (various coms.), Med. Soc. of N.Y. State (Continuing Med. Edn. award 1989-92, various coms.).

SULLIVAN, LOUIS WADE, former secretary health and human services, physician; b. Atlanta, Nov. 3, 1933; s. Walter Wade and Lubirda Elizabeth (Priester) S.; m. Eve Williamson, Sept. 30, 1955; children: Paul, Shanta, Halsted. B.S. magna cum laude, Morehouse Coll., Atlanta, 1954; M.D. cum laude, Boston U., 1958. Diplomate: Am. Bd. Internal Medicine. Intern N.Y. Hosp.-Cornell Med. Ctr., N.Y.C., 1958-59, resident in internal medicine, 1959-60; fellow in pathology Mass. Gen. Hosp., Boston, 1960-61; rsch. fellow Thorndike Meml. Lab. Harvard Med. Sch., Boston, 1961-63; instr. medicine Harvard Med. Sch., 1963-64; asst. prof. medicine N.J. Coll. Medicine, 1964-66; co-dir. hematology Boston U. Med. Ctr., 1966; assoc. prof. medicine Boston U., 1968-74; dir. hematology Boston City Hosp., 1973-75; also prof. medicine and physiology Boston U., 1974-75; dean Sch. Medicine, Morehouse Coll., Atlanta, 1975-89, pres., until 1989, 1993—; sec. Dept. of Health and Human Svcs., Washington, 1989-93; non-exec. dir. GM, 1993—; mem. sickle cell anemia adv. com. NIH, 1974-75; ad hoc panel on blood diseases Nat. Heart, Lung Blood Disease Bur., 1973, Nat. Adv. Rsch. Coun., 1977; mem. med. adv. bd. Nat. Leukemia Assn., 1968-70, chmn., 1970; researcher suppression of hematopoiesis by ethanol, pernicious anemia in childhood, folates in human nutrition. John Hay Whitney Found. Opportunity fellow, 1960-61; recipient Honor medal Am. Cancer Soc., 1991. Mem. Am. Soc. Hematology, Am. Soc. Clin. Investigation, Inst. Medicine, Phi Beta Kappa, Alpha Omega Alpha. Episcopalian. Office: Morehouse Sch Medicine Office of the Pres 720 Westview Dr SW Atlanta GA 30310-1495*

SULLIVAN, MARY K., nurse; b. Kansas City, Kans., Oct. 4, 1961; d. Robert W. and Ann J. (Cindrich) S. BS in Nursing, Creighton U., 1983. RN, Ariz., Kans., Nebr., R.N.C., C.A.R.N.; cert. psychiat.-mental health nurse; cert. addictions RN. Staff nurse Western Mo. Mental Health Ctr., Kansas City, 1983-84, Kansas City VA Hosp., 1984-85; shift supr. Ariz. State Hosp., Phoenix, 1986; staff nurse Camelback Hosp., Phoenix, Scottsdale, 1985-87, Carl T. Hayden VA Hosp., Phoenix, 1987—; chmn. psychiat. nursing com. Carl T. Hayden VA Hosp., 1988—; sexual assault nurse examiner. Mem. Fraternal Order of Police Aux. Mem. ANA (coun. psychiat. and mental health), Nat. Nurses Soc. Addictions, Internat. Assn. Forensics Nursing, Am. Coll. Forensic Examiners, Ariz. Nurses Assn. Roman Catholic. Office: Carl T Hayden V A Med Ctr 650 E Indian Sch Rd Phoenix AZ 85012

SULLIVAN, MICHAEL ALOYSIUS, radiologist; b. Washington, May 23, 1939; s. Albert Joseph and Bernadette (Durgin) S.; m. Karen Weigel, Aug. 29, 1964; children: Lauren Ann, Kristin Marie, Michael Durgin. BS, Tulane U., 1961, MD, 1964. Intern Phila. Gen. Hosp., 1964-65; resident Hosp. U. Pa., Phila., 1964-69; staff radiologist Ochsner Clinic and Found. Hosp., New Orleans, 1969—. Assoc. chmn., past pres. dad's club St. Martin's Episc. Sch., New Orleans, past dad's club rep. bd. trustees. Mem. Radiol. Soc. N.Am. (liaison for edn. 1990—, bd. dirs. 1990—, chair bd. dirs. 1995, pres.-elect 1996, pres. 1997). Roman Catholic. Home: 9104 Tanglewild Pl New Orleans LA 70123-2752 Office: Ochsner Clinic Med Found 1516 Jefferson Hwy New Orleans LA 70121-2429

SULLIVAN, PATRICIA EILEEN, physical therapist; b. Wilmington, Del., Mar. 5, 1946; 1 child, Kathryn. BS, Northeastern U., 1968; MS, Northwestern U., 1975; PhD, Boston U., 1989. Phys. therapist Mass. Gen. Hosp., Boston, 1968-69, 72-74, Kaiser Permanente, San Francisco, 1969-72; assoc. phys. therapy program Northwestern U. Med. Sch., Chgo., 1974-75; asst. prof. Boston U., 1975-88; assoc. prof., advisor internat. program Inst. Health Profls., Mass. Gen. Hosp., 1990—; lectr. dept. orthopedics Harvard Med. Sch.; cons. in field. Co-author: (textbooks) Integrated Approach to Therapeutic Exercise, 1982, Clinical Procedures in Therapeutic Exercise, 1986, Clinical Decision Making in Therapeutic Exercise, 1994, Clinical Procedures, 2nd edit., 1995. Mem. Phys. Therapy Assn. (v.p. Mass. chpt. 1990-92, sec. 1973-74, chief del. 1980-86). Office: Inst Health Profls 101 Merrimac St Boston MA 02114

SULLIVAN, ROBERT EMMETT, pediatric dentist, educator; b. Sioux City, Iowa, May 28, 1932; s. Joseph A. and Daisy B. (Stanieforth) S.; m. Mary Ann Sullivan, Sept. 22, 1961. BA, Morningside Coll., 1954; DDS, U. Nebr., 1961, MSD, 1963. Diplomate Am. Bd. Pediat. Dentistry. Prof., chair pediat. dentistry U. Nebr. Coll. Dentistry, Lincoln, 1963—; prof. pediats. U. Nebr. Coll. Medicine, Omaha, 1969—. Contbr. articles to profl. jours. Fellow Am. Acad. Pediat. Dentistry, Am. Coll. Dentists, Internat. Coll. Dentistry; mem. ADA, VFW, Am. Soc. Dentistry for Children, N.E. Nebr. Dental Assn., Lincoln Dist. Dental Assn. Democrat. Home: 1201 Piedmont Rd Lincoln NE 68510

SULLIVAN, ROBERT JOSEPH, lawyer; b. Ashville, N.C., Oct. 8, 1940; s. Daniel Joseph and Anne (McKann) S.; m. Paula Van Buskirk, Feb. 6, 1965; children: Robert Joseph Jr., Andrew Paul, Emily Elizabeth. AB, Stanford U., 1963; JD, UCLA, 1966. Bar: Calif. 1967, U.S. Dist. Ct. (ea. dist.) Calif. 1967, U.S. Ct. Appeals (9th cir.) 1967. Deputy atty. gen. Office Atty. Gen., Sacramento, Calif., 1967-71; staff, sr. counsel, chief counsel Calif. State Employees Assn., Sacramento, 1971-73; prin. Turner & Sullivan, Sacramento, 1973-91; ptnr. Nossaman, Gunther, Knox & Elliott, Sacramento, 1991—. Contbg. author: California Public Agency PRactice, 1988, California Adminstrative Mandamus, 1989. Bd. trustees Stanford Settlement, Sacramento, 1989; pro tem judge Sacramento Superior Ct., 1988—, arbitrator, 1980-88. Calif. Soc. Healthcare Attys. (bd. dirs. 1988—), Sacramento County Bar Assn. (chmn. healthcare law sect. 1990). Office: Nossaman Gunther Knox & Elliott 915 L St Ste 1000 Sacramento CA 95814-3705

SULLIVAN, STEPHEN GENE, psychiatrist, pharmacologist, administrator; b. Manchester, N.H., Feb. 27, 1947. BS, Georgetown U., 1970; MS, NYU, 1976, PhD, 1977, MD, 1984. Assoc. research scientist NYU Sch. Med., 1978-81, rsch. asst. prof. pharmacology, 1981-82, adj. asst. prof. pharmacology, 1984-91; intern Beth Israel Med. Ctr., N.Y.C., 1984, resident in psychiatry, 1984-88, physician-in-charge Clin. Psychopharmacology Lab., 1988-90; sci. dir. The Corp. for Clin. Psychopharmacology Research, N.Y.C., 1988—; pvt. practice N.Y.C., 1986—; instr. psychiatry Mt. Sinai Sch. Med. CUNY, 1986-88, asst. clin. prof. psychiatry, 1988-90. Contbr. numerous articles to profl. jours., author ten book chpts., 1976—. Med. scientist tng. program fellow NIH, 1970-76, 82-83, postdoctoral fellow, 1976-77. Mem. AAAS, AMA, Am. Psychiat. Assn., N.Y. Acad. Sciences. Office: Corp Clin Psychopharm Res 207 E 16th St Ste 4M New York NY 10003-3742

SULLIVAN, STEPHEN JEROME, retired psychologist; b. Wilmington, N.C., Apr. 13, 1943; s. Jerome John and Ann Elizabeth (Holmes) S. BA, St. John's U., 1965; MA, Cath. U. Am., 1968, PhD, 1971. Dir. dept. psychology Fairview Hosp. and Tng. Ctr., Salem, Oreg., 1971-74; psychologist Salem, 1974—. Adv. bd. Salem Airport, 1983-88, chmn. 1985-86; bd. dirs. Salem Area Mass Transit Dist., 1987-89. Mem. APA, Oreg. Psychol. Assn., Salem Psychol. Soc. (pres. 1990-91). Home: 63 Tull Dr Albany NY 12205-2415 Office: 635 Church St NE Salem OR 97301-2402

SULLIVAN, STUART FRANCIS, anesthesiologist, educator; b. Buffalo, July 15, 1928; s. Charles S. and Kathryn (Duggan) S.; m. Dorothy Elizabeth Faytol, Apr. 18, 1959; children: John, Irene, Paul, Kathryn. BS, Canisius Coll., 1950; MD, SUNY, Syracuse, 1955. Diplomate Am. Bd. Anesthesiology. Intern Ohio State Univ. Hosp., Columbus, 1955-56; resident Columbia Presbyn. Med. Ctr., 1958-60; instr. anesthesiology Columbia U. Coll. Physicians and Surgeons, N.Y.C., 1961-62, assoc., 1962-64, asst. prof., 1964-69, assoc. prof., 1969-73; prof. dept. anesthesiology UCLA, 1973-91, vice chair anesthesiology, 1974-77, exec. vice chair, 1977-90, acting chmn., 1983-84, 87-88, 90-91, prof. emeritus, 1991—. Served to capt. M.C., USAR, 1956-58. Fellow NIH, 1960-61; recipient research career devel. award NIH, 1966-69. Mem. Assn. Univ. Anesthetists, Am. Physiol. Soc., Am. Soc. Anesthesiologists. Home: 101 Foxtail Dr Santa Monica CA 90402-2047 Office: UCLA Sch Medicine Dept Anesthesiology Los Angeles CA 90024

SULLIVAN, SULLINS GRENFELL, surgeon, consultant; b. Stonewall, Okla., Oct. 6, 1912; s. Bedford Forrest and Jessie Eulalia (Lyles) S.; m. Alyce Idella Thomas, Oct. 6, 1937; 1 child, Thomas Joseph. BS in Medicine, U. Okla., 1933, MD, 1935. Diplomate Am. Bd. Surgery. Intern St. Joseph Hosp., Balt., 1935-36, resident in medicine, 1936-37, resident in surgery, 1937-39; chief resident in surgery Bon Secourse Hosp., —, 1939-40; chief of surgery Bon Secaurs Hosp., Balt., 1955-76, St. Joseph Hosp., Balt., 1976-83. With U.S. Army, 1942-46. Fellow ACS; mem. Med. Chirurg. Faculty of Md., (founder) Balt. Acad. of Surgery, Porsche Club Am. Home: 419 Oak Ln Baltimore MD 21286-7329 Office: 1129 Saint Paul St Baltimore MD 21202-2614

SULLIVAN, TONI J., dean; m. James T. Sullivan; children: Jill, James. BSN, Seaton Hall U., 1962; EdM, Columbia U., 1974, EdD, 1979. RN. Nursing inst. Seaton Hall U., South Orange, N.J., 1974-75, asst. prof., 1976-78; assoc. prof., dir. nursing program Felician Coll., Lodi, N.J., 1979-82; prof., chmn. nursing dept. U. Southern Calif., L.A., 1982-89; prof., dean U. Mo., Columbia, 1989—; assoc. dir. acad. nursing affairs, Norris Cancer Hosp. & Rsch. Inst., L.A., 1983-89, Univ. Mo. Hosps. and Clinics, 1989—. Contbr. articles to profl. jours. Chmn. Area Health Edn. Ctr. Cen. Region Adv. Coun., L.A., 1984-87, active Blue Ribbon Task Force Health Edn., 1985; active Sta. KCET Nat. Pub. TV adv. com., L.A., 1989. Recipient Outstanding Alumni award Seton Hall U. Coll. Nursing, 1988; fellow Am. Acad. Nursing, 1989. Mem. Sigma Theta Tau (Excellence in Leadership 1985), Rotary. Office: U Mo Columbia Sch Nursing S215 Sch Nursing Bldg Columbia MO 65211*

SULLIVAN, VICKI B., medical and surgical nurse, health facility administrator; b. St. Louis, June 29, 1946; d. Grover Alfred and Berneal Lola (Armstrong) Edmiston; m. Michael John Sullivan, July 11, 1966 (div. Dec. 1995); children: Shawn Michael, Tara Nicole. Nursing diploma, Moline (Ill.) Pub. Hosp. Sch., 1967; student, Blackhawk Coll., Moline, Western Ill. U., Coll. of St. Francis, Chgo. RN, Ill.; cert. oper. rm. nurse. Staff nurse, oper. rm. Moline (Ill.) Pub. Hosp., 1967-73; office/scrub nurse Dr. Richard Retz, Moline, 1973-78; staff nurse, oper. rm. Trinity Med. Ctr., Moline, 1980-91; dir. surg. svcs. Quad City Ambulatory Surgery, Moline, 1991—; mem. quality assurance com. Option Care Home Therapy, Moline, 1994-96. Mem. Am. Soc. Outpatient Surgeons, Federated Ambulatory Surgery Assn., Ill. Freestanding Surgery Ctr. Assn. (membership com. 1995-96), Quad City Assn. Oper. Rm. Nurses (multiple offices 1985-95). Office: Quad City Amb Surgery Ctr 520 Valley View Dr Moline IL 61265

SULLIVAN, WILLIAM E., gerontology nurse, administrator; b. Matawan, N.J., June 7, 1948; s. James C. and Mary C. Sullivan. Diploma, St. Margaret's Hosp., Kansas City, Kans., 1973; BS, St. Joseph's Coll., Standish, Maine, 1979; MS, SUNY, Buffalo, 1982. Cert. in nursing adminstrn., advanced. Instr. Daemen Coll., Buffalo; asst. adminstr. patient svcs. Terrace Health Care Ctr., Buffalo; dir. nursing svc. Niagara Geriatric Ctr., Niagara Falls, N.Y.; mem. N.Y. State Bd. for Nursing, 1987—. Mem. N.Y. State Nurses Assn., Sigma Theta Tau.

SULLIVAN, WILLIAM P., physician; b. Cheektowaga, N.Y., Aug. 13, 1965; s. William P. Jr. and Teresa (Ryan) S.; m. Michelle Snyderman, June 7, 1996. BA, Notre Dame U., 1987; DO, N.Y. Coll. Osteo. Medicine, 1992. Intern St. Barnabas Hosp., Bronx, N.Y., 1992-93; resident in emergency medicine/internal medicine Midwestern U., Downers Grove, Ill., 1993—; tchr. Chgo. Coll. Osteo. Medicine, Downers Grove, 1995—. Recipient Osteo. fellowship N.Y. Coll. Osteo. Medicine, 1991, 92. Mem. Am. Osteo. Assn., Am. Coll. Emergency Physicians. Home: PO Box 1415 Oak Park IL 60304

SULLY, ROBERT CAMERON, family practice physician; b. Toronto, May 5, 1956; came to the U.S., 1962; s. William and Irene D. Sully; children: Kenny, Naomi, Corinne, Brianna. BS in Biology, Loyola Marymount U., 1978; MD, U. Calif., Irvine, 1982. Intern, resident Kaiser Found. Hosp., Fontana, Calif., 1982-85; staff physician family practice So. Calif. Permanente Med. Group, Woodland Hills, Calif., 1985—. Office: So Calif Permanente Med Gro 5601 De Soto Ave Woodland Hills CA 91367

SULMASY, DANIEL PATRICK, internal medicine educator, bioethicist; b. N.Y.C., Jan. 28, 1956; s. Warren Joseph and Margaret Theresa (Quirke) S. AB, Cornell U., Ithaca, N.Y., 1978; MD, Cornell U., N.Y.C., 1982; PhD, Georgetown U., 1995. Vowed Franciscan friar Roman Cath. Ch., 1990; diplomate Am. Bd. Internal Medicine. Intern Johns Hopkins Hosp., Balt., 1982-83, resident in internal medicine, 1985-87, fellow, 1987-88, 89-91, chief resident, 1988-89; asst. prof. internal medicine Georgetown U. Med. Sch., Washington, 1991—; dir. ethics cons. svc. Georgetown U. Med. Ctr., 1993—, assoc. dir. Ctr. for Clin. Bioethics, 1995—. Mem. editl. bd. Annals Internal Medicine, 1995—; contbr. articles on med. ethics to med. jours. Co-chmn. pre-hosp. advance directives task force Washington Mayor's Adv. Subcom. on Emergency Medicine, 1992-95; trustee Siena Coll., Loudonville, N.Y., 1995—. Med. humanities scholar Culpeper Found., 1990-93. Mem. ACP (tchg. and rsch. scholar 1993-96), Soc. Gen. Internal Medicine, Washington Acad. Medicine. Office: Georgetown U Med Ctr Ctr for Clin Bioethics Washington DC 20007

SULTAN, JOHN M., internist; b. Highland Park, Ill., July 1, 1955; s. Robert M. and Shirley (Wigodner) S.; m. Susan P. Sultan, Dec. 8, 1991; children: Christine, Joshua. BA, Carleton Coll., Northfield, Minn., 1977; MD, U. Chgo., 1981. Diplomate Am. Bd. Internal Medicine, Am. Bd. Gerontology. Intern, resident Michael Reese Hosp. & Med. Ctr., Chgo., 1981-84; pvt. practice Highland Park, Ill., 1984-94; phywician Ravinia Assocs. in Internal Medicine, Highland Park, 1994—. Mem. ACP, AMA, Ill. State Med. Soc., Lake County Med. Soc., Phi Beta Kappa. Office: Ravinia Assocs in Internal Medicine 625 Roger Williams Ave Highland Park IL 60035

SULTANA, NAJMA, psychiatrist; b. Nirmal, Andhra, India; July 22, 1948; came to U.S. 1973; d. Khaja Moinuddin and Mujib (Unnisa) Begum; m. Khaja Mohiuddin, July 8, 1971 (div. 1978); m. M. Rashid Chaudhry, Oct. 16, 1981. M.B.B.S. Gandhi Med. Coll., Hyderaba, India, 1973. Resident in psychiatry SUNY/Kings County Hosp. Ctr., Bklyn., 1976-78, fellow child psychiatry, 1978-80; asst. clin. physician S. Beach Psychiat. Ctr., S.I., N.Y., 1980-81; asst. clin. prof. SUNY Downstate Med. Ctr., N.Y.C., 1981-94; attending psychiatrist King's County Hosp., Bklyn., 1981-94, Creedmoile Psychiatric Ctr., 1994—. Exec. bd. mem. Balkan Rape Response Team; co-pres. Coalition for Intervention Against Genocide in Bosnia; pres. Am. Fedn. of Muslims from India, v.p.; founding mem. G.O.P.I.O.; bd. dirs. T.O.U.C.H. Recipient Non-Resident Indian Internat. Women's award, 1992. Mem. Am. Psychiat. Assn. Democrat. Muslim.

SULTZER, BARNET MARTIN, microbiology and immunology researcher; b. Union City, N.J., Mar. 24, 1929; s. Moses Joseph and Florence Gertrude (Fischer) S.; m. Judith Ray Moreinis, Aug. 26, 1956; 1 child, Steven Bennett. BS, Rutgers U., 1950; MS, Mich. State U., 1951, PhD, 1958. Rsch.

assoc. Princeton (N.J.) Labs., Inc., 1958-64; from asst. prof. to prof. microbiology SUNY, Bklyn., 1964-94, prof. emeritus, 1994—, interim chmn. dept. microbiology, 1980-82; vis. scientist Karolinska Inst., Stockholm, 1971-72; vis. prof. Pasteur Inst., Paris, 1979-80; adj. prof. Fels Inst. of Cancer Rsch. and Molecular Biology, Temple U., Phila., 1995—. Assoc. editor Jour. of Immunology, 1983-86; contbr. book chpts. and over 50 articles to profl. jours. on microbiology and immunology; mem. editl. bd. Infection and Immunity, 1980-94. Pres. Tenants Assn. Gateway Plz., Manhattan, N.Y., 1990-92; mem. Cmty. Bd. #1, Manhattan, 1989-94. 1st lt. USMC, 1952-55. Pres.'s fellow Am. Soc. Microbiology, 1957; grantee USPHS, NIH, Office of Naval Rsch., 1967-94. Mem. AAAS, Am. Soc. Microbiology, Am. Assn. Immunologists, N.Y. Acad. Sci., Harvey Soc., Internat. Endotoxin Soc., Reticuloendothelial Soc., Sigma Xi. Office: SUNY Health Sci Ctr 450 Clarkson Ave Brooklyn NY 11203-2012

SUMERS, ANNE RICKS, ophthalmologist, museum director; b. Beverly, Mass., May 8, 1957; d. David Frank and Anne Russell (Russell) Ricks; m. Elliott H. Sumers, May 31, 1983; children: Ben, Ted. BA in English Lit. with honors, U. Mich., 1979; MD, U. Cin., 1983. Diplomate Am. Bd. Ophthalmology. Intern in internal medicine Mt. Auburn Hosp., Cambridge, Mass., 1984; resident in ophthalmology NYU/Bellevue Hosp., 1984-87; ptnr. Ridgewood (N.J.) Ophthalmology, PC, 1990—; dir. N.J. Childrens Mus., Paramus, N.J., 1992—; co-owner Saddle River (N.J.) Market, 1995—; team ophthalmologist N.Y. Giants Football Team, 1994—; state coord. N.J. Turn Off Your TV Week, 1994, 95, 96; spkr. in field. Author: The Offical M.D. Handbook, 1983; writer, host Channel 11/WPIX Wonder Zone, 1993; interviewed on Good Morning Am., Am.'s Talking, NJN Discover N.J., Comcast Cablevision, Cablevision, Fox Channel 5 Good Day N.Y., 1992-95, numerous radio shows. Named one of 10 N.J. Women of Yr., N.J. Woman Mag., 1993; profiled in AMA News, Med. Econs., The N.Y. Times, Star Ledger, Argus and other newspapers and mags. Fellow Am. Acad. Ophthalmology (media spokesperson, media info. com.); mem. AMA, Assn. Youth Museums, Alpha Omega Alpha. Office: Ridgewood Ophthalmology PC 1200 E Ridgewood Ave Ridgewood NJ 07451

SUMMANEN, PAULA ANNELI, ophthalmologist, educator; b. Ruokolahti, Finland, Oct. 9, 1952; d. Unto Kalervo Summanen and Aino (Luukkonen) Kuukka; m. Tero Kivelä; 1 child, Liia Matilda Kivelä. B Medicine, U. Kuopio, 1974, Lic. in Medicine, 1978. Jr. physician dept. pediatrics and cancer therapy Kotka Cen. Hosp., Finland, 1978-79; rsch. asst. Inst. Tropical Medicine, Khartoum, Dem. Republic Sudan, 1980; resident in ophthalmology Khartoum Eye Hosp., 1981; rsch. fellow King Khaled Eye Specialist Hosp., Nat. Eye Survey, Riyadh, Saudi Arabia, 1984; resident in ophthalmology Helsinki U. Eye Hosp., Finland, 1981-83, 85-87; cons. ophthalmologist Helsinki U. Eye Hosp., 1988—; clin. instr. ophthalmology U. Helsinki, 1989—; physician, Espoo Health Ctr. and Hosp., Finland, 1982. Named Tutor of Yr. by med. students U. Helsinki Faculty Medicine, 1993. Mem. Duodecim Soc., Finnish Med. Assn., Ophthalmol. Soc. Finland, David Livingstone Soc. (sec. 1988-92), European Macula Group, Finnish Diabetes Rsch. Soc. Home: Sepontie 1 D, FIN-02130 Espoo Finland Office: Helsinki U Eye Hosp, Haartmaninkatu 4C, FIN-00290 Helsinki Finland

SUMMER, GEORGE KENDRICK, medical educator, biochemist, researcher; b. Cherryville, N.C., May 8, 1923; s. Thomas Carlisle and Bessie Eunice (Kendrick) S.; m. Elizabeth Ann Koch, Aug. 27, 1952; children—David Elliott, Carol Ann. B.S. in Chemistry, U. N.C., 1944; M.D., Harvard U., 1951. Diplomate Am. Bd. Pediatrics. Intern medicine Vanderbilt U., Nashville, 1951-52; asst. resident in pediatrics Wake Forest U., Winston-Salem, N.C., 1952-53; sr. resident in pediatrics U. N.C.-Chapel Hill, 1953-54, fellow in pediatric metabolism, 1954-57, instr. in pediatrics, 1957-59, asst. prof. pediatrics, 1959-65, assoc. clin. prof. pediatrics, 1965—, asst. prof. biochemistry and nutrition, 1965, assoc. prof., 1966-72, prof., 1972-88, prof. emeritus dept. biochemistry and biophysics, 1988—; rsch. scientist Biol. Scis. Rsch. Ctr., Child Devel. Inst., 1971-88, dir. Automated Biochem. Systems Lab., 1965-88; vis. scientist human biol. genetics King's Coll., London and Galton Lab., Univ. Coll., London, 1962-63. Served with USNR, 1944-46. Recipient Research Career Devel. award Nat. Inst. Arthritis, Metabolic and Digestive Diseases, 1965-70. Fellow Am. Acad. Pediatrics; mem. N.C. Pediatric Soc., Am. Chem. Soc., Soc. Exptl. Biology and Medicine, Am. Inst. Nutrition, Am. Soc. Human Genetics. Contbr. numerous articles to profl. jours. Office: U NC CB #7260 Rm 405 Faculty Lab Office Bldg Chapel Hill NC 27599-7260

SUMMERS, JOHN M., physician; b. Booneville, Ind., July 8, 1924; s. Franklin Lyle and Mary Doris (Schurmeier) S.; m. Marylin Eileen Collins, 1947; 1 child, Jeffrey Murray; m. Julia Ann Howell, June 11, 1977. BS, Ind. U., 1944, MD, 1947. Internist pvt. practice, Springfield, Ohio, 1948-88; staff mem. Mercy Med. Ctr., Springfield, Ohio, 1951-88; chmn. dept. medicine City Hosp., Springfield, Ohio, 1954-57; med. dir. Credit Life Ins. Co., Springfield, Ohio, 1969-91; retired, 1991; founder, v.p. Western Ohio Health Care Found., Dayton, 1974-86; founder, charter mem. Western Ohio HMO, Dayton, 1980-86; assoc. clin. prof. Wright State U. Sch. Medicine, Dayton, 1978-94; trustee, mem. exec. com. Cmty. Hosp., Springfield, 1975-84. Elected city commr. City of Springfield, 1965-69. Col. USAR, ret. Mem. Springfield Country Club, Polo Club, Columbia Club Indpls., Wright-Patterson AFB Officer's Club, Cmty. Progress Coun. (pres. 1990), Co. of Mil. Collectors & Historians.

SUMMERS, WILLIAM COFIELD, science educator; b. Janesville, Wis., Apr. 17, 1939; s. Crosby Hungerford and Rebecca Delores (Cofield) S.; m. Wilma Jean Poos, July 24, 1965; 1 child, Emily Alexandra. BS, U. Wis., 1961, MS, 1963, Phd, MD, 1967; MA, Yale U., 1977. Post-doctoral fellow MIT, Cambridge, Mass., 1967-68; asst. prof. Yale U., New Haven, 1968-70, assoc. prof., 1970-77, prof., 1977—; cons. NIH, Bethesda, Md., 1976—. Editor Nucleic Acids Research Jour., 1977-79, Gene jour., 1984-91; contbr. articles to profl. jours. Cons. Anna Fuller Fund, New Haven, 1973-88, Searle Scholars Program, Chgo., 1980-84; trustee Leukemia Soc. Am., N.Y.C., 1981-85, Yale-China Assn., New Haven, 1982-88, 94—. Mem. Am. Soc. Biochemistry and Molecular Biology, Am. Soc. for Microbiology, History Sci. Soc., Am. Assn. Hist. Medicine. Office: Yale U Sch Medicine 333 Cedar St New Haven CT 06510-3206

SUMMERS, WILLIAM KOOPMANS, neuropsychiatrist, researcher; b. Jefferson City, Mo., Apr. 14, 1944; s. Joseph S. and Amy Lydia (Koopmans) S.; m. Angela Forbes McGonigle, Oct. 2, 1972(div. Apr. 1985); children: Elisabeth Stuart, Wilhelmina Derek. Student, Westminster Coll., Fulton, Mo., 1962-64; BS, U. Mo., 1966; MD, Washington U., St. Louis, 1971. Internal medicine intern Barnes Hosp-Washington U., St. Louis, 1971-72; resident in internal medicine Jewish Hosp., St. Louis, 1972-73; resident in psychiatry Rsch. Hosp., St. Louis, 1973-76; asst. prof. U. Pitts., 1976-78, U. So. Calif., L.A., 1978-82; asst. clin. prof. rsch. UCLA, 1982-88; rschr. Arcadia, Calif., 1988-92, Albuquerque, 1992—. Patentee in field. Mem. AMA, ACP, Am. Psychiat. Assn., Soc. Neurosci., N.Y. Acad. Scis., Am. Fedn. Clin. Rsch. Episcopalian. Office: 201 Cedar St SE Ste 404 Albuquerque NM 87106

SUMMITT, ROBERT LAYMAN, pediatrician, educator; b. Knoxville, Tenn., Dec. 23, 1932; s. Robert Luther and Mary Ruth (Layman) S.; m. Joyce Ann Sharp, Dec. 23, 1955; children: Robert Layman Jr., Susan Kelly Summitt Pridgen, John Blair. Student, Davidson Coll., 1950-51; MD, U. Tenn., 1955, MS in Pediatrics, 1962. Diplomate Am. Bd. Pediatrics, recert. in pediatrics, 1983, 92, Am. Bd. Med. Genetics (bd. dirs. 1985-89). Rotating intern U. Tenn. Meml. Research Ctr. and Hosp., Knoxville, 1956; asst. resident in pediatrics U. Tenn. Coll. Medicine and City of Memphis Hosp., 1959-60, chief resident, 1960-61; USPHS fellow in pediatric endocrinology U. Tenn. Coll. Medicine, Memphis, 1961-62; fellow in med. genetics U. Wis.-Madison, 1963; asst. prof. pediatrics, child devel. U. Tenn., Memphis, 1964-68, assoc. prof., 1968-71, prof. pediatrics and anatomy, 1971—, dean Coll. Medicine, 1981—, provost, 1988-91; cons. President's Commn. on Mental Retardation, 1979-80; CEO U. Tenn. Med. Group, 1983-93, chmn., 1983—; mem. Coun. on Grad. Med. Edn., 1990—. Lt. M.C., USN, 1957-59, rear admiral USNR, ret. 1992. NIH grantee, 1965—; recipient Alumni Pub. Service award U. Tenn. Alumni Assn., 1980-81, U. Tenn. Coll. Medicine Student Body Disting. Tchr. award, 1981-82, 82-83, 83-84, 84-85, 85-86, Outstanding Alumnus award U. Tenn. Coll. of Medicine, 1984. Fellow Am. Coll. Med. Genetics, Am. Acad. Pediatrics (Tenn. Pediatrician of Yr. Tenn. chpt. 1996); mem. AMA (rep. to accreditation coun. on grad. med. edn. 1995—), Tenn. Med. Assn., Memphis-Shelby County Med. Soc. (bd. dirs. 1994—), Am. Soc. Human Genetics, Soc. Pediatric Rsch., Coun. Deans of AAMC, Jour. Rev. Club (Memphis), Tenn. Pediatric Soc. (Tenn. Pediatrician of Yr. 1996). Office: U Tenn Coll Medicine 800 Madison Ave Memphis TN 38103-3400

SUMNER, DAVID SPURGEON, surgery educator; b. Asheboro, N.C., Feb. 20, 1933; s. George Herbert and Velna Elizabeth (Welborn) S.; m. Martha Eileen Sypher, July 25, 1959; children: David Vance, Mary Elizabeth, John Franklin. BA, U. N.C., 1954; MD, Johns Hopkins U., 1958. Diplomate Am. Bd. Surgery; cert. spl. qualification gen. vascular surgery, 1983, 93. Intern in surgery Johns Hopkins Hosp., Balt., 1958-59, resident in gen. surgery, 1960-61; resident in gen. surgery U. Wash. Sch. Medicine, Seattle, 1961-66; clin. investigator in vascular surgery VA Hosp., Seattle, 1967, 70-73; asst. surgery U. Wash. Sch. Medicine, Seattle, 1961-66, instr. surgery, 1966-70, asst. prof. surgery, 1970-72, assoc. prof. surgery, 1972-75; prof. surgery, chief sect. peripheral vascular surgery So. Ill. U. Sch. Medicine, Springfield, 1975-84, Disting. prof. surgery, chief sect. peripheral vascular surgery, 1984—; staff surgeon Seattle VA Hosp., 1973-75, Univ. Hosp., Seattle, 1973-75, St. John's Hosp., Springfield, 1975—, Meml. Med. Ctr., Springfield, 1975—; mem. VA Merit Review Bd. Surgery, 1975-78; mem. vascular surgery rsch. award com. The Liebig Found., 1990-95, chmn., 1994; bd. dirs. Am. Venous Forum Found., 1993-95; vis. prof. Cook County Hosp., Chgo., 1971, Washington U., St. Louis, 1976, U. Tex. San Antonio, 1978, Wayne State U., Detroit, 1978, U. Ind., Indpls., 1979, Ea. Va. Med. Sch., Norfolk, 1979, Case-Western Res. U., Cleve., 1980, U. Chgo., 1981, U. Manitoba, Winnipeg, Can., 1983, and others to present; dist. lectr. Yale U., 1982; guest examiner Am. Bd. Surgery, St. Louis, 1982, assoc. examiner, 1989, certifying examination gen. vascular surgery, 1993, 94; lectr. in field. Author: (with D.E. Strandness Jr.) Ultrasonic Techniques in Angiology, 1975, Hemodynamics for Surgeons, 1975, (with R.B. Rutherford, V. Bernhard, F. Maddison, W.S. Moore, M.O. Perry) Vascular Surgery, 1977, (with J.B. Russell) Ultrasonic Arteriography, 1980, (with F.B. Hershey, R.W. Barnes) Noninvasive Diagnosis of Vascular Disease, 1984, (with R.B. Rutherford, G. Johnson Jr., R.F. Kempczinski, W.S. Moore, M.O. Perry, G.W. Smith) Vascular Surgery, 3d edit., 1989, (with A.N. Nicolaides) Investigation of Patients With Deep Vein Thrombosis and Chronic Venous Insufficiency, 1991, (with R.B. Rutherford, G. Johnson, K.W. Johnston, R.F. Kempczinski, W.C. Krupski, W.S. Moore, M.O. Perry, A.J. Comerota, R.H. Dean, P. Gloviczki, K.H. Johansen, T.S. Riles, L.M. Taylor Jr.) Vascular Surgery, 4th edit., 1995; author 150 chpts. to books; mem. editl. adv. bd. Vascular Diagnosis and Therapy, 1980-84; mem. editl. bd. advisors Appleton Davies, Inc., 1983—; mem. editl. review bd. Jour. Soc. of Non-Invasive Vascular Tech., 1987—; mem. editl. bd. Jour. Vascular Surgery, 1987—; series editor Introduction to Vascular Tech., 1990—; mem. exec. editl. com. Phlebology, 1987-91; mem. Internat. Editl. Adv. Bd., 1991; mem. editl. com. Internat. Angiology, 1992—; contbr. over 140 articles to profl. jours. Lt. col. U.S. Army, 1967-70. Recipient fellowship in surg. rsch. Johns Hopkins U. Sch. Medicine, 1959-60, fellowship Am. Cancer Soc., Inc., 1965-66, Appleton-Century Crofts Scholarship award, 1956, Mosby Scholarship award, 1958. Fellow Am. Coll. Surgeons (Wash. chpt. 1971-75, Ill. chpt. counselor 1981-83), Cyprus Vascular Soc. (hon.); mem. AMA, Soc. Univ. Surgeons, Soc. Vascular Surgery (constn. and by-laws com. 1983, Wiley Fellowship com. 1990), Internat. Soc. Cardiovascular Surgery (N.Am. chpt. program com. 1985-88), Am. Surg. Assn., Am. Heart Assn. (stroke coun., cardiovascular surgery coun. 1978), Soc. Noninvasive Vascular Tech. (hon.), Vascular Surgery Biology Club, Am. Venous Forum (organizing com. 1987, founding mem. 1988, chmn. membership com. 1988-91, treas. 1992-95), Cardiovascular Sys. Dynamics Soc., Internat. Soc. Surgery, Vascular Soc. So. Africa (hon.), North Pacific Surg. Assn., Ctrl. Surg. Assn., Midwestern Vascular Surg. Soc. (counselor 1977-79, pres.-elect 1980-81, pres. 1981-82), Ill. Hea, Ill. State Med. Soc., Ill. Surg. Soc., Chgo. Surg. Soc., Seattle Surg. Soc., Sangamon County Med. Soc., Henry N. Harkins Surg. Soc., Harbinger Soc., Phi Eta Sigma, Phi Beta Kappa, Alpha Omega Alpha, Sigma Xi. Presbyterian. Home: 2324 West Lake Shore Dr Springfield IL 62707 Office: So Ill U Sch Medicine Dept Surgery 800 N Rutledge St Springfield IL 62781

SUMNER, EDWARD DONALD, retired pharmacy educator; b. Spartanburg, S.C., Mar. 21, 1925; s. James DuPre and Grace Frances (Harris) S.; m. Billie Janet Wallace, Sept. 7, 1947; children: Edward D. Jr., Melissa Sumner Kersey. BS in Chemistry, Wofford Coll., 1948; BS in Pharmacy, Med. U. S.C., 1950; MS, U. N.C., 1964, PhD, 1966. Lic. pharmacist, S.C. Pharmacist, mgr. Ind. Pharmacy, Mt. Pleasant, S.C., 1950-59; instr. U. N.C., Chapel Hill, 1959-65; from asst. to assoc. prof. U. Ga., Athens, 1965-75; prof. Med. U. S.C., Charleston, 1975-94, dir. geriatric pharmacy, 1989-94; co-founder Southeastern Conf. for Postgrad. Pharmacy Edn. and Tng., Athens, Ga., 1989. Author: Basic Concepts of Drugs Handbook of Geriatric Drug Therapy, 1970, Handbook of Geriatric Drug Therapy, 1983, Abstracts on Long Term Care Pharmacy, 1979. Chmn. adv. coun. United Way Area Agy. on Aging, Charleston, 1981, 91. With USN, 1943-46, PTO. Mem. Am. Assn. Colls. Pharmacy, S.C. Pharm. Assn., So. Gerontol. Soc., S.C. Gerontol. Soc. (pres. 1987-88), Ga. Soc. Hosp. Pharmacists (pres. 1972-73), Sigma Xi, Phi Kappa Phi, Rho Chi. Democrat. Methodist. Home: 514 Old Bridge Rd Mount Pleasant SC 29464-5019

SUNDBECK, GÖREL MARGARETH, medical educator, consultant; b. Jönköping, Sweden, Mar. 4, 1953; d. Johan and Karin Margaretha (Glimstedt) Westerberg; m. Anders Christer Sundbeck; children: Christina, Boel, Märta. MD, U. Gothenburg, 1978, PhD, 1991. Cert. specialist diploma in geriatric and internal medicine. Intern Hosp. Kungälo, Sweden, 1977-78; resident Hosp. Kungaelv, 1979-81; resident U. Hosp. Gothenburg, 1981-85, cons., 1986-90, 91—, tchr., 1991—. Fellow Swedish Med. Assn., Thyroid Group for Rsch. Home: Torsgatan 22, 43138 Melndal Sweden Office: Sahlgrenska Sjuknuset, Dept of Geriatric, Goteborg Sweden

SUNDERHAUS, EARL, ophthalmologist; b. Mt. Health, Ohio, July 17, 1932. BS, Ohio State U., 1956, MD, 1963; MBA, U. Mich., 1957, MS, 1968. Pvt. practice ophthalmology Asheville (N.C.) Eye Clinic. Home: 26 E Forest Rd Asheville NC 28805 Office: Asheville Eye Clinic 119 Tunnel Rd Asheville NC 28805-1800

SUNDERMAN, FREDERICK WILLIAM, physician, educator, author, musician; b. Altoona, Pa., Oct. 23, 1898; s. William August and Elizabeth Catherine (Lehr) S.; m. Clara Louise Baily, June 2, 1925 (dec. 1972); children: Louise (dec.), F. William, Joel B. (dec.); m. Martha-Lee Taggart, May 3, 1980. BS, Gettysburg Coll., 1919, ScD (hon.), 1952; MD, U. Pa., 1923, MS, 1927, PhD, 1929. Diplomate Am. Bd. Internal Medicine, Am. Bd. Pathology (v.p. 1944-50 life trustee 1950—), Nat. Bd. Med. Examiners. Intern, then resident Pa. Hosp., 1923-25; assoc. rsch. med. U. Pa., Phila., 1925-48; assoc. in chem. divsn. William Pepper Lab. U. Pa. Hosp., Phila., 1929-48; physician U. Pa. Hosp., 1929-48; med. dir. Office of Sci. R & D, 1943-46; physician, hon. pathologist Pa. Hosp., 1988—; mem. faculty U. Pa. Sch. Medicine, Phila., 1925-47; assoc. prof. research medicine, also lectr. U. Pa. Sch. Medicine; acting head med. dept. Brookhaven Nat. Lab., Upton, N.Y., 1947-48; chief chem. div. William Pepper Lab. Clin. Medicine, U. Pa. Med. Sch., 1933-47; prof. clin. pathology, dir. Temple U. Lab. Clin. Medicine, 1947-48; med. dir. govt. explosives lab. Carnegie Inst. Tech. and Bur. Mines, 1943-46; head dept. clin. pathology Cleve. Clinic Found., 1948-49; dir. clin. research M.D. Anderson Hosp. Cancer Research, Houston, 1949-50; dir. clin. labs. Grady Meml. Hosp., Atlanta, 1949-51; prof. clin. medicine Emory U. Sch. Medicine, 1949-51; chief clin. pathology Communicable Disease Center, USPHS, 1950-51; med. adviser Rohm & Haas Co., 1947-71; med. cons. Redstone Arsenal, U.S. Army Ordnance Dept., Huntsville, Ala., 1947-49; cons. clin. pathology St. Joseph's Hosp., Tampa, Fla., 1965-66; attending physician Jefferson Hosp., Phila., 1951—, dir. div. metabolic research, clin. prof. medicine, 1951-67, clin. prof. medicine, 1951-74, hon. clin. prof. medicine, 1975—; dir. Inst. Clin. Sci., 1965—; prof. pathology Hahnemann U. Med. Coll., 1970—, co-chmn. dept. lab. medicine, 1970-75, prof. emeritus, 1989; med. adviser and cons. bus. and industry, 1947—; dir. internat. seminars on clin. chemistry and pathology, 1947—; guest lectr. Beijing (People's Republic of China) Med. U., 1989. Author, editor 36 books on clin. chemistry and pathology; author: Our Madeira Heritage, 1979, Musical Notes of a Physician, 1982, Painting with Light, 1993; editor-in-chief Annals Clin. Lab. Sci., 1970—; mem. editl. bd. Am. Jour. Clin. Pathology, 1939-87, Am. Jour. Indsl. Medicine, 1979-85; cons. editor Am. Jour. Occupl. Medicine, 1979-85; also over 350 articles. Trustee Gettysburg Coll., 1967-89, chmn. bd. trustees, 1972-74, hon. life trustee, 1986—; bd. dirs. Mus. Fund Soc. Phila., 1938—, hon. life bd. dirs., 1993—; bd. dirs. Dwight D. Eisenhower Soc., 1984—, German Soc. Pa., 1986—, Geog. Soc. Phila., 1995; violin soloist Chautauqua Summer Series, Ea. U.S., 1919-20; guest soloist Concerto Soloists Pa., 1979, 83, 84, Pa. String Tchrs. Assn., Gettysburg, 1959, Westchester, 1962, 63, 67, 68, Trenton (N.J.) Tchrs. Coll. Orch., 1965; violin soloist Internat. String Conf. soloist World Congress on Arts and Medicine, Carnegie Hall, N.Y.C., 1992. Recipient Naval Ordnance Devel. award, 1946, cert. appreciation War Dept., 1947, Honor medal Armed Forces Inst. Pathology, 1964; recipient Meritorious Svc. award, 1979, Honor award Latin Am. Assn. Clin. Biochemistry, 1976, Disting. Svc. award Am. Soc. Clin. Pathology-Coll. Am. Pathologists, 1988, Life-time Achievement award in clin. chemistry Joint Congresses of IX Congresso Nacional de la Sociedad Espanola de Quimica Clin., 2d Internat. Congress Therapeutic Drug Monitoring and Toxicology, and 4th Internat. Congress on Automation and New Tech., Spain, 1990, John Gunther Reinhold award Phila. Sect. Am. Assn. for Clin. Chemistry, 1991, Jacob Ehrenzeller award Res. Assn. Pa. Hosp., 1993; named Disting. Alumnus Gettysburg Coll., 1963; Sunderman Seminar Rm. dedicated at Bermuda Biol. Sta. for Rsch., 1992; 1st ann. F. William Sunderman award for Disting. Community Svc. and Excellence in a ChoField of Endeavor established by Rho Deuteron chpt. Phi Sigma Kappa, Gettysburg Coll; recipient Nat. Phi Sigma Kappa Disting. Alumnus award, 1995. Fellow ACP (life), Royal Soc. Medicine (hon., life), Royal Soc. Health Great Britain (life); mem. Am. Assn. History Medicine, Am. Diabetes Assn., AMA, Am. Soc. Clin. Investigation, Royal Soc. Health, AAUP, Endocrine Soc., Am. Assn. Biol. Chemistry, AAAS, Am. Chem. Soc., Internat. Union Pure and Applied Chemistry (nickel subcom. Commn. on Toxicology), Inst. Occupational Health (Finland), Outokumpu Oy (Finland), Am. Assn. Clin. Chemists (award for outstanding efforts in edn. and tng. 1981, John Gunther Reinhold award 1991), Coll. Am. Pathologists (founding gov., Pathologist of Yr. award 1962, Pres.'s Honor award 1984), Am. Soc. Clin. Pathology (pres. 1951, archives com. 1977—, intersoc. pathology coun. 1976—, interpathology soc. coun. 1976—, Ward Burdick award 1975, Continuing Edn. Distinguished Service award 1976), Assn. Clin. Scientists (pres. 1957-59, dir. edn. 1959—, diploma honor 1960, ann. goblet award 1964, Gold-headed cane 1974), Coll. Physicians of Phila. (sec. 1946-48, hon. pres. arts medicine sect. 1995, Disting. Service award 1980, 85, 90, 95), Knight of Order of St. Vincent of Portugal (Disting. Svc. cross, Order of merit, (das Verdienstkreuz), Bundesrepublik Deutschland, 1989), Am. Indsl. Hygiene Assn., Am. Occupational Medicine Assn., Med. Soc. Pa., Nat. Soc. Med. Research, Nat. Acad. Clin. Biochemistry, Pan Am. Med. Assn., Pa. Assn. Clin. Pathology, Philadelphia County Med. Soc., Mus. Fund Soc. Phila. (hon. life), Soc. Toxicology, Brit. Assn. Clin. Biochemists (hon.), Soc. Pharm. and Environ. Pathologists (hon.), Internat. Union Pure and Applied Chemistry, Inst. Occupational Health Finland (nickel subcom. commn. toxicology), Phi Beta Kappa, Sigma Xi, Alpha Omega Alpha, Phi Sigma Kappa (1st annual F. William Sunderman award for Cmty. Svc Rho Deuteron chpt. Gettysburg Coll. 1995, Nat. Disting. Alumnus award grand chpt. 1995), Alpha Kappa Kappa. Lutheran. Home: 1833 Delancey Pl Philadelphia PA 19103-6606 Office: Pa Hosp Inst for Clin Sci 301 S 8th St Duncan Bldg 3A Philadelphia PA 19106-4014

SUNDLER, FRANK ESKIL GEORG, histology and cell biology educator, scientist; b. Hjärsås, Sweden, Apr. 5, 1943; s. Georg and Gulli (Sundell) S.; m. Kristina Larsson, Aug. 6, 1971; children: Martin, Linda, Emil, Frida. Cand. med., Lund (Sweden) U., 1965, PhD, MD, 1973. Amanuens dept. histology Lund U., 1965-71, rsch. asst., 1971-77, asst. prof., 1979-85, assoc. prof., 1986—, chmn. dept. med. cell rsch., 1987—, cons. dept. surgery, 1980-83; edtl. bd. Jour. Biol. Signals, Jour. Cell Vision. Asst. editor jour. Regulatory Peptides, 1984—; sect. editor jour. Acta Physiol. Scand., 1992—; mem. editl. bd. jour. Biol. Signals, 1992—, jour. Cell Vision, 1994—; mng. editor jour. Anat. Embryology, 1993—; cooperating editor jour. Cell Tissue Res., 1993—; contbr. articles to profl. publs. Mem. AAAS, N.Y. Acad. Scis., Soc. for Neurosci., Swedish Endocrine Soc., Swedish Royal Physiographic Soc., European Neuropeptide Club. Home: Vinkelvägen 4, 24010 Dalby Sweden Office: Lund U Dept Med Cell Rsch, Biskopsgatan 5, 22362 Lund Sweden

SUNDRY, CATHIE LEE, medical programs company executive, consultant; b. Kalamazoo, Mar. 27, 1946; d. James William Gilmartin and Geraldine Ann (Minckler) Jones; m. Charles Wayne Sundry, Nov. 20, 1977; children: Haakon Barrett, Cailin Dael. BSN cum laude, U. Pitts., 1968. RN; cert. pub. health nurse, Calif. Staff, charge nurse Magee Women's Hosp., Pitts., 1968-71; head nurse, unit dir. St. Vincent's Hosp., Portland, Oreg., 1971-73; instr., head nurse obstetrics Queens Med. Ctr., Honolulu, 1974-78; med. surg. instr. Kapiolani C.C., Honolulu, 1980-81; operating room, office nurse Plastic Surgeons Med. Group, Grossmont, Calif., 1982-83; med. sales rep., instr. Total Pharm. Care, Inc., San Diego, 1985-89; co-owner, regional v.p. Clin. Support Svcs., Inc., Fallbrook, 1989-91, v.p., 1991—; instr. Pitts. Organ. for Childbirth Edn., Pitts, 1969-71; panel coordinator, Hawaii Nurses Assn., Honolulu, 1975. Pres. Chula Vista Assn. for Gifted Children, 1993-95; mem. parent adv. com. on curriculum and instrn. Sweetwater Union H.S. Dist., 1992—, v.p., 1994-95, mem. gifted and talented edn. parent adv. com., 1992—. Mem. Am. Soc. Parenteral and Enteral Nutrition, Coun. Long Term Care Nurses of Calif., Coun. San Diego Health Care Assn. (assoc., bd. dirs. 1989, sec. 1990-91). Lutheran. Home: 778 Baylor Ave Chula Vista CA 91913-2002 Office: Clin Support Svcs Inc 1187 E Mission Rd Fallbrook CA 92028-2231

SUNG, KUOCHUN, pharmaceutical scientist; b. Taipei, Taiwan, Jan. 20, 1967. BS, Nat. Taiwan U., Taipei, Taiwan, 1988; MS, U. Kans., 1992, PhD, 111994. Rsch. asst. U. Kans., Lawrence, 1990-94; vis. scientist The Upjohn Co., Kalamazoo, Mich., 1994; assoc. prof. Chia-Nan Coll. of Pharmacy, Tainan, Taiwan, 1994-95; cons. Standard Pharm. Co., Tainan, 1994-95. Author: Effect of Polymer Swelling and Drug Diffusion on Drug Release, 1994. Recipient Gen. Predoctoral fellowship Genentech Co., 1993-94. Mem. Am. Assn. Pharm. Scientist, Controlled Release Soc. Home: No 20 An-E Road, Keelung Taiwan Office: Chia-Nan Coll of Pharmacy, Jen-Te Hsian, Tainan Taiwan

SUNG, SHEN-SHU, research scientist; b. Beijing, China; came to U.S., 1979; m. Lulu Xu, 1978; 1 child, Annie Xiaoyin. MS, Cornell U., 1981, PhD, 1984. Postdoctoral rsch. assoc. Brandeis U., Waltham, Mass., 1984-88; computational chemist SRI, Menlo Park, Calif., 1988-90; asst. staff Cleve. Clinic Found. Rsch. Inst., 1990—; asst. prof. Case Western Res. U., Cleve., 1995—. Contbr. articles to profl. jours. Mem. AAAS, Am. Chem. Soc., Am. Phys. Soc., Biophys. Soc., Protein Soc. Office: Cleve Clin Found Rsch Inst 9500 Euclid Ave FF3 Cleveland OH 44195

SUNTHARALINGAM, NAGALINGAM, radiation therapy physics educator; b. Jaffna, Sri Lanka, June 18, 1933; married; 3 children. BSc, U. Ceylon, 1955; MS, U. Wis., 1966, PhD in Radiol. Scis., 1967. Asst. lectr. physics U. Ceylon, 1955-58; from instr. radiol. physics to assoc. prof. radiology Thomas Jefferson U. Med. Coll., Phila., 1962-72, prof. radiology and radiation oncology (med. physics), 1972—, dir. divsn. med. physics, 1973—; vis. lect. grad. sch. medicine U. Pa., 1967-72, cons. dept. physics, 1968-72; cons. WHO, 1972. Recipient William D. Coolidge award Am. Assn. Physicists in Medicine, 1992. Fellow Am. Coll. Radiology, Am. Coll. Med. Physics (chmn. bd. dirs. 1988, Marvin M.D. Williams Profl. Achievement award 1995); mem. Am. Assn. Phys. Medicine (pres. 1983). Office: Thomas Jefferson University 111 S 11th St Philadelphia PA 19107

SUPERDOCK, KEITH R., nephrologist; b. Bloomsburg, Pa., Aug. 12, 1963; m. Jennifer Gale, Sept. 30, 1989; children: Matthew Carl, Michael Andrew. BS, Penn. State U., 1984; MD, Jefferson Med. Coll., 1986. Diplomate Am. Bd. Internal Medicine. Instr. medicine Nashville Dept. Vet. Affairs, 1992; nephrologist Lankenau Hosp., Wynnewood, Pa., 1993—; assoc. dir. transplant program Lankenau Hosp., 1993—; clin. asst. prof. medicine Jefferson Med. Coll., Phila., 1994—. Mem. AMA, Am. Soc. Transplant Physicians, Am. Coll. Physicians, Nat. Kidney Found., Alpha Omega Alpha, Hobart Amdry Hare Med. Honor Soc. Office: Nephrology Assocs Lankenau Med Bldg W Ste 130 Wynnewood PA 19096

SURACI, PATRICK JOSEPH, clinical psychologist; b. Rochester, N.Y., May 31, 1936; s. Frank and Josephine Rosalie (Marino) S. PhD in Psychology, New. Sch. for Social Rsch., N.Y.C., 1981. Cert. clin. psychologist, N.Y. Intern in clin. psychology Morrisania Neighborhood Family Care Ctr., Montefiore Hosp., N.Y.C., 1979-80; staff psychologist N.Y. Police Dept., 1981-83; pvt. practice N.Y.C., 1983—; adj. lectr. N.Y. Inst. Tech., N.Y.C., 1975-78, John Jay Coll. Criminal Justice, CUNY, 1973-81; adj. asst. prof. Baruch Coll. Psychology Dept., CUNY, 1983-92; vol. Manhattan Ctr. for Living, 1994—. Author: Male Sexual Armor. Erotic Fantasies and Sexual Realities of the Cop on the Beat and the Man in the Street, 1992. Mem. The Nat. Arts Club. With U.S. Army, 1959-62. Mem. APA, N.Y. State Psychol. Assn. (task force on AIDS), Actors Equity, Screen Actors Guild.

SURAMO, ILKKA, radiologist, educator; b. Teuva, Finland, Oct. 22, 1942; s. Otto and Aili (Muttilainen) S.; m. Marja-Liisa Järkkälä, Dec. 30, 1968; 1 child, Riikka Maria. MD, U. Turku, Finland, 1968; PhD, U. Oulu, 1973. Assoc. prof. roentgenology U. Oulu, Finland, 1980-84, prof. diagnostic radiology, 1990—; assoc. prof. radiology U. Helsinki, 1984-90, acting prof. radiology, 1985-89. Assoc. editor Acta Radiologica, Stockholm. Mem. Radiol. Soc. Finland (v.p. 1981-84, pres. 1988-89). Office: Univ of Oulu, Dept Diagnostic Radiology, Kajaanintie 50, 90220 Oulu Finland

SURAWICZ, CHRISTINA MATHILDA, physician; b. Munich, Jan. 4, 1948; d. Borys and Frida (Vanklaveren) S.; m. James Butler Bushyhead. BA, Barnard Coll., 1969; MD, U. Ky., 1973. Resident in medicine U. Wash. Affiliated Hosp., Seattle, 1973-76, asst. prof. medicine, 1981-86, assoc. prof. medicine, 1986—; chief gastroenterology Harborview Med. Ctr. Contbr. articles to profl. jours. Fellow ACP, Am. Coll. Gastroenterology (governor Wash. state 1989-93, sec. 1994-95, treas. 1995—). Office: Harborview Med Ctr 325 9th Ave Seattle WA 98104-2420

SURIA, AMIN MOHAMMED, neuropharmacologist, educator; b. Dhoraji, Bombay, India, Aug. 24, 1942; arrived in Pakistan, 1947; s. Mahammed Haroon and Halima (Motiwala) S.; m. Khair-Un-Nisa Vapiwala, Jan. 19, 1974; children: Nausheen, Sabrina, Raheel, Nida. BS in Chemistry with honors, U. Karachi, Pakistan, 1963, MSc in Chemistry, 1964; PhD in Pharmacology, Vanderbilt U., Nashville, 1970. Chemist incharge of lab. Hoechst, Ltd., Karachi, 1964-66; vis. fellow Nat. Heart & Lung Inst., NIH, Bethesda, Md., 1971-72; sr. staff fellow NIMH, Washington, 1972-75; asst. prof. pharmacology George Washington U., Washington, 1975-78, assoc. prof. pharmacology, 1978-80; assoc. prof. pharmacology King Saud U., Riyadh, Saudi Arabia, 1980-83; prof. pharmacology, chmn. dept. Med. Coll., Aga Khan U., Karachi, 1983—; cons. Pakistan Coun. Sci. and Indsl. Rsch., Karachi, 1984—, Postgrad. Inst. Chemistry, Karachi, 1988—; tech. adv. expert Pakistan Med. Rsch. Coun., Lahore, 1985—. Contbr. numerous articles to profl. jours. Pres. Dhoraji Youth Svcs., Karachi, 1989; trustee Dhoraji Found, Karachi, 1991. Fellow Pakistan Acad. Med. Scis.; mem. Am. Soc. Pharmacology and Exptl. Therapeutics, Med. Rsch. Soc. Pakistan (sec. 1985-89, treas. 1989-90, pres. 1991—). Office: Aga Khan U Med Coll, Po Box 3500 Stadium Rd, Karachi 74800, Pakistan

SURMAN, OWEN STANLEY, psychiatrist; b. Boston, Apr. 21, 1943; s. Aaron Harry and Edith Anne (Silver) S.; m. Lezlie Anne Humber, July 19, 1969 (dec. Nov. 5, 1994); children: Craig Bruce Hackett, Kathleen Bridget Lezlie. BSc with honors, McGill U., 1964, MD, CM, 1968. Diplomate Am. Bd. Psychiatry and Neurology. Intern in internal medicine Balt. City Hosp., 1968-69; clin. fellow in medicine Johns Hopkins U., Balt., 1968-69; resident in psychiatry Mass. Gen. Hosp., Boston, 1969-72; clin. fellow in psychiatry Harvard Med. Sch., Boston, 1969-72; clin. asst. in psychiatry Mass. Gen. Hosp., Boston, 1975-76, asst. in psychiatry, 1977-80, asst. psychiatrist, 1980-86, assoc. psychiatrist, 1986-89, psychiatrist, 1990—; instr. psychiatry Harvard U. Med. Sch., Boston, 1975-80, asst. prof., 1980-90, assoc. prof., 1990-94; mem., psychiat. cons. Boston Ctr. Heart Transplant, 1988-94; mem. ethics com. Mass. Ctr. Organ Transplantation, 1988—; mem. subcom. Human Studies, Mass. Gen. Hosp., 1982—, cons. transplant unit, 1975—; mem. Inst. for Study of Smoking Behavior and Policy, John F. Kennedy Sch. Govt., 1982-89. Mem. editorial bd. Jour. Geriatric Psychiatry and Neurology, 1988—; contbr. articles, letters and book revs. to med. jours., chpts. to books. Bd. dirs. Unitarian-Universalist Area Ch., Sherborn, Mass., 1983-86, 93-96; advancement officer troop 1 Boy Scouts Am., Sherborn, 1983-91. Lt. comdr. M.C., USNR, 1972-75. Milton Fund grantee, Upjohn Corp. grantee, Burroughs Wellcome Co. grantee, Eli Lily Corp. grantee, 1989. Fellow Am. Psychiat. Assn., Am. Acad. Psychosomatic Medicine (ethics com., awards com.); mem. AAAS, Mass. Med. Soc., N.Y. Acad. Scis., Hastings Ctr. (assoc.), Johns Hopkins Med. and Surg. Soc., Mass. ACLU, Libr. of Boston Athenaeum, Ford Hall Forum, New Eng. Poetry Club. Republican. Office: Mass Gen Hosp Wang ACC 815 15 Parkman St Boston MA 02114

SURPRISE, JUANEE, chiropractor, nutrition consultant; b. Gary, Ind., Apr. 28, 1944; d. Glenn Mark and Willia Ross (Vasser) Surprise; m. Peter E. Coakley, Feb. 12, 1966 (div. Jan. 1976); children: Thaddeus, Mariah, Darius; m. Robert T.Howell, Feb. 24, 1984. RN, Phila. Gen. Hosp. Sch. Nursing, 1965; DrChiropractic summa cum laude, Life Chiropractic Coll, Marietta, Ga., 1981. Diplomate Nat. Bd. Chiropractic Bd. Nutrition, Am. Acad. Pain Mgmt.; cert. clin. nutritionist; cert. in acupuncture, Thompson technique, Nimmo receptor tonus technique. Staff nurse Children's Hosp., Balt., 1966-67; charge nurse Melrose (Mass.)-Wakefield Hosp., 1967-68; hosp. adminstr. Animal Hosp. of Wakefield, Mass., 1967-79; chiropractor Chiropractic Clinic of Greenville, N.C., 1982-84, Chiropractice Rehab. Clinic, Denton, Tex., 1984—. Mem., chmn. Cmty. Planning Commn., North Reading, Mass., 1976-79; chmn. bldg. com. Immaculate Conception Ch., Denton, 1987-90, parish coun., 1990-92. Mem. ACA Coun. on Nutrition (sec.-treas.), Internat. and Am. Assns. Clin. Nutritionists, Internat. Assn. Pain Mgmt., Am. Chiropractic Assn., Am. Chiropractic Bd. on Nutrition (pres.), Tex. Chiropractic Assn., Tex. Chiropractic Assn. Coun. on Nutrition (sec.-treas.), Pi Tau Delta. Republican. Roman Catholic. Office: Chiropractic Rehabs Clinic 1100 Dallas Dr Denton TX 76205-5153

SURYANARAYANAN, RAJ GOPALAN, researcher, consultant; b. Cuddalore, Tamil Nadu, India, Apr. 19, 1955; came to U.S., 1985; s. Natesan and Pushpa (Subramanian) Rajagopalan; m. Shanti Venkateswaran, Nov. 24, 1985; children: Priya Mallika Sury, Meera Sindu Sury. B in Pharmacy, Banaras Hindu U., Varanasi, India, 1976, M in Pharmacy, 1978; MS, U. BC, Vancouver, Can., 1981, PhD, 1985. Mgmt. trainee Indian Drugs and Pharm. Lts., Rishikesh, India, 1978; supr. Roche Products, Bombay, India, 1979; teaching asst. U. BC, Vancouver, BC, Can., 1979, 82-83; asst. prof. pharmaceutics U. Minn., Mpls., 1985-92, assoc. prof., 1992—; dir. grad. studies, 1994—; cons. numerous pharm. cos. in U.S., 1987—. Contbr. articles to profl. jours.; patentee quantitative analysis of intact tablets. Recipient numerous grants for rsch., U.S., 1985—. Mem. Am. Assn. Pharm. Scientists, Am. Assn. Colls. Pharmacy. Hindu. Home: 1861 Moore St Saint Paul MN 55113-5530 Office: U Minn Coll of Pharmacy 308 Harvard St SE Minneapolis MN 55455-0353

SUSI, J. RICHARD, ophthalmologist; b. Sharon, Pa., Dec. 3, 1954; s. Edmond and Rose (Pancioni) S.; m. Cynthia Jane Murray, June 11, 1977; children: Christina Marie, William Richard. BA in Chemistry, Case We. Res. U., 1977; DO, Phila. Coll. Osteo. Medicine, 1981. Diplomate Am. Bd. Osteopathic Ophthalmology and Otorhinolaryngology. Pvt. practice Orange Eye Ctr., Orlando, Fla., 1985—. Home: 7326 Lake Underhill Rd Orlando FL 32822-6055

SUSKIND, SIGMUND RICHARD, microbiology educator; b. N.Y.C., June 19, 1926; s. Seymour and Nina Phillips S.; m. Ann Parker, July 1, 1951; children: Richard, Mark, Steven. A.B., NYU, 1948; Ph.D., Yale U., 1954. Research asst. biology div. Oak Ridge Nat. Lab., 1948-50; USPHS fellow NYU Med. Sch., N.Y.C., 1954-56; mem. faculty Johns Hopkins U., Balt., 1956—, prof. biology, 1965—, Univ. prof., 1983—, Univ. ombudsman, 1988-91, prof. emeritus, 1996—, dean grad. and undergrad. studies, 1971-78, dean Sch. Arts and Scis., 1978-83, prof. emeritus, 1996—; head molecular biology sect. NSF, 1970-71; cons. NIH, 1966-70, Coun. Grad. Schs., Mid States Assn. Colls. and Secondary Schs., 1973—, NSF, 1986; vis. scientist Weizmann Inst. of Sci., Israel, 1985; trustee Balt. Hebrew U., 1985-93; mem. adv. bd. La. Geriatric Ctr., 1990—. Author: (with P.E. Hartman) Gene Action, 1964, 69, (with P.E. Hartman and T. Wright) Principles of Genetics Laboratory Manual, 1965; editor: (with P.E. Hartman) Foundations of Modern Genetics series, 1964, 69; mem. sci. editorial bd. Johns Hopkins U. Press, 1973-76, 88-91. With USNR, 1944-46. NIH grantee, 1957-76. Fellow AAAS; mem. Am. Soc. Microbiology, Genetics Soc. Am., Am. Assn. Immunology, Am. Soc. Biol. Chemistry and Molecular Biology, Coun. Grad Schs., Assn. Grad. Schs., Northeastern Assn. Grad. Schs. (exec. com. 1975-76, pres. 1977-78). Office: Johns Hopkins U Dept Biology and McCollum-Pratt Inst 34th and Charles Sts Baltimore MD 21218

SUSSEX, JAMES NEIL, psychiatrist, educator; b. Northcote, Minn., Oct. 2, 1917; s. Rollo and Florence (Bartholomew) S.; m. Margaret Ann Garty, Apr. 25, 1943; children: Margaret Eileen, Mary Patricia, Barbara Lorraine, Teresa Virginia. AB, U. Kans., 1939, MD, 1942. Diplomate: Am. Bd. Psychiatry and Neurology (dir. for child psychiatry 1966-70, dir. 1975-83, pres. 1982). Commd. lt. (j.g.), M.C. U.S. Navy, 1943, advanced through grades to comdr., 1955; intern (Naval Hosp.), Chelsea, Mass., 1942-43; resident psychiatry (Naval Hosp.), Vallejo, Calif., 1946-49; fellow child psychiatry Phila. Guild Guidance Clinic, 1949-51; asst. chief neuropsychiatry Naval Hosp., Bethesda, Md., 1951-55; resigned, 1955; mem. faculty Med. Coll. Ala., 1955-68, prof. psychiatry, chmn. dept., 1959-68; psychiatrist-in-chief U. Ala. Hosps. and Clinics, 1959-68; faculty U. Miami Sch. Medicine, Fla., 1968—; prof. psychiatry U. Miami Sch. Medicine, 1970—, chmn. dept., 1970-83, chmn. emeritus, 1983—, spl. asst. to v.p. for med. affairs for geriatric medicine program, 1983-86; mem. adv. bd. Nat. Psychiat. Residency Selection Plan, 1965—; mem. Med. Adv. Bd. Ednl. Film Prodn., 1966—; cons. Bur. Rsch., U.S. office Edn., 1966-72; dir. Ala. Planning for Mental Retardation, 1964—; mem. psychiatry tng. rev. com. NIMH; mem. exec. com. Am. Bd. Med. Spltys., 1980-83. Editor: Jour. Ala. Soc. Med. History, 1957-63; editorial bd.: Jour. Am. Acad. Child Psychiatry, 1966-70. Mem. Am. Assn. Psychiat. Svcs. for Children (coun. 1966—, pres. 1972-74), Coun. Med. Specialty Socs. (pres. 1988-89), Accreditation Coun. for Grad. Med. Edn. (exec. com. 1989-94, chmn. 1992-93), Phi Beta Kappa, Nu Sigma Nu. Home: 6950 SW 134th St Miami FL 33156-6975

SUSSKIND, HERBERT, biomedical engineer, educator; b. Ratibor, Germany, Mar. 23, 1929; came to U.S., 1938; s. Alex and Hertha (Loewy) S.; m. E. Suzanne Lieberman, June 18, 1961; children: Helen J., Alex M., David A. BChE cum laude, CCNY, 1950; MChE, NYU, 1961. Engr., sect. supr. Brookhaven Nat. Lab., Upton, N.Y., 1950-77, biomed. engr., 1977-94, asst. to chmn. med. dept., 1989-94, rsch. collaborator, 1994—; assoc. prof. medicine SUNY, Stony Brook, 1979—. Co-inventor 3 patents in field. Co-founder, 1st pres. Huntington Twp. Jewish Forum, Huntington, N.Y., 1970-73; trustee Huntington Hebrew Congregation, 1970-78. Mem. Biomed. Engring. Soc., Soc. Nuclear Medicine, Am. Thoracic Soc., Am. Nuclear Soc. (exec. com., treas. L.I. Sect., 1978-83), Am. Inst. Chem. Engrs., CCNY Alumni Assn. (pres. 1982-84), CCNY Engring. & Architecture Alumni Assn., N.Y.C. (pres. 1963-65). Office: Brookhaven Nat Lab Box 5000 Bldg 490 Upton NY 11973-5000

SUSSMAN, MICHAEL DAVID, orthopedic surgeon; b. Balt., Feb. 20, 1943; s. Sidney and Leonora H. (Applebaum) S.; m. Nancy Evans Whiteley, Aug. 13, 1971; children: Evans, Tovah. AB, Washington and Lee U., 1963; MD, U. Md., Balt., 1967. Diplomate Am. Bd. Orthopaedic Surgery. Intern, jr. resident surgery Med. Coll. Va., Richmond, 1967-69; research assoc. NIH, Bethesda, Md., 1969-71; resident orthopaedic surgery Johns Hopkins Hosp., Balt., 1971-75; fellow pediatric orthopaedic surgery Childrens Hosp. Med. Ctr., Boston, 1975-76; from asst. prof. to prof. dept. orthopaedic surgery and dept. pediatrics U. Va., Charlottesville, 1976—, head div. pediatric orthopaedics, 1985—; mem. research adv. bd. Shrine Hosp., 1984—; mem. grant rev. bd. Orthopaedic Research Edn. Found., 1985—. Contbr. numerous articles to profl. jours. Bd. dirs. Bloomfield Inc., Ivy, Va., 1979-83, Dyslexia Ctr., Charlottesville, 1987—. Served to lt. commdr. USPHS, 1969-71. Frank Ober fellow, 1976, Gianestras-Schmerge Traveling fellow, 1978. Fellow Am. Acad. Orthopaedic surgery (mem. Com. on pediatric orthopaedics 1986—), Am. Acad. Cerebral Palsy and Devel. Medicine (sci. program com. 1986—, membership com. 1986—), Am. Acad. Pediatrics, Scoliosis Rsch. Soc.; mem. Pediatric Orthopaedic Soc. Democrat. Jewish. Office: U Va Childrens Rehab Ctr 2270 Ivy Rd Charlottesville VA 22903-4977

SUTCLIFFE, MARILYN CASE, retired research technician; b. New Haven, Apr. 20, 1936; d. Warren Evans and Esther Mary (Snow) Case; B.A. summa cum laude, U. Bridgeport, 1957; postgrad. Sorbonne, Paris, 1957-58, Duke U., 1958-59; m. William Manchester Sutcliffe, Dec. 27, 1958; children: Stacy Ellen, James Sheldon. Cert. practitioner Sancta Sophia Sem., Tahlequah, Okla, 1995. Substitute tchr. Broward County, Fla., 1966-67; tchr. chemistry Nova Sr. High Sch., Ft. Lauderdale, Fla., 1967-86; rsch. technician infectious diseases dept. biochemistry VA Med. Center, Nashville, 1986-94; ret., 1994. Fulbright scholar, 1957-58; James B. Duke fellow, 1958. Mem. Am. Soc. Microbiology. Republican. Contbr. articles to profl. jours. Home: 7705 Indian Springs Dr Nashville TN 37221-1128 Office: 1310 24th Ave S Nashville TN 37203

SUTER, DANIEL BLOSSER, biology educator, minister; b. Harrisonburg, Va., Apr. 25, 1920; s. John Early and Nettie Pearl (Blosser) S.; m. Frances Grace Fisher, June 25, 1941; children: Janice, David, Mary Louise, Daniel. BA, Bridgewater Coll., 1947; MA, Vanderbilt U., 1948; PhD, Med. Coll. Va., 1963. Ordained to min. Mennonite Faith, 1951. Biology dept. staff Eastern Mennonite U., Harrisonburg, 1948-85, registrar, 1957-60, biology prof., 1965-85, assoc. dean, 1976-77, prof. emeritus, 1985—. NIH fellow U. Calif., 1970-71. Home: 102 Old # 33 Harrisonburg VA 22801

SUTHERLAND, DONALD WOOD, cardiologist; b. Kansas City, Mo., July 29, 1932; s. Donald Redeker and Mary Frances (Wood) S.; m. Margaret Sutherland, Sept. 11, 1954 (div. 1994); children: Kathleen Massar, Ellen Baltus, Richard, Ann, Julia McMurchie; m. Roslyn Ruggiero Elms, Mar. 31, 1995. BA, Amherst Coll., 1953; MD, Harvard U., 1957. Intern, resident Mass. Gen. Hosp., Boston, 1957-60; fellow in cardiology U. Oreg., Portland, 1961-63; pvt. practice Portland, 1963—; assoc. clin. prof. medicine Oreg. Health Sci. U., Portland, 1967—; chief of staff St. Vincent Hosp. and Med. Ctr., Portland, 1971-72. Contbr. articles to profl. jours. Fellow Am. Heart Assn., Am. Coll. Cardiology (pres. Oreg. chpt. 1972); mem. Multnomah Athletic Club, North Pacific Soc. Internal Medicine (pres. 1985), Pacific Interurban Clin. Club. Home: 4405 SW Council Crest Dr Portland OR 97201 Office: Columbia Cardiology Ltd 9155 SW Barnes Rd # 233 Portland OR 97225

SUTKER, WILLIAM L., internist; b. Chgo., July 9, 1948; s. Robert H. and Carol (Levin) S.; m. Helen E. Horowitz, Dec. 20, 1970; children: Tara, Nikki, Cory. BS, U. Ill., 1970; MD, Chgo. Med. Sch., 1974. Diplomate Am. Bd. Internal Medicine, Infectious Diseases. Intern, resident internal medicine Baylor U. Med. Ctr., Dallas, 1974-77, fellow infectious diseases, 1977-79, attending physician, 1979—; dir. med. edn. Baylor U. Med. Ctr., Dallas, 1970—, chief infectious diseases, 1990—. Contbr. articles to profl. jours. Fellow ACP; mem. AMA, Am. Soc. Microbiology, Infectious Diseases Soc. Am., Assn. Program Dirs. Internal Medicine. Home: 7228 Arbor Oaks Dr Dallas TX 75248 Office: N Tex Infectious Dis Cons 3409 Worth St Ste 710 Dallas TX 75248

SUTTER, EMILY MAY GEESEMAN, psychologist, educator; b. St. Louis, Nov. 18, 1939; d. George Robert and Cora Hamilton (Glasgow) Geeseman; m. Gordon Frederick Sutter, Aug. 13, 1960; children: John Blaine, Steven George. BS, U. Pitts., 1960, M of Retailing, 1961; MEd, Wayne State U., 1965; PhD, U. Tex., 1967. Lic. psychologist, Tex. Chief psychologist Richmond State Sch., Houston, 1967-71; dir. Fairhill Sch., Houston, 1971-72; assoc. dir. Battin Clinic, Houston, 1972-81; from asst. to assoc. prof. U. Houston, Clear Lake, 1981-93, prof., 1993—, interim dean 1990-92; appointee Tex. State Bd. Examiners Psychologists, 1993—. Contbr. articles to profl. jours. Mem. Am. Psychol. Assn., Southwestern Psychol. Assn. (sec., treas. 1977-79), Tex. Psychol. Assn. (treas. 1978, liaison officer 1985-87, pres. 1990), Houston Psychol. Assn. (pres. 1976-77). Avocation: gardening. Home: 2110 Airline Dr Friendswood TX 77546 Office: U Houston 2700 Bay Area Blvd Houston TX 77058-1002

SUTTER, LINDA DIANE, health services administrator; b. Queens, N.Y., Oct. 6, 1948; d. Robert Henry Sutter and Mary Lillian (Knapp) Lavers; m. Steven Thomas Centore, Aug. 16, 1975. BA in Psychology, SUNY Binghamton, 1970; MEd in Counseling, Ohio U., 1973; MBA, U. Lowell, 1989; postgrad., Harvard U. Lic. mental health counselor, lic. nursing home adminstr.; cert. social worker; EMT. Asst. dean women, counselor Curry Coll., Milton, Mass., 1973-75; cons. self-employed Milton, Mass., 1975-80; dir. emergency and cmty. support svcs. Solomon Mental Health Ctr., Lowell, Mass., 1980-90; dir. cmty. svcs. Merrimack Valley Area Office/Dept. Mental Health, Lowell, Mass., 1990-92; asst. supt. for program and ops. Solomon Mental Health Ctr., Lowell, Mass., 1992-93, supt., 1993—. Mem. Am. Coll. Health Care Execs. (assoc.), Women in Health Care Mgmt. (steering com. 1994-96), Greater Boston EMT Assn. (bd. dirs. 1991-96). Democrat. Roman Catholic. Home: 735 Varnum Ave Lowell MA 01854 Office: Solomon Mental Health Ctr 391 Varnum Ave Lowell MA 01854

SUTTERBY, LARRY QUENTIN, internist; b. North Kansas City, Mo., Sept. 11, 1950; s. John Albert and Wilma Elizabeth (Henry) S.; m. Luciana Risos Magpuri, July 5, 1980; children: Leah Lourdes, Liza Bernadette. BA in Chemistry, William Jewell Coll., 1972; MD, U. Mo., Kans. City, 1976. Diplomate Am. Bd. Internal Medicine with qualifications in geriatric medicine. Resident in internal medicine Mt. Sinai Hosp., Chgo., 1976-79; physician Mojave Desert Health Svc., Barstow, Calif., 1979-86; pvt. practice Barstow, 1986—; med. dir. Rimrock Villa Convalescent Hosp., Barstow, 1995—, Mojave Valley Hospice, 1983—, VNA Hospice, Barstow, 1994—, Optioncare Home Health Svcs., 1995—. Recipient Loving Care award Vis. Nurse Assn. Inland Counties, 1988. Mem. AMA, ACP, Am. Med. Dirs. Assn., Am. Diabetes Assn., Calif. Med. Assn., San Bernardino County Med. Soc., Am. Soc. Internal Medicine, Am. Geriatric Soc., Acad. Hospice Physicians, Nat. Hospice Orgn., Internat. Coll. Hospice and Palliative Care, Soc. Gen. Internal Medicine, Am. Numismatic Assn., Combined Orgns. Numismatic Error Collectors Am. Democrat. Roman Catholic. Office: 209 N 2nd Ave Barstow CA 92311-2222

SUTTON, ANNIE TERESA, health information administrator; b. Springfield, Mass., July 14, 1940; d. Albert Ernest Jr. and Lois Miriam (Erskine) C.; m. John Martin Jr., May 5, 1962; children: Joyce Anderson, Joan, Joelle Wilkins, John III. RN, Maine, Mass.; Accredited Records Technician, ind. study, Am. Health Info. Mgmt. Assn., 1987. Med.-surg. staff nurse Malden (Mass.) Hosp., 1961-62, 67-68, Regional Meml. Hosp., Brunswick, Maine, 1969-71; ob-gyn. staff nurse Parkview Meml. Hosp., Brunswick, Maine, 1972-73; inpatient psychiatry staff nurse Eastern Maine Med. Ctr., Bangor, 1974-78; office asst. Dr. Anthony D'Andrea, South Portland, Maine, 1979-80; mobile technician Phys. Measurements, Inc., Falmouth, Maine, 1979-80; utilization rev. coord. Pine Tree Orgn., Augusta, Maine, 1979-80; dir. clin. info. svcs. Westbrook (Maine) Cmty. Hosp., 1980—. Chair liturgy com. Holy Martyr's Parish Coun., Falmouth, 1984-95, vice chair, 1987-95; mem., sec. Woodlands Homeowners Assn., Falmouth, 1991-96; v.p. Cumberland Hills Homeowners Assn., 1989-90; mem. Cancer Prevention and Control Adv. com., Augusta, Maine, 1989—, Mental Health Employer Consortium, Portland, 1993—, HIV Adv. Bd.-Legis. Commn., Augusta, 1995—. Mem. Am. Health Info. Mgmt. Assn., Maine Health Info. Mgmt. Assn. (pres.-elect 1989, pres. 1990, legis. com. chair 1992-96), Maine Assn. for Healthcare Quality, Am. Soc. Notaries, Informed Notaries Maine. Home: 64 Oakmont Dr Falmouth ME 04105

SUTTON, BETH HOWELL, physician; b. San Antonio, Mar. 23, 1950; m. Richard N. Sutton. BA, Baylor U., 1972, MD, 1976. Intern in surgery St. Paul Hosp., Dallas, 1976-77; resident Scott & White, Temple, Tex., 1977-81. Office: 1600 Brook Ave Wichita Falls TX 76301-5620

SUTTON, BEVERLY JEWELL, psychiatrist; b. Rockford, Mich., May 27, 1932; d. Beryl Dewey and Cora Belle (Potes) Jewell; m. Harry Eldon Sutton, July 7, 1962; children: Susan, Caroline. MD, U. Mich., 1957. Diplomate Am. Bd. Pediatrics, Am. Bd. Psychiatry and Neurology. Rotating intern St. Joseph Mercy Hosp., Ann Arbor, Mich., 1958; resident in child psychiatry Hawthorne Ctr., Northville, Mich., 1958-62; resident in pediatrics U. Hosp./U. Mich. Med. Ctr., Ann Arbor, 1959-61; resident in psychiatry Austin (Tex.) State Hosp., 1962-64, dir. children's svc., 1964-89, dir. psychiatric residency program, 1989—, dir. tng. and rsch., 1993—; cons. in field. Contbr. articles to profl. jours. Active numerous civic orgns. Recipient Outstanding Achievement award, YWCA, 1989, Jackson Day award, Tex. Soc. Child and Adolescent Psychiatry, 1989, Showcase award, Tex. Dept. Mental Health/Mental Retardation,1990, Disting. Svc. award, Tex. Soc. Psychiatric Physicians, 1990. Fellow Am. Acad. Child and Adolescent Psychiatry, Am. Psychiatric Soc., Am. Pediatric Assn.; mem. Tex. Soc. Child and Adolescent Psychiatry (pres. 1979-80), Tex. Soc. Psychiatric Physicians, AMA, Tex. Med. Soc., Am. Genetics Soc. Office: Austin State Hospital 4110 Guadalupe St Austin TX 78751-4223

SUTTON, DOUGLAS HOYT, nurse; b. McHenry, Ill., Oct. 27, 1962; s. Hoyt Douglas Sutton and Barbara (Sutton) Hensley. Cert. in emergency med. tech., Polk Community Coll., Winter Haven, Fla., 1985; ADN, SUNY, Albany, 1990, BS in Nursing, 1991, BS in Psychology, 1993; MSN, U. Fla., 1995; postgrad., U. S. Fla., 1995—. Cert. adv. nursing adminstrn., rehab. reg. nurse. Nurse adminstr. Bartow (Fla.) Meml. Hosp., 1991-94; paramedic Polk County Emergency Med. Svcs., Bartow, Fla., 1984-88; edn. cons. Moore Pubs., 1990-94; dir. subacute skilled care programs Columbia Healthcare, Inc., Gainesville, 1995—. Mem. Am. Assn. Rehab. Nurses, Am. Coll. Healthcare Execs., Sigma Theta Tau. Home: 7200 SW 8th Ave S-121 Gainesville FL 32607

SUTTON, GREGORY PAUL, obstetrician, gynecologist; b. Tokyo, Dec. 12, 1948; (parents Am. citizens); s. Vernon S. And Vonna Lou (Streeter) S.; m. Judith Craigie Holt, June 26, 1977; children: Anne Craigie, James Streeter. BS in Chemistry with honors, Ind. U., 1970; MD, U. Mich., 1976. Diplomate Am. Bd. of Ob/Gyn. Assoc. prof. and chief div. gynecologic oncology Ind. U. Sch. Medicine, Indpls., 1983—. Cancer Clin. fellow Am. Cancer Soc., Phila., 1981-83; recipient Career Devel. award Am. Cancer Soc., 1986-89. Fellow Am. Coll. Obstetrics and Gynecology; mem. Gynecologic Oncology Group (cert. Spl. Competence in Gynecologic Oncology 1985), Marion County Med. Soc., Ind. State Med. Soc., Bayard Carter Soc., Soc. of Gynecologic Oncologists, Gynecologic Oncology Group, Hoosier Oncology Group. Office: Ind U Hosp 926 W Michigan St Indianapolis IN 46202-5203*

SUTTON, JEFFREY PAUL, physician, scientist; b. N.Y.C., July 6, 1958. MD, U. Toronto, Ontario, Can., 1982, MSc in med. sci., 1985, PhD in physics, 1988. Intern U. Toronto, 1982-83, fellow in med. sci., 1983-84; fellow Can. Psychiat. Research Found., 1984-85; research fellow Med. Research Coun. of Can., 1985-88; clin. fellow in psychiatry Harvard Med. Sch., Boston, 1988-91; vis. scientist in brain and cognitive scis. MIT, Cambridge, 1988-95, rsch. affiliate in brain and cognitive scis., 1995—; instr. psychiatry Harvard Med. Sch., Boston, 1991-93, asst. prof., 1993—; dir. neural sys. group Mass. Gen. Hosp., 1995—. Recipient NIH Rsch. Career Scientist award, 1994—. Mem. AMA, Am. Phys. Soc., Am. Psychiat. Assn., Soc. for Neurosci. Office: Mass Gen Hosp Bldg 149 9th Fl 13th St Boston MA 02129

SUTTON, JOYCE ELAINE, medical records director; b. Chillicothe, Mo., Aug. 28, 1946; d. William Stanley and Helen Louise (Ashlock) Henderson; m. Ferold Rodrick Vermilyea, Jr., Feb. 7, 1964 (div. Aug. 1973); m. Ronald Eldon Sutton, Jan. 15, 1978; children: Sherra Wood, Janae Nezerka, Michael Sutton, Brian Sutton, Marcia Sandner. Accredited record technician. Ward clk. Heartland West Hosp. (formerly Meth. Med. Ctr.), St. Joseph, Mo., 1970-73; ward clk. Hedrick Med. Ctr., Chillicothe, 1973-74; med. records clk. Hedrick Med. Ctr., 1974-75, A.R.T. trainee, 1975-77, med. transcriber, 1977-82, asst. supr., 1982-85, med. records supr., 1985-89, med. records dir., 1989—, quality assurance cons., 1989-92, also med. staff sec., treas., coord.; dir. med. records Pershing Meml. Hosp., Pershing Regional Hosp., Brookfield-Marceline, Mo., 1992—, dir. admissions dept.; cons. Brookfield (Mo.) Nursing Ctr., 1987—, Excelsior Springs (Mo.) City Hosp., 1988—; dir. outpatient program, Hedrick Med. Ctr., Chillicothe, 1987—, dir. quality assurance/risk mgmt., 1988—. Mem. local civic orgns., Chillicothe, 1987—. Mem. Hedrick Med. Ctr. Aux. (life), Am. Med. Records Assn., Mo. Med. Records Assn., Kansas City Area Med. Records Assn. Republican. Baptist. Home: PO Box 114 Meadville MO 64659-0114 Office: Pershing Meml Hosp 130 E Lockling St Brookfield MO 64628-2337

SUTTON, LAURA BROWN, pharmacist; b. Portsmouth, Va., Oct. 18, 1967; d. Bobby Dean Reid and Lynda Leigh (Morris) Brown; m. Billy Frank Sutton, June 1, 1991; 1 child, Matthew Reid. BS in Biology, East Carolina U., Greenville, N.C., 1988; BS in Pharmacy, U. N.C., 1991, PharmD, 1994. Staff pharmacist Boone-Taylor Pharmacy, Ahoskie, N.C., 1991-92; relief pharmacist Revco Drug Stores, Sanford, N.C., 1992-94, Eckerd Corp., Sanford, 1994-96; drug info. resident Glaxo/U. N.C. Sch. Pharmacy, Research Triangle Park, 1994-95; drug info. assoc. Glaxo Wellcome, Inc., Research Triangle Park, 1995—. Republican. Baptist.

SUTTON, PHILIP D(IETRICH), psychologist; b. Ridgewood, N.J., June 20, 1952; s. Clifton C. and Ida-Lois (Dietrich) S.; m. Kathleen E. Duffy, June 17, 1973; children—Heather, Shivonne. B.A., So. Ill. U., 1974; M.A., U. Chgo., 1975; Ph.D., U. Utah, 1979. Lic. psychologist, Colo. Psychologist VA Hosp., Salt Lake City, 1975-76; psychology intern Salt Lake Community Mental Health Ctr., Salt Lake City, 1976-78; counselor, instr. Counseling Ctr., U. Utah, Salt Lake City, 1976-78; counselor, acting dir. spl. services program Met. State Coll., Denver, 1978-80; staff psychologist Kaiser-Permanente Health Plan, Denver, 1980-83; adj. prof. U. Colo., 1979-83; pvt. practice psychology, Boulder (Colo.) Med. Ctr., 1983—; cons. spl. programs for disadvantaged students in higher edn. Dept. HEW, 1980. Mem. Am. Psychol. Assn., Biofeedback Soc. Am., Soc. Behavioral Medicine. Home: 4185 Corriente Pl Boulder CO 80301-1626 Office: Boulder Med Ctr 2750 Broadway St Boulder CO 80304-3573

SUURMOND, DIRK, retired dermatology educator; b. Amsterdam, The Netherlands, Jan. 4, 1926; s. Jacobus Jan and Neeltje (Kater) S.; m. Hansje Van Leeuwen, Aug. 29, 1959. MD, U. Leiden (The Netherlands), 1953. Tng. in dermatology Mcpl. Hosp., The Hague, The Netherlands, 1955-59, mem. staff, 1959-62; lectr. dermatology dept. Univ. Hosp., Leiden, 1959-62, assoc. prof., 1965-78, prof., chmn. dept., 1978-88, prof. emeritus, 1988—; hosp. cons., 1989. Co-author: Synopsis and Atlas of Clinical Dermatology, 1983, 91; contbr. over 100 articles to sci. jours. With M.C., Dutch Army, 1953-55. Mem. Am. Assn. Dermatology, Dutch Assn. Dermatology (hon.), Dutch Health Coun. (UV com.). Home: 75 Plantsoen, 2311 KK Leiden The Netherlands

SUYETSUGU, GRACE TAMIKO, nurse; b. San Mateo, Calif., Feb. 16, 1957; d. Frank Takiji and Mitsuka (Shimizu) S. BS magna cum laude in Nursing, San Francisco State U., 1979. RN, Calif. Charge nurse med./surg. unit Peninsula Hosp. and Med. Ctr., Burlingame, Calif., 1979-84, staff nurse ICU, 1984-88, charge nurse ICU, 1988-91, staff nurse endoscopy and ICU, 1991-92, staff nurse recovery rm. and same day surgery, 1992—. Mem. AACN, Am. Soc. Post Anesthesia Nurses, Nat. Nurses Assn., Calif. Nurses Assn., Post Anesthesia Nurses Assn. Calif. Democrat. Buddhist. Avocations: travel, photography, cooking, needlework, sports. Home: 3682 Bobwhite Ter Fremont CA 94555-1524 Office: Peninsula Hosp and Med Ctr 1783 El Camino Real Burlingame CA 94010-3205

SUZUKI, JON BYRON, dean, periodontist, educator; b. San Antonio, July 22, 1947; s. George K. and Ruby (Kanaya) S. BA in Biology, Ill. Wesleyan U., 1968; PhD magna cum laude in Microbiology, Ill. Inst. Tech., 1971; DDS magna cum laude, Loyola U., 1978. Med. technologist Ill. Masonic Hosp. and Med. Ctr., Chgo., 1966-67; instr. lab. in histology and parasitology Ill. Wesleyan U., Bloomington, 1967-68; med. technologist Augustana Hosp., Chgo., 1968-69; rsch. assoc., instr. microbiology Ill. Inst. Tech., Chgo., 1968-71; clin. rsch. assoc. U. Chgo. Hosps., 1970-71; clin. microbiologist St. Luke's Hosp. Ctr., Columbia Coll., Physicians and Surgeons, N.Y.C., 1971-73; assoc. med. dir. Paramed. Tng. and Registry, Vancouver, B.C., Can., 1973-74; dir. clin. labs. Registry of Hawaii, 1973-74; chmn. clin. labs. edn. Kapiolani Community Coll., U. Hawaii, Honolulu, 1974; lectr. periodontics, oral pathology Loyola U. Med. Ctr., Maywood, Ill., 1974-90; lectr. stomatology Northwestern U. Dental Sch., Chgo., 1982-90; NIH rsch. fellow depts. pathology and periodontics Ctr. for Rsch. in Oral Biology, U. Wash.-Seattle, 1978-80; prof. dept. periodontics and microbiology U. Md. Coll. Dental Surgery, Balt., 1980-90; mem. attending faculty divsn. dentistry and oral and maxillofacial surgery The Johns Hopkins Med. Inst., Balt., 1985—; practice dentistry specializing in periodontics Balt., Pitts.; dean Sch. Dental Medicine, U. Pitts., 1989—; cons. Dentsply Internat., York, Pa., U.S. Army, Walter Reed Med. Ctr., Washington, U.S. Army, Ft. Gordon, Ga., USN, Nat. Naval Med. Command, Bethesda, The NutraSweet Co., Deerfield, Ill.; cons. Food and Drug Adminstrn., Rockville, Md.; mem. Oral Biology/medicine study sect. NIH, Bethesda, 1985-90; mem. nat. adv. dental rsch. coun. NIH/NIDR, Bethesda, 1994—; vis. scientist to Moscow State U., USSR, 1972, NASA, Houston, 1976-92; lectr. Internat. Congress Allergology, Tokyo, 1973; lab. dir. Hawaii Dept. Health. Author: Clinical Laboratory Methods for the Medical Assistant, 1974; mem. editorial bd. Am. Health Mag.; contbr. articles on research in microbiology, immunology and dentistry to sci. jours. Instr. water safety ARC, Honolulu, 1973-90. Recipient Pres.'s medallion Loyola U., Chgo., 1977; named Alumnus of Yr., Ill. Wesleyan U., 1977. Fellow Acad. Dentistry Internat., Am Coll. Dentists, Internat. Coll. Dentists, Am. Coll. Stomatognathic Surgeons; mem. AAAS, ADA (vice chair coun. sci. affairs), AAUP, Am. Acad. Periodontology (diplomate), Am. Inst. Biol. Scis., Internat. Soc. Biophysics, Internat. Soc. Endocrinologists, Ill. Acad. Sci. , Am. Internat. Assn. Dental Rsch. (pres. Md. chpt.), Am. Acad. Microbiology (diplomate), Am. Acad. Microbiology (diplomate, examiner), N.Y. Acad. Scis., Sigma XI, Omicron Kappa Upsilon (past nat. pres., exec. sec.), Beta, Beta, Beta Hon. Soc. Home: 3501 Terrace St Pittsburgh PA 15213-2523 Office: U Pitts Sch Dental Medicine Dean's Office Pittsburgh PA 15261

SUZUKI, TSUNEO, molecular immunologist; b. Nagoya, Aichi, Japan, Nov. 23, 1931; s. Morichika and Toshiko (Kita) S.; widowed; children: Riichiro, Aijiro, Yozo. BS, U. Tokyo, 1953, MD, 1957; PhD, U. Hokkaido, 1967. Asst. prof. U. Kans. Med. Ctr., Kansas City, 1970-79, assoc. prof., 1979-83, prof., 1983—, interim chair, 1994—; mem. NIH Study Sect., Washington, 1983-87. Contbr. articles to profl. jours. Postdoctoral fellows U. Wis., 1963-66, 69-70, U. Lausanne, Switzerland, 1966-67, U Toronto, 1969; recipient Fulbright Travel award, 1962, Sr. Investigator award, U. Kans. Med. Ctr., 1990. Mem. Am. Assn. Immunologists, Am. Soc. Biological Chemists (Travel award 1988). Home: 3620 W 73rd St Prairie Vlg KS 66208-2903 Office: U Kans Med Ctr Dept Microbiology 3901 Rainbow Blvd Kansas City KS 66160-0001

SVEEN, JANE HOFLAND, physician assistant; b. Bottineau, N.D., June 30, 1955; d. Norman Raymond and Gladys Marie (Carlson) H.; m. Marlo Jon Sveen, July 24, 1976; children: Thomas, William, Inga. BS in Biology, Minot (N.D.) State Coll., 1976; AS Physician Assistant, Pa. State U., Hershey, 1981. Cert. Nat. Commn. on Cert. of Physician Assts. Physician assistant, cardiology Heart and Lung Clinic, Bismarck, N.D., 1981—. Fellow Am. Assn. Physician Assts., N.D. Acad. Physician Assts. Republican. Evangelical Free Ch.

SVENSON, ERNEST OLANDER, psychiatrist, psychoanalyst; b. Duluth, Minn., Oct. 16, 1923; s. Ernest G. and Mabel A. (Benson) S.; m. Raquel Lefevre, 1954 (div. 1965); children: Ernest E., Stuart K.; m. Shirley Zupancic, 1982. BS, Wayne State U., 1948, MD, 1952; BA, Augustana Coll., 1948. Diplomate Am. Bd. Psychiatry and Neurology. Intern Gorgas Hosp., C.Z., 1952-53, staff physician, 1953-54; resident Charity Hosp., New Orleans, 1954-57; psychoanalytic trainee New Orleans Psychoanalytic Inst., 1958-62; pvt. practice, 1958—; assoc. prof. psychiatry La. State U., 1962-80, clin. prof. psychiatry, 1980—; chmn. dept. psychiatry Touro Infirmary, 1973-76; mem. Gov.'s Adv. Com., Mental Health, 1971-72; cons. S.E. La. State Hosp., 1958-61; sr. vis. physician, Charity Hosp., 1965—; clin. prof. psychiatry Tulane U. Med. Sch., 1983—. Bd. dirs. New Orleans Area/Bayou River Health Systems Agy., 1978-82, exec. com., 1979-82, chmn. project rev. com., 1978-79; mem. Area Health Planning, 1971-82. Lt. (j.g.) USNR, 1942-46. Recipient Disting. Alumni award Augustana Coll., 1990. Fellow Am. Psychiatric Assn.; mem. AAAS, Am. Psychoanalytic Assn. (com. new tng. facilities 1988-92), Internat. Psychoanalytic Assn., La. Med. Assn., Am. Coll. Psychiatrists, New Orleans Mental Health Assn. (bd. dirs. 1975-77), New Orleans Area Psychiatry Assn. (pres. 1969-70), La. Psychiatric Assn. (pres. 1969-71), New Orleans Psychoanalytic Soc. (pres. 1971-73), New Orleans Psychoanalytic Inst. (sec.-treas. 1975, tng. supr. analyst 1972—, pres. 1983-85, chmn. edn. com. 1983-85), N.Y. Acad. Scis., Alpha Omega Alpha. Home: 123 Walnut St Apt 1001 New Orleans LA 70118-4846 Office: 1301 Antonine St New Orleans LA 70115-3601

SVIKLA, ALIUS JULIUS, pharmacist; b. Merbeck, Germany, Jan. 12, 1947; came to U.S., 1949; s. Julius and Brone (Maksimavich) S. BS in Pharmacy, Northeastern U., Boston, 1973. Pharmacist Osco Drug, Cambridge, Mass., 1973-75; profl. sales rep. Pfizer Labs., N.Y.C., 1976-77; pharmacist, mgr. CVS Pharmacy, South Dennis, Mass., 1977—; drug abuse cons. Healthcare Assn., Boston, First Group of Boston, 1979-87; liason Kaunas Med. Acad., Lithuania. Served with USMC, 1965-68. Decorated Purple Heart. Mem. Am. Pharm. Assn., Internat. Pharm. Fedn., Mass. Pub. Health Assn., Mass. State Pharm. Assn., Lithuanian Am. Pharm. Assn., Mil. Order of Purple Heart (life), Fleet Res. Assn. (Cape Cod chpt. H.O.G., Boston chpt.). Republican. Roman Catholic. Home: 9 Seagrove Rd South Dennis MA 02660-2737 Office: CVS Pharmacy PO Box 715 Rte 134 Patriots Sq South Dennis MA 02660

SVOBODA, JERRY JOSEPH, vascular surgeon; b. Cleve., Aug. 23, 1951; s. Jerry Frank and Janet (Texler) S.; m. Adelaide Eizabeth Jones, Apr. 16, 1977; children: Elizabeth, Mark. AB in Biology magna cum laude, St. Louis U., 1973; MD, Hahnemann Med. Coll., 1977. Diplomate Am. Bd. Surgery in surgery and vascular surgery. Intern Mercy Med. Ctr., Denver, 1977-78; surg. resident Guthrie Cilnic/Robert Packer Hosp., Sayre, Pa., 1978-82; vascular surgery fellow Englewood (N.J.) Hosp., 1982-83; staff surgeon Mercy Med. Ctr., Denver, 1983-84; attending surgeon St. Mary's and Park Ridge Hosps., Rochester, N.Y., 1984—; med. staff pres. St. Mary's Hosp., 1996; cons. surgeon Lakeside Meml. Hosp., 1984—; cons. surgeon Rochester Gen. Hosp., 1984-90, courtesy staff, 1991—; clin. asst. prof. surgery U. Rochester Sch. Medicine and Dentistry, 1984—; mem. med. bd. St. Mary's Hosp., Rochester, 1989-93, 95-96, Park Ridge Hosp., Rochester, 1991-92. Contbr. articles to profl. jours. Sec. Christ Ch. Unity, Rochester, 1987-89. Recipient Physician Recognition award AMA, 1981-84, 84-87, 87-90, 90-93, 94—. Fellow ACS (apptd. to Young Surgeons Coun. 1996); mem. Soc. Clin. Vascular Surgery, Upstate N.Y. Vascular Soc., Ea. Vascular Soc., Monroe County Med. Soc. (asst. treas. 1990, sec. 1991-92), Rochester Vascular Soc. Home: 70 Brandywine Ln Rochester NY 14618-5602 Office: Rochester Vascular Surgery Assocs 503 Beahan Rd Rochester NY 14624-3403

SWAAB, DICK FRANS, physician, neuroscientist; b. Amsterdam, The Netherlands, Dec. 17, 1944; s. Leo Isaac and Helene Ans (Smit) S. MD, U. Amsterdam, 1968, PhD, 1970. Intern U. Clins. Amsterdam, 1958-71; gen. physician U. Amsterdam, 1972; acting dir. Netherlands Inst. Brain Rsch., Amsterdam, 1975-78, dir., 1978—; prof. neurobiology, med. faculty U. Amsterdam, 1979—; dir. Netherlands Brain Bank, 1985—. Contbr. articles to profl. jours. Recipient Snoo van't Hoogerhuijs prize, Utrecht, 1976, Citation Classic prize, 1990, Hugo van Poelgeest prize, 1990; named Holst lectr. T.U. Eindhover, 1987, Emil Kraeplin guest prof. Max Planck Inst. Psychiatry, 1996. Office: Netherlands Inst Brain Rsch, Meibergdreef 33, 11105 AZ Amsterdam The Netherlands

SWAAY, HENRI VAN, retired internist; b. The Hague, The Netherlands, Apr. 27, 1919; s. H.G.J.A. van and Aagje (Stam) S.; m. Kitty de Roos, July 16, 1946; children: Marieke Mathilde, Henriette, Henri, Aagje Marieke, Dirk Jan. MD, Leiden U., 1951. Intern, resident in internal medicine Univ. Hosp. Leiden/Amsterdam, Holland, 1945-51; cons. Royal Dutch Navy, Ankatan Laut, Indonesia, 1950-51; rhumatologist Bronovo Hosp., The Hague, 1951-57; cons. in internal medicine Sophia Ziekenhuis, Zwolle, 1957-75; pvt. practice Zwolle, 1975-96; cons. on med. ins. numerous cos. Contbr. articles to profl. jours.; editor: Congress Proceedings Contemporary Rheumatology, 1956; patentee in field. Lt. Netherlands Navy, 1950-51. Liberal Party. Home and Office: Kleine Veerweg 27, 8016 PA Zwolle The Netherlands

SWAFFORD, LESLIE EUGENE, physician assistant, consultant; b. Long Beach, Calif., Aug. 31, 1950; s. Leslie Eugene Swafford, Sr. and Kathryn Shirley (Gros) Jarvis; children: Jayson Patrick, Jonathan Allyn, Jude Christopher, Joshua Douglas; m. Cheryl Kaleen Killman, Apr. 10, 1993; 1 child, Lesli Tayte. BS in Allied Health, physician asst. degree of completion, George Washington U., 1978; postgrad. in Occupl. Medicine, U. Cin., 1994-95. Cert. physician's asst. NCCPA, ACLS, PALS, CDC AIDS Counselor, EBT (Alco-Sensor IV), EBT (EC/IR) QAP, TTT. Chief EEG technologist Group Health Assn., Washington, 1974-76; physician asst. Pediat. Assocs., Frederick, Md., 1978-81, Heart Inst. for Care, Amarillo, Tex., 1981-84, Maricopa Cmty. Medicine Assocs., Avondale-Goodyear, Ariz., 1984-89; mgr. Samarital Occupl. Health Svcs. Samaritan Health System, Phoenix, 1989—; adminstr. drug test program Samaritan Health Svcs., Phoenix, 1991; Mem. com. Ariz. Rural Health Conf., 1992-96; adj. asst. prof. physician asst. tng. program Kirksville Coll. of Osteo. Medicine, Phoenix, 1995—. Contbr. articles to profl. jours. Chmn. sex edn. com. North Ctrl. Accreditation-Aqua Fria H.S., Avondale, Ariz., 1991; physician asst. Camp Geronimo (Boy Scouts of Am.), Phoenix, 1989-94; team mem. Young People's Beginning Experience Grief Recovery Program for Children, Phoenix, 1989-93; mem. com. Ariz. Dept. Health Svcs.-Robert Wood Johnson Application, Phoenix, 1992-93. With USN, 1969-74. Recipient scholarship NIH, 1976, Squibb Pharm. Rural Physician Asst. of Yr. award honorable mention Am. Acad. Physician Assts., 1987, Dr. Paul L. Singer award for disting. cmty. svc. Samaritan Found., 1991. Fellow Ariz. State Assn. Physician Assts (pres.-elect 1990-91, pres. 1991-92, chmn. Ariz. physician asst. tng. program task force 1990-94). Republican. Roman Catholic. Home: 17305 Cactus Flower Dr Goodyear AZ 85338 Office: Samaritan Occupl Health Svcs Edwards Med Plz 1300 N 12th St Ste 407 Phoenix AZ 85006

SWAIM, JOHN FRANKLIN, physician, health care executive; b. Bloomingdale, Ind., Dec. 24, 1935; s. Max DeBaun and Edna Marie (Whitely) S.; m. Joan Dooley, Sept. 19, 1957 (div. Apr. 1979); children: John Franklin, Parke Allen, Pamela Ann; m. Peggy Lou Sankey, May 30, 1979; one child, Anne-Marie. BS cum laude, Ind. State U., 1959; MD, Ind. U., Indpls., 1963. Diplomate Am. Bd. Family Practice. Med. dir. Parke Clinic, Rockville, Ind., 1969—; pres. Parke Investments Inc., Rockville, 1972—, Vermillion Health Care Corp., Clinton, Ind., 1977—. Author: One Year and Eternity, 1978; also contbr. articles to profl. jours. Coroner, Parke County, Ind., 1972-82. Served to capt. USAF, 1963-67, Vietnam. Decorated Bronze Star. Mem. Am. Acad. Family Physicians, AMA, Ind. State Med. Assn. (dist. pres. 1986—), Midwest Fin. Assn. Republican. Club: Hoosier Assocs. (Indpls.). Lodges: Elks, Masons, Shriners. Home and Office: Parke Clinic PO Box 185 Rockville IN 47872-0185

SWAIM, MARK WENDELL, molecular biologist, gastroenterologist; b. Winston-Salem, N.C., Dec. 4, 1960; s. Donnie Lee and Bernice Earline (Brown) S. BA summa cum laude, U. N.C., 1983; MD, Duke U., 1990, PhD with honors, 1990. Diplomate Am. Bd of Internal Medicine. Resident Dept. of Med. Duke U. Med. Ctr., Durham, N.C., 1990-93; fellow gastroenterology Duke U. Med. Ctr., 1993—. Contbr. articles to profl. jours. Recipient Med. Sci. Training Program fellow Nat. Inst. of Health, 1983-90, numerous acad. scholarships. Mem. Am. Coll. Physicians, Reticuleondothelial Soc., Alpha Omega Alpha, Phi Beta Kappa, Sigma Xi. Home: 231-A Bridgefield Pl Durham NC 27705 Office: Duke Univ Medical Ctr PO Box 3913 Durham NC 27710

SWAIMAN, KENNETH F., medical educator; b. St. Paul, Minn.. BA magna cum laude, U. Minn., 1952, BS, 1953, MD, 1955. Diplomat Am. Bd. Pediatrics, Am. Bd. Psychiatry and Neurology, Am. Bd. Psychiatry and Neurology with Spl. Competence in Child Neurology. Intern Mpls. Gen. Hosp., 1955-56; fellow in pediatrics to chief resident U. Minn. Hosps., 1956-58; chief pediatrics U.S. Army Hosp., Ft. McPherson, Ga., 1958-60 spl. fellow in pediatric neurology U. Minn., 1960-63; pediatric neurology attending staff Hennepin County Med. Ctr., 1963—; dir. pediatric neurology tng. program U. Minn., 1968-94, various to interim head, dept. neurology, 1994—; vis. prof. numerous univs., including Children's Hosp. of Mich., Detroi, 1990, Univ. de Concepion, Chile, 1989, Xian Med. U., China, 1989, Beijing Med. U., China, 1989, Driscoll Children's Hosp., Corpus Christi, Tex., 1986, Hong Kong Child Neurology Soc., 1995, Inst. Nacional de Pediatria, Mexico City, 1986, U. Kyushu, Shiga, Nagoya, Tokyo, 1985, U. Ind. Med. Sch., 1983, Loyola U., 1982, U. N.Mex., 1982, others; lectr. in field; cons. in field; guest worker NIH, NICHD, Bethesda, Md., 1978-79, 79-81. Contbr. articles to profl. jours. and publs. Fellow Am. Acad. Neurology, Am. Acad. Pediatrics; mem. AAAS, Am. Chem. Soc., AMA, Am. Neurol. Assn., Am. Soc. Neurochemistry, Cen. Soc. Clin. Rsch., Cen. Soc. Neurol. Rsch., Child Neurology Soc. (1st pres.), Internat. Child Neurology Assn., Internat. Soc. Neurochemistry, Midwest Soc. Pediatric Rsch., Minn. Med. Found., Profs. of Child Neurology (1st pres.), Phi Beta Kappa, numerous others. Office: Univ Minn Med Sch Box 380 UMHC 420 Delaware St SE Minneapolis MN 55455

SWAIMAN, KENNETH FRED, pediatric neurologist, educator; b. St. Paul, Nov. 19, 1931; s. Lester J. and Shirley (Ryan) S.; m. Phyllis Kammerman Sher, Oct. 1985; children: Lisa, Jerrold, Barbara, Dana. B.A. magna cum laude, U. Minn., 1952, B.S., 1953, M.D., 1955; postgrad., 1956-58; postgrad. (fellow pediatric neurology), Nat. Inst. Neurologic Diseases and Blindness, 1960-63. Diplomate: Am. Bd. Psychiatry and Neurology, Am. Bd. Pediatrics. Intern Mpls. Gen. Hosp., 1955-56; resident pediatrics U. Minn., 1956-58, neurology, 1960-63; postgrad. fellow pediatric neurology Nat. Inst. Neurologic Diseases and Blindness, 1960-63; asst. prof. pediatrics, neurology U. Minn. Med. Sch., Mpls., 1963-66; asso. prof. Nat. Inst. Neurologic Diseases and Blindness, 1966-69; prof., dir. pediatric neurology U. Minn. Med. Sch., 1969—; interim head Dept. Neurology, U. Minn. Med. Sch., 1994-96; interim head dept. neurology U. Minn. Med. Sch., 1994—, mem. internship adv. council exec. faculty, 1966-70; interim head dept. neurology, 1994—; cons. pediatric neurology Hennepin County Gen. Hosp., Mpls., St. Paul-Ramsey Hosp., St. Paul Children's Hosp., Mpls. Children's Hosp.; vis. prof. Beijing U. Med. Sch., 1989. Author: (with Francis S. Wright) Neuromuscular Diseases in Infancy and Childhood, 1969, Pediatric Neuromuscular Diseases, 1979, (with Stephen Ashwal) Pediatric Neurology Case Studies, 1978, 2d edit., 1984, Pediatric Neurology: Practice and Principles, 1989; editor: (with John A. Anderson) Phenylketonuria and Allied Metabolic Diseases, 1966, (with Francis S. Wright) Practice Pediatric Neurology, 1975, 2d edit., 1982; mem. editorial bd.: Annals of Neurology, 1977-83, Neurology Update, 1977-82, Pediatric Update, 1977-85, Brain and Devel. (Jour. Japanese Soc. Child Neurology), 1980—, Neuropediatrics (Stuttgart), 1982-92; editor-in-chief: Pediatric Neurology, 1984—; contbr. articles to sci. jours. Chmn. Minn. Gov.'s Bd. for Handicapped, Exceptional and Gifted Children, 1972-76; mem. human devel. study sect. NIH, 1976-79, guest worker, 1978-81. Served to capt. M.C. U.S. Army, 1958-60. Fellow Am. Acad. Pediatrics, Am. Acad. Neurology (rep. to nat. council Nat. Soc. Med. Research); mem. Soc. Pediatric Research, Central Soc. Clin. Research, Central Soc. Neurol. Research, Internat. Soc. Neurochemistry, Am. Neurol. Assn., Minn. Neurol. Soc., AAAS, Midwest Pediatric Soc., Am. Soc. Neurochemistry, Child Neurology Soc. (1st pres. 1972-73, Hower award 1981, chmn. internat. affairs com., 1991—, mem. long range planning com. 1991—), Internat. Assn. Child Neurologists (exec. com. 1975-79), Profs. of Child Neurology (1st pres. 1978-80, mem. nominating com. 1986—), Japanese Child Neurology Soc. (Segawa award 1986, mem. nominating com. 1986—, chair internat. affairs com. 1991—, mem. long range planning com. 1991—), Soc. de Psiquiatria y Neurologia de la Infancia y Adolescencia, Phi Beta Kappa, Sigma Xi. Home: 420 Delaware St SE Minneapolis MN 55455-0374 Office: U Minn Med Sch Dept Pediatric Neurology Minneapolis MN 55455

SWAIN, JUDITH LEA, cardiovascular physician, educator; b. Long Beach, Calif., Sept. 24, 1948; m. Edward W. Holmes. BS in Chemistry with deptl. honors, UCLA, 1970; MD, U. Calif., San Diego, 1974. Diplomate Am. Bd. Internal Medicine, cardiovasc. disease; lic. physician Calif., Pa., N.C. Intern in medicine Duke U. Med. Ctr., 1974-75, resident in medicine, 1975-76, fellow in cardiology, 1976-80, assoc. in medicine, 1979-81, from asst. prof. medicine to assoc. prof. medicine, 1981-91, asst. prof. physiology, 1981-88, assoc. prof. microbiology & immunology, 1988-91, Herbert C. Rorer prof. med. scis., prof. genetics, 1991—, mem. molecular biology grad. group, 1991—, chief cardiovasc. divsn., 1991—; vis. asst. prof. dept. genetics Harvard Med. Sch., Boston, 1985-86; mem. search com. for dir. Ctr. for Aging, Duke U. Med. Ctr., 1991—, mem. exec. com. deptl. awards selection, 1992—, chmn. combined degree dir. search com., 1993, mem. clin. rsch. ctr. adv. com., 1993-94, mem. grad. student admissions com., 1993, mem. search com. for chief cardiovasc. surgery, 1992, dept. medicine intern selection com., 1992—; mem. instnl. rev. com. Pa. Muscle Inst., 1993; cardiology adv. com. Nat. Heart, Lung, & Blood Inst., 1989-93; dir. USA-Russia Cardiovasc. Rsch. Program, 1992—; mem. NIH Task Force on Heart Failure, 1992-93, dirs. standing com. on clin. rsch. NIH, 1995—; cons. Netherlands Rsch. Initiative in Molecular Cardiology, 1993; external adv. com. Ctr. for Prevention of Cardiovasc. Disease, Harvard Sch. Pub. Health, 1993—; adv. coun. NHLBI, 1995—, Friends of NHLBI com., 1996—, lectr. in field. Exec. editor: Trends in Cardiovascular Medicine, 1990-93; mem. editl. bd. Circulation Rsch., 1991—, Circulation, 1991—, Jour. Clin. Investigation, 1992—; cons. editor: Circulation, 1993—; contbr. articles to med. jours. Mem. exec. com. Coun. on Basic Sci., Am. Heart Assn., 1986-93, chmn. Katz Prize Award Com., 1989-92, rsch. rev. com., 1990-93, fellowship rsch. com., 1992—, program com., 1992—, mem. Levine Young Investigator Awards Com., Coun. on Clin. Cardiology, 1994—, mem. Basic Sci. Coun.; bd. dirs. Southeastern Pa. Heart Assn., 1992—. Recipient Bristol-Myers Squibb Cardiovasc. Achievement award, 1992, also numerous rsch. grants. Fellow Am. Coll. Cardiology (internat. edn. com. 1994—, chair cardiovasc. rsch. com. 1996—), Coll. Physicians of Phila.; mem. Assn. Univ. Cardiologists, Assn. Am. Physicians, Assn. Prof. of Cardiology, Am. Soc. Cell Biology, Am. Fedn. Clin. Rsch., Am. Soc. Clin. Investigation (pres.-elect 1994—, councilor 1991—), Internat. Soc. Heart Rsch. (councilor 1988—), Interurban Clin. Club, Clin. and Climitol. Soc., John Morgan Soc. Office: Hosp of Univ of Pa Cardiovasc Divsn 3400 Spruce St Philadelphia PA 19104

SWAIN, TERRY GIBB, mental health counselor, human resource consultant; b. Nassawadox, Va., July 8, 1951; d. Ivan Ward and Norma Elizabeth (Lewis) G.; m. Robert Franklin Swain, Apr. 21, 1972; children: Farah Tiffany Van Genderen, Melissa Swain Hicks. BA in Psychology, Salisbury State U., 1981, MA in Psychology, 1983. Lic. profl. counselor; cert. substance abuse counselor. Counselor Ea. Shore Substance Abuse Svc., Onancock, Va., 1982-90; outpatient clinician Ea. Shore Mental Health Ctr., Onancock, Va., 1990—; clin. dir., cons. Norac Humanitec, Inc., Accomac, Va., 1988—. Mem. AACD. Office: Norac Humanitec Inc PO Box 580 Accomac VA 23301-0580

SWALES, JOHN DOUGLAS, medical educator, consultant physician, editor; b. Leicester, Eng., Oct. 19, 1935; s. Frank and Doris Agnes (Flude) S.; m. Kathleen Patricia Townsend, Oct. 7, 1967; children: Philip, Charlotte. B.A., Cambridge U. (Eng.), 1957, M.B., B.Ch., 1961, M.D., 1973. Registrar Westminster Hosp., London, 1964-68; research fellow Royal Postgrad. Med. Sch., London, 1968-70; sr. lectr. U. Manchester, Eng., 1970-74; prof. U. Leicester, Eng., 1974—; dir. r&d Dept. Health, 1996—. Author: Sodium Metabolism in Disease, 1975; Clinical Hypertension, 1979; Platt Versus Pickering, 1985, Textbook of Hypertension, 1994; editor Clin. Sci., 1980-82; editor Jour. Hypertension, 1982-87, Jour. Royal Soc. Medicine, 1994—. Recipient Pasgham prize U. Cambridge, 1957, Mental Health Research Fund prize, 1958, Med. Writers prize for Best Textbook, 1995. Fellow High Blood Pressure Research Council, Royal Coll. Physicians (Harveian orator 1995); mem. Internat. Soc. Hypertension (council 1983-88), Assn. Physicians (council 1980-83), Brit. Hypertension Soc. (pres. 1983-85), Assn. Clin. Profs. Medicine (chmn. 1987-93), Fedn. Assn. Clin. Profs. (chmn. 1987-93), Club: Athenaeum. Home: 21 Morland Ave, Leicester LE2 2PF, England Office: Dept of Health, Richmond House 79 Whitehall, London SW1A 2NS, England

SWALES, RICHARD SCOTT, optometrist, health facility administrator; b. Clearfield, Pa., Feb. 23, 1951; s. Ernest Paul and Leetrice Joy (Halseth) S.; children: Chelle DeAnne, Cara Lee Swales Claxton, Richard Scott II. BS, U. Houston, 1973, DO, 1975. Pres. Primary Vision Care Svcs., Lawton, Okla., 1993—. mem. Drug Busters Southwest Okla., 1990—, pres. 1994; v.p. Lawton Coun. Camp Fire, Lawton, Okla, 1979, Black Beaver Coun., 1985—. Recipient Neefe Optical award, 1975. Mem. Okla. Optometrists Assn. (bd. dirs. 1978-80, 82-86), Rotary (pres. 1979-80). Home: 611 NW Waterford Dr Lawton OK 73505 Office: Primary Vision Care Svcs 2518 W Gore Blvd Ste C Lawton OK 73505

SWAN, JAMES H., sociology educator, health services researcher; b. Wichita, Kans., Sept. 14, 1946; s. William H. and Mary Madeline (Self) S.; m. Sandra J. Hiott, May 25, 1981; 1 hchild, Michael Joseph. BA, Wichita State U., 1969, MA, 1973; PhD, Northwestern U., 1981. Asst. rsch. sociologist U. Calif., San Francisco, 1977-87, assoc. rsch. sociologist, 1987-89; assoc. prof. Calif. State U., Long Beach, 1989-92; assoc. prof. dept. health svcs. Wichita State U., 1992—; mem. panel of experts EPPS study VA, Oak Brook, Ill., 1994. Sr. author: Serving the Mentally Ill. Elderly, 1987, Long Term Care Crisis, 1993; co-author: Long Term Care of the Elderly, 1985; contbr. chpt. to book. Faculty advisor Explorer Scouts, Boy Scouts Am., 1994—, com. mem. Cub Scouts, Wichita, 1994—; mem. Kans. Adv. Coalition for Children, Youth and Families, Topeka, 1994—; founding mem. Humanist Unitarian Universalists, Wichita, 1994—. Recipient Congl. award, 1989, Disting. Investigator award Inst. for Health and Aging, 1989. Mem. APHA (chair membership com. 1994—, mem. policy com. 1993—), Kans. Pub. Health Assn. (membership com. 1995—), Am. Sociol. Assn., Midwest Sociol. Soc., Calif. Sociol. Assn. Unitarian Universalist. Office: Wichita State U HSOP Box 43 Wichita KS 67260

SWAN, KENNETH CARL, surgeon; b. Kansas City, Mo., Jan. 1, 1912; s. Carl E. and Blanche (Peters) S.; m. Virginia Grone, Feb. 5, 1938; children: Steven Carl, Kenneth, Susan. A.B., U. Oreg., 1933, M.D., 1936. Diplomate: Am. Bd. Ophthalmology (chmn. 1960-61). Intern U. Wis., 1936-37; resident in ophthalmology State U. Iowa, 1937-40; practice medicine specializing in ophthalmology Portland, Oreg., 1945—; staff Good Samaritan Hosp.; asst. prof. ophthalmology State U. Iowa, Iowa City, 1941-44; asso. prof. U. Oreg. Med. Sch., Portland, 1944-45, prof. and head dept. ophthalmology, 1945-78; Chmn. sensory diseases study sect. NIH; mem. adv. council Nat. Eye Inst.; also adv. council Nat. Inst. Neurol. Diseases and Blindness. Contbr. articles on ophthalmic subjects to med. publs. Recipient Proctor Rsch. medal, 1953; Disting. Svc. award U. Oreg., 1963; Meritorious Achievement award U. Oreg. Med. Sch., 1968; Howe Ophthalmology medal, 1977; Aubrey Watzek Pioneer award Lewis and Clark Coll., 1979, Disting. Alumnus award Oreg. Health Scis. U. Alumni Assn., 1988, Disting. Svc. award, 1988; named Oreg. Scientist of Yr. Oreg. Mus. Sci. and Industry, 1959. Mem. Assn. Research in Ophthalmology, Am. Acad. Ophthalmology (v.p. 1978, historian), Soc. Exptl. Biology and Medicine, AAAS, AMA, Am. Ophthal. Soc. (Howe medal for distinguished service 1977), Oreg. Med. Soc., Sigma Xi, Sigma Chi (Significant Sig award 1977). Home: 4645 SW Fairview Blvd Portland OR 97221-2624 Office: Ophthamology Dept Oreg Health Scis U Portland OR 97201

SWAN, KENNETH GIRVAN, surgery educator; b. White Plains, N.Y., Oct. 2, 1934; s. Roy Craig and Ruth (Paxton) S.; m. Betsy Capwell, Jan. 30, 1965; children: Stephanie Alden, Kenneth G. Jr., Deborah Ruth. AB, Harvard U., 1956; MD, Cornell U., N.Y.C., 1960. Diplomate Am. Bd. Surgery, Am. Bd. Thoracic Surgery. Intern, resident in surgery N.Y. Hosp., N.Y.C., 1960-68; assoc. prof. surgery U. Medicine and Dentistry N.J., Newark, 1973, dir. sect. gen. surgery, 1973—, prof., 1976—, dir. sect. gen. surgery, 1973—; chief thoracic surgery Univ. Hosp., Newark, 1988—. Author: with (R.C. Swan) Gunshot Wounds, 1980, 2d edit., 1989. Capt. M.C., U.S. Army, 1968-73, Vietnam, col. Res., Persian Gulf. Fellow ACS, Am. Surg. Assn., Soc. for Vascular Surgery, Am. Assn. for Thoracic Surgery, Soc. Med. Cons. to Armed Forces (v.p. 1991-92, pres. 1992-93); mem. Alpha Omega Alpha. Presbyterian. Home: 666 Longview Rd South Orange NJ 07079-1109 Office: U Med & Dentistry NJ-NJ Med Sch 185 S Orange Ave # G590 Newark NJ 07103-2714

SWANK, ROY LAVER, physician, educator, inventor; b. Camas, Wash., Mar. 5, 1909; s. Wilmer and Hannah Jane (Laver) S.; m. Eulalia F. Shively, Sept. 14, 1936 (dec.); children: Robert L., Susan Jane (Mrs. Joel Keizer) Stephen (dec.); m. Betty Harris, May 23, 1987. Student, U. Wash., 1926-30; M.D., Northwestern U., 1935; Ph.D., 1935. House officer, resident Peter Bent Brigham Hosp., Boston, 1936-39; fellow pathology Harvard Med. Sch., 1938-39; mem. staff neurol. unit Boston City Hosp., 1945-48; asst. prof. neurology Montreal Neurol. Inst., McGill U., 1948-54; prof. medicine and neurology, head divsn. neurology Oreg. Med. Sch., 1954-75, prof. emeritus, 1975—; dir. Swank Multiple Sclerosis Clinic, Beaverton, Oreg., 1994—; prof. neurology, head divsn. neurology Oreg. Med. Sch., 1954-75; pres. Pioneer Filters, 1970-78. Served to maj. M.C. AUS, 1942-46. Recipient Oreg. Gov.'s award for research in multiple sclerosis, 1966. Mem. Am. Physiol. Soc., Am. Neurol. Assn., European Microcirculation Soc., Sigma Xi. Home: 789 SW Summit View Dr Portland OR 97225-6185 Office: Swank Multiple Sclerosis Clin 13655 SW Jenkins Rd Beaverton OR 97005

SWANN, KARL WINSTON, neurosurgeon; b. Iowa City, Feb. 4, 1955. BA, U. Mich., 1976, MD, 1979. Diplomate Am. Bd. Neurol. Surgery. Intern Mass. Gen. Hosp., Boston, 1979-80, resident, 1979-86; pvt. practice San Antonio, 1986—; staff Meth. Hosp., San Antonio, 1986—. Mem. Am. Assn. Neurol. Surgeons, Congress Neurol. Surgeons, Phi Beta Kappa, Alpha Omega Alpha. Office: 4410 Medical Dr Ste 610 San Antonio TX 78229-3755

SWANSON, AUGUST GEORGE, physician, retired association executive; b. Kearney, Nebr., Aug. 25, 1925; s. Oscar Valderman and Elnora Wilhelmina Emma (Block) S.; m. Ellyn Constance Weinel, June 28, 1947; children: Eric, Rebecca, Margaret, Emilie, Jennifer, August. BA, Westminster Coll., Fulton, Mo., 1951; MD, Harvard U., 1949; DSc (hon.), U. Nebr., 1979. Intern King County Hosp., Seattle, 1949-50; resident internal medicine U. Wash. Affiliated Hosp., 1953-55, neurology, 1955-57; resident neurology Boston City Hosp., 1958; dir. pediatric neurology, then dir. div. neurology U. Wash. Med. Sch., Seattle, 1958-67; assoc. dean acad. affairs U. Wash. Med. Sch., 1967-71; v.p. acad. affairs Assn. Am. Med. Colls., Washington, 1971-89, v.p. grad. med. edn., exec. dir. Nat. Resident Matching Program, 1989-91, ret., 1991; vis. fellow physiology Oxford (Eng.) U., 1963-64; cons. in field. Author articles brain function, physician edn., med. manpower. With USNR, 1943-46, 50-53. Markle scholar medicine, 1959-64; recipient Abraham Flexner awd. for Distinguished Service to Medical Education, Assn. of Am. Medical Coll., 1992. Mem. Inst. Medicine, Nat., Acad. Sci., Am. Neurol. Assn. Home: 3146 Portage Bay Pl E # H Seattle WA 98102-3878

SWANSON, KARIN, hospital administrator, consultant; b. New Britain, Conn., Dec. 8, 1942; d. Oake F. and Ingrid Lauren Swanson; m. B. William Dorsey, June 26, 1965 (div. 1974); children: Matthew W., Julie I., Alison K.; m. Sanford H. Low, Oct. 14, 1989. BA in Biology, Middlebury Coll., 1964; MPH, Yale U., 1981. Biology tchr. Kents Hill (Maine) Sch., 1964-66; laboratory instr. Bates Coll., Lewiston, Maine, 1974-78; asst. to gen. dir. Mass. Eye and Ear Infirmary, Boston, 1979-80; v.p. profl. services Portsmouth (N.H.) Hosp., 1981-83; v.p. Health Strategy Assn. Ltd., Chestnut Hill, Mass., 1983-85; v.p. med. affairs Cen. Maine Med. Ctr., Lewiston, 1986-89; health care mgmt. cons. Cambridge, Mass., 1989-91; CEO Hahnemann Hosp., Brighton, Mass., 1991-94; adminstr. Vencor Hosp., Boston, 1994-95; pres., CEO The Laser Inst. New Eng., Newton, Mass., 1996—. Mem. Phi Beta Kappa. Home: 198 Glen St Natick MA 01760-5606

SWANSON, ROBERT MARTIN, medical center administrator, ordained priest; b. Bell, Calif., Oct. 14, 1940; s. Harold M. and Elsie Lorraine (Allison) S.; AB, Long Beach (Calif.) State Coll., 1963; MA, U. Iowa, 1965; PhD, UCLA, 1970; m. Katharine Vivian Martin, Feb. 16, 1980. Dir., Office of Mental Health Rsch., U. Iowa, Iowa City, 1966-70; rsch. dir. Health Planning Coun., St. Paul, 1970-73; exec. dir. Kansas City (Mo.) Health Plan, 1973-75; asst. dir. St. Louis U. Hosps., 1975-80; asst. v.p. and chief planning officer St. Louis U. Med. Ctr., 1981-87, assoc. v.p., 1988—; pastor St. Basil the Great Orthodox Ch., 1987—; dir. Organizational Rsch. & Devel. Corp., Kansas City; dir., sec., chmn. awards com. Group Health Found. of Greater St. Louis; dir., sec., alliance for cmty. health; dir. Family Care Ctr. Carondelet; dir. Primary Care Coun. Greater St. Louis; clin. prof. St. Louis U. Grad. Sch. Pub. Health, 1980—; adj. prof. Webster Coll., St. Louis, 1975-82; spl. cons. to Kansas City (Mo.) Health Dept., 1974-75; tech. cons. Health Services Adminstrn., HEW, 1973-75; coord. St. Louis Cmty.-Univ. Conf., 1977-80; mem. health affairs task force Mo. Cath. Conf., 1977. Named Adm. in Nebr. Navy, 1971; State of Iowa grantee, 1969. Mem. Nat. Assn. Hosp. Devel. (cert.), Am. Mgmt. Assn., Soc. for Advancement Mgmt., N.Am. Soc. Corp. Planners, Internat. Platform Assn., Advt. Club Greater St. Louis, Zeta Beta Tau. Republican. Eastern Orthodox. Contbr. articles on health services to profl. jours. Office: 3556 Caroline St Saint Louis MO 63104-1008

SWANSON, RONALD BRADLEY, osteopath; b. Chgo., June 23, 1965; s. Ronald Federick and Sharon Marie (Hanzl) S.; m. Karin Teresa Alden, May 27, 1996. BS, U. South Fla., Tampa, 1987; DO, Nova Southeastern U., Davie, Fla., 1996. Lic. osteopath, Mich.; diplomate Am. Coll. Family Practitioners. Acct. Markham Nordin CPAs, Cape Coral, Fla., 1989, John Davis CPA, Ft. Myers Beach, Fla., 1990-92; resident Mt. Clemens (Mich.) Gen. Hosp., 1996—. Mem. Am. Osteo. Assn., Fla. Osteo. Assn., Fla. Inst. CPAs. Office: Mount Clemens Gen Hosp 1000 Harrington Blvd Mount Clemens MI 48043

SWARNER, SYLVIA MARTHA, nurse; b. Sacramento, Mar. 15, 1955; d. Arnold Joseph and Elisabeth (Hartmann) Guallini; m. David Lee Swarner, Nov. 1, 1980; children: Christopher Glenn, Jessica Reneé. Nursing diploma, Sacramento City Coll., 1978. RN, Calif. ICU nurse, relief charge nurse Sutter Cmty. Hosp., Sacramento, 1978—, mem. quality assurance com., 1987-93, mem. staff nurse coun., 1991-94, mem. collaborative care mgmt. com., 1991—, mem. critical care stds. com., 1985—, chairperson quality improvement com., 1992—, coord. complicated curriculum hosp. restructuring, 1993, coord. multidisciplinary timelines, 1993, chair ICU process improvement com., 1995—. Mem. Am. Assn. Critical Care Nurses. Home: 8818 Lambay Way Sacramento CA 95828-6141

SWARTWOUT, JOSEPH RODOLPH, obstetrics and gynecology educator, administrator; b. Pascagoula, Miss., June 17, 1925; s. Thomas Roswell and Marshall (Coleman) S.; m. Brandon C. Leftwich, Jan. 23, 1989. Student, Miss. Coll., 1943-44; MD, Tulane U., 1951. Intern Touro Infirmary, New Orleans, 1951-52; asst. in obstetrics and medicine Tulane U., 1952-53, instr., 1955-60; Nat. Found. fellow Harvard U., 1953-55; asst. in medicine Peter Bent Brigham Hosp., Boston, 1953-55; assoc. in obstetric rsch. Boston Lying-In-Hosp., 1953-55; asst. prof. U. Pitts., 1960-61; assoc. prof. Emory U., Atlanta, 1961-66; assoc. prof. ob-gyn. U. Chgo., 1967-80; chief ob-gyn. at Prime Health, also clin. assoc. prof. U. Kans. Sch. Medicine, 1978-80; prof. dept. ob-gyn. Mercer U. Sch. Medicine, Macon, Ga., 1980-95, prof. emeritus, 1995; dist. health dir. Dist. 5-2, Macon, Ga., 1996—; dist. dir. Ga. Divsn. Pub. Health, Macon, 1996—. Fellow Am. Coll. Obstetricians and Gynecologists, Am. Heart Assn. (coun. clin. cardiology), Am. Acad. Reproductive Medicine; mem. AAAS, AMA, APHA, Population Assn. Am., Med. Assn. Ga., Bibb County Med. Soc. Home: 1622 Peach Pkwy Fort Valley GA 31030

SWARTZ, MORTON NORMAN, medical educator; b. Boston, Nov. 11, 1923; s. Jacob H. and Janet (Heller) W.; m. Cesia Rosenberg, Sept. 18, 1956; children: Mark David, Caroline Joan. BA, Harvard Coll., 1945; MD, Harvard U., 1947; MD (hon.), U. Geneva, Switzerland, 1988. Diplomate Am. Bd. Internal Medicine (subsplty. exam. com. 1971-76, bd. govs. 1979-85). Med. intern and resident Mass. Gen. Hosp., Boston, 1947-50, chief resident in medicine, 1953-54; USPHS postdoctoral rsch. fellow Johns Hopkins U., McCollum-Pratt Inst. Enzymology, Balt., 1954-56; chief infectious disease unit Mass. Gen. Hosp., Boston, 1956-90, chief James Jackson Firm, dept. medicine, 1990—; assoc. prof. medicine Harvard Med. Sch., Boston, 1967-73, prof., 1973—; vis. assoc. prof. biochemistry, Stanford Med. Sch., Palo Alto, Calif., 1969-70. Author: (with others) Osteomyelitis, 1971; editor: Current Clinical Topics in Infectious Diseases, 1980—; assoc. editor New Eng. Jour. Medicine, 1981—; contbr. articles to profl. jours. 1st lt. U.S. Army, 1950-52. Sir MacFarlane Burnett lectr. Australasian Soc. Infectious Disease, 1981. Fellow ACP (master 1988, Disting. Tchr. award 1989); mem. Am. Soc. Biochemistry and Molecular Biology, Am. Soc. for Clin. Investigation, Assn. Am. Physicians, Infectious Diseases Soc. Am. (Bristol award 1984, Feldman award 1989), Inst. Medicine, Nat. Inst. Child Health and Devel. (bd. sci. counselors 1992—, chmn. 1995—). Jewish. Home: 54 Shaw Rd Chestnut Hill MA 02167-3122 Office: Mass Gen Hosp 32 Fruit St Boston MA 02114-2620

SWARTZ, WILLIAM MICHAEL, physician; b. Detroit, May 26, 1946; s. Harry Louis and Helen Louise (Kiley) S.; m. Cynthia Bennett, 1978. BA, Johns Hopkins U., 1968; BM in Sci., Dartmouth Med. Sch., 1970; MD, U. N.W. Colo., 1972. Diplomate Am. Bd. Plastic Surgery; CAQ Hand Surgery. Intern Mary Hitchcock-Dartmouth Affil. Hosp., 1972; surgery resident Mary Hutchcock-Dartmouth Affil. Hosp., 1973; intern Dartmouth-Hitchcock Affiliate Hosps., 1972; resident in gen. surgery Dartmouth-Hitchcock Hosp., 1973; resident in gen. surgery R.I. Hosp.-Brown U., 1974-75, resident in plastic surgery, 1976-78; asst. prof. surgery U. Pitts., 1980-86, clin. assoc. prof. surgery, 1992; assoc. prof. surgery Tulane U., New Orleans, 1986-89, prof. surgery, 1990; pvt. practice Pitts., 1990—. Author: Head and Neck Microsurgery, 1991. Lt. comdr. USNR, 1978-80. Mem. Am. Assn. Surgery of the Hand (treas. 1990-92), Am. Soc. Reconstructive Microsurgery (treas. 1992-94, pres. elect 1995), Am. Assn. Plastic Surgeons, Am. Soc. Plastic and Reconstructive Surgeons, Am. Soc. Surgery of the Hand. Home: 5030 Castleman St Pittsburgh PA 15232-2107 Office: 5750 Centre Ave Ste 180 Pittsburgh PA 15206-3761

SWASH, MICHAEL, neurologist, educator; b. Woodford, Essex, U.K., Jan. 29, 1939; s. Edwin Frank and Kathleen (Burton) S.; m. Caroline Mary Payne, Jan. 12, 1966; children: Jesse Edward, Thomas Henry, Edmond Joseph. MB BS, London U., 1962, MD, 1973. Neurology resident U. Hosp., Cleve., 1965-67, Case Western Res. U., Cleve., 1965-67; fellow Washington U., St. Louis, 1967-68; registrar, MRC rsch. fellow, sr. registrar London Hosp., 1968-72; cons. neurologist Royal London Hosp., 1972—; med. dir. Royal London Nat. Health Svc. Trust, 1990-94; sr. lectr. in neuropathology London Hosp. Med. Coll., 1976-95; prof. neurology St. Bartholomew's and Royal London Hosp. Sch. Medicine & Dentistry; adj. neurologist Cleve. Clinic Found., 1985—; healthcare planner Nat. Health Svc., U.K. Author: Clinical Neurology, 1991, Muscle Biopsy Pathology, 2d edit., 1992, Neuromuscular Disorders, 3d edit., 1996, Hutchison's Clinical Methods, 20th edit., 1995, others. Fellow Royal Coll. Physicians, Royal Coll. Pathologists; mem. Am. Neurolog. Assn. , Athenaeum Club, London Rowing Club. Office: Royal London Hosp, London E1 1BB, England

SWATEK, FRANK EDWARD, microbiology educator; b. Oklahoma City, June 4, 1929; s. Clarence Michael and Bessie (Doubek) S.; m. Mary Frances Over, Jan. 28, 1951; children: Frank Edward, Lorraine Beth Butcher, Martha Lynn Bradshaw, Susan Ann Denny, Cheryl Lee. B.S. in Zoology, San Diego State Coll., 1951; M.A. in Microbiology, UCLA, 1955, Ph.D., 1956. Mem. faculty Calif. State U. at Long Beach, 1956-92, prof. microbiology, 1962-82, chmn. dept., 1960-82; cons. to industry, 1953—; cons. dept. dermatology Long Beach VA Hosp., 1956—; lectr. postgrad. medicine U. So. Calif., 1958—; adj. prof. clin. med. U. Calif., Irvine, 1980—; mem. fuel sect. Coordinating Research Council, 1961—. Author: Textbook of Microbiology, 1967, Laboratory Manual and Workbook for General Microbiology, 1969; also articles. Fellow Royal Soc. Health, Am. Acad. Microbiology; mem. Am. Soc. Microbiology (chmn. bd. edn. and tng. 1980-85, Carski Found. Disting. Teaching award 1974), Internat. Platform Assn., Sigma Xi, Lambda Xi Alpha, Phi Kappa Phi. Club: Long Beach Aquatic (pres. 1963-65). Home: 812 Stevely Ave Long Beach CA 90815-5022

SWAYNGIM, DOWZELL MEDFORD, surgeon; b. Winston-Salem, N.C., Sept. 4, 1948; s. Dowzell M. and Lela Jane (Bullard) S.; m. Marilyn Rose Humenik, June 21, 1979; children: Robert, Elizabeth, Joseph Dale, Sarilyn, Merridth. BA in Sci. and Biology/Chemistry, Appalachian State U., 1970; MD, Bowman Gray Sch. Medicine, 1974. Resident in surgery Yale U., New Haven, Conn., 1974-76; resident, fellow Case Western Res. U./Luth. Med. Ctr., Cleve., 1976-80; peripheral vascular surgeon Sandusky, Ohio, 1980—; chmn. dept. surgery Firelands Cmty. Hosp., Sandusky, 1989—; asst. clin. prof. Ohio U., Athens, 1985—, Med. Coll. Ohio, Toledo, 1985—. Fellow ACS, Midwest Vascular Soc., Internat. Soc. for Endovascular Surgery, Orgn. Soc. for Clin. Vascular Surgery; mem. AMA. Republican. Home: 3414 Fox Rd Huron OH 44839 Office: Vascular Surgeons Sandusky 2525 Columbus Ave Sandusky OH 44870

SWAZEY, JUDITH POUND, institute president, sociomedical science educator; b. Bronxville, N.Y., Apr. 21, 1939; d. Robert Earl and Louise Titus (Hanson) Pound; m. Peter Woodman Swazey, Nov. 28, 1964; children: Elizabeth, Peter. AB, Wellesley Coll., 1961; PhD, Harvard U., 1966. Rsch. assoc. Harvard U., 1966-71, lectr., 1969-71, rsch. fellow, 1971-72; cons. com. brain scis. NRC, 1971-73; staff scientist neuroscis. rsch. program MIT, Cambridge, 1973-74; assoc. prof. dept. socio-med. scis. and community medicine Boston U., 1974-77, prof., 1977-80, adj. prof. Schs. Medicine and Pub. Health, 1980—; exec. dir. Medicine in the Pub. Interest, Inc., Boston and Washington, 1979-82, 89-93; pres. Coll. of the Atlantic, Bar Harbor, Maine, 1982-84, Acadia Inst., Bar Harbor, 1984—; mem. Army Sci. Bd., 1987-92. Author: Reflexes and Motor Integration, the Development of Sherrington's Integrative Action Concept, 1969, (with others) Human Aspects of Biomedical Innovation, 1971, (with R. C. Fox) The Courage to Fail, a Social View of Organ Transplants and Hemodialysis, 1975, rev. edit., 1978 (hon. mention Am. Med. Writers Assn., C. Wright Mills award Am. Sociol. Assn.), Chlorpromazine in Psychiatry, a Study of Therapeutic Innovation, 1974, (with K. Reeds) Today's Medicine, Tomorrow's Science, Essays on Paths of Discovery in the Biomedical Sciences, 1978; editor: (with C. Wong) Dilemmas of Dying, Policies and Procedures for Decisions Not to Treat, 1981, (with F. Worden and G. Adelman) The Neurosciences: Paths of Discovery, 1975, (with R. C. Fox) Spare Parts, Organ Replacement in American Society, 1992; assoc. editor IRB: A Jour. of Human Subjects Rsch., 1979—; mem. editl. bd. Sci. and Engring. Ethics, 1994—; contbr. articles to profl. jours. Mem. Maine Dept. Human Svcs. Bioethics Adv. Com. (chair 1991-94); mem. Commn. on Rsch. Integrity, 1994-95; bd. dirs. Maine Bioethics Network, 1994—. Wellesley Coll. scholar, 1961; Wellesley Coll. Alumnae fellow Harvard U., 1966, NIH predoctoral fellow, 1966, Radcliffe Coll. Coll. grad. fellow, 1966. Mem. AAAS (sci. freedom and responsibility com. 1986-89), Inst. Medicine NAS (mem. health scis. policy bd. 1986-89), Grad. Record Exam. (bd. dirs. 1987-91), Sherrington Soc., Phi Beta Kappa, Sigma Xi. Office: Acadia Inst PO Box 43 Bar Harbor ME 04609

SWEARINGEN, DAVID CLARKE, physician, musician; b. Shreveport, La., Apr. 23, 1942; s. David C. and Alverne (Walker) S.; m. Marion Joan Adams; children: David, Joy. BS, Centenary Coll., 1963; MD, La. State U., 1967. Intern Confederate Meml. Med. Ctr., Shreveport, 1967-68, resident in ophthalmology, 1968-71; staff ophthalmologist U.S. Naval Hosp., Memphis, 1971-73; pvt. practice in ophthalmology Shreveport, 1973-78; jr. officer of deck USS Halsey CG23, 1979; comdr. med. corps, head dept. ophthalmology, chmn. utilization rev. com. ophthalmology, family practice resident instr. opthalmology U.S. Naval Hosp., Jacksonville, Fla., 1981-84; med. dir. Bio Blood Components, Shreveport, 1985-88; dir. phys. health support svcs. Ctrl. La. State Hosp., Pineville, La., 1991—, exec. hosp. and med. exec. com., chmn. infection control and pharmacy, therapeutics com.; chmn. infection control com., pharmacy and therapeutic com.; pres. Shreveport Eye and Ear Soc., 1973-74; med. cons. Cenla Chem. Dependency Coun., Pineville, 1989—, Work Tng. Facility, Pineville, 1989—. Prin. bassoonist Cenla Symphonic Band, Pineville, 1988—; mem. Jacksonville Fla. Concert Choral, 1978-81; vestry mem. St. Michaels Ch., Pineville; active Am. Mus. Natural History Assocs. Recipient AMA Physician Recognition award for Continuing Med. Edn. Mem. Internat. Platform Assn., So. Med. Assn., Nat. Parks and Conservation Assn., N.Y. Acad. Scis., La. Wildlife Fedn., Wilderness Soc., Nature Conservancy, Smithsonian Assocs., Cousteau Soc., Soc. Hist. Preservation, Environ. Def. Fund, Planetary Soc., Nat. Audubon Soc., Am. Legion, Alpha Epsilon Delta, Gamma Beta Gamma, Nu Sigma Nu. Republican. Epsicopalian. Home: 10 Azalea Rd Pineville LA 71360-8004 Office: Ctrl La State Hosp PO Box 5031 242 W Shamrock Ave Pineville LA 71360-6439

SWEATT, JAMES LEONARD, III, surgeon; b. Ft. Worth, July 13, 1937; s. James L. Jr. and Jewell Juanita (Burnett) S.; m. Mary Lois Hudson, 1962; children: James IV, William, Alisa, Mary Elizabeth. BS in Chemistry, Middlebury Coll., 1958; MD, Washington U., 1962. Diplomate Am. Bd. Thoracic Surgery, Am. Bd. Surgery. Intern Cleve. Met. Gen. Hosp., 1962-63; resident U. Colo. Med. Ctr., 1965-69, U. Tex., Dallas, 1969-71; pvt. practice Ft. Worth, 1971, Dallas, 1972-85; physician James L. Sweatt III & Assoc., De Soto, Tex., 1985—; hosp. affiliations St. Paul Med. Ctr., Meth. Hosp. Dallas, Mesquite Cmty. Hosp., Dallas Family Hosp.; cons. Children's Med. Ctr., Dallas; instr. Parkland Meml. Hosp.; physician James L. Sweatt III & Assoc., Mesquite, Tex., 1986-92; spkr. in field. Trustee S.W. Med. Found. Mem. ACS, AMA, Dallas County Med. Soc. (bd. dirs. 1994, pres. 1995, del. Tex. Med. Assn.), Tex. Med. Assn. (bd. dirs. Texpac), Soc. Thoracic Surgeons, C.V. Roman Med. Soc. Home: 2745 Blackstone Dallas TX 75237 Office: Ste 102 2727 Bolton Boone Dr De Soto TX 75115-2019

SWEDENBORG, JESPER G.E., surgeon; b. Solna, Sweden, May 21, 1940; s. Jesper and Karin (Nilson) S.; m. Birgitta Hultgren, Aug. 2, 1987; children: Johanna, Jakob. MD, Karolinska Inst., Stockholm, Sweden, 1967, PhD, 1971. Postgrad. rsch. surgeon UCLA, 1968-69; resident Karolinska Hosp., Stockholm, 1969-70, chief divsn. vascular surgery, 1975—; resident Sabbatberg Hosp., Stockholm, N.Y., 1970-72; assoc. surgery U. Rochester, N.Y., 1973-74; chmn. ethical com. Karolinska Hosp., 1992-94, vice-chmn. dept. surgery, 1990—. Contbr. articles to profl. jours.; mem. editl. bd. European Jour. Vascular Surgery and Thrombosis Rsch. Mem. Swedish Soc. Vascular Surgery (chmn. 1996—). Office: Karolinska Hospital, Dept Surgery, 17176 Stockholm Sweden

SWEDLOW, BARRY LEONARD, podiatrist; b. N.Y.C., Apr. 10, 1944; s. William and Adele (Liebaum) S.; divorced; children: Andrew, Ryan. DPM, Ohio Coll. Podiatric Medicine, 1971. Diplomate Nat. Bd. Podiatry Examiners. Cons. podiatric medicine Va. Ctrl. Tng. Ctr., 1971—; podiatrist, founder Podiatric Clinic, Westminster-Canterbury, Va., 1986-89. Contbr. articles to profl. jours. Ad hoc nat. chmn. Stony Brook podiatry student emergency scholar fund NYU, 1976; mem. Va. regional bd., Anti-Defamation League of B'nai B'rith, 1987, exec. com., 1987, vice chmn. regional bd., 1989-91; past v.p. Agudath Sholom Congregation, Lynchburg, Va., mem. ho. com.; sec., bd. dirs. Abe Schewel Lodge #1211 B'nai B'rith; past chmn. bd. Va. Affiliate Am. Diabetes Assn.; past bd. dirs. Cen. Va. Diabetes Assn.; instc., asst. scoutmaster Boy Scouts Am., Troop 29; treas. Va. Hillel Found. Fellow Am. Coll. Foot Orthopedists, Am. Assn. Colls. Podiatric Medicine, Am. Coll. Foot Orthopedists, Am. Soc. Podiatric Medicine, Podiatry Polit. Action Com.; mem. APHA (podiatric health sect.), Am. Podiatric Med. Assn., Va. Podiatric Med. Assn. (past bd. dirs., editor newsletter, chmn. pub. rels., membership by-laws and institution and continuing edn. coms., v.p.), Chinese Med. Acad., Ohio Coll. Podiatric Medicine Alumni Assn. (life), NYU Alumni Assn. Office: Forest Hill Podiatry 3623 Old Forest Rd Lynchburg VA 24501-2906

SWEE, DAVID ETHAN, physician; b. N.Y.C., Sept. 3, 1947; s. Eugene and Joan (Shalit) S.; m. Karen Virginia Hermanson, Dec. 20, 1971; children: Kendra Olivia, Julia Elizabeth. BA, Grinnell Coll., 1969; MD, Dalhousie U., 1975. Diplomate Am. Bd. Family Practice. Dir. premed. programs dept. family medicine UMDNJ-Robert Wood Johnson Med. Sch., Piscataway, 1977-85, dir. fellowship program, 1985-87; med. dir. family practice ctr., vice chair dept. UMDNJ-Robert Wood Johnson Med. Sch., New Brunswick, 1987-91, prof., chmn. dept. family medicine, 1991—; item writer Am. Bd. Family Practice, Lexington, Ky., 1982—; chief dept. family medicine Robert Wood Johnson Univ. Hosp., Piscataway, 1991—; site surveyor Accreditation Coun. Continuing Med. Edn., Chgo., 1993—. Editor, main author: Teaching Family Medicine in Medical School: A Companion to Predoctoral Education in Family Medicine, 1991. Grantee Prudential Ins. Co., 1987-89, U.S. Dept. HHS, 1984-87, 91-94, 93-96. Fellow Am. Acad. Family Physicians; mem. Soc. Tchrs. Family Medicine (bd. dirs. 1985-89, group on predocotoral edn. 1984—, group on faculty devel. 1985—). Home: 259 Lawrence Ave Highland Park NJ 08904 Office: UMDNJ-RW Johnson Med Sch One Robert Wood Johnson Pl New Brunswick NJ 08903

SWEENEY, DONALD, psychiatrist, consultant; b. Medford, Mass., Aug. 14, 1937; m. Pamela J. Minella, Aug. 5, 1962; children—John, Kenneth, Ellen, Michael. A.B. in Philosophy, Holy Cross Coll., 1958; M.A. in Psychology, Fordham U., 1960, Ph.D. in Psychology, 1962; M.D., U. Rochester, 1970. Diplomate Am. Bd. Psychiatry and Neurology. Intern, Rochester Gen. Hosp. (N.Y.), Strong Meml. Hosp., 1970-71; resident in psychiatry Yale U., 1971-74; sole practice psychotherapy, 1974-78; cons. psychiatrist Lithium Clinic, Yale-New Haven Hosp., 1974-78; cons. psychiatrist Conn. Jr. Republic, Litchfield, 1974-78; assoc. psychiatrist Yale-New Haven Hosp., 1974-77, attending psychiatrist, 1976-77; asst. prof. psychiatry and assoc. chief research ward dept. psychiatry Yale U., 1974-78, lectr., 1978—; sr. cons. psychiatrist Whiting Forensic Inst., Middletown, Conn., 1976-78; cons. psychiatrist Muhlenberg Hosp., Plainfield, N.J., 1978—; clin. dir. Nueropsychiat. Evaluation Program, Fair Oaks Hosp., Summit, N.J., 1978-92; cons., lectr. in field; participant in profl. confs. Editor-in-chief Internat. Jour. of Psychiatry in Medicine, 1979-86. Assoc. editor The Psychiatric Hospital; contbr. articles to profl. jours. Fellow Am. Psychiat. Assn; mem. Am. Psychol. Assn., Am. Acad. Clin. Psychiatrists, N.J. Psychiat. Assn., N.J. Acad. Medicine, Phi Beta Kappa, Sigma Xi. Home: 8111 Bay Colony Dr # 1701 Naples FL 33963

SWEENEY, ELIZABETH ANN, healthcare consultant; b. Birmingham, Ala., Nov. 9, 1946; d. Huretta and Elizabeth (Whisenant) Chappell; children from previous marriage: Wesley, Hugh L. Mitchell. BSN, U. Ala., 1973, MSN, 1975; PhD, Friends Internat. Christian U., 1996. Staff nurse VA Med. Ctr., Birmingham, 1972-74; asst. prof. nursing Sch. Nursing U. Ala., Birmingham, 1975-79; coord. nursing svcs. Cen. City Mental Health Ctr., L.A., 1979-80; nurse educator VA Med. Ctr., L.A., 1980-88; asst. clin. prof. nursing Sch. Nursing U. Calif., L.A., 1984—; dir. med. ctr. edn. and tng. Kaiser Permanente Med. Ctr., Woodland Hills, Calif., 1989-93; asst. dir. edn. Kaiser Permanente Med. Ctr., Bellflower, Calif., 1988; guest faculty mem. Stanford U., Palo Alto, Calif., 1984; mem. conf. faculty United Nurses Assn. Calif., 1982, 83, 87, 95, Calif. Park and Recreation Soc. Conf., Sacramento, 1985, 86; EEO investigator VA, Washington, 1985—; faculty Hosp. Educators Confs., 1991. Contbr. articles to profl. jours; co-author rsch. grants. Recipient Commendation for Superior Performance Fed. Exec. Bd., Los Angeles, 1984. Mem. ANA (coun. on edn. 1989), NAFE, Ala. Nurses Assn. (exec. bd. dirs. 1976-79), Calif. Nurses Assn., Black Women's Network, Coun. Black Nurses, Culver City C. of C. Office: 10736 Jefferson Blvd #422 Culver City CA 90230

SWEENEY, LUCY GRAHAM, psychologist; b. Davenport, Iowa, Nov. 14, 1946; d. B. Graham and Dorothy (Lawson) S.; m. Richard N. Tiedemann, Dec. 2, 1978 (div. 1989); 1 child, Susan Lee. AA, William Woods Coll., 1966; BA with honors, U. Denver, 1968; MA in Devel. Psychology, Columbia U., 1977; PsyD, Rutgers U., 1990. Cert. family therapist. Profl. actress, 1968-73; dir. therapeutic play and recreation program St. Luke's Med. Ctr., N.Y.C., 1973-78; child life coord. St. Francis Hosp., Hartford, Conn., 1978-80; clinician Resolve Community Counseling Ctr., Scotch Plains, N.J., 1981-84; staff psychologist women's inpatient unit Lyons (N.J.) VA Med. Ctr., 1990; psychologist women's treatment program Fair Oaks Hosp., Summit, N.J., 1990-92; cons. Kessler Inst. for Rehab., East Orange, N.J., 1992-94, Resolve Community Counseling Ctr., Scotch Plains, N.J., 1992—; pvt. practice Westfield, N.J., 1993—. Contbr. articles to profl. jours. Recipient John Weyandt award for Outstanding Student in Theatre U. Denver, 1968. Mem. APA, N.J. Psychol. Assn., Phi Theta Kappa. Home: 21 Harwich Ct Scotch Plains NJ 07076-3165

SWEENEY, MARY LOUISE, biology educator; b. Canadian, Tex., Sept. 6, 1936; d. Clint L. and Ella Mae (Hext) Scott; m. W.B. Sweeney (div. Apr. 1966); 1 chld, Robin L. BA, Ariz. State U., 1967; MA, No. Ariz. U., 1970. Cert. secondary tchr., gifted tchr. Tchr. Casa Grande (Ariz.) Union High Sch., 1967—. Mem., vol. ad hoc com. Casa Grande Union High Sch., 1988. Recipient Caring, Sharing, Preparing award Outstanding Achievement, 1990, Outstanding Biology Tchr. award State of Ariz., 1996; named Tchr. of Yr., Casa Grande Union H.S., 1993-94. Mem. NEA (life), Nat. Assn. Biology Tchrs. (Ariz. state rep. 1989—), Ariz. Edn. Assn. (rep. 1967—, Outstanding Recruiter 1987), Ariz. Sci. Tchrs. Assn. (region VIII rep. 1986-89), Casa Grande Edn. Assn. (rep. 1967—), Environ. Def. Fund, Nature Conservancy, Wilderness Soc., World Wildlife Fund. Democrat. Office: Casa Grande Union High Sch 420 E Florence Blvd Casa Grande AZ 85222-4140

SWEENEY, MICHEL, chiropractor; s. Richard and Gisele S.; children: Alex, Gabe. BS in Biology, Va. Commonwealth U., 1979; BS in Anatomy, Nat. Chirpractic Coll., 1981, D of Chiropractic, 1983. Chiropractor Better Health Clinic, Vienna, Va., 1983—; adj. prof. Tex. Chiropractic Coll., 1984, 85, 86, 87, Palmer Chiropractic Coll., Iowa, 1987, 88, 92. Mem. Am. Chiropractic Assn., Va. Chiropractic Assn., No. Va. Chiropractic Soc. (pres. 1984), Rotary. Home: 6444 Jefferson Pl McLean VA 22101 Office: Better Health Clinic 268 Cedar Ln Vienna VA 22180

SWEENEY, ROSEMARIE, medical association administrator; b. Fall River, Mass., Sept. 2, 1950; d. John Francis and Phyllis (Field) S.; m. Edmund Burke Rice, Feb. 24, 1978; 1 child, Jonathan Field Rice. Student, Hillsdale Coll., 1968-69; BA, Am. U., 1972, MPA, 1978. Profl. staff mem. Office of Rep. Margaret Heckler, Washington, 1972-74; staff assoc. fed. agy. affairs Am. Osteo. Assn., Washington, 1974-78, govt. affairs rep., 1978-79; dir. Washington office Am. Acad. Family Physicians, Washington, 1979-82; v.p. socioeconomic affairs and policy analysis, 1992—; mem. family practice adv. com. George Washington U., Washington, 1990—. Vol. Montgomery County Sexual Assault Svc., Rockville, Md., 1984-93; mem. Glen Echo Fire Dept., Bethesda, Md., 1986-92, Victim Svcs. Adv. Bd., Md., 1987-93; chmn. victim svc. adv. bd. Montgomery County, Md., 1991-93; bd. dirs. Westmoreland Children's Ctr., Bethesda. Recipient Outstanding Svc. award Montgomery County Crisis Ctr., Md., 1986, Outstanding Performance award Montgomery County Sexual Assault Svc., Md., 1987, Recognition award Soc. Tchrs. Family Medicine, Kansas City, Mo., 1990, Govs.' Sixth Annual Victim Assistance award, Balt., 1991. Mem. Women in Govt. Rels. Office: Am Acad Family Physicians 2021 Massachusetts Ave NW Washington DC 20036-1011

SWEENY, RORY PATRICIA, nursing administrator, academic administrator, nursing educator; b. N.Y., Feb. 6, 1946. BSN cum laude, U. Bridgeport; MA, Columbia U. Teachers Coll., 1984, EdM, 1985, EdD, 1995. Cert. Health Edn. Specialist. Instr. Norwalk (Conn.) Community Coll.; instr. staff devel. Park City Hosp., Bridgeport, Conn.; dir. nursing Barnett Multi Health Care, Bridgeport, Conn.; asst. v.p. health svcs. M.D. Health Plan, New Haven, Conn.; asst. dir. nursing-edn. Bridgeport Hosp.; dir. patient care svcs., edn. and profl. devel. U. Medicine and Dentistry of N.J.-Univ. Hosp., Newark. Instr. CPR. Mem. ANA, Sigma Theta Tau, Sigma Delta Phi, Alpha Sigma Lambda. Home: 307 Prospect Ave 7G Hackensack NJ 07601

SWEET, ARTHUR, orthopedist; b. Chgo., Aug. 30, 1920; s. Mandel and Yetta (Spector) S.; m. Natalie Levy, Feb. 21, 1964; 1 child, Margaret Helaine. BS, U. Ill., 1941; MD, 1944. Diplomate Am. Bd. Orthopaedic Surgery. Instr. Northwestern U., 1947-52; mem. staff Decatur (Ill.) Meml. Hosp., 1954—, St. Mary's Hosp., Decatur, 1954—; cons. Wabash Hosp. Assn., Decatur, 1954—; instr. U. Ill., 1972—; pres. med. staff St. Mary's Hosp., Decatur, Ill. Capt. M.C., U.S. Army, 1946-48, 51-53, Korea. Mem. Acad. Orthopaedic Surgery, Decatur Club. Jewish. Home: 245 N Park Pl Decatur IL 62522-1951

SWEET, JAMES BROOKS, oral and maxillofacial surgeon; b. Darlington, Pa., Mar. 28, 1934; s. Lufay Anderson and Margaret Jean (Brooks) S.; m. N. Gayle Laird, Oct. 11, 1958; children: James Brooks II, Laird Anderson, Bradley Stephen. BA, Lafayette Coll., 1956; DDS, U. Pitts., 1964, DMD, 1974; MS in Dentistry, NYU, 1975. Aviation flight officer USNR, 1957; advanced through grades to dir. USPHS; rotating intern USPHS Hosp., Staten Island, N.Y., 1964-65, resident oral and maxillofacial surgery, 1970-73; chief dept. dentistry Fed. Correctional Inst. Hosp., Ashland, Ky., 1965-67, Terminal Island, Calif., 1967-70; chief oral and maxillofacial surgery Clin. Ctr. NIH, Bethesda, Md., 1973-80; chief dept. dentistry and oral and maxillofacial surgery USPHS Hosp., Nassau Bay, Tex., 1980-81; ret. USPHS, 1981; assoc. prof. dept. oral and maxillofacial surgery Health Sci. Ctr. U. Tex., Houston, 1981-84; prof., 1984—; asst. clin. prof. med. br. U. Tex., Galveston, 1980-; assoc. attending physicianBen Taub Gen. Hosp., Houston, 1984-; cons. oral and maxillofacial surgery self study guides, Stoma Press, Seattle, 1983-; cons. VA Hosp., Houston, 1986-. Contbr. articles to profl. jours.; editorial reviewer: Annals of Internal Medicine, 1977-. Coach basketball Olney (Md.) Boys Club, 1975-80; mem. aim rev. Tex. area USCG, 1981-82. Lt. USNR, 1957-64. Fellow Am. Assn. Oral and Maxillofacial Surgeons; mem. Tex. Soc. Oral and Maxillofacial Surgeons, Houston Soc. Oral and Maxillofacial Surgeons, Am. Assn. Dental Schs., USPHS Profl. Assn., NIH Sailing Club, Omicron Kappa Upslion (pres. Mu Mu chpt. 1993-94). Presbyterian. Office: U Tex Health Sci Ctr 6516 John Freeman St Houston TX 77030-3402

SWEET, JERRY JAMES, clinical psychologist; b. East Stroudsburg, Pa., Dec. 1, 1951; s. Waldo Thomas and Betty Jane (Flory) S.; m. Nancy Ann Sullivan, July 9, 1971; children: Christopher, Jamie. BS with distinction, Pa. State U., 1973; MS, Western Wash. U., 1975; PhD, U. S.D., 1979. Lic. clin. psychologist, Ill.; diplomate Am. Bd. Profl. Psychology in Clin. Neuropsychology. Sr. psychologist pain ctr., neuropsychologist dept. psychiatry Ill. Masonic Med. Ctr., Chgo., 1979-86; dir. psychol. evaluation and testing svc. Evanston (Ill.) Hosp., 1986-89, co-dir. Ctr. Psychol. Evaluation and Learning, 1989-91, dir. neuropsychology svc., 1991—; clin. assoc. prof. psychiatry med. sch. Northwestern U., adj. assoc. prof., 1982—, assoc. dir. clin. tng., 1986—; neuropsychology cons. Cook County Hosp., Chgo., 1983-87, 93—; lectr. psychology Loyola U., Chgo., 1983, 85, 87, 91; neuropsychol. seminar instr. Ill. State Psychiat. Inst., Chgo., 1986. Co-editor Handbook of Clin. Psychology in Med. Settings, 1991; founding assoc. editor Jour. Clin. Psychology in Med. Settings, 1993—; contbr. articles to profl. jours. and chpts. to profl. texts. Fellow Nat. Acad. Neuropsychology; mem. APA, Internat. Neuropsychol. Soc., Assn. Postdoctoral Tng. Programs in Clin. Neuropsychology. Office: Evanston Hosp Dept Psychiatry 2650 Ridge Ave Evanston IL 60201-1718

SWEET, WILLIAM HERBERT, neurosurgeon; b. Kerriston, Wash., Feb. 13, 1910; m. Paul Williams and Daisy Eleanor (Pool) S.; m. Elizabeth Jane Dutton, July 29, 1978; children: David Rowland, Gwendolyn Sweet Fletcher, Paula Sweet Carroll. SB, U. Wash., 1930; BSc, Oxford U., 1934, DSc, 1957; MD, Harvard U., 1936; DHC (hon.), Université Scientifique et Médicale de Grenoble, France, 1979. Diplomate Am. Bd. Psychiatry and Neurology, Am. Bd. Neurol. Surgery. Rhodes research fellow Nat. Hosp. for Nervous Disease, London, 1939; asst. in neurosurgery Mass. Gen. Hosp., Boston, 1945-47; asst. neurosurgeon Mass. Gen. Hosp., 1947-48, assoc. vis. neurosurgeon, 1948-57, vis. neurosurgeon, 1957-61, chief neurol. service, 1961-77, sr. neurosurgeon, 1977—; asst. in surgery Harvard U. Med. Sch., Boston, 1945-46; instr. surgery Harvard U. Med. Sch., 1946-47, assoc. in surgery, 1947-48, asst. prof. surgery, 1948-54, assoc. clin. prof., 1954-58, assoc. prof., 1958-65, prof., 1965-76, prof. emeritus, 1976—, cons., lectr. in field; trustee Neuro-Research Found. Inc., 1951—, pres., 1971—; trustee Neuroscis. Research Found. Inc., 1961—, pres., 1961-76. Author: (with J.C. White) Pain: Its Mechanisms and Neurosurgical Control, 1955, Pain and the Neurosurgeon: A Forty Year Experience, 1969; editor books in field; contbr. articles to profl. jours., chpts. to books, monographs in medicine. Sci. trustee Assoc. Univs. Inc. (AUI), rep. Harvard U., 1958-82, hon. trustee, 1982—. Served with AUS, 1941-45. Rhodes scholar, 1932-34; Arthur Tracy Cabot fellow Harvard U. Med. Sch., 1935-36; Commonwealth Fund fellow, 1940-41, Royal Coll. Surgeons of Edinburgh hon. fellow, 1986. Mem. Am. Acad. Arts and Scis., Am. Pain Soc., AAAS, Am. Acad. Surgery, Am. Acad. Neurology, ACS, Am. Assn. Neurol. Surgeons, Am. Neurol. Assn., Am. Physiol. Assn., Am. Surg. Assn., Assn. de chirgiens Suisses (corr.), Assn. for Research in Nervous and Mental Diseases, Congress Neurol. Surgeons (hon.), Electroencephalographic Soc., Halsted Soc., Internat. Assn. for Study Pain, Internat. Brain Research Orgn., Internat. Soc. Psychiat. Surgery, Internat. Soc. Surgery, Italian Neurosurg. Soc. (corr.), New Eng. Neurosurg. Soc., Research Soc. Neurol. Surgeons, Royal Soc. Medicine, Scandinavian Neurosurg. Soc. (corr.), Societe de Neuro-Chirurgie de Langue Francaise (hon.), Soc. Brit. Neurol. Surgeons, Soc. for Neurosci., Spanish-Portuguese Neurosurg. Soc. (hon.), Soc. Neurol. Surgeons, Egyptian Soc. Neurol. Surgeons (hon.). Office: 5 Longfellow Pl Ste 211 Boston MA 02114

SWEETMAN, BEVERLY YARROLL, physical therapist; b. Phila., Apr. 8, 1939; d. Albert Henry and Theresa (Payne) Yarroll; m. Denman John Sweetman, Apr. 1, 1961; children: Denman Eric, John Albert. BA in Biology, Hood Coll., 1961; cert. phys. therapist, Hahnemann U., 1983. Rsch. technician Mass. Gen. Hosp., Boston, 1961-62, Princeton (N.J.) U., 1965-66; part owner, phys. therapist Pain & Stress Control Ctr., Allentown. Pa., 1983-85; pvt. practice Body Ease Phys. Therapy Ctr., Grants Pass, Oreg., 1985; pvt. practice, pres. Body Ease Phys. Therapy Ctr., Staunton and Charlottesville, Va., 1986—; developer and co-presenter Total Body Concept Seminars; lectr. in field; pres. VMG Med., Staunton, 1988—; cons., co-presenter seminars Lossing Orthopedic, Mpls., 1985—. Fellow Am. Back Soc.; mem. Am. Phys. Therapy Assn. Office: Body Ease Phys Therapy Ctr 409 Walnut Hills Rd Staunton VA 24401-9467

SWENSEN, CLIFFORD HENRIK, JR., psychologist, educator; b. Welch, W.Va., Nov. 25, 1926; s. Clifford Henrik and Cora Edith (Clowis) S.; m. Doris Ann Gaines, June 6, 1948; children—Betsy, Susan, Lisa, Timothy, Barbara. B.S., U. Pitts., 1949, M.S., 1950, Ph.D., 1952. Diplomate Am. Bd. Profl. Psychology. Instr. U. Pitts., 1951-52; clin. psychologist VA, 1952-54; from asst. prof. to assoc. prof. U. Tenn., Knoxville, 1954-62; assoc. prof. psychology Purdue U., West Lafayette, Ind., 1962-65, prof., 1965—; dir. clin. tng. Purdue U., 1975-85; vice chair U. Senate, 1994-95; vis. prof. U. Fla., 1968-69, U. Bergen, Norway, 1976-77, 83-84; cons. VA, 1981 White House Conf. on Aging, others; Am. Psychol. Assn.-NSF Disting. Sci. lectr., 1968-69; Fulbright-Hays lectr., Norway, 1976-77. Author: An Approach to Case Conceptualization, 1968; Introduction to Interpersonal Relations, 1973; contbr. chpts. to books, articles to profl. jours. Served with USN, 1944-46. Recipient Gordon A. Barrows Meml. award for disting. contributions to psychology, 1990. Fellow APA (pres divsn. cons. psychology 1976-77), Am. Psychol. Soc., Soc. Personality Assessment, Am. Assn. Applied and Preventive Psychology, Acad. of Clin. Psychology; mem. Midwestern Psychol. Assn., Southeastern Psychol. Assn., Ind. Psychol. Assn., Gerontol. Soc., Sigma Xi, Psi Chi. Republican. Mem. Ch. of Christ. Home: 611 Hillcrest Rd West Lafayette IN 47906-2349 Office: Purdue U Dept Psychol Scis West Lafayette IN 47907

SWENSON, CHRISTINE ERICA, microbiologist; b. N.Y., Apr. 27, 1953; d. Oscar Adolf and Marjorie Claire (Wareing) S.; m. James Yasinski, Sept. 6, 1980; children: Jeffrey, Emma. BA, Middlebury Coll., 1975; PhD, Cornell U., 1980. Postdoctoral fellow Rockefeller U., N.Y., 1980-82, U. Calif., San Francisco, 1982-84; scientist The Liposome Co., Inc., Princeton, N.J., 1984-88, dir., 1988—. Office: The Lipsome Co Inc One Research Way Princeton NJ 08540

SWENSON, JAMES REED, physician, educator; b. Utah, Nov. 18, 1933; s. Reed K. and Ruth (Freebairn) S.; m. Sharon Coray, Aug. 21, 1953; children—Richard, Karen, Leslie, David, Julie. Student, Weber Coll., 1952-54; M.D., U. Utah, 1959. Intern, then resident in phys. medicine and rehab.; mem. faculty div. phys. medicine and rehab. U. Utah Sch. Medicine, Salt Lake City; chmn. div. U. Utah Sch. Medicine, 1965—, asso. prof., 1970-85, prof., 1985—. Chmn. bd. trustees U. Utah Sch. Alcoholism and Other Drug Dependencies; founder Miss Wheelchair Utah Pageant. Served to capt. M.C. U.S. Army, 1960-62. Mem. AMA, Utah State Med. Assn., Am. Acad. Phys. Medicine and Rehab., Assn. Acad. Physiatrists, Am. Spinal Injury Assn., Utah Soc. Phys. Medicine & Rehab., Am. Med. Soc. Alcoholism. Office: U Utah Med Ctr 50 N Medical Dr Salt Lake City UT 84132-0001

SWENSON, JON HALLIE, orthopedic surgeon; b. Davenport, Iowa, Dec. 10, 1957; s. Robert Earl and Bernice Charlotte Swenson; m. Christina Swenson; children: Nicholas, Eric, Hannah. BSME, Memphis State U., 1979; MD, U. Tex., 1985. Diplomate Am. Bd. Orthopedic Surgery. Intern Meth. Hosp., Memphis, 1986; resident Campbell Clinic, Memphis, 1990; with Riverside Regional Med. Ctr., Newport News, Va., Mary Immaculate Hosp., Newport News, Va. Recipient Physician's Recognition award AMA. Mem. Va. Orthopedic Soc., Med. Soc. Va., Newport News Med. Soc. Home: 201 Sylvia Yorktown VA 23693 Office: Hampton Rds Orthopedic Assocs Ltd 704 Thimble Shoals Blvd Newport News VA 23606

SWENSON, MICHAEL DAVID, internist; b. Willmar, Minn., July 19, 1960; s. Ronald L. and Mary Lou C. (Johnson) S.; m. Leslie J. Swenson, June 25, 1983; children: Rachel, Sara, David. BA, St. Olaf Coll., Northfield, Minn., 1982; PhD in Philosophy, U. Minn., Mpls., 1987, MD, 1987. Diplomate Am. Bd. Internal Medicine. Intern, resident U. Colo Health Science Ctr., Denver, 1987-91; staff physician Norton Sound Health Corp., Nome, Alaska, 1991—, dir. hosp. lab., 1991—; clin. asst. prof. U. Alaska, Fairbanks, 1994—. Contbr. articles to profl. jours. Coun. mem., v.p. Our Saviors Ch. Coun., Nome, 1993—; vol. Iditarod Trail Commn., Nome, 1992—. Fellow ACP; mem. Soc. Gen. Internal Medicine. Lutheran. Home: PO Box 1352 Nome AK 99762 Office: Norton Sound Health Corp PO Box 966 Nome AK 99762

SWENSON, ORVAR, surgeon; b. Halsingborg, Sweden, Feb. 7, 1909; s. Carl Albert and Amanda (Johnson) S.; m. Melva Criley, Sept. 1, 1941; children: Melva, Elsa, Wenda. AB, William Jewell Coll., 1933, DSc (hon.), 1993; M.D., Harvard U., 1937; Dr hc, U. Aix, Marseilles, France, 1975. Diplomate Am. Bd. Surgery. Intern Peter Bent Brigham and Children's hosps., Boston, 1939-41; chief resident Peter Bent Brigham Hosp., 1944-45; Arthur Tracy Cabot fellow Harvard Med. Sch., 1941-44; surgeon Peter Bent Brigham Hosp., 1945-50, Children's Hosp., Boston, 1947-50; surgeon-in-chief Boston Floating Hosp. Infants and Children, 1950-60; asso. surgery Harvard Med. Sch., 1947-50; prof. pediatric surgery Tufts U. Med. Sch., 1957-60; surgeon-in-chief Children's Meml. Hosp., Chgo., 1960-73; prof. surgery Northwestern U. Med. Sch., 1960-73, U. Miami, Fla., 1973-78; chmn. sect. surgery Am. Acad. Pediatrics, 1954-57; lectr. Alex Simpson Smith Lecture Inst. of Child Health, U. London, 1954, Blackfan Lecture Harvard Med. Sch., Boston Children's Hosp., 1958; spl. guest lectr. 16th Gen. Assembly, Japan Med. Congress, 1963; Felton Bequest vis. prof. surgery Univs. Sidney and Melbourne, 1959; vis. prof. U. Bombay, 1980. Author: Pediatric Surgery, 1958; mem. editorial bd. Pediatrics, 1962-68. Recipient Mead Johnson award, 1952, Ladd award Surg. sect. Am. Acad. Pediatrics, 1969, Achievement award Modern Medicine mag., 1971, Frank Billings award AMA, 1949; Swenson Vis. Professorship established in his honor Tufts U. Sch. Medicine, 1987, Swenson Chair in Pediatric Surgery established in 1990. Hon. fellow Royal Coll. Surgeons (Dublin, Ireland), Royal Coll. Physicians and Surgeons Can., Brit. Assn. Pediatric Surgeons (hon., Denis Brown medal 1979); mem. A.C.S., Am. Surg. Assn., Soc. Univ. Surgeons, Am. Pediatric Surg. Assn. (pres. 1973). Home: PO Box 41 Rockport ME 04856-0041 also: 172 Cabo de Lagos Fort Pierce FL 34951

SWENSON, WAYNE MORRIS, vascular surgeon; b. Dickinson, N.D., Oct. 13, 1930; s. Roy Leonard and Mildred Lucille (Morris) S.; m. Lois Corrine Havkebo, June 9, 1956; children: Maren, Erik, Britt, Taya, Kari. MS in Chemistry, N.D. State U., 1956; M Medicine, U. N.D., 1959; MD, Harvard U., 1961. Diplomate Am. Bd. Gen. Surgery; lic. physician, N.D. Intern U. Ill. Med. Sch.-Presbyn., St. Lukes Hosp., Chgo., 1961-62, resident gen. surgery, 1962-66; gen. surgeon Rogers-Gumper Clinic, Dickinson, N.D., 1966-69; active staff Medcenter One, Bismarck, N.D., 1970—; prof. surgery U. N.D. Sch. Medicine, 1986, asst. to chmn. dept. surgery, 1981—; mem. courtesy staff St. Alexius Med. Ctr., Bismarck, 1970—, Mandan (N.D.) Hosp., 1970—; coord. gen. surgery tng., family practice residency S.W. AHEC; mem. N.D. State Bd. Med. Examiners, 1958-95, chmn., 1987-88; mem. N.D. Med. Competency Bd.; bd. dirs. N.D. Blue Shield; mem. intensive care unit com. Medcenter One; mem. profl. edn. com. Am. Cancer Soc.; lectr., presenter various symposiums, confs. and meetings; mem. faculty acad. coun. U. N.D. Sch. Medicine, 1988-92, mem. libr. com., 1989-95, rsch. com., 1988—, mem. com. on acad. and profl. qualifications dept. surgery, 1981-90, mem. surgery residency selection com., 1982-92, mem. combined surgery/internal medicine faculty com., 1984—; mem. state adv. com. AIDS Edn. and Tng. Grant, 1989; mem. pub. rels. and advt. com. Blue Cross and Blue Shield N.D. Contbr. articles to profl. jours. Fellow ACS (pres. N.D. chpt. 1979-80, gov. 1988-94, mem. area screening com. of prospective candidates); mem. AMA, Soc. Clin. Vascular Surgery (exec. com. 1989, constitution and bylaws com. 1989, v.p. 1991-92, pres. elect 1992-93, pres. 1993-94), Rush Surg. Soc. (adv. coun. 1992), Internat. Cardiovascular Soc., Midwestern Vascular Surg. Soc., Assn. Acad. Surgery, Assn. Surg. Edn., N.D. 6th Dist. Med. Soc. (mem. corp. bd., mem.Commn. on Med. Edn., Western Surg. Soc. Home: 818 Ave C West Bismarck ND 58501 Office: U ND Sch Medicine 515 1/2 E Broadway Bismarck ND 58501

SWERSKY, ROBERT B., surgeon; b. Bklyn., Feb. 27, 1947; s. Harold and Ruth (Schatz) S.; m. Gail Brown (div.); children: Deborah, Lori; m. Jaon Swersky. BS, Cornell U., 1968; MD, Downstate Med. Ctr., 1972. Cardiothoracic and vascular surgeon St. Francis Hosp., Roslan, N.Y., 1982—, Cmty. Hosp. Glen Cove, N.Y., 1982—, L.I. Jewish Hosp., New Hyde Park, N.Y., 1982—, Little Neck (N.Y.) Cmty. Hosp., 1982—; pvt. practice Manhasset, N.Y., 1982—. Contbr. articles to profl. jours. Fellow Internat. Coll. Surgeons, Am. Coll. Surgeons, Am. Coll. Chest Physicians; mem. AMA, Ea. Vascular Soc., N.Y. Soc. Cardiovascular Surgery, Soc. Thoracic Surgeons. Office: 1201 Northern Blvd New York NY 10030

SWETLIK, WILLIAM PHILIP, orthodontist; b. Manitowoc, Wis., Jan. 31, 1950; s. Leonard Alvin and Lillian Julia (Knipp) S.; m. Cheryl Jean Klein, June 30, 1973 (div.); children: Alison Elizabeth, Lindsey Ann, Adam William Swetlik; m. Joyce M. Cmis, Mar. 10, 1995. Student, Luther Coll., Decorah, Iowa, 1968-70; DDS, Marquette U., 1974; MS in Dentistry, St. Louis U., 1977. Diplomate Am. Bd. Orthodontics. Resident in gen. dentistry USPHS, Norfolk, Va., 1974-75; practice dentistry specializing in orthodontics Green Bay, Wis., 1977—; instr. oral pathology NE Wis. Tech. Coll., Green Bay, 1979-86. Author: (with others) Orthodontic Headgear, 1977. Mem. Prevention Walking Club, Family Crisis Ctr. of Green Bay. Served as lt. USPHS, 1974-75. Fellow Coll. Diplomates Am. Bd. Orthodontics; mem. ADA, Am. Assn. Orthodontists, Wis. Dental Assn. (Continuing Edn. award 1986), Wis. Soc. Orthodontists, Orthodontic Edn. and Research Found., Brown Door Kewaunee Dental Soc. (program chmn. 1985-86, sec., treas. 1986-87, v.p. 1987-88, pres. 1988-89), St. Louis U. Orthodontic Alumni Assn. (pres. 1988-89), Acad. Gen. Dentistry, Violet Club of Am. Roman Catholic. Home: 2160 Green Leaf Rd DePere WI 54115-8621 Office: 2654 S Oneida St Green Bay WI 54304-5302

SWETS, JOHN ARTHUR, psychologist, researcher; b. Grand Rapids, Mich., June 19, 1928; s. John A. and Sara Henrietta (Heyns) S.; m. Maxine Ruth Crawford, July 16, 1949; children—Stephen Arthur, Joel Brian. B.A., U. Mich., Ann Arbor, 1950, M.A., 1953, Ph.D., 1954. Instr. psychology U. Mich., Ann Arbor, 1954-56; asst. prof. psychology M.I.T., Cambridge, 1956-60, assoc. prof. psychology, 1960-63; v.p. Bolt Beranek & Newman Inc., Cambridge, 1964-69, sr. v.p., 1969-74, gen. mgr. research, devel. and cons., dir., 1971-74; chief scientist BBN Labs., Cambridge, 1975—; lectr. dept. clin. epidemiology Harvard Med. Sch., 1985-88, dept. health care policy, 1988—; mem. corp. Edn. Devel. Ctr., Newton, Mass., 1971-75; vis. rsch. fellow Philips Labs., The Netherlands, 1958; Regents' prof. U. Calif., 1969; advisor vision com., com. on hearing and bioacoustics NAS-NRC, 1960-96; mem. Commn. on Behavioral Social Scis. and Edn., NRC, 1988-92, vice chair, 1992-93, chmn., 1993-96; sci. advisor, cons., lectr. numerous govtl. and profl. orgns. Author: Signal Detection Theory and ROC Analysis in Psychology and Diagnostics, 1996; co-author: (with D.M. Green) Signal Detection Theory and Psychophysics, 1966, (with R.M. Pickett) Evaluation of Diagnostic Systems: Methods From Signal Detection Theory, 1982; editor: Signal Detection and Recognition by Human Observers, 1964, (with L.L. Elliott) Psychology and the Handicapped Child, 1974, (with D. Druckman) Enhancing Human Performance, 1988; mem. editorial bd. Med. Decision Making, 1980-85, Psychol. Sci., 1989-94, Psychol. Rev., 1995—, Jour. Exptl. Psychology: Applied, 1995—; contbr. articles to profl. jours. Past mem. numerous civic orgns.; mem. corp. Winchester Hosp., Mass., 1981-84. Fellow AAAS (coun. 1986-89), APA (Disting. Sci. Contbn. award 1990), Am. Acad. Arts and Scis., Acoustical Soc. Am. (exec. coun. 1968-71), Soc. Exptl. Psychologists (chmn. 1986, exec. com. 1986-89, Howard Crosby Warren medal 1985), Am. Psychol. Soc.; mem. NAS (Troland award com. 1991, chmn. 1992), Psychonomic Soc., Psychometric Soc., Soc. Math. Psychology, Sigma Xi, Sigma Alpha Epsilon, Winchester Country Club. Congregationalist (moderator). Office: BBN Corp 10 Moulton St Cambridge MA 02138-1119

SWIBINSKI, EDWARD THOMAS, physician; b. Jersey City, Jan. 26, 1950; s. Stanley Adolph and Celina Frances (Szymanski) S.; BS Rutgers U., 1972; M.D., N.Y. Med. Coll., 1975. Diplomate Am. Bd. Internal Medicine, Am. Bd. Endocrinology and Metabolism. Resident in medicine N.Y. Med. Coll., N.Y.C., 1975-78; gen. internist Nat. Health Service Corp., Camden, N.J., 1978-79; fellow in endocrinology Hosp. of U. Pa., Phila., 1979-80, Robert Wood Johnson Med. Sch., Piscataway, N.J., 1980-81; assoc. clin. prof. medicine U. Medicine and Dentistry N.J.-Robert Woods Johnson Med. Sch.; div. chief Endocrniology , Our Lady of Loudes Ctr., pres.,1985, (v.p. 1993-94, 95— Phila Endocrinology soc.), bd. dir. Phila. Endocrinology soc., 1991-96, Phila. Endocrinology Soc. (sec.- treas.), Mem. A.C.P., Camden County Med. Soc., Phi Beta Kappa, Alpha Omega Alpha. Roman Catholic.. Office: 1305 Kings Hwy N Cherry Hill NJ 08034-1919

SWICK, HERBERT MORRIS, medical educator, neurologist; b. Baton Rouge, Nov. 22, 1941; s. Edgar Haight and Mary Ellen (Morris) S.; m. Mary Lynne McCluggage, June 29, 1963; children: Kristin Ann, Elizabeth May,

Diane Marie. BA with honors, Johns Hopkins U., 1963, MD Sch. Medicine, 1966. Cert. Am. Bd. Psychiatry and Neurology, Am. Bd. Pediatrics. Resident in pediatrics Johns Hopkins U., Balt., 1966-69; resident in neurology U. Ky., Lexington, 1971-74, asst. prof. neurology and pediatrics, 1974-75; asst. to assoc. prof. neurology and pediatrics Med. Coll. Wis., Milw., 1975-84, prof. neurology and pediats., 1984-94, asst. dean med. edn., interm chmn. dept. neurology, 1987-88, assoc. dean acad. affairs, 1988-91, sr. assoc. dean acad. affairs, 1991-93, sr. assoc. dean for acad. programs, 1993-94; prof. neurology, sr. assoc. dean acad. affairs Sch. Medicine U. Kans., Kansas City, 1994—, acting chmn. dept. history and philosophy of medicine Sch. Medicine, 1995, interim exec. dean Sch. Medicine, 1995—; chief dept. neurology Children's Hosp. Wis., Milw., 1981-87, acting chmn. dept. neurology, 1987-88; vis. prof. neurol. edn. Mayo Clinic and Found., Rochester, Minn., 1985. Contbr. numerous articles to profl. jours. Bd. dirs. Milw. Chamber Music Soc., 1982-88, pres. 1986-88. Served to lt. commdr., USN, 1969-71. Fulbright sr. scholar, 1978. Fellow Am. Acad. Neurology (edn. com., undergrad. edn. subcom. 1985-89); mem. Am. Assn. History Medicine, Child Neurology Soc. (archives and history com. 1981-88, exec. com. 1982-86, sci. selection com. 1983, 84), Columbia History of Medicine Club, Internat. Child Neurology Assn., Milw. Acad. Medicine (coun. 1993-94), Profs. of Child Neurology, Wis. Neurol. Soc. (sec.-treas. 1981-82, pres.-elect 1982-84, pres. 1984-85), Assn. Univ. Profs. in Neurology (undergrad. edn. com. 1979-86), Assn. Am. Med. Colls. (coun. deans 1995—).

SWIECICKI, MARTIN, neurosurgeon; b. Camden, N.J., June 29, 1934; s. Martin E. and Annetta Swiecicki; m. Gloria J. Whelpley; children: Diane, Annette, Karen, Sheryl, Martin C. BA, Colgate U., 1956; MD, Hahnemann Med. Sch., 1960. Diplomate Am. Bd. Neurol. Surgery. Intern West Jersey Hosp., Camden, 1960-61; resident in neurological surgery Jefferson U., Phila., 1961-65; mem. staff in neurol. surgery West Jersey Hosp., Camden, Berlin, N.J., 1967—, chief Neurol. Surgery, 1967-89; clin. assoc prof. Neurol. Surgery Hahnemann Med. Coll., Phila., 1977—. Contbr. articles to profl. jours. Recipient N.J. Gov.'s award for Outstanding Svcs., 1970, 71, 72, 73, Award for Support and Svc. Boy Scouts Am., 1992. Fellow ACS; mem. AMA, Camden County Med. Soc. (v.p.1993, pres. 1995), West Jersey Med. Soc., N.J. State Med. Soc., N.J. Neurosurg. Soc.(sec.-treas. 978-79, pres. 1981, chmn. peer rev. com. 1983-89, mem. peer rev. com. 1977—), Camden County Med. Soc. (exec. com. 1977—, v.p. 1993, pres.- elect 1994, pres. 1995), Soc. Air Force Clin. Surgeons, Am. Assn. Neurol. Surgeons. Office: Neurosurg Assocs NJ 2301 E Evesham Rd Ste 406 Voorhees NJ 08043-4505

SWIFT, ROBERT MICHAEL, psychiatrist, educator; b. Chgo., Mar. 8, 1951; s. Earl W. and Ellen E. Swift; m. Beatrice Hyson, Sept. 3, 1973; children: Rachel, Joshua, Ben. BA, U. Chgo., 1972, PhD, 1977, MD (hon.), 1979. Resident dept. psychiatry Yale U., New Haven, 1979-83; assoc. prof. Brown U. Med. Sch., Providence, 1991—; dir. psychiatry Roger Williams Gen. Hosp., Providence, 1984—. Grantee NIMH, 1972-76, Pharm. Mfg. Assn. grantee, 1985—, NIAAA grantee, 1987—. Mem. Am. Psychiat. Assn., Soc. Biol. Psychiatry, Rsch. Soc. Alcohol, Assn. for Med. Edn. and Research in Substance Abuse. Office: Roger Williams Gen Hosp 825 Chalkstone Ave Providence RI 02908-4728

SWIFT, STEVEN EDWARD, gynecologist, educator; b. Washington, Nov. 22, 1961; s. Hallock Freeman and Carol Ann (Nutter) S.; m. Alisa Marian Josef, Aug. 11, 1984; children: J. Dylan, W. Brooks. BA in Zoology cum laude, Miami U., Oxford, Ohio, 1983; MD, Ohio State U., 1987. lic., S.C. Fellow in urogynecology U. Calif., Irvine, 1991-93; resident in ob-gyn Med. U. S.C., 1987-91, asst. prof. ob-gyn, 1993—; v.p. Landacre Rsch. Soc., Columbus, 1986-87; presenter in field. Contbr. chpts. to books: Urogynecology and Urodynamics, 1996, Gynecologic Surgery, 1995, Ambulatory Gynecology, 1995; contbr. articles to profl. jours. including Obstetrics/Gynecology, Internat. Urogynecoiogy Jour. Core mem. Young Adult Catholics, Charleston, S.C., 1995; active Circle K Svc. Orgn., Oxford, Ohio, 1982. Fellow Am. Coll. Obstetricians-Gynecologists; mem. AMA, Am. Urogynecological Soc., Assn. Profs. Ob-Gyn, Donald Ostergard Gynecologic Soc. Home: 539 Flambeau Mount Pleasant SC 29464 Office: Med. U. S.C. Dept Ob-Gyn 171 Ashley Ave Charleston SC 29425

SWIFT, WILLIAM PORTER, psychologist, consultant; b. Albany, N.Y., Sept. 9, 1914; s. Cyrus Burgess and Georgia May (Fisher) S.; m. Jean S. MacPherson, June 19, 1943 (dec. 1978); children: Diane S., Neil Randolph, Frank Douglas; m. Jean Ruth Bennett, Aug. 18, 1979; stepchildren: Linda B. Simpson, Robert F. Snyder. AB, SUNY, Albany, 1936, MA, 1938; PhD, Cornell U., 1947. Lic. psychologist, N.Y., Pa.; lic. tchr., sch. psychologist, N.Y. Psychologist U.S. VA, Ithaca, N.Y., 1945-47, Syracuse (N.Y.) U., 1947-51; indsl. psychologist for various orgns. Phila., 1951-54; chair dept. psychology Ithaca Coll., 1954-59; cons. Hay Assocs., Phila., 1959-62; dir. psychol. svcs. Villanova (Pa.) U., 1962-64; clin. psychologist Broome County Mental Health Clinic, Binghamton, N.Y., 1965-75; prof., chair dept. psychology Broome Community Coll., Binghamton, 1965-83; pvt. practice N.Y., Pa., 1947-89; ret., 1989; cons. in field. Author 3 books.

SWILLER, RANDOLPH JACOB, internist; b. N.Y.C., Jan. 21, 1946; s. Abraham Irving and Helen (Emmer) S.; m. Florence Tena Davis, Sept. 3, 1967; children: Jeremy Adam, Rebecca Susan, Steven Eric. BA in Biology cum laude, Hofstra U., 1968; MD, Chgo. Med. Sch., 1972. Diplomate Am. Bd. Psychiatry and Neurology, Am. Bd. Med. Examiners. Intern Long Island Jewish-Hillside Med. Ctr., New Hyde Park, N.Y., 1972-73; psychiatric resident SUNY Downstate Med. Ctr., Bklyn., 1973-76; asst. attending psychiatrist Maimonides Med. Ctr., Bklyn., 1976-78; medical resident, mem. med. ethics com. Jewish Hosp. Med. Ctr. of Bklyn., 1978-80; fellow in hematology North Shore U. Hosp., Manhasset, N.Y., 1980-81; attending physician in internal medicine Fla. Med. Ctr., Lauderdale Lakes, 1982—, mem. med. utilization rev. com., 1986—, mem. credentials and qualifications com., 1990—; attending physician in internal medicine Coral Springs (Fla.) Med. Ctr., 1987—, mem. med. utilization rev. com., 1987-89. Mem. ACP, AMA, Am. Soc. Internal Medicine, Fla. Med. Assn., Broward County Med. Assn., Am. Psychiat. Assn. Democrat. Jewish. Office: 7710 NW 71st Ct Ste 304 Fort Lauderdale FL 33321-2932

SWIM, JESSE ROGENE, pharmacist; b. Matador, Tex., Nov. 30, 1945; s. Jesse Thomas Jr. and Imogene (Hastings) S.; m. Stella MArtin, June 6, 1965; children: Edward Wilson, Emily Sibyl. BS in Pharmacy, U. Tex., Austin, 1973. Pharmacist Sommer's Drugs, San Antonio, 1973-74, Berry Pharmacy, Austin, Tex., 1974-77, Tex. Dept. Health, Abilene, 1977-91; pharmacist cons. Am. Pharm. Svcs., Arlington, Tex., 1991-93; dir. pharmacy Sears Meth. Pharmacy, 1993-94; pharmacist cons. J.R. Swim Cons., 1994—. Author: Generic Drug Identification Guide, 1st edit., 1987, 2d edit., 1989, 3d edit., 1990. Mem. adminstrv. bd. Aldersgate United MEth. Ch., Abilene, 1991. With U.S. Army, 1966-69. Named Health Facility Surveyor of Yr. Assn. HEalth Facility Survey Agy. Dirs., 1986. Fellow Tex. Pharm. Assn. (dir. 1989-92); mem. Am. Pharm. Assn., Am. Soc. Con. Pharmacists', Big Country Pharm. Assn. Home and Office: 4841 Catclaw Dr Abilene TX 79606-4165

SWISTEL, ALEXANDER JULIAN, surgeon, researcher, educator; b. Munich, Jan. 18, 1949; came to U.S., 1950; s. George and Irene (Bohacka) S.; m. Patricia Lois Myskowski, July 31, 1976; children: Emily, Christopher (dec.), Gregory. AB, Harvard U., 1971; M Med. Sci., Rutgers U., 1973; MD, Brown U., 1975. Diplomate Am. Bd. Surgery. From resident to chief resident St. Luke's-Roosevelt Hosp., N.Y.C., 1975-81; fellow in surg. oncology Meml. Sloan-Kettering Cancer Ctr., N.Y.C., 1981-83; mem. attending staff, surgeon St. Luke's Roosevelt Hosp., N.Y.C., 1983—, Beth Israel Hosp., N.Y.C., 1984—; asst. clin. prof. surgery Columbia Coll. Physicans and Surgeons, N.Y.C., 1984-95; mem. attending staff, surgeon N.Y. Hosp.-Cornell Med. Ctr., 1996—; assoc. clin. prof. surgery Med. Sch. Cornell U.; assoc. dir. breast svc. N.Y. Hosp.-Cornell Med. Ctr. Contbr. articles to profl. jours. Bd. dirs. breast care program St. Luke's Hosp., N.Y.C. Rsch. grantee, prin. investigator State of N.Y., 1989-95. Fellow ACS (liaison physician cancer com. 1990—), Acad. Medicine N.Y.; mem. Am. Soc. Clin. Oncology, Soc. Head and Neck Surgeons, Assn. Acad. Surgeons, N.Y. Med. Soc., N.Y. Metro Breast Cancer Group (exec. com.). Office: 428 E 72nd St New York NY 10021-6001

SWITZ, DONALD MACLEAN, medical educator, internist, gastroenterologist; b. Orange, N.J., Mar. 1937; s. Theodore and Edith Faye (Pedersen) S.; m. Elise Hurd, May 22, 1965; children: Neil, Geoffrey, Katherine. BA, Carleton Coll., 1958; MD, U. Chgo., 1962. Intern U. Chgo. Hosp., 1962-63, resident in medicine, 1963-64; resident in medicine Univ. Hosp. Cleve., Western Res. U., 1964-66; fellow in gastroenterology Mayo Clinic, Rochester, Minn., 1968-70; asst. prof. medicine Med. Coll. Va., Richmond, 1970-73, assoc. prof. medicine, 1974-83, prof. medicine, 1984—, assoc. dean for ambulatory affairs, 1985—; vis. prof. Harvard Sch. Pub. Health, Boston, 1980-81; bd. dirs. State Bd. Med. Assistance Svcs. (Medicaid) Va., 1988—, chair state bd. liaison coun., 1993-94, chair 1995-96. Contbr. chpts. to books, articles to profl. jours. Chmn. Richmond Urban Inst., 1979-80. Lt. comdr. USN, 1966-68. Ford Found. scholar, 1952-54. Fellow ACP (councilor Va. coun. 1975—); mem. AAAS, Richmond Acad. Medicine (treas. 1990-92, 1st v.p. 1993-94, pres. 1996), Am. Gastroent. Assn., Am. Soc. for Gastrointestinal Endoscopy. Episcopalian. Office: Med Coll Va Dept Medicine Box 711 11th & Marshall Sts Richmond VA 23298-0711

SWOFFORD, JOHN BARNETT, anesthesiologist, medical educator; b. Yakima, Wash., Jan. 16, 1961; s. Peter Jay and Shirley Marie (Hollahan) S.; m. Minati Dolly Khuntia, May 24, 1987; children: 1 child, Connor Aneil. BS cum laude, Wash. State U., 1984; DO, Kirksville Coll. Osteo. Medicine, 1988. Diplomate Am. Bd. Anesthesiology; cert. DO, Am. Osteo Assn. Intern Doctors Hosp., Columbus, Ohio, 1988-89; resident in anesthesiology Ohio State U., Columbus, 1989-91, Ind. U., Indpls., 1991-92; clin. asst. prof. anesthesia Ind. U. Med. Ctr., Indpls., 1992—; mem. chronic pain staff Ind. U. Med. Ctr., Indpls., 1992—, mem. anesthesia residency selection com., 1992—. Named to Pres.'s Honor Roll, U.S. Govt., 1982-84. Mem. Am. Soc. Anesthesiologists, Ind. Soc. Anesthesiologists. Office: Ind U Anesthesia Assn Fesler Hall 1120 South Dr Indianapolis IN 46202

SWORT, ARLOWAYNE, retired nursing educator and administrator; b. Bartlesville, Okla., Dec. 9, 1922; d. Arlington L. and Clara E. (Church) S. Diploma, St. Luke's Hosp. Sch. Nursing, Kansas City, Mo., 1944; BSN, U. Colo., 1958; MS in Nursing, Cath. U. Am., 1961; EdD, Columbia U., 1973. Dean, prof. Sch. Nursing U. Tex. Health Scis. Ctr., Houston, 1977-83, prof. nursing, 1983-85; prof., assoc. in adminstrn. Johns Hopkins U. Sch. Nursing, Balt., 1985-87; prof., assoc. dean for adminstrn. and grad. acad. affairs Johns Hopkins U. Sch. Nursing, Balt., 1987-89, sr. assoc. dean, 1990-91. Recipient numerous rsrch. grants. Mem. ANA, NLN, APHA, AAUW, Am. Assn. for History of Nursing Soc., Am. Assn. Univ. Adminstrs., Am. Assn. for Higher Edn., Am. Nurses Found.-Century Club, Am. Assn. Nurse Execs., Nat. Gerontol. Nurses Assn., Found. for Nursing of Md., Inc., Sigma Theta Tau, Kappa Delta Pi. Home: 1317 Kollman Dr Hondo TX 78861-1014

SWORTZEL, TODD F., health facility administrator; b. Washington, Aug. 8, 1957; s. Robert Decker and Patty Lou (Farley) S.; m. Melissa Whitener, Aug. 3, 1979; children: Brad, Emily. Student, Radford U., 1975-77; BBA, Averett Coll., 1994; postgrad., Med. Coll. Va., 1995—. Lic. nursing home adminstr., Va. Entrepreneur T.F.S., Inc., Vienna, Va., 1980-88; real estate agt. Mount Vernon Realty, Alexandria, Va., 1988-90; br. mgr. HAMCO, Inc., Newton, N.C., 1990-93; asst. adminstr. Culpeper (Va.) Bapt. Ret. Cmty., 1993-94, adminstr., 1994—. Mem. Am. Coll. Health Care Adminstrn., Va. Assn. Nonprofit Homes for the Aging. Baptist. Office: Culpeper Bapt Ret Cmty PO Box 191 12425 Village Loop Culpeper VA 22701

SY, CLAUDE GO, internist; b. Manila, The Philippines, Apr. 13, 1964; came to the U.S., 1992; s. Mariano Tan and Purificacion (Go) S.; m. Annabelle M. Tan-Sy, Oct. 3, 1994; 1 child, Charles Marion. BS in Biology, U. Santo Tomas, Manila, 1985, MD, 1989. Co. physician Globe Hardware, Manila, 1991-92, Globesco, Inc., Manila, 1991-92, Impex Inc., Manila, 1991-92; intern internal medicine Mercy Hosp., Buffalo, N.Y., 1992-93; resident internal medicine Mercy Hosp., Buffalo, 1993-95, chief resident internal medicine, 1994-95; internal medicine physician Buffalo (N.Y.) Family Practice, 1995—. Mem. ASIM, ACP. Roman Catholic.

SY, FRANCISCO SANTOS, epidemiologist, educator; b. Manila, Philippines, Feb. 12, 1949; s. Hack Chan and Elena (Santos) S. BS, U. Philippines, 1970, MD, 1975; MS, Harvard U., 1981; DrPH, Johns Hopkins U., 1984. Asst. prof. parasitology U. Philippines, 1979-84; dir. Carolina AIDS rsch. and edn. project U. S.C., Columbia, 1987—, assoc. prof. epidemiology, 1985—; adj. assoc. prof. microbiology and immunology U. S.C., 1986—, adj. assoc. prof. preventive medicine, 1987—. Editor AIDS Edn. & Prevention-An Interdisciplinary Jour., 1989—. Named Outstanding Alumnus in Pub. Health Johns Hopkins U., 1990, Outstanding Alumnus in Med. Edn. U. Philippines, 1993; recipient J. Keith Outstanding Tchr. award U. S.C., 1991. Fellow Am. Coll. Preventive Medicine, Royal Soc. of Tropical Medicine and Hygiene, Am. Coll. of Allergy and Immunology; mem. AMA, Internat. Soc. for AIDS Edn. (founding pres. 1987-88, Svc. award 1988), Am. Coll. of Epidemiology, Am. Pub. Health Assn., Delta Omega. Home: 1915 College St Columbia SC 29201-3921 Office: U SC Sch Pub Health Dept Epidemiology Bios Columbia SC 29208

SYLVESTER, JAMES MILES, nuclear medicine physician; b. Springfield, Mo., July 23, 1952; s. Edgar Donald and Barbara Jean (Hedgecock) S.; m. Judith Ladine Schneider, Aug. 14, 1976; children: Jennifer Leigh, Janelle Marie. BS, S.W. Mo. State U., 1973; MD, Mo. U., 1988. Diplomate Am. Bd. Nuc. Medicine. Resident U. Mo., Columbia, 1993; broadcaster Midland TV, Inc., Springfield, Mo., 1973-75, Mark Twain Broadcasting, Springfield, 1975-77, Stauffer Comms., Springfield, 1977-79, Babcom, Inc., Springfield, 1979-80, KFRU, Inc., Columbia, 1980-83; rsch. asst. Info. Sci. Group, Columbia, 1983-84; pres. Nuc. Medicine Assocs., Baton Rouge, La., 1993—; cons. Orbis Broadcast Group, Chgo., 1994—; mem. med. adv. bd. America's House Call Network, Chgo., 1996—. Editor/host: (TV program/CNBC) Nuclear Medicine, 1994-95; author: (commentaries) Jour. Nuc. Medicine, 1994; contbr. articles to profl. jours. Recipient Student Summer Rsch. award March of Dimes, 1985. Fellow Am. Coll. Nuc. Physicians (chmn. profl. and pub. info. program 1995—); mem. AMA, Soc. Nuclear Medicine (Young Investigator's award Mo. Valley chpt. 1988), Nat. Assn. Physician Broadcasters. Office: Nuclear Medicine Assocs 5000 Hennessy Blvd Baton Rouge LA 70808

SYLVESTER, JOHN EDWARD, social worker; b. N.Y.C., Apr. 13, 1949; s. John and Esther (Larkin) S.; m. Dolores Alcantara, July 2, 1974. BA in Psychology, CUNY, 1975; cert. in social work, Fordham U., 1977. Program coord. Mid. Bronx (N.Y.) Sr. Citizen's Coun., 1980-82; assoc. editor N.Y.C. Self-Help Clearing House, 1978-80; case worker Cath. Guardian Soc., N.Y.C., 1982-83, Assn. for Advancement of the Blind, Queens, N.Y., 1984-86; probation officer N.Y.C. Dept. of Probation, Bronx, 1987-88; parole officer N.Y. State Div. of Parole, N.Y.C., 1988-92; program dir. Ehrlich Supported Housing Program for Homeless Univ. Consultation and Treatment Ctr. for Mental Hygiene, Bronx, 1992-95. Mem. Am. Servicemen's Union, N.Y.C., 1968; vol. ARC, N.Y.C., 1973. With USMC, 1967-70, Vietnam. Named one of Outstanding Young Men in Am., U.S. Jaycees, 1982. Mem. Assn. Black Social Workers, Amnesty Internat. Home: 2116 Clinton Ave Bronx NY 10457-3628

SYMCHOWICZ, SAMSON, biochemist; b. Krakow, Poland, Mar. 20, 1923; came to U.S., 1954; s. Chiel and Esther M. S.; m. Sarah R. Nussbaum, May 24, 1953; children: Esther, Beatrice, Caren. Chem. engr., Poly. Inst. Prague, Czechoslovakia, 1950; MS in Chemistry, Bklyn. Poly. Inst., 1956; PhD in Biochemistry, Rutgers U., 1960. Asst. biochemist McGill U., Montreal, Que., Can., 1951-54, SUNY, 1954-56; biochemist Schering-Plough Corp., Bloomfield, N.J., 1956-73, assoc. dir. biol. rsch., 1973-80, dir. drug metabolism, 1980-92. Editorial bd. Drug Metabolism and Disposition; contbr. over 90 sci. papers to profl. publs. Mem. Am. Soc. Microbiology, Am. Chem. Soc., N.Y. Acad. Sci., Soc. Pharmacology and Exptl. Therapeutics.

SYME, SHERMAN LEONARD, epidemiology educator; b. Dauphin, Man., Can., July 4, 1932; came to U.S., 1950; s. Robert and Rose (Bay) S.; m. Marilyn Elaine Egenes, July 28, 1932; children: Karen, David, Janet. BA, UCLA, 1953, MA, 1955; PhD, Yale U., 1957. Commd. USPHS, Washington, 1957-68; advanced through grades to chief Tng. Sta. USPHS, San Francisco, 1962-68; sociologist USPHS, Washington, 1957-60; exec. sec. NIH, Bethesda, Md., 1960-62; prof. emeritus epidemiology U. Calif., Berkeley, 1968—; chmn. Dept. Epidemiology, U. Calif., 1975-80; vis. prof. Teikyo U., Tokyo, 1977, York (Eng.) U., 1975, St. Thomas Sch. Medicine, London, 1980, U. London, 1989; expert adv. panels WHO, Geneva, 1975—. Co-editor Social Stress and Heart Disease, 1967, Social Support and Health, 1985; contbr. 115 articles to profl. jours. Fellow Am. Heart Assn., Soc. Epidemiol. Research; mem. Inst. Medicine, Am. Epidemiol. Soc. Office: U Calif Sch Pub Health Pub Health Biology & Epidemiology 140 Warren Hall Berkeley CA 94720*

SYMONDS, EDWIN MALCOLM, obstetrician, gynecologist, educator, dean; b. Adelaide, Australia, Nov. 6, 1934; arrived in Eng., 1972; s. Edwin Joseph and Eugenie Mary (Walker) S.; m. Beverley Sue Martin, Apr. 26, 1958 (div. Nov. 1992); children: Ian Martin, David Malcolm, Thomas Rex, Matthew Richard Edwin; m. Chloe Woolcott Simpson, Jan. 23, 1993. MB BS, U. Adelaide, 1957, MD, 1971. Sr. registrar, clin. lectr. U. Liverpool, Eng., 1962-66; sr. lectr. U. Adelaide, 1966-68, reader, 1968-71; Found. prof. ob-gyn. U. Nottingham, Eng., 1972-93, dean Faculty of Medicine, 1993—; non-exec. dir. Queen's Med. Centre Trust, Nottingham, 1993—; mem. coun. Med. Defence Union, London, 1975—, Gen. Med. Coun., London, 1993—; mem. Commonwealth Scholarships Commn., 1984-88. Author: (textbook) Essential Obstetrics and Gynecology, 1988; co-author: (textbook) Magnetic Resonance Imaging in Obstetrics and Gynecology, 1994; co-editor: (textbook) Gamete and Embryo Micromanipulation, 1993; editor. jour. Current Ob-Gyn., 1991—. Recipient Chesley award Internat. Soc. for Study of Hypertension in Pregnancy, Argentina, 1992; hon. fellow Faculty of Pub. Health Meidicne, Royal Coll. Physicians, U.K., 1996. Fellow Royal Coll. Ob-Gyn. (coun.), Royal Soc. Medicine, Am. Gynecol. and Obstet. Soc. (hon.), Italian Perinatal Soc. (hon.), Hungarian Ob-Gyn. Soc. (hon.), Car Colston Cricket Club of Nottinghamshire (v.p. 1992—). Office: Queen's Med Centre, Dept Ob-Gyn, Nottingham England

SYMON-GUTIERREZ, PATRICIA PAULETTE, dietitian; b. Orange, N.J., Jan. 21, 1948; d. Michael and Aneilia (Jablonski) Symon; m. Patrick William Campesi, Apr. 1970 (div. June 1974); m. Alfonso Pelayo Gutierrez, Jan. 20, 1990. Dietetic cert., N.Y. Inst. Dietetics, 1967; BS in Dietetics, Ga. Coll., 1978; MS in Nutrition and Dietetics, Finch U. Health Scis., Chgo., 1996. Lic. dietitian, Fla. Staff dietitian Landmark Learning Ctr., Opa-Loka, Fla., 1982-86; food svc. dir., dietitian Palm Ct. Nursing and Rehab. Ctr., Wilton Manors, Fla., 1986-87; food svc. dir. Canteen Co.-Dade County Juvenile Ctr., Miami, Fla., 1987-88; food svc. dir., dietitian Manor Care-Boca Raton, Fla., 1988-90, Manor Care-Plantation, Fla., 1990-92; dir. dietary svcs., dietitian Menorah House, Boca Raton, 1992—. Mem. Am. Dietetic Assn., Phi Sigma, Phi Upsilon Omicron. Episcopalian. Home: 8991 Sunset Strip Sunrise FL 33322-3737

SZABADI, ELEMER, psychiatry educator; b. Papa, Hungary, Feb. 23, 1939; s. Bela and Vilma (Bartha) S. MD, Semmelweis U., 1964, diploma in neurology, 1968; PhD, U. Edinburgh, 1978; D.Sc., U. Manchester, 1983. Lectr. neurology Semmelweis U. Sch. Medicine, Budapest, Hungary, 1964-69; rsch. fellow U. Edinburgh, 1970-73, sr. rsch. fellow, 1973-74, lectr. psychiatry, 1974-75; lectr. psychiatry U. Manchester, Eng., 1975-78, sr. lectr. psychiatry, 1978-82, reader in psychiatry, 1982-90; prof. U. Nottingham, Eng., 1991—; cons. South Manchester Health Authority, 1978-90, Nottingham Health Authority, 1991—. Editor: Adrenoceptors, 1991; contbr. articles to profl. jours. Fellow Royal Coll. Psychiatrists; mem. British Pharmacol. Socs. (edit. bd. 1981-87), British Assn. Psychopharmacology, Brain Rsch. Assn., Behavior Analysis Group. Office: Queens Med Ctr, Dept Psychiatry, Nottingham NG7 2UH, England

SZABO, ROBERT MORRIS, orthopedic surgeon, educator; b. N.Y.C., May 8, 1952; s. Gustav and Jette (Schulsinger) S.; m. Mary Lynne Talamo, May 7, 1977. BA in Psychobiology, NYU, 1973; MD, SUNY, Buffalo, 1977; MPH in Epidemiology, U. Calif., Berkeley, 1995. Diplomate Nat. Bd. Med. Examiners, Am. Bd. Orthopedics, Am. Bd. Orthopedic Surgery. Resident in gen. and orthopedic surgery Mt. Sinai Med. Ctr., N.Y.C., 1977-82; fellow in hand/microvascular surgery Univ. Calif. Hosp., San Diego, 1982-83; prof. orthopedics, chief hand/microvascular svc. Med. Ctr. U. Calif.-Davis Sch. Medicine, Sacramento, 1982—; Cons. rheumatology service Med. Ctr. U. Calif.-Davis. Contbr. articles to profl. jours. Bd. dirs. Californians for Safe Motorcycling, Sacramento, 1985. Grantee Am. Soc. Surgery of the Hand, U. Calif.-Davis Sch. Medicine, 1985, 86. Mem. Calif. Med. Assn. (adv. panel 1985—), AMA. Home: 1040 44th St Sacramento CA 95819-3729 Office: U Calif Davis Med Ctr 2230 Stockton Blvd Sacramento CA 95817-1419

SZABO, ZOLTAN, medical science educator, medical institute director; b. Szeged, Hungary, Oct. 5, 1943; came to U.S., 1967; s. Imre and Maria (Szikora) S.; m. Wanda Toy, Dec. 5, 1976; children: Eva, Maria. Student, U. Med. Sch., Szeged, 1962-65; PhD, Columbia Pacific U., 1983. Tech. dir. microsurgery lab. R.K. Davies Med. Ctr., San Francisco, 1972-80; dir. Microsurgery and Operative Endoscopy Tng. (MOET) Inst., San Francisco, 1980—; assoc. dir. advanced laparoscopic surgery tng. ctr. Sch. Medicine U. Calif., San Francisco, 1992—; rsch. assoc. oral and maxillofacial surgery U. of Pacific, San Francisco, 1980-83, adj. asst. prof., 1983—. Author: Microsurgery Techniques, vol. 1, 1974, vol. 2, 1984 (1st Place award for excellence in med. writing 1982); co-author: Tissue Approximation in Endoscopic Surgery, 1995; editor-in-chief Surgical Technology Internationa, Vol. 3, 1994, Vol. 4, 1995, Vol. 5, 1996; contbr. chpt. books, articles to profl. jours. With U.S. Army, 1969-71. Recipient cert. of Merit, AMA, 1978, commendation Accreditation Coun. for Continuing Med. Edn., 1984, 90, 94, Spl. Recognition award Sch. Medicine Cen. U. Venezuela, 1988, Sci. Poste Sessions Hon. Mention award Am. Urol. Assn., 1992, 1st prize Roundtable for New Techs. and Innovations we. sect., 1992, James Barrett Brown award Am. Assn. Plastic Surgeons, 1993. Fellow Internat. Coll. Surgeons (Disting. Svc. award 1994); mem. Hungarian Gynecol. Soc. (hon.), Medico-Dental Study Guild Calif., Internat. Microsurg. Soc., Soc. Am. Gastrointestinal Endoscopic Surgeons (hon., 1st prize Residents and Fellows Rsch. and Sci. Presentation 1992), Am. Fertility Soc., Am. Soc. Reconstructive Microsurgery (assoc.), Am. Soc. for Peripheral Nerve. Office: Microsurgery Operative Endoscopy Tng Inst 153 States St San Francisco CA 94114-1403

SZAP, MICHAEL DAVID, pharmacologist; b. Flushing, N.Y., July 6, 1945; s. Peter and Mary Sophie (Krucan) S.; m. Christine Fulco, June 27, 1970; children: Allison, Michael. BS, Long Island Univ., 1968, MS, 1970; PhD, N.Y. Univ., 1974; DhPh, British Inst. Homeopathic Med., England, 1995. Prof. City Univ., N.Y.C., 1968-70; researcher Dupont Pharmaceuticals, Long Island, 1970-86; mktg. Glaxo Pharmaceuticals, N.C., 1986—, Glaxo Wellcome Pharmaceuticals, N.C., 1986—; cons. St. John's Coll. Pharmacy, Queens, N.Y., 1985—; adv. bd. Arnold and Marie Schwartz Coll. Pharmacy, Bklyn., 1983—. Contbr. articles to profl. jours.; patentee in field. Fellow Am. Pharmaceutical; mem. Am. Chemist Soc., Am. Assn. Clinical Pharmacists, Am. Assn. Health Care Adminstrs. Roman Catholic. Office: 41-21 Glenwood St Little Neck NY 11363

SZAPOCZNIK, JOSÉ, psychiatry and psychology educator and researcher; b. Havana, Cuba, Aug. 15, 1947; s. Ydo and Basilia (Rzeznik) Nick. BS in Math., Physics, U. Miami, 1969, MS in Psychology, 1972, PhD in Clin. Psychology, 1977. Lic. psychologist, Fla. Instr. psychiatry U. Miami, Fla., 1974-77, rsch. asst. prof., 1978-80, rsch. assoc. prof., 1981-85, rsch. prof., 1985-94, rsch. prof. psychology, 1985-94, prof. psychiatry and psychology, 1994—; dir. Miami WHO Collaborating Ctr., 1983-92, Spanish Family Guidance Ctr., Miami, 1977—; dep. dir. Ctr. Biopsychosocial Study of AIDS, Miami, 1986-91; dir. Ctr. for Family Studies, 1991—; chmn. nat. Hispanic com. President's Commn. on Mental Health, Washington, 1978-79; nat. master trainer Nat. Coalition Hispanic Health, 9 U.S. cities, 1989-91; mem. search com. for commr. FDA, Washington, 1990, for dir. Nat. Inst. Drug Abuse, 1992, Ctr. for Substance Abuse Treatment, 1994, NIMH, 1994; mem. nat. adv. com. Coun. on Mental Health, NIMH/NIH, 1995—; ex-officio mem. AIDS rsch. adv. coun. NIH, 1996—. Author: (with others) Breakthroughs in Family, 1989; author: Psychoneuro. & HIV-1..., 1991; contbr. articles to profl. jours.; cons. editor Hispanic Jour. Behavioral Scis., 1978-84, 89—, Jour. Cons. and Clin. Psychology, 1989-92; adv. editor Psychotherapy Rsch., 1990—; mem. editorial bd. Jour. Family Psychology, 1991—, Jour. Family Dynamics and Addictions, 1991-93, Inst. of Cuban Studies, 1976-78. Chair Internat. Health Coun., Miami, 1986-88; mem. adv. com. AIDS program NIH, Rockville, Md., 1987-92; extramural sci. adv. bd.

Nat. Inst. Drug Abuse, Bethesda, Md., 1990—; adv. bd. N.S. Ctr. U. Miami, 1991-92; vice chmn. Confronting Cholera: A Global Response, WHO/PAHD and N.S. Ctr. Recipient Tavares Meml. Acad. Contbns. award Assn. Hispanic Mental Health Profls., N.Y., 1989, Outstanding Rsch. Publ. award Am. Assn. Marriage and Family, 1990, Innovative Contbns. award Am. Family Therapy Acad., 1993, Disting. Alumnus award U. Miami, 1993; physics fellow U. Miami, 1966-69, NDEA fellow, 1969-73. Mem. APA (minority affairs com. 1978-79, Disting. Profl. Contbns. to Pub. Svc. award 1991), Soc. Psychotherapy Rsch., Nat. Hispanic Psychol. Assn. (v.p. 1980-82), Nat. Coalition Hispanic Mental Health and Human Svcs. Orgn. (Nat. Leadership award for acad. excellence 1982, Cmty. Agy. award 1978), Nat. Hispanic Coun. on Aging (bd. dirs. 1983-86). Democrat. Jewish. Office: U Miami 1425 NW 10th Ave Fl 3D Miami FL 33136-1024

SZARKA, LASLO JOSEPH, pharmaceutical company executive; b. Hungary, Sept. 6, 1935; came to U.S., 1974; s. Geza and Ilona (Woditsch) S.; m. Violet Varkonyi; children: Monica, Lawrence. MS, U. Budapest, Hungary, 1961, PhD, 1967. Rsch. assoc. Chinoin, Budapest, 1963-64; sect. head Drug Rsch. Inst., Budapest, 1964-71; rsch. investigator E.R. Squibb & Sons, New Brunswick, N.J., 1974-81; asst. dir. E.R. Squibb & Sons, New Brunswick, 1981-86; dir. Bristol-Myers-Squibb, New Brunswick, 1986—. Patentee: 25 patents in Biotech.; contbr. articles to profl. jours. Com. mem. Sister Cities for New Brunswick, 1990—. Mem. AAAS, AIChE, N.Y. Acad. Sci., Am. Chem. Soc. Office: Bristol Myers Squibb PO Box 191 New Brunswick NJ 08903-0191

SZASZ, THOMAS STEPHEN, psychiatrist, educator, writer; b. Budapest, Hungary, Apr. 15, 1920; came to U.S., 1938, naturalized, 1944; s. Julius and Lily (Wellisch) S.; m. Rosine Loshkajian, Oct. 19, 1951 (div. 1970); children: Margot Szasz Peters, Susan Marie Szasz Palmer. AB, U. Cin., 1941, MD, 1944; DSc (hon.), Allegheny Coll., 1975, U. Francisco Marroquin, Guatemala, 1979. Diplomate: Nat. Bd. Med. Examiners, Am. Bd. Psychiatry and Neurology. Intern 4th Med. Service Harvard, Boston City Hosp., 1944-45; asst. resident medicine Cin. Gen. Hosp., 1945-46, asst. clinician internal medicine div. out-patient dispensary, 1946; asst. resident psychiatry U. Chgo. Clinics, 1946-47; tng. research fellow Inst. Psychoanalysis, Chgo., 1947-48; rsch. asst. Inst. Psychoanalysis, 1949-50, staff mem., 1951-56; practice medicine, specializing in psychiatry, psychoanalysis Chgo., 1949-54, Bethesda, Md., 1954-56, Syracuse, N.Y., 1956—; prof. psychiatry SUNY Health Sci. Ctr., Syracuse, 1956-90, prof. psychiatry emeritus, 1990—; vis. prof. dept. psychiatry U. Wis., Madison, 1962, Marquette U. Sch. Medicine, Milw., 1968, U. N.Mex., 1981; holder numerous lectureships, including C.P. Snow lectr. Ithaca Coll., 1970; E.S. Meyer Meml. lectr. U. Queensland Med. Sch.; Lambie-Dew orator Sydney U., 1977; Mem. nat. adv. com. bd. Tort and Med. Yearbook; cons. com. mental hygiene N.Y. State Bar Assn.; mem. research adv. panel Inst. Study Drug Addiction; adv. bd. Corp. Econ. Edn., 1977—. Author: Pain and Pleasure, 1957, The Myth of Mental Illness, 1961, Law, Liberty and Psychiatry, 1963, Psychiatric Justice, 1965, The Ethics of Psychoanalysis, 1965, Ideology and Insanity, 1970, The Manufacture of Madness, 1970, The Second Sin, 1973, Ceremonial Chemistry, 1974, Heresies, 1976, Karl Kraus and the Soul-Doctors, 1976, Schizophrenia: The Sacred Symbol of Psychiatry, 1976, Psychiatric Slavery, 1977, The Theology of Medicine, 1977, The Myth of Psychotherapy, 1978, Sex by Prescription, 1980, The Therapeutic State, 1984, Insanity: The Idea and its Consequences, 1987, The Untamed Tongue: A Dissenting Dictionary, 1990, Our Right to Drugs: The Case for a Free Market, 1992, A Lexicon of Lunacy, 1993, Cruel Compassion, 1994, The Meaning of Mind, 1996; editor: The Age of Madness, 1973; cons. editor of psychiatry and psychology: Stedman's Medical Dictionary, 22d edit, 1973; contbg. editor: Reason, 1974—, Libertarian Rev., 1986—; mem. editorial bd. Psychoanalytic Rev, 1965—, Jour. Contemporary Psychotherapy, 1968—, Law and Human Behavior, 1977—, Jour. Libertarian Studies, 1977—, Children and Youth Services Rev, 1978—, Am. Jour. Forensic Psychiatry, 1980—, Free Inquiry, 1980—. Comdr. M.C., USNR, 1954-56. Recipient Stella Feiss Hofheimer award U. Cin., 1944, Holmes-Munsterberg award Internat. Acad. Forensic Psychology, 1969; Wisdom award honor, 1970; Acad. prize Institutum atque Academia Auctorum Internationalis, Andorra, 1972; Distinguished Service award Am. Inst. Pub. Service, 1974; Martin Buber award Midway Counseling Center, 1974, Thomas S. Szasz award Ctr. Ind. Thought , 1990, Alfred R. Lindesmith award for achievement in field of scholarship and writing Drug Policy Found., 1991; others; named Humanist of Year Am. Humanist Assn., 1973; Hon. fellow Postgrad. Center for Mental Health, 1961, Mencken award, 1981, Humanist Laureate, 1984, Statue of Liberty-Ellis Island Found. Archives Roster, 1986. Fellow Am. Psychiat. Assn. (life), Am. Psychoanalytic Assn., Internat. Psychoanalytic Soc., Western N.Y. Psychoanalytic Soc. Home: 4739 Limberlost Ln Manlius NY 13104-1405 Office: 750 E Adams St Syracuse NY 13210-2306

SZCZEKLIK, ANDREW THADDEUS, physician, medical educator; b. Kraków, Poland, July 29, 1938; s. Edward and Marianna (Gruszczynska) S.; m. Maria Rejman, Nov. 4, 1967; children: Michael, Wojciech, Anna. Degree, Coll. Music, Kraków, 1955, Copernicus Acad. Medicine, Kraków, 1961; MD, Acad. Medicine, Wroclaw, Poland, 1966. Intern Monmouth (N.J.) Med. Ctr., 1962-63; from jr. rsch. asst. to sr. rsch. asst. dept. medicine Acad. Medicine, Wroclaw, 1964-71, chief lab. clin. enzymology, 1969-71; chmn. dept. allergy clin. immunology Copernicus Acad. Medicine, Kraków, 1972-89, chmn. dept. medicine, rector, 1990-93, vice-rector for sci. rsch., 1981-83; vice rector Jagiellonian U. for Med. Affairs, 1993-96; vis. prof. faculty medicine U. Sheffield, 1985. Author: Myocardial Infaction, 1971, 2d edit., 1974, 3d edit., 1981; contbr. articles to profl. jours. V.P. Solidarnosc U. Sch. Medicine, Kraków, 1980-90; active Civic Com., Warsaw, 1987-90. Recipient First prize Polish Soc. Internal Medicine, 1970, Polish Acad. Sci., 1974. Mem. Am. Acad. Allergy and Immunology, European Soc. for Clin. Investigation, N.Y. Acad. Sci., European Respiratory Soc. (Sadoul lectr. 1990), Polish Soc. Allergology, Am. Heart Assn., Internat. Union Angiology, Internat. Soc. Thrombosis and Haemostasis, Polish Soc. Cardiology, Polish Soc. Internal Medicine, Pontificia Acad. Scientiarium. Roman Catholic. Office: Jagiellonian Univ Sch Medicine Dept Medicine, Skawinska 8, Kraków 31-066, Poland

SZEDENIK, JOHANNES, chest physician; b. Vienna, June 16, 1963; s. Ludwig and Margarethe (Forjan) S.; m. Elisabeth Hillinger, June 10, 1988; children: Rafael, Pia. Doctor Medicine Univ., U. Vienna, 1987. With Vienna U. Aimes Gen. Hosp., 1987-90; asst. lung dept. Grimmenstein, Lower Austria, Austria, 1990-96; pvt. practice Klosterneuburg, Lower Austria, Austria, 1994-96; head sleep lab., Lower Austria, 1991. Mem. Austrian Soc. Lung Disease and Tuberculosis. Conservative Party. Roman Catholic. Home: Bauerngasse 26, 2435 Ebergassing Lower Austria, Austria Office: Stadtplatz 4, 3400 Klosterneuburg Austria

SZEFLER, STANLEY JAMES, pediatrics and pharmacology educator; b. Buffalo, Aug. 24, 1948; s. Stanley and Bernice Laura (Platt) S.; m. Christine M. Drezek, Dec. 26, 1970; children: David, Paul. BS, SUNY, Buffalo, 1971, MD, 1975. Resident pediatrics Children's Hosp. Buffalo, 1975-77; postdoctoral fellow in clin. pharmacology and allergy immunology SUNY, Buffalo, 1977-79, asst. prof. pediatrics and pharmacology, 1979-82; assoc. prof. pediatrics and pharmacology U. Colo., Denver, 1982-90, prof. pediatrics, pharmacology, 1990—; dir. clin. pharmacology Children's Hosp., Buffalo, 1979-82, Nat. Jewish Ctr. for Immunology and Respiratory Medicine, Denver, 1982—. Contbr. articles to profl. jours. Mem. steering com. asthma camp for children Am. Lung Assn., Denver, 1987—. Maj. USAR, 1979-88. NIH grantee, 1980-84, 90—, FDA grantee, Denver, 1988-91. Fellow Am. Acad. Allergy, Asthma and Immunology (chmn. asthma, rhinitis and respiratory disease interest sect.), Am.Acad. Pediats. (liaison mem. com. drugs). Office: Nat Jewish Ctr Dept Immunology/Respiratory Med 1400 Jackson St Denver CO 80206-2761

SZÉKELY, EUGENIA E., phlebotomist; b. Mexico City, Oct. 16, 1963; came to U.S., 1973; d. Luis Mauricio and Mary Louise (Davis) S. BS in Zoology cum laude, U. Mass., 1990; postgrad., Tufts U., 1996. EMT, Mass.; cert. paramedic, Calif. Lifeguard Marriott Hotel, Newton, Mass., 1980-82; EMT Chaulk Ambulance, Boston, 1982-83; paramedic Medevac Ambulance, L.A., 1984, Mobile Life Support/County of San Mateo, Calif., 1984-85, Baystate Ambulance, Malden, Mass., 1985-88, Chaulk Ambulance, Waltham and Newton, Mass., 1988-91; phlebotomist Damon Labs. Hyde Park Patient Svc. Ctr., 1992—; resident 1st yr. MacAllen Family Practice, Tex. Commonwealth scholar U. Mass., 1990. Mem. AMA, Mass. Med. Assn. Address: 83-1 Staniford St Newton MA 02166

SZEREMETA-BROWAR, TAISA LYDIA, endodontist; b. Geneva, N.Y., Mar. 21, 1957; d. Swiatoslaw Bohdan and Stefania (Melnyk) Szeremeta; m. Andrew Wolodymyr Browar, Sept. 19, 1981. BS in Dentistry, Case Western Res. U., 1978, DDS, 1980; cert. specialty endodontics magna cum laude, U. Ill., Chgo., 1982. Pvt. practice Hinsdale (Ill.) Periodontics and Endodontics, 1982—; asst. clin. prof. Northwestern U. Dental Sch., Chgo., 1986—. Counselor, mem. Plast-Ukrainian Scouting, 1963—; presenting team Worldwide Marriage Encounter, Chgo., 1985-94; mem. parish coun. Sts. Volodymyr and Olha, Chgo., 1985-94. E. Wach rsch. grantee U Ill., Chgo., 1980. Mem. ADA, Am. Assn. Endodontists, Am. Coll. Stomatologic Surgeons, Ukrainian Med. Assn. (chair membership 1983-88), Ill. Assn. Endodontists (pres. 1990-91), Ill. State Dental Soc., Chgo. Dental Soc. (sec. table clinic 1990, vice chair 1991, chair 1992), Hinsdale C. of C. Ukrainian Catholic. Office: Hinsdale Periodontics & Endodontics 40 S Clay St Ste 111W Hinsdale IL 60521-3257

SZILAGYI, D(ESIDERIUS) EMERICK, surgeon, researcher, educator; b. Nagykaroly, Hungary, June 20, 1910; came to U.S., naturalized, 1931; m. Martha Evelyn Fowlkes Harper (dec.); children: Martha, Christine; m. Sally Bolton, 1989. Diploma, Calvinist Coll., Klausenburg, Hungary, 1928; exam., U. Paris-Sorbonne; student, U. Debrecen; MD, U. Mich., 1935, MS, 1940; MD (hon.), Semmelweis Med. U., Budapest, Hungary, 1988. Diplomate Am. Bd. Surgery. Intern U. Mich. Hosp., Ann Arbor, 1935-36, asst. resident in surgery, 1936-37, instr. pathology, 1937-39; asst. resident in surgery Henry Ford Hosp., Detroit, 1939-42, chief resident, 1945, asst. surgeon, 1945-46, assoc. surgeon, 1946-49, chief div. II gen. surgery, 1949-66, chmn. dept. surgery, 1966-75, cons. vascular surgery, 1975—, chief of staff, 1968-71; emeritus clin. prof. surgery U. Mich. Med. Sch., Ann Arbor; dir. med. dept. Ford Rubber Plantations, Para, Brazil, 1942-45; Edwin A. Jarecki Meml. lectr. Albert Einstein Med. Ctr., Phila., 1964; David W. Yandell lectr. U. Louisville Med. Sch., 1973; William Mayo lectr. U. Mich., 1978; Matas Meml. lectr. XV Internat. Congress of Internat. Cardiovascular Soc., Athens, Greece, 1981. Editor Jour. Vascular Surgery, 1983—; contbr. articles to profl. jours. Mem. ACS, AMA, Am. Fedn. Clin. Rsch., Am. Surg. Assns., Am. Thyroid Assn., Ctrl. Surg. Assn. (past pres.), Internat. Soc. Cardiovascular Surgery (past chpt. pres.), Internat. Soc. Surgery, Midwestern Vascular Surg. Soc. (past pres.), Soc. Vascular Surgery (past pres.), Western Surg. Assn. (past v.p., pres.), Detroit Acad. Surgery, Detroit Surg. Assn., Mich. Med. Soc., Wayne County Med. Soc.; hon. mem. Sociedad Argentina de Angiologia, Sociedad Columbiana de Angiologia, Royal Australasian Coll. Surgeons, Deutsche Gesellschaft für Gefässchirurgie, Hungarian Soc. of Angiology. Home: 1008 Stratford Pl Bloomfield Hills MI 48304-2934 Office: Henry Ford Hosp 2799 W Grand Blvd Detroit MI 48202-2608

SZIRMAI, ENDRE ANREAS FRANZ, physician, writer; b. Budapest, Hungary, Aug. 21, 1922; s. Károly Péter and Erzsébet R. (Schwartz) S.; Dr.med., MD, Med. U. Szeged, Hungary, 1947; D in Sci. Medicine, PhD, Kobe U., Tokyo, 1961; Dr. med. lic., Innenministerium, Stuttgart, Germany, 1962; numerous hon. degrees from France, Hungary, Germany, Netherlands, Spain, U.S., Chile, Japan, Brazil, Ceylon, Mex., India, Italy, Can., Poland, Australia, USSR, New Zealand, Eng., others; m. Ilona Mikes, Feb. 13, 1945; children: Marta, Andrea. Specialist in lab. internal medicine, clin. pathology, biochemistry, nuclear and gen. hematology, ob-gyn, oncology, myology, hon. prof., 1954—; chmn. dept. nuclear hematology Inst. Nuclear Engring. and assoc. univs., London, 1960, Stuttgart, 1966—; prof. Univ. O.M.H. Sci , Des Moines, Iowa, 1965—, U. Louisville, 1975—, U. San Diego, 1985—, U.S. Internat. U.; dir. Inst. Stress Mgmt.; elected cons. Min. Sci. Zagreb, Croatia; founder Szirmai Archives; pres. bd. advisors Nobel Sci. Found., 1992. Proposed for Nobel Prize, 1969; recipient Letter of Appreciation Min. Sci. Croatia; Commemorative plaque Okayama U., Japan, others. Fellow Inst. Nuclear Engring. and Coll. Angiology of N.Y., Royal Soc. Medicine, Royal Soc. Chemists; mem. Internat. Nomenclature Com. (pres.), Germ. Ph. Acad. Sci., Hungarian Acad. Scis., Italian Acad. Scis., N.Y. Acad. Scis., Mex. Acad. Gerontology (hon.), also numerous med., nuclear, and lit. assns. Author books, poetry and novels transl. into 35 langs., numerous abstracts in 49 langs., publs. on med. atomic energy, linguistic arts; editorial bd. several jours.; research biochem. methods, drugs; developer myotonometer, angiomyograph, myograph, utero-embryo cardiotonograph, electrocoagulometer; developer theories in medicine, philosophy, music and art; established Rutherford Szirmai prize Szirmai Univ. Found.; Szirmai archives established librs. worldwide. Address: Adolf-Kroener Str 11, D-70184 Stuttgart Germany

SZIRMAI, JAN ALEXANDER, cell biologist; b. Ket, Czechoslovakia, Mar. 18, 1925; s. Jan and Helena (Concha) S.; m. Elsken Heesen, Apr. 11, 1952 (div. 1976); children: Henriette, Julia, Elena, Alexander; m. Mia de Gier, May 9, 1977. MD, U. Amsterdam, 1952, PhD, 1954. Assoc. prof. med. U. Bratislava, Czechoslovakia, 1945-47, U. Amsterdam, 1947-54; rsch. assoc. Inst. for Rheumatism Rsch., Leiden, The Netherlands, 1955-56; dir. Inst. for Rheumatism Rsch., Leiden, 1965-71; prof. med. U. Rotterdam, The Netherlands, 1966-68, U. Leiden, 1963-76. Contbr. over 70 articles to profl. jours. in bio-med. field. Recipient Izaak Korteweg and Anna Ida Overwaterfonds Netherland award for Med. Rsch., 1966. Mem. Netherlands Soc. for Histochemistry (founding mem., sec. 1960-65), Netherlands Soc. for Cell Biology (pres. 1965-69). Home: Beelaertslaan 16, 6861 AV Oosterbeek The Netherlands

SZIROVECZ, STEPHEN MICHAEL, optometrist; b. East Chicago, Ind., May 23, 1967; s. Michael Stephen Jr. and Alice Joan (Richards) S.; m. Brenda Kay Weirich, Sept. 3, 1994. BS in Optometry, Ind. U., 1989, OD, 1992. Diagnostic therapeutic cert. Ga. Bd. Optometry. Resident in ocular disease Omni Eye Svcs., Atlanta, 1992-93, staff optometrist, 1993—; adj. faculty in field, 1993—; lectr. in field. Mem. Am. Optometric Assn. (contact lens sect.), Ga. Optometric Assn., Ind. U. Alumni Assn., Golden Key Internat. Honor Soc., Alpha Lambda Delta. Office: Omni Eye Svcs Atlanta Ste 300 5505 Peachtree Dunwoody Rd Atlanta GA 30342 Office: 1800 Phoenix Blvd Ste 406 Atlanta GA 30349

SZYDLOWSKI, THADDEUS RAYMOND, physician; b. Shenandoah, Pa., Aug. 31, 1947; s. Thaddeus Francis and Leona (Jurewicz) S.; m. Susan Marion Mathews, Apr. 14, 1973; children: Kristen, Ellen. BS, Albright Coll., 1968; MD, Jefferson Med. Coll., 1972. Diplomate Am. Bd. Internal Medicine and Gastroenterology. Intern in internal medicine Reading (Pa.) Hosp., 1972-73; resident in internal medicine Abington (Pa.) Hosp., 1973-75; fellow in hepatology N.J. Coll. Medicine, Newark, 1975-76; fellow in gastroenterology Lankenau Hosp., Phila., 1976-77; staff physician Naval Regional Med. Ctr., Portsmouth, Va., 1977-79; physician Lebanon (Pa.) Internal Medicine Specialist, 1979—. Lt. comdr. USNR, 1977-79. Fellow Am. Coll. Gastroenterology, ACP; mem. AMA, Am. Soc. Gastrointestinal Endoscopy, Pa. Soc. Gastroenterology, Am. Gastroent. Assn., Bocus Alumni Internat. Soc. Gastroenterology. Home: 212 Spring Hill Ln Lebanon PA 17042-9055 Office: Lebanon Internal Medicine 508 Oak St Lebanon PA 17042-6245

SZYMANSKI, EDNA MORA, rehabilitation psychology and special education educator; b. Caracas, Venezuela, Mar. 19, 1952; came to U.S., 1952; d. José Angel and Helen Adele (McHugh) Mora; m. Michael Bernard, Mar. 30, 1973. BS, Rensselaer Poly. Inst., 1972; MS, U. Scranton, 1974; PhD, U. Tex., 1988. Cert. rehab. counselor. Vocat. evaluator Mohawk Valley Workshop, Utica, N.Y., 1974-75; vocat. rehab. counselor N.Y. State Office Vocat. Rehab., Utica, N.Y., 1975-80; sr. vocat. rehab. counselor N.Y. State Office Vocat. Rehab., Utica, 1980-87; rsch. assoc. U. Tex., Austin, 1988-89; asst. prof. U. Wis., Madison, 1989-91, assoc. prof., 1991-93, assoc. dean sch. edn., 1993—, dir. rehab. rsch. and tng. ctr., 1993-96, prof. rehab. psychology and spl. edn., 1993—; cons. Rsch. Assocs. Syracuse, N.Y., 1988-90. Co-author various book chpts.; co-editor: Rehabilitation Counseling Basics and Beyond, 1992; co-editor Work and Disability, 1996, Rehabilitation Counseling Bull., 1994—; contbr. articles to profl. jours. Mem. Pres.'s Com. on Employment of People with Disabilities, Washington, 1987—. Recipient Rsch. award Am. Assn. Counselor Edn. and Supr., 1991. Mem. ACA (chair rsch. com. 1992-94, Rsch. awards 1990, 93, 95), Am. Rehab. Counseling Assn. (pres. 1985-86, Rsch. award 1989, 94), Coun. Rehab. Edn. (chair rsch. com. 1990-95, v.p. 1993-95), Nat. Coun. Rehab. Edn. (chair rsch. com. 1992—, Rehab. Edn. Rschr. of Yr. 1993, New Career in Rehab. Edn. award 1990). Office: U Wis Dept Rehab Psychology and Spl Edn 432 N Murray St Madison WI 53706-1407

SZYMANSKI, THEODORE J., JR., physician; b. Detroit, Sept. 3, 1956; s. Theodore J. and Congetta (Parisi) S. BS, Mich. State U., 1978, DO, 1981. Diplomate Am. Bd. Emergency Medicine, Am. Bd. Osteo. Emergency Medicine. Vice-chmn. emergency svcs. St. Luke's Hosp.-Mayo Clinic, Jacksonville, Fla., 1984-88, chmn. emergency svcs., 1988—; assoc. prof. Mayo Med. Sch. Fellow Am. Coll. Emergency Physicians; mem. Am. Coll. Exec. Physicians, Phi Kappa Phi. Office: 4201 Belfort Rd Jacksonville FL 32216-1431

TABATZNIK, BERNARD, physician, educator; b. Mir, Poland, Jan. 8, 1927; came to U.S., 1959, naturalized, 1966; s. Max and Fay (Ginsberg) T.; m. Marjorie Turner, Jan. 8, 1956; children: Darron Mark, Keith Donald, Ilana Wendy; m. Charline Edwards Harmon, Aug. 7, 1992. B.Sc., U. Witwatersrand, South Africa, 1945; M.B., B.Ch., 1949. Intern Baragwanath Hosp., Johannesburg, South Africa, 1950-51, Hillingdon Hosp., Ashford Hosp., also research unit Canadian Red Cross Meml. Hosp., Taplow, Eng., 1951-54; med. registrar Ashford Hosp., 1954-56, Johannesburg Gen. Hosp., 1956-58; physician Baragwanath Hosp., 1958-59; fellow medicine Johns Hopkins Sch. Medicine, 1959-60, fellow cardiology, 1960-61, asst. prof. medicine, 1966—; head cardiopulmonary div. Sinai Hosp., Balt., 1961-72; asso. chief medicine Sinai Hosp., 1964-72; chief cardiology dept. North Charles Gen. Hosp., Balt., 1972; also dir. med. edn., dir. Postgrad. Inst., coordinator ambulatory services; med. dir. Nurse Practitioner-Physician Asst. Program, Ch. Hosp., Balt., 1987-90. Contbr. articles to profl. jours. Recipient Save-A-Heart Humanitarian award, 1977, Maimonides award, 1983, Shaarei Zion Humanitarian award, 1987. Fellow Royal Coll. Physicians (London); mem. South African Cardiac Soc., Am. Heart Assn., Md. Heart Assn. (chmn. health careers 1964-66), Laennec Cardiovascular Sound Group. Home: HC 3 Box 180 Monterey VA 24465-9313 Office: 8417 Bellona Ln Baltimore MD 21204-2014

TABAU, ROBERT LOUIS, rheumatologist, researcher; b. Marseille, France, May 10, 1928; s. Victor and Valentine Tabau; m. Mireille Thonney de Blonay, Sept. 18, 1962; children: Laurence, Valerie, Herve. Grad., Faculty Pharmacy Marseille, 1950, D of Pharmacology, 1952; MS, U. Aix-Marseille, France, 1950; MD, Faculty Medicine Marseille, 1959, M of Human Biology, 1960, diploma in human biology rsch. Cert. specialist in rheumatology, med. biology, thermal, climatic and nuclear medicine, homéopathie and acupuncture. Chief doctor U. Med. Clin. Ctr. Hosp. U. Vaudois, Lausanne, Switzerland, 1961-62; pvt. practice in rheumatology, thermal and climatic medicine Aix Les Bains, France, 1962—; rsch. worker, then rsch. supr. Nat. Inst. for Health and Med. Rsch., France, 1965; dir. rsch. ctr. in osteoarticulary pathology Nat. Inst. for Health and Med. Rsch., Marseille, 1965-79; asst. ctrl. lab. Hosp. de Conception, Marseille, 1952-56, head lab. of functional explorations, 1958-65; asst. radiobiology lab. Ctr. de Lutte contre Cancer, Marseille, 1953-57; med. cons. Hosps. in Marseille Ctr. Rheumatology, 1970-75; master rschr. and med. counselor Auvergne Thermale, Rhone Alpes Thermal. Co-author: Applied Radiations and Isotopes, 1957, Cesium 137 in Téléthé rapie, 1963, Goutte and Lithiase Urique, 1964, L'osteoporose, 1964, La Polyarthrite Rhumatoide, 1965; reporter various med. confs. and symposia. Named Chevalier for work in insecticides and pesticides Nat. Inst. Agronomic Rsch., 1966, Chevalier for svcs. to Edn. Govt. of France, 1980, Officer, Palmes Academiques, 1990, Chevalier Nat. Order of Merit, 1980, Officier, 1986, Chevalier Nat. Order legion of honor. Mem. French Chem. Soc., Barseille Soc. Pharmacis, Soc. Biology, Soc. Functional Medicine (hon.), Lyonais Group Med. Studies, Internat. Ctr. Auricular Medicine and Ancupuncture, European Coun. Drs. for Plurality in Medicine Brussels, Cir. of Rhematologists, French Soc. Clin and Biol. Rsch. (chmn. 1980—), Protuguese Inst. Rheumatology (hon.), Rotary (chmn. 1994—). Address: 23 Chem BELLEVUE. 73100 Aix les Bains France Office: Le Chambord 3 Roche du Roi, 73100 Aix les Bains France

TABBY, DAVID STUART, neurologist; m. Sara Ellen Marks; children: Dallas Heather, Ilana Zipporah, Genevieve Louise and Sabrina Carlotta (twins). AB, Princeton U., 1980; DO, Phila. Coll. Osteo. Medicine, 1984. Intern Met. Hosp. Parkview Divsn., Phila., 1984-85; resident Thomas Jefferson U. Hosp., Phila., 1985-87, chief resident, 1988; instr., lectr. neurology, cons. attending Jefferson Med. Coll. and Thomas Jefferson U. Hosp., Phila., 1988—; divsn. chmn., attending physician Parkview Hosp., Phila., 1988—; asst. prof., neurology, dept. internal medicine Phila. Coll. Osteo. Medicine, 1989—; attending physician Albert Einstein Med. Ctr., Phila., 1989—, Moss Rehab. Hosp., Phila., 1989—; sect. head neurology, attending physician Episcopal Hosp., Phila., 1990—; dir. Episcopal Memory Disorder Ctr., 1992—; attending physician Germantown (Pa.) Hosp., 1993—; instr. neurology Med. Coll. Pa. and Hahnemann U., Phila., 1995—; presenter and lectr. in field. Rsch. grantee Nat. Inst. Aging, 1992—, Consortium to Establish a Registry for Alzherimer's Disease, 1992-95, Parke-Davis Med. Rsch., 1993, 94—, Esai, America, 1993-95; recipient Sidney M. Kanev award Am. Coll. Neuropsychiatrists, 1989, Spl. recognition Alzheimer's Assn., Greater Phila. chpt., 1994. Mem. Am. Osteo. Assn., Am. Acad. Osteo. Neurologists and Psychiatrists, Am. Acad. Neurology, Pa. Osteo. Med. Assn., Phila. Neurol. Soc., Greater Phila. Pain Soc., Physicians for Social Responsibility, Thomas Jefferson U. Neurology Alumni Assn. Office: Episcopal Med Arts Bldg Ste 208 100 E Lehigh Ave Philadelphia PA 19125 also: Parkview Med Office Bldg Ste 3070 1331 E Wyoming Ave Philadelphia PA 19124

TABIBI, S. ESMAIL, pharmaceutical researcher, educator; b. Khoy, Iran, May 26, 1945; came to U.S., 1978; s. S. Ebrahim and Sharifeh Tabibi; m. Shahnaz Rahaie, Mar. 28, 1975; children: Shahrzad, Shirazeh, Shabnam. PharmD, U. Tabriz, Iran, 1969; PhD, U. Md., Balt., 1982. Lab. scientist I biochemistry dept. U. Md., 1979-82; vis. fellow Nat. Cancer Inst., Bethesda, Md., 1982-83; rsch. assoc. Roxane Labs., Inc., Columbus, Ohio, 1983-86; dir. pharm. R & D, H.G. Pars Pharm. Lab., Inc., Cambridge, Mass., 1986; dir. pharm. R & D MediControl Corp., Newton, Mass., 1986-89, v.p. R & D, 1989-90; v.p. R & D, mem. sci. adv. bd. Micro Vesicular Systems, Inc., Nashua, N.H., 1990-92; assoc. prof. pharms. dept. U. R.I., Kingston, 1992-93; project officer PRB, NCI, NIH, 1993—; adj. assoc. prof. Mass. Coll. Pharmacy, Boston, 1989-93; mem. sci. adv. bd. Cell Rsch. Corp., Newton, 1989-93; mem. equal employment opportunity adv. group Nat. Cancer Inst., 1996—. Contbr. articles to sci. jours., chpt. to book. Vice chmn. PTO, Chelmsford, Mass., 1991. Mem. Am. Pharm. Assn., Am. Assn. Pharm. Scientists (chmn. publ./newsletter com., biotech. sect. 1995—), Controlled Release Soc., Rho Chi. Office: Nat Cancer Inst-NIH Pharm Resources Br 6130 Executive Blvd Rockville MD 20852-4910

TABOR, EDWARD, physician, researcher; b. Washington, Apr. 30, 1947; married; 4 children. BA, Harvard U., 1969; MD, Columbia U., 1973. Intern and resident Columbia-Presbyn. Med. Ctr., N.Y.C., 1973-75; rsch. investigator Bur. Biologics, Bethesda, Md., 1975-83; dir. divsn. anti-infective drug products FDA, Rockville, Md., 1983-88; assoc. dir. for biol. carcinogenesis Nat. Cancer Inst./NIH, Bethesda, 1988-95; dir. divsn. transfusion transmitted diseases FDA, Bethesda and Rockville, Md., 1995—. Contbr. articles to more than 200 publs. Capt. USPHS, 1975—. Office: FDA/CBER HFM-310 1401 Rockville Pike Rockville MD 20852-1448

TABRISKY, JOSEPH, radiologist, educator; b. Boston, June 23, 1931; s. Henry and Gertrude Tabrisky; BA cum laude, Harvard U., 1952; MD cum laude, Tufts U., 1956; m. Phyllis Eleanor Page, Apr. 23, 1955; children: Joseph Page, Elizabeth Ann, William Page. Flexible intern U. Ill. Hosp., 1956-57; resident in radiology Fitzsimons Army Hosp., 1958-60; instr. radiology Tufts U. Med. Sch., 1964-65; cons. radiologist Swedish Med. Center, Denver, 1966-68; chief radiologist Kaiser Found. Hosp., Harbor City, Calif., 1968-72; mem. faculty UCLA Med. Sch., 1972—, prof. radiol. scis., 1975-92, prof emeritus, 1993—, vice chmn. dept., 1976-92 , exec. policy com. radiol. scis.; chmn. radiology dept. Harbor-UCLA Med. Ctr., 1975-92 , pres. faculty soc., 1979-80, exec. dir. MR/CT Imaging Ctr., bd. dirs. Rsch. Ednl. Inst., Harbor Collegium/UCLA Found.; chief exec. officer Vascular Biometrics Inc.; steering com. Harvard U., 1952; cons. L.A. County Dept. Pub. Health; chmn. L.A. County Radiol. Standards Com., 1979. Mem. Harvard-Radcliffe Schs. Com.; chmn., bd. dirs., treas., Harbor-UCLA Med. Found.; chmn.

UCLA Coun. for Ednl. Devel. Maj. M.C., U.S. Army, 1957-63. Recipient Silver Knight award Nat, Mgmt, Assn., 1992. Diplomate Am. Bd. Radiology. Fellow Am. Coll. Radiology, Univ. Radcom Assn. (chief exec. officer 1987-89); mem. Radiol. Soc. N. Am., Calif. Med. Assn., Calif. Radiol. Soc., L.A. Med. Assn., L.A. Radiol. Soc., Alpha Omega Alpha. Contbr. articles to med. jours. Office: 1000 W Carson St Torrance CA 90502-2004

TABRISKY, PHYLLIS PAGE, physiatrist, educator; b. Newton, Mass., Aug. 28, 1930; d. Joseph Westley and Alice Florence (Wainwright) Page; m. Joseph Tabrisky, Apr. 23, 1955; children: Joseph Page, Elizabeth Ann, William Page. BS, Douglass Coll., 1952; MD, Tufts U., 1956. Cert. phys. medicine and rehab. Intern U. Ill. Hosp., Chgo., 1956-57; phys. medicine and rehab. residency U. Colo. Sch. Medicine, Denver, 1958-60; gen. med. officer dept. pediatrics and medicine Coco Solo Hosp., Panama Canal Zone, 1961-62; staff physician dept. pediatrics Ft. Hood (Tex.) Army Hosp., 1963; instr. dept. rehab. medicine Boston (Mass.) U. Sch. Medicine, 1964-66; asst. prof. phys. medicine and rehab. U. Colo. Sch. Medicine, Denver, 1966-68; staff physician VA Med. Ctr., Long Beach, Calif., 1968-71; acting chief phys. medicine and rehab. VA Med. Ctr., Long Beach, 1971-73, asst. chief rehab. med. svcs., 1973-91, chief phys. medicine & rehab. svc., 1992—; asst. clin. prof. phys. medicine and rehab. U. Calif. Coll. Medicine, Irvine, 1970-75, assoc. clin. prof., 1975-80, prof., 1980—, vice chair dept. phys. medicine and rehab., 1985—, dir. residency tng., 1982—. Fellow Am. Acad. Phys. Medicine and Rehab. (mem. accreditation coun. grad. med. com. 1993—); mem. Am. Congress Rehab. Medicine, Assn. Acad. Physiatrists (bd. trustees 1995-97), Alpha Omega Alpha. Republican. Episcopalian. Office: VA Med Ctr 5901 E 7th St Long Beach CA 90822-5201

TACAL, JOSE VEGA, JR., public health official, veterinarian; b. Ilocos Sur, Philippines, Sept. 5, 1933; came to U.S., 1969; s. Jose Sr. and Cristina (Vega) T.; m. Lilia Caccam, 1959; children: Joyce, Jasmin, Jose III. DVM, U. Philippines, Quezon City, 1956; diploma, U. Toronto, 1964. Diplomate Am. Coll. Vet. Preventive Medicine; lic. vet., Calif. Provincial veterinarian Philippine Bur. Animal Industry, Manila, 1956-57; instr. vet. medicine U. Philippines, Quezon City, 1957-64, asst. prof., chmn. dept. vet. microbiology, pathology and pub. health, 1965-69; pub. health veterinarian San Bernardino (Calif.) County Dept. Pub. Health, 1970-83, sr. pub. health veterinarian, program mgr., sect. chief, 1984—; zoonotic diseases lectr. Calif. State U., San Bernardino, spring 1984; lectr. U. Calif. Extension, Riverside, spring, 1985; vis. prof. vet. pub. health U. Philippines at Los Banos, Laguna, 1988. Columnist L.A. Free Press, 1991, Pilipinas Times, 1993, Mabuhay Times, 1994-95; contbr. more than 50 articles to profl. jours. Pres. Filipino Assn. of San Bernardino County, Highland, Calif., 1979; charter mem. Greater Inland Empire Filipino Assn., Highland, 1986—; del. First Filipino Media Conf. N.Am., L.A., 1993. Recipient Donald T. Fraser Meml. medal U. Toronto, 1964, Cert. of Merit, Philippine Vet. Med. Assn., 1965, Cert. of Appreciation Calif. State Bd. Examiners in Vet. Medicine, 1979, 84, Cert. of Recognition, Congressman George E. Brown Jr., 42d Congl. Dist. Calif., 1994, Assemblyman Joe Baca, 62d Assembly Dist., Calif. State Legis., 1994, Colombo Plan Study fellow Can./Philippine Govts., 1963-64. Mem. AAAS, AVMA, Orange Belt Vet. Med. Assn., Western Poultry Disease Conf., Soc. for the Advancement of Rsch., Phi Kappa Phi, Phi Sigma. Office: San Bernardino County Dept Pub Health 351 N Mountain View Ave San Bernardino CA 92415-0010

TACHÉ, YVETTE FRANCE, medical research educator; b. Lyon, Rhone, France, Feb. 1, 1945; came to U.S., 1982; d. Lucien Joseph and Jeanne Marthe (Fouillat) Laurent; m. Jean Arthur Taché, June 1970 (dec. 1979); children: Stéphanie, Véronique. Baccalauréat, Lycee, Tarare, France, 1965; Maitrise, Faculty of Scis. U. C. Bernard, Lyon, 1968, DEA, 1969; PhD, U. Montreal, Que., Can., 1974. Asst. researcher U. Montreal, 1977-78, asst. research prof., 1980-81, assoc. research prof., 1981-82; assoc. prof. in residence UCLA, 1982-85, prof. medicine in residence, 1985—; vis. scientist Salk Inst., La Jolla, Calif., 1978-80; mem. selection com. Med. REsearch Council, Montreal, 1982. External referee Specialized Sci. Jours., 1977—, Med. Research Council, Quebec, 1981—; editl. bd. mem. Gastroenterology, Am. Jour. Physiology, Digestion Peptides, others; contbr. articles to profl. jours. Fellow MRC, Med. Research Council Que., Montreal and Ottawa, Can., 1974-78; centenial fellow MRC, Ottawa, 1978-80, scholar MRC, Ottawa, 1982; grantee FMRCQ, MRC, NIH, 1977—; Research Scientist award NIMH, 1988; named UCLA Woman of Sci., 1989. Mem. NIH (study sect. 1991-95, Merit award 1995—), Internat. Soc. Psychoneuroendocrinology, Endocrine Soc., Soc. Neurosci., Am. Physiol. Soc., Am. Gastroenterol. Soc., Hans Selye Found. (v.p. 1984), N.Y. Acad. Sci. Office: CURE VA Wadsworth Bldg 115 Rm 203 11301 Wilshire Blvd Los Angeles CA 90073

TACKEL, IRA S., biomedical engineer, consultant; b. N.Y.C., Apr. 3, 1954; s. Herman William and Aida (Link) T.; m. Sherry Dee Melker, Aug. 28, 1977; children—Elana Rachael, Joshua Chad. B.S. in Biomed. Engring., Rensselaer Poly. Inst., 1976, M in Biomed. Engring., 1977; postgrad. in intensive and coronary care units George Washington U., 1978, Emergency Care Research Inst., 1979, Ind. U. Sch. Medicine, 1979. Mech. engr. Olin Corp., chem. div., Lake Charles, La., 1974; biomed. engr. Helen Hayes Hosp., West Haverstraw, N.Y., 1975, Vets. Hosp., Albany, N.Y., 1976-77; dir. dept. clin. engring. Hosp. of U. Pa., Phila., 1977-85; dir. dept. biomed. instrumentation Thomas Jefferson U. Hosp., Phila., 1985—; cons. Biosonics, Inc., Phila., 1982-86, Integrated Techs. Resource Corp., 1983—; adj. faculty Temple U., Phila., 1979—, Drexel U., Phila., 1981—. Mem. editorial bd. Emergency Care Research Inst.-Health Devices, 1982—. Contbr. articles to profl. jours. Mem. Assn. Advancement Med. Instrumentation (mem. bd. dirs.), IEEE (Engring. Medicine and Biology), Phila. Area Med. Instrumentation Assn. (pres. 1982), Am. Hosp. Assn., Am. Soc. Hosp. Engrs. Home: 1327 Barton Dr Fort Washington PA 19034-1654 Office: Thomas Jefferson U Hosp 129 S 9th St Philadelphia PA 19107-5112

TACKETT, RANDALL L., pharmacology and toxicology educator; b. Jacksonville, Fla., Dec. 7, 1954; s. Roy Curtis and Elizabeth (Collier) T.; m. Ann Marie Aspinwall, Feb. 1, 1974; children: Laura Marie, Allison Lynn. BS, Jacksonville U., 1975; MS, Auburn U., 1977; PhD, U. Ga., 1979. Postdoctoral fellow Med. U. S.C., Charleston, 1979-81; asst. prof. U. Ga., Athens, 1981-85, assoc. prof., 1986-95, head dept. pharmacology, 1989-95, prof., 1995—; vis. sci. in exptl. biology Fedn. Am. Socs. Exptl. Biology Minority Access to Rsch. Careers, Miami, Fla., 1994. Contbr. articles to profl. jours. Mem. Am. Heart Assn. (mem. peer rev. com. 1992—, mem. circulation coun. 1994—, Grantee 1993-95), Internat. Soc. Hypertension in Blacks, Fedn. Am. Soc. Experimental Biology, Phi Delta Chi (advisor 1986—, Tchr. of Yr. 1983-84), Phi Kappa Phi. Office: U Ga Coll Pharmacy Athens GA 30602

TACKWELL, ELIZABETH MILLER, social worker; b. Caney, Kans., Mar. 14, 1923; d. Jesse Winfield and Mattie (Shuler) Miller; m. Joseph J. Tackwell, Dec. 13, 1946 (dec. Mar. 1988); children: Steven, Tiana Tackwell David, Christy Tackwell Reyner. BA, U. Okla., 1953, MSW, 1962. Bd. cert. diplomate Am. Bd. Examiners in Clin. Social Work; lic. social worker, Okla. Social worker Dept. Pub. Welfare, Tulsa/Cleve./Okla. County, Okla., 1958-59; med. social analyst Dept. Pub. Welfare, Okla., 1960-61; assoc. John Massey M.D. Clinic, Oklahoma City, 1964-69; clin. asst. prof. Okla. U. Sch. Social Work, Oklahoma City, 1964—; asst. prof., clin. instr. dept. psychiatry/behavioral scis. Okla. U. Health Scis. Ctr., Oklahoma City, 1963—; psychiat. social worker VA Med. Ctr., Oklahoma City, 1961—, chief mental health sect., 1976—, adminstrv. dir. day treatment ctr., 1993—; pvt. practice Oklahoma City, 1971—; VA Med. Ctr.; psychiat. surveyor Health Care Fin. Adminstrn., Dept. Human Svcs., Washington, 1985—. Recipient Svc. Commendation award DAV, 1980, Chi Omega Scholastic award, Awards Am. Ex-Prisoners of War, 1994, 95, 96. Mem. NASW (diplomate in clin. social work, pres. Okla. chpt. 1971-73, Social Worker of the Yr. Western Okla. chpt. 1975), Acad. Cert. Social Workers, Okla. Health and Welfare Assn. (conf. chmn. 1975—), Pi Gamma Mu. Home: 1328 Tarman Cir Norman OK 73071-4846 Office: Vets Affairs Med Ctr 921 NE 13th St Oklahoma City OK 73104-5007

TACTAC, ALBERT J., urologist; b. Lebanon, Feb. 19, 1927; came to U.S., 1953; s. Joseph and Catherine (Matook) T.; children: Catherine, Robert, James, Judith. MD, French Sch. of Medicine, Beirut, Lebanon, 1953. Diplomate Am. Bd. Urology. Pvt. practice, 1960—. Sponsor U.S. Support Group of Patient with Cancer of Prostate, Livonia, 1992—. Mem. AMA, ACS, Am. Urological Assn., Mich. State Med. Soc., Mich. Urological Soc., WCMS. Republican. Roman Catholic. Office: 15256 LeVan Rd Livonia MI 48154-5030

TAFELSKI, MICHAEL DENNIS, psychologist; b. Wyandotte, Mich., Apr. 12, 1949; s. Chester John and Veronica (Machcinski) T. BA in Sociology and Psychology, Wayne State U., 1973, MSW, 1975, MEd, 1976. Lic. med. social worker, Mich. Caseworker home attendent div. N.Y.C. Dept. Human Resouces, 1976-78; intake case mgr. Phoenix House Found., Inc., N.Y.C., 1978-81; ptnr. GR Social Svcs., Grand Rapids, Mich., 1982-84; founding ptnr. Tafelski, Tafelski & Gatz and predecessor firm Tafelski, Tafelski, Gatz & Robaskewicz, P.C., Grand Rapids, 1984—. Contbr. to Profl. Jour. of Social Work, 1984-86, DNC, 1992—. State of Mich. Higher Edn. grantee, Lansing, 1969. Mem. Polish Falcons Soc., KC (Grand Knight). Democrat. Roman Catholic. Office: Tafelski Tafelski Gatz 4254 Lamdale Ct SE Ste 9B Grand Rapids MI 49546-2403

TAFT, JOHN JOSEPH, counselor; b. Bklyn., Dec. 5, 1946; s. John Taft and Marie Eva Martineau; m. Susan M. Alfin (div. Nov. 1984); 1 child, Donna L.; m. Linda L. Bleecker, May 25, 1987. BS, C.W. Post Coll., 1993. Sr. dispatcher Village of Hempstead, N.Y., 1972-85; vets. counselor Nassau County, Plainview, N.Y., 1985—. Sgt. USMC, 1965-71. Decorated Purple Heart. Mem. VFW, DAV, Am. Legion, First Marine Divsn. Assn., Marine Corps League (past area vice commandant L.I. chpt., nat. chmn.), Mil. Order Devil Dogs (past pack leader, past pound keeper), Mil. Order Purple Heart, Nat. Amputation Found., Second Marine Divsn. Assn., Third Marine Divsn. Assn., Vets. Vietnam War, Vietnam Dog Handler Assn. (nat. v.p.). Home: 1261 Meadowbrook Rd North Merrick NY 11566-1512

TAFT, ROBERT MICHAEL, maxillofacial prosthodontist; b. Little Neck, N.Y., June 27, 1955; s. Robert Joseph and Georgette Marie (Danielson) T.; m. Camille Deanne Mancuso, June 12, 1980; children: Timothy, Christopher, Geoffrey. AS, Mohawk Valley C.C., 1975; BA, SUNY, Buffalo, 1977; DDS, Emory U., 1979; cert. in prosthodontics, Naval Dental Sch., 1990; cert. in maxillofacial prosthetics, Wilford Hall Med. Ctr., 1992. Diplomate Am. Bd. Prosthodontics. Sci. tchr. Grove Sch., Madison, Conn., 1977-79; commd. ens. USN, 1979, advanced through grades to comdr., 1994; clin. dir. USN, San Miguel, PI, 1984-86; prosthetic officer USN, Brunswick, Maine, 1986-88; lab. officer USN, Bethesda, Md., 1991-92; head maxillofacial prosthetics USN, San Diego, 1992—. Fellow Am. Acad. Maxillofacial Prosthetics (rschr. 1994), Am. Coll. Prosthodontists; mem. ADA, Am. Acad. Osseointegration. Home: 14660 Deerwood St Poway CA 92064 Office: Naval Med Ctr Bob Wilson Dr San Diego CA 92134

TAGER, MICHAEL GEORGE, urologist; b. Bklyn., Apr. 4, 1935; s. Harry L. and Rose B. (Brody) T.; m. Roberta Ann Kay, July 4, 1959; children: Jacqueline H., Elizabeth Stacey, Suzanne Kim. AB, Hamilton Coll., 1954; MD, N.Y. Med. Coll., 1958. Chief urology sect. Norwalk (Conn.) Hosp., 1972-80; urologist Urology Assocs. Norwalk. Recipient Air Def. Command Commendation medal USAF, 1962. Mem. ACS, Norwalk Med. Soc. (pres. 1978-79). Office: Urology Assocs Norwalk 12 Elmcrest Terr Norwalk CT 06850

TAGGART, LINDA DIANE, women's health nurse; b. Balt., June 14, 1940; d. Louis and Annie Helena (Heertje) Glick; divorced; 1 child, Keri Anne. AS in Nursing, Pensacola Jr. Coll., 1967; BA, U. West Fla., 1970; postgrad., St. Joseph's Coll., 1976-78. RN, Fla., Ala. Staff nurse Bapt. Hosp., Pensacola, Fla., 1967-70, head nurse, 1970-72; dir. in-svc. edn. Baycrest, Inc. Extended Care Facility, Pensacola, 1973, DON, 1973-74; DON Medica Media, Pensacola, 1974, clinic adminstr., 1974—; dir. Sex and Health Edn., Pensacola, 1974—; regional dir. Medica Media, ea. U.S., 1990; testified before Jud. com. U.S. Ho. of Reps., 1994 appeared on network Tv programs Dateline, 48 Hours, Turning Point, Nightline. Contbr.: The Gideon Project, 1993; contbr. articles to popular mags.; appeared on network TV programs including Dateline NBC, 48 Hours, Nightline, Turning Point, ABC, CNN. Bd. dirs. Rape Crisis Ctr., Pensacola, 1976-91, chair, 1980, 84, 89 (Addie Brooks award 1984); mem. exec. com. Lakeview Community Mental Health Ctr., Pensacola, 1989 (Expression of Appreciation award 1980-91). Recipient Pioneer/Heroe award Fla. Abortion Coun., 1989. Mem. NOW (Woman of Yr. award 1985, Women's Equity Day award 1986), NAFE, LWV, Am. Assn. Sex Educators, Counselors and Therapists (cert. sex educator), Religious Coalition for Reproductive Choice, People for Am. Way. Democrat. Presbyterian. Office: Medica Media 6770 N 9th Ave Pensacola FL 32504-7346

TAGLIARO, FRANCO, forensic pathologist; b. Verona, Italy, June 8, 1952; s. Remigio and Elsa (Zannoni) T.; m. Elena Saladino, Oct. 29, 1983; children: Chiara, Irene. Degree in medicine and surgery, U. Padua, 1978; degree in biochem. and clin. chem., U. Parma, 1981; degree in legal medicine, U. Verona, 1988. Asst. toxicol. lab. U. Brescia, Italy, 1978-80; from asst. to lectr. forensic medicine U. Verona Hosp., Italy, 1980—; vis. prof. grad. program forensic sci., dept. criminal justice, Sch. of Social and Behavioral Scis., U. Ala., Birmingham, 1994—. Editor: Developments in Analytical Methods in Pharmaceutical, Biomedical and Forensic Science, 1987; contbr. articles to profl. jours. Home: via Montorio 98, 37131 Verona Italy Office: Inst Forensic Medicine, Policlinico Borgo Roma, 37134 Verona Italy

TAHARA, EIICHI, pathologist, educator; b. Yokohama, Japan, July 19, 1936; s. Yoshinori and Sadako T.; m. Yoshie Shimamoto, Mar. 28, 1963; children: Hidetoshi, Makoto, Eiji. MD, Hiroshima U., 1963, PhD, 1968; dipolma nat. exam. dor med. practitioners. Asst. dept. pathology Hiroshima U. Sch. Medicine, 1968-72, asst. prof., 1972-77, assoc. prof., 1977-78, prof., chmn., 1978—; chief rsch. facilities for lab. animal sci. Hiroshima U., 1994—; councilor Hiroshima U., 1985-87; chief div. anatomical pathology Hiroshima U. Hosp., 1986-92; rep. Cancer Rsch. Project of Cancer Stromal Interaction, 1993—, Project of Gastric Intestinal Metaplasia, 1994—; chief rsch, fac, for lab. Animal Sci. of Hiroshima U., 1994—; mem. cancer Rsch. Project of genetic Instability in Human Cancer, 1994—. Author, editor: Gastric Cancer, 1993, Gann Monograph on Cancer Research, 1994; editor Differentiation, Jour. Cancer Rsch. and Clin. Oncology, Jour. Exptl. Therapeutics and Oncology, Jour. Pathology, Exptl. and Toxicologic Pathology, others; contbr. articles to profl. jours. Grantee Found. for Promotion Cancer Rsch., 1991, Princess Takamatsu Cancer Rsch. Fund, 1990, Ministry Health and Welfare, 1989-91, Ministry of Edn. Sci. and Cult., Japan, 1990-93, 94—; recipient award Hiroshima aMed. Assn., 1972. Mem. Interant. Soc. Differentiation (pres. elect 1994—, organizer 8th internat. conf. 1994), Japanese Soc. Pathology (bd. dirs. 1991-93, 95—), Japanese Cancer Assn. (dir., assoc. editor 1995—), Japanese Soc. for Gastric Cancer (sec.), Japan Soc. for Cancer Therapy (councilor), Hiroshima Soc. for Cancer Therapy (pres.), Japanisch-Deutsche Gesellschaft Hiroshima (v.p. 1990—), Hiroshima Humboldt Club (chmn.). Buddhist. Office: Hiroshima U Sch Medicine, 1-2-3 Kasumi Minami-ku, Hiroshima 734, Japan

TAICHMAN, NORTON STANLEY, pathology educator; b. Can., May 27, 1936; s. Louis and Frances (Kline) T.; m. Louise Sheffer, June 1, 1958; children: Russell, Susan, Darren, Leslie, Audrey. DDS, U. Toronto, 1961; Diploma in Periodontics, Harvard U., 1964; PhD, U. Toronto, 1967; MSc (hon.), U. Pa., 1972. Asst. prof. U. Toronto, 1967-69, assoc. prof., 1969-72; prof. pathology dept. sch. dental medicine U. Pa., Phila., 1972—, chmn. dept. pathology, 1972-95; assoc. dean acad. affairs, 1990-95. Recipient Birnberg award Columbia U., 1987, Disting. Alumnus award Harvard U., 1988. Mem. Internat. Assn. Dental Rsch. (Rsch. Basic Sci. award 1985), Am. Soc. Microbiology, Soc. for Leukocyte Biology. Office: U Pa Dept Dental Pathology 4010 Locust St Philadelphia PA 19104-6002

TAK, PAUL PETER, physician, educator; b. Hilversum, The Netherlands, Dec. 29, 1959; s. Paul and Johanna (Floor) T.; m. Danielle Marie Gerlag, Feb. 25, 1994; children: Olivier Paul, Willemijn Sophie. B cum laude, U. Amsterdam, 1982, M, 1984, MD cum laude, 1986; PhD, U. Leiden, The Netherlands, 1996. Resident Bronovo Hosp., The Hague, The Netherlands, 1986-90; fellow Leiden U. Hosp., 1990-93, clin. rschr., 1993-96, assoc. prof., 1996—; dir. MediPartners b.v., Leiden, 1991-96, mem. holding co., 1996—; mem. bd. VOAD, Amsterdam, 1993-95. Mem. Nederlandse Internisten Vereniging, Nederlandse Vereniging Voor Immunologie, Nederlandse Reumatologen Vereniging. Office: Leiden U Hosp, PO Box 9600, 2300 RC Leiden The Netherlands

TAKAHASHI, GARY WAYNE, internist, hematologist, oncologist; b. Honolulu, Jan. 2, 1959; s. Kenneth Kiyoshi and Grace Setsuko (Ishigure) T. BS in Math. and Biology, Stanford U., 1980; MS in Anatomy/Reproductive Biology, U. Hawaii, 1983; MD, John A. Burns Sch. Medicine, Honolulu, 1984. Diplomate Nat. Bd. Med. Examiners, Am. Bd. Internal Medicine (Hematology, Med. Oncology). Intern, resident Oreg. Health Scis. U., Portland, 1984-87; chief resident St. Vincent Med. Ctr., Portland, 1987-88; fellow hematology/oncology U. Wash., Seattle, 1988-93; physician Hematology Clinic, Seattle, 1993-94, Oreg. Hematology Oncology Assocs., 1994-95; clin. asst. prof. medicine Oreg. Health Scis. U., 1995—; clin. asst. prof. medicine Oreg. Health Scis. U., Portland, 1995—. Contbr. articles and abstracts to profl. publs. Recipient Achievement Rewards for Coll. Scientists scholarship, 1982, Merck, Sharp & Dohme Acad. award, 1982, Nat. Rsch. Svc. award fellowship NIH, 1990, March of Dimes Rsch. grant, 1993. Mem. Am. Coll. Physicians, Am. Soc. Hematology, Am. Soc. Clin. Oncology, Southwestern Oncology Group, Oreg. Med. Assn., Wash. Med. Assn., Oreg. Mycol. Soc. Office: Oreg Hematology Oncology Assocs 9155 SW Barnes Rd #530 Portland OR 97225

TAKAHASHI, JOSEPH S., neuroscientist; b. Tokyo, Dec. 16, 1951; s. Shigeharu and Hiroko (Hara) T.; m. Barbara Pillsbury Snook, June 28, 1985; children: Erika S., Matthew N. BA, Swarthmore (Pa.) Coll., 1974; PhD, U. Oreg., 1981. Pharmacology rsch. assoc. NIMH, NIGMS, Bethesda, Md., 1981-83; asst. prof. Northwestern U., Evanston, Ill., 1983-87; assoc. chmn. Neurobiology and Physiology Northwestern U., Evanston, Ill., 1988—, assoc. prof., 1987-91, prof., 1991-96; Walter and Mary Elizabeth Glass prof. life scis. Northwestern U., Evanston, Ill., 1996—; acting assoc. dir. Inst. for Neuroscience Northwestern U., Evanston, 1988-95; active NIMH Psychobiology and Behavior Rev. Com., 1988-92. Assoc. editor Neuron; mem. adv. bd. Jour. Biol. Rhythms, 1984—; contbr. over 90 articles to profl. jours. Grantee Bristol-Myers Squibb, 1995—; recipient Alfred P. Sloan award A.P. Sloan Found., 1983-85, Searl Scholars award Chgo. Cmty. Trust, 1985-88, Merit award NIMH, 1987, Honma prize in Biol. Rhythms Honma Found., 1986, Presdl. Young Investigator award NSF, 1985-90, 6th C.U. Ariens Kappers award Netherlands Soc. for Advancement Nat. Scis., Medicine and Surgery, 1995. Mem. AAAS, Soc. Neurosci., Assn. for Rsch. in Vision and Ophthalmology, Soc. for Rsch. on Biol. Rhythms (mem. adv. bd. 1986—), Mammalian Genome Soc. Office: Northwestern U Neurobiology 2153 North Campus Dr Evanston IL 60208-3520

TAKAHASHI, KAZUHIRO, physician, endocrinologist, molecular biologist; b. Fukushima, Japan, Mar. 18, 1959; s. Kanji and Kimi Takahashi; m. Izumi Miura Takahashi, Nov. 1, 1987; children: Kimihiro, Hidemi, Sayaka. MD, Tohoku U., Sendai, Japan, 1983. Med. diplomate. Resident Takeda Hosp., Aizuwakamatsu, Japan, 1983-85; rsch. fellow Royal Postgrad. Med. Sch., London, 1988-90, Tohoku Univ. Sch. Medicine, Sendai, 1985-88, 90, 92—; cons. physician Miyako (Japan) Hosp., 1991. Contbr. articles to profl. jours. Recipient rsch. grant Miyagi Kidney Assn. and Ministry Edn., Sci. and Culture of Japan. Mem. Japan Endocrine Soc., Japanese Soc. Internal Medicine, Japan Diabetes Soc., Internat. Soc. Neuroendocrinology, Japan Soc. for Dialysis Therapy, Japanese Soc. Biochemistry, The Endocrine Soc., N.Y. Acad. Scis., Japanese Soc. Nephrology, Japanese Soc. Molecular Biology. Office: Tohoku U Sch Med Dept Appl Physiology, 2-D Seiryo-cho Aoba-Ku, Sendai 980-77, Japan

TAKAHASHI, KEISUKE, orthopaedic surgeon; b. Fukuoka, Japan, Jan. 6, 1956; s. Shigeo and Sumiko (Gondoh) T.; m. Junko Abe, Dec. 16, 1984; children: Yuriko, Shinsuke. MD, Kanazawa U., 1981, PhD, 1988. Asst. Kanazawa (Japan) U., 1988-91, asst. prof., 1991-94; mem. med. staff Ishikawa Prefectural Ctrl. Hosp., Kanazawa, 1994—. Aithor: Lumbar Spinal Stenosis, 1992; contbr. articles to profl. jours. Kanzawa U. med. treatment of elderly grantee, 1992; Gothenburg (Sweden) U. fellow, 1990-91; recipient Sofamor Danek award, 1995, Japan Orthopaedics and Traumatology Found. award, 1992. Mem. Internat. Soc. Study Lumbar Spine, Japanese ORthopaedic Assn., Japan Spine Rsch. Soc. Office: Ishikawa Prefectural Ctrl Hosp, 153 Minami-shinbo, Kanazawa 920, Japan

TAKAHASHI, MASAYOSHI, medical sciences educator; b. Morioka, Iwate, Japan, Mar. 18, 1926; s. Goroku and Fuki Takahashi; m. Teruko, Nov. 21, 1965; children; Yoshimi, Masateru. MB, Nihon U., 1952, MD, 1956. Rsch. assoc. Sch. Medicine Nihon U., Tokyo, 1952-57, asst. prof., 1958-70, assoc. prof., 1970; prof. Sch. Medicine Kyorin U., Tokyo, 1970-92; councilor Japan Hosp. Assn., Tokyo, 1992-95; dir. corr. course Japan Hosp. Assn., Tokyo, 1972-92; bd. dirs. Japanese Soc. Hosp. Adminstrn. Researchers, Tokyo, 1989—. Author: Hospital Administration, 1988, Medical Record Administration, 1989, Health Information Administration, 1989, Health Care Administration, 1991; author, editor: Administrative Medicine, 1992. Mem. Health Stats. Spl. Com., Japanese Soc. on Hosp. Adminstrn. (mem. coun. 1970—, past pres.), Japanese Soc. of Med. Record Adminstrn. (mem. coun. 1975—, past pres.). Home: 5-29-13-704 Hongo, Bunkyo-ku Tokyo 113, Japan Office: Kyorin Univ, 6-20-2 Shinkawa, Mitaka Tokyo 181, Japan

TAKAHASHI, YASUO, psychiatrist; b. Sydney, Australia, Oct. 8, 1925; came to U.S., 1953; s. Goro and Chiyoko (Takekawa) T.; children: Nancy, Ken, Suzanne, Denise, Joy. Diploma, Shizuoka U., Japan, 1948; MD, Chiba U. Sch. of Medicine, Japan, 1952; postgrad., U. Pa. Diplomate Am. Bd. Psychiatry and Neurology 1960. Chief resident Dept. Psychiatry Med. Coll. of Va., Richmond, 1956-57; sr. psychiatrist Springfield Hosp. Ctr., Sykesville, Md., 1957-63; dir. Bur. Mental Health Prince Georges County Health Dept., Cheverly, Md., 1963-70; asst. prof. psychiatry Johns Hopkins U., 1971-82; med. dir. Team C, Adult Mental Health Clinic Dept. Addictions, Mental Health Svcs., Montgomery County, Md., 1989-91; med. dir. Mental Health Clinic, Kent County, Md., 1991—; pvt. practice psychiatry, 1964-91. Mem. AMA, Am. Psychiat. Assn., Am. Soc. Clin. Hyponosis. Home: 483 Heron Pt Chestertown MD 21620-1681

TAKALA, JUKKA ANTERO, anesthesiologist, educator, researcher; b. Turku, Finland, May 21, 1953; s. Matti Eliel and Astri Elina (Jaurela) T.; m. Marja-Leena Lähdetniemi, Oct. 6, 1977; children: Eeva-Leena, Meri-Leena. MD, U. Turku, 1978, PhD, 1982. Med. Lic. 1978, Spl. in Anesthesiology 1983, ECFMG 1985. Res. in Anesthesiology Turku U. Cen. Hosp., 1978-82, sr. staff anesthesiologist, 1983-85; research fellow Surg. Metabolism Program Columbia U., N.Y.C., 1984-86; assoc. prof. U. Turku, 1986—, U. Kuopio, Finland, 1987—; visiting prof. McGill U., Montreal, Canada, 1988, Albert Einstein Coll. of Med., N.Y.C., 1988; attending spl. dept. intensive care Dept. of Intensive Care, Kuopio U. Hosp., 1986—; also dir. critical care rsch. program Kuopio U. Hosp. Mem. European Soc. Intensive Care (exec. com. 1994—), European Soc. Parenteral and Enteral Nutrition (v.p. 1987-88, 89-90, pres. 1988-89). Office: Kuopio U Hosp, FIN-70210 Kuopio Finland

TAKASAKI, ETSUJI, urology educator; b. Tokyo, Apr. 24, 1929; s. Kuranosuke and Fumi Takasaki; m. Sachiko Shinkai, Nov. 1, 1960; children: Satoshi, Masumi, Hiromi. MD, U. Tokyo, 1955, D. Med. Sci., 1960. Instr. urology U. Tokyo, 1960-62, asst. prof., 1962-67; chief. urol. svc. Musashino Red Cross Hosp., Tokyo, 1967-69, Komagome Met. Hosp., Tokyo, 1969-74; prof. urology Dokkyo U. Sch. Medicine, Tochigi, Japan, 1974-95, emeritus prof., 1995—; lectr. U. Tokyo, 1969-74. Author: Urolithiasis, 1978; contbr. articles to Japanese Jour. Urology, 1960, Jour. Urology, 1986, Urologia Internat., 1989, 95, British Jour. Urology, 1994. Mem. Japanese Urol. Assn. (bd. dirs. 1963—), Japanese Soc. Andrology (bd. dirs. 1982—), Japanese Soc. Endourology and ESWL (bd. dirs. 1988—), Internat. Soc. Urology (Paris).

TAKASU, KATSUYA, plastic surgeon; b. Hazugun, Aichi-ken, Japan, Jan. 22, 1945; s. Shogo Matsuzaki and Toyoko Takasu; m. Shizu Hoshino, Nov. 23, 1969; children: Rikiya, Hisaya, Mikiya. MD, Showa U., Tokyo, 1969, PhD, 1973. Plastic surgeon Showa U. Hosp., Tokyo, 1969-73; plastic surgeon Takasu Hosp., Hazugun, Japan, 1973-76, sub-pres., 1973—; pres. Takasu Clinic, Tokyo, 1976—. Author: Atarashii Basuto Keiseijyutsu, 1992, Takasu Katsuya no Biyoseikei, 1994, Shimi Shiwa wo Jibun de Naosu Hon, 1996. Sub-pres. Japan Jr. Chamber, Inc., 1983. Recipient Yoneyama Kourousha prize Rotary Yoneyama Meml. Found., 1981, Shijuho prize Red Cross Soc. Japan, 1990; Paul Harris fellow Rotary Found. Mem. Am. Acad. Cosmetic Surgery (corr.), Am. Acad. Aesthetic & Restorative Surgery, Japanese Soc. Aesthetic Surgery, Japanese Soc. Plastic Surgery. Office:

Takasu Clinic Kokusai Shin Akasaka Bldg, Higashikan 2F 2-14-27 Akasaka, Minato-ku Tokyo 107, Japan

TAKATORI, TAKEHIKO, forensic medicine and toxicology educator; b. Nishimurayamagun, Yamagata, Japan, Dec. 2, 1938; s. Shuji and Tsuru T.; m. Yasuko Kanomori, Aug. 22, 1968. MD, Hokkaido U. Sch. Medicine, Sapporo, Japan, 1965, PhD, 1970. Instr. Hokkaido U., 1970-74, lectr., 1975-76, assoc. prof., 1977-79, prof., 1980-90; prof. U. Tokyo, 1991—. Author: Methods in Enzymology, 1982, Immunoassay for Trace chemical Analysis, 1991; mem. editorial bd. Forensic Sci. Internat., 1992—, Internat. Jour. Legal Medicine, 1996—. Mem. Medkco-legal Soc. Japan (editor-in-chief 1991-94), Japanese Soc. Compensation Medicine (editor-in-chief 1989-92), Japanese Assn. Forensic Toxicology (editor-in-chief 1988-90). Office: U Tokyo, Dept Forensic Medicine, Hongo 7-3-1, Bunkyo-Ku Tokyo, Japan

TAKEI, TOSHIHISA, otolaryngologist; b. L.A., Apr. 19, 1931; s. Taketomi and Mitsue (Hagihara) T.; m. Emiko Kubota, Jan. 25, 1955; children: H. Thomas, T. Robert. BA, UCLA, 1954; MD, Boston U., 1962. Diplomate, Am. Bd. Otolaryngology. Intern L.A. County Harbor Gen. Hosp., 1962-63; resident in otolaryngology L.A. County/U. So. Calif. Med. Ctr., 1963-67; staff physician Covina (Calif.) Ear, Nose & Throat Med. Group, 1968—; asst. prof. Sch. Medicine, U. So. Calif., L.A., 1968—. 1st lt. U.S. Army, 1955-56, Korea. Fellow Am. Acad. Otolaryngology, Royal Soc. Medicine. Republican. Buddhist. Office: Covina ENT Med Group Inc 236 W College St Covina CA 91723-1902

TAKES, PETER ARTHUR, immunologist; b. Albany, N.Y., May 1, 1957; s. Arthur Peter and Mary Nicholas (Marin) T.; m. Alexandra Kavourinos, Feb. 27, 1983; 1 child, Michael. BS, Clarkson U., 1979; PhD, Ind. State U., 1985. Rsch. immunologist Sigma Diagnostics, St. Louis, 1988-89; rsch. supr. Sigma Diagnostics, 1989-90, immunodiagnostics mgr., 1990-92; scientist, clin. studies coord. Sigma BioScis., St. Louis, 1992-96, regulatory assoc., 1995—; instr. BLS Am. Heart Assn., St. Louis, 1986-88; adj. prof. Webster U., 1993—; chmn. Joint Coun. Immunohistochem Mfrs., 1994—; mem. Nat. Com. Clin. Lab. Schs. Immunohistochemistry subcom. Author: Microwave Procedures Manual, 1990; contbr. articles to several profl. jours. Pres. Waterman Condo. Assn., St. Louis, 1987-90; basketball referee Mo. State High Sch. Athletic Assn., St. Louis, 1990—. U. fellow Ind. State U., 1979-84, Postdoctoral fellow Washington U. Sch. Medicine, St. Louis, 1985-87, Summer Rsch. fellow, AHEPA Cooley's Anemia Found., 1981. Mem. AAAS, Am. Assn. Clin. Chemistry, Nat. Soc. Histotechnology, N.Y. Acad. Scis., Assn. Med. Lab. Immunologists. Office: Sigma BioSciences PO Box 14508 Saint Louis MO 63178-4508

TAKESHIMA, YOICHI, psychology educator; b. Nankoku-shi, Japan, Feb. 13, 1952; s. Kenjiro and Tsuyako Takeshima. BS, U. Tsukuba, Tsukuba-shi, Japan, 1979, MS, 1982. Lectr. Kochi Jr. Coll., Kochi-shi, Japan, 1983-84, 91—, Kochi Gakuen Jr. Coll., Kochi-shi, 1986-89; clin. psychologist Geiyoin Hosp., Aki-shi, Japan, 1984-85; rschr. Kochi Med. Sch., Nankoku-shi, 1985—; lectr. Tosa Rehab. Coll., Kami-gun, 1994—, Kochi Rehab. Coll., Kochi-shi, 1995-96, Tosa Norse Coll., 1995-96, Kochi Sch. Allied Health and Med. Professions. Mem. Internat. Soc. Hypnosis, Japanese Soc. Hypnosis, Japanese Soc. Psychosomatic Medicine, Japanese Soc. Social Psychology, Japanese Psychol. Assn., Soc. for Psychical Rsch., Japanese Soc. Ednl. Psychology, Japanese Soc. for Parapsychology, Japanese Soc. Devel. Psychology. Home: 3-19 Ekimae-cho, Kochi-shi, Kochi-ken 780, Japan Office: Kochi Med Sch Dept Physiol, Okohcho, Kochi, Nankoku 781-51, Japan

TAL, JACOB, obstetrician, gynecologist; b. Iassi, Rumania, Oct. 9, 1945; came to U.S., 1976; s. Efraym and Esther (Bercovici) T.; m. Phyllis E., Nov. 7, 1974; children: Noa, Lara, Eric. Degree, Faculte Medicine, Lyon, France, 1969; MD, Sackler Sch. Medicine, Tel-Aviv, 1976. Diplomate Am. Bd. Ob-Gyn., 1982, recert. 1991. With Meml. City, Houston; resident ob-gyn. Albert Einstein Coll. Medicine, Bronx, N.Y., 1980; practice medicine specializing in ob-gyn. West Houston, and Katy, Tex., 1980-87; chief of staff Katy Community Hosp., 1987—. Fellow ACS, Am. Coll. Ob-Gyn, Tex. Assn. Ob-Gyn. Home: 618 Sandy Port St Houston TX 77079-2419 Office: Katy-W Houston Ob-Gyn Assn 5618 Medical Center Dr Katy TX 77494-6363

TALA, EERO OTTO, internist, chest diseases educator; b. Kiikka, Finland, Sept. 26, 1931; s. Otto Jalmari and Olga Maria (Järvinen) T.; m. Maija-Leena Teinilä, Dec. 4, 1955; children: Juhani, Leena, Marianna, Eeva. MD, U. Turku, Finland, 1957, DMS, 1967, Prof., 1970. Rsch. fellow in pharmacology U. Turku, 1958-61, resident in chest diseases and medicine, 1962-67; assoc. chief physician, chief physician Paimio Hosp., Preitilä, Finland, 1968-94; prof. diseases of chest U. of Turku, 1970-94, dean med. faculty, 1983-85; ret., 1994—; temporary expert WHO, Geneva, 1989—; pres. for Europe, Internat. Union Against Tb, 1982-90. Contbr. over 200 articles on pharmacology, medicine and chest diseases to med. jours. Decorated Order of White Rose (Finland). Mem. Finnish Lung Assn. (pres. Turku 1973-76), Hungarian Chest Assn. (hon.), Latin Am. Lung Assn. (hon.). Home: Myllyhaantie 4, FIN-21530 Paimio Finland Office: Paimio Hosp, FIN-21540 Preitilä Finland

TALAB, YOUNIS A., orthopedist, consultant; b. Beit Uwla, Hebran, Palestine, Dec. 26, 1946; arrived in Jordan, 1952; m. Mona M. Gad; 1 child, Maha. MB, BCh, Ain Shams U., Cairo, 1971. Cert. Am. Bd. Ortho. Surgery. Asst. prof. ortho. surgery U. Rochester, N.Y., 1978-79; cons. ortho. surgery ARAMCO, Dhahran, Saudi Arabia, 1979—, sr. cons. ortho. surgery, 1986—, chief ortho., 1992—. Fellow ACS, Am. Acad. Ortho. Surgery; mem. Am. Coll. Physician Execs. Office: ARAMCO, Box 8252, Dhahran 31311, Saudi Arabia

TALALAY, PAUL, pharmacologist, physician; b. Berlin, Mar. 31, 1923; came to U.S., 1940, naturalized, 1946; s. Joseph Anton and Sophie (Brosterman) T.; m. Pamela Judith Samuels, Jan. 11, 1953; children—Antony, Susan, Rachel, Sarah. S.B., Mass. Inst. Tech., 1944; student, U. Chgo. Sch. Medicine, 1944-46; M.D., Yale U., 1948; D.Sc. (hon.), Acadia U., 1974. House officer, asst. resident surg. services Mass. Gen. Hosp., Boston, 1948-50; asst. prof. surgery U. Chgo., 1950-51, asst. prof. biochemistry, 1955-57, asso. prof., then prof., 1957-63; asst. prof. Ben May Lab. Cancer Research, 1951-57, asso. prof., then prof., 1957-63; John Jacob Abel prof., dir. dept., pharmacology and exptl. therapeutics Johns Hopkins Sch. Medicine, 1963-75, John Jacob Abel Distinguished Service prof., 1975—, Am. Cancer Soc. prof., 1958-63, 77—; sr. asst. surgeon USPHS, 1951-53; vis. prof. Guy's Hosp. Med. Sch., London, 1970, 74-76; nat. adv. cancer council USPHS, 1967-71; vis. com. dept. biology Mass. Inst. Tech., 1964-67; bd. sci. advisers Jane Coffin Childs Meml. Fund for Cancer Research, 1971-80; bd. sci. consultants Sloan-Kettering Inst. Cancer Research, 1971-81. Hon. editorial adv. bd.: Biochem. Pharmacology, 1963-68; editorial bd.: Jour. Biol. Chemistry, 1961-66, Molecular Pharmacology, 1965-68, 71-80; editor-in-chief, 1968-71. Recipient Premio Internationale La Madonnina Milan, 1978; Med. Alumni Disting. Service award U. Chgo., 1978; Am. Cancer Soc. scholar, 1954-58; Guggenheim Meml. fellow, 1973-74. Fellow Am. Acad. Arts and Scis.; mem. AAAS (Theobald Smith award med. scis. 1957), Nat. Acad. Scis., Am. Philosophical Soc., Am. Soc. Biol. Chemists, Am. Soc. Clin. Investigation, Biochem. Soc., Am. Chem. Soc., Am. Soc. Pharm. and Exptl. Therapeutics, Phi Beta Kappa, Sigma Xi, Alpha Omega Alpha. Home: 5512 Boxhill Ln Baltimore MD 21210-2039 Office: Johns Hopkins U Sch Medicine Baltimore MD 21205

TALAMANTES, ROBERTO, developmental pediatrician; b. Juarez, Chihuahua, Chile, June 19, 1952; came to U.S., 1955; s. Cruz and Viviana (Monarez) T.; m. Blanca Yolanda Chavez, Aug. 19, 1972; children: Christian, Steven. BS in Biology, U. Colo., 1972; MD, U. Autonoma Ciudad Juarez, 1979. Rotating intern Baylor Coll. Medicine, Houston, 1980-81, pediat. resident, 1981-84, devel. pediat. fellow, 1984-86; pvt. practice Gen. Devel. Pediatrics, Las Cruces, N.Mex., 1986—; pres. IPA N.Mex., 1993-96; dir. Cimarron HMO, 1993-96; pres. elect med. staff Meml. Med. Ctr., Las Cruces, 1993-94, pres., 1994-95, sec., 1992-94. With U.S. Army, 1972-74. Fellow Am. Acad. of Pediatrics, Soc. of Devel. Pediatrics; mem. N.Mex. Podiatric Soc., N.Mex. Med. Soc. Republican. Office: Hillside Circle Las Cruces NM 88011

TALAMO, JONATHAN HASKELL, ophthalmologist, educator; b. Boston, Sept. 25, 1960. Student, Cornell U., 1978-80; AB, Johns Hopkins U., 1982, MD, 1986. Diplomate Am. Bd. Ophthalmology. Intern in medicine Children's Hosp. San Francisco-U. Calif., 1986-87; resident in ophthalmology Wilmer Ophthal. Inst., Johns Hopkins Hosp., 1987-90; clin. fellow ophthalmology, cornea and external disease Mass. Eye and Ear Infirmary-Harvard U. Med. Sch., Boston, 1990-91, asst. surgeon, 1992-95, assoc. surgeon, 1995—, dir. gen. eye and cataract consultation svc., 1992-94, dir. keratorefractice surgery unit, 1992-95, acting dir. cornea svc., 1994-95, dir. cornea and external disease fellowship program, 1994-95; pvt. practice, Providence, 1991-92, Boston, 1995—; rsch. fellow in ophthalmology Harvard U. Med. Sch., 1984-85, clin. fellow in ophthalmology, 1990-91, instr. ophthalmology, 1992-94, asst. prof., 1994-95, asst. clin. prof., 1995—; clin. fellow in ophthalmology Johns Hopkins U. Med. Sch., 1987-90; asst. clin. prof. dept. surgery Brown U. Sch. Medicine, Providence, 1991-93; attending surgeon Miriam Hosp., Providence, 1991-93, R.I. Hosp., Providence, 1991-93; mem. courtesy staff Milford (Mass.) Whitinsville Regional Hosp., 1993%; mem. active staff Winchester (Mass.) Hosp., 1995—; med. dir. New Eng. region New Vision Tech., Inc., Burlington, Mass., 1994-95; vis. prof. Cornell U. Med. Coll., 1995, U. Tex., San Antonio, 1995, St. Louis U., 1995; numerous guest lectures; ad hoc manuscript reviewer Am. Jour. Ophthalmology, Archives of Ophthalmology, Cornea, Jour. Cataract and Refractive Surgery, Jour. Refractive Surger, Investigative Ophthalmology and Visual Sci., Lasers in Surgery and Medicine, Ophthalmology, New Eng. Jour. Medicine, 1987—. Asst. editor Jour. Refractive Surgery, 1994—; mem. editl. bd. Ophthalmology Times, 1995—; contbr. articles and abstracts to med. jours., chpts. to books. Tng. grantee USPHS, 1984, travel grantee Assn. for Rsch. in Vision and Ophthalmology, 1985, N.E. Corneal Transplant Rsch. Fund, 1993, 94, Coherent Med., Inc., 1994, 95; fellow Fight for Sight, 1985, Heed Ophthalmic Found., 1990. Fellow Am. Acad. Ophthalmology (preferred practice patterns adv. panel 1996—); mem. AMA, Internat. Soc. Refractive Surgery (bd. dirs. 1995—), Am. Soc. Cataract and Refractive Surgery, Soc. Heed Fellows, New Eng. Ophthal. Soc., Mass. Soc. Eye Physiciand and Surgeons, R.I. Soc. Eye Physicians and Surgeons, Mass. Med. Soc.

TALARICO, DAVID J., plastic surgeon; b. Ft. Wayne, Ind., June 23, 1935; s. Joseph C. and Ruth (Bill) T.; m. Joan H. Talarico, June 12, 1965; children: David J., Deana. AB, Ind. U., 1957; MD, St. Louis U., 1962. Diplomate Am. Bd. Plastic Surgery. Pvt. practice South Miami, Fla., 1970-95, Ocala, Fla., 1995—. Capt. USAF, 1963-65. Republican. Office: 2801 SW State Rd 200 #23 Ocala FL 34474

TALBERT, JAMES LEWIS, pediatric surgeon, educator; b. Cassville, Mo., Sept. 26, 1931; s. William David and Frances (Lewis) T.; m. Alice Quintavell, July 25, 1958; children: William David, Alison Whitney. B.A., Vanderbilt U., 1953, M.D., 1956. Diplomate: Am. Bd. Surgery (with cert. of spl. competence in pediatric surgery), Am. Bd. Thoracic Surgery. Intern, then resident in surgery Johns Hopkins Hosp., 1956-64, resident in pediatric surgery, 1964-65, Harvey Cushing fellow, 1958-59; instr. surgery, Garrett scholar pediatric surgery Johns Hopkins U. Med. Sch., 1965-66, asst. prof., 1966-67; mem. faculty U. Fla. Med. Sch., Gainesville, 1967—; prof pediatric surgery, chmn. div., chief children's surgery U. Fla. Med. Sch., 1970—; mem. affiliated faculty VA Hosp., Gainesville; med. dir. Fla. Regional Med. Program for Diagnosis and Treatment Cancer in Children, 1970-73, N. Referal Center Children's Med. Service Program Fla., 1970-80; chmn Alachua County Emergency Med. Services Adv. Council, 1973-75; chmn. emergency med. services com. N. Central Fla. Health Planning Council, 1972-73; mem. Fla. Emergency Med. Services Adv. Council, 1973-75, 76-79. Author numerous articles in field; contbr. 16 chpts. to books. Served with USPHS, 1960-62. Recipient Founders medal, Roche award Vanderbilt U. Med. Sch., 1956. Fellow ACS (chmn. Fla. trauma com. 1969-77, gov.-at-large 1979-85, sec. bd. govs. 1982-85, rep. to Coun. of Med. Spl. Socs. 1988-89), Am. Acad. Pediatrics (exec. com. sect. oncology and hematology 1978-85); mem. AMA, Am. Pediatric Surg. Assn. (founding mem., chmn. trauma com. 1976-79), Pediatric Oncology Group (chmn. group retreat 1980), Am. Fedn. Clin. Rsch., Assn. Acad. Surgery, Soc. U. Surgeons, Soc. Pediatric Rsch., Am. Coll. Emergency Physicians, Am. Surg. Assn., Halsted Soc., Am. Assn. Surgery Trauma, Am. Burn Assn., Am. Pediatric Soc., Brit. Assn. Pediatric Surgeons, Soc. Internat. Chirurgie, So. Soc. Pediatric Rsch., So. Surg. Assn., Fla. Med. Assn., Fla. Heart Assn. (chmn. cardio-pulmonary resuscitation com. 1972-76), Fla. Assn. Pediatric Surgeons (pres. 1976-78), Fla. Assn. Pediatric Tumor Programs (pres. 1973—), Alachua County Med. Soc. (chmn. emergency med. svcs. adv. com. 1973-75), Phi Beta Kappa, Alpha Omega Alpha, Phi Eta Sigma. Office: J Hillis Miller Health Ctr PO Box 100286 Gainesville FL 32610-0286

TALBERT, LUTHER MARCUS, physician; b. Abington, Va., Dec. 30, 1926; s. Marcus Aurelius and Mary Elizabeth (Thompson) T.; m. Annie Brown Edmondson, Dec. 24, 1949; children: John T., Luther E., Martha C. B.A., Emory and Henry Coll., 1949, D.Sc. (hon.), 1980; M.D., U. Va., 1953. Med. intern U. Va., 1953-54, resident in Ob-Gyn, 1954-58, fellow in reproductive physiology, 1956-57; mem. faculty U. N.C. Med. Sch., Chapel Hill, 1958-92; prof. Ob-Gyn. U. N.C. Med. Sch., 1975-92, dir. div. reproductive endocrinology, 1975-84; dir. clin svcs. N.C. Ctr. for Reproductive Medicine, Cary, N.C. Served with USN, 1944-46. Mem. Assn. Profs. Ob-Gyn (pres. 1979-80), Soc. Gynecologic Investigation, Am. Gynecol. and Obstet. Soc., AAAS. Republican. Bapt. Home: 101 Stoneridge Dr Chapel Hill NC 27514-9733 Office: NC Ctr for Reproductive Medicine 204/60 Asheville Dr Cary NC 27514-4216

TALBOTT, JOHN A., psychiatrist, educator; b. Boston, Nov. 8, 1935; s. John H. and Mildred (Cherry) T.; m. Susan Webster, June 17, 1961; children: Sieglinde, Alexandra. AB, Harvard U., 1957; MD, Columbia U., 1961. Diplomate Am. Bd. Psychiatry and Neurology. Intern in medicine Rochester (N.Y.) Mcpl. and Strong Meml. Hosps., 1961-62; resident in psychiatry N.Y. State Psychiat. Inst. and Presbyn. Hosp., 1962-65, chief resident, 1964-65; prof., chair of psychiatry U. Md., Balt., 1985—, dir. Inst. Psychiatry & Human Behavior, 1985—; instr. Coll. Physicians and Surgeons, Columbia U., 1963-80, Cornell U. Med. Coll., 1975-85; psychiatrist Columbia-Presbyn. Med. Ctr., N.Y.C., N.Y. State Psychiat. Inst., Cmty. Svcs., N.Y.C., Ft. Bragg (N.C.) Mental Hygiene Consultation Ctr., U.S. Army in Viet Name, 935th Med. Detachment, Long Binh and 3d Field Hosp.; dir. cmty. psychiatry St. Luke's Hosp. Ctr., N.Y.C.; dep. dir., dir. tng. Meyer-Manhattan Psychiat. Ctr., N.Y.C.; dir. Dunlap-Manhattan Psychiat. Ctr., N.Y.C.; assoc. med. dir. Payne Whitney Psychiat. Clinic, N.Y.C. Author: The Death of the Asylum: A Critical Study of State Hospital Management, Services, and Care, 1978; mem. editor: Psychiatric Services formally Hosp. and Cmty. Psychiatry, 1978—; contbr. more than 200 articles to profl. jours., chpts. to books. Mem. mental health com., exec. com. Greater N.Y. Hosp. Assn.; mem. adv. com. on Viet Nam Vets ctrl. office VA; mem. task force on homelessness and severe mental illness, mem. adv. com. Dept. HHS; mem. com. to plan a major study of nat. long term care policies Inst. Medicine; mem. nat. adv. com. urban systems of care for the chronically mentally ill Robert Wood Johnson Found.; mem. sci. coun. Nat. Alliance for Rsch. on Schizophrenia and Depression; vice chmn. Nat. Com. on Youth Suicide Prevention; mem. PL 99-660 planning coun. State of Md.; mem. Mayor John Lindsay's Spl. Commn. on Prescription Drug Abuse; pres. Jimmy's Carter's Commn. on Mental Health, chmn. spl. study on chronic mental patients; mem. drug scheduling adv. com. chair N.Y. State Dept. on Health and Office of Drug Abuse; mem. profl. tech. adv. com. for long term care Gov. Hugh Carey's Health Adv. Coun.; mem. adv. com. Fed. Interdepartmental Task Force on Homelessness and Severe Mental Illness. Fellow Am. Psychiat. Assn. (pres. 1984-85), Am. Assn. Social Psychiatry, Am. Coll. Mental Health Adminstrn. (founder 1978—); mem. Am. Assn. Cmty. Mental Health Ctr. Psychiatrists (founding mem. 1984—), Am. Assn. Psychiat. Adminstrs. (pres. 1985-86), Am. Assn. Chairmen of Depts. of Psychiatry (pres. 1994-95). Home: 200 Goodwood Gardens Baltimore MD 21210 Office: U Md Sch Medicine 645 W Redwood St Baltimore MD 21201

TALCIK, JACKIE ELAINE, health facility administrator; b. Bakersfield, Calif., Feb. 5, 1945; d. Kenneth William and Marjorie Ruth (Skinner) Saupp; m. Joseph Martin Talcik, Aug. 2, 1969; children: Alexa, Grant. BS, U. Pa., 1969; MS, Syracuse U., 1974. RN, Pa., N.Y., Colo. Head nurse Hosp. of the Univ. of Pa., Phila., 1969-70; supr. Homestead Manor Nursing Home, Colorado Springs, Colo., 1971-72; instr. Sch. of Nursing Upstate Med. Ctr., Syracuse, N.Y., 1972-75, asst. prof. Sch. of Nursing, 1975-76; rev. adminstr. Profl. Stds. Rev. Orgn. of N.Y., Syracuse, 1976-77; assoc. exec. dir. Empire State Peer Rev. Orgn., Syracuse, 1977-87; dir. ops. Empire State Med., Sci. & Edn. Found., Syracuse, 1988; sr. v.p. for profl. svcs. Ctrl. N.Y. Hosp. Assn., Syracuse, 1988—; lectr., clerkship SUNY Health Sci. Ctr. Coll. of Medicine, Syracuse, 1986-87; lectr., instr. New Sch. for Social Rsch., Syracuse, 1988; bd. dirs. Transplant Donor Svcs. of N.Y., Syracuse, 1992—, Think First, Syracuse, 1995—. Fundraiser Burnet Park Zoo, Syracuse, 1985; subcom. chair and mem. Tecumseh Elem. Sch. Parent Tchr. Group, Syracuse, 1990-92; tchr. Sun. sch. Pebble Hill Presbyn. Ch., Syracuse, 1992—. Mem. Am. Coll. Healthcare Execs. (assoc.), Healthcare Mgmt. Assn. of N.Y.C., N.Y. State Nurses Assn. (Dist. #4 bd. dirs., legis. chair 1972—), Sigma Theta Tau Nat. Honor Soc., N.Y.C. NIV Steering Com. Republican. Presbyterian. Home: 5303 Aquarius Dr Syracuse NY 13224 Office: Ctrl NY Hosp Assn Inc 5740 Commons Pk Delphi Falls NY 13051

TALINGDAN, ARSENIO PREZA, health science administrator; b. Dolores, Abra, The Philippines, Mar. 30, 1930; came to U.S., 1973; s. Mariano T. and Candida (Tordil) Preza; m. Josefa Fernandez Biason. Apr. 21, 1954; children: Melda, Arsenio Jr., Jocelyn Almerick, Mario, Abe. AA, U. Philippines, 1951, AB, MPA, 1955; MAPA, The Am. U., 1956; BS, La Salle Extention U., Chgo., 1977; MBA, Century U., 1983. PhD, 1985. Cert. nursing home adminstr., life, health and securities underwriter. Job analyst, orgn. analyst, budget examiner Kroeger & Assocs. Project, Philippine Budget Commn., Manila, 1954-55; scholar, tech. asst., participant USA-ICA-NEC Program, 1955-56; supr. mgmt. analyst Philippine Budget Commn., Manila, 1957-59; asst. budget dir., IBM coordinator U. Philippines, Quezon City, 1959-65, mgmt. specialist, chief of studies, 1969-70; asst. v.p. for budget and mgmt. Sarmiento Enterprises, Inc., Makati, Rizal, Philippines, 1965-69; adminstr. Philippine Gen. Hosp., Manila, 1970-73; budget and facilities mgr. Hunter Coll., CUNY, N.Y.C., 1973-76; acctg. systems editor J.C. Penney Co., N.Y.C., 1977; regional med. care adminstr. N.Y. State Dept. Health, Office Health Systems Mgmt., N.Y.C., 1977-78; assoc. med. care adminstr., Medicaid mgmt. info. systems Dept. Health State of N.Y., N.Y.C., 1978—; with dental Medicaid program Dept. Health State of N.Y., 1978-82, with med. ops. br., 1982-84, with dental ops. br., 1984-91, with patient care investigations, long term care program, 1991—; asst. prof., chmn. social scis. dept. U.P. Coll., Manila, 1969-73; 1st Philippine tech. assistance fellow on orgn. and mgmt. U.S. Agy. for Internat. Devel., Washington, 1955-56; professorial lectr. U. Philippines, Manila, 1960-69. Co-author: Accounting, Auditing and Internal Auditing, 1964; author: Public Administration and Management, 1966, Management and Supervision, 1966, Work Simlification Handbook, 1957 and others; contbr. articles to profl. jours. Pres. Abra Varsitarians, Quezon City, 1949-53; founder, Dolores Young Men and Women's Assn., Manila, Abra, 1949-71; founder, pres. Philippine Execs. and Profls. Golf Assn., Quezon City, 1965-69, others. Maj. Res. Officer, Philippine Army, 1960-73. Recipient Hall of Nations award Am. U., 1956, Pub. Health Sci. award Del. Valley Assn. Philippines, 1980, Profl. award in Pub. Adminstrn. U. Philippines Alumni Assn. Am., 1991. Mem. Pub. Employees Fedn., U. of the Philippines Alumni Assn. in N.J. (founder, 1st pres. 1979-83), U. of the Philippines Alumni Assn. in Am. (founder, 1st pres. 1980-83), Filipino Am. Soc. of Teaneck (pres. 1983-84). Republican.

TALLENT, MARC ANDREW, clinical psychologist; b. Newport News, Va., Dec. 3, 1954; s. Norman and Shirley Dorothy (Rudman) T. BA, Columbia U., 1978; MA, Adelphi U., 1980, PhD, 1983. Lic. psychologist, N.Y. Pvt. practice N.Y.C., 1985—; psychoanalytic psychotherapist Ctr. for Modern Psychoanalytic Studies, N.Y.C., 1988—; supervising psychologist div. spl. edn. Bd. Edn. of N.Y.C., 1991—; cons. Big Bros./Big Sisters N.Y.C., 1988—, Task Force on AIDS N.Y. State Psychol. Assn., N.Y.C., 1989—. Editor: Modern Psychoanalysis, 1986—. Mem. APA, Nat. Assn. for Advancement of Psychoanalysis, N.Y. State Psychological Assn., Phi Beta Kappa. Office: Profl Ste B 51 Fifth Ave New York NY 10003-4320

TALLENT, SALLY M., counselor; b. Cochran, Ga., June 8, 1935; d. Tom Henry and Annie Gertrude (Gaillard) Crutchfield; m. James Kenneth Tallent, Aug. 15, 1960; children: James Kenneth Jr., Tammy Lisa. BS, Ga. State Coll., 1960. Cert. addiction counselor, Ga. Assn. Addiction Counselors, cert. risk reduction instr., PRI. Devel. planning mgr. Cardinal Industries, College Park, Ga., 1983-88; v.p., adminstr. Villager Lodge, Inc., Atlanta, 1989-92; substance abuse instr. Dept. Human Resources, Atlanta, 1992—; defensive driving instr. Ga. Dept. Pub. Safety, Atlanta, 1991—; risk reduction instr. Profl. Rsch. Inst., Lexington, Ky., 1992—; addiction counselor Coweta Substance Abuse, Newnan, Ga., 1993—. Democratic campaign worker, Atlanta, 1986. Recipient Bronze medal, Arthur Murray, Atlanta, 1957, Silver medal, 1958, gold medal, 1959. Mem. Alliance Mentally Ill., Ga. Addiction Counselor Assn. Mem. LDS Ch. Home: 8189 Park Ridge Dr Riverdale GA 30274 Office: Coweta Substance Abuse Ctr 107 Jefferson St Newnan GA 30263

TALLETT, ELIZABETH EDITH, biopharmaceutical company executive; b. London, Apr. 2, 1949; d. Edward and Edith May (Vickers) Symons; m. James Edward Wavle Jr.; children: James Edward Tallett, Alexander Martin Tallett, Christopher Andrew Wavle. BS with honors, U. Nottingham (Eng.), 1970. Ops. rsch. analyst So. Gas Bd., 1970-73; mgmt. svcs. mgr. Warner-Lamber (UK), Eastleigh, Eng., 1973-77, strategic planning mgr., 1977-81; internat. dir. strategic planning Warner-Lambert, Morris Plains, N.J., 1981-82, corp. dir. strategic planning, 1982-84; dir. mktg. ops. Parke-Davis, Morris Plains, 1984-87; exec. v.p. therapeutic products Centocor, Malvern, Pa., 1987-89, pres. pharms. div., 1989-92; pres., CEO Transcell Techs., Inc., Monmouth Junction, N.J., 1992-96, Dioscor, Inc., Stockton, N.J., 1996—; bd. dirs. Prin. Mut. Life Ins. Co., Varian Assoc., Inc.; dir. Biotech. Coun. N.J., Prosperity N.J., Inc. Contbr. articles to profl. jours. Apptd. by Gov. Christine Todd Whitman to Prosperity N.J. Commn., 1995—. Mem. Ch. of Eng.

TALLEY, JOSEPH EUGENE, psychologist; b. Springfield, Mass., May 27, 1949; s. Joseph Addison and Miriam Louise (Ayers) T.; m. Vibeke Absalon, Jan. 3, 1981; children: Kirsten, David, Jonathan. BA, U. Richmond, 1971; MA, Radford Coll., 1973; PhD, U. Va., 1978.Diplomate Am. Bd. Profl. Psychology; lic. psychologist, N.C.; cert. health svc. provider, N.C. Clin. faculty, psychologist Duke U., Durham, N.C., 1977—, coord. rsch., program evaluation and testing svcs., 1979—; gen. practice psychotherapy, Durham, 1980—. Author: Study Skills, 1981, Performance Prediction of Law Enforcement Personnel, 1990, The Predictors of Successful Very Brief Psychotherapy, 1992; author, editor: Counseling and Psychotherapy Services, 1985; Counseling and Psychotherapy with College Students: A Guide to Treatment, 1986; author, editor: Multicultural Needs Assessment with College and University Populations, 1995; contbr. articles to profl. jours. Bd. deacons Hillsborough Presbyn. Ch., N.C., 1983-85, chmn., 1985, bd. elders, 1987—, v.p. bd. trustees, 1992-94; bd. dirs. Orange County Mental Health Assn., Chapel Hill, N.C., 1982-83, mem. legis. com., 1983, site visitor for accreditation. Mem. APA, Acad. Counseling Psychology (pres. 1995—), Am. Bd. Profl. Psychology, N.C. Psychol. Assn., Nat. Soc. Clin. Hypnosis (cert. and approved cons., supr. and practitioner, ethics com.), Phi Kappa Phi, Omicron Delta Kappa, Psi Chi, Phi Kappa Sigma. Democrat. Presbyterian. Home: 134 E Tryon St Hillsborough NC 27278-2550 Office: Duke U Counseling & Psychol Svcs PO Box 90955 214 Page Bldg Durham NC 27708-0955

TALLEY, NICHOLAS JOSEPH, educator, scientist; b. Perth, Australia, Jan. 9, 1956; s. Nicholas Alexander and Irene Mary Talley; m. Penelope Ann Steele, Feb. 9, 1985; children: Nicholas Stephen, Matthew Jonathon. MB, BS, U. NSW, Sydney, Australia, 1979, MD, 1993; PhD, U. Sydney, 1987. Resident med. officer/registrar Prince of Wales Hosp., Sydney, 1979-83; rsch. fellow, prof. registrar Royal North Shore Hosp., Sydney, 1983-87; rsch. fellow Mayo Clinic, Rochester, Minn., 1987-88, asst. prof. medicine, 1988-91, assoc. prof., 1991-93; found. prof. Nepean Hosp., U. Sydney, 1993—. Author: (textbooks) Examination Medicine, 1985, 2nd edit., 1991, 3d edit., 1996, Clinical Examination, 1988, 2nd edit., 1992, 3d edit., 1996, Internal Medicine, 1990; asst. editor Am. Jour. Gastroenterology, 1992—; mem. editorial bd. Gastroenterology, 1993—; contbr. articles and revs. to profl. jours., chpts. to books. Pres. Miranda br. Young Liberals, Sydney, 1976. Postgrad. rsch. scholar Nat. Health and Med. Rsch. Coun., Australia, 1984-86. Fellow ACP, Royal Australasian Coll. Physicians, Am. Coll. Gastroenterology, Australian Faculty Pub. Health Medicine (founding mem.), Royal Coll. Physicians; mem. Am. Gastroent. Assn. (abstract selections com.

1991-94), Gastroent. Soc. Australia. Office: Univ Sydney Nepean Hosp, Clin Scis Bldg Penrith, Sydney 2751, Australia

TALLEY, ROBERT BOYD, physician; b. Scottsbluff, Nebr., Jan. 21, 1931; s. Richard Bedelle and Eloise Earline (Taylor) T.; m. Louise Carroll Settle, Dec. 28, 1954; children—Robert Boyd, Edwin T. Student, Northwestern U., 1949-52; M.D., U. Colo., 1956. Diplomate Am. Bd. Internal Medicine. Intern Wayne County Gen. Hosp., Eloise, Mich., 1956-57; resident State U. Iowa, Iowa City, 1959-62, instr. dept. internal medicine, 1962-63, postdoctoral fellow dept. internal medicine, 1962-63; practice medicine specializing in internal medicine and gastroenterology Stockton, Calif.; clin. instr. medicine U. Calif.-San Francisco, 1965-70; chief staff St. Joseph's Hosp., chief of medicine, 1975-77, trustee, 1984—; cons. Calif. HCSA Data Com.; mem. adv. com. on nat. health ins. Ways and Means Com., U.S. Congress, 1978-80 dir. Delta IPA, 1980—; v.p. statewide Calif. PPO, United Preferred Provider Orgn., 1982; mem. exec. com., sec. United Founds. for Med. Care, 1978-79, treas., 1980-82, v.p. 1982-84, pres., 1984—; pres. San Joaquin Found. for Med. Care, 1973-79. Served with USN, 1957-59. Packard undergrad. scholar in surgery, 1956. Fellow ACP (community service com. 1971-81, trustee Commn. on Profl. and Hosp. Activities 1973-82, pres., chmn. bd. 1979-81); mem. HMO's Group Health Assn. of Am. (tech. adv. com. 1982-84), Inst. Medicine of Nat. Acad. Scis., AMCRA (bd. dirs. 1984—), Calif. Acad. Medicine, San Joaquin Med. Soc., Calif. Med. Assn., Sigma Nu. Office: 1805 N California St Ste 201A Stockton CA 95204*

TALLEY, ROBERT COCHRAN, medical school dean and administrator, cardiologist; b. May 26, 1936; m. Katherine Ann Plocar; children: Andrew, Katherine, David. BS, U. Mich., 1958; MD, U. Chgo., 1962. Diplomate Nat. Bd. Med. Examiners (mem. medicine com. 1984-88, com. chair 1988-93), Am. Bd. Internal Medicine, subsplty. cardiovascular diseases. Asst. prof., dept. physiology and medicine U. Tex. Med. Sch., San Antonio, 1969-71, head, sect. cardiovascular diseases, 1971-75, assoc. prof., dept. medicine, 1971-75; acting chief medicine VA Hosp., San Antonio, 1974, chief cardiology service, 1973-75; chmn. dept. internal medicine U. S.D. Sch. Medicine, Sioux Falls, 1975-87, Freeman prof. medicine, 1984-87, interim v.p., dean, 1986-87, v.p., dean, 1987—. Contbr. 33 articles to med. jours. Served to surgeon USPHS, 1966-68. Teaching scholar Am. Heart Assn. U. Chgo., 1972-75; Outstanding Tchr. and Clinician award U. Tex., San Antonio, 1969-70, Ann. Teaching award for Best Clin. Instr., U. Tex., San Antonio, 1971-72, Anton Hyden Disting. Prof. award. U. S.D. Sch. Medicine, 1979, Faculty Recognition award U. S.D. Sch. Medicine, 1981. Fellow Am. Coll. Cardiology, ACP; mem. Am. Heart Assn. (bd. dirs. Dakota affiliate), Am. Fedn. Clin. Research, AMA. Home: 1305 Cedar Ln Sioux Falls SD 57103-4512 Office: U SD Sch Medicine 1400 W 22nd St Sioux Falls SD 57105-1570*

TALMAGE, DAVID WILSON, microbiology and medical educator, physician, former university administrator; b. Kwangju, Korea, Sept. 15, 1919; s. John Van Neste and Eliza (Emerson) T.; m. LaVeryn Marie Hunicke, June 23, 1944; children: Janet, Marilyn, David, Mark, Carol. Student, Maryville (Tenn.) Coll., 1937-38; BS, Davidson (N.C.) Coll., 1941; MD, Washington U., St. Louis, 1944. Intern Ga. Baptist Hosp., 1944-45; resident medicine Barnes Hosp., St. Louis, 1948-50; fellow medicine Barnes Hosp., 1950-51; asst. prof. pathology U. Pitts., 1951-52; asst. prof., then assoc. prof. medicine U. Chgo., 1952-59; prof. medicine U. Colo., 1959—, prof. microbiology, 1960-86, disting. prof., 1986—, chmn. dept., 1963-65, assoc. dean, 1966-68, dean, 1969-71; dir. Webb-Waring Lung Inst., 1973-83, assoc. dean for research, 1983-86; mem. nat. council Nat. Inst. Allergy and Infectious Diseases, NIH, 1963-66, 73-77. Author: (with John Cann) Chemistry of Immunity in Health and Disease; editor: Jour. Allergy, 1963-67, (with M. Samter) Immunological Diseases. Served with M.C. AUS, 1945-48. Markle scholar, 1955-60. Mem. NAS, Inst. Medicine, Am. Acad. Allergy (pres.), Am. Assn. Immunologists (pres.), Phi Beta Kappa, Alpha Omega Alpha. Office: U Colo Sch Med Box C321 Denver CO 80262

TAMAN, MAHMOUD SHAWKY, psychiatrist; b. Jan. 6, 1933; came to U.S., 1971; Married; 3 children. MD, Alexandria (Egypt) U., 1957; diploma in psychol. medicine, Bd. of Royal Coll. Physicians, Eng., 1969. Bd. cert. Royal Coll. Psychiatrists of Eng.; lic. MD Kans., S.D., Iowa, N.Y., Md., Wis. Intern Alexandria (Egypt) U. Hosp., 1957-58; house office in gen. medicine Kobba Gen. Hosp., Cairo, 1959-61; gen. practice Kobba Gen. Hosp., 1966-69; resident Banstead Hosp., Surrey, Eng., 1966-69; sr. resident tng. program Highcroft Hosp./Birmingham (Eng.) U., 1969-71; physician in charge of alcohol and drug abuse treatment Mental Health Inst., Clarinda, Iowa, 1971-72, chief psychiatrist, 1972-73; med. dir. Mental Health Ctr./Chippewa County Guidance Clinic, Chippewa Falls, Wis., 1973—; med. dir., chmn. psychiat. and chem. dependency unit Luther Hosp., Eau Claire, Wis., 1985-94; attending psychiatrist Sacred Heart Hosp., Eau Claire, 1995—; chmn. dept. psychiatry, med. dir. Sacred Heart Behavioral & Psychiat. Svcs., 1996—; past. pres. med. staff St. Joseph's Hosp., Chippewa Falls; cons. L.E. Phillips Alcohol and Drug Treatment Ctr., Chippewa Falls, 1976—. Mem. found. Peace Acad., Washington. Fellow APA; mem. Wis. Psychiat. Assn. (past chpt. pres.), Chippewa County Med. Soc. (past pres.), Islamic Med. Assn. (chpt. officer), Arab-Am. Psychiat. Assn. (past pres.). Home: 411 E Wisconsin St Chippewa Falls WI 54729 Office: 705 Bay St Chippewa Falls WI 54729

TAMAOKI, BUN-ICHI, retired endocrinology biochemistry educator; b. Tokyo, Japan, July 24, 1925; s. Bunjiro and Michi (Takeuchi) T.; children: Hidehiko, Shigeto. BS, U. Tokyo, 1947, PhD, 1958. Rsch. assoc. U. Tokyo, 1947-61; sect. chief Nat. Inst. Radiol. Science, Chiba, Japan, 1961-74; dir. div. pharm. sci. Nat. Inst. Radiol. Science, Chiba, 1974-86; prof. faculty of pharm. sci. Nagasaki (Japan) U., 1986-92. Recipient prize Ministry of Sci. & Tech., Japanese Govt., Tokyo, 1981, Decoration and diploma Emperor Japan, 1995, rsch. grantee, NIH, Washington, 1962-72. Home: 238-21 Sonno-cho, 263 Inageku Chiba-shi 263, Japan

TAMARIN, FRANK M., internist; b. New Rochelle, NY, Oct. 8, 1955; s. Sanford and Bernice (Warshaw) T.; m. Lisa Claire Stern, Oct. 27, 1990; children: Sandra, Mark. BA, Columbia Coll., 1977; MD, U. Auto. de Guadalajara, Mex., 1982. Diplomate Am. Bd. Internal Medicine. Medical resident New Rochelle (NY) Hosp. Med. Ctr., 1984-87, chief resident, 1987-88, attending in medicine, 1989—, ednl. coord. medicine, 1990—; pvt. practice New Rochelle, 1989—; cons. West Jewish Comm. Svcs., 1989—. Contbr. articles to profl. jours. including Chest, New Eng. Jour. Med., others. Mem. ACP, Am. Soc. Internal Medicine, N.Y. State Soc. Internal Medicine (alt. del. 1990). Home: 73 Ward Dr New Rochelle NY 19804 Office: 150 Lockwood Ave New Rochelle NY 10801

TAMASI, RAYMOND VALENTINO, health care facility administrator; b. Princeton, N.J., Mar. 7, 1942; s. Domenico and Pearl Irene (Toto) T.; m. Barbara Anne Scheutz, Sept. 21, 1968; children: David Christopher, Christina Lynn. BA in Econs., Rutgers U., 1963; MEd in Counseling, Health Care Adminstrn, Cambridge (Mass.) Coll., 1982. Lic. cert. social worker, Mass. Rsch. exec. Market Dynamics, Inc., Princeton, N.J., 1963-69; sr. projects mgr. Chesebrough Ponds, Inc., N.Y.C., 1969-70; dir. Falmouth (Mass.) Ecumenical Program for Youth, 1971-73; counselor Cape Cod Alcoholism Unit, Pocasset, Mass., 1973-76, asst. dir., 1976-80; dir. Cape Cod Alcoholism Unit/Gosnold on Cape Cod, Falmouth, 1980-88, v.p., 1988—, pres., CEO, 1992—, also bd. dirs.; instr. Cape Cod C.C., Barnstable, Mass., 1982—; mem. bd. incorporators Cape Cod Hosp., 1994—. Originator, broadcaster weekly radio svc. Looking at You and Alcohol, 1980-85. Mem. substance abuse com. Cape Cod Baseball League, Hyannis, Mass., 1986; chmn. Dennis (Mass.) Human Svcs. Com., 1989—; mem. Drug Free Campus Task Force, Hyannis, 1992, Barnstable County Health and Human Svcs. Coun., 1993—. Mem. Mass. Assn. Detox Dirs. (pres. 1981), Samaritans of Cape Cod (v.p. 1984-86), Employee Assistance Profls. Assn., Cert. Alcoholism Counselors Assn. Home: 2 Farm Hill Rd Dennis MA 02638-2453 Office: Gosnold on Cape Cod 200 Ter Heun Dr Falmouth MA 02540-2525

TAMBONE, GREGORIO, physician; b. Taranto, Italy, Aug. 10, 1963; came to U.S., 1980; s. Michael and Rosa (Pitarra) T.; m. Judie Lynn Threatt, Aug. 6, 1988 (div. Feb. 1990); m. Tracy L. Bryant, May 28, 1992; children: Michael, Isabella Rose. BS in Biology, Seton Hall U., 1986; DO, Kans. U. Health Scis., 1992. Resident St. John's Mercy Med. Ctr., St. Louis, 1992-95; physician Mercy Med. Group, St. Louis, 1995—. Vol. EMT Triboro Ambulance Corp., Park Ridge, N.J., 1983-85. Mem. AMA, Am. Coll. Physicians (assoc.). Office: 4700 Hwy 40/61 Saint Charles MO 63304

TAMBORLANE, WILLIAM V., JR., physician, biomedical researcher, pediatrics educator; b. N.Y.C., Aug. 25, 1946; s. William and Eleanor (Bernabo) T.; m. Kathleen Mary Blinn, Dec. 27, 1969; children: Melissa, Amy, James. BS, Georgetown U., 1968, MD, 1972. Diplomate Am. Bd. Pediatrics, Am. Bd. Pediatric Endocrinology. Attending physician Yale New Haven Hosp., 1977—; asst. prof. pediatrics Yale U., New Haven, 1977-81, dir. Children's Diabetes Ctr., 1977—; assoc. prof. pediatrics Sch. Medicine, New Haven, 1981-86; acting chief Pediatric Endocrinology, New Haven, 1982-83; chief pediatric endocrinology and diabetes Yale Sch. Medicine, 1985—, prof. prdiatrics, 1986—; program dir. Yale Children's Clin. Rsch. Ctr., N.H., Conn., 1986—; chmn. Lawson Wilkens Diabetes Com., 1988-89. Recipient Jonathan May award, Charles Best award Am. Diabetes Assn., 1979, Clin. Investigator award NIH, 1979-82. Mem. Am. Fedn. Clin. Rsch., Am. Soc. Clin. Investigation, Endocrine Soc., Soc. Pediatric Rsch., Phi Beta Kappa. Office: Yale U Sch Med Children's Clin Rsch Ctr 333 Cedar St New Haven CT 06510-3206

TAMI, THOMAS A., otolayringologist; b. Ridgway, Pa., Mar. 28, 1953; s. William D. and Ruth E. Beveridge T.; m. Molly Anne Toronski, Aug 14. 1976; children: Leigh Anne, Aaron Thomas. BS in Biochemistry, U. Pitts., 1975; MD, St. Louis U., 1979. Diplomate Am. Bd. Otolaryngology. Commd. 2d lt. USN, 1975, advanced through grades to commdr. med. corps, resigned, 1988; otolaryngology resident U.S. Naval Hosp., Oakland, Calif., 1981-86; staff otolaryngologist U.S. Naval Hosp., Portsmouth, Va., 1986-88; asst. prof. U. Calif., San Francisco, 1988-93; chief of otolaryngology San Francisco Gen. Hosp., 1990-92; assoc. prof. U. Cin. Coll. Medicine, 1993—; oral examiner Am. Bd. Otolaryngology, 1994—. Guest editor: (book) Otolaryngology Clinics of North America, 1992; contbr. numerous articles to Laryngoscope, Archives of Otolaryngology, Head and Neck Surgery, Otolaryngology. and others. Fellow ACS, Am. Acad. Otolaryngology; mem. Soc. Univ. Otolaryngologists. Office: Univ Cin PO Box 670528 Cincinnati OH 45267

TAMIN, AZAIBI, molecular virologist, researcher; b. Muar, Johor, Malaysia, Mar. 9, 1959; came to U.S., 1984; s. Hj Tamin Sahandan and Kamisah Hassan; m. Zabedah Ismail, Sept. 1, 1984; children: Adam Zulfaqar Azaibi, Afiq Zulfaiz Azaibi. BS in Microbiology with honors, U. Leeds, Eng., 1983; PhD in Microbiology, Oregon State U., 1989. Tutor in microbiology Nat. U. Malaysia, 1983-84; teaching asst. Oreg. State U., Corvallis, 1985-86; rsch. asst. Oregon State U., Corvallis, 1986-88; rsch. fellow U.S. NRC & Ctrs. for Disease Control & Prevention, Atlanta, 1989-91; rsch. scientist Ctrs for Disease Control & Prevention measles sect., Atlanta, 1991—. Contbr. articles to profl. jours. Capt. Outward Bound Sch., Malaysia (Merit award), 1978; boy-sgt. Royal Military Coll., Malaysia, 1978; pres. Malaysian Student Union, U. Leeds, Eng., 1983. Recipient scholarship Ministry of Edn., Malaysia, 1978-83, scholarship Dept. Pub. Svc., 1984-89, N.L. Tartar fellowship, 1989, postdoctoral fellowship U.S. NRC, CDC, 1989-91. Mem. AAAS, Am. Soc. Virology, Am. Soc. Microbiology, N.Y. Acad. Scis. Islamic. Office: Ctrs Disease Control & Prevention MS C22 Atlanta GA 30333

TAMKIN, ARTHUR S., psychologist; b. Montgomery, Ala., July 13, 1928; s. Sheer Sam Tamkin and Betha (Hirsch) Sofness; m. Ruth Helen Goldberg, Feb. 12,1950; children: Laura, Andrea Tamkin Bouchard, Jill, Roy. AB, Harvard U., 1950; PhD, Duke U., 1954; post doctoral study, Augusta (Ga.) Coll., 1990—. Cert. applied psychologist, Ga. Clin. psychologist VA Med. Ctr., Northampton, Mass., 1954-58; rsch. project dir. Dept. Mental Hygiene, Columbus, Ohio, 1958-59; chief psychologist VA Clinic, Hosp., Providence, R.I., 1960-73, Fuller Meml. Hosp., South Attleboro, Mass., 1973-79; psychologist Data Gen. Corp., Westboro, Mass., 1979-80; chief clin. psychologist VA Med. Ctr., Augusta, Ga., 1980-90; cons. Augusta Cor. Med. Inst., Grovetown, Ga., 1993; psychologist First Mental Health, Nashville, Tenn., 1994—; clin. psychologist pvt practice, Providence, R.I., 1959-79. Contbr. articles to Jour. Clin. Psychol., Psychol. Reports, Mil. Medicine. Mem. Augusta Area Psychol. Assn. Home: 3223 Crane Ferry Rd Augusta GA 30907 Office: PO Box 212323 Augusta GA 30917-2323

TAMLER, MARTIN S., physician; b. Indpls., Mar. 17, 1962; m. Patricia G. Ware, Oct. 18, 1987; children: Ilyssa Paige, Spencer Riley, Kendall Nicole. BA in Biology and Chemistry, Ind. U., 1984, MD, 1988. Diplomate Am. Bd. Physical Medicne and Rehab., Am. Bd. Electrodiagnostic Medicine, Nat. Bd. Med. Examiners. Intern William Beaumont Hosp., Royal Oak, Mich., 1988-89; resident in physical medicine and rehab. William Beaumont Hosp., Royal Oak, 1989-92, attending staff, 1992—; staff physician Beaumont Clinic Preventive Nutritional Medicine, 1990-92; dir. prosthetics and orthotics, co-dir. electrodiagnostics lab William Beaumont Hosp., Royal Oak, attending staff, Troy, Mich., 1992—; presenter in field. Contbr. articles to profl. publs. Supervising physician Mich. Wheelchair Games, 1990; field physician Troy Pub. Schs. Football program, 1991. Mem. AMA, Am. Acad. Physical Medicine and Rehab., Am. Assn. Electrodiagnostic Medicine, Am. Congress Rehab. Medicine, Assn. Academic Physiatrists (sec., mem. resident physician's coun. 1991-92), Physical Medicine Rsch. Found., Mich. Acad. Physical Medicine and Rehab., Mich. State Med. Soc., Oakland County Med. Soc., Phi Beta Kappa, Alpha Lambda Delta, Phi Eta Sigma. Office: 3535 W 13 Mile Rd Royal Oak MI 48073

TAMMINGA, CAROL ANN, neuroscientist; b. Grand Rapids, Mich., Jan. 26, 1946; d. Samuel William and Freda (Hekman) T.; children: Cristan Fredericka, Bonnie Michael. BS, Calvin Coll., 1966; student, U. Tubingen, Fed. Republic of Germany, 1966-67; MD, Vanderbilt U., 1971. Lic. physician, Ill., Md. Vivian Allen fellow Vanderbilt Med. Sch., 1968-71; intern in medicine Blodgett Meml. Hosp., Grand Rapids, Mich., 1971-72; resident in psychiatry U. Chgo., 1972-74, chief resident in psychiatry, 1974-75, instr. dept. psychiatry, 1975-77, asst. prof. psychiatry, 1978-79; assoc. prof. psychiatry U. Md., Balt., 1979-85, chief inpatient rsch. program, 1979—, prof. psychiatry, 1985—; chief clin. investigator Manteno (Ill.) State Hosp., 1975-79; chief clin. biochemsitry unit Nat. Inst. Neurologic & Communicative Diseases & Stroke NIH, Bethesda, Md., 1979-85; mem. treatment devel. and assessment rsch. rev. com. NIMH, 1981-85, 90-94, 96—; mem. FDA Psychopharm Adv. Com., 1990-92, chair, 1991-92; cons. in field. Author: Schizophrenia: Scientific Progress, 1988, Schizophrenia Research, 1989; editorial bd. Am. Jour. Psychiatry, Biol. Psychiatry, Jour. Nervous and Mental Diseases, Schizophrenia Bull., Schizophrenia Rsch., Functional Neurology, Progress in Neuroendocrinimmunology, Progress in Neuro-Psychopharmacology and Biol. Psychiatry; contbr. articles to Archive Gen. Psychiatry Sci., Am. Jour. Psychiatry, Jour. Neural Transmission, Lancet, Physiol. Behavior, and other. Recipient McAlpin award Nat. Assn. Mental Health, 1979; Beauchamp scholar, 1971; Found. for Rsch. in Psychiatry fellow, 1975-76, NIMH fellow, 1978-79. Mem. AAAS, Am. Psychiatric Assn., Am. Coll. Neuropharmacology, Internat. Psychoneuroendocrine Soc., Soc. Neurosci., Biol. Psychiatry. Office: U Md PO Box 21247 Baltimore MD 21228-0747

TAMPAS, JOHN P., radiologist; married; children: Jessica, Peter, Andrea, Christiana. BS, U. Vt., 1951, MD, 1954. Diplomate Am. Bd. Radiology. Radiology resident U. Vt., Burlington, 1957-60; teaching fellow pediat. radiology L.A. Children's Hosp., 1960-61; NIH Nat. Heart Inst. resident fellow cardiovascular radiology U. Ind., Indpls., 1961-62; attending radiology Med. Ctr. Hosp. Vt., Burlington, 1962—; asst. prof. radiology COll. Medicine U. Vt., 1962-70; prof. & chmn. dept. radiology Med. Ctr. Hosp. Vt., Burlington, 1970—. Contbr. articles to profl. jours. Recipient Karl Jefferson Thompson Meml. Excellence in Teaching award, 1969, 75; James Picker Found./NRC scholar, 1962-65. Fellow Am. Coll. Radiology (pres. 1987-88, bd. chancellors, emergency radiology com., accreditation com., chmn. mem. ins. com., adminstrv. affairs commn., radiologic practice commn., Gold medal 1996); mem. AMA, Soc. Pediat. Radiology, Am. Roentgen-Ray Soc. (pres. 1982-83), Radiol. Soc. N.Am., New Eng. Roentgen Ray Soc., Soc. Chmn. Acad. Radiology Depts., Assn. Univ. Radiologists, Vt. Radiol. Soc., Vt. Med. Soc., Alpha Omega Alpha. Office: Fletcher Allen Health Ctr 111 Colchester Ave Burlington VT 05401 also: Hosp Vt Med Ctr Dept Radiology Burlington VT 05401*

TAMURA, LORRAINE KEIKO, nurse; b. Honolulu, Aug. 16, 1964; d. Isami and Mitsue (Hayashida) T. AS in Nursing, U. Hawaii, 1985, BSN, 1987. Nurse aide Queens Med. Ctr., Honolulu, 1984-87, nurse, 1987—; instr. Info. Svcs., Honolulu, 1995—. Mem. Nurse Nat. Honor Soc., Sigma Theta Tau.

TAMURA, NEAL NOBORU, dentist, consultant; b. Honolulu, May 3, 1953; s. Tony T. and Doris (Fujiki) T.; m. Liana N.N. Pang, May 31, 1980 (div.); 1 child, Randi M.A. BS in Biology with distinction, U. Mo., Kansas City, 1975; DDS, Northwestern U., 1985. Resident asst. in counselling U. Mo., Kansas City, 1974-75; emergency med. technician Pacific Ambulance, Honolulu, 1975-77, mgr. ops., mobile intensive care technician, 1977-79; gen. practice dentistry Honolulu, 1985—; cons. Nuuanu Hale Hosp., Honolulu, 1985—, Hale Nani Hosp., Honolulu, 1990—, Dept. Corrections, State of Hawaii, 1987-89, Job Corps Hawaii, 1989-91, Lilina Healthcare Ctr., 1992—, Program for All Inclusivee Care for the Elderly Maluhia Hosp., 1993—. Vice chair mgmt. area hosps. State of Hawaii Bd. Commrs., Honolulu, 1987, chair, 1989, exec. com., 1989; mem. YMCA, Honolulu, 1987— (svc. award 1972, 73). Mem. ADA, Hawaii Dental Assn., Hawaii Implant Soc., Honolulu County Dental Soc., Papaniho Study Club (founder, sec. 1987-89), Phi Kappa Phi. Democrat. Home: 2016 Metcalf St Honolulu HI 96822-3333 Office: 1600 Kapiolani Blvd Ste 508 Honolulu HI 96814-3802

TAN, ALFONSO O., internist; b. Bay, Laguna, The Philippines, July 4, 1930; came to U.S., 1967; s. Miguel and Felicidad (Oliva) T.; m. Ameurfina Gatchialian; 1 child, Alfred. AA, U. Santo Tomas, Manila, 1949, MD, 1954. Diplomate Am. Bd. Internal Medicine. Intern St. Mary's Hosp., East St. Louis, Ill., 1955-56; resident in internal medicine Nashville Gen. Hosp., 1957-58, chief resident, 1958-59; fellow in cardiopulmonary disease Jewish Hosp., Cin., 1959-61; pvt. practice, Manila, 1961-67; staff physician Rutland Heights (Mass.) Hosp., 1967-69; asst. supt. Worcester County Hosp., Boyston, Mass., 1969-71; staff physician VA Med. Ctr., Columbia, S.C., 1971-78, Bonham, Tex., 1978-79, Roseburg, Oreg., 1979—. Mem. ACP, AMA, Mass. Med. Soc. Democrat. Home: 305 Thora Cir Winchester OR 97495 Office: VA Med Ctr Roseburg OR 97470

TAN, TJIAUW-LING, psychiatrist, educator; b. Pemalang, Java, Indonesia, June 2, 1935; came to U.S., 1967; naturalized, 1972; s. Ping-Hoey and Liep-Nio (Liem) T.; m. Esther Joyce Kho, June 2, 1961; children: Paul Budiman, Robert Yuling, Alice Ayling. BS, U. Indonesia Faculty Medicine, 1957, MD, 1961; postgrad. U. Indonesia, Jakarta, 1961-65, U. Calif. at L.A., 1967-71, Pa. State U., 1971-72. Diplomate Am. Bd. Psychiatry and Neurology, Am. Bd. Gen. Psychiatry, Am. Bd. Geriatric Psychiatry. Lectr. psychiatry U. Indonesia, Jakarta, 1965-67; psychiat. cons. Central Gen. Hosp., Jakarta, 1965-67; postdoctoral fellow U. Calif. at L.A. Brain Rsch. Inst., 1967-69; asst. rsch. psychiatrist, dept. psychiatry Neuropsychiat. Inst. U. Calif., L.A., 1969-70; asst. prof. psychiatry Pa. State U., 1972-87; assoc. prof. psychiatry Pa. State U., 1987—; chief inpatient psychiatry Univ. Hosp. Milton S. Hershey Med. Ctr., 1972—, dir. Behavioral Medicine Clinic, co-dir. Biofeedback Lab., 1975—; cons. psychiatry Family and Children's Svc. Lebanon County, Lebanon, Pa., 1971-79, Bd. dirs. Retarded Children's Assn. Dauphin County, Inc., 1971-73. Fellow Am. Psychiat. Assn.; mem. Pa. Psychiat. Soc., Central Pa. Psychiat. Soc., Assn. Advancement Behavior Therapy, Assn. Applied Psychophysiology and Biofeedback, Soc. Behavioral Medicine, Assn. Psychophysiol. Study of Sleep, Am. Acad. Sleep Disorder Medicine, Am. Assn. for Geriatric Psychiatry, Am. Geriatric Soc. Contbr. articles to profl. jours. Home: 1478 Bradley Ave Hummelstown PA 17036-9143 Office: Pa State U Coll Medicine Dept Psychiatry 500 University Dr Hershey PA 17033-2360

TANAKA, KOUICHI ROBERT, physician, educator; b. Fresno, Calif., Dec. 15, 1926; s. Kenjiro and Teru (Arai) T.; m. Grace Mutsuko Sakaguchi, Oct. 23, 1965; children—Anne M., Nancy K., David K. B.S., Wayne State U., 1949, M.D., 1952. Intern Los Angeles County Gen. Hosp., 1952-53; resident, fellow Detroit Receiving Hosp., 1953-57; instr. Sch. Medicine, UCLA, 1957-59, asst. prof. medicine, 1959-61, asso. prof. medicine, 1961-68, prof., 1968—; asso. chmn., chief hematology, dept. medicine Harbor-UCLA Med. Center, Torrance, Calif., 1961—. Served with AUS, 1946-48. Fellow ACP (gov. so. Calif. region I 1993—); mem. Am. Fedn. Clin. Rsch., Western Soc. Clin. Investigation, L.A. Soc. Internal Medicine (pres. 1971), Am. Soc. Hematology, Internat. Soc. Hematology, Western Assn. Physicians, Am. Soc. Clin. Investigation, Assn. Am. Physicians, Sigma Xi, Alpha Omega Alpha. Home: 4 Cayuse Ln Rancho Palos Verdes CA 90275-5172 Office: Harbor UCLA Med Ctr PO Box 2910 Torrance CA 90509-2910

TANAKA, MAKOTO, anesthesiologist; b. Tokyo, Nakano, Japan, Sept. 20, 1960; s. Junnichi and Sada (Kondo) T.; m. Tomoko Yamaguchi, May 24, 1989; children: Yutori, Tsuyoshi. MD, U. Tsukuba, Ibaraki, Japan, 1986. MD, Japanese Bd. Anesthesiologists. Resident anesthesiology U. Tsukuba Hosp., Ibaraki, 1986-89; resident anesthesiology and critical care medicine Johns Hopkins Hosp., Balt., 1989-91; instr. anesthesiology Inst. Clin. Medicine U. Tsukuba, Ibaraki, 1991-93; staff anesthesiologist Tsuchiura Kyodo Gen. Hosp., Ibaraki, 1993—. Contbr. articles to profl. jours. Mem. Internat. Anesthesia Rsch. Soc., Japan Soc. Anesthesiologists, Am. Soc. Anesthesiologists (cons., panelist task force on preanesthetic evaluation 1995—). Home: 4-419-406 Namiki, Ibaraki 305, Japan Office: Tsuchiura Kyodo Gen Hosp, Dept Anes/Crit Care Med, 11-7 Manabeshinnmachi, Ibaraki 300, Japan

TANAKA, STANLEY KATSUKI, optometrist, consultant; b. Honolulu, Sept. 19, 1932; s. Tomikichi and Hatsue T.; m. Esther K. Kokubun, Oct. 31, 1959; children: Glen A., Fay M. Student U. Hawaii, 1950-52; BS, U. Okla., 1952; OD magna cum laude (Jackson award), Ill. Coll. Optometry, 1956. Enlisted U.S. Army, 1957, advanced through grades to col. Res., 1981; optometrist Hawaii Permanente Med. Group, Honolulu, 1968—; cons. opthalmic firms. Named Hawaii Optometrist of Yr., 1984. Mem. Am. Optometric Assn., Hawaii Optometric Assn., Armed Forces Optometric Soc., Contact Lens Soc., Am. Optometric Found., Optometric Extension Program, Beta Sigma Kappa. Democrat. Club: Toastmasters. Home: 2645 Oahu Ave Honolulu HI 96822-1722 Office: 1831 S King St Honolulu HI 96826

TANDAN, BIRENDRA NATH, physician; b. Agra, India, Aug. 15, 1938; came to U.S., 1963; s. Harihar Nath and Urmila (Mehra) T.; m. Ursula R. Tandan, Jan. 9, 1965; children: Kurt N., Marc N. MBBS, Gandhi Med. Coll., 1961. Demonstrator in anatomy S.N. Med. Coll., Agra, India, 1963; intern Misericordia Hosp., Bronx, N.Y., 1963-64, resident in surgery, 1964-65; resident in urology N.Y. Med. Coll., 1965-66; resident in urology Akron (Ohio) City Hosp., 1966-67, chief resident in urology, 1967-68; urologist C.F.C. Hosp., Vrindaban, India, 1969-72, Ash Sharq Hosp., Al-Khobar, Saudi Arabia, 1972. Lt. col. ANG, N.J., 1980-89. Fellow Am. Coll. Surgeons, Internat. Coll. Surgeons; mem. Am. Geriatric Soc., Am. Urol. Assn., Am. Soc. Clin. Urol., AMA. Office: 560 Bellevue Ave Hammonton NJ 08037

TANDON, RAJIV, psychiatrist, educator; b. Kanpur, India, Aug. 3, 1956; came to U.S., 1984; s. Bhagwan Sarup and Usha (Mehrotra) T.; m. Chanchal Nammi Vohra; children: Neeraj, Anisha, Gitanjali. Student, St. Xavier's Coll., Bombay, India, 1974; BS, All India Inst., New Delhi, 1980; MD, Nat. Inst. of MH, India, 1983. Sr. resident Mental Health and Neuro-Scis., India, 1983-84; resident U. Mich. Hosps., Ann Arbor, 1984-87, attending psychiatrist, 1987—; dir. schizophrenia program U. Mich., Ann Arbor, 1987—, assoc. prof., 1993—; cons. Lenawee County Community Mental Health, Adrian, Mich., 1985—. Author: Biochemical Parameters of Mixed Affective States; Negative Schizophrenic Symptoms: Pathophysiology and Clinical Implications; contbr. more than 120 articles to profl. jours. Recipient Young Scientist's award Biennial Winter workshop on Schizophrenia, 1990, 92, Travel award Am. Coll. Neuropsychopharmacology/Mead, 1990, Rsch. Excellence award Am. Assn. Psychiatrists from India, 1993, Sci. award, Best Drs. in Am. award, 1994-95, Gerald Klerman award for outstanding rsch. by a Nat. Alliance for Rsch. in Schizophrenia and Depression young investigator, 1995. Mem. Am. Psychiat. Assn. (Wisniewski Young Psychiatrist Rschr. award 1993), World Fedn. Mental Health, Soc. for Neurosci., N.Y. Acad. Scis., Soc. Biol. Psychiatry, Mich. Psychiat. Soc. Democrat. Hindu. Office: U Mich Med Ctr Dept Psychiatry 1500 E Medical Center Dr # 8D Ann Arbor MI 48109-0999

TANENBAUM, MYRON, ophthalmic plastic surgeon; b. N.Y.C., July 26, 1955; s. Bernard and Beverly Tanenbaum; m. Monica Claire Caveny, Sept. 7, 1985; children: Geoffrey Marcus, Laura Melanie, Rebecca Elyse. BS, Tulane U., 1977; MD, Washington U., 1981. Intern Good Samaritan Med. Ctr., Phoenix, 1981-82; resident Bascom Palmer Eye Inst., U. Miami Sch. Medicine, Miami, Fla., 1982-85; instr. sch. medicine Emory U., Atlanta, 1985-86; clin. asst. prof. Bascom Palmer Eye Inst., U. Miami Sch. Medicine, 1986—; pvt. practice Miami, 1986—. Contbr. articles to profl. jours.; author, editor: Oculoplastic Surgery, 1987. Vol. Commun. Action Coun. Tulane U. Students, New Orleans, 1974-77, ARC, New Orleans, 1975-77. Emory U. fellow, 1985-86. Fellow ACP, ACS, Am. Acad. Ophthalmology, Am. Soc. Ophthalmic Plastic and Reconstructive Surgery; mem. AMA, Dade County Med. Assn., N.Y. Acad. Scis., Tau Epsilon Phi (pres. New Orleans chpt. 1976-77), Phi Beta Kappa. Office: 6280 Sunset Dr Miami FL 33143

TANENBAUM, STUART WILLIAM, biotechnologist, educator; b. N.Y.C., July 15, 1924; s. Julius and Anna (Saphirstein) T.; m. Hannah Mehler, Feb. 18, 1962; children: Jonas, Stefanie. BS, CCNY, 1944; PhD, Columbia U., 1951. Rsch. assoc. Stanford U., 1951-53; prof. microbiology Columbia Univ., Coll. of Physicians and Surgeons, N.Y.C., 1953-73; dean, Sch. Biology, Chemistry and Ecology SUNY-Coll. of Environ. Sci. & Forestry, Syracuse, 1973-85; assoc. mem. Polymer Rsch. Inst.; biotechnology prof. SUNY-Coll. of Environ. Sci. & Forestry, Syracuse, 1985-93, prof. emeritus, 1993—; adj. prof. microbiology SUNY Health Sci. Ctr., Syracuse, 1973—; vis. prof. Istituto Superiore di Sanità, Rome, 1963-64; program dir. biochemistry NSF, Washington, 1970-71; bd. dirs. Coll. Forestry Found., Syracuse, 1974-91; biotechnology cons., 1993—; chmn. ASI mtg. NATO, Sitges, Spain, 1990. Editor: Cytochalasins, 1978; contbr. over 150 articles to profl. jours.; patentee in field. Vis. scientist Fedn. Am. Socs. for Exptl. Biology Minorities Instns. Program, 1989. With U.S. Army, 1944-46; ETO. Decorated Combat Infantry award, U.S. Army, 1944; recipient Sigma Xi Faculty Rsch. award 1986, SUNY's Best Teaching award 1990, United Univ. Professions Excellence award, 1991. Mem. Am. Chem. Soc., Am. Soc. Biol. Chemists, Soc. for Indsl. Microbiology, Soc. Am. Microbiologists, Sigma Xi. Home: 7472 Armstrong Rd Manlius NY 13104-1418 Office: Coll Environ Sci & Forestry 310 Baker Labs Syracuse NY 13210

TANEY, BARRY STEPHEN, physician; b. Jersey City, N.J., June 24, 1953; s. Joseph and Cherie T.; m. Amy Brazen, Dec. 23, 1978. BS, Brown U., 1975; MD, Mt. Sinai Med. Coll., 1979. Resident in ophthalmology U. Cin., 1980-83; fellow in retina diseases Mayo Clinic, Rochester, Minn., 1983-84; pvt. practice physician, retina and vitreous diseases Ft. Lauderdale, Fla., 1984—; chief ophthalmologist, North Ridge Med. Ctr., Ft. Lauderdale, 1990-93. Mem. Am. Acad. Ophthalmology, Vitreous Soc., Am. Coll. Surgeons, Broward County Ophthalmology Soc. (pres. 1992-94). Office: Retina Vitreous Cons 5601 N Dixie Hwy Fort Lauderdale FL 33334 also: Ste 3CD 900 Glades Rd Boca Raton FL 33431 also: 3850 Hollywood Blvd Ste 403 Hollywood FL 33021

TANGUAY, PETER EUGENE, child and adolescent psychiatry educator; b. Quebec City, Que., Can., Nov. 6, 1935; came to U.S., 1960, naturalized, 1971; s. Oscar E. and Marion L. (Grady) T.; m. Margaret Fife, Dec. 22, 1960; children: Heather Louise, Gretchen Marie. BA, U. Ottawa, Ont., Can., 1956, MD, 1960. Diplomate Am. Bd. Psychiatry and Neurology (com. for cert. in child and adolescent psychiatry 1981-87, written exam. com. for child and adolescent psychiatry 1981-87, chmn. 1985-87, dir. 1990—). Intern Harper Hosp., Detroit, 1960-61; resident in psychiatry UCLA Med. Ctr.-Harbor Gen. Hosp., 1961-64; registrar in psychiatry Kingsway Hosp., Derby, Eng., 1966-68; fellow in child psychiatry UCLA Ctr. for Health Scis., 1968-70, from asst. prof. to assoc. prof., 1970-8076, prof., 1980-94, dir. child psychiatry clin. rsch. ctr., 1977-87, assoc. chief div., 1984-91, acting chief, 1992-94; Ackerly prof. child psychiatry U. Louisville Sch. Medicine, 1994—; tech. advisor Rainman, 1988; vis. prof. U. Tours, France, 1982, U. Hawaii, 1987, 90; Roy Grinker vis. prof. Michael Reese Hosp., Chgo., 1984; mem. gen. assembly Am. Bd. Med. Specialists, 1990—, rep. to Accreditation Coun. on Continuing Med. Edn., 1993—, mem. exec. com., 1994-96; bd. advisors Rieger Found., Santa Barbara, Calif., 1992—; mem. psychol. scis. rev. com. NIMH, 1976-80; lectr., presenter in field; editl. cons. EEG and Clin. Neurophysiology, 1979-85; numerous others. Author: (with Margaret Tanguay) Travel Adventure in Europe with Tent, Van or Motorhome, 1970; contbr. over 60 articles, abstracts and book revs. to sci. jours., over 20 chpts. to books. Mem. Clinton-Gore Nat. Leadership Coun., 1991-93. Recipient career sci. devel. award NIMH, 1970-75; grantee USPHS, 1977-87, 84-89, NIMH, 1980-95, MacArthur Found., 1983-88. Fellow Am. Psychiat. Assn. (coun. on rsch. 1980-95, vice chmn. 1981-94, mem. com. on chronically ill-emotionally handicapped child 1990-94), Am. Acad. Child and Adolescent Psychiatry (assoc. editor Jour. 1988—, co-chmn. task force on universal access to health care 1991—), Am. Coll. Psychiatry; mem. AMA, AAAS, Group for Advancement Psychiatry (chmn. child com. 1988—), Soc. for Rsch. in Child and Adolescent Psychopathology, Royal Coll. Psychiatry (Gt. Britain, affiliate). Democrat. Home: 1129 Cardinal Dr Louisville KY 40213-1363 Office: U Louisville Bingham Child Guidance Ctr 200 E Chestnut St Louisville KY 40202-1822

TANIGUCHI, ALICE MI YOUNG, diabetes nurse educator; b. Seoul, Republic of Korea, Feb. 15, 1948; d. Charles Chang Kee and Kerm Soon (Hahm) Hong; m. Ronald Toshio Taniguchi, Jan. 17, 1981. BSN, U. Hawaii, 1971, MPH, 1980. Cert. diabetes educator. Nurse coord., diabetes nurse specialist Straub Clinic and Hosp., Inc., Honolulu; project nurse coord. Pacific Health Rsch. Inst., Honolulu; diabetes nurse educator Straub, the Diabetes Ctr. of the Pacific, Honolulu; program coord. Hawaii State Diabetes Control Program; diabetes nurse educator Diabetes Treatment Clinic, Honolulu. Mem. Am. Assn. Diabetes Educators (bd. dirs. 1993—, Nat. Diabetes Educator of Yr. award 1991), Am. Diabetes Assn., Hawaii Assn. Diabetes Educators, Phi Kappa Phi, Sigma Theta Tau. Office: 1329 Lusitana St Ste 304 Honolulu HI 96813-2411

TANIGUCHI, TOKUSO, surgeon; b. Eleele, Kauai, Hawaii, June 26, 1915; s. Tokuichi and Sana (Omaye) T.; BA, U. Hawaii, 1941; MD, Tulane U., 1946; 1 son, Jan Tokuichi. Intern Knoxville (Tenn.) Gen. Hosp., 1946-47; resident in surgery St. Joseph Hosp., also Marquette Med. Sch., Milw., 1947-52; practice medicine, specializing in surgery, Hilo, Hawaii, 1955—; chief surgery Hilo Hosp.; teaching fellow Marquette Med. Sch., 1947-49; v.p., dir. Hawaii Hardware Co., Ltd. Capt. M.C., AUS, 1952-55. Diplomate Am. Bd. Surgery. Fellow Internat., Am. colls. surgeons; mem. Am., Hawaii med. assns., Hawaii County Med. Soc., Pan-Pacific Surg. Assn., Phi Kappa Phi. Contbr. articles in field to profl. jours. Patentee automated catheter. Home: 277 Kaiulani St Hilo HI 96720-2530

TANK, PATRICK WAYNE, anatomy educator; b. Charlotte, Mich., Jan. 9, 1950; s. Wayne Edward and Ruth Beryl (Towns) T.; m. Suzanne Kay Shaw, Dec. 29, 1973. BS in Biology, Western Mich. U., 1972; MS in Anatomy, U. Mich., 1973, PhD in Anatomy, 1976. NIH postdoctoral trainee U. Calif., Irvine, 1976-78; asst. prof. U. Ark. for Med. Scis., Little Rock, 1978-83, assoc. prof., 1983-89, prof., 1989—; dir. med. edn. U. Ark. for Med. Scis., 1989—. Contbr. over 40 articles to profl. jours. Rsch. grantee NSF, 1979, 83, 85, U. Ark. for Med. Scis., 1979, 88. Mem. Am. Assn. Anatomists, Am. Assn. Clin. Anatomists, Am. Soc. Zoologists, Soc. for Devel. Biology, Sigma Xi, Beta Beta Beta.

TANNEBAUM, IRA ROY, surgeon; b. Phila., May 23, 1945; s. David Mark and Rose Ruth (Eisenstein) T.; m. Elizabeth Jeanne Grogan, Aug. 19, 1973; children: Jonathan Ethan, Abigail Lea. BA, Ctrl. H.S., Phila., 1963; BS, Pa. State U., 1966; MD, Jefferson U., 1968. Diplomate Am. Bd. Surgery, Am. Bd. Colon and Rectal Surgery. Intern in surgery Columbia Presbyn., N.Y.C., 1968-69; resident in surgery Albert Einstein Coll.-Medicine, Bronx (N.Y.) Mcpl. Hosp., 1969-70, Thomas Jefferson U. Hosp., Phila., 1973-74; fellow in colon/rectal surgery Greater Balt. Med. Ctr., Towson, Md., 1984-85; surgeon Group Health Assn., Washington, 1977-94; pvt. practice, Washington, 1983—. Lt. comdr. M.C., USNR, 1973-77; capt. USNR ret. Fellow ACS, Am. Soc. Colon and Rectal Surgeons; mem. AMA, Am. Physicians Fellowship, Soc. Am. Gastroent. Endoscopic Surgeons, Washington Acad. Surgery. Jewish. Office: 1145 19th St NW Ste 313 Washington DC 20036

TANNEN, RICHARD LAURENCE, medical educator, nephrologist; b. N.Y.C., Aug. 31, 1937; s. Harold and Fannie (Rosenberg) T.; m. Elizabeth Whitney Harriman, Aug. 8, 1964 (div. Apr. 1990); m. Vivien Baraban, Nov. 17, 1990; children: Bradford, Whitney, Jennifer, Alison, Julie. Student, Vanderbilt U., 1957; MD, U. Tenn., Memphis, 1960. Rsch. internist Walter Reed Inst. Rsch., Washington, 1966-69; assoc. prof., co-dir. nephrology unit U. Vermont, Burlington, 1969-78; prof., chief nephrology divsn. U. Mich., Ann Arbor, 1978-88; prof., chmn. dept. medicine U. So. Calif., L.A., 1988-95; vice dean for rsch., prof. medicine U. Pa., Phila., 1995—; established investigator Am. Heart Assn., 1971-76. Co-editor: Fluids and Electrolytes, 1986, 3d edit., 1996; mem. editorial bd. Am. Jour. Medicine; contbr. more than 130 sci. articles to profl. jours. Maj. U.S. Army, 1966-69. Recipient Merit award NIH, 1986-94, Disting. Alumnus award U. Tenn., 1991. Fellow ACP; mem. Am. Soc. Nephrology (pres. 1991-92), Am. Soc. Clin. Investigation, Assn. Am. Physicians, Nat. Kidney Found. (regional v.p. 1984-87, Pres.'s award 1986). Jewish. Office: U Pa Health System 3400 Spruce St Philadelphia PA 19104*

TANNENBAUM, ABRAHAM J(OSEPH), psychologist, educator; b. N.Y.C., Jan. 5, 1924; s. Isaac and Miriam (Freeling) T.; m. Annette Schmerler, June 20, 1961; children: Alisa J. Schiff, M. David Tannenbaum, Nina S. Roisman. BA, Bklyn. Coll., 1946; MA, Columbia U., N.Y.C., 1948; PhD, Columbia U., 1960. Tchr. to prin. Yeshiva Elem. Sch., Bklyn., 1956-54; rsch. staff Tchrs. Coll., Columbia U., N.Y.C., 1954-59, prof. edn. and psychology, 1965-87, prof. emeritus, 1987—; coord. programs for gifted N.Y. State Edn. Dept., Albany, 1959-60; assoc. dean Grad. Sch. Edn. Yeshiva U., N.Y.C., 1960-65. Author: Adolescents' Attitudes, 1962, Gifted Children, 1983; co-editor: To Be Young and Gifted, 1992. Fulbright prof., 1968-69; recipient Cert. of Merit, U.S. Office of Edn., 1980. Mem. Am. Psychol. Assn., Am. Ednl. Rsch. Assn., Nat. Assn. for Gifted Children (Disting scholar 1985), Coun. for Children with Behavior Disorders (pres. 1975-76), Met. Assn. for Study of Gifted (pres. 1961). Home: 787 Caffrey Ave Far Rockaway NY 11691-5301

TANNENBAUM, STEVEN ROBERT, toxicologist, chemist; b. N.Y.C., Feb. 23, 1937; m. Carol Eigen, Sept. 6, 1959; children: Lisa, Mark. B.S. in Food Tech, MIT, 1958, Ph.D. in Food Sci. and Tech, 1962. Asst. prof. MIT, Cambridge, Mass., 1964-69; assoc. prof. MIT, 1969-74, prof. food chemistry, 1974-81, prof. chemistry and toxicology divsn. toxicology, registration and admissions officer, 1981-95; vis. prof. Hebrew U. of Jerusalem, 1973-74; BASF vis. prof. U. Kaiserslautern, 1994; mem. com. on food stds. and fortification policy NAS-NCR, 1970-73; mem. adv. com. on biochemistry and chem. carcinogenesis Am Cancer Soc., 1977-81; bd. sci. advisors divsn. cancer etiology, NCI, 1994-95, Frederick Cancer Sch. Facility, 1995—, Nat. Cancer Inst., 1989-93; mem. cancer spl. program adv. com., 1979-82; mem. peer rev. com. Nat. Toxicology Program, 1983-85; founder, bd. dirs. Vicam, Ltd., Partnership; mem. sci. adv. bd. Xenometrix, Inc., Transcend Pharmaceutics. Editor: (with R.I. Mateles) Single-Cell Protein, 1968, (with D.I.C. Wang) Single-Cell Protein II, 1975, (with others) The Economics, Marketing and Technology of Fish Protein Concentrate, 1974, (with J.R. Whitaker) Food Proteins, 1977, Nutritional Safety Aspects of Food Processing, 1979, (with others) Gastrointestinal Cancer: Endogenous Factors, 1981, (with R.A. Scanlan) N-Nitroso Compounds, 1981; mem. editl. bd. Japanese Jour. Cancer Rsch., 1986—, Chem. Rsch. Toxicology, 1988-91, 95—, Cancer Epidemiology, Prevention and Biomarkers, 1990—, Cancer Rsch., 1993—; contbr. over 300 articles to profl. jours. Mem. AAAS, Am. Chem. Soc., Inst. Food Technologists (sect. councillor N.E. chpt. 1966-69, Samuel Cate Prescott Rsch. award 1970, Babcock Hart award 1980), editorial bd. sci. jour. 1970-73, Am. Inst. Nutrition, Am. Assn. Cancer Rsch., Sigma Xi. Office: MIT Dept Chemistry Toxicology Bldg 16 Rm 822a 77 Massachusetts Ave Cambridge MA 02139-4301

TANNER, GEORGE ALBERT, physiology educator; b. Vienna, Austria, Aug. 2, 1938; came to U.S., 1939; s. Emil and Dora (Austein) T.; m. Judith Ann Shapiro, Dec. 2, 1962; children: Jonathan, Elizabeth. BA, Cornell U., 1959; PhD, Harvard U., 1964. Asst. prof. dept. physiology biophysics Ind. U. Sch. Medicine, Indpls., 1967-72; assoc. prof. Ind. U. Sch. Medicine, 1972-78, prof., 1978—; vis. prof. Physiology Inst., U. Heidelberg, Fed. Republic Germany, 1974-75. Contbr. to rsch. textbooks. Postdoctoral fellow, Cornell U., 1964-67, NIH Sr. Postdoctoral fellow, 1986-87; recipient Disting. Teaching award, Amoco Found., 1983. Mem. Am. Physiology Soc., Am. Soc. Nephrology, Internat. Soc. Nephrology, Phi Beta Kappa, Sigma Xi. Jewish. Home: 8086 Claridge Rd Indianapolis IN 46260-4910 Office: Ind U Sch Medicine Dept Physiology Biophysics 635 Barnhill Dr Indianapolis IN 46202-5126

TANNER, MARTIN ABBA, statistics and human oncology educator; b. Highland Park, Ill., Oct. 19, 1957; s. Meir and Esther Rose (Bauer) T.; m. Anat Talitman, Aug. 14, 1984; 1 child, Noam Ben. B.A., U. Chgo. 1978, Ph.D., 1982. Asst. prof. stats. and human oncology U. Wis., Madison 1982-87, assoc. prof., 1987-90, dir. lab., prof. and dept. chair dept. Biostatistics U. Rochester, 1990-94; prof. dept. of statistics Northwestern U., 1994—; cons. Kirkland & Ellis, 1980-82; mem. Nat. Inst. Allergy and Infectious diseases of NIH; reviewer NIH, NSF, VA. Assoc. editor Jour. Am. Stat. Assn., 1987—; contbr. articles to profl. jours. Recipient New Investigator Research award NIH, 1984, Mortimer Spiegelman award Am. Pub. Health Assn., 1993; NSF grantee, 1983, 95, NIH grantee, 1986—. Fellow Royal Statis. Soc.; mem. Am. Statis. Assn., AAAS, Mensa, Sigma Xi. Avocations: classical guitar; medieval poetry. Office: Northwestern U 2006 Sheridan Rd Evanston IL 60208

TANNO, RONALD LOUIS, dentist; b. San Jose, Calif., Dec. 17, 1937; s. George Anthony and Rose Marie (Manghisi) T. BS magna cum laude, Santa Clara U., 1959; DDS, U. of Pacific, 1963. Dentist Santa Clara County Health Dept., San Martin, Calif., 1965-67, Alameda County Health Dept., Oakland, Calif., 1965-67; pvt. practice San Jose, 1966—; dental cons. Found. Med. Care, San Jose, 1977-81, Dental Ins. Cons., Saratoga, Calif., 1980-88, Santa Clara County Sch. Dists. Dental Plan, San Jose, 1983—; cons. quality rev. Delta Dental Plan Calif., San Francisco, 1983—; mem. dental staff Los Gatos (Calif.) Community Hosp., 1978-94, chief dental dept., 1983, 84. Capt. USAF, 1963-65. Mem. ADA, Calif. Dental Assn., Santa Clara County Dental Soc., Elks, Lions, Xi Psi Phi, Omicron Kappa Upsilon. Office: 1610 Westwood Dr Ste 3 San Jose CA 95125-5110

TANSEY, ROBERT PAUL, SR., pharmaceutical chemist; b. Newark, Apr. 27, 1914; s. William Austin and Charlotte E. (Endler) T.; m. Natalie C. McMahon, Feb.22, 1941; children—Barbara, Carol, Robert, David. B.S., Rutgers U., 1938, M.S. in Pharm. Organic Chemistry, 1950. Sect. head Schering Corp., Bloomfield, N.J., 1953-58; mgr. research Strong Cobb Arner, Inc., Cleve., 1958-63; tech. dir., v.p. Vet. Labs., Inc., Lenexa, Kans., 1963-84, cons., 1984—. Registered pharmacist, N.J., Mo., Ohio. Contbr. articles to profl. jours. Patentee in field (5). Mem. Am. Pharm. Assn., Rho Chi, Kappa Psi. Club: Toastmasters (cert.). Home: 11141 Glen Arbor Rd Kansas City MO 64114-5118

TANYEL, FERIDUN CAHIT, medical educator, pediatric surgeon; b. Eskisehir, Turkey, Sept. 25, 1954; s. Muammer and Mefkure (Erguvan) T.; m. Nurhan Yildirim, June 27, 1979; children: Emre Doruk, Didem. MD, Hacettepe U., Ankara, Turkey, 1978. Diplomate Turkish Bd. Pediatric Surgery. Resident Hacettepe U., 1978-83; pediat. surgeon Children's Hosp., Ankara, 1983-85; hon. fellow U. Wis., Madison, 1990-91; asst. prof. Hacettepe U., 1987-89, assoc. prof., 1989-94, prof., 1995—. Contbr. over 60 articles to profl. jours. Surgeon Turkish Mil. Acad. Medicine, 1985-87. Hacettepe U. grantee, 1991; Fulbright scholar, 1990-91; Sci. and Tech. Rsch. grantee Coun. Turkey, 1994. Mem. Turkish Assn. Pediatric Surgeons, Hacettepe Assn. Pediatric Surgeons, Turkish Fulbright Assn. Office: Hacettepe U, Childrens's Hosp, Dept Pediatric Surgery, 06100 Ankara Turkey

TAPAWAN, LUCINO NATI, critical care nurse; b. Cavite, Philippines, Oct. 31, 1957; s. Alberto Corpuz and Paciencia Javier (Nati) T. Diploma, Emilio Aguinaldo Coll., Manila, 1979, BSN, 1980; MS, Columbia U., N.Y.C., 1991. CCRN, staff nurse Med. Ctr. Manila; head nurse U. Med. Ctr., Dasmarinas, Cavite, Philippines; staff nurse CCU St. Vincent's Hosp. & Med. Ctr., N.Y.C.; nursing practitioner emergency rm. St. Luke's-Roosevelt Hosp. Ctr., N.Y.C., clin. admistrv. liaison, emergency rm. nurse. Mem. AACN, N.Y. State Nurses Assn., Emergency Nurses Assn. Home: 412 W 110th St Apt 63 New York NY 10025-2404

TAPIA, FARZANA MOIEZ, mental health counselor; b. Hyderabad, India, Apr. 3, 1943; came to U.S., 1968; d. Feroze Husain and Malika (Begum) Arastu; m. Moiez Ahmed Tapia, Aug. 19, 1968. BA, Women's Coll. Osmania, Hyderabad, 1964; MA, Arts Coll. Osmania, Hyderabad, 1966; BJ, Osmania U., Hyderabad, 1968; MEd in Counseling, Ga. State U., 1972. Lic. mental health counselor, Fla. Fgn. student counselor Ga. State U., Atlanta, 1972; social worker Hampton (Va.) Dept. Social Svcs., 1973-74; mental health counselor Community Mental Health Ctr., Miami, Fla., 1974-75; coord. svcs. for elderly Community Health, Inc., Miami, 1975—; bd. dirs. H.O.M.E. Found., Miami, 1989, sec., 1990-91; bd. dirs. Inst. Islamic Rsch., Miami, 1989; treas. Hyderabad Assoc., 1990-91; advisor IQRA. Editor: Georgette mag., Vasudha, India, 1957-64, Inspirer mag., Hyderabad, Nama, 1976-89; contbr. articles to newspapers. Mem. Am. Assn. Counseling and Devel. Home: 5904 SW 64th Pl Miami FL 33143-2056 Office: Community Health Inc 11295 SW 216th St Miami FL 33170-2963

TAPPER, DAVID, pediatric surgeon; b. Balt., Aug. 26, 1945; s. Herman A. and Sylvia Phyllis (Golomb) T.; m. Susan Irene Wagner, June 25, 1968; children: Joellen, Erica, Jacalyn, Aaron. BS, U. Md., College Park, 1966; MD, U. Md., Balt., 1970. Surg. intern and resident U. Calif. San Francisco Med. Ctr., 1970-73; pediatric surg. rsch. fellow Boston Children's Hosp., 1973-75; sr. and chief surg. resident U. Calif., San Francisco, 1975-77; sr. and chief pediatric surg. fellow Children's Hosp., Boston, 1977-79; asst. prof. surgery Harvard Med. Sch., Boston, 1979-83; surgeon-in-chief Children's Hosp. Med. Ctr., Seattle, 1983—; prof. surgery and pediatrics U. Wash., Seattle, 1983—, vice chmn. dept. surgery, 1986—; bd. dirs. Am. Bd. Surgery, Phila., 1991—. Served to maj. USAR, 1971-82. Fellow ACS; mem. Am. Surg Assn., Am. Pediatric Surgery Assn. (bd. govs. 1993—), Soc. Univ. Surgeons, Pacific Coast Surg. Soc. Republican. Jewish. Office: Children's Hosp Med Ctr 4800 Sand Point Way NE Seattle WA 98105-3901

TARAN, RICHARD BRUCE, clinical psychologist; b. Ayer, Mass., Dec. 4, 1942; s. Albert and Sylvia Shirley (Silverman) T.; married, July 16, 1967; children: Andrew, Jason. BA in Clin. Psychology, L.I. U., 1964, MA in Clin. Psychology, 1967; PhD, Calif. Sch. Profl. Psychology, 1973. Lic. clin. psychologist, Tenn. Clin. dir. Multi County Mental Health Ctr., Tullahuma, Tenn., 1974-88; clin. psychologist Brentwood (Tenn.) Counseling Assocs., 1988—; clin. cons. Williamson County Schs., Franklin, Tenn., 1988—, Franklin City Schs., 1988—. Office: Brentwood Counseling Assocs 5111 Maryland Way Brentwood TN 37027-7513 Home: 906 Grapevine Ln Nashville TN 37221-4365

TARASKO, ALEXANDRA, nursing educator; b. Austria, Jan. 15, 1949; came to U.S., 1955; d. Peter Stephen and Alexandra (Narizna) Bazylewsky; m. Basil Paul Tarasko, Aug. 15, 1970; children: Andrei, Michael. BSN, Hunter Coll., 1973; MA in Nursing Edn., NYU, 1980; mental health/psychiat. nursing cert., Adelphi U., 1996. Psychiat. nurse Roosevelt Hosp., N.Y.C., 1974-76, head nurse, 1976-78; assoc. prof. Queensborough C.C., Bayside, N.Y., 1981—; recruiter nursing dept. Queensborough C.C., 1986-90; adj. lectr. NYU, N.Y.C., 1980; coord. Older Adults: Health Care '90's, Bayside, 1990, AIDS Conf., Bayside, 1991; participant TV and radio appearances, 1989, 91. Apptd. mem. Health Careers Task Force, N.Y.C., 1991, CUNY Health Professions Task Force, Psychosocial Svcs., 1994-95; leader Health Explorer post Boy Scouts Am., Queensborough C.C., 1988-90. Mem. Nat. League for Nursing. Home: 36-46 212th St Bayside NY 11361-2049 Office: Queensborough CC Springfield Blvd And Fifth Ave Flushing NY 11364

TARASZKIEWICZ, WALDEMAR, physician; b. Wilno, Poland, July 6, 1936; came to U.S., 1979; s. Michal Taraszkiewicz and Nina (Lutomska) Dylla; m. Teresa Barbara Szwarc, Oct. 15, 1966. MD, Med. Acad., Gdansk, Poland, 1961, internal medicine specialty, 1967, internal medicine specialty II, 1972. Diplomate Am. Bd. Family Practice. Family physician Out Patient Clinic, Sopot, Poland, 1962-64; resident doctor U. Hosp., Gdansk, 1965-71; allergist Clinic of Allergy, Gdansk, 1965-75; physician Cardiology Dept., Gdansk, 1971-75, Hôpital Civil, Telagh, Algeria, 1975-79; surg. asst. Hinsdale (Ill.) Hosp., 1979-82; resident physician St. Mary of Nazareth Hosp., Chgo., 1982-85, emergency room physician, 1984-85; family practice medicine Brookfield, Ill., 1985-88, Westmont, Ill., 1988-89, Chgo., 1987—; med. dir. Winston Manor Nursing Home, Chgo., 1989-90; clin. asst. prof. U. Ill. Med. Coll., 1994—; sr. asst. dept. cardiology Univ. Hosp., Gdansk, 1971-75; mem. adminstrv. com., pres. med. staff Hôpital Civil, Telagh, 1976-79. Contbr. articles to profl. jours. Recipient Bronze medal Polski Zwiazek Wedkarski, 1970, cert. 3d place, 1971. Fellow Am. Acad. Family Practice; mem. AMA (continuing edn. award), Ill. Med. Soc., Chgo. Med. Soc. (practice mgmt. com.), World Med. Assn., Am. Acad. Allergy and Immunology, Am. Coll. Allergy and Immunology, Polish Med. Alliance, N.Y. Acad. Scis. Office: Jefferson Park Med Bldg 4811 N Milwaukee Ave Ste 130 Chicago IL 60630-2103

TARDIF, ROBERT PAUL, obstetrician, gynecologist; b. July 18, 1959. DO, U. New Eng., Biddeford, Maine, 1988. Diplomate Am. Bd. Obstetrics and Gynecology. Rotating intern Osteopathic Hosp. of Maine, Portland, 1988-89; resident in ob-gyn. Albany (N.Y.) Med. Ctr., 1989-93; pvt. practice St. Mary's Regional Med. Ctr., Lewiston, Maine, 1993—. Office: St Marys Med Bldg 95 Campus Ave Lewiston ME 04240-6055

TARDIFF, KENNETH JOSEPH, psychiatrist; b. New Orleans, Oct. 20, 1944. MD with Honors, Tulane Med. Sch., 1969; MPH, Harvard U., 1973. Resident in psychiatry Mass. Gen. Hosp., Boston, 1970-73; asst. prof. psychiatry U. British Columbia, Vancouver, Canada, 1973-75; assoc. prof. psychiatry SUNY, Stony Brook, N.Y., 1975-81; assoc. dean Cornell Med. Coll., N.Y.C., 1981-87, assoc. prof. psychiatry and pub. health, 1981-90; prof. psychiatry and pub. health Cornell Med. Coll., 1990—; assoc. med. dir. Payne Whitney Clinic, N.Y.C., 1988—; cons. to instns. and lawyers on violence and suicide. Author: Assessment and Treatment of Violent Patients, 1996, Seclusion and Restraint, 1984, Violence-Psychiatric Clinics, 1988. Chmn. Am. Psychiat. Assn. Task Force on Seclusion and Restraint, Washington, 1981-85, Task Force on Clinician Safety, 1989—. Fellow Am. Psychiat. Assn., N.Y. Acad. Medicine; mem. Assn. Am. Med. Coll., Am. Acad. Psychiatry and Law, Assn. Acad. Psychiatry. Office: Cornell/Payne Whitney Box 147 525 E 68th St New York NY 10021-4873

TARDY, MEDNEY EUGENE, JR., otolaryngologist, facial plastic surgeon; b. Scottsburg, Ind., Dec. 3, 1934. MD, Ind. U., 1960. Diplomate Am. Bd. Otolaryngology (v.p. 1993, pres. 1994). Intern Tampa Gen. Hosp., 1960-61; resident in otolaryngology U. Ill. Hosp., 1963-67, fellow head, neck and plastic surgery, 1967-68; otolaryngologist St. Joseph Hosp., Chgo.; prof. clin. otolaryngology U. Ill.; pvt. practice Chgo.; dir. divsn. facial plastic and reconstructive surgery U. Ill.; prof. clin. otolaryngology Ind. U. Med. Ctr. Pres. Am. Bd. Otolaryngology; bd. govs., Chgo. Symphony Orch., Hubbard St. Dance Co. Mem. ACS, Am. Acad. Facial Plastic and Reconstructive Surgery, Am. Acad. Otolaryngology, Am. Laryngological Soc., Am. Rhinological Soc. Office: 2913 N Commonwealth Ave Ste 430 Chicago IL 60657-6224

TARGOVNIK, SELMA E. KAPLAN, physician; b. N.Y.C., Apr 22, 1936; d. Harry A. and Helen (Goodstein) Kaplan; m. Jerome H. Targovnik, Dec. 2, 1961; children: Nina Rebecca, Labe Eric (dec.), Diane Michelle. BA, NYU, 1957; MD, Albert Einstein Coll. Medicine, 1961. Diplomate Am. Bd. Dermatology. Intern Kaiser Found. Hosp., San Francisco, 1961-62; resident in internal medicine Bellevue Hosp., NYU Med. Ctr., 1962-63, U. Colo. Med. Ctr., Denver, 1963-64; rsch. fellow, resident in dermatology Boston U. Med. Ctr., 1964-66, mem. staff, 1968-69; mem. staff NYU Med. Ctr., 1966-68; practice medicine specializing in dermatology, Phoenix, 1969—; mem. staff St. Joseph's Hosp., Phoenix, St. Luke's Hosp., Phoenix, Columbia Hosp., Phoenix; mem. staff Good Samaritan Hosp., Phoenix, chief divsn. dermatology, 1985-90. Bd. dirs. ACLU, Ariz., 1973-78, 83-94, Congregation Beth El, Phoenix, 1971-75, Flagstaff Festival of the Arts, 1984-86; active Jewish Nat. Fund. Fellow Am. Acad. Dermatology, Assocs. for the Weizmann Inst. of Sci., Assocs. for the Technion Inst.; mem. Am. Technion Soc. (bd. dirs. 1988—, pres. Ariz. divsn. 1990-92), Dermatology Found., Sonoran Dermatologic Soc. Southwestern Dermatologic Soc., Pacific

Dermatologic Soc., Noah Worcester Dermatologic Soc., Phi Beta Kappa, Mu Chi Sigma, Pi Delta Phi, Beta Lambda Sigma. Democrat. Jewish. Home: 3706 E Rancho Dr Paradise Valley AZ 85253-5023 Office: 1300 N 12th St Ste 503 Phoenix AZ 85006

TARK, KWAN CHUL, plastic surgeon; b. Seoul, Korea, July 10, 1949; s. Won Chang and Soon Ok (Sohn) T.; m. Kyung Sook Han, Feb. 23, 1976; 3 children. BM, Yonsei U., Seoul, 1974, MA, 1977, PhD, 1985. Bd. cert. diplomate in plastic surgery. Plastic surgery resident Yonsei Univ. Med. Ctr., Seoul, 1975-79, asst. prof., 1982-91, assoc. prof., 1991-96, prof., 1996—; instr. NYU Med. Ctr., N.Y.C., 1987-88; chmn. Yonsei U. Wonju Christian Hosp., 1984-86. Author: Plastic Surgery, 1991; contbr. articles to profl. jours. Maj. Korean Army, 1979-82. Fellow ACS; mem. Am. Soc. Plastic and Reconstructive Surgeons, Am. Soc. for Reconstructive Microsurgery. Office: Yonsei Univ Med Ctr, Dept Plastic Surgery, CPO Box 8044, Seoul Korea

TARLOV, ALVIN RICHARD, former philanthropic foundation administrator, physician, educator, researcher; b. Norwalk, Conn., July 11, 1929; s. Charles and Mae (Shelinsky) T.; m. Joan Hylton, June 12, 1956 (div. 1976); children: Richard, Elizabeth, Jane, Suzanne, David. BA, Dartmouth Coll., 1951; MD, U. Chgo., 1956. Intern Phila. Gen. Hosp., 1956-57; resident in medicine U. Chgo. Hosps., 1957-58, 62-63, research assoc., 1958-61; asst. prof. medicine U. Chgo., 1963-68, assoc. prof., 1968-70, prof., 1970-84, chmn. dept. medicine, 1969-81; chmn. grad. med. edn. nat. adv. com. HHS, Washington, 1980; pres. Henry J. Kaiser Family Found., Menlo Park, Calif., 1984-90; sr. scientist New Eng. Med. Ctr., Boston, 1990—, exec. dir. The Health Inst., 1995—; prof. of Pub. Health Harvard U., Boston, 1990—; prof. of medicine Tufts U., 1990—. Pres. Med. Outcomes Trust, Inc., 1993—; chmn. bd., pres. Mass. Health Data Consortium, 1994—. Served to capt. U.S. Army, 1958-61. Recipient Research Career Devel. award NIH, 1962-67; John and Mary Markle Found. scholar, 1966-71. Mem. ACP (master), Inst. Medicine of Nat. Acad. Scis. Office: The Health Inst New Eng Med Ctr 750 Washington St # 345 Boston MA 02111-1533

TARPY, ELEANOR KATHLEEN, social worker; b. Pawtucket, R.I.; d. Stephen and Mary F. (Nolan) T. AB, Brown U., 1937; MS in Social Work, Boston U., 1947. Lic. social worker, Mass. Social worker R.I. Child Welfare, Providence, 1937-47, supr., 1947-49; supr. VA Regional Office, Providence, 1949-54, VA Med. Ctr., Brockton, Mass., 1954-90; ret., 1990. Contbg. author: Current Psychiatric Therapies, vol. 4, 1964. Mem. Nat. Assn. Social Work, (past com. chair). Home: 929 Armistice Blvd Pawtucket RI 02861-3321

TARRO, GIULIO, virologist; b. Messina, Italy, July 9, 1938; s. Emanuele and Emanuela (Iannello) T. MD, U. Naples, 1962, postgrad. in nervous diseases, 1968, PhD in Virology, 1971; postgrad. in med. and biol. scis., Roman Acad., 1979; hon. degree, U. Pro Deo, Albany, N.Y., 1989, St. Theodora Acad., N.Y., 1991. Asst. in med. pathology Naples U., Italy, 1964-66; rsch. assoc. divsn. virology and cancer rsch. Children's Hosp., Cin., 1965-68; asst. prof. rsch. pediat. U. Cin. Coll. Medicine, 1968-69; rsch. fellow Nat. Rsch. Coun., Naples, 1966-74, rsch. chief, 1974; prof. oncologic virology Coll. Medicine U. Naples, 1971-85, prof. microbiology adn immunology Sch. Specialization, 1972—; chief divsn. virology D. Cotugno Hosp. for Infectious Diseases, Naples, 1973—; dean faculty natural and phys. scis. Nobile Accademia di Santa Teodora Imperatrice, Capua, Italy, 1993—; sr. scientist Nat. Cancer Inst. Frederick (Md.) Ctr., 1973; project dir. Nat. cancer Inst., Bethesda, Md., 1971-75; edn. min. rep. Zool. Sta., Naples, 1975-79; cons. Italian Pharmacotherpic Inst., Rome, 1980—; pres. De Beaumont Bonelli Found. for Cancer Rsch., Naples, 1978—, nat. com. on bioethics, 1995—. Author: Virologia Oncologica, 1979 (award 1985), Patologia dell'AIDS, 1991, Con in Cancro si Puó Vivere, 1992, AIDS COsa Possiamo Fare Cosa Dobbiamo Sapere, 1994; contbr. over 300 sci. papers to profl. publs.; patentee in field. Pres. Sci. Cultural Com., Torre Annunziata, Italy, 1984, Tumor Prevention Assn., Rome, 1984; mem. acad. senate Constantinian U., Providence, 1990, U. Pro Deo, N.Y., 1994. Maj. Italian Navy, 1982-84, lt. col., 1993-95. Decorated Comdr. Nat. Order of Merit, 1991, Star of Europe, 1980; recipient Internat. Lenghi award Lincei Acad., 1969, Gold Microscope award Italian Health Min., 1973, Knights of Humanity award Internat. Register of Chivalry, Malta, 1978, gold medal of Culture, Pres. of Italian Republic, 1975, Culture award, 1985, 1st prize in Biomed. Rsch., Italian Acad. Arts and Scis., 1987, Castello di Pietrarossa award, Italy, 1991, gold Cesare award Padova, 1991, 20th Century award in Medicine, 1994, Knight of Grand Cross Sovereign Constantinian order of St George, 1993 Gold Little Horse , Transnat., European Federation, Rome 1996. Fellow AAAS; mem. Am. Soc. Microbiology, Internat. Assn. for Leukemias, Internat. League Drs. for Abolition of Vivisection (pres. 1992—), Italian Soc. Immuno-Oncology (v.p. 1975—, pres. 1990—), Italian Assn. for Viral Study and Rsch. (pres. 1995—), Assn. Res. Prevention of Cancer (mem. sci. com. 1995), N.Y. Acad. Scis., Lions (pres. Pompei chpt. 1987-89, vice gov. dist. 108y 1991-92, pres. to fight cancer 1992-94, pres. com. sci. and life 1994-95, pres. com. to fight drug addiction and AIDS 1995-96, Melvin Jones fellow 1993). Roman Catholic. Home: 286 Posillipo, 80123 Naples Italy Office: D Cotugno Hosp USL 41, 54 Quagliariello, 80131 Naples Italy

TARTAGLIA, ANTHONY PHILIP, dean, physician; b. Albany, N.Y., Sept. 14, 1932; s. Louis S. and Teresa (Vitale) T.; m. Jeanne Mochi; children: Robert, John, Catherine. BS, Union U., 1954; MD, Rochester (N.Y.) Med. Sch., 1958. Intern Univ. Hosps. Cleve., 1958-59; asst. resident Albany (N.Y.) Med. Ctr. Hosp., 1959-60, 1960-61, fellow in hematology, 1961-62, chief resident in medicine, 1962-63, asst. attending physician, asst. attending hematologist, 1963-70; chief hematologist Albany VA Hosp., 1970-75, attending physician, hematologist, 1975—, attending physician, 1963, cons. physician, 1970-75; cons. hematologist Children's Hosp., 1975—; chief of medicine St. Peter's Hosp., 1975-84; sr. v.p. patient and clin. affairs Albany Med. Ctr. Hosp., 1985, exec. v.p. patient care, 1985—, gen. dir., 1987-90; acting dean Albany Med. Coll., 1990, dean, 1990—; cons. hematologist Good Samaritan Hosp., 1975—. Contbr. numerous articles to profl. jours. Mem. State Bd. of Medicine, 1977-85; chmn. med. adv. com. blood program ARC, 1972-76, bd. dirs., 1976-82; chmn. med. adv. com. Leukemia Soc., Tri-Cities Cooley's Anemia Found., 1969-74; prin. investigator Nat. Polycythemia Vera Study Group; mem. task force on recredentialing and licensure N.Y. State Health Dept. and Bd. of Regents, 1986; mem. N.Y. State Coun. on Grad. Med. Edn., 1987-90, chmn. subcom. on consortial devel., 1989-90; mem. N.Y. State Hosp. Rev. and Planning Coun., 1990. Recipient Humanitarian of the Yr. award United Cerebral Palsy Ctr. for Disabled, 1982, Leone d'Oro award Sons of Italy in Am., 1989, Robert DeVillier's award Leukemia Soc. Am., 1989. Fellow ACP; mem. AMA, N.Y. State Med. Soc., Albany County Med. Soc. (sec. 1974-76, pres. 1978-80), Am. Soc. Hematology, Am. Fedn. Clin. Rsch., Northeastern Internal Med. Soc., Am. Internal Med. Soc., Phi Beta Kappa, Alpha Omega Alpha, Sigma Xi. Office: Albany Med Coll 47 New Scotland Ave Albany NY 12208-3412

TARTELL, ROBERT MORRIS, retired dentist; b. Bronx, N.Y., June 22, 1926; s. Julius and Ida (Saunders) T.; m. Lottie Haid Schachter, June 12, 1948; children: Ross Howard, Marc Sorrel, Adam Ethan. BA, N.Y.U., 1945, DDS, 1948. Lic. dentist, N.Y. V.p., dir. Medden, Inc., Valley Stream, N.Y., 1957-71; mng. ptnr. Profl. Investors, N.Y.C., 1957-91; pres., dir. Roberts Adv. Svc., Inc., N.Y.C., 1957-91; dir. postgrad. edn. Am. Soc. Study of Orthodontics, N.Y.C., 1971-72; mng. ptnr. RBT Co., Elmsford, N.Y., 1987-91; v.p., bd. dirs. Sport World of Am. Inc., West Chester, N.Y., 1992-94;, 1995. Prodr.: Gilbert and Sullivan Yiddish Light Opera Co., West Hempstead, N.Y., 1980—; co-copywriter: (operetta) H.M.S. Pinafore in Yiddish, 1986; prodr. (cassette record) Der Yiddisher Pinafore, 1994, Der Yiddisher Mikado, 1995. Pres. West Hempstead Sch. Commn. League, 1968-69; dir., founder West Hempstead Scholarship Fund, 1970-71. 1st lt. U.S. Army, 1952-54, Panama. Mem. Am. Dental Assn., N.Y. Acad. Scis., 1st Dist. Dental Soc., Gen. Semantics Inst., ACLU, Mensa, Common Cause, Mason, Gallatin. Jewish. Home: 690 Hawthorne St West Hempstead NY 11552-3112

TARTER, LARRY KELLY, optometrist; b. Greenville, Ky., Mar. 6, 1959; s. Loyd Kelly and Irene (Dwyer) T; m. Ruth Ann Hale, Jan. 23, 1988; children: Elizabeth, Zachary. Student, Murray State U., 1980; DO, So. Coll. Optometry, 1984. Optometrist Greenville, Ky., 1986—. Adv. bd. Muhlenberg County Opportunity Ctr., Greenville, 1993—, Greenville C. of C., Greenville, 1987-91. Mem. Am. Optometric Assn., Ky. Optometric Assn., Greenville Lions Club (pres., adv. bd. 1987—). Home: 243 Hickory Ln Greenville KY 42345 Office: 224 Hopkinsville St Greenville KY 42345

TARTTER, VIVIEN CAROL, psychology educator; b. Flushing, N.Y., June 13, 1952; d. John and Gertrude Phyllis (Ullmann) Rothman; m. Paul Ian Tartter, Oct. 13, 1972; children: Eric Walter, Alexander Charles. AB, Brown U., 1973, MA, 1975, PhD, 1977. Postdoctoral fellow Bell Labs., Murray Hill, N.J., 1977-79, cons., 1979-84; asst. prof. Rutgers U., Camden, N.J., 1979-84, assoc. prof., 1984-88, chmn. psychology, 1985; assoc. prof. psychology CCNY, 1988-90, prof., 1991; cons. Salk Inst., La Jolla, Calif., 1980, Air Force Aerospace Med. Rsch. Lab. Contract U. Dayton, 1984-86, Cochlear Implant Project Manhattan Eye and Ear Hosp., 1986-90; vis. rsch. assoc. dept. otolaryngology U. Melbourne, 1987. Author: Language Processes, 1986; contbr. articles to profl. jours. James Gordon Bennett Meml. scholar, 1969; grantee Deafness Rsch. Found., 1988, Nat. Inst. Deafness and Communication Disorders, 1991-95, predoctoral fellow, 1975-77; grantee U.S. Dept. Edn., 1992-96; Pub. Health Svc. predoctoral fellow, 1975-77, Fogarty Sr. Internat. fellow, 1987, grantee, 1991-95; recipient Charles Johanna Busch Meml. Fund award Rutgers U., 1985-87, Career Advancement award for women NSF, 1989. Mem. AAAS, Acoustical Soc. Am., Am. Psychol. Assn., Psychonomic Soc., N.Y. Acad. Scis. (chair linguistics sect. 1992—), Phi Beta Kappa, Sigma Xi. Democrat. Jewish. Avocations: cooking, sailing, scuba diving, hiking. Office: CCNY Dept Psychology 138th St & Convent Ave New York NY 10031

TARUI, SEIICHIRO, internal medicine educator, physician; b. Nishinomiya, Hyogo, Japan, July 23, 1927; s. Kasaburo and Katsuko (Shimada) T.; m. Yoshiko Iwasaki, Oct. 13, 1959; children: Jun, Makoto. MD, Osaka U., 1953, PhD Osaka U., 1959. Diplomate Ministry Health and Welfare of Japan. Intern Osaka U. Hosp. (Japan), 1953-54; asst. prof. clin. lab. Osaka U. Med. Sch., 1966-69, assoc. prof. internal medicine, 1969-78, prof., 1978-91, chmn. dept. internal medicine, 1978-91, prof. emeritus, 1991—; dir. Osaka U. Hosp., 1984-86, Otemae Hosp., 1992—; vis. prof. biol. chemistry U. Tex.-Dallas, 1970-71. Discoverer Glycogenosis Type VII, 1965, erythrocyte phosphofructokinase deficiency, 1969, myogenic hyperuricemia, 1986. Author numerous papers on metabolic myopathies, type I diabetes, textbook of Metabolic Diseases, 1984, Neuromuscular Diseases, 1984, Obesity, 1985, Insulitis and Type I Diabetes (Lessons from NOD mouse), 1986. Grantee Japan Med. Assn., Tokyo, 1973, Muscular Dystrophy Assn., N.Y., 1982, 86; recipient Spl. prize Japanese Med. Assn., 1990, Uehara prize Uehara Life Scis. Found., 1991, Takeda Med. prize Takeda Scis. Found., 1995. Mem. Japan Endocrine Soc. (com. mem. 1981-91), Japan Diabetic Soc. (com. mem. 1986—, Hagedorn prize 1990), Japan Soc. Internal Med. (com. mem. 1984-86), N.Y. Acad. Scis. Club: Nigawa Tennis (Nishinomiya), Rokko Country (Nishinomiya). Lodge: Rotary (Osaka). Home: 131 Nigawadai, Takarazuka, Hyogo 665, Japan Office: Otemae Hosp, 1-5-34 Otemae, Chuo-ku, Osaka 540, Japan

TARVONEN-SCHRÖDER, PIRJO SINIKKA, neurologist, researcher; b. Salo, Finland, June 2, 1961; d. Reijo Mauri Alfred and Orvokki Helena (Valta) Tarvonen; m. Kurt Rainer Schröder, Nov. 20, 1993; 1 child, Ella Cecilia Magdalena. Lic. Medicine, U. Turku, Finland, 1987, Specialist in Neurology, 1993; MD, U. Turku, 1995. Jr. physician Turku U. Hosp., 1989-93, jr. physician, rschr. geriatrics, 1991—. Author: Leuko-Araiosis, Clinical Presentation, Progression and Outcome, 1995. Mem. Finnish Neurol. Assn., Societas Gerontoogica Finnica. Home: Uimarinkatu 2 B 4, 20880 Turku Finland

TASHJIAN, DAVID NORMAN, dermatologist; b. Fresno, Calif., June 17, 1950; s. Karl Tashjian; m. Pam Tashjian; children: Jessica, Sarah. BS in Pharmacy cum laude, U. Pacific, 1973; MD, Baylor Coll. Medicine, 1980. Diplomate Am. Bd. Dermatology; lic. physician Calif., Wash., Tex.; lic. pharmacist Calif. Intern Baylor Coll. Medicine Affiliated Hosps., 1980-81; resident in dermatology Duke U. Med. Ctr., Durham, N.C., 1981-84; pvt. practice Fresno, Calif., 1985—; staff St. Agnes Med. Ctr., 1985—, Fresno Cmty. Hosp., 1985—, Clovis Cmty. Hosp., 1985—, Valley Children's Hosp., 1985—, Valley Med. Ctr., 1985—; asst. clin. prof. dermatology U. Calif.-San Francisco. Active skin cancer screening Am. Cancer Soc., Health Screening Clinic, Fresno County Health Dept., Calif. State U., Fresno. Recipient McKesson Robbins award, 1972; Long's Drugstore scholar, 1971-72. Mem. Am. Acad. Dermatology, Soc. Pediatric Dermatology, Calif. Med. Assn., Pacific Dermatologic Assn., Ctrl. Valley Dermatology Soc., Fresno-Madera Med. Soc., San Francisco Dermatology Soc., Rho Chi. Office: 1290 E Spruce Ave #101 Fresno CA 93720-3313

TASMAN, WILLIAM SAMUEL, ophthalmologist, medical association executive; b. Phila., 1929. MD, Temple U., 1955. Intern Phila. Gen. Hosp., 1955-56; resident in ophthalmology Wills Eye Hosp., Phila., 1959-61; fellow Mass. Eye and Ear Infirmary, Boston, 1961-62; prof., chmn. dept. ophthalmology Jefferson Med. Coll., Phila., 1985—; attending surgeon Wills Eye Hosp., Phila., 1974—, ophthalmologist-in-chief, 1985—. Mem. AMA, Am. Acad. Ophthalmologists (sec. ann. meeting 1992—), Pa. Acad. Ophthalmologists, Am. Ophthal. Soc. Office: Wills Eye Hosp 900 Walnut St Philadelphia PA 19107-5509

TASSE, JOSEPH MICHAEL, health facility administrator; b. Lakewood, Ohio, Dec. 5, 1952; s. Leo J. and Julia (Warcaba) T.; m. Karen Patricia Doyle, Nov. 12, 1983; children: Joseph Michael Jr., Anna Patricia Doyle. BSBA, John Carroll U., 1974; MBA, Cornell U., 1979. Diplomate Am. Coll. Healthcare Execs. Pers. mgmt. specialist U.S. Dept. Treasury, Cleve., 1974-77; assoc. adminstr. profl. svcs. U. Cin. Hosp., 1979-90; v.p. clin. and support svcs. Oakwood Hosp. and Med. Ctr., Dearborn, Mich., 1990—; instr. med. mgmt. series Oakwood Hosp. and Med. Ctr., 1993—; bd. dirs. Hosp. Emergency Med. System Inc., Dearborn, treas. 1996. Coord. pro-am tournament vols. Sr. Players' Championship PGA, Dearborn, 1993—; bd. visitors Adv. Bd. for Health Scis. Program Oakland U., 1996—. Fellow Nat. Assn. Pub. Hosps.; mem. Greater Detroit Area Health Coun. (regional heart consortium 1993—), Southeastern Mich. Health Execs. Forum, Cornell U. Sloan Program in Health Svcs. Adminstrn. Alumni (pres. 1996-97). Home: 45985 N Valley Northville MI 48167 Office: Oakwood Hosp Med Ctr 18101 Oakwood Blvd Dearborn MI 48123

TASSINARI, ROBIN BAKER, psychiatry educator; b. Hartford, Conn., Dec. 16, 1945; s. Harold Joseph Tassinari and Mildred Edith (Baker) Lloyd; m. Anne Marie O'Leary, Sept. 4, 1971; children: Kate, Samuel, Benjamin, Margaret, Jessica, Oliver, Cynthia, Alex. BS, Trinity Coll., 1967; MD, St. Louis U., 1971. Diplomate Am. Bd. Psychiatry and Neurology. Intern in medicine Albany (N.Y.) Med. Ctr. Hosp., 1971-72, resident in psychiatry, 1972-74, chief resident in psychiatry, 1974-75; instr. psychiatry Albany Med. Coll., 1975-77, asst. prof. medicine and psychiatry, 1977-82, assoc. prof., 1982-87, prof. psychiatry, 1987—, prof. medicine, 1989—; dir. student mental health Albany Med. Coll., 1975-92, cons. psychiatry, 1975—; lectr. in field. Town councilman, Austerlitz, N.Y., 1975-89. Capt. USAR, 1972-78. Fellow Am. Psychiat. Assn. Episcopalian. Office: Albany Med Ctr New Scotland Ave Albany NY 12208

TATOM, KENNETH DUKE, pharmacist; b. Dayton, Ohio, June 28, 1949; s. James William and Velma (Smith) T.; m. Susan Jean Wickham, Dec. 4, 1970; 1 child, Robert Allen. BS in Pharmacy, Ferris State Coll., 1972. Pharmacist Fidelity Prescriptions, Dayton, 1972-79, Eckerd Drugs, Palm Bay, Fla., 1979—; cons. pharmacy K & S Cons., Palm Bay, 1984—. Mem. Am. Pharm. Assn., Ohio State Pharm. Assn., Fla. Pharmacy Assn., Brevard County Pharmacist Assn. Home: 591 Minor Ave NE Melbourne FL 32907-2622 Office: Eckerd Drugs 4711 Babcock St NE Melbourne FL 32905-2805

TATSIS, GEORGE PETER, research laboratory administrative director; b. Charlotte, N.C., Dec. 7, 1958; s. Peter Demetrios and Antonia (Tzefos) T. BA, U. N.C., 1981; MS, U. N.C., Charlotte, 1989. Vol. Heineman Med. Rsch. Ctr., Charlotte, N.C., 1982; rsch. technician Heineman Med. Rsch. Ctr., Charlotte, 1982-85, rsch. assoc., 1985-87; adminstrv. dir. Laser and Applied Techs. Lab. div. Carolinas Med. Ctr., Charlotte, 1987—; dir. clin. rsch. Carolinas Heart Inst., Charlotte, 1993—; sec., treas. Assn. Biology Grad. Students, Charlotte, 1984-86. Contbr. articles to profl. jours. Tchr. Sunday sch., Charlotte, 1987—, ch. bd. dirs., 1992—, sec., 1992, v.p., 1993, 94, pres., 1995, 96. Mem. Am. Heart Assn., Am. Soc. for Laser Medicine and Surgery, Laser Inst. Am., Internat. Soc. for Optical Engring., Soc. for Rsch. Administrators, AAAS. Office: Carolinas Med Ctr Laser and Applied Techs Lab 1000 Blythe Blvd Charlotte NC 28203-5812

TATUM, JAMES L., nuclear medicine physician; b. Richmond, Va., July 28, 1947; s. Aubrey Stuart and Irene (Both) T.; m. Gail Enid Varela, June 26, 1970; children: Jennifer Gail, Melissa Ann, Emily Elizabeth. BS, Coll. William and Mary, 1969; MD, Med. Coll. Va., 1973. Diplomate Am. Bd. Radiology, Am. Bd. Nuc. Medicine. Intern in medicine Med. Coll. Va., Richmond, resident in diagnostic radiology; fellow in nuclear medicine Duke U., Durham, N.C.; asst. to assoc. radiology Med. Coll. Va., Richmond, 1978-87, prof. radiology, 1987—, prof. medicine, 1991—, chmn. nuc. medicine, 1992—, dir. nuc. cardiology, 1991—; mem. adv. bd. DuPont Pharm., Billerica, Mass., 1986-90; pres, CEO Health Resource Techs. of Va., Midlothian, 1995—; exec. bd. Va. Commonwealth U. Radiology, Inc., 1995—, Richmond; cons. Nuc. Imaging Sys., King of Prussia, Pa., 1995—. Co-author: Pulmonary Nuclear Medicine, 1987; contbr. articles to profl. jours. Recipient William Branch Poster award Med. Coll. Va., 1973; named one of the Best Doctor's in Am., 1992, 94. Fellow Am. Coll. Chest Physicians; mem. Soc. Nuc. Medicine (trustee 1992—, mid-eastern chpt. v.p. 1986-91, pres. 1992-94), Am. Soc. Nuc. Cardiology, Am. Coll. Nuc. Physicians, Radiol. Soc. N.Am., Orgs. United (liason). Republican. Episcopalian. Office: Med Coll Va Box 980001 Richmond VA 23298

TATUM, WILLIAM OTIS, IV, neurologist; b. Pitts., Oct. 21, 1957; s. Donald Edward Tatum and Eleanor (Kelsey) Kopf; m. Diane Diekman, May 26, 1990; 1 child, Kelsey Brooke. BA, Ohio No. U., 1979; DO, Coll. Osteopathic Medicine, Des Moines, 1985. Diplomate Am. Bd. Clin. Neurophysiologists, Am. Bd. Psychiatry & Neurology. Intern Suncoast Hosp., Largo, Fla., 1985-86; resident Hines Veterans Adminstrn. Hosp., Maywood, Ill., 1986-89; fellow Grad. Hosp. U. Pa., Phila., 1989-91; from staff neurologist to dir. epilepsy monitoring unit Tampa Gen. Hosp., 1994—; clin. asst. prof. dept. neurology U. South Fla. Coll. Medicine. Mem. AMA, Am. Acad. Neurology, Am. Osteopathic Assn., Am. Epilepsy Soc., Am. Encephalographic Soc. Home: 450 W Davis Blvd Tampa FL 33606 Office: Neurology Assocs 2919 Swann Ave Ste 401 Tampa FL 33609

TAUB, AARON MYRON, healthcare administrator, consultant; b. Jersey City, Dec. 21, 1935; s. Isadore and Beatrice (Grotsky) T.; m. Rosemary Elizabeth Dessel, July 24, 1967; children: Michael David, Deborah Anne. BS, Wagner Coll., 1960; PhD, SUNY, Buffalo, 1965. Mgr. med. svcs. Fisons Can., Toronto, 1969-72; mgr., dir. quality control Fisons Corp., Bedford, Mass., 1972-82, dir. regulatory affairs, 1982-84, sr. scientist, 1984, dir. project mgmt., 1985-88; dir. new product coord. Fisons Corp., Rochester, N.Y., 1988—. Mem., chmn. Bd. of Health, Stow, Mass., 1977-82. With USNR, 1953-55. Predoctoral fellow NIH, SUNY, 1960-64. Mem. Am. Assn. Aerosol Rsch., Sigma Xi. Home: 5 Glencannon Trail Pittsford NY 14534

TAUB, SHELDON JEFFREY, physician; b. Akron, Ohio, May 13, 1948; s. Hyman L. and Betty J. (Mirman) T.; m. Adrienne C. Belson, Jan. 6, 1974; children: Alyson Beth, Jason Scott. BA in Phys. Sci., Western Res. U., 1970; MD, Wayne State U., 1974. Resident internal medicine Emory U.-Affiliated Hosp., Atlanta, 1974-77; fellow gastroenterology U. Miami (Fla.)-Affiliated Hosp., 1977-79; chief of medicine Palm Beach Gardens (Fla.) Med. Ctr., 1983-84; chief of staff Jupiter (Fla.) Med. Ctr., 1987-88; pres. bd. trustees Jupiter (Fla.) Hosp., 1990-91, Jupiter (Fla.) Med. Ctr., 1994-95. Contbr. articles to profl. jours. V.p. West Palm Beach (Fla.) chpt., Am. Cancer Soc., 1989. Fellow ACP, Am. Coll. Gastroenterology; mem. Am. Gastroenterol. Assn., Am. Soc. Gastrointestinal Endoscopy, Fla. Soc. Gastrointestinal Endoscopy. Home: 103 Quayside Dr Jupiter FL 33477 Office: Koerner Taub Flaxman MD PA 3370 Burns Rd #205 Palm Beach Gardens FL 33410

TAUB, STANLEY, plastic surgeon, sculptor; b. N.Y.C., Aug. 15, 1931; s. Jacob and Estelle (Kounat) T.; m. Patricia Taub, Aug. 15, 1960 (div. 1975); 1 child, Ari. BS, NYU; MD, N.Y. Med. Coll. Diplomate Am. Bd. Plastic Surgery. Pvt. practice N.Y.C.; attending plastic surgeon Cabrini Med. Ctr., 1965—, Westchester Sq. Hosp. Med. Ctr., 1963—, Meadowlands Hosp. Med. Ctr., 1979—. Sculptor works include portrait commns., art works: Compassion, Blessed Spirit; sculpture commns. include portrait of Richard Giery, M.D., 1994, for the Richard Grossman Burn Ctr., 1996; inventor Taub oral panondoscope, 1963, artificial larynx "voicebak", 1968-78. Recipient Simone Barrequeh award Smith Kline French, 1963. Mem. Am. Soc. Plastic and Reconstructive Surgeons. Office: 737 Park Ave New York NY 10021

TAUBER, ALFRED IMRE, hematologist, immunologist, philosopher of science; b. Washington, June 24, 1947; s. Laszlo Nandor Tauber and Lilly Katherine (Manovill) Endrei; m. Susan Alice Swerdlow, Dec. 22, 1966; children: Joel, Dylan, Benjamin, Hannah. BS, Tufts U., 1969, MD, 1973. Intern, resident in internal medicine U. Wash., Seattle, 1973-75; clin. and research fellow in hematology Tufts-N.Eng. Med. Ctr., Boston, 1975-77; instr. in medicine Harvard Med. Sch., Boston, 1978-80; jr. assoc. in medicine Brigham and Women's Hosp., Boston, 1979-82; research assoc. Robert B. Brigham Hosp., Boston, 1979-82; asst. prof. medicine Harvard Med. Sch., Boston, 1980-82; assoc. prof. medicine, assoc. rsch. prof. biochemistry Boston U. Sch. Medicine, 1982-86, prof. medicine, 1986—, assoc. prof. pathology, 1985-87, prof. pathology, 1987—; prof. philosophy Boston U., 1992—, dir. Ctr. for Philosophy and History of Sci., 1993—; assoc. vis. physician Boston City Hosp., 1982-87, vis. physician, 1988—, chief hematology and oncology, 1982-91. Author: The Immune Self: Theory or Metaphor?, 1994; co-author: Metchnikoff and the Origins of Immunology, 1991; editor: Organism and the Origins of Self, 1991, The Elusive Synthesis: Aesthetics and Science, 1996; contbr. more than 150 articles on neutrophil biochemistry and history/philosophy of biology to profl. jours. Fellow Brandeis U. Waltham, Mass., 1978. Fellow ACP; mem. Am. Soc. Hematology, Reticuloendothelial Soc., Am. Assn. Immunology, Am. Soc. Cell Biology, Am. Assn. Biol. Chemistry and Molecular Biology, Am. Soc. Clin. Investigation, Assn. Am. Physicians, History of Sci. Soc., Am. Assn. History of Medicine, Am. Philos. Assn., Philosophy of Sci. Assn. Jewish. Office: Boston Univ 745 Commonwealth Ave Boston MA 02215-1401

TAUBER, JACOB ERIC, orthopaedic surgeon; b. Vineland, N.J., Dec. 4, 1951; s. Abraham and Regina (Schneiderman) T.; m. Nicole Lasher Franz, June 30, 1984 (div. Jan. 1989); 1 child, Jonathan Robert; m. Elizabeth Ann Ochsner, Jan. 15, 1995. BA magna cum laude, U. Pa., 1972; MD, Yale U., 1976. Diplomate Am. Bd. Orthopaedic Surgery. Intern Cornell U./N.Y. Hosp.; resident Yale New Haven Hosp.; pvt. practice orthopaedic surgeon Beverly Hills, Calif., 1980—; clin. faculty UCLA, 1980—; chief orthopaedic surgery Glendale Adventist, L.A., 1991-94, Brohman Med. Ctr., L.A., 1994—. Bd. mem. Jewish Big Bros., L.A., 1990-94; assoc. alumni trustee U. Pa., 1994—. Fellow Am. Acad. Orthopaedic Surgery; mem. AMA, Calif. Med. Assn., L.A. County Med. Assn., Yale Orthopaedic Assn., Western Orthopaedic Assn., Phi Beta Kappa. Republican. Jewish. Office: 9033 Wilshire Blvd #401 Beverly Hills CA 90211

TAUBMAN, MARTIN ARNOLD, immunologist; b. N.Y.C., July 10, 1940; s. Herman and Betty (Berger) T.; m. Joan Petra Mikelbank, May 30, 1965; children: Benjamin Abby, Joel David. B.S., Bklyn. Coll., 1961; D.D.S., Columbia U., 1965; Ph.D., SUNY, Buffalo, 1970. Asst. mem. staff Forsyth Dental Center, Boston, 1970—; head immunology dept. Forsyth Dental Center, 1972—, assoc. mem. staff, 1974-80, sr. staff mem., 1980—; asst. clin. prof. oral biology and pathophysiology Harvard U. Sch. Dental Medicine, 1976-79, assoc. clin. prof., 1979—; mem. oral biology and medicine study sect. NIH, 1980-84. Editor: (with J. Siots) Contemporary Microbiology and Immunology; contbr. articles to profl. jours, chpts. to books. Recipient Rsch. Career Devel. award, 1971-76, Fred Birnberg Alumni award for disting. dental rsch. Columbia U. Assn. Dental Alumni, Disting. Faculty award Harvard Sch. Dental Medicine, 1990, MERIT award NIH, 1991; USPHS fellow, 1962-63; postdoctoral fellow, 1966-70. Mem. Am. Soc. Microbiology, , Soc. Mucosal Immunology, Internat. Assn. Dental Research (Oral Biology award 1991), Am. Assn. Immunologists, Am. Assn. Dental Research (v.p. 1987—, pres. elect 1988, pres. 1989). Office: Forsyth Dental Ctr 140 Fenway Boston MA 02115-3782

TAUBTIN, JACQUES, orthopaedic surgeon; b. Moulins, France, Aug. 22, 1948; s. Jean and Denise (Jacon) T.; m. Chantal Gounot, June 12, 1976; children: Sophie, Berengere, Mayeul, Clemence. BA, Lycee Banville, Moulins, France, 1966; MD, U. Lyon, France, 1977, CES in Biomechanics and Kinesiology, 1979, CES in Gen. Anatomy and Organogenesis, 1980, MA in Human Biology, 1980. Cert. Orthopaedic Surgeon, 1983. Intern, resident Lyon, 1972-77, attache anatomie, 1974-77, chef de clinique, fellow, 1977-81; head orthopaedic surgery Hosp., Cannes, France, 1981—; expert pres. les Tribunaux, Aix En Provence, 1990; cons. Etablissement Francais Des Greffes, 1995; pres. Gradual Elongation Nail Com., 1996. Recipient Antonin Poncet prize U. Lyon, France, 1979. Mem. SOFCOT, SICOT, ESSKA, ESSES, European Hip Soc., Gerhard Kuntscher KREIS. Roman Catholic. Home: 8 Rue de Madrid, 06110 Le Cannet France Office: Centre Hospitalier, 13 Ave des Broussailles, 06401 Cannes France

TAUSCHER, JOHN WALTER, retired pediatrician, emeritus educator; b. LaSalle, Ill., Feb. 3, 1929; s. John Robert and Ella (Danz) T.; m. Mary Claire Cline, June 19, 1954 (dec. 1989); children—Michael, John, Claire, Mark, Matthew. B.S., U. Ill., 1952, M.D., 1954. Diplomate Am. Bd. Pediatrics. Intern Cook County Hosp., Chgo., 1954-55; resident in pediatrics Hurley Hosp., Flint, Mich., 1958-60; practice medicine specializing in pediatrics Flint, 1960-75; assoc. prof. human devel. Coll. Human Medicine, Mich. State U., East Lansing, 1975-80, prof. pediatrics and human devel., 1980-94, prof. emeritus, 1994; ret., 1994; v.p. After Hours Pediatric Care, P.C., Flint, 1972-87; chmn. pediatrics Hurley Med. Ctr., 1980-90, dir. pediatric edn., dir. primary care pediatrics, 1991-94; dir. clin. svcs. Mott Children's Health Ctr., 1981-85, v.p. health affairs, 1985-91. Served with USAF, 1955-58. Recipient Outstanding Teaching award Coll. Human Medicine, Mich. State U., 1977, 84, 85, Clin. Instr. of Yr. award St. Joseph Hosp., 1977, Disting. Community Faculty award Mich. State U., 1989. Mem. AMA, Genesee County Med. Soc. (pres. 1990), Mich. State Med. Soc., Northeastern Mich. Pediatric Soc., Am. Acad. Pediatrics. Roman Catholic. Home: 1069 Rayna Dr Davison MI 48423-2845 Office: Dept Pediatric Edn One Hurley Plaza Flint MI 48503-5905

TAVARES, JOSEPH FRANCIS, health facility administrator; b. N.Y.C., May 28, 1955. MD. With Sunbury (Pa.) Hosp. Mem. AMA, Am. Coll. Pathology, Am. Soc. Clin. Pathologists, Pa. Med. Assn. Office: Sunbury Hosp 300 N 11th St Sunbury PA 17801

TAVERAS, JUAN MANUEL, physician, educator; b. Dominican Republic, Sept. 27, 1919; came to U.S., 1944, naturalized, 1950; s. Marcos M. and Ana L. (Rodriguez) T.; m. Bernice Helen McGonigle, June 12, 1947 (dec. 1990); children: Angela Taveras Summers, Louisa Helen Taveras Koranda, Jeffrey Lawrence; m. Mariana Margarita Bucher, Mar. 18, 1991. BS, Normal Sch. Santiago, Dominican Republic, 1937; MD, U. Santo Domingo, Dominican Republic, 1943, U. Pa., 1949; MS honoris causa, Harvard Med. Sch., 1971; Dr. honoris causa, Univ. Nacional Pedro Henriquez Ureña, Dominican Republic, 1987; Doctor Honoris Causa, U. Catolica Madre Y Maestra, Santiago, Dominican Republic, 1992. Diplomate: Am. Bd. Radiology. Instr. anatomy U. Santo Domingo, 1943-44; fellow radiology Grad. Hosp. U. Pa., 1945-48; rotating intern Misericordia Hosp., Phila., 1949-50; asst. radiologist Presbyn. Hosp., N.Y.C., 1950-52; asst. attending radiologist Presbyn. Hosp., 1953-56, assoc. attending radiologist, 1956-60, attending radiologist, 1960-65; dir. radiology Neurol. Inst., N.Y.C., 1952-65; cons. USPHS Hosp., S.I., N.Y., 1952-65, Morristown (N.J.) Meml. Hosp., 1957-65, St. Barnabas Hosp., N.Y.C., 1959-65, VA Hosp., Bronx, N.Y., 1960-65; asst. instr. radiology U. Pa. Sch. Medicine, 1947-48; faculty Columbia Coll. Phys. and Surg., 1950-65, prof. radiology, 1959-65; prof. radiology, chmn. dept., dir. Mallinckrodt Inst. Radiology, Washington U. Sch. Medicine, St. Louis, 1965-71; radiologist-in-chief Barnes and Allied Hosps., St. Louis, 1965-71; cons. neuroradiology service Unit 1 St. Louis City Hosp., 1966-71; cons. radiology Jewish Hosp., St. Louis, 1966-71; prof. radiology Harvard Med. Sch., 1971-89, prof. radiology emeritus, 1989—; radiologist-in-chief Mass. Gen. Hosp., Boston, 1971-88; pres. VII Symposium Neuroradiologieum, 1964. Author: Neuroradiology, 1996; (with Ross Golden) Roentgenology of the Abdomen, 1961, (with Ernest H. Wood) Diagnostic Neuroradiology, 1964, 2d edit., 1976, (with Norman Leeds) Dynamic Factors in Diagnosis of Supratentorial Brain Tumors by Cerebral Angiography, 1969, (with F. Morello) Normal Neuroradiology, 1979, (with James Provenzale) Clinical Cases in Neuroradiology, 1994, (with Laszlo Szlavy) Noncoronary Angioplasty, 1994; editor: (with others) Recent Advances in the Study of Cerebral Circulation, 1970, Cysticercosis of the Central Nervous System, 1983, Radiology: Diagnosis, Imaging, Intervention, 1986; chief editor: Am. Jour. Neuroradiology, 1980-89; contbr. numerous articles to profl. jours. Bd. dirs. Edward Mallinckrodt, Jr. Found., 1980—. Decorated knight Order of Duarte Sanchez y Mella (Dominican Republic) 1972; Juan M. Taveras professorship established in his honor Harvard Med. Sch., 1988. Fellow Am. Coll. Radiology (gold medal 1985); mem. AMA, Am. Neurol. Assn., Am. Roentgen Ray Soc. (gold medal 1988), Radiol. Soc. N.Am. (gold medal 1981), Mass. Med. Soc., Inter-Am. Coll. Radiology, World Fedn. Neurology, Am. Soc. Neuroradiology (pres. 1962-64, gold medal, 1995), N.Y. Acad. Scis., Am. Assn. Neurol. Surgeons (assoc.), Assn. U. Radiologists (gold medal 1985), Mass. Radiol. Soc., New Eng. Roentgen Ray Soc.; pres. Iberian Latin Am. Soc. of Neurol. 1988-91, pres. IV Congress of Iberian Latin Am. Soc. of Neurol. 1992, hon. mem. Phila. Roentgen Ray Soc., Radiol. Soc. Venezuela, Rocky Mountain Radiol. Soc., Tex. Radiol. Soc., Radiol. Assn. Ctrl. Am. and Panama, Hungarian Radiologic Soc., European Soc. Neuroradiology (hon.), Alpha Omega Alpha. Republican. Home: 122 Glen Rd Wellesley MA 02181-1551 Office: Mass Gen Hosp Boston MA 02114

TAWA, NICHOLAS EDWARD, JR., surgical oncologist; b. Springfield, Mass., Feb. 14, 1956; s. Nicholas Edward and Michelina Maria (Siragusa) T.; m. Marianne Curran, Jan. 30, 1988. BA, U. Mass., 1977; PhD in Physiology, Harvard U., 1984; MD, Harvard Med. Sch., 1984. Cert. Am. Bd. Surgery, 1991. Assoc. surgeon Brigham and Women's Hosp., Boston, 1989-90, Beth Israel Hosp., Boston, 1991—; asst. prof. surgery, physiology Harvard Med. Sch., Boston, 1991—. Contbr. to books and articles to profl. jours. Warren-Whitman Alumni fellow, Harvard Med. Sch., 1990-91, Postdoctoral fellow, Am. Heart Assn., 1991-93; NIH Nat. Rsch. Svc. award, 1991-93. Fellow ACS (assoc.); mem. AAAS, Mass. Med. Soc., Assn. Acad. Surgery. Democrat. Office: Beth Israel Hosp Dept Surgery 330 Brookline Ave Boston MA 02215-5400

TAWADROS, AZMI MILAD, oral surgeon; b. Cairo, Egypt, Mar. 14, 1957; came to U.S., 1962; s. Milad A. and Sabah T.; m. Deborah Ann Hulderman, Apr. 16, 1988; children: Brianna, Alyssa. BS in Pharmacy, Purdue U., 1979; DDS, Indiana U., 1983; MD, Hahnemann U., 1990. Diplomate Am. Bd. Oral and Maxillofacial Surgery. Pharmacist Indpls., 1979-84; resident Emory U., Atlanta, 1984-85, Henry Ford Hosp., Detroit, 1985-88; pharmacist Phila., 1988-90; resident Ga. Baptist Med. Ctr., Atlanta, 1990-91; pvt. practice Acworth, Ga., 1991—. Mem. ADA, AMA, Northwest Dist. Dental Soc., Ga. Dental Assn. Home: 726 Creek Trl Kennesaw GA 30144-2132 Office: 5471 Bells Ferry Rd Ste 104 Acworth GA 30102-7520

TAWES, ROY LAWSON, surgeon; b. Dover, Del., Feb. 14, 1936; m. Joyce A. Tawes; children: Heather Gwynne, Ian Lawson. BA, Swarthmore Coll., 1958; MD, U. Pa., 1962; postgrad., Sch. Aerospace Medicine, 1963. Diplomate Am. Bd. Surgery; cert. gen. vascular surgery, thoracic surgery, Advanced Trauma Life Support. Intern Phila. Gen. Hosp., 1962-63; resident U. Calif., San Francisco, 1965-70; instr. surgery U. Pa., Phila., 1970; asst. clin. prof. U. Calif., San Francisco, 1971-86, assoc. clin. prof., 1986—; staff surgeon, Peninsula Hosp., Burlingame, Calif., Mills Meml. Hosp., San Mateo, Calif.; assoc. Seton Med. Ctr., Daly City, Calif., Sequoia Hosp., Redwood City, Calif., Chope Cmty. Hosp., San Mateo; instr. San Francisco Gen. Hosp.; vis. lectr. Royal Australasian Coll. Surgeons, 1991, Transfusion Soc. Japan, 1993, Health Care Ctr., Glasgow, Scotland, 1994; vis. prof. Guatemalan Surg. Soc., 1989. Author: Autotransfusion: Therapeutic Principles and Trends, 1994, (with W.H. Brown) Review Questions in General Vasvular Surgery, vol. 1, 1984, vol. 2, 1984, (with W.H. Brown and R.G. Scribner) Decision Making in Vascular Surgery, 1987, (with M.H. Braverman) Internation Surgical Technology, 1992, International Surgical Technology II, 1993, (with R.K. Spence) Seminars in Vascular Surgery. Blood Transfusion and the vascular surgeon, 1994; contbr. chapts. in books and articles to profl. jours. Flight surgeon USAF, 1963-65. Fellow Sidney Sussex Coll., 1961, Hosp. for Sick Children, 1967-68, Children's Hosp. Phila., 1970-71. Fellow ACS; mem. Internat. Soc. Cardiovascular Surgery, Michael E. DeBakey Internat. Surg. Soc., Ctrl. Am. Cardiovascular Assn. (Guatemalan chpt. hon.), European Vascular Soc., Am. Trauma Soc. (founder), Soc. Clin. Vascular Surgery (pres. 1989, exec. coun. 1984-93), Soc. Vascular Surgery, We. Trauma Soc., We. Surg. Soc., We. Vascular Soc. (founder), Pacific Coast Surg. Assn., Pan-Pacific Surg. Soc., Calif. Med. Assn., Calif. Acad. Scis., No. Calif. Vascular Soc. (program chmn. 1987-88, coun. 1990-93), San Francisco Surg. Soc. (v.p. 1982-83, 90-91), San Mateo Surg. Soc., Naffziger and Deaver Surg. Socs. Home: 1010 San Raymundo Rd Hillsborough CA 94010 Office: 1818 El Camino Real Ste 601 Burlingame CA 94010

TAYAR, RENE BENEDICT, radiologist, consultant; b. Sliema, Malta, Oct. 3, 1945; arrived in England, 1971.; s. Oscar and Violetta (Riccardi) T.; m. Margaret Rose Tortell, Jan. 25, 1971; 1 child, Benjamin. MD, Royal U. Malta. Registrar Bristol (England) Royal Infirmary, 1974-77, sr. registrar, 1977-81; cons. radiologist St. Helier Hosp., Carshalton, Surrey, England, 1981—, Parkside Hosp., Wimbledon, London, 1985—, St. Anthony's Hosp., Cheam, Surrey, 1995—; hon. sr. lectr. St. George's Hosp. Med. Sch., U. London, 1985—; vis. cons. Atkinson Morley's Imaging Ctr., Wimbledon, 1993—. Co-founder, organizer Sir Harry Secombe Ct. Scanner Fub. Appeal, 1985, Sir Harry Secombe M.R. Scanner Pub. Appeal, 1992. Fellow Coll. Radiologists (London); mem. Magnetic Resonance Radiologists Assn., Royal Automobile Club (Pall Mall).

TAYLOE, DAVID THOMAS, retired pediatrician; b. Washington, N.C., Oct. 12, 1925; s. David Thomas and Eleanor Winfield (Berry) T.; m. Erin Tuttle Woodall, June 18, 1947; children: David Thomas, Sally Tuttle, Elizabeth Berry, Ryal Woodall, Marcus Herndon. BA, U. N.C., 1946; MD, U. Pa., 1950. Intern Med. Coll. Va.; resident in pediatrics Duke U. Med. Ctr.; pvt. practice Washington, 1955-94; bd. dirs. 1st Citizens Bank & Trust, Washington; mem. local bd. health, chmn.; med. cons. Beaufort County Health Dept. Active local sch. bd., libr. bd., ch. bd., mental health bdtrustee U. N.C.; vice chmn. N.C. Med. Care Commn. Lt. USN, 1952-54. Mem. N.C. Pediatric Soc. (pres.), Am. Acad. Pediatrics (v.p., pres. N.C. chpt., Wyeth award). Democrat. Episcopalian. Home: 719 Short Dr Washington NC 27889-4731

TAYLOR, ANN SIEGRIST, psychologist; b. Lynchburg, Va., Feb. 17, 1953; d. Clifford Joseph Jr. and Bessie Lee (Garbee) Siegrist; m. Allen Richmond Taylor, June 21, 1975. BS with distinction, Va. Poly. Inst., 1975; MA, Cen. Mich. U., 1977; PhD, U. Tenn, 1986. Lic. psychologist, Mich.; cert. employee assistance profl. Psychology asst. Shawnee Mental Health Ctr., Portsmouth, Ohio, 1977-81; behavior specialist Ga. Highlands Ctr., Dalton, 1981-82; psychology intern VA Med. Ctr., Ann Arbor, Mich., 1985-86; adj. faculty Saginaw (Mich.) Valley State U., 1986; psychologist Psych Assocs., Saginaw, 1986-89; employee assistance program specialist Dow N.Am., Midland, Mich., 1989—. Bd. dirs., pers. com. chairperson Big Bros./Big Sisters, Midland, 1986-88. Cen. Mich. U. grad. fellow, 1975. Mem. APA, Soc. for Indsl. and Orgnl. Psychology, Employee Assistance Profls. Assn., Phi Kappa Phi. Office: Dow N Am 2020 Dow Ctr Midland MI 48674

TAYLOR, AUBREY ELMO, physiologist, educator; b. El Paso, Tex., June 4, 1933; s. Virgil T. and Mildred (Maher) T.; m. Mary Jane Davis, Apr. 4, 1953; children: Audrey Jane Hildebrand, Lenda Sue Brown, Mary Ann Smith. BA in Math. and Psychology, Tex. Christian U., 1960; PhD in Physiology, U. Miss., 1964; Postdoctoral fellow biophysics lab. Harvard U. Med. Sch., Boston, 1965-67; from asst. prof. to prof. dept. physiology U. Miss. Coll. Medicine, Jackson, 1967-77; prof., chmn. dept. physiology U. South Ala. Coll. Medicine, Mobile, 1977—, Louise Lenoir Locke eminent scholar; mem. pulmonary score com. Nat. Heart, Lung and Blood Inst., 1976; with Surgery and anesthesiology, 1979-82, and Manpower Com., 1985-95; chmn. RAP, 1983. Author 5 books; contbr. chpts. to books, 700 articles to profl. jours; assoc. editor Jour. Applied Physiology, 1984-94, Critical Care medicine, 1987—; mem. editorial bd. Circulation Rsch. Am. Jour. Physiology, Microvascular Rsch., Internat. Pathophysiology, Microcirculatory and Lymphatic Rsch., Microcirculation, Chinese Jour. of Physiology Jour. Biomed. Science, Jour. Biomed. Rsch., Am. Rev. Resp. and Critical Care. Served with U.S. Army, 1953-55. NIH grantee, 1967—; recipient Lederle Faculty award, 1967-70, Philip Dow award U. Ga., 1984, NIH Merit award, 1988—, Lucian award McGill U., 1988, John Whitney award U. Ark., 1990, Gelen award Intestinal Shock Soc., 1991; named Disting. Physiologist Am. Coll. Chest Physicians, 1994. Fellow AAAS, Am. Heart Assn. (circulation, coun., cardiopulmonary and critical care coun. 1977—, chmn. 1993—, chmn. So. regional rev. com. 1977-81, EIA Review Com. 1986-95, mem. pulmonary and devel. rev. com. 1987-95, chmn. grant/review com., 1994-95, chmn. med. student rsch. award com. 1992-94, nat. rsch. com. 1990-95, Dickson Richards award 1988, Bronze award Miss. AHA, 1976, Outstanding Alabaman AHA program 1993, sci. coun. achievement award, 1995, ACDP Svc. award, 1995), Royal Soc. Medicine, NAS (mem. com. for Internat. Union Physiol. Sci.); mem. Am Physiol. Soc. (coun. 1984-87, chmn. membership com. 1985-87, pres. 1987-90, Wiggers award 1987, chmn. Perkins fellow com., 1996—), Microcirculatory Soc. (coun. 1977-81, pres. 1981-83, Landis award 1985), Ala. Acad. Scis. (State Rsch. award 1988), Internat. Lymphology Soc., N.Am. Soc. Lymphology (pres. 1988-90, recipient First Cecil Drinker award 1988), Internat. Pathophysiology Soc. (v.p. 1991—), N.Y. Acad. Scis., Biophys. Soc., Fedn. Am. Socs. for Exptl. Biology (bd. dirs. 1988-90), Alpha Omega Alpha, Sigma Xi. Democrat. Presbyterian. Current work: Cardio-pulmonary physiology; fluid balance, edema, microcirculation and capillary exchange of solute and water. Subspecialties: Physiology (medicine); Pulmonary medicine. Home: 11 Audubon Pl Mobile AL 36606-1907

TAYLOR, BARRY LLEWELLYN, microbiologist, educator; b. Sydney, Australia, May 7, 1937; came to U.S., 1967; s. Fredrick Llewelyn and Vera Lavina (Clarke) T.; m. Desmyrna Ruth Tolhurst, Jan. 4, 1961; children: Lyndon, Nerida, Darrin. BA, Avondale Coll., Cooranbong, New South Wales, 1959; BSc with honors, U. New South Wales, Sydney, 1966; PhD, Case Western Res. U., 1973; postgrad., U. Calif., Berkeley, 1973-75. Vis. postdoctoral fellow Australian Nat. U., Canberra, 1975-76; asst. prof. biochemistry Loma Linda (Calif.) U., 1976-78, assoc. prof. biochemistry, 1978-83, prof. biochemistry, 1983—, prof., chmn. dept. microbiology and molecular genetics, 1988—, interim dir. Ctr. for Molecular Biology, 1989-94. Contbr. articles to profl. pubis. Rsch. grantee Am. Heart Assn., 1978-85, NIH, 1981—. Mem. Am. Soc. Microbiology, Am. Soc. Biochemistry and Molecular Biology. Office: Loma Linda U Dept Microbiology and Molecular Genetics Loma Linda CA 92350

TAYLOR, BERNARD FRANKLIN, laboratory administrator, microbiologist; b. Charles Town, W.Va., Mar. 21, 1930; s. Beverly Douglas and Harriet Elizabeth (Dotson) T.; m. Sylvia Adora Spriggs, Jan. 28, 1957; children: Bernard Franklin, Michael Lensen. Student Bluefield State Coll., 1951; BS in Biology cum laude, Storer Coll., 1952; MS in Microbiology and Pub. Health, Mich. State U., 1959, Rider Coll., 1961, Trenton Jr. Coll., 1964-65, Trenton State Coll., 1967; PhD in Microbiology, Rutgers U., 1972; MA in Adminstrn. Rider Coll., 1980; cert. Inst. Med. Rsch., Camden, N.J. 1974, 79, 81. Bacteriologist Bur. Virology, Dept. Health, State of Mich., Lansing, 1954-56, virologist, 1956-59; instr. sci., coach football Elizabeth City (N.C.) State Tchrs. Coll., 1959-60; virologist div. labs. Dept. Health State of N.J., 1960-61, sr. virologist, 1961-62, prin. virologist, 1962-67, chief virologist, 1967-79, dir. pub. health lab. svc. div. pub. health and environ. labs., 1979—; med. technologist Helene Fuld Hosp., Trenton, 1961-64; co-adj. dept. biology Trenton State Coll., 1972—; co-adj. Mercer County Community Coll., 1981. Contbr. articles to profl. jours. Mem. juvenile cof. com. County of Mercer (N.J.); chmn. United Way campaign N.J. Dept. Health, 1973; asst. scoutmaster troop 31 Boy Scouts Am., Charles Town, 1949; commr. Mercer County Improvement Authority, 1988—; govt. appointments include Nat. Def. Execution Reservist, Resource Mgmt. Officer, Office Def. Resources Fed. Emergency Mgmt. Agy. Recipient Ella P. Stewart Biology award, 1952. Mem. Am. Soc. Microbiologists, Am. Acad. Microbiologists (cert.), Am. Assn. for Lab. Animal Sci., Found. Infectious Disease, Assn. State and Territorial Pub. Health Lab. Dirs., Assn. Official Analytical Chemists, Am. Assn. for Clin. Chemistry, Am. Soc. Pub. Adminstrs., Am. Pub. Health Assn., Nat. Assn. Biology Tchrs., N.Y. Acad. Scis., Sigma Xi, Beta Kappa Chi, Alpha Phi Alpha. Democrat. Lodge: Masons. Home: 438 Walnut Ave Trenton NJ 08609-1534 Office: New Jersey State Dept Health CN 360 Trenton NJ 08625

TAYLOR, CARL ERNEST, physician, educator; b. Landour, Mussoorie, India, July 26, 1916; s. John C. and Elizabeth (Siehl) T.; m. Mary Daniels, Feb. 14, 1943; children—Daniel, Elizabeth, Henry. B.S., Muskingum Coll., 1937, D.Sc., 1962; M.D., Harvard, 1941, M.P.H., 1951, D.P.H., 1953; L.H.D. (hon.), Towson U., 1974. Diplomate: Am. Bd. Preventive Medicine. Intern, resident pathology, surg. staff, tropical disease research Gorgas Hosp., Panama C.Z., 1941-44; charge med. service Marine Hosp., Pitts., 1944-46; supt. Meml. Hosp., Fategarh, India, 1947-50; research assoc. Harvard Sch. Pub. Health, Boston, 1950-52; asst. prof. epidemiology Harvard Sch. Pub. Health, 1957-59, assoc. prof., 1959-61; prof. preventive and social medicine Christian Med. Coll., Ludhiana, Punjab, India, 1953-56; prof. internat. health Johns Hopkins Sch. Hygiene and Pub. Health, Balt., 1961-83; prof. emeritus Johns Hopkins Sch. Hygiene and Pub. Health, 1984—, chmn. dept. internat. health, 1961-83; Cons. AID, 1959—; UNICEF country rep. in China, 1984-87; mem. expert com. WHO, 1963, 66, 67, 70, 71, 72, 73, 75; mem. Inst. Medicine, Nat. Acad. Medicine, Nat. Adv. Commn. Health Manpower; chmn. Nat. Council for Internat. Health. Contbr. numerous articles to profl. jours. Fellow Royal Coll. Physicians (Can.), Royal Soc. Tropical Medicine and Hygiene, Am. Pub. Health Assn.; mem. Assn. Tchrs. Preventive Medicine, Am. Soc. Tropical Medicine and Hygiene, Indian Assn. for Advancement Med. Edn. Home: Bittersweet Acres 1201 Hollins Ln Baltimore MD 21209-2209

TAYLOR, CLAUDIA ANN, psychotherapist, nurse; b. Knoxville, Tenn., May 22, 1946; d. Darlene M. Moore; m. Kendryl S. Taylor (div. 1974). RN, Grady Nursing Sch., 1966; BSN, Ga. State U., 1979, MEd, 1982. Acting head nurse Grady Meml. Hosp., Atlanta, 1966, psychiatric clin. coordinator, 1969—; instr. in counseling Barbara King Sch. of Ministry, Atlanta, 1982-83; workshop, seminar coordinator and facilitator Atlanta, 1977—; pvt. practice psychotherapist, cons. C. Ann Taylor & Assocs., Atlanta, 1983—; assoc. trainer, counselor The Inst. for Effective Living, Trinidad, 1983—; producer Relationships on Cable Atlanta, 1984—; founder, CEO Inst. for Psychotherapy and Rsch. for HIV-Positive Women and, 1994—; cons. Ga. Inst. Tech., Atlanta, 1985-87, Psychiatric Inst. Atlanta, 1986-87, AT&T, Atlanta, 1988, IRS, Atlanta, 1988. Bd. dirs. Community Friendship, Inc., Atlanta; group leader Dept. Offender Rehab., Atlanta, 1980. Lt. col. USAFR, 1976—. Mem. NAFE, ASTD, Assn. Black Psychologists (chmn. 1986-88), Mental Health Assn., Ga. Nurses Assn., Res. Officers Assn., Internat. Transactional Analysis Assn., Nat. Coun. Negro Women (chmn. Atlanta 1983—, award of appreciation 1985, 87), Delta Sigma Theta (award of appreciation 1986). Democrat. Home: 410 Mary Erna Dr Fairburn GA 30213-2720 Office: Peachtree Psychol Svcs 600 W Peachtree St NW Ste 1430 Atlanta GA 30308-3603

TAYLOR, CLIFFORD AUBREY, psychiatrist; b. Asheville, N.C., Sept. 17, 1952; s. Mallie Clifford and Kathleen Estelle (Stepp) T.; m. Lynne Cecilia Smith, May 23, 1981; children: Whitney Leigh, Evan Andrew. BS, Harvard U., 1974; MD, Harvard Med. Sch., 1978. Diplomate Am. Bd. Psychiatry and Neurology. Resident in psychiatry N.Y. Hosp. Cornell Med. Ctr., N.Y.C., 1978-82; asst. clin. prof. psychiatry N.J. Med. Sch.; attending psychiatrist Morristown Meml. Hosp. Mem. Am. Psychiat. Assn. Home: 4 Midwood Ter Madison NJ 07940-2736 Office: 261 James St Ste 2E Morristown NJ 07960-6348

TAYLOR, CLOYD VERON, JR., psychologist, counselor; b. Ft. Bragg, N.C., Aug. 21, 1952; s. Cloyd Veron Sr. and Ruth Elisabeth (Peterson) T.; m. Mary Kay Huff, June 8, 1985; 1 child, Allen Cloyd. MA in New Testament, Abilene Christian U., 1979; ThM in Counseling, Harding Grad. Sch., 1984; MA in Psychology, Ga. State U., 1987, Ga. State U., 1987; PhD in Clin. Psychology, Ga. State U., 1989. Lic. psychologist, Conn., Va. Campus minister South Nat. Ch. of Christ, Springfield, Mo., 1974-75; instr. S.W. Mo. State U., Springfield, 1975; minister Storrs (Conn.) Ch. of Christ, 1977-82; counselor Ga. Agape, Smyrna, 1985-88; with Elmcrest Psychiat. Inst., Portland, Conn., 1988-89, Long Lane Sch, Middletown, Conn., 1989-92, N.E. Permanente Med. Group, East Hartford, Conn., 1992-95, Mid. Atlantic Permanente Med. Group, Merrifield, Va., 1995—. Vol. Am. Cancer Soc., Storrs, 1979, 80, chmn., 1981; vol. counselor Crisis Ctr., Memphis, 1983-84, Memphis Hosp. Trauma Ctr., 1983-84. Mem. Am. Assn. Marriage and Family Therapy, Am. Psychol. Assn., Campus Advance Club (pres. 1972-74), Phi Kappa Phi. Club: Campus Advance (pres. 1972-74). Home: 4403 Middle Ridge Dr Fairfax VA 22033-3651 Office: Kaiser-Permanente 8550 Lee Hwy Fairfax VA 22030

TAYLOR, DONNA BLOYD, vocational rehabilitation consultant; b. Louisville, Ky., July 15, 1958; d. Donald Ray Bloyd and Georgia Carmen (Bryant) Whitehead; 1 child, Stephanie Micah Taylor; m. Douglas A. Garner, June 6, 1992. BS, U. Louisville, 1981, MEd, 1982. Lic. profl. counselor, qualified rehab. provider, Ohio; cert. rehab. counselor U.S. Dept. Labor; qualified rehab. coord., Ky.; cert. disability mgmt. specialist; cert. case mgr., vocat. evaluator, nat. counselor; diplomate Am. Bd. Vocat. Experts; qualified mental retardation profl.; cert. vocat. evaluator, RAS. Program coord. Hazelwood ICF-MR, Louisville, 1981-83; lead vocat. therapist Rehab. Ctr. Southeastern Ind., Clarksville, 1983-85; regional supr., vocat. cons. Rehab. Coords., Inc., Louisville, 1985; asst. mgr., rehab. cons. Nat. Rehab. Cons., Cin., 1985-88; dist. mgr., vocat. cons. Recovery Unlimited, Inc., Cin., 1988-92; pvt. practice, Lawrenceburg, Ind., 1992—; vocat. expert Social Security Adminstrn. Co-author: (with Timothy Field and others) Study Guide to the CIRS Exam, 1992, The St. Thomas Resource on Certification, Ethics and Training for Private Sector Rehabilitation, 1993, CCM Study Guide, 1994. Vol. Am. Cancer Soc., mem. Rape Crisis Intervention Team. Mem. Nat. Assn. Rehab. Profls. in Pvt. Sector (past pres. Ky. chpt., SCRB com., co-chair internat. affairs divsn.), Nat Rehab. Assn., Nat. Forensic Ctr., Nat. Disting. Svc. Registry, Individual Case Mgmt. Assn., U. Louisville Alumni Assn., Disability Network Ohio-Solidarity, Rehab. Referral Network, Rehab. Internat., Phi Kappa Phi. Democrat. Methodist. Office: 15 Mary St Lawrenceburg IN 47025-1900

TAYLOR, DORIS DENICE, physician, entrepreneur; b. Indpls., Sept. 19, 1955; d. Eugene and Mary Catherine (Ryder) T. BA, U. Minn., 1976, cert. behavior analyst, 1977, MD, 1983; BS, Purdue U., 1979. Diplomate Nat. Bd. Med. Examiners. Pvt. practice Locumtenens, 1989—; mng. dir. Sebree-Watkins-Ovbokhan Meml. Cancer Fund, Indpls.; pres., CEO Taylors of Indy Corp., Indpls.; oncologic svcs. cons. and developer. Lange scholar, U. Minn., 1980, Joseph Collins Found. scholar, 1980-81, Nat. Med. Fellowship scholar, 1980-81. Mem. AMA, Am. Soc. for Therapeutic Radiology and Oncology, Am. Soc. Clin. Oncologists. Office: Taylors of Indy Corp 55 Monument Cir Ste 814 Indianapolis IN 46204

TAYLOR, DOUGLAS NIALL, psychologist; b. Mt. Vernon, N.Y., May 13, 1957; s. Edwin Douglas and Lois Johnstone (O'Neill) T. BA, McGill U., 1979; MA, U. Hartford, 1983; PhD, CUNY, 1991; cert. in biofeedback tng., 1988. Lic. psychologist, N.Y. Rsch. asst. McGill U., 1979-81; rsch. asst. U. Hartford, 1982-83; instr. CUNY, 1985-87, 88-89; predoctoral rsch. fellow Narcotic & Drug Rsch., Inc., N.Y.C., 1988-91, postdoctoral rsch. fellow, 1991-93; pvt. practice N.Y.C., 1988—. Contbr. numerous articles to profl. pubs.; has made many presentations on pyschol. topics. Mem. Am. Psychol. Soc., Assn. for Applied Psychophysiology and Biofeedback, N.Y. Soc. for Clin. Hypnosis.

TAYLOR, DOUGLAS ROBIN, respiratory medicine physician, consultant; b. Motherwell, Scotland, July 29, 1953; s. Robertson and Jessie More Kennedy (McGill) T. MB BChir, Aberdeeen U., Scotland, 1977; MD, Aberdeen U., Scotland, 1984. Reg. specialist in respiratory medicine New Zealand Med. Coun. House surgeon, registrar Queen's U., Royal Victoria Hosp., Belfast, 1977-83; fellow Canadian Lung Assn., UBC Hosp., Vancouver, Canada, 1983-85; sr. lectr. U. Otago, New Zealand, 1987—. Contbr. chpt. to book in field. Fellow Royal Coll. Physicians Can.; mem. Royal Coll. Physicians, Thoracic Soc. of Australia, British Thoracic Soc. Baptist. Office: U Otago Med Sch Dept Medicine, PO Box 913, Dunedin New Zealand

TAYLOR, DUNCAN PAUL, research neuropharmacologist; b. Bremerton, Wash., Feb. 4, 1949; s. Alan Earl and Barbara Eleanor (Thiel) T.; m. Jeanne

Louise Damgaard, Apr. 8, 1972; 1 child, Aubrey Elizabeth. BS in Chemistry, Calif. Inst. Tech., 1971; PhD in Biochemistry, Oreg. State U., 1977. Technician analytical svcs. Carnation Co. Rsch. Labs., Van Nuys, Calif., 1967-70; Peace Corps vol. Princess Margaret Secondary Sch., St. Johns, Antigua and Barbuda, 1971-73; grad. teaching and rsch. asst. biochemistry and biophysics Oreg. State U., Corvallis, 1973-77; rsch. assoc. sect. biochemistry and pharmacology NIMH, Bethesda, Md., 1977-79; scientist, neuropharmacologist, rsch. assoc. Pharm. div. Mead Johnson & Co., Evansville, Ind., 1979-80, sr. scientist, group leader, 1980-82; sr. scientist, group leader, neuropharmacologist Pharm. R & D div. Bristol-Myers Co., Evansville, 1982-83; sr. rsch. scientist, mgr. Pharm. R & D div. Bristol-Myers Co., 1983-85, rsch. fellow preclin. cen. nervous system rsch., 1985-89; sr. rsch. fellow preclin. cen. nervous system rsch. Pharm. Rsch. Inst. Bristol-Myers Squibb Co., Wallingford, Conn.; dir. pharmacology Symphony Pharms., Malvern, Pa., 1994-95; cons., 1995-96; analyst bus. devel. Pharmacia & Upjohn, Kalamazoo, Mich., 1996—; mem. external adv. bd. dept. chemistry U. So. Miss.; grant reviewer NSF, 1981, 2, Med. Rsch. Coun. Can., 1987, 88; frequent presenter to profl. confs. Contbr. numerous articles and abstracts to profl. jours. Bd. dirs. Posey County chpt. Am. Cancer Soc., 1983-85; mem. chancel choir 1st United Meth. Ch., Mt. Vernon, Ind., 1979-86, mem. adminstrv. bd., 1980-83, 84-86; mem. Tri-State Cursillo Community; mentor Horizons Leadership Acad., Evansville-Vanderburgh Sch. Corp., 1985; mem. adult choir South Congl. Ch., Middletown, Conn., 1986—, deacon, 1987-90, co-chmn., 1989-90, mem. coun., 1989-90, mem. task force on long-range planning, 1989-90; cons. Project Bus., Jr. Achievement, 1988. Scholar Carnation Co., 1967-70, Calif. State scholar, 1967-68, 70; rsch. fellow NSF, 1970, Cold Spring Harbor Labs., 1974. Fellow Am. Inst. Chemists; mem. AAAS, Am. Chem. Soc., Am. Soc. for Pharmacology and Exptl. Therapeutics, Soc. for Neurosci. (v.p. Conn. chpt. 1989-93), Brit. Brain Rsch. Assn., European Brain and Behavior Soc., Fedn. Am. Socs. for Exptl. Biology, Internat. Brain Rsch. Orgn.-World Fedn. Neuroscientists, Sigma Xi, Phi Lambda Upsilon. Democrat. Home: 8722 West F Ave Kalamazoo MI 49009

TAYLOR, EDNA JANE, employment program counselor; b. Flint, Mich., May 16, 1934; d. Leonard Lee and Wynona Ruth (Davis) Harvey; children: Wynona Jane MacDonald, Cynthia Lee Zellmer. BS, No. Ariz. U., 1963; MEd, U. Ariz., 1967. Tchr. high sch. Sunnyside Sch. Dist., Tucson, 1963-68; employment program counselor employment devel. dept. State of Calif., Canoga Park, 1968—. Mem. adv. coun. Van Nuys Cmty. Adult Sch., Calif., 1983—, steering com., 1989-91, leadership coun., 1991-92; mem. adv. coun. Pierce C.C., Woodland Hills, Calif., 1979-81; first aid instr., recreational leader ARC. Mem. NAFE, Internat. Assn. of Pers. in Employment Security, Calif. Employment Counselors Assn. (state treas. 1978-79, state sec. 1980), Delta Psi Kappa (life). Office: State of Calif Employment Devel Dept 21010 Vanowen St Canoga Park CA 91303-2804

TAYLOR, ELDON, psychologist researcher; b. Anchorage, Utah, Jan. 27, 1945; s. Blaine Eldon and Helen Gertrude (George) T.; m. Ravinder Kaur Sadana, June 17, 1990; children: Roy, Angela, Eric, Cassandra, Hillarie, Preston. Student, Weber State Coll., Ogden, Utah, 1971-74; BS, MS, DD, U. Metaphysics, L.A., PhD in Pastoral Psychology, 1986; PhD in Clin. Psychology, St. John's U., Springfield, La., 1990; HHD (hon.), Sem. Coll., 1987; PhD in Pastoral Psychology (hon.), World U. Roundtable, Benson, Ariz., 1988. Sales mgr. Sears, Roebuck & Co., Salt Lake City, 1964-76; v.p. mktg. Dictograph Security, Salt Lake City, 1976-77; dir. Bulwark, Salt Lake City, 1977-84; pres., dir. Progressive Awareness Rsch., Spokane, Wash., 1984—; bd. dirs. World U. Roundtable, Benson, Ariz.; co-founder Creative Living Inst., 1993; mem. adj. faculty St. John's U., 1989—. Author: Thinking Without Thinking, 1995, Subliminal Communication, 1986, Subliminal Learning, 1988, Simple Things and Simple Thoughts, 1989, Wellness: Just a State of Mind, 1993, others; contbr. numerous articles and poetry to various publs.; author numerous audiocassettes on self-improvement; patentee whole brain info. audio processor. Spiritual advisor Intermountain Hospice Ctr., Salt Lake City, 1987-88; counselor Utah State Prison, Draper, 1986-88; sports motivation trainer U.S. Judo Team, Colorado Springs, Colo., 1989—. Named Ky. Col., State of Ky., 1984; recipient Golden Poet award Am. Poetry Soc., 1985-87. Fellow Nat. Assn. Clergy Hypnotherapists; mem. Am. Psychol. Practitioners Assn., Am. Law Enforcement Officers Assn., Internat. Assn. for Forensic Hypnosis, Am. Counselors Soc., Internat. Soc. Stress Analysts, Am. Assn. Religious Counselors. Home: PO Box 13249 Spokane WA 99213 Office: Progressive Awareness Rsch 21203 W Beechwood Medical Lake WA 99002

TAYLOR, FRANK EUGENE, retired internist; b. Charleston, S.C., Sept. 18, 1923; s. Herbert Tyler and Minnie (Hyde) T.; m. Sarah Belle Smith, June 18, 1949; children: Sarah Taylor Hurley, Nancy Taylor Atkins, Frank E. Jr. BS magna cum laude, Hampden-Sydney Coll., 1943; MD, U. Va., 1950. Diplomate Am. Bd. Internal Medicine. Intern U. Va., Charlottesville, 1950-51; fellow in internal medicine Cleve. Clinic, 1951-53; sr. resident U. Va., Charlottesville, 1953-54, instr. internal medicine, 1954-55; pvt. practice internal medicine Roanoke, Va., 1955-61, Charlottesville, 1961-93; chief of staff Martha Jefferson Hosp., Charlottesville, 1975-76, bd. pres., 1981-82, part-time practice employee health and free clinic, 1993—; med. dir. Westminster Canterbury, Charlottesville, 1990-93. Sgt. U.S. Army, 1943-45. Recipient Gammon Cup Hampden-Sydney Coll., 1943. Fellow ACP; mem. AMA, Va. Med. Soc., Albemarle County Med. Soc. (pres. 1980), Albemarle County Rotary (charter 1970), Farmington Country Club (bd. dirs. 1990-93). Presbyterian.

TAYLOR, HUGH RINGLAND, ophthalmologist, educator; b. Melbourne, Victoria, Australia, Nov. 10, 1947; m. Elizabeth Mara Dax, Dec. 2, 1968; children: Kathryn Isabel, Bartholomew, Edward, Phoebe. B Med. Sci., U. Melbourne, 1969, MB, BS, 1971, MD, 1978. Resident med. officer Austin Hosp., Melbourne, 1972-73; ophthalmic registrar Royal Victorian Eye and Ear Hosp., Melbourne, 1974-76; assoc. dir. Nat. Trach. and Eye Health Program, R.A.C.O., Sydney, Australia, 1976-77; postdoctoral fellow Wilmer Inst., Balt., 1977-79; asst. prof. Johns Hopkins U., Balt., 1980-83, assoc. prof., 1983-90, prof. ophthalmology, 1990; prof. ophthalmology U. Melbourne, 1990—; cons. WHO, Geneva, 1979-90, dir. Collaborative Ctr. Prevention Blindness; cons. Mectizan Expert Com., Atlanta, River Blindness Found., Houston, Edna McConnell Clark Found., N.Y.C., Fred Hollows Found., Sydney. Recipient award Rsch. to Prevent Blindness, Inc., 1988, Internat. Orgn. Against Trachoma, 1990, Alcon Rsch. Inst. award, 1993. Fellow Royal Australian Coll. Surgeons; mem. Royal Australian Coll. Ophthalmologists, Internat. Agy. for Prevention of Blindness, Assn. for Rsch. in Vision and Ophthalmology (award 1981, 88), Rotary Internat. (Paul Harris fellow 1995). Home: 27 Kireep Rd, Balwyn Victoria 3103, Australia Office: U Melbourne Dept Ophthalmol, 32 Gisborne St, Melbourne Victoria 3002, Australia

TAYLOR, IRVING, surgeon, educator; b. Leeds, Eng., Jan. 7, 1945; s. Sam and Fay (Valkovich) T.; m. Berenice Penelope Brunner, July 31, 1969; children: Justine Samantha, Tamara Zoe, Gabrielle Rivka. MB ChB, U. Sheffield, Eng., 1968, MD, 1973, ChM, 1978. Sr. registrar Sheffield Hosps., 1973-77; sr. lectr., cons. surgeon U. Liverpool, 1977-81; prof. surgery, head dept. surgery U. Southampton, 1981-93, U. Coll., London, 1993—. Author: Complications of Lower Gastrointestinal Surgery, 1985; editor: Progress in Surgery, Vol. 1, 1984, Vol. 2, 1986, Vol. 3, 1987, Recent Advances in Surgery, Vol. 14, 1989, Vol. 15, 1991, Vol. 16, 1993; European Jour. Surg. Oncology. Fellow Royal Coll. Surgeons; mem. Surg. Rsch. Soc. (sec. 1986-88), Assn. Surgeons (editl. sec. 1986-91), Assn. Profs. Surgery (sec. 1987-90, editor-in-chief European Jour. Surg. Oncology), Brit. Assn. Surgical Oncology (pres.). Office: U Coll London Dept Surgery, 67-73 Riding House St, London W1P 7LD, England

TAYLOR, J(AMES) HERBERT, cell biology educator; b. Corsicana, Tex., Jan. 14, 1916; s. Charles Aaron and Delia May (McCain) T.; m. Shirley Catherine Hoover, May 1, 1946; children: Lynne Sue, Lucy Delia, Michael Wesley. B.S., So. Okla. State U., 1939; M.S., U. Okla., 1941; Ph.D., U. Va., 1944. Asst. prof. bacteriology and botany U. Okla., Norman, 1946-47; assoc. prof. botany U. Tenn., Knoxville, 1948-51; asst. prof. botany Columbia U., N.Y.C., 1951-54; assoc. prof. Columbia U., 1954-58, prof. cell biology, 1958-64; prof. biol. sci. Fla. State U., Tallahassee, 1964-83, Robert O. Lawton disting. prof. biol. sci., 1983-90, prof. emeritus, 1990—; assoc. dir. Inst. Molecular Biophysics, Fla. State U., 1970-79; dir. Inst. Molecular Biophysics, 1980-85; cons. Oak Ridge Nat. Lab., 1949-51; research collaborator Brookhaven Nat. Lab., 1951-58; nat. lectr. Sigma Xi Research Soc. Author: Molecular Genetics, Vol. 1, 1963, Vol. 2, 1965, Vol. 3, 1979; DNA Methylation and Cellular Differentiation, 1983; also papers on molecular genetics; contbr. over 100 articles in field to profl. jours. Pres. Unitarian Ch. Tallahassee, 1968-70. Served with M.C. U.S. Army, 1944-46, PTO. Recipient Meritorious Research award Mich. State U., 1960; Guggenheim fellow Calif. Inst. Tech., 1958-59. Mem. Nat. Acad. Scis., AAAS, Am. Inst. Biol. Sci., Am. Soc. Cell Biologists (pres. 1969-70), Biophysics Soc., Genetics Soc. Am. Democrat. Office: Fla State U Inst Molecular Biophysics Tallahassee FL 32306

TAYLOR, JIMMY LYNN, retired family practice physician, administrator; b. Franklin County, N.C., May 11, 1936; s. Herman Benjaman and Ruby Lynn (Perry) T.; m. Dorothy Keenum, Sept. 4, 1960; children: Gregory Scott, Sonya Lynn Taylor Loper. AA, Mars Hill Coll., 1956; BS, Wake Forest U., 1958; MD, Bowman Gray Med. Sch., 1962. Staff physician USPHS Indian Hosp., Pine Ridge, S.D., 1963-65, chief of obstetrics, 1964-65; family physician, co-owner Monroe (N.C.) Family Med. Ctr., 1965, family physician, ptnr., 1971-96; student physician Wingate (N.C.) U., 1987-94; med. dir. Brian Ctr. Nursing Facility, Monroe, 1992-95; med. dir. Brian Ctr. Long Term Care Facility, 1992-95. Lt. commdr. USPHS, 1963-65. Recipient Head Start Child Care Achievement award N.C. Head Start Assn., 1990. Fellow Am. Acad. Family Physicians; mem. Am. Bd. Family Practice (diplomate), N.C. Acad. Family Physicians, N.C. Med. Soc., Union County Med. Soc. (pres. 1976-97). Republican. Baptist. Home: 1657 Pageland Hwy Monroe NC 28112 Office: Monroe Family Med Ctr PA 1420 E Franklin St Monroe NC 28112

TAYLOR, JOYCE KNOX, nurse; b. Sewert AFB, Tenn., Mar. 21, 1955; d. George Phillipp II and Elspeth Ione (Kleinau) Knox; m. Chalres H. Taylor Jr.; children: Jason Bouchard, Michael Bouchard, Rebecca Bouchard, Zachary Falkenberry. AS in Nursing, DeKalb (Ga.) Coll., 1989. Obstetrics technician Humana Hosp. Gwinnett, Snellville, Ga., 1987-91, evening charge nurse labor and delivery room, 1991-95, labor and delivery charge nurse, operating rm. asst., 1996—. Mem. Nat. Student Nurses Assn. Lutheran. Home: 2820 Brookside Run Snellville GA 30278-5943 Office: Eastside Med Ctr 1700 Medical Way Snellville GA 30278

TAYLOR, KAREN ANNETTE, mental health nurse; b. Kinston, N.C., Oct. 7, 1952; d. Emmett Green and Polly Ann (Taylor) Tyndall; m. Paul Othell Taylor Jr., June 24, 1979; 1 child, Clarissa Anne. AA, Lenoir C.C., Kinston, 1972; Diploma, Lenoir Meml. Hosp. Sch. of, Nursing, 1984; student, St. Joseph's Coll., Windham, Maine, 1993-94. RN, N.C. Staff nurse Lenoir Meml. Hosp., 1984-86; staff nurse, relief patient care dir. Brynn Marr Hosp., Jacksonville, N.C., 1987-90; staff nurse, quality assurance Naval Hosp., Camp Lejeune, N.C., 1990-92. Recipient Meritorious Unit Commendation Am. Fedn. of Govt. Employees, 1992. Baptist.

TAYLOR, KENNETH MACDONALD, cardiac surgeon; b. Glasgow, Scotland, Oct. 20, 1947; s. Hugh Baird and Mary (Macdonald) T.; m. Christine Elizabeth Buchanan, May 14, 1971; children: Iain Buchanan, Kirstin Mairi. MB, ChB, U. Glasgow, 1970, MD, 1978. Hall fellow in surgery U. Glasgow, 1971-73; lectr. cardiac surgery Royal Infirmary, Glasgow, 1974-78; sr. lectr. cardiac surgery Royal Infirmary and Western Infirmary, Glasgow, 1979-83; prof. cardiac surgery, chief cardiac surgery U. London Royal Postgrad. Med. Sch., Hammersmith Hosp., London, 1983—; dir. Sch. Perfusion Scis., U.K., 1986—; mem. Specialist Adv. Com. in Cardiothoracic Surgery, U.K., 1986-95, chmn., 1992-95; mem. coun. cardiothoracic sect. Royal Soc. Medicine; dir. U.K. Heart Valve Registry, Dept. Health, 1986—, mem. working com. on cardiac waiting times; chmn. cardiac audit com. U.K. Dept. Health. Author: Cardiac Surgery, 1989; editor: Cardiopulmonary Bypass, 1986, Research Methods in Surgery, 1989, 2d edit., 1996, Perfusion, 1985—; co-editor: The Brain and Cardiac Surgery, 1992; mem. editorial adv. bd. Annals of Thoracic Surgery, 1991, Jour. Heart Disease, 1991—, Jour. Cardiovascular Anesthesia, 1993—; contbr. articles on cardiac surgery to profl. jours. Gov. Drayton Manor H.S., London, 1988—. Fellow Royal Coll. Surgeons Eng., Royal Coll. Physicians Edinburgh, Royal Coll. Physicians and Surgeons Glasgow (Fletcher prize 1978, Watson prize 1980, European Soc. Cardiology; mem. Brit. Cardiac Soc., Am. Assn. Thoracic Surgery, Soc. Thoracic Surgeons Am., European Assn. Cardiothoracic Surgery (chmn. database com.), Soc. Perfusionists Gt. Britain (pres. 1989-93). Home: 129 Argyle Rd Ealing, London W13 0DB, England Office: Royal Postgrad Med Sch, Ducane Rd, London W12, England

TAYLOR, LESLI ANN, pediatric surgery educator; b. N.Y.C., Mar. 2, 1953; d. Charles Vincent Taylor and Valene Patricia (Blake) Garfield. BFA, Boston U., 1975; MD, Johns Hopkins U., 1981. Diplomate Am. Bd. Surgery. Surg. resident Beth Israel Hosp., Boston, 1981-88; rsch. fellow Pediatric Rsch. Lab. Mass. Gen. Hosp., Boston, 1984-86; fellow pediatric surgery Children's Hosp. of Phila., Phila., 1988-90; asst. prof. pediatric surgery U. N.C., Chapel Hill, 1990—. Author: (booklet) Think Twice: The Medical Effects of Physical Punishment, 1985. Recipient Nat. Rsch. Svc. award NIH, 1984-86. Fellow Am. Coll. Surgeons; mem. AMA, Am. Acad. Pediatrics, Am. Pediat. Surg. Assn.

TAYLOR, MARY ELIZABETH, retired recreation administrator, retired dietitian; b. Medina, N.Y., Dec. 10, 1933; d. Glenn Aaron and Viola Hazel (Lansill) Grimes; m. Wilbur Alvin Fredlund, Apr. 12, 1952 (div. Jan. 1980); 1 child, Wilbur Jr.; m. Frederick Herbert Taylor, Mar. 15, 1981; children: Martha Dayton, Jean Grout, Beth Stern, Cindy Hey, Carol McLellan, Cheryl Dearborn, Robert. BS in Food and Nutrition, SUCB, Buffalo, 1973; MEd in Health Sci. Edn. and Evaluation, SUNY, 1978. Registered dietitian, 1977. Diet cook Niagara Sanitorium, Lockport, N.Y., 1953-56; cook Mount View Hosp., Lockport, N.Y., 1956-60, asst. dietitian, 1960-73, dietitian, food svc. dir., 1973-79, cons. dietitian, 1979-81; instr. Erie Community Coll., Williamsville, N.Y., 1979-81; sch. lunch coord. Nye County Sch. Dist., Tonopah, Nev., 1982-93; retired Nye County Sch. Dist., 1993; food svc. mgmt. cons., fin. mgmt. advisor pvt. practice, 1994—; activity dir. Preferred Equity Corp. Recreation Vehicle Resort, Pahrump, Nev., 1993-95; ret., 1996; cons. dietitian Nye Gen. Hosp., Tonopah, 1983-88; adj. instr. Erie Community Coll., Williamsville, 1978-79; nutrition instr. for coop. extension Clark County Community Coll., 1990—; cons. Group Purchasing Western N.Y. Hosp. Adminstrs., Buffalo, 1975-79, vice-chmn. adv. com., 1976-78; cons. BOCES, Lockport, 1979-81. Nutrition counselor Migrant Workers Clinic, Lockports, 1974-80; mem. Western N.Y. Soc. for Hosp. Food Svc. Adminstrn., 1974-81; nutritionist Niagara County Nutrition Adv. Com., 1977-81. Recipient Outstanding Woman of the Yr., YWCA-UAW Lockport, 1981, Disting. Health Care Food Adminstrn. Recognition award Am. Soc. for Hosp. Food Svc. Adminstrs., 1979, USDA award Outstanding Lunch Program in Nev. and Western Region, 1986, 91. Mem. Am. Assn. Ret. Persons, Am. Sch. Food Svc. Assn. (bd. dirs. 1987, 92-93, cert. dir. II 1987, 5-yr. planning com. 1990, mem. ann. confs. 1988-93), Am. Dietetic Assn. (nat. referral system for registered dietitians 1992-93), So. Nev. Dietetic Assn. (pres. 1985-86), Nev. Food Svc. Assn. (participant ann. meetings 1990-93), Nutrition Today Soc., Nev. Sch. Food Svcs. Assn. (dietary guidelines com. 1991-93). Republican. Baptist. Home: 481 N Murphy PO Box 656 Pahrump NV 89041-0656

TAYLOR, MARY KAY, geriatrics nurse; b. Knoxville, Iowa, Jan. 26, 1954; d. Wendell Shawver and Margery Ethel (Beebe) Kubli; m. Gregory Taylor, Sept. 4, 1993. ADN, Indian Hills Community Coll., 1979; BSN, Teikyo Marycrest U., 1993. RN, Iowa. Staff nurse Mercy Hosp., Des Moines, 1979-81, Knoxville Area Community Hosp., 1981-83, VA Med. Ctr., Knoxville, 1983—. Home: PO Box 646 Knoxville IA 50138-0646

TAYLOR, MICHAEL ALAN, psychiatrist; b. N.Y.C., Mar. 6, 1940; s. Edward D. and Clara D. T.; m. Ellen Schoenfield, June 28, 1963; children—Christopher, Andrew. B.A., Cornell U., 1961; M.D., N.Y. Med. Coll., 1965. Intern Lenox Hill Hosp., N.Y.C., 1965-66; resident N.Y. Med. Coll., 1966-69, asst. prof. psychiatry, 1971-73; asso. prof. SUNY Med. Sch., Stony Brook, 1973-76; prof. psychiatry Univ. Health Scis., Chgo. Med. Sch., 1976—, dept., 1976-94. Author: The Neuropsychiatric Mental Status Examination, 1981; sr. author: General Hospital Psychiatry, 1985, The Neuropsychiatric Guide to Modern Everyday Psychiatry, 1993; editor-in-chief Neuropsychiat., Neuropsychology and Behavioral Neurology Jour.; also numerous articles. Served to lt. comdr. M.C. USNR, 1969-71. Grantee NIMH, 1971-73; Grantee Ill. Dept. Mental Health, 1976-81; VA grantee, 1985-93. Fellow Am. Psychiat. Assn.; mem. AAAS, Am. Psychopath. Assn., Soc. Biol. Psychiatry, Ill. Psychiat. Assn. Office: FUHS Chgo Med Sch 3333 Green Bay Rd North Chicago IL 60064-3037

TAYLOR, MILTON WILLIAM, molecular biologist, consultant; b. Glasgow, Scotland, Dec. 10, 1931; s. Hyman L. and Jessie (Mitchell) T.; m. Miriam Reifer, Feb. 24, 1957; children: Yuval, Jonathan. BS, Cornell U., 1961; PhD, Stanford U., 1966. Asst. prof. Ind. U., Bloomington, 1967-70, assoc. prof., 1970-76, prof., 1976—; cons. Endotech., Indpls., 1987-89, Amgen, Thousand Oaks, Calif., 1989—, Cell Genesys, 1993, Transkaryotic Therapies, 1993—. Meyerhoff fellow Weizmann Inst., Rehovot, Israel, 1983-84; grantee USPHS, Am. Cancer Soc. Mem. Am. Soc. Microbiology, Fed. Am. Soc. Exptl. Biology, Am. Soc. Virology, Internat. Soc. Interferon Rsch. Office: Ind U Dept Biology Jordan Hall 343 Bloomington IN 47405

TAYLOR, PAUL PEAK, pediatric dentist, educator; b. Childress, Tex., May 11, 1921; s. Noah Peak and Lois T. (Vinson) T.; m. LaVerne Countryman, Aug. 11, 1945; children: Scott, Peri Ann. Student, W. Tex. State Coll., 1938-40; DDS, Baylor U., 1944; MS, U. Mich., 1951. Diplomate Am. Bd. Pediatric Dentistry (examining mem. 1977-84, chair 1983). Prof. Baylor U. Coll. Dentistry, Dallas, 1958-86, chmn. grad. pediatric dentistry, 1960-69, chmn. dept. pediatric dentistry, 1969-86, prof. emeritus, 1986—; dir. dental svcs. Children's Med. Ctr., Dallas, 1965-86, dir. emeritus dental svcs., 1986—; dir. dental svcs. Tex. Scottish Rite Hosp. for Children, Dallas, 1965-86, dir. emeritus dental svcs., 1986—. Contbr. articles to Jour. of Dentistry for Children, 1960-82; author (with others) Pediatric Dentistry, 1986, Current Therapy in Pediatric Infectious Disease, 1989; mem. edtl. and publs. com. Jour. Dentistry for Children. Capt. U.S. Army, 1951-53. Fellow Mott Found., 1949-51. Fellow Am. Coll. of Dentists (life); life mem. Am. Dental Assn., Tex. Dental Assn., Dallas County Dental Assn., Masons (life, Scottish Rite 32d degree Shriner). Episcopalian. Home: 2615 Briarcove Plano TX 75074

TAYLOR, ROBERT DALTON, microbiologist; b. Greenville, Ala., June 29, 1950; s. William Walter and Una Valise (Black) T.; m. Patricia Ann Dunhardt, Mar. 16, 1983. BS, Southeastern La. Univ., 1972, MS, 1973; PhD, La. State U., 1979. NIH postdoctoral fellow Va. Polytechnic Inst., Blackburg, 1979-82; asst. prof. microbiology U. So. Miss., Hattiesburg, 1982-83, asst. prof. biol. sci., 1983-87, assoc. prof. biol. sci., 1987; environmental microbiologist Krug Life Scis. at Johnson Space Ctr., Houston, 1987-89, group mgr. biomed. ops. and rsch. group, 1989-91, asst. to gen. mgr., 1991—; cons. Nat. Marine Fisheries Svc., Pascagoula, Miss., 1985-87; reviewer Soc. for Automotive Engring., 1988-92; mem. tech. staff The MITRE Corp., 1992-94; sr. assoc. Booz-Allen & Hamilton Inc. Contbr. articles to profl. jours. Mem. AAAS, Am. Soc. Microbiology, Air and Waste Mgmt. Assn., Am. Soc. for Testing and Materials, Inst. Food Tech., N.Y. Acad. Scis., Miss. Acad. Scis., Project Mgmt. Inst., Nat. Mgmt. Assn., Civitan, Sigma Xi. Home: PO Box 35514 San Antonio TX 78235-0514 Office: Booz-Allen & Hamilton Inc Ste 1250 300 Convent St San Antonio TX 78205

TAYLOR, RONALD FULFORD, physician; b. Bethesda, Md., Mar. 23, 1956; s. Harold Bernard and Evelyn (Stansbury) T.; m. Sharon Delyn Stevenson, Mar. 7, 1987; 1 child, Jonathan Bradford. BS, Frostburg (Md.) State Coll., 1978; MD, Med. Coll. Va., 1982. Intern Vanderbilt U., Nashville, 1982-83, resident, 1983-85, fellow in pulmonary and critical care medicine, 1985-87; practice pulmonary and critical care medicine Jackson (Tenn.) Clinic, 1987—. Contbr. articles to profl. jours. Bd. dirs. Am. Lung Assn. of Tenn., Nashville, 1987-95. Mem. AMA, Am. Coll. Chest Physicians. Office: Jackson Clinic 616 W Forest Ave Jackson TN 38301

TAYLOR, RONALD JOSEPH, psychiatrist, consultant, businessman; b. Atlantic City, Oct. 9, 1944. BA, Washington & Jefferson, 1966; MS, Yeshiva U., 1968; MD, U. Md., 1973; MBA, Loyola Coll., Balt., 1981. Cert. Am. Bd. Psychiatry and Neurology. Jr. asst. resident in psychiatry Inst. Psychiatry and Human Behavior U. Md. Hosp., Balt., 1973-74, asst. resident Inst. Pyschiatry and Human Behavior, 1974-75, chief resident Inst. Psychiatry and Human Behavior, 1975-76; coord. adolescent svcs. Taylor Manor Hosp., Ellicott City, Md., 1968-70; asst. chief psychiatry VA Hosp., Balt., 1976; prin., chief exec. officer, med. dir. Taylor Med. Group, Balt., 1976-88; exec. dir., chief operating officer Sheppard Pratt-Medlantic Alliance, Inc., Balt., 1988; pvt. practice psychiatry & bus. cons. Balt., 1988—; adj. asst. prof. psychiatry Sch. Medicine U. Md., 1978—; psychiatrist to ct. Cir. Ct. for Baltimore County, Md., 1993—; commr., vice chmn. Md. Commn. on Med. Discipline, Balt., 1984-88; psychiatric cons. counseling ctr. U. Md., 1994—. Contbr. articles to profl. jours. Treas. Confrerie de la Chaine des Rotisseurs, Balt., 1985-90; bd. dirs. Concert Artists Balt., 1987-89. Gov.'s citation Gov. of Md., 1971, 88. Fellow Am. Coll. Physician Execs., Am. Psychiat. Assn.; mem. Am. Physicians Fellowship (life), Med. and Chirurg. Faculty Md., U. Md. Club (pres. Balt. 1988-90), Zeta Beta Tau (nat. v.p. 1994—). Home and Office: 11 Regency Ct Baltimore MD 21208-1722

TAYLOR, ROSLYN DONNY, family practice physician; b. Columbia, S.C., Feb. 14, 1941; d. Otto Gary and Roslyn (Alfriend) Donny; children: Cynthia Gambill, Kevin Emory. BA, Emory U., 1963, MD, 1967. Diplomate Am. Bd. Family Practice. Intern USN, Jacksonville, Fla., 1967-68; resident in family practice Spartanburg (S.C.) Gen. Hosp., 1974-76; pvt. practice Green Cove Springs, Fla., 1968-70, Inman, S.C., 1976-78; student health physician U.S.C., Columbia, 1978-81; with faculty sch. med. U.S.C. Richland Meml. Hosp., 1979-87; vis. prof. family practice U. Utah, Salt Lake City, 1987-88, residency dir. family practice, 1988-94; assoc. prof. family medicine Mercer U. Sch. Medicine, Macon, Ga., 1990-94; assoc. dir. family practice residency Meml. Med. Ctr., Savannah, Ga., 1994—; med. dir. Woodrow Dormitory for Disabled U. S.C., 1984-86; attending physician pain therapy ctr. Richland Meml. Hosp., 1986-87. Rural physician fin. assistance com. State of Utah, 1990-94. Lt. comdr. USNR, 1967-68, 72-73. Named Physician of Yr. Mayor's Com. Employment of Handicapped, Columbia, 1984. Fellow Am. Acad. Family Physicians (Mead-Johnson awards com. 1985-87, commn. on continuing edn. 1988-94), Utah Acad. Family Physicians (alternate del. 1990-94, pres.-elect, pres. 1989-90),, Ga. Acad. Family Physicians (rsch. com., edn. com.); mem. AMA. Presbyterian. Office: Family Practice Ctr Dept Family Practice 1107 E 66th St Savannah GA 31404-5701

TAYLOR, SAMUEL DOUGLAS, psychiatrist; b. St. Helens, Ky., Nov. 28, 1924; s. Samuel Bailey and Ethel Marzine (Caudill) T.; m. Etta Lee Bayens, Aug. 1, 1950; children: Deborah Lynn Taylor Morgan, Elizabeth Ann Taylor Payne, Rebecca Leigh Taylor Watson. AB, U. Ky., 1947; MD, U. Louisville, 1951. Diplomate Am. Bd. Psychiatry and Neurology; cert. Am. Bd. Forensic Medicine. Gen. rotating intern St. Anthony's Hosp., Louisville, 1951-52; pvt. practice, Henderson, Ky., 1953-74; dir. lab. svcs. Henderson Clinic, 1958-74; chief staff Meth. Community Hosp., Henderson, 1963-65; resident in psychiatry Mental Health Inst., Cherokee, Iowa, 1976-79, chief adult female svcs., 1980-82, dir. psychiat. tng., 1982-89, dir. clin. svcs., 1989—. With USNR, 1942-45, PTO. Mem. AMA, Am. Psychiat. Assn., Iowa Psychiat. Soc., Alpha Omega Alpha. Democrat. Episcopalian. Home: 1230 W Cedar St Cherokee IA 51012-1511 Office: Mental Health Inst Cherokee IA 51012

TAYLOR, SAMUEL EDWIN, pharmacologist, educator; b. Tuskegee, Ala., Oct. 19, 1941; s. Grady Clifton and Annie Edna (Crapps) T.; m. Ouida Faye Oswalt, Aug. 12, 1961; children: Samuel Edwin Jr., Leslie Ann. BS, U. Ala., Tuscaloosa, 1963; PhD, U. Ala., Birmingham, 1971. Postdoctoral trainee dept. pharmacology U. Tenn., Memphis, 1971-72; asst. prof. dept. pharmacology dental sch. U. Oreg. Health Sci. Ctr., Portland, 1972-77; asst. prof. dept. pharmacology Baylor Coll. Dentistry, Dallas, 1977-78, assoc. prof., 1978-92, assoc. prof. dept. oral and maxillofacial surgery/pharmacol., 1993—; grad. faculty Baylor U., Waco, Tex., 1978—. Contbr. articles to profl. jours. Grantee Nat. Inst. Dental Rsch., 1986. Mem. Am. Soc. Pharmacol. Exptl. Therapeutics, Soc. Exptl. Biol. Medicine, Am. Assn. Dental Rsch. (mem. at large 1985), Am. Assn. Dental Schs. (sec. 1991, chair pharmacol. sect. 1993), Sigma Xi. Baptist. Office: Baylor Coll Dentistry 3302 Gaston Ave Dallas TX 75246-2013

TAYLOR, SANDRA LOUISE, nurse; b. Jacksonville, Fla., Jan. 27, 1960; d. Lonnie James and Inez (Sands) Taylor. ADN, Fla. Jr. Coll. Sch. Nursing, 1981; BS in Nursing, U. North Fla., 1988. RN, Fla.; cert. pediatric nurse, Nat. Certification bd. PNP. Nursing svc. technician Bapt. Med. Ctr., Jacksonville, 1980-81, staff nurse, 1981—, staff nurse rep. staff nurse com.; chmn. Pediatric Pain Resource Com., 1994—. Co-author: Collaborative Problem Intervention Manual, 1994. Mem. Sigma Theta Tau. Democrat. Baptist. Home: RR 2 Box 542-a Macclenny FL 32063-9542 Office: Bapt Med Ctr 800 Prudential Dr Jacksonville FL 32207-8202

TAYLOR, SHARON KAY, elementary school counselor; b. Ft. Worth, Oct. 13, 1954; d. Cecil James and Mary Evelyn (Careathers) Owens; m. Kenneth Carroll Taylor, May 21, 1977; children: Anna Marie, Scott Owens. BS, Howard Payne U., 1976; MEd, North Tex. State, 1986. Tchr. Elem. Pub. Sch., Belton, Tex., 1979-89; counselor Kelley Elem. Sch., Denver City, Tex., 1989—. Mem. Tex. Assn. Counseling and Devel., Tex. Sch. Counselors Assn., Assn. for Play Therapy, Beta Sigma Phi. Democrat. Baptist. Home: PO Box 486 Denver City TX 79323-0486 Office: Kelley Elementary School 500 N Soland Ave Denver City TX 79323-2824

TAYLOR, STEVEN JAMES, physician; b. Ogden, Utah, Mar. 9, 1946; s. James Reed and Fern (Parry) T.; m. Julie Hamilton, Nov. 8, 1972; children: Andrea, Brett. BA, Columbia U., 1968, MD, 1972. Diplomate Am. Bd. Family Practice, Am. Bd. Emergency Medicine. Resident family practice Med. U. S.C., Charleston, 1972-75; pvt. practice Logan, Utah, 1975-78; student health svc. physician Utah State U., Logan, 1978-80; emergency dept. physician Logan Regional Hosp., 1980-86, Bon Secours/St. Francis Xavier Hosp., Charleston, S.C., 1986—; med. dir. Cache County (Utah) Emergency Med. Svcs., Logan, 1983-86; bd. mem. advanced EMT com. Utah State Dept. Health, Salt Lake City, 1984-86. Fellow Am. Coll. Emergency Physicians (bd. dirs. Utah chpt. 1984-85); mem. AMA, S.C. Med. Assn. Republican. Mormon. Home: 304 Ocean Blvd Isle Of Palms SC 29451-2161 Office: Bon Secours St Francis Hosp Emergency Dept 135 Rutledge Ave Charleston SC 29401-1338

TAYLOR, THERESA EVERETH, registered nurse, artist; b. Carthage, N.Y., Aug. 9, 1938; d. Michael Patrick and Angelina (Cerroni) Evereth; m. James Edgar Taylor II, Mar. 12, 1966; children: Britt, Priscilla, Blackwell. Diploma in nursing, House of Good Samaritan Sch. Nursing, Watertown, N.Y., 1959; BFA summa cum laude, Ursuline Coll., 1992, postgrd., 1996—. RN, N.Y., Ohio. Home health nurse DON Brason's Willcare, Cleve., 1995—. Exhbns. in group shows. Pres. Wasmer Gallery Coun., Pepper Pike, Ohio, 1992-96; clk. vestry St. Christophers by the River, Gates Mills, 1979-81; treas. Welcome Wagon, Chesterland, Ohio, 1984-85; vol. artist Cleve. Ctr. Contemporary Art, 1993—; hospice vol.; art therapy intern. Home: 12060 Caves Rd Chesterland OH 44026-2104 Office: 6151 Wilson Mills Highland Heights OH 44143

TAYLOR, VICKIE TURNER, occupational health nurse; b. Kinston, N.C., Aug. 7, 1955; d. Jimmie James and Dolly Mae (Thompson) Turner; m. Clyde Ray Taylor, June 30, 1974; children: Bryan, Michael, Erin. Diploma in nursing, Lenoir Meml. Hosp., Kinston, 1976; BSN, Atlantic Christian Coll., Wilson, N.C., 1989. RN, N.C. Staff nurse Lenoir Meml. Hosp., 1976; staff nurse Greenville (S.C.) Gen. Hosp., 1976-78, Wilson (N.C.) Meml. Hosp., 1979, Wilson Clinic, 1981, Cherry Hosp., Goldsboro, N.C., 1990-91; occupational health nurse Standard Products Co., Goldsboro, 1991—. Mem. Am. Assn. Occupational Health Nurses, Sigma Theta Tau. Office: Standard Products Co 308 Fedelon Trail Goldsboro NC 27530-9001

TAYLOR, WARREN JUSTIN, thoracic surgeon; b. Boston, Nov. 2, 1921; s. William John and Virginia Stewart (Thompson) T.; m. Marjorie Marian Hutchins, Sept. 15, 1945; children: Wayne Jonathan, Leigh Whitham, Jane Stewart, Virginia Martha. AB, Dartmouth Coll., 1943; MD, Columbia U., 1945. Diplomate Am. Bd. Surgery, Am. Bd. Thoracic Surgery. Intern Mary Hitchcock Meml. Hosp., Hanover, N.H., 1945-46, resident anesthesia, 1948-49; resident surgery VA Hosp., White River Junction VA, Mary Hitchcock Meml. Hosp, 1949-52; chief surg. resident VA Hosp., White River Junction, 1952-53; surgeon VA Hosp., Rutland Heights, Mass., 1953-55; fellow thoracic surgery Malden (Mass.) Hosp., 1955-57, sr. surgeon, 1957-88, chief thoracic surgery, 1966-73, chief surgery, 1973-88; instr. surgery Harvard Med. Sch., 1961-68, clin. assoc. surgery, 1969-70, asst. clin. prof., 1970-74; clin. instr. Tufts Med. Sch., 1967—, assoc. clin. prof. surgery Boston U. Sch. Medicine, 1974-80, clin. prof., 1980—; mem. cons. staff numerous hosps. Contbr. articles to profl. jours. Mem. Winchester Bd. Health, 1963-75, 83-92. Maj., M.C., AUS, 1945-59. Fellow ACS, Am. Coll. Chest Physicians (treas. 1974-80), Am. Coll. Cardiology; mem. AMA, Mass. Med. Soc., Assn. Thoracic Surgeons, Soc. Thoracic Surgeons, Boston Surg. Soc. Home and Office: 209 Kinsman Franconia NH 03580

TAYLOR, WILSON H., diversified financial company executive. Grad., Trinity Coll. With Conn. Gen., 1954-82, sr. v.p., chief fin. officer, 1980-82; v.p. Aetna Ins. Co., 1975; exec. v.p. Cigna Corp., Phila., 1982-88, pres. property casualty group, 1983-88, corp. vice-chmn., chief operating officer, from 1988, chief operating officer, 1988, pres., chief exec. officer, 1988—, then chmn., pres., chief exec. officer, now chmn., chief exec. officer. Phi Beta Kappa. Office: Cigna Corp 1 Liberty Plz Philadelphia PA 19192-1550

TCHENG, JAMES ENLOU, physician; b. Covington, Ky., Sept. 15, 1956; s. John T.L. and Marlena Y.N. (Wang) T.; m. Mary Ann Powers, Aug. 13, 1983. BS, U. Cin., 1978; MD, Johns Hopkins U., 1982. Diplomate Am. Bd. Internal Medicine, Am. Bd. Cardiovascular. Intern Wash. U., St. Louis, 1982-83, resident, 1983-85; critical care physician DePaul Health Ctr., Bridgeton, Mo., 1985-86; fellow in cardiology Duke U. Med. Ctr., Durham, N.C., 1986-88, assoc. medicine, 1988-89, asst. prof. medicine, 1990—. Fellow Am. Coll. Cardiology; mem. ACP. Office: Duke U Med Ctr Box 3275 Durham NC 27710

TCHERTKOFF, VICTOR, pathologist; b. Lausanne, Switzerland, Aug. 7, 1919; s. Iekoussiel Gershon and Rose Schmuel (Dounaievsky) T.; m. Mildred Schwartz, June 25, 1942; children: Susan Antonelli, Adrienne Bonnie Glatzer. BS, CCNY, 1940; MD, N.Y. Med. Coll., 1943. Diplomate Am. Bd. Pathology. Intern N.Y. Beth Israel Hosp., Lincoln AFB, 1944-45; resident Met. Hosp., N.Y.C., 1946-48, fellow, 1948-49; acting chmn. pathology N.Y. Med. Coll., Valhalla, 1988-91; dir. labs. Met. Hosp., N.Y.C., 1961—, Luth. Hosp., Bklyn., 1965-70. Treas. med. bd. Met. Hosp., 1988-92, sec. med. bd., 1992-96. Capt. USAAF, 1944-46. Fellow Am. Soc. Clin. Pathologists, Coll. Am. Pathologists, Internat. Acad. Pathologists; mem. AMA, N.Y. State Soc. Medicine, N.Y. County Med. Soc., Pathologists Club of N.Y. (pres. 1974-75). Office: Met Hosp Ctr 1901 1st Ave New York NY 10029-7418

TEACHER, THEODORE MICHAEL, physician, neurologist; b. San Diego, Sept. 25, 1951; s. Theodore Abraham and Lucy (Musser) T.; m. Carol Jean Nelson, June 24, 1979; children: Eric Theodore, Fara Elizabeth. BA, U. Calif., San Diego, 1974; MD, Bowman Gray Sch. Medicine, 1978. Diplomate in neurology Am. Bd. Psychiatry and Neurology. Intern Tucson Hosps. Program, 1978-79; resident in neurology U. Ariz. Health Sci. Ctr., Tucson, 1979-82; fellow in EEG Harbor Gen./UCLA Med. Ctr., Torrance, 1982-83; physician, specializing in neurology Mission Viejo, Calif., 1983—. Mem. AMA, Calif. Med. Assn., Am. Acad. Neurology. Office: 27800 Med Ctr Rd # 226 Mission Viejo CA 92691

TEAGUE, ROBERT COLE, physician; b. Wayahachie, Tex., June 13, 1930; s. Isaac Lawson and Frances (Cole) T.; m. Virginia M. Teague, Nov. 11, 1960; children: Patrick, Michael. BA in Chemistry, Baylor U., Waco, Tex., 1951; MD, U. Tex., Galveston, 1955. Diplomate Am. Bd. Family Practice. Intern McLaren Hosp., Flint, Mich., 1955-56; med. officer USNR, 1956-58; physician family practice LaJolla, Calif., 1958-63, Phoenix, 1963—; med. dir. Vis. Nurse Svc., Phoenix; chmn. Family Practice Humana Hosp., 1984-86, Family Practice Good Samaritan Hosp., 1990-91. Mem. Ariz. Assn. Family Physicians (pres. 1988), Moon Valley C. of C. Republican. Episcopalian. Office: 1550 E Maryland Phoenix AZ 85014

TEASLEY, DEBORAH JOANN, healthcare administrator; b. Orlando, Fla., May 26, 1951. Diploma, Piedmont Hosp. Sch. Nursing, 1972; BS in Nursing, U. Tex., Galveston, 1978, MS in Nursing, 1980; PhDin Health adminstrn. edn., Tex. A&M U., 1986. Cert. critical care nurse. Staff nurse Barnes Hosp., St. Louis, 1972-74; head nurse Galveston County Meml. Hosp., Texas City, Tex., 1974-79; instr. Alvin (Tex.) Community Coll., 1980-81; instr. U. Tex. Med. Br., Galveston, 1981-82, asst. prof., 1982-84; asst. dir. nursing U. Tex. Med. Sch., Galveston, 1984-85; dir. nursing U. Tex. Med. Br., Galveston, 1985-86; assoc. exec. dir. West Jersey Health System, Camden, N.J., 1986-88; exec. dir. West Jersey Hosp., 1988-92; sr. v.p., COO Centra State Health System, Freehold, N.J., 1992—; tech. advisor videotape on nursing, 1985. Author (book chpt.) Mgmt. Concepts for Nurses, 1987; also articles. Vol. counselor Galveston Rape Crisis Ctr., 1979-80; chairperson task force on abused women NOW, Houston, 1982-83. Recipient Outstanding Faculty award U. Tex., Galveston, 1982; Kempner Found. grantee, 1983. Mem. Am. Heart Assn. (bd. dirs. Texas City chpt. 1975-77), Am. Coll. Healthcare Exec., Am. Hospital Assn. (regional policy bd. alternate delegate to bd. delegates), Sigma Theta Tau, Beta Sigma Phi. Office: Centra State Health System 901 W Main St Freehold NJ 07728-2537

TECE, SUNGUR ALP, psychiatrist; b. Tarsus, Turkey, Mar. 13, 1934; came to U.S., 1961; s. Ruhi and Ayse Tece; m. Renan Ozbilge, Nov. 30, 1942; children: Basak, Hande. MD, Med. Sch., Istabul, Turkey, 1960. Bd. cert. in psychiatry. Intern Hosp. Assn., Youngstown, Ohio, 1961-62; resident psychiatry Sch. Psychiatry, Wards Island, N.Y., 1963-64, 68-70; staff psychiatrist State Hosp., Gowanda, N.Y., 1962-63, Pilgrim State Hosp., West Brentwood, N.Y., 1963-65, 67-80, Mental Health Ctr., Brentwood, N.Y., 1971-85; staff psychiatrist State Hosp., Central Islip, N.Y., 1980-83, Kings Park, N.Y., 1985-95; staff psychiatrist Mental Health Ctr., Farmingville, N.Y., 1985-95. Mem. Turkish Am. Assembly, N.Y.C., 1988—. Lt. Turkish Army, 1965-67. Mem. Am. Psychiat. Assn. Home and office: 3 Dora Ct Commack NY 11725-2202

TEDDER, THOMAS FLETCHER, immunology educator, researcher; b. Chateauroux, France, May 14, 1956; came to U.S. 1959; s. Raymond Percy and Barbara (Hagemann) T. AA, Okaloosa-Walton Community Coll, Niceville, Fla., 1976; BS with honors, U. Fla., 1978, MS, 1980; PhD, U. Ala., Birmingham, 1984. Rsch. fellow in pathology Harvard Med. Sch., Boston, 1984-85, instr. pathology, 1986-88, asst. prof. pathology, 1988-93; assoc. prof. pathology Harvard U. Med. Sch., Boston, 1993; prof. immunology Duke U. Med. Ctr., Durham, N.C., 1993—, chmn. dept., 1993—; lectr. in immunology, Harvard Med. Sch., 1988—, prof. tumor immunology grad. course, 1990—. Assoc. editor Jour. Immunology, 1989-93, sect. editor, 1993—; contbr. numerous articles to med. jours., including Jour. Immunology, Cell Immunology, Jour. Gen. Virology. Recipient LeRoy Collins Disting. Alumnus award Fla. Assn. C.C.'s; named 25th Anniversary Disting. Alumnus, Okaloosa-Walton C.C., 1989; Damon Runyon-Walter Winchell rsch. fellow, 1985-87; scholar Leukemia Soc. Am., 1991-96, Stohlman scholar, 1995-96. Mem. Am. Soc. for Microbiology (Pres. Fellow 1982), Am. Assn. Immunologists, Sigma Xi, Phi Kappa Phi. Office: Duke U Med Ctr Dept Immunology PO Box 3010 Durham NC 27710

TEDESCO, FRANCIS JOSEPH, university administrator; b. Derby, Conn., Mar. 8, 1944; s. Lena (Tufano) Tedesco; m. Luann Lee Ekern, Aug. 1, 1970; 1 child, Jennifer Nicole. BS cum laude, Fairfield U., 1965; MD cum laude, St. Louis U., 1969. Asst. instr. Hosp. of U. Pa., Phila., 1971-72; asst. prof. Washington U. Sch. Medicine, St. Louis, 1974-75; asst. prof. U. Miami (Fla.) Sch. Medicine, 1975-77, co-dir. clin. research, 1976-78, assoc. prof., 1977-78; assoc. prof. Med. Coll. Ga., Augusta, 1978-81, chief of gastroenterology dept., 1978-88, prof., 1981—, acting v.p. clin. activities, 1984, v.p. for clin. activities, 1984-88, Interim dean Sch. of Medicine, 1986-88, pres., 1988—; cons. Med.-Letter/AMA div. drugs, Dwight D. Eisenhower Army Med. Ctr., Ft. Gordon, Ga., VA Med. Ctr., Augusta, Walter Reed Army Med. Ctr., Washington; mem. gastroenterology spl. study sect. NIH, Washington, 1982—, mem. nat. digestive disease adv. bd., 1985-88, vice chmn., 1986-87, chmn., 1987-88. Contbr. numerous articles to profl. jours. Bd. dirs. Augusta Country Day Sch., 1981-83, Am. Cancer Soc., Augusta, 1985—, v.p., 1986—; bd. dirs., exec. com. Ga. Coalition for Health, 1995—; chmn. Gov.'s Health Strategies Coun., 1992—. Capt. N.G., 1970-72. Recipient Eddie Palmer award for gastrointestinal endoscopy, 1983, cert. of appreciation Am. Cancer Soc., 1986, Outstanding Faculty award Med. Coll. Ga. Sch. Medicine, 1988, Profl. Achievement award Fairfield U., 1993; Avalon Found. scholar St. Louis U., 1968-69, Paul Harris fellow Rotary, 1990. Fellow ACP, Am. Fedn. Clin. Investigation, Am. Gastroent. Assn., Am. Soc. Gastrointestinal Endoscopy (treas. 1981-84, pres.-elect 1984-85, pres. 1985-86, Rudolph Schindler award 1993); mem. Am. Coll. Gastroenterology, So. Soc. Clin. Investigation, Richmond County Med. Soc., Med. Assn. Ga. Roman Catholic. Home 920 Milledge Rd Augusta GA 30912-7600 Office: Med Coll Ga Office Pres 1120 15th St Augusta GA 30912

TEDESCO, SUSAN MARY, pharmacy technician; b. Chgo., Sept. 22, 1954; d. Edmund L. and Viola M. (Cote) T. BA, U. St. Thomas, Houston, 1976. Cert. pharmacy technician. Sr. pharmacy technician, intravenous specialist Children's Meml. Hosp., Chgo., 1978—; pres., cons. Aseptech, Inc., Chgo., 1989—; instr., pharmacy technician educator South Suburban Coll., 1993—. Mem. Ill. Coun. Health-System Pharmacists (rep. bd. dirs. 1984-88, voting mem. bd. dirs. 1990-92, Pres.'s award 1987). Home: 2245 N Magnolia Ave Chicago IL 60614-3103 Office: Children's Meml Med Ctr 2300 N Childrens Plz Chicago IL 60614-3318

TEEL, THEODORE TREVANIAN, JR., physician; b. San Antonio, Sept. 21, 1928; s. Theodore Trevanian Sr. and Lola (Avery) T.; m. Barbara Bannen; children: Theodore Trevanian III, Stacy L., Robert B. BS, So. Meth. U., 1950; MD, Southwestern U. of Tex., 1952. Intern St. Albans Naval Hosp., N.Y.C., 1952-53; naval flight surgeon Opalorka, Fla., 1953—; pvt. practice Dallas, Fla., 1956—; grad. instr. Sch. Aviator Medicine, Pensacola, Fla., 1953—; with Baylor Hosp., Dallas, 1956—. Lt. USNR, 1952-56. Mem. AMA, Tex. Med. Soc., Dallas County Med. Soc., Alpha Omega Alpha, Phi Rho Sigma, Phi Delta Theta, Phi Beta Pi. Republican. Lutheran. Home: 4219 Glenwood Ave Dallas TX 75205-4318 Office: 2514 S Buckner Blvd Dallas TX 75227-8548

TEES, RICHARD CHISHOLM, psychology educator, researcher; b. Montreal, Que., Can., Oct. 31, 1940; s. Ralph Charles and Helen Winnifred (Chisholm) T.; m. Kathleen F. Coleman, Sept. 1, 1962; children: Susan M., Carolyn V. B.A., McGill U., 1961; Ph.D., U. Chgo., 1965. Asst. prof. U. B.C., Vancouver, 1965-67, assoc. prof., 1969-75, prof. psychology, 1975—; head dept. psychology U. B.C., 1984-94; rsch. prof. U. Sussex, Brighton, Eng., 1972-73, 77-78; chmn. grant selection panel Nat. Scis. and Engring. Rsch. Coun. Can., Ottawa, 1993-96, B.C. Health Care Rsch. Found., Vancouver, 1984-87; chmn. studentship com. Med. Rsch. Coun., Ottawa, 1985-92. Author: (with Kolb) Cerebral Cortex of the Rat, 1990; mem. editorial bd. Can. Jour. Exptl. Psychology, 1975-84, 87—; contbr. articles to profl. jours., chpts. to books. Research fellow Killam Found., 1972-73, 77-78; research fellow Can. Council, 1972-73. Fellow APA, Am. Psychol. Soc., Can. Psychol. Assn.; mem. Soc. for Neurosci., Psychonomic Soc., U. B.C. Senate, Faculty Club. Home: 1856 Acadia Rd, Vancouver, BC Canada V6T 1R3 Office: U BC, Dept Psychology, Vancouver, BC Canada V6T 1Z4

TEET, DANIEL ALBERT, plastic and reconstructive surgeon; b. Greensburg, Pa., Oct. 24, 1946; s. James John and Frances Rose (Policastro) T. BA, St. Vincent Coll., Latrobe, Pa., 1968; MD, Med. Coll. Ga., Augusta, 1975. Diplomate Am. Bd. Plastic Surgery. Intern in gen. surgery Mercy Hosp., Pitts., 1975-76, fellow in head & neck surgery, 1978-79; resident in gen. surgery West Pa. Hosp., Pitts., 1976-78; resident in plastic surgery Ohio State U., 1979-81; pvt. practice Mt. Pleasant, Pa., 1981—; mem. staff Frick Hosp., Mt. Pleasant, Monsom Med. Ctr., Jeannette, Pa., Wesmoreland Surg. Ctr., Mt. Pleasant, Lowry Surgi-Ctr., Jeanette. Fellow Am. Acad. Cosmetic Surgeons; mem. AMA, Am. Soc. Plastic Surgeons, Pa. County Med. Soc., Westmoreland County Med. Soc. Office: 601 S Church St Mount Pleasant PA 15666

TEETER, JAMES HERRING, surgeon; b. Taneytown, Md., Aug. 22, 1927; s. John Stuff and Margaret (Roop) T.; m. Mae McDaniel; children: Timothy, Paul, Jonathan, Mark. BA, Gettysburg Coll., 1950; MD, U. Md., 1954. Intern Mercy Hosp., Balt., 1954-55; resident Church Home Hosp., Balt., 1955-57, Franklin Sq. Hosp., Balt., 1957-59; attending surgeon Waynesboro (Pa.) Hosp., 1959—; clin. prof. surgery Hershey Med. Ctr., Pa. State U., 1988—; vol. World Med. Mission, Boone, N.C., 1963-92; attending surgeon Waynesboro Hosp., 1959—. Mem. bd. World Med. Mission, 1978—, United Brethren in Christ Missions, 1989-92. Fellow ACS (pres. Pa. chpt. 1988-89); mem. AMA, Christian Med. Soc., Pa. Med. Soc. Home: 11708 Country Club Rd Waynesboro PA 17268-9124 Office: Surg Assocs 45 Roadside Ave Waynesboro PA 17268-1924

TEEVAN, RICHARD COLLIER, psychology educator; b. Shelton, Conn., June 12, 1919; s. Daniel Joseph and Elizabeth (Halliwell) T.; m. Virginia Agnes Stehle, July 28, 1945; children—Jan Elizabeth, Kim Ellen, Clay Collier, Allison Tracy. B.A., Wesleyan U., Middletown, Conn., 1951; M.A., U. Mich., 1952, Ph.D., 1955. Rubber buffer Sponge Rubber Product Co., Derby, Conn., 1939-41; with U. Mich., 1951-57, teaching fellow, 1951-53, instr., 1953-57; asst. prof. Smith Coll., 1957-60; assoc. prof. Bucknell U., 1960-64, prof., 1964-69; chmn. psychology, prof. SUNY-Albany, 1969—; pres. Teevan Assocs., Cons., 1991—; cons. on coll. teaching, 1989—. Author: Reinforcement, 1961, Instinct, 1961, Color Vision, 1961, Measuring Human Motivation, 1962, Theories of Motivation in Learning, 1964, Theories of Motivation in Personality and Social Psychology, 1964, Motivation, 1967, Fear of Failure, 1969, Readings in Elementary Psychology, 1973; contbr. articles to sci. jours. Served to capt. AUS, 1941-47; prisoner of war 1943-45, Ger. Office Naval Research grantee, 1958-72; recipient Lindbach award Bucknell U., 1966. Mem. AAAS, AAUP, Am. Psychol. Assn. (Disting. visitor 1981-85), Eastern Psychol. Assn., Phi Beta Kappa, Sigma Xi. Home: 45 Pine St Delmar NY 12054-3413 Office: SUNY Dept Psychology 1400 Washington Ave Albany NY 12222-0100

TEGT, DAWN MARIE, medical surgical nurse, nursing administrator, intensive care nurse; b. Monroe, Wis., Mar. 7, 1972; d. Phillip John and Linda Mae (Shumway) T. ADN, Blackhawk Tech. Coll., 1993. RN, Ky. Staff nurse Meml. Cmty. Hosp., Edgerton, Wis., 1993—. Mem. Am. Legion Aux. (sec. 1991-92), Wis. Nurse Assn., Meml. Cmty. Hosp. Sunshine Com., Preceptor for Youth Apprentice Program, Meml. Cmty. Hosp. Lutheran. Home: 209 Front St Milton WI 53563 Office: Memorial Community Hospital 313 Stoughton Rd Edgerton WI 53534

TEGTMEIER, RONALD EUGENE, physician, surgeon; b. Omaha, Jan. 16, 1943; s. Harvey and Edna T.; children: Anne, Amy; m. Victoria Susan, June 28, 1985; children: Justina Becerra, Gregory Galvan, Mark Tegtmeier. AB, Dartmouth Coll., 1965; BMS, Dartmouth Med. Sch., 1966; MD, Harvard Med. Sch., 1968. Diplomate Am. Bd. Plastic Surgery. Internship in surgery U. Colo. Med. Ctr., Denver, 1968-69, residency in gen. surgery, 1969-70; plastic surgery preceptorship Kingston-upon-Hull, England, 1973; residency in plastic surgery U. Mexico, Albuquerque, 1974-76, fellowship, 1976; plastic surgeon pvt. practice Arvada, Colo., 1977—, Artistic Ctr. for Cosmetic Surgery, Golden, Colo., 1988—; pres. Clear Creek Valley Med. Soc., Lakewood, Colo., 1983-84; speaker of ho. Colo. Med. Soc., denver, 1985-87. Author: Aesthetica Tapes, 1988—; patentee in field; contbr. numerous papers and publs. to profl. jours. Named Outstanding Bus. Person, Arvada Jaycees, 1978; recipient Arvada Image award, 1981, Denver Post Gallery of Fame award, 1979. Mem. Am. Soc. Plastic and Reconstructive Surgeons, Am. Soc. for Aesthetic Plastic Surgery. Office: Artistic Ctr Cosmetic Surgery 14062 Denver West Pky Bldg 52 Golden CO 80401-3121

TEGTMEYER, CHARLES JOHN, radiologist, educator; b. Hamilton, N.Y., July 25, 1939; s. Charles Edwin and Eusebia (Petgrave) T.; BA (N.Y. Regents scholar) with honors, Colgate U., 1961; MD (USPHS Research scholar), George Washington U., 1965; m. Virginia Peters, June 1, 1965. Extern in surgery French Hosp., N.Y.C., 1964; surg. intern George Washington U. Hosp., Washington, 1965-66, surg. resident, 1966-68, resident in radiology, 1968-71; fellow in cardiovascular radiology Peter Bent Brigham Hosp., Boston, 1971-72; practice medicine specializing in interventional radiology, Charlottesville, Va., 1972—; asst. prof. of radiology U. Va. Med. Center, Charlottesville, 1972-75, asst. prof. anatomy, 1973-77, dir. radiology edn. for med. students, 1972-81, assoc. prof. radiology, 1975-78, prof., 1978—, assoc. prof. of anatomy , 1977-87—, prof. of anatomy and cell biology, 1987-92, dir. of angiography dept. radiology, 1974-87, prof. and chief div. angiography, internat. radiology and spl. procedures, 1987—; mem. staff U. Va. Hosp. Served to maj. AUS, 1966-72. Diplomate Am. Bd. Radiology (examiner June 1979, 81, 84, 86, 88), Nat. Bd. Med. Examiners. Fellow Am. Coll. Angiology, Am. Coll. Radiology (Va. chpt. bd. dirs. 1992—, alt. councilor 1993, pres.-elect 1994, pres. 1995), Soc. Cardiovascular and Interventional Radiology (fellow, sec.-treas. 1983, pres. 1986, exec. com. 1980-81, 83-87 and numerous other coms.); mem. Radiol. Soc. N.Am., Med. Soc. Va., Am. Roentgen Ray Soc., AMA, Albemarle County Med. Soc., Trout Unltd., Sigma Xi, Nu Sigma Nu, Sigma Chi, Alpha Omega Alpha. Editorial bd. Radiographics, 1982-87, Current Problems in Diagnostic Radiology, 1981-91; adv. editorial bd. Radiology, 1985-86, assoc. radiology editor 1985-86, Diagnostic Imaging, 1983-89; assoc. editor Jour. of Vascular and Interventional Radiology, 1990-92, cons. editor 1993-95; reviewer Radiology, Am. Jour. Radiology, CHEST, JAMA, Jour. Urology. Contbr. numerous articles on angiography and interventional radiology to med. jours.; inventor of lymph duct cannulator and the Tegwire low-profile percutaneous angioplasty balloon. Home: Bass Hollow 2040 Earlysville Rd Earlysville VA 22936-9667 Office: U Va Med Ctr Dept Radiology Charlottesville VA 22908

TEGUH, COLLIN, osteopathic physician, educator; b. Medan, Indonesia, Aug. 25, 1957; s. Tonga and Tsit Wati (Salim) T.; m. Lisa Hom; children: Justen W., Branden C. BA, U. Calif. San Diego, 1983; DO, U. Osteo. Medicine Des Moines, 1991. Rsch. asst. Scripp Meml. and Whittier Inst. for Endocrinology & Diabetes, LaJolla, Calif., 1983-87, U. Osteo. Medicine and Health Scis., Des Moines, 1988-90; intern, resident San Bernardino (Calif.) County Med. Ctr., 1991-93; staff physician, com. mem. Family Practice Assn. Med. Mgmt., San Diego, 1994—; asst. clin. prof. U. Calif. San Diego, LaJolla, 1995-96, Coll. Osteo. Medicine, Pomona, Calif., 1995-96. Contbr. articles to profl. jours. Mem. Am. Osteo. Assn., Am. Acad. Family Physician, San Diego Osteo. Med. Assn., San Diego Acad. Family Physicians, U. Calif. San Diego Alumni Assn., U. Osteo. Medicine and Health Scis. Alumni Assn. Office: Family Practice Assoc 3780 El Cajon Blvd San Diego CA 92105

TEICH, STEVEN, pediatric general surgeon; b. Long Beach, N.Y., Feb. 1, 1954; m. Esther M. Chipps, Aug. 6, 1993; children: Isaac Chipps, Jacob Teich. BS, Rensselaer Poly., 1976, MS, 1977; MD, SUNY, Buffalo, 1981. Asst. prof. surgery Ohio State U., Columbus, 1989-92; pediatric ge. surgeon Cols Pediatric Surg. Assn., Columbus, 1992—; edn. com. Am. Burn Assn., 1993—. Contbr. articles to profl. jours. Zoning and planning commn. mem. Village Powell, Ohio, 1995. Mem. Am. Coll. Surgeons, Am. Acad. Pediatrics, Am. Pediatric Surgery Assn., Columbus Surg. Soc., Tau Beta Pi. Office: Pediatric Surg Assn 555 S 18th St Ste S-6C Columbus OH 43205

TEICHER, MARTIN HERSCH, psychiatrist; b. Bklyn., May 17, 1951; s. James and Anna (Grassi) T.; m. Beverly Ann Willis, Aug. 4, 1973; children: Joseph Orrion, Emily Athena. BS, Rensselaer Poly. Inst., 1973; PhD highest distinctions, Johns Hopkins U., 1977; MD, Yale U., 1981. Diplomate Am. Bd. Med. Examiners, Am. Bd. Psychiatry and Neurology, Am. Bd. Adolescent Psychiatry. Clin. rsch. fellow Harvard U. Med. Sch., Boston, 1981-85, DuPont Warren fellow, 1984-85; chief resident psychopharmacology McLean Hosp., Belmont, Mass., 1984-85; asst. prof. Harvard U. Med. Sch., Boston, 1985-90, assoc. prof., 1990—; assoc. chief neuropharmacology lab. Mailman Rsch. Ctr., Belmont, 1986-88; dir. outpatient psychopharmacology McLean Outpatient Clinic, Belmont, 1986-88; assoc. psychiatrist McLean Hosp., 1988—; chief devel. psychopharmacology lab. Mailman Rsch. Ctr., 1988—; dir. devel. biopsychiatry progrm. McLean Hosp., 1988—; cons., reviewer NSF, USAF Office Sci. Rsch. March Dimes, 1980—; cons. pharmacology Bridgewater, Harry S. Solomon, Met. State Hosps., 1985-86; mem. com. chmn. NIMH rsch. com. on computers in mental health, 1984-86; mem. com. NIMH rsch. com. on neurobiology and psychopharmacology, 1988-92; rsch. com. neuropharmacology and neurochemistry, 1991—; developper objective diagnostic test for ADHD. Contbr. articles to profl. jours.; author (computer software) Apple-Ligand, Apple-Allfit, 1982, Cosifit, 1986, Mactivity, 1991; proposed relationship of fluoxetine to suicidal intention and violence. Recipient FIRST award. NIMH, 1988. Mem. Am. Psychiat. Assn., Soc. for Neurosci., Internat. Soc. Devel. Psychobiology, N.Y. Acad.

Sci., Soc. Light Treatment and Biol. Rhythms. Office: McLean Hosp 115 Mill St Belmont MA 02178-1041

TEIRSTEIN, PAUL SHEPHERD, physician, health facility administrator; b. N.Y.C., July 5, 1955; s. Alvin Stanley and Alice Teirstein. BA in Biology, Vassar Coll., 1976; MD, CUNY, 1980. Diplomate Am. Bd. Internal Medicine and Cardiovascular Diseases. With Lab. of Vision Rsch. NIH, Bethesda, Md., 1977-79; intern and resident Brigham & Women's Hosp., Boston, 1980-83; fellow in cardiology Stanford (Calif.) U., 1983-86; fellow in advanced coronary angioplasty Mid-Am. Heart Inst., Kansas City, Mo., 1986-87; fellow in stents, artherectomy and lasers NIH, Bethesda, 1987; dir. interventional cardiology Scripps Clinic and Rsch. Found., La Jolla, Calif., 1987—; presenter at Am. Coll. Cardiology, 1987-94, Am. Heart Assn., 1990-93, The French Hosp., San Luis Obispo, Calif., 1989, St. Luke's Med. Ctr., Phoenix, 1989, Cardiology for the Cons., Rancho Santa Fe, 1989, U. Calif., Irvine, 1989, ACP, Scottsdale, Ariz., 1989, Presbyn. Hosp., Whittier, Calif, 1989, St. Jude Med. Ctr., Fullerton, Calif., 1990, Oscala Med. Ctr., Osaka, Japan, 1992, Cedars-Sinai Med. Ctr., L.A., 1993, European Congress of Cardiology, Nice, France, 1993, Tokyo U., 1993, Lenox Hill Hosp., N.Y., 1993, Japanese Soc. Internat. Cardiology, 1994, Nat. Hindu Hosp., Bombay, 1994, G.B. Pant Hosp., Delhi, India, 1994, Escort's Hosp., 1994, B.M. Birla Hosp., Calcutta, 1994, Shaare Zedek Med. Ctr., Jerusalem, 1994, XV Gongresso da Sociedad de Cardiology de Sao Paulo, Ribeirao Preto, Brazil, 1994, and others. Grantee NSF, 1975. Fellow Am. Coll. Cardiology, Assn. for Rsch. in Vision and Ophthalmology, Beta Beta Beta, Alpha Omega Alpha. Office: Scripps Clinic & Rsch Found 10666 N Torrey Pines Rd La Jolla CA 92037-1027

TEITELBAUM, BALEGA RUTH, medical and surgical nurse, health facility administrator; b. Latrobe, Pa., Nov. 19, 1964; d. Stephen and Katherine R. (Moore) B.; m. Glenn Teitelbaum. BSN, U. Pitts., 1987, MSN, 1991. Cert. nursing adminstr. Staff nurse II Prebyterian U. Hosp., Pitts., 1987-91; adminstrv. supr. Albert Einstein Coll. Medicine, NYC, 1992—; Presenter in field. Univ. scholar, 1986-87. Mem. NAFE, Am. Orgn. Nurse Execs., Sigma Theta Tau. Home: 1056 Westwood Rd Woodmere NY 11598

TEIXEIRA DA CRUZ, ANTONIO, pharmaceutical company executive; b. Oporto, Portugal, Oct. 20, 1935; s. Antonio Júlio Jr. and Perfeita do Carmo (Teixeira) Cruz; m. Maria de Lourdes Amorim, Oct. 31, 1965; children: Maria Claudia, João. MD, U. Oporto, 1961; PhD in Biochemistry, U. Luanda, Angola, 1974. Intern in endocrinology U. Hosp., Oporto, 1962-63; asst. prof. Luanda U. Sch. Medicine, 1965-74; intern in endocrinology Karolinska Hosp., Stockholm, 1969; vis. researcher dept. biochemistry U. Stockholm, 1969-70; prof. biochemistry U. Lisbon, Portugal, 1974-76; sci. dir. Bayer-Portugal SA, Lisbon, 1976—. Contbr. articles to sci. jours. With M.C., Portugese Army, 1963-65. Grantee U. Luanda, 1969-70, 72. Office: Bayer Portugal SA, Rua da Quinta do Pinheiro, 1495 Lisbon Portugal

TEJADA, FRANCISCO, physician, educator; b. Moyobamba, San Martin, Peru, July 25, 1942; s. Francisco Tejada and Semiramis Reatequi; m. Barbara Ann Kotowski, Feb. 1, 1970; children: Anamaria, Semiramis, Barbara Lee, Francisco, James. BS, U. Nacional Mayor de San Marcos, Lima, Peru, 1961; MD, U. Peruana Cayetano Heredia, Lima, 1967. Diplomate Am. Bd. Internal Medicine, Am. Bd. Oncology. Resident in medicine Johns Hopkins U., Balt., 1969-72; sr. cancer researcher Nat. Cancer Inst., NIH, Bethesda, Md., 1972-75; asst. clin. dir. Comprehensive Cancer Ctr. Fla., Miami, Fla., 1975-80; asst. prof. U. Miami, 1975-79, assoc. prof., 1979-85, prof., 1985—; vis. prof. U. Peruana Cayetano Heredia, Lima, 1994—; sr. ptnr. Oncology Assocs., Miami, 1980-85; chief cancer control Papanicolaou Cancer Ctr., Miami, 1984-86; assoc. dir. AMC Cancer Rsch. Ctr., Denver, 1986-87; pres. Am. Oncology Ctrs., Miami, 1985—; prof. U. San Agustin, Arequipa, Peru, 1992—, U. Peruana Cayetano Heredia, Lima, Peru, 1994—; oncology expert Pan Am. Health Orgn., Washington, 1975-85, Nat. Cancer Inst., Bethesda, Md., 1984-86; dir. Miami Cancer Inst., 1980—; dir. Peruvian-Am. Endowment Inc., 1993—, v.p., 1995—. Editor Miami Med. Letter, 1986—; inventor cancer risk assessment. Mem. Beacon Coun., Miami, 1984, Latin Am. Cancer Info., Washington, 1976, Hispanic Cancer Rsch. Network, Washington, 1990; chpt. pres. Peruvian Am. Med. Soc., Miami, 1986. Lt. Peruvian Army, 1966-67. Recipient Gold Medal Merit award Ministry of Edn., Lima, 1959, Hipolito Unanue award Hipolito Unanue Inst., Lima, 1968. Fellow ACP, Johns Hopkins U., Nat. Cancer Inst.; mem. Colegio Medico del Perú, Am. Assn. Cancer Rsch., Am. Soc. Clin. Oncology, Am. Soc. Hematology, Bolivian Cancer Soc. (hon. mem.), Peruvian Cancer Soc. (hon. mem.), Chilean Soc. Cancer (hon. mem.), Argentinian Soc. Head and Neck Pathology (hon. mem.). Roman Catholic. Office: 1321 NW 14th St Ste 401 Miami FL 33125-1653

TELANG, NITIN T., cancer biologist, educator; b. Bombay, India, July 3, 1943; came to U.S., 1976; s. Trimbak Pandharinath and Madhumalati (Kanitkar) T. BSc, U. Poona, India, 1963, MSc, 1966, PhD, 1974. Assoc. rsch. scientist Tata Meml. Hosp. Cancer Rsch., Bombay, 1974-76; rsch. assoc. U. Nebr., Lincoln, 1976-78; staff fellow Am. Health Found., Valhalla, N.Y., 1978-81; rsch. assoc. Sloan-Kettering Inst., N.Y.C., 1981-85; asst. attending biochemist Meml. Sloan-Ketering Cancer Ctr., N.Y.C., 1985-91; assoc. prof. Cornell U. Med. Coll., N.Y.C., 1991—; dir. divsn. carcinogenesis & prevention Strang-Cornell Cancer Rsch. Lab., N.Y.C., 1991-95, dir. carcinogenesis and nutrition core lab., 1991—; dir. divsn. carcinogenesis and prevention Strong Cancer Rsch. Lab., The Rockefeller U., 1995—; vis. investigator The Rockefeller U., N.Y.C., 1985-89. Contbr. numerous articles to profl. jours. Mem. Am. Assn. Cancer Rsch., Am. Soc. Cell Biology, Am. Inst. Nutrition, European Assn. Cancer Rsch. Office: Strang Cancer Rsch Lab Rockefeller Univ 1230 York Ave New York NY 10021

TELFORD, SAM ROUNTREE, III, parasitologist, consultant; b. Gainesville, Fla., Aug. 29, 1961; s. Sam Rountree Jr. and Michiko (Miyazawa) T. BA, Johns Hopkins U., 1983; MS, Harvard U., 1987, DSc, 1990. Grad. rsch. asst. Harvard Sch. Pub. Health, Boston, 1984-90, instr., lectr., 1986—, rsch. fellow in tropical pub. health, 1990-92; instr. Harvard Med. Sch., Boston, 1987—; tchg. fellow, instr. Tufts U., Boston, 1986-88; instr. Marine Biol. Lab., Woods Hole, Mass., 1986-88, 91; lectr. in Tropical Pub. Health Harvard U., 1992—; lectr. Tufts U. Boston, 1986-88; cons. Becton Dickinson Co., Franklin Lakes, N.J., 1988—, Smith Kline Beecham Biologicals, Rixensart, Belgium, 1992—; spkr. in field. contbr. numerous articles to profl. jours. Grantee SmithKline Beecham Pharmaceuticals, 1993-94, 94, Gibson Island Corp., 1993—, NIH, 1995—. Mem. Am . Soc. Tropical Medicine & Hygiene, Am. Soc. Mammalogists, Am. Soc. Parasitologists, Herpetologist's League, Soc. Study of Amphibians Reptiles, Soc. Study of Evolution. Democrat. Office: Harvard Sch Public Health 665 Huntington Ave Boston MA 02115

TELLER, ANDREW SZANTO, physician; b. Nyiregyhaza, Hungary, Feb. 24, 1938; came to U.S., 1956; s. Imre and Agnes Szanto. BSE, U. Mich., 1960, MSE, 1962, PhD, 1966; MBA, NYU, 1969, MD, 1977. Diplomate Am. Bd. Internal Medicine. Asst. in rsch. U. Mich., Inst. Sci. and Tech., Ann Arbor, 1957-66; rsch. engr. Exxon Rsch. & Engring., Florham Park, N.J., 1966-74; resident Maimonides Med. Ctr., Bklyn., 1977-80; asst. instr. SUNY-Health Sci. Ctr., Bklyn., 1980-82, instr., 1983-94, clin. asst. prof. medicine, 1994—; attending physician Woodhull Med. and Med. Health Ctr., Bklyn., 1982—. Fellow ACP. Office: PO Box 200287 Brooklyn NY 11220-0287

TELLER, SONIA RUTH, internist; b. Bklyn., Apr. 16, 1938; d. Irving and Eva (Lehrman) Safir; m. David. N. Teller, Jan. 18, 1959. BS, Bklyn. Coll., 1958; PhD in Pharmacology, MD, U. Louisville, 1982. Diplomate Nat. Bd. Med. Examiners, Am. Bd. Internal Medicine. Rsch. asst. Sloan Kettering Inst., N.Y.C., 1959-62, Montiefiore Hosp., N.Y.C., 1962-68; rsch. scientist E. I. Dupont/Endo Labs., Garden City, N.Y., 1968-75; instr. dept. medicine U. Louisville, Ky., 1985-87; asst. prof. dept. medicine U. Louisville, 1987-90; asst. prof. clin. svcs. dept. medicine U. Louisville, 1990-94; assoc. prof. clin. svcs. dept. medicine U. Louisville, 1994—; dir. clin. diagnosis dept. medicine U. Louisville, 1985-95, dir. undergrad. edn., 1991-95; dir. clin. medicine dept. medicine, 1996—. Patentee antidepressant indoles, 1978; co-patentee process for preparation of indelobenzapine derivatives, 1974. Mem. AMA, Ky. Med. Assn. (chmn. sci. program com. 1990-95), Jefferson County Med. Soc., ACP. Home: 8013 Deronia Ave Louisville KY 40222-4847 Office: Dept Medicine U Louisville Ambulatory Care Bldg 3rd Fl Louisville KY 40292

TELLES, MARELYN V. TAYLOR, psychiatric clinical nurse specialist; b. N.Y.C., July 30; d. Edward J. and Mary J. (Byrnes) Taylor. Diploma, St. Mary's Hosp., Waterbury, Conn., 1963; AA in Psychology, San Diego Mesa Coll., 1980; BSN magna cum laude, U. San Diego, 1982, MSN, 1984. ARNP, N.H.; cert. adult psychiat. and mental health clin. nurse specialist ANCC. Psychiat. clin. nurse specialist VA Med. Ctr., San Diego, 1985-86, Manchester, N.H., 1986—; clin. adj. faculty Rivier Coll., Nashua, N.H., 1994—. Grantee NIMH, 1982-83; recipient award for disting. govt. svc. N.H. Fed. Execs. Assn., 1990. Mem. ANA, N.H. Nurses Assn. (editl. adv. bd. Nursing News 1986—, bd. dirs. 1986-91), Sigma Theta Tau. Home: 512 Bodwell Rd Manchester NH 03109-5007 Office: 718 Smyth Rd Manchester NH 03104-7004

TELTSCHER, HERRY OTTO, psychologist, consultant; b. Vienna, Austria; came to U.S., 1939, naturalized, 1943; s. Oskar and Elsa (Feiler) T.; m. Betti Sternfield, June 26, 1962; children: John, Nina; children from a previous marriage: Elizabeth, Susan. MA, N.Y. Sch. Social Research, 1954; PhD, Yeshiva U., N.Y.C., 1964. Pvt. practice psychology, N.Y.C., 1946—; lectr. Wayne U., Detroit, 1955; mem. faculty New Sch. Social Research, N.Y., 1976-83; cons. N.J. Dept. Human Services. Served with AUS, 1941-45. Recipient citation Mil. Intelligence War Dept., Cert. in Recognition of Disting. Contbns., 1986. Fellow Soc. Clin. and Exptl. Hypnosis; mem. Na. Register Health Svcs., Providers in Psychology, Am. Psychol. Assn., N.Y. State Psychol. Assn., Nat. Assn. Document Examines (Disting. Document Examiner of Yr. 1985), Manhattan Psychol. Assn. Author: Handwriting-An Introduction to Psycho-Graphology, 1942; Handwriting: Revelation of Self, 1970; contbr. articles to profl. jours. Address: 165 E 80th St New York NY 10021-0438

TEMELKOFF, VONDA LEE, counselor, therapist; b. Sharon, Pa., July 12, 1937; d. Edward Hopkins and Alberta (Hall; m. Thomas B. Temelkoff, Nov. 10, 1956; children: Linda Temelkoff Schuller, Thomas C., Timothy B., Todd A. BS in Edn., Youngstown State U., 1970, MS in Edn., 1986; postgrad., Kent State U., 1981, 90, 92, Akron State U., 1981, Mt. St. Joseph, Cin., 1987, Bowling Green State U., 1989, Ashland Coll., 1990, Drake U., 1990. Cert. sch. counselor, Ohio tchr., Ohio; nat. bd. cert. counselor; nat. bd. cert. sch. counselor; lic. profl. counselor, Ohio. Tchr. elem. Woodside Elem. Sch., Austintown, Ohio, 1971-84; tchr. Am. history Austintown Middle Sch., 1984-85; tchr. math. and sci. Frank Ohl Middle Sch., Austintown, 1986-87; guidance counselor five elem. schs. Austintown, 1987—; children's therapist Regional Assocs. in Counseling, Canfield, Ohio, 1987-91; presenter, trainer parent workshop Austintown Elem. Sch., winter 1989, 91; speaker Rotary and Kiwanis, 1987, 89; presentor, facillitator, speaker parenting and drug free schs. programs Communtiy Orgns. and Ohio Sch. Confs.; intern NEOUCOM Cancer Rsch. Ctr., Rootstown, summer 1986. Writer, prodr. (video) It's Your Choice, 1986. Youngstown State U. scholar, 1985-86, Jennings scholar, 1993-94. Mem. AAUW (bd. dirs. 1987, program v.p. 1988), NEA, Ohio Edn. Assn., Austintown Edn. Assn. (bldg. rep. 1978), Am. Counseling Assn., Ohio Assn. for Counseling and Devel., Internat. Reading Assn. (bd. dirs. membership com. 1989), Friends of Am. Art, Chi Sigma Iota, Delta Kappa Gamma Soc. Republican. Episcopalian. Home: 235 Topaz Cir Canfield OH 44406-9676

TEMPLE, BOBBY LOUIS, physician; b. Oklahoma City, Okla., Sept. 16, 1930; s. James Calvin and Grace Edna (Sitton) T.; m. Annagene Smith, Dec. 26, 1953; children: David John, Linda Diane, Robert Douglas. BA, U. Tex., 1952; MD, U. Tex., Galveston, 1954. Diplomate Am. Bd. Internal Medicine. Resident physician U. Tex. Southwestern Med. Sch.-Parkland Hosp., Dallas, 1957-60; pvt. practice internal medicine Douglas Ave. Med. Clinic, Dallas, 1960—; sr. mem. courtesy staff Parkland Meml. Hosp., 1962—; attending staff Presbyn. Hosp. Dallas, 1966—. Capt. U.S. Army, 1955-57. Fellow Am. Coll. Physicians; mem. AMA, Am. Soc. Internal Medicine, Tex. Med. Assn., Dallas County Med. Soc. Baptist. Office: Douglas Ave Med Clinic 3330 Douglas Ave Dallas TX 75219-2798

TEMPLE, DONALD, allergist, dermatologist; b. Chgo., May 21, 1933; s. Samuel Leonard and Matilda Eve (Riff) T.; m. Sarah Rachel Katz, Sept. 29, 1957; children: Michael A., Matthew D., Madeline B. AB in Biology cum laude, Harvard U., 1954; MD, U. Chgo., 1958. Am. Bd. Allergy and Immunology, Am. Bd. Dermatology, Nat. Bd. Med. Examiners; lic. Intern Michael Reese Hosp., Chgo., 1958-59; resident in dermatology U. Chgo. Hosps., 1959-62; clin. asst., dept. dermatology Boston U. Sch. Medicine, 1963-64; clin. instr. dermatology Stanford U. Sch. Medicine, 1965; preceptee in allergy Offices of Leon Unger, M.D., and Donald Unger, M.D., Chgo., 1965-69; practice medicine specializing in allergy and dermatology Des Plaines, Ill., 1969-76; mem. allergy dept. Glen Ellyn (Ill.) Clinic, 1972—; mem. dermatology and allergy staff, Louis A. Weiss Hosp., Chgo., 1965-73, allergy sect. Loyola U. Med. Ctr., Maywood, Ill., 1977-80, exec. and contract medicine coms. Glen Ellyn; clin. asst. prof. dermatology Abraham Lincoln Sch. Medicine, U. Ill., 1972-75; clin. asst. prof. medicine sect. allergy and dermatology, Loyola U., 1977-85; mem. staff Cen. DuPage Hosp., Winfield, Ill., 1973—, Glen Oaks Med. Ctr., Glendale Heights, Ill., Glendale Heights Community Hosp., 1980-92. Contbr. articles to profl. jours. Bd. dirs. Am. Lung Assn., DuPage, McHenry counties, 1980—; chmn. Contract Medicine, HMO Com., Glen Ellyn Clinic, 1985, mem. exec. com., 1988-92. Fellow Am. Coll. Chest Physicians, Am. Assn. Cert. Allergists, Am. Coll. Allergists, Am. Acad. Allergy, Ill. Soc. Allergy and Clin. Immunology, Chgo. Dermatol. Soc.; mem. AMA, Ill. State Med. Soc., DuPage County Med. Soc., Chgo. Med. Soc. Jewish. Home: 110 E Delaware Pl Apt 2004 Chicago IL 60611-1440 Office: Glen Ellyn Clinic 454 Pennsylvania Ave Glen Ellyn IL 60137-4402

TEMPLE, JOSEPH GEORGE, JR., retired pharmaceutical company executive; b. Bklyn., Aug. 29, 1929; s. Joseph George and Helen Frances (Beney) T.; m. Ann Elizabeth McFerran, June 21, 1952; children: Linda Jo, James, John. BSChemE, Purdue U., 1951, DEng (hon.), 1988. With Dow Chem. Co., Midland, Mich., 1951-89, v.p. mktg., 1976-78, dir., 1979-94; pres. Dow Chem. Latin Am., Coral Gables, Fla., 1978-80; group v.p. human health Dow Chem. Co., Cin., 1980-83; chief exec. officer, pres. Merrell Dow Pharms. Inc., Cin., 1983-87; exec. v.p. Dow Chem. Co., 1983-89; chief exec. officer, chmn. bd. dirs. Merrell Dow Pharms. Inc., Cin., 1988-89; chmn., chief exec. officer Marion Merrell Dow, Inc., Kansas City, Mo., 1989-92, also bd. dirs.; chmn. Marion Merrell Dow Pharms. Inc., 1992-94; vice chmn., 1994-95, ret., 1995; former trustee Com. for Economic Devel. Mem. pres.'s coun. Purdue U., 1978—; bd. fellows Saginaw Valley State U., 1987-89. Recipient Disting. Engr. Alumni award Purdue U., 1978, Outstanding Chem. Engr. award Purdue U., 1993. Mem. Am. Inst. Chem. Engrs., Soc. Plastics Industry (bd. dirs. 1980-82), Pharm. Mfrs. Assn. (bd. dirs. 1981-83), Mgmt. Assn. (Silver Knight award 1976, Gold Knight award 1982). Episcopalian.

TEMPLETON, JOHN MARKS, JR., pediatric surgeon, foundation executive; b. N.Y.C. Feb. 19, 1940; s. John Marks and Judith Dudley (Folk) T.; BA, Yale Coll., 1962; MD, Harvard U., 1968; m. Josephine J. Gargiulo, Aug. 2, 1970; children: Heather Erin, Jennifer Ann. Intern, Med. Coll. Va., Richmond, 1968-69, resident, 1969-73; prof. pediatric surgery U. Pa. and Children's Hosp. of Pa., 1995, dir. trauma program, 1989-95; chmn. bd. Templeton Growth Fund, Ltd. Assoc. editor: Textbook of Pediatric Emergencies, 1993. Chmn. health and safety, exec. bd. Cradle of Liberty Coun. Boy Scouts Am.; Ea. Coll., Nat. Recreation Found., Melmark Charitable Found.; nat. bd. dirs., pres. Pa. div. Am. Trauma Soc.; bd. dirs. Layman's Nat. Bible Assn.; pres. John Templeton Found. Served with M.C., USNR, 1975-77. Barclay fellow Templeton Coll. Oxford U. Mem. ACS, AMA, Am. Pediatric Surg. Assn., Am. Acad. Pediatrics, Am. Assn. Surgery of Trauma, Ea. Assn. Surgery of Trauma, Phila. Coll. Physicians, Union League, Nat. Layman's Bible Assn. (bd. dirs.), Merion Cricket Club. Republican. Evangelical. Office: 4 King St West, Toronto, ON Canada M5W 1M3

TEMPLETON, NEAL STEWART, anesthesiologist; b. Tulsa, Oct. 16, 1951; s. James B. and Phillis (Stewart) May; m. Carla Kay Mounts, Apr. 6, 1974; children: Kurt W., Katie L. BS, Okla. State U., Stillwater, 1974; DO, Okla. State U. Coll. Osteo., Tulsa, 1977. Diplomate Am. Bd. Anesthesiologists. Pvt. practice Enid, Okla., 1981-95; anesthesiologist Okla. Anesthesia Cons. Inc., Oklahoma City, 1995—. Mem. Am. Osteo. Assn., Am. Soc. Anesthesiologists, Soc. Ambulatory Anesthesia, Okla. Soc. Anesthesiologists, Okla. Osteo. Assn. Republican. Baptist. Home: 733 Hollowdale Edmond OK 73003-3012

TEMPLIN, ROBIN RONALD, chemical engineer, consultant; b. Lafayette, La., May 2, 1966; s. Gerald Leroy and Jane Ellen (Sever) T.; m. Helen F. Nishi, Oct. 10, 1992. BS in Biochemistry, UCLA, 1988. Microbiologist Amgen, Thousand Oaks, Calif., 1988-89, analytical biochemist, 1989-91; lead chemist Bot. Internat., Long Beach, Calif., 1992; chemist Gensia Labs., Ltd., Irvine, Calif., 1992-95, validation engr., 1995—; pres. Templin Techs., Huntington Beach, Calif., 1996—. Mem. Alpha Chi Sigma. Democrat. Roman Catholic. Office: Gensia Labs Ltd 19 Hughes Irvine CA 92718

TENENBAUM, ALLEN JEFFREY, psychologist; b. N.Y.C., July 18, 1946; s. William S. and Beatrice T.; Ph.D., U. Calif.-Berkeley, 1970. Sr. research and mktg. services mgr. Doyle Dane Bernbach, Inc., N.Y.C., 1975-77; assoc. dir. research and strategic planning J. Walter Thompson Co., N.Y.C., 1977-79; v.p. research and strategic planning Dancer Fitzgerald Sample Inc., N.Y.C., 1979-81; psychologist in pvt. practice, N.Y.C., 1981—. Mem. Am. Psychol. Assn. (life), Am. Assn. Public Opinion Research, Am. Mktg. Assn. Office: 44 E 32d St 11th Fl New York NY 10016

TENERY, ROBERT MAYO, JR., ophthalmologist; b. N.Y.C., Aug. 24, 1942; s. Robert Mayo and Barbara Nell (Koons) T.; m. Janet Jarratt, June 20, 1964; children: Robert Mayo III, Robyn Jarratt. BA, Franklin and Marshall Coll., 1964; MD, U. Tex. Med. Br., 1968. Ophthalmology resident Southwestern Med. Sch., Dallas, 1971-74; corneal & external disease fellow dept. ophthalmology U. Tex., San Antonio, 1974; pvt. practice, 1974—; chief surgery Med. City Dallas Hosp., 1980-81, chief of staff, 1982-83; monthly lectr. dept. ophthalmology U. Tex. Southwestern Med. Ctr., Dallas, 1978—; basic sci. lectr. dept. ophthalmology U. Tex. Med. Br., Houston, 1978—. Mem. Highland Park Presbyn. Ch., 1969—. Capt. U.S. Army, 1969-71. Recipient Ashbel Smith Disting. Alumnus award U. Tex. Med. Br., 1996, G. Frank Webber award, 1995. Mem. ACS, AMA (vice chmn. coun. on ethical and jud. affairs 1993—, monthly commentator Am. Med. News), Am. Acad. Ophthalmol. Assn., Tex. Med. Assn. (pres. 1993-94), Tex. Opthal. Assn., Dallas County Med. Soc. (pres. 1988), Dallas Acad. Ophthalmology (pres. 1981-82). Office: Med City Dallas Ste A-353 7777 Forest Ln Dallas TX 75230

TENG, SHENGYI, science researcher; b. Yuhuan, Zhejiang, People's Republic of China, Sept. 24, 1964; arrived in U.S., 1993; s. Fungkui and Aizhu (Zhuang) T.; m. Ying Jia Hu, Oct. 21, 1988; 1 child, Jesse. DDS, Zhejiang Med. U., 1985; M in Sci., West China U. Med. Scis., Chengdu, Sichuan, People's Republic of China, 1988. Intern Zhejiang Med. U., Hanzhou, 1983-85; resident West China U. of Med. Scis., Chengdu, 1985-91, lectr., 1991-93; rsch. assoc. U. Wash., Seattle, 1993—. Editor: (book) Practical Occlusion, 1990; author original rsch. Recipient 2nd prize for outstanding scientific rsch. Sichuan Province Govt., Chengdu, 1992. Mem. Internat. Assn. for Dental Rsch., Am. Assn. for Dental Rsch. Office: Univ of Wash Seattle WA 98195

TENJARLA, SRINI, pharmacy educator; b. India, Nov. 8, 1962. PhD, U. Houston, 1989. Asst. prof. Mercer U., Atlanta, 1990-95, assoc. prof., 1995—. Mem. AAPS. Office: Mercer Univ 3001 Mercer University Dr Atlanta GA 30341

TENNANT, JUANITA DORIS, physician assistant; b. Waycross, Ga., Feb. 7, 1948; d. Wilson Alexander and Doris (Harrell) T. BS in Edn., U. Ga., 1970; Physician Asst., U. Ala., 1975. Cert. physician asst. Physician asst. E.W. Knight, M.D., Pensacola, Fla., 1975-80, Rockledge, Fla., 1980-85; physician asst. U. Miami, Fla., 1985-86, Salim Osta, MD, Brunswick, Ga., 1986-88, U. Fla., Jacksonville, 1988—; mem. adv. coun. U. Fla. Health Scis. Ctr., Jacksonville, 1995—. Educator Am. Cancer Soc., Jacksonville, 1990—. Lt. comdr. USNR, 1982—. Fellow Am. Acad. Physician Assts.; mem. Naval Res. Assn., Fla. Acad. Physician Assts. Democrat. Home: 1920 Dunsford Rd Jacksonville FL 32207

TENNEY, STEPHEN MARSH, physiologist, educator; b. Bloomington, Ill., Oct. 22, 1922; s. Harry Houser and Caroline (Marsh) T.; m. Carolyn Cartwright, Oct. 18, 1947; children: Joyce B., Karen M., Stephen M. AB, Dartmouth; MD, Cornell U.; ScD (hon.), U. Rochester. From instr. to assoc. prof. of medicine and physiology U. Rochester Sch. Medicine, 1951-56; prof. physiology Dartmouth Med. Sch., Hanover, N.H., 1956-74; dean Dartmouth Med. Sch., 1960-62, acting dean, 1966, 73, dir. med. scis., 1957-59, chmn. dept. physiology, 1956-77, Nathan Smith prof. physiology, 1974-88, Nathan Smith prof. emeritus, 1988—; med. dir. Parker B. Francis Found., 1975-83, exec. v.p., 1984-89; Chmn. physiology study sect. NIH, 1962-65; tng. com. Nat. Heart Inst., 1968-71; mem. exec. com. NRC; mem. physiology panel NIH study Office Sci. and Tech.; mem. regulatory biology panel NSF, 1971-75; chmn. bd. sci. counselors Nat. Heart and Lung Inst., 1974-78; chmn. Commn. Respiratory Physiology Internat. Union Physiol. Scis. Asso. editor: Jour. Applied Physiology, 1976—, Handbook of Physiology; notes editor: News in Physiol. Sci., 1989—; editorial bd.: Am. Jour. Physiology, Circulation Research, Physiol. Revs; Contbr. articles to sci. jours. Served with USNR, 1947-49; sr. med. officer Shanghai. Markle scholar in med. sci., 1954-59; recipient Disting. Achievement award Dartmouth, 1994. Fellow Am. Acad. Arts and Scis., AAAS; mem. Inst. Medicine of Nat. Acad. Scis., Am. Physiol. Soc., Am. Soc. Clin. Investigation, N.Y. Acad. Scis., Gerontol. Soc., Am. Heart Assn., Assn. Am. Med. Colls., , Alpha Omega Alpha, Sigma Xi.

TENNEY, WILLIAM FRANK, pediatrician; b. Shreveport, La., June 5, 1946; s. William Bonds and Pat (Patton) T.; m. Elizabeth Carter Steadman, Oct. 4, 1973; children: Amy Karen, William Allen. BA, Vanderbilt U., 1968; MD, La. State U., New Orleans, 1972. Diplomate Am. Bd. Pediatrics, sub-Bd. Pediatric Nephrology. Intern Grady Meml. Hosp., Atlanta, 1972-73; resident in pediatrics Emory U. Affiliated Hosps., Atlanta, 1973-74, fellow in pediatric nephrology and inorganic metabolism, 1974-76; practice medicine specializing in pediatric nephrology St. Helens, Oreg., 1976-79, Shreveport, 1979-85, Seattle, 1985—; mem. staff Children's Orthopedic Hosp. and Med. Ctr., Seattle; chief dept. pediatrics Swedish Hosp. Med. Ctr., Seattle, 1987-90, 95—; clin. asst. prof. pediatrics La. State U. Sch. Medicine, 1979-85, U. Wash. Sch. Medicine, Seattle, 1985—; chmn. Renal com. Schumpert Med. Ctr., Shreveport, 1982, co-chmn. 1979-81, mem. 1983-84, co-dir. Renal Dialysis Unit, 1979-84, mem. renal transplantation com., 1984; cons. pediatric nephrology Shriner's Hosp. Crippled Children, Shreveport, 1979-84, Shreveport Regional Dialysis Ctr., 1979-84, Bossier Dialysis Ctr., Bossier City, La., 1983-84, Natchitoches (La.) Dialysis Facility, 1984. Author: (with others) Pediatric Case Studies, 1985; contbr. articles to profl. jours. Mem. Union Concerned Scientists, Cambridge, Mass., 1986—, Internat. Physicians for Prevention of Nuclear War, Boston, 1986—. Fellow Am. Acad. Pediatrics; mem. Am. Soc. Pediatric Nephrology, North Pacific Pediatric Soc., AMA, Wash. State Med. Assn., Internat. Soc. Peritoneal Dialysis, Empirical Soc. Emory U., King County Med. Soc., AAAS, Northwest Renal Soc., Southwest Pediatric Nephrology (mem. study group 1981-84). Home: 23915 SE 42nd Ct Issaquah WA 98027-7521 Office: 1221 Madison St Seattle WA 98104-1360

TEODORI, MICHAEL FELIX, cardiac surgeon; b. Pitts., Jan. 29, 1955; s. Peter A. and Philomena (Caste) T.; m. Janet Buonocore, Oct. 11, 1980; children: Nicholas, Teresa, Laura. BS, MIT, 1977; MD, U. Pa., 1981. Diplomate Am. Bd. Thoracic Surgery. Pvt. practice cardiac surgeon Phoenix, 1990—; chmn. dept. cardiac surgery Phoenix Children's Hosp., 1994—, St. Joseph's Hosp., 1996. Mem. Maricopa Med. Soc., Phi Beta Kappa. Office: 1144 E McDowell Rd # 204 Phoenix AZ 85006

TEPOEL, LOUIS DEAN, emergency physician; b. Hanna, Wyo., June 17, 1947; s. Dean Leon TeP.and Ardenia Marle (Maston) Gilbert; m. Donna Lee Fuller, July 4, 1974; children: Jamie, Sarah. BSEE, U. Colo., 1969, MS in Biomed. Engring., 1973, MD, 1977. Chief emergency medicine Campbell County Meml. Hosp., Gillette, Wyo., 1980-84; dir. emergency medicine St. Alexius Med. Ctr., Bismarck, N.C., 1984-88; staff emergency physician Bluefield (W.Va.) Regional Med. Ctr., 1988—, Welch (W.Va.) Emergemcy

Hosp., 1992—; owner, operator Mare's Run Farm, Tazewell, Va., 1990—. Home: 136 Ella Peery Rd Tazewell VA 24651

TEPPER, CLIFFORD, allergist, immunologist, educator; b. Schenectady, N.Y., Oct. 26, 1922; s. Solomon B. and Annette (Lifset) T.; m. Cynthia S. Tepper; children: Stewart, Nancy, Henry, Audrey. Chief allergy dept. Ellis Hosp., Schenectady, 1990—; chief allergy and immunology, clin. med. pharmacy dir. Comty. Health Plan, Latham, N.Y., 1992—; prof. pediatrics Albany (N.Y.) Med. Coll., 1973—; cons. allergist, clin. med. pharmacy dir. Cmty. Health Plan, Latham, N.Y. Trustee Schenectady Mus., 1987—, Schenectady Pub. Libr., 1985—. Mem. Coll. Allergy and Immunology, Am. Acad. Pediatrics, Am. Acad. Allergy and Immunology, New Eng. Soc. Allergy (pres. 1990-92), N.Y. State Allergy Soc. (treas. 1994—), Physicians for Social Responsibility. Home: 2216 Stone Ridge Rd Niskayuna NY 12309 Office: Cmty Health Plan 1201 Troy Schenectady Rd Latham NY 12110

TEPPER, ERIC R., podiatrist; b. Bklyn., Aug. 4, 1955; s. Bennett Jay and Shirley (Goldweitz) T.; married; children: Randall, Amy. BA, Queens Coll., 1977; DPM, Ohio Coll. Podiatric Medicine, 1981. Adj. prof. Ohio Coll. Podiatric Medicine, Houston, 1995—; mem. adv. bd. Nat. Edn. Ctr., Houston, 1990-94. Office: 3143 Hwy 6 S Sugarland TX 77478

TEPPER, LLOYD BARTON, physician; b. L.A., Dec. 21, 1931; m. Lamonte Leverage; children: Jeffrey Hamilton, Evan Clothier. AB, Dartmouth Coll., 1954; MD, Harvard U., 1957, MIH, 1960, ScD in Hygiene, 1962. Diplomate in occupational medicine Am. Bd. Preventive Medicine. Rsch. fellow Harvard Med. Sch., Boston, 1958-59; clin. fellow Mass. Gen. Hosp., Boston, 1958-60; rsch. assoc. MIT, Cambridge, 1959-61; physician U.S. AEC, Washington, 1962-65; prof. environ. health U. Cin., 1965-72; assoc. dir. Kettering Lab., Cin., 1965-72; assoc. commr. U.S. FDA, Washington, 1972-76; corp. med. dir. Air Products and Chems., Inc., Allentown, Pa., 1976—; dir. Chem. Industry Inst. Toxicology, Research Triangle Park, N.C., 1982-89; trustee Am. Bd. Preventive Medicine, vice chair, 1986-94. Editor Jour. Occupational Medicine, 1979-91. Fellow Am. Coll. Occupational and Environ. Medicine, Am. Acad. Occupational Medicine (pres. 1980-81). Office: Air Products and Chems Inc 7201 Hamilton Blvd Allentown PA 18195-1501

TERADA, HIROSHI, biochemist, educator; b. Dalien, China, Dec. 8, 1936; s. Shin-ichi and Toshiko (Miura) T.; m. Yukiko Miyatani, Aug. 29, 1969; children: Hiro-ichi, Kazu. BSc, Kyoto (Japan) U., 1960, MSc, 1962, PhD, 1962. Asst. prof. U. Tokushima, Japan, 1965-67, assoc. prof., 1967-85, prof. biochemistry, 1986—, faculty dean, 1992-96. Mem. com. Japan Ministry of Edn., Tokyo, 1994-96, Japan Ministry Environ. Protection, Tokyo, 1995—. Recipient Sci. award Tokushima Newspaper Press, 1987. Mem. Pharm. Soc. Japan (bd. dirs. 1994-96, award 1974), Biochem. Soc. Japan (bd. dirs. 1995—). Home: Myodo-cho 1-116-4, 770 Tokushima Japan Office: U Tokushima, Faculty Pharm Scis, Shomachi-1, 770 Tokushima Japan

TERAMOTO, RAE NAGAO, internist. AB, Cornell U., 1977; MS, U. Hawaii, 1980, MD, 1981. Diplomate Am. Bd. Internal Medicine, Endocrinology. Physician Ctrl. Med. Clinic, Honolulu, 1987—. Mem. AMA, ACP, Am. Diabetes Assn., Am. Assn. Clin. Endocrinologists, Alpha Omega Alpha. Office: Central Med Clinic 321 N Kuakini #201 Honolulu HI 96817

TERAO, TOSHIO, physician, educator; b. Shimizu, Japan, Jan. 18, 1930; s. Eiji and Mitsuko (Katagiri) T.; m. Setsuko Nishigaki, Nov. 13, 1961; children: Toshiya, Yasuo, Yoshio. Diploma U. Tokyo, 1953, M.D., 1960. Intern, Tokyo U. Hosp., 1953-54; sr. scientist Nat. Inst. Radiol. Sci., Chiba, Japan, 1963-67; research assoc. Mayo Clinic, Rochester, Minn., 1970-72; asst. U. Tokyo, 1972-77, lectr. in medicine 1977-79; prof. medicine Teikyo U., 1980-91, prof. neurology, 1991—; pres. Teikyo U. Med. Hosp., 1987-93, dean, 1993—. Author, editor in field. Mem. Am. Acad. Neurology, Japanese Soc. Internal Medicine, Japanese Soc. Neurology, Japanese Soc. Neuropathology, Japanese Soc. EEG and Electromyography, Japanese Soc. Psychiatry and Neurology, Japanese Soc. Cerebrovascular Disease, Sigma Xi. Office: Teikyo U, 2-11-1 Kaga Itabashiku, Tokyo 173, Japan

TERBIZAN, DONNA JEAN, physiology educator; b. Cleve., Feb. 2, 1953; d. Eugene P. and Evelyn R. (Gauley) T. BS, Cleve. State U., 1976; MA, Ohio State U., 1978, PhD, 1982. Grad. asst. Ohio State U., Columbus, 1978-82; instr. N.D. State U., Fargo, 1982-85, asst. prof., 1986-94, assoc. prof., 1994—; dir. corp./cmty. fitness N.D. State U., 1986—; sports medicine cons. Dakota Clinic, Fargo, 1984—, coord. sports medicine, 1985-86. Contbr. articles to profl. jours. Fellow Am. Coll. Sports Medicine (exercise test technician, pres. Northland chpt. 1989); mem. AAHPERD (Ctrl. Dist. Honor award 1995), N.D. Assn. Health, Phys. Edn., Recreation and Dance (pres. 1991, Honor award 1993), Am. Softball Assn., Nat. Strength and Conditioning Assn., Dakota Am. Heart Assn. (pres. Fargo Metro chpt. 1989-91). Office: ND State U Bentson Bunker Fieldhouse Fargo ND 58105

TERENZI, THOMAS JOHN, osteopathic physician, researcher; b. Port Chester, N.Y., Sept. 17, 1958; s. John R. and Agnes A. (Barbara) T. BS, SUNY; MA, Columbia U., 1986, MEd, 1989; MS, L.I. U., 1988; EdD, Columbia U., 1991; DC, N.Y. Chiropractic Coll., 1984; DO, N.Y. Coll. Osteo. Medicine, 1995. Gen. practice rehab. medicine Rye, N.Y., 1985—; rschr. in field. Contbr. articles to profl. jours. Mem. AMA, Am. Osteo. Med. Assn., Am. Chiropractic Assn. Office: 50 Harding Dr Rye NY 10580

TER HORST, GERRIT JOHANNES, neurobiologist; b. Den Ham, The Netherlands, Mar. 16, 1955; s. Engbertus and Hermina Johanna Femmigje (Gerrits) Ter H.; m. Ilse Yvonne Van der Poel, Dec. 29, 1988; children: Joris Thys, Victor Gys. Degree, U. Groningen, 1982. Product mgr. Janssen Pharmaceutica B.V., Tilburg, The Netherlands, 1986-87; asst. prof. dept. neurobiology U. Groningen, The Netherlands, 1987-92, asst. prof. dept. biol. psychiatry, 1992—; chmn. BCN program com. Inst. Behavioral and Cognitive Neurosci., Groningen, 199296. Editor: Clinical Pharmacology of Cerebral Ischemia; contbr. articles and revs. to profl. jours. and chpts. to books. Grantee Dutch Heart Found., 1991, ASTA-Medica, 1993, De Cook Found., 1992, Glaxo, Internat., 1995. Mem. Soc. for Neurosci., N.Y. Acad. Scis., European Neurosci. Assn., Dutch Pysiol. Soc., Royal Dutch Phys. Soc., Badminton Club Beyum (treas. 1982-86). Office: U Groningen Dept Biol Psych, Hanzeplein 1 PO Box 300001, 9700 RB Groningen The Netherlands

TER MAAT, MARILYN, nurse; b. Yankton, S.D., Feb. 3, 1954; d. Milton N. and Joyce A. (Boschma) Van Gerpen; m. Harry W. Ter Maat, Aug. 3, 1977. BSN, Mt. Marty Coll., 1975; MS, Drake U., 1985; MSN, U. Hawaii, 1989. RN, N.J., Iowa, Hawaii, Kans., Tex. Charge nurse St. Peter's Med. Ctr., New Brunswick, N.J., 1977-79; asst. dir. nursing Christian Health Care Ctr., Wyckoff, N.J., 1979-80; staff nurse Pella (Iowa) Cmty. Hosp., 1980-82; staff nurse VA Med. Ctr., Knoxville, Iowa, 1983, head nurse, 1983-85, nursing instr., 1985-86; dir. nursing Rehab. Hosp. of the Pacific, Honolulu, 1987-92; house supr. coord. Meml. Hosp., Manhattan, Kans., 1992-94; dir. patient care svcs. Health South, Midland, Tex., 1994—; cons. Divsn. of Cmty. Hosps., Honolulu, 1991-92; lectr. in nursing U. Hawaii, Hawaii Loa, Honolulu, 1991-92. Contbr. articles to profl. publs., chpt. to book. Mem. Assn. Rehab. Nurses (dir.-at-large 1993, cert. in rehab. nursing), Am. Orgn. Nurse Execs. (pres., sec.-treas. West Tex. chpt. 1995-96), Am. Assn. Spinal Cord Injury Nurses, Arthritis Found. Home: 5618 Crowley Blvd Midland TX 79707 Office: Health South Rehab Hosp 1800 Heritage Blvd Midland TX 79707

TERMINELLA, LUIGI, critical care physician, educator; b. Catania, Italy, Nov. 15, 1960; came to U.S., 1961; s. Roberto and Josephine (Bartolotta) T. MD summa cum laude, U. Catania, 1986. Pathology asst. Brotman Med. Ctr., Culver City, Calif., 1987-89; transitional resident Miriam Hosp./Brown U., Providence, 1989-90; resident in internal medicine U. Hawaii, Honolulu, 1990-92; tng. in critical care/internal medicine U. Hawaii/Queen's Med. Ctr., Honolulu, 1992-93; transfusion svc. physician Blood Bank of Hawaii, Honolulu, 1992-93; internal medicine physician Hawaii Physician Svcs., Honolulu, 1993—; critical care physician Queen's Med. Ctr., Honolulu, 1993—; mem. clin. faculty John H. Burns Sch. Medicine, U. Hawaii, Honolulu, 1994—; pres. Pualani Family Health, SRL, Corp., Honolulu. Recipient Clementi award U. Catania, 1986, others. Mem. ACP, AMA, Am. Soc. Internal Medicine, Hawaiian Soc. Critical Care, Soc. Critical Care Medicine. Office: Queen's Med Ctr 1301 Punchbowl QET 4B Honolulu HI 96813

TERNUS, JEAN ANN, nursing educator; b. Columbus, Nebr., Feb. 29, 1944; d. Maurice Henry and Marcella (Huntemer) T. BS in Nursing, Mt. Marty Coll., 1966; MS, Kans. State U., 1977. RN Kans., Mo., Nebr. Staff nurse Brian Meml. Hosp., Lincoln, Nebr., 1966-67; staff nurse VA Hosp., Milw., 1967-69, Kansas City, Mo., 1969-72; nursing instr. Kansas City (Kans.) Community Coll., 1973—; cardiovascular nurse specialist Meth. Hosp., Houston, 1973. Mem. AAUW, NEA, AACN, Kans. State Nurses Assn. (pres. dist. II 1980-82, chair dist. newsletter 1980—, 2d v.p. 1986-90, 1st v.p. 1990-92, sect. dist. II 1993—, v.p. 1993-95), NLN, Gerontol. Nurses Assn., Kans. Nurses Found. (bd. dirs. 1990-91, sec. 1992—, pres.-elect 1995—), Sigma Theta Tau, Delta Kappa Gamma. Democrat. Roman Catholic. Home: 5342 Juniper Dr Shawnee Mission KS 66205-2225 Office: Kansas City CC 7250 State Ave Kansas City KS 66112-3003

TERPINSKI, EVA ANTONINA, pharmaceutical company executive; b. Warsaw, Poland, Jan. 17, 1946; came to U.S. 1983; d. Stanislaw and Marianna (Lis) Zajaczkowski; m. Jacek Terpinski, Jan. 22, 1972; children: Peter, Agatha. MSc in Chemistry, Poly. U., Warsaw, 1969, MSc in Chem. Engring., 1969, PhD in Chemistry, 1977. Asst. Poly. U., Warsaw, 1969-73, sr. asst., 1973-78, asst. prof., 1978-83; lectr. Rutgers U., New Brunswick, N.J., 1983-84; sr. scientist Nat. Patent Co., New Brunswick, N.J., 1984-88; mgr. Nat. Patent Co., New Brunswick, 1988-90, dir., 1990—. Contbr. articles to profl. jours.; editor 5 books; patentee in field. Instr. Girl Scouts U.S.A., Perth Amboy, N.J., 1988—. Mem. AAAS, Am. Assn. Pharm. Scientists, Internat. Soc. Magnetic Resonance, Am. Chem. Soc. Office: Nat Patent Devel Co 783 Jersey Ave New Brunswick NJ 08901-3605

TERR, ABBA ISRAEL, allergist, immunologist; b. Cleve., 1930. MD, Case Western Res. U., 1956. Cert. in allergy and immunology; cert. internal medicine. Intern U. Wis. Hosps., Madison, 1956-57; resident in internal medicine U. Mich. Med. Ctr., Ann Arbor, 1957-60, fellow in allergy, 1960-62; physician Stanford (Calif.) U. Med. Ctr.; clin. prof. medicine Stanford U. Fellow ACP, Am. Acad. Allergy, Asthma, and Immunology; mem. Am. Thoracic Soc. Address: 450 Sutter St Ste 2534 San Francisco CA 94108-4204*

TERR, LENORE CAGEN, psychiatrist, writer; b. N.Y.C., Mar. 27, 1936; d. Samuel Lawrence Cagen and Esther (Hirsh) Cagen Raiken; m. Abba I. Terr; children: David, Julia. AB magna cum laude, Case Western Res. U., 1957; MD with honors, U. Mich., 1961. Diplomate Am. Bd. Psychiatry and Neurology. Intern Med. Ctr. U. Mich., Ann Arbor, 1961-62, resident Neuropsychiat. Inst., 1962-64, fellow Children's Psychiat. Hosp., 1964-66; from instr. to asst. prof. Med. Sch. Case Western Res. U., Cleve., 1966-71; pvt. practice Terr Med. Corp., San Francisco, 1971—; from asst. clin. prof. to clin. prof. psychiatry Sch. Medicine U. Calif., San Francisco, 1971—; lectr. law, psychiatry U. Calif., Berkeley, 1971—, U. Calif., Davis, 1974; bd. dirs. Am. Bd. Psychiatry and Neurology, Deerfield, Ill., 1988-96. Author: Too Scared to Cry, 1990, Unchained Memories, 1994; contbr. articles to profl. jours. Rockefeller Found. scholar-in-residence, Italy, 1981, 88; project grantee Rosenberg Found., 1977, 80-81, William T. Grant Found., 1986-87; recipient Career Tchr. award NIMH, 1967-69, Child Advocacy award, APA, 1994. Fellow Am. Psychiat. Assn. (Child Psychiatry Rsch. award 1984, Clin. Rsch. award 1987), Am. Coll. Psychiatrists (program chair 1991-92, Bowis award 1993), Am. Acad. Child and Adolescent Psychiatry (coun. 1984-87); mem. Group for Advancement Psychiatry (bd. dir. 1986-88), Phi Beta Kappa, Alpha Omega Alpha. Office: Terr Med Corp 450 Sutter St Rm 2534 San Francisco CA 94108-4204

TERRADAS, SHIRLEY ARNOLD, clinical psychologist; b. Great Bend, Kans., Apr. 12, 1963; d. Bobby Gene and Bettie Lou (Johnson) Arnold; married, June 5, 1993; 1 child, Will. AA, Mo. So. State Coll., 1984, BS, 1985; MS, Fla. Inst. Tech., 1987, Psychology D., 1989. Counselor various orgns. Mo., Fla., 1979-88; psychologist U.S. Army, Ft. Gordon, Ft. Stewart, Ga., 1988-90; chief div. mental health U.S. Army, Ft. Stewart, 1990-91; staff psychologist Fed. Bur. of Prisons, Jesup, Ga., 1991-92, chief psychologist, 1993—; psychologist suicide prevention team U.S. Army, 1989-91; mental health cons. hostage negotiation team Fed. Bur. Prisons, Jesup, 1991—. Capt. U.S. Army, 1989-91. Decorated Bronze Svc. Star (2), Appreciation Award. Mem. APA. Office: Fed Bur of Prisons Fci Hwy #3015 Jesup GA 31599

TERRELL, DAVID LAWRENCE, clinical psychologist, educator, consultant; b. Clarksville, Tenn., Oct. 25, 1935; s. David L. and Romania Jewell (Moreland) T.; m. Carolyn Rheba Hoover, Mar. 30, 1964; children: Toni Laurin, Steven Lawrence, Terri Lyn. BA, Tenn. State U., 1957, MS, 1958; PhD, U. Rochester, 1973. Diplomate Am. Bd. Profl. Psychology. Psychology intern Crownsville (Md.) State Hosp., 1958-60, clin. psychologist, 1960-63; youth counselor Washington Action for Youth, 1963-64; rsch. assoc. Howard U., Washington, 1964-69; cons. U. Rsch. Corp., Washington, 1964-70; supr. D.C. Govt., Washington, 1967-68; psychology intern U. Rochester, N.Y., 1970-72; dir. Fisk U.-Meharry Med. Coll., Nashville, 1972-83; prof. psychology Tenn. State U., Nashville, 1983—; adj. prof. Peabody Coll., Vanderbilt U., Nashville, 1974—; staff cons. VA Med. Ctr., Tuskegee, Ala., 1974—; psychotherapy cons. Meharry Med. Hosp., Nashville, 1990—; lectr. alcohol and drug prevention Nat. Conf. Rsch., 1990; bd. dirs. coun. Nat. Register Health Svc. Providers isn Psychology, 1992—. Mem. adv. bd. Operation Chem. Awareness of Nashville, 1985-94; bd. dirs. Crisis Intervention Ctr., Nashville, 1985-91; chair Mayor's Higher Edn. Task Force on Substance Abuse, Nashville, 1991. Recipient Plaque of Appreciation DAV, Washington, 1980; tng. grantee NIMH, 1973-82. Fellow APA, Acad. Clin. Psychology, Am. Psychol. Soc.; mem. Assn. Black Psychologists (pres 1981-82, plaque of appreciation 1987), Am. Orthopsychiat. Assn., Nat. Black Child Devel. Inst., Tenn. Psychol. Assn. Methodist. Home: 3710 Westport Dr Nashville TN 37218-1210 Office: Psychosocial Studies & Interventions Inc 1808 W End Ave Ste 1015 Nashville TN 37203-2516

TERRELL, HOWARD BRUCE, psychiatrist; b. Cleveland, Calif., Feb. 19, 1952. BS magna cum laude, Calif. State U., Hayward, 1974; MD, U. Calif., San Diego, 1980. Diplomate Am. Bd. psychiatry and Neurology, Am. Bd. Forensic Examiners. Intern. Kaiser Found. Hosp., Oakland, Calif., 1980-81; resident in psychiatry U. Calif., San Francisco/Fresno, 1982-85; staff psychiatrist Kings View Corp., Reedley, Calif., 1985-87, sr. staff psychiatrist, 1987-88, dir. outpatient psychiatry, 1988-89; dir. dual diagnosis and affective disorders programs Sierra Gateway Hosp., Clovis, Calif., 1989-91. Contbr. articles to profl. jours. Fellow Am. Coll. Forensic Psychiatry, Am. Bd. Forensic Examiners (diplomate); mem. Am. Acad. Psychiatry and the Law, Am. Psychiat. Assn., Ctrl. Calif. Psychiat. Soc. (pres. Sierra chpt. Office: 3100 Willow Ave Ste 102 Clovis CA 93612-4741

TERRELL, PAMELA SUE, pharmacist; b. Richmond, Ind., Feb. 1, 1965; d. Kenneth Duane and Phyllis J. (Preston) T. BS in Pharmacy with honors, PharmD, Purdue U., 1991. Registered pharmacist, Ind. Pharmacist Reid Hosp. and Health Care Svcs., Richmond, 1992-94, Owl Drugs, Muncie, Ind., 1994-95, Ball Meml. Hosp., Muncie, Ind., 1996—; resident in pharmacy practice Meth. Hosp. Ind., Indpls., 1995-96; adj. instr. pharmacy practice Butler U. Sch. Pharmacy and Health Scis., Indpls., 1995-96; cons. pharmacist H&R Healthcare Cons., Muncie, 1994-95. Mem. Am. Coll. Clin. Pharmacy (assoc.), Am. Soc. health-Sys. Pharmacists, Ind. Soc. Hosp. Pharmacists, Fellowship of Christian Pharmacists Internat., Ind. Coll. Clin. Pharmacy. Home: 2917 W Applewood Ct Muncie IN 47304 Office: Ball Meml Hosp 2401 Univ Ave Muncie IN 47303

TERRELL-MCDANIEL, ROBIN F., cardiac rehabilitation and critical care nurse; b. Charlton Heights, W.Va., May 9, 1961; d. Clarence E. Sr. and Dorothy Mae (Smith) T.; m. Charles Kevin McDaniel, Aug. 4, 1990. ADN, W.Va. Inst. Tech., 1982; BSN, W.Va. U., 1987. Emergency room charge nurse Montgomery (W.Va.) Gen. Hosp., 1982-87, nursing supr., 1987-88; coord. utilization rev. MedCert, Charleston, W.Va., 1988-89; vis. asst. prof. nursing W.Va. Inst. Tech., Montgomery, 1989-90; critical care nurse W.Va. Gen. Hosp., Montgomery, 1990—, cardiac rehab. nurse, 1995—. Mem. Am. Assn. Cardiovascular and Pulmonary Rehab. Home: PO Box 345 Pratt WV 25162-0345

TERRENATO, LUCIANO, geneticist, educator; b. Tripoli, Libya, May 10, 1939; s. Renato and Angela (Spyller) T.; m. Marina Frontali, Apr. 29, 1963; children: Nicola, Francesca. Degree in medicine, La Sapienza U., Rome, 1964, splty. in endocrinology, 1967. Lectr. U. Camerino, Italy, 1968-77, La Sapienza U., 1973-80; prof. U. Sassari, Italy, 1980-83; prof. population genetics Tor Vergata U., Rome, 1983—; chmn. degree course biol. sci. Tor Vergata U., 1985-88, dir. biomed. libr., 1988—; mem. com. genetic engring. NRC, Rome, 1989—; mem. com. human genome European Community, Brussels, 1991—. Editor Gene Geography, 1987—; assoc. editor Annals of Human Genetics, 1995—; contbr. articles to profl. jours. Mem. N.Y. Acad. Scis. Home: Piazza Goadar 14, 00199 Rome Italy Office: Tor Vergata U, Via O Raimondo, 00173 Rome Italy

TERRILL, KAREN STAPLETON, retired medical planning consultant; b. Milw., Mar. 21, 1939; d. Thomas John and Olive Patrea (Thorbjornsen) Stapleton; m. Max Kurt Winkler, Dec. 18, 1965 (dec. June 1976); m. Richard Terrill, Jan. 23, 1991 (dec. May 1991). BS in Nursing, U. Mich., 1961; MBA, U. Nev., 1974. RN, Calif. Project nurse Langley Porter N.P.I., San Francisco, 1962-64; asst. dir. nursing Milw. County Mental Health Ctr., 1964-66; instr. Fond du Lac (Wis.) Sch. Dist., 1966-67; sch. nurse Inglewood (Calif.) Sch. Dist., 1968-69; instr. nursing U. Nev., Reno, 1969-74; health planner manpower State of Nev. Comp B. Agy., Carson City, 1974-75; planning analyst St. Mary's Hosp., Reno, 1974-76; sr. system analyst U. Calif., San Francisco, 1976-79; med. planning cons. Stone Marraccini & Patterson, San Francisco, 1979-93. Mem. citizen's adv. group City of Richmond, Calif., 1987-88; founding dir. of B.O.A.T. non-profit corp. to promote ferry transit on San Francisco Bay. Mountain State Regional Planning Commn. grantee, 1973-74. Home: 1308 Mallard Dr Richmond CA 94801-4113

TERRILL, THOMAS EDWARD, health facility administrator; b. Mpls., Oct. 4, 1939; married. BS, U. Minn., 1961; M Health Care Adminstrn., U. Pitts., 1963, DS, 1970. Adminstrv. resident Homestead (Pa.) Hosp., 1962-63; adminstrv. asst. Truman Med. Ctr.-West, Kanasas City, Mo., 1963-65, asst. adminstr., 1965-67; asst. prof. U. Pitts., 1967-73, assoc. prof., 1973-74; dir. mktg. and planning Mountain States Regional Med. Program, Boise, Idaho, 1974-76, divsn. dir., 1976-77; v.p. Hollywood Presbyn. Med. Ctr., L.A., 1977; assoc. dir. Akron (Ohio) City Hosp., 1978-81, v.p. med. affairs, 1981-83; sr. mgr. Peat Marwick Mitchell, Phila., 1983-87; v.p. Network Inc., Randolph, N.J., 1987-90; exec. v.p. Univ. Health Sys., New Brunswick, N.J., 1990—. Contbr. articles to profl. publs. Home: Univ Health System Plaza 11 6009 Hunters Glen Dr Plainsboro NJ 08536 Office: Univ Health Sys 317 George St New Brunswick NJ 08901*

TERRIS, LILLIAN DICK, psychologist, association executive; b. Bloomfield, N.J., May 5, 1914; d. Alexander Blaikie and Herminia (Doscher) Dick; BA, Barnard Coll., 1935; PhD, Columbia U., 1941; m. Louis Long, Apr. 22, 1935 (dec. Sept. 1968), 1 son, Alexander Blaikie Long; m. Milton Terris, Feb. 6, 1971. Instr. psychology Sara Lawrence Coll., Bronxville, N.Y., 1937-40; jr. pers. tech. SSA, Washington, 1941; sr. pers. clk. OWI, N.Y.C., 1941-43; dir. profl. examination svc. Am. Pub. Health Assn., N.Y.C., 1943-70, pres., 1970-79, pres. emeritus, 1979—. Assoc. editor Jour. Pub. Health Policy, 1979—. Life mem., bd. dirs. Profl. Exam. Svc.; chair bd. VNA Chittenden County, Vt., 1989, mem. hon. bd., 1993—. Recipient Nat. Environ. Health Assn. award, 1976, Cert. of Svc. award Am. Bd. Preventive Medicine, 1979. Diplomate Am. Bd. Examiners in Profl. Psychology. Fellow Am. Psychol. Assn.; mem. Am. Pub. Health Assn., N.Y. State Psychol. Assn., Am. Coll. Hosp. Adminstrs. (hon. fellow), Phi Beta Kappa, Sigma Xi. Contbr. articles in field to profl. jours. Home: 208 Meadowood Dr South Burlington VT 05403-7401 Office: 475 Riverside Dr New York NY 10115-0122

TERRIS, MILTON, physician, educator; b. N.Y.C., Apr. 22, 1915; s. Harry and Gussie (Dokshitski) T.; m. Rema Lapouse, Nov. 23, 1941 (dec. Aug. 1970); children—Andrew David, Eugene Charles (dec.); m. Lillian Long, Feb. 6, 1971. A.B., Columbia, 1935; M.D., N.Y.U., 1939; M.P.H., Johns Hopkins, 1944. Intern Harlem Hosp., N.Y.C., 1939-41; resident Bellevue Hosp., N.Y.C., 1941-42; practice medicine specializing in preventive medicine Buffalo, 1951-58, N.Y.C., 1960-80, South Burlington, Vt., 1980—; asst. dean post-grad. edn. Sch. Medicine, U. Buffalo, 1951-58, assoc. 1952-54, asst. prof., 1954-55, assoc. prof. preventive medicine, 1955-58; prof. epidemiology Sch. Medicine, Tulane U., 1958-60; head chronic disease unit dept. epidemiology Pub. Health Research Inst., N.Y.C., 1960-64; prof. preventive medicine N.Y. Med. Coll., 1964-80, chmn. dept. community and preventive medicine, 1968-80; vis. prof. U. Toronto, 1984-93, U. Montreal, 1985—. Author: Goldberger on Pellagra, 1964, La Revolución Epidemiológica y la Medicina Social, 1980; Editor: Jour. Public Health Policy, 1980—. Recipient Abraham M. Lilienfeld award Am. Coll. Epidemiology. Fellow N.Y. Acad. Medicine, Am. Pub. Health Assn. (past pres.; Sedgwick Meml. award 1984); mem. Assn. Tchrs. Preventive Medicine (Duncan Clark award 1984; past pres.), Soc. Epidemiologic Research (past pres.), Nat. Assn. Pub. Health Policy (past pres.), Phi Beta Kappa, Alpha Omega Alpha, Delta Omega. Home and Office: 208 Meadowood Dr South Burlington VT 05403

TERRIS, SUSAN, physician, cardiologist; b. Morristown, N.J., Sept. 5, 1944; d. Albert and Virginia (Rinaldy) T. BA in History, U. Chgo., 1967, PhD in Biochemistry, 1975, MD, 1976. Diplomate Am. Bd. Internal Medicine, Am. Bd. Endocrinology and Metabolism, Am. Bd. Cardiovascular Disease. Resident in internal medicine Washington U., Barnes Hosp., St. Louis, 1976-78; fellow in endocrinology and metabolism U. Chgo., 1978-80, fellow cardiology, 1980-83; fellow cardiology U. Mich., Ann Arbor, 1983-85, instr. cardiology, 1985-86; head cardiac catheterization lab., head cardiology Westland (Mich.) Med. Ctr., 1985. Contbr. articles to Jour. Biol. Chemistry, Am. Jour. Physiology, Am. Jour. Cardiology, Jour. Clin. Investigation, other profl. publs. Grantee Juvenile Diabetes Found., 1978-80, NIH, 1978-79. Mem. AAAS, Am. Heart Assn., N.Y. Acad. Sci., Am. Women in Sci.

TERRY, BRIAN R., counselor, academic administrator; b. Providence, June 8, 1961; s. Edwin R. and Mary W. (Ahern) T.; m. Stephanie A. Fogli; children: Alexander Brian, Jarrod Stephen. AS in Bus. Adminstrn., Community Coll. of R.I., Warwick, 1982; BS in Bus. Adminstrn., Bryant Coll., 1984; MA in Agy. Counseling, R.I. Coll., 1990. Counselor Whitmarsh Corp., Providence, 1985-87, 87-90, supr., 1990-94; juvenile counselor Dept. of Children, Youth, and Families R.I. Tng. Sch., Cranston, R.I., 1988-90, acting dep. supt. for adminstrn. tng. sch. for youth, 1994—, cottage mgr., 1990—; social caseworker II Dept. for Children, Youth and their Families Divsn. of Direct Svcs., Cranston, R.I., 1990. Mem. Nat. Major Gang Task Force, New Eng. Coun. on Crime and Deliquency; vol. Spl. Olympics; former mem. Big Brothers. Acad. scholar Esterline Corp., acad. scholar City of Cranton, R.I., Tanner Meml. scholar. Am. Assn. for Counseling and Devel., Pub. Offender Counselor Assn., Nat. Ct. Appointed Spl. Advocate Assn., Am. Correctional Assn., Nat. Inst. for Reality Therapy (assoc., Northeast region), Community Leaders of Am., Juvenile Officers Assn., Phi Theta Kappa. Home: 115 E View Ave Cranston RI 02910-6505

TERRY, JOHN RICHARD, counselor; b. Cheyenne, Wyo., Sept. 1, 1945; s. Melvin Paul and Betty Eileen (Bailey) T.; m. Linda Louise Mueller, June 7, 1967 (div. May 1975); children: Leah Marie, Naomi Anne; m. Linda Lee Rice, May 19, 1975; children: Travis Clay, Dallas Michael. BS, USAF Acad., Colo., 1967; MS, Ea. Wash. U., 1983; postgrad., U. Mo. Lic. profl. counselor, Mo. Commd. USAF, 1967-87, advanced through grades to maj.; lic. prof. counselor in pvt. practice Columbia, Mo., 1987—. Decorated Silver Star, DFC (2), Air Medal (10); recipient Jorge Chavez Medal of Merit, Bolivian Govt., 1972. Mem. Mo. Assn. Counselors, Mo. Assn. Home-based Svcs. Home and Office: Cons for Positive Future 2815 Burrwood Columbia MO 65203

TERRY, LEON CASS, neurologist, educator; b. Northville, Mich., Dec. 22, 1940; s. Leon Herbert and Zella Irene (Boyd) T.; m. Suzanne Martinson, June 27, 1964; children: Kristin, Sean. Pharm. D., U. Mich., 1964; MD, Marquette U., 1969; PhD, McGill U., 1982, MBA, U. S. Fla., 1994. Diplomate Am. Bd. Psychiatry and Neurology, Am. Bd. Med. Mgmt. Intern, U. Rochester, N.Y., 1969-70; staff assoc. NIH, 1970-72; resident in neurology McGill U., Montreal, Que., Can., 1972-75, MRC fellow, 1975-78; assoc. prof. U. Tenn., Memphis, 1978-81; prof. neurology U. Mich., Ann Arbor, 1981-89, assoc prof. physiology, 1982-89; asst. chief neurology VA

Med. Ctr., Ann Arbor, 1982-89; prof. neurology and physiology, chmn. dept. neurology Med. Coll of Wis., Milw., 1989—; dir. clin. neurosci. ctr. and multiple sclerosis clinic, Med. Coll. Wis.; vice chief of staff Froedtert Hosp., 1994—. Contbr. articles to profl. jours., chpts. to books. Served to lt. comdr. USPHS, 1970-72. NIH grantee, 1981-92; VA grantee, 1980-92; VA Clin. Investigator award, 1980-81. Mem. AMA, Am. Soc. Clin. Investigation, Cen. Soc. Clin. Investigation, So. Soc. Clin. Investigation, Am. Neurol. Assn., Am. Coll. Physician Execs. (vice chmn. academic health ctr. soc. 1994-95, chair, 1995—, leader forum health care delivery 1995—), Am. Coll. Healthcare Execs., Endocrine Soc., Am. Acad. Neurology, Internat. Soc. Neuroendocrinology, Internat. Soc. Psychoneuroendocrinology, Soc. Neurosci, Soc. Rsch. Biol. Rhythms, Milw. Acad. Physicians, Wis. Neurol. Assn., Wis. State Med. Soc. (del.- elect 1995-96), Med. Soc. Milw. County, Milw. Neuropsychiatric Soc. (pres.-elect). Avocations: pilot, skiing, scuba diving, computers. Office: Med Coll Wis Dept Neurology Froedtert Hosp 9200 W Watertown Plank Rd Milwaukee WI 53226-3557

TERRY, RICHARD ALLAN, consulting psychologist, former college president; b. Lincoln, Nebr., June 4, 1920; s. Lester C. and Dorothy (Weeden) T.; m. Z. Inci Incikaya, June 3, 1959; 1 child, Deniz. A.B., U. Notre Dame, 1944; M.S., Catholic U. Am., 1950, Ph.D., 1954. Instr., asst. prof., chmn. psychol. dept. U. Portland, Oreg., 1953-59; prin. scientist, chief advanced research, life scis. North Am. Aviation, Downey, Calif., 1959-63; assoc. prof. indsl. engring., dir. systems research center U. Okla., Norman, 1963-69; prof., head dept. psychology U. Tulsa, 1970-73; prof. psychology SUNY Coll. at Oswego, 1973-75, dean grad. studies and research, 1973-75, acting v.p. acad. affairs, 1973-74; v.p. for instrn. and curriculum SUNY Coll. at Brockport, 1975-78; pres. Quinnipiac Coll., Hamden, Conn., 1978-86; sr. ptnr. Richard Allan Terry Assocs., Cons., Hamden, 1986-91; vis. prof. Hacettepe U., Ankara, Turkey, 1969-70; v.p. Found. for Study of Behavioral Scis., Downey, 1965-68; assoc. fellow Timothy Dwight Coll., Yale U., 1982—; v.p. Conn. Council Higher Edn., 1983-84, pres., 1984-85. Trustee Chamber Orch. of New Eng., 1979-82, chmn. bd., 1982-83; vice chmn. Mgmt. Study Group, Town of Hamden, 1982-83; bd. dirs. Urban League Greater New Haven, 1983-90, sec. 1988-90; chmn. oversight com. Study of Police-Media Rels., 1983-84; mem. steering com. New Haven Initiative for Excellence in Edn., 1986-90, steering com. Town of Hamden Plan for the Future, 1988-91, adv. bd. Conn. Small Bus. Devel. Ctr., 1989-91; mem. Town of Hamden Planning and Zoning Commn., 1991-93. Mem. Am. Psychol. Assn., Conn. Conf. Ind. Colls. (sec.-treas. 1983-86), Greater New Haven C. of C. (bd. dirs. 1982-86, chmn. jobs compact planning com., 1984-85, steering com. 1985-86) Sigma Xi. Democrat. Roman Catholic. Home: 24 Talon Dr Schenectady NY 12309-1839

TERRY, RICHARD B., surgeon; b. Nashville, Oct. 4, 1945; s. J. Fred and Margaret (Harris) T.; m. Sherry Lynn Bates, June 5, 1970; children: Katherine, Leigh. BA, U. of the South, 1967; MD, U. of Tenn., 1970. Diplomate Am. Bd. Surgery. Surg. resident U. of Miss. Med. Ctr., Jackson, 1970-75; staff surgeon USAF, Kirtland AFB, N.Mex., 1975-77, Bapt. Hosp., Nashville, 1977—, Centinal Hosp., Nashville, 1977—, St. Thomas Hosp., Nashville, 1985—; vis. surgeon Vanderbilt Hosp., Nashville, 1978—; sr. flt. surgeon Tenn. Air Nat. Guard, Nashville, 1995. Col. Air Nat. Guard, 1983—, cmdr. 118 Meds. Decorated Meritorious Svc. medal USAF, Commendation medal USAF. Fellow Am. Coll. Surgery, Soc. of Am. Gastroendoscopic Surgeons, Piedmont Colon Rectal Soc., S.E. Surg. Congress; mem. Am. Soc. Colon and Rectal Surgeons, Soc. Surgery of Alimentary Tract, Aerospace Med. Assn. Home: 414 Overton Park Nashville TN 37215 Office: 2011 Church St # 703 Nashville TN 37203

TERRY, ROGER, pathologist, consultant; b. Waterville, N.Y., May 8, 1917; s. Orrin and Mary Isabelle (Kennedy) T.; m. Eleanor Virginia, Dec. 13, 1942; children: Robin, Orrin. AB magna cum laude, Colgate U., 1939; MD, U. Rochester, 1944. Cert. anatomic pathologist. Intern then resident Strong Meml. Hosp., Rochester, N.Y., 1944-51; asst. prof. U. Rochester Sch. Medicine, 1951-56, assoc. prof., 1956-61, prof. pathology, 1961-69; prof. pathology U. So. Calif. Sch. Medicine, Los Angeles, 1969-82; pathologist San Gabriel (Calif.) Valley Med. Ctr., 1982—; exec. dir. Calif. Tumor Tissue Registry, Los Angeles, 1969-84. Contbr. articles to profl. jours. Served to capt. USAF, 1954-56. Fellow Am. Soc. Clin. Pathologists, Coll. Am. Pathologists; mem. AMA, Internat. Acad. Pathology (councilor 1973-76), Am. Assn. Pathologists, L.A. Soc. Pathologists, Am. Soc. Cytology, Phi Beta Kappa, Sigma Xi, Alpha Omega Alpha. Republican. Episcopalian. Home: 2841 Shakespeare Dr San Marino CA 91108-2230 Office: San Gabriel Valley Med Ctr 218 S Santa Anita Ave San Gabriel CA 91776-1154

TERUEL, JUAN JOSE, physician; b. Regina, Sask., Can., Oct. 26, 1966; came to U.S., 1984; s. Francisco and Manuela (Carretero) T.; m. Rebecca Dawn Cripps, July 13, 1991; children: Jeremy Juan, Rebecca Ruby. BS, Bob Jones U., 1988; DO, Chgo. Coll. Osteo. Medicine, 1993. Intern Sparrow Hosp.-Mich. State U., Lansing, 1993-94; resident in family practice E.W. Sparrow Hosp., Lansing, 1994-96; urgent care physician Mason (Mich.) Cmty. Health Ctr., 1994-96; med. resident Ingham County Health Dept., Lansing, 1994-96. Mem. Am. Osteo. Assn., Am. Acad. Family Physicians. Baptist. Office: Carle Clinic 1701 E College Ave Bloomington IL 61704

TERUYA, JUN, hematologist; b. Tokyo, Feb. 8, 1954; s. Kunimitsu and Yukiko T.; m. Naoko Taniguchi, Apr. 23, 1979; children: Ami, Miho. MD, Hokkaido U. Sch. Medicine, Sapporo, Japan, 1979; DSc, Teikyo U., Tokyo, 1988. Bd. cert. internal medicine, Japan, hematology, Japan, transfusion medicine, Japan; diplomate Am. Bd. Pathology, Internat. Bd. Acad. Clin. and Applied Thrombosis/Hemostasis; lic. physician, Mass. Resident dept. cardiovascular surgery Tokyo Women's Med. Coll., 1979-80, resident dept. medicine, 1980-82; instr. divsn. hematology dept. internal medicine Teikyo U. Sch. Medicine, Tokyo, 1983-86, asst. prof. divsn. hematology, 1986-89; rsch. fellow pathology Harvard Med. Sch., Boston, 1989-91; asst. prof. divsn. hematology Teikyo U. Sch. Medicine, Tokyo, 1991-92; clin. fellow pathology Harvard Med. Sch., Boston, 1992-95; assoc. prof. dept. transfusion medicine Juntendo U. Sch. Medicine, Tokyo, 1995—; asst. med. dir., assoc. med. dir. blood transfusion svc. Teikyo U. Sch. Medicine, Chiba, Japan, 1986-89, 91-92; resident, chief resident clin. pathology Mass. Gen. Hosp., Boston, 1992-94, acting asst. dir. blood transfusion svc., 1993-94, asst. dir. blood transfusion svc., 1994-95; assoc. med. dir. blood transfusion svc. Juntendo U. Hosp., Tokyo, 1995—; lectr. Teikyo U. Sch. Medicine, Tokyo, 1986-89, Mass. Gen. Hosp., Boston, 1993—. Author: Encyclopedia of Nursing, 2d edit., 1982; contbr. articles to profl. jours. Mem. AMA, Internat. Soc. Blood Transfusion, Am. Assn. Blood Banks, Am. Soc. Clin. Pathologists, Mass. Med. Soc., Coll. Am. Pathologists, Japanese Soc. Internal Medicine, Am. Soc. Apheresis, Japan Soc. Clin. Hematology, Japanese Soc. on Thrombosis and Hematosis, Japan Hematol. Soc., Japan Soc. Blood Transfusion, Japan Soc. Clin. Pathology, Internat. Acad. Clin. and Applied Thrombosis/Hemostasis. Office: Juntendo U Hosp Blood Transfusion Svc, 3-1-3 Hongo, Bunkyo-ku, Tokyo 113, Japan

TERZ, JOSE JUAN, physician, surgical educator; b. Buenos Aires, Apr. 18, 1929; came to U.S., 1954; s. Barbar and Eva (Alem) T.; m. Rosa Basilia Tomsich, Apr. 7, 1954; children: Roxanna, Joseph, David. BA, Sarmiento Coll., 1946; MD, U. Buenos Aires, 1952. Diplomate Am. Bd. Surgery. Intern Lincoln Hosp., 1954-55, resident in surgery, 1955-56; resident in surgery Mt. Sinai Hosp., 1956-59, Meml. Hosp. for Cancer and Allied Diseases and James Ewing Hosp., 1959-62; rsch. fellow Sloan-Kettering Inst. for Cancer Rsch., 1964-66; dir. dept. gen. and oncologic surgery City of Hope Med. Ctr., Duarte, Calif., 1980-91, chmn. div. surgery, 1988-91; prof. clin. surgery U. So. Calif., L.A., 1993—; mem. cancer clin. investigation review com. Nat. Cancer Inst., 1988-91; mem. Pacificare of Calif. Tech. Assessment Com., 1992-93; cons. Santa Teresita Hosp., Duarte, Calif., 1991-93, Meth. Hosp., Arcadia, Calif., 1991-93, Inter-Community Med. Ctr., Covina, Calif., 1991-93, Pomona (Calif.) Valley Hosp. Med. Ctr., 1991—, Queen of the Valley Hosp., West Covina, Calif., 1991—, Hosp. of Good Samaritan, L.A., 1991—, Kenneth Norris Jr. Cancer Hosp., L.A., 1993—, U. So. Calif. Univ. Hosp., L.A., 1993—, LAC/USC Med. Ctr., L.A., 1993—. Author, contbr. numerous chpts. and books; reviewer editl. bd. Jour. Surg. Oncology, 1989—, Cancer, 1992—; contbr. over 100 articles to profl. jours. Mem. AAAS, AMA, Am. Assn. for Cancer Rsch., Am. Coll. Surgeons, Am. Soc. Clin. Oncology, Internat. Soc. Surgery, Pacific Coast Surg. Assn., Soc. for Surgery of Alimentary Tract, Soc. Head and Neck Surgeons, Soc. Surg. Oncology, L.A. Surg. Soc., So. Calif. Acad. Clin. Oncology. Home: 700 S Lake Ave Apt 206 Pasadena CA 91106-3943 Office: Univ So Calif Med Ctr 1510 San Pablo St # 514 Los Angeles CA 90033-4586

TESK, ALOYSIUS, materials scientist; b. Chgo., Oct. 19, 1934; s. John August and Theresa Mary (Mattea) T.; m. Regina Sophia Budzyn, Dec. 10, 1966; 1 child, John A.W. BS in Engring. Sci., Northwestern U., 1957, MS in Metallurgy, 1960, PhD in Materials Sci., 1963. Asst. prof. U. Ill., Chgo., 1964-67; cons. Argonne (Ill.) Nat. Lab., 1964-67, asst. metallurgist, 1967-70; dir. rsch. Dental, Howmedica Inc., Chgo., 1970-77; dir. edn. svcs. Inst. Gas. Tech., Chgo., 1977-78; gen. phys. scientist, group leader, biomaterials coord. polymers divsn. Nat. Inst. Stds. & Tech., Gaithersburg, Md., 1978—; cons. Dentsply Internat., York, Pa., 1977-78; mem. review bd. Dental Sch. Case Western Res. U., Cleve., 1987-88; chmn. dental stds. ADA, Chgo., 1980-86; leader U.S. Del. Internat. Stds. Orgn., 1980-86; organizer confs. Holder 8 patents; editl. bd. Jour. Dental Materials, 1988-91, Jour. Oral Implantology, 1984—; contbr. chpts. to books and articles to profl. jours. Mem. bldg. com. Divine Savior Parish, Downers Grove, Ill., 1971-72; chmn. troop 737 Cub Scouts, Highland, Md., 1980; adult supr. youth group Saint Louis Parish, Highland, 1982-83. Fellow Acad. Dental Materials (exec. com. 1987-94); mem. Am. Phys. Soc., Am. Soc. Metals (exec. com. 1964-67, 78), Biomaterials Soc. (charter), Internat. Assn. Dental Rsch. (treas. dental materials group 1987-94), Tech. Materials Soc. (exec. com. 1965). Roman Catholic. Home: 6759 Cortina Dr Highland MD 20777 Office: Nat Inst Stds & Tech Rm A143 Bldg 224 Gaithersburg MD 20899

TESKE, JOHN ALFRED, psychology educator; b. Mpls., Oct. 20, 1953; s. Myron Max and Gloria J. (Steltz) T.; m. Diane Kavanagh Davis, May 21, 1983 (separated 1995); children: Johanna Kavanagh, Jacob Davis Steltz. BA, Ind. U., 1974; MA, Clark U., 1978, PhD, 1981. Rsch. asst. Lang. and Cognitive Devel. Ctr., Boston, 1980; rsch. cons. Dept. Family Medicine, Hershey (Pa.) Med., 1982; asst. prof. psychology and behavioral scis. Pa. State U., Harrisburg, 1980-86; rsch. cons. Philhaven Hosp., Mt. Gretna, Pa., 1986, Rsch. Communications, Boston, 1988; asst. prof. psychology Elizabethtown (Pa.) Coll., 1986-90, assoc. prof., 1990—, faculty sec., 1989, faculty v.p., 1990; founder Harrisburg (Pa.) Roundtable in Human Activity Res., 1985-88; assoc. Behavioral and Brain Scis., Princeton, N.J., 1985. Contbr. articles to profl. jours. Chair com. Luth. Task Force on Sci. and Tech., Chgo., 1987-90. Fellow NSF, 1975-79. Mem. APS, Eastern Psychol. Assn., Inst. for Study of Religion and Sci., Soc. Philosophy and Psychology, Soc. Advancement of Social Psychology, Soc. Personality and Psychology. Democrat. Office: Elizabethtown Coll 1 Alpha Dr Elizabethtown PA 17022-2298

TESKE, RICHARD HENRY, veterinarian; b. Christiansburg, Va., July 22, 1939; s. August Frank and Peggy Marie (Macomber) T.; m. Mary Helen Webb, June 11, 1961; children: Helen Desiree, Mary Michele. BS, Va. Tech. U., 1962; DVM, U. Ga., 1965; MS, U. Fla., 1966. Diplomate Am. Bd. Vet. Toxicology. Asst. prof. U. Fla., Gainesville, 1967; dir. toxicology Hill Top Rsch., Inc., Miamiville, Ohio, 1967-70; chief pharmacology/toxicology br. Ctr. for Vet. Medicine FDA, Beltsville, Md., 1971-77, dep. dir. div. med. rsch. Ctr. for Vet. Medicine, 1977-78, dir. div. vet. med. rsch. Ctr. for Vet. Medicine, 1978-82; assoc. dir. for sci. Ctr. for Vet. Medicine FDA, Rockville, Md., 1982-85, dep. dir. Ctr. for Vet. Medicine, 1985-95, assoc. dir. for policy, 1995—; mem. vet. med. adv. bd. panel U.S. Pharmacopeial Conv., Rockville, 1984—. Fellow Am. Acad. Vet. Pharms. and Therapeutics, Am. Acad. Vet. and Comparative Toxicology. Office: FDA Ctr for Vet Medicine 7500 Standish Pl Rockville MD 20855-2773

TESSLER, ARTHUR NED, physician; b. N.Y.C., Feb. 21, 1927; s. Isidore and Lillian (Josem) T.; m. Roslyn Chinitz, Feb. 14, 1953 (dec. May 1991); children: Daniel, Marc, Jonathan, Sara. AB, NYU, 1948, MD, 1952. Diplomate Am. Bd. Urology. Resident in urology NYU Med. Ctr., N.Y.C., 1956-59; intern Maimonides Hosp., 1952-54; resident in urology NYU Med. Ctr., N.Y.C., 1956-59; prof. clin. urology NYU Sch. of Medicine, N.Y.C., 1975—, assoc. dir. dept. urology, 1975-94. Feature editor: Urology Jour., 1973-92. Recipient med. award Kidney Disease Found., N.Y., N.J., 1984, Carl G. Hartman award Am. Fertility Soc., 1963. Fellow N.Y. Acad. Medicine (chmn. sect. urology 1977-78), Am. Coll. Surgeons; mem. AMA, N.Y. Sect. Am. Urol. Assn. (pres. 1983-84), Soc. Univ. Urologists, N.Y. Acad. Sci. Office: NYU Med Ctr 530 1st Ave New York NY 10016-6402

TESSLER, M. STUART, optometrist; b. Buffalo, N.Y., Aug. 10, 1949; s. M. Nelson and Ida (Goldsand) T. BS in Health Sci., SUNY, Buffalo, 1975; BS in Vision Sci., Pa. Coll. Optometry, Phila., 1976, OD, 1979. Pvt. practice, 1980—; founding ptnr. Homestead Park Vision Clinic, PC, Englewood, Colo, 1985—; mem. adv. bd. Rigid Gas Permeable Lens Inst., 1995-96; mem. bd. trustees Coll. Syntonic Optometry, 1996—. Fellow Coll. Syntonic Optometry; mem. Am. Optometric Assn., Colo. Optometric Assn., Nat. Eye Rsch. Found. Office: Homestead Park Vision Clinic 6979 S Holly Cir Englewood CO 80112

TESTER, LEONARD WAYNE, psychology educator; b. Nampa, Idaho, Aug. 21, 1933; s. Walter Vernon and Dora Dorothy (Peters) T. BTh, Kansas City Coll., Overland, Kansas, 1957; MA, Abilene Christian Coll. (now Abilene Christian U.), 1961; STB, Harvard U., 1969; EdM, Columbia U., 1971, EdD, 1976, MPhil, 1979, PhD, 1981. Lic. psychologist, N.Y. Pers. mgr. Boston Safe Deposit & Trust Co., 1966-69; adj. instr. clin. counseling N.Y. Inst. Tech., Westbury, 1971-80, adj. asst. prof., 1980-84, sr. counselor, 1980-92, assoc. prof., 1984-92, dir., 1992-95, sr. counselor, 1980-92, prof., 1992—, prof., chmn., 1992-93, prof., dir., 1993-95; cons., grad. asst. Bus. Sch. and Tchrs. Coll. Columbia U., 1977-81. Contbr. articles to profl. jours.; presenter workshops in field. Exec. dir. Ho. of the Carpenter, Boston, 1967-68; bd. dirs. Pierre (S.D.) Coun. of Arts, Counseling Ctr. Episcopal Ch., Great Neck, N.Y., Tech. Sch. in N.Y.C. William Wayne Jackson honors scholar Harvard Div. Sch. Fellow Am. Orthopsychiat. Assn.; mem. APA, N.Y. Soc. Clin. Psychologists, N.Y. Soc. Hypnosis and Psychotherapy, others. Home: PO Box 20107 New York NY 10023-1477 Office: NY Inst of Tech 1855 Broadway New York NY 10023-7602

TESTER, WILLIAM JOHN, oncologist; b. Aurora, Ill., July 2, 1950; s. William F. and Sylvia (Kish) T.; m. Linda M. Morante, July 30, 1972; children: Kristin, Marissa, Michael. BS, Rutgers Coll., 1972; MD, Hahnemann Coll., 1977. Diplomate Am. Bd. Hematology, Am. Bd. Med. Oncology, Am. Bd. Internal Medicine, Nat. Bd. Med. Examiners; lic. physician, Pa. Resident internal medicine Albert Einstein Med. Ctr., Phila., 1977-80, chief med. resident, 1979-80, attending physician, 1983—; assoc. dir. Albert Einstein Cancer Ctr., Phila., 1991-96, dir., 1996—; med. oncology fellow Nat. Cancer Inst., NIH, Bethesda, 1980-82; hematology fellow Georgetown U. Hosp., Washington, 1982-83. Editor PDQ, Nat. Cancer Inst., 1992—; contbr. articles to profl. jours. Mem. profl. edn. com. Am. Cancer Soc. Fellow ACP; mem. AMA (Physicians Recognition award), NIH Alumni Assn., Am. Soc. Clin. Oncology, Radiation Therapy Oncology Group, Nat. Surg. Adjuvant Breast Group, Ea. Coop. Oncology Group. Republican. Roman Catholic. Office: Albert Einstein Cancer Ctr Willowcrest Bldg 5501 Old York Rd Philadelphia PA 19141-3098

TETROKALASHVILI, MIKHAIL S., physician; b. Tbilisi, Georgia, Russia, July 4, 1945; came to U.S., 1992.; s. Shalva A. and Rachel (Chikvashvili) T.; m. Eteri I. Adjiashvili, July 4, 1967; 1 child, Mila Paltag. Grad., Donezk Med. Sch., Donezk, Ukraine, 1966; Grad., Tbilisi (Georgia, Russia) Med. Sch., 1968; postgrad., Moscow Instn. of Clin. and Exptl. Surgery, 1968-73; DO, N.Y. Coll. Osteo. Medicine, 1997. Surgeon City Hosp., Kirovsk, Ukraine, 1967-68; physician, rschr. Instn. of Surgery, Moscow, 1968-69; surgeon, chief rschr. Instn. of Tng. for Physicians, Tbilisi, 1973-78; surgeon, profl. asst. Postednl. Tng. Inst. for Surgeons, Tbilisi, 1979-92. Author: Noncalculose Cholecystitis, 1978; contbr. articles to profl. jours. and publs. in field; inventor in field. Mem. Am. Assn. Osteo. Physicians. Home: 120 de Kruif Pl Apt 15F Bronx NY 10475

TEUNIS, BERNARD SCOTT, surgeon; b. Washington, Wash., 1936. MD, U. Va., 1962. Diplomate Am. Bd. Plastic Surgery, Am. Bd. Surgery. Resident Washinton Hosp. Ctr., 1966-69, Mayo Clinic, Rochester, Minn., 1970-71; staff Fairfax Hosp., Falls Church, Va.; clin. prof. George Wash. U. Fellow ACS; mem. AMA, ASPRS. Office: Plastic Surgery Assocs 6845 Elm St Mc Lean VA 22101

TEUSCHER, EBERHARD, pharmacist; b. Halle, Germany, Dec. 9, 1934; s. Wolfram and Maria (Henke) T.; m. Gisela Hempel, July 30, 1964; 1 child, Franka. Degree in apothecary, U. Halle, 1958, dr. rer. nat., 1960; dr. habil., U. Greifswald, Germany, 1965; lectr., asst. prof., U. Greifswald, 1966. Lic. pharmacist. Asst. dept. pharmacognosy U. Halle, 1959-61; head asst. dept. botany U. Greifswald, 1962-68, asst. prof. dept. pharmacy, 1968-71, prof., 1971—; dean faculty natural scis. U. Greifswald, 1975-90. Author: Pharmacognosy, 1970, 78, 83, 88, 90, 96, Natural Toxins, 1988, 94. Mem. Soc. Med. Plant Rsch., Am. Soc. Pharmacognosy, German Pharm. Soc., N.Y. Acad. Sci. Office: U Greifswald, Jahnstrasse 15A, 17489 Greifswald Germany

TEUTSCH, CHAMPION KURT, psycho-geneticist; b. Leipzig, Germany, Feb. 10, 1921; came to U.S., 1939; s. Friedrich Wilhelm and Elizabeth (Babette) T.; m. Joel Marie Noel, Apr. 24, 1954 (dec. Mar. 1992); 1 child, Lee Brooks. BCE with high honors, U. Fla., 1942; degree, U. So. Calif., L.A., 1948-49, 57; postgrad., Harvard U., 1947-48; MS in Psychology, Calif. Coast U., Santa Ana, 1975, PhD in Psychology, 1976. Sr. engr., tech. writer, editor various aerospace firms, Columbus, San Francisco, L.A., 1946-60; cons., gene-physicist, psycho-geneticist L.A., 1960—; pres. Acad. Teutsch Ideal Method, L.A., 1981—; chmn. bd. dirs. Internat. Human Rsch. Ctr. Sunray, Moscow State U., 1993—; cons. med. clinics, law firms, real estate, computer, electronics ins. firms, automobile agys., entertainment orgns., various locations, 1964—; guest nat. and local TV programs, 1968—; cons. Bush Presdl. campaign, L.A., 1988; lectr. Moscow State U., 1993, U. St. Petersburg, 1993, Zaparoche, Ukraine, 1994, Med. Coll. U. Fla., 1994; vis. prof. medicine U. Fla., 1996—. Co-author: Understand and Raise Your Consciousness--From Here to Happiness!, 1959, 75, Victimology: An Effect of Consciousness, Interpersonal Dynamics and Human Physics, 1973, Stress, Genetics and Interpersonal Relationships--The Type D Complex, 1979, From Human Bondage to Liberty: An Introduction to Genephysics, 1993, A Nonmedical Andwer to Cancer and Other Diseases, 1994, Ideal Israel, Tel Aviv, 1996; developer (with J.M. Noel Teutsch) genogram and basic inner drive, direction or desire. Served to 1st lt. USAF, 1942-52. Mem. Friar's Club, Vikings Club, Optimist Internat. (pres. 1982). Home: Unit 401 2131 Century Park Ln Los Angeles CA 90067-3811 Office: Acad Teutsch Ideal Method Ste 2730 2049 Century Park E Los Angeles CA 90067-3202

TEXAN, FREDERICK GENE, pediatrician; b. N.Y.C., Sept. 16, 1938; s. Jack H. and Pearl A. (Chervesky) T.; m. Dec. 18, 1965; children: Fredrick II, Julie, Jonathan. AB, St. Peter's Coll., 1960; MD, Seton Hall, 1964. Diplomate Am. Bd. Pediatrics. Pvt. practice in pediatrics Rockville Ctr., N.Y., 1971—. Major U.S. Army, 1966-69. Fellow Am. Acad. Pediatrics; mem. Nassau Pediatric Soc. Roman Catholic. Office: Fred J Texan MD PC 36 Lincoln Ave Rockville Centre NY 11570

TEXTER, JOHN HENRY, JR., urologist, educator; b. Mohnton, Pa., June 13, 1936; s. John Henry and Florence Ellen (Hoyer) T.; m. Joyce Anette Turpin, Dec. 10, 1977; children: John Henry III, Rebecca Allison. BA, Johns Hopkins U., 1958, MD, 1962. Diplomate Am. Bd. Urology. Fellow Brady Urol. Inst., Balt., 1967-71; assoc. prof. surgery Med. Coll. Va., Richmond, 1971-81; prof., chmn. surgery dept. So. Ill. U. Sch. Medicine, Springfield, 1981—; cons. dept. surgery McGuire VA Hosp., Richmond, 1971-81. Author: (textbook) Master in Surgery0Urology, 1993, Complication in Surgery and Trauma, 1990, Shockwave, 1988. Lt. comdr. USN, 1958-66. Recipient Clin. Rsch. First prize Am. Urol. Assn., 1970, Grayson Carrol Essay Contest winner, 1973, Daken Hist. Essay First prize, 1984. Fellow ACS (instr. com. on trauma 1981—, del. 1987-93); mem. AMA, Ill. Urol. Soc. (program dir. 1981-95, pres. 1986-87), Springfield Med. Club. Home: 15 Centerwood Dr Springfield IL 62707 Office: So Ill U Sch Medicine 800 N Rutledge St Springfield IL 62794

THACKER, STEPHEN BRADY, medical association administrator, epidemiologist; b. Independence, Mo., Dec. 30, 1947; m. 1976; 2 children. AB, Princeton U., 1969; MD, Mt. Sinai Sch. Medicine, 1973; MSc, London Sch. Hygiene and Tropical Medicine, 1984. Chief consolidated surveillance and cmty. activity epidemiol. progress office Ctr. Disease Control, 1978-83, dir. surveillance and epidemiol. studies, 1983-86; asst. dir. sci. Ctr. Environ. Health and Injury Control, 1986-89; dir. epidemiol. progress office Ctr. Disease Control, 1989—; acting dir. Nat. Ctr. Environ. Health, 1993—; mem. steering com. Assn. Behavioral Sci. Med. Edn., 1971-74; assoc. Dept. Cmty. Medicine, Med. Ctr. Duke U., Durham, N.C., 1975-76; lectr. Cmty. Ctr. Mt. Sinai Sch. Medicine, N.Y.C., 1978—, Sch. Medicine Emory U., Atlanta, 1985-86; cons. epidemiology Arab Republic Egypt, 1979-91; clin. asst. prof. cmty. health Sch. Medicine Emory U., 1986—. Editor: Am. Jour. Epidemiology, 1990—. Clin. scholar Robert Wood Johnson Found., 1974-75; recipient Mosby Bood award for excellence, 1973, Saul Horowitz Jr. Meml. award, 1990, Supervisory award for contbr. advantage of women, 1991. Office: Ctr for Disease Control & Prevention MS C08 1600 Clifton Rd NE Atlanta GA 30333*

THADANI, UDHO, physician, cardiologist; b. Hydedrabad, India, Apr. 1, 1941; came to U.S., 1980; s. Vensimal Mulchand and Gopi Thadani; m. Dorothy Ann Thadani, 1979; 1 child, Emma Sarala. MBBS, All India Inst. Med. Scis., New Delhi, 1964. Lic. physician, Okla., Md., Ont., Can., Eng., India; cert. internal medicine, U.K., Can.; cert. cardiology, Can.; diplomate Am. Bd. Internal Medicine, subspecialty cardiovascular diseases. Intern All India Inst. Med. Scis., New Delhi, 1964-65, house physician, surgeon, 1965-66; house physician in medicine Joyce Green Hosp., Dartford, Kent, Eng., 1966-67; sr. house physician in medicine Kingston Gen. Hosp., Hull, Eng., 1967-69, registrar, rsch. fellow in medicine and cardiology, 1969-71; registrar, rsch. fellow in medicine and cardiology U. Leeds (Eng.), The Gen. Infirmary at Leeds, 1971-75; sr. rsch. fellow, clin. asst. medicine Queen's U., Kingston Gen. Hosp., Ont., Can., 1975-78; asst. prof. medicine Queen's U., Kingston, 1978-80; staff physician Kingston Gen. Hosp., 1978-80; assoc. prof. medicine U. Okla. Health Scis. Ctr., Oklahoma City, 1980-83; prof. medicine, vice chief cardiovascular sect. Okla. U. Health Scis. Ctr., Oklahoma City, 1983—, mem. cardiology fellowship com., 1980-82; dir. clin. cardiology Okla. U. Health Scis. Ctr. and VA Med. Ctr., Oklahoma City, 1980-87, vice chief cardiovascular sect., 1981—, dir. clin. rsch., 1987—; vice chmn. rsch. and devel. com. VA Med. Ctr., Oklahoma City, 1989-92, chmn. physiology-pharmacology categorical rev. com., 1989-94, chmn. rsch. and devel. com., 1992-94; sr. rsch. fellow Ont. Heart Found., 1978-80, rsch. fellow, 1976-78; rsch. fellow dept. medicine Queen's U., Kingston, Ont., 1975-76; rsch. fellow U. Leeds, Pub. Health and Ciba Found., dept. medicine and cardiovascular sect. Leeds Gen. Infirmary, 1971-75. Editor: Medical Therapy of Ischemic Heart Disease, 1992, Nitrates Updated, 1996; contbr. over 100 articles to profl. jours., chpts. to books; mem. editl. bd. panel Cardiology Drug Facts and Comparison, 1989; contbg. rev. panel Drug Facts and Comparisons, 1989—; mem. editl. bd. Internat. Jour. Cardiology, 1987-93, Cardiovascular Drugs and Therapy, 1987—; reviewer Circulation, Jour. Am. Coll. Cardiology, Am. Jour. Cardiology, Brit. Heart Jour., Internat. Jour. Cardiology, Can. Jour. Cardiology, European Heart Jour., Annals of Internal Medicine, New Eng. Jour. Medicine, Archives of Internal Medicine, Cardiovascular Drugs and Therapy, Drugs, European Jour. Pharmacology, Clin. Pharmacology and Therapeutics. Fellow Royal Coll. Physicians (Can.), Royal Soc. Medicine London, Am. Coll. Cardiology (mem. cardiovascular drug com. 1990-94), Royal Coll. Physicians (London), Clin. Coun. Cardiology Am. Heart Assn. (coun. rep. Okla. 1989—), Royal Coll. Physicians and Surgeons Can., N.Y. Acad. Med. Scis.; mem. Royal Coll. Physicians (U.K.), AAAS, Can. Cardiovascular Soc., Am. Fedn. Clin. Rsch., Phi Kappa Phi (mem. FDA cardiovascular and renal drugs adv. com. 1995—). Office: Okla U Health Sci Ctr Cardiology Sect 920 SL Young 5SP-300 Oklahoma City OK 73104

THAJEB, PETERUS (TAI TAU-EN), neurologist; b. Medan, Indonesia, June 18, 1957; s. Ishak (Tai Tjioe Tjuan) and Lily (Lie Li Ching); m. Shew-Tze Chang, June 26, 1982; children: Daniel Dailo, Maria D., Samuel D., David D. Grad. in Accordion, Medan Accordion Inst., Medan, Indonesia, 1973; MD, Taipei Med. Coll., Taiwan, 1982. Diplomate Taiwan Bd. Neurology. Intern Changhua Christian Hosp., Taiwan, 1981-82; family practice Mennonite Christian Hosp., Hwalien, Taiwan, 1982-84; resident in neurology Chang Gung Meml. Hosp., Taipei, 1984-87; vis. trainee in neuropathology U. Wash., Seattle, 1986; neurology fellowship Chang Gung Meml. Hosp., Taipei, 1987-88; attending physician, staff neurologist Cathay Gen. Hosp., Taipei, 1988—; chmn. 7th Asian and Oceanian Congress of

Neurology, Bali, Indonesia, 1987. Contbr. articles to profl. jours. Recipient award Exec. Yuan, Taiwan, 1976. Fellow Internat. Coll. Angiology; mem. Royal Soc. Medicine London (affiliate 1985-89), N.Y. Acad. Sci. (inaugural mem. Charles Darwin Assocs.), Am. Acad. Neurology (assoc.), Neurol. Soc. Republic of China. Office: Cathay Gen Hosp, 280 Sect 4 Jen Ai Rd, Taipei Taiwan

THAL, LEON JOEL, neuroscientist; b. N.Y.C., June 17, 1944; s. Bernard and Esther (Beller) T.; m. Donna Jean Norbo, June 25, 1967. MD, Downstate Med. Ctr., N.Y.C., 1969. Diplomate Am. Bd. Psychiatry and Neurology. Instr., asst. prof., assoc. prof. neurology Albert Einstein Coll. Medicine, Bronx, N.Y., 1975-85; assoc. prof. neuroscis. U. Calif. San Diego, 1985-89, prof. neuroscis., 1989—. Editor: Cognitive Disorders, 1992; contbr. chpts. in books and articles to profl. jours. Lt. comdr. USPHS, 1970-72. Home: 402 Brighton Ave Cardiff CA 92007 Office: Univ Calif Dept Neuroscience 9500 Gilman Dr La Jolla CA 92093-0624

THALER, MANNING MICHAEL, pediatrics educator; b. Poland, Sept. 29, 1934; came to U.S., 1965; s. Morris and Fanny Thaler; m. Libby L. Fuss, Jan. 24, 1966; children: Eva, Joshua. MD, U. Toronto, Can., 1958. Prof. pediatrics U. Calif., San Francisco, 1967-94, prof. emeritus pediatrics, 1994—, also dir. pediatric gastroenterology and nutrition, 1967-89; assoc. dir. liver ctr. U. Calif., San Francisco, 1975—; dir. NIH tng. program in pediatric gastroenterology and nutrition, 1972—. Contbr. articles to profl. jours. and chpts. to books. Pres. Holocaust Ctr. of No. Calif., San Francisco, 1982-93. Josiah Macy Jr. Found. scholar, 1974. Mem. Am. Soc. Biochemistry and Molecular Biology, Am. Pediatric Soc., Am. Soc. Clin. Investigation, Assn. for Study of Liver Disease, Soc. Pediatric Rsch., Am. Gastroenterol. Assn., Am. Assn. History of Medicine. Office: U Calif Dept Pediatrics San Francisco CA 94143-0136

THALER, PETER JACOB, orthopedic surgeon; b. N.Y.C., Apr. 15, 1935; s. Arthur H. and Molly K. (Wollner) T.; m. Loretta A. Calicchio, June 19, 1963. AB, Cornell U., 1956; MD, N.Y. Med. Coll., N.Y.C., 1960. Diplomate Am. Bd. Orthopaedic Surgeons. Intern Michael Reese Hosp., Chgo., 1960-61; gen. surgery tng. Bronx Mcpl. Ctr., N.Y., 1961-62, Cedars of Lebanon Hosp., L.A., 1965-66; resident in orthopedic surgery Wadsworth V.A. Hosp., L.A., 1966-69; orthopedic resident L.A. Orthopaedic Hosp., 1969-70; pvt. practice Peter J. Thaler, M.D, Inc., L.A., 1970—; tching. staff Orthopaedic Hosp., L.A., 1970—; asst. clin. prof. U. So. Calif. Sch. Medicine, L.A., 1978—; mem. quality control bd. Cooperative of Am. Physicians, L.A., 1989—; orthopedic surgeon L.A. Police and Fire Depts., 1971-76; med. advisor Industrial Indemnity Co., 1973-76. Speaker and presenter in field. Capt. U.S. Army Med. Corps. Fellow ACS, Am. Acad. Orthopaedic Surgeons; mem. Western Orthopaedic Assn., Calif. Orthopaedic Assn. (workers' compensation com. 1994—). Office: Peter J Thaler MD Inc 321 N Larchmont Blvd #404 Los Angeles CA 90004

THALLER, KARL E., psychologist, educator; b. Manhatten, Kans., Nov. 7, 1936; s. Howard Iran and Hilda (Bryant) T.; m. Barbara Doyle, Jan. 31, 1968; children: David, John. BA, U. Conn., 1960, MA, 1962, PhD, 1967. Rsch. asst. dept. psychology U. Conn., Storrs, 1961-65; instr. U. Conn. Sch. Edn., Storrs, 1965-66; assoc. prof. dept. psychology SUNY, Potsdam, 1967-77, prof. dept. psychology, 1978-80, chmn. dept. psychology, 1976-88, prof. dept. psychology, 1988—. Editor: Sexuality and the Mentally Retarded; contbr. articles to profl. jours. Pres., chmn. Transitional Living, Watertown, N.Y. Recipient SUNY grant, 1969, 74, NSF grant, 1969-71. Mem. Am. Psychology Assn., Ea. Psychology Assn., Undergraduate Psychology Instrs. Office: SUNY Potsdam Coll Dept Psychology Potsdam NY 13676

THAXTON, MARY LYNWOOD, psychologist; b. Detroit, Dec. 27, 1944; d. Osceola Alvin Jr. and Mary Phlegar (Penn) T. BA, Emory and Henry Coll., 1966; MLn, Emory U., 1967; AS, Ga. State U., 1978, MA, 1983, PhD, 1989. Reference libr. Coll. of William and Mary, Williamsburg, Va., 1967-71; reference libr., asst. prof. Ga. State U., Atlanta, 1971-77, social sci. bibliographer, assoc. prof., 1977-89; pvt. practice psychotherapy, gerontol cons., Tucker, Ga., 1989-91; gerontol. cons., psychotherapist in pvt. practice Marietta, Ga., 1991-95; Atlanta, 1996—. Editor bibliography: Metropolitan Atlanta Rapid Transit Authority, 1982, Community Mental Health Services to the Elderly, 1984 (Libr. award 1984); contbr. articles to profl. jours. Office: Ste 200 1970 Cliff Valley Way Atlanta GA 32329

THAYER, EDNA LOUISE, medical facility administrator, nurse; b. Madelia, Minn., May 21, 1936; d. Walter William Arthur and Hilda Engel Emily Ann (Geistfeld) Wilke; m. David LeRoy Thayer, Aug. 30, 1958; children: Scott, Tamara, Brenda. Diploma in nursing, Bethesda Luth., 1956; BS in Nursing Edn., U. Minn., 1960; MSN, Washington U., St. Louis, 1966; MS in Counseling, Mankato (Minn.) State U., 1972. Cert. nursing adminstr. advanced ANA. Nurse Bethesda Luth. Hosp., St. Paul, 1956-58, U. Minn. Hosp., Mpls., 1958; from nurse to asst. head nurse supr., edn. dir. Fairmont (Minn.) Community Hosp., 1959-63; instr. Alton (Ill.) Meml. Hosp., 1963-66; from nursing instr. to assoc. prof. and dean Sch. Nursing Mankato State U., 1966-77; asst. adminstr. Rice County Dist. One Hosp., Faribault, Minn., 1977-89; RN, adminstrv. supr. St. Peter (Minn.) Regional Treatment Ctr., 1990—; nurse surveyor Minn. Dept. Tech. Edn., St. Paul, 1980-93; mem. adv. co. LPN and MA programs Tech. Inst., Faribault, 1977—. Mem. Rice County Ext. Bd., Faribault, 1986-91, adult leader 4-H Club, Rice County and St. Paul, 1971—; advisor Med. Explorers, Faribault, 1977-89; mem. Rep. Rodosovich Health Com., Faribault, 1984-94; coun. mem. Our Savior's Luth. Ch., Faribault, 1984-87; mem. Rep. Boudreau Health Care Adv. Com., 1996—. Recipient alumni award Nat. 4-H Club, 1983, Disting. Friend of Nursing award Mankato State U., 1995. Mem. Minn. Orgn. Nurse Execs. (bd. dirs. 1987-89), Dist. F Nursing Svc. Adminstrs. (pres. 1980-82), Minn. Nurses Assn. (bd. dirs. 1982-87, Pres.'s award 1983, pres. 5th dist. 1974, 75, pres. 13th dist. 1984-86), AAUW, Sigma Theta Tau, Delta Kappa Gamma (pres. Pi chptr. 1982-84, Woman of Achievement award 1985), Hosp. Aux. Republican. Home: RR 1 Box 7B Elysian MN 56028-9731 Office: Saint Peter Regional Treatment Ctr 100 Freeman Dr Saint Peter MN 56082-2516

THEADO, GRACE COLETTE, community health nurse, administrator; b. Peoria, Ill., Nov. 11, 1952; d. Albert J. and Mary (Ansel) Theado. BSN, St. Xavier Coll., Chgo., 1974, MS in Rehab. Nursing, 1982. RN, Ill. Dir. profl. svcs. Community Home Health Svcs., Joliet, Ill., 1982-84; v.p. Home Care div. Combined Health Svcs. Am., Joliet, 1984-86; home care project dir. Joint Commn. on Accreditation of Health Care Orgns., Chgo., 1986-88; v.p. quality assessment Kimberly Quality Care, Boston, 1988-94; v.p. clin. svcs. Amicare Home Health Svcs., Farmington Hills, Mich., 1994—. Contbr. articles to profl. jours. Mem. ANA, Nat. League Nursing, Am. Assn. for Continuity Care, Sigma Theta Tau (scholarship).

THEIS, JAMES EDWARD, deaf counselor, interior designer; b. Bellville, Ill., May 23, 1963; s. Clement John and Alice Florence (Schoeppner) T. AA, Crafton Hills Coll., 1983; BS in Wildlife Mgmt., Humboldt State U., 1987; AOS in Culinary Arts, Calif. Culinary Acad., San Francisco, 1994. Wild animal trainer San Diego Zoo, 1983-84, Wild Animal Tng. Ctr., Riverside, Calif., 1980-85; jewelry salesperson J.C. Penney's, West Covina, Calif., 1987-88; display supr. Sherwood Mgmt., Inc., Bell Gardens, Calif., 1989-90; counselor State of Calif. Sch. for Deaf, Riverside, 1990—; mgr. fine jewelry Finlay Fine Jewelry Corp, Monclair, Calif., 1990; interior designer Theis Interiors, Calimesa, Calif., 1990-93; asst. banquet chef Ritz Carlton Hotel, Rancho Mirage, Calif., 1994-95; chef tournat Elcaris Restaurant, Palm Springs, Calif., 1995—. Scoutmaster Boy Scouts Am., Athens, Greece, 1985-86; fundraiser Desert AIDS Project. Sgt. USAF, 1985-86. Named to Outstanding Young Men Am., 1986. Republican. Roman Catholic. Home and office: Theis Catering 4018 Alabama # 2 San Diego CA 92104

THEN, RUDOLF LUDWIG, research scientist; b. Schweinfurt, Bavaria, Germany, Oct. 22, 1940; s. Ludwig and Angela (Ortner) T.; m. Roswitha M. Löhr, Aug. 23, 1969; children: Angela, Lothar, Ulrike, Rüdiger. Diploma biology, U. Mainz, Germany, 1966, D Natural Sci., 1969. Univ. asst. Inst. Microbiology U. Mainz, 1969-70; rsch. scientist F. Hoffmann LaRoche, Basel, Switzerland, 1970-83, group leader, 1984-87; dep. head dept. infectious diseases F. Hoffmann LaRoche, Basel, 1988-95, area head dept. infectious diseases, 1995—; vis. scientist Roche Inst. Molecular Biology, Nutley, N.J., 1974-75. Editor Jour. Chemotherapy, Florence, Italy, 1988—; contbr. articles to profl. jours., chpts. to books. Roman Catholic. Office: F Hoffmann La Roche Ltd, Grenzacherstrasse 124, 4070 Basel CH, Switzerland

THENABADU, PUJITHA NIHAL, cardiologist, consultant; b. Badulla, Uva, Sri Lanka, July 29, 1941; s. David de Silva and Ethel Mildred (Perera) T.; m. Shiranie Rukmal, Jan. 23, 1967; children: Shiyana Nilanthi, Tania Dinushi. MBBS, U. Ceylon, Colombo, Sri Lanka, 1965, MD, 1969. Intern med. officer Gen. Hosp., Colombo, 1966-67, sr. med. officer, 1967-68, physician in charge CIU, 1972-86, cons., 1986—; reader in medicine Faculty Medicine, Colombo, 1968-69; resident physician Ministry Health, Colombo, 1969-70; rsch. assn. VA Hosp., Little Rock, 1979-80; cons. Postgrad. Inst. Medicine, Colombo, 1980—, Nawaloka/Durdans Hosps., 1984—, North Colombo Med. Coll., 1985-87; cardiologist Inst. of Cardiology, Gen. Hosp. Colombo, 1986—; chief investigator WHO Rheumatic Fever Project, Sri Lanka. Contbr. articles to profl. jours. Commonwealth scholar Gen. Infirmary Royal P.G.M.S., Leeds, London, 1970-72. Fellow Royal Coll. Physicians, Am. Coll. Cardiology, Ceylon Coll. Physicians (editor jour. 1980-85, sec. 1980-86, pres. 1995); mem. Sri Lanka Assn. for Advancement of Sci., Asian Pacific Soc. Cardiac Pacing, Rotary (West Colombo). Buddhist. Home: # 4 Charles Dr, Colombo 3, Sri Lanka Office: Inst Cardiology GHC, Regent St, Colombo Sri Lanka

THEODORIDIS, GEORGE CONSTANTIN, biomedical engineering educator, researcher; b. Braila, Romania, Dec. 3, 1935; came to U.S., 1959; s. Constantin George and Anastasia (Haritopoulos) T.; m. Lilly Kate Hyman, Sept. 20, 1975; 1 child, Alexander. BS in Mechanical and Elec. Engring., Nat. Tech. U. Athens, 1959; DSc, MIT, Cambridge, Mass., 1964. Rsch. assoc. MIT, Cambridge, Mass., 1964; sr. scientist Am. Sci. Engring., Cambridge, Mass., 1964-68; assoc. prof. in residence U. Calif., Berkeley, 1968-70; biomedical engring. U. Va., Charlottesville, 1970—; prof. elec. engring. U. Patras, Greece, 1976-83; cons. Food and Drug Adminstrn., Washington, 1975-76, Applied Physics Lab, Columbia, Md., 1978-79. Author: Applied Math, 1983; contbr. articles to profl. jours. Den leader Boy Scouts Am., Charlottesville, Va., 1984-85. Fulbright fellow U.S. Govt., MIT, 1959-60; Nato fellow NATO, MIT, 1961-64; Spl. fellow NIH, U. Calif., 1968-70; recipient teaching award GE, MIT, 1963. Mem. Inst. Elec. and Electronics Engrs., Sigma Xi. Greek Orthodox. Home: 1817 Fendall Ave Charlottesville VA 22903-1613 Office: U Va Dept Biomed Engring Box 377 Medical Ctr Charlottesville VA 22908

THEOHARIDES, THEOHARIS CONSTANTIN, pharmacologist, physician, educator; b. Thessaloniki, Macedonia, Greece, Feb. 11, 1950; s. Constantin A. and Marika (Krava) T.; m. Efthalia I. Triarchou, July 10, 1981; children: Niove, Konstantinos. Diploma with honors, Anatolia Coll., 1968, BA in Biology and History of Sci. and Medicine, Yale U., 1972, MS in Immunology, 1975, MPhil. in Endocrinology, 1975, PhD in Pharmacology Yale U., 1978, MD Yale U., 1983. Asst. in rsch. biology Yale U., 1968-71, asst. in rsch. pharmacology, 1973-78, exec. sec. univ. senate, 1976-78, rsch. assoc. faculty clin. immunology, 1978-83; spl. instr. modern Greek Yale U., 1974, 77; vis. faculty Aristotelian U. Sch. Medicine, Thessaloniki, 1979; asst. prof. biochemistry and pharmacology Tufts U., 1983-88, co-dir. med. pharmacology curriculum, 1983-85, dir. med. pharmacology, 1985-93, assoc. prof. pharmacology, biochemistry and psychiatry, 1989-94, prof. pharmacology and internal medicine, 1995—, dir. grad. pharmacology, 1994—; clin. pharmocologist Commonwealth Mass. Drug Formulary Commn., 1985—; co-chmn. neuro-immunology 2d and 3d World Conf. on Inflammation, Monte Carlo, 1986, 89; mem. internat. adv. bd. 4th 5th and 6th World Conf. on Inflammation, Geneva, 1991, 93, 95; spl. cons. Min. of Health, Greece, 1993—; chmn. Internat. Com. to Upgrade Med. Edn. in Greece, 1994; bd. dirs., spl. cons. Inst. Pharm. Rsch. & Tech., Athens, 1994—. Trustee Anatolia Coll. 1984-85. Author books on pharmacology; mem. editorial bd. numerous jours.; contbr. articles to profl. jours.; patentee in field. Bd. dirs., v.p. for rels. with Greece, Krikos, 1978-79; sec. Assn. Greeks to Yale, 1974-79, pres., 1982-83. Recipient Theodore Cuyler award Yale U., 1972; George Papanicoalou Grad. award, 1977; Med. award Hellenic Med. Soc. N.Y., 1979, 83; M.C. Winternitz prize in pathology Yale U., 1980; Disting. Service award Tufts U. Alumni Assn., 1986, Spl. Faculty Recognition award Tufts U. Med. Sch., 1987, 88. Mem. Hellenic Biochem. and Biophys. Soc., AMA, AAUP, N.Y. Acad. Scis., Am. Inst. History Pharmacy, AAAS, Soc. Health and Human Values, Am. Assn. History Medicine, Am. Soc. Cell Biology, Soc. Neurosci., Am. Fedn. Clin. Research, Conn. Acad. Arts and Scis., Am. Soc. Pharmacology and Exptl. Therapeutics, Hellenic Soc. Cancer Research, Hellenic Soc. Med. Chemistry, Internat. Soc. Immunopharmacology, Am. Soc. Microbiology, Am. Assn. Immunologists, Internat. Soc. History of Medicine, Mass. Med. Soc., N.E. Hellenic Med. Soc. (sec. 1984-85, v.p. 1985-86, 94—, pres. 1986-87), Hellenic Sci. Assn. Boston (bd. dirs. 1985), Internat. Anatolia Alumni Assn. (sec. 1984-85). Alpha Omega Alpha (citation for excellence in teaching 1989, 90, 91, 92, 93, 94, 96), Sigma Xi. Research on mechanisms of release of secretory products; hormonal induction of ornithine decarboxylase and membrane functions of polyamines; pathophysiology of mast cells in neuroimmunoendocrine diseases such as irritable bowel syndrome, interstitial cystitis, migraines and multiple sclerosis. Home: 14 Parkman St Apt 2 Brookline MA 02146-3802 Office: Tufts U Sch Med Dept Pharmacology & Exptl Therapeutics 136 Harrison Ave Boston MA 02111-1800

THETFORD, SHARON RIFKIN, psychologist; b. Mont, N.J., Aug. 25, 1964; d. Gil Neal and Phyllis Janet (Egna) Rifkin; m. Jeffrey Earl Thetford, Nov. 25, 1994. BA, U. Ctrl. Fla., 1986; MS, Fla. Inst. Tech., 1988, D in Psychology, 1990. Lic. psychologist, Fla. Pvt. practice clin. psychology Altamonte Spring, Fla., 1990—. Mem. MADD (v.p., treas., bd. dirs. 1993—), Fla. Psychol. Assn. (chpt. edn. chair 1992-94, sec. 1992-93), Multiple Sclerosis Soc. (chpt. svcs. com. 1991—), Tourette Syndrome Assn. (pres., v.p., bd. dirs. 1984—). Office: 370 Whooping Loop #1160 Altamonte Springs FL 32701

THIBODEAU, GARY A., academic administrator; b. Sioux City, Iowa, Sept. 26, 1938; m. Emogene J. McCarville, Aug. 1, 1964; children: Douglas James, Beth Ann. BS, Creighton U., 1962; MS, S.D. State U., 1967, S.D. State U., 1970; PhD, S.D. State U., 1971. Profl. service rep. Baxter Lab., Inc., Deerfield, Ill., 1963-65; tchr., researcher dept. biology S.D. State U., Brookings, 1965-76, asst. to v.p. for acad. affairs, 1976-80, v.p. for adminstrn., 1980-85; chancellor U. Wis., River Falls, 1985—; mem. investment com. U. Wis., River Falls Found.; trustee W. Cen. Wis. Consortium U. Wis. System; bd. dirs. U. Wis. at River Falls Found.; mem. Phi Kappa Phi nat. budget rev. and adv. comm., Phi Kappa Phi Found. investment comm., comm. on Agrl. and Rural Devel., steering commn. Coun. of Rural Colls. and Univs., Joint Coun. on Food and Agrl. Scis., USDA. Author: Basic Concepts in Anatomy and Physiology, 1983, Athletic Injury Assessment, 1994, Structure and Function of the Body, 1996, The Human Body in Health and Disease, 1996, Textbook of Anatomy and Physiology, 1996. Mem. AAAS, Sigma Xi, Phi Kappa Phi, Gamma Sigma Delta, Gamma Alpha. Office: U Wis 116 N Hall River Falls WI 54022

THIENPONT, LOUIS A., pathologist, cytologist; b. Ghent, Belgium, June 5, 1943. MD, State U., Ghent, 1969; postgrad., Goormaghtigh Inst. Pathology, Ghent, 1974. Head histo. and cytopathology lab. Onze-Lieve-Vrouw Ziekenhuis, Aalst, Belgium. Mem. Belgian Soc. Clin. Cytology (pres.), Internat. Acad. Pathology, Internat. Acad. Cytology, Belgium Soc. Anatomo-Pathology (bd. dirs.). Office: OLV Ziekenhuis, Moorselbaan 164, B9300 Aalst Belgium

THIER, SAMUEL OSIAH, physician, educator; b. Bklyn., June 23, 1937; s. Sidney and May Henrietta (Kanner) T.; m. Paula Dell Finkelstein, June 28, 1958; children: Audrey Lauren, Stephanie Ellen, Sara Leslie. Student, Cornell U., 1953-56; MD, SUNY, Syracuse, 1960, DSc (hon.), 1987; DSc (hon.), Tufts U., 1988, Mt. Sinai Sch. Medicine, CUNY, 1988, George Washington U., 1989, Hahnemann U., 1989, U. Pa., 1994; LHD (hon.), Rush U., 1988, Va. Commonwealth U., 1992, Med. Coll. Pa., 1992, Brandeis U., 1994. Diplomate: Am. Bd. Internal Medicine (dir. 1977-85, exec. com. 1981-85, chmn. 1984-85). Intern Mass. Gen. Hosp., Boston, 1960-61; asst. resident Mass. Gen. Hosp., 1961-62, sr. resident, 1964-65, clin. and research fellow, 1965, chief resident, 1966; clin. asso. Nat. Inst. Arthritis and Metabolic Diseases, 1962-64; from instr. to asst. prof. medicine Harvard U. Med. Sch., 1967-69; prof. medicine, health care policy Harvard Med. Sch., 1994—; asst. in medicine, chief renal unit Mass. Gen. Hosp., Boston, 1967-69; asso. prof., then prof. medicine U. Pa. Med. Sch., 1969-72, vice chmn. dept., 1971-74; assoc. dir. med. svcs. Hosp. U. Pa., 1969-71; David Paige Smith prof. medicine Yale U. Sch. Medicine, 1978-81, Sterling prof. medicine, 1981-85, chmn. dept., 1975-85; pres. Inst. Medicine NAS, Washington, 1985-91; pres., Univ. prof. Brandeis U., Waltham, Mass., 1991-94; pres. Mass. Gen. Hosp., Boston, 1994—; pres. Ptnrs. HealthCare Sys., Inc., Boston, 1994-96, CEO, 1996—; chief medicine Yale-New Haven Hosp., 1975-85, trustee, 1978-85; bd. dirs. Conn. Hospice, Inc., 1976-82. Mem. editorial bd.: New Eng. Jour. Medicine, 1978-81; Contbr. articles to med. jours. Mem. adv. com. to the dir. NIH, 1980-85. Served with USPHS, 1962-64. Recipient Christian R. and Mary F. Lindback Found. Distinguished Teaching award, 1971. Fellow ACP (bd. regents 1982-85); mem. Assn. Am. Med. Colls. (adminstrv. bd. coun. acad. socs.), John Morgan Soc., Am. Fedn. Clin. Rsch. (pres. 1976-77), Am. Soc. Nephrology, Am. Physiol. Soc., Internat. Soc. Nephrology, Assn. Profs. Medicine, Assn. Am. Physicians, Interurban Clin. Club, Alpha Omega Alpha. Home: 99-20 Florence St Apt 4B Chestnut Hill MA 02167-1927

THIERRY, ROBERT CHARLES, microbiologist; b. Bcurtzwiller, France, Sept. 12, 1938; s. Emile G. and Lucie M. (Meyer) T.; m. Ruth A. Biehrer, Jan. 18, 1958; children: Isabelle, Michel, Christophe, Catherine, Pierre, Simon. Dr. Medicine, U. Strasbourg, 1968; cert. immunobiology, Inst. Pasteur, Paris, 1971; cert. microbiology, Inst. Pasteur, 1972. Asst. Med. High Sch., Strasbourg, France, 1970-73; chief of rsch. Med. High Sch., 1973-86, conf. master, 1986—. Mem. French Soc. Immunobiology, French Soc. Microbiology, Force Démocrate. Roman Catholic. Office: Faculte Medecine, 3 rue Koeberle, F 67000 Strasbourg France

THIGPEN, JAMES TATE, physician, oncology educator; b. Columbia, Miss., June 6, 1944; m. Louisa Berdie Kessler, June 14, 1969; children: Monroe Tate, James Howard, Samuel Calvin, Richard Allen, David Albert. BS, U. Miss., 1964, MD, 1969. Intern Strong Meml. Hosp., U. Rochester, N.Y., 1969-70; resident U. Miss. Sch. Medicine, 1970-71, fellow div. hematology/oncology dept. medicine, 1971-73, prof., dir. div. med. oncology dept. internal medicine, 1973—, also asst. prof. ob-gyn.; nat. med. del. from Miss. Am. Cancer Soc., 1983-85, mem. nat. pub. issues com., 1983-85; mem. cancer clin. investigations rev. com. Nat. Cancer Inst., 1990-95, chmn., 1993-95. Nat. bd. govs. ARC, 1981-87. Fellow ACP; mem. AMA, Miss. Med. Assn., Central Med. Soc., Jackson Acad. Medicine, Miss. Acad. Scis., SW Oncology Group, Gynecologic Oncology Group (group vice chmn. for sci. 1988—), Am. Fedn. Clin. Rsch., Am. Assn. Cancer Edn., Am. Soc. Clin. Oncology, Am. Assn. Cancer Rsch., Am. Soc. Hematology, Soc. Gynecologic Oncologists, So. Assn. for Oncology (pres. 1988-90), Am. Radium Soc. Baptist (deacon 1978—, Sunday sch. tchr. 1979-85). Club: Optimist (internat. v.p. 1983-84, internat. pres. 1990-91). Home: 3601 Kings Hwy Jackson MS 39216-3322 Office: 2500 N State St Jackson MS 39216-4500

THISTED, RONALD AARON, statistician, educator, consultant; b. L.A., Mar. 2, 1951; s. Dale Owen and Barbara Jean (Walker) T.; m. Linda Jeane Soder, Dec. 30, 1972; 1 child, Walker. BA, Pomona Coll., 1972; PhD, Stanford U., 1977. Asst. prof. statistics U. Chgo., 1976-82, assoc. prof. statistics, 1982-92, assoc. prof. anesthesia and critical care, 1989-92, prof. stats. and anesthesia and critical care, 1992—. Author: Elements of Statistical Computing, 1988; contbr. over 60 articles to profl. jours. Fellow AAAS, Am. Statis. Assn.; mem. Assn. for Computing Machinery, Inst. for Math. Stats., Soc. for Clin. Trials. Office: U Chgo 5734 S University Ave Chicago IL 60637-1514

THOBABEN, MARSHELLE, community and mental health nurse, educator. BS in Nursing, U. Portland, 1968; MS in Edn., Calif. State U., Fresno, 1976; postgrad., U. Rochester, 1980-81. RN, Calif.; lic. psychiat.-mental health nurse, nurse practitioner; cert. pub. health nurse, ARC community disaster nurse, AIDS educator. Asst. prof. dept. nursing W.Va. Wesleyan Coll., Buckhannon, 1977-78; lectr. Calif. State U., Fresno, 1978-80; clinic dir. Fresno County Dept. Health, 1979; ednl. cons. Am. Jour. Nursing Co., Chgo., 1980-82; fellow in primary care U. Rochester, N.Y., 1980-81; instr. psychiat. mental health nursing Case Western Res. U., Cleve., 1981-82; psychiat. nurse Natividad Med. Ctr., Salinas, 1982, 84; psychiat. nursing cons. Humboldt Sr. Resource Ctr., Eureka, Calif., 1983-87; psychiat. nursing cons., home health nurse Humboldt Home Health, Eureka, 1983-91; prof. Humboldt State U., Arcata, Calif., 1982—, mem. acad. senate, 1986—, mem. exec. com., 1987—; statewide acad. senator, 1990—; mem. Inst. Tchg. and Learning, 1990—, vice chair, 1995—; co-chair, statewide nursing discipline coord. Adult/Elder Abuse Task Force, 1988-92; mem. Humboldt Home Health Comty. Adv. Coun., 1986-91; manuscript reviewer Addison-Wesley Pub. Co., 1983-88; book reviewer Aspen, Lippincott. Author: Elder and Dependent Adult Abuse: Humboldt and Del Norte Guidelines for Mandated Reporters, 1988, 91, Elder Abuse: Practice and Policy, 1989; mem. editorial bd. Home Healthcare Nurse, 1984—, Caregiver: The Home Care Nursing Monitor, 1987-90, Jour. Home Health Care Practice & Mgmt., 1990—, Home Care Provider, 1996—; contbr. numerous articles to profl. jours. Recipient Honor award Calif. Nurse's Assn., 1989, Sr. Friends award Agy. on Aging, 1986, Scholar of Yr. award Humboldt State U., 1991; Traineeship award NIMH, 1973-74; named Outstanding Community Health Nursing Leader, Home Healthcare Nurse Jour.; Calif. Nurse's Assn. scholar, 1982-87. Mem. ANA, APHA, Calif. Faculty Assn. (v.p. 1986-90, exec. com. 1986—, pres. 1991—, stateside bd. dirs. 1991), Am. Psychiat. Nurses Assn., Am. Soc. on Aging, Phi Kappa Phi. Office: Humboldt State Univ Dept Nursing Arcata CA 95521

THOM, ALLAN RHODES, orthodontist; b. London, Feb. 18, 1941; s. William and Marjorie (Smith) T.; m. Heather Gillian Symons, Aug. 19, 1967; children: Emma, James. BDS, U. Coll. London, 1966, FDS, 1970, D of Orthodontics, 1971. Cons. orthodontist London, 1976—; cons. Govt. Malta, 1987—; registered expert witness, Eng., 1996—. Co-author: (textbook) Fixed Appliances Principles and Practice, 1996. Mem. Brit. Orthodontist Soc. (treas. 1995—, Spl. Svc. award 1995), World Fedn. Orthodontist (councillor). Home and Office: 52 Warwick Park, Tunbridge TN2 5EF, England

THOMA, RICHARD WILLIAM, chemical safety and waste management consultant; b. Milw., Dec. 7, 1921; s. Joseph Donath and Margaret Mary (Murphy) T.; A.A., U. Chgo., 1941; BS, U. Wis., Madison, 1947, MS in Biochemistry, 1949, PhD, 1951; m. Ida Mary Scharfschwerdt, Mar. 15, 1952; children: Adele, Richard W., Joseph O., John C. With E. R. Squibb & Sons, Inc., New Brunswick, N.J., 1951-82, sr. rsch. fellow, 1980-82; dir. process devel. New Brunswick Sci. Co., Inc., Edison, N.J., 1982-84; cons., 1984—. Commr. Somerset County Bd. Elections, 1981-84; mem. Bridgewater Town Coun., 1975-81, Environ. Commn., 1974-75, Sewerage Authority, 1975-76, Police Commn., 1977-81; chmn. Bridgewater Dem. Mcpl. Com., 1980-87; alderman St. Lucie Village, 1996—. Served with AUS, 1943-46. Mem. Am. Chem. Soc., Am. Soc. Safety Engrs., Nat. Safety Coun., Am. Soc. Microbiology, Am. Acad. Microbiology, N.Y. Acad. Scis., Am. Inst. Biol. Scis., Soc. Indsl. Microbiology, Soc. Gen. Microbiology (U.K.), St. Lucie County C. of C., Phi Beta Kappa, Sigma Xi, Phi Lambda Upsilon. Contbr. articles to sci. jours.; editor Industrial Microbiology, 1977; patentee microbiol. transformation of steroids. Home and Office: 3772 Outrigger Ct Fort Pierce FL 34946-1911

THOMADSEN, BRUCE ROBERT, physicist; b. Detroit, Nov. 9, 1948. BS, U. Mich., 1970; PhD, U. Wis., 1989. Diplomate Am. Bd. Radiology, Am. Bd. Health Physics, Am. Bd. Med. Physics. Resident in physics Henry Ford Hosp., Detroit, 1970-71; radiol. physicist Hurley Hosp., Flint, Mich., 1972-73; chief med. physicist St. Barnabas Med. Ctr., Livingston, N.J., 1974-75; physicist Midwest Ctr. for Radiol. Physics, Madison, Wis., 1975-77; radiation oncology physicist U. Wis., Madison, 1977—; cons. Internat. Atomic Energy Agy., Paraguay, Haiti and Vienna, 1989. Editor, author: Radiotherapu Safety, 1984. Mem. Am. Assn. Physicists in Medicine (bd. dirs. 1990-95), Health Physics Soc. Office: U Wis K4/B100 Clinical Sci Ctr Madison WI 53792-0600

THOMALSKE, R.E. GÜNTHER, neurosurgeon, educator; b. Hohkirch, Fed. Republic Germany, June 8, 1925; s. Paul E.M. and Eleonore O.E. (Pletz) T.; m. Anne This, July 11, 1958; children: Christine, Catherine. Student, U. Berlin, 1943, U. Freiburg, Germany, 1943-44, U. Prague, Czechoslovakia, 1944-45; MD, U. Marburg, Fed. Republic Germany, 1949. Asst. in Bacteriologic Inst. U. Marburg, 1949; with Psychiat. Hosp.,

Marburg, 1949-50; asst. in gen. surgery Town Hosp., Delmenhorst, Fed. Republic Germany, 1950-51, asst. in ob-gyn., 1951-52; asst. surg. U. Hosp., Mainz, Fed. Republic Germany, 1952; asst. neurosurgeon Pasteur Hosp., Colmar, France, 1952-58; resident neurosurgeon U. Frankfurt (Fed. Republic Germany) Main Hosp., 1958-64, head neurosurgeon, 1964-68, lectr. neurosurgery, 1969-72, prof., 1972—, dir. dept. functional neurosurgery, 1973-90. Author: (with Münzenberg) Leg Pain, 1986, (with Tilscher) Back and Low Back Pain, 1990; editor: Series Pain, VCH, 1986—, Pain Conference, 1984—, Non Pharmacological Treatment of Pain, 1990. Mem. Internat. Assn. Study of Pain (v.p. German chpt. 1978-93), German Soc. Neurosurgery, French Lang. Soc. Neurosurgery, German Soc. Neuroradiology, German Soc. Neurology, German EEG Soc., French Soc. EEG; corr. mem. Soc. Luso Expagnola Neurocir., French Soc. Neuroradiology, Swiss Soc. Neurosurgery. Home: Tulpenstr 12, D-63263 Neu-Isenburg Germany Office: Aerztehaus, D-63263 Isenburg Germany

THOMAN, MARK EDWARD, pediatrician; b. Chgo., Feb. 15, 1936; s. John Charles and Tasula Mark (Petrakis) T.; AA, Graceland Coll., 1956; BA, U. Mo., 1958, MD, 1962; m. Theresa Thompson, 1984; children: Marlisa Rae, Susan Kay, Edward Kim, Nancy Lynn, Janet Lea, David Mark. Intern, U. Mo. at Columbia, 1962-63; resident in pediatrics Blank Meml. Children's Hosp., Des Moines, 1963-65, chief resident, 1964-65; cons. in toxicology, 1966-67; chief dept. pediatrics Shiprock (N.Mex.) Navajo Indian Hosp., dir. N.D. Poison Info. Center, also practice medicine, specializing in pediatrics Quain & Ramstad Clinic, Bismarck, N.D., 1967-69; dir. Iowa Poison Info. Center, Des Moines, 1969—; pvt. solo practice pediatrics, Des Moines, 1969—; sr. aviation med. examiner, accident investigator FAA, 1976—, cons., lectr., 1977—; faculty Iowa State U., U. Iowa, U. Osteo. Sci. and Health; dir. Cystic Fibrosis Clinic, 1973-82; dir. Mid-Iowa Drug Abuse Program, 1972-76; mem. med. adv. bd. La Leche League Internat., 1965—; pres. Medic-Air Ltd., 1976—; aviation seminars lectr. Editor-in-chief AACTION, 1975-90. Bd. dirs. Polk County Pub. Health Nurses Assn., 1969-77, Des Moines Speech and Hearing Center, 1974-79, Ecumenical Coun. of Iowa, 1990—; bd. govs. Mo. U. Sch. Medicine Alumni, 1988—, pres.- elect, 1995. Served with USMCR, 1954-59; lt. comdr. USPHS, 1965-66; capt. USNR, 1993-96, ret. 1996; dir. Dept. Health Svcs. USNR. Recipient N.D. Gov.'s award of merit, 1969; Cystic Fibrosis Rsch. Found. award, 1975, Am. Psychiat. Assn. Thesis award, Diplomate Am. Bd. Pediatrics, Am. Bd. Med. Toxicology (examiner). 1962. Mem. AMA (del. 1970-88), NRA (life), Assn. Am. Physicians & Surgeons, Polk County Med. Soc., Iowa State Med. Assn., Aerospace Med. Assn., Res. Officers Assn., Civil Aviation Med. Assn., Am. Public Health Assn., 1986—, Soc. Adolescent Medicine, Inst. Clin. Toxicology, Internat. Soc. Pediatrics, Am. Acad. Pediatrics (chmn. accident prevention com. Iowa chpt. 1975—), Cystic Fibrosis Club, Am. Acad. Clin. Toxicology (trustee 1969-90, pres. 1982-84), Am. Assn. Poison Control Centers, U.S. Naval Inst. Republican. Elder mem. Reorganized Latter-Day Saints Ch. Clubs: Flying Physicians, Aircraft Owners and Pilots Assn., Nat. Pilots Assn. (Safe Pilot award), Hyperion Field and Country. Editor in chief AACTION, 1976-90. Home: 6896 Trail Ridge Dr Johnston IA 50131-1322 Office: 1426 Woodland Ave Des Moines IA 50309-3204

THOMAS, ALBERT GEORGE, obstetrician-gynecologist; b. N.Y.C., Nov. 9, 1957; s. Albert George and Curalee Victoria (White) T.; m. Stephanie M. LeMelle, May 30, 1987; childrenL Kaylin Marie, Aston Guillion. BS in Chemistry, Rensselaer Poly. Inst., 1979; MD, Mt. Sinai Med. Ctr., 1983. Diplomate Am. Bd. Obstetrics and Gynecology. Dir. family planning Mt. Sinai Med. Ctr., N.Y.C., 1989—; med. dir. The Door adolescent health ctr., N.Y.C., 1993%; lectr. in field. Contbr. articles to profl. jours. Fellow Am. Coll. Ob-Gyn.; mem. APHA, Assn. Pub. Health Professions, N.Am. Soc. Pediatric/Adolescent Medicine, Am. Assn. Gynecologic Laparoscopists, Am. Soc. Colposcopic Cervical Pathology, N.Y. Gynecologic Soc. Office: Mount Sinai Medical Ctr 5 E 98th St 5th Fl New York NY 10029

THOMAS, ANDRA CAROL, nurse, scientific studies administrator, health policy strategist; b. Decatur, Ill., Dec. 7, 1948; d. Elmer Jr. and Mary Katherine (Patteson) T. Diploma in Nursing, Barnes Hosp. Sch. Nursing, 1969; student, U. Md., 1971-72, Johns Hopkins U., 1976-79, Coll. Notre Dame, Md., 1980-81, SUNY, 1981—; grad. Minn. Mgmt. Inst., U. Minn., 1990. Staff nurse operating rooms Johns Hopkins Hosp., Balt., 1971-72, head nurse operating rooms, 1972-81; clin. rep. Intec Systems, Inc., Pitts., 1981-83, mgr. clin. research, 1983-85; mgr. clin. research implantable defibrillation devices Cardiac Pacemakers, Inc., St. Paul, 1985, mgr. clin. programs, 1985-88, mgr. sci. studies, 1988—. Mem. Pitts. Ballet Theater Guild, 1981-84; aux. vol. St. Margarets Meml. Hosp., Pitts., 1984-85. Mem. Am. Heart Assn. Clin. Couns., Assn. Operating Room Nurses, Am. Mgmt. Assn., NAFE, N.Am. Soc. Pacing and Electrophysiology, Nat. Health Lawyers Assn., Regulatory Affairs Profl. Soc. Office: Cardiac Pacemakers Inc 4100 Hamline Ave N Saint Paul MN 55112-5700

THOMAS, BARBARA ANN, medical sciences consultant; b. Stoke-on-Trent, Stafford, Eng., May 5, 1935; d. John and Annie (Jackson) Lockley; m. Michael Thomas, June 16, 1962; children: Karen Elizabeth, Christopher James. BA in Natural Scis., Tripos U., 1955, 56; MA, Newnham Coll., Cambridge, Eng., 1959; MB B, Middlesex Hosp. Med. Sch., London, 1959. Royal Coll. Radiologists, Royal Coll. Ob-Gyn. House officer Middlesex Hosp., 1959, casualty med. officer, 1960; gen. practice London, 1962-67; med. officer of health Harrow then Ealing, London, 1965-74; clin. med. officer Surrey, Eng., 1974-78; clin. coordinator Guildford (Eng.) Breast Screening Project, 1978-88; clin. dir. Jarvis Screening Ctr., Guildford, Eng., 1988—; trainer Nat. Breast Cancer Tng. Ctr., Guildford, 1988—; advisor, breast disease, Women's Nat. Cancer Control Campaign, Eng., 1987—. Advisor, interviewee: (video) Ray of Hope, 1988; contbr. articles to profl. jours. Recipient grants Dept. Health, 1979, Travel fellowship, Council of Europe, 1984, 89. Mem. European Group for Breast Cancer Screening (sec. 1986-88). Home: Copsen Knoll Rd, Frith Hill Godalming, Surrey GU7 2EL, England Office: Jarvis Screening Ctr, Stoughton Rd, Guildford GUI 1LJ, England

THOMAS, BRIAN LACY, anesthesiology educator; b. Kansas City, Mo., Apr. 27, 1959; m. Karen Primeaux, Mar. 30, 1985. BA in Chemistry, Baylor U., 1981; MD, U. Tex., Dallas, 1985. Diplomate Am. Bd. Anesthesiology. Intern Med. Coll. Va., 1985-86, surg. resident, 1986-89, resident in anesthesiology, 1989-91; resident in anesthesiology Emory U., Atlanta, 1991-92; fellow in cardiothoracic anesthesia Emory U. Sch. Medicine, Atlanta, 1992-93; asst. prof. anesthesia Emory U. Hosp., 1993—; cons. Abbott Labs., Abbott Park, Ill., 1995—. Contbg. author: Cardiopulmonary Bypass, 1995, Anesthesiology, 1995; contbr. numerous articles to med. jours. Recipient Peter J. Gingrass award Plastic Surg. Rsch. Coun., 1988, Bigger-Lehman awad Va. Surg. Soc., 1988. Mem. AMA, Am. Soc. Anesthesiology, Internat. Anesthesia Rsch. Soc., Soc. Cardiovasc. Anesthesiologists. Office: Emory U Hosp Dept Anes 1364 Clifton Rd Atlanta GA 30322

THOMAS, CARMEN CHRISTINE, physician, consultant administrator; b. Germany, Apr. 15, 1908; came to U.S., 1921; d. Paul Ernest and Huberta (Mohr) T. AB, U. Del., 1929; MD, Woman's Med. Coll. Pa., 1932; DSc, U. Pa., 1940. Diplomate Am. Bd. Dermatology. Asst. chief resident Phila. Gen. Hosp., 1934-35; fellow in dermatology U. Pa., Phila., 1936-39, asst. prof. dermatology, 1940-67; prof. dermatology Woman's Med. Coll. Pa., Phila., 1941-68, dir. dept. oncology, 1952-66, emeritus prof. dermatology, 1968—; chief dermatologist Phila. Gen. Hosp., 1944-77; pvt. practice Phila., 1939-77; cons. Vets. Hosp., Memor Hosp., Phila., 1950-77, Elwyn Inst., Devereux Sch., Delaware County, 1950-69. Contbr. articles to profl. jours. Fellow Phila. Coll. Physicians; mem. Am. Acad. Dermatology (life), Phila. Dermatol. Soc. (life, pres. 1942), Phila. County Med. Soc. (life), Phi Beta Kappa, Alpha Omega Alpha, Sigma Xi. Home: 600 E Cathedral Rd Apt G305 Philadelphia PA 19128-1929

THOMAS, CAROLE DOLORES, gerontologist; b. Huntington, Ind., Dec. 20, 1937; d. James Robert and Gladys Agnes (Walraven) Williams; m. Norman Day Thomas, Sept. 1, 1962 (separated); children: Diane Thomas Laucirica, Mark Alexander. BA in Polit. Sci., U. Ill., 1960; MA in Gerontology, U. South Fla., 1982. Human svcs. analyst Dept. Health and Rehab. Svcs., Tampa, Fla., 1987-94, adult protective investigator, 1994—; mem. Adult Protection Team, Tampa, 1990—, Bradenton, Fla., 1990—, Long Term Care Ombudsman Coun., Tampa, 1989—. Mem. Fla. Orch. Guild, Tampa, 1985—; guardian ad litem 13th Jud. Cir., Tampa, 1991—; vol. Performing Arts Ctr., Tampa, 1992—. Home: 14314 Diplomat Dr Tampa FL 33613-3107 Office: Dept Health & Rehab Svcs 4000 W Martin Luther King Blvd Tampa FL 33614-7012

THOMAS, CHARLES ALLEN, JR., molecular biologist, educator; b. Dayton, Ohio, July 7, 1927; s. Charles Allen and Margaret Stoddard (Talbott) T.; m. Margaret M. Gay, July 7, 1951; children: Linda Carrick, Stephen Gay. AB, Princeton (N.J.) U., 1950; PhD, Harvard U., 1954. Rsch. scientist Eli Lilly Co., Indpls., 1954-55; NCR fellow U. Mich., Ann Arbor, 1955-56, prof. biophysics, 1956-57; prof. biophysics Johns Hopkins U., Balt., 1957-67; prof. biol. chemistry Med. Sch. Harvard U., Boston, 1967-78; chmn. dept. cellular biology Scripps Clinic & Rsch. Found., La Jolla, Calif., 1978-81; pres., dir. Helicon Found., San Diego, 1981—; founder, CEO The Syntro Corp., San Diego, 1981-82; founder, CEO, now dir. of R&D Pantox Corp., San Diego, 1989—; mem. genetics study sect. NIH, 1968-72; mem. rsch. grants com. Am. Cancer Soc., 1972-76, 79-85. Mem. editorial bd. Virology, 1967-73, Jour. Molecular Biology, 1968-72, BioPhysics Jour., 1965-68, Chromosoma, 1969-79, Analytic Biochemistry, 1970-79, Biochim Biophys. ACTA, 1973-79, Plasmid, 1977—. With USNR, 1945-46. NRC fellow, 1965-66. Mem. AAAS, Am. Acad. Arts and Scis., Am. Fedn. Biol. Chemists, Genetics Soc. Am., Am. Chem. Soc. Home: 1640 El Paso Real La Jolla CA 92037-6304 Office: Helicon Foundation 4622 Santa Fe St San Diego CA 92109-1601

THOMAS, CLAUDEWELL SIDNEY, psychiatry educator; b. N.Y.C., Oct. 5, 1932; s. Humphrey Sidney and Frances Elizabeth (Collins) T.; m. Carolyn Pauline Rozansky, Sept. 6, 1958; children: Jeffrey Evan, Julie-Anne Elizabeth, Jessica Edith. BA, Columbia U., 1952; MD, SUNY, Downstate Med. Ctr., 1956; MPH, Yale U., 1964. Diplomate Nat. Bd. Med. Examiners, Am. Bd. Psychiatry. From instr. to assoc. prof. Yale U., New Haven, 1963-68, dir. Yale tng. program in social community psychiatry, 1967-70; dir. div. mental health service programs NIMH, Washington, 1970-73; chmn. dept. psychiatry U.M.D.N.J., Newark, 1973-83; prof. dept. psychiatry Drew Med. Sch., 1983—, chmn. dept. psychiatry, 1983-93; prof. dept. psychiatry UCLA, 1983-94, vice chmn. dept. psychiatry, 1983-93, prof. emeritus dept. psychiatry, 1994—; med. dir. Tokanui Hosp., TeAwamutu, N.Z., 1996; cons. A.K. Rice Inst., Washington, 1978-80, SAMSA/PHS Cons., 1991—; mem. L.A. County Superior Ct. Psych. Panel, 1991—. Author: (with B. Bergen) Issues and Problems in Contemporary Society, 1966; editor (with R. Bryce LaPorte) Alienation in Contemporary Society, 1976, (with J. Lindenthal) Psychiatry and Mental Health Science Handbook; mem. editorial bd. Internat. Jour. Mental Health, Adminstrn. In Mental Health. Served to capt. USAF, 1959-61. Fellow APHA, Am. Psychoanalytic Assn. (hon.), Am. Psychiat. Assn. (life), Royal Soc. Health, N.Y. Acad. Sci., N.Y. Acad. Medicine; mem. Am. Sociol. Assn. Home and Office: 30676 Palos Verdes Dr W Palos Verdes Peninsula CA 90274

THOMAS, CLINTON LAVURN, JR., obstetrician, gynecologist; b. Bogulusa, La., Jan. 31, 1943; s. Clinton Lavurn and Mattie Elizabeth (Pope) T.; m. Barbara Jane Brennan, July 23, 1976; children: Michelle Leigh, Melanie Kaye, Mattie Enola. BS, La. State U., 1966; MS, Southeastern La. U., 1971; PhD, Tex A&M U., 1975; MD, U. Autonama de Júarez, Mexico, 1981. Diplomate Am. Bd. Ob-Gyn. High sch. tchr. Parish Sch. Bds., New Orleans, 1966-71; asst. prof. U. New Orleans, 1977-79; resident LSU Med. Sch. Charity Hosp., New Orleans, 1981-85; pvt. practice ob-gyn. Slidell, La., 1985—; chmn. dept. ob-gyn. Slidell Meml. Hosp., 1988, 95. Fellow Am. Coll. Ob-Gyn.; mem. So. Med. Assn., La. State Med. Soc., Slidell C. of C. Democrat. Methodist. Office: 700 Gause Blvd Ste 206 Slidell LA 70458-2853

THOMAS, COLIN GORDON, JR., surgeon, medical educator; b. Iowa City, July 25, 1918; s. Colin Gordon and Eloise Kinzer (Brainerd) T.; m. Shirley Forbes, Sept. 14, 1946; children: Karen, Barbara, James G., John F. B.S., U. Chgo., 1940, M.D., 1943. Diplomate Am. Bd. Surgery. Intern U. Iowa Hosp., 1943-44, resident surgery, 1944-45, 47-50; assoc. in surgery U. Iowa Med. Sch., 1950-51, asst. prof., 1951-52; mem. faculty U. N.C. Med. Sch., Chapel Hill, 1952—, prof. surgery, 1961—, Byah Thomason Doxey-Sanford Doxey prof. surgery, 1982—, chmn. dept., 1966-84, chief div. gen. surg., 1984-89, part-time prof., 1991—. Contbr. surg. texts, numerous articles to med. jours. Served to capt., M.C. AUS, 1945-47. Recipient Prof. award U. N.C. Sch. Medicine, 1964, Disting. Svc. award U. Chgo., 1982, Med. Alumni Disting. faculty award U. N.C., 1984; Berryhill lectr. U. N.C., 1989; recipient Fleming Fuller award U. N.C. Hosps., 1994. Mem. AMA, ACS (Disting. Leadership award N.C. chpt. 1990), AAUP, Am. Thyroid Assn., Am. Assn. Cancer Research, Am. Assn. Endocrine Surgeons (pres. 1989-90), Soc. Univ. Surgeons, So. Surg. Assn. (v.p. 1989-90), N.Y. Acad. Scis., Halsted Soc., Ga. Surg. Soc., Soc. Exptl. Biology and Medicine, Am. Surg. Assn., Womack Surg. Soc. (pres. 1981-83), Soc. Internationale de Chirurgie, Soc. Surgery Alimentary Tract, N.C. Surg. Assn., Internat. Assn. Endocrine Surgeons, Alpha Omega Alpha. Episcopalian (warden 1961-62). Home: 408 Morgan Creek Rd Chapel Hill NC 27514-4934

THOMAS, CYNTHIA ELIZABETH, advanced practice nurse; b. Highland, Ind., Sept. 3, 1958; d. James William and Naomi Elizabeth (Rice) T. BS in Animal Sci., Purdue U., 1980; ADN, Purdue U. Calumet, 1986, BSN, 1988, MSN, 1990. RN, Ind.; cert. adult nurse practitioner, family nurse practitioner, clin. specialist in med.-surg. nursing. Med.-surg. open heart ICU/CCU staff nurse, charge nurse Porter Meml. Hosp., Valparaiso, Ind., 1986-94; med.-surg. clin. instr. Purdue U. North Ctrl., Westville, Ind., 1993-94; advanced practice nurse Cmty. Health Ctrs. Koontz Lake, LaCrosse, North Judson, Starke Meml. Hosp., Ind., 1994-95; advanced practice nurse Cmty. Health Ctrs.-Koontz Lake, LaCrosse, North Judson, Ind., 1994-95, Starke Meml. Hosp., Knox, Ind.; nurse practitioner/office coord. Hanna Family Med. Ctr., LaPorte Hosp./Lakeland Area Health Svcs., 1995-96; nursing instr. Bethel Coll., Mishawaka, Ind., 1995-96; adult medicine/pulmonary nurse practitioner Arnett Clinic, Lafayette, Ind., 1996—; med.-surg. clin. instr. Purdue U., Westville, Ind., 1993-94; nursing instr. Bethel Coll., Mishawaka, Ind., 1995-96; adult medicine/pulmonary nurse practitioner, Arnett Clinic, Lafayette, Ind., 1996—. Mem. AACN, Am. Acad. Nurse Practitioners, Alpha Zeta. Office: Pulmonary Dept Arnett Clinic 1500 Salem St Lafayette IN 47904

THOMAS, DANE RUSSELL, physical therapist; b. Modesto, Calif., Aug. 29, 1964; s. Russell Lee and Claudia Jane (Ebert) T.; m. Eva-Mari Lundin, Dec. 2, 1990; 1 child, Erik Jonathan. Student, Coll. Adventista de Sagunto, Spain, 1983-84, Pacific Union Coll., 1986-87; BS in Phys. Therapy, Loma Linda U., 1989; postgrad., Uppsala (Sweden) U., 1991. Cert. Nat. Strength and Conditioning Assn., U.S. Ski Coaches Assn. Staff phys. therapist gen. acute care dept. St. Charles Med. Ctr., Bend, Oreg., 1990; extremity/sports phys. therapist Orthopedic and Sports Phys. Therapy, Cupertino, Calif., 1990; post-surg. aquatic phys. therapist Vail (Colo.) Sports Medicine Phys. Therapy, 1990-93; dir. physical therapy Skilled Nursing Facility Beverly Manor, Stockton, Calif., summer 1992; dir. phys. therapy Steadman-Hawkins Clinic, Vail, 1993—; trainer U.S. Ski Team-Alpine, Saas Fee, Switzerland, 1990, Sysco Bicycle Racing Team, Idaho, 1990; spkr. Powder Mag. Performance, Colo., 1991-93; clin. advisor Am. Running and Fitness, 1992-94. Mem. Am. Phys. Therapy Assn. Office: Steadman-Hawkins Clinic 181 W Meadow Dr # 410 Vail CO 81657

THOMAS, EDWARD DONNALL, physician, researcher; b. Mart, Tex., Mar. 15, 1920; married; 3 children. BA, U. Tex., 1941, MA, 1943; MD, Harvard U., 1946; MD (hon.), U. Cagliari, Sardinia, 1981, U. Verona, Italy, 1991, U. Parma, Italy, 1992, U. Barcelona, Spain, 1994. Lic. physician Mass., N.Y., Wash.; diplomate Am. Bd. Internal Medicine. Intern in medicine Peter Bent Brigham Hosp., Boston, 1946-47, rsch. fellow hematology, 1947-48; NRC postdoctoral fellow in medicine dept. biology MIT, Cambridge, 1950-51; chief med. resident, sr. asst. resident Peter Bent Brigham Hosp., 1951-53, hematologist, 1953-55; instr. medicine Harvard Med. Sch., Boston, 1953-55; rsch. assoc. Cancer Rsch. Found. Children's Med. Ctr., Boston, 1953-55; physician-in-chief Mary Imogene Bassett Hosp., Cooperstown, N.Y., 1955-63; assoc. clin. prof. medicine Coll. Physicians and Surgeons Columbia U., N.Y.C., 1955-63; attending physician U. Wash. Hosp., Seattle, 1963-90; prof. medicine Sch. Medicine U. Wash., Seattle, 1963-90, head divsn. oncology Sch. Medicine, 1963-85, prof. emeritus medicine Sch. Medicine, 1990—; dir. med. oncology Fred Hutchinson Cancer Rsch. Ctr., Seattle, 1974-89, assoc. dir. clin. rsch. programs, 1982-89, mem., 1974—; mem. hematology study sect. NIH, 1965-69; mem. bd. trustees and med. sci. adv. com. Leukemia Soc. Am., Inc., 1969-73; mem. clin. cancer investigation review com. Nat. Cancer Inst., 1970-74; 1st ann. Eugene C. Eppinger lectr. Peter Bent Brigham Hosp. and Harvard Med. Sch., 1974; Lilly lectr. Royal Coll. Physicians, London, 1977; Stratton lectr. Internation Soc. Hematology, 1982; Paul Aggeler lectr. U. Calif., San Francisco, 1982; 65th Mellon lectr. U. Pitts. Sch. Medicine, 1984; Stanley Wright Meml. lectr. Western Soc. Pediatric Rsch., 1985; Adolfo Ferrata lectr. Italian Soc. Hematology, Verona, Italy, 1991. Mem. editl. bd. Blood, 1962-75, 77-82, Transplantation, 1970-76, Proc. of Soc. for Exptl. Biology and Medicine, 1974-81, Leukemia Rsch., 1977-87, Hematological Oncology, 1982-87, Jour. Clin. Immunology, 1982-87, Am. Jour. Hematology, 1985—, Bone Marrow Transplantation, 1986—. With U.S. Army, 1948-50. Recipient A. Ross McIntyre award U. Nebr. Med. Ctr., 1975, Philip Levine award Am. Soc. Clin. Pathologists, 1979, Disting. Svc. in Basic Rsch. award Am. Cancer Soc., 1980, Kettering prize Gen. Motors Cancer Rsch. Found., 1981, Spl. Keynote Address award Am. Soc. Therapeutic Radiologists, 1981, Robert Roesler de Villiers award Leukemia Soc. Am., 1983, Karl Landsteiner Meml. award Am. Assn. Blood Banks, 1987, Terry Fox award Can., 1990, Internat. award Gairdner Found., 1990, N.Am. Med. Assn. Hong Kong prize, 1990, Nobel prize in medicine, 1990, Presdl. medal of sci. NSF, 1990,. Mem. NAS, Am. Assn. Cancer Rsch., Am. Assn. Physicians (Kober medal 1992), Am. Fedn. Clin. Rsch., Am. Soc. Clin. Oncology (David A. Karnoksky Meml. lectr. 1983), Am. Soc. Clin. Investigation, Am. Soc. Hematology (pres. 1987-88, Henry M. Stratton lectr. 1975), Internat. Soc. Exptl. Hematology, Internat. Soc. Hematology, Academie Royale de Medicine de Belgique (corresponding mem.), Swedish Soc. Hematology (hon.), Swiss Soc. Hematology, Royal Coll. Physicians and Surgeons Can. (hon.), Western Assn. Physicians, Soc. Exptl. Biology and Medicine, Transplantation Soc., Nat. Acad. Medicine (hon.). Office: Fred Hutchinson Cancer Ctr 1124 Columbia St Seattle WA 98104-2015

THOMAS, FRANCIS THORNTON, surgeon, immunologist, consultant; b. Hibbing, Minn., June 24, 1939; s. Gerald M. and Patricia E. (Thornton) T.; m. Judith M. Jannino, June 20, 1968; children; Francis Scott, David Randolph, Jason Hunter. BS, U. Minn., 1960, MS, 1962, MD, 1964. Diplomate Am. Bd. Surgery, Am. Bd. Thoracic Surgery. Intern, resident, chief resident surgery N.Y.U.-Bellevue Med. Ctr., 1964-69; fellow cardiothoracic surgery Case-Western Res. U., 1969-71; instr. to assoc. prof. Med. Coll. of Va., Richmond, 1971-79; prof. surgery East Carolina Sch. Medicine, Greenville, N.C., 1979-95, U. Ala. Med. Ctr., Birmingham, 1995—. Served to capt. U.S. Army, 1965-69. Office: Univ Ala Med Ctr 728 Lyons Harrison Bldg 701 S 19th St Birmingham AL 35294-0016

THOMAS, FRANÇOIS PIERRE, health care consultant; b. Chartres, France, Sept. 26, 1957; s. René François and Nicole Andrée (Larrousse) T. MD, U. Paris, 1984, PhD, 1994; M in Mgmt., MIT, 1995. Bd. cert. med. oncology, France. Resident, fellow Hôpitaux de Paris, 1981-86; asst. prof. medicine Inst. Gustave Roussy, Villejuif, 1986-89; dir. R&D programs (SCRAS) Ipsen Beaufour, Paris, 1989-91; dir. R & D Ipsen Biotech., Paris, 1991-94; cons. for health care industry, founder Bioserve Ltd., U.K., Boulogne, France, 1994—, Bioserve Ltd., London, 1996—; guest researcher Nat. Cancer Inst., Bethesda, Md., 1987-88. Contbr. over 60 articles to profl. jours. Mem. Am. Soc. Clin. Oncology, Am. Soc. Cancer Rsch., N.Y. Acad. Sci., Am. Peptide Soc., Internat. Assn. Study Lung Cancer, Endocrine Soc., Assn. de Medecins de Industrie Pharmaceutique, Le Polo de Paris. Office: TEV Cons, 55 rue l'ancienne mairie, 92100 Boulogne France

THOMAS, FRANK JOSEPH, physician; b. Troy, N.Y., June 23, 1950; s. Frank Joseph Sr. and Marie (Graber) T.; m. Nancy E. O'Keeffe, Dec. 29, 1974. BS, Fordham U., 1972; MD, NYU, 1976. Diplomate Am. Bd. Radiology, Am. Bd. Radiation and Oncology. Intern Cin. Children's Hosp., 1976-77; resident U. Wis., Madison, 1977-80; fellow Cleve. Clinic, 1980, staff physician, 1981-83, chmn. radiation oncology, 1984-88; asst. prof. radiation oncology Case Western Res. U., Cleve., 1988-90; assoc. prof. Albany (N.Y.) Med. Coll., 1990-95; med. dir. Ellis Hosp., Schenectady. N.Y., 1990—. Contbr. various articleto profl. jours. Mem. AMA, Am. Soc. Therapeutic Radiology and Oncology, Am. Coll. Radiology (com. on radiation theraphy tech.), Phi Beta Kappa. Office: Ellis Hospital Dept Radiation Oncology 1101 Nott St Schenectady NY 12308

THOMAS, HERBERT CUSHING, JR., physician, teacher; b. Charlotte, N.C., Oct. 6, 1941; s. Herbert Cushing and Doris (Roberts) T.; m. Laureen Thompson, June 9, 1961 (div. 1983); children: Steven, Michael; m. Catherine Anne Campbell, Feb. 11, 1989. BA, U. Colo., 1963, MD, 1967; MS, U. Wash., 1976. Resident in surgery Swedish Hosp., Med. Ctr., Seattle, 1972-73; resident in otolaryngology U. Wash., Seattle, 1973-77; fellowship in otology Ear Rsch. Inst., L.A., 1977-78; pvt. practice Seattle, 1978—; attending physician Children's Hosp. and Med. Ctr., Seattle, 1985—, pres. med. staff, 1991-92; pres. Surg. Specialists, Inc., Seattle, 1988-90. Capt. USN, 1967-72, USNR, ret. Mem. AMA, Am. Acad. Otolaryngology, Wash. State Med. Soc., King County Med. Soc., Seattle Surg. Soc., N.W. Acad. Otolaryngology. Office: 4540 Sand Point Way NE Seattle WA 98105-3941

THOMAS, JAMES DAVID, cardiologist, medical educator; b. Oklahoma City, Apr. 6, 1955; s. Murrell Dee and Ruth Elizabeth (Rice) T.; m. Donna Marie Catanzano, May 19, 1984; children: Beth, Daniel. BA in Applied Math., Harvard U., 1977, MD, 1981. Diplomate Am. Bd. Internal Medicine, Am. Bd. Cardiology. Resident in internal medicine Mass. Gen. Hosp., Boston, 1981-84, rsch. fellow, 1986-88, clin. asst., 1988-89, asst. in medicine, 1989-92; fellow in cardiology U. Vt., Burlington, 1984-86; instr. medicine Harvard Med. Sch., Boston, 1988-89, asst. prof. medicine, 1989-92; dir. cardiovascular imaging Cleve. Clinic Found., 1992—; prof. med. and biomed. engring. Ohio State U., Columbus, 1993—; cons. NIH, Bethesda, Md., 1992—, Am. Heart Assn., Dallas, 1993—, FDA, Washington, 1993—, various Echo cos., 1988—. Contbr. over 190 articles to profl. jours. Recipient Young Investigator prize ACP, Washington, 1985. Fellow Am. Coll. Cardiology (editl. bd. 1984—, Young Investigator prize hon. mention 1988), Am. Heart Assn. (editl. bd.), Am. Soc. Echocardiography (bd. dirs., Young Investigator prize 1990); mem. IEEE, Computers in Cardiology (bd. dirs. 1986—), Phi Beta Kappa. Office: Cleve Clinic Dept Cardiology F15 9500 Euclid Ave Cleveland OH 44195

THOMAS, JAMES ROBERT, obstetrician-gynecologist, perinatologist; b. Lodi, Calif., Nov. 22, 1948; s. Harold Morse and Lillian Bertha (Litvin) T.; m. Mona Lee Mason, June 1, 1969; adopted children: Sarah Marie, Jesse Lee-Hwan, Hannah Shereé, Joseph Michael. BS, Loma Linda U., 1970, MD, 1977; PhD, U. Calif., Irvine, 1974. Cert. Am. Bd. Ob-Gyns, Nat. Bd. Med. Examiners. Intern in ob-gyn McGill U., Can., 1978-79; resident in ob-gyn Yale U., New Haven, 1979-82; fellow maternal-fetal medicine U. Vt., Burlington, 1982-84; dir. maternal-fetal medicine U. S.D., Sioux Falls, 1984-87, asst. prof. ob-gyn, 1984-87, assoc. prof., 1987; dir. maternal and fetal medicine Flagstaff (Ariz.) Med. Ctr., 1987-91, chmn. dept. ob-gyn, 1988; CEO Perinatal Assocs. No. Ariz., 1991-95. Mem. Ariz. Perinatal Trust, 1987—. Fellow ACOG (Mead Johnson clin. rsch. fellow 1984); mem. AMA, Soc. Perinatal Obstetrics, Am. Inst. Ultrasound in Medicine, Coconino County Med. Soc. (sec.-treas. 1994, pres. 1995-96), Wine Club Sioux Falls (charter pres. 1984-85), Alpha Omega Alpha. Home: RR 4 Box 736A 30 Wildrose Trail Flagstaff AZ 86001

THOMAS, JEAN MUELLER, psychiatrist. MS, Washington U., St. Louis, 1977, MD, 1981. Diplomate Am. Bd. Psychiatry, Child and Adolescent Psychiatry. Assoc. prof. psychiatry and pediatrics St. Louis U./Cardinal Glennon Children's Hosp. Office: Saint Louis Univ 1465 S Grand Blvd Saint Louis MO 63104

THOMAS, JOHN ARLEN, pharmacology educator, health science administrator; b. LaCrosse, Wis., Apr. 6, 1933; s. John M. and Eva Hazel (Nelson) T.; m. Barbara A. Fisler, June 22, 1957; children: Michael J., Jane L. BS in Sci. Edn., U. Wis., 1956; MA in Physiology, U. Iowa, 1958, PhD in Physiology, 1961. Diplomate Am. Acad. Toxicologic Sci. Instr., U. Iowa, Iowa City, 1961; asst. prof. U. Va., Charlottesville, 1961-64; assoc. prof. Creighton U., Omaha, 1964-67; assoc. prof. W.Va. U., Morgantown, 1968-69, prof. pharmacology 1970-80; asst. dean W.Va. Sch. Medicine, Morgantown, 1973-75, assoc. dean, 1973-80; v.p. corp. rsch. Baxter Internat. Travenol Labs, Round Lake, Ill., 1980-87; v.p. academic svcs. U. Tex.

Health Sci. Ctr., San Antonio, 1988—, prof. pharmacology dept. toxicology, 1988—. cons. NIH, Bethesda, Md., 1975, Nat. Libr. Medicine, Bethesda, Md., 1994; bd. dirs. ILSI, Washington, D.C., Tex. Soc. Biomedical Rsch., Austin, v.p., 1996. Author: (with M.G. Mawhinney) Synopsis of Endocrine Pharmacology, 1978; (with E.J. Keenan) Principles of Endocrine Pharmacl-nology, 1986; editor: (with others) Basic and Clinical Toxicology of Lead, 1985, Endocrine Toxicology, 1985; 1996, Drugs Athletes & Physical Performance, 1988, Biotechnicology and Safety Assessment, 1993, Endocrine Methods, 1996, Toxic Substances Mechanism Jour. Contbr. articles to profl. jours. Sgt. U.S. Army, 1951-53. Recipient Cert. Svc., U.S. EPA, 1977; Named Outstanding Alumnus, U. Wis.-La Crosse, 1978, Outstanding Tchr., W.Va. U., 1971. Mem. Endocrine Soc., Soc. Toxicology (councilor), Am. Soc. Pharmacology and Exptl. Therapeutics, Am. Coll. Toxicology (councilor, pres.-elect), Teratology Soc., Am. Acad. Vet. Pharmacology, Am. Chem. Soc. (pres. chem. toxicology pathology), Russian Acad. Med. Scis. (fgn.). Republican. Home: 219 Wood Shadow St San Antonio TX 78216-1633 Office: U Tex Health Sci Ctr 7703 Floyd Curl Dr San Antonio TX 78284-7722

THOMAS, JOHN MELVIN, retired surgeon; b. Carmarthen, U.K., Apr. 26, 1933; came to U.S., 1958; s. Morgan and Margaret (Morgan) T.; m. Betty Ann Mayo, Nov. 3, 1958; children: James, Hugh, Pamela. MB, BChir, U. Coll. Wales, U. Edinburgh, 1958. Intern Robert Packer Hosp., Sayre, Pa., 1958-59, chief surg. resident, 1963, pres. med. staff, 1968; assoc. surgeon Guthrie Clinic Ltd., Sayre, 1963-69, chmn. dept. surgery, 1969-91; pres. bd. dirs. Guthrie Clinic Ltd., 1972-89; trustee Robert Packer Hosp.; chmn. exec. com. Guthrie Healthcare Sys., 1990-92, dir., 1994—; guest examiner Am. Bd. Surgery, 1979, 81, 85; bd. dirs. Measurement Innovations Corp., Citizen Fin. Bank, Mansfield, Pa., Trianalytics Corp.; cons. The Hunter Group, 1995—. Bd. dirs. Donald Guthrie Found. for Rsch., pres., 1983—; bd. dirs. Pa. Trauma Sys. Found., 1984-90, pres., 1988, 89; chmn. licensure and accountability Gov.'s Conf., 1974; bd. dirs. Vol. Hosps. Am., 1993-95; trustee Mansfield (Pa.) U. Found., 1991—; trustee Mansfield Univ. Found., 1991-95. Mem. ACS (gov. 1985-91), AMA, Am. Group Practice Assn., Soc. for Surgery Alimentary Tract, Pa. Med. Soc., Bradford County Med. Soc., Cen. N.Y. Surg. Soc., Internat. Soc. Surgery, Soc. Surgery Alimentary Tract, Ea. Vascular Soc., Ithaca Country Club, Moselem Springs Golf Club. Presbyterian. Home: 383 Lansing Station Rd Lansing NY 14882-8606

THOMAS, JOHN WESLEY, psychiatrist; b. Birmingham, Ala., Feb. 13, 1932; s. James and Leila Mae (Berry) T.; m. Dorothy Thompson, 1955 (div. 1969); children: Courtland W., Stephen M. BA, Tenn. State U., 1953; MD, Meharry Med. Coll., Nashville, 1959. Intern McKeesport (Pa.) Hosp., 1959-60; resident Rollman Receiving Hosp. and Inst. of Psychiatry, Cin., 1960-61, Western Psychiat. Inst. and Clinic, Pitts., 1961-63; staff psychiatrist Mayview State Hosp., Bridgeville, Pa., 1963-66; med. dir. Adult Outpatient Svcs., St. Francis Mental Health Ctr., Pitts., 1971-89; supervising psychiatrist St. Francis Psychiatric Residency Prog., Pitts., 1982-89; field faculty dept. psychiatry Meharry Med. Coll., Nashville, 1980—; clin. instr. dept. psychiatry U. Pitts., 1963-89; pvt. practice psychiatry Pitts., 1963—; cons. in field. Fellow Am. Group Psychotherapy Assn.; mem. AMA, NAACP, Am. Psychiat. Assn., Nat. Med. Assn., Pa. Med. Soc., Pa. Psychiat. Soc., Tri-State Group Psychotherapy Soc., Alpha Phi Alpha, Chi Delta Mu. Office: 211 N Whitfield St Ste 392 Pittsburgh PA 15206-3031

THOMAS, JOSE HONORE, oncologist, internist; b. Oostende, Belgium, Nov. 17, 1946; s. Willy and Madeleine (Roose) T.; m. Christine Lommee, Mar. 23, 1974; children: Tom, Alexander. MD, Cath. U. Leuven, 1971. Internist UZ Leuven, 1971-76; resident U2 Leuven, 1976, joint chief of staff, 1977—; sec. EORTC Coop. Lymph Group, 1987—. Contbr. articles to profl. jours. Office: UZ GHB Leuven, Herestraat, B-3000 Leuven Belgium

THOMAS, JOSEPH PAUL, psychiatrist; b. Bioloxi, Miss., Oct. 11, 1947; s. William Lloyd and Myrtis (Farmer) T.; m. Sandra Kay Elam, Dec. 20, 1973; children: Stephen Paul, Ashlie Lauren, Emily Grace. BA, U. Ala., Tuscaloosa, 1968; MA, U. Ala., 1971; MD, U. Ala., Birmingham, 1979. Diplomate Am. Bd. Psychiatry and Neurology with added qualification in geriat. psychiatry, addiction psychiatry, forensic psychiatry, Am. Bd. Adolescent Psychiatry; cert. Am. Soc. Addiction Medicine. Tchr. Gadsden (Ala.) Pub. Schs., 1968-69, Birmingham Bd. Edn., 1969-75, 80; resident Univ. Hosps., Birmingham, 1980; intern Mayo Grad. Sch. Medicine, Rochester, Minn., 1980-81; resident Johns Hopkins Hosp., Balt., 1981-84; psychiatrist The Thomas Clinic, P.C., Mobile, Ala., 1984, Neuropsychiatric Assocs. of South P.C., Mobile, 1984—. Fellow Am. Psychiat. Assn.; mem. Ala. Psychiat. Soc. (pres. 1993-94), Am. Acad. Psychaitry and Law, Med. Soc. Mobile County (bd. censors). Office: Neuropsychiat Assocs South PO Box 8309 Mobile AL 36689-0309

THOMAS, KENNETH ALFRED, JR., biochemist, researcher; b. Oklahoma City, Nov. 28, 1946; s. Kenneth Alfred and Nellymae (DeWitt) T.; m. Theresa Ellen Behrens, Dec. 1, 1973; children: Kenneth Arthur, Christopher Alfred, Katharine Ann. BS in Chemistry, U. Del., 1969; PhD in Biochemistry, Duke U., 1974. Postdoctoral fellow Duke U., Durham, N.C., 1974-75, NIH, Bethesda, Md., 1975-77, Washington U., St. Louis, 1977-79; sr. rsch. scientist Merck Sharp & Dohme, Rahway, N.J., 1979-83, rsch. fellow, 1983-86, assoc. dir., 1986-88, dir., 1988—; corr. Trends in Biochem. Scis., 1988-93; co-organizer Keystone (Colo.) Symposium on Fibroblast Growth Factors and Angiogenesis, 1991; speaker Heidelberg (Germany) U. 600th Anniversary Symposium, 1986, NIH 100th Anniversary Symposium, 1987; session chmn., speaker Max-Planck Inst., Munich, 1988. Mem. editl. bd. Jour. Biol. Chemistry, 1991—; contbr. articles to profl. jours., patentee purification and characterization of fibroblast growth factor and vascular endothelial growth factor. Mem. AAAS, Am. Soc. Biol. Chemists, Protein Chemistry Soc., Am. Chem. Soc., N.Y. Acad. Scis., Sigma Xi. Office: Merck Rsch Labs Rm 42-300 West Point PA 19486

THOMAS, LEELAMMA KOSHY, women's health care nurse; b. Kerala, Kozhencherry, India, Feb. 10, 1936; naturalized Am. citizen, 1977; d. V.T. and Kunjamma (Koruth) Koshy; m. C.A. Thomas, Oct. 26, 1967; children: Linda Thomas Mathew, Lucie Thomas, John Thomas. BS in Nursing with honors, Coll. Nursing, Delhi, 1960; MA, Karnatak U., Dharwar Karnataka, Mysore, 1968. RN, Punjab, India, Tex.; RNC. PHN operational rsch. Nat. Tuberculosis Inst., Banglore, Mysore State, India, 1960-67; lectr. nursing Armed Forces Med. Coll., Maharstra State, India, 1971—; nurse labor and delivery U. Tex. Med. Br., nurse infant spl. care unit, nursing care coord. obgyn; head nurse U. Tex. Med. Br., Galveston, 1980-92, nurse clinician IV women and infants, 1993—; clin. instr. U. Tex. Sch. Nursing, Galveston, 1982—; presenter in field. Contbr. articles to profl. jours. Sunday sch. tchr. First Bapt. Ch., Galveston, Tex., 1982—. Recipient U. Tex. Med. Br. Maternal Health Coun. award, 1984; Am. Women's scholar. Mem. Sigma Theta Tau. Office: U Tex Med Br Ob-Gyn Nursing Svc Galveston TX 77550 also: U Tex Sch Nursing Galveston TX 77550

THOMAS, LEONA MARLENE, health information educator; b. Rock Springs, Wyo., Jan. 15, 1933; d. Leonard H. and Opal (Wright) Francis; m. Craig L. Thomas, Feb. 22, 1955 (div. Sept. 1978); children: Peter, Paul, Patrick, Alexis. BA, Govs. State U., 1982, MHS, 1986; cert. med. records adminstrn., U. Colo., 1954. Dir. med. records dept. Meml. Hosp. Sweetwater County, Rock Springs, Wyo., 1954-57; staff assoc. Am. Med. Records Assn., Chgo., 1972-77, asst. editor, 1979-81; statistician Westlake Hosp., Melrose Park, Ill., 1982-84; asst. prof. Chgo. State U., 1984—, acting dir. health info. adminstrn. program, 1991-92; acting dir. health info. Internat. Coll., Naples, Fla., 1994; dir. health info. adminstrn. program Chgo. State U., 1994—; chairperson Coll. Allied Health Pers., 1986-88; mem. rev. bd. network Newsletter of Assembly on Edn. Co-pres. Ill. Dist. 60 PTA, Westmont; liaison Ill. Trauma Registry, 1991; mem. adv. com. Health Info. Tech. Program Morraine Valley Cmty. Coll., Palos Hills, Ill., 1995—, Health Info. Tech. Program Robert Morris Coll., Orland Pk., Ill., 1995—, Wellness Ctr., Chgo. State U. Mem. Assembly on Edn., Am. Health Info. Mgmt. Assn., Am. Pub. Health Assn., Ill. Pub. Health Assn., Chgo. and Vicinity Med. Records Assn. (publicity com. 1989-90), Ill. Assn. Allied Health Profls., Gov.'s State Alumni Assn. Democrat. Methodist. Home: 6340 Americana Dr Apt 1101 Clarendon Hills IL 60514-2249 Office: Chgo State U Coll Nursin & Allied Health 95th at King Dr Chicago IL 60628

THOMAS, LOWELL PHILLIP, retired psychologist; b. Miami, Fla., Dec. 2, 1933; s. Phillip David and Florence (Lavery) T.; m. Shirley Buck, June 23, 1956 (div. Jan. 1979); children: Susan, Sharon, Kimberly Robe; m. Stephanie Glory Baker, Mar. 1, 1981; children: Victoria, Geoffrey. BS in Zoology, U. Miami, 1955, MS in Marine Biology, 1960, PhD in Marine Biology, 1965; PhD Clin. Psychology, Va. Tech., 1986. Lic. psychologist, Fla. Various faculty positions including prof. marine sci. U. Miami, Fla., 1960-83; forensic psychologist State of Fla. Prison System, Lawtey, 1987-88, New River, 1988-89; psychologist North Fla. Evaluation and Treatment Ctr., Gainesville, 1989-90, Naples (Fla.) Community Hosp., 1990-92. Contbr. articles to profl. jours. NSF grantee, 1966-80. Home: 75 Mentor Dr Naples FL 33942-1353

THOMAS, MARIANNE GREGORY, school psychologist; b. N.Y.C., Dec. 10, 1945. BS, U. Conn., 1985; MS, So. Conn. State U., 1987. Cert. sch. psychologist, Conn., N.Y. Sch. psychology intern Greenwich (Conn.) Pub. Schs., 1986-87; sch. psychologist Hawthorne (N.Y.)-Cedar Knolls, U.F.S.D., 1987-88, Darien (Conn.) Pub. Schs., 1988—. Mem. AAUW, NASP (cert.), Conn. Assn. Sch. Psychologists. Home: 154 Indian Rock Rd New Canaan CT 06840-3117

THOMAS, MARJORIE OLIVIENE, health care administrator; b. Spaldings, Jamaica, Sept. 5; came to U.S., 1971; d. Cedrick Milo and Avis Clair (Morgan) West; m. Carol Oswald Thomas, Sept. 10, 1977. children: Chandra, Brian. AA, Kendall Coll., 1973; BS, U. Ill.-Chgo., 1975; MPA, Roosevelt U., 1977. Asst. to dir. utilization rev. Bellevue Hosp., N.Y.C., 1977-81, risk mgr., 1981-83, assoc. dir./dir. quality assurance, 1983-85; dir. risk mgmt. svcs. Adminstrs. for the Professions, Inc., Manhasset, N.Y., 1985-93, v.p. risk mgmt. and underwriting, 1993—. Fellow Am. Soc. for Healthcare Risk Mgmt.; mem. Assn. Hosp. Risk Mgmt. N.Y. Mem. Christ Temple. Avocations: reading, writing, traveling.

THOMAS, MARK ALFRED BOWKER, nephrologist; b. London, Sept. 20, 1955; arrived in Australia, 1957; s. Ian Davies and Joan Helen (Bowker) T.; m. Susan Patricia Hogbin, July 2, 1980; children: Amanda, Michael, Kathy. MB BS, U. Sydney, Australia, 1979. Jr. med. officer Sydney Hosp., 1979-82; renal registrar Royal North Shore Hosp., Sydney, 1983-84; renal rsch. fellow Guys Hosp., London, 1985-87; staff nephrologist Royal Perth (Australia) Hosp., 1988-93, head dept. nephrology, 1994—. Fellow Royal Australasian Coll. Physicians; mem. Internat. Soc. Nephrology, Australian and New Zealand Soc. Nephrology. Office: Royal Perth Hosp, Dept Nephrology PO Box 2213, Perth 6001, Australia

THOMAS, MARY ELLEN, critical care nurse; b. South Whitley, Ind., Nov. 12, 1931; d. Harry R. Bollinger and Winnie Joyce Reed; m. Jack G. Thomas, Jan. 28, 1956 (dec. Oct. 1958); 1 child, Robert David. RN, Ball State U., 1955; student, Manchester Coll., 1949-52; cert. in coronary care, Ind. U., Indpls., 1971. RN, Ind.; cert. ACLS, BLS, EMT, Ind.; cert. CCRN, AACN. Staff medical-surgical nurse Huntington (Ind.) County Hosp., 1955-56; staff nurse obstetrics and nursery Home Hosp., Lafayette, Ind., 1955-57; staff surgical nurse Ball Meml. Hosp., Muncie, Ind., 1957-58; nurse medical floor, floater Whitley County Meml. Hosp., Columbia City, Ind., 1959-71, CCU, ICU nurse, 1971—, IV team nurse, 1982-94; nursing-pharmacy liaison Whitley County Hosp., Columbia City; tchr. IV technique Whitley County EMS, Columbia City, 1980; presenter inservices Whitley County Hosp., 1990—; CPR instructor. Active Heartbeats Festival, Columbia City, 1989, Let's Talk CCU Whitley County Nurses Assn., Columbia City, 1994. Mem. AACN. Mem. Brethren Ch. Home: 3769W 800S South Whitley IN 46787 Office: Whitley County Meml. Hosp. 353 Oak St Columbia City IN 46725

THOMAS, NORVIN EUGENE, internist; b. Marshall, Mo., Apr. 25, 1945; s. Jesse Dale and Irene Bell (Johnson) T.; m. Eva Sue Gibbons, Jan. 22, 1967 (div. June 1979); children: Sean E., Tiffany Sue; m. Sandra Marie Rotter, June 15, 1979; 1 child, Christopher Dale. BA, U. Mo., 1973; DO Kansas City Coll. Osteo. Medicine, 1978. Diplomate Am. Bd. Internal Medicine; cert. in internal medicine, pulmonary medicine and critical care medicine. Intern Kansas City Coll. Osteo. medicine, 1978-79; resident internal medicine U. Mo., Kansas City, 1979-82; fellow in pulmonary and environ. medicine Harry S. Truman VA Hosp., Columbia, 1982-84; practice osteo. medicine specializing in internal medicine Audrain Med. Ctr., Mexico, Mo., 1984—, dir. cardiopulmonary dept., 1984—; asst. prof. dept. medicine U. Mo., Columbia, 1985—. Served with USN, 1966-70; capt. USAR (inactive). Nat. Cancer Inst. grantee, 1975. Fellow ACP, Am. Coll. Chest Physicians; mem. Mexico C. of C., Sigma Sigma Phi. Republican. Roman Catholic. Home: 1400 Briarwood Pl Mexico MO 65265-1068 Office: 209 E Jackson St Mexico MO 65265-2820

THOMAS, PATRICK ROBERT MAXWELL, oncology educator, academic administrator; b. Exmouth, Devon, Eng., Feb. 23, 1943; came to U.S., 1976; s. Christopher Codrington and Aileen Daphne (Gordon) T.; m. Linda Sharon Rich, June 23, 1986 (dec. 1987), m. Geraldine M. Jacobson, Mar. 2, 1996. Diploma in biochemistry, London U., 1965, MB, BS, 1968. Lectr. Inst. Cancer Rsch., London, 1974-76; assoc. chief clinician Roswell Park Meml. Inst., Buffalo, 1976-79; asst. prof. Washington U., St. Louis, 1979-83, assoc. prof., 1983-89, prof., 1989-90; prof., chmn. Temple U., Phila., 1991—; extramural bd. PDQ, Bethesda, Md., 1989—; mem. in-svc. exam. com. Am. Coll. Radiology, Reston, Va., 1990—; examiner Am. Bd. Radiology, Louisville, 1990—. Fellow Am. Coll. Radiologists, Royal Coll. Physicians of London. Home: 106 Pier Five 7 N Columbus Blvd Philadelphia PA 19106-1422 Office: Temple U 3401 N Broad St Philadelphia PA 19140-5103

THOMAS, PAUL LOUIS, health services administrator; b. Hollis, N.Y., Feb. 28, 1950; s. Paul J. and Rita A. (Sheld) T.; m. Elizabeth A. O'Neil, Sept. 24, 1977; children: Alexander, Cassandra, Andrea. BSBA, Calif. State U., San Luis Obispo, 1972; M in Health Care Adminstrn., Va. Commonwealth U., 1983. Commd. 2d lt. USAF, 1973, advanced through grades to lt. col., 1990, ret., 1993; provider rels./network devel. MetLife Healthcare Corp., Richmond, Va., 1994-95; exec. dir. S.W. Ga. Healthcare Assn., Inc., Americus, Ga., 1995—; mem. Nat. Disaster Med. Sys. Adv. Bd., Washington, 1987-91. Recipient Sr. Health Policy fellowship Air Force Inst. Tech. and Am. Hosp. Assn., 1986-87, Cert. of Appreciation, Sec. Dept. Health and Human Svcs., 1990. Fellow Am. Coll. Healthcare Execs. (chmn. recruitment subcom./membership com. 1992-93); mem. Assn. Mil. Surgeons of U.S. (life), Am. Hosp. Assn., Ga. Soc. for Managed Care, Americus/Sumter County C. of C. Office: SW Ga Healthcare Assn Inc The Windsor Hotel 125 W Lamar St 4th Flr Americus GA 31709

THOMAS, PETER CHARLES, psychologist, educator; b. Houston, Sept. 24, 1947; s. Stephen and Eileen S. (Steyn) T.; m. Beverly J. Call, Aug. 30, 1969; children: Jonathan, Stephen, Katherine. BA in Psychology, Emory U., 1969; MEd in Sch. Psychology, Ga. State U., 1970, PhD in Sch. Psychology, 1978. Instr. Ga. State U., Atlanta, 1970-72; cons. Ga. Dept. Edn., Atlanta, 1972-73; field coord. U.S. Office Edn.: Exemplary Racial Discrimation Project, N.C., 1974; psychologist Dekalb County Sch. System, Atlanta, 1973-82; pvt. practice Atlanta, 1982—; cons. Decatur City Sch. Sys., 1982-86, Ga. Spl. Olympics Program, Atlanta, 1987, Fulton County Sch. Sys., 1984—; mem. adv. bd. Village of St. Joseph, Gables Acad., 1981-94, AIDS and Drug adv. bd. Met. Regional Ednl. Svc. Agy., Atlanta, The Howard Schs. Bd. dirs. Briarcliff Woods Civic Assn., Atlanta, 1982-84, North Atlanta Parents Coun., 1990—, Profl. Acad. Custody Evaluators, Doylestown Borough, Pa., 1993—; bd. dirs., pres. Briarcliff Woods Beach Club, Atlanta, 1980-82, 85-87. Recipient Service award Down Syndrome Assn. of Atlanta, 1986. Fellow Ga. Psychol. Assn. (Div. G chmn. 1985-87, Cert. of Merit for Outstanding Contbn. to Profession of Psychology, 1987); mem. APA, Nat. Acad. Neuropsychology, Soc. Personality Assessment, Assn. Children with Learning Disabilities, Ga. Assn. Sch. Psychologists (bd. mem. 1982-83). Home: 1821 Morris Landers Dr NE Atlanta GA 30345-4103 Office: 2900 Paces Ferry Rd NW C100 Atlanta GA 30339-5702

THOMAS, R. RUSSELL, JR., osteopath; b. Fort Worth, Aug. 27, 1953; s. Raymond Russell and Elfe-Luise (Martin) T.; m. Robin Joan Engstrom, June 26, 1976; children: Russell Barrett, Jacqueline Joan. BA, U. Tex., 1975; MPH, U. Tex., Houston, 1976; DO, Tex. Coll. Osteo. Medicine, 1980. Pvt. practice Eagle Lake, Tex., 1983—; med. dir. One Care-Thomas Clinic, Eagle Lake, 1995—; chief staff Rice Dist. Hosp., Eagle Lake, 1994-96. Active Tex. Trauma Tech. Adv., Austin, 1990-93. Grantee Ctr. for Rural Health Initiatives, 1992. Fellow Am. Acad. Family Physicians; mem. Tex. Acad. Family Physicians (dir. 19956), Tex. State Bd. Med. Examiners (v.p. 1995). Episcopalian. Office: Thomas Clinic 610 S Austin Rd Eagle Lake TX 77434

THOMAS, RICHARD JOSEPH, preventive and occupational medicine physician; b. Methuen, Mass., May 7, 1953; s. Frederic Joseph and Evelyn Margaret (McNiece) T.; m. Anne Lee Fitzhugh Dierdorff; children: James George, Ross Joseph. BS, U.S. Naval Hosp., Annapolis, Md., 1975; MD, Georgetown U., 1979; MPH, Johns Hopkins U., 1984. Diplomate Am. Bd. Med. Examiners, Am. Bd. Preventive Medicine in Occupl. Medicine, Am. Bd. Preventive Medicine in Pub. Health and Gen. Preventive Medicine; lic. MD, Va., Md. Intern U.S. Navy Regional Med. Ctr., Oakland, Calif., 1979-80; med. officer USS Guam, Norfolk, Va., 1980-81, Navy Regional Med. Ctr., Portsmouth, Va., 1981-82; med. officer Navy Environ. Health Ctr. Navy Environ. Health Ctr., Norfolk, Va., 1982-83, occupl. medicine physician, 1989-91; dep. dir. occupl. health Navy Environ. Health Ctr., 1991-92; resident in preventive medicine Johns Hopkins U., Balt., 1983-84; resident in occupl. medicine Johns Hopkins U., 1984-85; resident in preventive medicine Walter Reed Army Inst. Rsch., Washington, 1985-86; epidemiologist occupl. epidemiology divsn. Navy Environ. and Preventive Medicine Unit #6, Pearl Harbor, Hawaii, 1986-89; preventive medicine officer USNS Mercy, The Philippines and S. Pacific, 1987; preventive medicine officer, occupl. medicine physician III Marine Expeditionary Force and Naval Hosp., Okinawa, Japan, 1992-95; officer in charge Navy Environ. and Preventive Medicine Unit #2, Norfolk, 1995—; mem. adv. com. preventive medicine residency program Johns Hopkins Sch. Pub. Health, Balt., 1983-84; alt. mem. adv. com. preventive medicine residency program U. Hawaii Sch. Pub. Health, Honolulu, 1986-88, pres., 1988-89; mem. conf. planning com. Va. Occupl. Health Ea. Va. Med. Sch., Norfolk, 1991; mem. med. surveillance working group Dept. Def., Bethesda, Md., 1990-92, 95—; mem. Navy Epidemiology Bd., Norfolk, 1990-92. Co-author: Neuroepidemiology Theory and Method, 1993; contbr. articles to profl. jours. Scout leader Boy Scouts Am., Williamsburg, Va., 1989-92, 95—, Okinawa, 1992-95; vol. Internat. Red Cross, Okinawa, 1992-95. Capt. USN, 1975-95. Recipient Meritorious Svc. medal USN, 1989, 92. Fellow Am. Coll. Occupl. and Environ. Medicine; mem. Assn. Mil. Surgeons U.S., U.S. Naval Inst., Okinawa Med. Soc. (mil. chpt., sec.-treas. 1992-95), Va. Occupl. Med. Assn., Johns Hopkins Med. and Surg. Assn. Office: Navy Environ and Preventive Medicine Unit #2 1887 Powhatan St Norfolk VA 23511-3394

THOMAS, ROBERT JAMES, biology educator; b. Flint, Mich., July 5, 1949; s. Allan James and Ruth Pauline (Brandt) T. B.A. in Biology, U. Mich.-Flint, 1971; Ph.D. in Biology, U. Calif.-Santa Cruz, 1975. Asst. prof. biology Bates Coll., Lewiston, Maine, 1975-88, prof., 1988, chmn. dept., 1983-94 . Contbr. numerous articles to sci. jours. NSF research grantee, 1985—. Mem. Bot. Soc. Am., Am. Soc. Plant Physiology, Am. Bryological and Lichenlogical Soc. (sec., treas. 1994—). Avocations: folk music; nature photography; hiking. Office: Biology Dept Bates Coll Lewiston ME 04240

THOMAS, ROBERT MURRAY, educational psychology educator; b. Cheyenne, Wyo., July 28, 1921; s. Robert MacDonald and Elizabeth (Carson) T.; m. Shirley Louise Moore, July 3, 1948; children: Robert Gilmour, Kathryn Elizabeth. A.B., Colo. State Coll., 1943, M.A., 1944; Ph.D., Stanford U., 1950. Tchr. Kamehameha Schs., Honolulu, 1944-45; Tchr. Mid-Pacific Inst., Honolulu, 1945-47; instr. San Francisco State Coll., 1949-50; prof. State U. Coll., Brockport, N.Y., 1950-58, Padjadjaran (Indonesia) U., 1958-61, 64-65; prof. ednl. psychology U. Calif. at Santa Barbara, 1961-64, 69-91, prof. emeritus ednl. psychology, 1992—; dean U. Calif. at Santa Barbara (Grad. Sch.), 1965-69. Author: Judging Student Progress, 2d edit, 1960, Ways of Teaching, 1955, Integrated Teaching Materials, 2d edit, 1963, Individual Differences in the Classroom, 1965, Social Differences in the Classroom, 1965, Aiding the Maladjusted Pupil, 1967, A Chronicle of Indonesian Higher Education, 1973, Comparing Theories of Child Development, 1979, 4th edit., 1996, Japanese edit., 1985, Education in American Samoa-1700 to 1980, 1987, The Puzzle of Learning Difficulties-Applying a Diagnostic and Treatment Model, 1989, Counseling and Life-span Development, 1990, Classifying Reactions to Wrongdoing, 1995, An Integrated Theory of Moral Development, 1996, and numerous others; editor: Strategies for Curriculum Change: Cases from 13 Nations, 1968, Politics and Education: Cases from 11 Nations, 1983, Ency. of Human Development and Education, 1990, International Comparative Education, 1990, Education's Role in National Development Plans, 1992; co-author: Decisions in Teaching Elementary Social Studies, 1971, Curriculum Patterns in Elementary Social Studies, 1971, Penggunaan Statistik Dalam Ilmu Pengetahuan Sosial, 1971, Teaching Elementary Social Studies: Readings, 1972, Indonesian Education: An Annotated Bibliography, 1973, Social Strata in Indonesia, 1975, Political Style and Education Law in Indonesia, 1980, Schooling in the ASEAN Region, 1980, Schooling in East Asia, 1983, Schooling in the Pacific Islands, 1984, Die Entwicklung des Kindes, 1986, Educational Technology, 1987, Oriental Theories of Human Development, 1988, What Wrongdoers Deserve, 1993, Etude Comparée des Théories du Dévelopment de l'Enfant, 1994, Prevent, Repent, Reform, Revenge, 1995. Home: 1436 Los Encinas Dr Los Osos CA 93402-4520

THOMAS, STEVEN CLARK, surgeon; b. Salt Lake City, Sept. 27, 1955; s. E. Parry and Peggy Marie (Chatterton) T.; m. Karen Darlene Parker, Dec. 19, 1977; children: Sierra Juel, Corin Marie, Elina Parry. BA in Finance, U. Utah, 1979; MD, Johns Hopkins U., 1984. Resident in orthopaedic surgery U. Wash., Seattle, 1985-89, fellow in shoulder and elbow svc., 1989; pvt. practice Las Vegas, 1990—. Contbr. chpts. to books. Missionary LDS Ch., Lisbon, 1975-77; explorer scout post leader Boy Scouts Am., Las Vegas, 1995—. Alpha Kappa Psi scholar U. Utah, 1979. Mem. Nev. State Med. Assn., Clark County Med. Soc., Pres. Assocs. U. Nev. Las Vegas. Republican.

THOMAS, TERESA ANN, microbiologist, educator; b. Wilkes-Barre, Pa., Oct. 17, 1939; d. Sam Charles and Edna Grace T. BS cum laude, Coll. Misericordia, 1961; MS in Biology, Am. U. Beirut, 1965; MS in Microbiology, U. So. Calif., 1973. Tchr., sci. supr., curriculum coord. Meyers High Sch., Wilkes-Barre, 1962-64, Wilkes-Barre Area Public Schs., 1961-66; rsch. assoc. Proctor Found. for Rsch. in Ophthalmology U. Calif. Med. Ctr., San Francisco, 1966-68; instr. Robert Coll. of Istanbul (Turkey), 1968-71, Am. Edn. in Luxembourg, 1971-72, Bosco Tech. Inst., Rosemead, Calif., 1973-74, San Diego Community Coll. Dist., 1974-80; prof. math., sci. and engring. div. Southwestern Coll., Chula Vista, Calif., 1980—, pres. acad. senate, 1984-85, del., 1986-89; chmn., coord., steering com. project Cultural Rsch. Educational and Trade Exchange, 1991—, Southwestern Coll.-Shanghai Inst. Fgn. Trade; coord. Southwestern Coll. Great Teaching Seminar, 1987, 88, 89, coord. scholars program, 1988-90; mem. exec. com. Acad. Senate for Calif. C.Cs., 1985-86, Chancellor of Calif. C.Cs. Adv. and Rev. Council Fund for Instrnl. Improvement, 1984-86; co-project dir. statewide, coord. So. Calif. Biotech Edn. Consortium, 1993-95, steering com., 1993—; adj. asst. prof. Chapman Coll., San Diego, 1974-83; asst. prof. San Diego State U., 1977-79; chmn. Am. Colls. Istanbul Sci. Week, 1969-71; mem. adv. bd. Chapman Coll. Community Center, 1979-80; cons. sci. curriculum Calif. Dept. Edn., 1986—; pres. Internat. Relations Club 1959-61; mem. San Francisco World Affairs Coun., 1966-68, San Diego World Affairs Coun., 1992—; v.p. Palomar Palace Estates Home Owners Assn., 1983-85, pres. 1994—. mem. editorial rev. bd. Jour. of Coll. Sci. Teaching, NSTA, 1988-92; bd. dirs. San Diego-Leon Sister Cities Soc., 1991-94. Mem. Chula Vista Nature Interpretive Ctr. (life), Internat. Friendship Commn., Chula Vista, 1985—, vice chmn. 1989-90, chmn. 1990-92, Chula Vista, Calif., 1987-95; mem. U.S.-Mex. Sister Cities Assn., nat. bd. dirs., 1992-94, gen. chair 30th nat. conv., 1993; mem. City of Chula Vista Resource Conservation Commn., 1996—. NSF fellow, 1965; USPHS fellow, 1972-73; recipient Nat. Teaching Excellence award Nat. Inst. Staff and Orgnl. Devel., 1989; recognized at Internat. Conf. Teaching Excellence, Austin, 1989; Pa. Heart Assn. research grantee, 1962; named Southwestern Coll. Woman of Distinction, 1987. Mem. Am. Soc. Microbiology (So. Calif. Microbe Discovery Team 1995—), Nat. Sci. Tchrs. Assn. (life, internat. com., coord. internat. honors exchange lectr. competition sponsored with Assn. Sci Educators Great Britain, 1986), Nat. Assn. Biology Tchrs. (life), Soc. Coll. Sci. Tchrs. (life), S.D. Zool. Soc., Calif. Tchrs. Assn., NEA, Am. Assn. Community and Jr. Colls., Giraffes, Am.-Lebanese Assn. San Diego (chmn. scholarship com., pres. 1988-93), Am. U. of Beirut Alumni and Friends of San Diego (1st v.p. 1984-91), Lions Internat. (bull. editor 1991-93, best bull. award 1992, 93, 2nd v.p. 1992-93, 1st v.p. 1993-94, editor Roaring Times Newsletter 1993-94, chmn. dist. internat. rels. and cooperations com. 1993-95, pres. SW San Diego County chpt. 1994-95), Chula Vista-Odawara (Japan) Sister Cities Assn. (founding pres. 1995—), Kappa Gamma Pi (pres. Wilkes-Barre chpt. 1963-64, San Francisco chpt. 1967-68), Sigma Phi Sigma, Phi Theta Kappa (hon. mem. 1994—), Alpha Pi Epsilon (advisor Southwestern Coll. chpt. 1989-90, Am. Lebanese Syrian Ladies Club (pres. 1982-83). Office: Southwestern Coll 900 Otay Lakes Rd Chula Vista CA 91910-7223

THOMAS, WALTER HUGH TYRYNIS, surgeon; b. Llanelli, Wales, Dec. 20, 1935; s. Thomas Pegegrine Tyrynis and Irene Mary (Bowen) T.; m. Joann Marjorie Richards, Nov. 7, 1960; children: Owen Robert Tyrynis, Sian Catherine Tyrynis, Joana Angharad Tyrynis, Rhiannon Tyrynis. MBBS, St. Mary's Hosp., London, 1960; MD, Yale U., 1967. Rsch. fellow Hahnemann Hosp., Phila., 1964-65; sr. registrar MHS, London, 1965-66; rsch. assoc. Inst. Surgery Yale U., New Haven, 1966-68; con. surgeon St. Catherine's, Ont., Can., 1967-70; con. surgeon British Armed Forces, Berlin, 1970-76, Belfast, No. Ireland, 1974-78; con. surgeon MHS, Cardiff, Wales, 1978—; clin. tutor Med. Sch. Cardiff U., 1978. Author: The Murder of Rudolf Hess, 1978, Hess-A Tale of Two Murders, 1987, Doppelgangers, 1995. Col. Royal Air Med. Corps, 1970-78. Recipient Wallace Meml. medal Wright Fleming Inst. Fellow Royal Coll. Surgeons. Home: Muriau Cadarn Llan-Talyllyw, Breton LD3 7T9, Wales Office: Prince Charles Hosp, Merthyr Tydful, Glamorgan Wales

THOMAS, WILLIAM ORVILL, JR., retired obstetrician, gynecologist; b. Clinton, Wis., May 7, 1914; s. William Orvill and Eulah Mable (Howard) T.; m. Dorothy Mae Streedbeck, Aug. 18, 1941; children—William Orvill III, David Howard. Grad., Phillips Exeter Acad., 1933; A.B., Dartmouth Coll., 1937; M.D., Harvard U., 1941. Diplomate: Am. Bd. Ob-Gyn. Intern in surgery Boston City Hosp., 1941-42; intern Boston Lying-In Hosp., 1943-44, resident in obstetrics, 1947; asst. resident in gynecology Free Hosp. for Women, Brookline, Mass., 1942-43; asst. resident in pathology Free Hosp. for Women, 1947, resident in gynecology, 1948; clin. instr. ob-gyn U. Oreg., Portland, 1949-56; asso. clin. prof. U. Oreg., 1956-79, clin. prof., 1979—; active staff Emanuel Hosp., Portland, 1950—; courtesy staff Holladay Park Hosp., Portland, 1974—, St. Vincent's Hosp., 1976—, Providence Hosp., 1980—. Contbr. articles to profl. jours. Served to lt. M.C. USNR, 1944-46. Decorated Purple Heart. Fellow Am. Coll. Ob-Gyn (sec.-treas. dist. 1960-63, dist. chmn. 1969-72, nat. 2d v.p. 1975), A.C.S. (adv. council ob-gyn. 1972-76); mem. Pacific Coast Ob-Gyn Soc., Pacific NW Ob-Gyn Assn. (pres. 1973), Oreg. Soc. Obstetricians and Gynecologists (pres. 1958-59), Portland Soc. Obstetricians and Gynecologists (pres. 1964-65), Portland Planned Parenthood Assn., Assn. Planned Parenthood Physicians, AMA, Multnomah County Med. Assn., Oreg. Med. Soc., Am. Soc. Gynecol. Laparoscopists. Home: 2712 NE Regents Dr Portland OR 97212-1658

THOMASHOW, BYRON MARTIN, pulmonary physician; b. Bklyn., Apr. 19, 1949; s. Alexander Irwin and Emma (Zaslow) T.; m. Laurie Jo Kasoff, July 2, 1972; children: Samantha, Michael. BA, Columbia U., 1970, MD, 1974. Diplomate Nat. Bd. Med. Examiners, Am. Bd. Internal Medicine, subspecialty in pulmonary medicine. Med. intern Roosevelt Hosp., N.Y.C., 1974-75, med. resident, 1975-77, med. chief resident, pulmonary fellow, 1977-78; sr. pulmonary fellow Harlem Hosp., N.Y.C., 1978-79; asst. attending physician Presbyn. Hosp., Columbia Presbyn. Med. Ctr., N.Y.C., 1979-90, assoc. attending physician, 1991—; physician in charge Tbc Clinic Presbyn. Hosp., N.Y.C., 1983-90, attending physician Chest Clinic, 1979—; asst. prof. clin. medicine Columbia U., N.Y.C., 1979-90, assoc. clin. prof. medicine, 1990—; lectr. Englewood Hosp., 1988, ACP, 1986-92, Harlem Hosp., 1984, 93, Roosevelt Hosp., 1978, 86, 87, 88, 91, Columbia Presbyn. Hosp., 1980, 82-88, 90, 92, 93, 94, 95, 96, N.Y. Trudeau Soc., 1982, Columbia U. Coll. Physicians and Surgeons, 1980-96, Med. House staff Pulmonary Bd. Rev., 1980—, Emergency Med. Course, 1981—; mem. Presbyn. Hosp. Med. Bd., 1995—; mem. exec. com. Soc. of Practitioners Columbia Presbyn. Med. Ctr., 1993—; chmn. quality care com. Soc. of Practitioners, 1994—; med. co-dir. emphysema lung reduction program Columbia Presbyn. Med. Ctr., 1995—. Stony Wold-Herbert Fund fellowship grantee, 1978-79. Fellow ACP, Am. Coll. Chest Physicians; mem. Am. Thoracic Soc., N.Y. Trudeau Soc. (exec. com. 1992-94, chmn. membership com. 1992-94), Soc. Practitioners (exec. com. 1994—, chmn. quality care com. 1995—). Office: 161 Fort Washington Ave New York NY 10032-3713

THOMAS-MOSS, VIVIAN CAROL, physician associate; b. Titusville, Fla., Feb. 27, 1947; d. Wesley Lee and Mildred E. (Hazzard) Campbell; m. Ira Eric Moss, May 24, 1969 (div. Sept. 1977); children: Eric, Jamal, Olivia; m. Eugene Thomas, Sept. 21, 1988; 1 child, Tracy. BS, New Sch. for Social Rsch.; postgrad., Fordham U., Queens Coll. Fed. women's mgr. Met. Corr. Ctr., N.Y.C., 1977-87, physician's asst., 1977-87, asst. hosp. adminstr., 1983-84; mental retardation profl. Washington Square Behavioral Pro Specialist, Titusville, Fla., 1989-93; FEEA/NUSA rep. Orlando, Fla., 1991; exec. dir. Word of Life, Inc., Titusville, 1992, founder, pastor, 1992—; treas. Precious Space Coast chpt., Titusville, 1995-96; mem. PA/RN Orgn., India Atlantic, Fla., 1991—. Rep. Nat. United Svc., Washington, 1990-92, Fed. Edn. Employment Assn., Washington, 1990—. Home: 1660 Rice Ave Titusville FL 32796

THOMASON, PAULA SUE, medical and surgical nurse; b. Cuyahoga Falls, Ohio, Aug. 11, 1953; d. Herman Vincent and Mary Alice (Weigand). Diploma, Mercy Sch. Nursing, Canton, Ohio, 1974. RN, Ohio; cert. med.-legal nurse cons. Organizer, head skin care com. med. telemetry fl. Cuyahoga Falls (Ohio) Gen. Hosp. Preceptor Stark Tech. Coll. Nursing, Canton. Recipient Excellence in Nursing 1995 award. Mem. ANA (cert. med.-surg. nurse), Assn. Advancement Wound Care. Home: 3804 Eakins Rd Cuyahoga Falls OH 44223-2620

THOMAS-SANCHEZ, AMY LEE, nurse; b. Davenport, Iowa, Mar. 15, 1955; d. Raymond Milton Jr. and Doris May (Johnston) Thomas; m. Manuel Frank Sanchez, Apr. 29, 1983; 1 child, Raymond Daniel. AA, Ill. Cen. Coll., 1976; AS, U. Albuquerque, 1979. RN, N.Mex. Staff nurse Presbyn. Hosp., Albuquerque, 1979, staff nurse, rehab. nurse for brain damaged babies newborn nursery, 1981-84; staff nurse U. N.Mex. Hosp., Albuquerque, 1980-81; charge nurse, emergency coord. LaVida Llena Retirement Ctr., Albuquerque, 1984; maternity nurse Heights Gen. Hosp., Albuquerque, 1984-87; cons. nursing Neuro Infant Rehab. and Stimulation, Albuquerque, 1985—; pediatrics nurse Carrie Tingley Hosp., Albuquerque, 1989-91; maternity nurse U. N.Mex. Hosp., Albuquerque, 1991-94; staff nurse Transition Hosp. Corp., Albuquerque, 1995-96, Prudental Healthcare Precerto, 1996—; instr. childbirth maternal and infant project U. N.Mex., Albuquerque, 1987-88. Playwright Whose Child is This, 1986; songwriter The Unmailed Letter; author poems. Arranger, tenor Thomas Family Singers, 1974—; poet, co-arranger Gospel Chapel Radio Ministries, 1980—; mem. Resolve Through Sharing. Mem. Assn. Rehab. Nurses, Gospel Music Assn., Alpha Mu Gamma. Republican. Mem. Assembly of God. Home: 6705 Carney NW Albuquerque NM 87120 Office: Neuro Infant Rehab Stimulation PO Box 27157 Albuquerque NM 87125-7157

THOMASSEN, PAULINE F., medical, surgical nurse; b. Cleve., Jan. 19, 1939; d. Henry Clifford and Mabel Pauline (Hill) Nichols; m. Ruben Thomassen, Nov. 10, 1979; children: Rhonda, Terry, Diana, Philipp, Jody, Barbara. AA in Nursing, So. Colo. State Coll., 1974, BA in Psychology with distinction, 1975; BSN magna cum laude, Seattle Pacific U., 1986. RN, Wash. Staff nurse III orthopedic unit, preceptor orientation RNs and student RNs Swedish Hosp. Med. Ctr., Seattle, 1975—; mem. planning task force and faculty National Nurses Conference, The Nurse and Spinal Surgery, Cleve. Author: Spinal Disease and Surgical Interventions. Mem. Nat. Assn. Orthop. Nurses.

THOMLEY MILES, WESLEY, urologist; b. Calgary, Alberta, Can., Mar. 24, 1915; s. Gustave M. and Ruth R. (Ludwick) T.; m. Elizabeth Johnson, Nov. 19, 1941; children: Alan, Julia, Karen. BS, U. Wis., 1937, MD, 1941. Diplomate Am. Bd. Urology. Maj. U.S. Army, 1942-46, ETO. Fellow Am. Coll. Surgeons, Am. Urol. Assn.; mem. Fla. Urol. Soc. Republican. Home: 1711 Turnberry Cir Orlando FL 32804

THOMM, MICHAEL WOLFGANG, microbiologist; b. Bad Reichenhall Bayern, Oberbayern, Germany, Jan. 29, 1951; s. Friedrich and Elisabeth Maria (Schöller) T. Diploma biology, U. Munich, 1980; PhD, U. Regensburg (Germany), 1983. Postdoctoral fellow U. Regensburg, 1983-88, dozent, 1988-91; prof. microbiology U. Kiel, Germany, 1991—. Mem. AAAS, Vereinigung Allgemeine und Angewandte Mikrobiologie, Am. Soc. Microbiology. Office: U Kiel, Am Botanischen Garten 1-9, 24118 Kiel, Schleswig-Holstein Germany

THOMPSON, ALVIN J., internist; b. Washington, 1924; m. Faye Thompson; children—Michael, Donna, Kevin, Susan, Gail. MD, Howard U., 1946. Diplomate Am. Bd. Internal Medicine. Intern St. Louis City Hosp. (Phillips), 1946-47, resident, 1947-51; pvt. practice medicine specializing in internal medicine, gastroenterology, 1957—; mem. attending staff Providence Hosp., Swedish Hosp. Med. Ctr.; attending physician VA Hosp., Univ. Hosp., Harborview Med. Ctr.; founder, dir. Gastroenterology Lab. Providence Hosp., Seattle, 1963-77, chief of medicine, 1972-74, pres. med. staff, 1970-71, hosp. trustee, 1974-75; clin. prof. U. Wash. Sch. of Medicine, Seattle, 1972—; physician, gastroenterologist VA, Seattle, 1953-57; bd. dirs. Puget Sound Health Planning Bd., 1974-76, Puget Sound Health Systems Agy., 1974; v.p., acting pres. King County Comprehensive Health Planning Council, 1973; mem. Nat. Commn. Corretional Health Care, 1987—; trustee King County Blue Shield, 1972-74, Northwest Kidney Ctr., 1981—, Hospice of Seattle, 1987—; mem. Wash. State Profl. Services Rev. Orgn. and PRO/W, 1982—; mem. community medicine study group for health care needs of the poor U. Wash. Sch. of Pub. Health and Community Medicine, 1982—; mem. Wash. State Health Coordinating Council, 1979—, Gov.'s Task Force on Health Planning, 1982—, Gov.'s Task Force on the Costs of Med. Care, 1983—, Nat. Commn. on Correctional Health Care, 1987—; mem. vis. com. Schs. of Nursing and Social Work U. Wash. Editorial bd. Jour. Jail and Prison Health; contbr. articles to Archives of Internal Medicine, Northwest Medicine, other profl. jours. Pres. bd. dirs. East Madison YMCA, 1956; trustee Seattle Urban League, 1958-59, Seattle Goodwill Industries, 1986—, Providence Med. Ctr. Found., Travelers Aid Soc., 1960-64, Civic Unity Com., 1960-64, Anti-Tb League, 1961-62, Hospice of Seattle, 1987—; mem. vestry Christ Ch., Seattle, 1958-60; mem. Emmanuel Ch., Mercer Island, 1963—; treas. Boy Scout Troop 451, Mercer Island, 1965-68; mem. Fair Housing Com. City of Mercer Island, 1961—; mem. and cast Gilbert and Sullivan Soc., 1954-57; trustee Seattle Ballet Assn., 1968-69; mem. adv. com., chmn. human services com. Salvation Army, 1979-82, also mem. lay bd.; co-chmn. King County Medic I Com., 1979; mem., trustee Pacific Sci. Ctr. Found., 1980—; vis. com. U. Wash. Sch. Social Work, 1985—. Apptd. U.S. Naval Acad., 1940; chief med. service U.S. Air Force, Ramey AFB Hosp., 1951-53; served to maj. USAFR, 1953-59. Recipient Kappa Cup for Superior Scholarship Howard U., 1941; Robert H. Williams Superior Leadership award Seattle Acad. Internal Medicine, 1979; award Seattle C. of C., 1983; award for Outstanding Contbns. in Health Nat. Assn. Med. Minority Educators, 1983; named Philanthropist of Yr. Washington Gives, 1989. Mem. AMA (del. 1980—), NAS, ACP (Wash. and Alaska ,gov. 1974-78), Wash. State Med. Assn. (trustee 1969-70, pres. 1977-78, past. pres., chmn. exec. com. 1978-79), Wash. State Soc. Internal Medicine (ASIM del. 1969-70, pres. 1970-71), King County Med. Soc. (del. 1969-71, trustee 1969-71, pres. 1974), Seattle Acad. Internal Medicine (sec.-treas. 1970-71, pres. 1972-73), ACP, Am. Gastroenterologic Assn., Am. Soc. for Gastrointestinal Endoscopy, North Pacific Soc. Internal Medicine, Am. Soc. Internal Medicine, Nat. Med. Assn., Inst. of Medicine, Wash. State Assn. Biomed. Rsch. (pres. 1988—), , Wash. State Assn. Black Profls. in Health Care (chmn. 1980—), Seattle C. of C. (mem. health care policy com. 1976-79), NAACP (life). Lodge: Rotary (Seattle). *

THOMPSON, ARLENE RITA, nursing educator; b. Yakima, Wash., May 17, 1933; d. Paul James and Esther Margaret (Danroth) T. BS in Nursing, U. Wash., 1966, Masters in Nursing, 1970, postgrad., 1982—. Staff nurse Univ. Teaching Hosp., Seattle, 1966-69; mem. nursing faculty U. Wash. Sch. Nurses, Seattle, 1971-73; critical care nurse Virginia Mason Hosp., Seattle, 1973—; educator Seattle Pacific U. Sch. Nursing, 1981—; nurse legal cons. nursing edn., critical care nurse. Contbr. articles to profl. jours. USPHS grantee, 1969; nursing scholar Virginia Mason Hosp., 1965. Mem. Am. Assn. Critical Care Nurses (cert.), Am. Nurses Assn., Am. Heart Assn., Nat. League Nursing, Sigma Theta Tau, Alpha Tau Omega. Republican. Presbyterian. Home: 2320 W Newton St Seattle WA 98199-4115 Office: Seattle Pacific U 3307 3rd Ave W Seattle WA 98119-1940

THOMPSON, CAROLYN WYNELLE, psychologist, behavioral healthcare executive; b. Birmingham, Ala., Oct. 15, 1939; d. Davis Hunt and Margaret Wynelle (Doggett) T.; m. James Robbin Cochrane (div.). BA, Emory U., 1961; MA, U. Chgo., 1963, PhD, 1968. Lic. psychologist, 1971; diplomate in clin. psychology Am. Bd. Profl. Psychology. Postdoctoral student Gestalt Inst., Chgo., 1970-73; counselor U. Chgo., 1968; acting dir. Am. Inst. for Rsch., Chgo., 1970-71; asst. prof. DePaul U., Chgo., 1968-72; dir. psychol. svcs. Family Svc. Ctrs., Flossmoor, Ill., 1972-78; pres., CEO Family Svc. Ctrs., Matteson, Ill., 1978—; comm. prof. Govs. State U., University Park, Ill., 1973, 75, 76; cons. Met. Sanitary Dist. Chgo., 1969; bd. dirs. Great Lakes Fin. Resources, Inc., First Nat. Bank Blue Island. Contbr. articles to profl. jours. Mem. Ill. Assn. Cmty. Mental Health Agys. (pres. 1994-95, bd. dirs. 1991-95), Rotary Club Chicago Heights. Home: 565 Aberdeen Dr Crete IL 60417-1202 Office: Family Svcs Ctrs 19530 Kedzie Flossmoor IL 60422

THOMPSON, CHARLES WESLEY, oral surgeon; b. Bladenboro, N.C., Dec. 21, 1925; s. Frederick Weaver and Cecile Agnes (LeQueux) T.; m. Virginia Lee Vogt, June 12, 1954; children: Charles Wesley Jr., Paula Suzanne Thompson Collins, William Frederick. MD, Emory U., 1952. Diplomate Am. Bd. Oral and Maxillofacial Surgery. Pvr. practice gen. dentistry Decatur, Ga., 1952-53; pvt. practice Atlanta, 1956-95; instr. oral surgery Emory Sch. Dentistry, Atlanta, 1956-80, Grady Meml. Hosp., Atlanta, 1956-82. Mem. adv. bd. Fulton County div. Am. Cancer Soc., Atlanta, 1985--86; elder Mt. Paran Ch. of God, Atlanta, 1960-91. With USN, 1943-46. Fellow Am. Assn. Oral Surgeons; mem. ADA (life), Ga. Dental Assn. (life), No. Dist. Dental Soc. (life), S.E. Soc. Oral Surgeons. Republican. Home: 525 Cameron Manor Way NW Atlanta GA 30328-6202 Office: 1136 Cleveland Ave Atlanta GA 30344-3618

THOMPSON, CHARLOTTE ELLIS, pediatrician, educator, author; b. Sept. 5, 1928; d. Robert and Ann Ellis; divorced; children: Jennifer Ann, Geoffrey Graeme. BA, Stanford U., 1950, MD, 1954. Diplomate Am. Bd. Pediat. Intern Children's Hosp., San Francisco, 1953-54; resident UCLA, 1960-61, L.A. Children's Hosp., 1962-63; pvt. practice La Jolla, Calif., 1963-75; dir. Muscle Disease Clinic, Univ. Hosp.-U. Calif. Sch. Medicine, San Diego, 1969-80, asst. clin. prof. pediat., 1969—; dir. Ctr. for Handicapped Children and Teenagers, San Francisco, 1981—; cons. U.S. Naval Hosp., San Diego, 1970-91; dep. dir. Santa Clara County Child Health and Disability, Santa Clara, Calif., 1974-75; dir. Ctr. for Multiple Handicaps, Oakland, Calif., 1976-81; co-dir. Muscle Clinic Children's Hosp., San Diego, 1963-69. Author: Raising a Handicapped Child: A Helpful Guide for Parents of the Physically Disabled, 1986, 4th edit., 1991, Allein leben: Ein umfassendes Handbuch für Frauen, 1993, Making Wise Choices: A Guide for Women, 1993; contbr. articles to med. jours., including Clin. Pediat., New Eng. Jour. Medicine, Neurology, Jour. Family Practice, Mothering, Jour. Pediatric Orthopedics, Pediatrician, Am. Baby, Pediatric News, also chpts. to books. Mem. Calif. Children's Svc. Com., 1977—. Fellow Am. Acad. Pediatrics; mem. Am. Women's Med. Assn., Internat. Music Box Soc. Office: Ctr for Handicapped Children and Teenagers 2000 Van Ness Ave Ste 307 San Francisco CA 94109

THOMPSON, DAVID GEORGE, gastroenterologist, educator; b. London, May 4, 1948; s. George David and Margaret (Lewington) T.; m. Hilary Harrison, Nov. 26, 1972; children: Toby, Catherine. BSc, London Hosp., 1969, MB, BS with honors, 1972; MD, London U., 1980. House officer London Hosp., 1973, lectr., 1975-82, sr. lectr., 1982-86; house officer Whittington (Eng.) Hosp., 1974, Hammersmith Hosp., Eng., 1975; rsch. fellow Mayo Clinic, Rochester, Minn., 1980-81; sr. lectr. U. Manchester, Eng., 1987—; asst. prof. U. N.C., 1980—; cons. physician Home Hosp., Salford, Eng. Mem. Brit. Soc. Gastroenterology (sec. 1990-92, rsch. medalist 1988), Am. Gastroenterology Assn. Home: Belmont Rd, Hale WA15 9PT, England Office: Hope Hosp, Dept Medicine, Salford M6 8HD, England

THOMPSON, DENNIS PETERS, plastic surgeon; b. Chgo., Mar. 18, 1937; s. David John and Ruth Dorothy (Peters) T.; m. Virginia Louise Williams, June 17, 1961; children: Laura Faye, Victoria Ruth, Elizabeth Jan. BS, U. Ill., 1957, BS in Medicine, 1959, MS in Physiology, MD, 1961. Diplomate Am. Bd. Surgery, Am. Bd. Plastic Surgery. Intern Presbyn.-St. Lukes Hosp., Chgo., 1961-62; resident in gen. surgery Mayo Clinic, Rochester, Minn., 1964-66, fellow in gen. surgery, 1964-66; resident in gen. surgery Harbor Gen. Hosp., Los Angeles, 1968-70; resident in plastic surgery UCLA, 1971-73, clin. instr. plastic surgery, 1975-82, asst. clin. prof. surgery, 1982—; practice medicine specializing in plastic and reconstructive surgery, Los Angeles, 1974-78, Santa Monica, Calif., 1978—; chmn. plastic surgery sect. St. John's Hosp., 1986-91; mem. staff Santa Monica Hosp., UCLA Ctr. Health Scis.; chmn. dept. surgery Beverly Glen Hosp., 1978-79; pres. Coop. of Am. Physicians Credit Union, 1978-80, bd. dirs., 1980—, chmn. membership devel. com., 1983—, treas., 1985—. Contbr. articles to med. jours. Moderator Congl. Ch. of Northridge (Calif.), 1975-76, chmn. bd. trustees, 1973-74, 80-82; bd. dirs. L.A. Bus. Coun., 1987-90. Am. Tobacco Inst. research grantee, 1959-60. Fellow ACS; mem. AMA (Physicians Recognition award 1971, 74, 77, 81, 84, 87, 90, 93), Calif. Med. Assn., L.A. County Med. Assn. (chmn. bylaws com. 1979-80, chmn. ethics com. 1980-81, sec.-treas. dist. 5 1982-83, program chmn. 1983-84, pres. 1985-86, councilor 1988-96), Pan-Pacific Surgical Assn., Am. Soc. Plastic and Reconstructive Surgeons, Calif. Soc. Plastic Surgeons (chmn. bylaws com. 1982-83, chmn. liability com. 1983-85, councilor 1988-91, sec. 1993-95, v.p. 1995-96, pres.-elect 1996—), L.A. Soc. Plastic Surgeons (sec. 1980-82, pres. 1982—), Lipoplasty Soc. N.Am. (chmn. bylaws com. 1995—), UCLA Plastic Surgery Soc. (treas. 1983-84), Am. Soc. Aesthetic Plastic Surgery, Am. Assn. Accreditation of Ambulatory Surg. Facilities (bd. dirs. 1995—), Western Los Angeles Regional C. of C. (bd. dirs. 1981-84, 86-89, chmn. legis. action com. 1978-80), Phi Beta Kappa, Alpha Omega Alpha, Nu Sigma Nu, Phi Kappa Phi, Delta Sigma Delta, Omega Beta Pi, Phi Eta Sigma. Republican. Office: 2001 Santa Monica Blvd Santa Monica CA 90404-2102

THOMPSON, EDWARD IVINS BRAD, biological chemistry and genetics educator, molecular endocrinologist, department chairman; b. Burlington, Iowa, Dec. 20, 1933; s. Edward Bills and Lois Elizabeth (Bradbridge) T.; m. Lynn Taylor Parsons; children: Elizabeth Lynn, Edward Ernest Bradbridge. BA with distinction, Rice U., 1955; postgrad., Cambridge U., 1957-58; MD, Harvard U., 1960. Intern The Presbyn. Hosp., N.Y.C., 1960-61, asst. resident internal medicine, 1961-62; rsch. assoc. Nat. Inst. Mental Health, NIH, Bethesda, Md., 1962-64; rsch. scientist Nat. Inst. Arthritis and Metabolic Diseases, NIH, Bethesda, Md., 1964-68; rsch. scientist Lab of Biochemistry, Nat. Cancer Inst., NIH, Bethesda, Md., 1968-73, sect. chief, 1973-84; I.H. Kempner prof. U. Tex. Med. Br., Galveston, 1984, prof., chmn. dept. human biol. chemistry and genetics, 1984—, prof. internal medicine, 1984—; attending physician Nat. Naval Med. Ctr., Bethesda, 1978-80; chmn. hormones and cancer task force NIH, Bethesda, 1978-80; co-chmn. Gordon Research Conf., 1980; mem. adv. com. on Biochem. & Chem. Carcinogenesis, Am. Cancer Soc., 1982-86; mem. revision com. Endocrinology adv. panel U.S. Pharmacopoeial Conv., Inc., 1980-85; mem. council for clin. investigation and research awds., Am. Cancer Soc., 1989-93; bd. scientific overseers Pennington Nutrition Rsch. Ctr. La. State U., 1991—; Fulbright prof., Marburg, Germany. 1992-93. Co-editor Gene Expression and Carcinogenesis in Cultured Liver, 1975, Steroid Receptors and the Management of Cancer, 1979, DNA: Protein Interactions and Gene Regulation, other vols. in field; assoc. editor Cancer Rsch. jour., 1976-86; corr. editor Jour. Steroid Biochemistry, 1977-85; founding editor-in-chief Molecular Endocrinology Jour., 1985-92; contbr. over 200 sci. articles to profl. jours. Mem. troop com. Girl Scouts U.S., Rockville, Md., 1970-76; mem. PTA, Rockville, 1967-77, Wilderness Soc., Washington, 1964-75; initiator sci. edn. liaison program Galveston Pub. Schs., 1991; mem. pres.'s cabinet U. Tex. Med. Br. Served as med. dir. USPHS, 1962-84. Grantee NIH, Walls Rsch., Nat. Inst. Diabetes and Digestive and Kidney Diseases, Nat. Cancer Inst.; Am. Cancer Soc. scholar, 1992-93; Fulbright scholar. Mem. Am. Soc. Cell Biology, Am. Assn. Cancer Rsch., Am. Soc. Biol. Chemists, Endocrine Soc., Am. Soc. Microbiology, Am. Coll. Med. Genetics (affiliate), Tissue Culture Assn., S.W. Environ. Mutagen Soc., Rotary Internat., The Yacht Club, Racquet Club, Harvard Club, Pres.'s Clubs of Rice U. and U. Tex. Med. Br., Phi Beta Kappa, Alpha Omega Alpha. Office: U Tex Med Br Dept Human Biol Gene Galveston TX 77555

THOMPSON, ELBERT ORSON, retired dentist, consultant; b. Salt Lake City, Aug. 31, 1910; s. Orson David and Lillian (Greenwood) T.; m. Gayle Larsen, Sept. 12, 1935; children: Ronald Elbert, Karen Thompson Toone, Edward David, Gay Lynne. Student, U. Utah, 1928-30, 33-35; DDS, Northwestern U., 1939; hon. degree, Am. Coll. Dentistry, Miami, Fla., 1958, Internat. Coll. Dentistry, San Francisco, 1962. Pvt. practice dentistry Salt Lake City, 1939-78; ret., 1978; inventor, developer and internat. lectr. postgrad./undergrad. courses various dental schs. and study groups, 1953-83; developer, tchr. Euthenics Dentistry Concept; also, sit-down dentistry, four handed dentistry, lounge-type dental chair, washed field dentistry, euthenics dental operating chair; cons. in field. Contbr. numerous dental articles to profl. jours. Life mem. Rep. Presdl. Task Force, Washington, 1985—. Recipient Merit Honor award U. Utah, 1985; named Dentist of the Yr. Utah Acad. Gen. Dentistry, 1991, Father of Modern Dentistry, 1991. Mem. ADA (life), Utah Dental Assn. (life, sec. 1948-49, Disting. Svc. award 1980, E.O. Thompson Recognition award 1995, 96), Salt Lake City Dental Soc. (life, pres. 1945-46), Utah Dental Hygiene Soc. (hon.), Am. Acad. Dental Practice Adminstrn. (life, pres. 1965-66), Internat. Coll. Dentists, Am. Coll. Dentists, Sons of Utah Pioneers (life), Dinorators Club (charter), Northwestern U. Alumni Assn. (Merit award 1961), Omicron Kappa Upsilon. Mormons. Home: 5672 S 960 E Ogden UT 84405

THOMPSON, ELEANOR DUMONT, nurse; b. Derry, N.H., May 26, 1935; d. Louis Arthur and Florence Berthae (Gendreau) D.; m. Carl Hugh Thompson, Aug. 22, 1959; children: Justine, Julie. Student, Dartmouth Hitchcock Nur. Sch., 1956; BA, New Eng. Coll., 1977; MS, Drake U., 1984. Registered art therapist. Pediatric instr. Hanover (N.H.) Sch. Practical Nursing, 1958-61; pub. W.B. Sanders Co., Phila., 1962—; pediatric instr. St. Joseph Hosp., Nashua, N.H., 1978-81; cert. clin. nurse specialist Mercy Hosp. Med. Ctr., Des Moines, 1987-90; clin. nurse specialist HCA Portsmouth (N.H.) Regional Hosp., 1991—; pvt. practice Silverman & Assoc., Inc., 1991-93; puppeteer St. Joseph's Hosp. Sch. Nursing, Nashua, 1981-82; created and conducted shows on hospitalization for children; nursing cons. Hospice Cen. Iowa, Des Moines, 1982-89. Author: Pediatric Nursing An Introductory Text, 1965, 6th edit., 1992, Introduction to Maternity and Pediatric Nursing, 1990, 2d edit., 1995. Vol. nurse Vietnam Vets. Ctr., Des Moines, 1985-87, Camp Apanda Childrens Cancer Camp Boone, Iowa, 1984-86; organist Holy Trinity Ch. Des Moines, 1982, St. Pius Ch., Des Moines, 1982. Mem. ANA, Am. Psychiat. Nurses Assn., Am. Art Therpy Assn., N.H. Art Therapy Assn., Drake Alumnae Assn., N.H. Nurses Assn. Democrat. Roman Catholic. Home: 13 Sherman Ave Brentwood NH 03833-6225

THOMPSON, HAROLD J., health care company executive. Student, Ind. U., 1961-65. Co-founder Koala Ctrs., Carmel, Ind., 1973-89; pres. Health Mgmt. Internat. and Seniors Unlimited, Inc., Carmel, 1989—; treas., bd. dirs. Nat. Assn. for Children of Alcoholics, Laguna Beach, Calif., 1987-92; bd. dirs. Diva Prodns.; broadcast affiliate The Peoples Network. Bd. dirs. Carmel Bd. Zoning Appeals, 1988-91. Lt. U.S. Army, 1961-67. Mem. Am. Soc. Aging (bd. dirs.), Hudson Inst., World Trade Club, Rotary Internat. (Paul Harris fellow). Office: 11711 N Meridian St Ste 580 Carmel IN 46032-4548

THOMPSON, HAROLD JEROME, counselor, mental retardation professional; b. Oklahoma City, May 5, 1947; s. John Caldwell and Marian Louree (Cejda) T.; m. Donna Marie Steed, May 13, 1967 (div. Feb. 1977); children: Treva Marie, Derek Martin; m. Clydia Dee Nichols, Aug. 11, 1984 (div. Apr. 1993). BA, Langston U., 1983; MS, Northea. Okla. State U., 1985. Lic. profl. counselor; qualified mental retardation profl.; cert. behavior analyst. Sales rep. Jones-Newly Supply Co., Oklahoma City, 1969-72, Jones-Newby Supply Co., Tulsa, 1972-74; ins. sales agt. ind. brokers, Tulsa, 1974-77; sales rep. Empire Plumbing Supply, Tulsa, 1977-79, 81-82, Amfac Mech. Supply, Tulsa, 1979-81; chmn. citizens adv. bd. Tulsa Psychiat. Ctr., 1982-83; counselor Horizon Program Shadow Mountain Inst., Tulsa, 1983-90; psychologist Hissom Meml. Ctr., Sand Springs., Okla., 1985-91; pvt. practice Tulsa, 1990—; cons., vol. counselor to mentally retarded, Denver, 1987. With U.S.

Army, 1966-68. Mem. Am. Assn. on Mental Deficiency, Nat. Assn. Masters in Philosophy. Republican. Roman Catholic. Office: Behavioral Solutions 7217 S Columbia Tulsa OK 74136

THOMPSON, HERBERT STANLEY, neuro-ophthalmologist; b. Shansi, China, June 12, 1932; came to U.S., 1949, naturalized, 1955; s. Robert Ernest and Ellen (Mulligan) T.; m. Delores Lucille Johnson, June 27, 1953; children: Geoffrey, Peter, Kenneth, Philip, Susan. Student, Methodist Coll., Belfast, No. Ireland, 1947-49; B.A., U. Minn., 1953, M.D., 1961; M.S., U. Iowa, 1966. Diplomate Am. Bd. Ophthalmology (assoc. examiner 1972-88, bd. dirs. 1989-96, chmn. ABO 1996). Intern U. Iowa, Iowa City, 1961-62; resident in ophthalmology U. Iowa, 1962-66; fellow in pupillography Columbia Coll. Physicians and Surgeons, 1962; fellow in clin. neuro-ophthalmology U. Calif., San Francisco, 1966-67; prof. ophthalmology U. Iowa, Iowa City, 1976—; dir. neuro-ophthalmology unit U. Iowa, 1967—; practice medicine specializing in neuro-ophthalmology Iowa City, 1967—. Editor: Topics in Neuro-opthalmology, 1979; assoc. editor Am. Jour. Ophthalmology, 1981-84, book rev. editor, 1984-91; cons. Stedman's Med. Dictionary, 26th edit. Served with AUS, 1954-55. NIH spl. fellow, 1966-67; research career devel. awardee, 1968-72. Fellow Am. Acad. Ophthalmoogy, N.Am. Neuro-ophthalmol. Soc.; mem. Am. Ophthalmol. Soc., Cogan Ophthalmic History Soc. (Charles Snyder lectr. 1995). Office: U Iowa Dept Ophthalmology Iowa City IA 52242

THOMPSON, HILAIRE JANE, neurosurgical nurse; b. Columbus, Ohio, May 13, 1968. BS in Biology, Mary Washington Coll., Fredericksburg, Va., 1991; BSN, Cath. U. Am., 1992; MS in Med./Surg. Nursing, Va. Commonwealth U., 1996. RN, Va. Staff neurosurg. nurse Med. Coll. Va. Hosps., Richmond, 1992-93, clinician, 1993—; staff med. ICU nurse Mary Washignton Hosp., 1995-96. Author pamphlet and booklets. Mem. Am. Assn. Neurosci. Nurses, Sigma Theta Tau. Office: Med Coll Va Hosps Main 11 West Box 7 MCV Station Richmond VA 23201

THOMPSON, JEFFERY ELDERS, health care administrator, minister; b. Bremen, Ga., Feb. 21, 1951; s. Jack Elders and Jewell Dean (Hutto) T.; m. Pamela Jennette Watson, Aug. 26, 1972; children: Rebecca Lynn, Joshua Elders. BA, Auburn U., 1973; MDiv, So. Bapt. Theol. Sem., 1977, DMin, 1991. Ordained to ministry So. Bapt. Conv., 1977. Youth min. Calder Bapt. Ch., Beaumont, Tex., 1977-79, First Bapt. Ch., Florence, S.C., 1979-82; chaplain Ga. Regional Hosp., Augusta, Ga., 1982-84; dir. pastoral care East Ala. Med. Ctr., Opelika, 1984—. Pres. Hospice of Lee County, Opelika, 1986-87, bd. dirs., 1987-91; bd. dirs. Widowed Person Svc., Opelika; mem. Leadership Lee County, 1991; scoutmaster Boy Scouts Am., 1991-94, Explorer advisor, 1995—, mem. dist. com., 1994—. Fellow Coll. Chaplains; mem. Lions Club (chaplain Opelika club 1985, Outstanding Lion 1985, 1st v.p. 1994, pres. 1995-96). Office: East Ala Med Ctr 2000 Pepperell Pky Opelika AL 36801-5452

THOMPSON, JESSE ELDON, vascular surgeon; b. Laredo, Tex., Apr. 7, 1919; s. Jesse Eathel and Sara Gail (Bolton) T.; m. Madeleine Jane Curtis, Sept. 18, 1944; children: Sally C., Jesse E., Janet E., Diane B. BA, U. Tex., 1939; MD, Harvard U., 1943; Rhodes scholar, Oxford U., 1949-50. Intern Mass. Gen. Hosp., Boston, 1943; resident in surgery Mass. Gen. Hosp., 1944-48; practice medicine specializing in surgery, tchr. surgery Boston U., 1949-54; practice medicine specializing in surgery, tchr. vascular surgery Baylor Hosp., Dallas, 1954—; chief vascular surgery Baylor Hosp., 1980-86; clin. prof. surgery U. Tex. Southwestern Med. Sch., Dallas; attending surgeon Baylor Hosp., 1954—; chief surgery Baylor Hosp., Dallas, 1982-86; Mem Tex. and Dist. Rhodes Scholar Selection Coms. Author: Surgery for Cerebrovascular Insufficiency, 1968; editorial bd.: Surgery, 1975-89, Jour. Cardiovascular Surgery, 1975—; sr. editor Jour. Vascular Surgery, 1984-86; contbr. numerous articles to profl. jours. Served to capt. M.C. AUS, 1945-47. Fulbright sr. fellow, 1949-50. Fellow ACS (treas.); mem. Am. Surg. Assn., So. Surg. Assn., Tex. Surg. Soc., Soc. Vascular Surgery, Internat. Cardiovascular Soc., Internat. Soc. Surgery, So. Assn. for Vascular Surgery, Dallas Petroleum Club, Dallas Country Club, Masons. Methodist. Home: 3705 Stanford Ave Dallas TX 75225-7204 Office: 712 N Washington Ave Ste 509 Dallas TX 75246-1635

THOMPSON, JOHN ALBERT, JR., dermatologist; b. Austin, Tex., June 5, 1942; s. J. Albert Sr. and Elizabeth (Brady) T. BA, Georgetown U., 1963; MD, Bowman Gray Sch. Medicine, 1967; Dermatology Fellowship, U. N.C., 1971-73. Diplomate Am. Bd. Dermatology. Resident in internal medicine N.C. Baptist Hosp., Winston-Salem, N.C., 1967-69; resident in dermatology N.C. Meml. Hosp., Chapel Hill, N.C., 1971-73; pvt. practice Charlotte, N.C., 1974—; clin. prof. dermatology Dept. Dermatology, U. N.C. Sch. Medicine, Chapel Hill, 1974—. Author profl. papers. Lt. comdr. USNR, 1969-71, Vietnam. Mem. Am. Acad. Dermatology (chmn. subcom. for sch. health edn. 1976-79, task force--nat. health ins.), Carolinas-Va. Dermatology Assn. (adv. bd. council rep. 1976-79), Charlotte Dermatology Assn., Mecklenburg County Med. Soc., N.C. Med. Soc., North Am. Clin. Dermatology Soc. Southern Med. Assn., Southeastern Consortium for Continuing Dermatol. Edn. (steering com. 1983—), South Cen. Dermatol. Congress (organizing com. 1982-86), Am. Soc. Dermatol. Surgery, Am. Dermatol. Soc. Allergy and Immunology. Democrat. Episcopalian. Home: 2633 Richardson Dr Apt 8A Charlotte NC 28211-3346 Office: 2310 Randolph Rd Charlotte NC 28207-1526

THOMPSON, JOHN TILYNN, ophthalmologist, educator; b. Ann Arbor, Mich., June 8, 1956; s. John Morgan and Dorothy Georgene (Kinne) T.; m. Mary Ann Serpi; children: Lauren Alexis, John Michael. Student, Oberlin Coll., 1973-75; BA cum laude, Johns Hopkins U., 1977, MD, 1980. Diplomate Am. Bd. Ophthalmology, 1985. Intern Cedars-Sinai Med. Ctr., L.A., 1980-81; resident Wilmer Ophthalmologic Inst., Balt., 1981-84, asst. chief svc., 1986; asst. prof. Yale U., New Haven, Conn., 1986-90, assoc. prof., 1990-91; assoc. clin. prof. U. Md., Balt., 1993—; ptnr. The Retina Inst. Md., Balt., 1991—; dir. retina sect. Yale U., 1986-91. Contbr. articles to profl. jours. Grantee Conn. Lions Eye Found., 1986-91, The Hearst Found., 1989-90; Wilmer Ophthalmologic Inst. fellow, 1984-85, Heed Found. fellow, 1984; recipient Lamport award Biomed. Rsch. Johns Hopkins U., 1978. Fellow Am. Acad. Ophthalmology (honor award 1988); mem. AMA, Assn. Rsch. in Vision & Ophthalmology, The Retina Soc., The Macula Soc., The Vitreous Soc., Phi Beta Kappa. Office: The Retina Inst Md 7505 Osler Dr Ste 103 Baltimore MD 21204-7737

THOMPSON, JOSEPH WARREN, physician; b. Wichita Falls, Tex., June 27, 1950; s. Allen Dulaney and Norma Helen (Rinabarger) T.; m. Linda K. Sparks, Mar. 19, 1988. BS, S.E. Mo. State U., 1972; DO, U. Health Scis., Coll. Osteo. Medicine, Kansas City, Mo., 1976. Diplomate Am. Coll. Gen. Practitioners, Nat. Bd. Osteo. Med. Examiners. Intern Normandy Hosp., St. Louis, 1976-77, resident in family practice, 1977-79; pvt. practice medicine, St. Louis, 1979—; program dir. family practice residency, 1982-93, chief of staff, Normandy Osteo. Hosps. North and South, 1986-87; pres. of bd. Comprehensive Family Health Plan, Inc., 1987-90; apptd. staff mem. Deaconess Med. Ctr.-West, 1979—, De Paul Health Ctr., St. Louis, 1988—, med. dir. PHO 1995—, Mo. Bapt. Med. Ctr., 1992—, Deaconess Med. Ctr., 1992—; med. dir. DePaul Home Health, 1994—; mem. adv. bd. Olsten Home Health Svcs., 1991-94. Major M.C., USAFR. Mem. Mo. Osteo. Assn. (polit. action com., jud. com. 1986-88, physician licensure com. 1987-90, Young Physician of Yr. 1985), Am. Osteo. Assn. (com. on edn. and evaluation, 1985-86), Nat. Libr. of Medicine, Region IV, (mem. adv. coun. 1987-91), Am. Coll. Osteo. Family Physicians, Mo. Assn. Osteo. Physicians and Surgeons, St. Louis Dist. Assn. Osteo. Physicians and Surgeons, Elks, Masons, Shriners, Phi Theta Kappa. Methodist.

THOMPSON, JOSIE, nursing administrator, nurse; b. Ark., Apr. 16, 1949; d. James Andrew and Oneda Fay (Watson) Rhoads; m. Mark O. Thompson, Feb. 14, 1980. Diploma, Lake View Sch. Nursing, 1970; student, Danville C.C., 1974-75, St. Petersburg Jr. Coll., 1979. RN, Ill., Wyo. Staff nurse St. Elizabeth Hosp., Danville, Ill., 1970-78, Osteopathetic Hosp., St. Petersburg, Fla., 1980-81, Wyo. State Hosp., Evanston, 1981-83; staff nurse Wyo. Home Health Care, Rock Springs, 1984—, adminstr., 1986-95; pres. Home Health Care Alliance Wyo., 1991-92. Mem. nursing program adv. bd. Western Wyo. Community Coll.; mem. Coalition for the Elderly, Spl. Needs Com. Sweetwater County, 1992-93. Home: 2704 S Greeley Hwy Cheyenne WY 82007

THOMPSON, JUDITH KASTRUP, nursing researcher; b. Marstal, Denmark, Oct. 1, 1933; came to the U.S., 1951; d. Edward Kastrup and Anna Hansa (Knudsen) Pedersen; m. Richard Frederick Thompson, May 22, 1960; children: Kathryn Marr, Elizabeth Kastrup, Virginia St. Claire. BS, RN, U. Oreg., 1958, MSN, 1963. RN, Calif., Oreg. Staff nurse U. Oreg. Med. Sch., Eugene, 1957-58; staff nurse U. Oreg. Med. Sch., Portland, 1958-61, head staff nurse, 1960-61; instr. psychiat. nursing U. Oreg. Sch. Nursing, Portland, 1963-64; rsch. asst. U. Oreg. Med. Sch., Portland, 1964-65, U. Calif., Irvine, 1971-72; rsch. assoc. Stanford (Calif.) U., 1982-87; rsch. asst. Harvard U., Cambridge, Mass., 1973-74; rsch. assoc. U. So. Calif., L.A., 1987—. Contbg. author: Behavioral Control and Role of Sensory Biofeedback, 1976; contbr. articles to profl. jours. Treas. LWV, Newport Beach, Calif., 1970-74; scout leader Girl Scouts Am., Newport Beach, 1970-78. Named Citizen of Yr. State of Oreg., 1966. Mem. Soc. for Neurosci., Am. Psychol. Soc. (charter), ANA, Oreg. Nurses Assn. Republican. Lutheran. Home: 28 Sky Sail Dr Corona Del Mar CA 92625-1436 Office: U So Calif University Park Los Angeles CA 90089-2520

THOMPSON, KAY FRANCIS, dentist; b. Pitts.; d. Lony C. and Betha E. (Porter) T.; m. Ralph P. Krichbaum, Jan. 10, 1959. BS, U. Pitts., 1951, DDS, 1953. Pvt. practice dentistry Pitts., 1953—; assoc. prof. U. Pitts., Behavioral Sci., Dentistry, Pitts., 1970-80, W.Va. U. Sch. Dentistry and Sch. of Medicine, Morgantown, 1980—; dentist for handicapped Robinson Devel. Ctr., McKees Rocks, Pa., 1976—; cons. NIH, Washington, 1975-90, VA Hosp., Pitts., 1978—; lectr., educator various med., dental and psychol. assns. Contbr. articles to profl. jours. Chmn. Dental Legis. Fund Pa., Pitts., 1981-83; mem. World Affairs Coun., Pitts., 1980—, Pa. Dental Polit. Action Com., Harrisburg; bd. dirs. Am. Dental Polit. Action Com., Washington, 1985-90; trustee U. Pitts., 1988-91; mem. Amdental Assoc. Govt. Svcs., 1990-93. Recipient Erickson award De Nederlands Vereniging voor Hypnotherapie, 1983, Bicentennial Medallion of Distinction U. Pitts., 1988, Alumnae of Yr. 1991, Erickson Found. Lifetime Achievement award, 1992. Fellow Am. Coll. Dentists, Internat. Coll. Dentists, Am. Soc. Clin. Hypnosis (pres. 1972-73, scientific 1970), Soc. Clin. and Exptl. Hypnosis (exec. bd. 1976-80), Pierre Fauchard Acad.; mem. ADA (trustee 1993—), Am. Assn. Women Dentists (trustee 1982-88, Pres.'s award 1986), Pa. Dental Assn. (sec. 1984-88, pres. 1989-90), U. Pitts. Dental Alumni Assn. (pres. 1988-91). Lutheran. Office: PO Box 16152 Pittsburgh PA 15242-0152

THOMPSON, KENNETH RICHARD, critical care nurse; b. Manhattan, Kans., Nov. 28, 1956; s. Hugh Erwin and Jean Grace (Link) T.; m. Elisabeth Thiel, Sept. 17, 1988; children: Katherine Anne, Elke Cassandra, Karl Erwin. Student, U. Kans., 1974-76, Kans. State U., 1977-81; grad. lic. practical nurse, Manhattan Area Vocat.-Tech Sch., 1980; ADN, Cloud County Community Coll., 1982. Staff nurse ICU St. Francis Hosp., Topeka, 1982-83; mem. ICU staff Upjohn Health Care Agy., Topeka, 1983-85; staff nurse ICU, CCU Doctors Hosp., Conroe, Tex., 1985-87; staff nurse ICU Dartmouth Hitchcock Med. Ctr., Hanover, N.H., 1987-91, New London (N.H.) Hosp. Assn., 1991-93, Brooksdale Nursing Home, Vt., 1994-95, Mt. Ascutney Hosp., Windsor, Vt., 1995—; former supr. for 400-bed nursing home. Mem. AACN. Home: RR 2 Box 121-W West Lebanon NH 03784-9601

THOMPSON, LARRY GENE, anesthesiologist; b. Columbia, S.C., Aug. 20, 1941; s. John Madison and Virginia Faye (Findley) T.; m. Janet Elaine Rawles, Jan. 18, 1970; children: Michelle Aileen, David John, Mark Alan. BA, U. Indpls., 1963; MD, Ind. U., 1967. Diplomate Am. Bd. Anesthesiologists. Rotating intern Meml. Hosp., South Bend, Ind., 1967-68, staff anesthesiologist, 1974—; resident anesthesiology Ind. U. Sch. Medicine, Indpls., 1968-71; anesthesiology dir. USAF/RAF Lakenheath, Eng., 1971-74; staff anesthesiologist Michiana Anesthesia Care, South Bend. Bd. dirs. Meml. Hosp., 1987-93, South Bend Symphony, 1993—, Univ. Indpls., 1994—. Maj. USAF, 1971-74. Mem. Am. Soc. Anesthesiologists (dist. dir. 1994-95), Internat. Anesthesia Rsch. Soc., Ind. Soc. Anesthesiologists (pres. 1996—), St. Joseph County Med. Soc. (pres. 1986-88), St. Joseph Acad. Anesthesiologists (dir. 1985-91). Republican. United Methodist. Office: Michiana Anesthesia Care 605 Portage Ave South Bend IN 46616

THOMPSON, LEONARD RUSSELL, pediatrician; b. Columbus, Ohio, Sept. 29, 1934; s. Oliver Bernard and Christina (Nichols) T.; m. Candice Elizabeth Brisken, Dec. 6, 1980; children: Ryan, Deron, Hillary, Jon, Christina, Lisa. BA, Ohio State U., 1956, MD, 1960. Diplomat Am. Bd. Pediatrics. Intern Fitzsimmons Gen. Hosp., Denver, 1960-61, resident, 1961-63; chief pediatrics Ireland County Hosp., Ft. Knox, Ky., 1965-66; chmn. dept. pediatrics Fresno (Calif.) Med. Group, 1966-80; pediatrician pvt. practice, Fresno, 1990—; pres. med. staff Valley Children's Hosp., Fresno, 1992. Maj. U.S. Army, 1960-66. Fellow Am. Acad. Pediatrics. Office: 5305 N Fremont St #110A Fresno CA 93710

THOMPSON, LEWIS WILLIAM, plastic surgeon; b. South Portsmouth, Ky., Apr. 27, 1933; s. Lewis Madison and Anna Louise (Scheible) T.; m. Ruth Ann Lee, June 8, 1955; children: Brenda, Sharon, Margaret. AB, Asbury Coll., 1955; MD, Wake Forest U., 1960. Intern U. Va. Hosp., Charlottesville, 1960-61, resident, 1961-64, chief resident, 1964-65; resident Ind. U. Med. Ctr., Indpls., 1965-66, chief resident, 1966-68; asst. prof. surgery, asst. dir. plastic surgery Ind. U. Sch. Medicine, Indpls., 1968-71; assoc. prof. plastic surgery George Washington U. Sch. Medicine, Washington, 1972-82, chmn. plastic surgery, 1972-80; chmn. plastic surgery Children's Hosp. Nat. Med. Ctr., Washington, 1972-82; prof. surgery, chmn. plastic surgery Oral Roberts U. Sch. Medicine, Tulsa, 1982-89; plastic surgeon pvt. practice, Tulsa, 1989—; vis. prof. Norfolk (Va.) Ctr., 1973, Howard U., Washington, 1978, St. Vincent's Med. Ctr., N.Y.C., 1979, others; guest speaker Am. Acad. Mexillofacial Prostetics, 1974, No. Va. Pediatric Soc. Ann. Meeting, 1981, Met. Washington Dental Soc., 1981, others; guest lectr. Greater Balt. Soc. Speech Pathologists, 1975, Japanese Teaching Hosp., 1991, others; researcher in field. Author: (chpts.) Cleft Lip and Palate, 1972, Surgery in Cancers of the Head and NEck, 1972, Plastic Surgery and Its Relationship to MAxillofacial Prosthesis, 1972; contbr. articles to profl. jours. Youth coun. Chevy Chase United Meth. Ch., 1974-82, youth coord., 1975-82, coun. on ministries, 1975-82, long range planning com., 1976-77, adminstrv. bd., 1976-82, staff-parish com., 1979-80, lay leader, 1981-82; Appalachian svc. project United Meth. Ch., 1984, ethics com. Okla. Ann. Conf., 1992—; pres. Boston Ave. United Meth. Ch., 1985, v.p., 1984, adminstrv. bd., 1984-88, chmn. evangelism work area, 1985-88, interfaith work area, 1996, fin. com., 1989—; mem. Thomas Gilcrease Mus. Assocs., 1984—, Philbrook Mus. Art, 1985—. Am. Cancer Soc. Clin. fellow, 1964-65, Plastic Surgery Rsch. fellow, 1966-67, Frederick H. Coller Soc. fellow, 1967. Mem. AMA, Am. Acad. Pediatrics (sect. plastic surgery), Am. Assn. Hand Surgery, Am. Assn. Pediatric Plastic Surgeons, Am. Assn. Plastic Surgeons, Am. Assn. for Surgery of Trauma, Am. Cleft Palate Assn., Am. Coll. Physician Execs., Am. Coll. Surgeons, Am. Burn Assn., Am. Soc. Aesthetic Plastic Surgeons, Am. Soc. Plastic and Reconstructive Surgery, Am. Trauma Soc., So. Med. Assn., Okla. State Med. Assn., Okla. Regional Soc. Plastic Surgeons, Tulsa County Med. Soc., Tulsa Soc. Plastic Surgeons, Tulsa Surg. Soc., Assn. Acad. Surgery, Christian Med. Dental Soc., William H. Muller Jr. Surg. Soc., Plastic Surgery Acad. Forum, Plastic Surgery Edal. Found., Plastic Surgery Rsch. Coun., Sigma Xi, Phi Chi. Republican. Office: 1560 E 21st St Ste 200 Tulsa OK 74114

THOMPSON, LOIS JEAN HEIDKE ORE, psychologist; b. Chgo., Feb. 22, 1933; d. Harold William and Ethel Rose (Neumann) Heidke; m. Henry Thomas Ore, Aug. 28, 1954 (div. May 1972); children: Christopher, Douglas; m. Joseph Lippard Thompson, Aug. 3, 1972; children: Scott, Les, Melanie. BA, Cornell Coll., Mt. Vernon, Iowa, 1955; MA, Idaho State U., 1964, EdD, 1981. Lic. psychologist, N.Mex. Tchr. pub. schs. various locations, 1956-67; tchr., instr. Idaho State U., Pocatello, 1967-72; employee/orgn. devel. specialist Los Alamos (N.Mex.) Nat. Lab., 1981-84, tng. specialist, 1984-89, sect. leader, 1989-93; pvt. practice indsl. psychology and healthcare, Los Alamos, 1988—; sec. Cornell Coll. Alumni Office, 1954-55, also other orgns.; bd. dirs. Parent Edn. Ctr., Idaho State U., 1980; counselor, Los Alamos, 1981-88. Editor newsletter LWV, Laramie, Wyo., 1957; contbr. articles to profl. jours. Pres. Newcomers Club, Pocatello, 1967, Faculty Womens Club, Pocatello, 1968; chmn. edn. com. AAUW, Pocatello, 1969. Mem. APA, ACA, N.Mex. Psychol. Assn. (bd. dirs. divsn. II 1990, sec. 1988-90, chmn. 1990), N.Mex. Soc. Adlerian Psychology (pres. 1990, treas. 1991-95, bd. dirs. 1996—), Soc. Indsl. and Orgn. Psychology, Assn. for Adult Devel. and Aging. Mem. LDS Ch. Home and Office: 340 Aragon Ave Los Alamos NM 87544-3505

THOMPSON, LYNN RENEE, chiropractor; b. Rockford, Ill., Sept. 19, 1955; d. James LeRoy Sturz and Juanita June (Longanecker) Youderian; m. John Michael Thompson, Aug. 27, 1975 (div. Feb. 1985); 1 child, Jennifer Marie. AD med. lab. technologist, Chippewa Valley Tech., 1979; BA, Midwestern State U., 1985; D of Chiropractic, Palmer Coll. Chiropractic, Davenport, Iowa, 1993. Lic. chiropractor Iowa, Ill., Wis. Med. lab. technician Laughlin Osteo. Hosp., Kirksville, Mo., 1979-82; med. technologist Hamilton Hosp., Olney, Tex., 1982-83, Bethania Regional Hosp., Wichita Falls, Tex., 1983-87, St. Clare Hosp., Baraboo, Wis., 1987-88, Samaritan Health Care, Clinton, Iowa, 1993-95; chiropractor Yours For Health Chiropractic, Chippewa Falls, Wis., 1995—; owner Conant Chiropractic Clinic, LeClaire, Iowa, 1993—; bd. advisors Iowa Commn. on Persons with Disabilities, Davenport, 1993-94; bd. dirs. Quint Cities Handicap Group, Davenport, 1989-94, Sigma Phi Chi, Davenport. Mem. Internat. Chiropractors Assn., Am. Soc. Clin. Pathologists (cert.), Am. Med. Technologists (cert.). Lutheran. Office: Yours For Health Chiropract 109 Bay St Chippewa Falls WI 54729

THOMPSON, MARI HILDENBRAND, medical staff services professional; b. Washington, Apr. 26, 1951; d. Emil John Christopher Hildenbrand and Ada Lythe (Conklin) Hildenbrand-Kammer; m. R. Marshall Thompson, Sept. 27, 1970 (div. June 1981); 1 child, Jeremy Marshall. BA in Secondary Edn., Am. U., 1976, BA in Performing Arts, 1976. Cert. med. staff coord.; cert. profl. credentialing specialist. Employment interviewer Scripps Meml. Hosp., La Jolla, Calif., 1977-81; office mgr. Jacksina & Freedman Press Office, N.Y.C., 1982-83; staffing coord., med. staff asst. Am. Med. Internat. Clairemont Hosp., San Diego, 1983-85; adminstrv. asst. Am. Med. Internat. Valley Med. Ctr., El Cajon, Calif., 1985-88; med. staff coord. Sharp Meml. Hosp., San Diego, 1988-92; adminstrv. asst. Grossmont Hosp., La Mesa, Calif., 1992-93, coord. Sharp family practice residency program, 1993-94; ops. coord. Sharp Meml. Hosp. med. staff svcs., San Diego, 1994—; wardrobe mistress various community theatres, San Diego, 1978-79, actress, San Diego, 1979-81. Appeared N.Y.C. (N.Y.) Playreaders Group, 1981-83, N.J. Shakespeare Theatre, Madison, 1982, Good Humor Improv Co., N.Y.C., 1982-83; contbg. writer to Poetry Revival: An Anthology, 1994. Mem. NOW, 1995, World Wildlife Fedn., Calif., 1991, Greenpeace, Calif., 1991, Sierra Club, Calif., 1991, 92, Audubon Soc., Calif., 1991, 92, Internat. Wildlife Fedn., 1992, Smithsonian, 1993, 94, Dem. Nat. Com., 1996. Included in Outstanding Young Women of Am., 1986. Mem. NAFE, AFTRA, Nat. Assn. Med. Staff Svcs., Calif. Assn. Med. Staff Svcs., San Diego Assn. Med. Staff, Nat. Assn. Health Care Quality, Assn. Family Practice Adminstrs. Democrat. Home: 7951 Beaver Lake Dr San Diego CA 92119-2610

THOMPSON, MAVIS SARAH, physician; b. Newark, June 22, 1927; d. Nathaniel Albert and Mavis Carolyn (Smart) T.; m. James Blaize, Apr. 17, 1955; children: Clayton, Marcia, Sidney, Ronald, Kevin. BA Hunter Coll., 1947; MD, Howard U., 1953. Intern, then resident in internal medicine Kings County Hosp., Bklyn., 1953-57; pvt. practice medicine specializing in internal medicine, Bklyn., 1957-76; med. dir. Lyndon B. Johnson Health Complex, Inc., Bklyn., 1970-71, 74-76; sch. med. insp. N.Y.C. Bd. Edn., Bklyn., 1962-85; family physician Kingsboro Med. Group, Bklyn., 1976-95; cons., 1986—; tchr. dept. nursing Medgar Evers Coll., 1975-76; mem. adv. com. Gerontol. Svcs. Adminstrn. program New Sch. Social Rsch., N.Y.C.; cons. in field. Contbr. articles to med. jours. Bd. dirs. Camp Minisink, 1973-85, Episcopal Health Svcs., Diocese of L.I., 1990—, Bklyn. Plz. Med. Ctr., 1991—; active local Boy Scouts Am.; lic. lay reader St. George's Eplsc. Ch., Bklyn., vestry mem., 1985-88. Recipient Community Svc. award St. Mark's Meth. Ch., N.Y.C., 1973, Bishops Cross, 1990; Alberta T. Kline Svc. award Camp Minisink, 1980, Svc. award Provident Clin. Soc., 1995. Mem. Am. Public Health Assn. (pres. Black caucus health workers 1976-77), Nat. Med. Assn., Am. Mgmt. Assn., Am. Geriatrics Soc., Am. Med. Women's Assn., Kings County Med. Soc., Delta Sigma Theta. Episcopalian.

THOMPSON, PAUL BANKS, philosophy educator; b. Springfield, Mo., July 22, 1951; s. Richard Elliot and Joan (Banks) T.; m. Edith Diane Lanier, Mar. 28, 1975; children: Eudora Diane, Walker Lanier. BA, Emory U., 1974; MA, SUNY, Stony Brook, 1979, PhD, 1980. Asst. prof. philosophy Tex. A&M U., College Station, 1981-87, assoc. prof., 1987-92, George R. and Maria Julia Jordan prof. pub. policy, 1990-92, prof., 1992—, dir. Ctr. for Biotech., Policy and Ethics, 1990—; cons. animal well-being Coun. Agrl. Sci. Tech., agrl. curriculum devel. USDA, Washington, 1985-89, agrl. rsch. policy USAID, Washington, 1986-88, ethics and devel. Office of Tech. Assessment, Washington, 1988-89; mem. U.S. Agrl. Biotech. Rsch. Adv. Com., 1994-96; fellow Agrarian Studies Program, Yale U., 1994-95. Author: 2 books; co-author: 3 books; contbr. articles to profl. jours. Internat. Affairs fellow Coun. Fgn. Rels., 1986-87; resident fellow Resources for the Future, Washington, 1987; grantee; Rockefeller Found., 1987-93, Kellogg Found., 1984-94, NSF, 1988-96, USDA, 1990—. Mem. AAAS, Am. Philos. Assn., Am. Polit. Sci. Assn., Am. Agrl. Econs. Assn., Soc. Food Agr. and Human Values (v.p. 1987-89, pres. 1990-91). Democrat. Mem. United Ch. of Christ. Office: Tex A&M U Dept Philosophy Ctr for Biotech Policy College Station TX 77843-4355

THOMPSON, PAUL BRETT, anesthesiologist; b. Union, W.Va., Mar. 26, 1964; s. James Paul and Audrey Frances (Williams) T. Student, Concord Coll., 1982-85; DO, W.Va. Sch. Osteo. Medicine, 1989. Intern Cuyahoga Falls (Ohio) Gen. Hosp., 1985-86; clin. instr. Bellevue Hosp. Med. Ctr., N.Y.C., 1989—, NYU Med. Ctr., N.Y.C., 1989—. Mem. Am. Soc. Anesthesiologists, N.Y. State Soc. Anesthesiologists. Office: NYU Med Ctr Dept Anesthesiology 550 1st Ave Rm 626 New York NY 10016

THOMPSON, PETER LINDSAY, cardiologist, educator; b. Perth, Australia, Dec. 26, 1941; s. Reginald and Veronica (Donoghue) T.; m. Andrea Jane Stimson, Aug. 16, 1969; children: James, Alexandrea, Angus. MBBS, U. Western Australia, Perth, 1965; MD, U. Western Australia, 1989. Diplomate Am. Bd. Internal Medicine. Intern Royal Perth Hosp., 1965-67; asst. in medicine Peter Bent Brigham Hosp., Boston, 1970-72; cardiologist Sir Charles Gairdner Hosp., Perth, 1972—, head cardiology, 1989—; pvt. practice medicine specializing in cardiology Perth, 1973—; clin. prof. medicine U. Western Australia, 1990—; med. registrar Walter and Eliza Hall Inst., Melbourne, Australia, 1968; cardiology registrar Royal Melbourne Hosp., 1969. Author: Prognosis of Heart Attack, 1987, Coronary Care Manual, 1996; contbr. articles to med. jours. Fellow Royal Australasian Coll. Physicians, ACP, Am. Coll. Cardiology; mem. Nat. Heart Found. (bd. dirs. 1986—, chmn. heart attack com. 1987—), Australian Med. Assn. (pres. Western Australin br. 1986-87), Cardiac Soc. Australia and New Zealand (coun. 1986-91, pres. 1994-96). Roman Catholic. Clubs: Royal Freshwater Bay Yacht, Weld. Home: 10 Hobbs Ave Dalkeith, Perth 6009, Australia Office: 100 Outram St, West Perth 6005, Australia

THOMPSON, RANDALL CHESHIRE, cardiologist; b. Atlanta, Aug. 27, 1954; s. Robert T. and Elaine (Cheshire) T.; m. Martha M. Thompson, May 17, 1986; children: Adam M., Elaine C. BA, Emory U., 1976, MD magna cum laude, 1980. Diplomate in internal medicine and cardiovascular diseases Am. Bd. Internal Medicine; lic. physician, Fla., Minn. Intern Mass. Gen. Hosp., Boston, 1980-81, resident in internal medicine, 1981-83; clin. and rsch. fellow in medicine (cardiology) Mass. Gen. Hosp./Harvard Med. Sch., 1983-86; cons. cardiovascular diseases Mayo Clinic, Rochester, Minn., 1986-

87; cons. cardiovascular diseases, assoc. prof. medicine Mayo Clinic, Jacksonville, Fla., 1987-95; cons. cardiologist Mid Am. Heart Inst., Kansas City, Mo., 1995—. Contbr. articles to profl. jours. Fellow Am. Coll. Cardiology; mem. AMA. Am. Heart Assn., Duval County Med. Soc., Paul Dudley White Soc., Am. Soc. Nuclear Cardiology (founding), Alpha Omega Alpha. Office: 8901 W 74th St Ste 281 Shawnee Mission KS 66204

THOMPSON, RICHARD FREDERICK, psychologist, neuroscientist, educator; b. Portland, Oreg., 1930; s. Frederick Albert and Margaret St. Clair (Marr) T.; m. Judith K. Pedersen, May 22, 1960; children: Kathryn M., Elizabeth K., Virginia St. C. B.A., Reed Coll., 1952; M.S., U. Wis., 1953, Ph.D., 1956. Asst. prof. med. psychology Med. Sch. U. Oreg., Portland, 1959-63, assoc. prof., 1963-65, prof., 1965-67; prof. psychobiology U. Calif., Irvine, 1967-73, 75-80; prof. psychology Harvard U., Cambridge, Mass., 1973-74; Lashley chair prof. Harvard U., Cambridge, 1973; prof. psychology, Bing prof. human biology Stanford U., Palo Alto, Calif., 1980-87; Keck prof. psychology and biol. scis. U. So. Calif., L.A., 1987—, dir. neuroscience program, 1989—. Author: Foundations of Physiological Psychology, 1967, (with others) Psychology, 1971, Introduction to Physiological Psychology, 1975; Psychology editor (with others), W.H. Freeman & Co. publs., chief editor, Behavioral Neurosci., 1983—; editor: Jour. Comparative and Physiol. Psychology, 1981-83; regional editor: (with others) Physiology and Behavior; contbr. (with others) articles to profl. jours. Fellow AAAS, APA (Disting. Sci. Contbn. award 1974, governing coun. 1974—), Soc. Neurosci. (councilor 1972-76); mem. NAS, Am. Acad. Arts and Scis., Internat. Brain Rsch. Orgn., Psychonomic Soc. (gov. 1972-77, chmn. 1976), Am. Psychol. Soc. (pres. 1994-96), Western Psychol. Assn. (pres. 1994-95), Soc. Exptl. Psychology (Warren medal). Office: Univ of So Calif Neuroscis Program HNB 122 Univ Park Los Angeles CA 90007

THOMPSON, ROBERT BRUCE, medical products executive; b. Jackson, Tenn., Nov. 24, 1959; s. Robert Eugene and Jean Clara (Childers) T. BS in Acctg., Freed Hardeman U., 1981. CPA, Tenn. Staff acct. Ernst & Whinney, Memphis, Tenn., 1981-82; equity specialist Econocom USA, Memphis, 1983-86; chief exec. officer, owner Thompco Med., Inc., Memphis, 1986—, Medcor X-Ray Systems, Inc., Memphis, 1990—. Bd. dirs., chmn. West Tenn. Agape, 1987-93; bd. dirs. West Tenn. March of Dimes, 1987-91, TN-AK-MS Girl Scouts Coun., 1988-93, Freed Hardeman Coll. Adv. Bd., Henderson, Tenn., 1988—. Named to Outstanding Young Men of Am., 1981-88. Mem. Am. Assn. Equipment Lessors, Computer Dealers and Lessors Assn., Univ. Club of Memphis, Phoenix Club, Carnival Memphis (bd. dirs., pres. 1993, chmn. bd. 1994), Racquet Club Memphis (bd. dirs., v.p. 1989-92). Republican. Church of Christ. Office: Thompco Med Inc 5050 Poplar Ave Ste 2407 Memphis TN 38157

THOMPSON, ROBERT LEE, internist; b. Covington, Ohio, Nov. 2, 1939; s. Judson H. and Velma E. Thompson; m. Patty Lou Draher, June 12, 1968 (dec. May 1990); m. Hedy Sue Deems, Sept. 28, 1991. BA, Ohio State U., 1965, MD, 1968. Intern Riverside Meth. Hosp., Columbus, Ohio, 1968-69, resident, 1969-72; attending staff Riverside Meth. Hosp., 1974—, med. coord. intensive care unit, 1976-81; pvt. practice W.F. Millhon Med. Clinic, Columbus, 1974—; continuing med. edn. Riverside Meth. Hosp., 1979-81, med. care evaluation com., 1978-81, emergency svcs. com., 1974-80, smoking com., 1975-83, intensive care com., 1974-85, pharmacy and therapeutics chmn. 1979-93, com. to evaluate clin. competence, 1976—, chmn. critical care com. 1993-95, quality enhancement of the med. staff, 1993-95, in patient transformation com. co-chair 1994—; cons. staff Harding Hosp., 1990-95; clin. asst. prof. Dept. Medicine Ohio State U., 1981-94, clin. assoc. prof., 1994—; clin. asst. prof., 1981—; pres. Riverside Meth. Hosp. staff, 1996-97; bd. dirs. U.S. Health Corp. Contbr. articles to profl. jours. Maj. U.S. Army, 1972-74. Mem. ACP, AMA, Ohio State Med. Assn., Am. Soc. of Internal Medicine, Am. Coll. of Chest Physicians, Am. Heart Assn., Ohio Thoracic Soc., Columbus Soc. of Internal Medicine, Ctrl. Ohio Lung Assn., Am. Thoracic Soc. Home: 110 Kenyon Brook Dr Worthington OH 43085

THOMPSON, ROBY CALVIN, JR., orthopedic surgeon, educator; b. Winchester, Ky., May 1, 1934; s. Roby Calvin and Mary Davis (Guerrant) T.; m. Jane Elizabeth Searcy, May 2, 1959; children: Searcy Lee, Roby Calvin, III, Mary Alexandria. BA, Va. Mil. Inst., 1955; MD, U. Va., 1959. Diplomate Am. Bd. Orthopaedic Surgery (mem. bd. 1983). Intern Columbia Presbyn. Med. Center, N.Y.C., 1959-60; asst. resident, then resident in orthopedic surgery Columbia Presbyn. Med. Center, 1963-67; instr. orthopaedic surgery Coll. Phys. and Surg. Columbia U., 1967-68; mem. faculty Med. Sch. U. Va., 1968-74, prof. orthopaedic surgery, vice chmn. dept. Med. Sch., 1973-74; prof., chmn. dept. Med. Sch. U. Minn., 1974-95; chief med. officer U. Minn. Health Sys., 1995—; mem. merit rev. bd. VA, 1977-80; mem. study sect. on applied physiology and orthopedics NIH, 1980-83; adv. council mem. NIH, Nat. Inst. Arthritis, Musculoskeletal Disease and Skin, 1987—. Trustee Jour. Bone and Joint Surgery, 1988—, chmn. bd. trustees, 1991—; contbr. articles to med. jours. Capt. M.C. USAR, 1960-61. Grantee John Hartford Found., NIH. Mem. ACS, Orthopaedic Rsch. and Edn. Found. (bd. trustees 1990-96), Am. Acad. Orthopaedic Surgeons (bd. dirs. 1975-76, 83-90, pres. 1986), Orthopaedic Rsch. Soc. (pres. 1978), Am. Orthopaedic Assn., Musculoskeletal Tumor Soc. (pres. 1988-89), U. Va. Med. Alumni Assn. (bd. dirs. 1979-84), Woodhill Club (Wayzata). Republican. Presbyterian. Office: U Minn Hosps & Clinic Haward St at E River Rd Minneapolis MN 55455

THOMPSON, RONALD MACKINNON, family physician, artist, writer; b. N.Y.C., Oct. 19, 1916; s. George Harold and Pearl Anita (Hatfield) T.; m. Ethel Joyce Chastant, June 30, 1950; children: Phyllis Anita, Walter MacKinnon, Charles Chastant, Richard Douglas. BS, U. Chgo., 1947, MS, 1948, MD, 1949. Diplomate Am. Bd. Family Practice. Intern U. Mich., Ann Arbor, 1950-51; resident in psychiatry U. Tex., Galveston, 1951-52; pvt. practice, family and internal medicine South Dixie Med. Ctr., West Palm Beach, Fla., 1952-85; instr. Anatomy, U. Chgo., 1946-47, Pharmacology, 1948-49. Contbr. articles to profl. jours.; exhibited in 7 one-man shows (over 30 awards for painting in regional and nat. shows); represented in permanent collections at 5 mus. Mem. Civitan Club W. Palm Beach, Fla., 1951; former bd. dirs. Norton Gallery Mus. of Art, West Palm Beach. Mem. Fla. Nat. Guard, 1936-40; cadet Army Air Force, 1943-44. Over thirty awards for painting in juried regional and nat. shows. Fellow Am. Acad. Family Physicians; mem. AMA, Fla. Med. Assn., Fla. Acad. of Family Physicians, Palm Beach County Med. Soc., Nat. Watercolor Soc., Ariz. Watercolor Soc. Republican. Episcopalian. Home: 308 Leisure World Mesa AZ 85206-3142

THOMPSON, SETH CHARLES, retired oral and maxillofacial surgeon; b. Whittemore, Mich., Aug. 12, 1927; s. Seth Charles and Annie Ernestine (Washburn) T.; m. Effie Valore Garland, Jan. 20, 1954; children: Seth Charles III, David Garland. BS, Mich. State U., 1949; DDS, U. Mich., 1952, MS, 1959. Pvt. practice oral and maxillofacial surgery Midland, Mich., 1959-95; ret., 1995. Discoverer surgical treatment for trigeminal neuralgia, 1976. Bd. dirs. Midland (Mich.) Christian Sch., 1971-72, Inst. for Achievement of Human Potential, Midland, 1970-71. Served to capt. USAF, 1953-55. Fellow Am. Assn. Oral and Maxillofacial Surgery; mem. ADA, Mich. Dental Assn., Mich. Assn. Oral and Maxillofacial Surgery, Midland County Med. Soc. Republican. Baptist. Lodge: Rotary. Home and Office: 2728 Parrish Rd Midland MI 48642-9601

THOMPSON, TIMOTHY CHARLES, research scientist; b. Indpls., Apr. 9, 1951; s. Charles Avery and Gladys Kathryn T.; m. Sang Hee Park, Feb. 9, 1988; 1 child, Benjamin Paul. AB, Ind. U., 1974; PhD, Colo. U., 1985; postdoctoral fellow, Imperial Cancer Rsch. Fund, London, 1988. Asst. prof. Dept. of Urology and Cell Biology Baylor Coll. of Medicine, Houston, 1988-92, dir. rsch. Scott Dept. of Urology, 1992—, assoc. prof. Dept. of Urology, Cell Biology and Radiology, 1992—; cons. reviewer for acad. jours. Cancer Rsch., 1991—; mem. pathology B study sect. NIH, Bethesda, Md., 1993—; cons. Oncor, Inc., Gaithersburg, Md., 1994—, UroCor, Inc., Oklahoma City, 1995—. Contbr. numerous articles to profl. jours. and chpts. to books. Adult class Sun. sch. tchr. Rice Temple Bapt. Ch., Houston, 1992—. Grantee NIH, 1989—. Mem. Soc. of Basic Urological Rsch. (program com. 1989—), CaP CURE (bd. sci. dir. 1993—), Metastasis Rsch. Soc., Keystone Symposia (co-organizer 1996 Symposium). Democrat. Office: Baylor Coll of Medicine One Baylor Plz Houston TX 77030

THOMPSON, VANCE MICHAEL, ophthalmologist; b. San Diego, Dec. 18, 1959; s. Marion George and Judy Lee (Assam) T.; m. Jana Sue Kapaska, May 5, 1984; children: Blake, Joel, Lauren. BS in Chemistry, U. S.D., 1982, MD, 1986. Resident U. Mo., Columbia, 1989-90; ophthalmologist Ophthalmology Ltd., Sioux Falls, S.D., 1991—. Contbr. articles to profl. jours., chpts. to books. Refractive & Corneal Surgery fellow Hunkeler Eye Clinic, Kansas City, 1990. Fellow Am. Acad. Ophthalmology; mem. AMA, Internat. Soc. Refractive Surgery. Republican. Lutheran. Office: Ophthalnology Ltd 1200 S Euclid Sioux Falls SD 57105

THOMPSON, VETTA LYNN SANDERS, psychologist, educato; b. Birmingham, Ala., Sept. 7, 1959; d. Grover and Vera Lee (King) S.; m. Cavelli Andre Thompson, May 27, 1990; children: Olajuwon, Malik Rashad, Kimberlyn, Assata Iyana. BA, Harvard U., 1981; MA, Duke U., 1984, PhD, 1988. Cert. psychologist and health svc. provider, State of Mo. Com. Psychologists. Psychology intern Malcolm Bliss Mental Health Ctr., St. Louis, 1985-86; psychotherapist, testing coord. Washington U. Child Guidance Clinic, St. Louis, 1986-87; psychologist, treatment team coord. Hawthorn Children's Psychiatric Hosp., St. Louis, 1987-89; asst. prof. U. Mo., St. Louis, 1989-95, assoc. prof., coord. black studies, 1995—; tchg. asst. Duke U., Durham, N.C., 1982-84, rsch. asst., 1984-85; chairperson monitoring com. crisis access sys. Ea. Regional Adv. Coun. Dept. Mental Health, St. Louis, 1995-96; chairperson African Am. Task Force on Mental Health, Jefferson City, Mo., 1995—. Editl. adv. bd. A Turbulent Voyage: Readings in African American Studies, 1995-96; contbr. articles to profl. jours. Mem. adv. com. on violence prevention and investment in youth Mo. House, Jefferson City, 1995; mem. managed care steering com. Dept. Mental Health, Jefferson County, 1995-96. Kellogg Found.-Mo. Youth Initiative fellow, 1991-93; Ctr. for Great Plains Studies fellow U. Nebr., 1995—. Mem. APA (divsns. 1, 45), Assn. Black Psychologists. Methodist. Office: U Mo 8001 Natural Bridge Rd Saint Louis MO 63121

THOMPSON, WILLIAM BENBOW, JR., obstetrician, gynecologist, educator; b. Detroit, July 26, 1923; s. William Benbow and Ruth Wood (Locke) T.; m. Constance Carter, July 30, 1947 (div. Feb. 1958); 1 child, William Benbow IV; m. Jane Gilliland, Mar. 12, 1958; children: Reese Ellison, Belinda Day. AB, U. So. Calif., 1947, MD, 1951. Diplomate Am. Bd. Ob-Gyn. Resident Gallinger Mun. Hosp., Washington, 1952-53; resident George Washington U. Hosp., Washington, 1953-55; asst. ob-gyn. La. State U., 1955-56; asst. clinical prof. UCLA, 1957-64; assoc. prof. U. Calif.-Irvine Sch. Med., Orange, Calif., 1964-92; dir. gynecology U. Calif.-Irvine Sch. Med., 1977-92; prof. emeritus U. Calif.-Irvine Sch. Med., Orange, 1993—; vice chmn. ob-gyn. U. Calif.-Irvine Sch. Med., 1978-89; assoc. dean U. Calif.-Irvine Coll. Med., Irvine, 1969-73. Inventor: Thompson Retractor, 1976; Thompson Manipulator, 1977. Bd. dirs. Monarch Bay Assn. Laguna Niguel, Calif. 1969-77, Monarch Summitt II A ssn. 1981-83. With U.S. Army, 1942-44, PTO. Fellow ACS, Am. Coll. Ob-Gyn. (life), L.A. Ob-Gyn. Soc. (life); mem. Orange County Gynecology and Obstetrics Soc. (hon.), Am. Soc. Law and Medicine, Capistrano Bay Yacht Club (commodore 1975), Internat. Order Blue Gavel. Office: UCI Med Ctr OB/GYN 101 City Blvd W Orange CA 92668-2901

THOMPSON, WILLIAM MOREAU, radiologist, educator; b. Phila., Oct. 20, 1943; s. Charles Moreau and Aileen (Haddon) T.; m. Judy Ann Seel, July 27, 1968; children—Christopher Moreau, Thayer Haddon. B.A., Colgate U., 1965; M.D., U. Pa., 1969. Diplomate Am. Bd. Radiology. Intern, Case Western Res. U., Cleve., 1969-70; resident in radiology Duke U., Durham, N.C., 1972-75, asst. prof. Duke U. Med. Center, 1976-77, assoc. prof., 1977-82, prof. radiology, 1982-86; prof., chmn. dept. radiology, Vilhelmina and Eugene Gedgared chair in Radiology, U. Minn. Hosp. and Clinic, Mpls., 1986—. Served with USPHS, 1970-72. Recipient James Picker Found. Scholar in Acad. Medicine award, 1975-79; research and devel. grantee VA, 1977-86. Fellow Am. Coll. Radiology; mem. AMA, Radiology Soc. N.Am. (program chmn. 1994—), Minn. Med. Soc., Am. Roentgen Ray Soc., Assn. Univ. Radiologists (pres. 1989-90), Soc. Gastrointestinal Radiology (pres. 1995), Sigma Xi. Republican. Presbyterian. Contbr. chpts. to books, articles to profl. jours. Home: 18700 Woolman Dr Minnetonka MN 55345-3164 Office: U Minn Med Sch UMHC Box 292 Harvard Street Rd Minneapolis MN 55455-0361

THOMPSON, WILLIAM WEST, allergist, immunologist, pediatrician; b. Hallsboro, N.C., Apr. 6, 1921. MD, Duke U., 1947. Diplomate Am. Bd. Allergy and Immunology, Am. Bd. Pediatrics. Intern Mountainside Hosp., Montclair, 1947-48; resident in pediatrics Duke Hosp., Durham, N.C., 1948-49, Jefferson Davis Hosp., Houston, 1949-50; fellow in allergy Ark. Allergy Clinic, Little Rock, 1956-57; staff mem. Humana Hosp., Fort Walton Beach, Fla.; pvt. practice. Mem. AMA, Am. Acad. Allergy and Immunology, Am. Acad. Pediatrics, Am. Coll. Allergy and Immunology. Office: 906A Mar Walt Dr Fort Walton Beach FL 32547-6752

THOMS, NORMAN WELLS, carduivascular and thoracic surgeon; b. Bahrain, Nov. 5, 1934; (parents Am. citizens); m. Anna J. Holmes, June 22, 1962; 3 children. BA, Oberlin Coll., 1955; MD, U. Mich., 1959. Diplomate Am. Bd. Surgery, Am. Bd. Thoracic Surgery. Rotating intern Blodgett Meml. Hosp., Grand Rapids, Mich., 1959-60; resident in gen. surgery Detroit Gen. Hosp., 1960-62, 66-68, resident in thoracic surgery, 1968-70; instr. surgery Wayne State U. Sch. Medicine, Detroit, 1968-70, asst. prof., 1970-74, assoc. prof., 1974-75; pvt. practice, Topeka, 1975—; active staff Stormont-Vail Health Care, Topeka, St. Francis Hosp. and Med. Ctr., Topeka; participant state and local med. meetings. Contbr. articles to med. jours. Officer M.C., U.S. Army, 1962-64. Recipient Regents' award for best sci. exhibit Am. Coll. Chest Physicians, 1972, Bal Jeffrey award Stormont-Vail Found., 1995. Fellow ACS; mem. AMA, Internat. Soc. Heart Transplantation, Kans. Med. Soc., Shawnee County Med. Soc., Soc. Thoracic Surgeons. Office: Cardiovasc & Thoracic Surgeons PA 901 SW Garfield St 2d Fl Topeka KS 66606-1670

THOMSEN, STEPHEN, physician; b. Jersey City, Feb. 15, 1950; s. Harold E. and Muriel C. (Kelly) T.; m. Lois A. Von Atzingen, Sept. 23, 1973; children: David, Kerri. BS in Chemistry, St. Peter's Coll., Jersey City, 1972; MD, U. Rome, 1977. Diplomate Am. Bd. Internal Medicine. Pvt. practice Union City, N.J., 1982—. Mem. AMA, ACP, Am. Soc. Nephrology, Internat. Soc. Nephrology, Renal Physician Assn., Am. Informatics Assn., Am. Soc. Internal Medicine. Office: S Thomsen MD PA 316 Monastery Pl Union City NJ 07087

THOMSON, ELIZABETH REDMAN, managed care executive; b. Detroit, Apr. 13, 1951; d. William Joseph and Doreen Marie (Brodeur) Redman; m. Bruce Scott Thomson; children: Brianna, Kathryn. BA cum laude, Siena Heights Coll., 1992. Bus. adminstr. Macomb Clinton Med. Ctr., Clinton Twp., 1985-86; managed care coord. Oakland Gen. Hosp., Madison Hghts., Mich., 1988-94; bus. adminstr. Oakland Gen. Assn., Madison Hghts., 1988-94; exec. dir. PHO of Mercy Macomb, Clinton Twp., 1994—; adv. bd. First Am. Home Health, 1994—. Coach AYSO Macomb, Clinton Twp., 1993, 95. Mem. Healthcare Fin. Mgmt. Assn. (Ea. Mich. chpt., mgd. care com. 1995—). Office: PHO of Mercy-Macomb 15855 19 Mile Rd Clinton Township MI 48038

THOMSON, GERALD EDMUND, physician, educator; b. N.Y.C., 1932; s. Lloyd and Sybil (Gilbourne) T.; m. Carolyn Webber; children: Gregory, Karen. M.D., Howard U., 1959. Diplomate Am. Bd. Internal Medicine (bd. govs. 1985-92, exec. com. 1988-91, chmn.-elect 1990-91, chmn. 1991-92). Intern SUNY-Kings County Hosp. Center, Bklyn., 1959-60; resident in medicine SUNY-Kings County Hosp. Center, 1960-62, chief resident, 1962-63, N.Y. Heart Assn. fellow in nephrology, 1964-65, asst. vis. physician, 1963-70, clin. dir. dialysis unit, 1965-67; practice medicine specializing in internal medicine N.Y.C., 1963—; attending physician SUNY Med. Bklyn. Hosp., 1966-70; instr. in medicine SUNY, Bklyn., 1963-68; clin. asst. prof. medicine SUNY, 1968-70; asso. chief med. services Coney Island Hosp., Bklyn., 1967-70; attending physician Presbyn. Hosp., 1970—; dir. nephrology Harlem Hosp. Center, N.Y.C., 1970-71; dir. med. services Harlem Hosp. Center, 1971-85, pres. med. bd., 1976-78; assoc. prof. medicine Columbia Coll. Physicians and Surgeons, 1970-72, prof., 1972—, Samuel Lambert prof. medicine, and chief of staff, 1980—; exec. v.p. for profl. affairs, chief of staff Columbia-Presbyn. Med. Ctr., 1985-90; assoc. dean Coll. Physicians and Surgeons, Columbia U., N.Y.C., 1990—; mem. Health Rsch. Coun. City N.Y., 1972-75; mem. med. adv. bd. N.Y. Kidney Found., 1971-82; mem. Health Rsch. Coun., State N.Y., 1975-81; mem. hypertension info. and edn. adv. com. NIH, 1973-74, N.Y. State Adv. Com. on Hypertension, 1977-80; com. on non-pharm. treatment of hypertension Inst. of Medicine, Nat. Acad. Scis., 1980; mem. med. adv. bd. Nat. Assn. Patients on Hemodialysis and Transplantation, 1973-83; mem. adv. bd. Sch. Biomed. Edn., CUNY, 1979-83, Med. News Network, 1993-95; mem. com. on mild hypertension Nat. Heart and Lung Inst., 1976, mem. clin. trials rev. com., 1980-85, mem. rev. panel, 1979; bd. dirs. N.Y. Heart Assn., 1973-81, chmn. com. high blood pressure, 1976-81, Primary Care Devel. Corp.; chmn. com. hypertension N.Y. Met. Regional Med. Program, 1974-76; mem. adv. com. Heart and Hypertension Inst. of N.Y. State, 1984; mem. N.Y. Gov.'s Health Adv. Coun., 1981-84, pub. Health Coun., N.Y., 1983-95, Joint Nat. Com. High Blood Pressure NIH, 1983-84, 87-88, mem. rev. panel hypertension detection and monitoring bd. study cardiovasc. risk factors in young Nat. Heart, Lung and Blood Inst., 1984-90; mem. panel on receiving and withholding med. treatment ACLU, 1984-88; mem. Grad. Med. Edn. Commn., State of N.Y., 1984-86, mem. Commn. on End-State Renal Disease, 1985, 89-90; pres. Washington Heights-Inwood Ambulatory Care Network Corp., 1986-91; bd. dirs. Primary Care Devel. Corp., 1993—. Mem. adv. bd. Jour. Urban Health, 1974-80, Med. News Network, 1993-94. Chmn. ad hoc com. on access to nursing homes Pub. Health Council State of N.Y.; pres. Washington Heights-Inwood Ambulatory Care Network Corp., 1986-91; chmn. Federated Coun. Internal Medicine, 1991-92; mem. Mayor's Commn. Health and Hosps. Corp.; dir. Harlem Ctr. for Health Promotion and Disease Prevention; bd. dirs. Primary Care Devel. Corp. Recipient Nat. Med. award Nat. Kidney Found., N.Y., 1984, Outstanding Alumnus award Howard U., 1987, Dean's Outstanding Tchg. award Coll. Physicians and Surgeons Columbia U., 1986. Fellow ACP (Gov.'s coun. downstate region 1982-89, chmn. com. health pub. policy N.Y. chpt. 1982-89, health care professions com. 1987-90, bd. regents 1990-97, chmn. nat. health and pub. policy com. 1993-94, pres.-elect 1994-95, pres. 1995-96), N.Y. Acad. Medicine (mem. com. medicine in soc. 1974-76); mem. AAAS, N.Y. Soc. Nephrology (pres. 1973-74), Am. Fedn. Clin. Rsch., Federated Coun. for Internal Medicine (chmn. 1991-92, 95-96), Soc. Urban Physicians (pres. 1972-73), Am. Soc. Artificial Internal Organs, Assn. Program Dirs. in Internal Medicine, Pub. Health Assn. N.Y.C. (dir. 1983-86), Physicians for Social Responsibility of N.Y. (dir. 1983-85), Assn. Acad. Minority Physicians (pres. 1988-90). Home: Premium Pt New Rochelle NY 10801-5327 Office: Coll Physicians & Surgeons Columbia U New York NY 10032

THOMSON, JAMES ADOLPH, medical group practice administrator; b. Kansas City, Mo., Feb. 25, 1924; s. Edward Wilkins and Gladys Lucile (Opperman) T.; m. Patricia Jane Herron, Jan. 24, 1943; children: Linda Lee Thomson Schwartz, Kenneth Leroy, James Howard. BBA, Rockhurst Coll., Kansas City, 1950. Cost acct. Standard Brands, Inc., Kansas City, 1950-52; asst. comptroller Menorah Med. Ctr., Kansas City, 1952-56; comptroller Holzer Hosp. and Clinic, Gallipolis, Ohio, 1956-63; bus. mgr. Oberlin (Ohio) Clinic, Inc., 1963-71; adminstr. and treas. Thompson, Brumm & Knepper Clinic, Inc., St. Joseph, Mo., 1971-80; bus. mgr. Cin. Neurological Assocs., Inc., 1980-89; ret., 1989; cons. med. groups, Ohio, 1968-70. V.p. St. Joseph (Mo.) Area C. of C., 1976-78; pres. Oberlin Health Commn., 1968-69; bd. dirs. St. Joseph Sheltered Workshop, 1978-80. Served with M.C. U.S. Army, 1943-46, ETO. Recipient Disting. Svc. award St. Joseph Area C. of C., 1979. Fellow Am. Coll. Med. Group Adminstrs.; mem. Am. Assn. Hosp. Accts. (charter, pres. 1954-56), Mo. Med. Group Mgmt. Assn. (charter, pres. 1978-79), Med. Group Mgmt. Assn., Ohio Med. Group Mgmt. Assn., Cin. Med. Group Mgmt. Assn. (pres. 1983-84), Rotary (pres. Oberlin and St. Joseph clubs), Lions (pres. 1962-63), KC, Masons, Shriners (clown, asst. circus dir. Syrian Shrine 1993, 94, 95). Republican. Lutheran.

THOMSON, NEIL CAMPBELL, allergist; b. Kilmarnock, Scotland, Apr. 3, 1948; s. Adam Simpson Turnbull and Margaret Campbell (Templeton) T.; m. Lorna Jean Fraser, Aug. 16, 1973; children: David, Andrew, Jennifer. MbChB, U. Glasgow, 1972, MD, 1980. Jr. house officer Western Infirmary, Glasgow, United Kingdom, 1972-73, sr. house officer, 1973-75, registrar, 1975-78, sr. registrar, 1978-80, cons. physician, 1982—; rsch. fellow McMaster U., Hamilton, Canada, 1980-81. Co-editor: Asthma: Basic Mechanisms and Clinical Management, 2d edit., 1992, Manual of Asthma Management, 1995; co-author: Handbook of Clinical Allergy, 1990; mem. editl. bd. Pulmonary Pharmacology, 1988-95; assoc. editor Thorax, 1987-90. Travel grantee Am. Acad. Allergy, 1980. Mem. Brit. Thoracic Soc. (hon. sec. 1990-92, chmn. scientific meeting com. 1990-92). Office: West Glasgow Hosps, U NHJ Trust, Glasgow G12 0YN, Scotland

THOMSON, PHILIP DEPOYSTER, microbiologist; b. San Angelo, Tex., Mar. 13, 1943; s. John Throckmorton and Hazel (Parnell) T.; m. Margaret Jean Hoffmaster, July 29, 1967; 1 child, Philip DePoyster. AA, San Angelo Coll., 1963; BS, Angelo State Coll., San Angelo, 1968; MS, Mont. State U., 1972, PhD in Microbiology/Immunology, 1974. Rsch. asst. in ophthalmology Wilmer Inst., Johns Hopkins U., Balt., 1964-66; grad. fellow Mont. State U., Bozeman, 1968-74; postdoctoral fellow U. Tex. Med. Br., Galveston, 1974-76; chief microbiology divsn. Shriners Burns Inst., Galveston, 1976-83; dir. Burn Ctr. Labs. U. Mich. Hosps., Ann Arbor, 1983-92; asst. dir. technol. planning Mallinckrodt Med., Inc., St. Louis, 1992-94, assoc. dir. technol. planning, 1994—; chair tissue com. Organ Procurement Agy., Mich., 1988-92; mem. grant rev. com. NIDDR/U.S. Dept. Edn., Washington, 1991—; dir. skin bank U. Mich. Hosps., 1983-92. Editor/co-editor 5 books; contbr. chpts. to books, numerous articles to profl. jours. Mem. Am. Burn Assn., Internat. Soc. Burn Injuries, Wound Healing Soc., N.Am. Burn Soc., Phi Theta Kappa. Office: Mallinckrodt Med Inc 675 McDonnell Blvd Box 5840 Saint Louis MO 63134

THON, PATRICIA FRANCES, pediatrics nurse, medical/surgical nurse; b. Portland, Oreg., Sept. 25, 1959; d. Anthony William and Catherine Mary (Scully) Brenneis; m. Eric Phillip Thon, Apr. 30, 1988. AS, Johnson County C.C., 1980; BSN, U. Kans., Kans. City, 1982; MA, Webster U., 1992; postgrad., Portland State U., 1977; grad., St. Louis U., 1994. Staff nurse in pediatrics and oncology St. Luke's Hosp., Kansas City, Mo., 1982-84; commd. nurse officer USAF, 1984, advanced through grades to maj., 1988; staff nurse USAF, Scott AFB, Ill., 1984-88; flight nurse USAF, Scott AFB, 1988-91, sr. staff nurse in pediatrics and orthopedics, 1992; head nurse, flight chief maternal/child health Pediatric Clinic, Altus AFB, Okla., 1994—. Office: 97 MDG/SGOB 301 N 1st St Altus AFB OK 73523-5005

THOPPIL, CECIL KOSHEY, pediatrician, educator; b. Trivandrum, India, Aug. 4, 1961; m. Jennifer Carrol Gallego, Apr. 25, 1992; 1 child, Cecilia Ruth. Pre-degree, Mar Ivanios Coll., Trivandrum, Kerala, India, 1979; MB, BS, Med. Coll. Hosp., Trivandrum, 1984. Diplomate Am. Bd. Pediat.; cert. instr. neonatal advanced life support, pediat. advanced life support, BLS. Compulsory rotating internship Med. Coll. Hosp., Trivandrum, Kerala, India, 1985-86; postgrad. tng. pediatric medicine dept. child health S.A.T. Hosp., Trivandrum, Kerala, India, 1986-87; postdoctoral rsch. assoc. dept. perinatal pediatrics U. Tex. Med. Br., Galveston, 1987-89; pediatric internship Univ. Hosps. Cleve. Rainbow Babies and Children's Hosp., 1989-90; pediatric residency dept. pediatrics Scott & White Meml. Hosp./Tex. A&M U. Coll. Medicine, Temple, 1990-92; pediatrician Surry County Health Dept., Dobson, N.C., 1992-94, Med. Assocs. of Surry, Carolina Medicorp Inc., Mt. Airy, N.C., 1994—; physician cons. Surry County Sch. Health Adv. Coun., Surry Pre-sch. Interagy. Coun., Surry County Day Care Assn.; pediat. cons. Surry Smart Start Task Force. Contbr. articles to profl. jours. Provider for "Caring" Program; mem. Haymore Bapt. Ch. Recipient Father Kuncheria Goldmedal for First Rank in Loyola Sch. for Matriculation. Fellow Am. Acad. Pediat.; mem. AMA, N.C. Med. Soc., N.C. Pediat. Soc., Surry-Yadkin Med. Soc. Home: 860 Cross Creek Dr Mount Airy NC 27030-9229 Office: Med Assocs of Surry 865 W Lake Dr Mount Airy NC 27030

THOR, KARL BRUCE, neuropharmacologist, researcher; b. Pitts., Mar. 30, 1954; s. Milo and Marian (Golden) T.; m. Karen Leslie Booth, Aug. 8, 1981; children Michael Gregory, Jennifer Ann. BS, Pa. State U., 1976; PhD, U. Pitts Sch. Medicine, 1985. Post doctoral fellow NRSA Univormed Svcs. U. Health Scis., Bethesda, Md., 1985-88; sr. staff fellow Nat. Inst. Neurologic Diseases and Stroke, NIH, Bethesda, 1988-90; sr. scientist Eli Lilly & Co., Indpls., 1990—. Contbr. articles to profl. jours., chpts to books. Recipient predoctoral fellowship Pharm. Mfrs. Assn. Found., 1983; postdoctoral fellowship Am. Heart Assn., 1986. Mem. Soc. for Neurosci., Soc. for

Urodynamics, Internat. Continence Soc. Office: Eli Lilly & Co. Lilly Corp Ctr Indianapolis IN 46285

THORARENSEN, ODDUR C.S., pharmacist; b. Reykjavik, Iceland, Apr. 26, 1925; s. Stefan and Ragnheidur (Hafstein) T.; m. Asta Baldvinsdottir, Oct. 24, 1948 (div. Aug. 1956); children: Stefan, Baldvin Hafsteinn; m. Unnur Arny Long Thorarensen, Nov. 27, 1958; children: Ragnheidur Katrin, Sigridur Elin, Unnur Alma. Grad. diploma, Reyjavik Latin Sch., Iceland, 1945; examinatus Pharmaciae, U. Iceland, 1948; candidatus Pharmaciae, Royal Danish Coll. Pharmacy, Copenhagen, Denmark, 1949, 53, 54; student, P.C.P. & S., Phila., 1950. Proprietary Pharmacist, 1963. Asst. pharmacist Laugavegs Apotek, Reykjavik, Iceland, 1950-51, chief pharmacist, 1954-57, owner, mgr., 1963—; gen. mgr. Efnagerd Reykjavikur Ltd., Reykjavik, Iceland, 1957-69; mng. dir. Torenco Ltd., Iceland, 1981—. Chmn. and diverse other positions, Independence Party, Local Orgn., Gardabaer, Reykjavik, Iceland, 1980-90; mem. Diverse Comnx., Min. Health, Reykjavik, Iceland, 1970—, Parish Bd. Gardar Ch., Gardabaer, Reykjavik, Iceland, 1972-84. Mem. Iceland C. of C. (bd. electors 1974-91), Gimli Lodge, Masonic Nat. Grand Lodge Iceland, Iceland Pharmacist Union (sec. 1955-56, chmn. 1956-57), Iceland Proprietary Pharmacist Assn. (sec. 1973-74, 77-80), Reykjavik Proprietary Pharmacist Assn. (chmn. 1974-77, sec. 1977-78). Lutheran. Office: Laugavegs Apotek, 16 Laugavegi PO Box 477, 121 Reykjavík Iceland

THOREN, LARS OLOF, surgeon, educator; b. Gothenburg, Sweden, Nov. 18, 1921; s. Lars Einar and Anna Juliana (Thorn) T.; m. Ingrid Tyra; children: Birgitta, Gunnar, Karin, Gunilla. MD, U. Uppsala, Sweden, 1949, PhD, 1957. Chmn. dept. surgery Orebro (Sweden) Hosp., 1964; prof. surgery, chmn. dept. surgery U. Hosp. Uppsala, 1965-87, prof. emeritus, 1988-. Contbr. articles to profl. jours. Fellow Am. Coll. Surgeons (hon.); mem. Swedish Surg. Soc. (hon.), Swedish Soc. Med. Scis. (hon.), Finnish Surg. Soc. (hon.), Finnish Med. Soc. (hon.). Home: Bruksvg 1, 75241 Uppsala Sweden Office: Univ Hosp, Uppsala Sweden S 75185

THORÉN, MARJA CHRISTINE, endocrinologist; b. Stockholm, Mar. 29, 1938; d. S. Rudolf and Gunnel (Staverfelt) Lundstam; m. Stig O.G. Thorén, June 16, 1962; children: Katarina, Malin. B.Medicine, Karolinska Inst., Stockholm, 1967. Asst. physician Med. Clinic, Ersta Hosp., Stockholm, 1967-71, sr. physician, 1975-78; asst. physician dept. endocrinology Karolinska Hosp., Stockholm, 1972-75, sr. physician dept. endocrinology, 1978—, assoc. prof., 1985—. Contbr. articles to profl. jours. Mem. Swedish Soc. Medicine. Office: Dept Endocrinology, Karolinska Hosp., Stockholm Sweden S10401

THORNBURY, JOHN ROUSSEAU, radiologist, physician; b. Cleve., Mar. 16, 1929; s. Purla Lee and Gertrude (Glidden) T.; m. Julia Lee McGregor, Mar. 20, 1955; children: Lee Allison, John McGregor. A.B. cum laude, Miami U., Oxford, Ohio, 1950; M.D., Ohio State U., 1955. Diplomate: Am. Bd. Radiology. Intern Hurley Hosp., Flint, Mich., 1955-56; resident U. Iowa Hosps., Iowa City, 1958-61; instr., asst. prof. radiology U. Colo. Med. Center, Denver, 1962-63; practice medicine specializing in radiology Denver, 1962-63, Iowa City, 1963-66, Seattle, 1966-68, Ann Arbor, Mich., 1968-79, Albuquerque, 1979-84, Rochester, N.Y., 1984-89, Madison, Wis., 1989-94; mem. staff U. Wisconsin Hosp., Madison, prof. radiology, chief sect. of body imaging, Med. Sch., 1989-94, prof. emeritus, 1994—; asst. prof. radiology U. Iowa Hosps., 1963-66, U. Wash. Hosp., Seattle, 1966-68; assoc. prof. radiology U. Mich. Med. Ctr., 1968-71, prof. radiology, 1971-79; prof. radiology, chief divsn. diagnostic radiology dept. radiology Sch. Medicine, U. N.Mex., 1979-84; prof. radiology U. Rochester Sch. Medicine, 1984-89, acting chmn., 1985-87; chmn. sci. com. on efficacy studies Nat. Coun. on Radiation Protection, 1980-95; rapporteur/mem. sci. group on indications/limitations of x-ray diagnostic procedures WHO, 1983; cons. com. on efficacy of magnetic resonance nat. health tech. adv. panel Australian Inst. Health, 1986; invited U.S. cons. MRI program, Nijmegen, The Netherlands, 1992; lectr. in field; cons. tech. assessment and outcomes rsch., 1994—; cons. to Am. Soc. of Neuroradiology, 1995-97. Co-author/cons. Clin. Efficacy Assessment Project, Am. Coll. Physicians, 1986-89; assoc. editor: Yearbook of Radiology, 1971-82; editorial bd.: Contemporary Diagnostic Radiology, 1977-84, Urologic Radiology, 1977-84. Served to capt., M.C. USAF, 1956-58. Grantee Agy. Health Care Policy and Rsch., 1986-91, U. Rochester, 1986-89, U. Wis., Madison, 1989-91. Fellow Am. Coll. Radiology; mem. Soc. Uroradiology (pres. 1976-77, dir. 1977-79), Assn. Univ. Radiologists (pres. 1980-81), Radiol. Soc. N.Am., Am. Roentgen Ray Soc. (Caldwell medal 1993), Colo. Radiol. Soc., Phi Beta Kappa, Delta Tau Delta, Omicron Delta Kappa, Phi Chi. Republican. Lutheran. Home: 185 Morgan Pl Castle Rock CO 80104-9061

THORNE, FRANK LEADLEY, plastic surgeon; b. Rochester, N.Y., 1933. MD, U. Pa., 1957. Diplomate Am. Bd. Plastic and Reconstructive Surgery. Intern U. Mich., Ann Arbor, 1957-58; resident surgery U. Wash., Seattle, 1962-65; resident plastic surgery Duke U., Durham, N.C., 1965-68; surgeon Swedish Hosp., Seattle; clin. prof. plastic surgery U. Wash., Seattle; pres. Am. Assn. Hand Surgery, 1977-78, Plastic Surgery Ednl. Found., 1988-89; gov. ACS, 1990-96; dir. Am. Bd. Plastic Surgery, 1990-96, vice chmn., 1995-96. Fellow Am. Coll. Surgeons; mem. AMA, Am. Assn. Hand Surgeons, Am. Soc. Plastic and Reconstructive Surgery. Office: 1229 Madison St Ste 790 Seattle WA 98104-1381

THORNE, GARY MARVIN, surgeon; b. Great Bend, Kans., Feb. 22, 1948; s. Marvin E. and Annebeth L. (Oeser) T.; m. Margarita Salazar, May 3, 1975; children: Mary, Marci. BA, Pasadena Coll., 1970; MD, U. Ariz., 1974. Diplomate Am. Bd. Surgery. Intern U. Tex., San Antonio, 1974-75; resident in surgery U. Calif., Davis, 1975-79; pvt. practice Lewiston, Idaho, 1980—; attending surgeon Tri-State Meml. Hosp., Clarkston, Wash., 1979—, chief of staff, 1983; attending surgeon St. Joseph's Regional Med. Ctr., Lewiston, 1979—, chief of surgery, 1987, chief of staff, 1995—. Fellow ACS; mem. Idaho Med. Assn., North Idaho Dist. Med. Soc., U. Calif.-Davis Surg. Assn. Republican. Nazarene. Home: 1624 Swallows Nest Loop Clarkston WA 99403 Office: Gary M Thorne MD 307 Saint John s Way Lewiston ID 85301

THORNTON, ELAINE SERETHA, oncology nurse; b. N.Y.C., Mar. 25, 1967; d. Jerry Richard and Shelia (Beckford) T. BS, Syracuse U., 1990, postgrad. Cert. in gerontology. Staff nruse, clin. nurse I New Rochelle (N.Y.) Hosp. Med. Ctr., 1990-92, staff nurse, clin. nurse II, 1993-96, staff nurse drug and alcohol detoxification unit, 1996—; RN lab. asst. Sch. Nursing Coll. New Rochelle, 1992—; adj. prof. Coll. New Rochelle, Borough Manhattan C.C., N.Y.C., 1985—; vol. Am. Cancer Soc. Vol. Cancer Info. Svc., N.Y.C., 1991-92, Liz Holzman for Senate, N.Y.C., 1992, Clinton/Gore Presdl. campaign, 1992, Dole for Pres. Campaign, 1995; vol. providing cancer screening, blood pressure screening Pelham (N.Y.) Sr. Ctr., 1992; pub. info. rep. to economically disadvantaged Am. Cancer Soc., bd. dirs. Westchester divsn., 1993-95, 95—, pres. So. unit; organizer 1st & 2d ann. Cmty. Health Fair, New Rochelle. Recipient Orthobiotech. Quality of Life award, Pub. Educator award Westchester divsn. Am. Cancer Soc. Mem. Oncology Nursing Soc. (Hudson Valley chpt., nominating com. 1992-93, treas. 1993-94, pres. elect Hudson Valley chpt. 1995—), Black Nurses Assn., Am. Psychiat. Nurses Assn., Oncology Nursing Soc. (corr.), CTME (nat. membership). Republican. Home: 50 Guion Pl Apt 5K New Rochelle NY 10801-5517

THORNTON, JOHN LEMUEL, nuclear medicine physician; b. Warrenton, Va., Feb. 2, 1927; s. John Lemuel and Pearl Kinder (Champe) T.; m. Marjorie Mae Lucas, Nov. 5, 1949; children: John Lemuel, Anne Ellerson, Margaret Lucas Thornton Lammers. MD, Med. Coll. Va., 1949; internship, U.S. Naval Hosp., Phila., 1949-50; residency, Pathology Med. Coll. of Va., 1952-55. Diplomate Am. Bd. Pathology, Am. Bd. Nuc. Medicine. Instr. in pathology Med. Coll. Va., Richmond, 1955-56; dir. Va. Blood Bank, Richmond, 1953-63; pathologist Johnston-Willis Hosp., Richmond, 1963-70; pres. Physicians Clin. Labs., Richmond, 1970-79, Clin. Lab. Consultants, Richmond, 1970—, Johnston-Willis Hosp., Richmond, 1985-95, Chippenham & Johnston-Willis Hosps., Richmond, 1995—; chmn. Va. Blood Svcs., Richmond, 1974—, Am. Blood Commn., Washington, 1988-90; dir. Hosp. Corp. Am., Nashville, 1985-94. Lt. Comdr. USN, 1945-52. Democrat. Office: 1401 Johnston-Willis Hosp Richmond VA 23235

THORNTON, PHYLLIS JEAN, pathologist; b. Muncie, Ind., Nov. 18, 1940; d. Clem Eldon and Geraldine DeBride (Evans) Findley; m. Samuel Junior Thornton, Aug. 21, 1965. BS in Med. Tech., Ind. U., 1962; MEd, Howard U., 1969; MD, U. Mich., 1976. Resident in pathology LAC-U. So. Calif. Med. Ctr., L.A., 1976-80; physician specialist pathology LAC-Olive View Med. Ctr., Sylmar, Calif., 1980-86; sr. physician pathology Olive View-UCLA Med. Ctr., Sylmar, 1986—; from clin. instr. to clin. prof. U. So. Calif. Sch. Medicine, L.A., 1977—; trustee, treas., exec. bd. Olive View Edn. and Rsch. Inst., Sylmar, 1981-91; observer guidelines devel. Nat. Com. Clin. Lab. Standards, Villanova, Pa., 1990—; CompHealth scholar mgmt. in health care U. N.C. Kenan-Flagler Bus. Sch., Chapel Hill., 1994-95; moderator/speaker women's health forum SmithKline Beecham Clin. Labs., N.Y.C., 1992. Mem. resource bd. Safe Harbor Women's Clinic, L.A., 1992. Cytology quality assurance grantee NIH, 1989; named Outstanding Doping Control Coord. L.A. Olympics Com., 1984. Fellow Am. Soc. Clin. Pathologists; mem. Acad. Clin. Lab. Scientists and Physicians, Group Rsch. in Pathology Edn., Am. Coll. Physician Execs. Home: 76 N Arroyo Blvd Pasadena CA 91105

THORNTON, SANDRA DENISE, oncology nurse; b. Ft. Myers, Fla., Feb. 12, 1966; d. Jesse Terry and Ora Esther (Bauman) T. BSN, U. Tex., Houston, 1991; MS in Nursing Oncology, U. Tex. at Houston, 1995. RN, Tex. Clinician, charge nurse M.D. Anderson Cancer Ctr., Houston, 1991-94, clinician, 1994—; nursing supr. Vitas Healthcare Corp., 1994-95; clin. nurse specialist and outcomes mgr. Oncology Houston Northwest Med. Ctr., 1995—. Mem. speakers bur. Am. Cancer Soc., Houston, 1994—. Mem. Oncology Nursing Soc. (historian 1994-95), Pearl Moore Career Devel. award from Oncology Nursing Soc., 1995. Roman Catholic.

THORNTON, SPENCER P., ophthalmologist, educator; b. West Palm Beach, Fla., Sept. 16, 1929; s. Ray Spencer and Mae (Phillips) T.; m. Annie Glenn Cooper, Oct. 6, 1956; children: Steven Pitts, David Spencer, Ray Cooper, Beth Ellen. BS, Wake Forest Coll., 1951, MD, 1954. Diplomate: Am. Bd. Ophthalmology. Intern Ga. Bapt. Hosp., Atlanta, 1954-55; resident gen. surgery U. Ala. Med. Center, 1955-56; resident ophthalmology Vanderbilt U. Sch. Medicine, 1960-63; practice medicine specializing in ophthalmic surgery Nashville, 1960—; med. dir. Thornton Eye Ctr., 1995—; mem. staff Bapt. Hosp., chief ophthalmology svc., 1982-87; guest prof., vis. lectr. U. Toronto, 1990, 91, 92, U. Paris, 1989, Rothchilds Inst., Paris, 1992, 94, U. Pretoria, 1991, 93, others; instr. Moscow Inst. Eye Microsurgery, 1981; instr. ophthalmic surgery Am. Acad. Ophthalmology Ann. Courses; lectr. lens implant symposiums Eng., Spain, Australia, Switzerland, Can., Sweden, Greece, Germany, France, Republic of South Africa, Japan; Berzelius lectr. U. Lund, Sweden, 1992; P.J. Hay Gold medal lectr., North of Eng. Ophthal. Soc., Scarborough, 1992. King Features syndicated newspaper columnist, 1959-60, feature writer, NBC radio and TV, 1958-60; author, co-author textbooks on cataract and refractive surgery; mem. editl. bd. Jour. Refractive and Corneal Surgery, Jour. Cataract and Refractive Surgery, Video Jour. Ophthalmology, Ocular Surgery News (Ophthalmologist of Yr. 1996), Ophthalmic Practice (Can.), Eye Care Tech. Mag. (Lifetime Achievement award 1996); contbr. articles to profl. jours.; inventor instruments and devices for refractive and lens implant surgery. Named among Outstanding Young Men of Yr., U.S. Jaycees, 1965; recipient Honor award Can. Implant Assn., 1993, Outstanding Achievement award Bowman Gray Sch. Medicine, 1995. Fellow ACS, Am. Acad. Ophthalmology (Honor award 1995); mem. Am. Soc. Cataract and Refractive Surgery (pres.-elect 1995, chmn. internat. com. stds. and quality control for ophthalmic instruments and devices), Am. Med. Soc. Vienna (life), South African Intraocular Implant Soc. (life), Can. Implant Soc. (life), Tenn. Soc. Medicine, Nashville Acad. Medicine, Internat. Refractive Surgery Club (v.p. 1994), Phi Rho Sigma, Delta Kappa Alpha. Baptist. Home: 5070 Villa Crest Dr Nashville TN 37220-1425 Office: 2010 Church St Nashville TN 37203-2012

THORSON, ALAN GLEN, surgeon; b. Omaha, June 20, 1952; s. E. Wallace and Vendela Marie (Havenstein) T.; m. Nancy Lois Maricle, Apr. 18, 1981; children: Alicia Marie, Scott Alan, Katherine Elizabeth. BS in Agrl. Econs., U. Nebr., 1974, BA in Internat. Rels., 1976; MD, U. Nebr., Omaha, 1979, cert. gen. surgery, 1984. Diplomate Am. Bd. Med. Examiners. Am. Bd. Surgery, Am. Bd. Colon and Rectal Surgery. Intern gen. surgery U. Nebr. Hosp., Omaha, 1979-80, resident gen. surgery, 1980-84; fellow colon and rectal surgery U. Minn., Mpls., 1984-85; sec. Colon and Rectal Surgery, Inc., Omaha, 1987-89, v.p., 1989—; clin. asst. prof. surgery U. Nebr. Coll. Medicine, Omaha, 1985-93, clin. assoc. prof. of surgery, 1993—; clin. asst. prof. surgery Creighton U. Sch. Medicine, Omaha, 1986-88, asst. prof. surgery, 1989-92, assoc. prof. surgery, 1992—, program dir. sect. colon and rectal surgery, 1988—; v.p. Todd Valley Farms, Inc., Mead, Nebr., 1988—; med. advisor United Ostomy Assn., Omaha chpt., 1986—; assoc. examiner Am. Bd. Colon and Rectal Surgery, 1993—. Contbr. articles to profl. jours. Bd. dirs. Nebr. divsn. Am. Caner Soc., 1991-96, pres. Nebr. divsn., 1995-96, bd. dirs. Heartland divsn., 1996—; mem. adminstrv. bd. Faith Westwood United Meth. Ch., Omaha, 1988-92; trustee Nebr Satellite, Crohn's Colitis Found. of Am., 1992-93. Fellow ACS, Am. Soc. Colon and Rectal Surgeons, Southwestern Surg. Conf., Soc. Surg. Oncology; mem. AMA, Am. Soc. Gastrointestinal Endoscopy, Soc. Surgery Alimentary Tract, Soc. Am. Gastrointestinal Endoscopic Surgeons, Wilderness Med. Soc., Omaha Midwest Clin. Soc., Assn. Program Dirs. for Colon and Rectal Surgery. Office: Colon and Rectal Surgery 711 Profl Tower 105 S 17th St Omaha NE 68102-1401

THORSON, PAMELA MANCE, family practice and pediatrics nurse; b. Huntsville, Ala., May 20, 1950; d. Fred and Mildred Virginia (Ellett) Mance; m. Roy Wayne Thorson, Apr. 10, 1971; children: Stewart, Blake. ADN, J.C. Calhoun Coll., Decatur, Ala., 1975; BS in Health Sci., Athens (Ala.) State U., 1991. RN, Ala.; cert. BCLS instr. Dir. nursing Madison Manor Nursing Home, Madison, Ala., 1975-77; staff nurse Med. Ctr. Hosp., Huntsville, 1977-79; supr. North Ala. Home Health, Huntsville, 1979-82; head nurse Dept. Army, Redstone Arsenal, Ala., 1982—; asthma educator Fox Army Hosp., Redstone Arsenal, 1995—. Home: 225 Hartside Rd Owens Cross Roads AL 35763

THORSTAD, MICHAEL GARDNER, orthodontist; b. Detroit, Oct. 21, 1945; s. Merrill J. and Carol Elissa (Gardner) T.; m. Janice Lee Gibbs, Aug. 5, 1966; children: Erik Gardner, Carol Elissa, William Michael, James Matthew. BS, U. Ala., 1966; DDS, Columbia U., 1976, postgrad., 1976-77. Orthodontist U. Miss., Jackson, 1977-78; pvt. practice orthodontics West Palm Beach, Fla., 1978—. Lt. (j.g.) USN, 1966-69. Mem. ADA, 1st Dist. Dental Soc. Home: 110 El Pueblo Way Palm Beach FL 33480 Office: 1911 N Flagler Dr West Palm Beach FL 33407

THORSTENSON, MICHAEL ERVIN, surgeon; b. Rhinelander, Wis., July 2, 1947; s. Ervin Lawrence and Doris Ruth (Strolk) T.; divorced; children: Erin, Michelle, Erik, Mark. BA in Psychology, U. Wis., 1971, MD, 1978. Diplomate Am. Bd. Surgery. Intern, resident in gen. surgery Henry Ford Hosp., Detroit, 1979-84; staff surgeon Wilkinson Clinic S.C., Oconomowoc, Wis., 1984—. With U.S. Army, 1967-69. Fellow ACS; mem. Milw. Acad. Surgery. Home: 1419 N Summit Ave Oconomowoc WI 53066 Office: Wilkinson Clinics SC 915 E Summit Ave Oconomowoc WI 53066

THORVINGER, BJÖRN OLOF STURE, interventional radiologist; b. Malmö, Sweden, Aug. 9, 1947; s. Sture Nils and Stina Rut (Hansson) T.; m. Berit Lisbeth Fredriksson, Aug. 17, 1979; children: Emilia, Elin. B Medicine, U. Lund, Sweden, 1972, BA, 1972, MD, 1978, PhD, 1990. Asst. prof. dept. diagnostic radiology U. Lund, 1986-92, assoc. prof., 1992—; cons. Swedish Med. Bd., 1992. Author: Diagnostic and Interventional Radiology of Gynecologic Neoplasms, 1990, Interventional Radiology, 1990. Mem. Swedish Soc. Interventional Radiology, Swedish Soc. Interventional Cardiology. Home: Bärsärkagången 5, 22475 Lund Sweden Office: U Lund, Dept Diagnostic Radiology, S-22185 Lund Sweden

THRALL, JAMES HUNTER, radiology educator; b. Ann Arbor, Mich., 1943. BA, U. Mich., 1964, MD, 1968. Intern Walter Reed Army Med. Ctr., Washington, 1968-69, resident in radiology, 1969-72, fellow in nuclear medicine, 1972-73, asst. chief nuclear med. svc. dept. radiology, 1973-75 asst. prof. radiology and nuclear medicine U. Mich., Ann Arbor, 1975-78, assoc. prof., 1978-81, prof., 1981-83; now Juan M. Taveras prof. radiology Harvard U., Cambridge, Mass.; cons. nuclear medicine Ann Arbor VA Hosp.; chmn. radiology dept. Henry Ford Hosp., Detroit, 1983; radiologist in chief, Mass. Gen. Hosp., Boston, 1983—. Maj. M.C., U.S. Army, 1968-75. Office: Mass General Hosp Fruit St Boston MA 02114

THRASH, MELVIN LAWRENCE, psychiatrist; b. Asheville, N.C., June 29, 1940; s. Augustus Pinkney and Margaret Frances (Ball) T. AB, Duke U., 1962, MD, 1967. Diplomate Am. Bd. Psychiatry. Intern UCLA, 1967-68; resident Ea. Pa. Psychiat. Inst., Temple U. Svc., 1968-70; fellow in child psychiatry St. Christopher's Hosp. for Children, Temple U., 1970-71, Columbia U., 1975-76; chief exec. officer Halgarth Behavioral Scis. Inst., Falmouth, Mass., 1973-75; chief day treatment svcs. Roosevelt Hosp.-Columbia U., N.Y.C., 1976-78; assoc. med. dir. Pfizer Labs., N.Y.C., 1978-79; dir. neuropsychiatric drug devel. Ayerst Labs., N.Y.C., 1979-82; dir. psychiat. ambulatory svcs. Bellevue Hosp. Ctr., N.Y.C., 1982-89; prof. psychiatry NYU, 1982—, exec. dir. for health affairs, 1989-91; med. dir. Value Behavioral Health, N.E. Region, Troy, N.Y., 1992-94, South Oaks Hosp./Broadlawn Manor Nursing Care Ctr., Amityville, N.Y., 1994—; med. advisor Sports Tng. Inst., N.Y.C., 1976—; cons. psychiatry and sports medicine, 1976-86, N.Y. Times, Vogue mag., Self mag., 1978—; v.p., bd. dirs. Mary Duke Biddle Found., Durham, N.C., 1983—. Deacon, The Riverside Ch., N.Y.C., 1984-88. Maj. USAF, 1971-73. Fellow Am. Psychiat. Assn.; mem. Coll. Sports Medicine, Am. Ortho Psychiatric Assn., AAAS, N.Y. Acad. Medicine, N.Y. Athletic Club. Democrat. Methodist. Office: The Long Island Home LTD 400 Sunrise Hwy Amityville NY 11702

THRASHER, JACK D., toxicologist, researcher, consultant; b. Nashville, Kans., Aug. 13, 1936; s. Harold A. and Margaret E. (Bolin) T.; m. Diane L. Walton, June 29, 1963; children: Traci L., Kristen I. BS, Longbeach State U., 1959; PhD, UCLA, 1964. Asst. prof. U. of Colo. Sch. of Medicine, Denver, 1964-66, UCLA Sch. of Medicine, L.A., 1966-72; application specialist Millipore Corp., Bedford, Mass., 1973-75; cons. Thrasher and Assocs., L.A., 1975-92, Alto, N. Mex., 1992—; mem. faculty E. N. Mex. U., RuiDoso, 1992—; mentor Columbia Pacific U., San Rafael, Calif., 1992—; bd. dirs., chmn. Internat. Inst. Rsch. for Chem. Hypersensitivity, Alto, N. Mex., 1991-94; advisor Chem. Impact Project Mill Valley, Calif., 1993—. Author: (books) Cellular and Molecular Renewal in the Mammalian Body, 1971, The Poisoning of our Homes and Work Places, 1990; editor-in-chief Informed Consent, 1993-94. Grantee: USPHS, NIH, 1966-69. Home and Office: Thrasher and Assocs PO Box 879 110 Raven Corners Alto NM 88312

THRASHER, JAMES BRANTLEY, surgeon; b. Anderson, S.C., Sept. 9, 1960; s. James Douglas and Margaret Ann (Erskine) T.; m. Laura Lesslie Church, Aug. 26, 1989; children: James Brantley Jr., Madeline Lee. BS, Clemson U., 1982; MD, Med. U. S.C., 1986. Diplomate Am. Bd. Urology, Nat. Bd. Med. Examiners. Attending urologist Fitzsimmons Army Med. Ctr., Aurora, Colo., 1991; cons. urol. surgery VA Hosp., Durham, N.C., 1991-92; attending urologist Madigan Army Med. Ctr., Tacoma, Wash., 1992-95, program dir. urology svc., 1995—; cons. Am. Lake VA Med. Ctr., Tacoma, 1992—; clin. asst. prof. surgery Uniformed Svcs. U. Health Scis., Bethesda, Md., 1993-96, U. Wash., Seattle, 1993—; cons. urol. surgery Naval Regional Med. Ctr., Bremerton, Wash., 1994—. Decorated army achievement medal, 1995. Mem. AMA, Am. Assn. Clin. Urologists, Am. Coll. Surgeons, Am. Urol. Assn., Soc. Govt. Svc. Urologists, Assn. Mil. Surgeons U.S., N.C. Med. Soc., Northwest Urol. Soc., Phi Kappa Phi. Office: Madigan Army Med Ctr MCHJ-SU Tacoma WA 98431

THRASHER, ROSE MARIE, critical care and community health nurse; b. Urbana, Ohio, Jan. 19, 1948; d. Jesse and Anna Frances (Clark) T. Student, Mercy Med. Ctr. Sch. Med. Tech., 1966-67, Wittenberg U., 1969-70; BSN, Ohio State U., 1974, BA in Anthropology, 1994, postgrad., 1994—. RN, Ohio; cert. cmty. health nurse ANA; cert. provider BCLS and ACLS, Am. Heart Assn. Pub. health nurse Columbus (Ohio) Health Dept., 1977-78; critical care nurse VA Med. Ctr., San Francisco, 1981, Staff Builders Health Care Svc., Oakland, Calif., 1975-76, 81-85; supr., case mgr. home health nurse passport program and intermittent care program Interim Health Care (formerly Med. Pers. Pool), Columbus, 1976-77, 85—. Recipient numerous acad. scholarships Wittenberg U. and Ohio State U.; mem. Nat. Women's Hall of Fame. Mem. AACN, ANA (coun. cmty. health nursing), AAUW, Ohio Nurses Assn., Intravenous Nurses Soc., Ohio State U. Alumni Assn., Am. Anthropol. Assn., Ohio Acad. Sci., Ohio State U. Coll. of Nursing Alumni Soc.

THUESON, DAVID OREL, pharmaceutical executive, researcher, educator, writer; b. Twin Falls, Idaho, May 9, 1947; s. Orel Grover and Shirley Jean (Archer) T.; m. Sherrie Linn Lowe, June 14, 1969; children: Sean, Kirsten, Eric, Ryan, Todd. BS, Brigham Young U., 1971; PhD, U. Utah, 1976. Postdoctoral fellow U. Tex. Med. Br., Galveston, 1976-77, asst. prof., 1977-82; sr. rsch. assoc. Parke-Davis Pharms., Ann Arbor, Mich., 1982-88; dir. pharmacology Immunetech Pharms., San Diego, 1988-90; dir. immunopharmacology Tanabe Rsch. Labs., San Diego, 1990-92; v.p. discovery Cosmederm Techs., San Diego, 1992—. Contbr. articles to profl. jours.; patentee in field. Scout leader Boy Scouts Am., Mich., Tex. and Calif., 1979—. NIH grantee, 1978-81. Mem. Am. Acad. Allergy and Clin. Immunology, Am. Assn. Immunologists, Am. Thoracic Soc. Republican. Mormon. Home: 12740 Boxwood Ct Poway CA 92064-2643 Office: Cosmederm Techs 3252 Holiday Ct Ste 226 San Diego CA 92037

THUESON, SHARON, physician assistant; b. Jerome, Idaho, June 17, 1956; d. Constant Walter and Mary (Tyler) Thueson; m. Keith Gustav Tanner, Apr. 6, 1991; children: Kristofer, Ashlee, Haylee. AA Physician Asst., Pa. State U., 1981. Physician asst. John M. Garrity, M.D., Lovell, Wyo., 1981-82, Graham Med. Clinic, Newville, Pa., 1982-87, St. Benedict's Hosp., Ogden, Utah, 1987-89, Kaiser Permanente, Longview, Wash., 1989—; lactation cons. mother baby program Kaiser Permanente, 1995—, drug utilization rev. com., 1993-94. Office: Kaiser Permanente 1230 7th Ave Longview WA 98623

THURBER, ROBERT EUGENE, physiologist, researcher; b. Bayshore, N.Y., Oct. 11, 1932; s. Hallett Elliot and Mary Jean (Winkler) T.; m. Barbara Meyer, June 24, 1953 (div. 1982); children: Robert, Joseph, Karl, Michael; m. Linda Boyd, Mar. 4, 1984; stepchildren: Janet, Barbara, Karen, Robert. BS, Holy Cross Coll., Worcester, Mass., 1954; MS, Adelphi U., 1961; PhD, U. Kans., 1964. Rsch. assoc. Brookhaven Nat. Lab., Upton, N.Y., 1956-61; rsch. asst. Iowa State U., Ames, 1961-62; asst. prof. Med. Coll. Va., Richmond, 1964-69; assoc. prof. Jefferson Med. Coll., Phila., 1969-70; prof., chmn. physiology Sch. Medicine East Carolina, Greenville, N.C., 1970-94, prof., 1994—. Contbr. articles to profl. jours. Sgt. U.S. Army, 1954-56, Korea. Predoctoral fellow USPHS, 1962, postdoctoral fellow NEH, 1977. Mem. Am. Physiol. Soc., Assn. Chairmen Depts. Physiology (councilor 1989-91), Am. Heart Assn. (pres. N.C. affiliate 1979), Greenville Country Club, River Bend Country Club. Home: 108 Hyde Ct New Bern NC 28562-3724 Office: E Carolina U Sch Medicine Dept Physiology Greenville NC 27858

THURER, RICHARD JEROME, surgeon, educator; b. Amityville, N.Y., June 1, 1936; s. Carl and Rose (Friedman) T.; m. Priscilla Arlen, Sept. 1, 1940; children: Margaret Anne, Katherine Arlen. AB, Princeton U., 1957; MD, Columbia U., 1961. Diplomate Am. Bd. Surgery, Am. Bd. Thoracic Surgery. Intern in surgery Columbia Presbyn. Med. Ctr., N.Y.C., 1961-62; resident in gen. surgery Coilumbia Presbyn. Med. Ctr., N.Y.C., 1964-68, resident in thoracic and cardiovascular surgery, 1968-70; Instr. surgery Coll. of Physicians & Surgeons, Columbia U., N.Y.C., 1970; assoc. surgery U. Pa., Phila., 1970-71; asst. prof. surgery U. Miami, Miami, 1971-77, assoc. prof. surgery, 1977-83; dir. Thoracic Surgery Jackson Meml. Hosp., Miami, 1978—; prof. surgery U. Miami, Miami, 1983—. Author and co-author several scientific articles; author several book chapters. Bd. dirs. Am. Heart Assn. Greater Miami, 1985-92; mem. Miami Com. on Fgn. Rels., 1988-90. Lt. USNR, 1982-84. Recipient Student Fellowship Arthritis and Rheumatism Found. 1960. Fellow ACS, Am. Coll. Chest Physicians, Am. Coll. Cardiology; mem. Am. Assn. Thoracic Surgery, Am. Thoracic Soc. (Fla. rep. coun. of chpt. N.Y.C. 1987-93), Soc. Thoracic Surgeons, Princeton Club South Fla. (officer 1985-87). Democrat. Jewish. Home: 7400 SW 133rd St Miami FL 33156-6836 Office: U Miami R-114 Divsn Cardiothroacic Surgery PO Box 016960 Miami FL 33101

THURMAN, ADDISON EUGENE, JR., urologist; b. Pawnee, Okla., Apr. 27, 1943; s. Addison Eugene and Cathleen Lee (Irwin) T.; m. Eileen Lee Ittmann, Aug. 10, 1968; children: Scott Addison, Sally Ann. BS, Southwestern State Coll., Weatherford, Okla., 1965; MS, Tulane U., 1967; D. of Medicine, U. Okla., Oklahoma City, 1971. Diplomate Am. Bd. Urology. Intern in surgery Bexar County Hosp. Dist., San Antonio, 1971-72, resident in urology, 1972-77; maj., dept. urology USAF Carswell AFB Hosp., Ft. Worth, 1977-79; pvt. practice in urologic surgery Tex., 1979-85; mem. staff Ft. Worth Urol. Clinic, 1985—; chief dept. surgery St. Joseph Hosp., Ft. Worth, 1989-90. Maj. USAF, 1977-79. Fellow ACS, Tex. Surg. Soc.; mem. AMA, Am. Urol. Assn., Tex. Med. Assn., Alpha Omega Alpha. Home: 2111 Pembroke Dr Fort Worth TX 76110-1239 Office: Fort Worth Urol Clinic 1415 Pennsylvania Ave Fort Worth TX 76104-2113

THURMAN, JOHN NEAL, internist; b. Lansdowne, Pa., Nov. 1, 1941; s. Edgar Neal and Julia Gardner (Ross) T.; m. Claire Ellen Naselli, July 9, 1966; children: Neal, Dawn. BA in Zoology, Swarthmore Coll., 1963; MD, U. Pa., 1967. Diplomate Am. Bd. Internal Medicine, Nat. Bd. Med. Examiners. Intern Geisinger Med. Ctr., Danville, Pa., 1967-68, resident in internal medicine, 1970-73; physician Media (Pa.) Clinic, 1973-81, Bell-Thurman Assocs., Media, 1981-95, Clin. Care Assocs., Media, 1995—; clin. asst. prof. of medicine Hosp. U. Pa., Phila., 1996—; chief subdivsn. endocrinology Riddle Meml. Hosp., Media, 1981—, chmn. divsn. medicine, 1983-96, mem. med. exec. com., 1983-96, bd. dirs., 1993-95; active staff Riddle Meml. Hosp., Hosp. of U. Pa., Phila. Acad. advisor A Better Chance, Swarthmore, 1993—; deacon Swarthmore Presbyn. Ch., 1996—. Lt. USNR, 1968-70. Recipient Legion of Honor Chapel of the Four Chaplains, 1980. Fellow ACP; mem. Am. Soc. Internal Medicine, Pa. Soc. Internal Medicine, Pa. Med. Soc., Delaware County Med. Soc., Am. Diabetes Assn., Alpha Omega Alpha. Office: Bell-Thurman Clin Care Asso Outpatient Pavilion 340B 1098 W Baltimore Pike Media PA 19063

THURMAN, RALPH HOLLOWAY, health care company executive; b. Chgo., July 28, 1949; s. Joseph Ralph and Jean (Holloway) T.; m. Karen Ann Eisenhart, Mar. 14, 1980; children: Kelly Ann, Kaitlin Leigh, Kyle Joseph. BA, Va. Poly. Inst., 1971; MA, Webster U., 1974; postgrad., USAF Air Command and Staff Coll., 1974. Dir. orgn. Exxon Corp., N.Y.C., 1976-82; dir. personnel Pepsico Internat., Purchase, N.Y., 1982-84; pres. Rhone-Poulenc Rorer, Ft. Washington, Pa., 1984-94; CEO Corning Life Scis., N.Y.C., 1994—, 1994—; bd. dirs. Immune Response Corp., Enzon Corp., Hannaman U., Fox Chase Cancer Ctr.; cons. on resource mgmt. Contbr. articles to profl. publs. Bd. dirs. Jr. Achievement, 1984, Phila. Bus. Attraction Commn., 1987—, Univ. City Sci. Ctr., Phila., 1987—; mem. Greater Phila. Econ. Devel. Coalition, 1987—. Capt. USAF, 1971-76, Vietnam combat pilot. Home: 1483 Ponus Rdg New Canaan CT 06840-3400 Office: Corning Life Scis 450 Park Ave New York NY 10022-2605

THURMAN, WILLIAM GENTRY, medical research foundation executive, pediatric hematology and oncology physician, educator; b. Jacksonville, Fla., July 1, 1928; s. Horace Edward and Theodosia (Mitchell) T.; m. Peggy Lou Brown, Aug. 11, 1949 (div. 1978); children—Andrew E., Margaret Anne, Mary Allison; m. Gabrielle Anne Martin, Jan. 22, 1980; 1 step child, Stephanie Anne. B.S., U. N.C., 1949; M.S., Tulane U. Sch. Pub. Health, 1960; M.D.C.M., McGill U., Montreal,, 1954. Prof. pediatrics Cornell U. Sch. Medicine, N.Y.C., 1962-64; prof. pediatrics U. Va., Charlottesville, 1964-73; dean sch. medicine Tulane U., New Orleans, 1973-75; provost Health Scis. Ctr. U. Oklahoma, Oklahoma City, 1975-80; pres., chief exec. officer Okla. Med. Research Found., Oklahoma City, 1979—; sr. cons. pediatrics Surgeon Gen. USAF, Washington, 1964—; mem. Diet and Nutrition Study Com., Nat. Cancer Inst., Bethesda, Md., 1969—, Profl. Edn. Com., Am. Cancer Soc., N.Y.C., 1973—. Author: (with others) Bone Tumors in Children, 1963, Pediatric Malignant Disease, 1964; contbr. articles to profl. jours. Bd. dirs. United Way, Oklahoma City, 1977—, chmn., 1994, Community Found., Oklahoma City, 1975—, ARC, Oklahoma City, 1992—; bd. dirs. C. of C., 1984—, chmn. 1995. Served with U.S. Army, 1944-46, ETO. Markle scholar, 1959-64. Fellow Am. Acad. Pediatrics (dir. 1969-72); mem. Am. Pediatric Soc., Soc. Pediatric Rsch. (councillor 1971-75), Soc. Mil. Cons., Assn. Ind. Rsch. Insts. (pres. 1985-87), Oklahoma City C. of C. (dir. 1979, chmn. 1994-95), Alpha Omega Alpha. Baptist. Club: Petroleum. Home: 1213 Larchmont Ln Oklahoma City OK 73116

THURMOND, STEPHEN ROBERT, optometrist; b. Atlanta, Nov. 25, 1952; s. Robert Hugh and Dorothy H. (Pulliam) T.; m. Gwen Martin, May 14, 1994; 1 child, Rebecca Leah. BS, Ga. Coll., 1974; postgrad., U. Ala., 1986-88; OD, So. Coll. Optometry, 1992. Lic. optometrist Ga. State Bd. Examiners. Optometrist Clayton (Ga.) Family Eye Care PC; bd. dirs. Hospice of N.E. Ga., Clayton, Rhapsody in Rabun, Dillard, Ga. Pres. student govt. So. Coll. Optometry, Memphis, 1990-91, bd. mem. Trustees of So. Coll. Optometry, 1990-92; chair Rabun Youth Inc. Cmty. hero Olympic torchbearer, Clayton, 1996. Mem. Ga. Optometric Assn. (trustee 1994—), Rotary Club Clayton (pres.-elect 1994—, pres. 1995-96). Presbyterian. Office: Clayton Family Eye Care PC 164 W Warwoman Rd Clayton GA 30525

THURSTON, R(OBERT) SCOTT, cardiovascular surgeon; b. Atlanta, Nov. 3, 1953; s. Robert Moore and Phyllis (Miller)T.; m. Chyrl Lynn Lowe, Jan. 1979; m. Joann Margaret Waldie, May 23, 1987; children: Elizabeth, Matthew. BA cum laude, Rice U., 1975; MD, Baylor Coll. Medicine, Houston, 1978. Diplomate Am. Bd. Surgery, Am. Bd. Thoracic Surgery. Resident in surgery Baylor Coll. Medicine, 1978-86, instr. surgery, 1984-86; pvt. practice, McAllen, Tex., 1986-88, Baton Rouge, 1988—. Bd. dirs. La. State U. Sch. Music; deacon Presbyn. Ch., Baton Rouge, 1994—. Fellow Soc. Thoracic Surgeons, Am. Assn. Thoracic Surgery, Am. Coll. Chest Physicians; mem. Pelican Yacht Club (bd. dirs.). Republican. Office: CVT Surg Ctr 7777 Hennessy Blvd Ste 108 Baton Rouge LA 70808

THYSEN, BENJAMIN, biochemist, health science facility administrator, researcher; b. N.Y.C., July 27, 1932; s. Bernard and Clara (Linietsky) Tissenbaum; m. Joan Albin; 1 child, Julie Ann, Gregory Eden. BS, CCNY, 1954; MS, U. Mo., 1963; PhD, St. Louis U., 1967. Instr. St. Louis U. Med. Sch., 1967-68; sr. research scientist Technicon Instrument Corp., Ardsly, N.Y., 1968-69; group leader Technicon Instrument Corp., Tarrytown, N.Y., 1969-70; asst. prof. lab., med., and ob-gyn depts. Albert Einstein Coll. Medicine, Bronx, N.Y., 1971-86, assoc. prof. lab. med. and ob-gyn depts., 1986—, dir. endocrine labs., 1971—; cons. Technicon Instrument Corp., Tarrytown, 1979-81, Albert Einstein Coll. of Medicine, Bronx, 1969-70. Contbr. articles to profl. jours. Served with U.S. Army, 1956-58. Recipient Cancer Research award St. Louis U., 1967-68; fellow NIH, 1963-67. Mem. AAAS, Assn. Clin. Scientists, Soc. Study of Reproduction, Endocrine Soc., Sigma Xi.

TICHENOR, MARY WILLINGHAM, non-profit advocacy organization administrator; b. Columbia, S.C., Mar. 15, 1944; d. Aaron and Mary F. (Klettner) Willingham; m. Clarence B. Tichenor, Aug. 3, 1967; 1 child, James. BS, Winthrop U., Rock Hill, S.C., 1966; MSW, U. S.C., 1993. Lic. master social worker. Exec. dir. S.C. Alliance for Mentally Ill, Columbia, 1988—. Mem. S.C. Mental Health Transition Coun., Columbia, 1989—, S.C. Protection and Advocacy for Mentally Ill, Columbia, 1987—, S.C. Disability Coalition, 1996. Office: SC Alliance Mentally Ill 1223 Bull St Columbia SC 29201

TICKLE, SAMUEL MILTON, physician, publisher; b. Johnson City, Tenn., Mar. 26, 1933; s. John Crockett and Nora Nannie (Witcher) T.; m. Phyllis Alexander, June 14, 1955; children: Nora Katherine, Mary Gammon, Laura Lee, John Crockett II, Samuel Milton Jr., Philip Wade, Rebecca Rutledge. BS, East Tenn. State U., 1954; MD, U. Tenn., 1957. Chief resident U. Tenn. Coll. Medicine, Memphis, 1964-65, fellow pulmonary medicine, 1966-68; acting chair pulmonary medicine U. Tenn., Memphis, 1968-69; ptnr. Fountain & Tickle, P.C., Memphis, 1969-74; pres. Pulmonary Physicians, P.C., Memphis, 1974—; clin. assoc. prof. medicine U. Tenn. Coll. Medicine, Memphis, 1969—; bd. dirs. Peachtree Pubs., Atlanta; CEO Tickle Publs. Group dba Shelby House, Osler House, Memphis, 1983-91, St. Luke's Press, Iris Press, Memphis, 1983-90. Mem. editl. bd. U. Tenn. Med. Alumnus, 1988—. Bd. dirs. Tenn. Lung Assn., Nashville, 1966-78, Pub. Assn. of the South, Albany, Ga., 1985-88. Mem. AMA, Tenn. Med. Assn., Memphis/Shelby Med. Soc. Episcopalian. Office: Pulmonary Physicians 1407 Union Ave Ste 401 Memphis TN 38104-3616

TIEMAN, SUZANNAH BLISS, neurobiologist; b. Washington, Oct. 10, 1943; d. John Alden and Winifred Texas (Bell) Bliss; m. David George Tieman, Dec. 19, 1969. AB with honors, Cornell U., 1965; postgrad., MIT, 1965-66, Calif. Inst. Tech., 1971-72; PhD, Stanford U., 1974. Postdoctoral fellow dept. anatomy U. Calif., San Francisco, 1974-77; rsch. assoc. Neurobiology Rsch. Ctr. SUNY, Albany, 1977-90, sr. rsch. assoc., 1990—, assoc. prof. dept. biomed. scis., 1988-95, prof., 1995—, rsch. prof. dept. biol. scis., 1990—. Contbr. articles to profl. jours., chpts. to books in field. Rsch. grantee Nat. Eye Inst., SUNY, Albany, 1979-83, NSF, SUNY, 1983-86, 88-92, 92—; predoctoral fellow NSF, NIH, Stanford U., 1970-73, 73-74, postdoctoral fellow Nat. Eye Inst., U. Calif., San Francisco, 1974-77. Mem. AAAS, Soc. for Neurosci. (steering com. Hudson Berkshire chpt. 1980-81, pres. 1991-93), Assn. Rsch. in Vision and Ophthalmology, Am. Assn. Anatomists, Assn. Women in Sci., Fedn. Am. Socs. Exptl. Biology, Women in Neurosci., Nat. Audubon Soc., Nature Conservancy. Office: SUNY Neurobiology Rsch Ctr 1400 Washington Ave Albany NY 12222-0100

TIENGHI, AMELIA, oncologist; b. Ravenna, Italy, Oct. 8, 1955; d. Uvio and Iride (Tassinari) T. MD, Bologna U., Italy, 1980. Specialization in oncology Bologna (Italy) U., 1980-83; specialization in internal medicine Parma (Italy) U., 1983-88; asst. oncology dept. City Hosp., Ravenna, 1985—. Contbr. articles to profl. jours. Mem. Am. Soc. Clin. Oncology, Assn. Italian Oncology Medicine, European Soc. Med. Oncology. Office: City Hosp Oncology Dept, v Missiroli 10, 48100 Ravenna Italy

TIERNO, PHILIP MARIO, JR., microbiologist, educator, researcher; b. Bklyn., June 5, 1943; s. Philip M. and Phyllis (Tringone) T.; m. Josephine Martinez, Apr. 2, 1967; children: Alexandra Lorraine, Meredith Anne. BS, Bklyn. Coll. Pharmacy/R.L. Conolly Coll., L.I. U., 1965; MS, NYU, 1974, PhD, 1977. Microbiologist, Luth. Med. Ctr., Bklyn., 1965-66; chief research microbiologist hemodialysis unit VA Hosp., Bronx, N.Y., 1966-70; dir. microbiology div. NYU Med. Ctr. Goldwater Meml. Hosp., F.D. Roosevelt Island, N.Y., 1970-81; assoc. and cons. microbiologist Maimonides Med. Ctr., Bklyn., 1970-79; dir. microbiology dept. Tisch-Univ. Hosp., NYU Med. Ctr., 1981—; adj. asst. prof. CUNY, 1974-76, Bloomfield (N.J.) Coll., 1975-82; assoc. prof. microbiology and pathology NYU Med. Sch., 1981—; cons. Office Atty. Gen. N.Y. State, NIH, Coll. of Am. Pathologists, and Dept. Health City of New York, 1981—. Pres., Flushing Taxpayers Assn., 1973-77; bd. dirs. Comprehensive Health Planning Agy. City N.Y., 1974-75, Norwood Bd. Adjustment, N.J., 1978-83, 86—, Norwood Bd. Edn., 1983-86; chmn. Norwood Environ. Commn., 1986—; co-founder, bd. dirs. Found. Sci. Research in Pub. Interest, S.I., N.Y., 1985—. Mem. AAAS, N.Y. Acad. Scis., Am. Acad. Microbiology, Am. Pub. Health Assn., Am. Soc. Microbiology, Phi Sigma, Alpha Epsilon Delta. Club: Optimists (v.p. Norwood 1978—). Lodge: Knights of Malta. Contbr. articles to profl. jours. and books. Home: 30 Carter St Norwood NJ 07648-1518 Office: Tisch Hosp-Microbiology Dept NYU Med Ctr 560 1st Ave New York NY 10016

TIERSKY, TERRI S., dentist, lawyer; b. Chgo., July 25, 1959; d. Morris D. and Joan R. (Berets) T.; m. Roland D. Davidson. BA, U. Ill., 1982; DDS, Loyola U., Chgo., 1986; JD, John Marshall Law Sch., 1991. Bar: Ill., 1991. Pvt. practice dentistry Chgo., 1986—; staff mem. Meth. Hosp., Chgo., 1988—. Mem. ABA, ADA, Chgo. Bar Assn., Chgo. Dental Soc., Ill. State Dental Soc.

TIETKE, WILHELM, gastroenterologist; b. Niengraben, Germany, Oct. 15, 1938; came to U.S., 1969, naturalized, 1979; s. Wilhelm and Frieda (Schmeding) T.; m. Imme Schmidt, Oct. 15, 1965; children: Cornelia, Isabel. MD, U Goettingen (West Germany), 1968. Diplomate Am. Bd. Internat. Medicine, Am. Bd. Gastroenterology. Intern Edward W. Sparrow Hosp., Lansing, Mich., 1970; resident in internal medicine Henry Ford Hosp., Detroit, 1971-73; fellow in gastroenterology, 1973-75; practice medicine specializing in gastroenterology, Huntsville, Ala., 1975—; mem. vol. faculty, cons. U. Ala., Huntsville, 1976; clin. assoc. prof. internal medicine, 1979—; v.p. Huntsville Gastroenterology Assocs., P.C., 1979—. Fellow Coll. Gastroenterology; mem. AMA, Ala. Med. Soc., Am. Coll. Physicians, Am. Soc. Gastrointestinal Endoscopy. Lutheran. Lodge: Rotary. Home: 2707 Westminister Way SE Huntsville AL 35801-2241 Office: 119 Longwood Dr Huntsville AL 35801-4205 also: PO Box 2169 Huntsville AL 35804-2169

TILBE, LINDA MACLAUCHLAN, nursing administrator; b. Bangor, Maine, Mar. 1, 1950; d. John and Ruby Mae (Dorr) MacLauchlan; married; children: William, Robert, Grant. BSN, U. Maine, 1973; M in Healthcare Adminstrn., Quinnipiac Coll., 1988. RN, Conn., Fla. Ob-gyn. staff nurse Yale New Haven Hosp., 1973-79, med. ICU nurse, 1979-83, post anesthesia staff nurse, 1983-88; adminstrv. mgmt. intern Shirley Frank Found., New Haven, 1987-88; clin. nurse adminstr. pain mgmt. Yale U., New Haven, 1988-92; nurse mgr., arthritis and pain ctrs. North Broward Med. Ctr., 1992-95; clin. nurse supr. Pain Mgmt. Ctr. Doctors Hosp. Sarasota (Fla.), 1995—. Author: A Manual for Acute Postoperative Pain Management, 1992; author and editor: Acute Pain Mechanisms and Management, 1992; contbr. articles to profl. jours. Mem. Internat. Assn. Study of Pain, Am. Pain Soc., Am. Soc. Post Anesthesia Nurses, Am. Soc. Pain Mgmt. Nurses (founder), Conn. Soc. Post Anesthesia Nurses. Home: 4414 Winner's Cir Apt 2514 Sarasota FL 34238 Office: Doctors Hosp Sarasota Pain Mgmt Ctr 5741 Bee Ridge Rd Sarasota FL 34233

TILDAHL, KARLA LOUISE, women's health nurse; b. Chandler, Minn., Apr. 13, 1939; d. Victor H. and Anne (Swart) Bruemmer; m. Brent Stuart Tildahl, Dec. 22, 1961; children: Bradley Stuart, Michael James. BSN, U. Minn., 1962. RN, Wis. Staff nurse Fairview Hosp., Mpls., 1960; mgr. ctrl. svc. St. Andrews Hosp., Mpls., 1961; operating rm. nurse Fairview Hosp., 1962-64; emergency rm. nurse Methodist Hosp., St. Louis Park, Minn., 1964-65; office nurse Wayzata (Minn.) Clinic, 1965-66; staff nurse Crestview Nursing Home, Mpls., 1967-71, Golden Years Nursing Home, Walworth, Wis., 1971-73; staff med./surg. nurse Lakeland Med. Ctr., Elkhorn, Wis., 1973-78; nurse educator Gateway Tech. Coll., Elkhorn, Wis., 1976-79; obstetrics nurse, nurse supervisor Lakeland Med. Ctr., Elkhorn, 1978-87; coord. women's health Lakeland Med. Ctr., 1987—; adv. bd. Wis. Breast Cancer Coalition, Milw., 1995—. Author, editor (newsletter) Communique, 1988-96. Organist Faith Lutheran Ch., Walworth, 1981—; advocacy com. Am. Cancer Soc., 1987—, state chair Resources Info. & Guidance com., 1996—, local chair patient svcs. com., 1987—. Mem. Nat. Osteoporosis Found., Nat. Arthritis Found., Nat. Endometriosis Assn., Nat. Assn. Women's Health Profls., Nat. Breats Cancer Coalition, Wis. Breats Cancer Coalition, Wis. Assn. Women's Health, Nat. Women's Health Network, Older Women's League. Lutheran. Home: 770 Odsila Way Fontana WI 53125 Office: Lakeland Med Ctr Hwy NN Box 1002 Elkhorn WI 53121

TILLACK, ROBERT CHARLES, physician; b. Rochester, N.Y., June 11, 1952; s. Henry Philip and Elizabeth Jane (Helfer) T.; m. Diane Lynn Switlyk, Apr. 25, 1981; children: Lindsey Ann, Sandra Michelle. BS in Biology, Rensselaer Poly. Inst., 1976; MD, Albany Med. Coll., 1976. Diplomate Nat. Bd. Med. Examiners, Am. Bd. Emergency Medicine. Resident in gen. surgery Albany (N.Y.) Med. Ctr., 1976-77, resident in neurosurgery, 1977-78; attending physician Samaritan Hosp., Troy, N.Y., 1979-85, Columbia Meml. Hosp., Hudson, N.Y., 1979-85, Somerset (N.J.) Med. Ctr., 1985—; ptnr. Emergency Med. Assocs., Livingston, N.J., 1985—; instr. advanced cardiac life support Am. Heart Assn., 1988—. Fellow Am. Coll. Emergency Physicians. Republican. Lutheran. Office: Emergency Med Assocs 651 W Mt Pleasant Ave Livingston NJ 07039-1609

TILLACK, THOMAS WARNER, pathologist; b. Jacksonville, Fla., Nov. 16, 1937; s. Warner S. and Charlotte G. T.; m. Lynne Anne Beam, Oct. 30, 1970; children—Jonathan Allan, Allison Anne. B.A., U. Rochester, 1959; M.D., Yale U., 1963. Diplomate: Diploma Am. Bd. Pathology. Intern Barnes Hosp., St. Louis, 1963-64; resident Barnes Hosp., 1964-66; staff asso. NIH, Bethesda, Md., 1966-69; sr. staff fellow NIH, 1969-71; asst. prof. pathology Washington U., St. Louis, 1971-73; assoc. prof. Washington U., 1973-76; Walter Reed prof., chmn. dept. pathology U. Va. Med. Center, 1976—. Served with USPHS, 1966-69. Mem. Am. Soc. Investigative Pathology, U.S. and Can. Acad. Pathology, Am. Soc. Cell Biology, Assn. Pathology Chairs, Phi Beta Kappa. Home: PO Box 376 Ivy VA 22945-0376 Office: U Va Med Ctr Dept Pathology PO Box 214 Charlottesville VA 22908-0001

TILLEY, SHERMAINE ANN, molecular immunologist, educator; b. Shawnee, Okla., Feb. 22, 1952; d. Cecil Fern and Zona Emma (Evans) T. BA in Chemistry summa cum laude, Okla. City U., 1973; PhD in Biochemistry, The Johns Hopkins U., 1980. Rsch. assoc. Albert Einstein Coll. Medicine, Bronx, 1980-85; rsch. asst. prof. NYU Sch. Medicine, N.Y.C., 1985-94; rsch. assoc. prof., 1994—; asst. mem. Pub. Health Rsch. Inst., N.Y.C., 1985-93, assoc. mem., 1994—; ad hoc reviewer SBIR grants NIH, 1989—; sec., staff coun. adv. com. Pub. Health Rsch. Inst., N.Y.C., 1990-95. Contbr. articles to profl. jours.; patentee in field. Recipient Letzeiser medal, Okla. City U., 1973; Nat. Arthritis Found. fellow, 1982-85; Life and Health Ins. Med. Rsch. Fund grantee, 1986-89; NIH grantee, 1988—. Mem. AAAS, Am. Assn. Immunologists, Am. Soc. Microbiology. Office: Pub Health Rsch Inst 455 1st Ave Rm 1133 New York NY 10016-9189

TILLMAN, ELIZABETH CARLOTTA, nurse, educator; b. Md., Aug. 31, 1929; d. Walter Monroe and Mozelle Virginia (Shugars) Brown; m. Lloyd A. Tillman, Apr. 16, 1949; children: Lloyd A. Jr., William L., Susan E. Tillman Chaires. Diploma, Md. Gen. Hosp. Sch. Nursing, 1950; student, Towson State U., U. Md., Loyola Coll., Balt., Howard C.C. RN. Psychiatric nurse Spring Grove Hosp. Ctr., Catonsville, Md., 1950; pvt. duty home health nurse Md., 1951-60; dir., tchr., nurse Doughoregan Manor Day Sch., Ellicott City, Md., 1960-80; med.-surg. nurse Woman's Hosp., Balt., 1964, Md. Gen. Hosp., Balt., 1980; nursing instr. Howard County Dept. Edn., Ellicott City, 1981-91; nursing educator Howard County Sch. Tech., 1981-91, Howard County Gen. Hosp., 1981-91; geriatric nurse Lorien Columbia (Md.) Nursing & Rehab. Ctr., 1981-91; home health nurse Md., 1992—. Mem. NEA, Md. State Tchrs. Assn., Md. Gen. Hosp. Alumni Assn., Am. Vocat. Assn., Health Occupations Educators, Md. Vocat. Assn., Phi Eta Sigma, Iota Lambda Sigma. Home: 10002 Reed Ln Ellicott City MD 21042-2238

TILLMAN, MARY ANNE TUGGLE, pediatrician; b. Bristow, Okla., Sept. 4, 1935; d. Thomas Gus and Ruthie (English) Tuggle; B.S., Howard U., 1956, M.D., 1960; postgrad. Harvard Grad. Med. Sch., 1965; m. Daniel Tillman, Apr. 20, 1957; children: Dana, Daniel. Intern, Homer G. Phillips Hosp., St. Louis, 1960-61, resident pediatrics, 1961-63; practice medicine, specializing in pediatrics, St. Louis, 1963—; dir. nurseries Homer G. Phillips Hosp., St. Louis, 1964-79, St. Louis City Hosp., 1979-85; mem. staffs St. Louis Children's, Deaconess, Barnes, Jewish hosps.; assoc. prof. Washington U. Sch. Medicine, St. Louis, 1963—, pediatric cons. Project Head Start, 1969-72. Recipient Woman of Year award Zeta Phi Beta, 1970; Woman of Achievement, St. Louis Globe Democrat, 1982. Diplomate Am. Bd. Pediatrics. Fellow Am. Acad. Pediatrics (nat. com. adoptions 1969-75); mem. Am., Nat. med. assns., Am. Med. Women's Assn. Presbyterian. Contbr. articles to profl. publs. Home: 26 Washington Ter Saint Louis MO 63112-1914 Office: Northland Office Bldg 330 W Florissant At Lucas Hu Saint Louis MO 63136

TILLOTSON, JAMES RICHARD, medical educator; b. Berkeley, Calif., Oct. 3, 1933; s. Robert Russell and Betty (Bailey) T.; m. Dorothy Louise Wormack, Aug. 20, 1966 (div. 1975); children: Sonya Laruen, Dirk; m. Elizabeth Ann Barbuto, Feb. 26, 1982. BA, Lehigh U., Bethlehem, Pa., 1955; MD, U. Calif., San Francisco, 1959; postgrad., SUNY, 1985-89. Lic. physician, Calif., N.Y. Intern Detroit Receiving Hosp., 1959-60, resident, 1962-64; sr. asst. surgeon USPHS, St. Louis, 1960-62; fellow infectious disease medicine Wayne State U. Med. Sch., Detroit, 1964-66; fellow infectious diseases Boston City Hosp., 1966-68, rsch. fellow in medicine, 1966-68, clin. fellow II and IV Med. Svc., 1966-68; instr. medicine Harvard Med. Sch., Boston, 1967-68; asst. prof. medicine U. Mich. Med. Sch., Ann Arbor, 1968-70; dir. infectious disease section Wayne County Gen. Hosp., Eloise, Mich., 1968-70; head divsn. infectious diseases Albany Med. Coll., 1970-86, asst. prof., assoc. prof., prof., clin. prof., 1970-95; cons. in infectious diseases, med. edn., infection control and legal medicine, Mendocino, Calif., 1994—; hon. sr. rsch. fellow U. Dundee, Scotland, 1984. Contbr. articles to profl. jours, chpts. to books. Fellow Infectious Disease Soc. Am., Am. Coll. Clin. Pharmacology; mem. Am. Fedn. Clin. Rsch., Assn. Am. Med. Colls., Assn. for Study of Med. Edn., Assn. Med. Edn. of Europe. Home and Office: 14221 Headlands Dr Mendocino CA 95460

TILONSKY, SAMUEL IRVING, optometrist; b. Phila., Mar. 21, 1954; s. Isadore and Adele (Kushner) T.; m. Judith Eve Narrow, June 29, 1980; children: Avi Narrow-Tilonsky, Perri Narrow-Tilonsky. AB in Chemistry, Temple U., 1978; OD, Pa. Coll. Optometry, 1982. Chief Contact Lens Clinic, asst. chief optometry svcs. USAF Med. Ctr., Scott AFB, Ill., 1982-84; chief optometry svcs. USAF Clinic, McGuire AFB, N.J., 1984-87; pvt. practice Westmont, N.J., 1986—; chief optometry svcs. 166 MDS, Del. Air Nat. Guard, New Castle, 1987—; staff optometrist Camden (N.J.) Optometric Eye Ctr., 1987—; cons. child health confs. Camden County Divsn. Health, 1987—. Lt. col. Air NG, 1973—. Mem. Armed Forces Optometric Soc., Nat. Guard Assn. U.S., Nat. Guard Assn. Del., Air Nat. Guard Optometric Soc. Jewish. Office: 10 Haddon Ave Westmont NJ 08108-2706

TILSON, KATHERINE ANNE, medical practice manager; b. Cin., Mar. 21, 1951; d. Paul Joseph Walter and Anne Elizabeth (Kleemann) Centner; m. Dennis Bascombe Tilson, II, June 8, 1974. B.S. in Nursing, Med. Ctr. U. Kans.-Kansas City, 1973; M.B.A., Avila Coll., 1983. R.N., Kans., Mo. Staff nurse U. Kans. Med. Ctr., Kansas City, 1973-76, Menorah Med. Ctr., Kansas City, 1976-78; nursing coordinator Kelly Health Care, Inc., Kansas City, 1978, nursing supr., 1978-79, br. mgr., service dir., 1979-83; mgr. ServiceMaster Home Health Care Services, Kansas City, 1983, adminstr., 1983-84; cons. Am. Nursing Resources, Inc., Kansas City, 1984, adminstr. Am. Nursing Resources Home Health Agy., Inc., 1985-88, exec. dir. Am. Nursing Resources, Inc., Kansas City, Mo., 1984-88; med. practice mgr. Drs. Brothers and Centner, Kansas City, 1988—; jr. faculty liaison for home health nursing practice residency tng. program S.S.M. Family Practice, Kansas City, 1982-83; mem. in-home services com. Johnson County Area Agy. on Aging, 1982-83. Mem. Challinor Guild, St. Andrew's Episcopal Ch., 1981-89, choir, 1980—, Scola Cantorum, 1984-85, Metro Discharge Planners Group, 1985-88, Mayor's Corps of Progress for Greater Kansas City, 1980-83. Mem. Am. Assn. Occupational Health Nurses, Mo. Assn. Occupational Health Nurses, Greater Kansas City Assn. Occupational Nurses, Broadway Bus. Assn., Mid-Am. Regional Council (in-home services task force 1980-87, in-home services com. 1979-87), Kansas City Regional Home Health Assn. (bd. dirs. 1979-83, mem., chmn. coms.), Kansas City C. of C. Republican. Avocations: piano; singing; sailing; swimming; sports; sewing; gardening. Home: 4600 W 66th St Shawnee Mission KS 66208-1652 Office: Midwest Occupational Medicine 3037 Main St Ste 201 Kansas City MO 64108-3323

TILSON, M(ARTIN) DAVID, surgeon, scientist, educator; b. Texarkana, Tex., Aug. 25, 1941; s. M. David and Leta (Martin) T.; m. Joan E. Stanescki, 1974; children: William Thomas, John Wainwright, Martin David III. BA, Rice U., 1963; MD, Yale U., 1967. Diplomate Am. Bd. Surgery, Nat. Bd. Med. Examiners. Surg. intern Yale U., 1967-68; resident in surgery U. New Haven, 1968-72; asst. to assoc. prof. Yale U., New Haven, 1974-83, prof., 1983-89; Alisa Mellon Bruce prof. of surgery Columbia U., N.Y.C., 1989—. Contbr. articles to profl. jours. Maj. USAF, 1972-74. Rsch. grantee NIH, 1983-94. Mem. ACS, Soc. Univ. Surgeons, Am. Surg. Assn., Soc. Vascular Surgery, Internat. Soc. Cadiovasc. Surgery, Halsted Soc. Office: St Lukes Roosevelt Hosp 1000 10th Ave New York NY 10019-1105 Home: 104 Edgemont Rd Scarsdale NY 10583

TILSTRA, SALLY ANN, clinical laboratory scientist; b. Rapid City, S.D., Jan. 26, 1958; d. George Orland and Virginia Katherine (French) Kaubisch; m. Ronald Gary Tilstra, July 12, 1980; 1 child, Kara Renae. BS in Med. Tech., U. S.D., 1980; MBA, 1994. Cert. specialist in hematology. Med. tech. generalist Sioux Valley Hosp., Sioux Falls, S.D., 1980-82; med. tech. hematology Sioux Valley Hosp., Sioux Falls, 1982-89, med. tech. instr., 1989-95; outreach mgr. lab. Weiner Meml. Med. Ctr., Marshall, Minn., 1995—. Active mem. First United Meth. Ch., Sioux Falls, 1982. Mem. Am. Soc. for Clin. Pathology, Am. Soc. for Med. Techs., Nat. Cert. Agy., Beta Gamma Sigma. Home: 6512 Cheyenne Dr Sioux Falls SD 57106-1646

TIMBERS, KATHLEEN COMEAU, psychiatric nurse specialist; b. Boston, June 15, 1952; d. John Francis and Catherine Marie (Fallon) Comeau; m. Robert Timbers, May 9, 1982; children: Amelia, Elizabeth. BS, Cornell U., 1974; MSN, Yale U., 1981. RN, Calif.; cert. psychiat. clin. specialist, drug abuse counselor. Counselor Mainline Crisis Ctr., Ithaca, N.Y., 1973-74;

program dir. Am. Heart Assn., Andover, Mass., 1975-76; educator community health Pathways Counseling Ctr., San Diego, 1976-78; psychotherapist Conn. Mental Health Ctr., New Haven, 1979-81; specialist psychiat. clin. Tufts New Eng. Med. Ctr., South Boston, 1981-83; clin. nurse specialist McLean Hosp., Belmont, Mass., 1983-88; instr. psychiat. nursing Northeastern U., Boston, 1988; dir. regional exec. Calif. Nurses Assn., Napa, Calif., 1988; pvt. practice psychotherapy Belmont, Mass.; administv. coord. alcohol and drug dependency svcs. CPC Redwoods Hosp., Santa Rosa, Calif., 1992; mental health counselor San Luis Rey Hosp., Encinitas, Calif., 1976; ICU nurse Yale New Haven Hosp., 1980; courtesy faculty Boston U., 1985-86; outpatient therapist Psycho. Ctr., Lawrence, Mass., 1988; head nurse First Hosp., Vallejo, Calif., 1988-90; cons., creator psychiat. nursing home care program Care Home Health, 1996; mem. Sonoma County Drug Adv. Bd., 1992—; ptnr. New Options Outpatient Chem. Dependency Program, 1993-94; psychiat. nursing coord. Petaluma Valley Hosp., 1993—; bd. registered nursing diversion com., 1994—; assoc. Psychstrategies, Inc., 1996—. Contbr. articles to profl. jours. Co-chair Sex Edn. by and for Cornell Students, 1971; bd. dirs. Planned Parenthood Tompkins County, 1972-74; program dir. Am. Heart Assn., Northeast Mass., 1975-76; organizer High Blood Pressure Coun., 1975-76; chair Health Task Force Community Congress San Diego, 1978. Mem. DSA (nat. bd. 1982, New Haven chair 1978-80, Boston chair 1982-83), Calif. Nurses Assn., Mass. Nurses Assn. (legis. commn. 1983-87), Nat. Consortium of Chem. Dependency Nurses. Democrat. Methodist.

TIMM, KENT EDWARD, exercise scientist, physical therapist; b. Wisconsin Rapids, Wis., Oct. 21, 1958; s. Reuben E.A. and Harriet B. (Schleich) T.; m. Deborah J. Cicinelli, Sept. 27, 1986; children: Kenzie Michele, Karen Jean. BA in Biology, BA in Sports Medicine, Ripon (Wis.) Coll., 1981; BS in Phys. Therapy, MS in Sports Medicine, U. Pitts., 1982, MS in Athletic Tng., 1983, MS in Orthopaedic Phys. Therapy, 1984; PhD in Exercise Sci., Columbia-Pacific U., 1986. Certt. sports phys. therapist, athletic trainer, back specialist, orthophys. therapist. Athletic trainer Pitts. Steelers, 1981-82, Carnegie-Mellon U., Pitts., 1981-83; sports phys. therapist Pitts. Penguins, 1981-83, Podiatry Hosp. Pitts., 1983-84, Ohio Inst. for Sports, Columbus, 1984; indsl. medicine coordinator St. Luke's Hosp., Saginaw, Mich., 1984—, asst. dir. phys. therapy, 1988—, leader athletic med. team, 1996—; lectr. Andrews U., Berrien Springs, Mich.; cons. Saginaw Gens., 1985—, Ripon (Wis.) Coll., 1981—, Cybex Corp., Ronkonkoma, N.Y., 1983—, Universal Gym Equipment, Cedar Rapids, Iowa, 1987—; adj. instr. U. Mich., Flint, 1985—, U. Indpls.; sports and indsl. medicine cons. St. Luke's Healthcare Assn., 1989—. Editor IsoKinetics and Exercise Sci.; mem. editorial bd. Jour. Orthopaedic Sports Phys. Therapy, LaCrosse, Wis., 1986—; contbr. articles to profl. jours. Recipient Presdl. Sports award Pres.'s Council on Phys. Fitness and Sports, 1977. Fellow Am. Back Soc.; mem. Am. Coll. Sports Medicine, Am. Phys. Therapy Assn. (Mich. Northeastern dist. treas. 1984-88, chmn. 1988—, sports sect., orthopaedic sect.), Mich. Phys. Therapy Assn. (pres. 1993—), Am. Bd. Phys. Therapy Specialties, Nat. Athlete Trainers Assn., Acad. Clin. Electrodynography, Planetary Soc., Mensa, Saginaw Bridge Club, Phi Beta Kappa, Phi Delta Theta, Beta Beta Beta. Republican. Lutheran. Home: 4809 Brook Dr Saginaw MI 48603-5649 Office: St Luek's Hosp OSF 600 Irving Ave Saginaw MI 48602-5375

TIMMERMANN, SANDRA, educational gerontologist, communications specialist; b. Orange, N.J., Mar. 25, 1941; d. Bernhard and Matilda (Schaaf) T.; m. George W. Bonham. BA with honors, U. Colo., 1963; MA, Columbia U., 1967; EdD, 1979. Account exec. Rowland Co., N.Y.C., 1964-67; dir. pub. info. The N.Y. TV Network. SUNY, N.Y.C., 1967-72; asso. Hoefer/Amidei Pub. Relations/Mktg., 1972-74; asso. dean Inst. Lifetime Learning, Am. Assn. Ret. Persons, Washington, 1974-76, dir. Inst., 1976-84, dir. geriatric edn., 1984-86 ; exec. dir. Peninsula Ctr. for the Blind, Palo Alto, Calif., 1986-88; dir. western states region Am. Found. for the Blind, San Francisco, 1988—; bd. dirs. Calif. Council of Gerontology and Geriatrics, 1988-90; edn. and tng. cons. Am. Soc. on Aging, 1994—, dir. edn. 1990-94; mem. tng. com. Nat. Ctr. for Black Aged; mgr. older adults sect. HEW Lifelong Learning Project; cons. Brookdale Ctr. on Aging, Hunter Coll.; cons. to bus. and industry; adv. com. nat. project on counseling older people Am. Personnel and Guidance Assn.; nat. adv. com. vocat. edn. and older adults U.S. Dept. Edn. Trustee, chmn. adv. com. on later years Am. Found. for the Blind; commr. Commn. on Status of Women, San Mateo County, Calif.; mem. bd. dirs. Sr. Coastsiders. Kellogg fellow. Chmn. Youth and Edn. Community United Meth. Ch., Half Moon Bay, Conn. Mem. Am. Soc. on Aging (dir. edn., tng. San Francisco chpt.), Am. Assn. Adult and Continuing Edn. (editor Edn. and Aging newsletter, chmn. commn. on aging, bd. dirs.), Coalition Adult Edn. Orgns. (dir., pres. 1984-85), Pi Beta Phi, Pi Lambda Theta, Kappa Delta Pi, Phi Delta Kappa. Club: Capital Speakers. Contbr. articles to profl. jours. and newspapers. Home: 371 Cypress Point Rd Half Moon Bay CA 94019-2242

TIMMERS, RICHARD LAWRENCE, psychotherapist; b. Green Bay, Wis., Sept. 28, 1931; m. Marilyn Jane Opal, Sept. 12, 1964; children: Josh Francis, Sarah Christine. BS, U. Wis., Madison, 1957; MSW, U. Wis., Milw., 1962. Lic. social worker, Maine. Mem. faculty Sch. Social Work U. Wis., Madison, 1967-86; sex therapist Midwest Sex Counseling and Psychotherapy Ctr., Madison, 1973-86; social worker, coord. sex offender program S.C. Dept. Corrections, Columbia, 1986-90; psychotherapist, coord. sex offender program Community Health and Counseling Svcs., Bangor, Maine, 1990-95; psychiatric clinician Acadia Hosp., Bangor, Maine, 1995—. With U.S. Army, 1950-53, Korea. Mem. Acad. Cert. Social Workers, Nat. Assn. Social Workers, Am. Assn. Sex Edn. Counselors and Therapists (cert.). Home: 16 Bowdoin St Bangor ME 04401-5910 Office: Acadia Hosp 268 Stillwater Ave Bangor ME 04401

TIMMONS, EVELYN DEERING, pharmacist; b. Durango, Colo., Sept. 29, 1926; d. Claude Elliot and Evelyn Allen (Gooch) Deering; m. Richard Palmer Timmons, Oct. 4, 1952 (div. 1968); children: Roderick Deering, Steven Palmer. BS in Chemistry and Pharmacy cum laude, U. Colo., 1948. Chief pharmacist Meml. Hosp., Phoenix, 1950-54; med. lit. rsch. librarian Hoffman-LaRoche, Inc., Nutley, N.J., 1956-57; staff pharmacist St. Joseph's Hosp., Phoenix, 1958-60; relief mgr. various ind. apothecaries, Phoenix, 1960-68; asst. then mgr. Profl. Pharmacies, Inc., Phoenix, 1968-72; mgr. then owner Mt. View Pharmacy, Phoenix and Paradise Valley, Ariz., 1972—; pres. Ariz. Apothecaries, Ltd., Phoenix, 1976—; mem. profl. adv. bd., bereavement counselor Hospice of Valley, 1983—; mem. profl. adv. bd. Upjohn Health Care and Svcs., Phoenix, 1984-86; bd. dirs. Am. Council on Pharm. Edn., Chgo., 1986-92, v.p. 1988, 89, treas., 1990-91. Author poetry; contbr. articles to profl. jours. Mem. Scottsdale (Ariz.) Fedn. Rep. Women, 1963; various other offices Rep. Fedn.; mem. platform com. State of Ariz., Nat. Rep. Conv., 1964; asst. sec. Young Rep. Nat. Fedn., 1963-65; active county and state Rep. coms.; fin. chmn. Internat. Leadership Symposium:Woman in Pharmacy, London, 1987; treas. Leadership Internat. Women Pharmacy, 1991—. Named Outstanding Young Rep. of Yr., Nat. Fedn. Young Reps., 1965, Preceptor of Yr., U. Ariz./Syntex, 1984; recipient Disting. Public Svc. award Maricopa County Med. Soc., 1962, Disting. Alumni award Wasatch Acad., 1982, Career Achievement award, 1983, Leadership and Achievement award Upjohn Labs., 1985-86, Outstanding Achievement in Profession award Merck, Sharp & Dohme, 1986, award of Merit, 1988, Disting. Coloradoan award U. Colo., 1989, Vanguard award, 1991, Pharmacist of the Yr. award Profl. Compounding Corp. of Am., 1995, 96. Fellow Am. Coll. of Apothecaries (v.p. 1982-83, pres. 1984-85, chmn. bd. dirs. 1985-86, adv. coun. 1986-92, Chmn. of Yr. 1980-81 Victor H. Morganroth award 1985, J. Leon Lascoff award 1990); mem. Ariz. Soc. of Hosp. Pharmacists, Am. Pharm. Assn. (Daniel B. Smith award 1990, U.S. pharmacoepial conv. expert adv. com. on compounding pharms. 1992—), Ariz. Pharmacy Assn. (Svc. to Pharmacy award 1976, Pharmacist of Yr. 1981, Bowl of Hygeia 1989, 1st Innovative Pharmacy award 1994), Maricopa County Pharmacy Assn. (pres. 1977, Svc. to Pharmacy award 1977), Am. Soc. of Hosp. Pharmacists, Aux. to County Med. Soc. (pres. 1967-68), Am. Aircraft Owners and Pilots Assn., Air Safety Found., Nat. Assn. of Registered Parliamentarians, Kappa Epsilon (recipient Career Achievement award 1986, Vanguard award 1991, Unicorn award 1993). Lodge: Civinettes (pres. Scottsdale chpt. 1960-61). Avocations: flying, skiing, swimming, backpacking, hiking. Office: Mt View Pharmacy 10565 N Tatum Blvd Ste B-118 Paradise Valley AZ 85253

TIMMONS, GERALD DEAN, pediatric neurologist; b. Rensselaer, Ind., June 1, 1931; s. Homer Timmons and Tamma Mildred (Spall) Rodgers; m. Lynne Rita Matrisciano, May 29, 1982; 1 child, Deanna Lynne; children from previous marriage: Jane Christina Timmons Mitchell, Ann Elizabeth, Mary Catherine. AB, Ind. U., 1953, MD, 1956. Diplomate Am. Bd. Psychiatry and Neurology. Intern Lima (Ohio) Meml. Hosp., 1956-57; resident Ind. U. Hosp., Indpls., 1957-59, 61-62; instr. neurology dept. Ind. U., Indpls., 1962-64; practice medicine specializing in psychiatry and neurology Indpls., 1962-64; practice medicine specializing in pediatric neurology Akron, Ohio, 1964—; chief pediatric neurology Children's Hosp. Med. Ctr., Akron, 1964—; chmn. neurology subcouncil Coll. Medicine Northeastern Ohio Univs., Rootstown, 1978—; chief examiner Am. Bd. Neurology and Psychiatry. Contbr. articles to profl. and scholarly jours. Served to capt. USAF, 1959-61. Mem. Summit County Med. Soc., Ohio Med. Soc., AMA, Am. Acad. Pediatrics, Am. Acad. Neurology (practice com. 1980-86), Child Neurology Soc. (chmn. honors and awards com. 1978—), Am. Soc. Internal Medicine, Am. Electroencephalographic Soc. Republican. Methodist. Office: Akron Pediatric Neurology 300 Locust St Ste 460 Akron OH 44302-1804

TIMMRECK, THOMAS C., health sciences and health administration educator; b. Montpelier, Idaho, June 15, 1946; s. Archie Carl and Janone (Jensen) T.; m. Ellen Prusse, Jan. 27, 1971; children: Chad Thomas, Benjamin Brian, Julie Anne. AA, Ricks Coll., 1968; BS, Brigham Young U., 1971; MEd, Oreg. State U., 1972; MA, No. Ariz. U., 1981; PhD U. Utah, 1976. Program dir. Cache County Aging Program, Logan, Utah, 1972-73; asst. prof. div. health edn. Tex. Tech U., Lubbock, 1976-77; asst. prof. dept. health care adminstrn. Idaho State U., Pocatello, 1977-78; program dir., asst. prof. health services program No. Ariz. U., Flagstaff, 1978-84; cons., dir. grants Beth Israel Hosp., Denver, 1985; prof. dept. health scis. and human ecology, coordinator grad. studies, coordinator health adminstrn. and planning Calif. State U., San Bernardino, 1985—; pres. Health Care Mgmt. Assocs., 1985—; presenter at nat. confs.; mem. faculty Loretto Heights Coll., Denver, Dept. Mgmt. U. Denver, Dept. Mgmt. and Health Adminstrn. U. Colo., Denver, dept. bus. adminstrn. U. Redlands (Calif.), U. So. Calif., L.A. Author: Dictionary of Health Services Management, rev. 2d edit., 1987, Health Services Cyclopedic Dictionary, 3d edit., An Introduction to Epidemiology, 1994, Planning and Program Development and Evaluation: A Handbook for Health Promotion, Aging, and Health Services, 1995; mem. editl. bd. Jour. Health Values, 1986—, Basic Epidemiological Methods and Biostats., Dictionary of Epidemiology and Public Health; contbr. numerous articles on health care adminstrn., behavioral health, gerontology and health edn. to profl. jours. Chmn., bd. dirs. Inland Counties Health System Agy.; mem. strategic planning com. chmn. Vis. Nurses Assn. of Inland Counties; bd. dirs. health svc. orgns. With U.S. Army, 1966-72, Vietnam. Mem. Assn. Advancement of Health Edn., Am. Acad. Mgmt., Assn. Univ. Programs in Health Care Adminstrn., Healthcare Forum. Republican. Mormon. Office: Calif State U Dept Health Scis and Human Ecology San Bernardino CA 92407

TIMONEN, KIRSI LIISA, epidemiologist, researcher; b. Kuopio, Finland, Mar. 10, 1964. MD, U. Kuopio, 1989. Asst. physician Kainuu Ctr. Hosp., Kajaani, Finland, 1991-92; acting sr. lectr. dept. physiology U. Kuopio, 1992-93; rschr. unit environ. epidemiology Nat. Pub. Health Inst., Kuopio, 1994—. Chmn. cross-country skiing unit Puijo Ski Club, Kuopio, 1995—. Office: Nat Pub Health Inst Unit Environ Epidemiology, PO Box 95, 70701 Kuopio Finland

TINAWI, MOHAMMAD, physician; b. Damascus, Syria, Oct. 20, 1966; came to U.S., 1990; s. Ahmad Rateb and Khetam (Tahan) T.; m. Kinda Baghdadi, Nov. 26, 1994. MD, Damascus U., 1989. Diplomate Am. Bd. Internal Medicine. Resident Mich. State U., East Lansing, 1990-93; clin. fellow St. Louis U. Hosp., 1993-95; staff physician Gentry County Meml. Hosp., Albany, Mo., 1995—. Contbr. articles to profl. jours. Mem. ACP, Am. Soc. Nephrology. Office: Gentry County Meml Hosp 1607 E US Hwy 136 Albany MO 64402

TINDALL, GEORGE TAYLOR, neurosurgeon, educator; b. Magee, Miss., Mar. 13, 1928; s. George Earl and Lyda (Smith) T.; children: Catherine, George Taylor Jr., Suzanne, Annelle. BA, U. Miss., 1948; MD, Johns Hopkins U., 1952. Diplomate Am. Bd. Neurol. Surgery. Intern Johns Hopkins Hosp., Balt., 1952-53; resident in neurosurgery Duke U., Durham, N.C., 1955-61, asst. prof. neurosurgery, 1961-67, assoc. prof., 1967-68; chief neurosurgery Durham VA Hosp., 1961-68; prof., chief div. neurosurgery U. Tex. Med. Br., Galveston, 1968-73; prof. surgery, chief neurosurgery Emory U., Atlanta, 1973-95; pvt. practice specializing in neurosurgery Atlanta, 1973—. Capt. USAF, 1953-55. Mem. Am. Acad. Neurol. Surgery (editor Jour. 1971-74)), Am. Assn. Neurol. Surgeons (pres. 1988-89), Congress Neurol. Surgeons (pres. 1973-74), Soc. Neurol. Surgeons, Neurosurg. Soc. Am., Soc. Univ. Neurosurgeons (pres. 1966), ACS, AMA (vice chmn. coun. neurol. surgery 1972—), Ga. Med. Assn., Johns Hopkins Med. and Surg. Assn., Alpha Omega Alpha. Home: 869 Lullwater Pky NE Atlanta GA 30307-1233 Office: 1365B Clifton Rd NE Atlanta GA 30307-1013

TINDLE, JEFFREY ALAN, hospital association executive; b. Sedalia, Mo., Apr. 19, 1955; married. BS, U. Mo., 1977, M Healthcare Adminstrn., 1980. Adminstrv. resident Audrain Med. ctr., Mexico, Mo., 1980-81; asst. adminstr. Nevada (Mo.) City Hosp., 1981-83; assoc. adminstr. Nevada City Hosp., 1983-84; exec. dir. Assn. Ind. Hosps., Kansas City, Mo., 1984-87, pres., CEO, 1987—; mem. Mark Twain Bancshares Health Bd.; bd. dirs. Cabot Westside clinic. Active various civic and cmty. orgns. Mem. Assn. Healthcare Execs., Assn. Healthcare Enterprises, Am. Coll. Healthcare Execs. (assoc.), Mo. Hosp. Assn. Office: Assn Ind Hosps 8300 Troost Ave Kansas City MO 64131*

TINER, DONNA TOWNSEND, nurse; b. Memphis, Dec. 14, 1947; d. Jack Edwin and Anne Coolidge (Burleigh) Townsend; m. Clinton William Matson, Aug. 30, 1969 (div. 1976); m. Dow David Tiner, Apr. 15, 1978; children: Jeffrey David, Cynthia Leigh, Catherine Renee. Grad., Bapt. Meml. Hosp. Sch. Nursing, Memphis, 1969. RN, Ark.; cert. ACLS. Nurse Bapt. Meml. Hosp., Memphis, 1969, 71-72, New Bern (N.C.) Surg. Assocs., 1970-71, Meml. Hosp., Little Rock, 1972-73, Bapt. Med. Ctr., Little Rock, 1974-87; practice nursing specializing in post-anesthesia care Little Rock, 1987-89; post-anesthesia care specialist Little Rock Surgery Ctr. (formerly Freeway Surgery Ctr.), 1989—. Instr., ARC, 1975—; leader Park Hill Bapt. Ch., 1986—. 1st. lt. U.S. Army Med. Unit 1976-79. Mem. Am. Soc. Post Anesthesia Nurses (chartered), Ark. Post Anesthesia Care Nurses, Alumnae Assn. Bapt. Hosp. Sch. Nursing. Republican. Home: 12 Knights Bridge Rd North Little Rock AR 72116-6535

TING, ALBERT CHIA, bioengineering researcher; b. Hong Kong, Sept. 7, 1950; came to U.S., 1957; s. William Su and Katherine Sung (Bao) T.; m. Shirley Roung Wang, July 30, 1988. BA, UCLA, 1973; MS, Calif. State U., L.A., 1975, Calif. Inst. Tech., 1977; PhD, U. Calif., San Diego, 1983. Rsch. asst. Calif. Inst. Tech., Pasadena, 1975-77, U. Calif., San Diego, 1982-83; sr. staff engr. R&D Am. Med. Optics, Irvine, Calif., 1983-86; project engr., rsch. Allergan Med. Optics, Irvine, Calif., 1987-89; sr. project engr., rsch., 1989-92, sr. project engr., engring., 1993-94; bioengr. cons. Pharmacia Iovision, Inc., Irvine, Calif., 1995—. Inventor med. and optical devices, recipient patent awards 1988, 89, 91, 92, 93; contbr. articles to sci. jours. Mem. AAAS, Biomed. Engring. Soc., Assn. for Rsch. in Vision and Ophthalmology, Biomed. Optics Soc.

TING, ARTHUR J., orthopaedic surgeon; b. San Francisco, Sept. 9, 1951; m. Marilyn Ting, Oct. 15, 1975; children: Rich, Brandon, Ryan. BS in Biology, Occidental Coll., L.A.; MD, St. Louis U., 1980. Diplomate Am. Bd. Orthop. Surgery, Am. Bd. Arthroscopy (bd. dirs., test devel. com.); lic. physician, Calif.; cert. ALS in CPR. Intern in gen. surgery Los Angeles County-U. So. Calif. Med. Ctr., L.A., resident in orthopedic surgery; fellow in sports medicine Kerian & Jobe Orthop. Med. Group, Inglewood, Calif.; pvt. practice specializing in sports medicine Fremont, Calif.; orthop. surgeon Neurosport Rehab. Assocs., Fremont, Disability Reporters, Oakland, Calif., Palo Alto Med. Clinic; staff El Camino Hosp., Sunnyvale, Calif., O'Connor Hosp., Sunnyvale, Sequoia Hosp., Redwood City, Calif., Stanford U. Med. Ctr., Washington Hosp., Fremont; head team physician San Jose Sharks NHL Hockey, 1991-95, Menlo Coll., Woodside H.S., Menlo H.S., Can. Jr. Coll., San Francisco Blackhawks Profl. Soccer Team, San Jose Bandits Minor League Football, 1988-90, Oakland Skates Pro Roller Hockey, San Jose Rhinos Pro Roller Hockey, San Jose Grizzlies Pro Indoor Soccer, San Jose Storm Pro Volleyball, U.S. Track and Field Goodwill Games, Washington, 1990, U.S. Track and Field Pan Am. Games, Winnipeg, Can., 1993, San Jose Sabercats Profl. Arena Football, 1995—, USA Track and Field Pan Am. Games, Gateshead, Eng., 1994; mem. med. staff 1984 Summer Olympics, L.A., U.S. Olympic Trials, Indpls., 1988, U.S. Olympic Trials, New Orleans, 1992; med. cons. 1990 Profl. Beach Volleyball, Roger Craig's Tng. Video; assoc. to head team physician San Francisco 49ers NFL Football Team, 1986-91; med. dir. Ctr. for Sports Health, Sequoia Hosp., 1992—; lectr. in field; sports medicine cons. Yamaha Motor Sports, Jaguar Motor Sports Racing Team; team physician San Jose Giants Baseball/San Francisco Giants affiliate. Editl. rsch. bd. The Physician and Sports Medicine, 1986; contbr. articles to profl. jours. Adv. bd. The Champs Found. Recipient North Coast sect. Calif. Interscholastic Honor Physician award, 1991. Mem. AMA, Am. Coll. Sports Medicine, Am. Acad. Orthop. Surgeons, Am. Running and Fitness Assn., Bay Area Knee Soc., Am. Acad. Sports Physicians, Nat. Hockey League Teams Physician Soc. Home: 350 Jane Dr Woodside CA 94062 Office: Palo Alto Medical Clinic Dept Sports Medicine 300 Homer Ave Palo Alto CA 94301 Office: 40928 Fremont Blvd Fremont CA 94538

TING, IRWIN PETER, biology educator; b. San Francisco, Jan. 13, 1934; s. Peter Clare and Amanda Rose (Whitthorne); m. Donna Mead, Mar. 13, 1976; children: Coleen, Diane. BS, U. Nev., 1960, MS, 1961; PhD, Iowa State U., 1964. Prof. U. Calif., Riverside, 1965—, chmn. dept. botany, 1983-87; chair faculty acad. senate U. Calif., Riverside, 1994-96. Author: (with W. Jennings) Deep Canyon, A Desert Wilderness for Science, 1976, Plant Physiology, 1982; contbr. over 180 articles to profl. jours. Served in USN, 1956-60. Office: Univ Calif Dept Botany & Plant Scis Riverside CA 92521

TINGELSTAD, JON BUNDE, physician; b. McVille, N.D., Jan. 15, 1935; s. Sophus B. and Mabelle (Bunde) T.; m. Marcia Ayers, Dec. 17, 1960; children: Paul, Catherine, David. B.A., U. N.D., 1957, B.S., 1958; M.D., Harvard U., 1960. Diplomate Am. Bd. Pediatrics. Intern Children's Hosp. Med. Ctr., Boston, 1960-61, resident, 1961-62; resident U. Colo. Med. Ctr., Denver, 1962-63; fellow in pediatric cardiology Children's Hosp., Buffalo, 1965-67; asst. prof. pediatrics Med. Coll. Va., Richmond, 1967-71, assoc. prof., 1971-76; prof., vice chmn. pediatrics East Carolina U. Sch. Medicine, Greenville, N.C., 1976-77, prof., chmn. pediatrics, 1977—. Mem. Greenville City Bd. Edn., 1978-82, chmn., 1981-82. Served to capt. USAF, 1963-65. Fellow Am. Acad. Pediatrics, Am. Coll. Cardiology; mem. AAAS, AMA, So. Soc. Pediatric Rsch., Assn. Med. Sch. Pediatric Dept. Chairmen, Am. Bd. Pediatrics (bd. dirs.), Phi Beta Kappa, Phi Eta Sigma. Home: 208 Chowan Rd Greenville NC 27858-6321 Office: E Carolina U Sch Med Dept Pediatrics Greenville NC 27858-4354

TINGEY, CAROL, psychologist, educator; b. St. James, Mo., Sept. 24, 1933; d. Willis Alma and Lola (Madsen) T.; children: Richard, Blaine, James, Neil, Trish. BS magna cum laude, U. Utah, 1970, MEd, 1971, PhD, 1976. Tchr. public schs., Salt Lake City, 1970, spl. edn. tchr., 1971-72; clin. instr. spl. edn. U. Utah, Salt Lake City, 1972-74; dir. staff devel. Utah State Tng. Sch., American Fork, Utah, 1974-75; asst. prof. spl. edn. U. No. Iowa, Cedar Falls, 1975-77; asst. prof. spl. edn. Trinity Coll., Washington, 1977-78; asst. prof. spl. edn. of severely handicapped George Mason U., Fairfax, Va., 1978-79; assoc. prof. edn. and tng. physically and multi-handicapped Northwestern State U. of La., Natchitoches, 1979-81; assoc. prof. spl. edn. Ill. State U., Normal, also coordinator program for physically handicapped, 1981-83; assoc. prof. psychology Utah State U., Logan, 1983-88; psychologist Bear River Mental Health, Brigham City, Utah, 1988-90; psychologist Western Rehab. Inst., Salt Lake City, 1990—; pvt. practice, Salt Lake City, 1990—; psychologist U. Med. Ctr., 1993—; bd. dirs. Nat. Down Syndrome Congress; researcher, cons. in field. Fellow Am. Assn. on Mental Retardation (sec. Utah chpt. 1975, edn. chmn. region VIII 1976-77, treas. edn. div. 1979-80, editorial com., chair Down Syndrome Spl. Interest Group, mem. edit. adv. bd., 1989—) mem. Assn. for Severely Handicapped, Council for Exceptional Children (pres. Utah chpt. 1974-75), Assn. for Retarded Citizens, Phi Delta Kappa, Phi Kappa Phi. Author: Home and School Partnerships in Exceptional Education; Handicapped Infants and Children: Handbook for Parents and Professionals; New Perspectives on Down Syndrome; Down Syndrome: A Resource Handbook; Implementing Early Intervention; contbr. articles to profl. jours.; recorded albums: Self Help Skills, Adaptive Behavior; Socialization Skills; Adaptive Behavior; Daily Living Tasks, Housekeeping Skills, Vocational Awareness, Community Helpers; editorial adv. bd. Exceptional Parent mag., Infants and Young Children mag. Office: 50 N Medical Dr Salt Lake City UT 84132

TINGLEY, FLOYD WARREN, physician; b. Charlotte, N.C., Nov. 22, 1933; s. Floyd Warren Sr. and Janie (Suggs) T.; m. Sandra Carpenter, Aug. 20, 1955 (div. Dec. 1984); children: Sheryl Tingley Hagen, David Alan; m. Johnette Hill, Apr. 5, 1985. BA in English, Emory U., 1955, MD, 1959. Diplomate Am. Bd. Internal Medicine (bd. govs. 1986-92). Intern USAF Hosp., Lackland AFB, Tex., 1959-60; resident in internal medicine Parkland Meml. Hosp., Dallas, 1963-65, fellow in cardiology, 1965-66; pvt. practice specializing in internal medicine Arlington, Tex., 1966-88; med. dir. southwestern region Met. Life Ins. Co., Irving, Tex., 1988-90; regional practice leader William M. Mercer Inc., 1990-91; v.p., sr. med. dir. Provident Life and Accident Co., Chattanooga, 1991-92; v.p., nat. med. dir. Travelers Ins. Cos., Hartford, Conn., 1992-94; sr. v.p., chief med. officer Kemper Nat. Svcs., Plantation, Fla., 1995—; apptd. Tex. Commn. on Health Care Reimbursement Alternatives, 1987; bd. dirs. Riverside Nat. Bank, Grand Prairie, Tex. Contbr. articles to profl. jours. Pres. Arlington YMCA, 1971; chmn. budget com. Family Services, Ft. Worth, 1973; participant Health Policy Agenda for Am. People, Chgo., 1984-87; trustee Tex. Med. Liability Trust, Austin, 1987-88. Capt. USAF, 1958-63. Fellow ACP (pres. Tex. chpt. 1981); mem. AMA (chmn. sect. coun. internal medicine, 1979-88), Am. Soc. Internal Medicine (pres. 1986-87), Tex. Med. Assn. (treas. 1978-85, alt. del. to AMA 1985-91, commendation 1985), Tarrant County Med. Soc. (pres. Arlington br. 1974, del. to Tex. Med. Assn., Community Svc. award 1983). Presbyterian. Home: 7588 NW 51st Pl Coral Springs FL 33067 Office: Kemper Nat Svcs Inc 1601 SW 80th Terr Plantation FL 33324-4036

TINKER, JOHN HEATH, anesthesiologist, educator; b. Cin., May 18, 1941; s. Leonard Henry and Georgia (Reeves) T.; m. Martha Iuen (div. Jan., 1989); children: Deborah H. Lynne, Karen Sue, Juliette Kay; m. Bonnie Howard, Mar. 18, 1989. BS magna cum laude, U. Cin., 1964, MS summa cum laude, 1968. Diplomate Am. Bd. Anesthesiology (sr. examiner 1976—). Surg. intern, resident Harvard Med. Sch., Peter Bent Brigham Hosp., Boston, 1969-70, resident in anesthesiology, 1970-72; cons. anesthesiology Mayo Clinic, Rochester, Minn., 1974-83, chief cardiovascular anesthesiology, 1978-83; prof. anesthesiology U. Iowa Coll. Medicine, Iowa City, 1983—, chmn. dept., 1983—; mem. pharm. scis. rev. com., NIH, Bethesda, Md., 1986—; dir. Matrix Med. Inc., Orchard Park, N.Y., 1988—; frequent guest lectr. Author: Controversies in Cardiopulmonary Bypass, 1989 (monograph award Soc. Cardiovascular Anesthsiologists); editor: Anesthesia and Analgesia, Jour. Internat. Anesthesiology Rsch. Soc., 1983—; contbr. over 185 articles to profl. jours. Maj. U.S. Army, 1972-74. NIH grantee, 1977-87. Fellow Royal Coll. Surgeons Australia; mem. Am. Soc. Anesthesiologists (active numerous coms. 1972—), Soc. Cardiovascular Anesthesiologists, Assn. Univ. Anesthetists. Office: U Iowa Hosps & Clinics 450 Newton Rd Iowa City IA 52242*

TINKOFF, GLEN HERMAN, trauma and general surgeon; b. Baumholder, Germany, Apr. 5, 1955; came to the U.S., 1956; s. Bernard and Norma Rose (DeCastro) T.; m. Lauren Williams, Jan. 9, 1988; children: Gregory, Andrea, Jeffrey. BA, Williams Coll., 1977; MD, U. Cin., 1982. Diplomate Am. Bd. Surgery. Resident in gen. surgery Med. Coll. Pa., Phila., 1982-84; resident in gen. surgery Lankenau Hosp., Phila., 1984-86, chief surg. resident, 1986-87; fellow in surg. critical care U. Hosp., Stony Brook, N.Y., 1987-88; trauma rsch. fellow Lehigh Valley Hosp., Allentown, 1988-89, assoc. dir. trauma, 1989-92; gen./trauma surgeon Surg. Assocs. Lehigh Valley, Allentown, 1989-92; dir. trauma Med. Ctr. Del., Newark, 1992—, assoc. dir. surg. critical care, 1992—; lectr. in field. Contbr. articles to profl. jours. Fellow ACS (chmn. com. of trauma Del. chpt.); mem. AMA, Soc. Critical Care Medicine, Am. Trauma Soc., Ea. Assn. for Surgery of Trauma, Am. Soc. Parenteral and Enteral Nutrition, Del. Med. Soc., New Castle County Med. Soc., Blood Bank Del. (bd. dirs.). Office: Med Ctr Del Christiana Hosp Rm 4214 4755 Ogletown-Stanton Rd Newark DE 19718

TINNER, FRANZISKA PAULA, social worker, artist, designer, educator; b. Zurich, Switzerland, Sept. 18, 1944; came to U.S., 1969; d. Siegfied Albin and Gertrude Emilie (Sigg) Maier; m. Rolf Christian Tinner, Dec. 19, 1976; 1 child, Eric Francis. Student, U. Del., 1973-74, Va. Commonwealth U., 1974; BFA, U. Tenn., 1984; BA of Arts, U. Ark., Little Rock, 1991, postgrad. Lic. real estate broker. Dominican nun Ilanz, Switzerland, 1961-67; waitress London, 1967-68; governess Bryn Mawr, Pa., 1969; saleswoman, 1970-90, model, 1983; artist, designer Made For You, Kerrville, Tex. and Milw., 1984—; realtor Century 21, Milw., 1987-91; intern Birch Community Ctr., 1992-93. Designer softsculptor doll Texas Cactus Blossom, 1984. Ombudsman Action 10 Consumerline, Knoxville, Tenn., 1983-84; foster mother, Powhatan, Va., 1976-81; vol. ARC, Knoxville, 1979, Va. Home for Permanently Disabled, 1975; vol., counselor Youth For Understanding-Fgn. Exch., Powhatan, Va., 1975-77; tchr. pager/archiving host, mentor, area expert on Am. On Line; vol. Interactive Ednl. Svc. Recipient Art Display award U. Knoxville, 1983, Prof. Choice of Yr. award, 1983, Outstanding Achievemnt award TV Channel 10, Knoxville, 1984, 1st place award for paintings and crafts State Fair Va., Tenn., 1st place award Nat. Dollmakers, 1985, finalist Best of Coll. Photography, 1991, Achievement award Coll. Scholar af Am., 1991, Achievement cert. in technique of anger therapy, 1993, Achievement cert. in crisis response team tng., 1994; named One of Outstanding 1000 Women, 1995, Woman of Yr., 1995. Mem. NASW, NAFE, Milw. Bd. Realtors, Homemakers Club (pres. 1979-80), Newcomers Club, Bowlers Club (v.p.), Internat. Platform Assn.

TINSWORTH, STEVEN HOWARD, orthodontist; b. Williamsburg, Va., Nov. 22, 1945; s. Arvil Howard and Blanche Dehoney (Cheatham) T.; m. Jane Deanne Bayliss, Dec. 23, 1968 (div. Aug. 1985); children: Christin, Summer; m. Barbara Ruth Methven, June 11, 1988; stepchildren: Andrew Daniel Mobley, Ian Frazer Mobley; 1 child, John Steven Tinsworth. Student, Murray (Ky.) State U., 1963-66; DMD, U. Ky., 1970; cert. in orthondontics, La. State U., 1974. Orthodontist in pvt. practice Bradenton, Fla., 1974—; advisor, lectr. Manatee Vocat./Tech. Ctr.; state dir. Fla. Orthodontic Testing Program, 1990-93. Mem. Manatee Symphony Guild of Fla. West Coast Symphony, Bradenton, 1977, sec. bd. dirs. parent orgn., 1979; pres. Manatee Players Theatre, Bradenton, 1980; founding bd. dirs. Cmty. Concerts Assn.; chmn. dental div. United Way Manatee County, 1978, 88; pres. Am. Cancer Soc., Manatee, 1987; mem. president's coun. Am. Lung Assn.; bd. dirs. ARC, Manatee, 1987-93; Sunday sch. tchr. Christ Episcopal Ch., 1984, 86, 87, 94; cub scout leader Sunnyland coun. Boy Scouts Am., 1989-93. Capt. USAF, 1970-72. Mem. ADA, Fla. Dental Assn., West Coast Dental Assn., Manatee Dental Soc. (pres. 1980-81, exec. bd.), Am. Assn. Orthodontists, So. Assn. Orthodontists (Fla. alternate del. to Am. Assn. Orthodontists 1995—), Fla. Assn. Orthodontists (bd. dirs. 1988—, sec. 1991-92, pres. 1993-94), Am. Lingual Orthodontic Assn. (charter), Internat. Assn. Esthetic Orthodontics, Fla. Cleft Palate Assn., Manatee C. of C. (bd. dirs. 1984-87). Republican. Home: 509 65th Street Ct NW Bradenton FL 34209-1640 Office: 1500 59th St W Bradenton FL 34209-4634

TIPP, KAREN LYNN WAGNER, school psychologist; b. Chgo., Feb. 15, 1947; d. Harry and Sarah (Damask) Wagner; m. Michael Harvey, Dec. 30, 1973; children: Brenda Alyse, Brandon Philip. BA in Gen. High Sch. Edn., Roosevelt U., 1971; B of Jewish Studies, Spertus Coll., 1973, cert. in sch. psychology, 1981, MA in Jewish Studies, 1993; MS in Ednl. Theory, Nat. Louis U., 1974, CAS, 1981. Cert. psychologist, Ill.; nat. cert. sch. psychologist. Tchr. Niles Twp. High Sch., Skokie, Ill., 1971-72; mgr. travel agy. Chgo., 1983-85; tchr. spl. edn. No. Cook County, Ill., 1972-90; tchr. Hebrew Chgo. Bd. Jewish Edn., 1969-90, interim prin. religious sch., 1989-90; sch. psychologist Chgo. Pub. Schs., 1990—; ind. ednl. therapist, Chgo., 1973—; contract psychologist N.W. Suburban Chgo., 1981-90; cons. learning disabled Chgo. Bd. Jewish Edn., 1983-90; mem. adv. bd. Tchr.'s Task Force, 1993—. Pres. Truman Coll. (City Coll. Chgo.) Coun., 1985-87, 93-95, nom. chair, 1990—; exec. sec. North Town Cmty. Coun., Chgo., 1984-86, pres., 1989-91, v.p., 1991-93, treas., 1993-96, v.p., 1996—; pres. dist. 2 coun. Chgo. Bd. Edn., 1987-89, spl. edn. chair, 1990-92; exec. sec. North Town Civic League, 1978-80, pres., 1981-84; mem. coop. extension youth coun. U. Ill., sec., 1985-91, exec. coun., 1990-91; charter mem. Hild Culture Ctr., membership chair; beat rep. Chgo. Police Dept.; vice chair Head Start, Salvation Army, Dewey Day Care Evanston, 1972-75, Rogers Park Montessori Sch., 1979-80; corr. sec. Day Care Ctr. Bd.-Evanston, 1978-81, Rogers Park Mental Health Coun.; youth chair Indian Boundary Playground Bldg., 1986-89; mem. steering com. Rogers Park Centennial, 1991-93; mem. state coms. 4-H, 1982-88, Chgo./Cook County 4-H Coun., 1984-95; mem. North Town Post Office Adv. Coun., 1995—. Master Tchr. grantee Jewish Bd. Edn., Chgo., 1981-89, 20 Yr. award, 1990; recipient Cmty. Leadership award Dept. Human Svcs., Chgo., 1985, North Town-Dorothy LeRoy Cmty. Svc. award, 1992. Fellow Am. Orthopsychiat. Assn.; mem. NASP, Coun. Exceptional Children (liaison 1972-86), Assn. Ednl. Therapist, Ill. Psychol. Assn. (Sch. Psychologist of Yr. 1991), Family Resource Ctr. on Disabilities (spl. edn. com. 1990—, bd. dirs. 1993—), Profls. in Learning Disabilities (legis. chair 1987—), Children with Attention Deficit Disorder, Learning Disabilities Assn., Ill. Sch. Psychologists Assn. (Practitioner of Yr. 1991, child study com.), Chgo. Assn. Sch. Psychologists (rec. sec. 1995—, v.p. 1996—), Greater Uptown Youth Network, Family Resource Handicapped (spl. edn. com.), Family Resource (bd. dirs. 1993—), Ill. 4-H Found., Edn. Therapists, Samoyed Club Am. (bd. dirs. 1996—), Samoyed Club Am., Prairieland Samoyed Club (legis. chair 1995—, membership chair). Home: 6730 N Maplewood Ave Chicago IL 60645-4620

TIPPENS, JACK KELVIN, orthopedic surgeon; b. Canton, Ga., June 2, 1939; s. Joseph Walter and Leola (Cown) T.; m. Lynda Louella Holcombe; children: Terry Lee, Traci Anne. BS, N. Ga. Coll., 1961; MD, Med. Coll. Ga., 1965. Diplomate Am. Bd. Orthopaedic Surgery. Intern Med. Ctr. Hosp., Columbus, Ga., 1965-66; orthopaedic resident Letterman Army Med. Ctr., San Francisco, 1968-71; commd. 2d lt. U.S. Army, 1961, advanced through grades to col., 1980; orthopaedic surgeon U.S. Army Hosp., Camp Zama, Japan, 1966-68; pediatric orthopaedic surgeon U.S. Army Hosp., Ft. Gordon, Ga., 1972-75; chief orthopaedic surgery Eisenhower Army Med. Ctr., Ft. Gordon, 1975-83, dep. comdr., 1987—; chief orthopaedic surgery Walter Reed Army Med. Ctr., Washington, 1983-87; dir. S.E. Health Support Area, Ft. Gordon, Ga., 1994—; orthopaedic cons. Office of Army Surgeon Gen., Washington, 1983-92. Contbr. articles to profl. publs. Decorated Legion of Merit. Fellow Am. Acad. Orthopaedic Surgeons (mil. affairs com. 1984-90, bd. councilors 1985-89), ACS; mem. Soc. Orthopaedic Mil. Surgeons (treas. 1983-87), Rotary. Republican. Methodist. Home: 205 Chatham Rd Augusta GA 30907-3707 Office: SE Health Support Area Eisenhower Army Med Ctr Fort Gordon GA 30905

TIPTON, BARBARA MARY, physical therapist; b. Detroit, Oct. 15, 1965; d. Paul and Helen (Viola) Mendola; m. David Tipton, Oct. 8, 1988; 1 child, Nicholas Warren. BS in Phys. Therapy cum laude, Wayne State U., 1988; M of Health Sci., U. Indpls., 1993. From phys. therapist to co-mgr. rehab. svcs. Hutzel Hosp., Detroit, 1988-94; phys. therapy supr. Macomb Hosp. Ctr., Warren, Mich., 1994—; rehab. svcs. orthopedic coord. Hutzel Hosp., 1990-94; student clin. instr. Wayne State U., Detroit, 1989-94; conf. spkr. Nat. Assn. Orthop. Nurses, Detroit, 1992. Co-author: Total Joint Replacement, 1993. Hosp. chair March of Dimes Walk Am., Detroit, 1989-90. Mem. NAFE, Am. Phys. Therapy Assn. (adminstrn., orthop. sect.), Am. Acad. Med. Adminstrs., Am. Coll. Neuromusculoskeletal Adminstrn., Exec. Womens Golf League. Republican. Roman Catholic. Office: Macomb Hosp Ctr Phys Rehab Svcs 27450 Schoenherr Rd Warren MI 48093

TIPTON, REUBEN RYDER, III, ophthalmologist; b. Memphis, Oct. 31, 1949; s. Reuben Ryder II and Mary (Mayo) T.; m. Sally Normert Horne; children: Lauren, Ryder. BA, Rhodes Coll. (formerly Southwestern at Memphis), 1971; MD, U. Tenn., 1974. Diplomate Am. Bd. Ophthalmology, Am. Bd. Eye Surgery. Intern Meth. Hosp., Memphis, 1975; emergency rm. physician Aiken (S.C.) Cmty. Hosp., 1976-77; resident Birmingham (Ala.) Eye Found. Hosp., 1977-80; pvt. practice ophthalmology, ptnr. Ea. Carolina Regional Eye Ctr., Myrtle Beach, S.C., 1980—. Fellow Am. Acad. Ophthalmology; mem. AMA, Am. Coll. Eye Surgeons, S.C. Soc. Ophthalmology, Found. N.Am. Wild Sheep (life). Methodist. Office: E Carolina Regional Eye Ctr 900 Medical Circle Myrtle Beach SC 29572

TIRER, SAMUEL, physician; b. Haifa, Israel, Oct. 8, 1950; s. Morris and Sabina (Davidson) T.; m. Margaret Sheila Sullivan, Apr. 14, 1978; children: Alexandra, Daniel. BSc with honors, McGill, Montreal, Can., 1972, MD, CM, 1976. Intern Hosp. U. Pa., Phila., 1976-77; staff physician Mt. Sinai Hosp., Ste Agathe, Que., Can., 1977-78; resident Hosp. U. Pa., Phila., 1978-81; asst. prof. U. Pa., Phila., 1981-83; staff anesthesiologist Frankford Hosp., Phila., 1984-85; asst. prof. U. Pa., Phila., 1985-89, clin. asst. prof., 1989—; med. dir. Short Procedure Unit, Presbyn. Med. Ctr., Phila., 1990—. Contbr. articles to profl. jours. Mem. Town Watch, Lower Merion, Pa., 1991, Mus. Com. Wood Libr., Park Ridge, Ill., 1990—. Fellow Coll. Physicians Phila., 1989. Mem. McGill Soc. Phila. (pres. 1982—).

TIRIBELLI, CLAUDIO, medical educator; b. Mestre-Venezia, Veneto, Italy, Oct. 6, 1946; s. Mario and Adele (Brusa) T.; m. Rita Russo, May 27, 1972; 1 child, Mario. MD, U. Padua, Italy, 1971; PhD in Gastroenterology, U. Trieste, Italy, 1975. Rsch. assoc. U. Trieste, 1972-74, asst. prof. medicine, 1974-80, rsch. prof. medicine, 1980-89, prof. medicine, 1982-89; vis. scientist U. Groningen, The Netherlands, 1982; vis. prof. Poly. U., Bklyn., 1989—, U. Toronto, 1995—. Mem. European Assn. for Study of Liver (sec. 1983-85, sec. edn. com. 1992—), Internat. Assn. for Study of Liver (councillor 1986-90), N.Y. Acad. Sci., Fondo Studi Fegato (pres. 1992—), Sigma Xi. Office: U Trieste Centro Studi, Fegato Dept BBCM, via Giorgeri 1, 34127 Trieste Italy

TIRNAUER, LAWRENCE THEODORE, psychologist, psychotherapist; b. N.Y.C., Apr. 15, 1933; s. Samuel and Rose Tirnauer; m. Sandra Smathers (div.); children: Jennifer, Karen, Diana, Eric. BA, Otterbein Coll., 1954; MS, Pa. State U., 1955, PhD, 1959. Lic. psychologist, Washington. Staff psychologist St. Elizabeth's Hosp., Washington, 1959-60; psychologist Child Guidance Clinic D.C. Health Dept., Washington, 1960-63, chief psychologist children's program area C, 1963-64, chief psychologist adolescent program area C, 1964-65; chief psychologist Bur. Infant and Maternal Care, Washington, 1965-68; pvt. practice psychology and psychotherapy Washington, 1968—; cons. McFarland Child Guidance Clinic, Washington, 1965-68, Washington Free Clinic, 1970-75, Pastoral Counseling Ctrs., 1965-85. Editorial bd. Voices: The Art and Sci. of Psychotherapy, 1977—; assoc. editor The Psychotherpay Patient, 1984—; contbr. articles on psychotherapy to profl. jours., chpts. to books. Mem. APA, Am. Acad. Psychotherapists (pres. 1986-88, chair rsch. com. 1992—), Am. Group Psychotherapy Assn., D.C. Psychol. Assn. Office: 5225 Connecticut Ave NW Washington DC 20015-1845

TISCHFIELD, JAY ARNOLD, genetics educator; b. N.Y.C., June 15, 1946; s. Max and Ethel Barbara (Smith) T.; m. Donna Marie Mitchell, Aug. 29, 1978; children: Max Alexander, Samuel Eli, David James. BS, Bklyn. Coll., 1967; MPH, Yale U., 1969, PhD, 1973. Diplomate Am. Bd. Med. Genetics. Asst. prof. Case Western Reserve U., Cleve., 1972-78; assoc. prof., prof. Med. Coll. of Ga., Augusta, 1978-87; prof., dir. molecular genetics Ind. U. Sch. Medicine, Indpls., 1987—; sci. adv. bd. Genetrix Inc., Scottsdale, Ariz., 1986—, Biodex Inc., Cambridge, Mass. Contbr. articles to profl. jours. Undergrad. admissions mem. Assn. Yale Alumni, Ind., 1987—; mem. Ind. Corp. for Sci., Technology, 1987—. Named Disting. Alumnus, Bklyn. Coll., 1990; NIH postdoctoral fellow, 1967-72; grantee NIH, 1972—, NSF, 1983-85. Mem. Am. Soc. for Human Genetics, Am. Soc. for Microbiology, AAAS, Sigma Xi, Yale Club of Ind. Office: Ind U Sch of Medicine 975 W Walnut St Indianapolis IN 46202-5181

TISCHLER, GARY LOWELL, psychiatrist, educator; b. N.Y.C., Oct. 30, 1935; s. Louis and Dorothy (Green) T.; m. Judith Post, Aug. 18, 1957; children: Laurie Dee, Marc David, Rachel Mara. AB, Hamilton Coll., 1957; MD, U. Pa., 1961; MS, Yale U., 1975. Intern Kings County Hosp., Bklyn., 1961-62; resident in psychiatry Yale U. Sch. Medicine, New Haven, 1962-65, asst. prof., 1967-70, assoc. prof., 1970-75, prof. psychiatry, 1975-90; prof., chmn. dept. psychiatry and biobehavioral scis., dir. neuropsychiatric inst. UCLA Sch. Medicine, 1990-95; chmn. dept. psychiatry Yale U. Sch. Medicine, New Haven, 1986-87; dir. Yale Psychiatric Inst., New Haven, 1978-87; chief psychiatry Yale-New Haven Hosp., 1986-87; clin. dir. Hill-West Haven div. Conn. Mental Health Ctr., New Haven, 1968-70, dir., 1970-77; prof. psychiatry UCLA, 1990-95; prof., exec. vice chair dept. psychiatry Cornell U. Med. Coll., 1996—; dir. Westchester divsn., dir. mental health programs N.Y. Hosp., 1994—, dir. Payne Whitney Clinic, 1996—; study dir. Pres.'s Commn. on Mental Health, Washington, 1977-79; cons. Arthur D. Little Inc., Boston, 1973-75, IBM Corp., Armonk, N.Y., 1986-87; mem. profl. adv. com. Am. Med. Internat., L.A., 1984-86; mem. bd. mental health and behavioral medicine Inst. Medicine, Washington, 1986—, com. on clin. evaluation, 1990-94. Author: Quality Assurance Thru Utilization and Peer Review, 1982; editor: Patient Care Evaluation in Mental Health, 1985, Diagnosis and Classification in Psychiatry, 1987; contbr. articles to profl. jours. Mem. Gov.'s transition staff on mental health, Conn., 1975; vice chmn. Bd. Mental Health State of Conn., 1986. Served to capt. U.S. Army, 1965-67, Vietnam. Fellow Am. Psychiat. Assn., Am. Coll. Mental Health Adminstrn., Am. Assn. for Social Psychiatry, Am. Coll. Psychiatry. Home: 36 Rock Hill Rd Bedford NY 10506-1522 Office: NY Hosp-Cornell Med Ctr 21 Bloomingdale Rd White Plains NY 10605

TITILOYE, VICTORIA MOJIRAYO, pediatrics nurse; b. Okemesi Ekiti, Nigeria, Nov. 17, 1955; d. Ezekiel Ajiboye and Julianah Oyindaola (Atitebi) T. Diploma, Lagos U. Teaching Hosp., 1977; BS, SUNY, Bklyn., 1981; MA, NYU, 1983, PhD valedictory rep., 1988. Cert. occupational therapist, Nigerian nurse, RN. Asst. nursing supt. adult med. and surg. wards Wesley Guild Hosp., Unife-Complex, Ilesha, Oyo, 1977-78; sr. occupational therapist United Cerebral Palsy, Bklyn., 1982-85; occupational therapist con., Sch. for Multiply Handicapped Children, Vis. Therapist Assocs., Bklyn., 1985-89; rsch. assoc. NYU, N.Y.C., 1989-90; asst. dir. occupational therapy Cobble Hill Nursing Home, Bklyn., 1991-92; asst. prof. occupl. therapy SUNY Health Sci. Ctr., Bklyn., 1994—; dir. occupl. therapy dept. Sts. Joachim and Ann Residence, Bklyn., 1992-93; cons. drs. office occupl. therapy dept. U. Medicine and Dentistry N.J., 1993; clin. and rsch. cons. League Therapeutic Ctr., Bklyn., 1993—; rsch. cons. Kessler Inst. Rehab., East Orange, N.J., 1993—; adj. asst. prof. dept. life scis. N.Y. Inst. Tech., 1993-94; clin. and rsch. cons. League Therapeutic Ctr., Bklyn., 1993—; rep. NYU Sch. Edn., Health, Nursing and Arts Professions; reviewer articles and proposals for profl. jours. and confs. Contbr. articles to profl. jours. Food coord. Food Program for the Homeless, Sts. Ann and George, Bklyn.; reviewer conf. proposals. Recipient scholarships Nigerian govt., NYU Grad. Sch., Downstate Acad. Achievement. Mem. ANA, Am. Occupational Therapy Assn., Am. Soc. on Aging, N.Y. Acad. Scis., Nigerian Nurses Assn., MEDART Internat.

TITKO, KRISTIN KIMBERLY, surgeon; b. Hamilton, Ohio, Aug. 16, 1967; d. Jerry L. and Phyllis E. (Wolfli) T. DPM, Ohio Coll. Podiatric Medicine, 1992. Podiatric surgeon Podiatry Svcs. Cin., 1994—; team podiatric physician Cin. Silverbacks and Cyclones, 1995—; chairperson provider coun. Cin. Health Plan, 1995—. Mem. Am. Diabetes Assn., Am. Podiatric Med. Assn., Am. Coll. Foot and Ankle Surgeons, Am. Coll. Podiatric Sports Medicine, So. Ohio Acad. Podiatrists (sec., bd. dirs. 1995-96). Office: Podiatry Svcs Cin 10475 Reading Rd # 306 Cincinnati OH 45241

TITUS, CHARLES OTIS, health care medical director; b. Augusta, Maine, Jan. 26, 1927; s. Charles O. Titus and Effie M. Douphinelt; m. Joan M. Myles, Dec. 27, 1954; children: Donna, William, Elizabeth, Joseph, Mary, Melinda, Karen. BS, BA, U. Ottawa, Can., 1951, MD, 1956. Cert. Am. Bd. Ophthalmology. Intern Ottawa (Can.) Gen. Hosp., 1955-56; resident Northwestern Med. Ctr., Chgo., 1956-59; commd. 2d lt. USAF, 1959, advanced through grades to col., 1966; pvt. practice Washington, 1966-74; hosp. comdr. Air Nat. Guard, Washington, 1973-84; med. dir. Bausch & Lomb, Rochester, N.Y., 1974-94, ret., 1994; med. cons. Bausch & Lomb, 1994-95. Fellow Am. Coll. Surgeons, Am. Acad. Ophthalmologists; mem. Contact Lens Assn. Ophthalmologists, Pan-Am. Med. Assn., Soc. Mil. Ophthalmologists. Home: 12 Niblick Ct Penfield NY 14526-2815

TITUS, JACK L., pathologist, educator; b. South Bend, Ind., Dec. 7, 1926; s. Loren O. and Rutha B. (Orr) T.; m. Beverly Harden, June 18, 1949; children—Jack, Elizabeth Ann Titus Engelbrecht, Michael, Matthew, Joan. B.S., Notre Dame U., 1948; M.D., Washington U., St. Louis, 1952; Ph.D., U. Minn., 1962. Practice medicine Rensselaer, Ind., 1953-57; fellow in pathology U. Minn., 1957-61; assoc. prof. pathology Mayo Grad. Sch., Rochester, Minn., 1961-72; prof. pathology Mayo Med. Sch., 1971-72, coordinator pathology tng. programs, 1964-72; W.L. Moody Jr. prof., chmn. dept. pathology Baylor Coll. Medicine, Houston, 1972-87; chief pathology service Meth. Hosp., Houston, 1972-87; pathologist-in-chief Harris County Hosp. Dist., Houston, 1972-87; chmn. dept. pathology Med. Ctr. Hosp., Conroe, Tex., 1982-87, Woodlands Community Hosp., 1984-87; dir. registry for cardiovascular diseases United Hosps., 1987-95; clin. prof. pathology U. Minn., 1987—; adj. prof. pathology Baylor Coll. Medicine, 1987—; sr. cons. in pathology U. Tex. System Cancer Ctr., Houston, 1974—. Mem. editl. bd. Circulation, 1966-72, Am. Heart Jour., 1972-77, Modern Pathology, 1987-95, Human Pathology, 1988—, Am. Jour. of Cardiovascular Pathology, 1987-94, Cardiovascular Pathology, 1991—; contbr. articles to med. jours. Served with U.S. Army, 1945-47. Recipient Billings gold medal AMA, 1968, Hoektoen gold medal, 1969, Disting. Achievement award Soc. Cardiovascular Pathology, 1993, Scholarly Achievement award Houston Soc. Clin. Pathology, 1993. Mem. Internat. Acad. Pathology, Am. Assn. Pathologists, Am. Soc. Clin. Pathologists, AAAS, AMA, Am. Heart Assn., Coll. Am. Pathologists, Minn. Med. Assn., Minn. Heart Assn., Minn. Soc. Clin. Pathologists, Ramsey County Med. Soc., Sigma Xi, Alpha Omega Alpha. Methodist. Office: 255 Smith Ave N Ste 200 Saint Paul MN 55102-2518

TIZES, REUBEN, preventive health physician, educator; b. Ploesti, Romania, 1930; m. Carol Wiener, Nov. 27, 1959; children: Bruce R., Andrea C. Tizes-Feinberg, Simone M. MD, Hebrew U., Jerusalem, 1956; MPH, Columbia U., 1969. Diplomate Am. Bd. Preventive Medicine. Rotating intern Kaplan Hosp., Rehovoth, Israel, 1955-56, Samaritan Hosp., Troy, N.Y., 1959-60; resident in internal medicine Queens Gen. Hosp., Jamaica, N.Y., 1960-61; resident in internal medicine and pulmonary disease Kings County Hosp. Ctr., Bklyn., 1961-62, clin. asst., vis. physician, 1964-70, Tb coord., 1964-69; resident in renal and gastrointestinal disease Met. Hosp., N.Y.C., 1962-63; internal medicine staff Franklin Hosp. Med. Ctr., Valley Stream, N.Y., 1964—; dir. ambulatory care Newark Beth Isreal Med. Ctr., 1974; clin. asst. instr. SUNY, Bklyn., 1965-70, asst. prof. environ. medicine and community health, 1970-75, assoc. prof., 1975—; commr. health Orange County Dept. Health, Goshen, N.Y., 1972-73; physician-in-charge Williamsburg-Greenpoint Chest Clinic, N.Y.C., 1964-69; clinician Bur. Tb N.Y.C. Dept. Health, 1964-69; dir. respiratory diseases and Tb control program Nassau County Dept. Health, Mineola, N.Y., 1969-71; dir. ambulatory care svcs. and community medicine Kingsbrook Jewish Med. Ctr., Brklyn., 1974-77; dir. med. rehab. divsn. Peninsula Hosp. Ctr., Far Rockaway, N.Y., 1977-83. Maj. M.C. Israeli Army, 1957-59. Fellow ACP, APHA, Am. Coll. Angiology, Am. Coll. Chest Physicians, Am. Coll. Preventive Medicine; mem. Am. Thoracic Soc., Am. Soc. Internal Medicine. Address: Hewlett Bay Pk 49 Piermont Ave Hewlett NY 11557-2109

TJIAN, ROBERT TSE NAN, bichemistry educator, biology resercher, virology researcher; b. Hong Kong, Sept. 22, 1949; naturalized Brit. citizen.; m. 1976. BA, U. Calif., Berkeley, 1971; PhD in Molecular Biology, Harvard U., 1976. Staff investigator molecular virology Cold Spring Harbor Lab., 1976-79, Robertson fellow, 1978; prof. biochemistry U. Calif., Berkeley, 1979—. Named Passano Found. laureate; recipient Lewis S. Rosentiel award for disting. work in basic med. rsch. Brandeis U., 1995. Mem. NAS (Molecular Biology award 1991). Office: Univ Calif Dept Biochemistry 401 Barket St Berkeley CA 94720

TOADVINE, JOANNE ELIZABETH, physical therapy foundation executive; b. Covington, Ky., Nov. 29, 1933; d. Ralph and Myrtle (Wasson) Bailer; children: Daniel, Michael, Patrick, Michell, Joseph. Student, St. Benedict Coll. Bus. Sch., 1948; PhD, U. for Humanistic Studies, Las Vegas, Nev., 1986. Cert. rehab. technician in functional elec. stimulation, Nev. Founder, pres. Help Them Walk Again Found., Inc., Las Vegas, 1976—. Contbr. articles to profl. jours. Mem. State of Nev. Dem. Cen. Com., Clark Clunty (Nev.) Dem. Cen. Com. Recipient Humanitarian award Chiropractic Assn. Ariz., Channel 3 Spirit award, Humanitarian award Dr. Otto Kestler, Key to City, Las Vegas, 1992; named to Honorable Order Ky. Cols., Mother of Yr. Clark County, 1988, Disting. Women of So. Nev., 1989-95; recognized in The Congl. Recorder, 1980; Congrl. recognition, 1992; Senatorial recognition, 1993. Mem. Am. Acad. of Neurol. Orthopedic Surgeons (nat. coordinating council on spinal cord injury), Nat. Coordinating Coun. on Spinal Cord Injury, Las Vegas C. of C. (Women's Achievement award in health care), VFW, NAFE, The Pilot Club Internat. Office: Help Them Walk Again Found 5300 W Charleston Blvd Las Vegas NV 89102-1307

TOBACK, F(REDERICK) GARY, nephrologist, cell biologist; b. Bklyn., Oct. 23, 1941; s. Israel (Henry) and Evelyn Adele (Friedman) T.; m. Phyllis Ruby Brooks, June 9, 1963; children: David Andrew, Alison Rachel, Jonathan Daniel. AB cum laude, Columbia U., 1963; MD, NYU, 1967; PhD in Biochemistry, Boston U., 1974. Diplomate Am. Bd. Internal Medicine, also Sub-bd. Nephrology. Intern and resident Cleve. Met. Gen. Hosp., 1967-69; rsch. assoc. Sch. Medicine Boston U., 1970-73; fellow in nephrology Sch. Medicine Harvard U., Boston, 1974; asst. prof. medicine U. Chgo., 1974-79, assoc. prof. medicine, 1980-85, prof. medicine and cell physiology, 1985—; investigator Am. Heart Assn., Chgo., 1980-85. Contbr. articles to profl. jours. Bd. dirs. Congregation Rodfei Zedek, Chgo., 1991—. Lt. comdr. USN, 1979-80. Nat. Kidney Found. fellow, 1971, USPHS fellow Boston U., 1972-73; named Am. Cancer Soc. scholar Salk Inst. for Biol. Studies, San Diego, 1979-80; grantee USPHS, NIH, 1975—. Mem. Assn. Am. Physicians, Am. Soc. Clin. Investigation, Am. Physiol. Soc., Am. Soc. Nephrology, Internat. Soc. Nephrology, Ctrl. Soc. for Clin. Rsch. Jewish. Office: U Chgo 5841 S Maryland Ave MC 5100 Chicago IL 60637-1463

TOBEÑA, ADOLF, psychiatry researcher, educator, writer; b. Graus, Huesca, Spain, July 26, 1950; s. Pere and Roser (Pallarés) T.; children: Anna, Jordi. MD, U. Barcelona, Spain, 1972, PhD cum laude, 1977. Diplomate Spanish Bd. Psychiatry. Rsch. asst. U. Barcelona, 1972-74; rsch. asst. Autonomous U. Barcelona, Bellaterra, Spain, 1975-77, lectr. in psychology, 1978-80, assoc. prof. psychology, 1980-85, prof. psychiatry, 1985—, dir. behavior lab., 1975-77, dir. animal lab. psychopharmacology, 1980-96, dir. dept. psychiatry and toxicology Sch. Medicine, 1996—; cons. psychiatrist Hosp. Del Mar, Barcelona, 1982-84; prin. rschr. Digiyt-Fis, Madris, 1982—; cons. rsch. Upjohn Pharm. S.A., 1985-91; collaborator Sci. Mus. Barcelona 1986-91; vis. prof. Inst. Psychiatry, London, 1988. Author 6 books on anxiety disorders, neurobiology and social issues; contbr. over 100 articles to neuroscience jours.; regular appearances on various radio and TV programs, 1987-96. Recipient Marti I Julia award Inst. Catalan Studies, 1986, 89, Serra Moret award Regional Govt. of Catalonia, 1990, 94, Avui award for articles in catalan press, 1991, City of Barcelona Sci. award, 1992. Mem. AAAS, Spanish Soc. Neurosci., Catalan Soc. Biology (Best Article 1990), Catalan Soc. Behavior Rsch. and Therapy (award 1990), N.Y. Acad. Scis.

TOBEY, MARTIN ALAN, cardiologist; b. Dallas, Tex., Sept. 24, 1947; s. Nathan Gene and Rose Marcus T.; m. Judith Helane Ross, Mar. 10, 1974; children: Daniel, Rachel. BS with highest distinction, Pa. State U., 1968; MD, Jefferson Med. Coll., 1970. Diplomate Am. Bd. Internal Medicine, Am. Bd. Cardiovascular Diseases. Intern Phila. Gen. Hosp., 1970-71; resident in internal medicine Parkland Meml. Hosp., Dallas, 1971-74; fellow in cardiology U. Tex. Southwestern Med. Sch., Dallas, 1976-78; cardiologist Cardiology Assocs. of Fort Worth, Tex., 1978—; mem. med. bd. Harris Hosp. Meth., Ft. Worth, 1988-90, chmn. cardiology divsn., 1988-90. Author (software) Workshops in Coronary Angioplasty, 1984. Major U.S. Army, 1974-76. Fellow Am. Coll. Cardiology (regional rep. Tex. chpt. 1996—), Am. Heart Assn., Alpha Omega Alpha. Office: Cardiology Assocs Ft Worth 1300 W Rosedale Fort Worth TX 76104

TOBIAN, LOUIS, JR., medical educator; b. Dallas, Jan. 26, 1920; s. Louis and Isabelle (Franklin) T.; m. Frances Williams, Oct. 18, 1951; 1 child, Anne Simpson. BA, U. Tex., 1940; MD, Harvard Med. Sch., 1943. Diplomate Am. Bd. Internal Medicine. Intern Brigham-Womens Hosp., Boston, 1944; resident U. Calif. Hosp., San Francisco, 1944-45, Parkland Hosp., Dallas, 1945-46; fellow in medicine U. Tex. Southwestern Med. Sch., Dallas, 1946-49, rsch. fellow, 1949-51, asst. prof. medicine, 1951, 54; rsch. fellow biol. chemistry Harvard Med. Sch., Boston, 1951-53; assoc. prof. medicine U. Minn. Hosp. and Med. Sch., Mpls., 1954-64, prof. medicine, 1964—. Contbr. over 200 articles to profl. jours. Chmn. NIH Task Force on

Hypertension, 1972-73, Coun. for High Blood Pressure Rsch., AHA, 1974-76. Franz Volhard award Internat. Soc. Hypertension, 1988. Mem. Am. Assn. Physicians, Am. Soc. Clin. Investigation, Am. Physiol. Soc. (chmn. circulation group 1977), Am. Soc. Hypertension (pres. 1992-94, Richard Bright award 1992), Am. Soc. Nephrology (John P. Peters award 1990), Coun. for High Blood Pressure Rsch. (chmn. 1974-76). Home: 1437 E River Rd Minneapolis MN 55414 Office: U Minn Hosp & Clinic Box 285 420 Delaware St SE Minneapolis MN 55455

TOBIAS, RANDALL L., pharmaceutical company executive; b. Lafayette, Ind., Mar. 20, 1942; m. Marilyn Jane Salyer, Sept. 2, 1966 (dec. May 1994); children: Paige Noelle, Todd Christopher; m. Marianne Williams, July 15, 1995; stepchildren: James Russell Ullyot, Kathryn Lee Ullyot. BS in Mktg., Ind. U., 1964; LLD (hon.), Galuedette U.; D of Engring. (hon.), Rose Hulman Inst. Tech. Numerous positions Ind. Bell, 1964-77, Ill. Bell, 1977-81; v.p. residence mktg. sales and service AT&T, 1981-82, pres. Am. Bell Consumer Products, 1983, pres. Consumer Products, 1983-84, sr. v.p., 1984-85; chmn., CEO AT&T Comm., N.Y.C., 1985-91, AT&T Internat., Basking Ridge, N.J., 1991-93; vice chmn. bd. AT&T, N.Y.C., 1986-93; chmn., CEO Eli Lilly & Co., Indpls., 1993—; bd. dirs. Eli Lilly & Co., Kimberly-Clark, Knight-Ridder, Phillips Petroleum; active U.S.-Japan Bus. Coun., U.S.-China Bus. Coun., Indpls. Cmty. Leaders Allied for Superior Schs. Trustee Duke U.; vice chmn. Colonial Williamsburg Found.; bd. govs. Skyline Club, Indpls. Mus. Art; bd. dirs. Indpls. Symphony Orch., Ind. U. Found., Econ. Club Indpls. Mem. Bus. Coun. Indpls. Corp. Cmty. Coun., Coun. Fgn. Rels., Bus. Roundtable, Meridian Hills Country Club (Indpls.), Woodstock Club (Indpls.), Columbia Club (Indpls.), Athletic Club (Indpls.), Univ. Club (Indpls.), Amwell Valley Conservancy, Theta Chi. Office: Eli Lilly & Co Lilly Corp Ctr Indianapolis IN 46285

TOBIN, ILONA LINES, psychologist, marriage and family counselor, educator, consultant; b. Trenton, Mich., Apr. 15, 1943; d. Frank John and Marjorie Cathalean (Lines) Kotyuk; m. Roger Lee Tobin, Aug. 20, 1966. BA, Ea. Mich. U., 1965; MA, 1968; MA, Mich. State U., 1975; EdD, Wayne State U., 1978. Diplomate Am. Bd. of Sexology; cert. marriage, family counselor; cert. sex educator and counselor; cert. sex therapist. Tchr., counselor Willow Run Pub. Schs., Ypsilanti, Mich., 1966-72; prof. Macomb County Community Coll., Mt. Clemens, Mich., 1974-79; psychotherapist Identity Ctr., Inc., Mt. Clemens, 1974-79; dir. treatment Alternative Lifestyles, Inc., Orchard Lake, Mich., 1979-80; psychologist Profl. Psychotherapy and Counseling Ctr., Farmington Hills, Mich., 1980-83; pvt. practice clin. psychology, Birmingham, Mich., 1983—; lectr. Wayne State U., Detroit, 1977-88; tchr., lectr. med. edn. St. Joseph's Hosp., Pontiac, Mich., 1993—; recruitment dir. Upward Bound Ea. Mich. U., Ypsilanti, 1969-72. Creator Doc's Dolls. Co-chmn. Birmingham Families in Action, 1982-83; bd. dirs. HAVEN-Oakland County's Phys. and Sexual Abuse Ctr. and Oakland Area Counselors Assn., 1984-85; mem. exec. bd., v.p. pres. Birmingham Community Women's Ctr., 1984-85, also bd. dirs.; mem. adv. bd. Woodside Med. Ctr. for Chemically Dependent Women, 1984-86. NIMH fellow, 1976-78; Wayne State U. scholar, 1976-78. Mem. Am. Psychol. Assn., Mich. Psychol. Assn. (mass media cons. 1983—, mem. crisis intervention network, legis. com. 1992-94), Am. Assn. Sex Educators, Counselors and Therapists, Am. Assn. for Counseling and Devel., Pi Lambda Theta, Phi Delta Kappa. Jewish.

TOBIN, MARLA JANEEN, family physician; b. Independence, Mo., Feb. 12, 1954; d. Howard I. and Doris M. (Farmer) Tobin; m. Ronald G. Bowman, June 22, 1985. BA in Biology, U. Mo., 1975, MD, 1980. Diplomate Am. Bd. Family Practice. Family practice resident Duke U., Durham, N.C., 1980-83; family physician Kelling Clinic, Waverly, Mo., 1983-85, Family Practice Assocs., Higginsville, 1985—; pres. Family Practice Assn. West Ctrl. Mo., Higginsville, 1987—; speaker in field. Mem. editorial bds. various publs.; contbr. chpts. to books, articles to profl. jours. Vol. sch. and civic projects. Fellow Am. Acad. Family Physician (Mead Johnson award 1982); mem. Am. Med. Women's Assn., Mo. State Med. Soc., Assn. Reproductive Health Profls., Mo. Acad. Family Physicians (pres. 1993-94). Office: Family Practice Assocs West Ctrl Mo 1200 W 22d St Higginsville MO 64037

TOBIN, PATRICK JOHN, dermatologist; b. Bay City, Mich., Sept. 20, 1938; s. John Howard and Dorothy Ida (De Matio) T.; m. Suzanne Lane Bumstead, Apr. 11, 1959; children: Jennifer Lane, Suzanne Lane, Benjamin Lane. AS, Bay City Jr. Coll., 1958; MD, U. Mich., 1964. Diplomate Am. Bd. Dermatology. Intern Munson Med. Ctr., Traverse City, Mich., 1964-65, mem. active staff, 1970—; resident Univ. Hosp., Ann Arbor, Mich., 1965-68. Lt. comdr. USN, 1968-70. Fellow Am. Acad. Dermatology; mem. Mich. State Med. Soc., AMA, Am. Soc. for Dermatologic Surgery, Alpha Omega Alpha, Grand Traverse Yacht Club (commodore 1977), Grand Traverse Ski Club (pres. 1975). Home: 7777 Truesdale Ln Traverse City MI 49686 Office: Northwestern Mich Dermatol 1105 E Front St Traverse City MI 49686

TOBIN, THOMAS VINCENT, biology educator; b. Plymouth, Pa., Apr. 8, 1926; s. James Vincent and Mary (Evans) T.; m. Dolores Mary Chewey, Nov. 27, 1947; 1 child, Cynthia Joan. BS cum laude, King's Coll., 1951; MS in Biology, Boston Coll., 1953. Grad. asst. in biology Boston Coll., 1951-52; instr. biology King's Coll., Wilkes'Barre, Pa., 1952-54, asst. prof. biology, 1955-61, natural sci. div. chmn., 1971-77, chmn. dept. biology, 1985-91, assoc. prof. biology, 1962—, chief health professions advisor, 1989—; dir. clin. lab. sci. program King's Coll., 1990—; lectr. biology Pa. State U., University Park, 1972-77; lectr. biology Coll. Misericordia, Dallas, Pa., 1977-78. With USAAF, 1943-46. NSF sci. faculty fellow, 1960, summer sci. fellow, 1961; named O'Hara Desting. Svc. Prof. of Sci. King's Coll., 1984. Mem. Nat. Assn. Advisors for the Health Professions, Penna Soc. Medical Tech. Democrat. Roman Catholic. Home: 124 Forest Rd Wilkes Barre PA 18707-1320 Office: King's Coll Dept Biology Wilkes Barre PA 18711-0801

TOBIS, JEROME SANFORD, physician; b. Syracuse, N.Y., July 23, 1915; s. David George and Anna (Feinberg) T.; m. Hazel Weisbard, Sept. 18, 1938; children: David, Heather, Jonathan. B.S., CCNY, 1936; M.D., Chgo. Med. Sch., 1943. Diplomate: Am. Bd. Phys. Medicine and Rehab. Intern Knickerbocker Hosp., 1943-44; resident Bronx VA Hosp., 1946-48; med. dir. state fever therapy unit USPHS, Brookhaven, Miss., 1944-46; practice medicine N.Y.C., 1948-70; prof. dir. dept. phys. medicine and rehab. N.Y. Med. Coll., Flower and Fifth Av. Hosps., 1948-61; prof. rehab. medicine Albert Einstein Coll. of Medicine, 1963-70; chief div. rehab. medicine Montefiore Hosp., 1961-70; dir. vis. physician Met., Bird S. Coler hosps., 1952-61; prof., chmn. dept. phys. medicine and rehab. Calif. Coll. Medicine, U. Calif. at Irvine, 1970-82, prof., dir. program in geriatric medicine and gerontology, 1980-86; mem. adv. com. Acad. Geriatric Resource program, 1984-86, 95—; mem. expert med. com. Am. Rehab. Found., 1961-70; cons. Dept. Health, N.Y.C., Long Beach VA Hosp., 1970—, Fairview State Devel. Ctr., 1976—; mem. adv. coun. phys. medicine and rehab. for appeals com. Calif. Med. Assn., 1971-74, adv. com. U. Calif. Acad. Geriatric Resource Program, 1995—; NIH Internat. Fogarty fellow, hon. lectr., dept. geriatric medicine U. Birmingham, 1979-80; chair ethics com. U. Calif.-Irvine Med. Ctr., 1986—. Mem. editorial bd.: Heart and Lung, 1973-76, Geriatrics, 1975-80, Archives of Phys. Medicine and Rehab, 1958-73. Named Physician of the Year, 1957; recipient Distinguished Alumnus award Chgo. Med. Sch., 1972, Acad. award Nat. Inst. on Aging, 1981-86; named hon. faculty mem. Calif. Zeta chpt. Alpha Omega Alpha, 1981; Leavitt Meml. lectureship Baylor Coll. Medicine, 1983, Griffith Meml. lectureship Am. Geriatric Soc., 1984; Australian Coll. Rehabilitation Medicine, 1984; Jerome S. Tobis Ann. Conf. on Geriatric Medicine established in his name, U. Calif. at Irvine, 1986. Fellow ACP, Am. Coll. Cardiology; mem. AMA (mem. residency rev. com. Coun. Med. Edn. 1973), AAAS, Am. Acad. Cerebral Palsy, Am. Acad. Phys. Medicine and Rehab. (Disting. Clinician award 1993), Am. Congress Rehab. Medicine (pres. 1962), Calif. Coun. Gerontology and Geriatrics (bd. dirs. 1980-86, pres. 1985), N.Y. Acad. Medicine, N.Y. Acad. Sci., Orange County Med. Soc. Home: 1115 Goldenrod Ave Corona Del Mar CA 92625-1508 Office: U Calif Dept Phys Medicine & Rehab Irvine CA 92668

TOBOLOWSKY, DAVID MARTONE, psychiatrist; b. Dallas, July 22, 1953; s. Jake and Helen B. Tobolowsky; m. Patrice Marie Tobolowsky, Dec. 28, 1980; children: Joseph, Pamela, Hilary. BS, So. Meth. U., 1974; MD, U. Tex. Southwestern Med. Sch., Dallas, 1978. Diplomate Am. Bd. Psychiatry and Neurology. Chief resident dept. psychiatry U. Miami (Fla.) Sch. Medicine, 1981-82, resident in psychiatry, 1978-82; pvt. practice psychiatry Miami, 1982—; chmn. dept. psychiatry Healthsouth Larkin Hosp., South Miami, 1989-90, 93-94; part-time med. dir. Jackson Meml. Hosp., Inst. 2, Miami, 1982-83; part-time cons. State of Fla. Dept. Health and Rehab. Svcs., Office of Disability Determination, Miami, 1984-88; part-time psychiatrist Fellowship House, South Miami, Fla., 1994—. Bd. dirs. Temple Samuel Or Olom, Miami, 1991—. Recipient Exemplary Psychiatrist award Nat. Alliance for the Mentally Ill, 1994. Fellow Am. Psychiat. Assn.; mem. AMA, Fla. Med. Assn., Dade County Med. Assn., South Fla. Psychiat. Soc. (sec. 1992-94, v.p. 1994-95), Alpha Omega Alpha. Office: 7400 N Kendall Dr # 310 Miami FL 33156

TOBON, HECTOR, gynecologic pathologist, educator; b. Aranzazu, Colombia, Sept. 20, 1934; came to U.S., 1962; MD, Univ. de Caldas, Colombia. Diplomate Am. Bd. Anatomic and Clin. Pathology. Intern Hosp. San Juan de Dios Armenia; resident Inst. Nat. Cancer, Hosp. San Juan de Dios Bogota; resident in pathology Meml. Hosp., Danville, Va., 1962-65, Presbyn. U. Hosp./U. Pitts. Med. Ctr., 1965-66; assoc. prof. pathology U. Pitts., 1967—; assoc. chief pathology Magee Womens Hosp., Pitts., 1986—. Office: Magee Womens Hosp 300 Halket Office 4606 Pittsburgh PA 15213

TOCZYNSKI, JANET MARIE, oncological nurse; b. Toledo, Sept. 21, 1953; d. William J. and Patricia B. (Daugherty) Meyer; m. Daniel J. Toczynski, May 21, 1988; children: Aaron, Stephanie, Christie; children by previous marriage: Brooke, Shana. Diploma, St. Vincent's Sch Nursing, 1974. RN, Ohio. Float nurse ICU, CCU, burn care ctr. St. Vincent Med. Ctr., Toledo, 1974-80, head nurse orthopedics, 1980-83, ops. analyst, 1983-87; staff nurse Mercy Hosp., Toledo, 1987-92; oncology nurse Med. Coll. Ohio, Toledo, 1992—. Mem. Intravenous Nursing Soc., Toledo Area Oncology Nurses Soc., St. Vincent Alumni Assn. Home: 2160 Kingston Dr Maumee OH 43537-1153 Office: Med Coll Ohio 3000 Arlington Ave Toledo OH 43614-2595

TODARO, GEORGE JOSEPH, pathologist; b. N.Y.C., July 1, 1937; s. George J. and Antoinette (Piccinni) T.; m. Jane Lehv, Aug. 12, 1962; children: Wendy C., Thomas M., Anthony A. BS, Swarthmore Coll., 1958; MD, NYU, 1963. Intern NYU Sch. Medicine, N.Y.C., 1963-64, fellow in pathology, 1964-65, asst. prof. pathology, 1965-67; staff assoc. Viral Carcinogenesis br. Nat. Cancer Inst., Bethesda, Md., 1967-70, head molecular biology sect., 1969-70; chief Viral Carcinogenesis br. Nat. Cancer Inst. (Lab. Viral Carcinogenesis), 1970-83; sci. dir., pres. Oncogen, Seattle, 1987-90; sr. v.p. exploratory biomed. rsch. Bristol-Myers Squibb Pharm. Rsch. Inst., 1990; adj. prof. pathology U. Wash., Seattle, 1983—, chmn. dept. pathobiology, 1991—; sr. v.p., sci. dir. Pathogenesis Corp., Seattle, 1992-95; mem. Fred Hutchinson Cancer Rsch. Ctr., Seattle, 1991-93. Editor: Cancer Research, 1973-86, Archives of Virology, 1976—, Jour. Biol. Chemistry, 1979—; contbr. articles to profl. jours. Served as med. officer USPHS, 1967-69. Recipient Borden Undergrad. Research award, 1963, USPHS Career Devel. award, 1967, HEW Superior Service award, 1971, Gustav Stern award for virology, 1972, Parke-Davis award in exptl. pathology, 1975; Walter Hubert lectr. Brit. Cancer Soc., 1977. Mem. Nat. Acad. Scis., Am. Soc. Microbiology, Am. Assn. Cancer Research, Soc. Exptl. Biology and Medicine, Am. Soc. Biol. Chemists, Am. Soc. Clin. Investigation. Home: 1940 15th Ave E Seattle WA 98112 Office: U Wash Dept Pathobiology 101 Elliott Ave W Ste 428 Seattle WA 98119*

TODD, KAREN DAWN, ophthalmologist; b. New Orleans, Oct. 23, 1958; d. George David and Helen Mildred (Luthi) T.; m. A. Mark Gambee, Oct. 20, 1982. BA, Vanderbilt U., 1980; MD, Johns Hopkins U., 1984. Diplomate Am. Bd. Ophthalmology. Intern Mercy Hosp. Med. Ctr., San Diego, 1984-85; resident in ophthalmology U. Calif., San Francisco, 1985-88; fellow in glaucoma U. South Fla., Tampa, 1988-89; ophthalmologist Fla. Eye Inst., Vero Beach, Fla., 1989—. Fellow Am. Coll. Surgeons; mem. AMA, Fla. Med. Assn., Indian River Med. Soc., Am. Acad. Ophthalmology, Am. Soc. Cataract and Refractive Surgery, Internat. Soc. Refractive Surgery, Alpha Omega Alpha, Phi Beta Kappa, Tau Beta Phi. Office: Fla Eye Inst 2750 Indian River Rd Vero Beach IL 32960

TODD, KENNETH S., JR., parasitologist, educator; b. Three Forks, Mont., Aug. 25, 1936; s. Kenneth S. and Anna Louise (Seeman) T. BS, Mont. State U., 1962, MS, 1964; PhD, Utah State U., 1967. Asst. prof. U. Ill., Urbana, 1967-71, assoc. prof., 1971-76, prof. vet. parasitology, 1976-94, chmn. div. parasitology, 1983-90, asst. head vet. pathobiology, 1984-87, prof. vet. programs in agr., 1984-94, acting head vet. pathobiology, 1987-90, head, 1990-94; prof. emeritus, 1994; affiliate scientist Ill. State Natural History Survey, 1987—; adj. prof. microbiology Mont. State U. Served with USAF, 1954-58. NSF grad. fellow, 1966-67. Mem. AVMA, Am. Assn. Vet. Parasitologists, Am. Micros. Soc., Am. Soc. Parasitologists, Am. Soc. Tropical Medicine and Hygiene, Helminthologic Soc. Washington, Midwest Conf. Parasitologists, Wildlife Disease Assn., Soc. Protozoologists. Office: Mont State U Dept Microbiology Bozeman MT 59715

TODD, LARRY THOMAS, orthopedic surgeon; b. St. Joseph, Mo., Feb. 18, 1969; s. Larry Thomas and Rose Marie (Lawhon) T.; m. Catherine Lee Zanone, Dec. 19, 1992. BA in Biology, Mo. U., 1991; DO, U. Osteo. Medicine and Health, 1995. Letter writing campaign Nat. Wildlife Fedn., 1993-95. Mem. Nat. Audobon Soc., Pi Kappa Alpha (scholastic and philanthropy com. 1989-90, chmn. 1990-91), Sigma Sigma Phi. Home: 2305 Bradley Dr Saint Joseph MO 64503 Office: Doctors Hosp 1087 Dennison Ave Columbus OH 43201

TODD, LINDA MARIE, air traffic-weather advisor, nutritional researcher, financial consultant; b. L.A., Mar. 30, 1943; d. Ithel Everette and Janet Marie (Zito) Fredricks; m. William MacKenzie Cook, Jan. 11, 1962 (div. Oct. 1989); m. Robert Oswald Todd, Apr. 8, 1990; 1 child, Jesse MacKenzie Todd. BA in Psychology and Sociology, U. Colo., 1969; student Psychology Grad. work, U. No. Colo., 1970. Pilot lic., weather cert., FCC lic., Calif. life ins. lic., coll. teaching credential; registered with Nat. Assn. Securities Dealers. Counselor Jeffco Juvenile Detention Ctr., Golden, Colo., 1969-71; communications Elan Vital, Denver, 1971-81; legal sec. Fredman, Silverberg & Lewis, San Diego, 1980-82; escrow supr. Performance Mktg. Concepts, Olympic Valley, Calif., 1982-85; mgmt. commn. instr. Sierra Coll., Truckee, Calif., 1986-87; regional mgr. Primerica Fin. Svcs., Reno, 1987-91; air traffic, weather advisor Truckee (Calif.) Tahoe Airport Dist., 1986—; student tour leader, air show organizer Truckee (Calif.) Tahoe Airport; fin. cons. Primerica Fin. Svcs., Truckee, 1987-91; gen. agt. TTS Fin., 1992—; co-founder Todd Nutrition, 1995—. Editor: (newsletter) Communications, 1975. Sec. gen. Arapahoe H.S. Model UN, Littleton, Colo., 1965; del. State Model UN, Colo., 1966; conv. del. Elan Vital, The Ninety-Nines Inc. Recipient Univ. scholarship Littleton (Colo.) Edn. Assn., 1966, flight scholarship The Ninety-Nines Inc., Reno, 1990; named Recruiter of Month, Al Williams Primerica, Reno, 1987. Mem. Elan Vital, Plane Talkers, The Ninety Nines, Planetary Soc. Home and Office: PO Box 1303 Truckee CA 96160-1303

TODD, LUIS, pediatrician; b. Juarez, Mexico, May 17, 1960; came to U.S., 1976; s. Oscar and Bertha (Romero) T.; m. Dorothea Alexandra Diamos, Jan. 12, 1980; children: Mackenzie, Alexandra. BS, Coll. of the Ams., Jurarez, Mex., 1980; MD, U. AG, Guadalajara, Mex., 1985. Diplomate Am. Bd. Pediatrics. Attending physician Wesley Chapel (Fla.) Pediatric Assn., 1990-91; panel physician U.S. State Dept., Juarez, Mex., 1992-94; cons. Immigration and Naturalization Svc., El Paso, Tex., 1992-95. Fellow AMA, Tex. Med. Assn., El Paso County Med. Soc., Tex. Pediatrics Soc., Am. Assn. Pediatricians. Roman Catholic. Office: Sunrise Childen's Hosp 6301 Mountain Vista Ste 209 Henderson NV 89014

TODD, SUSAN, nurse, midwife; b. Chgo., Jan. 17, 1951; d. Maurice and Harriet (Heda) Goodwin; m. Daniel H. Todd, Apr. 25, 1982; children: Bonnie, Sheri. BSN, No. Ill. U., 1973; MSN, U. Ill. Med. Ctr., 1976. Staff midwife Links, Northfield, Ill., 1976-81; nurse midwife AWMC, Chgo., 1981-85; pvt. practice Buffalo Grove, Ill., 1985—; adj. faculty U. Ill. Med. Ctr., Chgo.; lactation cons. Medela Products, Buffalo Grove. Vol. Make a Wish Found., 1993—; vol. nurse-midwife The Arc, Chgo., 1990-95. Mem. Am. Coll. Nurse-Midwives. Home: 425 Park Chester Rd Buffalo Grove IL 60089 Office: 1213 W Dundee Rd Ste 100 Buffalo Grove IL 60089

TODD, WILLIAM MICHAEL, counselor, educator; b. Dayton, Ohio, Jan. 4, 1957; s. J.T. and Bessie Kate (Lowe) T.; children: Lukas, Leigh. BA in Psychology, Ottawa U., 1993, MA in Profl. Counseling, 1994. Cert. cmty. coll. tchr., 1995. Counselor Arrowstar Counseling, Phoenix, 1992—; prof. psychology Glendale (Ariz.) C.C., 1994; bus. owner Antique Market, MT Constrn., Arrowstar Cons., Phoenix, 1983—. Assoc. pastor Nazarene Ch., Phoenix, 1991-93, youth min., 1993; counselor Boys and Girls Club, Phoenix, 1993-94. Mem. Am. Counselors Assn., Am. Clin. Mental Health Assn., Marriage and Family Counseling Assn., Phi Theta Kappa. Home: 3507 E Windsor Ave Phoenix AZ 85008 Office: Arrowstar Counseling 3520 E Indian School Rd Phoenix AZ 85018-5115

TODHUNTER, JOHN ANTHONY, toxicologist; b. Cali, Valle, Colombia, Oct. 9, 1949; s. John Arthur and Teresa Maria (Torres) T.; divorced, 1986; children: Jennifer, Julia; m. Donna Kay Wilson, Apr. 19, 1986; 1 child, Jacqueline Rose. BSc, UCLA, 1971; MSc, Calif. State U., 1973; PhD, U. Calif., Santa Barbara, 1976. Diplomate Am. Bd. Toxicology, Am. Bd. Forensic Examiners; regulatory affairs cert. Instr. Calif. State U., L.A., 1972-73; rsch. asst. U. Calif., Santa Barbara, 1973-76; fellow Roche Inst. Molecular Biology, Nutley, N.J., 1976-78; asst. prof. Cath. U. Am., Washington, 1978-81; chmn. biochemistry program, 1980-81; asst. adminstr. U.S. EPA, Washington, 1981-83; cons. Sci. Regulatory Svcs. Internat., Washington, 1983-91; pres. SRS Internat. Corp., 1991—, SRS Internat. Health Care Group, 1995—; expert advisor European regional office WHO, Stockholm, 1984; mem. Hazardous Waste Siting Bd., Annapolis, Md., 1980-81. Contbr. articles to profl. jours. Bd. dirs. Reagan Alumni Assn., Washington, 1985—; vol. Am. Cancer Soc., Washington, 1988—; mem. Presdl. Transition Team, Washington, 1980. U. Calif. Bd. Regents fellow, 1975, B.R. Baker Meml. fellow dept. chemistry U. Calif., Santa Barbara, 1976. Fellow Am. Inst. Chemists (dir. at large 1989-92, vice chmn. bd. 1992); mem. Soc. of Toxicology, Am. Chem. Soc., Soc. for Risk Analysis, N.Y. Acad. Sci. Office: SRS Internat 1625 K St NW # 1000 Washington DC 20006-1604

TOFFEL, PAUL HASKELL, maxillofacial surgeon, educator; b. Los Angeles, Mar. 3, 1943; s. Harry and Estelle Charlotte (Kandel) T.; m. Beverly Diane Peterson, June 12, 1965; children: Nicole, Hope, Erica. Student Stanford U., 1961-62; MD, U. So. Calif., 1968. Intern, L.A. County-U. So. Calif. Med. Center, 1968-69, resident in otolaryngology, 1969-73; practice medicine specializing in otolaryngology and maxillofacial surgery, L.A., 1975—; mem. staff Daniel Freeman Med. Center, Centinela Valley Med. Center, Orthopedic, U. So. Calif. U. Hosp., Verdugo Hills hosps.; clin. prof. U. So. Calif. Med. Sch., 1974—; mem. med. emergency team L.A. County Sheriff's Dept., 1973—; head facial plastics div., med. adv. com. Calif. Athletic Commn.; chief med. officer equestrian events 1984 L.A. Olympiad. Served to lt. comdr. M.C., USNR, 1973-75. Fellow Am. Acad. Otolaryngology, Am. Rhinologic Soc. (bd. dirs. 1991—), Soc. Mil. Otolaryngologists, ACS, Am. Acad. Facial, Plastic and Reconstructive Surgery; mem. AMA, Calif., L.A. County med. assns., Salerni Collegium. Office: 2080 Century Park E Ste 610 Los Angeles CA 90067-2001 also: 1808 Verdugo Blvd Ste 418 Glendale CA 91208-1408

TOFT, JÜRGEN HERBERT, orthopedic surgeon; b. Berlin, May 4, 1943; s. Herbert and Erna (Milczinsky) T.; m. Waltraud Toft, Dec. 27, 1968; children: Philip, Felix, Frederike, Maurizio. Grad., Humboldt U., Berlin, 1971; MD, Saarland U., Homburg, Germany, 1976. Intern County Hosp., Biberach, Germany, 1972-75; resident Orthopedic Clinic, Tailfingen, Tübingen, 1975-76; orthopedic surgeon Ingolstadt, Golstadt, Germany, 1976-80, Remscheid, Germany, 1980-84; cons. pvt. practice Germany, 1976—; chief, knee specialist Ambulatory Surg. Ctr., Munich, Germany, 1985—; pres., founding mem. Wissenschaftliche Gesellschaft für Arthroskopische Chirurgie, Munich, 1984—. With inf. German Armed Forces, 1962-65. Mem. Internat. Knee Soc., Internat. Arthroscopy Assn., Deutsche Gesellschaft für Orthopädie und Traumatology. Office: Ambulantes Operationszentrm, Effnerstrasse 38, 81925 Munich Germany

TOHMO, HARRI ILMARI, physician, anesthesiologist; b. Turku, Finland, Dec. 12, 1957; s. Lasse Olavi and Elise Kristiina (Kaunisto) T.; m. Marja Helena Hiltunen, July 25, 1986; children: Sakari, Erkka. MD, Turku (Finland) U., 1983, Specialist in Anesthesiology, 1990, PhD, 1995. Resident internal medicine Selkämeri Dist. Hosp., Finland, 1984-85; resident anesthesiology Turku (Finland) U. Hosp., 1986-90, staff anesthesiologist, 1991; staff anesthesiologist Kymenlaakso Ctrl. Hosp., Finland, 1992-94; chief anesthesiologist Lounais-Häme Dist. Hosp., Finland, 1995—; cons. anesthesiologist Hamina (Finland) Hosp., 1992-94. Contbr. articles to profl. jours. Grantee Emil Aaltonen Found., Finland, 1989, 94, Turku U. Found., 1990, 91, Merck and Co. Human Health divsn., 1990. Mem. Finnish Med. Assn., Finnish Soc. Anesthesiologists, Scandinavian Soc. Anesthesiologists. Lutheran. Home: Kartanonkatu 16 A 11, 30100 Forssa Finland Office: Lounais-Häme Dist Hosp, Dept Anesthesiology, 30100 Forssa Finland

TOI, MASAKAZU, surgeon; b. Hiroshima, Japan, Oct. 19, 1957; s. Kimikazu and Chihoko (Okada) T.; m. Kazuko Kadota, Sept. 24, 1984; children: Hirokazu, Hidekazu, Erie. MD, Sch. Medicine, Hiroshima U., 1982, PhD, 1988. Resident fellow Hiroshima U., 1982-83, rsch. asst., 1983-87, rsch. assoc., 1988-90; rsch. assoc. Kyushu Cancer Ctr. Hosp., Fukuoka, 1987-88; acad. visitor Oxford U., United Kingdom, 1990-92; med. staff, dep. of surgery Tokyo Met. Komagome Hosp., 1992-94, dep. dir., dept. surgery, 1994—; cons. Japanese Breast Cancer Soc., Tokyo 1992—; lectr. human genetics Tokyo U. Inventor imaging of breast cancer, prognostic factor of breast cancer; editor Oncology Reports, 1992—. Recipient Sapporo Biosci. Found. award, 1993. Mem. Adjuvat Chemoendocrine Theray for Breat Cancer (com. 1988-92), Found. for Multidisciplinary Treatment of Cancer (com. 1988-90), World Congress on Advanced Oncology, Am. Assn. for Cancer Rsch., Japan Soc. for Gastro Intestinal Surgery (bd. dirs. 1990—), Japan Soc. Surgery, N.Y. Acad. Scis. Home: 3-37-1-202 Narimasu, Itabashi-ku, Tokyo 175, Japan Office: Tokyo Met Komagome Hosp, 3-18-22 Honkomagome Bunkyo-ku, Tokyo 113, Japan

TOIVANEN, PAAVO UURAS, immunologist, microbiologist, educator; b. Tuupovaara, Finland, June 14, 1937; s. Vilho Pekka and Suoma Helena (Silvennoinen) T.; m. Auli Marjaana Pirilä, Nov 3, 1961; children: Laura, Otto, Pekka, Hannes, Suoma. BS, Turku (Finland) U., 1958, MD, 1962, D Med. Scis., 1966. Asst. physician Dept. Med. Microbiology Turku U., 1961-69, docent, 1968-69, assoc. prof., 1969-78, prof. bacteriology, serology, 1978—; mem. Basel Inst. for Immunology, 1979-80, mem. internat. adv. bd., 1991-95, chmn. internat. adv. bd., 1994-95. Editor: Avian Immunology, Basis and Practice, 1987, Reactive Arthritis, 1988. Mem. Finnish Soc. Immunology (pres. 1979-82), Am. Assn. Immunologists, Am. Soc. Microbiology, Transplantation Soc., Finnish Soc. Pathology, Finnish Soc. Hematology, Scandinavian Soc. Immunology (treas. 1978-82). Lutheran. Office: Turku U Dept Microbiolo, Kiinamyllynkatu 13, FIN20520 Turku Finland

TOKOLY, MARY ANDREE, microbiologist; b. Manila, Dec. 4, 1940; (parents Am. citizens) d. Robert Francis Tokoly and Ruby Waunita (Shriner) Kaderli. BS, Tex. Woman's U., 1962, MS, 1964, PhD, 1974. Instr Victoria (Tex.) Coll., 1964-66; asst. prof. Kans. State Coll., Pittsburg, 1966-68, Kans. Newman Coll., Wichita, 1974-75; grad. teaching asst. Tex. Woman's U., Denton, 1968-74; microbiologist Nix Hosp., San Antonio, 1975-77, Met. Meth. Hosp., San Antonio, 1977—. Sec. Bexar County chpt. Czech Heritage Soc. Tex., San Antonio, 1988. Robert A. Welch Found. grantee, 1971, 72. Mem. AAUW, Am. Soc. Clin. Pathologists (registered microbiologist), Tex. Soc. Microbiology, South Tex. Assn. Microbiology Profls., Am. Soc. Med. Tech., N.Y. Acad. Scis., S.W. Assn. Clin. Microbiologists, Sigma Xi. Roman Catholic. Office: Met Meth Hosp 1310 Mccullough Ave San Antonio TX 78212-5601

TOLAN, ROBERT WARREN, pediatric infectious disease specialist; b. Bowling Green, Ohio, Nov. 20, 1960; s. Robert Warren Tolan and Margaret Delores (Petter) Cardwell; m. Lenita Kay Newberg, May 15, 1983. BA, Ind. U., 1982, MA, 1983; MD, Washington U., St. Louis, 1987. Diplomate Nat. Bd. Med. Examiners, Am. Bd. Pediatrics, sub-bd. of pediat. infectious diseases. Resident in pediatrics Riley Hosp. for Children, Indpls., 1987-90; fellow in infectious diseases St. Louis Children's Hosp., 1990-94. Co-author: Fever of Unknown Origin in Children, 1991; contbr. articles to Clin. Infectious Diseases, Pediatric Infectious Diseases Jour., Infection and Immunity, Jour. Clin. Microbiology. Nat. Merit scholar Pitts. Plate Glass, 1978; Pediatric Scientist Devel. Program fellow, 1990-94. Fellow Am. Acad. Pediatrics; mem. AMA, Am. Soc. Microbiology, Infectious Diseases Soc. Am., Pediatric Infectious Diseases Soc., Soc. for Preservation and Encouragement of Barbershop Quartet Singing in Am., Physicians for Social Responsibility. Democrat. Episcoplian. Office: St Louis Childrens Hosp Rm 1102 One Childrens Pl Saint Louis MO 63110-1093

TOLBERT, BERT MILLS, biochemist, educator; b. Twin Falls, Idaho, Jan. 15, 1921; s. Ed. and Helen (Mills) T.; m. Anne Grace Zweifler, July 20, 1959; children—Elizabeth Dawn, Margaret Anne, Caroline Joan, Sarah Helen. Student, Idaho State U., 1938-40; B.S., U. Calif. at Berkeley, 1942, Ph.D., 1945; postgrad., Fed. Inst. Tech., Zurich, Switzerland, 1952-53. Chemist Lawrence Radiation Lab., Berkeley, 1944-57; faculty U. Colo., Boulder, 1957-89, prof., 1961-89, prof. emeritus, 1989—, assoc. chmn. dept. chemistry and biochemistry, 1980-88; bd. dirs. Hauser Chem. Rsch., Boulder, 1983—; vis. prof. IAEA, Buenos Aires, Argentina, 1961-62; Biophysicist U.S. AEC, Washington, 1967-68; cons. pvt. cos, govt. agys. Author: (with others) Isotopic Carbon, 1948; contbr. (with others) articles to profl. jours. Fellow AAAS; mem. Am. Chem. Soc., Am. Soc. Biochemistry and Molecular Biology, Radiation Rsch. Soc., Soc. for Exptl. Biology and Medicine. Home: 444 Kalmia Ave Boulder CO 80304-1732

TOLCHIN, JOAN GUBIN, psychiatrist, educator; b. N.Y.C., Mar. 10, 1944; d. Harold and Bella (Newman) Gubin; m. Matthew Armin Tolchin, Sept. 1, 1966; 1 child, Benjamin. AB, Vassar Coll., 1964; MD, NYU, 1972. Diplomate Am. Bd. Gen. Psychiatry, Am. Bd. Child Psychiatry. Rsch. asst. Albert Einstein Coll. Medicine, N.Y.C., 1964-68; instr. psychiatry med. coll. Cornell U., N.Y.C., 1977-78, clin. instr., 1978-86, clin. asst. prof., 1986—. Contbr. articles to profl. jours. Fellow Am. Acad. Child and Adolescent Psychiatry; mem. APA, Am. Acad. Psychoanalysis, N.Y. Coun. Child and Adolescent Psychiatry (bd. dirs. 1992-96, pres. 1994-95), Alpha Omega Alpha. Office: 35 E 84th St New York NY 10028-0871

TOLCHINSKY, PAUL DEAN, organization design psychologist; b. Cleve., Sept. 30, 1946; s. Sanford Melvin and Frances (Klein) T.; m. Laurie S. Schermer, Nov. 3, 1968 (div. Jan. 1982); m. Kathy L. Dworkin, June 19, 1988; children: Heidi E., Dana M. BA, Bowling Green State U., 1971; PhD, Purdue U., 1978. Bd. dirs. Temple Tiferth Israel, Cleve., 195. With U.S. Army, 1966-69, Vietnam. Mem. APA, Acad. Mgmt. Democrat. Jewish. Office: Dannemiler Tyson Assocs Box 22987 Beachwood OH 44122

TOLIA, BHUPENDRA MANILAL, urologist; b. Jamnagar, India, Dec. 21, 1936; came to U.S., 1967; s. Manilal Premji and Prabhavati Manilal (Mehta) T.; m. Chandrika J. Lakhani, Jan. 7, 1967; children: Nameeta B., Chirag B. MB BS, Med. Coll. Baroda, India, 1962; MS, Med. Coll. Baroda, 1966. Diplomate, Am. Bd. Urology. Resident in gen. surgery SSG Hosp., Baroda, India, 1962-66, Nazareth Hosp., Phila., 1967-68; resident in urology Thomas Jefferson U. Hosp., Phila., 1968-71; spl. fellow in urology Meml. Sloan-Kettering Cancer Ctr., N.Y.C., 1971-72; spl. trainee spinal cord injury svc. VA Hosp., Bronx, N.Y., 1972-73; dir. urology clinic Bronx Mcpl. Hosp. Ctr., 1973-80; attending urologist Albert Einstein Hosp., Bronx, 1973—; clin. instr. urology, then asst. prof. urology Albert Einstein Coll. Medicine, Bronx, 1973-80, assoc. prof. urology, 1980-91, assoc. clin. prof. urology, 1991—; attending urologist Westchester Sq. Med. Ctr., 1992—, Our Lady of Mercy Med. Ctr., 1992—; cons. urologist, Dr. Martin Luther King Jr. Health Ctr., Bronx. Fellow ACS (Bronx chpt. treas. 1988-90, pres.-elect 1990-91, pres. 1991-92), N.Y. Acad. Medicine, Internat. Coll. Surgeons; mem. Am. Urol. Assn., Soc. Univ. Urologists, Societe Internat. d'Urologie. Republican. Jain. Office: 1695 Eastchester Rd Apt 306 Bronx NY 10461-2330

TOLL, DAVID, pediatrician; b. Cleve., May 6, 1925; s. Herman I. and Mollie (Neuger) T.; B.A., Harvard U.; M.D., Western Res. U., 1948; m. Bridget Ann Fryer; children: Job, Abel, Seth. Intern, Children's Hosp., Boston, 1948-50; resident in pediatrics Mass. Gen. Hosp., 1951-52; practice medicine specializing in pediatrics, St. Johnsbury, Vt., 1952; med. dir. Child Health Center, St. Johnsbury, 1952—; cons. Vt. Health Dept., N.H. Health Dept., 1952—; preceptor Stanford, Dartmouth, Case Western Res., U. Vt. med. schs. Mem. AMA, Vt. Med. Assn., Am. Acad. Pediatrics, New Eng. Pediatric Soc., Am. Acad. Med. Dirs. Home: RR 2 Saint Johnsbury VT 05819-9802 Office: 95 Main St Saint Johnsbury VT 05819-2211

TOLL, ROBERTA DARLENE (MRS. SHELDON S. TOLL), clinical psychologist; b. Detroit, May 14, 1944; d. David and Blanche (Fischer) Pollack; married, Aug. 11, 1968; children: Candice, John, Kevin. B.A., U. Mich., 1966; M.S.W., U. Pa., 1971; PhD, 1990. Dir. counselors Phila. Family Planning, Inc., 1971-72; psychologist Lafayette Clinic, Detroit, 1972-73; social worker Project Headline, Detroit, 1973-75; pvt. practice clin. psychology, Bloomfield Hills, Mich., 1975—; adj. prof. U. Detroit, Oakland Community Coll. Past bd. dirs. Detroit chpt. Nat. Council on Alcoholism.; bd. dirs. Merill Palmer Inst., Child Abuse Coun.; pres. Mich. Women Psychologist. Cert. social worker, Mich. Fellow Masters and Johnson Inst.; mem. APA, Nat. Assn. Social Workers. Democrat. Club: Franklin Hills Country. Home and Office: 640 Lone Pine Hl Bloomfield Hills MI 48304-2822

TOLLIVER, KEVIN PAUL, dentist; b. Ft. Wayne, Ind., Mar. 17, 1951; s. Herbert and Norma Jean (Scheele) T.; m. Melanie Beth Johnson, May 5, 1973; children: Chad, Joshua, Jordan, Ashley. BA, Ind. U., 1973; DDS, Ind. U., Indpls., 1977. Lic. dentist, Ind. Gen. practice dentistry Indpls., 1977—. Pres. Williston Green Assn., Indpls., 1983, 85; vol. Pan Am. Games, Indpls., 1986-87; vol., com. mem. Campaing. for Ind. Named one of Outstanding Young Men of Am., 1984. Fellow Acad. Functional Prosthodontics, Acad. Physiologic Dentistry; mem. ADA, Internat. Acad. Laser Dentistry, N.Am. Acad. Laser Dentistry, Acad. Sports Dentistry, Am. Acad. Cosmetic Dentistry, Acad. Gen. Dentistry, Ind. Dental Assn., Indpls. Dist. Dental Soc., Chgo. Dental Soc., Ind. U. Well House Soc., Ind. U. Hoosier Hundred. Home: 648 Suffolk Ln Carmel IN 46032-8660 Office: 3390 W 86th St Ste S-1 Indianapolis IN 46268-1991

TOLMAN, WILLIAM BAKER, chemistry educator; b. Cleve., May 20, 1961; s. Stephen and Sherlane J. (Feih) T.; m. Bonnie C. Gruen, Aug. 13, 1989; children: Sarah Francis, Claire Rachel. BA in Chemistry, Wesleyan U., 1983; PhD in Chemistry, U. Calif., Berkeley, 1987. Postdoctoral fellow MIT, Cambridge, 1987-90; asst. prof. U. Minn., 1990-94, assoc. prof., 1994—. Contbr. articles to profl. jours. Recipient Nat. Young Investigator award NSF, 1993—, Searle Scholar award Chgo. Cmty. Trust, 1992-95, Rsch. award Alfred P. Sloan Found., 1993—, Camille and Henry Dreyfus Found., 1994—; grantee NIH, NSF, 1990—. Mem. Am. Chem. Soc., AAAS. Jewish. Home: 3517 Fremont Ave S Minneapolis MN 55408 Office: U Minn Dept Chemistry 207 Pleasant St SE Minneapolis MN 55455

TOLMAS, HYMAN CYRIL, pediatrician; b. New Orleans, Feb. 1, 1922; s. Charles and Cecile (Bressler) T.; B.S., Tulane U., 1943; M.D., Tulane Med. Sch., 1945; m. Constance D. Cohen, July 9, 1950; children—Jean Ann, Alan Leon. Intern, Charity Hosp. La., New Orleans, 1945-46, resident pediatrics, 1946, 48-50; practice medicine specializing in pediatrics, New Orleans, 1950—; mem. med. adv. com. New Orleans Speech & Hearing Center, 1964—; chief, coordinator pediatrics Hotel Dieu Hosp., New Orleans, 1960-65; sr. vis. pediatrician Touro Infirmary, New Orleans, 1950—, dir. adolescent unit, 1978—; mem. staff Mercy, East Jefferson Gen., Lakeside Hosps., New Orleans; pres. med. staff Mercy Hosp., 1972, trustee, 1973—, v.p. bd., 1976-77, pres., 1977—; clin. prof. emeritus pediatrics Tulane Med. Sch., 1995—, clin. prof. of pediatrics LSU. Bd. dirs. ARC, 1953-54; coordinator med. center Tulane Alumni Fund. Served to lt. (j.g.) USNR, 1946-48. Recipient Med. award City of New Orleans, 1963, Orleans Parish Med. Soc., 1967. Fellow Am. Acad. Pediatrics (exec. com. adolescent sect. 1981-84, now program dir. adolescent sect., chmn. com. on adolescence, state chpt. 1978—, Outstanding Contbr. award in adolescent medicine 1985); mem. New Orleans Pediatric Soc. (pres. 1963-65), La. Pediatric Soc. (sec. 1968-70), Orleans Parish Med. Soc., AMA, La. Med. Soc., New Orleans Grad. Med. Assembly, Tulane Med. Alumni Assn. (dir. 1981-84, pres., 1989-90, Lifetime Achievement award 1995), Am. Soc. Pub. Service (Thomas Jefferson award 1982). Club: Bacchus Carnival (New Orleans). Contbr. articles to nat. jours.; mem. editorial bd. Internat. Jour. Adolescent Medicine; mem. editl. adv. com. Adolescent Medicine: State of the Art Reviews. Home: 466 Crystal St New Orleans LA 70124-2622 Office: 2017 Metairie Rd Metairie LA 70005-3832

TOMA, GEORGE E., ophthalmologist; b. Cleve., Mar. 9, 1943. BA in Chemistry, Ohio Wesleyan U., 1964; MD, Ohio State U., 1968. Diplomate Am. Bd. Ophthalmology. Intern N.C. Meml. Hosp., Chapel Hill, 1968-69; fellow, then resident in ophthalmology Ohio State U., Columbus, 1969-70, 72-75; pvt. practice Charleston (W.Va.) Eye Care Assocs., Inc., 1975—; clin. asst. prof. Ohio State U., Columbus, 1972—, W.Va. U., Morgantown, 1978—. Lt. USN Med. Corps, 1970-72. Fellow ACS; mem. AMA, Am. Acad. Ophthalmology, W.Va. State Med. Assn., W.Va. Acad. Ophthalmology. Office: Charleston Eye Care Assocs 331 Laidley St Ste 102 Charleston WV 25301

TOMAR, RUSSELL HERMAN, pathologist, educator, researcher; b. Phila., Oct. 19, 1937; s. Julius and Ethel (Weinreb) T.; m. Karen J. Kent, Aug. 29, 1965; children: Elizabeth, David. BA in Journalism, George Washington U., 1959, MD, 1963. Diplomate Am. Bd. Pathology, Am. Bd. Allergy and Immunology, Am. Bd. Pathology, Immunopathology. Intern Barnes Hosp., Washington U. Sch. Medicine, 1963-64, resident in medicine, 1964-65; asst. prof. medicine SUNY, Syracuse, 1971-79, assoc. prof., 1979-88, assoc. prof. microbiology, 1980-84, prof., 1984-88, asst. prof. pathology, 1974-76, assoc. prof., 1976-83, prof., 1983-88, dir. immunopathology, 1974-88, attending physician immunodeficiency clinic, 1982-88, acting dir. microbiology, 1977-78, 82-83, interim dir. clin. pathology, 1986-87; dir. clin. labs., prof. pathology and lab. medicine U. Wis. Ctr. for Health Scis., Madison, 1988-95; dir. div. lab medicine U. Wis., Madison, 1988-95, dir. immunopathology, 1995—; past mem. numerous coms. SUNY, Syracuse, U. Wis., Madison; mem. exec. com., chair and med. cons. AIDS Task Force Cen. N.Y., 1983-88. Assoc. editor Jour. Clin. Lab. Analysis; contbr. articles, rev. to profl. jours. Mem. pub. health com. Onondaga County Med. Soc., 1987-88. Lt. comdr. USPHS, 1965-67. Allergy and Immunology Div. fellow U. Pa. Fellow Coll. Am. Pathologists (diagnostics immunology rsch. com. 1993—, stds. com. 1995—), Am. Soc. Clin. Pathology (com. on continuing edn. immunopathology 1985-91, pathology data presentation com. 1976-79), Am. Acad. Allergy (penicillin hypersensitivity com. 1973-77); mem. AAAS, Am. Assn. Immunologists, Am. Assn. Pathology, Acad. Clin. Lab. Physicians and Scientists (com. on rsch. 1979-81, chairperson immunology 1979), Clin. Immunology Soc. (clin. lab. immunology com., chair coun. 1991-96). Office: U Wis Clinical Sci Ctr Rm B4-251 Madison WI 53792-2472

TOMASHEFSKY, PHILIP, biomedical researcher, educator; b. Bklyn., May 4, 1924; s. Harry and Mae (Shapiro) T.; m. Rhoda Tanenbaum, Oct. 31, 1948; children—Clark Steven, Michael Allen. B.S., CCNY, 1947, M.S., 1951; M.S., NYU, 1963, Ph.D., 1969. Chemist Funk Found., N.Y.C., 1947-65; biochemist U.S. Vitamin, N.Y.C., 1966; asst. prof. clin. pathology Columbia U., N.Y.C., 1975-89 . Contbr. articles to profl. jours. Served with U.S. Army, 1943-45, ETO. Mem. N.Y. Acad. Scis., Sigma Xi. Avocations: travel, photography, gardening. Office: Columbia Univ Dept Urology 630 W 168th St New York NY 10032

TOMASZESKI, JOSEPHINE GALLAS, retired nursing educator; b. Manchouli, Manchuria, China, Jan. 18, 1919; d. Paul Fedorovich Kislitzin and Barbara Matveevna (Borodeev) Kislitzin-Meisel; m. John Joseph Gallas, Jan. 22, 1953 (dec. Feb. 1966); m. Julian Stephen Tomaszeski, June 10, 1972; stepchildren: Julie Ann, Mary Jane, Wayne Michael, John William. Student, Mary Washington Coll., 1937; diploma, St. Mary's Coll. Nursing, 1941; BS in Pub. Health Nursing, Cath. U. Am., 1943; MSN, U. Calif., Berkeley and San Francisco, 1960. RN, Calif.; cert. pub. health nurse, tchr., Calif. Nurse, charge nurse Children's Hosp., Washington, 1941-43; pub. health nurse Dept. Pub. Health, Washington, 1943-45; dir. outpatient clinic, nurse instr. Mary's Help Hosp., San Francisco, 1946-49; nurse, pub. health nurse, nurse instr. VA Med. Ctr. and Gen. Clinics, San Francisco, 1949-54; nurse instr. St. Mary's Hosp., San Francisco, 1954-55; asst. prof. nursing U. San Francisco, 1954-72; medicine and treatment nurse Schutz Am. Sch., Alexandria, Egypt, 1972-73; newspaper corr. Representative, Calmar, Alta., Can., 1975-81; medicine and treatment nurse Hillhaven Convalescent Hosp., San Rafael, Calif., 1982. Vol. nurse County Health Dept., Sausalito, Calif., 1956-63; vol. pollworker City of Sausalito, 1962-65; vol. city coun. campaigns, Sausalito, 1962-65; vol. Santa Ventia Cmty. Orgn., San Rafael, Calif. Fed. Nursing grantee Cath. U. Am., 1942-43; Fed. scholar U. Calif., Berkeley, 1959-60. Mem. ANA, AAUP, Nursing Alumni Bd. U. San Francisco (voting vol. 1982-94), NLN (sec. 1956-60), Sigma Theta Tau, Alpha Phi Sigma. Republican. Roman Catholic. Home: 61 Labrea Way San Rafael CA 94903-3065 also: 5114 49th Ave, PO Box 444, Calmar, AB Canada T0C 0V0

TOMASZUNAS, STANISLAW, medical officer, scientist, researcher; b. Pinsk, Poland, July 31, 1927; s. Lucjan and Stanislawa (Lutowicz) T.; m. Teresa Brzozowska, Apr. 2, 1961; children: Joanna, Monika. Dipl., Med. Acad. Gdansk (Poland), 1952, Dr.hab.med., 1974; MD, Polish Acad. Scis., Warsaw, 1959; DTM and H, Sch. Hygiene & Tropical Med., London, 1963. Intern, then resident Clinic of Infectious Diseases Gen. Hosp./Med. Acad. of Gdansk, Gdynia, 1953-54; asst. Inst. Maritime and Tropical Medicine, Gdansk, Poland, 1953-54, rsch. fellow, 1955-59, chief of unit, 1959-66, chief Health Ctr. for Seafarers, 1972-74, 82-83, dep. dir. tropical health, 1984—; dir. WHO Collaborating Ctr. on Maritime Occupational Health, Gdynia, 1990—; med. officer WHO Malaria Eradication Program, various countries, 1967-71, WHO Smallpox Eradication and Immunization Program, New Delhi, 1974-81; cons. WHO Geneva, India, Burma, Bangladesh, Korea, 1982, 83, 84, 87; mem. ILO-WHO Joint Com. on the Health of Seafarers. Author: Tropical Hygiene and Travel Medical Guide, 1985, 2d rev. edit., 1991; editor: Medical Guide for Ships, 1987; contbr. numerous articles to profl. jours. Served to lt. Polish Infantry, 1944-45. Polish Acad. Scis. grantee, 1953-57; recipient Honorary cert. WHO, 1975. Mem. Polish Soc. Epidemiologists, Internat. Soc. Travel Medicine. Office: Inst Maritime and Tropical Medicine, Powst Stycz St 9b, 81-519 Gdynia Poland

TOMBOLINI, VINCENZO, radiologist, educator; b. Macerata, Marche, Italy, May 11, 1952; s. Mario and Adriana (Rutolini) T.; m. Laura Marsicola, June 26, 1982. MD, U. La Sapienza, 1976, oncologist, 1982, radiotherapist, 1980. House phys., asst. U. La Sapienza, Rome, 1976-91, assoc. prof., 1994—; cons. Mil. Cecchignola, Rome, 1990, ICOT, Latina, Italy, 1982. Contbr. articles to profl. jours. Mem. Soc. Italian Radiology Medica, Assn. Italian Radiotherapy, Assn. Italian Radiobiology. Roman Catholic. Home: via Arenula N 41, 00186 Rome Italy Office: U La Sapienza, V le Regina Elena N 324, 00161 Rome Italy

TOMITA, KANAKO MARGARET, optometrist; b. Okinawa, Japan, July 8, 1967; came to U.S., 1970; d. Teruo and Yoko (Hagiwara) Tomita; m. Vincent Hong Wong, Sept. 3, 1995. BS in Biochemistry, U. Calif., Riverside, 1989; BS in Visual Sci., U. Calif., Berkeley, 1991, OD, 1993. Optometrist in pvt. practice Stockton, Calif., 1993-94; optometrist Eyecare Assocs./Ctr. for Sight, Sacramento, 1993-95; optometrist in pvt. practice Rocklin, Calif., 1993—, Roseville, Calif., 1994—; vol. at vision screenings Sacramento Valley Optometric Soc., 1993—. Mem. Am. Optometric Assn., Calif. Optometric Assn., Sacramento Valley Optometric Soc.

TOMITA, TADANORI, neurosurgeon; b. Osaka, Japan, Nov. 19, 1945; s. Tadao and Noriko (Ikeda) T.; m. Kathryn Morley, June 28, 1980; children: Tadaki M., Kenji W., Dan Y. MD, Kobe (Japan) U., 1970. Diplomate Am. Bd. Neurol. Surgery. Attending neurosurgeon Children's Meml. Hosp., Chgo., 1981—, dir. neurosurg. oncology, 1984—; prof. Northwestern U. Med. Sch. Contbr. articles to profl. jours. Recipient Sherry Kallick award Northwestern Meml. Hosp., 1979, Frank Notides award Children's Meml. Hosp., Chgo., 1980. Fellow ACS, Am. Acad. Pediatrics; mem. Am. Assn. Neurol. Surgeons, Congress Neurorol. Surgeons, Am. Soc. Pediatric Neurosurgery, Soc. Pediatric Neurosurgery. Office: Childrens Meml Hosp 2300 N Childrens Plz Chicago IL 60614-3318

TOMLINSON, STEPHENSON ANTHONY, surgeon; b. Cayman Islands, W.I., Nov. 14, 1950; s. Anthony Daniel and Chrissie Bell (Martin) T.; m. Margaret Evans, Jan. 1, 1973 (div. 1976). BChir, Univ. W.I., 1973. House med. officer Univ. W.I. Hosp., Kingston, Jamaica, 1973-74, emergency officer, 1974-75, anesthetist, 1975-76; gen. surgeon Queen Elizabeth Hosp., Bridgetown, Barbados, 1976-77, East Birmingham (Eng.) Hosp., 1977-78, Wordsley (Eng.) Hosp., 1978-79; med. officer Cayman Islands Hosp., Grand Cayman, 1979-83; pvt. practice medicine specializing in gen. surgery Grand Cayman, 1983—; advisor Grand Cayman Cancer Support Soc., 1985-87. Elected mem. parliament Govt. of Cayman Islands, 1992—; organizer Grand Cayman Pks. Programme, 1987. Mem. Brit. Med. Assn., Cayman Island Med. and Dental Soc. (exec. officer 1980-81, pres. 1990—), Grand Cayman C. of C. (adv. officer health com. 1984-85). Home and Office: PO Box 273, Grand Cayman Cayman Islands

TOMONAGA, SUSUMU, anatomy educator; b. Yamaguchi, Japan, Feb. 14, 1939; s. Nobuichi and Tomiko Tomonaga; m. Hideko Tomonaga, May 17, 1966; children: Atsuko, Junko, Izumi. BS, Yamaguchi (Japan) U., 1962, DMS, 1973. Asst. prof. Yamaguchi U., 1966-69, lectr., 1969-76, assoc. prof., 1976-81, prof., 1981—; rsch. fellow Australian Nat. U., Canberra, 1973-75. Recipient Nakamura award Yamaguchi U. Sch. Medicine, Ube, 1980. Mem. Internat. Soc. Devel. and Comparative Immunology, Histochem. Soc. (U.S.), N.Y. Acad. Scis., Japanese Assn. for Devel. and Comparative Immunology. Home: 2-16-9 Minami-Obayama, Ube, Yamaguchi 755, Japan Office: Yamaguchi U, Sch Allied Health Scis, 1144 Kogushi, Ube, Yamaguchi 755, Japan

TOMPKINS, JAMES LANGHORNE, pediatrician; b. Richmond, Va., Sept. 30, 1948; s. James Langhorne Sr. and Martha Anne (Glazebrook) T.; m. Beverly Jo Thomas, June 20, 1970; children: Stephanie, Elizabeth, Katherine. BS, Hampden-Sydney (Va.) Coll., 1970; MD, Vanderbilt U., 1974. Diplomate Am. Bd. Pediatrics. Intern in pediat. Med. Coll. Va., Richmond, 1974-75, resident in pediat., 1975-77; pvt. practice Bedford, Va., 1979-81; pediatrician Fuller-Roberts Clinic, South Boston, Va., 1981—. Lt. comdr. USNR, 1977-79. Fellow Am. Acad. Pediatrics; mem. Med. Soc. Va., So. Med. Assn., Halifax Med. Soc., South Boston Lions Club (past pres.). Office: Fuller-Roberts Clinic 2212 Wilborn Ave South Boston VA 24592

TOMPKINS, ROBERT GEORGE, physician; b. Portland, Oreg., May 29, 1923; s. George Henry and Minnie (Davies) T.; m. Rosemarie Nowicki, June 6, 1948 (dec. 1960); children: Timothy Michael, Mary Eileen, George Henry, Robert George. B.S., U. Wash., 1943; M.B., Northwestern U., 1947, M.D., 1949; M.S., U. Minn., 1954. Diplomate Am. Bd. Internal Medicine. Intern King County Hosp., Seattle, 1948-49; resident King County Hosp., 1949-50; fellow, 1st asst. Mayo Found., Rochester, Minn., 1950-54; practice medicine specializing in cardiology and internal medicine Tulsa, 1954—; mem. staff St. Francis Hosp., chief staff, 1964, med. dir., 1968-86; clin. prof. medicine Tulsa Med. Coll. and U. Okla. Med. Coll.; v.p., med. dir. Wiliam K. Warren Med. Rsch. Inst., med. chmn. Guatemala Mission Hosp., Diocese Oklahoma City and Tulsa; coord. planning program Okla. Regional Med. Program; mem. Tulsa Health and Hosp. Planning Coun.; bd. dirs. Okla. Ctr. Molecular Medicine; med. dir. Laureate Hosp. Rsch. Inst.; pres. Tulsa Med. Edn. Found., 1980-82; bd. dirs. Laureate Psychiatric Clinic and Hosp.; founding mem. bd. dirs. Am. Bank and Trust, Tulsa. Contbr. articles to profl. jours; editor: Jour. Okla. State Med. Assn, 1974-86. Pres. Oklahoma Cath. Health Conf., 1981-82; bd. dirs. St. Francis Hosp., Tulsa. Decorated Knight of the Grand Cross (Equestrian Order Holy Sepulchre of Jerusalem, Knight (Sovereign Mil. Order of Malta); recipient Dean's award U. Okla., 1991, diploma of Merit and Honor, Municipality of Santiago, Atitlau, Guatemala. Fellow ACP, Royal Coll. Medicine, Am. Coll. Cardiology; mem. AAAS, AMA, Am. Diabetic Assn., Am. Acad. Med. Dirs. (bd. dirs.), Am. Heart Assn., Tulsa County Heart Assn. (pres. 1959), Am. Rheumatism Assn., Mayo Alumni Assn., KC, Alpha Kappa Kappa. Home: 6551 S Darlington Ave Tulsa OK 74136-2002 Office: 6465 S Yale Ave Tulsa OK 74136-7822

TOMPKINS, RONALD GARY, surgeon, educator, biomedical investigator; b. Many, La., Sept. 24, 1951; s. Horace and Ruby (McFerrin) T.; m. Denise Marie Clougherty, Mar. 7, 1985; children: Megan Elizabeth, Ryan Coleman, Caitlin Maureen. BS in Chemistry summa cum laude, Tulane U., 1972, MD, 1976; SM in Chem. Engring., MIT, 1983, ScD in Med. and Chem. Engring., 1983. Diplomate Am. Bd. Surgery (bd. dirs. 1994—), Am. Bd. Surg. Critical Care. Intern in surgery Mass. Gen. Hosp., Boston, 1976-77, asst. resident, then resident, 1977-79, 83-85, asst. in surgery, 1985-87, asst. surgeon, 1988-90, assoc. chief trauma and burn svcs., 1987-90, chief, 1990—, assoc. vis. surgeon, then vis. surgeon, 1991—; clin. fellow in surgery Harvard Med. Sch., Boston, 1977-79, 92-85, instr., then asst. prof. surgery, 1985-90, assoc. prof., 1990—; rsch. assoc. MIT, Cambridge, Mass., 1985-86; asst. in surgery Shriners Burns Inst., Boston, 1987-88, asst. surgeon, 1988-90, chief staff, 1990—; vis. asst. prof. Rutgers U. Sch. Engring., 1988-91; surg. cons. Spaulding Rehab. Hosp., Boston, 1987-88; numerous presentations in field at regional, nat. and internat. orgns. Mem. editl. bd. Critical Care Medicine, 1991—, Jour. Tissue Engring., 1994—, Jour. Am. Soc. Artificial Internal Organs, 1994—; contbr. over 100 articles and revs. to med. jours., chpts. to books; patent pending for culturing liver cells. DuPont fellow MIT, 1979-80, E.R. Gilliland fellow, 1980-81, William Prince fellow, 1981-83; Edward D. Churchill rsch. fellow Mass. Gen. Hosp., 1981-82, fellow Am. Surg. Assn. Found., 1987-88; grantee Link Found., 1985—, NIH, 1987-91, Whitaker Found., 1988-91, Nat. Inst. Gen. Med. Scis., 1992—, Nat. Inst. Digestive Diseases and Kidney, 1987-94, Shriners Hosps., 1988—. Fellow ACS; mem. AMA, AAAS, AIChE, Assn. for Acad. Surgery, Am. Chem. Soc., Am. Burn Assn., Am. Fedn. for Clin. Rsch., Soc. Critical Care Medicine, Surg. Infection Soc., Am. Soc. for Artificial Internal Organs, Shock Soc., Am. Assn. for Surgery of Trauma, Am. Soc. for Laser Medicine and Surgery, Soc. for Cryobiology, Soc. Univ. Surgeons, Am. Assn. for Study Liver Diseases, Am. Trauma Soc., New Eng. Surg. Soc., Cell Transplant Soc., Phi Beta Kappa, Alpha Omega Alpha, numerous others. Home: 16 Emerson Pl Boston MA 02114-2251 Office: Mass Gen Hosp Fruit St Boston MA 02114*

TOMS, KATHLEEN MOORE, nurse; b. San Francisco, Dec. 31, 1943; d. William Moore and Phyllis Josephine (Barry) Stewart. RN, AA, City Coll. San Francisco, 1963; BPS in Nursing Edn., Elizabethtown (Pa.) Coll., 1973; MS in Edn., Temple U., 1977; MS in Nursing, Gwynedd Mercy Coll. 1988; m. Benjamin Peskoff; children from previous marriage: Kathleen Marie Toms Myers, Kelly Terese Toms. Med.-surg. nurse St. Joseph Hosp., Fairbanks, Alaska, 1963-65; emergency room nurse St. Joseph Hosp., Lancaster, Pa., 1965-69, blood, plasm and components nurse, 1969-71; pres. F.E. Barry Co., Lancaster, 1971—; dir. inservice edn. Lancaster Osteo. Hosp., 1971-75; coord. practical nursing program Vocat. Tech. Sch., Coatesville, Pa., 1976-77; dir. nursing Pocopson Home, West Chester, Pa., 1978-80, Riverside Hosp., Wilmington, Del., 1980-83; assoc. Coatesville VA Hosp., 1983-89; chief Nurse, 1984-89; with VA Cen. Office; supr. psychiat. nursing Martinez (Calif.) VA Med. Ctr., 1989-94; assoc. chief nursing svc. edn. VA No. Calif. Sys. Clinics, Pleasant Hill, Calif., 1994—; trainee assoc. chief Nursing Home Care Unit, Washington; mem. Pa. Gov.'s Council on Alcoholism and Drug Abuse, 1974-76; mem. Del. Health Council Med.-Surg. Task Force, 1981-83; dir. Lancaster Cmty. Health Ctr., 1973-76; lectr. in field. Col. Nurse Corps, USAR. Decorated Army Commendation medals (5), Meritorious Svc. medals (2); recipient Cmty. Svc. award Citizens United for Better Public Relations, 1974; award Sertoma, Lancaster, 1974; Outstanding Citizen award Sta. WGAL-TV, 1975; U.S. Army Achievement award, 1983. Mem. Elizabethtown, Temple U. Alumni Assns., Pa. Nurses' Assn. (dir.), Sigma Theta Tau, Beta Gamma. Inventor auto-infuser for blood or blood components, 1971. Home: 208 Sea Mist Dr Vallejo CA 94591-7748 Office: VA No Calif System of Clinics 2350 Contra Costa Blvd Pleasant Hill CA 94523-3930

TONEGAWA, SUSUMU, biology educator; b. Nagoya, Japan, Sept. 5, 1939; came to U.S., 1963; s. Tsutomu and Miyoko (Masuko) T.; m. Mayumi Yoshinari, Sept. 28, 1985; children: Hidde, Hanna, Satto. BS, Kyoto U., Japan, 1963; PhD, U. Calif., San Diego, 1968. Rsch. asst. U. Calif., San Diego, 1963-64, teaching asst., 1964-68; mem. Basel (Switzerland) Inst. Immunology, 1971-81; prof. biology MIT, Cambridge, 1981—; investigator Howard Hughes Med. Inst., 1988—; dir. MIT Ctr. for Memory and Learning, 1994; professorship Amgen, Inc., 1994. Editorial bd. Jour. Molecular and Cellular Immunology. Decorated Order of Culture, Emperor of Japan; recipient Cloetta prize, 1978, Avery Landsteiner prize Gesselschaft für Immunologie, 1981, Louisa Gross Horwitz prize Columbia U., 1982, award Gardiner Found. Internat., Toronto, Ont., Can., 1983, Robert Koch Found. prize, Bonn., Fed. Republic Germany, 1986, co-recipient Albert Lasker Med. Rsch. award, 1987, Nobel prize in Physiology or Medicine, 1987; named Person with Cultural Merit Japanese Govt., 1983. Mem. NAS (fgn. assoc.), Am. Assn. Immunologists (hon.), Scandinavian Soc. Immunology (hon.). Office: MIT 77 Massachusetts Ave Cambridge MA 02139-4301

TONELLI, GIOVANNA MARIE, professional development consultant, social worker; b. Phila., Nov. 13, 1951; d. Peter Paul and Mary Rita (Campagna) T. AAS, Community Coll. of Phila., 1972; B of Social Work, Temple U., 1974, MSW, 1981. Lic. social worker, Pa. Med. social worker Bio-Med. Applications, Phila., 1976-79; with foster care program Tabor Children's Svcs., Doylestown, Pa., 1981; with adoption program, cons. Tabor Children's Svcs., Doylestown, 1982; social worker City of Phila., 1982; program dir. Italian Home for Children, Boston, 1983-87; trainer, cons. Temple U., Phila., 1987; social worker Support Ctr. for Child Advocates, Phila., 1987-88; trainer/ cons. profl. devel. Becoming, Phila., 1987—; mem. exec. bd. Today's Child, Boston, 1985-87 ; mem. network speakers USA, Inc., Pigeon Forge, Tenn., 1991; convenor Gathering Bus. Women in South Phila., 1991—. Vol. Boston Dept. Social Svcs., 1986-87; adv. Nat. Abortion Rights Action League, Phila. and Boston, 1974-89. Recipient Achiever award Success Motivation Inst., Inc., Waco, Tex., 1988. Mem. Nat. Assn. Social Workers (mem. child welfare task force 1984-87), NAFE, Bus. Women's Network. Home and Office: Becoming 905 Mountain St Philadelphia PA 19148-1117

TONG, DEAN BRIAN, medical technologist, consultant, author, speaker; b. Boston, July 22, 1956; s. Kenneth Gilbert and Claire (Gardner) T.; children: Christine, Kenny. BS, Northeastern U., 1979; postgrad., U. St. Lucia, W.I., 1983-84. Lic. MT, Fla. Med. technologist Lawnwood Med. Ctr., Ft. Pierce, Fla., 1980-83, MEDPRO Clin. Labs. Sales, Orlando, Fla., 1984-85; biol. scientist MEDTECH/State Dept. Health/Rehab. Svcs. Lab., Jacksonville, Fla., 1985-86; med. technologist Upson County Hosp., Thomaston, Ga., 1986-87; med. technologist generalist Mayo Clinic-St. Luke's Hosp., Jacksonville, 1987-93; med. technologist stat. lab. Meml. Med. Ctr., Jacksonville, 1993; med. technologist hematology U. Med. Ctr., Jacksonville, 1993-95, Lab. Corp. Am., Tampa, 1995—; pres. cons. VOCAL (Victims of Child Abuse Laws), Jacksonville, 1992—; mem. adv. bd. Coalition for Preservation of Fatherhood, Boston, 1996—; author, spkr., cons., activist on false child abuse allegations. Author: Don't Blame ME, Daddy: False Accusations of Child Sexual Abuse, 1992, Ashes to Ashes...Families to Dust, 1996. Pres. Tampa Bay VOCAL, 1995—, Jacksonville VOCAL, 1992-94; mem. Children's Rights Coun., Washington, 1992—, Internat. Spkrs. Network, Sevierville, Tenn., 1995—. Recipient Cert. of Achievement, DADS Assisting Dads, 1994. Mem. Am. Med. Technologists, Fla. Soc. Med. Technologists. Home: 6102 Webb Rd # 811 Tampa FL 33605 Office: Valuing Our Children and Laws (VOCAL) 6102 Webb Rd # 811 Tampa FL 33615

TONG, RICHARD DARE, anesthesiologist; b. Chgo., Oct. 20, 1930; s. George Dare and June (Jung) T.; student U. Calif., Berkeley, 1949-52; MD, U. Calif., Irvine, 1956. m. Diane Helene Davies, Apr. 12, 1970; children: Erin, Jason; m. Deanna Johnson, Jan. 5, 1993; stepchildren: Jeffery Johnson, Ryan Johnson. Intern, Phoenix Gen. Hosp., 1956-57; resident in anesthesiology UCLA, 1965-67; pvt. practice, Lakewood, Calif., 1967—; clin. instr. UCLA Sch. Medicine, 1968—. Dep. sheriff reserve med. emergency team, L.A. County. With USNR, 1947-53. Diplomate Am. Bd. Anesthesiology. Fellow Am. Coll. Anesthesiology; mem. Am. Soc. Anesthesiologists, AMA, Calif. Med. Assn., L.A. County Med. Assns. Office: PO Box 1131 Lakewood CA 90714-1131

TONG, THEODORE G., pharmacy educator, dean; b. La Jolla, Calif., Oct. 8, 1942; s. Raymond and Guey Kay (Dear) T.; m. Esther D. Lee, June 29, 1968. BS, U. So. Calif., 1964, Oreg. State U., 1965; DPharm, U. Calif., 1969. Licentiate pharmacy, Ariz., Calif.; Diplomate Am. Bd. Applied Toxicology. Clin. instr. Sch. Pharmacy U. Calif., San Francisco, 1969-70, asst. clin. prof. Sch. Pharmacy, 1970-78, assoc. clin. prof. Sch. Pharmacy, 1978-82, prof. Coll. Pharmacy, 1982—; assoc. dean Coll. Pharmacy U. Ariz., Tucson, 1987—; exec. dir. Ariz. Poison Control Sys., Tucson, 1984—; mem. non prescription durgs adv. com. FDA/DHHS, Rockville, Md., 1994—, adv. panel substance abuse and clin. toxicology U.S. Pharmacopeia, Rockville, 1990—. Contbr. 29 chpts. to books, 52 articles to profl. jours. Recipient Disting. Leadership Dr. Martin Luther King Jr. Ctr. U. Ariz., 1992, Outstanding Faculty Asian Am. Faculty Staff Alumni Assn. U. Ariz., 1994. Fellow Am. Acad. Clin. Toxicology; mem. Am. Pharm. Assn., Am. Coll. Clin. Pharmacy, Am. Assn. Poison Control Ctrs., Am. Assn. Colls. Pharmacy. Office: Coll Pharmacy U Ariz 1701 Mabel St Tucson AZ 85721

TONKENS, REBECCA A., maternal women's health nurse; b. Searcy, Ark., Dec. 17, 1943; d. William T. and Velda M. (Goodloe) McAfee; m. Richard E. Morris, June 24, 1960 (div. Nov. 1980); children: Terri L. Morris Bomar, Toni L. Morris Carroll; m. Solvin W. Tonkens, Dec. 22, 1986. LPN, Area Vocat. Tech. Sch., Kansas City, Kans., 1973; ADN, Kansas City C.C., 1980; BSN, Webster U., 1992. RN, Kans., Mo. Area Vocat. Tech. Sch.; Staff nurse Providence-St. Margaret Hosp., Kansas City, 1973-80; indsl. nurse, office mgr. Kansas City Indsl. Clinic, 1980-81; staff nurse Bethany Med. Ctr., Kansas City, 1981—; active community rels. diabetes unit Bethany Med. Ctr., 1983-86. Officer, v.p., bd. dirs. Cambridge Townhouse Assn., Leawood, Kans., 1989-92; chaperone Rose Bud (Ark.) Band at Presdl. Inauguration, Washington, 1992; mem. adv. bd. Kansas City Kans. C.C. Day Care Ctr.; vol. Habitat for Humanity, Salvation Army, others. Recipient Cert. of Appreciation, Salvation Army, 1994. Mem. ANA, Am. Coll. Occupational and Environ. Medicine (aux.). Episcopalian. Home and Office: 12861 Cambridge Ter Leawood KS 66209-1634

TONKIN, INA LYNN DYER, cardiovascular radiologist, educator; b. Louisville, Apr. 26, 1944; d. Robert S. and Nancy E. (Camp) Dyer; m. Allen K. Tonkin, June 29, 1968; children—Allison Elizabeth-Ann, Keith Allen. B.A., DePauw U., 1966; M.D., U. Louisville, 1970. Diplomate Am. Bd. Radiology. Intern U. Fla., Gainesville, 1970-71, resident in radiology, 1971-73, fellow in cardiovascular radiology, 1974-75; asst. prof. U. Ariz. Health Sci. Ctr., Tucson, 1975-77, U. Ala.-Birmingham, 1977-79; assoc. prof. radiology U. Tenn., Memphis, 1979-84, prof., 1984—, prof. pediatrics, 1985—; exec. com. LeBonheur Children's Med. Ctr., Memphis, 1981-85, chief of med. staff, 1987. Editor: (book) Pediatric Cardiovascular Imaging, 1992; contbr. chpts. to books, rsch. articles to profl. jours. Fellow Am. Heart Assn. (exec. com. Council Cardiovascular Radiology 1980-82), Soc. Cardiovascular and Interventional Radiology, Am. Coll. Radiology; mem. Soc. Pediatric Radiology (treas.), Jour. Rev. Club of Memphis (sec. 1984, pres. 1985). Methodist. Home: 3415 Chambers Chapel Rd Lakeland TN 38002-9508 Office: LeBonheur Children's Med Ctr 50 N Dunlap Memphis TN 38103-2821

TONKONOGY, JOSEPH MOSES, physician, neuropsychiatrist, researcher; b. Belaya Tserkov, Kiev, Ukraine, Oct. 22, 1925; came to U.S., 1979, naturalized, 1985; s. Moysey Iosifovich and Beyla (Gdalievna (Schvachkina) T.; married; children: Vitaly, Milla, Bella. MD, Military Med. Acad., Leningrad, USSR, 1947; PhD, All Union Acad. Med. Sci., Moscow, 1956; DSc, 1st Med. Inst., Leningrad, 1966. From asst. to assoc. prof. The Bechterev Inst., Leningrad, 1956-66, prof., chmn., 1966-78; assoc. Boston U. Sch. Medicine, 1980-81; physician VA Med. Ctr., Northampton, Mass., 1981-87; assoc. prof. U. Mass. Med. Ctr., Worcester, 1987-95, prof., 1995—; dir. neuropsychiatry svc. Worcester State Hosp., Mass., 1989—. Author: Introduction to Clinical Neuropsychology, 1973, Vascular Aphasia, 1986; editor: Problems of Contemporary Psychoneurology, 1966, Psychological Experiment in Psychiatry and Neurology, 1969, Mathematical Methods in Psychiatry and Neurology, 1971, Current Problems of Clinical Psychology, 1975; cons.: (book) Soviet Military Psychiatry, 1986; contbr. numerous articles to profl. jours. Capt. Med. Corps, Germany, 1947-48. Recipient The Bechterev Prize, All Union Acad. Med. Scis., Moscow, 1974. Fellow The Royal Soc. Medicine (U.K.); mem. Am. Neuropsychiat. Assn., Am. Acad. Neurology, Internat. Neuropsychol. Soc., Soc. Neurosci., Internat. Psychogeriatric Soc. Jewish. Office: U Mass Med. Ctr Dept of Psychiatry 55 Lake Ave N Worcester MA 01655-0002

TONN, ELVERNE MERYL, pediatric dentist, dental benefits consultant; b. Stockton, Calif., Dec. 10, 1929; s. Emanuel M. and Lorna Darlene (Bryant) T.; m. Ann G. Richardson, Oct. 28, 1951; children: James Edward, Susan Elaine Tonn Yee. AA, La Sierra U., Riverside, Calif., 1949; DDS, U. So. Calif., 1955; BS, Regents Coll., U. State N.Y., 1984. Lic. dentist; cert. tchr., Calif., dental ins. cons. Pediatric dentist, assoc. Walker Dental Group, Long Beach, Calif., 1957-59, Children's Dental Clinic, Sunnyvale, Calif., 1959-61; pediatric dentist in pvt. practice Mountain View, Calif., 1961-72; pediatric dentist, ptrn. Pediatric Dentistry Assocs., Los Altos, Calif., 1972-83; pediatric dentist, ptnr. Valley Oak Dental Group, Manteca, Calif., 1987—; from clin. instr. to assoc. prof. U. Pacific, San Francisco, 1964-84; assoc. prof. U. Calif., San Francisco, Calif., 1984-86; ; pediatric dental cons. Delta Dental Plan, San Francisco, 1985—; chief dental staff El Camino Hosp., Mountain View, 1964-65, 84-85; lectr. in field. Weekly columnist Manteca Bull., 1987-92; producer 2 teaching videos, 1986; contbr. articles to profl. jours. Lectr. to elem. students on dental health Manteca Unified Sch. Dist., 1982—; dental health screener Elem. Schs., San Joaquin County Pub. Health, 1989-92; dental cons. Interplast program Stanford U. Sch. Medicine. Capt. U.S. Army, 1955-57. Fellow Internat. Coll. Dentists, Am. Acad. Pediatric Dentistry, Am. Coll. Dentists, Royal Soc. Health (Eng.), Acad. of Dentistry for Handicapped, Pierre Fauchard Acad., Acad. Dental Materials; mem. ADA, Internat. Assn. Pediatric Dentistry, Internat. Assn. Dental Rsch., Fedn. Dentaire Internationale, Am. Soc. Dentistry for Children, Am. Assn. Dental Cons., Calif. Dental Assn., Calif. Soc. Dentistry for Children (pres. 1968), Calif. Soc. Pediatric Dentists, N.Y. Acad. Scis., Calif. Acad. Sci., Rotary Internat., Am. Bd. Quality Assurance and Utilization Rev. Physicians (diplomate, cert. dental benefits cons.), Nat. Assn. for Healthcare Quality. Republican. Home: 374 Laurelwood Cir Manteca CA 95336-7122 Office: Valley Oak Dental Group Inc 1507 W Yosemite Ave Manteca CA 95337

TONN, MELISSA DAWN, physician; b. Ardmore, Okla., Nov. 18, 1959; d. Elsworth and Mildred (Buck) T. BA, Rice U., 1982; MD, U. Tex. Health Sci. Ctr., 1986; MBA, Rice U., 1989; MPH, U. Tex. Health Sci. Ctr., 1990. Resident Baylor Coll. Medicine, Houston, 1986-87; pvt. practice Houston, 1987-89; resident occupational medicine Univ. Tex. Health Sci. Ctr., 1989-90; med. dir. occupational health svcs. Meml. Healthcare System, Houston, 1990—; cons. occupl. health svcs., delivery sys. Mem. AMA, Am. Coll. Physician Execs., Tex. Med. Assn., Am. Coll. Occupl. and Environ. Medicine, Harris County Med. Assn., Houstonian Network Assn., Rice U. Alumni Assn., Alpha Omega Alpha. Home: 651 Bering Dr Apt 1601 Houston TX 77057-2135

TONN, ROBERT JAMES, entomologist; b. Watertown, Wis., June 23, 1927; s. Harry James and Elise (Foogman) T.; m. Noemi C. Tonn; children: Sigrid M., Monica E. BS, Colo. State U., 1949, MS, 1950; MPH, Okla. Med. Sch., 1963; PhD, Okla. State U., 1959. Rsch. assoc La. State U., Costa Rica/New Orleans, 1961-63; dir. Taunton Field Sta., Taunton, Mass., 1963-65; chief PMO unit WHO, various locations, 1965-87; adj. prof. of parasitology U. Tex.-El Paso, 1988—; cons. USAID/VBC, 1987—. Contbr. numerous articles to profl. jours. Mem. Am. Soc. Tropical Medicine, Soc. Vector Ecology (pres. 1984), Am. Mosquito Control Assn., U.S./ Mex. Border Health Assn., Royal Soc. Tropical Medicine and Hygiene. Masons. Congregationalist. Home: RR 3 Box 505 Park Rapids MN 56470-9363

TOOLE, JAMES FRANCIS, medical educator; b. Atlanta, Mar. 22, 1925; s. Walter O'Brien and Helen (Whitehurst) T.; m. Patricia Anne Wooldridge, Oct. 25, 1952; children: William, Anne, James, Douglas Sean. BA, Princeton U., 1947; MD, Cornell U., 1949; LLB, LaSalle Extension U., 1962. Intern, then resident internal medicine and neurology U. Pa. Hosp., Nat. Hosp., London, Eng., 1953-58; mem. faculty U. Pa. Sch. Medicine, 1958-62; prof. neurology, chmn. dept. Bowman Gray Sch. Medicine Wake Forest U., 1962-83; vis. prof. neuroscis. U. Calif. at San Diego, 1969-70; vis. scholar Oxford U., 1989; mem. Nat. Bd. Med. Examiners, 1970-76; mem. task force arteriosclerosis Nat. Heart Lung & Blood Inst., 1970-81; chmn. 6th and 7th Princeton confs. cerebrovascular diseases; cons. epidemiology WHO, Japan, 1971, 73, 93, USSR, 1968, Ivory Coast, 1977, Japan, 1993; mem. Lasker Awards com., 1976-77; chmn. neuropharmacologic drugs com. FDA, 1979; co-chair Commn. on Presdl. Disability, 1994—; cons. NASA, 1966. Author: Cerebrovascular Disorders, 4th edit., 1990; editor: Current Concepts in Cerebrovascular Disease, 1969-73, Jour. Neurol. Sci., 1990—; mem. editorial bd. Annals Internal Medicine, 1968-75, Stroke, 1972-91, Jour. AMA 1975-77, Ann. Neurology, 1980-86, Jour. Neurol. Soc., 1990; mem. editorial bd. Jour. of Neurology, 1985-89. Pres. N.C. Heart Assn., 1976-77. Served with AUS, 1950-51; flight surgeon USNR, 1951-53. Decorated Bronze Star with V, Combat Med. badge. Fellow ACP (life), AAAS (life); mem. AMA, Am. Clin. and Climatol Assn. (life), Am. Heart Assn. (chmn. com. ethics 1970-75), Am. Physiol. Soc., Am. Neurol. Assn (sec.-treas. 1978-82, pres. 1984-85, archivist, historian 1988—), World Fedn. Neurology (sec.-treas. 1982-89, mgmt. com. 1990—), Am. Acad. Neurology, Am. Soc. Neuroimaging (pres. 1992-94), Internat. Stroke Soc. (exec. com. 1989—, program chmn. 1992), Nat. Stroke Assn. (bd. dirs. 1993—, exec. com. 1994—, co-chmn. Commn. on U.S. Presdl. Disability 1994—); hon. mem. Assn. Brit. Neurologists, German Neurol. Soc., Austrian Soc. Neurology, Irish Neurol. Assn. Home: 1836 Virginia Rd Winston Salem NC 27104-2316

TOOMEY, HUGH EDWARD, orthopedist, surgeon; b. Visalia, Calif., Dec. 6, 1934; s. David J. and Catherine M. (Creegan) T.; m. Mary Patricia McGavick, June 28, 1958; children: Elizabeth, Patricia, Steven, Sean. BS, Wash. State U., 1956; MD, UCLA, 1963. Diplomate Am. Bd. Orthop. Surgery. Intern Harborview Hosp., Seattle, 1963-64; resident U. Wash., 1964-69; orthop. surgeon Orthop. Phys. Assocs., Seattle, 1969—. With U.S. Infantry, 1957-58. Office: Orthop Physicians Assocs 1229 Madison Ste 1600 Seattle WA 98104

TOOMEY, JOHN CHRISTOPHER, biologist, research scientist; b. Sewickley, Pa., Nov. 17, 1964; s. William Shenberger and Nancy (Mangin) T.; m. Jennifer Mullen, Nov. 4, 1989; children: Ariel Elizabeth, Chase Evan. BS in Biology, Allegheny Coll., 1987. Assoc. rsch. engr. Medex, Inc., Dublin, Ohio, 1988-89, project engr., 1989-95, sr. project engr., 1995; mem. emergency response team Medex, Inc., Dublin, 1990—. Mem. ASM Internat., Am. Soc. for Microbiology. Office: Medex Inc 6250 Shier Rings Rd Dublin OH 43016-1295

TOOMEY, LAURA CAROLYN, psychologist; b. Manchester, Conn., Mar. 29, 1929; d. David Clark and Olive (Hutchinson) T. BS, Bates Coll., 1950; MA, U. Conn., 1954, PhD, 1961. Lic. psychologist, Conn. Psychologist Community Child Guidance Clinic, Manchester, 1959-64; from psychologist to chief psychologist Springfield (Mass.) Hosp., 1964-73; with Conn. Valley Hosp., Middletown, 1973—, acting dir. psychol. svcs., 1986-87, dir. clin. internship tng., 1974-92, asst. chief of psychol. svcs., 1987-91. Co-author: Evaluation of Changes Associated with Psychiatric Treatment, 1959; contbr. chpts. in books and articles to profl. jours. Justice of the peace Town of Bolton, Conn., 1954-89; mem. Bolton Town Commn. on Aging, 1972-76, Bolton Bd. Health, 1993—, sec., 1995—; sec. Bolton Property Owners Assn., 1964-76. Mem. Am. Psychol. Assn. (treas. div. clin. psychology 1982-90), Conn. Psychol. Assn. (coun. bd. dirs. 1975-86). Republican. Home: PO Box 9486 40 Steeles Crossing Rd Bolton CT 06043 Office: Conn Valley Hosp Middletown CT 06457

TOOMEY, RICHARD KIRK, health facility administrator; b. Greenville, S.C., Oct. 21, 1954; s. Robert Edward and Laurette Pearl (Creighton) T. AB, Duke U., 1977, MHA, 1979. Diplomate Am. Coll. Healthcare Execs. Resident Leigh Meml. Hosp., Norfolk, Va., 1979-80; adminstrv. asst. Norfolk Gen. Hosp., 1980-81; v.p. Toomey Co., Inc., Greenville, S.C., 1981-85; mgr. Amherst Assocs. Inc., Tampa, Fla., 1986-88; sr. mgr. Ernst & Whinney, Tampa, 1988; sr. cons. TriBrook Group, Inc., Chgo., 1988-89; v.p. Nash Gen. Hosp., Rocky Mount, N.C., 1989-92; exec. v.p., COO Nash Gen. Hosp., Rocky Mount, 1992-95, pres., 1996—; pres. Duke U. Hosp. and Health Alumni Assn., Durham, N.C., 1993; bd. dirs. Duke U. Alumni Assn., Durham, 1993-95. Named Outstanding Young Man of Am., 1985. Mem. Tar River Kiwanis. Office: Nash Gen Hosp 2460 Curtis Ellis Dr Rocky Mount NC 27804

TOPFER, STEVEN A., anesthesiologist; b. Allentown, Pa., Jan. 27, 1961; s. Bernard Julian and Minna Ruth (Rothstein) T.; m. Geri Ruth Schlessel, July 5, 1961; children: Jacob Spencer, Sydney Michele. BA, Emory U., 1984; DO, Phila. Coll. Osteo. Medicine, 1987. Diplomate Am. Bd. Anesthesiology. Resident, then chief resident Hackensack (N.J.) Med. Ctr., 1988-92; attending anesthesiologist Rahway (N.J.) Hosp., 1992—. Mem. Am. Soc. Anesthesiology. Office: Rahway Hosp 865 Stone St Rahway NJ 07065

TOPPOZADA, MOKHTAR KHAIRY, obstetrician, gynecologist, educator; b. Giza, Egypt, Mar. 11, 1939; s. Hussein Khairy and Fadila Ibrahim (Aref) T.; m. Jane Antoine Bonnet; children: May, Tarek. MBBCh, Alexandria Faculty Medicine, 1962, diploma in ob-gyn., 1964, diploma in surgery, 1966, MD, 1968. Lectr. in ob-gyn. Alexandria (Egypt) U., 1969-74, assoc. prof., 1974-79, prof., 1979—; temporary advisor, bd. mem., cons. WHO, Geneva, 1974-91; cons. U.S. Congress Population, Washington; mem. adv. bd. Ford Found., 1977-79; cons. Indian Coun. Med. Rsch., New Delhi, 1979-85; mem. bd. dirs. Alexandria Med. Ctr. Contbr. articles to profl. jours. and chpts. to books; mem. editl. bd. several jours. Recipient Nat. award for scientific activities Nat. Acad. for Rsch. and Tech., 1975, Dr. F. Mekkawy award, 1988, 1st Class Govt. Decoration for Scis. and Art, 1976. Office: Shatby Univ Hosp, Alexandria Egypt

TORACK, RICHARD MAURICE, neuropathologist; b. Passaic, N.J., July 23, 1927; s. Geza J. and Margaret E. (Voros) T.; m. Catherine N. Reagan, Apr. 18, 1953; children: Richard M., James W., Thomas A., Margaret K., William P. MS, Seton Hall U., 1948; MD, Georgetown U., 1952. Asst. pathologist Montefiore Hosp., N.Y.C., 1958-60; asst. prof. pathology Cornell Med. Coll., N.Y.C., 1962-65, assoc. prof. pathology, 1965-68; assoc. attending pathologist N.Y. Hosp., N.Y.C., 1962-68; assoc. prof. pathology Washington U. Sch. Medicine, St. Louis, 1968-70, prof. pathology, 1970—. Author: Pathology Physiology of Dementia,1978, Your Brain Is Younger Than You Think, 1981. Capt. USAF, 1953-55. Mem. Am. Assn. Neuropathology, Am. Assn. Pathology and Bacteriology, Am. Geriatric Soc., N.Y. Acad. Sci. Office: Washington U Sch Medicine 660 S Euclid Ave # 8118 Saint Louis MO 63110-1010

TORBICKI, ADAM RYSZARD, medical educator; b. Warsaw, Feb. 7, 1953; s. Ryszard and Emilia (Wozniak) T.; m. Grazyna Loska, June 6, 1981. MD, Med. Acad. Warsaw, PhD. Asst. prof. dept. hypertension & angiology Med. Acad. Warsaw, 1978-87, assoc. prof., 1987—, head echocardiographic lab., 1981—. Co-author: Pulmonary Embolism, 1994; contbr. articles to profl. jours. Fellow European Soc. Cardiology; mem. Polish Cardiac Soc. Home: Al Roz 7/2, PL-00556 Warsaw Poland Office: Med Acad. Warsaw, Banacha 1, 02-097 Warsaw Poland

TORELLI, JULIUS NICHOLAS, cardiologist; b. Detroit, Mar. 30, 1960; s. Antonio and Anna Lidia (Pettinaro) T.; m. Maria Cristina Noyola, July 2, 1983; children: Jessica, Daniel. BS, U. Miami, 1982; MD, U. South Fla., 1986. Diplomate Am. Bd. Internal Medicine in Cardiovascular Disease. Intern Cleve. Clinic, 1986-87, resident, 1987-89, fellow, 1989-92, resident in internal medicine, 1986-89, fellow in cardiovascular disease, 1989-92; cardiologist LeBauer & Assocs., Greensboro, N.C., 1992—. Fellow Am. Coll. Cardiology. Office: 520 N Elam Ave Greensboro NC 27403

TORGENRUD, TERRY WAYNE, pediatrician; b. Wahpeton, N.D., Sept. 6, 1942; s. Lyle Jerome and Maxine Bird (Hoffman) T.; m. Janet Marie Kuchera, Aug. 1, 1965; children: Timothy, Matthew, Andrew. BS, U. N.D., 1964, BS in Medicine, 1966; MD, Bowman Gray Sch. Medicine, 1968. Diplomate Am. Bd. Pediatrics. Intern Madigan Army Med. Ctr., Tacoma, 1968-69, resident in pediatrics, 1969-72; fellow in adolescent medicine U. Wash., Seattle, 1971-72, chief adolescent svc., 1972-74; pediatrician University Pl. Pediatric Clinic, Seattle, 1974—; chief of staff Mary Bridge Children's Hosp., Tacoma, 1978. Chmn. Citizens for Better Dental Helath, Tacoma, 1991-92. Maj. M.C., U.S. Army, 1968-74. Fellow Am. Acad. Pediatrics; mem. North Pacific Pediatric Soc., Wash. State Med. Soc., Pierce County Med. Soc. (chair sch. health, pub. health com., Cmty. Svc. award 1994). Roman Catholic. Home: 4216 Bayview Pl W Tacoma WA 98466 Office: Univ Pl Pediatric Clinic 1033 Regents Blvd Ste 102 Fircrest WA 98466-6030

TORJMAN, MARC CLAUDE, medical researcher; b. Marakech, Morocco, Dec. 29, 1954; s. Jacques and Rachel T.; m. Gayle Berman, Aug. 13, 1995; 1 child, Yariv. BS, Temple U., 1976, MEd, 1987, PhD, 1997. Rschr. Jefferson Med. Coll., Phila., 1985—. Mem. Internat. Anesthesia Rsch. Soc. Home: 14007 Clifford Ln Philadelphia PA 19116 Office: Jefferson Med Coll Dept Anesthesiology 111 S 11th St Philadelphia PA 19107

TORMOLLAN, GARY GORDON, health facility administrator, physical therapist; b. Plainfield, N.J., Feb. 23, 1954; s. Gordon William and Doris Evelyn (Palmer) T.; m. Stacey Lee Cole, Aug. 20, 1983; children: Brian, Kristin. BS in Health Edn., Trenton (N.J.) State Coll., 1976; cert. in phys. therapy, Hahnemann U., 1982; MEd, Trenton State Coll., 1987. Lic. phys. therapist, Maine, Pa.; lic. athletic trainer, N.J. Athletic trainer Princeton (N.J.) High Sch., 1976-81; phys. therapist Holy Redeemer Hosp., Huntington Valley, Pa., 1982-83, Phys. Therapy of Princeton, 1984-86; sports medicine coord. Omni-Fit, Mt. Laurel, N.J., 1986-87; dir. rehab. svcs. Med. Coll. of Pa., Phila., 1987-90; dir. phys. therapy Mid-Maine Med. Ctr., Waterville, 1990-92; pres., CEO Maine Phys. Therapy, Waterville, 1993—; cons. Burnt Mill Med. Ctr., Cherry Hill, N.J., 1983; mem. clin. faculty Temple U., Phila., 1989-90; cons., mem. adv. bd. phys. therapy asst. program Kennebec Valley Tech. Coll., Fairfield, Maine, 1990-94. Deacon Ewing (N.J.) Presbyn. Ch., 1989; coach Waterville Little League, Waterville (Maine) Youth Soccer Assn. Mem. Am. Phys. Therapy Assn., Nat. Athletic Trainers Assn., Waterville Rotary. Congregationalist. Home: 31 Messalonskee Ave Waterville ME 04901-5352 Office: Maine Physical Therapy 28 College Ave Waterville ME 04901-6105

TORNATORE-MORSE, KATHLEEN MARY, pharmacy educator; b. Oneida, N.Y., Feb. 25, 1955; d. James Joseph and Concetta Barbara (Crimi) T.; m. Gene Morse; two children. BS in Pharmacy cum laude, Union U., 1978; PharmD, SUNY, Buffalo, 1981. Registered pharmacist, N.Y. Hosp. pharmacy residency U. Nebr. Med. Ctr., Omaha, 1978-79; pharmacist Health Care Plan, West Seneca, N.Y., 1979-80; lab. instr. Profl. Practice Lab. Sch. of Pharmacy SUNY, Buffalo, 1979-80, instr. in pharmacology nurse practitioner program, 1982-85, 87-91, clin. pharmacokinetics fellow, 1983-85, clin. instr. Sch. of Pharmacy, 1981-83, rsch. asst. prof. pharmacy Sch. of Pharmacy, 1985-87, asst. prof. pharmacy, 1987-90, clin. asst. prof. pharmacy, 1990-91, asst. prof. pharmacy, 1991-95; assoc. prof. pharmacy, 1995—; lectr. and presenter in field; pharmacokinetics cons. VA Med. Ctr., Buffalo, 1986-91; curriculum com. mem. Sch. of Pharmacy, SUNY, Buffalo, 1990-91, mem. Ctr. for Clin. Pharmacy Rsch., 1989—, mem. substance abuse com., 1990—, mem. Doctor of Pharmacy Student Rsch. com., 1987—, mem. curriculum com. Doctor of Pharmacy program, 1984-86, mem. policy and implementation com., 1984-86; quality assurance com. Buffalo Gen. Hosp. Corp., 1981-82, investigational rev. bd., 1982-83; mem. med. adv. com. West N.Y. Kidney Found., 1994—. Contbr. chpts. to Textbook of Pharmacology, 1991; contbr. numerous articles to profl. jours. including Transplantation, Clin. Pharmacology and Therapeutics, Clin. Nephrology, Clin. Transplantation, others. Recipient Outstanding Young Women of Am. award, 1984, Achievement award Albany Coll. Pharmacy, 1984; grantee Upjohn, 1984-86, 88, 90-91, 93, 95. Mem. AAAS, AAUW, Internat. Soc. Immunopharmacology, Am. Coll. Clin. Pharmacy, (mem. devel. and steering com. N.Y. state chpt. 1990-91, other coms. 1991-93), Am. Soc. Hosp. Pharmacists, Am. Assn. Colls. Pharmacy, Am. Fedn. Aging Rsch., Rho Chi. Office: SUNY Sch of Pharmacy Dept Pharmacy Practice 313 Cooke Hall Buffalo NY 14260-1200

TOROK, JOHN ANTHONY, III, dentist, financial analyst, portfolio manager; b. Cin., July 16, 1952; s. John Anthony Jr. and Anne Champ (Busch) T.; m. Jacquelyn Ann Zeiser, Aug. 26, 1977; children: Amanda, Morgan. BS in Biology with honors, U. Cin., 1974; DDS, Ohio State U., 1977; MBA in Fin., U. Cin., 1986, postgrad. in law, 1986—. Gen. practice dentistry Cin., 1977—; pres. Torok Investment Counsel, 1989—; gen. ptnr. Anthony Alexander and Assocs., 1989—. Cardio Pulmonary Resuscitation instr. Am. Heart Assn., Lake County, Ill., 1977-79. Served to lt. USN, 1977-79. Recipient Disting. Service award Lake County Heart Assn., 1979, Disting. Service award United Appeal Assn, 1981; named one of Outstanding Young Men Am., U.S. Jaycees, Cin., 1983. Mem. ADA, Ohio Dental Assn., Cin. Dental Soc., Assn. Am. Mil. Surgeons, Ohio State U. Alumni Assn. for Dentists, Mensa. Republican. Roman Catholic. Club: U. Cin. Vets. Lodge: KC.

TORRADO RIDGLEY, BEATRIZ M., physician; b. Santa Monica, Calif., Oct. 28, 1965; d. Antonio and Evangelina (Laino Rios) Torrado; m. Erik Duke Ridgley, Aug. 1, 1992; 1 child, Jacqueline Eve. BA in Cell Biology and Biochemistry, U. Calif., San Diego, 1988, BA in Spanish Lit., 1988; DO, U. New Eng., 1994. Resident Downey (Calif.) Cmty. Hosp., 1994—. Republican. Roman Catholic. Home: 11356 Burnham St Los Angeles CA 90049

TORRES, ISRAEL, oral and maxillofacial surgeon; b. El Paso, Tex., Sept. 5, 1934; s. Francisco Mendoza and Manuela (Gallardo) T.; m. Karen Marie Hensley, Aug. 22, 1970; children: Michael, George Stanley, Dianna. BS, Tex. Western Coll., 1958; DDS, U. Tex.-Houston, 1963; postgrad. Health Sci. Ctr., Houston, 1963-66; diploma (hon.) XX Reunion de Provincia, Juarez, Chihuahua, Mexico, 1970, Ateneo Odontologica Mexicano, Valle de Bravo, Mexico, 1973, Colegio de Cirujanos Mexicanos, Juarez, 1975, 84. Cert. instr. Advanced Cardiac Life Support, 1986—. Diplomate Am. Bd. Oral and Maxillofacial Surgery. Resident in oral surgery Methodist Hosp., Houston, 1963-64, Ben Taub Hosp., Houston, 1964-65, Hermann Hosp., Houston, 1965-66; practice dentistry specializing in oral and maxillofacial surgery, El Paso, 1966—; mem. staff Sun Towers Hosp., chief oral and maxillofacial surgery, 1975, 76, 77, 93; gov. appointee Tex. State Bd. Dental Examiners, 1993-95; instr. pathology El Paso C.C., 1975-76; lectr. in field; OMS cons. Latuna Fed. Correct Inst. Author, editor: Magnificent Obsession: In Quest of High Mountain Game, 1990; contbg. author Asian Hunter, 1989; contbr. articles to Jour. Oral/Maxillofacial Surgery. Bd. dirs. Am. Cancer Soc., El Paso, 1971-73, El Paso Cancer Treatment Ctr., 1971-74; bd. dirs. West Tex. Health Systems Agy., 1980-82, chmn., 1981-82; med. adv. com. W. Tex. Council of Regional Health. Recipient Bowie Exes award, El Paso, 1982, Mexican Consul Gen. Award of Appreciation, 1986, Mexican Social Security Service Award of Appreciation, 1986. Fellow Am. Coll. Oral and Maxillofacial Surgeons, Am. Assn. Oral and Maxillofacial Surgeons, Internat. Assn. Oral and Maxillofacial Surgeons, Southwest Soc. Oral and Maxillofacial Surgeons, Acad. Internat. Dental Studies, Pan Am. Med. Assn., EPSDT (dental adv. and rev. com. 1985-86), Tex. Soc. Oral and Maxillofacial Surgeons, The Explorers Club; mem. El Paso Dist. Dental Soc. (pres. 1979), U. Tex. Dental Br. Alumni Assn. (life), Nat. Rifle Assn. (life), Tex. Rifle Assn. (life), Am. Found. for N.Am. Wild Sheep, Internat. Sheep Hunting Assn. Republican. Roman Catholic. Clubs: Anthony Rod and Gun, Grand Slam (life). Avocations: high mountain sheep hunting; outdoor activities. Home: 6632 Westside Dr El Paso TX 79932-2623 Office: 1201 E Schuster Ave Bldg 4A El Paso TX 79902-4646

TORRES, JAMES C., II, emergency physician; b. Englewood, N.J., Nov. 13, 1959; s. James C. Torres and Margaret (Kee) Devan. MD, Mount Sinai Med. Sch., 1985. Attending physician emergency medicine Providence/Gen. Hosp. Ctr., Everett, 1991—; med. dir. Shannon Ambulance, Snohomish, Wash. Recipient Congl. Medal of Merit, 1977.

TORRES-AYBAR, FRANCISCO GUALBERTO, medical educator; b. San Juan, P.R., July 12, 1934; s. Francisco and Maria (Aybar) Torres; m. Elga Arroyo; children: Elga, JoAnn Marie. BS, U. P.R., 1956; MD, U. Barcelona, Spain, 1963. Diplomate Am. Bd. Pediatrics. Chief pediatric cardiology Ponce (P.R.) Dist. Hosp., 1970-91, chmn. dept. pediatrics, 1971-91, med. dir., 1980, prog. dir. pediatric tng. prog., 1970-91; prof., chmn. dept. pediatrics Cath. Univ. Sch. of Medicine, Ponce, 1978-80; chmn., dept. pediatrics Damas Hosp., Ponce, 1985—; prof., chmn. dept. pediatrics Ponce Sch. of Medicine, 1980—. Mem. editl. bd. Sci.-Ciencia jour., ponce, 1975-95; contbr. articles to profl. jours. Fellow Am. Acad. Pediatrics, Am. Coll. Physicians, Am. Coll. Cardiology, Am. Coll. Internat. Physicians, British Royal Soc. Health, InterAm. Coll. Physicians and Surgeons; mem. AAUP, Phi Delta Kappa. Republican. Roman Catholic. Home: A26 Jacaranda Ponce PR 00731 Office: 13 Calle Mayor Ponce PR 00731-5025

TORRESE, DANTE MICHAEL, prosthodontist, educator; b. Yonkers, N.Y., Feb. 12, 1949; s. Dante Angelo and Matilda (Dal Lago) T.; m. Camille Patricia DiPaola, Aug. 7, 1982. BS in Biology, Manhattan Coll., 1971; DDS, Columbia U., 1975; prosthodontic cert. NYU, 1983. Resident in dentistry Presbyn. Hosp., N.Y.C., 1975-76; clin. instr. dentistry Columbia U., N.Y.C., 1976-78, asst. clin. prof. dentistry, 1978—; pvt. practice dentistry, Yonkers, N.Y., 1976—; attending dentist Presbyn. Hosp., N.Y.C., 1976-86; lectr. in field. Recipient Am. Acad. Oral Pathology Grad. award, 1975; Densply Corp. award for removable prosthodontics, 1975; Psi Omega Scholastic Achievement award, 1975. Fellow Am. Coll. of Dentists, Royal Soc. Health; mem. NRA (life), Yonkers Dental Soc., 9th Dist. State Dental Soc., Invested Baker St. Irregular, Sherlock Holmes Wireless Soc., Yonkers Amateur Radio Club, Westchester Astronomy Club, Exch. Club (sec. 1979—), Three Garridebs of Westchester County Club, Priory Scholars of N.Y.C. Club, Montague Street Lodgers of Bklyn. Club, Omicron Kappa Upsilon. Office: 984 N Broadway Ste 503 Yonkers NY 10701-1308

TORRES-GIL, FERNANDO M., federal official; b. Salinas, Calif., June 24, 1948. BA in Polit. Sci., San Jose State U., 1970; MSW, Brandeis U., 1972, PhD, 1976. Spl. asst. to sec. Dept. Health, Edn. and Welfare, Washington, 1978-79; spl. asst. to sec. Dept. Health and Human Svcs., Washington, 1979-80, asst. sec. for aging, 1993—; prof. gerontology and pub. adminstrn. U. So. Calif., 1981-91, assoc. dir. Nat. Resource Ctr. on Minority Aging Populations, 1988-92, prof. social welfare, 1991-93; staff dir. Select Com. on Aging, U.S. Ho. of Reps., Washington, 1985-87. Contbr. articles to profl. jours. White House fellow, 1978-79. Mem. Am. Soc. Aging (pres. 1989-92). Office: Dept Health and Human Svcs 200 Independence Ave SW Washington DC 20201-0004

TORRES MEDINA, EMILIO, oncologist, consultant; b. Mexico, Aug. 8, 1934; s. Manuel Torres and Juana Medina; m. Luisa Torres Dec. 6, 1966; children: Patricia, Ana Luisa, Veronica, Jesus Manuel. MD, U. Mex., 1958-64. Cert. Consejo Mexicano de Radioterapia and Consejo Mexicano de Oncologia. Internist Hosp. of Nutrition, Mex., 1965-67; oncologist Hosp. of Oncology, Mex., 1967-70; chief dept. radiation Clin. of Parque, Chih, Mexico, 1970-80, chief of med. edn., 1974-78; chief dept. radiation Centro Oncologico del Norte, Juarez, Mexico, 1981-95; chief. of med. edn. I.S.S.S.T.E., Juarez, Mexico, 1984-85; oncologist I.S.S.S.T.E., Juarez, 1981-85; oncology prof. Uach Y Uacj, Juarez, Mexico, 1981-92; mem. med. coun. Pensiones Civiles del Edo., Juarez, Chih., 1985-90; med. dir. Pensionesl Civiles del Edo., Juarez, Chih., 1982-88, Electronic Diagnosis of Juarez, 1981-92; oncologist cons. Gen. Hosp. of Juarez City, 1988-95. Author: Policitemia on Rats by Hemolizates, 1965, Alkil beta-d Glicosias on Human Lymphs, 1970. Advisor Juarez Cancer Soc., 1986-95. Mem. ASTRO, ASCO, Soc. Mex. Est. Oncol. Capitulo Chihuahua (pres. 1990-92), Soc. Medicina Interna Cd. Juarez (pres. 1992). Office: Centro Oncologico del Norte, Plutarco Elias Calles 1235, 32350 Juarez Mexico

TORRES MORERA, LUIS, anesthesiologist, researcher; b. Sevilla, Spain, Apr. 13, 1953; s. Luis Torres and Angeles Morera; m. M. Jose Terrero, Mar. 18, 1978; children: Luis, M. Jose. Physician, Med. Sch., Sevilla, Spain, 1976; MD, Med. Sch., Badajoz, Spain, 1983. Resident in anesthesiology Insalud, Badajoz, 1977-80, staff anesthesiology, 1980-87; head dept. SAS, Cadiz, Spain, 1987—, dir. pain unit, 1989—; staff Asociacion Andaluza Extremeña de Anestesifologia y Reanimacion, 1993—. Editor: Tratamiento Del Dolor En Atencion Primaria, 1996, Medicina Del Dolor, 1996; editor sec. Jour. Algia; dir. Spanish Pain Soc. Jour., 1994—. Named El Medico Author of the Yr., 1996. Mem. Sociedad Andaluza del Dolor spain (pres. 1996—), Spanish Pain Soc., Spanish Anesthesiology Soc., IASP. Roman Catholic. Home: Avenida de Cadiz 58A, 11500 El Puerto de Santa Maria Cadiz, Spain Office: H U Puerta Del Mar, Avenida Ana De Viya 21, 11009 Cadiz Spain

TORRIENTE, LUIS RAFAEL, physician; b. Palma Soriano, Oriente, Cuba, Aug. 19, 1932; came to U.S., 1957; s. Luis and Zoila Marina (Marti) T.; m. Dolores Melba Guinart, July 19, 1957 (div. Jan. 1984; m. Margaret Claire Rank, Jan. 11, 1984; children: Suzanne Luisa, Daniel Luis. MD, U. Havana, Cuba, 1957. Diplomate Am. Bd. Internal Medicine. Pvt. practice Chgo., 1962-78, Melbourne, Fla., 1984—. Lt. col. USAF, 1978-84. Roman Catholic. Home: 548 Rio Pino N Indialantic FL 32903 Office: 1430 Valentine St Melbourne FL 32901

TORRUELLA, JUAN EUGENIO, clinical psychologist, consultant; b. Ponce, P.R., Oct. 25, 1960; s. Guillermo J. Torreulla and Ileana Maria Soler. BA, DePauw U., 1980; MS with distinction, Caribbean Ctr. Advanced Studies, 1983, PsyD with distinction, 1990; MA, Columbia U., 1988. Nat. cert. sch. psychologist; lic. psychologist P.R.; lic. bilingual sch. psychologist N.Y.; diplomate Am. Bd. Med. Psychotherapists, Am. Bd. Vocat. Neuropsychology. Psychoednl. cons. Transitions Ednl. Svcs., Inc., Rio Piedras, P.R., 1981-83; chief exec. officer Sistema Delta Corp., San Juan, P.R., 1983-85; bilingual staff psychologist, coord. consultation svcs. Worcester (Mass.) Youth Guidance Ctr., 1985-86; bilingual sch. psychologist com. of handicapped N.Y.C. Bd. Edn., 1986-88; pvt. practice clin. and neuropsychology, Rio Piedras, 1982-83, 88—; bilingual psychologist, cons. East Harlem Consultation Svcs., N.Y.C., 1987-88; mental health cons. Office Human Devel. Svcs., HHS, 1989-92; clin. psychologist Dept. Anti-Addiction Svcs., Rio Pedras, 1989-91; psychoednl. cons. Nat. Sch. Svcs., Inc., 1991-92; clin. psychologist Administrn. Juvenile Instns., Guaynabo, P.R., 1990-92; part time prof. psychology Intra-Am. U. Grad. Sch. Behavioral Scis., P.R., 1993. Adv., cons. Parent's Adv. Coun., Worcester, 1985-86. Recipient N.Y. State Senate Scholastic Achievment award, 1987; fellow Am. Bd. Vocat. Experts, 1987—; Nat. Hispanic scholar, 1986-88. Mem. NASP, Assn. Children and Adults with Attention Deficit Disorder, P.R. Psychol. Assn., Am. Bd. Vocat. Experts. Roman Catholic. Home: Austral 4 Altamira Rio Piedras PR 00920 Office: Cond Iberia I Ste G-1 Altamira San Juan PR 00920

TORVIK, PATRICIA ANN, health facility executive; b. Ivanhoe, Minn., Oct. 3, 1938; d. Carl Elmo and Wilma Gertrude (Weigert) Nyhus; m. Peter John Torvik, Sept. 20, 1958; children: Peter John, Jr., Carl Fredric. BS, Wright State U., 1972, MEd, 1977; PhD, Ohio State U., 1983. Cert. mental health adminstr. Tchr. Dayton (Ohio) Pub. Schs., 1972-78; teaching asst. Ohio State U., Columbus, 1978-80; supr. teaching Dayton Mental Health Ctr., 1980-82, program dir., 1982-84, asst. to supt., 1984-86, supt., 1986-89, chief exec. officer, 1989—; clin. prof. Schs. Medicine and Profl. Psychology, Wright State U., Dayton, 1986—. Bd. dirs. Met. Chs. United, Dayton, 1978-86; mem. Dayton Women's Coalition, 1984-88; office chairperson Montgomery County United Way, Dayton, 1986. Named one of Ten Top Women local newspapers, 1985. Mem. Internat. Assn. Psychosocial Rehab. Services, Assn. Mental Health Adminstrs., Ohio Assn. Mental Health Adminstrs., Ohio Supt.'s Assn. Democrat. Presbyterian. Home: 1866 Winchester Rd Xenia OH 45385-9740 Office: Dayton Mental Health Ctr 2611 Wayne Ave Dayton OH 45420-1833

TOSCANO, ARNOLD J., emergency nurse, educator; b. Newark, Oct. 22, 1957; s. Arnold Richard and Mariana Carmella (D'Ameico) T. BSN, Wilkes Coll., Wilkes-Barre, Pa., 1983. Cert. emergency nurse, emergency med. technician, trauma, BLS, advanced burn life support, TNCC instr., ENPC. Asst. head nurse, emergency dept. Robert Wood Johnson U. Hosp., New Brunswick, N.J., Beth Israel Med. Ctr., Newark; charge nurse, emergency dept. St. Joseph's Hosp. and Med. Ctr., Paterson, N.J.; asst. nurse mgr. emergency dept. St. Joseph's; nurse mgr. emergency dept. Med. Ctr. Del.; clin. preceptor in paramedic tng. program. Capt. USAFR. Mem. AACN, Emergency Nurses Assn., Am. Men in Nursing, Am. Trauma Soc., Nat. Flight Nurses Assn.

TOSCANO, JAMES VINCENT, medical institute administration; b. Passaic, N.J., Aug. 8, 1937; s. William V. and Mary A. (DeNigris) T.; m. Sharon Lee Bowers; children: Shawn, Lauren, David Brendan, Dania. A.B. summa cum laude, Rutgers U., 1959; M.A., Yale U., 1960. Lectr. Wharton Sch., U. Pa., 1961-64; chief opinion analyst Pa. Opinion Poll, 1962-64; mng. dir. World Press Inst., St. Paul, 1964-68; exec. dir. World Press Inst., 1968-72; dir. devel. Macalester Coll., St. Paul, 1972-74; v.p. resource devel. and public affairs Mpls. Soc. Fine Arts, 1974-79; pres. Minn. Mus. Art, 1979-81; exec. v.p. Park Nicollet Med. Found., 1981-95; corp. sec. Park Nicollet Med. Ctr., 1983-86; sr. v.p. Am. Med. Ctrs., Inc., 1985-87; exec. v.p. Inst. for Rsch. and Edn. Health Sys. Minn., Mpls., 1996—; adj. prof. sch. of mgmt. U. St. Thomas, 1989—. Author: The Chief Elected Official in the Penjerdel Region, 1964; co-author, co-editor: The Integration of Political Communities, 1964. Bd. dirs., exec. com., World Press Ins., 1972—; bd. dirs., chmn. Southside Newspaper Mpls., 1975-79; chmn. com. to improve student behavior St. Paul Pub. Schs., 1977-79; bd. dirs. Planned Parenthood St. Paul, 1965-72; emeritus dir. Help Enable Alcoholics Receive Treatment; mem. St. Paul Heritage Preservation Commn., 1979-82, vice chmn., 1981; mem. Citizens Adv. Com. on Cable Comm.; bd. dirs. Citizens League, 1980, Park Nicollet Med. Found., 1981-95, Inst. for Rsch. and Edn., Health Sys. Minn., 1996. African-Am. Culture Ctr., 1979-82, Minn. Composers Forum, 1981-85, St. Paul Chamber Orch., 1976-80, 83-89, United Theol. Sem., 1985-88; bd. dirs., mem. exec. com. Med. Alley Assn., 1986—; mem. task force on tech. assessment Med. Alley, 1992-93; mem. health affairs adv. com. Acad. Health Ctr. U. Minn., 1988-95; bd. dirs. Mother Cabrini House, 1985-92, Minn. Civil Justice Coalition, 1987-91, also chmn.; chmn. Gov.'s Task Force on Health Care Promotion, 1985-86, mem. Gov.'s Com. Promotion Health Care Resources, 1986-87; chmn. bd. Minn. Fin. Counseling Svcs., Inc., 1990-93; mem. task force cost effectiveness Med. Alley, 1994-95. Mem. Minn. Newspaper Found. (bd. dirs. 1987-92), Minn. Coun. Nonprofits (bd. dirs. 1989-95, bd. mem. Plymouth Music series 1993-96, alt. Minn. Healthcare Commn., 1993-95, mem. Minn. Healthcare Commn., 1995—, chair task force on med. edn. and rsch. costs 1994-96; chair com. on med. rsch. and edn. costs, 1996—, liaison health tech. adv. com. 1993—), Skylight Club, Informal Club. Address: 1982 Summit Ave Saint Paul MN 55105-1460 Office: Inst for Rsch and Edn Health Sys Minn 3800 Park Nicollet Blvd Minneapolis MN 55416

TOSKES, PHILLIP PAUL, physician, educator, clinical researcher; b. Balt., Md., Jan. 4, 1940; s. John F. and Mary R. (Vonelli) T.; m. Patricia A. Sponsel, June 3, 1961; children: Tammy Lynn Price, Tracey Lynn, Steven D. BA, Johns Hopkins U., 1961; MD, U. Md., 1965. Diplomate Am. Bd. Internal Medicine (bd. dirs.), Am. Bd. Gastroenterology. Intern, resident U. Md. Hosp., Balt., 1965-68; fellow in gastroenterology Hosp. U. Pa., Phila., 1968-70; asst. prof. medicine U. Fla., Gainesville, 1973-75, assoc. prof. medicine, 1975-78, prof. medicine, 1978—, dir. divsn. gastro, hepatology, 1978—; chief gastro sect. Gainesville VA Med. Ctr., 1973-92; mem. adv. bd. Lederle Labs, Pearl River, N.Y., 1986—, Solvay Labs, Marietta, Ga., 1990—, Martek Inc., Columbia, Md., 1991—; chmn. Nat. Digestive Disease Adv. Bd., Washington, 1992-94. Author chpts. to books. Maj. U.S. Army, 1970-73. Recipient Disting. Achievement award Can. Gastroenterol. Assn., 1982. Fellow ACP (Meade Johnson scholar 1966-68); mem. Am. Soc. Clin. Investigation, Am. Fedn. Clin. Rsch., Am. Gastroenterol. Assn. Home: 202 NW 114th Way Gainesville FL 32607-1122 Office: U Fla Box 100214 1600 SW Archer Rd Gainesville FL 32610

TOSTESON, DANIEL CHARLES, physiologist, medical school dean; b. Milw., Feb. 5, 1925; s. Alexis H. and Dilys (Bodycombe) T.; m. Penelope Kinsley, Dec. 17, 1949 (div. 1969); children: Carrie Marias, Heather Tosteson, Tor, Zoe Losada; m. Magdalena Tieffenberg, July 8, 1969; children: Joshua, Ingrid. Student, Harvard U., 1942-44, MD, 1949; DSc (hon.), U. Copenhagen, 1979; Dr. hon. causa, U. Liege, 1983; DSc (hon.), Med. Coll. Wis., 1984, NYU, 1992; DHL (hon.), Johns Hopkins U., 1993; Dr. honoris causa, Cath. U. Louvain, 1996, Duke U., 1996, Emory U., 1996. Fellow physiology Harvard Med. Sch., 1947-48; intern, then asst. resident medicine Presbyn. Hosp., N.Y.C., 1949-51; research fellow medicine Brookhaven Nat. Lab., 1951-53; lab. kidney and electrolyte metabolism Nat. Heart Inst., 1953-55, 57; research fellow biol. isotope research lab. Nat. Heart Inst., Copenhagen, 1955-56; research fellow Physiol. Lab., Cambridge, Eng., 1956-57; assoc. prof. physiology Washington U. Sch. Medicine, St. Louis, 1958-61; prof., chmn. dept. physiology and pharmacology Duke U. Sch. Medicine, 1961-75, James B. Duke Distinguished prof., 1971-75; dean div. biol. scis., dean Pritzker Sch. Medicine U. Chgo., Lowell T. Coggleshall prof. med. scis., v.p. for Med. Center, 1975-77; dean and Caroline Shields Walker prof. physiology Harvard Med. Sch., Boston, 1977—; pres. Med. Center Harvard Med. Sch., 1977; mem. molecular biology panel NSF, 1959-62; cons. sci. rev. com. NIH, 1964-67, nat. adv. gen. med. scis. coun., 1982-86; mem. U.S. Office Tech. Assessment, 1976; ethics adv. bd. HEW, 1977-80; nat. adv. gen. med. scis. coun. NIH, 1982—; mem. governing bd. NRC, 1977; mem. sci. com. Found. pour l'Etude du Systeme Nerveux Central et Peripherique, 1982—; nat. adv. com. biomed. scis. PEW Scholars Program, 1984-87. Mem. Inst. Medicine NAS (coun. 1975-78, adv. bd. PEW scholars program 1984-85), AAAS, Am. Physiol. Soc. (council 1967-75, pres. 1973-74), Soc. Gen. Physiologists (pres. 1968-69), Biophys. Soc. (council 1970-73), Assn. Am. Med. Colls. (chmn. coun. acad. socs. 1969-70, chmn. assembly 1973-74, chmn. physician supply task force 1988-90, Abraham Flexner award 1991), Assn. Am. Physicians, Red Cell Club, Soc. Health and Human Values, Danish Royal Soc. (fellow), Alpha Omega Alpha. Office: Harvard Med Sch 25 Shattuck St Boston MA 02115-6027

TOSTI, DONALD THOMAS, psychologist, consultant; b. Kansas City, Mo., Dec. 6, 1935; s. Joseph T. Tosti and Elizabeth M. (Parsons) Tosti Addison; m. Carol J. Curless, Jan. 31, 1957 (dec. 1980); children: Rene, Alicia, Roxanna, Brett, Tabitha, Todd Marcus; m. Annette Brewer, Dec. 29, 1989. BS in Elec. Engring., U. N. Mex., 1957, MS in Psychology, 1962, PhD in Psychology, 1967. Chief editor Teaching Machines Inc., Albuquerque, 1960-64; div. mgr. Westinghouse Learning Corp., Albuquerque, 1964-70; founder, sr. v.p. Ind. Learning Systems, San Raphael, Calif., 1970-74, pres., 1974-76; chmn. bd. Omega Performance, San Francisco, 1976-77; pres. Operants Inc., San Rafael, 1978-81; v.p. Forum corp., San Rafael, 1981-83; mng. ptnr. Vanguard Cons. Group, San Francisco, 1983—. Author: TMI Programmed Arithmetic Series, 1960-63; Behavior Technology, 1970; A Guide to Child Development; Tactics of Communication; co-author: Learning Is Getting Easier, 1973; Introductory Psychology, 1981, Performance Based Management, Positive Leadership, 1986, Strategic Alliances, 1990, The Professional Manager, 1995, Power and Governance, 1996. Mem. APA, Internat. Soc. for Performance Improvement (v.p. rsch. 1983-85; outstanding mem. award 1984, life membership award 1984, outstanding product award 1974). Home: 41 Marinita Ave San Rafael CA 94901-3443

TOTER, KIMBERLY MROWIEC, nurse; b. Chgo., Apr. 22, 1956; d. A. Kenneth and Megan Dawson (Schiefer) Mrowiec; m. William Frank Toter, Dec. 16, 1978; children: William Kenneth, Kimberly Helen, Tod Frank, Matthew Jonathan, Haley Victoria, Toria Megan. BS in Biology, Millikin U., 1978; cert. sch. nursing, Decatur (Ill.) Meml. Hosp., 1978. RN, Ill.; cert. operating room nurse. Oper. room nurse Riddle Meml. Hosp., Media, Pa., 1979-89; pres., chief exec. officer Towic Med., Inc., Park Ridge, Ill., 1986—; staff nurse oper. room Luth. Gen. Hosp., Park Ridge, 1991; perioperative nurse, 1991—; instr. Delaware Community Coll., Media, 1986; reviewer, cons. Perioperative Nursing Care Planning; speaker laparoscopy seminar Luth. Gen. Hosp., 1992, 93. Contbg. author: Decision Making in Perioperative Nursing, 1987; also articles; patentee gastric drainage system. Cheerleading coach St. Paul of the Cross, 1993—. Recipient Young Alumnus of Yr. award Millikin U., 1991. Mem. Assn. Operat. Rm. Nurses (v.p. Southeast Pa. chpt. 1983-85, pres.-elect 1985-86, pres. 1986-87, ednl. chmn. 1983-85, chmn. bylaw and policy com. 1987—, bd. dirs. 1983-89, chmn. 1987-89, bd. dirs. NW suburban chpt. 1995—), Pa. Coun. Oper. Rm. Nurses, Am. Tech Mgmt. (bd. dirs. 1989—), Am. Reprographics Mgmt. (bd. dirs. 1989—), Pi Beta Phi. Roman Catholic.

TOTH, BENEDICT JOHN, physician; b. Vasboldogasszony, Hungary, Nov. 28, 1910; came to U.S., 1937, naturalized, 1942; s. Benedek Joseph and Maria (Doka) T.; M.D., U. Budapest, 1936; m. June Eileen Riley, Feb. 16, 1946; children—John Thomas. Intern, Univ. Hosps., Budapest, 1935-36; resident New Rochelle (N.Y.) Hosp., 1937-42; instr. pathology U. Budapest, 1935-36; chief radiology dept. St. Francis Hosp., Olean, N.Y., 1941-56, Salamanca Dist. Hosp., 1941-56, Tri-county Meml. Hosp., Gowanda, N.Y., 1953-70, Gowanda State Hosp., 1955-70, Cuba (N.Y.) Meml. Hosp., 1942-71, Chaffee Meml. Hosp., Springville, N.Y., 1956-70, Port Allecany Hosp., 1948-68, Wellsville (N.Y.) Meml. Hosp., 1943-47; cons. radiologist Cuba Meml. Hosp., 1971-82; chmn. com. N.Y. State Hosp. and Schs., 1965-66. Diplomate Am. Bd. Radiology. Mem. Cattaraugus County Med. Soc. (pres. 1961), N.Y. Radiol. Soc., Am. Coll. Radiology, AMA, N.Y. Med. Soc., Buffalo Radiol. Soc., Pa. Radiol. Soc., Radiol. Soc. N.Am., Am. Cancer Soc., Nat. Gastroent. Soc. Republican. Presbyterian. Club: Coral Gables (Fla.) Country. Contbr. articles in field to profl. jours. Address: 5317 Orduna Dr Coral Gables FL 33146-2640

TOTH, IMRE GERHARD, internist; b. Breslau, Germany, June 8, 1937; came to U.S., 1956; s. Laszlo Zoltan and Johanne Margarete (Boese) T.; m. Eleanor Mae Hodgins, May 15, 1965; children: Kimberly Michelle Genest, Randall Kenneth, Natalie Darlene. AB in Math., Harvard Coll., 1960; MD, NYU, 1964. Diplomate Am. Bd. Internal Medicine, Am. Bd. Internal Medicine, Am. Bd. Gastroenterology and Geriatrics, Am. Bd. Med. Mgmt. Intern Montefiore Hosp., Bronx, 1964-65; resident in medicine Boston VA Hosp., 1967-69, resident in gastroenterology, 1969-70, chief resident in hepatology, 1970-71; pvt. practice Hudson, Mass., 1971-95; v.p. medical affairs, med. dir. Healthsource Mass. Inc., Worcester, 1995—; asst. med. dir., cons. Tufts Associated Health Plan, Waltham, Mass., 1986-93, regional med. dir., 1993-95; pres., founder Assabet Valley Ind. Practice Assn., Marlborough, Mass., 1983-94; pres. med. staff Marlborough Hosp., 1983-84, v.p. clin. svcs., 1993-95; co-founder, chmn. New Health Enterprises, Inc., Marlborough, 1984-95; pres. Marlborough Physician Svcs. Corp., 1992-95. Pres. 1st Congl. Unitarian Ch., Harvard, Mass., 1990-93; coach Nashoba Regional High Sch. Chess Club, Bolton, Mass., 1980—. Lt. USNR, 1965-67, Vietnam. Master, postal chess U.S. Chess Fedn., 1989. Mem. AMA, Am. Gastroent. Assn., Am. Coll. Physician Execs., New Eng. Endoscopy Soc., Mass. Med. Soc. Unitarian-Universalist. Home: 37 Flanagan Rd Bolton MA 01740-1038 Office: Healthsource Mass Inc Ste 300 100 Front St Worcester MA 01608

TOTH, PAUL W., psychotherapist; b. Oct. 21, 1961. BS, St. Vincent Coll., 1983; MS, Hahnemann U., 1985; PhD, Union Inst., 1996. Cert. med. psychotherapist, cert. addiction counselor (CAC), internat. cert. addiction counselor. Pvt. practice Health Profl. svcs., Phila., Pa.; clin. coord. Eagleville (Pa.) Hosp.; cons., psychotherapist, Health Profl. Svcs., Phila., psychotherapist, Eagleville (Pa.) Hosp. Mem. APA, ACA, Nat. Assn. for the Advancement Psychoanalysis, Am. Assn. Counseling and Devel., Am. Bd. Med. Psychotherapists, Del. Valley Group Psychotherapy Soc., Phila. Soc. for Psychoanalytic Psychology, Pa. Chem. Abuse Cert. Bd. Home: 63 Lynn Dr Norristown PA 19403-2934

TÓTH, ZOLTÁN ÁGOSTON, biologist, researcher; b. Budapest, Hungary, Mar. 31, 1968; s. Ágoston and Ágostonné (Lukács) T.; m. Krisztina Gál, Aug. 1, 1992; children: Gergely, Viktória. Biology degree, Eötvös U., Budapest, 1992; expert in gen. radiation protection, Postgrad. Med. U., Budapest, 1993. Prof.'s asst. dept. plant anatomy Eötvös U., Budapest, 1992-96; project mgr. Chem. Works Gedeon Richter, Budapest, 1996—. Mem. Hungarian Pharm. Soc. Office: Chem Works Gedeon Richter, Gyomroi u 19 21, 1103 Budapest Hungary

TOUCHARD, JACQUES JEAN HENRY, retired physician; b. Bordeaux, Gìronde, France, Mar. 17, 1921; s. Georges Pierre and Ellen Louise (Labroue) T.; m. Alice Colette Theilacker, Jan. 11, 1945; children: Yves, Kathleen, Florence, Marie-Pierre, Frédéric. MD, U. Bordeaux, 1947, diploma in radiology, 1957. Asst. radiologist Bergonié Inst., Bordeaux, 1957-67, chief dept., 1967-87; ret., 1987; mem. edn. and rsch. com. for oncology. Hon. councilor Clairac, Lot et Garonne, 1955. Mem. Radiotherapie section de Soc. Française de Radiologie, European Soc. Therapeutic Radiology and Oncology. Home: rue Bertrand de Goth 152, 33800 Gironde Bordeaux, France Office: Bergonié Inst, rue de Saint Genes 180, 33076 Gironde Bordeaux, France

TOUR, ROBERT LOUIS, ophthalmologist; b. Sheffield, Ala., Dec. 30, 1918; s. R.S. and Marguerite (Meyer) T.; m. Mona Marie Elien, Oct. 3, 1992. Chem.E., U. Cin., 1942, M.D., 1950. Intern, U. Chgo. Clinics, 1950-51; resident U. Calif. Med. Center-San Francisco, 1951-54; practice medicine, specializing in ophthalmology, occupational medicine and plasmapheresis, San Francisco, 1954-76, Fairbanks, Alaska, 1976-79, Phoenix, 1979—; clin. prof. ophthalmology U. Calif.-San Francisco, 1974-76. Maj. AUS, 1942-45. Diplomate Am. Bd. Ophthalmology. Fellow ACS, Am. Acad. Ophthalmology; mem. AMA, MENSA, Ariz. Ophthal. Soc., Phoenix Ophthal. Soc., Calif. Assn. Ophthalmology, Contact Lens Assn. Ophthalmologists, Pacific Coast Oto-Ophthal. Soc., Ariz. Med. Assn., Maricopa County Med. Soc. , F.C. Cordes Eye Soc., Masons, K.T., Lions, Shriners, Sigma Xi, Nu Sigma Nu, Alpha Tau Omega, Tau Beta Pi, Alpha Omega Alpha, Phi Lambda Upsilon, Omicron Delta Kappa, Kappa Kappa Psi. Home: 2201 E Palmaire Ave Phoenix AZ 85020-5633

TOURETZ, LILLIAN CAROLE CONRAD, psychotherapist; b. N.Y.C., Oct. 17, 1923; d. Philip and Rose Helen Stetsky;m. Martin Conrad, June 3, 1944; children David, Donna; m. 2d, Arthur Touretz, May 28, 1977. BA, Hunter Coll., 1944; MSW, NYU, 1968. Diplomate Am. Bd. Examiners

Social Work. Asst. mgr. N.Y.C. Housing Authority, 1946-49; pres. Profl. Workers AFL-CIO, 1947-49; lectr., cons. in field, 1952-78; psychotherapist Pelham (N.Y.) Family Svc., 1968-77; pvt. practice psychotherapy, Hartsdale, N.Y., 1977—; field instr. Adelphi U., 1972-77. Chmn. United Jewish Appeal; v.p. regional bd. B'nai B'rith, chpt. pres., 1981-84, pres. Coun. of Pres. Mem. Nat. Assn. Social Workers (diplomate), Soc. Clin. Social Work Psychotherapists, Hunter Coll. Alumni Assn., NYU Alumni Assn. Democrat. Address: 55 Edgewood Rd Hartsdale NY 10530-1223

TOURLENTES, THOMAS THEODORE, psychiatrist; b. Chgo., Dec. 7, 1922; s. Theodore A. and Mary (Xenostathy) T.; m. Mona Belle Land, Sept. 9, 1956; children: Theodore W., Stephen C., Elizabeth A. BS, U. Chgo., 1945, MD, 1947. Diplomate Am. Bd. Psychiatry and Neurology (sr. examiner 1964-88, 90). Intern Cook County Hosp., Chgo., 1947-48; resident psychiatry Downey (Ill.) VA Hosp., 1948-51; practice medicine specializing in psychiatry Chgo., 1952, Camp Atterbury, Ind., 1953, Ft. Carson, Colo., 1954, Galesburg, Ill., 1955-71; staff psychiatrist Chgo. VA Clinic, 1952; clin. instr. psychiatry Med. Sch., Northwestern U., 1952; dir. mental hygiene consultation service Camp Atterbury, 1953-54, Ft. Carson, 1953-54; asst. supt. Galesburg State Research Hosp., 1954-58, supt., 1958-71; dir. Comprehensive Community Mental Health Ctr. Rock Island and Mercer Counties; dir. psychiat. services Franciscan Hosp., 1971-85; chief mental health services VA Outpatient Clinic, Peoria, Ill., 1985-88; clin. prof. psychiatry U. Ill., Chgo. and Peoria, 1955—; preceptor in hosp. adminstrn. State U. Iowa, Iowa City, 1958-64; councilor, del. Ill. Psychiat. Soc.; chmn. liaison com. Am. Hosp. and Psychiat. Assns., 1978-79, chmn. Quality Care Bd., Ill. Dept. Mental Health, 1995—. Contbr. articles profl. jours. Mem. Gov. Ill. Com. Employment Handicapped, 1962-64; zone dir. Ill. Dept. Mental Health, Peoria, 1964-71; mem. Spl. Survey Joint Commn. Accreditation Hosps.; chmn. Commn. Cert. Psychiat. Adminstrs., 1979-81; pres. Knox-Galesburg Symphony Soc., 1966-68; bd. dirs. Galesburg Civic Music Assn., pres., 1968-70; chair Knox county United Way Campaign, 1989; pres. Civic Art Ctr., 1990-92. Capt. M.C. AUS, 1952-54. Fellow AAAS, AMA, Am. Psychiat. Assn. (chair hosp. and cmty. psychiatry award bd. 1989-90), Am. Coll. Psychiatrists, Am. Coll. Mental Health Adminstrs.; mem. Ill. Med. Soc. (chmn. aging com. 1968-71, coun. on mental health and addictions 1987-89), chair mental health substance abuse com. 1987-89), Ill. Psychiat. Soc. (pres. 1969-70), Am. Pub. Health Assn., Soc. Biol. Psychiatry, Ill. Hosp. Assn. (trustee 1968-70), Am. Coll. Hosp. Adminstrs., Assn. for Rsch. Nervous and Mental, Am. Assn. Psychiat. Adminstrs. (pres. 1980). Home and Office: 138 Valley View Rd Galesburg IL 61401-8524

TOURLITSAS, JOHN CONSTANTINE, radiologist; b. Cavala, Greece, Oct. 4, 1926; came to U.S., 1956; s. Constantine Nacos and Marica Constantine (Athanasiou) T. MD, U. Athens, 1955. Diplomat Am. Bd. Radiology. Intern Sioux Valley Hosp., Sioux Falls, S.D., 1956-57; resident Midway Hosp., Mpls.-St. Paul, 1957-59, New Eng. Deaconess Hosp., Harvard MEd. Sch., Boston, 1959-60, Boston U. Med. Ctr., Mass. Meml. Hosps., 1960-62, Royal Victoria Hosp., McGill U., Montreal, Can., 1963-65; attending, cons. radiologist Bronx-Lebanon Hosp. Ctr., Albert Einstein Coll. Medicine, 1968-95; retired, 1995; instr. radiology Albert Einstein Coll. Medicine, 1972-77. Joslin Clinic fellow, Boston, 1959, rsch. fellow U. Toronto, 1962-63. Fellow Am. Coll. Chest Physicians; mem. Am. Coll. Radiology, Am. Roentgen Ray Soc., Radiol. Soc. N.Am., N.Y. State Med. Soc. Episcopalian.

TOURNEY, GARFIELD, psychiatrist, educator; b. Quincy, Ill., Feb. 6, 1927; s. Guy and Rose Dora (Werner) T.; m. Helen Winifred Wohler, Apr. 4, 1950; children: Carolyn Tourney Florek, Patricia Ann, Catherine Tourney Hughes. BS, U. Ill., 1946, MD, 1948; MS, U. Iowa, 1952; DLitt (hon.), Quincy U., 1992. Intern Univ. Hosps., Iowa City, 1948-49; resident in psychiatry Psychopathic Hosp., Iowa City, 1949-52; instr. Colo. Psychopathic Hosp., Denver, 1952-53; instr., asst. prof. U. Miami, Fla., 1953-55; from asst. prof. to prof. Lafayette Clinic, Wayne State U., Detroit, 1955-67; prof. U. Iowa, Iowa City, 1967-71; prof., vice chmn., chmn. dept. psychiatry Wayne State U., 1971-78; prof. dept. psychiatry U. Miss., Jackson, 1978-92, prof. emeritus, 1992—; part-time cons. in psychiatry, 1992—; psychiat. cons. VA hosps. and others, Iowa, Mich., Miss., 1955—; chief dept. psychiatry Harper Hosp., Detroit, 1971-78. Contbr. numerous chpts. to books and articles and revs. to profl. jours. Bd. dirs. Northeast Mental Health Ctr., Detroit, 1974-78. Fellow Am. Psychiat. Assn. (libr. and history com. 1985-90, chmn. 1989-90, cons. on 150th anniversary 1990-94, Garfield and Helen W. Tourney Rare Books Rm. of Libr. and Archives dedicated in his honor 1994); mem. AMA, Am. Osler Soc., Mich. Psychiat. Soc. (Presdl. award 1977). Home and Office: 106 Cherry Hills Dr Jackson MS 39211-2507

TOURTELLOTTE, CHARLES DEE, physician, educator; b. Kalamazoo, Aug. 28, 1931; s. Dee and Helen May (Lotz) T.; m. Barbara Richwine, June 25, 1955; children: Daniel DeWitt, Elizabeth Anne, William Charles, Scott David. AB, Johns Hopkins U., 1953; MS in Biochemistry, MD, Temple U., 1957. Diplomate Am. Bd. Internal Medicine. Intern, resident in medicine U. Mich. Hosp., Ann Arbor, 1957-60; fellow in rheumatology Temple U. Hosp., Phila., 1960-61; fellow in biochemistry Rockefeller U., N.Y.C., 1961-63; faculty Sch. Medicine, Temple U., 1963—, prof. medicine, 1972—; chief rheumatology Temple U. Hosp., 1966—, pres. med. staff, bd. govs., 1984-86; dir. Greater Delaware Valley Arthritis Control Program, 1974-77; pres. Eastern Pa. chpt. Arthritis Found., 1972-74; mem. active/cons. staff 10 area and regional hosps. Contbr. chpts. to textbooks, articles to profl. jours.; Editorial Bd.: Arthritis and Rheumatism, 1969-77, 19th-24th Rheumatism Revs, 1969-81. Mem. Haddonfield (N.J.) Bd. Edn., 1968-74, pres., 1974; mem. Borough of Haddonfield Environ. Comm., 1975-87, chmn., 1977-85; mem. Haddonfield Civic Assn., 1963—; South N.J. chmn. Johns Hopkins U. Alumni Schs. Com., 1975-90; trustee Bobby Fulton Meml. Fund, 1979—. Served with AUS, 1953-61. Helen Hay Whitney Found. fellow, 1962-63; Arthritis Found. fellow, 1963-66. Fellow ACP, Phila. Coll. Physicians, Am. Coll. Rheumatology (founding fellow); mem. AMA, Am. Fedn. for Clin. Rsch., Am. Soc. Internal Medicine, Pa. Soc. Internal Medicine, Pa. Med. Soc., Phila. County Med. Soc., Babcock Surg. Soc., Phila. Rheumatism Soc. (pres. 1968-69), Pa. Rheumatology Soc. (founding pres. 1985-86), N.J. Soc. of Pa., Huguenot Soc. Pa., Tavistock County Club (N.J.), Little Egg Harbor Yacht Club, Med. Club of Phila. (bd. dirs. 1991—), Diamond Club (Yale U.), Sigma Xi, Alpha Omega Alpha, Delta Upsilon, Phi Chi. Republican. Presbyterian. Clubs: Tavistock Country (N.J.); Little Egg Harbor Yacht, Med. of Phila. (bd. dirs. 1991—); Johns Hopkins; Diamond (Temple U.). Home: 6 Lane of Acres Haddonfield NJ 08033-3505 Office: Temple Univ Hosp Dept Rheumatology Philadelphia PA 19140-5192

TOURTELLOTTE, WALLACE WILLIAM, neurologist; b. Great Falls, Mont., Sept. 13, 1924; s. Nathaniel Mills and Frances Victoria (Charlton) T.; m. Jean Esther Toncray, Feb. 14, 1953; children: Wallace William, George Mills, James Millard, Warren Gerard. PhB, BS, U. Chgo., 1945, PhD, 1948, MD, 1951. Intern Strong Meml. Hosp. U. Rochester (N.Y.) Sch. Medicine and Dentistry, 1951-54; resident in neurology U. Mich. Med. Ctr., Ann Arbor, 1954-57, asst. prof. neurology, 1957-59, assoc. prof., 1959-66, prof., 1966-71; prof., vice chmn. dept. neurology UCLA, 1971—; chief neurology service West Los Angeles VA Med. Ctr., 1971—; vis. assoc. prof. Washington U., St. Louis, 1963-64; mem. med. adv. bd. Nat. Multiple Sclerosis Soc., 1968—, So. Calif. Multiple Sclerosis Socs., 1972—; dir. Multiple Sclerosis Rsch. and Treatment Ctr., Nat. Neurol. Rsch. Specimen Bank, 1971—. Author: Multiple Sclerosis, Clinical and Pathogenetic Basis, 1997; mem. editorial bd. Jour. Neurol. Sci., Revue Neurologica, Italian Jour. Neurol. Sci., Multiple Sclerosis Jour. Lt. (j.g.) M.C., USN, 1952-54. Recipient Disting. Alumni Service award U. Chgo., 1982. Fellow Am. Acad. Neurology (S. Weir Mitchell Neurology Reseach award 1959); mem. AAUP, Am. Neurol. Assn. (counselor 1982—, v.p. 1992), World Fedn. Neurology (founding mem.), Am. Assn. Neuropathologists, Internat. Soc. Neurochemsitry (founding mem.), Am. Soc. Pharmacology and Exptl. Therapeutics, Am. Soc. Neurochemistry (founding mem.), Soc. Neurosci., Conferie de la Chaine des Rotisseur (chevalier Los Angeles chpt.), Argentier du Baillage de Los Angeles, Ordre Mondial des Gourmets Degustateurs Etats-Unis, Pasadena Wine and Food Soc., Physician Wine & Food Soc., Soc. Med. Friends of Wine, Sigma Xi. Republican. Presbyterian. Home: 1140 Tellem Dr Pacific Palisades CA 90272-2244 Office: West Los Angeles VA Med Ctr 11301 Wilshire Blvd Los Angeles CA 90073

TOURTILLOTT, ELEANOR ALICE, nurse, educational consultant; b. North Hampton, N.H., Mar. 28, 1909; d. Herbert Shaw and Sarah (Fife) T. Diploma Melrose Hosp. Sch. Nursing, Melrose, Mass., 1930; BS, Columbia U., 1948, MA, 1949; edn. specialist Wayne State U., 1962. RN. Gen. pvt. duty nurse, Melrose, Mass., 1930-35; obstet. supr. Samaritan Hosp., Troy, N.Y., 1935-36, Meml. Hosp., Niagara Falls, N.Y., 1937-38, Lawrence Meml. Hosp., New London, Conn., 1939-42, New Eng. Hosp. for Women and Children, Boston, 1942-43; dir. H. W. Smith Sch. Practical Nursing, Syracuse, N.Y., 1949-53; founder, dir. assoc. degree nursing program Henry Ford Community Coll., Dearborn, Mich., 1953-74; dir. pioneering use of learning techs. via mixed media USPHS, 1966-71; prin. cons., initial coord. Wayne State U. Coll. Nursing, Detroit, 1975-78; cons. curriculum design, modular devel., instructional media Tourtillott Cons., Inc., Dearborn, Mich., 1974—; condr. numerous workshops on curriculum design, instructional media at various colls., 1966—; mem. Mich. Bd. Nursing, 1966-73, chmn., 1970-72, mem. rev. com. for constrn. nurse tng. facilities, div. nursing USPHS, 1967-70, mem. nat. adv. coun. on nurse tng., Dept. Health Edn. and Welfare, 1972-76. Author: Commitment-A Lost Characteristic, 1982; contbg. co-author: Patient Assessment-History and Physical Examination, 1975-78; contbr. chpts., articles, speeches to profl. publs. Served to capt. Nurse Corps, U.S. Army, 1943-47; ETO. Recipient Disting. Alumnae award Tchrs. Coll. Columbia U., 1974, Spl. tribute 77th Legislature Mich., 1974, Disting. Alumnae award Wayne State U., 1975, Disting. Service award Henry Ford Community Coll., 1982; established and endowed Eleanor Tourtillott Outstanding Student Nurse of Yr. award at Henry Ford C.C., 1993. Mem. DAR, ANA, Nat. League Nursing (chmn. steering com. dept. assoc. degree programs 1965-67, bd. dirs. 1965-67, 71-73, mem. assembly constituent leagues 1971-73, council assoc. degree programs citation 1974, Mildred Montag Excellence in Leadership award coun. assoc. degree programs 1994), Mich. League for Nursing (pres. 1969-71), Mich. Acad. Sci., Arts and Letters, Am. Legion, Tchrs. Coll. Alumnae Assn., Wayne State U. Alumnae Assn., Phi Lambda Theta, Kappa Delta Pi.

TOVAR, JUAN ANTONIO, pediatric surgeon, educator; b. Salamanca, Spain, June 30, 1944; s. Antonio Tovar and Consuelo Larrucea m. Annick Lefaure, Dec. 7, 1968; children: Daniel, Clara. MD, U. Salamanca, 1966; PhD, U. Valladolid, 1970. Cert. specialist in pediats. and pediat. surgery. Attending surgeon Hosp. La Paz, Madrid, 1971-76; rsch. fellow Childrens Hosp., L.A., 1974; chief surgeon Hosp. Aranzazu, San Sebastian, Spain, 1977-91; chief surgeon, chief dept. pediat. surgery Hosp. La Paz, Madrid, 1992—; prof. pediats. U. Pais Vasco, San Sebastian, 1980-91, U. Autonoma, Madrid, 1992—. Contbr. numerous sci. articles and book chpts. to profl. publs. Lt. Sanidad, 1967. Mem. French Assn. Pediat. Surgeons, Brit. Assn. Pediat. Surgeons, Spanish Assn. Pediat. Surgeons (pres. 1996-98), Polish Assn. Pediat. Surgeons (hon.), Can. Assn. Pediat. Surgeons (hon.), Asociacion Española de Pediatria (hon.). Home: Calendula 192, 28109 Soto de la Moraleja Madrid, Spain Office: Hosp Infantil La Paz, Castellana 261, 28046 Madrid Spain

TOWER, ALTON G., JR., pharmacist; b. Buffalo, N.Y., Jan. 15, 1927; m. Nan R. Spinner, Aug. 15, 1953; children: Adrienne, Michele, Renee. BS in Pharmacy, U. Buffalo, 1953. Registered pharmacist. Pharmacist Woldmans Drug Store, Buffalo, 1946-53; med. svc. rep. Strasenburgh Lab., Rochester, N.Y., 1953-66; pharmacist, mgr. Eckerd Drugs, Clearwater, Fla., 1966—. Bd. dirs. Am. Cancer Soc. Pinellas County, Fla., 1976—, pres., 1988-89, Life Saver award, 1988, life mem., 1995—, dir. cmty. affairs Pinellas Pharmacist Soc.; charter mem. Smoke Free Class of 2000, Pinellas County, 1988—. Recipient Vol. of Yr. award Am. Cancer Soc. Pinellas County, 1987, Life Saver award Am. Cancer Soc. Pinellas County, 1988, James Beal award Pharmacist of the Yr., Fla. Pharm. Assn., 1992; named Hon. Life Mem., Am. Cancer Soc. Pinellas County Unit, 1995. Mem. Am. Pharm. Assn., Fla. Pharmacy Assn. (bd. dirs. 1981-85, speaker ho. of dels. 1986, R.Q. Richards award 1989, Bowl of Hygeia award 1990, Sid Simkowitz Involvement award 1991), Pinellas County Pharmacy Soc. (life; dir. 1968-73, 78-81, 89-91, pres. 1973, 88, Pharmacist of Yr. 1973). Office: Eckerds # 2332 Pinellas Park FL 34666

TOWERS, BERNARD LEONARD, medical educator; b. Preston, Eng., Aug. 20, 1922; s. Thomas Francis and Isabella Ellen (Dobson) T.; m. Carole Ilene Lieberman (div. 1992); 1 child, Tiffany Sabrina; children from previous marriage: Helena Marianne, Celia Marguerite, Julie Carole. M.B., Ch.B., U. Liverpool, 1947; M.A., U. Cambridge, 1954. House surgeon Royal Infirmary, Liverpool, 1947; lectr. U. Bristol, 1949-50, U. Wales, 1950-54, Cambridge U., 1954-70; fellow Jesus Coll., 1957-70, steward, 1961-64, tutor, 1964-69; dir. med. studies, 1964-70; prof. pediatrics UCLA, 1971-84, prof. anatomy, 1971-91, prof. psychiatry, 1983-91, prof. emeritus anatomy and psychiatry, 1991—, convenor, moderator medicine and soc. forum 1974-89; pvt. practice integrative medicine, 1991—; co-dir. Program in Medicine, Law and Human Values, 1977-84; cons. Inst. Human Values in Medicine, 1971-84; adv. bd. Am. Teilhard Assn. for Future of Man, 1971—; v.p. Teilhard Centre for Future Man, London, 1974—. Author: Teilhard de Chardin, 1966, Naked Ape or Homo Sapiens?, 1969, Concerning Teilhard, 1969; also articles, chpts. on sci. and philosophy.; Editor anat. sect.: Brit. Abstracts Med. Scis, 1954-56, Teilhard Study Library, 1966-70; adv. bd.: Jour. Medicine and Philosophy, 1974-84. Served to capt. RAMC, 1947-49. NIH grantee, 1974-78; NEH grantee, 1977-83. Fellow Cambridge Philos. Soc., Royal Soc. Medicine; mem. Brit. Soc. History of Medicine, Soc. Health and Human Values (pres. 1977-78), Anat. Soc. G.B., Worshipful Soc. Apothecaries London, Am. Assn. for Study Mental Imagery, Western Assn. Physicians, Societe Europeene de Culture Venise. Office: 436 N Bedford Dr Ste 302 Beverly Hills CA 90210-4320

TOWERS, CRAIG V., physician; b. Lynwood, Calif., Oct. 13, 1955; m. Kelly Towers, May, 21, 1983; children: Rachel, Brian, Charles. BS in chemistry, Whittier Coll., 1977; MD, U. Kans., 1981. Diplomate Am. Bd. Ob-Gyn., Maternal Fetal Medicine. Intern Wesley Med. Ctr. U. Kans. Sch. Medicine, Wichita, 1981-82, resident ob-gyn., 1982-84, chief resident, 1984-85; assoc. prof. U. Calif., Irvine, 1993—, clin. instr. dept. ob-gyn., 1985-87, asst. prof., 1987-93; med. dir. perinatal svcs. Hoag Meml. Hosp. Presbyn., Newport Beach, Calif., 1987—; dir. perinatalogy Long Beach (Calif.) Women's Hosp., 1987—; maternal fetal med. fellows edn. coord. U. Calif., Irvine, 1994—, LBMMC, Long Beach, 1994—. Contbr. articles to profl. jours. Recipient Munzer Family award Excellence in Tchg. and Rsch. Meml. Med. Ctr. Found., 1993; C.V. Mosby scholar, 1981. Fellow Am. Coll. Ob-Gyn.; mem. AMA, Soc. Perinatal Obstetricians, L.A. Ob-Gyn. Soc., Omicron Delta Kappa, Alpha Omega Alpha. Office: MMCLB Perinatal Ctr 2801 Atlantic Ave Long Beach CA 90801

TOWLE, DAVID WALTER, osteopath; b. Greenwich, Conn., Feb. 15, 1955; s. Walter Raymond and Patricia (Bailey) T.; m. Janet Lillian Anderson, July 1, 1978; children: Christopher, Daniel. BS in Microbiology, U. Conn., 1977, MS in Pathobiology, 1979; DO, U. Osteo Medicine-Health Sci., Des Moines, 1986; MPH, La Salle U., Mandeville, La., 199. Microbiologist Madigan Army Med. Ctr., Tacoma, intern, 1986-87, resident in family practice, 1988-90; pvt. practice, Johnson City, N.Y., 1993—; dir. med. edn. United Health Svcs., Johnson City, 1993—; dep. dir. residency Wilson Family Practice Residency, Johnson City, 1993—; bd. dirs.HMO-CNY Blue Cross/Blue Shield N.Y., 1994, v.p., 1995—; v.p. Family Practice Assocs. PC, Berlin, Wis., 1986—; vice chmn. dept. family medicine UHS, 1994—. Patentee for leptospira growth media, mycoplasma lypholysation media. Officer M.C., U.S. Army; lt. col. USAR. Mem. Am. Acad. Family Physicians (pres. So. Tier chpt. N.Y. State), Broome County Med. Soc. Office: Johnson City Family Care 40 Arch St Johnson City NY 13790

TOWNE, ALAN RAYMOND, neurologist, educator; b. Malden, Mass., July 9, 1948; s. Allen Newman and Carmelia (Foskin) T.; m. Elizabeth Ann Hull. BA, Hobart Coll., 1970; Cert. d'etudes in French Lit., U. d'Anger, France, 1972; MD with honors, U. Aix-Marseille, France, 1981. Diplomate Am. Bd. Psychiatry and Neurology; lic. MD, Va. Intern in neurology Hosp. Ste. Anne, Toulon, France, 1979-80; fellow in neuroimaging and neurophysiology U. Aix-Marseille, France, 1980-81; rotating intern Med. Coll. Va., Richmond, 1981-82, resident in neurology, chief resident in neurology, 1982-85, 84-85, fellow in neurophysiology, 1985-86, asst. prof. neurology dept. neurology, 1986-94, assoc. prof. neurology, 1994—, co-dir. clin. neurophysiology labs., 1994—, dir. ambulatory EEG svc. monitoring lab., 1988—, attending physician epilepsy monitoring unit, 1988—, dir. status epilepticus rsch. program, 1988—; chmn. dept. neurology residency recruitment program Med. Coll. of Va., 1989—; guest reviewer Epilepsia; guest lectr. in field. Contbr. articles to profl. publs. and chpts. to books. Usher com. Episcopal Ch. of the Redemmer, 1988—, spl. events com., 1992—; organizing com. Boy Scouts Am., Robert E. Lee Coun., 1992; com. chmn. Pack 811, Boy Scouts Am., 1992—. Grantee Abbott Labs., 1990, 92-93, 91-93, 92—, Burrough Wellcome, 1989-90, 90—, Janssen Rsch. Found., 1989-91, Merrell Dow Pharms. Inc., 1990-92, Marion Merrell Dow, 1991-92, 92—, Carter-Wallace Labs., 1992-93, 92—, Dainippon Pharm. Co., 1993—, NIH, 1987—. Mem. Am. Assn. for Study of Headache, Am. Acad. Neurology, Richmond Acad. Medicine, Am. Epilepsy Soc., Va. Neurol. Soc., Soc. for Neurosci., Am. Electroencephalographic Soc., Am. Acad. Clin. Neurophysiology. Episcopalian. Home: 10103 Cutter Dr Richmond VA 23235 Office: Va Commonwealth U Med Coll Va Dept Neurology Box 599 Richmond VA 23298

TOWNE, SARAH PATTON, physician; b. Fountain Hill, Pa., Aug. 28, 1953; d. William Frank and Arline Rose (Patton) T. Degree in Nursing, Geisinger Med. Ctr., Danville, Pa., 1973; BS magna cum laude, Kutztown U. Pa., 1988; DO, Phila. Coll. Osteo. Medicine, Phila., 1992; MSc in Family Practice, Ohila. Coll. Osteo. Medicine, 1995. Diplomate Nat. Bd. Osteo. Med. Examiners. Psychiatric nurse Allentown (Pa.) State Hosp., 1973-76, N.W. Inst. Psychiatry, Ft. Washington, Pa., 1976-78; RN, psychotherapist Boulder (Colo.) County Mental Health Ctr., 1979-85; intern Phila. Coll. Osteo. Medicine, 1992-93, resident in family practice, 1993-95; physician Troup (Tex.) Family Practice, 1995—; physician Harleysville (Pa.) Med. Assn., 1993-95. Bd. dirs. Boulder County Rape Crisis Team, 1979-81. Mem. Am. Osteo Assn., Am. Coll. Family Practitioners, Am. Coll. Osteo. Family Practitioners (bd. cert.), Pa. Osteo. Med. Assn., Pa. Osteo. Gen. Practitioners Soc., Tex. Med. Assn. Home: 1901 S Chilton St Tyler TX 75701 Office: Troup Family Practice 201 S Railroad St Troup TX 75789

TOWNE, SUSAN L., pediatric nursing educator; b. San Francisco, Oct. 10, 1950; d. Philip Neldon and Betty Dawn (Gilpin) Leavitt; chidren: Charles F., Steven E., Sarah M. BSN, U. Utah, 1974; MS in Nursing Edn., Idaho State U., 1995. RN, Idaho. Lamaze instr. Childbirth Edn. Assn.; staff RN St. Vincent's Med. Ctr., Jacksonville, Fla.; staff RN primary Bannock Regional Med. Ctr., Pocatello, Idaho, 1985-93; prof. nursing Ricks Coll., Rexburg, Idaho, 1993—; neonatal resusitation instr. Am. Acad. Pediat., 1989—, pediat. advanced life support instr., 1990—. V.p. Naval Officers Wives Club, Naval Air Sta., Guam, 1982; pres. Young Women's Ch. Orgn., Idaho Falls, 1994—. Office: Ricks Coll Rexburg ID 83460-0620

TOWNSEND, ERNEST JOSEPH, health care executive; b. Albany, N.Y., Aug. 11, 1940; s. G. Dewey and Genevive (Fierro) T. BA, Siena Coll., 1966; MA in Social Work, Syracuse U., 1968; M in Pub. Adminstrn., NYU, 1979, D in Pub. Adminstrn., 1981. Program analyst N.Y. State Mental Hygiene, Albany, 1970-74; chief of service Capital Dist. Psychiat. Ctr., Albany, 1974-79, dep. dir., 1979-80, acting dir., 1981; assoc. prof. psychiatry Albany Med. Coll., 1980-81; supt. N.H. Hosp., Concord, 1981-85; adj. assoc. prof. Dartmouth Med. Sch., Hanover, N.H., 1982-86; exec. dir. N. Cen. Human Services, Inc., Gardner, Mass., 1985-88; dir. Ulster County Mental Health Dept., Kingston, N.Y., 1988—; chmn. managed care com. N.Y. State Conf. Mental Health Dirs. Contbr. articles to profl. jours. Served with USAF, 1958-62. Mem. NASW. Home: 45 Pine Grove St Woodstock NY 12498-1509 Office: Ulster County Dept Mental Health 239 Golden Hill Rd Kingston NY 12401-0800

TOWNSEND, FRANK MARION, pathology educator; b. Stamford, Tex., Oct. 29, 1914; s. Frank M. and Beatrice (House) T.; m. Gerda Eberlein, 1940 (dec. div. 1944); 1 son, Frank M.; m. Ann Graf, Aug. 25, 1951; 1 son, Robert N. Student, San Antonio Coll., 1931-32, U. Tex., 1932-34; MD, Tulane U., 1938. Diplomate: Am. Bd. Pathology. Intern Polyclinic Hosp., N.Y.C., 1939-40; commd. 1st lt. M.C., U.S. Army, 1940, advanced through grades to lt. col., 1946; resident instr. pathology Washington U., 1945-47; trans. to USAF, 1949, advanced through grades to col., 1956; instr. pathology Coll. Medicine, U. Nebr., 1947-48; asso. pathologist Scott and White Clinic, Temple, Tex., 1948-49; asso. prof. pathology Med. Br. U. Tex., Galveston, 1949-59; flight surgeon USAF, 1950-65; dir. labs. USAF Hosp. (now Wilford Hall USAF Hosp.), Lackland AFB, Tex., 1950-54; cons. pathology Office of Surgeon Gen. Hdqrs. USAF, Washington, 1954-63, chief cons. group Office of Surgeon Gen. Hdqrs., 1954-55; dep. dir. Armed Forces Inst. Pathology, Washington, 1955-59; dir. Armed Forces Inst. Pathology, 1959-63; vice comdr. aerospace med. divsn. Air Force Systems Command, 1963-65; ret., 1965; practice medicine specializing in pathology San Antonio, 1965—; dir. labs. San Antonio State Chest Hosp.; consulting pathologist Tex. Dept. Health hosps., 1965-72; clin. prof. pathology U. Tex. Med. Sch., San Antonio, 1969-72; prof., chmn. dept. pathology Health Sci. Ctr. U. Tex. Med. Sch., 1972-86, emeritus chmn., prof., 1986—; cons. U. Tex. Cancer Ctr.-M.D. Anderson Hosp., 1966-80, NASA, 1967-75; mem. adv. bd. cancer WHO, 1958-75; mem. Armed Forces Epidemiology Bd., 1983-91; bd. govs. Armed Forces Inst. Pathology, 1984-95. Mem. editorial bd. Tex. Med. Jour., 1978-86; contbr. articles to med. jours. Mem. adv. coun. Civil War Centennial Commn., 1960-65; bd. dirs. Alamo Area Sci. Fair, 1967-73. Decorated D.S.M., Legion of Merit; recipient Founders medal Assn. Mil. Surgeons, 1961. Recipient Comdr.'s award Armed Forces Epidemiol. Bd., 1990; F.M. Townsend Chair of Pathology endowed in his honor by faculty of Dept. Pathology, U. Tex. Health Sci. Ctr., 1987. Fellow ACP, Coll. Am. Pathologists (edn. advisor on accreditation, commr. lab. accreditation South Ctrl. States region 1971-84), Am. Soc. Clin. Pathologists (Ward Burdick award 1983), Aerospace Med. Assn. (H.G. Mosely award 1962); mem. AMA, AAAS, Tex. Med. Assn., Internat. Acad. Aviation and Space Medicine, Tex. Soc. Pathologists (Caldwell award 1971), Am. Assn. Pathologists, Internat. Acad. Pathology, Acad. Clin. Lab. Physicians and Scientists, Soc. Med. Cons. to Armed Forces, Torch Club. Home: PO Box 77 Harwood TX 78632-0077 Office: U Tex Health Sci Ctr Dept Pathology 7703 Floyd Curl Dr San Antonio TX 78284-7750

TOWNSEND, JAMES WILLIS, computer scientist; b. Evansville, Ind., Sept. 9, 1936; s. James Franklin and Elma Elizabeth (Galloway) T.; m. Leona Jean York, Apr. 20, 1958; 1 child, Eric Wayne. BS in Arts and Scis., Ball State U., 1962; PhD, Iowa State U., 1970. Rsch. technologist Neuromuscular div. Mead Johnson, Evansville, 1957-60; chief instr. Zoology dept. Iowa State U., Ames, 1965-67; asst. prof. Ind. State U., Evansville, 1967-72; cons. electron microscopy Mead Johnson Rsch. Ctr., Evansville, 1971-73; mgr. neurosci. Neurosci. Lab., Kans. State U., Manhattan, 1974-76; head electron microscopy Nat. Ctr. for Toxicology Rsch., Jefferson, Ark., 1976-82; dir. electron microscopy U. Ark. Med. Sci., Little Rock, 1982-87; dir. computer ops. pathology dept. Univ. Hosp., Little Rock, 1987—; workshop presenter Am. Soc. Clin. Pathology, 1980-81, Nat. Soc. Histotechnologists, 1984-88. With USAF, 1957. Contbr. articles to profl. jours.; reviewer Scanning Electron Microscopy, 1977-78. Nat. Def. fellowship NDEA, Iowa State U., 1962-65; recipient Chgo. Tribune award Chicago Tribune, 1955. Mem. Sigma Xi, Sigma Zeta. Baptist. Home: 4 Breeds Hill Ct Little Rock AR 72211-2514 Office: Univ Ark for Med Sci Dept Pathology Slot 517 4301 W Markham St Little Rock AR 72205-7101

TOWNSEND, ROBERT GLENN, JR., family physician; b. Grayson, Ky., Aug. 30, 1929; s. Robert Glenn and Lois Jaunita (Jackson) T.; m. Mina Jean Hensley, Aug. 2, 1958; children: Susan Elizabeth Townsend Barnes, Robert Glenn III. BS, Wake Forest Univ., 1957; MD, U. Louisville Sch. of Medicine, Louisville, 1961. Diplomate Am. Bd. Family Practice. Intern Indpls. Gen. Hosp., 1961-62; owner, prin. R. G. Townsend Jr., MD, Raeford, N.C., 1964-92; clin. prof. family medicine East Carolina Sch. of Medicine, Greenville, N.C., 1982—; assoc. prof. family medicine Duke U., Durham, N.C., 1992—. Officer Raeford (N.C.) United Meth. Ch., 1964—; pres. Raeford C. of C., 1966-67, bd. dirs., 1965-67; bd. dirs. Southeastern Econ. Devel. Commn., 1967-77, Fayetteville Area Health Edn. Ctr., 1987-91, pres., 1990-91. Mem. AMA, N.C. Med. Soc. (vice counselor 1989-95), N.C. Acad. Family Physicians (v.p. 1980-81, pres. 1982-83, N.C. Family Physician of Yr. 1988), Am. Acad. Family Physicians (alt. del. 1988-93, del. 1992-96), Hoke County Bd. Health, Cardinal Health Svcs. (bd. dirs. 1981-88), Fayetteville Family Life Ctr. (bd. dirs. 1976-79), Hoke County Med. Soc., N.C. Cancer Inst. (bd. dirs. 1970-73). Democrat. Office: 405 S Main St Raeford NC 28376-3222

TOY, KAREN W., army nurse; b. Tokyo, Aug. 3, 1962; d. Edward S. and Toku (Koasa) Wall; m. Robert P. Toy, May 30, 1989. AA, N.Mex. Mil. Inst., 1982; postgrad., U. Hawaii, 1987; BS in Biology, Tex. Tech U., 1985. Commd. USAR, 1982, advanced through grades to capt.; mobilization officer USAR, Harrisburg, Pa.; supply distbn. officer Hawaii Army NG, Honolulu. With Operation Desert Shield/Desert Storm, 1991. Recipient undergrad. physics rsch. scholarship. Mem. Sigma Theta Tau, Gamma Psi (at large). Home: 46-259 Kahuhipa St apt B100 Kaneohe HI 96744 Office: Tripler Army Medical Ctr Honolulu HI 96859

TOYAMA, KEISUKE, neurobiologist; b. Nagoya, Japan, Oct. 27, 1935; s. Takaji and Chiyoko Toyama; m. Kayoko Yamada; children: Akiko, Tetsuya. MD, Nagoya U., Japan, 1960, PhD, 1965. Researcher NHK Broadcasting Sci. Insts., Japan, 1960-74; assoc. prof. U. Tokyo, 1974-81; prof. Kyoto Prefectural U., Japan, 1981—. Home: 356-2 Kamigamo-Motoyama, Kamigyo Kyoto 603, Japan Office: Kyoto Prefectural U, Kawaramachi-Hirokohji, Kyoto 602, Japan

TOYE, RICHARD CHARLES, psychologist; b. Marion, Ohio, June 24, 1958; s. Robert James and Fenella LaFern (Fairall) T.; m. Mary Katherine Hogan, Oct. 5, 1985; children: Brian Andrew, James Edward. BA cum laude, Rice U., 1979; MSc, Brown U., 1980; PhD, U. Ill., Chgo., 1984. Diplomate Am. Bd. Profl. Psychology, Am. Bd. Forensic Examiners; lic. psychologist, Mass., Maine, Nebr., N.H., N.C. Sr. psychologist N.H. Hosp., Concord, 1985-88; pvt. practice Exeter, N.H., 1988-92; psychologist VA Med. Ctr., Fayetteville, N.C., 1992-94, chief psychologist, 1994-96; geriatric neuropsychologist Hastings Regional Ctr., Mich., 1996—; cons. Head Injury Treatment Program, Dover, N.H., 1987-89. Contbr. articles to profl. publs. Mem. consumer adv. coun. Vocat. Rehab., Nashua, N.H., 1990, sch. budget adv. com., Exeter, 1989-92. Recipient Excellence in Psychology award Houston Psychol. Assn., 1979; NSF fellow, 1979. Fellow N.H. Psychol. Orgn. (chair continuing edn. 1987-89, pres. 1990-92); mem. APA, Soc. Personality Assessment, Nat. Eagle Scout Assn., Phi Kappa Phi. Office: 4200 2d St Hastings NE 68902

TOYOMURA, AKIKO CHARLOTTE, health administrator, nurse; b. Kahuku, Hawaii, Sept. 14, 1923; d. Torajiro and Mika Nakamura; m. Dennis T. Toyomura, May 29, 1949; children: Wayne J., Gerald F., Amy J., Lyle D. Diploma, St. Francis Hosp., Honolulu, 1945; postgrad. certs., Cook County Med. Hosp., Chgo., 1949; Assoc. degree, Kapiolani C.C., U. Hawaii, 1981, cert. of achievement, 1980, 81. RN HI, Ill.; sch. health aide; cert. first aid ARC, CPR, Hawaii. Head nurse Women's & Children's Hosp., Chgo., 1949-51; nurse civil svc. U.S. Army, Honolulu, 1952-53; school nurse Luth. Evang. School, Chgo., 1953-58; nurse Rehab. Hosp., Honolulu, HI, 1962-63, Kaiser Med. Ctr., 1963-66; sr. health aide State of Hawaii, Honolulu, 1983—; developer basic health and nursing program Luth. Evang. Sch., Chgo., 1953-58. Home: 2602 Manoa Rd Honolulu HI 96822-1703 Office: State of Hawaii 1240 7th Ave Honolulu HI 96816-2644

TRACHTE, GEORGE JOSEPH, pharmacology educator; b. Pottsville, Pa., Oct. 29, 1953; s. Arthur and Frances Mary (Sharkey) T.; m. Patricia Ann O'Neill, June 30, 1979; children: Gregory Alexander, Samantha Ann. BS, Pa. State U., 1975; Phd, Thomas Jefferson U., Phila., 1979. Postdoctoral fellow U. Va. Med. Sch., Charlottesville, 1979-82; vis. scientist Pharmakologisches Inst., Koln, Germany, 1982; asst. prof. U. Minn. Duluth Sch. Medicine, 1982-88, assoc. prof., 1988-94, prof., 1994—; mem. adv. bd. Eicosanoids, Germany, 1990-92. Mem. Am. Physiol. Soc., Am. Soc. Pharm. & Exp. Therapeutics, Sigma Xi (pres. U. Minn. Duluth chpt. 1995-96). Methodist. Office: U Minn Dept Pharm Sch Medicine 10 University Ave Duluth MN 55812

TRACY, JOHN MICHAEL, III, speech pathology educator; b. Whittier, Calif., Apr. 29, 1949; s. John Michael and Roberta Josephine (Clay) T.; m. Diane Elaine Kafka, June 21, 1971. BA, Whittier Coll., 1971; MS, Oreg. Coll. Edn., 1974; PhD, U. Oreg., 1983; Cert. in Healthcare Adminstrn., Concordia Coll., Portland, Oreg., 1995. Cert. clin. competence in speech-lang. pathology. Speech clinician Medford (Oreg.) Pub. Sch., 1974-76; speech pathologist Providence Hosp., Medford, 1977-80, Home Health Agy., Eugene, Oreg., 1981-84; assoc. prof. Western Oreg. State Coll., Monmouth, 1984-88; supr. speech and lang. pathology Salem (Oreg.) Hosp., 1988-91, program mgr. outpatient rehab. svcs., 1991—. Mem. Am. Speech-Lang. Hearing Assn., Oreg. Speech-Lang. and Hearing Assn. (editor newsletter 1982-84, pres. 1986-87. clin. and pvt. practice cons. 1995—).

TRACY, JOSEPH IGOE, clinical psychologist; b. Orange, N.J., Apr. 11, 1954; s. William Irwin and Virginia Mary (Igoe) T.; m. Carol Susan Busacca, May 29, 1982; children: Ryan, Lauren, Nicole. BA, Bowdoin Coll., 1976; MA, Columbia U., 1981; PhD, New Sch. Social Rsch., 1990. Program dir. Carrier Found., Belle Meade, N.J., 1990-91; asst. prof. Med. Coll. Pa./E.P.P.I., Phila., 1991—; vis. asst. prof. Ctr. Alcohol Studies Rutgers U., Piscataway, N.J., 1990—. Recipient Alvin Johnson fellowship New Sch. for Social Rsch., 1987, Nat. Assn. for Rsch. on Schizophrenia and Depression Young Investigator award. Fellow McDonnell-Pew Inst. for Cognitive Neuroscience; mem. APA (dissertation rsch. award 1988), Internat. Neuropsychol. Soc., Cognitive Neurosci. Soc. Office: Med Coll Pa Dept Psychiatry 3200 Henry Ave Philadelphia PA 19129-1137

TRACY, RICHARD E., medical educator; b. Klamath Falls, Oreg., Apr. 30, 1934. BA, U. Chgo., 1955, MD, PhD, 1961. Diplomate Am. Bd. Anatomic Pathology. Prof. Sch. Medicine La. State U., New Orleans, 1967. Office: Sch of Medicine La State U Med Ctr New Orleans LA 70112

TRACZYK, WŁADYSŁAW ZYGMUNT, physiology educator, researcher; b. Warsaw, Poland, June 27, 1928; s. Zygmunt Teodor and Władysława Kazimiera (Dzikiewicz) T.; m. Zdzisława Andrysik, Dec. 7, 1954; 1 child, Zdzisław Władysław. MD, Med. U. Warsaw, Poland, 1951, DMS, 1962; PhD, 1st Sch. Medicine, Moscow, 1955. Asst. to head Lab. Physiology, Polish Acad. Scis., Warsaw, 1956-62; assoc. prof. physiology Med. U. Warsaw Sch. Medicine, 1963; prof., chmn. dept. Med. U. Łódź (Poland) Sch. Medicine, 1963—, dir. Inst. Physiology and Biochemistry, 1973—; rsch. supr. project on neuroendocrinology Polish Acad. Scis., 1976-90. Author: Neurohormones, 1970, Outline of Human Physiology, 5th edit., 1992; author, editor Human Physiology for Medical Students, 1989-90, 2d edit. Neuropeptides and Neural Transmission, 1980; editor-in-chief Annales Academiae Medicae Lodzenses, 1976—. Mem. coun. Polish Ministry Health, Warsaw, 1982-86, Coun. Sci. and Univ. Edn., Warsaw, 1986-90; chmn. glossary commn. physiol. terms Polish Acad. Scis., 1986—. Decorated chevalier and officer Order Polonia Restituta, Order Educator of Merit; recipient award Ministry Health and Social Welfare, 1971, 76, 90. Mem. Polish Physiol. Soc. (chmn. Łódź br. 1963-72), Polish Soc. EEG and Clin. Neurophysiology (pres. 1981-85), Internat. Brain Rsch. Orgn., Internat. Neuroendocrinology Soc., Assn. Authors Med. Books (pres. 1993—). Home: ul Bernardyńska 4 m 13, 02-904 Warsaw Poland Office: Med U Łódź Dept Physiol, ul Lindleya 3, 90-131 Łódź Poland

TRADUP, JANETTA FREEMAN, nursing educator; b. Pawhuska, Okla., Jan. 12, 1951; d. Foy Eugene and Cora Ellen (Anderson) Freeman; m. Steven William Tradup, Aug. 10, 1969 (div. Oct. 1977); 1 child, Gregory Mark. AD in Nursing, U. Albuquerque, 1979; BS in Nursing, West Tex. State U., 1982; MS in Nursing, U. Tex. Health Sci. Ctr., 1984. Staff nurse Lubbock (Tex.) Gen. Hosp., 1979-80, charge nurse, 1980-82; staff nurse Meth. Hosp., Lubbock, 1982, instr. Sch. Nursing, 1985-89, sec. faculty, 1985-86; head nurse Health Sci. Ctr. Tex. Tech. U., Lubbock, 1983; asst. prof. Tex. Tech U. Health Scis. Ctr. Sch. Nursing, Lubbock, 1989-94; assoc. prof. Tex. Tech. U. Health Scis. Ctr. Sch. Nursing, Lubbock, 1994—. Contbr. articles to profl. jours. Com. mem. Boy Scouts Am., Lubbock, 1982; caseworker Family Outreach, Lubbock, 1986; nurses com. Am. Cancer Soc., 1990—; vol. Am. Cancer Soc. Reach to Recovery, 1992-93. Mem. ANA (cert. high risk perinatal nurse), Tex. Nursees Assn. (faculty cons. student's assn. 1986—, treas. local dist. 1986, v.p. 1988-89, state fin. com. 1988-95, state treas., chair TNA state fin. com., treas. Tex. Nurses Found.), NLN, Tex. League for Nursing, Sigma Theta Tau (pres. Iota Mu chpt. 1995—). Home: 4209 40th St Lubbock TX 79413-2533 Office: TTUHSC Sch Nursing Lubbock TX 79430

TRAGER, WILLIAM, biology educator; b. Newark, Mar. 20, 1910; s. Leon and Anna (Emilfork) T.; m. Ida Sonnow, June 16, 1935; children—Leslie, Carolyn, Lillian. B.S., Rutgers U., 1930, Sc.D. (hon.), 1965; M.A., Harvard U., 1931, Ph.D., 1933; Sc.D. (hon.), Rockefeller U., 1987. Fellow Rockefeller U., N.Y.C., 1934-35, mem. faculty, 1935—, assoc. prof., 1950-64, prof. biology, 1964-81, prof. emeritus, 1981—; guest investigator West African Inst. Trypanosomiasis Research, 1958-59, Nigerian Inst. Trypanosomiasis Research, 1973-74; vis. prof. Fla. State U., 1962, U. P.R. Med. Sch., 1963, U. Mex. Med. Sch., 1965; mem. study sect. parasitology and tropical medicine Nat. Inst. Allergy and Infectious Diseases, 1954-58, 67-70, mem. tng. grant com., 1961-64, mem. microbiology and infectious diseases adv. com., 1978-79; mem. malaria commn. Armed Forces Epidemiol. Bd., 1965-73; mem. study group parasitic diseases Walter Reed Army Inst. Research, 1977-79; chmn. sci. adv. council Liberian Inst. Tropical Medicine, 1965-66; rapporteur 6th, 7th Congresses Tropical Medicine; pres. Am. Found. for Tropical Medicine, 1966-69; mem. steering com. Malaria Immunology Group, WHO, 1977-80; cons. WHO, Bangkok, 1978, Panama, 1979, Shanghai, 1979; hon. pres. Asia and Pacific Conf. on Malaria, 1985. Author: Symbiosis, 1970, Living Together: The Biology of Animal Parasitism, 1986; editor Jour. Protozoology, 1954-65; contbr. articles on insect physiology and exptl. parasitology to profl. jours. Served to capt. AUS, 1943-45. Recipient Leuckart medal Deutsche Gesellschaft fur Parasitologie, 1982, First Rameshwardas Birla Internat. award in Medicine, 1982, Darling medal WHO, Manson medal Royal Soc. Tropical Medicine and Hygiene, 1986, Prince Mahidol award in Med. Sci., 1994; fellow NRC, 1933-34, Guggenheim Found., 1973-74, Avivah Zuckerman fellow Kuvin Ctr. Infections and Tropical Diseases, Hebrew U., 1982. Fellow AAAS, N.Y. Acad. Scis.; mem. Nat. Acad. Sci., Am. Soc. Parasitologist (council 1956-57, v.p. 1973, pres. 1974), Soc. Protozoologists (pres. 1960-61), Am. Soc. Tropical Medicine and Hygiene (pres. 1978-79, Le Prince medal 1991). Office: Rockefeller U York Ave At 66th St New York NY 10021

TRAIL, MERVIN L., health facility administrator; b. Cumberland, Md., Dec. 2, 1933; s. Watson Daniel and Lelah Blanche (Deahl) T.; m. Edythe Marie Wenger, June 8, 1958; children: Shelby, Lisa, Kelly, Kristi. BA, Bridgewater Coll., 1955; MD, U. Md., 1959; PhD, U. New Orleans, 1994. Intern U.S. Naval Hosp., Portsmouth, Va., 1959-60; resident in otolaryngology, head and neck surgery Johns Hopkins Hosp., Balt., 1967-68; asst. prof., dir. clin. tng. dept. otorhinolaryngology U. New Orleans, 1968-70, assoc. prof., 1970-74, clin. prof., 1974-92, prof. dir., 1992-93, prof., chmn., 1993-94; dir. Stanley S. Scott Cancer Ctr., New Orleans, 1991-94; chancellor La. State U. Med. Ctr., New Orleans, 1994—; bd. dirs. Drs. Hosp., Metairie, La., La. State U. Med. Ctr. Found., New Orelans Regional Med. Ctr. Contbr. articles to profl. jours. Pres. Greater New Orleans Tourist and Conv. Commn., 1987-88; co-chmn. media and hospitality com. Rep. Nat. Conv., New Orleans, 1988; chmn. exec. com. New Orleans Sports Found., 1988-94; pres. Ernest N. Morial Exhbn. Hall Authority, New Orleans, 1992-95. Lt. USN, 1959-63. Mem. Assn. Acad. Health Ctrs., Alpha Omega Alpha. Office: La State U Med Ctr 433 Bolivar St New Orleans LA 70112

TRAINA, VINCENT MICHAEL, pharmaceutical company executive; b. L.I., N.Y., May 8, 1943; s. John Joseph and Anne (Copertino) T.; m. Lynn R. Miko, Aug. 20, 1978; children: Allison, Kimberly, Brent. BA in Biology, Rutgers U., 1965, MS in Biology, 1970, PhD in Physiology, 1973. Diplomate Am. Bd. Toxicology. Research investigator in toxicology Squibb Inst., New Brunswick, N.J., 1966-74; mgr. toxicology Ciba-Geigy Corp., Summit, N.J., 1974-79, assoc. dir. toxicology and pathology, 1979-82, dir. toxicology, 1982-84, exec. dir. toxicology and pathology, 1984-88, v.p. toxicology/pathology, 1988-92; v.p. toxicology/pathology/metabolism Ciba-Geigy Corp., Summit, 1992; v.p. and head preclinical safety worldwide Ciba-Geigy Pharm. Div., Summit, 1992—; mem. indsl. rels. and negotiation com. Ciba-Geigy Corp., Summit, 1986—; faculty Residential Sch. of Medicinal Chemistry, Drew U., 1989—. Mem. Am. Coll. Toxicology, Soc. Toxicology, Environ. Mutagen Soc., Am. Inst. Biol. Scis., Soc. Sigma Xi. Republican. Roman Catholic. Office: Ciba-Geigy Corp 556 Morris Ave Summit NJ 07901-1330

TRAISMAN, HOWARD SEVIN, pediatrician; b. Chgo., Mar. 18, 1923; s. Alfred Stanley and Sara (Sevin) T.; m. Regina Gallagher, Feb. 29, 1956; children—Barry D. Lifschultz, Edward S., Kenneth N. B.S. in Chemistry, Northwestern U., 1943, M.B., 1946, M.D., 1947. Intern Cook County Hosp., Chgo., 1946-47; resident in pediatrics Children's Meml. Hosp., Chgo., 1949-51; attending physician div. endocrinology Children's Meml. Hosp., 1951—; mem. faculty Northwestern U. Med. Sch., 1951—, prof. pediatrics, 1973—. Author articles in field, chpts. in books. Served to capt. M.C. AUS, 1943-46, 47-49. Mem. Am. Diabetes Assn. (Disting. Service award 1976), Am. Pediatric Soc., Am. Acad. Pediatrics, Endocrine Soc., Lawson Wilkins Pediatric Endocrine Soc., AMA, Midwest Soc. Pediatric Research, Ill. Med. Soc., Chgo. Pediatric Soc., Chgo. Med. Soc., Inst. Medicine Chgo. Democrat. Jewish. Office: 1325 Howard St Evanston IL 60202-3766

TRAM, KENNETH KHAI KT, internist; b. Saigon, Vietnam, Oct. 29, 1961; came to U.S., 1978; s. Felix Ngan and Lisa Hong (Pham) T.; m. Christine Tram-Hong Tran, June 19, 1993. BS summa cum laude, U. Calif., Irvine, 1984; MD, UCLA, 1988. Diplomate Am. Bd. Internal Medicine, Am. Bd. Geriatric Medicine. Resident in internal medicine UCLA-San Fernandy Valley, 1988-91; geriatric medicine fellow UCLA Sch. Medicine, 1992-94; clin. instr./assoc. investigator Sepulveda (Calif.) VA Med. Ctr., 1991-94, acting med. dir., 1994; internist Facey Med. Group, Sepulveda, 1994—. Contbr. articles to profl. jours. Mem. CPAG/CHOMS, Calif., 1991—. Recipient Solomon Scholars Resident award UCLA Sch. Medicine, 1991, Nat. Kidney Found. Fellowship award, 1991-92, VA Rsch. and Devel. Career Devel. award, 1992-94. Mem. ACP, AAAS, AMA, Am. Soc. for Bone and Mineral Rscl:., U.S. Table Tennis Assn., Nat. Geog. Soc., Mus. Heritage Soc. Home: 6 Malaga Irvine CA 92714-7304 Office: Facey Medical Group Inc 11211 Sepulveda Blvd Mission Hills CA 91345-1115

TRAN, HENRY BANG Q., social work case manager; b. Binh Dinh, Vietnam, Dec. 28, 1952; came to U.S., 1975; s. Mau Dinh and Ho Thi Tran; m. Thuhong T. Ngo; children: John, Michael, Robert, Richard, Jennifer. BA, Northeastern Ill. U., 1977, MA, 1978. Cert. social worker, real estate broker. Social worker Tex. Dept. Human Svcs., Houston, 1980—; founder, pres. Texo Properties, Inc., Houston, 1984-85; pres. N.E.W.S. Properties, Houston, 1985—; case mgr. Tex. Workforce Commn., 1996—; instr. math. City Colls. Chgo., 1977, Vietnamese lang. U. Houston, 1985. V.p. Buddhist Assn. for Services of Humanity in Am., Houston, 1985—; pres. Quang Trung Mut. Assistance Assn., Houston, 1984—. Fellow U. Miami, 1979. Mem. Nat. Assn. Realtors, Tex. Pub. Employee Assn., Dalat U. Alumni Assn., Asia Soc., Houston Vietnam Lions Club (pres. 1991).

TRAN, JOHN, osteopathic physician; b. Binhdinh, Vietnam, Apr. 5, 1964; came to U.S., 1983; s. Dung Dang and To-Wuan (Ta) T. BS in Chemistry, U. Okla., 1988; DO, Okla. State U., 1996. Mem. Am. Coll. Family Physicians. Home: 9509 Maybrook Oklahoma City OK 73159

TRANCHEMONTAGNE, TERESA BODWELL, osteopath; b. Nashua, N.H., Feb. 19, 1964; d. Paul and Rachel (Watier) T.; m. Jeremy S. Bodwell, Aug. 21, 1993; children: Joseph, Jennifer. BS in Chemistry, Rivier U., 1990; DO, U. New England Coll. Osteo. Medicine, 1995. Respiratory therapist St. Joseph Hosp., Nashua, 1986-89; rsch. technician Deaconess Hosp., Boston, 1989-90; intern Med. Ctr. Meml., Worcester, Mass., 1995—. Asst. coach Nashua Youth Soccer, 1994-95.

TRANQUADA, ROBERT ERNEST, medical educator, physician; b. Los Angeles, Aug. 27, 1930; s. Ernest Alvro and Katharine (Jacobus) T.; m. Janet Martin, Aug. 31, 1951; children: John Martin, James Robert, Katherine Anne. B.A., Pomona Coll., 1951; M.D., Stanford U., 1955; D.Sc. (hon.), Worcester Poly. Inst., 1985. Diplomate Am. Bd. Internal Medicine. Intern in medicine UCLA Med. Center, 1955-56, resident in medicine, 1956-57; resident Los Angeles VA Hosp., 1957-58; fellow in diabetes and metabolic diseases UCLA, 1958-59; fellow in diabetes U. So. Calif., 1959-60, asst. prof. medicine, 1960-63, assoc. prof., 1964-68, chmn. dept. community medicine, 1967-70; med. dir. Los Angeles County/U. So. Calif. Med. Center, 1969-74; regional dir. Central Region, Los Angeles County Dept. Health Services, 1974-76; assoc. dean UCLA Sch. Medicine, 1976-79; chancellor and dean U. Mass. Med. Sch., 1979-86; dean U. So. Calif. Sch. Medicine, 1986-91; prof. medicine U. So. Calif., L.A., 1986-92, Norman Topping/Nat. Med. Enterprises prof. medicine and pub. policy, 1992—. mem., chair L.A. County Task Force on Health Care Access, 1992-94. Trustee Pomona Coll., 1969—, vice chmn., 1987-91, chmn. 1991—; mem. bd. fellows Claremont U. Ct., 1971-79, 91—; corporator Worcester Art Mus., 1980-86; bd. dirs. Nat. Med. Fellowships, Inc., 1973—, chmn. 1980-85; trustee Charles Drew U. Med. and Sci., 1968-79, 86-95, Orthopaedic Hosp., 1986-91, Barlow Hosp., 1987-89; bd. dirs. Worcester Acad., 1984-86, Worcester County Inst. for Savs., 1982-86, U. So. Calif. Univ. Hosp., 1988-91, Alliance for Childrens Rights, 1991-95; bd. dirs. Good Hope Med. Found., 1994—; mem. Ind. Commn. on L.A. Police Dept., 1991-92; mem. gover ing bd. L.A. County Local Initiative Health Authority, 1994—. Milbank faculty fellow, 1967-72. Fellow AAAS, Am. Antiquarian Soc.; mem. AMA, Am. Diabetes Assn., Western Soc. Clin. Investigation, Los Angeles County Med. Assn., Los Angeles Acad. Medicine, Calif. Med. Assn., Inst. Medicine of Nat. Acad. Scis., Phi Beta Kappa, Sigma Xi, Alpha Omega Alpha. Office: U So Calif VKC # 368A Los Angeles CA 90089-0041

TRAPP, ROBERT GREIG, rheumatologist; b. Lincoln, Ill., Nov. 7, 1948. BA, Earlham Coll., Richmond, Ind., 1970; MD, Northwestern U., Chgo., 1974. Diplomate Am. Bd. Internal Medicine, Am. Bd. Rheumatology. Resident in internal medicine Evanston (Ill.) Hosp., 1974-77; fellow in intensive care/ambulatory medicine St. Joseph's Hosp., Chgo., 1977-78; fellow in immunology U. cin., 1978-80; fellow in rheumatology U. Manchester, Eng., 1980-81; asst. prof./chief rheumatology So. Ill. U. Sch. Medicine, Springfield, Ill., 1981-89; med. dir. The Arthritis Ctr., Springfield, 1989—. Author: Basic and Clinical Biostatistics, 1990, 2d edit., 1994. Fellow ACP, Am. Coll. Rheumatology; mem. Heberdon Soc., Phi Beta Kappa. Office: Arthritis Center 2528 Farragut Dr Springfield IL 62704

TRAUB, TODD STEVEN, anesthesiologist; b. Bklyn., Sept. 2, 1952; s. Paul and Lynn (Gordon) T.; m. Janice K. Traub, Dec. 18, 1977; children: Adam, Randi, Alyssa. BA, Alfred (N.Y.) U., 1974; MD, Universidad Autonoma Juarez, Mex., 1982. Diplomate Am. Bd. Anesthesiology, Am. Acad. Pain Mgmt. Intern Westchester County Med. Ctr., Valhalla, N.Y., 1982-83, resident in anesthesiology, 1983-85; attending anesthesiologist Oil City (Pa.) Health Ctr., Inc., 1985-89, dir. anesthesiology, 1986-89; physician advisor Keystone Peer Review Orgn., Lemoyne, Pa., 1986-89; attending anesthesiologist Broward Gen. Med. Ctr. and others, Fort Lauderdale, Fla., 1989-94; dir. anesthesiology Columbia St. Petersburg Med. Ctr., 1994—, med. dir. Comprehensive Pain Mgmt. Ctr., 1996—; dir. anesthesiology Oil City Area Health Ctr., 1986-89. Active ARC, 1986, YMCA. Mem. AMA (Physicians Recognition award 1994), Am. Soc. Anesthesiology, Fla. Soc. Anesthesiologists, Fla. Med. Soc., Pinellas County Med. Soc., Soc. for Ambulatory Anesthesia. Office: Columbia St Petersburg Med Ctr 6500 38th Ave Worth Saint Petersburg FL 33710

TRAUGH, MARK WILLIAM, physician assistant; b. Denver, Feb. 13, 1953; s. William Harry and Carol Jay (Osborn) T.; m. Janice Dee Crane, Apr. 28, 1973; children: Scott C., Jennifer B. AA in Emergency Med. Tng., El Paso C.C., Colorado Springs, Co., 1975; AA, A Gen. Studies, Pikes Peak C.C., Colorado Springs, 1980; AA in Gen. Studies, Azusa (Calif.) Pacific Coll., 1980; AA in Emergency Medicine, C.C. of Air Force, 1981; BS, U. Okla., Oklahoma City, 1983. Cert. Nat. Commn. on Cert. Physician Assts.; lic. physician asst., Ga., Calif., Tenn.; cert. ACLS. Enlisted man USAF, 1973, advanced through grades. to capt., 1987; med. technician USAF Acad., Colorado Springs, 1973-78, Mountain Home AFB, Idaho, 1978-80; staff physician asst. Robins Air Force Hosp., Warner Robins, Ga., 1983-89; chief physician asst. McClellan AFB Clinic, Sacramento, 1989-93; ret., 1993; chief physician asst. Internal Medicine Assocs., Warner Robins, 1993-94, Unionville Clinic, Macon, Ga., 1994-96, Dresden (Tenn.) Med. Assocs., 1996—; presenter in field; cons. to surgeon gen. on physician asst. affairs Air Force Logistics Command, 1991, 92, Air Force Materiel Command, 1993; mem. staff Houston County Med. Ctr., Warner Robins, 1993-96, Mid. Ga. Hosp., Macon, 1994-96, Macon Med. Ctr., 1994-96; pres., owner SJT Enterprises, Warner Robins, 1986-96. Contbr. articles to profl. jours. Recipient Order of Arrow, Boy Scouts Am., 1976. Fellow Am. Acad. Physician Assts., Soc. Air Force Physician Assts. Republican. Office: Dresden Med Assocs 130 E Locust St Dresden TN 38225

TRAUGHBER, SAM HENDLEY, cardiologist; b. Maysville, Ky., Nov. 29, 1935; s. Samuel Bradley and Rose Ellen (Hendley) T.; m. Blanche Polley Traughber, June 2, 1956; children: Samantha Lyn, James Bradley. BME with hons., Murray (Ky.) State U., 1957; MME, U. Kans., 1959; MD with hons., U. Louisville, 1965. Lic. physician, Ky., Tenn.; diplomate Am. Bd. Internal Medicine. Intern and resident Vanderbilt U., Nashville, 1965-69; pvt. practice cardiology Hopkinsville, Ky., 1969—; mem. staff Jennie Stuart Med. Ctr., Hopkinsville, Ky., Caldwell County War Meml. Hosp., Princeton, Ky., Trigg County Hosp., Cadiz, Ky.; bd. dirs. Ky. affiliate Am. Heart Assn., 1985—, pres., 1991-92; bd. dirs. Ky. Peer Rev. Orgn., 1980-85; assoc. prof. clin. medicine U. Ky., Lexington; Fed. Black Lung examiner, 1985—; dir. Jennie Stuart Med. Ctr. Dialysis Unit, 1969-90, Ren Ctr. Dialysis, Hopkinsville, Ky., 1990—; prin. investigator Gusto Trial, 1991-93. Contbr. articles to profl. jours. Mem. Gov.'s Adv. Council for Kidney Disease, 1969;l bd. dirs. Pennyrile Mental Health and Retardation, 1969; trustee 1st Meth. Ch., 1990. With U.S. Army, 1959-61. Recipient Physicians Recognition award AMA, 1980, 85, 87. Fellow ACP (Laureate award 1992), Am. Coll. Cardiology; mem. Ky. Med. Assn. (coun. for continuing med. edn. 1987-88, claims and utilizations rev. com., sci. com., membership com.), Am. Soc. Echocardiography, Pennyrile Med. Soc. (past pres.), Alpha Omega Alpha. Methodist. Home: 202 James Lyn Dr Hopkinsville KY 42240-9033 Office: 1910 S Virginia St # 1 Hopkinsville KY 42240-3692

TRAUPMAN, ARNOLD FRANK, ophthalmologist; b. Allentown, Pa., Nov. 19, 1947; s. Arnold and Katherine (Didovitz) T.; m. Barbara Zylwitis, Aug. 1, 1970; children: Jonathan, Matthew, C. Gabriel, Emily. BS, St. Joseph's U., 1969; MD, Thomas Jefferson U., 1973. Diplomate Am. Bd. Ophthalmology. Intern Chestnut Hill Hosp., Phila., 1973-74; ophthalmology resident Thomas Jefferson U., Phila., 1974-77; ophthalmologist St. Luke's Hosp., Bethlehem, Pa., 1977—; instr. Thomas Jefferson U., Phila., 1977-96; adv. bd. Lehigh Valley Lung Assn., Allentown, 1980-83. Dist. chmn. Boy Scouts Am., 1988-92; v.p. Minsi Trails Coun., Lehigh Valley, Pa., 1992—; bd. dirs. Northampton Cmty. Blind Assn., Bethlehem, 1978-81. Recipient Silver Beaver award Boy Scouts Am., 1991, St. George award Cath. Com. Scouting, 1988. Fellow Am. Acad. Ophthalmology; mem. Pa. Med. Soc., Northampton County Med. Soc., Pa. Acad. Ophthalmology, Lehigh Valley Ophthalmology Soc. (treas. 1983-88). Democrat. Roman Catholic. Office: 1313 Center St Bethlehem PA 18018

TRAVAGLINI, FIORENZO HUGO, orthopaedic surgeon; b. Reggio, Emilia, Italy, June 14, 1930; s. Irmo and Anna (Bosella) T.; m. Laura Manetti, June 7, 1980. MD, Sch. Medicine, Bologna, Italy, 1954. Cert. Bd. Orthopaedic Surgery, Italy, Bd. Physiotherapy, Italy; cert. prof. orthopaedic surgery, Italy. Resident Tuscany Inst. Orthopaedics, Florence, Italy, 1955-58, sr. resident, 1958-65, asst. prof., 1965-71, prof., chief surgeon dept. scoliosis and allied disorders, 1971—. Contbr. numerous papers to sci. jours. Fellow Internat. Coll. Surgery; mem. Internat. Soc. Orthopaedic Surgery, Scoliosis Rsch. Soc., Royal Soc. Medicine (affiliate). Office: Tuscany Inst Orthopaedics, 41 Viale Michelangelo, 50125 Florence Italy

TRAVERS, ROSE ELAINE, nursing supervisor; b. Aberdeen Proving Grounds, Md., July 30, 1956; d. Calvin Mace and Margaret Rose (Duncan) T. AA, Harford Community Coll., Bel Air, Md., 1976; BS magna cum laude, Towson State U., 1985; MSA, Cen. Mich. U., 1992. Nursing asst. Brevin Nursing Home, Havre de Grace, Md., 1973, Citizen's Nursing Home, Havre de Grace, 1974; staff nurse Harford Meml. Hosp., Havre de Grace, 1976-84; RN supr. Keswick Home, Balt., 1985—.

TRAVERS, W. LAWRENCE, health care executive; b. Syracuse, N.Y., Nov. 1, 1943; s. Walter Roy and Elizabeth Laurene (Hicks) T.; BS, Coll. of Emporia (Kans.), 1965; MSW, Syracuse U., 1972. Diplomate in clin. social work, cert. alcoholism counselor, master addiction counselor. N.Y. Cons. alcoholism treatment Hutchings Psychiat. Ctr. of N.Y. State, Office of Mental Health, Syracuse, 1972-73, program dir. alcoholism rehab. unit,

1973-76, program dir. psychogeriatric day treatment/outpatient services, 1976-80, mental health outpatient service, 1980-86, program dir. mentally ill. chem. abuse sr. adv. panel, 1986-91; rehab. coord. Capital Dist. Psychiat. Ctr., Albany, N.Y, 1991-94; edn. and tng. cons., 1994—; pvt. practice, Marietta, N.Y.; bd. dirs. Franklin Med. Lab. Sch., Westbury, N.Y., 1980. Dem. party official, 1974-76. Recipient sci. achievement award Chem. Rubber Co., 1965. Fellow Am. Orthopsychiat. Assn.; mem. Acad. Cert. Social Workers (diplomate), Nat. Assn. Social Workers (clin. register), Am. Coll. Addiction Treatment Adminstrs., Am. Bd. Examiners in Clin. Social Work, Am. Coll. Health Care Exec. Presbyterian. Home: Empire View 204 196 Morton Ave Albany NY 12202 Office: Capital Dist Psychiatric Ctr 75 New Scotland Albany NY 12208

TRAVIS, MARLENE O., healthcare management executive; b. Edmonton, Alta., Can.; Came to U.S. 1959.; d. LeRoy David and Della Jessie (Campbell) T.; m. Gary T. McIlroy, Aug. 20, 1962; children: Jennifer Renee, Montgomery Travis. Student (mass comms.), St. Cloud State U., 1974-76; exec. edn., U. Pa., Stanford U., 1989-92. Cert. exec. edn. Owner Travis Communications, Brainerd, Minn., 1975-77; co-founder, operating officer Midwest Lab. Assoc., Mpls., 1977-80; dir., corp. v.p. Meidinger-HRM (MHRM), Mpls., 1981-83; co-founder, exec. v.p., bd. dirs. Health Risk Mgmt. Inc., Mpls., 1977—, dir., pres., COO, 1986—; chair of bd., CEO HRM Ltd. (Can.), 1989—; founder, chair CEO Inst. Healthcare Quality, Mpls., 1991—; vice-chair Med. Alley, 1994—, bd. dirs. Co-author Self Health Guide to Laboratory Tests, 1982. Chmn. Minn. Task Force on Battered Women, 1977-79; bd. dirs. Minn. Task Force on Sexual Assault, 1974-76; co-founder, chair Mid Minn. Women's Ctr. Brainerd, 1975; founder, chair Crow Wing County Task Force on Sexual Assault, Brainerd, 1974-77; founder Crow Wing County Task Force to Support Battered Women, 1974; mem. Minn. Commr. of Edn.'s Task Force to Eliminate Sexism in Edn., 1973-74; mem. leadership group Amnesty Internat., 1990—, mem. exec. com., 1990—, com. of 200, 1991—. Named Cornerstone Leader in Giving United Way Mpls., 1992-95. Mem. AAUW, NOW (convenor Marshfield, Wis. chpt. 1972, Brainerd area chpt. 1974), C-200 Found. (mentor contbr.), Nat. Assn. Corp. Dirs., Toastmasters (sponsor 1988), Phi Beta Gamma. Office: Health Risk Mgmt Inc 8000 W 78th St Minneapolis MN 55439-2534

TRAVIS, TRACY LEIGH, emergency physician; b. Lynchburg, Va., Aug. 27, 1957; d. Charles C. Jr. and Mildred (Lindsay) T.; 1 child, Jennifer Koecke. BS in Biology, Lynchburg Coll., 1979; MD, Eastern Va. Med. Sch., 1982. Diplomat Am. Bd. Emergency Medicine. Resident Butterworth Hosp., Grand Rapids, Mich., 1987; emergency physician Mary Washington Hosp., Fredericksburg, Va., 1988-93, Expresslane, Stafford, Va., 1992—. Fellow Am. Coll. Energency Physicians; mem. Phi Kappa Phi. Home: 710 Virginia Ave Fredericksburg VA 22401 Office: Expresslane 422 Gairisonville Rd Stafford VA 22554

TREANOR, JOHN J., psychiatrist; b. Kenmore, N.Y., Oct. 12, 1931; s. William Michael and Margaret (Power) T.; m. Sarah Ellen Januale, June 1, 1968; children: Joseph, Margaret, William. BA in Physics, U. Buffalo, 1961; MD, SUNY, Buffalo, 1967; MPH, U. Hawaii, 1973. Diplomate Am. Bd. Preventive Medicine, Am. Bd. Psychiatry and Neurology; lic. physician, N.Y., Hawaii, Ala., Ga., Pa. Intern Buffalo Gen. Hosp., 1967-68; aerospace medicine resident Brooks AFB, San Antonio, 1973-74; psychiatry resident Eisenhower Army Med. Ctr., Ft. Gordon, Ga., 1978-81; staff psychiatrist Arden Hill Hosp., Mental Health Unit, Goshen, N.Y., 1981-87; inpatient ward psychaitrist Buffaloo Psychiatric Ctr., 1987-88; cons. in forensic psychiatry Erie County, N.Y., 1988—; clin. dir., psychiatrist III Buffalo Psychiatric Ctr., 1988—; clin. asst. prof. U. Buffalo, 1988—; investigator in clin. psychiatry, 1988—; psychiatric cons. Occupations, Inc., Scotchtown, N.Y., 1985-87, Castle Point VA Med. Ctr., Beacon, N.Y., 1985-87. Contbr. articles to profl. jours. Col. U.S. Army, 1951-87, Persian Gulf war, 90-91. Named Aerospace Medicine Specialist of the Yr., Soc. U.S. Army Flight Surgeons, 1976, Order of Mil. Med. Merit, Order of Aeromed. Merit, 1991; decorated Legion of Merit, Bronze Star (with 2 oak leaf clusters), Army Commendation Medal, Air Medal. Fellow Am. Psychiat. Assn., Aerospace Med. Assn., Am. Bd. Preventive Medicine, Am. Bd. Family Practice; mem. Am. Soc. Mil. Surgeons. Democrat. Roman Catholic. Home: 756 Richmond Ave Buffalo NY 14222-1159 Office: Buffalo Psychiat Ctr 400 Forest Ave Buffalo NY 14213-1207

TREECE, TIMOTHY A., plastic surgeon; b. Columbus, Ohio, Oct. 3, 1957; s. Florin and Dorothy (Orr) T.; m. Sharon Millhon; children: Tyler, Dylan, Luke. BS, Ohio State U., 1979, MD, 1982. Diplomate Am. Bd. Surgery, Am. Bd. Plastic Surgery. Chief surg. svcs. USAF Hosp., Dhaw AFB, S.C., 1989-90; plastic surgeon resident Ohio State U., 1990-92; staff surgeon Riverside Meth. Hosp., Childrens Hosp., Columbus, 1992—; clin. asst. prof. Ohio State U. Maj. USAF, 1987-90. Decorated Meritorious Svc. medal USAF, 1990. Fellow ACS (assoc.); mem. Am. Soc. Plastic and Reconstructive Surgeons. Republican. Presbyterian. Office: 3555 Olentangy Rd Columbus OH 43214

TREFZ, BRUCE ROBERT, oral and maxillofacial surgeon; b. Milw., Oct. 20, 1946; s. Robert Henry and Lois (Murphy) T.; m. Linda Sue Trefz, June 24, 1972; children: Leann Sue, Robert Bruce. BS, U. Mich., 1968, DDS, 1973, MS in Oral Surgery, 1977, MS in Neurosci., 1979. Diplomate Am. Bd. Oral and Maxillofacial Surgery. Grad. rsch. asst. U. Mich., Ann Arbor, 1968-75, clin. instr., 1973-77; asst. prof. U. Detroit, 1977-81, dir. pain control clinic, 1977-81; pvt. practice oral and maxillofacial surgery Gastonia, N.C., 1981—; mem. surg. staff Gaston Meml. Hosp., Gastonia, 1982—; med. missionary, cons. in oral and maxillofacial surgery Hosp. of Light, Bonne Fin, Haiti, 1979—, Regional and Children's Hosp., Vladimir, Russia, 1993—. Contbr. articles to profl. jours.; editor Oakland County Dental Rev., 1979-81. Pres. Gaston County Cancer Soc., 1986; internat. rep. Piedmont coun. Boy Scouts Am., 1991—; founder Gaston Cmty. Concert Band, Gastonia, 1993. Recipient E.H. Hatton Rsch. award Internat. Assn. Dental Rsch., 1972; predoctoral rsch. fellow NIH, 1972, postdoctoral rsch. fellow, 1973-75. Fellow Am. Assn. Oral and Maxillofacial Surgeons; mem. ADA (bd. dirs. 1969—), N.C. Soc. Oral and Maxillofacial Surgeons (pres. 1981—), Chalmers J. Lyons Acad. of Oral and Maxillofacial Surgeons (sec.-treas. 1977—), Christian Med. Dental Soc., Rotary Club of Gastonia (bd. dirs., officer 1984—). Office: 1041 X-Ray Dr Gastonia NC 28054

TREFZGER, RICHARD CHARLES, surgeon; b. Peoria, Ill., Jan. 27, 1948; s. John Dennis and Marilyn Lestilie (Wilson) T.; m. Nancy Ellen Guy, Dec. 19, 1971; children: Emily Jean, Michael Guy. BS, U. Ill., 1970, MD, 1973. Diplomate Am. Bd. Surgery. Intern in surgery Med. Coll. Wis., Milw., 1973-74, resident in surgery, 1974-75; resident in surgery Presbyn.-St. Luke's Hosp., Chgo., 1975-78; instr. surgery Rush Med. Coll., Chgo., 1977-78; med. dir. Westminster Village Retirement Ctr., Bloomington, Ill., 1980-84, St. Joseph's Trauma Ctr., Bloomington, 1986-96, BroMenn Regional Trauma Ctr., Normal, Ill., 1994-96; chief surgery Bromenn Regional Med. Ctr., Normal, Ill., 1987-88, 94-96; chief surgery St. Joseph's Med. Ctr., Bloomington, 1989-91, pres. med. staff, 1991-92; clin. instr. U. Ill. Coll. Medicine, 1980—; chmn. bd. dirs. BroMenn Physician Hosp. Orgn., 1995-96; bd. dirs. Cmty. Cancer Ctr., 1996—. Mem. Ill. State U. Civic Chorale, Normal, 1991—; bd. dirs. Barton Stone Christian Home, Jacksonville, Ill., 1979-82, Cmty. Cancer Ctr., Bloomington, 1996—. Fellow ACS (councilor Ill chpt. 1986-88, mem. Ill. chpt. com. on trauma 1996—); mem. AMA, Ill. Surg. Soc. (gov. 1990-94), Rotary (dir. 1982-85, 94—, sec. 1995-96, v.p. 1996—, mem. bd., Paul Harris fellow 1989, band-saxophone), Masons, Scottish Rite, Alpha Omega Alpha. Mem. Christian Ch. Home: 41 Pendleton Way Bloomington IL 61704-6243 Office: Surg Assocs 1404 Eastland Dr Bloomington IL 61701-3517

TREJO, JOANN, medical researcher; b. Stockton, Calif., Jan. 23, 1964. BS, U. Calif., Davis, 1986; PhD, U. Calif., San Diego, 1992. Postdoctoral fellow Cardiovascular Rsch. Inst., U. Calif., San Francisco, 1992—; undergrad. rsch. asst. Lawrence Berkeley Lab. Divsn. Biology and Medicine, 1983-86; teaching asst. dept. environ. toxicology U. Calif., Davis, 1986, dept. pharmacology, San Diego, 1988-91, dept. biology, 1989. Contbr. articles to profl. jours. Katherine Larcara, Jack O'Keefe and Kiwanis Club Undergrad scholar, 1982; San Diego and Grad. Opportunity fellow, 1986-88, Dissertation fellow Nat. Rsch. Coun. Ford Found., 1991-92, Pres.'s Postdoctoral fellow U. Calif., 1993-95; recipient Nat. Hispanic Scholarship Fund award, 1990-91, Minority Scientist Career Devel. award Am. Heart Assn., 1995; Tng. grantee NIH/NHLBI Cardiovascular Rsch. Inst., 1992-93. Mem. AAAS, LWV, Am. Soc. Cell Biology, Soc. Advancement of Chicanos and Native Americans in Sci. Home: 215 Upper Terrace Apt B San Francisco CA 94117 Office: U Calif Cardiovascular Rsch Inst 505 Parnassus Ave San Francisco CA 94143-0130

TRELLES, LUIS ANTONIO, neurology educator; b. Lima, Peru, Sept. 3, 1942; s. Julio Oscar and Maria (Montero) T.; m. Cecilia Thorne; children: Maria Veronica, Maria Del Pilar, Maria Del Carmen. Medicine, Cayetano Heredia U., Lima, 1968; neurolgoy, Born-Bunge Inst. Anvers, Belgium, 1970-71; student, Salpetreiere Hosp., Paris, 1971-75; MD, Cayetano Heredia U., 1977. Med. diplomate. Resident St. Toribio Neurol. Hosp., Lima, 1968-70; fellowship Born-Bunge Inst. Anvers, Belgium, 1970-71; resident Paris (France) Hosp., Hosp. de la Salpetriere, 1971-73; asst., neurology prof. Lhermitte Hosp. Salpetriere, Paris, 1973-75; asst. in neuroanatomy Faculty Medicine Broussais-Hotel Dieu, Paris. 1971-75; neurologist Sto. Toribio Neurol. Hosp., Lima, 1976—; prof. neurol. scis. Cath. U., Lima, 1976—; head rsch. dept. Nat. Inst. Neurol. Sci., Lima, 1983-90, dir., 1990-93; prof. neurology U. Cayetano Heredia, Lima, 1991—; bd. dirs. Revista de Neuropsiquiatria, Lima, editor, 1977—; bd. dirs. Clinica Santa Clara S.C.R. Ltd., Lima. Vice min. Pub. Health, Peru, 1985. Recipient Leignel Lavastine prix U. Paris, 1975, Gran Cruz Hipolito Unanue, Peruvian, 1985, Gran Cruz Daniel Alcides Carrion, Peruvian, 1985. Mem. Soc. Francaise Neurology, Am. Neurol. Assn., Am. Acad. Sci., Club Francais Neuropathologie, Soc. Peruana Neurologia. Office: Clinica Santa Clara SCR Ltd, Km 11.500 Carretera Ctrl, Lima 1977, Peru

TRELSTAD, ROBERT LAURENCE, pathology educator, cell biologist; b. Redding, Calif., June 16, 1940; s. Bertram Laurence and Dorothy (Axt) T.; m. Barbara Stanton Henken, Aug. 27, 1961; children: Derek, Graham, Brian, Jeremy. BA, Columbia U., 1961; MD, Harvard U., 1966. From asst. to assoc. prof. Harvard Med. Sch., Boston, 1972-81; chief pathology Shriners Burns Inst., Boston, 1975-81; staff pathologist Mass. Gen. Hosp., Boston, 1972-81; prof., chair pathology Robert Wood Johnson Med. Sch., Piscataway/New Brunswick, N.J., 1981—; mem. study sect. NIH, Bethesda, Md., 1971-75, 86-90; mem. adv. coun. Nat. Inst. Child Health and Human Devel., 1993—. Co-founder, editor-in-chief: Keyboard Publishing, Inc., 1990; past mem. editorial bd. various profl. jours. including Jour. Cell Biology, Am. Jour. Pathology, Devel. Biology, Devel. Dynamics. Lt. comdr. USPHS, 1967-69. Helen Hay Whitney Found. fellow, 1969-72; recipient Rsch. Faculty award Am. Cancer Soc., 1972-76, Disting. Tchr. in Basic Scis. award Alpha Omega Alpha and Assn. Am. Med. Colls., 1992. Mem. Am. Soc. Cell Biology (sec. 1982-88), Soc. Devel. Biology (pres. 1983). Home: 35 Westcott Rd Princeton NJ 08540-3038 Office: Robert Wood Johnson Med Sch Dept Of Pathology Piscataway NJ 08854

TREMBLAY, ALBERT T., health facility administrator; b. Nashua, N.H., Jan. 18, 1954; s. Henry G. and Jeanette (Robidas) T. m. Maureen P. Tremblay, June 15, 1982; children: William, Krystina, Lucas. Diploma, Lowell Gen. Hosp., 1981; BSN, U. State N.Y., Albany, 1993; postgrad., U. Vt., 1995—. Staff nurse intensive care burn unit Mass. Gen. Hosp., Boston, staff nurse neonatal ICU, ECMO nurse coord., nurse coord.; cath lab. instr. Med. Ctr. Hosp. Vt., Burlington; clin. dir. special care unit Fanny Allen Hosp., Colchester, Vt., clin. dir. inpatient svc., interim dir. nursing svc., 1991-92, adminstr. nursing svcs., 1992-93; adminstrv. nurse coord. Med. Ctr. Hosp. Vt., Burlington, 1994—. Mem. ANA, AACN, Am. Orgn. Nurse Execs., Vt. Orgn. Nurse Execs., Vt. Orgn. Nurse Mgrs., Vt. State Nursing Assn. Sigma Theta Tau.

TREMBLAY, JANINE MARIE, psychologist; b. Cambridge, Mass., Aug. 11, 1949; d. Henry Joseph and Marie Therese (Fradette) T.; m. George Royal Albert Johns, Nov. 20, 1993. PhD, St. John's U., 1983; postdoctorate, Adelphi U., 1994. Lic. psychologist, N.J., Fla., N.Y. Staff psychologist Rahway State Prison, Avenel, N.J., 1978-81; from staff psychologist to dir. psychology Greystone Park (N.J.) Hosp., 1981-91; pvt. practice psychology Morristown, N.J., 1985—; cons. Johnstone Tng. & Rsch., Bordentown, N.J., 1979-85; faculty Contemporary Ctr. for Advanced Psychoanalytic Studies, 1995—. Edtl. bd. N.J. Psychologist, 1981-93. Mem. APA, N.J. Acad. Psychology (trustee 1991-94), N.J. Psychol. Assn. (com. mem. 1987-93), Adelphi Soc. for Psychoanalysts and Psychotherapy. Home and Office: 150 Madison Ave Morristown NJ 07960

TREMBONE, AUDREY C., obstetrical, nursery nurse; b. Apr. 7, 1958; d. Martin James Glynn and Arlene Dorothy (Jacques) Hennessey; m. Samuel Trembone, Oct. 28, 1983; children: Courtney James, Samantha Joan, Victoria Elizabeth. Diploma, St. Vincent's Sch. Nursing, Staten Island, N.Y., 1993. Floor nurse Silver Lakes Nursing Home, Staten Island, N.Y., 1993; home health nurse Carefull Steps Inc., Staten Island, 1993—; obstetrics, nursery nurse Passasic (N.J.) Gen. Hosp., 1994—. Home: 39 Bement Ave Staten Island NY 10310 Office: Passaic Gen Hosp 350 Boulevard Passaic NJ 07055

TREMPER, KEVIN KEEFE, anesthesiologist, educator; b. Phila., Jan. 5, 1948; s. Henry Stever and Sheila Tremper; m. Amy Louise Opheim, Dec. 19, 1987; children: Theodore Tyler, Connor Keefe. BSChemE, U. Denver, 1971; MS in Chem. Engring., U. Calif., Berkeley, 1973, PhD in Chem. Engring., 1975; MD, U. Calif., Irvine, 1978. Diplomate Am. Bd. Anesthesiologists; lic. physician, Mich., Calif. Intern/surg. resident Harbor/UCLA Med. Ctr., 1978-79, surg. ICU rsch. fellow, 1979-81; resident in anesthesiology UCLA Sch. Medicine, 1981-83; asst. prof. anesthesiology U. Calif., Irvine, 1983-84, assoc. prof., chmn. dept. anesthesiology, 1984-90; prof., chmn. dept. anesthesiology U. Mich., Ann Arbor, 1991—; extensive lectr. in field. Editl. bd. Anesthesiology News, Critical Care Medicine, Jour. Clin. Monitoring, Jour. Clin. Anesthesia, Seminars in Anesthesia, Jour. Intensive Care Monitoring, 1986-88; reviewer for AIChE Jour., Anesthesiology, Anesthesia and Analgesia, Chest, Critical Care Medicine, IEEE Transactions, Jour. Applied Psychology, Jour. Clin. Engring., Jour. Clin. Anesthesia, Pediatrics. Pediatric Rsch., Obstetrics and Gynecology, Med. Instrumentation, Sugery; contbr. 89 articles and 500 abstracts to profl. jours., 33 chpts. to books; author: Perfluorochem. Oxygen Transport, 1985, Advances in Oxygen Monitoring, 1987. With USAR, 1971-77. Fellow Am. Coll. Chest Physicians, Am. Coll. Anesthesiologists; mem. AMA, Am. Soc. Anesthesiologists (chmn subcom. on equip., monitoring and engring. tech. 1992—, adj. mem. com. on sci. papers 1992—), Internat. Anesthesia Rsch. Soc., Mich. Soc. Anesthesiologists, Internat. Soc. of Oxygen Transport to Tissue, Am. Soc. Critical Care Anesthesiologists, Calif. Med. Assn. (sci. adv. panel 1984-90). Orange County Anesthesia Soc. (treas. 1985-86, pres. 1986-87), Alpha Omega Alpha. Republican. Home: 7227 Pleasant Lake Rd Ann Arbor MI 48103 Office: U of Mich Med Sch 1301 Catherine St Ann Arbor MI 48109-0600

TRENT, BRUCE EDWIN, transplant coordinator; b. Huntington, W.Va., June 27, 1953; s. David Edwin and Garnet Elizabeth (Francis) T.; m. Angela Dawn Suiter, June 14, 1974; children: Nicholas Ryan, Natalie Dawn. Student, Ohio U., 1971-74, Ohio State U., 1974-75; diploma in nursing, St. Mary's Sch. Nursing, 1986; BA, Marshall U., 1987. RN, W.Va., Ky., Ohio; cert. transplant coord. Pharmacy clk. Arrington-Wyant Pharmacy, Proctorville, Ohio, 1970-73; pharmacist intern Arrington-Wyant Pharmacy, Proctorville, 1973-78; lab. mgr. Riverside Coal Co., Proctorville, 1978-80; lab. technician Barboursville (W.Va.) Testing Lab., 1980-83; pharmacy clk. St. Mary's Hosp., Huntington, W.Va., 1983-86; RN St. Mary's Hosp., Huntington, 1986-87; transplant coord. Ky. Organ Donor Affiliates, Huntington, 1987-90, 91-96; med. sales cons. Support Sys. Internat., Charleston, W.Va., 1990-91; trauma nurse coord. Cabell Huntington Hosp., Huntington, 1996—; mem. organ donor com. King's Daughter's Med. Ctr., Ashland, Ky., 1991—, St. Mary's Hosp., Huntington, 1991—, Cabell Huntington (W.Va.) Hosp., 1991—. Clk.-treas. Village of Proctorville, Ohio, 1980—. Recipient Good Neighbor award ARC, W.Va. chpt., 1986, Spl. Life Saving commendation, S.E. Ohio Emergency Med. Svcs., 1990. Mem. AACN, Am. Bd. Transplant Coords., N.Am. Transplant Coords. Assn. Republican. Baptist. Home: PO Box 297 304 Wilgus St Proctorville OH 45669 Office: Ky and WVa Organ Donor Aff 1401 6th Ave Ste 202 Huntington WV 25701

TREPMAN, ELLY, orthopaedic surgeon; b. Montreal, Quebec, Can., June 14, 1956. BS (hon.), McGill U., 1977; MD cum laude, Harvard Med. Sch.-MIT, 1982. Diplomate Am. Bd. Orthopaedic Surgery. Intern in gen. surgery Beth Israel Hosp., Boston, 1982-83, jr. resident, 1983-84; chief resident Brigham & Women's Hosp., Boston, 1987; fellow in sports medicine Children's Hosp., Boston, 1988; orthopaedic surgeon Harvard Cmty. Health Plan, Boston, 1989-90; asst. prof. orthopaedics Yale U., 1990-93, co-dir. foot and ankle svc., dir. health svcs., 1990-93; orthopaedic surgeon, assoc. dir. Boston Foot & Ankle Ctr. New Eng. Bapt. Hosp., Boston, 1993-95, co-dir. Boston Foot & Ankle Ctr., 1995—. Assoc. editor, subsection editor Foot & Ankle Internat. (editor's award 1995); contbr. articles to profl. jours. Foot and ankle fellow New England Bapt. Hosp., Boston, 1992-93. Fellow Am. Acad. Orthopaedic Surgeons, Am. Orthopaedic Foot & Ankle Soc.; mem. Am. Coll. Sports Medicine, Internat. Assn. Dance Med. Sci. Office: Boston Foot & Ankle Ctr 70 Parker Hill Ave Boston MA 02120

TRESALTI, EMILIO, physician; b. Rome, June 25, 1935; s. Ettore and Fernanda (Persi) T. MD, U. Rome, 1959, diploma in endocrinology, 1963, MPH, 1970. Jr. resident U. Rome Med. Faculty, 1959-60, sr. resident, 1961-63; cons. internal and occupational medicine St. Barbara Hosp., Gela, Italy, 1963-69; dep. med. dir. Cath. U. "A. Gemelli" Hosp., Rome, 1969-76; prof. epidemiology and preventive medicine, med. faculty Somali Nat. U., Mogadishu, Somalia, 1977-80; chmn. community health dept. Somali Nat. U., 1979-80; med. dir. Cath. U. "A. Gemelli" Hosp., Rome, 1980-94; prof. hygiene and health mgmt. Catholic U. Med. Faculty, Rome, 1980—; cons. health dept. Coun. Europe, Strasbourg, France, 1985-88, dept. for cooperation to devel. Ministry Fgn. Affairs, Rome, 1977-82; v.p. Assn. Studi Am. Latina, Rome, 1989; cons. Congregation for Consecrated Life and Apostolic Socs., Hole See, 1991. Author: Epidemiologia e Medicina Preventive, 1980, Igiene e Tecnica Ospedaliera, 1988, Daryeelka Caafimaadka Beesha, 1980; contbr. articles to profl. jours. Sec. gen. Conf. Mondiale des Instituts Seculiers, Rome, 1972-80. Lt. Italian mil., 1960-61. Named Knight Commander Order St. Silvester, Pope John Paul II, 1981, Order St. Gregory the Great, 1993, Knight Order Merito della Repubblica, Pres. Italy, 1985. Fellow Societa Italiana de Igiene Medicina Preventiva e Sanita Pubblica, Royal Soc. Tropical Medicine and Hygiene London, Internat. Soc. on Disaster Medicine Geneva, Fondation Hygie Geneve (sci. com. 1989). Roman Catholic. Home: Via Capodistria 15, 00198 Rome Italy Office: U Cattolica S Cuore, Facolta Medicina Chirurgia, Largo F Vito 1, 00168 Rome Italy

TRESELER, KATHLEEN MORRISON, retired nursing educator; b. Tacoma, Wash., Apr. 28, 1925; d. Charles T. and Elizabeth M. (McDermott) Morrison; m. Donald K. Treseler, July, 1949; children: Michael S., C. Maureen, Patrick A. BS, Seattle Coll., 1946; MSN, U. Wash., 1966. Prof. Seattle U. Sch. Nursing, 1968-91, prof. emeritus, 1991—. Author: Clinical Laboratory and Diagnostic Tests, 1982, 3d edit., 1995. Home: 17401 17th Pl NE Shoreline WA 98155-5201

TRESSER, MELVIN, physician; b. N.Y.C., Oct. 31, 1931; s. Max and Hannah (Levy) T.; m. Bella Kerner, Feb. 11, 1956; children: Debra Ilene, Steven Jeffrey, Andrea Michel. AB, Columbia Coll., 1952; MD, NYU, 1956. Diplomate Am. Bd. Internal Medicine. Intern, Montefiore Hosp., N.Y.C., 1956-57, resident, 1957-58, 61-62; resident in gastroenterology Mt. Sinai Hosp., N.Y.C., 1960-61; practice medicine specializing in gastroenterology and internal medicine, Orlando, Fla., 1962—; chief gastroenterology Orlando Regional Med. Ctr., 1977-83. Capt. USAF, 1958-60. Fellow Am. Coll. Gastroenterology; mem. Am. Soc. Gastrointestinal Endoscopy, ACP, AMA, So. Med. Assn., Fla. Gastroenterologic Soc., Orange County Med. Soc., Am. Heart Assn. Office: 1720 S Orange Ave Ste 305 Orlando FL 32806

TRESTMAN, ROBERT LEE, psychiatrist, educator; b. New Orleans, June 4, 1953; s. Anschel and Mae (Schwendelson) T.; m. rosanna Gene Liebman, Oct. 9, 1988; children: Lior Anschel, Morris Elia. BS, Carnegie Mellon U., 1975; PhD, U. Tenn., 1981, MD, 1985. Diplomate Am. Bd. Psychiatry and Neurology., 1990-95; Intern, then resident Mt. Sinai Med. Ctr., N.Y.C., 1985-89, rsch. fellow, 1988-90, assoc. in psychiatry, 1988-90, asst. prof. psychiatry, 1990-95, assoc. prof. psychiatry, 1995—, dir. rsch. fellowship tng., 1990-95, dep. chmn. dept. psychiatry, 1995—; clin. dir. dept. psychiatry, 1996—; co-dir. outpatient psychiatry Bronx (N.Y.) VA Med. Ctr., 1990-95; Ginsburg fellow Group for the Advancement of Psychiatry, Phila., 1987-89. Co-inventor chainless bicycle transmission. Am. Coll. Neuropsychopharmacology travel fellow, 1993. Mem. AMA, Soc. for Biol. Psychiatry, Am. Psychiat. Assn., Assn. for Personality Disorders (pres. 1995—). Democrat. Jewish. Office: Mt Sinai Med Ctr 1 Gustave L Levy Pl # 1230 New York NY 10029-6504

TREXLER, SUZANNE FRANCES, geriatrics nurse; b. Harrisburg, Pa., Feb. 8, 1963; d. Walter Richard and Catherine Frances (Mourawski) Markham; m. Barry Kenneth Trexler, Nov. 9, 1991; children: William Chester, Brittany Nancy, Katye Iona. LPN, Harrisburg Stelton Highs, Sch. Practical Nursing, 1984; ADN, Harrisburg (Pa.) Area C.C., 1984; BA in Long Term Care Adminstrn., St. Joseph Coll., 1994, postgrad., 1994—; BSN, York (Pa.) Coll., 1996. Nurse ICU and critical care unit Meml. Hosp., York, Pa., 1987-88; staff nurse emergency dept. Polyclinic Med. Ctr., Harrisburg, 1988-91; assoc. prof. Nat. Edn. Ctr.-Jr. Coll., Harrisburg, 1991; dir. nursing Camp Hill (Pa.) Care Ctr., 1991-92; resident assessment supr. Susquehanna Ctr., Harrisburg, 1992-94; dir. nursing Susquehanna Luth. Village, Millersburg, Pa., 1994-95; asst. adminstr. Dauphin Manor, Harrisburg, 1995—; ACLS, CPR instr. Am. Heart Assn., Harrisburg, 1989—; BCLS, CPR instr. ARC, Harrisburg, 1992—; RN, paramedic Lebanon (Pa.) County First Aide and Safety Patrol, 1992—. Sec. Little People PTA, Harrisburg, 1991-92; pres. Student Human Resource Mgmt. Club, York (Pa.) Coll., 1992—. Recipient Nurse of Hope award Am. Cancer Soc., Dauphin County, Harrisburg, 1983-84. Mem. AACN, Pa. Nurses Assn., Pa. Dir. Nursing Assn. for Long Term Care, PANPHA (advocate). Roman Catholic. Office: Dauphen Manor Paxton St Harrisburg PA 17111

TREZZA, VICENTE, pediatrician; b. Barranquilla, Colombia, Nov. 12, 1931; came to the U.S., 1960; s/ Vincenzo and Amparo (Pacheco) T.; m. Anita Lucia, Sept. 5, 1964; children: Vanessa Lynn, Paul Gregory, Alan Todd. BS, Barranquilla Coll., 1953; degree in painting and sculpture, Sch. Fine Arts, Colombia, 1952; MD, U. Cartagena, 1959. Diplomate Am. Bd. Pediatrics. Pediatric chief resident Queens Hosp. Ctr., N.Y.C., 1963; lectr. Hispanoam. Med. Congress, N.Y.C., 1990. Author: (novel in Spanish) Under Pontius Pilate, 1993, (short stories) The Same Land, 1979, (poetry) Exaltation, 1950. Fellow Am. Acad. Pediatrics; mem. Spanish Am. Med. Soc. (bd. dirs. 1990-91, 94-95, scientific com. 1993-94), Lions (bd. dirs. 1994—, pres. 1978-80), Masons (master 1994—), Alpha Beta Ki. Republican. Roman Catholic. Office: 40 36 82 St Jackson Heights NY 11373

TRIANTAPHYLLIDIS, CONSTANTINOS DEMETRIOS, biology and genetics educator; b. Drama, Macedonia, Greece, Sept. 5, 1940; s. Demetrios Constantinos and Aspasia John (Moutaftse) T.; m. Zenobia Achilleas Petalopoulou, Nov. 14, 1968; children: Demetra, Alexandros. Diploma in Natural Scis., Aristotle U., Thessaloniki, Greece, 1963, PhD in Biology, 1971; postgrad., U. Tex., 1978. Teaching asst. Aristotle U., Thessaloniki, Greece, 1966-72; postdoctorate U. Tex., Austin, 1973-75; instr. Aristotle U., Thessaloniki, 1975-78, sr. lectr., 1978-83, assoc. prof., 1983-86, prof., 1986—; prof. U. Newcastle Upon Tyne, U.K., 1988; head dept. genetics Aristotle U., Thessaloniki, 1984-87, chmn. sch. biology, 1989-95. Author 9 books on genetics; contbr. more than 55 articles to profl. jours. Sgt. inf. Greek Army, 1963-66. Scholar Greek Nat. Forum, 1959-63, U. Tex., 1973-75, Brit. Coun., 1985; grantee, 1975-76. Mem. Internat. Assn. Human Biologists, Assn. Greek Biologists. Greek Orthodox. Home: Phanariou 28 Kalamaria, 55 133 Thessaloniki Greece

TRIARHOU, LAZAROS CONSTANTINOS, neurobiologist, educator; b. Thessaloniki, Greece, June 23, 1957; s. Constantinos and Penelope (Georgiades) Triarhou. MD, Aristotelian U., Thessaloniki, 1981; MSc in Neurosci., U. Rochester, 1984; PhD in Neurobiology, Ind.-Purdue U., 1987. Rsch. asst. in neurosci. Ctr. for Brain Rsch., U. Rochester, N.Y., 1981-84; postdoctoral fellow in neuropathology and neurobiology Ind. U. Med. Ctr., Indpls., 1984-88, asst. prof. neuropathology and med. neurobiology, 1988-94; assoc. prof., 1994—; Mem. Internat. Parliament for Safety and Peace (dep. 1991—). Referee Brain Rsch., Exptl. Neurology, Cell Transplantation; contbr. numerous sci. reports to profl. jours. including Arch. Neurology, Experientia, Proc. Nat. Acad. Sci. USA, Jour. Comparative Neurology, Anatomy and Embryology, Nature Med., others. Recipient Honourable Weil award Am. Assn. Neuropathologists, 1987, First award U.S. Dept. of

HHS, 1990, Scientific award in medicine Bodossaki Found., 1995. Fellow Am. Soc. Neural Transplantation; mem. Brit. Brain Rsch. Orgn., Soc. for Neurosci. (mem. exec. com. Indpls. chpt. 1986-88), European Brain and Behaviour Soc., European Neurosci. Assn., Internat. Brain Rsch. Orgn., Hellenic Soc. for Neurosci., Med. Assn. Thessaloniki, N.Y. Acad. Scis., World Fedn. Neuroscientists, John Shaw Billings History of Medicine Soc., Internat. Union Psychol. Sci. Office: Ind U Sch Medicine Med. Sci Bldg A-128 Indianapolis IN 46202

TRICHOPOULOS, DIMITRIOS VASSILIOS, epidemiologist, educator; b. Volos, Greece, Dec. 9, 1938; s. Vassilios Konstantinou and Alexandra Dimitrios (Kataropoulou) T.; m. Antonia Athanasiou Polychronopoulou, June 17, 1967. MD, Athens U., Greece, 1963, PhD, 1971; MS, Harvard Sch. Pub. Health, 1968; MD honoris causa, Uppsala (Sweden) U., 1994. Diplomate Am. Coll. Epidemiology. Lectr. preventive medicine U. Athens Med. Sch., 1965-67, prof., chair preventive medicine, 1972-89; lectr. epidemiology Harvard Sch. Pub. Health, Boston, 1969-70, prof., chair epidemiology, 1989-96; prof., dir. Harvard Ctr. Cancer Prevention, Boston, 1994—; chmn. health group Coun. European Union, Brussels, 1988. Editor: Teaching Epidemiology, 1992; contbr. numerous articles to profl. jours. Decorated officier Ordre Palmes Academiques (France). Mem. Royal Acad. Medicine Belgium (corr., fgn.), Nat. Acad. Medicine France (corr., fgn.), Harvard Club, Athens Club. Greek Orthodox. Office: Harvard Sch Pub Health 677 Huntington Ave Boston MA 02115

TRICK, JUDY A., nurse manager; b. Great Falls, Mont., May 13, 1954; d. Charles M. and Kathleen M. (Devine) T. LPN, Great Falls Vocat. Tech.; ADN, Regents Coll. Rehab. supr. Walla Walla, Wash., 1980-82; staff nurse Oddfellows Home, Walla Walla, 1982-84; floor nurse Hearthstone, Medford, Oreg., 1984-86, mgr. rehab. svcs., 1986-90, staff devel./edn. nurse, 1990-91, Alzheimers unit mgr., 1991-94; nurse mgr. Rogue Valley Serenity Ln., Central Point, Oreg., 1994—; mem. nurse adv. com. Rogue C.C., Grants Pass, Oreg., 1995—. Democrat. Roman Catholic. Home: 719 Palm Medford OR 97501 Office: Rogue Valley Serenity Ln 600 S 2d St Medford OR 97502-2704

TRICKETT, JENNIFER BEATRICE, medical and surgical nurse; b. Takoma Park, Md., July 17, 1957; d. Kenneth William and Sigrid Annette (Engelke) T. AA, Hopkinsville (Ky.) C.C., 1981; BA in Psychology, U. Ctrl. Fla., Orlando, 1985; ASN, Valencia C.C., Orlando, 1992. RN, Fla.; cert. med.-surg. nurse; cert. BLS. Staff nurse Leesburg (Fla.) Regional Med. Ctr., 1992-93; multi-skilled practitioner Lakeland Regional Med. Ctr., Fla., 1993-94; shift supr. Winter Haven (Fla.) Hosp., 1994—. Red Cross vol. Tripler Army Med. Ctr., Honolulu, 1973. Served to sgt. Signal Corps, U.S. Army, 1979-83, to capt. Med. Svc. Corps, 1986—. Decorated Army Commendation medal, Achievement medal (2); scholarship ROTC. Mem. Phi Theta Kappa. Lutheran. Home: 200 Ave K SE # 29 Winter Haven FL 33880-4005

TRICOULIS, DIMITRIOS, ophthalmologist; b. Poulithra, Arcadia, Greece, Sept. 25, 1933; s. Ioamis and Heleni (Chiotis) T.; m. Eugenia Perakis, Mar. 11, 1967; children: Heleni, Christina. MD, Athens (Greece) Med. Coll., 1959; postgrad., Inst. Ophthalmology, London, 1965; Doctorat, Salonica (Greece) Med. Coll., 1968. Asst. on ophthalmology Evangelismos Hosp., Athens, 1961-65, sr. registrar, 1966-73, attending physician, 1973-75; cons. Greek Church's Hosp., Athens, 1975-86; prof. Nursing Sch. Athens, 1975-86; pvt. practice, 1986—. Contbr. articles to profl. publs. Officer Greek Army, 1959-61. Mem. Royal Coll. Ophthalmologists U.K. (affiliate), Helenic Ophthalmol. Soc. Greek Orthodox. Home: Othonos 24, 15231 Chalandri Greece Office: 55 Skoupha, 10672 Athens Greece

TRIDENTE, GIUSEPPE, immunologist, educator; b. Triggiano, Puglia, Italy, Apr. 16, 1939; s. Nicola and Vincenza (Campobasso) T.; m. Sara Dal Dosso; children: Gaia, Ginerva. MD, Univ. Bari, Italy, 1963, postgrad. in pathology, 1966; postgrad. in hematology, U. Padua, Italy, 1968. Med. Diplomate specialist. Jr. researcher, fellow Lady Tata Meml. Fund., U. Bari, 1965-68, Italian Minister Pub. Instrn., U. Bari, 1966; sr. rsch. fellow Dutch Nat. Rsch. Coun., Risswisk, The Netherlands, 1968-69; asst. in pathology lab. Civil Hosp. and Univ., Padua, 1969-70; sr. scientist, asst. prof. transplant immunology & pathology Univ. Edmonton, Alberta, Can., 1971; prof. without tenure immunopathology U. Verona, Italy, 1971-75; prof. immunopathology U. Verona, 1975-82; mem. bd. adminstrn., 1986-87, mem. acad. senate, 1991-94; prof., dir. immunology U. Verona, 1983-90; dir. Inst. Immunology and Infectious Diseases, Univ. Verona., 1991—, dean med. faculty, 1994—; dean of med. faculty, 1994—. Author: Immunology and Immunpathology, 1979; editor: Jour. of Immunolgy Rsch., 1989; contbr. over 250 publs. to med. and sci. jours. and books. Mem. city hall coun. City of Verona, 1990-91. Office: Inst Immunology & Infectious Diseases, Policlinico B Roma, 37100 Verona Veneto, Italy

TRIGG, JACK WALDEN, JR., physician; b. Birmingham, Ala., Apr. 18, 1932; s. Jack Walden Sr. and Florine (Hagood) T.; m. Dorothy Wynne, June 3, 1958; 1 child, James Albert. BS, Va. Mil. Inst., 1953; MD, Med. Coll. of Ala., 1958. Diplomate Am. Bd. Internal Medicine. Intern in medicine Duke U. Hosp., Durham, N.C., 1958-59; resident in medicine Univ. Hosp., Birmingham, 1959-62; physician So. Med. Group, Birmingham, 1964—; pres. med. staff St. Vincent's Hosp., 1986. Capt. USAF, 1962-64. Fellow ACP; mem. AMA, Birmingham Soc. of Internists, Jefferson County Med. Soc. Republican. Episcopalian. Home: 2006 Garden Pl Birmingham AL 35223-1156

TRIGGLE, DAVID JOHN, university dean, consultant; b. U.K., Apr. 5, 1935; came to U.S., 1962; s. William John and Maud F. (Henderson) T.; m. Ann. M. Jones, Sept. 22, 1959; children: Andrew B., Jocelyn A. BSc in Chemistry, U. Southampton, United Kingdom, 1956; PhD, U. Hull, United Kingdom, 1959. Research fellow U. Ottawa, Ont., Can., 1959-61, U. London, 1961-62; asst. prof. SUNY Sch. of Pharmacy, Buffalo, 1962-65, assoc. prof., 1965-69, prof., 1985-95, chmn. dept., 1971-85, dean, 1985-95, Disting. prof., vice-provost for grad. edn., 1990—. Author: Chemical Aspects of Autonomic Nervous System, 1965, Neurotransmitter-Receptor Interactions, 1971, Chemical Pharmacology of the Synapse, 1976. Recipient Volwiler Rsch. Achievement award Am. Assn. Colls. Pharmacy, 1988, 89, George Koepf award Biomed. Rsch. Med. Found. Buffalo, 1994. Fellow AAAS; mem. Am. Chem. Soc., Am. Soc. Pharmacology and Therapeutics (Otto Krayer award 1995), Soc. Neurosci., Brit. Pharmacology Soc. Office: SUNY Grad Sch 410 Capen Buffalo NY 14260

TRIGIANO, LUCIEN LEWIS, physician; b. Easton, Pa., Feb. 9, 1926; s. Nicholas and Angeline (Lewis) T.; children: Lynn Anita, Glenn Larry, Robert Nicholas. Student Tex. Christian U., 1944-45, Ohio U., 1943-44, 46-47, Milligan Coll., 1944, Northwestern U., 1945, Temple U., 1948-52. Intern, Meml. Hosp., Johnstown, Pa., 1952-53; resident Lee Hosp., Johnstown, 1953-54; gen. practice, Johnstown, 1953-59; med. dir. Pa. Rehab. Center, Johnstown, 1959-62, chief phys. medicine and rehab., 1964-70; fellow phys. medicine and rehab. N.Y. Inst. Phys. Medicine and Rehab., 1962-64; dir. rehab. medicine Lee Hosp., 1964-71, Ralph K. Davies Med. Center, San Francisco, 1973-75, St. Joseph's Hosp., San Francisco, 1975-78, St. Francis Meml. Hosp., San Francisco, 1978-83; asst. prof. phys. medicine and rehab. Temple U. Sch. Medicine; founder Disability Alert. Served with USNR, 1944-46. Diplomate Am. Bd. Phys. Medicine and Rehab. Mem. AMA, A.C.P., Pa., San Francisco County Med. socs., Am. Acad. Phys. Medicine and Rehab., Am. Congress Phys. Medicine, Calif. Acad. Phys. Medicine, Nat. Rehab. Assn., Babcock Surg. Soc. Author various med. articles. Home: 1050 North Point St San Francisco CA 94109-8302 Office: 1150 Bush St Ste 4B San Francisco CA 94109-5920

TRIGOBOFF, DANIEL HOWARD, psychologist; b. Bklyn., Jan. 21, 1953; s. Philip and Eileen G. (Dubin) T.; m. Eileen Hazel Ruff, Mar. 30, 1985. BA, SUNY, 1974; MA, U. Iowa, 1978, PhD, 1980. Lic. clin. psychologist. Clin. psychologist VA, Buffalo, 1980-87; program dir. Buffalo Psychiat. Ctr., 1988-89; program coord. Buffalo Gen. Hosp., 1989-92; adj. prof. SUNY, Buffalo, 1984—; clin. psychologist pvt. practice Amherst, N.Y., 1982—; cons. Mid-Erie Mental Health Svcs., Buffalo, 1980-89. Mem. adv. bd. Langston Hughes Inst., Buffalo, 1986. Mem. Am. Psychol. Assn. Jewish.

TRILLI, JAMES VICTOR, podiatrist; b. Pitts., July 15, 1950; s. Giberto Luigi and Virginia Marie (Magone) T.; m. Suzanne Marie Walos, June 3, 1972; 1 child, Jonathan Christopher. BS in Bus. Mgmt., Point Park Coll., 1972; BS in Chemistry, Biology, California (Pa.) State U., 1978; D Podiatric Medicine, Ohio Coll. Podiatric Medicine, 1982. Diplomate Am. Bd. Podiatric Surgery. Sales mgr. Culligan Soft Water Svc., Star Junction, Pa., 1972-74; substitute tchr. Douglas Sch. Bus., Monessen, Pa., 1974-78; coal miner Consol. Coal, Library, Pa., 1974-78; resident Podiatry Hosp. Pitts., 1983-84; pvt. practice Monessen, 1984—; med. staff Podiatry Hosp. Pitts.; med. staff Monongahela Valley Hosp., mem. credentials com., laser com.; team podiatrist Mon-Valley Cath. High Sch. football team. Vol. Monessen March of Dimes, 1984-91; bd. dirs. Monongahela (Pa.) YMCA, 1988-92, Monessen United Way, 1991-92, Am. Diabetes Assn. Fellow Am. Coll. Foot Surgeons; mem. Am. Podiatric Med. Assn., Pa. Podiatric Med. Assn., Am. Running and Fitness. Democrat. Roman Catholic. Office: Eastgate Family Foot Care Eastgate 15 Ste 1-h Monessen PA 15062

TRINOSKY-LIND, PATRICIA, nursing educator; b. Louisville, Feb. 9, 1953; d. Frank George and Katherine Elizabeth (Miller) Trinosky. BSN, U. N.Mex., 1975; MS, U. Colo., Denver, 1979. Cert. provider and instr. ACLS. Staff nurse med. and neurol. units VA Hosp., San Diego; staff nurse ICU Mercy Hosp., San Diego; part-time staff nurse Rose Med. Ctr., Denver, 1978-79; mem. faculty BSN program Beth-El Coll. Nursing, Colorado Springs, Colo., 1979—. Contbr. articles to profl. jours. Mem. AACN.

TRIPP, JOHN HOWARD, pediatrician, consultant, educator; b. Dartford, Kent, England, Nov. 16, 1944; s. George Frederic and Ann (Buckingham) T.; m. Judy Margaret Peskett; children: Melanie Ruth, Esther Anne. BSc, London, 1965; MBBS, Guys Hosp., London, 1969; MD, London. House officer Guy's Hosp., London, 1968-69; sr. house officer Great Ormond St. Children's Hosp., London, 1971; registrar Hosp. for Sick Children, London, 1971-73, sr. registrar, 1977-80; rsch. fellow Inst. Child Health, London, 1973-76; cons. pediatrician Royal Devon & Exeter (England) Hosp., 1980—; sr. lectr. U. Exeter, 1984—. Editor: Manual of Pediatric Gastroenterology & Nutrition, 1992; contbr. articles to profl. jours. Rsch. grantee Joseph Rountree Found., 1990, 92, NHS Exec. Fellow Royal Coll. Physicians of England; mem. Brit. Pediat. Assn. Home: Pixie Cottage Alphington, EX2 8TD Exeter Devon, England Office: U Exeter Hosp Dept Child Health, Church Rd Heavitree, EX2 5SQ Exeter Devon, England

TRIPP, THOMAS EUGENE, psychotherapist; b. Albany, N.Y., Sept. 23, 1950; s. Thomas E. and Anne (Viola) T.; m. Barbara Anna Scheublein, June 12, 1971; 1 child, Sarah Jeanne. B.S., Union Coll., Schenectady, 1972; M.S.W., U. Kans., 1976. Cert. clin. social worker, N.H.; lic. clin. social worker, Mass., Vt., diplomate. Caseworker, St. Agnes Sch. for Children, Sparkill, N.Y., 1972-74; counselor East Central Kans. CAP, Ottawa, 1975; clinician Family and Children's Service, Lebanon, Pa., 1976-78; sr. clinician Family Services, Keene, N.H., 1978-86; pvt. practice psychotherapy, Keene, 1981—. Mem. NASW, N.H. Soc. for Clin. Social Work, Phi Kappa Phi. Office: Therapy Center 82 Court St Keene NH 03431-3408

TRIPPET, SUSAN ELAINE, nursing educator; b. Princeton, Ind., Nov. 3, 1946; d. Charles Kightly and Isabel (Key) T. AA, Ind. U., Indpls., 1971, MS in Nursing, 1983; DS in Nursing, U. Ala., Birmingham, 1988. Lectr. Ind. U., Indpls., 1976-83, asst. prof., 1983-84; CNS perinatal div. U. Hosps., Birmingham, 1984-85; assoc. prof. U. So. Miss., Hattiesurg, 1988-94; pres. D.J.S. Resources P.A., 1995—; pres. D.J.S. Resources P.A.; various presentations on older women, relationship issues, mothers & daughters, and therapeutic use of music. Mem. Am. Nursing Assn., So. Nursing Rsch. Soc., Internat. Coun. Women's Health Issues, Sigma Theta Tau, Sigma Tau Delta.

TRISTÁN, MICHAEL PETER, physician, educator, researcher; b. Mexico, Mexico, Sept. 19, 1928; Came to the U.S., 1930; s. Jose Maria Tristán Fernandez and Katharine Atherton (Russell) Tristán; m. Margaret L. Cook, Aug. 1, 1948 (div. April 1961); m. Irmgard M. Stuhlmiller, Aug. 25, 1962 (div. Aug. 1984); children: Julia Short Tristán, Sarah C. Tristán, Peter Tristán, Lisa Graichen Yoram, Mark E. Tristán, Marina P. Tristán, Andrew R. Tristán; m. Pamela Marie Shepard Berger, April 22, 1989; 1 child, Benjamin H. J. Berger. BA, Nebr. Wesleyan U., Lincoln, Nebr., 1949; MD, Boston U. Sch. Medicine, 1953; MPH, U. Tex. Sch. Pub. Health, Houston, 1975. Diplomate Am. Bd. Pediatrics. Intern Mary Hitchcock Meml. Hosp., Dartmouth Med. Sch., Hanover, N.H., 1953-54; resident in pediatrics Boston City Hosp., 1954-55, 57-58; pvt. practice Sudbury, Mass., 1958-62, Laredo, Tex., 1962-68; med. dir. pediatrics Driscoll Found. CHN's Hosp., Corpus Christi, Tex., 1968-73; various positions Dept. of Cmty. Medicine, Baylor Coll. of Medicine, Houston, 1974—. Capt. U.S. Army Med. Corps, 1955-58. Recipient Spl. award for contbns. in behav. scis. and health edn. Coalition of Spanish Speaking Health & Mental Health Orgns., 1975. Democrat. Office: Baylor Coll Medicine Dept Cmty Medicine 1 Baylor Plz Houston TX 77030

TRISTRAM-NAGLE, STEPHANIE ANN, research biologist; b. N.Y.C., Nov. 21, 1948; d. Edward Wells and Marguerite Ann (Doner) Tristram; m. John Frederick Nagle, Dec. 31, 1980; children: Julia Courtney, Lara Kimberly. BA in French, Rutgers U., 1970; postgrad., U. Mass., 1972-75; PhD in Comparative Biochemistry, U. Calif., Berkeley, 1981. Clin. research lab. tech. Clin. Assays, Cambridge, Mass., 1972-75; chemistry tutor U. Mass., Boston, 1974-75; lab. asst. U. Calif., Berkeley, 1975-80, teaching asst., reader, 1976-80; postdoctoral research biologist Carnegie Mellon U., Pitts., 1982-86, research biologist, 1986—. Contbr. articles to profl. jours. Fundraiser Wightman Sch. Preservation Soc., Pitts., 1986-89, 3d Presbyn. Ch., 1983—. Samuel & Emma Winters grantee, 1985, 90. Mem. Assn. Women in Sci. Biophys. Soc., Sigma Xi (membership sec. CMU chpt. 1990-93, v.p. 1993-94, pres. 1994-95). Democrat. Presbyterian. Home: 504 Glen Arden Dr Pittsburgh PA 15208-2809 Office: Carnegie Mellon U 4400 5th Ave Pittsburgh PA 15213-2617

TRITTON, THOMAS RICHARD, pharmacology educator; b. Lakewood, Ohio, Dec. 20, 1947; s. William Frank and Margie Jean (Galbraith) T.; m. Louise Meschter Tritton; children: Lara, Christiana. BA, Ohio Wesleyan U., 1969; PhD, Boston U., 1973. Asst. prof. Yale Med. Sch., New Haven, Conn., 1975-80; assoc. prof. Yale U., New Haven, Conn., 1980-85; prof. U. Vt., Burlington, 1985—, vice provost, 1991—; mem. NIH Exptl. Therapeutics Study Sect., 1988-92. Editor books; mem. editorial bd. 5 profl. jours.; contbr. numerous scientific papers to profl. jours. Rsch. grantee NIH, Am. Cancer Soc. Mem. Am. Assn. Cancer Rsch. (com. mem.), Am. Soc. Biol. Chemists. Mem. Soc. of Friends. Home: 28 Oakhill Rd Shelburne VT 05482-7279 Office: Univ of Vermont Med Sch Dept Of Pharmacology Burlington VT 05405

TRITTSCHUH, JOHN RICHARD, ophthalmologist; b. Tipton, Ind., Jan. 13, 1942; s. Frank Wilbur and Edna Pearl (Darrow) T.; m. Carol L. Turbeville, Dec. 16, 1967; children: Emily H., Alison L., Erica L. AB, Ind. U., 1964; MD, Ind. U., Indpls., 1967. Diplomate Am. Bd. Ophthalmology. Intern SMAHEC, Kalamazoo, 1967-68; resident Wills Eye Hosp., Phila., 1970-73, fellow, 1973-74; ophthalmologist Kalamazoo Ophthalmology, 1974-93, Eye Care Physicians & Surgeons, Kalamazoo, 1993—. Bd. Dirs. Bronson Health Found., Kalamazoo, 1993—. Capt. USAF, 1968-70. Fellow ACS; mem. AMA, Am. bd. Ophthalmology, Mich. Med. Soc. Office: EyeCare Physicians & Surgeons P C 4016 W Main Kalamazoo MI 49006

TROCKI, STANLEY THOMAS, nursing home administrator; b. Revere, Mass., Aug. 7, 1944; s. Stanley Thomas and Alice Kathleen (Hayes) T.; m. Loretta Mary Hetnar, Sep. 8, 1993; children: Lisa Marie, Deborah Denise, David Joseph, Steven Thomas, Daniel Stanley, Robert Russel Wile, Jr., Ana Dziadosz Wile. AS nursing home, hosp., No. Essex Cmty. Coll., Haverhill, Md., 1976; BS in human svcs., Merrimac Coll., North Andover, Md., 1979; MBA, Anna Maria Coll., Paxton, Md., 1991. lic. nursing home administrn. Medic USAF, 1964-71; clin. lab. tech. Cable Mem. Hosp., Ipswich, Mass., 1970-72; head dept. chemistry Addison Gilbert Hosp., Gloucester, Md., 1972-75; staff chemistry, blood banking Hunt Hosp., Danvers, Mass., 1975-77; nursing home administr. Country Manor Convalescent Home, Newbury Port, Mass., 1977-84, Glynn Mem. Nursing Home, Haverhill, Mass., 1984-95, Den-Mar Rehab. & Nursing Ctr., Rockport, Mass., 1995—; bd. dirs. Haverhill VNA, 1991-94; Coun. on Aging, Rockport, 1995-96. With USAF, 1964-71. Mem. Am. Coll. Healthcare Administrs., New Eng. Healthcare Assembly, New Eng. Gerontological Assn., Rotary, Polish Legion of Am. Vets. (chaplain 1989—). Democrat. Roman Catholic. Home: 6 Heatherside Ln Ipswich MA 01938 Office: Den-Mar Rehab Nursing Ctr 44 South St Rockport MA 01966

TROFATTER, KENNETH FRANK, obstetrician, gynecologist; b. Bklyn., Nov. 7, 1951; s. Kenneth Frank and Lorraine (Lewald) T.; m. Anna Michele Offutt, Nov. 6, 1992; 1 child, Maren Kendall; children from previous marriage: Peter Blair, Benjamin Cleland, Kenneth Parker. BS in Zoology, Duke U., 1973, PhD in Pathology, MD, 1979. Diplomate Am. Bd. Ob-Gyn. Intern and resident in ob-gyn. Duke U. Med. Ctr., Durham, N.C., 1979-83, fellow in maternal-fetal medicine, 1983-85, asst. prof., 1985-87; asst. prof. U. Tenn. Med. Ctr., Knoxville, 1987-89, assoc. prof., dir. reproductive immunology, 1989-93; prof., 1993—; dir. maternal-fetal medicine U. Tenn. Med. Ctr., 1990-94; dir. East Tenn. Regional Perinatal Program, 1990—; cons. Burroughs-Wellcome Corp., Rsch. Triangle Pk., N.C., 1985-87, Hoffman-LaRoche Labs., Nutley, N.J., 1988—, 3M Pharm., St. Paul, 1991—; mem. FDA Adv. Com. on Microbiol. Devices, Washington, 1989-92. Contbr. articles, chpts. to med. publs. Grantee Burroughs-Wellcome Corp., 1985-87, Hoffman-LaRoche Labs., 1987, 3M Pharmaceuticals, 1991—. Fellow Am. Coll. Ob.-Gyn.; mem. Soc. Perinatal Obstetricians, Tenn. Perinatal Assn., Am. Soc. for Immunology of Reproduction, AMA, So. Med. Assn., AAAS. Democrat. Methodist. Home: 713 Andover Blvd Knoxville TN 37922-1531 Office: U Tenn Med Ctr 1924 Alcoa Hwy Knoxville TN 37920-1511

TROLIO, WILLIAM MICHAEL, health care executive, educator; b. Amsterdam, N.Y., July 12, 1947; s. Morino Fiorello and Jeanne Estelle (Lawrence) T.; m. Judith Mary Starr, Sept. 27, 1969; children: Kristen Marie, Matthew Lawrence. A in Applied Sci., Hudson Valley Community Coll., Troy, N.Y., 1968; BS, SUNY, Albany, 1972; MBA, Northland U., Toronto, Ont., 1983. Lic. clin. lab. scientist. Med. technician Faxton Hosp., Utica, N.Y., 1968-69; mktg. devel. specialist GE, Milw., 1969-74; mktg. devel mgr. Bio Data Corp., Hatboro, Pa., 1974-79; lab. mgr. Cen. Maine Med. Ctr., Lewiston, 1979-80; gen. mgr. lab. svcs. Mary Imogene Basset Hosp. and Clinic, Cooperstown, N.Y., 190-92, lab. adminstr., 1992-94; asst. adminstr. clin. svcs. Bassett Hosp. of Schoharie County, 1994—; adj. clin. prof. med. tech. Utica Coll., Syracuse U., 1980—; adj. clin. faculty Broome County Community Coll., Binghamton, N.Y., 1984—; officer advt. dir. Beaver Valley Music Festival, 1988-89; mem. N.Y. State com. on profl. and pers. standards Clin. Lab. Pers.; mem. mgmt. evaluation com. Nat. Cert. Aging for Clin. Labr. Pers., clin. lab. pers. N.Y. State Profession Pers. Standards Com., project exec. Bassett U. Health Edn. Consortium. Editor; Cen. N.Y. Clin. Lab. Assn. bull., 1984-88; contbr. articles to profl. jours. Asst. leader Webelos, Boy Scouts Am., 1988-90; bd. dirs. Cooperstown Baseball Fields Assn.; mem. bldg. and grounds com. St. Mary's Ch. 1st lt. Med. Svc. Corps, USAR. Fellow Bus. Adminstrn. Can. Sch. Mgmt., 1983. Mem. Northeastern N.Y. Hosp. Assn., Hosp. Assn. N.Y. (rep.), Clin. Lab. Mgmt. Assn. (chpt. pres. 1987-88, legis. liaison bd. 1984), Iroquois Hosp. Consortium (various coms. 1985-92), Am. Soc. Clin. Pathologists (assoc.), Mid Atlantic Health Congress, N.Y. Acad. Sci., Vol. Hosp. Assn. (lab. task force 1990—), CSM Alumni Club, Am. Coll. Healthcare Execs. Republican. Roman Catholic. Home: RR 1 Box 23D Fly Creek NY 13337-9722 Office: Bassett Healthcare/BHSC One Atwell Rd 41 Grandview Dr Cobleskill NY 12043

TROLL, LILLIAN ELLMAN, psychologist, educator; b. Chgo., Sept. 24, 1915; d. Morris C. and Bertha H. (Holland) Ellman; divorced; children: Kathren, Jeanne, Gregory. BS in Psychology, U. Chgo., 1937, MA in Human Devel., 1966, PhD in Human Devel., 1967. Pers. technician U.S. War Dept., Washington, 1941-45; sch. psychologist Newton (Mass.) Pub. Schs., 1957-63; cons. State Calif., San Francisco, 1964-65; sr. rsch. assoc. Merrill-Palmer Inst., Detroit, 1967-70; assoc. prof. psychology Wayne State U., Detroit, 1970-75; prof. Rutgers U., New Brunswick, N.J., 1975-86; adj. prof. human devel. and aging, med. anthropology U. Calif., San Francisco, 1986—; vis. prof.; lectr. in field 47 convs. and invited talks. Author: Family Issues in Current Gerontology, 1986, Continuations: Development After 20, 1982, Development in Early and Middle Adulthood, 1975, rev. edit., 1985, 32 chpts. in other books; co-author: (with Joan and Kenneth Israel) Looking Ahead: A Woman's Guide to the Problems and Joys of Growing Older, 1977, (with Nancy Schlossberg) Perspectives on Counseling Adults, 1978, (with Sheila Miller and Robert Atchley) Families of Later Life, 1979, (with Barbara Turner) Women Growing Older, 1994; contbr. over 30 articles to profl. jours. Recipient Eminent Women in Psychology award, 1988, Disting. Contbn. Div. Adult Devel. and Aging award APA, 1989, Women's Heritage Inst. award, 1992, Disting. Creative Contbn. to Gerontology award, 1993. Fellow APA (sec.-treas. 1973-76, 84-87, pres. 1986-87), Gerontol. Soc. Am. (sec.-treas. behavioral and soc. scis. sect. 1981-87). Home: 1001 Shoreline Dr Apt 302 Alameda CA 94501-5925 Office: U Calif 1350 7th Ave San Francisco CA 94122-2508

TROLL, RALPH, biology educator; b. Reinheim, Hesse, Germany, Oct. 8, 1932; came to U.S., 1947; s. Johann Christian and Nelly (Bentheim) T.; m. Loretta Frieda Glaser, June 28, 1958; children: Michael B., Karen N., Krista A. BS, U. Ill., 1957, MS, 1958; PhD, U. Minn., 1965. Instr. biology Augustana Coll., Rock Island, Ill., 1959-63, asst. prof., 1963-66, assoc. prof., 1966-72, prof., 1972—. Author: Life of Marcello Malphigi, 1989; contbr. articles to profl. jours. With U.S. Army, 1952-54, Japan. Recipient NSF summer fellow, U. Ariz., 1959, Duke U., 1960, U. Minn., 1961, Oreg. State U., 1966. Mem. Ill. State Acad. Sci., Nat. Assn. Biology Tchrs., Am. Fern Soc. Office: Augustana Coll Dept Biology Rock Island IL 61201

TROMPETER, RICHARD SIMON, pediatrician; b. London, Jan. 27, 1946; s. Nysen and Betty (Rubin) T.; m. Barbara Ann Blum, Mar. 26, 1978; children: Sara, Alexander, Nicholas, Rebecca. BS, Guys Hosp., London, 1970. Sr. house officer Various Hosps., London, 1971-74; registrar Hosps. for Sick Children, Great Ormond St. & London, 1975-78; sr. registrar Guys Hosp., London, 1978-83; cons., pediatrician Royal Free Hosp., London, 1983-89; cons., pediatrician, pediatric nephrologist Hosp. for Sick Children, London, 1989—. Contbr. articles to profl. jours. Fellow Royal Coll. Physicians. Office: Hosps for Sick Children, Great Ormond St, London WC1 3JH, England

TRONGONE, RICHARD JAMES, physician; b. N.Y.C., Mar. 26, 1953; s. Michael Anthony Sr. and Anne Marie (Capra) T.; m. Joann Alice De Santis, July 14, 1979; 1 child, Christina Marie. BS, Fordham U., 1975; MD, Mt. Sinai Sch. Medicine, 1981. Diplomate Am. Bd. Ob-gyn. Resident North Shore U. Hosp., Manhasset, N.Y., 1981-84, chief resident, 1984-85, attending staff, 1985—; clin. instr. Cornell Med. Coll., N.Y.C., 1985—. Mem. Am. Coll. Ob-gyn., Am. Assn. Gynecologic Laparascopists, Med. Soc. State of N.Y., Nassau County Med. Soc., Soc. of Laparoendoscopic Surgeons, North Hempstead Country Club. Republican. Roman Catholic. Office: Kubec and Trongone MD LLP 1615 Northern Blvd Manhasset NY 11030

TRONVOLD, LINDA JEAN, occupational therapist; b. Yankton, S.D., Dec. 8, 1950; m. Marvis D. Tronvold, July 7, 1976; children: Marcie, Tami, Kristi, Bradley, Cindy. Student, Mt. Marty Coll., 1989; AS, Kirkwood Community Coll., Cedar Rapids, Iowa, 1989; BS, Creighton U., 1991. Registered occupl. therapist, S.D., Neb., Iowa. Psychiatric aide S.D. Human Svcs. Ctr., Yankton, 1969-74, mental health technician, 1974-85, occpul. therapist asst., 1985-89, occupl. therapist, 1991-92; mem. edn. svc. unit Human Svcs. Ctr., Yankton, 1991-93; asst. program dir. occupl. therapy Western Iowa Tech. C.C., Dakota Dunes, S.D., 1993—; dir. occupl. therapy Nova Care, Inc., 1993—; guest speaker Creighton U., Omaha, U. S.D., Vermillion; mem. student staff Upward Bound, Omaha, 1989-91,. Scout leader Boy Scouts Am., Hartington, Nebr., 1977-80, Girl Scouts USA, Yankton, 1986-89; Sunday sch. tchr. United Ch. of Christ, Yankton, 1984-88; mem. spl. populations staff YWCA, Cedar Rapids, Iowa, 1987-88. Mem. Am. Occupl. Therapy Assn., S.D. Occupl. Therapy Assn., Nebr. Occupl. Therapy Assn., Iowa Occupl. Therapy Assn., Creighton U. Student Occupl. Therapy Assn., VFW Aux., Sq. Dance Club (pres. 1979-81), Alpha Tri Ota Club. Home: 705 Broadway St Yankton SD 57078-3923 Office: 350 W Anchor Dr Ste 500 Dakota Dunes SD 57049-5153

TROPP, RORY, emergency medicine physician; b. Queens, N.Y., May 10, 1958; s. Murray and Elaine (Backerman) T.; m. Shelley Ames, May 25, 1986; children: Lauren, Joshua, Dustin, Jessica. B in Chemistry, Bklyn. Coll.,

1979; MD, Downstate Med. Ctr., Bklyn., 1983. Diplomate Am. Coll. Emergency Physicians. Intern, resident Albany (N.Y.) Med. Ctr., 1983-85; resident emergency medicine L.I. Jewish Hosp., New Hyde Park, N.Y., 1987-90; attending ED Saratoga, Saratoga Springs, N.Y., 1985-87; attending chmn. ED and clin. instr. QA Com. L.I. Jewish and Queens Hosp. Ctr., New Hyde Park, N.Y., 1990-92; attending chair of QA St. ELizabeth's Hosp., Utica, N.Y., 1992-93; ED attending interim dir. Rome (N.Y.) Hosp., 1993—. Fellow Am. Coll. Emergency Physicians; mem. Oneida County Med. Soc. Office: Rome Meml Hosp 1500 N James St Rome NY 13440

TROSHINSKY, CHARLES HILARY, psychiatrist; b. Washington, Mar. 31, 1932; s. Israel and Ida (Charen) T.; married 1953; children: Kathryn, Lisa, Matthew, Kenneth. BA, George Washington U., 1954, MD, 1958. Diplomate, Am. Bd. Psychiatry and Neurology. Intern USPHS Hosp., S.I., N.Y., 1958-59; resident Norristown (Pa.) State Hosp., 1959-61; fellow Phila. Child Guidance Clinic, 1961-63; pvt. practice Bethesda, Md., 1964—; chief of child guidance clinic, D.C. Mental Health Dept., 1964-70; assoc. clin. prof. Med. Sch., Georgetown U., Washington, 1965—; cons. to NIMH, Bethesda, 1975—; cons., Walter Reed Army Hosp., Washington, 1986—. Lt. (j.g.), USPHS, 1957-59. Fellow Am. Psychiat. Assn. (lfie), Am. Acad. Child and Adolescent Psychiatry; mem. Alpha Omega Alpha. Home and Office: 6300 Carnegie Dr Bethesda MD 20817-1702

TRÖSTER, ALEXANDER I., neuropsychologist, educator; b. Vienna, Austria, Oct. 16, 1960; came to U.S., 1984; s. Guy W. and Christine U. (Rieder) T.; m. Kristy A. Straits. BSc in Psychology with honors, U. Zimbabwe, Harare, 1983; MS, N.D. State U., 1986; PhD, San Diego State U. & U. Calif., San Diego, 1991. Lic. psychologist, Kans., Mo. Asst. prof. psychology Wash. State U., Pullman, 1991-93; asst. prof. neurology U. Kans. Med. Ctr., Kansas City, 1993—; external grant reviewer Dept. Vets. Affairs Rsch. Svc., Md., 1995—; ad hoc reviewer Jour. Neuropsychiatry and Clin. Neurosci., Washington, 1995—, Brain and Cognition, San Diego, 1995—, Jour. Clin. and Exptl. Neuropsychology, The Netherlands, 1994—; presenter in field. Contbr. numerous articles to profl. jours., chpts. to books. Fellow Epilepsy Found. Am., 1988, 89; recipient Butters award for rsch. contbns. to clin. neuropsychology Nat. Acad. Neuropsychology, 1993. Mem. APA, Internat. Neuropsychol. Assn., Am. Neuropsychiat. Assn., Behavioral Neurology Soc., Am. Epilepsy Soc., Movement Disorder Soc. Office: U Kans Med Ctr Neurology Dept 3901 Rainbow Blvd Kansas City KS 66160

TROTOT, PIERRE MARCEL, radiologist; b. Paris, Jan. 24, 1942; s. Raymond P. and Françoise (Houdard) T.; children: Juliette, Flore, Nicolas, Alice; m. Sylvie Barjaud; 1 child, Edouard. MD, U. Paris, 1970. Externist Hosp. Paris, 1963-67, internist, 1967-72; asst. Hosp. St. Joseph, Paris, 1972-82, radiologist, 1977; chief dept. radiology Inst. Pasteur, Paris, 1982—; radiologist Maison de Sante des Gardiens de la Paix, Paris, 1975-83, Found. Cognacq Jay, Paris, 1979-83, Electricite de France Gaz de France, Paris, 1977—. Editor: Risque Infectieux, 1986, Imagerie du SIDA, 1988 (prize CERM 1989), Imaging of AIDS, 1991; editor, mgr. RMV, video mag., 1985. Administr. Aide aux Malades Désemparés, Paris, 1978—; v.p. Assn. pour la Formation, L'Animation et la Recherche, Paris, 1980; pres. Assn. Clinique et Recherche en Imagerie, Paris, 1989. Mem. Soc. Française Radiologie, Engrs. Soc. Neuro-Radiology, Soc. Forensic Imaging, Soc. Française Chirurgie Pedatique (assoc.), Radiol. Soc. N.Am. (corr.). Office: Inst Pasteur, Rue de Vaugirard 2ll, 75015 Paris France

TROTTER, JOHNNY RAY, physician; b. Detroit, Aug. 30, 1950; s. Robert Terris and Johnnie Mae (Ivory) T.; m. Nadine Frances Simpson, July 7, 1973; children: Johnny Ray II, Charissa Nadine, David Louis, Jason Aaron. BA, U. Mich., 1972, MD, 1976. Diplomate Am. Bd. Family Practice. Resident Bon Secours Hosp., Grosse Pointe, Mich., 1976-79; instr. in family medicine Wayne State U., Detroit, 1979-82; pres., dir., physician Grace Family Health Ctr., P.C., Detroit, 1982—; bd. dirs. Physician Lab. Svcs., Inc., Southfield, Mich., 1987—; mem. adv. com. dept. family practice Grace Hosp.; physician cons. Nat. Cons. Panel, Boulder, Colo., 1988—; speaker in field. Nat. Med. fellow, 1972; recipient Semmes award Sisters of Bon Secours, 1979. Fellow Am. Acad. Family Physicians; mem. Mich. Acad. Family Physicians (chmn. minority affairs com. 1983-87), Detroit Med. Soc. Democrat. Office: Grace Family Health Ctr PC 20905 Greenfield Ste 303 Southfield MI 48075

TROTZER, JAMES P., psychologist; b. Wausau, Wis., May 20, 1943; s. Roger E. and Betty J. (Hoeft) T.; m. Antoinette B. Nardini, Nov. 22, 1969; children: Traci Ann, Daniel Roger, Benjamin James. BA, U. Wis., Eau Claire, 1965; MA, U. Colo., 1967, PhD, 1969. Cert. psychologist, N.H. Tchr. English and history Starbuck Jr. H.S., Racine, Wis., 1965-66; prof. counselor edn. U. Wis., River Falls, 1969-83; exec. dir. Renew Counseling Ctr., Rye, N.H., 1983-93; pvt. practice, Exeter, N.H., 1993—. Author: Marriage and Family: Better Ready Than Not, 1986, The Counselor and the Group, 1989, Renewing Your Mind: Meditations for Mental Health, 1993; contbr. articles to profl. jours. NDEA fellow U. Colo., 1966-69. Fellow Assn. for Specialists in Group Work (Exemplary Svc. award 1989, Exemplary Practice of Group Work award 1996); mem. APA, ACA, Internat. Assn. for Marriage and Family Counseling, N.H. Psychol. Assn. Office: 5 Buzell Ave Exeter NH 03833

TROUPIN, ALLAN S., neurologist; b. N.Y.C., May 29, 1935; s. James Leonard and Beatrice Joyce (Perlman) T. BA, Columbia Coll., 1956, MD, 1960. Diplomate Am. Bd. Psychiatry and Neurology. Asst. prof. neurol. surgery U. Washington, Seattle, 1972-78; assoc. prof. neurology U. Pa., Phila., 1978-81, UCLA, L.A., 1981-85; assoc. prof. U. S. Fla., Tampa, 1986-87; neurology dir. Fairview Tng. Ctr., Salem, Oreg., 1987-89; clin. assoc. prof. neurology Oreg. Health Scis. U., Portland, 1987-89; prof. neurology La. State U., New Orleans, 1989—, dir. EEG and epilepsy programs, 1989—. Contbr. numerous articles to profl. jours., chpts. to books. Capt. U.S. Army, 1966-68. Recipient Best Controlled Drug Trial prizes Internat. League Against Epilepsy, 1977, 81. Fellow Am. Acad. Neurology, Am. EEG Soc.; mem. Western EEG Soc. (bd. dirs. (1996-98), Am. Epilepsy Soc. Office: La State U Dept Neurology 1542 Tulane Ave New Orleans LA 70112

TROUSDALE, ROBERT T., orthopedist; b. St. Paul, Apr. 25, 1961; s. Elmer B. Trousdale; m. Mary B. Coogan, May, 1983; children: Kate, Rob, Elli, Will. BS, U. Notre Dame, 1983; MD, St. Louis U., 1987. Resident orthopedic surgery Mayo Clinic, Rochester, Minn., 1987-92; fellow orthopedic surgery U. Bern, Switzerland, 1992; cons. reconstructive orthopedic surgery Mayo Clinic, Rochester, 1992—. Contbr. chpts. in books and articles to profl. jours. Fellow Am. Acad. Orthopedic Surgeons; mem. AMA, Minn. Med. Assn. Office: Mayo Clinic Rochester MN 55905

TROUT, MONROE EUGENE, hospital systems executive; b. Harrisburg, Pa., Apr. 5, 1931; s. David Michael and Florence Margaret (Kashner) T.; m. Sandra Louise Lemke, June 11, 1960; children: Monroe Eugene, Timothy William. AB, U. Pa., 1953, MD, 1957; LLB, Dickinson Sch. of Law, 1964, JD, 1969; LLD (hon.), Dickinson Sch. Law, 1996, Bloomfield Coll., 1994, Dickinson Sch. Law, 1996. Intern Great Lakes (Ill.) Naval Hosp., 1957-58; resident in internal medicine Portsmouth (Va.) Naval Hosp., 1959-61; chief med. dept. Harrisburg State Hosp., 1961-64; dir. drug regulatory affairs Pfizer, Inc., N.Y.C., 1964-68; v.p., med. dir. Winthrop Labs., N.Y.C., 1968-70; med. dir. Sterling Drug, Inc., N.Y.C., 1970-74, v.p., dir. med. affairs, 1974-78, sr. v.p., dir. med. affairs, bd. dirs., mem. exec. com., 1978-86; pres., CEO Am. Healthcare Sys., Inc., 1986-95, chmn., 1987-95; also bd. dirs. Am. Healthcare Systems, Inc.; chmn. emeritus Am. Healthcare Sys., Inc., 1995—; interim CEO Cytran Inc., 1996—; bd. dirs. Baxter Internat., SAIC, Gensia, Inc., West Co., Inc., Cytyc, Inc.; chmn. bd. dirs. Am. Excess Ins. ltd., 1990-95; adj. assoc. prof. Bklyn. Coll. Pharmacy; spl. lectr. legal medicine, trustee Dickinson Sch. Law, 1970-93; trustee Ariz. State U. Sch. Health Adminstrn., 1988-91; mem. Sterling Winthrop Rsch. Bd., 1977-86, Joint Commn. Prescription Drug Use, 1976-80; sec. Commn. on Med. Malpractice, HEW, 1971-73, cons., 1974; co-chmn. San Diego County Health Commn., 1992-94; dir. Biotransplantation, Inc., 1994-95. Mem. editl. bd. Hosp. Formulary Mgmt., 1969-79, Forensic Sci., 1971—, Jour. Legal Medicine, 1973-79, Reg. Tox. and Pharmac, 1981-87, Med. Malpractice Prevention, 1985—; editl. reviewer Annals of Internal Medicine; contbr. articles to profl. jours. Exec. com. White House Mini Conf. on Aging, 1980; Rep. dist. leader, New Canaan, Conn., 1966-68; active Nat. Health Adv. Bd. AAA, N.Y. State Commn. Substance Abuse, 1978-80, Town Coun., New Canaan, 1978-86, vice chmn., 1985-86; bd. dirs. New Canaan Interchurch Svc. Com., 1965-69, Athletes Kidney Found., Circle in Sq. Theatre Inc., 1984-86; trustee U. Calif.-San Diego Thornton Hosp. and Med. Ctr., Albany Med. Coll., 1977-86, St. Vincent DePaul Ctr. for the Homeless, 1987-90, Cleve. Clinic, 1971-87; trustee, vice chmn. Morehouse Med. Sch., 1980-89; assoc. trustee U. Pa.; bd. visitors U. Pa. Sch. Nursing, 1988-92; pres. U. Calif.-San Diego Edn. Bd. Trustees, 1994—; vice chmn. Med. Commn. for Food and Shelter, Inc.; chmn. bd. Am. Coll. Legal Medicine Found., 1983-87; chmn. Internat. B'nai B'rith Dinner, 1989, 94. Recipient Alumni award of merit U. Pa., 1953, Disting. Alumni award Dickinson Sch. Law, 1989, Nat. Healthcare award Internat. B'nai B'rith, 1991, Entrepreneur of Yr. award San Diego, 1994, Horatio Alger award, 1995, Salvation Army Tradition of Caring award, 1996; named to Hon. Order Ky. Cols., Tenn. Cols. Fellow Am. Coll. Legal Medicine (v.p., pres., bd. govs.); mem. AMA (Physician's Recognition awards 1969, 72, 76, 82, 85, 88, 92), Med. Execs. (pres. 1975-76), Delta Tau Delta (Alumni Achievement award 1996). Lutheran Office: Box 8052 Rancho Santa Fe CA 92067

TROUT, ROSCOE MARSHALL, JR., health care and insurance executive; b. Alexandria, La., July 24, 1944; s. Roscoe Marshall Sr. and Clara (de la Croix) T.; m. Myra Susan Segerson; children: Heather Renee, Tiffany Linnea. BA, NW State U., Natchitoches, La., 1967; MA, NW State U., 1973; EdD, U. No. Colo., 1976; postdoctoral study, U. Pa., 1986. Cert. med. rehab. counselor; registered health underwriter, registered employee benefits cons. Regional ops. dir. Tex. edn. Agy., Beaumont, Tex., 1976-77; mgmt./ops. cons. Tex. Dept. Mental Health-Mental Retardation, Austin, 1977-79; CEO Mytro, Inc., Shreveport, La., 1979-84; COO, CEO, NME Health Plans, New Orleans, 1985-88; v.p. mktg. HSI Health Plans, Ft. Collins, Colo., 1989-92; pres. TSOP Fin. Strategies, Austin, Tex., 1989-93; state dir. coordinated health care Tex. Dept. of Health, 1992-93; CEO Providence Health Alliance, Waco, Tex., 1994—; cons. HEW, Denver, 1975, U.S. Dept. Labor, Denver, 1975; mem. Colo. Task Force on Health Care Reform. Com. mem. Shreveport (La.) C. of C., 1980-83; mem. New Orleans Health Adminstrs., 1986-88, Greater No. La. C. of C., New Orleans, 1985-88; com. mem. Exchange Club, Mandeville, La., 1987-88, Ft. Collins C. of C., 1988-89; bd. dirs. Medicom Internat. (Med. Interface), 1989—. Recipient Leading Producers Round Table Insurance award, 1989; La. State Legis. scholar, 1962, Colo. State Legis. scholar, 1976. Mem. New Orleans Assn. Health Underwriters (bd. dirs. 1987-88), Employee Benefit Planners New Orleans, New Orleans Assn. Health Care Adminstrs., Colo. Assn. Health Underwriters (bd. dirs. 1990-92), No. Colo. Assn. Health Underwriters (pres. 1992-93), Rotary (Waco, Tex.). Mem. Ch. of Christ.

TROUTWINE-BRAUN, CHARLOTTE TEMPERLEY, psychologist, educator, writer; b. Newton, Mass., Nov. 27, 1906; d. Joseph and Libbie (Kempton) Temperley; m. Arklay S. Richards, Nov. 28, 1928 (div. 1942); children: Whitman Albin, Lincoln Kempton, Sylvia Caroline; m. Harry Troutwine, May 3, 1945 (div. 1954); m. Charles E. McCrum, 1961 (div. 1965); m. Lester Lewis Walsh, Feb. 16, 1968 (div. Feb. 1972); m. George Braun, Feb. 6, 1975 (dec. Oct. 1975). BS, Simmons Coll., 1927; postgrad. Boston U., 1947-49; MA, Northeastern U., 1966; BES, Internat Ch. Ageless Wisdom, 1981. Pvt. sec. pres. Hygrade Sylvania Electric Corp. Salem, Mass., 1927-28; pvt. and dept. exec. sec. Dr. Stanley Cobb, Bullard prof. neuropathology Harvard U. Med. Sch., 1928-31; part-time caseworker Friends of Framingham Reformatory, 1928-31, others, 1931-51; organizer, exec. dir. Postgrad. Med. Inst. under Mass. Med. Soc., Boston, 1951-57; mgr. Postgrad. Information Services, Lederle Labs. div. Am. Cyanamid Co., Pearl River, N.Y., 1957-61; exec. dir. postgrad. med. edn. Hahnemann Med. Coll. and Hosp. also exec. dir. Mary Bailey Inst. Cardiovascular Research, 1961; counselor, tchr. psychology Holliston High Sch., 1965-65. Counselor Falmouth (Mass.) High Sch., 1966-74 psychotherapist Hallgarth Clinic, 1974-75. Speaker for Am. Epilepsy League. Mem. Mass. Tchrs. Assn. (life), Spiritual Frontiers Assn. (life), N.E.A. (life), Nat. Ret. Tchrs. Assn. (life), Nat. Assn. Sch. Counselors (charter, life), Assn. Research Enlightenment, Soc. Mayflower Descs. (life), Simmons Coll. Alumnae Assn., AAUW, Med. Soc. Execs. Assn. (emeritus), Am. Soc. Psychical Research, States Med. Postgrad. Assn. (past sec.), Mass. Psychol. Assn. (life), Spiritual Frontiers Fellowship (life), World Fedn. Healers (healer mem.), Mass. Healers Assn. Author: Practicing the Silence, 1978, 5th edit., 1992, Open Windows, 1994; contbr. numerous articles in med., spiritual and psychol. fields. Mem. Soc. of Friends. Home: 83 Falmouth Ct Bedford MA 01730-2912

TROWBRIDGE, PHILLIP EDMUND, surgeon, educator; b. Hartford, Conn., Oct. 17, 1930; s. John Henry and Isabelle Story (Warner) T.; m. Fay Elaine Russell, June 23, 1956; children: Kimberly, Heather, Allison, John, David. BA, Trinity Coll., 1952; postgrad, Harvard U., 1955; MD, Tufts Med. Sch., 1959. Diplomate Am. Bd. Surgery. Intern Hartford Hosp., 1959-60, resident in gen. surgery, 1960-65, from mem. surg. staff to sr. surgeon, 1965—; clin. asst. prof. Surgery U. Conn. Med. Sch., Farmington, 1986—; adj. asst. prof. Surgery Dartmouth Med. Sch., Hanover, N.H., 1986—. Contbr. 17 articles to profl. jours. Corporator Hartford Sem., Hartford, 1975-77, 86—, trustee, 1977-86; dir. West Hartford Street Ministry, 1974-79. With USAF, 1952-54. Mem. ACS, Hartford Med. Soc. (pres. 1988, trustee 1989-93, Loving Cup award 1994), Am. Soc. Gen. Surgeons (chmn. Conn. chpt. 1993—), New Eng. Surg. Soc., New Eng. Cancer Soc., Internat. Surg. Soc., Soc. for Surgery Alimentary Tract. Republican. American Baptist. Home: 11 Lucy Way Simsbury CT 06070-2534 Office: 85 Seymour St Hartford CT 06106-5501

TROWELL-HARRIS, IRENE, nurse; b. Aiken, S.C., Sept. 20, 1939; d. Frank and Irene (Battle) Trowell; m. Benoni Harris, Oct. 2, 1978 (div. May 1983). BA, Jersey City State U., 1971; RN, Columbia Hosp., 1959; MPH, Yale U., 1973; MEd, Columbia U., 1983, EdD, 1983. Staff nurse Talmadge Hosp., Augusta, Ga., 1959-60; head nurse N.Y. Hosp., N.Y.C., 1960-64; pediatric supr. Brookdale Hosp., N.Y.C., 1964-66; adminstr. HEA Maimonides Hosp., Bklyn., 1966-71; adminstr., coordinator Misericordia Hosp., Bklyn., 1974-85; policy devel. Am. Nurses Assn., Kansas City, Mo., 1985-87; advisor USAF Nurse Corps., Bolling AFB, D.C., 1987-93; dir. VA, Washington, 1993—. Contbr. articles to profl. jours. Mem. leadership com., chief of staff to Gov. N.Y., Latham, 1986-93; AIDS advisor ARC, 1987—. Served to brig. gen. N.Y. ANG, 1963—. Mem. ANA (congl. dist. coord. 1981-85, task force on AIDS 1986-93), APHA, N.Y. State Nurses Assn., Nat. Guard Assn. U.S., Res. Officers Assn. (life), NAACP (life), Kappa Delta Pi. Democrat. Baptist. Club: Yale (N.Y.C.). Home: 2582 S Arlington Mill Dr # G Arlington VA 22206-3352 Office: VA/OIG 810 Vermont Ave NW Washington DC 20420

TROY, FREDERIC ARTHUR, II, medical biochemistry educator; b. Evanston, Ill., Feb. 16, 1937; s. Charles McGregor and Virginia Lane (Minto) T.; m. Linda Ann Price, Mar. 23, 1959; children: Karen M., Janet R. BS, Washington U., St. Louis, 1961; PhD, Purdue U., 1966; postdoctoral, Johns Hopkins U., 1968. Asst. prof. U. Calif. Sch. Medicine, Davis, 1968-74, assoc. prof., 1974-80, prof., 1980—, chmn., 1991-94; vis. prof. Karolinska Inst. Med. Sch., Stockholm, 1976-77; cons. NIH, Bethesda, Md., 1974—, NSF, Washington, 1975—, Damon Runyon Cancer Found., N.Y.C., 1980-81, VA, Washington, 1984-88. Mem. editl. bd. Jour. Biol. Chem., 1988—, Glycobiol., 1990—; contbr. articles to profl. jours. Recipient Research Cancer Devel. award Nat. Cancer Inst., 1975-80; Eleanor Roosevelt Internat. Cancer fellow Am. Cancer Soc., 1976-77. Mem. AAAS, Am. Soc. Biol. Chemistry and Molecular Biology, Am. Assn. Cancer Rsch., Am. Chem. Soc., Am. Soc. Enologists, Biochemistry Soc., Biophysics Soc., Am. Fedn. for Clin. Rsch., N.Y. Acad. Scis., Soc. for Glycobiol. (pres. 1991-92), Am. Med. and Grad. Sch. Dept. Biochem. (pres.-elect 1995—), Sigma Xi. Office: U Calif Sch Medicine Davis CA 95616

TROY, LEO JOSEPH, JR., orthopaedic surgeon; b. Melrose, Mass., Mar. 19, 1950; s. Leo Joseph and Jeanne Marie (McNally) T.; m. Susan Scully, Oct. 1, 1977; children: Caroline Moira, Nicholas Leo, Joanna Kathleen. BS, U.S. Mil. Acad., 1972; MD, Harvard U., 1979. Diplomate Am. Bd. Orthopaedic Surgery. Intern in gen. surgery Walter Reed Army Med. Ctr., 1980, orthopaedic resident, 1984; commd. 2d lt. U.S. Army, 1668, advanced through grades to lt. col., 1992; orthopaedic surgeon 130th Sta. Hosp., Heidelberg, Germany, 1984-88, Harvard Cmty. Health Plan, Boston, 1988—; pvt. practice Wellesley, Mass., 1989—; mem. staff Brigham & Womans Hosp., Newton Wellesley Hosp., Faulkner Hosp., Mt. Auburn Hosp. Fellow Am. Acad. Osteopathic Surgeons. Roman Catholic. Office: Assocs Ortho Sports Med 422 Worcester St Wellesley MA 02181

TRPIS, MILAN, vector biologist, scientist, educator; b. Mojsova Lucka, Slovakia, Dec. 20, 1930; came to U.S., 1971, naturalized, 1977; s. Gaspar and Anna (Sevcikova) T.; m. Ludmila Tonkovic, Dec. 15, 1956; children: Martin, Peter, Katarina. M.S., Comenius U., Bratislava, 1956; Ph.D., Charles U., Prague, 1960. Research asst. Slovak Acad. Sci., Bratislava, 1953-56; sci. asst. Slovak Acad. Sci., 1956-60, scientist, 1960-62, ind. scientist, 1962-69; ecologist-entomologist East Africa-Aedes Rsch. Unit WHO, Dar es Salaam, Tanzania, 1969-71; asst. faculty fellow dept. biology U. Notre Dame, 1971-73, assoc. faculty fellow, 1973-74; assoc. prof. med. entomology Johns Hopkins U. Sch. Hygiene and Pub. Health, 1974-78, prof., 1978—, dir. labs. med. entomology; med. entomology; rsch. assoc. U. Ill., Urbana, 1966-67, Can. Dept. Agr., Lethbridge, Alta., 1967-68; dir. Biol. Rsch. Inst. Am., 1971-79; external dir. rsch. Liberiran Inst. Biomed. Rsch., 1981-89; dir. AID project on transmission of river blindness in areas of Liberia and Sierra Leone; dir. WHO rsch. grant; tech. adv. com. AID Vector Biology and Control Project, 1986-91; dir. Johns Hopkins U./Fed. U. Tech. Akure Onchocerciasis Project in Nigeria, 1991-94, Johns Hopkins U./Organisation de Coordination et de Cooperation pour la Lutte les Grandes Endemies-Pierre Richet Inst. Onchocerciasis Project, Bouaké, Ivory Coast, 1993-96; dir. Johns Hopkins U./Pierre Richet Inst./ORSTOM onchocerciasis project in Ivory Coast, 1993-96; prof.-advisor doctoral students, Africa, Asia, Cen. Am., 1979—. Editor: Jour. Biologia, 1956-71, Jour. Entomol. Problems, 1960-72; zool. sect.: Jour. Biol. Works, 1960-71; Contbr. articles to profl. jours. Dir. WHO project on prophylactic drugs for river blindness, Liberia, 1985-87. Recipient Slovak Acad. Sci., 1st prize for research project. Mem. AAUP, AAAS, Am. Inst. Biol. Sci., Am. Mosquito Control Assn., Am. Soc. Parasitologists, Helminthol. Soc. Washington, Am. Soc. Tropical Medicine and Hygiene, Entomol. Soc. Am., Am. Genetic Assn., Soc. of Vector Ecology, N.Y. Acad. Scis., Johns Hopkins U. Tropical Medicine Club, Smithsonian Assocs., Royal Soc. Tropical Medicine and Hygiene, Royal Entomol. Soc. of London, Sigma Xi, Delta Omega (Alpha chpt.). Home: 1504 Ivy Hill Rd Cockeysville MD 21030-1418 Office: Johns Hopkins U 615 N Wolfe St Baltimore MD 21205-2103

TRUAX, JAMES FRANCIS, pharmacologist; b. Neptune, N.J., Jan. 21, 1948; s. Stanley John and Phyllis (Rauso) T.; m. Gail Roberts, Nov. 22, 1988; 1 child, Jamie Caitlin. BS in Biol. Sci., Quincy (Ill.) Coll., 1969; MA in Physiology/Pharmacology, Duke U., 1978. Rsch. asst. Burroughs Wellcome Co., Research Triangle Park, N.C., 1970-78; jr. rsch. pharmacologist Burroughs Wellcome Co., 1978-84, assoc. pharmacologist, 1984-87, sr. assoc. pharmacologist, 1987-94, sr. rsch. pharmacologist, 1994-96; sr. scientist Glaxo Wellcome, Inc., Research Triangle Park, 1996—. Contbr. articles to profl. jours., chpts. to books. Mem. Inflammation Rsch. Assn. Home: 1605 E Hardscrabble Dr Hillsborough NC 27278-9740 Office: Glaxo Wellcome Inc 3030 W Cornwallis Rd Durham NC 27709-2700

TRUDEL, MICHEL, virologist; b. Montreal, Feb. 5, 1944; married, 1981; 3 children. BA, U. Montreal, 1965, BSc, 1968, MSc, 1970; PhD in Cell Biology, U. Sherbrooke, 1973. Fellow cell membranes Nat. Cancer Inst., 1973-74, asst. prof., 1974-75; prof. virology Inst. Armand-Frappier, Laval, Que., 1975—; also dir. ctr. virology, 1989-94, scientific dir., 1994—; grants, formation rschr. Ministry of Edn., Que., 1976-78, 88-91, Health and Welfare, Can., 1976-78, Nat. Rsch. Coun. Can., 1978-81, 84-93, 93—, Can. Med. Rsch. Coun., 1992—, conseil de recherches en peche et agroalimentaire, Que., 1985-89. Mem. Am. Soc. Virologists, Internat. Soc. Antiviral Rsch., Can. Assn. Clin. Microbiology Infectious Diseases, Can. Soc. Microbiologists. Office: Armand-Frappier Inst, 531 Blvd des Prairies Po 100, Laval, PQ Canada H7N 4Z3

TRUITT, GARY ARTHUR, pharmacologist; b. Boulder, Colo., Mar. 31, 1947; s. Arthur Leonard and Dorothy Velma (Reese) T.; m. Theresa Patricia-Ann Striegel, May 7, 1982; children: Kelley Catherine, Christian Alec. BA, Pitts. State U., Kans., 1970; PhD, U. Kans. Med. Ctr., 1975. Postdoctoral fellow Baylor Coll. Medicine, Houston, 1975-78; NSF fellow Nat. Naval Med. Ctr., Bethesda, Md., 1979-80; postdoctoral fellow Thomas Jefferson U., Phila., 1980-82; sr. scientist Hoffmann-La Roche, Inc., Nutley, N.J., 1982-87, rsch. investigator, 1987—. Contbr. articles to profl. jours.; patentee in field. Fellow Kelsey Leary Found., Houston, 1976-78. Mem. AAAS, Fedn. Am. Socs. for Exptl. Biology and Medicine, N.Y. Acad. Sci., Am.Assn. Immunology, Sigma Xi. Office: Hoffmann LaRoche Inc 340 Kingsland St Nutley NJ 07110-1150

TRUITT, ROBERT LINDELL, immunologist, researcher, pediatrics educator; b. Carbondale, Ill., July 26, 1946; s. Arthur G. and Verna A. (Lingle) T.; m. Dawn M. Kowalkiewicz, Sept. 2, 1967; children: Cabrina M., Valerie L., Tiffany D., Andrea L., Lyndell M. BA, So. Ill. U., 1968, PhD, 1973. Rsch. assoc. Mt. Sinai Med. Ctr., Milw., 1975-77, sr. scientist, 1977-83, assoc. dir. Winter Rsch. Lab., 1983-84; rsch. assoc. prof. Med. Coll. of Wis., Milw., 1984-88, rsch. prof., 1988-91; prof., 1991—; cons. NIH, Bethesda, Md., 1978—, Netherlands Cancer Found., The Hague, VA. Reviewer Blood, Bone Marrow Transplantation, Jour. Immunology; editor: Cellular Immunotherapy of Cancer, 1987. Bd. trustees Leukemia Soc. Am., Wis., 1986-90, 1991—. United Cancer Coun. fellow, 1972-73, Damon Runyon Meml. Fund fellow, 1973-75, Leukemia Soc. Am., Inc. fellow, 1976-78, scholar, 1978-83. Mem. Am. Soc. for Microbiology, Assn. for Gnotobiotics (bd. dirs. 1980-83, 91—, pres. 1981-82), Internat. Soc. for Exptl. Hematology, Am. Assn. Immunologists. Office: Med Coll of Wis Dept of Pediatrics 8701 W Watertown Plank Rd Milwaukee WI 53226-3548

TRULL, DAVID JOHN, hospital administrator; b. Lowell, Mass., Mar. 15, 1947; m. Cynthia. BA, U. Notre Dame, 1970; MBA, Cornell U., 1972. From assoc. dir. to exec. v.p., COO New England Med. Ctr., Boston, 1972-94; pres., CEO Faulkner Hosp., Boston, 1994—. Office: Faulkner Hosp 1153 Centre St Boston MA 02130

TRULOCK, ELBERT POWELL, III, academic pulmonary clinician; b. Bainbridge, Ga., Sept. 25, 1946; s. Elbert P. Jr. and Mildred (Ward) T.; m. Phyllis Mary De Roberts, Aug. 8, 1971; children: Brian David, Alison Mary. BS cum laude, Emory U., 1968, MD cum laude, 1978. Diplomate Am. Bd. Internal Medicine, Am. Bd. Pulmonary Disease. Intern and resident in medicine Barnes Hosp.-Washington U. Med. Ctr., St. Louis, 1978-81, fellow in pulmonary medicine, 1981-83, chief resident in medicine, asst. dir. med. svc., 1983-84, asst. physician, 1984—, med. dir. pulmonary function lab., 1984-93, asst. prof. medicine respiratory and critical care divsn., 1984-92, assoc. prof., 1992—, med. dir. pulmonary bronchoscopy ste., 1984—, med. dir. lung transplantation program, 1988—, interim med. dir. respiratory care svcs., 1992-93; lectr. numerous profl. orgns. and seminars; mem. adv. bd. dirs., govt. rels. com. and med. com. Am Lung Assn. Ea. Mo., 1989-90, mem. med.-rsch. rev. bd., 1992—. Contbr. articles, revs. and abstracts to med. jours., chpts. to books. Lt. USN, 1969-74. Fellow ACP, Am. Coll. Chest Physicians; mem. AMA, Am. Thoracic Soc. (program com. for sci. assembly on clin. problems 1992-93), Internat. Soc. Heart and Lung Transplantation, Barnes Hosp. Soc. (coun. 1988-92, v.p. 1991-92), Phi Beta Kappa, Alpha Omega Alpha. Office: Washington U Sch Medicine Divsn Pulmonary-CC Medicine 660 S Euclid Ave Saint Louis MO 63110

TRULUCK, JAMES PAUL, JR., dentist, vintner; b. Florence, S.C., Feb. 6, 1933; s. James Paul and Catherine Lydia (Nesmith) TruL; m. Kay Bowen (dec. Oct. 1981); children: James Paul III, David Bowen, Catherine Ann; m. Amelia Nickels Calhoun, Apr. 26, 1983; 1 child, George Calhoun. BS, Clemson (S.C.) U., 1954; DMD, U. Louisville, 1958. Pvt. practice Lake City, S.C., 1960—; founder, pres. TruLuck Vineyards & Winery, Lake City, 1976, Chateau TruLuck Natural Water Co., Lake City, 1990. Member bd. advisors Clemson U., 1978-84; mem. bd. visitors Coker Coll., Hartsville, S.C., 1978-84; pres., bd. dirs. Lions, Lake City, 1960-73; chmn. Greater Lake City Lake Commn., 1967-84. Capt. USAF, 1958-67. Recipient S.C. Bus. and Arts Partnership award S.C. State Arts Commn., 1988. Mem. ADA, Am. Assn. Vinters (bd. dirs. 1982-86), Am. Wine Soc. (nat. judge 1982-88), Am. Soc. Clin. Hypnosis (emeritus), Internat. Acad. Laser Dentistry (chartered), S.C. Dental Assn., Florence County Dental Assn., Soc. First Families of S.C. (exec. sec. 1991—), Descs. Colonial Govs. of Am., Descs. Magna Carta Barons Runnymede, Soc. Gem Cutters Am. Episcopalian.

Home: 1036 Mccutcheon Rd Lake City SC 29560-5616 Office: 125 Epp St Lake City SC 29560-2449

TRUMP, BECKY ANN, hospital administrator; b. Lancaster, Pa., Oct. 28, 1955; d. John Raymond and Shirley Ann (Hess) Snyder; m. Peter Martin Trump, June 26, 1976 (div. Mar. 1984); children: Gretchen Marie, Savannah Lee. Diploma in nursing, St. Joseph Hosp., Lancaster, 1976; BS summa cum laude, Chapman Coll., Orange, Calif., 1981; MBA in Health Adminstrn., St. Joseph's U., Phila., 1989. RN. Mem. nursing staff Bass Meml. Bapt. Hosp., Enid, Okla., 1976-77, Columbus (Miss.) Hosp., Inc., 1982-83; supr. nursing Beverly Manor, Riverside, Calif., 1978-82; charge nurse Lancaster Gen. Hosp., 1984-85; from head nurse mental health to dir. clin. support svc. Ephrata (Pa.) Community Hosp., 1985-89, asst. v.p. for planning and ancillary svcs., 1989-91, aux. treas., 1990-91; adminstrv. dir. physical medicine and rehabilitation Lancaster (Pa.) Gen. Hosp., 1991-94, nurse mgr. child and adolescent psychiatry, 1994-95; pres. Schreiber Pediat. Rehab. Ctr. Lancaster County, Lancaster, 1996—. Recipient Great Am. Family award Children and Youth Svcs. County of Lancaster, 1987. Republican. Lutheran. Home: 1517 Springside Dr Lancaster PA 17603-6320 Office: Schreiber Pediat Rehab Ctr 555 N Duke St 625 Community Way Lancaster PA 17603

TRUMP, LISA ELLEN, obstetrical nurse; b. Warsaw, Ind., Jan. 1, 1971; d. Robert S. and Nancy E. (Koch) T. BSN, Ind. U., 1993. RN, Ind. Mem. nursing staff Kosciusko Cmty. Hosp., Warsaw, Ind., 1993—. Republican. Baptist. Home: 5909 S 1000 S Mentone IN 46539

TRUNNELL, THOMAS NEWTON, dermatologist; b. Waterloo, Iowa, May 7, 1942; s. Thomas Lyle and Vivian (Dahl) T.; m. Patricia Rautiala, Aug. 2, 1974; children: Suzanne, Thomas, Sarah. AB cum laude, Princeton U., 1964; MD, U. Iowa, 1968. Diplomate Am. Bd. Dermatology. Intern U. So. Calif., L.A., 1969; resident NYU, 1972; pvt. practice dermatology Tampa, Fla., 1974—; asst. clin. prof. U. S. Fla., Tampa, 1975—; pres. Dermcorp., 1995, 96; pres. DermCorp, 1995—. Contbr. articles to profl. jours. Maj. USAF, 1972-74. Mem. AMA, Am. Acad. Dermatology, Am. Assn. Dermatol. Surgeons, Fla. Med. Assn., Fla. Soc. for Dermatol. Surgeons (pres. 1993), Fla. Dermatol. Soc., Hillsborough County Med. Assn., Cutaneous Therapy Soc., Ducks Unltd. (organizing com. North Tampa chpt. 1988—). Republican. United Methodist. Office: 13801 Bruce B Downs Blvd Tampa FL 33613-3946

TRUPO, FRANK J., plastic surgeon; b. N.Y.C., Oct. 15, 1957; s. Frank and Rose T.; m. Gail Stringer, May 22, 1987; children: Stephanie, Thomas. BS, Bethany Coll., 1979; MD, W.Va. U., 1984. Diplomate Nat. Bd. Med. Examiners, Am. Bd. Plastic Surgery. Resident gen. surgery Charleston (W.Va.) Area Med. Ctr., 1984-87; resident plastuc, reconstructive, cosmetic, maxillofacial and head and neck surgery Kans. U. Med. Ctr., Kansas City, 1987-89; pvt. practice plastic surgery Charleston, W.Va., 1990—; chief sect. plastic surgery St. Francis Hosp., Charleston, 1993—, co-chmn. credentials com., 1993—, med. adv., peer reviewer, 1994—; med. advisor, peer reviewer W.Va. Med. Inst., Mountain State BC/BS, Primary One, Inc. Fellow ACS, Am. Soc. Lasers in Medicine & Surgery; mem. Am. Soc. Aesthetic Plastic Surgery, So. Med. Assn., Kanawha Med. Soc. (pres. elect 1995), Am. Soc. Plastic and Reconstructive Surgeons. Office: 331 Laidley St Ste 510 Charleston WV 25301

TRUPP, ROBIN J., nursing administrator; b. Cin., Dec. 19, 1953; d. Jack Raymond and Barbara Jean (Huff) Shaw; m. Robert W. Trupp; children: Robert J., Amanda E. RN, Jewish Hosp. Sch. Nursing, Cin., 1975; BSN, Miami U., Oxford, Ohio, 1991; MSN, U. Cin., 1996. RN, Ohio; CCRN. Staff nurse Providence Hosp., Cin., 1975-79; RN cardiac catheterization lab Deaconess Hosp., Cin., 1983-88; ICU staff nurse Mercy Fairfield (Ohio) Hosp., 1979-83, dir. cardiac catheterization lab., 1988-91; nat. account exec. McFaul & Lyons, Inc., 1992-94; dir. critical care Deaconess Hosp., Cin., 1994-95; nurse mgr. CICU Miami Valley Hosp., Dayton, 1995—. Advanced cardiac life support instr. Am. Heart Assn., 1988—. Mem. Am. Nurses Assn., Ohio Nurses Assn., Am. Assn. Critical Care Nurses, Ohio Hosp. Assn., Ohio Orgn. Nurse Execs., Sigma Theta Tau. Home: 6069 Eaglet Dr West Chester OH 45069

TRUSHKOWSKY, RICHARD DENNIS, dentist; b. Bklyn., Dec. 6, 1945; s. Morris and Helen (Dubrow) T. BA, Bklyn. Coll., 1966; DDS, NYU, 1971. Dentist various dental offices, 1973-79; pvt. practice, 1979—; attending dentist S.I. (N.Y.) Univ. Hosp., 1981-92, dir. operative dentistry, 1992; clin. evaluator for several dental mfrs.; faculty postgrad. program in esthetic dentistry Buffalo and Baylor; lectr. in field. Mem. editl. bd. Practical Periodontics and Aesthetic Dentistry; reviewer Jour. of the Acad. Gen. Dentistry; contbr. articles to profl. jours. Capt. U.S. Army, 1971-73. Fellow Acad. Dental Materials, Acad. Gen. Dentistry; mem. Am. Prosthodontic Soc., Am. Acad. Osseointegration, Am. Acad. Cosmetic Dentistry, Internat. Assn. Dental Rsch., Richmond County Dental Soc. (sec. 1996). Democrat. Jewish. Office: 483 Jefferson Blvd Staten Island NY 10312

TRUTHAN, CHARLES EDWIN, physician; b. Cleve., Mar. 30, 1955; s. Jordan Alexander and Jean Marie (Knoll) T.; m. Joyce Lynn Miller, Dec. 4, 1982; children: Jennifer Ann, Patricia Jean, Kristine Marie. BA in Psychology, U. Toledo, 1979; DO, Ohio U., 1986. Diplomate Nat. Bd. Osteo. Med. Examiners; bd. cert. Am. Coll. Osteo. Family Practitioners. Instr. anatomy and physiology Hocking Tech. Coll., Nelsonville, Ohio, 1980-81; intern Brentwood Osteo. Hosp., Cleve., 1986-87; resident in family practice Davenport (Iowa) Med. Ctr., 1987-88; pvt. practice Wisconsin Dells, Wis., 1989-93; chief med. svcs. Troop Med. Clinic #1, Ft. McCoy, Wis., 1992-93; med. adviser Maple Heights (Ohio) Fire Dept., 1986-87; instr. ACLS, Am. Heart Assn., 1985—; instr. EMT tng. MATC, Madison, Wis., 1989-93; med. dir. Wis. BTLS, 1990-93, bd. dirs., 1992-93; v.p. med. staff Patient Care Specialists, 1994-96, Flight Physician Aeromed., 1994-96. Firefighter, paramedic Willoughby Hills (Ohio) Fire Dept., 1973-84; firefighter Springfield Twp. Vol. Fire Dept., Toledo, 1977-79; EMT instr. Dept. Vocat. Edn., Trade and Indsl. Edn., Ohio, 1976-83; vol. APPAL Corps, Athens, Ohio, 1980; bd. dirs. S.E. Ohio Regional Coun. on Alcoholism, Athens, 1980-81; med. dir. Quad City Air Show, Devenport, 1988. Comdr. USPHS, active duty with U.S. Coast Guard, 1988-89, res., 1989—. Mem. Am. Osteo. Assn., Wis. Assn. Osteo. Physicians and Surgeons (sec.-treas. 1991-92, pres.-elect 1992-93, pres. 1993-94), Wis. Soc. Am. Coll. Osteo. Family Physicians (pres. 1992-93), Mich. Assn. Osteo. Physicians and Surgeons, Mich. Assn. Osteo. Family Physicians, Am. Acad. Family Practitioners, Assn. Mil. Osteo. Physicians and Surgeons, Assn. Mil. Surgeons U.S., Am. Coll. Physician Execs., Aircraft Owners and Pilots Assn., Exptl. Aircraft Assn., Res. Officers Assn. (life). Office: Patient Care Specialists Ste 370 21 Michigan NE Ste 370 Grand Rapids MI 49503

TRYBA, MICHAEL, anesthesiologist, researcher; b. Walsum, Germany, July 21, 1950; s. Bernhard and Johanna Tryba; m. Jacoba Sperschneider, Dec. 31, 1975; children: Christiane, Carmen. MD, U. Hannover, 1977. Resident U. Hannover, 1977-83, sr. physician, 1983-84, oberarzt, 1985-86, lectr., 1984-86; vice chmn. U. Hosp. Bergmannsheil, Bochum, 1987—; lectr. Ruhr U., Bochum, 1987-90, prof., 1990—. Author: Prevention of Stress Bleeding–A New Concept, 1988; contbr. articles to profl. jours. Mem. European Acad. Anesthesiologists, European Soc. Anesthesiologists (Brussels), European Soc. Regional Anesthesia (Hans Killian award 1987), Am. Soc. Regional Anesthesia, European Soc. Intensive Care Medicine (Brussels), Internat. Assn. of the Study of Pain. Roman Catholic. Home: Kleekamp 10, D-44797 Bochum Germany Office: U Hosp Bergmannsheil, Buerkle-de-la-Camp-Platz 1, D-44789 Bochum Germany

TRYON, WARREN WILLARD, psychologist, educator; b. Schenectady, N.Y., May 26, 1944; s. Willard Harold and Dorothy Elizabeth (Hill) T.; m. Georgiana Shick, July 31, 1970; 1 child, Elizabeth. BA, Ohio Northern U., 1966; MA, Kent State U., 1969, PhD, 1970. Diplomate Am. Bd. Profl. Psychology. Asst. prof. Fordham U., Bronx, N.Y., 1970-77, assoc. prof., 1977-83, prof., 1983—. Editor: Behavioral Assessment in Behavior Medicine, 1985, Ethics in Applied Dev. Psychology; author: Activity Measurement in Psychology and Medicine, 1991. Social Security grantee, 1988, NIH grantee, 1988, Nat. Multiple Sclerosis Soc. grantee, 1988, Nat. Inst. Disability and Rehab. Rsch., 1993. Fellow APA (divsn. 12); mem. N.Y. Psychol. Assn., Assn. Advancement Behavior Therapy, Ea. Psychol. Assn. Office: Fordham U Psychology Dept 338 Dealy Hall Bronx NY 10458-5198

TRZASKO, JOSEPH ANTHONY, psychologist; b. Jamaica, N.Y., June 4, 1946; s. Joseph Anthony and Lottie Marion (Nadraus) T.; B.A. cum laude, U. N.H., 1967; M.A., U. Vt., 1969, Ph.D., 1972; m. Ann Elizabeth Kidd, June 26, 1971; 1 son, Joshua Damon. Cert. behavioral therapy, 1976. Prof. dept. psychology Mercy Coll., Dobbs Ferry, N.Y., 1969—; postdoctoral internship Ridge State Home and Tng. Sch., Colo. Dept. Insts., 1980; staff psychologist St. Dominic's Intermediate Care Facility for Developmentally Disabled, Blauvelt, N.Y., 1980—; cons. psychologist Jewish Guild for Blind, N.Y.C., 1983—, Orange County A.H.R.C., Middletown, N.Y., 1985—; pvt. practice clin. psychology. Contbg. author: Working with Visually Impaired Young Children: A Curriculum Guide for Birth -3 Year Olds, 1992. NDEA fellow U. Vt., 1967-69; NSF faculty research participation grantee Ednl. Commn. States/Nat. Assessment Ednl. Progress, 1976. Mem. Am. Psychol. Assn., AAUP, N.Y. State Psychol. Assn. Roman Catholic. Home and Office: 30 Lake Dr Somers NY 10589-2420

TSAI, CHI-CHENG, dentist, researcher; b. Taiwan, Sept. 4, 1942; m. Fong-Mei Chen, Dec. 15; children: Karen, Rodger. DDS, Kaohsiung (Taiwan) Med. Coll., 1967; PhD, U. Toronto, Can., 1975. Cert. MT-ASCP, dentist, Taiwan, Pa.; cert. periodontist and oral pathologist, Taiwan. Rsch. asst. prof. Sch. Dental Medicine U. Pa., Phila., 1977-80, rsch. assoc. prof. Sch. Dental Medicine, 1980-84; prof. Sch. Dentistry Kaohsiung Med. Coll., 1984—, dir., dean Grad. Inst. Dental Scis., Sch. Dentistry, 1986—, dir. Coll. Hosp.-Dental, 1986-93; adj. prof. Sch. Dental Medicine, U. Pa., Phila., 1994—. Vice-chief-editor: (periodical) The Kaohsiung Jour. Medicine, 1985-89. Recipient Distinction in Tchg. award Ministry of Edn., 1988, Distinction in Rsch. award Nat. Sci. Coun., 1988. Fellow Acad. Oral Pathology Republic of China; mem. Acad. Periodontology Republic of China (pres. 1995—), Internat. Assn. Dental Rsch. Home: 5F-4 93 Chung-Shan Herng Rd, 801 Kaohsiung Taiwan Office: Kaohsiung Med Coll, Sch Dentistry, 100 Shih-Chuan 1st Rd, 807 Kaohsiung Taiwan

TSAI, CLARK S., ophthalmologist. BE, CCNY, 1983; MD, Albert Einstein Coll. Medicine, 1988. Intern medicine Bronx (N.Y.) Mcpl. Hosp., 1988-89; fellow glaucoma Kresge Eye Inst., Detroit, 1989-90, resident ophthalmology, 1990-93; fellow glaucoma U. Calif.-San Diego, La Jolla, 1993-94; pvt. practice San Jose, Calif., 1994—. Contbr.: The Claucomas, 2nd edit., 1996. Recipient Heed fellowship Heed Ophthalmic Found., Cleve., 1993-94, travel fellowship Nat. Eye Inst., Balt., 1994.

TSALIKIAN, EVA, physician; b. Piraeus, Greece, June 22, 1949; came to U.S., 1974; d. Vartan and Arousiak (Kasparian) T. M.D., U. Athens, 1973. Research fellow U. Calif.-San Francisco, 1974-76; resident pediatrics Children's Hosp., Pitts., 1976-78, fellow endocrinology, 1978-80; research fellow Mayo Clinic, Rochester, Minn., 1980-83; asst. prof. dept. pediatrics U. Iowa, Iowa City, 1983—. Fellow Juvenile Diabetes Found., 1978-80, Heinz Nutrition Found., 1980-81; recipient Young Physician award AMA, 1977. Mem. Am. Diabetes Assn. Home: 1217 Dolen Pl Iowa City IA 52246-4524 Office: U Iowa Dept Pediatrics Iowa City IA 52242

TSAMBASSIS, NICHOLAS ALEXANDER, pediatrician; b. Evanston, Ill., Sept. 3, 1956; s. Alexander Nicholas and Katharine (Voulelis) T. BS, Calif. U. Pa., 1979; MD, Ross U., 1985. Diplomate Am. Bd. Pediatrics. Intern Trenton (N.J.) Affiliated Hosps., 1985-86; resident Lincoln Med. and Mental Health Ctr., Bronx, N.Y., 1986-89; pvt. practice Gardner Healthcare Initiative, Portland, Tenn., 1990, Centerville (Pa.) Clinics, Inc., 1991—; med. dir. South Fayette Nursing Ctr., Markleysburg, Pa., 1993-95. Active Rock Out Censorship, Jewett, Ohio, 1992, ACLU, N.Y.C., 1994, People for the Am. Way, Washington, 1994, Ams. United, Washington, 1995. Mem. Pa. Med. Soc., Assn. Am. Physicians and Surgeons. Home: 107 Skyline Dr California PA 15419 Office: Centerville Clinics Inc 1070 Old National Pike Fredericktown PA 15333

TSE, FRANCIS LAI-SING, pharmaceutical company executive; b. Hong Kong, Jan. 20, 1952; s. Yuen-Hong and Li-Ing (Shone) T.; m. Irene Chong-Hwa Chow, Mar. 23, 1979; 1 dau., Clara Kwok-Fong. Student Wis. State U., 1969-70; BS with honors U. Wis., 1974, MS, 1975, PhD, 1978. Lectr., Sch. Pharmacy, U. Wis., Madison, 1978; asst. prof. pharmaceutics Rutgers U., Piscataway, N.J., 1978-80, sr. scientist, unit head Sandoz Research Inst., East Hanover, N.J., 1981-84, mem. sr. sci. staff, 1985-86, fellow 1987-90, assoc. dir., 1991-95, dir., 1996. Recipient Oscar Rennebohm Teaching award U. Wis., 1974-75; grantee Rutgers U. Research Council, 1979, 80, Biomed. Research Support, 1979, 80, Western Electric Found., 1980, Nat. Inst. on Drug Abuse, 1980-81. Fellow Am. Coll. Clin. Pharmocology, Am. Pharm. Assn., Acad. Pharm. Rsch. and Sci., Am. Assn. Pharm. Scis.; mem. N.Y. Acad. Scis., Internat. Soc. for Study Xenobiotics, Am. Soc. for Clin. Pharmacology and Therapeutics, Sigma Xi. Mem. editorial bd. Antimicrobial Agts. and Chemotherapy, 1984—: author 5 books on pharmacokinetics; contbr. numerous articles to profl. jours. Home: 19 Arbor Way Morristown NJ 07960-6030 Office: Sandoz Research Inst Route 10 Drug Metabolism Dept Hanover NJ 07936

TSE, KELVIN ANTHONY, dentist; b. Cleve., Dec. 29, 1962; s. Kenneth K. and Joyce (Auyeung) T.; m. Cynthia Lee Weideman, Aug. 20, 1994; 1 child, Carleen Ann. BS in Marine Biology, Loyola Marymount U., 1984; DDS, U. Pacific, 1989; cert. esthetic dentistry, UCLA, 1994. Lic. dentist, Calif. Pvt. practice Alhambra, Calif., 1990-94, Citrus Heights, Calif., 1995—; dir. Am. Soc. Dentistry for Children. Mem. ADA, Am. Acad. Cosmetic Dentistry, Internat. Congress Oral Implantologists, Sacramento Dist. Dental Soc., Rotary Club. Office: 7916 Pebble Beach Dr #103 Citrus Heights CA 95610

TSENG, MICHAEL TSUNG, medical educator; b. Chung King, China, Jan. 25, 1944; came to U.S., 1962; s. Yung Sen and Mo-Jen (Liu) T.; m. Shirley Ch. H. Lu, Feb. 14, 1970; 1 child, Sophia Y.W. BS, Iowa State U., 1967; PhD, SUNY, Buffalo, 1973. Asst. prof. SUNY Upstate Med. Ctr., Syracuse, 1974-78; assoc. prof. U. Louisville, 1978-86, prof. anatomy and neurobiology, 1987—, dir. tumor evaluation lab., 1982—; vis. prof. Nat. Def. Med. Ctr., Taipei, Republic of China, 1989-90. Bd. dirs. Orgn. Chinese Ams., Louisville, 1991. Named Hon. Prof. Henan (Zhengzhou, Peoples Republic China) Med. U., 1987. Mem. Am. Assn. Cancer Rsch., Assn. Rsch. in Vision and Ophthalmology, Am. Assn. Anatomist, Sigma Xi (pres. U. Louisville chpt. 1991-92). Office: U Louisville Louisville KY 40292

TSENG, WEN-PING, cardiologist; b. Chang-Hwa, Taiwan, Republic of China, Jan. 15, 1924; s. Chi-Chin and Chin-Kwei (Chang) T.; m. Tsui-Wei, Chou, Sept. 7, 1945; children—Hui-Jen, Yea-Fan, Ham-Min, Tzy-Mei. M.D., Nat. Taiwan U., Taipei, 1953; D.Med. Sci., Osaka Mcpl. Med. Ctr. (Japan), 1960. Resident Nat. Taiwan U. Hosp., Taipei, 1953-57, staff physician, 1958—, vice supt., 1978-83, instr. medicine Med. Coll., 1961-67, assoc. prof., 1967-75, prof., 1975-88, supt. Tzu-Chi Buddhist Gen. Hosp., 1989—; prof., chmn. Sch. Rehab., 1980-86. Author: Blackfoot Disease, 1979. Fellow Am. Coll. Cardiology, Am. Coll. Chest Physicians, Internat. Coll. Angiology, Am. Coll. Angiology, Royal Soc. Medicine; mem. Am. Heart Assn., Internat. Soc. Cardiology, N.Y. Acad. Sci., Republic China Soc. Cardiology, Formosan Med. Assn., Chinese Med. Assn., Chinese Med. Info. and Service Assn. (chmn. 1981), Chinese Hypertension Assn. (chmn. 1986). Home: 2d Floor Lane 109 Sect 1, An-Ho Rd, Taipei 106 China Office: Tzu Chi Buddhist Gen Hosp, 8 Hsin Sheng S Rd, Hualien Taiwan Republic of China

TSIEN, RICHARD WINYU, biology educator; b. Tating, Kweichow, People's Republic China, Mar. 3, 1945; s. Hsue-Chu and Yi-Ying (Li) T.; m. Julia Shiang Aug. 29, 1971; children: Sara Shiang-Ming, Gregory Shiang-An, Alexa Tsien-Shiang. BS, MIT, 1965, MS, 1966; DPhil, Oxford U., Eng., 1970. Rsch. student Eaton Peabody Lab. Auditory, Physiology, Mass. Eye and Ear Infirmary, 1966; asst. prof. dept. physiology, Yale U. Sch. Medicine, New Haven, 1970-74, assoc. prof., 1974-79, prof., 1979-88; George D. Smith prof. molecular and cellular physiology Stanford (Calif.) U., 1988—, chmn. dept., 1988—; established investigator Am. Heart Assn., 1974-79. Author: Electric Current Flow in Excitable Cells, 1975. Recipient Otsuka award Internat. Soc. Heart Rsch., 1985; Rhodes Scholar, 1966; Weir Rsch. fellow, 1966-70 Univ. Coll., Oxford, 1966-70, lecturing fellow Balliol Coll., Oxford, 1969-70. Mem. Soc. Gen. Physiologists (pres. 1988), Biophys. Soc. (Kenneth S. Cole award 1985), Soc. for Neurosci. Democrat. Home: 866 Tolman Dr Palo Alto CA 94305-1026 Office: Stanford U Dept Molecular and Cellular Physiology 300 Pasteur Dr Stanford CA 94305*

TSIEN, ROGER YONCHIEN, chemist, cell biologist; b. N.Y.C., Feb. 1, 1952; s. Hsue Chu and Yi Ying (Li) T.; m. Wendy M. Globe, July 30, 1982. AB summa cum laude in Chemistry and Physics, Harvard Coll., 1972; PhD in Physiology, U. Cambridge, 1977. Rsch. asst. U. Cambridge, Eng., 1975-78; asst. prof. Dept. Physiology-Anatomy U. Calif., Berkeley, 1981-85, assoc. prof., 1985-87, prof., 1987-89; prof. Pharmacology and Chemistry, investigator Howard Hughes Med. Inst. U. Calif., San Diego, 1989—; T.Y. Shen vis. prof. Medicinal Chem., MIT, 1991. Mem. editorial bds. Jour. Biological Chemistry, Molecular Biology of the Cell; contbr. chpts. to books, articles to profl. jours. Recipient Lamport prize N.Y. Acad. Scis., 1986, Javits Neurosci. Investigator award Nat. Inst. Neurol. Disorders and Stroke, 1989—, Young Scientist award Passano Found., 1991, W. Alden Spencer Neurobiology award Columbia U., 1991, Bowditch lectureship Am. Physiol. Soc., 1992; Gairdner Found. Internat. award, 1995; Comyns Berkeley Rsch. fellow Gonville & Caius Coll., 1977-81; Marshall scholar British Govt., 1972-75, Searle scholar, 1983-86. Mem. Phi Beta Kappa. Office: U Calif Howard Hughes Med Inst M-047 Cellular & Molecular Medicine La Jolla CA 92093-0647*

TSIOTOS, GREGORY G., surgeon; b. Athens, Greece, Aug. 29, 1961; came to U.S., 1990; s. George V. and Eleni (Ktistop) T.; m. Julia Macris, Feb. 10, 1991; 1 child, George. BA, Athens Coll., 1980; MD, Aristotelion U., 1986. Resident gen. surgery Mayo Clinic, Rochester, Minn., 1991-95; scholar gastrointestinal surgery Mayo Clinic, Rochester, 1995-97. Contbr. articles to profl. jours. Med. officer Greek Air Force, 1989-90. Mem. AMA, ACS, Minn. Med. Assn., Zumbro Valley Med. Assn., Athens Med. Assn. Office: Mayo Clinic 200 First St SW Rochester MN 55905

TSIVITIS, MARIE IRENE, epidemiologist, medical technologist; b. N.Y.C., May 1, 1962; d. Guy Frank Ciacco and Eleni Bacola; m. James Tsivitis; 1 child. BS in Med. Technology, SUNY, Stony Brook, 1984; MPH in Infectious Disease Epidemiology, Yale U., 1986. Cert in infection control, med. technologist Am. Soc. Clin. Pathologists. Coord. infection control St. Clare's Hosp. & Health Ctr., N.Y.C., 1986-90, Meml. Sloan Kettering Cancer Ctr., N.Y.C., 1990-92, L.I. State Vets. Home/SUNY, Stony Brook, N.Y., 1992—; mem. Infection Control Adv. Com. N.Y. State Dept. Health, Albany, 1995—; mem. Job Analysis Com./Certification Bd. for Infection Control, Lenexa, Kans., 1990-91, 96. Contbr. chpt. to book, articles to profl. jours. Mem. APHA, Am. Soc. Microbiology, Assn. for Profls. in Infection Control and Epidemiology (nat. rsch. com. 1990-92). Greek Orthodox. Office: LI State Vets Home SUNY 100 Patriots Rd Stony Brook NY 11790

TSOU, WALTER HAI-TZE, physician; b. Boston, Nov. 1, 1952; s. Kwan Chung and Teresa (Lee) T. BA, U. Pa., 1974, MD, 1978; MPH, Johns Hopkins U., 1988. Diplomate Am. Bd. Internal Medicine. Resident in internal medicine Presbyn. U. Pa. Med. Ctr., Phila., 1978-81; clinician Phila. Dept. Pub. Health, 1981-84, clin. dir., 1984-91; med. dir. Montgomery County Health Dept., Norristown, Pa., 1991—, dep. dir. personal health svcs., 1991—; asst. prof. Med. Coll. Pa., Phila., 1990—; mem. Phila. AIDS Consortium, 1991-93; mem. profl. and edn. com. Am. Cancer Soc., Phila., 1991—. Contbg. editor Physicians News Digest, Narberth, Pa., 1989—. Mem. fund distbn. com. United Way of S.E. Pa., Phila., 1994—; co-chair Physicians for a Nat. Health Program, Phila., 1991—. Recipient John C. Hume award Johns Hopkins Sch. Pub. Health, 1988. Fellow Coll. Physicians of Phila. (chair com. pub. health 1994—); mem. APHA, ACP, Pa. Pub. Health Assn., Chinese-Am. Med. Soc., Delta Omega. Office: Montgomery County Hlth Dept 1 Lafayette Pl Ste 325 Norristown PA 19401

TSUANG, MING TSO, psychiatrist, educator; b. Tainan, Taiwan, Nov. 16, 1931; came to U.S., 1971; s. Ping Tang and Chhun Kuei (Lin) T.; m. Snow Huei S. Ko, Nov. 24, 1958; children—John, Debby, Grace. M.D., Nat. Taiwan U., Taipei, 1957; Ph.D. in Psychiatry, Ph.D. (Sino-Brit. Fellowship Trust scholar); certs. in epidemiology and stats., population genetics, psychiat. genetics, U. London, 1965; D.Sc. in Psychiat. Genetics and Epidemiology, Faculty of Sci., U. London, 1981. Intern Nat. Taiwan U. Hosp., 1956-57, resident in psychiatry, 1957-61, assoc. prof. psychiatry, staff psychiatrist, 1968-71; collaborating investigator Internat. Pilot Study of Schizophrenia, WHO, 1966-71; vis. assoc. prof. psychiatry Washington U. Sch. Medicine, St. Louis, 1971-72; assoc. prof., staff psychiatrist U. Iowa Coll. Medicine, Iowa City, 1972-75; prof. psychiatry U. Iowa Coll. Medicine, 1975-82, prof. psychiat. epidemiology, 1978-82; clin. tchr., lectr. to residents, med. students; cons. psychiatrist VA Hosp., Iowa City, 1972-82; prof., vice chmn. sect. of psychiatry and human behavior Brown U., Providence, 1982-85; assoc. med. dir. Butler Hosp., Providence, 1982-85, dir. psychiat. epidemiology research unit, 1982-85; prof. psychiatry Harvard Inst. Psychiat. Epid. and Genetics Harvard U. Med. Sch. and Harvard Sch. Pub. Health; dir. psychiat. epidemiology and genetics Mass. Mental Health Ctr., Boston; chief psychiatry, chmn. Ctr. for Mental Health Brockton-West Roxbury VA Med. Ctr., 1985-94; head and supt. dept. psychiatry Harvard U. at Mass. Mental Health Ctr., 1992—; Stanley Cobb prof. Psychiatry Harvard U., 1993—; mem. epidemiol. studies rev. com. NIMH, 1976-79, mem., chmn. rsch. scientist devel. rev. com. NIMH, 1982-86, chmn. epidemiologic studies rev. com., 1989-90; mem. extramural sci. adv. bd. NIMH, 1990—; mem. med. rsch. svc. planning coun. Vets. Health Svcs. and Rsch. Adminstrn., VA Cen. Office, 1990—; vis. prof. psychiatry (Josiah Macy faculty scholar award) Oxford U., Eng., Warneford Hosp., 1979-80; chmn. mental health policy working group, div. health and policy research and edn. Harvard U., 1986—. Author: (with R. Vandermey) Genes and The Mind: Inheritance of Mental Illness, 1980, Schizophrenia: The Facts, 1982, (with S.V. Faraone) The Genetics of Mood Disorders, 1990; co-editor: Schizoaffective Psychoses, 1986, Handbook of Schizophrenia, vol. 3, 1988, Affective and Schizoaffective Disorders, Similarities and Differences, 1990, also monographs.; contbr. chpts. to books, numerous articles to profl. jours. Recipient Clin. Rsch. award Am. Acad. Clin. Psychiatrists, 1983, Rema Lapous award APHA, 1984, Stanley Dean award for rsch. on schizophrenia Am. Coll. Psychiatrists, 1989, Lifetime Achievement award Internat. Soc. Psychiat. Genetics, 1995, Taiwanese-Am. award for Achievement in Sci. and Engring., 1995. Mem. Psychiat. Rsch. Soc., Am. Psychopathol. Assn., Soc. for Life History Rsch. in Psychopathology (steering com. 1989—, Inst. of Medicine/NAAS, Sigma Xi. Home: 354 Dudley Rd Newton MA 02159-2829 Office: 940 Belmont St Brockton MA 02401-5596

TSUCHIYA, MASAHARU, internal medicine educator; b. Niigata, Japan, Apr. 8, 1928; parents Haruki and Ukiko Tsuchiya; m. Toshiko Tsuchiya. Degree in medicine, Keio Y., Tokyo, 1953; hon. degree, Acad. Nat. de Médicine, France, 1988. Asst. prof. medicine Keio U., Tokyo, 1974-77, prof., 1977-94, prof. emeritus, 1994—; pres. IV World Congress Microcirculation, Tokyo, 1987, IV Internat. Congress Mucosal Immunology, Tokyo, 1990; hon. pres. 1st Asian Congress for Microcirculation, 1993. Recipient Légion d'Honneur, 1980. Mem. AAAS, N.Y. Acad. Scis. Home: 5-8-16 Aobaku, Utsukushigaoka, Yokohama Japan Office: Keio U Hosp, 35 Shinanomachi Shinjuku, Tokyo Japan

TSUI, LAP-CHEE, molecular genetics educator; b. Shanghai, Dec. 21, 1950; arrived in Can., 1981; s. Jing Lue Hsue and Hui Ching Wang; m. Ellen Lan Fong, Feb. 11, 1977; children: Eugene, Felix. BS, Chinese U. Hong Kong, 1972, MPhil, 1974, DSc (hon.), 1991; PhD, U. Pitts., 1979; DCL (hon.), U. King's Coll., Halifax, N.S., Can., 1991; DSc (hon.), U. N.B., Can., 1991; DLL (hon.), U. St. Francis Xavier, Antigonish, N.S., Can., 1994. Postdoctoral investigator Oak Ridge (Tenn.) Nat. Lab., 1979-80; postdoctoral fellow Hosp. for Sick Children, Toronto, Ont., Can., 1981-83, geneticist-in-chief, 1996—, Sellers chair cystic fibrosis rsch., 1990—; asst. prof. depts. genetics and med. genetics U. Toronto, Ont., Can., 1983-88, assoc. prof., 1988-90, prof., 1990—, univ. prof., 1994—; chmn. chromosome 7 subcom. Human Gene Mapping Workshop, 1986—; mem. mammalian genetics study sect. NIH, Bethesda, Md., 1988-93; dir. Cystic Fibrosis Rsch. Ctr., Hosp. for Sick Children Spl. Rsch. Ctr., 1994—; scientist Med. Rsch. Coun. Can., 1989—; advisor European Jour. Human Genetics, 1992—, Molecular Medicine Today, 1995—. Editor Cytogenetics and Cell Genetics, 1988-92, Internat. Jour. Genome Rsch., 1990—; assoc. editor Am. Jour.

Human Genetics, 1990-93, Genomics, 1994—; mem. editl. bd. Mammalian Genome, 1990, Clin. Genetics, 1991—, Human Molecular Genetics, 1991—; communicating editor Human Mutation, 1995—, Molec. Medicine Today; contbr. over 200 articles to sci. jours.; co-discoverer cystic firbrosis gene, 1989. Trustee Edn. Found., Fedn. Chinese Canadian Profls., Toronto, 1987—. Recipient Paul di Sant Agnese Disting. Achievement award Cystic Firbosis Found., 1989, Gold medal of honor Pharm. Mfrs. Assn. Can., 1989, award of excellence Genetics Soc. Can., 1990, Gairdner Internat. award 1990, Cresson medal Franklin Inst., 1992, E. Mead Johnson award, 1992, Disting. Scientist award The Canadian Soc. Clin. Investigators, 1992, Canadian Conf. medal 1992, Sarstedt Rsch. prize, 1993, Sanremo Internat. award for Genetic Rsch., 1993, J.P. Lecocq prize Inst. de France, 1994, Henry Frieson award The Canadian Soc. for Clin. Investigation and the Royal Coll. of Physicians and Surgeons of Can.; named scholar Can. Cystic Fibrosis Found., 1984-86. Fellow Royal Soc. Can., Royal Soc. London, Academia Sinica; mem. Human Genome Orgn., Am. Soc. Human Genetics. Office: Hosp for Sick Children, 555 University Ave, Toronto, ON Canada M5G 1XG

TSUKAMOTO, NAOKI, gynecologic oncologist; b. Kobe, Kyogo-ken, Japan, Oct. 6, 1940; s. Yoshitaka and Yuriko (Nagafuchi) T.; m. Shizuko Noda, Sept. 18, 1969; children: Naotaka, Eriko. MD, Kyushu U. Faculty Medicine, Fukuoka, Japan, 1965, D of Med. Sci., 1985. Lic. in Japan. Intern Buffalo Gen. Hosp., N.Y., 1967-68; resident in ob-gyn. U. Hosp., Cleve., 1968-72; asst. in ob-gyn. faculty of medicine Kyushu U., Fukuoka, Japan, 1972-76, asst. prof., 1979-83, assoc. prof., 1983-93; fellow in gynecologic oncology Meml. Sloan-Kettering Cancer Ctr., N.Y.C., 1976-78; dir. Nat. Kyushu Cancer Ctr., Fukuoka, Japan, 1993—. Contbr. articles to profl. jours. Fellow ACOG; mem. Japan Soc. Ob-Gyn., Soc. Gynecologic Oncologists, Soc. Meml. Gynecologic Oncologists, Internat. Gynecologic Cancer Soc. Home: Wakamiya 5-5-3 Higashi-ku, Fukuoka 813, Japan Office: Nat Kyushu Cancer Ctr, Notame 3-1-1, Minami-ku, Fukuoka 815, Japan

TSUNEJI, NAGAI, pharmaceutics educator; b. Shikishima, Gumma, Japan, June 10, 1933; s. Ushinosuke and Take (Kogure) N.; m. Kiyoko Usui, May 5, 1964. BS, U. of Tokyo, 1956, MS, 1958, PhD, 1961. Lic. pharmacist. Rsch. and teaching assoc. U. of Tokyo, 1961-71; postdoct. fellow Columbia U., N.Y.C., 1965-66, U. Mich., Ann Arbor, 1966-67; prof. pharmaceutics Hoshi U., Tokyo, 1971—; Chmn. bd. trustees The Nagai Found., Tokyo, 1986—; dir. FIP Found. for Edn. and Rsch., The Hague, The Netherlands, 1983—, Iwaki Found., Tokyo, 1985—. Author numerous books, papers and articles in field; inventor 55 patents. Trustee Hoshi U., Tokyo, 1979-91; mem. adv. com. Ministry of Health and Welfare, Tokyo, 1967-83, Ministry of Fgn. Affairs, Tokyo, 1981-87, Ministry of Edn. Culture and Sci., Tokyo, 1981-83; spl. mem. Japan Accredidation Assn., Tokyo, 1981—. Recipient Japan Invention prize Japan Invention Assn., Tokyo, 1984, Most Prestigious Rsch. prize Pharm. Soc. Japan, Tokyo, 1987; William Evans fellow U. Otago, Duneden, New Zealand, 1993. Mem. Acad. Pharm. Sci. and Tech. (founding pres. 1985-87), Internat. Pharm. Fedn. (v.p. 1986-94, Host-Madsen medal 1986), Controlled Release Soc. (del., pres. 1996—), Japan Soc. Drug Delivery (pres., chmn. bd. dirs. 1994—), Soc. of Cyclodextrins Japan (founding pres.), Internat. House of Japan. Home: 1-23-10-103 Hon-Komagome, Bunkyo-ku, Tokyo 113, Japan Office: Hoshi U Dept Pharmaceutics, 2-4-41 Ebara, Shinagawa-ku, Tokyo 142, Japan

TSUTSUI, HIROYUKI, cardiologist; b. Kitakyushu, Fukuoka, Japan, Oct. 12, 1957; s. Terumi Koshino, July 7, 1990. MD, Kyushu U., Fukuoka, 1982, PhD, 1992. Resident Kyushu U., Fukuoka, 1982-84, rsch. fellow, 1984-87, fellow, 1992-94, lectr., 1994—; rsch. fellow Med. U. S.C., Charleston, 1990-92. Contbr. articles to profl. jours. Home: 902 Jousui-Dori Parkhomes, 4-6-7 Yakuin, Chuo-ku, Fukuoka Japan Office: Kyushu U, 3-1-1 Maidashi, Higashi-ku, 812-82 Tukuoka Japan

TSYKIN, ANNA, molecular biologist, researcher; b. Moscow, June 10, 1961; d. Eugene and Galina (Dvorkina) T. BSc (hon.), Monash U., Melbourne, Australia, 1985; PhD, U. Melbourne, 1994. Rsch. officer Macfarlane Burnet Ctr. for Med. Rsch., Melbourne, 1994—; rschr. in acute-phase response, liver regeneration, thyroid hormone transport, HIV/AIDS, 1987—. Contbr. articles to profl. jours. Supporter environ. protection movements. Mem. Australasian Soc. for HIV Medicine. Office: Macfarlane Burnet Ctr, PO Box 254, Fairfield Vic 3078, Australia

TUBLIN, IRA NATHAN, physician; b. Balt., Feb. 8, 1929; s. Morris and Rose (Cohen) T.; m. Marilyn Claire Scherlis, June 13, 1954; children: Marjorie Grossman, Robert, Gary, Eric. BS, U. Md., College Park, 1950; MD, U. Md., Balt., 1954. Diplomate Am. Bd. Internal Medicine; cert. geritrics, nephrology. Intern D.C. Gen. Hosp., Washington, 1954-55, resident, 1957-59; fellow in nephrology VA Hosp., Washington, 1959-60; pvt. practice Silver Spring, Md., 1960—; clin. assoc. prof. medicine George Washington U. Med. Ctr., Washington, 1977—; cons. Montgomery Gen. Hosp., Olney, Md., 1970-87; bd. dirs. Nat. Kidney Found., D.C. Capt. AUS, 1955-57. Fellow Am. Coll. Physicians; mem. Montgomery County Med. Soc. (named Clinician of Yr. 1986), Am. Soc. Nephrology, Internat. Soc. Nephrology. Hebrew. Home: 1210 N Belgrade Rd Silver Spring MD 20902-3024 Office: 8830 Cameron Ct Silver Spring MD 20910-4114

TUBOKU-METZGER, ALBERT JAMES, pediatric cardiology educator; b. Freetown, Sierra Leone, Jan. 5, 1941; came to U.S., 1984; s. Samuel John and Edith Frances (Roberts) T.-M.; m. Catherine Burke, July 18, 1969; children: Akinsope, Frances, Jennifer. MD, U. Toronto, Ont., Can., 1967. Diplomate Am. Bd. Pediatrics. Intern St. Joseph's Hosp., McMaster U. Med. Sch., Hamilton, Ont., 1967-68; resident in gen. pediats. Sick Children's Hosp., U. Toronto Med. Sch., 1972-74; fellow in pediat. cardiology Case Western Res. U., Rainbow Babies & Children's Hosp., Cleve., 1974-77; specialist pediatrician Children's Hosp., Freetown, 1977-80, sr. specialist pediatrician, 1980-84; fellow in pediatric cardiology Emory U., Atlanta, 1984-85, asst. prof. pediatrics, 1985-95, assoc. prof., 1995—. Contbr. articles and abstracts to med. jours. Fellow Am. Coll. Pediatrics, Am. Coll. Cardiology (diplomate), West African Coll. Physicians. Episcopalian. Home: 3618 Preakness Dr Decatur GA 30034 Office: Emory U Dept Pediatrics 89 Butler St Atlanta GA 30303

TUCCI, JAMES M., health facility administrator; b. Teaneck, N.J., July 31, 1949; s. Peter Anthony and Ann Francis (McGoldrick) T.; m. Phyllis Mary Amato, June 22, 1974 (div. Dec. 1992); m. Judy Ann Lamoreaux, July 23, 1994; children: James Jr., Peter. BA in Philosophy, Fordham U., 1974; MD, Rutgers U., 1978. Diplomate Am. Bd. Psychiatry and Neurology, Am. Bd. Sleep Medicine. Chief neurology sect. Naval Regional Med. Ctr., Jacksonville, Fla., 1982-87; chair neurology dept. The Ochsner Clinic, New Orleans, 1987-91, Lovelace Health Sys., Albquerque, 1991-94; v.p. health plans Lovelace/Cigna Health Plans, Albquerque, 1994-95; chief med. officer, sr. v.p. mgmt. Aetna Healthcare, Dallas, 1995—. Lt. comdr. USN, 1978-86. Fellow Am. Acad. Neurology, Am. EEG Soc., Am. Sleep Disorder Assn., Phi Beta Kappa, Alpha Omega Alpha. Episcopalian.

TUCCI, NICHOLAS, psychologist; b. Reading, Pa., Dec. 22, 1936; s. Alfonzo and Angelina (Masciotti) T.; m. Patricia Ann Miller; children: Gregory Colin, Pamela Ann. BS, Kutztown (Pa.) State Coll., 1959, MS in Edn., 1966; postgrad., Temple U., 1973. Lic. psychologist, sch. psychologist, Pa. Tchr. pub. schs. Scotch Plains, N.J., 1959-61; tchr., dept. head Fleetwood (Pa.) Area Schs., 1962-73; psychologist Berks County Intermediate Unit, Reading, 1973-91, Wilson Sch. Dist., West Lawn, Pa., 1991—; cons. Montgomery County Intermediate Unit, Norristown, Pa., 1976—, Cath. Social Agy., Reading, 1983—, Family Life Svcs., Topton, Pa., 1986-88. Mem. adv. bd. Cath. Social Agy., Allentown, Pa., 1980-90, chmn. 1986-90. Mem. APA, Berks Area Psychol. Soc. (treas. 1980-84, pres. 1983-84), Pa. Psychol. Soc., Berks County Intermediate Edn. Assn. (treas. 1975-91), Victor Emmanuel Benificial Soc., Phi Delta Kappa. Democrat. Roman Catholic. Home: 400 Friedensburg Rd Reading PA 19606-1513

TUCKER, ASHLEY ROBERT, III, thoracic and cardiovascular surgeon; b. Maryville, Mo., Nov. 27, 1944; m. Lois Jean Tucker; children: Ashley Jean, Noah Scott. BA in Zoology, U. Mo., 1966, MD, 1970. Diplomate Am. Bd. Thoracic and Cardiovasc. Surgery. Intern in surgery U. Va., 1970; resident in surgery U. Mo., 1971-72; resident in surgery U. Va., 1972-74, chief resident in surgery, 1974-75, resident in thoracic cardiovascular surgery, 1975-77; attending physician Winchester (Va.) Med. Ctr., 1979—. Trustee, bd. dirs. Shenandoah U., Winchester. Maj. USAF, 1977-79. Fellow ACS, Am. Coll. Chest Physicians, So. Thoracic Surg. Assn., Soc. Thoracic Surgery; mem. Va. Surg. Soc., Muller Surg. Soc., Med. Soc. Va., No. Va. Med. Soc., Am. Med. Soc. Home: 139 Academy Ln Winchester VA 22601 Office: Winchester Surg Clinic Ltd 20 S Stewart St Winchester VA 22601

TUCKER, ERNEST SHREEVES, III, pathologist, scientific and health care consultant; b. Birmingham, Ala., Mar. 23, 1933; s. Ernest Shreeves, Jr. and Lillian Ione (Williams) T.; m. Carlyn Loyl Collins, Aug. 4, 1957 (Dec. 28, 1977); 1 child, Ernest Shreeves IV; m. Joanne Elizabeth Powell, May 17, 1980; 1 child, Stephanie Lynn Grader. Deep Springs Coll., 1950-53, Cornell U., 1953-54; MD, U. Ala., 1958. Diplomate Am. Bd. Pathology, Am. Bd. Anatomic Pathology, Am. Bd. Clin. Pathology, Am. Bd. Immunopathology. Intern U. Ala. Med. Ctr., Birmingham, 1958-59; resident in pathology U. Ala. Med. Ctr., 1959-62; asst. prof. pathology U. Ala. Sch. Medicine, Birmingham, 1964-67; NIH fellow exptl. pathology Scripps Clinic and Rsch. Found., La Jolla, Calif., 1967-69; assoc. prof. pathology U. Wis. Med. Sch., Madison, 1969-70; co-dir. pathology dept. Grossmont Hosp., La Mesa, Calif., 1970-74; lab. dir., pres. Immunodiagnostics, Inc., San Diego, 1974-75; dir. immunology reference lab. The Scripps Rsch. Inst., La Jolla, Calif., 1977-88; chair pathology Calif. Pacific Med. Ctr., San Francisco, 1989-92, Scripps Clinic, La Jolla, Calif., 1992—; trustee, bd. dirs. Scripps Health, La Jolla, 1993—, mem. strategic planning com., 1996; bd. dirs., sci. cons. Abaxis, Inc., Sunnyvale, Calif., 1995—. Contbr. articles to profl. jours. and chpts. to books. Pres. Telluride Assn., Ithaca, N.Y., 1961-62; trustee, CFO Deep Springs Coll., Calif., 1994—. Capt. MC USAR Armed Forces Inst. Path, 1962-64. Recipient Disting. Alumnus award Alumni Assn. U. Ala. Sch. Medicine, 1993. Mem. NAS (subcom. on immunotoxicology 1989-92), Am. Soc. Clin. Pathologists (pres., v.p., bd. dirs., disting. svc. award 1980, Ward Burdick award for disting. svc. to clin. pathology 1996), Coll. Am. Pathologists (mem. pub. affairs com.), Am. Soc. Investigative Pathology, Calif. Soc. Pathologists, Sigma Xi. Office: Scripps Clinic Pathology 211C 10666 N Torrey Pines Rd La Jolla CA 92037

TUCKER, GARY JAY, physician, educator; b. Cleve., Mar. 6, 1934; s. Isadore Martin and Blanche Hanna (Luftig) T.; m. Sharon Ruth Pobby, June 10, 1956; children: Adam, Clare. AB, Oberlin Coll., 1956; MD, Case Western Res. U., 1960; postdoctoral fellow, Yale U., 1961-64; MA (hon.), Dartmouth Coll., 1977. Diplomate Am. Bd. Psychiatry and Neurology. Asst. prof. psychiatry Sch. Medicine Yale U., New Haven, 1957-70, assoc. prof. psychiatry, 1970-71; with Dartmouth Med. Sch., Hanover, N.H., 1971-85, prof. psychiatry, 1974-85, chmn. dept., 1978-85; prof., chmn. psychiatry and behavioral scis. Sch. Med. U. Wash., Seattle, 1985—; bd. dirs. Am. Bd. Psychiatry and Neurology. Co-author: Rational Hospital Psychiatry, 1974, Behavioral Neurology, 1985; contbr. articles to profl. jours. Lt. Commdr. USN, 1964-67. Fellow Am. Psychiat. Assn.; mem. W. Coast Coll. Biol. Psychiatry, Sigma Xi, Alpha Omega Alpha. Democrat. Jewish. Office: Univ of Washington Dept of Psychiatry Box 356560 Seattle WA 98195

TUCKER, GARY W., psychiatric care nurse; b. Oct. 2, 1956; s. Clayton Wilson Jr. and Jewell (Shelton) T. ADN, Cleveland (Tenn.) State Community Coll., 1980; BSW, Lamar U., Beaumont, Tex., 1991; MPH, U. Tex. Sch. Pub. Health, 1996. CCRN, ACLS. Nurse, relief shift supr. Moccasin Bend Mental Health Inst., Chattanooga, 1980-81; staff nurse pediat. ICU Thompson Childrens', Chattanooga, 1981-83; nurse, cons. King Fahad Hosp., Riyadh, Saudi Arabia, 1983; staff nurse ICU/ CCU Beaumont Med.-Surg. Hosp., 1984-88; charge nurse CCU Bapt. Hosp. S.E. Tex. Beaumont, 1988—, staff nurse, hemodialysis, 1988—, cardio-vascular nurse educator, 1988—, cardiac rehab. coord., head edn., 1988—. mem. AACN, Southeast Tex. Cardiopulmonary Rehab. Profls., Alpha Delta Mu. Home: 501 22nd St Beaumont TX 77706-4915

TUCKER, IRVING FRANCIS, psychology educator; b. Lynn, Mass., Mar. 26, 1933; s. Walter Edward and Hazel Lynn (Lobdell) T.; m. Jeanne Lynn Weber, Mar. 20, 1982; 1 child, Lauren Frances. BA, U. Mass., 1959; MA, U. Iowa, 1960, PhD, 1962. Lic. psychologist, W.Va.; diplomate Am. Bd. Adminstrv. Psychology. Asst. prof. La. State U., New Orleans, 1962-65; assoc. prof. Am. U. Beirut, 1965-68; mem. faculty psychology dept. Shepherd Coll., Shepherdstown, W.Va., assoc. prof., 1977—, chmn. dept., 1979—; lectr. U. Md., College Park, 1968—; pres. Logosphere, Shepherdstown, 1987—; supr. licensure candidates W.Va. Bd. Examiners Psychologists. Author: Adjustment: Models and Mechanisms, 1973, Jungian Personality Types, 1994. Recipient Prof. of Yr. award Faculty Merit Found. W.Va., 1989. Mem. APA, W.Va. Psychol. Assn., Assn. Psychol. Type. Office: Shepherd Coll Psychology Dept Shepherdstown WV 25443

TUCKER, NEIL THOMAS, pediatrician, gastroenterologist, educator; b. Balt., Sept. 15, 1949; s. Samuel and Helen Sylvia (Kotler) T.; m. Aline Evelyne Gontcharuk, Mar. 26, 1976; children: David, Alex. BS, U. Md., 1971; MD, Free U. Brussels, 1980. Intern and resident Ea. Va. Grad. Sch. Medicine, Norfolk, Children's Hosp. King's Daughters, Norfolk; fellow in pediatric gastroenterology Children's Hosp. Buffalo; asst. prof. pediatrics U. Tex. Health Sci. Ctr., San Antonio, 1985-88, clin. asst. prof. pediatrics, 1988—; pvt. practice San Antonio, 1988-94; clin. assoc. prof. pediatrics U. Tex. Health Sci. Ctr., San Antonio, 1995—. Contbr. articles to med. jours. Fellow Am. Acad. Pediatrics; mem. AMA, Tex. Med. Assn., Tex. Pediatric Soc., San Antonio Pediatric Soc., N.Am. Soc. Pediatric Gastroenterology and Nutrition. Home: 303 Post Oak Way San Antonio TX 78230 Office: 2829 Babcock Rd Ste 515 San Antonio TX 78229-6013

TUCKER, N(IMROD) H(OLT), III, physician; b. Columbus, Ga., Nov. 22, 1947; s. Nimrod Holt Jr. and Sarah Elizabeth (King) T.; m. Kathryn Gail Waddle, June 6, 1976; children: Jennifer Leigh, Nimrod Holt IV. BS, Auburn (Ala.) U., 1969; MD, U. Ala., 1973. Diplomate Am. bd. Internal Medicine. Intern and resident ednl. program Jacksonville Hosp. U. Fla., 1973-76; pvt. practice Jacksonville, Fla., 1976—; mem. med. staff St. Vincent's Hosp., Jacksonville, 1976—; bd. dirs. Profl. Found. for Health Care, Tampa, Fla. Bd. dirs. Fla. Community Coll. Found., Jacksonville, 1986—, St. Vincent's Hosp. Heart and Lung Inst., 1989—. Mem. ACP (bd. dirs. Fla. chpt. 1988—), Fla. Soc. Internal Medicine (bd. dirs 1988—), AMA, Fla. Med. Assn. (del. 1987, 89), Duval County Med. Soc. (bd. dirs., ex officio), Jacksonville C. of C., Timuquana Country Club, Fla. Yacht Club, River Club. Methodist. Office: 2149 Saint Johns Ave Jacksonville FL 32204-4418

TUCKER, ROBERT DENNARD, health care products executive; b. Tifton, Ga., July 18, 1933; s. Robert Buck and Ethel Margaret (Dennard) T.; m. Peggy Angelyn Smith, June 23, 1957; children: Robert Barron, Jennifer Lee. BBA, Ga. State U., 1958. With sales and sales mgmt. Johnson & Johnson Inc., New Brunswick, N.J., 1958-68; v.p., gen. mgr. ASR Med. Industries, N.Y.C., 1968-72, Howmedica Suture div. Pfizer Inc., N.Y.C., 1972-75; exec. v.p., chief operating officer R. P. Scherer Corp., Detroit, 1976-79; pres., chief operating officer Scherer Sci. Inc., Atlanta, 1980-95, also bd. dirs; chmn., chief exec. officer Scherer Health Care Inc., Atlanta, 1980-95, also bd. dirs.; bd. dirs. Nat. Travel Mgmt., Atlanta Biofor Inc., Waverly, Pa., Clean Air Corp. Am., Atlanta, U.S. Environ. Compliance Corp., Atlanta, Body Care Inc., Atlanta; chmn., CEO Throwleigh Techs., LLC, 1995—. Pub: Tuckers of Devon, 1983; author, pub.: Descendants of William Tucker of Throwleigh, Devon. Chmn. bd. Health Industries Mfrs. Assn. polit. action com., Washington, 1983-85; trustee, past pres. Ga. Horse Found., Atlanta; trustee Brenau Coll., Gainesville, Ga., 1985—. Served with USN, 1951-54, Korea. Decorated Knight of Malta, Imperial Russian Order of St. John; recipient Disting. Service award Brenau Coll., 1987. Mem. Nat. Assn. Mfrs., Health Industries Mfrs. Assn. (bd. dirs. 1979-86, disting. service recognition 1981, 86), Pharm. Mfrs. Assn., Thoroughbred Owners and Breeders Assn. Ky. and Ga. (Man of Yr. 1984). Republican. Methodist. Clubs: Cherokee (Atlanta); Big Canoe (Ga.). Home: 405 Townsend Pl NW Atlanta GA 30327-3037 Office: Scherer Healthcare Inc 2859 Paces Ferry Rd NW Ste 300 Atlanta GA 30339-5701

TUCKER, SCOTT L., plastic and hand surgeon; b. Bonne Terre, Mo., Nov. 1, 1954; s. William L. and Ruth Gene (Leming) T.; m. Patricia Simmons Haynes, May 3, 1985; 1 child, Sally Anne. BA cum laude, U. Mo., 1976, MD, 1982. Diplomate Am. Bd. Plastic and Reconstructive Surgery, Am. Bd. Med. Examiners. Resident in gen. surgery Wake Forest U. Bowman Gray Sch. Medicine, Winston-Salem, N.C., 1982-86, resident in plastic surgery, 1986-88; fellow in hand surgery U. So. Calif.-Rancho los Amigos Hosp., Downey, 1985; pvt. practice, Winston-Salem, 1988—; chief plastic surgery Forsyth Meml. Hosp., Winston-Salem, 1990—; pres. exec. com. Hawthorne Surgery, Winston-Salem, 1994-95. Bd. dirs. Childrens Cancer Support Group, N.C Bapt. Hosp., 1995. Fellow ACS; mem. AMA, Am. Soc. Plastic and Reconstructive Surgeons, So. Med. Assn., N.C. Plastic Surgery Soc., Alpha Omega Alpha. Office: Salem Plstic Surgery 175 Charlois Blvd Ste 102 Winston Salem NC 27103

TUCKER, SHERWIN MORGAN, podiatrist; b. Bklyn., Aug. 3, 1956; s. Edwin and Gladys T.; m. Elaine Jacobs; children: Jillian, Alyson, Brandon, Molly. BA, Boston U., 1978; DPM, Pa. Coll. Podiatric Med., Phila., 1982. Pvt. practice West Hartford, Conn., 1983—. Mem. Hartford County Podiatric Med. Assn. Office: 81 South Main St West Hartford CT 06107

TUCKER-OSBORNE, ANNETTE LA VERNE, nursing home administrator; b. N.Y.C.; d. Roy L. and Gwendolyn (Cush) Tucker; m. Andrew H. Osborne; 1 child, Aaron Nathaniel. Diploma in Nursing, Misericordia Sch. Nursing, 1976; BS in Health Care Adminstrn. with distinction, Iona Coll., 1984; M in Profl. Studies, New Sch. for Social Research, 1988; postgrad., LaSalle U., 1995—. Cert. long term care mgmt., 1988. Charge nurse Jacobi Hosp., 1976-77; charge nurse pediatrics Bronx (N.Y.) Mcpl. Hosp., 1977-78, asst. head nurse neonatal ICU, 1978-83, coord. utilization rev., 1983-84; charge nurse hematology Van Etten Hosp., Bronx, 1984-85; asst. dir. Salem Home Care, N.Y.C., 1985-87, dir., 1987-90. Fellow Hunter-Brookdale Coll. on Aging; mem. Am. Assn. Homes for the Aging (assoc.), Am. Coll. Health Care Adminstrs., Nat. Caucus and Ctr. on Black Aged.

TUDOR, JOHN COLIN, ophthalmic surgeon; b. St. Albans, Herts, Eng., Sept. 3, 1941; s. Colin Ewert and Alma Frances (Service) T.; m. Sandra Tudor; children: Catharine, Alison, John William. MA, St. Catharine's Coll., Cambridge, Eng., 1963; MB, BChir, St. Bartholomews Hosp., London, 1966. Intern opthalmology St. Bartholomews Hosp., London, 1967; registrar opthalmology Bristol Eye Hosp., 1968; sr. registrar opthalmology Southampton Eye Hosp., 1973; cons. ophthalmic surgeon Queen Alexandra Hosp., Cosham, Hants, Eng., 1977—; hon. tutor Southampton U., 1977—. Fellow Royal Coll. Surgeons Eng., Royal Coll. Surgeons Edinburgh, fellow of Coll. Ophthalmologists, Hayling Island Lodge (organist). Home: Winton House, Portsdown Hill Rd, Portsmouth PO6 1BE, England Office: 38 Saint Edward Rd Hants, Portsmouth PO5 3DJ, England

TUERK, JONATHAN DAVID, psychiatrist; b. Balt., Mar. 22, 1939; s. Isadore and Helen Tuerk; m. Catherine Lucille Miller, 1964; children: Joshua, Jennifer. BA, Dartmouth Coll., 1960; MD, U. Md., 1964; cert., Balt.-D.C. Inst.Psychoanalysis, 1980. Diplomate Am. Bd. Psychiatry and Neurology. Intern in internal medicine U. Md. Hosp., Balt., 1964-65; resident in internal medicine U. of Md. Hosp., Balt., 1965-66; resident in psychiatry Yale U., New Haven, 1966-69; staff psychiatrist Chestnut Lodge Hosp., Rockville, Md., 1972-94; asst. clin. dir. Chestnut Lodge Hosp., Rockville, 1994—; asst. clin. prof. dept. psychiatry George Washington U. Sch. Medicine, Washington, 1982-91, assoc. clin. prof. 1991—. Maj. U.S. Army, 1969-72. Mem. Am. Psychiat. Assn., AMA, Washington Psychiat. Assn. Democrat. Jewish. Office: Chestnut Lodge Hosp 500 W Montgomery Ave Rockville MD 20850-3892

TUFTE, MARILYN JEAN, microbiology educator, consultant; b. Iron Mountain, Mich., Nov. 20, 1939; d. John Vincent and Frances Mary (Vitton) Zanardi; m. Fredric Wayne Tufte, Aug. 12, 1972. BA in Biology, No. Mich. U., 1961; MS in Bacteriology, U. Wis., 1965, PhD in Bacteriology, 1968. Asst. prof. biology U. Wis., Platteville, 1968-71, assoc. prof., 1971-79, prof., 1979—; vet. cons., med. cons., dairy industry cons., Wis., 1970—; biotech. cons., 1991——; reviewer Lab. Manual for Microbiology, 1991, Lab. Manual for Zoology, 1991, biotech. text., 1991. Contbr. electron micrographs to textbooks; rsch. on effects of electrolytes on colon carcinoma in mice. Bd. dirs. U. Wis. Found., Platteville, 1980-95. Recipient Tchg. Excellence award U. Wis., 1990, 94. Mem. Nat. Edn. Network of Am. Soc. for Microbiology, Phi Kappa Phi, Sigma Xi. Office: Univ Wis Platteville Dept Biology 1 University Plz Platteville WI 53818-3012

TUFTON, JANIE LEE (JANE TUFTON), dental hygienist, animal rights lobbyist, activist; b. Allentown, Pa., Jan. 6, 1949; d. Robert Harry and Jean Lorraine (Seng) T. BS in Edn., Indiana U. Pa., 1979; postgrad. in English, 1979-82. Registered dental hygienist, Pa., N.J., Calif.; cert. tchr., Pa. Dental hygienist pvt. dental practices, Pa., N.J., Calif., 1976-90. Author bd. game for dental health edn., 1974. Lobbyist, activist for animal rights; bd. dirs. and pub. rels. Lehigh Valley Animal Rights Coalition, 1984-93; active civil rights movement, cultural events, literacy programs, detoxification units for drug and alcohol abuse, venereal disease clinics, practical-life workshops for the cognitively impaired, suicide hotlines, YWCA, Girl Scouts U.S. Recipient recognition Pa. Dental Hygienists Assn., 1974; named Internat. Woman of Yr., Internat. Biog. Ctr., 1992-93, Internat. Profl. and Bus. Women's Hall of Fame, Am. Biog. Inst., Inc., 1994, Woman of Yr., Am. Biographical Inst., Inc., 1994. Mem. Am. Anit-Vivisect. Soc., Nat. Humane Edn. Soc., The Fund for Animals, The Humane Soc. of the U.S., Nat. Alliance for Animals, Internat. Soc. for Animal Rights, Physicians Com. for Responsible Medicine, Culture and Animals Found., Animal Legal Def. Fund, People for the Ethical Treatment of Animals, Farm Animal Reform Movement, Farm Sanctuary, Com. to Abolish Sport Hunting, Animal Rights Mobilization, In Def. of Animals, United Animal nations, Internat. Platform Assn., Internat. Network for Religion and Animals. Home: 2102 S Lehigh Ave Whitehall PA 18052-5532

TUGGLE, JEAN FRANCES, health facility administrator; b. Westerly, R.I., Nov. 6, 1946; d. John William and Dorothy Ann (Bendele) Schmitz; m. Stephen John McAneeny, June 17, 1967 (div. 1979); children: Patrick Michael, Sean Ryan; m. Warren Mullen Tuggle, Aug. 7, 1993. RN, Joseph Lawrence Sch. Nursing, 1967; BS in Long Term Care Adminstrn., Quinnipiac Coll., 1981. Cert. nursing home adminstr. Nursing asst. Mary Kenny Nursing Home, Waterford, Conn., 1965-67, staff nurse, 1968, 76, evening supr., 1969-70, asst. dir. nursing, 1976-77, dir. nursing svcs., 1977-82; staff nurse Green Grove Nursing and Convalescent Ctr., Neptune, N.J., 1968; staff nurse intensive care unit Lawrence and Meml. Hosp., New London, Conn., 1973-76; adminstr. Canterbury Villa of Waterford, 1982-87, Bayview Health Care Ctr., 1989-94; quality assurance cons. Aid and Assistance, New London, 1985-87. Contbr. articles to profl. jours. Active Planning and Zoning Commn., New London, 1983-85; bd. dirs. Am. Heart Assn., 1980-82, S.W. Conn. divsn. ARC, New London, 1978-82. Grantee S.E. Conn. Job and Industry Coun., 1994, 93; named one of Outstanding Young Women Am., 1973; recipient Cert. of Appreciation ARC, 1973, 75, 77, 83. Mem. Am. Coll. Health Care Adminstrs., Harbor Heights Civic Assn., AARP, Quinnipiac Coll. Alumni Assn. Democrat. Roman Catholic. Home: 3450 Dover Dr Punta Gorda FL 33983

TUHRIM, STANLEY, physician, neurologist; b. N.Y.C., Jan. 26, 1954; m. Betty Jane Mintz, Feb. 8, 1981; 1 child, Richard J. BA in Psychology, Haverford Coll., 1975; MD, Mt. Sinai Sch. Medicine, 1979. Intern U. Pa. Hosp., Phila., 1979-80; resident in neurology Mt. Sinai Hosp., N.Y.C., 1980-83; stroke fellow U. Md. Hosp., 1983-84; asst. prof. dept. neurology U. Md., Balt., 1985-87; asst. prof. dept. neurology Mt. Sinai Hosp., N.Y.C., 1987-90, assoc. prof. dept. neurology, 1991—; assoc. prof. dept. geriatrics and adult devel. Mt. Sinai Med. Ctr., N.Y.C., 1994—. Contbr. articles to profl. jours. Recipient Tchr.-Investigator award NINCDS, 1984, Bressler Rsch. award U. Md., 1985; NINDS clin. investigator, 1988. Mem. Soc. Critical Care Medicine, Am. Med. Informatics Assn., Nat. Stroke Assn., Am. Acad. Neurology. Office: Mt Sinai Med Ctr One Gustave Levy Pl Box 1137 New York NY 10029

TULLOCH, BRIAN ROBERT, endocrinologist; b. Chunya, Tanzania, May 30, 1938; came to U.S., 1977; s. Robert Graeme and Audrey Madelein (Bremner) T.; m. Elizabeth Watkins Rogg, Jan. 26, 1980; children:

Nathaniel, Genevieve. BSc, Natal U., S. Africa, 1959, MSc, 1961; BM, BCh, Oxford (Eng.) U., 1966. FRCP, FACP, London. House physician to specialists in gen., plastic, thoracic surgery, Univ. Coll. Hosp., London, 1965-66; house physician to specialist in gen. and renal medicine Radcliffe Infirmary, Oxford, Eng., 1966-67; house physician to cardiologist Hammersmith Hosp., London, 1967; house physician Brompton Chest Hosp., London, 1967-68; med. registrar Nat. Heart Hosp., London, 1968-69; clin. rsch. fellow, sr. registrar, clin. tutor, cons. Med. Rsch. Coun. endocrine unit Royal Postgrad. Med. Sch., London, 1969-72; Wellcome sr. rsch. fellow dept. medicine Royal Postgrad. Med. Sch., London, 1972-74; sessional cons. in endocrinology and diabetes St. Charles Hosp., London, 1973-74; hon. lectr. in medicine Hammersmith Hosp., London, 1972-74; sr. lectr. in medicine, hon. cons. physician Manchester (Eng. Royal Infirmary), 1974-77; endocrinologist Diagnostic Clinic, Houston, 1977—; clin. assoc. prof. internal medicine and ophthalmology U. Tex. Med. Sch., Houston, 1977—, M.D. Anderson Hosp. and Tumor Inst., Houston, 1977—; attending physician, Diagnostic Ctr. Hosp., Houston, Hermann Hosp., Houston, Park Plaza Hosp., Houston; mem. student promotions com. U. Tex.. tissue com. Hermann Hosp.; NIH site visitor, Diabetes Rsch and Tng. Ctr., NIH advisor Diabetes Epidemology in Egypt; invited participant NIH Conf. on flushing, markers for Type II Diabetes Mellitus, 1980, Conf. on Lipoprotein Physiology, San Diego, 1981, Lipid Metabolism, N.Y., 1985; reviewer Diabetologia, Hormone and Metabolic Rsch., Clin. Sci., Cardiovascular Rsch., Biochem. Pharmacology, Artery, Metabolism: Clin. and Exptl.; advisor Ministry of Health, Kuwait, 1976-78, ICI Internat., 1976-78; for rev. lectures given to Univs. Cairo, Ain Shams, Assyut, Mansoura and Alexandria in Egypt; invited disting. guest lectr. Sudan Assn. Physicians, Khartoum, 1978. Contbr. numerous articles and abstracts to profl. jours.; speaker to nat. and internat. sci. confs. as well as lay groups on diabetes and related health care topics. Recipient Caltex scholarship, 1955-59, Coun. for Sci. and Indsl. Rsch. scholarship, 1960-61, Charelick Salemon scholarship, 1960-61, Rhodes scholarship, St. Johns Coll. Oxford U., 1961-64, Croxon fellowship, 1964-65, Convenators Trust, 1964-65, Preventive Cardiology Acad. award; grantee: MRC (heavy equipment grant), Manchester Regional Rsch. Fund, 1975, U. Tex., 1977, Am. Diabetes Assn., Warner Lambert-Parke Davis, 1979-81, CO-Pl, 1979-82, 1983-86. Fellow Am. Endocrine Soc., Am. Diabetes Assn. (pres. Houston chpt. 1982-83, pres. Tex. affiliate 1984-86); mem. Royal Coll. Physicians, Brain-Pituitary Soc. (treas. 1981-86), Houston-Galveston Endocrine Assn., Am. Heart Assn., The Endocrine Soc., Harris County Med. Soc., Harveian Soc. London, Manchester Med. Soc., Med. Rsch. Soc., Soc. for Endocrinology, European Assn. for Study of Diabetes, Brit. Diabetic Soc., Royal Soc. Medicine London (com. mem. endocrine sect.), Royal Ocean Racing Club London, Hellenic Travelers Club London, Egypt Exploration Soc. London, Houston Yacht Club (fleet surgeon 1983-84), Tex. Offshore Racing Club, Galveston Bay Cruising Assn. Republican. Episcopalian. Office: Diagnostic Clinic 6448 Fannin St Houston TX 77030

TULLOS, HUGH SIMPSON, orthopedic surgeon, educator; b. Waco, Tex., Aug. 7, 1935; s. Hugh Simpson and Roberta (Thomas) T.; m. Marcelle Gaye Unger; children: Paul R., Hugh S. III. Student, Vanderbilt U., 1952-55; MD, MS in Cancer Biology, Baylor U., 1960. Diplomate Am. Ed. Orthopaedic Surgeons (examiner 1974—). Intern Jefferson Davis Hosp., Houston, 1960-61; gen. surgery resident Baylor Coll. Medicine, Houston, 1961-62, orthopedic surgery residnet, 1964-67; successively asst. instr., instr., asst. prof. to assoc. prof. Div. Orthopedic Surgery, Baylor Coll. Medicine, 1967-75; pvt. practice Fonden Orthopedic Group, Houston, 1967-88; head div. orthopedic surgery Tex. Med. Ctr., Houston, 1989—, Wilhemina Barnhart chmn., prof. dept. orthopedic surgery, 1991—; chief orthopedic svc. Meth. Hosp., Houston, 1974, Ben Taub Gen. Hosp., Houston, 1974; clin. assoc. prof. dept. surgery U. Tex. Med. Sch. Health Sci. Ctr., Houston, 1975; vis. lectr. sports medicine symposium Hosp. for Joint Diseases, N.Y.C., 1982; vis. prof. Peruvian Orthopaedic Soc., 1978, U. Miami Sch. Medicine, 1979, Health Sci. Ctr., Tex. Tech U., 1983, Rex Dively Lecturship, Kansas City, Mo., 1985; presenter numerous instructional courses, profl. symposia, meetings; Murray S. Danforth surgeon-in-chief pro tempore Brown U., R.I. Hosp., Providence, Nov., 1988. Author: (with others) Principles of Sport Medicine, 1984, The Elbow, 1985, Injuries to the Throwing Arm, 1985, Art of Total Hip Arthoplasty, 1987, other books, also Instructional Course Lectures Am. Acad. Orthopaedic Surgeons, vols. 25, 33, 1984, 86; editorial bd. Jour. of Arthroplasty, 1988; bd. assoc. editors Clin. Orthopaedics and Related Rsch., 1986—; cons. to editor Tex. Medicine; contbr. numerous articles, abstracts to profl. jours.; presenter exhibits, films med. meetings. Patentee orthopedic devices. Capt. U.S. Army, 1961-63. Fellow Am. Acad. Orthopaedic Surgeons (bd. dirs. 1976, sec. com. sports medicinew 1974-81, com. instructional courses 1987—, chmn. 1988; mem. AMA, Am. Orthopaedic Assn., Am. Orthopaedic Soc. Sports Medicine (founding, chmn. nominating com. 1980, chmn. ann. meeteing 1982), Assn. Bone and Joint Surgeons, Assn. Orthopaedic Chmn., Clin. Orthopaedic Soc., Harris County Med. Soc., Houston Orthopaedic Assn., Houston Surg. Soc., Internat. Congress Knee Surgeons, Internat. Soc. of the Knee (founding, bd. dirs. 1983-88, sec.-treas. 1989), Mid-Am. Orthopaedic Assn., Orthopaedic Rsch. Soc., Pan Am. Med. Assn., Soc. Am. Shoulder and Elbow Surgeons, 20th Century Orthopaedic Soc. (chmn. ann. meeting 1987), Tex. Soc. Athletic Team Physicians (pres. 1978), Tex. Med. Assn., Tex. Orthopaedic Assn., Tex. Rheumatism Soc., The Knee Soc., Baylor Orthopaedic Alumni Assn. (pres. 1970—). Office: Tex Med Ctr Div Orthopedic Surgery 6565 Fannin St Ste 2525 Houston TX 77030-2704*

TULLY, CHRISTOPHER CARL, retired physician, hospital administrator; b. Charleston, W.Va., June 22, 1913; s. Christopher Columbus and Eva Lena (Lanham) T.; BS magna cum laude, Morris Harvey Coll., 1937; BS, W.Va. U., 1945; MD, Med. Coll. Va., 1947; m. Virginia Belle Tully, Apr. 9, 1937 (dec. 1963); children: Christopher Carl II, Richard R.; m. 2d, Margaret A. Plumley, Oct. 29, 1966. With Charleston Fire Dept., 1935-39, U.S. P.O., Charleston, 1939-43; intern U.S. Marine Hosp., 1947-48; gen. practice medicine, South Charleston, W.Va., 1948-79; mem. staff H. J. Thomas Meml. Hosp., South Charleston, 1948-93, pres., 1966, med. coordinator, 1979-81; med. coordinator St. Francis Hosp., Charleston, W.Va., 1981-93; ret. 1993; prof. family practice Kanawha Valley Family Practice Center, 1973-79; bd. dirs., mem. exec. com. First Nat. Bank of South Charleston. Mem. South Charleston Recreation Com.; chmn. South Charleston Park Bd.; mem. Kanawha County Bd. Edn., 1959-70, pres., 1963-64; mem. Charter Bd. South Charleston, W.Va.; pres. W.Va. div. Am. Cancer Soc., 1981-83. Served with U.S. Army, 1944-46, 47-48, 51-53, 71. Diplomate Am. Bd. Family Practice. Fellow Am. Acad. Family Physicians; mem. Am. Acad. Family Practice (pres. Kanawha chpt. 1962-63; pres. W.Va. chpt. 1969-70, chmn. bd.), W.Va. Acad. Family Practice (dir. 1960-64), AMA, W.Va., Kanawha med. socs., So. Med. Assn., Am. Soc. Contemporary Medicine and Surgery, Phi Beta Pi. Lodges: Masons, Shriners, Lions (pres. Spring Hill 1957-58, Citizen of Yr. South Charleston 1956-57). Home: 4530 Spring Hill Ave Charleston WV 25309-2213

TULLY, SUSAN BALSLEY, pediatrician, educator; b. San Francisco, July 12, 1941; d. Gerard E. Balsley Sr. and Norma Lilla (Hand) Carey; m. William P. Tully, June 19, 1965; children: Michael William, Stephen Gerard. BA in Premed. Studies, UCLA, 1963, MD, 1966. Diplomate Am. Bd. Pediatrics, Am. Bd. Pediatric Emergency Medicine. Intern L.A. County-U. So. Calif. Med. Ctr., 1966-67, jr. resident pediatrics, 1967-68; staff pediatrician, part-time Permanente Med. Group, Oakland, Calif., 1968; sr. resident pediatrics Kaiser Found. Hosp., Oakland, 1968-69; sr. resident pediatrics Bernalillo County Med. Ctr., Albuquerque, 1969-70, chief resident pediatric outpatient dept., 1970; instr. pediatrics, asst. dir. outpatient dept. U. N.Mex. Sch. Medicine, 1971-72; asst. prof. pediatrics, dir. (ambulatory pediatrics) U. Calif., Irvine, 1972-76, asst. prof. clin. pediatrics, vice chair med. edn., 1977-79; staff pediatrician Ross-Loos Med. Group, Buena Park, Calif., 1976-77; assoc. prof. clin. pediatrics and emergency medicine U. So. Calif. Sch. Medicine, 1979-86; dir. pediatric emergency dept. L.A. County/U. So. Calif. Med. Ctr., 1979-87; prof. clin. pediatrics and emergency medicine U. So. Calif. Sch. Medicine, 1986-89; dir. ambulatory pediatrics L.A. County/U. So. Calif. Med. Ctr., 1987-89, L.A. County-Olive View/UCLA Med. Ctr., 1989—; clin. prof. pediatrics UCLA, 1989-93, prof. clin. pediatrics, 1993—, dir. ambulatory pediatrics, 1989—, interim chief pediatrics, 1996—; pediatric toxicology cons. L.A. County Regional Poison Control Ctr. Med. Adv. Bd., 1981—; faculty exec. com., clin. faculty rep. UCLA Sch. Medicine, 1992-93, strategic planning action com. subcom. on ednl. structure, 1992-93, dept. pediatrics alliance-wide rev. and appraisal com., 1992-93, steering com., 1993—; pediatric liaison dept. emergency medicine Olive View/UCLA Med. Ctr., 1989—, dir. lead poisoning clinic, 1993—, L.A. County Dept. Health Svcs., 1990—; mem. quality assurance com. L.A. County Community Health Plan, 1986-89; mem. survey team pediatric emergency svcs. L.A. Pediatric Soc., 1984-86; mem. adv. bd. preventive health project U. Affiliated Program Children's Hosp. L.A., 1981-83; active numerous coms. Author: (with K.E. Zenk) Pediatric Nurse Practitioner Formulary, 1979; (with W.A. Wingert) Pediatric Emergency Medicine: Concepts and Clinical Practice, 1992; (with others) Educational Guidelines for Ambulatory/General Pediatrics Fellowship Training, 1992, Physician's Resource Guide for Water Safety Education, 1994; reviewer Pediatrics, 1985-89; editorial cons. Advanced Pediatric Life Support Course and Manual, 1988-89; dept. editor Pediatric Pearls Jour. Am. Acad. Physician Assts., 1989-94; tech. cons., reviewer Healthlink TV Am. Acad. Pediatrics, 1991; reviewer Pediatric Emergency Care, 1992—; question writer sub-bd. pediatric emergency medicine Am. Bd. Pediatrics, 1993—; cons. to lay media NBC Nightly News, Woman's Day, Sesame Street Parents, Parenting, Los Angeles Times; author numerous abstracts; contbr. articles to profl. jours. cons. spl. edn. programs Orange County Bd. Edn., 1972-79; mem. Orange County Health Planning Coun., 1973-79; co-chairperson Orange County Child Health and Disability Prevention Program Bd., 1975-76; mem. Orange County Child Abuse Consultation Team, 1977-79; mem. project adv. bd. Family Focussed "Buckle Up" Project, Safety Belt Safe, U.S.A., 1989—;. Fellow Am. Acad. Pediatrics (life, active numerous sects. and coms., active Calif. chpt.); mem. APHA, Ambulatory Pediatric Assn., L.A. Pediatric Soc. (life), L.A. Area Child Passenger Safety Assn. Democrat. Office: Olive View UCLA Med Ctr Pediatrics 3A108 14445 Olive View Dr Sylmar CA 91342-1495

TUMA, STANISLAV JOSEF, radiologist; b. Mělník, Czech Republic, Mar. 30, 1934; s. Josef and Marta (Panochová) T.; m. Vanda Langrová, May 10, 1954 (div. 1966); children: Zuzana, Ondřej, Magdalena; m. Jitka Fabichová, Nov. 2, 1990. MD, Charles U., Prague, Czech Republic, 1958, cert. pediat. I, 1962, cert. radiology I, 1964, CSc, PhD, 1970. Med. registrar Dist. Hosp., Šumperk, Czech Republic, 1958-60, Clinic of Pediat., Prague, 1960-64, X-Ray Dept., Prague, 1964-70; rsch.fellow Pediat. Cardiocenter, Prague, 1970-90; head Clinic Imaging Methods, Prague, 1990—. Editor: Congenital Anomalies, 1995; contbr. articles to profl. jours. Office: Clinic for Imaging Methods, U Hosp Motol, V Uvalu 84, CZ 15018 Prague 5, Czech Republic

TUMOSA, NINA, neuroscientist, educator; b. Dover-Foxcroft, Maine, Oct. 12, 1951; d. Frank John and Mary (Green) T.; m. Dennis Connors, May 26, 1973 (div. Mar. 1976); m. Paul Kerlinger, July 5, 1982 (div. Apr. 1990). BS in Biology, Rensselaer Poly. Inst., 1973, MS in Biology, 1974; PhD in Neuroscience, SUNY, Albany, 1982. Postgrad. fellowship Alta. Heritage Fund Med. Rsch., Calgary, Can., 1982-84; NIH fellowship U. Wis., Madison, 1985-87, rsch. assoc., 1987-88; scis. engring. fellow AAAS, Washington, 1988-89; asst. prof. U. Mo., St. Louis, 1988—; cons. Agy. for Internat. Devel., Washington, 1988—. Contbr. articles to Sci., Jour. Neurophysiology, Jour. Comparative Neurology, Brain Rsch., Visual Neuroscience, Jour. Neurosicence. Office: U Mo Sch Optometry 8001 Natural Bridge Rd Saint Louis MO 63121-4401

TUNBERG, THOMAS CHAS, surgeon. BS, U. N.D., 1972; MD, U. Minn., 1979. Diplomate Am. Bd. Surgery, Nat. Bd. Med. Examiners; lic. physician, Minn., Ind., Wis. Intern Tufts-New Eng. Med. Ctr., Boston, 1979-80; gen. surgery resident Med. Coll. Wis., Milw., 1980-81; gen. surgery resident St. Joseph's Hosp., Milw., 1983-86, chief resident, 1985-86; pvt. practice Cambridge (Minn.) Med. Ctr., 1986—; assoc. (oral) examiner Am. Bd. Surgery certifying exam, Mpls., 1995; clin. instr. surgery U. Minn., Mpls., 1995, Ind. U. and Meth. Hosp., Indpls., 1986-88; surgery peer rev. cons. Minn. Bd. Med. Practice, 1993—, Found. for Health Care Evaluation, 1993—; lectr. in field. Contbr. articles to profl. jours. With USAF N.G. and Res. Alworth Meml. Scholar, 1968-72. Fellow ACS; mem. AMA (Physician Recognition award 1995—), Minn. Med. Assn. (peer rev. program, cons. com. 1993—), Minn. Surg. Soc. (exec. com. bd. dirs. 1994—), Am. Soc. Gen. Surgeons, Soc. Am. Gastrointestinal Endoscopic surgeons, Soc. Laparoendoscopic Surgeons, Am. Soc. Colon and Rectal Surgeons, Christian Med. and Dental Soc., East Ctrl. Minn. Med. Soc., Alpha Omega Alpha. Home: Goldenwood 2630 Joy Ct Cambridge MN 55008 Office: Cambridge Medical Ctr Dept Surgery 701 S Dellwood Cambridge MN 55008

TUNBRIDGE, WILLIAM MICHAEL GREGG, physician, consultant; b. Leeds, Yorkshire, Eng., June 13, 1940; s. Ronald Ernest and Dorothy (Gregg) T.; m. Felicity Katherine E. Parrish, Aug. 28, 1965; children: Clare Katherine, Anne Jacqueline. BA, Cambridge (Eng.) U., 1961, MB, BCh, 1964, MD, 1977. House physician, house surgeon U. Coll. Hosp., London, 1964-65; sr. house officer Mpilo Hosp., Bulawayo, Zimbabwe, 1965-66; sr. house officer Manchester (Eng.) Royal Infirmary, 1967-68, tutor in medicine, 1970-72; registrar Hammersmith Hosp., London, 1970-72; rsch. fellow U. Newcastle upon Tyne, Eng., 1972-75, U. Liege, Belgium, 1976-77; sr. registrar Newcastle U. Hosps., 1975-77; cons. physician Newcastle Gen. Hosp., 1977-94; dir. postgrad. med. edn. and tng. Oxford U., England, 1994—; cons. physician John Radcliffe Hosp., Oxford, 1994—. Author: Diabetes and Endocrinology in Clinical Practice, 1991. Fellow Royal Coll. Physicians of London; mem. European Thyroid Assn. (com. 1980-84). Office: Oxford U Med Sch Offices, John Radcliffe Hosp, Oxford 0X3 9DU, England

TUNE, BRUCE MALCOLM, pediatrics educator, renal toxicologist; b. N.Y.C., Aug. 26, 1939; s. Buford M. and Sylvia (Newman) T.; m. Nancy Carter Doolittle, Sept. 13, 1969; children: Sara E., Steven M. AB, Stanford U., 1963, MD, 1965. Diplomate Am. Bd. Pediatrics, Am. Bd. Pediatric NeOhrology, Nat. Bd. Med. Examiners. Intern in medicine and pediatrics Strong Meml. Hosp., Rochester, N.Y., 1965-66; rsch. assoc. Lab. Kidney and Electrolyte Metabolism, Nat. Heart Inst., NIH, Bethesda, Md., 1967-69, clin. assoc., 1968-69; resident in pediatrics Stanford (Calif.) U. Sch. Medicine, 1966-67, chief resident, 1969-70, fellow in pediatric renal and metabolic disease, 1970-71, asst. prof., 1971-77, assoc. prof., 1977-83, prof., 1983—, acting chmn. dept., 1991-93, dir. pediatric nephrology, 1971—; attending physician, chief pediatric renal svcs. Stanford U. Hosp., Palo Alto, Calif., 1971-91, Children's Hosp. at Stanford, Palo Alto, 1971-91; cons. physician Santa Clara Valley Med. Ctr., San Jose, Calif., 1973—; attending physician, chief pediatric renal svcs. Lucile Salter Packard Children's Hosp. at Stanford, 1991—, acting chief pediatric medicine, 1991-93; mem. rev. panel internat. study kidney diseases in children NIH, N.Y.C., 1973, 74, polycystic kidney disease study group, Albuquerque, 1984; mem. spl. study sect. on genetics and kidney maturation, Bethesd, Md., 1992; cons. Lilly Rsch. Labs., Indpls., 1980, Merck Sharp and Dohme Labs., Rahway, N.J., 1980, Bristol Labs., Syracuse, N.Y., 1982, ICI Pharms., Cheshire, Eng., 1992, Gilead Scis., Foster City, Calif., 1993, Zeneca Pharms., Mereside, Eng., 1994—; organizing mem., chmn. session on antibiotics NIH and EPA Conf. on Nephrotoxicity of Drygs and Environ. Toxicants, Pinehurst, N.C., 1981; co-dir. Coop. Study Therapy of Steroid-Resistant Focal Glomerulosclerosis in Children, 1988—; mem. rsch. grant rev. panel Ont. (Can.) Ministry Health, 1992—, Wellcome Trust, London, 1994—; reviewer bd. environ. studies and toxicology NRC, 1994. Mem. editl. bd. Am. Jour. Kidney Diseases, 1981-94; guest editor Contemporary Issues in Nephrology, 1984, Jour. Am. Soc. Nephrology, 1991; contbr. articles to med. jours. Grantee NIH, 1985-89, 90-95. Mem. Am. Soc. Nephrology, Internat. Soc. Nephrology, Am. Soc. Pediatric Nephrology (coun. 1978-82, rsch. subcom. 1993—), Internat. Pediatric Nephrology Assn., Western Soc. for Pediatric Rsch., Soc. for Pediatric Rsch., Am. Pediatric Soc., Am. Heart Assn. (coun. on kidney diseases, grantee 1985-88, 89-92), Am. Soc. for Pharmacology and Exptl. Therapeutics, Am. Soc. Renal Biochemistry and Metabolism, Phi Beta Kappa, Alpha Omega Alpha. Office: Stanford U Sch Medicine Dept Pediatrics 300 Pasteur Dr Palo Alto CA 94304-2203

TUNIS, SCOTT WILLIAM, ophthalmologist; b. Boston, May 24, 1955; s. William David Tunis and Mary Elaine (Stewart) Dickerson; m. Susan Ellen Tunis, Sept. 10, 1983; children: Joshua William, Alaina Stewart. BA, Amherst Coll., 1977; MD, U. Va., 1981. Diplomate Am. Bd. Ophthalmology. Intern Eastern Va. Grad. Sch. of Med., 1981-82; resident Medical U. of S.C., Charleston, 1982-85; pvt. practice, Ft. Lauderdale, Fla., 1985-95, Boca Raton, Fla., 1995—; chief ophthalmology Holy Cross Hosp., Ft. Lauderdale, 1988-90,. Holds 2 patents for appartus and methods of inserting intraocular lenses. Fellow ACS, Am. Acad. Ophthalmology; mem. Am. Soc. Cataract and Refractive Surgery. Office: Clear Vision Laser Consultants 301 Yamato Rd Ste 3190 Boca Raton FL 33431

TUNNESSEN, WALTER WILLIAM, JR., pediatrician; b. Hazleton, Pa., July 25, 1939; s. Walter William and Grace Louise (Schaller) T.; m. Nancy Louise Layton, Aug. 24, 1963; children: Walter William III, Anne L. BA, Lafayette Coll., Easton, Pa., 1961; MD, U. Pa., 1965. Diplomate Am. Bd. Pediatrics (bd. dirs. 1986—). Resident Children's Hosp. of Phila., 1965-67; chief resident in pediatrics Hosp. U. Pa., Phila., 1967-68; isntr., dir. newborn nurseries Hosp. U. Pa./U. Pa. Sch. Medicine, Phila., 1970-72; from asst. prof. to assoc. prof. pediatrics SUNY Health Sci. Ctr., Syracuse, 1972-81, prof. pediat., 1981, acting chair dept., 1985-86; assoc. prof. pediatrics and dermatology Johns Hopkins U. Sch. Medicine, Balt., 1986-90, dir. pediatric dermatology, dir. pediatric diagnostic clinic, 1986-90; assoc. chmn. for med. edn. Children's Hosp. of Phila., 1990-95; prof. pediatrics U. Pa. Sch. Medicine, Phila., 1990-95; sr. v.p. Am. Bd. Pediatrics, Chapel Hill, N.C., 1995—; Robert Wood Johnson clin. Scholar Yale U. Sch. Medicine, New Haven, 1978-79; mem. Nat. Bd. Med. Examiners, 1989-91; mem. sci. bd. Nat. Found. for Ectodermal Dysplasia, 1989-93. Author: Signs and Symptons in Pediatrics, 1983, 2d edit., 1988; editor monthly jour. sects. Capt. USAF, 1968-70. Mem. Am. Acad. Pediats. (sect. on dermatology exec. com. 1993-95), Soc. for Peidat. Dermatology (pres. 1988-89, bd. dirs.), Am. Pediat. Soc. Office: Am Bd Pediatrics 111 Silver Cedar Ct Chapel Hill NC 27514-1651

TUPIN, JOE PAUL, psychiatry educator; b. Comanche, Tex., Feb. 17, 1934; m. Betty Thompson, June 19, 1955; children: Paul, Rebecca, John. BS in Pharmacy, U. Tex., 1955, postgrad., 1955; MD, U. Tex., Galveston, 1959, Wash. Sch. Psychiatry, 1962, NIH Grad. Sch., 1962-64. Lic. physician, Tex., Calif. Intern U. Calif. Hosps., San Francisco, 1959-60; resident U. Tex. Med. br., Galveston, 1960-62, asst. prof. psychiatry, 1964-68, mem. staff John Sealy Hosp., 1964-69, dir. psychiatric consultation service, 1965-66, dir. psychiatric research, 1965-69, asst. dean medicine, 1967-68, assoc. prof., 1968-69, assoc. dean, 1968-69; resident NIMH div NIH, 1963-64; assoc. prof. psychiatry U. Calif., Davis, 1969-71, mem. staff Davis Med. Ctr., 1969—, vice-chmn. dept. psychiatry, 1970-76, prof., 1971-93, prof. emeritus, 1993, acting chmn. dept. psychiatry, 1977, acting dir. admissions sch. medicine, 1977-78, chmn. dept. psychiatry, 1977-84; med. dir. U. Calif. Davis Med. Ctr., 1984-93; cons. staff St. Mary's Infirmary, Galveston, 1967-69, Moody House Retirement Home for the Aged, Galveston, 1967-69, VA Hosp., Martinez, 1977-82, Yolo Gen. Hosp., 1980-81; dir. psychiatric consultation service U. Calif., Davis, 1969-74, co-director 1974-77; vis. prof. King's Coll. Med. Sch., London, 1974; acting dir. admissions sch. medicine, U. Calif., Davis, 1977-78; chief div. mental health U. Calif. Davis Med. Ctr., 1977-84, also mem. quality care com., 1979-85, chmn. com., 1981-85; med. dir. and assoc. dir. Hosp. and Clinics U. Calif., Davis, 1984-93; cons. U. Calif., Davis, 1993. Referee and book reviewer numerous publs.; mem. sci. editorial bd. Am. Jour. Forensic Psychiatry, 1985-88, Jour. Clin. Psychopharmacology, 1981—, Psychiatry, 1985, Tex. Reports on Biology and Medicine, 1965-67, 68-69; Western Jour. Medicine, 1979-89; contbr. numerous articles to profl. jours. Mem. Academically Talented Child com. Galveston City Sch. Bd., 1966-67; chmn. bd. dirs. William Temple Found., Galveston, 1967-68; bd. dirs. Citizens for Advancement of Pub. Edn., Galveston, 1967-69, pres., 1968-69, Moody House Retirement Home for the Aged, 1968, Cal Aggie Athletic Assn., 1978-82; mem. Davis Master Plan com., 1971. Served to lt. commdr. USPHS, 1962-64, with Res. 1964-80. Recipient Career Teaching award NIMH, 1964-66; named to Friars Soc. U. Tex., 1954; Mosby scholar U. Tex., Ginsberg fellow Group for Advancement of Psychiatry, 1960-62, Nat. Found. Infantile Paralysis fellow, 1957; grantee U. Tex. Med. br., 1964-69, NIMH, 1965-68. Fellow Am. Psychiat. Assn., Am. Coll. Psychiatrists (mem. com., editorial com.); mem. AMA, Yolo County Med. Assn. (chmn. credentials com. 1974-75, nominating com. 1980-84), Calif. Med. Assn. (sec. psychiatry sect. 1977-78, 78-79, sci. adv. panel on psychiatry 1975-80, psychiatry adv. sect. 1977-80, sci. adv. bd. 1978-80), Titus Harris Soc., Cen. Calif. Psychiat. Soc. (chmn. mem. com. 1970-73, pres. 1976), AAAS, Soc. Health and Human Values (exec. council 1970-73), Am. Acad. Psychiatry and the Law, AAUP, West Coast Coll. Biol. Psychiatries Com., Sigma Xi, Rho Chi, Alpha Omega Alpha. Home: 108 Kent Dr Davis CA 95616 Office: U Calif Davis Med Ctr Office of Med Scis 2315 Stockton Blvd Sacramento CA 95817-2201

TUPPER, CHARLES JOHN, physician, educator; b. Miami, Ariz., Mar. 7, 1920; s. Charles Ralph and Grace (Alexander) T.; m. Mary Hewes, Aug. 4, 1942; children: Mary Elizabeth, Charles John. B.A. in Zoology, San Diego State Coll., 1943; M.D., U. Nebr., 1948. Diplomate: Am. Bd. Internal Medicine. Intern U. Mich. Hosp., Ann Arbor, 1948-49; asst. resident U. Mich. Hosp., 1949-50, resident, 1950-51, jr. clin. instr., 1951-52; pvt. practice specializing in internal medicine Ann Arbor, 1954-66; practice medicine specializing internal medicine Davis, Calif., 1966—; rsch. asst. Inst. Indsl. Health, U. Mich., 1951-52, rsch. assoc., 1954-56, instr. internal medicine, 1954-56, asst. prof., 1956-59, assoc. prof., 1959-66, sec. Med. Sch., 1957-59, asst. dean, 1959-61, assoc. dean, 1961-66, dir. periodic health appraisal program univ. faculty, 1956-66; prof. internal medicine Sch. Medicine U. Calif., Davis, 1966-90, prof. emeritus cmty. health & family medicine, 1990—, dean, 1966-80, prof. cmty. health, 1980-90, prof. family practice, 1981-90, acting chair cmty. health, 1989-91, 94-95; mem. adv. bd. Golden State Svcs. Dir. consultation services U. Mich. Health Service, 1956-66, 73-76; pres. Calif. Med. Assn., 1979-80; vice chmn. U. Calif. Davis Found., 1993—, Sacramento Regional Found., 1993. Served from 1st lt. to capt. USAF, 1952-54. Fellow ACP; mem. AMA (trustee 1985-89, pres. elect 1989-90, pres. 1990-91, immediate past pres. 1991-92, chmn. coun. sci. affairs 1977-79, coun. sect. med. schs. 1977-78), Internat., Am., Calif. socs. internal medicine, Am. Coll. Health Assn., Assn. Am. Med. Colls., Am. Assn. Automotive Medicine, Yolo County Med. soc., Calif. Med. Assn. (pres. 1979-80, chmn. sci. bd. 1970-78, chmn. liaison to state bar com., chmn. com. on state legislation 1975-85, del. to AMA 1975-85), Sci. Rsch. Club. Club: El Macero Country (dir.). Home: PO Box 2007 El Macero CA 95618-0007 Office: U Calif Med Sch Dept Cmty Health Davis CA 95616

TUPPER, DAVID EDWARD, neuropsychologist; b. Brockton, Mass., Sept. 17, 1955; s. John F. and Carol A. (Hammerquist) T.; m. Sharon Theresa Bateman, Sept. 3, 1977; children: Jonathan David, Ashley Michelle. BA in Psychology, Boston U., 1977; MA in Psychology, U. Hartford, 1979; PhD in Neuropsychology, U. Victoria, 1982. Diplomate Am. Bd. Profl. Disability Cons.; lic. psychologist, N.Y., Minn. Postdoctoral fellow Henry Ford Hosp., Detroit, 1982-83; sr. neuropsychologist Lifestyle Inst., John F. Kennedy Ctr., Edison, N.J., 1983-86; clin. care coord. The Head Injury Ctr. at Highgate, Troy, N.Y., 1986-88; dir. clin. svcs. New Medico Rehab. Ctr., Troy, 1988-92; dir. neuropsychology Hennepin County Medical Ctr., Mpls., 1993—. Editor: Soft Neurological Signs, 1987, The Neuropsychology of Everyday Life, Vol. I, 1990, Vol. II, 1991; co-author: Human Developmental Neuropsychology, 1984. Mem. Internat. Neuropsychol. Soc., Internat. Acad. for Rsch. in Learning Disabilities, Nat. Acad. Neuropsychology (membership com. 1988—), Am. Psychol. Assn., Am. Congress Rehab. Medicine, Minn. State Psychol. Assn., Soc. for Cognitive Rehab., N.Y. State Head Injury Assn. (bd. dirs. 1990-92), N.J. Head Injury Assn. (adv. bd. 1985-86). Home: 6540 Quail Xing Chanhassen MN 55317-9248 Office: Neuropsychology Hennepin County Medical Ctr 701 Park Ave Minneapolis MN 55415-1623

TURCOTTE, JEREMIAH GEORGE, physician, surgery educator; b. Detroit, Jan. 20, 1933; s. Vincent Joseph and Margaret Campau (Meldrum) T.; m. Claire Mary Lenz, July 5, 1958; children: Elizabeth Margaret, Sarah Lenz, John Jeremiah, Claire Meldrum. BS with high distinction, U. Mich., 1955, MD cum laude, 1957. Diplomate Am. Bd. Surgery (dir. 1982-88); added qualification in surg. critical care, 1986. Intern U. Mich. Med. Ctr., 1957-58, resident in surgery, 1958-60, 61-63; research asst. USPHS grant U. Mich. surgery dept., 1960-61; mem. faculty U. Mich. Med. Sch., 1963—, prof. surgery, 1971—, chmn. dept., 1974-87, head sect. gen. surgery, 1974-81; mem. residency rev. com. for surgery Am. Coun. for Grad. Med. Edn., 1980-86; dir. Transplant and Health Policy Ctr., U. Mich., 1985-95, dir. Organ Transplant Ctr. and Liver Transplant Program, 1984—; chmn. ethics com. United Network for Organ Sharing, 1987-91. Author 8 books, 51 book chpts. contbr. some 185 articles to profl. jours. Recipient Henry Russell award U. Mich., 1970, Mich. State Med. Soc. award, 1991. Fellow ACS (gov. 1982-92, pres. Mich. chpt. 1979-80); mem. Transplantation Soc. Mich. (pres. 1973-75), Assn. Acad. Surgeons, Am. Surg. Assn., Soc. Univ. Surgeons, Internat. Transplantation Soc., Ctrl. Surg. Assn. (pres. 1990-91),

Midwest Surg. Assn., Am. Gastroenterol. Assn., Western Surg. Assn., Soc. Surgery Alimentary Tract, Am. Soc. Transplant Surgeons (pres. 1979-80, chmn. ethics com. 1991-94), Frederick A. Coller Soc. (pres. 1982-83), Am. Trauma Soc. (founder), Halsted Soc., Mich. State Med. Soc. (Pres.'s award 1991), Am. Liver Found., Am. Coun. on Transplantation (bd. dirs. 1987-90), Ctrl. Surg. Assn. Found. (executor and sec. 1992—). Roman Catholic. Home: One Regent Dr Ann Arbor MI 48104-1738

TURCOTTE, MARGARET JANE, retired nurse; b. Stow, Ohio, May 17, 1927; d. Edward Carlton and Florence Margaret (Hanson) McCauley; R.N., St. Thomas Hosp., Akron, Ohio, 1949; m. Rene George Joseph, Nov. 24, 1961 (div. June 1967); 1 son, Michael Lawrence. Mem. nursing staff St. Thomas Hosp., 1949-50; pvt. duty nurse, 1950-57; polio nurse Akron's Children Hosp., 1953-54; mem. nursing staff Robinson Meml. Hosp., Ravenna, Ohio, 1958-67, head central service, 1963-67; supr. central service Brentwood Hosp., Warrensville Heights, Ohio, 1967-93; emergency med. technician. Mem. aux. Robinson Meml. Hosp., also hosp. vol.; active RSVP. Mem. St. Thomas Hosp. Alumni Assn. Democrat. Roman Catholic. Home: 6037 Highview St Lot 14-F Ravenna OH 44266

TURCZYN-TOLES, DOREEN MARIE, pharmaceutical consultant; b. Chelsea, Mass., Aug. 5, 1958; d. Francis Henry and Rosalie (Lomba) Turczyn; m. Ronald Eugene Toles, Oct. 19, 1986. BA cum laude, Boston U., 1981; MA, U. Chgo., 1984. Programming subcontr. Abbott Labs., Abbott Park, Ill., 1983-84; programmer, analyst Nat. Opinion Research Ctr., Chgo., 1984-88; statis. computing analyst G.D. Searle & Co., Skokie, Ill., 1988-90; supr. Parke-Davis Pharms., Ann Arbor, Mich., 1990-92; mgr. applications programming Univax Biologics, Inc., Rockville, Md., 1993-95; asst. project dir. Apache Med. Sys., Inc., McLean, Va., 1995-96; sr. systems analyst Westat, Inc., Rockville, Md., 1996—. Mem. Nat. Assn. Female Execs., NOW. Democrat. Roman Catholic.

TURER, GARY EVANS, ophthalmology; b. Bronx, N.Y., June 28, 1959; s. Gerald Alan and Allene (Vogel) T.; m. Nancy Rosman, July 5, 1982; children: Jason Aaron, Carly Melissa, David Ethan. BS, Union Coll., 1981; MD, NY Med. Coll., 1985. Diplomate Am. Bd. Ophthalmology. Pvt. practice medicine White Plains, N.Y., 1989—. Mem. Am. Acad. Ophthalmology, N.Y. State Med. Soc., Westchester County Med. Soc. Office: 303 North St White Plains NY 10605

TURESKY, SAMUEL, dentist, educator; b. Portland, Maine, Feb. 22, 1916; s. Philip and Gertrude (Perlin) T.; m. Barbara Proner, Nov. 23, 1952; children: Andrew, Jon, Robert, Philip, Lisa. AB, Harvard U., 1937; DMD, Tufts U., 1941. Resident in dentistry Mary Fletcher Hosp., Burlington, Vt., 1941-42; pvt. practice Dorchester, Mass., 1945-70, Brookline, Mass., 1970-92; from rsch. asst. to assoc. rsch. prof. Tufts U. Dental Sch., Boston, 1946-68, rsch. prof., 1968—; cons. dental rsch. oral hygiene divsn. Gillette Corp., Boston, 1987-94. Contbr. articles to profl. jours. Capt. USAF, 1942-45. Recipient citation for rsch. and acad. contbns. Tufts U. Dental Sch. Alumni Assn., 1996. Mem. AAAS, Internat. Assn. for Dental Rsch., Omicron Kappa Upsilon. Jewish. Home: 84 Wallis Rd Chestnut Hill MA 02167-3173

TURIEL, MAURIZIO, cardiologist; b. Milan, Italy, Oct. 16, 1948; s. Isacco and Lina (Zagdoun) T. Student, Pharmacology Inst., Milan, 1972-73; MD, U. Milan, 1973. Italian govt. rsch. grantee II Med. Clinic of U. Milan, 1974, specialist in pneumology, 1976, in cardiology, 1978, in hygiene and preventive medicine, 1985; rsch. fellow I Med. Pathology Inst., 1981; dir. Echo lab Med. Pathology Inst., 1987; rsch. fellow Cardiovascular Rsch. unit Royal Postgrad. Med. Sch., London, 1986—; chief Hewlett Packard Tng. Echo Ctr., U. Milan. Contbr. articles to profl. publs. U.S. Rsch. fellow U. Milan, 1981—. Mem. Italian Soc. Cardiology, Societas Europaea Physiologial Clinical Respiratoriae. Jewish. Home: Via Frua 24, 20146 Milan Italy

TURINO, GERARD MICHAEL, physician, medical scientist, educator; b. N.Y.C., May 16, 1924; s. Michael and Lucy (Arciero) T.; m. Dorothy Estes, Aug. 25, 1951; children: Peter, Phillip, James. A.B., Princeton U., 1945; M.D., Columbia U., 1948. Diplomate: Am. Bd. Internal Medicine. Intern Columbia U., Bellevue Hosp., 1948-49, asst. resident in medicine, 1949-50; resident in medicine New Haven Hosp., 1950-51; chief resident in medicine Columbia U. div. Bellevue Hosp., 1953-54; sr. fellow N.Y. Heart Assn., 1956-60; career investigator Health Research Council City of N.Y., 1961-71; asst. prof. medicine Columbia U., 1960-67, assoc. prof., 1967-72, prof. medicine, 1973-83, John H. Keating prof. medicine, 1983—; mem. staff Presbyn. Hosp., N.Y.C., 1960—; attending physician Presbyn. Hosp., 1983—; dir. med. svcs. St. Lukes-Roosevelt Hosp., N.Y.C., 1983-92; cons. on sci. affairs Am. Thoracic Soc., 1992—; mem. sci. adv. com. Nat. Heart, Lung, and Blood Inst., Am. Lung Assn., Am. Heart Assn., N.Y. Lung Assn., N.Y. Heart Assn.; mem. staff divsn. med. sci. Nat. Rsch. Coun., Washington; cons. VA Hosp., East Orange, N.J., 1962-67; cons. in medicine Englewood (N.J.) Hosp., Hackensack (N.J.) Hosp., pres.-elect Am. Bur. Med. Advancement in China, 1994, pres., 1994—. Contbr. articles to med. jours. Mem. Bd. Edn., Alpine, N.J., 1960-67. Served to capt. USAF, 1951-53. Recipient Joseph Mather Smith prize Columbia U., 1965, Alumni medal, 1983; Silver medal Alumni Assn. Coll. Physicians and Surgeons Columbia U., 1979, gold medal, 1986. Fellow AAAS; mem. Assn. Am. Physicians, Am. Soc. Clin. Investigation, Harvey Soc., Am. Thoracic Soc. (pres. 1987-88), Am. Fedn. Clin. Rsch., Am. Physiol. Soc. (chmn. steering com. respiration sect.), Am. Heart Assn. (award of merit 1980, Disting. Achievement award 1989, bd. dirs.), N.Y. Heart Assn. (pres. 1981-83, dir.), N.Y. Lung Assn. (dir.), N.Y. Med.-Surg. Soc. (pres. 1995), N.Y. Clin. Soc., Princeton Club (N.Y.C.), Maidstone Club, Devon Yacht Club, Century Assn. Club. Home: 66 E 79th St New York NY 10021-0217 Office: St Lukes-Roosevelt Hosp W 114th St and Amsterdam Ave New York NY 10025

TURK, DENNIS CHARLES, psychologist; b. Bklyn., Mar. 15, 1946; s. Irving and Rose (Beskin) T.; m. Lorraine Meichenbaum, Sept. 7, 1969; children: Kenneth Matthew, Katharine Elizabeth. BA, U. Fla., 1967; MA, U. Waterloo, 1975, PhD, 1978. Asst. prof. Yale U., New Haven, 1977-81, assoc. prof., 1981-85; prof. psychiatry U. Pitts. Sch. Medicine, 1985—; dir. Pain Evaluation and Treatment Inst., Pitts.; cons. Boehringer-Mannheim, Indpls., 1983-87, Paradigm Health Corp., Concord, Calif., 1993-95; Time Life Med., 1996—, Astra Merck, 1996—, Janssen, 1996—; attending psychologist VA, West Haven, 1980-85; chair profl. adv. bd. Am. Chronic Pain Assn., 1993—; councilor Internat. Assn. Study Pain, 1994—; bd. dirs. Am. Pain Soc., 1995—. Author: Pain and Behavioral Medicine, 1983, Facilitating Treatment Adherence: Practitioners Guide, 1987; editor: Health, Illness and Families, 1985, Psychosocial Assessment in Terminal Care, 1986, Chronic Pain, 1986, Reasoning, Inference and Judgement in Clinical Psychology, 1988, Handbook of Pain Assessment, 1992, Noninvasive Approach to Treatment of Pain in the Terminally Ill, 1992, Annals of Behavioral Medicine, 1993—, Psychological Approaches to Pain Management: A Practitioner's Handbook, 1966. Recipient Nat. award Am. Assn. Diabetes Educators, 1981; Merit Rev. grantee VA, 1982, 84; grantee Nat. Inst. Dental Research, 1985—, Nat. Inst. Arthritis and Musculoskeletal and Skin Diseases, 1987-95, Nat. Ctr. Health Statistics, 1990-92, Nat. Headache Found., 1993—, Arthritis Found., 1995—. Fellow Soc. Behavioral Medicine, Acad. Behavioral Medicine Research; mem. Internat. Assn. for Study of Pain, Am. Pain Soc., Am. Psychol. Assn. (Outstanding Sci. Contbn. to Health Psychology award 1993), Agy. Health Care Policy and Rsch. Low Back Problems (guideline devel. panel 1992-95). Home: 2163 Poor Richard Ln Pittsburgh PA 15237-4282 Office: U Pitts Sch Medicine Pain Evaluation and Treatment 4601 Baum Blvd Pittsburgh PA 15213

TURK, ROBERT LOUIS, radiologist; b. Lima, Ohio, Oct. 30, 1940; s. Herman Matthew and Daphne Carol (Stout) T.; m. Penelope Bryant, Mar. 25, 1964; children: Marjorie Carol Turk Desmond, Susan Elizabeth Turk Charles. BA, Stanford U., 1962; MD, UCLA, 1966. Diplomate Am. Bd. Radiology, Am. Bd. Nuclear Medicine. Rotating intern U. Iowa, Iowa City, 1966-67; resident in radiology Harbor Gen.-UCLA Hosp., Torrance, Calif., 1967-70; radiologist, chief staff, vice chief, head radiology El Cajon (Calif.) Valley Hosp., 1972-83; pvt. practice, El Cajon, 1983—. Elder Presbyn. Ch., 1966—. Maj. M.C., USAR, 1970-72, Vietnam. Mem. Am. Coll. Radiology, Radiol. Soc. N.Am., Calif. Radiol. Soc., San Diego Radiol. Soc. (pres. 1990-91, past treas., rep.), Calif. Med. Soc., San Diego Med. Soc. Democrat. Home: 1760 Key Ln El Cajon CA 92021 Office: El Cajon X-Ray Imaging 1663 Greenfield Dr El Cajon CA 92021

TURK, ROBERT PETER, surgeon; b. Hopelawn, N.J., June 29, 1931; s. Joseph and Ethel (Zoldi) T. BS, U. Ala., 1956; MD, Med. Coll. Ala., 1960. Diplomate Am. Bd. Surgery. Physician, surgeon USAF, Washington, 1959-79; clin. prof. surgery Wright State U. Sch. Medicine, Dayton, Ohio, 1979—. Decorated Legion of Merit USAF, 1979. Fellow Am. Coll. Surgeons; mem. AMA, Dayton Surg. Soc., Alpha Epsilon Delta, Alpha Omega Alpha. Home: 5235 Mad River Rd Dayton OH 45429 Office: St Elizabeth Med Ctr 627 Edwin C Moses Blvd Dayton OH 45408

TURKA, LAURENCE A., medical educator, researcher. BA in Biochemistry summa cum laude, Colgate U., 1978; MD cum laude, Yale U., 1982. Diplomate Am. Bd. Internal Medicine, Am. Bd. Nephrology. Intern in medicine Yale-New Haven Hosp., Conn., 1982-83, resident in medicine, 1983-85; fellow in nephrology Brigham and Women's Hosp.-Harvard Med. Sch., Boston, 1985-88; asst. prof. U. Mich., 1988-93, assoc. prof., 1993-94; dir. immunobiology and tumor immunology program U. Mich. Cancer Ctr., 1993-94; staff physician U. Mich. Med. Ctr., 1988-94; assoc. prof. U. Pa., 1994—, dir. immunology programs Inst. for Human Gene Therapy, 1994—; staff physician Hosp. U. Pa., 1994—; adj. assoc. prof. Wistar Inst., 1995—. Ad hoc reviewer: Transplantation, 1990-96, Blood, 1992—, Kidney Internat., 1993—, Diabetes, 1994—, Gastroenterology, 1994—, Arthritis and Rheumatism, 1994—, Immunology Today, 1994—, Jour. Clin. Investigation, 1994—, Proceedings of NAS, 1995—, Internat. Immunology, 1995—; mem. editl. bd. Transplantation, 1996—; assoc. editor: Jour. Immunology, 1992—; lectr. in field; contbr. articles to profl. jours., chpts. in books. Recipient Established Investigator award Am. Heart Assn., 1995. Mem. Am. Fedn. for Clin. Rsch. Am. Soc. Transplant Physicians (young investigator award 1988), Am. Assn. Immunologists, Am. Soc. Nephrology (ad hoc reviewer Jour. Am. Soc. Nephrology 1994-96, mem. editl. bd. Jour. Am. Soc. Nephrology, 1996—, young investigator award 1996), Am. Soc. Hematology, Phi Beta Kappa. Office: U Pa 409 Stellar Chance Labs 422 Curie Blvd Rm 409 Philadelphia PA 19104-6100*

TURKEWITZ, GERALD, psychology educator; b. N.Y.C., Feb. 25, 1933; s. Morris and Jean (Mintz) T.; m. Myrna Genuth, Nov. 23, 1955; children—Barbara, Neil, Aaron, Joel. B.A., CCNY, 1955, M.S., 1957; Ph.D., NYU, 1967. Research asst. Am. Mus. Natural History, N.Y.C., 1955-61; research assoc. A. Einstein Coll. Medicine, Bronx, 1961-67, assoc. prof., 1967-68; assoc. prof. Hunter Coll., N.Y.C., 1971-76; vis. prof. A. Einstein Coll. Medicine, 1985—; prof. Hunter Coll., N.Y.C., 1976—. Author: Advances in the Study of Behavior, 1984, Evolution and Lateralization of the Brain, 1977, Infant Stress Under Intensive Care, 1985; Neuropsychology of Face Perception, 1985, Developmental Psychobiology, 1992, Developmental Time and Timing, 1993. Pres. Internat. Soc. for Infant Studies. Fellow Am. Psychol. Assn.; mem. Internat. Conf. on Infant Studies, Eastern Psychol. Assn., Internat. Soc. Devel. Psychobiology, Soc. for Research in Child Devel. Avocations: nature study. Home: 900 Lydig Ave Bronx NY 10462-2149 Office: Hunter Coll 695 Park Ave New York NY 10021

TURKISH, LANCE, physician, ophthalmologist; b. Jersey City, Aug. 6, 1949; s. Solomon and Rosalyn (Lieb) T.; m. Karen Rose Stern, Mar. 10, 1984; children: Hallie Greer, Lainie Brett, Evan Spencer. AB, Case Western Res. U., 1970, MD, 1973. Diplomate Am. Bd. Ophthalmology. Intern Charity Hosp.-Tulane U., New Orleans, 1973-74; resident in ophthalmology 5th Ave. Hosp.-N.Y. Med. Coll., 1974-77; fellow in diseases and surgery of the vitreous and retina Vitreoretinal Rsch. Found., Memphis, 1977; pvt. practice New Orleans, 1978—; co-investigator Early Treatment Diabetic Retinopathy Study, NEI-NIH, 1983-89. Contbr. articles to profl. jours. Chmn. bd. Communal Hebrew Sch., New Orleans, 1993-96; mem. bd. dirs. Juvenile Diabetes Found., La., 1985—, Am. Diabetes Assn., New Orleans, 1980-93, Anti-Defamation League of B'nai B'rith, New Orleans, 1990—. Recipient scholarship Omicron Delta Kappa. Fellow Am. Acad. Ophthalmology, ACS, Internat. Coll. Surgeons. Jewish. Home: 3700 Edenborn Matairie LA 70002 Office: 3600 Chestnut St 3d Fl New Orleans LA 70115

TURKO, ALEXANDER ANTHONY, biology educator; b. Bridgeport, Conn., Aug. 19, 1943; s. Alexander I. and Elizabeth K. (Kulesar) T.; m. Nancy Bally Hoinacky, Dec. 30, 1967; children: Michelle Lynn, Mark A. BA, So. Conn. State U., 1965, MS, 1967, postgrad., 1976. Assoc. prof. So. Conn. State U., New Haven, 1965—. Mem. AAUP. Home: 11 Birchwood Ln Monroe CT 06468-1025

TURKULA-PINTO, LOUISE DIANE, plastic surgeon; b. St. Paul, Alta., Can., Sept. 28, 1955; m. Manuel Reimao Pinto, Feb. 10, 1984; children: Manuel Stefano, Sophia Tereza. BS, U. N.D., 1977, BS in Medicine, 1979; MD, Washington U., 1981. Bd. cert. Am. Bd. Plastic Surgery. Intern straigth gen. surgery Mayo Clinic, Rochester, Minn., 1981-82; resident gen. surgery Mayo Clinic, Rochester, 1982-86, resident plastic surgery, 1986-88; microvascular and breast reconstructive surgery staff Drs. J. Fisher and G.P. Maxwell, Nashville, 1989; sr. house officer burn unit Bangour Gen. Hosp., Scotland, 1989; staff Fargo (N.D.) Clinic, 1989—, Plastic Surgery of Mpls., 1990-92; ptnr. Edina (Minn.) Plastic Surgery Ltd., 1992—; presenter in field. Contbr. articles to profl. jours. Mem. ACS, Am. Soc. Plastic and Reconstructive Surgeons, Am. Med. Women's Assn., Minn. Soc. Plastic and Reconstructive Surgeons, Minn. Med. Assn., Hennepin County Med. Soc. Office: Edina Plastic Surgery Ltd 3625 W 65th St Ste 150 Edina MN 55435

TURMAN, TRACY PENN, health facility administrator; b. Stuart, Va., Nov. 26, 1967; s. Dexter Penn and Judy Jean (Webb) T.; m. Amy Brooke Key, May 16, 1992. BA in Polit. Sci. and Comm., James Madison U., 1990. Adminstr. (4 locations) Med. Facilities of Am., Roanoke, Va., 1990-95; adminstr. Willow Creek Health Care Ctr., Midlothian, Va., 1995—; bd. dirs. Ctrl. Va. Health Planning. Registered lobbyist rep. Nursing Home Industry, Richmond, Va., 1993-95. Mem. Am. Health Care Assn., Va. Health Care Assn. (Richmond chpt. vice chair 1995-96, publ. rels. com.). Home: 11801 Pleasanthill Ct Richmond VA 23236 Office: Willow Creek Health Care 11611 Robious Rd Midlothian VA 23113

TURNBULL, ALAN DAVID MACKAY, surgeon, educator; b. Montreal, Que., Can., June 25, 1936; came to the U.S., 1967; s. George David and Jane Kerr (Mackay) T.; m. Nancy Elizabeth Black, June 24, 1967. BSc, McGill U., Montreal, 1957, MD, BChir, 1961, MSc, 1965. Diplomate Am. Bd. Surgery. Intern Royal Victoria Hosp., Montreal, resident; fellow Meml. Hosp. for Cancer & Allied Diseases Sloan-Kettering Cancer Ctr., N.Y.C., attending surgeon Meml. Hosp. for Cancer & Allied Diseases, 1971—; prof. surgery Cornell Med. Sch., N.Y.C., 1971—. Fellow ACS, Royal Coll. Surgeons (Can.), Am. Coll. Critical Care Medicine. Office: Meml Hosp 1275 York Ave New York NY 10021

TURNBULL, H. RUTHERFORD, III, law educator, lawyer; b. N.Y.C., Sept. 22, 1937; s. Henry R. and Ruth (White) T.; m. Mary M. Slingluff, Apr. 4, 1964 (div. 1972); m. Ann Patterson, Mar. 23, 1974; children: Jay, Amy, Katherine. BA, Johns Hopkins U., 1959; LLB with hon., U. Md., 1964; LLM, Harvard U., 1969. Bar: Md., N.C. Law clerk to Hon. Emory H. Niles Supreme Bench Balt. City, 1959-60; law clerk to Hon. Roszel C. Thomsen U.S. Dist. Ct. Md., 1962-63; assoc. Piper & Marbury, Balt., 1964-67; prof. Inst. Govt. U. N.C., Chapel Hill, 1969-80, U. Kans., Lawrence, 1980—. Editor-in-chief Md. Law Review. Cons., author, lectr., co-dir. Beach Ctr. on Families and Disability, U. Kans.; pres. Full Citizenship Inc., Lawrence, 1987-93; spl. staff-fellow U.S. Senate subcom. on disability policy, Washington, 1987-88; bd. dirs. Camphill Assn. N.Am., Inc., 1985-87; trustee Judge David L. Bazelon Ctr. Mental Health Law, 1993-96. With U.S. Army, 1960-65. Recipient Nat. Leadership award Nat. Assn. Pvt. Residential Resources, 1988, Nat. Leadership award Internat. Coun. for Exceptional Children, 1996; Public Policy fellow Joseph P. Kennedy, Jr. Found., 1987-88. Fellow Am. Assn. on Mental Retardation (pres. 1985-86); mem. ABA (chmn. disability law commn. 1991-95), U.S.A. Assn. for Retarded Citizens (sec. 1981-83), Assn. for Persons with Severe Handicaps (treas. 1988), Nat. Assn. Rehab. Rsch. and Tng. Ctrs. (chair govt. affairs com. 1990-93), Internat. Assn. Scientific Study of Mental Deficiency, Internat. League of Assns. for Persons with Mental Handicaps, Johns Hopkins U. Alumni Assn. Democrat. Episcopalian. Home: 1636 Alvamar Dr Lawrence KS 66047-1714 Office: U Kans 3111 Haworth Hall Lawrence KS 66045

TURNDORF, HERMAN, anesthesiologist, educator; b. Paterson, N.J., Dec. 22, 1930; s. Charles R. and Ruth (Blumberg) T.; m. Sietske Huisman, Nov. 24, 1957; children: David, Michael Pieter. A.B., Oberlin Coll., 1952; M.D., U. Pa., 1956. Diplomate: Am. Bd. Anesthesiology. Instr. anesthesiology U. Pa. Hosp., 1957-59; asst. anesthetist med. sch. Harvard U., Mass. Gen. Hosp., Boston, 1961-63; assoc. attending anesthesiologist, asst. dir. dept. anesthesiology Mt. Sinai Hosp., N.Y.C., 1963-70; clin. prof. anesthesiology Mt. Sinai Hosp., 1966-70; prof., chmn. dept. anesthesiology W.Va. U. Sch. Medicine and Med. Center, Morgantown, 1970-74, NYU Sch. Medicine, 1974—; dir. anesthesiology NYU Hosp., 1974—; pres. med. bd., med. dir. Bellevue Hosp. Med. Center, 1990—; cons. in anesthesiology Manhattan VA Hosp., Armed Forces Sch. Medicine, 1974-77. Co-author: Anesthesia and Neurosurgery, 2d edit., 1986, Trauma, Anesthesia and Intensive Care, 1990; contbr. articles to profl. jours. Served to lt. M.C. USNR, 1959-61. Fellow Am. Coll. Chest Physicians, Am. Coll. Anesthesiologists (bd. govs. 1977-85, chmn. bd. govs. 1984), N.Y. Acad. Medicine; mem. AMA, Am. Soc. Anesthesiologists, Assn. Univ. Anesthetists, Internat. Soc. Study of Pain, Soc. Acad. Anesthesia Chairmen, Soc. Critical Care Medicine, Soc. Neurosurgical Anesthesia and Neurologic Supportive Care, N.Y. Acad. Scis., N.Y. State Soc. Anesthesiologists. Home: 105 Harbor Dr Unit 118 Stamford CT 06902-7456 Office: NY Univ Dept Anesthesiology 550 1st Ave New York NY 10016-6481*

TURNDORF, JAMIE, clinical psychologist; b. Boston, July 12, 1958; d. Gary Owen and Sharon (Sandow) T.; m. Emile Jean Pin, Jan. 2, 1988. AB in Am. Culture, Vassar Coll., 1980; MSW, Adelphi U., 1983; PhD, Calif. Coast U., 1994. Lic. social worker, N.Y. Pvt. practice psychology N.Y.C. and Millbrook, N.Y., 1981—; lead creative movement and psychodrama program Lincoln Farms Work Camp, Roscoe, N.Y., 1976; with Astor Child Guidance Clinic, Poughkeepsie, N.Y., 1982-83; leader various pgroups Braig House Hosp., Beacon, N.Y., 1982-87, developer, dir. eating disorders program, 1984-86; founder, dir. INC.TIMACY, 1990—, J.T. Developers, Inc., Poughkeepsie, 1983-91; dir. Hudson Valley br. Ctr. for Advancement Group Studies, Ctr. for Emotional Comm., Millbrook, 1990—. Author: (with Emile Jean Pin) The Pleasure of Your Company: A Socio-Psychological Analysis of Modern Sociability, 1985; columnist Dr. Love various newspapers; relationship advice on world wide web; host Ask Dr. Love, Sta. WEVD, N.Y.C., 1992; creator, inventor LoveQuest: The Game of Finding Mr. Right, 1990 (one of best new games award Fun and Games mag. 1991). Mem. NASW, N.Y. State Soc. Clin. Social Work Psychotherapists. Home and Office: PO Box 475 Millbrook NY 12545-0475

TURNER, CHARLES HALL, biomedical engineer, educator; b. Roswell, N.Mex., Nov. 29, 1961; s. Bob Franklin and Mary (Hall) T.; m. Nancy Jo Wieczorek, Mar. 13, 1993. BSME, Tex. Tech. U., 1983; PhD, Tulane U., 1987. Rsch. asst. biomed. engring. Tulane U., New Orleans, 1984-87; dir. biomechanics, asst. prof. oral biology Creighton U., Omaha, 1987-91; asst. prof. mech. engring. Purdue U., Indpls., 1991—; asst. prof. orthopaedic surgery, dir. orthopaedic rsch. Ind. U., Indpls., 1991—. Contbr. articles to Jour. Biomechanics, Jour. Biomech. Engring., Jour. Materials Sci. Recipient Morris F. Miller award Health Future Found., Omaha, 1987, FIRST award NIH, 1991; Whitaker Found. grantee, 1989. Mem. ASME, Orthopaedic Rsch. Soc., Soc. Biomechanics. Office: Ind U 541 Clinical Dr Indianapolis IN 46202-5233

TURNER, CHRISTOPHER EDWARD, cell biology educator; b. Birmingham, Eng., Sept. 17, 1961; came to U.S., 1987; s. Frank and Brenda Turner; m. Susan Benoit, Sept. 2, 1989. BSc, Sheffield (Eng.) U., 1983; DPhil, Oxford (Eng.) U., 1986. Postdoctoral fellow U. N.C., Chapel Hill, 1987-91; asst. prof. cell biology SUNY Health Sci. Ctr., Syracuse, 1991—. Contbr. articles to Jour. Cell Biology, Jour. Cell Sci., Jour. Biol. Chemistry. Rsch. grantee NIH, 1991—, Muscular Dystrophy Assn., 1992—; established investigator Am. Heart Assn., 1995-2000. Mem. AAAS, Am. Soc. for Cell Biology, Brit. Soc. for Cell Biology. Office: SUNY Health Sci Ctr 750 E Adams St Syracuse NY 13210-2306

TURNER, DAVID B., health facility administrator; b. McAllen, Tex., Dec. 2, 1949; s. Robert B. and Kathryn F. (Houghton) T.; m. Telma Barahona, Dec. 28, 1988; children: David Gene, Kelyn Sarahi, Cathryn L., William James. AAS, U. Tex., Edinburg, 1980. RN, Tex. Nursing supr. Mission (Tex.) Mcpl. Hosp., 1981-85; house supr. Willacy County Hosp. Dist., Raymondville, Tex., 1985-86; staff nurse psychiatry McAllen Med. Ctr., 1990-91, 92—; house supr. Dolly Vinsaint Meml. Hosp., San Benito, Tex., 1986-90, Edin Gen. Hosp., Edinburg, Tex., 1991-92; instr. anatomy. instr. anatomy, CBM Edn. Ctr., San Benito, Tex., 1985-89; with USAF, 1972-76. Home: 311 N 13th St Donna TX 78537-2815

TURNER, DAVID ROBERT, pathology educator, consultant histopathologist; b. Barnehurst, Eng., Feb. 26, 1939; s. Harry James and Vera (Jackson) T.; m. Doreen Mary Duncombe (div. 1980); children: Karen Mary, Ian Keith, Sarah Ann, Judith Dawn; m. Juliet Mary Heaton, Dec. 22, 1980; children: Mark John, Nils Alexander. B of Medicine, BS, Guy's Hosp., 1962, PhD, 1969. Lectr. in anatomy Guy's Hosp., London, 1963-69, lectr. in pathology, 1969-72, sr. lectr. in pathology, 1972-75, reader in pathology, 1975-80, prof. histopathology, 1980-81; cons. histopathologist Musgrove Park Hosp., Taunton, Eng., 1981-82; prof. pathology Nottingham (Eng.) U., 1983—; vice dean Nottingham Med. Sch., 1984-87; cons. histopathologist Univ. Hosp., Nottingham, 1983—; com. on classification of Glomerula Diseases WHO, 1976—. Author: An Atlas of Renal Pathology, 1980; author sci. papers on glomerulonephritis and metalloproteinases and their inhibitors in tumor invasiveness. Fellow Royal Coll. Pathologists; mem. Assn. Profs. Pathology (sec. 1988-91, chmn. 1991-94), Fedn. Assns. of Clin. Profs. (chmn. 1994—). Anglican. Office: Univ Hosp Queen's Med Ctr, Clifton Blvd, Nottingham NG7 2UH, England

TURNER, EDWIN ARNOLD, JR., occupational health physician; b. Plainfield, N.J., Nov. 29, 1937; s. Edwin Arnold and Ruth Alice (Carter) T.; m. Jean Marie Cooper, Dec. 27, 1964; children: Suzanne Marie, Scott Cooper. BS in Zoology, Wheaton Coll., 1959; MD, Cornell U. Med. Coll., 1963. Diplomate Am. Bd. Preventive Medicine/Occupational Medicine; lic. N.J., N.Y. Resident, gen. surgery U.S.P.H.S. Hosps., Staten Island and Gallup, N.Mex., 1964-68; physician City of Plainfield, 1971—; corp. med. dir. Ethicon, Inc. (divsn. Johnson & Johnson), Somerville, N.J., 1969-75, Western Union, Upper Saddle River, N.J., 1975-85, Sterling Drug, Inc. (divsn. Eastman Kodak), N.Y.C., 1985-91, L&F Products (divsn. Eastman Kodak), Montvale, N.J., 1992-95; chief occupational health svcs. Ctrl. N.J. Med. Group, New Brunswick, 1993; dir. occupational medicine Princeton (N.J.) U., 1994; regional med. dir. IMC Health Care-Continental Airlines, Newark Airport, 1995—; cons. Carrier Found., Bellemead, N.J.; clin. asst. prof. Robert Wood Johnson Med. Sch., Univ. of Medicine and Dentistry of N.J., Piscataway, 1985—. Surgeon USPHS, 1967-69. Fellow Am. Coll. Occupational Medicine (bd. dirs. 1986-91), Am. Coll. Preventive Medicine; mem. AMA, Am. Soc. Legal and Indsl. Medicine (bd. govs. 1985-92), Med. Execs. (exec. bd., pres. 1985-86), Nat. Soc. to Prevent Blindness (bd. dirs. 1985-95, del. 1991), Med. Soc. N.J. Republican. Home: 1045 Oak Ln Plainfield NJ 07060-3429

TURNER, H(ARRY) SPENCER, preventive medicine physician, educator; b. Dayton, Ohio, July 25, 1938; s. Eli and Daphne (Cunagin) T.; children: Michael, Mary, Daniel. BA, Manchester Coll., North Manchester, Ind., 1960; MD summa cum laude, Ohio State U., 1963, MS in Preventive Medicine, 1968. Diplomate Am. Bd. Preventive Medicine. Resident in preventive (aerospace) medicine Ohio State U., Columbus, 1966-69, chief resident, 1968-69, clin. asst. prof. dept. preventive medicine, 1969-80, dir. Univ. Health Svc., 1970-80; pvt. practice Dayton, 1980-90; head team physician U. Ky., Lexington, 1991—, prof. preventive medicine and environ. health, 1991—. Contbr. articles and papers to profl. jours. and meetings. Bd. dirs. Blue Shield, 1981-86; mem. Cin. Internat. Chorale, 1989-94. Capt. U.S. Army, 1964-66. Fellow Am. Coll. Preventive Medicine, Am. Coll. Health Assn. (pres. 1980, Ruth Boynton award 1982, Edw. Hitchcock award 1996), Alpha Omega Alpha. Episcopalian. Office: U Ky Coll Medicine Univ Health Svc Lexington KY 40536

TURNER, JOHN BUNYAN, surgeon, family physician; b. Iuka, Miss., Oct. 22, 1916; s. John Henry and Ida Mozell (Goodrich) T.; m. Lillian Burton, June 5, 1948; children: John Lee, Suzann Turner Vermillion, James Burton, William David. Student, Union U., Jackson, Tenn., 1937-39, Peabody Coll., 1949-51; BS, U. Tenn., 1954, MD, 1955; attended, Vanderbilt U. Cert. Am. Bd. Family Practice. Pvt. practice Springfield, Tenn., 1955—; chief staff Jesse Holman Jones Hosp., Springfield; med. dir. Springfield Health Care Nursing Home. Capt. USAF, 1941-45. Decorated Air medals, USA Ribbon, African Ribbon. Mem. AMA, Tenn. Med. Assn., Am. Acad. Family Practice, Geriatric Soc. Assn., Tenn. Acad. Family Practice, Robertson County Med. Assn., Rotary, Am. Legion, POW Soc. of Sagan, Germany, Shriners (32d degree). Office: 541 N Pawnee Dr Springfield TN 37172-2204

TURNER, JOHN SIDNEY, JR., otolaryngologist, educator; b. Bainbridge, Ga., July 25, 1930; s. John Sidney and Rose Lee (Rogers) T.; m. Betty Jane Tigner, June 5, 1955; children: Elizabeth, Rebecca, Jan Marie. BS, Emory U., 1952, MD, 1955. Diplomate Am. Bd. Otolaryngology. Intern U. Va. Hosp., 1955-56; resident in otolaryngology Duke U. Med. Ctr., 1958-61; prof. otolaryngology Emory U., Atlanta, 1961-95, chmn. dept., 1961-95; cons. Healthcare Partnership Cons., Atlanta, 1995—; ear specialist, chief otolaryngology Emory Clinic, 1961-95; area cons. in field U.S. 3d Army, 1962-69; assoc. dir. heart disease control program Fla. Bd. Health, 1956-58; Ga. state chmn. Deafness Rsch. Found., 1968—; v.p. Clifton Casualty Ins. Co., Atlanta, 1975-95. Mem. internat. editl. bd. Drugs Jour., 1982—, Ethicals in Med. Progress, 1982—, Dialogue Jour., 1988-95; mem. editl. bd. Otolaryngolog—Head and Neck Surgery, 1991; contbr. chpts. to books, articles to profl. jours. With USPHS, 1956-58. Recipient Appreciation award Children of Fulton County and Fulton County Health Dept., 1975, Citation for Disting. Svc., Fla. divsn. Am. Cancer Soc., 1957, Lester A. Brown award Ga. Soc. Otolaryngology—Head and Neck Surgery, 1995. Mem. AMA, So. Med. Assn. (chmn. otolaryngology sect. 1974, cert. of appreciation 1974), Am. Acad. Otolaryngology--Head and Neck Surgery (Honor award 1994), Triological Soc. (v.p., chmn. so. sect. 1991—), Am. Acad. Otolaryngic Allergy, Ga. Soc. Otolaryngology (pres. 1973), Med. Assn. Ga., Med. Assn. Atlanta, Assn. Acad. Depts. Otolaryngology, Optimists (pres. Atlanta 1975), Alpha Omega Alpha. Democrat. Methodist. Home: 1388 Council Bluff Dr NE Atlanta GA 30345-4132

TURNER, LILLIAN ERNA, nurse; b. Coalmont, Colo., Apr. 22, 1918; d. Harvey Oliver and Erna Lena (Wackwitz) T. BS, Colo. State U., 1940, Columbia U., 1945; cert. physician asst., U. Utah, 1978. Commd. 2d lt. Nurse Corps, U.S. Army, 1945; advanced through grades to lt. comdr. USPHS, 1964; 1st lt. U.S. Army, 1945-46; U.S. Pub. Health Svc., 1964-69; dean of women U. Alaska, Fairbanks, 1948-50; head nurse Group Health Hosp., Seattle, 1950-53; adviser to chief nurse Hosp. Am. Samoa, Pago Pago, 1954-60; head nurse Meml. Hosp., Twin Falls, Idaho, 1960-61; shift supr. Hosp. Lago Oil and Transport, Siero Colorado, Aruba, 1961-63; nurse adv. Province Hosp., Danang, South Vietnam, 1964-69, Cho Quan Hosp., South Vietnam, 1970-72; chief nurse, advisor Truk Hosp., Moen, Ea. Caroline Islands, 1972-74; nurse advisor Children's Med. Relief Internat., South Vietnam, 1975; physician's asst. U. Utah, 1976-78, Wagon Circle Med. Clinic, Rawlins, Wyo., 1978-89, Energy Basin Clinic Carbon County Meml. Hosp., Hanna, Wyo., 1989-96. Named Nat. Humanitarian Pa. of Yr., 1993, Wyo. Pa. of Yr., 1992. Mem. Wyo. Acad. Physician Assts. (bd. dirs. 1982-83), Am. Acad. Physician Assts., Nat. Assn. Physician Assts. Home: PO Box 337 Hanna WY 82327-0337

TURNER, MARK DUDLEY, orthopaedic surgeon, army officer; b. Knoxville, Tenn., Oct. 6, 1954; s. Donald Lee and Geraldine (Roach) T. BA, U. Tenn., 1976; MD, Uniformed Scvs. U. Health Scis., 1982. Diplomate Am. Bd. Orthopaedic Surgery. Commd. officer U.S. Army, 1978, advanced through grades to lt. col.; intern Eisenhower Army Med. Ctr., Ft. Gordon, Ga., 1982-83, resident in orthopaedic surgery, 1983-87; fellow in pediatric orthopaedics U. Miami (Fla.)-Jackson Meml. Hosp., 1987-88; staff orthopaedic surgery 97th Gen. Hosp., Frankfurt, Germany, 1988-89, chief orthopaedic svc., 1989-91; asst. chief orthopaedic surgery Evans Army Cmty. Hosp., Ft. Carson, Colo., 1991—. Fellow ACS, Am. Acad. Orthopaedic Surgeons; mem. Soc. Mil. Orthopaedic Surgeons.

TURNER, NATHAN WEBB, clinical psychologist; b. Berkeley, Calif., Mar. 1, 1931; s. James C. and Jennie E.; m. Marjorie Beth Vinz, Aug. 14, 1954; children: Steven, David. B.A., U. Redlands, 1953; M.Div., Berkeley Bapt. Div. Sch., 1956; M.Ed., Temple U., 1970, Ed.D., 1976. Ordained to ministry Am. Bapt. Conv., 1956; diplomate Am. Bd. Profl. Psychology, Am. Bd. Sexology. Active local chs., 1956-61; assoc. dir. youth ministry Am. Bapt. Churches, U.S.A., 1961-63, dir. adult edn., 1963-69, dir. marriage and family life edn., 1969-72; assoc. family study in psychiatry dept. psychiatry, U. Pa. Sch. Medicine, Phila., 1972-76, 84—; asst. prof. psychiatry and human behavior Jefferson Med. Coll., Phila., 1976—; faculty Drexel U., 1972-73, Eastern Coll., 1972-74; adj. prof. counseling Ea. Bapt. Theol. Sem., 1976—; cons. Scott Paper Co., First Pa. Bank., Bell of Pa.; bd. dirs. Am. Bd. Family Psychology, 1995-97. Prin. investigator research grants Assn. for Creative Change, 1972-73, Assn. Theol. Schs., 1978-79. Mem. APA, Acad. Family Psychology (pres. 1993-94), Am. Mgmt. Assn., Pa. Psychol. Assn. (clin.), Am. Assn. Marriage and Family Therapy (approved supr.), Am. Assn. Sex Educators, Counselors and Therapists (cert. sex educator and sex therapist, approved supr.), Am. Soc. Clin. Hypnosis. Democrat. Author: Effective Leadership in Small Groups, 1977; book reviewer The Family Psychologist, The Jour. of Marital and Family Therapy; contbr. articles in behavioral sci. and religion to publs.

TURNER, RAYMOND SCOTT, neurologist, neuroscientist; b. Manchester, Eng., Oct. 5, 1957; came to U.S., 1965.; s. Derek and Barbara (Edwards) T.; m. Arlene Christine Minar, Oct. 8, 1983; children: Kathryn Alexandra, Alex Edmund. PhD, Emory U., 1984, MD, 1988. Diplomate Am. Bd. Psychiatry & Neurology. Intern, resident, fellow in neurology Hosp. of the Univ. Pa., Phila., 1988-95; asst. prof. neurology U. Mich./VA Med. Ctrs., Ann Arbor, 1995—. Mem. Am. Acad. Neurology, Soc. for Neurosci. Episcopalian. Home: 2626 Pin Oak Dr Ann Arbor MI 48103 Office: VAMC GRECC 2215 Fuller Rd Ann Arbor MI 48105

TURNER, THOMAS CREAGHER, orthopaedic surgeon; b. Eupora, Miss., Aug. 5, 1924; s. Thomas C. and Mallie Mae (Kimbriel) T.; m. Mary Jane Prowell, Apr. 19, 1953; children: Martha Kimbriel, Mary Darrah, Thomas C. Jr. BS, U. Miss., 1945; MD, Jefferson Med. Coll., 1948; MS, U. Tenn., 1955. Diplomate Am. Bd. Orthopaedic Surgery. Intern Jefferson Med. Coll. Hosp., Phila., 1948-50; resident Willis C. Campbell Clinic, Memphis, 1952-55; pvt. practice, Jackson, Miss., 1955-93; ret. Author: Treatment of Tennis Elbow, 1986. Lt. USN, 1949-52. Fellow Am. Acad. Orthopaedic Surgery; mem. Mid-Am. Orthopaedic Assn. Republican. Baptist. Home: 4104 N Honeysuckle Ln Jackson MS 39211-6544

TURNER, THOMAS RICHARD, neurologist; b. Arp, Tex., May 19, 1917; s. Leonard Walton and Rosamond (Dean) T.; m. Donnie Martha Goodner, Aug. 29, 1941 (dec. Sept. 1993); children: Nancy Ethel, Ann Rosamond, Richard Leonard. BA, Baylor U., Waco, Tex., 1938; MD, Baylor U., Dallas, 1941; MS, U. Minn., St. Paul, 1945. Diplomate Am. Bd. Psychiatry and Neurology. Intern in medicine Baylor U. Hosp., Dallas, 1941-42; fellow in neurology Mayo Clinic, Rochester, Minn., 1942-45, 1st asst. in neurology, 1945; pvt. practice neurology and psychiatry Springer Clinic, Tulsa, 1945-60; pvt. practice, Tulsa, 1960-80; mem. med. staff St. John's Hosp. and Med. Ctr., Tulsa, 1945—, Hillcrest Hosp. and Med. Ctr., Tulsa, 1945—, St. Francis Hosp., Tulsa, 1960-80. Fellow Am. Acad. Neurology (sr. mem.), Am. Psyhciat. Assn. (life); mem. AMA (life), Okla. State Med. Assn., Tulsa County Med. Soc., Am. Med. EEG Assn. (life), Petroleum Club Tulsa. Republican. Episcopalian. Home: 1831 E 31st Pl Tulsa OK 74105

TURNER, WELD WINSTON, industrial psychologist; b. St. Paul, July 25, 1931; s. Frank and Hazel Thirza (Weld) Prevratil; B.S. Commerce, Okla. State U., 1954; M.S., Purdue U., 1955, Ph.D. in Indsl. Psychology, 1959; m. Helen Theo Kralicek, June 12, 1953 (div. 1969); children: Jean Ann, Alan Weld. Personnel evaluation asso. Gen. Motors Inst., Flint, 1955-60; supr. personnel research B.F. Goodrich Co., Akron, 1960-67; sr. manpower adv. Mobil Oil Corp., N.Y.C., 1967—; lectr. adult edn. div. U. Akron, part-time. With U.S. Army, 1951-52. Mem. Am. Psychol. Assn., Am. Psychol. Soc., Sigma Xi, Phi Kappa Phi, Pi Gamma Mu. Home: 601 Rosery Rd E Apt 3905 Largo FL 33770-3829

TURNER, WILLIAM JOSEPH, retired psychiatrist; b. Wilkinsburg, Pa., Sept. 22, 1907; s. William Moore and Phoebe Emma (Smith) T.; m. Kathryn Morrow, Aug. 12, 1925 (div. May 1959); children: William Morrow, James Quigly. BS, Pa. State Coll., 1927; MA, Johns Hopkins U., 1933. Cert. in medicine. Rotating intern Harriburg Hosp., Harrisburg, Pa., 1933-34; asst. resident pathology Balt. City Hosp., 1934-35; asst. resident medicine Billings Hosp., U. Chgo., 1935-36; staff physician Cresson The Hosp., Cresson, Pa., 1936-37; staff psychiatrist VA Hosp., N. Little Rock, Ark., 1937-40; psychiatrist VA Hosp., L.A., 1940-41, Northport, N.Y., 1941-50; rsch. psychiatrist Cen. Islip State Hosp., Cen. Islip, N.Y., 1954-76, SUNY, Stony Brook, 1976-82; prof. emeritus psychiatry, 1982-90, ret.; med. dir. Dreyfus Med. Found., N.Y.C., 1964-68, cons., 1966—. Author papers on subjects in field. Pres., various positions Suffolk County Dist. br. Am. Psychiat. Assn., 1960-92; chmn. com. for liaison with lay groups S.C.D.P. Lt. col. U.S. Army, 1943-46. Fellow Am. Psychiat. Assn. (life); mem. AMA (life), Am. Coll. Neuropsychopharmacology (life), AAAS, N.Y. Acad. Sci., Am. Chem. Soc., Soc. Biol. Psychiatry.

TURNER, WILLIAM REDD, urologist, educator; b. Portsmouth, Va., June 20, 1936; s. William Redd and Mary (Rudd) T.; m. Kathleen Bouldin Stevenson; children: William Redd, Randall Williams, John Persons. BS, Davidson Coll., 1958; MD, Med. U. S.C., 1962. Diplomate Am. Bd. Urology. Resident in urology Med. U. S.C., Charleston, 1962-68, asst. prof. urology, 1970-74, assoc. prof. pediat., urology, 1978-80, prof. urology and pediat., 1980—; chief divsn. urology Charleston VA Hosp., 1970-75; dir. Am. Ravenel Meml. lectureships dept. urology Med. U. S.C., 1971-75, acting chmn. dept. urology, 1974-75, chmn. faculty senate, 1976-77, chief divsn. pediat. urology, 1978-87, chmn. univ. grievance com., 1980-84, acting chmn. dept. urology, 1988-91, chmn. dept. urology, 1991—; assoc. med. dir. Med. U. S.C. Hosp., 1986-88; cons. urology VA, Roper Hosp., Bon Secours St. Francis Xavier Hosp., Charleston Meml. Hosp. Contbr. over 50 articles to profl. jours. Trustee Charleston Mus., 1974-75, 93—, mem. exec. com., 1975-84, v.p., 1980-85; trustee Am. Found. for Urologic Disease; ruling elder First Scots Presbyn. Ch., 1975-82, 84—, clk. of session, 1980-82; exec. com. Charleston Presbytery, 1983-84, chmn. Presbytery boundary com., 1984-86, vice chmn. exec. com., 1984, chmn. exec. com., 1985-86, exec. com. Cursillos in Christianity, 1989—, ; bd. dirs. Friends of State Mus., 1986-87; mem. Charles Webb Easter Seal Ctr. Cmty./Profl. Adv. Coun., 1989—. Capt. maj. USMC, 1968-70. Recipient Trident Vol. Physician of Yr. award, 1989. Fellow ACS, Am. Acad. Pediat.; mem. AMA (Merit award 1974), Am. Urol. Assn. (sec. 1992—, bd. dirs. 1988—, sec. S.E. sect. 1985-87, pres. sect. 1987-88), Am. Assn. Clin. Urologists, Soc. Univ. Urologists, Soc. for Pediat. Urology, S.C. Med Soc., Soc. Internat. D'Urologie, Carolina Urol. Assn., Charleston County Med. Soc., So. Soc. Pediat. Urologists, So. Soc. Urol. Surgeons, S.C. Urol. Assn., Brit. Assn. Urologic Surgeons (hon.), Alpha Omega Alpha. Office: Med Univ SC Dept Urology 171 Ashley Ave Charleston SC 29425-0001

TURO, JOANN K., psychoanalyst, psychotherapist, consultant; b. Westerly, R.I., Feb. 13, 1938; d. Angelo and Anna Josephine (Drew) T. BS in Biology and Chemistry, U. R.I., 1959; MA in Human Rels. and Psychology, Ohio U., 1964; postgrad., NYU, 1966-71, N.Y. Freudian Inst., N.Y.C., 1977-85, Mental Health Inst., N.Y.C., 1977-80. Rsch. asst. biochemistry studies on schizophrenia Harvard U. Med. Sch., Boston, 1959-60; indsl. psychology asst. studies on managerial success N.Y. Telephone Co., N.Y.C., 1964-66; staff psychologist Testing and Advisement Ctr. NYU, 1966-70; psychology intern Kings County Hosp., Bklyn., 1970-71; staff psychologist M.D.C. Psychol. Svcs., N.Y.C., 1971-72; clin. dir. Greenwich House Substance Abuse Clinic, N.Y.C., 1973-76; cons. psychotherapist Mental Health Consultation Ctr., N.Y.C., 1977-82; pvt. practice psychoanlysis and psychotherapy N.Y.C., 1981—; mental health cons. Bklyn. Ctr. for Psychotherapy, 1976-78; with Psychoanaltyic Consultation Svcs., 1994—; presenter in field. Mem. Itnernat. Psychoanalytic Assn. (cert., presenter fall meeting 1995), Soc. for Personality Assessment (cert.), N.Y. Freudian Soc. (cert., co-chmn. grad. com. 1985-86, mem. continuing edn. com. 1986—, pub. rels. com. 1992-93, psychoanalytic consult svc. 1994—, tng. and supr. psychoanalyst 1995), N.Y. Coun. Psychoanalytic Psychotherapists (cert.), Met. Assn. for Coll. Mental Health Practitoners (cert.). Office: 175 W 12th St Apt 9H New York NY 10011-8221

TUROCK, JANE PARSICK, nutritionist; b. Peckville, Pa., Apr. 15, 1947; d. Paul Charles and Elizabeth Dorothy (Mistysyn) Parsick; m. Michael John, July 12, 1968; children: Eric Matthew, Nathan Andrew, J. Seth, Melanie Kay. BS, Marywood Coll., Scranton, 1969; MS, Marywood Coll., 1982. Registered dietitian; cert. nutrition specialist. Registered dietitian Jane P. Turock, Scranton, Pa., 1985--; founder and chief dietitian Gastric Bubble, Scranton, Pa., 1986--; prof. Penn State Coll., Scranton, Pa., 1987--; dietitian & presenter WNEP TV Healthwatch, Avoca, Pa., 1988--; dir. & chief dietitian Vascular Inst. of Northeast Pa., Pa., 1989--; owner, mgr. Nutrition...Plus/Fitness Unlimited, Scranton, Pa., 1991—; cons. Home Health Care Assn., Clarks Summit, 1985—; dietitian Clarks Summit, 1985—; founder Nat. Nutrition Month Bakeoff; dir. Camp Jane. Treas. Lackawanna County Med. Soc. Aux., 1974-76, pres., 1979-80, bd. dirs., 1980-81; allocations com. United Way Lackawanna County, 1990—; mem. bd. dirs. Lupus Found., 1995, St. Francis of Assissi Kitchen, 1995. Mem. Am. Dietic Assn., Northeast Dist. Pa. Dietic Diet Therapy, Consulting Nutritionists in Pvt. Practice, Am. Diabetic Assn., Northeast Womens Network, Allied Wedding Firm. Republican. Roman Catholic. Office: Nutrition Plus Fitness Unltd 815 Smith St Scranton PA 18504-3150 also: Abington Family Svcs 211 N State St Clarks Summit PA 18411-1087 also: Lady Jane Inc dba The Ski Habit Elk Mountain PA 18470

TURPEINEN, URSULA LEILA, clinical chemist; b. Helsinki, Finland, Nov. 28, 1950; d. Osmo Kalervo and Aili Ester (Nuppola) T. BS, Helsinki U., 1972, MS in Biochemistry, 1975, PhD in Biochemistry, 1984. Asst. dept. biochemistry Helsinki U., 1976-83; asst. chemist Helsinki U. Cen. Hosp., 1982-86, chemist, 1986—; invited reviewer Am. Assn. Clin. Chemistry, 1991—. Office: Helsinki U Cen Hosp, Lab Haartmaninkatu 2, 00290 Helsinki Finland

TURRELL, EUGENE SNOW, retired psychiatrist; b. Hyattsville, Md., Feb. 27, 1919; m. Denise Deuprey, Dec. 26, 1942 (div. Jan. 1976); children: David Hillyer, Gregory Sherman (dec.); m. Zenobia A. Hopper, Apr. 16, 1988; stepchildren: Elizabeth Ann Crofoot, Mary Jane Cooper. BS, Ind. U., 1939, MD, 1947. Diplomate Am. Bd. Psychiatry and Neurology. Intern Peter Bent Brigham Hosp., Boston, 1947-48; resident physician Kandakee (Ill.) State Hosp., 1948-49; clin. asst. psychiatry U. Calif., San Francisco, 1949-51; asst. prof. Ind. U. Sch. Medicine, 1952-53, assoc. prof., 1953-58; prof., chmn. dept. psychiatry Marquette U. Sch. Medicine, 1958-63, clin. prof. psychiatry, 1963-69; lectr. U. Calif., San Francisco, 1969-75; assoc. prof. Ind. U., 1975-80, prof., 1980-89, prof. emeritus, 1989—; dean emeritus San Diego County Psychiat. Hosp., 1995—, 1995—; assoc. clin. prof. U. Calif., San Diego, 1991-95; ret., 1995; mem., bd. dirs. Community Addictions Svcs. Agy, Indpls., 1975-79, pres. bd., 1976-77. Contr. articles to profl. jours. Lt. USNR, 1950-52. Recipient Certs. of Appreciation Office Sci. Rsch. and Devel., 1945, VA, 1964, Ind. U. Found., 1966. Fellow Am. Psychiat. Assn. (life); mem. AMA (Physician's Recognition award 1978-96), AAAS, Calif. State Med. Assn., Calif. State Psychiat. Assn., San Diego County Med. Soc., San Diego County Soc. Psychiat. Physicians, Sigma Xi, Alpha Omega Alpha. Democrat. Episcopalian.

TURRILL, FRED LOVEJOY, surgeon; b. Redlands, Calif., Sept. 14, 1922; s. Gardner Stilson and Virginia Marie (Johnson) T.; m. Edith Mae Brown, Mar. 17, 1951; children: Brian Casey, Kevin Michael, Ann Louise, Mark. AS, Glendale Coll., 1942; BSE, U. Mich., 1944; MD, U. So. Calif., 1950. Diplomate Am. Bd. Surgery. Intern L.A. County/U. So. Calif. Med. Ctr., 1950-52, resident surgery, 1952-56; surgeon Turrill, Shader & Myles, Glendale, Calif., 1956—; prof. surgery U. So. Calif., L.A., 1974—. Contbr. articles to profl. jours. With U.S. Army, 1942-46. Grantee USPS, 1956-57. Mem. ACS (gov. 1977-84), Collegium Internat. Chirurgiae, Pacific Coast Surg. Assn. (councillor 1980-83), We. Surg. Assn., Soc. Grad. Surgeons (life hon., pres. 1970-71), L.A. Surg. Soc. (pres. 1975). Republican.

TURTIL, LAWRENCE CHARLES, psychiatrist; b. N.Y.C., Dec. 30, 1951; s. Joseph Fredric and Estelle Rebecca (Heifferman) T. BA cum laude, U. Pa., 1972; MD, Georgetown U., 1977. Diplomate Am. Bd. Psychiatry and Neurology, Am. Bd. Internal Medicine, Am. Bd. Adolscent Psychiatry. Resident in internal medicine Lenox Hill Hosp., N.Y.C., 1977-80, attending physician emergency svc., 1980-81, attending physician dept. psychiatry, 1989-90; asst. chief inpatient psychiatry unit Lenox Hill Hosp., 1990-94; resident in psychiatry Cornell, N.Y. Hosp., White Plains, 1981-84; attending physician N.Y. Hosp., Westchester div., 1984-85; med. dir. Four Winds Hosp., Katonah, N.Y., 1985-89; pvt. practice N.Y.C. & Katonah, N.Y.; attending psychiatrist Manhattan Psychiatric Ctr., N.Y.C., 1994; med. dir. Four Winds Hosp., Katonah, N.Y., 1994—. Mem. Am. Psychiat. Assn. Office: 65 E 76th St Ste 1B New York NY 10021

TURTLE, WILLIAM JAMES, pediatrician; b. Providence, July 28, 1959; s. Quentin Charles and Albina Esther (Cestrone) T.; m. Jean Marie Smith, Oct. 3, 1987; 1 child, William Raymond. ScB, Brown U., Providence, 1981; MD, U. Rochester, N.Y., 1985. Diplomate Am. Bd. Pediatrics. Pediatric resident R.I. Hosp., Providence, 1985-88, chief pediatric resident, 1988-89; pediatrician East Bay Pediatrics, Barrington, R.I., 1989-93, Harvard Cmty. Health Plan, Warwick, R.I., 1993—; asst. clin. instr. pediatrics R.I. Hosp., Providence, 1989-96. Mem. St. Luke's Cath. Ch., Barrington, 1990—. Fellow Am. Acad. Pediatrics. Roman Catholic. Office: Harvard Cmty Health Plan 400 Bald Hill Rd Warwick RI 02806

TUTKO, ROBERT JOSEPH, radiology administrator, educator; b. Buffalo, Nov. 18, 1955; s. Robert Edward and Agatha (Pagliaccio) T.; m. Susan Joy Biddle, Oct. 29, 1976; children: Suzan Denise, Nicola Marie. Student, SUNY, Brockport, 1973-74; AAS, Trocaire Coll., 1982; BS, Pacific Western U., 1992, MS, PhD, 1995. Dir. X-ray svcs. Fla. Ctr. for Knee Surgery, Clearwater, 1985-86; surgery X-ray technologist St. Joseph's Hosp., Tampa, Fla., 1986-90; dir. radiology Met. Gen. Hosp., Pinellas Park, Fla., 1990-91; dir. med. imaging Univ. Gen. Hosp. and Women's Med. Ctr., Seminole, Fla., 1991-92; program dir. Sch. Radiology St. Joseph Hosp., Memphis, 1992-94; physician asst. DeSoto Family Practice, Olive Branch, Miss., 1995—; founder, dir. continuing edn. TCB Med. Edn., Palm Harbor, Fla., 1985-91, pres., CEO, Germantown, Tenn., 1992—; tchr. Hillsborough County Schs., Tampa, 1989-92; lectr. profl. confs.; nat. radiology specialist Concorde Career Colls., Inc., Kansas City, Mo., 1994-95. Author: Limited X-Ray Course and Curriculum, 1995; contbr. articles to profl. jours. County chmn. radiology group Pinellas County Non-Profit Hosp. Venture Group, 1990-91; lectr. Pinellas County Sch. System, 1984-91. Sgt. U.S. Army, 1974-75. Recipient commendation letter Pinellas Park Police Dept., 1991. Mem. Am. Legion, Am. Educators Radiol. Scis., Am. Soc. Radiol. Technologists, Tenn. Soc. Radiol. Technologists, Fla. Soc. Radiol. Technologists, Ga. Soc. Radiol. Technologists, Colo. Soc. Radiol. Technologists, Am. Healthcare Radiology Adminstrs., KC (treas. 1989-91, Knight of Month Dec. 1989). Democrat. Roman Catholic. Home and Office: 4701 Falling Oak Cove Memphis TN 38125-4723

TUTT, NANCY JEAN, physical therapist; b. Washington, July 4; d. Lewis Jackson and Louise Monroe (Abbott) T. BS, U. Ky., 1947; MA, Columbia U., 1951, Cert. in Phys. Therapy, 1952. Staff Columbia-Presbyn. Med. Ctr., N.Y.C., 1952-54, 56-57; sr. phys. therapist St. Vincent's Hosp., N.Y.C., 1957-60; staff Hans Kraus, M.D., N.Y.C., 1955-56; pvt. practice N.Y.C., 1955-63; phys. therapist James Ewing Hosp., N.Y.C., 1962-63; sr. phys. therapist Inst. Phys Rehab., N.Y.C., 1963-66, Mt. Sinai Hosp./Elmhurst City Hosp., N.Y., 1966-68; asst. dir. phys. rehab. U. N.C. at Dix Hosp., Raleigh, 1968-70, Medictr., Raleigh, 1970-71; pres. Therapeutic Home Care Assocs., Inc., Raleigh, 1970-72, Tammy Lynn Ctr., Raleigh, 1971-72; with Rex Hosp. Wellness Ctr., Raleigh, 1991—. Vol. VA Hosp., Durham, N.C., 1980-82, Rex Hosp., Raleigh, 1983-84, Duke Inst. for Learning in Retirement, Durham, 1985—. With WAC, 1943-45. Named Ky. Col.; March of Dimes scholar, 1951-52. Mem. AAUW, DAV, Am. Soc. on Aging, Am. Phys. Therapy Assn. Home: PO Box 51536 Durham NC 27717-1536

TUTTLE, JACQUELINE CORA, pediatrician; b. Boston, Mar. 1, 1948; d. David F. and Becky H. Tuttle. DO cum laude, Tex. Coll. Osteo. Medicine, 1983; MA in Spanish, Stanford U., 1971. Diplomate Am. Bd. Pediatrics. Intern in pediats. U. Chgo. Hosps./Clinics, Los Gatos, Calif., 1983-85; resident Children's Meml. Hosp., Chgo., 1985-86, St. Francis Med. Ctr.-U. Ill., Peoria; pvt. practice Los Gatos, Calif.; clin. asst. prof. pediats. Kirksville Coll. Osteo. Medicine; preceptor in pediats.physicians asst. program U. So. Calif. Sch. Medicine, 1991, clin. lectr., 1992. Mem. Am. Assn. Pediatrics, Am. Osteo. Assn. Home: 713 Alvarado Row Rear Stanford CA 94305-1010 Office: 700 W Parr Ste A1 Los Gatos CA 95030

TUTTLE, JEREMY BALLOU, neurobiologist; b. N.Y.C., Oct. 9, 1947; s. John Bauman and Charlotte Marion (Root) T.; m. Sara Jane Stasko, Mar. 23, 1971. AB, U. Rochester, 1969; PhD, Johns Hopkins U., 1977. Postdoctoral fellow U. Conn., Storrs, 1976-79, vis. asst. prof., 1980, asst. prof. in residence, 1981-84; asst. prof. physiology U. Va., Charlottesville, 1984-87, asst. prof. neuroscience, 1987-90, rsch. asst. prof., 1990-93, assoc. prof. urology neuroscience, 1993—. Contbr. articles to Devel. Biology, Synapse, Jour. Neurochemistry, others. Chmn. mem. Common Area Planning Commn., 1984-87; pres. bd. Earlysville Forest Homeowner's Assn., 1986-89, Earlysville, Va. U. Rochester Hon. scholar, 1965-69, Regent's scholar for Medicine, 1969, NIH predoctoral fellow, 1971-75, Nat. Rsch. Svc. fellow, 1976-79, Nat. Spinal Cord Injury Found. rsch. fellow, 1979-80; recipient Rsch. Career Devel. award NINCDS/NIH, Muscular Dystrophy Assn. Rsch. award, 1990—; Am. Heart Assn. grantee, 1987-89, 90—. Home: 900 Stillwater Ln Earlysville VA 22936-9538 Office: U Va Med Sch PO Box 230 Charlottesville VA 22902-0230

TUTTLE, LAURA SHIVE, healthcare educator, administrator; b. Morristown, N.J., Nov. 19, 1962; d. Richard Byron and Patricia (Butler) Shive; m. Richard Lawrence Tuttle, Dec. 15, 1984; 1 child, Marissa Lynn. BSN, Skidmore Coll., 1984; postgrad., Northeastern U., 1992—. RN. Pub. health nurse Navy Relief Vis. Nurse, San Diego, 1985-86; home health nurse Trend Home Health, San Diego, 1986-87, Scripps Home Health Care, San Diego, 1987, Community Health and Counseling Svcs., Bangor, Maine, 1988-89; clin. svcs. coord. Bangor Dist. Nursing Assn., 1989-91; clin. supr. Spl. Care Home Health Svcs., Woburn, Mass., 1991; br. dir. Spl. Care Home Health Svcs., Quincy, Mass., 1991-92; founder, pres. Career Visions, Inc., Brockton, Mass., 1992—; nursing instr. Eastern Maine Tech. Coll., Bangor, 1988-89; pub. speaker Maine Vets. Homes, Augusta, 1991, Bangor Dist. Nursing Assn., 1990-91. Co-author: Clinical Care of the Geriatric Patient, 1991. Mem. NAFE, Prof. Ski Instrs. Assn. (cert. 1982). Republican.

TUTTON, ROGER HEADLEY, radiologist; b. Decorah, Iowa, Feb. 25, 1931; s. Robert Millard and Marion (Church) T.; m. Kathryn Stumme, June 10, 1955 (dec. 1985); m. Janet Brady, Mar. 21, 1987. BA, State U. Iowa, 1951, MD, 1955; MS, U. Minn., 1962. Radiologist Harrisburg (Pa.) Hosp., 1962-63, Ochsner Clinic and Found. Hosp., New Orleans, 1963—. Fellow Am. Coll. Radiology, Radiol. Soc. N.Am., Roentgen Ray Soc. Episcopalian. Office: Ochsner Clinic 1514 Jefferson Hwy New Orleans LA 70121-2429

TUTUSKA, PETER JAMES, cardiac surgeon; b. Bethpage, N.Y., Sept. 12, 1956; s. Peter John and Frances Charlotte (Gorski) T.; m. Deborah Lynn Millett, May 21, 1983; children: Breana Elyce, Ryne Peter. BSEE, Northwestern U., 1978; MD, Albany Med. Coll., 1982. Diplomate Am. Bd. Surgery, Am. Bd. Thoracic Surgery. Resident in gen. surgery Northwestern U., Chgo., 1982-87; resident in cardiac surgery Case-Western Res. U., Cleve., 1987-89; cardiothoracic surgeon Stormont Vail Regional Med. Ctr., Topeka, 1989—. Fellow ACS; mem. IEEE, STS, FACCP, FACC, Tau Beta Pi, Eta Kappa Nu. Office: Cardiothoracic Surgery PA 901 SW Garfield Ave Topeka KS 66606-1670

TUXEN, ANDERS MORCH, physician; b. Svoldrup, Denmark, May 17, 1930; s. Harry Viggo and Esther (Trier Morch) T.; m. Inger Jensen, July 5, 1953; children: Marianne, Anette, Troels. Degree in pharmacy, Royal Sch. Pharmacy, Copenhagen, 1953; MD, U. Copenhagen, 1961, U. Lund, Sweden, 1962. Scientific asst. U. Chgo., 1954-55; med. dir. Hoffman-La Roche, Basle, Switzerland, 1963-68, Merck Sharp & Dohme, Copenhagen, 1968-76; shipsdoctor Trainingship Danmark, Copenhagen, 1981, Royal Viking Star, Bergen, Norway, 1984; med. attachment Danmarks Radio, Copenhagen,

1965—. Author seven med. books; med. editor Lademann's Leksikon, Copenhagen, 1977-80, Lademann's Medicinskabet, Copenhagen, 1977—, Morgenavisen Jyllands-Posten, Aarhus, Denmark, 1987—. Decorated Order Ouissam Alouit Cherifien, Ridder at Dannebrog. Mem. Danish Sci. Writers Assn. (bd. dirs. 1991-93), Med. Soc. Copenhagen (v.p. 1991-93, pres. 1993-95). Home: Dronninggaards Alle 93, DK 2840 Holte Denmark Office: Laegerne over Virum Apotek, Frederiksdalsvej 75, DK 2830 Virum Denmark

TUZIL, TERESA JORDAN, clinical social worker, psychotherapist; b. N.Y.C., May 13, 1948; d. Lester Francis and Kathleen Geraldine (Brady) Jordan; B.A., St. John's U., 1970; M.S.W., Hunter Coll., 1973, certified in gerontology, 1977; m. Joseph Stephen Tuzil, Jan. 15, 1972; children—Joseph IV, Brian Joseph. Social worker Salvation Army Foster Care and Adoption Services, N.Y.C., 1971-72; sr. caseworker Jewish Assn. for Services to the Aged, N.Y.C., 1973-78; program cons. Community Council of Greater N.Y., N.Y.C., 1978-79; pvt. practice individual and family psychotherapy, Seaford, N.Y., 1976—; caseworker Nassau County Dept. Social Services Children's Protective Service, 1983-90, Pennsula Counseling Ctr. Outpatient Alcoholism Treatment Ctr.; adj. clin. instr. Hunter Grad. Sch. Social Work, 1975-78; field instr. Grad. Sch. Social Work, Rutgers U., 1975-77; program cons. Assn. for Services to Aged, Bklyn., 1981—. Certified, registered clin. social worker, N.Y. Mem. Nat. Assn. Social Workers, Acad. Certified Social Workers. Editor: Jour. of Gerontological Social Work, 1977—; contbr. articles to profl. publs. in field. Home and Office: 3859 Tiana St Seaford NY 11783-3508

TWEDDELL, JAMES SCOTT, surgeon; b. Cin., Sept. 2, 1959; s. Richard and Marie (Bowen) T.; m. Sue Ellen Stamper, June 1, 1985; children: Sarah, Alison, Caroline. BA in Zoology, Miami U., 1981; MD, U. Cin., 1985. Resident in surgery NYU Med. Ctr., 1985-87; rsch. fellow Washington U. Med. Ctr., St. Louis, 1987-89, resident in surgery, 1989-91, fellow in cardiothoracic surgery, 1991-93; asst. prof. surgery and pediatrics Med. Coll. Wis., Milw., 1993—. Contbr. articles to profl. jours. Mem. ACS, Soc. Thoracic Surgery, Am. Heart Assn., Alpha Omega Alpha, Phi Beta Kappa. Office: Childrens Hosp Wis MS 715 9000 W Wisconsin Ave Milwaukee WI 53201

TWEEDY, ROBYN K., healthcare institute administrator; b. Cape Girardeau, Mo., Dec. 19, 1966; d. Ron and Lois (Hitt) T. BBA, U. Miss.; MHA, Washington U., St. Louis. Adminstrv. fellow Clarkson Hosp., Omaha, 1992-93, dir. cancer inst., 1993—. Office: Clarkson Hosp 44th and Dewey Ave Omaha NE 68105

TWISDALE, HAROLD WINFRED, dentist; b. Roanoke Rapids, N.C., Apr. 28, 1933; s. James Robert and Elma (Smith) T.; m. Barbara Ann Edmonds, Aug. 2, 1958 (div. Apr. 1974); children: Harold Winfred, Leigh Ann.; m. Frances Jean Winstead, July 1983. B.S. in Dentistry, U. N.C., 1955, D.D.S., 1958. Individual practice dentistry Charlotte, N.C., 1961—; head, dept. dental prosthetics Meml. Hosp., 1964-66; lectr. dental subjects.; pres., gen. mgr. WCTU-TV, Charlotte Telecasters, Inc., 1967-69, WATU-TV, Augusta, Ga., Augusta Telecasters, Inc., 1968-69, Television Presentations, Inc., Charlotte, 1967-69; partner Twisdale and Steel Assos., Charlotte, 1965-70; propr. Twisdale Enterprises, Charlotte, 1965-70; Pres. Memphis Telecasters, Inc., 1966-76, Va. Telecasters, Inc., Richmond, 1966—, Durham-Raleigh Telecasters, Inc., Durham, N.C., 1966-70, Gentil Elite, Inc., 1979—. Transp. chmn. Miss N.C. Pageant, 1965; v.p. N.C. Jaycees, 1963-64; Trustee Boys Home, Lake Waccomaw, N.C., 1966-67. Served to capt. USAF, 1958-60. Recipient various awards Charlotte Jaycees, 1962-66. Mem. ADA, N.C. Dental Found., N.C. Dental Soc., Charlotte Dental Soc. (chmn. various coms. 1961—), Am. Analgesia Soc., Internat. Analgesic Soc. (dir. 1980-85), N.C. Dental Soc. Anesthesiology (v.p. 1983-84), Charlotte Analgesia Study Club (co-founder 1970), N.C. 2d Dist. Dental Soc., Metrolina Dental Soc. (founder 1994, pres. 1994-95), U. N.C. Dental Alumni Assn., Southeastern Analgesia Soc. (founder 1972, pres. 1972-74), Lambda Chi Alpha, Delta Sigma Delta. Republican. Methodist. Home: 4212 Burning Tree Dr 2221 Streatley Ln Matthews NC 28105-6648 Office: 6623 Executive Circle #110 PO Box 25528 Charlotte NC 28212

TWIST-RUDOLPH, DONNA JOY, neurophysiology and psychology researcher; b. Cape May, N.J., Dec. 3, 1955; d. Donald and Mary Ann (Johnson) Twist; m. Daniel Jay Rudolph, Jan. 10, 1981; children: Andrew, Adam, Matthew. BS, Boston U., 1978; MA, SUNY, Stony Brook, 1984; PhD, SUNY, 1986. Licensed phys. therapist, N.Y., Conn. Teaching asst., dept. phys. therapy N.Y. U., 1980; teaching asst., dept. psychology SUNY, Stony Brook, 1982-83, teaching asst., dept. grad. psychology, 1984; intern, dept. rehab. medicine N.Y. U. Med. Ctr., Rusk Inst. Rehab. Medicine, N.Y.C., 1984-86, postdoctoral fellow, rsch. scientist, 1986-87; dir. rsch. and edn., chief of phys. therapy Norwalk (Conn.) Hosp., 1987-96; dir. rsch. and dir. rehab. svcs. Norwalk (Conn.) Hosp.-ACRM, 1994—; state bd. examiner N.Y. State Phys. Therapy Licensing Exam. Profl. Svcs., Albany, 1986—; adj. asst. prof. Mt. Sinai Sch. Med., N.Y.C., 1990—. Exec. prodr. All the King's Horses, All the King's Men: How to Prevent Head Injury in Our Children (Gold award Houston Internat. Film Festival 1992). Named Outstanding Young Woman Am., 1981, 83; grantee Easter Seal Rsch. Found., 1985-87, Rehab. Svcs. Adminstr. Dept. Edn., 1991; recipient Therapeutic Techs. Ins. award, 1989. Mem. Am. Phys. Therapy Assn., Am. Congress Rehab. Medicine, N.Y. Acad. Scis. Home: 381 Hemlock Rd Fairfield CT 06430-1857 Office: Norwalk Hosp 24 Stevens St Norwalk CT 06850-3813

TWITTY, H. R., hospital official; b. Columbia, S.C., May 9, 1941; s. Archie Hazel Twitty and Sara (Murphy) Avritt; m. Marlene Faye Wingate, June 9, 1961; children: William Thomas, Michael David. BA, Tenn. Temple Coll., 1964. Cert. profl. for hosp. material mgmt. Mgr. store room Erlanger Hosp., Chattanooga, 1961-69; purchasing agt. Meml. Hosp., Chattanooga, 1969-71, dir. material, 1972—, bd. dirs. credit union, 1986-92. Chmn. bd. deacon Duncan Park Bapt. Ch., Chattanooga, 1983, 88, deacon, 1986-88, 90-92, 95-96, leadership com., 1995-96. Mem. Am. Hosp. Assn. Purchasing Mgrs. (cert. sr.), Internat. Hosp. Soc. Material Mgrs. (Disting. Profl.), Tenn. Hosp. Soc. Material Mgrs. (bd. dirs. region III 1979-82, pres. 1983-84, 89-92, Mgr. of Yr. award 1991, bd. dirs. 1994—), Chattanooga Area Purchasing Soc. (pres. 1985-87), Optimist. Home: 2017 Prater Rd Rossville GA 30741 Office: Meml Hosp 2525 Desales Ave Chattanooga TN 37404-1161

TWOMBLY, PATRICIA DUDLEY, healthcare executive; b. Haverhill, Mass., Sept. 26, 1946; d. Eugene Cyrus and Mary Ellen (Gould) Dudley; m. Milton G. Twombly, July 26, 1969; 1 child, Kathryn. RN, Boston City Hosp., 1967; BA, Emmanuel Coll., 1976; M in Pub. Health, Boston U., 1981; JD, New England Sch. Law, 1992. RN, Mass; bar: Mass. 1992. Head nurse surg. dept. Boston City Hosp., 1967-72; nurse epidemiologist Mass. Dept. Pub. Health, 1972-74; utilization specialist Blue Cross/Blue Shield of Mass., 1975-76; mgr. rev., mgr. tng., spl. projects mgr., UR supr. Ea. Mass. Profl. Stds. Rev. Orgn., Inc., 1976-83; dir. admitting Holy Family Hosp., 1983-84; dir. med. rev. systems Peer Rev. Analysis, Inc., 1984-87; mgr. utilization mgmt./quality assurance Tufts Associated Health Plan, 1987-95; dir. utilization mgmt. Healthsource Inc., 1995—. Mem. Mass. Bar Assn. (health law divsn.), Am. Soc. of Law (medicine and ethics com.). Office: Healthsource Inc 2 College Park Dr Hooksett NH 03106-1636

TYBURCZY, JOHN ADRIAN, surgeon; b. Alameda, Calif., Dec. 24, 1953; s. Joseph Andrew and Irene Janet (Christo) T. BS, Lewis and Clark Coll., 1975; MD, N.Y. Med. Coll., 1979. Diplomate Am. Bd. Surgery. Resident in gen. surgery Oreg. Health Scis. U., Portland, 1979-83; resident in gen. surgery San Joaquin Gen. Hosp., Stockton, Calif., 1985-87, chief resident, 1987-88; pvt. practice, Elko, Nev., 1989—; chief surgery Elko Gen. Hosp., 1992-94, chief staff, 1994-95. Vice pres. for med. affairs Elko chpt. Am. Cancer Soc., 1990-92. Fellow ACS (participant 2d group of 100 1995), Southwestern Surg. Congress; mem. Am. Soc. Gen. Surgeons (charter), Boondocks Med. Soc. Office: Elko Clinic 762 14th St Elko NV 89801

TYCKOSKI, STACEY ALLISON, optometrist; b. Flint, Mich., Dec. 23, 1965; d. Louis James and Marily Frances (Benson) Alaria; m. William Gerald Tyckoski, Oct. 8, 1994. AS, Ferris State U., 1986; OD, Ill. Coll. Optometry, 1990. Optometrist Lapeer (Mich.) County Vision Ctr., 1990—. Mem. Flint Symphonic Wind Ensemble, 1990-95. Mem. Zonta Club (corr. sec. 1995). Office: Opticare Vision Ctr 700 S Main St Ste 105 Lapeer MI 48446 Address: 5457 Old Franklin Rd Grand Blanc MI 48439-8623

TYDELL, PATRICIA ANN, nurse, researcher; b. Chgo., Jan. 2, 1949; m. Arnold J. Tydell, June 26, 1971; children: Jill, Scott. BSN, No. Ill. U., 1971; MSN, Loyola U., 1974; MPH, U. Ill., Chgo., 1993. RN, Ill.; CPHQ, Ill. Staff nurse ICU/Critical Care Unit Resurrection Hosp., Chgo., 1971-73; staff nurse open heart unit St. Francis Hosp., Evanston, Ill., 1973-74; instr., mgr. Luth. Gen. Hosp., Park Ridge, Ill., 1974-84; staff devel./QI Condell Hosp., Libertyville, Ill., 1984-89; mktg./comm. rels. St. Therese Hosp., Waukegan, Ill., 1989-91; QI/rschr. VA Med. Ctr., North Chicago, Ill., 1991—; instr. health mgmt. Nat. Louis U., Evanston, Ill., 1987-89; CPR, ACLS instr., 1986—; cmty. educator, 1986-91. Chmn. allocations com. United Way of Lake County, Green Oaks, Ill., 1991—. Office: North Chicago VA Med Ctr 3001 Green Bay Rd North Chicago IL 60061

TYGSTRUP, NIELS, hepatology educator; b. Vejle, Denmark, May 27, 1926; s. Svend Linde and Thora Katrine (Tork) T.; m. Inge Sort, May 27, 1950; children: Pernille, Frederik. MD, U. Copenhagen, 1952, DSc, 1966. Cert. specialist in internal medicine, clin. physiology. Intern Copenhagen Hosps., 1952-53, 57-65; rsch. fellow med. dept. B Rigshospitalet U. Hosp., 1953-56; asst. prof. med. dept. A Rigshospital, U. Copenhagen, 1965-69, chmn., 1976—; prof. internal medicine U. Copenhagen, 1969—. Editor books on hepatology; contbr. aritcles on hepatology to profl. jours. Pres. Royal Danish Med. Rsch. Found., Copenhagen, 1977-79; mem. Gov. Com. Assessment Medicine, 1977-85. Recipient Benzon Found. prize, Copenhagen, 1966, Klein Found. prize, Copenhagen, 1972, Novo Found. prize, Copenhagen, 1976, Bolte Found. prize, 1987. Mem. Swedish Soc. Gastroenterology (hon.), German Soc. Gastroenterology (hon.), Royal Danish Acad. Scis. and Letters, European Assn. Study of Liver (pres. 1995), Internat. Assoc. Study of Liver (pres. 1974-78), Danish Soc. Internal Medicine (pres. 1971-74, Hagedorn prize 1983). Home: 6 Wiedeweltsgade, DK 2100 Copenhagen Denmark Office: Rigshospitalet, 9 Blegdamsvej, DK 2100 Copenhagen Denmark

TYHACH, RICHARD JOSEPH, medical products executive, researcher; b. N.Y.C., Aug. 14, 1949; s. Joseph and Pauline Tyhach; m. Elaine Barbara Goral, Nov. 11, 1973; children: Jeffrey, Matthew. BA, CUNY 1970, MA, 1973, PhD, 1976. Postdoctoral fellow Med. Sch. Harvard U., Cambridge, Mass., 1976-78; rsch. scientist diagnostics div. Miles Inc., Elkhart, Ind., 1978-81, staff scientist diagnostics div., 1981-85, supr. R & D diagnostics div., 1985-87, mgr. R & D diagnostics div., 1987-89, dir. urine chemistry products R & D diagnostics div., 1989-92, dir. reagt. devel./instrument engring., urine chemistry unit, 1992-95; dir. new products urine chemistry unit Bayer Corp. Bus. Group Diagnostics, Elkhart, 1995—. Inventee in field. Damon Runyon-Walter Winchell Cancer Fund fellow, 1976. Mem. Am. Assn. for Clin. Chemistry, Am. Chem. Soc., Phi Beta Kappa, Sigma Xi. Office: Bayer Corp Business Group Diagnostics 1884 Miles Ave Elkhart IN 46514-2201

TYLER, DARLENE JASMER, dietitian; b. Watford City, N.D., Jan. 26, 1939; d. Edwin Arthur and Leola Irene (Walker) Jasmer; BS, Oreg. State U., 1961; m. Richard G. Tyler, Aug. 26, 1977 (dec.); children: Ronald, Eric, Scott. Clin. dietitian Salem (Oreg.) Hosp., 1965-73; sales supr. Sysco Northwest, Tigard, Oreg., 1975-77; clin dietitian Physicians & Surgeons Hosp., Portland, Oreg., 1977-79; food svc. dir. Meridian Park Hosp., Tualatin, Oreg., 1979—. Registered dietitian. Mem. Am. Dietetic Assn., Oreg. Dietetic Assn., Portland Dietetic Assn., Am. Soc. Hosp. Food Svc. Adminstrs. Episcopalian. Home: 9472 SW Hume Ct Tualatin OR 97062-9039 Office: 19300 SW 65th St Tualatin OR 97062

TYLER, DONALD EARL, urologist; b. Ontario, Oreg., Oct. 3, 1926; s. Charles Maurice and Iva (Hess) T.; 1 child, Paul Donald. MD, U. Oreg. Med. Sch., 1950; JD, U. Denver Coll. Law, 1967. Diplomate Am. Bd. Urology, Am. Coll. Legal Medicine. Fellow in gen. surgery, urology The Mayo Found., Rochester, Minn., 1953, 55-58; clin. instr. in urology U. Utah Med. Sch., Salt Lake City, 1959-64. Author: A New and Simple Theory of Gravity, 1970, Originations of Life from Volcanoes and Petroleum, 1983, The Other Guy's Sperm: The Cause of Cancer and Other Diseases, 1994. Served to lt. USNR, 1944-45, 53-55, WWII, Korea. Mem. Alpha Omega Alpha, Phi Eta Sigma. Home: 1092 SW 2d Ave Ontario OR 97914

TYLER, GAIL MADELEINE, nurse; b. Dhahran, Saudi Arabia, Nov. 21, 1953 (parents Am. citizens); d. Louis Rogers and Nona Jean (Henderson) Tyler; m. Alan J. Moore, Sept. 29, 1990; 1 child, Sean James. AS, Front Range C.C., Westminster, Colo., 1979; BS in Nursing, U. Wyo., 1989. RN. Ward sec. Valley View Hosp., Thornton, Colo., 1975-79; nurse Scott and White Hosp., Temple, Tex., 1979-83, Meml. Hosp. Laramie County, Cheyenne, Wyo., 1983-89; dir. DePaul Home Health, 1989-91; field staff nurse Poudre Valley Hosp. Home Care, 1991—. Avocations: collecting internat. dolls, sewing, reading, travel.

TYLER, H. RICHARD, physician; b. Bklyn., Oct. 16, 1927; s. Max M. and Beatrice F. T.; m. Joyce Colby, June 17, 1951; children—Kenneth, Karen, Douglas, Lori. AB, Syracuse U., 1947; BS in Medicine, Washington U., 1951, MD, 1951; MA (hon.), Harvard U., 1989. Diplomate Am. Bd. Neurology and Psychiatry. Intern Peter Bent Brigham Hosp., Boston, 1951-52; resident in neurology Boston City Hosp., 1952-54; public health fellow Neurol. Inst., Queen's Sq., London, Salpêtrière, Paris, 1954-55; asst. in pediatrics and neurology Johns Hopkins Hosp., Balt., 1955-56; neurologist Peter Bent Brigham Hosp., Boston, 1956-74; asst. in neurology Harvard Med. Sch., Boston, 1956-59; assoc. in neurology Harvard Med. Sch., 1959-61, instr., 1961-64, asst. prof., 1964-68, assoc. prof., 1968-73, prof., 1974—; sr. physician Brigham and Women's Hosp., Boston, 1974—, dir. neurol. svc., 1979-88. Co-editor: Current Neurology I and II, 1979, 80; mem. editorial bd.: Jour. Neurology, 1979-84, Classics on Neurology and Neurosurgery Libr., 1983—; contbr. articles in field to profl. jours. Trustee Brookline Pub. Library, 1970—, chmn. bd. trustees, 1985-86, 90-91. Served with U.S. Army, 1946-47. Mem. Am. Neurol. Assn., Am. Acad. Neurology, Mass. Med. Soc. Office: 1 Brookline Pl Brookline MA 02146-7224

TYMON, RANDY, physician assistant, medical illustrator; b. N.Y.C., Dec. 11, 1953; d. David and Hannah (Grossman) T. BA in History, U. Rochester, 1975; Physician Asst. Cert., Cornell U., 1977. Registered physician asst., N.Y. Surg. physician asst. in plastic surgery Cornell U. Med. Ctr.-N.Y. Hosp., N.Y.C., 1978-83, surg. physician asst. in renal transplant, 1983-85; sr. physician asst. vascular surgery, tech. dir. vascular lab. L.I. Jewish-Hillside Med. Ctr., New Hyde Park, N.Y., 1986-94; sr. physician asst. vascular surgery Beth Israel Med. Ctr., N.Y.C., 1995—, renal-vascular surg. coord., coord. dir. all vascular labs, 1995—. Illustrator: Breast Reconstruction (by Randolph Guthrie), 1979, Modern Vascular Surgery (by John B. Chang), 1991, Lecture Series in Vascular Surgery (by Jon R. Cohen), 1992; illustrator Jour. Plastic and Reconstructive Surgery, 1979-81. Mem. Am. Acad. Physicians Assts., N.Y. State Soc. Physicians Assts., Am. Assn. Cardiovascular Physician Assts. Office: Beth Israel Med Ctr Dept Surgery 16th St and 1st Ave New York NY 10003

TYNDALL, RICHARD LAWRENCE, microbiologist, researcher; b. Mt. Joy, Pa., Mar. 29, 1933; s. William Leroy and Reba May (Ream) T.; m. Thelma Mae Sherk, June 19, 1955; children: Sharon Tyndall Headley, Michael L., Sandra Tyndall Holland. BS in Microbiology, Pa. State U., 1955, MS in Microbiology, 1959, PhD in Microbiology, 1961. Rsch. staff biology div. Oak Ridge (Tenn.) Nat. Lab., 1961-73; rsch. staff med. div. Oak Ridge Assoc. Univs., 1973-76; assoc. prof. rsch. zoology dept. U. Tenn., Knoxville, 1976-87; adj. rsch. assoc. Biology and Environ. Scis. div. Oak Ridge Nat. Lab., 1976-87; rsch. staff mem. Health and Safety Rsch. div. Oak Ridge Nat. Lab., 1988—; founder, CEO Microbial Monitoring, Clinton, Tenn., 1985—; co-founder Reprotech Inc., Knoxville, 1981; cons. in field. Contbr. numerous articles to profl. jours.; patentee in field. Mem. com. for control of Legionella, State of Wis. With U.S. Army, 1955-57. AEC postdoctoral fellow. Fellow Am. Acad. Microbiology; mem. AAAS, ASHRAE (subcom. on Legionella), Am. Soc. Microbiology, Phi Sigma, Gamma Sigma Delta (awards). Methodist. Home: 209 Woodland View Rd Clinton TN 37716

TYNES, BAYARD SHIELDS, internist; b. Birmingham, Ala., Oct. 28, 1929; s. William Doric and Carolyn (Shields) T.; m. Carolyn Dickinson, June 16, 1956; children: Bayard Jr., Ingram, Norman, Cary. BS, Sewanee U., 1951; MD, Emory U., 1956. Diplomate Am. Bd. Internal Medicine. Intern U. Ala. Med. Ctr., Birmingham, 1956; ptnr. Southview Internists, Birmingham, 1961—; clin. prof. medicine U. Ala. Med. Ctr., Birmingham, 1975-89, ret.; clin. assoc. NIAID NIH, Bethesda, Md., 1957-59, sr. asst. surgeon, 1961. Lt. commdr. USPHS, 1959-61. Republican. Episcopalian. Home: 33 Ridge Dr Birmingham AL 35213-3633 Office: Southview Internists Ste 300 833 Saint Vincent Dr Birmingham AL 35205

TYREE, DARLENE RAE, art therapist, artist; b. Chgo., Jan. 28, 1953; d. LeRoy and Grace Thelma (Alves) T.; m. Guy Pla, Nov. 8, 1990. BA, So. Ill. U., 1975; MFA, No. Ill. U., 1983. Caseworker, aid to the aged, blind, disabled Ill. Dept. Pub. Aid, Chgo., 1975-79; rsch., teaching asst. dept. art No. Ill. U., DeKalb, 1979-81, coord. art therapy workshop, 1981, speaker, exhibitor art edn. for the handicapped and gifted, 1979-80, mem. testing staff, 1981-87; field worker art therapy Ben Gordon Community Mental Health Ctr., DeKalb, 1979-80; coord. art by art therapists Ill. Art Therapy Assn., Chgo., 1987; art therapist Elgin (Ill.) Mental Health Ctr., 1987—. Exhibited in group shows So. Ill. U., Carbondale, 1972-74, No. Ill. U., DeKalb, 1979-83, DuSable Mus. African-Am. History, Chgo., 1975-76, Artists' Guild Chgo., 1976, Southside Community Art Ctr., Chgo., 1976, Mus. Sci. and Industry, Chgo., 1976-77, 87, Art Inst. Chgo., 1977-79, Elgin (Ill.) C.C., 1989, Atlanta Life Ins., 1990, A.R.C. Gallery, Chgo., 1991, Found. African Am. Life and Culture, Dallas, 1991, Biennial Ark. Exhbn., Pine Bluff, 1985, 57th St. Exhbn., Chgo, 1985-88, Hyde Park Art Ctr., Chgo., 1985, Independence Bank, Chgo., 1984, U. Ill., Chgo., 1980, Vaughn Cultural Ctr., St. Louis, 1983, Von Isser Gallery, Elgin, 1988. Rhoten Smith fellow No. Ill. U., 1979-81; recipient purchase award Nat. Exhbn. African-Am. Art, 1990; named to Outstanding Young Women of Am., 1982, 87. Mem. Am. Art Therapy Assn., Ill. Art Therapy Assn. Office: Elgin Mental Health Ctr 750 S State St Elgin IL 60123-7612

TYRELL, LORNE S., dean. Dean U. Alberta. Office: U Alberta Faculty Medicine, 2J2 Ma Kenzie Health Sci, Edmonton, AB Canada T6G 2R7*

TYROLER, HERMAN ALFRED, epidemiologist. Grad., NYU Sch. medicine. Lic. to practice, N.C. Prof., now alumni disting. prof. dept. epidemiology U. N.C. Mem. Inst. of Medicine, Nat. Acad. Scis. Office: U NC Dept Epidemiology Chapel Hill NC 27514*

TYRRELL, ELEANORE DAY, health program evaluation specialist; b. Phila., Aug. 9, 1938; d. Peter Aloysius Tyrrell and Elsie Amelia Day. BA in Psychology, U. Richmond, 1960; MA in Psychology, Pepperdine U., 1980. Rsch. assoc. U. Pa. Med. Sch., Phila., 1961-62; with UCLA, 1962-91; rsch. assoc. to lab. supr. to co-adminstr. Marijuana Rsch. Program, coord. Program in Psychiatry, Law & Human Sexuality; program and policy analyst Alzheimer's Disease Program, Ctr. for Gerontology, Calif. Dept. Health Svc.-Inst. for Health and Aging, U. Calif., San Francisco, 1991—; exec. dir. Ctr. for Drug Edn. and Brain Rsch., L.A., 1987-88; cons. rschr. Beverly Hills Headache & Pain Med. Group, L.A., Los Alamos (N.Mex.) Nat. Labs., SUNY, Stony Brook, So. Calif. Neuropsychiat. Inst., La Jolla, others. Contbr. articles and rsch. papers to profl. jours. Pres. The Opera Assocs., L.A.; dir. publicity and pub. rels. L.A. and western regions Met. Opera Nat. Coun. Auditions. Recipient Adminstrv. and Profl. Staff award U. Calif. San Francisco, 1994, Outstanding Performance award U. Calif. San Francisco, 1996. Mem. Sacramento Area Pepperdine U. Alumni (v.p.), Psi Chi. Home: 3421 Toledo Way Sacramento CA 95821-2437

TZARNAS, CHRIS DIMITRI, plastic surgeon; b. Washington, Aug. 30, 1949; m. Ellie Kelepouris, 1976; children: Stephanie, Alexa. BA, Northwestern U., 1970; MD magna cum laude, U. Athens, Greece, 1975. Diplomate Am. Bd. Surgery, Am. Bd. Plastic Surgery. Intern in surgery Presbyn.-U. Pa. Med. Ctr., Phila., 1975-76, resident in surgery, 1976-80, chief resident in surgery, 1980-81; resident in plastic surgery U. Pa., Phila., 1981-82, chief resident in plastic surgery, 1982-83; clin. instr. in surgery U. Pa. Sch. Medicine, Phila., 1982-83, clin. assoc. in plastic surgery, 1985—; instr. in surgery Jefferson Med. Coll., Phila., 1986—; dir. surg. edn., program dir. Mercy Cath. Med. Ctr., Darby, Pa., 1993—; clin. asst. prof. surgery Med. Coll. Pa., 1994—; attending surgeon Mercy-Cath. Med. Ctr., Darby, 1984—; chief plastic surgery Mercy Fitzgerald Med. Ctr., 1991—; attending surgeon Taylor Hosp., Ridley Park, Pa., 1984—; assoc. attending surgeon Lankenau Hosp., Phila., 1984—; attending surgeon Del. County Meml. Hosp., Drexel Hill, Pa., 1985—, Jefferson U. Hosp., Phila., 1985—; assoc. chief plastic surgery Phila. V.A. Hosp., 1985-90; clin. affiliate Children's Hosp. Phila., 1986—; attending surgeon Chestnut Hill Hosp., Phila., 1988—, Presbyn. Med. Ctr., Phila., 1994—; vis. prof., speaker in field; cons. plastic surgery Inst. Treatment Poisonous Snakebite. Contbr. articles to profl. jours. Fellow Am. Coll. Surgeons; mem. AMA (Physician;s Recognition award 1987-90, 90-93), Am. Soc. Plastic and Reconstructive Surgeons, Northeastern Soc. Plastic Surgeons, Robert H. Ivy Soc., Phila. Soc. Plastic Surgeons, Lipoplasty Soc. N.Am., Pa. Med. Soc., Phila. County Med. Soc., Am. Med. Writers Assn., Assn. Program Dirs. of Surgery, Assn. Surg. Edn. Home: 541 Howe Rd Merion PA 19066 Office: Mercy Fitzgerald Med Office 1501 Lansdowne Ave Ste 206 Darby PA 19026

UCHIDA, TAKAHIRO, virology educator; b. Muroran, Hokkaido, Japan, Dec. 9, 1929; s. Kohtoku and Miki (Fukushima) U.; m. Mikiko Narumi, Sept. 28, 1955; 1 child, Yuko. MD, Sapporo (Japan) Med. Coll., 1954, DMS, 1962. Rsch. assoc. Sapporo Med. Coll., 1955-60, lectr., 1961-66; rsch. assoc. MIT, Cambridge, Mass., 1960-62; assoc. prof. Sapporo Med. Coll., 1966-75; UICC fellow Salk Inst. Biol. Studies, San Diego, Calif., 1969-70; prof. U. Tokushima, Japan, 1975-95, prof. emeritus, 1995—; discover new spotted fever group rickettsia in Japan (Rickettsia japonica). Fellow Rockefeller Found., Internat. Union Against Cancer (Eleanor Roosevelt Internat. Cancer fellow 1969); mem. N.Y. Acad. Scis., Soc. Japanese Virologists. Home: 13-7 Tainohata-higashimachi, Sumaku Kobe 654-01, Japan

UDEN, DAVID ELLIOTT, cardiologist, educator; b. Montreal, Sept. 7, 1936; s. Reginald and Elsie Ada (Elliott) U.; children: Thomas Elliott, Linda Ann, Christopher Elliott. BSc, McGill U., 1958; MD, McGill U., Quebec, Can., 1962. Diplomate Am. Bd. Internal Medicine; cert. cardiovascular disease. Attending cardiologist Toronto Western Hosp., 1972-93, The Wellesley Hosp., Toronto, 1990-93; asst. prof. medicine U. Toronto, 1975-93; chief of cardiology Oconee Meml. Hosp., Seneca, S.C., 1993—, chief of medicine, 1994-96. Contbr. articles to sci. and profl. jours. With RCAF, 1963-66. Fellow Am. Coll. Cardiology, Am. Heart Assn. Coun. on Clin. Cardiology. Office: 103 Omni Dr # B Seneca SC 29672-9448

UDIN, SUSAN BOYMEL, neurobiology educator; b. Phila., Aug. 11, 1947; d. Jules and Pauline (Friedman) Boymel; m. David Udin, June 3, 1967; children: Rachel, Michael. BS, MIT, 1969, PhD, 1975. Sr. staff scientist Nat. Inst. for Med. Rsch., London, 1978-79; asst. prof. neurobiology SUNY-Buffalo, 1979-85, assoc. prof. physiology, 1985-92, prof. physiology, 1992—. Contbr. articles to profl. jours. Mem. ad hoc study sects. NIH, 1991—. NIH grantee, 1980—; NAS grantee, 1980; March of Dimes grantee, 1983-85, 89-93; Burroughs Wellcome travel grantee, 1980, 81; Howard Hughes Med. Found. grantee, 1993-94. Mem. Nat. Eye Inst. Visual Scis. B. Study Sect. 1986-90, Women in Neurosci., Soc. for Neurosci., AAAS, Sigma Xi. Avocations: embroidery, gardening. Office: SUNY Dept Physiology 313 Cary Hall Buffalo NY 14214

UDOLF, ROY, psychology educator, lawyer; b. N.Y.C., Aug. 7, 1926; s. Barney and Esther (Kadis) U.; m. Marcelle Temkin, July 1, 1950; children—Bruce Lee, Penny Jill, Brad Robert, David William. B.E.E., NYU, 1950; J.D. cum laude, Bklyn. Law Sch., 1954; M.A., Hofstra Coll., 1963; Ph.D., Adelphi U., 1971. Bar: N.Y. 1954, U.S. Dist. Ct. (so. and ea. dists.) N.Y., 1954, U.S. Supreme Ct. 1958; diplomate Am. Bd. Forensic Psychology. Practice, East Meadow, N.Y., 1954-56; test engr. Arma Corp., Garden City, N.Y., 1956-63; asst. dept. head Gyrodyne Co., St. James, N.Y., 1963-67; prof. psychology New Coll. of Hofstra U., Hempstead, N.Y., 1967—. Author: Criminal Justice System and its Psychology, 1979; Handbook of Hypnosis, 1981; Forensic Hypnosis, 1983. Served with USMC, 1944-46, PTO. Home: 2777 Granz Ct East Meadow NY 11554-4302 Office: Roosevelt Hall New Coll of Hofstra U Hempstead NY 11550

UEMURA, TERUKI, child brain developmentalist; b. Tokyo, Mar. 25, 1944; came to U.S., 1973; s. Kiichi and Teru (Koizumi) U. BA, Keio U., Tokyo, 1967, diploma in bus. adminstr., 1972; M Mgmt., Northwestern U., 1975; postgrad., U. Pa., 1976-81. Mem. staff Aichi Steel Works, Ltd., Nagoya, Japan, 1967-81; coord. Insts. for Achievement Human Potential, Phila., 1984—; vice dir. intellectual growth at The Children's Ctr. The Children's Ctr., Phila., 1984-91; vice dir. The Children's Ctr. Insts. for Achievement Human Potential, Phila., 1991-94; vice dir. Insts. Achievement of Intellectual Excellence, Phila., 1994—; rsch. asst. Harvard U., Cambridge, Mass., 1972-74, U. Pa., Phila., 1979-81; translator U.S. State Dept., Washington, 1980—. Program coordinator Coun. Internat. Visitors, Phila., 1978-81. Recipient Brazilian Gold medal of Humanities, World Orgn. for Human Potential, 1984, 88, Sakura Koro Sho award, 1986, Leonardo da Vinci award, 1993. Fellow Internat. Acad. Child Brain Devel., Japan Group II. Office: Inst for the Achievement Human Potential 8801 Stenton Ave Wyndmoor PA 19038-2319

UENO, AKIRA, pharmacology educator, professor emeritus; b. Fukuoka, Kyushu, Japan, Jan. 16, 1929; s. Shigeru and Natsu Ueno; married, Mar. 31, 1958; children: Isao, Kei. MD, Nagasaki (Japan) U., 1952, PhD, 1956. Med. diplomate. Rsch. assoc. U. Ill., Urbana, 1956-58; asst. Sch. Medicine Nagasaki U., 1952-55, lectr., 1956, assoc. prof., 1959-74, prof., 1974-94, chmn. dept. pharmacology, 1994—; prof. emeritus, 1994—. Home: 11-18-405 Shiratorimachi, 52-69 Minego Nagayo-cho, Nagasaki 859-06, Japan Office: Kohfuudai Hosp, 12-4 Sakamotomachi, 1-45 Narumidai, Nagasaki 851-22, Japan

UFEMA, JOHN WILLIAM, radiologist, educator; b. Johnstown, Pa., July 31, 1946; s. George and Loretta Cecilia (Bent) U.; m. Mary Jo Federici, June 21, 1980; 1 child, Anthony M. Oliver. Student, Johns Hopkins U., 1964-67; MD, Emory U., 1971; MBA, Nova U. Adminstrn. Studies Ctr., 1987. Cert. in Diagnostic Radiology, 1975. Intern in internal medicine Emory affiliated hosps., 1971-72, resident in diagnostic radiology, 1972-75; attending physician Ponce de Leon Infirmary, Atlanta, 1972-75; clin. assoc. Emory U., Atlanta, 1976; attending radiologist Diagnostic Clinic, Largo, Fla., 1977-80; pres., chmn. Med. Imaging Services, Port Charlotte, Fla., 1980-88; mng. gen. ptnr. Ufema Capital Equipment Leasing, Port Charlotte, 1984-89; med. dir. Palm Harbor (Fla.) Imaging, 1988-92; pres. Diagnostic Imaging, Palm Harbor, 1992-94; sr. staff radiologist Scott and White Clinic, College Station, Tex., 1994—; asst. prof. radiology Tex. A&M U. Coll. Medicine, 1994—; pres. Physician's Reference Lab. Charlotte County, 1987-88. Contbr. numerous articles to profl. jours. Mem. Soc. for Entertainment and Arts Devel., Port Charlotte, 1984-88. Maj. USAF, 1975-77. Mem. AMA (Physicians' Recognition award in Continuing Med. Edn.), Am. Coll. Radiology, Radiol. Soc. N.Am., Tex. Radiol. Soc., Tex. Med. Assn., Brazos-Robertson Counties Med. Soc., Mensa, NRA (life). Republican. Roman Catholic. Office: 1600 University Dr East College Station TX 77842

UGLAND, DAVID NELS, ophthalmologist; b. Midland, Tex., Jan. 2, 1954; s. Lloyd Eugene and Sally Ann (Baird) U.; m. Lisa Ann Frey, Dec. 4, 1982; children: Leslie Ann, Jennifer, Eric. BA in Math., U. Tex., 1976; MD, Baylor Coll. Medicine, 1980. Diplomate Am. Bd. Ophthalmology. Medical intern Brackenridge Hosp., Austin, 1980-81; resident in ophthalmology Emory U., 1981-84, chief resident, 1983-84; fellow corneal and external disease Baylor Coll. Medicine, 1984-85; ptnr. Gaskin Eye Clinic, Charlotte, 1985—; bd. dirs. Retinitis Pigmentosis Found., Charlotte, N.C., 1993—, bd. dirs. Macklenburg County Med. Soc., Charlotte, 1994—, treas., 1996; dir. Eye Bank, Life Share of the Carolinas, 1994—. Fellow Am. Acad. Ophthalmology, Paton Corneal Soc.; mem. Am. Soc. Cataract and Refractive Surgeons, N.C. Med. Soc. Office: Gaskin Eye Clinic 100 Queens Rd Charlotte NC 28204

UHDE, GEORGE IRVIN, physician; b. Richmond, Ind., Mar. 20, 1912; s. Walter Richard and Anna Margaret (Hoopes) U.; m. Maurine Elizabeth Whitley, July 27, 1935; children—Saundra Uhde Seelig, Thomas Whitley, Michael, Janice. M.D., Duke U., 1936. Diplomate: Am. Bd. Otolaryngology. Intern Reading (Pa.) Hosp., 1936-37, resident in medicine, 1937-38; resident in otolaryngology Balt. Eye, Ear, Nose and Throat Hosp., 1938-40, U. Oreg. Med. Sch., Portland, 1945-47; practice medicine specializing in otolaryngology Louisville, 1948—; asst. prof. otolaryngology U. Louisville Med. Sch., 1945-62, prof. surgery (otolaryngology), head dept., 1963-92, prof. emeritus, 1992—, dir. otolaryngology services, 1963—; mem. staffs Meth., Norton's-Children's, Jewish, St. Joseph's, St. Anthony's, St. Mary and Elizabeth's hosps.; cons. Ky. Surg. Tb Hosp., Hazlewood, VA Hosp., Louisville, U. Louisville Speech and Hearing Center. Author 4 books.; Contbr. articles to profl. jours. Bd. dirs. Easter Seal Speech and Hearing Ctr. Lt. col. M.C. U.S. Army, 1940-45, ETO, Gen. Eisenhower staff, 1943-45. Recipient Disting. Service award U. Louisville, 1972. Fellow A.C.S., Am. Acad. Ophthalmology and Otolaryngology, So. Med. Soc.; mem. N.Y. Acad. Scis., Am. Coll. Allergists, Am. Acad. Facial Plastic and Reconstructive Surgery, AAAS, Assn. U. Otolaryngologists, AAUP, Assn. Mil. Surgeons U.S., Am. Laryngol., Rhinol. and Otol. Soc., Am. Audiology Soc., Soc. Clin. Ecology, Am. Soc. Otolaryngology Allergy, Centurian Otol. Research Soc. (Ky. rep.), Am. Council Otolaryngology (Ky. rep. 1968—), Hoopes Quaker Found., SAR (life), Gen. Soc. Colonial Wars (hereditary mem.), Alpha Kappa Kappa. Democrat. Methodist. Clubs: Filson, Big Spring Country, Jefferson. Home: 708 Circle Hill Rd Louisville KY 40207-3627 Office: Med Towers Louisville KY 40202

UHDE, THOMAS W., psychiatry educator, psychiatrist; b. Louisville, Jan. 6, 1948; s. George I. and Maurine U.; m. Marlene Ann Kraus, Oct. 22, 1977; Miles August, Katherine Kraus. BS, Duke U., 1971; MD, U. Louisville, 1975. Pvt. practice in psychiatry Bethesda, Md., 1979-93; attending staff Clin. Ctr. NIH, Bethesda, 1982-93; chmn. Dept. Psychiatry Detroit Receiving Hosp., Detroit, Mich., 1994—; psychiatrist in chief Detroit Med. Ctr., 1993—; clin. prof. Uniformed Svcs. U.S. USUHS Scb. of Medicine, Bethesda, Md., 1991—; prof., chmn. of psych. dept. Wayne State U. Sch. of Medicine, Detroit, 1993—; mem. sci. adv. com. Bethesda, Md., 1990—; cons. Assessment (DATTA) program AMA, Chgo., 1991—; exec. bd. ADDA, chair ADDA sci. adv. bd., Rockville, Md., 1991-93. Editor-in-chief (jour.) Anxiety; mem. edtl. bd. Actualities Medicales Internationales en Psychiatrie, 1983, Jour. of Affect. Dis., 1986, Jour. of Anxiety Disorders, 1987-95. Capt. USPHS, 1979-93. Recipient Brain, Body & Mind award USPHS, Recognition award ADAA. Mem. Am. Assn. Chmn. Depts. Psychiatry, Am. Coll. Psychiatry, Soc. of Clin. Psychopharmomcology, Internat. Brain Rsch. Orgn., Sleep Rsch. Soc., ACNP. Office: Wayne State Sch Medicine 4201 Saint Antoine 9B UHC Detroit MI 48201

UHLENHUTH, EBERHARD HENRY, psychiatrist, educator; b. Balt., Sept. 15, 1927; s. Eduard Carl Adolph and Elisabeth (Baier) U.; m. Helen Virginia Lyman, June 20, 1952; children: Kim Lyman, Karen Jane, Eric Rolf. BS in Chemistry, Yale U., 1947; MD, Johns Hopkins U., 1951. Intern Harborview Hosp., Seattle, 1951-52; resident in psychiatry Johns Hopkins Hosp., Balt., 1952-56; asst. psychiatrist in charge outpatient dept. Johns Hopkins Hosp., 1956-61, psychiatrist in charge, 1961-62; chief adult psychiatry clinic U. Chgo. Hosps. Clinics, 1968-76; instr. psychiatry Johns Hopkins U., 1956-59, asst. prof., 1959-67, assoc. prof., 1967-68; assoc. prof. U. Chgo., 1968-73, prof., 1973-85, acting chmn., 1983-85; prof. psychiatry U. N.Mex., Albuquerque, 1985—, vice chmn. for edn., 1991-94; cons. in field; mem. clin. psychopharmacology rsch. rev. com. NIMH, 1968-72, treatment devel. and assessment rev. com., 1987; mem. psychopharmacology adv. com. FDA, 1974-78; mem. adv. group to Treatment of Depression Collaborative Rsch. Program, NIMH, 1978-92; study rev. com. Xanax Discontinuation Program, The UpJohn Co., 1988-92, Nat. Adv. Coun. on Drug Abuse, NIDA, 1989-92, Coop. Studies Evaluation Com., VA, 1989-92. Mem. editl. bd. Jour. Affective Disorders, 1978—, Psychiatry Rsch., 1979-96, Behavioral Medicine, 1982—, Neuropsychopharmacology, 1992-94, Exptl. and Clin. Psychopharmacology, 1992—, Anxiety, 1993—; contbr. articles to profl. jours. Recipient Research Career Devel. award USPHS, 1962-68, Research Scientist award, 1976-81. Fellow Am. Coll. Neuropsychopharmacology (pres. 1986), Am. Psychiat. Assn., Am. Psychopath. Assn.; mem. Balt.-Washington Soc. for Psychoanalysis, Collegium Internat. Neuro-Psychopharmacologicum, Psychiat. Rsch. Soc. Office: U NMex Dept Psychiatry 2400 Tucker NE Albuquerque NM 87131

UHR, JONATHAN WILLIAM, immunologist, educator, researcher; b. N.Y.C., Sept. 8, 1927; s. Jacques Stanley Uhr and Mary Wetsman; m. Roberta Joy Klibanoff (div.); children: Jacqueline, Sarita. AB, Cornell U., 1948; MD, NYU, 1952. Diplomate Am. Bd. Internal Medicine. Dazian fellow dept. microbiology NYU Med. Ctr., 1955-56; chief resident in medicine Mt. Sinai Hosp., N.Y.C., 1956-57; instr. dept. microbiology NYU Sch. Medicine, 1957-58, asst. prof. medicine, 1958-62, assoc. prof., 1962-68, prof., 1968-72; prof., chmn. dept. microbiology U. Tex. Southwestern Med. Ctr., Dallas, 1972—; dir. Irvington House Inst. for Rheumatic Fever and Allied Diseases, N.Y.C., 1962-72; vis. prof. microbiology Yale U., 1970-72; assoc. attending physician Univ. Hosp., N.Y.C., 1963-72; assoc. vis. physician Bellevue Hosp., N.Y.C., 1959-72; cons. internal medicine Manhattan Vet.'s Hosp., 1964-74. Contbr. articles to profl. publs. With USN, 1945-46. Recipient Newcomb Cleveland prize AAAS, 1963, Squibb award Infectious Diseases Soc. Am., 1971, NAS award, 1984, Faculty medal Med. Sch. Montpellier, France, 1984; Commonwealth fellow Walter and Eliza Hall Inst. Med. Rsch., 1961-62. Mem. Am. Assn. Immunologists (pres. 1989—), Am. Assn. Pathologists, Am. Soc. Clin. Investigation, Transplantation Soc., Assn. Am. Physicians. Office: U Tex Southwestern Med Ctr Dept of Microbiology 5323 Harry Hines Blvd Dallas TX 75235-8576*

UKAH, FERDINAND OKE, surgeon; b. Mgbowo, Enugu, Nigeria, July 26, 1957; came to U.S., 1976; s. Lawrence Nwosu and Benedette Lewe (Chukwu) U.; m. Cynthia Marie Payne, Aug. 8, 1987; children: Adanna, Nneka, okechukwu Jr., Chike. BS with honors, Portland State U., 1980; MD, Howard U., 1985. Diplomate Nat. Bd. Med. Examiners, Am. Bd. Surgery. Resident Howard Hosp., Washington, 1985; transplant fellow U. Pitts., 1992; asst. prof. U. Iowa Hosp. and Coll., Iowa City, 1993-96; staff surgeon VA Med. Ctr., Iowa City, 1993-96; dir. transplantation U. South Ala., Mobile, 1996—; adv. bd. Discovery/Minority in Health Sci., Pitts., 1991-92. Reviewer Iowa Found. for Med. Care, 1993—; editor: Synapse/Howard U. publ., 1986-87; contbr. articles to profl. jours. and publs. Physician mentor Student Nat. Med. Assn., Iowa City, 1993-96. Acad. scholar Portland State U., 1986-89; rsch. grantee Ctr. for Advanced Studies, Iowa City, 1994; recipient Alexander Clark award Black Law Students Assn., Iowa City, 1995. Fellow ACS; mem. AMA, AAAS, World Assn. Hepatobiliary Surgery, Cell Transplant Soc., Internat. Liver Transplant Soc. Home: 2820 Churchbell Ct Mobile AL 36695

ULETT, GEORGE ANDREW, psychiatrist; b. Needham, Mass., Jan. 10, 1918; s. George Andrew and Mabel Elizabeth (Caswell) U.; m. Pearl Carolyn Lawrence; children: Richard Carlton, Judith Anne, Carol Lynn. BA in Psychology, Stanford U., 1940; MS in Anatomy, U. Oreg., 1943, PhD in Anatomy, 1944, MD, 1944. Diplomate Am. Bd. Psychiatry and Neurology. Asst. psychiatrist Barnes Hosp., St. Louis, 1950-64; med. dir. Malcolm Bliss Hosp., St. Louis, 1951-61; dir. Mo. Div. Mental Health, Jefferson City, Mo., 1962-72; prof., chair Mo. Inst. Psychiatry, St. Louis, 1964-73; dir. psychiatry Deaconess Hosp., St. Louis, 1973-94; interim dir. Mo. Inst. of Mental Health, St. Louis, 1990-91; assoc. dir. for policy and ethics Mo. Inst. of Mental Health, 1991-94; clin. prof. dept. family and cmty. medicine St. Louis U. Sch. Medicine, 1995—; mem. adv. coun. Mental Health Assn. St. Louis, 1965-66, 69-70, mem. profl. adv. com., 1965; chair health and hosp. com. Health & Welfare Coun. St. Louis, 1960; mem. alcohol rev. com., psychopharmacology study sect., alcoholism study sect., 1993, grants rev. com. for alternative medicine NIMH, Rockville, Md.; prof. psychiatry Washington U. Sch. Medicine, St. Louis, 1956-61; clin. prof. cmty. and family medicine St. Louis U. Sch. Medicine, 1981-89, U. Mo. Sch. Medicine, 1990—. Author eight books; contbr. over 200 articles to profl. jours. Capt. U.S. Air Force, 1946-47. Recipient Ann. award Mo. Assn. for Mental Health, 1966, Recognition award, 1970, AMA Honorable Mention award Foster Com. Exhibit, 1974, Pax Mundi Fellowship award for profl. excellence, 1989; named hon. mem. Turkish Coll. Neuropharmacology, 1969. Fellow Am. Psychiat. Assn.; mem. Am. Soc. Acupuncture (past pres.), Am. Soc. of Med. Psychiatry (past pres.), Mo. Acad. Psychiatry (past pres.). Office: Mo Inst Mental Health 5247 Fyler Ave Saint Louis MO 63139-1300

ULICNY, KARL STEPHEN, II, surgeon; b. Salem, Ohio, June 20, 1957; s. Karl Stephen and Twila May (Eister) U.; m. Tracy Tiller, May 13, 1989; children: Ann Kennon, Elisabeth Lloyd. AB, Vassar Coll., 1979; MD, U. Cin., 1984. Diplomate Am. Bd. Thoracic Surgery, Am. Bd. Surgery, Nat. Bd. Medical Examiners. Resident internal medicine The Jewish Hosp. Cin., 1984-85, resident gen. surgery, 1985-89, chief resident gen. surgery, 1989-90; rsch. fellow Univ. N.C., Chapel Hill, 1990-91, chief resident thoracic surgery, 1991-92, chief resident cardiac surgery, 1992-93; assoc. Will & Robinson MD, Inc., Edgewood, Ky., 1993—; reviewer The Annals of Thoracic Surgery, 1993, Advanced Cardiac Life Support Am. Heart Assn., 1985; instr. Advanced Trauma Life Support Am. Coll. Surgeons, 1987; vascular surgery recredentialing com. Jewish Hosp. Cin., 1994, intensive care com. St. Elizabeth South Hosp., 1994; attending staff St. Elizabeth South, 1993, St. Elizabeth North, 1993, The Christ Hosp., 1993, St. Luke Hosp., 1993, Bethesda Hosps., 1993. Contbr. numerous articles to profl. jours. Recipient Sidney A. Peerless Resident award, 1987, Spirit of Surgery award, Jewish Hosp. Cin., 1989. Mem. AMA, Ohio State Medical Assn., Hamilton County Medical Assn., Cin. Acad. Medicine, Am. Coll. Surgeons, Soc. Thoracic Surgeons, Nathan A. Womack Surgical Soc. Office: Will & Robinson Inc Ste 204 20 Medical Village Dr Edgewood KY 41017 Home: 713 Avon Fields Ln Cincinnati OH 45229

ULLAND, L. ARLIE, internist, nephrologist; b. Ledgerwood, N.D., Apr. 3, 1944; s. Harold Kenneth and Lorraine Ruth (Rensby) U.; m. Diane Ulland, Nov. 17, 1986. BS in Chemistry summa cum laude, U. N.D., 1966; PhD in Chemistry, U. Calif., Davis, 1970; MD, U. Tex. Southwestern, 1978. Diplomate Am. Bd. Internal Medicine, Am. Bd. Critical Care, Am. Bd. Nephrology. Project chemist Dow Corning Group, Midland, Mich., 1971-74; nephrologist Ocala (Fla.) Critical Care and Kidney Group, 1983—; chief medicine Marion Comty. Hosp., Ocala, 1987-89, chief staff, 1994-96; dir. Ocala Regional Dialysis Ctr., 1986. Mem. AMA, Am. Coll. Physicians, Soc. Critical Care Physicians, Phi Beta Kappa. Home: 2709 SE 16th St Ocala FL 34471 Office: Ocala Critical Care & Kidney Group 2980 SE 3rd Ct Ocala FL 34478

ULMER, EVONNE GAIL, health science administration admission executive; b. Bagley, Minn., Sept. 12, 1947; d. John Ferdinand and Elsie Mabel (McCollum) Lundmark; m. G. Bryan Ulmer, Jan. 11, 1969; 1 child, G. Bryan. Diploma, St. Luke's Hosp., Duluth, Minn., 1968; BS, St. JOseph's Coll., N. Windam, Maine, 1981; MHA, U. Minn., 1984; student, T.M. Cooley Law Sch., 1996—. Staff nurse Baton Rouge Gen., 196970, St. Luke's Hosp., Duluth, Minn., 1968-69, 71-72; asst. adminstr. Hickory Heights Care Ctr., Metarie, La., 1972--73; asst. head nurse Eisenhower Hosp., Colorado Springs, Colo., 1973-74; dir. pt. care svcs. St. Vincent's Gen. Hosp., Leadville, Colo., 1974-78; inservice, quality assurance dir. Watsatch Hosp., Heber City, Utah, 1979; adminstr. Prospect Park Living Ctr., Estes Park, Colo., 1982-84; asst. adminstr. Estes Park Med. Ctr., Colo., 1979-84; chief exec. officer Weston Co. Hosp. and Manor, Newcastle, Wyo., 1984-92; ceo Ionia (Mich.) County Meml. Hosp., 1992—; pres. Ionia County Health Sys., 1995—. Mem. Am. Hosp. Assn. Chgo. (tech. sml. and rural governing coun., past del. region and policy be., past chair sml. and rural governing com., mem. leadership com.), Medicare Geographic Reclassification Rev. Bd. Republican. Lutheran. Home: 536 Skyview Dr Ionia MI 48846-9776 Office: Ionia County Meml Hosp Ionia MI 48846

ULNICK, KEITH MITCHELL, physician, health care administrator; b. L.A., Sept. 11, 1962; s. Melvin Arthur and Helane (Pearlman) U.; m. Sheryl Lynn Ward, June 25, 1988; 1 child, Katrina Mykelle. AA in Liberal Arts, SUNY, Albany, 1985; BS in Health Care Mgmt. with honors, So. Ill. U., 1986; MS in Health Care Adminstrn., Calif. State U., Northridge, 1988; DO, Coll. of Osteo. Medicine of the Pacific, 1992. Diplomate Am. Bd. Osteopathy. Commd. USN, 1980, advanced through grades to lt., 1992; leading petty officer ENT Naval Hosp. Phila., 1981-83; leading petty officer Naval Weapons Sta. Br. Clinic, Colts Neck, N.J., 1983-84; leading petty office ENT Naval Hosp. Long Beach, Calif., 1984-86; adminstn./tng. officer Naval Hosp. Camp Pendleton Det 819, Santa Barbara, Calif., 1986-87; officer-in-charge Med. Det "D" wd Bn. 23d Marines, Los Alamitos, Calif., 1987-88; student med. sch. COMP, Pomona, Calif., 1988-92; intern in surgery Portsmouth (Va.) Naval Hosp., 1992-93; bn. surgeon 1st Tank Bn., Twenty-nine Palms, Calif., 1993-95; regimental surgeon 7th Marine Regiment, Twenty-nine Palms, Calif., 1995—; mem. exec. ocm. med. staff Naval Hosp., Twenty-nine Palms, 1995-96; resident Otorhynolaryngology Madigan ARmy med. Ctr., Ft. Lewis, Wash. Mem. admissions/interview com. Coll. Osteopathci Medicine of the Pacific, Pamona, 1993—. Ensign USNR, 1986. Mem. Assn. Mil. Osteo. Physicians and Surgeons, Assn. of Mil. Surgeons of U.S., Am. Osteo. Assn., Golden Key Honor Soc. Republican. Roman Catholic. Home: 4002 214th St Ct E Spanaway WA 98387 Office: Madigan Army Med Ctr Ft Lewis WA

ULRICH, JOHN AUGUST, microbiology educator; b. St. Paul, May 15, 1915; s. Robert Ernst and Mary Agnes (Farrell) U.; m. Mary Margaret Nash, June 6, 1940 (dec. May 1985); children: Jean Anne, John Joseph, Robert Charles, Karl James, Mary Ellen, Lenore Alice; m. Mary Matkovich, July 19, 1986. BS, St. Thomas Coll., 1938; PhD, U. Minn., 1947. Instr. De La Salle High Sch., Mpls., 1938-41; rsch. asst. U. Minn., Mpls., 1941-45, 49, Hormel Inst., U. Minn., Austin, 1945-49; instr. Mayo Clinic, U. Minn., Rochester, 1949-55; asst. prof. Mayo Found., U. Minn., Rochester, 1955-66; assoc. prof. U. Minn., Mpls., 1966-69; prof. U. N.Mex., Albuquerque, 1969-82, prof. emeritus, 1982—; chmn. Bacteriology & Mycology Study Sect., NIH, Washington, 1961-64, Communicable Diseases Study Sect., Atlanta, 1968-69; rsch. chmn. in field. Chmn. Zumbry Valley Exec. Bd., Boy Scouts Am., Rochester, 1953-55; mem. Gamehaven Exec. Bd., Boy Scouts Am., Rochester, 1952-62, Dem. Com., Olmsted County, Minn., 1964-69. Recipient Silver Beaver award Boy Scouts Am., 1962, Bishop's award Winona Diocese, 1962, Katahli award U. N.Mex., 1980. Mem. Am. Soc. Microbiology, Am. Chem. Soc., Am. Bd. Med. Mycology, Am. Acad. Microbiology, Am. Acad. Dermatology (affiliate) Elks. Democrat. Roman Catholic. Home: 3807 Columbia Dr Longmont CO 80503-2122

ULRICH, ROGER STEFFEN, healthcare facility design educator, researcher; b. Birmingham, Mich., Feb. 20, 1946; s. Victor Frederick and Eunice (Williams) U.; m. Ann-Margret Gunilla Nilsson, July 18, 1970; children: Kenneth, Michael. BA in Econs., U. Mich., 1968, MA in Geography, 1971, PhD in Geography, 1973. Asst. prof. geography U. Del, Newark, 1974-78, assoc. prof., 1979-88; prof., depts. arch. and landscape arch. Tex. A&M U., College Station, 1988—, assoc. dean for rsch. Coll. Architecture, 1988—; vis. prof. Lund (Sweden) Inst. Tech., 1977-78; vis. rschr. dept. clin. psychology Uppsala (Sweden) U., 1984-85; numerous presentations in field; mem. urban ecosystems directorate U.S. man and biosphere program, Dept. State and UNESCO, 1987-91; mem. exec. bd. Archtl. Rsch. Ctrs., Consortium, 1992—; mem. Healthcare Design Rsch. Com., 1992—; reviewer sci. and design jours. Author: Scenery and the Shopping Trip: The Roadside Environment as a Factor in Route Choice, 1974; mem. editl. bd. Man-Environ. Sys., 1978-83, Urban Ecosystems, 1995—; mem. editl. adv. bd. Landscape Rsch., 1982-96, also numerous articles. Recipient nat. award for exemplary team leadership in higher edn. Am. Assn. Univ. Adminstrs., 1990; rsch. fellow Nat. Swedish Coun. for Bldg. Rsch., 1977-78, 84-85. Mem. APA (population-environ. divsn.), Environ. Design Rsch. Assn., Landscape Rsch. Group, Assn. Am. Geographers. Office: Tex A&M U Coll Architecture College Station TX 77843-3137

UMBREIT, WAYNE WILLIAM, bacteriologist, educator; b. Markesan, Wis., May 1, 1913; s. William Traugott and Augusta (Abendroth) U.; m. Doris McQuade, July 31, 1937; children: Dorayne Loreda, Jay Nicholas, Thomas Hayden. B.A., U. Wis., 1934, M.S., 1936, Ph.D., 1939. Instr. soil microbiology Rutgers U., 1937-38; faculty U. Wis., Madison, 1938-44; asst. prof. bacteriology and chemistry U. Wis., 1941-44; faculty Cornell U., 1944-47, prof. bacteriology, 1946-47; head dept. enzyme chemistry Merck Inst., Rahway, N.J., 1947-58; asso. dir., 1958; chmn. dept. bacteriology Rutgers U., New Brunswick, N.J., 1958-75; prof. microbiology, dir. grad. programs Rutgers U., 1969-83, prof. emeritus microbiology, 1983—; dir. labs. So. Br. Watershed Assn., 1983-89. Author: (with Burris, Stauffer) Manometric Techniques, 1945, 5th edit., 1972, (with Oginsky) An Introduction to Bacterial Physiology, 1954, Metabolic Maps, 1960, Modern Microbiology, 1962, Essentials of Bacterial Physiology, 1976; Editor: Advances in Applied Microbiology, vols. 1-10, 1959-68; Contbr. articles to profl. jours. Recipient Biochem. Congress Symposium medal Paris, France, 1952. Fellow Am. Acad. Microbiology, N.Y. Acad. Sci., A.A.A.S.; mem. Am. Soc. for Microbiology (Eli Lilly award in bacteriology 1947, Carski Found. award for distinguished teaching 1968), Soc. Biol. Chemists, Am. Chem. Soc., Theobald Smith Soc. (Waksman award in microbiology 1957, past pres.), AAUP, Sigma Xi. Home: 826 Covered Bridge Rd Holland PA 18966

UME-EZEOKE, PHILIP CHUKWUDI, surgeon; b. Onitsha, Anambra, Nigeria, June 14, 1951; s. Philip Orji and Angelina Enu (Okolo) U.; m. Edith Ijeoma Nonyelu, Feb. 16, 1980; children: Kasie, Odera, Chinedu. M.B.B.S., U. Ibadan, Nigeria, 1977. Surgery registrar Univ. Hosp., Enugu, Nigeria, 1979-80, Health Bds., Galway/Limerick, Ireland, 1981-86; surgery specialist Ministry of Health, Najran, Saudi Arabia, 1986-90; cons. surgeon Bukayriyah (Saudi Arabia) Hosp., 1990—; sr. cons. surgeon Al Hamadi Hosp. Ops., Riyadh, Saudi Arabia, 1994—; cons. Al Hanouf Health Svcs., Riyadh, 1990-94. Advisor Obiagu Social Youth Club, Amichi, Nigeria, 1978. Fellow Royal Coll. Surgeons Edinburgh, Internat. Coll. Surgeons; mem. Med. Informatics Club Bukayriyah. Mem. Xtian Faith. Office: Bukayriyah Gen Hosp, Box 177, Hospital Rd, Bukayriyah Gassim, Saudi Arabia

UMPIERREZ, GUILLERMO E., medical educator; b. Guayaquil, Ecuador, Jan. 4, 1954; came to the U.S., 1982; s. Leopoldo and Maria (Garcia) U.; m. Monica Umpierrez, Mar. 7, 1980; children: Denise, Erica. MD, U. Guayaquil, Ecuador, 1979. Diplomate Am. Bd. Internal Medicine, Am. Bd. Endocrinology and Metabolism. Intern in internal medicine Emory U. Sch. Medicine, Atlanta, 1982-83, resident internal medicine, 1983-85, fellow endocrinology and metabolism, 1985-88; pvt. practice Guayaquil, 1989-91; asst. prof. medicine Emory U., Atlanta, 1992—; instr. medicine Cath. U. Guayaquil, 1980-82, U. Guayaquil, 1980-82; staff endocrinologist Social Security Hosp., Guayaquil, 1981-82; coord. tchg. divsn., staff endocrinologist Hosp. Clinica Kennedy, Guayaquil, 1988-92; staff physician Hosp. Luis Vernaza, Guayaquil, 1990-92, Emory U. Hosp. and affiliated hosps., 1992—, Grady Meml. Hosp., 1992—, med. dir. metabolic and intermediate care unit, 1994—. Contbr. articles to profl. jours. Recipient Nat. Rsch. Svc. award NIH grantee, 1987-88; rsch. grantee Emory Med. Care Found., 1993, 94-95. Mem. ACP, Am. Diabetes Assn. (chmn. youth com. 1994, pres. Atlanta chpt. 1995—), Am. Fedn. Clin. Rsch., Endocrine Soc., Ecuatorian Coll. Physicians, Ecuatorian Soc. Endocrinology, Alpha Omega Alpha. Roman Catholic. Home: 1486 Vernon North Dr Dunwoody GA 30338 Office: Emory Univ Sch Medicine 69 Butlers St Atlanta GA 30303

UNAKAR, NALIN JAYANTILAL, biological sciences educator; b. Karachi, Sindh, Pakistan, Mar. 26, 1935; came to U.S., 1961; s. Jayantilal Virshankar and Malati Jaswantrai (Buch) U.; m. Nita Shantilal Mankad; children: Rita, Rupa. BS, Gujerat U., Bhavnagar, India, 1955; MSc, Bombay U., 1961; PhD, Brown U., 1965. Research asst. Indian Cancer Research Ctr., Bombay, 1955-61; USPHS trainee in biology Brown U., Providence, 1961-65; research assoc. in pathology U. Toronto, Ont., Can., 1965-66; asst. prof. biology Oakland U., Rochester, Mich., 1966-69, assoc. prof., 1969-74, prof., chmn. biology dept., 1974-87; prof., 1974—; adj. prof. biomed. scis. Oakland U., Rochester, Mich., 1984—; mem. coop. cataract research group Nat. Eye Inst., Bethesda, Md., 1977—; mem. visual scis. study sect. NIH, Bethesda, 1982-86, mem. cataract panel, 1980—. Mem. vis. bd. Lehigh U., Bethlehem, Pa., 1986-89. Grantee Nat. Cancer Inst., NIH, 1967-70, Nat. Eye Inst., NIH, 1976—. Mem. AAAS, Am. Soc. Cell Biology, Assn. Rsch. in Vision and Ophthalmology, Sigma Xi. Home: 2822 Rhineberry Rd Rochester Hls MI 48309-1912 Office: Oakland U Dept Of Biol Scis Rochester MI 48309

UNANUE, EMIL RAPHAEL, immunopathologist; b. Havana, Cuba, Sept. 13, 1934; married, 1965; 3 children. B.Sc., Inst. Secondary Edn., 1952; M.D., U. Havana Sch. Medicine, Cuba, 1960; M.A., Harvard U., 1974. Assoc. exptl. pathology Scripps Clin. and Research Found., 1960-70; intern in pathology Presbyn. Univ. Hosp., Pitts., 1961-62; research fellow in exptl. pathology Scripps Clin. and Research Found., 1962-65; research fellow immunology Nat. Inst. Med. Research, London, 1966-68; from asst. prof. to assoc. prof. pathology Harvard U. Med. Sch., Boston, 1971-74, prof., 1974-77, Mallinckrodt prof. immunopathology, 1977—; prof., chmn. dept. pathology Washington U. Sch. Medicine, St. Louis, 1988—. Recipient T. Duckett Jones award, Helen Hay Whitney Found., 1968, Park-Davis award, Am. Soc. Exptl. Pathology, 1973, Albert Lasker Award for Basic Med. Rsch., 1995. Office: Washington U Sch Medicine Dept of Pathology PO Box 8188 Saint Louis MO 63156-8188*

UNDERWOOD, ALFRED H., JR., dentist; b. Detroit, Jan. 31, 1930; s. Alfred H. Sr. and Eleanor (Lowry) U.; m. Annette Iho, Oct. 10, 1958; children: Alan H., Lee Alfred. Student, U. Miami, 1948-50, Emory U., 1950-53, 55-58; DDS, Emory U., 1958. Registered dentist, Fla. Pvt. practice Miami, 1958—; chair, organizer DCDRC sect. Orthodontics for the Gen. Dentist, 1977-84, co-chmn. D.C.D. rsch. chair sect., 1984—; clin. assoc. prof. U. Miami Sch. Medicine, 1982—; bd. dirs. Dade County Dental Rsch. Clinic, Miami, 1980—, pres. 1982-83; pres. S.E. Fla. Acad. Gen. Dentistry, Miami, 1990-92, rep. S.E. Fla. Acad. Dentistry, on bd. dirs. Fla. Acad. Gen. Dentistry 1992—; del. to Acad. Gen. Dentistry from Fla. Acad. Gen. Dentistry, 1994—. With U.S. Army, 1953-55, Korea. Fellow Acad. Gen. Denistry, 1980. Mem. ADA, Fla. Dental Assn., Greater Miami Dental Soc. (pres. 1983-84), North Miami Cmty. Band (exec. bd. property mgr. 1992—), Am. Legion (exec. bd. post 29 1992, 1st vice comdr. 1993-96, comdr. 1996—). Office: 1399 NW 17th Ave Miami FL 33125-2349

UNDERWOOD, BENJAMIN HAYES, health care executive; b. Savannah, Ga., Mar. 10, 1942; s. Frank Callaway and Marion Elizabeth (Hayes) U.; m. Sheri Lynn Vennell, Dec. 1984; children: Ashley Hayes, Benjamin Hayes, Kasey McDaniel. AA, Ga. Mil. Coll., 1962; BBA, U. Ga., 1964. Chief exec. officer Met. Psychiatric Ctr., Atlanta, 1965-76, Ridgeview Inst., Atlanta, 1976-82; cons., pres. BHU, Inc., Atlanta, 1984-86; pres., chief exec. officer Anchor Hosp., Atlanta, 1986—; bd. dirs. Talbott Recovery System. Bd. dirs. Cobb County C. of C., Atlanta, 1981-84, Caduceus Found. Named Boss of Yr., Am. Bus. Women's Assn., 1973. Fellow Am. Acad. Med. Adminstrs.; mem. Ga. Hosp. Assn. (trustee), Nat. Assn. Addiction Treatment Providers (bd. dirs. 1988—, exec. com., chmn.), Am. Coll. Healthcare Execs. (bd. dirs.), Am. Coll. Addiction Treatment Adminstrs. (cert., Outstanding Achievement award 1992), Assn. Mental Health Adminstrs. (cert.), Eagles Landing Golf Club, Rotary (bd. dirs., treas. 1980-84). Baptist. Home: 200 Riviera Ct Mc Donough GA 30253-4249 Office: Anchor Hosp 5454 Yorktowne Dr Atlanta GA 30349-5317

UNDERWOOD, BRENDA S., microbiologist, grants administrator; b. Oak Ridge, Tenn., Mar. 19, 1948; d. William Henry Hensley and Maudell (Walker) Townsend; m. Thomas L. Janiszewski, Feb. 14, 1984; 1 child, Thomas Zachary Janiszewski. BS, U. Tenn., 1970; MS, Hood Coll., 1980; MBA, Mt. St. Mary's Coll., 1993. Scientist I chem. carcinogenesis Frederick (Md.) Cancer Rsch. Ctr., 1977-84; microbiologist NCI/NIH, Bethesda, Md., 1984-86; sci. tech. writer Engring. and Econs. Rsch., Germantown, Md., 1987-88; spl. asst. to dir., program dir. grants div. Cancer Biology Diagnosis Ctrs., NCI/NIH, Bethesda, 1988-91; indexer, div. extramural activities Rsch. Analysis and Evaluation br. NCI/NIH, Bethesda, 1991—. Vol. Riding for the Handicapped, Frederick, 1990-96; mem., recreational sec. Capital Hill Equestrian Soc., Washington, 1988. Mem. AAAS, Am. Soc. for Microbiology, Am. Assn. for Cancer Rsch., Women in Cancer Rsch., Federally Employed Women. Office: NCI-NIH RAEB Divsn Extramural Activ Bethesda MD 20892

UNDERWOOD, JACK LAWRENCE, psychiatrist; b. Cleve., Mar. 13, 1928; s. Walter Kenneth and Agnes (Nolan) U.; m. JoBerta Louise Beauchamp, June 15, 1952; children: Janice Lynn, Jay Lawrence. AB, Duke U., 1951; MD, Howard U., 1958. Intern Albany Med. Ctr., Albany, N.Y., 1958-59; resident Albany Med. Ctr., Albany, 1959-62; pvt. practice Schenectady, N.Y., 1962—; staff psychiatrist Conifer Park, Scotia, N.Y., 1984-88; cons. Liberty Enterprises, Inc., Amsterdam, N.Y., 1984—. Med. com. Planned Parenthood of S.A.C. (name now Planned Parenthood Health Svcs. of Northeastern N.Y., Inc.), Schenectady, 1962—; chmn. northeast region, Planned Parenthood of Am., N.Y.C., 1972-75. Lt. (j.g.) USN, 1946-47, 1951-54. Mem. AMA, Am. Psychiatry Assn. Libertarian. Unitarian. Office: 1565 Union St Schenectady NY 12309-6047

UNDERWOOD, PAUL BENJAMIN, obstetrician, educator; b. Greer, S.C., Aug. 8, 1934; s. Paul Benjamin and Gladys (Guest) U.; m. Peggy Joyce Outen, July 7, 1957; children: Paul Benjamin III, Mary Barton. MD, Med. U. S.C., 1959. Diplomate Am. Bd. Ob-Gyn, Am. Bd. Gynecol. Oncology. Intern Med. U. S.C., Charleston, 1959-60, resident, 1960-64; fellow M.D. Anderson Hosp. and Tumor Inst., Houston, 1966-67; asst. prof. U. S.C., 1967-70, assoc. prof., 1970-74, prof., 1974-79; chmn. dept. ob-gyn U. Va. Sch. Medicine, Charlottesville, 1979—. Contbr. numerous articles to med. jours. With USN, 1964-66. Recipient Alumni of Yr. award Med. U. S.C., 1989. Mem. Am. Coll. Ob-Gyn., Soc. Gynecol. Oncologists (coun. 1972-75, v.p. 1977-78, pres. 1983), Am. Assn. Ob-Gyn. (sec. 1992-95), Felix Rutledge Soc. (pres. 1977), Am. Gynecol. Club (pres. 1996), So. Med. Soc., Charlottesville Med. Soc., S.C. Ob-Gyn. Soc., Thegos Soc., Alpha Omega Alpha. Office: U Va School Medicine Med Ctr PO Box 387 Charlottesville VA 22908

UNDERWOOD, ROBERT WILLIAM, physician assistant; b. Bridgton, Maine, Oct. 8, 1942; s. Robert Dana and Gloria Alice (Dunn) U.; m. Charlotte French, Oct. 15, 1962; children: Lisa, Dana. Student, Gorham State Tchrs. Coll. Oper. rm. technician Maine Med. Ctr., 1965-72; physician asst. Franklin Family Practice, Farmington, Maine; mem. state legislation com. for physician asst., Maine. Mem. Maine Soc. Physician Assts., N.Y. Soc. Physician Assts., Shriners, Masons (past master Farmington lodge 1981, 93). Republican. Methodist. Home: 34 Main St Farmington ME 04938 Office: Franklin Family Practice Rts 2 and 4 Farmington ME 04938

UNGARO, MARIO, pathologist, educator; s. Fabricio Ungaro and Enriquetta Zevallos. MB, Nat. U. San Marcos, Peru, 1954, MD. Bd. diplomate in pathology. Intern Marymount Hosp., Cleve., 1954-55; resident St. Vincent Charity Hosp., Cleve., 1955-57; resident in pathology New Britain Gen. Hosp., 1958-59, Roswell Park Meml. Inst., Buffalo, 1959-60; fellow forensic pathology Frank E. Bunts Ed. Inst., Cleve., 1957-58; asst. pathologist Mercy Hosp., Buffalo, 1960-61; prof. pathology Nat. U. Trujillo, Peru, 1961—; chmn. pathology Hosp. Regional Tchg. Hosp., Trujillo, 1980—; prof. emeritus Nat. U. Trujillo, 1992. Mem. Peruvian Assn. Pathology, Peruvian Med. Assn., Nat. Club, Golf Country Club. Office: Hosp Regional Tchg Hosp, Trujillo Peru

UNGER, ROGER HAROLD, physician, scientist; b. N.Y.C., Mar. 7, 1924; s. Lester and Beatrice (Raphael) U.; m. Barbara Latz, June 28, 1946; children: Christine, Craig, Jimmy; m. Marlise Mantel, Dec. 16, 1981; 1 child, Romy-Michelle. BS, Yale U., 1944; MD, Columbia U., 1947; MD (hon.), U. Geneva, 1976, U. Liège, Belgium, 1980. Diplomate Am. Bd. Internal Medicine. Asst. prof. internal medicine U. Tex. Med. Sch., Dallas, 1959-64, assoc. prof., 1964-69, prof., 1969—; dir. Ctr. for Diabetes Research, U. Tex. Health Sci. Ctr., Dallas, 1985—; Disting. chair diabetes rsch Touchstone/West, 1989—; sr. med. investigator VA Med. Ctr., Dallas, 1979—; mem. Nat. Diabetes Adv. Bd., Bethesda, Md., 1985—. Editor: Glucagon, 1972, Glucagon Physiology etc., 1981; assoc. editor (jour.) Diabetes, 1979-84, mem. editorial bd., 1975-79; mem. editorial bd. (jour.) Endocrinology, 1976-81; author 50 chpts. in textbooks, 300 papers for scientific jours. Served with USPHS, 1950-52. Recipient Lilly award Am. Diabetes Assn., 1964, Banting medal Am. Diabetes Assn., 1975, David Rumbough award Juvenile Diabetes Assn., 1975, Joslin medal Harvard U., 1979, Claude Bernard award European Assn. for Study Diabetes, 1979, Fred Conrad Koch award Endocrine Soc., 1983. Mem. NAS, Am. Acad. Arts and Scis., Am. Assn. Physicians, Am. Soc. for Clin. Investigation (emeritus). Office: Ctr for Diabetes Research 5323 Harry Hines Blvd Dallas TX 75235-7200

UNGOS, ERWINA QUINTO, emergency medicine physician; b. Mapandan, Philippines, Sept. 7, 1963; d. Eugenio Penuliar and Catalina (Quinto) U.; m. Michael Anthony Arroyo, June 3, 1993. BS, Calif. State U., Long Beach, 1987; OD, Coll. Osteo. Medicine Pacific, 1992. Intern William Beaumont Army Med. Ctr., El Paso, 1992-93; resident in emergency medicine Joint Mil. Med. Ctrs., San Antonio, 1993—. Capt U.S. Army, 1992—. Mem. Am. Coll. Emergency Physicians, AMA, Am. Assn. Women Emergency Physicians.

UPADHYAY, YOGENDRA NATH, physician, educator; b. Gorakhpur, India, Dec. 21, 1938; came to U.S., 1963; s. Murlidhar and Vansraji (Pande) U.; m. Cecile R. Yonish; children: Asha, Sameer, Sanjay. MB, BS, All India Inst. Med. Scis., New Delhi, 1962. Diplomate Am. Bd. Psychiatry and Neurology, Am. Bd. Pediatrics. Instr. in pediatrics Johns Hopkins U. Sch. Medicine, Balt., 1969-71; fellow in child psychiatry Johns Hopkins Hosp./Johns Hopkins U., Balt., 1971-72; resident, then sr. resident in psychiatry Albert Einstein Coll. Medicine/Bronx Mcpl. Hosp. Ctr., 1972-74, fellow in child psychiatry, 1974-75; chief, partial hosp. program for children, dept. psychiatry Brookdale Hosp., Bklyn., 1976-77; med. dir. West Nassau Mental Health Ctr., Franklin Sq., N.Y., 1977-80; asst. prof. clin. psychiatry SUNY, Stony Brook, 1978-92; dir. child and adolescent psychiatry Nassau County Med. Ctr., East Meadow, N.Y., 1980-92; sr. psychiatrist South Oaks Hosp., Amityville, N.Y., 1992—, pres. med. staff, 1995—, pres. medical staff, 1995—. Fellow Am. Psychiat. Assn. Sons. task force treatments psychiat. disorders 1989—), Am. Acad. Child and Adolescent Psychiatry, Allmsonians of Am. (founding pres. 1982-86). Office: 400 Sunrise Hwy Amityville NY 11701-2508

UPSHUR, CAROLE CHRISTOFK, psychologist, educator; b. Des Moines, Oct. 18, 1948; d. Robert Richard and Margaret (Davis) Christofk; 1 child, Emily. AB, U. So. Calif., 1969; EdM, Harvard U., 1970, EdD (NIMH fellow), 1975. Lic. psychologist, Mass. Planner, Mass. Com. on Criminal Justice, Boston, 1970-73; licensing specialist, planner, policy specialist Mass. Office for Children, Boston, 1973-76; asst. prof. Coll. Public and Cmty. Svc., U. Mass., Boston, 1976-81, assoc. prof., 1982-93, prof., 1993—, chmn. Ctr. for Cmty. Planning, 1979-81, 84-86, 1995-96, sr. rsch. fellow Maurice Gaston Inst. Latino Pub. Policy, 1993—, Ctr. Social Devel. & Edn., 1991—, sr. rsch. fellow Gerontology Inst., 1996—, dir. PhD in Pub. Policy program, 1995—; cons. to govt. and cmty. agys. on mental health and social svc. policy and mgmt., 1970—; cons. Harvard Family Rsch. Project, 1983-93; assoc. in pediatrics, sr. rsch. assoc. U. Mass. Med. Sch., 1983-94; adj. prof. Heller Sch. Social Welfare, Brandeis U., 1985—. Commr. Brookline Human Rels.-Youth Resources Commn., 1988-91, Gov's. Commn. on Facility Consolidation, 1991-92, Mass. Healthcare Adv. Com., 1993—. Fellow Mass. Psychol. Assn.; mem. APA, Am. Assn. on Mental Retardation (cons. editor Mental Retardation, Amer. Jour. on Mental Retardation 1981—, AJMR Monographs. Office: PhD Program in Public Policy U Mass Boston MA 02125

UPSON, KATHERINE WOLFF CORCORAN, critical care nurse; b. Waterbury, Conn., May 7, 1953; d. Edward A. and Lucy M. (Guarrera) Wolff; children: John, James, Matthew; m. Thomas F. Upson. AS in Nursing, U. Bridgeport (Conn.), 1974; BSN, U. Conn., Torrington, 1991. Cert. critical care nurse. Staff nurse Meriden (Conn.)-Wallingford Hosp., 1981-85, St. Mary's Hosp., Waterbury, 1974-81, 86—. Mem. AACCN, Conn. Nurses Assn. (Search for Excellence award 1990), Sigma Theta Tau (Mu chpt.). Home: 827 Oronoke Rd 10-1 Waterbury CT 06708

UPSON, ROGER BALLARD, healthcare executive; b. Isleworth, Middlesex, Eng., Apr. 13, 1938; s. Albert and Olive (Ballard) U.; m. Jean Leach, June 30, 1962; children: Karen, Anne, Kristen, Mary Kay. BSc in Econs., London Sch. Econs., 1960; MBA, U. Mich., 1961, PhD, 1965. Fin. analyst Esso Petroleum, London, 1962-64, Exxon Corp., N.Y.C., 1965-67; assoc. prof. U. Minn., Mpls., 1967-73; prof. fin. U. Minn., 1973-83, assoc. dean Sch. Bus., 1972-78, dir. MBA prog. Sch. Mgmt., 1978-83; chief fin. officer Park Nicollet Med. Ctr., Mpls., 1983-86; sr. v.p., chief fin. officer Am. Medcenters, Mpls., 1984-87; sr. v.p., COO Managed Care divsn. Health One, Mpls., 1987-93; Minn. care officer and physician clinic cons. Healthspan Health Systems Corp., Mpls., 1993-94; v.p. fin., Minn. care officer Allina Health System, Mpls., 1994—; chmn. bd. dirs. Preferred One, Inc, St. Paul, 1990-92, Preferred One Mgmt. Corp., St. Paul, 1987-93; chmn. bd., dir. Minn. Hosp. Capitation Consortium, Mpls., 1988-89. Author: Returns in OTC Stock Markets, 1973; contbr. articles to profl. jours. Mem. program and budget com. Episcopal Diocese, Mpls., 1985—, chmn., 1991—. Rackham predoctoral fellow, 1964-65; Harkness fellow, 1960-62. Mem. Am. Econs. Assn.

UPTON, ARTHUR CANFIELD, experimental pathologist, educator; b. Ann Arbor, Mich., Feb. 27, 1923; s. Herbert Hawkes and Ellen (Canfield) U.; m. Elizabeth Bache Perry, Mar. 1, 1946; children: Rebecca A., Melissa P., Bradley C. Grad., Phillips Acad., Andover, Mass., 1941; BA, U. Mich., 1944, MD, 1946. Intern Univ. Hosp., Ann Arbor, 1947; resident Univ. Hosp., 1948-49; instr. pathology U. Mich. Med. Sch., 1950-51; pathologist Oak Ridge (Tenn.) Nat. Lab., 1951-54, chief pathology-physiology sect., 1954-69; prof. pathology SUNY Med. Sch. at Stony Brook, 1969-77, chmn. dept. pathology, 1969-70, dean Sch. Basic Health Scis., 1970-75; dir. Nat. Cancer Inst., Bethesda, Md., 1977-79; prof., chmn. dept. environ. medicine NYU Med. Sch., N.Y.C., 1980-92, prof. emeritus, 1993—; clin. prof. radiology U. N.Mex. Sch. Medicine, 1993—, clin. prof. pathology, 1992-95; clin. prof. environ. and cmty. medicine U. Medicine and Dentistry N.J.-Robert Wood Johnson Med. Sch., 1995—; attending pathologist Brookhaven Nat. Lab., 1969-77; dir. Inst. Environ. Medicine, Med. Sch., NYU, 1980-91; mem. various coms. nat. and internat. orgns.; lectr. in field. Assoc. editor: Cancer Research; mem. editorial bd.: Internat. Union Against Cancer. Served with AUS, 1943-46. Recipient Ernest Orlando Lawrence award for atomic field, 1965, Comfort-Crookshank award for cancer rsch. Inst. Med., NAS, 1979, Claude M. Fuess award 1980, Sarah L. Poilley award for pub. health, 1983, CHUMS Physician of Yr. award 1985, Basic Cell Rsch. in Cytology Lectureship award 1985, Fred W. Stewart award, 1986, Ramazzini award, 1986, Lovelace Med. Found. award, 1993; Sigma Xi nat. lectr., 1989-91. Fellow Soc. Risk Analysis, N.Y. Acad. Sci.; mem. Am. Assn. Pathologists and Bacteriologists, Internat. Acad. Pathology, Inst. Medicine NAS, Radiation Rsch. Soc. (councilor 1963-64, pres. 1965-66), Internat. Assn. Radiation Rsch. (pres. 1983-87), Am. Assn. Cancer Rsch. (pres. 1963-64), Am. Soc. Exptl. Pathology (pres. 1967-68), AAAS, Gerontol. Soc., Sci. Rsch. Soc. Am., Soc. Exptl. Biology and Medicine, Peruvian Oncology Soc. (hon.), Japan Cancer Assn. (hon.), N.Y. State Health Rsch. Coun. (chmn. 1982-90), Internat. Assn. Radiation Rsch. (pres. 1983-87), Assn. Univ. Environ. Health Sci. Ctrs. (pres. 1982-90), Ramazzini Inst. (pres. 1992—), Phi Beta Kappa, Phi Gamma Delta, Alpha Omega Alpha, Nu Sigma Nu, Sigma Xi. Home: Apt 12B 401 E 86th St New York NY 10028 Office: 681 Freylinghuysen Rd Piscataway NJ 08855-1179

UPTON, GERALD WILLIAM, oral and maxillofacial surgeon, infectious diseases researcher; b. Washington, Mar. 5, 1949; s. William Bruce, Jr. and Addie Morine (Williams) U.; m. Nancy Gail Henshaw, Dec. 11, 1976; children: Elizabeth Chandler Henshaw, Richard William Henshaw. B.S. in Biology, Va. Mil. Inst., 1971; M.S. in Microbiology, Med. Coll. Va., 1975, D.D.S., 1975; Ph.D. in Exptl. Pathology, U. N.C., 1981. Diplomate Am. Bd. Oral and Maxillofacial Surgery. Resident oral and maxillofacial surgery U. N.C., Chapel Hill, N.C., 1977-80, AAOMS post doctoral research fellow, 1980-81; practice of oral and maxillofacial surgery, Raleigh, N.C., 1981—; adj. prof. U. N.C. Sch. Dentistry, Chapel Hill, 1984—; prin. investigator Clin. Research Study, Burroughs-Wellcome Co., Raleigh, N.C., 1984—; bd. dirs. Blue Ridge Ambulatory Surgery Ctr., Raleigh, N.C., 1983-95. Mem. Va. Mil. Inst. Alumni Assn. (new cadet recruiting chmn. Central Carolina chpt. 1983-84, v.p. Central Carolina chpt. 1985), ADA, N.C. Dental Soc., Raleigh-Wake County Dental Soc., Am. Assn. Oral and Maxillofacial Surgeons (recipient research fellow 1979), Omicron Kappa Upsilon, Sigma Zeta, Mu Beta Psi. Avocations: snow skiing; jogging Office: 2310 Myron Dr Raleigh NC 27607-3358

UPTON, PETER DODDS, physician; b. Burlington, Vt., May 18, 1936; s. Hiram Eugene and Doris Atwater (Dodds) U.; m. Kathleen Ovitt; children: Michael Dodds, Timothy Ovitt, Louise Alice. AB, Dartmouth Coll., 1958; MS, U. Vt., 1961, MD, 1963. Cert. Am. Bd. Neurol. Surgery, 1972. Intern Colo. Gen. Hosp., Denver, 1963-64, resident neurology, 1964-65; resident neurosurgery Med. Ctr. Hosp. of Vt., Burlington, 1965-69; practice of neurosurgery Rutland (Vt.) Regional Med. Ctr., 1969—. Mem. Rutland Regional Med. Ctr., Rutland County Med. Soc., Vt. State Med. Soc., New England Neurosurgical Soc., Alpha Omega Alpha. Home: 34 S Main St Wallingford VT 05773 Office: 231 Mussey St Rutland VT 05701-4843

UPTON, THOMAS VERNON, medical educator; b. Antigo, Wis., Apr. 27, 1948; s. Laverne Leo and Mildred Helen (Burmeister) U.; m. Teresa Anne Ugis, June 11, 1977; children: Mark, Paul, Catherine, Marie. BA, Cath. U. Am., MA, 1972, PhD, 1977. Assoc. prof. Gannon U., Erie, Pa., 1977-83, 84—; vis. prof. Cath. U. Am., Washington, 1983-84; cons. in field. Contbr. articles to profl. jours. Basselin Found. scholar, 1968-71; J.K. Ryan Found. fellow, 1974-77, NEH fellow, 1980, 83, 86, 88. Mem. Am. Philos. Assn., Cath. Philos. Assn. (bd. dirs. 1984-86), Soc. Ancien. Republican. Roman Catholic. Office: Gannon U Box 209 Erie PA 16541

URBACH, FREDERICK, physician, educator; b. Vienna, Austria, Sept. 6, 1922; s. Erich and Josepha (Kronstein) U.; m. Nancy Ann Phillips, Dec. 20, 1952; children: Erich J., Gregory M., Andrew D. AB cum laude, U. Pa., 1943; MD, Jefferson Med. Coll., 1946; MD (hon.), U. Göttingen, Fed. Republic Germany, 1987. Diplomate: Am. Bd. Dermatology. Intern Jefferson Hosp., 1946-47; fellow in dermatology U. Pa. Hosp., 1949-52; fellow pediatric dermatology Children's Hosp., Phila., 1950-52; asst. vis. physician Phila. Gen. Hosp., Skin and Cancer Hosp., U. Pa. Hosp., 1952-54; assoc. chief cancer research (dermatology) Roswell Park Meml. Inst., Buffalo, 1954-55, chief cancer research (dermatology), 1955-58; asst. med. dir. Skin and Cancer Hosp. Phila., 1958-67, med. dir., 1967-88; research prof. physiology U. Buffalo Grad. Sch., 1955-58; assoc. prof. dermatology Temple U. Sch. Medicine, 1958-60, prof. research dermatology, 1960-67, chmn. dept. dermatology, 1967-88; dir. Ctr. for Photobiology, 1977-89, prof. dermatology emeritus, 1989—; dep. dir. Health Rsch. Inc., Buffalo, 1954-58; mem. U.S. nat. com. photo-biology Nat. Acad. Sci., 1973-80. Author: The Biology of Cutaneous Cancer, 1963, The Biologic Effects of Ultraviolet Radiation, 1969, (with Parrish, Anderson and Pitts) UVA, 1978; (with Gange) Biologic Effects of UVA Radiation, 1985, Responses to UVA Radiation, 1992; contbr. articles to profl. jours. Served with AUS, 1943-46; with USAAF, 1947-49. Recipient Ritter Meml. medal German Dermatology Soc., 1980. Fellow AAAS, N.Y. Acad. Sci.; mem. AMA, ACP, FACP, Am. Soc. Photobiology (councilor 1973-76, pres. 1977), Am. Assn. Cancer Rsch. Soc. Exptl. Biology and Medicine, Internat. Soc. Tropical Dermatology, Internat. Assn. Photobiology (v.p. 1976-79, pres. 1980-84, Finsen medal 1992); hon. mem. Danish Soc. Dermatology, Swedish Soc. Dermatology (Hellerstoöm medal 1977), Polish Soc. Dermatology, Austrian Soc. Dermatology, German Soc. Dermatology, Philippine Soc. Dermatology. Home: 438 Clairemont Rd Villanova PA 19085-1706 Office: Temple Med Practices 220 Commerce Dr Fort Washington PA 19034-2404

URBANIAK, JAMES RANDOLPH, orthopedic surgeon; b. Fairmont, W.Va., May 15, 1936; s. Cecil and Patricia (Morgan) U.; m. Martha Helen Shawger, Dec. 20, 1970; children: Julie Kathleen, Michael James. BS, U. Ky., 1958; MD, Duke U., 1962. Diplomate Am. Bd. Orthop. Surgery, Am. Bd. Hand Surgery. Intern Duke U., Durham, N.C., 1962-63; resident in orthopaedic surgery Duke U. Hosps., Durham, N.C., 1965-69; asst. prof. Div. Orthopaedic Surgery, Duke U., Durham, 1969-73, assoc. prof., 1973-77, prof., 1977—, chief, 1985—; chief orthopaedics VA Med. Ctr., Durham, 1969-76; dir. replantation team, orthopaedic research Duke U. Med. Ctr. Editor: Microsurgery, 1987; co-editor: AAOS Symposium Microsurgery, 1979; contbr. over 110 articles to profl. jours. and 30 chpts. to books. Served to lt. comdr. USN, 1963-65. Camp Orthopaedic Travel fellow, 1968, Am. Orthopaedic Assn. Travel fellow; named N.C. Physician of Yr., 1985; recipient Disting. Alumni award U. Ky., 1985. Mem. Am. Soc. Reconstructive Microsurgery (founder, pres. 1985), Am. Soc. for Surgery of Hand (sec. 1985—), Am. Bd. Orthopaedic Surgery (bd. dirs. 1985, pres.-elect. 1988—), Joint Com. of Surgery of Hand (chmn. exam. com. 1986), Am. Orthopaedic Assn., Am. Acad. Orthopaedic Surgeons, Eastern Orthopaedic Assn. (pres. 1981), Phi Beta Kappa, Alpha Omega Alpha. Home: 2600 Vintage Hill Ct Durham NC 27712-9492 Office: Duke U Med Ctr Box 2912 Durham NC 27710*

URE, JORGE ALBERTO, neurologist, consultant; b. Buenos Aires, Mar. 13, 1948; s. Carlos Maria and Maria Ines (Ottolenghi) U.; m. Carmela Salto, Feb. 7, 1985. Grad. faculty of medicine, Buenos Aires U., 1970, MD, 1984. Med. resident Policlínico Castex, Buenos Aires, 1971-74; mÉdico de planta Hosp. Churruca, Buenos Aires, 1979-84; chief divsn. Policlínico UPM Cen., Buenos Aires, 1983-85; asst. prof. neurology Buenos Aires U., 1984; chief of sect. Hosp. Borda, Buenos Aires, 1984-90; chief of svc. Inst. Antártida, Buenos Aires, 1985—, Hosp. Borda, Buenos Aires, 1990—; perito mÉdico neurólogo, Poder Jud., Buenos Aires, 1989—; v.p. XXXII Congreso de la Soc. Neurology Argentina, 1993. Author: (book, invention) Urgencias en Psiquiatría, 1986; contbr. papers to profl. jours. Mem. Gente de Letras, Buenos Aires, 1982. Scholar Consejo de Investigaciones Cientificas, IN-IBIBB, Bahia Blanca, 1981, XV World Congress of Neurology, Vancouver, Can., 1993, Assn. Médica Hosp. Borda, 21 Epilepsy Congress, Sydney, Australia, 1995. Fellow Royal Soc. Medicine U.K., Am. Acad. Neurology (corr.); mem. Argentine Soc. Escritores, Soc. Neurology Argentina, Liga Argentina contra la Epilepsia, Argentine Med. Assn. Roman Catholic. Home: Monte Grande, Eugenio Rebizo 455, 1842 Buenos Aires Argentina Office: Hosp Borda, Ramon Carrillo 375, 1275 Buenos Aires Argentina

URIBE, JOHN W., orthopedist, surgeon, educator; b. Bogota, Columbia, Sept. 29, 1949; came to U.S., 1952; s. William and Lola (Ferraira) U.; m. Nancy, Feb. 16, 1985; children: Alex, Michael, Julia. BS in Chemistry, The Citadel, 1969; MD, U. N.C., 1976. Diplomate Am. Bd. Orthop. Surgery. Orthop. surgeon U.S. Army Med. Ctr., Frankfurt, Germany, 1981-84; fellow in sports medicine Hughston Clinic, Columbus, Ga., 1984-85; chief orthop. surgery Tripler Army Med. Ctr., Honolulu, 1985-87; assoc. prof. U. Miami, Fla., 1987—; chief sports medicine Sch. Medicine; cons. Wright Med., Memphis, 1992—, Innouasive Devices, Boston, 1995—, Arthro Care Corp., San Francisco, 1995—; team physician U. Miami, Miami Dolphins, Fla. Marlins. Contbr. articles to profl. jours. Bd. dirs. Touqueville Soc. United Way, 1987—. Lt. col. U.S. Army, 1981-87. Named Physician of Yr., Health South, 1994. Fellow Am. Acad. Orthop. Surgeons (sports medicine com.). Office: Univ Miami 1150 Campo Sano Ave Coral Gables FL 33146

URICCHIO, WILLIAM ANDREW, biology educator; b. Hartford, Conn., Apr. 21, 1924; s. William and Mary (Donadio) U.; m. Velma Mathias, June 12, 1950; children: William, MaryLynn, Barbara, Robert, Michael. AB, Cath. U. Am., 1949, MS, 1951, PhD, 1953. From asst. to assoc. prof. Carlow Coll., Pitts., 1953-61, prof., 1961-94, prof. emeritus, 1994—; chmn. dept. biology Carlow Coll., Pitts., 1953-87, chmn. divsn. natural sci., 1987—; cons. edn. divsn. Xerox, Pitts., 1967-75; assoc. program dir. NSF, Washington, 1967-68. Author: Microbiology for Nurses, 1966, Independent Research in the Sciences, 1975; editor: Nat. Family Planning Proc., 1973, Pa. Acad. Sci. jour., 1963-67. Bd. dirs. Duquesne U., Pitts., 1973—, McGuire Meml., Pitts., 1972—, Human Life Found., Washington, 1968-80. With U.S. Army, 1943-46. Named Knight of St. Gregory, Pope Paul VI, 1967; recipient Pa. Sci. Edn. award Pa. Jr. Acad. Sci., 1976. Fellow AAAS; mem.

Pa. Acad. Sci. (editor, pres. 1970-72), Am. Grad. and Profl. Com. (pres. 1970-74), Internat. Fedn. for Family Promotion (hon., bd. dirs. 1978—), Serra Club (pres. 1970-71), Delta Epsilon Sigma (nat. lectr. 1985, pres. 1960-82). Roman Catholic. Home: 300 Fox Chapel Rd Pittsburgh PA 15238 Office: Carlow Coll 3333 5th Ave Pittsburgh PA 15213-3109

URLAUB, CHARLES JOSEPH, hospital administrator; b. Rochester, N.Y., Dec. 22, 1956; s. Warren Gerald and Elaine (Ringelstein) U.; m. Susan Lee Gorman, Sept. 12, 1981; children: Kaitlyn Marie, Morgan Lee. BS, Rensselear Poly Tech. Inst., 1979, MBA, 1981. Project specialist St. Mary's Hosp., Rochester, N.Y., 1979-80; asst. v.p. St. Mary's Hosp., Rochester, 1981-84, v.p. ops., 1984-88; asst. v.p. Buffalo Gen. Hosp., 1988-93, v.p. continous quality improvement, 1993—; adminstrv. adv. bd. D'Youville Coll. Health Svcs., 1982—; guest lectr. Sch. Mgmt., SUNY, Buffalo; guest lectr. univs. Hungary, 1995. Bd. dirs. 19th Ward Cmty. Orgn., Rochester, 1984-85; loaned exec. United Way Rochester, 1982, hosp. chmn. and liaison, 1983-87, allocations com., Buffalo, 1991—, mem. chmn.'s campaign staff. Mem. Am. Coll. Healthcare Execs., Western N.Y. Healthcare Exec. Forum (chmn. membership com.), Am. Soc. Quality Control, Western N.Y. Hosp. Assn. (com. mem., support network steering com. chair), Greater Buffalo Community Quality Coun., Nat. Assn. Rocketry, Tripoly Rocketry, Canadaigua Emergency Squad (Perington Ambulance/Southeast Quadrant Advanced Life Support 1980-84, Nat. Ski Patrol 1972-78), Epsilon Delta Sigma, Phi Mu Delta (v.p. fin. 1978-79). Republican. Roman Catholic. Home: 255 Glen Oaks Dr East Amherst NY 14051-1252 Office: Buffalo Gen Hosp 100 High St Buffalo NY 14203-1126

UROSEVICH, WILLIAM BLAZO, optometrist, educator; b. Hazleton, Pa., Aug. 8, 1954; s. George Thomas and Marija (Vukcevich) U.; m. Patricia Reilly, June 18, 1977; children: Alexander, Katharine. BA in Chemistry, Wilkes U., Wilkes-Barre, Pa., 1976; MS, U. So. Calif., 1979; DO, Pa. Coll. Optometry, Phila., 1983. Asst. chief optometry DeWitt Army Hosp., Ft. Belvoir, Va., 1983-86, Keller Army Hosp., West Point, N.Y., 1986-89; asst. prof. Pa. Coll. Tech., Williamsport, 1993—; owner Urosevich Eye Assocs., Lewisburg, Pa., 1989—; owner Urosevich Eye Seminars, Lewisburg, 1995—. Author: Ocular Disease Update, 1989. Liaison officer U.S. Mil. Acad., West Point, 1989—; cons. U.S. Army ROTC, Lewisburg, 1989—. Lt. col. U.S. Army, 1976—. Decorated Meritorious Svc. medal; named Disting. Young Alumnus, Wilkes U., 1989. Fellow Am. Acad. Optometry; mem. Am. Optometric Assn., Armed Forces Optometric Soc., Masons, Scottish Rite. Home: 1585 Monroe Ave Lewisburg PA 17837 Office: Urosevich Eye Assocs 1722 W Market St Lewisburg PA 17837

URREA, PAUL T., physician; b. L.A., Aug. 1, 1955; s. Gilberto Soto and Sofia (Tirado) U.; m. Nora Alicia Macias, Dec. 19, 1981; children: Oliva Raquel, Isabella Beatriz, Julian Pablo. BA, Yale U., 1977; MD, UCLA, 1982, M in Pub. Health, 1982. Diplomate Am. Bd. Ophthalmology. Intern flexible ophthalmology LAC-USC Med. Ctr., 1982-86, resident ophthalmology Doheny Eye Inst., 1982-86; fellow pediat. ophthalmology and strabismus Jules Stein Eye Inst., 1986-87; physician John J. McDermott, M.D., Claremont, Calif., 1987-90; pvt. practice Monterey Park, Calif., 1990—; Mem. adv. bd. Inst. Families of Blind Children, 1990-95; bd. dirs. L.A. chpt. Am. Diabetes Assn.; lectr. ophthalmology U. So. Calif. Sch. Medicine Cmty. Hosp. Network, 1989—; mem. physicians adv. group U. So. Calif. U. Hosp., 1989—. Contbr. chpts. to books, articles to profl. jours. Mem. adv. bd. San Gabriel Valley Head Start program, 1992—; bd. dirs. St. Edmund's Episcopal Ch. Nursery Sch., San Marino, Calif., 1989-91, Youth Opportunities Scholarship Found., 1989—; med. dir. So. Calif. Lions-Doheny Eye Found., 1991—. Merit Scholar Henry J. Kaiser Family Found., 1982; recipient Cmty. Svc. award Ciba Pharm. Co., 1979, Medicine/Health award Coun. Recognition of Hispanics, 1984, Physician Leadership award U. Calif. Irvine Coll. Medicine Found., 1988, Scientific Participation award XVII Mexican Nat. Congress Ophthalmology, 1988, Resident Tchg. dept. ophthalmology White Meml. Med. Ctr., 1991. Mem. Am. Acad. Ophthalmology (cons. pub. info. com. 1989—), Am. Assn. Pediat. Ophthalmology and Strabismus (cons. pub. info. com. 1988-91), AMA, Am. Pub. Health Assn., Am. Soc. Cataract and Refractive Surgery, Calif. Assn. Ophthalmology (bd. dirs. 1986—, v.p. pub. edn. 1988-89), Calif. Hispanic-Am. Med. Assn. (bd. dirs. 1989-91, First Annual scholarship 1981, chmn. scholarship com. 1986-91), Calif. Med. Assn., L.A. County Med. Assn., UCLA Med. Alumni Assn. Office: 850 S Atlantic Blvd Monterey Park CA 91754

URSANO, ROBERT JOSEPH, psychiatrist; b. Heidelberg, Ger., May 26, 1947; s. James Joseph and Neoma Faye (Summers) U.; m. Diane T. Ursano; children: Amy, Anna. BS magna cum laude, U. Notre Dame, 1969; MD, Yale U., 1973; grad., Washington Psychoanalystic Ins, 1986. Diplomate Nat. Bd. Med. Examiners, Am. Bd. Psychiatry and Neurology; lic. physician N.Y., Tex., Md. Resident in psychiatry Wilford Hall USALF Med. Ctr., 1973-75; postdoctoral fellow in psychiatry Yale U./Yale Psychiat. Inst., 1975-77; staff psychiatrist USAF Sch. Aerospace Medicine, Brooks AFB, Tex., 1977-79; clin. asst. prof. U. Tex. Health Sci. Ctr., San Antonio, 1977-79; asst. prof. and dir. third yr. clerkships Dept. psychiatry, Uniformed Svcs. U. Health Scis., Bethesda, Md., 1979-81; assoc prof. and dir. 3rd yr. clerkships Dept. psychiatry, Uniformed Svcs. U. Health Scis., 1981-83, assoc. prof. and assoc. chmn. dept. psychiatry, 1983-86, prof. and assoc. chmn. dept. psychiatry, 1987-82; prof., chair dept. psychiatry Uniformed Svcs. U. Health Scis., Bethesda, Md., 1992—; examiner Am. Bd. Psychiatry and Neurology, 1984—; asst. prof. Nat. Naval Med. Ctr Dept. Psychiatry, Georgetown U. Sch. Medicine, Washington, 1980-84, assoc. prof., 1984-88, prof., 1988—. Editor: Concise Guide to Psychodynamic Psychotherapy, Individual and Community Responses to Trauma and Disaster: The Structure of Human Chaos, Emotional Aftermath of The Persian Gulf War: Veterans, Families, Communities and Nations; reviewer Am. Jour. Psychiatry, Jour. Nervous and Mental Disease, Psychosomatics, Psychiatry, Jour. Applied Social Psychology, Archives of Gen. Psychiatry, Hosp. and Community Psychiatry, all 1986—, Jour. Neuropsychiatry and Clin. Neurosci., 1988—, Jour. Traumatic Stress, 1989—; contbr. numerous articles to profl. jours., chpts. to books. Decorated Air Force Commendation medal, Dept. Def. Humanitarian Svc. medal; recipient William C. Porter award AMSUS. Fellow Am. Psychiat. Assn.; mem. Am. Psychoanalytic Assn., Internat. Psychoanalytic Assn., Am. Psychosomatic Soc., Washington Psychiat. Soc., Washington Psychoanalytic Soc., Soc. of USAF Psychiatrists (v.p. 1981-82), Assn. for Acad. Psychiatry, Am. Coll. Psychiatrists, Alpha Epsilon Delta, Phi Beta Kappa. Home: 3900 Cleveland St Kensington MD 20895-3804 Office: Uniformed Svcs U Health Sci 4301 Jones Bridge Rd Bethesda MD 20814-4712

URSCHEL, JOHN DOUGLAS, thoracic surgeon; b. Edmonton, Alberta, Can., Oct. 19, 1958; 1 child, John Cameron. MD, U. Alberta, Edmonton, 1982. Intern Misericordia Hosp., Edmonton, 1982-83; resident in gen. and thoracic survery U. Alta., Edmonton, 1983-90; resident in thoracic surgery U. Man., Winnipeg, 1990-91; thoracic surgeon U. Alberta, Edmonton, Can., 1991-93, Roswell Pk. Cancer Inst., Buffalo, 1993—. Contbr. over 50 articles to profl. jours. Fellow Royal Coll. Surgeons of Can., Royal Coll. Surgeons of Edinburgh. Office: Roswell Pk Cancer Inst Elm & Carlton Sts Buffalo NY 14263-0001

URSO, PAUL, immunologist; b. Sicily, Italy, Aug. 3, 1925; came to U.S., 1930, naturalized, 1936; s. Paolo and Melchiorra (Garufi) U.; children: Theresa M. Urso Schweizer, Peter J.; m. Shirley F. Cockrell, Apr. 13, 1996. BS, St. Francis Coll., 1950; MS, Marquette U., 1952; PhD, U. Tenn., 1961. Grad. asst. Marquette U., 1950-52; instr. Cardinal Stritch Coll., Milw., 1952-53; biologist NIH, 1953-55; jr. biologist Dept. Biology, Oak Ridge Nat. Lab., 1955-58, Rsch. assoc. 1958-59; predoctoral fellow U. Tenn., Oak Ridge Inst., Nuclear Studies, 1959-61; asst. and assoc. prof. biology Seton Hall U., S. Orange, N.J., 1961-71; sr. scientist/immunologist Oak Ridge Assoc. U., Oak Ridge, 1971-81; asst. prof. microbiology/immunology Morehouse Sch. Medicine, Atlanta, 1981-89, assoc. prof., 1989—; cons. ORNL, 1961-63, ORAU, 1963-70, USAID Wash. III program, 1987—; mem. com. NIH, 1983—. Adv. grads. Seton Hall U. 1965-70; bd. dirs. Oak Ridge Community Playhouse, 1979-80, Cath. High, Knoxville, 1974-75; mem. St. Mary's Ch. choir, Oak Ridge, 1974-81, Sacred Heart Ch. Choir, Atlanta, 1982—, treas., 1991-94; baseball coach Oak Ridge Boys Club, 1971-74, Our Lady of Sorrows, Tacoma Park, Md. 1953-55. With Signal Corps, U.S. Army, 1944-46, PTO. ORINS at U. Tenn. predoctoral fellow, 1959-61; NIH grantee, 1964-67; Dept. Energy/EPA Co., grantee, 1978-81; grantee NIH/MBRS, 1983-87, 87—, AID, 1985-86, 87-88., 89-91, 91-93, 93—, RCMI-AIDS (NIH) program, 1989—, EPA grantee, 1989—. Mem. Am. Assn. Immunologists, Soc. Leukocyte Biology, Transplantation Soc., Internat. Soc. Exptl. Hematologists, Internat. Soc. Devel. and Comparative Immunology, Clin. Immunological Soc., Am. Assn. Cancer Rsch., Soc. Toxicology, Radiation Rsch. Soc., Parents without Ptnrs. (v.p. Oak Ridge 1979), Oak Ridge Community Playhouse, Pi R Sqs. Sq Dance, Honey Creek Golf Club, Sigma Xi (v.p. 1968-69, pres. 1969-70). Contbr. articles to profl. jours. Home: 371 Clubland Cir Conyers GA 30208 Office: Morehouse Sch Med 720 Westview Dr SW Atlanta GA 30310-1458

USDAN, JAMES MORRIS, health care executive; b. Englewood, N.J., Nov. 3, 1949; s. Leo Judah and Selma (Goldfein) U.; m. Vinette Ann Carknard, June 8, 1980. AB, Harvard U., 1971. Gen. mgr. Some Place Else Restaurant, Schuylerville, N.Y., 1972-77; v.p. Meth. Hosp., Houston, 1977-83, Health Resources Corp. Am., Houston, 1983-84; pres., chief exec. officer Behavioral Health Systems, Houston, 1984-87; exec. v.p., chief operating officer Rehab. Hosp. Services Corp., Camp Hill, Pa., 1987-88; pres., chief exec. officer Am. Transitional Care, Inc., Houston, 1987-90; cons. Rehab Care Corp., St. Louis, 1988, pres., chief exec. officer, dir., 1990—; dir. Maryville Univ., St. Louis, 1996—. Dir. Met. Employment & Rehab. Svc.; pres. bd. dirs. Laumeir Sculpture Park, 1995. Mem. Houston Philos. Soc., Harvard Club, St. Louis Club. Home: 1019 S Mcknight Rd Saint Louis MO 63117-1009 Office: Rehab Care Group Inc # 1700 7733 Forsyth Blvd Ste 1700 Saint Louis MO 63105-1817

USHERWOOD, PETER NORMAN RUSSELL, science educator; b. Gravesend, Kent, Eng., Oct. 7, 1936; s. Donald Mann and Elsie Daphne (Russell) U.; m. Gloria Marina Hopton, Sept. 27, 1958; children: Keri Andrew, Russell David, Stephen Paul, Lisa Jane. BS, U. Wales, 1958; PhD, U. Glasgow, 1962. From asst. lectr. to lectr. U. Glasgow, Scotland, 1960-68, sr. lectr., 1968-74; prof. U. Nottingham, Eng., 1974—; com. chmn. Sci. and Engring. Rsch. Coun., U.K., 1976-93; exec. editor Sheffield (Eng.) Acad. Press, 1994—; cons. Blackie & Sons Ltd., Glasgow, 1968-89, Pharmaceutic and Pesticide Ind. Worldwide, 1966-94. Author: Nervous Systems, 1973; editor: Simple Nervous Systems, 1975, Insect Muscle, 1975, Neurotox '84, 1985. Mem. Children's Panel, Scotland, 1972; mem. adv. com. Ministry Agr. and Fisheries, London, 1974. Fulbright fellow, Columbia U., 1963. Fellow Royal Soc. Edinburgh, Inst. Biology, Zool. Soc. London, Soc. for Exptl. Biology (pres. 1980), Brit. Pharmacological Soc., Brit. Physiological Soc., Brit. Soc. for Chemistry Industry. Home: 35 Normanby Rd, Nottingham NG7 2RD, England Office: U Nottingham, University Park, Nottingham NG7 2RD, England

USINGER, MARTHA PUTNAM, counselor, educator; b. Pitts., Dec. 10, 1912; d. Milo Boone and Christiana (Haberstroh) Putnam; m. Robert Leslie Usinger, June 24, 1938 (dec Oct. 1968); children: Roberta Christine (dec.), Richard Putnam. AB cum laude, U. Calif., Berkeley, 1934; postgrad., Oreg. State U., 1935, U. Ghana, 1970, Coll. Nairobi, 1970. Tchr. Oakland (Calif.) Pub. Schs., 1936-38; tchr. Berkeley (Calif.) Pub. Schs., 1954-57, dean West Campus, counselor, 1957-78; lectr., photographer in field. Author: Ration Books and Christmas Crackers, 1989. Mem. DAR, Berkeley Ret. Tchrs., U. Calif. Emeriti Assn., U. Calif. Alumnae Assn., Prytanean Alumnae Assn. (pres. 1952-54), Mortar Bd., Delta Kappa Gamma.

USUI, MASAMICHI, orthopaedic surgeon; b. Akan, Hokkaido, Japan, Jan. 11, 1943; s. Masuo and Tori (Akutsu) U.; m. Etsuko Hara, Oct. 10, 1970; children: Kyouko, Takuma, Yumi. MD, Hokkaido U., Sapporo, Japan, 1967, PhD, 1978. Lic. med. dr., Japan. Lectr. Hokkaido U., Noboribetsu, Japan, 1978-83, Sapporo, 1983-84; assoc. prof. Sapporo Med. U., 1984—. Contbr. articles to med. jours. Grantee Edn. Ministry, 1980, 84, Welfare Ministry, 1995. Mem. Japanese Soc. Reconstructive Microsurgery (pres. 1991-92). Office: Sapporo Med U, Minami 1-jo, nishi-16-cho-me, 060 Sapporo Hokkaido, Japan

USUKI, SATOSHI, physician, educator; b. Ehime, Japan, July 2, 1944; s. Wataru and Chieko (Doi) U.; m. Yoshie Inage, Aug. 8, 1974; children: Hiromune, Yoshimune, Chiemi. MD, Yokohama (Japan) City U., 1971, U. Tokyo, 1981. Ednl. asst. U. Tokyo, 1971-78; asst. prof. U. Tsukuba, Japan, 1978-93, assoc. prof., 1993—; fellow, prof. of distinction Inst. Advanced Rsch. in Asian Sci. and Medicine, WHO, Hempstead, N.Y., 1990-91; lectr. Hüddinge U. Hosp., Karolinska Inst., Sweden, 1992; councilor The Japan Endocrine Soc., The Japan Soc. for the Study of Toxemia of Pregnancy, The Japan Soc. of Fertility and Sterility, The Japan Menopause Soc., The Japan Soc. for Comparative Endocrinology, The Japan Soc. of Obstetrics and Gynecology. Promoter East Asian Econ. Caucus; trustee Minamiuwakai; mem. Japan-North Am. Med. Exch. Found., 1987, Internat. Human Resources Inst. Network. Recipient Japan-China Med. Assn. award, 1988, Li Shi Zhen Outstanding Manuscript award Hong Kong Inst. Promotion Chinese Culture, 1993. Fellow Inst. Advanced Rsch.; mem. AAAS, N.Y. Acad. Sci., Inter-Am. Sci. Hypertension, Fallopius Internat. Soc., Am. Inst. Ultrasound in Medicine, Internat. Soc. Gynecol. Endocrinology, Am. Assn. Gynecol. Laparoscopists, Inst. Growth Sci. Assn. (assoc., Japan), Am. Roentgen Ray Soc., Internat. Soc. Amino Acid Rsch., Am. Soc. Hypertension, Am. Pituitary Soc., Internat. Study Group for Steroid Hormones, Internat. Soc. Cardiovascular Pharmacotherapy, Internat. Menopause Soc., Internat. Soc. Infectious Diseases, Planetary Soc., Nat. Geographic Soc., Internat. Soc. Outer Space Law. Home: Kurakake 725-3, Tsukuba Ibaraki 305, Japan Office: U Tsukuba Inst Clin Medicine, Tennodai 1-1-1, Tsukuba Ibaraki 305, Japan

UTAIN, MARSHA, marriage, family, and child counselor, author, lecturer; b. Phila., Oct. 16, 1947; d. Charles and Diana Green; m. Arthur Melville, May 28, 1978. BA in English, Beaver Coll., 1969; MS in Counseling, Calif. State U., Long Beach, 1979. Lic. marriage family child counselor, Calif.; cert. high sch. and jr. coll. tchg., Calif. Tchr. Neshaminy (Pa.) Sr. H.S., 1969-71, spl. project tchr. Sch. Without Walls, 1971-72; chair dept. English-Reading Garden Gate Alternative H.S., L.A., 1976-79; co-tchr., spl. clin. supr. Calif. State U., Long Beach, 1979-81, co-tchr. Sch. Nursing Continuing Edn., 1980-81; co-host mental health mag. KFOX Radio, L.A., 1987-89; pvt. practice Long Beach, 1980—; cons. Orange County Dept. Mental Health, Laguna, Calif., 1983, Long Beach Psychiat. Clinic for Children, 1985; lectr./trainer U.S. Jour. Tng., Inc., Deerfield Beach, Fla., 1989-91; presenter Calif. Consortium for Prevention of Child Abuse, 1992; clin. dir. So. Calif. Youth Offender Recovery Program, 1991—. Author: (pamphlet) Stepping Out of Chaos, 1989; co-author: The Healing Relationship, 1989; contbg. author: The Partnership Way, 1990. Charter mem. Orange County Task Force on Organized Abuse of Children, Costa Mesa, Calif., 1991-93. Mem. ACA (clin. mem.), Calif. Assn. Marriage Family Therapists (clin. mem.), Phi Kappa Phi, Phi Delta Kappa, Kappa Delta Pi, Phi Alpha Theta (past sec.). Office: 5520 E 2nd St Ste K Long Beach CA 90803-3957

UTELL, MARK JEFFREY, medical educator; b. N.Y.C., July 25, 1946; m. Lois Brooks; 1 child, Michael Jon. BA cum laude, Dartmouth Coll., 1968; MD, Tufts U., 1972. Diplomate Am. Bd. Internal Medicine. Intern St. Elizabeth's Hosp., Boston, 1972-73, resident in internal medicine, 1973-75; from instr. to prof. sch. medicine U. Rochester, N.Y., 1975-92; prof. sch. medicine U. Rochester, 1992—; dir. respiratory and med. ICUs Strong Meml. Hosp., Rochester, 1977-89, mem. intensive care com., 1977-87; co-dir. pulmonary and CCU sch. medicine U. Rochester, 1984-91, occupl. medicine program, 1988—, assoc. chmn. clin. affairs dept. environ. medicine, 1992—, dir. occupl. and environ. medicine divsn., 1992—; cons. VA, 1977—, EPA, 1980—, mem. clean air sci. adv. com., 1988-94; reviewer site visit com. NIH, 1982, outside reviewer respiratory and applied physiology sect. NHLBI, 1982; mem. rev. study sect. Nat. Inst. Environ. Health Scis., 1990-94, mem. task force for rsch. planning; mem. health rsch. com. Health Effects Inst., 1985-94; mem. N.Y. State Commr.'s Panel on Tuberculosis, Syracuse, 1988; mem. commn. life scis. NRC, NAS, 1989; mem. panel airborne particulate matter in spacecraft NASA, 1987, mem. environ. health scis. working group, 1993-94. Co-author: Inhalation Toxicology of Air Pollution: Clinical Research Considerations, 1985, Susceptibility to Inhaled Pollutants, 1989; co-editor: Advances in Controlled Clinical Inhalation Studies, 1993; mem. editl. bd. Jour. Aerosol Medicine, Annals of Internal Medicine, Inhalation Technology; guest reviewer various jours.; contbr. over 100 articles to profl. jours. Bd. dirs. Am. Lung Assn. N.Y. State, 1986-88. Grantee NASA, Nat. Inst. Environ. Health Scis., Nat. Heart Lung and Blood Inst., Elec. Power Rsch. Inst., Ctr. Indoor Air Rsch., Dow Corning Corp., Allied Signal, Inc. Fellow AAAS, ACP, Am. Coll. Chest Physicians (mem. steering com. sect. environ. occupl. health 1983-87, assessment asthma in workplace com. 1994); mem. Am. Physiol. Soc., Am. Thoracic Soc. (chmn. scientific assembly on environ. and occupl. health 1987, mem. planning com., 1992-94, respiratory protective guidelines com., 1993-95, other coms.), Am. Coll. Occupl. Environ. Medicine, N.Y. Trudeau Soc. (pres. 1986). Home: 16 Framingham Ln Pittsford NY 14534 Office: Dept Medicine Pulmonary CCU Box 692 U Rochester Sch Medicine Rochester NY 14642-8692*

UTHMAN, BASIM MOHAMMAD, neurologist, epileptologist, consultant; b. Tripoli, Lebanon, Sept. 25, 1958; came to the U.S., 1984; s. Mohammad Assa'ad and Mariam Mohammad (Moukalled) U. BSc, Am. U. Beirut, 1978, MD, 1984. Diplomate Am. Bd. Psychiatry and Neurology, Am. Bd. Clin. Neurophysiology. Intern Am. Univ. Beirut Med Ctr., Lebanon, 1983-84; resident in neurologyDept. Neurology U. Cin., 1984-87, preceptor, 1987-88, clin. fellow in neurophysiology, epilepsy, 1987-88; clin. rsch. fellow in epilepsy, neurophysiology and neuropharmacology U. Fla., Gainesville, 1988-90, clin. instr., 1990-91; vis. assoc. prof. dept. neurology U. Fla., 1991-92; asst. prof. dept. neurology, brain inst. U. Fla., Gainesville, 1992-96, assoc. prof. dept. neurology, brain inst., 1996—; staff neurologist VA Med. Ctr., Gainesville, 1990—, asst. chief neurology svc., dir. status epilepticus team, 1990-95, contracting officers tech. rep., 1990-92, acting chief neurology svc., 1993, dir. clin. neurophysiology lab. EEG/EP, 1991—; chmn. Adminstrv. Bd. Investigation VA Med. Ctr., Gainesville, 1993; attending epileptologist Shands Hosp., 1993—; permanent mem. U. Fla. Instnl. Rev. Bd. Health Sci. Ctr., 1994—. Ad hoc referee U.S. Pharmacopeial Conv., 1988-89, Drug Evaluations, 1990, Epilepsia, 1990—, Jour. Neuroimaging, 1990—, Drugs, 1993—; contbr. articles to profl. jours., chpts. to books. Active emergency blood donation campaign, Beirut, 1982-83, worker war disaster plan, 1982-83; vol. Lebanese Red Cross, Beirut, 1982-83; organizer children's med. ednl. presentations, 1984; profl. adv. bd. Epilspsy Found. Fla., 1992-93, chmn., 1993—. A.S. Khalidi scholar Am. U. Beirut, 1978, Azeez B. Ajloini scholar, 1979, Tamari-Saab scholar, 1979, Dr. Haddad, 1980; fellow Bowman Gray Med. Sch., Winston-Salem, N.C., 1987; grantee Epilepsy Rsch. Found. Fla., 1988-90, Cyberonics, 1989—, Coop. Studies Program Coordinating Ctr., 1990—, VA Affairs Med. Ctr. Allotment, 1991-92, Abbott Labs., 1991—, U. Fla., 1991-92, Ceiba-Geigy, 1991-94, U. Fla. Brain Inst., 1992, Parke-Davis 1993—. Mem. AMA, Am. Acad. Neurology, Am. Epilepsy Soc., Am. Sleep Disorders Assn., Am. Electroencephalographic Soc., Am. Soc. Neurophysiological Monitoring, Am. Coll. Internat. Physicians, Nat. Stroke Assn., So. Clin. Neurol. Soc., So. Electroencephalographic Soc., Fla. Med. Assn., Alachua County Med. Soc., Nat. and Internat. Spkrs. Bur. (Parke-Davis, Marion Merryl Dow, Burroughs Wellcome, Abbott Labs., Ciba-Geigy, Cyberonics 1993—). Moslem. Office: VA Med Ctr-Neurology Svc 127 1601 SW Archer Rd Gainesville FL 32608-1135

UTLEY, DONNA LAVELLE, healthcare human resources administrator; b. Tulare, Calif., June 30, 1948; d. Donald Raymond and Vivian Lee (Baber) Rogers; married, July 23, 1970. BS, Calif. State U., Fresno, 1970; MPA, U. So. Calif., 1985. Resources and devel. asst. Concentrated Employment Program, Fresno, 1970-72; pers. analyst Fresno County Pers. Dept., 1972-74; pers. mgr. Fresno County Health Dept., 1974-79; pers. dir. Merced (Calif.) Cmty. Med. Ctr., 1979-81; dir. human resources Bay Area Hosp., Coos Bay, Oreg., 1981-85; asst. adminstr. human resources St. Elizabeth Med. Ctr., Yakima, Wash., 1985-90; dir. human resources Washoe Med. Ctr., Reno, 1990-92, Mercy Am. River/Mercy San Juan Hosp, Carmichael, Calif., 1992—; bd. dirs. Enterprise for Progress in the Cmty., 1986-90, sec., 1989-90, chair pers. com., 1987, 88, 89, 90. Mem. Am. Soc. Healthcare Human Resources Adminstrn., Soc. for Human Resources Mgmt., Healthcare H.R. Mgmt. Assn. Calif. Republican. Methodist. Office: 6501 Coyle Ave Carmichael CA 95608

UTTING, JOHN EDWARD, anesthesiologist, educator; b. Liverpool, Eng., Mar. 17, 1932; s. Henry Alphege and Theresa Gladys (Mullins) U.; m. Jean Oliver Gerrard, Sept. 27, 1958 (dec. June 1991); children: Clare Helen, Mary Elizabeth Utting White, Catherine Utting Grace, James Henry. MA, Cambridge (Eng.) U., 1955, MB BCh, 1957. Home surgeon, house physician Broadgreen Hosp., Liverpool, 1957-58; Christiana Hartley rsch. fellow U. Liverpool, 1959-60; sr. registrar Mercy region Mercy Region Hosp. Bd., 1960-62; lectr. in anesthesia, cons. anesthetist U. Liverpool, 1962-70, sr. lectr. in anesthesia, 1970-77, prof., head dept. anesthesia, 1977-94, pro-vice chancellor, 1987-90, emeritus prof., 1994—; v.p. Liverpool Coll., 1995—; chmn. Linacre Ctr. for Study of Bioethics, London, 1989-95. Co-author: General Anaesthesia, 5th edit., 1989. Justice of peace, Merseyside Commn., Liverpool, 1975—. Fellow Royal Coll. Anesthetists (Hewitt lectr. 1985). Conservative. Roman Catholic. Home: Sanjo Green Ln, L18 2EP Liverpool England Office: Univ Liverpool, PO Box 147, L69 36X Liverpool England

UTZ, SARAH WINIFRED, nursing educator; b. San Diego; d. Frederick R. and Margaret M. (Gibbons) U.; BS, U. Portland, 1943, EdM, 1958; MS, UCLA, 1970; PhD, U. So. Calif., 1979. Clin. instr. Providence Sch. Nursing, Portland, Oreg., 1946-50, edn. dir., 1950-62; edn. dir. Sacred Heart Sch. Nursing, Eugene, Oreg., 1963-67; asst. prof. nursing Calif. State U., L.A., 1969-74, assoc. prof., 1974-81, prof., 1981—, assoc. chmn. dept. nursing, 1982—; cons. in nursing curriculum, 1978—; healthcare cons., 1991—; past chmn. ednl. adminstrs., cons., tchrs. sect. Oreg. Nurses Assn., past pres. Oreg. State Bd. Nursing; mem. rsch. program Western Interstate Commn. on Higher Edn. in Nursing; chmn. liaison com. nursing edn. Articulation Coun. Calif. Author articles and lab manuals. Served with Nurse Corps, USN, 1944-46. HEW grantee, 1970-74, Kellogg Found. grantee, 1974-76, USDHHS grantee, 1987—; R.N., Calif., Oreg. Mem. Am. Nurses Assn., Calif. Nurses Assn. (edn. commr. region 6 1987—, chair edn. interest group region 6 , 1987—), Am. Ednl. Rsch. Assn., AAUP, Phi Delta Kappa, Sigma Theta Tau. Formerly editor Oreg. Nurse; reviewer Western Jour. Nursing Rsch. Home: 1409 Midvale Ave Los Angeles CA 90024-5454 Office: 5151 State University Dr Los Angeles CA 90032

UY, FELIPE RATUNIL, internist; b. Misamis Oriental, Philippines, Jan. 24, 1942; came to U.S., 1969; s. Ching Toh and Modesta (Ratunil) Uy; m. Ester Rodriquez Lambujon, May 22, 1971; children: Christine, Melanie, Vincent. AA, Cebu Inst. Tech., Philippines, 1962; MD, Southwestern U., Philippines, 1968. Cert. Am. Bd. Internal Medicine. Med. intern St. John Episcopal Hosp., Bklyn., 1969-70; med. resident Beekman Downtown Hosp., N.Y.C., 1970-72; anesthesia resident Kings County Hosp., Bklyn., 1972-74; fellow pulmonary medicine VA Hosp., East Orange, N.J., 1974-75; med. attending Charles Drew Health Ctr., Bklyn., 1975-77; med. specialist Kingsboro Psychiat. Hosp., Bklyn., 1977—; dir. emergency med. svc. Kingsboro Psychiat. Ctr., Bklyn., 1985—. Editor: (manual) Practical Guide on Advanced Cardiac Life Support,1987. Mem. Kingsboro Emergency Preparedness Com., Bklyn., 1992. Fellow Am. Coll. Anesthesiologists; mem. Am. Bd. Anesthesiology (diplomate). Roman Catholic. Home: 76-22 172nd St Flushing NY 11366-1409 Office: Kingsboro PC 681 Clarkson Ave Brooklyn NY 11203-2125

UY, HARRY LIM, physician, educator; b. Manila, The Philippines, Feb. 4, 1961; came to U.S., 1988; s. Kim and Felisa (Lim) U.; m. Jemelle Rodriguez, June 11, 1989; children: Natalie Frances, Stephanie Nicole, Hans Mitchell. BS in Biology, U. Phillipines, 1981, MD, 1986. Diplomate Am. Bd. Internal Medicine, and subsplty. Endocrinology, Diabetes and Metabolism. Intern, resident Mercy Hosp., Buffalo, N.Y., 1988-91; endocrinology fellow U. Tex. Health Sci. Ctr., San Antonio, 1991-94; asst. prof. Univ. Tex. Health Sci. Ctr., San Antonio, 1994—; physician Audie L. Murphy Veterans Hosp., San Antonio, 1994—; chief VA endocrine clinic Audie L. Murphy VA, San Antonio, 1995—; bd. dirs. internat. alliance Univ. Tex. Health Sci. Ctr., San Antonio, 1994—, dir. clin. endocrine fellowship program, 1995—. Contbr. articles to profl. jours. Grantee San Antonio Cancer Inst., 1994, Am. Cancer Soc., 1994-95, NIH, 1995—. Mem. AMA, ACP, Am. Soc. Bone and Mineral Rsch., Am. Soc. Internal Medicine, Endocrine Soc. Roman Catholic. Office: U Tex Health Sci Ctr-SA 7703 Floyd Curl Dr San Antonio TX 78284-7877

UYAMA, EIICHIRO, neurologist, educator; b. Aino-cho, Nagasaki, Japan, June 29, 1955; s. Mamoru and Miyoko (Iwanaga) U.; m. Makiko Kokumai, Nov. 24, 1984; children: Chisako, Rika. MD, Miyazaki Med. Coll., Japan,

1981; PhD, Kumamoto (Japan) U., 1993. Asst. prof. Kumamoto (Japan) U. Sch. Medicine, 1985—; vis. rsch. fellow Montefiore Med. Ctr., N.Y., 1994-95. Contbr. articles to neurosci. jours. Sci. rsch. grantee Japanese Ministry Edn., 1990, 91, 93-95. Mem. Japanese Soc. Neurology (diplomate), Japanese Soc. Internal Medicine (diplomate), Japanese Soc. Neuropathology, Japanese Soc. Rehab. Medicine, N.Y. Acad. Scis. Home: B-104 2-3-57 Tsukide, Kumamoto 862, Japan Office: Kumamoto Univ Sch Medicine, 1-1-1 Honjo, Kumamoto 860, Japan

UYEHARA, CATHERINE FAY TAKAKO (YAMAUCHI), physiologist, educator, pharmacologist; b. Honolulu, Dec. 20, 1959; d. Thomas Takashi and Eiko (Haraguchi) Uyehara; m. Alan Hisao Yamauchi, Feb. 17, 1990. BS, Yale U., 1981; PhD in Physiology, U. Hawaii, Honolulu, 1987. Postdoctoral fellow SmithKline Beecham Pharms., King of Prussia, Pa., 1987-89; asst. prof. in pediatrics U. Hawaii John Burns Sch. Medicine, Honolulu, 1991—; rsch. pharmacologist Kapiolani Med. Ctr. for Women and Children, Honolulu, 1990—; statis. cons. dept. clin. investigation Tripler Army Med. Ctr., Honolulu, 1984-87, 89—, chief rsch. pharmacology sect., 1991—, dir. coop. rsch. and devel. projects, 1995—; asst. prof. pharmacology U. Hawaii John A. Burns Sch. Medicine, 1993—; grad. faculty Interdisciplinary Biomed. Sci. program, 1995—. Contbr. articles to profl. jours. Mem. Am. Fedn. Clin. Rsch., Am. Physiol. Soc., Soc. Uniformed Endocrinologists, Endocrine Soc., We. Soc. Pediatric Rsch., N.Y. Acad. Scis. Democrat. Mem. Christian Ch. Office: Tripler Army Med Ctr Dept Clin Investigation MCHK-CI 1 Jarrett White Rd Bldg 40 Rm 131 Honolulu HI 96859-5000

UZSOY, PATRICIA J., nursing educator and administrator; b. Corning, Ark.; m. Namik K. Diploma, Mo. Bapt. Hosp. Sch. Nursing, St. Louis, 1960; BSN, Washington U., St. Louis, 1962; MEd, Lynchburg Coll., 1977, EdS, 1981; MS in Nursing, U. Va., 1987. RN, Va. Dir. sch. nursing Lynchburg (Va.) Gen. Hosp., dir. Mem. ANA, NLN, Va. Nurses Assn. (Nurse of Yr. dist. III 1987).

VAAL, JOSEPH JOHN, JR., psychologist; b. St. Louis, Nov. 19, 1947; s. Joseph John and Dorothy Jane (Collett) V.; m. Patricia Gail Winkler, Apr. 24, 1982; 1 child, Lauren Elizabeth. BA, Lawrence U., 1969; MA in Psychology, Western Mich. U., 1971; PhD, Columbia Pacific U., 1981. Tchr. spl. edn. KVISD Title VI Program, Kalamazoo, 1970, Mannheim Pub. Schs., Franklin Park, Ill., 1971; sch. psychologist Wheaton (Ill.) Pub. Schs., 1971-79; dir. office continuing edn. Rush-Presbyn.-St. Luke's Med. Ctr., Chgo., 1979-81; adj. instr. Grad. Sch. Nat. Coll. Edn., Evanston, 1972—; spl. edn. due process hearing officer Ill. Bd. Edn., Springfield, 1978—; dir. ednl. svcs. Healthcare Fin. Mgmt. Assn., Oak Brook, Ill., 1981-84; psychologist Sch. Assn. Spl. Edn. in DuPage, Addison, Ill., 1984-87; asst. dir. Sch. Assn. for Spl. Edn. in DuPage, Addison, Ill., 1987-89; dir. planning No. Suburban Spl. Edn. Dist., Highland Park, Ill, 1989-90; sch. psychologist Dept. Pediatrics Luth. Gen. Children's Hosp., Park Ridge, Ill., 1990—. Mem. Ill. Sch. Psychologists Assn., Nat. Assn. Sch. Psychologists. Office: Luth Gen Children's Hosp Yacktman Pavillion 1675 W Dempster St Park Ridge IL 60068

VACCA, DANTE F., neurosurgeon; b. Las Vegas, Nev., May 26, 1957; s. Don J. and Olga (Dicowicz) V.; m. Terry A. Pionk, July 10, 1988; children: Brandon, Sarah, Rachel. BS, U. Notre Dame, 1979; MD, U. Nev., 1983. Diplomate Am. Bd. Neurol. Surgeons. Intern. gen. surgery Henry Ford Hosp., Detroit, 1983-84, resident neurosurgery, 1984-89; asst. clin. prof. surgery U. Nev. Sch. Medicine, Reno, 1990—; staff neurosurgeon Washoe Med. Ctr. & St. Mary's Regional Med. Ctr., Reno, 1989—. Mem. AMA, Am. Assn. Neurol. Surgeons; Congress Neurol. Surgeons, Nev. State Med. Soc., Washoe County Med. Soc., Alpha Omega Alpha. Republican. Roman Catholic. Office: Sierra Neurosurgery Group 850 Mill St 3d Fl Reno NV 89502

VACCARELLA, PAUL JOSEPH, optometrist; b. Red Bank, N.J., Aug. 9, 1965; s. Peter and Patricia V.; m. Dale Elizabeth Ruffino, Apr. 4, 1994; 1 child, Krista Ann. BS, King's Coll., 1987; D Optometry, New Eng. Coll. Optometry, Boston, 1991. Therapeutic optometrist, N.J. State Bd. Optometrists. Optometrist N.J. State Bd. Optometrists, Newark, 1991—; staff optometrist Profl. Eyecare Svcs., Edison, N.J., 1991—; cons./adminstr. Busy Bumble Bee Child Care Ctr., Bedminster, N.J., 1994—; field doctor N.J. State Commn. for the Blind and Visually Impaired, Toms River, N.J., 1993—. Trustee Edison Sheltered Workshop, 1994—. Mem. Am. Optometric Assn., N.J. Optometric Assn., Mid Jersey Optometric Assn. Office: Profl Eyecare Svcs 940 Amboy Ave Edison NJ 08837

VACCARO, DONATO, psychologist, researcher; b. Bronxville, N.Y., July 19, 1957; s. Luke Francis and Corina Delores (Carapella) V. BA, SUNY, Potstdam, 1979; PhD, Adelphi U., 1987. Computer cons. Adelphi U., Garden City, N.Y., 1979-83, 1979-83; instr. Albert Einstein Coll. Medicine, Bronx, N.Y., 1990-94; assoc. instr. psychology Adelphi U., Garden City, N.Y., 1983-86; rsch. asst. Albert Einstein Coll. Medicine, Bronx, N.Y., 1985-86, instr., 1990-94; behavioral psychotherapist Fairfield Behavioral Med. Inst., Fairfield, Conn., 1986-88; rsch. assoc. Am. Health Found., N.Y.C., 1988-94, Consumers Union/Pub. Consumer Reports, Yonkers, N.Y., 1994—; prof. psychology Fairfield (Conn.) U., 1987-88; cons. in field. Contbr. articles to profl. jours. Mem. APA, Soc. for Behavioral Medicine, Delta Kappa Theta. Home: 1 Garrett Pl 4C Bronxville NY 10708 Office: Consumer's Union Survey Rsch Dept 100 Truman Ave Yonkers NY 10703

VACCARO, PATRICK SAMUEL, vascular surgeon, educator; b. Steubenville, Ohio, Apr. 30, 1949; s. Angelo Joseph and Eva Maria (Bonafede) V.; m. Therese Marie Abel, June 14, 1980; children: Michael John, Daniel Patrick, Thomas Benjamin, Alex Christopher, Hope Elizabeth. BS, Yale U., 1971; MD, U. Cin., 1975. Diplomate Am. Bd. Surgery. Intern and resident, gen. surgery Ohio State U., Columbus, 1975-80; fellow in cardiovasc. surgery Baylor Coll. Medicine, Houston, 1980-81; assoc. prof. surgery Ohio State U., Columbus, 1981-88, clin. assoc. prof. surgery, 1988—; dir. surg. edn. Grant Med. Ctr., Columbus, 1988—; bd. dirs. IPA U.S. Health Orgn., Columbus. Contbr. articles to profl. jours., chpts. to books. Bd. dirs. Franklin County Bd. Mental Retardation, Columbus, 1991-95. Fellow ACS; mem. Internat. Soc. Cardiovascular Surgery, Ctrl. Surg. Assn., Peripheral Vascular Surgery Soc., Midwestern Vascular Surgery Soc., Alpha Omega Alpha. Roman Catholic. Office: Peripheral Vascular Surgery 300 E Town St Columbus OH 43215

VACHHER, PREHLAD SINGH, psychiatrist; b. Rawalpindi, Punjab, Pakistan, Nov. 30, 1933; came to U.S., 1960; s. Thakar Singh and Harbans Kaur (Ghai) V.; m. Margaret Mary Begley, Oct. 9, 1963; children: Paul, Sheila, Mary Ann, Eileen, Mark. Grad., Khalsa Coll., India, 1950; MD, Panjab U., Amritsar, India, 1956. Diplomate Am. Bd. Psychiatry. Staff N.J. State Hosp., Trenton, 1965-66, Wayne County Gen. Hosp., Eloise, Mich., 1966-68; pvt. practice Livonia, Mich., 1966-75, Woodstock, Va., 1991—; pres. Vachher Psychiat. Ctr., P.C., Livonia, 1975-91; dir. community psychiatry Northville (Mich.) State Hosp., 1968-71; cons. staff Kingswood Hosp., Ferndale, Mich., 1967-72, Annapolis Hosp., Wayne, 1967-88, St. Joseph Mercy Hosp., Ann Arbor, 1970-89; westland staff Margaret Montgomery Hosp., 1988-91; bd. dirs. Oakland Rental Housing Assn., 1990-91; med. dir. mental health unit Shenandoan County Meml. Hosp., Woodstock, Va., 1991-94. Mem. Am. Psychiat. Assn., Va. Psychiat. Soc., Sikh Physicians in Mich. (bd. dirs. 1987), Canton C. of C. (pres. 1975), Sikh Bus. Profl. Coun. (pres. 1988—), Rotary (Canton and Plymouth, Mich., Woodstock), Prince William County C. of C. Office: 14573 Potomac Mills Rd Woodbridge VA 22192

VACHON, LOUIS, psychiatrist, educator; b. Montreal, June 15, 1932; m. Monique Blain, June 25, 1960; children: Philip, Dominique. BA, U. Montreal, 1952, MD, 1958. Diplomate Am. Bd. Psychiatry and Neurology. Intern Hotel Dieu de Montreal, Que., 1957-58, resident in psychiatry, 1958-61; intern Hotel Dieu de Montreal, 1957-58; psychiat. resident Instiut Albert Prevost, Montreal, 1958-61; sr. physician Medfield (Mass.) State Hosp., 1961-62; rsch. assoc., then instr. Boston U. Med. Sch., 1962-68, asst. prof., then assoc. prof., 1968-87, interim chmn. div. psychiatry, 1985-87, prof., chmn. div. psychiatry, 1987-96; dir. psychiatry outpatient svc. Univ. Hosp., Boston, 1978-85, interim psychiatrist-in-chief, 1985-87, psychiatrist-in-chief, vis. physician in psychiatry, 1987—. Contbg. author: Comprehensive Textbook of Psychiatry, 1989. Fellow Am. Psychiat. Assn.; mem. Boston Psychoanalytic Soc. Inst., Am. Psychoanalytic Assn., Internat. Psychoanalytic Assn., Mass. Psychiat. Soc., Am. Psychosomatic Soc., Mass. Med. Soc., Boston. Office: Boston U Sch Medicine 720 Harrison Ave Rm 914 Boston MA 02118-2334

VACIK, JAMES PAUL, university administrator; b. North Judson, Ind., Nov. 30, 1931; s. George J. and Elsie E. (Paulsen) V.; m. Dorothy M. Nobles, Dec. 27, 1967; children: Deborah, Pamella, James, Stephen, Joshua, Jonathan. BS in Pharmacy, Purdue U., 1955, MS in Medicinal Chemistry, 1957, PhD in Bionucleonics, 1959. Cert. hazard control mgr.; registered biosafety profl., registered pharmacist, Ind., N.D., Ala. Asst. prof. bionucleonics dept. Purdue U., Lafayette, Ind., 1959-60; assoc. prof., dept. chmn. pharm. chemistry & bionucleonics N.D. State U., Fargo, 1960-63; prof., dept. chmn. pharm. chemistry & bionucleonics N.D. State U., 1963-76; assoc. prof. pharmacology Univ. S. Ala., Mobile, 1976-82; adj. prof., dir. environ. safety Univ. S. Ala., 1982—; Pub. Health Svc. grant dir. N.D. State U., Fargo, 1963-71; VA Hosp. cons. VA Hosp. System, Washington, 1966; vis. prof. Nat. Reactor Testing Sta., Idaho Falls, Idaho, 1968; pvt. cons. to various indsl. firms, 1970—. Contbr. articles to profl. Mem., first dir. "Showboat on the Red," Jaycees, Fargo, 1965. With U.S. Army, 1949-52, ETO. Named Outstanding Educator Am., Fuller & Dees, Washington, 1975. Mem. Am. Chem. Soc., Am. Pharm. Assn., Health Physics Soc. (chmn. com.), Am. Biol. Safety Assn. (bd. dirs. 1985-87), Health Physics Soc. (pres., treas., bd. dirs. Ala chpt. 1977—, pres., bd. dirs. N. Ctrl. chpt. 1969—), Masons. Baptist. Home: 1220 Vendome Dr W Mobile AL 36609-3326 Office: U South Ala CC CB 307 University Blvd N Mobile AL 36688-3053

VAGLEY, RICHARD THOMAS, plastic surgeon; b. Charleroi, Pa., Dec. 11, 1945; m. Mary C. Carroll, Apr. 3, 1976; children: Sarah E., Adam S., Andrew C., Christian C. BS, Pa. State U., 1966; MD, Jefferson Med. Coll., Phila., 1968. Diplomate Am. Bd. Plastic Surgery. Pvt. practice Pitts., 1968—. Lt. USN, 1969-71. Fellow ACS. Office: Pitts Inst Plastic Surgery 532 S Aiken Ave Pittsburgh PA 15232-1572

VAGUE, JEAN MARIE, physician; b. Draguignan, France, Nov. 25, 1911; s. Victor Francois and Marie (Voiron) V.; m. Denise Marie Jouve, Sept. 3, 1936; children: Philippe, Thierry, Irene (Mrs. Claude Juhan), Maurice. Baccalaureat, Cath. Coll., Aix en Provence, France, 1928; MD, Marseilles (France) U., 1935. Intern, Hotel Dieu Conception, Marseilles, 1930, resident, 1932-39; practice medicine specializing in endocrinology, Marseilles, 1943—; assoc. prof. Marseilles U., 1946-57, prof., clinic endocrinology, 1957—. Dir. Ctr. Alimentary Hygiene and Prophylaxis Nutrition Diseases Nat. Rys. Mediterranean region, 1958—; expert chronic degenerative diseases (diabetes) WHO, 1962—. Served to lt. French Army, 1939-40. Decorated Cross Legion Honor, Acad. Palms, knight pub. health, knight mil. merit, War Cross. Mem. Endocrine Soc. U.S., Am. Diabetes Assn., Royal Soc. Medicine (London), European Assn. for Study Diabetes, Spanish, Italian French (past pres.) socs. endocrinology, French Acad. Medicine, Spanish Acad. Medicine, Italian Acad. Medicine, Belgian Acad. Medicine, French Lang. Diabetes Assn. (past pres.). Author: Human Sexual Differentiation, 1953, Notions of Endocrinology, 1965, Obesities, 1991, Dawn on Iaboc's Ford, History of Man, History of Men, 1993, others. Achievements include first identification of the metabolic and vascular complications of android obesity and their mechanism; research in demonstration of diabetogenic and atherogenic power of obesity with topographic distbn. fat in upper and deep part of body, evolution of android diabetogenic obesity from 1st stage of efficacious hyperinsulinism to less efficacious hyperinsulinism and hypoinsulinism-neurogerminal degeneration, degenerative lesions of germinal epithelium and nervous system. Home: 6 Prado Parc, 411 Ave du Prado, 13008 Marseille France Office: Hopital U Timone Clin Endocrinologique, Blvd Jean-Moulin, 13385 Marseilles France

VAITUKAITIS, JUDITH LOUISE, medical research administrator; b. Hartford, Conn., Aug. 29, 1940; d. Albert George and Julia Joan (Vaznikaitis) V. BS, Tufts U., 1962; MD, Boston U., 1966. Investigator, med. officer reproductive rsch. Nat. Inst. Child Health and Human Devel., NIH, Bethesda, Md., 1971-74; assoc. dir. clin. rsch. Nat. Ctr. Rsch. Resources NIH, Bethesda, Md., 1986-91, dir. gen. clin. rsch. ctr., 1986-91, dep. dir. extramural rsch., 1991; acting dir. Nat. Ctr. Rsch. Resources NIH, Bethesda, 1991-92, dir., 1993—; from assoc. prof. to prof. medicine Sch. Medicine Boston U., 1974-86, assoc. prof. physiology, 1975-80, assoc. prof. ob-gyn., 1977-80, program. dir. gen. clin. rsch. ctr., 1977-86, prof. physiology, 1980-86; head sect. endocrinology and metabolism Boston City Hosp., 1974-86. Mem. editorial bd. Jour. Clin. Endocrin. and Metabolism, 1973-80, Proc. Soc. Exptl. Biol. and Medicine, 1978-87, Endocrine Rsch., 1984-88. Author: Clinical Reproductive Neuroendocrinology, 1982; contbr. articles to profl. jours. Recipient Disting. Alumna award Sch. Medicine, Boston U., 1983, Mallincrodt award for Inv. Rsch. Clin. Radiossay Soc., 1980. Mem. Am. Fedn. Clin. Rsch., Endocrine Soc., Am. Soc. Clin. Rsch., Soc. Exptl. Biology and Medicine, Assn. Am. Physicians. Office: Nat Ctr Rsch Resources NIH Bldg 12A Rm 4007 12 South Dr MSC 5662 Bethesda MD 20892-5662

VAKAY, LLOYD RICHARD, prosthodontist, dentist; b. Port Jefferson, N.Y., Dec. 16, 1946; s. George Percy Vakay and Beverly Enid Freeman; m. Abigail Fordham Dietrick, Mar. 30, 1990; 1 child, Conor. Student, Suffolk County C.C., 1964-66; BA, U. W.Va., 1968; DDS, W.Va. U., 1972; MEd, U. So. Calif., 1976, cert. in prosthodontics, 1976. Commd. 2d lt. USAF, 1972, advanced through grades to lt. col., 1990; gen. dentist USAF, Washington and Thailand, 1972-74; resigned USAF, Bolling AFB, 1980; pvt. practive prosthodontics Washington, 1980—. Lt. col. USAFR, 1980—. Fellow Am. Coll. Prosthodontists; mem. ADA, Am. Acad. Osseointegration. Am. Acad. Implant Dentistry. Office: 2440 M St NW # 610 Washington DC 20037

VALDEZ, ARNOLD, dentist; b. Mojave, Calif., June 27, 1954; s. Stephen Monarez Jr. and Mary Lou (Esparza) V.; m. Brandy Radovich, Dec. 31, 1994; children: Bayleigh, Briton. BS in Biol. Sci., Calif. State U., Hayward, 1976; BS in Dental Sci. and DDS, U. Calif., San Francisco, 1982; MBA, Calif. State Poly. U., 1985; BS and JD, Pacific West Coll. Law, 1995. Cert. ind. med. examiner, qualified med. examiner, Calif. Pvt. practice specializing in temporomandibular joint and Myofascial Pain Dysfunction Disorders Pomona, Calif., 1982, Claremont, Calif., 1982—; CEO Valcom, 1994—; CEO Valcom-A Telecom. Corp.; mem. adv. com. dental assisting program Chaffey Coll., Rancho Cucamonga, Calif., 1982—; mem. staff Pomona Valley Hosp. Med. Ctr. Vol. dentist San Antonio Hosp. Denal Clinic, Rancho Cucamonga, 1984—, Pomona Valley Assistance League Dental Clinic, 1986—; bd. dirs. Pacific West Coll. Law, 1993—, v.p. fgn. devel., 1996—. Fellow Acad. Gen. Dentistry (mastership 1994); mem. ADA, Calif. Dental Assn., Tri-County Dental Soc. (co-chmn. mktg. 1986, chmn. sch. screening 1987, Golden Grin award), Acad. Gen. Dentistry, U. Calif.-San Francisco Alumni Assn., U. So. Calif. Sch. Dentistry Golden Century Club, Psi Omega, Delta Theta Phi. Democrat. Roman Catholic. Home: 515 Seaward Rd Corona Del Mar CA 92625 Office: 410 W Baseline Rd Claremont CA 91711-1607

VALDEZ, JOANNE MARINDA, critical care, medical and surgical nurse; b. Moundsville, W.Va., Nov. 12, 1935; d. Byron L. and Marinda Gould (Thompson) Dunn; m. Joseph V. Valdez, Dec. 24, 1953; children: Joseph V. II, M. Louise, Alice, Robert, Richard, Michael, Elizabeth. Lic. practical nurse, St. Vincent's Sch., Santa Fe, 1974; ADN, No. N.Mex. Community Coll., 1985; BSN, U. N.M., 1992. Lic. practical nurse, N.Mex.; RN, N.Mex.; cert. in BLS, ACLS, Pediatric Life Support. Practical nurse post cardiac unit St. Vincent's Hosp., Santa Fe, 1974-77, practical nurse ICU, 1977-80, practical nurse CCU, practical nurse renal and med.-surg. floor, 1983-86, nurse oncology floor and med.-surg. unit, 1986-87, nurse post anesthesia care unit, 1987-96; ret., 1996; participant N.Mex. Gov.'s Conf. on Nursing, 1989. Recipient 20-yr. Svc. award St. Vincent's Hosp., 1989. Mem. ANA, NAFE, Nat. League Nursing, Post Anesthesia Nurse Assn. N.Mex. Home: 1013 Calle La Resolana Santa Fe NM 87505-5112

VALDEZ, MARIA DEL ROSARIO, perinatal nurse; b. San Antonio, Nov. 4, 1955; d. Guadalupe Garza and Beatrice Consuelo (Martinez) V. BS in Nursing, BA in Psychology, Incarnate Word Coll., San Antonio, 1978; MS in Nursing, U. Tex. Health Sci. Ctr., San Antonio, 1986; postgrad., Tex. Woman's U. RN, Tex. Nurse, team leader Santa Rosa Med. Ctr., San Antonio, 1979-81, Met. Gen. Hosp., San Antonio, 1981-85; childbirth educator Santa Rosa Hosp., 1985-87, obstetrics clin. educator, 1987-94; instr. nursing Incarnate Word Coll., 1989-94; part-time perinatal staff nurse several nursing agys., Houston, 1994—; instr. in Basic Life Support/CPR, Am. Heart Assn., 1985—, Prepared Childbirth, Coun. of Childbirth Edn. Specialists, 1985, instr. neonatal resucitation, 1989, instr.; mem. adv. bd. Hispanic Nurse Practice in Medically Underprivileged Areas, Ctr. for Health Policy Devel., San Antonio, 1989-91, Tex. Works Together program United Way, San Antonio, 1990—. Mem. ANA, NAACOG, Tex. Nurses' Assn., Nat. Assn. Hispanic Nurses, Am. Soc. Psychoprophy Obstets., Internat. Childbirth Edn. Assn., Coun. Childbirth Edn. Specialists, Sigma Theta Tau. Roman Catholic. Home: 7332 Staffordshire St Apt 1 Houston TX 77030-5155

VALDIVIA, HECTOR H., medical educator; b. Loreto, Mex., Aug. 23, 1958; married. MD, Nat U. Mex., 1982, PhD, 1987. Teaching asst. Nat. U. Mex. Sch. Medicine, Mexico City, 1980-86; rsch. assoc. Baylor Coll. Medicine, Houston, 1986-89; assoc. scientist U. Wis. Sch. Medicine, Madison, 1989-92; rsch. asst. prof. U. Md. Med. Sch., Bapt., 1992-94; asst. prof. dept. physiology U. Wis. Med. Sch., Madison, 1994—; lectr. and researcher in field. Contbr. articles to profl. jours., chpts. to books. Cystic Fibrosis Found. fellow, 1989-91. Mem. Am. Heart Assn. (scintific coun. 1995—), Biophys. Soc. U.S.A. Office: U Wis Med Sch Dept Physiology 1300 University Ave Madison WI 53706*

VALE, MARGO ROSE, physician; b. Balt., June 16, 1950; d. Henry and Pauline Esther (Koplow) Hausdorff; m. Michael Allen Vale, Aug. 22, 1971; children: Edward, Judith. BA magna cum laude, Brandeis U., 1971; MD, Albert Einstein Coll. Medicine, 1975. Diplomate Am. Bd. Dermatology. Resident in internal medicine and dermatology NYU, N.Y.C., 1975-79, Bellevue Hosp., N.Y.C., 1975-79, VA Hosp., N.Y.C., 1975-79; staff physician HIP Greater N.Y., Bay Shore, 1979-81; pvt. practice medicine Huntington, N.Y., 1981—; cons. in dermatology Huntington Hosp., 1981—, Gurwin Jewish Geriatric Ctr., Commack, N.Y., 1990—. Contbr. articles to profl. jours. Mem. Am. Acad. Dermatology, Med. Soc. State N.Y., Long Island Dermatology Soc., Suffolk County Med. Soc., Suffolk Dermatology Soc. (pres. 1990-92), Phi Beta Kappa. Office: 205 E Main St Huntington NY 11743-2923

VALEGA, THOMAS MICHAEL, retired health scientist; b. Linden, N.J., May 23, 1937; s. Paul and Anna (Vakalar) B.; m. Mary Margaret Orr, Aug. 30, 1958 (div. Dec., 1992); children: Margaret, Thomas, Vinson, Catherine; m. Heidi Hughes, Dec. 31, 1992. BS, Rutgers U., 1959, PhD, 1963. Chemist USDA, Beltsville, Md., 1963-67; grants assoc. NIH, Bethesda, Md., 1968; health science adminstr. NIAMD-NIH, Bethesda, 1969-72, NIDR-NIH, Bethesda, 1972-94; ret., 1994; sec.-treas. Implantology Rsch. Group, IADR/AADR, Washington, 1985-91. Contbr. articles to profl. jours.; editor symposium proceedings, 1977. Fellow Soc. for Biomaterials (chmn. awards com. 1977, Spl. award 1984), Am. Bat Conservation Soc. (pres. 1992—). Home: 724 Galloway Ct Winter Springs FL 32708

VALENSI, PAUL ELIE, physician, researcher, educator; b. Tunis, Tunisia, Mar. 14, 1953; arrived in France, 1958; s. Guy David Victor and Dora Allegra (Luisada) V.; m. Joelle Suzanne Maquaire, Sept. 19, 1981; children: Marine, Audrey, Alexandre. BA, Lycee Jacques Decourt, Paris, 1969; MA in Physiology, U. Paris, 1979, MA in Immunology, 1983, MA in Biochemistry, 1985. Specialist in nutrition, cardiology, internal medicine, endocrinology and metabolic diseases. Resident various hosps. Pub. Assistance, Paris, 1978-82; sr. resident various hosps. Pub. Assistance, Bobigny and Bondy, France, 1982—; univ. lectr. Univ. Paris-Nord, 1982—, research team, 1982—, prof. nutrition, 1993—; expert in clin. and pharmacological trials in the fields of diabetlogy, nutrition, endocrinology, hypertension, coronary heart disease, Bondy, 1982—; sci. counselor for rev. of Diabetology, Paris, 1988—; expert for internat. reviews of Diabetology and Cardiology; assoc. dir. Dept. of Endocrinology-Diabetology-Nutrition, Jean Verdier Hosp., Bondy, 1993—; dir. lab. for rsch. in nutrition U. Paris Nord, 1995—. Contbr. articles on diabetes, obesity, cardiovascular diseases microcirculation and thyroid function to profl. jours. Mem. Council of Adminstrn., U. Paris-Nord, 1986—, Council of Mgmt, Faculty of Medicine of Bobigny, 1987—. Officer Air Army, 1977-78, France. Recipient silver medal Faculty Lariboisiere, Paris, 1982, prize French Assn. for Study Diabetes and Metabolic Diseases, 1989. Mem. French Assn. for the Study Diabetes and Metabolic Diseases (adminstrn. coun.), European Assn. for the Study Diabetes, French Soc. Endocrinology, French Soc. Nutrition and Dietetics (adminstrn. coun.), French Soc. Microcirculation, Diabetes Edn. Study Group (pres. French sect.). Office: Hopital Jean Verdier, Avenue du 14 Juillet, 93140 Bondy France

VALENSTEIN, ARTHUR F., psychiatrist, educator; b. N.Y.C., Jan. 15, 1914; s. Abraham and Jennie (Friedman) V.; m. Katrina Ely Burlingham, Dec. 29, 1958; 1 child, David Arthur. BA, Cornell U., 1934, MD, 1938. Diplomate Am. Bd. Psychiatry and Neurology. Intern Cin. Gen. Hosp., 1938-39; resident Boston Psychopathic Hosp. (now The Mass. Mental Health Ctr.), 1939-40, sr. physician, 1941-42; resident Bellevue Hosp., N.Y.C., 1940-41; from instr. to clin. prof. psychiatry Harvard U. Med. Sch., Boston, 1948-84; clin. prof. emeritus Med. Sch. Harvard U., Boston, 1984—; asst. chief psychiatry Mental Health Clinic VA Med. Ctr., Boston, 1946-49; from assoc. psychiatrist to hon. psychiatrist Beth Israel Hosp., Boston, 1949—; from assoc. in psychiatry to physician Brigham and Women's Hosp. (formerly Peter Bent Brigham Hosp.), Boston, 1949—; pvt. practice Cambridge, Mass., 1949—; cons. psychiatrist Mt. Auburn Hosp., Cambridge, 1975—, Mass. Gen. Hosp., Boston, 1994—; attending child psychiatrist McLean Hosp. Mass. Gen. Hosp., Belmont, 1975—; John B. Turner vis. prof. psychiatry Coll. Physicians and Surgeons, Columbia U., 1968-69; Freud Anniversary Birthday lectr. Anna Freud Ctr., London, 1990, mem. internat. adv. coun., 1980—. Contbr. articles to profl. jours., chpts. to books on psychiatry and psychoanalysis. Maj. M.C., USAAF, 1942-46, PTO. Fellow Am. Psychiat. Assn.; mem. Am. Psychoanalytic Assn. (com. 1963-81), Internat. Psychoanalytic Assn. (v.p. 1971-77), Psychoanalytic Inst. New Eng. East (tng. and supervising analyst 1975—), Boston Psychoanalytic Soc. and Inst. (pres. 1974-75). Office: 140A Foster St Cambridge MA 02138-4746

VALENTI, RHONDA KAY, medical technologist; b. Austin, Pa., Aug. 29, 1960; d. William Homer and Dixie Lee (Stuckey) Ripple; m. John William Valenti, May 12, 1984; children: Marcia Theresa, Karina Helen. BS in Med. Tech., U. Pitts., 1982. Lab. technologist Charles Cole Meml. Hosp., Coudersport, Pa., 1982—, high sch. career advisor for health-related professions, 1985—. V.p. sch. bd. Austin Area Sch., 1993—. Mem. Am. Assn. Med. Technologists.

VALENTINE, JOHN PHILLIP, retired hospital executive; b. Evanston, Ill., Jan. 11, 1923; s. Frank B. and Margaret (Purdy) V.; m. Gloria M. Nelson, 1948; 1 child, James A. (dec.). BA, San Francisco State Coll., 1956; MBA, Syracuse U., 1958; D of Hosp. Adminstrn., George Washington U., 1965. Enlisted U.S. Army, 1943, advanced through grades to col., 1965, with Field Med. Svc., 1943-51, exec. officer Kyoto Army Hosp., 1952-54; spl. asst. to comptr. Office Surgeon Gen. U.S. Army, Washington; comptr. Office of Surgeon Hdqrs. 5th Army U.S. Army, Chgo.; comptr. Office of Surgeon Hdqrs. 6th Army U.S. Army, Persidio, Calif., 1955-64; dir. U.S. Army-Baylor Univ. Program, Ft. Sam Houston, Tex., 1965-70; ret. U.S. Army, 1969; adminstr. Loudon Meml. Hosp., Leesburg, Va., 1970-75; owner, operator Valentines, The Bahamas; prof. hosp. adminstrn. Baylor U., Waco, Tex.; dean Sch. Hosp. Adminstrn., Baylor U.; appointee health care adv. coun., appointee for study of health care-related legislation Gov. of State of Va.; bd. dirs. Lee Meml. Hosp., Ft. Myers, Fla. Bd. dirs. S.W. Fla. Symphony, ARC, Handicapped Riders; active Sanibel-Captiva Audubon Soc., 1983—, J.N. "Ding" Darling Wildlife Soc., Sanibel, 1983—. Decorated Bronze star with two bronze oak leaf clusters, Army Commendation medal with three bronze oak leaf clusters, Legion of Merit. Fellow Am. Coll. Health Care Execs., Am. Acad. Med. Adminstrs. (diplomat); mem. Nat. Trust for Hist. Preservation (pres.), Lions (Sanibel-Captiva club). Home: 5299 Ladyfinger Lake Rd Sanibel FL 33957-2437

VALENTINE, MARK CONRAD, dermatologist; b. Parkersburg, W.Va., Sept. 26, 1948; s. Sestel and Margaret ELaine (Sabolo) V.; m. Elizabeth Michelle Monezis, Apr. 21, 1975; children: Perry Martin, Owen Mark. BA, W.Va. U., 1970; MD, Johns Hopkins U., 1974. Intern, resident U. Hosps.

Cleve., 1974-76, resident, 1976-79; dermatologist pvt. practice, Everett, Wash., 1979—; clin. assoc. prof. U. Wash., Seattle, 1979—; active med. staff Providence Gen. Med. Ctr., Everett, 1979—. Bd. dirs., sec. City Libr. Bd., Mukilteo, Wash., 1994—; bd. dirs., v.p. Everett Symphony Bd., 1982-85; bd. dirs. Book Arts Guild, Seattle, 1988-90. Nat. Merit scholar, 1966. Mem. AMA, Am. Acad. Dermatology (adv. coun. 1983-86), Wash. State Dermatological Assn. (pres.-elect 1996), Seattle Dermatology Soc. (pres. 1985-86), Combined Med. Staff Everett (sec./treas. 1986-87), Soc. Dermatologic Surgery, Phi Beta Kappa. Office: 3327 Colby Ave Everett WA 98201

VALENTINE, PEGGY ANN, allied health educator; b. Danville, Va., Oct. 12, 1950; d. Nelson R. and Odessa M. (Echols) Valentine; 1 child, Terrence J. Teal. AA, Washington Tech. U., 1972; BS, Howard U., 1981, MA, 1983; EdD, Va. Poly. Inst. and State U., 1987. RN, D.C.; cert. physician asst. Staff nurse Sibley Hosp., Washington, 1972-85, nursing coord., 1979-85; physician asst. George Washington U., Washington, 1979-80; instr. Howard U., Washington, 1980-83, asst. prof., 1983-87, chmn. dept., 1983-89, assoc. prof., 1987—, dir. AIDS project, 1991—; cons. Charles Drew U., L.A., 1983-85, Nat. AIDS Edn. Tng. Ctrs.-HRSA; site visitor Com. Allied Health Edn. and Accreditation/AMA for Physician Asst. Programs, Chgo., 1983—; grant reviewer Dept. HHS/Physician Asst. Tng., Rockville, Md., 1985—. Mem. editl. bd. Jour. of Am. Acad. Physician Assts., 1993—. Project dir., nurse trainer World AIDS Found., Zimbabwe, 1993—. Grantee physician asst. tng. Dept. HHS, 1986-89, CDC, 1990—, Pa. Found. of Am. Acad. Physician Assts., 1991. Mem. Am. Acad. Physician Assts. (chmn. minority affairs com. 1991-94), D.C. Acad. Physician Assts. (pres. 1988-89). Office: Howard Univ CAHS Annex II Washington DC 20059

VALENTINE, WILLIAM NEWTON, physician, educator; b. Kansas City, Mo., Sept. 29, 1917; s. Herbert S. and Mabel W. (Watson) V.; m. Martha Hickman Winfree; children: William, James, Edward. Student, U. Mich., Ann Arbor, 1934-36, U. Mo., Columbia, 1936-37; MD, Tulane U., New Orleans, 1942. Diplomate: Am. Bd. Internal Medicine. Intern Strong Meml. Hosp., Rochester, N.Y., 1942-43, asst. resident in medicine, 1943, chief resident in medicine, 1943-44; specialist, attending physician in internal medicine Wadsworth Hosp., L.A., 1949-88, VA Ctr., L.A., 1949-88; specialist, attending physician in internal medicine Ctr. Health Scis. UCLA, 1949—, prof. medicine, 1957-88, chmn. dept., 1963-71; prof. emeritus medicine UCLA, Los Angeles, 1988—. Contbr. articles to profl. jours. Served to capt. MC, AUS, 1944-47. Recipient Mayo Soley award for excellence in research Western Soc. Clin. Research, 1978; 53d Annual UCLA faculty research lectr., 1978; Henry Stratton lectr. Am. Soc. Hematology, 1978; John Phillips Meml. award for Disting. Achievements in Internal Medicine, ACP, 1979. Fellow Am. Soc. Hematology, Internat. Soc. Hematology (v.p. U.S. 1976-80); mem. Am. Bd. Internal Medicine, ACP (master), Am. Soc. Clin. Investigation (v.p. 1962), Assn. Am. Physicians, Nat. Acad. Scis., Western Assn. Physicians (pres. 1969-70), Western Soc. Clin. Research, Am. Acad. Arts and Scis. Republican.

VALJEE, KRISHNA DAMODAR, surgeon; b. Durban, South Africa, July 25, 1949; came to the U.S., 1975; s. Damodar and Shanta (Varela) V.; m. Bernadette Lorraine Enicker, June 17, 1975; children: Kiren, Jashan. MD, U. Natal, 1973. Intern King Edward VIII Hosp., Durban, 1974; intern in gen. surgery Henry Ford Hosp., Detroit, 1975-76, resident, 1976-80, fellow in colon and rectal surgery, 1980-81; pvt. practice as gen. and colonrectal surgeon St. Clair, Mich., 1981-84, Cape Coral, Fort Myers, Fla., 1984-92, Port Huron, Mich., 1992—. Fellow ACS, Internat. Coll. Surgeons. Home: 4176 Gratiot Ave Port Huron MI 48060 Office: Saint Clair Surg Group PC 2609 Electric Ave Ste C Port Huron MI 48060

VALLE, MICHAEL JOHN, neurologist; b. Wyandotte, Mich., Dec. 24, 1959; s. Eraldo John and Grace G. (Stonier) V.;m.Cyntitia L. Valle, Nov. 20, 1992; 1 child, Lauren N.; 1 stepchild, Brandon R. Seifert. BS in Microbiology, Mich. State U., 1982, DO, 1986. Intern osteopathy Garden City (Mich.) Hosp., 1986-87, resident neurology, 1987-90; neurologist Dayton Ctr. Neurol. Disorders, Centerville, Ohio, 1990—; chmn. dept. neurology Grandview Hosp., Dayton, Ohio, 1994-96; resident dir. neurology residency, 1996—, med. dir. EEG, 1990—; med. dir. EEG Greene Meml. Hosp., Xenia, Ohio, 1994—. Mem. Am. Coll. Osteopathic Neurologists and Psychiatrists, Am. Acad. Neurology, Am. Osteo. Assn., Am. Sleep Disorders Assn., Dayton Neurol. Assn. Office: Dayton Ctr Neurol Disorders 1504 Yankee Park Pl Centerville OH 45458

VALLERGA, LOIS PETERS, healthcare manager, nutritionist; b. St. Louis, Sept. 30, 1954; d. John and Frances Mary (Justice) P. BS in human nutrition, food mgmt., U. Mo., 1977. Registered dietitian. Clinical interventionist St. Louis Heart Assn., St. Louis, Mo., 1977-79; clinical dietitian St. Charles Med. Ctr., Bend, Oreg., 1979-86; pvt. practice Bend, Oreg., 1979-86; edn. mgr. St. Charles Med. Ctr., 1986-93, adminstrn. and human resources cluster mgr., 1993—, dir. edn., tng. & orgnl. devel., 1996—. Commn. Bend Urban Area Planning Comm., 1992-95; bd. liaison Bend Devel. Bd., 1992-94; bd. dirs. Child Care Coun., Bend, 1979-81, Women, Infants and Children adv. bd., Bend, 1979-81; bd. dirs., exec. com. Am. Heart Assn., 1986-89, Area Health Edn. Ctr., 1991—. Recipient Cert. of Appreciation Oreg. Health Svcs., 1990. Mem. Am. Coll. Healthcare Execs., Am. Soc. Healthcare, Edn. and Traning, Am. Soc. Human Resources Adminstrn., Bend Rotary Club (com. chair 1988), Bend C. of C. (com. chair. 1987—, Pres. award 1988). Roman Catholic. Office: St Charles Med Ctr 2500 NE Neff Rd Bend OR 97701-6015

VALLET, JEAN-MARIE P., health care company executive; b. Laval, France, Oct. 21, 1955; s. Jacques Vallet and Françoise Daussy; m. Evelyne P. Gouilloud, Apr. 28, 1987; children: Marine, Cyril. PhD, U. Geneva, 1986, MBA, 1989. Tchg. asst. U. Geneva, Switzerland, 1981-85; project leader genetic engring. Battelle Inst., Geneva, 1985-88; dir. export Jouan SA, Nantes, France, 1989-90; from asst. to sr. vice dir. Pierre Fabre SA, Toulouse, France, 1990-92; dir. adm. & fin. clin. dept. Parke Davis GmbH, Freiburg, Germany, 1992-94; sr. dir. planning investment dept. Warner-Lambert & Co., Morris Plains, N.J., 1994-96; v.p. bus. devel. Europe Bristol-Myers-Squibb, 1996—. Home: 5 Sinclair Terr Madison NJ 07940

VALLEY, THOMAS, physician assistant; b. Eau Claire, Wis., Apr. 18, 1952; s. Randall Iee and Mary Jean (Hoehn) V.; m. Bonnie Beth Hong, Jan. 8, 1972; children: Trisha J. Studer, Christa B., Katina L., Tommi Lynn. AS, Chapman Coll., 1977; BS, U. Wis., 1981; cert. physicians asst., Marshfield Med. Found., 1980. Family practice, surg. physicians asst. Merrill (Wis.) Med. Assn., 1981-83; high sch. football coach Hayfield (Minn.) Schs., 1992-95; trauma physicians asst. Mayo Clinic, Rochester, Minn., 1991-95; high sch. varsity football coach Barron (Wis.) Area H.S., 1995; physicians asst. Midelfont Clinic, Barron, 1995—; high sch. varsity football coach Cameron H.S., 1996—; adj. clin. prof. medicine U. Nebr. Med. Sch., Omaha, 1990-91; pres. Co. Grade Officers Coun., Eielson AFB, 1987. Pres. Parish Coun., Eilson AFB, 1986; selection com. U. Wis. LaCrosse Physicians Asst. Program, 1996. Capt. USAF, 1983-91. Recipient Arthur C. Storz award Air Force Assn., 1991. Fellow Am. Acad. of Physicians Assts. (del. 1987-92), K.C. (treas. 1986-87), Am. Legion,. Roman Catholic. Home: 677 85th St Amery WI 54001 Office: 1220 E Woodland Ave Barron WI 54812

VALLIANOS, FRED, psychology educator; b. N.Y.C., Aug. 4, 1935; s. Spyros and Rodomanthe (Livanis) V.; m. Bessie T. Zezefillis, June 10, 1962; children: Marc, Rosemond. BS, NYU, 1957; MA in Psychology, East Carolina Coll., 1966; EdD in Ednl. Psychology, U. Va., 1969. Grad. instr. East Carolina U., Greenville, N.C., 1960-61; asst. prof., chmn. acting dept., dir. testing and counseling U. N.C., Wilmington, 1961-65; instr. U. Va., Charlottesville, 1965-68; assoc. prof. psychology U. West Fla., Pensacola, 1969-71, chmn. dept. ednl. leadership, 1977-79, chmn. dept. psychology, 1983-86; dir. Eglin and Ft. Walton Beach (Fla.) ctrs. U. West Fla., 1986—, chmn. dept. psychology, 1993—; also chmn. faculty senate and acad. coun.; assoc. dir. pers. and faculty rels. State Univ. System Fla., 1976-77; presenter in field, 1974—; grant reviewer Fla. Dept. Edn., 1976. Bd. dirs. West Fla. Community Care Ctr., Milton, 1988—; mem. N.W. Fla. Health Coun., Panama City, 1985—, Alcohol, Drug Abuse and Mental Health Planning Coun., Pensacola, 1985—; chmn. Health & Human Svcs. Bd.; past pres. Mental Health Assn. Escambia County, Mental Health Assn. Fla.; v.p. Mental Health Assn. Okaloosa County; past chmn. Task Force to Revise Community Mental Health Act Fla.; mem. Statewide Health Coun.; arbitrator Juvenile Justice System, Escambia, Santa Rosa, Oscaloosa counties. Sgt. U.S. Army, 1957-59. Recipient Founders Day award NYU, 1958, Disting. Svc. award Nat. Mental Health Assn., 1979, U. West Fla., 1983, Leadership award N.W. Fla. Health Coun., 1985, Presdl. award Mental Health Assn. Fla., 1976, svc. award Dist. I Mental Health Bd., 1981; Disting. Leadership award Mental Health Assn. Escambia County, 1975, Vol. of Yr. award, 1980, Disting. Svc. and Leadership award, 1982; Dupont fellow, 1966. Mem. APA, Southeastern Psychol. Assn., N.W. Fla. Psychol. Assn., Beta Gamma Sigma, Pi Delta Epsilon, Kappa Delta Pi, Psi Chi, Phi Delta Kappa, Phi Kappa Phi. Democrat. Greek Orthodox. Home: 1407 Sound Retreat Dr Navarre FL 32566-7509 Office: U West Fla Dept of Psychology 11000 University Pky Pensacola FL 32514-5732

VALLITTU, PEKKA KALEVI, dentist, researcher; b. Mikkeli, Finland, May 11, 1965; s. Seppo and Sinikka Mirja (Kärkkäinen) V.; m. Anna-Maija Kaislamäki, June 27, 1992. Dental technician, Inst. Dental Tech., Finland, 1988; DDS, PhD, U. Kuopio, Finland, 1994; docent in prosthodontic material sci., U. Turku, Finland, 1995. Lectr. Inst. Dental Tech., Kuopio, 1989-93; acting lectr. U. Kuopio, 1992, rsch. worker, 1993, lectr., 1994-96; vis. scientist Scandinavian Inst. Dental Meterials, Haslum, Norway, 1995—; part-time pvt. practitioner, Kuopio, 1995-96; reviewer Am. Jour. Orthodontics and Dentofacial Orthopaedics, 1996—, Jour. Prosthodontics, 1996—. Reviewer Finnish Dental Jour., 1995—, asst. editor in prosthodontics, 1995—; contbr. articles to profl. jours.; inventor in field. Mem. ADA, Finnish Dental Soc. (responsible for continuing edn. of prosthodontics 1995—), Internat. Assn. Student Clinicians, European Prosthodontic Assn., Internat. Assn. for Dental Rsch., Am. Acad. Dental Materials, Scandinavian Soc. for Prosthetic Dentistry, 1995—. Office: Scand Inst Dental Materials, PO Box 70, N-1344 Haslum Norway

VALO, MARTHA ANN, hospital dietary executive, consultant; b. West Aliquippa, Pa., Apr. 6, 1938; d. George and Susan Helen (Pollak) V.; m. John Daniel Dempsey, Dec. 17, 1974. B.S., Carlow Coll., 1960; MS, U. Pa., 1991. Registered dietitian; disting. health care food svd. adminstr. Food service mgr. Stouffer's Mgmt. Co., Phila., 1960-76; restaurant mgr. Strawbridge & Clothier, Phila., 1976-78; food service dir. Saunders House, Phila., 1978-80; dir. food/nutrition svcs. U. Med. Ctr., Stratford, N.J., 1980-93, adminstrv. dir. supply svcs., 1993—; adj. faculty Camden County Coll., Blackwood, N.J., 1985—. Mem. Am. Soc. for Hosp. Food Service Adminstrs., Am. Coll. Health Care Execs., Nat. Soc. Healt Care Food Svcs. Mgrs., So. N.J. Nutritional Coun., N.J. Dietetic Assn., Amer. Dietetic Assn. Home: 135 Fenway Ave Atco NJ 08004-3016 Office: Kennedy Meml Hosps Univ Med Ctr 18 Laurel Rd E Stratford NJ 08084-1327

VALSAMIS, MARIUS PETER, neuropathologist, educator; b. N.Y.C., Feb. 23, 1932; s. Peter Christ and Anna (Demetrokopoulous) V.; m. Nancy Weems, June 16, 1957; children: Helen Anna, Demetrios Peter, Ariadne Irene. AB, Columbia Coll., 1953; MD, SUNY, Bklyn., 1957. Intern Hosp. St. Raphael, New Haven, Conn., 1957-58; resident physician King's County Hosp., Bklyn., 1958-59; NIH tng. fellow SUNY Downstate Med. Ctr., Brklyn., 1959-63, clin. asst. prof. pathology, nueropathology, 1967-69; surgeon Off. Surg. Gen. PHS, Bethesda, Md., 1963-65; instr. Neurology, Pathology Jefferson Med. Coll., Phila., 1965-69; chief of labs. Bklyn. State Hosp., 1967-69; assoc. prof. Pathology (Neuropathology) Albert Einstein Med. Coll., The Bronx, N.Y., 1969-74; prof. neuropathology, dir. pathophysiology course N.Y. Med. Coll., Valhalla, N.Y., 1974-91; cons. neuropathology Lincoln Hosp., Bronx, N.Y., 1993—, Med. Examiners Office of Westchester County, 1992—; cons. Anatomic Pathology Cert. Nat. Cancer Inst., Bethesda, Md., 1964—, Clin. Ctr. Nat. Inst. Health, Bethesda, 1981—. Author (with others) AIDS (chapt. on neuropathology); contbr. articles sci. jours. Chmn. Med. Commn. U.S. Fencing Assn., Colorado Springs, Colo., 1972-84, 87-92; mgr. Pan Am. Olympic Fencing Team, Colorado Springs, 1975, 79, U.S. Olympic Fencing Team, 1976, 80; mem. Commn. Medicale Fed. Internat. d'Escrime, Paris, 1978—. Fellow AAAS, N.Y. Acad. Scis.; mem. Am. Assn. Neuropathologists (archivist), Internat. Soc. Greek Neuroscientists (pres. 1995-96), The Fencers' Club (bd. dirs. N.Y. 1969-91). Home: 375 Vanderbilt Ave Brooklyn NY 11238-1010 Office: NY Med Coll Valhalla NY 10595

VALSECCHI, ROSSANO HERMES, dermatologist, researcher; b. Andalo, Sondrio, Italy, Jan. 22, 1946; s. Ermenegildo Valsecchi and Dalia Guzzi; m. Marina Riva, Apr. 21, 1969; children: Massimiliano, Stefania. MD, U. Pavia, Italy, 1973. Specialist in dermatology, allergology and immunology. Asst. dermatologist Gen. Hosp., Bergamo, 1974, vice chmn. dermatology dept., 1985; head dept. dermatology allergy unit Gen. Hosp., 1989. Author, editor: Orticaria-Angioedema, 1991; editor Dermo-Time, 1989. Home: Via Pignolo 56, 24100 Bergamo Italy Office: Gen Hosp Dept Dermatology, Largo Barozzi 1, 24100 Bergamo Italy

VAMVAKETIS, CAROLE, health services administrator; b. Bklyn., Mar. 1, 1943; d. William and Helen (Calacanis) Vamvaketis; 1 child, William. AA, Packer Collegiate Inst., Bklyn., 1962; BS, Columbia U., 1964; MA, Columbia Tchrs. Coll., 1969; AAS in Nursing, Rockland C.C., Suffern, N.Y., 1981; BSN, Dominican Coll., 1991. Tchr. elem. sch. A. Fantis Parochial Sch., 1964-67; tchr. Adelphi Acad., 1967-72, girls dean, 1968-72; nurse Nyack (N.Y.) Hosp., 1981-91; nurse mgr. Kings Harbor Care Ctr., 1991-93; assoc. dir. nursing Port Chester Nursing Home, 1993-94; CQI/edn. coord. Highbridge Woodycrest Ctr., 1994-95; profl. svcs. cons. Multicare Cos., Inc., Nanuet, N.Y., 1995—, personal svcs. cons., 1995-96, divsn. dir. clin. svcs., 1996—. Home and Office: 102 Poplar St Nanuet NY 10954-2007

VAN, GEORGE PAUL, international money management consultant; b. Isle Maligne, Que., Can., Feb. 12, 1940; s. Raymond Murdoch and Germaine Marie (Brassard) V.; m. Janine Marie Irene Therese Yvette Boily, Sept. 15, 1962; children: John, Robert, Caroline. BA, McGill U., 1961; DHA, U. Toronto, 1963. Sr. cons. Agnew Peckham and Assos., Toronto, Ont., Can., 1963-65; chief exec. officer, exec. dir. Misericordia Corp., Edmonton, Alta., Can., 1965-68; chief operating officer, exec. v.p. Texpack, Ltd., Brantford, Ont., 1968-70, also bd. dirs.; group v.p. Will Ross, Inc., Milw., 1970-73; exec. v.p. Nortek, Inc., Cranston, R.I., 1973-77, also bd. dirs.; pres., chief operating officer Hosp. Affiliates Internat. Inc. subs. INA Corp., Nashville, 1977-80, also bd. dirs.; chmn., pres., chief exec. officer Health Group Inc., Nashville, 1980-84; chmn., chief exec. officer Columbia Corp. (formerly Franklin Corp.), Nashville, 1984-88; pres. Grinders Switch Farms, Grinders Switch Shooting Club, Centerville, Tenn., 1990—; chmn. Van Hedge Fund Advisors, Inc., Nashville, 1992—. Bd. dirs. Tulane U. Med. Ctr., 1977-80, Nashville Inst. for the Arts, 1987-88, Nashville Symphony, 1987-88, Fedn. Internat. de Tir aux Armes Sportives de Chasse, Paris, 1990-92; mem. Internat. Tech. Commn. for Sporting Clays, Paris, 1990; bd. overseers U. Pa. Sch. of Nursing, 1979-82, 84-88, assoc. trustee U. Pa., 1979-82, 84-88; chmn. internat. com. U.S. Sporting Clays Assn., 1989-92; active pres.'s coun. Andrew Jackson Inst., 1993—; adv. bd. Fin. Mktg. Rsch. Ctr. Vanderbilt U. Recipient several scholarships. Mem. Westside Club, Grinders Switch Club. Contbr. articles to profl. jours. Home and Office: 1608 Chickering Rd Nashville TN 37215-4906

VANARSDALE, DIANA CORT, social worker; b. N.Y.C., Oct. 27, 1934; d. Arthur and Augusta Deutsch; B.S., N.Y.U., 1955; M.S.W., Columbia U., 1957; m. Leonard Van Arsdale, Sept. 17, 1978; children by previous marriage—Hayley, Daniel. Clinician, Payne Whitney Clinic, N.Y. Hosp., N.Y.C., 1957-59, psychiat. clinic Jewish Bd. Guardians, N.Y.C., 1959-61; founder, pres. Big Six Towers Nursery Sch., N.Y.C., 1962-67; dir. intake and social service L.I. Consultation Center, Forest Hills, N.Y., 1966-84, clin. dir., coordinator clin. services, 1984-86; supr., faculty mem. L.I. Inst. Mental Health, 1973-86; cons. in social work Bergen Ctr. for Child Devel., 1981-87; dir. Seniors Option Service, Allendale, N.J., 1980-90. Author: Transitions A Woman's Guide to Successful Retirement, 1991. Mem. Nat. Assn. Social Workers, N.Y. Soc. Clin. Social Workers. Home: 47-30 61st St Woodside NY 11377-5763

VAN ARSDALE, GARY LEE, health services administrator; b. Columbus, Ohio, Sept. 1, 1948; s. Charles and Barbara Lee (Lindinmeyer) Van A.; m. Marcia Anne Tetreault, Sept. 1, 1969; children: Jessica Lee, Becky Ellen. BS in Edn., Ashland U., 1970; MA in Adminstrn., Ohio State U., 1972. Activity dir., athletic dir. Columbus Pub. Schs., 1970-79; rsch. devel. dir. George W. Wimpey, Inc., Columbus, 1979-81; sales mgr. Ctrl. Benarts, Columbus, 1981-85; COO Physicians Health Plan, Columbus, 1985-90; pres. Eggert Van Arsdale Agy., Columbus, 1990—, E-V Benefits Mgmt., Columbus, 1990—. Chmn. bd. dirs. Ctrl. Ohio Health Care Commn., Columbus, 1988-90; chmn. City County, Westerville, 1979-87, mayor, 1986; dir. Campus Drug Rehab., 1986-88; pres. PTA, Columbus, 1978; chmn. Cable TV Commn., Westerville, 1984. Named Young Man of Yr., Jr. C. of C., 1987. Mem. Rotary. Republican. Roman Catholic. Home: 4990 Harlem Rd Galena OH 43021

VAN ARSDALE, STEPHANIE KAY LORENZ, cardiovascular clinical specialist, nursing educator, researcher; b. Butte, Mont., June 20, 1952; d. Hubert Nelson and Pauline Anna (Tebo) Lorenz; m. Roy Burbank Van Arsdale, June 18, 1978; children: Christopher, Erica. Diploma, St. Johns McNamara, Sch. Nursing, 1975; BSN cum laude, U. Utah, 1978, MSN, 1979; EdD, U. Ark., 1993. RN, Ark.; cert. ACLS instr., Am. Heart Assn.; cert. BLS instr.-trainer, Am. Heart Assn. Staff nurse cardiovascular surg. ICU Presbyn. Hosp. Ctr., Albuquerque, 1975-76; staff nurse surg. ICU and CCU U. Utah Med. Ctr., Salt Lake City, 1976-78; clin. specialist residency LDS Hosp., Salt Lake City, 1979; asst. prof. dept. Baccalaureate Nursing Ea. Ky. U., Richmond, 1980-84; staff nurse critical care unit Pattie A. Clay Hosp., Richmond, 1981-83; med. clinician Washington Regional Med. Ctr., Fayetteville, Ark., 1985; cardiovascular clin. specialist VA Med. Ctr., Fayetteville, 1985-93; assoc. prof. U. Memphis, 1993-96; asst. prof. U. Ark. for Med. Scis., Little Rock, 1996—; CPR instr. in cmty., Fayetteville and Richmond, 1980-93; mem. adj. faculty div. nursing Northeastern State U., Tahlequah, Okla., 1986-93, U. Ark., Fayetteville, 1989-93; mem. adj. clin. faculty U. Ark. for Med. Scis. Coll. Nursing, Little Rock, 1988-93; charter mem., spkr. N.W. Ark. Critical Care Consortium Area Health Edn. Ctr., Fayetteville, 1989-93; presenter in field. Contbr. articles to profl. jours. Coord., vol. Home Meals Delivery Program, Richmond, Ky., 1981-84; adminstrv. bd., Sunday sch. tchr., sec. adult forum Ctrl. United Meth. Ch., Fayetteville, 1986-87; troop leader Girl Scouts Am. NOARK Coun., Fayetteville, 1987-90; sound sys. operator Christ United Meth. Ch., 1993—. Recipient Nurse of Yr. award for excellence in nursing practice Dist. 9, Ark. State Nurses Assn., 1987; grantee Ctrl. U.S. Earthquake Consortium, 1993, U.S. Geologic Survey, 1994, Miss. Emergency Mgmt. Agy., 1996. Mem. ANA (v.p. Dist. 9 1985-86, pres. 1987-88, mem. image com. 1990-93, chmn. program com. 1986-87, state 2d v.p. 1988-90, clin. nurse specialist coun. 1991—), AACN (CCRN; bd. dirs., chpt. sec. program com. 1994—), Nat. League for Nursing (mem. nominating com. Ky. 1984-85), Sigma Theta Tau. Methodist. Home: 8872 Farmoor Rd Germantown TN 38139-6517 Office: Univ Ark for Med Scis Little Rock AR 72205

VANARSDALL, ROBERT LEE, JR., orthodontist, educator; b. Crewe, Va., Feb. 7, 1940; s. Robert Lee Sr. and Margie Mae (Jenkins) V.; m. Sandra E. Hoffman, Aug. 11, 1962; children: Robert Lee III, Lesley, Ashley. BA in Econs., Coll. William and Mary, 1962; DDS, Med. Coll. Va., 1970; cert. Orthodontics and Periodontics, U. Pa., 1973. Diplomate Am. Acad. Periodontology, Am. Bd. Orthodontics. Staff Children's Hosp., Phila., 1973—; prof. orthodontics, chmn. dept. orthodontics U. Pa., Phila., 1981—; prof. dentistry, chmn. Med. Coll. Pa., Phila., 1989—; bd. dirs. Nat. Dental Ins. Co., Denver. Editor: Internat. Jour. Adult Orthodontics and Orthognathic Surgery, 1986—, Orthodontoics: Current Principles and Techniques, 2d edit., 1994; editorial bd. profl. jours.; contbr. articles to profl. jours. Bd. dirs. Phila. Soc. William and Mary Alumni Assn. Lt. USNR, 1962-65. Fellow Coll. Physicians of Phila. 1978, Am. Coll. Dentistry 1980. Mem. ADA, Am. Assn. Orthodontists, Stomatological Club Phila., Angle Soc. Orthodontists, Phila. Soc. Orthodontists (pres. 1989, chmn. sci. affairs coun. 1990—). Roman Catholic. Home: 208 Ashwood Rd Villanova PA 19085-1504 Office: Sinkler Bldg 588 E Lancaster Ave Radnor PA 19087-5235

VAN ASSENDELFT, ONNO WILLEM, hematologist; b. Brummen, The Netherlands, Aug. 23, 1932; came to U.S. 1976; s. Frederik and Anna Maria (Veenbaas) Van A.; m. Theodora Henriette Teunissen, July 15, 1960; children: Anne C.E., Frederik H.B., Albert H.P., Diederik A.A., Catharina E.E. MD, U. Groningen, 1959, PhD, 1970. Rsch. scientist, assoc. prof. Lab. Regulatory Physiology, Groningen, 1961-76; sec., dean Groningen Med. Sch., 1973-75; supervisory med. rsch. officer Ctrs. for Disease Control and Prevention, Atlanta, 1976—; cons. FDA, 1979—; bd. secretariat Internat. Com. Standardization in Hematology, 1978—, chmn. secretariat, 1994—; bd., exec. com. Nat. Comm. Clin. Lab. Stds., Villanova, Pa., 1982-96, pres., 1992-94; chmn. U.S. delegation to ISO/TC 212 on clin. lab. testing and in vitro diagnostic test sys., 1995—. Author: Spectrophotometry of Hemoglobin Derivatives, 1970; editl. bd. ECRI Healthcare Product Comparison System, Lab. Hematology; contbr. articles to profl. jours., chpts. to books. Capt. Royal Netherlands Army, 1959-61. Recipient Sec. Group award USPHS, 1986, Bronze plaque Ministry of Health, Chile, 1983, Russel J. Eilers award Nat. Com. for Clin. Lab. Stds., Villanova, 1988, Spl. award Nat. Hemophilia Found., 1992. Mem. AAAS, Am. Soc. Hematology, Internat. Soc. Lab. Hematology, N.Y. Acad. Scis. Office: Ctrs Disease Control Prevention 1600 Clifton Rd NE Atlanta GA 30329-4018

VANATTA, JOHN CROTHERS, III, physiologist, physician, educator; b. Lafayette, Ind., Apr. 22, 1919; s. John Crothers and Ida Lahr (Raub) V.; m. Carol Lee Geisler, July 30, 1944; children: Lynn Ellen, Paul Richard. B.A., Ind. U., 1941, M.D., 1944. Intern Wayne County Gen. Hosp., Eloise, Mich., 1944-45, resident in internal medicine, 1946-47; fellow in physiology, pharmacology Southwestern Med. Coll., Dallas, 1947-48, fellow in exptl. and internal medicine, 1948-49; instr. physiology U. Tex. Southwestern Med. Sch., 1949-50, asst. prof., 1950-53, assoc. prof., 1953-57, prof. physiology, 1957—, Robert W. Lackey prof. physiology, 1987-89; prof. physiology So. Meth. U. Dallas, Dallas, 1969-80, Baylor Coll. Dentistry, Dallas, 1992-96; mem. staff Parkland Meml. Hosp., Dallas, 1953-57, VA Hosp., Dallas, McKinney, Tex., 1956-58; cons. div. nuclear edn. tng. AEC, 1964-67. Author: Oxygen Transport, Hypoxia and Cyanosis, 1974, Fluid Balance - A Clinical Manual, 1988; contbr. articles to profl. jours. Scouter, Circle 10 council Boy Scouts Am., Dallas, 1963-78; v.p. Luth. Health Care Council N. Tex., 1975-80, pres., 1980-81. Served as lt. (j.g.) M.C., USNR, 1945-46, PTO. Mem. AMA, AAAS, Am. Physiol. Soc., Soc. Exptl. Biology and Medicine, Phi Beta Pi, Sigma Xi, Delta Tau Delta. Lutheran (councilman 1951-91, v.p. 1974-75). Home: 10416 Remington Ln Dallas TX 75229-5262

VAN ATTA, RALPH EDWARD, clinical psychologist, consultant; b. Columbus, Ohio, July 24, 1933; s. Clarence Dell and Wilma (Davidson) V.; m. JoAnn Luce, Sept. 15, 1962; children: Katherine, Karen, Ralph Davidson, Sarah. BS, Ohio State U., 1955, MA, 1960, PhD, 1964. Lic. psychologist, W.Va.; diplomate Am. Bd. of Psychotherapy. Intern, Ohio State Counseling Ctr., Columbus, 1962; clin. psychology intern Norwich (Conn.) Hosp., 1963; asst. prof., psychologist U. Tex., 1964-69; assoc. prof., psychologist, So. Ill. U., Carbondale, 1969-72; dir., prof. dept. psychol. services U. Wis., Milw., 1972-80; exec. dir. Behavioral Medicine Assocs., Waukesha, Wis., 1978-87; pres. Behavioral Medicine Wis., Ltd., 1984-86; mem. panel forensic experts Counties of Waukesha and Milwaukee, Wis., 1978-89; chief psychologist Louis A. Johnson VA Med. Ctr., Clarksburg, W.Va., 1990—; clin. asst. prof. Sch. Medicine W.Va. U., 1990—; adj. prof. Grad. Coll. W.Va., 1994—. 1st lt. U.S. Army, 1955-57. Named Disting. Mil. Student Ohio State U., 1955. Mem. APA, Am. Soc. Clin. Hypnosis (Clin. Research award 1987), Assn. Va. Chief Psychologists, Am. Acad. Forensic Examiners, Phi Delta Kappa, Psi Chi. Contbr. articles to profl. jours. Office: Louis A Johnson VA Med Ctr Clarksburg WV 26301

VANAUKER, LANA LEE, recreational therapist, educator; b. Youngstown, Ohio, Sept. 19, 1949; d. William Marshall and Joanne Norma (Kimmel) Speece; m. Dwight Edward VanAuker, Mar. 16, 1969 (div. 1976); 1 child, Heidi. BS in Edn. cum laude, Kent (Ohio) State U., 1974; MS in Edn., Youngstown (Ohio) U., 1989. Cert. tchr., Ohio; nat. cert. activity cons. Phys. edn. instr. St. Joseph Sch., Campbell, Ohio, 1973-75; program dir. YWCA, Youngstown, 1975-85; exercise technician Youngstown State U., 1985-86; health educator Park Vista Retirement Ctr., Youngstown, 1986-87; sch. tchr. Salem (Ohio) City Sch., 1987-88; recreational therapist Trumbull Meml. Hosp., Warren, Ohio, 1988—; activity cons. Mahoning/Trumbull Nursing Homes, Warren, 1990-92; adv. bd. rep. Ohio State Bur. Health Promotion Phys. Fitness, 1996—; mem. adv. bd. Ohio State Executive Physical Fitness Dept. Health, 1996. Producer chair exercise sr. video Excercise is the Fountain of Youth, 1993; photographer, choreographer. Vol. Am. Cancer Soc., 1980—, Am. Heart Assn., 1986—, Dance for Heart, 1980-

86; mem. State of Ohio Phys. Fitness Adv. Bd., 1996. Youngstown State U. scholar, 1986-89. Mem. AAHPERD, Youngstown Camera Club (social chair 1989-90, pres. 1993-95), Resident Activity Profl. Assn. (pres. 1994, 95, 96), Pa. Activity Profl. Assn., Kappa Delta Pi. Democrat. Presbyterian. Home: 385 N Broad St Canfield OH 44406-1256 Office: Trumbull Meml Hosp 1350 E Market St Warren OH 44483-6608

VAN BADEN, MARC, surgeon; b. Leuven, Brabant, Belgium, Mar. 23, 1940; s. Maurice and Lily (Symons) Van B.; m. Lieve Dessers, Apr. 24, 1965; children: Ann, Karin, Kristin. Degree in Greek and Latin Humanities, O.L. Vr. Coll., Antwerp, Belgium, 1958; MD, Cath. U. Leuven, 1965, degree in surgery, 1971. Intern A.Z. St. Josef, Mortsel, Belgium, 1965-68, surgeon, 1971-82, head dept. surgery, 1983—; intern Univ. Lyon, Hôpital Ed. Hérriot, Lyon, France, 1969, St. Josefkliniek, Brugge, Belgium, 1970; resident Stuyvenberggasthuis, Antwep, Belgium, 1971-72; vis. prof. U. Iasi, Romania, 1995. Contbr. articles to profl. jours. Mem. Belgian Genootschap Heelk (corr.), Soc. Royale Belge Gastroenterologists (assoc.), Belgian Genootschap Gastroenterol., Internat. Coll. Surgeons, Internat. Gastro-Surg. Club (corr.), European Assn. Endoscopic Surgery, Assn. Francaise Chirurgie. Home: F Williotstraat 16, Antwerp Belgium

VANBENTHUYSEN, RICHARD, JR., physician assistant; b. Goldsboro, N.C., Dec. 28, 1946; s. Richard and Helen Grace (Sauls) VanB.; m. Lavonda Kay Thomas, July 20, 1969; children: Betsy Kay, Richard III. BS in biology, Mars Hill Coll., 1969; PA, Bowman Gray Sch. Medicine, 1972. Lic. physician asst., N.C. Biology instr. Goldsboro, 1969-70; physician asst. Ben R. Boyette, Jr., MD, Goldsboro, 1972-73, Clinton (N.C.) Med. Clinic, 1973, Fred S. Gachet, Jr., MD, Hickory, N.C., 1973-76, Woodward (Okla.) Hosp., 1994-95, Seagrove (N.C.) Med. Clinic, 1995-96, Randolph Med. Assocs., Asheboro, N.C., 1996—; rep. G.D. Searle Pharm., Durham, N.C., 1976-79; hosp. rep. McNeil Pharm., Goldsboro, 1979-94. Com. chmn. Boy Scouts Am., Goldsboro, 1988-90, baseball coach, 1982-84. Fellow Am. Acad. Physicians Assts., N.C. Acad. Physician Asst. Republican. Episcopalian. Home: 2331 Northmont Dr Asheboro NC 27203 Office: Randolph Med Assocs 132-A W Miller St Asheboro NC 27203

VAN BOCKSTAELE, ELISABETH JEANNE, neuroscientist, researcher; b. Paris, Jan. 4, 1965; d. Pierre Georges and Kathleen Mary (Garrish) Van B.; m. Erol Veznedaroglu, June 27, 1993; 1 child, Lauren Kincal. BA, Sarah Lawrence Coll., Bronxville, N.Y., 1985; MS, N.Y.U., 1989; PhD, 1991. Grad. student N.Y.U., 1986-91; postdoctoral fellow Cornell U. Med. Coll., N.Y.C., 1991-93, instr. in Neuroscience, 1993-94, asst. prof. Neuroscience, 1994—. Author: Central Neural Mechanisms in Cardiovascular Regulation, 1991; contbr. articles to profl. jours. Named NARSAD Young Investigator Nat. Alliance for Rsch. on Schizophrenia and Depression, 1994-96; recipient NIDA First award Nat. Inst. on Drug Abuse, 1994-99, Established Investigatorship award Am. Heart Assn., 1996. Mem. Soc. for Neuroscience. Office: Cornell University Med Coll 411 E 69th St New York NY 10021-5603*

VAN BRUNT, EDMUND EWING, physician; b. Oakland, Calif., Apr. 28, 1926; s. Adrian W. and Kathryn Anne (Shattuck) Van B.; m. Claire Monod, Feb. 28, 1949; children: Karin, Deryk, Jahn. BA in Biophysics, U. Calif., Berkeley, 1952; MD, U. Calif., San Francisco, 1959; ScD, U. Toulouse, France, 1978. Postdoctoral fellow NIH, 1961-63; rsch. assoc. U. Calif., San Francisco, 1963-67; staff physician Kaiser Permanente Med. Ctr., San Francisco, 1964-91; dir. div. rsch. Kaiser Permanente Med. Program, Oakland, Calif., 1979-91; assoc. dir. Kaiser Found. Rsch. Inst., Oakland, 1985-91, sr. cons., 1991—; adj. prof. U. Calif., San Francisco, 1975-92; chmn. instnl. rev. bd. Kaiser Found. Rsch. Inst., 1986—; pres. bd. trustees French Found. Med. Rsch. and Edn., San Francisco, 1992—. Contbr. articles to profl. books and jours. With U.S. Army, 1944-46. Fellow ACP, Am. Coll. Med. Informatics; mem. AAAS, Calif. Med. Assn., U. Calif. Emeritus Faculty Assn., Sigma Xi. Office: 131 Tamalpais Rd Berkeley CA 94708

VAN BRUNT, MARCIA ADELE, social worker; b. Chgo., Oct. 21, 1937; d. Dean Frederick and Faye Lila (Greim) Slauson; student Moline (Ill.) Pub. Hosp. Sch. Nursing, 1955-57; BA with distinguished scholastic record, U. Wis., Madison, 1972, MSW (Fed. tng. grantee), 1973; M.O.E. Bartholomew; children: Suzanne, Christine, David. Social worker div. community services Wis. Dept. Health Social Services, Rhinelander, 1973, regional adoption coordinator, 1973-79, chief adoption and permanent planning no. region, 1979-83, asst. chief direct services and regulation no. region, 1983-84, adminstr., clin. social worker No. Family Services, Inc., 1984—; counselor, psychotherapist, public speaker, cons. in field of clin. social work. Home: 5264 Forest Ln Rt 1 Rhinelander WI 54501 Office: 5 W Frederick PO Box 237 Rhinelander WI 54501-0237

VAN BURKLEO, BILL BEN, osteopath, emergency physician; b. Tulsa, Nov. 21, 1942; s. Walter Russell and Joan Vera (Brimm) Van B.; m. Paula Mae Brinkley, Mar. 5, 1965 (div. Feb. 1974); children: Baron, Kristy and Kelly (twins). BS, U. Tulsa, 1965; DO, Okla. State U., 1981. Diplomate Nat. Bd. Osteo. Examiners. Defensive back, quarterback, punter Can. Football League, Ottawa, Calgary, 1966-73; dir. sports and spl. events Tulsa Cable TV, 1974-78; rotating intern Corpus Christi (Tex.) Osteo. Hosp., 1981-82; family physician Antlers (Okla.) Med. Clinic, 1982-90, Colbert (Okla.) Med. Clinic, 1989-90; dir. dept. emergency Valley View Regional Hosp., Ada, Okla., 1990-94; regional med. dir. Okla., N.Mex., Ariz., So. Calif. Okla. Spectrum Emergency Care, Inc., 1994—; mem. clin. faculty Coll. Osteo. Medicine, Okla. State U. Author newspaper column, several computer programs. Mem. Rep. Senatorial Inner Ctr., Washington, 1990-91 (medal of Freedom 1994); affiliate faculty Am. Heart Assn. Named to Alltime Greats of Okla., Jim Thorpe Award Com., 1975. Fellow Assn. Emergency Physicians; mem. Am. Osteo. Assn., Am. Coll. Gen. Practitioners, Okla. Osteo. Assn., S.W. Okla. Osteo. Assn. (pres. 1990-91). Home: PO Box 2740 Ada OK 74821-2740

VANCE, CYNTHIA LYNN, psychology educator; b. Norwalk, Calif., Mar. 31, 1960; d. Dennis Keith and Donna Kay (Harryman) V. BS, U. Oreg., 1982; MS, U. Wis., Milw., 1987, PhD, 1991. Teaching asst. U. Wis., Milw., 1983-89; computer graphics mgr. Montgomery Media, Inc., Milw., 1987-92; asst. prof. Cardinal Stritch Coll., Milw., 1992-93, Piedmont Coll., Demorest, Ga., 1993—. Contbr. articles to profl. jours. Vol. Dunwoody (Ga.)-DeKalb Kiwanis Club, 1993—. Mem. AAUP, APA, Assn. Women in Psychology, S.E. Psychol. Assn., Am. Psychol. Soc., Am. Assn. Higher Edn. Office: Piedmont Coll PO Box 10 Demorest GA 30535-0010

VANCE, RALPH BROOKS, oncologist and educator; b. Jackson, Miss., Dec. 4, 1945; s. Brooks C. and Chrystine G. (Gober) V.; m. Mary Douglas Allen, June 18, 1979; children: Brooks, Barrett. BA in Biology and German, U. Miss., 1968, MD, 1972. Asst. prof. medicine U. Miss., Jackson, 1978-86, assoc. prof. medicine, 1986-93, prof. medicine, 1993—; chief of staff U. Miss. Hosp. and Clinics, Jackson, 1989-90; pres. faculty senate Univ. Med. Ctr., Jackson, 1986-87, univ. clin. assoc., pres., 1987-89. Author (with others) Development in Molecular Virology: Herpes Virus DNA, 1982; contbr. numerous articles and abstracts to profl. jours. Bd dirs. Am. Cancer Soc., Atlanta, nat. bd. dirs., exec. com.; bd. dirs. ARC, Jackson; med. adv. bd. Blue Cross/Blue Shield, Jackson, 1989-92. Named to Hall of Fame, U. Miss., 1968. Mem. Am. Assn. for Cancer Edn., Am. Fedn. for Clin. Rsch., Am. Soc. Clin. Oncology, Am. Assn. for Cancer Rsch., Miss. Acad. Scis., S.W. Oncology Group, Sigma Xi. Episcopalian. Office: Univ of Miss Sch Medicine 2500 N State St Jackson MS 39216-4505

VAN CITTERS, ROBERT LEE, medical educator, physician; b. Alton, Iowa, Jan. 20, 1926; s. Charles and Wilhemina (Heemstra) Van C.; m. Mary E. Barker, Apr. 9, 1949; children: Robert, Mary, David, Sara. A.B., U. Kans., 1949; M.D., U. Kans. Med. Ctr., Kansas City, 1953; Sc.D. hon., Northwestern Coll., Orange City, Iowa, 1977. Intern U. Kans. Med. Ctr., Kansas City, 1953-54, resident, 1955-57, fellow, 1957-58; research fellow Sch. Medicine, U. Wash., Seattle, 1958-61, asst. prof. physiology and biophysics, 1962-65, assoc. prof, 1965-70, prof., 1970—; prof. medicine Sch. Medicine, U. Wash., 1970—, assoc. dean Sch. Medicine, 1968-70, dean Sch. Medicine, 1970-81; mem. staff Scripps Clinic and Research Found., La Jolla, Calif., 1961-62; exchange scientist joint U.S.-U.S.S.R. Sci. Exchange, 1962; mem. Liason Commn. on Med. Edn., Washington, 1981-85; mem. various coms., nat. adv. research council NIH, Bethesda, Md., 1980-83; mem. Va. Spl. Med. Adv. Commn., 1974-78, chmn., 1976-78; chmn. working group on mech. circulatory support systems Nat. Heart, Lung and Blood Inst. NIH, 1985—, mem. adv. coun. clin. applications and prevention, 1985-89. Contbr. numerous articles to profl. jours. Served to 1st lt. U.S. Army, 1943-46, PTO; to capt. M.C., USAF, 1953-55. Recipient research career devel. USPHS. Fellow AAAS; mem. Assn. Am. Med. Colls. (adminstrv. bd. and exec. council 1972-78, Disting. Service mem.), Am. Coll. Cardiology (Cummings medal 1970), Nat. Acad. Sci. Inst. Medicine, Am. Heart Assn., Wash. State Med. Assn. (hon. life). Office: U Wash Sch Medicine Seattle WA 98195

VANCURA, STEPHEN JOSEPH, radiologist; b. Norton, Kans., June 26, 1951; s. Cyril William J. and Clara Mae (Ruthstrom) V.; BA in Chemistry magna cum laude, Kans. State U., 1972; MD, Kans. U., 1976; m. Lydia Acker, Dec. 10, 1976. Intern in medicine Letterman Army Med. Center, San Francisco, 1976-77, resident in radiology, 1977-80; practice medicine specializing in radiology, 1980—; chief dept. radiology Darnall Army Hosp., Ft. Hood, Tex., 1980-82; pvt. practice diagnostic radiology, 1982—; chief of staff Metroplex Hosp., 1985-86, 88-90. Served to maj. M.C., U.S. Army, 1976-82 Recipient Ollie O. Mustala award in clin. pharmacology Kans. U. Med. Center, 1974; A. Morris Ginsberg award in phys. diagnosis Kans. U. Med. Center, 1975; Resident Tchr. of Yr. award Letterman Army Med. Center, 1979; Staff Tchr. of Yr. award Darnall Army Hosp., 1982. Trembly Meml. scholar, 1972. Diplomate Am. Bd. Radiology. Mem. Am. Coll. Radiology, Radiologic Soc. N. Am., AMA, Tex. Med. Assn., Tex. Radiol. Soc., Ind. Med. Practitioners Assn. Ctrl. Tex. (pres.), Clinical Magnetic Resonance Soc., Sigma Xi, Alpha Chi Sigma, Alpha Omega Alpha. Home: 3302 Walnut Cir Harker Heights TX 76542 Office: Metroplex Hosp Dept Radiology 2201 Clear Creek Rd Killeen TX 76548-4110

VANDEBERG, JOHN LEE, scientist, geneticist, educator; b. Appleton, Wis., June 14, 1947; s. Gale LeRoy and Zona Idell (Raine) V.; m. Jane Frances Barr, Mar. 29, 1975; children: Jason Cash, James Robert. BS in Genetics, U. Wis., 1969; BS in Genetics with honors, La Trobe U., Melbourne, Australia, 1970; PhD in Genetics, Macquarie U., Sydney, Australia, 1975. Instr., tutor Macquarie U., Sydney, 1973-75; rsch. assoc., postdoctorate fellow U. Wis., Madison, 1975-79, asst. scientist Wis. Regional Primate Rsch. Ctr., 1979-80; prof. depts. pathology and cellular and structural biology U. Tex., San Antonio, 1982—; chmn., scientist dept. genetics S.W. Found. Biomed. Rsch., San Antonio, 1980-93, scientific dir., 1993—; adj. prof. divsn. life scis. U. Tex., San Antonio, 1990—. Contbr. over 150 articles to profl. jours. Trustee Mind Sci. Found., San Antonio, 1990—. Fulbright fellow U.S. Dept. State, 1969-70. Mem. AAAS, Am. Heart Assn., Am. Soc. for Biochemistry and Molecular Biology, Am. Heart Assn. Coun. on Arteriosclerosis, Am. Soc. for Human Genetics, Am. Soc. Primatologists, Genetics Soc. Am. Office: SW Found Biomed Rsch 7620 Northwest Loop # 410 San Antonio TX 78228-5301

VAN DECKER, WILLIAM ARTHUR, cardiologist; b. Passaic, N.J., May 27, 1957; s. William and Louise Adelaide (Meli) Van D.; m. Generosa Grana; children: Stephanie, William, Christopher. BS in Biology summa cum laude, Fairfield (Conn.) U., 1979; MD, Georgetown U., 1983. Bd. cert. internal medicine, bd. cert. cardiovascular diseases. Intern Temple U. Hosp., Phila., 1983-84, resident internal medicine, 1984-86, cardiology fellow, 1986-88, non-invasive cardiology imaging tng./rsch. fellow, 1988-89; assoc. dir. Non-Invasive Imaging, dir. Cardiology Clinic Med. Coll. Pa., Phila., 1989-95, asst. prof. medicine and cardiology, 198 —, dir. Heart Sta., 1990—; mem. com. on radiation safety Med. Coll. Pa., hila., 1990—, chmn. com. on radiation safety, 1993—, mem. pharmacy ar l therapeutics com., 1992—, chmn. pulmonary and therapeutics com. 1993- -, mem. continuing med. edn. com., 1992—, vice-chmn. quality assurance com., 1993—, group leader freshman bioethics, 1992—, med. student advi or, 1992—; presenter in field. Manuscript Peer reviewer Annals of Internal Medicine, 1993—; contbr. articles to profl. jours. Fellow Am. Heart Assı , Am. Coll. Cardiology, Am. Coll. Chest Physicians; mem. AMA, ACP, Aı . Soc. for Echocardiography, Am. Fedn. for Clin. Rsch., Pa. Med. Soc., Soc. Nuclear Medicine, Am. Assn. for Nuclear Cardiology (founding mem.), A n. Soc. Nuclear Cardiology (founding mem.), Philadelphia County Med. oc. (standing com. 1992—), Alpha Epsilon Delta, Alpha Omega Alpha. O ice: Med Coll Pa 3300 Henry Ave Philadelphia PA 19129-1121

VANDE KEMP, HENDRIKA, psychology educator; b. Voorthuizen, Gelderland, the Netherlands, Dec. 13, 1948; d. Hendrik and Petronella (Van Peursem) van de Kemp. BA, Hope Coll., 197 ; MS, U. Mass., 1974, PhD, 1977. Lic. psychologist, Calif. Instr. psy hology Fuller Theol. Sem., Pasadena, Calif., 1976-77, asst. prof., 1977-81 assoc. prof., 1981-91, prof., 1991—. Author: Psychology and Theology i Western Thought 1672-65, 1984; series co-editor: (book series) Christian Explorations in Psychology; contbr. articles to profl. jours. Mem., speak So. Calif. C.S. Lewis Soc., Pasadena, 1979—; mem. com. on preparatio for ministry Presbyn. Ch. USA, 1984-89; program chair Western Assn of Christians for Psychol. Studies, Malibu, Calif., 1978. Christian Wo ker's Found. scholar Hope Coll., 1970-71. Fellow Am. Psychol. Assn. (s c.-treas. Psychologists Interested in Religious Issues div. 36 1985-88, pre Psychologists Interested in Religious Issues div. 36 1988-89, William Bi r award 1990), Psychology Grad. Union/Fuller Theol. Sem. (Commu ity Bldg. award 1990). Democrat. Home: 219 N Primrose Ave Mon ovia CA 91016-2118 Office: Fuller Theol Sem 180 N Oakland Ave Pasade a CA 91101-1714

VAN DE LEUV, JOHN HENRI, emergency n edicine physician; b. Batavia, East Indies, Oct. 1, 1926; came to U.S., 1962; s Henri Richard and Cornelia Wilhelmina (Kleef) van de L.; m. Johanna N. an Beekum, Aug. 21, 1951 (dec. Jan. 1980); children: Jacqueline, Mark, Mo ique, Erik; m. Theresa Ann Dudash, Nov. 7, 1980; children: Jonathan, Ada . BSc, Sir George Williams U., Montreal, Que., Can., 1953; MD, CM, M cGill U., Montreal, 1957. Diplomate Am. Bd. Emergency Medicine. Int rn, then resident in ob-gyn. Detroit Meml. Hosp., 1957-59; corp. med. dir. C oastal Govt. Svcs., Durham, N.C., 1990-94; lead physician Portsmouth (a.) Naval Hosp., 1990-94; emergency physician Greensville Meml. Hosp. Editor, author: Management of Emergency Services, 1987. Fellow Am. Col Emergency Physicians (bd. dirs. 1968-73, chmn. coms. 1968-79, James Mil s award 1986). Home: 820 Quail Point Cv Virginia Beach VA 23454-3156

VANDEN AKKER, ROB, industrial pharmac st; b. Amsterdam, July 9, 1956; m. Marianne Bramson, Aug. 27, 1993; 1 child, Bram. M Pharmacy cum laude, U. Amsterdam, 1982, cert. pharmacy 1984. Head stability group Solvay Duphar, Weesp, The Netherlands, 1987- 1, pharmacy project leader, 1991—; cons. medicine use Medicyn Winkel, A nsterdam, 1986-91. 1st lt. M.C., Royal Dutch Army, 1984-85. Mem. Ro l Dutch Soc. for Advancement of Pharmacy, Soc. Dutch Indsl. Pharmaci s. Home: Rustenburgh 18, 1111 VE Diemen The Netherlands Office: Solvay Duphar, CJ Van Houtenlaan 36, 1381 Weesp The Netherlands

VAN DEN BERG, JAN HENDRIK, psychia ist, education educator; b. Deventer, The Netherlands, June 11, 1914; s. L mbertus Van den Berg and Aleida Krudde; m. Louise Johanna van Everdil gen, 1943 (dec. 1980); children: Ewoud, Janrik, Tuja. MD summa hon., U Utrecht, The Netherlands, 1946; MD (hon.), U. the Orange Free State, B oemfontein, Rep. of South Africa, 1984; EdD (hon.), U. South Africa, P etoria, 1991. Prof., head psychiatric clinic U. Utrecht, 1947, prof. pastora psychology, theol. faculty, 1951; lectr. psycho-pathology U. Utrecht S h. Medicine, 1948; prof. psychology U. Leyden, 1954; vis. prof. Duquesi U., Pitts., 1967, summer, 1970, 73, U. South Africa, Pretoria, 1971-72, Bl ck U. the North, Sovenga, No. Transvaal, Republic of South Africa, 1974 Medunsa U., Republic of South Africa, 1982; lectr. Republic of South Afr a, 1969, 80, U.S.A., 1975-77, 92, Can., 1975, Eng., 1977, Centennial Duqu sne U., Pitts., 1978, Japan, 1981, U.S., 1992, Second m. Alida de Gier 193 1987. Author 25 books; contbr. articles to profl. jours. Home: Hoogstra 46, 4285 AJ Woudrichem The Netherlands

VAN DEN BERGH, CORNELIUS JACOB, h alth services administrator; b. Johannesburg, South Africa, Feb. 10, 1942; s. Barend Jacobus and Esther Leonora (Brink) V.; m. Andriesa Gerhardina N , May 3, 1969 ; children: Barend Jacobus Petrus, Hendrik Johannes, Ja oba Maria, Esther Leonora. M.B.Ch.B., U. Pretoria, South Africa, 1 68, M.Prax. Med., 1973, D.H.S.M., 1995. Intern H.F. Verwoerd Hosp., retoria, 1968; med. officer Pietersburg (South Africa) Hosp., 1969; supt. Th song Hosp., Lichtenburg, South Africa, 1969-71, Paul Kruger Meml. Hosp., Rustenburg, South Africa, 1971—. Mem. Coll. Medicine South Africa. Mem. Dutch Ref. Ch. (elder).

VAN DEN BOOM, ESPERANZA (HOPE VAN DEN BOOM), speech and language pathologist, educator; b. Adrian, Mich., Aug. 31, 1953; d. Bennito Christino Hernandez and Enriqueta Mendez; m. Wayne Jerome Van Den Boom; children: Sean, Kristine. AA, Delta Coll., 1974; BS in Spl. Edn., Ea. Mich. U., 1977, M Spl.Edn. SLI, 1978, M Spl. Edn., 1986; postmasters cert. in Early Intervention, U. Mich. Cert. speech and lang. pathologist, tchr. of learning impaired, art and early childhood tchr. Tchr's. aide Bay City (Mich.) Pub. Schs., 1972-74; receptionist Cen. Mich. U., Mt. Pleasant, Mich., 1974, Ea. Mich. U., Ypsilanti, Mich., 1975-76; dir. speech pathology Emma L. Bixby Hosp., Adrian, Mich., 1981-83; learning disability tchr. Utica (Mich.) Community Schs., 1986; speech lang. pathologist Grand Ledge (Mich.) Pub. Schs., 1978-81, Rochester (Mich.) Community Schs., 1986—; early intervention 0-3 speech pathologist, dir. speech dept. E. L. Bixby Hosp., Adrian, 1981-83; supr. tchr. tng. in learning disabilites Oakland U., Rochester, 1988—. Mem. Women's Bus. Assn., Grand Ledge, Mich., 1978-81, U. Mich. Hosp. Med. Rsch. Team,Ann Arbor, Mich., 1981-83. MemNEA, Mich. Edn. Assn., Mich. Speech Hearing and Lang., Oakland County Speech and Hearing Assn., Macomb St. Clair Speech and Hearing Assn., Mich. Assn. Learning Disabilities Educators, Mich. Assn. for Learning Disabled, Coun. for Exceptional Child (mental retardation div., communication disorder div., learning disabilities div., early childhood div.), Mich. Infant Mental Health Assn. Home: 46347 Franks Ln Shelby Township MI 48315-5309 Office: Rochester Community Schs 501 W University Dr Rochester MI 48307-1944

VANDENBOS, GARY ROGER, psychologist, publisher; b. Grand Rapids, Mich., Dec. 16, 1943; s. Paul Martin and Irene (Dorenbos) V.; m. Jane Annunziata, Dec. 16, 1983; 1 child, Bret. BS, Mich. State U., 1967, MA, 1969; PhD, U. Detroit, 1973. Dir. Howell (Mich.) Area Community Mental Health Ctr., 1973-77; dir. nat. policy studies Am. Psychol. Assn., Washington, 1977-82, exec. dir. for publs., 1984—; prof. U. Bergen, Norway, 1982-84; project cons. Rand Corp., Santa Monica, Calif., 1984-89; bd. dirs. Am. Biodyne Found., San Francisco; newspaper pub. APA Monitor, 1985—. Author: Psychotherapy with Schizophrenic, 1981; editor Pscyhology and National Health Insurance, 1979; assoc. editor Am. Psychologist Jour. Office: Am Psychol Assn 750 1st St NE Washington DC 20002-4241

VANDENBURG, MARY LOU, psychologist; b. Passaic, N.J., Dec. 18, 1943; d. Nicholas and Louise (Rosiello) Yacono; m. James Joseph Vandenburg, Jr., July 2, 1966; 1 child, James Joseph III. BA, William Paterson, 1965; MA, Montclair Coll., 1982; MS, Pace U., 1986, D of Psychology, 1988. Cert. tchr., sch. guidance counselor; lic. psychologist. Elem. tchr. various, 1966-67, 76-80; therapist Pequannock Valley Mental Health Ctr., 1985-90; sch. psychologist Andover Schs., 1988—; pvt. practice Butler, N.J., 1989—; lectr. ednl. enrichment programs, 1980—; psychotherapist various schs., clinics, hosps. Author children's books; contbr. articles to profl. jours. Recipient honor cert. Freedom Found., Valley Forge, Pa., Merit Scholarship, Pace U. Mem. N.J. Assn. Sch. Psychologists, Nat. Assn. Sch. Psychologists, Am. Psychol. Assn., Sussex County Assn. Sch. Psychologists, Morris County Assn. Psychologists. Home: 404 E Lakeshore Dr Highland Lakes NJ 07422 Office: 1395 State Rte 23 Butler NJ 07405-1736

VAN DEN HAAG, ERNEST, psychology law and sociology educator; b. The Hague, Netherlands, Sept. 15, 1914; came to U.S., 1940, naturalized, 1947; s. Max and Flora (van den Haag) van den H. Student, U. Naples, Italy, 1937-38, U. Florence, Italy, 1937-38, Sorbonne U., Paris, 1938-40; M.A., State U. Iowa, 1942; Ph.D., NYU, 1952. Lectr., 1955-65, CCNY, Bklyn Coll., U. Minn., U. Colo., U. Calif.-Berkeley, Columbia U., Yale U., Harvard U.; adj. prof. social philosophy NYU, 1965-75; lectr. psychology and sociology New Sch. Social Research, N.Y.C., 1965-80; adj. prof. law N.Y. Law Sch., 1978-80; practice psychoanalysis N.Y.C., 1955-82; vis. Disting. prof. Queens Coll., CUNY, 1974-75; vis. prof. criminal justice SUNY-Albany, 1977-78; vis. prof. sociology Vassar Coll., 1969-70; John M. Olin prof. jurisprudence and pub. policy Fordham U., N.Y.C., 1982-88; Disting. scholar Heritage Found., 1981—; Freud Meml. lectr. Phila. Assn. Psychoanalysis, 1964. Author: The Fabric of Society, 1957, Education as an Industry, 1956, Passion and Social Constraint, 1963, The Jewish Mystique, 1969, Political Violence and Civil Disobedience, 1972, Punishing Criminals: Concerning a Very Old and Painful Question, 1975, Capitalism: Sources of Hostility, 1979, (with John P. Conrad) The Death Penalty: A Debate, 1983, (with John P. Conrad) The U.N.: In or Out?, 1987, (with Tom J. Farer) U.S. Ends and Means in Central America: A Debate, 1988; contbr. articles to profl. jours. Guggenheim fellow, 1967; NEH sr. fellow, 1973. Fellow Royal Econ. Soc., Am. Sociol. Assn.; mem. Mont. Pelerin Soc., Profl. Psychoanalytic Assn., Phila. Soc. (past pres.), Nat. News Council, Council on Fgn. relations. Home and Office: 118 W 79th St New York NY 10024-6445

VAN-DEN-NOORT, STANLEY, physician, educator; b. Lynn, Mass., Sept. 8, 1930; s. Judokus and Hazel G. (Van Blarcom) van den N.; m. June Le Clere, Apr. 17, 1954; children: Susanne, Eric, Peter, Katherine, Elizabeth. A.B., Dartmouth, 1951; M.D., Harvard, 1954. Intern then resident Boston City Hosp., 1954-56, resident neurology, 1958-60; research fellow neurochemistry Harvard, 1960-62; instr. medicine Case Western Res. U., Cleve., 1962-66; asst. prof. Case Western Res. U., 1966-69, assoc. prof., 1969-70; prof. neurology U. Calif., Irvine, 1970—; chair dept. neurology U. Calif., 1970-72, 86—, assoc. dean Coll. Medicine, 1972-73, dean, 1973-85; mem. cons. staff U. Calif., Irvine Med. Center; mem. Long Beach (Calif.) Meml. Hosp., Long Beach VA Hosp.; mem. com. of revision U.S. Pharmacopoeial Conv., 1990-95. Mem. med. adv. bds., Nat. Multiple Scierosis Soc./Myasthenia Gravis, 1971—, Orange County chpt. Nat. Multiple Scierosis Soc., 1971—, Orange County Health Planning Coun., 1971-85, Nat. Com. Rsch. in Neurol. Disease, 1982-87. Lt. M.C. USNR 1956-58. Fellow ACP, Am. Acad. Neurol.; mem. AAUP, AMA, Am. Neurol. Assn., Orange County Med. assn., Calif. Med. Assn., Am. Heart Assn. Home: 17592 Orange Tree Ln Tustin CA 92680-2353 Office: U Calif Dept Neurology 100 Irvine Hall Irvine CA 92697-4275

VANDER AARDE, STANLEY BERNARD, retired otolaryngologist; b. Orange City, Iowa, Sept. 26, 1931; s. Bernard John and Christina (Luchtenberg) Vander A.; m. Agnes Darlene De Beer, June 19, 1956; children: Paul, David, Debra, Mary. BA, Hope Coll., 1953; MD, Northwestern U., 1957. Diplomate Am. Bd. Otolaryngology. Intern Cook County Hosp., Chgo., 1957-59; resident in otolaryngology Northwestern U. Hosp., Chgo., 1966-70; mem. staff Mary Lott Lyles Hosp., Madanapalle, India, 1961-66, 71-87; mem. staff Affiliated Med. Clinic, Willmar, Minn., 1987-95, ret., 1995. Served to capt., USAF, 1959-60. Fellow ACS, Am. Bd. Otolaryngology, Am. Acad. Otolaryngology. Republican. Mem. Reformed Church in America. Home: 708 2nd St SE # 112 Orange City IA 51041-2156 Office: Affiliated Med Clinic 101 Willmar Ave SW Willmar MN 56201-3556

VANDER ARK, GARY DUANE, neurosurgeon; b. Ellsworth, Mich., Aug. 3, 1937; s. Harry G. and Dorothy W. (Horrenga) Vander A.; m. Phyllis J. Quist, May 31, 1958; children: Tom, Jillane. BS, Calvin Coll., 1958; MD, U. Mich., 1962. Diplomate Am. Bd. Neurosurgery. Intern, then resident U. Hosp., Ann Arbor, Mich., 1962-68; pvt. practice, Englewood, Colo.; chief neurosurgery Denver Gen. Hosp., 1971-76; pres. Colo. Neurol. Inst., Denver, 1988—. Author: A Primer of EEG, 1970; contbr. over 50 articles to med. jours., chpts. to books. Pres. Doctors Care, Denver, 1988—. Maj. MC., U.S. Army, 1968-71. Recipient Robbins cmty. svc. award Colo. Med. Soc., 1990, svc. to manking award local, dist. and regional Sertoma, 1992, Disting. Alumni award Calvin Coll., 1993. Fellow ACS; mem. Am. Assn. Neurol. Surgeons, Western Neurosurg. Soc., Colo. Nerosurg. Soc. (pres. 1995-96), Arapahoe Med. Soc. (pres. 1985-86). Republican. Mem. Christian Reformed Ch. Home: 79 Glenmoor Dr Englewood CO 80110 Office: Colo Neurol Inst 701 E Hampden Ave Ste 510 Englewood CO 80110

VANDERBILT, CLARA EVANS, physician assistant; b. Orange County, N.C., Oct. 28, 1940; d. Otha Willis and Hazel Gladys (Jones) Evans; children: Robin M. Dawson Storch, Robert Wayne Dawson Jr., Kimberly Vanderbilt Fried. Cert. physician asst., Duke U., 1971; BS in Philosophy, SUNY, 1982. Cert. physician asst., Pa. Physician asst. surg. resident

Montefiore Med. Ctr./Albert Einstein Coll. Medicine, Bronx, N.Y., 1971-78, dir. physician asst. surg. residency, 1978—; preceptor physician asst. student surg. clerkship physician asst. program Touro Coll, Dix Hills, N.Y., 1985-95, Harlem Hosp., CUNY, N.Y.C., 1980-95. Recipient Disting. Alumnus award Duke U. Physician Asst. Alumni, 1993. Fellow Am. Acad. Physician Assts. (v.p. 1975-76, 10th Anniversary Appreciation award 1989), N.Y. State Soc. Physician Assts. (founding pres. 1975, pres. 1976), Am. Acad. Physician Assts. (bd. dirs. 1972, 74), Nat. Commn. Cert. Physician Assts. (bd. dirs. 1977-84). Office: Montefiore Med Ctr 111 E 210th St Bronx NY 10467

VANDERGON, DIRK DENIER, physician, cardiologist; b. Mpls., Apr. 11, 1953; s. Keith Gordon and Sally (Brooks) V.; m. Joyce Lynn Burkholder, May 31, 1983; children: Austin, Alexander. BS in Zoology, U. N.D., 1975, BS in Medicine, 1978; MD, U. Ariz., 1980. Diplomate in internal medicine and cardiovascular disease Am. Bd. Internal Medicine. Resident in internal medicine U. Nev., Reno, 1980-83; fellow in cardiology U. Calif. Davis, Sacramento, 1984-86; staff physician Reno VA Med. Ctr., 1983-84; cardiologist Corvallis (Oreg.) Clinic, 1986-87, Cardiology Assocs., Reno, 1987-92, Reno Heart Physicians, 1992—. Fellow Am. Coll. Cardiology. Office: Reno Heart Physicians 236 W 6th St Reno NV 89503

VANDER HEYDEN, YVAN, pharmacist, researcher; b. Ninove, Belgium, May 27, 1964; s. Ernest and Maria (Van De Sijpe) V.H.; m. Carine Vannecke, Sept. 18, 1993. Clin. technician, IHR-CTL, Gent, Belgium, 1986; pharmacist, YUB, Brussels, 1991. Asst. rschr. YUB, Brussels, 1991—. Contbr. articles to profl. jours. Home: Lebecke 56, 9650 Denderholtem Belgium Office: YUB, Laarbeeklaan 103, 1090 Brussels Belgium

VANDERHOST, LEONETTE LOUISE, psychologist; b. Phila., June 11, 1924; d. Charles and Pauline (McGhaney) V. BA, CUNY, 1945; MA, NYU, 1949, PhD, 1966. Lic. psychologist, N.Y. Intern staff Lincoln (Ill.) State Sch., 1951-52; staff Evansville (Ind.) State Hosp., 1953-54, Children's Guidance Ctr., Dayton, Ohio, 1954-56; psychotherapist Hempstead (N.Y.) Consultation Services, 1963-66; staff, sr. psychologist Hillside Hosp., Glen Oaks, N.Y., 1957-64; sr. psychologist, chief West Nassau Mental Health Ctr., Franklin Sq., N.Y., 1959-63; pvt. practice psychologist N.Y.C., 1959—; cons. Big Sisters, N.Y., 1960-62, Health Ins. Planning, N.Y., 1962-64, Head Start, N.Y., 1967-73. Mem. Am. Psychol. Assn., Am. Orthopsychiatric Assn.

VANDER KOLK, CRAIG A., plastic surgeon; b. Ann Arbor, Mich., Mar. 15, 1954; s. Anno M. Vander Kolk and Claire Elizabeth (Wierenga) Monsma; m. Mary Anne Berrevoets, Aug. 23, 1975; children: Christopher R., Jonathan A., Elliott H. BA, Hope Coll., Holland, Mich., 1976; MD, U. Mich., 1980. Diplomate Am. Bd. Plastic Surgery. Intern U. Mich., 1980, resident in plastic surgery, 1983-86; fellow Craniofacial Children's Hosp., Phila., 1986-87; asst. prof. surgery Johns Hopkins U., Balt., 1987-93, asst. prof. pediatrics, 1989—, assoc. prof. surgery, 1993—. Office: Johns Hopkins U 601 N Caroline St Baltimore MD 21287

VAN DER LAARSE, ARNOUD, biochemist, educator and researcher; b. Bogor, Indonesia, Dec. 7, 1948; arrived in Netherlands, 1954; s. Pieter and Clara Johanna Jacoba (Scholten) V.; m. Machelina Berdina Maria Veling, Feb. 18, 1977; children: Matthys, Jeroen. MS, U. Amsterdam, 1972, PhD, 1978. Postdoctoral fellow dept. cardiology U. Leiden, The Netherlands, 1976-79, rschr. dept. cardiology, 1980-85, asst. prof. dept. cardiology, 1985-91; prof. cardiobiochemistry Interuniv. Cardiology Inst of the Netherlands, Utrecht, 1991—; head lab. of cardiobiochemistry faculty of medicine U. Leiden, 1985—; sci. bd. mem. Netherlands Heart Found., 1988—. Editor Netherlands Jour. Cardiology, 1990—; contbr. numerous articles to profl. jours., chpts. to books. Recipient Marie Parys prize U. Leiden, 1982. Fellow European Soc. Cardiology, 1994—; mem. N.Y. Acad. Scis. Home: 18 Leeuwerikstraat, Leiden 2333VZ, The Netherlands Office: Univ Hosp, Rynsburgerweg 10, Leiden 2333AA, The Netherlands

VAN DER MEER, JAN, hematologist; b. Leeuwarden, Friesland, The Netherlands, Sept. 19, 1950; s. Jacob and Margaretha Helena Maria (Wolters) van der M.; m. Pyteke Goslinga, July 6, 1972; children: Jacob Sebastiaan, Paul Jan, Robert Louis. MD, PhD, U. Groningen, The Netherlands, 1972. Head of coagulation lab. U. Hosp. Groningen, The Netherlands, 1976-78, head div. of haemostasis thrombosis and rheology, 1983—, head haemophilia ctr. Groningen, 1983—, head of lab. for haemostasis thrombosis and rheology, 1983—, head sect. thrombosis and thrombolysis Thorax Ctr., 1989—, gen. dir. ctr. for clin. drug rsch., 1990—; assoc. prof. U. Groningen, The Netherlands, 1996—; bd. dirs. Cent. Haematology Labs. U. Hosp. Groningen, The Netherlands; coord. Dutch Rsch. Group for Coronary Bypass Surgery, Interuniversity Cardiologic Inst. of the Netherlands, 1986-87; mem. cardiovascular rsch. group Thorax Ctr., U. Hosp. Groningen, 1988—; adv. bd. angiology, 1988—; mem. scientific adv. bd. Fedn. of Dutch Thrombosis Svcs., The Hague, 1990—; scientific adv. bd Dutch Thrombosis Found., 1990—; Dutch adv. bd. for prevention of cardiovascular events, The Netherlands, 1995-96. Contbr. numerous articles to profl. jours. Recipient Lorex Synthélabo Cardiology award, 1995. Mem. Dutch Soc. on Internal Medicine, Dutch Soc. on Haematology, Dutch Soc. on Haemophilia Treatment, Benelux Soc. on Microcirculation (bd. dirs.), Dutch Soc. on Thrombosis and Haemostasis, Internat. Soc. on Thrombosis and Haemostasis, Mediterranean League against Thromboembolic Diseases. Office: Univ Hosp, Hanzeplein 1, 9713 GZ Groningen The Netherlands

VAN DER MEULEN, JOSEPH PIERRE, neurologist; b. Boston, Aug. 22, 1929; s. Edward Lawrence and Sarah Jane (Robertson) VanDer M.; m. Ann Irene Yadeno, June 18, 1960; children—Elisabeth, Suzanne, Janet. A.B., Boston Coll., 1950; M.D., Boston U., 1954. Diplomate: Am. Bd. Psychiatry and Neurology. Intern Cornell Med. div. Bellevue Hosp., N.Y.C., 1954-55; resident Cornell Med. div. Bellevue Hosp., 1955-56; resident Harvard U., Boston City Hosp., 1958-60, instr., fellow, 1962-66; assoc. Case Western Res. U., Cleve., 1966-67; asst. prof. Case Western Res. U., 1967-69, assoc. prof. neurology and biomed. engring., 1969-71; prof. neurology U. So. Calif., L.A., 1971—; also dir. dept. neurology Los Angeles County/U. So. Calif. Med. Center; chmn. dept. U. So. Calif., 1971-78, v.p. for health affairs, 1977—, dean Sch. Medicine, 1985-86, 95—, vice dean med. affairs, 1995—; vis. prof. Autonomous U. Guadalajara, Mex., 1974; pres. Norris Cancer Hosp. and Research Inst., 1983—. Contbr. articles to profl. jours. Mem. med. adv. bd. Calif. chpt. Myasthenia Gravis Found., 1971-75, chmn., 1974-75, 77-78; med. adv. bd. Amyotrophic Lateral Sclerosis Found., Calif., 1973-75, chmn., 1974-75; mem. Com. to Combat Huntington's Disease, 1973—; bd. dirs. Calif. Hosp. Med. Ctr., Good Hope Med. Found., Doheny Eye Hosp., House Ear Inst., L.A. Hosp. Good Samaritan, Children's Hosp. of L.A., Barlow Respiratory Hosp., USC U. Hosp., chmn., 1991—; bd. govs. Thomas Aquinas Coll.; bd. dirs. Assn. Acad. Health Ctrs., chmn., 1991-92; pres. Scott Newman Ctr., 1987-89; pres., bd. dirs. Kenneth Norris Cancer Hosp & Rsch. Inst. Served to lt. M.C. USNR, 1956-58. Nobel Inst. fellow Karolinska Inst., Stockholm, 1960-62; NIH grantee, 1968-71. Mem. AMA, Am. Neurol. Assn., Am. Acad. Neurology, L.A. Soc. Neurology and Psychiatry (pres. 1977-78), L.A. Med. Assn., Mass. Med. Soc., Ohio Med. Soc., Calif. Med. Soc., L.A. Acad. Medicine, Alpha Omega Alpha (councillor 1992—), Phi Kappa Phi. Home: 39 Club View Ln Palos Verdes Peninsula CA 90274-4208 Office: U So Calif 1540 Alcazar St Los Angeles CA 90033-1058

VANDERPLOEG, JAMES M., preventive medicine physician; b. Upland, Calif., Nov. 22, 1950. BA, U. Iowa, 1975. Intern U. Hosp./U. Calif., San Diego, 1975-76; resident in otolaryngoloty U. Iowa Hosps., Iowa City, 1978-79; resident in occupational medicine U. Tex. Sch. Pub. Health, Houston, 1980-82, assoc. prof. occupational health; mem. staff St. John Hosp., Nassau Bay, Tex.; pvt. practice, ptnr. group practice; part-time med. adminstr. Mem. Am. Coll. Occupational Medicine, ACPrM-AerosMA. Office: Ctr for Aerospace &Occupational Medicine 700 Gemimi Ave Ste 110 Houston TX 77068*

VANDERPLOEG, RODNEY DIRK, clinical psychologist; b. Upland, Calif., Nov. 17, 1953; s. James and Carolyn Nelle (DeWit) V.; m. Sandra Gailya Logan, Aug. 22, 1981. BA, Calvin Coll., 1975; MA, Fuller Theol. Sem., Pasadena, Calif., 1981, PhD, 1982. Psychology intern Lafayette Clinic, Detroit, 1981-82; psychology intern St. Louis VA Med. Ctr., 1982-83, rsch. clin. neuropsychologist, 1985-87; instr. med. psychology dept. psychiatry Washington U. Med. Sch., St. Louis, 1982-85; staff psychologist Malcolm Bliss Mental Health Ctr., St. Louis, 1982-85; asst. clin. prof. dept. neurology Coll. Medicine, U. South Fla., Tampa, 1987—; clin. neuropsychologist psychology svc. James A. Haley Vets. Hosp., Tampa, 1987—, cir. clin. tng. psychology svc., 1989—; pvt. practice, Tampa, 1989—; workshop presenter U. No. Colo., Greeley, 1991; presenter in field, 1980—. Contbr. articles to profl. jours., 1980—. Co-chairperson nat. stroke symposium James A. Haley Vets. Hosp., 1989. Mem. APA, Internat. Neuropsychol. Soc., Calif. Scholarship Fedn. (life). Democrat. Lutheran. Home: 1401 Shell Flower Dr Brandon FL 33511-8370 Office: James A Haley Vets Hosp Psychology Svc # 116B Tampa FL 33612

VANDER SCHRAAF, ANNA HENRIETTE, physician; b. Indonesia, May 22, 1928; d. Nicholas H. and Anna B.C. (Dumas) Altman; m. Eric E. Vander Schraaf; children: A. Marian, Dorine B. de Mena, Robert C., Walter D. MD, U. Amsterdam, The Netherlands, 1952. Cert. Am. Bd. Psychiatry and Neurology, child psychiatry. Pvt. practice child/adolescent & adult psychiatry Morristown, N.J., 1973—; attending dept. psychiatry Morristown Meml. Hosp., 1973—; clin. instr. Mt. Sinai Sch. Medicine, N.Y.C., 1973—; asst. psychiatrist Mt. Sinai Hosp., N.Y.C., 1973—; clin. asst. prof. Robert Wood Johnson Med. Sch. U. Medicine & Dentistry, Piscataway, N.J., 1973—; cons. Morristown Sch. System, 1976-79. Co-author: Borderline Conditions in Children: Clinical Handbook of Child Psychiatry, 1979. Fellow Am. Acad. Child and Adolescent Psychiatry, Am. Soc. Adolescent PsychiatryAm. Psychiat. Assn.; mem. AMA, N.J. Coun. Child and Adolescent Psychiatry (past pres.). Office: 21 Perry St Morristown NJ 07960-5241

VANDERVEEN, JOHN E., federal agency administrator; b. Prospect Park, N.J., May 13, 1934; m. Ernestine Neuhardt, June 3, 1967; children: Keith Bradley, Kimetha Leigh. BS, Rutgers U., 1956; PhD, U. N.H., 1961. Nutritionist USAF, 1961-75; dir. divsn. nutrition FDA, Washington, 1975-92, dir. office plant & dairy foods and beverages, 1992—. Served to 1st lt. USAF, 1961-64. Office: FDA Ctr Food Safety and Applied Nutrition 200 C St SW Washington DC 20204-0001

VAN DER WERF, SJOERD DIRK JOSEPH, gastroenterologist; b. The Netherlands, Dec. 30, 1945; s. Dirk and Anna Henrietta Josepha van der Werf; m. Martha Maria Cornelia Reuver, Feb. 17, 1971; children: Michiel Adrianus, Erik Sebastiaan, Paulus Johannes. MD, Cath. U., Nymegen, 1971, specialist internal medicine, 1981; PhD, Cath. U., 1983. Asst. surgeon, gynecologist St. Carolus Hosp., Den Bosch, The Netherlands, 1971-72; med. officer health Machakos, Meru, Kenya, 1972-75; trainee internal medicine Cath. U., Nymegen, The Netherlands, 1975-84; trainee gastroenterology, rsch. fellow Municipal Hosp., Arnhem, The Netherlands; cons. internal medicine and gastroenterology Westeinde Hosp., The Hague, The Netherlands, 1984—. Editor: New Eng. Jour. Medicine, 1986. Mem. Netherlands Soc. Gastroenterology, Netherlands Soc. Internal Medicine, European Soc. Clin. Investigation. Roman Catholic. Home: Helmlaan 4, Wassenaar 2244 AZ, The Netherlands Office: Westeinde Hosp, Lynbaan 32, The Hague 2501 CK, The Netherlands

VAN DER WOUDE, FOKKE JOHANNES, physician; b. Leeuwarden, The Netherlands, Sept. 30, 1953; m. H. Griesen, Jan. 14, 1978; children: Joanne, Diane. MD, State U. Groningen, 1977, PhD, 1984. Intern State Univ. Hosp. Groningen, 1975-77, resident, 1977-82; jr. staff mem. Renal Transplantation Unit, Groningen, 1982-85; postdoctoral fellow dept. pediatrics U. Minn., Mpls., 1985-87; head renal transplant unit, assoc. prof. medicine Univ. Hosp., Leiden, The Netherlands, 1987-95; prof., dir. V Med. Clinic U. Heidelberg, Germany, 1995—; full prof. U. Heidelberg; head V Med. Clin., Klinikum Mannheim, Germany; project leader European ANCA Study Group, EEC, Brussels, 1989-95. Contbr. articles to profl. jours. Postdoctoral fellow Dutch Kidney Found., 1985. Fellow Royal Soc. Medicine; mem. Dutch Soc. Nephrology, Dutch Soc. Immunology, Dutch. Soc. Transplantation, British Transplant Assn., Internat. Soc. for Nephrology, Am. Soc. Nephrology, Tranplantation Soc. Office: V Med Clinic Mannheim, Rynsburgerweg 10, Theodore Kutzer Uferi-3, 68135 Mannheim Germany

VAN DEUSEN, WAYNE JOHN, pediatric and family practice physician assistant; b. Manchester, Conn., Aug. 5, 1957; s. Charles John and Marjorie Ann (Kocum) Van D.; m. Petronella Lyda Francisca van Deusen-Scholl, Dec. 30, 1980; 1 child, Noely Ashley Maya. AA, U. Fla., 1978, BA in Psychology, 1982; physician asst.-student, U. Calif., Davis, 1993. Lab. asst. pediatric renal clin. rsch. lab. Shands Tchg. Hosp., 1975-77, nursing asst., equipment technician emergency rm., 1978-79, clin. rsch. asst. divsn. renal pediatrics, 1980-83; clin. asst. Nephrology Assocs., Ft. Pierce, Fla., 1991; physician asst. resident in pediatrics U. So. Calif., L.A. County Hosp., 1993-94; rsch. assoc. U. Calif., San Francisco, 1994; rsch. rev. bd. Children's Hosp. Oakland, Calif., 1996—, mulitcultural planning com., 1996—; vol. Berkeley Primary Care Access Clinic. Contbr. articles to profl. jours.; presenter in field. Kellogg scholar, 1992. Fellow Am. Acad. Physician Assts.; mem. Class Nat. Am. Assn. Physician Asst. (chpt. pres. 1993), Rotary Club Internat. (activities chmn. 1983), Phi Eta Sigma Nat. Honor Soc. (activities com. chmn. 1976), Alpha Lambda Delta, Phi Delta Theta. Democrat. Roman Catholic. Home: 7222 Blake St El Cerrito CA 94530

VAN DEVEERE, KATHLEEN, medical facility administrator; b. Seattle, Nov. 8, 1935; d. Joseph Anderson and Dorothy Mabel (Burke) Dailey; m. Warren Craig Van DeVeere, Dec. 22, 1957 (div. Aug. 1989); children: Mary Van DeVeere Deatherage, Joseph Earl. AA, U. Calif., Berkeley, 1955; BS, U. Calif., San Francisco, 1958; MPA, U. Denver, 1983. Program dir. Dept. Vet. Affairs Med. Ctr., Denver; creator Cancer Comfort Line, 1989. Mem. Feed the Children, Box Project. Recipient Dale Tooley Award of Hope, Am. Cancer Soc., 1988. Mem. Colo. Assn. Home Health Agys., Order of Ea. Star. Office: Dept Vets Affairs Med Ctr 1055 Clermont Denver CO 80220

VAN DOREN, RICHARD WITT, counseling psychologist, career consultant; b. Mpls., Mar. 27, 1946; s. William Ogden and Janet Jane (Pierce) Van D.; m. Nancy Whitman, June 8, 1968; children: Peter Davis, Katherine. BA, Macalester Coll., 1968; MA, Ball State U., 1972, EdD, 1975. Doctoral fellow Ball State U., Muncie, Ind., 1973-75; postdoctoral intern Counseling Ctr. Shippensburg (Pa.) State Coll., 1975-76; postdoctoral intern Elmcrest Psychiat. Inst., Portland, Conn., 1976-77; counseling assoc., adj. prof. Rider Coll., Lawrenceville, N.J., 1977-80; sr. cons., dir. interview tng. Mainstream Access, Inc., N.Y.C., 1981-87; regional dir. counseling svcs. Fuchs, Cuthrell and Co., N.Y.C., 1987-89; v.p. Minsuk, Macklin, Stein and Assocs., Princeton Junction, N.J., 1989-93, Manchester Ptnrs. Internat., Princeton, N.J., 1993—; speaker in field. Contbg. author: Career and Life Planning, 1975, E-SPAN Career Management Forum, 1995—; author: Evaluation Interview Training Trainers Manual, 1987. Asst. cubmaster, troop com. Belle Mead (N.J.) area Boy Scouts Am., 1977-83; bd. dirs. Family Svc. Agy. Princeton, N.J., 1978-81; trustee Historic Morven, Inc., Princeton, 1986-93. Capt. USAF, 1968-73. Mem. Am. Psychol. Assn., Masons, Scottish Rite 33d degree, Royal Order Scotland. Presbyterian. Home: 47 Jamestown Rd Belle Mead NJ 08502-5224 Office: 5 Independence Way Princeton NJ 08540

VAN DYCK, PETER CUYLER, health services administrator, pediatrics educator; b. Dec. 9, 1939; married; 3 children. BA in Physiology, U. Ill., 1962; MS in Physiology, U. Ill., Chgo., 1966, MD, 1966; MPH in Maternal and Child Health, U. Calif., Berkeley, 1973. Diplomate Nat. Bd. Med. Examiners; med. lic., Utah. Intern, then resident in pediatrics Children's Meml. Hosp., Chgo., 1966-68, chief resident, 1968-89; instr. Med. Sch. Northwestern U., Chgo., 1968-89; chief pediatrics Frankfurt (Fed. Republic Germany) Health Clinic, U.S. Army, 1969-71; primary nursery physician 97th Gen. Hosp., U.S. Army, Frankfurt, 1971-72; pediatric cons. Internat. Red Cross, Amman, Jordan, 1973; dir. maternal and child health Utah State Div. Health, Salt Lake City, 1973-74, dir. div. family health svcs., 1974-92, acting exec. dir., 1984-85, acting dir. div. health care financing (Medicaid), 1986-87; sr. med. advisor to adminstr. HRSA, 1992-93; asst. prof. Med. Ctr. U. Utah, Salt Lake City, 1976-82, prof. Med. Ctr., 1991—; sr. med. advisor to dir. Maternal & Child Health Bur., 1993-94; dir. Office of State & Com. Health Maternal & Child Health Bur., 1994—; adj. assoc. prof. health Univ. Utah, Salt Lake City, 1975—, adj. asst. prof. Coll. Nursing, 1976—; mem. adv. com. U. Utah Coll. Nursing, 1976-80, Albert Einstein Coll. Medicine, Ctr. for Disease Control, 1983-86, U.S. Sen. Orrin Hatch, 1979—, John F. Kennedy Child Devel. Ctr., Denver, 1979-82; faculty coord. Crippled Children's Svcs. Advanced Inst., Children's Hosp., Columbus, Ohio, 1983—; mem. maternal and child health/Medicaid tech. assistance group Health Care Financing Adminstrn., 1987—; mem. planning com., faculty Surgeon Gens. Conf., 1987; mem. various coms. and task forces; presenter, cons., reviewer in field; cons. Interagy. Efforts Children Spl. Health Needs Federated States Micronesia, 1991, Third Pacific Basin Interagy Conf. Individuals Spl. Health Care Needs No. Marianas Islands, 1992; faculty mem. Med. Ctr. Georgetown U., Washington, 1993; chief party U.S. Del. Third Regional Follow-up Meeting World Summit Children, Antigua, Guatemala, 1995. Contbr. articles to profl. jours. Co-chmn. sch. health com. Utah State Bd. Edn., Utah Dept. Health, 1974—, statewide immunization action com. Awareness Com., 1977-78; project dir. Sudden Infant Death Syndrome Regional Ctr., Utah, 1975-80; chmn. Govs. Adv. Coun. for Developmentally Disabled Children, 1976-78; mem. task force on svcs. to presch. handicapped children Utah State Legis., 1984, tech. adv. coun. Utah Children, 1985-88, adv. bd. Jr. League, 1985-88; bd. dirs. Exceptional Child Ctr., Utah, 1975-80. Recipient Nat. Leadership award Dept. Health and Human Svcs., 1989, Nat. Achievement award Healthy Mothers, Healthy Babies, 1991; named one of 500 Most Influential Healty Policymakers Health Care 500, 1992; grantee U.S. Dept. Health and Human Svcs., Ctrs. for Disease Control., Devel. Diabetes Coun., Bur. Edn. for the Handicapped, Bur. Community Health Svcs.; WHO fellow, 1995. Mem. APHA (mem. various coms., chmn. maternal and child health sect. 1988—, Ross award 1977), Nat. Acad. for State Health Policy (mem. steering com. 1987—), Nat. Found. March of Dimes (chmn. med. adv. bd. 1975—, Plaque for Outstanding Svc. 1977-78), Nat. Early Childhood Tech. Assistance System (mem. nat. adv. com. 1988—), Am. Acad. Pediatrics (mem. various coms.), Nat. Assn. of State Bds. Edn. (mem. task force on adolescent pregnancy 1979-80), Nat. Assn. State and Territorial Maternal and Child Health and Crippled Children Dirs. (pres. 1978-80), March of Dimes Birth Defect Found. (mem. nat. chpt. grants rev. com. 1988—), Intermountain Pediatrics Soc. (mem. legis. and child abuse coms. 1974-76), Utah Pub. Health Assn. (mem. various coms., pres. 1984-86, mem. editorial bd. 1976-77, Beaty award 1985). Office: Maternal & Child Health Bur Parklawn Bldg Rm 1820 5600 Fishers Ln Rockville MD 20857

VAN DYKE, CRAIG, psychiatrist; b. Detroit, Oct. 4, 1941; married; two children. BS, U. Wash., 1963, MD, 1967. Asst. prof. psychiatry Yale U., New Haven, Conn., 1974-78; from assoc. to prof. psychiatry U. Calif., San Francisco, 1979-86, prof., chmn. dept. psychiatry, 1994—. Mem. Am. Psychosom. Soc., Internat. Coll. Psychosom. Medicine, Soc. Neurosci., Internat. Neuropsychol. Soc. Office: U Cal San Francisco Langley Porter Psychiatric Inst 401 Parnassus Ave San Francisco CA 94143*

VAN DYKE, DANIEL L., geneticist; b. Paterson, N.J., Mar. 1, 1947. PhD, Ind. U., 1976. Cert. med. genetics and clin. cytogenetics Am. Bd. Med. Genetics. Divsn. head genetics labs. Henry Ford Hosp., Detroit, 1975—; faculty U. Mich. Med. Sch., Detroit, 1978—, Case Western Res. U., Cleve., 1994—. Address: Henry Ford Hospital Cytogenetics Lab 2799 W Grand Blvd Detroit MI 48202-2608

VANE, JOHN ROBERT, pharmacologist; b. Worcestershire, Eng., Mar. 29, 1927; s. Maurice and Frances Florence V.; m. Elizabeth Daphne Page, Apr. 4, 1948; children: Nicola, Miranda. BSc in Chemistry, U. Birmingham, 1946; MSc in Pharmacology, Oxford U., 1949, D Phil., 1953, DSc, 1970; MD (hon.), U. Cracow, Poland, 1977, Copernicus Acad. Medicine, Cracow; Hon. doctorate, Rene Descartes U., Paris, 1978; DSc (hon.), CUNY, 1980, Aberdeen U., 1983, N.Y. Med. Coll., Birmingham U., U. Surrey, 1984, Camerino U., Italy, 1984, Louvain, 1986, Buenos Aires, 1986; D honoris causa in Medicine and Surgery, U. Florence; DSc (hon.), U. London, 1995. Fellow Therapeutic Rsch. Coun., Oxford U., 1946-48; rsch. worker Sheffield U., 1948-49; rschr. worker Nuffield Inst. Med. Rsch., Oxford U., 1949-51; Stothert rsch. fellow Royal Soc., 1951-53; instr., then asst. prof. pharmacology Yale U. Med. Sch., 1953-55; mem. faculty Inst. Basic Med. Scis., Royal Coll. Surgeons Eng., 1955-73, prof. exptl. pharmacology, 1966-73; group R & D dir. Wellcome Found. Ltd., Beckenham, Kent, 1973-85; dir.-gen. William Harvey Rsch. Inst. St. Bartholomew's/Royal London Sch. of Medicine/Dentistry, Queen Mary/Westfield Coll, U. London, 1986—; bd. dirs. Vanguard Medica Ltd., Sparta Pharms. Inc., U.S. Co-editor: Adrenergic Mechanisms, 1960, Prostaglandin Synthetase Inhibitors, 1974, Metabolic Functions of the Lung, Vol. 4, 1977, Handbook of Experimental Pharmacology, 1978, Prostacyclin, 1979, Interactions Between Platelets and Vessel Walls, 1981, Endothelin I, 1989, II, 1991, III, 1993, IV, 1995; contbr. numerous articles to profl. jours. Freeman City of Scranton (Pa.), 1988, Taipei (Taiwan), 1989, New Orleans, 1995. Decorated knight bachelor; recipient Baly medal Royal Coll. Physicians; Albert Lasker Basic Med. Rsch. award; Peter Debye prize; Nuffield Gold medal; Ciba Geigy Drew medal Soc. for Endocrinology, 1981; Nobel prize in physiology or medicine, 1982; Galen Medal Worshipful Soc. Apothecaries, 1983; Louis Pasteur Found. prize, Santa Monica, Calif., 1984. Fellow ACP (hon.), Inst. Biology, Royal Soc. (Royal medal 1989), Brit. Pharm. Soc. (hon.), Royal Coll. Pathologists (hon.); mem. NAS (fgn. assoc.), Polish Pharm. Soc. (hon.), Physiol. Soc. (hon.), Royal Acad. Medicine Belgium, Royal Netherlands Acad. Arts and Scis., Polish Acad. Scis. (fgn.), Am. Acad. Arts and Scis. (fgn. hon.), Soc. Drug Research, Alpha Omega Alpha (hon.). Office: William Harvey Rsch Inst, St Bartholomew/Royal London, U London/Queen Mary Coll, London EC1M 6BQ, England

VAN EENENAAM, JEFFREY ALAN, dentist; b. St. Joseph, Mich., Oct. 10, 1957; s. Robert Dale and Mary Catherine (Johnson) Van E.; m. Bonnie Lynn Boyer, May 17, 1986; children: Abigail Irma, Alex Raymond. BA, U. Colo., 1979; DDS, U. Detroit, 1983. Pvt. practice dentistry Kalamazoo, 1983—. Asst. scoutmaster Boy Scouts Am., Portage, Mich., 1984-94, cub scout den leader, 1994—; campaign mgr. City Councilman Dale Shugars, Portage, 1983, 85, 89. Named Eagle Scout Boy Scouts Am., 1969. Mem. ADA, Mich. Dental Assn., Kalamazoo Valley Dist. Dental Assn. Republican. Club: Kalamazoo Ski (pres. 1985-88), Nat. Ski Patrol. Lodge: Lions (v.p. 1986, pres. 1987). Home: 3045 Kalarama Rd Portage MI 49024 Office: 525 Pleasant Home Ct Kalamazoo MI 49008-3205

VAN ETTEN, EDYTHE AUGUSTA, retired occupational health nurse; b. Arthur, N.D., Oct. 13, 1921; d. Lacy Edward and Emma Erna (Mundt) Roan; m. Robert Scott Van Etten, Feb. 12, 1944; children: Ronald, Cynthia Czernysz, Martin, Roger, Randall, Janet K. Diploma, Mt. Sinai Hosp. Sch. Nursing, Chgo., 1945; AS, Waubonsee Community Coll., Sugar Grove, Ill., 1978; BSN, No. Ill. U., 1981. Cert. occupational health nurse; RN, Ill. Occupation health nurse Barber-Greene Co., Aurora, Ill., 1965-82; occupational health relief nurse No. Ill. Gas Co., Naperville, Ill., 1983-85; supr. or staff nurse Michealsen Health Ctr., Batavia, Ill., 1982-93; occupational health relief nurse The Dial Corp., Montgomery, Ill., 1982-94; occupational health nurse cons. AT&T Svc. Ctr., West Chicago, Ill., 1988-94. Mem. adminstrv. bd. Ch. of the Good Shepherd Meth., Oswego, Ill., 1988-94; active Fox Bend Ladies Golf League, United Meth. Women; mem. Lyric Opera of Chgo. Mem. Suburban Chgo. Assn. Occupational Health Nurses, Dist. 2 Ill. Nurses Assn. (del. state conv. 1985, Award for Excellence in Nursing Practice 1993), Sr. Svcs. Assn. Inc. (adv. 1983-87, Humanitarian award 1985), Oswegoland Women's Civic Club (bd. dirs. 1985—). Republican. Home: 427 S Madison St PO Box 1 Oswego IL 60543

VAN ETTEN, PETER WALBRIDGE, hospital administrator; b. Boston, May 10, 1946; s. Royal Cornelius Van Etten and Peggy June (Walbridge) Hutchins; m. Mary Peters French, Oct. 13, 1968; children: Molly, Clarissa, Ellen. BA, Columbia U., 1968; MBA, Harvard U., 1973. Br. mgr. BayBanks, Brookline, Mass., 1968-71; loan officer Bank of Boston, 1973-76; CFO Univ. Hosp., Boston, 1976-79; exec. v.p., CFO New Eng. Med. Ctr., Boston, 1979-89; pres., CEO Transitions Systems, Boston, 1986-89; dep. chancellor U. Mass. Med. Ctr., Worcester, 1989-91; CFO Stanford (Calif.) U., 1991-94; pres., CEO Stanford Univ. Hosp., 1994—. Bd. dirs. The Hosp. Fund, New Haven, 1989—. Office: Stanford Hosp Pasteur Dr Stanford CA 94305*

VAN FURTH, RALPH, physician; b. The Hague, The Netherlands, Apr. 30, 1929; m. Anne Ghiliane Henriette Vreede; children: Eric Frank, Anne Marceline, Wouter Ralph. MD, U. Leiden, 1955, PhD cum laude, 1964.

Asst. psychiatry U. Utrecht, 1955; resident St. Elisabeth's Hosp., 1957-61; chief resident Univ. Hosp., Leiden, 1961-63, head lab. cellular immunology dept. infectious diseases, 1967-94; prof. internal medicine and infectious diseases U. Leiden, 1975-94; prof. emeritus, 1994; guest investigator Rockefeller U., N.Y., 1964-67, 72-75, vis. assoc. prof., 1972, vis. prof., 1974, 85; vis. prof. Ruitinga Found., Acad. Med. Centrum, Amsterdam, 1986. Mem. editorial bds. various immunological and infectious disease jours. Fulbright fellow, 1985; recipient Lister award, Edinburgh, 1974, Alexandre Besredka prize U. Munster, 1987, Dr. Frederich Sasse Found. award, U. Berlin, 1988, Order of Knighthood of Dutch Lion, others. Fellow Infectious Disease Soc. Am., Royal Coll. Physicians; mem. Am. Soc. Immunologists, Am. Soc. Microbiology, British Soc. Immunology, Dutch Soc. Immunology, Dutch Soc. Internal Medicine, European Soc. Clin. Investigation, European Soc. Clin. Microbiology and Infectious Diseases, N.Y. Acad. Scis., Infectious Diseases Soc. of The Netherlands and Flanders (hon., founder 1975, sec. 1976-82, chmn. 1983-91), Infectious Diseases Club The Netherlands (founder 1970, sec. 1970-76), Royal Acad. of Med. of Belgium (fgn. hon.), and others.

VAN GELDER, HUGH MAURICE, cardiothoracic surgeon; b. London, May 3, 1958; came to U.S., 1959; s. Michael Alan and Patricia Rose (Morley) van G.; m. Susan Amy Seldin, July 24, 1983; children: Stephanie, Jennifer, Brittany. BS, Emory U., 1980; MD, Cornell U. Med. Coll., 1985. Diplomate Am. Bd. Thoracic Surgery, Am. Bd. Surgery. Resident in gen. surgery Emory U., Atlanta, 1985-90; resident in thoracic surgery U. Fla., Gainesville, 1990-92; attending surgeon All Children's Hosp./Bayfront Med. Ctr., St. Petersburg, Fla., 1992—; surg. director cardiac transplantation, vice-chmn. dept. cardiac svcs. All Children's Hosp. Fellow Am. Coll. Cardiology, Am. Coll. Chest Physicians, Am. Coll. Surgeons, Southeastern Surg. Congress. Office: Cardiothoracic Surg Assocs 603 7th St S Ste 450 Saint Petersburg FL 33701

VAN GILDER, JOHN CORLEY, neurosurgeon, educator; b. Huntington, W.Va., Aug. 14, 1935; s. John Ray and Sarah Pool (Corley) Van G.; m. Kerstin Margarita Olesson, Mar., 1965; children: Sarah, John, Rachel, David. BA, W.Va. U., 1957, BS, 1959; MD, U. Pitts., 1961. Diplomate Am. Bd. Neurol. Surgery. (examiner 1976, 79, 84). Intern Pa. Hosp., Phila., 1961, asst. resident in surgery, 1964-65; asst. resident in surgery Wilkes-Barre (Pa.) Hosp., 1962; asst. resident neurosurgery Barnes Hosp., St. Louis, 1966-68, sr. resident, 1968-69; instr. neurosurgery Yale U. Sch. Medicine, New Haven, 1970, asst. prof., 1970-73, assoc. prof., 1973-76; prof. neurosurgery U. Iowa, Iowa City, 1976—, chmn. div. neurosurgery, 1976—, exec. com. dept. surgery, 1978-81; fellow neurosurgery Wash. U. Sch. Medicine, St. Louis, 1965 -66, instr., 1966; attending neurosurgeon VA Hosp., New Haven, 1970-73, cons. 1973-76; assoc. to attending neurosurgeon Yale-New Haven Med. Ctr., 1970-76; cons. VA Hosp., Iowa City, 1976—; mem. clin. coordinating com. U. Iowa Cancer Ctr., 1979—; presenter numerous papers at profl. meetings., confs., symposia; vis. prof. U. Tenn., 1984, Tufts U. Med. Ctr., Boston, 1986, U. Tex., San Antonio, 1987, U. Mich., Ann Arbor, 1988, People's Republic China at Hunan Med. Coll., Beijing Neurol. Inst., Tianjin Med. Coll. Hosp., Tiantan Xili, Xian Gen. Hosp., 2d Mil. Coll., Shanghai, Suzhou Med. Coll. Shanghai, 1985, USSR at Burdenk Inst., Kiev Neurol. Inst., Leningrad Neurol. Soc., 1989, Western Reserve U., Cleve., 1993, Yale U., New Haven, Conn., 1994. Author: (with others): Principles of Surgery, 2d edit., 1973, Brief Textbook of Surgery, 1976, Aneurysmal Subarachnoid Hemorrhage, 1981, Operative Meurosurgical Techniques, Indications, Methods, and Results, 1982, Sports Medicine, 1982, Neurosurgery, 1982, Clinical Neurosurgery, 1982, Operative Neurosurgical Technique, Vol. II, 1982, 88, Vol. III, 1995, Current Therapy in Neurosurgical Surgery, 1985, 2d edit. , 1987, Craniovertebral Junction Abnormalities, 1987, Decision Making in Neurological Surgery, 1987, Neurological Surgery, 3d edit., 1988, Anterior Cervical Spine Surgery, 1993, Brain Surgery: Complication Avoidance and Management, 1993, Neurosurgical Emergencies, 1994, Techniques of Spinal Fusion and Instrumation, 1995, Somatic Gene Therapy, 1995; contbr. numerous articles and abstracts to profl. jours.; co-author teaching films; mem. editorial bd. Neurosurgery jour., 1978-84. Capt. USAF, 1962-64. Grantee NIH, 1973-78, Nat. Cancer Inst., 1980-88. Fellow ACS (membership com. Iowa dist. #1 1983—); mem. AMA (Physicians Recogniton award), Am. Physiol. Soc., Congress Neurol. Surgeons (resident placement com. 1970), Am. Assn. Neurol. Surgeons (bd. dirs. 1986-90, awards com. 1986-87, chmn. 1987-88), Rsch. Soc. Neurol. Surgeons, Neurol. Soc. Am. (long range planning com. 1984—, v.p. 1985), Iowa Med. Soc., Johnson County Med. Soc. (program com. 1984-88, chmn. 1985-86), Iowa-Midwest Neurosurg. Soc. (pres. 1978-79), Soc. Neurol. Surgeons (chmn. membership com. 1986-87, treas. 1991—, pres. elect 1996), Midwest Surg. Assn., Am. Acad. Neurol. Surgery (v.p. 1995—), Ga. Neurosurg. Soc. (hon. life), Am. Bd. Neurol. Surgery (dir. 1992—, residency rev. com.-neurol. surgery 1995—), Sigma Xi. Home: 330 S Summit St Iowa City IA 52240-3220 Office: U Iowa Hosps & Clinics Dept Neurosurgery 200 Hawkins Dr Iowa City IA 52242

VAN HEMELRIJCK, JAN HERMAN, anesthesiologist; b. Asse, Brabant, Belgium, Aug. 2, 1953; s. Jozef Philip Van Hemelrijck and Lucovica Irene Verheyden; m. Lydia Maria VanLoock, Aug. 6, 1976; children: Katrien, Joris, Valerie, Elise. MD, Cath. U. Leuven, Belgium, 1978, PhD, 1992. Cert. anesthesia and reamination, Belgium. Staff anesthesiologist Univ. Hosp. Cath. U. Leuven, 1982—; fellow in clin. rsch. in anesthesiology Washington U., St. Louis, 1989-90; assoc. prof. anesthesiology Cath. U. Leuven, 1993—. Mem. European Acad. Anesthesia, Belgian Soc. Anaesthesia and Reamination. Office: Univ Hosps Cath U Leuven. Dept Anesthesiology, 3000 Leuven Belgium

VAN HERIK, JUDITH, psychology and religion educator; b. Rochester, Minn., Aug. 18, 1947; d. Martin and Jeanette (Wilchinski) Van H. AB, U. Chgo., 1968, MA in Teaching, 1971, MA in Divinity, 1973, PhD in Divinity, 1978. Instr. Pa. State U., University Park, 1977-78, asst. prof., 1978-84, assoc. prof., 1985—. Author: Freud on Femininity and Faith, 1982; contbr. articles to profl. jours. Mem. Am. Acad. Religion, Am. Psychol. Assn., Pa. Humanities Coun. (acad. mem. referee for jours., presses and founds. 1986—). Office: Pa State U 318 Weaver Bldg University Park PA 16802-5503

VANHOOK, PATRICIA M., family nurse practitioner, consultant; b. East Stone Gap, Va., Dec. 23, 1953; d. James Pierson and Thelma Lorraine (McFarland) McKenzie; m. Guy Phillip Vanhook, May 9, 1975; children: Andrew Phillip, Alicia Lorraine. AAS, Mt. Empire C.C., Big Stone Gap, Va., 1982; BSN, East Tenn. State U., 1991, MSN, 1994. Staff nurse spl. care unit Lonesome Pine Hosp., Big Stone Gap, 1973-82, dir. emergency rm.-spl. care unit, 1982-91; instr. critical care Indian Path Med. Ctr., Kingsport, Tenn., 1991-93; projects adminstr. Indian Path. Med. Ctr., Kingsport, Tenn., 1993-95, FNP, 1994—; projects adminstr. FNP Physician Access, Duffield, Va., 1995—; mem. assoc. faculty Mt. Empire C.C.; pres. McKenzie-Vanhook, PC, Big Stone Gap, Pa., 1995—. Mem. AACN (bd. dirs. S.W. Va. chpt., cert. crit. care nurse), Am. Heart Assn. (cert. instr. ACLS, Tenn. affiliate faculty), ENA (cert. trauma nurse), Rho Nu Nursing Club (past pres.), ANA (cert. FNP), Sigma Theta Tau, Tenn. Nurses Assn., Am. Acad. Family Nurse Practitioners.

VAN HOOSIER, GERALD LEONARD, veterinary science educator; b. Weatherford, Tex., June 4, 1934; s. Gerald L. Sr. and Louise (Ashcroft) Van H.; m. Marlene M., Aug. 2, 1959; children: Gunther, Paul. DVM, Tex. A&M, 1957. Diplomate Am. Coll. Lab. Animal Medicine. Postdoctoral fellow U. Calif., Berkeley, 1959-60, Wash. State U., Pullman, 1969-71; chief applied virology NIH, Bethesda, 1960-62; assoc. prof. Baylor U. Coll. Medicine, Houston, 1962-69; assoc. prof., dir. Wash. State U., Pullman, 1969-75; prof., chmn. U. Wash., Seattle, 1975—; cons. VA Med. Ctr., Seattle, Tacoma, Boise, Seattle Biomed. Rsch. Inst. Editor: Laboratory Hamsters, 1987; contbg. author: The Hamster, Clin. Chemistry of Lab. Animals, 1989; contbr. articles to profl. jours. With USPHS Res., 1959—. Recipient Disting. Alumni award Tex. A&M, 1991, Animal Investigation and Diagnosis Lab award NIH, 1979-91, Comparative Med. Tng. NIH, 1982-91. Mem. Am. Assn. Lab. Animal Sci. (pres. 1991-92, Charles A. Griffin award 1986). Office: U Wash Dept Comparative Med S # 42 Seattle WA 98195*

VAN HORN, O. FRANK, counselor, consultant; b. Grand Junction, Colo., Apr. 16, 1926; s. Oertel F. and Alta Maude (Lynch) Van H.; m. Dixie Jeanne MacGregor, Feb. 1, 1947 (dec. Nov. 1994); children: Evelyn, Dorothy. AA, Mesa Coll., 1961; BA, Western State Coll., 1963; MEd, Oreg. State U., 1969. Counselor, mgr. State of Oreg.-Employment, Portland and St. Helens, 1964-88; pvt. practice counselor and cons. St. Helens, 1988—; chair Task Force on Aging, Columbia County, 1977-79; advisor Western Interstate Commn. on Higher Edn., Portland, 1971, Concentrated Employment and Tng., St. Helens, 1977, County Planning Bd. Columbia County, Oreg., 1977-80, City Planning Bd., St. Helens, 1978, Youth Employment Coun., St. Helens, 1978, Task Force on Disadvantaged Youth, St. Helens, 1980; counselor Career Mgmt. Specialists Internat.; instr. Portland C.C. Mem. ACA, Oreg. Counseling Assn., Internat. Assn. Pers. in Employment Svc. (Outstanding Achievement award 1975), Nat. Employment Counselors Assn. Democrat. Home: 1111 St Helens St Saint Helens OR 97051

VAN HORN, REBECCA ANN, presentation specialist; b. Cleve., Feb. 10, 1957; d. Ross Edward and Virginia Mary (Connell) V. BA, Ohio State U., 1979. Dental hygienist Dr. Michael Zimmerman DDS, Columbus, Ohio, 1980-85, St. Mary of Nazareth Hosp. Dental Ctr., Chgo., 1985-87, Dr. Katherine Lauterbach DDS, Chgo., 1985-87; profl. programs area mgr. Oral-B Lab., Chgo.; pres., Ohio State U. Dental Hygiene Alumni Assn., Columbus, Ohio, 1982-83; adv. bd. Dental Hygiene Program Kalamazoo Cmty. Coll. Mem. Am. Dental Hygienists Assn., Ill. Chgo. Dental Hygienists Assn.

VAN HOUTEN, MARILYN, health facility administrator; b. Lafayette, Ind., Jan. 15, 1947; d. George and Barbara (Lutz) Smith; m. Edward Van Houten, May, 1978 (dec.); 1 child, John J. Coonen III. BS in Nursing, U. Miami, 1969; MS, Nova U., 1984. Cert. nursing adminstr., cert. case mgr. Regional case mgr. Rehab. Svcs., Winter Park, Fla.; case mgr. VPS Case Mgmt., Ft. Lauderdale, Fla.; dir. nurse South Dade Home Health, Miami, Fla.; patient care coord. Hospice, Inc., Miami; pres. Rehab. Case Mgmt., Inc., Miami. Mem. ANA (cert. ins. rehab specialist), Am. Pub. Health Assn., Fla. Nurses Assn., Am. Acad. Pain Mgmt., Case Mgmt. Soc. Am. (Fla. govt. affairs chair, pres.-elect), Fla. Assn. Rehab. Providers in Pvt. Sector, Am. Assn. Rehab. Nurses, Am. Assn. Legal Nurse Cons. Home: 11620 SW 99th Ct Miami FL 33176-4127

VAN HOUZEN, RUSSELL NEIL, physician; b. Detroit, Nov. 29, 1949; s. Russell David and Margaret Jean (Alspaugh) Van H.; m. Susan Carol Hubanks, Aug. 7, 1971; children: Nathan, Jennifer, Jessica. Student, U. Mich., 1967-70; MD, Wayne State U., 1974. Diplomate Am. Bd. Internal Medicine. Intern Hutzel Hosp., Wayne State U., Detroit, 1974-75, resident, 1975-77; staff physician Munson Med. Ctr., Traverse City, Mich., 1977%; chief internal medicine sect. Munson Med. Ctr. Traverse City, 1981-85, chief medicine svc., 1985-88, med. dir. cardiac rehab., 1992—. Contbr. articles to profl. pubs. Elder Faith Reformed Ch., Traverse City, 1986-89, 92-94. Fellow ACP; mem. Am. Soc. Internal Medicine, Mich. Soc. Internal Medicine, Mich. State Med. Soc., Grand Traverse County Med. Soc., Alpha Omega Alpha. Office: Russell Van Houzen MD FACP 1100 Sixth St Traverse City MI 49684

VAN KIRK, JOHN ELLSWORTH, cardiologist; b. Dayton, Ohio, Jan. 13, 1942; s. Herman Corwin and Dorothy Louise (Shafer) Van K.; m. Patricia L. Davis, June 19, 1966 (div. Dec. 1982); 1 child, Linnea Gray. BA cum laude, DePauw U., Greencastle, Ind., 1963; BS, Northwestern U., Chgo., 1964, MD with distinction, 1967. Diplomate Am. Bd. Internal Medicine, Am. Bd. Internal Medicine subspecialty in cardiovascular disease; cert. Nat. Bd. Med. Examiners. Intern Evanston (Ill.) Hosp., 1967-68; staff assoc. Nat. Inst. of Allergy & Infectious Diseases., Bethesda, Md., 1968-70; resident internal medicine U. Mich. Med. Ctr., Ann Arbor, 1970-72, fellow in cardiology, 1972-74, instr. internal medicine, 1973-74; staff cardiologist Mills Meml. Hosp., San Mateo, Calif., 1974—, vice-chief medicine, 1977-78, dir. critical care, 1978—, critical care utilizaton rev., 1978—, dir. pacemaker clinic, 1976—; mem. active staff Peninsula Hosp. and Med. Ctr.; mem. courtesy staff Sequoia Hosp. Contbr. rsch. articles to profl. jours. Recipient 1st prize in landscaping Residential Estates, State of Calif., 1977, Physician's Recognition award AMA, 1968, 72, 75, 77, 80, 82, 85, 87, 89, 93. Fellow Am. Coll. Cardiology; mem. AMA, Calif. Med. Assn., San Mateo County Med. Soc., Am. Heart Assn., San Mateo County Heart Assn. (bd. dirs. 1975-78, bay area rsch. com. 1975-76, edn. com. 1975-77, pres. elect 1976-77, pres. 1977-79), Alpha Omega Alpha. Republican. United Brethren. Office: Unified Med Clinics of Peninsula 50 S San Mateo Dr Ste 270 San Mateo CA 94401-3859

VAN KIRK, ROBERT JOHN, nursing case manager, educator; b. Jersey City, N.J., Sept. 18, 1944; s. Robert and Doris V.; m. Marjorie Ann Carroll, Mar. 23, 1968 (div. Nov. 30, 1993); children: Walter, Michael, Robert Jr., Peggy; m. Nancy A. Fix, Aug. 31, 1996. BA cum laude, U. Conn., 1974; MEd, Kent State U., 1983; D of Nursing, Case Western Reserve U., 1986. RN. Sales mgr. Nutmeg Home Protection, Middlebury, Conn., 1972-74; theater mgr. SBC Mgmt. Corp., Boston, 1974; dist. supr. Selected Theatres Mgmt. Corp., Lyndhurst, Ohio, 1974-86; nat. sales mgr. ZBS Video, Inc., Lyndhurst, Ohio, 1981-82; staff nurse Cleve. Clinic Found., 1986-87, clin. instr., 1987-88, head nurse, 1988-93; case mgr., 1993—; asst. clin. prof. Case Western Reserve U., Frances Payne Bolton Sch. Nursing, Cleve., 1990—; case mgr. Cleve. Clin. Home Care, 1993—. Health officer Lake County (Ohio) Bd. Alcohol, Drug Addiction and Mental Health Svcs., 1991—; co-chmn. United Way, Cleve., 1991-93. Staff sgt. U.S. Army, 1964-71, Vietnam. Recipient Achievement award Greater Cleve. Nurses Assn., 1986. Mem. AACN, Am. Assn. Tchrs. German, Am. Assn. Tchrs. Portuguese and Spanish, Assn. Specialists in Aging, Frances Payne Bolton Sch. Nursing Alumni Assn. (pres. 1992-93), Kappa Delta Pi, Sigma Theta Tau. Home: 5011 Nob Hill Dr Apt 9C Chagrin Falls OH 44022 Office: Cleve Clinic Found 9555 Rockside Rd Valley View OH 44125

VÁNKY, FARKAS TAMÁS, medical educator; b. Székelyudvarhely, Romania, July 3, 1931; s. Kálmán János and Mária (Váró) V.; m. Anna Márta Szentkirályi, June 13, 1936; children: Eszter, Farkas, Péter. MD, Sch. Medicine, Tirgu-Mures, Romania, 1957; DMS, Karolinska Inst., Stockholm, 1979. Dist. med. officer Uliesul Dist., Romania, 1957-62; orthopedic surgeon fellow Tirgu-Mures, 1962-65, asst. surgeon clin. orthopedics, 1965-69; asst. surgeon Karolinska Hosp., Stockholm, 1969-70; rsch. fellow Karolinska Inst., Stockholm, 1970-82, assoc. prof., 1982—. Mem. EACR, Scandinavian Soc. for Immunology. Calvinist. Home: Rymstarsvägen 24, 162 24 Vällingby Sweden Office: Karolinska Inst, Microbio and Tumor Bio Ctr, Solna vägen 1, 171 77 Stockholm Sweden

VAN MILLIGEN, JAMES MICHAEL, health care administrator; b. Chgo., Feb. 12, 1949; s. Alferd C. and H. Patricia Van M.; m. Jane, May 5, 1971. B of Health Sci., Wichita State U., 1977, M of Health Sci., 1984. Physician asst. Wichita Osteo. Clinic, 1977-84; data mgr. Preferred Health Care, 1984-85; dir. network devel. Equicor, 1986-87; chief oper officer WPAA, Inc., 1987—, WPPA-HMO, Inc., 1995—. Pres. Wichita Ind. Neighborhoods, 1994-95, Fairmount Neighborhood Assn., Wichita, 1984-96; advisor United Sch. Dist. #249 Bus. & Tech. Com., Wichita, 1993-94, Mayor's Adv. Coun., Wichita, 1989-92. With U.S. Army, 1970-73, Vietnam. Mem. Nat. Assn. Health Underwriters (Journalism award 1991), Kans. Assn. Health Underwriters, Ctrl. Kans. Assn. Health Underwriters, Med. Soc. Sedgewick County (assoc. exec. dir. 1987—, Wichita Area C. of C. Home: 1717 Fairmount Wichita KS 67208 Office: WPPA Inc 1102 S Hillside Wichita KS 67211

VAN MOFFAERT, MYRIAM MARCELLE, psychiatrist; b. Ghent, Belgium, May 8, 1943; d. Jean Van Moffaert and Marie-Madeleine De Buck; m. Marc de la Ruelle, Dec. 9, 1975. MD, Ghent, 1969. Prof. Univ. Hosp., Ghent, 1970-91, investigator psychopharmacology, 1985—; bd. dirs. Psychomatic Centrum, Ghent, 1988-91, Psychodermatology Ctr., Ghent, Sleep Disorders Ctr. Editor: Anxiety and Panic, 1991. Mem. Flemish Assn. Psychiatry and Neurology (pres. 1989-91), Belgian Assn. for Liaison Psychiatry (v.p. 1989—). Roman Catholic. Home: Wauendreef 24, 9831 Latem Deurle Belgium Office: Univ Hosp, Dept Psychosomatics, 9000 Ghent Belgium

VAN NIMAN, CYNTHIA MARIE, family physician, artist; b. Cin., Feb. 5, 1958; d. Kempton Charles and Colette Catherine (Ast) Van N.; m. Daniel John Wissel, July 27, 1980 (div. Oct. 1985); children: Catherine Marie, Stephanie Ann; m. David Alan Hart, May 20, 1995; 1 stepchild, Kyle Michael Hart; 1 child, Patrick Matthew. Diploma in German studies, U. Vienna, Ströbl, Austria, 1978; BA summa cum laude, Edgecliff Coll., Cin., 1980; MA in Art Therapy, Wright State U., 1983, MD, 1991. Diplomate Am. Bd. Med. Examiners, Am. Bd. Family Practice; cert. ACLS, PALS, ATR, neonatal resuscitation. Reservationist Gogo Tours, Cin., 1975-81; primary tchr. German, St. Agnes Sch., Cin., 1977-78; asst. counselor Living Arrangements for Developmentally Disabled, Cin., 1977-78; art therapist U. Cin. Med. Ctr., 1983-87, Millcreek Psychiat. Ctr. for Children, Cin., 1987; resident in family practice St. Elizabeth Med. Ctr., Dayton, Ohio, 1991-94, mem. staff, 1994-95; pvt. practice Beavercreek, Ohio, 1995—; pvt. practice Ohio Valley Family Physicians, Hillsboro, Ohio, Sabina, Ohio, 1994-95; keynote speaker Assn. for Edn. Young Children, Cin., 1987. One-woman show Emery Art Gallery, Cin., 1980. Judge Montgomery County Sci. Fair, 1988. Acad. presdl. and German studies scholar, 1976, activity scholar Edgecliff Coll., 1978, grad. scholar Wright State U., 1982, Cornaro scholar, 1990. Mem. Am. Acad. Family Practice, Ohio Med. Assn., Greene County Med. Soc., Chi Sigma Iota, Kappa Gamma Pi, Psi Chi. Roman Catholic. Office: Forest View Family Practice 1911 N Fairfield Rd Dayton OH 45432-2754

VAN NOORDWIJK, JACOBUS, retired pharmacologist; b. Amsterdam, Netherlands, Jan. 3, 1920; s. Arie Johannes and Agatha Cornelia (Weber) van N.; m. Johanna Catharina Van Veen, Aug. 26, 1946; children: Arie Johannes, Meine, Maria Agatha. Lic. med. practice, U. Groningen, 1947; MSc in Biochemistry, U. Western Ont., London, Can., 1949; MD, U. Amsterdam, 1956. Registered pharmacologist, Netherlands. Chief asst. scientific civil svcs. U. Amsterdam, 1950-63; head unit biol. standards Nat. Inst. Public Health, Bilthoven, 1963-85, dir. div. of pharmacology, 1964-85; prof. pharmacology U. Utrecht, 1967-80; mem. drug lic. bd. Ministry of Public Health, Rijswijk, 1963-85; chmn. groups of experts European Pharmacopoeia, Strasbourg, 1984—; mem. Netherlands delegation to European Pharmacopoeia, Strasbourg, 1984—; chmn. com. LD50 Health Coun. of the Netherlands, The Hague, 1981-89. Author, editor (with others) Algemene Farmacotherapie, 1962—. Chmn. Algemeen Humanistisch Trefpunt, Oegstgeest, 1982-91. Recipient Wallhäusser prize for reduction of animal use in quality control of pharmaceuticals, 1994. Mem. Koninklyke Nederlandse Maatschappy Bevordering Pharmacie.

VAN NOOTEN, GUIDO JAN, surgeon; b. Ekeren, Belgium, Feb. 5, 1953; s. Victor Felix and Elisabeth Maria (Wernerus) V.N.; m. Fabienne Jopen, Nov. 20, 1978 (div. 1994); children: Maya, Wendy, Joyce; m. Marleen Bogaert, June 20, 1994; children: Chris, Axelle. MD, U. Brussels, 1977, diploma in surgery, 1982. Resident in surgery U. Brussels, 1977-87; assoc. chef de clinique cardiac surgery U. Hosp., Brugmann, Brussels, 1987-89, chief cardiac surgery, 1989-90; prof., chief cardiac surgery U. Ghent, Belgium, 1990—, pres. dept. surgery, 1995—; bd. dirs. European Homograft Bank, Brussels. Contbr. articles to profl. jours. Mem. Soc. Thoracic Surgery, European Assn. Thoracic Surgery, Internat. Assn. Cardiovascular Surgery (European chpt.), Belgian Soc. Cardio-Thoracic Surgery (bd. dirs. 1995—). Office: U Hosp Ghent, De Pintelaan 185, 9000 Ghent Belgium

VAN ORMAN, COLIN BLAIR, child neurologist, educator, consultant; b. Taber, Alta., Can., July 1, 1952; came to U.S., 1992; s. Van Demar and Bird (Mendenhall) Van O.; m. Janeen Anne Chisholm, June 18, 1977; children: Thomas, Eliza, Kathryn, Daniel, Camilla, Sarah. BA, U. Lethbridge, Alta., 1975; MD, U. Calgary, Alta., 1978. Diplomate Am. Bd. Pediatrics, Am. Bd. Psychiatry and Neurology. Resident in pediatrics U. Utah, 1979-81; intern U. Calgary, 1978-79, chief resident in pediatrics, 1981-82, resident in pediatric neurology, 1982-85; asst. clin. prof. U. Alta., Edmonton, 1985-87; asst. prof. U. Calgary, 1987-92; child neurologist Primary Children's Med. Ctr., Salt Lake City, 1992—; assoc. clin. prof. U. Utah, Salt Lake City, 1992—. Pres. PTA, Calgary, 1988-89. Fellow Royal Coll. Physicians and Surgeons (Can.); mem. Can. Assn. Child Neurologists, Am. Acad. Neurology, Utah Med. Assn. Mem. LDS Ch. Office: Primary Children's Med Ctr 1000 N Medical Dr Salt Lake City UT 84113

VAN PELT, ARNOLD FRANCIS, JR., biologist, educator, researcher; b. Orange, N.J., Sept. 24, 1924; s. Arnold Francis and Fredericka Emma (Kleiber) VanP.; m. Gladys Mae Smith, June 24, 1947; children: Stephen Arnold, Susan Frances. BA, Swarthmore Coll., 1945; MS, U. Fla., 1947, PhD, 1950. Assoc. prof. biology Appalachian State U., Boone, N.C., 1950-54; prof. Tusculum Coll., Greeneville, Tenn., 1954-63; prof. Greensboro (N.C.) Coll., 1963-88, chmn. dept. sci. and math., 1964-71, 82-83, dir. Allied Health programs, 1975-89, chmn. div. sci. math., 1983-86, Moore prof. biology, 1980-88, Moore disting. prof. emeritus, 1988—; cons. entomology and ecology, Tex., Greensboro, 1989—; adj. faculty mem. nursing U. N.C., Greensboro, 1974, Moses H. Cone Meml. Hosp., Greensboro, 1975, 77, 83-89, Forsyth Meml. Hosp., Winston-Salem, 1972-89; cons., rschr. Big Bend Nat. Pk., 1982-95. Grantee: NSF, Research Corp., N.Y., Big Bend (Tex.) Nat. Hist. Soc., Piedmont U. Ctr., Winston-Salem, Oak Ridge Nat. Lab., Savannah River Ecology Lab., S.C., Greensboro Coll. Mem. AAAS, Entomol. Soc. Am., S.W. Assn. Naturalists, S.W. Entomol. Soc., Sigma Xi. (Greensboro chpt. treas. 1978-79, sec. 1980-81, pres. 1983). Quaker. Contbr. articles to profl. jours. Recipient Alpha Chi award, 1987. Arnold Van Pelt Best Biology Sr. Award established in his honor Greensboro Coll., 1991. Home: 203 Howell Pl Greensboro NC 27455-1712

VAN POZNAK, ALAN, anesthesiology and pharmacology educator; b. Newark, Dec. 30, 1927; s. Aaron and Florence (Danzis) Van P.; m. Dorothy Beatrice Lehmann, June 10, 1950; children: Christina, Theodore, John, Catherine. BA, Cornell U., 1948, MD, 1952. Diplomate Am. Bd. Anesthesiology. Prof. Med. Coll. Cornell U., N.Y.C., 1974—; adj. prof. N.Y. State Coll. Vet. Medicine, Ithaca, N.Y., 1981—; legal cons. various lawyers, 1975—. 1st lt. M.C., USAR, 1953-55. Mem. Am. Soc. Anesthesiologists, Assn. U. Anesthesiologists. Republican. Presbyterian. Home: 28 Northrop Ln Tenafly NJ 07670-2428 Office: NY Hosp Cornell Med Ctr 1300 York Ave New York NY 10021-4873

VAN REEN, ROBERT, nutritionist, educator; b. Paterson, N.J., June 12, 1921; s. Cornelius and Martha (Miller) Van R. BA, State Tchrs. Coll., Montclair, N.J., 1943; PhD, Rutgers U., 1949. Assoc. biochemist Brookhaven Nat. Lab., Upton, N.Y., 1949-51; rsch. assoc. Johns Hopkins U., Balt., 1951-53, asst. prof. biology, 1953-56; supr., chemist Naval Med. Rsch. Inst., Bethesda, Md., 1956-61; head nutritionist div. biochemistry Naval Med. Rsch. Inst., Bethesda, 1961-70; prof. nutrition U. Hawaii at Manoa, Honolulu, 1970-85, chmn. dept. nutrition, 1979-83, prof. emeritus, 1985—; USN rep. nutrition study sect. NIH, Bethesda, 1964-70, mem. panel, 1970-74; vis. assoc. prof. Ramathibodi Hosp., Bangkok, 1968-79; cons. WHO, Geneva, 1971-72, editor symposium, 1971-72. Contbr. articles to profl. jours. 1st lt. U.S. Army,1943-46. Recipient McLester award Assn. Mil. Surgeons, 1959. Mem. Am. Inst. Nutrition (ret.), Am. Soc. Biol. Chemists (ret.), U.N. Assn. Hawaii (pres. 1975-76). Home: 1054 Green St Apt 108 Honolulu HI 96822-3692 Office: U Hawaii Manoa Dept Food Sci Nutritio Honolulu HI 96822

VAN REENEN, JANE SMITH, speech and language pathologist; b. Baton Rouge, Sept. 16, 1949; d. William Robert and Mary Jane (Laidlaw) Smith; m. Dirk Andries van Reenen, Mar. 3, 1973; children: Andrea Lee, Erika Lynn. BS in Speech Pathology, La. State U., 1971; MEd in Speech Pathology, Ga. State U., 1984. Cert. clin. competence Am. Speech-Lang.-Hearing Assn.; lic. Ga.; cert. tchr. Ga. Speech-lang. pathologist Livingston Parish Schs., La., 1971-73, Gwinnett County (Ga.) Schs., 1973-75, 95—; pvt. practice speech-lang. pathology Norcross, Ga., 1975—; speech-lang. pathologist Nova Care, Atlanta, 1979—, Gwinnett County Schs., 1994—; grad. asst. Ga. State U., Atlanta, 1983-84, substitute clin. supr., 1988-90, interim clinic coord., 1991; speech-lang. pathologist Americana Nursing Home, Decatur, 1984; chairperson Atlanta (Ga.) Orofacial Myology Study Group, 1987-89; adv. com. Comm. Disorders Program, Atlanta, 1990-94; mem. Ga. Supervision Network, 1991—; mem. Cognitive Remediation Interest Group, Atlanta, 1993—. Mng. editor: Internat. Jour. Orofacial Myology, 1989-91; contbr. articles to profl. jours. Ruling elder Northminster Presbyn. Ch., Roswell, Ga., 1981; mem. local sch. adv. com. Pinckneyville Middle Sch., Norcross, 1987-92, co-founder sch. based drug/alchol abuse prevention program, 1988; v.p. Parent Tchr. Student Assn. Norcross High Sch., 1990-91; pres. River Valley Estates Homeowners Assn., Norcross,

1991; local sch. adv. com. Norcross High Sch., 1993—, AIDS rep. PTSA, 1993-96, drug/alcohol abuse rep., 1993-96, care team, 1993—. Recipient Positive Parenting awards Ga. State Supt. of Schs., Atlanta, 1987-88, 88-89; named Outstanding Sch. Vol., Gwinnet County Bd. Edn., Lawrenceville, Ga., 1989-90. Mem. Am. Speech-Lang.-Hearing Assn. (congl. action contact com. 1991—), Ga. Speech-Lang.-Hearing Assn. (honors and ethics com. 1989-91), Internat. Assn. Orofacial Myology (mng. editor 1989-91). Republican. Home and Office: 3992 Gunnin Rd Norcross GA 30092-1953

VAN RIPER, CHARLES, III, biology educator; b. Mahopac, N.Y., Sept. 24, 1943; s. Charles II and Dorothy (Wilson) van R.; m. Sandra Jean Guest, June 4, 1977; children: Charles IV, Jacqueline, Kimberley, Carena. BS in Zoology, Colo. State U., 1966, MS in Sci., 1967; PhD in Zoology, U. Hawaii, 1978. Biol. tech. Colo. Fish, Game & Pks. Dept., Colo., 1963; instr. Mahopac (N.Y.) High Sch., 1967-68, Hawaii Prep. Acad., Kamuela, 1968-72; teaching asst. U. Hawaii, Honolulu, 1972-74, rsch. asst., 1974-75, asst. rsch. prof., 1975-76; wildlife biologist Dept. Interior, U.S. Fish & Wildlife, Hawaii, 1977-79; unit leader Coop. U. Calif., Davis, 1979-89; unit leader, Coop. Pk. Studies Unit No. Ariz. U., Flagstaff, 1990—, prof., biol. scis., 1990—; mem. Western U.S. Peregrine Falcon recovery team, U.S. Fish & Wildlife Svc., 1982—, Hawaii endangered species recovery team, 1974—. Leader 4-H, Davis, Calif., 1974-90, sheep leader, Flagstaff, 1990—. Grantee McInery Found., Internat. Coun. Bird Preservation, 1973; recipient Frank M. Chapman Meml. award Fund Am. Mus. Natural History, 1973, 79. Fellow Ecol. Soc. (grantee 1974, 78); mem. Nat. Wildlife Soc. (Hawaii rep.), Am. Ornithologists Union (life., chmn. com. career opportunities in ornithology 1985-86), Aviculturists Soc. (life), Field Ornithologists (life), Cooper Ornithology Soc. (bd. dirs. 1986-89), Soc. Am. Naturalists, Western Bird-banding Assn. (life), Wilson Ornithology Soc. (life), Wildlife Disease Assn. (asst. editor 1986-91), Wildlife Soc., Sigma Xi (grantee 1979). Home: 12750 Stockmens Flagstaff AZ 86004-9108 Office: No Ariz Univ Dept Biol Scis PO Box 5614 Flagstaff AZ 86011

VANSANT, JOHNATHAN PAUL, medical educator; b. Atlanta, May 14, 1947; s. Henley Adams and Lynne M. (Johnson) V.; m. Rhonda Joy Edwards, Sept. 13, 1972; children: Melanie Noel, Joanna Joy. BS in Chemistry, U. Ga., 1969; MD, Med. Coll. Ga., 1973. Diplomate Am. Bd. Internal Medicine, Am. Bd. Rheumatology, Am. Bd. Nuclear Medicine. Chief internal medicine Med. Ctr. Family Practice Program, Columbus, Ga., 1977-82; asst. prof. medicine Med. Coll. Ga., Augusta, 1977-82; clin. asst. prof. medicine EMory U. Med. Sch., Atlanta, 1977-90, Med. Coll. Ga., 1982-90, Vanderbilt U. Hosp., Nashville, 1988-90; asst. prof. radiology Emory U. Med. Sch., 1990-95, asst. prof. internal medicine, 1990—, assoc. prof. radiology, 1995—; intern in internal medicine Med. Coll. Ga., 1993-94; resident in internal medicine, fellow in rheumatology Vanderbilt U., 1994—, fellow in nuclear medicine, 1988-90; dir. clin. cardiac imaging Emory U. Sch. Medicine, 1993—, dir. residenty tng. program dept. radiology, 1992-95; spkr., cons. DuPont Lab. Author: Cardiology (#2), 1994; editor: Correlative Imaging, 1992. Founding mem. Rep. Nat. Com., Washington, 1988—; mem. Zoo Atlanta, 1994—. Fellow Am. Coll. Cardiology; mem. Ga. Rheumatism Soc. (sec./treas. 1979-80, pres. 1984-86), Soc. Nuclear Medicine (southeastern chpt. treas. 1993-95, coun. 1995—), Soc. Nuclear Medicine (correlative imaging coun. sec. 1991-93), Nat. Audubon Soc., Wilderness Soc., World Wildlife Fund. Republican. Home: 1419 Waterford Green Dr Marietta GA 30068 Office: Emory U Hosp Dept Radiology 1364 Clifton Rd NE Atlanta GA 30322

VAN SCOY, GARY, social services administrator; b. Williamsport, Pa., Feb. 12, 1950; s. Thomas Van Scoy and Velma Lee (Coats) Valentine; m. Paula Maria Kovach, May 31, 1975; 1 child, Justin. BA in Sociology, King's Coll., 1972; MSW, Marywood Coll., 1974. Lic. social worker. Child abuse specialist Childrens Bur. Lehigh County, Allentown, Pa., 1974-76; program founder Parents Anonymous, Wilkes-Barre, Pa., 1976-78; family counselor Cath. Social Svcs., Wilkes-Barre, 1976-80, program dir., 1980-86; asst. dir. Cath. Social Svcs., Scranton, Pa., 1986-91; exec. dir. Cath. Social Svcs., Scranton, 1991-93; sr. outpatient therapist Children Svc. Ctr., Wilkes-Barre, Pa., 1993—, dir. managed care, 1994—; bd. dirs. Child Devel. Coun., Wilkes-Barre, 1978-86; bd. dirs. Child Welfare Luzerne County, Wilkes-Barre, 1976-80, pres., 1978-80. Bd. dirs. St. Michael's Sch., Tunkhannock, Pa., 1986-89; alumni mem. Leadership Wilkes-Barre, 1984. Named Outstanding Young Citizen, Scranton Jaycees, 1988; recipient award of harmony Barbershops Singers, 1980, Disting. Svc. award Wilkes-Barre Jaycees, 1980, Benjamin Rush award Luzerne County Med. Soc., 1980, 449th Daily Point of Light award Pres. of U.S., 1991. Mem. NASW (Social Worker of Yr. award 1989), KC (4 degree). Democrat. Roman Catholic. Home: 300 Chapel St Wilkes Barre PA 18704-1966 Office: Children Svc Ctr 335 S Franklin St Wilkes Barre PA 18702-3808

VANSELOW, NEAL ARTHUR, university administrator, physician; b. Milw., Mar. 18, 1932; s. Arthur Frederick and Mildred (Hoffmann) V.; m. Mary Ellen McKenzie, June 20, 1958; children: Julie Ann, Richard Arthur. AB, U. Mich., 1954, MD, 1958, MS, 1963. Diplomate: Am. Bd. Internal Medicine, Am. Bd. Allergy and Immunology. Intern Mpls. Gen. Hosp., 1958-59; resident Univ. Hosp., Ann Arbor, Mich., 1959-63; instr. medicine U. Mich., 1963-64, asst. prof., 1964-68, assoc. prof., 1968-72, prof., chmn. dept. postgrad. medicine and health professions edn., 1972-74; dean Coll. Medicine U. Ariz., Tucson, 1974-77; chancellor med. ctr. U. Nebr., Omaha, 1977-82, v.p., 1977-82; v.p. health scis. U. Minn., 1982-89, prof. internal medicine, 1982-89; chancellor Tulane U. Med. Ctr., New Orleans, 1989-94; prof. internal medicine, adj. prof. health sys. mgmt. Tulane U., New Orleans, 1989—; chmn. Joint Bd. Osteo. and Med. Examiners Ariz., 1974-77; chmn. coun. on Grad. Med. Edn., Dept. Health and Human Svcs., 1986-91; mem. com. on educating dentists for future Inst. Medicine, NAS, 1993-95, chairperson com. on future of primary care, 1994-96, co-chairperson com. on the U.S. physician supply, 1995-96, scholar in residence, 1994-95. Bd. dirs. Devel. Authority for Tucson's Economy, 1975-77, Minn. Coalition for Health Care Costs, 1983-87, La. Health Care Authority, 1989-90, United Way Greater New Orleans Area, 1992—; mem. exec. com. United Way Midlands, 1980-82, vice chmn. 1981 campaign; bd. dirs., mem. exec. com. Health Planning Coun. Midlands, Omaha, 1978-82, v.p., 1981-82; bd. dirs. Minn. High Tech. Coun., 1983-86; mem. commn. on Health Professions Pew Charitable Trusts, 1990-92; mem. Gov.'s Pan Am. Commn., La., 1991-92; mem. mktg. mgmt. governing coun. U. Hosp. Consortium, 1993-95. Fellow ACP, Am. Acad. Allergy, Am. Coll. Physician Execs.; mem. Assn. Acad. Health Ctrs. (bd. dirs. 1983-89, chmn. bd. dirs. 1988), Soc. Med. Adminstrs., Phi Beta Kappa, Sigma Xi, Alpha Omega Alpha, Beta Theta Pi, Nu Sigma Nu. Home: 1828 Palmer Ave New Orleans LA 70118-6216 Office: Tulane U 1430 Tulane Ave New Orleans LA 70112-2699

VAN SLOOTEN, DALE ALLEN, surgeon; b. Washington, Nov. 5, 1945; s. David John and Blanche (Wiegers) V.; m. Kay Ann Young, Nov. 3, 1969 (div. Apr. 1990); children: Christina, Chad Allen; m. Marian Elaine Black, June 1, 1991. BA, Rutgers U., 1967; MD, SUNY, Buffalo, 1971. Diplomate Am. Bd. Surgery. Intern in surgery Monmouth Med. Ctr., Long Branch, N.J., 1971-72; resident in surgery Monmouth Med. Ctr., 1972-75; pvt. practice surgeon Lewisburg, Tenn., 1975-85; ptnr. Family Surgery Ctr., Greer, S.C., 1985—. Recipient Physician Recognition award AMA, 1996. Fellow ACS, Southeastern Surg. Congress; mem. Am. Soc. Breast Surgeons (regional dir.), Rotary (pres. Lewisburg, Tenn. chpt. 1982-83). Presbyterian. Office: Family Surgery Ctr 556A Memorial Dr Ext Greer SC 29651

VAN SLOOTEN, RONALD HENRY JOSEPH, dentist; b. Paterson, N.J., July 12, 1937; s. Henry and Edythe (De Marco) Van S.; m. Joyce Elenor Mandel, 1962 (div. 1969); children: Ronald Henry Jr., Timothy Jay, Lauren; m. Barbara Rose Durante, July 1, 1979; children: Jonathon Henry, Brian Joseph. DDS, Farleigh Dickinson U., 1962; FAGD, Acad. Gen. Dentistry, 1986. Dentist pvt. practice, Paterson, N.J., 1965-76, Ridgewood, N.J., 1969-78, Ho Ho Kus, N.J., 1978—; staff mem. Bainert Meml. Hosp., Paterson, 1966-75, Ridgewood Valley Hosp., 1975—; assoc. prof. Fairleigh Dickinson Dental Sch., Hackensack, N.J., 1973-90; pres. Van Slooten Harbour Marina Inc., Port Henry, N.Y., 1989—; cons. N.J. Mfrs. Ins. Co., Trenton, 1966—. Pres. Fairleigh DIckinson Sch. Dentistry Alumni Assn., 1976-77. Lt. USN, 1962-65. Fellow Acad. Gen. Dentistry, Acad. Dentistry Internat.; mem. Am. Dental Assn., Internat. Dental Health Found., N.J. Dental Soc., Bergen County Dental Soc. (Chmn. Nat. Dental Health Week citation 1970), Moriah C. of C. Republican. Roman Catholic. Office: Ho Ho Kus Profl Bldg 110 Warren Ave Ho Ho Kus NJ 07423-1561

VANSTEENKISTE, JOHAN FILIP, chest physician; b. Izegem, Belgium, June 1, 1957; m. Myriam Vermeire, Sept. 14, 1990. MD, Cath. U. Louvain, Belgium, 1982, Pneumologist, 1989. Resident in internal medicine and pheumology Univ. Hosp., Louvain, 1982-89; pvt. practice, Antwerp, Belgium, 1991-94; pneumologist Univ. Hosp., Louvain, 1994—.

VANSTRAELEN, LUC CLEMENT, radiologist; b. St Truiden, Limburg, Belgium, Sept. 19, 1951; s. Albert Louis and Marie-Louise Renee (Heynen) V.; m. Hilda Seraphina Lefevre, Apr. 28, 1977; children: Caroline Hilde, Annelies Isabelle. MD magna cum laude, U. Leuven, Leuven, Belgium, 1976; cert. specialist in radiology, U. Hosp., Leuven, 1979, cert. specialist in vascular radiology, 1980. Radiologist H. Hart Hosp., Mol, Belgium, 1980—; sec. med. coun. Hosp. Mol, 1981-87, pres., 1988-91; mem. gen. assembly Social Security for Med. Drs., Brussels, 1989—. Active gen. assembly Cath. Edn., Mol, 1982—. Fellow Belgium Veren Radiologie; mem. Syndicate of Radiologists, Orde V.D. Prince (pres. local divsn. 1993-96. Home: Kapellestraat 11, 2400 Mol Belgium

VANTASH, CATHERINE ANN, medical and surgical nurse; b. Bryn Mawr, Pa., Sept. 9, 1966; d. Robert J. and Margaret T. (Esher) Bell. ADN, Delaware County Community Coll, Media, Pa., 1988; BSN, Thomas Jefferson U., 1995. Cert. ACLS. Nurse's aide Broomall (Pa.) Presbyn. Nursing Home, Riddle Meml. Hosp., Media; staff nurse med. respiratory intensive care unit Thomas Jefferson U. Hosp., Phila. Mem. Nat. League Nurses, Sigma Theta Tau. Home: 2371 Donna Ln Pottstown PA 19464-2664

VANUNO, DANIEL G., surgeon; b. Asuncion, Paraguay, Apr. 4, 1968; s. David and Hilda (Paluch) V. MD, U. Nacional de Asuncion, 1992. Intern Hosp. de Clinicas, U. Nacional de Asuncion, 1992; pathology resident W.Va. U. Hosps., Morgantown, 1993-94; surgery resident Western Res. Care Sys., Youngstown, Ohio, 1994-95, Met. Group Hosps./U. Ill., Chgo., 1995—. Miami U. Sch. Medicine scholar, 1991. Fellow AMA; mem. ACS, Am. Coll. Pathologists (jr. mem.), Am. Soc. Clin. Pathologists (jr. mem.).

VAN VORST, B. CHARLES, health facility administrator; b. Harvey, Ind., June 22, 1943; s. John William and Bessie (Borg) Van V.; m. June A. Van Vorst; children: Krista Ann, Dirk Brian. BS in Bus. Mgmt., U. Evansville, 1966; MBA in Health Care Adminstrn., George Washington U., 1968. Adminstrv. resident Meth. Hosp., Indpls., 1967-68, adminstrv. asst., 1968-69, asst. adminstr., 1969-71, v.p. ops., 1972-79; pres., CEO The Carle Found., Urbana, Ill., 1979-90, Carle Found. Hosp., Urbana, Ill., 1979-90, Santa Rosa Health Care Corp., San Antonio, 1991—; clin. asst. prof. Coll. Medicine U. Ill., Urbana; mem. affiliate faculty Trinity U.; tchr. bus. adminstrn. Ind. Ctrl. U.; bd. dirs. Millard Fillmore Hosps., 1993—, exec. com., 1993—; chmn., bd. dirs. Millard Fillmore Surgery Ctr., 1993—; bd. dirs., exec. com. Millard Fillmore Health, Edn. & Rsch. Found., 1993—; bd. dirs. Vis. Nursing Assn. HomeCare Group, Western N.Y. Healthcare Assn., chmn. pub. rels. task force, 1993—, edn. com., 1993—; chmn. pub. rels. task force Western N.Y. Hosp. Assn., 1993—; bd. dirs. Health Sys. Agy. Western N.Y., Health Care Industries Assn., Buffalo State Coll. Found., CarleCare, Inc.; mem. Greater Buffalo Partnership-Cmty. Coun., 1993—, The Amherst Group, 1994—; mem. nat. adv. com. pub. health tng. Dept. Tng. HEW, NIH. Adv. bd. San Antonio M.D. mag.; contbr. articles to profl. jours. Mem. D'Youville Coll. Pres.'s Adv. Coun., 1993—; mem. strategic planning com. United Way of Buffalo & Erie County, 1995—; mem. Welfare to Work Coun., Buffalo, 1993—, City of Buffalo Neighborhood Revitalization Corp., 1994—; bd. dirs. San Antonio Econ. Devel. Found.; treas. Alpha Home Assn.; mem. med. adv. com., long range planning com. United Meth. Home, Franklin, Ind.; chmn. fin. com. Cmty. Addiction Svcs. Agy.; bd. dirs. Med. Destination, Tex. Hosp. Edn. and Rsch. Found., 1992—; med. and bus. subcom. BCMS; chmn. Champaign-Urbana Areawide Svcs. Coun.; trustee Ill. Provider Trust; mem. allocation com., chmn. profl. svcs. divsn. United Way, 1982. Recipient Excellence cert. U. Evansville Alumni Assn., 1973, Bus. First Pathfinders award, 1995, The Frederick H. Gibbs award for Excellence in Grad. Edn.; WHO fellow, 1973. Fellow Am. Coll. Healthcare Execs.; mem. Am. Hosp. Assn., Am. Assn. Hosp. Planning (bd. dirs.), Health Issues Study Soc. (past pres.), Cath. Hosp. Assn., Tex. Hosp. Assn. (chair coun. human rels.), Tex. Conf. Cath. Health Care Facilities (bd. dirs., trustee), Ill. Health Care Cost Containment Coun. (bd. dirs., vice chmn.), Ill. Hosp. Assn. (teaching hosps. coun., gov. bd., trustee, sec. exec. com., cost containment com.), George Washington U. Alumni Assn. Health Care (chmn. curriculum adv. com.), Urbana Downtown Promotion Assn., Urbana C. of C. (long range planning com., mem. fin. and econ. devel. coms.), Sonterra Country Club, Rotary. Republican. Methodist. Office: Millard Fillmore Fillmore Health Sys 901 Washington St Buffalo NY 14203

VAN ZANDT, DORIS YUKIKO, pediatric rehabilitation nurse; b. Portland, Oreg., Nov. 25, 1955; d. George Tetsuro and Takako (Ohashi) Kimura; m. Charles Winne Van Zandt, Jan. 4, 1992. BS in Nursing, U. Wash., 1979. Cert. Rehab. Registered Nurse. Staff nurse inpatient rehab. unit Children's Hosp. & Med. Ctr., Seattle, 1979-82, rehab./urology/birth defects nurse clinician, 1982-87, urology nurse clinician, 1987-89, rehab. nurse clinician, 1989—. Author, co-author book chpts., training manual. Swim coach Shadow Seals disabled children's team, Seattle, 1992—; com. chair adaptive aquatics Pacific Northwest Swimming, 1995—. Mem. Assn. Rehab. Nursing, Wheelchair Sports USA, Am. Assn. Spinal Cord Injury Nurses, Spina Bifida Assn. Puget Sound. Office: Children's Hosp & Med Ctr 4800 Sand Point Way NE Seattle WA 98105

VARANO, JOSEPH ROBERT, physician assistant; b. Shamokin, Pa., July 13, 1948; s. Joseph N. and Patricia F. (Mellowship) V. BS, Alderson-Braddus Coll., 1973; MS, U. Hartford, 1986. Physician asst. So. Phila. Med. Group, Phila., 1973-77, Oncology Assoc. Ltd., Phila., 1977-85, Mt. Sinai Hosp., Hartford, Conn., 1985-86, Children's Hosp., Washington, 1986-87, Mt. Sinai Hosp.-St. Francis Hosp., Hartford, Conn., 1987-89, 90-94, Duke U. Hosp., Durham, N.C., 1989-90, U. Conn. Health Ctr., Farmington, Conn., 1994—. Fellow Am. Acad. Physician Assts., Pa. Soc. Physician Assts. (pres. 1977-79), Conn. Acad. Physician Assts. (pres. 1993-94).

VARDI, JOSEPH ROBERT, gynecologist, oncologist; b. Israel, Dec. 6, 1933; came to U.S., 1972; s. Hoshe and Zehava Vardi. MD, Hebrew U., 1967. Resident U. California, Davis; gynecologic oncology fellow Tufts U., Boston; dir. gynecol.-oncology St. Lukes Hosp., N.Y.C., 1977-78; dir. Gynecologic Oncology Boston Univ. Med. Sch., 1978-80; dir. gynecologic-oncologic Maimonides Med. Ctr., Bklyn., 1980—; clin. prof. health sci. ctr. SUNY, Bklyn. Contbr. articles to profl. jours. Office: 941 48th St Brooklyn NY 11219-2919

VARGAS, JUAN ANTONIO, internist; b. Madrid, July 1, 1960; s. Juan Antonio and Maria Mercedes (Nunez) V.; m. Maria Jose Tabuenca, June 20, 1986; children: Maria, Juan. BS, Sagrado Corazon, 1976; MD, U. Complutense, 1984, PhD, 1991. Resident Insalud, Madrid, 1985-89, asst., 1990—. Contbr. articles to profl. jours. Mem. Internal Medicine Soc., Analytical Cytology Soc. Office: Clinica Puerta de Hierro, San Martin de Porres 4, 28035 Madrid Spain

VARGAS, LENA BESSETTE, nursing administrator; b. Hardwick, Vt., Dec. 26, 1922; d. Leon Alphonse and Dorilla Leah (Boudreau) Bessette; m. Jose Emilio Vargas, Sept. 3, 1949; children: Jose Emilio, Maria del Carmen, J. Ramon, Vicente Andres, Yolanda Teresa. BS in Nursing Edn., U. Vt., 1949. Instr. basic nursing Mary Fletcher Hosp., Burlington, Vt., 1947-49; clin. instr. St. Francis Hosp., Evanston, Ill., 1949-50; nurse participant streptomycin therapy research H.M. Biggs Meml. Hosp., Ithaca, N.Y., 1950-51; supr. ancillary personnel Providence Hosp., Washington, 1953-55, asst. dir. nursing, 1965—. Mem. coun., del. coop. congress Greenbelt Coop., Savage, Md., 1983-86; bd. dirs. Providence Hosp. Fed. Credit Union, Washington, 1977-80, v.p. bd. dirs., 1983-85. Mem. AAUW (chmn. various coms., chair Kensington del. to nat. conv. 1991, gift to Ednl. Found. named in her honor by Kensington br. 1992, del. US/China Conf. on Women's Issues, Beijing 1995), Am. Nurses Assn. (cert. nursing adminstr.), Nat. League for Nursing, Christ Child Soc. Roman Catholic. Avocations: bridge, travel, real estate, horseback riding. Home: 10706 Keswick St Garrett Park MD 20896-0130 Office: Providence Hosp 1150 Varnum St NE Washington DC 20017-2180

VARGO, CHARLES RICHARD, health facility administrator; b. Pitts., Apr. 18, 1959; s. George J. and Lois I. (Sammer) V.; m. Joyce A. Carey, July 25, 1987; children: Charles G., Richard J., Julianne R. BSBA, Duquesne U., 1981; M of Health Adminstrn., U. Pitts., 1984. Adminstrv. resident and fellow Mercy Hosp. Pitts., 1983-85, adminstrv. asst. for med. affairs, 1985-88; dir. profl. svcs. Mercy Hosp. Pitts., 1988-92; v.p. Mercy Hosp. Pitts., 1992—; bd. dirs. Global Links, Pitts.; mem. bd. ops. Ctr. for Emergency Medicine, Pitts., 1987—; mem. adv. bd. Duquesne U. Sch. Health Scis., Pitts., 1992—, Bus. Consortia for Sch. to work Opportunities, Pitts., 1994—, Salud y Misericordia en Peru Program, Radnor, Pa., 1995—. Gov., treas. Duquesne U. Alumni Assn., Pitts., 1986-93; bd. dirs. Nat. Neurofibromatosis Found.-Pitts. chpt., 1986-88, preceptor Robert Morris Coll., Pitts., 1992—, Pa. State U., University Park, 1993—. Roman Catholic. Home: 5059 Carlyn Dr Pittsburgh PA 15236 Office: Mercy Hosp Pitts 1400 Locust St Pittsburgh PA 15219

VARIA, MAHESH AMRATLAL, radiation oncologist, oncology educator; b. Kampala, Uganda, June 7, 1943; came to U.S. 1972; s. Amratlal and Dhiraj V.; m. Indira M. Ghatalia, Dec. 3, 1969; children: Rachna, Nisha, Smita. MB, Ch.B, U. Liverpool, Eng., 1967. Diplomate Am. Bd. Radiology. Resident Hahnemann Med. Coll. and Hosp., Phila., 1973-76; asst. prof. U. N.C., Chapel Hill, 1976-83, assoc. prof., 1983—, dir., div. radiation oncology, 1987-88, assoc. chmn., dept. radiation oncology, 1988—. Contbr. articles to profl. jours. Pres. Jain Study Ctr. N.C., 1986; v.p. Orange County, N.C. Am. Cancer Soc., 1988-89. Fellow Am. Coll. Radiology (exec. com. gynecol. oncology group 1996-99); mem. AMA, Am. Soc. Therapeutic Radiology and Oncology, Am. Coll. Radiology, Am. Soc. Clin. Oncology, N.C. Med. Soc. (alt. del. 1992-95), Coun. Affiliated Regional Radiation Oncology Socs. (pres. N.C. chpt. 1989-90). Office: U NC Dept Radiation Oncology Cb # 7512 Chapel Hill NC 27599

VARJU, DEZSOE, biologist, educator; b. Gasztony, Hungary, May 22, 1932; arrived in Germany, 1956; s. Johann and Anna (Hirschmann) V.; m. Heide Agner. Diploma Physics, U. Budapest, Hungary, 1956; PhD, U. Goettingen, Germany, 1958; univ. tchr., U. Tuebingen, Germany, 1967. Rsch. asst., rsch. assoc. Max Planck Inst., Tuebingen, 1958-59, 60-68; postdoctoral fellow Calif. Tech., Pasadena, 1959-60; prof. U. Tuebingen, 1968—. Author: Systems Theory, 1977; editor: Localisation and Orientation in Biology and Engineering, 1984; co-editor: Biological Cybernetics Jour., 1993; mem. adv. bd. Jour. Comp. Physiology. Office: U Tuebingen, Auf der Morgenstelle 28, 72076 Tuebingen Germany

VARMUS, HAROLD ELIOT, government health institutes administrator, educator; b. Oceanside, N.Y., Dec. 18, 1939; s. Frank and Beatrice (Barasch) V.; m. Constance Louise Casey, Oct. 25, 1969; children: Jacob Carey, Christopher Isaac. AB, Amherst Coll., 1961, DSc (hon.), 1984; MA, Literature, Harvard U., 1962; MD, Columbia U. Med. Sch., 1966. Lic. physician, Calif. Intern, resident Presbyn. Hosp., N.Y.C., 1966-68; clin. assoc. NIH, Bethesda, Md., 1968-70; lectr. dept. microbiology U. Calif., San Francisco, 1970-72, asst. prof., depts. microbiology and immunology, biochemistry and biophysics, 1972-74, assoc. prof., 1974-79, prof., 1979-83, Am. Cancer Soc. research prof., 1984-93; dir. NIH, Bethesda, Md., 1993—; chmn. bd. on biology NRC. Editor: Molecular Biology of Tumor Viruses, 1982, 85; Readings in Tumor Virology, 1983; assoc. editor Genes and Development Jour., Cell Jour.; mem. editorial bd. Cancer Surveys. Named Calif. Acad. Sci. Scientist of Yr., 1982; co-recipient Lasker Found. award, 1982, Passano Found. award, 1983, Armand Hammer Cancer prize, 1984, GM Alfred Sloan award 1984, Shubitz Cancer prize, 1985, Nobel Prize in Physiology or Medicine, 1989. Mem. AAAS, NAS, Inst. Medicine of NAS, Am. Soc. Virology, Am. Soc. Microbiology, Am. Acad. Arts and Scis. Democrat. Office: National Istitutes of Health Bldg 1 Rm 126 1 Center Dr MSC 0148 Bethesda MD 20892-0148*

VARNER, CHARLEEN LAVERNE MCCLANAHAN (MRS. ROBERT B. VARNER), nutritionist, educator, administrator, dietitian; b. Alba, Mo., Aug. 28, 1931; d. Roy Calvin and Lela Ruhama (Smith) McClanahan; student Joplin (Mo.) Jr. Coll., 1949-51; BS in Edn., Kans. State Coll. Pittsburg, 1953; MS, U. Ark., 1958; PhD, Tex. Woman's U. 1966; postgrad. Mich. State U., summer, 1955, U. Mo., summer 1962; m. Robert Bernard Varner, July 4, 1953. Apprentice county home agt. U. Mo., summer 1952; tchr. Ferry Pass Sch., Escambia County, Fla., 1953-54; tchr. biology, home econs. Joplin Sr. H.S., 1954-59; instr. home econs. Kans. State Coll., Pittsburg, 1959-63; lectr. foods, nutrition Coll. Household Arts and Scis., Tex. Woman's U., 1963-64, rsch. asst. NASA grant, 1964-66; assoc. prof. home econs. Central Mo. State U., Warrensburg, 1966-70, adviser to Colhecon, 1966-70, adviser to Alpha Sigma Alpha, 1967-70, 72, mem. bd. advisers Honors Group, 1967-70; prof., head dept. home econs. Kans. State Tchrs. Coll., Emporia, 1970-73; prof., chmn. dept. home econs. Benedictine Coll., Atchison, Kans., 1973-74; prof., chmn. dept. home econs. Baker U., Baldwin City, Kans., 1974-75; owner, operator Diet-Con Dietary Cons. Enterprises, cons. dietitian, 1973—, Home-Con Cons. Enterprises. Mem. Joplin Little Theater, 1956-60. Mem. NEA, Mo., Kans. state tchrs. assns., AAUW, Am., Mo., Kans. dietetics assns., Am., Mo., Kans. home econs. assns., Mo. Acad. Scis., AAUP, U. Ark. Alumni Assn., Alumni Assn. Kans. State Coll. of Pittsburg, Am. Vocat. Assn., Assn. Edn. Young Children, Sigma Xi, Beta Sigma Phi, Beta Beta Beta, Alpha Sigma Alpha, Delta Kappa Gamma, Kappa Kappa Iota, Phi Upsilon Omicron, Theta Alpha Pi, Kappa Phi. Methodist (organist). Home: PO Box 1009 Topeka KS 66601

VARNUM, JAMES WILLIAM, hospital administrator; b. Grand Rapids, Mich., May 29, 1940; s. Robert Otto and Jeannette (Badger) V.; m. Lucinda Hotchkiss, June 6, 1964; children: Kenneth James, Susan Lucinda. A.B., Dartmouth Coll., 1962; M.Hosp. Adminstrn. with honors, U. Mich., 1964. Adminstrv. asst. U. Wis. Hosps., Madison, 1963-64; asst. supt. U. Wis. Hosps., 1964-68, asso. supt., 1968-69, supt., 1969-73; hosp. adminstr. U. Wash. Hosp., Seattle, 1973-78; pres. Mary Hitchcock Meml. Hosp., Lebanon, N.H., 1978—; prof. Med. Sch., Dartmouth Coll., 1978—. Mem. Am. Hosp. Assn. (bd. trustees 1994—), The Hitchcock Alliance (pres. 1983—). Home: 7 Woodcock Ln Etna NH 03750-4403 Office: Mary Hitchcock Meml Hosp 1 Medical Center Dr Lebanon NH 03756-0001

VARONA-FRANCO, LUIS, neurologist, consultant; b. Bilbao, Spain, Mar. 13, 1965. Med. degree, Licentiate with honors, Basque Country U., Bilbao, 1989. Bd. cert. in neurology, Spain, European Union. Intern in gen. medicine Hosp. Basurto, Bilbao, 1987-89; resident in neurology Hosp. Cruces, Baracaldo, Vizcaya, Spain, 1991-94; cons. neurologist Hosp. Galdakao, Spain, 1995, Hosp. Basurto, Bilbao, Spain, 1996—. Collaborative author: Zarranz's Neurologiía, 1993. Mem. Drs. Without Frontiers, 1994, Amnesty Internat., 1991. Mem. European Neurol. Soc., Spanish Soc. Neurology. Home: Julio Urquijo 17 8oC, 48014 Bilbao Spain

VARRASSI, GIUSTINO, anesthesiologist; b. L'Aquila, Italy, Jan. 30, 1948; s. Emilio and Clorinda (Nolletti) V.; m. Petra Böhmig, Jan. 29, 1976; children: Matteo, Simone. Degree in medicine, U. Rome, 1973. Diplomate Italian Bd. Anesthesia and Intensive Care, Italian Bd. Pulmonary Diseases. Rschr. Med. Sch. U. Rome, 1974-76; rschr. Med. Sch. L'Aquila (Italy) U., 1976-77, asst. prof. dept. anesthesia, 1977-85, assoc. prof., chmn. dept. anesthesia, 1985—, cons. Med. Sch., 1976-85. Author: Physical Fitness, 1986, Obstetrie Analgia and Anesthesia, 1992; editor 13 books in field. CNR grantee. Mem. Italian Soc. Anesthesiologists, Internat. Assn. for Study of Pain (sec. European Fedn. 1993—), European Soc. Obstetric Anesthesists. Home: 67010 Preturo Italy Office: U L'Aquila Dept Anesthesia, via Vetoro, 67100 L'Aquila Italy

VARRIALE, PHILIP, cardiologist; b. N.Y.C., July 30, 1934; s. John J. and Florence (Ferrara) V.; m. Eileen D. Rubencamp, Dec. 28, 1968; children: Donna, Philip, David. BA, NYU, 1955; MD, SUNY, 1959. Attending physician Dept. of Medicine, St. Vincent Hosp., 1963—; chief of cardiology Cabrini Med. Ctr. of N.Y., 1964—. Co-author: Textbook of Vectorcardiography, 1970; author: Cardiac Pacing, A Concise Guide to Clinical Practice, 1979. Lt. col. U.S. Army Med. Corps, 1968-70. Fellow ACP, Am. Coll. of Cardiology, Am. Coll. of Chest Physicians. Home: 37 North Rd Bronxville NY 10708 Office: 222 E 19th St New York NY 10003

VARRICCHIO, CLAUDETTE GOULET, nursing educator, researcher; b. Fall River, Mass., Apr. 13, 1940; d. Joseph Wilfred Goulet and Imelda R. Barrette; m. Frederick E. Varricchio, Dec. 28, 1962; children: Nicole, Erika. BS, Boston Coll., 1961; MS, U. Md., Balt., 1977; DSN, U. Ala., Birmingham, 1983. Cert. Oncology Nurse. Asst. prof. N.W. La. State U., Shreveport, 1978-80; assoc. prof. Loyola U., Chgo., 1980-91; rsch. assoc. NIH, Nat. Cancer Inst., 1989-90, program dir., nurse cons., 1992—. Recipient Chgo. Lung Assn. grant 1989-91. Mem. ANA, Oncology Nursing Soc., Am. Acad. Nursing, Am. Pain Soc., Am. Soc. Clin. Oncology, Sigma Theta Tau. Office: NIH Nat Cancer Inst DCPC EPN300 9000 Rockville Pike Bethesda MD 20892-0001

VARTANIAN, ISABEL SYLVIA, dietitian; b. Duquesne, Pa.; d. Apel and Mary (Kasparian) V. BS, U. Ala., 1957; MS, Columbia U., 1962. Registered dietitian. Dietetic intern N.Y. Hosp./Cornell Med. Ctr., N.Y.C., 1957-58; therapeutic dietitian Vets. Affairs Med. Ctr., Bronx, N.Y., 1958-60, adminstrv. dietitian, 1960-62, nutrition clinic dietitian, 1962-63; rsch. and nutrition clinic dietitian Vets. Affairs Med. Ctr., Coral Gables, Fla., 1963; nutrition clinic dietitian Vets. Affairs Med. Ctr., Richmond, Va., 1963-66, chief nutritional therapy edn. and rsch. sect., 1966-83, nutrition support dietitian, 1983—. Bd. dirs. Richmond Cmty. Action Program, 1978-83; adv. com. Social Svcs., Hopewell, Va., 1991—. Recipient Outstanding awards Vets. Affairs Med. Ctr., Superior Performance awards, Outstanding award. Mem. Richmond Dietetic Assn. (chairwoman diet therapy sect. 1966-67, pres.-elect 1967-68, pres. 1968-70, chairwoman Dial-A-Dietitian 1972-74, chairwoman pub. rels. 1973-74, 78-81, chairwoman Divsn. Cmty. Dietetics 1983-85, chairwoman program planning com. 1985), Va. Dietetic Assn. (chairwoman career guidance com. 1963-65, ednl. exhibits 1967, Dial-A-Dietitian 1972-74, pub. rels. 1982-84, visibility campaign 1984, exhibit com. 1984, program planning com. 1988, divsn. cmty. dietetic 1989-91), Va. Soc. Parenteral and Enteral Nutrition (chairwoman program planning com. 1988-89, membership com. 1990), Am. Dietetic Assn. (life, membership com.), Nat. Kidney Found. (renal nutrition sect.), Am. Soc. Parenteral and Enteral Nutrition. Home: 2005 Jackson St Hopewell VA 23860-3633 Office: VA Med Ctr 1201 Broad Rock Blvd Richmond VA 23249-0001

VARTOUKIAN, QUEENIE, social worker. BA, Rutgers U., Newark, N.J., 1973; MA, Montclair State Coll., 1977; MSW, NYU, 1984. Cert. social worker, N.Y., alcoholism counselor, N.Y.; lic. clin. social worker, N.J.; diplomate clin. social work. High sch. math. tchr. Newark Bd. Edn., 1973-82; social work intern Human Resources Adminstrn., N.Y.C., 1982-83; psychiat. social worker St. Vincent's Hosp., N.Y.C., 1984-86, Fair Oaks Hosp., Summit, N.J., 1986-93; pvt. practice Summit, Rutherford, N.J., 1987—. mem. Nat. Assn. Social Workers. Office: 118 Union Ave Rutherford NJ 07070 also: 28 Beachwood Rd Summit NJ 07901

VARY, THOMAS CRISPIN, physiologist; b. Fountain Hill, Pa., Sept. 15, 1954; s. George Crispin and Clairebette (Folk) V.; m. Kathleen Ann O'Neal, May 3, 1991; 1 child, Katherine Ann; stepchildren: Jennifer Taverna, Charles Taverna. BA, Johns Hopkins U., 1976; MS, Lehigh U., 1978; PhD, Pa. State U., 1982. Postdoctoral fellow Pa. State U. Coll. Medicine, Hershey, 1982; British-Am. rsch. fellow Nuffield dept. clin. biochemistry U. Oxford, England, 1982-83; asst. prof. Md. Shock Trauma Ctr., Balt., 1983-88; asst. prof. dept. cells and molecular physiology Pa. State U., 1988-90, assoc. prof., 1995-96, prof., 1996—; vis. scientist INRA, Clermont-Ferrand, France, 1996—. Editl. bd.: Shock; contbr. articles to profl. jours. and chpts. to books. Coach Hampden Area (Pa.) Youth Soccer, 1990—, Hampden Area Little League, 1990—. NIH grantee, 1989—, Career Devel. award, 1990—. Mem. Shock Soc., Internat. Soc. for Heart Rsch., Am. Physiol. Soc. (editorial bd. 1990—), Am. Soc. Biol. Chemists, Hershey Country Club. Republican. Episcopalian. Office: Pa State U Coll Medicine Dept Cellular Molecular Physiology Hershey PA 17033

VASQUEZ, EVA MARIE, pharmacotherapist; b. Houston, Sept. 12, 1963; d. Michael and Evangeline (Arce) V. PharmD, U. Ill., 1989. Fellow in transplant pharmacotherapy U. Ill. Med. Ctr., Chgo., 1989-91, pharmacotherapist, 1991—; clin. asst. prof. U. Ill. Coll. Pharmacy, Chgo., 1991—; adv. panelist Sandoz Corp., Raritan, N.J., 1993. Mem. AAAS, Am. Coll. Clin. Pharmacy, Am. Soc. Health Sys. Pharmacists, Am. Assn. Colls. Pharmacy, Ill. Coll. Clin. Pharmacy, Transplantation Soc. Office: U Ill Coll Pharmacy 833 S Wood St M/C 886 Chicago IL 60612

VASSILOPOULOU-SELLIN, RENA, medical educator; b. Dec. 29, 1949. MD, Albert Einstein Coll. Medicine, 1974. Resident Montefiore Hosp., Bronx, 1974-77; fellow Northwestern U., Chgo., 1977-80; prof. Univ. Tex., Houston, 1980—. Fellow ACP, Am. Assn. Clin. Endocrinol.; mem. AAAS, AMA, Am. Soc. Bone and Mineral Rsch., Am. Diabetes Assn., Am. Soc. Clin. Oncology, Endo Soc. Office: Anderson Cancer Ctr 1515 Holcombe Blvd # 15 Houston TX 77030-4009

VASUDEVAN, DAMODARAN MADHAVI, biochemist; b. Manjeri, India, June 6, 1942; s. Damodaran and Madhavi (Mangalath) V.; m. Devi Kannath Kesavan, Dec. 11, 1968. MBBS, Med. Coll. Calicut, 1967; MD, All India Inst. Med. Scis., 1971. Tutor biochemistry Med. Coll., Calicut, 1968-74, asst. prof. biochemistry, 1974-79; assoc. prof. rsch. Regional Cancer Ctr., Trivandrum, India, 1979-82; rsch. dir. Amala Cancer Rsch. Ctr., Trichur, India, 1982-87; prof. biochemistry Med. Coll., Kottayam, India, 1987-89, Trichur, 1989—; vice prin. Med. Coll., Trichur, 1992—; editl. bd. Jour. Exptl. and Clin. Cancer Rsch., 1993—. Author: Textbook of Biochemistry for Medical Students, 1995; contbr. articles to profl. jours. Eleanor Roosevelt Cancer Found. fellow, 1973. Fellow Nat. Acad. Med. Scis., Royal Coll. Pathology (London), Coll. Allergy and Applied Immunology, Indian Acad. Med. Specialties; mem. Indian Immunology Soc. Hindu. Office: Med Coll, Dept Biochemistry, 680596 Trichur India

VATTER, RUSSELL KENNETH, hospital administrator; b. Memphis, Jan. 5, 1947; s. Kenneth Louis Vatter and Dixie Lou (Pope) Shaw; m. Vicky Glenda Gray, Aug. 4, 1967; children: Shelley, Jack, Nathan. BBA, Memphis State U., 1969, MBA, 1977. Hosp. attendant Bapt. Meml. Hosp., Memphis, 1965-68; staff acct. Bernard J. Garfinkel, CPA, Memphis, 1968-69; state auditor State of Tenn., Nashville, 1969-73; bus. mgr. Western Mental Health Inst., Bolivar, Tenn., 1973-77; chief fin. mgmt. TDMH/MR, Nashville, 1977-78; hosp. adminstr. Memphis Mental Health Inst., 1978-80, Western Mental Health Inst., Bolivar, 1980-89; hosp. supt. Moccasin Bend Mental Health, Chattanooga, 1989—; Mem. exec. com. Tenn. Mental Health Planning, Nashville, 1992-94; v.p. West Tenn. Hosp. Coun., Jackson, 1988-89. Author: Grains of Sand, 1988. Pres. Bolivar Civitan Club, 1985; allocation United Way of Greater Chattanooga, 1994-95. With U.S. Army, 1970-71. Mem. Mental Health Assn. Bapitst. Office: Moccasin Bend Mental Health 100 Moccasin Bend Rd Chattanooga TN 37343

VAUDO, KENNETH A., health services administrator; b. Cambridge, Mass., Nov. 21, 1951; s. Albert Anthony and Gloria Shelton Vaudo; m. Margaret Elizabeth Vaudo, Feb. 26, 1971; children: Kimberley Anne, Barbara Elizabeth. BSBA, McNeese State U., 1977; MHA, Washington U., St. Louis, 1980. Diplomate Am. Coll. Health Care Execs. EMT West Cal-Cam. Hosp., Sulphur, La., 1975-78; patient coord. St. Louis Children's Hosp., 1978-80; adminstrv. resident St. Anthony's Hosp., Louisville, 1980-81; asst. v.p., v.p. gen. svcs. Emma L. Bixby Hosp., Adrian, Mich., 1981-85; asst. adminstr. Eye Found. Hosp., Birmingham, Ala., 1985—. Pres. Vestivia Hills (Ala.) H.S. Band Parent Assn., 1993-94, publicity chair, 1994-95, 3d v.p., 1995—. Sgt. USAF, 1971-73. Mem. Birmingham Regional Health Care Exec. Forum (sec. 1990-91, pres. 1991-92, bd. dirs. 1992-94), Lions (Vestiva Hills club, publicity chair 1994—, 3d v.p. 1995—). Methodist. Home: 3337 Shallowford Rd Birmingham AL 35216 Office: Eye Found Hosp 1720 University Blvd Birmingham AL 35233

VAUGHAN, CHRISTOPHER D., research scientist; b. Camden, N.J., July 22, 1944; s. Forrest E. Vaughan; children: David T., Daniel W. BS, Fairleigh Dickinson U., 1974; MBA, NYU, 1978. Lab. asst. Smith Kline & French Labs., Phila.; tecnician Rohm & Haas Co., Phila.; chemist Avon Products, Suffern, N.Y.; tech. mgr. Kolmar Labs., Port Jervis, N.Y.; tech. dir. Pvt. Label Cosmetics, inc., Fairlawn, N.J.; rsch. group leader Cosmair L'oreal, Clark, N.J.; v.p. Sun Pharms., Inc., Pompano Beach, Fla.; pres. S.P.F. Cons. Labs., Inc., Pompano Beach, Fla.; program chair, moderator Fla. Sunscreen Symposium, Nassau Bay and Orlando, Fla., 1989-91, 93; tech. speaker Cosmeticos Nuevos-Latin Tech. Co..., Miami, Fla., 1993. Author: Rheological Properties of Cosmetics and To...tries, 1993; patentee in field. Judge Fla. State Sci. and Engring. Fair, 1...0-96. Fellow Soc. Cosmetic Chemsitrs (chpt. chair 1990-91); mem. Am...Chem. Soc. Office: SPF Consulting Labs Inc 1425 SW 1st Ct Pompano Beach FL 33069-3247

VAUGHAN, EDWIN DARRACOTT, ...R., urologist, surgeon; b. Richmond, Va., May 13, 1939; s. Edwin Dar...cott and Blanche V. (Bashaw) V.; m. Virginia Anne Lloyd, June 30, 1962; ...ildren: Edwin Darracott III, Barbara Anderson. BS, Washington and Le... U., 1961; MD, U. Va., 1965, MS, 1969; DSc, Washington and Lee U., 198... Diplomate Am. Bd. Urology (trustee, v.p. 1988, pres. 1989). Intern Vande...ilt U., 1965-66, asst. resident, 1966-67; chief resident in urology U. Va., 19...-71, asst. prof. urology, 1973-75, assoc. prof., 1975-78, prof., 1978; clin. ...search fellow Columbia U., 1971-72, research assoc. dept. medicine, 1972-...; James J. Colt prof. urology, chmn. dept. urology Cornell U. Med. Coll., ...Y.C. and; attending urologist-in-chief N.Y. Hosp., N.Y.C., 1978—; sr. asso... dean clin. affairs Cornell U. Med. Coll., N.Y.C., 1993—, chmn. dept. urol...y, 1993—; mem sci. adv. bd. Nat. Kidney Found., 1977-81; sec.-treas. U...ogy Coun., 1977-80, chmn., 1980-81; mem. med. adv. bd. Coun. High ...ood Pressure, 1977. Editor: Seminars in Urology, 1983-95; assoc. editor ...vestigative Urology, 1977-78, mem. editorial bd., 1978-94; editor Campbel... Urology; contbr. articles on obstructive uropathy, renal hemodynamics, ...pertension to profl. jours. Recipient Research Career Devel. award NI... 1976-78; NIH tng. grantee, 1967-68; USPHS grantee, 1971-73, 74-77; Am. Heart Assn. grantee, 1976-79. Mem. ACS, AAAS, N.Y. Acad. Scis., Soc. Univ. Urologists, Am. Urol. Assn. (chmn. rsch. com. 1980-91, treas. N.Y. ...t. 1985, v.p. N.Y. sect. 1986, pres. N.Y. sect. 1987, Golden Cystoscope a...rd 1981, bd. dirs. 1992-96, Disting. Contbn. award 1992), Urol. Soc. A...stralasia (hon.), Soc. Exptl. Biology and Medicine, Soc. Univ. Surgeons, Soc. Internat. Urology, Am. Found. Urol. Disease (pres. 1987-92), Nat. K...ney and Urol. Disease Adv. Bd. (dep. chmn.), Intersoc. for Kidney and Urol. Disease Rsch. (chmn. 1987), Am. Assn. Genito-Urinary Surgeons ...arringen medal 1993), Am. Surg. Assn., Sigma Xi, Alpha Omega Alpha ...ward 1976), Omicron Delta Kappa (award 1981). Home: 1165 Park Ave ...t 6A New York NY 10128-1210 Office: 525 E 68th St New York NY 10... -4873

VAUGHAN, JONATHAN, psychologist; b. ...w Haven, June 10, 1944; s. Victor Clarence and Deborah (Cloud) V.; m. ...irginia Gray, July 2, 1968; children: Joseph, Alexander. BA, Swarthmore Coll., 1966; MA Brown U., 1968, PhD, 1970. Prof. Hamilton Coll., Clin..., N.Y., 1971—; vis. scholar Univ. Oreg., 1981-83, Univ. Mass., 1987-94, Pa. State U., 1995—; computing psychology dir. Carnegie Mellon Univ., 1990—. Predoctoral fellow NSF, Brown Univ., 1967-70; Rsch. grantee NIMH, Hamilton Coll., 1974, 76-80; recipient Rsch. Svc. award NIMH, Univ. Oreg. 1981-83, Rsch. Opportunity award NSF, Univ. Mass., 1988—. Mem. APA, Am. Psychol. Soc., Psychonomics Soc., Soc. for Computers in Psychol...y (pres. 1990-91). Office: Hamilton Coll Psychology Dept Clinton NY 13323

VAUGHAN, VICTOR CLARENCE, III, ph...ician, educator; b. Toledo, July 19, 1919; s. Warren Taylor and Emm... Elizabeth (Heath) V.; m. Deborah Cloud, Dec. 27, 1941; children: Jona..., Judith (dec.), Sarah Fox Sayre, Joanna; m. Iris Figarsky Litt, June 14, 1...7. A.B., Harvard U., 1940, M.D., 1951. Diplomate Am. Bd. Pediatrics (c... 1960-65, 68-73 sec. 1963-65, pres. 1973), Am. Bd. Allergy and Immunc...gy (treas. 1978-80). Intern Mass. Gen. Hosp., Boston, 1943; resident in ...iatrics New Haven Hosp., 1944-47; research fellow in pediatrics Harvar... Children's Hosp., Boston, 1947-49; instr., then asst. prof. pediatrics Yale U. Sch. Medicine, 1949-52; assoc. prof. pediatrics Temple U. Sch. Medic..., 1952-57, prof., 1964-87, chmn. dept., 1964-76; prof., chmn. dept. pediat... Med. Coll. Ga., Augusta, 1957-64; adj. prof. pediatrics U. Pa. Sch. M...icine, 1985-87; clin. prof. pediatrics Stanford U. Sch. Medicine, Calif., ...88—; med. dir. St. Christopher's Hosp. for Children, Phila., 1964-76; ... fellow Nat. Bd. Med. Examiners, 1977-81, sr. med. evaluation officer, 19...-87; cons. Nat. Inst. Child Health and Human Devel., NIH, 1963-70. Me... AMA, Am. Pediatric Soc., Soc. Pediatric Research (v.p. 1964-65), Am. ...d. Pediatrics, Am. Acad. Allergy and Immunology, Am. Soc. for Human ...enetics, Friends Med. Soc. Mem. Soc. of Friends. Address: 350 El Camin... Carmel Valley CA 93924-9635

VAUGHAN KROEKER, NADINE, psycholog...; b. Tampa, Fla., Aug. 30, 1947; d. Joseph Marcus and Velna Pearl (Jones) Williams; m. E.L. Vaughan III, 1966 (div. Aug. 1976); children: E.L. ...ughan, Heather Vaughan Oyarzun; m. Dennis Wayne Kroeker, Apr. 9, 1...2 (div. Jan. 1994); 1 child, Melanie Sage. BA in Criminal Justice, U. South... Fla., 1974, MA with honors in Rehab. Counseling, 1975; PhD in Psycholog... Saybrook Inst., 1990. Lic. clin. psychologist, Calif., Wash. Co-founder Women's Resource Ctr., Tampa, Fla., 1973—; exec. dir. Vocare Found... Oakland, Calif. 1976-78; cmty. and organizational devel. specialist State of Calif., Berkeley, Sacramento, 1978-82; cons., trainer N. Vaughan K...ker, PhD, 1982—, APA Hope Program, 1994—; mem. adj. faculty psych...gy Peninsula Coll. Mem. APA, Divsns. Health Psychology and Humanist... Psychology. Democrat.

VAUGHEN, JUSTINE L., rehabilitation hosp... medical professional; b. Wilmington, Del., Apr. 21, 1930; d. John Victo... and Charlotte (Leicht) V.; m. Richard M. Fry, June 26, 1955; children: Martha Hilary Morrow, Amanda Tung. BS, Stetson U., 1950; MD, Te...ple U., 1954. Diplomate Am. Bd. Physical Medicine and Rehab. Reside... physical medicine, rehab. U. Mich., Ann Arbor, 1954-59; asst. prof. physic... medicine, rehab. U. Mich. Hosp., Ann Arbor, 1959-60; private practice Ga...esville, Fla., 1961—; chief rehab. med. svc. VA Med. Ctr., Gainesville, Fla., ...971—; med. dir. Upreach Rehab. Hosp., Gainesville, Fla., 1986-95; co-clin. prof. U. Fla., Gainesville, 1967—; cons. Vocat. Rehab., State Fla., 1986—; adv. coun. State Divsn. Vocat. Rehab., Tallahassee, 1980-95. Pres. D.A...E., Gainesville, 1992-94; bd. dirs. Altrusa House, Gainesville, 1991—. Me... AMA, Am. Acad. Phys. Medicine and Rehab., Fla. Soc. Phys. Medicine and Rehab. (pres. 1992-94), Fla. Med. Assn., Altrusa Internat., Am. Assn. E...ctrodiagnostic Medicine. Office: Rehab Medicine Assoc 4881 NW 8th Ave ... 2 Gainesville FL 32605

VAUGHN, ANDREW I.S., occupational heal... physician; b. Mwanza, Tanzania. BS magna cum laude, U. Ga., 1974; MD, Med. Coll. Ga., 1978; MPH, Johns Hopkins U., 1989. Diplomate Am. ... Internal Medicine, Am. Bd. Preventive Medicine. Staff internist Royal A... Force Base, Lakenheath, England, 1982-84; dir. spl. care unit, chief intern... medicine USAF Hosp., Portsmouth, N.H., 1984-88; fellow in occpl. me...cine Johns Hopkins U., Balt., 1991; sr. occupl. physician Eastman Kodak, Rochester, N.Y., 1991—. Fellow Am. Coll. Preventive Medicine; mem. Am. Coll. Occupation & Environ. Medicine (sect. pres. 1993-94), N.Y. Upstat... Coll. Occupl. & Environ. Medicine (pres. 1995-96).

VAUGHN, DONALD REID, urologist; b. Me...phis, Jan. 17, 1944; s. Darwin Penn and Dorothy Jane (Fuller) V.; m. ...ice Marie Hart, July 5, 1969; children: Joel, Jeremy, Amanda. BS in Eng...g., USAF Acad., 1966; M in Aerospace Ops. Mgmt., U. So. Calif., 1969; MD, U. Tenn., Memphis, 1975. Diplomate Am. Bd. Urology. Intern Bapt... Hosp., Memphis, 1975-76; resident in urology U. Tenn., Memphis, 1976-...; officer USAF Satellite Test Facility, Sunnyvale, Calif., 1966-70; urologi... pvt. practice Drs. Long and Vaughn, PA, Greenville, S.C., 1980—; chmn. dept. urology Greenville Meml. Hosp., 1994-95, St. Francis Hosp., 1994-95. Bd. dirs. Child Evangelism Fellowship, 1992—, S.C. Physician's Resource Coun., 1996—. Fellow Am. Coll. Surgeons; mem. AMA, S.C. Med. Ass..., Am. Urol. Assn. Baptist. Office: Drs Long & Vaughn PA 18 Memorial ...edical Dr Greenville SC 29605

VAUGHN, LISA DAWN, family physician, educa...; b. Ashland, Ky., May 10, 1961; d. Charles Clinton and Mildred Darl...e (Cantrell) V. AS in Biology, U. Ky., 1981, BS in Zoology, 1983; DO, W.Va. Sch. Osteo. Medicine, 1988. Diplomate Nat. Osteo. Med. E... Gen. intern Doctors Hosp. Inc., Massillon, Ohio, 1988-89; family practi... resident Doctors Hosp. Inc., Massillon, 1989-91; emergency room phys...an Coastal Emergency Svcs., Snowpark, Ohio, 1989-90; urgent care phys...an Acute Care Specialists, Akron, Ohio, 1991; physician Portage Fami... Practice Clinic, North Canton, Ohio, 1991-95, First Care Family Health... Immediate Care Ctr., Canton, Ohio, 1995-95; dir. occupl. medicine Fir... Care, Canton, 1996—; clin. asst. faculty Ohio U. Coll. Medicine, Athens, ...90-91, adj. clin. faculty, 1992—; asst. dir. family practice residency Ohio U. Coll. Medicine-Doctors Hosp. Inc., Massillon, 1992-95; urgent CARE physician First Care, Canton, Ohio, 1995—; med. dir. family home health svc. Doctors Hosp., 1992-94, chmn. dept. family medicine, 1994-95; med. advisor Boy Scouts Med. Explorers, Massillon, 1989-90; med. career advisor Girl Scouts Career Day, Canton, 1990; affiliate physician Cleve. Clinic, 1991—. Contbr. poems. Col. Ky. Cols. Assn., Ashland, 1989—; vol. United Way of Stark County, 1990-91. Mem. Cleve. Clinic Found. (affiliate physician), AMA, Am. Coll. Gen. Practitioners, Am. Osteo. Assn. (cert.), Ohio State Med. Assn., W.Va. Soc. Osteo. Medicine, Stark County Med. Soc., Sigma Sigma Phi (sec. 1985-86). Democrat. Office: First Care 4612 Tuscarawas St W Canton OH 44708

VAUGHT, RICHARD LOREN, urologist; b. Ind., Oct. 28, 1933; s. Loren Judson and Bernice Rose (Bridges) V.; widowed, July 1987; children: Megan, Niles, Barbara, Mary; m. Nancy Lee Gusa, Aug. 1992. AB in Anatomy and Physiology, Ind. U., 1955; MD, Ind. U., Indpls., 1958. Diplomate Am. Bd. Urology. Intern, then resident in gen. surgery U.S. Naval Hosp., St. Albans, N.Y., 1958-60, resident in urology, 1960-63; spl. fellow Sloan Kettering Meml. Hosp. for Cancer and Allied Diseases, N.Y.C., 1962; pediatric urology observer Babies Hosp., Columbia-Presbyn. Med. Ctr., N.Y.C., 1962; head urology U.S. Naval Hosp., Beaufort, S.C., 1963-65. asst. chief urology, head pediatric urology U.S. Naval Hosp., San Diego, 1965-68; pvt. practice Plaza Urol., Sioux City; med. dir. dept. hyperbaric medicine St. Luke's Regional Med. Ctr., Sioux City, 1988-95; pres., chmn. bd. dirs. Care Choices of Siouxland, Sioux City, 1987-94; med. dir. Male Impotence Clinic, Marian Health Ctr., Sioux City, 1995—. Organizer telecommunications system for deaf, Siouxland, 1983. Lt. comdr. USN, 1958-68. Fellow ACS, Internat. Soc. Cryosurgery, Am. Acad. Pediat.; mem. Am. Urol. Assn., Soc. Pediatric Urology, European Soc. Pediatric Urology (corr.), Undersea and Hyperbaric Medicine Soc., Am. Coll. Hyperbaric Medicine, Am. Soc. Laser Medicine and Surgery, Am. Lithotripsy Soc., Woodbury County Med. Soc. (pres.), Am. Confedn. Urology, Sertoma (Sertoman of Yr. award 1983). Home: 10 Cottonwood Landing South Sioux City NE 68776 Office: Plaza Urol PC 2800 Pierce St Ste 308 Sioux City IA 51104-3759

VAUX, DIANE RITCHEY, clinical psychologist; b. Cambridge, Mass., Nov. 2, 1942; d. John Arthur and Frances (Curtis) Ritchey; m. Walter Gregson Vaux, Jan. 15, 1983. BA, Ind. U., 1964, MA, 1965; MS, Drexel U., 1968, U. Pitts., 1975; PhD, U. Pitts., 1979. Lic. psychologist, Pa. Tchr. secondary Pitman (N.J.) High Sch., 1965-66; jr. cataloguer Drexel Library, Phila., 1966-67; reference librarian Free Library of Phila., 1968-69, coordinator young adult services, 1969-72; mental health therapist S.W. Communities Mental Health/Mental Retardation Ctr., Pitts., 1977-82; coordinator stepfamily services Families in Transition, Pitts., 1982-85; pvt. practice specializing in psychology Murrysville, Pa., 1985—. Charter mem. West Pa. Task Force on Women and Addictions, Pitts., 1981-86. Fellow Am. Psychol. Assn., Pa. Psychol. Assn.; mem. Acad. of Family Psychology, Am. Assn. of Marital and Family Therapists (clin.). Home: 3491 Ivy Ln Murrysville PA 15668-1606 Office: 4051 Old William Penn Hwy Murrysville PA 15668-1258

VAUX, DORA LOUISE, sperm bank official, consultant; b. White Pine, Mont., Aug. 8, 1922; d. Martin Tinus and Edna Ruth (Pyatt) Palmlund; m. Robert Glenn Vaux, Oct. 25, 1941; children: Jacqueline, Cheryl, Richard, Jeanette. Grad. high sch., Bothell, Wash. Photographer Busco-Nestor Studios, San Diego, 1961-68; owner, mgr. Vaux Floors & Interiors, San Diego, 1968-82; cons., mgr. Repository for Germinal Choice, Escondido, Calif., 1983-91; adminstr. Found. for the Continuity of Mankind, Spokane, 1991—. Republican. Home: 2727 S Skipworth Rd Spokane WA 99206 Office: Found Continuity of Mankind 1209 W 1st Ave Spokane WA 99204-0601

VAVALA, DOMENIC ANTHONY, medical scientist, educator, retired air force officer; b. Providence, Feb. 1, 1925; s. Salvatore and Maria (Grenci) V. BA, Brown U., 1947; MS, U. R.I., 1950; MA, Trinity U., San Antonio, 1954; PhD in Physiology, Accademia di Studi Superiori "Minerva", Italy, 1957; MEd, U. Houston, 1958; DSc (hon.), Nobile Accademia di Santa Teodora Imperatrice, Rome, 1966, DMS (hon.), 1970; DPH (hon.), Nobile Accademia di Santa Teodora Imperatrice, 1983; D Pedagogy (hon.), Studiorum Universitas Constantiniana of Sovrano Ordine Constantiniano di San Giorgio, Rome, 1966; DEd (hon.), Imperiale Accademia di San Cirillo, Pomezia, Italy, 1977; LittD, Univ. Internazionale Sveva "Frederick II", Bergamo, Italy, 1979; D Health Scis. (hon.), Johnson & Wales U., 1993. Research asst. tumor research U. R.I., also asst. entomol. research, 1950; research asst. pharmacology Boston U. Sch. Medicine, 1950-51; commd. 2d lt. med. service USAF, 1951, advanced through grades to lt. col., 1968; physiologist cold injury research team Army Med. Research Lab., Osaka (Japan) Army Hosp., 1951-52; research aviation physiologist USAF Sch. Aviation Medicine, Randolph AFB, Tex., 1952-54, 3605th USAF Hosp., Ellington AFB, Tex., 1955-57; chief physiol. tng. 3605th USAF Hosp., 1957; cons. aviation physiology, film prodn. dept. U. Houston, 1956; research aviation physiologist, head acad. sect. dept. physiol. tng. USAF Hosp., Lackland AFB, Tex., 1957-58; vis. prof. physiology Incarnate Word Coll., San Antonio, 1958; research aviation physiologist, chief physiol. tng. comdr. 832d Physiol. Tng. Flight, 832d Tactical Hosp., Cannon AFB, N.Mex., 1958-65; adj. faculty mem. Eastern N.Mex. U., Portales, 1959-64; instr. adult edn. div. Clovis (N.Mex.) mcpl. schs., 1960; research aviation physiologist, comdr. 15th Physiol. Tng. Flight, 824th USAF Dispensary, Kadena Air Base, Okinawa, 1965-66; research scientist, directorate fgn. tech., aerospace med. div. Brooks AFB, Tex., 1966-68; chief R & D support and interface div., dep. dir. for fgn. tech., 1968-70; adj. instr. Johnson & Wales U., Providence, 1973-74; instr. humanities Johnson and Wales U., Providence, 1974-75, asst. prof. humanities, 1975-77, prof. health scis. and nutrition, 1977-93, prof. emeritus, 1993—, coord. biomed. and behavioral scis. Day Coll. div., 1973-75, psychology coord. vets. div. Coll. Continuing Edn., 1974-76, assoc. dean adj. faculty, 1975, dean faculty, 1975-77, coord. acad. devel., 1977-78, dir. musical series, 1990—, curator Chapel Empress St. Theodora, 1992—; pres. corp., chmn. bd. Sovereign Constantinian Order of St. George, Inc., R.I., 1986—; pres. R.I. Corp., chmn. bd. dirs., 1988; instr. anatomy, physiology and med. terminology R.I. Hosp., Providence, R.I., 1987-90. Writer, producer: (TV Series) Your Body in Flight, Sta. KUHT, Houston, 1956; (TV series) Highway to Health, Okinawa, 1965; editor-in-chief: NADUS Jour., 1963-85; compiled and edited: Fifty Years of Progress of Soviet Medicine, 1917-67; abstractor: Am. Chem. Soc., 1963-74. Contbr. articles to profl. jours. Trustee, Gov. Ctr. Sch., Providence, 1979-85; mem. scholarship com. St. Sahag and, St. Mesrob Armenian Apostolic Ch., Providence. Served with AUS, 1943-44. Recipient Disting. Svc. award Clovis (N.Mex.) Jaycees, 1959, Acad. Palms Gold medal Accademia di Studi Superior "Minerva", 1960, citation from chief chaplains USAF, 1970, commendation medal USAF, 1970, chief biomed. scientist insignia, biomed. scis. corps USAF Med. Svc., 1970, spl. faculty citation Johnson and Wales U., 1981; academician divsn. scis. Accademia di Studi Superiori "Minerva", 1960; Min. Plenipotentiary for U.S. of Nobile Accademia di Santa Teodora Imperatrice, Rome, 1967, rector pro tempore, 1980; decorated knight grand officer Merit Class, Sovereign Constantinian Order St. George, Rome, 1969, Knight of Grand Cross with Constantinian neckchair, Justice Class, Sovereign Constantinian Order of St. George, 1969, Knight of Grand Cordon Justice Class, Order of Teutonic Knig Sao Paulo, 1986, Knight of Grand Cross Justice Class, Mil. Order St. Gereon, Sao Paulo, 1986, Knight of Grand Cross Justice Class, Mil. and Hospitalier Order St Jean d'Acre and St. Thomas, Capua, Italy, 1987, Knight of Grand Cross Justice Class, Mil. and Hospitalier Order St. Mary of Bethlehem, Capua, 1987, Ednl. Professionalism award Domei Toastmasters Internat., 1965; named Magnificent Rector and Pres. of the Constantinian U. (Studiorum Universitas Constantiniana), Italy, 1970. Fellow AAAS, Tex. Acad. Sci., Royal Soc. Health (London), Am. Inst. Chemists; mem. Assn. Mil. Surgeons U.S., Nat. Assn. Doctors U.S. (founder 1958, sec.-treas. 1958-85, editor-in-chief The Nadus Jour. 1963-68), Accademia di San Cirillo Italy (hon.), N.Y. Acad. Scis., Phi Sigma, Kappa Delta Pi, Phi Kappa Phi, Alpha Beta Kappa (charter mem., pres. R.I. Alpha chpt. Johnson & Wales U. 1984-92). Home: 30 Oaklawn Ave Apt 219 Cranston RI 02920-9319

VAZIRI, NOSRATOLA DABIR, internist, nephrologist, educator; b. Tehran, Iran, Oct. 13, 1939; came to U.S., 1969, naturalized, 1977; s. Abbas and Tahera V. M.D., Tehran U., 1966. Diplomate: Am. Bd. Internal Medicine, Am. Bd. Nephrology. Intern Cook County Hosp., Chgo., 1969-70; resident Berkshire Med. Ctr., Pittsfield, Mass., 1970-71, Wadsworth VA Med. Ctr., 1971-72, UCLA Med. Ctr., 1972-74; prof. medicine U. Calif.-

Irvine, 1979—, chief nephrology div., 1977—, dir. hemodialysis unit, 1977—, vice chmn. dept. medicine, 1982—; chmn. dept. medicine, 1994—; mem. sci. adv. council Nat. Kidney Found., 1977—. Contbr. numerous articles to med. jours. Recipient Golden Apple award, 1977; named outstanding tchr. U. Calif-Irvine, 1975, 78, 79, 80, 82. Fellow ACP; mem. Am. Soc. Nephrology, Am. Paraplegia Soc. (pres. 1992-94), Western Assn. Physicians, Assn. Profs. of Medicine, Alpha Omega Alpha. Home: 66 Balboa Cv Newport Beach CA 92663-3226 Office: U Calif Irvine Med Ctr Div Nephrology Dept Medicine 101 City Dr Orange CA 92668

VÁZQUEZ, LOUIE, psychology educator, counselor, family therapist; b. Luquillo, P.R., Aug. 28, 1934; s. Isidoro and Sabat Vázquez; m. Evropi Aslanidou, June 3, 1960; children: Alèxandros, Myron, Margarita. BA in Psychology, Temple U., 1963; MEd, U. Tenn., Chattanooga, 1967. Cert. profl. counselor, Tenn. Psychiat. social worker Moccasin Bend Health Inst., Chattanooga, 1954-64; caseworker Travelers Aid Soc., Chattanooga, 1964-67; counselor, asst. prof. psychology Cleveland (Tenn.) C.C., 1976—; cons., workshop and seminar presenter Dept. Pub. Health, Chattanooga, Tenn. Commn. on Aging, Athens (Tenn.) Convalescent Ctr., Bradley County Nursing Home, Cleveland, numerous others. Past pres. Cen. High Sch. PTA, Chattanooga; soloist, Sunday sch. tchr. United Meth. Ch., Chattanooga. With USN, 1954-58. Recipient Gov.'s Outstanding Tennessean award, 1974, Employee of Yr. award Tenn. Dept. Mental Health, 1974, Outstanding Profl. in Human Svcs. award. Fellow Internat. Coun. on Sex Edn. and Parenthood; mem. AAUP, Am. Assn. Marriage and Family Therapists, Internat. Club (pres.). Home: 9205 Ramblewood Dr Harrison TN 37341-9506 Office: Cleveland State C C Adkisson Dr Cleveland TN 37311

VAZQUEZ-PLARD, JULIAN, endocrinologist; b. San Juan, P.R., Oct. 8, 1937; s. Julian and Maria (Plard) V.; m. Wilma Vincenty, Nov. 12, 1962; children: Ricardo and Laura. BS, U. P.R., San Juan, 1959, MD, 1963. Diplomate Am. Bd. Internal Medicine. Intern Upstate Med. Ctr., Syracuse, N.Y., 1963-64; resident in internal medicine U. P.R., 1964-66, fellow in endocrinology, 1966-67, 69-70, instr., 1970-73, clin. asst. prof., 1973-76; pvt. practice San Juan, 1971—; dir. med. edn. Auxilio Mutuo Hosp., San Juan, 1976-80, head endocrinology, asst. chief medicine, 1984—. Fellow ACP (bd. dirs. 1991), mem. Am. Diabetes Assn., P.R. Med. Assn., Soc. Endocrinologia P.R. Office: 730 Ponce de Leon San Juan PR 00918

VEATCH, JOHN WILLIAM, speech pathologist; b. Mitchell, S.D., Dec. 9, 1923; s. William Homer and Helen Gwendolyn (Lowther) V.; m. Doris Lavelle Guthrie (dec. 1978); children: Dean, Joan; m. Winnifred Ann Sawin, 1982 (div. 1992); m. Joy Sullivan, Aug. 21, 1993. BA in Speech, Wash. State U., 1946, BEd, 1951; MA in Speech, U. Wash., 1950; DEd, U. Idaho, 1970. Pvt. practice speech pathology Spokane, Wash., 1950-79; pvt. practice speech pathology and ednl. cons. Tacoma, 1980—; dir. rsch., edn. & bus. Sullivan Ctr. & Phys. Therapy, Puyallup, Wash., 1993—; dir. rsch. edn. and bus. Sullivan Ctr. & Physical Therapy, Puyallup, Wash., 1993—; lectr. in speech pathology Gonzaga U., Spokane, Wash., 1963-70; adj. prof. Wash. State U., 1972-77, Applied Psychology, Eastern Wash. U., 1977; chief exec. officer and dir. rsch. Espial Inst., Tacoma, 1982-92; mem. home health adv. bd. Spokane County Health Dept., past. pres. Wash. State Health Dept. Crippled Children's Svc. Adv. Bd. Maxillofacial Defects; co-dir. Sullivan Ctr., 1992—; cons. in field; workshops and training in alternative medicine techniques; co-developer V.E.A.T.C.H. Technique. Author: (with D. Hughes) Teacher Qualities, 1947; (test profiles) Personal Stress Balance Profile, 1982, Info. Processing Style, 1984, The Deep Screening Profile of Tongue Thrusting Activity, 1985, The Tongue Thrust Screening Test, 1986, Learning Style Profile, 1986; writer, contbr. guides, workbooks, studies and films in field. Fellow Northwest Acad. Speech Pathology (pres. 1978-82, 86-91); mem. Am. Speech-Lang.-Hearing Assn. (life, pres. bd. Oakbridge U. 1989-90). Office: 2717 E Main Ave Puyallup WA 98372-3165

VECCHIARELLI, LORETTA MARIE, physician assistant, educator; b. Springfield, Mass., Mar. 15, 1957; d. Richard Nicholas and Therese Marie (Craven) V. BS, Alderson-Broaddus Coll., Philippi, W. Va., 1979; MS, Springfield Coll., 1986, cert. advanced grad. studies, 1986. Rehab. counselor Hartford (Conn.) Easter Seals, 1986-89, Am. Internat. Health and Rehab. Svcs., Andover, Mass., 1989-90; med. case mgr. The Rehab. Hosp. Western New Eng., Ludlow, Mass., 1990-93; dir. med. case mgmt. CompWorks, Springfield, Mass., 1993-94; asst. prof. allied health scis. Springfield Coll., 1994—; consumer rep. Agy. for Health Care Policy and Rsch., Washington, D.C., 1990-94. Fellow Am. Acad. Physician Assts., Mass. Assn. Physician Assts., Nat. Rehab. Assn. Office: Springfield Coll 263 Alden St Springfield MA 01109-3797

VEDDER, NICHOLAS BLAIR, surgeon, researcher; b. Chgo., Mar. 27, 1955; s. Beverly Blair and Geraldine (Bovbjerg) V.; m. susan Russell Heckbert, June 26, 1978; children: Katherine Anne, Nicholas Russell. BS with distinction in Biology, Stanford U., 1977; MD, Case Western Res. U., 1981. Diplomate Am. Bd. Surgery with added qualification in hand surgery, Am. Bd. Plastic Surgery, Nat. Bd. Med. Examiners; lic. physician, Wash., Mass. Resident in surgery U. Wash., Seattle, 1981-86, NIH rsch. fellow, 1986-88, hand surgery fellow, 1990-91, asst. prof. plastic surger and orthop., 1991-95, assoc. prof., 1995—; resident in plastic surgery Mass. Gen. Hosp., Boston, 1988-90; attending surgeon U. Wash. Hosps., 1990—, Harborview Med. Ctr., U. Wash. Med. Ctr., Children's Hosp. and Med. Ctr., VA Med. Ctr.; lectr. in field; vis. prof. Johns Hopkins U., Balt., 1991, Nat. Heart and Lung Inst., London, 1991, So. Ill. U., 1991. Contbr. numerous articles to profl. jours., chpts. to books; referee Jour. Clin. Investigation, Am. rev. of Respiratory Diseases, Jour. Surg. Rsch., Jour. Pharmacology and Exptl. Therapeutics, Jour. of trauma, Plastic and Reconstructive Surgery, Annals of Plastic Surgery. Recipient Peter Gingrass award Plastic Surgery Rsch. Coun., 1995; ACS First Prize Nat. scholar, 1987; grantee NIH, 1988-89, 89-94, 91-92, 95—, Genentech, Inc., 1991-93, Biomembrante Inst., 1993-94, Cell Therapeutics, Inc., 1995-96, CDC, G.D. Searle, Inc., 1995-96. Fellow ACS; mem. AAAS, Henry N. Harkins Surg. Soc., N.W. Soc. Plastic Surgeons, Wash. Soc. Plastic Surgeons, seattle Surg. Soc., King County Med. Soc., Wash. Med. Soc., Assn. Acad. Chmn. Plastic Surgery, Am. assn. Hand Surgery, Assn. Acad. Surgery, Am. Soc. Plastic and Reconstructive Surgeons (Robert H. Ivy award 1994), Am. Soc. Surgery or the Hand, Plastic Surgery Ednl. Found., Sigma Xi. Office: Harbor View Med Ctr Surg ZA Seattle WA 98104*

VEGA, ELI SAMUEL, nurse anesthetist; b. Guayama, P.R., Oct. 26, 1945; came to U.S., 1979; m. Maria J. Ramos, Apr. 22, 1972; children: Marieely, Samarys. Diploma in Nursing, Bella Vista Sch. Nursing, Mayaguez, P.R., 1971; cert. in Anesthesia, Damas Hosp., Ponce, P.R., 1973; posgrad., U. West Fla., 1990-92. RN. Staff nurse Bella Vista Hosp., Mayaguez, P.R., 1974-79; commd. lt. (j.g.) USN, 1979, advanced through grades to comdr., 1993; staff nurse anesthetist U.S. Naval Hosp., San Diego, 1979-81; head anesthetiology dept. U.S. Naval Hosp., Twentynine Palms, Calif., 1981-84; staff nurse anesthetist U.S. Naval Hosp., Jacksonville, Fla., 1984-87; asst. anesthesia dept. head U.S. Naval Hosp., Rota, Spain, 1987-90; staff nurse anesthetist U.S. Naval Hosp., Pensacola, Fla., 1990-94; asst. anesthesia dept. head Naval Hosp. Keflavik, Iceland, 1994-95; sr. nurse anesthetist Naval Hosp., Pensacola, Fla., 1995—, 1996—. Developer, instr. intravenous therapy program U.S. Naval Hosp., Rota, Spain, 1989. Decorated two Navy commendation medals. Mem. Am. Assn. Nurse Anesthetists, Fla. Nurse Anesthetist Assn., P.R. Nurse Anesthetist Assn. (v.p. 1976-77). Home: 3691 Monteigne Dr Pensacola FL 32504-4538

VEGA, JOSE GUADALUPE, psychologist, clinical director; b. San Benito, Tex., June 4, 1953; s. Jose Guadalupe and Bertha (Saenz) V.; children: Lilian Anna, Jose Guadalupe III; m. Alberta L. Valdez, Oct. 5, 1990. BA, Pan. Am. U., Edinburg, Tex., 1975; MA, U. Denver, 1976, PhD, 1979. Lic. psychologist, Colo., 1983, profl. counselor, Tex., 1982; diplomate Am. Bd. Med. Psychotherapists, Am. Bd. Vocat. Neuropsychology, Am. Bd. Profl. Disability Cons., Am bd., Forensic Examiners; cert. adminstrn. Halstead-Reitan Neuropsychology test batteries. With Oasis of Chandala, Denver, 1978-79, Maytag-Emrick Clinic, Aurora, Colo., 1979; psychologist Spanish Peaks Mental Health Ctr., Pueblo, Colo., 1980-85; pvt. practice Assocs. for Psychotherapy and Edn., Inc., 1985-86; co-owner Affiliates in Counseling, Psychol. Assessment and Consultation, Inc., Pueblo, 1986-87; psychologist Parkview Psychol. Testing Clinic, Pueblo, 1987-93, Colo. Dept. Corrections, 1994—; pvt. practice, Pueblo, 1993—; mem. state grievance bd. Psychology Augment Panel, 1988-95. Active Colo. Inst. Chicano Mental Health Community Youth Orgn., Boys Club Pueblo. Mem. Am. Psychol. Assn., Nat. Acad. Neuropsychology, Internat. Neuropsychol. Soc., Colo. Neuropsychol. Soc., Am. counseling Assn., Health and Human Services Com. City of Pueblo, Colo. Psychol. Assn. (bd. dirs. non-metro rep. 1995—), Nat. Hispanic Psychol. Assn., Hispanic Neuropsychological Soc., Phi Delta Kappa, Kappa Delta Pi. Democrat. Roman Catholic.ocrat. Roman Catholic. Office: 2705 N Elizabeth St Pueblo CO 81003-3643

VEHAUN, MARSHALL JERRY, emergency services director; b. Asheville, N.C., Jan. 17, 1943; s. Marshall Rom and Bernez (Lominac) VeH.; m. Gail Stepp, Apr. 1, 1970 (div.); m. Genieve Elizabeth Penland, Aug. 10, 1974. Grad., U. N.C., Asheville, 1963, Gupton Coll., 1964. Mortician Anders-Rice Funeral Home, Asheville, 1964-66, Morris Funeral Home, Asheville, 1966-70; mgr. Tamiami Plumbing Co., Miami, Fla., 1970-72; dir. emergency svcs. County of Buncombe, Asheville, 1972—; mem. emergency med. svcs. adv. coun. State of N.C., Raleigh, 1985-93; chmn. bd. Asheville Area Resque Squad, 1988-95; mem. environ. affairs bd. County of Buncombe. Pres. Western N.C. Kidney Found., Asheville, 1975-76; co-chmn. N.C. 2000 Com., Asheville, 1982-83; bd. dirs. MANNA Food Bank, Asheville, 1978-80, N.C. State Emergency Response Commn., 1992-94. Mem. Am. Soc. Profl. Emergency Planners, Nat. Coordinating Coun. on Emergency Mgmt. (pres. region IV 1991-92, pres. 1995-96), N.C. Assn. Emergency Med. Svc. Adminstrs. (treas. 1987-89), We. Carolina Safety Coun. (bd. dirs. 1978—), N.C. Emergency Mgmt. Assn. (pres. 1976, 84), Kiwanis (pres. 1964—), Mason, Moose. Republican. Baptist. Home: 35 Beverly Rd Asheville NC 28806-4506

VEILLE, JEAN-CLAUDE, maternal-fetal medicine physician, educator; came to U.S., 1982; m. Beatrice Buehler; children: Olivier, Xavier, Patrique. BS, McGill U., 1971; MD, U. Montpellier, France, 1977. Fellow in maternal-fetal medicine Oreg. Health Scis., Portland, 1982-84; from asst. prof. to assoc. prof. Case Western Res. U., Cleve., 1984-90; chief maternal, fetal medicine Case Western Reserve U., Cleve., 1989-90; assoc. prof., dir. maternal fetal med. fellowship program Bowman Gray Sch. Medicine, Winston-Salem, N.C., 1990-95, prof., 1995—. Contbr. articles to med. jours. Grantee NIH, 1991—. Office: Bowman Gray Sch Medicine Medical Center Blvd Winston Salem NC 27157

VEIS, JUDITH H., nephrologist; b. Chgo., Apr. 11, 1958; d. Arthur and Eve (Zenner) V.; m. Andrew I. Gavil, Oct. 15, 1983; children: Justin Veis Gavil, Noah Veis Gavil. BS, Northwestern U., 1980; MD, Northwestern U., Chgo., 1982. Resident Northwestern U., Chgo., 1982-86; renal fellow U. Colo. Health Scis., Denver, 1986-89; nephrologist, dir. dialysis Dept. Vets. Affairs Med. Ctr., Washington, 1989-95; assoc. dir. nephrology Washington Hosp. Ctr., 1995—; profl. adv. bd. mem. Nat. Kidney Found. (Capital area), 1990-95, chair women's health task force, 1991—, edn. com., 1995—. Fellow ACP; mem. Am. Soc. Nephrology, Alpha Omega Alpha. Office: Washington Hosp Ctr 110 Irving St NW Washington DC 20010

VEIT, BRUCE CLINTON, immunologist, educator; b. Cleve., Aug. 22, 1942; s. Roland William and Rosalyn (Slater) V.; m. Carol Ann Greene, June 18, 1968 (div. July 1989); children: Heather Noel Veit Tyler, Brian Matthew; m. Linda Ve Moon. BA, Wittenberg U., 1965; MS, U. Cin., 1969, PhD, 1972. Postdoctoral fellow Scrips Clinic and Rsch. Found., La Jolla, Calif., 1972-76; asst. mem. St. Jude Children's Rsch. Hosp., Memphis, 1976-84; chief immunology and microbiol sect. William Beaumont Army Med. Ctr., El Paso, Tex., 1984—; adj. asst. prof. U. Tenn. Ctr. Health Sci., Memphis, 1976-85; adj. assoc. prof. U. Tex., El Paso, 1985—; cons. Tobacco Health Rsch. Inst., Lexington, 1983—; rev. bd. mem. El Paso Inst. Med. Rsch., 1988—. Contbr. articles to profl. jours. USPHS Cancer Rsch. fellow NIH, 1974-75; grantee Am. Cancer Soc., 1978-80, NIH, 1979-82. Mem. Am. Assn. Immunologists. Home: 2990 Trawood Dr Apt 13H El Paso TX 79936-4234 Office: William Beaumont Med Ctr Dept Clin Investigation El Paso TX 79920

VEIT, CLAIRICE GENE TIPTON, measurement psychologist; b. Monterey Park, Calif., Feb. 20, 1939; d. Albert Vern and Gene (Bunning) Tipton; children: Steven, Barbara, Laurette, Catherine. BA, UCLA, 1969, MA, 1970, PhD, 1974. Asst. prof. psychology Calif. State U., L.A., 1975-77, assoc. prof. psychology, 1977-80; rsch. psychologist The Rand Corp., Santa Monica, Calif., 1977—; rsch. cons. NATO Tech. Ctr., The Hague, The Netherlands, 1980-81; faculty Rand Grad Sch., Santa Monica, 1993—. Developer subjective transfer function (STF) method to complex sys. analysis. Mem. LWV, NOW, Mil. Ops. Rsch. Soc. Am., Inst. Mgmt. Sci., Soc. Med. Decision-Making, Soc. for Judgement and Decision-Making, L.A. World Affairs Coun., L.A. Opera League. Office: The Rand Corp 1700 Main St Santa Monica CA 90401-3208

VEKEMANS, MARCEL G.J., obstetrician/gynecologist; b. Mechelen, Belgium, Feb. 8, 1944; s. Emiel Veklemans and Georgina De Prins; m. Claire Verougstraete; children: Marc, Johan. MD, U. Libre Brussels, 1969. Cert. in tropical medicine, in epidemiology, stats., pub. health. Asst. gynecology St.-Pierre Hosp., Brussels, 1969-80, adj. chef clin., 1980—; aspirant Fonds Nat. Rsch. Sci., Belgium, 1973-76; resident advisor Rwanda John Snow Inc., 1993-95; charge de cours U. Libre Brussels, 1987—; cons. SHO, UNFPA, U.S. AID. Co-author: L-Avortement en Belgique et Dans Les Pays Voisins, 1992; editor, co-author: Planification Familiale Dans Les Pays en Voie de Developpement, 1993. Office: Hopital Saint-Pierre, Rue Haute 322, 1000 Brussels Belgium

VELANOVICH, VIC, surgeon; b. Dearborn, Mich., Jan. 17, 1961; s. Bogoljub and Rosa (Pavlovich) V.; m. Sara Nur Yildiz, July 2, 1984 (div. Feb. 1992); m. Lynda Kinsell Wright, Sept. 4, 1994; children: Irina Marie, Thomas Alexander. BA, U. Chgo., 1983; MD, Wayne State U., 1987. Diplomate Am. Bd. Surgery. Resident in surgery Madigan Army Med. Ctr., Tacoma, Wash., 1987-92; staff surgeon Ireland Army Hosp., Ft. Knox, Ky., 1992-96; sr. staff surgeon Henry Ford Hosp., Detroit, 1996—; clin. asst. prof. Uniformed Svcs. U., Bethesda, Md., 1993—. Served to maj. U.S. Army, 1987-96. Fellow Am. Coll. Surgeons, Southeastern Surg. Congress; mem. AMA, Soc. Am. Gastrointestinal Endoscopic Surgeons, Assn. Mil. Surgeons (Sir Henry Wellcome Prize, 1995). Office: Divsn Gen Surgery Henry Ford Hosp 2799 W Grand Blvd Detroit MI 48202-2689

VELARDE, ROBERT M., nurse, hospital administrator, educator; b. Tampa, Fla., Oct. 28, 1950; s. Jesus Manuel and Angela (Velasco) V. Surg. technician, St. Petersburg Jr. Coll., 1969; AS in Nursing, Hillsborough C.C., Tampa, 1972; BSN, Samford U., 1975; M. Pub. Adminstrn., Golden Gate U., 1980. RN, Fla., Ala.; cert. in nursing adminstrn. advanced Am. Nurses Assn.; cert. surg. technologist Assn. Surg. Technologists. Surg. technologist attendant Centro Espanol Hosp., Tampa, 1965-72, nursing supr., 1972-74, asst. adminstr. patient svcs., 1975-85, adminstr., chief exec. officer, 1985-87; charge nurse emergency room Brookwood Med. Ctr., Birmingham, Ala., 1974-75; dept. chair health sci. edn. Brewster Tech. Ctr., Tampa, Fla., 1989—; health occupations instr. Armwood H.S., Seffner, Fla., 1988-89; nurse clinician-Critical Care Am., 1989-94; mem. blue ribbon task force to Fla. Bd. Nursing, 1982-83; mem. adv. bd. Fla. Nursing News. Recipient award from bd. dirs. Centro Espanol Hosp., 1977; Contbns. to Nursing award Minority Nurses Assn., 1979. Mem. ASCD, AVA (health occupations edn. divsn., policy bd. 1994—), FNA (Dist. #4, sec. 1993-95), Nursing Educators Assn. Tampa, Health Occupations Students Am., Am. Orgn. Nurse Execs., Tampa Bay Orgn. Nurse Execs., ANA, Nat. Assn. Health Occupations Tchrs., Fla. Nurses Assn., Nurses House, Inc., Am. Vocat. Assn., ARC, Fla. Vocat. Assn., Health Occupations Educators Fla. (state sec. 1990-91, pres. elect 1993-95, pres., 1995—), Fla. Assn. Supervision & Curriculum Devel., Hillsborough Tech., Career, Adult Assn., Assn. Nurses in AIDS Care, Sigma Theta Tau (chpt. v.p. 1983-84). Democrat. Home: 2618 W St John St Tampa FL 33607-2942

VELARDO, JOSEPH THOMAS, molecular biology and endocrinology educator; b. Newark, Jan. 27, 1923; s. Michael Arthur and Antoinette (Iacullo) V.; m. Forresta M. Monica Power, Aug. 12, 1948 (dec. July 1976). AB, U. No. Colo., 1948; SM, Miami U., 1949; PhD, Harvard U., 1952. Rsch. fellow in biology and endocrinology Harvard U., Cambridge, Mass., 1952-53; rsch. assoc. in pathology, ob-gyn. and surgery Sch. Medicine Harvard U., Boston, 1953-55; asst. in surgery Peter Bent Brigham and Women's Hosp., Boston, 1954-55; asst. prof. anatomy and endocrinology Sch. Medicine, Yale U., New Haven, 1955-61; prof. anatomy, chmn. dept. N.Y. Med. Coll., N.Y.C., 1961-62; cons. N.Y. Fertility Inst., 1961-62; dir. Inst. for Study Human Reprodn., Cleve., 1962-67; prof. biology John Carroll U., Cleve., 1962-67; mem. rsch. and edn. divs. Saint Ann Obstetric and Gynecologic Hosp., Cleve., 1962-67; head dept. rsch. Saint Ann Hosp., Cleve., 1964-67; prof. anatomy Stritch Sch. Medicine Loyola U., Chgo., 1967-88, chmn. dept. anatomy Stritch Sch. of Medicine, 1967-73; pres. Internat. Basic and Biol.-Biomed. Curricula, Lombard, Ill., 1979—; course moderator laparoscopy Brazil-Israel Congress on Fertility and Sterility, and Brazil Soc. of Human Reproduction, Rio de Janeiro, 1973; organizer, chmn. symposia in field. AUthor: (with others) Annual Reviews Physiology, Reproduction, 1961, Histochemistry of Enzymes in the Female Gential System, 1963, The Ovary, 1963, The Ureter, 1967, rev. edit., 1981; editor, contbr.: Endocrinology of Reproduction, 1958; cons. editor, co-author: The Uterus, 1959; contbr. Progestational Substances, 1958, Trophoblast and Its Tumors, 1959, The Virginia, 1959, Hormonal Steroids, Biochemistry, Pharmacology and Therapeutics, 1964, Human Reproduction, 1973; co-editor, contbr.: Biology of Reproduction, Basic and CLinical Studies, 1973; contbr. articles to profl. jours.; live broadcasts on major radio and TV networks on subjects of bioscis., biomed. careers, biomed. subjects of bioscis., biomed careers, biomed. subjects; co-author movie on human reprodn. The Soft Anvil. Apptd. U.S. del. to Vatican, 1964; charter mem. U.S. Rep. Presdl. Task Force, 1988—; rep. U.S. Senate Inner Circle, 1988—, U.S. Rep. Senatorial Commn., 1991—. With USAAF, 1943-45. Decorated Presdl. Unit citation, 2 Bronze Stars; recipient award Lederle Med. Faculty Awards Com., 1955-58; named hon. citizen City of Sao Paulo, Brazil, 1972; U.S. del. to Vatican, 1964. Fellow AAAS, N.Y. Acad. Scis. (co-organizer, chmn., consulting editor internat. symposium The Uterus), Gerontol. Soc., Pacific Coast Fertility Soc. (hon.); mem. Am. Assn. Anatomists, Am. Soc. Zoologists (organizer symposium The Uterus 1973), Am. Physiol. Soc. (vis. prof. 1962), Endocrine Soc., Soc. Endocrinology (Gt. Britain), Soc. Exptl. Biology and Medicine, Am. Soc. Study Sterility (Rubin award 1954), Internat. Fertility Assn., Pan Am. Assn. Anatomy (co-organizer symposium Reproduction 1972), Midwestern Soc. Anatomists (pres. 1973-74), Mexican Soc. Anatomy (hon.), Harvard Club, Sigma Xi, Kappa Delta Pi, Phi Sigma, Gamma Alpha, Alpha Epsilon Delta. Office: 607 E Wilson Ave Lombard IL 60148-4062

VÉLEZ, EILEEN MCLELLAN DE, social worker; b. Boston, Apr. 26, 1955; d. Robert Francis and Mary Joan (McNulty) McLellan; m. Luis Arnaldo Vélez-Cortés. Bachelor in Journalism, Suffolk U., 1977; BS in Journalism. Cert. in cultural understanding in child welfare, substance abuse and family violence. Eligibility worker Dept. Pub. Welfare, Quincy, Mass., 1977-78; adminstrv. asst. Dept. Pub. Welfare, Quincy, 1978-80; sr. interviewer Div. Employment Security, Boston, 1980; social work tech. Dept. Social Services, Quincy, 1980-81, social worker III, 1981—, supr. B of Social Work student interns, 1990-94; hotline counselor Survival Crisis Lines, Quincy, 1978-80. Vol. spl. events, cmty. outreach coord. for fundraising AIDS Action Com., Boston, 1988—, asst. dir. of acquisitions Acad. Awards Night Fundraiser, 1992; mem. com. women's concerns, eucharistic minister Dignity-Boston, exec. bd., sec., 1993-95, mem.-at-large, 1995-96; active Greater Boston Bus. Coun., 1992-94, 500 Club-AIDS Walk for Life, 1991-96, Greenpeace, 1994-95; mem. Human Rights Campaign, 1996, Call to Action, Catholics Speak Out, 1995—; union stewart SEIU Local 509, 1990—. Named Social Worker of Yr., Mass. Foster Parent Assn., 1989. Mem. NOW, Parents and Friends Lesbians and Gays, Dignity-Boston, Suffolk U. Alumni Ambs., Gamma Sigma Sigma. Democrat. Roman Catholic. Home: 1153 Hyde Park Ave Hyde Park MA 02136-2808 Office: Dept Social Svcs 541 Main St Weymouth MA 02190-1845

VELICER, JANET SCHAFBUCH, elementary school educator; b. Cedar Rapids, Iowa, Aug. 27, 1941; d. Allan J. and Geraldine Frances (Stuart) Schafbuch; m. Leland Frank Velicer, Aug. 17, 1963; children: Mark Allan, Gregory Jon, Daniel James. BS, Iowa State U., 1963, MS, 1966; cert. Elem. Edn., Mich. State U., 1976. Tchr. chemistry Prendergast High Sch., Upper Darby, Pa., 1964-65; tchr. home econs. Cardinal O'Hara High Sch., Springfield, Pa., 1965-66; substitute tchr. Pa., Mich., 1967-76; elem. tchr. Winans Elem. Sch., Waverly, Mich., 1976-78, Wardcliff Elem. Sch., Okemos, Mich., 1978-94; tchr. gifted and talented alternative program grades 4 and 5 Hiawatha Elem. Sch., Okemos, 1994-95; tchr. grade 4 Wardcliff Elem. Sch., 1995—; computer coord., Great Books coord.; dist. com. mem. math, computer, substance abuse, cable TV, evaluation revision Okemos Pub. Schs., Instructional Coun. Author: (video) Wardcliff School Documentary, 1982, The Integrated Arts Program of the Okemos Elementary Schools, 1983. Citizens adv. com. to develop a five-yr. plan, 1982-83, Bldg. utilization adv. com., 1983-84, Community use of schs. adv. com., 1984-85, Strategic planning steering com., 1989-90, Taking our schs. into tomorrow com., 1990-91, Bonding election steering com., 1991; chmn. wellness com. Okemos Pub. Schs., 1993-95. Recipient Classrooms of Tomorrow Tchr. award Mich. Dept. Edn., 1990. Mem. NEA, NAFE, Mich. Edn. Assn., Inst. Noetic Scis., Okemos Edn. Assn., Phi Kappa Phi, Mich. Coun. Tchrs. Math., Omicron Nu, Iota Sigma Pi. Democrat. Home: 2678 Blue Haven Ct East Lansing MI 48823-3804 Office: Okemos Pub Schs 4406 Okemos Rd Okemos MI 48864-2553

VELICK, STEPHEN H., medical facility administrator. BS, Wayne State U., 1970, MS, 1980. Mgr. billing Henry Ford Hosp., Detroit, 1970-72, 72-74, mgr. patient svcs., 1974-75, asst. dir. bus., 1975-76, dir. bus. office, 1976-78, assoc. adminstr., 1978-83, group v.p., COO, 1990—; exec. dir. Greenfield Health Sys. Corp., Detroit, 1983-86; chief adminstrv. officer Henry Ford Med. Group, Detroit, 1986-90; adv. bd., bd. dirs. various healthcare orgns. Active various cmty. orgns. Mem. Am. Coll. Healthcare Execs. (assoc.). Office: Henry Ford Hosp 2799 W Grand Blvd Detroit MI 48202*

VELIGDAN, ROBERT GEORGE, dentist; b. Rochester, Pa., Mar. 3, 1949; s. George and Mary (Vinc) V. BS, U. Pitts., 1971, DMD, 1975; postgrad., U. Pa., Phila. Chemistry lab. asst. St. Margaret's Hosp., Pitts., 1971-72; asst. autopsies Montifiore Hosp., Pitts., 1972-74; pvt. practice dentistry N.Y.C., 1975—; clin. instr. Columbia U. Dental Sch., N.Y.C., 1976-82, asst. clin. prof., 1982—; advisor cons. Queens, N.Y. Pub. Schs., 1977-79; lectr. dental esthetics U.S. and abroad, 1984—; asst. attending dentist Presbyn. Hosp., N.Y.C., 1986—; self-help seminars given to vol. working for homeless men, N.Y.C., 1989, 90; staff Ctr. for Alternative/Complimentary Medicine Columbia U., 1994—; organizer Nat. Health Care Network in Dentistry, 1995. Author, producer, dir. (videos) Esthetics and Etched Porcelain Veneers, 1985; contbr. articles to profl. jours. Recipient Recognoition award Greater N.Y. Dental Meeting, N.Y.C., 1985. Mem. Am. Dental Assn., Acad. Gen. Dentistry, Acad. Oral Rehab., Internal Conf. Oral Implantology, Acad. Esthetic Dentistry, I Franklin Miller Study Club. Home: 40 W 72d St Apt # 25 New York NY 10023-7253 Office: 30 Central Park S Ste 7A New York NY 10019-1628

VELLER, MARGARET PAXTON, retired obstetrician, gynecologist; b. Beaver Dam, Ky., Dec. 14, 1925; d. Darrell K. and Gladys (Myers) V.; BA, Vanderbilt U., 1947, MD, 1950. Intern, resident Vanderbilt U. Hosp., Nashville, 1950-54; practice medicine, 1954—. Mem. AMA, Miss. Med. Assn. (com. maternal and child care 1956-72), Homochitto Valley Med. Assn., Miss. Ob-Gyn. Soc., Phi Beta Kappa, Alpha Omega Alpha. Baptist. Club: Pilgrimage Garden. Home: 28 S Circle Dr Natchez MS 39120-4053

VELMAHOS, GEORGE, physician, surgeon; b. Athens, Mar. 23, 1962; came to U.S., 1994; s. Constantinos and Elpida (Valakis) V.; m. Irene Souter, June 20, 1993; 1 child, Elpida. MD, Athens Sch. Medicine, 1985, PhD, 1991. Resident in surgery Hippokration Hosp., Athens, 1986-91; surgeon in rural svc. Kalamata (Greece) Gen. Hosp., 1991-92; trauma fellow Baragwanath Hosp., Johannesburg, South Africa, 1991-94; asst. prof. in surgery L.A. County/U. So. Calif. Med. Ctr., L.A., 1994—. Contbr. articles to Am. and internat. jours. Fellow Royal Coll. Surgeons Edinburgh, Royal Coll. Surgeons Glasgow. Office: Los Angeles Co-USC Med Ctr 1200 N State St Los Angeles CA 92204

VENABLE, JAMES E., optometrist; b. Monroe, Mich., May 25, 1963; s. Joe Lynn and Flora Mae (Hicks) V.; m. Anne Margaret Booth, Dec. 27, 1991; 1 child, James Chandler. BS, East Tenn. State U., 1985; D Optometry, So. Coll. Optometry, Memphis, 1989. Pvt. practice, owner Disease & Vision of the Eye, Knoxville, Tenn., 1989-91; dir. pediatrics and spl. svcs. The Kahn & Diehl Ctrs. for Progressive Eye Care, Toledo, Ohio, 1991—; Mem. low vision/low income clinic com. The Sight Ctr., Toledo, 1993-95; mem. Am. Found. for Vision Awareness, St. Louis, 1995; mem. Optometric Ext. Program Found., St. Louis, 1991-95. Assoc. dir. Theatre Works of N.W. Ohio, Toledo, 1993-95. Recipient Irvin M. Borish award Am. Optometric Found., Memphis, 1989, award for clin. excellence in vision therapy Coll. Optometrists in Vision Therapy, Chula Vista, Calif., 1989. Fellow Coll. of Optometrists in Vision Devel. Republican. Lutheran. Home: 3425 Chiltenham Rd Toledo OH 43606 Office: Kahn & Diehl Ctrs Prog Eye Care 1835 S Reynolds Rd Toledo OH 43614

VENABLES, PATRICK JOHN WOODGATE, immunorheumatology educator, consultant; b. Devizes, Wiltshire, Eng., Feb. 17, 1948; s. Raymond and Doris Venables. MA in Medicine, Cambridge (Eng.) U., 1969, MB BChir, 1972, MD, 1986. House physician, surgeon St. Bartholomews Hosp., London, 1972-73, sr. house officer medicine, 1973-74; sr. house officer medicine Northwick Pk. Hosp., London, 1974-76; registrar in medicine St. Stephen's Hosp., London, 1976-77; rsch. fellow, lectr. Kennedy Inst., London, 1977-86, reader in immunorheumatology, 1986—. Contbr. numerous articles and papers to profl. jours. Grantee Arthritis and Rheumatism Coun. and Nuffield Found. Fellow Royal Coll. Physicians London, Royal Soc. Medicine (sec. 1995—). Office: Kennedy Inst, 6 Bute Gardens, London W67DW, England

VENEZIA, ANTONIO JOSEPH, JR., orthodontist; b. New Orleans, Dec. 20, 1932; s. Antonio J. and Suelene Venezia; m. Joan L. Venezia; children: Stephen, Kimberly, Natalie, Christopher, Terence, Stacy, Jennifer. Student, Memphis State U., 1949-51; DDS, U. Tenn., 1954; MS, Northwestern U., 1961. Diplomate Am. Bd. Orthodontists. Enlisted U.S. Army, 1954, advanced through graded to lt. col., 1954-67; pvt. practice Chgo., 1966—; asst. clin. prof. Northwestern U., Evanston, Ill., 1970-78, guest lectr., 1978—; vis. lectr. U. Detroit Dental Sch., 1976-81; presenter in field. Fellow Am. Coll. Dentists, Chgo. Inst. Medicine, Internat. Coll. Dentists; mem. ADA (del. 1985, alt. del. 1986, coun. on journalism 1985-86, coun. on govtl. affairs and fed. dental svcs. 1986-88), Am. Assn. Orthodontists, Royal Soc. Medicine Eng., Fedn. Dentaire Internat., Ill. State Dental Soc. (trustee 1993-96), Ill. Soc. Orthodontists, Edward H. Angle Soc. Orthodontists, Richard Doggert Dean Hon. Odontol. Soc., Assn. Dental Editors, Chgo. Dental Soc. (treas. 1997, dir. 1981-84, pres. Progressive Club 1981-82, 82-83, 83-84, South Suburban Br. treas. 1974-75, sec. 1975-76, v.p. 1976-77, pres. 1977-78, sci. editor 1971-93, chmn. sci. rev. com. 1993—), Odontographic Soc. Chgo., Pierre Fauchard Acad. (Man of Yr. Ill. sect. 1993), Delta Sigma Delta, Sigma Phi Epsilon. Office: Orthodontic Assocs Ltd 19815 Governors Hwy Flossmoor IL 60422-0189 Also: 845 N Michigan Ave #943 W Chicago IL 60611

VENGER, BENJAMIN HERSCHEL, neurosurgeon, medical consultant; b. Dearborn, Mich., Dec. 27, 1957; s. Norman and Sally Rita (Friedman) V. BA in Zoology, Pomona Coll., 1979; MD, U. Tex., Houston, 1983. Diplomate Am. Bd. Neurol. Surgery. Surg. intern Baylor Coll. Medicine, Houston, 1983-84; neurosurg. resident Baylor Coll. Medicine, Houston, 1984-89; pvt. practice Las Vegas, 1989—. Co-author: Guide to Human Anatomy, 1985; contbr. articles to profl. jours., chpts. to books. Fellow ACS; mem. AMA, Am. Assn. Neurol. Surgeons, Congress of Neurol. Surgeons, Nev. State Mental Assn., Clark County Med. Soc., Phi Beta Kappa, Sigma Xi, Alpha Omega Alpha. Office: Ste 265 3006 S Maryland Pkwy Las Vegas NV 89121

VENGROW, MICHAEL IAN, neurologist; b. Brookline, Mass., Apr. 10, 1949; s. Max and Mary V.; m. Lucy Lee Smith, Aug. 4, 1979; children: Robert David, Mary Elizabeth. BS in Chemistry magna cum laude, U. Mass., 1971; MD, U. Mass., Worcester, 1977. Diplomate Am. Bd. Psychiatry and Neurology, Am. Bd. Clin. Neurophysiology, Am. Bd. Electrodiagnostic Medicine, Am. Acad. Pain Mgmt., Nat. Bd. Med. Examiners. Rsch. chemist, asst. KFA-Julich, West Germany, 1970; rsch. chemist, asst. biomed. svcs. divsn. Damon Corp., Needham, Mass., 1971-72; rsch. chemist, head Shrine Burn Inst., Boston, 1972-73; intern Naval Regional Med. Ctr., San Diego, 1977-78; battalion med. officer Third Combat Engr. Battalion, Third Marine Divsn., Okinawa, Japan, 1978-79; resident, chief resident in neurology Nat. Naval Med. Ctr., Bethesda, Md., 1979-82; fellow in clin. neurophysiology Walter Reed Army Med. Ctr., Washington, 1982-83; neurologist, head divsn. diagnostic neurophysiology Naval Hosp. San Diego, 1983-85; neurologist Neurology Ctr. No. Ariz., Flagstaff, 1985-96, Neurology Cons. of Dallas, 1996—; sr. reviewer Ariz. Long Term Care Sys., Phoenix, 1986-94; dir. Alzheimer's unit Kachina Point Health Ctr., Sedona, Ariz., 1986-93, dir. neurol. rehab. unit, 1989-93; dir. neurophysiology lab. Kingman Regional Med. Ctr., 1985-95, Flagstaff Med. Ctr., 1985-95, Cmty. Med. Edn. dir., 1988, chief medicine, 1989; mem. profl. adv. bd. Epilipsy Soc., Phoenix, 1987-96, Multiple Sclerosis Soc., Phoenix, 1989-96, Quantum Health Resources; cons. First Western Med. Group, Fresno, Calif., 1991-93, Long Term Care Program Ariz. Long Term Care System, 1987-95, Marcus J. Lawrence Hosp., Cottonwood, Ariz., Pub. Health Svcs. Hosp., Tuba City, Ariz.; ind. med. examiner, Ariz.; agreed med. examiner, qualified med. examiner, electromyographer BH Mgmt. Med. Group, Fresno, 1993—; instr. emergency medicine L.A. C.C. Overseas, Uniformed Svcs. U. Health Scis., Bethesda; clin. lectr. dept. neurology sch. health scis. U. Ariz., Tucson; clin. tchr. U. Tex. Southwestern Med. Sch.; rschr. in field; presenter in field. Contbr. articles to profl. pubs. Bd. dirs. Flagstaff Symphony, 1991-94; sponsor Am. Youth Soccer Orgn., 1988-90. LCDR, USN, 1978-85, capt. M.C., USNR. Pub. Health scholar, 1975, State Bd. Higher Edn. Scholar, 1967-71, 75, Armed Forces Health Svcs. Profl. scholarship, 1975-77, Religious High Edn. scholar, 1965; recipient letter commendation Operation Desert Storm, 1991. Fellow Am. Acad. Neurology (govt. section), Am. EEG Soc. (practice com.), Am. Assn. Electrodiagnostic Medicine, Am. Electromyographic Soc.; mem. AMA, Ariz. Med. Assn., Am. Mil. Surgeons U.S., Am. Epilepsy Soc., Uniformed Svcs. Neurology U.S., U.S. Navy Neurol. Soc., Am. Soc. Clin. Evoked Potentials, Am. Soc. Neuroimaging, Am. Med. EEG Assn., Naval Res. Assn., Am. Biographical Inst. Rsch. Assn., (life, dep. gov., bd. govs.), Am. Biographical Inst. (Man of Yr., 1992), Phi Eta Sigma, Phi Kappa Phi, Phi Beta Kappa. Home: 5945 W Parker Rd # 3112 Plano TX 75093

VENKATAKRISHNA, KANAKAPURA N., nephrologist; b. Kollegal, India, Apr. 13, 1954; s. Kanakapura Narayanaswamy and Jyothi Ramachandra Subba Rao; m. Jyothi Ramachangdra, Dec. 23, 1987; 1 child, Varsha. MBBS, Govt. Med. Coll., Mysore, India, 1978. Intern, resident in internal medicine, fellow nephrology Hahnemann Univ. Hosp., Phila., 1987-92; staff physician Alvin C. York VA Med. Ctr., Murfreesboro, Tenn., 1993—. Mem. Internat. Soc. Nephrology, Nat. Kidney Found. Home: 602 Independence Way Murfreesboro TN 37129 Office: Alvin C York Med Ctr 3400 Lebanon Rd Murfreesboro TN 37130

VENKATASESHAN, SURYA VENKATA, pathologist; b. Rajahmundry, India, Sept. 3, 1952; came to U.S., 1976; d. Lakshminarayana Sastry and Ramana Venkata (Hota) Lanka; m. Thirumoorthi Venkata Seshan, Feb. 23, 1975; children: Karthik Siva, Nandini Lakshmi. Grad., Govt. Med. Coll., 1969, B of Medicine and Surgery, 1974. Intern Med. Coll. Affiliated Hosps., Mysore, India, 1974-75, K.R. Hosp., Mysore, India, 1975; physician Johnston-Willis Hosp., Richmond, Va., 1977-78; resident pathology N.Y. Hosp. Coll., Met. Hosp. Ctr., N.Y.C., 1978-82, chief resident anatomic pathology, 1979-80, chief resident clin. pathology, 1981; assoc. clin. prof. Mt. Sinai Sch. Medicine; attending pathologist, assoc. dir. labs. Barnert Hosp., Paterson, N.J.; guest lectr. and cons. in field. Author: The Kidney in Collagen-Vascular Diseases, 1993, WHO Classification of Glomerular Diseases, 2d edit., 1994; contbr. articles to profl. jours. Rsch. fellow Parkinson Disease Found. Coll. Physicians and Surgeons, Columbia U., 1977, Renal Pathology fellow Barnert Hosp., 1982-84, Vis. fellow Mt. Sinai Hosp., 1982-84. Fellow Am. Soc. Clin. Pathologists, Coll. Am. Pathologists; mem. AMA, Am. Soc. Nephrology, Renal Pathology Soc., Nat. Kidney Found., Internat. Acad. Pathology, Women in Nephrology, N.J. Soc. Pathology. Office: Barnert Hosp Dept Pathology 680 Broadway Paterson NJ 07514-1422

VENNING, MICHAEL CHARLES, renal physician; b. London, Sept. 25, 1948; s. Geoffry Richard and Mary Ruth (Barker) V.; m. Pamela Mary Berryman, Aug. 7, 1982; children: Noel Clive, Max Tristan. BA, Oxford U., 1969; MA, Cornell U., Ithaca, N.Y., 1971, PhD, 1975; BM, BCh, Oxford U., 1979. House physician Radcliffe Infirmary, Oxford, 1979-80 sr. house officer Hammersmith Hosp., London, 1980, Guy's Hosp., London, 1980, Brompton Hosp., London, 1981, London Chest Hosp., London, 1981; rsch. fellow Hammersmith Hosp., London, 1982-[illegible] registrar Royal Victoria Infirmary, Newcastle-upon-Tyne, 1984-86; lectr. renal medicine U. Newcastle-upon-Tyne, 1986-90; cons. renal physician Univ. Hosp. of South Manchester, 1990—; cons. Baxter Healthcare, 1991—. Contbr. articles to profl. jours. Scholar, Winchester Coll., 1960, Balliol Coll., Oxford, 1966. Fellow Royal Coll. Physicians Gt. Britain; mem. European Dialysis and Transplant Assn., Renal Assn. U.K., Am. Soc. Nephrology, Brit. Soc. Immunology, U.K. Renal Sr. Registrars Club (pres. 1988-89). Office: Withington Hosp, Nell Ln, Manchester M20 8LR, England M2 8[illegible]

VENTRESCA, DEBORAH ANNE, nurse; b. Boston, Oct. 12, 1948; d. H. Vincent and M. Helen (Butler) Strout; m. Anthony L. Ventresca Jr.; 1 child, Amy L. AS in Nursing, North Shore Community Coll., 1980; BS in Nursing summa cum laude, U. Mass, 1986, MSN, 1991. Staff nurse J.B. Thomas Hosp., Peabody, Mass., 1980-87; staff nurse home health J.B. Thomas Home Care/Vis. Nurses, Peabody, 1987; staff devel. coord. Lenox Hill Nursing and Rehabilitative Care Facility, Lynn, Mass., 1987-88; community health nurse J.B. Thomas Health Care, Peabody, 1988-90, Vis. Nurses Assn. of Greater Lynn, 1990-92; RN coord. Lyman Adult Day Health Program E. Boston Neighborhood Health Ctr., 1992-93; clin. coord. All Care VNA of Greater Lynn, 1993-96, v.p. clin. svcs., 1996—. Vol. nurse Make Today Count, Beverly, Mass., 1982-8[illegible]; nurse admission assessment Hospice North Shore, 1983, vol. coord., 198[illegible]-8[illegible], bd. dirs. 1984-86; bd. dirs. Am. Cancer Soc., Lynn, 1987-92; vol. facilitator Parents Anonymous Group, 1994—. Margaret Anderson Meml. scholar U. Mass., 1989; recipient Academic Excellence award, U. Mass, 1991. Mem. Sigma Theta Tau (treas. Theta Alpha chpt.). Home: 836 Humphrey St Swampscott MA 01907-2339 Office: 16 City Hall Sq Lynn MA 01901-100[illegible]

VENTRY, PAUL GUERIN, physician, government official; b. Ossining, N.Y., Sept. 1, 1934; s. Victor and Catherine (Dillon) V.; BS Manhattan Coll., 1957; MD, Syracuse U., 1962; m. Betty-Anne Baildon, Aug. 20, 1960. Diplomate Am. Bd. Profl. Disability Cons., Am. Bd. Forensic Medicine. Commd. 1st lt. M.C., U.S. Army, 1962, advanced through grades to lt. col., 1971; intern Walter Reed Gen. Hosp., 1962-63, resident in internal medicine, 1963-66, fellow in immunology, 196[illegible], fellow in allergy, 1967, chief med. outpatient clinic, 1971, allergy cons. to Surgeon Gen., Europe, 1967-70, ret., 1971; chief adult services Montgomery County Health Dept. (Md.), 1972; med. dir. Goddard Space Flight Ctr., NASA, 1973; ptnr. Med. Assocs. D.C., Washington, 1974; med. dir. Civilian Employees Health Svc., Dept. Def., Washington, also med. dir. Pentagon Drug and Alcohol Program and dir. Dept. Def. Blood Donor Program, 1975-[illegible]3 prin. med. cons. to Office Hearings and Appeals, Social Security Adminstrn., Arlington, Va., 1983—; asst. clin. prof. medicine George Washington U., 1973-79; chief med. cons. Social Security Adminstrn., 1983—; med. dir. Nat. Coun. Social Security Adminstrn. OHA, 1991, Am. Fedn. Govt. Employees # 3615, 1991—, Nat. Coun. Social Security Employees, Am. Fed. Govt. Coun. 215. Fellow Am. Occupl. Med. Assn., Am. Coll. Occupational and Environ. Medicine, Am. Acad. Disability Evaluating Physicians; mem. ACP, Fed. Physicians Assn. (treas.), Am. Pub. Health Assn., Am. Acad. Allergy, Royal Soc. Medicine, Brit. Allergy Soc., Am. Acad. Civil Svc. Physicians (treas.), Am. Coll. Physician Execs., Am. Bd. Forensic Examiners, Potomac C. of C., Washington Performing Arts Soc., D.C. Med. Soc., Montgomery County Med. Soc., Alpha Kappa Kappa. Contbr. articles to med. jours. Home: 7813 Masters Dr Potomac MD 20854

VENTURA, HECTOR OSVALDO, cardiologist; b. Buenos Aires, Mar. 21, 1951; came to U.S., 1981; s. Osvaldo Domingo and Nelida (Scocczza) V.; m. Laurie Anne Zeringue, Apr. 21, 1990; children: Austin Alejandro, Leighton Leandro, Kendra Mariel. BS, Nat. No. 10 Coll. Buenos Aires, 1968; MD, U. Buenos Aires, 1974. Diplomate Am. Bd. Internal Medicine with subspecialty in cardiovascular diseases. Resident in internal medicine Mil. Hosp., Argentina, 1975-78; rsch. fellow hypertension Ochsner Found., New Orleans, 1981-84; internal medicine resident Ochsner Found. Hosp., New Orleans, 1984-86, cardiology fellow, 1986-88; heart failure/heart transplant fellow Loyola U., Chgo., 1989; co-dir. heart failure heart transplant Oshsner Med. Inst., New Orleans, 1989—, transplant adv. bd., 1992—, mem. ethics com., 1995—; assoc. prof. medicine La. State U. Sch. Medicine, New Orleans; jour. manuscript reviewer. Editl. bd. Jour. Heart & Lung Transplantation, 1994; contbr. articles to profl. jours. 1st lt. Argentine Army, 1974-80. Ochsner Found. fellow, 1985, 86. Fellow Am. Coll. Cardiology; mem. Am. Soc. Transplant (organ thoracic com. 1993—), Am. Heart Assn. Roman Catholic. Home: 3900 Wheat Dr Metairie LA 70002 Office: Ochsner Med Instn 1514 Jefferson Hwy New Orleans LA 70[illegible]

VENTURATOS, STEVE GEORGE, gastroenterologist; b. Pitts., Mar. 5, 1952; s. George Steve and Aphrodite (Bon) V.; m. Carol Marie Amerland, June 15, 1974; children: Lauren Marie, Georg Philip. BA, Tulane U., 1974, MD, 1978. Diplomate Am. Bd. Internal Medicine, Am. Bd. Gastroenterology. Staff mem. West Jefferson Hosp., Marrero, La., 1983—; gastroenterologist Met. Gastroenterology Assocs., Marrero, La., 1983—. Fellow Am. Coll. Gastroenterology; mem. Am. Gastroenterology Assocs., Am. Soc. Gastrointestinal Endoscopy. Mem. Greek Orthodox Ch. Office: Met Gastroenterology Assocs Ste 450 1111 Medical Ctr Blvd Marrero LA 70072

VENZKE, RAY FRANK, psychotherapist; b. Wood County, Wis., Sept. 7, 1933; s. Herman A. and Christina (Sojka) V.; m. Dawn Woltman, June 14, 1953 (div. Feb. 1972); 1 child, Diane W. Doerson; m. Joy Leadbetter, June 21, 1972 (div. Nov. 1985); m. DeMaris Hafner Unruh, May 31, 1986. BA in Ednl. Psychology, Wartburg Coll., 1955; MDiv, Trinity Sem., Columbus, Ohio, 1959; MA in Psychology, U. N.D., 1974. Lic. clin. profl. counselor, Mont. Pastor Bearlake Luth. Parish, Twin Lakes, Minn., 1959-63; missionary Thailand Luth. Mission, 1963-64; pastor First Luth. Parish, Washburn, N.D., 1965-67; addiction counselor Heartview Found., Mandan, N.D., 1971-74; therapist, program evaluator Badlands Human Svc. Ctr., Dickinson, N.D., 1975-85; psychotherapist Dickinson, N.D., 1985-87, Chrysalis Counseling Svcs., Helena, Mont., 1988—; cons. Lewis and Clark County Law Enforcement Chaplains, Helena, 1988-95. Narrator Mont. Libr. for the Blind, Helena, 1990—; chair task force CISM Mont. Dept. Disaster, 1994—; mem. Mont. Gov.'s Task Force on Mental Health/Medicaid, Helena, 1993—. Mem. Am. Counselors Assn., Am. Mental Health Counselors, Mont. Clin. Mental Health Counselors (treas. 1992-94, counselor of yr. award 1996), Mont. Counselors Assn., Lions (Dist. Gov. 5NW award 1983), Am. Philatelic Soc. Home: 2019 Missoula Ave Helena MT 59601-3245 Office: Chrysalis Counseling Svc Apt 201 3117 Cooney Dr Helena MT 59601-0200

VENZOR, OSCAR, JR., internal medicine physician; b. San Antonio, Apr. 19, 1946; s. Oscar Villabos and Flora (Felan) V.; m. Sherl A. Daniels (div.); children: Samara, Michael; m. Jean Ann Franklin, Oct. 13, 1982; children: John, David. BA, St. Mary's U., 1968; DO, Kirksville Coll. Osteo., 1975. Rotating internship Doctor's Hosp., Tucker, Ga., 1975-76; pvt. practice Milan, Mo., 1976-80; resident in internal medicine Tucson Gen. Hosp., 1981-84; pvt. practice Tampa, Fla., 1984—; dir. med. edn. Univ. Cmty. Hosp., Tampa, 1986—, chmn. med. edn. com., 1986—, chmn. dept. internal medicine, 1991-92, 86-88; PSRO advisor Sullivan County Meml. Hosp., Milan, 1980-81. 1st lt. U.S. Army, 1969-71. Mem. Am. Osteo. Assn., Am. Coll. Osteo. Internists, Fla. Osteo. Med. Assn., Fla. Med. Assn., Hillsborough County Med. Assn. Office: Carrollwood Internal Medici 14003 N Dale Mabry Tampa FL 33618

VERBOUT, JAMES PAUL, recreational therapist; b. Sterling, Ill., July 7, 1957; s. Louis Pius and Agnes (Rajnowski) V.; m. Loretta Margaret Jaquet, May 30, 1981; children: Kimberly Noel, Brandon James. BS in Therapeutic Recreation, U. Wis., LaCrosse, 1979. Cert. therapeutic recreation specialist. Recreational therapist Glenwood (Iowa) State Hosp., 1979-80; recreational therapist Mayo Med. Ctr., Rochester, Minn., 1980—, lead recreational therapist, 1988—; S.E. Minn. dir. Minn. Therapeutic Recreation steering com., Burnsville, 1988-90. Bd. dirs. Rochester Area Disabled Athletics and Recreation, Inc., 1986-95, vice sec., 1986-87, v.p., 1991, pres., 1992-93. Recipient Spirit award Rochester Area Disabled Athletics and Recreation, 1989-90, Outstanding Bd. Mem. award Rochester Area Disabled Athletics and Recreation, 1995. Mem. Am. Therapeutic Recreation Assn., Minn. Park and Recreation Assn., Nat. Closed Head Injury Found., State Closed Head Injury Found., S.E. Minn. Head Injury Support Group, KC (3d degree). Democrat. Roman Catholic. Home: 4911 22nd Ave NW Rochester MN 55901-2033 Office: Mayo Med Ctr 200 1st St SW Rochester MN 55905-0001

VERDESCA, ARTHUR SALVATORE, internist, corporate medical director; b. Cliffside Park, N.J., May 25, 1930; s. Cosimo Theodore and Giulia Elvira (DeLipsis) V.; m. Ann Edith Copping, June 24, 1961; children: Stephen, Julia, Edith. AB, Columbia U., 1951, MD, 1955. Diplomate Am. Bd. Internal Medicine. Intern St. Luke's Hosp., N.Y.C., 1955-56, resident, 1956-57, 59-60, fellow Nat. Heart Inst., 1960-61; staff physician Western Electric, N.Y.C., 1961-63, assoc. hdqrs. med. dir., 1963-65, hdqrs. med. dir., 1965-85; corp. med. dir. Am. Internat. Group, N.Y.C., 1985—. Author: Live, Work and Be Healthy, 1980. Capt. USAF, 1957-59. Fellow ACP, Am. Acad. Occupational Medicine; mem. N.Y. Occupational Med. Assn. (pres. 1979-80). Roman Catholic. Home: 19 Randolph Dr Morristown NJ 07960-5319 Office: Am Internat Group Inc 70 Pine St New York NY 10270-0002

VERDI, ANTHONY FRANK, psychologist; b. Phila., Dec. 20, 1956; s. Frank P. and Carmela J. (Massaro) V. BA, U. Pa., 1978; MEd, Temple U., 1981, PhD, 1991. Lic. psychologist, Pa. Dir. psychology Rolling Hill Hosp., Elkins Park, Pa., 1981-91; dir. rehab. svcs. and psychology Mt. Sinai Hosp., Phila., 1991—; cons. Ctr. for Psychoeducational Processes, Temple U., Phila., 1987-91, rsch. Group and Orgnl. Rsch. Ctr., 1988—; adj. faculty Widener U., Chester, Pa., 1992—; process cons. The Wharton Sch., Phila., 1993-94. Author: The Group Development Observation System, 1994; contbr. articles to jours. and chpt. to book. Recipient The Sylvia Kunreuther award Temple U., 1990. Mem. Am. Psychol. Assn., Pa. Psychol. Assn. Roman Catholic. Home: 420-C Fitzwater St Philadelphia PA 19147-3109 Office: Mount Sinai Hosp Fourth & Reed Sts Philadelphia PA 19147

VERDI, GERALD DELANO, plastic surgeon; b. N.Y., Mar. 8, 1936; s. James and Ann (Calise) V.; m. Charlene Anne Bedell, Dec. 16, 1967; children: Michael, Sean, Marc, Christopher. DDS, U. Pa., 1960; MD, Albany Med. Coll., 1965. Diplomate Am. Bd. Surgery, Am. Bd. Plastic Surgery. Oral surgery intern Bellevue Hosp., N.Y.C., 1960-61; resident oral surgery Nassau County Med. Ctr., 1961; surg. intern Columbia Presbyn. Med. Ctr., N.Y.C., 1965-66, resident in surgery, 1968-69; resident in surgery Nassau County Med. Ctr., 1969-71, resident in plastic surgery, 1971-73; pvt. practice plastic surgery Louisville, 1973—. Chmn. sch. bd. Anchorage Sch., 1984-86. Lt. USNR, 1966-68. Fellow ACS. Office: 250 E Liberty St #504 Louisville KY 40202

VERDOORN, TODD ALLEN, neuroscientist, educator; b. Madison, Wis., Dec. 12, 1960; s. Donald Leroy and Shirley Arlene (Tuinstra) V.; m. Patricia Ann Deppe, Mar. 26, 1983; children: Benjamin Arie, Logan Todd, Carlyn Elizabeth. BA in Chemistry, Ctrl. U. Iowa, 1983; PhD of Neurobiology, U. N.C., 1988. Rsch. asst. Nat. Inst. Environ. Health Scis., Research Triangle Park, N.C., 1984; postdoctoral fellow Max-Planck Soc., Heidelberg, Germany, 1988-91; asst. prof. pharmacology dept. Vanderbilt U., Nashville, 1991—. Editl. bd. mem. Molecular Pharmacology, 1995-97, Jour. Biol. Chemistry, 1996-98; reviewer jours. in field; contbr. chpts. in books and articles to profl. jours. Recipient Established Investigator award Am. Heart Assn., 1995; fellow NSF, 1983, Pharm. Mfrs. Assn. Found., 1987-88, Alexander von Humboldt Found., 1988-90; grantee NIH, 1992-93, 93-96, Coun. Tobacco Rsch., 1992-95, NeuroSearch A/S, 1995, Am. Heart Assn., 1995-2000, Pharm. Mfrs. Assn. Found., 1992-94, 91. Mem. N.Am. Soc. Neurosci. Office: Vanderbilt U Sch Medicine 23d Ave at Pierce Nashville TN 37232-6600*

VERDUGO ALONSO, MIGUEL ANGEL, psychology eductor; b. Valladolid, Spain, Apr. 6, 1954; s. Pedro and Carmen (Alonso) V. MEd, Columbia U., 1982; PhD, U. Autonoma, Madrid, Spain, 1987. Primary tchr. Ministerio de Educación, Valladolid, Spain, 1977-79, speech pathologist, 1979-80, 83-84, sch. prin., 1984-86, spr., 1986-88; Fulbright scholar Columbia U., N.Y.C., 1980-82; prof. psychology U. Salamanca, Spain, 1988—; dir. Master in Integration of Persons with Disabilities: Habilitation & Rehab., Salamanca; vice rector U. Salamanca, 1994—. Recipient Nat. Award in Rsch. Ministerio de Educación, 1988. Mem. APA. Home: El otero 2 Urb El Viso, Villares de la Reina 37184, Salamanca 47001

VEREBEY, KARL GEZA, toxicologist, pharmacologist, educator; b. Budapest, Hungary, Mar. 12, 1938; came to U.S., 1956; s. Karoly and Etelka (Szabo) V.; m. Debra Adler, Feb. 22, 1962; children: Rita, Todd, Marc. AA, Eotvos J. Gimnazium, Budapest, Hungary, 1956; BA, Hunter Coll., 1965; MA, CUNY, 1968; PhD, Cornell U. Med. Coll., 1972. Diplomate Am. Bd. Forensic Toxicology; cert. clin. lab. dir. Am. Bd. Bioanalysis; lic. clin. lab. dir., N.Y., N.J., Ill., Md., Vt. Dir. clin. pharmacology State of N.Y., N.Y.C., 1973-88; dir. clin. lab. Psychiat. Diagnostic Lab. Am., South Plainfield, N.J., 1982-89; chief toxicologist City of N.Y., 1989-92; dir. toxicology N.Y. State Inst. Basic Rsch., S.I., 1992-95; pres., dir. Leadtech Corp., North Bergen, N.J., 1992—; assoc. prof. SUNY Health Sci. Ctr., 1978; mem. exec. com. Drug Abuse Adv. Bd., N.Y. State Dept. Health, 1985; advisor subcom. on trace metals analysis to Nat. Com. on Clin. Lab. Stds., 1992; insp. Nat. Lab. Cert. Program HHS, 1989. Mem. editl. bd. Jour. Addictive Diseases, 1981; contbr. over 100 articles to sci. jours., chpts. to books. With U.S. Army, 1961-63. Rsch. fellow USPHS, 1968-73; grantee Cornell U. Med. Coll., 1974-77, Narcotic and Drug Rsch., Inc., 1974-76, 79-81, DuPont Pharm., 1985; inductee Hunter Coll. Hall of Fame, 1989. Fellow Am. Acad. Forensic Sci.; mem. N.Y. Acad. Sci., Am. Soc. Pharmacology and Exptl. Therapeutics, Soc. Forensic Toxicologists. Home: 638 Debchar Ct River Vale NJ 07675-6409

VERECZKEY, GÁBOR, anesthesiologist, therapist, cardiologist, consultant; b. Budapest, Nov. 25, 1958; s. György and Éva (Keleti) V.; m. Cosima Verebély, June 10, 1988; children: Döme Dávid Sonó, Luca Lili Maku. MD, Semmelweis Med. U., Budapest, 1984; Specialist in Anaesthesia and Intensive Care, Postgrad. Med. U., Budapest, 1989. Diplomate European Acad. Anaesthesiology. Registrar Wexham Park Hosp., Slough, E. Berkshire, England, 1989-92; med. dir. Pfizer, Budapest, 1993-95; head of ICU HIETE Postgrad. Faculty Internal Med. and Cardiovascular Ctr. Heart and Vascular Surgery Clinic, Budapest, 1995—; cons. Hewlett-Packard Med., Budapest, 1992-94, Radiometer, Budapest, 1992—, Ask-Boeringer, Budapest, 1995—. Author: Tissue Oxygenation in Critical Care The Radiometer Concept, 1996, What is Impedance Cardiography?, 1996; co-author Inodilator Therapy, 1996. Mem. European Acad. Anaesthesiology. Home: 24 Országház Utca, H-1014 Budapest Hungary Office: HIETE Postgrad Faculty Internal & Cardivascular Ctr, 35 Szabolcs Utca, H-1135 Budapest Hungary

VERGONA, KATHLEEN DOBROSIELSKI, biology educator, researcher; b. Pitts., Dec. 6, 1948; d. Raymond Henry and Sophie Bernice (Rabazinski) Dobbs; m. Ronald Joseph Vergona, Sept. 1, 1973; 1 child, Raymond. BS, U. Pitts., 1970, PhD, 1976. Rsch. fellow Cancer Rsch. Ctr. Allegheny Gen. Hosp., Pitts., 1976; rsch. fellow dept. anatomy and cell biology Sch. Medicine U. Pitts., 1977-79, asst. prof. dept. anatomy and histology Sch. Dental Medicine, 1976-81, assoc. prof. dept. anatomy and histology, 1982—, rsch. asst. prof. dept. neurobiology, anatomy and cell sci. Sch. Dental Medicine, 1982—, chmn. dept. anatomy/histology, 1990-92; lectr. Carnegie Mus. of Natural History, Pitts., 1984-85; faculty fellow Geriatric Edn. Ctr., Pitts., 1986—, dental curriculum coord. Editor: The Biology of Salivary Glands; contbr. articles to profl. jours. Judge Pa. Jr. Acad. of Sci., Pitts., 1976—, Am. Student Dental Assn., Pitts., 1978—. Recipient Achievement of Excellence award Geriatric Edn. Ctr. Pa., 1987, Outstanding Instr. award Am. Student Dental Assn., 1981, 83; Nat. Inst. on Aging rsch. fellow, 1976. Mem. Am. Soc. Cell Biology, Am. Assn. Oral Biologists (founding mem., pres.), Am. Assn. Dental Rsch. (councilor Pitts. chpt. 1989-92), Am. Assn. Dental Schs. (chair anatomic scis. sect. 1995-96), Tissue Culture Assn., Salivary Rsch. Group, Sigma Xi, Beta Beta Beta. Democrat. Roman Catholic. Home: 4943 Oakhurst Ave Gibsonia PA 15044 Office: U Pitts Sch Dental Medicine 615-1 Salk Hall Pittsburgh PA 15261-1906

VERHAEGHE, PIERRE JACQUES, surgeon, educator; b. Lille, Nord, France, July 14, 1947; s. Jacques Etienne and Thérèse Fernande (Lebecque) V.; m. Martine Biancamaria, July 1, 1978; children: Celia, Thibault, Etienne. MD, Lille U., 1971; PhD, U. Picardy-Jules Verne. Resident in surgery Amiens, France, 1971-72, 74-77, chef de clinique-asst., 1977-82; asst. prof. rsch. unit R. Stoppa, Amiens, 1978-82; gen. surgeon C.H.U. d'Amiens, 1982-88; prof. gen. surgery U. Picardy-Jules Verne, Amiens, 1988—; dir. unit of dept. gen. surgery Hosp. Nord, Amiens, 1992—; mem. ethical com. Picardie's Region, Amiens, 1991—; dir. rsch. group DREDE ER 122, 1992—; bd. Clin. Rsch. Regional Delegation, 1994—; v.p. Emergency Coun. of Univ. Hosp., Amiens, 1995—. Author: (videotape collection) To Live Daily with Osteogenesis Imperfecta, 1992-95; coord. of monograph: Osteogenesis Imperfecta, 1991; assoc. editor Internat. Surgery, 1987-95. Funding mem. FILMED (internat. med. videoforum), Amiens, 1988; vol. svc. physician Civic Svc., Martinique, 1972-74. French Found. for Med. Rsch. grantee, 1979. Mem. Internat. Soc. Surgery, Osteogenesis Imperfecta Fedn. Europe (v.p. 1993—), Assn. French Surgeons (adjoint gen. sec. 1990—), French Acad. Surgery. Roman Catholic. Office: Hospital Nord, Service de Chirurgie Gen, 80054 Amiens France

VERHESEN, ANNA MARIA HUBERTINA, counselor; b. Heerenveen, Friesland, Netherland, Dec. 6, 1932; came to U.S., 1968; d. Hendrikus H. and Henrika C. (Kluessjen) V. BS, Mercy Coll. of Detroit, 1981; MA, Sienna Height, Adrian, Mich., 1992. Childcare worker Schiedam, Netherland, 1952-54; social worker Rotterdam Halfweg, Netherland, 1954-59; childcare worker Mt. St. Ann's Home, Worcester and Lawrence, Mass., 1968-70; chem. dependency social worker St. Vincent Med. Ctr., Toledo, Ohio, 1970-75; social worker St. Joseph Hosp., Nashua, N.H., 1975-78; vocation dir. Grey Nuns, Lexington, Mass., 1978-79; coord. community svcs. St. Vincents Med. Ctr., Toledo, 1981-91; pvt. practice clin. therapist Sylvania, Ohio, 1992—; alcohol/drug addiction/mental health counselor for ex-prisoners; founder St. Vincent Med. Ctr. Alcoholism Detox and Rehab. Unit, Toledo, 1970-75. Co-founder Transitional Residences for the Homeless, Toledo, 1981-90, Ohio Coalition for the Homeless, Columbus, 1982-89; co-founder of a home for persons with AIDS; co-chair City of Toledo Housing Policy, 1985-90; coord. Housing Now, Toledo, 1988-90. Recipient Woman of Achievement award Women in Communication, Toledo, 1986, Spirit of '87 award N.W. Ordinance and U.S. Constn. Bicentennial Commn., Toledo, 1987, Gov.'s Spl. Recognition award, 1988, Man for Others award St. John's High Sch., 1991; named Woman of Toledo, St. Vincent Med. Ctr. Aux., 1988, Ohio Ho. of Reps., 1987; featured in various mags. Roman Catholic. Home: 219 Page St Toledo OH 43560-1430 Office: Elliott and Assocs Inc 5600 Monroe St Sylvania OH 43560-2701

VERHEY, JOSEPH WILLIAM, psychiatrist, educator; b. Oakland, Calif., Sept. 28, 1928; s. Joseph Bernard and Anne (Hanken) V.; BS summa cum laude, Seattle U., 1954; MD, U. Wash., 1958; m. Darlene Helen Seiler, July 21, 1956. Intern, King County Hosp., Seattle, 1958-59; resident Payne Whitney Psychiatric Clinic, N.Y. Hosp., Cornell Med. Center, N.Y.C., 1959-62, U. Wash. Hosp., Seattle, 1962-63; pvt. practice, Seattle, 1963-78; mem. staff U. Providence Hosp., 1963-78, Fairfax Hosp., 1963-78, VA Med. Center, Tacoma, 1978-83, chief inpatient psychiatry sect., 1983—; clin. instr. psychiatry U. Wash. Med. Sch., 1963-68, clin. asst. prof. psychiatry, 1968-82, clin. assoc. prof., 1982—; cons. psychiatry U.S. Dept. Def., Wash. State Bur. Juvenile Rehab.; examiner Am. Bd. Psychiatry and Neurology. Diplomate Am. Bd. Psychiatry and Neurology. Fellow N. Pacific Soc. Psychiatry and Neurology, Am. Psychiat. Assn.; mem. AMA, Am. Fedn. Clin. Rsch., World Fedn. Mental Health, Soc. Mil. Surgeons of U.S., Wash. Athletic Club, Swedish Club (life). Home: 1100 University St Seattle WA 98101 Office: VA Med Ctr Tacoma WA 98493

VERHEYEN, MARCEL MATHIEU, homeopathist, consultant; b. Stokkem, Belgium, Dec. 11, 1951; s. Rene and Maria (Peeters) V.; m. Nicole Stevens Verheyen, July 17, 1974; children: Renee, Rachel. MD, K.U.L Cath. U., Leuven, Belgium, 1979; student, Joszef Coll., Hasselt, Belgium, 1970. Medical Doctor. Editor Beter, 1983; cons. Enterprises for rsch. and devel. of natural med., The Netherlands, 1982; rscher. Homoepathy and Phytotherapy, Switzerland, 1988. Author: Homeopathy For the Whole Family, 1986, Stop Stress, 1995; editor: Gezondheidsnieuws, 1983. Mem. Nederlandse Vereniging voor Fytotherapie, Belgische Vereniging vor Fytotherapie, European Sci. Coop. for Phytotherapy. Home: 5 Trolieberg-plein, 3010 Leuven Belgium Office: Ctr for Natuurgeneeskunde Prev Medicine/Homeopathy, 1 Cortenstraat, 6211 HT Maastricht The Netherlands

VERKAUF, BARRY STEPHEN, obstetrician, gynecologist; b. Tampa, Fla., Dec. 28, 1940; s. Oscar and Rose (Freeman) V.; m. Arline Laviage, Aug. 20, 1964; children: Stefanie, Leslie. MD, Tulane U., 1965. Resident and fellow in ob-gyn. Johns Hopkins U., Balt., 1966-72; asst. prof. U. South Fla. Med. Sch., Tampa, 1974-79, assoc. prof., 1979—; pvt. practice, Tampa, 1981—. Editor, author: Congenital Anomalies in the Female Reproductive Tract, 1993; mem. editl. bd., ad hoc editor Fertility and Sterility, 1990—. Mem. CADRE, Tampa, 1976—. Maj. M.C., U.S. Army, 1972-74. Fellow ACOG; mem. Am. Fertility Soc. (com. chmn. 1971—), Soc. Reproductive Endocrinologists, Soc. Reproductive Surgeons, South Atlantic Assn. Obstetricians and Gynecologists, Fla. Soc. Reproductive Endocrinologists (pres.), Omicron Delta Kappa. Republican. Jewish. Office: 2919 Swann Ave Tampa FL 33629

VERMA, RAM SAGAR, geneticist, educator, author, administrator; b. Barabanki, India, Mar. 3, 1946; came to the U.S., 1972; s. Gaya Prasad and Late Moonga (Devi) V.; m. Shakuntala Devi, May 4, 1962; children: Harendra K., Narendra K. BSc, Agra U., India, 1965, MSc in Quantitative Genetics, 1967; PhD in Cytogenetics, U. Western Ont., London, Ont., Can., 1972; diploma clinical cytogenetics, The Royal Coll. Pathologists, London, 1984. Diplomate The Royal Coll of Pathologists, London; lic. dir. clin. Cytogenetics, N.Y.C. and N.Y. state. Rsch. and teaching asst. dept. plant scis. U. Western London, Ont., Can., 1967-73; postdoctoral rsch. assoc. cytogenetics U. Colo. Dept. of Pediatrics, Denver, 1973-76; instr. to prof. human cytogenetics dept. of medicine Health Sci. Ctr. SUNY, Bklyn., 1976—, prof. dept. anatomy and cell biology, 1988—; chief cytogenetics div. hematology and cytogenetics Interfaith Med. Ctr. (formerly Jewish Hosp. and Med. Ctr. Bklyn.), 1980-86; chief div. genetics L.I. Coll. Hosp., Bklyn., 1986—; cons. WHO, Switzerland, 1982, Nat. Geog. Soc., Washington, 1982, Phototake, 1982-87; mem. cytogenetic adv. com. Prenatal Diagnosis Lab. N.Y.C. Dept. Health, 1978-90, Genetic Task Force N.Y. State, N.Y.C., 1976—; reviewer grants Nat. and Internat. Health Agys. and Socs.; lectr. colls., univs. and profl. assns. Author: Heterochromatin: Molecular and Structural Aspects, 1988, The Genome, 1990, (with A. Babu) Human Chromosomes: Manual of Basic Techniques, 1989, Human Chromosomes: Principles and Techniques; editor-in-chief: Advances in Genome Biology, 1989; contbr. over 350 abstracts and presentations and over 300 articles to profl. publs. including Am. Jour. Ob.-Gyn., Blood, Jour. Med. Genetics, Japanese Jour, Human Genetics, Oncology, Cytobios, Am. Jour. Human Genetics, Am. Jour. clin. Oncology, Internat. Jour. Cancer, Chromosoma, Cytogenetics. Apptd. to Adv. Coun. to Asst. Commr. City of N.Y. Dept. Health, Bur. Lab. Svcs., 1988. Nat. Merit scholar Gov. India, 1964-67, 1965-67; rsch. scholar Nat. Rsch. Coun. Can. and U. Western Ont., 1967-72, also teaching assistantship, 1972-73; rsch. grantee N.Y. State Dept. Health, Albany, 1985, 85-86, Cancer Treatment Fund, Cornell Med. Coll., 1985-86, United Leukemia Fund, Cornell Med. Coll., 1985-86, 86-87, Nat. Cancer Inst. of Health, Md., 1985-86, 86-87, 97-88, 88-90, Nat. Cancer Inst., 1976-77, 77-78, 78-80. Fellow AAAS, Royal Coll. Pathologists London, Assn. Clin. Scientists, The Inst. of Biology, N.Y. Acad. Scis., N.Y. Acad. Medicine (assoc.); mem. Am. Assn. Clin. Rsch., Am. Fedn. Clin. Rsch., Am. Genetic Assn. (life), Am. Soc. Cell Biology, Am. Soc. Human Genetics (life), European Soc. Human Genetics, Fedn. Am. Scientists, Genetic Soc. Am., Genetic Soc. Can., Genetic Toxicology Assn., Internat. Assn. Human Biologists, Indian Soc. Human Genetics (life), Soc. Exptl. Biology and Medicine. Home: 45-38 Springfield Blvd Bayside NY 11361-3556 Office: The L I Coll Hosp Div of Genetics Divsn Genetics Brooklyn NY 11201

VERMETTE, RAYMOND EDWARD, clinical laboratories administrator; b. Lewiston, Maine, June 30, 1942; s. Edward Louis and Anna Lucy (Raymond) V.; m. Ernestine Pero, Dec. 28, 1963; children: Tamara, Gregory. BS in Bacteriology, U. Maine, 1964; MS in Biochemistry, U. Wis., 1966; cert. personnel mgmt. Va. Dept. Edn., Fairfax, 1969; MBA, Temple U., 1973; master tchrs.' cert., Cath. Diocese of Boston, 1981. Supr. animal toxicology Hazleton Labs., Vienna, Va., 1967-71; personnel mgr. Damon Clin. Lab., Phila., 1971-73, ops. mgr., 1973-75, gen. mgr., Needham, Heights, Mass., 1975-90; v.p. ops. Damon Corp., Needham Hts., 1983-87, corp. v.p., 1987-89, sr. v.p., 1990-93; sr. v.p., gen. mgr. Corning/MetPath, Westwood, Mass., 1994-95; ret. 1995; vis. lectr fin. mgmt. and bus. adminstrn. Framingham State Coll., 1978-84; instr. mgmt. Newbury Jr. Coll., Boston, 1976-79. Author: (with B. Kliman and E. Kolowrat) What You Should Know About Medical Lab Tests, 1979. V.p. fin. com. Framingham, Mass., 1982-84; mem. capital budget com., Town of Framingham, 1987; mem.-elect, Town Meeting, 1987—; chmn. bd. religious edn. Cath. Ch., Framingham, 1981-84, co-chmn. Pre-Marriage Preparation Council, 1981—, organist, 1979—. Democrat. Home: 11 Willowbrook Dr Framingham MA 01701-5515

VERNAGLIA, PAUL ALBERT, ophthalmologist; b. Medford, Mass., July 19, 1941; s. John and Madeline (Baruffaldi) V.; m. Lydia Freitas; children: Lawrence, Brian. MD, N.Y. Med. Coll., 1968. Intern St. Barnabas Med. Ctr., N.Y.C., 1968-69; resident Boston U./Tufts Med. Ctr., 1969-72. Office: 63 Shore Rd Ste 22 Winchester MA 01890

VERNER, PETR, biomedical analyst, consultant; b. Prague, Czech Republic, Jan. 22, 1953; s. Alexej and Augustina (Valtova) V.; m. Hanka Simova, Apr. 14, 1979; children: Jonathan, Mikolas, Kristof, Rebecca. BS, H.S. Chem. Tech., Prague, 1972; MS, Tech. U., Prague, 1977; PhD, Inst. Pharmacy & Biochemistry, Prague, 1983. Rsch. head Charles U., Prague, 1983-92; vis. scientist Med. Rsch. Coun., Harrow, Eng., 1992-93; biomed. analyst, cons. Spectronex, Prague, 1993—; cons. Ctr. for Metabolic Disorders, Prague, 1993—. Co-author: Inherited Metabolic Disorders, 1989; contbr. revs. to profl. jours. Mem. Spectroscopy Soc., Mass Spectrometry Soc. (head 1992-95), Purkyně Med. Soc. Mem. Brathren Ch. Home: Dvouletky 47, 100 00 Prague 10, Czech Republic Office: Spectronex, Nad Santoškou 18, 150 00 Prague 5, Czech Republic

VERNON, ANDREW ANTHONY, epidemiologist; b. Atlanta, Jan. 12, 1948; s. Anthony G. Vernon and Helen M. (Weiner) Banks; m. Janice L. Callaway, Oct. 18, 1986; children: David, Benjamin, Anna. BA, Harvard U., 1971, MD, 1975; M Health Scis., Johns Hopkins U., 1987. Diplomate Am. Bd. Internal Medicine, Am. Bd. Infectious Disease, Nat. Bd. Med. Examiners. Commd. lt. USPHS, 1978, advanced through grades to capt., 1992; intern Cambridge (Mass.) Hosp., 1975-76, resident, 1976-77; resident Grady Meml. Hosp. and Emory U. Sch. Medicine, Atlanta, 1981-82; fellow in medicine and epidemiology Johns Hopkins U. Sch. Medicine, Balt., 1983-86, instr. medicine, 1986-87; epidemic intelligence svc. officer Ctrs. for Disease Control, Atlanta, 1978-80, staff epidemiologist, 1980-81, field epidemiologist Internat. Health Program Office,, 1987-90, asst. dir. for sci., 1990-91, dir. tech. support div., 1991-93; chief TB epidemiology unit Ga. De. Human Resources, Atlanta, 1993-95; med. epidemiologist divsn. TB elimination Ctrs. for Disease Control, Atlanta, 1995—. Contbr. articles on pub. health and medicine to med. jours. Mem. APHA, Am. Thoracic Soc., Soc. Epid. Rsch., Phi Beta Kappa. Office: Ctrs for Disease Control Mailstop E-10 Atlanta GA 30333

VERNON, CHARLES ROBERTSON, psychiatrist; b. Morganton, N.C., Aug. 21, 1926. BA, U. N.C., 1948; MD, Western Reserve U., 1952; postgrad. studies, Washington Psychoanalytic Inst., 1957-60. Diplomate Am. Bd. of Psychiatry and Neurology. Intern and resident N.C. Meml. Hosp., Chapel Hill, 1952-56; instr. dept. psychiatry U. N.C., Chapel Hill, 1856-59, asst. prof., 1959-60, clin. asst. prof., 1960-62, clin. assoc. prof., 1962—; pvt. practice Durham, N.C., 1963-68, Wilmington, N.C., 1968—; bd. dirs. SE Mental Health Ctr.; staff psychiatrist Counseling and Psychotherapy Ctr., Wilmington, N.C.; dir. profl. tng. N.C. Hosps. Bd. Control; dir. Cmty. Mental Health Svcs., N.C. Dept. Mental Health; dep. dir. N.C. Mental Health Region; dir. psychiat. edn. Area Health Edn. Ctr., Wilmington. Contbr. articles to profl. jours. Bd. dirs. N.C. Mental Health Coun., 1962-66, Southea. Mental Health Ctr. N.C., 1993—; mem. med. rev. bd. N.C. Divsn. Motor Vehicles, 1968-71, med. cons. panelist, 1971—; pres. George C. Ham Soc., 1984-85; active other civic orgns. Fellow Am. Coll. Psychiatrists (charter), Am. Psychiat. Assn.; mem. AMA, New Hanover County Med. Assn., N.C. Med. Soc. (com. on mental health 1987-94, other coms.), N.C. Psychiat. Assn. (pres. 1967), N.C. Group Behavior Soc., other health and mental health orgns. Home: CB 3411 116 Captains Ct Wrightsville Beach NC 28480 Office: Counsel & Psychotherapy Ctr 7230 Wrightsville Ave Wilmington NC 28403-7223

VERPOORTE, ROBERT, pharmacognosy and biotechnology educator; b. Eindhoven, the Netherlands, May 17, 1946; s. Pieter Marinus and Johanna Wilhelmina Frederika (van Dyk) V.; m. Jeannette van den Berge, Nov. 10, 1972; children: Kim M., Wencke F. MSc in Pharmacy, U. Leiden (the Netherlands), 1972, PhD in Pharmacy, 1976. Rsch. asst. U. Stockholm, 1970; rsch. asst. U. Leiden, 1972-76, lectr., 1976-87, prof., 1987—; vis. prof. U. Uppsala (Sweden), 1979, 80, U. Reims, France, 1992. Author: Chromatography of Alkaloids A and B, 1983, 84; contbr. numerous articles to profl. jours. Recipient Koninklyke Nederlandse Maatschappy Bevordering Pharmacie prize, 1970. Mem. Am. Soc. Pharmacognosy, Gesellschaft für Arzneipflanzenforschung, Internat. Assn. Plant Tissue Culture, Phytochem. Soc. Europe (chmn.). Home: Spanjaardslaan 7, 2352 AK Leiderdorp The Netherlands Office: Ctr for Bio Pharm Sci, PO Box 9502, 2300 RA Leiden The Netherlands

VERRET, JOSEPH MARC, psychiatrist; b. Port au Prince, Haiti, Sept. 2, 1953; came to U.S., 1981; s. Louis C. and Mrie Therese (Martelly) V.; m. Nicole Desir, Mar. 29, 1980; children: Mrie Christine, Joseph Marc Jr. BS, Petit Seminaire Coll., Haiti, 1972; MD, State U. Haiti, 1978; MPH, Columbia U., 1983. Rotating intern State U. Haiti Hosp., Port-au-Prince, 1977-78; resident in internal medicine State U. Haiti Hosp., 1978-81; resident in psychiatry Harlem Hosp./Columbia U., N.Y.C., 1983-87; attending physician, psychiatrist St. Joseph Hosp. and Med. Ctr., Paterson, N.J., 1987—; chief outpatient dept., psychiat. emergency room St. Joseph Hosp. and Med. Ctr., 1989-90; med. chief substance abuse svcs. Elizabeth (N.J.) Gen. Med. Ctr., 1990—; attending psychiatrist St. Joseph Hosp. and Med. Ctr., 1990—; cons. Office of Minority of Mental Health, Washington, 1989—. Fellow Acad. Medicine N.J., Coll. Forensic Examiners; mem. AMA, NRA (life), Am. Psychiat. Assn., Am. Pub. Health Assn., Am. Coll. Forensic Examiners (life), Am. Soc. Addiction Medicine. Office: Elizabeth Gen Med Ctr Substance Abuse Svcs East Bldg 655 E Jersey St Elizabeth NJ 07206

VERRILLO, RONALD THOMAS, neuroscience educator, researcher; b. Hartford, Conn., July 31, 1927; s. Francesco Paul and Angela (Forte) V.; m. Violet Silverstein, June 3, 1950; children—Erica, Dan, Thomas. B.A., Syracuse U., 1952; Ph.D., U. Rochester, 1958. Asst. prof. Syracuse U., 1957-62, research assoc., 1959-63, research fellow, 1963-67, assoc. prof., 1967-74, prof., 1974-94, prof. emeritus, 1995, assoc. dir. Inst. Sensory Research, 1980-84, dir., 1984-93, dir. grad. neurosci. program, 1984-93; advisor com. on hearing, bioacoustics and biomechanics NRC. Author: Adjustment to Visual Disability, 1961 (award 1962). Contbr. many chpts. to books, articles to profl. jours. Served with USN, 1945-46. Fellow Am. Found. for Blind, 1956, NATO, 1970; grantee NSF, 1969-72, 84-87, NIH, 1972—. Fellow Acoustical Soc. Am.; mem. Soc. for Neurosci. N.Y. Acad. Scis., Sigma Xi (research award 1982). Home: 312 Berkley Dr Syracuse NY 13210-3031 Office: Syracuse U Inst Sensory Rsch Merrill Ln Syracuse NY 13244

VERSCHOOR, JOHN, IV, physician assistant; b. Phoenix, Mar. 19, 1949; s. John Verschoor III and Dorothy (Killman) Hibbard; m. Nancy Lorel Welsh, Jan. 24, 1970; children: Bianca Dawn, Jared Moroni, Renee Ann, Benjamin Thayer. AS, Ariz. Western Coll., Yuma, 1972; Assoc. Med. Sci., Emory U., 1975; MD, Spartan Health Sci. U., St. Lucia, West Cast, 1985. Lic. nurse, Ariz., Ga., Tex., physician asst., Ariz. Orderly Yuma Regional Med. Ctr., 1967-68, emergency rm. nurse, 1970-72; commd. U.S. Army, 1972, advanced through grades to maj., 1990; physician asst. S.W. Med., Yuma, 1975-80; comdr. 12th Spl. Force Group, Albuquerque, 1980-85; exec. officer 996th Med. Co., Glendale, Ariz., 1985-88; bn. comdr. indsl. facility Fitzsimmons Army Hosp., 1988-92; physician asst. Deseret Diagnostic Ctr., Mesa, Ariz., 1990—; med. svc. officer CIA, Langley, Va., 1988—; exec. officer Tripler Army Med. Ctr., 1995—; Lectr. U. Utah, Salt Lake City, 1990-94; bd. dirs. Lazerus Group, Inc., Las Vegas, 1989—. V.p. Clnica de Mormona, Guadalajara, Mexico, 1981. Mem. Wilderness Med. Soc., Am. Acad. Physician Assts. Republican. LDS Ch. Office: Deseret Diagnostic Ctr 215 S Power Rd # 106 Mesa AZ 85206

VERSIC, LINDA JOAN, nurse educator, research company executive; b. Grove City, Pa., Aug. 27, 1944; d. Robert and Kathryn I. (Fagird) Davies; m. Ronald James Versic, June 11, 1966; children: Kathryn Clara, Paul Joseph. RN, Johns Hopkins Sch. of Nursing, 1965; BS in Health Edn., Ctrl. State U., 1980. Asst. head nurse Johns Hopkins Hosp., Balt., 1965-67; staff Nurse Registry Miami Valley Hosp., Dayton, Ohio, 1973-90; instr. Miami Jacobs Jr. Coll. Bus., Dayton, 1977-79; pres. Ronald T. Dodge Co., Dayton, 1979-86, chmn. bd., 1987—; chmn. bd. dirs. A-1 Travel, Inc. instr. Warren County (Ohio) Career Ctr., 1980-84, coord. diversified health occupations, 1984—. Coord. youth activities, mem. steering com. Queen of Apostles Cmty. Recipient Excellence in Tchg. award, 1992, award for Project Excellence, 1992. Active Miami Valley Mil. Affairs Assn., Glen Helen, Friends of Dayton Ballet, Dayton Art Inst., Cin. Art Mus. Mem. Ohio Vocat. Assn., Am. Vocat. Assn., Vocat. Indsl. Clubs Am. (chpt. advisor 1982—). Roman Catholic. Club: Johns Hopkins, Yugoslav of Greater Dayton. Home: 1601 Shafor Blvd Dayton OH 45419-3103 Office: Ronald T Dodge Co PO Box 630 Dayton OH 45459-0630

VER STEEG, DONNA LORRAINE FRANK, nurse, sociologist, educator; b. Minot, N.D., Sept. 23, 1929; d. John Jonas and Pearl H. (Denlinger) Frank; m. Richard W. Ver Steeg, Nov. 22, 1950; children: Juliana, Anne, Richard B. BSN, Stanford, 1951; MSN, U. Calif., San Francisco, 1967; MA in Sociology, UCLA, 1969, PhD in Sociology, 1973. Clin. instr. U. N.D. Sch. Nursing, 1962-63; USPHS nurse rsch. fellow UCLA, 1969-72; spl. cons., adv. com. on physicians' assts. and nurse practitioner programs Calif. State Bd. Med. Examiners, 1972-73; asst. prof. UCLA Sch. Nursing, 1973-79, assoc. prof., 1979-94, asst. dean, 1981-83, chmn. primary ambulatory care, 1976-87, assoc. dean, 1983-86, prof. emeritus, 1994—, chair primary care, 1994-96; co-prin. investigator PRIMEX Project, Family Nurse Practitioners, UCLA Extension, 1974-76; assoc. cons. Calif. Postsecondary Edn. Commn., 1975-76; spl. cons. Calif. Dept. Consumer Affairs, 1978; accredited visitor Western Assn. Schs. and Colls., 1985; mem. Calif. State Legis. Health Policy Forum, 1980-81; mem. nurse practitioner adv. com. Calif. Bd. RNs, 1995—. Contbr. chpts. to profl. books. Recipient Leadership award Calif. Area Health Edn. Ctr. System, 1989, Commendation award Calif. State Assembly, 1994; named Outstanding Faculty Mem. UCLA Sch. Nursing, 1982. Fellow Am. Acad. Nursing; mem. AAAS, ANA (interim chair Calif. 1995-96), Am. Soc. Law and Medicine, Nat. League Nursing, Calif. League Nursing, N.Am. Nursing Diagnosis Assn., Am. Assn. History Nursing, Assn. Health Svcs. Rsch., Stanford Nurses Club, Sigma Theta Tau (Gamma Tau chpt. Leadership award 1994), Sigma Xi. Home: 708 Swarthmore Ave Pacific Palisades CA 90272-4353 Office: UCLA Sch Nursing 700 Tiverton Ave Box 956919 Los Angeles CA 90095

VERSTRAETE, MARC, hematologist, educator; b. Brugge, Belgium, Apr. 1, 1925; s. Louis and Jeanne (Coppin) V.; m. Bernadette Moyersoen, July 12, 1955; children: Anneli, Benedicte, Luc, Frances, Beatrijs. MD with great honors, U. Leuven, Belgium, 1951, PhD, 1955; doctorate (hon.), U. Cordora, Argentina, 1983, U. Bologna, Italy, 1988, U. Bordeaux, France, 1989, U. Edinburgh, Scotland, U. London, 1996. Lectr. U. Leuven, 1957-61, asst. prof., 1961-63, assoc. prof., 1963-68, full prof., 1968—; rsch. fellow U. Oxford, U.K., 1955, Cornell U., N.Y.C., 1956. Author numerous books including Thrombosis, 1980, Bleeding Disorders, 1982; contbr. articles to profl. jours. Col. Belgium Army res. Decorated enobled baron, 1996. Fellow ACP, Am. Coll. Cardiology (hon.), Royal Coll. Medicine Edinburgh and London (hon.); mem. Internat. Soc. on Thrombosis and Hemostosis (pres. 1986-88), Internat. Soc. Hematology, European Soc. Cardiology. Home: Minderbroedersstraat 29, B-3000 Leuven Belgium Office: U Leuven Ctr Molecular & Vascular Rsch, Herestraat 49, B-3000 Leuven Belgium

VERTUA, RODOLFO, pharmacology educator; b. Milan, July 17, 1932; m. Boeuf Alda, Oct. 14, 1964; children: Valerio, Maria, Andrea. MD, U. Milan, 1957, PhD in Pharmacology, 1963. Asst. prof. U. Milan, 1958-63; vis. asst. prof. U. Detroit, 1961; assoc. prof. U. Trieste, Italy, 1969-73, prof., 1973—, dir. Inst. Pharmacology, 1976-95. Editor: Progress in Biochemical Pharmacology, 1965. Cons. State for Commn. for Drugs, Regione Friuli-Venezia Giulia, Trieste, 1980—. Mem. Rotary. Office: U Trieste Dept Biomed Scis, Via L Giorgieri 7, 34100 Trieste Italy

VERVILLE, TIMOTHY RAMOND, managed care executive; b. Pontiac, Mich., Apr. 23, 1954; s. Francis Raymond and Rosemarie Katherine (Rankin) V.; m. Johnnie Chris McCullar (div.); m. Ellen Catherine Kukulski, Sept. 23, 1983; children: Krystle Rose, Jennifer Lee, Victoria Alyce. Grad. h.s., Fountain Valley, Calif. Mgr. corp. devel. FHP, Fountain Valley, 1985-90; dir. HMO compliance Lincoln Nat. Corp., Ft. Wayne, Ind., 1990-92; mgr. specialty billing United Health Care, Minnetonka, Minn., 1992-93; network mgr. Principal Health Care, Ft. Wayne, 1993-95; managed care specialist Continental Health Systems, Ft. Wayne, 1995-96; v.p. managed care Drake Ctr., Cin., 1996—. With USCG, 1972-75. Home: 1632 Westley Ct Fort Wayne IN 46845

VESPER, LEE JOSEPH, dermatologist; b. Newport, Ky., July 5, 1937; s. Lee Joseph and Delma (Ranft) V.; m. Rose Marie Heiselmann, Aug. 19, 1961; children: Stephanie, Jennifer, Jessica. BS in Zoology, U. Cin., 1957, MD, 1961; MS, U. Minn., 1966. Intern Jackson Meml. Hosp., Miami, Fla., 1961-62; dermatology resident Mayo Clinic, Rochester, Minn., 1962-65; pvt. practice Cin., 1967—. Capt. USAF, 1965-67. Mem. Acad. Medicine Cin. (past pres. 1985-86), Ohio State Med. Assn., AMA. Republican. Roman Catholic. Home: 1174 Watkins Hill Rd New Richmond OH 45159 Office: 1127 Fehl Ln Cincinnati OH 45230

VESPER, TIMOTHY MICHAEL, critical care nurse, emergency nurse; b. Livonia, Mich., Sept. 23, 1972; s. Donald Lowell and Toni Maria (Talarico) V.; m. Andrea Lynn Kitson, May 21, 1994. Student, U. Mich., 1990-91; degree, Hurley Med. Ctr. Sch. Nursing, 1993. RN, Mich.; Am. Heart Assn. cert. BLS instr., ACLS provider. Staff nurse St. Mary's Med. Ctr., Saginaw, Mich., 1993—; agency nurse Nurse Corps Inc., Washington, Mich., 1994—. Firefighter, Swartz Creek (Mich.) Area Fire Dept., 1990—; emergency med. technician, Durand-Vernon Ambulance, Swartz Creek, 1990—, dispatcher, Durand, Mich., 1994—; citizen rep., Met. Alliance, Genesee County, Mich., 1994—. Home: 5021 School St Swartz Creek MI 48473

VEST, STEVEN LEE, gastroenterologist, hepatologist, internist; b. Mpls., July 30, 1948; s. Lee Herbert and Marian Mize (Rains) V.; m. Gayle Maureen Southworth, Nov. 27, 1971; 1 child, Matthew Steven. BA, U. Minn., 1970, MD, 1974. Diplomate Am. Bd. Intenal Medicine, Am. Bd Gastroenterology. Intern internal medicine Milw. County Hosp., 1974-75; resident internal medicine So. Ill. U., Springfield, 1975-77; fellow in gastroenterology and hepatology Duke U. Med. Ctr., Durham, N.C., 1978-80; gastroenterology-hepatology and internal medicine cons. Lonesome Pine Hosp., Big Stone Gap, Va., 1980—; gastroenterology and internal medicine cons. St. Mary's Hosp., Norton, 1983, Norton Community Hosp., Norton, Va., 1985—; chmn. med. care evaluation, Lonesome Pine Hosp., Big Stone Gap, 1984-88; chief of medicine Norton Community Hosp., 1991-93, bd. dirs., 1993—. Fellow ACP, Am. Coll. Gastroenterology; mem. Am. Gastroent. Assn., Am. Soc. Internal Medicine, Va. Med. Soc. (state del. 1992), Wise County Med. Soc. (treas. 1984-86, v.p. 1991-92, pres. 1992-93), Am. Assn. Christian Counselors. Methodist. Home: Powell Valley 1800-B Egan Rd Big Stone Gap VA 24219 Office: NCH Med Arts Bldg #2 98 15th St NW Ste 202 Norton VA 24273

VESTAL, KATHERINE WHEELER, nurse, administrator, consultant; b. N.C., June 27, 1947; d. Sheldon and Katherine (Hall) Wheeler; m. Rudy Janota; 1 child, Rick Vestal. BSN, Tex. Christian U., 1970; MS, Tex. Women's U., 1975; PhD, Tex. A&M U., 1983; postgrad., St. Thomas U., 1987. Prof. U. Tex., Galveston; assoc. exec. dir. Hermann Hosp., Houston; v.p. Northwestern Meml. Hosp., Chgo.; ptnr. Ernst and Young, Dallas, Hay Mgmt. Cons. Author: Pediatric Critical Care, 1982, Perinatal Critical Care, 1984, Management Concepts for the New Nurse, 1987, 94. Fellow Am. Acad. Nursing; mem. Nat. League for Nursing, Am. Coll. of Healthcare Execs. Home: 122 Meadowcreek Rd Coppell TX 75019-4019

VESTAL, ROBERT ELDEN, physician, clinical gerontologist, pharmacologist; b. Auburn, Calif., Oct. 25, 1945; s. Elden Hall and Mary Ethel (Gerth) V.; m. Bonita Helen Klahn, Sept. 7, 1968; children: Zachary Robert, Sarah Ruth. BA in Biology with great distinction, Stanford U., 1967; MD, U. Calif., San Francisco, 1971. Diplomate Nat. Bd. Med. Examiners, Am. Bd. Internal Medicine with subspecialty in geriatric medicine, Am. Bd. Clin. Pharmacology (charter); lic. physician Md., Tenn., Idaho. Intern U. Colo. Med. Ctr., Denver, 1971-72, asst. resident, 1972-73; clin. assoc. Gerontology Rsch. Ctr. Nat. Inst. Aging/NIH, Balt., 1973-76; fellow divsn. clin. pharmacology Vanderbilt U., Nashville, 1975-77; chief clin. pharmacology and gerontology rsch. unit VA Med. Ctr., Boise, Idaho, 1978—, co-dir. fellowship in gerontology/geriatric medicine, 1983-95, assoc. chief of staff for R & D, 1985—, chief clin. pharmacology sect., 1987—; dir. Mountain States Med. Rsch. Inst., Boise, 1994—; summer rsch. fellow Electron Microscope Lab., U. Calif.-San Francisci, 1968, Metabolic Rsch. unit, 1969; vis. physician Balt. City Hosp., 1973-75; med. cons. Md. Poison Info. Svcs., Sch. Pharmacy, U. Md., Balt., 1974-75; active staff internal medicine svc. Vanderbilt U. Hosp., Nashville, 1976-77; med. dir. Idaho Vets. Nursing Home, Boise, 1981-83, assoc. med. dir., 1983-87; instr. depts. pharmacology and medicine Vanderbilt U., Nashville, 1976-77; asst. prof. dept. medicine U. Wash., Seattle, 1977-81, assoc. prof. dept. medicine, 1981-88, adj. assoc. prof. dept. pharmacology, 1987-88, adj. prof. dept. pharmacology, 1988—, prof. dept. medicine, 1988—; clin. prof. (affiliate) Coll. Health Scis., Boise State U., 1984—; prof. (affiliate) dept. pharm. scis. Coll. of Pharmacy, Idaho State U., Pocatello, 1987—; participant and rapporteur WHO Tech. Group Meeting on Use of Medicaments by Elderly, Geneva, 1980; participant numerous confs.; lectr. in field; ad hoc adv. com. aging pharmacology program Nat. Inst. Aging, NIH, 1981-86; adv. panel on geriatrics gen. com. of revision U.S. Pharmacopeial Conv., Inc., 1981—, chmn., 1990—; mem. pharmacy and therapeutics adv. com. Pharm. Assistance Contract for the Elderly, Dept. Aging, Commonwealth of Pa., 1992—; tech. adv. group Abt Assocs., 1993—; sci. adv. bd. Collaborative Clin. Rsch., Inc., 1994—; mem. generic drugs adv. com. FDA, Dept. Health and Human Svcs., 1994-95; mem. Medco Geriatric Drug Utilization Adv. Bd., Merck Rsch. Labs., 1995—; pharm. scis. adv. com. FDA, 1996—; mem. acad. selection panel Pfizer Vis. Professorship Program in Clin. Pharmacology, 1996—. Editl. bd. Geriatrics, 1980-85, Jour. Gerontology, 1981-85, Jour. Am. Geriatrics Soc., 1982-85, 87-89, Clin. Pharmacokinetics, 1984—, Clin. Pharmacology and Therapeutics, 1986—, Jour. Gerontology, 1988-95, Rsch. Comm. in Chem. Pathology and Pharmacology, 1989-94, Drugs and Aging, 1990—, Jour. Pharmacology and Exptl. Therapeutics, 1992—, PharmacoEcons., 1992—, Drugs and Therapy Perspectives, 1993—, Rsch. Comm. in Molecular Pathology and Pharmacology, 1994—; contbr. numerous articles and abstracts to profl. jours., chpts. to books. Mem. Project Independence Task Force, Gov. Idaho, 1979-80; bd. trustees and exec. com. Mountain States Med. Rsch. Inst., Boise, 1994—, mem. rsch. com., 1994—. With USPHS, 1975-77. Recipient Arthur S. Flemming award, 1982; Alfred P. Sloan Found. scholar, 1963-67; grantee VA, 1978—, NIH, 1980-87, 91-94, Am. Heart Assn., 1980-85, 89-91, Clin. Rsch. Internat., 1987-89, Merck Sharp & Dohme, 1989-90, 92-95, Squibb Pharm. Group, 1990-92, Apotex Inc., 1992-93, Hoechst-Roussel Pharm., Inc., 1991-94, Sandoz Pharm. Corp., 1993-95, Immunex Corp., 1995. Fellow AAAS, ACP, Gerontol. Soc. Am., Am. Geriat. Soc., Am. Coll. Clin. Pharmacology, Molecular Medicine Soc.; mem. Am. Fedn. Clin. Rsch., Am. Soc. Clin. Pharmacology and Therapeutics (v.p. 1987-88, 92-93, bd. dirs. 1987—, pres.-elect 1996-97), Brit. Pharm. Soc., Idaho Acad. Sci., Am. Heart A80-88, rsch. com. 1980-85, pres. 1984-86, mem. edn. com. 1986—, govt. affairs com. 1989—, mem. coun. on basic sci. 1993—, others), Am. Soc. for Pharmacology and Exptl. Therapeutics (mem. exec. com. clin. pharmacology divsn. 1985-90, chmn. 1986-90, selection com. for Otto Krayer award 1989), Western Soc. for Clin. Investigation, Am. Fedn. for Aging Rsch., Western Assn. Physicians, Am. Thoracic Soc., Western Pharmacology Soc., N.Y. Acad. Scis., Ada County Med. Soc., Idaho Med. Ass., Soc. for Exptl. Biology and Medicine, Phi Beta Kappa, Alpha Omega Alpha. Office: VA Medical Center 500 W Fort St Boise ID 83702-4501

VETSCH, RAYMOND, physician; b. Zurich, Switzerland, Apr. 2, 1955; m. Susan Vetsch; children: Maria Nicole, Sean Phillip, Madeline Rochelle, Siena Rae. Degree in natural sci., Premed. Coll., Aarau, Switzerland, 1971-75; MD, U. Basel, Switzerland, 1981. Diplomate Am. Bd. Surgery, Am. Bd. Thoracic Surgery; cert. ATLS instr. Intern Med. Sch. U. Basel, 1980-81; resident in gen. surgery State Hosp., Aarau, 1982-84; intern Med. Coll. Wis., Milw., 1984-85, resident in gen. surgery, 1985-90; resident in cardiothoracic surgery and cardiac transplant U. Utah, Salt Lake City, 1990-92; fellow in pediatric congenital heart surgery Hosp. for Sick Children, Toronto, Ont., Can., 1992; pvt. practice adult and pediatric cardiac thoracic surgery N.Mex. Heart Inst., PA, Albuquerque, 1993—; co-dir. pediatric cardiac surgery program Presbyn. Hosp., Albuquerque, 1993—; presenter in field. Contbr. articles to profl. publs. Fellow ACS (assoc.); mem. Assn. for Acad. Surgery, Am. Thoracic Soc., Greater Albuquerque Med. Assn. Home: 9801 Modesto Rd NW Albuquerque NM 87122

VETTER, HERBERT OTTO, cardiac surgeon; b. Tiefenbach, Baden, Germany, Aug. 29, 1955; s. Alfred Josef and Helga (Tauer) V.; m. Heidi Zensen; children: Sabrina, Miriam. MD, U. Heidelberg, Germany, 1982; PhD, U Munich, Germany, 1996. Rsch. fellow Albert-Einstein Coll. Medicine, Bronx, N.Y., 1984; registrar Groote Schuur Hosp., Capetown, South Africa, 1985; resident German Heart Ctr., Berlin, 1986, St. Gertrauden Hosp., Berlin, 1987-89; resident Grosshadern Hosp., Munich, 1990-94, cons., 1995—. Author: (with Hetzer and Schmutzler) Ischemic Mitral Incompetence, 1991. Office: Grosshadern Hosp U Munich, Dept Cardiac Surgery, 81366 Munich Germany

VEZERIDIS, MICHAEL PANAGIOTIS, surgeon, educator; b. Thessaloniki, Greece, Dec. 16, 1943; came to U.S., 1974; s. Panagiotis and Sofia (Avramidis) V.; m. Therese Mary Statz; children: Peter Statz, Alexander Michael. MD, U. Athens, 1967; MA (hon) ad eundem, Brown U., 1989. Diplomate Am. Bd. Surgery. Fellow surg. rsch. Harvard Med. Sch./Mass. Gen. Hosp., Boston, 1974-77; resident U. Mass., Worcester, 1977-80; fellow in surg. oncology Roswell Park Meml. Inst., Buffalo, 1980-81, attending surgeon, 1981-82; staff surgeon VA Med. Ctr., Providence, 1982-84; asst. prof. surgery Brown U., Providence, 1982-88; chief surg. oncology VA Med. Ctr., Providence, 1984—, assoc. chief surgery, 1986—; cons. in surgery R.I. Hosp., Providence, 1987—; surg. oncologist Roger Williams Med. Ctr., Providence, 1989—; assoc. dir. div. surg. oncology Brown U., Providence, 1989—, assoc. prof. surgery, 1988-94, prof., 1994—; chmn. profl. edn. com. R.I. div. Am. Cancer Soc., Providence, 1987-89, bd. dirs., 1987—, pres.-elect 1989-91, pres. 1991-93, del. dir. to nat. bd. dirs., 1993—; vis. prof. U. Patras (Greece) Med. Sch., 1988; mem. sci. adv. com. Clin. Rsch. Ctr., Brown U., Providence, 1989-91. Contbr. articles to profl. jours. and chpts. in med. books. Mem. parish coun. Ch. of Annunciation, Cranston, R.I., 1985-91; v.p. Hellenic Cultural Soc. Southeastern New Eng., Providence, 1987-89. Decorated Navy Commendation medal; named Profl. Fed. Employee of Yr., R.I. Fed. Exec. Coun., 1987; recipient St. George medal Am. Cancer Soc.; Merit Rev. Cancer Rsch. grantee VA, 1983-89. Fellow ACS; mem. Soc. Surg. Oncology, Assn. for Acad. Surgery, Am. Soc. Clin. Oncology, N.Y. Acad. Scis. (life), Soc. for Surgery Alimentary Tract, Am. Assn. for Cancer Rsch., Collegium Internat. Chirurgiae Digestivae, Soc. for Metastasis Rsch., New Eng. Cancer Soc., New Eng. Surg. Soc., Quidnessett Country Club. Greek Orthodox. Home: 50 Limerock Dr East Greenwich RI 02818-1643 Office: Roger Williams Med Ctr 825 Chalkstone Ave Providence RI 02908-4728

VICDAN, KUBILAY, obstetrician, gynecologist; b. Malatya, Turkey, Nov. 28, 1964; s. Mehmet and Yuksel (Aksoy) V.; m. Nedjme Arzu Dicleli, Oct. 14, 1989; 1 child, Umut. MD, Ankara U., 1988. Resident Ministry of Health, Ankara, 1988-93, chief resident, specialist, 1994-95; specialist Sevgi Hosp., Ankara, 1996—; cons. Ministry of Health, 1993-94. Contbr. articles to profl. jours. Recipient award Turkish Sci. and Rsch. Inst. for Encouraging Internat. Scientific Publications, 1994-95. Mem. Turkish Med. Assn., Turkish Perinathology and Endocrinology Soc., Turkish Gynecology Soc. Home: Guvenlik Caddesi Alidede So, Ankara 06540, Turkey Office: Sevgi Hosp, Tunus Caddesi No 28, Ankara 06680, Turkey

VICE, JON EARL, hospital executive; b. Fairfield, Ala., July 1, 1947; s. Jon Walker Vice and Martha Ann (Lee) Cain; m. Sara Rose Romano Marino, July 26, 1967 (div. Feb. 1975); children: Jon E. Jr., Lisa Ann; m. Joanne Katherine Richter, June 28, 1975 (div. Mar. 1992); children: Jeffrey Walker, Jessica Lynn. BS, U. Ala., Tuscaloosa, 1970; MS, U. Ala., Birmingham, 1974. Asst. to adminstr. Children's Hosp. Ala., Birmingham, 1971-72, adminstr., chief operating officer, 1977-79; assoc. adminstr. Children's Hosp. Med. Ctr., Cin., 1972-76; exec. v.p., chief operating officer Children's Hosp. Wis., Milw., 1979-84, pres., chief exec. officer, 1984—; chmn., bd. dirs. Milw. Regional Med. Ctr., 1985—, Child Health Corp. Am., Kansas City, Mo.; pres., bd. dirs. Total Care Health Plan (HMO), Milw., 1985-87; mem. Greater Milw. Com.; bd. dirs. Milw. Ednl. Trust. Named Outstandng Alumnus Grad. Program in Health Adminstrn., U. Ala.-Birmingham Alumni Assn., 1987. Mem. Am. Coll. Healthcare Execs., Nat. Assn. Childrens Hosps. (exec. coun., bd. dirs. 1986—, chmn. 1989—), Westmoore Country Club (v.p. bd.), Univ. Club. Presbyterian. Office: Children's Hosp Wis PO Box 1997 Milwaukee WI 53201-1997

VICK, DAVID ARTHUR, osteopathic physician; b. Denver, Feb. 25, 1937; s. Morris M. Vick and Gladys Marie Hamilton; m. Suzanne Evans, June 14, 1959; children: Paul David, Douglas Eugene, Gregory Allen, Cynthia Ann. BS, N.E. Mo. State U., Kirksville, 1963; DO, Kansas City Coll. Osteopathy, 1963. Intern Mt. Clemens (Mich.) Gen. Hosp., 1963-64; resident in internal medicine Flint (Mich.) Osteo. Hosp., 1964-67; pvt. practice internal medicine Mesa, Ariz., 1967-72, Lubbock, Tex., 1972-79, Worland, Wyo., 1979-87, Dallas, 1987-88; asst. prof. Tex. Coll. Osteo. Medicine, Ft. Worth, 1988-96; assoc. prof., chmn. dept. manipulative medicine U. North Tex. Health Sci. Ctr., Ft. Worth, 1996—. Fellow Am. Acad. Osteopathy; mem. Cranial Acad., Am. Osteo. Assn., Am. Coll. Osteo. Internists, Rho Sigma Chi. Home: 4254 Barcelona Dr Fort Worth TX 76133 Office: U North Tex Health Sci Ctr 3500 Camp Bowie Blvd Fort Worth TX 76107

VICK, NICHOLAS A., neurologist; b. Chgo., Oct. 3, 1939. MD, U. Chgo., 1965. Diplomate Am. Bd. Neurology. Intern U. Chgo. Hosps., 1965, resident in neurology, 1966-68; fellow in neurology NIH, Bethesda, Md., 1968-70; staff Evanston (Ill.) Hosp., 1975—; prof. neurology Northwestern U. Med. Sch., Evanston, Ill., 1978—. Office: Evanston Hosp Div Neurology 2650 Ridge Ave Evanston IL 60201-1718

VICKERMAN, KEITH, biologist; b. Huddersfield, U.K., Mar. 21, 1933; s. Jack and Mabel (Dyson) V.; m. Moira Dutton, Sept. 16, 1961; 1 child, Louise Charlotte. BSc, U. Coll. London, 1955; PhD, London U., 1960, DSc, 1970. Wellcome rsch. fellow U. Coll. London, 1958-63, tropical rsch. fellow of the Royal Soc., 1963-68; reader in zoology U. Glasgow, Scotland, 1968-74; prof. zoology U. Glasgow, 1974-84, Regius prof. zoology, 1984—; cons. expert WHO Panel on Parasitic Diseases, 1973—. Author: (with F.E.G. Cox) The Protozoa, 1967; contbr. numerous articles to profl. jours. Fellow Royal Soc., Royal Soc. Edinburgh, U. Coll. London, Leeuwenhoek lectr., 1994. Fellow Royal Soc. Tropical Medicine and Hygiene, Linnean Soc. (Gold medalist 1996); mem. Soc. Protozoologists (hon. mem., Brit. sect. pres. 1977-80). Home: 16 Mirrlees Dr, Glasgow Scotland G12 0SH Office: Univ of Glasgow, Glasgow Scotland G12 8QQ

VICKERS, MARK ADRIAN, hematologist, researcher; b. Tunbridge Wells, Kent, Eng., Mar. 13, 1959; s. Peter Vickers and Mira (Sunderland) Howard; m. Julie Anne Collins; children: Timothy, Anna, Andrew. MA, Oxford (Eng.) U., 1980, MB BChir, 1983, MD, 1992. Tng. fellow Med. Rsch. Coun., Oxford, 1986-90; registrar Hammersmith Hosp., London, 1990-92; sr. registrar Royal Berkshire, Reading, Eng., 1992-94, John Radcliffe, Oxford, 1994-96; sr. lectr. Aberdeen (Scotland) U., 1996—. Contbr. articles to profl. jours. Mem. Royal Coll. Physicians, Royal Coll. Pathologists, Brit. Soc. Hematology. Office: Aberdeen Univ, Dept Med & Therapeutics, Polwarth Bldg Foresterhill, Aberdeen AB9 27D, Scotland

VICKERY, ROBERT KINGSTON, JR., biology educator; b. Saratoga, Calif., Sept. 18, 1922; s. Robert Kingston Sr. and Ruth (Bacon) V.; m. Marcia Agnes Hoak, July 7, 1951; children: David Kingston, Peter Hoak. AB in Engring., Stanford U., 1944, MA in Biology, 1948, PhD in Biology, 1952. Instr. botany Pomona Coll., Claremont, Calif., 1950-51; asst. prof. biology U. Utah, Salt Lake City, 1952-57, assoc. prof., 1957-64, chair genetics dept., 1962-65, prof., 1964-93, prof. emeritus, 1994—; vis. assoc. prof. biology Harvard U., Cambridge, Mass., summer 1961; mem. fellow panel NIH, Bethesda, Md., 1964-69; leader field trips to Galapagos Islands, 1989-93. Author: Manuel of Native Plants of Salt Lake Region, 1963; assoc. editor: Evolution, 1968-72; contbr. over 90 articles to profl. publs. 1st lt. USAF, 1943-46, PTO. Rsch. fellow Calif. Inst. Tech., Pasadena, 1955. Mem. Internat. Orgn. Plant Biosystematists (officer 1973-85), Soc. for Study of Evolution (1st v.p. 1977-78), Calif. Bot. Soc. (2d v.p. 1983-88), Sigma Xi (chpt. pres. 1973-74). Home: 3376 Louise Ave Salt Lake City UT 84109-4267 Office: U Utah Dept Biology Salt Lake City UT 84112

VICKREY, HERTA MILLER, microbiologist; b. San Gregorio, Calif.; d. John George and Hertha Lucy (Mehrstedt) Miller; m. William David Vickrey; children: Ellean H., Carlene L. Smith, Corrine A. Pochop, Arlene A.; m. Robert James Fitzgibbon, Dec. 28, 1979. BA, San Jose State U., 1957; MA, U. Calif., Berkeley, 1963, PhD in Bacteriology and Immunology, 1970. Cert. immunologist, pub. health microbiologist, med. technologist. Pub. health microbiologist Viral & Rickettsial Diseases Lab., Calif. Dept. Pub. Health, Berkeley, 1958-60, 61-62, 1964; postgrad. rsch. bacteriologist dept. bacteriology U. Calif., Berkeley, 1963-64; bacteriologist Children's Hosp. Med. Ctr. No. Calif., Oakland, 1958-70; asst. prof. U. Victoria, B.C., Can., 1970-72; rsch. assoc. rsch. dept. Wayne County Gen. Hosp., Wayne, Mich., 1972-83; lab. supr. med. rsch. and edn. U. Mich., Ann Arbor, 1977-83; pub. health lab. dir. Shasta County Pub. Health Svcs., Redding, Calif., 1983-84; sr. pub. health microbiologist, med. technologist Tulare County Pub. Health Lab., Tulare, Calif., 1984—; tech. supr. Tulare County Pub. Health Lab., Visalia, Calif., 1992-93; med. technologist Tulare County Pub. Health Lab., Tulare, Calif., 1994—; vis. scientist MIT, Cambridge, 1982; organizer, lectr. mycology workshop Tulare County Health Dept. Lab., Visalia, 1988; USPHS trainee U. Calif., Berkeley, 1965, 66. Author: Isolation and Identification of Mycotic Agents, 1987-88; contbr. articles to profl. jours. Fundraiser Battered Women's Shelter, Redding, 1983, Real Opportunities for Youth, Visalia, 1985, 86, Open Gate Ministries, Dinuba, Visalia, 1987-94. Fellow NIH, 1966-69, Dr. E.E. Dowdle rsch. fellow, U. Calif., 1969-70; grantee U. Victoria, 1970-72, Med. Rsch. and Edn. and Med. Adminstrn., U. Mich., 1973-83. Mem. No. Calif. Assn. Pub. Health Microbiologists, Calif. Scholarship Soc., Am. Soc. Clin. Pathologists (assoc.), Phi Beta Kappa, Delta Omega, Phi Kappa Phi, Beta Beta Beta. Home: 3505 W Campus Ave Apt 5 Visalia CA 93277-1869 Office: Tulare County Pub Health Lab 1062 S K St Tulare CA 93274

VICTOR, JAY, dermatologist; b. Detroit, Dec. 4, 1935; s. Ben and Pauline (Meisel) V.; m. Elawa S. Lepler, Mar., 1965 (div. Aug., 1977); children: Pamela C., Daryl B.; m. Marianne Cook, sept. 4, 1978; children: Jonah A., Lauren. BA, U. Mich., 1958, MD, 1962. Diplomate Am. Bd. Dermatology. Intern Henry Ford Hosp., Detroit, 1962-63, resident, 1963-66; asst. prof. drematology Wayne State U. Sch. of Medicine, Detroit, 1958-68; pvt. practice in dermatology Allen Park, Mich., 1966—; mem. active staff Oakwood Hosp., Dearborn, Mich., 1967—, courtesy staff Detroit Med. Ctr., 1967—; cons. Heritage Hosp. Taylor, Mich., 1980—. Fellow Am Acad. Dermatology; mem. AMA, Mich. State Med. Soc. (del. 1980—) Wayne County Med. Soc. (del. 1980—), Mich. Dermatology Soc.. Jewish. Office: Jay Victor MD 15201 Southfield Allen Park MI 48101

VICTOR, LORRAINE CAROL, critical care nurse; b. Duluth, Minn., June 14, 1953; d. George E. and Phyllis M. (Pierce) Drimel; m. Robert G. Victor. BA in Nursing, Coll. St. Scholastica, 1975; MS in Nursing, U. Minn., 1984. Cert. regional trainer for neonatal resuscitation program. Staff nurse St. Mary's Hosp., Rochester, Minn., 1975-79, 80-81, U. Wis. Hosp., Madison, 1979-80, U. Minn. Hosps., Mpls., 1981-84, 85-86; clin. instr. neonatal ICU, Children's Hosp. Inc., St. Paul, 1984-86; clin. nurse specialist neonatal ICU, Orlando (Fla.) Regional Med. Ctr., 1986-88, Children's Hosp. St. Paul, 1988—. Mem. AACN (Critical Care Nurse of Yr. award Greater Twin Cities chpt. 1992, cert. neonatal intensive care nursing), Nat. Cert. Corp. (cert. in neonatal intensive care nursing), Nat. Assn. Neonatal Nurses, Sigma Theta Tau. Office: Children's Health Care St Paul Birth Ctr 345 N Smith Ave Saint Paul MN 55102-2392

VIDELL, JARED STEVEN, cardiologist; b. Phila., Apr. 9, 1947; s. Harry and Rose (Malken) V.; m. Cyla Trocki, Dec. 27, 1969; children: Haviv Elana, Mikhael Alon, Samara Pilar. AA, Miami-Dade Jr. Coll., Opalocka, Fla., 1966; BEd, U. Miami, 1969; DO, Phila. Coll. Osteo. Medicine, 1976. Resident and chief resident in internal medicine Atlantic City (N.J.) Med. Ctr., 1976-79; fellow in cardiovascular diseases Albert Einstein Med. Ctr., Phila., 1979-81; rsch. fellow in nuclear cardiology Deborah Heart and Lung Ctr., Browns Mills, N.J., 1981-82; dir. employee health svcs. Deborah Heart and Lung Ctr., Browns Mills, 1982-84; asst. dir. cardiology Pritikin Longevity Ctr., Downington, Pa., 1984-87; cardiologist, dir. clin. lab. Physician Care, P.C., Towanda, Pa., 1987-90; from co-chmn. intensive care to dir. cardiac stress lab. Meml. Hosp., Towanda, 1987-90; dir. house staff, intensive/cardiac care Lower Bucks Hosp., Bristol, Pa., 1992-94; dir. house staff ICU-Critical Care Unit North Phila. Health Systems, 1994—; med. dir. Am. Cancer Soc. chpt., 1989-90; mem. state peer rev. KEPRO, 1989-90. Contbr. rsch. articles to profl. jours. Fellow Am. Coll. Angiology; mem. AMA, Am. Coll. Chest Physicians, Am. Soc. Internal Medicine, Internat. Soc. Internal Medicine, Internat. Soc. Endovascular Surgery, Internat. Platform Assn., Pa. Med. Soc., Phila. County Med. Soc., Alumni Assn. Phila. Coll. Osteo. Medicine. Jewish. Home: 408 N Exeter Ave Margate City NJ 08402

VIDOVICH, DANKO VICTOR, neurosurgeon, researcher; b. Zagreb, Croatia, Dec. 29, 1958; came to U.S., 1991; s. Mladen and Zdenka (Radonichich) V. MD, Zagreb U., Croatia, 1982, MSc in Biology, 1990. Neurosurgeon Clin. Hosp. Sisters of Mercy, Zagreb, Croatia, 1986-91; sr. rschr. Allegheny Singer Rsch. Inst., Pitts., 1991—. Contbr. articles to profl. jours. Office: Allegheny Gen Hosp 320 E North Ave Pittsburgh PA 15212-4746

VIEDERMAN, MILTON, psychiatrist, educator; b. N.Y.C., Feb. 17, 1930. BA, Columbia U., 1951; MD, Harvard U., 1955; cert. in psychoanalysis, Columbia U., 1964. Diplomate Am. Bd. Psychiatry and Neurology, 1967. Intern Peter Bent Brigham Hosp., 1955-56, Columbia-N.Y. State Psych. Inst., 1956-57, 60-62; instr., assoc. in psychiatry Columbia U. Coll. Physicians and Surgeons, N.Y.C., 1962-71, asst. clin. prof., 1967-71; pvt. practice N.Y.C.; dir. consultation-liaison svcs. N.Y. Hosp., N.Y.C., 1975—; tng. and supervising analyst Columbia Psychoanalytic Ctr. for Tng. and Rsch., N.Y.C., 1969—; assoc. prof. clin. psychiatry Cornell U. Med. Coll., N.Y.C., 1975-78, prof., 1980—; cons. Rockefeller U. Hosp., N.Y.C., 1984—, Meml. Sloan-Kettering Inst., N.Y.C.; disting. lectr. Radcliff Hosp., Oxford (Eng.) U. Sch. Medicine, 1982. Contbr. articles to med. jours. Capt. M.C., U.S. Army, 1957-60. Recipient Outstanding Tchr. award N.Y. Hosp. Westchester div., 1979, PWC, 1980, 84. Office: 525 E 68th St New York NY 10021-4873

VIEIRA, LINDA MARIE, endoscopy technician; b. San Jose, Calif., July 8, 1961; d. Albert Sequeira and Catherine Marie (Souza) Vieira; m. John Bettencourt Ramos, June 12, 1982 (div. July 1993). AA, De Anza Coll., 1986; BA, St. Mary's Coll. Calif., Moraga, 1988. Cert. gastrointestinal clinician, aerobic instr. Endoscopy technician O'Connor Hosp., San Jose, 1979-94, Good Samaritan Health Sys., Los Gatos, Calif., 1994—, Alexian Bros. Hosp., San Jose, Calif., 1995—; aerobic instr. Mountain View (Calif.) Athletic Club, 1984-95, Decathlon Club, Santa Clara, 1991—, Golds Gym, Mountain View, 1994—, Silicon Valley Athletic Club, Santa Clara, 1995—. Contbr. articles to profl. jours. Vol. O'Connor Hosp., 1975-79; active campaign Santa Clara City Council, 1980-81. Fellow Irmandade Da Festa Do Espirito Santo (sec. 1974-82, queen 1975-76), Soc. Gastrointestinal Assts., No. Soc. Gastrointestinal Assts., Soc. Espirito Santo of Santa Clara, Luso Am. Fraternal Fedn. (state youth pres. 1979-80, youth leader local coun. Santa Clara Mountain View 1979-87, scholar, 1979, founder, organizer Mountain View-Santa Clara chpt. 1980, pres. local region 1980-84, state 20-30 pres. 1984-85, state dir. youth programs 1988-94, state dir. 1994—); mem. Aerobics and Fitness Assn. Am. Republican. Roman Catholic. Home: 1618 Roll St Santa Clara CA 95050-4024 Office: Good Samaritan Health Sys 15066 Los Gatos Almaden Rd Los Gatos CA 95032-3909

VIETA, PAUL ANTHONY, obstetrician, gynecologist; b. N.Y.C., July 8, 1940; s. John O. and Henrietta E. (Countiss) V.; m. Leila May, May 28, 1966; children: Kathryn, Amy, Paul, Laura. BA, Columbia Coll., 1962; MD, N.J. Coll. Medicine, 1966. Diplomate Am. Bd. Ob-Gyn. 1st ltd. U.S. Army, 1962, advanced through grades to col., 1980; intern Cooper Hosp., Canden, N.J., 1966-67; resident N.Y. Med. Coll., Met. Hosp. Ctr., 1967-71; physician, dep. chief 279th Sta. Hosp., Berlin, Germany, 1971-74; physician Walson Army Hosp., Ft. Dix, N.J., 1974-75; chief ob-gyn. 3274th USAH, Durham, N.C., 1975-92; physician Womack Army Hosp., 1990-91, Highland Ob-Gyn Clinic, Fayetteville, 1975—. Fellow Am. Coll. Ob-Gyn., Royal Coll. Medicine; mem. AMA, Am. Med. Soc., N.C. Med. Soc. Home: 2906 Skye Dr Fayetteville NC 28303 Office: Highland Ob-Gyn Clinic 911 Hay St Fayetteville NC 28305

VIEWEG, BRUCE WAYNE, mental health researcher; b. Westminster, Mass., July 30, 1947; s. Herman C. and Ardath (Woollacott) V.; m. JoAnne Rawlings, Dec. 19, 1970; children: Emily, Anna. BMus Ed, U. Lowell, 1969; MSEd, So. Ill. U., 1975. Tchr. Hampshire Country Sch., Rindge, N.H., 1969-71; rsch. technician U. Mo. Inst. Psychiatry, Columbia, 1972-75, rsch. specialist, 1975-80, rsch. asst., 1980-84, rsch. assoc., 1984-94, dir. computer lab., 1987-94; dep. dir. for quality of treatment Mo. Dept. of Mental Health, Jefferson City, 1994-95, dir. of office of info. systems, 1995—. Author: (with others) several sci. books; contbr. articles profl. jours. Treas. Hand in Hand Presch., St. Charles, Mo., 1980; pres. Becky-David Elem. Sch. PTO, St. Charles, 1988, 89; long-range planning coun. Francis Howell Sch. Dist., 1988-94, long-range study com. on tech., 1990, long range task force on faculty compensation, 1990, mem. bd. edn., 1992-94, pres. 1993; steering com. Knights of Excellence North H.S., 1990. Recipient Howell of Fame award Francis Howell Sch. Dist., 1990. Mem. Silver Key. Home: 1017 Mayfair Rd Saint Charles MO 63303-4024 Office: Mo Dept Mental Health 1706 E Elm St Jefferson City MO 65102

VIGEN, KATHRYN L. VOSS, nursing administrator, educator; b. Lakefield, Minn., Sept. 24, 1934; d. Edward Stanley and Bertha C. (Richter) Voss; m. David C. Vigen, June 23, 1956 (div. 1977); children: Eric. E., Amy Vigen Hemstad, Aana Marie. BS in Nursing magna cum laude, St. Olaf Coll., 1956; MEd, S.D. State U., 1975; MS, Rush U., 1980; PhD, U. Minn., 1987. RN. Staff nurse various hosps., Mpls, Boston, Chgo., 1956-68; nursing instr. S.E.A. Sch. Practical Nursing, Sioux Falls, S.D., 1969-74; statewide coord. upward mobility in nursing Augustana Coll., Sioux Falls, S.D., 1974-78; cons./researcher S.D. Commn. Higher Edn., 1974-79; gov. appointed bd. mem. S.D. Bd. Nursing, 1975-79; RN upward mobility project dir., chair/dir. div. of nursing Huron Coll. S.D. State U., 1978-79, mobility project dir., 1980-84; head dept. nursing, assoc. prof. Luther Coll., Decorah, Iowa, 1984-94; prof. nursing Graceland Coll., Independence, Mo., 1994—; cons. in field; developer outreach MSN programs Graceland Coll.; governing bd. mem. Midwest Alliance in Nursing, 1984-92; founder Soc. for Advancement of Nursing, Malta, 1992; developer Health Care in the Mediterranean Study Abroad Program, Greece and Malta, 1994, 96; developer summer internship for Maltese nursing students Mayo Med. Ctr. and Luther Coll.; presenter on internat. collaboration with Malta for nursing leadership 2d Internat. Acad. Congress on Nursing, Kansas City, 1996. Author: Role of a Dean in a Private Liberal Arts College, 1992; devel. and initiated 3 nursing programs in S.D., 1974-84 (named Women of Yr., 1982). Lobbyist Nursing Schs. in S.D., 1974-79; task force mem. Sen. Tom Harkin's Nurse's Adv. Com., 1986-94. Fellow to rep. U.S.A. ANA cand. in internat. coun. nursing 3M, St. Paul, 1978; recipient Leadership award Bush Found., St. Paul, 1979; tenure Luther Coll., 1986; Faculty fellow Minn. Area Geriatric Edn. Ctr. U. Minn., 1990-91; recipient Fulbright award Malta Coun. Internat. Exch. of Scholars, Washington, 1992—. Mem. AAUW, ANA, Am. Assn. Colls. Nursing (exec. devel. subcom. 1990—), Internat. Assn. Human Caring, Iowa Nurse's Assn. (bd. dirs. 1989-92, mem. nursing edn. com. 1989—, co-pres. 1989—), Midwest Alliance in Nursing (gov. bd. rep. Iowa 1989-92, chair membership com. 1989-92, S.D. gov. bd. rep. 1984-86, Rozella Schlotfeldt Leadership award 1993), Iowa Acad. Sci., Iowa Assn. Colls. Nursing Soc., Gerontol. Soc. Am., Rotary, Sigma Theta Tau. Democrat. Lutheran. Home: 4316 Northern Ave Apt 2633 Kansas City MO 64133-7249 Office: Graceland Coll Divsn Nursing 221 W Lexington Ave Independence MO 64050-3707

VIGMO, JOSEF, retired geriatrician; b. Reykjavík, Iceland, Nov. 12, 1922; arrived in Sweden, 1956; s. Olaf Johan Olsen-Vigmostad and Aline Josefine (Zachariassen) Hervik; m. Soffia Axelsdóttir, Jan. 24, 1953; children: Terje, Sylvi Aline. MD, U. Iceland, 1953; postgrad., U. Gothenburg, Sweden, 1960. Lic. in internal medicine, cardiology, geriatrics, Sweden. Asst. med. officer Sandträsks Tuberculosis Sanatorium, Sweden, 1953-54; resident in pulmonary diseases Sandträsks Tuberculosis Sanatorium, 1956-57; rotating intern White Meml. Hosp. and Clinic, Loma Linda U., L.A., 1954-55; resident in internal medicine Piteå County Hosp., Sweden, 1958-59, Kalix and Skene County Hosps., Norrköping Gen. Hosp., Sweden, 1961-65; sub-chief med. officer Hultafors Health Ctr., Sweden, 1960; sub-chief med. officer geriatric dept. Borås Gen. County Hosp., Sweden, 1966-77; chief med. officer geriatric dept. Borås Gen. County Hosp., 1977-87; ret., 1987; consulting cardiologist, Borås Gen. County Hosp., 1978—, lectr. Sch. Nursing, 1967—. Recipient Gold medal Älvsborg County Council, 1987. Mem. Swedish Med. Assn., Swedish Geriatrics Assn., Swedish Assn. Chief Med. Officers, South-Älvsborg County Assn. Chief Med. Officers. Lutheran. Home: Bâleröd, Sjövägen 1, S-452 97 Strömstad Sweden

VILARDELL, FRANCISCO, gastroenterologist, educator; b. Barcelona, Spain, Apr. 1, 1926; s. Jacinto Vilardell and Mercedes Viñas; m. Leonor March; children: Mercedes, Carmen, Xavier. MD, U. Barcelona, 1949, DSc, 1961; DSc in Medicine, U. Pa., Phila., 1962; PhD (hon.), U. Toulouse, France, 1974, U. Zaragoza, Spain, 1990. Resident medicine Hosp. del Mar, Barcelona, 1949-52; fellow gastroenterology Hosp. de la Santa Cruz & San Pablo, 1952-55, chief gastroenterology svc., 1963—; fellow gastroenterology Grad. Hosp., Phila., 1959-62; prof., dir. Postgrad. Sch. Gastroenterology U. Barcelona, 1970—; pres. European Assn. Study Liver, 1975-76, Coun. Internat. Orgns. Med. Scis. coms., 1987-91; sec.-gen. World Orgn. Gastroenterology, 1974-82, pres., 1982-90. Author: Enfermedades Difusas del Estomago, 1962, others; assoc. editor Bockus Gastroenterology, 3rd edit., 1972, editl. cons., 4th edit., 1986; contbr. articles to profl. jours. Asst. dir. gen. med. edn. Spanish Ministry Health, 1978-80, dir. gen. health planning, 1980-82, mem. med. rsch. coun., 1982-91. Fellow ACP, Royal Coll. Physicians, Royal Coll. Physicians Edinburgh, Am. Coll. Gastroenterology; mem. Catalan Soc. Bioethics (pres. 1994-96); hon. mem. French Gastroenterology Soc., Brit. Gastroenterology Soc., German Gastroenterology Soc., Japanese Gastroenterology Soc., Spanish Gastroenterology Soc., Polish Gastroenterology Soc., Hungarian Gastroenterology Soc., Portuguese Gastroenterology Soc., Argentinian Gastroenterology Soc., Colombian Gastroenterology Soc. Home: Johann Sebastian Bach 11, 08021 Barcelona Spain Office: Hosp Santa Cruz & San Pablo, 08025 Barcelona Spain

VILCHES, ANTONIO RICARDO, nephrologist; b. N.Y.C., Apr. 29, 1946; s. Antonio Manuel and Maria (San Esteban) V.; m. Liliane Raquel Petcho, Dec. 29, 1983; 1 child, Aline Mercedes. MD, U. Buenos Aires, 1970. Intern U. Buenos Aires, 1970, med. resident, 1971-74, chief resident, 1975; renal fellow Guy's Hosp., London, 1977-81; prof. medicine U. Buenos Aires, 1988—; med. dir. Eli Lilly & Co., Buenos Aires, 1984—; bd. dirs. Med. Edn. and Clin. Rsch. Ctr., Argentina, 1990—. Recipient Belaustegui award Acad. of Surgery, Argentina, 1974, Interamericana, Guemes and Sivori awards for rsch. in cardiology and nephrology; named Outstanding Youth, Argentina C. of C., 1983. Fellow Argentine Soc. Nephrology. Home: Av Libertador 2235 4o A, 1425 Buenos Aires Argentina Office: Eli Lilly & Co, Reconquista 656 7o P, 1003 Buenos Aires Argentina

VILCHES, GUSTAVO M., cardiologist; b. Santiago, Chile, Mar. 20, 1947; s. Humberto R. and Mercedes R. (Tarradella) V.; m. Cecilia C. Riumallo, Apr. 22, 1971; 3 children. MD, U. Chile, Santiago, 1971. Diplomate Am. Bd. Internal Medicine; cert. cardiologist Nat. Commn. on Med. Specialties Cert. Intern U. Chlie Sch. Medicine, 1973-74; resident internal medicine Baroness Erlanger Clin. Edn. Ctr., Chattanooga, 1974-76, chief med. resident, 1976-77; attending cardiologist Naval Hosp., Valparaiso, Chile, 1978—, chief Catheterization Lab., 1980-93. Home: 10 Norte 882, Viña Del Mar Chile

VILES, HENRY, pathologist; b. Cali, Colombia, Dec. 24, 1938; s. Pedro and Tulia V.; M.D., U. del Valle (Colombia), 1968; m. Mary Jo Oliver, Oct. 10, 1980; children—Maurice, Andrés, Tabatha, Joshua. Rotating intern Hosp. U. del Valle, Cali, 1967-68; resident in pathology Stamford (Conn.) Hosp., 1971-75, chief pathology resident, 1975-76; dir. labs. Mayfield (Ky.) Community Hosp./ Columbia Pinelake Regional Hosp., 1976—. Diplomate Am. Bd. Pathology. Fellow Coll. Am. Pathologists; mem. AMA, Am. Soc. Clin. Pathologists, Am. Soc. Microbiology, AAAS. Home: 309 Lakeview Dr Mayfield KY 42066 Office: 1099 Medical Center Cir Mayfield KY 42066-2200

VILLAR-PALASI, CARLOS, pharmacology educator; b. Valencia, Spain, Mar. 3, 1928; came to U.S., 1963; s. Vicente Villar Bolinaga and Teresa (Palasi-Pinazo); m. Amparo Gosalvez-Sobrino, Aug. 17, 1957 (dec. July 1978); children: Victor, Carlos, Juan Jose, María Amparo. MS in Chemistry, U. Valencia, Spain, 1951; PhD in Biochemistry, U. Madrid, Spain, 1955; MS in Pharmacy, U. Barcelona, Spain, 1962. Rsch. fellow med. sch. U. Hamburg, Fed. Republic of Germany, 1953-54, Spanish Rsch. Coun., Madrid, 1954-57, Case Western Res. U., Cleve., 1960-63; rsch. assoc. Spanish Rsch. Coun., Madrid, 1960-63, Case Western Res. U., Cleve., 1963-64; rsch. assoc. U. Minn., Mpls., 1964-65, asst. prof., 1965-69; assoc. prof. U. Va., Charlottesville, 1969-72, prof., 1972—; invited speaker Fedn. European Biochem. Soc., 1969, 96. March Found. fellow, 1957; recipient Rsch. award Cleve. Diabetes Found., 1960, NIH, 1967-69. Mem. AAAS (Rsch. award 1960-62), Am. Soc. Pharmacology, Am. Soc. Biol. Chemistry. Roman Catholic. Home: PO Box 101 Ivy VA 22945-0101 Office: U Va Med Sch Dept Pharmacology 1300 Jefferson Park Ave Charlottesville VA 22903-3363

VILLAVECES, JAMES WALTER, allergist, immunologist; b. San Luis Obispo, Calif., Nov. 4, 1933; s. Robert and Solita (Combariza) V. BA, UCLA, 1955; MD, U. Calif. Med. Sch., 1960. Cert. Am. Bd. Allergy and Immunology, recert. Rotating intern Santelle VA Hosp., L.A., 1960-61; preceptorship adult allergy L.A. County Hosp., Los Angeles, 1964-66; fellow allergy White Meml. CCM, L.A., 1966-67; chief allergy div. Ventura (Calif.) Med. Ctr., 1969-87; practice medicine specializing in allergy-immunology Ventura, 1984-96; cons. Bio-Dynamics Co., Ventura, 1975-80, Norwich-Eaton and Pharmacia and Fisons, Ventura, 1980-85; lectr. in field. Bd. dirs. Am. Lung Assn., Ventura, 1969-85, pres., 1974, advisor air pollution control com., 1971-74; judge Ventura Sci. Fair, 1970-85. Recipient Commendation, County Bd. Suprs., Ventura, 1974. Fellow Am. Acad. Allergy, Am. Coll. Allergists; mem. Am. Headache Soc., Calif. Soc. Allergy-Immunology, Calif. Med. Assn., Gold Coast Tri-County Allergy Soc. (pres. 1987), CAL Club (hon.), Ventura County Sports Hall of Fame (founder), Mensa. Republican. Home: 88 Eugenia Dr Ventura CA 93003-1502 Office: Dudley Profl Ctr 4080 Loma Vista Rd Ste M Ventura CA 93003-1811

VILLECCO, JUDY DIANA, substance abuse, mental health counselor, director; b. Knoxville, Tenn., Jan. 19, 1948; d. William Arthur and Louise (Reagan) Chamberlain; m. Tucker, June 10, 1965 (div. 1974); children: Linda Louise (Tucker) Smith, Constance Christine; m. Roger Anthony Villecco, May 3, 1979. BA in Psychology, U. West Fla., 1988, MA in Psychology, 1992. Lic. mental health counselor, Fla.; cert. addiction profl., Fla.; internat. cert. alcohol and drug counselor. Counselor Gulf Coast Hosp., Ft. Walton Beach, Fla., 1986-87; peer counselor U. West Fla., Ft. Walton Beach, 1987-89; family and prevention counselor Okaloosa Guidance Clinic, Ft. Walton Beach, 1988-89; family svc. dir. Anon Anew of Tampa (Fla.), Inc., 1989-91; dir. Renew Counseling Ctr., Ft. Walton Beach, 1990-92; substance abuse dept. dir. Avalon Ctr., Milton, Fla., 1992-93; adult coord. Partial & Rivendell, Ft. Walton Beach, 1994-95; pvt. practice Emerald Coast Psychiat. Care, P.A., Fort Walton Beach, 1994-95, Associated Psychotherapists, Ft. Walton Beach, 1995—; internat. substance abuse counselor, dir. and presenter in field. Author: Co-dependency Treatment Manual, 1992; creator Effective Treatment for Codependants, 1992. Named Outstanding Mental Health Profl. of Yr., Nat. Mental Health Assn., 1994. Mem. Internat. Assn. for Offender Counselors, Fla. Alcohol, Drug, Substance Abuse Assn. (bd. dirs., regional rep., Regional Profl. of Yr. 1992-93, 95—), Am. Counseling Assn. (alt. rep.), Internat. Assn. for Marriage and Family Counseling, Phi Theta Kappa, Alpha Phi Sigma. Office: 348 Miracle Strip Pky Ste 38 Fort Walton Beach FL 32548

VINAY, PATRICK, academic dean. Dean Faculty Medicine Univ. Montreal, Quebec, Can. Office: Univ Montreal, PO Box 6128 Sta A, Montreal, PQ Canada H3C 3J7

VINCENS, LOUIS-FRANÇOIS, surgeon; b. Treignac, France, June 11, 1939; s. Robert and Marie-Françoise (Maurin) V.; m. Catherine Laire, Apr. 3, 1970; 1 child, Xavier. MD, U. Clermont-Ferrand, France, 1968, student urology, 1971. Hosp. extern Clermont-Ferrand, France, 1959-63; hosp. intern Clermont-Ferrand, 1965-68, asst. hosp. clin. chief, 1969-71, practice medicine specializing in surgery, 1971—; gen.-pres., dir. Clinique des Domes, Clermont-Ferrand, 1987; expert Arreal Tribunal, Riom, 1975. Mem. French Assn. Urology. Roman Catholic. Lodge: Rotary. Home: Les Malieves, 63114 Montpeyroux France Office: 99 Avenue de la Republique, 63000 Clermont France

VINCENT, CHARLES ANTHONY, psychologist; b. London, July 12, 1952; s. Anthony Peyton and Angela Mary (Tingay) V.; m. Angela Emma Phillips; 1 child, Rhianne. BA, Oxford U., 1975; MPhil, London U., 1978; PhD, U. Coll. London, 1987. Clin. psychologist British Nat. Health Coun., London, 1979-84; rsch. psychologist U. Coll. London, 1985-88, lectr. psychology, 1988-94, sr. lectr., 1994—; cons. World Health Orgn., 1995. Editor: Clinical Risk Management, 1995; co-editor: Medical Accidents, 1993; contbr. articles to profl. jours. Office: U Coll London, Gower St, London WC1E 6BT, England

VINCENT, FREDERICK MICHAEL, SR., neurologist, educational administrator; b. Detroit, Nov. 19, 1948; s. George S. and Alyce M. (Borkowski) V.; m. Patricia Lucille Cordes, Oct. 7, 1972; children: Frederick Michael Jr., Joshua Peter, Melissa Anne. BS in Biology, Aquinas Coll., 1970; MD, Mich. State U., 1973. Diplomate Am. Bd. Psychiatry and Neurology (neurology and clin. neurophysiology), Am. Bd. Electrodiagnostic Medicine, Nat. Bd. Med. Examiners, Am. Bd. Forensic Examiners, Am. Bd. Forensic Medicine. Intern St. Luke's Hosp., Duluth, Minn., 1974-75; resident in neurology Dartmouth Med. Sch., Hanover, N.H., 1975-77, instr. dept. medicine, chief resident neurology, 1977-78; chief, neurology sect. Munson Med. Ctr., Traverse City, Mich., 1978-84; asst. clin. prof. medicine and pathology Mich. State U., East Lansing, 1978-84, chief sect. neurology Coll. Human Medicine, 1984-87; clin. prof. psychiatry and internal medicine Mich. State U., 1989—; clin. prof. medicine, 1990—; pvt. practice Neurology, Neuro-oncology and Electrodiagnostic Medicine, Lansing, Mich., 1987—; clin. and research fellow neuro-oncology Mass. Gen. Hosp., Boston, 1985; clin. Fellow in neurology Harvard Med. Sch., Boston, 1985; cons. med. asst. program Northwestern Mich. Coll., Traverse City, 1983-84; neurology cons. radio call-in show Sta. WKAR, East Lansing, 1984—, Sta. WCMU TV, 1987, 1993—. Author: Neurology: Problems in Primary Care, 1987, 2d edit., 1993; contbr. articles to profl. jours. Fellow NSF, 1969, Nat. Multiple Sclerosis Soc., 1971. Fellow ACP, Am. Acad. Neurology (mem. program accreditation and devel. subcom. 1993—), Am. Assn. Electrodianostic Medicine (mem. computer and electronics com. 1995—); mem. Am. Coll. Legal Medicine, Am. Acad. Clin. Neurophysiology, Am. Heart Assn., Am. Soc. Clin. Oncology, Am. EEG Soc., Am. Fedn. Clin. Rsch., Am. Soc. Neurol. Investigation, Am. Epilepsy Soc., Soc. for NeuroSci., N.Y. Acad. Scis., Am. Bd. of Forensic Examiners, Am. Soc. for Neuro-Rehab., Movement Disorders Soc., Univ. Club, Alpha Omega Alpha. Roman Catholic. Office: 1515 Lake Lansing Rd Ste F1 Lansing MI 48912-3703

VINCENT, JAMES LOUIS, biotechnology company executive; b. Johnstown, Pa., Dec. 15, 1939; s. Robert Clyde and Marietta Lucille (Kennedy) V.; m. Elizabeth M. Matthews, Aug. 19, 1961; children: Aimee Archelle, Christopher James. BSME, Duke U., 1961; MBA in Indsl. Mgmt., U. Pa., 1963. Mgr. Far East div. Tex. Instruments, Inc., Tokyo, 1970-72; pres. Tex. Instrument Asia, Ltd., Tokyo, 1970-72; v.p. diagnostic ops., pres. diagnostics div. Abbott Labs., North Chgo., Ill., 1972-74, group v.p., bd. dirs., 1974-81, exec. v.p., COO, bd. dirs., 1979-81; corp. group v.p., pres. Allied Health and Sci. Products Co. Allied Corp., Morristown, N.J., 1982-85; CEO Biogen, Inc., 1985—; also bd. dirs. Bd. trustees Duke U.; bd. dirs. Found. for the Nat. Tech.; bd. overseers Wharton Grad. Bus. Sch. U. Pa. Recipient Young Exec. Achievement Young Execs. Club, Chgo., 1976, Disting. Alumni award Duke U., 1988. Mem. Biotech. Industry Orgn. (bd. dirs.), Econ. Club Chgo., Shoreacres Country Club, Algonquin Club, Boston Club, Chgo. Club, The Links (N.Y.C.). Republican. Presbyterian. Office: Biogen Inc 14 Cambridge Ctr Cambridge MA 02142-1401

VINCENT, MICHAEL BAYARD, ophthalmologist; b. Wilmington, Del., July 26, 1954; s. Bayard Richard and Berneta McKee) V.; m. Eileen Lord, Oct. 25, 1980; children: Richard Lord, Andrew Michael Lord. BA in Biology, Franklin & Marshall Coll., 1975; MD, Jefferson Med. Coll., 1979. Diplomate Am. Bd. Ophthalmology. Med. intern Med. Ctr. of Del., Wilmington, 1979-80, dir. residency dept. ophthalmology, 1985—; ophthalmology resident N.Y. Eye and Ear Infirmary, N.Y.C., 1980-83; pvt. practice ophthalmology Vincent & Vincent, MD, P.A., Wilmington, 1983—; sec. med. staff St. Francis Hosp., Wilmington, 1995—. Treas. Ophthalmology PAC, Wilmington, 1986—. Fellow Am. Acad. Ophthalmology; mem. AMA, Med. Soc. of Del. (bd. dirs. 1995—), Del. Acad. Ophthalmology. Office: Vincent & Vincent MD PA 1711 Woodlawn Ave Wilmington DE 19806

VINCENT, MICHAEL PAUL, plastic surgeon; b. Ottawa, Ontario, Can., Aug. 8, 1950; s. Dale Leon and Mildred (Havird) V.; m. Mary Margaret Glennon, July 28, 1973; children: Kathryn Blair, Jonathan Michael, Marc Andrew, Caroline Wyatte. BA, Duke U., 1972, MD, 1976. Diplomate Am. Bd. Surgery, Am. Bd. Plastic Surgery. Internship in surgery Bethesda Naval Hosp., Bethesda, Md., 1976-77; gen. surgery residency Bethesda Naval Hosp., Bethesda, 1977-81; plastic surgery fellowship Eastern Va. Sch. of Medicine, Norfolk, Va., 1982-84; chief, plastic surgery Bethesda Naval Hosp., Bethesda, 1984-92; plastic surgeon pvt. practice, Rockville, Md., 1992—; assoc. prof. of clin. surgery, Uniformed Svcs. U. of the Health Scis., Bethesda, 1989—; clin. cons. plastic surgery NIH, 1987—; also speaker, advisor. Contbr. chpts. to books: Eyelid Reconstruction, 1987, 91, 92, Ptosis Surgery, 1988; contbr. chpt. to book and articles to profl. jours.; co-editor Flap Dissection Workshop, 1984. Active Operation Smile, Washington, 1986—, St. Francis Episcopal Ch., Potomac, Md., 1986—; vet. Operation Desert Shield/Storm. With USN, 1972-92. Recipient Physician Recognition award, AMA, 1985, 89, 94. Fellow ACS; mem. Plastic Surgery Ednl. Found., Am. Soc. Plastic and Reconstructive Surgeons, Am. Soc. Aesthetic Plastic Surgery, Nat. Capital Soc. Plastic Surgeons, Phi Beta Kappa. Episcopal. Home: 11812 Piney Glen Ln Potomac MD 20854-1413 Office: Chief Plastic Surgery 9715 Med Ctr Dr Ste 315 Rockville MD 20850

VINCENT, STEPHEN K., oral and maxillofacial surgeon; b. N.Y.C., June 7, 1956; s. Donald E. and Laura W. (Lillard) V.; m. Rhonda R. Collins; children: Natalie A., Stephen A., Bailey A. BA in Chemistry, U. Mo., Kansas City, 1979, DDS, 1983. Diplomate Am. Bd. Oral and Maxillofacial Surgery. Resident in oral and maxillofacial surgery Truman Med. Ctr.-U. Mo., 1983-87, resident in gen. surgery, 1984-85; resident in oral and maxillofacial surgery St. Luke's Hosp.-U. Mo., 1983-87; pvt. practice oral and maxillofacial surgery, Lawrence, Kans., 1987—; examiner oral and maxillofacial surgery Kans. Dental Bd., Topeka, 1995—. Contbr. articles to dental jours. Mem. Pierre Fauchard Acad., Omicron Kappa Upsilon, Phi Kappa Phi. Office: 346 Maine St Lawrence KS 66044

VINER, DONALD LEE, surgeon; b. Hardy, Ark., Sept. 7, 1930; s. Ernest Donald and Cova L. (Hastings) V.; m. Lila J. Oates, Aug. 12, 1959; children: Paul Marshal, Melissa A. BS, Ark. Tech., 1956; MD, U. Ark., 1961. Diplomate Am. Bd. Surgery. Internship Baptist Hosp., Little Rock, Ark., 1961-62; residency Va. Hosp., Little Rock, 1962-66; staff surgeon Saline Meml. Hosp., Benton, 1966—. Fellow ACS. Home: 105 Mcneil St Benton AR 72015-3345

VINER, NICHOLAS ANDRÉ, physician, urologist; b. Bridgeport, Conn., Jan. 10, 1942. AB, Holy Cross Coll., 1964; MD, Vanderbilt U., 1968. Diplomate Am. Bd. Urology. Rotating intern Greenwich (Conn.) Hosp., 1968-69, resident in gen. surgery, 1969-70; resident in urology Vanderbilt U., 1970-74; chief of urology Scott AFB, Belleville, Ill., 1974-76, Bridgeport Hosp., 1983—; pres. Bridgeport Health Network, 1990-95. Maj. USAF, 1974-76. Fellow ACS. Office: Urol Assocs of Bridgeport 160 Hawley Ln Trumbull CT 06611

VINGOE, FRANCIS JAMES, clinical and forensic psychologist, consultant; b. San Diego, Oct. 20, 1931; arrived in Wales, 1975; s. Alfred and Mary Ellen (James) V.; m. Dolores Marguerite Chevillard, Apr. 1957 (div. 1965); 1 child, Sylvie Lamorna; m. Grace Roberta Cameron, Apr. 15, 1966; children: Lisa Michelle, Wendy Sue, Michael Jan. BA with honors, Calif. State U., San Diego, 1956; MA, Calif. State U., San Francisco, 1960; PhD, U. Oreg., 1965. Diplomate in hypnosis Am. Bd. Psychol. Examiners; chartered clin. psychologist, forensic psychologist. Teaching asst. U. Nebr., Lincoln, 1956-57; instr. math. Cogswell Poly. Coll., San Francisco, 1959-61; ednl. psychologist Bremerton (Wash.) Pub. Schs., 1961-63; instr. psychology Olympic Coll., Bremerton, 1961-63; clin. psychology intern Napa State Hosp., 1963-64; lectr. Napa Coll., 1963-64; counselor, psychometrist, instr. U. Oreg., Eugene, 1964-65; rsch. assoc. State of Oreg., 1965; asst. prof. psychology Colo. State U., Ft. Collins, 1965-68; assoc. prof. psychology SUNY, Cortland, 1968-71; sr. lectr. clin. psychology U. Groningen, The Netherlands, 1971-75; prin. clin. psychologist Univ. Hosp. Wales, Cardiff, 1975-85; lectr. U. Wales Coll. Medicine, Cardiff, 1975-92; pvt. practice cons. clin. and forensic psychologist, 1994—; cons. clin. psychologist Univ. Hosp. Wales, Cardiff, 1985-94; cons. Poudre R-1 Schs., Ft. Collins, 1966-68, Tri County Head Start Programme, Torrington, Wyo., 1967-68; vis. lectr. Wells Coll., Aurora, N.Y., 1968-70. Author: Clinical Psychology and Medicine, 1981; cons. editor Internat. Jour. Clin. and Exptl. Hypnosis; assoc. editor Brit. Jour. Exptl. and Clin. Hypnosis, 1982, Jour. Contemporary Hypnosis, 1991; clin. editor Brit. Jour. Exptl. and Clin. Hypnosis, 1982; contbr. articles to profl. jours. With USN, 1949-53. Faculty Rsch. fellow SUNY, Cortland, 1970; Faculty Rsch. grantee Colo. State U., 1968. Fellow Brit. Psychol. Soc.; mem. Brit. Soc. Exptl. and Clin. Hypnosis (chmn. Wales and West of Eng. br. 1982-85), Brit. Soc. Clin. and Exptl. Hypnosis (chmn. 1985, spl. group clin. neuropsychology). Home and Office: 87 Blackoak Rd Cyncoed, Cardiff CF2 6QW, Wales

VINOCUR, EDWARD WILLIAM, nursing home administrator; b. Cleve., Mar. 4, 1951; s. Harry and Goldie (Brown) V.; m. Debra Gilbert, Dec. 21, 1960; children: Jonathon Harry, Alicia Gilbert, Joel Gilbert. BA, Ohio State U., 1974; MPA, North Tex. State U., 1983, cert. in aging, 1984. Lic. nursing home adminstr. Exec. dir. student community projects Columbus, Ohio, 1971-73; asst. adminstr. Heritage House, Columbus, 1974-77; exec. dir. Heritage Tower, Columbus, 1977-79; ops. adminstr. Heritage Village, Columbus, 1980-84; exec. dir. Menorah Manor, St. Petersburg, Fla., 1984-88, Montefiore Home, Cleve., 1988—; pres., COO Montefiore Found., Cleve., 1995—. Com. mem. Jewish Fedn. Pinellas County, Clearwater, Fla., 1984-88. Named one of Outstanding Young Men in Am., 1984. Mem. Am. Assn. Homes for Aging, Fla. Assn. Homes for Aging (mem. nursing home com. 1984-88), Ohio Assn. Homes for Aging (treas. 1982-83, v.p. 1983-84, bd. dirs. 1993—), North Am. Assn. Jewish Homes (Outstanding Young Exec. 1991), Gerontol. Assn., Nat. Coun. on Aging, Ohio State U. Alumni Assn., North Tex. State U. Alumni Assn. Home: 2165 Campus Rd Cleveland OH 44122-1216 Office: The Montefiore Home One David N Myers Pkwy Beachwood OH 44122-1101

VINSANT, GEORGE O'NEAL, surgery educator; b. Lafollette, Tenn., July 19, 1951; s. George Finley and Cleo Alta (O'Neal) V.; m. Ortrun E. Bonsiepe, Mar. 5, 1991; 1 child, Oliver O'Neal. BS, Lincoln Meml. U., 1974; MD, U. Tenn., Memphis, 1983. Intern U. Tenn. Med. Ctr., Knoxville, 1983-84, resident, 1984-87, chief resident surgery, 1987-88; trauma fellow, instr. surgery U. Fla. Health Sci. Ctr., Jacksonville, 1988-89, asst. prof. surgery, 1989—, med. dir. trauma ICU, 1989-93, chmn. nutrition com., 1990—, med. dir. Trauma One Flight Program, 1992-93. Contbr. articles to profl. jours. Mem. AMA, Am. Trauma Soc., Ea. Assn. Surgery Trauma (assoc.), Southeastern Surg. Congress (gold medal paper 1985), Fla. Med. Assn., Duval Med. Soc. Home: 5259 Alloaks Ct Jacksonville FL 32258-2299 Office: U Fla Health Sci Ctr 653 W 8th St Jacksonville FL 32209-6511

VINSON, DAVID BERWICK, neuropsychologist; b. Houston, Oct. 7, 1917; s. David Berwick and Norma (Calhoun) V.; m. Helen Patricia Freiday, Dec. 28, 1940; children: David Berwick III (dec.), Helen Catharine. BA, UCLA, 1941; PhD, U. London, 1952. Dir. Tex. Acad. Advancement Life Scis., 1954-89; pres. Microset, Inc., Tex., 1978-87, Factor, Inc., Tex., 1986—, Assessment Systems, Inc., Tex., 1968—; cons. in field. Capt. USAF, 1941-43, ETO. Fellow AIAA; mem. APA, IEEE, Soc. Biol. Psychiatry, Sigma Xi. Lutheran. Home and Office: 161 Schattenbaum Dr Fredericksburg TX 78624-6130

VIOLET, WOODROW WILSON, JR., retired chiropractor; b. Columbus, Ohio, Sept. 19, 1937; s. Woodrow Wilson and Alice Katherine (Woods) V.; student Ventura Coll., 1961-62; grad. L.A. Coll. Chiropractic, 1966; m. Judith Jane Thatcher, June 15, 1963; children: Woodina Lonize, Leslie Alice. Pvt. practice chiropractic medicine, Santa Barbara, Calif., 1966-73, London, 1973-74, Carpinteria, Calif., 1974-84; past mem. coun. roentgenology Am. Chiropractic Assn. Former mem. Parker Chiropractic Rsch. Found., Ft. Worth. Served with USAF, 1955-63. Recipient award merit Calif. Chiropractic Colls., Inc., 1975, cert. of appreciation Nat. Chiropractic Antitrust Com., 1977. Mem. Nat. Geog. Soc., L.A. Coll. Chiropractic Alumni Assn., Scripps Rsch. Coun., Delta Sigma. Patentee surg. instrument.

VIOLETTE, PETER J., optometrist; b. Fort Kent, Mass., Mar. 12, 1960; s. James Philip and Jacqueline Patricia (Rinquette) V.; m. Hope Marie Blette, Oct. 4, 1986; children: Brian James, Nicholas Charles, Mark Jeffrey. BA, Hofstra U., 1982; OD, New Eng. Coll. Optometry, 1986. Staff optometrist Kenneth F. Nuzzo, Augusta, Maine, 1986-87, Harvard Cmty. Health Plan, Wellesley, Mass., 1987-89; pvt. practice Wakefield, Mass., 1989—. Cons. Lions of Wakefield, 1992—. Recipient achievement award New Eng. Coun. Optometrists, 1992. Mem. Mass. Soc. Optometrists (dist. chair 1990-93). Office: 446 Main St Wakefield MA 01880

VIRGILIO, JOANNE, oncologist, hematologist; b. Bklyn., Sept. 9, 1958; d. James and Rita (Rakowski) V.; m. George D. Gromke, May 13, 1989; children: Megan, Mikaela, George. BA in Biology, NYU, 1981; DO, Chgo. Coll. Osteo. Medicine, 1986. Diplomate Nat. Bd. Osteopathic Medicine in Internal Medicine, Oncology, Hematol ogy. Intern Grandview Hosp., Dayton, Ohio, 1986-87; resident in internal medicine Grandview Hosp., Dayton, 1987-89; fellow in oncology U. Cin., 1989-91; fellow in hematology-oncology U. S. Fla., Tampa, 1991-92; pvt. practice Grand Junction (Colo.) Oncology Group, 1992—. Mem. Am. Osteopathic Assn. Roman Catholic. Office: St Marys Hosp 2635 N 7th St Grand Junction CO 81502

VIRGO, KATHERINE SUE, health services researcher; b. East Alton, Ill., Feb. 14, 1959; d. John William and Doris Ann (Spencer) Ulmrich; m. John Michael Virgo, Sept. 6, 1980. BSBA, So. Ill. U., 1981, MBA, 1983; PhD in Health Svcs. Rsch., St. Louis U., 1991. Asst. coord. Atlantic Econ. Soc., Edwardsville, Ill., 1978-79, exec. asst., 1979-81, exec. adminstr., 1981-86; co-founder, exec. adminstr. Internat. Health Econs. and Mgmt. Inst., Edwardsville, Ill., 1983-87; rsch. asst. VA Med. Ctr., St. Louis, 1986-91, health sci. specialist, 1991-93; clin. rsch. coord. St. Louis U., 1993—, asst. prof., 1991-96, assoc. prof., 1996—; bd. dirs. Internat. Health Econs. and Mgmt. Inst., Edwardsville, 1983-87. Assoc. editor Atlantic Econ. Jour., 1994—; dep. editor Internat. Advances in Econ. Rsch., 1995—; contbr. articles to profl. jours. Mem. Am. Pub. Health Assn., Acad. Mgmt., Assn. for Health Svcs. Rsch., Health Econs. Rsch. Orgn., Am. Stats. Assn. Democrat. Roman Catholic. Home: 5277 Lindell Blvd Saint Louis MO 63108-1223 Office: VA Med Ctr 112JC 915 N Grand Blvd Saint Louis MO 63106-1621

VISCO, DENISE MARIE, research fellow; b. Winthrop, Mass., July 27, 1957; d. Joseph Anthony and Patricia Ann (Koeppe) V. BS, U. N.H., 1979; MS, U. Tenn., 1981; PhD, Purdue U., 1987. Rsch. assoc. Med. Ctr. anatomy dept. Ind. U., Indpls., 1988-89, postdoctoral fellow Med. Ctr. anatomy dept., 1989; sr. rsch. scientist Miles Rsch. Ctr., Inst. for Bone and Cartilage Metabolism, West Haven, Conn., 1989-91, 1989-91, 91-93; rsch. fellow, dept. pharmacology Merck Rsch. Labs., Rahway, N.J., 1993—; vis. asst. prof. Med. Ctr., Ind. U., 1987-88. Contbr. articles to profl. jours. Grantee Canine Disease Rsch. Funds, 1984, USDA Formula Fund, 1984, NIH, 1988. Mem. AAAS, Orthopaedic Rsch. Soc., Am. Coll. Sports Medicine, Osteoarthritis Rsch Soc., Sigma Xi (assoc.), Gamma Sigma Delta (assoc.). Roman Catholic. Office: IBCM Merck & Co Inc PO Box 2000 R 804-140 400 Morgan Ln Rahway NJ 07065-0900

VISCO, FERDINAND JOSEPH, cardiologist, educator; b. Bklyn., July 8, 1941; s. Joseph Thomas and Susan (Baratta) V.; m. Laurie Judith Glass, Sept. 18, 1983; 1 child, Melissa; children by previous marriage, Ruth, Joseph, Jennifer. BS in Biology, Fairfield U., 1963; MD, U. Padua, Italy, 1969. Diplomate Am. Bd. Internal Medicine, specialty cardiovascular disease; lic. physician and surgeon, N.Y. Intern medicine Flushing (N.Y.) Hosp., 1969-70; jr. and sr. resident medicine Cath. Med. Ctr., Queens Hosp. Ctr., Jamaica, N.Y., 1970-72; fellow cardiology Nassau County Med. Ctr., East Meadow, N.Y., 1972-74; dir. medicine Freeport (N.Y.) Hosp., 1975; instr. medicine SUNY, Stony Brook, 1973-75; instr. medicine Albert Einstein Coll. Medicine, Bronx, N.Y., 1975-78, asst. prof. medicine, 1978—; attending physician St. John's Queens Hosp., Cath. Med. Ctr., Bklyn., 1975—, dir. non-invasive cardiology lab., 1975-96; assoc. dir. cardiology Bronx Lebanon Hosp., 1993-96. Fellow Am. Coll. Cardiology, ACP, Coun. Clin. Cardiology; mem. Am. Soc. Echocardiography. Office: St Johns Queens Hosp Divsn Cardiology 90-02 Queens Blvd Elmhurst NY 11373

VISCO, GIUSEPPE, physician; b. Sorrento, Italy, Oct. 28, 1927; s. Vincenzo and Teresa (Gargiulo) V.; m. Ubalda Comandini, Apr. 26, 1954; children: Vincenzo, Ubaldo. MD, U. La Sapienza, Rome, 1950, Med. Clinics Master, 1955, Hematology Master, 1958, Hygiene Master, 1963; Toxicology Master, U. Florence, 1968; postgrad., U. Tor Vergata, 1990-93, U. La Sapienza, 1994—. Intern Med. Clinics U., Rome, 1950-52, resident, 1952-61, prof. infectious diseases, 1960—; asst. cardiology dept. S. Giovanni Hosp., Rome, 1961-62; sub-chief med. officer infectious diseases dept. Spedali Riuniti, Brescia, Italy, 1962-63; sub-chief med. officer hygiene and toxicology S. Camillo Hosp., Rome, 1964-71; chief med. officer infectious diseases dept. L. Spallanzani Hosp., Rome, 1972—, chief med. office hepatology, 1974—; chief med. officer hygiene, pub. health and labor med. United Sanitaria Locale/RM 10 local Health Authority, Rome, 1980-94, with epidemiology dept., 1988-90; mem. Nat. AIDS Commn., Health Ministry, Rome, 1989—; cons. in field. Author: AIDS Epidemia del Secolo, 1989; editor jour. AIDS Notizie, 1988-90; editor: Pagina ANLAIDS, ISIS Bull, 1991-93; co-editor: Il Policlinico, 1960—; contbr. more than 300 sci. papers, 1950—. Recipient award Nat. Inst. Cancer, 1975, Istituto Superiore di Sanitá, 1988-92, Regione Lazio Assn. Sanitá, 1988, 89, 93. Mem. Soc. Italian Infectious Diseases, Soc. Italian Internal Medicine, Internat. Soc. for Infectious Diseases (gen. sec. 1982-86, bd. dirs. 1982-92), Am. Soc. Microbiology, Assn. Nat. Lotta Contro AIDS (gen. sec. 1986—), Enviro Italia Assn. (pres. 1975—), Rotary (life), Mai soli (pres. 1990—). Office: Via Flaminia 195, 00196 Rome Italy

VISKUM, KAJ, physician; b. Frederiksberg, Denmark, Mar. 10, 1938; s. Henrik and Thyra (Vang) V.;m. Birgitte Herborg, Oct. 7, 1961; children: Sara, Louise, Frauke. MD, U. Copenhagen, 1963; degree internal and pulmonary medicine, Danish Med. Bd., 1973; PhD, U. Aarhus, 1977. Intern Trinity Luth. Hosp., Kansas City, Mo., 1963-64; resident Bispebjerg Hosp., copenhagen, 1964-75; chief dept. Vejle Hosp., 1975-77; chief dept. pulmonary medicine Bispebjrg Hosp., Copenhagen, 1977-96; chief of dept. of pulmonary medicine Rigshospitalet, Copenhagen, 1996—; cons. Zurich Ins., Forensic Coun., EEC Monospeciaist Sect., Whittaker. Contbr. articles to profl. jours. Mem. Danish Soc. Pneumonology, Danish Soc.Allergology, Danish Soc. Internal Medicine. Office: Bispebjerg Hosp, Bispebjerg Bakke 23, Copenhagen 2400 NV, Denmark

VISLOSKY, FRANK MICHAEL, nursing educator; b. Pueblo, Colo., Sept. 29, 1957; s. Frank and Frances Eleanor (Kochevar) V. Dipoma, Mass. Gen. Hosp. Sch. Nursing, 1978; BS in Physiology, MIT, 1985; student, Harvard Med. Sch., 1987. Registered cardiovascular technologist. Staff nurse surg. ICU Boston City Hosp., 1978-79; staff nurse Mass. Gen. Hosp., Boston, 1979-80, 85-87, tchr. nursing, 1980-82, clin. rsch. nurse, 1982-84, head nurse, unit tchr., 1984-85, hemodynamic monitoring specialist, 1987-89, cons. critical care, staff nurse, 1989-90; head nurse cardiovascular ICU St. Mary-Corwin Regional Med. Ctr., Pueblo, Colo., 1990-91, head nurse cardiovascular svcs., 1991, educator nursing, cardiac clinician, 1991—. Contbr. articles to profl. jours. Mem. AACN, Am. Assn. Oper. Rm. Nurses, Am. Heart Assn., Emergency Nurses Assn. Roman Catholic. Home: 1425 Claremont Ave Pueblo CO 81004-3009 Office: St Mary Corwin Hosp 1008 Minnequa Ave Pueblo CO 81004-3733

VITALE, FREDERICK R., safety and environmental professional; b. Kenilworth, N.J., Sept. 2, 1941; s. Ferdinand Paul and Rita Patricia (Moretti) V.; B.S., Rutgers U., 1967; Ph.D., N.Y.U., 1978; m. Anna M. Franchak, May 7, 1961; children—F. Richard, J. Steven, J. Christopher. Regional indsl. hygienist Nat. Loss Control Service Corp., Summit, N.J., 1969-74; supr. indsl. hygiene and safety Occupational Safety and Health Adminstrn., Belle Meade, N.J., 1974-76; mgr. safety and environ. affairs Ciba-Geigy, Summit, N.J., 1976-79; dir. safety and environ. affairs Revlon, Inc., N.Y.C., 1979-86; v.p. Enviro Scis., Inc., Rockaway, N.J., 1986-87; dir. safety and environ. affairs Sterling Drug Co., 1987-95; v.p. Travel World, 1989—; pres. Vitran, Inc., 1975—; ptnr. Hampton Mgmt., Mount Holly, N.J. Real estate devel., 1970—; constrn. and zoning officer North Hanover Twp. (N.J.), 1970-74, safety officer, 1974-76, health officer, 1973-75. Served with USAF, 1960-64. Cert. safety profl., hazard control mgr. Mem. Am. Indsl. Hygiene Assn., Am. Soc. Safety Engrs., N.J. Safety Council, N.Y. Safety Execs., N.A.M., Pharm. Safety Group. Club: Masons.

VITALE-GREGORACE, STACY ANN, neurologist; b. Bronx, N.Y., Mar. 5, 1965; d. Anthony Peter and Athena (Anthony) V.; m. Joseph George Gregorace, June 27, 1992. BA, SUNY, 1988; DO, N.Y. Coll. Osteopathic Medicin, 1993. Diplomate Am. Bd. Nat. Osteopathic Medical Examiners. Neurology resident Long Island Jewish Medical Ctr., New Hyde Park, N.Y., 1993—. Vol., crew chief StonyBrook Amb. Corps., 1986-88; EMT basic sci. instr. Suffolk County, N.Y., 1987-89. Mem. N.Y. Medical Soc., AOA, AMA, Am. Acad. Neurology. Office: L I Jewish Medical Ctr Lakeville Rd New Hyde Park NY 11040

VITETTA, ELLEN SHAPIRO, microbiologist educator, immunologist. BA, Conn. Coll.; MS, NYU, 1966, PhD, MD, 1968. Prof. microbiology Southwestern Med. Sch., U. Tex., Dallas, 1976—; dir. Cancer Immunobiology Ctr., U. Tex., Dallas, 1988—; Sheryle Simmons Patigian Disting. chair in cancer immunobiology Southwestern Med. Sch., U. Tex., Dallas, 1989—; bd. sci. coun. NCI Cancer Treatment Bd., 1993; sci. adv. bd. Howard Hughes Med. Inst., 1992—; Kettering selection com. GM Cancer Rsch. Foun., 1987-88; task force NIAID in Immunology, 1989-90; mem. sci. bd. Ludwig Inst., 1983—. Mem. editl. bd.: Advances in Host Defense Mechanisms, 1983—, Annual Review of Immunology, 1991—, Bioconjugate Chemistry, 1989-93, Cellular Immunology, 1984-93, Current Opinions in Immunology, 1992—, FASEB Journal, 1987—, Internat. Jour. of Oncology, 1992—, Internat. Soc. Immunopharmacology, 1989—, Jour. of Immunology, 1975-78, Molecular Immunology, 1978-93; assoc. editor Cancer Research, 1986—; Immunochemistry sect. editor: Jour. of Immunology, 1978-82; co-editor in chief: Therapeutic Immunology, 1992—. Recipient Women's Excellence in Sci. award Fedn. Am. Soc. Exptl. Biology, 1991, Taittinger Breast Cancer Rsch. award Komen Found., 1983, Pierce Immunotoxin award, 1988, NIH Merit award, 1987—, U. Tex. Southwestern Med. Sch. Faculty Teaching awards 1989, 91, 92, 93, 94, FASED Excellence in Sci. award, 1991, Abbot Clinical Immunology award Am. Soc. Microbiologists, 1992, Past State Pres. award Tex. Fed. Bus. Profl. Women's Club, 1993. Richard and Hinda Rosenthal Found. award Am. Assn. Cancer Rsch 1995. Mem. Am. Assn. Immunologists (pres. 1993—), Nat. Acad. Scis. (Rosenthal award AACR 1995). Office: Univ of Texas Southwestern Medical Ctr Cancer Ctr 6000 Harry Hines Blvd Dallas TX 75235-5303

VITRO, FRANK THOMAS, JR., psychologist, educator; b. Westerly, R.I., Oct. 21, 1941; s. Frank Thomas Sr. and Angeline (Pendola) V.; m. Elaine Catherine Vitro, Aug. 29, 1964; children: Thomas Michael, Sheri Susan. BS in Pre-Med. Studies, U. Notre Dame, 1963; MA Experimental Psychology, Boston Coll., 1966; PhD in Ednl. Psychology, U. Iowa, 1969. Lic. psychologist, Tex.; bd. cert. sch. psychologist. Instr. psychology Chamberlayne Jr. Coll., Boston, 1964-66, Parsons Coll., Fairfield, Iowa, 1966-67; sch. psychologist Iowa City Ind. Sch. Dist., 1967-69; asst. prof. edn. U. Maine, Orono, 1969-72, assoc. prof. psychology and edn., 1972-78; prof. psychology Tex. Woman's U., Denton, Tex., 1978—, chmn. Dept. Psychology, 1982-85, 91—; presenter seminars and workshops throughout Maine and Tex.; sch. cons. in field. Contbr. articles to profl. jours. Pres. Bangor (Maine) Golf Assn., 1977-78, Denton, Tex., 1985-86. Mem. APA, S.W. Psychol. Assn., Dallas Psychol. Assn., Nat. Assn. Sch. Psychologists. Roman Catholic. Home: 3200 Dunes St Denton TX 76201-1471 Office: Tex Woman's U Psychology Dept PO Box 22996 Denton TX 76204-0996

VITS, DARRIN GILBERT, optometrist; b. Pana, Ill., Oct. 11, 1968; s. Donald Eugene and Judith Ann (Barringer) V.; m. Inez Marie Marley, May 27, 1995. BS in Biology, BA in Music, Ill. Coll., 1991; OD, U. Mo., St. Louis, 1995. Lic. optometrist, Ill., Mo. Optometrist Internat. Eyecare Ctr., Girard, Ill., 1995—. Mem. Lions Club, Girard, 1995. Mem. Am. Optometric Assn., Ill. Optometric Assn., Mid-State Optometric Soc. Roman Catholic. Office: Internat Eyecare Ctr 130 W Center Girard IL 62640

VITT, DAVID AARON, medical manufacturing company executive; b. Phila., Aug. 3, 1938; s. Nathan and Flora B.; m. Renee Lee Salkever, Oct. 20, 1963; children: Nadine Lori Einiger, Jeffrey Richard. BS, Temple U., 1961. Sales engr. Picker X-Ray Corp., Phila., 1961-65; sales engr. Midwest Am., Chgo., 1965-67, product mgr., 1967-68, product mgr. regional sales, 1968-70; dir. mktg. Valtronic & Living Wills, Bronx, N.Y., 1970-74; v.p. Siemens Med. Systems Inc., gen. mgr. dental div., Iselin, N.J., 1974-86, past corp. v.p.; CEO, pres. Pelton & Crane, Charlotte, N.C., 1986-89; v.p. govt. sales Siemens Med. Systems Corp. Officers, ret., 1994; founder, pres., CEO D.A.V., Inc., 1995—; industry rep. to Am. Nat. Standards Inst.; co. rep. U.S.-USSR Trade and Econ. Coun.; mem. exec. com. Jr. Achievement, Charlotte. Bd. dirs. Am. Fund for Dental Health; apptd. mem. Charlotte Mecklenburg Community Relations Com.; mem. bd. visitors, bd. vis. U. N.C., Charlotte; Jr. Achievement exec com. mem., officer. Served in USAR, 1961-68. Mem. Am. Mgmt. Assn. (bd. dirs. N.J. chpt.), Am. Mktg. Assn., Am. Dental Trade Assn. (bd. dirs.), Dental Mfrs. Am. (past pres.), Am. Acad. Dental Radiology, Charlotte C. of C. (bd. advisors), Acad. Gen. Dentists (bd. mem. found.), Masons (32 deg.), Shriners. Republican.

VITTONE, BERNARD JOHN, psychiatrist, researcher; b. Latrobe, Pa., Oct. 5, 1951; s. Felix Edward and Jessie (Mosso) V.; 1 child, Matthew. BS in Psychology, Georgetown U., 1969-73, DMS, 1973-77. Diplomate Am. Bd. Psychiatry and Neurology. Intern in flexible medicine, then resident in psychiatry St. Vincent's Hosp and Med. Ctr., N.Y.C., 1977-82; resident in ophthalmology Wills Eye Hosp., Phila., 1978-79; staff psychiatrist Phila. State Hosp., Phila., 1979; med. staff fellow NIMH, Bethesda, Md., 1982-84; dir. Nat. Ctr. for Treatment of Phobias, Anxiety, and Depression, Washington, 1985—; cons. Roundhouse Sq. Psychiat. Ctr., Alexandria, Va., 1984-85; guest rschr. NIMH, 1984-93; mem. tng. com. St. Vincent's Hosp. and Med. Ctr., N.Y.C., 1980-81; mem. attending staff Dominion Hosp., 1991-92; featured expert Nightline, Washington Post, Newsweek, numerous other TV and newspaper pieces. Contbg. author to profl. jours. and books. Mem. instnl. rev. bd. Inst. for Behavior and Health, Rockville, Md., 1988-91; dir. adv. bd. Am. Against Drugs, 1990-94. Recipient Outstanding achievement award in microbiology, Georgetown Univ., 1976. Mem. AMA, Am. Psychiat. Assn., Washington Psychiat. Soc., D.C. Mental Health Counselors Assn., Anxiety Disorders Assn. of Am., Alpha Omega Alpha. Office: NCTPAD 1755 S St NW Washington DC 20009-6107

VITULLI, WILLIAM FRANCIS, psychology educator; b. Bklyn., July 17, 1936; s. William S. and Sadie Rosaria (Stallone) V.; m. Betty Jean Sheubrooks, June 15, 1961; children: Paige Vitulli Baggett, Quinn Anthony, Sherik Denise. BA, U. Miami, 1961, MS, 1963, PhD, 1966. Lic. psychologist, Ala. Grad. asst. U. Miami, Coral Gables, Fla., 1961-65; asst. prof. psychology U. South Ala., Mobile, 1965-69, assoc. prof., 1969-75, prof., 1975—; v.p. Ala. Bd. Examiners in Psychology, Montgomery, 1982-84; rsch. cons. Drug Edn. Coun., Mobile, 1988-94. Mem. editorial bd. Jour. Sport Behavior, 1978—; contbr. articles to profl. jours. Mem. adv. bd. Contact Mobile, 1987-92. Named Prof. of Quar., Alpha Lambda Delta, Faculty Mem. of Yr., 1993-94; recipient Outstanding Prof. award Alumni Assn., 1994. Mem. APA, Southeastern Psychol. Assn., Ala. Psychol. Assn. (pres. 1975), Italian-Am. Cultural Soc. South Ala. (chair hist.-cultural com. 1982), Sigma Xi, Psi Chi (faculty adviser U. South Ala. chpt. 1972-80). Roman Catholic. Home: 2025 Maryknoll Ct Mobile AL 36695-3829 Office: U South Ala 307 University Blvd N Mobile AL 36688-3053

VIVEK, SEETH, psychiatrist; b. Jabalpur, India, May 18, 1951; came to U.S. 1976; s. Muthu and Bharathi (Paul) Seetharaman; m. Anupama Reddy Vivek. MD, U. Madras, India, 1972; DPM, Nat. Inst. Mental Health, Bangalore, 1974. Diplomate Am. Bd. Psychiatry and Neurology. Resident Mt. Sinai Hosp. Svcs., 1976-79; fellow Montefiore Hosp., Bronx, 1979-81; staff psychiatrist Booth Meml. Hosp., Flushing, N.Y., 1981-83; dir. psychiatry Bapt. Med. Ctr., Bklyn., 1983-86; chmn. psychiatry Jamaica Hosp., N.Y., 1986—. Recipient Leo Davidoff award Albert Einstein U. Med. Sch., 1980. Mem. Am. Psychiatric Assn., Am. Assn. Group Psychotherapy qand Psychodrama. Office: Jamaica Hosp 8900 Van Wyck Expy Jamaica NY 11418

VIVERA, ARSENIO BONDOC, allergist; b. Cebu City, Philippines, Oct. 29, 1931; s. Arsenio R. and Ramona del Mar (Bondoc) V.; A.A., Cebu Coll., U. Philippines, 1950, M.D., 1954. Intern, Philippines Gen. Hosp., 1954-55; resident in medicine Beekman-Downtown Hosp., N.Y.C., 1955-57, Detroit Meml. Hosp., 1957-58; resident in allergy Robert A. Cooke Inst. Allergy, Roosevelt Hosp., N.Y.C., 1958-59, fellow in allergy, 1959-61; sr. cons. scientist Philippines Nat. Inst. Sci. and Tech., Manila, 1961-62; practice medicine specializing in allergy, N.Y.C.; chief allergy dept. attending physician N.Y. Polyclinic Med. Sch. and Health Center, 1972-77, adj. prof., 1972-77; clin. attending physician Robert A. Cooke Inst. Allergy, 1969—; asst. attending physician N.Y. Infirmary, N.Y.C., 1969—; chief allergy, attending St. Vincent's Hosp. and Med. Center, N.Y.C., 1977—. Diplomate Am. Bd. Allergy and Immunology. Fellow Am. Acad. Allergy, Am. Coll. Allergists, Am. Assn. Clin. Immunology and Allergy; mem. N.Y. Allergy Soc., AMA, Am. Assn. Cert. Allergists, N.Y. Acad. Scis., N.Y. Acad. Medicine, Am. Geriatric Soc., N.Y. State Med. Soc., N.Y. County Med. Socs. Office: 211 E 53rd St P-3 New York NY 10022-2625

VIZZI, RUSSELL FRANK, home health company executive; b. Passaic, N.J., Sept. 3, 1928; s. Frank and Sadie (Bunetta) V.; m. Esther Miriam Wolf, Feb. 8, 1953 (div. 1985); m. Katie Lee Burkhalter, Jan. 16, 1987; children: Michael Glenn, Ellen Beth, Rusane, Denise Lynn Vizzi Covert. AA, Fairleigh Dickinson Coll., 1951, BS, 1953; postgrad., Stevens Inst. Tech., 1981—. Adminstrv. engr. Curtiss-Wright Corp., Woodridge, N.J., 1954-56; quality engr. Am. Standard Co., New Orleans, 1956-58; with ITT-Fed. Electric Corp., various locations, 1958-70; dir. project ops. ITT-Fed. Electric Corp., Huntsville, Ala., 1965-70; mgr. internat. proposal ops. Gen. Electric Corp., Huntsville, 1970-73; pres. MidSouth Comprehensive Home Health and Hospice, Memphis, 1973-87, MidSouth Staffing Services, Inc., Memphis, 1986-87, MidSouth Caring, Inc., Memphis, 1986-87, RKV of Broward County, Inc. dba Classic Shapes, Lauderhill, Fla., 1988—. Mem. ad hoc com. on home health service, Memphis United Way, 1975; chmn. programs and long range planning com. Memphis Sr. Citizens, 1976; del. Citizens Ambassador Program, People's Republic of China, 1987. Mem. Tenn. Assn. Home Health (bd. dirs., chmn. Medicare liaison com. 1984-87), Miss. Home Health Assn. (bd. dirs. 1983-87), Nat. Assn. Home Care (bd. dirs. 1984-85, chmn. awards com. 1987, mem. numerous coms.), West Tenn. Regional Home Health Council (legis. cons. 1984-85), Home Health Council Greater Memphis (chmn. 1980). Home: 7009 NW 49th Pl Fort Lauderdale FL 33319

VLADECK, BRUCE CHARNEY, charitable organization executive; b. N.Y.C., Sept. 13, 1949; s. Stephen Charney and Judith (Pomarlen) V.; m. Fredda Wellin, Aug. 5, 1973; children—Elizabeth Charney, Stephen Isaiah, Abigail Sarah. B.A., Harvard U., 1970; M.A., U. Mich, 1972, Ph.D. in Polit. Sci., 1973. Assoc. social scientist N.Y.C.-Rand Inst., 1973-74; asst. prof. Columbia U., N.Y.C., 1974-78; assoc. prof. Columbia U., 1978-79; asst. commr. health planning and resources devel. N.J. Dept. Health, Trenton, 1979-82; asst. v.p. Robert Wood Johnson Found., Princeton, N.J., 1982-83; pres. United Hosp. Fund, N.Y.C., 1983—; now admstr. Dept. Health & Human Services, Washington; adj. prof. pub. adminstrn. NYU, 1984—; cons. U.S. Gen. Acctg. Office, other agys., Washington, 1984—; mem. N.Y. State Coun. on Health Care Financing, Albany, 1978—; mem. com. on nursing home regulation Inst. Medicine, Washington, 1983-85, chmn. com. on health care for homeless people, 1986-88, mem. prospective payment assessment com., 1986—. Author: Unloving Care: The Nursing Home Tragedy, 1981. Contbr. numerous articles to profl. publs. Fellow N.Y. Acad. Medicine; mem. Inst. Medicine, Nat. Acad. Scis., Phi Beta Kappa. Home: 161 W 15th St New York NY 10011-6720 Office: Dept of Health & Human Services Healthcare Financing Admin 200 Independence Ave SWRm 314G Washington DC 20201-0004*

VLADUTIU, ADRIAN O., clinical pathologist, pathology educator; b. Bucharest, Romania, Aug. 5, 1940; came to U.S., 1969, naturalized 1974; s. Octavian and Veturia (Chirescu) V.; m. Georgirene D. Therrien; children: Christina Lynn, Catherine Joy. MD, Sch. Medicine, Bucharest, 1962; PhD, Sch. Medicine, Jassy, Romania, 1968. Diplomate Am. Bd. Pathology. Asst. prof. physiopathology Sch. Medicine, Bucharest, 1968-71; assoc. prof. pathology SUNY Sch. Medicine, Buffalo, 1978-81, prof. pathology, 1981—; pathologist Buffalo Gen. Hosp., 1974—, dir. clin. labs., 1982—, prof. microbiology, 1982—, prof. medicine, 1985—; cons. Niagara Falls (N.Y.) Meml. Hosp., 1976-82, Tri-County Hosp., Gowanda, N.Y., 1991-93; acting head dept. pathology Buffalo Gen. Hosp., 1985-86. Med. Rsch. Coun. Can. fellow, 1968, Buswell fellow, 1969; recipient rsch. award NIH, 1985. Fellow Am. Coll. Physicians, Coll. Am. Pathologists; mem. Am. Soc. Immunologists, Am. Soc. Investigative Pathology, N.Y. Acad. Scis. Home: 80 Oakview Dr Buffalo NY 14221-1420

VLAOVIC, MILAN STEPHEN, pathologist; b. Novi Sad, Yugoslavia, Feb. 1, 1936; came to U.S., 1970; s. Stevan and Olga (Kantardzic) V.; m. Sharon Helen Rabatich, July 24, 1969; children: Stevan Alexander, Sofija Ann, Peter Michael. DVM, U. Belgrade, Yugoslavia, 1961; MS, U. Sask., Saskatoon, Can., 1970; postgrad., Wash. State U., 1970-71; PhD, U. Mo., 1974. Veterinarian Prosina, Beli Manastir, Yugoslavia, 1961-63; head technologist Banatski Karlovac (Yugoslavia) Meat Plant, 1963-65; pvt. practice vet. medicine various cities, Fed. Republic Germany, 1965-67; insp. various meat plants, Winnipeg, Man., Can., 1967-68; mgr. Frederick (Md.) Cancer Rsch. Ctr., 1974-77; toxicologic pathologist Indsl. Bio-Test, Decatur, Ill., 1977-78; mgr. toxicology support Eastman Kodak Co., Rochester, N.Y., 1978—. Mem. Soc. Toxicologic Pathologists, Soc. Vet. Immunologists. Serbian Orthodox. Home: 7 Dixon Woods Honeoye Falls NY 14472 Office: Eastman Kodak Co 1100 Ridgeway Ave # 320B Rochester NY 14615-3712

VLAY, STEPHEN CHARLES, cardiologist, electrophysiologist; b. N.Y.C., July 25, 1950; s. Stephen and Rose Vlay; m. Linda C. Vlay. AB, NYU, 1971; MD, Yale U., 1975. Diplomate Am. Bd. Internal Medicine. Prof. medicine SUNY, Stony Brook; dir. Stony Brook Arrhythmia Study/Sudden Death Prevenvtion Ctr. Editor: Manual of Cardiac Arrhythmias, 1988, Medical Care of the Cardiac Surgical Patient, 1992, A Practical Approach to Cardiac Arrhythmias, 1996. Fellow ACS, Am. Heart Assn. (coun. on clin. cardiology), Am. Coll. Cardiology; mem. N.Am. Soc. Pacing and Electrophysiology. Office: SUNY Health Sci Ctr N T17 020 Stony Brook NY 11794

VLIETINCK, ARNOLD JOZEF, pharmacy educator; b. Brugge, Flanders, Belgium, Oct. 23, 1941; s. René and Paula (Zwaenepoel) V.; m. Flora Loos, Aug. 10, 1968; children: Hans, Tom, Eefje. B Pharmacy, U. Leuven (Belgium), 1964, PhD in Pharmacy, 1968, Degree in Indsl. Pharmacy, 1969, Degree in Clin. Biology, 1973. Sr. asst. U. Leuven, Belgium, 1969-73; rsch. asst. Sch. Pharmacy, Madison, Wis., 1973-74; prof. pharmacy U. Antwerp (Belgium), 1974—; Expert European Pharmacopoeia Com., Strasbourg, France, 1974—; coord. Edn. Project, Butare-Rwanda, 1981—; chmn. Natural Products Rsch. Inst. WHO Collaboration Centre for Traditional Medicine, Antwerp, 1991. Author 3 books; patentee in field. Fulbright-Hays grantee, Brussels, 1973-74; postdoctoral fellowships WHO, Gent, 1973-74, NATO, Brussels, 1973-74. Home: Boswachtersdreef 26, B-2920 Kalmthout Belgium Office: U Antwerp, Universiteitsplein 1, 2610 Antwerp Belgium

VO, HUU DINH, pediatrician, educator; b. Hue, Vietnam, Apr. 29, 1950; came to U.S., 1975; s. Chanh Dinh and Dong Thi (Pham) V.; m. Que Phuong Tonnu, Mar. 22, 1984; children: Katherine Hoa-An, Karyn Bao-An. MD, U. Saigon, 1975. Diplomate Am. Bd. Pediatrics. Adminstr. bilingual vocat. tng. Community Care and Devel. Svc., L.A., 1976-77; resident in pediatrics Univ. Hosp., Jacksonville, Fla., 1977-80; physician, surgeon, chief med. officer Lanterman Devel. Ctr., Pomona, Calif., 1980-92, chief med. staff, 1984-88, coord. med. ancillary svc., 1984-88, 91—; physician Pomona Valley Community Hosp., 1988-90; asst. clin. prof. Loma Linda (Calif.) Med. Sch., 1985-92; chief med. officer So. Reception Ctr.and Clinic., Norwalk, Calif., 1992—; bd. dirs. Pomona Med. Clinic Inc. Pres. Vietnamese Cmty. Ponoma Valley, 1983-85, 87—, chmn., 1993—; nat. co-chair mem. Vietnamese Am. Cmty. in USA, 1993—; bd. dirs. YMCA, Ponoma, 1988—, Sch.-Cmty. Partnership, Ponoma, 1988—. Mem. AMA (Physician recognition award 1989, 1992), L.A. Pediatrics Soc., Vietnamese-Am. Physicians Assn. La. and Orange County (founding mem., sec. 1982-84, bd. dirs. 1987-90). Republican. Buddhist. Home: 19036 Stonehurst Ln Huntington Beach CA 92647 Office: So Reception Ctr and Clinic 13200 Bloomfield Ave Norwalk CA 90650-3253

VODKIN, MICHAEL HAROLD, geneticist; b. Boston, Dec. 4, 1942; s. Hyman and Eva (Weiner) V.; m. Lila Ott, June 28, 1975. BS, Boston Coll., 1964, MS, 1966; PhD, U. Ariz., 1971. Postdoctoral fellow Cornell U., Ithaca, N.Y., 1971-73; asst. prof. U. S.C., Columbia, 1973-80; sr. fellow Nat. Inst. Allergy and Infectious Disease/NIH, Bethesda, Md., 1980-82; chemist U.S. Army Med. Rsch. Inst. Infectious Disease-Ft. Detrick, Frederick, Md., 1982-87; staff scientist U. Ill., Urbana, 1987—. Contbr. articles to profl. jours. Mem. Genetics Soc. Am., Am. Soc. for Microbiology. Democrat. Jewish. Home: 2522 Brett Dr Champaign IL 61821-5752 Office: U Ill Dept Vet Pathobiology Urbana IL 61801

VOELKER, MARGARET IRENE (MEG VOELKER), gerontology, medical, surgical nurse; b. Bitburg, Germany, Dec. 31, 1955; d. Lewis R. and Patricia Irene (Schaffner) Miller; 1 child, Christopher Douglas. Diploma, Clover Park Vocat.-Tech., Tacoma, 1975, diploma in practical nursing, 1984; ASN, Tacoma (Wash.) C.C., 1988; postgrad., U. Washington Tacoma, Tacoma, 1992-95; student nurse practitioner program, U. of Wash., 1995—. Cert. ACLS. Nursing asst. Jackson County Hosp., Altus, Okla., 1976-77; receptionist Western Clinic, Tacoma, 1983; LPN, Tacoma Gen. Hosp., 1984-88, clin. geriatric nurse, 1988-90, clin. nurse post anesthesia care unit perioperative svcs., 1990—; pre-admit clinic nurse, 1995—; mem. staff nurse coun. Tacoma Gen. Hosp., 1990-91. Recipient G. Corydon Wagner endowment fund scholarship. Mem. PostAnesthesia Nurses Assn., Phi Theta Kappa, Sigma Theta Tau.

VOELKERS, GERARD JOSEPH, JR., neurosurgeon; b. South Bend, Ind., Aug. 3, 1930; s. Gerard Joseph and Annis Marion (Daly) V.; m. Joy Angela Leppert, Sept. 6, 1952 (div. Sept. 1989); children: William, Robert; m. Linda Kay Xezonatos, May 17, 1992. BA, Mo. U., 1953; MD, Ind. U., 1957. Diplomate Am. Bd. Neurologic Surgery. Resident in neurosurgery U. Mo., Columbia, 1960-65; pvt. practice neurosurgery Bakersfield, Calif., 1965—. Capt. USAF, 1958-60. Fellow ACS; mem. Am. Assn. Neurologic Surgeons, Congress Neurologic Surgeons, Calif. Assn. Neurologic Surgeons, Alpha Omega Alpha. Republican. Baptist. Office: Kern Neurosurgery Med Group 2129 17th Bakersfield CA 93301

VOGEL, BRUCE GREGORY, geriatrics services professional, physician; b. Minn., Feb. 12, 1940; s. Rudolph and Margaret (Helland) V.; m. Beverly Kay Soetaert, Aug. 24, 1968; children: Tara Lee, Tami Joe. BA, Olivet Nazarene U., 1962; DO, U. Health Scis., 1970. Cert. Am. Assn. Profl. Specialist Family Practice, Geriat. Intern Parkview Osteo. Hosp., Toledo, 1971, chief of staff, 1980, 81; physician USCG Mcht. Marines, Toledo, 1978-85; assoc. prof. geriat. Ohio U., Athens, 1985-92; med. dir. geriat. Riverside Hosp., Toledo, 1990-92; med. dir. Belmont Nursing Home, Perrysburg, Ohio, 1987-92; exec. bd. Parkview Osteo. Hosp., Toledo, 1975-82. Contbr. articles to profl. jours. Mem. Kiwanis (sec. 1994). Republican. Home: 530 S 208 Hwy Yerington NV 89447

VOGEL, GERHARD, HANS, pharmacologist, toxicologist; b. Bucarest, Roumania, Sept. 9, 1927; s. Eugen Georg and Emilie Katharina (Sturm) V.; m. Anna Theresia Zoller, Dec. 23, 1988. Pharmacist degree, U. Erlangen, 1951; physician degree, U. Tubingen, 1955; assoc. prof. degree, U. Marburg,

1967; honorary prof. degree, U. Frankfurt, 1979. Resident City Hosp., Heidenheim, Germany, 1956-57; senior scientist endocrinology lab. Dept. of Pharmacology, Hoechst AG, Frankfurt, Germany, 1958-69, dir., 1967-78; dir. Pharma Rsch. Experimental Medicine, Hoechst AG, Frankfurt, Germany, 1977-79, Pharma Preclinical Evaluation and Devel., Hoechst AG, Frankfurt, Germany, 1980-88, Decision Bd. on Pharm. Devel., Hoechst AG, Frankfurt, Germany, 1989-90; cons. Pharmaceutical and Medical Rsch. Devel., Hofheim, Germany, 1990—; mem. several scientific assns., Germany/ USA, 1970—; cons. in drug evaluation and devel. Editor several books on workshop confs. and symposia; contbr. over 100 articles on biomechanics to profl. jours. Home: Mainzer Strasse 40, D 65719 Hofheim Germany Office: Hoechst AG, Bruening Strasse, D 65926 Frankfurt am Main Germany

VOGEL, H. VICTORIA, psychotherapist, educator. BA, U. Md., 1968; MA, NYU, 1970, 1975; MEd, Columbia U., 1982, postgrad., 1982—; cert., Am. Projective Drawing Inst., 1983. Art Therapist Childville, Bklyn., 1962-64; tchr., Montgomery County (Md.) Jr. H.S., 1968-69; with H.S. div. N.Y.C. Bd. Edn., 1970—, guidance counselor, instructor, psychotherapist in pvt. practice; clinical counseling cons. psychodiagnosis and devel. studies, art/play therapy, The Modern School, 1984—; art/play therapist Hosp. Ctr. for Neuromuscular Disease and Devel. Disorders, 1987—; employment counselor-adminstr. N.Y. State Dept. Labor Concentrated Employment Program, 1971-72; intern psychotherapy and psychoanalysis psychiat. divsn. Cen. Islip Hosp., 1973-75; with Calif. Grad. Inst., L.A.; Columbia U. Tchrs. Coll., N.Y. intern psychol. counseling and rehab. N.J. Coll. Medicine, Newark, 1979. Mem. com. for spl. events NYU, 1989; participant clin. and artistic perspectives Am. Acad. Psychoanalysis Conf., 1990, participant clin. postmodernism and psychoanalysis, 1996; auxilary police officer N.Y. Police Dept. Precinct 19, N.Y.C., 1994—; chair bylaws com. Columbia U., 1995—. Mem. APA, AAAS, Am. Psychol. Soc., Am. Orthopsychiat. Assn., Am. Soc. Group Psychotherapy & Psychodrama (publs. com. 1984—), Am. Counseling Assn., N.Y.C. Art Tchrs. Assn., Art/Play Therapy, Assn. Humanistic Psychology (exec. sec. 1981), Tchrs. Coll. Adminstrv. Women in Edn., Phi Delta Kappa (editor chpt. newsletter 1981-84, exec. sec. Columbia U. chpt. 1984—, chmn. nominating com. for chpt. officers 1986—, nominating com. 1991, pub. rels. exec. bd. dirs. 1991, rsch. rep. 1986—), Phi Delta Kappa (v.p. programs NYU chpt. 1994—). Author: The Never Ending Story of Alcohol, Drugs and Other Substance Abuse, 1992, Variant Sexual Behavior and the Aesthetic Modern Nudes, 1992, Psychological Science of School Behavior Intervention, 1993, Joycean Conceptual Modernism: Relationships and Deviant Sexuality, 1995, Electronic Evil Eyes, 1995.

VOGEL, LAWRENCE CABELL, physician; b. Oak Park, Ill., Oct. 1, 1948; s. John Cabell and Joyce Veronica (Stewart) V.; m. Linda M. Bernas, May 22, 1983; children: Michael, Rebecca, Alexander, Katrina. BA, Northwestern U., 1969; MD, U. Ill., Chgo., 1973. Pediatric residency Yale-New Haven Hosp., 1973-76; fellow Michael Reese Hosp., 1976-78; asst. prof. pediatrics U. Chgo., 1978-79; assoc. attending physician Michael Reese Hosp., Chgo., 1978-79; attending physician, program dir. Mercy Hosp., Chgo., 1979-80; asst. prof. pediatrics U. Ill., Chgo., 1979-86; attending physician, dir. pediats. Shriners Hosp. for Children, Chgo., 1981—; asst. prof. pediatrics Rush U., Chgo., 1987—; cons. Marianjoy Rehab. Ctr., Wheaton, Ill., 1988—. Fellow Am. Acad. Pediats., Am. Spinal Injury Assn., Inst. Medicine Chgo., Am. Paraplegic Soc.; mem. AMA, Am. Soc. Microbiology, Am. Acad. Cerebral Palsy and Devel. Medicine, Chgo. Pediat. Soc., Alpha Omega Alpha. Office: Shriners Hosp 2211 N Oak Park Ave Chicago IL 60635-3351

VOGEL, MARY STALGAITIS, dentist, dental educator; b. Hazleton, Pa., Aug. 2, 1949; d. Joseph George and Sylvia (Nicholas) Stalgaitis. BS, Pa. State. U., 1974; DMD, U. Pitts., 1974. Dental extern Home for Crippled Children, Pitts., 1973-75; pres. Mary Vogel, D.M.D., P.C., Pitts., 1976—; asst. clin. prof. Sch. Dental Medicine U. Pitts., 1974—; panel discussant on Women's Careers, Pa. Sect. Edn., Indiana U. Pa. Demonstrator dental procedures TV, 1981. Troop leader Girls Scouts U.S.A., Forrest Hills, P.A., 1983; active health fair booth Women's Task Force on Alcoholism, Pitts., 1982; keynote speaker Marian High., Tamaqua, Pa., 1981. Mem. Am. Assn. Women Dentists (v.p. Pitts. br. 1982-83), ADA, Pa. Dental Assn. (del. 1980), East End Pitts. Odontol. Soc. (pres. 1978-79), Acad. Oral Medicine, (Sr. Dental Student award 1974), U. Pitts. Dental Alumni (exec. com. 1977—), Nat. Assn. Women's Bus. Owners. Home and Office: Suite 340 Gateway Towers Pittsburgh PA 15222

VOGEL, STEPHEN NORMAN, emergency physician, consultant, author; b. Buffalo, Feb. 4, 1946; s. Henry E. and Rosalind G. (Garten) V.; m. Esther Strossberg, Aug. 16, 1969; children: Michelle, Jonathan. BA, Columbia U., 1967; MD, SUNY, Buffalo, 1971. Diplomate Am. Bd. Emergency Medicine. Intern Millard Fillmore Hosp., Buffalo, 1971-72; resident in emergency medicine Northwestern U., Evanston (Ill.) Hosp., 1974-76; sr. attending physician emergency rm. Evanston Hosp., 1976—; clin. asst. prof. Northwestern U. Sch. of Medicine, Chgo., 1976—; med. dir. Occupational Medicine Evanston-Glenbrook Assn., Glenview, Ill., 1986—; publisher EMT, Inc., Wilmette, Ill., 1984-95.; founding ptnr. Inspe Assocs., Ltd. Chgo., 1981—, Evanston-Glenbrook Emergency Assn., Evanston, 1984—; sec. v.p. EMT, Inc., Wilmette, 1984-95. Author: (books) Emergency Medical Treatment- Children, 1984, Emergency Medical Treatment- Infants, 1989, Emergency Medical Treatment- Adults, 1992; editor: Outdoor Emergencies, 1996; contbr. articles to profl. jours. Capt. USAF, 1972-74. Fellow Am. Coll. Emergency Physicians. Office: Evanston Hosp Emergency Rm 2650 Ridge Evanston IL 60201

VOGEL, SUSAN MICHELLE, physician; b. London, June 17, 1961; d. John P. and Mary A. (Murphy) V.; m. Marco R. Siqueiros, Oct. 27, 1990; children: Nicholas, Alexander Maxwell. BS, Syracuse U., 1983; MD, SUNY, Syracuse, 1987. Resident U. Tex. Med. Sch., Houston, 1990-91, asst. prof., 1991—; pres., mng. physician Houston Internal Medicine Assocs., Houston, 1992-96; pres. Susan M. Vogel & Assocs. P.A., 1996—; pres. South East Tex. IPA, Houston, 1995-96; bd. dirs. St. Joseph Hosp., Houston. Mem. Tex. Med. Assn., Preaclarus. Office: 1315 Calhoun #1605 Houston TX 77002

VOGEL, THOMAS TIMOTHY, surgeon, health care consultant, lay church worker; b. Columbus, Ohio, Feb. 1, 1934; s. Thomas A. and Charlotte A. (Hogan) V.; m. M.M. Darina Kelleher, May 29, 1965; children: Thomas T., Catherine D., Mark P., Nicola M. AB, Coll. of Holy Cross, 1955; MS, Ohio State U., 1960, PhD, 1962; MD, Georgetown U., 1965. Pvt. practice surgery Columbus, 1971—; chmn. liturgy com., pres. parish coun. St. Catharine Parish, Columbus, 1971-73; chmn. diocesan adminstrn. com. Diocesan Pastoral Coun., Columbus, 1972-73, chmn., 1973-75; vice prefect Sodality of Holy Cross, 1953-55; mem. Ohio Bishop's Adv. Coun., Columbus, 1976-79; clin. asst. prof. surgery Ohio State U., Columbus, 1974—; mem. med. adv. com. Ethix Corp., Dublin, Ohio; past trustee Peer Rev. Systems, Inc. Contbr. articles to profl. jours. Bd. dirs. St. Vincent's Children's Ctr., 1975-83, chmn., 1981-82; past chmn. bd. trustees St. Joseph Montessori Sch. Recipient Layman's award Columbus Ea. Kiwanis, 1972. Mem. Am. Coll. Surgeons, Am. Physiol. Soc., Assn. for Acad. Surgery, Ohio Med. Assn., Columbus Acad. Medicine, Sigma Xi, Delta Epsilon Sigma. Roman Catholic. Home: 247 S Ardmore Rd Columbus OH 43209-1701 Office: 621 S Cassingham Rd Columbus OH 43209-2403

VOGEL, VICTOR GERALD, medical educator; b. Bethlehem, Pa., Mar. 14, 1952; s. Victor Gerald Jr. and Margaret Moser (Smith) V.; m. Saralyn Sue Schaffner, June 25, 1977; children: Heather Marie, Christiaan Keith. Diplomate Am. Bd. Internal Medicine, Nat. Bd. Med. Examiners. Resident in internal medicine Balt. City Hosps., 1978-81; fellow in med. oncology Johns Hopkins Oncology Ctr., Balt., 1983-86; Andrew W. Mellon fellow Johns Hopkins Sch. Hygiene Pub. Health, Balt., 1984-86; asst. prof. medicine and epidemiology U. Tex./M.D. Anderson Cancer Ctr., Houston, 1986-93, assoc. prof. clin. cancer prevention, 1993-95; asst. prof. epidemiology U. Tex. Sch. Pub. Health, Houston, 1987-95; prof. medicine and epidemiology U. Pitts. Cancer Inst./Magee-Women's Hosp., 1996—, dir. comprehensive breast cancer program, 1996—; epidemiologist Tex. breast screening project Am. Cancer Soc., 1986—; Susan G. Komen Found. rsch. fellow, 1989; lectr. in field. Contbr. articles to profl. jours. Served with USPHS, 1981-83. Named Med. Vol. of Yr., Am. Cancer Soc., 1983, award 1987, career devel. award, 1990-93. Fellow Am. Coll. Preventive Medicine, ACP; mem. Am. Soc. Clin. Oncology, Am. Soc. Preventive Oncology, Christian Med. and Dental Soc. Republican. Methodist. Office: University of Pittsburgh Cancer Inst 802 Kaufmann Bldg 3471 Fifth Ave Pittsburgh PA 15213-3221

VOGELSTEIN, BARRY NORMAN, orthopaedic surgeon; b. Balt., May 22, 1950; m. Eve Lawrence; children: Hana Rose, Daniel J., Claire Frances, Harvey Fishel. BS in Psychology, U. Pa., 1971; MD, U. Md., 1976. Diplomate Am. Bd. Orthopedic Surgery; lic. physician, N.Y., Md. Intern Temple U. Health Sci. Ctr., Phila., 1976-77; resident Orthopedic Inst./Hosp. for Joint Diseases Med. Ctr., N.Y.C., 1977-81; pvt. practice Clin. Assocs., P.A., Towson, 1981—; clin. instr. dept. orthopedics Mt. Sinai Med. Ctr., N.Y.C., 1977-81; asst. dir. sports medicine Nassau County Med. Ctr., L.I., N.Y., 1981-87; assoc. orthopedist Balt. Orioles at Camden Yards, 1994—; staff physician Temple U. Health Sci. Ctr., Phila., 1976-77, Orthop. Inst. Hosp. for Joint Diseases Med. Ctr., N.Y.C., 1977-81, Mt. Sinai Med. Ctr., N.Y.C., 1981—, Greater Balt. Med. Ctr., 1986-87, Franklin Square Hosp., Balt., 1987-89, Good Samaritan Hosp., Balt., 1987—, St. Joseph Hosp., Balt., 1987—, Mercy Hosp., Balt., 1989—, Children's Hosp., Balt., 1989—, N.W. Gen. Hosp., Balt., 1990—. Contbr. articles to profl. jours. Recipient Batcock Award for Surg. Excellence, 1976. Fellow ACS, Internat. Coll. surgeons, Am. Orthop. Soc.; mem. AMA, Internat. Arthroscopic Assn., N.Y. Med. Soc., Md. Orthop. Assn., Ea. Orthop. Assn., Am. Acad. Orthop. Surgeons, Arthroscopic Assn. N.Am. Office: Clinical Assocs PA 515 Fairmount Ave #530 Towson MD 21286 also: 750 Main St Reisterstown PA 21136

VOGELSTEIN, BERT, oncology educator. BS, U. Pa., 1970; MD, Johns Hopkins U. Rsch. assoc. Nat. Cancer Inst., 1976-78; prof. dept. oncology Johns Hopkins U. Sch. Medicine, Balt., 1978—; advisor Nat. Insts. Health Scientific Review Groups, Nat. Cancer Inst. Assoc. editor Genes, Chromosomes and Cancer; mem bd. reviewing editors Science Magazine; contbr. article to profl. jours. Recipient Anne & Jason Farber Lecture award Am. Acad. Neurology, 1991, Gairdner Found. Internat. award Gairdner Found., 1992, Medal of Honor Am. Cancer Soc., 1992, Richard Lounsbery award Nat. Acad. Scis., 1993, Baxter Rsch. award Assn. Am. Med. Coll., 1994. G.H.A. Clowes Meml. award Am. Assn. Cancer Rsch. 1995; laureates Passano Found., 1994. Mem. NAS, Am. Acad. Arts Scis. Office: Johns Hopkins U Sch Med Dept Oncology 720 Rutland Ave Baltimore MD 21205-2109*

VOGELZANG, NICHOLAS JOHN, medical oncologist; b. Holland, Mich., Dec. 13, 1949. AB, Trinity Christian Coll., 1971; MD, U. Ill., Chgo., 1974. Diplomate Am. Bd. Internal Medicine and Med. Oncology. Intern, resident, chief resident Rush Presbyn. St. Lukes, Chgo., 1974-78; fellow, instr. U. Minn., Mpls., 1978-82; asst. and assoc. prof. U. Chgo., 1982-93, prof., attending physician, 1993—; attending physician Bernard Mitchell Hosp., Chgo., investigator, vice chmn. data audit com., exec. com. Cancer and Leukemia Group B., Boston, prostate cancer chmn.; cons., contractor Roche, Schering, Zeneca, Bristol-Myers Squibb Vical, Ciba, U.S. Biosci., Immunex, Eli Lilly, UpJohn. Mem. editl. adv. bd. Cancer, Jour. Clin. Oncology; contbr. over 100 articles to profl. jours. Named Alumnus of Yr. Trinity Christian Coll., 1991. Fellow ACP; mem. Am. Cancer Soc. (bd. dirs. Ill. divsn. 1986—, pres. 1994-96), Am. Assn. Cancer Rsch., Am. Soc. Clin. Oncology (mem. program com. 1985, nat. bd. dirs. 1993-96), Am. Urol. Assn. Home: 5108 Fair Elms Ave Western Springs IL 60558-1808 Office: U Chgo Sect Hematology/Oncology MC 2115 5841 S Maryland 5841 S Maryland Chicago IL 60637-1470

VOGL, EDWARD, cardiologist; b. Prague, Czechoslovakia, July 9, 1948; s. Frank and Edith (Furth) V.; m. Shahla Danesh, 1974. Degree in medicine, U. London, 1971. Intern The London Hosp., London, 1971; residency North Staffordshire Royal Infirmary UK, 1974-77, Prince Henry/Prince of Wales Hosps., Sydney, Australia, 1977-81; vis. specialist in cardiology/ medicine Illawarra Health Svc., Wollongong, Australia, 1981—. Fellow Royal Australian Coll. Physicians; mem. AMA, Cardiac Soc. Australia and New Zealand, Royal Coll. Physicians. Address: 20 Loftus St, Wollongong 2500, Australia

VOHS, JAMES ARTHUR, health care program executive; b. Idaho Falls, Idaho, Sept. 26, 1928; s. John Dale and Cliff Lucille (Packer) V.; m. Janice Hughes, Sept. 19, 1953; children: Lorraine, Carol, Nancy, Sharla. B.A., U. Calif., Berkeley, 1952; postgrad., Harvard Sch. Bus., 1966. Employed by various Kaiser affiliated orgns., 1952-92; chmn., pres., CEO Kaiser Found. Hosps. and Kaiser Found. Health Plan, INc., Oakland, Calif., 1975-92, chmn. emeritus; chmn. bd. dirs. Holy Names Coll., 1981-92; chmn. Marcus Foster Inst., 1981—; bd. dirs. Clorox Co.; dep. chmn. Fed. Res. Bank San Francisco, chmn., 1991-94. Bd. dirs. Oakland-Alameda County Coliseum Complex, Bay Area Coun., 1985-94, chmn., 1991-92; mem. Oakland Bd. Port Commrs. With AUS, 1946-48. Mem. NAS, Inst. Medicine. Office: Kaiser Center Ordway Bldg Oakland CA 94612

VOIPIO-PULKKI, LIISA MARIA, medical administrator; b. Helsinki, Finland, Apr. 4, 1955; m. Kari Johannes Pulkki; children: Anni-Maria, Eveliina. MD, U. Helsinki, 1979; PhD, U. Turku, Finland, 1986. Head med. intensive care and critical care unit Turku U., Ctrl. Hosp., 1996—; clin. investigator Finnish Acad., 1995. Editor: Jour. Finnish Cardiac Soc., 1995—, (procs.) Book of the Symposium Med. Application of Cyclotrons VI, 1992. Mem. Finnish Soc. for Internal Medicine (sec. 1993-95). Lutheran. Office: U Turku, Dept Medicine, FIN20520 Turku Finland

VOJTECKY, MARK ANTHONY, health educator; b. Natrona Heights, Pa., June 18, 1958; s. Joseph Stephen and Margaret Mary (Hrnciar) V.; m. Shirley Ann Harold, May 28, 1983. BS, Pa. State U., 1980, MS, 1985; MPH, U. Pitts., 1986. Rsch. assoc. U. Pitts., 1986-87; dir. health edn. Western Res. Care System, Youngstown, Ohio, 1987-90; resource mgmt. officer USAF Med. Ctr., Wright-Patterson AFB, Ohio, 1990-91; health educator Pa. State U., Pitts., 1986-88; resource mgr. USAF Med. Ctr., Wright Patterson AFB, Ohio, 1990-91; asst. dir. managed health care Wright-Patterson Med. Ctr., Wright-Patterson AFB, 1991—; asst. dir. total quality mgmt. Wright-Patterson Med. Ctr., Wright-Patterson AFB, Ohio, 1991-93; med. flight comdr. USAF Recruiting, Pitts., 1993-95; dir. ops. Tricare, 89th Med. Group, Andrews AFB, Md., 1995—. Planner AIDS Task Force Edn., Youngstown, 1987, Hypertension Task Force, Youngstown, 1987; vol. ARC, Youngstown, 1988. Capt. USMC, 1981-87. Named Outstanding Young Am., 1987. Fellow Soc. Pub. Health Edn. (state coordinator interest group 1987-88); mem. Am. Pub. Health Assn., Pa. Pub. Health Assn., Ohio Pub. Health Assn., Internat. Brotherhood Magicians. Republican. Roman Catholic. Home: 10694 Ashford Cir Waldorf MD 20603 Office: Tricare 89th Medical Group Andrews Air Force Base MD 20762

VOLK, STEPHAN ALBERT, psychiatry, neurology, and psychotherapy educator; b. Frankfurt Am Main, Germany, July 20, 1955; s. Hans Joachim and Gertrud Amalie (Ahlborn) V.; m. Sigrid Anne Meyer, Aug. 26, 1983; children: Jan-Eric, Robin John. MD in Psychiatry and Neurology, Heidelburg (Germany) U., 1981. Postgrad. work Max Planck Inst., Munich, 1981-83; jr. physician Univ. clinics, Frankfurt, 1983-88, sr. physician, 1988—; head sleep disorders dept. Univ. Clinics, Frankfurt, 1988, outpatient dekpt., 1990; instr. psychiatry Frankfurt U., 1990. Author: Obsessive-Compulsive Disorders, 1994; contbr. articles to profl. jours. Max Planck Soc. rsch. fellow, 1981. Mem. Internat. Soc. of Brain Imaging in Psychiatry, World/European/German Sleep Rsch. Socs. (spkr. edn. in sleep medicine sect. 1988, 89, 90).

VOLK, WESLEY AARON, microbiologist; b. Mankato, Minn., Nov. 23, 1924; s. Albert Lee and Della Margret (Buelow) V.; m. Rose Marjorie Keller, Feb. 24, 1945 (dec. July 1, 1966); children: Bradley George, Pamela Lee; m. Joan Ryan, Jan. 29, 1969; stepchildren: Kurt Franke, Fritz Franke. BS in Chemistry, U. Wash., 1948, BS in Food Technology, 1948, MS in Microbiology, 1949, PhD in Microbiology, 1951. Prof. of microbiology U. Va. Sch. Medicine, Charlottesville, 1951-95; researcher NIH, Bethesda, Md., 1963-64, Max Planck Inst. fur Immunobiologie, Freiburg, Germany, 1969-70, Pasteur Inst., Paris, 1983-84; ret., 1995. Author: Basic Microbiology, 1964, 8th edit., 1997, Essentials of Medical Microbiology, 1976, 5th edit., 1996. Lt. USNR, 1943-46. Recipient Robert Bennett Bean award for Excellence in Teaching, 1982. Mem. Am. Soc. for Microbiology, Am. Soc. for Biochemistry and Molecular Biology, AAAS. Home: 5 Cove Cir Palmyra VA 22963-2015

VOLKMAN, ALVIN, pathologist, researcher, educator; b. Bklyn., June 10, 1926; s. Henry Phillip and Sarah Lucille (Silverstein) V.; m. Winifred Joan Grinnell, June 12, 1947 (div. Aug. 1967); children: Karl Frederick, Nicholas James, Rebecca Jane Evans, Margaret Rose Werrell, Deborah Ann Falls; m. Carol Ann Fishel, Jan. 26, 1973 (dec. Sept. 1992); 1 child, Natalie Fishel; 1 stepchild Jeffrey C. Moore. BS, Union Coll., 1947; MD, U. Buffalo, 1951; D.Philosophy, U. Oxford (Eng.), 1963. Diplomate Nat. Bd. Med. Examiners, Am. Bd. Pathology. Intern, Mt. Sinai Hosp., Cleve., 1951-52; research fellow dept. anatomy Western Res. U. Sch. Medicine, 1952-54; resident, then sr. resident, then asst. in pathology Peter Bent Brigham Hosp., Boston, 1956-60; asst. prof. pathology Columbia U. Coll. Physicians and Surgeons, 1960-66; asst. mem., then assoc. mem. Trudeau Inst., Saranac Lake, N.Y., 1966-67; prof. dept. pathology East Carolina U. Sch. Medicine, Greenville, N.C., 1977—, acting chmn. dept. pathology, 1989-90, assoc. dean for rsch. and grad. studies, 1989-95, prof. emeritus, 1995—; mem. NIH study sect. immunological scis., 1975-79, chmn., 1977-79. Served to lt. USNR, 1954-56. Am. Cancer Soc. scholar, 1961-63; Arth and Rheumat Found. fellow 1952-54. Mem. AAAS, Am. Soc. Investigative Pathology, Am. Assn. Immunologists, Am. Soc. Hematology, Reticuloendothelial Soc., Am. Soc. Microbiologists, N.Y. Acad. Scis., Soc. Leukocyte Biology (hon. life). Contbr. articles to sci. jours. Office: East Carolina U Sch Medicine Brody Bldg Greenville NC 27858

VOLKMAR, FRED ROBERT, psychiatrist, educator; b. Highland, Ill., Mar. 26, 1950; s. Fred Harwood and Ella Josephine (Smith) V.; m. Elizabeth Anne Wiesner, Sept. 2, 1984; 1 child Lucy Amelia. B.S., U. Ill., 1972; M.A., Stanford U., 1976, M.D., 1976. Diplomate Am. Bd. Psychiatry and Neurology. Resident in psychiatry Stanford U., Calif., 1976-80; fellow in child psychiatry Yale U., New Haven, 1980-82, asst. prof. Child Study Ctr., 1982-88, Harris assoc. prof. Child Study Ctr., 1988—; cons. psychiatrist Benhaven Sch., New Haven, 1984-85; med. dir., 1982-85; mem. sci. com. Nat. Ctr. for Clin. Infant Programs, Washington, 1985. Recipient Sandoz award, 1980; Faculty Scholar award, William T. Grant Found., 1982; Research Career award NIMH, 1983. James scholar, Phi Beta Kappa, 1972; Laughlin fellow, 1982. Mem. Soc. for Research in Child Devel., Am. Acad. Child Psychiatry. Democrat. Avocations: photography; astronomy; sailing. Office: Yale U Child Study Ctr 230 S Frontage Rd New Haven CT 06519-1124

VOLLUCCI, PAUL ANTHONY, teaching fellow; b. Bellflower, Calif., May 28, 1967; s. Eugene Edward and Barbara Ann (Turner) V.; m. Deinyell Marie Vizcaino, May 2, 1992. BS in Biol. Scis., U. Calif., Irvine, 1990, BA in Psychology, 1991; postgrad., Coll. Osteo. Medicine Pacific, 1992—. Tchr. Pacific Shores Pvt. H.S., Laguna Niguel, Calif., 1991-92; undergrad. tchg. fellow Coll. Osteo. Medicine Pacific, Pomona, 1994—. Mem. AMA, Am. Acad. Family Physicians, Am. Osteo. Assn., Calif. Med. Assn. Home: 31 Briarglen Irvine CA 92714

VOLPE, JOSEPH JOHN, pediatric neurologist, educator; b. Salem, Mass., Dec. 17, 1938; s. John Rosario and Anne Eleanor (Femino) V.; m. Sara Lee Solov, June 2, 1980; children from previous marriage: Joanna Marie, Joseph Anthony, John Matthew. BA, Bowdoin Coll., 1960; MD, Harvard U., 1964. Diplomate Am. Bd. Pediatrics, Am. Bd. Neurology and Psychiatry with spl. competence in child neurology. Pediatric intern Mass. Gen. Hosp., Boston, 1964-65, pediatric resident, 1965-66, neurology and pediatric resident, 1968-71; rsch. assoc. Nat. Inst. Child Health and Human Devel., Bethesda, Md., 1966-68; asst. prof. pediatrics and neurology Washington U. Med. Sch., St. Louis, 1971-76, assoc. prof. pediatrics and neurology, 1976-79, prof. pediatrics and neurology, 1979—, prof. biol. chemistry, 1980-90, dir. div. pediatric neurology, 1984-90; Bronson Crothers prof. neurology Harvard Med. Sch., Boston, 1990—; neurologist in chief Children's Hosp., Boston, 1990—. Author: Neurology of the Newborn, 1981, 2d edit., 1987, 3d edit., 1995; contbr. over 240 articles to profl. jours. Capt. USPHS, 1966-68. Recipient Weinstein-Goldenson award United Cerebral Palsy Assn., 1985; rsch. grantee NIH, 1973—, March of Dimes Nat. Found., 1985-87. Office: Children's Hosp 300 Longwood Ave Boston MA 02115-5724

VOLPÉ, ROBERT, endocrinologist, researcher, educator; b. Toronto, Mar. 6, 1926; s. Aaron G. and Esther (Shulman) V.; m. Ruth Vera Pullan, Sept. 5, 1949; children: Catherine, Elizabeth, Peter, Edward, Rose Ellen. MD, U. Toronto, 1950. Intern U. Toronto, 1950-51, resident in medicine, 1951-52, 53-55, fellow in endocrinology, 1952-53, Nat. Rsch. Coun. fellow, 1955-57, sr. rsch. fellow dept. medicine, 1957-62, McPhedran fellow, 1957-65, asst. prof., 1962-68, assoc. prof., 1968-72, prof., 1972-92, prof. emeritus, 1992—, dir. div. endocrinology and metabolism, 1987-92, chmn. Centennial Com., 1987-88; attending staff St. Joseph's Hosp., Toronto, 1957-66; active staff Wellesley Hosp., Toronto, 1966—; dir. endocrinology rsch. lab. Wellesley Hosp., 1968—, physician-in-chief, 1974-87; trans-Atlantic vis. prof. Caledonia Endocrine Soc., 1985; Hashimoto Meml. lectr. Kyushu U., Fukuoka, Japan, 1992; K.J.R. Wightman vis. prof. Royal Coll. Physicians, Can., 1994; celebratory lectr. commemorating 200th anniversary of birth of Robert Graves, Dublin, Ireland, 1996. Author: Systematic Endocrinology, 1973, 2d edit., 1979, Thyrotoxicosis, 1978, Auto-immunity in the Endocrine System, 1981, Auto-immunity and Endocrine Disease, 1985, Thyroid Function and Disease, 1987, Autoimmunity in Endocrine Disease, 1990; also over 300 rsch. articles mostly on immunology of thyroid disease; past editl. bd. Jour. Clin. Endocrinology and Metabolism, Clin. Medicine, Clin. Endocrinology, Annals Internal Medicine, Endocrine Pathology; editl. bd.: Am. Jour. Physiology, Opinions in Endocrinolgy Metabolism, Thyroid. Served with Royal Can. Naval Vol. Res., 1943-45. Recipient Goldie medal for med. rsch. U. Toronto, 1971, Novo-Nordisk prize Irish Endocrine Soc., 1990; Med. Rsch. Coun. Can. grantee, 1960—. Fellow Royal Coll. Physicians Can. (coun. 1988—, chmn. ann. meetings com. 1988-94, sci. program com. 1988-94, chmn. rsch. com. 1994—, v.p. medicine 1994—), Royal Coll. Physicians Edinburgh and London, Royal Soc. Medicine (editl. bd.), ACP (gov. for Ont. 1978-83); mem. AAAS, Can. Soc. Endocrinology and Metabolism (past pres., Sandoz prize lectr. 1985, disting. svc. award 1990), Toronto Soc. Clin. Rsch. (Baxter prize lectr. 1984), Can. Soc. Clin. Investigation, Am. Thyroid Assn. (pres. 1980-81, disting. scientist award 1991), Assn. Am. Physicians, Endocrine Soc., Am. Fedn. Clin. Rsch., Can. Soc. Nuclear Medicine (Jamieson prize lectr. 1980), Can. Inst. Acad. MEdicine, N.Y. Acad. Sci., European Thyroid Assn. (corr.), Latin Am. Thyroid Assn. (corr.), Soc. Endocrinology and Metabolism of Chile (hon.), Caledonia Soc. Endocrinology (hon.), Japan Endocrine Soc. (hon., gold medal 1986), F+Donalda Club, Alpine Ski Club (bd. dirs. 1987-89), U. Toronto Faculty Club. Home: 3 Daleberry Pl, Don Mills, ON Canada M3B 2A5 Office: Wellesley Hosp, Toronto, ON Canada M4Y 1J3

VON ARB, JOHN J., dentist; b. Davenport, Iowa, Oct. 15, 1952; s. Doris Ann Baehnk; m. Phyllis Helen Marshall, Aug. 20, 1976. AS, Palmer Jr. Coll., 1975; BS, U. Iowa, 1978, DDS, 1982. Resident in dentistry USA Dentac, Ft. Bragg, N.C., 1982-83; chief operative dentistry USA Dentac, Bremerhaven, Fed. Republic Germany, 1983-86; practice gen. dentistry USA Dentac, Ft. Carson, Colo., 1986-88, 89—; div. dental surgeon F Co 704 Support Bn. 4th Inf. Div., Ft. Carson, 1988-89; chief operative dentistry Bremerhaven Dental Clinic, 1985-86; chief endodontics Larson Dental Clinic, Ft. Carson, 1987. Lt. col. Iowa Army Nat. Guard. Lutheran. Home: 625 Western Ave Davenport IA 52803 Office: USADENTAC 1304 Brady St Davenport IA 52803

VONAU, PATRICIA ANN, critical care nurse; b. New Orleans, Dec. 22, 1944; d. Richard Joseph Sr. and Violet Mary (Lizana) Melancon; m. Louis Francis Vonau, Oct. 9, 1965; children: Deborah, Lisa, Robert, Elizabeth. Student, U. New Orleans, 1962-64, U. Southwestern La., 1974-76; BSN, William Carey Coll., 1977. RN, Colo. Staff nurse critical care unit Highland Park Hosp., Covington, La., 1977-78; staff nurse ICU Pendleton Meml. Meth. Hosp., New Orleans, 1978, Slidell (La.) Meml. Hosp., 1978; staff nurse cardiology lab. Med. Ctr. East New Orleans, 1978-80; staff nurse ICU Presbyn. Aurora (Colo.) Hosp., 1988-89, Swedish Med. Ctr., Englewood, Colo., 1989-91; staff nurse gastro-intestinal lab. Swedish Med. Ctr., Englewood, 1991-94.

VON BEHREN, RUTH LECHNER, adult day health care specialist, retired; b. Dubuque, Iowa, Apr. 10, 1933; d. Adolph J. and Elva M. (Fedeler) Lechner; m. Donald D. Von Behren, Dec. 16, 1952 (div. 1965); children: Debi, Jerry, LuAnn. BS, Ill. State U., 1965, MA, 1968; PhD, U. Calif., Davis, 1972. Tchr. Centennial Sch., El Paso, Ill., 1962-65; grad. asst. Ill. State U., Normal, 1967-68; assoc. in History U. Calif., 1968-71; rsch. asst. Calif. Health and Welfare Agy., Sacramento, 1972-74; asst. prof. Sacramento State U., 1970-71, 78-79; analyst Calif. Dept. Health Svcs., Sacramento, 1974-75, sect. chief adult day health care, 1975-80; project dir. State Health and Welfare Agy., Sacramento, 1980-82; adult day health care specialist On Lok Sr. Health Svcs., San Francisco, 1982-95; ret., 1995; cons. adult day health care various orgns. Author: Adult Day Care in America, 1986, Adult Day Care: A Program for the Functionally Impaired, 1989, (with others) Planning and Managing Adult Day Care, 1989; contbr. articles to profl. jours. Sec. Yolo County Hist. Soc., Woodland, Calif., 1976-80; dir. Yolo County Mus. Assocs., Woodland, 1980-82. Recipient Adult Day Health Care Tech. Assistance award Kaiser Found., 1983-86, Rural Adult Day Care Model award Sierra Found., 1988-89. Mem. Nat. Coun. on Aging, Inc., Nat. Inst. on Adult Day Care (chair 1988-90, Ruth Von Behren award for Outstanding Dedication to Growth and Devel. of Adult Day Care, Nat. Inst. on Adult Day Care, 1992), Phi Alpha Theta, Alpha Phi Gamma, Alpha Psi Omega, Kappa Delta Phi, Phi Kappa Phi. Home: 1813 Chapman Pl Davis CA 95616

VON BURG, MARY M., advocate, social services administrator; b. Montezuma, Ind., Feb. 13, 1937; d. Jesse and Gertrude (wilburn) Thomas; m. Raymond E. Von Burg; 1 child, Raymond E. BS in Edn., Ind. U., Indpls., 1980; MS in Counseling and Student Personnel, Ind. U., 1984, postgrad., 1989—. Rsch. asst., faculty sec. Sch. Pub. & Environ. Affairs, Ind. U., Indpls., 1980-81; adminstrv. sec. Sch. Medicine, Ind. U., Indpls., 1981-85; counseling Marion County Prosecutor's Alternative Runaways Program, 1984-85; instr. Ind. U., Indpls., 1984-85; sec. Dept. Pediatrics; exec. sec. dept. pediatrics Sch. Medicine Ind. U., Indpls., 1985-88; project mgr. Regionalization Care for Abused Children, Indpls., 1988—; coord. adminstrn. Cmty. Child Abuse Project., 1985—, Liaison Child Abuse Forum, Indpls., 1988—; mem. com. Child Advocacy Ind. U. Hosp., Indpls., 1989—; delegation to Russia and Lithuania Citizen Amb. Program People to People Internat., 1994; pres. Domestic Violence Network, 1994-96. Contbr. numerous articles to profl. jours. Mem. violence awareness com. Wishard Meml. Hosp., 1995—; chair battered women's protocol com. Marion County, 1994—, statewide tng., 1994—, mem. prevention of child abuse and neglect through dental awareness coalition, 1994—. Recipient Glenn W. Irwin Jr. award Ind. U., Purdue U., 1992. Mem. Child Welfare League Am., Nat. Assn. Counsel Children, Am. Assn. Protecting Children, Nat. Com. Prevention Child Abuse and Neglect (Ind. chpt.), Sigma Pi Alpha. Office: Ind U Comm Child Abuse Projects 1001 W 10th St Myers Bldg D503 Indianapolis IN 46202-2859

VON COLLANI, GERNOT ULRICH, psychology educator, researcher; b. Swinemuende, Germany, Apr. 25, 1942; s. Hans-Joachim and Gertraude Karoline (Schmidt) von C.; m. Sonja Setiawaty Surya, July 7, 1980; children: Marcel Niklas, Patrice Dominic. B.A., Univ. Hamburg, 1966, M.A., 1969; Ph.D., Tech. Univ., Braunschweig, Fed. Republic Germany, 1973;Dr. rer. nat. habil., 1986. Research asst. dept. stats. Univ. Konstanz, Fed. Republic Germany, 1969-72; univ. asst. dept. psychology Univ. Braunschweig, 1972-81, asst. prof. dept. psychology, 1981-85, prof., 1992; prof. U. Leipzig, 1993. Author: Social Network Analysis, 1987; contbr. articles to profl. jours. Lutheran. Avocations: sports, photography, letters. Office: Inst Psychology, Spielmannstrasse 19, D 38106 Braunschweig Germany

VONDERHEID, ARDA ELIZABETH, nursing administrator; b. Pitts., June 19, 1925; d. Louis Adolf and Hilda Barbara (Gerstacker) V.; diploma Allegheny Gen. Hosp. Sch. Nursing, 1946; B.S. in Nursing Edn., Coll. Holy Names, Oakland, Calif., 1956; M.S. in Nursing Adminstrn., UCLA, 1960. Head nurse Allegheny Gen. Hosp., Pitts., 1946-48; staff nurse Highland-Alameda County Hosp., Oakland, Calif., 1948-51, staff nurse poliomyelitis units, 1953-55; pvt. duty nurse Directory Registered Nurses Alameda County, Oakland, 1951-53; adminstrv. supervising nurse Poliomyelitis Respiratory and Rehab. Center, Fairmont, Alameda County Hosp., Oakland, 1955-58; night supr., relief asst. dir. nursing Peninsula Hosp., Burlingame, Calif., 1960, adminstrv. supr., 1961-62, inservice educator, 1963-69; staff nurse San Francisco Gen. Hosp., 1969, asst. dir. nurses, 1969-72; mem. faculty continuing edn. U. Calif., San Francisco, 1969-71; dir. nursing services Kaiser Permanente Med. Center, South San Francisco, 1973-1982, asst. adminstr. Med. Center Nursing Services, 1982-85; asst. adminstr. Kaiser Hosp., San Francisco, 1985-87; ret. 1987. Chmn. edn. com. San Mateo County (Calif.) Cancer Soc., 1962-69; bd. dirs. San Mateo County Heart Assn., 1968-71; mem., foreman pro tem San Mateo County Civil Grand Jury, 1982-83; mem. San Mateo County Health Council, 1982-85, vice chmn., 1984; mem. all ch. coms. Cert. advanced nursing adminstrn. Mem. San Mateo County (dir. 1964-69, pres. elect 1967-68, pres. 1968-70), Golden Gate (1st v.p. 1974-78, dir. 1974-78), Calif., Am. nurses assns., Nat. League Nursing, Soc. for Nursing Service Adminstrs., State Practice and Edn. Council, AAUW, Maui Hospice Assn. (vol.), San Mateo County Grand Jury Assn., Calif. Grand Jury Assn., AARP (chpt. 3184 Lahaina, Hawaii 1995—), Maui Christian Women's Club (bd. dirs. 1995—), Sigma Theta Tau. Republican. Club: Kai-Perm. Contbr. articles in field to profl. jours. Home: 150 Puukolii Rd Apt 47 Lahaina HI 96761-1961

VON DOEPP, CHRISTIAN ERNEST, psychiatrist; came to U.S., 1949; s. Philip and Elizabeth von Doepp; m. Janet Carol Brown, Jan. 2, 1994; children: Heidi Louise von Doepp Lemon, Peter Anders, Niels Christian. Student, U. Heidelberg, Germany, 1955; BA, DePauw U., 1957; MD, Stanford U., 1961; intern, Boston City Hosp., Tufts U., 1962. Diplomate Am. Bd. Psychiatry and Neurology, Nat. Bd. Med. Examiners. Resident psychiatry Langley Porter Psychiat. Inst. U. Calif., San Francisco, 1968; house call physician Permanente Med. Group, San Francisco, 1966-68; consulting psychiatrist Somerville (Mass.) Child Guidance Ctr., 1969; brig psychiatrist and cons. to correctional program Boston Naval Sta., 1968-69; lectr. and preceptor Calif. Dept. Health, Health Tng. Resource Ctr., Berkeley, Calif., 1970-77; dir. day hosp. and aftercare programs San Mateo (Calif.) Ctrl. County Psychiat. Svcs., 1970-87; sr. psychiatrist San Mateo County Mental Health Divsn., 1987—; cons. psychiatrist Calif. Med. Facility,CDC, Vacaville, 1995—; fellow Inst. Pathology, U. Freiberg, Germany, 1960, Lab. Cmty. Psychiatry, Harvard Med. Sch., Boston, 1969; supr., coord. cmty. psychiatry rotation for residents U.S. Naval Hosp., Oakland, Calif., 1970-81; med. examiner State of Calif., 1971-78; cons. Counseling and Assistance Ctr., U.S. Naval Sta., Treasure Island, Calif., 1974-76; asst. clin. prof. dept. psychiatry U. Calif., San Francisco, 1971—; chmn. or mem. numerous coms. San Mateo County Mental Health Div., 1970—. Bd. dirs. Tahoma Meadows Homeowners Assn., 1986-92, pres., 1980-81; pres. Tahoma Mut. Water Co., 1978-80. With M.C., USN, 1962-65; capt. USNR, 1965—. Mem. Am. Psychiat. Assn., No. Calif. Psychiat. Soc., San Mateo County Psychiat. Soc. (sec.-treas. 1987-89, bd. dirs. 1987-93), Calif. Med. Assn., San Mateo County Med. Assn., Faculty-Alumni Assn. Dept. Psychiatry U. Calif. San Francisco (bd. dirs. 1985-90). Office: 19 W 39th Ave Ste 4 San Mateo CA 94403

VON FELDT, FRANCIS JAMES, physician, corporate medical administrator; b. Austin, Minn., Dec. 3, 1940; s. John Leo and Rose Louise (Bedard) Von F.; m. Audrey Ann Youso, Apr. 4, 1964; children: Christine Louise, Matthew James, Luke Donald. BS, St. Thomas Coll., St. Paul, 1964; MD, Med. Coll. Wis., 1968; MPH, U. Minn., 1977. Diplomate Am. Bd. Preventive Medicine, Occupational and Aerospace Medicine. Resident in internal medicine Mayo Clinic, Rochester, Minn., 1972-73; asst. regional flight surgeon FAA, FArmington, Minn., 1973-77; dir. med. svcs. Prudential Ins. Co., Mpls., 1977-79; asst. med. dir. 3M Corp., St. Paul, 1980-83; regional med. dir. Unocal, Schaumburg, Ill., 1983-84; corp. med. dir. Paccar Inc., Bellevue, Wash., 1984—. Maj. USAF, 1969-72; lt. col. USARNG, 1977-83. Fellow Am. Coll. Occupl. Medicine; mem. AMA, King County Med. Soc., Am. Pub. Health Assn., Genealogy Assn. Home: 13817 180th Ave NE Redmond WA 98052-1217 Office: Paccar Inc 777 106th Ave NE Bellevue WA 98004-5001

VON FRIEDERICHS-FITZWATER, MARLENE MARIE, health communication educator; b. Beatrice, Nebr., July 14, 1939; d. Paul M. and Velma B. (von Friederichs) Fitzwater; children: Richard Nielson, Kevin T. Young, James L. Nielson, Paul M. Nielson. BS, Westminster Coll., 1981; MA, U. Nebr., Omaha, 1981; PhD, U. Utah, 1987; cert. in death edn., Temple U., 1982. Various pub. rels., writing and editing positions, 1957-78; teaching fellow in communication U. Nebr., Omaha, 1978-83; teaching fellow in communications U. Utah, Salt Lake City, 1978-83; asst. prof. mass communications U. So. Colo., Pueblo, 1983-85; prof. communication studies Calif. State U., Sacramento, 1985—; asst. clin. prof. family practice Sch. Medicine U. Calif., Davis, 1987—; condr. workshops on communication skills for health care profls. Bergan Mercy Hosp., Omaha, 1980-81, Mercy Care Ctr., Omaha, 1980-81, Am. Cancer Soc., 1981-82, Hospice of Salt Lake, Utah, 1981-82; condr. seminars, workshops and courses on health communication, death and dying, patient edn. and compliance, other related topics, 1983—; presenter in health communication various profl. orgn. meetings and confs., 1981—; dir., co-founder The Health Communication Rsch. Inst., Sacramento, 1988—. Contbr. articles to profl. jours. Trainer United Way, Sacramento, project mgr., 1986—; pres. bd. dirs. Hospice Care Sacramento, Inc., 1986-87; instr. vol. tng. program Hospice Consortium Sacramento; hospice vol. 1980—. Recipient numerous state, regional and nat. awards for writing, editing, publ. design and photography. Fellow Am. Acad. on Physician & Patient; mem. Internat. Communication Assn. (health communication div., newsletter editor 1987—, sec. 1989—), AAUP, Assn. Behavioral Scis. and Med. Edn., Assn. Women in Sci., Pub. Rels. Soc. Am. (bd. dirs. Calif. Capital chpt. 1987—), Soc. Tchrs. Family Medicine, Soc. Health Care Pub. Rels. and Mktg. No Calif. Home: 5020 Hackberry Ln Sacramento CA 95841-4765 Office: Calif State U Communication Studies Dept 6000 J St Sacramento CA 95819-2605

VON GIERKE, HENNING EDGAR, biomedical science educator, former government official, researcher; b. Karlsruhe, Germany, May 22, 1917; came to U.S., 1947, naturalized, 1977; s. Edgar and Julie (Braun) Von G.; married; 2 children. Dipl. Ing., Karlsruhe Tech., 1943, Dr. Engr., 1944. Asst. in acoustics Karlsruhe Tech., 1944-47, lectr., 1946; cons. Aerospace Med. Research Labs, Wright-Patterson AFB, Ohio, 1947-54; chief bioacoustics br. Aerospace Med. Research Labs, 1954-63, dir. biodynamics and bionics div., 1963-88; assoc. prof. Ohio State U., 1963-88; clin. prof. Wright State U., 1980—; mem. com. hearing bioacoustics and biomechanics NRC, 1953-93, chmn. 1990-93, bio-astronaut com., 1959-61; mem. adv. com., flight medicine and biology NASA, 1960-61. Author over 160 tech. publs., book chpts.; patentee in field. Recipient Def. Disting. Civilian Svc. award, 1963, Hubertus Strughold medal, 1980, Meritorious and Disting. Exec. Presdl. rank Pres. of U.S., 1980, 81, H.R. Lissner award ASME, 1983, Lord Rayleigh medal, 1988. Fellow Acoustical Soc. Am. (pres. 1979-80, Silver medal 1981), Aerospace Med. Assn. (v.p. 1966-67, E. Liljenkrantz award 1966, A.D. Tuttle award 1974), Inst. Environ. Scis. (hon.), Internat. Acad. Aviation and Space Medicine; mem. NAE, Inst. Noise Control Engring., Biomed. Engring. Soc., Internat. Acad. Astronautics. Home: 1325 Meadow Ln Yellow Springs OH 45387-1219 Office: Armstrong Aerospace Med Rsch Lab Dayton OH 45433

VON HEIMBURG, ROGER LYLE, surgeon; b. Chgo., Feb. 5, 1931; s. Franklin Dederick and Alice Julia (Zebuhr) von H.; m. Mary Ellen Janson, July 12, 1952; children: Mary Deborah, Donald Franklin. AB, Johns Hopkins U., 1951, MD, 1955; MS in Surgery, U. Minn., Rochester, 1964. Diplomate Am. Bd. Surgery. Intern Johns Hopkins Hosp., Balt., 1955-56; resident in surgery Mayo Clinic, Rochester, 1958-62, chief resident in surgery, 1962, asst. to staff in surgery, 1962-64; practice medicine specializing in surgery Green Bay, Wis., 1964-94; staff St. Vincent Hosp., Green Bay, 1964-94, Bellin Meml. Hosp., Green Bay, 1964-94; ret., 1994. Contbr. articles to profl. jours. Mem. state Bd. of Health Care Info., 1988-91; reapptd., 1991-95. Lt. USNR, 1956-58. Fellow ACS; mem. State Med. Soc. Wis. (bd. dirs. 1980-89, vice-chmn. 1983-87, chmn. 1987-89, pres.-elect 1989-90, pres. 1990-91), Wis. Chpt. ACS (v.p. 1985-86, pres.-elect 1986-88, pres. 1988-90), Brown County Med. Soc. (pres. 1986), Wis. Surg. Soc. (coun. mem. 1987-90). Republican. Methodist. Home: 344 Terraview Dr Green Bay WI 54301-1523

VON HILSHEIMER, GEORGE EDWIN, III, neuropsychologist; b. West Palm Beach, Fla., Aug. 15, 1934; s. George E. Jr. and Dorothy Sue (Bridges) Von H.; m. Catherine Jean Munson, Dec. 27, 1968 (div. Oct. 1987); children: Dana Germaine, George E. IV, Alexandra; m. Jonnie Mae Warner, June 29, 1991. BA, U. Miami, 1955; PhD, Saybrook Inst., 1977. Diplomate Acad. Psychosomatic Medicine, Am. Bd. Behavioral Medicine, Am. Acad. Pain Mgmt., Am. Bd. Cert. Managed Care Providers, Am. Acad. Psychol. Treating Addiction, Nat. Register Neurofeedback. Sr. minister Humanitas, N.Y.C., 1959-64; cons. Pres. Kennedy's Commn. Nat. Vol. Svc., Juv. Del., Migration Labor, 1963-64; headmaster Summerlane Sch., North Branch, N.Y., 1964-69; supt. Green Valley Sch., Orange City, Fla., 1969-74; neuropsychologist Growth Insts., Twyman's Mill, Va., 1974-79, Growth Inst., DeLand, Fla., 1980-82; assoc. health profl. Maitland, 1982—; cons. Sci. Adv. Bd. EPA, Washington, 1974-84; chmn. Certification Bd., Internat. Coll. Environ. Medicine, 1991-94; mem. Bd. Assn. Diagnostic Efficiency and Brief Therapy, dir. curriculum, 1993-94. Author: How to Live With Your Special Child, 1970, Understanding Problems of Children, 1975, Allergy, Toxins and the LD Child, 1977, Psychobiology of Delinquents, 1978, Depression Is Not a Disease, 1989, Brief Therapy, 1993, Brief Therapy: Antecedent Scientific Principles, 1994; editor Human Learning, Washington. Mem. spl. bd. Fla. Symphony Orch., 1992-93. With U.S. Army, 1957-59. Fellow Royal Soc. Health (life), Internat. Coll. Applied Nutrition, Acad. Psychosomatic Medicine; mem. Toastmasters, Phi Kappa Phi, Omicron Delta Kappa, Alpha Sigma Phi. Mem. Ch. of Brethren. Home: 160 W Trotters Dr Maitland FL 32751-5736 Office: AAT 175 Lookout Pl # 1 Maitland FL 32751-4494

VON HOLDEN, MARTIN HARVEY, psychologist; b. Bronx, N.Y., May 29, 1942; s. Leon and Gertrude (Fishbein) Von H.; m. Virginia T. Brown, Dec. 17, 1971; 1 child, Mark Walter; children by previous marriage: Sandi Gwen Bitton, David Lawrence; 1 stepchild, Theresa Ann Brilli-Rogers. B.A., NYU, 1964; M.A., U. Toledo, 1965; D.P.A., NYU, 1981. Sr. psychologist N.Y. State Dept. Mental Hygiene, Rockland State Hosp., Orangeberg, 1966-67, team leader, 1970-71, dir. interdisciplinary tng. team, 1971-73; chief of service Metro Unit Harlem Valley Psychiat. Ctr., Wingdale, N.Y., 1973-74, dep. dir. programs, 1974-75; dep. dir. treatment services Pilgrim Psychiat. Ctr., West Brentwood, N.Y., 1975-76; dir. Matteawan State Hosp., Beacon, N.Y., 1977, Central N.Y. Psychiat. Ctr., Marcy, N.Y., 1977-82; exec. dir. Rochester Psychiat. Ctr., Rochester, N.Y., 1982—; assoc. dir. Inst. for Motivation Rsch., Croton-on-Hudson, N.Y., 1965-73; dir. Martin H. Von Holden Assocs., motivation rsch., Fairlawn, N.J., 1970-74; cons. psychologist, group therapist Green Haven Correctional Facility, Stormville, N.Y., 1970-77; cons. psychologist, group therapist Auburn Correctional Facility, N.Y., 1977-94, Butler Correctional Facility, 1994—; clin. assoc. prof. dept. psychiatry Sch. Medicine, U. Rochester, 1983—; speaker nat. and internat. profl. confs. including 2d World Congress on Prison Health Care, 1983. Contbr. articles to profl. jours. Mem. adv. coun. N.Y. State Commn. Quality Care to Mentally Disabled, 1989—. Capt. MSC, U.S. Army, 1967-70. Recipient James Gordon Bennett prize NYU, 1964, Outstanding Achievement award United Way of N.Y. State, 1994. Fellow Am. Assn. Mental Health Adminstrs. (cert. mental health adminstr.); mem. Am. Psychol. Assn., Am. Correctional Assn., Am. Assn. Correctional Psychologists, Assn. Facility Dirs. N.Y. State Office Mental Health (pres. 1984-85), Order of Arrow, Psi Chi. Jewish. Home: 15 Waterbury Ln Rochester NY 14625-1361

VON HOLT, LAEL POWERS, psychotherapist, psychiatric social worker; b. Boston, Apr. 9, 1927; d. Merritt Adams and Rea Francisca (Hunt) Powers; m. Henry William Von Holt, Jr., Sept. 18, 1954; children: Gardner, Dudley, Edward. BA, U. Mass., 1950; MSW, U. Mo., 1972, postgrad., 1978; postgrad. Menninger Found., Topeka, 1977-85. Diplomate Bd. Clin. Social Work, Internat. Acad. of Behavioral Medicine Counseling and Psychotherapy; lic. clin. social worker, Mo. Psychiat. social worker N.Y. Dept. Mental Hygiene, Wingdale, 1950-51, Mass. Dept. Mental Health, Worcester, 1951-54; instr., social worker U. Oreg., Eugene, 1954-59; psychiat. social worker Mo. Dept. Mental Health, Fulton State Hosp., 1973-81, Columbia (Mo.) Regional Hosp. Psychiat. Svcs., Inc., 1977-82, Family Mental Health Ctr., Jefferson City, Mo., 1982-91; mental health cons. Midland Counseling Ctrs., Inc., Hermann, Mo., 1991—; field instr. U. Mo., Columbia, 1988. Bd. dirs. PTA, 1970-74, 77-78; mem. health com. Boone County Cmty. Svcs. Coun., 1975-76; vol. Meals on Wheels, 1972-75, 76-79; den mother Boy Scouts Am., 1968-69, 71-72; mem. by-laws com. Springdale Neighborhood Assn., 1977. Named Social Worker of Yr. Cen. Mo., 1986. Mem. Nat. Assn. Social Workers, Acad. Cert. Social Workers, LWV (state bd. dirs. 1995—, city coun. observor 1976-82, chmn. local action com. 1979-80, sec. 1974-77, chmn. Observer Corps 1981-83, chmn. com. mental health 1988-89, chair health com. 1991-94, co-pres. 1992-94), Stephens Coll. Faculty Wives (pres. 1979-80, 89-90), Kappa Kappa Gamma. Republican. Methodist. Home: 378 Crown Pt Columbia MO 65203-2242 Office: Midland Counseling Ctrs Inc 18th And Wein St Hermann MO 65041

VON KEHL, INGE, toxicologist, pharmacologist; b. Frankfurt, Main, Germany, Jan. 16, 1933; came to U.S., 1954; BS in Chemistry, Biology, NE Mo. State U., 1959; MS, U. Idaho, 1963; PhD in Eurotech. Rsch., Southhampton U., 1988. Prof. Kirksville Mo. Coll. of Medicine & Surgery, 1963-85; prof. pharmacy U. San Marco, Lima, Peru, 1985-87; instr. chemistry U. SW La., Lafayette, 1987-88; rsch. assoc. U. Mo., Kansas City, 1988-90; quality assurance officer Heritage Found., Kansas City, 1990-93; prof. pharmacology health sci. program Midwest Sci. Found., Kansas City, Kans., 1993—. Editor: The Biology and Chemistry of Hydroxamic acids, 1982; contbr. articles to profl. jours.; editorial cons. Jour. Am. Osteopathic Assn., 1971-82; abstractor Am. Chem. Soc. Nat. Def. Act fellow U.S. Govt., 1961. Mem. Am. Chem. Soc., Am. Soc. Exptl. Pharmacology. Home: 10012 Oakdell St Kansas City MO 64114-4145

VONNEGUT, BERNARD, retired chemist, scientist, educator; b. Indpls., Aug. 29, 1914; s. Kurt and Edith Sophia (Lieber) V.; m. Lois Gloria Bowler, Dec. 25, 1943; children: Peter, Scott, Terry, Kurt, Alex. BS in Chemistry, MIT, 1936, PhD in Chemistry, 1939. Rsch. sci. Hartford (Conn.) Empire Co., 1939-41, MIT, Cambridge, Mass., 1941-46, Gen. Electric Co., Schenectady, N.Y., 1946-54, Arthur D. Little Inc., Cambridge, 1954-67; prof. U. Albany, N.Y., 1967, prof. emeritus, 1985—. Fellow Am. Meteorol. Soc., Am. Geophys. Union. Home: 35 Norwood St Albany NY 12203

VON PRINCE, KILULU MAGDALENA, occupational therapist, sculptor; b. Bumbuli, Lushoto, Tanzania, Jan. 9, 1929; came to U.S., 1949; d. Tom Adalbert and Juliane (Martini) Von P. BA in Occupational Therapy, San Jose State U., 1958, MS in Occupational Therapy, 1972; EdD, U. So. Calif., 1980. Registered occupational therapist; cert. work evaluator, work adjustment specialist. Commd. 2d lt. U.S. Army, 1959, advanced through grades to lt. col.; staff asst. U.S. Army, Denver, 1959-62; hand rehab. asst., hand therapy Walter Reed Army Med. Ctr., 1962-65; hand rehab. asst. occupational therapist 97th Gen. Hosp., U.S. Army, Frankfurt, Fed. Republic Germany, 1965-68; occupational therapist Inst. Surg. Rsch. U.S. Army, Ft. Sam Houston, Tex., 1967-70; occupational therapy dir., cons. U.S. Army, Honolulu, 1972-75; adminstr. occupational therapy clinic, cons. LAMC U.S. Army, Presido, Calif., 1975; asst. evening coll. program San Jose (Calif.) C.C., 1976-77; postdoctoral fellow allied health adminstrn. SUNY, Buffalo, 1978, Commonwealth U., Richmond, Va., 1978-79; project dir. Ctr. of Design, Palo Alto, 1980; part-time staff project developing pre-retirement program older adults De Anza Coll., Cupertino, Calif., 1980-81; part-time instr. Stroke Activity Ctr. Cabrillo Coll., Santa Cruz, Calif., 1981; dir. occupl. therapy Presbyn. Med. Ctr., 1981-86; ptnr., mgr. retail store, 1986-89; dir. rehab. therapy Merrithew Meml. Hosp. Contra Costa Med. Ctr., Martinez, Calif., 1990-93; sculptor, 1993—; part-time activity program coord. Calif. Women's Detention Facility, Chowchilla, Calif., 1994—; researcher, presenter workshops and seminars in field. Co-author: Splinting of Burned Patients, 1974; producer videos: Elbow Splinting of the Burned Patient, 1970, Self-Instruction Unit: Principles of Elbow Splinting, 1971; contbr. articles to profl. jours. Decorated Legion of Merit; recipient Disting. Alumni Honors award San Jose State U., 1982; grad. scholar U.S. Surgeon Gen.; Kellogg Found. postdoctoral fellow, 1979. Mem. Am. Occupational Therapy Assn., Occupational Therapy Assn. Calif. (award of excellence 1986, v.p. 1981-84, state chair pers. 1981-84, state chair continuing edn. 1984-86, Lifetime Achievement award 1994), Am. Soc. Hand Therapists (hon., life). Home: 36141 Manon Ave Madera CA 93638-8613 Office: Calif Women's Detention Facility Chowchilla CA 93610-1501

VON REYN, C. FORDHAM, infectious disease physician; b. Montour Falls, N.Y., Sept. 24, 1945; m. Janet Elizabeth Goldberger, June 18, 1967; children: Leah Edana, Adam Daniel, Charles Alexander. AB, Dartmouth Coll., 1967, BMS, 1969; MD cum laude, Harvard U., 1971. Diplomate Am. Bd. Internal Medicine, Am. Bd. Infectious Diseases. Intern in medicine Beth Israel Hosp., Boston, 1971-72, jr. resident in medicine, 1972-73, sr. asst. resident in medicine, 1975-76; clin. fellow in infectious disease Beth Israel Hosp., Children's Hosp. Med. Ctr., Dana-Farber Cancer Ctr., Boston, 1976-77; clin. assoc. in medicine U. N.Mex. Sch. Medicine, Albuquerque, 1973-75, clin. assoc. in family & cmty. medicine, 1974-75, outpatient attending dept. medicine, 1976-77, inpatient attending dept. medicine, 1978-79; instr. epidemiology sch. medicine Tufts U., Boston, 1974, 76; adj. asst. prof. clin. medicine Dartmouth Med. Sch., Hanover, N.H., 1978-85, lectr. microbiology, 1978—, adj. assoc. prof. clin. medicine, 1986-87, assoc. prof. clin. medicine, 1988-91; attending physician infectious disease svc. dept. medicine, co-dir. infectious disease block scientific basis of medicine Dartmouth Med. Sch., 1988—; assoc. prof. medicine Dartmouth Med. Sch., Hanover, N.H., 1991-94, prof. medicine, 1994—; dir. microbiology, hosp. epidemiologist infectious disease dept. Concord (N.H.) Hosp., 1977-88; cons. staff Mary Hitchcock Meml. Hosp., Hanover, 1977-88, clin. staff, 1988—; hosp. epidemiologist, chief infectious disease section Dartmouth-Hitchcock Med. Ctr., Hanover, 1988—; cons. physician infectious diseases Vets. Adminstrn. Hosp., White River Junction, Vt., 1990—; asst. physician Harvard U. Health Svcs., Cambridge, 1975-77; pres. Concord Clinic Inc., 1984-85; section chief internal medicine Concord divsn. Hitchcock Clinic, 1985-88; cons. global program on AIDS World Health Orgn., 1987. Mem. editl. bd. Current Issues in Public Health, 1993—; mem. internat. editl. adv. bd. AIDS and Society, 1989—; contbr. articles to profl. jours. and chpts. in books. Pres. Frontiers of Knowledge Found., Concord, N.H., 1982-83; v.p. Concord Cmty. Music Sch., 1984-85, pres., 1986-88; trustee Am. Red Cross, Concord, 1986-88, N.H. AIDS Found., Manchester, 1989—; chmn. N.Mex. Task Force on Rabies, 1974, U.S. del. Congress of the Internat. Physicians for the Prevention of Nuclear War, Helsinki, 1984; mem. N.H. AIDS Adv. Com., 1985-87; mem. Commr.'s Task Force on HIV/AIDS Divsn. of Pub. Health Svcs., N.H., 1990— and numerous others. Med. officer USPHS, 1973-75. Recipient Gov.'s Spl. award for Pub. Svc., Santa Fe, N.Mex., 1975. Fellow Infectious Disease Soc. Am.; mem. Am. Soc. Microbiology, Internat. Immunocomprised Host Soc., Internat. AIDS Soc., Northern New England Infectious Disease Soc. (v.p. 1990-92, pres. 1992-94), Physicians for Social Responsibility, Soc. for Hosp. Epidemiology Am., Alpha Omega Alpha. Home: 44 Waterman Hill Rd Norwich VT 05055 Office: Dartmouth-Hitchcock Med Ctr Infectious Disease Sect One Medical Ctr Dr Lebanon NH 03756

VON ROENN, KELVIN ALEXANDER, neurosurgeon; b. Louisville, Dec. 5, 1949; s. Warren George and Catherine Jean (Bauer) Von R.; m. Jamie Hayden, June 24, 1979; children: Erika Marie, Lisa J., Alexander H., Karl G. BS, Xavier U., 1971; MD, U. Ky., 1975. Diplomate Am. Bd. Neurol. Surgery. Instr. neurosurgery Rush-Presbyn. St. Luke's Med. Ctr., Chgo., 1980-83, asst. prof. neurosurgery, 1983—; cons. neurosurgery Shriner's Hosp. for Crippled Children, Chgo., 1988—, attending neurosurgeon, 1990—; lectr. sect. of neurosurgery U. Ill. Coll. Med., 1996. Named one of Outstanding Young Men of Am., 1986. Fellow ACS; mem. Congress Neurologic Surgeons, Am. Assn. Neurol. Surgeons, Ill. Neurosurg. Soc. (v.p. 1994-95, pres. 1995-96), Alpha Sigma Nu, Alpha Omega Alpha. Office: Assocs in Neurol Surgery 1725 W Harrison St # 1117 Chicago IL 60612-3828

VON SANDOR, COUNT ROBERT, optometrist, educator, researcher; b. Budapest, Hungary, Apr. 16, 1929; s. Louis and Irene (Bauer) von S.; m. Anita Bernice Johansson, Apr. 4, 1952; children: Jan-Douglas, Helen Bernice. PhD, U. Ariz., 1987; LittD (hon.), U. Found., Del., 1987; HHD (hon.), Albert Einstein Acad. Found., Kans., 1990. Diplomate in social anthropology, diplomate in visual optics and physiology. Dean Coll. of Optometry, Stockholm, 1954-67; head of info. Coun. of Info. of Visual Scis., Stockholm, 1967-85; sr. lectr., rschr. Coll. Applied Visual Scis., Sigtuna, Sweden, 1985—; head of info. Hoya-Optikslip, Stockholm, 1985-96; bd. dirs. Ethnographical Mus., Stockholm, 1990—, Optichistorical Mus. Sweden, 1996—; chief rsch. Inst. Japanology, Teckomatorp, Sweden, 1991—, adj. prof. clin. optometry, visual scis. and physiol. optics, 1992. Author 5 textbooks in visual optics and optometry and 15 handbooks in Japanology, 1952—; contbr. more than 270 articles to profl. jours. Pres. The Japanese The-Ceremony Found., Stockholm, 1990—, Japanese Token and Bijutsu Ctr., Stockholm, 1980—. Recipient Gullstrand medal, 1979, Peace medal Albert Einstein Acad. Found., 1988, Alfred Nobel medal Internat. Acad. Found., 1991, Gold medal of merits Swedish Sport Fedn., 1980, Swedish Judo Assn., 1964, Medal of merit U. Medicine, Budapest, 1947, The Einstein Acad. Cross of Merit, 1992. Fellow Am. Acad. Optometry, N.Y. Acad. Scis.; mem. Swedish Optometric Assn. (bd. dirs. 1985-90, Medal of Merit 1985), Internat. Fedn. Japanese Fencing (v.p. 1970-80, Gold medal 1989), European Kendo Fedn. (h. pres. 1982, Medal of Merit 1982), Judo Club Stockholm (pres. 1960-74, Gold medal 1974), Budo Club Lidingo (pres. 1970—, Medal of Merit 1990), European Assn. Japanese Fencing (pres. 1970-82), Swedish Budo Fedn. (pres. 1980-82, Medal of Merit 1985), Stockholm-Sergel Rotary Club (pres. 1990-91).

VON SCHÉELE, CHRISTIAN CARL, physician; b. Stockholm, June 29, 1940; s. Carl-Adam Götrik and Christian Elisaeth (Hamilton) von S.; m. Ingela Birgitta Kristiansen, May 15, 1991. MD, U. Lund, Sweden, 1970. Resident gen. internal medicine, 1970-75; cons. dept. medicine Gen. Hosp., Säffle, Sweden, 1975-77, Sollefteå, Sweden, 1977-88; cons. dept. medicine Gen. Hosp., Östersund, Sweden, 1988—, head edn., gen. internal medicine, 1992—, cons. clin. labs., 1995—. Co-author and author 2 books of poetry; contbr. articles to profl. jours. Affiliate Swedish Orgn. Against U.S. War Campaign in Vietnam, 1968-75. Mem. Swedish Med. Assn., Soc. Neurology (head ctrl. no. Sweden 1980). Home: Storgatan 4B, S-831 30 Östersund Sweden Office: Gen Hosp, Dept Medicine, S-831 83 Östersund Sweden

VON SEGESSER, LUDWIG KARL, cardiovascular surgeon, educator; b. Lucerne, Switzerland, Mar. 15, 1952; s. Ludwig and Mathilde (Glutz) von S.; m. Marie Dinh, June 27, 1979; children: Ludwig, Jeanne. MD, U. Basel, Switzerland, 1979, PD, 1989. Cert. Surg. Bd. Switzerland, 1985. Resident Kantonsspital Obwalden, Sarnen, Switzerland, 1979; resident Univ. Hosp., Geneva, 1980-83, mem. staff cardiovascular surgery, 1983-85; fellow cardiovascular surgery Tex. Heart Inst., Houston, 1986; staff surgeon Clinic for Cardiovascular Surgery Univ. Hosp., Zurich, Switzerland, 1987-96; acad. appointee Zurich (Switzerland) U., 1989-96; prof., chief dept. cardiovascular surgery Univ. Hosp. Lausanne, Vaud, Switzerland, 1996—; Mem. European Bd. of Cardiovascular Perfusion, chmn. 1993—; clin. prof., 1996—; head clinic cardiovascular surgery CHUV U. Hosp., Lausanne, Switzerland, 1996; gen. sec. Union Swiss Surg. Socs., 1996. Author: Arterial Grafting for Myocardial Revascularization, 1990; asst. editor Perfusion, 1992—, European Jour. Cardio-Thoracic Surgery, 1994—; contbr. over 300 articles to profl. jours. Recipient Goetz-Preis award U. Zurich, 1991, award Swiss Cardiology Found., 1991. Fellow ACS; mem. Swiss Soc. Thoracic and Cardiovascular Surgery (sec. 1989—), Swiss Soc. Surgery, Union Swiss Surg. Socs. (gen. sec. 1996—), Swiss Soc. of Cardiology, German Soc. Thoracic and Cardiovascular Surgery, European Assn. Cardio-Thoracic Surgery, European Soc. Artificial Organs, Soc. Critical Care Medicine, Internat. Soc. Heart & Lung Transplantation, Internat. Soc. Surgery, The Soc. Thoracic Surgeons, Assn. Advancement Med. Instrn., Am. Soc. Artificial Internal Organs, Internat. Soc. Artificial Organs. Office: Univ Hosp-CHUV, Dept Cardiovascular Surgery, CH-1011 Lausanne Switzerland

VON STRANDTMANN, MAXIMILIAN, chemist; b. Grodno, Poland, Apr. 17, 1927; came to U.S., 1957; s. Sophia (Kurloff) Von S.; m. Olga Lockhart, 1986 (dec. Apr. 15, 1993); children: Marina, Vera, Marimilian, Sophia; m. Agnieszka Anna Badowska, Oct. 10, 1993; 1 child, Alexander. PhD in Organic Chemistry, U. Erlangen, Nürenberg, Germany, 1955. Scientist Chemistry Fabrik Pfleger, Baberg, Germany, 1955-57; assoc. dir. organic chemistry Warre-Lambert Rsch. Inc., Morris Plains, N.J., 1957-76; prin. chemist Imperial Chem. Industries, Wilmington, Del., 1977-79; v.p. Custum Chem. Labs. Inc., Indpls., 1980-84; pres. Medea Rsch. Labs. Inc., Port Jefferson Sta., N.Y., 1985—. Contbr. articles to profl. jours. Holder number of patents in medicinal chemistry. Recipient Cystinosis Found. award, 1991, NIH grant SBIR Phase I, 1989, NIH grant SBIR Phase II, 1992, N.Y. Rsch. Found. grant, 1991. Russian Orthodox. Home: 33 Brookhaven Blvd Port Jefferson Station NY 11776 Office: Medea Rsch Labs Inc 200 Wilson St Port Jefferson Station NY 11776

VON STREMPEL, ARCHIBALD HEINRICH, spine surgeon, consultant, researcher; b. Velbert, Germany, Apr. 28, 1950; s. Gustav-Adolf and Liselotte (Hoerder) von S.; m. Sabine Maria Franke; children: Maja, Alexandra-Charlotte. D in Engring., U. Berlin, 1984, MD, 1986. Med. asst. Prof. Ruecker, Berlin, 1982, Dr. Zielke, Bad Wildungen, 1983-85; asst. physician Dr. Pueschel and Dr. Eckhardt, Vogtareuth, 1985-87, Prof. Refior, Munich, 1987-89; orthopaedist Munich, 1989; asst. med. dir. Prof. Wirth, Hanover, 1989-94; med. dir. Annastift e.V., Hanover, 1995—. Author: Invitro Untersuchungen an Menschlichen Wirbeksaeulen zur Stabilitaetsbestimmung von Bogenwurzelschrauben, 1992, Die Instabilitaet des Lumbosakralen Scharniers, 1992, Operative Behandlung der Spondylolisthesis durch Distrahierende und Transpedikulaere Stabilisierung ueber Sakralknieaufbau nach Zielke, 1986; inventor segmental spinal correction system. Mem. Deutsche Gesellschaft fuer Orthopaedie und Traumatologie, European Spine Soc. Office: Annastift eV Klinik III, Heimchenstrasse 1-7, 30625 Hannover Germany

VON TAAFFE-ROSSMANN, COSIMA T., physician, writer, inventor; b. Kuklov, Slovakia, Czechoslovakia, Nov. 21, 1944; came to U.S., 1988; d. Theophil and Marianna Hajossy; m. Charles Boris Rossmann, Oct. 19, 1979; children: Nathalie Nissa Cora, Nadine Nicole. MD, Purkyne U., Brno, Czechoslovakia, 1967. Intern Valtice (Czechoslovakia) Gen. Hosp., 1967-68, resident ob-gyn, 1968-69; med. researcher Kidney Disease Inst., Albany, N.Y., 1970-71; resident internal medicine Valtice Gen. Hosp., 1972-73; gen. practice Nat. Health System, Czechoslovakia, 1973-74; pvt. practice West Germany, 1974-80; med. officer Baragwanath Hosp., Johannesburg, South Africa, 1984-85, Edendale Hosp., Pietermaritzburg, South Africa, 1985-86; pvt. practice Huntingburg, Ind., 1988-90, Valdosta, Ga., 1990—; med. researcher, 1966—. Contbr. articles on medicine to profl. jours.; inventor, patentee in field. Office: 2301 N Ashley St Valdosta GA 31602-2620

VON ZUR MÜHLEN, ALEXANDER MEINHARD, physician, internal medicine educator; b. Riga, Latvia, May 13, 1936; arrived in Germany, 1939; s. Alexander and Kira (Velitschkowski) von zur M.; m. Karen Berg, 1958 (div. 1977); children: Insa, Friederike, Patrick; m. Ulrike Warnecke, 1977; children: Constantin, Nicolas. Grad., Med. Sch. Freiburg, Fed. Republic Germany, 1963. Asst. Med. Sch. Göttingen, Fed. Republic Germany, 1965-74, sr. asst., 1974; prof. Internal Medicine Med. Sch. Hannover, Fed. Republic Germany, 1974—. Contbr. articles to profl. jours. Mem. German Soc. Endocrinology, German Soc. Internal Medicine. Office: Med Hochschule Hannover, Konstanty-Gutschow Str 8, D-30625 Hannover Germany

VOOGT, JAMES LEONARD, medical educator; b. Grand Rapids, Mich., Feb. 8, 1944; married; 3 children. Student, Calvin Coll., 1962-64; BS in Biological Sci., Mich. Tech. Univ., 1966; MS in Physiology, Mich. State Univ., 1968, PhD in Physiology, 1970. Postdoc. fellow, lectr. dept. physiology U. Calif., San Francisco, 1970-71; asst. prof. dept. physiology and biophysics U. Louisville Sch. Medicine, 1971-77, assoc. prof. dept. physiology and biophysics, 1977; assoc. prof. dept. physiology U. Kans. Sch. Medicine, 1977-82, prof. dept. physiology, 1982—; assoc. in psychology, assoc. in oncology U. Louisville, 1973-77; assoc. dean rsch. U. Kans. Sch. Medicine, 1982-84, acting chmn. dept. physiology, 1987, chmn. dept. physiology, 1993—; vis. prof. Erasmus U., 1985. Mem. editl. bd. Endocrinology, 1984-86, 89-92, Am. Jour. Physiology, 1984-88, Doody's Jour., 1995—; ad hoc reviewer Neuroendocrinology, Sci., Biology of Reproduction, Life Scis., Jour. Endocrinology, Molecular Cellular Neuroscis., PSEBM, biochm. endocrinology study sect. NIH, 1992—, reproductive endocrinology study sect., 1994—; reviewer grants NSF; editor scientific proceedings Research Week, 1982, 83; contbr. over 120 articles to prof. publs., 4 chpts. to books. Grantee NIH, 1972-80, 80-81, 82-85, 88—, 90-93, 94—, NSF, 1985-86, 91-94, Ctr. on Aging, 1988, Nat. Inst. Drug Abuse, 1991-93; fellow Japan Soc. Promotion of Sci., 1993; recipient Outstanding Young Alumni award Mich. Tech. Univ., 1974, Honors in Edn., Med. Student Voice, 1990. Mem. AAAS, Endocrine Soc., Internat. Soc. Neuroendocrinology (charter mem.), Am. Physiol. Soc. (pub. affairs adv. com. 1983-87) Soc. Neuroscis., Phi Kappa Phi, Sigma Xi. Office: Dept Physiology U Kans Med Ctr 3901 Rainbow Blvd Kansas City KS 66160-7401*

VOORHEES, JOHN JAMES, dermatologist. B.S., Bowling Green U., 1959; M.D., U. Mich., 1963. Intern U. Mich., 1963-64, resident in dermatology, 1966-69; asso. prof. dermatology U. Mich., Ann Arbor, 1972-74; prof. U. Mich., 1974—; chief dermatology service Univ. Hosp., Ann Arbor, 1975; chmn. dept. dermatology U. Mich., 1975—. Contbr. articles to profl. jours., chpts. in books. Recipient Taub Internat. Meml. award for psoriasis research, 1973, 86, Henry Russel award U. Mich., 1973; Herzog fellow Am. Dermatol. Assn., 1968-70. Mem. Am. Soc. Clin. Investigation, Am. Soc. Pharmacology and Exptl. Therapeutics, Am. Assn. Pathologists, Central Soc. Clin. Research, Soc. Investigative Dermatology, Dermatology Found., Skin Pharmacol. Soc., Assn. Profs. Dermatology, Am. Soc. Cell Biology, Am. Acad. Dermatology, Am. Dermatol. Assn., Alpha Omega Alpha. Office: U Mich Med Ctr Dept Dermatology 1910 Taubman Health Care Ctr Ann Arbor MI 48109

VORHIES, JACK MCKIM, orthodontist; b. Indpls., Feb. 19, 1923; s. Bacil Jacob and Irene M. (Arbuckle) V.; m. Georgia Thelma Reese, Nov. 2, 1943; children: Lawrence, Brent Carl, Scott, Mark, Joyce, Rhonda. DDS with honors, Ind. U., Indpls., 1950; student, Muskingum Coll., 1943; MS, Ind. U., Indpls., 1953. Diplomate Am. Bd. Orthondontic. Gen. practice dentistry specializing in orthodontics Greenwood, Ind., 1952-92; ret., 1992; instr. Ind. U., 1949-53; dental cons. Conn. Gen., Indpls., 1983-84. Bd. dirs. Am. Internat. Charolais Assn., 1965-72, treas. 1969-71. Served to cpl. U.S. Army, 1943-45, ETO. Decorated Bronz Star. Mem. ADA, Am. Assn. Orthodontics, Ind. Soc. Orthodontics (past pres.), Acad. Internat. Dentistry, Orthodontic Edn. and Researce Found., Tweed Found. Orthodontic Research, Edward H. Angle Soc. Orthondotists, Omicron Kappa Upsilon. Republican. Methodist. Lodge: Rotary, Scottish Rite.

VORLICKY, LOREN NEIL, pediatrician; b. Chewelah, Wash., Aug. 12, 1934; s. Henry T. and Marjorie (Beshaw) V.; m. Marie T. Halloran, May 30, 1959; children: Loren Marie, Susan, Ann, Margaret, Jessica. BS, Gonzaga U., 1955; MD, Marquette U., 1959. Diplomate Am. Bd. Pediatrics. Intern USN Hosp., Camp Pendleton; resident USN Hosp., Oakland, Stanford U., Palo Alto, Calif.; pediatric oncologist Park Nicolett Med. Ctr., Mpls., 1966-86; pres. Med. Ctr. Health Plan, Mpls., 1972-86, med. dir., 1972-85; v.p. med. affairs Am. Med. Ctrs., Mpls., 1984-86; nat. med. dir. Ptnrs. Nat. Health Plan, Dallas, 1986-90; sr. v.p. Lahey Hitchcock Clinic, Bedford, N.H., 1990—; adj. prof. pediatrics Dartmouth Med. Sch., Hanover, N.H., 1991—. Lt. comdr. USN, 1959-66. Fellow Am. Acad. Pediatrics, Am. Coll. Physician Execs., Am. Soc. Pediatric Hematology-Oncology. Office: 1 Bedford Farms Bedford NH 03110-6524

VOROSCAK, ROBERT ANTHONY, rehabilitation specialist, educator; b. Blakely, Pa., Aug. 1, 1938; s. Stephen Joseph and Theresa Evangeline (DelleDonne) V.; m. Theresa Josephine Paternoster, Aug. 27, 1960; 1 child, Stacey Lydia. B.A., U. Conn., 1960; M.S., U. Bridgeport, 1962, EdD, 1988; CAGS, NYU, 1974. Tchr. math. Masuk High Sch., Monroe, Conn., 1960-66; chmn. dept., 1966-67; sr. counselor Bur. Rehab. Services div. Vocation Rehab. Conn., Norwalk, 1967-73, vocat. rehab. supr., Bridgeport, 1973-75, coordinator facilities sect., bur. planning, evaluation and tng., Hartford, 1975-86 ; coordinator Planning and Program Devel. and Human Resource Devel., Orgnl. Support, 1986-95; tng. coord. region I (New England) rehab. cont. edn. program for cmty. based providers U. Hartford, 1995—. Mem. adj. faculty, cons. Assumption Coll., Worcester, Mass., U. Hartford. Mem. Hartford Area Rehab. Exec. Com., 1978-82. Named Man of Yr., Am. Sch. for Deaf, West Hartford, 1978; George Washington U. Inst. Ednl. Leadership fellow, 1980-81; Disting. Svc. award Easter Seal Soc. of Conn., 1988, Pres.'s award Conn. State Employee's Assn., 1988. Mem. Conn. Assn. Rehab. Facilities (Disting. Service award 1986), Conn. Rehab. Assn. (treas. 1989-90, bd. dirs., E.P. Chester award 1985, Robert W. Bain award 1995), Farmington Valley Assn. Retarded and Handicapped (bd. dirs.), Conn. Rehab. Adminstrs. Assn. (bd. dirs.), Nat. Rehab. Assn., Nat. Rehab. Counseling Assn., Conn. Rehab. Counseling Assn., Conn. Rehab. Adminstrs. Assn., Northeast Rehab. Assn. (Conn. coun. on devel. disabilities 1991-96, Meritorious service award 1985). Republican. Roman Catholic. Avocations: Skiing; swimming; travelling; gardening; reading. Home: 11 Michael Rd Simsbury CT 06070-1921 Office: U Hartford-Regional Continuing Edn Program Auerbach Hall Rm 228 200 Bloomfield Ave Hartford CT 06117

VOSBURGH, VICTORIA LYNN, rehabilitation services executive; b. Putnam, Conn., Aug. 7, 1965; d. Douglas Warren Vosburgh and Margaret Jean (Grenier) Baggetta; m. Michael R. DeNardis, Aug. 7, 1988. Paralegal diploma, Westchester Sch., 1985. Adminstrv. asst. Hospitality House T.C., Inc., Albany, N.Y., 1985-87; exec. adminstr. Hospitality House T.C., Inc., Albany, 1987-91; human immunodeficiency virus issues coord. Hospitality House T.C., Inc., Albany, N.Y., 1989-91, dir. adminstrn., 1991—. Mem. North Shore Animal League, Divers Alert Network. Home: 203 Blue Barns Rd Burnt Hills NY 12027-9527 Office: Hospitality House TC Inc 271 Central Ave Albany NY 12206-2611

VOSS, WERNER, dermatologist; b. Hagen, Germany, Apr. 6, 1949; s. Karl and Herta (Koch) V.; m. Barbara Finke, June 16, 1973; children: Viola, Marcel. MD, Univ. Hosp., Muenster, 1973. Resident in dermatology Univ. Hosp., Muenster, 1973-78; pvt. practice Muenster, 1978—; pres. Dermatest Rsch. Co., Muenster, 1983—; pres. Med. Data Svc. Co., Muenster, 1987—. Home: Birkenweg 4, D-48155 Muenster Germany Office: Dermatest GmbH, Birkenweg 4, D-48155 Muenster Germany

VOSSLER, DAVID GREGG, neurologist; b. Wellsville, N.Y., May 22, 1957; s. Charles Martin and Virginia Mae (Ford) V.; m. Michele Andrea Janis Vossler, Aug. 9, 1980; children: William Michael, Jonathan Carl. BA magna cum laude, U. Rochester, 1979; MD cum laude, Jefferson Med. Coll., 1983. Intern Thomas Jefferson U., Phila., 1983-84; resident in neurology Boston U., 1984-87; fellow in clinical neurophysiology U. Wash., Seattle, 1987-89, instr. neurology, 1989-90, clin. asst. prof., 1990—; dir. neurol. svc. epilepsy ctr. Swedish Med. Ctr., Seattle, 1992—. Contbr. articles to profl. jours. and chpts. to books. Chmn. profl. adv. bd. Epilepsy Assn. Wash., Seattle, 1992—. Mem. Am. Acad. Neurology, Am. Epilepsy Soc., Am. Electroencephalographic Soc., Western Electroencephalographic Soc. (bd. dirs. 1990—), Am. Bd. Registration of EEG Technologists (examiner 1991—), Alpha Omega Alpha. Office: Swedish Med Ctr Epilepsy Ctr 801 Broadway Ste 830 Seattle WA 98122

VOTH, DOUGLAS W., academic dean. Exec. dean U. Okla. Coll. Medicine, Oklahoma City. Office: U Okla Coll Medicine PO Box 26901 Rm 357-BMSB Oklahoma City OK 73190*

VOTTELER, THEODORE PAUL, pediatric surgeon; b. Portland, Oreg., Aug. 2, 1927; m. Vermelle McCain, Sept. 4, 1958. BS, U. Tex., Austin, 1947; MD, Tulane U., 1951. Diplomate Am. Bd. Surgery, Am. Bd. Pediatric Surgery. Intern Parkland Meml. Hosp., Dallas, 1951-52, resident, 1952-57; pediat. surgery fellow Children's Hosp., Phila., 1956-57; pres. Pediat. Surg. Assocs., Dallas, 1957—. Author: Practical Pediatric Therapy, 1985, Current Therapy in Pediatrics, 2d edit., 1989, Pediatric Therapy, 3d edit., 1993; contbr. articles to profl. jours. With USNR, 1945-47. Recipient Disting. Svc. award Children's Med. Ctr., 1993. Mem. Tex. Pediatric Surg. Soc. (pres. 1975), Tex. Med. Assn. (chmn. surg. sect. 1975), Tex. Surg. Soc. (v.p. 1985), Dallas Soc. Gen. Surgeons (pres. 1984-85), Doctor's Club (pres. 1982-83). Office: Pediatric Surgical Assocs 8226 Douglas Ste 547 Dallas TX 75225

VOTTO, JOHN JOSEPH, physician; b. New Haven, Conn., Sept. 8, 1951; s. Francis Joseph and Gloria Adrian (Fuggi) V.; m. Brenda Sue Newman, Oct. 27, 1978; children: Peter, Stephen, Leah. BA, U. Conn., 1973; DO, Kansas City Coll. Osteo., 1978. Resident USPHS Hosp., Staten Island, N.Y., 1978-81; asst. prof. pulmonary medicine U. Conn. Health Ctr., Farmington, 1984-95; assoc. prof. clin. medicine, 1995—; dir. intensive care Bradley Meml. Hosp., Southington, Conn., 1985-90, chief staff, 1988-89; chief pulmonary medicine Hosp. Spl. Care, New Britian, Conn., 1990—, v.p. med. affairs, 1992—. Contbr. articles to profl. jours. Pulmonary medicine fellow U. Conn. Health Ctr., 1981-83. Fellow Am. Coll. Chest Physicians; mem. Conn. Thoracic Soc. (chmn. credentials com. 1991, exec. com. 1992, chmn. planning com. 1992, sec. 1993, v.p. 1994, pres. 1995), Hartford County Med. Soc. (alt. del.), European Respiratory Soc. Independent. Roman Catholic. Office: Hosp Spl Care 2150 Cerbin Ave New Britain CT 06070

VOYLES, BARBARA JEAN, social worker, consultant; b. Desloge, Mo., Aug. 14, 1938; d. Walter Edward and Glena Mae (Moyer) V. AA, Flat River Jr. Coll., 1959; BS, Mo. Valley Coll., 1968; MSW, Washington U., 1980. Cert. tchr., Mo.; lic. clin. social worker, Mo. Social worker Family Svcs. Div. State of Mo., St. Genevieve, 1960-66; nurse Mo. Valley Health Svcs., Marshall, Mo., 1966-68, Fitzgibbon Hosp., Marshall, 1966-68; tchr. sci. Farmington (Mo.) Sch. Dist., 1968-72; tchr., sch. nurse, counselor R 14 Sch. Dist., Lonedell, Mo., 1972-75; social worker, clinician Family Svcs. Div. State of Mo., St. Louis, 1975-93; dir. social svcs. Mineral ARea Regional Med. Ctr., Farmington, Mo., 1993—; pvt. practice therapy, St. Louis, 1975—; cons. juvenile ct., St. Louis, 1980—, State of Mo. Licensing Bd., 1994; social worker home health, 1995. Contbr. articles to profl. jours., books. Mem. NASW, Acad. Cert. Social Workers, Mo. Assn. Social Workers, Mo. Assn. Prevention Adult Abuse, St. Louis County Juvenile Justice Assn., Washington U. alumni Assn., Order Ea. Star. Home: 309 Sycamore Desloge MO 63601 Office: Mineral Area Regional Med Ctr 1212 Weber Rd Farmington MO 63640-3309

VRABEC, MICHAEL PAUL, ophthalmologist, educator; b. Beaver Dam, Wis., July 29, 1957; s. Andrew Paul and Cecelia (Dolan) V.; m. Stephanie Howard, Oct. 9, 1982; children: Sara, Rachel. BS with distinction, U. Wis., 1979, MD, 1983. Diplomate Am. Bd. Ophthalmology. Intern in flex surgery Pres./St. Lukes, Denver, 1983-84; resident in ophthalmology U. Wis., 1984-87; fellow in cornea/ext. Ds U. Iowa, 1987-88; fellow in ref. surgery Hunkeler Eye, 1992; asst. prof. ophthalmology U. Vt., Burlington, 1988-94, assoc. prof., 1994; pvt. practice, Appleton, Wis., 1995; asst. clin. prof. U. Wis., Madison, 1995—. Author: Ophthalmic Essentials, 1993, Photographic Case Studies in Ophthalmology, 1995; contbr. over 50 articles to med. jours. Recipient physician's recognition award AMA, 1994. Fellow ACS, Am. Acad. Ophthalmology; mem. Midwest Cornea Soc., Alpha Omega Alpha. Office: Valley Eye Assocs 21 Park Pl Appleton WI 54915-8872

VREDEVOE, DONNA LOU, research immunologist, microbiologist, educator; b. Ann Arbor, Mich., Jan. 11, 1938; d. Lawrence E. and Verna (Brower) V.; m. John Porter, Aug. 22, 1962; 1 child, Verna. B.A. in Bacteriology, UCLA, 1959, Ph.D. in Microbiology (Univ. fellow, USPHS fellow), 1963. USPHS postdoctoral fellow Stanford U., 1963-64; instr. bacteriology UCLA, 1963, postgrad. research immunologist dept. surgery Center Health Scis., 1964-65, asst. research immunologist dept. surgery Center Health Scis., 1964-67; asst. prof. Sch. Nursing, Center Health Scis., 1967-70, asso. prof., 1970-76, prof., 1976—, asso. dean Sch. Nursing, 1976-78, acting assoc. dean Sch. Nursing., 1985-86, asst. dir. space planning Cancer Center, 1976-78, dir. space planning, 1978-90, cons. to lab. nuclear medicine and radiation biology, 1967-80; acting dean Sch. Nursing Center Health Scis., 1995—. Contbr. articles to profl. publs. Postdoctoral fellow USPHS, 1963-64; Mabel Wilson Richards scholar UCLA, 1960-61; research grantee including Am. Cancer Soc.; Calif. Inst. Cancer Research; Calif. div. Am. Cancer Soc.; USPHS; Am. Nurses Found.; Cancer Research Coordinating Com. U. Calif.; Dept. Energy. Mem Am. Soc. Microbiology, Am. Assn. Immunologists, Am. Assn. Cancer Research, Nat. League Nursing (2d v.p. 1979-81), Sigma Xi, Alpha Gamma Sigma., Sigma Theta Tau (nat. hon. mem.). Home: 355 21st Pl Santa Monica CA 90402-2503 Office: UCLA Sch Nursing Los Angeles CA 90024-6918

VREELAND, JAMES CHESTER, hospital administrator, consultant; b. Binghamton, N.Y., Mar. 29, 1940; s. James Quinn and Laura (Barrus) V.; m. Mary Louise Meighan, Aug. 13, 1963; children: Tracy L. Vreeland Flynn, James S. BSBA, King's Coll., Wilkes-Barre, Pa., 1962; MBA in Hosp. Adminstrn., Xavier U., Cin., 1964. Adminstrv. asst. Westmoreland Hosp., Greensburg, Pa., 1964-66; asst. exec. dir. Eye and Ear Hosp., Pitts., 1969-71; pres., CEO, Meml. Hosp. Bedford County, Everett, Pa., 1971—; cons. in field, 1991—. Mem. adv. bd. King's Coll. McGowan Sch. Bus., 1990—; chmn. bd. Hosp. Assn. Pa., 1994. Capt. USAR, 1966-69. Hosp. wing named in his honor Meml. Hosp. Bedford County, 1992; recipient Outstanding Support and Leadership award Hosp. Assn. Pa., 1995. Fellow Am. Coll. Healthcare Execs.; mem. Rotary (pres. 1981-82). Home: 605 Hammer St Bedford PA 15522 Office: Meml Hosp Bedford County RD 1 Box 80 Everett PA 19937

VRIESENDORP, FRANCINE J., neurologist; b. Rotterdam, The Netherlands, Feb. 8, 1947; came to U.S., 1980; m. Huibert Vriesendorp, June 6, 1970; 1 child, Corine. MD, U. Leiden, 1969. Diplomate Am. Bd. Psychiatry & Neurology, Am. Bd. Clin. Neurophysiology. Asst. prof. neurology U. Md., Balt., 1988-92, U. Tex., Houston, 1992—. Office: U Tex Health Sci Ctr 6431 Fannin Ste 7044 Houston TX 77030

VRIS, THOMAS W., surgeon; b. Elkins, W.Va., Apr. 27, 1951; s. Thomas and Barbara (Johns) V.; m. Donna Merrill, Oct. 6, 1973; children: Tracy, Courtney. BA, Columbia U., 1973; MD with honors, NYU, 1979. Diplomate Am. Bd. Otolaryngology. Resident Harvard Sch. Medicine, Boston, 1979-81, Yale U., New Haven, Conn., 1982-85; attending surgeon Norwalk (Conn.) Hosp., 1985—. Mem. Norwalk Med. Soc. (treas. 1991—, pres. 1994—), The Riding Club Wilton (Con.), Yale Club, Columbia Club, Am. Acad. Otolaryohology Head and Neck Surgery. Republican. Episcopalian. Office: Norwalk Hosp 10 Mott Ave Norwalk CT 06850-3320

VROLIX, MATHIAS CHRISTIAAN, cardiologist, researcher; b. Mortsel, Antwerp, Belgium, July 12, 1958; s. Hubert J. Vrolix and Maria E. Ruttens; m. Carine E. Steylaerts, May 22, 1981; children: Joel, Myrrhine, Gaelle, Dominique. MD, K.U. Leuven, Belgium, 1983, cardiology degree, 1988. Cert. interventional cardiologist. Resident in cardiology Leuven, 1988-90, supr. cardiology, 1990-92; dir. cath. lab. Genk, Belgium, 1992—; cons. SciMed Europe, 1995-96, Meditronic, 1995-96. Contbr. articles to profl. jours. Capt. Belgian Army, 1996. Mem. SCA&I, Belgian Working Group Interv. Cardiology (sec. 1996-2000). CVP. Roman Catholic. Home: Rietbeemdstraat 8, 3600 Genk Belgium Office: St Jans Hosp, Dept Cardiology, Schiepse Bos 2, 3600 Genk Belgium

VU, NANCY T., neurologist; b. Saigon, Vietnam, July 15, 1955; came to the U.S., 1971; m. Quy V. Nguyenphuc, 1986; children: Melody, Andrew. BA in Chemistry, Barnard Coll., 1977; MD, SUNY, Buffalo, 1981. Intern internal medicine Millard Fillmore Hosp., Buffalo, 1981-82; neurology resident PGY1 SUNY, Stony Brook, 1982-83; neurology resident PGY2-3 UCIMC, Orange, Calif., 1983-85; fellowship in electrodiagnostics UCIMC, Orange, 1985-86; staff neurologist FHP, Inc., Fountain Valley, Calif., 1986-95, Talbert Med. Group, Fountain Valley, 1996—. Mem. Am. Acad. Neurology. Office: 13918 Brookhurst St #B Garden Grove CA 92643

VUCKOVIC, STEVAN ALEXANDAR, emergency medicine physician; b. Berwyn, Ill., Mar. 28, 1964; s. Simeon and Milka (Hrnjak) V.; m. Norma Kay Van Milligan, June 13, 1993; 1 child, Alexandra Marie. BA, Trinity Christian Coll., 1987; DO, Chgo. Coll. Osteo. Medicine, 1992. Cert. paramedic Vandenberg Ambulance, Tinley Park, Ill., 1983-94; emergency physician Midwestern U., Downers Grove, Ill., 1993—; firefighter, paramedic Crestwood (Ill.) Fire Dept., 1984-87; med. coord., flight paramedic Air Ambulance Network, Miami, 1986-88; chief resident dept. emergency medicine Midwestern Univer. Chgo. Coll. Osteopathic Medicine, 1995-96. Vol. surg. team Christian Med. Soc., Honduras, 1986; vol. Tinley Park Emergency Svcs. and Disaster Agy., 1983-96. Mem. Am. Osteopathic Assn., Am. Coll. Osteopathic Emergency Physicians, Am. Coll. Emergency Physicians, Emergency Medicine Residents Assn. Home: 7001 W Plymouth Ct Tinley Park IL 60477

VUKSTA, MICHAEL JOSEPH, surgeon; b. Pitts., Apr. 25, 1926; s. Michael and Mary Sarah (Hanulya) V.; m. Dorothy Ann Bosak, Sept. 12, 1953; children: Patricia, Michael, Carol, Janet. BA, Youngstown State U., 1949; MD, Ohio State U., 1957. Diplomate Am. Bd. Surgery. Enlisted USN, advanced through grades to capt., 1974; intern St. Elizabeth Hosp., Youngstown, Ohio, resident in gen. surgery, 1958-62; pvt. practice gen.

surgery Youngstown, 1962-89; head blue team surgery Oak Knoll U.S. Naval Hosp., Oakland, Calif., 1989-93. Capt. USN retired. Fellow ACS, Am. Coll. Sports Medicine, Southwestern Surg. Congress; mem. Nat. Athletic Trainers Assn. (advisor). Byzantine Catholic. Home: 131 Lovett Pl Pensacola FL 32506-5265

VUTURO, ANTHONY FRANCIS, physician, educator; b. Louisville, Aug. 6, 1940; s. Anthony and Della (Meena) V., Sr.; m. Joan Margaret McGuinness, June 20, 1964; children—Jennifer, Jane, Steve, Matt, Kate. A.B. in Philosophy and Biology, Bellarmine U., 1962; M.D., U. Ky., 1966; M.P.H., Harvard U., 1971. Diplomate Am. Bd. Family Practice, Am. Bd. Preventive Medicine, Am. Bd. Med. Mgmt. Intern, resident St. Joseph's Hosp. and SUNY-Syracuse, 1966-68; dir. pub. health U.S. Civil Adminstrn., Ryakya, Japan, 1968-71; sr. adviser Whittaker Corp., Los Angeles, 1974-77; assoc. dean Coll. Medicine, U. Ariz., Tucson, 1977-79, prof., chmn. dept. family medicine, 1979—, assoc. dean health affairs, 1989—; cons. Whittaker Corp., Westinghouse, CIGNA, Consortuim for Internat. Devel., U.S. AID, WHO; dir. continuing edn. Am. Health Vons., Atlanta, 1986—. Editor Am. Med. Reports, Emergency Medicine Reports, Internal Medicine Reports, Physicians Marketing Reports, 1980-84. Contbr. articles, reports, book revs. to profl. publs. Bd. dirs. Pima County Bd. Health, Tucson, 1981-85, Pima Council on Aging, Tucson, 1981-85. Served to maj. U.S. Army, 1968-70. WHO fellow, 1973. Fellow Am. Acad. Family Physicians, Am. Coll. Physician Execs.; mem. ACP, AMA, AAFP, Am. Mgmt. Assn., Med. Dirs., Recipient of the Thomas Johnson Award, 1989, Outstanding acheivement in FP Education, 1996, distinguished Allumna award, 1996; Democrat. Roman Catholic. Office: U Ariz Coll Medicine Dept Family Community Tucson AZ 85724

WAALKES, T. PHILLIP, physician, educator; b. Belmond, Iowa, Oct. 30, 1919; s. Albert Herman and Grace (Prins) W.; m. Frances Elizabeth Brewster, Aug. 18, 1945 (dec. Nov. 1988); children: Richard Hugh, Steven Albert, Michael Phillip, Robert Louis Brewster, Kelly, Marian; m. Helen Hayes Smith, Apr. 11, 1992. A.B. magna cum laude, Hope Coll., 1941; Ph.D. in Chemistry, Ohio State U., 1945; M.D. with honors, George Washington U., 1951. From grad. asst. to instr. dept. chemistry Ohio State U., 1941-48; asst. scientist Res. USPHS, Nat. Cancer Inst., Bethesda, Md., 1948-51; intern USPHS Hosp., Balt., 1951-52; resident in medicine USPHS Hosp., 1952-55; clin. staff Nat. Heart Inst., Bethesda, 1955-58; spl. asst. to chief cancer chemotherapy Nat. Service Center, Bethesda, 1958-59; chief clin. br. Nat. Service Center, 1959-63; assoc. dir. charge collaborative research Nat. Cancer Inst., 1963-65, charge extramural ops., 1965—; prof. oncology Med. Sch., John Hopkins U., 1976—; now prof. emeritus; Pres., Md. chpt. Am. Cancer Soc. Served to med. dir. USPHS, 1959—. Mem. AMA, AAAS, APHA, Am. Soc. Clin. Oncology, Am. Assn. for Cancer Rsch., Internat. Histamine Club, Sigma Xi, Phi Lambda Upsilon, Phi Chi. Home: 9801 Kendale Rd Potomac MD 20854-4246 Office: Johns Hopkins Oncology Center Johns Hopkins Oncology Ctr Baltimore MD 21205

WACHTEL, THOMAS LEE, surgeon; b. Mansfield, Ohio, July 25, 1938; s. Earl J. and Lorena Fredona (Lehman) W.; m. Carolyn Coleman, May 15, 1965; children: John Matthew, David Earl-Martin, Julianne Maria. AB, Western Res. U., Cleve., 1960; MD, St. Louis U., 1964; NFS, Naval Flight Sch., Pensacola, Fla., 1970. Diplomate Am. Bd. Surgery; cert. added qualification in surg. critical care. Pvt. practice Hamilton & Wachtel, Corbin, Ky., 1973-74; mem. surg. faculty U. N.Mex., Albuquerque, 1974-77; mem. surg. faculty U. Calif., San Diego, 1978-80, burn dir., 1980-84, head trauma divsn., 1982-84; med. dir. trauma Samaritan Regional Med. Ctr., Phoenix, 1984-90; program dir. Phoenix Integrated Surg. Residency, 1986-90; med. dir. trauma Sharp Meml. Hosp., San Diego, 1990—. Author: Medical Exploring, 2 edits., 1973, 76, Current Topics in Burn Care, 1983, Burns of the Head and Neck, 1984; editor: A Symposium on Burns, 1985. Mem. Nat. Commn. on Exploring Boy Scouts Am., Arlington, Tex., 1972-95; mem. Flynn Found. on Commn. on Med. Manpower, Phoenix, 1987-88. With USN, 1969-73, capt. Res. Recipient Family Practice Teaching award Am. Acad. Family Practice, Phoenix, 1985; rsch. grantee U.S. Army, NIH, HSA-HEW. Fellow ACS, Am. Assn. Surgery of Trauma, Am. Coll. Critical Care Medicine; mem. Am. Burn Assn. (pres. 1973-95). Roman Catholic. Office: Sharp Meml Hosp 7901 Frost St San Diego CA 92123

WACKER, WARREN ERNEST CLYDE, physician, educator; b. Bklyn., Feb. 29, 1924; s. John Frederick and Kitty Dora (Morrissey) W.; m. Ann Romeyn MacMillan, May 22, 1948; children: Margaret Morrissey, John Frederick. Student, Georgetown U., 1946-47; M.D., George Washington U., 1951; M.A. (hon.), Harvard, 1968. Intern George Washington U. Hosp., 1951-52, resident, 1952-53; resident Peter Bent Brigham Hosp., Boston, 1953-55; Nat. Found. Infantile Paralysis fellow, 1955-57; investigator Howard Hughes Med. Inst., Boston, 1957-68; mem. faculty Harvard Med. Sch., Boston, 1955—; assoc. prof. medicine Harvard Med. Sch., 1968-71, Henry K. Oliver prof. hygiene, 1971-89, prof. hygiene, 1989-95, dir. univ. health services, 1971-89; Henry K. Oliver prof. hygiene emeritus, 1995; acting master Mather House Harvard Med. Sch., 1974-75, acting master Kirkland House, 1975-76, master Cabot House, 1978-84; sr. med. cons. Risk Mgmt. Found. of the Harvard Med. Instns., Cambridge, 1992—; vis. scholar St. Mary's Hosp. Med. Sch., 1964; vis. prof. U. Tel Aviv, 1987; chmn. bd. Applied mgmt. Sys., Burlington, Mass., Millipore Corp., Bedford, Mass., 1971-94; mem. editorial adv. bd. Toxilogical and Environ. Chemistry. Author: Magnesium and Man, 1981; sec., editorial adv. bd.: Biochemistry, 1962-76; assoc. editor: Magnesium; contbr. articles to med. and sci. jours. Vestryman St. Paul's Episc. Ch., Brookline, Mass., 1965-68, 76-79, 91-94; bd. dirs. Harvard Cmty. Health Plan, Boston, 1973-84, mem. fin. com., 1984-86, mem. corp., 1986—; bd. dirs. Bishop Rhinelander Found., Cambridge, 1973-76, 78-84, Controlled Risk Ins. Co., 1976-78; pres. bd. overseers Peter Bent Brigham Hosp., Boston, 1979-84; trustee Brigham and Women's Hosp., Boston, 1984-89,Risk Mgmt. Found., 1979-92; mem. mgmt. bd., med. bd. MIT, 1985-95; mem. corp. Mt. Auburn Hosp., Cambridge, 1986—; mem. adv. bd. hospitality program Episc. Diocese Mass., 1989—. 1st lt. USAAF, 1942-45. Decorated Air medal, D.F.C., Liberation medal (Greece); named Disting. Alumnus, George Washington U., 1963; recipient Cert. of Merit, Soc. Magnesium Research, 1985. Mem. AMA, Am. Chem. Soc., Am. Soc. Biol. Chemistry, Am. Soc. Clin. Investigation, Mass. Med. Soc., A.C.P., Am. Coll. Health Assn. (pres. 1981, Boynton award 1986), Biochemistry Soc. (London), Am. Coll. Nutrition, Sigma Xi, Alpha Omega Alpha, Harvard Club (Boston). Home: 91 Glen Rd Brookline MA 02146-7764 Office: Risk Mgmt Found 840 Memorial Dr Cambridge MA 02139-3771

WADDEL, DOUGLAS HOWARD, family physician; b. Bluff City, TN, May 6, 1943; s. Cecil Howard and France Daisy (Boling) W.; m. Luz Isabel Garza, Jan 2, 1971; children: Amy, Christopher, Brandon. BS in Biology, Chemistry, Carson-Newman Coll., Jefferson City, Tenn., 1965; MD, U. Tenn., 1969. Diplomate Am. Bd. Family Practice. Physician, owner Launey Med. Clinic, Dallas, 1971-82, Beltline North Med. Clinic, Dallas, 1983-85, Atrium Med. Clinic, Dallas, 1985—. Fellow Am. Acad. Family Physicians; mem. Tex. Med. Assn., Dallas County Med. Soc., Tex. Acad. Family Physicians (bd. dirs. state assn., past sec., treas., v.p., pres. Dallas chpt.), Am. Coll. Occupational and Environ. Medicine. Republican. Baptist. Home: 10473 Epping Ln Dallas TX 75229 Office: Atrium Med Clinic 14465 Webbs Chapel Rd # 111 Dallas TX 75234

WADDELL, WILLIAM JOSEPH, pharmacologist, toxicologist; b. Commerce, Ga., Mar. 16, 1929; s. John Daniel and Lillian Marie (Vollrath) W.; m. Grace Carolyn Marlowe, Oct. 19, 1974; children: William Joseph, James Glenn, Martin Christie, Amy Alison. A.B. in Chemistry, U. N.C., 1951, M.D., 1955. Postdoctoral research fellow U. N.C. Sch. Medicine, 1955-58, asst. prof. pharmacology, 1958-62, asso. prof., 1962-72; asso. prof. oral biology U. N.C. Sch. Medicine (Dental Research Center), 1967-69, prof., 1969-72, asso. dir., 1968-72; prof. pharmacology U. Ky. Coll. Medicine, Lexington, 1972-77; prof., chmn. dept. pharmacology and toxicology U. Louisville, 1977—; Centennial Alumni Disting. vis. prof. U. N.C. Sch. Medicine, 1979. Contbr. articles to profl. jours. Fellow Acad. Toxicological Scis.; mem. Am. Soc. for Pharmacology and Exptl. Therapeutics, Am. Physiol. Soc., Am. Teratology Soc., Internat. Soc. for Study Xenobiotics, Soc. for Exptl. Biology and Medicine, Soc. Toxicology, Sigma Xi. Home: 14300 Rose Wycombe Rd Prospect KY 40059-9024 Office: U Louisville Dept Pharmacology Louisville KY 40292

WADDEN, THOMAS ANTONY, psychologist, educator; b. Richmond, Va., Sept. 3, 1952; s. Thomas Antony Jr. and Mary Lloyd (Cradock) W.; m. Jan Robin Linowitz, Nov. 11, 1984; children: David Joseph, Michael James, Steven Zachary. AB magna cum laude, Brown U., 1975; PhD, U. N.C., 1981. Psychology intern Boston VA Med. Ctr., 1980-81; instr. in psychology U. Pa. Sch. Medicine, Phila., 1981-82, asst. prof. psychology, 1982-87, assoc. prof. psychology, 1987-91, prof. psychology, 1994—; prof. psychology, dir. clin. tng. Syracuse (N.Y.) U., 1992-93; clin. dir. Obesity Rsch. Group, U. Pa., Phila., 1983-91, dir. Weight and Eating Disorders Program, 1994—; dir. Ctr. for Health and Behavior, Syracuse U., 1992-93. Assoc. editor Annals of Behavioral Medicine, 1990-93; mem. editl. bd. Behavior Theraphy, Internat. Jour. Eating Disorders, Jour. Cons. and Clin. Psychology Obesity Rsch.; editor: (with T.B. VanItallie) Treatment of the Seriously Obese Patient, 1992, (with A.J. Stunkard) Obesity: Theory and Therapy, 1993; contbr. chpts. in books; writer numerous sci. papers. Recipient Nat. Rsch. Svc. award NIMH, 1983-85, Rsch. Scientist Devel. award, 1987-91, 94—. Mem. APA, Soc. Behavioral Medicine (bd. dirs. 1987-90), Assn. for Advancement of Behavior Therapy (New Rschr. award 1986), Acad. Behavioral Medicine, Phi Beta Kappa, Sigma Xi. Democrat. Home: 433 Bolsover Rd Wynnewood PA 19096-1301 Office: U Pa 3600 Market St Fl 738 Philadelphia PA 19104-2611

WADDLE, AUDREY STERLING, rehabilitation nurse; b. Gloucester County, Va., June 20, 1932; d. James Edward and Ethel Haydon (Williams) Sterling; RN, Riverside Sch. Profl. Nursing, 1952; student Hampton Inst., 1971-72, Thomas Nelson Community Coll., 1973; BS in Health Adminstrn., St. Joseph's Coll., 1980; m. Travis Gene Waddle, May 4, 1952; children: Pamela Gayle Waddle Furr, Anita Darlene Smith. RN, Va. Cert. trainer, course developer, supr. trainer, Va. Head nurse Riverside Hosp., Newport News, 1953, Onslow County Hosp., Jacksonville, N.C., 1954 pvt. duty, relief dir. Gray's Clinic & Hosp., Springhill, La., 1955-57; gen. duty nurse Ea. State Hosp., Williamsburg, Va., 1957-58, head nurse, 1958-59, nurse supr., 1959-65, mental health nurse instr. and tng. coord., 1965-68, chmn. ward manual com., 1967-81, nursing coord., 1988-92, employee health nurse, 1992—. Adv. bd. and selection com. Lafayette Practical Nurse Program, Williamsburg, 1972-82; mem. State of Va. Dept. Mental Health/Mental Retardation Individualized Treatment Planning Com., 1979-80; chmn. Ea. State Hosp. United Fund drive, 1978-79; mem. G.S.H. Tardive Dyskinesia Tng. Com., 1988—. U. Md. grantee, 1964. Mem. ANA (cert.), Va. Govt. Employees Assn., Nat. Soc. Registered Nurses. Presbyterian. Developer psychiat. practical nurse program Eastern State Hosp., 1967. co-author manuals. Home: 5100 Greenwich Mews Williamsburg VA 23188-8515 Office: Drawer A Williamsburg VA 23187

WADE, KENNETH ALAN, physician assistant; b. Salt Lake City, Oct. 22, 1948; s. Lester Heber and Carol (Braby) W.; m. Denice Stratford, Dec. 17, 1970; children: Kenneth Andrew, Dennis Curtis, Christopher Aaron. BS, Okla. Univ., 1981, U. Utah, 1973; AS, Weber State Coll., 1971. Staff acct. Elwood & Barnes, CPAs, Salt Lake City, 1973-79; physician asst. U.S. Army, 1979-81, Utah Army Nat. Guard, Salt Lake City, 1981—; mgr. Logan (Utah) Med. Ctr., 1983—; adj. instr. U. Utah, Salt Lake City, 1982-87; physician's asst. Logan Woman's Clinic, 1981—. Co-author: Prenatal Development. Bd. dirs. Cache County Sch. Bd., North Logan, 1992—, Cache Edn. Found., North Logan, 1992—. Fellow Am. Acad. Physician Assts., Utah Acad. Physician Assts.; mem. Assn. Mil. Surgeons U.S. Mem. Ch. Jesus Christ Latter Day Saints. Home: 175 W 100 S Smithfield UT 84341 Office: Logan Women's Clinic 550 E 1400 N Ste K Logan UT 84341

WADE, SAMUEL DAVID, medical products company executive; b. Hempstead, N.Y., Dec. 6, 1949; s. Samuel Davis and Pauline L. (Watkins) W.; m. Dorothy Elizabeth Dodge; 1 child, Alexander Andrew. BS, Colo. State U., 1971. Dir. internat. quality assurance and regulatory affairs Boston Scientific Internat., Watertown, Mass., 1982-89; dir. quality assurance and regulatory affairs Bard Vascular Systems divsn. C.R. Bard, Billerica, Mass., 1989-91, St. Jude Med., Chelmsford, Mass., 1991-94; v.p. quality and regulatory affairs Infusaid divsn. Pfizer Inc., Norwood, Mass., 1994-95; prin. The Acton (Mass.) Group, 1995—; bd. dirs. On Site Acad. Selectman Town of Maynard, Mass., 1982-84, mem. bd. of health, 1974-81; mem. adv. bd. County of Middlesex, Maynard, 1983; active Stow (Mass.) Conservation Commn., 1986. Recipient Community Svc. awards Mass. Ho. of Reps., 1984, Mass. Senate, 1984. Mem. Regulatory Affairs Profl. Soc., Am. Soc. for Quality Control, Soc. for Clin. Trials, Critical Incident Stress Debriefing Team, Am. Meteorol. Soc., N.Y. Acad. Scis. Home: 12 Grasshopper Ln Acton MA 01720-4607

WADLE, ROY BRENT, osteopathic physician; b. Arlington, Tex. Sept. 12, 1965; s. Roy Dean and Gennie V. (Brooks) W.; m. Glenda Gay Throckmorton, June 29, 1991; 1 child, Jacob Thomas. BS in Clin. Lab. Sci., Tex. Tech U., Lubbock, 1989; DO, Tex. Coll. Osteo. Medicine, Ft. Worth, 1994. Med. technologist Meth. Hosp., Lubbock, 1988-89, Meth. Med. Ctr., Lubbock, 1989-90; resident in family practice St. Anthony Hosp., Oklahoma City, 1994—. Mem. Am. Osteo. Assn., Am. Assn. Family Practitioners, Am. Coll. Family Practitioners, Okla. Osteo. Assn., Tex. Osteo. Med. Assn. Mem. Assembly of God Ch. Office: St Anthony Hosp Family Practice Residency 608 NW 9th St Ste 1000 Oklahoma City OK 73102

WADLEY, FREDIA STOVALL, state commissioner; b. Winchester, Tenn.. BS, Tenn Tech U., 1967; MD, U. Tenn., 1969; MSHPA, U. Cin., 1978. Diplomate Am. Bd. Pediats. Pediat. intern City of Memphis Hosp., 1970, pediat. resident, 1971-72; clin. instr. pediats. dept. pediats. U. Tenn. Ctr. for Health Scis., Memphis, 1973-74; pvt. practice Winchester, Tenn., 1974-75; instr. phys. assessment course dept. nursing U. Tenn., Chattanooga, 1975-76; dir. med. svcs. Dept. Health and Environ. Southeast Region, Chattanooga, 1975-80, regional dir., 1981-83; chief med. officer Dept. Health and Environ. Commr.'s Office, Nashville, 1984-87; dir. Met. Health Dept., Nashville, 1987-95; commr. Dept. Health, Nashville, 1995—; clin. asst. prof. dept. pediats. Meharry Med. Coll., 1985—; mem. faculty staff preventive medicine divsn. Quillen Dischner Med. Coll., 1985-87; vol. faculty mem. dept. nursing U. Tenn. Ctr. for Health Scis., Memphis, 1977-83, U. Tenn., Knoxville, 1977-83; mem. preventive medicine resident adv. com. Meharry Family Medicine Dept., 1988—; adj. assoc. prof. nursing dept. family and cmty. health Vanderbilt U., 1988—; presenter in field. Contbr. articles to profl. jours. Mem. HSA III Task Force on Ambulatory Health Care Problems, 1977, HSA III Bd., 1981-82; mem. southeast Tenn. regional placement com. Tenn. Med. Loan Scholarship Program, 1978-79; bd. dirs. Southeast Tenn. Chpt. Kidney Found., 1981, Vol. Healthcare Sys., Inc., 1988-90, Vanderbilt AIDS Project, 1990, United Way Mid. Tenn., 1992-95, ARC, 1992; mem. Tenn. Sch. health Coalition, 1985—, Cmty. Coalition for Minority Health, 1988, Mayor's Substance Abuse Action Team, 1990; active Brentwood United Meth., Sunday Sch. tchr. 6th grade, 1984-87; chmn. Tenn. AIDS Adv. Com., 1987-88, Davidson County Child Fatality Rev. Team, 1994-95, others. Mem. AMA, APHA (Charles G. Jordan award for outstanding accomplishments in field of pub. health so. br. 1981), Southern Health Assn. (chmn. awards com. and governing coun. 1981-83, pres. 1989-90, spl. meritorious award for outstanding contbns. to orgn. and pub. health 1992), Tenn. Pub. Health Assn. (pres. 1990-91, spl. meritorious award 1993), Tenn. Health Officers, Tenn. Pediat. Soc., Tenn. Med. Assn., Nashville/Davidson County Acad. Medicine, Davidson County Pediat. Soc. Address: 909 Lakemont Dr Nashville TN 37220

WADLINGTON, WALTER JAMES, law educator; b. Biloxi, Miss., Jan. 17, 1931; s. Walter and Bernice (Taylor) W.; m. Ruth Miller Hardie, Aug. 20, 1955; children: Claire Hardie, Charlotte Taylor Griffith, Susan Miller, Derek Alan. AB, Duke U., 1951; LLB, Tulane U., 1954. Bar: La. 1954, Va. 1965. Pvt. practice New Orleans, 1954-55, 58-59; asst. prof. Tulane U., 1960-62; mem. faculty U. Va., 1962—, prof law, 1964—, James Madison prof., 1970—; prof. legal medicine U. Va. Med. Sch., 1979—; Harrison Found. rsch. prof. U. Va., 1990-92; tutor civil law U. Edinburgh, Scotland, 1959-60; vis. Tazewell Taylor prof. law Coll. William and mary, spring 1986; program dir. Robert Wood Johnson Med. Malpractice Program, 1985-91; mem. adv. bd. Robert Wood Johnson clin. scholars program, 1989—; chmn. nat. adv. bd. Improving Malpractice Precention and Compensation Sys., 1994—; Disting. Health Law Tchr. Am. Soc. Law, Medicine and Ethics. Author: Cases and Materials on Domestic Relations, 1970, 3d edit., 1995; (with Waltz and Dworkin) Cases and Materials on Law and Medicine, 1980; (with Whitebread and Davis) Children in the Legal System, 1983; editor-in-chief Tulane U. Law Rev., 1953-54. Fulbright scholar U. Edinburg. Mem. Va. Bar Assn., Am. Law Inst., Inst. Medicine of NAS, Order of Coif. Home: 1620 Keith Valley Rd Charlottesville VA 22901-3018 Office: U Va Sch Law Charlottesville VA 22903

WAECHTER, WALTER LESLIE, general surgeon; b. Fort Worth; m. Laura Bryan; children: Graham, Emily. BS in Pre-med., U. Tex., Arlington, 1972; MD, U Tex. Southwestern Med. Sch., Dallas, 1976. Lic. surgeon Tex. State Bd. Med. Examiners. Gen. surgeon pvt. practice Arlington, Tex., 1981—. Fellow ACS, Am. Soc. for Laser Medicine and Surgery; mem. AMA, Tex. Med. Assn., Tarrant County Med. Soc., Southwestern Surgical Congress. Office: 515 W Mayfield Rd Ste 402 Arlington TX 76014

WAELSCH, SALOME GLUECKSOHN, geneticist, educator; b. Danzig, Germany, Oct. 6, 1907; came to U.S., 1933, naturalized, 1938; d. Ilya and Nadia Gluecksohn; m. Heinrich B. Waelsch, Jan. 8, 1943; children: Naomi Barbara, Peter Benedict. Student, U. Konigsberg, Germany, U. Berlin, 1927-28; PhD, U. Freiburg, Germany, 1932; DSc (hon.), Columbia U., 1995. Rsch. assoc. in genetics Columbia U., 1936-55; assoc. prof. anatomy Albert Einstein Coll. Medicine, 1955-58, prof., 1958-63, prof. molecular genetics, 1963—, chmn. dept. genetics, 1963-76; mem. study sects. NIH. Contbr. numerous articles on devel. genetics. Recipient Nat. Medal of Sci., Pres. Clinton, 1993. Fellow AAAS, Am. Acad. Arts and Scis.; mem. NAS, N.Y. Acad. Scis. (hon. life), Am. Soc. Zoologists, Am. Assn. Anatomists, Genetics Soc., Soc. Devel. Biology, Am. Soc. Naturalists, Am. Soc. Human Genetics, The Royal Soc. (fgn. mem.), Sigma Xi. Office: Albert Einstein Coll Med Dept Molecular Genetics 1300 Morris Park Ave Bronx NY 10461-1926

WAFFENSCHMIDT, PATRICIA HUNT, osteopathic physician; b. Bronx, N.Y., May 4, 1961; d. John Patrick and Barbara (Levine) Hunt; m. Robert Waffenschmidt, Aug. 16, 1991. BS, Polytech. Inst., 1983; DO, N.Y. C.C., 1988. Attending physician Woodhull Hosp., Bklyn., 1992-95; clin. staff Columbia Sch. Medicine, N.Y.C., 1993—; med. dir. Betances Family Unit Beth Israel Hosp., N.Y.C., 1995—. Editor: Med. Tribune, 1990; contbr. articles to profl. jours. Mem. League Women Voters, Kew Gardens, N.Y., 1994—. Nat. Health Svc. scholar, 1984-88. Mem. Am. Coll. Physicians (com. women internists 1994—). Office: Beth Israel Hosp Betances Family Unit 280 Henry St New York NY 10002

WAGENAAR, JAMES S., osteopathic physician; b. Grand Rapids, Mich., June 30, 1961; s. Jacob and Rosina Doreen (House) W.; m. Lynne Ann Severo, Mar. 6, 1985; children: Jessica Lynne, Douglas James. BS magna cum laude, Aquinas Coll., 1983; DO, Mich. State Coll. Medicine, 1985. Diplomate Am. Coll. Osteopathic Internists. Gen. internist Cmty. Action Orgn., Ironton, Ohio, 1991-92; emergency medicine physician Ashland (Ky.) Emergency Med. Assn., 1992—; lectr. and rschr. Genentech Corp. , 1989-91, Merck Corp., West Point, Pa., 1991-92. Active mem. Rep. Party Ky. and Nat. level, 1994—. Mem. Am. Osteopath. Assn., Ky. Med. Assn., So. Med. Assn., Fraternal Order of the Elks. Republican. Lutheran. Home: 6636 Hickory Hills Dr Ashland KY 41102

WAGENBERG, HAROLD ROSS, dermatologist; b. Windsor, Ont., May 28, 1934; s. Ansel and Celia (Price) W.; m. Elaine S. Forbes, Aug. 24, 1986; children: Jeffrey, Todd, Scott. Student, U. Western Ont., London, 1952-54, MD, 1958. Intern Harper Hosp., Detroit, 1958-59; pediatric resident Akron (Ohio) Children's Hosp., 1962-64; fellow in pediatric hematology Children's Hosp. of Mich., Detroit, 1964-65; pvt. practice Met. Assn. of Pediatricians, Detroit, 1965-78; resident in dermatology Wayne State U., Detroit, 1978-80; pvt. practice Assocs. in Dermatology, Southfield, Mich., 1980—. Capt. M.C., U.S. Army, 1960-62. Fellow Am. Acad. Dermatology, Am. Acad. Pediatrics, Am. Acad. of Dermatology and Dermatopathology; mem. AMA. Home: 500 Overhill Rd Bloomfield Hills MI 48301-2566 Office: Assocs in Dermatology 22250 Providence Dr Ste 301 Southfield MI 48075-6211

WAGENER, JOHANN, therapist, consultant; b. France, June 6, 1941. BS, Calif. State U., L.A., 1981; MS, U. So. Calif., 1985. Cert. coll. addiciton treatment adminstr. Mgr., buyer Woolworth/G.R. Kinney Corp., 1963-73; security dir. Am. Protection Systems, L.A., 1973-75; owner, operator Advanced Prtoections Systems, Inc., Marina Del Rey, Calif., 1975-76; cons., dir. Peninsula Groupe, Redondo Beach, Calif., 1981—; program dir. Advanced Recovery Inst., Torrance, Calif., 1985-88, Vista Health Corp., El Segundo, Calif., 1988-90; primary therapist Charter Hosp., Torrance, 1983-85; pvt. practice therapy Redondo Beach, Calif., 1983—. Bd. mem. Alliance for Formerly Abused. Mem. ACLU, Am. Psychol. Assn. (assoc.), Am. Psychol. Soc. (affiliate), Am. Coll. Addiction Treatment Adminstrs., N.Y. Acad. Scis., Calif. Assn. Marriage and Family Therapists (affiliate), South Bay Coalition on Drugs and Alcohol, Coalition for Outpatient Treatment of Chem. Dependency, Calif. Personnel and Guidance Counseling Assn., South Bay Coalition for Alternatives to Domestic Violence, Californians Preventing Violence, U. Soc. Calif. Alumni Assn. (dir. 1988—), Psi Chi. Office: Pen Con Inc PO Box 530 Redondo Beach CA 90277-0530

WAGER, STEVEN GARY, psychiatry educator; b. Cleve., Nov. 29, 1952; s. William Charles and Ruth Ray (Joseph) W.; m. Lisa Klein, July 19, 1986; children: Rachel, Matthew. AB, Washington U., St. Louis, 1974; MD, Case Western Res. U., 1980. Diplomate Am. Bd. Psychiatry and Neurology. Intern U. Hosps. Cleve., 1980-81; resident Columbia Presbyn. Med. Ctr. & N.Y. State Psychiat. Inst., N.Y.C., 1981-84; rsch. psychiatrist N.Y. State Psychiat. Inst., N.Y.C., 1986-90; asst. clin. prof. Columbia U. Coll. Physicians & Surgeons, N.Y.C., 1987-94; dir. clin. psychopharmacology St. Luke's-Roosevelt Hosp. Ctr., N.Y.C., 1990—, dir. edn. dept. psychiatry, 1993—; assoc. clin. prof. psychiatry Columbia U. Coll. Physicians & Surgeons, N.Y.C., 1994—. Contbr. articles to profl. jours. Psychiat. rsch. fellow Columbia Presbyn. Med. Ctr. & N.Y. State Psychiat. Inst., 1984-86. Mem. Am. Psychiat Assn., Am. Soc. Clin. Psychopharmacology, Am. Assn. Dirs. of Psychiatric Residency Tng. Office: St Lukes Roosevelt Hosp Ctr Dept Psychiatry 1111 Amsterdam Ave New York NY 10025

WAGNER, ALLAN RAY, psychology educator, experimental psychologist; b. Springfield, Ill., Jan. 6, 1934; s. Raymond August and Grace (Johnson) W.; m. Barbara Rae Meland, Nov. 21, 1959, (dec. Nov. 1994); children: Krystn Rae, Kathryn Rae. B.A., U. Iowa, 1956, M.A., 1958, Ph.D., 1959; M.A. hon., Yale U., 1970. Asst. prof. psychology Yale U., New Haven, 1959-64, assoc. prof., 1964-69, prof., 1970-89, chmn. psychology dept., 1983-89, James Rowland Angell prof. psychology, 1990—, chmn. philosophy dept., 1991-93, dir., divsn. of the soc. sci., 1992—; cons. NIMH, 1968-71; mem. Pres. Biomed. Research Panel, 1975-76; adv. bd. Cambridge Ctr. Behavioral Studies, 1982—; mem. psychobiology panel NSF, 1984-85, com. on basic research in behavioral and social scis. NRC, 1984-87. Author: Reward and Punishment, 1965; assoc. editor: Learning and Motivation, 1969-74, Animal Learning and Behavior, 1972-74; editor: Jour. Exptl. Psychology, 1974-81, Quantitative Analyses of Behavior, Vol. 3, 1982, Vol. 4, 1983, Vol. 7, 1988. Fellow NSF, 1958 (grantee 1960—), NIMH, 1963. Fellow APA, AAAS (mem. coun. 1988-91), Soc. Exptl. Psychologists (Howard Crosby Warren medal 1991), Am. Psychol. Soc.; mem. NAS, Psychonomic Soc., So. Quantitative Analysis of Behavior (sec. 1983-92), Ea. Psychol. Assn. (bd. dirs. 1985-88), Sigma Xi, New Haven Law Club. Home: 1405 Ridge Rd North Haven CT 06473-3051 Office: Yale U Dept Psychology PO Box 208205 New Haven CT 06520-8205

WAGNER, BRETT ALAN, biologist; b. Waterloo, Iowa, Apr. 19, 1959; s. Larry Gene and Karen Kay (Mitchell) W.; m. Pamela Sue Morehead, Aug. 10, 1991. BA, U. No. Iowa, 1983, MA, 1987. Rsch. asst. III U. Iowa Hosps. and Clinics, Iowa City, 1987—. Contbr. articles to Biochemistry, Med. Oncology and Tumor Pharmacotherapy, Jour. Lipid Rsch., Cancer Rsch. Mem. Sigma Xi (assoc.). Office: U Iowa 357 MRF Iowa City IA 52242

WAGNER, GÜNTER PAUL, biologist educator; b. Vienna, Austria, May 28, 1954; came to U.S., 1991; s. Otto Karl and Käthe Auguste (Birk) W.; m. Herta Ruttner Brinkmann, Dec. 31, 1978 (div. 1985); 1 child, Susanne Karoline; m. Michaela Sabine Hauser, July 19, 1985; 1 child, Veronika Eszter. PhD, U. Vienna, 1979; MA (hon.), Yale U., 1992. Asst. prof. U. Vienna, Austria, 1985-90; assoc. prof. U. Vienna, 1990-91; prof. Yale U., New Haven, 1991—; bd. dirs. Orgn. for Tropical Studies; vis. prof.

Northwestern U., Evanston, Ill., 1987-88, U. Basel. Switzerland, 1991, U. Leiden, The Netherlands, 1995; Gompertz lectr. U. Calif., Berkeley, 1993; disting. lectr. Internat. Inst. for Applied Sys. Analysis, 1995; Sewell Wright lectr. U. Chgo., 1996. Publ. com. mem. Yale U. Press, New Haven, 1992-95; contbr. articles to profl. jours. Bd. dirs. Ctr. Computational Ecology, New Haven. Recipient MacArthur prize MacArthur Found., 1992. Mem. AAAS, European Soc. Evolutionary Biology (editl. bd. 1988-92), Soc. for Study of Evolution (assoc. editor 1994—), Soc. Systematic Biology, German Zool. Soc. Lutheran. Office: Yale Univ 165 Prospect St New Haven CT 06520-8104

WAGNER, GUSTAV ALFRED, retired medical educator; b. Hannover, Germany, Jan. 10, 1918; s. Gustav and Anna Wagner; m. Inge Winiarz, Dec. 6, 1941; 1 child, Klaus-Dieter. MD, U. Berlin, 1944. Resident physician Mcpl. Dermatol. Hosp., Hannover, 1946-51; asst. prof. U. Dermatol. Hosp., Kiel, Fed. Republic of Germany, 1951-64; prof. medicine, dir. German Cancer Research Ctr., Heidelberg, Fed. Republic of Germany, 1964-86; ret. German Cancer Research Ctr., Heidelberg, 1986. Author/editor over 60 books and 300 jours. articles. Recipient Ernst von Bergmann medal Chamber German Physicians, 1980. Mem. German Soc. of Med. Informatics (hon.), European Fed. of Med. Informatics (hon.), Internat. Working Group of Bone Tumours (hon.), Assn. German Medical Press. (hon.). Home: Bluetenweg 64, 6905 Schriesheim Baden Wurtt Germany

WAGNER, HENRY NICHOLAS, JR., physician; b. Balt., May 12, 1927; s. Henry N. and Gertrude Loane W.; m. Anne Barrett Wagner, Feb., 1951; children—Henry N., Mary Randall, John Mark, Anne Elizabeth. A.B., Johns Hopkins U., 1948, M.D., 1952; D.Sc. (hon.), Washington Coll., Chestertown, Md., 1972, Free U., Brussels, 1985; M.D. (hon.), U. Gottingen, 1988. Chief med. resident Osler Med. Service, Johns Hopkins Hosp., Balt., 1958-59; asst. prof. medicine, radiology Johns Hopkins Med. Instns., 1959-64, asso. prof., 1964-65, prof., dir. divs. nuclear medicine and radiation health sci., 1965—. Author numerous books in field.; contbr. articles to med. jours. Served with USPHS, 1955-57. Recipient Georg von Hevesey medal, 1976. Fellow ACP; mem. Inst. Medicine of NAS, AMA (coun. sci. affairs, Sci. Achievement award 1991), Balt. City Med. Soc. (past pres.), World Fedn. Nuclear Medicine and Biology (past pres.), Am. Bd. Nuclear Medicine (founding mem.), Soc. Nuclear Medicine (past pres.), Am. Fedn. Clin. Research (past pres.), Research Socs. Council (past pres.), Assn. Am. Physicians, Am. Soc. Clin. Investigation, Phi Beta Kappa. Home: 5607 Wildwood Ln Baltimore MD 21209-4520 Office: 615 N Wolfe St Baltimore MD 21205-2103*

WAGNER, JEAN-CLAUDE, gastroenterologist; b. Paris, Oct. 15, 1941; s. Jean-Jacques and Renée (Diamant) W.; m. Anne-Marie Gatel, Sept. 21, 1967; children: Claire, Marc, Serge. BS, Lycee de Troyes, 1958; MD, MEC, Paris, 1962. Extern Hopitaux de Paris, 1965-68; intern Region Sanitaire de Paris, 1968-71, Assistance Publique, Paris, 1971-75; chief de clinique A.P. Paris, 1975-79; chef de svc. Hopital Troyes, France, 1979-81, 81—; attandie Assistance a Publique, 1979—. Home: 17 Rue E Perochon, 10600 La Chapelle Saint Lu France Office: Centre Hospitalier de Troye, 101 Ave A France, 10003 Troyes France

WAGNER, KATHRYN P., medical center administrator; b. Cripple Creek, Va., Apr. 5, 1947; d. Stephen Lawson and Lois Marie (Andrew) Porter; m. Norbert Peter Wagner, Sept. 27, 1967 (div. Oct. 1981); children: Angela Denise, Stephen Lawson Porter. AS, Daytona Beach (Fla.) C.C., 1987. A.R.T., A.H.I.M.A., Fla. Med. records analyst Parrish Med. Ctr., Titusville, Fla., 1980-88; med. records dir. Hoots Meml. Hosp., Yadkinville, N.C., 1988-91, Sycamore Shoals Hosp., Elizabethton, Tenn., 1991-93, Health South Rehab., Kingsport, Tenn., 1993-94, Johnson County Hosp., Mountain City, Tenn., 1994-95; v.p. quality improvement Stewart Marchman Ctr., Daytona Beach, Fla., 1995—. Mem. Am. Health Info.Mgmt., Ocean Regional Health Info. (del. 1996—), Toastmasters Internat. Home: 1911 Sugar Tree Circle New Smyrna Beach FL 32169 Office: Stewart Marchman Ctr 3875 Tiger Bay Rd Daytona Beach FL 32124

WAGNER, MAHLON WHITNEY, psychology educator; b. Chaffee, N.Y., Aug. 23, 1935; s. Rafael Wayne and Tillie Alicia (Rakoska) W.; m. Peggy Ann Almekinder, Aug. 25, 1960 (div. 1976); children: April Christine, Anneliese Cay, Theron Mahlon, Kathryn Rose; m. Iris E. Richards, Aug. 6, 1983. B.S. in Chemistry, Bucknell U., 1957; Ph.D. in Psychology, U. Rochester, 1961. Instr. in psychology U. Mass., Amherst, 1961-64; asst. prof. Valparaiso U., Ind., 1964-66, assoc. prof., 1966-67; assoc. prof. SUNY-Oswego, 1967-72, prof., 1972—; guest prof. U. Saarland, Saarbruecken, Fed. Republic Germany, 1973-74, 81. Contbr. articles to profl. jours. Elder Faith Luth. Ch., Cicero, N.Y., 1985-88. Recipient Richard Merton Stipend German Research Soc., 1973-74; Saarland Friends of Univ. fellow, 1972; NSF grantee, N.Y. State grantee; recipient Fulbright Research award U. Giessen, Fed. Republic of Germany, 1989. Mem. Eastern Psychol. Assn., Midwestern Psychol. Assn., German Soc. for Sci. Study of Border Sci., Parapsychol. Assn., Psychonomic Soc., Sigma Xi. Democrat. Lutheran. Avocations: history, phrenology, psychic animals, Saarland history. Home: 3720 Black Brant Dr Liverpool NY 13090-1060 Office: SUNY Dept Psychology Oswego NY 13126

WAGNER, MARVIN, general and vascular surgeon, educator; b. Milw., Feb. 20, 1919; s. Benjamin and Ella (Drotman) W.; m. Shirley Semon; children: Terry, Jeffrey, Penny. MD, Marquette U., 1944, MS, 1951. Diplomate Am. Bd. Surgery. Intern Mt. Sinai Med. Ctr., Milw., 1944-45, jr. and sr. resident in surgery, 1945-46, 47-50; pvt. practice Milw., 1950—; mem. staff Columbia, Milw. Children's, Milwaukee County Gen., St. Joseph's, VA, Froedtery Meml. Luth. hosps., Good Samaritan Med. Ctr., Sinai-Samaritan Ctr.; chmn., chief dept. surgery St. Michael's Hosp., 1965-69, pres. med. staff, 1981-82; vascular cons. Trinity Meml. Hosp., Waukesha (Wis.) Meml. Hosp.; clin. prof. surgery, adj. prof. anatomy Med. Coll. Wis., Milw.; mem. occupational adv. com. Milw. Area Tech. Coll., 1982-83; lectr., condr. workshops, site visitor in field; also others. Author: (with T. Lawson) Segmental Anatomy: Applications to Clinical Medicine, 1982 (Most Outstanding Book in Health Scis. award Assn. Am. Pubs. 1982), Atlas of Chest Imaging; contbr. over 85 articles to med. jours. including Surgery, Wis. Med. Jour., Am. Jour. Obstet. Surg. Gynecology, Modern Medicine, AMA Archives Surgery, Marquette Med. Rev., Am. Jour. Gastroenterology, Surg. Gynecology and Obstetrics, Sci., Transplantation Bull., Angiology, Abdominal Surgery, Am. Jour. Surgery, Archives Surgery, Jour. AMA. Mem. United Way Corp., 1975-78; chmn. physicians div. United Fund, 1972, bd. dirs., 1973-76, chmn. profl. div., 1973, co-chmn. doctor's div., 1977; mem. agy. facilities rev. com. and steering com. Southeastern Wis. Health Systems Agy., 1976-77; mem. adlumni fund raising com. Marquette U., 1971-72; mem. fund rasing com. project 75, Med. Coll. Wis., 1975-76. Recipient Disting. Svc. award Med. Coll. Wis., 1980, Alumnus of Yr. award, 1985, citation Milw. County Bd. Supervisors, 1988; Marvin Wagner endowed chair in anatomy and cellular biology named in his honor, 1988-91; grantee Am. Heart Assn., 1957-59, Milw. Cancer Soc., 1959-60, Wis. Heart Assn., 1960, USPHS, 1960-62, 86-89, NIH, 1960-62, Taitel, 1961, 62, 64, 65, 66, 3M Corp., 1968, Med. Coll. Wis., 1972, Winters Rsch. Found., 1976-80, McMillan Pub. Co., 1979-82, Tisshberg Found., 1985. Fellow ACS (sci. exhibit award 1957, 70); mem. AAUP, AMA (Physician's recognition award 1980-85, 89), Am. Assn. Anatomists, Cen. Surg. Soc., Collegium Internat. Chirurglae Digestivae, Soc. for Surgery Alimentary Tract, Am. Assn. Clin. Anatomists, Milw. Acad. Medicine, Milw. Acad. Surgery (coun. 1973-76), N.Y. Acad. Scis., Western Surg. Assn., Wis. Heart Assn., Wis. Surg. Soc. (coun. 1973-76), Med. Soc. Milwaukee County (pres. 1975, President's citation 1975), Alpha Omega Alpha. Office: Med Coll Wis Anatomy and Cellular Biology 8701 W Watertown Plank Rd Milwaukee WI 53226-3548

WAGNER, MURIEL GINSBERG, nutrition therapist; b. N.Y.C., Apr. 6, 1926; d. Irving A. and Anna Ginsberg; divorced; 1 child, Emily Lucinda Faith. BA, Wayne State U., 1948, MS, 1951; PhD, U. Mich., 1982. Registered dietitian. Nutritionist Merrill-Palmer Inst., Detroit, 1951-74; pvt. practice, nutritional therapist Southfield, Mich., 1976—; cons. select com. on nutrition U.S. Senate, 1973-74, Ford Motor Co., Dearborn, Mich., 1975-78, Detroit Dept. Consumer Affairs, 1979—; adj. faculty mem. Wayne State U., Detroit, 1970-80, U. Mich., Dearborn, 1974-79. Author: (cookbook) Tun...ahhh, 1993; contbr. articles to profl. publs. Vol. Am. Heart Assn. of Mich.; also various local and nat. govtl. groups. Recipient Outstanding Cmty. Svc. award Am. Heart Assn., 1990; named Outstanding Profl., Mich. Dietetic Assn., 1974. Fellow Am. Dietetic Assn. (organizer Dial-A-Dietitian); mem. Soc. Nutrition Edn., Am. Diabetes Assn. Office: 4400 Town Ctr Ste 275 Southfield MI 48075

WAGNER, ROBERT RODERICK, microbiologist, oncology educator; b. N.Y.C., Jan. 5, 1923; s. Nathan and Mary (Mendelsohn) W.; m. Mary Elizabeth Burke, Mar. 23, 1967. A.B., Columbia U., 1943; M.D., Yale U., 1946. Intern, asst. resident physician Yale-New Haven Med. Center, 1946-47, 49-50; research fellow Nat. Inst. Med. Research, London, Eng., 1950-51; instr., then asst. prof. medicine Yale U., 1951-55; asst., then assoc. prof. medicine Johns Hopkins U., Balt., 1956-59, assoc. prof. microbiology, 1959-64, asst., then assoc. dean med. faculty, 1957-63, prof. microbiology, 1964-67; vis. fellow, mem. Common Room All Souls Coll. Oxford U., 1967, 76; prof. microbiology U. Va., 1967—; chmn. dept. microbiology, 1967-94; Marion McNulty Weaver and Malvin C. Weaver prof. oncology U. Va., 1984—; dir. Cancer Ctr., 1984-94; vis. scientist Chinese Acad. Med. Scis., 1982; vis. prof. Univs. Giessen and Wuerzburg (W. Ger.), 1983; Cons. Am. Cancer Soc. Mem. coms.; USPHS, NSF, Assn. Am. Med. Colls., AMA, Nat. Bd. Med. Examiners.; bd. dirs. W. Alton Jones Cell Sci. Center, Lake Placid, N.Y., 1982—. Editor-in-chief: Jour. Virology, 1966-82. Served to lt. USNR, 1947-49. Rockefeller Found. resident scholar Villa Serbelloni, Bellagio, Italy, 1976; Macy Found. Faculty scholar Oxford U., 1976; recipient Disting. U.S. Scientist award Alexander von Humboldt Found., 1983. Fellow AAAS (councillor); mem. Assn. Am. Physicians, Am. Soc. Clin. Investigation, Am. Soc. Biol. Chemists, Am. Assn. Immunologists, Am. Soc. for Microbiology (councillor), Assn. Med. Sch. Microbiology Chmn. (pres. 1974), Am. Soc. Virology (pres. 1984). Office: Univ of Va Dept Microbiology Box 441 Charlottesville VA 22908

WAGNER, RUDOLPH STEVEN, ophthalmologist, educator; b. Passaic, N.J., Aug. 5, 1952; s. Rudolph Jospeh and Helen Loretta (Rzucidlo) W.; m. Jean Ann Wagner, June 6, 1981; children: Katherine, Elizabeth, Julie, Christine. BS, U. Notre Dame, 1974; MD, N.J. Med. Sch., Newark, 1978. Diplomate Am. Bd Ophthalmology. Attending physician St. Barnabas Med. Ctr., Livingston, N.J., Univ. Hosp., Newark; intern Thomas Jefferson U. Hosp. of Medicine, 1978-79; resident in ophthalmology N.J. Med. Sch., Newark, 1979-82; fellow pediatric ophthalmology Wills Eye Hosp., Phila., 1983; dir. pediatric ophthalmology Children's Hosp. N.J., Newark, 1983—; assoc. prof. clin. ophthalmology and pediatrics N.J. Med. Sch., 1983—. Editor: Strategment Surgery, 1984. Fellow Am. Acad. Ophthalmology; mem. N.Y. Soc. Pediatric Ophthalmology and Strategment (pres. 1995—). Office: Children s Eye Care Ctr 15 S 9th St Newark NJ 07107

WAGNER, SHELDON LEON, clinical toxicologist, agricultural chemistry educator; b. Merrill, Wis., Apr. 4, 1929; s. Louis and Frieda (Charne) W.; m. Linda Wessel, May 28, 1960; children: Diane, Deborah. BS, U. Wis., 1954, MD, 1957. Intern Wayne County Hosp., Detroit, 1957-58; resident VA Rsch. Hosp., Chgo., 1958-61; fellow Northwestern U., Chgo., 1961-63; pvt. practice physician Corvallis, Oreg., 1963-70; prof. in agrl. chemistry Oreg. State U., Corvallis, 1970—; cons. Oreg. Dept. Agrl., Salem, 1970, Oreg. Health Scis. U., Portland, 1978—, EPA, Washington, 1986, Oreg. Health Divsn., Portland, 1979—; adminstr. Nat. Pesticide Med. Monitoring Program, 1986—; assoc. adminstr. Nat. Pesticide Telecom. Network, 1995—. Author: Clinical Toxicology Emergencies, 1984, Acute Health Hazards of Pesticides, 1985, Indoor Air Pollution of Pesticides, 1995; contbr. articles to profl. publs. Mem. curriculum com. Corvallis Sch. Dist., 1968; committeeman Benton County Hospice Program, Corvallis, 1990; chmn. ethics com. Good Samaritan Hosp., Corvallis, 1989. Sgt. USAF, 1946-49. Mem. Am. Coll. Occupational and Environ. Medicine, Soc. Toxicology, Am. Soc. Internat. Medicine, Oreg. Med. Assn., Rotary. Home: 1684 NW Crest Pl Corvallis OR 97330-1812 Office: Oreg State U Dept Agrl Chemistry Agrl and Life Scis 1007 Corvallis OR 97331-7301

WAGNER, TERRY JOHN, family practice physician; b. Barberton, Ohio, Oct. 3, 1967; s. John Dale and Ruth Catherine (Clark) W. BS in Biology, Akron U., 1990; DO, Ohio U., 1994. Resident family practice Akron (Ohio) Gen. Med. Ctr., 1994—, chief resident family practice, 1996—; mem. curriculum com. West Side Family Practice, Akron, 1995—. Mem. Am. Acad. Family Physicians. Home: 280 W Heatherwood Barberton OH 44203 Office: West Side Family Practice 400 Wabash Ave Akron OH 44307

WAGNER, WILLIAM EDWARD, surgeon; b. Beech Grove, Ind., Dec. 2, 1946; s. Wilbur Edward and Eva Elizabeth (Johnson) W.; m. Marilyn Kay Higgins, Nov. 22, 1974; children: Michael William, Jennifer Lynn. BA, U. Kans., 1968; MD, U. Tex., Galveston, 1972. Diplomate Am. Bd. Surgery. Resident in surgery U. S.D., Yankton and Sioux Falls, 1973-78; pvt. practice, Marshall, Minn., 1980—; chief staff Weiner Meml. Med. Ctr., Marshall, 1988-90; bd. dirs. Affiliated Cmty. Med. Ctrs., Willmar, Minn., 1991-94. Vol. team physician Marshall H.S., 1980—, S.W. State U., Marshall, 1980—; prin. cellist S.W. Minn. Orch., Marshall, 1980—; lay reader, chalice bearer Episcopal Diocese of Minn., St. Paul, 1987—. Maj. M.C., U.S. Army, 1978-80. Fellow ACS (pres. Minn. chpt. 1991-92); mem. AMA, Minn. Med. Assn., Minn. Surg. Soc. (pres. 1992-93, presenter, lectr. in field), Lyon-Lincoln Med. Soc. (pres., sec. 1980-82), Rotary. Republican. Office: Affiliated Cmty Med Ctrs 300 S Bruce Marshall MN 56258

WAGONER, DALE EUGENE, geneticist, educator; b. Niagara Falls, N.Y., Oct. 12, 1936; s. Harvey Eugene and Jessie Gladys (Sare) W.; m. Lorraine Joyce Samuel, Dec. 10, 1974; children: Lisa Michele, Libra Marie, Justin Dale. AB in Music, Ind. U., 1959, AB in Zoology, 1959, MA in Zoology, 1964, PhD in Genetics, 1965. Sr. rsch. scientist Metabolism and Radiation Rsch. Lab, Entomology Rsch. Div., USDA, Fargo, N.D., 1964-75; prof. biology Maharishi Internat. U., Fairfield, Iowa, 1975-83; self employed Sarasota, Fla., 1983-88; tchg. lab specialist New Coll. U. South Fla., Sarasota, 1988-91, sr. tchg. lab. specialist, 1991-93; asst. in natural scis. New Coll. U. South Fla., 1993—; asst./assoc. prof., grad. faculty N.D. State U., Fargo, N.D., 1968-75. Contbr. articles to profl. jours. Granted predoctoral fellowship, Nat. Inst. Health, Bloomington, In., 1960-64. Mem. Am. Genetics Assn., Sigma Xi. Home: 4427 Violet Ave Sarasota FL 34233-1826 Office: U South Fla 5700 N Tamiami Trl Sarasota FL 34243-2146

WAGONFELD, JAMES B., gastroenterologist; b. Bronx, N.Y., Jan. 30, 1946; m. Judith Wagonfeld; children: Temira Lital, Ariella Lirit. BA, NYU, 1966; MD, U. Health Scis., Chgo., 1970. Diplomate Nat. Bd. Med. Examiners, Am. Bd. Internal Medicine, Am. Bd. Internal Med. subsplt. gastroenterology cert.; lic. M.D. Ill., Oreg., Wash. Med. intern Duke U. Med. Ctr., Durham, N.C., 1970-71; jr. asst. resident in medicine U. Chgo. Hosps. and Clinics, 1971-72, sr. asst. resident in medicine, 1972-73, NIH fellow in gastroenterology, 1973-75, instr. medicine, 1975-76; asst. prof. medicine U. Oreg. Health Scis. Ctr., Portland, 1976-78; attending physician Portland VA Hosp., 1976-78; pvt. practice Digestive Disease Consultants, Inc. P.S., Tacoma; dir. gastrointestinal study unit Allenmore Hosp., Tacoma, 1979-93, Tacoma Gen. Hosp., 1987—; co-dir. gastrointestinal diagnostic nit St. Joseph Hosp. and Health Care Ctr., 1988-90; cons. FDA panel on rev. of vitamins, minerals, and hematinic drug products, 1974-75. Contbr. articles to profl. jours. Physician Benita Juarez Clinic, Chgo., 1971-73, Cardiac Rehab. Program Tacoma-Pierce County Family YMCA, 1980-84; advisor Portlan dAssn. for Childbirth Edn., 1976-78, RESOLVE, An Advocacy Orgn. for Infertile Couples, 1976-78, Colon Cancer Screening in Sr. Citizens, Multinomah County Pub. Health Dept. and Southwest Wash. Health Dist., 1977-78; scientific advisor Shaw Meml. Lecture series, Oreg. Med. Assn., 1977-78; bd. med. advisors Pacific Northwest Soc. of Gastrointestinal Assts., 1982; trustee Charles Wright Acad., 1984-87, chmn. devel. com., 1985-87, chmn. edn. fund, 1985-86. Recipient NIH rsch. award, 1975-76. Fellow ACP, Am. Coll. Gastroenterology; mem. AMA, Am. Gastroenterologic Assn., Am. Soc. for Gastrointestinal Endoscopy, Pacific Northwest Endoscopy Soc., The Wilderness Med. Soc., Wash. State Med. Assn., Med. Soc. Pierce County, Alpha Omega Alpha. Office: Digestive Disease Cons 1901 S Union #B-4006 Tacoma WA 98405

WAGSHUL, ALAN MICHAEL, neurologist; b. Bklyn., Apr. 20, 1941; s. David Lieb and Rose (Pfeiffer) W.; m. Marilyn Jane Abbott, May 27, 1966; children: Joelle Alyse, Bradley Scott. BS cum laude, Bklyn. Coll., 1962; MD, SUNY, Buffalo, 1966. Diplomate Am. Bd. Psychiatry and Neurology. Intern Ben Taub Gen. Hosp. and VA Hosp., Houston, 1966-67; resident in neurology E.J. Meyer Meml. Hosp., Buffalo, 1967-68, Jackson Meml. Hosp., Miami, Fla., 1968-70; intern Baylor U., 1966-67; neurologist Neurol. Cons., Miami, Fla., 1972—; bd. dirs., bd. dirs. devel. South Miami (Fla.) Hosp., 1988-93; ct. apptd. arbitrator Cir. Ct. Dade County, Fla., 1985—. Maj. USAF, 1970-72. Mem. AMA, Fla. Med. Assn., Dade County Med. Assn., Fla. Soc. Neurologists, Soc. Computerized Tomography and Neuroimaging, So. Med. Assn. Office: Neurologic Cons 7330 SW 62d Pl South Miami FL 33143

WAHL, RICHARD LEO, radiologist, educator, nuclear medicine researcher; b. Iowa, July 13, 1952; s. Max Henry and Josephine Elizabeth (Hogan) W.; m. Sandra K. Moeller, June 28, 1975; children: Daniel, Matthew, Peter, Katherine. BA in Chemistry, Wartburg Coll., 1970-74; MD, Washington U., St. Louis, 1974-78. Intern U. Calif., San Diego, 1978-79; resident in Radiology Mallinckrodt Inst. Washington U., 1979-82; fellow in nuclear medicine and immunology Washington U., St. Louis, 1982-83; asst. prof. U. Mich. Med. Ctr., Ann Arbor, 1983-87, assoc. prof., 1987-90, prof., 1990—; mem. exptl. immunology study sect. NIH, Bethesda, Md., 1990-94. Contbr. 100 articles to profl. jours., chpts. to books. Recipeint Jerome W. Conn rsch. award U. Mich., 1989; rsch. grantee NIH, ACS, 1985—. Mem. AMA, Soc. Nuclear Medicine (Marc Tetalman award 1986, Berson and Yalow rsch. award 1992, Hounsfield rsch. award 1992), Radiol. Soc. N.Am., Am. Soc. for Clin. Investigation, Am. Assn. for Cancer Rsch., Am. Coll. Nuclear Physicians. Office: U Mich Med Ctr 1500 E Med Ctr Dr Ann Arbor MI 48109-0001*

WAHL, STEVEN ALAN, podiatric physician and surgeon; b. Jersey City, Mar. 27, 1953; s. Harold Irving and Libby Rose (Stiskin) W.; m. Jordanna Kyle Lenter, Feb. 2, 1990. BS in Biology, Upsala Coll., 1975, Ill. Coll. Podiatric Medicine, 1979; D Podiatric Medicine, Ill. Coll. Podiatric Medicine, 1979. Diplomate Nat. Bd. Podiatry Examiners; lic. podiatrist, N.J., Pa. With Ill. Coll. Podiatric Medicine Clinic, Chgo., 1976-78, 78; podiatrist Mt. Sinai Hosp., Englewood Health Ctr., Henrotin Hosp., Chgo., 1978—; asst. chief resident dept. surgery div. podiatry Coney Island Hosp., Bklyn., 1979-80; pvt. practice, Paterson, N.J., 1980-81, Englewood, N.J., 1980-81, Millburn, N.J., 1981—; clin. instr., attending podiatry staff, asst. chief dept. St. Michael's Med. Ctr., Newark, 1987—; mem. adj. clin. faculty Pa. Coll. Podiatric Medicine, Phila.; mem. exec. com. div. podiatry West Essex Gen. Hosp., Livingston, N.J., 1983-88; attending podiatry staff Roseland (N.J.) Surg. Ctr.; former attending Irvington Gen., South Bergen, No. Community, Bergen Pines, Barnet hosps.; former editorial cons. Current Podiatry; former cons. Wood Crest Ctr. Nursing Home, Camp Nejeda. Podiatric screener Health Fair, Millburn and Maplewood Twps., 1981—. Fellow Am. Soc. Podiatric Medicine, Am. Acad. Podiatric Microsurgery (charter), Am. Assn. Hosp. Podiatrists; mem. APHA, Am. Podiatric Med. Assn., Am. Coll. Podopediatrics (assoc.), Am. Acad. Podiatric Sports Medicine (assoc.), N.J. Podiatric Med. Soc. (ho. of dels. ea. div. 1982-85, pres. 1984-85), N.J. Pub. Health Assn., Am. Physicians Fellowship for Medicine in Israel, N.Y. Acad. Scis., Ill. Coll. Podiatric Medicine Alumni Assn., Upsala Coll. Alumni Assn., Nat. Honor Soc., Beta Beta Beta. Office: 120 Millburn Ave Ste 205 Millburn NJ 07041-1935

WAHLERS, THORSTEN, thoracic and cardiovascular surgeon, educator; b. Germany, Feb. 8, 1958; married; 2 children. Grad. in Basic Med. Sci., U. Dusseldorf, Germany, 1979; grad. in Clin. Medicine, U. Cologne, Germany, 1983. Diplomate German Bd. Surgery. Resident in thoracic and cardiovascular surgery Hannover Med. Sch., 1983-84, resident in traumatology, 1985-86, resident in gen. surgery, 1987-89, resident in cardiothoracic surgery, 1989-90, staff surgeon div. thoracic and cardiovascular surgery, 1989—, assoc. co-dir. transplantation program, 1989—. Recipient fellowship Harefield Hosp., 1986-87. Mem. German Soc. for Thoracic and Cardiovascular Surgery (Ethicon prize 1992, Franz Köhler prize 1993), German Surg. Soc., Internat. Soc. for Heart and Lung Transplantation (Pres.'s award 1989), European Soc. for Heart and Lung Transplantation, German Soc. Transplant Ctrs. Home: Lahriede 74, 30916 Isernhagen Germany Office: Med Sch Hannover, Dept Thoracic Surgery, 30623 Hannover Germany

WAHLI, WALTER ARTHUR, biology educator; b. Moutier, Berne, Switzerland, May 23, 1946; s. Ernest and Jeannette (Portenier) W.; m. Marguerite Eicher, Oct. 12, 1968; children: Olivier, Isaline, Muriel. Tchr. diploma, Ecole normale d'instituteurs, Porrentruy, 1967; biology diploma, U. Berne, 1975, PhD, 1977. Tchr. Ecole primaire de Corcelles, Switzerland, 1967-69; biology tchr. Gymnase francais de Bienne, Switzerland, 1972-73; asst. U. Berne, 1973-77; postdoctoral fellow dept. embryology Carnegie Instn. of Washington, Balt., 1977-78; vis. fellow NIH, Nat. Cancer Inst., Bethesda, Md., 1978-79, vis. assoc., 1979-80; prof. biology U. Lausanne, Switzerland, 1980—, dir. Inst. Animal Biology, 1980—. Mem. editl. bd. Molecular and Cellular Endocrinology,1993—, Molecular Endocrinology, 1994—; corr. editor Procs. of Royal Soc. London, 1990-93; mem. adv. bd. European Jour. Biochemistry, 1996—. Elected to Inst. Jurassien des Scis., des Lettres et des Arts, 1987. Home: Chemin du Baillon, CH-1112 Echichens Switzerland Office: U Lausanne, Inst Animal Biology, Bâtiment de Biologie, CH-1015 Lausanne Switzerland

WAINERDI, RICHARD ELLIOTT, medical center executive; b. N.Y.C., Nov. 27, 1931; s. Harold Roule and Margaret (Greenhut) W.; m. Angela Lampone, June 2, 1956; children: Thomas Joseph, James Cooper. B.S. in Petroleum Engring, Okla. U., 1952; M.S., Pa. State U., 1955, Ph.D., 1958. Registered profl. engr., Tex. Research asst., fellow petroleum engring. Pa. State U., 1953-55; mem. faculty Tex. A. and M. U., College Station, 1957-77; prof. chem. engring. Tex. A. and M. U., 1961-77, assoc. v.p. acad. affairs, 1974-77, also founder, head activation analysis lab., 1957-77; sr. v.p. 3D/Internat., Houston, 1977-82; coord. nuclear activities Dresser Industries Inc., Dallas, 1956-57; head Nuclear Sci. Ctr. Tex. Engring. Expt. Sta., 1957-59; pres. Gulf Research & Devel. Co. div. Gulf Oil Corp., Houston, 1982-84; pres., chief exec. officer Tex. Med. Ctr., Houston, 1984—. Author: Modern Methods of Geochemical Analysis, 1971; regional editor: Internat. Jour. Radioanalytical Chemistry; contbg. editor: Producers Monthly, 1957-69; assoc. editor: Radiochemical and Radioanalytical Letters; mem. editorial adv. bd. Talanta jour., 1969; contbr. to profl. jours. Served with USAF, 1952-53. Recipient 1st pl. presentation award Am. Inst. Chem. Engrs. and Chem. Inst. Can., 1961, faculty disting. rsch. award Tex. A. and M. U., 1962, George Hevesy medal, 1977, others. Mem. Am. Nuclear Soc. (chmn. isotopes and radiation divsn. 1964), Internat. Union Pure and Aplied Chemistry (chmn. com. on analytical radiochemistry), Am. Chem.. Soc., River Oaks Country Club, Ramada Club, Sigma Xi, Tau Beta Pi, Phi Kappa Phi, Sigma Tau, Pi Epsilon Tau, Phi Eta Sigma. Office: Tex Med Ctr 406 Jesse H Jones Libr Bldg Houston TX 77030

WAISMAN, JERRY, pathologist, educator; b. Borger, Tex., Sept. 14, 1934; s. Sammie and Lillie W.; m. Jane B. Atkins, June 15, 1958 (div. 1985); children: Eric A., Nina A. A., John C.; m. Lenore V. Gale, Mar. 24, 1990. BA, U. Tex., 1956; MD, U. Tex., Galveston, 1960. Diplomate Am. Bd. Pathology. Intern medicine SUNY, Bklyn., 1960-61; resident pathology U. Utah, Salt Lake City, 1961-62, fellow pathology, 1964-66, instr. pathology, 1967-68; asst. prof. to prof. pathology UCLA, 1968-81; prof. pathology NYU, N.Y.C., 1981—. Contbr. chpts. to books and articles to profl. jours. Capt. USAF, 1962-64. Mem. Am. Soc. Clin. Pathology, Am. Assn. Investigative Pathology, Am. Soc. Cytology, Electron Microscopy Soc. Am., N.Y. Pathol. Soc. (v.p. 1991), N.Y. State Bd. Profl. Med. Conduct, Coll. Anat. Pathology, N.Y. Pathol. Soc. (pres. 1993-95). Office: NYU Med Ctr Dept Pathology 560 1st Ave New York NY 10016-6402

WAISMAN, MORRIS, dermatologist; b. St. Louis, Sept. 2, 1911; s. Abraham and Dora (Kaner) W.; m. Rachel Katz, Sept. 15, 1933; children: Alice, Margaret, Roemy. BS, U. Ill., Chgo., 1933, MD, 1935; MS, U. Minn., 1940. Diplomate Am. Bd. Dermatology; cert. in dermatopathology. Adj. prof. dermatology U. Miami, Fla., 1958—; clin. prof. dermatology U. S. Fla., Tampa, 1973—. Author: Pharmaceutical Therapeutics in Dermatology, 1968; co-author (with R.L. Sutton) The Practitioner's Dermatology, 1975. Capt. Med. Corps. USAF, 1943-46. Named Practitioner of Yr. Dermatology Found., 1977. Mem. Am. Acad. Dermatology (v.p. 1976), Am. Dermatol. Assn. (v.p. 1981), Fla. Soc. Dermatology (pres. 1953, Outstanding Dermatologist, 1974, 88), Southeastern Dermatol. Assn. (pres. 1970), So. Med. Assn. (chmn. dermatology sect. 1964). Home: 33 Ladoga Ave Tampa FL 33606-3803 Office: 220 E Madison St Tampa FL 33602

WAIT, RICHARD BRUCE, surgeon, researcher, educator; b. Montclair, N.J., Apr. 23, 1950; s. Herman Warren and Mary Naomi (Smith) W.; m. Mary Jean Alster, June 10, 1972; children—Casey, Michael, Robert. B.S., St. Lawrence U., 1972; M.D., U. Vt., 1978, Ph.D., 1979. Diplomate Am. Bd. Surgery. Intern, Med. Ctr. Hosp. Vt., Burlington, 1978-79, resident, 1979-83; instr. anatomy U. Vt., Burlington, 1979-83; prof. and chmn. dept surgery SUNY-Health Sci. Ctr., Bklyn.; chief of surgery King's County Hosp. Ctr., Bklyn.; chmn. clin. practice mgmt. plan SUNY-Health Sci. Ctr., 1994—; pres. Univ. Physicians of Brooklyn, 1994—; cons. Hall, Decker, McGibben Inc., N.Y.C., 1984—. Contbr. articles to profl.jours. Grantee NIH, 1983—. Mem. AMA, ACS, Bklyn. Surg. Soc., Assn. for Acad. Surgery, Soc. Univ. Surgens (exec. council), N.Y. Surg. Soc., Soc. Surg. Alimentary Tract, N.Y. Med. Soc., Soc. Breast Surgeons, Assn. Program Dirs. in Surgery, Soc. Surg. Chmn. Republican. Methodist. Avocations: photography; sports; woodworking. Office: SUNY-Downstate Med Ctr Dept Surgery 450 Clarkson Ave # 40 Brooklyn NY 11203-2012

WAITE, LAWRENCE WESLEY, osteopathic physician; b. Chgo., June 27, 1951; s. Paul J. and Margaret E. (Cresson) W.; m. Courtnay M. Snyder, Nov. 1, 1974; children: Colleen Alexis, Rebecca Maureen, Alexander Quin. BA, Drake U., 1972; DO, Coll. Osteo. Medicine and Surgery, Des Moines, 1975; MPH, U. Mich., 1981. Diplomate Nat. Bd. Osteo. Examiners. Intern Garden City Osteo. Hosp., Mich., 1975-76; practice gen. osteo. medicine, Garden City, 1979-82, Battle Creek, 1982-96, La Crosse, Wis., 1996—; assoc. clin. prof. Mich. State U. Coll. Osteo. Medicine, East Lansing, 1979—; dir. med. edn. Lakeview Gen. Osteo. Hosp., Battle Creek, Mich., 1983-87; cons. Nat. Bd. Examiners Osteo. Physicians and Surgeons, 1981-88; chief med. examiner Calhoun County, 1991-93. Writer TV program Cross Currents Ecology, 1971; editor radio series Friendship Hour, 1971-72. Bd. dirs., instr. Hospice Support Services, Inc., Westland, Mich., 1981-86; mem. profl. adv. council Good Samaritan Hosp., Battle Creek, 1982-83; bd. dirs. Neighborhood Planning Council 11, Battle Creek, 1982-92; mem. population action council Population Inst., 1984—; exec. bd. officer Battle Creek Area Urban League, 1987-91; vestryman St. Thomas Episcopal Ch., 1990-93; leader Boy Scouts Am. Served to lt. comdr. USN, 1976-79. State of Iowa scholar, 1969. Mem. AMA, APHA, Aerospace Med. Assn., Nat. Eagle Scouts Assn. (life), Am. Osteo. Assn., S. Cen. Osteo. Assn. (officer, state del. 1983-96), Am. Acad. Osteopathy, Bermuda Hist. Soc. (life). Avocations: geography, medieval history, genealogy. Home: 2110 Evenson Dr Onalaska WI 54650-8772 Office: Gunderson Clinic Ltd 1836 South Ave La Crosse WI 54601

WAITE, SHIRLEY ELEANOR, retired nurse and administrator; b. Gloucester, Mass., Jan. 4, 1925; d. Walter Dunlap and Ida Estelle (Robinson) Collins; R.N., Truesdale Hosp. Sch. Nursing, Fall River, Mass., 1946; student Miami Dade C.C., 1963-68, Fla. Internat. U., Miami, 1974-77; cert. in nursing adminstr., 1980; m. Horatio Simmons Waite, Feb. 15, 1946; children: Bruce F., Cheryl J. Waite Kapit, Charles W., David W., Gayle I.W. Molnar. Staff nurse, St. Luke's Hosp., New Bedford, Mass., 1946; nurse premature and new born nursery Union Hosp., Fall River, Mass., 1947-48; supr. Newport (R.I.) Hosp., 1951-52; staff nurse, supr. Jackson Meml. Hosp., 1953-63; supr. Meml. Hosp., Hollywood, Fla., 1964-65; supr., asst. dir. nursing, dir. nurse recruitment Cedars of Lebanon Health Care Center, Miami, Fla., 1966-77; head nurse North Miami Gen. Hosp., 1978; v.p. nursing service DeSoto Meml. Hosp., Arcadia, Fla., 1978-87, staff RN med. surgery, 1987-89; mem. adv. com. South Fla. C.C.; Charlotte Vo-Tech. Sch., DeSoto LPN Sch.; 2d v.p. Cedars of Lebanon Credit Union., geog. rep. Desoto County commn. Future of Nursing in Fla. Contbr. articles to profl. jours. Mem. Nat. League Nursing, Fla. League Nursing, Fla. Orgn. Nursing Execs., Fla. Nurses Assn. Dist. 19 (v.p. 1992-95), Charsoto Council Continuing Edn. for Nurses (pres. 1981-82), Dade County Practitioners in Infection Control (past v.p.). Avocations: calligraphy, philately. Home: 11162 SE Herbert Ave Arcadia FL 34266-7668

WAITES, ELIZABETH ANGELINE, psychologist; b. Rockmart, Ga., Oct. 20, 1939; d. Oscar Louis and Willie (Phillips) W.; children: Nicholas Graham, Emily Diane. AB, Ala. Coll., 1961; PhD, U. Mich., 1965. Lic. psychologist, Mich. Lectr. psychology dept. U. Mich., Ann Arbor, 1966; psychology counselor U. Mich., Flint, 1970-73; psychologist Cath. Charities, N.Y.C., 1968-69; pvt. practice psychology Ann Arbor, 1976—; chmn. bd. Octagon House, Ann Arbor, 1975. Author: Trauma and Survival: Post-Traumatic and Dissociative Disorders in Women, 1993; contbr. articles to psychol. jours. Research assoc. Mich. House Dem. Research Staff, Lansing, 1975; mem. adv. com. Mich. Women's Commn., Lansing, 1978. Mem. NOW. Office: 103 E Liberty St # 208 Ann Arbor MI 48104-2136

WAITKEVICZ, H. JOAN, physician; b. N.Y.C., Dec. 18, 1946; d. Peter J. and Helen (Zakiewicz) W. BA, Goucher Coll., 1966; MD, Tufts U., 1970. Diplomate Am. Bd. Internal Medicine. Intern Rochester (N.Y.) Gen. Hosp., 1970-71; resident to chief resident Lincoln Hosp., Bronx, N.Y., 1970-74, attending physician, 1975-76, chief, Geriatric Clinic, 1977-81; asst. attending physician Montefiore Hosp., Bronx, 1977-81; physician People's Health Ctr., Bronx, 1974-81, St. Mark's Women's Health Collective, n.Y.C., 1974-95; asst. attending physician N.Y. Downtown Hosp., N.Y.C., 1981—, pvt. practice, internal medicine, 1981—. Mem. Am. Coll. Physicians, ACLU, Am. Med. Women's Assn., Internat. Physicians for the Prevention of Nuclear War, Nat. Lesbian and Gay Health Assn. Democrat. Office: 13 East 15th St New York NY 10003

WAJGT, ANDRZEJ MACIEJ, neurologist; b. Warsaw, Poland, Jan. 10, 1942; s. Ludwik and Barbara (Strzelecka) Weigt; m. Anna Wiktorowicz, June 25, 1965 (div. 1976); children: Katarzyna, Michal; m. Urszula Stachowiak, Apr. 4, 1980; 1 child, Maciej. Physician, Sch. of Medicine, Poznan', Poland, 1965, Neuropathologist, 1967, Neurologist, 1973. Lic. MD. Physician dept. neurology Sch. medicine, Poznan', 1965-71, MD, 1971-81, dr. habit of medicine, 1981-84; chief dept. neurology Silesian Med. Sch., Katowice, Poland, 1984—; prof. neurology, chief dept. Silesian Med. Sch., Katowice, 1990—; mem. internat. med. adv. bd. Internat. Fedn. Multiple Sclerosis Socs., 1983—; mem. Country Cons. Bd. for Neurology, Warsaw, 1987—. Author: Diagnostyka Roznicowa Objawow Chorobowych, 1990; inventor in field of neuroimmunology. Fulbright Hays scholar, 1974, 75. Mem. Polish Soc. Neurology (leading bd., v.p. Silesian sect. 1984-87, 90—), Poznan' Soc. of Friendship of Sci., Solidarity, Royal Soc. Medicine. Home: Pietrusinski St 5a, 40-842 Katowice Poland Office: Silesian Med Sch, Medykow St 14, 40-752 Katowice Poland

WAKABAYASHI, TETSUO, physician, educator; b. Tokyo, Dec. 15, 1949; s. Kazuji and Sachiko Wakabayashi; married, June 13, 1982. Student, Tokyo Med. and Dental U., 1969. Med. diplomate. Physician Aoyama Tokyo Met. Hosp., 1976-85; with Tokyo Med. and Dental U., 1975-76, researcher, 1985-93; physician Sangiin Shokuin Shinroujo, Tokyo, 1993—. Active Foster Plan Japan, 1987. Mem. Internat. Diabetes Fedn., Japan Diabetes Assn., Am. Diabetes Assn., Japanese Soc. Internal Medicine. Office: Sangiin Shokuin Shinryoujo, 1-11-16 Nagata-cho Chiyoda-ku, Tokyo 100, Japan

WAKAYAMA, YOSHIHIRO, medical educator; b. Ohgaki, Gifu, Japan, Apr. 30, 1945; s. Mitsuhiro and Toshiko (Sakaida) W.; m. Kikuko Nemoto, 1972; children: Koji, Tatsuji. Office: Showa U Fujigaoka Hosp, 1-30 Fujigaoka Aoba-ku, Yokohama 227, Japan

WAKE, MADELINE MUSANTE, nursing educator. Diploma, St. Francis Hosp. Sch. Nursing, 1963; BS in Nursing, Marquette U., 1968, MS in Nursing, 1971; PhD, U. Wis., Milw., 1986. Clin. nurse specialist St. Mary's Hosp., Milw., 1971-74, asst. dir. nursing, 1974-77; dir. continuing nursing edn. Marquette U., Milw., 1977-92, asst. prof., 1977-90, assoc. prof., 1991—, dean Coll. Nursing, 1993—. Chmn. bd. dirs. Trinity Meml. Hosp., Cudahy, Wis., 1991-96. Recipient Profl. Svc. award Am. Diabetes Assn.-Wis. affiliate, 1978, Excellence in Nursing Edn. award Wis. Nurses Assn., 1989; named Disting. Lectr. Sigma Theta Tau Internat., 1991. Fellow Am. Acad. Nursing; mem. ANA, AACN, Am. Orgn. Nurse Execs. Office: Marquette Univ Sch Nursing Milwaukee WI 53201-1881

WAKEFIELD, DONALD LEE, cardiologist; b. South Bend, Ind., Jan. 11, 1944; s. Wayne Willis and Margaret Ellen (Lefforge) W.; m. Suzanna, Apr. 15, 1967; children: Heather, Elizabeth, Donald Markam. BA, Ind. U., 1965; MD, Ind. U., Indpls., 1969. Intern, resident, fellow Ind. U. Sch. Medicine, Indpls., 1969-76; ptnr. Cardiology Assocs., Lexington, Ky., 1976—. Maj. USAF, 1971-77. Fellow ACP, Am. Coll. Cardiology, Am. Coll. Chest Physicians; mem. AMA, Am. Coll. Nuclear Cardiology (founding mem.), Am. Soc. Echocardiology, Alpha Omega Alpha. Office: Cardiology Assocs Lexington 1401 Harrodsburg Rd A300 Lexington KY 40504

WAKEFIELD, THOMAS WILLIAM, vascular surgeon, educator; b. Toledo, Jan. 28, 1954; s. William Henry and Doris Alice (Antolini) W.; m. Mary Margaret Reas, June 17, 1977; children: Andrew Thomas, Victor Walter. BA, U. Toledo, 1975; MD, Med. Coll. of Ohio at Toledo, Toledo, 1978. Lic. gen. surgeon, Mich.; lic. vascular surgeon, Mich.; lic. surg. critical care, Mich. Instr. surgery Med. Ctr. U. Mich., Ann Arbor, 1984-86, asst. prof., 1986-92; assoc. prof. U. Mich., Ann Arbor, 1992—. Author: (with others) Techniques in Arterial Surgery, 1990, Clinical Ischemic Syndromes, 1990, Textbook of Surgery: Scientific Principles, 1993, Current Therapy in Vascular Surgery, 3d edit., 1995, others; contbr. numerous articles to profl. jours. Recipient Gov.'s award Am. Coll. Cardiology, 1972, 3d Pl. award for Rsch. in Venous Disease, Am. Venous Forum, 1991. Fellow ACS; mem. Soc. Univ. Surgeons, European Soc. Vascular Surgery, Ctrl. Surg. Assn., Frederick A. Coller Surg. Soc. (Conrad Jobst award for vascular surgery rsch. 1982), Assn. Acad. Surgery, Midwest Vascular Surg. Soc., Internat. Soc. for Cardiovascular Surgery (N.Am. chpt.), Western Surg Assn., Am. Venous Forum, Soc. Vascular Surgery, Phi Kappa Phi (grad. scholar 1975). Roman Catholic. Office: U Mich Med Ctr 1500 E Medical Center Dr Ann Arbor MI 48109-0329

WAKELEE, ADAH MAE, microbiologist; b. Conneaut, Ohio, Apr. 6, 1935; d. Walter Ivan and Arleen Louise (Beach) Terrill; B.S. in Med. Tech., Wittenberg U., 1960; m. Robert L. Wakelee. Jr., May 23, 1963; children—Kieth Robert, Kent Walter. Staff technologist, Mercy Hosp. Lab., Springfield, Ohio, 1959-63, Grant Hosp. Lab., Columbus, Ohio, 1963-64, J. Mark Handley, M.D., Santa Maria, Calif., 1965-69; microbiologist Rome (N.Y.) City Hosp. Lab., 1972-79; chief technologist MDS Health Systems Inc. (formerly Lorkim Labs.), Rome, 1980-85; asst. lab. supr. Slocum Dickson Med. Group, 1985—; cons. in microbiology Rose Hosp., Rome, Slocum-Dickson Med. Group, Utica, N.Y. Mem. Oneida County Profl. Adv. Council, 1977, 78; trustee Rome Acad. Scis., 1978—, pres., 1979-81, 92-95; mem. Rome Mayor's Water Com., 1983-85; Cert., registered Am. Soc. Clin. Pathologists; lic. clin. med. technologist, Calif. Mem. Am. Soc. Clin. Pathology, Am. Soc. Microbiology, Mohawk Valley Engrs. Exec. Council (chmn. 1981-82, sec. 1983-84), AAUW (pres. Rome br. 1980-82). Republican. Congregationalist. Clubs: Order Eastern Star, Daus. of the Nile. Determined causes of illnesses, Rome, 1975, Holland Patent (N.Y.) area, 1976; co-author article in field for profl. jour. Home: 123 Glen Rd S Rome NY 13440-1929

WAKEMAN, RICHARD JOHN, psychologist, neuropsychologist; b. Chgo., Ill., Apr. 3, 1948; s. Richard Frank and Leilani Margaret (Wongwai) W.; m. Pamela Anne Bonura, May 26, 1973; children: Jared John, Devin John. BA with honors, Loyola U., New Orleans, 1970; MA with honors, U. of Southern Miss., 1973, PhD with honors, 1975. Diplomate Am. Bd. Psychology; cert. in neuropsychology, La. and Tex. Internship Walter Reed Army Med. Ctr., Washington, 1974-75; asst. chief, psychology Brooke Army Med. Ctr., San Antonio, 1975-80; head of dept. psychology Ochsner Clinic, New Orleans, 1980—; Mem. State Bd. of Examiners, State of La., Baton Route, 1984-85; cons. Dupont Corp., Delisle, Miss., 1986—, Entergy Corp., New Orleans, 1988—, Mobil Oil Co., New Orleans, 1993—. Contbr. articles and editor for prof. jours. Capt. U.S. Army Med. Svc. Corp., 1974-80. Fellow Am. Acad. Clinical Psychology, 1994; recipient Milton H. Erickson award Am. Soc. of Clinical Hypnosis, 1979, 1988. Mem. Am. Psychol. Assn., Internat. Neuropsychological Soc., Southeastern Psychol. Assn., La. Psychol. Assn. Republican. Roman Catholic. Home: 1907 Octavia St New Orleans LA 70115-5651

WAKIL, SALIH JAWAD, biochemistry educator; b. Kerballa, Iraq, Aug. 16, 1927; s. Jawad and Milook (Attraqchi) W.; m. Fawzia Bahrani, Nov. 30, 1952; children: Sonya, Aida, Adil, Youssef. B.Sc., Am. U., Beirut, 1948; Ph.D., U. Wash., 1952. Research fellow U. Wash., 1949-52; research fellow U. Wis., Madison, 1952-56, asst. prof., 1956-59; asst. prof. Duke U., 1959-60, assoc. prof., 1960-65, prof., 1965-71; prof. biochemistry, chmn. dept. Baylor Coll. Medicine, Houston, 1971—, Lodwick T. Bolin prof., chmn. dept. biochemistry, 1984—, prof. biotechnology, 1986-95, Disting. Svc. prof., 1990—. Recipient Paul Lewis award in enzyme chemistry Am. Chem. Soc., 1967, Disting. Duke Med. Alumnus award 1973, Chilton award U. Tex. Southwestern Med. Ctr., Dallas, 1985, Kuwait prize Kuwait Found. Advancement Sci., 1988, Disting. Svc. award Arab Am. Med. Assn., 1990, Supelco Rsch. award Am. Oil Chemists Soc., 1993; John Simon Guggenheim fellow, 1968-69. Fellow Am. Acad. Microbiology; mem. NAS, Assn. Med. and Grad. Depts. Biochemistry (pres. 1988-89). Office: Baylor Coll Medicine Biochemistry Dept 1 Baylor Plz Houston TX 77030-3411

WAKSMUNDZKA-HAJNOS, MONIKA VEVA, science educator; b. Lublin, Poland, May 23, 1950; d. Andrzej and Antonina (Greczek) Waksmundzka; m. Mieczysław Kazimierz Hajnos, July 1, 1972; children: Michael, Agnieszka. MS, U. Maria Curie-Skłodowska, Lublin, 1973, PhD, 1980. Student asst. Med. Acad., Lublin, 1973-74, asst., 1974-80, adj., 1980—. Co-author: Polish-German Agrophysics Dictionary, 1989; contbr. numerous articles to sci. jours. Mem. Solidarnośc, 1981—. Recipient Sci. Group award Min. Health, 1987, 93, Sci. awards Rector Med. Acad., Chromatography Rsch.; scholar U. Vienna, 1982-83. Mem. Polish Pharm. Soc. Roman Catholic. Home: Namysłowskiego 4a, 20-709 Lublin Poland Office: Med Acad, Dept Inorganic/Analyt Chem, Staszica 6, 20-081 Lublin Poland

WALBERG, HERBERT JOHN, psychologist, educator, consultant; b. Chgo., Dec. 27, 1937; s. Herbert J. and Helen (Bauer) W.; m. Madoka Bessho, Aug. 20, 1965; 1 child, Herbert J. III. BE in Edn. and Psychology, Chgo. State U., 1959; ME in Counseling, U. Ill., 1960; PhD in Ednl. Psychology, U. Chgo., 1964. Instr. psychology Chgo. State U., 1962-63, asst. prof., 1964-65; lectr. edn. Rutgers U., New Brunswick, N.J., 1965-66; asst. prof. edn. Harvard U., Cambridge, Mass., 1966-69; assoc. prof. edn. U. Ill., Chgo., 1970-71, prof., 1971-84, rsch. prof., 1984—, external examiner, 1981; external examiner, 1981; ednl. cons. numerous orgns.; external examiner Monash U., 1974, 76, Australian Nat. U., 1977; speaker in field; former coord. worldwide radio broadcasts on Am. Edn. Voice of Am., USIA, Office Pres. U.S., cons. Ctr. for Disease Control U.S. Pub. Health Svcs., 1985-90. Author, editor 49 books; chmn. editl. bd. Internat. Jour. Ednl. Rsch., 1985—; contbr. over 350 articles to profl. jours., chpts. to books. Mem. Chgo. United Edn. Com., also other civic groups, 1971-86; bd. dirs. Family Study Inst., 1987; chmn. bd. dirs. Heartland Inst., 1995. Nat. Inst. Edn. rsch. grantee, 1973, NSF rsch. grantee, 1974, March of Dimes rsch. grantee, 1976, numerous others. Fellow AAAS, Am. Psychol. Assn., Royal Statis. Soc.; mem. Internat. Acad. Edn. (founding), Am. Ednl. Rsch. Assn., Assn. for Supervision and Curriculum Devel., Brit. Ednl. Rsch. Assn., Nat. Soc. for Study Edn., Evaluation Rsch. Soc., Internat. Acad. Scis., Phi Delta Kappa (Disting. Rsch. award U. Chgo. chpt. 1971, cert. of recognition 1985), Phi Kappa Phi (hon.). Lutheran. Home: 180 E Pearson St Apt 3607 Chicago IL 60611 Office: U Ill PO Box 4348 Chicago IL 60680-4348

WALBURN, JOHN CLIFFORD, mental health services professional; b. Marion, Ind., Apr. 6, 1945; s. Rex Raymond and Norma Jane (Clifford) W.; m. Linda Sue Spall, Sept. 21, 1968 (div. Dec. 1987); 1 child, Geoffrey Jacob; m. Mitzi Lynn Johnson, June 20, 1992; 1 child, Abigail Rae. BS, Ball State U., 1969, MA, 1975; JD, I.U., Indpls., 1991. Bar: Ind. 1992. Planner Metro. Planning Commn., Muncie, Ind., 1970-72; dir. adult svcs. Del. County Assn. for Retarded, Muncie, Ind., 1972-76; exec. dir. Fayette-Union Assn. for Retarded, Connersville, Ind., 1976-83; cons. Ind. Protection and Advocacy, Indpls., 1984-86; case mgr. Ind. Dept. Mental Health, Indpls., 1986-87; v.p. Cardinal Svc. Mgmt., New Castle, Ind., 1987—; ofcl. Ind. Spl. Olympics, 1973—; chmn. Ind. Residential Mgmt. Com., 1991—; cons. DLG Cons. and Mktg. Svc., Ind., 1992. Co-author: Feldman/Walburn Habilitation System, 1988; photo, drawing artist, 1978—. With USN, 1965-67. Named Ky. Col., Commonwealth of Ky., 1978. Mem. Am. Assn. Mental Retardation (bd. dirs. 1991—). Home: 1121 Indiana Ave New Castle IN 47362-4620 Office: Cardinal Svc Mgmt Inc PO Box 505 New Castle IN 47362-0505

WALCHER, DWAIN NEWTON, pediatrician; b. Ill., Apr. 7, 1915; s. Jesse Leroy and Lucile Agnes (Newton) W.; m. Emily Jane Jones, Dec. 31, 1939; children—Susan Dair Walcher Reed, David Newton. Student Blackburn Coll., 1933-35; B.S., U. Chgo., 1938, M.D., 1940. Diplomate Am. Bd. Pediatrics. Intern, Ind. U. Med. Ctr., Indpls., 1940-41; intern, asst. resident, then resident in pediatrics Yale U. Sch. Medicine, New Haven Hosp., 1941-44; instr. pediatrics Yale U. Sch. Medicine, 1943-46; asst. prof. pediatrics Ind. U., 1946-52, assoc. prof., 1952-62, prof., 1962-63, clin. prof. health administrn. and pediatrics, 1980-82, clin. prof. pediatrics, 1982-85, clin. prof. emeritus, 1985—; dir. growth and devel. program Nat. Inst. Child Health and Human Devel., NIH, Bethesda, Md., 1963-66, assoc. dir. program planning and evaluation, 1966-69, dir. Inst. Study Human Devel., 1969-78; spl. asst. to provost Pa. State U., 1971-74, sr. adv. for coll. devel. and relations, 1978-80, prof. human devel., 1969-80, prof. emeritus, 1980—; spl. asst. for med. ops. Ind. State Bd. Health, Indpls., 1980-85 ; mem. program com. Nat. Easter Seal Soc., 1969-71; cons. Nat. Inst. Child Health and Human Devel., 1969-74; trustee Nat. Easter Seal Research Found., 1968-76, chmn. bd. trustees, 1971-75. Recipient Disting. Service medal Université Rene Descartes, Academie de Paris, 1977; Disting. Alumnus award Blackburn Coll., 1982. Emeritus mem. numerous profl. assns., including Internat. Orgn. for Study Human Devel. (exec. sec.-treas. 1969-82). Presbyterian. Contbr. articles to profl. jours.; co-editor books, including: Mutations: Biology and Society, 1978; Food, Nutrition and Evolution, 1981. Home: 2610 E 2nd St Bloomington IN 47401-5349

WALCOTT, DEXTER WINN, allergist; b. Greenville, Miss., Dec. 20, 1954; s. Charles DeWitt and Ruth LaFon (Stillions) W.; m. Virginia Shackelford, Sept. 20, 1980; children: Arrington, Winn. Grad. cum laude, U. Miss., 1977; postgrad., U. Miss. Sch. Medicine, 1978-82. Diplomate Am. Bd. Pediatrics, Am. Bd. Allergy and Immunology; lic. physician, Miss. Intern U. Miss. Med. Ctr., Jackson, 1982-83, resident in pediatrics, 1983-85; pvt. practice Oxford, Pa., 1985-91; with Miss. Asthma and Allergy Clinic, Jackson, 1993—; pres. house staff U. Med. Ctr., 1984-85, U. Med. Ctr. del. to Miss. State Med. Soc., 1985; ethics com. mem. North Miss. Retardation Ctr.; rev. physician Miss. Found. for Med. Care; participant vis. clinician program LeBonheur Children's Hosp.; mem. staff Miss. Bapt. Med. Ctr., Meth. Med. Ctr., River Oaks Hosp., St. Dominic's Med. Ctr., U. Med. Ctr. dept. pediatrics divsn. allergy/immunology; spkr. in field. Allergy/Immunology fellow La. State U. Med. Ctr., 1991-93. Fellow Am. Bd. Allergy and Immunology; mem. AMA, Am. Coll. Allergy/Immunology, Am. Acad. Allergy and Immunology, Am. Acad. Pediatrics, Miss. State Med. Assn., Miss. State Acad. Pediatrics, Ctrl. Miss. Med. Soc. (exec. com. mem. 1994—), Ctrl. Miss. Pediatric Soc. (pres. 1996), Alpha Epsilon Delta, Order of Omega, Eta Sigma Phi, Beta Beta Beta, Sigma Alpha Epsilon (pres. 1976-77). Office: Miss Asthma & Allergy Clin 940 N State St Jackson MS 39202-2646

WALD, GEORGE, biochemist, educator; b. N.Y.C., N.Y., Nov. 18, 1906; s. Isaac and Ernestine (Rosenmann) W.; m. Frances Kingsley, May 15, 1931 (div.); children: Michael, David; m. Ruth Hubbard, 1958; children: Elijah, Deborah. B.S., NYU, 1927, D.Sc. (hon.), 1965; M.A., Columbia U., 1928, Ph.D., 1932; M.D. (hon.), U. Berne, 1957, U. Leon, Nicaragua, 1984; D.Sc. (hon.), Yale U., 1958, Wesleyan U., 1962, McGill U., 1966, Amherst Coll., 1968, U. Rennes, 1970, U. Utah, 1971, Gustavus Adolphus U., 1972, Hamline U., 1977, Columbia U., 1990; D.H.L. (hon.), Kalamazoo Coll., 1984. NRC fellow at Kaiser Wilhelm Inst. Berlin and Heidelberg, U. Zurich, U. Chgo., 1932-34; tutor biochem. scis. Harvard U., 1934-35, instr. biology, 1935-39, faculty instr., 1939-44, assoc. prof. biology, 1944-48, prof., 1948-77, Higgins prof. biology, 1968-77, prof. emeritus, 1977—; vis. prof. biochemistry U. Calif., Berkeley, summer 1956; Nat. Sigma Xi lectr., 1952; chmn. divisional com. biology and med. scis. NSF, 1954-56; Guggenheim fellow, 1963-64; Overseas fellow Churchill Coll., Cambridge U., 1963-64; participant U.S.-Japan Eminent Scholar Exchange, 1973; guest China Assn. Friendship with Fgn. Peoples, 1972; v.p. Permanent Peoples' Tribunal, Rome, 1980—. Co-author: General Education in a Free Society, 1945, Twenty Six Afternoons of Biology, 1962, 66, also sci. papers on vision and biochem. evolution. Recipient Eli Lilly prize Am. Chem. Soc., 1939, Lasker award Am. Pub. Health Assn., 1953, Proctor medal Assn. Rsch. in Opthalmology, 1955, Rumford medal Am. Acad. Arts and Scis., 1959, Ives medal Optical Soc. Am., 1966, Paul Karrer medal in chemistry U. Zurich, 1967, T. Duckett Jones award Helen Hay Whitney Found., 1967, Bradford Washburn medal Boston Mus. Sci., 1968, Max Berg award, 1969, Priestley medal Dickinson Coll., 1970, Columbia U. award for Disting. Achievement, 1991; co-recipient Nobel prize for physiology or medicine, 1967. Fellow NAS, Am. Acad. Arts and Scis., Am. Philos. Soc.; mem. Optical Soc. Am. (hon.). Home: 21 Lakeview Ave Cambridge MA 02138-3325 Office: Harvard U Dept Biology Cambridge MA 02138

WALD, NIEL, medical educator; b. N.Y.C., Oct. 1, 1925; s. Albert and Rose (Fischel) W.; m. Lucienne Hill, May 24, 1953; children: David, Philip. A.B., Columbia U., 1945; M.D., NYU, 1948. Sr. hematologist Atomic Bomb Casualty Commn., Hiroshima, Japan, 1954-57; head biologist health physics div. Oak Ridge Nat. Lab., 1957-58; med. rsch. and teaching specializing in radiation medicine and cytogenetics Pitts., 1958—; mem. faculty U. Pitts. Grad. Sch. Pub. Health and Med. Sch., 1958—, prof. radiation health, 1962-91, prof. environ. and occupational health, 1991—, prof. radiology, 1965—; prof. human genetics U. Pitts., 1991—; chmn. dept. radiation health U. Pitts. Grad. Sch. Pub. Health and Med. Sch., 1969-76, 77-89, chmn. dept. occupational health, 1975-76, chmn. dept. indsl. environ. health scis., 1976-77; dir. radiation medicine dept. Presbyn.-Univ. Hosp., 1966—; med. dir. Cllin. Cytogenetics Lab., U. Pitts., 1982—; cons. U.S. Nuclear Regulatory Commn. Office of Nuclear Materials Safety and Safeguards, mem. adv. panel for decontamination of Three Mile Island Nuclear Power Sta. Unit 2, 1981-93, cons. adv. com. on reactor safeguards, 1989-94; mem. U.S. working group on health effects, U.S.-USSR Joint Coordinating Com. for Civilian Nuclear Reactor Safety, 1989-92; cons. USN, nuclear industries and utilities; chmn. radiol. health study sect. USPHS, 1967-71; mem. Nat. Coun. Radiation Protection and Measurements, 1969-81, consociate mem., 1981—; mem. Gov. Pa. Adv. Com. Atomic Energy Devel. and Radiation Control, 1966-84, chmn., 1974-76; mem. Pa. Dept. Environ. Protection adv. com. on low level radioactive waste disposal, 1985—. Contbr. numerous articles to sci. and med. publs. Served to capt. M.C. USAF, 1952-54. Recipient Health Physics Faculty Rsch. award U.S. Dept. Energy, 1992-95. Mem. Health Physics Soc. (pres. 1973-74), Am. Pub. Health Assn. (governing council 1971-73, program devel. bd. 1973-74), Radiation Rsch. Soc. (assoc. editor jour. 1965-68), Soc. Nuclear Medicine (assoc. editor jour. 1959-69), Am. Soc. Human Genetics, Am. Coll. Occupational & Environ Medicine, AAAS, AMA, Internat. Soc. Hematology. Office: U Pitts Grad Sch Pub Health A-744 Crabtree Hall Pittsburgh PA 15261

WALDE, PETER JOHANN, chemist; b. Martigny, Switzerland, Nov. 24, 1956; s. Hans and Adelheid (Sacher) W.; m. Vera Clivio, Oct. 30, 1993. Diploma in chemistry, Swiss Fed. Inst. Tech., Zurich, 1979, Dr.sc.nat., 1983, PD, 1992. Postdoctoral U. Auckland, New Zealand, 1984-85, U. Nagasaki, Japan, 1985-86; asst. ETH, Zurich, 1986-88, higher asst., 1989-91, privatdozent, 1992—. Fellowship Auckland U., 1984-85, Matsumae Internat. Found., 1985-86. Mem. Controlled Release Soc., European Colloid and Interface Soc., Neue Schweizerische Chemische Gesellschaft, Swiss Socs. for Exptl. Biology. Roman Catholic. Home: Kindergartenstrasse 6, CH-5200 Windisch Switzerland Office: ETH Zurich, Universitaetstr 6, CH-8092 Zurich Switzerland

WALDECKER, THOMAS RAYMOND, social worker; b. Monroe, Mich., Sept. 4, 1950; s. Henry Stephen and Martha Louise (Skinner) W.; m. Lilian Marlene Ames, Nov. 19, 1983; 1 child, Sean. AA, Monroe County C.C., 1970; BS, Ea. Mich. U., 1973; MSW, U. Mich., 1977. Cert. social worker. Tng. and vol. coord. Monroe County (Mich.) Helpline, 1970-74; substance abuse and employee assistance svcs. coord. Monroe County, Monroe, 1978-81; employee counselor Kelsey Hayes Co., Romulus, Mich., 1981-82; outreach counselor Flower Meml. Hosp., Sylvania, Ohio, 1983-86; regional mgr. Managed Health Network, Inc., Dearborn, Mich., 1986—; bd. dirs. Southeastern Mich. Substance Abuse, 1981—; mktg. cons. Counseling Associates, Southfield, 1985—. Vice chmn. bd. dirs. Monroe County C.C.;bd. dirs. Monroe County Mental Health Bd., 1986-91. Mem. NASW, Employee Assistance Soc. N.Am. (pres. Mich. chpt.), Am. Coll. Mental Health Administrn., Dearborn C. of C. Democrat. Home: 634 W 9th St Monroe MI 48161-4004 Office: Managed Health Network 23400 Michigan Ave Dearborn MI 48124-1915

WALDHAUSEN, JOHN ANTON, surgeon, educator; b. N.Y.C., May 22, 1929; s. Max. H. and Agnes H. (Stettner) W.; m. Marian Trescher, June 4, 1957; children: John H., Robert Rodney, Anthony Gordon Scarlett. B.S. magna cum laude, Coll. Great Falls, 1950; M.D., St. Louis U., 1954. Diplomate Am. Bd. Surgery (bd. dirs. 1985-88), Am. Bd. Thoracic Surgery (bd. dirs. 1989—). Intern Johns Hopkins Hosp., 1954-55, resident, 1955-57; clin. asst. Nat. Heart and Lung Inst., NIH, 1957-59; resident Hosp. U. Pa., 1959, Ind. U. Med. Center, 1960-62; practice medicine specializing in cardiothoracic surgery Indpls., 1962-66, Phila., 1966-70; mem. staff Milton S. Hershey (Pa.) Med. Ctr., 1969-96; from instr. to asst. prof. Ind. U. Med. Ctr., 1962-66; assoc. prof. surgery U. Pa., Phila., 1966-70; prof. surgery Pa. State U. Coll. Medicine/Milton S. Hershey Med. Ctr., Hershey, 1966-83, 94—, J.W. Oswald prof., 1983-94, assoc. dean and dir. Univ. Physicians, 1993-96, sr. mem. grad. faculty, 1970—, chmn. dept. surgery, 1969-94, vice chmn. med. policy bd., 1971-72, interim provost, dean, 1972-73, assoc. dean health care, 1973-75. Mem. editl. bd. Jour. Cardiovascular Surgery, 1985-93, Jour. Pediatric Surgery, 1972-78, Jour. Thoracic and Cardiovascular Surgery, 1982, editor, 1994; cons. editor Archives of Surgery, 1972-74; contbr. chpts. to books and articles to med. jours. Served with USPHS, 1957-59. Recipient Career Devel. award USPHS, 1964. Mem. AMA, AAAS, ACS (chpt. pres. 1974-75, gov. 1979-85, chmn. adv. coun. Conn. surgery 1992—), Am. Acad. Pediatrics, Am. Assn. Surgery of Trauma, Am. Coll. Cardiology (sec. 1981-82, trustee 1984-89, mem. editorial bd. jour. 1983, assoc. editor 1986-89), Am. Fedn. Clin. Rsch., Am. Heart Assn., Am. Physiol. Soc., Am. Soc. Artificial Internal Organs, Am. Assn. Thoracic Surgery (1st v.p. 1990-91, pres., 1991-92), Am. Surg. Assn. (1st v.p. 1984-85), Central Surg. Assn., Internat. Cardiovascular Soc. (chpt. recorder 1969-74), Pa. Assn. Thoracic Surgery (pres. 1977-78), Thoracic Surgery Dirs. Assn. (pres. 1977-79), Societe International de Chirurgie (membership chmn. 1987-92, treas. 1992-94), Soc. Clin. Surgery (treas. 1971-80, v.p. 1981-82, Pres. 1982-83), Soc. Surg. Chairmen, Soc. Thoracic Surgeons, Soc. Univ. Surgeons, Soc. Vascular Surgery, So. Surg. Assn., Sigma Xi, Alpha Omega Alpha. Home: RR 1 Box 158G Annville PA 17003-9704 Office: Pa State U Coll Med MS Hershey Med Ctr PO Box 850 Hershey PA 17033-0850

WALDMAN, KENNETH ROBERT, psychologist; b. Houston, Aug. 22, 1947; s. Nelson F. and June (Friedberg) W.; m. Karen L. Waldman, July 27, 1986; children: Lisa K., Eric M., Alyson A. Bodai, David Z. Bodai. BA, Washington U., St. Louis, 1969, MA, 1971; PhD, U. Tex., 1975. Psychologist SUNY, Oswego, 1975-76, U. Tex., San Antonio, 1976-87; dir. psychol. svcs., tng. dir. U. Houston Counseling & Testing Svc., 1987—; examiner oral licensing exam for psychologists Tex. State Bd. Examiners Psychology, Austin, 1986—. Mem. APA, Am. Assn. Marriage and Family Therapy (clin. mem.), Tex. Psychol. Assn., Houston Psychol. Assn., Bexar County Psychol. Assn. (pres. 1982-83). Democrat. Jewish. Office: U Houston Counseling & Testing Svc Houston TX 77204-3242

WALDMANN, KATHARINE SPRENG, public health physician; b. Cleve., Nov. 22, 1927; d. Dwight Sinclair and Elizabeth Partridge (Dial) Spreng; m. Thomas Alexander Waldmann, Mar. 29, 1958; children: Richard Allen, Robert James, Carol Ann. AB, Oberlin Coll., 1950; MD, Case-Western Res. U., 1954. Diplomate Am. Bd. Internal Medicine. Intern, then resident in internal medicine Mass. Gen. Hosp., Boston, 1954-57; resident in psychiatry U. Md. Hosp., Balt., 1957-58; instr. internal medicine Georgetown U., Washington, 1958-62; sch. health physician Montgomery County Health Dept., Rockville, Md., 1961-88, disease control physician, 1985—, chief physician, 1985—; med. cons. Green Acres Sch., Rockville, 1962-80, Georgetown Day Sch., Washington, 1974-84; sci. adv. Washington Regional AIDS program, 1993—; satellite prin. investigator Women's Interagy. HIV Study Georgetown U., 1993—. Trustee Am. Heart Assn., Bethesda, Md., 1967-69, Montgomery Hospice Soc. Ethics, Health and Human Svcs. Ethics Com. Fellow ACP; mem. APHA, Md. Pub. Health Assn., Greater Washington Infectious Disease Soc., Silver Spring Garden Club, Alpha Omega Alpha, Phi Beta Kappa. Congregationalist. Home: 3910 Rickover Rd Silver Spring MD 20902-2329 Office: Montgomery Cty Hlth Hum Svcs 2000 Dennis Ave Silver Spring MD 20902-4136

WALDMANN, ROBERT, hematologist; b. Budapest, Hungary, Aug. 17, 1935; s. Gyula and Elizabeth (Vajda) W.; m. Denise Bartz, Dec. 24, 1960; 1 child, Rodena. BS, St. Louis Coll. Pharmacy, 1958; DO, Kansas City Coll. Osteo., 1967. Diplomate Am. Bd. Internal Medicine, Am. Bd. Hematology. From resident internal medicine to staff hematologist Henry Ford Hosp., Detroit, 1971-82; staff Sinai Hosp., Detroit, 1982—; staff Harper Hosp., Detroit, 1986—; staff St. Joseph Mercy Hosp., Detroit, 1982—, chmn. dept. medicine, 1990-92. Bd. dirs. Children's Leukemia Found., Detroit, 1983-86. Mem. AMA, Am. Soc. Hematology, Am. Soc. Clin. Oncology, Am. Osteopathic Assn., Mich. Med. Assn., Mich. Assn. Osteopathic Physicians. Democrat. Jewish. Home: 1288 W Long Lake Bloomfield Hills MI 48302 Office: 43555 Dalcoma Clinton Township MI 48038

WALDMANN, THOMAS ALEXANDER, medical research scientist, physician; b. N.Y.C., Sept. 21, 1930; s. Charles Elizabeth (Sipos) W.; m. Katharine Emory Spreng, Mar. 29, 1958; children—Richard Allen, Robert James, Carol Ann. A.B., U. Chgo., 1951; M.D., Harvard U., 1955; PhD (hon.), U. Med. Sch., Debrecin, Hungary, 1991. Diplomate Am. Bd. Allergy and Immunology. Intern Mass. Gen. Hosp., Boston, 1955-56; clin. assoc. Nat. Cancer Inst. NIH, Bethesda, Md., 1956-58, sr. investigator, 1958-68, head immunophysiology sect., 1968-73, chief metabolism br., 1971—; cons. WHO, 1975, 78; bd. dirs., v.p. Found. for Advanced Edn. in Scis., Bethesda, 1980—, treas., 1988-90, v.p., 1990-92; William Dameshek vis. prof. U. Calif., Irvine, 1984; mem. med. adv. bd. Howard Hughes Med. Inst., 1987-93; vis. com. mem. Harvard Med. Sch., Boston, 1988-94; mem. sci. adv. com., chmn. Mass. Gen. Hosp., 1992-96; cons. HealthCare Investment Corp., Edison, N.J., 1986—. Author: Plasma Protein Metabolism, 1970; contbr. over 570 articles to profl. jours. With USPHS, 1956-58, 59-63, 75-94. Recipient Henry M. Stratton medal Am. Hemotology Soc., 1977; named Man of Yr. Am. Leukemia Soc., 1980; recipient G. Burroughs Mider award NIH, 1980; Disting. Service medal Dept. Health and Human Services, 1983. Fellow Am. Acad. Allergy (Bela Schick award 1974, John M. Shelton award 1984, Lila Gruber prize 1986, Simon Shubitz prize 1987, CIBA-GEIGY Drew award 1987, Milken Family Med. Found. Disting. Basic Scientist prize, Artois Latour Internat. Rsch. prize 1991, Bristol-Myers Cancer prize 1992); mem. NAS (chmn. 1985—), Am. Acad. Arts and Scis., Inst. Medicine, Nat. Acad. Scis., Assn. Am. Physicians, Am. Soc. Clin. Investigation (mem. editorial bd. 1978-80, 83-88), Clin. Immunology Soc. (pres. 1988). Office: Nat Inst Health 9000 Rockville Pike Bethesda MD 20892-0001

WALDRON, ROBERT LEROY, II, physician; b. Carbondale, Ill., Feb. 6, 1936; s. Robert Leroy and Violet Mae (Thompson) W.; m. Sandra Sellers; children: Richard, Robert Leroy III, Ryan, Burton Johnson. AB, Princeton U., 1958; MD, Harvard U., 1962. Diplomate Am. Bd. Radiology; cert. added qualifications in neuroradiology. Intern, Mass. Gen. Hosp., Boston, 1962-63; resident in radiology Columbia-Presbyn. Med. Center, N.Y.C., 1965-68; instr. radiology Coll. Physicians and Surgeons, Columbia U. and spl. fellow in neuroradiology Neurol. Inst., N.Y.C., 1968-69; clin. asst. in radiology Harvard Med. Sch., asst. radiologist Mt. Auburn Hosp. and MIT, Cambridge, 1969-71; assoc. prof. clin. radiology Coll. Physicians and Surgeons, 1971-73; dir. radiology French Hosp. and French Med. Clinic, San Luis Obispo, 1973-80, v.p., dir., 1976-77; assoc. clin. prof. radiology Loma Linda U. Sch. Medicine, 1977-80; dir. radiology Richland Meml. Hosp., Columbia, S.C., 1980-90; chief radiology svcs. Richland Meml. Hosp., 1982-90, trustee, 1990—; prof. radiology U. S.C. Sch. Medicine, Columbia, 1985—; mng. ptnr. Richland Radiol. Assn., Columbia, 1988-90; founder Chilean N.Am. Hosp. Corp., 1989; pres. MedBill; Bd. dirs. Am. Cancer Soc., San Luis Obispo. With USPHS, 1963-65. Recipient grants James Picker Found., Am. Cancer Soc., NRC, Nat. Acad. Scis., Nat. Cancer Inst. Fellow Am. Coll. Radiology, Soc. Internat. Med. Sci. Cooperation; mem. AMA, Am. Roentgen Ray Soc., Radiol. Soc. N.Am., Am. Soc. Neuroradiology, Western Neuroradiol. Soc., Southeastern Neuroradiol. Soc., S.C. Med. Assn., San Luis Obispo County Med. Soc. (pres. 1979), Columbia Med. Soc., Sierra-Cascade Trauma Soc. (pres. 1983-84), S.C. Radiol. Soc. (pres. 1992-93). Republican. Methodist. Clubs: Ivy of Princeton; Wildewood, Capital City (Columbia). Contbr. articles to profl. jours. Home: 1420 Adger Rd Columbia SC 29205-1406 Office: 1814 Bull St Columbia SC 29201-2506

WALDROP, CHARLES WESLEY, physician; b. Murray, Ky., Sept. 15, 1933; m. Margie Whitmer, 1957; children: Charles W. III, Heather. BA, Murray State U., 1955; MD, U. Louisville, 1959; postgrad., U. Miami, 1959-60. Diplomate Am. Bd. Family Practice. Pvt. practice Lancaster, Tex. Pres. Lancaster C. of C.; pres. Lancaster Ind. Sch. Bd., 1971-83; mem. Lancaster City Coun., 1965-67. With USAF, 1960-62. Co-recipient Golden Gather award Lancaster C. of C., 1985; named Citizen of Yr. Lancaster C. of C., 1972. Mem. Am. Acad. Family Physicians (pres. Dallas chpt., 1973), Tex. Acad. Family Physicians (bd. dirs. 1984-88), U. Louisville Alumni Assn. (Dallas chpt. 1973), Sigma Chi. Office: 2700 W Pleasant Run Rd Lancaster TX 75146-1012

WALENGA, JEANINE MARIE, medical educator, researcher; b. Evergreen Park, Ill., Nov. 21, 1955; d. Eugene Adam and Therese Marie (Podsiadlik) W. BS, U. Ill., Chgo., 1978; Diplome d'Etudes Approfondies, U. Paris VI, 1984, PhD, 1987; postgrad., Loyola U., Maywood, Ill., 1981-84. Cert. med. technologist. Med. technologist MacNeal Hosp., Berwyn, Ill., 1978-79; rsch. asst. Loyola U. Med. Ctr., Maywood, 1979-80, hemostasis rsch. lab. supr., 1980-87, co-dir. hemostasis rsch. lab., 1987—, asst. prof. thoracic/cardiovascular surgery/pathology, 1988-94, assoc. prof., 1994—; mem. Cardiovascular Inst., Loyola U., 1995—; cons. in field; lectr. in field; observer Nat. Com. for Clin. Lab. Stds., 1988—; del. US Pharmacopeia, 1990—. Contbr. articles to profl. jours. Named Alumnus of Yr., U. Ill., 1990; NHLBI rsch. grantee, 1989—; recipient Investigator Recognition award, 1993. Fellow Am. Coll. Angiology; mem. Internat. Inst. for Thrombotic Diseases (sec. 1989—), Am. Assn. Pathologists, Am. Soc. Hematology, Internat. Soc. Thrombosis and Hemostasis (sci. and standardization subcom. on heparin 1990-93), Am. Soc. Clin. Pathologists, Am. Heart Assn., Am. Soc. Med. Tech.

WALENTIK, CORINNE ANNE, pediatrician; b. Rockville Centre, N.Y., Nov. 24, 1949; d. Edward Robert and Evelyn Mary (Brinskele) Finno; m. David Stephen Walentik, June 24, 1972; children: Anne, Stephen, Kristine. AB with honors, St. Louis U., 1970, MD, 1974, MPH, 1992. Diplomate Am. Bd. Pediatrics, Am. Bd. Neonatal and Perinatal Medicine. Resident in pediatrics St. Louis U. Group Hosps., 1974-76, fellow in neonatology, 1976-78; neonatalogist St. Mary's Health Ctr., St. Louis, 1978-79; co-dir. neonatal unit St. Louis City Hosps., 1979-83, dir. neonatal unit, 1983-85; dir. neonatology St. Louis Regional Med. Ctr., 1985—; asst. prof. pediatrics St. Louis U., 1980-94, assoc. clin. prof., 1994—; supr. nursery follow up program Cardinal Glennon Children's Hosp., 1979—. Contbr. articles to profl. jours. Mem. adv. com. Mo. Perinatal Program., 1983-86. Fellow Am. Acad. Pediats.; mem. APHA, Mo. Pub. Health Assn. (pres. St. Louis chpt. 1995-96), Mo. Perinatal Assn. (pres. 1983), Nat. Perinatal Assn. (coun. 1984-87), Mo. State Med. Assn., St. Louis Met. Med. Soc. Roman Catholic. Home: 7234 Princeton Ave Saint Louis MO 63130-3027 Office: St Louis Regional Med Ctr 5535 Delmar Blvd Saint Louis MO 63112-3005

WALETSKY, LUCY ROCKEFELLER, psychiatrist; b. N.Y.C., Mar. 9, 1941; d. Laurance Spelman and Mary Billings (French) Rockefeller; m. Jeremy Peter Waletsky (div. 1984); children: Jacob Peter, Naomi French. BA, Wellesley Coll., 1963; MD, Columbia U., 1968. Cert. Am. Bd. Psychiatry and Neurology. Pvt. practice Chevy Chase, Md., 1975-81; co-dir., co-founder Med. Illness Counseling Ctr., Chevy Chase, Md., 1982-95; asst. dir. Stress Medicine Group, Pleasantville, N.Y., 1995—; founder, pres. DateABLE, Chevy Chase, 1987—. Fellow Am. Psychiatric Assn. (Significant Achievement award 1993), Am. Holistic Med. Assn., Am. Soc. Psycho-oncology/AIDS. Episcopalian. Office: Stress Medicine Group 444 Bedford Rd Pleasantville NY 10570

WALINSKY, PAUL, cardiology educator; b. Phila., June 21, 1940; s. Aaron and Bess (Kleiman) W.; m. Stephanie Sosenko, Nov. 27, 1971; children: Shira, Daniel. BA, Temple U., 1961; MD, U. Pa., 1965. Cert. Nat. Bd. Med. Examiners, Am. Bd. Internal Medicine Cardiovascular. Instr. medicine Thomas Jefferson U., Phila., 1973-75, asst. prof. medicine, 1975-79, assoc. prof. medicine, 1979-82, prof. medicine, 1982—; cons. EP Technologies, Mountain View, Calif., 1991-93, Baxter Edwards, Irvine, Calif.,1 988-91, C.R. Bard, Billerica, Mass., 1994. Contbr. articles to profl. jours.; inventor method for high frequency ablation, percutaneous microwave catheter angioplasty. Capt. USAF, 1967-69. Fellow Am. Coll. Cardiology, ACP; mem. AMA, Pa. Med. Soc., Phila. County Med. Assn. Office: Thomas Jefferson U 111 S 11th St Philadelphia PA 19107-4824

WALIZE, REUBEN THOMPSON, III, health research administrator; b. Williamsport, Pa., May 28, 1950; s. Reuben Thompson Jr. and Marion Marie (Smith) W.; m. Kathleen Anne Smith, Aug. 13, 1979; children: Heather, Amanda, Reuben IV. BS, Pa. State U., 1972; MPH magna cum laude, U. Tenn., 1975; cert. exec. mgmt., Boston U., 1978. Manpower planner North ctrl. Pa. Area Health Edn. Sys. The Inst. for Med. Edn. and Rsch. Geisinger Med. Ctr., Danville, Pa., 1975-76; asst. dir. Northcentral Pa. Area Health Edn. System, Danville, 1976, exec. dir., 1976-78; health mgr. Seda-Cog, Timberhaven, Pa., 1978; exec. asst. VA Med. Ctr., Erie, Pa., 1978-81; trainee VA Med. Ctr., Little Rock, 1981; adminstrv. officer rsch. svc. VA Med. Ctr., White River Junction, Vt., 1981-88; mgmt. analyst Dept. Vets. Affairs Med. Ctr., Roseburg, Oreg., 1988-90, health systems specialist, 1990-92; adminstrv. officer rsch. Vets. Affairs Med. Ctr. Am. Lake, Tacoma, 1992-95; EEO investigator Tacoma, 1995—; adminstrv. officer rsch. dept. vets. affairs Am. Lake divsn. VA Puget Sound Health Care System, Tacoma, 1995—; mem. Pa. Coun. Health Profls., 1975-77, Ctrl. Pa. Health Sys. Agy. Manpower Com., 1975-77; mem. Interagy. Coun. Geisinger Med. Ctr., Danville, 1976-78; liaison for rsch. Dartmouth Med. Sch., Hanover, N.H., 1981-88; mem. instnl. rev. bd. Madigan Army Med. Ctr., 1994—; EEO investigator; cons. in field. Recipient Man of Achievement award Queens Coll., Eng., 1978, Student Am. Med. Assn. Found. award, 1975; 1st pl. Douglas County Lamb Cooking Contest, 1992. Mem. APHA, AAAS, N.Y. Acad. Scis., Soc. Rsch. Adminstrs., Assn. Hosps., Pa. State Alumni Assn., Nat. Audubon Soc., Steamboaters, Nat. Wildlife Fedn., Record Catch Club, VIP Club. Home: 1103 25th Ave SE Puyallup WA 98374-1362

WALK, DAVID, neurologist; b. Pitts., June 19, 1958; s. Leonard E. and Florence (Zweig) W.; m. Missy Jensen, Jan. 3, 1987; children: Daniel, Sarah. BA, Brown U., 1980, MD, 1984. Resident in neurology U. Chgo., 1986-89; fellow in electrophysiology Michael Reese Hosp., Chgo., 1989-90; asst. prof. neurology U. Ill., Chgo., 1990—; dir. neuromuscular clinic U. Ill., 1992—. Fellow Am. Acad. Neurology, Am. Assn. Electrodiagnostic Medicine. Office: U Ill Chgo 912 S Wood St Chicago IL 60601

WALK, RICHARD DAVID, retired psychology educator; b. Camp Dix, N.J., Sept. 25, 1920; s. Arthur Richard and Elsie (Roberts) W.; m. Lois MacDonald, Apr. 1, 1950; children: Joan MacDonald Scharf, Elizabeth Walk Robbins, Richard David Jr. AB, Princeton U., 1942; MA, U. Iowa, 1947; PhD, Harvard U., 1951. Research assoc. Human Resource Research Office, George Washington U., Washington, 1952-53, from assoc. prof. to prof., 1959-91; asst. prof. Cornell U., Ithaca, N.Y., 1953-59, prof. emeritus, 1991—; vis. prof. MIT, Cambridge, 1965-66, London Sch. Econs., U. London, 1981. Author: Perceptual Development, 1981; editor: (with H.L. Pick Jr.) Perception and Experience, 1978, Chinese edit., 1987, Intersensory Perception and Sensory Integration, 1981; contbr. articles to profl. jours., chpts. to books. Served to 1st lt. U.S. Army, 1942-45, ETO, 1951-52. Fellow AAAS, Am. Psychol. Soc.; mem. Am. Psychol. Assn., Soc. for Rsch. in Child Devel., Psychonomic Soc., Brit. Psychol. Assn. (fgn. assoc.), Sigma Xi, Vet. OSS. Democrat. Episcopalian. Club: Princeton Terrace (N.J.); Princeton, Harvard (Washington). Home: 7100 Oakridge Ave Chevy Chase MD 20815-5170

WALKER, ABRAHAM LINCOLN, physician assistant; b. Savannah, Ga., June 1, 1944; s. Abraham Walker and Elizabeth (Cooper) Fields; m. Yvonne Theresa Harris; m. Joan Cassandra Blakem Feb 2, 1980; children: Sarah Elizabeth, Jonathan Blake. AA, Harbor Coll., Harbor City, Calif., 1972; AS, Carson (Calif.) Coll., 1974; BA, Calif. State U., Dominguez Hills, 1977; MA, Azusa Pacific U., 1986. Cert. physician asst., Ga. Microbiology technician St. Luke's-Presbyn.-Rush Hosp., Chgo., 1969-70; med. lab. asst. Harbor Gen. Hosp., Torrance, Calif., 1971-74; clin. instr. trainee Charles R. Drew Postgrad. Sch., L.A., 1974; physician asst. to emergency care physician Kaiser Permanente Med. Ctr., Carson, 1974-75; physician asst. to orthopaedic surgery dept. Long Beach (Calif.) VA Med. Ctr., 1975-86, lead EEO counselor, 1984-86; staff therapist Affiliated Counseling Svc., Costa Mesa, Calif., 1984-86; psychol. asst. Parkway Regional Med. Ctr., Lithia Springs, Ga., 1986-87; physician asst. VA, Decatur, Ga., 1987—, physcian asst. in substance abuse, dept. psychiatry, 1989-94, physician asst. in primary care/ambulatory care, 1994-95, physician asst. in orthopedic surgery, 1995—; EEO counselor VA, Long Beach, Atlanta, 1984-92, EEO investigator, Atlanta, 1992—, facilitator's trainer, Decatur, 1993, facilitator of diversity, Atlanta, 1995; EEO backup mgr. VA Med. Ctr., Atlanta, 1994; instr. A-I Defensive Driving Sch., Atlanta, 1992—. Mem. task force Ga. Coun. Child Abuse, Atlanta, 1989—. With U.S. Army, 1966-69. Recipient cert. of appreciation Long Beach VA Med. Ctr., 1986. Mem. Optimists (v.p. Decatur 1992-93, pres. 1993-94). Home: 2812 Rainbow Forest Dr Decatur GA 30034 Office: VA Med Ctr 1670 Clairmont Rd Decatur GA 30033

WALKER, BAILUS, JR., environmental scientist, dean, health facility administrator. MPH, U. Mich., 1959, PhD in Occupl. and Environ. Health, 1975. Environ. health scientist, adminstr. Environ. Health Svc., Washington, 1972-79; dir. occupl. health standard U.S. Dept. Labor, 1979-81; commr. pub. health Commonwealth Mass., 1983-87; toxicologist Sch. Pub. Health SUNY, Albany, 1987-90; prof. dept. occupl. and environ. health, dean coll. pub. health U. Okla. Health Sci. Ctr., 1990—; now prof. Howard U; head U.S. Exch. Mission to Japan, collaborator U.S.-Japanese efforts in occupl. medicine, 1980; mem Physicians Human Rights Mission, South Korea, 1987, Mozambique Health Assessment Mission, 1988, Sec.'s Coun. Health Prom & Dis Prev U.S. Dept. Health & Human Svc., Commn. Study Future Pub. Health U.S. NAS. Fellow Royal Soc. Health; mem. Inst. Medicine NAS. Office: Cancer Ctr 2041 Gorgia Ave NW Washington DC 20059*

WALKER, CLARENCE EUGENE, psychology educator; b. Monongahela, Pa., Jan. 8, 1939; s. Lewis G. Walker and Olga T. Brioli; divorced; children: Chad Eugene, Kyle Lewis, Cass Emanuel. BS in Psychology summa cum laude, Geneva Coll., 1960; MS in Clin. Psychology, Purdue U., 1963, PhD in Clin. Psychology, 1965. Lic. psychologist, Okla. Asst. prof. Westmont Coll., 1964-68; pvt. practice clin. psychology Santa Barbara, Calif., 1965-68; from asst. prof. to assoc. prof. Baylor U., 1968-74; pvt. practice clin. psychology Waco, Tex., 1970-74; assoc. prof. med. sch. U. Okla., Oklahoma City, 1974-80; chief pediatric psychology svc. Okla. Children's Meml. Hosp., 1974-80, dir. out-patient pediatric psychology clinic, 1974-80; prof. med. sch., dir. pediatric psychology tng. program U. Okla., Oklahoma City, 1980—; assoc. chief mental health svcs. Children's Hosp. Okla., 1980—; intern in clin. psychology Riley Children's Hosp., West 10th St. VA Hosp., Indpls., 1963-64; psychology trainee West 10th St. VA Hosp., Indpls., 1963; cons. Head Start Program, Waco, 1968-70, VA Hosp, Waco, 1969-74, VA Ctr., Temple, Tex., 1969-74, Region XII Ednl. Svc. Ctr., Waco, 1971-74, Rusk (Tex.) State Hosp., 1972-74, Bapt. Children's Home, Oklahoma City, 1975-79; rsch. cons. Los Alamos (N.Mex.) Pub. Schs., 1975-79; chmn. div. edn. and psychology Westmont Coll., 1966-68. Author: Learn to Relax, 1975, 2nd edit., 1991, (with P. Clement, A. Hedberg and L. Wright) Clinical Procedures for Behavior Therapy, 1981, (with B.L. Bonner and K. Kaufman) The Physically and Sexually Abused Child, 1988, others; editor: The History of Clinical Psychology in Autobiography, Vol. I, 1992, Vol. II, 1993, (with M.C. Roberts) Handbook of Clinical Child Psychology, 1992; contbr. articles to profl. jours. Fellow APA; mem. AAAS, Southwestern Psychol. Assn. (pres. 1977), Okla. Psychol. Assn. (pres. 1983), Soc. Pediat. Psychology (pres. 1986), Ctrl. Tex. Psychol. Assn. (pres. 1973), Sigma Xi. Office: U Okla Med Sch Po Box 26901 920 S L Young Blvd Oklahoma City OK 73190

WALKER, DONALD WILLIAM, home health care nurse, critical care nurse; b. Ft. Smith, Ark., June 27, 1964; s. Donald Edward Walker and Nancy Coradelia (Simpson) Pigg; m. Barbara J. Jester, May 3, 1986 (div. May 1990); 1 child, Christopher Michael Shane; m. Deborah Jo Hiner, July 26, 1991. LPN, Ark. Valley Vocat.-Tech. Inst., 1988; ADN, Westark Community Coll., 1994. LPN, Ark., Okla.; RN, Ark., Okla. LPN ICU nurse St. Edwards Mercy Med. Ctr., Ft. Smith, 1988-90; home health field nurse Med. Home Health Inc., Sallisaw, Okla., 1990-92; home health aid liaison Med. Home Health Inc., Spiro, Okla., 1992-94; field nurse Med. Home Health Inc., Sallisaw, Okla., 1994-95; home health aide supr. Med. Home Health, Inc., Poteau, Okla., 1995—. Cub scout leader Boy Scouts Am. With USAF, 1982-85. Recipient Achievement medal USAF, 1982-83; Ark. Valley Vocat.-Tech. Inst. scholar, 1987. Democrat.

WALKER, DOUGLASS WILLEY, retired pediatrician, medical center administrator; b. Thomaston, Maine, Aug. 3, 1913; s. Lee Wilson and Eliza Ann (Willey) W.; m. Janet Franklin Stockbridge, Mar. 21, 1942; children: Barbara, Elizabeth, Ann. BS, Bowdoin Coll., 1935, ScD (hon.), 1977; MD, Yale U., 1939. Diplomate Am. Bd. Pediatrics. Resident in pediatrics Yale Med. Sch.-New Haven Hosp., 1939-41, 46; pvt. practice, Laconia, N.H., 1946-63; pres. Laconia Clinic, 1963; asst. prof., asst. dean Johns Hopkins U. Med. Sch., Balt., 1963-67, assoc. prof., assoc. dean, 1967-70; med. dir. Maine Med. Ctr., Portland, 1970-75, v.p. med. affairs, 1975-78, corporator, 1970—; ret., 1978; assoc. clin. prof. Tufts U. Med. Sch., Boston, 1970-78; trustee Penobscot Bay Med. Ctr., Rockport, Maine, 1985-91; incorporator N.E. Health, Camden, Maine, 1985—. Mem. editl. bd. History of Preventive Medicine, World War II, 8 vols., 1955-76. Chmn. child health com. N.H. White House Conf., 1960; mem. adv. bd. So. Maine Vocat. Tech. Inst., South Portland, 1978-84; bd. mgrs. Park Danforth Home, Portland, 1980-82; sec., past pres. Martin Point Improvement Assn. Lt col. M.C., AUS, 1941-46. Decorated Legion of Merit. Mem. New Eng. Pediatric Soc. (past pres.). Republican. Methodist. Home: PO Box 40 Friendship ME 04547-0040

WALKER, DUARD LEE, medical educator; b. Bishop, Calif., June 2, 1921; s. Fred H. and Anna Lee (Shumate) W.; m. Dorothea Virginia McHenry, Aug. 11, 1945; children: Douglas Keith, Donna Judith, David Cameron, Diane Susan. A.B., U. Calif. - Berkeley, 1943, M.A., 1947; M.D., U. Calif. - San Francisco, 1945. Diplomate Am. Bd. Microbiology. Intern, U.S. Naval Hosp., Shoemaker, Cal., 1945-46; asst. resident internal medicine Stanford U. Service San Francisco Hosp., 1950-52; asso. prof. med. microbiology and preventive medicine U. Wis., Madison, 1952-59; prof. med. microbiology U. Wis., 1959-88, prof., chmn. med. microbiology, 1970-76, 81-88, Paul F. Clark prof. med. microbiology, 1977-88, prof. emeritus, 1988—; cons. Naval Med. Rsch. Unit., Gt. Lakes, Ill., 1958-74; mem. microbiology tng. com. Nat. Inst. Gen. Med. Scis., 1966-70; mem. nat. adv. Allergy and Infectious Diseases Coun., 1970-74; mem. adv. com. on blood program rsch. ARC, 1978-79; mem. study group on papovaviridae Internat. Com. on Taxonomy of Viruses, 1976-90; mem. vaccines and related biol. products adv. com. FDA, 1985-89. Mem. editorial bd. Infection and Immunity, 1975-83, Archives of Virology, 1981-83, Microbial Pathogenesis, 1985-90. Served to lt. comdr. USNR, 1943-46, 53-55. NRC postdoctoral fellow virology Rockefeller Inst. Med. Research, N.Y.C., 1947-49; USPHS fellow immunology George Williams Hooper Found., U. Calif. - San Francisco, 1949-50. Fellow Am. Pub. Health Assn., Am. Acad. Microbiology, Infectious Diseases Soc. Am.; mem. NAS, Am. Assn. Immunologists, Am. Soc. Microbiology, AAAS, Soc. Exptl. Biology and Medicine (editorial bd. Procs.), Reticulendothelial Soc. AAUP, Am. Soc. Virology, Wis. Acad. Scis., Arts and Letters. Home: 618 Odell St Madison WI 53711-1435 Office: U Wis Med Sch 1300 University Ave Madison WI 53706-1510

WALKER, FRANK BANGHART, pathologist; b. Detroit, June 14, 1931; s. Roger Venning and Helen Frances (Reade) W.; m. Phyllis Childs; children: Nancy Anne, David Carl, Roger Osborne, Mark Andrew. BS, Union Coll., N.Y., 1951; MD, Wayne State U., 1955, MS, 1962. Diplomate Am. Bd. Pathology (trustee 1982-94, treas. 1984-91, v.p. 1991-92, pres. 1993-94). Intern Detroit Meml. Hosp., 1955-56; resident Wayne State U. and affiliated hosps., Detroit, 1958-62; pathologist, 1962-93; dir. labs. Detroit Meml. Hosp., 1984-87, Cottage Hosp., Grosse Pointe, Mich., 1984-93; pathologist, dir. labs. Macomb Hosp Ctr. (formerly South Macomb Hosp.), Warren, Mich., 1966-93, Jennings Meml. Hosp., Detroit, 1971-79, Alexander Blain Hosp., Detroit, 1971-85; ptnr. Langston, Walker & Assocs., P.C., Grosse Pointe, 1968-93; instr. pathology Wayne State U. Med. Sch., Detroit, 1962-72, asst. clin. prof., 1972-94, assoc. clin. prof., 1994—. Pres. Mich. Assn. Blood Banks, 1969-70; mem. med. adv. com. ARC, 1972-83; mem. Mich. Higher Edn. Assistance Authority, 1975-77; trustee Alexander Blain Meml. Hosp., Detroit, 1974-83, Detroit-Macomb Hosp. Corp., 1974-93, 95—; bd. dirs. Wayne State Fund, 1971-83. Capt. M.C., U.S. Army, 1956-58. Recipient Disting. Svc. award Wayne State U. Med. Sch., 1990. Fellow

Detroit Acad. Medicine (pres.-elect 1995-96); mem. AMA (coun. on long-range planning and devel. 1982-88, vice chmn. 1985-87, chmn. 1987-88, trustee 1988—), Coll. Am. Pathologists (Disting. Svc. award 1989), Am. Soc. Clin. Pathologists (sec. 1971-77, pres. 1979-80, Disting. Svc. award 1989), Mich. Soc. Pathologists (pres. 1980-81), Wayne County Med. Soc. (pres. 1984-85, trustee 1986-91, chmn. 1990-91), Mich. Med. Soc. (bd. dirs. 1981-90, vice chmn. 1985-88, chmn. 1988-90), Am. Assn. Blood Banks, Mich. Assn. Blood Banks, Wayne State U. Alumni Assn. (bd. govs. 1968-71), Wayne State U. Med. Alumni Assn. (pres. 1969, trustee 1970-85, Disting. Alumni award 1974), Econ. Club Detroit, Detroit Athletic Club, Lochmoor Club, Mid-Am. Club, Alpha Omega Alpha, Phi Gamma Delta, Nu Sigma Nu. Republican. Episcopalian. Home and Office: 14004 Harbor Place Dr Saint Clair Shores MI 48080-1528

WALKER, GAIL JUANICE, electrologist; b. Bosque County, Tex., Sept. 3, 1937; d. Hiram Otis and Hazel Ruth (Carmichael) Gunter; cert. Shults Inst. Electrolysis, 1971; children—Lillian Ruth, Deborah Lynn. In quality control Johnson & Johnson, San Angelo, Tex., 1962-70; owner, pres., electrologist Ariz. Inst. Electrolysis, Scottsdale, 1979—; ednl. cons. Gail Walker's Internat. Sch. Electrolysis, Tokyo, 1980; area corr. Hair Route mag., 1981; co-founder Gailshay Worldwide Bio-Tonique and Epluche Skin Care Products. participant continuing edn. program in electrology Shelby State Coll., 1981. Editor Electrolysis World. Cert., Pvt. Bus. and Tech. Schs., State of Ariz. Mem. Ariz. Assn. Electrologists (pres. 1980—), Am. Electrolysis Assn., Internat. Guild Profl. Electrologists, Nat. Fedn. Ind. Businessmen, Ariz. Assn. Electrologists (organizer 1980). Republican. Baptist. Club: Order of Eastern Star. Co-developed Bio-Tonique Skin Care product line, 1990, pvt. label Epluche Skin Care product line, 1994.

WALKER, GRAHAM CHARLES, biology educator; b. Boston, Feb. 8, 1948; s. Charles Bertram and Margaret Elizabeth (Biehn) W.; m. Janet Elizabeth Haliburton, May 30, 1970; 1 child, Gordon Andrew. BSc with honors, Carleton U., Ottawa, Ont., Can., 1970; PhD, U. Ill., 1974. Asst. prof. biology MIT, Cambridge, Mass., 1976-80, assoc. prof. biology, 1980-86; prof. biology MIT, Cambridge, 1986—. Editor-in-chief Jour. Bacteriology, 1991—, editor, 1985-91; editorial bd. Mutation Rsch., Amsterdam, Netherlands, 1982—; contbr. articles to Procs. NAS USA, Cell, Microbiology Rev. Housemaster McCormick Hall, MIT, Cambridge, 1986-92. Margaret MacVicar Faculty fellow MIT, 1992-2002, John Simon Guggenheim Meml. fellow, 1984, Woodrow Wilson fellow, 1970; recipient Rita Allen Career Devel. award, 1978-83. Mem. Am. Soc. for Microbiology, Genetics Soc. Am., Am. Chem. Soc., Environ. Mutagen Soc. Office: MIT Biology Dept 77 Massachusetts Ave Cambridge MA 02139-4301

WALKER, H. KENNETH, medical educator; b. Washington, Ga., Oct. 4, 1936. AB, Emory U., 1958, MD, 1963. Diplomate Am. Bd. Internal Medicine, Psychiatry and Neurology. Prof. medicine Emory U., Atlanta. Author: Clinical Methods, 2d edit., 1988, Medical Management of the Surgical Patient, 3d edit., 1995. Capt. USAF, 1965-67. Office: Emory Univ Dept Medicine 69 Butler St SE Atlanta GA 30303

WALKER, HARVEY CAPERS, urologist; b. Eatonton, Ga., Aug. 25, 1931; s. Frank Anderson and Julia Belle (Dennis) W.; m. Caroline Griffith, Aug. 24, 1954 (div. 1961); children: Harvey Capers Jr., John Griffith; m. Henrietta Clanton, Aug. 21, 1968; 1 child, Valerie Anderson. BS, U. Ga., 1957; MD, Med. Coll. Ga., 1961. Diplomate Am. Bd. Urology. Intern Univ. Hosp., Augusta, Ga., 1961-62; resident in gen. surgery and pathology Med. Coll. Ga. Hosps., Augusta, 1962-63, resident in urology, 1963-66; pvt. practice, Anderson, S.C., 1967—; active med. staff Anderson Meml. Hosp., 1967—, Greenville (S.C.) Meml. Hosp., 1987—, St. Francis Hosp., Greenville, 1989—. Staff sgt. USAF, 1951-54. Fellow ACS; mem. Am. Urol. Assn. Home: 1913 Lynn Ave Anderson SC 29621-2038 Office: 1113 N Fant St Anderson SC 29621-4819

WALKER, JAMES DAVID, physician; b. Watford, Eng., Dec. 9, 1957; s. Paul Hubert and Marion Joan (Farrow) W.; m. Olivia Marie Schofield, July 5, 1986; children: George, Imogen, Fiona, Eleanor. BSc, U. London, 1979, MB, BS, 1982, MD, 1994. Registar The London Hosp., 1983-87; rsch. registrar Guy's Hosp., London, 1987-89; sr. med. registrar St. Bartholomew's Hosp., London, 1989-94; rsch. fellow Juvenile Diabetes Found. Internat. U. Minn. Hosp. and Clinic, Mpls., 1991-93; cons. physician Royal Infirmary of Edinburgh, 1994—. Contbr. articles to profl. jours. Mem. Royal Coll. Physicians of Edinburgh and London, Royal Coll. Physicians U.K., Brit. Diabetic Assn., European Assn. for Study of Diabetes. Office: Royal Infirmary Edinburgh, Lauriston Pl, Edinburgh EH39YW, Scotland

WALKER, JEWEL LEE, health facility administrator, consultant; b. Columbus, Ohio, Jan. 4, 1950; d. Zerold and Frieda Arlene (Tolliver) Sizemore; m. David Walker (div. Sept. 1984). AS, Mt. Vernon (Ohio) Nazarene Coll., 1970; diploma in Nursing, Mansfield (Ohio) Gen. Hosp., 1974; BSBA summa cum laude, Franklin U., 1983; postgrad., U. Dayton, 1985; MSA in Health Care Adminstrn., Cen. Mich. U., 1991. RN Ohio. Nurse Martin Meml. Hosp., Mt. Vernon, 1974-75, Ohio State U. Hosp., Columbus, 1974-78; chief registrar Nurses Profl. Registry, Columbus, 1978-82, cons., 1982-84; dir. nurses Bryden Manor Nursing Home, Columbus, 1982-83; health svcs. coord. Nat. Nursing Corp., Columbus, 1983-86, corp. dir. nursing svcs., 1986-88; pvt. practice nursing cons. Columbus, 1988—; shift dir. Columbus Community Hosp., 1991-95; clin. svcs. coord. Care Connections Inc., Columbus, 1995—; clin. svcs. dir. Care Connections, Inc., Columbus. Callvac, Columbus, 1988, Columbus Arthritis Found., 1988. Mem. NOW, ANA (cert. in nursing adminstrn. 1989), NAFE. Democrat. Home and Office: 1407 Royston Dr Columbus OH 43204-1532

WALKER, JODI LYNN, nurse; b. Hartford, Conn., Jan. 12, 1961; d. Lazarus and Selma (Rome) G. BS in Nursing, U. Miami, 1983. RN. Student nurse VA Hosp., West Haven, Conn., 1982, Miami, Fla., 1982-83; lic. practical nurse Coral Gables (FLa.) Hosp., 1983; RN in neurosurgery George Washington Hosp., Washington, 1984-86; nurse evaluator, marketer New Medico Assocs., Lynn, Mass., 1986-90; case mgr. Kimberly Quality Care, Silver Spring, Md., 1991-92; liaison nurse Inova Home Care, Washington, 1992—. Home: 12912 Cedar Glen Ln Herndon VA 22071-2951

WALKER, LESLIE C., mental health center administrator; b. New Haven, June 23, 1962; d. George Toms and Linda Rose (Mort) Curry; m. John Joseph Walker, Oct. 10, 1987. BA in Polit. Sci., Tufts U., 1984; postgrad., Yale U., 1988; MPH, U. Conn., Farmington, 1991. Rsch. asst. Yale Med. Sch., New Haven, 1984-86; med. quality assurance investigator State Dept. Health, Hartford, Conn., 1986-89, health program assoc., 1989-92; rsch. project coord. Braceland Ctr. for Mental Health & Aging, Hartford, 1992, assoc. dir., 1993, acting dir., 1995—, dir., 1996—; asst. prof. medicine U. Conn., Farmington, 1995—, asst. prof. cmty. medicine, 1993—; prin. investigator Robert Wood Johnson/State of Conn., Hartford, 1995; co-prin. investigator Retirement Rsch. Found., 1995. Adv. bd. North Ctrl. Area Agy. on Aging, Hartford, 1995—; mem. strategic planning com. Hartford Alzheimer's Assn., 1995—. Hamilton fellow in health mgmt. Capital Area Health Consortium, 1993. Mem. APHA, Am. Geriatrics Soc., Gerontol. Soc. Am., Alzheimers Assn. Office: Braceland Ctr Mental Health 400 Washington St Hartford CT 06106

WALKER, L.G., JR., general surgeon, educator; b. Alexander City, Ala., July 26, 1931; s. L.G. Sr. and Madge (Bailey) W.; m. Diane Hathaway Holmes, Aug. 10, 1957 (div. 1972); children: Susan, Lisa, Patricia, Ann, Jane; m. Mary Dianne Melton, Sept. 30, 1972; 1 child, L.G. III. AS, Marion (Ala.) Mil. Inst., 1951; postgrad., U. Va., 1951-52; MD, U. Ala., Birmingham, 1956. Diplomate Am. Bd. Surgery, 1964. Intern U. Va., Charlottesville, 1956-57; resident U. Mich., Ann Arbor, 1959-60, George Washington U., Washington, 1960-62, Emory U., Atlanta, 1962-63; staff surgeon VA Hosp., Iron Mountain, Mich., 1963-64; staff surgeon VA Hosp., Atlanta, 1964-67, asst. chief surgery, 1967-69; pvt. practice surgery Charlotte, N.C., 1969-86; chair dept. surgery Carolinas Med. Ctr., Charlotte, 1986—; instr., assoc. in surgery Emory U. Sch. Medicine, Atlanta, 1964-66, asst. prof., 1967-69; from clin. asst. prof. to clin. prof. surgery U. N.C., Chapel Hill, 1988—. Lt. USN, 1957-59. Fellow ACS; mem. Assn. for Acad. Surgery, Soc. Surgery Alimentary Tract, Soc. Int. de Chir., Assn. Program Dirs. in Surgery, Am. Assn. for History of Medicine, Assn. for Surg. Edn., Alpha Omega Alpha. Baptist. Home: 1053 Bolling Rd Charlotte NC 28207 Office: Carolinas Med Ctr Dept Gen Surgery 1000 Blythe Blvd Charlotte NC 28232

WALKER, MARK LAMONT, medical educator; b. Bklyn., Jan. 5, 1952; s. Philip David and Ann (Boston) W.; m. Alicia Louise Watson, Nov. 1975; children: Kweli, Akilah, Olabisi, Rashanna, Sharufa, Rahsaan. BS, CCNY, 1973; MD, Meharry Med. Coll., 1977. Diplomate Am. Bd. Surgery; bd. cert. surg. critical care. Intern Howard U. Hosp., Washington D.C., 1977-78, resident, 1978-82; instr. Howard U. Hosp., Washington, 1983-85; asst. prof. Morehouse Sch. Medicine, Atlanta, 1985-87, clin. asst. prof., 1987-90, assoc. prof., 1990—, chmn. dept. surgery, 1990-94, program dir., 1990—; developer Morehouse Surg. Svc. at Grady Hosp., 1988-90, Morehouse Surg. Residency Program, 1990—. Developer radio show on health Sta. WCLK, Atlanta, 1985-90; founder Violence Prevention Task Force, Atlanta, 1987. Named Physician of Yr., Atlanta Med. Assn., 1992. Fellow ACS; mem. Soc. Critical Care Medicine, Surg. Infection Soc., Nat. Med. Assn. (William Sinkler award surg. sect. 1992), Assn. for Acad. Surgery, Ea. Assn. for Surgery of Trauma, Alpha Omega Alpha. Office: Morehouse Sch Medicine 22 Piedmont Ave Atlanta GA 30335

WALKER, MARY ELLA, nurse; b. St. Louis, Aug. 23, 1945; d. Earl Earnest and Myrtle Emma (Agnew) W.; BS in Nursing, Tex. Christian U., 1967; MS in Nursing, U. Tex., 1972, PhD, 1976. Staff nurse, asst. head nurse, head nurse Barnes Hosp., St. Louis, 1967-71; staff nurse Brackenridge Hosp., Austin, Tex., 1972; rsch. assoc. U. Tex. System, 1973-74; rsch. assoc. Ctr. Study of Human Resources, Austin, 1975-76, So. Regional Coun., Inc., Atlanta, 1975-76; nurse cons. Tex. Med. Found., Austin, 1976-77; vis. lectr. U. Wis., Oshkosh, 1977-78; program dir. S.W. Rural Health Field Svcs. Program Nat. Rural Ctr., Austin, 1977-78; program dir. Tex. Rural Health Field Svcs. Program, 1979-85; program devel. officer Tex. Office of Rural Health, 1987; health care cons., 1986—; lectr. U. Tex., 1979-85, 87-88; project dir. Health Care Options for Rural Communities, 1989-93, LBJ Sch. of Pub. Affairs, lectr., 1989-91; exec. dir. Tex. Hosp. Trustees Found., 1993—. Mary Gibbs Jones scholar, 1976; Meadows fellow, 1983-85. Fellow Am. Acad. Nursing; mem. ANA, Nat. Rural Health Assn., Tex. Rural Health Assn. (past pres.), Sigma Theta Tau, Phi Kappa Phi. Contbr. articles in field to profl. jours.

WALKER, MATTHEW, III, biomedical engineer; b. Newark, Nov. 10, 1964; s. Matthew Walker Jr. and Ramona Muldrow; m. Kellye Williams, Mar. 13, 1993. BSE in Biomed. Engring. with honors, U. Tenn., 1987, MS in Biomed. Engring., 1991; postgrad., Vanderbilt U., 1991-95, Tulane U., 1995—. Biomed. engr. in tng., rsch. fellow in space medicine NASA, Lyndon B. Space Ctr., Houston, 1982-86; grad. teaching asst. Vanderbilt U. Grad. Sch., Nashville, 1991-92; instr. U. Tenn., Knoxville, 1990; rsch. fellow in surgery Cornell Med. Ctr.-Meml. Sloan Kettering Cancer Ctr., N.Y.C., 1992—. Big bro. Ch. of Christ, Knoxville, Tenn., 1985-87, Evangelism Sunday sch. tchr., Nashville, 1990—; advisor, tutor Black Cultural Ctr., 1987-91; leader, mentor YMCA, Nashville, 1993-94. Recipient NASA Biomed. Engring. rsch. award 1982, Coop. Engring. Outstanding Achievement award, 1987, Delta Sigma Theta Outstanding Grad. Student award, 1990; U Tenn. Engring. Acad. scholar, 1982, James King Acad. scholar, 1985; Vanderbilt U. fellow and acad. rsch. award, 1990, Patricia Harris Nat. Acad. Grad. fellow, 1989-91, Tulane Chancellor's fellow, Grad. Med. Acad. fellow, Exptl. Biology NIDOR Travel fellow. Mem. Biomed. Engring. Soc. (pres. 1982-87), Minority Engring. Scholars (advisor), Master's Music City Swim Club, Nashville Sportsman Club, Am. Physiol. Soc., Student Nat. Med. Assn., Mortar Bd., Alpha Epsilon Delta (pres. 1986-87). Avocations: golf, hunting, fishing, swimming, philosophy.

WALKER, MICHAEL CHARLES, SR., retirement services executive; b. Rochester, N.Y., Mar. 4, 1940; s. Charles Boyle and Evelyn Esther (Young) W.; m. Patricia Ann Camelio, Feb. 2, 1963; children: Michael Charles Jr., Lyn, Lea, Matthew. BA, U. Colo., 1962; MBA, Columbia Pacific U., 1982, DBA, 1984. Adminstrv. trainee Lincoln Rochester (N.Y.) Trust Co., 1962-64, mktg. officer, 1964-68; asst. v.p. Lincoln First Bank of Rochester, 1968-72, v.p., 1972-77; pres. M.C. Walker Co., Inc., Spencerport, N.Y., 1977-80; exec. dir. The Valley Manor, Rochester, 1980-85; pres., CEO Presbyn. Residence Ctr. Corp., Rochester, 1985—; lectr. SUNY, Brockport, 1982-89; v.p., dir. Kilian and Caroline Schmitt Found., Rochester, 1985—. mem. adv. bd. Chase Lincoln 1st Bank, Rochester, 1989-92; trustee Rochester Hearing and Speech Ctr., 1989-95, chmn., 1993-94; bd. dirs. Genesee Region Home Care Assn., Rochester, 1990—, chmn., 1995—; trustee Greater Rochester Metro C. of C., 1981-89. Author: Introduction to Bank Marketing Research, 1969, rev. edit., 1972, Practical Handbook of Marketing Definitions, 1970; contbr. articles to profl. jours. Leader task force Spencerport Ctrl. Schs. Bd. Edn., 1977, 80-81, 85; chmn. Monroe County Svs. Bond Com., Rochester, 1972—; mem. United Way Evaluation Team, 1990-94; mem. bus. adv. bd. SUNY, Brockport, 1993—; mem. N.Y. State Bd. Profl. Med. Conduct, 1993—; mem. profl. adv. com. Self Help for Hard of Hearing, 1994—. Recipient Pres.'s Geneseekers award Rochester Area C. of C., 1979, Innovation of Yr. award NYAHSA, 1989. Mem. Am. Assn. Homes for Aging (various coms.), Am. Mktg. Assn. (pres. Rochester chpt. 1969-70), N.Y. State Bankers Assn. (pres. residential mortgage com. 1975-76), N.Y. Assn. Homes and Svcs. for Aging (various coms.), Ridgemont Country Club, Rochester Rotary. Episcopalian. Home: Spencerport NY 14559 Office: Presbyn Residence Ctr Corp 1570 East Ave Rochester NY 14610-1610

WALKER, MICHAEL JAMES, surgeon, educator; b. Washington, July 11, 1946; s. James Willard and Dorothy Elizabeth (Townsend) W. BSc, U. Toronto, Ont., Can., 1968; MD, SUNY, Syracuse, 1972. Diplomate Am. Bd. Med. Examiners, Am. Bd. Surgery. Intern R.I. Hosp., Providence, 1972-73; resident U. Ill. Hosp., Chgo., 1975-82; surgical oncology fellow U. Ill. Hosp., 1982-83; instr. surgery U. Ill., Chgo., 1979-82, asst. prof., 1982-88, assoc. prof., 1988-89; assoc. prof. surgery Ohio State U., Columbus, 1989—. Contbr. articles to profl. jours. Am. Cancer Soc. jr. faculty fellow, 1983-86; NIH Physician Investigator, 1984-87. Fellow ACS; mem. Soc. Univ. Surgeons, Cen. Surg. Assn., Soc. of Surg. Oncology, Am. Soc. Clin. Oncology, Soc. for Exptl. Biology and Medicine, Am. Assn. for Cancer Rsch. Office: OSU Dept Surg Oncology N904 Doan Hall 410 W 10th St Columbus OH 43210

WALKER, MILDRED ANN, home health nurse; b. Baldwyn, Miss., Nov. 13, 1955; d. Charlie D. Hurd and Helen A. (Crump) Grizzard; m. James E. Walker, Aug. 8, 1974; children: Jay R., K. Jamar. ADN, Northeast C.C., Booneville, Miss., 1975; BSN, U. No. Ala., 1989. Cert. nursing adminstr. Staff RN Magnolia Hosp., Corinth, Miss., 1975-76, charge nurse, 1976-78, head nurse, 1978-82, unit mgr., 1982-89; instr. staff devel. Magnolia Regional Health Ctr., Corinth, Miss., 1989-92; clin. dir. Supr. Home Health & Hospice, Corinth, Miss., 1992—; mem. spkrs. bur. Magnolia Regional Health Ctr., Corinth, 1994—. Adv. bd. mem. Alcorn County Vocat. Program, Corinth, 1989—, Northeast C.C. ADN, Booneville, 1990—, Northeast Ext. Ctr. LPN program, Corinth, 1991—; bd. dirs. Neighborhood Cmty. Ctr., Cornith, 1990-95; bd. dirs., treas. Project Attention, Corinth, 1992—; mem. Leadership Alcorn, 1990; founder, charter mem. Cornith Alcorn Parents Assn., 1993. Mem. NAACP (mem. exec. com.), Miss. Nurses Assn. (nurse educator of yr. dist. 26 1990, home health nurse of yr. dist. 26 1991), Miss. Home Health Assn. (mem. edn. com.), Miss. Hospice Orgn. (mem. ethics com.). Democrat. Office: Supr Home Health & Hospice 3001 Hwy 72 E Corinth MS 38834

WALKER, PAUL CHRISTOPHER, pharmacist; b. Detroit, Aug. 25, 1957; s. Albert and Barbara Pauline (Miller) W.; m. Kathy McCluster, June 12, 1982; children: Lauren Elyse, Jillian Michelle. BS in Pharmacy with distinction, Wayne State U., 1980, Dr. Pharmacy, 1982. Registered pharmacist, Mich. Asst. prof. pharmacy practice Wayne State U., Detroit, 1983-88; clin. coord. drug info. Children's Hosp. of Mich., Detroit, 1983-85, mgr. clin. svcs., 1992—; clin. coord. pediatric svcs. Henry Ford Hosp., Detroit, 1985-88; dir. pharmacy Lafayette Clinic, Detroit, 1988-92; adj. assoc. prof. Wayne State U., 1988—; clin. asst. prof. U. Mich., Ann Arbor, 1995—; instr. Wayne County C.C., Detroit, 1987—, mem. pharmacy tech. adv. bd., 1995—; lectr. in field. Assoc. editor Pediatric Therapeutic Newsletter, 1984-85; contbg. editor: Administration of Intravenous Medications to Pediatric Patients, 3d edit., 1988, contbg. editor and rev. 5th edit., 1995; editl. rev. panel: The Handbook of Non-Prescription Drugs, 9th edit., 1990, 10th edit., 1993, 11th edit., 1996; editl. adv. bd. Pain Management: Patient Education Manual, 1995; reviewer Am. Jour. Hosp. Pharmacy, Clin. Pharmacy, Devel. Pharmacology and Therapeutics, Am. Jour. Pharm. Edn., Annals of Pharmacotherapy; contbr. articles to profl. jours. Bd. dirs. Am. Lung Assn., Southfield, Mich., 1986-90; allocations panel mem. United Way of Southeastern Mich., Detroit, 1989—; bd. dirs. Project Health on Wheels, Detroit, 1990-92, Alliance for Mental Health Svcs., Detroit, 1989-92; ministerial staff Deliverance Temple, 1989—. Grantee Durley Y. Dista Corp., 1981, Plough, Inc., 1983, Am. Assn. Colls. of Pharmacy, 1985, Roche Labs., 1985, Wayne State U., 1985, Henry Ford Hosp. Rsch. Fund, 1987. Mem. Am. Soc. Health Sys. Pharmacists, Southeastern Mich. Soc. Hosp. Pharmacists, Nat. Pharm. Assn. (coord. spl. programs for student assn. 1986-88, faculty advisor student chpt. 1983—), Detroit Pharmacists' Guild, Wayne State U. Alumni Assn. (Coll. of Pharmacy bd. dirs. 1988-93). Office: Children's Hosp of Mich 3901 Beaubien Blvd Detroit MI 48201

WALKER, RICHARD, JR., nephrologist, internist; b. Dayton, Ohio, Sept. 1, 1948; m. Madeleine Ann Walker. BS cum laude, Ohio State U., 1970, MD, 1973. Diplomate Nat. Bd. Med. Examiners, internal medicine, nephrology, critical care medicine Am. Bd. Internal Medicine. Intern medicine U. Tex. Southwestern, Dallas, 1973-74, resident internal medicine, 1974-76, fellow nephrology, 1976-78; staff nephrologist and internist Bay Med. Ctr., Panama City, Fla., 1978—, HCA Gulf Coast Hosp., Panama City, 1978—; pres., med. dir., CEO Panama City Artificial Kidney Ctr., 1978—, North Fla. Artificial Kidney Ctr., 1993—. Mem. AMA, ACP, Soc. Critical Care Medicine, Fla. Physicians Assn., The Bays Med. Soc., Fla. Med. Assn., Am. Soc. Nephrology, Internat. Soc. Nephrology, Fla. Soc. Nephrology, Renal Physicians Assn., Am. Soc. Internal Medicine, Fla. Soc. Internal Medicine, Nat. Kidney Found., Alpha Omega Alpha. Home: 320 Bunkers Cove Rd Panama City FL 32401-3912 Office: Nephrology Assocs PA 504 N Macarthur Ave Panama City FL 32401-3636

WALKER, RICHARD HUGH, orthopaedic surgeon; b. Elgin, Ill., Jan. 29, 1951; m. Wendy Allen; children: Ashley Elizabeth, Blake Allen, Emily Paige. AB cum laude, Occidental Coll., 1973; MD, U. Chgo., 1977. Diplomate Nat. Bd. Med. Examiners, Am. Bd. Orthopaedic Surgery. Jr. resident in surgery UCLA, 1977-79; jr. resident in orthopaedic surgery Stanford (Calif.) U., 1979-81, sr. resident, 1981-82, chief resident, 1982-83; clin. mem. divsn. orthopaedic surgery, sect. lower extremity reconstructive surgery Scripps Clinic and Rsch. Found., La Jolla, Calif., 1983—, co-dir. lower extremity reconstructive surgery fellowship, divsn. orthopaedic surgery, 1989—, assoc. head. divsn. orthopaedic surgery, 1990—; staff physician dept. surgery Green Hosp. of Scripps Clinic, La Jolla, 1983—, chief of staff, 1995—; staff physician Pomerado Hosp., Poway, Calif., 1983-92; team physician San Diego Padres, 1983-86, 95—; clin. instr. dept. orthopaedics and rehab. U. Calif., San Diego, 1983-92, asst. clin. prof., 1992—; mem. bd. dirs. Scripps Clinic Med. Group, La Jolla; mem. bd. govs. Scripps Clin. and Rsch. Found., 1992—, mem. joint exec. bd., 1992-93; mem. joint coun. Scripps Health, 1995—; mem. physicians coun. Scripps Insts. of Medicine and Sci., 1995—; presenter, lectr. in field. Cons. reviewer Clin. Orthopaedics and Related Rsch., 1989—, Jour. Bone and Joint Surgery, 1994—; contbr. articles to profl. jours. Mem. AMA, Am. Acad. Orthopaedic Surgeons, We. Orthopaedic Assn. (program chmn. San Diego chpt. 1994-95, treas. 1995-96, Resident Paper award 1983), Calif. Orthopaedic Assn., Assn. Arthritic Hip and Knee Surgery (charter mem. 1991), Am. Assn. Hip and Knee Surgeons, Assn. Bone and Joint Surgeons. Office: Scripps Clinic and Rsch Found Divsn Orthopaedic Surgery 10666 N Torrey Pines Rd La Jolla CA 92037-1027 also: Scripps Clinic and Rsch Found 15025 Innovation Dr San Diego CA 92128-3409

WALKER, ROBERT DONALD, lawyer; b. Sacramento, Calif., Dec. 4, 1937; s. Charles L. and Sylvia S. Walker; m. Shirley M. Walker; children: Michael C., Catherine D., William C. Student, Dartmouth Coll., 1955-58; BS, U. So. Calif., 1959; JD, UCLA, 1962. Bar: Calif. 1963, U.S. Dist. Ct. (so., cen. and no. dists.) Calif., Nev. 1989, U.S. Ct. Appeals (9th cir.), 1989. Mem. firm Brill, Hunt, DeBuy & Burby, L.A., 1963-68, Belcher, Henzie & Biegenzahn, 1968-74, Harney & Moore, 1974-78, Belcher, Henzie, Biegenzahn & Walker, 1978-85; sole practice, L.A., 1985—. Mem. ABA, Am. Soc. Law & Medicine, Am. Soc. Forensic Examiners, Assn. Bus. Trial Lawyers, Calif. Bar Assn., Nev. Trial Lawyers Assn., L.A. County Bar Assn., Pasadena Bar Assn., Am. Bd. Trial Advs., Am. Bd. Profl. Liability Attys. Republican.

WALKER, WILLIAM EASTON, surgeon, educator, lawyer; b. Glasgow, Scotland, Aug. 7, 1945; came to U.S., 1969; s. William Telfer and Josephine Blair (Easton) W.; m. Mary Fraley Cooley, June 23, 1973; children—Sarah Cooley, Blair Easton, Denton Arthur Cooley, William Easton, II. M.D., Glasgow U., Scotland, 1968; Ph.D., Johns Hopkins U., 1975; JD, South Tex. Coll Law, 1993. Diplomate Am. Bd. Surgery, Am. Bd. Thoracic Surgery, Am. Bd. Vascular Surgery. Intern, resident Johns Hopkins U., Balt., 1969-75; resident Vanderbilt U., Nashville, 1976-79; assoc. prof., dir. div. thoracic and cardiovascular surgery U. Tex. Med. Sch., Houston, 1979—; cons. M.D. Anderson Hosp., Houston, 1979—. Recipient Harwell Wilson award Vanderbilt U., Nashville, 1979. Fellow ACS, So. Surg. Assn., Royal Coll. Surgeons, Am. Coll. Cardiology; mem. Am. Assn. Thoracic Surgery, Coun. Fgn. Rels., Confrèrie de la Chaine de Rôtisseurs, Houston Country Club, Belle Meade Country Club, Cosmos Club (Washington), Krewe of Endymion (New Orleans), Phi Beta Kappa, Sigma Xi. Republican. Presbyterian. Home and Office: 2831 Sackett St Houston TX 77098-1125

WALL, MICHAEL, neurologist, ophthalmologist; b. Flint, Mich., Jan. 4, 1950; s. Kurt Edwin and Harriet Klein (Podolsky) W.; m. Susan Dale; children: Eric Joseph, Kurt Eldon, Brian Martin. BS, Tulane U., 1972, MD, 1976. Diplomate Am. Bd. Psychiatry and Neurology. Asst. prof. neurology Tulane U. Sch. Medicine, New Orleans, 1981-88, assoc. prof. neurology, ophthalmology, neurosurgery, 1988-91, prof. neurology and ophthalmology, 1991; assoc. prof. neurology and ophthalmology U. Iowa, Iowa City, 1991-96, prof. neurology and ophthalmology, 1996—; cons. Stereo Optical Co., Chgo., 1986—, Randwal Instrument Co., South Bridge, Mass., 1986-89. Author: (with Montgomery and Henderson) Introduction to Neurologic Diagnosis, 1985; editor: (with Sadun) New Methods of Sensory Visual Testing, 1989. Fellow Am. Acad. Neurology; mem. Am. Neurol. Assn., Phi Beta Kappa. Home: 354 Lexington Ave Iowa City IA 52246-2415 Office: U Iowa Coll Medicine Dept Neurology Iowa City IA 52242

WALL, MIRIAM L., nursing home administrator; b. Savannah, Ga., Aug. 16, 1962; d. Herbert and Charlotte (Rosenthal) W.; 1 child, Jonathan Reitz. AS, Med. Coll. Ga., 1983; B.of Gen. Studies, Armstrong State U., 1992; M.Health Sci., Ga. So. U., 1993. Lic. nursing home adminstr., Ga. Nursing home adminstr. Hillhaven's Savannah Rehab. and Nursing Ctr., 1993-95, So. Care's Heritage Park of Savannah, 1995—. Mem. Traveler's Protective Assn., Savannah. Mem. Am. Coll. Health Care Adminstrs., Ga. Coun. Notaries Pub. Office: Southern Care Corp 12825 White Bluff Rd Savannah GA 31419

WALL, SONJA ELOISE, nurse administrator; b. Santa Cruz, Calif., Mar. 28, 1938; d. Ray Theothornton and Reva Mattie (Wingo) W.; m. Edward Gleason Holmes, Aug. 1959 (div. Jan. 1968); children: Deborah Lynn, Lance Edward; m. John Aspesi, Sept. 1969 (div. 1977); children: Sabrina Jean, Daniel John; m. Kenneth Talbot LaBoube, Nov. 1, 1978 (div. 1989); 1 child, Tiffany Amber. BA, San Jose Jr. Coll., 1959; BS, Madonna Coll., 1967; student, U. Mich., 1968-70; postgrad., Wayne State U., 1968-70. RN, Calif., Mich., Colo. Staff nurse Santa Clara Valley Med. Ctr., San Jose, Calif., 1959-67, U. Mich. Hosp., Ann Arbor, 1967-73, Porter and Swedish Med. Hosp., Denver, 1973-77, Laurel Grove Hosp., Castro Valley, Calif., 1977-79, Advent Hosp., Ukiah, Calif., 1984-86; motel owner LaBoube Enterprises, Fairfield, Point Arena, Willits, Calif., 1979—; staff nurse Northridge Hosp., L.A., 1986-87, Folsom State Prison, Calif., 1987; co-owner, mgr. nursing registry Around the Clock Nursing Svc., Ukiah, 1985—; critical care staff nurse Kaiser Permanente Hosp., Sacramento, 1986-89; nurse Snowline Hospice, Sacramento, 1989-92; carepoint home care and travel nurse Hosp. Staffing Svcs. Inc., Placerville, Calif., 1992-94, interim home health nurse, 1994-95; owner Sunshire Manor Resdl. Care Home, Placerville, Calif., 1995—; owner Royal Plantation Petites Miniature Horse Farm. Contbr. articles to various publs. Leader Coloma 4-H, 1987-91; mem. mounted divsn. El Dorado County Search and Rescue, 1991-93; docent Calif. Marshall Gold Discovery State Hist. Park, Coloma, Calif. Mem. AACN, NAFE, Soc. Critical Care Medicine, Am. Heart Assn. (CPR trainer, recipient awards), Calif. Bd. RNs, Calif. Nursing Rev., Calif. Critical Care Nurses, Soc. Critical Care Nurses, Am. Motel Assn. (beautification and remodeling award 1985), Nat. Hospice Nurses Assn., Cmty. Residential Care Assn. Calif., Soroptimist Internat. Calif., Am. Miniature Horse Assn. (winner nat. grand championship 1981-82, 83, 85, 89), DAR (Jobs Daus. hon. mem.), Cameron Park Country Club. Republican. Episcopalian. Home and Office: Around the Clock Nursing Svc 3112 Washington St Placerville CA 95667

WALLACE, ANDREW GROVER, physician, educator; b. Columbus, Ohio, Mar. 22, 1935; s. Richard Homes and Eleanor Bradley (Grover) W.; m. Kathleen Barrick Altvater, June 22, 1957; children: Stephen Andrew, Michael Bradley, Kathleen Claude. BS, Duke, 1958, MD, 1959. Diplomate Am. Bd. Internal Medicine. Intern medicine Duke U., Durham, N.C., 1959-60, asst. resident, 1960-61; fellow NIH, 1961-63; chief resident medicine Duke U., Durham, 1963-64, asst. prof., 1965-67, assoc. prof., 1967-71, chief, div. cardiology, 1970, prof. medicine, 1971, Walter Kempner prof. medicine, 1973; vice chancellor health affairs, chief exec. officer Duke U. Hosp., Durham, 1981; v.p. Duke U., 1987; dean Dartmouth Med. Sch., Hanover, N.H., 1990—; v.p. for health affairs Dartmouth Coll., 1990; cons. program project com., cardiology adv. com. and pharmacology study sect. Nat. Heart and Lung Inst., cardiovascular merit rev. bd. VA. Mem. editorial bd. Am. Jour. of Physiology, 1965-70, Jour. of Pharmacology and Exptl. Therapeutics, 1966-71, Jour. of Molecular and Cellular Cardiology, 1970-75, Jour. of Clin. Investigation, 1973-78. Pres. Durham YMCA Swim Assn., 1975-77. Markle scholar, 1965-70. Mem. AAMC, COD, Am. Fedn. for Clin. Rsch., Am. Soc. Clin. Investigation, Am. Heart Assn. (coun. on clin. cardiology), Am. Physiol. Soc., Biomed. Engring. Soc., Assn. U. Cardiologists, Am. Assn. Physicians, Soc. Med. Adminstrs. Home: 62 Oak Ridge Rd West Lebanon NH 03784-3113 Office: Dartmouth Coll Med Sch Office of Dean Hanover NH 03755-3833

WALLACE, DANIEL JEFFREY, rheumatologist; b. L.A., Oct. 27, 1949; s. Leon and Fern (Wixen) W.; m. Janice Brock. BS, U. So. Calif., 1970, MD, 1974. Diplomate Am. Bd. Med. Examiners, Am. Bd. Internal Medicine. Med. intern R.I. Hosp., Providence, 1974-75; med. resident Cedars-Sinai Med. Ctr., L.A., 1975-77; rheumatology fellow UCLA Sch. of Medicine, 1977-79; chief rheumatology cons. City of Hope Med. Ctr., Duarte, Calif., 1980-88; chief of rheumatology, cons. physician Century City Hosp., 1982-84; clin. chief of rheumatology Cedars Sinai Med. Ctr., L.A., 1992—; divsn. of rheumatology reappointment/peer rev. Cedar Sinai Med. Ctr., L.A., 1988—, hospital peer rev. com., 1986-89, 92-94, med. adv. com., 1985-88, 92—, intern selection com., 1979-93, chmn. med. peer rev., 1985-87, mem. 1982-89, attending physician; assoc. clin. prof. UCLA Sch. of Medicine, 1988—, asst. clin. prof., 1981-88, asst. clin. prof. U. So. Calif., 1979-81. Editl. bd. Jour. of Clin. Apheresis, 1982—; reviewer Jour. of Rheumatology, Lupus, Arthritis and Rheumatism, Jour. of Clin. Apheresis, Artificial Organs, Jour. of Musculoskeletal Medicine, Annals of Internal Medicine, New England Jour. of Medicine, Scandanaivan Jour. of Rheumatology; editor Current Opinion in Rheumatology, 1994—; co-author: Dubois Lupus Erythematosus, 3rd edit., 1987, 4th edit., 1993, The Lupus Book, 1995; contbr. numerous articles to profl. jours. Fellow ACP, Am. Coll. Rheumatology (com. on rheumatologic practice 1982-85, lupus coun. 1986—, chmn. 1990-91, nomination com. 1991—, rsch. and edn. found bd. dirs. 1993—, chmn. 1995—); mem. AMA, Royal Coll. of Physicians, L.A. County Med. Assn., Calif. Med. Assn., So. Calif. Rheumatism Soc., Gerontology Soc., Lupus Found of Am. (bd. dirs. 1991—, nat. med. adv. bd. 1988—, L.A. chpt. med. adv. bd., co-chair 1989—), Am. Lupus Soc. (nat. med. adv. bd. 1988—, L.A. chpt. chief med. advisor, San Fernando valley chpt. med. adv. bd.), Am. Soc. for Apheresis (med. exec. com. 1987-89, editor ASFA newsletter 1987-89), Am. Fibromyalgia Syndrome Assn. (med. adv. bd. 1994—), United Scleroderma Found. (bd. dirs. 1990—), Arthritis Found. (L.A. metro com. chmn. 1989-94, cmty. svcs. com. 1989-94, med. and scientific com. 1989-94, institutional grants com. 1989-94, fibromyalgia subcom. 1988—, chmn. 1990-95, rep. nat. ho of dels. 1987, 90, bd. dirs. So. Calif. 1994—). Home: 8737 Beverly Blvd Ste 203 Los Angeles CA 90048

WALLACE, HAROLD JAMES, physician; b. Burlington, Vt., Dec. 2, 1960; s. Harold James and Dorothy Ann (Green) W.; m. Micaela Ellen Sorrell, Oct. 1, 1961; children: Aislinn Anne, Audrey Elizabeth, Eleanor Clare. BA in Zoology, U. Vt., 1983, MD, 1988. Diplomate Am. Bd. Radiology. Radiation oncologist Cape Code Hosp., Hyannis, Mass., 1992-94, St. Alphonsus Cancer Treatment Ctr., Boise, Idaho, 1994—; clin. asst. prof. U. Wash., Seattle, 1994—; med. dir. Horizon Hospice, Meridian, Idaho, 1995—. Mem. Am. Coll. Radiation Oncologists, Am. Coll. Radiology, Am. Soc. Clin. Oncology, AMA, Alpha Omega Alpha. Office: St Alphonsus Cancer Trt Ctr 1055 North Curtis Rd Boise ID 83706

WALLACE, HELEN MARGARET, physician, educator; b. Hoosick Falls, N.Y., Feb. 18, 1913; d. Jonas and Ray (Schweizer) W. AB, Wellesley Coll., 1933; MD, Columbia U., 1937; MPH cum laude, Harvard U., 1943. Diplomate Am. Bd. Pediatrics, Am. Bd. Preventive Medicine. Intern Bellevue Hosp., N.Y.C., 1938-40; child hygiene physician Conn. Health Dept., 1941-42; successively jr. health officer, health officer, chief maternity and new born div., dir. bur. for handicapped children N.Y.C. Health Dept., 1943-55; prof., dir. dept. pub. health N.Y. Med. Coll., 1955-56; prof. maternal and child health U. Minn. Sch. Pub. Health, 1956-59; chief profl. tng. U.S. Children's Bur., 1959-60, chief child health studies, 1961-62; prof. maternal and child health U. Calif. Sch. Pub. Health, Berkeley, 1962-80; prof., head divsn. maternal and child health Sch. Pub. Health San Diego State U., 1980—; Univ. Research lectr. San Diego State U., 1985—; cons. WHO numerous locations, including Uganda, The Philippines, Turkey, India, Geneva, Iran, Burma, Sri Lanka, East Africa, Australia, Indonesia, China, Taiwan, 1961—, traveling fellow, 1989—; cons. Hahnemann U., Phila., 1993, Ford Found., Colombia, 1971; UN cons. to Health Bur., Beijing, China, 1987; fellow Aiiku Inst. on Maternal and Child Health, Tokyo, and NIH Inst. Child Health and Human Devel., 1994; dir. Family Planning Project, Zimbabwe, 1984-87. Author, editor 10 textbooks; contbr. 325 articles to profl. jours. Mem. coun. on Disabled Children to Media, 1991; dir. San Diego County Infant Mortality Study, 1989—, San Diego Study of Prenatal Care, 1991. Recipient Alumnae Achievement award Wellesley Coll., 1982, U. Minn. award, 1985; Ford Found. study grantee, 1986, 87, 88; fellow World Rehab. Fund, India, 1991-92, Fulbright Found., 1992—, NIH Inst. Child Health and Human Devel., 1994, Aiiku Inst. of Maternal-Child Health, Tokyo, 1994. Fellow APHA (officer sect., Martha May Eliot award 1978), Am. Acad. Pediatrics (Job Smith award 1980, award 1989); mem. AMA, Assn. Tchrs. Maternal and Child Health, Am. Acad. Cerebral Palsy, Ambulatory Pediatric Assn., Am. Sch. Preventive Medicine. Home: 850 State St San Diego CA 92101-6046

WALLACE, HERBERT WILLIAM, physician, surgery educator, researcher; b. Bklyn., Dec. 11, 1930; s. Philip and Jean (Brand) W.; m. Rosalie Sandra Becker, Dec. 18, 1954; children: Ira, Ellen, Lisa. AB, Harvard U., 1952; MD, Tufts U., 1956, MS, 1960; MBA, U. Pa., 1981, MA (hon.), 1973. Diplomate Am. Bd. Surgery, Am. Bd. Thoracic Surgery. Resident in gen. surgery Tufts U.-New Eng. Med. Ctr., Boston, 1956-61; thoracic and cardiovascular surg. resident Mt. Sinai Hosp., N.Y.C., 1963-65; assoc. in surgery and physiology U. Pa., Phila., 1966-70, asst. prof. surgery, 1970-72, assoc. prof. surgery, physiology and bioengring., 1972-76, prof., 1976—; chief div. thoracic and cardiovascular surgery Grad. Hosp. U. Pa., 1976-79; assoc. in univ. seminar on biomaterials Columbia U., N.Y.C., 1972—. Contbr. over 100 articles to profl. jours. Rsch. grantee NIH, 1965—. Fellow Am. Coll. Surgeons, Am. Heart Assn.; mem. Am. Assn. Cancer Rsch., Am. Assn. Thoracic Surgery, Am. Thoracic Soc., Biomedical Engring. Soc., Soc. Thoracic Surgeons, others. Home: 255 Harrogate Rd Wynnewood PA 19096-3131 Office: U Pa Dept Surgery One Graduate Pla Philadelphia PA 19146

WALLACE, JAMES GILBERT, plastic and reconstructive surgeon; b. Charlotte, N.C., May 20, 1943; m. Monte Hyatt Nicholson, Aug. 3, 1966; children: Monte, Sara Spicer, Ben, Shepard. BS, Davidson Coll., 1965; MD, U. N.C., 1969. Diplomate Am. Bd. Plastic and Reconstructive Surgery. Intern U. Fla. Tchg. Hosp., 1969-70; resident Emory U., Atlanta, 1973-76, resident in plastic and reconstructive surgery, 1976-78; chief plastic surgeon Pinehurst (N.C.) Surg. Clinic, 1978-82; instr. divsn. plastic surgeon MVSC Sch. of Medicine, Charleston, 1982—; assoc. prof. surgery USC Sch. of Medicine, Columbia, 1988—; cons. plastic surgery Shriner's Hosp., 1982—; attending plastic surgeon Greenville (S.C.) Hosp. System, 1982—, St. Francis Hosp., Greenville, 1982—; surg. tchg. staff Greenville Hosp. System, 1982—; mem. occpl. medicine com. S.C. Workmen's Compensation Bd., 1986—; chmn. cancer care com. Greenville Hosp. System, 1986-87, chmn. dept. of plastic surgery Greenville Hosp. System and St. Francis Hosp., 1988-89, 92-94; facilities inspector Am. Assn. for Accreditation of Ambulatory Plastic Surgery Facilities, 1993—; sug. facilities co-dir. ambulatory surgery-Plastic Surgery Assocs.; clin. assoc. prof. surgery, dept. surgery U. S.C. Sch. of Medicine, 1993—; presenter in field; mem. S.C. State Bd. of Med. Examiners, 1994—. Contbr. articles to profl. jours. Youth soccer coach YMCA, 1984-87, youth basketball coach, 1983-86, youth baseball, 1984-87; coach St. Mary's Ch. Youth Basketball, 1986-92, Greenville county Little League Baseball, 1987-92. Maj. U.S. Army, 1970-73. Fellow ACS (S.C. chpt.); mem. AMA, Am. Soc. of Plastic and Reconstructive Surgeons, Southeastern Soc. of Plastic and Reconstructive Surgeons, S.C. Med. Assn., Greenville County Med. Soc., S.C. Soc. of Plastic and Reconstructive Surgeons (pres. 1986), S.C. Surg. Soc., Am. Soc. for Laser Medicine and Surgery, Inc., Am. Soc. for Aesthetic Plastic Surgery, Inc., Christian Med. and Dental Soc. Home: 412 Crescent Ave Greenville SC 29605 Office: Plastic Surgery Assocs 24 Memorial Medical Dr Greenville SC 29605

WALLACE, KARL KENNETH, JR., physician, radiologist; b. Farmville, Va., June 12, 1932; s. Karl Kenneth and Frances Virginia (Newman) W.; m. Patricia Laughbaum, June 19, 1954; children: Karl Kenneth III, Elizabeth, John, Patricia. BA, Hampden-Sydney Coll., 1954; MD, Med. Coll. Va., 1958. Diplomate Am. Bd. Radiology, Am. Bd. Nuclear Medicine; lic. in medicine and surgery, Va. Rotating intern Coll. Va. Hosps., 1958-59; radiology resident Duke U., 1959-62; chmn. dept. radiology Virginia Beach (Va.) Gen. Hosp., 1963-91; prof. radiology U. Va., Charlottesville, 1992—. Bd. dirs. Va. divsn. Am. Cancer Soc., Richmond, 1973-84. Fellow Am. Coll. Radiology (pres. 1994-95, chmn. bd. chancellors 1992-94); mem. Radiol. Soc. N.Am., Coun. Med. Splty. Socs., Am. Roentgen Ray Soc., Soc. for Nuclear Medicine, Am. Inst. Ultrasound in Medicine, Med. Soc. Va. (speaker ho. of dels. 1976-80), Soc. Thoracic Radiology. Office: U Va Dept Radiology Box 170 HSC Charlottesville VA 22908

WALLACE, LEON, internist, educator; b. N.Y.C., Aug. 12, 1920; s. Abraham and Rose (Burstein) W.; m. Fern Wixen, July 13, 1945; children: Daniel, Laura. BA, U. So. Calif., 1940, MD, 1944. Diplomate Am. Bd. Internal Medicine. Intern Los Angeles County Gen. Hosp., L.A., 1944-45; fellow in cardiovascular medicine Michael Reese Hosp., Chgo., 1945-46, fellow in pathology, 1947-48; resident in medicine Bellevue Hosp., N.Y.C., 1946-47; pvt. practice, Beverly Hills, Calif., 1948—; asst. prof. medicine U. So. Calif. Sch. Medicine, L.A., 1949—; attending physician Cedars-Sinai Hosp., L.A., 1950—; cons. in medicine U.S. Army Ft. MacArthur Hosp., San Pedro, Calif., 1955-57. Contbr. articles to med. jours. Capt. M.C., U.S. Army, 1953-55. Fellow ACP, Am. Coll. Cardiology. Office: 435 N Roxbury Dr Ste 303 Beverly Hills CA 90210

WALLACE, LOUISE MARGARET, clinical coordinator; b. Norwich, Conn., June 15, 1942; d. Irving Clifford and Helen Lucille (Fain) Hayden; m. R.D. Wallace, Dec. 2, 1967; 1 child, Donald Orville. Grad., Joseph Lawrence Sch. Nursing, Conn., 1963; student, Miami-Dade (Fla.) Jr. Coll., 1966-67, Yavapai Coll., 1970. RN, Ariz., Mo., D.C., Fla., Conn., New Zealand; ACLS, ABLS. Nurse ICU and ob-gyn. dept. George Washington U. Hosp., Washington, 1964-65; nurse pediatrics dept. Jackson Meml. Hosp., Miami, Fla., 1965-66; nurse ICU Bapt. Hosp., Miami, 1966-67; nurse ICU and CCU N. Shore Hosp., Miami, 1967-71; nurse ICU and CCU VA Med. Ctr., Prescott, Ariz., 1971-84; nurse ICU and CCU VA Med. Ctr., Poplar Bluff, Mo., 1984-93, relief clin. coord., 1991-92; clin. coord., 1993—; instr. nursing Miami-Dade Jr. Coll., 1968-69; instr. basic CPR, Prescott, 1975-81. Mem. Am. Diabetes Assn. Home: HC 1 Box 76 Grandin MO 63943-9602

WALLACE, PAUL EDWARD, JR., health services management; b. Balt.; s. Paul E. and Frances (Tindal) W.; children from previous marriage: Gregory, Demetria, Denise, Eli. BS, Morgan State U., 1974; MA, U. Pitts., 1976, PhD, 1979, MPH, 1981. Adminstrv. fellow Mercy Hosp., Pitts., 1980-81; asst. adminstr. Norfolk (Va.) Gen. Hosp., 1981-85; v.p. profl. svc. Forsyth Meml. Hosp., Winston, N.C., 1985-88; chmn., assoc. prof. Howard U., Washington, 1988—; cons. OAS, Washington, 1989-91. Bd. dirs. Am. Heart Assn., Washington, 1991-95, Franciscan Health Sys., Aston, Pa., 1994. Recipient Recognition award Area Health Edn. Ctr., 1985, J.B. Johnson award Am. Heart Assn., 1992. Fellow Am. Coll. Healthcare Execs. (regent 1994). Presbyterian. Office: Urban Med Inst 2600 Liberty Heights Ave Baltimore MD 21215

WALLACE, ROBERT BRUCE, surgeon; b. Washington, Apr. 12, 1931; s. William B. and Anne E. W.; m. Betty Jean Newel, Aug. 28, 1955; children: Robert B., Anne E., Barbara N. B.A., Columbia U., 1953, M.D., 1957. Diplomate: Am. Bd. Surgery, Am. Bd. Thoracic Surgery. Chmn., prof. dept. surgery Mayo Clinic and Mayo Med. Sch., Rochester, Minn.; bd. govs. Mayo Clinic, 1968-79; prof. dept. surgery Georgetown U. Sch. Medicine, 1980—, chmn. dept. surgery, 1980-95, surgeon and chief univ. hosp., 1980-95. Trustee Mayo Found., 1970-78. Mem. ACS (bd. govs. 1975-79), Am. Surg. Assn., Soc. Clin. Surgery, Am. Assn. Thoracic Surgery (pres. 1994-95), Internat. Cardiovascular Soc., Soc. Vascular Surgery. Home: 1322 Darnall Dr Mc Lean VA 22101-3009 Office: Dept Surgery Georgetown U Hosp 3800 Reservoir Rd NW Washington DC 20007-2196

WALLACE, SIBYLLE ADELINE, pediatrician, child neurologist; b. Berlin, Jan. 3, 1938; d. Wilhelm and Irmgard (Steinhaus) Bauer; m. Michael J. Wallace, Jan. 15, 1966; children: Christine, Stefan, Michael. MD, U. Munich, 1962. Diplomate Am. Bd. Pediatrics, Am. Bd. Psychiatry and Neurology with subspecialty in child neurology. Intern St. Mary's Hosp., Passaic, N.J., 1964-65; resident in pediat. Misericordia Hosp. and Fordham Hosp., Bronx, N.Y., 1968-70; pediat. neurol. fellow Mt. Sinai Hosp., N.Y.C., 1972-74; pvt.practice N.Y.C.; asst. prof. Mt. Sinai Hosp., N.Y.C., 1972—; attending physician St. Joseph's Med. Ctr., Paterson, N.J., 1972-78. Translator: (German to English) Peripheral Nerve Lesions, Anatomy of the Cervical Spine. Mem. Epilepsy Soc., Child Neurology Soc., Acad. Pediatrics, Acad. Neurology, North Jersey Philharmonic Soc. (bd. dirs. 1995). Office: Mount Sinai Hospital 5 E 98th St New York NY 10029

WALLACH, EDWARD ELIOT, physician, educator; b. N.Y.C., Oct. 8, 1933; s. David Abraham and Madeleine (Spiro) W.; m. Joanne Levey, June 24, 1956; children: Paul, Julie. BA, Swarthmore Coll., 1954; MD, Cornell U., 1958; MA (hon.), U. Pa., 1970. Diplomate Am. Bd. Ob-gyn. (bd. dirs. 1989—, dir. divsn. reproductive endocrinology 1989—), subcert. in reproductive endocrinology. Intern 2d med. div. Bellevue Hosp., N.Y.C., 1958-59; resident obstetrics and gynecology Kings County Hosp., Bklyn., 1959-63; asst. instr. State U. N.Y. Downstate Med. Center, Bklyn., 1962-63; mem. faculty U. Pa. Sch. Medicine, 1965-84, prof. obstetrics and gynecology, 1971-84, chief endocrinology sect., div. human reprodn., dept. obstetrics and gynecology, 1968-71, mem. admissions com., 1970-73, mem. community health com., 1966-71, mem. student adv. com., 1966-84, mem. com. for appointments and promotions, 1972-77, chmn., 1974-77; dir. dept. obstetrics and gynecology Pa. Hosp., 1971-84, sec., treas. profl. staff, 1972-75; prof., chmn. dept. ob-gyn. Johns Hopkins U. Sch. Medicine, 1984-94, chmn. med. staff, 1991-94, prof., 1984-94; vis. prof. ob-gyn. U. Kyoto Sch. Medicine, 1981; vis. prof. Keio U. Sch. Medicine, 1987; mem. fertility and maternal health drugs adv. com. FDA, 1992-96. Assoc. editor: Fertility and Sterility, 1974—; co-editor: Modern Trends in Infertility and Conception Control; editor-in-chief Postgrad. Obstetrics and Gynecology, 1980—; mem. editorial bd. Fertility and Sterility, 1970—, Obstetrics and Gynecology, 1976-79, Contemporary Obstetrics and Gynecology, 1976—, Biology of Reproduction, 1978-84; editor-in-chief Current Opinion in Obstetrics and Gynecology, 1989-93; contbr. to med. jours. Trustee Marriage Council Phila., 1970-78; chmn. finance com. Phila. Coordinating Council for Family Planning, 1972-73, chmn. med. adv. com., 1973-76; trustee Balt. Chamber Orch., 1989—. Served as surgeon USPHS, 1963-65. Trainee NIH, 1961-62; recipient Lindback Found. Disting. Teaching award U. Pa., 1971. Fellow Am. Coll. Ob-Gyn., Am. Fertility Soc. (dir. 1977-81, pres. 1985-86); mem. AAAS, Am. Gynecol. and Obstet. Soc. (v.p. 1983-84), Endocrine Soc., Soc.Gynecol. Investigation (pres. 1986-87), Am. Bd. Ob-Gyn. (bd. dirs. 1989—, dir. divsn. reproductive endocrinology 1989—), Phila. Endocrine Soc., Obstet. Soc. Phila. (program chmn. 1969-70, 70-71, 71-72, mem. coun. 1972-83, v.p. 1976-77, pres. 1979-80), Soc. Study Reprodn., Inst. Medicine/NAS, Alpha Omega Alpha. Office: Johns Hopkins Med Instn Houck Bldg Rm 201 600 N Wolfe St Dept Gyne-Ob Baltimore MD 21287-1201

WALLACH, STANLEY, medical educator, consultant, administrator; b. Bklyn., Dec. 10, 1928; s. Abraham and Ida Helen (Pevin) W.; m. Pearl Small, 1973; children: Sara Lynn, Rhonda, Peter, Francine, Shellie, Allen, Corinne, Mara. AB, Cornell U., 1948; MA in Phys. Chemistry, Columbia U., 1949; MD, SUNY Downstate Med. Ctr., 1953. Diplomate Am. Bd. Internal Medicine, Am. Bd. Endocrinology and Metabolism. Intern Kings County Hosp., Bklyn., 1953-54; resident in internal medicine VA Hosp./Salt Lake Gen. Hosp., Salt Lake City, 1954-56; fellow in endocrinology and metabolism Mass. Gen. Hosp., Boston, 1956-57; attending physician Kings County Hosp., Bklyn., 1957-73, SUNY Hosp., Bklyn., 1966-73, Albany (N.Y.) Med. Ctr., 1973-83; chief of med. svc. VA Med. Ctr., Albany, 1973-83, Bay Pines, Fla., 1983-90; cons. VA Med. Ctr., Tampa, Fla., 1991-92; attending physician Tampa Gen. Hosp., 1991—, Moffitt Cancer Ctr., 1991-92; dir. med. edn. Cath. Med. Ctr., Jamaica, N.Y., 1992-93; dir. endocrinology and osteoporosis ctr. Hosp. for Joint Diseases, N.Y.C., 1993—; instr. in medicine SUNY Downstate Med. Ctr., 1957-58, from asst. prof. to assoc. prof., 1960-71, prof., 1971-73; prof., asst. chmn. dept. medicine Albany Med. Coll., 1973-77, prof., assoc. chmn. dept. medicine, 1977-83; prof. internal medicine Coll. Medicine U. South Fla., 1983-92, assoc. chmn. dept. internal medicine, 1988-92; exec. dir. Am. Coll. Nutrition, 1993—; clin. prof. medicine NYU Sch. Medicine, N.Y.C., 1995—; pres. Certification Bd. for Nutrition Specialists, 1992—; career scientist Health Rsch. Coun., City of N.Y., 1967-71; program dir. USPHS Clin. Rsch. Ctr., SUNY Downstate Med. Ctr., 1966-73; rsch. collaborator Brookhaven Nat. Lab., Upton, N.Y., 1970-82; vice-chmn. Gordon Rsch. Conf. on Magnesium in Biochem. Processes and Medicine, 1987, chmn., 1990; cons. NIH, NSF, USDA, Nat. Osteoporosis Found., Nat. Arthritis Found., U.S. Pharmacopeial Conf. Mem. editl. bd. Jour. Am. Coll. of Nutrition, 1981—, Magnesium and Trace Elements, 1982—, Jour. Trace Elements in Exptl. Medicine, 1987—; reviewer Am. Jour. Medicine, Annals of Internal Medicine, Archives of Internal Medicine, Jour. Clin. Endocrinology and Metabolism, Endocrinology, Metabolism, Calcified Tissue Internat., Jour. Bone and Mineral Rsch., Osteoporosis Internat., Procs. of Soc. Exptl. Biology and Medicine, Jour. Nutritional Biochemistry; contbr. numerous articles to profl. jours. Capt. USNR, 1957-88. Co-recipient Hektoen Silver award AMA Conv., 1959, John B. Johnson award Paget's Disease Found., 1989. Fellow ACP (emeritus), Am. Coll. Clin. Pharmacology, Am. Coll. Endocrinology, Am. Coll. Nutrition (bd. dirs. 1982—, v.p. 1983-85, pres.-elect 1985-87, pres. 1987-89, sec., treas. 1991-93); mem. Assn. Am. Physicians, Am. Soc. for Clin. Investigation (emeritus), Am. Fedn. Clin. Rsch. (emeritus), Am. Soc. for Magnesium Rsch., Am. Soc. Bone and Mineral Rsch., Am. Soc. for Clin. Nutrition, Am. Inst. of Nutrition, Am. Assn. Clin. Endocrinology, Endocrine Soc., Confedn. of Nutrition Socs., European Calcified Tissue Soc., Paget's Disease Found. (bd. dirs. med. adv. panel), Internat. Conf. on Calcium Regulating Hormones, Internat. Soc. Trace Element Rsch. in Humans, Nat. Orgn. Rare Disorders, Harvey Soc. (emeritus), Sigma Xi. Office: Hosp for Joint Diseases 301 E 17th St New York NY 10003-3804

WALLENBURG, HENK CORNELIS SILVESTER, obstetrician, gynecologist; b. Den Ham, The Netherlands, May 10, 1938; s. Cornelis S. and Cornelia M. (Van Zyll) W.; m. Frouwkjen F. Haagsma; children: Sjoukje C., Branka, Cees, Fronwkjen H. MD, Free U., Amsterdam, The Netherlands, 1961, PhD, 1971; DSc, U. Warsaw, Poland, 1993. Intern Free U., Amsterdam, 1961-63, resident, 1965-70, asst. prof., 1970-71; assoc. prof. U. Pitts., 1971-72; assoc. prof. Erasmus U., Rotterdam, The Netherlands, 1972-77, prof., 1977—; dir. dept. ob-gyn. Erasmus U. Hosp., Rotterdam, 1978—. Capt. Royal Dutch Army, 1963-65. Named Hon. Citizen, Poznan, Poland, 1986. Fellow Royal Coll. Obstetricians and Gynecologists U.K. Office: Erasmus U Sch Med &Hlth Scis, PO Box 1738, 3000 DR Rotterdam The Netherlands

WALLER, BRUCE FRANK, physician, researcher; b. Austin, Minn., Oct. 18, 1947. BA, Luther Coll., 1969; MD, U. Minn., 1973, MS, 1976. Resident in medicine Mayo Clinic, Rochester, Minn., 1973-76; fellow in cardiology Georgetown U., Washington, 1976-78; with pathology div. Nat. Heart, Lung and Blood Inst., Bethesda, Md., 1978-82; prof. Ind. U. Med. Ctr., Indpls., 1982-89; clin. prof., also dir. cardiovascular pathology registry St. Vincent Hosp., Indpls., 1989—. Author books. Office: Nasser Smith Pinkerton Cardiology 8333 Naab Rd Ste 400 Indianapolis IN 46266-0001

WALLER, JOHN LOUIS, anesthesiology educator; b. Loma Linda, Calif., Dec. 1, 1944; s. Louis Clinton and Sue (Bruce) W.; m. Jo Lynn Marie Haas, Aug. 4, 1968; children: Kristina, Karla, David. BA, So. Coll., Collegedale, Tenn., 1967; MD, Loma Linda U., 1971. Diplomate Am. Bd. Anesthesiology. Intern Hartford (Conn.) Hosp., 1971-72; resident in anesthesiology Harvard U. Med. Sch.-Mass. Gen. Hosp., Boston, 1972-74, fellow, 1974-75; asst. prof. anesthesiology Emory U. Sch. Medicine, Atlanta, 1977-80, assoc. prof., 1980-86, prof., chmn. dept., 1986—; svc. chief anesthesiology Emory Univ. Hosp., Atlanta, 1986-94, med. dir., 1993-95; assoc. v.p. info. svcs. Woodruff Health Scis. Ctr., 1995—; chief info. officer Emory U. System Healthcare, Atlanta, 1995—; cons. Arrow Internat., Inc., Reading, Pa., 1988—; bd. dirs. Clifton Casualty Co., Colo.; mem. adv. com. on anesthetic and life support drugs FDA, Washington, 1986-92; numerous vis. professorships and lectures. Contbr. articles to med. jours. Maj. M.C., USAF, 1975-77. Recipient cert. of appreciation Office Sec. Def., 1983. Fellow Am. Coll. Anesthesiologists, Am. Coll. Chest Physicians; mem. AMA, Am. Soc. Anesthesiologists, Soc. Cardiovascular Anesthesiologists (pres. 1991-93), Internat. Anesthesia Rsch. Soc. (trustee 1984—, sec. 1993—), Assn. Univ. Anesthetists, Soc. Acad. Anesthesia Chairmen (councillor 1989—), Assn. Cardiac Anesthesiologists. Office: Emory U Hosp Dept Anes 1364 Clifton Rd NE Atlanta GA 30322-1059

WALLER, MARILYN JEAN, podiatric surgeon, educator; b. Mpls., Nov. 30, 1950; m. John w. Niewold, Aug. 19, 1995; children: Skot Waller, Richard Waller, Khrystofer Waller, Daniel Waller, Rebekah Waller. Student, Bethel Coll., 1969-71; BS, U. Minn., 1975; postgrad., Calif. Poly., 1983-86; DPM, Calif. Coll Podiatric Medicine, 1990. Cert. foot and ankle surgeon Calif. Bd. Podiatric Medicine. Instr. h.s. Minn., 1975-78, Arroyo Grande, Calif., 1980-83; resident in surgery VA Med. Ctr., San Francisco, 1990-92; rsch. fellow VA Med. Ctr./Travis AFB, San Francisco, 1992-93; pvt. practice Hayward, Calif., 1993—; wound advisor St. Rose Hosp. Phys. Rehab., Hayward, 1994—. Mem. Am. Podiatric Med. Soc., Am. Diabetes Assn., Am. Assn. Women Podiatrists, Calif. Podiatric Med. Soc., Alameda-Contra Costa Podiatric Med. Soc., Omicron Nu. Office: Calaroga Surg Ctr 27225 Calaroga Ave Hayward CA 94545

WALLERSTEIN, BETTY COOPER, clinical social worker; b. Ohio, Mar. 24, 1936; d. Joseph and Adele (Haberfeld) Cooper; m. David D. Wallerstein, May 31, 1966; children: Andrew Jonathan, Susan Eva. AB, Goucher Coll., 1958; MSW, Howard U., 1960; postgrad. cert. in adminstrn., Hunter Coll., 1980. Cert. clin. social worker. Caseworker Mass. SPCC, Boston, 1960-62; psychotherapist Jewish Bd. of Guardians, Manhattan, N.Y., 1962-65; caseworker Georgetown Adolescent Clinic, Washington, 1965; family therapist Family Mental Health Clinic of Jewish Family Svcs., Manhattan, 1966-71; pvt. practice N.Y.C., 1971—; casework supr. Jewish Family Svcs., 1968; guest lectr. various colls. presenter Am. Orthopsychiat. Assn., others in field. Co-chmn., founder Coalition to Save City and Suburban Housing, Inc., N.Y.C., 1985-94; founder, pres. 36 Blocks E 79 St. Neighbor Assn., N.Y.C., 1984-96; cmty. orgn./devel. activities various civic and social welfare bds.; apptd. Cmty. Bd. 8, others; vol. civic/cmty. devel. Recipient Disting. Pub. Svc. award Goucher Coll., Our Town Leadership awards, Mayor's award for Vol. Leadership Excellence, Boro Pres. award for Vol. Pub. Svc., Manhattan, 1988, others. Mem. Nat. Assn. Social Workers.

WALLERSTEIN, JUDITH SARETSKY, marriage and divorce researcher; b. N.Y.C., Dec. 27, 1921; d. Samuel Saretsky and Augusta (Tucker) Weinberger; m. Robert S. Wallerstein, Jan. 27, 1949; children—Michael, Nina, Amy. B.A., Hunter Coll., N.Y.C., 1943; M.S., Columbia U., 1946;

Ph.D. in Psychology, Lund U. (Sweden) 1978. Sr. lectr. U. Calif.-Berkeley, 1966-91, sr. lectr. emeritus, 1991—; dir. Calif. Children of Divorce Project, Marin County, Calif., 1971—; mem. task force on family equity Calif. Senate, 1986; exec. dir. Ctr. for the Family in Transition, Corte Madera, Calif., 1980-93. Prin. investigator follow-up study Effects of Divorce on Children and Their Parents. Mem. adv. com. on family law Calif. Senate Subcom. on Adminstrn. of Justice, 1977-79; mem. task force on Family equity Calif. State Senate, 1986. Author 3 books; contbr. 80 articles to profl. jours. Recipient Koshland award in Social Welfare San Francisco Found., 1975, Geri Taylor Meml. award No. Calif. Psychiat. Soc., 1993, Presdl. Citation Am. Psychol. Assn. Divsn. of Family Psychol., 1995; others. Fellow Ctr. Advanced Study in the Behavioral Scis., Stanford, Calif., 1979-80, Rockefeller Found. Study Ctr., Bellagio, Italy, 1992. Mem. NASW, Am. Psychoanalytic Assn. (hon.), N.Y. Freudian Soc. (hon.), San Francisco Psychoanalytic Soc. (interdisciplinary mem.), Am. Orthopsychiatric Assn., Assn. Child Psychoanalysis (mem. exec. council 1977-80), Assn. Family Conciliation Courts, Phi Beta Kappa.

WALLERSTEIN, RALPH OLIVER, physician; b. Dusseldorf, Germany, Mar. 7, 1922; came to U.S., 1938, naturalized, 1944; s. Otto R. and Ilse (Hollander) W.; m. Betty Ane Christensen, June 21, 1952; children: Ralph Jr., Richard, Ann. A.B., U. Calif., Berkeley, 1943; M.D., U. Calif., San Francisco, 1945. Diplomate: Am. Bd. Internal Medicine. Intern San Francisco Hosp., 1945-46, resident, 1948-49; resident U. Calif. Hosp., San Francisco, 1949-50; research fellow Thorndike Meml. Lab., Boston City Hosp., 1950-52; chief clin. hematology San Francisco Gen. Hosp., 1953-87; faculty U. Calif., San Francisco, 1952—; clin. prof. medicine U. Calif., 1969—. Served to capt. M.C. AUS, 1946-48. Mem. AMA, ACP (gov. 1977-87, chmn. bd. govs. 1980-81, regent 1981-87, pres. 1988-89), Am. Soc. Hematology (pres. 1978), San Francisco Med. Soc., Am. Clin. and Climatol. Assn., Am. Fedn. Clin. Rsch., Am. Soc. Internal Medicine, Am. Bd. Internal Medicine (bd. govs. 1975-83, chmn. 1982-83), Am. Assn. Blood Banks, Inst. Medicine, Calif. Acad. Medicine, Internat. Soc. Hematology, Western Soc. Clin. Rsch., Western Assn. Physicians, Gold Headed Cane Soc. Republican. Home: 3447 Clay St San Francisco CA 94118-2008 Office: 3838 California St Rm 707 San Francisco CA 94118-1509

WALLERSTEIN, ROBERT SOLOMON, psychiatrist; b. Berlin, Jan. 28, 1921; s. Lazar and Sarah (Guensberg) W.; m. Judith Hannah Saretsky, Jan. 26, 1947; children—Michael Jonathan, Nina Beth, Amy Lisa. B.A., Columbia, 1941, M.D., 1944; postgrad., Topeka Inst. Psychoanalysis, 1951-58. Assoc. dir., then dir. rsch. Menninger Found., Topeka, 1954-66; chief psychiatry Mt. Zion Hosp., San Francisco, 1966-78; tng. and supervising analyst San Francisco Psychoanalytic Inst., 1966—; clin. prof. U. Calif. Sch. Medicine, Langley-Porter Neuropsychiat. Inst., 1967-75, prof., chmn. dept. psychiatry, also dir. inst., 1975-85, prof. dept. psychiatry, 1985-91, prof. emeritus, 1991—; vis. prof. psychiatry La. State U. Sch. Medicine, also New Orleans Psychoanalytic Inst., 1972-73, Pahlavi U., Shiraz, Iran, 1977, Fed. U. Rio Grande do Sul, Porto Alegre, Brasil, 1980; mem., chmn. rsch. scientist career devel. com. NIMH, 1966-70; fellow Ctr. Advanced Study Behavioral Scis., Stanford, Calif., 1964-65, 81-82, Rockefeller Found. Study Ctr., Bellagio, Italy, 1992. Author 14 books and monographs; mem. editl. bd. 19 profl. jours; contbr. over 230 articles to profl. jours. Served with AUS, 1946-48. Recipient Heinz Hartmann award N.Y. Psychoanalytic Inst., 1968, Disting. Alumnus award Menninger Sch. Psychiatry, 1972, J. Elliott Royer award U. Calif., San Francisco, 1973, Outstanding Achievement award No. Calif. Psychiat. Soc., 1987, Mt. Airy gold medal, 1990, Mary Singleton Sigourney award, 1991. Fellow ACP, Am. Psychiat. Assn., Am. Orthopsychiat. Assn.; mem. Am. Psychoanlytic Assn. (pres. 1971-72), Internat. Psychoanalytic Assn. (v.p. 1977-85, pres. 1985-89), Group for Advancement Psychiatry, Brit. Psycho-Analytical Soc. (hon.), Phi Beta Kappa, Alpha Omega Alpha. Home: 290 Beach Rd Belvedere CA 94920-2472 Office: 655 Redwood Hwy Ste 261 Mill Valley CA 94941-3011

WALLERSTEIN, SETH MICHAEL, dentist; b. Newark, Feb. 6, 1960; s. Sheldon Melvin Wallerstein and Jeanne Alice (Rothenberger) Kushinsky; m. Lisa Mary Calvani, June 21, 1986; 1 child, Genna Marie. BA, Haverford (Pa.) Coll., 1982; DMD, U. Pa., 1986. Resident in dentistry John F. Kennedy Meml. Hosp., Edison, N.J., 1986-87; gen. practice dentistry Edison, 1987—; mem. staff dental dept. John F. Kennedy Meml. Hosp., 1987—. Mem. ADA, Acad. Gen. Dentistry, Alpha Omega. Jewish. Home: 33 Tower Rd Edison NJ 08820-3513

WALLGREN-PETTERSSON, CARINA, physician; b. Helsinki, Uusimaa, Finland, July 26, 1956; d. Henrik Wallgren and Carin Forsius-Wallgren; m. Tom E. Pettersson, 1980; children: Tobias, Katarina. MD, U. Helsinki, 1982, PhD, 1990, Specialist in Med. Genetics, 1994. Lic. physician, 1982. House officer in paediatrics Helsinki, 1982-84; researcher Children's Hosp./Univ. Helsinki, 1984-90; sr. registrar dept. med. genetics Väestöliitto, Helsinki, 1990-91; rsch. fellow Inst. Med. Genetics/Univ. Wales, Cardiff, U.K., 1991-92; sr. registrar Dep. Clin. Genetics Univ. Helsinki, 1992-94, researcher, 1994—; head of genetics The Folkhälsan Dept., 1995—; coord. ENMC Internat. Consortium on Myotubular Myopathy, 1993—, ENMC Internat. Consortium on Nemaline Myopathy, 1996—. Contbr. articles to profl. jours. Mem. European Soc. Human Genetics, Clin. Genetics Soc. Office: Univ Helsinki Dept Med Genetics, PO Box 21 Haartmaninkatu 3, FIN00014 Helsinki Finland

WALLIN, GUNNAR BENGT, neurophysiologist; b. Karlstad, Sweden, Oct. 26, 1936; s. Ragnar and Elsa (Källström) W.; m. Ann Marie Lindbom, Aug. 6, 1960; children: Maria, Johan, Staffan. MD, U. Uppsala, Sweden, 1963. Rsch. physiologist U. Calif., San Francisco, 1963-64; staff mem. dept. clin. neurophysiology U. Uppsala, 1969-84; prof. clin. neurophysiology U. Göteborg, Sweden, 1984—; chmn. dept. clin. neurosci. U. Göteborg, 1993-95; vis. prof. Va. Commonwealth U., Richmond, 1980, Baker Med. Rsch. Inst., Melbourne, Australia, 1991, Prince of Wales Med. Rsch. Inst., Sydney, Australia, 1995; em. Commn. on Autonomic Nervous System, Internat. Union Physiol. Scis., 1982-90, Commn. on Clin. Physiology, 1995—. Contbr. over 150 sci. articles to profl. jours. and books; mem. editl. bd. several profl. jours.; assoc. editor Acta Physiologia Scandinavica, 1993—. Recipient Australian-European award Australian Govt., Canberra, 1988-89. Mem. Swedish Soc. Medicine (Alvarenga's prize 1988), Swedish Soc. Clin. Neurophysiology (chmn. 1988-90). Office: Univ Göteborg Sahlgren Hosp, Dept Clin Neurophysiology, Göteborg S-41345, Sweden

WALLIN, JOHN DAVID, internal medicine educator, naval officer; b. Pasadena, Calif., June 30, 1932; s. Nathaniel Charles and Florence Elizabeth (Wade) W.; m. Karen Elder, June 20, 1959 (div. Apr. 1990); children: John David Jr., Nancy Caren. BS, Stanford U., 1958; MD, Yale U., 1962. Diplomate Am. bd. Internal Medicine, Am. Bd. Nephrology. Enlisted USN, 1961, advanced through grades to capt.; served as intern Naval Hosp., San Diego, 1962-63; resident in internal medicine Naval Hosp., Oakland, Calif., 1963-66; chief internal medicine Naval Hosp., Roosevelt Roads, 1966-70; chief clin. investigation Oakland, 1972-78; fellow nephrology Southwestern Med. Sch., Dallas, 1970-72; prof., chief sect. nephrology Med. Sch. Med. Sch. Tulane U., New Orleans, 1978-90, La. State U., New Orleans, 1990—. Contbr. articles to profl. jours. Fellow ACP; mem. Am. Soc. Nephrology, Internat. Soc. Nephrology, Am. Soc. Hypertension, Am. Fedn. Clin. Rsch., So. Soc. Clin. Investigation. Office: La State U Med Sch 1542 Tulane Ave New Orleans LA 70112-2825

WALLING, JOHN FRANCIS, JR., gastroenterologist; b. Detroit, Oct. 26, 1960; s. John Francis and Joan Therese (Grider) W.; m. Angela Sue Bozzo, Sept. 23, 1995. BS, Madonna Coll., 1982; DO, U. Health Scis., 1986. Diplomate Am. Bd. Internal Medicine, Am. Bd. Gastroenterology, Am. Osteopathic Bd. Internal Medicine. Intern Mount Clemens (Mich.) Gen. Hosp., 1986-87; resident in internal medicine Botsford Gen. Hosp., Farmington Hills, Mich., 1987-90, fellow in gastroenterology, 1990-92; asst. clin. prof. Coll. Osteo. Medicine Mich. State U., East Lansing, 1992—; gastroenterologist Mid-Mich. Gastroenterology Specialists, East Lansing, 1992—. Mem. AMA, Am. Osteo. Assn., Am. Coll. Gastroenterology, Am. Soc. Gastrnintestical Endoscientists, Crohns and Colitis Found. Roman Catholic. Office: Mid Mich GastroenterologySpecs 2035 Asher Ct Ste 200 East Lansing MI 48823

WALLIS, ROBERT JOE, pharmacist, retail executive; b. Lawton, Okla., Dec. 26, 1938; s. John L. and Bertha Leora (Blake) W.; m. Rubena Ann Hennessee, June 1, 1958; children: Jeffrey Allen, Joseph Robert, Justin Matthew. BS in Pharmacy, Okla. U., 1962. Pharmacist, mgr. Hyde Drug, Oklahoma City, 1962-77, v.p., mgr., 1977-82, pres., 1982—; mem. McKesson Drug Co. Small Chain Adv. Bd., San Francisco, 1986-87. Bd. mgmt. YMCA, 1989—. Mem. Oklahoma City Profl. Businessmen's Assn. (pres. 1962, 72), Nat. Assn. chain Drug Stores (sml. chain com. 1991—). Republican. Methodist. Office: Hyde Drug Inc 5108 N Shartel Ave Oklahoma City OK 73118-6025

WALLSKOG, JOYCE MARIE, nursing educator, psychologist; b. Melrose Park, Ill., Apr. 20, 1942. BSN, Alverno Coll., 1977; MSN, U. Wis., Milw., 1982; PhD, Marquette U., 1992. RN, Wis.; lic. psychologist. Staff nurse St. Mary's Hill Hosp., Milw., 1977-78; Staff nurse Waukesha (Wis.) Meml. Hosp., 1978-80, clin. nurse specialist, 1980-87; asst. prof. nursing Marquette U., Milw., 1986—; psychotherapist Psychiat. Assocs. Comprehensive Services, Ltd., Milw., 1982-85; nurse psychotherapist Counseling and Wellness Ctr., Waukesha, 1982—; cons. Alverno Coll., Milw., 1983-84, Health Care Cons., Sussex, Wis., 1985—; coord. Waukesha Premenstrual Syndrome Program, 1980—; nurse psychotherapist Stress Mgmt. and Mental Health Svcs., Waukesha, 1991-94; co-founder Turning Point Mental Health and Cons. Svcs., Waukesha, 1994—. Contbr. articles to profl. jours. Bd. dirs. Waukesha County Mental Health Assn., 1982; mem. Waukesha County Unified Svcs., 1984; advisor Resolve Through Sharing, 1986—, Women's Health Svcs., 1987—; advisor Parish Nurse Program. Mem. ANA (coun. psychiat. and mental health nursing), Wis. Nurses Assn. (rep. Wis. Coalition on Sexual Misconduct by Psychotherapists and Counselors 1988-93), Delta Upsilon Sigma, Phi Lambda Delta. Office: Turning Point Mental Health & Cons Svcs Waukesha WI 53188

WALLUM, BRAD JOY, endocrinologist; b. Mitchell, S.D., Oct. 17, 1955; s. Joy L. and Delores J. (Barringer) W; m. Connie J. Swettanam, June 11, 1994; 1 child, Sarah Joy. BS, U. S.D., 1977, MD, 1981. Resident Mayo Clinic, Rochester, Minn., 1981-84; fellow U. Wash., Seattle, 1984-87; physician Eastside Endocrinology and Diabetes, Bellevue, Wash., 1986—. Office: Eastside Endocr & Diabetes 2020 116th Ave NE # 150 Bellevue WA 98004

WALMAN, JEROME, psychotherapist, publisher, consultant, critic; b. Charleston, W.Va., June 19, 1937; s. Joe and Madeline Minnie (Levy) W.; m. Mary Joan Granara, Sept. 5, 1960. Student, U. W.Va.; student, Boston U., Berkley Sch. Music, Boston. Producer, composer, writer mus. compositions Carnegie Hall, Broadway Theatre, 1962, 63; pvt. practice psychotherapy in spl. hypnosis and music therapy, 1964—; designer Jerome Walman Systems Applied Hypnosis, 1969; travel-restaurant-wine-entertainment critic Sta. WNCN-FM Radio; critic travel, food, wine Sta. WNCN-FM Radio, Fodor's N.Y. restaurant sect.; marriage and family counselor; lectr. dir. tng. programs in memory improvement and speed reading; cons. personal image, wine and food Dept. Def., NYU; cons., dir. Cooking for Relaxation and Wieght Control; restaurant publicist; condr. courses in wine appreciation and food; restaurant, wine and food critic Sta. WCNC-GAF Radio; host travel, restaurant and wine show Sta. WEVD Radio. Dir., producer syndicated TV show Enterprises Unltd., 1978—; producer, composer I Murdered Mary, N.Y.C., 1976, Last Call, N.Y.C., 1977, TV Mag., 1978; lectr. East-West Ctr., N.Y.C., 1978, Actors Tng. and Acting Therapy Ctr. Am., Westwinds Learning Ctr., The Learning Exchange, 1986; editor Punch In Internat. Electronic Travel, Wine and Restaurant mag.; pub. Wine On Line mag., The Computer User's Survival Newsletter and Syndicated Column; originator facimile news svc. Fax It To Me; author papers on hypnosis, psychic phenomena and memory, music therapy, biofeedback and meditation application; featured in various publs. including Fortune, Gentleman's Quar., Cosmopolitan, Leaders mag., Mademoiselle; editor Punch in Internat. Wine, Restaurant and Travel Electronic mag.; syndicated columnist travel and wine Cab Mag.; reviewer Wine-on-Line Internat. Wire Svc., The Computer User's Survival Newsletter; contbg. writer Chocolatier Mag., Troika Mag.; contbr. The Official Airline Guides Electronic Edition, Fodor's N.Y. Sunday in N.Y. and Pocket N.Y. Travel Guide. Mem. Music Therapy Internat. Meditation and Mental Devel. Ctr. N.Y., Memory Improvement and Concentration Ctr. Am., Delphi-Gen. Videotex Svc.-Nynex Info-Logic, Internat. Foods, Wine & Travel Writers Assn. Office: Punch In Syndicate 400 E 59th St Apt 9F New York NY 10022-2344

WALMSLEY, ROBERTA CHAPIN, social worker; b. Blytheville, Ark., Sept. 1, 1933; d. John Arnett and Ruth (Pollock) Chapin; m. Arthur Edward Walmsley, Dec. 29, 1954; children: Elizabeth, John. AB, Washington U., St. Louis, 1955; MSW, U. Conn., 1979. Lic. social worker ACSW, Conn. Social worker sch. systems Wallingford, Conn., 1979-86; coord. Clergy Family Project, Hartford, Conn., 1986-89, project dir., 1990—; v.p. bd. Bklyn. Kindergarten Soc., 1962-74; cons. Family Life Com. of Episcopal Ch., N.Y.C., 1967-69. Co-author: Clergy Family in the 80's, Manual for Clergy Family Committees, Health Clergy, Wounded Healers: Their Families and Their Ministries, 1996. mem. children's network com. Dio of N.H., 1994—; bd. dirs. N.H. Family Resource Coalition, 1995—. Democrat. Home: RR 1 Box 224 Hillsboro NH 03244-9333

WALROND, ERROL RICARDO, surgeon; b. Mar. 19, 1936; m. Beverley Walrond; children: Maurice, Maya. BS in Anatomy with honors, London U., 1958; Degree, Conjoint Coll. Royal Coll. Physicians and Surgeons Eng., 1960; MB, BS, London U., 1961; FRCS, Royal Coll. Surgeons Eng., 1964. House physician Guy's Hosp., London, 1960-61, ENT house surgeon, 1961; house surgeon Putney Hosp., London, 1961-62, casualty officer, 1962-63; surg. registrar Alton (Eng.) and Lord Mayor Treloars Hosp., 1963-65; sr. surg. registrar Queen Elizabeth Hosp., Barbados, 1965-66, U. Hosp., Jamaica, 1966-67; commonwealth fellow thoracic surg. dept. Guy's Hops., London, 1967-68; lectr. dept. surgery U. W.I., Mona, Jamaica, 1968—, sr. lectr. dept. surgery, 1971-76, prof. surgery, 1976-96; vice-dean faculty of medicine U. W.I., Barbados, 1977-86, dean faculty med. scis., 1986-92; sci. sec. of Commonwealth Caribbean Med. Rsch. coun., 1973—; appt. mem. expert adv. panel health manpower WHO, 1980-92; mem. coun. Caribbean Rsch. and Epidemiology Ctr., 1979—; chmn. Med. Coun., Barbados, 1985-87, 92-96. Editor: BAMP Bulletin, 1983-85; contbr. numerous articles to profl. jours. sci. sec. of Commonwealth Caribbean Med. Rsch. coun., 1973—; appt. mem. expert adv. panel health manpower WHO, 1980-92; mem. coun. Caribbean Rsch. and Epidemiology Ctr., 1979—; chmn. Med. Coun., Barbados, 1985-87, 92-95. Fellow ACS; mem. Assn. Surgeons Jamaica (sec. 1964-73), Barbados Assn. Med. Practitioners (v.p., chmn. ethical com. 1975-76, pres. 1976-82, v.p. 1982-87, chmn. task force on AIDS, nat. adv. com. on AIDS 1987-94, Companion of Honor Barbados 1990). Home: 34 Sandy Ln, Saint James Barbados Office: U WI, Faculty Med Scis, Bridgetown Barbados

WALSH, ANTHONY FRANCIS, microbiologist; b. London, Dec. 17, 1930; came to U.S., 1956; s. Archibald Edward and Irene Mary (Hendry) W.; m. Mamie Rae Lewis, June 15, 1957; children: Clare, Anne. BS, U. Fla., 1965, MS, 1966, PhD, 1970. Profl. microbiologist, med. technologist. Microbiologist Pittsfield (Mass.) Gen. Hosp., 1956-57, Orange (Fla.) Meml. Hosp., 1957-62; rsch. technologist U. Fla., Gainesville, 1962-70; chief microbiologist Orland Regional Med. Ctr., 1970—; assoc. prof. U. Cen. Fla., 1972—; cons. Flowers Chem. Labs, Altamonte Springs, Fla., 1972—. Pres. Fla. Right to Life Com., Orlando, 1975; community resource vol. Orange County Sch. System, 1975—. With Royal Army Med. Corps, 1949-51, Eng. Mem. Fla. Acad. Scis. (treas. 1972—), Inst. Med. Labs Scis. (assoc. mem.), Canadian Soc. Med. Lab Technicians, Am. Soc. Microbiology. Roman Catholic. Home: 5636 Satel Dr Orlando FL 32810-4954

WALSH, ARTHUR CAMPBELL, psychiatrist; b. Vancouver, B.C., Can., Dec. 21, 1919; came to U.S., 1964; s. William Charles and Kathleen (Patterson) W.; m. Bernice Martha Hessom, Dec. 26, 1944; children: Kathleen, David, Thomas. MD, U. Alta., Edmonton, 1943. Intern Vancouver Gen. Hosp., B.C., 1943; pvt. practice Vancouver, B.C., 1945-64; resident psychiatry U. Pitts., 1964-67, clin. asst. prof. psychiatry, 1967-89; pvt. practice Pitts., 1968—; pres. Ctr. Senility Studies Alzheimer Treatment Rsch. Ctr., Pitts., 1969—; psychiat. cons. VA, Pitts., 1969-89, Woodville State Hosp., Pitts., 1969-86. Author: Conquering Senility; co-author: Mental Capacity: Medical Legal Aspects of Assessment and Treatment, 1975, 2d edit., 1994; contbr. med. articles to profl. jours. With Royal Can. Army Med. Corps, 1943-45. Mem. AMA, Am. Psychiat. Assn., Am. Assn. Geriatric Psychiatry, Pa. Med. Soc. Home: 307 S Dithridge St Apt 202 Pittsburgh PA 15213-3514 Office: Alzheimer Treatment Rsch Ctr Ctr Senility Studies 161 N Dithridge St Pittsburgh PA 15213-2646

WALSH, CHRISTOPHER THOMAS, biochemist, department chairman; b. Boston, Feb. 16, 1944; married; 1 child. BA, Harvard U., 1965; PhD in Life Sci., Rockefeller U., 1970. Helen Hay Whitney Found. fellow Brandeis U., 1970-72; from asst. prof. to prof. chemistry and biology MIT, 1972-87, assoc. dir. Whitaker Coll. Mgmt., 1979-82, Uncas and Helen Whitaker prof., 1980-85, Karl Taylor Compton prof., 1985-87, chmn. chemistry dept., 1982-87; David Wesley Gaiser prof. Harvard U., 1987-91, chmn. dept. biol. chemistry and molecular pharmacology Med. Sch., 1987—, Hamilton Kuhn prof., 1991—; pres. Dana-Farber Cancer Inst., Boston, 1992-95; cons. Merck, Sharp & Dohme Rsch. Labs., 1975-81, Monsanto Corp. Res. Labs., 1980-81, Johnson & Johnson, 1982-83, Hoffman LaRoche, 1982—, Genzyme & Bioinfo Assocs., 1983—, Firmenich, S A, 1986-90, Enzymatics, 1988—, Biotage, 1989—; mem. panel rsch. grants study NSF, 1977-79, panel study sect. biochemistry NIH, 1978-82, gen. med. coun., NIH, 1983-85, Chemal Rsch. Group, WHO, 1984-86; co-chmn. Gordon Rsch. Conf. Enzymes, Coenzymes & Molecular Biology, 1978, Conf. Methanogenesis, 1984; chmn. study sect. biochemistry NIH, 1982—; lectr. in field. Alfred P. Sloan Found. fellow, 1975-77, Camille and Henry Dreyfus Tchr.-Scholar grantee, 1976-80; recipient Eli Lilly award, 1979. Mem. NAS, Inst. Medicine-NAS, Am. Acad. Arts & Sci., Am. Soc. Biol. Chemists, Am. Chem. Soc., Am. Soc. Microbiology. Office: Harvard Med Sch Dept Bio Chem & Molecular Pharmacology Boston MA 02215*

WALSH, DEIRDRE V., physician; b. Phila., Jan. 18, 1962; d. Raymond Michael and Dolores (Porretta) Victor; m. Matthew Joseph, June 8, 1986; children: Jason, Adam, Joseph. BA in Biology, Swarthmore Coll., 1983; MD, Hahneman U., 1987. Resident in internal medicine Temple Hosp., Phila., 1987-90; fellow in cardiology Hahneman Hosp., Phila., 1990-93; pvt. practice cardiology St. Mary Hosp., Langhorne, Pa., 1993—. Contbr. articles to profl. jours. Recipient Rsch. prize Am. Hosp. Assn., 1987. Fellow Am. Coll. Cardiology; mem. AMA, Am. Coll. Physicians, Phi Beta Kappa, Alpha Omega Alpha (chpt. pres. 1987). Home: 904 Sturgis Ln Lower Gwynedd PA 19002 Office: Bucks County Cardiology Assocs Ste 204 1205 Langhorne-Newtown Rd Langhorne PA 19047

WALSH, JAMES ANTHONY, psychology educator; b. Portland, Oreg., Apr. 13, 1938; s. James Anthony and Mary Norine (O'Shea) W.; m. Roberta Annette Blake, Sept. 17, 1957; children: Jennifer, Robert. BS, U. Wash., 1960, MS, 1961, PhD, 1963. Lic. psychologist, Mont. (mem. licensing bd. 1981-82, chmn. 1982-84). Asst. prof. psychology and stats. Iowa State U., Ames, 1965-66, assoc. prof., 1966-69, prof., 1969-72; prof. psychology Mont. State U., Missoula, 1972—, chmn. dept., 1972-76; cons. Mont. Gov., Helena, 1976-77, Mont. C. of C., Helena, 1978, Casey Family Program, Helena, 1980-87, McKenzie, Steele, Briggs, Crown Corp., Brandon, Man., Can., 1985, Rsch. and Tng. Ctr. on Rural Rehab. Svcs., Missoula, Mont., 1988—, Confederated Salish and Kootenai Tribal Health Dept., St. Ignatius, Mont., 1988, 90—; vis. lectr. Com. Pres. Statis.Socs., 1976-86. Author: Quality Care for Tough Kids; developer: Comprehensive Social Desirability Scale for Children, 1974; contbr. articles and revs. to profl. jours. Mem. Missoula Pub. Schs. Adv. Council, 1974-76; mem. program. com. Comprehensive Devel. Ctr., Missoula, 1980-83; bd. dirs. Crisis Ctr. of Missoula, 1984-85. Postdoctoral fellow NIMH, 1963-64, Soc. Sci. Research Council, 1970-71. Fellow APA, Am. Psychol. Soc.; mem. Am. Statis. Assn., Psychometric Soc., Biometric Soc., Sigma Xi. Democrat. Office: U Mont Dept Psychology Missoula MT 59812

WALSH, JOSEPH BRENNAN, ophthalmologist; b. Troy, N.Y., Mar. 6, 1941; s. Joseph Edward and Edna Margaret (Molloy) W. BS in Biology, Georgetown U., 1962, MD, 1966. Diplomate Am. Bd. Ophthalmology. Intern in medicine SUNY Upstate Med. Ctr., Syracuse, 1966-67; resident in medicine Univ. Hosp., Boston, 1967-68; resident in ophthalmology The N.Y. Eye and Ear Infirmary, N.Y.C., 1970-73; retina fellow Montefiore Hosp. and Med. Ctr./Albert Einstein Coll. Medicine, Bronx, 1973-74; from instr. to assoc. prof. dept. ophthalmology Montefiore Med. Ctr./Albert Einstein Coll. of Medicine, Bronx, N.Y., 1973-88; chmn., prof. dept. ophthalmology N.Y. Eye and Ear Infirmary/N.Y. Med. Coll., N.Y.C., 1988—. Capt. USAF, 1968-70, Vietnam. Fellow N.Y. Acad. Medicine, N.Y. Acad. Sci., Royal Coll. Ophthalmologists; mem. Am. Acad. Ophthalmology, Assn. for Rsch. in Vision and Ophthalmology, Ophthalmic Laser Surg. Soc. (pres. 1991-94), Macula Soc., Retina Soc., N.Y. Soc. for Clin. Ophthalmology (pres. 1993-95), Am. Soc. Order of St. John Ophthalmic Hosp. (knight). Office: NY Eye and Ear Infirmary 310 E 14th St New York NY 10003

WALSH, KENNETH ANDREW, biochemist; b. Sherbrooke, Que., Can., Aug. 7, 1931; s. George Stanley and Dorothy Maud (Sangster) W.; m. Deirdre Anne Clarke, Aug. 22, 1953; children: Andrew, Michael, Erin. BSc in Agr., McGill U., 1951; MS, Purdue U., 1953; PhD, U. Toronto, 1959. Postdoctoral fellow U. Wash., Seattle, 1959-62, from asst. prof. to assoc. prof. Biochemistry, 1962-69, prof. Biochemistry, 1969—, chair, 1990—. Author (book) Methods in Protein Sequence Analysis, 1986. Mem. The Protein Soc. (sec.-treas. 1987-90), Am. Soc. Biochemistry/Molecular Biology. Office: U Wash Dept Biochem Box 357350 Seattle WA 98195

WALSH, KENNETH BRIAN, pharmacology educator; b. N.Y.C., Mar. 18, 1956; s. Martin F. and Dorothy K. (Martin) W.; m. Gina D. Walsh; children: Cari E., Thomas M. BA, Bard Coll., 1978; MA, SUNY, 1981; PhD, Univ. Cin., 1986. Post-doctoral fellow Univ. Rochester, Rochester, N.Y., 1986-89; asst. prof. Univ. S.C., Columbia, 1989-95, assoc. prof., 1995—; editorial bd. Current Drug Review, London, 1995—. Contbr. articles to profl. jours. Institutional Animal Care and Use com. Univ. S.C., 1994—; reviewer Am. Heart Assn., Columbia, 1995—. Recipient First award Nat. Heart, Lung & Blood Inst., 1992—, Shannon Award, 1991-92, Grant-in-Aid Am. Heart Assn., 1992-94, Venture award Univ. S.C., 1995-96. Mem. Biophysical Soc., Am. Soc. Pharmacology & Experimental Therapeutics. Office: Univ SC Sch Medicine Columbia SC 29208

WALSH, KEVIN KANE, psychologist, consultant, researcher; b. Phila., Feb. 28, 1950; s. George F. and Dora Louise (Galbiati) W.; m. Janet Ellen Calovi, Oct. 30, 1971; children: Amanda, Douglas, Edward, Elizabeth. BS in Psychology, Mt. St. Mary's Coll., Emmitsburg, Md., 1972; MA in Psychology, U. Akron, 1978, PhD in Psychology, 1982. Grad. rsch. asst. U. Akron, Ohio, 1975-80; assoc. staff psychologist Broome Svcs.-State of N.Y., Binghamton, 1980-81; dir. residential svcs. The Tng. Sch. at Vineland, N.J., 1981-83, dir. psychology/habilitation, 1984-86, asst. exec. dir., 1988-91; cons. psychologist Vineland, 1991—; dir. rsch. Devel. Disabilities Ctr. of Morristown (N.J.) Meml. Hosp., 1992—; mem. rsch. com. N.J. Divsn. Devel. Disabilities, Trenton, 1989—. Author: (with others) Role of Institutions in Community Services, 1987, Developmentally Disabled People Grow-Up, 1991; editor: Threads of Change: Historical Readings, 1988; assoc. editor Mental Retardation; contbr. numerous articles to profl. jours. Sec., bd. trustees Ellison Sch., Vineland, 1983-85; bd. dirs. Sun Nat. Bank, Vineland, 1990—; mem. Cumberland Unit Assn. Retarded Citizens, 1992—, pres. 1995—; bd. dirs. Am. Assn. Mental Retardation, Washington, 1993-95; region v.p. ARC, N.J., 1993-95. Named Intern in Community Svc., State of N.J., 1970; DeGraff scholar, Akron, 1979-80. Mem. APA, Am. Assn. Mental Retardation (chair region psychol. divsn. 1985-90, region chair 1992, nat. bd. dirs. 1993-94). Home: 2490 Vine Rd Vineland NJ 08360-2520

WALSH, MARIE LECLERC, nurse; b. Providence, Sept. 11, 1928; d. Walter Normand and Anna Mary (Ryan) Leclerc; m. John Breffni Walsh, June 18, 1955; children: George Breffni, John Leclerc, Darina Louise. Grad., Waterbury Hosp. Sch. Nursing, Conn., 1951; BS, Columbia U., 1954, MA, 1955. Team leader Hartford (Conn.) Hosp., 1951-53; pvt. duty nurse St. Luke's Hosp., N.Y.C., 1953-57; sch. nurse tchr. Agnes Russel Ctr., Tchrs. Coll. Columbia U., N.Y.C., 1955-56; clin. nursing instr. St. Luke's Hosp., N.Y.C., 1957-58; chmn. disaster nursing ARC Fairfax County, Va., 1975; course coord. occupational health nursing U. Va. Sch. Continuing Edn., Falls Church, 1975-77; mem. disaster steering com. No. Va. C.C., Annandale, 1976; adj. faculty U. Va. Sch. Continuing Edn., Falls Church, 1981; disaster svcs. nurse ARC, Wichita, Kans., 1985-90; disaster svcs. nurse Seattle-King County chpt. ARC, Seattle, 1990-96; rsch. and statis. analyst U. Va. Sch. Continuing Edn. Nursing, Falls Church, 1975; rsch. libr. Olive

Garvey Ctr. for Improvement Human Functioning, Inc., Wichita, 1985. Sec. Dem. party, Cresskill, N.J., 1964-66; county committeewoman, Bergen County, N.J., 1965-66; pres., v.p., Internat. Staff Wives, NATO, Brussels, Belgium, 1978-80; election officer, supr. Election Bd., Wichita, 1987, 88. Mem. AAAS, AAUW, N.Y. Acad. Sci., Pi Lambda Theta, Sigma Theta Tau. Home: 8800 Prestwould Pl Mc Lean VA 22102

WALSH, PATRICIA REGINA, trauma nurse, educator; b. Phila., Nov. 16, 1955; d. William Aloysius and Patricia Delores (Smith) W.; 1 child, William. BSN, West Chester U., 1977; MSN, Widener U., 1987. RN, Pa.; cert. ACLS, BCLS Am. Heart Assn.; cert. basic trauma life support provider, instr. Am. Coll. Emergency Physicians. Staff nurse Hosp. of U. Pa., Phila., 1977-80, asst. head nurse, head nurse neuro-med. unit, 1980-82, advanced clin. staff nurse neuro-med. unit, 1982-84, staff nurse oper. rm., 1984-87; coord. trauma edn. Thomas Jefferson U. Hosp., Phila., 1987—; adj. faculty Widener U., 1988, Thomas Jefferson U., 1990; presenter at profl. confs. Contbr. to profl. publs. Mem. Am. Trauma Soc. (Pub. Svc. award 1990, Disting. Svc. award 1993), Delaware Valley Trauma Nurses Consortium, Sigma Theta Tau. Home: 800 Gainsboro Rd Drexel Hill PA 19026-1614 Office: Jefferson U Hosp Trauma Ctr 118 S 11th St Philadelphia PA 19107-4801

WALSH, PATRICK CRAIG, urologist; b. Akron, Ohio, Feb. 13, 1938; s. Raymond Michael and Catherine N. (Rodden) W.; m. Margaret Campbell, May 23, 1964; children—Christopher, Jonathan, Alexander. A.B., Case Western Res. U., 1960, M.D., 1964. Intern in surgery Peter Bent Brigham Hosp., Boston, 1964-65; asst. resident in surgery Peter Bent Brigham Hosp., 1965-66; asst. resident in pediatric surgery Children's Hosp. Med. Center, Boston, 1966-67; resident in urology U. Calif.-Los Angeles Med. Center, 1967-71; dir. Brady Urol. Inst., urologist-in-chief Johns Hopkins Hosp., Balt., 1974—; prof., dir. dept. urology Johns Hopkins U. Sch. Medicine, 1974—. Contbr. articles to med. jours. Served to comdr. M.C. USN, 1971-73. Recipient Charles F. Kettering medal GM Cancer Rsch. Found., 1996. Mem. Soc. Univ. Surgeons, Am. Assn. Genitourinary Surgeons, Clin. Soc. Genitourinary Surgeons, Am. Urol. Assn., Endocrine Soc., Am. Surg. Assn. Inst. Medicine of NAS, Alpha Omega Alpha. Roman Catholic. Office: Johns Hopkins Med Inst 600 N Wolfe St Baltimore MD 21205-2110

WALSH, RAYMOND JOHN, medical educator; b. Dec. 13, 1947; married; 2 children. BS in Zoology, U. Mass., 1969; PhD in Anatomy, Tufts U., 1976. Rsch. asst. dept. comparative pathology New Eng. Regional Primate Rsch. Ctr., 1969-72; postdoctoral rsch. fellow dept. ob-gyn. Royal Victoria Hosp., McGill U., Montreal, 1976-78; asst. prof. anatomy George Washington U., Washington, 1978-82, assoc. prof., 1982-91, interim chmn. anatomy, 1990-95, prof. and chmn. anatomy, 1995—; participant numerous ednl. confs.; lectr. in field; sponsor Ednl. Commn. for Fgn. Med. Grads., Quaid-i-Azam Med. Coll. Bahawalpur, Pakistan, 1992-93; external examiner dept. anatomy Kuwait U., 1993, 94. Contbr. numerous articles and abstracts to profl. jours. Chmn. anatomical bd. Dept. Human Svcs., D.C. Govt., 1992—. Grantee Biomed. Rsch. Support, 1978-79, 85-86, 90-91, NINCDS, 1979-83, 83-85, NSF, 1986-90, Souers fund, 1994-95. Mem. Am. Assn. Anatomists (local organizing com. ann. meeting 1987), Soc. Neurosci., Internat. Brain Rsch. Orgn., Soc. for Applied Learning Tech., Am. Assn. Neurol. Surgeons (local organizer workshop 1994), Washington Soc. for Electron Microscopy (chmn. sponsor site orgn. com. 1980). Office: George Washington Univ Dept Anatomy 2300 I St NW Washington DC 20037*

WALSH, THOMAS JOSEPH, neuro-ophthalmologist; b. N.Y.C., Sept. 18, 1931; s. Thomas Joseph and Virginia (Hughes) W.; m. Sally Ann Maust, June 21, 1958; children—Thomas Raymond, Sara Ann, Mary Kelly, Kathleen Meghan. BA, Coll. Fordham, 1954; MD, Bowman Gray Med. Sch., 1958. Intern St. Vincent's Hosp., N.Y.C., 1958-59; resident ophthalmology Bowman Gray Med. Sch., Winston-Salem, N.C., 1961-64; fellow neuro-ophthalmology Bascom Palmer Eye Inst., Miami, Fla., 1964-65; practice medicine specializing in neuro-ophthalmology Stamford, Conn., 1965—; dir. neuro-ophthalmology service, asst. prof. ophthalmology and neurology Yale Sch. Medicine, New Haven, 1965-74; assoc. prof. Yale Sch. Medicine, 1974-79, prof., 1979—, also bd. permanent officers; dir. ophthalmology Stamford Hosp., 1978-83; mem. staff St. Joseph Hosp., Yale New Haven Hosp.; cons. to surgeon gen. army in neuro-ophthalmology Walter Reed Hosp., Washington, 1966—, VA Hosp., West Haven, 1965—, Silver Hill Found., New Canaan, Conn., 1974—; frequent lectr. various univs. Contbr. articles to various publs. Mem. adv. bd. Stamford Salvation Army, 1972-92; mem. med. bd. Darien Nurses Assn., Conn., 1972—; surgeon Darien Fire Dept., 1969—. With AUS, 1959-61. Decorated Knight of Malta, 1983; Centennial fellow Johns Hopkins, 1976. Mem. AMA, Conn., Fairfield County med. socs., Acad. Ophthalmology, Oxford Ophthal. Congress, Acad. Neurology, Am. Assn. Neurol. Surgeons, Internat. Neuro-Ophthalmology Soc., Soc. Med. Cons. to Armed Forces, Cosmos Club (Washington), Darien County Club, Yale Club (N.Y.C), Lions, Army-Navy Club. Office: 1100 Bedford St Stamford CT 06905-5301

WALSH, THOMAS RAYMOND, surgeon; b. N.Y.C., Mar. 28, 1959; s. Thomas Joseph and Sara Ann (Maust) W.; m. Elizabeth Ann Douglass, Nov. 26, 1983; children: Molly Elizabeth, Mallory Ann, Thomas De Berry. BA magna cum laude, Wake Forest U., 1980, MD, 1984. Diplomate Am. Bd. Surgery, Nat. Bd. Med. Examiners. Intern in surgery Hosps. of U. Health Ctr. of Pitts., 1984-85, resident in surgery, 1985-87, rsch. fellow in transplantation surgery, 1987-89, sr. resident in surgery, 1989-90, chief resident in surgery, 1990-91; surgeon Westwood Surg. Assn., High Point, N.C., 1991-95, Cornerstone Health Care, PA, High Point, N.C., 1995—; also bd. dirs., 1995—; clin. faculty Bowman Gray Sch. of Medicine, Winston-Salem, N.C., 1991—; founding bd. dirs., exec. med. dir. Practice Directions, High Point, 1993-95; dir., bd. dirs. Comprehensive Cancer Program, High Point Regional Hosp., 1993-95; mem. steering com. Triad Managed Care Orgn., High Point/Greenboro/Winston-Salem, 1995-96; presenter in field. Contbr. articles to profl. jours. Vice chairperson parish coun. Immaculate Heart of Mary Parish, High Point, 1992-93, chairperson, 1993-94; bd. dirs. Am. Cancer Soc., High Point, 1993—, v.p., 1994-95; vol. physician Cmty. Clinics of High Point, 1993-95. Recipient Rsch. Svc. award NIH, 1988-90, Rsch. award U. Pitts., 1988-89, Lederle Traveling Fellowship award Soc. Univ. Surgeons, 1990; named one of Outstanding Young Men of Am., 1982, 83. Fellow Am. Coll. Surgeons (Lederle Traveling Fellowship award 1989); mem. AMA, Am. Coll. Physician Execs., N.C. Med. Soc., High Point Med. Soc., Carolina Vascular Soc., Mark Ravitch Surg. Soc., Rotary, KC, Friendly Sons of St. Patrick, Alpha Epsilon Delta, Kappa Sigma. Roman Catholic. Home: 1269 Westminster Dr High Point NC 27262 Office: Cornerstone Health Care PA 624 Quaker Ln Ste 101-C High Point NC 27262

WALSH, WILLIAM JOSEPH, orthopedic surgeon; b. N.Y.C., Apr. 19, 1938; s. William Joseph and Rosemary Frances (Healy) W.; m. Nancy Claire Stoldt, July 16, 1966 (div. Nov., 1993); children: Colleen Joan, William Joseph, Kevin Stoldt, Ryan Patrick; m. Melinda Mathias, Apr. 8, 1994. BS, Coll. of Holy Cross, 1960; MD, N.Y. Med. Coll., 1964. Intern St. Vincent's Hosp., N.Y.C., 1964-65, resident, 1965-66; resident N.Y.U. Bellevue Ctr., N.Y.C., 1968-71; attending orthopedist St. Agnes Hosp., White Plains, N.Y., 1971—, White Plains Hosp., 1971—; Westchester Med. Ctr., Valhalla, N.Y., 1971—; assoc. prof. N.Y. Med. Coll., Valhalla, 1975—; trustee St. Vincent's Hosp., Harrison, N.Y., 1989-95, St. Agnes Hosp., White Plains, N.Y., 1994-96; acting chmn. orthopedics dept. N.Y. Med. Coll., Valhalla, 1994-95. Chmn. Westchester Triathalon, Rye, N.Y., 1988-94; com. mem. Cath. Hosp. Network, N.Y.C., 1994-95. Lt. USNR, 1966-68, Vietnam. Fellow Am. Acad. Orthop. Surgery; mem. AMA, Westchester Med. Soc. (pres.), N.Y. State Orthop. Soc. (bd. dirs.), N.Y. State Med. Soc. (del.), Irish-Am. Orthop. Soc. Republican. Roman Catholic. Office: 311 North St White Plains NY 10605

WALSMITH, CHARLES RODGER, psychologist, educator; b. Denver, May 19, 1926; s. Joseph Francis and Florence Ophelia (Brown-Smith) W.; children: Karen Frances, Cynthia Ann, Erik Konrad. BA (Chancellor's Ednl. scholar), U. Denver, 1956, MA, 1962; postgrad. U. Wash., 1968-76; PhD, Stanton U., 1976. Rsch. psychologist Personnel Tng. and Rsch. Ctr., Maintenance Lab., USAF Lowery AFB, Denver, 1956; rsch. asst. U. Colo. Med. Ctr., Denver, 1956-57, rsch. assoc., 1957-64; assoc. prof. psychology North Park Coll., Chgo., 1965-66; sr. human engring. analyst, psychoacoustics Boeing Co., Seattle, 1965-68; instr. psychology dept. behavioral scis. Bellevue (Wash.) Community Coll., 1968-87, chmn. dept., 1968-75, 79-82, Phi Theta Kappa adviser, 1981-87, instr., chmn. dept. emeritus, 1987—. Resident trainer Gestalt Inst. of Can., Lake Cowichan, B.C., summers 1969-71, assoc., 1969—; dir. Gestalt Inst. of Wash., Bellevue, 1970—. Dem. precinct chmn., Renton, Wash., 1966-68. With USNR, 1944-46. Mem. NEA, Phi Beta Kappa, Psi Chi. Home: Gestalt House 14909 SE 44th Pl Bellevue WA 98006-2421

WALSTON, LOLA INGE, dietitian; b. Chgo., Jan. 26, 1943; d. Willy and Ingeborg (Smith) Neumann; m. Steven Ward Walston, Aug. 5, 1967; children: Bradley, Scott. BS, No. Ill. U., 1965; MS, U. Iowa, 1967. Registered, lic. dietitian. Asst. dietary dir. Alaska Hosp. Med. Ctr., Anchorage, 1975-78; cons. dietitian Mercer County Hosp., Coldwater, Ohio, 1979; profl. service cons. Health Care and Retirement Corp. Am., Lima, Ohio, 1981-84; dietary dir. Estes Health Care Ctr., Montgomery, Ala., 1979-80, Mercy Meml. Hosp., Urbana, Ohio, 1984-86, Dairy & Nutrition Council Mid East, Dayton, Ohio, 1987-89; cons. Sharonview Nursing Home, South Vienna, Ohio, 1987—; Miami Health Care Ctr., Troy, Ohio, Columbia House, Springfield, Ohio, SCOPE Nutrition Program for the elderly, Fairborn, Ohio, CLS Nutrition Program, Bellefontaine, Ohio, 1987-90, Westview Acres Care Ctr., Eaton, Ohio, 1988—, St. John's Nursing Home, Springfield, 1989—, Oakwood Village, Springfield, 1989—, Villa Springfield, Springfield, Ohio, 1990—, Covington (Ohio) Care Ctr., 1990-91, Champaign Nursing Home, 1993—, Covenant House, 1993. Mem. com. Tecumseh council Boy Scouts Am., 1984—, Tri-County Community Action Commn./CLS Nutrition, Bellefontaine, Ohio, 1987-90. Mem. Am. Dietetic Assn., Ohio Dietetic Assn., Ohio Cons. Dietitians Health Care Facilities (chmn. 1982-84, treas.-elect 1996—), Dayton Dietetic Assn. (treas. 1995-96), AAUW. Club: Hilltoppers (Fairborn, Ohio) (pres. 1982-83). Avocations: camping, sewing, knitting, crocheting, cooking.

WALTA, DOUGLAS CRAIG, gastroenterologist, clinic executive; b. Arlington, S.D., Apr. 23, 1943; s. John P. and Elizabeth (Kranz) W.; m. Trudi Walta; children: Maren, Krin. BS, St. John's U., Collegeville, Minn., 1965; MD, U. Minn., 1968. Bd. cert. Am. Bd. Internal Medicine; subspecialty bd. gastroenterology. Intern W.Va. U., Morgantown, 1968-69; fellow in gastroenterology U. Minn., 1971, 74-75; pvt. practice, 1975—; clin. instr. medicine U. Oreg. Health Scis. Ctr.; cons. gastroenterology Portland VA Hosp.; staff Providence Med. Ctr., Holladay Park Med. Ctr.; mem. med. morals com. Providence Med. Ctr.; vis. lectr. Kelowna (B.C., Can.) Gen. Hosp., 1986, 92, North Pacific Soc. Internal Medicine, N.W. Conf. Radiologic Technologists, 1993, Portland C.C. Radiography Program, 1993, Practices in Advances in Internal Medicine, Providence Med. Ctr., 1994. With U.S. Army, 1971-73. Fellow Am. Coll. Gastroenterology; mem. AMA, Am. Gastroenterology Assn., Oreg. Med. Assn. (bd. trustees, task force financing health care), North Pacific Soc. Internal Medicine, Multnoman County Med. Soc. (1st v.p., sec., exec. com., ethics com., chmn. bioethics com. 1991, trustee), Pacific Interurban Clin. Club. Home: 3415 SW Heather Ln Portland OR 97201-1680 Office: Oreg Clinic GI Divsn Ste 611 5050 NE Hoyt Portland OR 97213-2988

WALTER, ERIC G., podiatrist; b. Long Island City, N.Y., Feb. 16, 1964; s. Gerd Emil and Aloisia Maria (Knaus) W.; m. Daphne Frances Reinhardt, Nov. 24, 1990 (div. Oct. 1995). BS in Biology, Boston Coll., 1986; DPM, N.Y. Coll. Podiatric Medicine, 1990. Podiatric med. resident postgrad. program N.Y. Coll. Podiatric Medicine, N.Y.C., 1990-91, podiatric surg. resident postgrad. program, 1991-93; pvt. practice Bronx & Westchester, 1993—; cons. podiatrist Running Sch. Inc., Dix Hills, N.Y., 1990-94; attending clinician St. Barnabus Hosp., Bronx, N.Y., Our Lady of Mercy Med. Ctr., Bronx. Fellow Am. Assn. Podiatric Sports Medicine; mem. Am. Podiatric Med. Assn., N.Y. State Podiatric Med. Assn., Am. Coll. Foot and Ankle Surgeons, Am. Coll. Sports Medicine. Roman Catholic. Home: 2172 Central Pk Ave Yonkers NY 10710-1826

WALTER, MELINDA KAY, health department evaluator; b. Taylorville, Ill., Aug. 6, 1957; d. Ray and Betty (Jones) W.; m. Laurence M. Nakrin, Dec. 21, 1983. BA, Millikin U., 1979; MPA, Sangamon State U., 1981. Acctg. intern Archer Daniels Midland, Decatur, Ill., 1978; econ. devel. intern City of Decatur, 1979; resident dir. Millikin U., Decatur, 1978-79; classification analyst Ill. Dept. Personnel, Springfield, 1979-81; rules analyst Ill. Gen. Assembly, Springfield, 1981-84; regulatory cons. Ill. Dept. Pub. Health, Chgo., 1984-85; asst. to div. chief Ill. Dept. Pub. Health, 1985-88; health planner Lake County Health Dept., Waukegan, Ill., 1988-89; program evaluator Lake County Health Dept., 1989—; cons., Waukegan St. People Task Force, 1990-91; mem. pub. health com., Lake County Coalition for Homeless, Grayslake, Ill., 1990-91; legis. com. mem., Ill Pub. Health Assn., Springfield, 1989-90. Named Student Marshall, Sangamon State U., 1981, Outstanding Young Women Am., 1983. Mem. Am. Soc. Pub. Adminstrn. (exec. bd. Springfield, Chgo. 1983-84), Am. Evaluation Assn., Ill. Pub. Health Assn., Ill. Farmers Union, Chgo. Area Health Planning Mktg. Assn. Home: 801 Browning Ct Vernon Hills IL 60061-1401 Office: Lake County Health Dept 3010 Grand Ave Waukegan IL 60085-2321

WALTER, NORMAN EUGENE, orthopedic surgeon; b. Flint, Mich., Sept. 13, 1946; s. Marshall Eugene and Eva Bernice (Nielsen) W.; m. Mary Jo Carr, Dec. 17, 1966; children: Julie, Jennifer, Norman II. BA, U. Mich., Flint, 1969; MD, Wayne State U., 1974. Diplomate Am. Bd. Orthopedic Surgeons. Orthopedic surgeon Family Orthopedic Assoc., Flint, 1978—; orthopedics cons. Wright Med. Ctr., Memphis, 1995—. Vol. physician Genesee Free Care Clinic; trustee United Meth. Ch., Byron, Mich., 1992—. With USN, 1964-66. Fellow Am. Acad. Orthopedic Surgery; mem. Clin. Orthopedic Soc., Orthopedic Rsch. Soc., Assn. Arthritic Hip and Knee Surgeons, Acad. Orthopedic Soc. Methodist. Office: Family Orthopedic Assocs G-4466 W Bristol Rd Flint MI 48507

WALTERS, ARTHUR SCOTT, neurologist, educator, clinical research scientist; b. Balt., Feb. 20, 1943; s. Charles Henry and Jean Vivian (Scott) W.; m. Bokyun Kim, May 18, 1985 (div. Oct. 1992); m. Lesley J. Gill, Dec. 19, 1992. BA, Kalamazoo Coll., 1965; MS, Northwestern U., 1967; MD, Wayne State U., 1972. Diplomate Am. Bd. Psychiatry and Neurology; diplomate Am. Bd. Sleep Medicine. Intern Oakwood Hosp., Dearborn, Mich., 1972-73; resident in neurology SUNY Downstate Med. Ctr., Bklyn., 1976-79; movement disorder fellow Neurol. Inst., N.Y.C., 1982-84; asst. prof. neurology Robert Wood Johnson Med. Sch., U. Medicine & Dentistry N.J., New Brunswick, 1984-91, assoc. prof. neurology, 1991—; asst. chief divsn. neurology Lyons (N.J.) VA Med. ctr., 1985-89, neurology cons., 1984—; nat. chmn. med. adv. bd. Restless Legs Syndrome Found., 1992—; organizer Internat. Restless Legs Study Group, 1992—; head Restless Legs Syndrome and Periodic Limb Movement Coun. for the Nat. Sleep Found., 1994—; neurology cons. Coney Island Hosp., Bklyn., Bklyn. Jewish Hosp., 1980-81; presenter in field. Contbr. articles, abstracts, to profl. publs., chpts. to books, organizer symposia. Grantee UMDNJ, 1984-86, VA RAG, 1985-86, Sandoz Corp., 1985-88, VA Merit Rev., 1989—, Clemente Found., 1994-95. Fellow Am. Acad. Neurology, Am. Sleep Disorders Assn.; mem. AAAS, Sleep Rsch. Soc., Movement Disorder Soc., N.Y. Acad. Scis., N.J. Sleep Soc. (sec. 1995—). Home: 207 S Adelaide Ave Highland Park NJ 08904-1605 Office: UMDNJ-Robert Wood Johnson Med Sch Dept Neurology CN19 1 Robert Wood Johnson Pl New Brunswick NJ 08903-0019

WALTERS, DORIS LAVONNE, pastoral counselor; b. Peachland, N.C., Feb. 24, 1931; d. H. Lloyd and Mary Lou (Helms) W. BA cum laude, Carson-Newman Coll., 1961; MRE, Southwestern Bapt. Theol. Sem., 1963; MA in Pastoral Counseling, Wake Forest U., 1982; DMin in Pastoral Counseling, Southeastern Bapt. Theol. Sem., 1988. Min. of edn. and youth First Bapt. Ch., Orange, Tex., 1963-66; assoc. prof. Seinan Jo Gakuin Jr. Coll., Japan, 1968-72; dir. Fukuoka (Japan) Friendship House, 1972-88, pastoral counselor, chaplain, 1983-86; Tokyo lifeline referral counselor (in English) Hiroshima-South, Fukuoka, 1983-86; supr. Japanese and Am. staff Fukuoka Friendship House, 1972-86; with chaplaincy Med. Coll. Va., Richmond, 1976; resident chaplain N.C. Bapt. Hosp., Winston-Salem, 1981-82, counselor-in-tng. pastoral care dept., 1986-88; dir. missionary counseling and support svcs. Pastoral Care Found. N.C. Bapt. Hosp., Winston-Salem, 1989-93; dir. Missionary Family Counseling Svcs., Inc., Winston-Salem, 1993—; mem. Japan Bapt. Mission Exec. Com., Tokyo, 1973-76. Author: An Assessment of the Reentry Issues of the Children of Missionaries, 1991; translator: The Story of the Craft Dogs, 1983. J.M. Price scholar Southwestern Bapt. Theol. Sem., 1962; First Bapt. Ch. Blackwell grantee Southeastern Sem., 1986-88. Mem. Assn. for Clin. Pastoral Counselors (assoc.), Am. Assn. Pastoral Counselors (pastoral affiliate). Democrat. Home: 208 Oakwood Sq Winston Salem NC 27103-1914 Office: Missionary Family Counseling Svcs Inc 514 S Stratford Rd Winston Salem NC 27103-1823

WALTERS, GEORGE JOHN, oral and maxillofacial surgeon; b. Balt., June 16, 1956; s. George John Sr. and Henrietta Jean (Parker) W.; m. Melanie Ann Goodreau, June 23, 1989. BS, Loyola Coll., 1978; DDS, U. Md., 1983; postgrad., John Hopkins, 1991, U. Pa., 1992, U. Pa., 1993. Cert. argon laser. Rsch. asst. dept. otolaryngology The Johns Hopkins Sch. Medicine, Balt., 1978-79; ind. learning ctr. technician Balt. Coll. Dental Surgery, Dental Sch., U. Md., 1980-81; audio-visual technician U. Md. Law Sch., Balt., 1981-82, res. material circulation asst., 1982-83; resident gen. practice residency York (Pa.) Hosp., 1983-84; resident dept. anesthesia The Med. Coll. of Pa. and Hosp., Phila., 1984-85; resident dept. dentistry div. oral and maxillofacial surgery U. Md. Med. System, Balt., 1985-89, chief adminstrv. resident dept. dentistry, 1988-89; assoc. in oral and maxillofacial surgery Miller Oral Surgery and Pa. Jaw Treatment Ctr., Harrisburg, Pa., 1989-91; ptrn. Oral and Maxillofacial Surgery, Panama City, Fla., 1991-95; individual practice oral and maxillofacial surgery Panama City, Fla., 1995—; explorer advisor for health career explorer post Balt. Coll. Dental Surgery, Dental Sch., U. Md., 1981, dental rsch. student com., 1982, vol. for recruitment of minority students, 1983; testifier Sen. House Com. on Medicaid Funding, State House, Annapolis, Md., 1987-88; lectr. Gulf Coast C.C., 1991—. Copntbr. to profl. jours. Health vol. overseas Nepal Mission for Cleft Lip and Palate, 1989; vol. Guatemala Med. Mission Cleft Lip and Palate, 1994. John Hopkins fellow 1989. Mem. ADA, Am. Assn. Oral and Maxillofacial Surgery, Mid. Atlantic Soc. Oral and Maxillofacial Surgery, Bay County Dental Soc., Fla. Dental Soc., N.W. Dental Soc. Fla., Fla. Soc. Oral and Maxillofacial Surgery, Gorgas Odontological Soc., Rotary, Bay County Civil War Roundtable, Gamma Pi Delta. Roman Catholic. Home: PO Box 27473 1702 Wahoo Cir Panama City FL 32411-7230 Office: 2202 State Ave Ste 200 Panama City FL 32405

WALTERS, GRETA ALITA, nurse; b. Mandeville, Jamaica, Sept. 28, 1933; arrived in U.S., 1969; d. Hubert Augustus and Adina Wilhelmina Denton; m. Calwood Alexander Walters, Oct. 12, 1957 (dec.); children: Calwood, Michael, Paul, Stephen, Robert. Diploma, St. Alfege's Hosp., 1958. Staff nurse Meml./Brook Gen. Hosp., London, 1961-65, Percy Jr. Hosp., Jamaica, 1965-69; charge nurse St. Barnabas Hosp., Bronx, N.Y., 1969-95. Mem. Coll. Care & Armed Forces Com. (pres. 1984-90), St. Luke's Guild, Lamplighters, North Bronx Democratic Club. Democrat. Episcopalian. Home: 3400 Tiemann Ave Bronx NY 10469

WALTERS, JUDITH RICHMOND, neuropharmacologist; b. Concord, N.H., June 20, 1944; d. Samuel Smith and Hazel Albertina (Stewart) Richmond; m. James Wilson Walters, Aug. 23, 1969 (div. 1992); children: James Richmond, Gregory Stewart, Douglas Powers. BA, Mt. Holyoke Coll., 1966; PhD, Yale U., 1972. Postdoctoral fellow dept. psychiatry Yale U. Med. Sch., New Haven, rsch. assoc. dept. pharmacology, asst. prof. dept. psychiatry; unit chief neurophysiol. pharmacology sect. exptl. therapeutics br. Nat. Inst. Neurol. Disease and Stroke, Bethesda, Md., 1976-81, sect. chief physiol. neuropharmacology sect. exptl. therapeutics br.; mem. sci. adv. bd. Hereditary Disease Found., L.A., 1977-80, 82-86, Tourette Syndrome Assn., 1992—; mem. bd. sci. counselors Nat. Inst. on Alcohol Abuse and Alcoholism, 1992-95; mem. Inst. of Medicine Com. to Raise the Profile of Rsch. on Substance Abuse, 1995-96. Sect. editor Neuroscience.net, 1996—; contbr. more than 100 articles on neuropharmacology and neurophysiology to profl. jours. Recipient NIH Dir.'s award, 1994. Mem. Am. Soc. Pharmacology and Exptl. Therapeutics, Soc. for Neurosci. (mem. com. 1995-98). Home: 3615 Littledale Rd Kensington MD 20895-3435 Office: NIH Bldg 10 Rm 5C106 Bethesda MD 20892

WALTERS, NANCY LU, medical services educator; b. Luverne, Minn., Sept. 25, 1938; d. H. Calvin and Bijou (Stockton) Knock; divorced; children: Mary Patricia, Anthony Thomas, Deborah Kay. AB, Lindenwood Coll., 1960. Med. technologist St. Joseph Hosp., Kirkwood, Mo., 1960-63, Good Samaritan Hosp., Vincennes, Ind., 1963-65; chief med. technologist Johnson County Meml. Hosp., Franklin, Ind., 1965-68; health occupations coord. Ind. Vocat. Tech. Coll., Tippewa Tech. Inst., Lafayette, Ind., 1968-70; head allied health dept. Cin. Tech. Coll., 1970-76, coord. med. assts., 1976—. Mem. profl. edn. com. Am. Cancer Soc., Cin., 1976-82; bd. dirs. ACLU, Cin., 1988—; bd. dirs. ACLU Ohio, 1992, sec. exec. com., 1993-95, pres., 1995—; bd. dirs. Cin. chpt. Ind. Voters Ohio, 1975-77, Cin. Women's Polit. Caucus, 1994—; mem. various coms. Hyde Park Cmty. United Meth. Ch., Cin., 1986—, chmn. singles com., 1983-86, chmn. stewardship com., 1983-86, chmn. coun. on ministries, 1987-90, lay del. to ann. conf., 1992—, chmn. adminstrv. bd., 1994—. Recipient Drummer's award Cin. Conv. and Vis. Bur., 1978. Mem. Am. Soc. Allied Health Professions (bd. dirs. 1976-79), Am. Assn. Med. Assts. (curriculum rev. bd. 1993—, vice chmn. 1994—), Ohio Soc. Allied Health Professions (pres. 1981-82), Ohio Soc. Med. Assts. (sec. 1993-94), Ohio Soc. Med. Technologists, Woman's City Club (women's com. 1993—), Single Parent Ctr. Club (group leader). Democrat. Home: 1317 Grace Ave Cincinnati OH 45208-2427 Office: Cin Tech Coll 3520 Central Pky Cincinnati OH 45223-2612

WALTERS, NICK ALLEN, family physician; b. Glendale, Calif., Dec. 14, 1961; arrived in Singapore, 1996; s. George Conrad and Norma Lee (Acuff) W.; m. Phosfe Ornopia, Dec. 20, 1987; children: Christopher Robin Ornopia, Ian Nicholas Ornopia. Student, Loma Linda U., Riverside, Calif., 1980-81; BS in Human Biology, Pacific Union Coll., 1985; MD, Loma Linda U., 1989. Diplomate Am. Bd. Family Physicians; cert. I, II, III, Nat. Bd. Med. Examiners. Lab. instr. biology dept. Pacific Union Coll., Angwin, Calif., 1983-85, biology tutor biology dept., 1985; venipuncture Loma Linda (Calif.) U. Med. Ctr., 1986-87; mem. faculty Fla. Hosp. Family Practice Residency, Orlando, 1992; physician Orange County Health Dept./State of Fla., Orlando, 1990-92; staff physician Youngberg Adventist Hosp., Singapore, 1992-96; missionary physician Guam Seventh-Day Adventist Clinic, Tamuning, 1996—; pharmacy dir. Youngberg Adventist Hosp., Singapore, 1985—, asst. dir. med. staff, 1995—; lectr. S.E. Asia Union Coll., Singapore, 1993—; lectr. ann. meeting Indonesian Soc. Cardiologists, 1993. Elder Seventh-Day Adventist Ch., Singapore, 1995—. Recipient Physician Recognition award AMA, 1990-92. Mem. Am. Acad. Family Physicians, Singapore Med. Assn. Home: #04-01, Avon Park Apt 1 Youngberg, 1335 Singapore Singapore Office: Guam Seventh-Day Adventist Clinic, 388 Ypao Rd, 96911 Tamuning Guam

WALTERS, NORMAN EDWARD, hospital administrator; b. Williamsburg, Ky., Nov. 21, 1941; s. Winford and Dorothy Florence (Clifford) W.; m. Elizabeth Lou Custer, Sept. 7, 1963; children: Pamela Denise, Scot Edward. BS, Southeastern U., 1969; MS, St. Joseph's U., Windham, Maine, 1991. Br. mgr. GEICO, Chevy Chase, Md., 1965-68; asst. dept. head, internal audit mgr., dir. of fin. Commonwealth of Va., Alexandria and Richmond, 1968-77; asst. contr. Cumberland County Hosp. System, Fayetteville, N.C., 1978-81; contr., asst. adminstr. Hosp. Mgmt. Assoc., Williamson, W.Va., 1981; asst. adminstr. Advanced Health System, Inc., Marlow and Elk City, Okla., 1981-87; asst. adminstr., CFO Taylor County Hosp., Campbellsville, Ky., 1987—; v.p. Pikeville (Ky.) Meth. Hosp., 1991—; govt. cons. healthcare com. Health Care Fin. Mgmt. Assn., Campbellsville, 1991. Contbr. articles to profl. jours. Member Christian Profl. Bus. Men, Alexandria, 1970-80, Lions, Marlow and Elk City, 1981, 83God. Jim Hunt's Health Care Task Force, Raleigh, N.C., 1980; ; treas. Rotary, Campbellsville, 1987. Capt. USAF, 1959-65. Decorated Hon. Order of Ky. Cols. Mem. Am. Mgmt. Assn. (chmn. 1968-75, 88-89), Health Care Fin. Mgmt. Assn. (nat. matrix 1978—, health care task force com. Charleston, W.Va. chpt. 1981-82, program chmn. N.C. chpt. 1980-81, health care reform task force Ky. chpt. 1991-92, mem. adv. com. health care task force nat. com., Leffer Plaque 1981), Health Law Mgmt. Assn. (assoc. chmn. Ky. chpt. 1988-89, Leffer Plaque 1989, 90). Democrat. Baptist. Home: 224 College St Apt 2A Pikeville KY 41501-1771

WALTERS, REBA NELLE, nursing educator, administrator; b. Lenox, Ga., Apr. 20, 1933; d. John Roy and Essie (Barton) Rowan; m. Charles Ray Walters, Sept. 3, 1955; children: Charles Ray, Jr., Nancy Walters Harman, J. Douglas. BSN, U. N.C., 1969; EdM., N.C. State U., 1973; MSN, East

Carolina U., 1982, postgrad. Nova, 1989—. RN, N.C. Staff nurse Monongalia Gen. Hosp., Morgantown, W.Va., 1955-56, Vincent Pallotti, Morgantown, 1957; Kingston Hosp., N.Y., 1960-65; nursing instr. Rex Hosp., Raleigh, N.C., 1969-75, Wake Tech. Coll., Raleigh, 1975-82; chairperson health edn., dir. nursing edn. Vance Granville C.C., Henderson, N.C., 1982-87, chairperson, 1988—, health, human svcs., dir. nursing edn. Piedmont C.C.; active Assoc. Degree Nursing Coun. Recipient Best Ob Nurse award Crawford Long, 1955. Mem. ANA (pres. dist. 13 1979-80, bd. dirs. 1980-82), Am. Vocat. Assn. (v.p. C.C. and tech. edn. div. 1977-79), ADN dir., Assoc. Degree Nursing Dirs. (sec., treas 1989-91, mem. nominating com. 1994-95, coun.), Alpha Kappa Delta, Sigma Theta Tau. Democrat. Baptist. Avocation: gardening. Home: 303 Country Club Rd Roxboro NC 27573 Office: Piedmont CC PO Box 1197 Roxboro NC 27573

WALTERS, REBECCA RUSSELL YARBOROUGH, medical technologist; b. Lancaster, S.C., Mar. 9, 1951; d. William Peurifoy and Anna Beth (Cheatham) Yarborough; m. Thomas Edward Walters, Oct. 15, 1983; 1 child, Katherine Rebecca. BA, Winthrop Coll., 1972; postgrad. in med. tech., Bapt. Med. Ctr., Columbia, S.C., 1974; MA, Cen. Mich. U., 1978. Diplomate in Lab. Mgmt. ASCP. Teaching asst. in biology Winthrop Coll., Rock Hill, S.C., 1972-73; microbiology technologist Bapt. Med. Ctr., 1974-76, night shift supr., 1976-77, asst. adminstrv. dir., 1977—, tchr. Sch. Med. Tech., 1974—; article reviewer Med. Lab. Observer; mem. Nat. Cert. Agy. for Med. Lab. Personnel. Hycel, Inc. scholar, 1976, 77. Mem. Am. Soc. for Med. Tech. (scholar 1977), S.C. Soc. Med. Tech. (pres. 1979-80, scholar 1976), Am. Soc. Clin. Pathologists (assoc.), Clin. Lab. Mgmt. Assn., Beta Beta Beta, Alpha Mu Tau (scholar 1977). Republican. Presbyterian. Home: 155 Shawn Rd Chapin SC 29036-9215 Office: Bapt Med Ctr Taylor At Marion Columbia SC 29220

WALTERS, ROLAND A, III, ophthalmologist; b. Oklahoma City, Apr. 18, 1943; s. Roland A. Jr. and Marie V. (Rogers) W.; m. Kelsey Price, June 24, 1964; children: Michele, Allison. Student, Stanford U., 1964; MD, U. Okla., 1968. Emergency physician St. Anthony Hosp., Oklahoma City, 1969-70; resident U. Okla. Health Scis. Ctr., Oklahoma City, 1970-73; ophthalmologist pvt. practice, Oklahoma City, 1973—. Pres. Lyric Theatre Okla., Oklahoma City, 1992, bd. dirs. Capt. USAFR, 1969-74. Fellow Am. Acad. Ophthalmology (councillor 1986-89); mem. Am. Soc. cataract and Refractive Surgery, Okla. State Med. Soc. (bd. trustees 1995-96), Okla. State Soc. Eye Surgeons and Physicians (pres. 1982), Okla. County Med. Soc. (pres. 1993), Vis. Nurses Assn. (pres. 1996). Republican. Episcopalian. Home: 1607 Guilford Ln Oklahoma City OK 73120 Office: 5701 N Portland #101 Oklahoma City OK 73112

WALTERS, STEVEN D., medical educator, consultant; b. Grand Forks, N.D., Feb. 1, 1959; s. Alfred G. Walters and Loretta Ruth (Gulbranson) Walters-Hiestand; m. Vicky Jo Newman, June 2, 1979; children: Ben, Jessica, Monica. BS in Radiologic Tech., Andrews U., Berrien Springs, Miss., 1983; MS in Adminstrn., U. Notre Dame, 1989. Cert. RT (R), ARRT. Staff radiographer St. Joseph's Med. Ctr., South Bend, Ind., 1981-84; clin. instr. radiography Meml. Hosp., South Bend, 1984-88, dir. radiography, 1988-90; dir. radiography Ind. U., South Bend, 1990—; mem. med. adv. bd. Edumed Corp., Mpls., 1994—; mem. exam com. ARRT, Mpls., 1992—. Facilitator Men to Men support group Am. Cancer Soc., South Bend, 1995-96. Mem. Assn. Educators in Radiologic Scis. (treas. 1991-92), Ind. Soc. Radiologic Technologists (editor jour. 1992-93, pres.-elect 1994-95, pres. 1995-96). Home: 2518 Locust Rd South Bend IN 46614 Office: Ind U 1700 Mishawaka Ave South Bend IN 46634

WALTHER, JOSEPH EDWARD, health facility administrator, retired physician; b. Indpls., Nov. 24, 1912; s. Joseph Edward and Winona (McCampbell) W.; m. Mary Margaret Ruddell, July 11, 1945 (dec. July 1983); children: Mary Ann Margolis, Karl, Joanne Landman, Suzanne Conran, Diane Paczesny, Kurt. BS, Ind. U., 1936, MD, 1936; postgrad., U. Chgo., Harvard U., U. Minn., 1945-47. Diplomate Nat. Bd. Med. Examiners, Am. Bd. Internal Medicine, Am. Bd. Gastroenterology. Intern Meth. Hosp. and St. Vincent Hosp. of Indpls., 1936-37; physician, surgeon U.S. Engrs./Pan Am. Airways, Midway Islands, 1937-38; chief resident, med. dir. Wilcox Meml. Hosp., Lihue, Kauai, 1938-40; internist, gastroenterologist Meml. Clinic Indpls., 1947-83, med. dir., pres., chief exec. officer, 1947—; founder, pres. Doctors' Offices Inc., Indpls., 1947—; founder, pres., chief exec. officer Winona Meml. Found. and Hosp. (now Walther Cancer Inst.), Indpls., 1956—; clinical asst. prof. medicine Ind. U. Sch. Medicine, Indpls., 1948-93, clin. asst. prof. emeritus, 1993—. Author: (with others) Current Therapy, 1965; mem. edit. rsch. bd. Postgrad. Medicine, 1982-83; contbr. articles to profl. jours. Bd. dirs. March of Dimes, Marion County div., 1962-66, Am. Cancer Soc., Ind. div., 1986—. Col. USAAF, 1941-47, PTO. Decorated Bronze Star, Silver Star, Air medal; recipient Clevenger award Ind. U. 1989;, Disting. Alumnus award Ind. U. Sch. Med., 1990, Sagamore of Wabash award State of Ind., 1995; Dr. Joseph E. Walther Disting. Physician's award named in honor Winona Meml. Hosp., 1995. Master Am. Coll. Gastroenterology (pres. 1970-71, Weiss award 1988); mem. AMA (del. 1970-86), Soc. Cons. to Armed Forces, Ind. Med. Assn., Marion County Med. Assn., Ind. U. Alumni Assn. (life), Hoosier Hundred (charter), Highland Golf and Country Club (hon.), Waikoloa Golf and Country Club (Hawaii), Indpls. Athletic Club, 702 Club. Republican. Home: 4266 N Pennsylvania St Indianapolis IN 46205-2613 Office: Walther Cancer Inst 3202 N Meridian St Indianapolis IN 46208-4646

WALTON, CARMELITA NOREEN, retired nurse; b. Chgo., Nov. 15, 1926; d. Elmo Augusta and Evelyn Mae (Terry) Desobrey; student St. Marys Coll., U. Notre Dame, 1943-45; grad. Cook County Sch. Nursing, 1949; BA DePaul U., 1993; children from previous marriage—Michael Jerome. Cert. correctional health profl. Head nurse, supr., nurse clinician Cook County Hosp., Chgo., 1951-71; supr. U. Chgo. Hosps./Clinics, 1963-68; dir. nursing Woodlawn Child Health Center, Chgo., 1968-69; dir. nursing prison health care Cermak Health Services, Cook County Jail, Chgo., 1973-93; ret., 1993; nurse cons. Quality Mgmt., In-Svc. Edn.; med.-surg. staff nurse; cons., surveyor Nat. Commn. on Correctional Health Care, speaker 13th ann. conv., 1989, apptd. to bd. certification correctional health, 1991—. Contbr. articles to profl. jours. Recipient Superior Pub. Service award City of Chgo., 1984. Mem. Am. Nurses Assn. (cert. in nursing adminstrn., mem. Council Nursing Adminstrn.), Ill. Nurses Assn., Nat. League Nursing, Am. Pub. Health Assn. Democrat. Roman Catholic. Home: 5050 S Lake Shore Dr Chicago IL 60615-3205

WALTON, CAROLE LORRAINE, clinical social worker; b. Harrison, Ark., Oct. 20, 1949; d. Leo Woodrow Walton and Arlette Alegra (Cohen) Armstrong. BA, Lambuth Coll., Jackson, Tenn., 1971; MA, U. Chgo., 1974. Diplomate Clin. Social Work, Acad. Cert. Social Workers; bd. cert. diplomate; lic. clin. social worker. Social worker Community Mental Health, Flint, Mich., 1971-72; clin. social worker Community Mental Health, Westchester, Ill., 1974-76; dir. self-travel program Chgo. Assn. Retarded Citizens, 1973; coord. family svcs. Inner Harbors Psych. Hosp., Douglasville, Ga., 1976-83; sr. mental health clinician Northside Mental Health Ctr., Atlanta, 1983—. Mem. NASW, Ga. Soc. for Clin. Work (pres. 1981-82, pres. 1993-95). Office: Northside Mental Health Ctr 5825 Glenridge Dr NE Bldg 4 Atlanta GA 30328-5387

WALTON, DONALD CAMERON, JR., obstetrician, gynecologist; b. Providence, R.I., Apr. 11, 1934; s. Donald Cameron and Ebba Louise (Anderson) W.; m. Mary Jane Gibbons, Sept. 17, 1960; children: Kathleen Ann, Kyle Marie, Donald Cameron III, James Joseph, Diane Jeanne. BA, Bowdoin Coll., 1955; MD, Tufts U., 1959. Diplomate Am. Bd. Obstetrics and Gynecology. Intern Maine Med. Ctr., Portland, 1959-60; resident in gen. surgery Maine Med. Ctr., 1960-61; residency in ob/gyn Tufts-New England Med. Ctr./Carney and St. Margaret's Hosps., Boston, 1963-66; pvt. practice North Andover, Andover, Mass., 1966-73; physician Montgomery County Health Dept., Rockville, Md., 1973-95; pvt. practice Rockville, Md., 1995—. Capt. U.S. Army, 1961-63, Germany. Fellow Am. Coll. Obstetricians and Gynecologists; mem. Mass. Med. Soc., Am. Soc. for Reproductive Medicine. Republican. Roman Catholic.

WALTON, KIMBERLY ANN, medical laboratory technician; b. Balt., June 16, 1965; d. Lucian Wayne and Arlene Catherine (Hopkins) W. AA in med. lab. tech., Essex Coll., 1985. Med. technician Balt. Rh Typing Lab., Balt., 1985-94; med. technician HelixCare at Towson, 1993—, Chesapeake Diagnostic Lab., 1995—. Mem. AAAS, Am. Soc. Clin. Lab. Science, Am. Soc. Clin. Pathologists (cert.), Am. Assn. Blood Banks. Office: HelixCare at Towson 7801 York Rd Towson MD 21204

WALTON, RALPH GERALD, psychiatrist, educator; b. Darlington, Eng., Aug. 18, 1942; came to U.S., 1950; s. Kenneth and Paula (Weissman) W.; m. Ellen Paula Liebling, Feb. 15, 1970 (div. 1980); children: Deborah, Rachel; m. Mary Elaine Hultburg, Sept. 27, 1981; children: Lisa, Jonathan. AB, U. Rochester, 1963; MD, SUNY, Syracuse, 1967. Diplomate Am. Bd. Psychiatry and Neurology. Intern Strong Meml. Hosp., Rochester, N.Y., 1967-68, resident in psychiatry, 1968-71; asst. prof. psychiatry Sch. Medicine U. Rochester, N.Y., 1973-76; chief psychiatry Jamestown (N.Y.) Gen. Hosp., 1976-88; commr. mental health Chautauqua County, Jamestown, 1985-88; chmn. dept. psychiatry Western Res. Care System, Youngstown, Ohio, 1988—; prof. psychiatry N.E. Ohio Univs. Coll. of Medicine, Rootstown, Ohio, 1988—; med. dir. Profl. Recovery Plus Alcoholic Clinic, Youngstown, 1992—. Contbr. chpt. to: Dietary Phenylalanine and Brain Function, 1988; contbr. foreword to: Katherine It's Time, 1989; contbr. articles to profl. jours., 1972—. Maj. U.S. Army, 1971-73, Panama. Fellow Am. Psychiat. Assn. Jewish. Office: 725 Boardman Canfield Rd Youngstown OH 44512-4380

WALTON, RICHARD ALLYN, JR., psychologist; b. Pitts., Aug. 4, 1951; s. Richard Allyn and Corinne Ann (Hemeter) W.; m. Sherilyn Gay Cheatam, Aug. 6, 1976; children: Aaron Allyn. Andrew B., Tucker Hall. BS, U. Tulsa, 1977; MS in Psychology, St. Louis U., 1981, PhD in Clin. Psychology, 1986. Lic. health svc. psychologist, Okla. Child care worker Dillon Family & Youth Svcs., Tulsa, 1976; intern Children's Med. Ctr., Tulsa, 1981-82; hosp. program dir. Shadow Mountain Inst., Tulsa, 1982-84, adminstr. children's residential treatment ctr., 1984-87; pvt. practice Tulsa, 1987—; ptnr. Family Resource Group of Eastern Okla., Inc., Tulsa, 1996—; gen. mgr. Behavioral HealthCare Assocs., Tulsa, 1994—; bd. trustees Palmer Drug Abuse Program, Tulsa, 1991-94. Mem. Am. Psychol. Assn., Okla. Psychol. Assn. (pres. divsn. health svc. providers 1996, treas. 1994). Office: Family Resource Group Eastern Okla Inc 5110 S Yale Ste 102 Tulsa OK 74135-7438

WALTON, ROBERT LEE, JR., plastic surgeon; b. Lawrence, Kans., May 30, 1946; s. Robert L. and Thelma B. (Morgan) W.; m. Laura Lake, May 1, 1971; children: Marc, Morgan, Lindsey. BA, U. Kans., 1968; MD, U. Kans., Kansas City, 1972. Diplomate Am. Bd. Surgery, Am. Bd. Plastic Surgery. Resident in surgery Johns Hopkins Hosp., Balt., 1972-74, Yale-New Haven (Conn.) Hosp., 1974-78; chief of plastic surgery San Francisco Gen. Hosp., 1979-83; prof. and chmn. dept. plastic surgery U. Mass. Med. Ctr., Worcester, 1983-94; prof., chmn. dept. plastic surgery U. of Chicago, 1994—. Contbr. articles to profl. jours. Founder Federico Trilla Hosp. Found. for Handicapped Children, Carolina, P.R., 1990. Mem. Am. Assn. Plastic Surgery, Am. Coll. Surgeons, Am. Soc. Plastic and Reconstructive Surgery, Am. Soc. Surgery of the Hand, Alpha Omega Alpha. Office: Div Plastic Surgery U of Chicago 5841 S Maryland Chicago IL 60637*

WALTZ, MARCUS ERNEST, retired prosthodontist; b. Brownsville, Oreg., July 29, 1921; s. Roswell Starr and Eva Ione (Cherrington) W.; m. Constance Jean Elwood, May 31, 1952 (div. Nov. 1973); children: Melody Ann, Martha Louise, Kathryn Jean, Holly Jay, Joy Evalyn, Ross Elwood; m. Shelby Annette Schwab, June 10, 1975. AB, Willamette U., 1942; DMD, U. Oreg., 1945. Cert. Nev. State Bd. Dental Examiners. Practice dentistry specializing in prosthodontics Forest Grove, Oreg., 1946-52; practice dentistry specializing in prosthodontics Reno, 1954-95, ret., 1995; councillor Pacific Coast Dental Conf.; pres. Pacific Coast Soc. of Prosthodontics, 1983. Mem. State of Nev. Selective Svc. Appeals Bd., 1970-76, pres., 1974-76. Lt. USN, 1945-46, 52-54, Korea. Decorated Combat Medics award, Battle Stars (oak leaf cluster). Fellow Internat. Coll. Dentistry, Acad. Dentistry Internat.; mem. ADA, Northern Nev. Dental Soc. (pres. 1959), Nev. Dental Assn., Nev. Acad. Gen. Dentistry (pres. 1974), Sigma Chi, Omicron Kappa Upsilon. Democrat. Methodist. Club: Reno Exec. (dir. 1960-66, pres. 1964-65). Lodges: Sigma Tau (pres. 1941-42), Masons (32 degree), Shriners. Home: 715 Manor Dr Reno NV 89509-1944

WALTZER, WAYNE CHARLES, surgery educator; b. Bklyn., Apr. 18, 1948; children: Aaron, Gregory, Michael. BA, Pa. State U., 1969; MD, U. Pitts., 1973. Intern Presbyn. Univ. Hosp., Pitts., 1973-74, resident, 1974-78; fellow Mayo Clinic, Rochester, Minn., 1978-79; instr. surgery dept. surgery SUNY, Stony Brook, 1979-81, asst. prof. dept. urology and surgery, 1981-84, assoc. prof. dept. urology and surgery, 1984-89, prof. dept. urology and surgery, 1989—; prof., chmn. dept. urology, 1993—. Office: SUNY HSC T-9 Dept Urology Stony Brook NY 11794

WALWORTH, EDWARD ZINSSER, surgeon; b. Washington, Jan. 30, 1945; s. Edward Henry and Nancy Knowlton (Zinsser) W.; m. Candace Wentworth Cooper, Dec. 27, 1969; children: Elizabeth Zinsser, Nancy Cooper. AB, Princeton U., 1966; MD, Columbia U., 1970. Diplomate Am. Bd. Surgery. Intern Dartmouth-Hitchcock Med. Ctr., Hanover, N.H., 1970-71, resident surgery, 1971-75; pvt. practice Lewiston, Maine, 1977—; mem. active med. staff St. Mary's Regional Med. Ctr., Lewiston, Maine, 1977—, pres. med. staff, 1989—; mem. active med. staff Cen. Maine Med. Ctr., Lewiston, 1983—. Mem. bd. LA Arts, Lewiston-Auburn, Maine, 1991—, pres., 1995-96. Lt. comdr. USNR, 1975-77. Fellow ACS (pres. Maine chpt. 1988-89, gov. Maine 1991—); mem. AMA, New Eng. Surg. Soc., Maine Med. Assn., County Med. Assn. (pres. 1982). Democrat. Congregationalist. Office: Androscoggin Clin Assocs 710 Main St Lewiston ME 04240-5801

WALZ, BRUCE JAMES, radiation oncologist; b. Waterloo, Ill., Sept. 18, 1940; s. George Frederick and Alberta Emma (Heyl) W.; m. Renata T. Jaeger, Mar. 8, 1970; children: Jennifer Mara Walz Kuhn, Rachel Elizabeth. A.B., Washington U., 1962, M.D., 1966. Diplomate Am. Bd. Radiology Therapy. Intern, St. Luke's Hosp., St. Louis, 1966-67; resident Washington U. St. Louis, 1969-72; instr. Harvard Med. Sch., Boston, 1972-74; asst. prof. Washington U., 1974-82, assoc. prof., 1982-86, clin. assoc. prof., 1986—; dir. radiation therapy St. Anthony's Med. Ctr., St. Louis. 1986—. Contbr. articles to profl. jours. Active med. adv. com. Medicare, 1992—. Served to lt. comdr. USNR, 1967-69, Vietnam. Harvard Med. Sch. fellow, 1972-73. Fellow Am. Coll. Radiology; mem. AMA, Am. Cancer Soc. (bd. dirs. Mo. divsn. 1992-96), Mo. Med. Soc. (ho. of dels. 1975—), Mo. State Radiol. Soc. (bd. dirs. 1982-87, sec.-treas. 1987-90, v.p. 1990-91, pres. 1991-92, ACR counselor 1995—), St. Louis Metro Med. Assn. (councilor 1987-89), Greater St. Louis Soc. Radiologists (chair therapy sect. 1985, sec.-treas. 1988-89, pres. elect 1989-90, pres. 1990-91), Am. Soc. Therapeutic Radiologists and Oncologists, Am. Coll. Radiology, Am. Soc. Clin. Oncologists, Arab-Am. Med. Soc. Presbyterian. Clubs: Whittemore House (Clayton, Mo.). Avocations: gardening, travelling, scuba diving. Office: St Anthony's Med Ctr Div Radiation Therapy Saint Louis MO 63128

WALZ, BRUCE JOHN, emergency services administrator; b. Balt., Mar. 28, 1953; s. John Louis and Dorothy Elizabeth (Redulski) W. BA, Western Md. Coll., 1975; MA, Hood Coll., 1982; PhD, U. md., 1985. Mem. Nat. Registry of EMTs. Sr. instr. Md. Fire Rescue Inst., College Park, Md., 1979-87; asst. prof. U. Md. Baltimore County, 1987-94, assoc. prof., 1994—, interim chmn., 1994-95, chmn., 1995—; CE coord. Jems Comms., Delmar, Calif., 1990-94. Contbr. articles to profl. jours. Officer, paramedic Mt. Airy Vol. Fire Co., Mt. Airy, Md., 1990—, Winfield Comm. VFD, Md., 1970-89. Recipient EMS Svc. award Md. Chpt. Am. Coll. Emergency Physicians, 1994; grantee md. Inst. for EMS, 1993. Mem. Nat. Assn. for Search and Rescue (v.p. edn. affairs 1988-89, dir. 1987-90), Ind. Fire Svc. Tng. Assn. (com. 1985-93). Home: 1134 Oak View Dr Mount Airy MD 21771 Office: UMBC 1000 Hilltop Circle Baltimore MD 21250

WAN, LIVIA SHANG-YU, obstetric gynecologist, educator; b. Nanking, China, May 27, 1932; came to U.S., 1958; d. Shih-hsang and Yen-hsa (Hsu) W.; m. Francis Lui, Dec. 2, 1967; children: Lawrence Lui, Yvonne Lui. MD, Nat. Taiwan U., 1958. Diplomate Am. Bd. Ob-Gyn. Rsch. assoc. U. Pa., Phila., 1967-69; asst. prof., assoc. prof. NYU, 1969-80, prof., 1980—; dir. family planning divsn., attending physician Bellevue Hosp., N.Y.C., 1969—, dir. divsn. endoscopic pelvic surgery, 1995—; attending physician Tisch Hosp., NYUMC., 1969—; med. adv. com. mem. Planned Parenthood, N.Y.C., 1973—, Cmty. Family Planning Coun. N.Y.C., 1990—; nat. med. bd. mem. Planned Parenthood Fedn. Am., N.Y.C., 1977-80; mem. Population Coun., N.Y.C., 1979—; cons. Chinatown Health Clinic, N.Y.C., 1975-80. Contbr. chpts. in books and articles to profl. jours. Recipient Certificate of Appreciation Am. Med. Women's Assn., 1994. Fellow Am. Coll. Obs./Gyn., Am. Fertility Soc.; mem. Am. Assn. Gynecol. Laparoscopists, Internat. Soc. Gynecol. Endoscopists, Soc. Laparoscopic Surgeons, N.Y. Ostetrical Soc. (pres. 1996-97). Democrat. Office: NYU Med Ctr 550 First Ave New York NY 10016

WANAMAKER, WILLIAM MEADE, neurologist; b. Seattle, Wash., Sept. 30, 1938; s. Clarence Ira and Grace Charlotte (Meade) W.; m. Sonja Jane Recker; children: Thomas Meade, Anne Hastings, John MacAndrew. MD, Creighton Univ., 1964. Assoc. prof. neurology Univ. Wis., Madison, 1970-75, Univ. Nebr., Omaha, 1975-78; neurologist Neurology Assocs. NE Wis., Green Bay, 1978-95, GreenBay Neurology, Green Bay, 1995—. Contbr. articles to profl. jours. With U.S. Air Force, 1968-70. Mem. Acad. Neurology, Am. Acad. Electrodig. Office: Green Bay Neurology Ltd 1901 S Webster Ave Green Bay WI 54301

WANEBO, CLIFFORD KEVIN, urologist; b. Denver, Mar. 12, 1937; s. Clifford Paul and Jo Ann Marie (Curtin) W.; m. Marian Joyce May, Feb. 23, 1963; children: Charles Patrick, Kathleen Louise, Kevin Thomas, Cheryl Jeanne, Karen Marie. BS in Biology and Chemistry, Regis Coll., 1959; MD, U. Colo., 1963. Diplomate Am. Bd. Urology. Intern Bellevue Hosp., N.Y.C., 1963-64, resident in internal medicine, 1964-65; resident in gen. surgery U. Colo. Med. Ctr., Denver, 1967-68, resident in urologic surgery, 1968-71; rschr. NIH, Hiroshima, Japan, 1965-67; pvt. practice physician Wanebo, Simons, Roy & Beshai, P.C., Grand Junction, Colo. Chmn. selection com. Jude Scholarship Program, Grand Junction, 1982—. Lt. comdr. USPHS, 1965-67. Fellow ACS (local selection com. 1990-96); mem. AMA, Am. Urol. Assn., Colo. State Med. Soc., Mesa County Med. Soc. (pres. 1983-84). Roman Catholic. Home: 810 Mazatlan Dr Grand Junction CO 81506 Office: Wanebo Simons Roy & Beshai PC 790 Wellington Grand Junction CO 81501

WANEK, RONALD MELVIN, orthodontist; b. Richland Center, Wis., Nov. 3, 1938; s. Melvin Leo and Mary Esther (Picha) W.; m. Janet Eleanor Lundquist, June 22, 1974; children: Lynn Ann, Mark Ronald. Student, U. Wis., 1956-60; DDS, Marquette U., 1964, MS, 1969. Practice dentistry specializing in orthodontics Madison, Wis., 1969—. Served to lt. USNR, 1964-67, Vietnam. Mem. ADA, Wis. Dental Assn., Dane County Dental Assn., Am. Assn. Orthodontists, Wis. Soc. Orthodontists, Midwest Soc. Orthodontists, Omicron Kappa Upsilon. Republican. Methodist. Office: 4915 Monona Dr Madison WI 53716-2665

WANG, ALLAN ZUWU, cell biologist, pharmacologist; b. Shanghai, China, June 1, 1939; came to U.S., 1982; m. Qin-Yu Chen, Mar. 30, 1968; 1 child, George Qi. MD, Shanghai Med. U., 1962; PhD, Chinese Acad. Scis., 1966. Rsch. assoc. Chinese Acad. Sci., Shanghai, 1966-80; postdoctoral rsch. fellow Imperial Cancer Rsch. Fund, London, 1980-82; assoc. rsch. scientist U. Tex. System Cancer Ctr., Houston, 1982-83; assoc. prof. Chinese Acad. Scis., 1983-85; Stanley Reimann rsch. scientist Fox Chase Cancer Ctr., Phila., 1987-90; acting scientific dir. Western Pa. Hosp. Found. Rsch. Inst., Pitts., 1990-91, dir. rsch. dept. medicine, sr. faculty scientist, 1990—; faculty collaborator NSF Sci. and Tech. Ctr. Carnegie Mellon U., 1990—; vis. assoc. prof. Med. Coll. Pa., 1986-87; mem. rsch. bd. advisors Am. Biophys. Inst., N.C., 1989—, Internat. Biophys. Ctr., Cambridge, Eng., 1989—; com. mem. Instnl. Animal Care and Use Com., Western Pa. Found., 1990—. Contbr. articles to 115 profl. jours. Mem. AAAS, Am. Coll. Rheumatology, Inflammation Rsch. Assn., Am. Soc. Cell Biology, Am. Assn. Cancer Rsch., Brit. Soc. Cell Biology, Brit. Assn. Cancer Rsch., Inflammation Rsch. Assn. Office: Western Pa Hosp Found 4800 Friendship Ave Pittsburgh PA 15224-1722

WANG, CHING CHUNG, biochemistry educator; b. Beijing, People's Republic China, Feb. 10, 1936; came to U.S., 1960; m. Alice Lee, Apr. 6, 1963; 1 child, Charlotte I-Ting. BSc in Chemistry, Nat. Taiwan U., Taipei, Republic China, 1958; PhD in Biochemistry, U. Calif., Berkeley, 1966. Rsch. assoc. Columbia U., N.Y.C., 1966-67, Princeton (N.J.) U., 1967-69; sr. investigator Merck Inst., Rahway, N.J., 1969-81; prof. chemistry U. Calif., San Francisco, 1981—. Mng. editor: Molecular Biochem. Parasitology, 1988-96; contbr. articles to profl. jours. Vice-chmn. Golden Gate Regional Ctr. for the developmentally disabled, San Francisco, 1982-88. Recipient Molecular Parasitology award Burroughs Wellcome Fund, 1983. Fellow AAAS; mem. Academie Sinica (Taiwan), Am. Soc. Biochem. Molecular Biologists, Soc. Chinese Bioscientists in Am. (pres. 1986-87). Office: U Calif Sch Pharmacy San Francisco CA 94143

WANG, DEHUA, chemist; b. Shaoxing, China, Sept. 27, 1937; m. Xiaolong Xu, Nov. 7, 1967; children: Kathy Yu, Wendy Lu. PhD, Syracuse U., 1985. Spectroscopist Atlanta U., 1985-86; prof. Wuhan Inst. Physics, China, 1986-89; vis. prof. Coll. Staten Island, N.Y., 1989-90; NMR rsch. scientist Kimberly-Clark Corp., Roswell, Ga., 1990—. Office: Kimberly-Clark Corp 1400 Holcomb Br Rd Roswell GA 30076

WANG, EVA MAYE, optometrist; b. Queens, N.Y., May 12, 1963; d. Koon Chun and Sunshine (Wong) W. BS, St. John's U., Jamaica, N.Y., 1985; OD, New Eng. Coll. Optometry, 1989. Pvt. practice, Flushing, N.Y., 1990—, N.Y.C., 1994-95; student advisor New Eng. Coll. Optometry, Boston, 1994—. Mem. Am. Optometric Assn. Republican. Office: Better-Sight Vision Ctr 42-02 Main St Flushing NY 11355

WANG, FREDERICK MARK, pediatric ophthalmologist, medical educator; b. N.Y.C., Feb. 17, 1948. Student, Northwestern U., 1968; MD, Yeshiva U., 1972. Diplomate Am. Bd. Ophthalmology, Am. Bd. Pediats., Nat. Bd. Med. Examiners. Intern in pediats. H.C. Moffitt-U. Calif. San Francisco Hosps., 1972-73; resident in pediats. Bronx Mcpl. Hosp. Ctr.-Albert Einstein Coll. Medicine, 1973-74, resident in ophthalmology, 1976-79; Heed fellow in ophthalmology and strabismus Children's Hosp. Nat. Med. Ctr., Washington, 1979-80; asst. prof. ophthalmology Albert Einstein Coll. Medicine, Bronx, 1980-82, asst. clin. prof., 1982-85, assoc. clin. prof., 1985-95, clin. prof., 1995—, asst. prof. pediats., 1980-82, asst. clin. prof. pediats., 1982-92; dir. pediat. ophthalmology and strabismus svc. Montefiore Med. Ctr., Bronx, 1980-90; cons. ophthalmologist Children's Evaluation & Rehab. Ctr., Rose Kennedy Ctr. for Rsch. in Mental Retardation and Human Devel., Bronx, 1980—, Craniofacial Ctr., Montefiore Med. Ctr., Bronx, 1980—; attending physician in ophthalmology Bronx Mcpl. Hosp./Montefiore Med. Ctr., 1980—; asst. attending physician in ophthalmology North Ctrl. Bronx Hosp., 1980—; assoc. attending physician in ophthalmology N.Y. Eye & Ear Infirmary, N.Y.C., 1982—; attending physician Strabismus Svc., N.Y. Eye & Ear Infirmary, N.Y.C., 1982—; mem. dept. ophthalmology Lenox Hill Hosp., N.Y.C., 1988—; sci. reviewer Jour. Am. Acad. Ophthalmology, 1980-86; mem. profl. adv. bd. Found. for Children with Learning Disabilities, N.Y.C., 1983-89; mem. sci. adv. bd. The Glaucoma Found., N.Y.C., 1986—; mem. profl. adv. bd. Nat. Assn. for Visually Handicapped, N.Y.C., 1988—; coord. pediat. sect. Greater N.Y. Ophthalmology Clin. Lectr. Series, 1990-93; mem. Velo-Cardio-Facial Syndrome Ednl. Found., 1994—, nominating com., 1995—. Contbr. chpts. to books and articles to profl. jours. Maj. med. officer USAF, 1974-76. Mem. Am. Acad. Pediats., Am. Acad. Ophthalmology, Am. Assn. for Pediat. Ophthalmology and Strabismus, N.Y. Soc. for Pediat. Ophthalmology and Strabismus (program chmn. 1987-89, pres. 1990-92), N.Y. Soc. for Clin. Ophthalmology (corr. sec. 1988-90, membership chmn. 1990-91, program chmn. 1991-92, pres. 1992-93), N.Y. Acad. Medicine (sec. sect. on ophthalmology 1993-94), Alpha Omega Alpha. Office: Pediat Ophthalmology of NY 30 E 40th St New York NY 10016

WANG, GWO JAW, university educator. Recipient U. Va. Pres.'s Report award, 1992. Office: U Va Sch Medicine Charlottesville VA 22906

WANG, JI-PING, pharmacist, researcher; b. Tang-Shan, Hebei, China, Sept. 13, 1948; came to U.S., 1981; d. Shao-Hsun and Liang-Shou (Hu) W.; m. Si Luo, Feb. 16, 1978; 1 child, Lai Laura Luo. BS in Pharmacy, U. Wash., 1987, MS, 1992. X-ray technician Xin-Xian Hosp., Shanxi, People's Republic of China, 1972-73; pharmacist Drug Inspection Inst., Beijing, People's Republic of China, 1978-81; rsch. technician U. Wash., Seattle, 1985-87; pharmacist Luke's Pharmacy, Seattle, 1988-91; rsch. scientist U. Washington, Seattle, 1991—. Contbr. articles to Jour. of Chromatography, Pharm. Rsch., Clin. Pharmacology and Therapeutics. Recipient Scholastic Achievement award U. Wash., 1985, Merck award, 1986. Mem. Am. Pharm. Assn., Rho Chi (Achievement award 1985). Office: U Washington Box 357610 Seattle WA 98195

WANG, JONAS CHIA-TSUNG, pharmaceutical executive; b. Canton, People's Republic of China, July 21, 1944; came to U.S., 1977; s. Gin-Han and Gin (Lai) W.; m. Huey-Wen An, Nov. 15, 1969; children: Jeremy, Joseph, JoAnn. BS in Pharmacy, Nat. Def. Med. Ctr., Taipei, Republic of China, 1967; PhD in Phys. Pharmacy, U. Iowa, 1982. Registered pharmacist, Republic of China. Instr. in pharm. chemistry Nat. Def. Med. Ctr., 1968-77; chief quality control dept. Ret. Serviceman's Pharm. Plant, Taipei, 1968-77; teaching asst. U. Iowa, Iowa City, 1977-81; assoc. dir. R & D Bristol-Myers Squibb, Buffalo, 1981-88; dir. R & D Johnson & Johnson Consumer Products, Inc., Skillman, N.J., 1988-94, v.p. Applied Rsch. and Tech. Rsch. Ctr., 1994—; adj. prof. cosmetic sci. program Coll. Pharmacy, U. Cin., 1985—; mem. coun. biology dept. Canisius Coll., Buffalo, 1984-88; reviewer Pharm. Rsch., 1986-94; mem. faculty spl. seminar IV Internat. Symposium on Psoriasis, Stanford U., 1986; tech. cons. Western N.Y. Tech. Transfer Com., 1984-88; lectr., presenter in field; vis. prof. Sch. Pharmacy Nat. Def. Med. Ctr., 1986. Contbr. articles to profl. publs.patentee in field. Maj. Rep. of China armed forces, 1965-67. Mem. Acad. Pharm. Sci., Soc. Cosmetic Chemists (mem. Merit award com. 1991), Am. Assn. Pharm. Scientists, Am. Acad. Dermatology, Nat. Def. Med. Ctr. Alumni Assn. (pres. N.Y. chpt. 1991-93), Chinese Pharm. Soc., Asian Pharm. Assn. Home: 23 Ellsworth Dr Robbinsville NJ 08691-9006 Office: Johnson & Johnson Consumer Products Inc Grandview Rd Skillman NJ 08558

WANG, JOSEPH, education educator, scientist; b. Haifa, Israel, Jan. 8, 1948; came to U.S., 1978; s. Moshe and Elka Wang; m. Ruth Wang, Mar. 2, 1976; 1 child, Sharon. BSc, Technion, Israel, 1972, MS, 1974, DSc, 1978. Rsch. assoc. U. Wis., Madison, 1978-80; asst. prof. N.Mex. State U., Las Cruces, 1980-84, assoc. prof., 1984-88, prof., 1988—. Author 4 books and 400 papers in field; chief editor Electroanalysis, 1988—; mem. editl. bd. 6 jours. Office: NMex State U Dept Chem Las Cruces NM 88003

WANG, NING, biologist, educator, consultant; b. Shenyang, Liaoning, China, Nov. 29, 1956; came to the U.S., 1984; s. Dui and Derun (Liu) W.; m. Hong Tian, Dec. 18, 1984; 1 child, Richard Ning. BS, Huazhong U. Sci. & Tech., Wuhan, Hubei, China, 1982, MS, 1984; ScD, Harvard U., 1990. Vis. fellow NIH, Bethesda, Md., 1984-86; vis. fellow Harvard Sch. Pub. Health, Boston, 1986-87, rsch. fellow, 1987-90, rsch. assoc., 1990-94, asst. prof., 1994—; vis. prof. U. Paris XII, Creteil, France, 1994, Huazhong U. Sci. and Tech., 1994—; cons. C.P. Li Biomed. Rsch. Corp., Arlington, Va., 1993—. Contbr. articles to profl. jours.; inventor in field. Mem. Am. Soc. for Cell Biology, Am. Physiol. Soc. (Scholander award 1991, Caroline tum Suden Profl. Opportunity award 1991). Office: Harvard Sch Pub Health 665 Huntington Ave Boston MA 02115-6021

WANG, SHAOKE, agriculturist, educator; b. Shanghai, China, Apr. 30, 1952; came to U.S., 1984; s. Chuan and Wen (Zhu) W.; m. Ping Dou, Dec. 9, 1981; children: Su, Collins D. BS, Suzhou Agrl. Univ., China, 1977; MS, Chinese Acad. Agrl. Scis., Beijing, 1982; PhD, Colo. State U., 1987. Tchg. asst. Shzhou Agrl. U., 1977-79; asst. prof. Chinese Acad. Agrl. Scis., Beijing, 1982-84; postdoc. fellow Colo. State U., Ft. Collins, 1987-92; gen. mgr. rsch. Seedex Inc., Longmont, Colo., 1992—; internat. coord. Intern Soc. Barley Genetics, Colo. State U., Ft. Collins, 1989-92, faculty affiliate, 1992—. Contbr. articles to profl. jours. Rockefeller Found. fellow, 1984-87. Mem. Am. Soc. Agronomy, Crop Sci. Soc. Am., Am. Soc. Sugarbeet Tech. Home: 2431 Cucharas Ct Fort Collins CO 80525 Office: Seedex Inc 1350 Kansas Ave Longmont CO 80501

WANG, SHIH-CHANG, radiologist, researcher; b. London, Apr. 10, 1957; arrived in Australia, 1968; s. Gungwu and Margaret Ping-Ting (Lim) W.; m. Jennifer Anne McCrorey, Aug. 14, 1982; children: Sebastian, Ryan. BSc in Medicine, U. Sydney, Australia, 1978, M.B.B.S. with honors, 1981. Resident med. officer Royal Prince Alfred Hosp., Sydney, 1981-82; registrar in radiology Royal North Shore Hosp., Sydney, 1983-86, staff specialist, 1987-94, sr. staff specialist, 1995—; rsch. fellow U. Calif., San Francisco, 1988; sr. clin. lectr. radiology U. Sydney, 1995—; vis. lectr. Hong Kong Sanatorium Hosp., 1990; luminary vis. lectr. GE, Tsingtao, Suzhou, China, 1992. Author: Chirurgie Thoracique Générale, 1989; co-author: (with P. Razemon) Chirurgie du Mediastin, 1970; contbr. articles to profl. jours. Contbg. sponsor Bell Shakespeare Theatre Co., Sydney, 1995. Decorated Legion of Honor, Palmes Academiques Ministry Edn. (France); recipient Prix Nat. for med. surgery film Cannes Festival, Pri De z Dubar, 1956. Fellow Royal Australasian Coll. Radiologists; mem. Radiol. Soc. N.Am., Soc. of Magnetic Resonance. Office: Royal North Shore Hospital, Dept Diagnostic Radiology, Sydney Saint Leonards 2065 NSW, Australia

WANG, WEIQUN, cancer researcher, biochemist; b. Tai-Zhou, Jiang-Su, China, June 20, 1961; s. Min-sun and Houlin (Zou) W.; m. Qianqian Su; children: Sushu, Sophie. BS, Nanjing U., 1983; MS, Nanjing Agrl. U., 1987, PhD, 1990. Rsch. assoc. Biol. Rsch. Inst. Shanghai, 1983-85; asst. prof. in biology Nanjing (China) U., 1990-91; postdoctoral fellow in animal sci. U. Hawaii, Honolulu, 1991-92; jr. rschr. Cancer Rsch. Ctr. Hawaii, Honolulu, 1992—; summer presenter, spkr. U. Hawaii, Honolulu, 1992, 93, 95, 96, Ann. Biomed. Scis. Symposium, Honolulu, 1994, Third Internat. Conf. on Phytoestrogens, Little Rock, 1995. Contbr. articles to profl. jours. Grantee Am. Heart Assn., 1995—, Am. Assn. Cancer Rsch., 1994; Mead Johnson award, 1994, Travel award, 1995. Mem. NEA, AAAS, Am. Assn. Cancer Rsch. Home: 707 16th Ave Honolulu HI 96816 Office: Cancer Rsch Ctr Hawaii 1236 Lauhala St Honolulu HI 96813

WANG, YANG, cardiology educator, researcher; b. Tangshan, China, May 12, 1923; s. Yu-Shen and Jun-Rong (Bo) W.; m. Helen S. Huang, June 18, 1966; children: Dale, Cynthia, Jennifer, Heather. MB, Nat. Shanghai Med. Coll., 1948; MD, Harvard U., 1952. Diplomate Am. Bd. Internal Medicine; cert. cardiovascular diseases. Intern, then resident Mass. Gen. Hosp., Boston, 1952-57, fellow in cardiology, 1957-58; fellow in physiology Mayo Found., Rochester, Minn., 1958-59; from instr. to prof. of medicine (cardiology) U. Minn. Med. Sch., Mpls., 1959—. Contbr. over 100 articles to sci. jours. Bd. dirs. Minn. Mus. Art, St. Paul, 1984-90; session elder Presbyn. Ch., St. Paul. Capt. Med. Corps USAF, 1954-56. Fellow ACP, ACC, AAAS, Am. Heart Assn. (cons., mem. internat. program com., mem. Great Plains com., pres., bd. dirs. Mpls. chpt. 1973-74); mem. Assn. Univ. Cardiologists, Ctrl. Soc. Clin. Rsch. Office: U Minn Hosp & Clinic Box 83 UMHC 420 Delaware St SE Minneapolis MN 55455-0374

WANG, YI-XIN, physiologist; b. Shanghai, People's Republic of China, Aug. 13, 1956; s. Jia-Jing Wang and Feng-Xia Yuan; m. Wei Xia, Feb. 5, 1986; 1 child, Xia-Hui Wang. MD, Shanghai Coll. Traditional, Chinese Medicine, 1982; MS in Physiology, Shanghai Med. U., 1985. Rsch. asst. Shanghai Med. U., 1985-87, lectr. physiology, 1987-88; postdoctoral fellow Boston U. Sch. of Medicine, 1988-89, rsch. assoc., 1989-91; sr. postdoctoral scientist SmithKline Beecham Pharms., 1991-93; asst. prof. dept. physiology and biophysics The U. Tenn., 1993—. Contbr. articles to profl. jours. Home: 389 Spruce Glen Dr Cordova TN 38018 Office: Univ Tenn Dept Physiology 894 Union Ave Memphis TN 38163

WANGENSTEEN, STEPHEN LIGHTNER, surgery educator; b. Mpls., Aug. 30, 1933; s. Owen Harding and Sarah (Davidson) W.; m. Lita Laura Lindley, Sept. 12, 1935; children: Christine, Stephen, Philip, William. BA, BS, U. Minn., 1955; MD, Harvard U., 1958. Diplomate Am. Bd. Surgery. Resident surgeon Columbia-Presbyn. Hosp., N.Y.C., 1958-65; asst. prof./assoc. prof. surgery U. Va., Charlottesville, 1967-72; prof. surgery U. Va., 1972-76; prof./chmn. dept. surgery U. Ariz., Tucson, 1976-87; prof. surgery U. South Fla., Tampa, 1987—; dep. chmn. dept. surgery, 1989-90. Contbr. articles to profl. jours. Fellow ACS; mem. Am. Surg. Assn., So. Surg. Assn., University Surgeons, Halsted Soc., Field Club (Sarasota, Fla.). Home: 82 Red Bank Rd Rembert SC 29128 Office: U South Fla 12901 Bruce B Downs Blvd Tampa FL 33612-4742

WANSER, DAVID RAY, health facility administrator, psychotherapist; b. Oak Park, Ill., Dec. 7, 1947; s. Raymond and Ruth (Tobey) W.; m. Debra Richison, Oct. 17, 1987; 1 child, Erin. BA in Journalism, U. Okla., 1972, MA in Human Rels., 1973, PhD in Psychology, 1989. Nat. bd. cert. counselor; lic. profl. counselor. Clin. supr. Cleve. County Youth & Family Ctr., Norman, Okla., 1977-81; psychologist Cen. Okla. Community Mental Health Ctr., Gen. Oklahoma Community Mental Health Ctr., Cen. State Hosp., Norman, 1980-87; program cons. Tex. Dept. Mental Health and Mental Retardation, Austin, 1987-88, program rev. coord., 1988-90, asst. dep. commr., 1991-93; assoc. commr., 1993-95; dir. policy and program devel. managed care Tex. Dept. Mental Health and Mental Retardation, Austin, 1995—; psychotherapist Norman, Austin, 1981-93. Bd. dirs. Lake Travis Ind. Sch. Dist. Edn. Found., Austin, 1990-92, mem. adv. bd. Gifted and Talented Program, 1991. Mem. APA, Greater Austin C. of C. (quality award examiner 1991-92). Office: Tex Dept Mental Health PO Box 12668 Austin TX 78711-2668

WAPNER, KEITH LESLIE, orthopedic surgeon, educator; b. Phila., Sept. 27, 1953; s. Paul Mordecai and Evelyn (Locke) W.; m. June Carosia, Jan. 16, 1982; children: Peter, Charles. BA, U. Pa., 1976; MD, Temple U., 1980. Diplomate Am. Bd. Orthopedic Surgery. Intern in surgery Hosp. of U. Pa., 1980-81; fellowship in orthop. U. Pa., 1981-82; resident in orthop. surgery Hosp. of U. Pa., 1982-85; asst. prof. Thomas Jefferson U., Phila., 1986-93, assoc. prof., 1993-95; prof. Allegheny U., Phila., 1996—; lectr. in field. Mem. editl. bd. Seminars in Arthroplasty, 1990, Operative Techniques in Orthopaedics, 1990, Foot and Ankle, The Official Jour. of Am. Orthop. Foot and Ankle Soc., 1992, Clin. Orthops. and Related Rsch., 1993; reviewer Am. Jour. Sports Medicine, 1993; contbr. numerous articles to profl. jours. Bd. dirs. Oheo Shalom Hebrew Sch., Wallingford, Pa., 1995. Fellow Am. Coll. Surgeons, Am. Acad. Orthop. Surgery, Am. Orthop. Foot and Ankle Soc.; mem. Am. Diabetes Soc., Pa. Med. Soc., Phila. Med. Soc., Phila. Orthop. Soc., Phila. Rheumatism Soc. Office: Hahnemann Univ Dept Orthop Surgery 219 N Broad St 5th Fl Philadelphia PA 19107

WAPPNER, REBECCA SUE, pediatrics educator; b. Mansfield, Ohio, Feb. 25, 1944; d. William Henry and Helen Elizabeth (Gilmore) W. BS in Zoology, Ohio U., 1966; MD, Ohio State U., 1970. Cert. Am. Bd. Pediatrics, clin. and clin. biochem. Am. Bd. Med. Genetics. Intern in pediatrics The Children's Hosp., Ohio State U., Columbus, 1970-71, resident in pediatrics, 1971-72, asst. chief resident, 1972-73; fellow in pediatric metabolism and genetics Ind. U. Sch. Medicine, Indpls., 1973-75, asst. prof. dept. pediatrics, 1975-78, assoc. prof. dept. pediatrics, 1978-92, prof. dept. med. & molecular genetics, 1993—, prof. pediats., 1992—. Mem. Am. Acad. Pediatrics, Am. Soc. for Human Genetics, Soc. for Inherited Metabolic Disease, Soc. for the Study of Inborn Errors of Metabolism, Soroptimist Internat., Mortar Bd., Iota Sigma Pi, Sigma Xi, Phi Beta Kappa. Office: Riley Hosp 702 Barnhill Dr Rm 0907 Indianapolis IN 46202-5225

WARD, BRIAN SCOTT, psychologist; b. Hartford, Conn., Oct. 19, 1946; s. James Donald and Patricia Agnes (Giacomini) W.; m. Janina Deirdre Beach, Feb. 12, 1982. BA in Psychology, Baldwin-Wallace Coll., 1968; MEd, U. Hartford, 1971; MSW, U. Conn., 1981. Cert. sch. social worker; lic. psychologist. Staff psychologist Northeast Kingdom Mental Health Ctr., St. Johnsbury, Vt., 1971-77; psychologist, pvt. practice St. Johnsbury, Burlington, and, Montpelier, 1977—, stress mgmt. cons., 1983—; profl. adv. bd. Caledonia Home Health, St. Johnsbury, 1979-80, adv. bd. St. Johnsbury Youth Svc. Bur., 1976-78. Contbg. author: Child Custody Visitation Law and Practice, 1981. Mem. Vt. Psychol. Assn. (N.E. rep. 1995).

WARD, DONNA SUE, quality manager, nurse; b. Dallas, Feb. 18, 1957; d. Donald G. Cameron and Sue (Dodd) Werner; m. William R. Ward Jr., Dec. 9, 1989. BSN, U. Tex., 1979, MSN, 1987. RN, Tex.; cert. healthcare quality bd. RN, staff nurse to clin. mgr. Baylor Med. Ctr., Dallas, 1980-88; utilization quality coord. Aetna Health Plan, Dallas, 1989-93; quality mgr. CIGNA Health Care, Dallas, 1994—. Mem. Nat. Assn. of Healthcare Quality. Office: CIGNA Healthcare of Tex 600 E Las Colinas Ste 1100 Irving TX 75039

WARD, EVAN, JR., pharmacist; b. Selma, Ala., Sept. 13, 1942; s. Evan and Hattie Mae (Hunter) W.; children from previous marriage—Donna Janine, Jennifer Lynn, Christopher Evan; m. Mattie Mobley, Oct. 13, 1995; children—Nicholas Cameron, Dustin Roman. B.S., Fla. A&M U., 1965. Pharmacist, Triangle Prescription, Atlanta, 1966-70; pharmacist, asst. mgr. Walgreen Drugs, Atlanta, 1968-70; pharmacist, pres. Medics Drug Marts, Inc., Atlanta, 1970—; exec. v.p., founder W&W Pharms., Atlanta, 1982-84; cons. Sadie Mays Nursing Home, Atlanta, 1973-77; staff pharmacist McClendon Hosp., Atlanta, 1976-79; mem. adv. com. State Ga., 1984—. Mem. United Negro Coll. Fund, 1985, Nat. Urban League, 1985. Recipient Bus. Man of Year award Atlanta Bus. League, 1970, Cert. Appreciation award CETA, 1980. Mem. Ga. Pharm. Assn., Nat. Assn. Retail Druggists, Fla. A&M Sch. Pharmacists Alumni Assn. (pres. 1973, Pharmacist of Year 1973), Fla. A&M Alumni Assn. (Disting. Service award 1984), C. of C., Kappa Alpha Psi. Baptist. Office: Medics Drug Marts Inc 75 Piedmont Ave NE Atlanta GA 30303-2508

WARD, JACQUELINE ANN BEAS, nurse, healthcare administrator; b. Somerset, Pa., Oct. 23, 1945; d. Donald C. and Thelma R. (Wable) Beas; divorced; children: Charles L. Jr., Shawn M. BS in Nursing, U. Pitts., 1966; MA in Counseling and Guidance, W.Va. Coll. Grad. Studies, 1976; MBA, Columbus Coll., 1983. Cert. in advanced nursing adminstrn. Staff nurse W.Va. U. Hosp., Morgantown, 1966-67; staff nurse, head nurse Meml. Hosp. Charleston, W.Va., 1967-69; staff nurse Santa Rosa Hosp., San Antonio, 1969; staff nurse, supr. Bexar County Hosp., San Antonio, 1970; charge, staff nurse Rocky Mountain Osteo. Hosp., Denver, 1971; staff nurse Charleston Area Med. Ctr., 1971-74, asst. dir. nursing, 1974-82; dir. nursing H.D. Cobb Meml. Hosp., Phenix City, Ala.; clin. instr. Chattahoochee Valley C.C., Phenix City, 1982-84; v.p. nursing Venice (Fla.) Hosp., 1984-90, v.p. ops., 1990-94, exec. dir., v.p. Life Counseling Ctr., Osprey, Fla., 1994-95, dir. skilled unit and spl. projects Bon Secours/Venice Hosp., 1995—. Mem. Am. Coll. Healthcare Exec., Fla. Hosp. Assn., Nat. League Nursing, Articulation Coun. Sarasota and Manatee Counties, Am. Orgn. of Nurse Execs. (pres. region II south Fla. 1985-86, 90-94), Fla. Orgn. Nurse Execs., Fla. Commn. on Nursing. Office: Bon Secours-Venice Hosp 540 The Rialto Venice FL 34285

WARD, JAMES V., ophthalmologist; b. Malvern, Ariz., Nov. 29, 1928; s. Elmer Vernon and Eva Mae (Yates) W.; m. Rosemary Elizabeth Cereghino, Aug. 15, 1955; children: Richard W., Chris A. BS with honors, U. Ark., 1951; MD, U. Ark., Little Rock, 1952. Diplomate Am. Bd. Obstetrics-Gynecology, Am. Bd. Ophthalmology. Clin. asst., prof. ophthalmologist La. State U. Sch. Medicine, Shreveport, 1969—. Contbr. articles to profl. jours. Lt. comdr. USN, 1957-59. Mem. AMA, Am. Acad. Ophthalmology, So. Med. Assn., Shreveport Country Club, Phi Beta Kappa. Episcopalian. Office: 2121 Fairfield Ave Shreveport LA 71104-2057

WARD, JOHN WESLEY, retired pharmacologist; b. Martin, Tenn., Apr. 8, 1925; s. Charles Wesley and Sara Elizabeth (Little) W.; m. Martha Isabelle Hendley, Dec. 7, 1947; children: Judith Carol, Charles Wesley, Richard Little. A.A., George Washington U., 1948, B.S., 1950, M.S., 1955; Ph.D., Georgetown U., 1959. Research assoc. in pharmacology Hazleton Labs., Falls Church, Va., 1950-55; head dept. pharmacology Hazleton Labs., 1955-58, chief depts. biochemistry and pharmacology, 1958-59; with A. H. Robins Co., Richmond, Va., 1959-90, dir. biol. research, 1978-80, dir. research, 1980-82, v.p. research, 1982-89, v.p., gen. mgr. R & D div., 1989-90; ret., 1990; lectr. in pharmacology Med. Coll. Va., 1960-64, adj. assoc. prof. pharmacology, 1982-90; guest lectr. Seminar on Good Lab. Practices, FDA, Washington, 1979, Chgo., 1979, San Francisco, 1979; apptd. expert pharmacologue toxicologue, France, 1986. Contbr. articles on pharmacology, toxicology and medicinal chemistry to profl. publs. Served with USMC, 1943; Served with USN, 1944-46; Served with U.S. Army, 1944. Mem. AAAS, N.Y. Acad. Sci., Va. Acad. Sci., Am. Chem. Soc., Soc. Toxicology (charter), Am. Soc. Pharmacology and Exptl. Therapeutics, Internat. Soc. Regulatory Toxicology and Pharmacology (charter), Pharm. Mfrs. Assn. (chmn. animal care and use com. 1971-88), Am. Assn. for Accreditation Lab. Animal Care (chmn. bd. trustees 1976-80), Sigma Xi. Clubs: Willow Oaks (Richmond); Cosmos (Washington), Masons (Washington). Home: 10275 Cherokee Rd Richmond VA 23235-1107

WARD, KATHERINE NORA, medical virologist, educator; b. Brighton, Sussex, Eng., Mar. 14, 1948; d. Wilfred and Nancy Ward. BSc with honors, U. London, 1969, PhD, 1973; MB BChir, U. Cambridge, Eng., 1983, MA, 1990. Registered med. practitioner. Fellow Kennedy Rheumatology Inst., London, 1972-74; rsch. assoc. pathology dept. U. Cambridge, 1974-79; house officer Gen. and Addenbrooke's Hosps., Newmarket and Cambridge, 1984-85; registrar Pub. Health Lab., Manchester, Eng., 1985-87; clin. lectr. U. Cambridge, 1987-91; hon. sr. registrar Addenbrooke's Hosp., Cambridge, 1987-91; fellow, dir. studies Christ's Coll., Cambridge, 1987-91; sr. lectr., hon. cons. Royal Postgrad. Med. Sch./Hammersmith Hosp., London, 1991—; mem. nat. standing sci. com. on virology Pub. Health Lab. Svc., 1966—. Contbr. sci. papers to internat. jours. Rsch. grantee U.K. Med. Rsch. Coun., U.K. Action Rsch. Mem. Royal Coll. Pathologists, Brit. Soc. for Immunology, Soc. for Gen. Microbiology, London Virus Group. Office: Dept Virology Royal Postgrad Med Sch, Ducane Rd, London W12 OHS, England

WARD, KENNETH LEE, recreation therapist; b. Lincoln, Nebr., Nov. 29, 1961; s. Philip Asher and Elaine Delores (Harms) W.; m. Vanessa Gaye Colby, June 25, 1988; children: Hannah, Elaine, Caleb Lee. BA, U. Nebr., 1985; postgrad. in agr., Tex. A&M U., 1986-87. Recreation therapist VA Med. Ctr., Grand Island, Nebr., 1987—. Bd. dirs. Presbyn. Presch., Ctrl. Nebr. Coun. on Alcoholism. Mem. Nat. Recreation and Parks Assn., Nat. Therapeutic Recreation Assn., Am. Therapeutic Recreation Assn., Grand Island Employees Assn. Presbyterian. Home: 4049 Horseshoe Pl Grand Island NE 68803-1517

WARD, LOUIS EMMERSON, retired physician; b. Mt. Vernon, Ill., Jan. 19, 1918; s. Henry Ben Pope and Aline (Emmerson) W.; m. Nan Talbot, June 5, 1942; children—Nancy, Louis, Robert, Mark; m. Marian Mansfield, Jan. 27, 1979. A.B., U. Ill., 1939; M.D., Harvard, 1943; M.S. in Medicine, U. Minn., 1949. Intern Ill. Research and Ednl. Hosp., Chgo., 1943; fellow medicine Mayo Found., 1946-49; cons. medicine, rheumatology Mayo Clinic, 1950-83, chmn. bd. govs., 1964-75. Contbr. articles to profl. jours. Vice chmn. bd. trustees Mayo Found., 1964-76; past bd. dirs. Fund for Republic, Ctr. for Study Democratic Instns., Arthritis Found.; mem. Nat. Council Health Planning and Devel., 1976-83. Recipient U. Ill. Alumni Achievement award, 1968; recipient disting. alumnus award Mayo Found., 1983. Master Am. Coll. Rheumatology (pres. 1969-70); mem. AMA, Nat. Soc. Clin. Rheumatologists (pres. 1967-69), Ctrl. Soc. Clin. Rsch., Minn. Med. Soc., Zumbro Valley Med. Soc., So. Minn. Med. Assn., Phi Beta Kappa, Sigma Xi, Alpha Omega Alpha, Phi Delta Theta. Home: 30 Raeburn Ct Port Ludlow WA 98365-9796

WARD, MADONNA LEE, physicians assistant; b. Bemidji, Minn., July 8, 1940; d. Everett Howard and Vera Blanch (Brown) Bair; m. M. Wayne Ward, Sept. 18, 1939; children: Michael Gene, Patricia Roseada. BS, Wichita State U., 1980; MA, Webster U., 1994. Mem. surg. scrub, heart team St. Francis Hosp., Wichita, Kans., 1960-72; physicians asst Wichita VA Med. Ctr., 1974—. Advisor for Career Day, Derby (Kans.) H.S., 1980—. Fellow Am. Acad. Physician Assts., Kans. Acad. Physician Assts., VA Physician Assts. Assn. Home: 1100 Woodlawn Heights Ct Derby KS 67037-0797

WARD, MARCIA DIANE, marketing professional; b. Detroit, Oct. 13, 1945; d. Edsel Denton and Lois Irene (Hunley) W.; m. Michael L. Ward, Nov. 19, 1966 (div. Oct. 1987); 1 child, Christian Michael. ADN, Purdue U., Ft. Wayne, Ind., 1977. RN, Ind., Ga.; cert. case mgr. Critical care nurse Parkview Meml. Hosp., Ft. Wayne, 1977-79, St. Joseph's Hosp., Atlanta, 1979-83; bus. owner M/K Diagnostics, Inc., Atlanta, 1984-88; ind. legal nurse cons. Atlanta, 1988-90; med. case mgr. Travelers Ins. Co., Atlanta, 1990-93; managed care/med. law tchr./cons. Atlanta, 1993—; market segment mgr. IBM Healthcare Solutions, Atlanta, 1994—; mem. adv. bd. for Nat. Home Health Care Congress. Mem. editl. adv. bd. The Case Mgmt. Advisor; contbr. articles to profl. jours., chpt. to book. Vol. ARC, Atlanta Shelter for Homeless. Recipient Outstanding Svc. award Nursing in Bus. Assocs., Atlanta, 1988. Mem. Am. Legal Nurse Cons. Assn., Ind. Case Mgmt. Assn., Case Mgmt. Soc. Am. (track developer disease mgmt. 1996), Purdue Alumni Club, Am. Managerial Care Nurses Assn. Home: 110 Glenleaf Dr Norcross GA 30092 Office: IBM Healthcare Solutions SG14A Bldg G 3200 Windy Hill Rd Atlanta GA 30339

WARD, MELVIN A., nursing educator; b. Tonkawa, Okla., June 4, 1940; s. Franklin Daniel and Lottie Mae (Abel) W.; m. Sharon Lynn Ward, July 3, 1969; children: Alyssa Elizabeth, Robert Benjamin. BA, Okla. State U., 1962; MS, U. hawaii, 1964, PhD, 1969. Postdoctoral fellow U. Hawaii, Honolulu, 1969-70, Purdue U., 1970-71; teaching asst. biochemistry U. Hawaii, 1962-64; prof. biology Hawaii Loa Coll., Kaneohe, 1971-92, Hawaii Pacific U., Hawaii Loa Campus, 1992—; dir. health sci. prog. Hawaii Loa Coll., 1976-92; advisor pre-med. program Hawaii Pacific U., 1994—. Contbr. articles to profl. jours. NDEA fellow, 1964-67. Mem. Nat. Assn. Advisors Health Professions, Sigma Xi. Home: 1415 Kupau Pl Kailua HI 96734-3637 Office: Hawaii Pacific U 45-045 Kamehameha Hwy Kaneohe HI 96744-5221

WARD, NEIL O., otolaryngologist; b. Chippewa Falls, Wis., 1934. MD, George Washington U., 1963. Rotating intern LDS Hosp., Salt Lake City, 1963-64; resident in gen. surgery Wadsworth/VA Hosp., L.A., 1964-65, resident in otolaryngoloty, 1965-68; mem. staff Good Samaritan Hosp., Phoenix; pvt. practice. Mem. AMA, ACS, AAO-HNS, ASHNS. Office: Ariz Phys Ctr 1331 N 7th St # 375 Phoenix AZ 85006-2772*

WARD, PATRICIA ANN, radiographer; b. Vincennes, Ind., Aug. 12, 1956; d. Harold Edgar and Thelma Lucille (Mason) Hudson; m. Steven Joe Ward, Aug. 31, 1974; children: Jennifer Jo, Jade Steven. Student, Vincennes U., 1984; diploma in radiologic tech., Good Samaritan Sch. Radiologic Tech., Vincennes, 1986; BS in Mgmt., Oakland City U., 1992. Nat. cert. radiologic technician; cert. radiologic technologist, Ind. Clin. mgr., chief radiographer Orthopaedic Assocs. Princeton, Inc., Evansville, Ind., 1989—. Vol. United Cerebral Palsy Ind., Vincennes, 1983, VFW, Newburgh, 1995, Colonnade Club, Delta Zeta, Evansville, 1994—; cons. Girl Scouts U.S.A., Bicknell, Ind., 1984; parent vol. Castle H.S., Newburgh, Ind., 1992—; mem. Comdr.'s Club, DAV, Newburgh, 1995—. Mem. Am. Soc. Radiologic Technologists, Ind. Soc. Radiologic Technologists (mem. dist. 8 radiologic technologists). Home: 3177 Graceland Ct Newburgh IN 47630

WARD, PETER ALLAN, pathologist, educator; b. Winsted, Conn., Nov. 1, 1934; s. Parker J. and Mary Alice (McEvoy) W. B.S., U. Mich., Ann Arbor, 1958, M.D., 1960. Diplomate: Am. Bd. Anat. Pathology, Am. Bd. Immunopathology. Intern Bellevue Hosp., 1960-61; resident U. Mich. Hosp., Ann Arbor, 1961-63; postdoctoral fellow Scripps Clinic, La Jolla, Calif., 1963-65; chief immunobiology br. Armed Forces Inst. Pathology, Washington, 1967-71; prof. dept. pathology, chmn. dept. U. Conn. Health Center, Farmington, 1971-80; prof., chmn. dept. pathology U. Mich., Ann Arbor, 1980—; interim dean U. Mich. Med. Sch., 1982-85, 1st Godfrey D. Stobbe prof. pathology, 1987; Disting. faculty lectr. U. Mich. Biomed. Rsch. Coun., 1989; cons. VA Hosp., 1980—; mem. rsch. rev. com. NHLBI, NIH, Bethesda, Md., 1978-82, Inst. Medicine/NAS, 1990—; trustee Am. Bd. Pathology, 1988—, pres., 1996; bd. dirs. Univs. Assoc. for Rsch. and Edn. in Pathology, Inc., 1978—, pres. bd. dirs., 1988-90; chmn., mem. sch. adv. bd. Armed Forces Inst. Pathology, Washington, 1981-83; mem. pathology A study sect. NIH, 1972-76, chmn., 1976-768; pres.-elect U.S./Can. Acad. Pathology, 1991-92, pres., 1992-93, past pres., 1993-94. Capt., M.C. U.S. Army, 1965-67. Recipient Borden Research award U. Mich. Med. Sch., Ann Arbor, 1960; recipient Research and Devel. award U.S. Army, 1969, Meritorious Civilian Service award Dept. Army, 1970, Parke-Davis award Am. Soc. Exptl. Pathology, 1971. Mem. Am. Assn. Pathologists (pres. 1978-79), Am. Soc. Clin. Investigation, Am. Assn. Immunologists, U.S./Can. Acad. Pathologists (past pres. 1993-94), Assn. Pathology Chmn., Mich. Soc. Pathologists. Office: U Mich Med Sci I PO Box 0602 1301 Catherine Rd #M5240 Ann Arbor MI 48109-0602

WARD, ROBERT JUDE, surgeon; b. N.Y.C., June 30, 1952; s. Robert L. and Helen (Stopford) W.; m. Margaret A. Moxness, May 19, 1984; children: Christine, Valerie. BS, Fairfield U., 1974; MD, Columbia U., 1978. Diplomate Am. Bd. Surgery with subspecialty in surg. critical care. Intern dept. surgery St. Vincent's Hosp. and Med. Ctr. of N.Y., 1978-79, resident dept. surgery, 1979-82, chief resident dept. surgery, 1982-83; asst. dir. dept. surgery North Shore U. Hosp., Manhasset, N.Y., 1983-86, dir. trauma svcs. and gen. surgery, 1985—, co-dir. dept. surgery, 1986-88, program dir. dept. surgery, 1985-92, chief divsn. gen. surgery, 1988—; clin. instr. in surgery NYU, 1982-83, N.Y. Med. Coll., 1983; instr. clin. surgery Cornell U. Med. Coll., N.Y.C., 1983-86, asst. prof. surgery, 1987-93, assoc. prof. clin. surgery, 1993—, course dir. ATLS. Contbr. articles to profl. publs. Fellow ACS (mem. membership com. Bklyn./L.I. chpt., chmn. sci. com.), N.Y. Acad. Medicine; mem. AMA, Nassau Surg. Soc., Am. Assn. Clin. Anatomists, Nassau County Med. Soc., Soc. Critical Care Medicine, Soc. Internat. Surgery, Soc. Am. Gastrointestinal Endoscopic Surgeons, Am. Soc. Gen. Surgeons. Office: North Shore U Hosp 300 Community Dr Manhasset NY 11030

WARD, VERNON GRAVES, internist; b. Palisade, Nebr., Mar. 5, 1928; s. Charles Bennett and Mildred Belle (Graves) W.; m. Eleanore Mae Farstveet, Aug. 28, 1952; children: Margo, Alison, Barry. BA, Nebr. Wesleyan U., 1948; MD cum laude, U. Nebr., Omaha, 1954. Diplomate Am. Bd. Internal Medicine. Instr. in anatomy Columbia U., N.Y.C., 1948-50; intern U. Wis., Madison, 1954-55, resident internal medicine, 1955-58, chief resident, physician, 1957-58; fellow in neurophysiology and psychosomatic medicine U. Okla., Oklahoma City, 1960-61; asst. clin. prof. medicine U. Wis., Madison, 1961-62; pvt. practice internal medicine Kearney, Nebr., 1962-67; asst. prof. U. Nebr. Coll. Medicine, Omaha, 1967-69; assoc. clin. prof. medicine U. Nebr., Omaha, 1969—; pvt. practice internal medicine Omaha, Nebr., 1969—; chmn. dept. internal medicine Clarkson Hosp., Omaha, 1976-78, 96—. Contbr. articles to profl. jours. including JAMA, Nebr. State Med. Jour., Wis. State Med. Jour., Am. Heart Jour., Postgrad. Medicine. Pres. Nebr. chpt. Arthritis Found., 1969-71. Lt. Commdr. USNR, 1958-60. Named Hutton Traveling Scholar Coll. of Physicians, 1965. Fellow ACP, Am. Coll. Rheumatology; mem. AMA, Nebr. State Med. Soc., Omaha Med. Soc., Am. Soc. Internal Medicine, Am. Psychosomatic Soc., Nebr. Soc. Internal Medicine (pres. 1980-82, Disting. Internist award 1990), Phi Kappa Phi, Alpha Omega Alpha (pres. Nebr. chpt. 1984-85), Phi Chi (grand sec.-treas. 1986—, co-chmn. nat. conv. Omaha 1953), Phi Kappa Tau. Republican. Lutheran. Home: 302 N 54th St Omaha NE 68132-2813 Office: 201 S Doctor's Bldg Omaha NE 68131

WARD, WALLACE DIXON, medical educator; b. Pierre, S.D., June 30, 1924; s. Edmund Dixon and Thelma Marie (Hill) W.; m. Edith Marion Bystrom, Dec. 27,1949; children: Edith Marion IV, Laurie Elizabeth, Kathryn Christine, Holly Lydene. BS in Physics, S.D. Sch. Mines and Tech., 1944, DSc, 1971; PhD in Exptl. Psychology, Harvard U., 1953. Research engr. Baldwin Piano Co., Cin., 1953-54; research assoc. Cen. Inst. for Deaf, St. Louis, 1954-57; assoc. dir. research Noise Research Ctr., Am. Acad. Ophthalmology and Otolaryngology, Los Angeles, 1957-62; prof., depts. communication disorders, otolaryngology, pub. health and psychology U. Minn., Mpls., 1962—; mem. com. on hearing, bioacoustics and biomechanics NRC, 1960-92, mem. exec. coun., 1970-75, chmn., 1971-73; mem. communicative scis. study sect. div. rsch. grants NIH, 1969-73; sci. adviser Callier Hearing and Speech Ctr., Dallas, 1968-86; cons. U.S. Army, 1972-88, EPA Office Noise Abatement and Control, 1973; mem., co-chmn. Internat. Sci. Noise Teams, 1973—. Editor: Noise as a Public Health Hazard, 1969, Noise as a Public Health Problem, 1974, Noise and Hearing Conservation Manual, 1986; contbr. articles to tech. jours. Served with USNR, 1944-46. Recipient Research Career Devel. award NIH, 1962. Fellow Acoustical Soc. Am. (mem. exec. coun. 1978-81, pres. 1988), Am. Speech and Hearing Assn.; mem. AAAS, Am. Audiology Soc. (v.p, 1973-75, pres. 1976), Internat. Soc. Audiology (governing bd., pres. 1978-80), Am. Otol. Soc., Am. Indsl. Hygiene Assn., Mensa, Triangle, Soc. for Music Perception and Cognition (v.p. 1992), Sigma Xi, Sigma Tau. Libertarian. Home: 1666 Coffman St #315 Falcon Heights MN 55108-1340 Office: U Minn Med Sch Dept Otolaryngology 2001 6th St SE Minneapolis MN 55455-3007

WARD, WILLIAM QUINCY, dermatologist; b. Albany, Ga., Mar. 17, 1924; s. Joseph Quincy and Vivan Lillian (Atwater) W.; m. Janet Brown; children: Stephen Q., Robert T., Beth Lynn Ward Dillard, Patricia Ann Ward Pace. Student, Emory U., 1944-47. Diplomate Am. Bd. Internal Medicine, Am. Bd. Dermatology. Intern resident Baptist Meml. Hosp., Memphis, 1947-51; pvt. practice internal medicine Van Nuys, Calif., 1953-56; physician internal medicine Meml. Clin., Russellville, Ala., 1956-68; resident dermatology Johns Hopkins Hosp., Balt., 1968-70; pvt. practice dermatology Birmingham, Ala., 1970-80; assoc. prof. dermatology U. Ala., Birmingham, 1980-89; dermatologist Diagnostic Clin., Largo, Fla., 1990—. Contbr. articles to profl. jours. 1st Lt. U.S. Army, 1945-53. Fellow Am. Acad. Dermatology, Am. Coll. Physicians; mem. N. Am. Clin. Dermatology, Southern Med. Assn., Southeastern and South Central Dermatology Assn., Fla. Med. Assn., Fla. Dermatological Soc.

WARDE, DONAL ANTHONY, cardiologist; b. Dublin, Ireland, Aug. 7, 1948; came to U.S., 1972; s. Constantine and Mary Margaret (Gibbons) W.; m. Mary Esther Duane, July 5, 1972; children: Conor Thomas, Deirdre Marie. BA, U. Dublin, 1970, MD, 1972. Resident Allegheny Gen. Hosp., Pitts., 1972-74, 75-76, Federated Dublin Vol. Hosp., 1974-75; fellow cardiology Temple U. Health Scis. Ctr., Phila., 1976-78; staff physician Allegheny Gen. Hosp., Pitts., 1978—, pres. med. staff, 1993-94. Fellow Am. Coll. Cardiology; mem. Allegheny County Med. Soc. (adv. bd. managed care 1995—), Univ. Club Pitts., Teutonia Maennerchor Pitts. Office: Carlton Cardiology Assocs 490 E North Ave Ste 301 Pittsburgh PA 15212

WARDELL, JOE RUSSELL, JR., pharmacologist; b. Omaha, Nov. 11, 1929; s. Joe Russell and Marie Hamilton (Waugh) W.; m. Leta Harris, July 14, 1952 (div. Oct. 1981); children: Michael R., Susan E., John D.; m. Doris Erway, Aug. 27, 1983. BS in Pharmacy, Creighton U., 1951; MS in Pharmacology, U. Nebr., Omaha, 1959, PhD in Pharmacology, 1962. Lic. pharmacist Nebr. Pharmacist Osco Drug, Waterloo, Iowa, 1953-56; grad. asst. Coll. of Medicine U. Nebr., Omaha, 1956-62; sr. pharmacologist Smith Kline & French Labs., Phila., 1962-64, advanced to assoc. dir. biol. rsch., 1974-78; dir. R & D compound acquistions R&D, 1978-86; pres. Wardell Assocs., Park City, Utah, 1986—. Author: more than 40 articles in profl. pubs.; inventor/co-inventor 4 patents respiratory and cardiovascular drugs. Asst. scoutmaster, Boy Scouts of Am., N.J., 1969-75. Recipient Merck Award Creighton U., 1951. Mem. Soc. of Parmacology & Experiemental Therapeutics, Am. Acad. of Pharmaceutical Scis., Am. Chem. Soc., Licensing Exec. Soc., Am. Arbitration Assn. Panel Neutrals. Home and Office: Wardell Assocs 55 Thaynes Canyon Dr Park City UT 84060-6713

WARDEN, CLARK GERARD, surgeon; b. New Orleans, July 29, 1960; s. Merlin M. and Carmen C. (Carra) Warden; m. Emma Miller, May 13, 1989; 1 child, Parker Dayton. BS, Tulane U., 1980, MD, 1984. Diplomate Am. Bd. Surgery. Intern, resident, chief resident in surgery N.C. Meml. Hosp., Chapel Hill, 1984-89; pvt. practice surgery Pascagoula, Miss., 1989—. Office: 4211 Hospital St Ste 312 Pascagoula MS 39581-5318

WARDEN, HERBERT EDGAR, surgeon, educator; b. Cleve., Aug. 30, 1920; s. Fred Edgar and Eva Alethea (Powers) W.; m. Audrey Eleanor Flaten, June 14, 1958; children: Karen Eleanor, Bradford Edgar, Douglas Edward, Suzanne Elise. BS, Washington and Jefferson Coll., 1942, DSc (hon.), 1996, ScD, 1996; MD, U. Chgo., 1946. Diplomate Am. Bd. Surgery, Am. Bd. Thoracic Surgery. Intern U. Chgo. Clinics, 1946-47; med. officer U.S. Naval Hosp., Mare Island, Calif., 1947-49; surgeon USAF Hosp., Travis AFB, Calif., 1949-50; asst. resident in surgery U. Minn., Mpls., 1951-56, rsch. asst. cardio vascular surgery, 1953-56, chief resident, 1956-57, instr., 1957-60; assoc. prof. surgery W.Va. U., Morgantown, 1960-62, head cardiovascular surgery, 1960-82, prof., 1962—, vice chmn. dept. surgery, 1968-76; cons. Louis A. Johnson VA Hosp., Clarksburg, W.Va., 1962—; bd. dirs. W.Va. U. Med. Corp., Morgantown, 1987—; physician football team W.Va. U.; bd. dirs. First Nat. Bank, Morgantown. Contbr. articles to profl. jours. Trustee Drummond Chapel, Morgantown, 1974-78, Washington and Jefferson Coll., Washington, Pa., 1974—; bd. dirs. Am. Heart Assn., 1968-73. Lt. M.C., USNR, 1947-49. Recipient Albert Lasker award APHA, 1955, Disting. Svc. awards W. Va. Heart Assn., 1973, W. Va. U., 1976; named to the Order of Vandalia, W.Va. U., 1995; named Disting. Alumnus Washington and Jefferson Coll., 1968. Fellow ACS (gov. 1988—), Am. Coll. Cardiology (gov. 1982-85), Southeastern Surg. Congress; mem. AMA (Hektoen Gold medal 1957), Am. Surg. Assn., Am. Assn. Thoracic Surgery, Soc. Univ. Surgeons, Soc. Thoracic Surgeons (founder, chair program com. 1983-84, Chamberlin award 1985), So. Thoracic Surg. Assn., Halsted Soc., Lillehei Surg. Soc. (pres. 1988), Alpha Kappa Alpha, Alpha Omega Alpha, Sigma Xi. Republican. Methodist. Home: 616 Schubert Pl Morgantown WV 26505-2330 Office: Health Scis Ctr N W Va U Morgantown WV 26505

WARDROP, RICHARD MARK, nursing educator, gerontology nurse; b. Ashland, Mass., Aug. 26, 1949; s. Frederick D. and Shirley E. (Boyd) W.; m. Janice Milzarek, June 19, 1971; children: Joshua, Sarah. BA, U. Mass., Amherst, 1972; ADN, Quinsigamond Community Coll., Worcester, Mass., 1976; BSN, Framingham State Coll., 1993; MSN, U. Mass., Worcester, 1996. RN, Mass.; cert. adult nurse practitioner; cert. CPR and First Aid instr. Staff nurse dept. pub. health Cushing Hosp., Framingham, Mass., 1976-79, head nurse, 1979-81, safety officer, 1982-89, nursing instr., 1981-92; nurse mgr. Mary Ann Morse Nursing Home, Natick, Mass., 1992—; staff nurse Greater Milford-Northbridge Vis. Nurses Assn., Mendon, Mass., 1992—; instr. and researcher in field. Mem. ANA (cert. gerontol. nurse), Mass. Nurses Assn., Nat. Environ. Health Assn. Home: 84 High St Milford MA 01757-4006

WARDZALA, LAWRENCE JOSEPH, internist; b. Chgo., Sept. 25, 1953; s. Joseph Eugene and Marie Victoria (Bartolph)) W. BA, Northwestern U., 1974; PhD, Dartmouth Coll., 1979; MD, U. Vt., 1987. Postdoctoral fellow Laboratoire de Recherches Metabolique, Geneva, Switzerland, 1979-81; staff fellow NIH, Bethesda, Md., 1981-83; rsch. assoc. INSERM, Paris, 1983; fellow NIH, Bethesda, 1987-88; house officer internal medicine Wash. Hosp. Ctr./Jackson Meml. Hosp., 1988-91; pvt. practice internist HIV/AIDS medicine Washington, 1991-92, Ft. Lauderdale, 1991—; med. dir. spl. Immunology Imperial Point Med. Ctr., Ft. Lauderdale. Mem. Broward County HIV Planning Coun., Ft. Lauderdale, 1994-96. Capt. U.S. Army, 1984-87. Mem. AMA, Am. Soc. Internal Medicine, Fla. Med. Assn., Broward County Med. Assn. Office: 6405 N Federal Hwy Ste 205 Fort Lauderdale FL 33308

WARE, JAMES LATANÉ, plastic surgeon; b. Richmond, Va., Mar. 31, 1934; s. Harry Hudnall Jr. and Mary Warren (Williams) W.; m. Betsy Schaeffer Jones, June 7, 1958; children: James Latané Jr., Elizabeth Schaeffer. BA, U. Va., 1955; MD, Med. Coll. Va., 1959. Surg. intern Duke Hosp., Durham, N.C., 1959-60, jr. asst. resident in surgery, 1960-61; asst. resident, resident in surgery Grady Hosp., 1961-64; asst. resident, resident plastic surgery Duke Hosp., 1964-67; plastic surgeon USN, Bethesda, Md., 1967-69, Drs. Smith and Ware, Richmond, 1969-77, Plastic Surg. Ctr. Richmond, Va., 1977—. Comdr. USNR, 1967-69. Fellow ACS; mem. AMA, Am. Soc. Plastic and Reconstructive Surgeons, Southeastern Soc. Plastic and Reconstructive Surgeons, Va. Soc. Plastic and Reconstructive Surgeons (pres.), Am. Soc. Aesthetic Plastic Surgery, Med. Soc. Va., Richmond Acad. Medicine (pres.). Office: Plastic Surgery Ctr Richmond 5855 Bremo Rd Ste 606 Richmond VA 23226

WAREHAM, NEALE COLIN, chemist; b. Grimsby, Eng., Dec. 29, 1960; s. David Eric and Jill (MacDonald) W.; m. Helen Margaret Gerlack, May 12, 1984; children: Colin Scott, Caroline Christina, Catherine Irene, Cameron James, Clare Philippa. BSc with honors in Analytical Chemistry, U. Hertfordshire, Eng., 1991. Jr. sci. officer Stoke Mandeville Hosp., Aylesbury, Eng., 1980-84; analyst Wellcome Found., Berkhamsted, Eng., 1984-91, Stiefel Labs., Berkshire, Eng., 1991-93; sr. analyst Stiepel Labs., Berkshire, Eng., 1993-95, sect. leader, 1995—. Patentee in field. Office: Stiefel Labs Whitebrook Park, Lower Cookham Rd, Maidenhead SL6 8XY, England

WARGO, ANDREA ANN, public health official, commissioned officer; b. Pottsville, Pa., Dec. 27, 1941; d. John Andrew and Anna Mary (Blischok) W.; m. Roger Fredrick Sies, Mar. 31, 1981. B.S. in Biology, Chestnut Hill Coll., 1972; Ph.D. in Biology, Georgetown U., 1978. Educator, adminstr. Catholic Archdiocese Phila., 1961-74; teaching asst. Georgetown U., Washington, 1974-78, postdoctoral fellow, 1978-80; acting br. chief FDA, Silver Spring, Md., 1980-86, acting chief gen. hosp. and personal use devices, 1986-88; assoc. adminstr. Agy. for Toxic Substances and Disease Registry, Washington, 1988—. Contbr. articles to sci. publs. Grantee NSF, 1972, 73, Kidney Found., 1979-80. Mem. Assn. Women in Sci. (treas. Washington-Balt. chpt. 1979-80), Commd. Officers Assn., Georgetown U. Alumni Assn., Toastmistress Club (pres. Bethesda, Md. chpt. 1978-79), Pub. Health Service (scientist profl. adv. com., exec. sec. 1984-86, vice-chmn 1986-87, chairperson 1987-88), Sigma Xi. Avocations: gardening; computers; financial planning; handwriting analysis. Home: 15521 Quail Run Dr North Potomac MD 20878 Office: 200 Independence Ave SW Washington DC 20201-0004

WARICK, LAWRENCE HERBERT, psychiatrist; b. Warsaw, Poland, May 2, 1936; came to U.S., 1949, naturalized, 1954; s. Joseph and Marsha (Beck) W.; m. Elaine Ruth Christensen, Feb. 24, 1963; children: Catherine Ann, David Mark. BS, CCNY, 1956; MD, Albert Einstein Coll. Medicine, 1960; PhD, So. Calif. Psychoanalytic Inst, 1980. Diplomate Am. Bd. Psychiatry and Neurology. Rotating intern L.A. County Gen. Hosp., 1960-61; resident neurology U. So. Calif. Sch. Medicine, L.A. County Gen. Hosp., 1961-62, resident psychiatry, 1962-65; clin. assoc. Sc. Calif. Psychoanalytic Inst., L.A., 1973-80, instr., 1981—; pvt. practice L.A., 1980—; asst. clin. prof. psychiatry UCLA Sch. Medicine, 1967—; instr. faculty Psychoanalytic Inst. So. Calif., L.A., 1980—. Contbr. chpts. to books and articles to profl. jours. Capt. USAF, 1962-68. Mem. Am. Psychiat. Assn., Am. Acad. Psychiatry and Law, So. Calif. Psychiatry Soc., So. Calif. Psychoanalytic Soc., Phi Beta Kappa. Office: 2444 Wilshire Blvd Ste 418 Santa Monica CA 90403-5808

WARING, MARY LOUISE, social work administrator; b. Pitts., Feb. 15, 1928; d. Harold R. and Edith (McCallum) W. AB, Duke U., 1949; MSS, Smith Coll., 1951; PhD, Brandeis U., 1974. Lic. clin. social worker, Tenn. Sr. supervising social worker Judge Baker Guidance Ctr., Boston, 1955-65; dir. social svc. Cambridge (Mass.) Mental Health Ctr., 1965-70; assoc. prof. Sch. Social Work Fla. State U., Tallahassee, 1974-77; prof. Fordham U., N.Y.C., 1977-82; cons. Dept. Human Svc., N.J., 1983-84; cons., sr. staff mem. Family Counseling Svc. Bergen County, Hackensack, N.J., 1984-86; dir. Step One Employee Assistance Program Fortwood Ctr., Inc., Chattanooga, 1986—; mem. ethics com. Chattanooga Rehab. Hosp., 1995. Contbr. articles to profl. jours. Mem. Citizen Amb. Program Human Resource Mgmt. Delegation to Russia, 1993; active Nat. Trust for Hist. Preservation, Nature Conservancy, Hunter Mus. Am. Art, Chattanooga Symphony and Opera Assn., Friends of Hamilton County Bicentennial Libr. Recipient Career Tchr. award Nat. Inst. Alchohol and Alchohol Abuse, 1972-74; traineeship NIMH, 1949-51. Mem. NASW (charter), Acad. Cert. Social Workers, Nat. Mus. Women in Arts (charter), Smithsonian Assocs., Cmty. Svcs. Club Greater Chattanooga (pres. 1995, 96, v.p. 1994, 97). Office: Fortwood Ctr Inc 1028 E 3rd St Chattanooga TN 37403-2107

WARITZ, RICHARD STEFAN, toxicologist; b. Portland, Oreg., Apr. 1, 1929; s. Anton John and Theresa (Stegelmaier) W.; m. Ruth Evelyn White, June 7, 1950; children—Joyce E., Gary S., Sharon J., Carol L. B.A., Reed Coll., 1951; Ph.D., Stanford U., 1957. Diplomate Am. Bd. Toxicology, Acad. Toxicological Scis. Sr. research scientist E.I. DuPont de Nemours & Co., Wilmington, Del., 1957-64, mgr. inhalation toxicology, 1964-72, mgr. bioscis., 1972-75; sr. toxicologist Hercules Inc., Wilmington, 1975-80, mgr. toxicology, 1980-92; pres. BioSante Internat., Inc., 1992—; mem. grad. toxicology edn. adv. bd. Rutgers U., Piscataway, N.J., 1980—; mem. life scis. adv. bd. and toxicology peer rev. bd. U.S. Army, Aberdeen, Md., 1982—; vis. prof. toxicology Rutgers U., 1993—. Contbr. articles to profl. jours. Mem. Soc. Toxicology (treas. 1981-85, pres. Mid-Atlantic chpt., 1989), Internat. Union Toxicol. Socs. (councillor 1983-88), Am. Indsl. Hygiene Assn., Am. Chem. Soc. Roman Catholic. Club: Hercules Country (bd. dirs. 1985-90). Avocations: golf, surf fishing. Home and Office: 2613 Turnstone Dr Wilmington DE 19808-1638

WARNCKE, ESBERN, scientist, editor, writer; b. Sønderborg, Denmark, Aug. 1, 1939; s. Carl and Naomi Katrine (Kjeldsen) W.; m. Else Callesen, Aug. 18, 1962; children: Claus W., Mette W., Ole W. BSc in Forestry, Agrl. U. Copenhagen, 1961; MSc in Biology, U. Aarhus, Denmark, 1968, DSc in Ecology, 1980. Asst. prof. U. Aarhus, 1966-68, assoc. prof., 1968—; head Local Trade and Industries Coun., Hornslet, Denmark, 1987-91. Editor-in-chief Jour. Lindbergia, 1974-79. Mem. taxation adv. bd. Municipality of Rosenholm/Hornslet, Denmark, 1984-88. Sgr. Danish infantry, 1959-61. Mem. Woodlands Assn. (chmn. 1988-95), Rotary (pres. Rosenholm chpt. 1985-86). Liberal. Lutheran. Home: Egelund Sdr Mosevej 21, DK-8543 Hornslet Denmark Office: U Aarhus, Nordlandsvej 68, DK-8240 Risskov Aarhus Denmark

WARNER, HEIDI C., clinical research nurse; b. Thomasville, N.C., Nov. 7, 1962; d. Walter Vance and Virginia Ruth (Beck) Warner. BSN, N.C. U., Charlotte, 1985. RN, N.C.; cert. in audiometry. Clin. rsch. assoc. tng. The Blethen Group, Research Triangle Park, N.C.; clin. rsch. nurse Olsten-Kimberly Quality Care, Kalamazoo, Mich.; clin. cons. Pathogenesis Corp., Seattle. Walter C. Teagle Found. nursing scholar, Exxon Co. USA. Mem. Nat. Assn. Female Execs., Phi Eta Sigma. Republican. Methodist.

WARNER, HOMER R., physiologist, educator; b. Salt Lake City, Apr. 18, 1922; married, 1946; 6 children. BA, U. Utah, 1946, MD, 1949; PhD in Physiology, U. Minn., 1953; Doctorate (hon.), Brigham Young U., 1971, U. Linkoping, Sweden, 1990. Intern Parkland Hosp., Dallas, 1949-50; resident in medicine U. Minn. Hosp., 1950-51; fellow Mayo Clinic, 1951-52, U. Minn., 1952-53; rsch. instr. dept. internal medicine U. Utah, Salt Lake City, 1953-54, asst. rsch. prof. dept. physiology, 1957-64, prof., chmn. dept. biophysiology and bioengring., 1964-73, rsch. prof. dept. surgery, 1966-83, spl. asst. info. mgmt. to v.p. health sci., 1983-93, prof., chmn. dept. medicine informatics, 1973—, dir., chmn. computer health sci., 1993—; dir. cardiovasc. lab. Latter-Day Sts. Hosp., 1954-70; mem. adv. com. computers NIH, 1961-63, chmn. computer rsch. study sect., 1963-66; vis. prof. U. Hawaii, 1968, U. So. Calif., 1972; mem. Biomed. Libr. Rev. Com., Nat. Libr. Medicine, 1982-86, chmn. grant rev. study sect., 1985-86. Recipient James E. Talmage Sci. Achievement award, 1968. Mem. Inst. Medicine-NAS (sr.), Am. Physiol. Soc., Am. Coll. Med. Informatics (pres. 1989). Office: U Utah Sch Medicine Dept Med Informatics AB193 Med Ctr Salt Lake City UT 84132*

WARNER, PATRICIA JOAN, psychotherapist; b. Greenville, N.C., Mar. 5, 1947; d. Joseph Ophir and Florence Genevieve (Jenkins) Teel; m. Richard Barr Cayton, May 21, 1971 (div. 1978); 1 child, Heather Jeanine; m. Michael Roy Warner, Jan. 9, 1987. BS in Elem. Edn., East Carolina U., 1968, MA in Guidance an Counseling, 1969. Lic. profl. counselor, Ga., Tenn.; nat. cert. counselor. Mental retardation counselor Pineland Mental Health, Jesup, Ga., 1983-85; mental health counselor Jesup, 1985-89; therapist, adolescence substance abuse Sci. Applications Internat., Nuernberg, Germany, 1989-92; adolescent therapist Harriett Cohn Ctr., Clarksville, Tenn., 1992—; chairperson Troubled Childrens Com., Baxley, Ga., 1988; presenter Am. Women's Activities in Germany, 1989. Recipient Letter of Commendation Comdr. U.S. Army Europe, 1991. Mem. Am. Counseling Assn., Erlangen Amateur Radio Soc. (sec. 1990-92), Clarksville Amateur Transmitting Soc., Assn. of Specialists in Group Work. Democrat. Home: 447 Winding Way Rd Clarksville TN 37043-5191 Office: Harriett Cohn Mental Health Ctr 511 8th St Clarksville TN 37040-3093

WÄRNERYD, KARL-ERIK, economic psychology educator; b. Sweden, Dec. 20, 1927; s. Werner Hjalmar and Nanny Hildegard (Andersson) W.; m. Eila Anna Marita Nystrom, Aug. 9, 1957; children: Karl Mikael, Jan Erik. MBA, Stockholm Sch. Econs., 1950; PhD, U. Chgo., 1955; D in Econs. honoris causa, Helsinki Swedish Sch. Bus., 1989. Rsch. asst. Stockholm Sch. Econs., 1950-52, asst. prof., 1955-63, prof. econ. psychology, 1963-92; ret., 1992; rsch. asst. Psychometric Lab., U. Chgo., 1953-55; dep. chmn., chmn. Sci. Adv. Group, Commn. for Switching to Right-Hand Driving, Stockholm, 1964-67; expert Commn. on Advt., Stockholm, 1967-74; rsch. fellow Ctr. for Econ. Rsch., Tilburg U., The Netherlands. Co-editor: Handbook of Economic Psychology, 1988, Ethics and Economic Affairs, 1994. Mem. Internat. Assn. Rsch. in Econ. Psychology (bd. mem. 1981—), Internat. Assn. Applied Psychology (pres. div. econ. psychology 1984-90), Swedish Psychol. Assn. Home: Wollmar Ykullsgatan 14, S-11850 Stockholm Sweden Office: Stockholm Sch Econs, Sveavägen 65, S-11383 Stockholm Sweden

WARNICK, JORDAN EDWARD, pharmacologist; b. Boston, Mar. 21, 1942; s. Samuel William and Ruth Barbara (Hite) W.; m. Hazel Augusta Cohen, Aug. 16, 1970; 1 child, Meredith Nicole. BS in Pharmacy, Mass. Coll. Pharmacy, 1963; PhD in Pharmacology, Purdue U., 1968. Registered pharmacist, Mass. Grad. teaching asst. Purdue U., West Lafayette, Ind., 1963-65; grad. rsch. asst. Purdue U., West Lafayette, 1965-68; post-doctoral fellow SUNY, Buffalo, 1968-70, NIH spl. awardee, 1970-71, asst. prof. Sch. of Pharmacy, 1971-74; asst. prof. U. Md. Sch. Medicine, Balt., 1974-80, assoc. prof., 1980-94, prof., 1994—, dir. short term rsch. tng. programs, 1983-94, dir. rsch. programs Office Student Rsch.; dir. office of student rsch. U. Md. Sch. Medicine, Balt., 1983—. Contbr. numerous articles, abstracts to profl. jours., chpts. to books. Chmn. Balt.-Rotterdam Sister City Com., 1991—. Grantee Nat. Sci. Found., 1987-92, Am. Heart Assn., 1989-96, NIH, 1985-95, 1996—. Mem. Am. Soc. for Pharmacology and Exptl. Therapeutics, Soc. for Neurosci. Office: U Md Sch Medicine Office Student Rsch 685 W Baltimore St Baltimore MD 21201-1509

WARR, OTIS SUMTER, JR., physician; b. Memphis, Mar. 30, 1914; s. Otis S. Sr. and Ethel (Boyce) W.; m. Vivian Barnett, Apr. 23, 1938; children: Otis S. III, Virginia W. Rubin, Robert B., Margaret W. Stewart, Edward L. BS, U. Va., 1935; MD, U. Tenn., Memphis, 1937. Diplomate Am. Bd. Internal Medicine, Nat. Bd. Med. Examiners. Intern Pa. Hosp., Phila., 1938, Geisinger Meml. Hosp., Danville, Pa., 1938-39; resident in internal medicine John Gaston Hosp., Memphis, 1939-41; pvt. practice internal medicine Memphis, 1945-92; ret. from pvt. practice, 1992; instr. to assoc. prof. internal medicine U. Tenn. Coll. Medicine, Memphis, 1945-79, ret., 1979; chmn. dept. medicine Bapt. Meml. Hosp., Memphis, 1954-55; pres. Memphis Acad. Internal Medicine, 1967-68; pres. Shelby County Tuberculosis and Health Assn., 1957-58, Memphis Heart Assn., 1950-51; pres. Tenn. Heart Assn., Nashville, 1958-59, chmn. bd., 1959-60. Pres. Memphis Civitan Club, 1954-55; past chmn. bd. St. John's Meth. Ch. Lt. col. M.C. U.S. Army, 1941-45. Fellow ACP; mem. AMA, Tenn. State Med. Soc., Memphis Med. Soc., Shelby County Med. Soc., Memphis Acad. Internal Medicine, Tenn. Lung Assn., Univ. Club Memphis. Methodist. Home: 1521 Central Ave Memphis TN 38104-4907

WARREN, DONALD WILLIAM, physiology educator, dentistry educator; b. Bklyn., Mar. 22, 1935; s. Sol B. and Frances (Plotkin) W.; m. Priscilla Girardi, June 10, 1956; children: Donald W. Jr., Michael C. BS, U. N.C., 1956, DDS, 1959; MS, U. Pa., 1961, PhD, 1963; d Odontology honoris causa, U. Kuopio, Finland, 1991. Asst. prof. dentistry U. N.C., Chapel Hill, 1963-65, dir. Craniofacial Ctr., 1963—, assoc. prof., 1965-69, prof., 1969-80, chmn. dept. dental ecology, 1970-85, Kenan prof., 1980—, rsch. prof. otolaryngology, 1985—; cons. NIH, Bethesda, Md., 1967—, R. J. Reynolds-Nabisco, Winston-Salem, N.C., 1986—. Contbr. articles to profl. jours. Recipient Honor award Am. Cleft Palate Assn./Craniofacial Assn., 1992, O. Max Garner award U. N.C. Bd. Govs., 1993. Fellow AAAS, Internat. Coll. Dentists, Am. Speech and Hearing Lang. Assn., Internat. Assn. Dental Rsch., Acoustical Soc. Am., Am. Cleft Palate Assn. (pres. 1981-82, Disting. Svc. award 1984), Am. Cleft Palate Edn. Found. (pres. 1976-77). Home: PO Box 1356 Southern Pines NC 28388-1356 Office: U NC Sch Dentistry CB # 7450 Chapel Hill NC 27599

WARREN, JEFFRY CLARY, clinical psychologist; b. Burbank, Calif., Nov. 1, 1949; s. Bernard W. and Florence S. W.; children: Adam Bernard, Eric Casey; student Valley Coll., 1967-79; BA, U. Calif.-Santa Barbara, 1971; PhD in Clin. Psychology, Calif. Sch. of Profl. Psychology, 1976. Registered psychologist Tech. Research, San Diego, 1976-78; developer, coordinator grad. tng. program Edwards Inst. for Advanced Studies, San Diego, 1980, dir. profl. and acad. tng., 1980; clin. psychologist TRI-Cmty. Svc. Systems, San Diego, 1979-83; pvt. practice, La Jolla, Calif., 1983—; sr. v.p., dir. Grid Research Corp., 1982-83; cons. and educator in family therapy and child abuse; cons. sports psychology; forensic psychologist, 1976—. Developer task force on child abuse, San Diego, 1978-80. Mem. Am. Psychol. Assn., Nat. Register of Health Service Providers in Psychology, Calif. State Psychol. Assn., Acad. San Diego Psychologists, Western Psychol. Assn. Jewish.

Contbr. papers to profl. assn. confs. Office: 7755 Fay Ave Ste I La Jolla CA 92037-4314

WARREN, JOHN ROBIN, physician, pathologist; b. Adelaide, Australia, June 11, 1937; s. John Roger Hogarth and Helen Josephine (Verco) W.; m. Winifred Teresa Williams, May 5, 1962; children: John Campbell, David Daniel, Patrick Stephen, Andrew Timothy, Rebecca Ruth, Eliza. Grad., St. Peters Coll., Adelaide, 1954; MB, BChir, U. Adelaide, 1961. Resident med. officer Queen Elizabeth Hosp., Adelaide, 1961; registrar Inst. Med. and Vet. Sci., Adelaide, 1962; lectr. pathology Univ. Adelaide, 1963; registrar pathology Royal Melbourne (Victoria, Australia) Hosp., 1964-67; cons. pathologist Royal Perth (Western Australia) Hosp., 1968—. Contbr. articles to profl. jours. Recipient plaque in recognition of major contribution in gastroduodenal disease, 1991, Warren Albert Found. prize Harvard U., 1994, award Australasian Med. Assn., 1995. Fellow Royal Coll. Pathologists of Australasia (Disting. Fellows award 1995, Western Pacific Helicobacter Conf. Inaugural award 1996, Paul Ehrlich award 1997); mem. Internat. Acad. Pathology, Australian Soc. Cytology. Office: Royal Perth Hosp, GPO Box X2213, Perth 6001, Australia

WARREN, JONATHAN TURNER, immunologist; b. Portsmouth, Va., Sept. 20, 1950; s. Robert Warren and Janice Tyre von Trapp; m. Elizabeth Huber, June 16, 1973 (div. 1988); m. Heather Hanson, Aug. 24, 1990; stepchildren: Matthew Aaron Napier, Sarah Jane Napier. BS, Baldwin-Wallace Coll., 1973; postgrad., Johns Hopkins U., 1988; MS, Hood Coll., Frederick, Md., 1980; PhD, U. Pa., 1985. Cert. med. lab. technologist. Med. lab. technologist Lorain (Ohio) Community Hosp., 1975; med. lab. rsch. specialist U.S. Army, USAMRIID, Frederick, Md., 1976-80; profl. musician (violinist) Frederick, Md., 1976—; rsch. scientist, fellow Nat. Cancer Inst.-FCRDC, Frederick, Md., 1988-90; immunologist AIDS Vaccine Evaluation Group The Emmes Corp., Potomac, Md., 1990—. Contbr. articles to profl. jours., chpts. to books. Co-founder, concertmaster Frederick Symphony Orch., 1976-94. NIH fellow, 1980-85, 86-88. Mem. AAAS, Am. Soc. Clin. Pathologists, Am. String Tchrs. Assn., N.Y. Acad. Scis., Clin. Immunology Soc., Johns Hopkins Immunology Coun. Home: 2047 Fire Tower Ln Ijamsville MD 21754-8737 Office: The Emmes Corp 11325 Seven Locks Rd Ste 214 Potomac MD 20854-3205

WARREN, KENNETH S., medical educator, physician; b. N.Y.C., June 11, 1929; m. Sylvia Marjorie Rothwell, Feb. 14, 1959; children: Christopher Harwood, Erica Marjorie. AB, Harvard U., 1951, MD, 1955; DSc (hon.), Mahidol U., Thailand, 1990. Intern, Harvard service Boston City Hosp., 1955-56; research assoc. Lab. Tropical Diseases, NIH, Bethesda, Md., 1956-62; asst. prof. medicine Case Western Res. U., 1963-68, asso. prof., 1968-75, prof., 1975-77, prof. library sci., 1974-77; dir. health scis. Rockefeller Found., N.Y.C., 1977-87, assoc. v.p., 1988-89; adj. prof. Rockefeller U., 1977-89; prof. medicine NYU, 1977—; dir. sci. Maxwell Communication Corp., Maxwell Found., N.Y.C., 1989-92; Heath Clark lectr. London Sch. Hygiene and Tropical Medicine, 1988; adj. prof. medicine Tufts U., 1990—; cons. ed. Charles Scribner's Sons, 1992-93; CEO Comprehensive Med. Sys., Inc., 1992-94; v.p. acad. affairs Picower Inst. Med. Rsch., 1993—; chmn. Harvard Internat. Med. Libr., Inc. 1994—; mem. Inst. Medicine, Nat. Acad. Scis.; bd. dirs. Immunotherapy, Inc.; cons. WHO. Author: Schistosomiasis: The Evolution of a Medical Literature, Selected Abstracts and Citations, 1852-1972, 1973, Geographic Medicine for the Practitioner, 2d edit., 1985, Scientific Information Systems and the Principle of Selectivity, 1980, Coping with the Biomedical Literature, 1981, Tropical and Geographical Medicine, 2d edit., 1990, Immunology and Molecular Biology of Parasitic Infections, 1993, Doing More Good Than Harm, 1993; founding editor: Jour. Molecular Medicine; contbr. numerous articles to profl. jours. Recipient Career Devel. award NIH, 1966-71, Mary Kingsley medal Liverpool Sch. Tropical Med., 1987, Frohlich award N.Y. Acad. Sci., 1988, Van Thiel medal Dutch Soc. Parasitology, 1989. Fellow ACP, Royal Coll. Physicians, N.Y. Acad. Scis. (bd. govs. 1991-93); mem. Am. Soc. Clin. Investigation, Assn. Am. Physicians, Am. Assn. Immunologists, Am. Assn. Study Liver Diseases, Am. Soc. Tropical Medicine and Hygiene (Bailey K. Ashford award 1974), Infectious Diseases Soc. Am. (Squibb award 1975), Royal Soc. Tropical Medicine and Hygiene, Internat. Fedn. Sci. Editors (exec. bd.), N.Y. Acad. Scis. (bd. govs. 1991-93), Royal Soc. Medicine Found. (bd. dirs. 1992—, treas. 1994—), Internat. Molecular Medicine Soc. (founding sec., treas.). Office: Picower Inst Med Rsch 350 Community Dr Manhasset NY 11030-3849

WARREN, RICHARD WAYNE, obstetrician and gynecologist; b. Puxico, Mo., Nov. 26, 1935; s. Martin R. and Sarah E. (Crump) W.; m. Rosalie J. Franzola, Aug. 16, 1959; children: Lani Marie, Richard W., Paul D. BA, U. Calif., Berkeley, 1957; MD, Stanford U., 1961. Intern, Oakland (Calif.) Naval Hosp., 1961-62; resident in ob-gyn Stanford (Calif.) Med. Ctr., 1964-67; practice medicine specializing in ob-gyn, Mountain View, Calif., 1967—; mem. staff Stanford and El Camino hosps.; pres. Richard W. Warren M.D., Inc.; assoc. clin. prof. ob-gyn Stanford Sch. Medicine. Served with USN, 1961-64. Diplomate Am. Bd. Ob-Gyn. Fellow Am. Coll. Ob-Gyn; mem. AMA, Am. Fertility Soc., Am. Assn. Gynecologic Laparoscopists, Calif. Med. Assn., San Francisco Gynecol. Soc., Peninsula Gynecol. Soc., Assn. Profs. Gynecology and Obstetrics, Royal Soc. Medicine, Shufelt Gynecol. Soc. Santa Clara Valley. Contbr. articles to profl. jours. Home: 102 Atherton Ave Menlo Park CA 94027-4021 Office: 2500 Hospital Dr Mountain View CA 94040-4106

WARREN, TONY EDWIN, internist; b. Macon, Ga., Nov. 13, 1952; s. Willie B. Warren and Lucy M. (Mullis) Woodall; m. Nell Hester Reed, Apr. 2, 1977; children: Alison S., Spencer. MD, Emory U., 1977. Diplomate in pulmonary diseases and critical care Am. Bd. Internal Medicine. Intern Naval Hosp., San Diego, 1977-78, resident, 1978-80, fellow, 1980-82, staff physician, 1982-84; asst. prof. medicine Ebert Sch. of Medicine, Bethesda, Md., 1985-86; pvt. practice physician Harbin Clinic, Rome, Ga., 1986—; chmn. dept. medicine Redmond Regional Med. Ctr., Rome, 1988-90, pres. med. staff, 1992-93. Comdr. USNR, 1977-86. Fellow Am. Coll. Chest Physicians; mem. ACP, AMA, Am. Thoracic Soc. Office: Harbin Clinic 1825 Martha Berry Blvd Rome GA 30165-1644

WARRICK, KENNETH RAY, dermatologist, cosmetic surgeon; b. Charleston, S.C., Dec. 15, 1946; s. Ray Lawrence and Evelyn Lila (Hughes) W.; m. Linda Diane Painter, Oct. 11, 1975; 1 child: Michael Todd. BS in Chemistry, Coll. of Charleston, S.C., 1967. Diplomate Am. Bd. Dermatology. Pvt. practice dermatology Charleston, 1975—; clin. instr. dermatology Med. U. S.C., Charleston, 1976-85, clin. assoc. prof. dermatology; med. adv. bd. Am. Electrolysis Assoc.; cons. S.C. Bd. Cosmetology; co-chmn. S. C. Gov.'s Adv. Com. Bd. on Medicaid Formulary. Recipient Pres.'s Award, Am. Electrolysis Assn., 1986. Fellow Am. Acad. Dermatology; mem. S.C. Med. Assn., S.C. Dermatol. Assn. (pres. 1986-87), Charleston County Med. Soc. United Methodist. Lodge: Rotary (North Charleston). Office: Ashley Cooper Dermatology and Cosmetic Surgery Clinic 9304 Medical Plaza Dr Charleston SC 29406-9143 also: Atlantic Dermatology 2021 N Myrtle Point Blvd North Myrtle Beach SC 29582

WARRINER, RICHARD BASCOMB, III, pediatric dentist; b. Corinth, Miss., July 8, 1947; s. Richard Bascomb Jr. and Ellen Lowery (Hayes) W.; m. Dale Galbraith Dalton, Jan. 25, 1969; children: Laurie Trice, Dale Dalton. BA, U. Miss., 1970, MBA, 1972; DDS, U. Tenn., Memphis, 1975. Chemist Texaco, Port Arthur, Tex/., 1968-72; dental educator U. Tenn., Memphis, 1975-76; resident, fellow Cin. Children's Hosp., 1976-78, part-time pvt. practice, 1976-78; practice pediatric dentistry Children's Dental Clinic, Tupelo, Miss., 1978—; chmn. dental dept. North Miss. Med. Ctr., Tupelo, 1983-84, 90—. Bd. dirs. Tupelo Symphony Orch., 1984—, Area coun. Boy Scouts Am., 1980—; chmn. bd. Miss. affiliate Am. Diabetes Assn., Jackson, 1985. With U.S. N.G., 1969-75. Named Outstanding Vol., Am. Diabetes Assn., 1985; recipient McFarland Spl. Svc. award Am. Diabetes Assn., 1988. Mem. ADA, Am. Acad. Pediatric Dentistry (mem. com. 1985-87), Tupelo Kiwanis Club (chair com. 1988—). Republican. Methodist. Home: 735 N Madison St Tupelo MS 38801-2017 Office: Children's Dental Clinic 155 Medical Park Circle Tupelo MS 38801-3732

WARSCHAUSKY, JUDITH SUE, clinical psychologist; b. Ann Arbor, Mich., May 29, 1957; d. Sidney Warschausky and Lorraine Nadelman; 2 children. BA cum laude, Brandeis U., 1979; MA, Boston U., 1983, PhD in Clin. Psychology, 1988. Lic. psychologist, Ill. Psychiat. counselor inpatient unit Cambridge (Mass.) Hosp., 1979-81; rsch. analyst Mass. Gen. Hosp., Boston, 1981-85; psychology trainee Douglas A. Thom Clinic, Boston, 1982-83; psychology fellow Danielsen Inst., Boston, 1984-85; assessment coord. House of Affirmation, Hopedale, Mass., 1986-87; mem. staff Ill. Masonic Med. Ctr., Chgo., 1987-92; pvt. practice, Chgo., 1987—. Vol. organizer Mothers-in-Touch, Evanston, Ill., 1990-95. Mem. APA. Democrat. Jewish. Office: 55 E Washington St Ste 3301 Chicago IL 60602-2207 also: Ste 328 1618 Orrington Ave Evanston IL 60201

WARSHAW, ANDREW LOUIS, surgeon, researcher; b. N.Y.C., Feb. 18, 1939; s. David and Florence (Rand) W.; m. Brenda Rose Flavin, Jan. 4, 1986; children: Jordan, Abigail, Daniel; stepchildren: Heather, Gretchen, Brenda. AB, Harvard U., 1959, MD, 1963. Diplomate Am. Bd. Surgery. Intern in surgery Mass. Gen. Hosp., Boston, 1963-64, resident in surgery, 1964-65, 67-70, rsch. fellow in medicine, 1970, chief resident in surgery, 1971; clin. assoc. in gastroenterology NIH, Bethesda, Md., 1965-67; from instr. surgery to prof. surgery Harvard Med. Sch., Boston, 1972-90, Harold & Ellen Danser prof. surgery, 1990—; assoc. chief surg. svcs. Mass. Gen. Hosp., Boston, 1990—, chief gen. surgery, 1992—. Editor: Pancreatitis, 1989, Current Practice of Surgery, 1993; contbr. over 220 articles to med. jours., revs., 8 med. ednl. films, videos. Lt. comdr. USPHS, 1965-67. Mem. Am. Bd. Surgery (chmn. 1992-93, dir. 1985-93), New Eng. Surgical Soc. (pres. 1993-94), Am. Coll. Surgeons (pres. Mass. chpt. 1991-92). Office: Mass Gen Hosp WACC-336 Boston MA 02114

WARSHAW, JOSEPH BENNETT, pediatrician, educator; b. Miami Beach, Fla., July 17, 1936; s. Phillip Robert and Mona (Monashefsky) W.; m. Cynthia Ann Stober, June 6, 1961; children: Deborah, Kathryn, Lawrence. B.S., U. Fla., 1957; M.D., Duke U., 1961; M.S. (hon.), Yale U., 1976; M.D. (hon.), Catholic U.; Josiah Macy Jr. faculty scholar, U. Oxford, 1979-80. Diplomate Am. Bd. Pediatrics., subsplty bd. in neonatal-perinatal medicine. Intern, resident in pediatrics Strong Meml. Hosp., Rochester, N.Y., 1961-63; resident in pediatrics Duke Hosp., Durham, N.C., 1963-64; research assoc. NIH, 1964-66, Retina Found., Boston, 1966-68; assoc. in pediatrics Harvard U., 1968-71, asst. prof. pediatrics, 1971-72, assoc. prof., 1972-73; assoc. prof. pediatrics and ob-gyn Yale U., 1973-76, prof. pediatrics and ob-gyn, 1976-82; prof., chmn. dept. pediatrics U. Tex. Health Sci. Ctr., Dallas, 1982-87; chief staff Children's Med. Ctr., Dallas, 1982-87; chief pediatrics Parkland Meml. Hosp., Dallas, 1982-87; prof., chmn. dept. pediatrics Yale U. Sch. Medicine, New Haven, 1987—; physician-in-chief Children's Hosp. at Yale New Haven Hosp., 1987—, dep. dean for clin. affairs, 1995—; mem. human embryology and devel. study sect. NIH, 1974-78, nat. adv. council nat. inst. child health and human devel., 1987-91. Editor: Seminars in Perinatology, Principles and Practice of Pediatrics; contbr. articles on pediatrics, perinatology, devel. biology and biochemistry to profl. jours. Clin. research adv. com. Nat. Found. March of Dimes, 1978-92; mem. rsch. com. United Cerebral Palsy, 1987—. Served with USPHS, 1964-66. Fellow Am. Acad. Pediatrics; mem. Inst. Medicine of NAS, Am. Pediatric Soc. (coun. mem. 1988-94), Am. Soc. Clin. Investigation, Am. Soc. Biol. Chemistry, Am. Soc. Cell Biology, Soc. Devel. Biology, Soc. Pediatric Rsch. (pres. 1981-82), Assn. Am. Physicians, Internat. Pediatric Rsch. Found. (chmn. bd. 1989-93), Conn. Acad. Arts and Scis., Conn. Acad. Sci. & Engring. Home: 350 Vineyard Point Rd Guilford CT 06437-3255

WARTENBERG, ALAN ARTHUR, physician; b. Bklyn., Apr. 7, 1947; s. Oscar and Natalie (Rimmer) W.; m. Carol Ann Rahn, Sept. 23, 1978; children: Eve Stephanie, Ruth Jessica. BA, NYU, 1967; MD, Med. Coll. Wis., 1972. Med. intern UCLA-Harbor Med. Ctr., Torrance, Calif., 1973; med. resident Med. Coll. Wis., Milw., 1980; social caseworker N.Y.C. Dept. Social Svcs., Bklyn., 1967-68; pvt. practice Bklyn., 1973-77; staff physician Northpoint Med. Group, West Allis, Wis., 1980-81; asst. prof. medicine Med. Coll. of Wis., Milw., 1981-84, career tchr. in chem. dept., 1982-84; med. dir. Alcohol Dependence Treatment Program/VA Hosp., Providence, R.I., 1984-88; med. dir. Substance Abuse Treatment Ctr. Roger Williams Hosp., Providence, 1989-91; asst. prof. of medicine Brown U., Providence, 1984-91; med. dir., addiction recovery program Faulkner Hosp., Boston, 1991—; asst. prof. medicine Tufts U., Boston, 1991—; med. dir. Ctr. for Behavioral Health, Johnston, R.I., 1989—, Discovery House, Providence, 1991—, Addiction Treatment Ctr., Brighton, Mass., 1995—. Contbg. author: HIV Disease: A Clinical Manuel, 1996, Clinical Aspects of Aging, 4th edit., 1995, Principles of Addiction Medicine, 1994. Chmn. bd. dirs. Marathon House, Providence, 1986-91; v.p. Cong. Agudas Achim, Attleboro, Mass., 1994—, pres., 1996—. Recipient Pfizer scholarship Med. Coll. Wis., 1969. Fellow Am. Coll. Physicians; mem. Am. Soc. Addiction Medicine (bd. dirs. 1994-97), Soc. for Gen. Internal Medicine, Assn. for Med. Edn. in Substance Abuse, AMA, Mass. Med. Soc. Democrat. Jewish. Office: Faulkner Hosp Addiction Recovery 1153 Centre St Boston MA 02130

WARTENBERG, MARTIN B., physician, educator; b. Cali, Columbia, Apr. 14, 1944; s. Bertram and Haydee (Villegas) W.; m. Virginia Correa, Dec. 20, 1975; children: Federico, Juan Sebastian, Alejandro. MD, U. del Valle, 1969. Diplomate Am. Bd. Internal Medicine, Am. Bd. Cardiovascular Disease. Intern Princeton (N.J.) Hosp., 1971; resident in internal medicine Tulane U., New Orleans, 1974-76, fellow in cardiology, 1976; assoc. prof. medicine U. del Valle, Cali, Columbia, 1976—; exec. dir. Fundacion Valle del Lilli, Cali, 1983-85, med. dir., 1985—; dir. ICU Hosp. Univ. Valle, Cali, 1977-80; exec. sec. X Congreso Colombia Cardiology, Cali, 1983. Assoc. editor Revista Colombiana Cardiology, Bogota, Columbia, 1984—. Fellow Am. Coll. Cardiology (assoc.); mem. Musser-Burch Soc., Soc. Colombian Medic-Interna, Soc. Colombiana de Cardiology, N.Y. Acad. Scis. Liberal. Roman Catholic. Clubs: Campestre (Cali) (bd. dirs. 1980-83), Colombia. Home: Carrera 2 B Oeste # 7-40, Cali Colombia Office: Fundaction Valle del Lili, Carrera 2 B Oeste # 7-40, Cali Colombia

WARTH, JAMES ARTHUR, physician, researcher; b. N.Y.C., Apr. 30, 1942; s. Peter and Anne (Furgang) W.; m. Maria Archer Russell, May 3, 1969; children: David M., Andrew A. BS, Tufts U., 1963, MD, 1967. Diplomate Am. Bd. Internal Medicine, Am. Bd. Hematology, Am. Bd. Oncology. Hematologist Harvard Health Svcs. Harvard U., Cambridge, Mass., 1976-77, officer, 1976-77; attending hematologist Harper-Grace Hosps., Detroit, 1977-84; asst. prof. medicine Wayne State U., Detroit, 1977-84; rsch. scientist New England Med. Ctr., Boston, 1984-86; attending hematologist-oncologist The Faulkner Hosp., Boston, 1986—; asst. prof. medicine Tufts U. Sch. Medicine, Boston, 1986—; course dir. phys. diagnosis Faulkner Hosp., Boston, 1992—; cons. NIH, Bethesda, Md., 1980-83, 87, Mass. Profl. Rev. Orgn., Waltham, 1991-93, in hematology and oncology Medfield (Mass.) State Hosp., 1993—; vis. prof. Yale U., New Haven, 1986; invited lectr. Columbia U., 1982, Harvard U., 1984, SUNY, Syracuse, 1991, Tufts U., New Eng. Med. Ctr., 1992; med. grand rounds spkr. Faulkner Hosp., 1986, 88, 92, 96; mem. case devel. com., problem base learning Tufts U. Sch. Medicine, 1994-95, faculty advisor, 1991—; rsch. lectr. NIH, Tarrytown, N.Y., 1986; bd. dirs. Faulkner Physicians Assn., Inc., Boston, 1994—; mem. pharmacy and therapeutics com. Faulkner Hosp., Boston, 1991—, chmn. subcom. on anticoagulation of pharmacy and therapeutics; mem. melanoma adv. bd. N.E. region Schering-Plough Co., Kenilworth, N.J., 1995. Contbg. author: (textbook) Hematologic Disorders in Maternal-Fetal Medicine, 1990; reviewer Am. Jour. Hematology, 1986, Jour. Andrology, 1990-92; contbr. articles to profl. jours.; guest appearance NBC affiliate TV news program, Detroit, 1980. Maj. U.S. Army, 1969-71. Rsch. grantee NIH, 1980-83, 83-86, spl. fellowship, 1974-76. Fellow ACP; mem. Am. Soc. Hematology, Am. Fedn. Clin. Rsch., Biomembranes in Sickle Cell Rsch. Group. Office: Faulkner Hosp 1153 Centre St Rm 5950 Boston MA 02130-3446

WASDEN, WAYNE WILLIAM, health services administrator; b. Murray, Utah, Oct. 6, 1954; s. Jed William and Deon (Childs) W.; m. Nancy Gwen Gerber, Mar. 16, 1987; children: Elissa Nancy, Jedidiah William. BS in Polit. Sci., U. Utah, 1980; M Health Care Adminstrn., Brigham Young U., 1982. Cert. profl. in healthcare quality. Health planner, mktg. rschr. Intermountain Health Care, Inc., Salt Lake City, 1981-82; dir.quality assurance Mid-Atlantic states region Kaiser Permanente, Washington, 1986-87; adminstrv. dir. quality assessment dept. Kettering Med. Ctr., 1987-92; v.p. quality Alexian Bros. Med. Ctr., Elk Grove Village, Ill., 1992—; pres. Quality Cost Solutions Inc., McHenry, Ill., 1990—; cons., condr. various seminars. Contbr. articles to profl. jours. With USN, 1982-86. Mem. Nat. Assn. Healthcare Quality, Am. Coll. Med. Quality, Am. Med. Peer Rev. Assn., Internat. Soc. Quality Assurance in Health Care, Am. Hosp. Assn. Soc. Health Planning and Mktg., Ill. Assn. Healthcare Quality, Cath. Health Alliance Met. Chgo., Am. Soc. Pub. Adminstrn., Nat. Com. Health Care, Canadian Assn. Quality, Phi Sigma Alpha. Office: Alexian Bros Med Ctr 800 Biesterfield Rd Elk Grove Village IL 60007

WASFIE, TARIK JAWAD, surgeon, educator; b. Baghdad, Iraq, July 1, 1946; m. Barina Y. Wasfie, Mar. 11, 1975; children: Giselle, Nissan. BS, Central U., Iraq, 1964; MD, Baghdad Med. Sch., 1970. Cert. gen. surgeon. Surg. rsch. assoc. Sinai Hosp. of Detroit/Wayne State U., 1981-85; clin. fellow Coll. Phys. & Surg., Columbia U., N.Y.C., 1985-91, postdoctoral rsch. scientist, 1987-91; attending surgeon Mich. State U./McLaren Hosp., Flint, 1991—. Contbr. articles to profl. jours. NIH grantee, 1984. Fellow ACS (assoc.), Internat. Coll. Surgeons; mem. AMA, Mich. State Med. Soc., Flint Acad. Surgeons, Am. Soc. Artificial Internal Organs, Internat. Soc. Artificial Organs, Soc. Am. Gast. Endoscopic Surgeons. Home: 1125 Kings Carriage Rd Grand Blanc MI 48439-8715

WASHINGTON, JOHN AUGUSTINE, physician, pathologist; b. Istanbul, Turkey, May 29, 1936; (parents Am. citizens); s. Samuel Walter and Simone (Fleisher) Washington; m. Maaja Harms, July 11, 1959; children: Stephen L., Richard R., Mikaela A. BA with honors, U. Va., 1957; MD, Johns Hopkins U., 1961. Diplomate Am. Bd. Pathology, (Clin. Pathology, Med. Microbiology). Intern Duke U. Med. Ctr., Durham, N.C., 1961-62, resident in surgery, 1962-63; resident in clin. pathology NIH, Bethesda, Md., 1965-67, asst. chief microbiology svc., 1966-67; assoc. cons. microbiology Mayo Clinic, Rochester, Minn., 1967-68, dir. bacteriology lab., 1968-71, head sect. clin. microbiology, 1971-86; chmn. dept. microbiology Cleve. Clinic Found., 1986-92, vice chmn. divsn. pathology and lab. medicine, 1992-96, chmn. dept. clin. pathology, 1992-96, head microbiology sect., 1992—; trustee Am. Bd. Pathology, Tampa, Fla., 1989-94. Mem. editl. bd. European Jour. Clin. Microbiology and Infectious Diseases; sect. editor Infectious Diseases in Clin. Practice; contbr. more than 300 articles to profl. jours.; author numerous chapters in books. Lt. comdr. USPHS, 1963-67. Fellow ACP, Coll. Am. Pathologists, Am. Soc. Clin. Pathologists, Am. Coll. Chest Physicians, Infectious Diseases Soc. Am., Am. Acad. Microbiology. Democrat. Office: Cleve Clin Found 9500 Euclid Ave Cleveland OH 44195-5140

WASHINGTON, MARGARET SMITH, medical association administrator; b. Pitts., Oct. 31, 1935; d. Walter C. and Anna Mae (Harris); m. Charles E., Nov. 24, 1956; 1 child, Charles Michael. BA, Chatham Coll., Pitts., 1957; MSW, U. Pitts., 1970, M in Med. and Hosp. Admin, 1974. Interviewer Unemployment Compensation Claims, Pa., 1963-67; caseworker Allegheny County Bd. of Assistance, 1963-67; dir. of social svcs. and adult edn. Brushton Inner-City Project, Pitts., 1963-67; dir. Brushton Inner-City Encouragement Project, 1967-68; cons. Maurice Falk Med. Fund, 1967-80; dir. ambulatory programs Mercy Hosp., 1968-70; dir. of training Homewood-Brushton Neighborhood Health Ctr., Pitts., 1968-70; dir. cmty. programs Mercy Hosp., 1970-77; exec. dir. ESRD NEtwork 4, 1977—. Bd. dirs. Am. Kidney Found., Commn. on Workforce Excellence, United Way Allegheny County; Rodman St. Missionary Bapt. trustee. Named One of 25 Outstanding Black Women in Pitts., Talk mag., 1976, Pitts. Most Imfluential Women, Talk mag., 1995, Vol. of Yr., United Way, 1989; recipient Harold B. Gardner Citizen award Allegheny County Med. Soc., 1975, Cmty. Health award Nat. Coun. NEgro Women, Inc., 1977, appreciation award Urban League Pitts., 1982, Urban League Guild Pitts., 1982, Leadership for the Professions award Greater Pitts. YWCA, 1992. Office: Univ of Pitts Med Ctr De Soto & O'Hara Sts 200 Lothrop St Pittsburgh PA 15213

WASHINGTON, VALERIE BRYANT, nursing administrator; b. N.Y.C., Aug. 20, 1952; d. David and Lucy B. (Hairstone) Bryant; m. Emmanuel M. Samuels, July 1, 1971 (div. June 1986); children: Christopher D., Diantha L.; m. Joe L. Washington, Oct. 26, 1991. Student, Sch. Performing Arts, 1970; AA, Eugenio Marie de Hostos Coll., 1972; BS, Herbert Lehmann Coll., 1974; postgrad., St. Joseph Coll., 1985. RN. RN Fordham Hosp., N.Y.C., 1972-76; charge RN Albert Einstein Coll. Medicine, N.Y.C., 1976-77, coord., 1977-80; coord. Good Samaritan Hosp., N.Y.C., 1980-83; head nurse Booth Meml. Hosp., N.Y.C., 1983-86, nursing dir. renal svcs., 1986-89, acting dir., 1986-89; nurse mgr. renal svcs. Good Samaritan Hosp., West Islip, N.Y., 1989-95, cmty. health nurse, 1995—; nurse cons. Harbor Nephrology, Fla., 1979-83, Good Samaritan Hosp., Bayshore, N.Y., 1983-85, nurse mgr. renal svcs., 1989; nurse cons. South Shore Renal Hosp., Hempstead, N.Y., 1984-86; v.p. JoVal Fin. Mgmt., 1994; lectr. in field. Mem. exec. bd. Roosevelt vol. div. Salvation Army. Mem. NAACP, NAFC, Nat. Assn. Patients on Hemodialysis and Transplantation (exec. bd.), Am. Assn. Nephrology Nurses, Texarkana Nat. Dialysis Assn. (exec. bd. patient and staffing issues), Lions (dep. dist. gov. 1990-92). Republican. Lodge: Lions Internat. (Roosevelt, N.Y.), (sec. 1985-87, pres. 1987-91, Lioness of yr. 1986, first female pres. 1987-90, region chmn. 1990-92, treas. 1992—). Home: 11 Long Beach Ave Roosevelt NY 11575-1911 Office: Good Samaritan Hosp Home Care Divsn 181 W Main St Babylon NY 11702

WASHINGTON-KNIGHT, BARBARA J., military officer, nurse; b. Chgo., July 13, 1948; d. Lewis and Carrie Mae (Randolph) Washington; m. William S. Knight, Aug. 23, 1986; children: Carlton, Carrie. Diploma, St. Elizabeth's Hosp., Chgo., 1971; B in Health Scis., Chapman Coll., 1979, postgrad. CCRN; cert. instr., advanced cardiac life support provider and instr. Commd. lt. USAF, 1972, advanced through grades to lt. col.; asst. head nurse med. unit USAF, Fairfield, Calif., 1976-78, asst. head nurse orthopedic unit, 1978-79; asst. head nurse spl. care unit USAF, Montgomery, Ala., 1979-80, head nurse spl. care unit, 1980-82; head nurse spl. care unit USAF, Riverside, Calif., 1982-85; head nurse surg. ICU USAF, San Antonio, 1985-87, clin. supr. dept. of critical care, 1987-88; head nurse spl. care unit USAF, Riverside, Calif., 1988-91, coord. quality improvement, 1990-92; asst. chief nurse, clin. nurse specialist inpatient svcs. USAF, Tinker AFB, Oklahoma City, 1992-93; clin. nurse post critical care unit Moreno Valley (Calif.) Cmty. Hosp., 1993—. Mem. Soc. Retired Air Force Nurses, Am. Assn. Critical Care Nurses, Air Force Assn., Air War Coll. Assn., Women's Meml. Found.

WASS, HANNELORE LINA, educational psychology educator; b. Heidelberg, Germany, Sept. 12, 1926; came to U.S., 1957, naturalized, 1963; d. Hermann and Mina (Lasch) Kraft; m. Irvin R. Wass, Nov. 24, 1959 (dec.); 1 child, Brian C.; m. Harry H. Sisler, Apr. 13, 1978. B.A., Tchrs. Coll., Heidelberg, 1951; M.A., U. Mich., 1960, Ph.D., 1968. Tchr. W. Ger. Univ. Lab. Schs., 1958-60; mem. faculty U. Mich., Ann Arbor, 1958-60, U. Chgo. Lab. Sch., 1960-61, U. Mich., 1963-64, Eastern Mich. U., 1965-69; prof. ednl. psychology U. Fla., Gainesville, 1969-92; prof. emeritus, 1992—; faculty assoc. Ctr. for Gerontol. Studies U. Fla., Gainesville; cons., lectr. in thanatology. Author: The Professional Education of Teachers, 1974, Dying-Facing the Facts, 1979, 2d edit., 1988, 3d edit., 1995, Death Education: An Annotated Resource Guide, 1980, vol. 2, 1985, Helping Children Cope With Death, 1982, 2d edit., 1984, Childhood and Death, 1984; founding editor (jour.) Death Studies, 1977—; cons. editor: Ednl. Gerontology, 1977-92, (book series) Death Education, Aging and Health Care; contbr. approximately 200 articles to profl. jours. and chpts. in books. Mem. Am. Psychol. Assn., Gerontol. Soc., Internat. Work Group Dying, Death and Bereavement (bd. dirs.), Assn. Death Edn. and Counseling. Home: 6014 NW 54th Way Gainesville FL 32653-3265 Office: U Fla 346 Norman Hall Gainesville FL 32611-2053

WASSEEN, MARJORIE, rehabilitation nurse, administrator; b. Kylertown, Pa., Jan. 3, 1944; d. Raymond George and Dorcas Carolyn (Hoover) Watts; m. James Wasseen, Sept. 17, 1966; children: Melissa, James II, Julie. Diploma, York (Pa.) Hosp. Sch. Nursing, 1966. Cert. rehab. nurse. Head nurse oper. rm. Broaddus Hosp., Philippi, W.Va.; dir. nursing Camelot Hall Nursing Home Med. Facilities of Am., Richmond, Va.; nurse mgr. med.-surg. unit Richmond Meml. Hosp.; nurse mgr., dir. clin. support svcs. Sheltering Arms Rehab. Hosp., Richmond. Mem. Am. Orgn. Nurse Execs., Assn. Rehab. Nurses, Va. Assn. Rehab. Nurses.

WASSER, LAWRENCE JAY, pediatrician; b. Bronx, N.Y., Dec. 7, 1948; s. Arnold Charles and Miriam (Klein) W.; m. Rhonda Friedman (div. 1987); children: Emily, Jacob; m. Sharon Elmore, June 5, 1993; stepchildren: Dustin, Jenna. BS, Yale U., 1970; MD, Johns Hopkins U., 1974. Diplomate Am. Bd. Pediat. Intern, then resident Children's Hosp. Med. Ctr., Boston, 1974-77; fellow child devel. unit Children's Hosp. Med. Ctr., 1977-79; pvt. practice Louisville, Ky., 1979—; assoc. prof. pediat. U. Louisville, 1980—; chmn. infant care com. NKC, Inc., 1983—; cons. pediat. team Hospice of Louisville, 1984—. Mem. med. bd. Planned Parenthood, 1983-91; active Alliant Med. Ethics Coun., MEH Ethics Com. Nat. Merit Assn. scholar, 1966. Fellow Am. Acad. Pediatrics; mem. Phi Beta Kappa. Jewish. Home: 2123 Edgeland Ave Louisville KY 40204-1422 Office: Seligman & Wasser PSC 506 Med Towers N Louisville KY 40202

WASSER EDELSTEIN, VICKI, optometrist; b. N.Y.C., Apr. 11, 1963; d. Seymour and Gertrude (Bernstein) Wasser; m. Gary Steven Edelstein, Aug. 27, 1988; 1 child, Hailey Ilyse Edelstein. BA in Biology, SUNY, Buffalo, 1985; OD, Pa. Coll. Optometry, 1989. Frame stylist Eyelab, Carle Place, N.Y., summer 1984; resident Indian Health Svcs., Rosebud, S.D., 1988, William Feinbloom Ctr.-Low Vision, Phila., 1988, Drs. Margaretten & Mazur, North Miami Beach, Fla., 1988-89, Drs. DeLuca, Connors & Kline, New Haven, Conn., 1989; optometrist Dr. G. Klein, Princeton, N.J., 1989-90; pvt. practice Maple Shade, N.J., 1991—. Mem. Am. Optometric Assn. (contact lens sect.), Vol. Optometrists to Svc. Humanity (mem. student chpt. San Luis Potasi, Mexico 1989), N.J. Optometric Assn., Rotary, Lions. Office: 38 W Main St Maple Shade NJ 08052-2432

WASSERMAN, DAVID H., medical educator, researcher; b. New Orleans, Aug. 24, 1957; m. Doris S.; children: Micah Joseph, Mira Rose. BSc in Kinesiology, UCLA, 1979, MSc in Kinesiology, 1981; PhD in Physiology, U. Toronto, 1985. Rsch. asst. dept. respiratory physiology and medicine UCLA, 1979-81, tchg. asst. gen. physiology dept. kinesiology, 1980-81; tchg. asst. gen. physiology dept. physiology U. Toronto, 1982-84; rsch. assoc. dept. molecular physiology and biophysics Vanderbilt U. Sch. Medicine, Nashville, 1985-87, lab. instr. med. sch. physiology dept. molecular physiology and biophysics, 1986-88, course coord., lectr. exercise physiology dept. molecular physiology and biophysics, 1986—, rsch. instr. dept. molecular physiology and biophysics, 1987-88, asst. prof. dept. molecular physiology and biophysics, 1988-92, lectr. tutorials in physiology dept. molecular physiology and biophysics, 1989-90, lectr. metabolic regulation in vivo dept. molecular physiology and biophysics, 1989—, lectr. history physiology dept. molecular physiology and biophysics, 1991-92, assoc. prof. dept. molecular physiology and biophysics, lectr. med. sch. physiology dept. molecular physiology and biophysics, 1992—, lectr. interdisciplinary grad. program physiology dept. molecular physiology and biophysics, 1992-94, course coord. interaction cell sys. sect. interdisciplinary grad. program, 1994—, course coord., instr. tutorials in physiology dept. molecular physiology and biophysics, 1995—. Mem. editl. bd. Am. Jour. Physiology: Endocrinology and Metabolism, 1992—, Jour. Applied Physiology, 1996—; assoc. editor: Metabolism, 1996—. Mem. Am. Diabetes Assn. (mem. rsch. coun. on exercise 1988—, co-advisor tech. report on diabetes and exercise 1993-94, mem. grant review panel 1993-96), Am. Coll. Sports Medicine, Am. Physiol. Soc. (mem. program adv. com. 1988-92, head organizing com. interactions of endocrine and cardiovasc. sys. in health and disease 1989-91, sec./treas. endocrinology and metabolism sect. 1992-95, mem. organizing com. integrated biology of exercise 1993—), Juvenile Diabetes Found. Internat. (bd. dirs. Tenn. chpt. 1995—, chmn. govt. rels. com. Tenn. chpt. 1996—), European Assn. for Studies in Diabetes. Office: Vanderbilt U Med Sch Dept Molecular Physiology and Biophysics Med Rsch Bldg Rm 702 Nashville TN 37232

WASSERMAN, EUGENE M., pediatrician; b. Bklyn., Mar. 2, 1931; s. Jacob and Lena (Kartell) W.; m. Nancy C. Ziluck, Sept. 1, 1959; children—Brett D., A. Michael, Julie B. A.B., Columbia U., 1952; M.D., Chgo. Med. Sch., 1956. Rotating intern Kings County Hosp. Med. Ctr., Bklyn., 1956-57; resident in pediatrics, Mt. Sinai Hosp., N.Y.C., 1957-59; practice medicine specializing in pediatrics, Mamaroneck, N.Y., 1961—; chmn. pediatrics United Hosp., Port Chester, N.Y., 1975-80; asst. attending in pediatrics St. Agnes Hosp., White Plains, N.Y., 1975—. Chmn. doctors' com. Village of Mamaroneck, 1975-85. Served as capt. M.C., U.S. Army, 1959-61. Fellow Am. Acad. Pediatrics; mem. Med. Soc. N.Y. Jewish. Avocation: cabinet making. Office: 1600 Harrison Ave PO Box 186 Mamaroneck NY 10543-0186

WASSERMAN, JACK F., exercise science educator; b. Dayton, Ohio, July 29, 1941; s. Lee Simond and Louise (Cockerill) W.; m. Susan Ainsworth, June 5, 1965 (div. May 1975); children: Ric, Andrea; m. Betty M. McClain, July 29, 1978; 1 child, Michel. BS, Purdue U., 1964; MS, U. Cin., 1971, PhD, 1975; cert. physician asst., Cin. Tech. Coll., 1977. Registered profl. engr., Ohio. Assoc. prof. U. Tenn., Knoxville, 1979—, cons. Meml. Rsch. Ctr. Hosp., 1979—, adj. assoc. prof. Inst. Agr., 1983—, prof., 1986, adj. prof. exercise sci., 1996—; pres. ops., acting v.p. Hydro Force Corp.; adj. assoc. prof. U. Cin., 1975-79, rsch. assoc., 1975-79; vis. prof. U.S. Army Aeromed. Rsch. Lab., Ft. Rucker, Ala., summer 1984. Inventor acoustic aneurysm detector and associated method. Mem. Am. Acad. Physician's Asst., Am. Soc. Biomechanics, ASME (membership chmn., biomed. divsn.), Acoustic Soc. Am., Orthopedic Rsch. Soc., Tenn. Acad. Scis. Home: 4512 Westover Ter Knoxville TN 37914 Office: U Tenn MAES Dept 310 Perkins Hall Knoxville TN 37996-2030

WASSERMAN, LISA MICHELLE, physician; b. N.Y.C., Apr. 29, 1968; d. Alan L. and Isabel (Kravitz) Choleff; m. Michael Andrew Wasserman, Aug. 27, 1995. BS, N.Y. Inst. Tech., 1990; DO, N.Y. Coll. Osteopathic Med, 1993. Intern Tripler Army Med. Ctr., Honolulu, 1993-94; chief, phys. exams. U.S. Army Health Clinic, Schofield Barracks, Hawaii, 1994; physician Family Practice #2, Schofield Barracks, 1994—; mem. staff Allergy/Immunizations Clinic, Schofield Barracks, 1995—. Mem. Am. Osteo. Assn., Assn. Mil. Osteo. Physicians and Surgeons. Jewish. Home: 94-1133 Nanilihilihi St Waipahu HI 96797 Office: Family Practice #2 US Army Health Clinic Schofield Barracks HI 96857

WASSERMAN, MARTIN P., human health administrator; m. Barbara; children: Brad, Torrey. Grad., John Hopkins Sch. Medicine, 1968. Dir. pediat. care on Navajo reservation Gallup, N.Mex.; med. dir. Mt. Washington Pediat. Hosp., Balt.; dir. pediat. outpatient clinic and emergency room U. Md. Hosp., 1974-76; health officer Montgomery County, Md., Prince George's County, Md.; dir. human svcs. Arlington County, Va.; sec. Md. Dept. Health and Mental Hygiene; chair U.S. Surgeon Gen.'s Lifestyles Task Force. Mem. APHA, ABA, APHA, Am. Acad. Pediats. Office: Dept Health and Mental Hygiene 201 W Preston St Baltimore MD 21201

WASSERMAN, ROBERT HAROLD, biology educator; b. Schenectady, Feb. 11, 1926; s. Joseph and Sylvia (Rosenberg) W.; m. Marilyn Mintz, June 11, 1950; children: Diane Jean, Arlene Lee, Judith Rose. B.S., Cornell U., 1949, Ph.D., 1953; M.S., Mich. State U., 1951. Research assoc. AEC project U. Tenn., Oak Ridge, 1953-55; sr. scientist med. div. Oak Ridge Inst. Nuclear Studies, 1955-57; asso. prof. dept. phys. biology N.Y. State Vet. Coll., Cornell U., 1957-63, prof., 1963—, James Law prof. physiology, 1989—, acting head phys. biology dept., 1963-64, 71, 75-76, chmn. dept. / sect. physiology, 1983-87, mem. exec. com. div. biol. sci., 1983-87; vis. fellow Inst. Biol. Chemistry, Copenhagen, 1964-65; chmn. Conf. on Calcium Transport, 1962; co-chmn. Conf. on Cell Mechanisms for Calcium Transfer and Homeostasis, 1970; mem. adv. bd. Vitamin D Symposia, 1976—; mem. adv. bd. Symposia Calcium-Binding Proteins, 1977-88, chmn., 1977; mem. food and nutrition bd. NRC; cons. NIH, Oak Ridge Inst. Nuclear Studies; mem. pub. affairs com. Fedn. Am. Socs. Exptl. Biology, 1974-77 ; chmn. com. MPI, NRC. Bd. editors: Calcified Tissue Research, 1977-80, Procs. Soc. Exptl. Biol. Medicine, 1970-76, Cornell Veterinarian, Jour. Nutrition; contbr.: articles to profl. jours. Served with U.S. Army, 1944-45. Recipient Mead Johnson award, 1969, Andre Lichtwitz prize INSERM, 1982, W.F. Neuman award Am. Soc. Bone and Mineral Rsch., 1990, merit award NIH, 1993-96; Guggenheim fellow, 1964-65, 72, fellow NSF-OECD, 1964-65. Fellow Am. Inst. Nutrition, mem. Am. Physiol. Soc., Soc. Exptl. Biology and Medicine, AAAS, Nat. Acad. Scis., Sigma Xi, Phi Kappa Phi, Phi Zeta. Home: 207 Texas Ln Ithaca NY 14850-1758

WASSERMAN, STEPHEN IRA, physician, educator; b. Los Angeles, Dec. 17, 1942; m. Linda Morgan; children: Matthew, Zachary. BA, Stanford U., 1964; MD, UCLA, 1968. Diplomate Am. Bd. Internal Medicine, Am. Bd. Allergy and Immunology. Intern, resident Peter B. Brigham Hosp., Boston, 1968-70; fellow in allergy, immunology Robert B. Brigham Hosp., Boston, 1972-75; asst. prof. medicine Harvard U., Boston, 1975-79, assoc. prof., 1979; assoc. prof. U. Calif.-San Diego, La Jolla, 1979-85, prof., 1985—, chief allergy tng. program Sch. Medicine, 1979-85, chief allergy div. Sch. Medicine, 1985-93, acting chmn. dept. medicine, 1986-88, chmn. dept. medicine, 1988—, Helen M. Ranney prof., 1992—; co-dir. allergy sect. Robert B. and Peter B. Brigham Hosps., 1977-79; dir. Am. Bd. Allergy and Immunology, Am. Bd. Internal Medicine. Contbr. articles to profl. jours. Served to lt. comdr. USPHS, 1970-72, San Francisco. Fellow Am. Acad. Allergy and Immunology; mem. Am. Soc. Clin. Investigation, Assn. Am. Physicians, Am. Assn. Immunologists, Collegium INternationale Allergologicum, Phi Beta Kappa, Alpha Omega Alpha. Office: U Calif Med Ctr 402 Dickinson St Ste 380 San Diego CA 92103-6902

WASSERMANN, HERBERT EDWARD, ophthalmologist, oculoplastic surgeon; b. Mannheim, Germany, Nov. 30, 1936; came to U.S., 1946; s. Emil and Edith (Linz) W.; m. Runa Sleipnaes, Nov. 16, 1969; children: Jessica, Jonathan. Student, Rutgers U., 1955-57; BSc, Ohio State U., 1959; MD, U. Chgo., 1964. Diplomate Am. Bd. Ophthalmology. Intern Barnes Hosp.-Washington U., St. Louis, 1964-65; resident in ophthalmology Cornell U.-N.Y. Hosp., N.Y.C., 1967-71; fellow in oculoplastics Manhattan Eye and Ear Hosp., N.Y.C., 1971-72; ophthalmologist Project Hope, Natal, Brazil, 1972; pvt. practice, West Hartford, Conn., 1972—; sr. attending physician Hartford (Conn.) Hosp., 1972—, Mt. Sinai Hosp., Hartford, 1972—; assoc. attending physician U. Conn. Med. Sch., Farmington, 1972—. Lt. M.C., USNR, 1965-67. NIH fellow U. Chgo., 1959-60. Fellow ACS, Internat. Coll. Surgeons, Am. Acad. Ophthalmology; mem. AMA, New Eng. Ophthal. Soc., Conn. Med. Soc., Hartford County Med. Soc. Office: Affiliated Eye Cons 8 Ellsworth Rd West Hartford CT 06107-2313

WASTERLAIN, CLAUDE GUY, neurologist; b. Courcelles, Belgium, Apr. 15, 1935; s. Desire and Simone (De Taeve) W.; m. Anne Marguerite Thomsin, Feb. 28, 1967; 1 child, Jean Michel. Cand. Sci., U. Liege, 1957, MD, 1961; LS in Molecular Biology, U. Brussels, 1969. Resident Cornell U. Med. Coll., N.Y.C., 1964-67, instr. neurology, 1969-70, asst. prof., 1970-75, assoc. prof., 1975-76; assoc. prof. UCLA Sch. Medicine, 1976-79, prof., 1979—, vice chair dept. neurology, 1976—; chief neurology svc. VA Med. Ctr., Sepulveda, Calif., 1976—; cons. neurologist Olive View Med. Ctr., Sylmar, Calif., 1976—; attending neurologist UCLA Ctr. Health Scis., 1976—. Author, editor: Status Epilepticus, 1984, Neonatal Seizures, 1990, Molecular Neurobiology and Epilepsy, 1992; contbr. articles to med. jours. William Evans fellow, U. Auckland, New Zealand, 1984; recipient N.Y. Neurol. Soc. Young Investigator award, 1965, Rsch. Career Devel. award NIH, 1973-76, Worldwide AES award, 1992. Fellow Am. Acad. Neurology; mem. Am. Neurol. Assn., Am. Soc. Neurochemistry (coun. mem. 1991—), Internat. Neurochemistry, Am. Epilepsy Soc., Royal Soc. Medicine. Office: VA Med Ctr 1611 Plummer St Sepulveda CA 91343

WATANABE, KOUICHI, pharmacologist, educator; b. Manchuria, Japan, Aug. 26, 1942; s. Tetsuya and Mine W.; m. Harumi Miyamoto; children: Toshikazu, Yoshihiro, Motohiro. BS, Tokyo Coll. Pharmacy, 1966; MS, Osaka U., 1968; PhD, 1971; LPIBA, 1986; DSc (hon.) Internat. U. Found., 1987, World U. Roundtable, 1988. Vis. fellow reprodn. rsch. br. Nat. Inst. Child Health and Devel., NIH, Bethesda, Md., 1971-73; vis. scientist dept. pharmacology Coll. Medicine, Howard U., Washington, 1973-75, asst. prof., 1975-83; asst. prof. pharmacology U. Hawaii, 1983-96; drug info. mgr. med. info. dept. Minophagen Pharm. Co., Tokyo, 1993-96. Contbr. articles to sci. jours. Am. Cancer Soc. grantee, 1980-81. Hon. mem. adv. coun. Internat. Biog. Ctr. (named man of year 1991,92); hon. mem. rsch. bd. advisors Am. Biog. Inst. (named man of year 1991,93,95), Mem. Am. Soc. Pharmacology and Exptl. Therapeutics, N.Y. Acad. Scis. (inaugural mem.), Am. Soc. Hypertension (charter). Subspecialties: Chemotherapy; Molecular pharmacology. Current work: Mechanism of action of various antineoplastic agts. on calmodulin. Vinca alkaloids found to be calmodulin inhibitors. Suggested that amounts of calmodulin or its binding proteins may be endogenous regulators of antineoplastic action or transport of these drugs. Died Mar. 20, 1996. Home: Tokyo Japan

WATANABE, MARK DAVID, pharmacist, educator; b. Santa Monica, Calif., Dec. 7, 1955; s. Jack Shigeru and Rose Nobuko (Iida) W. BA in Chemistry, U. Calif., Irvine, 1977, BS in Biol. Sci., 1978; PharmD, U. Calif., San Francisco, 1982, PhD in Pharm. Chemistry, 1990. Lic. pharmacist, Calif., Oreg., Tex., Ill. Pharmacy intern various locations, San Francisco, 1979-82; pharmacist Kaiser Permanente, San Francisco, 1981-87; clin. scis. rsch. fellow in psychiat. pharmacy U. Tex.. Austin, 1987-89; clin. asst. prof. pharmacy practice U. Ill., Chgo., 1989—; rsch. asst. U. Calif., San Francisco, 1980-87; clin. pharmacy cons. Ill. Dept. Mental Health & Devel. Disabilities, 1994—. Regents scholar U. Calif., San Francisco, 1979-82; recipient Excellence in Teaching award Long Found., San Francisco, 1984. Mem. Am. Coll. Clin. Pharmacy, Am. Soc. Health-Sys. Pharmacists, Am. Assn. Colls. Pharmacy, Am. Pharm. Assn., Amnesty Internat., Mensa, Rho Chi. Unitarian Universalist. Home: 636 W Barry Ave Apt 1 Chicago IL 60657-4568 Office: U Ill 1601 W Taylor St Rm 534 W Chicago IL 60612-4310

WATANABE, RONALD KIYOSHI, optometrist, educator; b. Hollywood, Calif., Apr. 17, 1965; s. Sadao and Terumi (Fujimoto) W. BS in Biology, UCLA, 1986; OD, So. Calif. Coll. Optometry, Fullerton, 1991. Lic. optometrist, Calif., Mass., N.H. Optometrist N.H. Eye Assocs., Manchester, 1993—; asst. prof. optometry New Eng. Coll. Optometry, Boston, 1992—; dir. contact lens svc. New Eng. Eye Inst., 1994—. Contbr. articles to profl. jours. Future Focus grantee Bausch & Lomb, 1994. Fellow Am. Acad. Optometry; mem. Am. Optometric Assn. Office: New Eng Coll Optometry 424 Beacon St Boston MA 02115

WATANAKUNAKORN, CHATRCHAI, medical educator, physician, researcher; b. Bangkok, Sept. 6, 1935; came to U.S., 1962; m. Eleanor Irene Good, June 3, 1967; children: Maria Irene, Paul William. MD, Chulalongkorn U., Bangkok, 1961. Fellow in infectious diseases Coll. Medicine, U. Cin., 1966-68, instr., 1968-70, asst. prof., 1970-72, assoc. prof., 1972-76, prof., 1976-79; dir. infectious diseases St. Elizabeth Hosp. Med. Ctr., Youngstown, Ohio, 1979—; prof. internal medicine Northeastern Ohio U. Coll. of Medicine, Rootstown, 1979—. Cons. editor Am. Jour. Medicine, 1977-78; mem. editl. bd. Infections in Medicine, 1985—; editor Abstracts in Infectious Disease, 1991-93; contbr. 25 chpts. to books and over 230 articles to profl. jours. Fellow ACP (Master tchr. award Ohio chpt. 1994), Am. Coll. Chest Physicians, Am. Coll. Internat. Physicians (Disting., Internat. Physician award 1995), Infectious Diseases Soc. Am.; mem. Am. Soc. for Microbiology, Am. Fedn. for Clin. Rsch., Soc. for Healthcare Epidemiology Am., N.Y. Acad. Scis., Ctr. Soc. for Clin. Rsch., Am. Heart Assn., Sigma Xi. Home: 8003 Forest Lake Dr Youngstown OH 44512-5912 Office: St Elizabeth Health Ctr 1044 Belmont Ave Youngstown OH 44501

WATERER, HENRY CHRISTMAS, cardiologist; b. Greenwood, Miss., Mar. 9, 1959; s. Henry Christmas Jr. and Alice Jane (Patton) W.; m. Rebecca Joy Rieves, June 16, 1985; children: Joy Kate, Hank. BS, Miss. State U., 1981; MD, U. Miss., 1985. Diplomate Am. Bd. Internal Medicine. Intern Univ. Med. Ctr., Jackson, Miss., 1985-86, resident, 1986-88, fellow in cardiology, 1989-92; staff emergency physician Vicksburg (Miss.) Med. Ctr., 1986-90; instr. in medicine U. Med. Ctr., Jackson, Miss., 1991-92, asst. prof., 1992—. Contbr. articles to profl. jours. Fellow Am. Coll. Cardiology, Am. Hosp. Assn. (pres. Hinds County affiliate 1995-96). Home: 4760 W Cheryl Dr Jackson MS 39211 Office: U Med Coll Heart Sta 2500 N State St Jackson MS 39216

WATERS, DANIEL JAMES, cardiovascular surgeon; b. Phila., May 6, 1955; s. James Charles and Miriam May (Dadino) W.; m. Pamela Ann Higgins, Nov. 22, 1985; children: Jessica Lynn, Michael Colin, John Thomas. BS in Biology, St. Joseph's Coll., Phila., 1977; DO, UMDNJ/Sch. Osteo. Medicine, 1982. Bd. cert. thoracic/cardiovascular surgery, gen. surgery Am. Osteo. Bd. Surgery. Intern U. Med. Ctr., Stratford, N.J., 1982-83; resident gen. surgery Des Moines Gen. Hosp., 1983-87; fellow cardiac surgery Cleve. Clinic Found., 1987-89; staff surgeon Des Moines Gen. Hosp., 1989-90, Mercy Heart Ctr., Mason City, Iowa, 1990—; chmn. dept. cardiovascular and thoracic surgery Mercy Heart Ctr., Mason City, 1995—; med. dir. C.V.R.U. North Iowa Mercy Health Ctr., Mason City, 1995—. Author: A Heart Surgeon's Little Instruction Book, 1995; editor-in-chief Iowa Osteo. Med. Assn., 1990-95; contbr. articles to books. Fellow Am. Coll. Osteo. Surgeons (Resident Achievement award 1985, Resident Literary Achievement award 1985), Am. Coll. Chest Physicians, Am. Coll. Cardiology; mem. AMA, Am. Osteo. Assn., U.S. Rowing Assn. Office: Mason City Clinic Mercy Heart Ctr 250 S Crescent Dr Mason City IA 50401

WATERS, SUZANNE HOPFENSPIRGER, critical care nurse, educator; b. Albany, N.Y., Sept. 24, 1952; d. Joseph William and Jeanne Marie (Houghtaling) Hopfenspirger; m. Bryon Edward Waters, May 7, 1977; children: Jennifer Anne, Jonathan Rhodes, Christopher Joseph, Joshua Matthew, Rebecca Suzanne Marie. BSN, Russell Sage Coll., 1995. RN, N.Y. Staff nurse med., surg. unit and geriatrics VA Hosp., Albany, 1975-78; staff nurse med., surg. St. Peter's Hosp., Albany, 1978-80; sch. nurse Rensselaer (N.Y.) City Sch. Dist., 1980-81; nurse counselor One to One Weight Mgmt. Sys., Albany, 1981, Weight Control Ctr., Inc., Vails Gate, N.Y., 1982-84; telemetry staff RN Benedictine Hosp., Kingston, N.Y., 1989-90; critical care educator St. Luke's Hosp., Newburgh, N.Y., 1990—; clinical instr. Orange County C.C., Middletown, N.Y., 1984, Ulster County C.C., Stone Ridge, N.Y., 1989-90. mem. Mid-Hudson Consortium Assn. Regents Alternate in Nursing scholar, Vets. of Foreign Wars scholar, 1971; recipient letter of commendation Rensselaer City Youth Bureau, 1981. Mem. N.Y. State Nurses Assn., AHA (BLS instr., ACLS instr.), Emergency Cardiac Care Task Force, Staff Devel. Educators Assn. (past treas.), Sigma Theta Tau (Mu Epsilon chpt.). Republican. Roman Catholic. Home: PO Box 241 Fox Hollow Dr Blooming Grove NY 10914 Office: St Lukes Hosp 70 Dubois St Newburgh NY 12550

WATERS, ZACK J., JR., surgeon; b. Myersville, Md., Aug. 2, 1934; s. Zack J. and Minnie (Helms) W.; m. Deborah Taylor; children: Mark, Michael, Gregory, James Matthew. BS, U. N.C., 1956; MD, U. Md., 1961. Intern Spartanburg (S.C.) Gen. Hosp., 1961-62, resident, 1962-65; resident Talmadge Meml. Hosp., Augusta, Ga., 1965-68; gen. surgeon Craven Hosp., New Bern, N.C., 1969-77, North Trident Regional Hosp., Charleston, S.C., 1977-79, Beaufort County Hosp., Washington, N.C., 1979—. Lt. comdr. USN, 1968-86. Fellow ACS; mem. Pamlico Albemarle Med. Soc. Office: 1110 Highland Dr Washington NC 27889

WATHNE, CARL NORMAN, hospital administrator; b. Johnstown, Pa., Oct. 16, 1930; s. Odd and Alice (Anderson) W.; m. Alice Adele Tucker, Jan. 25, 1958; children: John M., Carl K. BS, U. Pitts., 1952; MS, Columbia U., 1958. Asst. adminstr. Bayonne (N.J.) Hosp., 1958-60; assoc. adminstr. Binghamton (N.Y.) Gen. Hosp., 1960-63; chief exec. officer Putnam Community Hosp., Carmel, N.Y., 1963-65; v.p. A.J.J. Rourke, Inc., New Rochelle, N.Y., 1965-72; exec. dir. Lahey Clinic, Boston, 1972-79; pres., chief exec. officer Leonard Morse Health System, Natick, Mass., 1980-85, Leominster (Mass.) Health System, 1985-92; pres. Wathne Health Strategists, 1992—; adj. asst. prof. Boston U., 1981—; pres. Cen. New Eng. PHO, Leominster, 1991-92; hosp. cons. Contbr. articles to profl. jours. Mem. Mass. Hosp. Assn. (pres. 1987-88, chmn. 1987), New Eng. Hosp. Supts. Club (pres. 1986-88), North Cen. Mass. C. of C. (dir. 1988-91). Home: 6 Colony Rd Lexington MA 02173-2004 Office: Wathne Health Strategists 6 Colony Rd Lexington MA 02173-2004

WATKINS, CHARLES REYNOLDS, medical equipment company executive; b. San Diego, Oct. 28, 1951; s. Charles R. and Edith A. (Muff) W.; children: Charles Devin, Gregory Michael. BS, Lewis and Clark Coll., 1974; postgrad., U. Portland, 1976. Internat. salesman Hyster Co., Portland, Oreg., 1975-80, Hinds Internat. Corp., Portland, 1980-83; mgr. internat. sales Wade Mfg. Co., Tualatin, Oreg., 1983-84; regional sales mgr. U.S. Surg., Inc., Norwalk, Conn., 1984-86; nat. sales mgr. NeuroCom Internat., Inc., Clackamas, Oreg., 1986-87; pres. Wave Form Systems, Inc., Portland, 1987—; bd. dirs. U.S. Internat., Inc., Portland, Clearfield Med., Minorax, Inc. Bd. dirs. Portland World Affairs Coun., 1980. Mem. Am. Soc. Laser Medicine and Surgery, Am. Fertility Soc., Am. Assn. Gynecol. Laparoscopists, Portland City Club. Republican. Office: Wave Form Systems Inc PO Box 3195 Portland OR 97208-3195

WATKINS, CLIFTON EDWARD, JR., psychology educator; b. Westminster, S.C., Sept. 9, 1954; s. Clifton Edward and Betty (Land) W.; m. Wallene Grantland, Aug. 14, 1976. AA, Anderson Coll., 1974; BA, Carson-Newman Coll., 1976; MA in Edn., Western Carolina U., 1977; PhD, U. Tenn., 1984. Psychol. technician Knoxville Counseling Ctr., Tenn., 1977-78; psychotherapist Cherokee Mental Health Ctr., Morristown, Tenn., 1978-79; counselor Coll. Counseling Ctr., Jefferson City, Tenn., 1980-82; psychology intern VA Med. Ctr., Durham, N.C., 1983-84; asst. prof. psychology North Tex. State U., Denton, 1984-87, assoc. prof., 89—; asst. prof. counseling psychology Kent (Ohio) State U., 1987-89. Mem. edit. bd. Jour. Counseling and Devel., 1987-93; contbr. chpts. to books, articles to profl. jours. Mem. editorial bd. Individual Psychology Jour., 1984-87, Am. Mental Health Counselors Assn. Jour., 1984-87. Mem. exec. bd. Denton County Mental Health Ctrs., 1984-86. Mem. Am. Assn. for Counseling Devel., Am. Psychol. Assn. Home: 1705 Westchester Denton TX 76201-0602 Office: U North Tex Psychology Dept Denton TX 76203

WATKINS, EUGENE LEONARD, surgeon, educator; b. Worcester, Mass., Jan. 4, 1918; s. George Joseph and Marcella Katherine (Akels) W.; A.B. with honors in biology, Clark U., 1940; M.D. (Hood scholar), Harvard U., 1943; m. Victoria Peake, Sept. 23, 1944; children—Roswell Peake, Priscilla Avery. Intern, Roosevelt Hosp., N.Y.C., 1944; resident in surgery, 1944-46, sr. asst. resident in surgery, 1948-49, resident surgery, 1949-50; fellow in surgery, clin. research fellow, Mass. Gen. Hosp., Boston, 1947-48; practice medicine specializing in surgery, N.Y.C., 1950-56, Morristown, N.J., 1950—, Denville, N.J., 1956-85, Boonton, N.J., 1961-85; mem. staff Morristown Meml. Hosp., 1950, vice chmn. dept. surgery, 1974-77, chmn., 1959-61, mem. corp.; cons. surgeon St. Clare's Hosp., Denville, N.J., Riverside Hosp., Boonton, N.J., Community Med. Center, Morristown; courtesy surg. staff St. Luke's-Roosevelt Hosp. Center, N.Y.C.; asst. clin. prof. surgery Rutgers U. Coll. Medicine and Dentistry, New Brunswick, N.J., 1972-85; asst. clin. prof. surgery Columbia Coll. Phys. and Surg., 1985—; v.p. chmn. fin. com. Morristown Bd. Health, 1954-56. Served to 1st lt., AUS, 1946. Diplomate Am. Bd. Surgery. Fellow ACS (chmn. N.J. Adv. Com. 1965-77, chmn. N.J. State com. Trauma, 1960); mem. N.J., Morris County med. socs., AMA, Soc. Surgeons N.J. (1st v.p. 1982, pres. 1983), Am. Thoracic Soc., AAAS, Harvard Med. Soc. N.Y. (pres. 1960-61), West Side Med. Soc., Roosevelt Hosp. Alumni Assn. Republican. Presbyterian. Clubs: Harvard (N.Y.C.), Morristown, Morristown Field. Development spring-loop surg. suture holder. Home: PO Box 1037 Buffalo WY 82834-1037

WATKINS, JEFFREY CLIFTON, neuroscientist; b. Perth, Australia, Dec. 20, 1929; s. Colin Hereward and Amelia Miriam (Smith) W.; m. Beatrice Joan Thacher, Apr. 5, 1973; children: Timothy Douglas, Katherine Helen. BS, U. Western Australia, Perth, 1949, BS with honors, 1950, MS, 1954; PhD, U. Cambridge, U.K., 1954. Rsch. fellow chemistry U. Cambridge, 1954-55, Yale U., New Haven, 1955-57; rsch. fellow in physiology Australian Nat. U., Canberra, 1958-65; vis. rsch. scientist Agrl. Rsch. Coun., Inst. Animal Physiology, Babraham, U.K., 1963-64, sci. officer, 1965-67; sci. staff mem. Neuropsychiatry Unit, Med. Rsch. Coun., Carshalton, Surrey, U.K., 1968-73; sr. rsch. fellow in physiology/pharmacology U. Bristol, U.K., 1973-83, hon. sr. rsch. fellow in pharmacology, 1983-89; hon. prof. pharmacology U. Bristol, 1989—; cons. Sandoz Pharma, Berne, Switzerland, 1983-94, Tocris Neuramin Ltd., Bristol, 1985-94, dir., 1992-94; cons. and dir. Tocris-Cookson Ltd., Bristol and Southampton, 1994—. Co-editor: The NMDA Receptor, 1989, 2d edit. 1994; contbr. articles to profl. jours.; patentee in field. Recipient Wakeman Found. award, 1992, Charles A. Dana Found. award, 1994, Bristol-Myers Squibb award, 1995. Recipient Wakeman Found. award, 1992, Charles A. Dana Found. award, 1994, Bristo-Myers Squibb award, 1995. Fellow Royal Soc. London; mem. Internat. Brain Rsch. Orgn., Brit. Physiol. Soc., Brit. Pharmacol. Soc., Am. Soc. for Neurosci., Academia Europaea. Home: 8 Lower Court Rd, Lower Almondsbury, Bristol BS12 4DX, England Office: Pharmacology Dept, Univ Bristol Sch Med Scis, Bristol BS8 1TD, England

WATKINS, JUDITH ANN, nurse administrator; b. Chgo., Mar. 11, 1942; d. Russell and Louise Bernadine (Aloy) Keim; m. Thomas H. Watkins III, Dec. 24, 1961; children: Tamara Sue, Randall Scott. Grad. in nursing, Knapp Coll. Nursing, Santa Barbara, Calif., 1963; BSN, Pacific Union Coll., 1991, PHN cert., 1991; MHA, U. LaVerne, 1995. Cert. CPR instr., vocat.

edn. instr. Obstetrics supr. Bowling Green (Ky.) Warren County Hosp., 1963-67; clin. staff nurse Chula Vista (Calif.) Med. Clinic, 1967-69; nurse aide instr. Sawyers Coll., Ventura, Calif., 1972; ob-gyn. supr. Westlake (Calif.) Community Hosp., 1972-77; RN acute patient care Medical Personnel Pool, Bakersfield, Calif., 1984; med. asst. instr., dir. of allied health San Joaquin Valley Coll., Bakersfield, 1984-88; dir. nurses Bakersfield Family Med. Ctr., 1988-91, dir. client svcs., 1991-94, asst. adminstr. clin. svcs., 1994—. Named Mother of the Yr., Frazier Pk. (Calif.) Community Ch., 1979, Instr. of the Yr., 1986. Mem. Kern County RN Soc., Kern County Trade Club, Pine Mt. Golf Club (founder Lilac Festival 1982, Lady of the Yr. 1983) Sundale Country Club, Seven Oaks Country Club, Toastmasters Internat. Home: 9513 Steinbeck Ln Bakersfield CA 93311-1445 Office: Bakersfield Family Med Ctr 4580 California Ave Bakersfield CA 93309-1104

WATREL, WARREN GEORGE, pharmaceutical company executive; b. N.Y.C.; s. John and Julia (Rock) W.; children: Marc, Justin, Stephen. BS, Syracuse U., 1957, MS, 1958, postgrad., 1958; postgrad., Columbia U. Gen. sales mgr. Pharmacia AB Sweden, Piscataway, N.J., 1964-65, dir. mktg. and sales, gen. mgr., 1965-72; v.p., gen. mgr. Damon Corp., Vineland, N.J., 1972-74; ops. and mktg. exec. Pharmachem Corp., Bethlehem, Pa., 1974-75; exec. v.p., chief operating officer Newton (N.J.) Industry Inc., 1976-79; v.p. Seton Co., Newark, N.J., 1980-84, George Warren Assocs., Hasbrouck Heights, N.J., 1984—; bd. dirs. Newton Industries, 1976-79; cons. ITT, Paramus, N.J., 1971-72, Jay Holland-Moritz Inc., Hillside, N.Y., 1975, Xonics Inc., L.A., 1975; instr. bacteriology Syracuse (N.Y.) U., 1958. Author: Encyclopedia of Chemistry, 3d edition., 1971. Capt. U.S. Army, 1959-60. Mem. Am. Chem. Soc., AAAS, Am. Soc. Microbiology, N.Y. Acad. Scis., Inst. Chemists. Home: 506 Collins Ave Hasbrouck Heights NJ 07604-2232

WATRELOT, ANTOINE-ANDRE, surgeon, gynecologist; b. Lille, France, Jan. 28, 1952; s. Pierre and Therese (Borel) W.; children: Audrey, Pierre-Antoine, Amelia; m. R.M. Tortiget Nadette, June 18, 1996. BA, U. Grenoble (France), 1969; MD, Med. U. Grenoble, 1975. Resident Univ. Hosp., Grenoble, 1974-78, head clinic, 1978-81; asst. St. Joseph Hosp., Lyons, France, 1981-82, head assoc., 1982-87; dir. Ctr. for Rsch. and Treatment Sterility, Lyons, 1985—; surgeon, head gynecol. dept. Red Cross Hosp. Lyons, 1989—; gen. sec. Tubal Transplantation Meeting, Grenoble, 1979, 80; pres. Ist Internat. Congress on Gift, Lyons, 1988; cons. Gyne-Dips, 1981—. Author: Microsurgery in Infertility, 1980; contbr. articles to med. jours. Mem. French Procreation Assn. (v.p.), Am. Assn. Gynecol. Laparoscopists, Spanish Microsurg. Assn. (hon.), also numerous French gynecol. assns. Roman Catholic. Office: Ctr Rsch & Treatment Steril, 85 Cours Albert Thomas, 69003 Lyon France also: Medicare Fr, 3 Harrington Gardens, London SW7 4JJ, England

WATRING, WATSON GLENN, gynecologic oncologist, educator; b. St. Albans, W.Va., June 2, 1936; m. Roberta Tawell. BS, Washington & Lee U., 1958; MD, W.Va. U., 1962. Diplomate Am. Bd. Ob-Gyn, Am. Bd. Gynecol. Oncology. Intern The Toledo Hosp., 1963; resident in ob-gyn Ind. U., Indpls., 1964-66, Tripler Gen. Hosp., Honolulu, 1968-70; resident in gen. and oncologic surgery City of Hope Nat. Med. Ctr., Duarte, Calif., 1970-71, assoc. dir. gynecol. oncology, sr. surgeon, 1973-77; fellow in gynecol. oncology City of Hope Nat. Med. Ctr. and UCLA Med. Ctr., 1972-74; asst. prof. ob-gyn UCLA Med. Ctr., 1972-77; assoc. prof., sr. gynecologist, sr. surgeon Tufts New Eng. Med. Ctr. Hosp., Boston, 1977-80, asst. prof. radiation therapy, 1978-80; practice medicine specializing in ob-gyn Boston, 1980-82; assoc. prof. ob-gyn U. Mass., Worcester, 1982; regional dir. gynecol. oncology So. Calif. Permanente Med. Group, Los Angeles, 1982—, asst. dir. residency tng., 1985—; dir. gynecol. oncology St. Margarets Hosp. for Women, Dorchester, Mass., 1977-80; clin. prof. ob-gyn U. Calif., Irvine, 1982—. Contbr. articles to profl. jours. Mem. ch. council Luth. Ch. of the Foothills, 1973-75. Served to lt. col. M.C., U.S. Army, 1965-71. Fellow Am. Coll. Ob-Gyn, Los Angeles Obstet. and Gynecol. Soc.; mem. AAAS, ACS (Calif. and Mass. chpts.), Boston Surg. Soc., AMA, Mass. Med. Soc., Mass. Suffolk Dist. Med. Soc., Internat. Soc. Gynecol. Pathologists, Western Soc. Gynecologists and Obstetricians, Am. Soc. Clin. Oncology, Soc. Gynecol. Oncologists, Western Assn. Gynecol. Oncologists (sec.-treas. 1976-81, program chmn. 1984, pres. 1985—), New Eng. Assn. Gynecol. Oncologists (chmn. charter com.), New Eng. Obstet. and Gynecol. Soc., Obstet. Soc. Boston, Am. Radium Soc., Soc. Study Breast Disease, New Eng. Cancer Soc., Internat. Gynecol. Cancer Soc., Daniel Morton Soc., Sigma Xi. Republican. Office: So Calif Permanente Med Group 4950 W Sunset Blvd Los Angeles CA 90027-5822

WATSON, ANDREW SAMUEL, psychiatry and law educator; b. Highland Park, Mich., May 2, 1920; s. Andrew Nicol and Eva Arvel (Barnes) W.; m. Catherine Mary Osborne, Sept. 1942; children: Andrew Nicol, John Lewis, David Winfield, Steven; m. Joyce Lynn Goldstein, July 21, 1967. BS in Zoology, U. Mich., 1942; MD, Temple U., 1950, M in Med. Sci., 1954. Intern, U. Pa. Grad. Hosp., 1950-51; resident in psychiatry Temple U., Phila., 1951-54; spl. lectr. Sch. Social Work, Bryn Mawr Coll., 1955-59; mem. med. faculty U. Pa., 1954-59, law faculty, 1955-59; prof. psychiatry U. Mich., Ann Arbor, 1959-80, mem. law faculty, 1959-90, prof. emeritus psychiatry and of law, 1990; pvt. practice medicine, specializing in psychiatry, Ann Arbor, 1959—. Mem. Mich. Law Enforcement and Criminal Justice Commn., 1968-72. Served to capt. Med. Service Corps, AUS, 1942-46. Recipient Issac Ray award Am. Psychiat. Assn., 1978. Mem. Am. Psychiat. Assn., Am. Coll. Psychiatry, ABA (assoc.). Democrat. Unitarian. Author: Psychiatry for Lawyers, rev. edit., 1978; The Lawyer in the Interviewing and Counseling Process, 1976; others. Home: 21 Ridgeway St Ann Arbor MI 48104-1739 Office: 555 E William St Apt 21D Ann Arbor MI 48104-2427

WATSON, BEVERLY ANN, nurse; b. Springfield, Mass., Aug. 31, 1948; d. Paul Michael and Ann Theresa (Wheeler) Urekew; m. Kenneth A. Watson Jr., Dec. 17, 1977. Diploma in Nursing, Framingham Union Hosp., 1970. RN; cert. nursing supr., Ga. Staff nurse Hartford (Conn.) Hosp.; charge nurse Ridgeview Nursing Home, Springfield, Vespers Nursing Home, Wilkesboro, N.C.; asst. dir. nurses North Macon Health Care, Macon, Ga.; medical supr. Hospitality Care Ctr., Macon, Ga. Mem. ANA, Ga. Nurses Assn. Address: PO Box 13144 Macon GA 31208-3144

WATSON, DARCIE ANN, speech pathologist; b. Van Nuys, Calif., July 22, 1965; d. Robert Jerome and Marie Eugene (Pryzbyla) Duba; m. John Michael Watson, Nov. 5, 1994. BS, U. Nev., 1987, MA, 1989. Cert. clin. competence. Sr. speech pathologist Sierra Rehab. Svc., Reno, Nev., 1989-92, Alameda (Calif.) Hosp., 1992-94; mgr. so. region, speech pathologist Tolfa Corp., Mountain View, Calif., 1994-95. Republican. Roman Catholic.

WATSON, DAVID GOULDING, pediatric cardiologist, pediatrics educator; b. Toronto, Ont., Can., May 7, 1929; came to U.S., 1959; s. George Herbert and Hazel Elizabeth (Goulding) W.; m. Frances Louise Richards, Oct. 4, 1957 (dec. Sept. 1959); 1 child, Patrice; m. Aileen Ingrid Fors, Sept. 12, 1961; children: Carmen, Eric, Joanna, Andrew. MD, U. Toronto, 1952. Diplomate Am. Bd. Pediatrics; cert. in paediatrics, Can. Intern St. Michael's Hosp., Toronto, Can., 1952-53; sr. intern St. Michael's Hosp., Toronto, 1958-59; pediatric intern Hosp. for Sick Children, Toronto, 1953-54; residency in pathology Children's Hosp. of Mich., Detroit, 1954-55; asst. residency in pediatrics Hosp. for Sick Children, Toronto, 1955-56; Mayo fellow in pediatrics U. Minn., 1956-57; fellow in cardiology Hosp. for Sick Children, Toronto, 1957-58, 59; asst. prof. Sch. Medicine, U. Miss., Jackson, 1959-62, assoc. prof., 1962-75, prof., 1975-93; fellow in cardiovascular radiology NIH, Gainesville, Fla., 1972-73; prof. emeritus, 1993—. Contbr. articles to profl. jours. Treas. Ronald McDonald House, Jackson, 1985-93. Fellow Am. Acad. Pediatrics (chmn. Miss. chpt. 1981-83), Am. Coll. Cardiology (gov. for Miss. 1978-80), Royal Coll. Physicians and Surgeons Can.; mem. Can. Paediatric Soc. Episcopalian. Home: 2036 Southwood Rd Jackson MS 39211-6031

WATSON, DAVID MATHEW, pharmacy director; b. Hobbs, N.Mex., Apr. 13, 1956; s. William Floyd and Billie Dean (Mathew) W.; m. Mary Elizabeth Gordon, Aug. 14, 1982; children: Michal Anne, Meg. BS in Biology, Abilene Christian U., 1978; BS in Pharmacy, S.W. Okla. State U., 1980. Registered pharmacist. Staff pharmacist St. Joseph Hosp., Ft. Worth, 1980-82, pharmacy supr., 1982-85; dir. pharmacy Baylor Med. Ctr., Grapevine, Tex., 1985—; pres. MedData, Ft. Worth, 1985—. Programmer computer software, Pharm I, Lab I, Super Bill, Pharm Comm. Pharmacist Camp Pathfinder, Tarrant County Epilepsy Assn., Ft. Worth, 1981—. Named to Hall of Champions: innovation, Baylor Health Affiliates Group, 1990; named one of Outstanding Young Men of Am., 1985, 87. Mem. Am. Soc. Hosp. Pharmacists, North Cen. Tex. Soc. Hosp. Pharmicists (treas. 1987-89). Mem. Ch. of Christ. Home: 8609 Terrell Dr North Richland Hills TX 76180-2433

WATSON, DENISE SANDER, medical products sales executive; b. Bellville, Tex., July 19, 1960; d. Charles Morris and Corinne Olive (Bakke) S. Assoc., S.W. Tex. State U., 1981, BS in Allied Health Mgmt., 1982. Cardiodiagnostician Katy Community Hosp., Katy, Tex., 1982-84; staff cardiodiagnostician Sharpstown Gen. Hosp., Houston, 1984-85; cardiodiagnostician, noninvasive lab. supr. W. Houston Med. Ctr., Houston, 1985-86; with Pro-Tech Med. Assocs., Houston, 1985-86; clinical applications specialist Hewlett-Packard Co., Houston, 1986-87; field application specialist Acuson, Houston, 1987-92; dist. medical product sales rep. Acuson, St. Louis, 1992—. Named Field Application Specialist of Yr., Western Cardiology Region, 1990. Fellow Am. Registry Diagnostic Med. Sonographers, Am. Soc. Diagnostics Med. Sonographers, Am. Soc. Echocardiography, Soc. Vascular Tech.; mem. Ctrl. West End Assn., Bluebonnet Soc. Bellville, Alpha Delta Pi. Republican. Episcopalian. Office: Acuson 1899 Powers Ferry Rd Ste 100 Atlanta GA 30339-5653

WATSON, DONALD CHARLES, cardiothoracic surgeon, educator; b. Fairfield, Ohio, Mar. 15, 1945; s. Donald Charles and Pricilla H. Watson; m. Susan Robertson Prince, June 23, 1973; children: Kea Huntington, Katherine Anne, Kirsten Prince. BA in Applied Sci. Lehigh U., 1968, BS in Mech. Engring., 1968; MS in Mech. Engring., Stanford U., 1969; MD, Duke U., 1972. Diplomate Am. Bd. Thoracic Surgery, Am. Bd. Surgery. Intern in surgery Stanford U. Med. Ctr., Calif., 1972-73, resident in cardiovascular surgery, 1973-74, resident in surgery, 1976-78, chief resident in heart transplant, 1978-79, chief resident in cardiovascular and gen. surgery, 1978-80; clin. assoc. surgery br. Nat. Heart and Lung Inst., 1974-76, acting sr. surgeon, 1976; assoc. cardiovascular surgeon dept. child health and devel. George Washington U., Washington, 1980-84, asst. prof. surgery, asst. prof. child health and devel., 1980-84, attending cardiovascular surgeon dept. child health and devel., 1984-89; assoc. prof. surgery, 1984-89; assoc. prof. pediatrics U. Tenn.-Memphis, 1984-90, prof. surgery, 1989—, prof. pediatrics, 1990—, chmn. cardiothoracic surgery, 1984—; mem. staff Le Bonheur children's Med. Ctr., Memphis, chmn. cardiothoracic surgery, 1984—; mem. staff William F. Bowld Med. Ctr., Memphis, Regional Med. ctr. at Memphis, Baptist Meml. Med. Ctr., Memphis; cons. in field; instr. advanced trauma life support; profl. cons., program reviewer HHS. Contbr. chpts., numerous articles, revs. to profl. publs. Bd. dirs. Internat. Children's Heart Found., Child Health Alliance of the Mid-South. Served to lt. comdr. USPHS, 1974-76. Smith Kline & French fellow Lehigh U., 1967; NSF fellow Lehigh U., 1968; univ. interdepartmental scholar and univ. scholar Lehigh U., 1968. Fellow Am. Coll. Cardiology, Am. Coll. Chest Physicians (forum cardiovascular surgery, council critical care), Southeastern Surg. Congress, Am. Acad. Pediatrics (surgery sect.), ACS; mem. Assn. Surg. Edn., Am. Assn. Thoracic Surgery, Soc. Thoracic Surgeons, So. Thoracic Surg. Assn., Am. Thoracic Soc., Assn. Acad. Surgery, Internat. Soc. Heart Transplantation, Am. Fedn. Clin. Research, Found. Advanced Edn. in Scis., Andrew G. Morrow Soc., Norman E. Shumway Soc. (multiple bd. dirs.). Council on Cardiovascular Surgery of Am. Heart Assn., Soc. Internat. di Chirig, AAAS, N.Y. Acad. Sci., AMA, NIH Alumni Assn., Stanford U. Med. Alumni Assn., Duke U. Med. Alumni Assn., Duke U. Alumni Assn., Stanford U. Alumni Assn., Lehigh U. Alumni Assn., Smithsonian Assocs., Sierra Club, U. Tenn. Pres.'s Club, LeBonheur Pres.'s Club, U.S. Yacht Racing Assn., Pilots Internat. Assn., Nat. Assn. Flight Instrs., Aircraft Owners and Pilots Assn., Order Ky. Cols., Phi Beta Kappa, Tau Beta Pi, Pi Tau Sigma, Phi Gamma Delta. Republican. Presbyterian. Club: Crescent. Avocations: sailing, racquet sports, flying, computers. Office: The Heart Ctr 777 Washington Ave Ste 215 Memphis TN 38105-4567

WATSON, JAMES DEWEY, molecular biologist, educator; b. Chicago, Ill., Apr. 6, 1928; s. James Dewey and Jean (Mitchell) W.; m. Elizabeth Lewis, 1968; children: Rufus Robert, Duncan James. BS, U. Chgo., 1947, DSc (hon.), 1961; PhD in Zoology, Ind. U., 1950, DSc (hon.), 1963; LLD (hon.), U. Notre Dame, 1965; DSc (hon.), L.I. U., 1970, Adelphi U., 1972, Brandeis U., 1973, Albert Einstein Coll. Medicine, 1974, Hofstra U., 1976, Harvard U., 1978, Rockefeller U., 1980, Clarkson Coll., 1981, SUNY, 1983; MD (hon.), U. Buenos Aires, Argentina, 1986; DSc (hon.), Rutgers U., 1988, Bard Coll., 1991, U. Cambridge, 1993, Fairfield U., 1993, U. Stellenbosch, 1993, U. Oxford. Rsch. fellow NRC, U. Copenhagen, 1950-51; Nat. Found. Infantile Paralysis fellow Cavendish Lab., Cambridge U., 1951-52, 55-56; sr. rsch. fellow biology Calif. Inst. Tech., 1953-55; asst. prof. biology Harvard U., 1955-58, assoc. prof., 1958-61, prof., 1961-76; dir. Cold Spring Harbor Lab., N.Y., 1968—, pres., 1994—; assoc. dir. Nat. Ctr. for Human Genome Rsch. NIH, 1988-89, dir. Nat. Ctr. for Human Genome Rsch., 1989-92; Newton-Abraham vis. prof. Oxford U., 1994. Author: Molceular Biology of the Gene, 1965, 4th edit., 1986, The Double Helix, 1968, (with John Tooze) The DNA Story, 1981, (with others) The Molecular Biology of the Cell, 1983, 2d edit., 1989, 3d edit. 1994, (with John Tooze and David Kurtz) Recombinant DNA, A Short Course, 1983, 2d edit., 1992. Named Hopn. fellow Clare Coll., Cambridge U.; recipient (with F.H.C. Crick) John Collins Warren prize Mass. Gen. Hosp., 1959, Eli Lilly award in biochemistry Am. Chem. Soc., 1959, Albert Lasker prize Am. Pub. Health Assn., 1960, (with F.H.C. Crick) Rsch. Corp. prize, 1962, (with F.H.C. Crick and M.H.F. Wilkins) Nobel prize in medicine, 1962, Presdl. Medal of Freedom, 1977, Kaul Found. award for excellence, 1993, Nat. Biotech. Venture award, 1993, Copley Medal, 1993, Royal Society. Mem. NAS (Carty medal 1971), Am. Philos. Soc., Am. Assn. Cancer Rsch., Am. Acad. Arts and Scis., Am. Soc. Biol. Chemistry, Royal Soc. (London) (Copley medal 1993), Acad. Scis. Russia, Danish Acad. Arts and Scis. Home: Bungtown Rd Cold Spring Harbor NY 11724 Office: Cold Spring Harbor Lab PO Box 100 Cold Spring Harbor NY 11724-0100

WATSON, MARY ELLEN, ophthalmic technologist; b. San Jose, Calif., Oct. 29, 1931; d. Fred Sidney and Emma Grace (Capps) Doney; m. Joseph Garrett Watson, May 11, 1950; children: Ted Joseph, Tom Fred, Pamela Kay Watson. Cert. ophthalmic med. technologist and surg. asst. Ophthalmic technician Kent W. Christoferson, M.D., Eugene, 1965-80; ophthalmic technologist, surg. asst., adminstr. I. Howard Fine, M.D., Eugene, 1980—; course dir. Joint Commn. Allied Health Pers. in Ophthalmolgy, 1976—, lectr., mem. faculty, 1983—, skill evaluator and site coord., Eugene, 1988—; internat. instr. advanced surgical techniques. Contbr. articles to profl. jours. Recipient 5-Yr. Faculty award Joint Commn. for Allied Health Pers. in Ophthalmology, 1989. Mem. Allied Tech. Pers. in Ophthalmology, Internat. Women's Pilots Assn. Home: 2560 Chaucer Ct Eugene OR 97405-1217 Office: I Howard Fine MD 1550 Oak St Eugene OR 97401-7701

WATSON, RALPH EDWARD, physician, educator; b. Cin., Apr. 4, 1948; s. John Sherman and Evelyn (Moore) W.; m. Demetria Rencher, Sept. 9, 1972; children: Ralph, Jr., Monifa. BS, Xavier U., 1970; MD, Mich. State U., 1976. Diplomate Am. Bd. Internal Medicine. Intern, U. Cin. Med. Ctr., 1976-77; resident in internal medicine U. Cin. Med. Ctr., 1977-79, asst. clin. prof., internal medicine, 1980-88; asst. prof. internal medicine Mich. State U., 1988-94, assoc. prof., 1994—, attending physician in hypertension clinic, 1991-94, assoc. dir. hypertension clinic, 1995—, dir. Hypertension Clinic, 1991—, program dir. transitional residency; asst. dir. programs internal medicine residency. Fellow Am. Assn. Black Cardiologists; mem. ACP, Nat. Med. Assn., Am. Soc. Internal Medicine, Am. Soc. Hypertension, Internat. Soc. Hypertension in Blacks, U.S. Dept. Health Human Svc. Office Minority Health Resource Person Network, Xavier U. Alumni Assn. Home: 4199 Shoals Dr Okemos MI 48864-1315 Office: Mich State U 338B Clinical Ctr East Lansing MI 48824-1313

WATSON, ROBERT JOHN, surgeon, consultant; b. Iserlohn, Germany, Feb. 9, 1954; s. Robert and Joan (Barrow) W.; m. Judy Carling, Dec. 22, 1986; children: Holly, Robert, Allie. MB, BS, U. Newcastle Upon tyne, Eng., 1977; ChM, U. Manchester, Eng., 1987. Fellow Royal Coll. Surgeons (Eng.). Home: Four Trees, 159 Ribchester Rd, Blackburn BB1 9EE, England Office: Blackburn Royal Infirmary, Bolton Rd, Blackburn Lancashire, England

WATSON, SHARON GITIN, psychologist, executive; b. N.Y.C., Oct. 21, 1943; d. Louis Leonard and Miriam (Myers) Gitin; m. Eric Watson, Oct. 31, 1969; 1 child, Carrie Dunbar. B.A. cum laude, Cornell U., 1965; M.A., U. Ill., 1968, Ph.D., 1971. Psychologist City N.Y. Prison Mental Health, Riker's Island, 1973-74; psychologist Youth Services Ctr., Los Angeles County Dept. Pub. Social Services, Los Angeles, 1975-77, dir. clin. services, 1978, dir. Youth Services Ctr., 1978-80; exec. dir. Crittenton Ctr. for Young Women and Infants, Los Angeles, 1980-89, Assn. Children's Svcs. Agys. of So. Calif., L.A., 1989-92, L.A. County Children's Planning Coun., 1992—. Contbr. articles to profl. jours. Mem. Commn. for Children's Svcs. Family Preservation Policy Com., Mayor's Com. on Children, Youth and Families, L.A. Learning Ctrs. Design Team, Interagy. Coun. Child Abuse and Neglect Policy Com., L.A. Unified Sch. Dist. Bd. Edn.'s Com. on Student and Health and Human Svcs.; bd. dirs. L.A. Roundtable for Children, 1988-94, Adolescent Pregnancy Childwatch, 1985-89; trustee L.A. Ednl. Alliance for Restructuring Now; co-chmn. Los Angeles County Drug and Alcohol Abuse Task Force, 1990; mem. Cmty. Adv. Coun. Dept. Children's Svcs., 1989-90; mem. steering com. western region Child Welfare League Am., 1985-87. Mem. APA, Calif. Assn. Svcs. for Children (sec.-treas. 1983-84, pres. elect 1985-86, pres. 1986-87), Assn. Children's Svcs. Agys. So. Calif. (sec. 1981-83, pres. elect 1983-84, pres. 1984-85), Town Hall Calif., U.S. Figure Skating Assn. (bd. dirs., chair, membership com. 1994, sanctions and eligibility 1993-96), Pasadena Figure Skating Club (bd. dirs., pres. 1985-87, 89-90). Home: 4056 Camino Real Los Angeles CA 90065-3928 Office: LA County Children's Planning Coun 500 W Temple St Rm B-26 Los Angeles CA 90012-2713

WATSON, SHARON SUE, nurse; b. Greensburg, Ky., Sept. 28, 1946; d. Everett Ezra and Violet Mossie (Taylor) Gupton; m. Bobby L. Watson, Aug. 24, 1985; 1 child, Robert Daniel. Diploma, St. Joseph Infirmary, 1966. Cert. in infection control. Staff nurse, infection control, employee health insvc.coord. Jane Todd Crawford Meml. Hosp., Greensburg, Ky., 1965-86; charge nurse, staff nurse Lake Cumberland Home Health, Somerset, Ky., 1986-91; insvc. coord., infection control, employee health, educator Westlake Cumberland Hosp., Columbia, Ky., 1990—; mem. adv. coun. Tim Lee Carter Vocat. Sch. Health Occupations Dept., Greensburg, 1970-80. Active Dem. Women's Club, Greensburg, 1970's. Mem. Assn. Profls. in Infection Control and Epidemiology. Roman Catholic. Home: 3517 Blowing Spring Rd Greensburg KY 42743 Office: Westlake Cumberland Hosp 100 Westlake Dr Columbia KY 42728

WATT, JOHN WILLIAM HEDDLE, anesthesiologist; b. Perth, Scotland, Feb. 5, 1950; s. Ian Stuart and Enid Louise (Heddle) W. M.B.Ch.B., U. Liverpool, U.K., 1973, MD, 1981; FFARCS, London, 1975. Cons. anesthetist, Southport Spinal Injuries Unit Southport-Formby NHS Trust Hosp., Southport, Eng., 1981—. Contbr. articles to profl. jours., chpts. to books. Office: Southport-Formby NHS Trust, Town Ln, Southport PR8 6PN, England

WATT, THOMAS LORNE, dermatologist; b. Denver, July 14, 1935; s. Sherman Alvin and Lois May (Hitt) W.; m. Mette Arup, Aug. 22, 1959; children: Charles Thomas, Sherman Alexander, Kathryn Anne. AB, Dartmouth Coll., 1957; D, Harvard U., 1960. Diplomate Am. Bd. Dermatology. Intern, resident Dartmouth-Hitchcock Hosp., Hanover, N.H., 1960-65; dermatologist Monroe (Wis.) Clinic, 1965-71, U.S. Army Med. Corps, El Paso, Tex., 1968-70; pvt. practice, dermatology Bangor, Maine, 1971—; head, sect. dermatology, Ea. Maine Med. Ctr., Bangor, 1973—; mem. Maine Bd. Registration in Medicine, Augusta, 1987-93. Bd. dirs., pres., Bangor Symphony Orch., 1988-94. Lt. col. U.S. Army Med. Corps, 1968-69, Viet Nam. Decorated Bronze Star. Fellow New England Dermatol. Soc. (pres. 1996—), Am. Acad. Dermatology, Can. Dermatology Assn.; mem. Penobscot County Med. Soc. (pres. 1971—). Republican. Episcopalian. Office: 263 State St Bangor ME 04401

WATTERS, TERESA MARIE, health care administrator; b. Columbus, Ohio, Dec. 11, 1961; d. James Lilburn Banner and Eleanor Jane (Lewis) Smith; m. Jerome Wendell Watters, Sept. 9, 1989; 1 child, Ashley Lauren. BS, Howard U., 1984; M in Health Svc. Adminstrn., George Washington U., 1991. From adminstrv. asst. to exec. asst. for clin. ops. George Washington U. Med. Ctr., Washington, 1987-91; from exec. assoc. to dir. bus. ops. VITAS Healthcare Corp., Miami, Fla. and Ft. Worth, 1991-93; regional dir. bus. ops. VITAS Healthcare Corp., Dallas, Ft. Worth, 1993-95; branch dir. Olsten Kimberly Quality Care, Dallas, 1995—. Coord. D.C. CARE Health Directory, 1989. Adminstrv. vol. Dept. Health and Human Svcs., Washington, 1987. Mem. Am. Coll. Healthcare Execs. (assoc. 1991—), Nat. Assn. Healthcare Exec., Nat. Hospice Assn., Tex. Hospice Assn. Home: 717 Bear Run Dr Grapevine TX 76051

WATTS, CHARLES DEWITT, surgeon, corporate medical director; b. Atlanta, Sept. 21, 1917; s. Lewis G. and Ida H. (Hawes) W.; m. Constance Merrick, Jan. 5, 1945; children: Eileen Constance Watts Welch, Deborah Hill (dec.), Charles D., Winifred Anita Watts Hemphill. B.S., Morehouse Coll., 1938; M.D., Howard U., 1943; LHD (hon.), St. Pauls Coll., 1984; DSc (hon.), Duke U., 1991. Diplomate: Am. Bd. Surgery. Practice medicine specializing in surgery Durham, N.C., 1950—; med. dir. N.C. Mut. Life Ins. Co., Durham, 1960—; mem. faculty dept. surgery Howard U. Coll. Medicine, 1947-50; instr. surgery Howard U., Washington; asst. clin. prof. surgery Duke Med. Center; attending surgeon Durham County Gen. Hosp.; chmn. bd. Capital Health Systems Regional Agy., 1976; founder, dir. Lincoln Community Health Center, Durham, 1970. Trustee Howard U., Washington. Fellow Am. Coll. Surgery; mem. Inst. of Medicine of NSF. Home: 829 E Lawson St Durham NC 27701-4534

WATTS, DAVID MICHAEL, physician, educator; b. Salt Lake City, July 7, 1956; s. Elwood Lester and Carolyn W.; m. Marilyn Baum, April, 1979; children: John, Daniel, Melissa, Robert, Laura, Emily. BS, Brigham-Young U., 1981; MD, Uniformed Svc. U. Health Scis., 1985. Diplomate Am. Bd. Surgery. Commd. officer U.S. Army, 1981, advanced through grades to maj., 1991; intern Madigan Army Med. Ctr., Tacoma, Wash., 1985-86, staff surgeon, 1993—; resident gen. surgery Tripler Army Med. Ctr., Honolulu, 1986-90; chief gen. surgery svc. Irwin Army Cmty. Hosp., Ft. Riley, Kans., 1990-93; clin. asst., prof. surgery Uniformed Svcs. U. Health Scis., Bethesda, Md., 1994—. Contbr. articles to profl. jours. Fellow Am. Coll. Surgeons. Mem. LDS Ch. Office: Madigan Army Med Ctr Gen Surgery Svc Tacoma WA 98431

WATTS, DON SANDFORD, psychotherapist; b. Dallas, Apr. 23, 1951; s. Howard William and Jewell Maurice (Skinner) W.; children: Belinda Dawn, Kimberly Renee, Donald William. BA, U. Tex., Dallas, 1977, MS, 1979; PhD, Calif. Coast U., 1994. Lic. marriage and family therapist, Tex. State Bd. Marriage and Family Therapists, profl. counselor, Tex. State Bd. Staff therapist Dallas Psychiat. Assn., 1980-83, Brookwood Hosp., Wilmer, Tex., 1983; pvt. practice psychotherapist Dallas, 1979—; adj. prof. Dallas County Community Coll. Dist., 1979-89; seminar leader, L.A., 1983. With U.S. Army, 1968-71. Named to Nat. Disting. Svc. Registry for Counseling and Devel., Libr. of Congress, 1990. Methodist. Office: Dallas Psychotherapy Group 6750 Hillcrest Plz Ste 106 Dallas TX 75230-1415

WATTS, JAN SCHRODER, mental health nurse; b. New Haven, Sept. 14, 1942; d. James Edward and Mildred (Gardner) Schroder; m. Stephen Frank Watts, Aug. 7, 1982; 5 children. AA, Chesapeake Coll., 1977; BSN, Salisbury State U., 1979; MS, U. Md., 1990. RN, Md. Staff nurse State of Md., Balt., 1979, Meml. Hosp., Easton, Md., 1979-81, MIEMSS, Balt., 1981-82; acting head nurse North Charles Hosp., Balt., 1982-83; clin. mgr. Md. Gen. Hosp., Balt., 1983-90; clin. specialist State of Md., 1990-91; dir. mental health Carroll County Gen. Hosp., Westminster, Md., 1991-92; instr. Union Meml. Hosp. Sch. Nursing, 1992—; cons. ednl. psychotherapy JSW and Assocs., Sykesville, md., 1991—; mem. Carroll County Mental Health Bur., 1992; clin. specialist Vis. Nurses Assn., 1994—. Mem. ANA (cert. psychiat. nurse), Am. Psychiat. Nurses' Assn., Toastmasters Internat., Sigma Theta Tau. Baptist. Home: 5408 Huckleberry Ln Sykesville MD 21784-8939

WATTS, JANET HAWKINS, educator, occupational therapist; b. Richmond, Va., Feb. 23, 1951; d. Redfield Bayne and Kathleen Ballew (Powell) Hawkins; m. Robert Allen Watts Jr., July 2, 1977; children: Robert Allen III, Kathleen Virginia. BA, Coll. of William & Mary, 1973; MS, Va.

Commonwealth U., 1977, cert. in Aging Studies, 1986. Spl. activities leader Richmond Day Treatment Ctr., 1977-78; occupational therapist community support program Chesterfield (Va.) Dept. Mental Health, 1978-80; asst. prof. occupational therapy Va. Commonwealth U., Richmond, 1980-87, assoc. prof., 1987—. Author: (with others) Psychosocial Occupational Therapy: Practice in a Pluralistic Arena, 1983, Bodies of Knowledge in Psychosocial Practice, 1988, Occupational Therapy in Psychosocial Practice, 1988; editor, author: (with others) Instrument Development in Occupational Therapy, 1988; contbg. author: A Model of Human Occupation, 1985; contbr. articles to profl. jours. Recipient Dissertation Rsch. award The Am. Occupational Therapy Found., 1996. Mem. Va. Occupational Therapy Assn. (exec. bd., chmn. pub. affairs com. 1985-87), Am. Occupational Therapy Assn. Office: Med Coll Va MCV Box 980008 VMI Bldg 10th and Marshall MCV Box 8 Richmond VA 23298-0008

WATTS, JOHN COMER, JR., pediatrician; b. Camden, Ark., Mar. 12, 1931; s. John Comer and Elizabeth (Owen) W.; m. Edna Garnet Montgomery; children: John III, Coralle Elizabeth, Field Montgomery. BS, U. Ark., 1952; MD, Tulane U., 1956. Pediatrician Bost & Watts, Ft. Smith, Ark., 1962-65, pvt. practice, Ft. Smith, Ark., 1965-71, Watts & Aclin, Ft. Smith, Ark., 1971-92, Holt Korck Pediatrics, Ft. Smith, Ark., 1994—; staff physician Ark. Crippled Children's Svcs., Ft. Smith, 1962-67; chief pediatrics Sparks Regional Med. Ctr., Ft. Smith, St. Edwards Mercy Med. Ctr., Ft. smith. Contbr. articles to profl. jours. Pres. bd. dirs. Suspected Child Abuse & Neglect, Ft. Smith, 1984; sr. warden St. Bartholomow's Episcopal Ch., Ft. Wmith, 1988; camp dr. Full Fill A Dream, Ft. Wmith, 1986-88. Capt. U.S. Army, 1958-60. Mem. Am. Acad. Pediatrics, Ark. Pediatric Soc.

WATTS, MALCOLM L., chemist; b. Bristol, Somerset, Eng., Oct. 23, 1937; came to U.S., 1979; s. Geoffrey H. and Lillian Florence (Pye) W.; m. Lovat Simpson, June 28, 1992; children: George, Isla, Elizabeth, Claire. BSc in Chemistry with honors, Bristol U., 1958, PhD in Chemistry, 1961. Plant supr. ICI, North Yorishire, Eng., 1961-64, plant start-up supr., 1964-67, sr. plant start-up supr., 1968-70, project mgr., 1971-76, sect. mgr., 1977-79; tech. dir. ICI, Houston, 1980-84; program mgr. ICI, Wilmington, Del., 1985—. Mem. IEEE, Am. Chem. Soc. Home: 807 Lisa Dell Dr Kennett Square PA 19348-1303 Office: ZENKA Concord Pike Wilmington DE 19803*

WATTS, PAUL GRAHAM, oral and maxillofacial surgeon, consultant; b. Hull, Yorkshire, Eng., Jan. 17, 1949. B Dental Surgery, U. Dundee, Scotland, 1972. House officer Dundee Dental Hosp., 1972-73; sr. house officer Doncaster Royal Infirmary, Eng., 1973-77; registrar Addenbrookes Hosp., Cambridge, Eng., 1977-79; sr. registrar Kings Coll. Hosp., London, 1979-81, John Radcliffe Hosp., Oxford, Eng., 1981-87; cons. Kings Mill Centre, Sutton-in-Ashfield, Eng., 1988—; hon. clin. tutor U. Sheffield, Eng., 1991—; examiner Part II FDS Royal Coll. Surgeons, Edinburgh, 1989—; chmn. hosp. med. com. Kings Mill Centre, Sutton-in-Ashfield, 1995—, vice chmn. theatre users com., 1993—; mems. rep. on coun. Brit. Assn. Oral and Maxillofacial Surgeons, London, 1986-88. Contbr. articles to profl. jours. Fellow Brit. Assn. Oral and Maxillofacial Surgeons, Royal Soc. Medicine, Royal Coll. Surgeons Edinburgh (fellow in dental surgery 1978, Ethicon Found. Fund award 1984); mem. Hosp. Cons. and Specialists Assn. Office: Kings Mill Centre, Mansfield Rd, Sutton NG17 4JL, England

WATTS, RICHARD ARTHUR, rheumatologist, consultant; b. London, Dec. 18, 1956; s. Richard We and Joan Em Watts; m. Lesley Diana Watts, Apr. 23, 1983; children: Oliver, Isobel. BA, Oxford (Eng.) U., 1978, MA, MB BChir, 1982, MD, 1992. Rsch. fellow Middlesex Hosp., London, 1985-90; sr. registrar Adderbrooke Hosp., Cambridge, Eng., 1990-92, Norwich (Eng.) Hosp., 1992-94; cons. rheumatologist Ipswich, Eng., 1994—. Contbr. papers to profl. publs. Fellow Am. Coll. Rheumatology; mem. Brit. Soc. for Rheumatology, Brit. Med. Assn., Royal Coll. Physicians. Home: Bury Hill House Woodbridge, Suffolk IP1L 1JD, England

WATTS, ROBERT GLENN, retired pharmaceutical company executive; b. Norton, Va., Apr. 28, 1933; s. Clifford Amburgey and Stella Lee (Cornette) W.; m. Doris Juanita Slaughter, Aug. 29, 1953 (dec. 1980); children: Cynthia L. Watts Waller, Robert Glenn, Kelly L.; m. Sara Lowry Childrey, Aug. 20, 1982; stepchildren: J. Eric Alexander, Matthew R. Alexander. B.A., U. Richmond, 1959. Dir. ops. A.H. Robins Co., Inc., Richmond, Va., 1967-71, asst. v.p., 1971-73, v.p., 1973-75, sr. v.p., 1975-79, exec. v.p., 1979-92; ret., 1992; bd. dirs. Little Oil Co., Richmond, Fidelity Fed. Savs. Bank, Richmond. Bd. dirs. United Way, Richmond, 1982—; Pvt. Industry Council, Richmond, 1983—; sec. YMCA, Richmond, 1984—. Served with USN, 1952-56. Mem. Met. Richmond C. of C. (chmn. 1985-86), Bull and Bear Club, Hermitage Country. Episcopalian. Home: 2409 Islandview Dr Richmond VA 23233-2525

WAUGH, THEODORE ROGERS, orthopedic surgeon; b. Montreal, Sept. 21, 1926; s. Theodore Rogers and Anne Maude (Lawlor) W.; children: Susanne Rogers, Margaret Stewart, Theodore Rogers. BA, Yale U., 1949; MD, CM, McGill U., 1953; D Med.Sci., U. Goteborg, Sweden, 1968. Diplomate Am. Bd. Orthopaedic Surgery. Intern Royal Victoria Hosp., Montreal, 1953-54; asst. resident in pathology McGill U., 1954-55; asst. resident in surgery N.Y. U. Bellevue Med. Center, 1955-56; asst. resident, resident, fellow N.Y. Orthopedic Hosp., Columbia U., 1958-62, instr., clin. asst. prof. orthopedic surgery, 1962-68; asst. attending Presbyn. Hosp., N.Y.C., 1962-68; prof., chief div. orthopedic surgery U. Calif., Irvine, 1968-78; prof., chmn. dept. orthopedic surgery N.Y. U. Med. Center, 1978—. Contbr. numerous articles to profl. jours. Capt., M.C. USAF, 1956-58. Fellow ACS, Royal Coll. Surgeons (Can.), Am. Acad. Orthopaedic Surgeons, Scoliosis Research Soc., Assn. Bone and Joint Surgeons, Am. Orthopaedic Assn., Am. Orthopaedic Soc. for Sports Medicine.; mem. Soc. Colonial Wars, Alpha Omega Alpha. Presbyterian. Club: 20th Century Orthopedic. Office: NYU Med Ctr 550 1st Ave New York NY 10016-6481

WAUTERS, LISA LACROIX, nurse; b. Lantana, Fla., Nov. 15, 1964; d. Albert Joseph Lacroix and Victoria Ann (Traynor) Cowles; m. James Stephen Wauters, Apr. 18, 1981 (div.); children: Kimberly Marie, James Joseph, Daniel Allan. ADN, Indian River C.C., Ft. Pierce, Fla., 1994. RN, Fla. Nurse physician's office, Ft. Pierce, 1991; staff nurse, cardiac nurse Med. Ctr. of Port St. Lucie, Fla., 1991—. Republican. Presbyterian. Home: 1115 S Brocksmith Rd Fort Pierce FL 34945 Office: Port St Lucie Med Ctr 1800 Tiffany Ave Port Saint Lucie FL 34952

WAVLE, JAMES EDWARD, JR., pharmaceutical company executive, lawyer; b. N.Y.C., July 19, 1942; s. James Edward and Florence Marie (Kehoe) W.; children from previous marriage: James Edward, William Patrick, Robert Thomas, Stephanie Elizabeth; m. Elizabeth Edith Symons Tallett; 1 child, Christopher Andrew; stepchildren: James E. Tallett, Alexander M. Tallett. B.A., Adelphi U., 1964; J.D., Georgetown U., 1967; LL.M., N.Y. U., 1968. Bar: N.Y. bar 1967. With Warner-Lambert Co., Morris Plains, N.J., 1968-87; internat. counsel Warner-Lambert Co., 1971-74, assoc. gen. counsel, 1974-77, v.p., gen. counsel, 1977-80, sr. v.p., gen. counsel, 1980-81; corp. sr. v.p. and pres. Parke-Davis Group, 1982-87; pres., CEO Centocor Inc., Malvern, Pa., 1987-92; chmn. Dioscor Inc., Stockton, N.J., 1993—. Mem. Am. Bar Assn. Clubs: Lake Mohawk Golf, Stamford Yacht. Office: Dioscor Inc PO Box 531 Stockton NJ 08559

WAWROSE, FREDERICK EUGENE, psychiatrist; b. Binghamton, N.Y., Jan. 23, 1929; s. John Joseph and Marie Johanna (Anton) W.; m. Dorothy Jean Stewart, Sept. ll, 1954; children: John, David, Susan, Stephen, Dorothy. AB cum laude, U. Colo., 1950; MD, U. Pa., 1954. Diplomate Am. Bd. Psychiatry and Neurology, Am. Bd. Child Psychiatry. Dir. pre-sch. unit Child Study Ctr., Phila., 1963-64, dir. Ctr., 1964-70; psychiatrist J.C. Blair Hosp., Huntingdon, Pa., 1970-94, dir., 1986—; intern Univ. Pa. Hosp., 1954-55; resident in adult psychiatry Inst. of the Pa. Hosp., 1958-61; resident in child psychiatry Child Study Ctr. Phila., 1961-63; psychiatrist State Correctional Inst., Huntington, 1971—, Juniata Valley Mental Health-Mental Retardation Program, Huntington, 970—. Capt. M.C., U.S. Army, 1955-57. Fellow Am. Acad. Child Psychiatry; mem. AMA (physicians recognition award 1988), Am. Psychiat. Assn., Am. Cad. Psychiatry and Law.

WAX, ARNOLD, physician; b. Bklyn., Mar. 11, 1949; s. Emanuel and Eleanor (Greenfield) W.; m. Francine Wax; children: Erin, Racheal, Adam, Benjamin. BS in Pharm. Scis., Columbia U., 1971; MD, SUNY, Buffalo, 1976. Diplomate Nat. Bd. Med. Examiners, Am. Bd. Internal Medicine, Am. Bd. Quality Assurance and Utilization Rev. Physicians, Am. Acad. Pain Mgmt.; lic. physician, Fla., Calif., N.D., Minn., N.Y., Nev., Ariz. Intern, resident Millard Fillmore Hosp., Buffalo, 1976-79; clin. asst. instr. SUNY, 1977-79; instr. medicine U. Rochester, N.Y., 1979-81; dir. internal medicine U. N.D., Grand Forks, 1982-83, clin. asst. prof., 1982-85; pvt. practice Las Vegas, Nev., 1987—; mem. staff Sunrise Hosp., Las Vegas, Desert Springs Hosp., Las Vegas, Nathan Adelson Hospice, Las Vegas, Valley Hosp., Las Vegas, U. Med. Ctr., Las Vegas, St. Rose Dominican Hosp., Henderson, Nev., Lake Mead Hosp., North Las Vegas. Contbr. articles to profl. jours. Grantee So. Nev. Cancer Rsch. Found., Ea. Coop. Oncology Group, Gynecol. Oncology Group, North Ctrl. Cancer Treatment Group, S.W. Oncology Group. Mem. AMA, ACP, Am. Cancer Soc. (fellow 1979), Am. Soc. Clin. Oncology, Nev. Med. Soc., Clark County Med. Soc. (trustee, peer rev. com.), Nev. Peer Rev. Orgn., U. Nev. Las Vegas Found., Nev. Dance Theater, Nev. Opera Theater, Las Vegas Symphony, Nev. Inst. Contemporary Art, Lied Mus., Allied Arts Coun., James Platt White Soc., U. Buffalo Found., Rho Chi (Bronze medal 1971). Home: 2224 Chatsworth Ct Henderson NV 89014 Office: 3920 S Eastern Ave # 202 Las Vegas NV 89119

WAXLER, BEVERLY JEAN, anesthesiologist, physician; b. Chgo., Apr. 11, 1949; d. Isadore and Ada Belle (Gross) Marcus; m. Richard Norman Waxler, Dec. 24, 1972; 1 child, Adam R. BS in Biology, No. Ill. U., 1971; MD, U. Ill., Chgo., 1975. Diplomate Am. Bd. Anesthesiology, Am. Bd. Pathology. Intern dept. pathology Northwestern U., Chgo., 1975-76, resident, 1976-79; instr. Rush Presbyn. St. Luke's Med. Ctr., Chgo., 1979-81; asst. prof. pathology Loyola U., Maywood, Ill., 1981-84; resident dept. anesthesiology Cook County Hosp., Chgo., 1984-87, attending anesthesiologist, 1987—; clin. asst. prof. U. Ill., Chgo., 1988-95, Rush Med. Coll., Chgo., 1996—. Contbr. papers to Tissue and Cell, British Jour. Exptl. Pathology, Biochem. Medicine, Calcified Tissue Internat., Jour. Lab. Clin. Med. Recipient B.B. Sankey Anesthesia Advancement award Internat. Anesthesia Rsch. Soc., 1989; Nat. Rsch. Svc. award fellow Nat. Cancer Inst., 1980; grantee Varlen Corp., 1982. Mem. AAAS, Internat. Anesthesia Rsch. Soc., Am. Soc. Anesthesiologists, Sigma Xi. Home: 7615 Church St Morton Grove IL 60053-1618 Office: Cook County Hosp Chicago IL 60612

WAXMAN, JONATHAN, oncologist; b. London, Oct. 31, 1951; s. David and Shirley (Friedman) W.; m. Clare Petronella Taylor; children: Thea, Frederick. BSc, U. Coll. London, 1972, MB BS, 1975; MD, U. London, 1986. House surgeon, intern U. Coll. London, 1975; house physician Addenbrooke Hosp., Cambridge, Eng., 1975-76; sr. house officer U. Coll. Hosp., London, 1977-78; registrar, resident St. Mary's Hosp., London, 1979-81; sr. registrar, sr. resident St. Bartholomew's Hosp., London, 1981-86; reader oncology Royal Postgrad. Med. Sch., London, 1986—. Editor: Molecular Endocrinology of Cancer, 1995; co-editor: Urological Oncology, 1992, Interleukin 2, 1992, Molecular Biology of Career, 1988, The New Endocrinology of Cancer, 1985; contbr. articles to profl. jours. Fellow Royal Coll. Physicians (London); mem. Assn. Physicians Am. Soc. Clin. Oncology, Am. Assn. for Cancer Rsch. Office: Dept Oncology, Royal Postgrad Med Sch, Du Cane Rd, London W12 ONN, England

WAXMAN, KENNETH STEVEN, surgeon; b. San Francisco, Aug. 16, 1949; s. Robert and Lois (Glazer) W.; m. Shirley Wareing, Apr. 16, 1977; children: Ryan, Stephanie. BA, U. Calif., Berkeley, 1971; MD, U. Chgo., 1975. Asst. prof. UCLA, 1975-76; prof. surgery U. Calif., Irvine, 1976-95; dir. surgery Santa Barbara (Calif.) Cottage Hosp., 1995—; dir. Trauma Ctr., UCI, Orange, Calif., 1976-95. Contbr. articles to profl. jours. Organizer Orange County (Calif.) Youthful Drunk Driver Program, 1988-55. Fellow ACS; mem. Soc. Univ. Surgeons, Pacific Coast Surg., Western Surg., Am. Assn. for Surgery of Trauma. Office: Santa Barbara Cottage Hosp PO Box 689 Santa Barbara CA 93102

WAXMAN, STEPHEN GEORGE, neurologist, neuroscientist; b. Newark, Aug. 17, 1945; s. Morris and Beatrice (Levitch) W.; m. Merle Applebaum, June 25, 1968; children: Matthew, David. AB, Harvard U., 1967; PhD, Albert Einstein Coll. Med., Yeshiva U., 1970, MD, 1972; MA (hon.), Yale U., 1986. Rsch. fellow in neurosci. Albert Einstein Coll. Medicine, Bronx, N.Y., 1970-72; clin. fellow Boston City Hosp., 1972-75; asst. prof. neurology Med. Sch. Harvard U., Boston, 1975-77, assoc. prof., 1977-78; prof. Stanford (Calif.) U., 1978-86; chief neurology unit Palo Alto (Calif.) VA Hosp., 1978-86; prof., chmn. dept. neurology Yale U., New Haven, 1986—; chief neurology Yale-New Haven Hosp., 1986—; vis. asst. prof. biology MIT, Cambridge, 1975-77, vis. assoc. prof., 1977-78; vice chmn. dept neurology Stanford, 1981-86, chmn. neurosci. program, 1982-86; mem. adv. bd. Regeneration Programs VA, Washignton, 1982-86; mem. sci. adv. com. Nat. Spinal Cord Injury Assn., 1982-87, Paralized Vets Am., 1981-91; dir. Ctr. Rsch. Neurol. Disease, VA Med. Ctr., West Haven, Conn., 1986—; mem. corp. Marine Biol. Labs., Woods Hole, Mass., 1988; mem. sci. adv. coun. Am. Paralysis Assn., 1988-92, mem. bd. sci. counselors NINDB, 1990-92; mem. bd. neurosci. and behavior Inst. Medicine, 1990; Geschwind vis. prof. Harvard U., 1996. Author: Spinal Cord Compression, 1990, Correlative Neuroanatomy, 1995, The Axon, 1995; editor: Physiology and Pathbiology of Axons, 1978; editor-in-chief The Neuroscientist; assoc. editor Jour. Neurol. Scis.; mem. editl. bd. Brain Rsch., Muscle and Nerve, Internat. Rev. Neurobiology, Annals of Neurology, Jour. Neurol. Rehab., Glia, Devel. Neurosci., Jour. Neurotrauma, Neurobiology of Disease, Cerebrovascular Disease, Synapse. Recipient Trygve Tuve Meml. award NIH, 1973, Rsch. Career Devel. award NIH, 1975, Disting. Alumnus award Albert Einstein Coll. Medicine, 1990; rsch. fellow Univ. Coll., London, 1969; Nat Multiple Sclerosis Soc. established investigator, 1987; numerous vis. lectureships. Fellow Royal Soc. Medicine (Gr. Britain), Am. Heart Assn. (stroke coun.); mem. Am. Soc. Cell Biology, Am. Acad. Neurology, Internat. Brain Rsch. Orgn. (U.S. nat. com.), Soc. Neurosci., Am. Neurol. Assn. (counsillor 1980), World Fedn. Neurology, Assn. Rsch. in Nervous and Mental Diseases (trustee, pres. 1992), Assn. Univ. Profs. Neurology. Office: Yale U Sch Medicine 33 Cedar St New Haven CT 06519-2314

WAY, JAMES LEONG, pharmacology and toxicology educator; b. Watsonville, Calif., Mar. 21, 1926; s. Wong Bung Wee and Wow Wee (Wong) W.; m. Diana Chen, Dec. 20, 1991; children: Lani, Jon, Lori. BA, U. Calif., Berkeley, 1951; PhD, George Washington U., 1955. Asst. prof. U. Wis., Madison, 1959-62; assoc. prof. Marquette Med. Sch., Milw., 1962-67; prof. Washington State U., Pullman, 1967-82; endowed Shelton prof. pharmacology Tex. A&M U., College Station, 1982—; mem. toxicology study sect. NIH, Bethesda, Md., 1974-78; mem. toxicology data bank peer rev. com., NIH-NLM, 1978-85; mem. environ. health sci. study sect. NIEHS, 1985-90; vis. prof. pharmacology Nat. Def. Med. Ctr, Taipei, Taiwan, 1981-82; mem. toxicology data bank NLM, 1976-85; vis. scientist Med. Rsch. Coun./Nat. Inst. Med. Rsch., London, 1973-75. Contbr. over 200 articles to profl. jours. Recipient rsch. career devel. award NIH, 1959-72; Greenwald scholar U. Calif., Berkeley, 1960, Disting. scholar of U.S. NAS, 1986-88; N.Am. Baxter fellow, 1954-55, fellow NIH, 1979-80, Nat. Cancer Inst., 1955-58, also others. Mem. Am. Soc. Pharmacology and Exptl. Therapeutics (treas. 1989-90), Soc. Toxicology, Western Pharmacology Soc. (pres. 1978-79, mem. editorial bd. Toxicology and Applied Pharmacology 1978-90, Ann. Rev. Pharmacology and Toxicology 1986-91, assoc. editor 1991—), Internat. Soc. Resealed Erthrocyte (pres. 1994-96). Office: Tex A&M U Health Sci Ctr Dept Med Pharmacology Med Sci Bldg College Station TX 77843-1114

WAY, WILSON SPENCER, retired osteopathic physician and surgeon; b. Guatemala City, Guatemala, Feb. 24, 1910; s. Wilson Spencer and Lydia Caroline (Walker) W.; m. Louise Edrington, May 20, 1938 (div. May 1953); children: Flora Ann Way Arnold, Wilson Edrington; m. Olga Cheves, May 25, 1953 (dec. 1990); m. Annie Mae Hardesty, 1991. DO, Kirksville Coll. Osteo. Medicine, 1941; PhD, Donsbach U., 1979; D. Christian Lit. (hon.), Freedom U., 1984. Gen. practice osteo. medicine, Orlando, Fla., 1941; staff Orlando Gen. Hosp., 1941-72; cert. instr. Dale Carnegie, Orlando, 1957-63. Author: Total Life, 1978; Miracle of Enzymes, 1979. Bd. dirs. Sta. WTGL-TV, Cocoa-Orlando, 1980—; deacon Assembly of God Ch. Fellow Internat. Coll. of Applied Nutrition; mem. Am. Osteo. Assn., Fla. Osteo. Med. Assn., Fla. Acad. Osteopathy, Nat. Acad. Osteopathy, Internat. Acad. of Preventive Medicine. Democrat. Lodge: Toastmasters Internat. (pres. Orlando, Fla. 1966-67). Avocation: fishing.

WAYLAND, MARILYN TICKNOR, medical researcher, evaluator, educator; b. Detroit, Sept. 12, 1949; d. George Gary and Vera Virginia (Lux) Rieckhoff; m. William James Wayland, Sept. 22, 1979; children: Jessica, James. BA, Wayne State U., 1972, PhD, 1983. Project dir. Oakland County Emergency Med. Svcs., Pontiac, Mich., 1980-81, Wayne State U. Med. Sch., Detroit, 1981-84; dir. clin. rsch. St. John Hosp. Med. Ctr., Detroit, 1984—; assoc. Grad. Faculty Ctrl. Mich. U., Detroit, 1994—. Contbr. articles to Acad. Medicine, Michigan Hosps., Jour. Med. Edn., Med. Bull.; editor Med. Bull., 1984—. Grantee Mich. Health Care Edn. & Rsch. Found., Detroit, 1986, '89. Mem. Am. Assn. Med. Colls., Am. Pub. Health Assn., Am. Ednl. and Rsch. Assn., Mich. Assn. of Med. Educators. Office: St John Hosp & Med Ctr 22101 Moross Rd Grosse Pointe MI 48236-2148

WAYNE, MARVIN ALAN, emergency medicine physician; b. Detroit, Dec. 11, 1943; s. Jack I. and Marian M. (Berk) W.; m. Joan A. Tobin, Dec. 30, 1971; children: Michelle, Dana. MD, U. Mich., 1968. Diplomate Am. Bd. Emergency Medicine. Fellow St. Bartholomew's Hosp., London, 1968, Virginia Mason Hosp., Seattle, 1973-74; resident in surgery U. Colo. Med. Ctr., Denver, 1968-71; pvt. practice Bellingham, Wash., 1974—; staff emergency dept. St. Joseph's Hosp. (merger St. Joseph's Hosp. and St. Luke's Hosp.), Bellingham, Wash., 1974—, vice chmn. dept. emergency medicine, 1980-83, chmn., 1984-86; med. dir. Emergency Med. Svcs., Bellingham, Wash., 1975—; assoc. clin. prof. sch. medicine U. Wash., Seattle, 1986—; vice chmn. emergency med. svcs. com. State of Wash., 1982-83, chmn., 1983-86; med. dir. Med-Flight Helicopter, 1980—, Inst. for Pre-Hosp. Medicine, 1980—; pres. Whatcom County Emergency Med. Svcs. Coun., 1979; med. advisor Mt. Baker Ski Patrol; spkr. nat. and internat. edn. programs; founder, owner Dr. Cookie Inc., Edmonds, Wash., 1985—. Contbr. articles to med. jours. Bd. dirs. YMCA, Bellingham, 1980-84. Maj. M.C., U.S. Army, 1971-73, Vietnam. Recipient Outstanding Achievement award Whatcom County Emergency Med. Svcs. Coun., 1980, Outstanding Ednl. Achievement award Abbott Labs., 1982, Outstanding Advanced Life Support System award State of Wash., 1983, Emergency Med. Svc. rsch. award Wash. Assn. Emergency Med. Technicians and Paramedics, 1983. Fellow Am. Coll. Emergency Physicians (bd. dirs. Wash. chpt. 1977-84, pres. 1978, sci. meetings com. 1984, Outstanding Ednl. Achievement award 1982), Royal Soc. Medicine (Eng.); mem. Wash. State Med. Soc. (emergency med. svc. adv. com. 1978--), Whatcom County Med. Soc., Univ. Assn. for Emergency Medicine, Soc. Critical Care Medicine, Am. Trauma Soc. (founding), Nat. Assn. Emergency Med. Svc. Physicians, Am. Soc. Automotive Medicine, Nat. Assn. Emergency Med. Technicians. Office: Emergency Med Svcs 1800 Broadway Bellingham WA 98225-3133

WAYNE, ROBERT, surgeon; b. N.Y.C., Aug. 14, 1943; s. William and Dorothy (Gear) W.; m. Jean Wayne. Diplomate Am. Bd. Surgery. Resident in surgery Creighton U., Omaha, 1971-74; pvt. practice, Astoria, Oreg., 1978—. Office: 2055 Exchange St Astoria OR 97103

WAYNE, VICTOR SAMUEL, cardiologist; b. Melbourne, Australia, Jan. 7, 1953; s. Mark Isaac and Anita (Selzer) W.; m. Karen Susan Eisinger; children: Fairlie, Stephanie. MB, BS with honors, Monash U., 1976. Diplomate Australian Soc. Ultrasound in Medicine. Intern, resident med. officer, registrar Alfred Hosp., Melbourne, 1976-79, cardiology registrar, 1980-81; advanced cardiology fellow St. Vincent Hosp., Worcester, Mass., 1982-83; instr. medicine U. Mass., Worcester, 1982-83; sr. cardiologist St. Francis Xavier Cabrini Hosp., Epworth Hosp., Melbourne, 1983—; vis. physician, cardiologist Alfred Hosp., Monash U., Melbourne, 1983—; lecturer in field. Contbr. articles to profl. jours; co-author books. Grantee Nat. Heart Found., Alfred Hosp., 1982. Fellow Royal Australasian Coll. Physicians, Am. Coll. Chest Physicians, Internat. Acad. Chest Physicians and Surgeons, N.Y. Acad. Scis., Am. Coll. Cardiology, Internat. Coll. Angiology, European Soc. Cardiology; mem. Cardiac Soc. Australia and New Zealand, Australian Soc. Echocardiography, Internat. Soc. and Fedn. Cardiology. Jewish. Club: Nat. Golf of Australia. Home: 44 Grange Rd, Toorak Victoria 3142, Australia Office: Cabrini Med Ctr, Isabella St Malvern, Melbourne Victoria 3144, Australia

WAYNIK, CYRIL, psychiatrist; b. Cape Town, South Africa, May 3, 1928; came to U.S., 1963; s. Louis and Leah (Yuter) W.; m. Loraine Katz; children: Mark, Melanie. MB ChB, U. Cape Town, 1950. Diplomate, Am. Bd. Psychiatry and Neurology. Intern Groote Schuur Hosp., Cape Town, 1951-52; family practice Cape Town, 1952-62; resident psychiatry Groote Schuur Hosp., Cape Town, 1962, Fairfield Hills Hosp., Newtown, Conn., 1962-64; pvt. practice psychiatry Fairfield, Conn., 1967—; dir. out-patient clinic, Bridgeport (Conn.) Hosp., 1966, 67; chmn. psychiatry, Park City Hosp., Bridgeport, 1970-79. Fellow Am. Psychiat. Assn.; mem. Conn. Psychiat. Soc. (pres. 1979-80). Office: 52 Beach Rd Fairfield CT 06430-6017

WAZEN, JACK JOSEPH, otolaryngologist, educator; b. Beirut, Sept. 9, 1954. BS in Biology with Distinction, Am. U. Beirut, 1974, MD, 1978. Intern Am. U. Beirut Hosp., 1977-78, resident in otolaryngology, 1978-79, resident in gen. surgery, 1979-80; resident in otolaryngology Columbia Presbyn. Med. Ctr., N.Y.C., 1980-83; fellow in otology, neurotology Ear Rsch. Found. Fla., Sarasota, 1983-84; asst. prof. dept. speech and lang. pathology Columbia U., N.Y.C., 1984, course dir. otolaryngology, 1984-90, asst. prof., 1984-90, assoc. prof., 1990—, assoc. dir. clin. affairs dept. otolaryngology-head & neck surgery, 1996—, med. dir. speech & hearing dept.; assoc. prof. clin. otolaryngology/neurol. surgery Columbia Presbyn. Med. Ctr., N.Y.C., 1995—; assoc. attending physician Columbia Presbyn. Med. Ctr., N.Y.C., 1990—, asst. attending physician, 1984-90, dir. divsn. neurotology, 1984-88, dir. otology-neurotology, 1988—; cons. dept. otolaryngology Englewood (N.J.) Hosp., 1991—. Contbr. articles to profl. jours.; mem. editorial rev. bd. Otolaryngology: Head and Neck Surgery, 1991—, Internat. Tinnitis Jour. Rsch. grantee N.Y. Ear Found., 1990. Fellow Am. Acad. Otolaryngology Head and Neck Surgery, Am. Neurotology Soc., ACS; mem. AMA, N.Y. Acad. Sci., Deafness Rsch. Found., Assn. for Rsch. in Otolaryngology, Ear Rsch. Found., N.Y. Acad. Medicine, N.Y. Otological Soc., Soc. Univ. Otolaryngologists Head and Neck Surgeons, Am. Laryngological, Rhinological and Otological Soc, Inc., Am. Otological Soc. Office: Columbia U 630 W 168th St New York NY 10032-3702

WAZIR, TADAR JIHAD, chaplain, small business owner; b. Kansas City, Mo., Dec. 28, 1944; s. Roosevelt and Osceola (Moore) Byers; m. Kay Frances Kyle-Byers, May 17, 1969; children: Tarik, Ibrahim; 1 adopted child, Ajamu. AA in Adminstrn. of Justice, Penn Valley Community Coll., Kansas City, 1977. Ins. salesperson Western & So. Life Ins. Co., Kansas City, 1968-69, N.Y. Life Ins. Co., Kansas City, 1969; supr. check transit dept. First Nat. Bank, Kansas City, 1969-70, methods analyst, 1971-72; paramedic St. Joseph's Hosp., Kansas City, 1974-77; owner W. K. Enterprises, Kansas City, 1977-79; ins. salesperson Roosevelt Nat. Life, Independence, Mo., 1978-79; pvt. mcht., Kansas City, 1980-81, Marshall, Mo., 1989—; bd. dirs. Welcome Home, Inc. 1994—; real estate salesperson Mid-Western Realty, Kansas City, 1980-86; chaplain, hostage negotiator, Mo. Dept. of Corrections, Jefferson City, 1982—; speaker, cons. Masjid Omar, Inc., Kansas City, 1977-92, Islamic Life Mission, 1992—; contract chaplain, cons. U.S. Med. Ctr. Fed. Prison, Springfield, Mo., 1979—; co-chmn. report the drug pusher Ad-Hoc Group Against Crime, Kansas City, 1978-82, pres. A.U. (African Unity, Inc.) 1994—, (Qadi) spl. master of the Jackson County, Mo. cir. ct., 1992. Chaplain chpt. 393, Vietnam Vets. Assn. Am. Jefferson City, 1991; Mo. st. coun. of the Vietnam Vets. of Am. co-chaplain 1991, treas. 1992-94; With USMC, 1962-66; mem. U.S. affiliate Islamic African Relief Agy. Mem. Am. Corrections Assn., Mo. Corrections Assn., Mo. Assn. Social Welfare, Nat. Assn. Muslim Chaplains, NAACP (pres. Marshall-Saline chpt. 1989-90, v.p., 1990-91, polit. action com. chmn. 1994—), Mid.-Am. Coun. Imams, Islamic Soc. N.Am., Optimists (chaplain Marshall 1990-91, chmn. community svcs. 1991-92, co-organizer ROTC program Ark. AM&N Coll.). Home: 456 W Porter St Marshall MO 65340-1358 Office: Mo Dept of Corrections 2729 Plaza Dr Jefferson City MO 65109-1146

WEAR, SHERYL A., pharmacist; b. Eugene, Oreg., June 10, 1955; d. Swan Edward and Maureen Ellen (Vaughn) Hodges; m. John Lewis Welsh, July 31, 1977 (div. June 1987); m. Britt Milton Wear, July 5, 1989; 1 child,

Kienan Milton. BS, Oreg. State U., 1979. Cert. pharmacist, Oreg. Pharmacist Bimart Retail, North Bend, Oreg., 1979-85, Oregon City, Oreg., 1979-85; pharmacist Kaiser Permanente, Portland, Oreg., 1985—. Recipient Excellence in Edn. award, OSHP, 1994. Office: Home Infusion Pharmacy 2701 NW Vaughn S Ste 140 Portland OR 97210

WEARY, PEYTON EDWIN, medical educator; b. Evanston, Ill., Jan. 10, 1930; s. Leslie Albert and Conway Christian (Fleming) W.; m. Janet Edsall Gregory, Aug. 23, 1952; children—Terry, Conway Christian, Carolyn Fielder. B.A., Princeton U., 1970; M.D., U. Va., 1955. Diplomate: Am. Bd. Dermatology (dir. 1978-88, pres. 1987-88). Intern, case Western Res. U. Hosps., Cleve., 1955-56; rotating intern Univ. Hosp. Cleve., 1955-56; asst. resident dermatology U. Va., Charlottesville, 1958-60; resident dermatology U. Va., 1960-61, instr. dept. dermatology, 1961-62, asst. prof., 1962-65, asso. prof., 1965-70, prof., chmn. dept. dermatology, 1970-93; mem. staff Univ. Hosp., mem. cancer com., 1979—, sec.-treas.; Univ. Hosp. house staff, 1960-61, clin. staff, 1965-66, pres. clin. staff, 1966-67. Mem. editorial bd. Jour. Am. Acad. Dermatology, 1978-87; editorial adv. bd. Skin and Allergy News, 1978—; contbr. articles to profl. jours. Bd. dirs. Lupus Found. Am., 1980-84; trustee, mem. exec. com. Dermatology Found., 1975-79; pres. Albemarle County unit Am. Cancer Soc., 1967-69. Served from 1st lt. to capt., M.C. U.S. Army, 1956-58. Mem. Nat. Assn. Physicians Environ. (pres. 1995—), Va. Dermatol. Soc. (sec.-treas. 1965-71), Am. Acad. Dermatology (hon. bd. dirs. 1973-76, Gold medal 1990, pres. 1993-95), Soc. Investigative Dermatology (bd. dirs. 1976-81, v.p.1985, hon. mem. 1996), Assn. Profs. Dermatology (sec.-treas. 1976-79), Am. Dermatol. Assn. (bd. dirs. 1987-93, pres. 1992-93), Dermatology Found., Albermarle County Med. Soc., Med. Soc. Va., So. Med. Assn., Reven Soc., Am. Bd. Med. Specialties (v.p. 1988, pres-elect 1989, pres. 1990-92), Coun. Med. Specialty Socs. (bd. dirs. 1989-92, sec. 1992-95), Alpha Omega Alpha, Sigma Xi. Republican. Presbyn. Club: Boar's Head Sports. Home: 110 Magnolia Dr Charlottesville VA 22901-2015 Office: Dept Dermatology Univ Va Hosp Charlottesville VA 22908

WEATHERBY, LAURA BETH, medical/surgical nurse; b. Wilmington, Del., Nov. 2, 1969; d. David George and Geraldine Marie (Burnett) W. BSN, U. Del., Newark, 1992. RN, Pa. Clin. nurse Citadel MCH Svcs., Narberth, Pa., 1993-94; staff nurse Maternal/Child, Pediatrics, Med./Surg/ Hosp. Homecare of Greater Phila., 1994—; developer devel. program Citadel MCH Svcs., Narberth, 1993—, Girl Scout leader. Home: Apt S-10 3131 Meetinghouse Rd Boothwyn PA 19061

WEATHERFORD-BATMAN, MARY VIRGINIA, rehabilitation counselor, educator; b. St. Louis, Mar. 28; d. John Ely and Virginia Louise (Cox) Weatherford; m. Aug. 28, 1965 (div. Jan. 1976); 1 child, Christopher James Batman. Cert. med. technologist, Jackson Meml. Hosp., Miami, Fla., 1966; BS, Barry U., 1984, MBA, 1986, EdS, 1992; postgrad., Union Inst. Cert. rehab. counselor; cert. case mgr. Crossmatch technologist John Elliott Blood Bank, Miami, 1966-68; nurse D. E. Fortner MD, P.A. Gutlohn MD, Miami, 1969-75; allergy technologist Dadeland Allergy, Ear, Nose and Throat Assocs., Miami, 1975-78; tech. mgr. Morris Beck MD, Miami, 1978-86; sales rep. Glaxo, Inc., Research Triangle Park, N.C., 1987-88; med. ctr. specialist Wyeth Ayerst, Phila., 1988-90; hosp. rep. Allen & Hanburys, Div. Glaxo, Inc., Research Triangle Park, 1990; sales cons. Profl. Detailing Network, Princeton, N.J., 1991—; adj. prof. Union Inst., Miami, 1993—; chief psychology intern Miami Heart Inst., 1994-95; rehab. counselor Nat. Health and Rehab. Cons., Inc., Miami, 1991-94; therapist Ctrs. for Psychol. Growth, 1994; chief psychology intern Miami Heart Inst., 1994-95. Vocat. devel. vol. Jackson Meml. Hosp., U. Miami, 1991—; vol. Crippled Children's Soc., Miami, 1968-69, South Miami Hosp., 1959-63. Recipient award DAR, 1962; Tng. scholar NIH, 1962, Lucille Funk Keely Trust scholar, 1991, 92. Mem. ACA, APA, Assn. for Adult Devel. and Aging, Am. Rehab. Counseling Assn., Fla. Counseling Assn., Fla. Assn. for Adult Devel. and Aging (pres.), Fla. Soc. Med. Technologists, Barry U. Counseling Assn., Toastmasters Internat. Inc., Miami Parrot Club, Country Club of Coral Gables, Delta Epsilon Sigma. Methodist. Office: PO Box 141217 Coral Gables FL 33114-1196

WEAVER, ARTHUR LAWRENCE, physician; b. Lincoln, Nebr., Sept. 3, 1936; s. Arthur J. and Harriet Elizabeth (Walt) W.; BS (Regents scholar) with distinction, U. Nebr., 1958; MD, Northwestern U., 1962; MS in Medicine, U. Minn., 1966; m. JoAnn Versemann, July 6, 1980; children: Arthur Jensen, Anne Christine. Intern U. Mich. Hosps., Ann Arbor, 1962-63; resident Mayo Grad. Sch. Medicine, Rochester, Minn., 1963-66; practice medicine specializing in rheumatology and internal medicine, Lincoln, 1968—; mem. staff Bryan Meml. Hosp., chmn. dept. rheumatology, 1976-78, 82-85, 89-91, vice-chief staff, 1984-87; bd. dirs. Bryancare (PHO), 1995-96, chmn. fin. com., 1995-96; mem. courtesy staff St. Elizabeths Hosp., Lincoln Gen. Hosp.; mem. cons. staff VA Hosp.; chmn. Juvenile Rheumatoid Arthritis Clinic, 1970-88; asst. prof. dept. internal medicine U. Nebr., Omaha, 1976-88, assoc. prof., 1988-95, prof., 1995—; med. dir. Lincoln Benefit Life Ins. Co., Nebr., 1972-90; bd. dirs. Lincoln Mutual Life Ins., Co., 1994—, med. dir., 1995—; mem. exam. bd. Nat. Assn. Retail Druggists; mem. adv. com. Coop. Systematic Studies in Rheumatic Diseases III. Bd. dirs. Nebr. chpt. Arthritis Found., 1969—; mem. tech. cons. panel for rheumatology Harvard Resource Based Relative Value Study; trustee U. Nebr. Found., 1974—. Served to capt., M.C., U.S. Army, 1966-68. Recipient Outstanding Nebraskan award U. Nebr., 1958, also C.W. Boucher award; Philip S. Hench award Rheumatology, Mayo Grad. Sch. Medicine, 1966. Diplomate Am. Bd. Internal Medicine, Am. Bd. Rheumatology. Fellow ACP (Nebr. council 1983—), Am. Rheumatism Assn. (com. on rheumatologic practice 1983-87, pres.-elect Cen. region 1983-84, pres. Cen. region 1984-85); mem. AMA, Am. Coll. Rheumatology (sec. 1991-93, 1st Paulding Phelps award, bd. dirs. 1985—, planning com. 1987—, exec. com. 1991—, sec. 1991-93, pres. rsch. and edn. found. 1991-93, 2nd v.p. 1993-94, 1st. v.p., pres. elect. 1994-95, pres. 1995-96), Am. Soc. Internal Medicine (coord. com. physician payment svcs. 1988-93), Nebr. Soc. Internal Medicine (Internist of Yr., 1988), Nebraska Rheumatism Assn., Nebr. Med. Assn., Lancaster County Med. Soc., Mayo Grad. Sch. Medicine Alumni Assn., Arthritis Health Professions Assn. (com. on practice 1984-87), Nat. Soc. Clin. Rheumatology (program chairperson 1986-87, 88, exec. com. 1987-92), Midwest Cooperative Rheumatic Disease Study Group, (chmn. exec. com. 1986-92), Arthritis Found. (profl. del.-at-large 1987-88, 89, 90, 95-96, Nat. Vol. Svc. citation, 1988, blue ribbon rsch. com. 1995—), Phi Beta Kappa, Sigma Xi, Alpha Omega Alpha, Pi Kappa Epsilon, Phi Rho Sigma. Republican. Presbyterian. Editorial bd. Nebr. Med. Jour., 1982—; contbr. articles to med. jours. Home: 4239 Calvert Pl Lincoln NE 68506-4252 Office: 2121 S 56th St Lincoln NE 68506-2111

WEAVER, ARTHUR WILLARD, surgeon; b. Arpin, Wis., Nov. 29, 1923; s. Ernest Perry and Olive Bell (Stevenson) W.; m. Natalie Jean Wheeker, June 26, 1945; children: Karen, Donald, Sharon, Robert, Susan, Ellen. BA, Pacific Union Coll., 1948; MD, Loma Linda U., 1952. Diplomate Am. Bd. Surgery. Pvt. practice surgeon Pontiac, Mich., 1956-61; chief surgery Karachi (Pakistan) Adventist Hosp., 1961-66; prof. Wayne State U., Detroit, 1966—; chief surg. svc. VA Med. Ctr., Allen Park, Mich., 1970-75, chief head and neck surgery, 1973-93. Contbr. over 61 articles to profl. jours. and book chpts. to 23 publs. Pres. Better Living Seminar, Plymouth, Mich., 1975-95. Named Layman of the Yr., Mich. Conf. of Seventh-Day Adventist, 1970, Man of Yr., Mich. Cancer Found., 1970, Michiganian of Yr., Detroit News, 1986. Fellow ACS; mem. AMA, Soc. Head and Neck Surgeons (exec. com. 1971-75). Seventh-Day Adventist. Home: 49285 Ridge Ct Northville MI 48167 Office: Wayne State U 4201 Saint Antoine St Detroit MI 48201

WEAVER, DAVID ELLIS, cardiologist; b. Amarillo, Tex., May 3, 1958; s. Vernon Ellis and Freda (Spencer) W.; m. Ann Elizabeth Martin, Oct. 15, 1988; children: Lauren Elizabeth, Andrew Spencer. BA, U. Tex., 1980; MD, Southwestern U., Dallas, 1984. Diplomate Am. Bd. Internal Medicine, Am. Bd. Cardiovascular Diseases. Intern Baylor U. Med. Ctr., 1984-85, resident, 1986-88; fellow cardiology U. N.C., Chapel Hill, 1988-91; cardiologist Tex. Cardiology Cons., Dallas, 1991—. Fellow Am. Coll. Cardiology; mem. AMA, Phi Beta Kappa. Office: 5939 Harry Hines # 630 Dallas TX 75235

WEAVER, DOUGLAS KENT, hospital executive; b. Delta, Colo., Nov. 1, 1955; s. Jerry James and Orpha Lee (Guin) W.; m. Jacqueline Sue Key, Oct. 20, 1979; children: Jaclyn, Kyle. AS, Seward County C.C., 1976; BS in Pharmacy, Southwestern Okla. State U., 1979; MBA, Wayland Bapt. U., 1993. Lic. pharmacist, Okla., Kans. Dir. pharmacy/material mgmt. Meml. Hosp., Guymon, Okla., 1980-88, asst. adminstr., 1988-90, CEO, 1990-94; CEO Meml. Hosp., Frederick, Okla., 1994—; chairperson Okla. Telemedicine Network, 1994—; mem. Med. Tech. and Rsch. Authority, Okla., 1994—; bd. dirs. Meml. Hosp., Frederick. Mem. Am. Coll. Healthcare Execs., Frederick C. of C. (bd. dirs. 1994—). Southern Baptist. Office: Meml Hosp 319 E Josephine St Frederick OK 73542

WEAVER, ESTHER RUTH, medical and surgical, geriatrics and oncology nurse; b. Kansas City, Mo., Mar. 20, 1951; d. Fred Bicknell and Mary Elizabeth (Williams) Crigler; 1 child, Scott Lee McPhee; m. Charles Edward Weaver, June 10, 1995; stepchildren: Alan Bower, Ward. ADN, Eastern N.Mex. U., Roswell, 1989. Cert. chemotherapy nurse. Staff nurse med. floor St. Mary's Hosp., Roswell, Eastern N.Mex. Med. Ctr., Roswell; night nurse Sunset Villa Care Ctr., Roswell; nurse supr. Turtle Creek Health Care Ctr., Jacksonville, Fla.; oncology staff nurse, active with dept. corrections unit Meml. Med. Ctr., Jacksonville. Mem. Merrill Rd. Bapt. Ch.; dir. children's ch. Merrill Rd. Comty. Ch. Nursing Found. scholar. Mem. N.Mex. Nurses Assn. (publicity chmn. Dist. 5), Oncology Nurses Soc., Phi Theta Kappa (v.p.).

WEAVER, KENNETH, gynecologist, researcher; b. Whitetop, Va., Dec. 4, 1933; s. Grover Cleveland and Violet Elaine (Baldwin) W.; children: Teresa Marie, Janice Eileen, Beverly Lynn, Pamela Jean, Cynthia Ann; m. Shelby Jean Davis, June 15, 1966. BA, U. N.C., 1957, MD, 1960. Diplomate Am. Bd. Ob-Gyn. Intern U.S. Pub. Health Svc., Boston, 1960-61; med. officer Cherokee (N.C.) Indian Hosp., 1961-64; gen. physician Haywood County Hosp., Waynesville, N.C., 1964-70; obstetrician, gynecologist Haywood County Hosp., Waynesville, 1974-77; resident U. Ark. Med. Ctr., Little Rock, 1970-74; asst. prof. U. Ark., Little Rock, 1977-78, acting chmn., dept. ob-gyn., 1978; pvt. practice Johnson City, Tenn., 1978—; mem. Gov. Com. on Cancer, Raleigh, N.C., 1970-71; dir. Maternity and Infant Care, Little Rock, 1977-78; assoc. prof. James H. Quillen Coll. Medicine, Johnson City, 1978-83. Contbr. articles to sci. jours. Fellow Am. Coll. Ob-Gyn., Am. Coll. Nutrition, Am. Asson. Gynecol. Laparoscopists, N.Y. Acad. Scis. Home: 377 Tavern Hill Rd Jonesborough TN 37659-5026 Office: 1103 Jackson Blvd Jonesborough TN 37659

WEAVER, LOIS JEAN, physician, educator; b. Wheeling, W.Va., May 23, 1944; d. Lewis Everett and Ann (Novak) W. BA, Oberlin Coll., 1966; MD, U. Chgo., 1970. Pulmonary fellow Northwestern U., Evanston, Ill., 1975-77; trauma fellow U. Wash. Harborview Hosp., Seattle, 1977-79, research assoc., instr. medicine, 1979-81, clin. asst. prof. medicine, 1983—; clin. research fellow Virginia Mason Med. Research Ctr., Seattle, 1981-82; mem. med. staff Swedish Hosp., Seattle, 1984-92; pulmonary cons. Fred Hutchinson Cancer Research Inst., Seattle, 1984-86, regional med. advisor and med. cons., disability quality br. Social Security, Seattle, 1985—. Contbr. sci. articles to profl. jours. La Verne Noyes scholar U. Chgo., 1966; Parker B. Francis fellow Northwestern U., 1975. Mem. AMA, Am. Thoracic Soc., Wash. Lung Assn., Sigma Xi. Home: PO Box 2098 Kirkland WA 98083-2098 Office: 2201 6th Ave # 53 Seattle WA 98121-1836

WEAVER, MARK A., optometrist; b. Lake Charles, La., Oct. 17, 1962; s. Richard Parks and Ann Elizabeth (Nezzio) W.; m. Sheree Faye Lamb, June 15, 1991 (div.); 1 child, Franco Solomon. BS, McNeese State U., 1984; OD, U. Houston Coll. Optometry, 1994. From phlebotomist to coroner's asst./surg. technologist St. Patrick's Hosp., Lake Charles, 1982-87; asst. reference lab. supervisor Smith-Kline Biosci. Lab., Austin, Tex., 1988-89, Clearlake Regional Med. Ctr., Houston, 1990-94; optometrist Round Rock Optical, Austin, 1994-96, Vision Quest Eye Ctr., Austin, 1996—; co-owner Weaver Enterprises, Baton Rouge, 1991—. Adv. bd. Men's Health Network, Austin, 1996; mem. Children's Rights Coalition, Austin, 1996. Mem. Am. Optometric Assn., Tex. Optometric Assn. Democrat. Roman Catholic.

WEAVER, MICHAEL GLENN, pharmacist; b. Tuscola, Ill., Sept. 11, 1955; s. Glen H. and Margaret I. (Long) W.; m. Catherine A. (Paynic), Sept. 30, 1978; children: Jennifer L., Michelle R., Gregory M. BS, St. Louis Coll. of Pharmacy, 1978; MBA, So. Ill. U., 1989. Registered pharmacist. Clin. coordinator, staff pharmacist St. Elizabeth Med. Ctr., Granite City, Ill., 1975-87; dir. pharmacy Freeport (Ill.) Meml. Hosp., 1987-92, dir. pharmacy and info. systems, 1992—; dir. Ill. State Bd. Pharmacy, 1995—. Am. Soc. Hosp. Pharmacists, Ill. Pharm. Assn., Am. Soc. Parenteral and Enteral Nutrition, Ill. Coun. Hosp. Pharmacists (dir. ednl. affairs 1991-94), Am. Coll. Healthcare Execs., Phi Kappa Phi, Beta Gamma Sigma, Delta Sigma Theta. Republican. Mem. United Church of Christ. Home: 1346 Carriage Hill Ln Freeport IL 61032-6168 Office: Freeport Meml Hosp 1045 W Stephenson St Freeport IL 61032-4864

WEAVER, ROBERT PATRICK, urologist; b. Birmingham, Ala., Sept. 16, 1959; s. Thomas Richard and Mildred Louise (Young) W.; m. Mary Lynn Heggeman, Dec. 21, 1985; 1 child, Robert Mackenzie. BS, U. Ala., 1981; MD, U. South Ala., 1985. Diplomate Am. Bd. Urology. Intern in gen. surgery U. Tex.-Parkland Hosp., Dallas, 1985-86; resident U. S.C., Columbia, 1986-87; resident in urologic surgery U. Kans., Kansas City, 1987-90; fellow in urologic oncology Baylor Coll. Medicine, Houston, 1990-91; pvt. practice Orlando, Fla., 1991—; bd. dirs. Orlando Surgery Ctr. V.p. Orlando metro unit Am. Cancer Soc., 1995; bd. dirs. Fla. State Golf Assn., Sarasota, 1996; dir. Man to Man Prostate Cancer Support Group, Orlando, 1993-96. Fellow ACS, Soc. Surg. Oncology; mem. Am. Soc. Clin. Oncology, Am. Urol. Assn., AMA, Fla. Urol. Soc. Roman Catholic. Home: 1108 Lancaster Dr Orlando FL 32806 Office: Butler Hodge and Weaver MD 3824 Oakwater Circle Orlando FL 32806

WEAVER, THOMAS HAROLD, health facility administrator; b. Asheville, N.C., July 21, 1943; s. Thomas Harold and Evelyn (Morris) W.; m. Marsha Va Fossen, Dec. 17, 1982; 1 child, Sallie Jayne. BA, Va. Mil. Inst., 1964; MEd, U. Ga., 1970; MAHA, George Washington U., 1973. Vol. EMS, various locations, 1965-94; mgmt. analyst VA Med. Ctr., Martinez, Calif., 1972-74; health planner VA Ctrl. Hdqs., Washington, 1974-76, sr. health sys. specialist, 1976-79; asst. dir. VA Med. Ctr., Lexington, Ky., 1979; COO, assoc. dir. VA Med. Ctr., Ft. Howard, Md., 1980-82; sr. exec. sys. specialist VA Med. Ctr., Durham, N.C., 1982-85; COO, assoc. med. dir. VA Med. Ctr., Pitts., 1985-89; CEO, med. ctr. dir. VA Med. Ctr., Martinsburg, W.Va., 1989-94; CEO, dir. VA Med. Ctr., Bay Pines, Fla., 1994—; v.p., bd. dirs. Berkeley County Emergency Ambulance Authority, Martinsburg, 1989-94; pres., chmn. bd. Bedington Vol. Fire and Rescue Dept., 1989-93; disting. vis. lectr. W.Va. U., 1992-94; lectr., cons. in field. Contbr. articles to profl. jours. Emergency med. svcs. instr. various locations, 1967-94, W.Va., 1990-94; bd. dirs. Pinellas County EMS Med. Control Bd., 1995-96, Hurricanes and Health Care Consortium, 1994-96. Recipient Nat. Cmty. Svc. award Sec. Vets. Affairs, Washington, 1975, Cert. of Merit, Geico Pub. Svc., Washington, 1985, Spl. Act Commendation award DVA and County Commn. for outstanding actions during cmty. disaster, 1993. Fellow Am. Coll. Healthcare Execs. (Fed. Exec. of Yr. W.Va. chpt. 1994); mem. Nat. Registry EMTs, Rotary. Office: Dept VA Affairs Med Ctr 10000 Bay Pines Bay Pines FL 33504

WEBB, CHARLES HOWARD, internist, geriatrician; b. Lima, Ohio, Dec. 1, 1945; s. Howard Floyd and Carol Jean (Black) W.; married; children: Maria Lee, Paul Howard. BA, Coll. of Wooster, 1967; MD, Ohio State U., 1973. Diplomate Am. Bd. Internal Medicine. Vol. Peace Corps., Eseka, Cameroun, 1967-69; case worker Dept. Pub. Aid, Chgo., 1969-70; intern Ohio State Univ. Hosps., Columbus, 1973-74, jr. asst. resident, 1974-75, sr. asst. resident, 1975-76; asst. prof. medicine Ohio State U., Columbus, 1976-79; asst. prof. internal medicine U. Fla., Gainesville, 1979-82; med. officer Peace Corps., Niamey, Niger, 1982-83; assoc. chief of staff VA Med. Ctr., Hampton, Va., 1983-87, staff physician, assoc. prof. internal medicine, 1987—, dir. geriatric evaluation and mgmt. unit, 1992—; dir. med. pathology conf. VA Med. Ctr., Hampton, 1988-92. Historian Hist. Hilton Village, Inc., Newport News, Va., 1985—; elder Presbyn. Ch., 1992—. Mem. ACP, Soc. Gen. Internal Medicine, Hampton Med. Soc., Am. Geriatric Soc. Home: 67 Main St Newport News VA 23601-4140 Office: Dept Vets Affairs 590-111 Emanicaption Dr Hampton VA 23667

WEBB, H. WARNER, pediatric surgeon; b. Columbus, Ga., Feb. 17, 1933; s. Howard Warner Webb and Doris Lillian (McNeice) Bushong; m. Shirley Ann Cox, Dec. 14, 1957 (dec. 1979); children: Daniel W., Patrick J., Julia C.; m. Carolyn Lucille Kirkland, Oct. 5, 1980. B, U. Ga., 1953; MD, Emory U., 1957. Diplomate Am. Bd. Surgery. Intern Grady Meml. Hosp., Atlanta, 1957-58, resident in surgery, 1958-60, 62-63; chief resident surgeon Grady Meml. Hosp, Atlanta, 1963-64; resident in pediatric surgery Children's Hosp., Pitts., 1964-66; ptnr. Pediatric Surg. Assocs., Jacksonville, Fla., 1966-86; surgeon-in-chief, asst. med. dir. The Nemours Children's Clinic, Jacksonville, 1986-96; clin. prof., Mercer U. Sch. Med., Macon, Ga., 1984-92, U. Fla., Gainesville, Fla., 1989; chmn. dept. children's surg. svcs. Jacksonville Wolfson Children's Hosp., Jacksonville, Fla., 1984-92. Contbr. articles to profl. jours. Chmn., Mayor's Commn. on Children and Youth, Jacksonville, Fla., 1989-90, Mayor's Task Force on Child Health, Jacksonville, 1989-90. Capt. U.S. Army, 1960-62. Take the Time Vol. award Jacksonville Wolfson Children's Hosp., 1990. Fellow Am. Coll. Surgeons, Am. Acad. Pediatrics; mem. Am. Pediatric Surg. Assn. (charter), Fla. Assn. Pediatric Surgeons (pres. 1972-76), Rotary. Republican. Episcopalian. Home: 5242 Sea Chase Dr Unit 1 Amelia Island FL 32034 Office: Nemours Children's Clinic Jacksonville FL 32207

WEBB, LENORE LORRAINE, medical records administrator; b. Pontiac, Mich., Apr. 10, 1952; d. Robert James and Maribeth Ann (Mentzer) Slonaker; m. John Edward Webb, Jr., June 16, 1979; children: Jennifer Leigh, Jeffrey Edward, Anthony Joseph. BS in Med. Record Adminstrn., Mercy Coll. Detroit, 1976. Registered record administr. Dir. med. record svcs. Mercy Hosp., Port Huron, Mich., 1976-80; dir. med. records Morgan County Meml. Hosp., Martinsville, Ind., 1980—; clin. practice supr. med. record adminstrn. program Ind. U. Sch. Medicine, Indpls., 1989—; directed practice supr. med. record adminstrn. program Mercy Coll. Detroit, 1976-80; adv. com. mem. med. secretarial program St. Clair Community Coll., Port Huron. Mem. Ind. Health Info. Assn. (pres. 1996—, pres.-elect 1995-96, del. 1993-95, chmn. project devel. com. 1991-92, chmn. nominating and credentials com. 1990-91, sec. 1989-90, pub. rels. com. 1989-90, procedures com. 1982-83, bylaws com. 1981-82), Southeastern Ind. Med. Record Assn. (chmn. continuing edn. com. 1989-90, pres. 1988-89, chmn. bylaws com. 1987-88, sec.-treas. 1984-85), Mich. Record Assn. (edn. com. 1978-80). Home: 300 Bailliere Dr Martinsville IN 46151-4306 Office: Morgan County Meml Hosp 2209 John R Wooden Dr Martinsville IN 46151-1840

WEBB, O(RVILLE) LYNN, physician, pharmacologist, educator; b. Tulsa, Aug. 29, 1931; s. Rufus Aclen and Berla Ophelia (Caudle) W.; m. Joan Liebenheim, June 1, 1954 (div. Jan. 1980); children—Kathryn, Gilbert, Benjamin; m. Jeanne P. Heath, Aug. 24, 1991. B.S., Okla. State U., 1953; M.S., U. Okla., 1961; Ph.D. in Pharmacology, U. Mo., 1966, M.D., 1968. Diplomate Nat. Bd. Med. Examiners, Am. Bd. Family Practice. Research assoc. in pharmacology U. Okla., 1959-61; research fellow NIH, 1962-66; instr. pharmacology U. Mo., Columbia, 1966-68, asst. prof., 1968-69; intern, U. Mo. Med. Center, 1968-69; family practice, New Castle, Ind., 1969-89, med. dir. VA Clinic, Lawton, Okla., 1989-94, Comanche County Hosp., 1994—; clin. assoc. prof. family medicine U. Okla. Coll. Medicine, 1989—; adj. assoc. prof. pharmacology U. Okla. Coll. Medicine, 1989—; mem. U. Okla. Coll. Medicine Admissions Bd., 1995—; mem. staff Henry County Meml. Hosp., New Castle, 1969-89; guest prof. pharmacy and pharmacology Butler U. Coll. Pharmacy, Indpls., 1970-75; owner, dir. Carthage Clinic, 1975-89; clin. assoc. prof. family medicine Ind. U. Coll. Medicine, 1986-89; county physician, jail med. dir. Henry County, Ind., 1976-89. Bd. dirs. Lawton Philharmonic, 1990-95. Recipient Cert. of merit in Pharmacol. and Clin. Med. Research, 1970; Med. Student Research Essay award Am. Acad. Neurology, 1968. Fellow Am. Acad. Family Physicians, Am. Coll. Physician Execs.; mem. AMA (ann. award recognition 1975—), Ind. State Med. Assn., Am. Coll. Sports Medicine, AAAS, N.Y. Acad. Sci., Am. Soc. Contemporary Medicine and Surgery, Festival Chamber Music Soc. (bd. dirs. Indpls. 1981-87), Nat. Fraternity Eagle Scouts, Mensa, Phi Sigma, Sigma Xi. Clubs: Columbia, Skyline (Indpls.), Country, Kiwanis. Lodge: Elks. Author: (with Blissitt and Stanaszek, Lea and Febiger) Clinical Pharmacy Practice, 1972; contbr. 30 articles to profl. jours. Home: 30 Quail Creek Dr NW Lawton OK 73501-9026

WEBB, PAUL, physician, researcher, consultant, educator; b. Cleve., Dec. 2, 1923; s. Monte F. and Barbara (Webb) Bourjaily; m. Eileen Whalen, Mar. 13, 1948; children: Shaun P., Paul S. Webb Womacks. BA, U. Va., 1943, MD, 1946; MS in Physiol., U. Wash., 1951. Asst. prof. physiol. U. Okla. Sch. Medicine, Oklahoma City, 1952-54; chief environ. sect. Aeromed. Lab., Wrights-Patterson AFB, Ohio, 1954-58; prin. assoc. Webb Assocs., Yellow Springs, Ohio, 1959-82; vis. scientist INSERM, Paris, 1983; vis. prof. U. Limburg, Maastricht, The Netherlands, 1986, U. Uppsala, Sweden, 1988-89; clin. prof. Wright State U. Sch. Medicine, Dayton, Ohio, 1980—; cons. aerospace and undersea medicine, Yellow Springs, Ohio, 1958-90; cons. energy balance and thermal physiology, Yellow Springs, 1980—. Author: Human Calorimeters, 1985; contbr. articles to profl. jours. Village councilman Village of Yellow Springs, Ohio, 1969-75; mem. Air Force Scientific Adv. Bd., Washington, 1984-88. Recipient Ely award Human Factors Soc., 1972. Fellow Aerospace Med. Assn. (Aerospace Indsl. Life Scis. Assn. award 1969), Am. Inst. Med. and Biol. Engring.; mem. Am. Physiol. Soc., Am. Soc. for Clin. Nutrition, Undersea Med. Soc. (oceaneering internat. award 1979, pres. 1980-81). Home and Office: 370 Orton Rd Yellow Springs OH 45387

WEBB, PETER JOHN, surgeon; b. London, Mar. 10, 1947; s. Jack and Margaret Florence (Marden) W.; m. Pamela Dorothy Burch, Sept. 20, 1975; children: Ian, Kathryn, Clare. MB BS, Middlesex Hosp. Med. Sch., London, 1972; MS, London U., 1977. Cert. recognised tchr., examiner in surgery U. London. H.S. Middlesex Hosp., 1972-73; surg. resident Grenfell Assn., St. Anthony, Can., 1974-75; SHO Radcliffe Infirmary, Oxford, Eng., 1975; registrar Orset Hosp., Essex, Eng., 1975-81; registrar Kings Coll. Hosp., London, 1975-81, sr. registrar, 1981-86; cons. surgeon Medway NHS Trust, Kent, Eng., 1986—. Co-author: The Clinical Anatomy of Practical Procedures, 1975; co-author surgeons-in-tng. ednl. program, 1995. Mem. oun. Grenfell Assn. of Gt. Britain and Ireland, 1985—. Fellow Royal Coll. Surgeons; mem. Brit. Med. Assn., Brit. Assn. of Surg. Oncologists, Assn. Surgeons. Office: St Bartholomews Hosp, New Rd, Rochester ME1 1DS, England

WEBB, ROBERT MARK, psychiatrist; b. Ft. Leonardwood, Mo., Sept. 1, 1953; s. Robert O. and Betty Jo (Griffin) W.; m. Patricia Holland, Oct. 10, 1981; 2 children. BS in Microbiology, Ohio State U., 1975, MD, 1980. Intern U. Pitts. Hosp./Western Psychiat. Inst. and Clinic, 1981; resident in psychiatry Western Psychiat. Inst. and Clinic, Pitts., 1981-84; fellow in consultation and liaison psychiatry Western Psychiat. Inst. and Clinic, 1985; instr. psychiatry Western Psychiat. Inst. and Clinic, Pitts., 1985, asst. prof. psychiatry, 1986-89; neuropsychiatrist Allegheny Neuropsychiat. Inst., Oakdale, Pa., 1989-90; pvt. practice, 1990—; clin. researcher in treatment of depression in primary care WPIC, 1991-94; psychiat. cons. East Liberty Family Health Care Ctr., Pitts., 1983-84; cons. neurology clinic U. Pitts., 1984-85, Montefiore Hosp., Pitts., 1986-87, memory clinic Alzheimer Disease Rsch. Ctr., Pitts., 1986-89; clin. adj. asst. prof. psychiatry Med. Coll. of Pa., Allegheny Campus, 1990—; med. dir. Pitts. Pastoral Inst., 1992—; presenter in field. R.T. Lewis scholar, 1971-75, Kellogg scholar, 1975-80. Mem. Am. Psychiat. Assn., Pa. Psychiat. Assn. Episcopalian. Office: 230 N Craig St Pittsburgh PA 15213-1565

WEBB, TIMOTHY ALLAN, podiatrist; b. Paintsville, Ky., Oct. 13, 1961; s. Charles Otis and Emma Sue (Wells) W.; m. Mary Kathryn Givan, Aug. 3, 1985; children: Brittany Suzanne, Mary Katelyn, Hannah Rose. BS, Morehead (Ky.) State U., 1983; D in Podiatric Medicine, Ohio Coll. Podiatric Medicine, Cleve., 1987. Diplomate Am. Bd. Podiatric Surgery. Preseptor Office of Roderick Fuller, Columbus, Ohio, 1987-88; resident VA Med. ctr., Huntington, W.Va., 1989-90; co-owner Foot Care Assocs., Paintsville, Ky., 1990—; mem. staff Our Lady of Bellefonte Hosp., Ashland, Ky., 1990—, Highlands Regional Med. Ctr., Prestonsburg, Ky., 1990—; cons. H.R.M.C. Diabetic Ctr., Prestonsburg, Ky., 1992—. Pres. sch. bd. our Lady of the Mountain Sch., Paintsville, Ky., 1994-95. Fellow Am. Coll. Foot and Ankle Surgeons; mem. Am. Podiatric Med. Assn. Office: Foot Care Assocs. 1110 S Mayo Trail Paintsville KY 41240

WEBBE, FRANK MICHAEL, psychology educator; b. Vero Beach, Fla., Oct. 13, 1947; s. Richard St. Clare and Virginia Peggy (Buckles) W.; m. Ellen Marie Kane, Sept. 6, 1969; children: Elizabeth St. Clare, Tristan Kane. BA in Psychology, U. Fla., 1969, MS in Psychology, 1971, PhD in Psychology, 1974. Diplomate Am. Bd. Adminstrv. Psychology. Interim asst. prof. U. Fla., Gainesville, 1974-75; research assoc. U. Miss., University, 1975-78; research asst. prof. U. Miss., 1976-78; asst. prof. Fla. Inst. Tech., Melbourne, 1978-80; assoc. prof. Fla. Inst. Tech., 1980-86, prof. psychology, 1986—, chmn. dept. psychology, 1979-85, dean Sch. Psychology, 1985-93. Author: Food Addiction: Understanding the Problem, 1988; contbr. articles to profl. jours. Prin. investigator Food Addiction Hot Line, Melbourne, 1987-94; pres. Crisis Svcs., Brevard, Inc., Rockledge, Fla., 1992; chmn. E. Ctrl. Fla. Memory Disorder Clinic. NSF traineeship, 1970-74. Mem. Am. Psychol. Assn., Nat. Acad. Neuropsychology, Human Factors Soc., Southeastern Psychol. Assn. Democrat. Home: 1687 Henley Rd NW Melbourne FL 32907-6328 Office: Sch Psychology Fla Inst Tec 150 W University Blvd Melbourne FL 32901-6982

WEBBER, JOHN BENTLEY, orthopedic surgeon; b. Morritown, N.J., Jan. 27, 1941; s. George Bentley and Gladys (Moody) W.; m. Mary Christina Thometz, Feb. 25, 1978; children: John Bentley, Edward Alan. B.A., Lehigh U., 1962; M.D., Temple U., 1966. Intern Rochester Gen. Hosp., N.Y., 1966-67; resident Temple U. Med. Ctr., Phila., 1967-70; Stelrling Bunnell fellow in hand surgery Pacific Med. Ctr., San Francisco, 1971; practice medicine specializing in orthopedic surgery and surgery of hand Phila., 1973—; assoc. prof. orthopedic surgery and rehab. Hahnemann Med. Coll. and Hosp., Phila., 1973—, chief sect. on hand surgery, 1973—; attending surgeon St. Christopher's Hosp. for Children, Phila., 1996—; cons. in hand surgery Mcpl. Med. Svcs., Phila., 1973-87, USPHS, Phila., 1973-76, burn ctr. St. Agnes Med. Ctr., Phila., 1973—, Phila. unit Shriners' Hosp. for Crippled Children, 1979-95. Served to maj. USAF, 1971-73. Fellow ACS (Pa. com. on trauma), Am. Acad. Orthopedic Surgeons; mem. AMA, Am. Soc. for Surgery of Hand, Bunnell Hand Club (pres. 1978-80), Assn. for Acad. Surgery, Eastern Orthopedic Soc., Pa. Med. Soc., Phila. Orthopedic Soc., Phila. Hand Soc. (pres. 1987-89), Phila. County Med. Soc., Phila. Coll. Physicians, Meigs Med. Assn., Rotary, Union Leauge, Riverside Yacht Club (fleet surgeon), Phila. Country Club, Delaware Valley Ducks Unltd. (chmn. 1983-88). Republican. Congregationalist. Home: 1139 Rock Creek Rd Gladwyne PA 19035-1439 Office: 221 N Broad St Philadelphia PA 19107-1511

WEBBER, LARRY STANFORD, biostatistician, researcher; b. New Orleans, Apr. 1, 1945; s. Abraham and Fanny (Stone) W.; m. Rhoda Marsha Binder, Aug. 13, 1967; children: David H., Howard A. BS, La. State U., 1967; MPhil, Yale U., 1970, PhD, 1973. Rsch. assoc. Community Health Care Ctr. Plan, New Haven, 1971-72; statistician Atomic Bomb Casualty Commn., Hiroshima, Japan, 1972-74; asst. prof. biostats. La. State U. Med. Ctr., New Orleans, 1974-79, assoc. prof., 1979-84; prof. La. State U. Med. Ctr., 1984-91; prof., chair dept. biostat. and epidemiology Tulane U. Sch. Pub. Health and Tropical Medicine, New Orleans, 1991—; cons. Brooks County Heart Study, Corpus Christi, 1983-86; grant reviewer Nat. Heart, Lung, Blood Inst., Bethesda, Md., 1983—. Author: Cardiovascular Risk Factors in Children, 1980; editor monograph; reviewer Preventive Medicine, 1988—, Pediatrics, 1987—. Nat. Heart, Lung, Blood Inst. grantee, 1987—. Mem. APHA, Am. Heart Assn., Biometric Soc., Sigma Xi. Democrat. Jewish. Office: Tulane U Sch Pub Health and Tropical Medicine 1501 Canal St New Orleans LA 70112-2817

WEBER, ADELHEID LISA, former nurse, chemist; b. Cottbus, Germany, June 1, 1934; came to the U.S., 1958; d. Johannes Gustav Paul and Johanna Katinka (Askevold) Haertwig; m. Joseph Cotrell Weber (dec. 1986), Oct. 25, 1957; children: Robert Andreas, Miriam Lisa. RN, Stadtisches Hosp., Dortmund, Germany, 1956; BS in Distributive Sci., Am. U., 1983; MBA, U. Md., 1991. RN. Nurse Krankenhaus, Wuppertal, Germany, 1956-57; pvt. nurse Wellesley, Mass., 1969-74; lab. tech. Microbiol. Assoc., Bethesda, Md., 1979-84; switchboard operator Best Products Co., Bethesda, 1983-87; lab. tech. Uniformed Svcs. U. Health Scis., Bethesda, 1984-90; info. rsch. tech. Info. Rsch. Internat. Inc., Bethesda, 1987; chemist USDA, Beltsville, Md., 1990-93; ret., 1993. Vol. Sibley Meml. Hosp., Washington, 1991. Recipient Cert. award County of Montgomery, Md., 1988, Whitman Walker Clinic, 1987. Mem. NAFE, Soc. for Rsch. Adminstrs., Am. Chem. Soc., Nat. Assn. for Amputees, Soc. for Applied Spectroscopy, Nat. Trust for Historic Preservation, Hemlock Soc. Nat. Capital Area, Nat. Mus. for Women in Arts, Wash. Performing Arts Soc. Home: 23 Sunset Ln Osterville MA 02655-2035

WEBER, CAROL MARTINEZ, physician; b. N.Y.C., May 5, 1950; d. Eduardo and JAcqueline Martinez; children: Julia, Andres. Student, Mt. Holyoke Coll., 1968-70; BA, Williams Coll., 1972; MD, Tufts U., 1981. House officer Mt. Sinai Hosp., N.Y.C., 1981-83; house officer St. Vincents Hosp., N.Y.C., 1983-84, chief resident, 1984-85, attending physician, 1985—; asst. prof. N.Y. Med. Coll., Valhalla, 1986—; cons. in field. Contbr. articles to profl. jours. and chpts. to books. Bd. trustees Corleais Sch., N.Y.C., 1987. Grantee N.Y. State Dept Health, N.Y.C., 1993-94, 94-95, 95, McKinnoy Healthcare for Homeless, N.Y.C., 1993-94, USPHS, N.Y.C., 1995. Fellow Am. Coll. Physicians, Am. Coll. Preventive Medicine; mem. Am. Acad. Physicians, Physicians for Social Responsibility, Physicians for Prevention of Nuclear War, Alpha Omega Alpha. Office: St Vincents Hosp 153 W 11th St New York NY

WEBER, CHARLES ALFRED, II, internist, rheumatologist; b. Harrisburg, Pa., Apr. 9, 1953; s. Otto Roy and Alberta May (Finch) W.; m. Kathy Anne Shearman, June 19, 1982; children: Charles Alfred, Drew Thomas, Alexia Anne, Chad Christian. BA in Physics and Math., Franklin and Marshall Coll., 1974; MS in Physics, Lehigh U., 1976; MD with honors, Autonomous U. Guadalajara, Mex., 1981; postgrad., U. Medicine and Dentistry N.J., 1981-82. Diplomate Am. Bd. Internal Medicine, Am. Bd. Rheumatology. Tchg. asst. in physics Lehigh U., Bethlehem, Pa., 1974-76; intern in medicine Jersey Shore Med. Ctr., Neptune, N.J., 1982-83, resident in medicine, 1983-85, asst. and assoc. attending dept. medicine and rheumatology, 1987-96, attending, 1996—; pvt. practice, Neptune, 1987—; instr. medicine U. Medicine and Dentistry Robert Wood Johnson Med. Sch., Piscataway; cons. in internal medicine (rheumatology) Point Pleasant (N.J.) divsn. Med. Ctr. Ocean County, 1987—, Brick divsn., Bricktown, 1987—; mem. pateint svcs. com. N.J. chpt. Arthritis Found., Iselin, 1994—. Contbr. articles to med. jours. Fellow Am. Coll. Rheumatology; mem. AMA, ACP, AAAS, N.J. Rheumatism Soc., N.J. Med. Soc., Monmouth County Med. Soc., Space Studies Inst., N.Y. Acad. Scis., Sigma Pi Sigma. Roman Catholic. Office: Shore Rheumatology Assocs 10 Neptune Blvd Ste 106 Neptune NJ 07753

WEBER, CHARLES WALTER, nutrition educator; b. Harold, S.D., Nov. 30, 1931; s. Walter Earl and Vera Jean (Scott) W.; m. Marylou Merkel Adam, Feb. 3, 1961; children: Matthew, Scott. BS, Colo. State U., 1956, MS, 1958; PhD, U. Ariz., 1966. Research asst. U. Ariz., Tucson, 1963-66, asst. prof., 1966-68, assoc. prof., 1969-72, prof. nutrition, 1973—; cons. Hermosillo, Mex., 1970-74, Inst. of Health, Cairo, 1981-82, U. Fortaleza, Rio de Janiero, 1986. Contbr. articles to sci. jours. Served as cpl. U.S. Army, 1952-54. Mem. Am. Assn. Cereal Chemists, Am. Inst. Nutrition, Inst. Food Technologists, N.Y. Acad. Scis., Am. Soc. Clin. Nutrition, Poultry Sci. Assn., Ariz. Referees Assn., Sigma Xi. Club: Randolph Soccer (Tucson) (pres. 1976-79). Home: 4031 E Calle De Jardin Tucson AZ 85711-3410 Office: U Ariz Dept Nutritional Sci 309 Shantz Bldg Tucson AZ 85721

WEBER, GEORG FRANZ, immunologist; b. Erlangen, Germany, July 7, 1962; came to U.S., 1989; s. Otto and Margret (Hartung) W.; m. Chitra Edwin, Sept. 21, 1991; 1 child, Ramona Sara. BS, Ohm-Gymnasium, Erlangen, Germany, 1981; MD, Julius Maximilians U., Wuerzburg, Germany, 1988, PhD, 1988. Rsch. assoc. U. S. Ala., Mobile, 1989; rsch. fellow dept. biochemistry and Dana-Farber Cancer Inst. Harvard U., Boston, 1990-91, rsch. assoc. dept. pathology and Dana-Farber Cancer Inst., 1991-93, instr., 1993—. Contbr. articles to profl. jours. Mem. Amnesty Internat., N.Y.C., 1991--. Deutsche Forschungsgemeinschaft fellow, 1989-91. mem. AMA, Deutscher Aerzteverband, Oxygen Soc. Office: Dana-Farber Cancer Inst 44 Binney St Boston MA 02115-6013

WEBER, JAN RICHARD, cardiologist; b. Manotowoc, Wis., Feb. 23, 1948; s. Joseph John and Geraldine Lillian (Novak) W.; m. Doreen Lea Newell, Aug. 14, 1981; children: Courtney Beth, Andrew Jameson. BA with honors, U. Wis., 1970, MD, 1974. Bd. cert. in internal medicine, cardiovascular diseases. Internal medicine intern Hahnemann Hosp., Phila., 1974-75, internal medicine resident, 1975-77, cardiovascular diseases fellow, 1977-79; dir. noninvasive cardiology Grad. Hosp., Phila., 1979-84; dir. cardiac ultrasound lab. Presbyn. Med. Ctr., Phila., 1984-91; chief divsn. cardiology Our Lady of Lourdes Med. Ctr., Camden, N.J., 1991—; med. dir. N.J. Heart Inst., Our Lady of Lourdes Med. Ctr., Camden, 1992—; dir. cardiovascular fitness One-on-One Sports Tng. Ctr., Phila., 1985-88. Author chpts. to books; mem. editl. bd. Jour. Med. Edn., 1973-75, Med. Info. Sys., 1979-80; contbr. articles to profl. jours. Bd. dirs. Am. Heart Assn., Camden County, N.J., 1993-94; master com. Peer Review Orgn. of N.J., East Brunswick, 1994—. Recipient Harry Farrell Tchg. award Grad. Hosp., Phila., 1981. Fellow Am. Coll. Cardiology, Am. Heart Assn. (bd. dirs. Camden County 1993-94), Am. Coll. Physicians; mem. Am. Coll. Physician Execs., Am. Soc. Echocardiography, Camden County Med. Soc. Republican. Presbyterian. Home: 1125 Rock Creek Rd Gladwyne PA 19035 Office: Our Lady of Lourdes Med Ctr 1600 Haddon Ave Camden NJ 08103

WEBER, JANET M., nurse; b. Lansdale, Pa., Mar. 12, 1936; d. Russell H. and Naomi (dec.) Moyer W. Diploma in nursing, Washington County Hosp. Sch. Nursing, 1959; B.S. in Nursing, Grace Coll., 1960; M.Ed., Duquesne U., 1969. Staff nurse, supr. Murphy Med. Ctr., Warsaw, Ind., 1959-60; coll. nurse Grace Coll., Winona Lake, Ind., 1959-60; med. surg. nursing instr. Washington County Hosp. Sch. Nursing, Hagerstown, Md., 1961-64; pvt. duty nurse Washington County Hosp., Hagerstown, 1964; chmn. found. of nursing Presbyn. Univ. Hosp. Sch. Nursing, Pitts., 1964-72; curriculum coordinator Albert Einstein Med. Ctr. Sch. Nursing, Phila., 1972-73; assoc. dir. Albert Einstein Med. Ctr. Sch. Nursing, 1973-74, acting dir., 1974, dir., 1974-87; staff nurse ARC Penn-Jersey Blood Drive Donor Services, Phila., 1988-92, asst. nurse mgr., 1992—; nurse mgr. ARC Penn-Jersey Blood Drive Donor Svcs., Phila., 1992—; cons. Md. Bd. Higher Edn., 1981-82. Author: The Faculty's Role in Policy Development, 1981, Assisting Students with Educational Deficiencies, 1975. Mem. Washington County Hosp. Nurses Alumni Assn. (pres. 1962-64), Grace Coll. Alumni Assn., Duquesne U. Alumni Assn. Republican. Home: 5640 Arbor St Philadelphia PA 19120-2502 Office: ARC Blood Donor Svcs 700 Spring Garden St Philadelphia PA 19123-3508

WEBER, LINDA FICKLIN, clergy, therapist; b. Columbia, Mo., Mar. 11, 1926; d. Nathan Clyde and Helen Othelia (Erickson) Ficklin; m. Joseph Ralph Weber, Sept. 29, 1946; children: Barry, Cynthia, Amy, Gwen. BA cum laude, Elmhurst Coll., 1968; MS, No. Ill. U., 1975; grad., Gestalt Inst. of Chgo., 1982; D Ministry, Bethany Theol. Sem., Oakbrook, Ill., 1993. Ordained to ministry Ch. of the Brethren, 1995. Tchr. Dist. #45 Schs., Villa Park, Ill., 1968-74, counselor, 1974-84; therapist Linda Weber & Assocs., Villa Park, 1982-85; adminstrv. sec. Washington office Ch. of the Brethren, 1985-88; counselor Washington Pastoral Counseling Svc., 1988-89. Pres., Women for Meaningful Summits, Washington, 1985—; caucus chair Nat. Women's Conf. Com., 1989—; mem. Dist. 45 Sch. Bd. Mem. AACD, Am. Assn. Pastoral Counselors, Alpha Xi Delta. Home: 806 E 13th St Lombard IL 60148-4739

WEBER, PAUL A., opthalmologist, medical educator, researcher; b. Olney, Ill., Aug. 2, 1949; m. Lesley Jones; children: Justin, Tory. Student, Ohio State U., 1967-70; MD, Northwestern U., 1974. Diplomate Am. Bd. Ophthalmology. Chief resident Ohio State U., Columbus, 1977-78, assoc. prof. ophthalmology, 1978-84, prof. ophthalmology, 1989—, chmn. dept. opthalmology, 1989—. Contbr. numerous articles to profl. jours., chpts. to books. Recipient rsch. grants Burroughs-Wellcome Co., SISA, Inc., Snyder Fund, Schering Corp., The Bremer Fund, Am. Med. Optics, Nat. Eye Inst. NIH, H.G. PARS Pharm. Labs., Inc.. Mem. Am. Acad. Ophthalmology, Assn. Rsch. in Vision and Ophthalmology, Am. Glaucoma Soc., Columbus and Franklin County EENT Soc., Columbus and Franklin County Acad. Medicine, Ohio Soc. Prevention of Blindness (voting mem.), Ohio Lions Eye Rsch. Found., Alpha Omega Alpha. Home: 1624 Essex Columbus OH 43221 Office: Glaucoma Consultants Inc 456 West 10th Ave Columbus OH 43201

WEBER, PAUL FREDERICK, medical services manager, pharmacist, educator; b. Cleve., Mar. 21, 1960; s. Paul Henry and Anna (Papastathis) W.; m. Ann Marie Vinci, June 29, 1985. BS, Rutgers Coll. Pharmacy, 1983; MD, U. Med. Dental N.J., 1987. Diplomate Am. Bd. Internal Medicine; reg. pharmacist, N.J. Pharm. scientist Parke-Davis divsn. Warner-Lambert Co., Morris Plains, N.J., 1983; staff pharmacist Wallkill Valley Gen. Hosp., Sussex, N.J., 1984; rsch. asst. UMDNJ-Robert Wood Johnson Med. Sch., Piscataway, N.J., 1985; clin. asst. prof. medicine UMDNJ-Robert Wood Johnson Med. Sch., New Brunswick, N.J., 1990—; asst. med. dir. Health and Scis. Rsch., Inc., Englewood, N.J., 1990, assoc. med. dir., 1990-92, safety officer, 1991-92; dir. clin. rsch. Medicis Pharm. Co., Phoenix, 1992-93; v.p. med. affairs Girgenti, Hughes, Butler and McDowell, Inc., N.Y.C., 1993-95; med. svcs mgr. Hoffmann-La Roche, Inc., Nutley, N.J., 1995—. Recipient Roche Patient Communication award Rutgers U., 1983; Rotary Achievment scholar, 1981. Mem. ACP, AMA, Am. Coll. Physician Execs. Office: Hoffman-La Roche Inc 340 Kingsland St Nutley NJ 07110

WEBER, RALPH, cardiologist; b. Balt., Mar. 11, 1929; s. Jacob and Pearl (Schmuckler) W.; m. Suzan Babitt, Mar. 27, 1960; 1 child, Clifford. BS, Franklin & Marshall Coll., 1949; MD, Temple U., 1954. Diplomate Am. Bd. Internal Medicine, Cardiovascular Diseases. Intern, resident Sinai Hosp. Balt., 1954-57; resident surgeon USPHS Hosp., S.I., N.Y., 1957-59; fellow cardiology Johns Hopkins Hosp., Balt., 1959-61; cardiologist Johns Hopkins Hosp., Sinai Hosp., Balt., 1961-90; staff physician Johns Hopkins Med. Svcs. Corp., Balt., 1990-92; cardiologist Sinai Hosp. Balt., 1992—; dir. coronary care unit Luth. Hosp. Md., Balt., 1975-80; cons. Social Security Adminstrn., Balt., 1961-92. Contbr. chpts. in books and articles to profl. jours. Co-prin. investigator NIH, 1994—. Fellow Am. Coll. Cardiology (cons.), Am. Heart Assn. Coun. Clin. Cardiology; mem. Am. Soc. Internal Medicine, Am. Soc. Echocardiography, Md. Soc. Cardiology, Johns Hopkins Med. and Surg. Assn. Home: 6 Barstad Ct Lutherville MD 21093 Office: Hoffberger Profl Bldg 2435 W Belvedere Ave Baltimore MD 21215

WEBER, ROY RICHARD, internist; b. Independence, Kans., Dec. 11, 1946; s. Raymond Albert and Betty Jean (Banning) W.; m. Connie Jeanne Toews, June 2, 1973; children: Sarah Louise, Michael Thomas. BA in Chemistry, U. Kans.; MD, U. Kans., Kansas City, 1973. Intern, then resident St. Francis Hosp., Wichita, Kans., 1973-74, resident, 1974-76; pvt. practice Newton, Kans., 1976-85; clin. pharm. fellow U. Chgo., 1985-87; internist Hertzler Clinic, Halstead, Kans., 1987—. Fellow ACP; mem. Am. Soc. Hypertension, Am. Autonomic Soc. Home: 720 NE 36th Newton KS 67114 Office: Hertzler Clinic 327 Chestnut Halstead KS 67056

WEBER, STEVEN JOHNSON, emergency flight nurse; b. Frankfort, Ky., May 11, 1962; s. Robert Lee and Alice (Dews) W. Diploma, Appalachian Sch. Practical Nursing, 1982; ADN, Ky. State U., Frankfort, 1988. RN, Ky.; cert. flight RN, CEN; cert. BCLS, ACLS, ACLS instr., PALS, BTLS, TNCC ENPC instr. Staff nurse med./surg. unit King's Daus. Meml. Hosp., Frankfort, 1982-88; staff nurse pediatric ICU U. of Ky. Med. Ctr., Lexington, 1988-89; charge nurse emergency dept. U. Ky. Albert B. Chandler Med. Ctr., Lexington, 1989-92; flight nurse Careflight Air Med. St. Joseph Hosp., Lexington, 1992-94, chief flight nurse, 1994-96; flight nurse Life Flight, Duke U. Med. Ctr., Durham, N.C., 1996—. Mem. AACN, Emergency Nurses Assn., Nat. Flight Nurses Assn. Home: 5110 Copper Ridge Dr #6-101 Durham NC 27707

WEBSTER, CATHERINE ALICE, nurse, auditor; b. San Rafael, Calif., Apr. 5, 1958; d. Robert E. and Helen L. (Niemeyer) W. AS in Nursing, Coll. of Marin, 1979; BS in Nursing, Sonoma State U., 1982. RN, Calif.; cert. pub. health nurse, Calif.; cert. trainer, auditor. Nurses aide Profl. Nurses Bur., San Rafael, 1978-79; staff nurse Novato Community Hosp., Calif., 1979-84; allergy nurse, office mgr., Novato, 1984-93; ind. contractor, ins. examiner Hooper-Holmes, Inc., Hayward, Calif., 1983-86, Am. Paraprof. System, Walnut Creek, Calif., 1985-86, Phys. Measurements Info., San Ramon, Calif.; med. records auditor, external audit coordinator Am. Cons. Inc., Las Vegas, Nev., 1986-89; R.N. evaluator Am. Claims Evaluations, Inc., Los Angeles, 1984-91, hosp. bill auditor for Equifax Svcs. (now Equifax Cost Mgmt. Sys. HBA divsn.), San Francisco Metroplex, San Ramon, Calif., 1987—. Avocations: miniatures, stamps, crafts, reading. Home: 10 Bret Ct Novato CA 94947-3904

WEBSTER, DOUGLAS PETER, emergency physician; b. Chgo., July 4, 1957; s. David Ferguson and Margaret Webster; m. Mariruth K. Burkhart, Sept. 25, 1989. BA in Chemistry, BS in Psychology, Loyola U., Chgo., 1978; MS in Chem. Physics, Wayne State U., 1980; DO, Chgo. Coll. Osteo. Medicine, 1985. Diplomate in emergency medicine Am. Osteo. Bd. Emergency Medicine, Am. Bd. Forensic Examiners. Intern Chgo. Coll. Osteo Medicine, 1985-86; resident in gen. surgery Sinai Hosp. Detroit, 1986-87; resident in emergency medicine Chgo. Coll. Osteo Medicine, 1988-90; clin. asst. prof. emergency medicine Chgo. Coll. Osteo. Medicine, 1990-93, clin. assoc. prof., 1993—; assoc. chmn. dept. emergency medicine, 1995—; assoc. chmn. emergency medicine Chgo. Coll. Osteo. Medicine, 1995—; assoc. dir. emergency svcs. Olympia Fields (Ill.) Osteo Med./Trauma Ctr., 1990-91; dir. emergency svcs. St. Anthony Hosp., Chgo., 1991-93; sr. ptnr. Med. Rev. Assocs., S.C., 1992—; chmn., med. dir. emergency medicine Little Co. of Mary Hosp., Evergreen Park, Ill., 1993-95; med. dir. Trauma Ctr. Columbia Olympia Fields (Ill.) Osteo. Med. Ctr., 1996—; assoc. clin. coord., cons. Crescent Counties Found. for Med. Care, 1992—; speaker in field. Diplomate in emergency medicine Am. Osteo. Bd. Emergency Medicine, Am. Bd. Forensic Examiners, Am. Bd. Forensic Medicine. Recipient award Disting. Physicians Am., 1991, Family Medicine award Lemmon Pharm. Found., 1985, others; Univ. Grad. fellow Wayne State U., 1979. Fellow Am. Coll. Osteo. Emergency Physicians; mem. Am. Bd. Forensic Examiners, Am. Bd. Forensic Medicine, Am. Coll. Emergency Physicians, Am. Osteo. Assn., Phi Lambda Upsilon, Alpha Epsilon Delta. Home: 4439 Cascara Ln Lisle IL 60532-4368 Office: Columbia Olympia Fields Osteo Med Ctr 20201 S Crawford Olympia Fields IL 60461

WEBSTER, EDWARD WILLIAM, medical physicist; b. London, Apr. 12, 1922; came to U.S., 1949, naturalized, 1957; s. Edward and Bertha Louisa (Cornish) W.; m. Dorothea Anne Wood, June 24, 1961; children: John Stein, Peter Wood, D. Anne, Edward Russell, Mark Vincent, Susan Victoria. BSc in Elec. Engring., U. London, 1943, PhD, 1946; postgrad., MIT, 1949-51, 65-66, Columbia U., 1966; AM (hon.), Harvard U., 1989. Diplomate: Am. Bd. Radiology in radiol. physics (examiner 1958-84, chmn. physics com. 1966-76), Am. Bd. Health Physics. Research engr. English Electric Co., Stafford, Eng., 1945-49; travelling fellow lab. for nuclear sci. MIT, 1949-50, staff scientist, 1950-51; lectr. U. London, 1952-53; physicist Mass. Gen. Hosp., Boston, 1953—, chief radiol. scis. div., 1970—; prof. radiology Harvard U. Med. Sch., Boston, 1975—; prof. radiology div. health scis. and tech. Harvard-MIT, 1978-86; Langham lectr. U. Ky. Coll. Medicine, 1989; mem. biol. effects of ionizing radiation com. NAS, 1977-80; adv. com. on environ. hazards VA, 1985—, Med. Use of Isotopes, U.S. Nuclear Regulatory Commn., 1971-93; U.S. del. UN Sci. Com. on Effects of Atomic Radiation, 1987—; lectr. Harvard Sch. Pub. Health, 1971-86; cons. Radiation Effects Rsch. Found., Hiroshima, Japan, 1988; Taylor lectr. Nat. Coun. on Radiation Protection, 1992, mem., 1965-89, hon. mem., 1989—, cons. Presdl. Adv. Com. on Human Radiation Experiments, 1994-95. Author: A Basic Radioisotopes Course, 1959, Atlas of Radiation Dose Distributions, 1965, Radiation Safety Manual of MGH, 1965, Physics in Diagnostic Radiology, 1970; co-author: Instrumentation and Monitoring Methods for Radiation Protection, 1978, Low-level Radiation Effects, 1982; co-editor: Advances in Medical Physics, 1971, Biological Risks of Medical Irradiations, 1980; inventor composite shields against low energy X-rays, 1970. Robert Blair travelling fellow London County Council, 1949; USPHS fellow, 1965; NIH grantee, 1958-80. Fellow Health Physics Soc. (Landauer award 1985, Failla award 1989), Am. Coll. Radiology (commn. mem. 1963—, Gold medal 1991), Am. Assn. Physicists in Medicine (dir. 1958-65, pres. 1963-64, Coolidge medal 1983); mem. Soc. Nuclear Medicine (trustee 1973-77), Radiol. Soc. N.Am. (v.p. 1977-78), New Eng. Roentgen Ray Soc. (hon., exec. com. 1976-77), Radiation Rsch. Soc., Sigma Xi (nat. lectr. 1988-89). Office: Mass Gen Hosp Fruit St Boston MA 02114-2620

WEBSTER, HENRY DEFOREST, neuroscientist; b. N.Y.C., Apr. 22, 1927; s. Leslie Tillotson and Emily (deForest) W.; m. Marion Havas, June 12, 1951; children: Christopher, Henry, Sally, David, Steven. AB cum laude, Amherst Coll., 1948; MD, Harvard U., 1952. Intern Boston City Hosp., 1952-53, resident, 1953-54; resident in neurology Mass. Gen. Hosp., 1954-56, research fellow in neuropathology, 1956-59; prin. investigator NIH research grants for electron microscopic studies of peripheral neuropathy, 1959-69; mem. staffs Mass. Gen., Newton-Wellesley hosps.; instr. neurology Harvard Med. Sch., 1959-63, assoc. in neurology, 1963-66, asst. prof. neuropathology, 1966; assoc. prof. neurology U. Miami Sch. Medicine, 1966-69, prof., 1969; head sect. cellular neuropathology Nat. Inst. Neurol. Diseases and Stroke, Bethesda, Md., 1969—; assoc. chief Lab. of Neuropathology and Neuroanat. Scis., 1975-84; chief Lab. Exptl. Neuropathology, 1984—; disting. scientist, lectr. dept. anatomy Tulane U. Sch. Medicine, 1973; Royal Coll. lectr. Can. Assn. Neuropathologists, 1982; Saul Korey lectr. Am. Assn. Neuropathologists, 1992; chmn. Winter Conf. on Brain Rsch., 1985, 86; head neuropathology delegation to visit China in 1990, Citizen Amb. Program, People to People Internat.; mem. exec. com. rsch. group on neuromuscular disease World Fedn. Neurology, 1986-93. Author: (with A. Peters and S.L. Palay) The Fine Structure of the Nervous System, 1970, 76, 91; contbr. articles to sci. jours. Recipient Superior Svc. award USPHS, 1977, A. von Humboldt award Fed. Republic Germany, 1985, Sci. award Peripheral Neuropathy Assn., 1994; named hon. prof. Norman Bethune U. of Med. Scis., Chanchun, China, 1991. Mem. Am. Assn. Neuropathologists (v.p. 1976-77, pres. 1978-79, Weil award 1960), Internat. Soc. Neuropathology (councillor 1976-80, v.p. 1980-84, exec. com. 1980-84, 86-94, pres. 1986-90), Internat. Congress Neuropathology (sec. gen. VIII 1978), Peripheral Nerve Study Group (exec. com. 1975-93, chmn. 1977 meeting), Japanese Soc. Neuropathology (hon.), Am. Neurol. Assn., Am. Acad. Neurology, Am. Soc. Cell Biologists, Am. Assn. Anatomists, Soc. Neurosci., Rotary Internat., Washington Ctr. Photography, Ausable Club. Office: NIH Bldg 36 Rm 4A 29 Bethesda MD 20892

WEBSTER, JAMES RANDOLPH, JR., physician; b. Chgo., Aug. 25, 1931; s. James Randolph and Ruth Marian (Burtis) W.; m. Joan Burchfield, Dec. 28, 1954; children: Susan, Donovan, John. B.S., U. Chgo.-Northwestern U., 1953; M.D., M.S., Northwestern U., 1956. Diplomate: Am. Bd. Internal Medicine (sub bd. pulmonary disease and geriatrics). Resident in medicine, NIH fellow in pulmonary disease Phila. Gen. Hosp., 1956-57; resident in medicine and fellow in pulmonary disease Northwestern U., 1957-60, 62-64; asst. chief medicine Northwestern Meml. Hosp., Chgo., 1968-73; chief medicine Northwestern Meml. Hosp., 1973-88; prof. medicine Northwestern U. Med. Sch., 1977—, chief gen. med. sect. Dept. Medicine, 1987-88; chief exec. officer Northwestern Med. Group Practice, 1978-88; dir. ctr. on aging/geriatrics Northwestern U. Med. Ctr., 1988—; chief staff Northwestern Meml. Hosp., 1988-90. Contbr. chpts. to books, articles to med. jours. Served with U.S. Army, 1960-62. Recipient Outstanding Clin. tchr. award Northwestern U. Med. Sch., 1974, 77, 84, 86, Alumni Merit award Northwestern U., 1979. Mem. Am. Fedn. Clin. ACP (gov. for Ill. 1988-92, chair sub-com. on aging 1993—, Claypoole award 1994), Am. Thoracic Soc., Am. Geriatrics Soc., Ill. Geriatrics Soc. (pres. 1992-94), Soc. Rsch. and Edn. in Geriatrics. Home: 227 E Delaware Pl Chicago IL 60611-1713 Office: 750 N Lake Shore Dr Rm 601 Chicago IL 60611-4403

WEBSTER, JOHN KINGSLEY OHL, II, health administrator, rehabilitation manager; b. L.A., July 27, 1950; s. John Kingsley Ohl and Inez (Gilbert) W.; m. Marcia Lanier McKnight, June 16, 1977; children: David Lilly, Jason Kingsley McKnight. AA, Pasadena (Calif.) City Coll., 1973; BS, San Jose (Calif.) State U., 1975; MS, Calif. State U., L.A., 1989. Registered occupational therapist, Calif. Supervising occupational therapy cons. San Gabriel Valley Regional Ctr., 1976-79; supr. II occupational therapy cons. San Diego Regional Ctr., 1979-83; sr. occupational therapist Mesa Vista Hosp., 1983-84; pvt. practice Vista, Calif., 1983-85; occupational therapy cons. Calif. Children Svcs., State Dept. Health Svcs., L.A., 1985-86, regional adminstrv. cons., 1986-90; dir. occupational therapy Eureka Gen. Hosp., 1990; dir. ops. and mktg. Life Dimensions Inc., Newport Beach, Calif., 1990; occupational therapy cons., licensing and cert. Calif. Dept. Health Svcs., 1990-93; program dir. rehab. svcs. Scripps Meml. Hosp., Encinitas, Calif., 1993-94; dir. rehab. Vista (Calif.) Knoll, 1994; clin. dir. occupational therapy

Sundance Rehab., San Diego, 1994-95; regional dir. ops. Quest Rehab, L.A., 1995—; area mgr. Am. Therapy Svc.; cons. Hopi and Navajo Tribes, Winslow, Ariz., 1978; dir. Imperial County SPRANS grant, El Centro, Calif., 1986-88; pres., owner Kingsley Constrn., Vista, 1988—. Artist (sculpture) Free Form (3d pl. award 1973), (oil painting) Jamaican Woman (3d pl. award 1979). Recipient Esquire title Lady Elliott of STOBS, Edinburough, Scotland, 1973, spl. dept. recognition Calif. State U., 1989. Mem. Am. Occupational Therapy Assn., Inst. Profl. Health Svc. Adminstrs., Student Assn. of Am. Coll. Health Care Execs.

WEBSTER, LESLIE TILLOTSON, JR., pharmacologist, educator; b. N.Y.C., Mar. 31, 1926; s. Leslie Tillotson and Emily (de Forest) W.; m. Alice Katharine Holland, June 24, 1955; children—Katharine White, Susan Holland, Leslie Tillotson III, Romi Anne. B.A., Amherst Coll., 1947, Sc.D. (hon.), 1982; student, Union Coll., 1944; M.D., Harvard U., 1948. Diplomate: Am. Bd. Internal Medicine. Rotating intern Cleve. City Hosp., 1948-49, jr. asst. resident in medicine, 1949-50; asst. resident medicine Bellevue Hosp., N.Y.C., 1952-53; research fellow medicine Harvard and Boston City Hosp. Thorndike Meml. Lab., 1953-55; from demonstrator to instr. Sch. of Medicine Western Res. U., 1955-60; research assoc. to sr. instr. biochemistry Case Western Res. U. Sch. Medicine, 1959-60, asst. prof. medicine, 1960-70, asst. prof. biochemistry, 1960-65, asst. prof. pharmacology, 1965-67, asso. prof., 1967-70, prof. pharmacology, 1976-92, chmn. pharmacology dept., 1976-91, prof. pharmacology dept. emeritus, 1992, prof. medicine, 1980-86; prof., chmn. pharmacology dept. Northwestern U. Med. and Dental Sch., 1970-76. Served to lt. USNR, 1950-52. Russell M. Wilder fellow Nat. Vitamin Found., 1956-59; Sr. USPHS Research fellow, 1959-61; Research Career Devel. awardee, 1961-69; Macy faculty scholar, 1980-81. Mem. ACP (life), Central Soc. Clin. Rsch. (emeritus), Am. Soc. Clin. Investigation (emeritus), Am. Soc. Biochemistry and Molecular Biology (emeritus), Assn. Med. Sch. Pharmacology (emeritus), Am. Soc. Pharmacology and Exptl. Therapeutics (emeritus). Home: 2728 Leighton Rd Cleveland OH 44120-1325 Office: Univ Hosps of Cleve Rainbow Babies and Childrens Hosp 2074 Abington Rd Cleveland OH 44106-2602

WEBSTER, RAYMOND EARL, psychology educator, psychotherapist; b. Providence, Dec. 3, 1948; s. Earl Harold and Madeline (D'Antuono) W.; m. Angela Grenier, Jan. 31, 1984; children: Matthew Raymond, Patrick Gregory, Timothy Andrew. BA, R.I. Coll., 1971, MA, 1973; MS, Purdue U., 1976; PhD, U. Conn., 1978. Diplomate Am. Bd. Forensic Examiners; lic. psychologist, N.C. Dir. pupil svcs. and spl. edn. Northeastern Area Regional Edn. Svcs., Wauregan, Conn., 1978-79; dir. alternative vocat. sch. Capital Region Edn. Coun., West Hartford, Conn., 1979-83; prof. psychology, dir. sch. psychology program East Carolina U., Greenville, N.C., 1983—; rsch. assoc. edni. psychology U. Conn., Storrs, 1976-78; cons. Bolton (Conn.) Pub. Schs., 1976-78, Columbia (Conn.) Pub. Schs., 1976-78, N.C. Dept. Instrn., Raleigh, 1983—; speaker at profl. meetings. Guest reviewer Jour. Applied Behavior Analysis, 1975, Clin. Psychology Pub. Co., 1992, Psychol. Reports, 1993—, Perceptual and Motor Skills, 1993—; mem. editl. bd. Psychology in Schs., 1987—; contbr. numerous articles to profl. jours., chpts. to books. Trustee N.C. Ctr. for Advancement of Teaching, Cullowhee, 1990-93. Sgt. U.S. Army Spl. Forces N.G., 1969-75. Recipient spl. distinction award Conn. Assn. Sch. Psychologists, 1983. Mem. APA, Am. Coll. Forensic Examiners (cert. Forensic Examiner), Nat. Assn. Sch. Psychologists (cert., alt. del. 1985-86, spl. distinction in profl. devel. 1982, 83), Nat. Acad. Neuropsychology, Sigma Xi. Methodist. Home: 200 Williams St Greenville NC 27858-8712 Office: East Carolina U Rawl Bldg Greenville NC 27834-4353

WEBSTER, STEPHEN BURTIS, physician, educator; b. Chgo., Dec. 3, 1935; s. James Randolph Webster and Ruth Marion (Burtis) Holmes; m. Katherine Griffith Webster, Apr. 4, 1959; children: David Randolph, Margaret Elizabeth, James Lucian. BS, Northwestern U., 1957, MD, 1960. Diplomate Am. Bd. Dermatology. Intern Colo. Gen. Hosp., Denver, 1960-61; resident Walter Reed Gen. Hosp., Washington, 1962-65; staff physician Henry Ford Hosp., Detroit, 1969-71, Gundersen Clinic, La Crosse, 1971—; assoc. clin. prof. U. Wis., Madison, 1976—, U. Minn., Mpls., 1978—. Lt. col. U.S. Army, 1962-69. Fellow Am. Acad. Dermatology (sec.-treas. 1985-88, pres. 1991), Am. Bd. Dermatology (dir. 1992—); mem. AMA, Am. Dermatol. Assn., Wis. State Med. Soc., La Crosse County Med. Soc., Soc. Investigative Dermatology, Alpha Omega Alpha. Republican. Congregationalist. Home: 2062N Wedgewood Dr E La Crosse WI 54601 Office: Gundersen Clinic Ltd 1836 South Ave La Crosse WI 54601-5429

WEBSTER, THOMAS GLENN, psychiatrist; b. Topeka, Jan. 23, 1924; s. Guy Welland and Iva Amanda (Keefover) W.; m. Mary Tupper Dooly, June 27, 1948; children—Warnie Louise, Guy Weyman, David Michael. AB, Ft. Hays State Coll., 1946; MD, Wayne State U., 1949. Intern Los Angeles County Gen. Hosp., Calif., 1949-50; resident in psychiatry Mass. Mental Health Ctr., Boston, 1953-55, resident in child psychiatry, 1955-56; resident in child psychiatry James Jackson Putnam Children's Ctr., Boston, 1956-58; dir. presch. program for retarded children Greater Boston, 1958-62; coordinator 3d yr. med. student psychiatry clerkship Harvard U. Med. Sch.-Mass. Mental Health Ctr., Boston, 1960-63; practice medicine specializing in psychiatry Boston, 1953-62, Bethesda, Md., 1963-72, Washington, 1972—; tng. specialist psychiatry, then chief continuing edn. br. NIMH, Bethesda, Md., 1963-72; prof. psychiatry George Washington U., Washington, 1972-86, chmn. dept. psychiatry and behavioral scis., 1972-75, prof. emeritus, 1986—; vis. prof. Harvard U. Med. Sch., 1980-83, McLean Hosp., 1980-86; U.S.-Poland exchange health scientist, 1981. Pres. Woodhaven Citizens Assn., 1971-72. Served with AUS, 1943-46; as sr. asst. surgeon USPHS, 1951-53. Fellow Am. Psychiat. Assn., Am. Coll. Psychiatrists, Am. Coll. Psychoanalysts; mem. Assn. Acad. Psychiatry (pres. 1976-78), Group Advancement Psychiatry. Home: 8506 Woodhaven Blvd Bethesda MD 20817-3117 Office: 2112 F St NW Washington DC 20037-2715

WECHSLER, ARNOLD, osteopathic obstetrician, gynecologist; b. N.Y.C., June 10, 1923; s. David and Eva (Kirsch) W.; m. Marlene Esta Jurnovoy, Sept. 11, 1955 (div. Sept. 1986); children: Diane, Paul, Stewart. Grad., Rutgers U.; DO, Phila. Coll. Osteo. Medicine, 1952. Diplomate Am. Bd. Osteo. Obstetricians and Gynecologists; lic. physician, Pa., N.Y., Fla. Intern Hosps. of Phila. Coll. Osteo. Medicine, 1952-53, resident in obstetrics/gynecology and gen. surgery, 1953-56; lectr. in obstetrics and gynecology Nursing Sch. Phila. Coll. Osteo. Medicine; founder, mem. staff Tri County Hosp., Delaware County, Pa., from 1960, chief staff, 1960-62, chief dept. obstetrics and gynecology surgery, 1960-77, dir. med. edn., 1968-71; attending and cons. in obstetrics and gynecol. surgery Met. Hosp., Phila., 1956-60, 71-75; chief dept. obstetrics and gynecology Humana Hosp.-South Broward, Hollywood, Fla., 1980-84; cons. and attending in gynecol. surgery Drs. Hosp. of Hollywood, 1982-86; insp. for intern and resident tng. programs Bur. Hosps. of Am. Osteo. Assn., 1965-66; founder, med. dir. Women's Med. Svcs., 1973-77, Nutrients Inc., Phila., 1977-79, Supplements Inc., Phila., 1979-80, Alternative Lifestyle Ctr., Fla., 1983-86; founder, dir. A.W. Profl. Consultants, Inc.; cons. Practice Mgmt. Group, Med Temps Plus, Plantation, Fla.; provider ambulatory gyn. surgery for multiple gyn ctrs. in Dade, Broward and Palm Beach Counties, Fla. Author: Dr. Wechsler's New You Diet, 1978. Staff Sgt. Signal Corps, USAF, 1942-46, PTO, Japan. Fellow Am. Coll. Osteo. Obstetricians and Gynecologists, Internat. Coll. Applied Nutrition; mem. Am. Osteo. Assn., Pa. Osteo. Med. Assn., Philadelphia County Osteo. Soc., Fla. Osteo. Med. Assn., Broward County Osteo. Med. Assn., Am. Soc. Bariatric Physicians, Assn. Maternal and Child Welfare, Internat. Acad. Preventive Medicine, Inst. Food Technologists, Coun. for Responsible Nutrition, Internat. Coll. Gynecologic Laparoscopists, Assn. Reproductive Health Profls.

WECHSLER, JAMES STEPHEN, anesthesiologist; b. N.Y.C., June 6, 1943; s. Leonard and Ruth Shirley (Cain) W.; m. Eva Veronica Erdos, July 23, 1972; children: David, Mark, Carolyn. BS, U. Chgo., 1965; PhD, Loyola U., Chgo., 1969; MD, Med. Coll. Wis., 1973. Diplomate Am. Bd. Anesthesiology, Pain Mgmt. Rsch. assoc. dept. anesthesiology Med. Coll. Wis., Milw., 1969-73; resident Mass. Gen. Hosp., Boston, 1973-74, 75-76; intern Cambridge (Mass.) Hosp., 1974-75; staff anesthesiologist South Shore Hosp., S. Weymouth, Mass., 1976—; clin. fellow Harvard Med. Sch., Boston, 1973-76; cons. anesthesiology New Eng. Sinai Hosp., Stoughton, Mass., 1987—, Braintree (Mass.) Hosp., 1989—. Contbr. articles to profl. jours. Fellow Am. Coll. Anesthesiologists; mem. AMA (Physician's Recognition award), Soc. Critical Care Medicine, Soc. Critical Care Anesthesiologists (founder), Reflex Sympathetic Dystrophy Syndrome Assn., Mass. Soc. Anesthesiologists. Jewish. Office: South Shore Anesthesia Inc 74 Pleasant St South Weymouth MA 02190

WECKEL, GLENN W., chiropractor; b. Towanda, Ga., May 1, 1960; s. Glenn A. and Barbara A. (Mesley) W.; m. Leigh Anne Leatherwood, Aug. 13, 1983; children: Jason Mark, Jessica Leigh, Alicia Nicole. BS, Bob Jones U., 1982; DC, Nat. Coll. Chiropractic, 1986. Pvt. practice Wilmington, N.C., 1987—. Active bd. Wilmington Christian Acad., 1992-94. Mem. Am. Chiropractic Assn., N.C. Chiropractic Assn. Republican. Baptist. Home: 7611 Mallow Rd Wilmington NC 28405 Office: 3015 Market St Wilmington NC 28403

WECKER, WILLIAM A., preventive medicine physician, neuropsychiatrist; b. N.Y.C., Mar. 14, 1923; s. Philip and Ruth (Frumkin) W.; m. Norma Cairney (dec. 1993); 1 child, Lyle Jeffery. BA, NYU, 1943, MD, 1946; MPH in Adminstrn., Harvard U., 1950; diploma Sch. Aviation Medicine, USAF, 1953. Lic. physician, surgeon, psychiatrist, N.Y.; cert. treating physician N.Y. State Workmen's Compensation Bd.; qualified psychiatrist N.Y. State Dept. Mental Health. Intern Bellevue Hosp., N.Y.C., 1946, Bayonne Gen. Hosp., 1946-47; health officer N.Y.C. Health Dept., 1948-50; dist. health officer N.Y. State Health Dept., Albany, 1950-52; pvt. practice medicine N.Y.C., 1954-59; grad. Sch. Aviation Medicine USAF, 1953; resident in psychiatry U.S. VA Hosp., N.Y.C., 1959-62, psychiatrist, 1962-64; psychiatrist Riverside Hosp., N.Y.C. Hosp. Dept., 1964-65, Postgrad. Ctr. for Mental Health, N.Y.C., 1964-65; pvt. practice preventive medicine, neuropsychiatry N.Y.C., 1948—; advisor Pan Am. Med. Assn., N.Y.C., 1952-55; cons. World Med. Assn., N.Y.C., 1954-61; staff physician Meml. Hosp., Queens, N.Y., 1955-64, Springfield (Mass.) Hosp., 1970-71; civil def. lectr. N.Y.C. Dept. of Health, 1955-58; advisor, charter mem. Acad. Religion and Mental Health, N.Y.C., 1959-62; psychiatrist, mgmt. cons., advisor in staff devel. program Youth House, N.Y.C., 1963-71; psychiatrist, cons. Mahoney Health Ctr., N.Y.C. Dept. Health, Bklyn., 1964-71; psychiatrist N.Y. State Narcotic Addiction Control Commn., 1970-71; med. examining physician N.Y.C. Workers Compensation Bd., 1971-76. Author: 3rd World Economics, 1981, Psychecology for Everybody, 1983, Comprehensive Psychenomics, 1983, American Confetti, 1990, Anatomy of an Asylum, 1968, The Story of "H", 1971, The Honduran Syndrome, 1973, Devil's Den, 1978, Growing Up in Honduras, 1980. Cons. Allen Haus, Zurich, 1990-91; advisor English Gentlemen's Club, Zurich, 1982-87, Centro Cultural, Honduras, 1978-82; corr. Harry Schulz Internat. Newsletter, Switzerland and monaco, 1983-91. 2d lt. U.S. Army, 1943-45, ATO, capt. MC-USAF, 1952-54, ETO. Fellow Nat. Poliomyelitis Found., 1949-50, U.S. VA, 1960-61, NIMH fellow Postgrad. Ctr. for Mental Health, N.Y.C., 1964-65; recipient 50th Anniversary cert. NYU, 1996. Mem. Acad. Medicine Bklyn. (life), Nat. Inst. Mental Health, N.Y. State Med. Soc. (life, citation for 50 yrs. of svc. 1996), N.Y. Coun. Child Psychiatry, Kings County Med. Soc. (life), Royal Soc. Health (London). Home and Office: 52 Macdougal St # 1-a New York NY 10012-2937

WEDBERG, STANLEY EDWARD, microbiology educator; b. Bridgeport, Conn., Aug. 28, 1913; s. Frank Enock and Anna Mathilda (Osterlund) W.; m. Mary Elizabeth Stewart, June 28, 1941; children: Karen Elizabeth Wedberg Miller, Robin Carol Wedberg Brown. BS, U. Conn., 1937; PhD, Yale U., 1940. Instr. Yale U. Med. Sch., New Haven, Conn., 1941; instr. U. Conn., Storrs, 1941-43, asst. prof. microbiology, 1946-50, assoc. prof., 1950-59, prof., 1959-69, head dept., 1955-66; microbiologist Southwestern Coll., Chula Vista, Calif., 1969-80; free-lance lectr. and cons. San Diego, 1980—; pres. Conn. Pub. Health Assn., Hartford, 1960-61, Conn. Adv. Com. Food and Drugs, Hartford, 1952-53, 62-63, mem. 1952-69; host 39-week TV series Survival, Channel 8, New Haven, 1968-69. Author: (texts.) Microbes & You, 1954, Paramedical Microbiology, 1963, Introduction to Microbiology, 1966; author 13 biographies of scientists World Book Ency., 1962; contbr. articles to profl. jours. V.p. Conn. Adv. Clean Air Task Force, Hartford, 1968-69; mem. Conn. Gov.'s Clean Water Task Force, Hartford, 1967-68. Served to capt. U.S. Army, 1943-46, ETO, lt. col. Res. ret. Recipient Outstanding Tchr. award U. Conn., 1963. Fellow Am. Acad. Microbiology (charter); mem. AAAS, Zool. Soc. San Diego, Mil. Order World Wars, Phi Kappa Phi, Soc. Sigma Xi. Republican. Presbyterian. Club: Friends of Classics (San Diego) (dir. 1984—). Home and Office: 3361 Ullman St San Diego CA 92106-2426

WEDEL, CHERYL STRUM, social worker; b. Richmond, Va., Nov. 7, 1963; d. Michael David and Sylvia Marie (Arthurs) Strum; m. Stuart William Wedel, Oct. 17, 1992; 1 child, Joshua. BS in Social Work, Va. Commonwealth U., 1986, MSW, 1989. Social worker VA Med. Ctr., Hunter Holmes McGuire Hosp., Richmond, 1988-89, Libbie Convalescent Ctr., Richmond, 1989-90; social worker, discharger planner Riverside Tappahannock (Va.) Hosp. & Skilled Nursing Home, 1990-91; case mgr., social worker Healthsouth Med. Ctr. Rehab. Unit, Richmond, 1991-92; admissions coord. Marshall (Va.) Manor, 1993; social worker, discharge planner Prince William Hosp., Manassas, Va., 1993—. Mem. NASW, Va. Orgn. Hosp. Social Workers, Prince William Interfaith Vol. Caregivers (bd. 1994-95).

WEDNER, H. JAMES, physician, researcher; b. Pitts., May 12, 1941; s. Benjamin Mayer and Lucille Ruth (Jacobs) W.; m. Maureen Patricia Martin, June 18, 1978; children: Bryna Kimberly, Jason Oliver. BS, Cornell U., 1963; MD, Cornell Med. Coll., N.Y.C., 1967. Intern Barnes Hosp., St. Louis, 1867-68; resident internal medicine Washington U. Med. Sch., St. Louis, 1970-71; fellow allergy and immunology Wash. U. Med. Sch., 1971-73; lt. comdr. USPHS, Govenor's Island, N.Y., 1968-70; dir. tng. program allergy and immunology Washington U. Med. Sch., St. Louis, 1986-95, chief clin. allergy and immunology, 1988—, prof. medicine, 1990—; vis. prof. Am. Coll. of Allergy and Immunology, Little Rock, Ark., 1991; prin. investigator psychosocial aspects of asthma, St. Louis Asthma Study Unit; chmn. steering com. Nat. Coop. Inner City Asthma Study. Editor: Allergy: Theory and Practice, 1984, 2d rev. edit., 1991; mem. editl. bd. Jour. Immunology, 1980-82, Jour. Allergy and Clin. Immunology, 1991-96. Fellow Am. Acad. Allergy Asthma Immunology; mem. Internat. Soc. Immunopharmacology, Am. Coll. Allergy Asthma Immunology, Am. Ass. Immunology, Clin. Immunology Soc. Office: Washington U Med Sch Campus Box 8122 600 S Euclid Ave Saint Louis MO 63110-1010

WEED, LAWRENCE L., pharmacology educator; b. Troy, N.Y., Dec. 26, 1923; married, 1952; 5 children. BA, Hamilton Coll., 1945; MD, Coll. Physicians & Surgeons, 1947. Asst. prof. medicine and pharmacology Sch. Medicine Yale U., 1954-56; dir. medicine edn. Eastern Maine Gen. Hosp., Bangor, 1956-60; asst. prof. microbiology Case Western Reserve U., 1961-64, assoc. prof., 1964-69; prof. cmty. medicine U. Vt., 1969-82, emeritus prof. Coll. Medicine, 1982—; pres. PKC Corp., 1984—; prof. medicine, dir. outpatient clinic Cliv. Met. Gen. Hosp., 1964-69; dir. Promis Lab., 1969-81; chief scientist Promis Info. Sys., Inc., 1981-82. Recipient Gustav O. Lienhard award, 1995. Mem. Am. Coll. Physicians, Am. Soc. Microbiology. Address: RFD 1 Box 630 Cambridge VT 05444-9611 Office: U Vt Burlington VT 05405

WEED, ROGER OREN, rehabilitation educator and counselor; b. Bend, Oreg., Feb. 2, 1944; s. Chester Elbert and Ruth Marie (Urie) W.; m. Paula J. Keller; children: Nicholette, Andrew. BS in Sociology, U. Oreg., 1967, MS in Rehab. Counseling, 1969; PhD in Rehab. Counseling, U. Ga., 1986. Cert. rehab. counselor; cert. disability mgmt. specialist; lic. profl. counselor. Vocat. rehab. counselor State of Alaska, Anchorage, 1969-71; instr. U. Alaska, Anchorage, 1970-76; counselor Langdon Psychiat. Clinic, Anchorage, 1971-74; from asst. dir. to exec. dir. Hope Cottages, Anchorage, 1974-79; owner Profl. Resources Group, Anchorage, 1978-80; mng. ptnr. Collins, Weed & Assocs., 1980-84; assoc. dir. Ctr. for Rehab. Tech. Ga. Tech. U., Atlanta, 1986-87; catastrophic injury rehab. Weed & Assocs., Atlanta, 1984—; assoc. prof. Ga. State U., Atlanta, 1987—; adj. faculty Ga. Inst. Tech. Co-author: Vocational Expert Handbook, 1986, Transferable Work Skills, 1988, Life Care Planning: Spinal Cord Injured, 1989, 94, Life Care Planning: Head Injured, 1994, Life Care Planning for the Amputee, 1992, Rehab Consultant Handbook, 1994; mem. editl. bd. Jour. of Pvt. Sector Rehab., Athens, Ga., 1986—; mem. Disting. Editl. Bd. Vanguard Series in Rehab., Athens, 1988—; contbr. articles to profl. publs. Recipient Gov.'s award Gov.'s Com. on Employment, Alaska, 1982, Goldpan Svc. award Gov.'s Com. on Employment, Alaska, 1978, Profl. Svcs. award Am. Rehab. Counselors Assn., 1993. Fellow Nat. Rehab. Assn. (chair legis. com., bd. dirs. met. Atlanta chpt. 1988—, pres. Pacific region 1983-85, pres.'s award Pacific region 1986), Nat. Assn. Rehab. Profls. in Pvt. Sector (chair resh. and tng. com. 1988-93, pres. 1994-95, Educator of the Yr. award 1991), Nat. Brain Injury Assn., Pvt. Rehab. Suppliers Ga., Rehab. Engring. Soc. N.Am., Anchorage Amateur Radio Club. Republican. Methodist. Office: 9th Fl College of Education Ga State U Dept Counseling Atlanta GA 30303

WEEDER, RICHARD STOCKTON, surgeon; b. Phila., Sept. 2, 1936; s. Stephen Dana and Caroline Denny (Nixon) W.; m. Areta Oebel Parle, May 17, 1987; children by previous marriage: Erica Crispin, Megan Alexandra; 1 stepchild, Annika Oebel. BA, Princeton U., 1958; MD, U. Pa., 1962. Diplomate Am. Bd. Surgery. Intern Germantown Hosp., Phila., 1962-63; surg. resident Geisinger Med. Ctr., Danville, Pa., 1963-67; gen. surgeon Hunterdon Med. Ctr., Flemington, N.J., 1969—. Author: Surgeon: The View From Behind the Mask, 1988, 91. Trustee Princeton Day Sch., 1982-85; founding trustee Princeton Friends Sch., 1987-91. Fellow ACS. Mem. Soc. Friends. Home: 45 Green Ave Lawrenceville NJ 08648-1623 Office: Hunterdon Med Ctr Dept Surgery Flemington NJ 08822

WEEKER, ELLIS, emergency physician; b. New Orleans, June 7, 1944; s. Harry and Marion W.; m. Gail Otis, July 3, 1982; children: Michael, Lisa, Elizabeth, Matthew. BS, Tulane U., 1966; MD, La. State U., 1970. Diplomate Am. Bd. Emergency Medicine. Intern Kaiser Found. Hosp., Oakland, 1970-71, resident in internal medicine, 1972-73; resident in internal medicine Highland Gen. Hosp., Oakland, 1972-73, assoc. chief emergency svcs., 1973-75; staff physician Calif. Emergency Physicians Med. Group, Oakland, 1975—, also bd. dirs.; med. dir. capitation svcs. Calif. Emergency Physicians/Medamerica, 1994—; med. dir. Calif. Emergency Physicians Med. Group, Oakland, 1976-95, regional med. dir., 1978—, chmn. bd. dirs., 1979-87; mem. staff Good Samaritan Hosp., San Jose, Calif., 1975—, chmn. emergency dept., 1977-82; mem. staff South Valley Hosp., Gilroy, Calif., 1990—. Commnr. Emergency Med. Care Commn., Santa Clara County, Calif., 1990-92. Mem. Am. Heart Assn. (chmn. bd. Santa Clara chpt. 1991-92, pres. 1988-89, nat. affiliate faculty ACLS 1982-91). Republican. Roman Catholic. Office: Calif Emergency Physicians Med Group 588 Blossom Hill Rd San Jose CA 95123

WEEKS, BOB LEE, osteopathic physician; b. Merced, Calif., July 30, 1942; s. Frank Lee and Beatrice Mae (Lawrence) W.; m. Kathleen Kay Sears, Nov. 22, 1972 (div. June 1974); m. Karen Frances Terry, June 21, 1977 (dec. Mar. 1991); children: Teresa Dawn Torres, Bonny Lee; m. Lynda Joyce Wheeler, Aug. 21, 1993. BS, East Cen. State U., 1965; MS, U. Okla., Oklahoma City, 1975; DO, Okla. State U., 1978; DD (hon.), Universal Life Ch., Modesto, Calif., 1988. Diplomate Am. Bd. Forensics, Am. Bd. Forensic Medicine. Chemist SunRay DX Oil Co., Tulsa, 1965; linguist USAF, Frankfort, Fed. Republic Germany, 1965-69, Athens, Greece, 1965-69; chemist Sun Oil Co., Tulsa, 1969-72; rsch. asst. U. Okla. Health Scis. Ctr., Oklahoma City, 1972-75; med. sch. intern Coll. Osteo. Medicine Okla. State U., Tulsa, Oklahoma City, 1975-79; pvt. practice osteopathy Oklahoma City, 1979-84; emergency room physician Coastal Emergency Svc./SW Med. Assn., Wichita Falls, Victoria, Tex., 1984-86; pvt. practice osteopathy Porum, Quinton, Okla., 1986-88, Edmond, Okla., 1989—; assoc. teaching staff Coll. of Osteopathy, Okla. State U., Oklahoma City, 1979-84; dir. emergency svc. Hillcrest Hosp., Oklahoma City, 1979-80, Bethania Regional Med. Ctr., Wichita Fall, Tex., 1984-85. Capt. USAR, 1983-86. Decorated Nat. Def. medal, Air medal. Mem. Am. Coll. Forensic Examiners (bd. cert. forensic examiners, bd. cert. forensic medicine), Am. Coll. Gen. Practitioners in Osteo. Medicine, Exptl. Aircraft Assn. Home and Office: 10012 Cedar Trl Edmond OK 73034-8661

WEEKS, GWENDOLEN BRANNON, nurse, educator; b. Durham, N.C., Aug. 23, 1943; d. Gus Travers and Valerie Dunster (Baker) B.; m. John Luther Weeks, May 28, 1983; step-children: Cynthia Weeks Kelly, John Luther Weeks Jr. BS in nursing, U. N.C., 1967; MS, Med. Coll. Va., 1971. Maternity staff nurse N.C. Meml. Hosp., Chapel Hill, 1967-68; obstetrics instr. Watts Hosp. Sch. Nursing, Durham, N.C., 1968-69; maternity instr. U. N.C., Greensboro, N.C., 1971-72; clin. specialist Petersburg (Va.) Gen. Hosp., 1972-77; assoc. prof. J. Sargeant Reynolds Community Coll., Richmond, Va., 1977—; clin. assoc., staff nurse St. Mary's Hosp., Richmond, 1969-83. Bd. dirs. Jr. League of Richmond, 1969—; hospitality bd. dirs. Hist. Richmond Coun., 1987-93. Mem. Nat. AWOHN (cert. inpatient obstetric nursing 1987—), Nurses Assn. Am. Coll. Ob-Gyn. (Richmond sect. chmn. 1972-74), Nat. Soc. for Colonial Dames, George Mason Meml. Soc., Sigma Theta Tau (sec. 1974-77). Home: 3803 Timber Ridge Rd Midlothian VA 23112-4539 Office: J S Reynolds Community Coll 8th Jackson St Richmond VA 23232

WEEKS, LIONEL EDWARDS, orthopedic surgeon; b. Rockville Ctr., N.Y., Jan. 19, 1947; m. Sue Jensen, 1973; childen: Edward Jesse, Lionel Tyler. AB magna cum laude, Williams Coll., 1968; MD, Columbia U., 1973. Diplomate Am. Bd. Orthop. Surgery, Am. Bd. Emergency Medicine. Pvt. practice emergency medicine Wasatch Emergency Physicians, Salt Lake City, Utah, 1975-82; pvt. practice orthop. surgery Orthop. Specialty Hosp., Salt Lake City, 1985—; clin. instr. orthop. surgery U. Utah Sch. of Medicine, Salt Lake City, 1986-91, clin. asst. prof., 1991—; chmn. shoulder guidelines com. Utah State Indsl. Commn., 1994-95. Fellow Am. Acad. Orthop. Surgeons; mem. Western Orthop. Assn., Arthroscopy Assn. N. Am., Internat. Coll. Surgeons, N.Y. Orthop. Hops. Alumni Assn. Home: 1485 Alta Cir Salt Lake City UT 84103 Office: Orthop Specialty Hosp 5848 S 300 E Salt Lake City UT 84107

WEEKS, PAUL MARTIN, plastic surgeon, educator; b. Clinton, N.C., June 11, 1932; m. Doris Hill, Apr. 28, 1956; children: Christopher, Heather, Paul, Thomas, Susan, Phillip. AB, Duke U., 1954; MD, U. N.C., 1958. Diplomate Am. Bd. Surgery, Am. Bd. Plastic Surgery. Intern N.C. Meml. Hosp., Chapel Hill, 1959-62, asst. resident in surgery, 1962-63, chief resident in gen. surgery, 1962-63, chief resident in plastic surgery, 1963-64; from instr. to asst. prof. surgery U. Ky., Louisville, 1964-68, assoc. prof. surgery, 1968-70; prof. surgery, plastic and reconstructive surgery, head of div. Washington U. Sch. Medicine, St. Louis, 1971—; plastic surgeon-in-chief Barnes Hosp., St. Louis, 1971—, St. Louis Children's Hosp., 1971—. Assoc. editor Jour. Hand Surgery, 1976—, Plastic and Reconstructive Surgery, 1978-84; contbr. articles to profl. jours. Mem. AMA, ACS (gov. 1991—), Soc. Univ. Surgeons, So. Med. Assn., Am. Surg. Assn., So. Surg. Assn., Assn. Academic Surgeons, Am. Cleft Palate Assn., Am. Soc. Plastic and Reconstructive Surgeons, Am. Soc. Surgery of the Hand, Plastic Surgery Research Council, Am. Burn Assn., Am. Assn. Plastic Surgeons (pres. elect 1990-91, pres. 1991-92), Am. Assn. Plastic and Reconstructive Surgeons, Mo. State Med. Assn., St. Louis Med. Soc., Canadian Soc. Plastic and Reconstructive Surgeons, Nathan Womack Soc. Republican. Home: 6470 Ellenwood Ave Saint Louis MO 63105-2229 Office: Barnes Hosp Barnes Hospital Plz Saint Louis MO 63110

WEEKS, ROBERT J., microbiologist, researcher, consultant; b. Quapaw, Okla., Feb. 19, 1929; s. Robert Orvill and Mildred E. (Davis) W.; m. Betty Sue Martin, May 10, 1949; children: Joseph Earl, Karen Sue, Patricia Robin. BS, S.W. Mo. State U., 1961. Correctional officer U.S. Dept. Justice, Springfield, Mo., 1955-62; mycology microbiologist Ctr. for Disease Control HEW, Kansas City, Kans., 1962-73; microbiologist, mem. licensure and proficiency testing staff Ctr. for Disease Control HEW, Atlanta, 1973-79; mycology microbiologist Ctr. for Disease Control U.S. Dept. Health & Human Svcs., Atlanta, 1979-85; cons. Rogers, Ark., 1985—; chief soil ecology unit Ecol. Investigations Program, Ctr. for Disease Control, Kansas City, 1962-73, head soil ecology lab. Mycotic Div., 1979-85. Contbr. chpts. to books, over 70 articles to profl. jours. 1st lt. U.S. Army, 1946-48, 50-52, Korea. Mem. Mycological Soc. Am. (emeritus). Home and Office: 12790 We Be Ln Rogers AR 72756-7969 also: 720 S Scott St Republic MO 65738-2223

WEEKS, SANDY CLAIRE, medical researcher; b. Adelaide, Australia, Sept. 18, 1950; d. Henry Vernon and Valda Dorothy (Wahlqvist) W. Student in med. sci., U. So. Australia, Adelaide, 1977-82. Justice of the Peace. Surgical rsch. asst. Adelaide U., 1968-76; surgical rsch. asst. Flinders U. Med. Ctr., Adelaide, 1976-81, med. rsch. scientist, 1982-88, sr. med. rsch. scientist, 1989—; lectr. in biol. scis. So. Australian Colls. for Advanced Edn.,

Adelaide, 1973-78; dir. Flinders Credit Union, 1985—; devel. cons. Diagnostic Rsch. Labs., Australia, 1987-90; spkr. Asian & Pacific Fedn. Cancer Rsch. and Control, Bangkok, 1993. Author: The Anti-Cancer Cookbook, 1990, 2d edit., 1993, How Not to Take Medicine, 1995; contbr. articles to profl. jours. Cmty. preceptor in preventive cancer edn. Mem. N.Y. Acad. Scis., Australian Inst. Med. Scientists (spkr.), Internat. Soc. Preventive Oncology (spkr.), Australian and New Zealand Soc. Cell Biology. Office: Flinders U Dept Pathology, Flinders Med Ctr, Bedford Park 5042, Australia

WEEMS, ALAN M., neurosurgeon; b. Jonesboro, Ark., Nov. 24, 1952; m. Karen R. Martin, July 11, 1987. BA, U. Ark., 1977; MD, U. Ark., Little Rock, 1981. Diplomate Am. Bd. Neurol. Surgery. Resident in neurosurgery Tulane U. Affiliated Hosps., New Orleans, 1981-87; asst. clin. dir. Charity Hosp., New Orleans, 1987; pvt. practice neurol. surgery Columbus, Ga., 1987-88, Oak Ridge, Tenn., 1988—. Fellow ACS; mem. AMA, Tenn. Med. Assn., So. Med. Assn., Am. Assn. Neurol. Surgeons, Congress Neurol. Surgeons, Phi Beta Kappa, Alpha Omega Alpha. Office: Neurol Surgery of Oak Ridge 200 New York Ave # 350 Oak Ridge TN 37830

WEG, JOHN GERARD, physician; b. N.Y.C., Feb. 16, 1934; s. Leonard and Pauline M. (Kanzleiter) W.; m. Mary Loretta Flynn, June 2, 1956; children: Diane Marie, Kathryn Mary, Carol Ann, Loretta Louise, Veronica Susanne, Michelle Celeste. BA cum laude, Coll. Holy Cross, Worcester, Mass., 1955; MD, N.Y. Med. Coll., 1959. Diplomate: Am. Bd. Internal Medicine. Commd. 2nd lt. USAF, 1958, advanced through grades to capt., 1967; intern Walter Reed Gen. Hosp., Washington, 1959-60; resident, then chief resident in internal medicine Wilford Hall USAF Hosp., Lackland AFB, Tex., 1960-64; chief pulmonary sect. Wilford Hall USAF Hosp., 1964-66, chief inhalation sect., 1964-66, chief pulmonary and infectious disease service, 1966-67; resigned, 1967; clin. dir. pulmonary disease div. Jefferson Davis Hosp., Houston, 1967-71; from asst. prof. to assoc. prof. medicine Baylor U. Coll. Medicine, Houston, 1967-71; assoc. prof. medicine U. Mich. Med. Sch. Univ. Hosp., Ann Arbor, 1971-74; prof. U. Mich. Med. Sch. Univ. Hosp., 1974—; physician-in-charge pulmonary div., 1971-81, physician-in-charge pulmonary and critical care med. div., 1981-85; cons. Ann Arbor VA, 1971—, Wayne County Gen. hosps., 1971-84; mem. adv. bd. Washtenaw County Health Dept., 1973—; mem. respiratory and nervous system panel, anesthesiology Sect. Nat. Ctr. Devices and Radiol. Health, FDA, 1983—, chmn., 1985-88. Contbr. med. jours., reviewer, mem. editorial bds. Decorated Air Force Commendation medal; travelling fellow Nat. Tb and Respiratory Disease Assn., 1971; recipient Aesculpaius award Tex. Med. Assn., 1971. Fellow Am. Coll. Chest Physicians (chmn. bd. govs. 1976-79, gov. Mich. 1975-79, chmn. membership com. 1976-79, prof.-in-residence 1972—, chmn. critical care coun. 1982-85), Am. Coll. Chest Physicians and Internat. Acad. Chest Physicians (exec. council 1976-82, pres. 1980-81), ACP (chmn. Mich. program com. 1974); mem. AAAS, Am. Fedn. Clin. Rsch., AMA, Am. Thoracic Soc. (sec.-treas. 1974-76), Am. Assn. Inhalation Therapy, Air Force Soc. Internists and Allied Specialists, Soc. Med. Consultants to Armed Forces, Internat. Union Against Tb, Mich. Thoracic Soc. (pres. 1976-78), Mich. Lung Assn. (dir., Bruce Douglas award 1981), Am. Lung Assn., Rsch. Club U. Mich., Assn. Advancement Med. Instrumentation, Central Soc. Clin. Rsch., Am. Bd. Internal Medicine (subsplty. com. on pulmonary disease 1980-86, critical care medicine test com. 1985-87, critical care medicine policy com. 1986-87), N.Y. Med. Coll. Alumni Assn. (medal of honor 1990), Alpha Omega Alpha. Home: 3060 Exmoor Rd Ann Arbor MI 48104-4132 Office: B I H 245 Box 0026 1500 E Medical Center Dr Ann Arbor MI 48109-0026

WEGMAN, MYRON EZRA, physician, educator; b. Bklyn., July 23, 1908; s. Max and Nettie (Finkelstein) W.; m. Isabel Howe, July 4, 1936; children: Judith (Mrs. John A. Hirst), David Howe, Jane (Mrs. David D. Dunatchik), Elizabeth Gooding (Mrs. Ralph A. Petersen). A.B., CCNY, 1928; M.D. cum laude, Yale U., 1932; M.P.H., Johns Hopkins U., 1938. Diplomate Am. Bd. Preventive Medicine, Am. Bd. Pediatrics (ofcl. examiner). Intern, asst. resident, resident in pediatrics New Haven Hosp., 1932-36; instr. pediatrics Yale U., 1933-36; cons. pediatrics Md. State Health Dept., 1936-41; asst. prof. child hygiene sch. Tropical Medicine, San Juan, P.R., 1941-42; dir. research and tng. in child health, dir. sch. health N.Y.C. Health Dept., 1942-46; instr. pediatrics and lectr. public health adminstrn. Johns Hopkins U., 1939-46; asst. prof. pediatrics and pub. health Cornell U., 1942-46; asst. prof. pub. health Columbia U., 1940-46; prof. pediatrics, head dept. La. State U., 1946-52; pediatrician-in-chief Charity Hosp., New Orleans, 1946-52; prof. public health Sch. Public Health, U. Mich., Ann Arbor, 1960-74; dean Sch. Public Health, U. Mich., 1960-74, dean emeritus, 1974—; prof. pediatrics U. Mich. Med. Sch., 1961-78, prof. emeritus, 1978—, chmn. div. health sci., 1970-74; John G. Searle prof. public health, 1974-78, emeritus, 1978—; vis. prof. U. Malaya, 1974, Centro Universitario de Salud Publica, U. Autónoma Madrid, 1990—, U Cin., 1993; external examiner Nat. U. Singapore, 1983; cons. Internat. Sci. and Tech. Inst., 1986—, Sch. Pub. Health U. Kinshasa, Zaire, 1987, Schs. Pub. Health Jakarta, Surabaya, Ujung Pandang, Medan, Semarang, Indonesia, 1988; coord. Mich.-Madrid Sch. Pub. Health collaboration, 1990—. Editor: Public Health in the People's Republic of China, 1973; author: also pediatrics and public health textbooks, articles in med. jours. Status of Pan American Centers; mem. editorial bd. Revista Mexicana de Salud Publica, 1990—. Chief divsn. edn. and tng. Pan-Am. San. Bur., Regional Office for Ams., WHO, 1952-56; sec. gen. Pan-Am. San. Bur., WHO Regional Office, 1957-60; pres. Assn. Schs. Pub. Health, 1963-66; pres. Comprehensive Health Planning Coun., S.E. Mich., 1970-74; trustee Pan-Am. Health and Edn. Found., 1970-85, 86-92, 94—, pres., 1984-85, chmn. devel. com., 1991—, v.p., 1996—; trustee Nat. San. Found., 1969-84, emeritus trustee, 1984—; pres. Physicians for Social Responsibility, Ann Arbor, 1987-92; mem. com. on carcinogenesis of pesticides Nat. Acad. Sci., 1977-79, com. on advanced study in China, 1978-82; chmn. Task Force in Nat. Immunization Policy, HEW, 1975-76; adv. com. Kellogg Nat. Fellowship Program, 1982—; rsch. adv. com. Resources for Future, 1978-84, spl. cons. State U. System Fla., 1982-87; mem. com. on prevention ctrs. CDC, 1986-84. Recipient Man of Yr. award CCNY, 1955; Clifford G. Grulee award Am. Acad. Pediatrics, 1958; Townsend Harris medal CCNY, 1961; Bronfman prize Am. Public Health Assn., 1967; Disting. Service award Mich. Public Health Assn., 1974; Walter P. Reuther award for disting. service United Auto Workers, 1974; Sedgwick medal Am. Pub. Health Assn., 1974; Outstanding Alumnus award Johns Hopkins Sch. Hygiene, 1982; Disting. Service award Delta Omega Soc., 1982; Spes Hominum award Nat. Sanitation Found., 1986, Disting. Alumnus award Yale U. Med. Sch., 1987; Spl. award Korean Soc. Preventive Medicine, 1989. Fellow AAAS, Royal Soc. Health (hon.); mem. Am. PEdiatric Soc., Soc. Pediatric Rsch., Am. Acad. Pediatrics, Am. Assn. World Health (v.p. 1979-82, 85-88, pres. 1982-84), Am. Pub. Health Assn. (chmn. exec. bd. 1965-70, pres. 1971-72), Fedn. Assn. Schs. Health Professions (1st pres. 1968-70), Soc. Exptl. Biol. and Medicine, Peruvian, Eduadorian, Artentinian Pediatric Socs. (hon.), P.R. Pub. Health Assn. (hon.), Sigma Xi, Alpha Omega Alpha, Delta Omega, Phi Kappa Phi, Phi Beta Kappa (hon.). Club: Cosmos (Washington). Home: 2760 Overridge Dr Ann Arbor MI 48104-4049 Office: Sch Public Health U Mich Ann ArbMI 48109-2029

WEGMILLER, DONALD CHARLES, health care corporation executive; b. Cloquet, Minn., Sept. 25, 1938; m. Janet A. Listerud, Apr. 27, 1957; children: Katherine, Mark, Dean. BA, U. Minn., 1960, MHA, 1962. Asst. adminstr. Fairview Hosp., Mpls., 1962-65; asst. adminstr. Fairview-Southdale Hosp., Mpls., 1965-66, adminstr., 1966-76; sr. v.p. Health Central System, Mpls., 1976-78; pres. Health Central, Inc., Mpls., 1978-80, Health Central Corp., Mpls., 1980-87; pres., CEO Health One Corp., Mpls., 1987-92; pres. HealthSpan, Mpls., 1992-93; pres. & CEO Mgmt. Compensation Group/HealthCare, Mpls., 1993—; preceptor clin. faculty U. Minn., 1975—; lectr., adj. faculty U. Mich., 1980—; clin. faculty, lectr. Duke U., 1981—; cons. div. med. services U.S. Dept. State, Washington, 1975; bd. dirs. Health Providers Ins. Co., Hosp. Rsch. and Ednl. Trust, Med. Graphics Corp., HBO & Co., G.D. Searle & Co., Minn. Power, Profile Group, LifeRate; U.S. del. King's Fund Internat., 1979-85, nat. coord., 1985; U.S. Internat. Hosp. Fedn., 1987; keynote speaker Australian Pvt. Hosps. Assn. 10th Nat. Congress, 1990; mem. leadership adv. com. Am. Coll. Healthcare Execs., 1994. Mem. adv. bd. Health Mgmt. Quar. mag.; editorial bd. of Frontiers an Am. Coll. of Healthcare Execs. publ.; contbr. articles to profl. jours. Chmn. Bd. Edn., Richfield, Minn., 1971-74; staff asst. to Presidents Nixon, Ford and Reagan, 1972-89; adv. com. Sen. Durenberger's Health Care, Mpls., 1979—; trustee Nat. Adv. Coun. on Social Security, 1989—, Nat. Com. for Quality Health Care. Recipient Outstanding Pres. of Yr. award Mpls. Jaycees, 1969, Young Man of Yr. award, 1971, Nat. Healthcare award B'nai B'rith, 1987, Merit award Duke U. Program in Healthcare Adminstrn. Alumni Assn., 1990. Fellow Am. Coll. Health Care Execs. (Robert S. Hudgen's award 1969), Am. Hosp. Assn. (chmn. bd. trustees 1987), Minn. Hosp. Assn. (Disting. Svc. award 1988). Republican. Methodist. Lodge: Rotary. Home: 7871 Chesshire Ln N Maple Grove MN 55311-2207 Office: Mgt Compensation Group Health Care 608 2nd Ave S Ste 370 Minneapolis MN 55402-1906

WEHMEIER, HELGE H., chemical, health care and imaging technologies company executive; b. Goettingen, Germany, 1943; married; 2 children. Attended, Internat. Mgmt. Devel. Inst., Switzerland, Inst. Europeen d'Adminstrn. des Affaires, France. With Bayer AG, 1965; mktg. synthetic fibers U.S. and Can. Mobay, N.Y.C., 1969; mktg. mgr. Leverkusen, Ger., 1974-78; gen. mgr. U.K., 1978-80; mgr. organic chem. divsn., 1981-84; head indsl. photographic divsn. Agfa-Gevaert AG subs. Leverkusen, 1984-89; pres., CEO Agfa Corp., Ridgefield Park, N.J., 1989-91; also bd. dirs., exec. com. Agfa Corp., Ridgefield Park, N.J.; pres., CEO Bayer Corp. (formerly Miles Inc.), 1991—; bd. dirs. PNC Bank Corp. Bd. dirs. Pitts. Symphony Soc.; mem. exec. com., officer Allegheny Conf. Cmty. Devel.. Pitts.; mem. Conf. Bd., Trilateral Commn. Mem. Chem. Mfrs. Assn. (exec. com., internat. com.). Office: Bayer Corp One Mellon Bank Ctr 500 Grant St Pittsburgh PA 15219-2502

WEHNER, ALFRED PETER, inhalation toxicologist, biomedical scientist; b. Wiesbaden, Germany, Oct. 23, 1926; came to U.S., 1953, naturalized, 1958; s. Paul Heinrich and Irma (Schulze) W.; m. Ingeborg Hella Miller, Aug. 30, 1955; children: Patricia Ingeborg, Alfred Peter, Jr., Jackie Diane, Peter Hermann. Cand. med., Johannes Gutenberg U., 1949, Zahnarzt DDS, 1951, D.M.D. cum laude, 1953. Diplomate Acad. Toxicol. Scis., 1988. Individual practice dentistry Wiesbaden, 1951-53; fellow clin. pedodontia Guggenheim Dental Clinic, N.Y.C., 1953-54; dentist 7100th Hosp., USAF, 1954-56; rsch. asst. Mobil Oil Co., Dallas, 1957-62; sr. rsch. scientist Biometrics Instrument Corp., Plano, Tex., 1962-64; pres. Electro-Aerosol Inst., Plano, Tex.; dir. Electro-Aerosol Therapy Centers, 1964-67; prof., chmn. dept. sci. U. Plano, 1966-67; sr. rsch. scientist biology dept. Battelle Pacific Northwest Labs., Richland, Wash., 1967-78; mgr. environ. and indsl. toxicology Battelle Pacific Northwest Labs., 1978-80, project dir., task leader indsl. toxicology, 1980-89; founder, pres. Biomed. & Environ. Cons., Inc., 1989—; cons. VA Hosp., McKinney, Tex., 1963-65; chmn., guest speaker 16 internat. sci. congresses and symposia. Author: From Hitler Youth to U.S. Citizenship, 1972; more than 120 sci. publs., including chpts. to books.; editor-in-chief: Am. Inst. Biomed. Climatology Bull.; editor: MEDICEF Direct Information (Federal Republic of Germany); reviewer various sci. jours.; patentee in field. Chmn. citizen adv. bd. Richland Police Dept. Fellow Internat. Soc. Med. Hydrology, Tex. Acad. Sci.; mem. Am. Inst. Biomed. Climatology (bd. dirs. 1972-90, sec. 1972-83, pres. 1984-90), Accademia degli Abruzzi per le Scienze e le Arti, Italy (hon. academician, v.p.), Pacific N.W. Assn. Toxicologists, Internat. Soc. of Biometeorology (USA rep. 1972-79), Internat. Soc. Aerosols in Medicine (exec. bd. 1970-80, diploma for highest merits in med. sci. 1980), Dallas County Dental Soc. (hon.), Internat. Assn. Aerobiology, Sigma Xi.

WEHNER, HENRY OTTO, III, pharmacist, consultant; b. Birmingham, Ala., Mar. 3, 1942; s. Henry O. Jr. and Carolyn (Kirkland) W.; m. Sammye Ruth Murphy, June 8, 1974 (div. July 1989). AA, Daytona Beach Community Coll., 1967; BS in Biology, North Ga. Coll., Dahlonega, 1971; BS in Pharmacy, U. Ga., 1978. Registered pharmacist, Fla., Ga.; cert. sci. tchr. grades 7-12, Ga. Tchr. biology Irwin County High Sch., Ocilla, Ga., 1971-75; extern Eckerd Drugs, Athens, Ga., 1977; intern/extern St. Mary's Hosp., Athens, 1977; pharmacy intern Button Gwinnett Hosp., Lawrenceville, Ga., 1978; co-owner, mgr. Hiawassee (Ga.) Pharmacy, 1978-79; staff pharmacist Dyal's Pharmacy, Daytona Beach, Fla., 1979, Little Drug Co., New Smyrna Beach, Fla., 1979-80; staff pharmacist, mgr. Super X Drugs, New Smyrna Beach, 1980-81; staff pharmacist Fish Meml. Hosp., New Smyrna Beach, 1981-92, Halifax Med. Ctr., Daytona Beach, Fla., 1992—. With USAF, 1961-65. Mem. Am. Pharm. Assn., Fla. Soc. Hosp. Pharmacists, Volusia County Pharm. Assn., Ea. Shores Soc. Hosp. Pharmacists (charter, pres. 1995-96), Eastern Shores Fla. Soc. Hosp. Pharmacists, Phi Lambda Sigma, Phi Theta Kappa. Methodist. Office: Halifax Med Ctr PO Box 1350 303 N Clyde Morris Blvd Daytona Beach FL 32114-2709

WEHRLE, KATHERINE EPPLER, obstetrical and gynecological nurse practitioner, consultant; b. Balt., Aug. 27, 1951; d. William Brandt and Katherine (Goldsborough) Eppler; m. R. Craig Wehrle, Mar. 16, 1990; children by previous marriage: Kenneth W. Knapp Jr., Katherine B. Knapp. AA, Marymount Coll., 1971; BSN, Towson State U., 1982; postgrad., U. Pa., 1985-88. RN, cert. RN practitioner, controlled drug substance lic., Md. Oper. rm. nurse St. Joseph's Hosp., Towson, Md., 1982-83; rsch. nurse div. clin. rsch. dept. ob-gyn. Sinai Hosp. of Balt., Inc., 1982-83; coord. rsch., nurse practitioner div. reproductive medicine Homewood Hosp. Ctr./ Johns Hopkins Health System, Balt., 1983-89; nurse practitioner ob.-gyn. Columbia Freestate Health System, Balt., 1989—; pvt. practice, cons. Balt., 1985—; ob-gyn. nurse practitioner, dept ob-gyn. U. Maryland Med. System, Balt., 1990—; vis. prof. Wyeth-Ayerst Labs., 1988—; presenter at profl. confs. Contbr. articles to profl. jours. and reports. Mem. Am. Coll. Obstetricians and Gynecologists (ednl. affiliate), Am. Coll. Nurse Practitioners, Am. Coll. Nutrition, Assn. Reproductive Health Profls., Nat. Assn. Nurse Practitioners in Reproductive Health, Nurse Practitioner Assn. Md., Jacobs Inst., N.Y. Acad. Scis., Gailhac Honor Soc., Sigma Theta Tau, Alpha Theta Zeta (pres.), Sigma Tau. Home: 100 Yorkleigh Rd Towson MD 21204-7511 Office: 8508 Loch Raven Blvd Towson MD 21286-2308

WEHRMACHER, WILLIAM HENRY, physiology educator, clinical cardiologist; b. Waterloo, Iowa, May 17, 1921. Student, Wartburg Coll., 1939-41; BA, State U. Iowa, 1943; MD, Iowa State U., 1945. Diplomate Am. Bd. Internal Medicine, Am. Bd. Cardiovascular Diseases. Intern U.S. Naval Hosp., Norfolk, Va., 1946; resident in internal medicine U.S. VA Hosp., Dearborn, Mich., 1948-50; resident in internal medicine Wayne State U. Med. Sch., Detroit, 1948-50, instr., 1948-50; instr. State U. Iowa Coll. Medicine, 1950-51, Northwestern U. Med. Sch., Chgo., Ill., 1951-71; clin. prof. medicine Stritch Sch. Medicine Loyola U., Chgo., 1971—, adj. prof. dept. physiology, 1975—; adj. prof. dept. physiology, 1975—; affiliated with U.S. Naval Hosp., Oceanside, Calif., 1950-51, Ravenswood Hosp., Chgo., 1951-61, Passavant Meml. Hosp., Chgo., 1952-71, U.S. VA Rsch. Hosp., Chgo., 1955-70, St. Joseph Hosp., Chgo., 1963. Editor Internal Med. Digest, 1974-75; assoc. editor Current Med. Digest, 1966-75; mem. editorial bd. Am. Heart Jour., 1977-81, Internal Medicine for the Specialist, 1981-91, Data Centrum, 1984-87, Postgrad. Medicine, 1988—; book rev. editor Chgo. Medicine, 1975—; contbr. articles to Jour. Iowa Med. Soc., Arch. Phys. Med., Am. Jour. Physiol., U.S. Armed Forces Med. Jour., JAMA, Circulation, Am. Jour. Cardiology, Minn. Medicine, Chgo. Medicine. others. Fellow Am. Coll. Cardiology, Am. Coll. Physicians, Internat. Acad. Clin. and Applied Thrombosis/Hemostasis; mem. AMA, Am. Fedn. for Clin. Rsch., Am. Heart Assn. (fellow coun. clin. cardiology 1963-75), Am. Med. Soc. Vienna, Chgo. Med. Soc., Chgo. Soc. Internal Medicine, Ill. Med. Soc., Inst. Medicine Chgo., Pan Am. Med. Assn., Soc. Med. History Chgo., Alpha Kappa Kappa, Alpha Omega Alpha, Sigma Xi. Home: 5706 Capulina Ave Morton Grove IL 60053-3034 Office: 55 E Washington Ste 1622 Pittsfield Bldg Chicago IL 60602

WEI, FONG, physician, medical administrator; b. Shanghai, May 2, 1941; came to U.S., 1941; s. Tseh Heen and Waling (Chung) W.; m. Theodora Mary Zopko, July 16, 1966; children: Christopher, Alexander. BA, Yale U., 1963; MD, Tufts U., 1967. Diplomate Am. Bd. Internal Medicine, Am. Bd. Nephrology. Intern Boston City Hosp., 1967-68, resident, 1968-69; resident Bronx (N.Y.) Mcpl., 1969-70; fellow U. N.C., Chapel Hill, 1970-72; nephrologist Princeton (N.J.) Med. Group, 1974—, pres., 1980—; prin. investigator Merck and Co., Princeton, 1988—, Bristol Myers Squibb, Princeton, 1984—; cons. Princeton U., 1990—; clin. assoc. prof. Robert Wood Johnson Med. Sch., New Brunswick, N.J., 1975—; pres. med. staff Med. Ctr. Princeton, 1981-82. Med. advisor Princeton Regional Homemakers Assn., 1975—. Fellow Am. Coll. Physicians; mem. Am. Soc. Nephrology, Internat. Soc. Nephrology, Am. Soc. Hypertension. Office: Princeton Med Group 419 N Harrison St Princeton NJ 08540

WEIANT, ELIZABETH ABBOTT, retired biology educator; b. New Britain, Conn., July 4, 1913; d. William Armstrong and Flora (Abbott) W. BS, MS, Tufts U., 1943; MA, Radcliffe Coll., 1952; EdD, Boston U., 1970. Instr. biology Tufts Coll., Medford, Mass., 1943-56, asst. prof., 1957-61; asst. prof. biology Simmons Coll., Boston, 1961-71, assoc. prof., 1972-79, chmn. dept., 1977-79, ret., 1979; corr. Evening Citizen, Laconia, N.H., 1987—, Franklin-Tilton Telegram, Franklin, N.H., 1990—; rsch. OSRD, USPHS, NSF, 1943-61; sr. rsch. fellow Max-Planck Inst., Seewiesen, Fed. Republic Germany, 1958; physiologist for product validation Cordis Corp., Miami, Fla., 1970;. Contbr. articles to profl. jours. Mem. Hist. Dist. Commn., Sanbornton, N.H., 1979-83; sec., mem. Sanbornton Conservation Commn., 1979-83, Trustees of Trust Fund, Sanbornton, 1985-96; bd. dirs., sec. N.H. affiliate Am. Heart Assn., Manchester, 1981-85; bd. dirs., mem. coms. Franklin (N.H.) Regional Hosp., 1984-91; pres. Sanbornton Hist. Soc., 1980-82; publicity chmn. Friends N.H. Music Festival. Recipient Disting. Svc. award Tufts U., 1970, Tower award Westbrook Coll., Portland, Maine, 1974, Woman of Yr. award Tilton-Northfield Bus. and Profl. Women, 1980, Heart of Gold award Am. Heart Assn., 1986, award for Pub. Svc. Belknap County Pomona Grange, 1990, Gov.'s Outstanding Vol. award, 1992. Mem. Am. Inst. Biol. Scis., Sigma Xi (sec. 1947-59), Grange. Republican. Home: PO Box 11 Sanbornton NH 03269-0011

WEIBEL, EWALD RUDOLF, anatomy educator, medical scientist; b. Buchs, AG, Switzerland, Mar. 5, 1929; s. Jakob and Berthe Méry (Pilet) W.; m. Anna Verena Trachsler, Mar. 30, 1932. MD, U. Zurich, Switzerland, 1955; DSc (hon.), U. Edinburgh, Scotland, 1988. Medical diplomate. Asst. anatomy U. Zurich, 1955-58, asst. prof. anatomy, 1963-66; rsch. fellow dept. pathology Yale U., New Haven, Conn., 1958-59; rsch. assoc. Columbia U., N.Y.C., 1959-61, Rockefeller U., N.Y.C., 1961-63; prof., chmn. dept. anatomy U. Berne, Switzerland, 1966-94; prof. emeritus Inst. of Anatomy U. Berne, Switzerland; chmn. Swiss Med. Rsch. Coun., Switzerland, 1974-80; rector, U. Berne, 1984-85. Author: (book) Morphometry of Human Lung, 1963, Stereological Methods, 1979, Pathway for Oxygen, 1984; editor: Lung: Scientific Foundations, 1991. Recipient Marcel Benoist prize Swiss Govt., Berne, 1974, medal Am. Coll. Chest Physicians, 1982, Anders Retzius medal Swedish Med. Soc., Stockholm, 1987, Perkynje Gold medal, Prague, 1993. Fellow AAAS, Royal Microscopical Soc. London (hon.); mem. U.S. nat. Acad. Sci. (fgn. assoc.), Polish Acad. Scis., Royal Soc. UPPSALA (Sweden), Acad. Scis. Leopoldina,Swiss Acad. Med. Scis.. Office: M E Muller Found, Murtenstrasse 41 PO Box 620, CH-3000 Berne 9, Switzerland

WEICHLER, NANCY KAREN, pediatric nurse; b. Pitts., Feb. 19, 1959; d. John James and Ruth Catherine (Miller) Janosko; m. Kevin William Weichler, June 4, 1983; children: Kara Lenore, Karleigh Josephine. BSN, Villanova U., 1981; MSN, U. Pitts., 1987. RN, Pa. Nurse's aide Negley House, 1978; nurse technician Shadyside, 1980; nurse's aide United Presbyn. Nursing Home, Wilkinsburg, Pa., 1979; surg./transplant staff nurse Children's Hosp. Pitts., 1981-87, clin. nurse facilitator, 1987-89, amb., 1988, renal clin. nurse specialist, 1989-95; pediatric ICU staff nurse, educator Brandon (Fla.) Hosp., Fla., 1995—; adj. faculty nursing care children grad. program U. Pitts., 1988-95; lectr. nursing Carlow Coll., Pitts., 1989-90; researcher and presenter in field. Contbr. articles to profl. and med. jours. March of Dimes scholar, 1977; Disting. Nursing Alumni award Villanova U., 1994. Mem. Am. Nephrology Nurses Assn., Soc. Pediatric Nephrology Nurses, Hosp. Asn. Pa. (Achievement award 1988), Villanova Sch. Nursing Alumni Assn. (recruiter 1987-89), Sigma Theta Tau. Roman Catholic.

WEICHSELBAUM, RALPH R., oncologist chairman. BS, U. Wis., 1967; MD, U. Ill., Chgo., 1971. Intern Alameda County Hosp., Oakland, Calif., 1971-72; resident in radiation therapy Harvard Med. Sch., Boston, 1972-75; assoc. prof. radiation therapy Harvard Med. Ctr., Boston, 1980-84; assoc. prof. dept. cancer biology Harvard Sch. Public Health, Boston, 1983-84; prof., chmn. dept. radiation and cellular omcology Pritzker Sch. Medicine U. Chgo., 1984—, Harold H. Hines Jr. prof., chmn., 1990; head Michael Reese/ U. Chgo. Ctr. Radiation Therapy, 1984—. Contbr. articles to profl. jours. Office: Ctr for Radiation Therapy Pritzker Sch of Medicine 5841 S Maryland Ave Chicago IL 60637-1463*

WEICHT, FORD ROBERT, physician assistant; b. Niagara Falls, N.Y., June 17, 1956; s. Harold and Nancy Ann (Hanna) W.; m. Teresa Ann Meller, June 25, 1983; children: Kimberly, Courtney. BS in Biology, Lenoir-Rhyne Coll., 1978; BS, Baylor Coll. Medicine, 1980. Cert. physician asst., Tex. Physician asst. Abilene (Tex.) Diagnostic Clinic, 1980-92, John H. Judd MD, Abilene, 1993—; v.p. Abilene Med. Transcription, 1990—. Asst. scoutmaster Boy Scouts Am., Abilene, 1983-85, scoutmaster, 1985-94, troop com., 1994—. Recipient Eagle Scout Boy Scouts Am., 1972, Dist. award of merit, 1993. Mem. Am. Acad. Physician Assts., Tex. Acad. Physician Assts., West Ctrl. Tex. Physician Asst. Soc. (co-founder, treas. 1981—). Lutheran. Home: 182 County Rd #332 Abilene TX 79606

WEIDENBAUM, MARK, surgeon; b. Corning, N.Y., Mar. 27, 1955; m. Lisa Berke; children: Rachel, Emily, Martina. BS in Chemistry, U. Conn., 1977; MD, Columbia U., 1981. Gen. surg. intern Roosevelt Hosp., N.Y.C., 1981-82, gen. surg. resident, 1982-83; orthopaedic surg. resident N.Y. Orthopaedic Hosp., Columbia Presbyn., N.Y.C., 1983-86; spine surgery fellow Rush Presbyn. St. Luke's Med. Ctr., Chgo., 1986-87; asst. prof. orthopedic surgery Columbia U. Coll. Physicians and Surgeons, N.Y.C., 1987-94, assoc. prof., 1994—; asst. attending in orthopedic surgery N.Y. Orthopaedic Hosp. Columbia Presbyn. Med. Ctr., N.Y.C., 1987-94, assoc. attending, 1994—; chmn. program com. 12th Internat. Congress Groupe Internat. Cotrel-Dubousset, Asheville, N.C., 1995. Contbr. articles to profl. jours. Rsch. grantee Orthopaedic Rsch. and Edn. Found., 1991-93; recipient Career Devel. award Orthopaedic Rsch. and Edn. Found., 1994-96, Frank Stinchfield award N.Y. Orthopaedic Hosp., 1985, Parke-Davis Resident award, 1986. Mem. Scoliosis Rsch. Soc. (rsch. com. 1993-95, nominating com. 1992-93), Orthopaedic Rsch. Soc., Am. Acad. Orthopaedic Surgeons, N.Am. Spine Soc. Office: NY Orthopaedic Hosp 161 Fort Washington Ave New York NY 10032

WEIDENBRUCH, ANNA MAE, nurse; b. Owosso, Mich., July 26, 1926; d. Robert Harry and Della Jane (Gander) Thompson; m. Manley Lavern Nixon, Aug. 3, 1946 (div. 1961); children: Terry Lee, Douglas Kent, LaVerna Ann, Norma Jean; m. Donald F. Clewley, Aug. 27, 1961 (dec. 1973); m. Heinz Weidenbruch, 1984. ADN, Lansing (Mich.) C.C., 1983; BS in Health Studies, Western Mich. U., Kalamazoo, 1993. RN, Mich. Staff nurse Sparrow Hosp., Lansing, 1958-62, Ingham Med. Hosp., Lansing, 1962-64, Lansing Gen. Hosp., 1964-66, 77-88, Hazel I. Findlay Country Manor, St. Johns, Mich., 1987-89, Staff Builders, Okemos, Mich., 1990—. Democrat. Home: 2123 Northwest Ave Lansing MI 48906-3653

WEIDENFELLER, GERALDINE CARNEY, speech and language pathologist; b. Kearny, N.J., Oct. 12, 1933; d. Joseph Gerald and Catherine Grace (Doyle) Carney; BS, Newark State U., 1954; postgrad. Northwestern U., summer 1956, U. Wis., summer 1960; MA, NYU, 1962; m. James Weidenfeller, Apr. 4, 1964; children: Anne, David. Lic speech/language pathologist, N.J. Speech pathologist Kearny (N.J.) Public Schs., 1954-61, North Brunswick (N.J.) Public Schs., 1961-65, Bridgewater (N.J.) Public Schs., 1969-72; speech therapist Somerset County Ednl. Commn., 1983-88; real estate agt., N.J., 1982-89; pvt. practice speech therapy, Somerville, N.J., 1980-92; speech therapist no. br. Midland Sch., 1989, No. Plainfield, N.J., 1989-90. V.p. Rosary Soc., Hillsborough, N.J., 1986—; Rep. county com. woman, 1989-96, chmn. scholarship com.; chmn. fedn. of Rep. women program com., Somerset, program chmn., scholarship chmn. 1991—; dancer Hillsborough Rockettes, 1994—; tudor Literacy Vol. of Am., 1993-96; storyteller Cath. Charities, 1992-93. Mem. Am. Speech and Hearing Assn., N.J. Speech and Hearing Assn. Roman Catholic. Club: Toastmasters (winner dist. humorous speech contest 1984, sec. 1985, advanced Toastmaster 1986). Home: 3 Banor Dr Somerville NJ 08876-4501

WEIDENTHAL, DANIEL, retinal surgeon; b. Aug. 29, 1932; s. Clarence and Ann Weidenthal; m. Judith Weidenthal, June 8, 1934; children: Jeff, David. BA, Dartmouth Coll., Hanover, N.H., 1954; MD, Case Western Res. U., 1958. Diplomate Am. Bd. Ophthalmology; lic. physician, Ohio, Calif. Intern Mt. Sinai Hosp., Cleve., 1958-59; resident in ophthalmology Kresge Eye Inst. and Detroit Receiving Hosp., 1959-62; fellow Armed Forces Inst. Pathology, Washington, 1962, Children's Hosp., Washington,

1962, Mass. Eye and Ear Infirmary, Boston, 1963-64; chief divsn. retinal surgery St. Luke's Med. Ctr., Cleve., 1970—, dir. divsn. ophthalmology, 1985—; assoc. clin. prof. ophthalmology Case Western Res. U., Cleve.; lectr. in field. Home: # 10 Pepper Creek Pepper Pike OH 44124

WEIDMANN, SILVIO, medical educator emeritus; b. Berne, Switzerland, Apr. 7, 1921; m. Ruth Brandenberger, Mar. 14, 1947; children: Marcus, Bernhard, Simon. MD, U. Berne, 1947; Dr. (hon.), U. Paris, 1976; MD (hon.), U. Uppsala, Sweden, 1977; DSc (hon.), U. Leicester, Eng., 1982. Post-doctoral fellow U. Uppsala, 1947-48, U. Cambridge, Eng., 1948-50; vis. prof. SUNY, Bklyn., 1954-55; assoc. prof. U. Berne, 1958-68, chmn. dept. physiology, 1968-86, prof. emeritus, 1986—; rector U. Berne, 1974-75. Contbr. articles to profl. jours.

WEIGEL, OLLIE J., dentist, former mayor; b. Guthrie County, Iowa, Sept. 29, 1922; s. Verne Noble and Ethel Rebecca (Johnson) W.; m. Mary Kathryn Finnegan, June 3, 1944; children: John, Marilyn, Larry, Susan. DDS, U. Iowa, 1951. Practice dentistry Ankeny, 1951-94; mayor City of Ankeny, 1974-93; mem. Metro Planning Orgn., 1995—; bd. dirs. Brenton Bank of Ankeny, Neveln Resource Ctr. Mem. Ankeny City Coun., 1966-73, Des Moines Area C.C. Found. Bd., 1993—, Des Moines Area Metro Forum, 1985-93, found. bd. On With Life, 1994—; life mem. Ankeny Indsl. Devel. Corp. 2d lt. USAAF, 1943-45, ETO. Mem. ADA (life), Iowa Dental Assn. (life), Des Moines Dist. Dental Assn., Ankeny C. of C. (life, pres., Outstanding Citizen 1976, 93), Mid Iowa Assn. Local Govts. (chmn. 1983), League of Iowa Municipalities (pres. 1976-77), Ctrl. Iowa Regional Govts. (pres. 1978), Am. Legion, Lions. Republican. Methodist. Home and Office: 2506 NW 4th St Ankeny IA 50021-1002

WEIGLE, WILLIAM OLIVER, immunologist, educator; b. Monaca, Pa., Apr. 28, 1927; s. Oliver James and Caroline Ellen (Alsing) W.; m. Kathryn May Lotz, Sept. 4, 1948 (div. 1980); children—William James, Cynthia Kay; m. Carole G. Romball, Sept. 24, 1983. B.S., U. Pitts., 1950, M.S., 1951, Ph.D., 1956. Research assoc. pathology U. Pitts., 1955-58, asst. prof. immunochemistry, 1959-61; assoc. div. exptl. pathology Scripps Rsch. Inst., La Jolla, Calif., 1961-62, assoc. mem. div., 1962-63; mem. dept. exptl. pathology Scripps Rsch. Inst., La Jolla, 1963-74, mem. dept. immunopathology, 1974-82, chmn. dept. immunopathology, 1980-82, mem., vice chmn. dept. immunology, 1982-85, mem. dept. immunology, 1982—, chmn. dept. immunology, 1985-87; adj. prof. biology U. Calif., San Diego; McLaughlin vis. prof. U. Tex., 1977; mem. adv. bd. Immunetech Pharms., San Diego, 1988—; cons. in field. Author: Natural and Acquired Immunologic Unresponsiveness, 1967; assoc. editor: Clin. and Exptl. Immunology, 1972-79; Jour. Exptl. Medicine, 1974-84; Immunochemistry 1964-71; Procs. Soc. Exptl. Biology and Medicine, 1967-72; Jour. Immunology, 1967-71; Infection and Immunity, 1969-86, Aging: Immunology and Infectious Disease, 1987—; sect. editor: Jour. Immunology, 1971-75; editorial bd.: Contemporary Topics in Immunobiology, 1971-93; Cellular Immunology, 1984—; contbr. articles to profl. jours. Emeritus Coun. of the Trustees, Lovelace Inst., Albuquerque, 1996—. Pub. Health Research fellow, Nat. Inst. Neurol. Diseases and Blindness, 1956-59; NIH sr. research fellow, 1959-61, Research Career award, 1962. Mem. Am. Assn. Immunologists, Am. Soc. Exptl. Pathology (Parke Davis award 1967), Am. Soc. Microbiology, N.Y. Acad. Scis., Am. Assn. Pathologists, Soc. Exptl. Biology and Medicine. Home: 688 Via De La Valle Solana Beach CA 92075-2461 Office: Scripps Rsch Inst Dept Immunology IMM9 10666 N Torrey Pines Rd La Jolla CA 92037-1027

WEIKEL, MALCOLM KEITH, health care company executive; b. Shamokin, Pa., Mar. 9, 1938; s. Malcolm J. and Marian Eleanor (Faust) W.; m. Barbara Joan Davis, Dec. 17, 1960; children: Richard, Kristin. BSc, Phila. Coll. Pharmacy and Sci., 1960; MSc, U. Wis., 1962, PhD, 1966. Mgr. Roche Labs., 1966-70; commr. health svcs. HEW, Washington, 1970-77; v.p. Am. Med. Internat., 1978-82, pres., CEO, 1982-84; exec. v.p., COO, Manor Healthcare Corp., Silver Spring, Md., 1984-86; exec. v.p. Health Care & Retirement Corp., Toledo, 1986-88, sr. exec. v.p., COO, 1988—. Recipient sec.'s spl. citation HEW, 1975, 77. Mem. Am. Health Care Assn. (v.p. 1990—, chmn. multifacility group 1990-93). Office: Health Care & Retirement Corp One SeaGate Toledo OH 43604-2616

WEIL, MARVIN LEE, pediatric neurologist; b. Gainesville, Fla., Sept. 28, 1924; s. Joseph and Ann (Abrams) W.; m. Joyce Sari Zimmerman, May 2, 1954; children: Daniel Ivan, Clifford Felix, Meredith. BS with high hons., U. Fla., 1943; MD, Johns Hopkins Sch. Medicine, 1946. Diplomate Am. Bd. Pediatrics, Am. Bd. Neurology with spl. competence in child neurology. Intern in pediatrics Duke U., Durham, N.C., 1946-47, resident in pediatrics, 1947-48; asst. chief neurotropic virus sect., div. virus and rickettsial diseases Army Med. Dept. Rsch. and Grad. Sch., Washington, 1948-50; resident in pediatrics Cin. Children's Hosp., 1950-52; clin. instr. in pediatrics U. Cin., 1952-53; clin. asst., prof. pediatrics U. Miami Sch. Medicine, 1954-65; asst. prof. pediatrics and neurology UCLA Sch. of Medicine, 1968-72, assoc. prof. pediatrics and neurology, 1972-78, prof. pediatrics and neurology, 1978-89, prof. emeritus, 1989—; acad. vis. dept. biochemistry U. Oxford, U.K., 1989—; cons. Torrance (Calif.) Sch. Dist., 1983-89; acting dir. Harbor Regional Ctr. for Developmentally Disabled, L.A., 1973-74; physician specialist chief, div. pediatric neurology, Harbor-UCLA Med. Ctr., Torrance, 1968-89. Contbg. author books in field; contbr. articles to profl. jours. Capt. AUS, 1948-50. Spl. fellow Nat. Inst. Neurol. Diseases and Blindness, Johns Hopkins U., UCLA, 1965-66, 66-68; sr. internat. fellow Fogarty Internat. Ctr./NIH, Karolinska Inst., Stockholm, Sweden, 1976-77. Fellow AAAS, Am. Acad. Pediatrics, Am. Acad. Neurology; mem. Am. Pediatric Soc., Child Neurology Soc. (bd. dirs. 1980-82), Am. Assn. Immunologists, Am. Assn. Mental Deficiency (exec. bd. region II 1971-76, chmn. region II 1973-74), Internat. Child Neurology Soc., L.A. Soc. Neurology and Psychiatry (sec./treas. 1978-80, pres. elect 1980, pres. 1981, bd. dirs. 1982-84), Western Soc. Pediatric Rsch., Calif. Child Neurology Soc., Dade County Med. Assn., N.Y. Acad. Sci. Democrat. Home: 82 Thames St, Oxford OX1 1SU, England Office: Dept Biochemistry/U Oxford, South Parks Rd, Oxford OX1 3QU, England

WEILBURG, DONALD KARL, orthodontist; b. N.Y.C., Apr. 12, 1936; s. John and Esther Edith (Alexandre) W.; m. Sally Rae Curwood, Sept. 5, 1937; children: Heidi Maria, Burkley Curwood, Lindsay Alexandre. AB, Dartmouth Coll., 1958; DMD, U. Pa., Phila., 1967, orthodontic cert., 1968. Clin. instr. oral medicine U. Pa. Sch. Dental Medicine, Phila., 1967; clin. instr. oral hygiene U. R.I. Sch. Oral Medicine, Kingstown, 1969; pvt. practice orthodontics Westerly, R.I., 1969—. Del. Dem. Nat. Conv., Miami, Fla., 1972, mem. rules com., Washington, 1972; mem. exec. com. Westerly Dem. Town Com., 1972-85, R.I. Dem. Com., Providence, 1972-84; bd. dirs. Trinity Square Reperatory Theater, Providence, 1976-82. With USPHS, 1966. Mem. Am. Assn. Orthodontics, ADA, Fedn. Dentaire Internat., R.I. Dental Assn., South County Dist. Dental Soc. (pres. 1974-75), Watch Hill (R.I.) Yacht Club (bd. dirs. 1975-80), Westerly Yacht Club, Omicron Kappa Upsilon. Democrat. Unitarian. Home: 19 Timothy Dr Westerly RI 02891-3211 Office: 5 Crestview Dr Westerly RI 02891-2907

WEILL, TERRY LISTER, psychiatrist; b. Newark, Mar. 23, 1949. BFA, Carnegie-Mellon U., 1971; postgrad., NYU, 1974-76; MD, Hahneman Med. Coll., 1980. Diplomate Am. Bd. Psychiatry and Neurology. Rotating intern in medicine, neurology and psychiatry Mount Sinai Med. Ctr., 1980-81, resident psychiatrist, 1981-83, chief resident, outpatient and inpatient psychiatry, 1983-84, attending staff, 1984—, asst. prof., 1996; grad. psychoanalyst N.Y. Psychoanalytic Inst., 1983-91; staff psychiatrist The Bridge, Inc., N.Y., 1984-86, Met. Ctr. for Mental Health, N.Y., 1985-88; attending psychiatrist Breast Cancer Support Group, Beth Israel Hosp. North, N.Y., 1986—, Gracie Square Hosp., N.Y., 1987—; mem. profl. adv. bd. Epilepsy Inst., 1986. Mem. AMA, Am. Med. Women's Assn., Am. Psychiat. Assn., Am. Psychoanalytic Assn.,Acad. Psychosomatic Medicine, N.Y. Psychoanalytic Soc. and Inst. Address: 350 Central Park West New York NY 10023

WEIMAR, ROBERT HENRY, counselor, clinical hypnotherapist; b. Chgo., July 4, 1946. BA in Psychology, U. Ill., 1968; MS in Community Mental Health, No. Ill. U., 1971. Cert. med. hypnotherapist, cert. clin. mental health counselor. Cons., edn. coord. No. Community Mental Health Ctr., Ashland, Wis., 1978-79; pvt. practice counselor and cons. Ashland, 1981-88; alcohol prevention coord. Bad River Chippewa Tribe, Odanah, Wis., 1982-88; prodr. freelance radio programs Ashland, Wis., 1984-90, Lynchburg, Va., 1984-90; mental health counselor Ctrl. Health (Bridges), Lynchburg, 1988-90, mental health cons. 1990—; coord. Va. Divsn. Drug Abuse Control, Richmond, 1972-74; planner N.Y. State Drug Abuse Control Commn., N.Y.C., 1974-75. Contbr. numerous articles to profl. jours. Recipient Outstanding Svc. award Nat. Indian Bd. on Alcohol and Drug Abuse, 1987. Office: Hypnotist For Health 3313 Old Forest Rd Lynchburg VA 24501

WEIN, ALAN JEROME, urologist, educator, researcher; b. Newark, Dec. 15, 1941; s. Isadore R. and Jeanette Frances (Abrams) W. A.B. cum laude, Princeton U., 1962; M.D., U. Pa., 1966. Diplomate emeritus Am. Bd. Urology. Intern mixed surgery Hosp. U. Pa., Phila., 1966-67, resident surgery, 1967-68; resident urology U. Pa., Phila., 1969-72, fellow Harrison Dept. Surg. Rsch. Urology Sch. Medicine, 1968-69, asst. instr. surgery Sch. Medicine, 1967-68, asst. instr. urology, 1969-71, instr., 1971-72, asst. prof., 1974-76, assoc. prof., 1976-83, prof., 1983—, asst. chief urology, 1974-79, dir. Urodynamic Evaluation Ctr., 1974—, chmn. div. urology, 1981—, chief urology, 1981—; dir. resident edn. com. div. urology Sch. Medicine U. Pa., 1976—, coord. program urologics oncology, 1976—; chief urology VA Hosp., Phila., 1974-82, attending urologist, 1982—; asst. surgeon Children's Hosp. Phila., 1974—; cons. CDC Coun. Incontinence, 1990—; assoc. surgeon Pa. Hosp., Phila., 1977—; attending urologist Grad. Hosp., Phila., 1980—. Author: (with D.M. Barrett) Controversies in Neuro-Urology, 1984, Voiding Function and Dysfunction: A Logical and Practical Approach, 1988, 2d edit., 1995, (with A.R. Mundy and T.P. Stephenson) Urodynamics: Principles, Practice and Application, 1984, 2d edit., 1994, (with P.M. Hanno) A Clinical Manual of Urology, 1987, 2d edit., 1994, (with Hanno, Staskin and Krane) Interstitial Cystitis, 1990; editl. bd. asst. Urol. Survey, 1978-81; editl. bd. cons. Investigative Urology, 1978-81; mem. editl. bd. World Jour. Urology, 1982—, Am. Urol. Assn. Update series, 1983—, Urol. Survey, 1987—, Internat. Jour. Impotence Rsch.: Basic and Clin. Studies, 1989—, Urology, 1991—; ad hoc reviewer Cancer, 1985—; cons. editor Sexuality and Disability, 1985—; asst. editor Jour. Urology, 1980-89, ad hoc reviewer clin. sect., 1989—, editl. bd. investigative sect., 1989—; assoc. editor Neurourlogy and Urodynamics, 1982—; contbr. over 560 articles and abstracts to profl. jours. Mem. coun. urology Nat. Kidney Found., Inc.; mem lectrs. bur. Am. Cancer Soc., 1984—; mem. adv. panel Nat. Assn. for Incontinence, 1987—; mem. adv. bd. Simon Found., 1987—; mem. med. adv. bd. Institial Cystitis Assn., 1987—; chmn. bladder health coun. Am. Found. Urologic Disease, 1990—; trustee Am. Bd. Urology, 1990-96. Maj. MC, U.S. Army, 1972-74. Grantee VA, 1974-79, 79, 81, 81-84, 82-85, 85-88, 88-92, Eaton Labs., 1975-76, 78-80, McCabe Rsch. Fund, 1975-82, 87-88, Merrell Nat. Labs., 1979-82, 1980-82, Nat. Kidney Found., 1980-81, NIH, 1980-83, 83-88, 84-87, 87—, Roche Labs., 1981, Smith Kline and French Labs., 1982, 86-88, Eli Lilly Labs., 1986-88, 91, Found. Interstitial Cystitis, 1986-87, 87-88, Sterling Drug Co., 1991. Fellow ACS; mem. AAAS, AMA (cons. com. drug evaluation 1977—), Am. Acad. Clin. Neurophysiology, Am. Assn. Surgery of Trauma, Am. Assn. Clin. Urologists, Am. Assn. Genito-Urinary Surgeons, Am. Fertility Soc., Am. Inst. Ultrasound in Medicine, Am. Soc. Pharmacology and Exptl. Therapeutics, Am. Soc. Andrology, Am. Soc. Clin. Oncology, Am. Urol. Assn. (chmn. practical cases urology 1982—, rsch. com. 1985—, editl. com. mid-Atlantic sect. 1988—), Assn. Acad. Surgery, Can. Urol. Assn., Clin. Soc. Genito-Urinary Surgeons, Ea. Coop. Oncologic Group, Endourol. Soc., Internat. Continence Soc., Nat. Assn. VA Physicians, N.Y. Acad. Scis., Coll. Physicians Phila., John Morgan Soc., Pa. Med. Assn., Pa. Oncologic Soc., Phila. Acad. Surgery, Phila. County Med. Soc., Phila. Profl. Standards Rev. Orgn., Phila. Urologic Soc. (pres. 1990-91), Ravdin-Rhoads Surg. Soc., Urol. Assn. Pa., Radiation Therapy Oncology Group (genitourinary working com. 1980—), Royal Soc. Medicine, Soc. Internat. d'Urologie, Soc. Basic Urologic Rsch., Soc. Sex Therapy and Rsch., Soc. Govt. Svc. Urologists, Soc. Pelvic Surgeons, Soc. Univ. Surgeons, Soc. Univ. Urologists, Soc. Urologic Oncology, Univ. Urologic Forum, Urodynamics Soc. (exec. com. 1980—), Urologic Rsch. Soc., Uroloe: 609 Robinson Ln Haverford PA 19041-1921 Office: Hosp U Pa 1 Rhoads Pavilion 3400 Spruce St Philadelphia PA 19104

WEIN, ROBERT MICHAEL, obstetrician, gynecologist; b. Beckley, W.Va., May 30, 1947; s. Isadore R. and Jeanette Frances (Abrams) W.; m. Judith Lorraine Diamond, June 12, 1970; children: Robert Jr., Jennifer, Scott, Noell, Erin. BS in Biology, Washington & Lee U., 1968; MD, U. Va., 1972. Diplomate Am. Bd. Ob-Gyn. Intern U. Va. Hosp., Charlottesville, 1972-73, resident in ob-gyn, 1975-78; pvt. practice, Greensboro, N.C., 1979—; assoc. clinical prof. U. N.C.; chief ob-gyn. staff Moses Cone and Women's Hosps., Greensboro, 1991—, sec. med. bd., 1991-92, v.p. med. bd., 1992-93, pres. med. bd. 1994-95. With USPHS, 1973-75. Mem. AMA, N.C. Ob-Gyn. Soc., N.C. Med. Soc., Greensboro Soc. Medicine, S. Atlantic Assn. of Obstetricians and Gynecologists. Home: 300 Willoughby Blvd Greensboro NC 27408-3829 Office: Green Valley Ob-Gyn. 721 Green Valley Rd Ste 201 Greensboro NC 27408-7013

WEINBAUM, GEORGE, medical educator; b. Bklyn., July 27, 1932; s. Hyman Al and Sarah Ruth (Kaplan) W.; m. Carol Miriam Rosenblatt, June 19, 1963; children: Eve, Cindy, Laura, Elliot. BA in Chemistry, U. Pa., 1953; MS in Biochemistry, Pa. State U., 1955, PhD in Biochemistry, 1957. Vis. researcher Marine Biol. Labs., Woods Hole, Mass., 1970-80; rsch. assoc. prof. microbiology Temple U., Phila., 1973-81, rsch. prof. microbiology, 1981—; rsch. assoc. prof. medicine U. Pa. Sch. Medicine, Phila., 1983-88, rsch. prof. medicine, 1988—; asst. chmn. for rsch., dir. rsch. div. dept. medicine The Grad. Hosp., Phila., 1982—; dir. rsch. div. dept. medicine Albert Einstein Med. Ctr., Phila., 1980-82, full mem., 1969-82; dir. biochem. sect. dept. pathology Geisinger Med. Ctr., Danville, Pa., 1957-61; lectr. in field. Contbr. articles to profl. jours. Grantee Nat. Heart, Lung and Blood Inst., 1972-91. Mem. Am. Soc. Biochemistry and Molecular Biology, Am. Assn. Pathologists, Am. Soc. for Microbiology, Am. Thoracic Soc. (bd. dirs. 1986-89), Sigma Xi, Gamma Sigma Delta, Phi Lambda Upsilon. Jewish. Home: 6532 N 12th St Philadelphia PA 19126-3640 Office: The Grad Hosp 415 S 19th St Philadelphia PA 19146-1464

WEINBERG, MARCY, psychologist; b. Detroit; m. Michael Eugene Weinberg, June 1, 1966. BA, Northeastern Ill. U., 1977; MA, Northwestern U., 1978; PhD, Nova Univ., 1989. Lic. psychologist. Psychology intern Broward Gen. Med. Ctr., Ft. Lauderdale, Fla., 1984-85; psychology resident U. Miami Sch. Medicine, 1989-90; psychologist Marcy Weinberg, Hollywood, Fla., 1991—; adj. prof. dept. psychiatry U. Miami, 1991-92; diagnostician Cen. Agy. for Jewish Edn., Miami, 1981-87; invited lectr., guest WLRN-TV, Miami, 1987, 90, Hollywood Meml. Hosp. Contbg. author: Pediatric Nephrology, 1991; author computer prog., 1985. Fundraiser Transplant Found. of South Fla., Miami, 1989—; invited speaker Dialysis/Organ Transplant Support Groups, Miami, Boca Raton, 1990. Recipient Svc. award Stratford Ctr. Sch., Highland Park, Ill., 1977. Fellow Am. Orthopsychiat. Assn.; mem. APA, Fla. Psychol. Assn. Office: 3990 Sheridan St Ste 204 Hollywood FL 33021-3656

WEINBERG, MILTON, JR., cardiovascular, thoracic surgeon; b. Sumter, S.C., Aug. 8, 1824; s. Milton and Ethel (Harper) W.; m. Joan Ehrenstrom, Nov. 24, 1956; children: Caryl, Susan, Amy. Student, Duke U., 1941-43, MD, 1947. Diplomate Am. Bd. Surgery, Am. Bd. Thoracic Surgery. Attending surgeon Rush Presbyn.-St. Luke's Med. Ctr., Chgo., 1957-90, emeritus attending, 1990—; attending surgeon Cook County Hosp., Chgo., 1956—, Luth. Gen. Hosp., Park Ridge, Ill., 1986—; mem. governing coun., 1996—; assoc. prof. Rush Med. Coll., Chgo., 1969-78, prof. surgery, 1978-90, emeritus prof., 1990—; clin. prof. U. Chgo., 1990—; chmn. dept. surgery Luth. Gen. Hosp., Park Ridge, 1988-94, vice-chmn. dept. surgery, 1994—; pres. med. staff Rush Med. Ctr., Chgo., 1977-79; presenter movies at mtgs. ACS. Mem. editorial bd. Annals of Thoracic Surgery, 1968-79; contbr. articles to profl. jours., chpts. to surg. textbooks. Trustee The Presbyn. Home, Evanston, Ill., 1984-94; bd. dirs. Chgo. Symphony Orch., 1985-95; adv. Charitable Found., 1996—. Maj. U.S. Army, 1951-53. Decorated Bronze Star. Fellow ACS, Am. Coll. Chest Physicians, Am. Coll. Cardiology; mem. Am. Assn. Thoracic Surgery, Soc. Thoracic Surgeons, Soc. Vascular Surgery, Internat. Cardiovascular Soc., Ctrl. Surg. Soc. Home: 2550 Princeton Ave Evanston IL 60201-4941 Office: Luth Gen Hosp 1775 Dempster St Park Ridge IL 60068-1143

WEINBERG, SAMUEL, pediatric dermatologist; b. N.Y.C., Jan. 12, 1926; s. Harry and Rose (Stecher) W.; m. Pearl Oksner, Dec. 12, 1948; children: Ronald Andrew, Robin Ann. MB, Chgo. Med. Sch., 1947, MD, 1948. Clin. asst. prof. dermatology to prof. dermatology Med. Ctr. NYU, N.Y.C., 1961—. Author: Color Atlas of Pediatric Dermatology, 1975, 2d rev. edit., 1990. Capt. USAF, 1951-53. Fellow Am. Acad. Pediatrics, ACP, Am. Acad. Dermatology (chmn. pediatric dermatology sect. 1978-81, com. dermatolog. subspecialties 1984-86, task force pediatric dermatology 1981-84); mem. Soc. Pediatric Dermatology (charter, pres. 1980-81). Office: NYU Med Ctr 530 1st Ave New York NY 10016-6402

WEINBERG, SAUL ABRAM, psychiatrist; b. Hartford, Conn., Aug. 13, 1925; s. Hyman P. and Rose May (Apter) W.; m. Ethel Schwartz, Aug. 30, 1959; children: David, Diane. BA, Yale U., 1948; MS in Social Svc., Boston U., 1951; MD, U. Pa., 1956. Diplomate, Am. Bd. Psychiatry and Neurology. Pvt. practice Phila., 1960-80; psychiatric consultation liason dir. Albert Einstein Med. Ctr., Phila., 1980-86; clin. assoc. prof. Sch. Medicine Temple U., Phila., 1984-86; staff psychiatrist Baystate Med. Ctr., Springfield, Mass., 1986-92; pvt. practice Springfield, 1992—; clin. assoc. prof. Sch. Medicine Sch. Medicine Tufts U., Boston, 1989-94, clin. prof. psychiatry, 1994—; lectr. dept. psychiatry U. Pa., Phila., 1976-80. Mem. arts com. Mattoon Arts Festival, Springfield, 1987-90; pres. Mattoon St. Hist. Preservation Assn., Springfield, 1989-91; mem. adv. bd. springfield Fine Arts Mus., 1991—; fin. com. Springfield Libr. and Mus. Assn., 1994—. Mem. AMA, Am. Psychiat. Assn., Mass. Med. Soc., West Mass. Psychiat. Soc., Connecticut Valley Yale Club (sec.), Realty Club, Springfield Cen. (bd. dirs.), Stagewest (bd. dirs.), Phi Beta Kappa. Jewish. Office: 780 Chestnut St Springfield MA 01107

WEINBERGER, JESSE M., neurologist; b. Rochester, N.Y., July 1, 1947; s. Irving L. and Adele (Silver) W.; m. Ronnie F. Cohen, Nov. 8, 1975; children: Evan Lawrence, Amanda Susan. BA, U. Pa., 1967; MD, Johns Hopkins U., 1971. Rsch. assoc. cerebrovascular rsch. U. Pa., Phila., 1977-78; from asst. prof. to prof. medicine Mt. Sinai Sch. Medicine, N.Y.C., 1983—; chief neurology Worth Gen. Hosp., N.Y.C., 1985—. Author: Noninvasive Imaging of Cerebrovascular Disease, 1988; contbr. articles to profl. jours. Lt. cmdr. U.S. Navy, 1975-77. Fellow Stroke Coun., Am. Heart Assn.; mem. Am. Acad. Neurology, Soc. Neurosci., Soc. Neuroimaging. Democrat. Jewish. Home: 11 Baldwin Ln Scarsdale NY 10583 Office: Mt Sinai Sch Medicine 1 Gustave Levy Pl New York NY 10029

WEINBERGER, MILES M., physician, pediatric educator; b. McKeesport, Pa., June 28, 1938; divorced; 4 children; m. Leslie Kramer, Aug. 22, 1992. A.B., U. Pitts., 1960, M.D., 1965. Diplomate Am. Bd. Pediatrics, Am. Bd. Allergy and Immunology, Am. Bd. Pediatric Pulmonology. Intern U. Calif. Med. Ctr., San Francisco, 1965-66, pediatric resident, 1965-67; research assoc NIH, Bethesda, Md., 1967-69; allergy and pulmonary fellow U. Colo., Denver, 1969-71; staff Ross Valley Med. Clinic, Greenbrae, Calif., 1971-73; clin. pharmacology fellow U. Colo., Denver, 1973-75; div. chmn. U. Iowa, Iowa City, 1975—; cons. D.C.Hosp. for Sick Children, 1967-69, allergy and immunology Family Practice Program, Sonoma County Community Hosp., U. Calif. Sch. Medicine, 1972-73; clin. instr. pediatrics Georgetown U. Sch. Medicine, Washington, 1967-69; staff pediatrician part-time West Side Neighborhood Health Ctr., Denver, 1970-71; pediatric sr. staff mem. Nat.Jewish Hosp. and Research Ctr., 1973-75; clin. asst. U. Colo. Med.Ctr., 1974-75; assoc. prof. pediatrics, chmn. pediatric allergy and pulmonary div. U. Iowa Coll. Medicine, 1975-80, assoc. prof. pharmacology, 1975-79, dir. Cystic Fibrosis Ctr., 1977—, prof. pediatrics, 1980—, dir. pediatric allergy and pulmonary div., 1975—. Author: Managing Asthma, 1990; contbr. numerous articles to profl. jours., chpts. to books, also audio-visual materials, commentaries, pub. letters and presentations in field. Recipient Clemens von Pirquet award Am. Coll. Allergy, 1974; grantee NIH, 1980-85, Cystic Fibrosis Ctr., Pharm. Mfrs. Assn. Fellow Am. Acad. Pediatrics (allergy sect. 1972, sect. on clin. pharmacology and therapeutics 1978, diseases of chest 1978); mem. Am. Acad. Allergy, Am. Soc. Clin. Pharmacology and Therapeutics, Soc. for Pediatric Rsch., Am. Thoracic Soc. (pres. Iowa Thoracic Soc. 1992-93), Camp Superkids of Iowa (adv. bd. 1981—), Am. Lung Assn. (pediatric pulmonbary ctr. task force com. 1984-86). Home: 7 Cottage Grove Dr NE Iowa City IA 52240-9171 Office: U Iowa Dept Pediatrics Iowa City IA 52242

WEINBERGER, STEVEN ELLIOTT, internist; b. Phila., Jan. 28, 1949; s. Leon and Ruth (Shoemaker) W.; m. Janet Harrison Brauer, June 14, 1970; children: Eric, Mark. AB, Princeton U., 1969; MD, Harvard U., 1973. Diplomate Am. Bd. Internal Medicine, Am. Bd. Pulmonary Disease, Am. Bd. Critical Care Medicine. Intern, then resident U. Calif. Med. Ctr., San Francisco, 1973-75; intern U. Calif. Med. Ctr., San Francisco, Md., 1973-74; resident U. Calif. Med. Ctr., San Francisco, 1974-75; fellow Nat. Heart Lung and Blood Inst., NIH, 1975-78; attending physician Beth Israel Hosp., Boston, 1978—, clin. dir. pulmonary and critical care div., 1986-94; chief pulmonary and critical care divsn., 1994—, assoc. chmn. dept. medicine, 1992—; instr. Harvard Med. Sch., Boston, 1978-80, asst. prof., 1980-89, assoc. prof., 1989-95, prof., 1995—. Author: Principles of Pulmonary Medicine, 1986, 2d edit., 1992. Fellow ACP, Am. Coll. Chest Physicians. Office: Beth Israel Hosp 330 Brookline Ave Boston MA 02215-5400

WEINER, BARRY M., optometrist, consultant; b. Balt., Jan. 20, 1944; s. Harry and Lillian (Cooper) W.; m. Clare Ann Wilson, June 21, 1981; children: Sean Michael, Courtney Lynn. AA, Balt. Jr. Coll., 1963; BS, Pa. Coll. Optometry, Phila., 1965, OD, 1967. Clin. asst. U. Md. Med. Sch., Balt., 1973-86, asst. prof., 1986-93; pvt. practice Phoenix, Md., 1968—; assoc. Eye Cons. of Md., Balt., 1993—; adj. faculty Johns Hopkins Med. Sch., Balt., 1994—; cons. Refractive Ctrs., Internat., Boston, 1993—; dir. Contact Lens Clinic, U. Md. Hosp., 1973-93; chief contact lens sect. Katzen Eye Group Mercy Hosp., 1980-85; mem. Cooper Vision Optics Adv. Panel, 1984—; cons. So. Optical Co., 1984—; adv., panel Alcon Pharms., 1990—, Poly. Tech., 1991—; mem. Sherman Adv. Panel, 1992, Ciba Adv. Panel, 1992; guest lectr. in field. Contbr. numerous articles to profl. jours. Bd. dirs. Md. Soc. for Prevention of Blindness, 1986—; mem. Summit Tech. Ophthalmology Commn., 1994. Fellow Am. Acad. Optometry (contact lens sect. coun. mem. 1993—); mem. Am. Optometric Assn., Md. Optometric Assn., Contact Lens Assn. of Ophthalmology, Nat. Eye Rsch. Found., Internat. Orthokeratology Soc., Contact Lens Assn. of Ophthalmology. Office: 3421 Sweet Air Rd Phoenix MD 21131

WEINER, CLARE FRANCES, social worker, psychotherapist; b. Phila., Dec. 3, 1929; d. Jack and Jessie (Rosengarten) Weinbaum; m. George C. Wheeler, Jan. 21, 1978; children by previous marriage: Justin M., Kate J., Lucian J. BS, Temple U., 1951; MSW, U. Wis., 1967. Diplomate Am. Bd. Examiners in Clin. Social Work. Social worker Ohio Valley Mental Retardation Evaluation Unit, Athens, Ohio, 1968-69; social worker inpatient psychiat. svc. VA Hosp., Albany, N.Y., 1969-70; chief social worker Schenectady County Outpatient Mental Health Clinic, 1970-76; adult treatment team leader, supervising social worker Saratoga County Mental Health Ctr., N.Y., 1976-81; pvt. practice psychotherapy individuals, couples, families Schenectady and Albany, 1975—. Fellow N.Y. State Soc. for Clin. Social Workers (diplomate), Nat. Assn. Social Workers (diplomate); mem. Gestalt Inst. Cleve., Thursday Mus. Soc. Office: 29 Front St Schenectady NY 12305-1301

WEINER, FERNE, psychologist; b. N.Y.C., June 14, 1928; d. Irving Kapp and Peggy (Finkelstein) Hessberg; m. Howard Weiner, July 20, 1948; children: Irving Kenneth, Laurie. BA, Skidmore Coll., 1965; MA, Sarah Lawrence Coll., 1971; PhD, U. Hawaii, 1975. Lic. psychologist, Conn., Hawaii. Asst. prof. West Oahu Coll. U. Hawaii, Honolulu, 1975-77; staff psychologist Cmty. Guidance Clinic, Manchester, Conn., 1978-83; chief cons. psychologist Consultation and Evaluation Ctr., Meriden, Conn., 1984-85; psychologist cons. Disability Determination Svcs., Hartford, Conn., 1986-87, Honolulu, 1988—; police psychologist Honolulu Police Dept., 1988; pvt. practice, Greenwich, Conn., 1983-87, Honolulu, 1988—; cons. Adopt-A-Sch. Project, Honolulu, 1991-94; interviewer, therapist Sexual Abuse Treatment Team, Manchester, 1979-83; cons., trainer Conn. schs., day care, ch. groups, 1979-87. Contbr. articles to profl. jours. Active Disaster Assistance Mgmt. Team, Hawaii, 1994-95; v.p., sec. Queens Court at Kapiolani Bd., Honolulu, 1992-95; admissions rep. Hawaii Sarah Lawrence Coll., Honolulu, 1970-80; cons. to adoptees search Orphan Voyage, Conn., 1980-87; mentor Girl Scout Coun. Am., Oahu, 1993-94. Mem. Am. Psychol. Assn. (clin. psychotherapy and neuropsychology divsn.), Hawaii Psychol. Assn., Nat. Registry Health

Svcs. Providers, Outrigger Canoe Club, Honolulu Club. Democrat. Jewish. Home: 3004 Hibiscus Dr Honolulu HI 96815 Office: Behavior Therapy Clinic Kahala Office Ctr 4211 Waialae Ave Honolulu HI 96816 also: Disability Determination Br 1580 Mataloa St Honolulu HI 96814

WEINER, GERSHON RALPH, physician; b. Detroit, Apr. 12, 1935; s. Morris and Phyllis (Lemberg) W.; m. Myra H. Levenson, July 1956 (div. May 1972); children: Bruce J., Sandra C. Mishory, Stuart J. (dec.); m. M. Jean (Jeannie) Mann, Dec. 31, 1975; 1 child, Joel Edward Jackson. BS, Wayne State U., 1955; DO, Coll. Osteopathic Medicine and Surgery, 1963. Diplomate Nat. Bd. Examiners, Am. Osteo Bd. Rehab. Medicine (bd. examiner 1982-91). Intern Mt. Clemens (Mich.) Gen. Hosp., 1963-64; family practice Detroit and Warren, Mich., 1964-71; practice in emergency medicine Macomb (Mich.) County hosps., 1964-73; dep. med. examiner Macomb County, 1965-74; resident, fellow in physical medicine and rehab. Wayne State U. Sch. Medicine, Detroit, 1971-74; practice medicine specializing in physical medicine and rehab. Wayne and Macomb Counties, 1974—; team physician wheelchair basketball team Detroit Sparks, 1971-72; rehab. med. cons. Detroit League Handicapped Goodwill Industries, 1972-76; lectr. phys. therapy Wayne State U., 1972-74; postgrad. trainer, lectr., cons., staff psychiatrist BiCounty Cmty. Hosp., Warren, Riverside Osteo. Hosp., Trenton, Mich., 1974—; spkr. in field. Contbr. articles to profl. jours. Served to capt. USAF, 1955-58. Fellow Am. Osteo. Coll. Rehab. Medicine (trustee 1982-89, pres. 1984-85); mem. Am. Osteo. Assn., Am. Congress Rehab. Medicine, Macomb County Osteo. Assn. Jewish.

WEINER, HAROLD M., radiologist; b. Phila., Apr. 30, 1937; s. Louis A. and Anna (Becker) W.; divorced; children: Lori, Julie. BA summa cum laude, Temple U., 1958, MD with hons., 1962. Diplomate Am. Bd. Radiology, Nat. Bd. Med. Examiners. Intern Polyclinic Hosp., Harrisburg, Pa., 1962-63; resident in pathology VA Hosp., Phila., 1965, resident in radiology, 1966-68; staff radiologist Sacred Heart Hosp., Norristown, Pa., 1969-73, chief radiologist, 1973-94; chmn. infectious disease com., 1976-77, patient care com., 1977-80, med. audit com., 1981-87; sec.-treas. med. staff, 1982-85; radiologist Suburban Gen. Hosp., Norristown, Pa., 1994-95. Presenter numerous papers med. meetings. Served to capt. M.C. USAF, 1963-65. Decorated Legion of Honor Chapel of Four Chaplains. Mem. AMA, Am. Heart Assn. (coun. on cardiovascular radiology), Pa. Radiologic Soc., Pa. Med. Soc., Montgomery County Med. Soc. (chmn. continuing edn. com. 1980-84, bd. dirs. 1983-89, v.p. 1983-84, pres. 1985-86, del. to Pa. Med. Soc. 1979-92, chair nominating com. 1988-89), Phila. Coll. Physicians and Surgeons, Phila. Roentgen Ray Soc., Am. Coll. Radiology (alt. councilor 1983-85), N.Y. Acad. Scis., Soc. for Magnetic Resonance Imaging, Radiolog. Soc. N.Am., World Affairs Coun., Alpha Omega Alpha.

WEINER, IRWIN M., medical educator, college dean, researcher; b. N.Y.C., Nov. 5, 1930; s. Samuel and Pearl (Levine) W.; m. Lois M. Fuxman, Apr. 18, 1961 (div. 1980); children: Stefanie F., Jeffrey N.; m. Lieselotte Roth, June 20, 1981. AB, Syracuse U., 1952; MD, SUNY-Syracuse, 1956. Postdoctoral fellow Johns Hopkins Sch. Medicine, Balt., 1956-58, instr., 1958-60, asst. prof., 1960-66; assoc. prof. SUNY, Upstate Med. Ctr., Syracuse, 1966-68, prof., chmn. dept., 1968-87, v.p. rsch., 1982-88, dean Coll. Medicine, 1987-91, v.p. for med. and biomed. edn., 1988-91; dean Coll. Medicine SUNY Health Sci. Ctr., Bklyn., 1991-96; emeritus prof. pharmacology SUNY Health Sci. Ctr., Syracuse, 1995—; vis. asst. prof. Albert Einstein Coll Medicine, Bronx, N.Y., 1964-65; cons. Sterling-Winthrop Rsch. Inst., N.Y., 1968-82, mem. rsch. bd., 1973-76; mem. study sect. Pharmacology and Exptl. Therapeutics "A", NIH, 1965-72, ad hoc com. on comparative pharmacology, Nat. Inst. Gen. Med. Scis., 1966-68, ad hoc com. rsch. career devel. awards and fellowships pharmacology, 1975-76; mem. consensus devel. panel analgesic associated kidney disease NIH, 1984; mem. pharmacology com. Nat. Bd. Med. Examiners, 1977-82; mem. rsch. com. Am. Heart Assn., 1969-74, chmn., 1969-74; mem. pharmacology adv. com. Pharm. Mfrs. Assn. Found., 1981—, chmn. basic pharmacology adv. com., 1987—; mem. N.Y. State Health Rsch. Coun., 1987—, chmn., 1991—. Field editor for renal pharmacology Jour. Pharmacology & Exptl. Theapeutics, 1965-72, editorial adv. bd., 1981-86; editorial bd. Life Scis. jour., 1973-79, renal, fluid and electrolyte physiology Am. Jour. Physiology, 1982-86; editorial com Ann. Rev. Pharmacology and Toxicology, 1982-86; contbr. over 90 articles to profl. jours., chpts. to books. Trustee Loretto Geriatric Ctr., 1989-91; bd. regents L.I. Coll. Hosp., 1993—; bd. dirs. Rsch. Found. SUNY, 1994—. Predoctoral fellow in physiology SUNY Upstate Med. Ctr., 1953-54; recipient numerous fed. fellowships, grants, 1956—, Rsch. Career Devel. award NIH, 1964-65. Mem. AAAS, Am. Soc. Pharmacology and Exptl. Therapeutics (bd. publs. trustees 1973-79), N.Y. Acad. Scis., Am. Soc. Nephrology, Internat. Soc. Biochem. Pharmacology, Internat. Soc. Nephrology, Assn. Med. Sch. Pharmacologists, N.Y. Acad. Medicine. Democrat. Jewish. Home: 39 Plaza St W Apt 10A Brooklyn NY 11217-3932 Office: State Univ NY Health Sci Ctr Bklyn Coll Med 450 Clarkson Ave Box 97 Brooklyn NY 11203

WEINER, IVAN JAY, urologist, educator; b. Alexandria, La., Jan. 4, 1934; s. Elias and Pauline (Mossoff) W.; m. Barbara Friedman, Sept. 4, 1960; children: David Alan, Robert Scott, Ellen Sue, Julie Ann. AB, Hamilton Coll., 1954; MD, Tulane U., 1958. Diplomate Am. Bd. Urology. Rotating intern Meadowbrook Hosp., Hempstead, N.Y., 1958-59; resident in gen. surgery Queens Hosp. Ctr., Jamaica, N.Y., 1959-60, resident in urology, 1960-63; pvt. practice, L.I., N.Y., 1963-66, 68, New Orleans, 1969—; clin. prof. urology Tulane U. Sch. Medicine, New Orleans, 1969—; mem. active staff Touro Infirmary, New Orleans, 1969—, Elmwood Med. Ctr., Jefferson, 1988—; mem. activee staff St. Charles Gen. Hosp., New Orleans, New Orleans, 1972—, chief staff, 1993—; mem. assoc. staff Tulane U. Hosp., 1996—. Capt. M.C., U.S. Army, 1966-68, Vietnam. Fellow ACS; mem. Am. Urol. Assn., S.E. Sect. Am. Urol. Assn., So. Med. Assn. Jewish.

WEINER, LESLIE PHILIP, neurology educator, researcher; b. Bklyn., Mar. 17, 1936; s. Paul Larry and Sarah (Paris) W.; m. Judith Marilyn Hoffman, Dec. 26, 1959; children: Patrice Weiner Miller, Allison Hope, Matthew, Jonathan. BA, Wilkes Coll., 1957; MD, U. Cin., 1961. Diplomate Am. Bd. Psychiatry and Neurology. Intern in medicine SUNY, Syracuse, 1961-62; resident in neurology Johns Hopkins Hosp., Balt., 1962-65, fellow, 1967-69; resident Balt. City Hosp., 1962-63; fellow in virology Slow Virus Lab., Nat. Inst. Neurol and Communicative Disorders-Stroke, NIH, Balt., 1969; asst. prof. neurology Johns Hopkins U., 1969-72, assoc. prof., 1972-75; prof. neurology and microbiology U. So. Calif. Sch. Medicine, L.A., 1975—, chmn. dept. neurology, 1979—, Richard Angus Grant Sr. chair in neurology, 1987—; chief neurologist U. So. Calif. Univ. Hosp., 1991, mem. bd. govs.; chief neurologist L.A. county-U. So. Calif. Med. Ctr., 1979-94; chmn. U. So. Calif. Gen. Clin. Res. Ctr., 1994-95; bd. dirs. John Douglas French Found., L.A., 1987—; mem. neurosci. tng. study sect. NIH, 1990-93, chmn., mem. sci. adv. bd. Hereditary Disease Found., 1992—, chmn., 1994-96. Contbr. over 120 articles on neurology, immunology and virology to med. jours., chpts. to books; mem. editl. bd. Infectious and Geographic Neurol., 1994—; assoc. editor: Neurobase. Bd. dirs. Starbright Found., L.A., 1991. Capt. M.C., U.S. Army, 1965-67. Grantee NIH, 1995-99, Kenneth Norris Found., 1995-97, Conrad Hilton Found., 1995-97. Fellow Am. Acad. Neurology; mem. AAAS, Am. Health Assistance Found., Am. Neurology Assn., Soc. Neurosci., Johns Hopkins U. Soc. Scholars, L.A. Acad. of Medicine, Assn. of Univ. Profs. of Neurology, Alpha Omega Alpha. Democrat. Jewish. Home: 625 S Rimpau Blvd Los Angeles CA 90005-3842 Office: U So Calif Sch Medicine 1510 San Pablo St Ste 646 Los Angeles CA 90033-4606

WEINER, MAURICE, health services administrator; b. Bklyn., Aug. 18, 1930; s. Charles and Esther (Brand) W. BBA, CUNY, 1951; postgrad., New Sch. for Social Rsch., N.Y.C., 1952-54. Housing adminstrv. asst. N.Y.C. Housing Authority, 1953-60; methods & planning analyst Citizens Nat. Bank, L.A., 1960-62; adminstrv. asst. L.A. City Unified Sch. Dist., 1962-65; dep. to city coun. mem. Tom Bradley, L.A., 1965-73; chief of staff Mayor Tom Bradley, 1973-76; adminstr. Tarzana Treatment Ctr., L.A., 1976—k; chmn. bd. dirs. San Fernando Valley Partnership for Prevention of Drug Abuse, L.A., 1993—; bd. dirs. The Alliance for Prevention of Drug Abuse, L.A., 1993—, Therapeutic Cmtys. of Am., Washington, 1992—. V.p. commn. Mcpl. Improvement Corp. of L.A., 1990—; coord. Californians for Liberal Representation, L.A., 1962-72; pres. So. Calif. Ams. for Dem. Action, L.A., 1985-86. Mem. AARP (chmn. health com. of state legis. com. 1992—, pres.'s commendation 1994). Democrat. Jewish. Home: 18307 Burbank Blvd # 228 Tarzana CA 91356 Office: Tarzana Treatment Ctr 18646 Oxnard St Tarzana CA 91356

WEINER, MURRAY, medical educator, pharmaceutical researcher; b. N.Y.C., Apr. 18, 1919; s. Samuel O. and Gussie (Begun) W.; m. Marilyn R. Greenberg, Jan. 14, 1951 (dec. 1973); children: Eve Gail Weiner Shauer, George Jay, Joan Sally Weiner Tarasar; m. Barbara Samuelson, Oct. 17, 1990. BS, CCNY, 1939; MS in Biochemistry, MD, NYU, 1943. Diplomate Am. Bd. Internal Medicine. Intern Sinai Hosp., Balt., 1944; resident, fellow NYU/Goldwater Meml. Hosp., N.Y.C., 1946-49, clin. researcher, 1946-70; from instr. to prof. NYU, N.Y.C., 1946-70; dept. head, v.p. Geigy Pharms., Ardsly, N.Y., 1956-70; v.p. rsch. Merrell-Nat. Labs., Cin., 1970-80; prof. medicine U. Cin., 1970—; pvt. practice, N.Y.C. and Plainveiw, N.Y., 1949-70; pres. Weiner Cons., Inc., Cin., 1980—; cons. in field. Author: The Medicine Makers, 1979, Nicotinic Acid, 1983, Side Effects to Exipients, 1989; editor: Clinical Pharmacology, 17 vols., 1986-91. Chmn. Cin. chpt. Project Hope, 1978-82. Capt. U.S. Army, 1944-46. Office: U Cin Med Ctr Cincinnati OH 45267

WEINER, MYRON FREDERICK, psychiatrist, educator; b. Atlantic City, June 4, 1934; s. Jack and Eva (Friedman) W.; m. Jeanette Harmon; children: Daniel, Gary, Darrel, Holli. MD, Tulane U., 1957. Diplomate Am. Bd. Psychiatry, qualifications in geriatric psychiatry. Intern Parkland Hosp., Dallas, 1957-58, resident, 1960-63; fellow in geriatrics and adult devel. Mt. Sinai Med. Ctr., N.Y.C., 1984-85; clin. instr. to assoc. prof. U. Tex. Southwestern Med. Ctr., Dallas, 1963-77, prof. psychiatry, 1980—; head geriatric psychiatry U. Tex Southwestern Med. Ctr., Dallas, 1985—; asst. prof. neurology U. Tex. Southwestern Med. Ctr., Dallas, 1989, head clin. core Alzheimer Disease Ctr., 1988—, vice-chair clin. affairs, 1993—. Author: Techniques of Group Psychotherapy, 1984, Practical Psychotherapy, 1986; editor: The Dementias: Diagnosis and Management, 1991, 2d edit., 1996; co-author: The Psychotherapist Patient Privilege, 1987. Mem. Tex. Alzheimer's Coun., 1991—. Capt. USAF, 1958-60. Mem. AMA, Am. Psychiatric Assn., Am. Assn. Geriatric Psychiatry, Tex. Soc. Psychiatry Physicians (pres. 1985-86). Office: U Tex Southwestern Med Ctr 5323 Harry Hines Blvd Dallas TX 75235-7200

WEINER, NORMAN, pharmacology educator; b. Rochester, N.Y., July 13, 1928; m. Diana Elaine Weiner, 1955; children: Steven, David, Jeffrey, Gareth, Eric. BS, U. Mich., 1949; MD, Harvard U., 1953. Diplomate Am. Bd. Med. Examiners. Intern 2d and 4th Harvard Med. Svc., Boston City Hosp., 1953-54; rsch. med. officer USAF, 1954-56; instr. dept. pharmacology-biochemistry Sch. of Aviation Medicine, San Antonio, 1954-56; from instr. to asst. prof. Harvard Med. Sch., Boston, 1956-67; prof. pharmacology U. Colo. Health Sci. Ctr., Denver, 1967—, disting. prof., 1989, chmn. dept. pharmacology, 1967-87; vis. prof. U. Calif., Berkeley, 1973-76; interim dean U. Colo. Sch. Medicine, 1983-84; Allan D. Bass lectr. sch. medicine Vanderbilt U., Nashville, 1983, divsn. v.p. Abbott Labs., Abbott Park, Ill., 1985-87; Pfizer lectr. Tex. Coll. Osteo. Medicine, Ft. Worth, 1985; disting. prof. UCHSC, 1989. Editor: Drugs and the Developing Brain, 1974, Structure and Function of Monoamine Enzymes, 1977, Regulation and Function of Monoamine Enzymes, 1981, Neuronal and Extraneuronal Events in Autonomic Pharmacology, 1984. Recipient Rsch. Career Devel. award USP HS, 1963, Kaiser Permanente award, 1974, 81, Otto Krayer award Am. Soc. Pharmacology and Exptl. Therapeutics, 1985; Spl. fellow USPHS, London, 1961-62; Disting. Volwiler Rsch. fellow Abbott Labs., 1988; Norman Weiner Festschrift, 1993; Julius Axelrod medal for outstanding scholarship in catecholamine rsch., 1993. Mem. AAAS, Am. Soc. for Pharmacology and Exptl. Therapeutics (Otto Krayer award 1985), N.Y. Acad. Scis., Assn. Med. Sch. Pharmacology, Am. Soc. Neurochemistry, Western Pharmacology Soc., Am. Coll. Neuropsychopharmacology, Soc. Neurosci., Biochem. Soc., Internat. Brain Rsch. Orgn., Internat. Soc. Neurochemistry, Rsch. Soc. on Alcoholism, Phi Beta Kappa, Sigma Xi, Alpha Omega Alpha, Phi Eta Sigma, Phi Lambda Upsilon, Phi Kappa Phi. Office: U Colo Health Sci Ctr Pharmacology Dept 4200 E 9th Ave Denver CO 80262-0236

WEINER, RICHARD DAVID, psychiatrist, researcher; b. N.Y.C., Nov. 25, 1945. BS, MIT, 1967; M of Systems Engring., U. Pa., 1969; MD, PhD, Duke U., 1973. Diplomate Am. Bd. Psychiatry and Neurology. Assoc. prof. psychiatry Duke U. Med. Ctr., Durham, N.C., 1984—, dir. electroconvulsive therapy program, 1991—; chief, psychiatry svc. VA Med. Ctr., Durham, N.C., 1993—. Recipient Merit award NIMH, 1988. Mem. Am. Psychiat. Assn. (chmn. electroconvulsive therapy task force 1987—). Office: Duke U Med Ctr PO Box 3309 Durham NC 27710-3309

WEINER, RICHARD LENARD, hospital administrator, educator, pediatrician; b. N.Y.C., May 23, 1951; s. Irving and Martha E. (Pell) W. AB in Biology, NYU, 1972; MD, Albert Einstein Coll. Medicine, 1975. Diplomate Am. Bd. Pediatrics. Instr. in pediat. Albert Einstein Coll. of Medicine, Bronx, N.Y., 1978-80, asst. prof. pediat., 1980-95, assoc. prof. pediat., 1995—, dir. divsn. faculty practice dept pediat., 1993—; pediatrician New Rochelle (N.Y.) Hosp. Med. Ctr., 1978-80; asst. dir. pediat. Hosp. of Albert Einstein Coll. of Medicine, Bronx, 1980-86; assoc. dir. pediat. Einstein-Weiler Hosp. MMC, Bronx, 1986—; dir. pediat. evaluation unit Einstein-Weiler Hosp., Bronx, 1990-95; coord. pediatric med. edn. New Rochelle Hosp., 1978-80; chmn. pvt. practice governance coun. dept. pediatrics Albert Einstein Coll. of Medicine, 1988-91; pres. Temple Beth Abraham Tarrytown, N.Y., 1995-96. Mem. editorial adv. bd. Primary Care/Emergency Decisions, 1984-88; contbr. articles to Jour. Pediatrics, Pediatrics, Pediatric Infectious Diseases, Emergency Decisions. Recipient Physician's Recognition award AMA, 1982, 86. Mem. Phi Beta Kappa, Beta Lambda Sigma. Jewish. Office: Einstein Hosp 1825 Eastchester Rd Bronx NY 10461-2373

WEINER, RICHARD S., healthcare administrator; b. Yonkers, N.Y., July 14, 1951; s. Joseph and Muriel (Zucker) W.; m. Kathryn, Aug. 25, 1985; children: Jason C., Rebecca E. BA, U. Del., 1976, MC, 1978, PhD, 1981. Nat. cert. counselor, crt. behavioral medicine, mediator; diplomate med. psychotherapy, profl. counseling; diplomate in pain mgmt. Exec. dir. Inst. Pain Mgmt., Ceres, 1983-90; assoc. dir. planning Meml. Hosp., Ceres, Calif., 1987-90; exec. dir. Am. Acad. Pain Mgmt., 1988—. Contbr. articles to profl. jours. Hon. citizen ambassador Med. Exch. Program to People's Republic China, coleader to Russia, Czechoslovakia, Hungary, Vietnam, Singapore, Thailand. Mem. Am. Pain Soc. (profl. edn. com.), Am. Mental Health Counseling (editorial rev. bd.). Home: 19240 Michigan Dr Twain Harte CA 95383-9794

WEINER, ROBERT HAROLD, clinical psychologist; b. Dallas, Aug. 3, 1951; s. Abe Arnold and Lillian Weiner; m. Doris Kephart, Mar. 20, 1994. BA, Northwestern U., 1973; PhD, Tex. Tech U., 1983. Lic. psychologist, health svc. provider, Tex. Staff psychologist Tex. Back Inst., Plano, 1984-86, dir. psychol. svcs., 1986-87; pvt. practice Plano, 1987—. Intern Human Rights Rsch. Coun., Crownpoint, N.Mex., 1974. Recipient Am. Jurisprudence award U. Tex. Sch. Law, 1974. Mem. APA, Tex. Psychol. Assn., Collin County Psychol. Assn., North Tex. Soc. Clin. Hypnosis, Assn. Applied Psychophysiology and Biofeedback, Physicians for a Nat. Health Program, Acad. Cert. Neurotherapist. Office: 2801 Regal Rd Ste 107 Plano TX 75075-6315

WEINER, SY, endodontist; b. Bklyn., Aug. 13, 1949; s. Alvin and Lee (Belkin) W.; m. Carol Ellen Sattler, May 13, 1952; children: Marisa, Erica. BS in Biology, SUNY, Stony Brook, 1971; DDS, Georgetown U., 1975. Diplomate Am. Bd. Endodontics. Resident in endodontics Med. Coll. Ga. Sch. Dentistry, Augusta, 1977-79; pvt. practice Pembroke Pines & Sunrise, Fla., 1979—; co-chmn. endodontics Dade County Dental Rsch. Ctr., Miami, Fla., 1979-84; instr. Broward County Dental Rsch. Ctr., Davie, Fla., 1985. Capt. U.S. Army Dental Corp., 1975-77. Mem. ADA, Am. Assn. Endodontics, Fla. Dental Assn., Broward County Dental Soc., South Broward Dental Soc. (pres.-elect), South Fla. Endodontic Study Club (pres. 1987-88), West Broward Dental Study Club (pres. 1984-85). Office: Ste 12 2500 N University Dr Fort Lauderdale FL 33322-3003

WEINERT, JEROME RAYMOND, nursing educator; b. Dayton, Ohio, Jan. 23, 1951; s. Fredrick J. Sr. and Eileen M. (Amann) W. ADN, Sinclair Community Coll., Dayton, 1981. Cert. massage therapist, neuromuscular therapist. ICU relief charge nurse Pardee Hosp., Hendersonville, N.C., 1982-83; program dir. Heart Path Cardiac Rehab. Program, Asheville, N.C., 1983-86; dir. outpatient svcs. Thoms Rehab. Hosp., Asheville, 1986-88; dir. Integrated Health Consultants, Sylva, N.C., 1988-94; faculty mem. Phoenix Therapeutic Massage Coll., 1994-95; pvt. practice wellness counseling & neuromuscular therapy, 1994—; faculty mem. Desert Inst. Healing Arts, 1995—. Sgt. USAF, 1970-74. Mem. Nat. Assn. Nurse Massage Therapists (Western regional dir.), Am. Massage Therapy Assn.

WEINGARTEN, KATHY, clinical psychologist; b. Bklyn., Jan. 13, 1947; d. Victor and Violet (Brown) W.; m. Hilary Goddard Worthen, June 15, 1969; children: Benjamin, Miranda Eve. BA, Smith Coll., 1969; PhD in Arts and Sci., Harvard U., 1974. Pvt. practice Newton, Mass., 1974—; asst. prof. dept. psychology Wellesley (Mass.) Coll., 1975-78; rsch. assoc. Wellesley (Mass.) Coll. Ctr. for Rsch. on Women, 1975-79; founder, dir. family tng. program, Dept. Psychiatry Judge Baker Children's Ctr. Harvard Med. Sch., Boston, 1979-87, teaching assoc., cons. Dept. Psychiatry, 1979-94; asst. prof. psychology dept. psychiatry Harvard Med. Sch., Boston, 1994—; co-dir. program in systemic therapies Family Inst. of Cambridge, Watertown, Mass., 1982-90, co-dir. program in narrative therapies, 1991—; presenter for psychol., med. and family therapy orgns. Author: The Mother's Voice: Strengthening Intimacy in Families, 1994; co-author: Sooner or Later: The Timing of Parenthood in Adult Lives, 1982; editor: Cultural Resistance: Challenging Beliefs About Men, Women and Therapy, 1995; editl. bd. Family Process, Jour. of Feminist Family Therapy; contbr. articles to profl. jours. Fellow Mass. Psychol. Assn.; mem. APA, Am. Assn. Marriage and Family Therapists (bd. dirs.), Am. Family Therapy Assn., Nat. Register Health Svc. Proficers, Soc. for Family Therapy and Rsch. Office: Family Inst of Cambridge 51 Kondazian St Watertown MA 02172-2830

WEINGEIST, THOMAS ALAN, ophthalmology educator; b. N.Y.C., Jan. 28, 1940; s. Samson and Fausta (Haim) W.; m. Carol Perera, Mar. 19, 1963 (div. Aug. 1977); children: Aaron P., Rachel; m. Catherine McGregor, Aug. 18, 1977; children: Robert M., David M. BA, Earlham Coll., 1963; PhD, Columbia U., 1969; MD, U. Iowa, 1972. Resident in ophthalmology U. Iowa, 1972-75, fellow in retina, 1976; asst. prof. ophthalmology U. Iowa, Iowa City, 1976-80, assoc. prof., 1980-83, prof., 1983—, prof., head dept. ophthalmology, 1986—. Mem. editl. bd. Documenta Ophthalmologica, The Netherlands, 1989-94, Ophthalmology World News, vice chair, 1994. Fellow Am. Acad. Ophthalmology (editorial bd. jour. 1982—, Honor award 1979, Sr. Honor award 1989, assoc. sec. for self-assessment 1988-93, sec. continuing edn. 1993—, trustee 1993—, sr. sec. clin. edn. 1994—); mem. Macula Soc., Retina Soc., Vitreous Soc., Am. Medico-Legal Found., Assn. Univ. Profs. Ophthalmology (bd. dirs., pres.-elect. 1994, pres. 1995). Home: 3 Heather Ct Iowa City IA 52245-3226 Office: U Iowa Dept Ophthalmology Iowa City IA 52242

WEINGOLD, ALLAN B., obstetrician, gynecologist, educator; b. N.Y.C., Sept. 2, 1930; s. Irving and Evelyne (Gold) W.; m. Marjorie Nassau, Dec. 21, 1952; children: Beth, Roberta, Matthew, Daniel. B.A., Oberlin Coll., 1951; M.D., N.Y. Med. Coll., 1955. Diplomate Am. Bd. Ob-Gyn. Instr. N.Y. Med.Coll., N.Y.C., 1960-63, asst. prof., 1963-67, assoc. prof., 1967-70, prof., 1970-73; prof., chmn. dept. ob-gyn George Washington U., Washington, 1973-92, v.p. med. affairs and exec. dean, 1992—; cons. NIH, Bethesda, Md., 1974—, Walter Reed Army Med. Ctr., Washington, 1974—. Author: Principles and Practices of Clinical Gynecology, 1988; editor: Monitoring the Fetal Environment, 1969, Surgical Complications of Pregnancy, 1984. Bd. dirs. Mayor's Adv. Bd. Maternal Health, Washington, 1981-87; mem. host com. John Glenn Campaign Com., Washington, 1983-85. Maj. U.S. Army, 1957-66. Recipient Alumni award N.Y. Med. Coll., 1974. Fellow Am. Coll. Obstetricians and Gynecologists (program chmn. 1975-77), Am. Gyn.-Ob. Soc. (coun. 1988-90); mem. Assn. Profs. Ob-Gyn. (sec. 1981-84, pres. 1985-86), Soc. Perinatal Rsch. Republican. Office: George Washington U 2300 I St NW Washington DC 20037-2396

WEINGRAD, DANIEL NEAL, oncologist, surgeon; b. N.Y.C., Mar. 11, 1947; s. Irving R. and Sylvia G. (Garfinkel) W.; m. Elizabeth Mary Gilbert, July 31, 1972; children: Julie, Marc, Rachel. BA, Columbia Coll., 1969; MD, Harvard U., 1973. Diplomate Am. Bd. Surgery. Intern then resident Peter Bent Brigham Hosp., Boston, 1973-75; clin. assoc. Nat. Cancer Inst., Bethesda, Md., 1975-77; resident U. Md. Hosp., Balt., 1977-79; fellow surg. oncology Meml. Sloan-Kettering Cancer Ctr., N.Y.C., 1979-81; surgical oncologist Miami (Fla.) Cancer Inst., 1981—. Contbr. articles to profl. jours. Pres. Am. Cancer Soc., Dade County, Fla., 1981—, mem. profl. edn. research com. Fla. div., 1985—, pres-elect Fla. divsn. Fellow Am. Cancer Soc., N.Y., 1979-81; named Rookie of Yr., 1984. Fellow ACS; mem. Fla. Med. Assn. (del. 1986-89), Soc. Surg. Oncology, Am. Soc. Clin. Oncology. Office: Mt Sinai Comprehensive Cancer Ctr 4306 Alton Rd Miami Beach FL 33140

WEINHOFF, MARTIN LEONARD, ophthalmologist; b. Chgo., May 17, 1945; s. David and Rose (Zelner) W.; m. Bonnie Dale Brilliant; children: Gregory, Debra. MD, U. Ill., 1970. Diplomate Am. Bd. Ophthalmology. Intern Montefiore Hosp., Bronx, N.Y., 1970-71; resident in ophthalmology Montefiore Hosp./Einstein Coll. Medicine, Bronx, 1973-76; asst. clin. prof. Albert Einstein Coll. of Medicine, Bronx, N.Y., 1976—; pvt. practice Hewlett, N.Y., 1976—. Fellow ACS, Am. Acad. Ophthalmology; mem. AMA, N.Y. Ophthalmology Soc., Nassau Med. Soc., N.Y. State Med. Soc., L.I. Ophthalmology Soc., Alpha Omega Alpha. Office: Martin L Weinhoff 1705 Broadway Hewlett NY 11557

WEINHOUSE, SIDNEY, biochemist, educator; b. Chgo., May 21, 1909; s. Harry and Dora (Cutler) W.; m. Sylvia Krawitz, Sept. 15, 1935 (dec. Aug. 1957); children: Doris Joan, James Lester, Barbara May; m. Adele Klein, Dec. 27, 1969. B.S., U. Chgo., 1933, Ph.D., 1936; D.M.S. (hon.), Med. Coll. Pa., 1973; D.Sc. (hon.), Temple U., 1976, U. Chieti, Italy, 1979, Jefferson Med. Coll., 1983. Eli Lilly fellow U. Chgo., 1936-38, Coman fellow, 1939-41; staff OSRD, 1941-44; with Houdry Process Corp., 1944-47; biochem. research dir. Temple U. Research Inst., 1947-50, prof. chemistry, 1952-77; emeritus prof. biochemistry Temple U. Med. Sch., 1977—; emeritus prof. Jefferson Med. Coll., 1991; sr. scientist Lankenau Med. Research Ctr., 1987—; head dept. metabolic chemistry Lankenau Hosp. Research Inst. and Inst. Cancer Research, 1950-57; chmn. div. biochemistry Inst. Cancer Research, 1957-61; assoc. dir. Fels Research Inst., Temple U. Med. Sch., Phila., 1961-64, dir., 1964-74; mem. bd. sci. advisers Inst. Environ. Health, NIH. Contbr. articles on original research to sci. jours.; editor: Jour. Cancer Research, 1969-79. Bd. dirs. Am. Cancer Soc. Mem. Am. Chem. Soc., Am. Soc. Biol. Chemists, Am. Assn. Cancer Research, Nat. Acad. Sci. Home: 1919 Chestnut St Phildelphia PA 19103-3401 Office: Lankenau Med Rsch Ctr 100 E Lancaster Ave Wynnewood PA 19096-3411 also: Jefferson Cancer Inst Rm 1034 273 S 10th St Philadelphia PA 19107

WEINLAND, ROBERT LOGAN, emergency physician; b. Fayetteville, N.C., Apr. 19, 1951; s. George C. and Mary (Morrison) W.; m. Victoria Regina Rocca, Sept. 7, 1975; children: James, Joanna, Madeline. BA in Chemistry, Ind. U., 1973, MD, 1977. Diplomate Am. Bd. Emergency Medicine, 1984. Intern and residency in family practice Community Hosp. of Indpls., 1977-78; staff physician J.F. Kennedy Med. Ctr., L.A., 1982-85, Huron Meridia, Cleve., 1985-86, Hillcrest Meridia, Cleve., 1985—; dir. Community Urgent Care Ctr., Manhattan Beach, Calif., 1983-85; pvt. practice emergency medicine Cleve., 1985—; paramedic coord. Mayfield Village, Cleve., 1989—. Capt. USPHS, 1978-81. Fellow Am. Coll. Emergency Physicians; mem. Soc. Emergency Medicine N.E. Ohio. Home: 2888 Manchester Rd Cleveland OH 44122-2571 Office: Hillcrest Meridia Hosp 6780 Mayfield Rd Cleveland OH 44124-2203

WEINLANDER, MAX MARTIN, retired psychologist; b. Ann Arbor, Mich., Sept. 9, 1917; s. Paul and Emma Carol (Lindemann) W.; BA, Ea. Mich. Coll., 1940; MA, U. Mich., 1942, PhD, 1955; M.A., Wayne U., 1951; m. Albertina Adelheit Abrams, June 4, 1946; children: Bruce, Annette. Psychometrist, VA Hosp., Dearborn, Mich., 1947-51; sr. staff psychologist Ohio Div. Corrections, London, 1954-55; lectr. Dayton and Piqua Centers, Miami U., Oxford, Ohio, 1955-62; chief clin. psychologist Child Guidance Clinic, Springfield, Ohio, 1956-61, acting dir., 1961-65; clin psychologist VA Center, Dayton, Ohio, 1964-79; cons. Ohio Divsn. Mental Hygiene; summer guest prof. Miami U., 1957, 58, Wittenberg U., 1958; adj. prof. Wright State

U., Dayton, 1975-76; cons. State Ohio Bur. Vocat. Rehab., Oesterlen Home Emotionally Disturbed Children. Pres. Clark County Mental Health Assn., 1960, Clark County Health and Welfare Club, 1961; mem. Community Welfare Coun. Clark County, 1964; chmn. Comprehensive Mental Health Planning Com. Clark County, 1964; trustee United Appeals Fund, 1960. Mem. citizens adv. coun. Columbus Psychiat. Inst., Ohio State U. Served as sgt. AUS, 1942-46. Fellow Ohio Psychol. Assn. (chmn. com. on utilization of pscyhologists; treas., exec. bd. 1968-71); mem. Am. Psychol. Assn., Ohio Psychol Assn., Mich. Psychol. Assn., DAV, U. Mich. Pres. Club, Pi Kappa Delta, Pi Gamma Mu, Phi Delta Kappa. Republican. Lutheran. Lodge: Kiwanis. Contbr. 18 articles to psychology jours. Home: 17185 Valley Dr Big Rapids MI 49307-9523

WEINMAN, JOEL B., optometrist; b. Bklyn., Jan. 8, 1937; s. Frank and Rose (Sobel) W.; student U. Pitts., 1954-56; BS, DO, Pa. Coll. Optometry, 1960; m. Gretchen FonDersmith, Sept. 20, 1970; children by previous marriage-Jay, Michael, Richard. Practice optometry, Kutztown, Pa., 1960—; pres. Kutztown Optical, Inc.; instr. Reading Area Community Coll.; cons., lectr. rehab. of partially sighted children Kutztown State Coll.; mem. council sports and vision Bausch & Lomb. Mem. Gov.'s Council to Study Health Trend in State of Pa., 1970; mem. opticianary sci. adv. com. Reading Area C.C.; bd. dirs. N.E. chpt. Cystic Fibrosis, 1989—. Diplomate Nat. Bd. Optometric Examiners. Fellow Am. Acad. Optometry; mem. APHA, Am. Optometric Assn. (charter mem. sect. contact lenses), Pa. Optometric Assn. (vision screening chmn. 1966-67, chmn. practice mgmt. 1967-68, 73—), Berks County Optometric Soc. (pres. 1968-69), Berkeleigh Optometric Profl. Assn. (pres. 1970—), Vision Conservation Inst., Am. Optometric Found., Assn. Kremer Laser Eye Ctr. Postoperative Mgmt. Surgery, Beta Sigma Kappa. Jewish (dir. temple 1967-69). Clubs: Lions, Rotary. Home: PO Box 268 Kutztown PA 19530-0268

WEINMANN, JUDY MUNGER, nurse; b. Georgetown, Tenn., June 1, 1943; d. Paul and Martha Edith (Smith) Powell; m. David Finley Munger, Dec. 6, 1963 (div. June 1985); children: David Finley Jr., Robert Powell. G-rad., Erlanger Hosp., Chattanooga, 1964; AS, Cleveland (Tenn.) State Coll., 1982; BS, U. Tenn., 1984. RN, Tenn.; cert. occupational health nurse, Tenn. Med. staff nurse Bradley Meml. Hosp., Cleveland, 1964; office nurse William I. Proffitt, M.D., Cleveland, 1964-65; occupational health nurse Singer-Cobble Co., Chattanooga, 1966-67, Burlington Woolens Co., Cleveland, 1967-68, Am. Uniform Co., Cleveland, 1972-73; sch. nurse Cleveland State Coll., 1968-72, Bradley High Sch., Cleveland, 1973-79; occupational health nurse M&M/Mars, Cleveland, 1979-91; dir. nursing Open Arms Care Corp., Ooltewah, Tenn., 1992-93, Tenn. Home Health, Hixson, Tenn., 1993; dir. cmty. edn./case mgmt. Med. Shares Home Care, Chattanooga, Tenn., 1994—; presenter in field. Nurse ARC, Cleveland, 1979—; chmn. Bradley County Substance Abuse Com., Cleveland, 1980-87; com. mem. Am. Cancer Soc., Chattanooga, 1984—. Recipient Schering award as Tenn. outstanding occupational health nurse Schering-Plough Co., 1989. Mem. Chattanooga, Tenn. Nurses Assn., Tenn. Occupational Health Nurses Assn. (bd. dirs. 1986—), Chattanooga Occupational Health Nurses Assn. (v.p., bd. dirs., Pres.'s award 1989), Cleveland Area Safety Coun. (Safety award 1988). Democrat. Baptist. Home: 1200 King Arthur Rd Chattanooga TN 37421

WEINMANN, ROBERT LEWIS, neurologist; b. Newark, Aug. 21, 1935; s. Isadore and Etta (Silverman) W.; m. Diana Weinmann, Dec. 13, 1980 (dec. Dec. 1989); children: Paul, Chris, Dana, Paige. BA, Yale U., 1957; MD, Stanford U., 1962. Diplomate Am. Bd. of EEG and Neurophysiology, v.p.; diplomate Am. Acad. Pain Mgmt., Am. Bd. Forensic Medicine. Intern Pacific Presbyn. Med. Ctr., San Francisco, 1962-63; resident in neurology Stanford U. Hosp., 1963-66, chief resident, 1965-66; pvt. practice San Jose, Calif., 1969—. Chmn. editorial bd. Clin. EEG Jour.; mem. editorial bd. Jour. Am. Acad. Pain Mgmt.; formerly mem. editorial bd. Clin. Evoked Potentials Jour.; contbr. articles to various publs. Capt. M.C., U.S. Army, 1966-68, Japan. Award recipient State of R.I., Santa Clara County Med. Soc., Epilepsy Soc., other orgns.; fellow Univ. Paris, 1957-58. Union of Am. Physicians and Dentists (pres. 1990—, bd. dirs. 1972—, pres. Calif. fedn. 1990—). Office: Union Am Physicians & Dentists 1330 Broadway Ste 730 Oakland CA 94612-2506

WEINMANN, ROBERTO, molecular biologist, educator; b. Buenos Aires, Dec. 30, 1941; came to U.S., 1967; s. Bernardo and Gerda (Tobias) W.; m. Nury Vicens, Dec. 25, 1967 (div.); children: Guillermo, Joslyne. Bachelor's degree, Nat. Coll. Buenos Aires, 1960; Lic. in Biology, Sch. of Scis., Buenos Aires, 1967; PhD, Iowa State U., 1972. Postdoctoral fellow Washington U. Sch. Medicine, St. Louis, 1972-76; asst. prof. to assoc. prof. Wistar Inst., Phila., 1976-93; from asst. to assoc. prof. molecular biology grad. group Med. Sch. U. Pa., 1976—; rsch. fellow Bristol-Myers Squibb PRI, Princeton, N.J., 1993—; vis. sr. rsch. scientist dept. molecular biology, Princeton U., 1993—; cons. Pew Latin Am. Fellows Program, San Francisco, 1991-95. Mem. editorial bd. Gene Expression, 1990—; contbr. rsch. articles to sci. jours. Humboldt fellow Inst. for Genetics, U. Cologne, West Germany, 1975, INSERM fellow Pasteur Inst., Paris, 1983. Mem. Internat. Cell Rsch. Orgn., Am. Soc. Virology, Am. Soc. Microbiology. Office: Bristol-Myers Squibb PO Box 4000 Princeton NJ 08543-4000

WEINREB, ARI, physician, geneticist; b. Columbus, Ohio, Oct. 20, 1962; s. Irwin and Reneé (Leder) W.; m. Jane E., March 29, 1987; 1 child, Joshua Tobyn. BS, U. So. Calif., 1983; MD, Albert Einstein Coll. Medicine, Bronx, N.Y., 1990, PhD, 1990. Diplomate Am. Bd. Internal Medicine. Resident in internal medicine New Eng. Med. Ctr. at Tufts Univ., Boston, 1990-93; fellow in med. genetics UCLA, 1993—. reviewer Jour. Arteriosclerosis, Thrombosis and Vascular Biology, L.A., 1994—; contbr. articles to profl. jours. Grantee Multipurpose Arthritis and Musculoskeletal Disease Ctr. NIH, 1993. Mem. ACP, Phi Beta Kappa, Alpha Omega Alpha. Jewish. Office: Dept Medicine Divsn Cardiology 047-123 CHS UCLA Los Angeles CA 90095

WEINREB, ROBERT NEAL, ophthalmologist, educator; b. N.Y.C., Nov. 23, 1949; s. David and Ruth (Kramer) W. S.B., MIT; M.D., Harvard U., 1975. Diplomate Am. Bd. Ophthalmology. Resident in ophthalmology U. Calif.-San Francisco, 1976-80, fellow in glaucoma, 1981; mem. faculty U. Calif.-San Diego, La Jolla, 1984—, prof. ophthalmology, 1984—, vice chair, 1984—, chief glaucoma div., 1984—. Chief editor Focus on Glaucoma, 1986—; assoc. editor Jour. Glaucoma, 1992—. Recipient Hogan prize U. Calif.-San Francisco, 1981, Alcon prize Alcon Rsch. Inst., 1983, 92. Fellow Am. Acad. Ophthalmology (Honor award 1986, Sr. Honor award 1996); mem. Internat. Soc. Eye Rsch., Assn. Rsch. in Vision and Ophthalmology (Helmholtz award 1979). Office: U Calif San Diego Glaucoma Ctr and Rsch Labs 9415 Campus Point Dr La Jolla CA 92093

WEINRICH, ALAN JEFFREY, occupational hygienist; b. Passaic, N.J., Aug. 24, 1953; s. Erwin Hermann and Ann Elizabeth (Gall) W.; m. Nina Kathryn Hooker, Jan. 14, 1983; 1 child, Sheena Elizabeth Rochelle. BS with high honors, Rutgers U., 1975; MS, U. Iowa, 1988, postgrad., 1988-89. Cert. Am. Bd. Indsl. Hygiene, cert. environ. trainer Nat. Environ. Tng. Assn. Indsl. hygienist Tenn. Dept. Labor, Nashville, 1975-78; health info. specialist occupl. health program U. Tenn., Memphis, 1980-82; vol. tchr. Internat. Sch. Moshi, Tanzania, 1982-84; sr. rsch. asst. agrl. medicine rsch. facility U. Iowa, Iowa City, 1985-89; sr. indsl. hygienist PSI Energy, Inc., Plainfield, Ind., 1989-92; asst. dir. health & safety programs environ. mgmt. and edn. Purdue U., West Lafayette, 1992-94; assoc. dir. tech. affairs Am. Conf. Govtl. Indsl. Hygienists, Cin., 1994—. Co-editor book supplement: Documentation of the Threshold Limit Values and Biological Exposure Indices, 1996. Mem. healthy cities com. Butler-Tarkington Neighborhood Assn., Indpls., 1992-94. Mem. Am. Acad. Indsl. Hygiene, Am. Conf. Govtl. Indsl. Hygienists (column editor newsletter 1995—), Am. Indsl. Hygiene Assn. (v.p. Mid-South sect. 1981-82, bd. dirs. Iowa-Ill. sect. 1987-89, bd. dirs. Ind. sect. 1991-94, pres. Ind. sect. 1994-95), Internat. Occupl. Hygiene Assn., Am. Soc. Assn. Execs. Democrat. Office: Am Conf Govtl Indsl Hygienists 1330 Kemper Meadow Dr Cincinnati OH 45240-1634

WEINSTEIN, ALBERT, ophthalmologist; b. Bridgeport, Conn., June 16, 1932; s. Samuel L. and Jennie (Rome) W.; m. Helen Sue Berger, July 5, 1959; children: Kenneth Louis, Richard Bruce, Jeffrey Paul. BA, Wesleyan U., 1954; MD, Boston U. Sch. Medicine, 1958. Diplomate Am. Bd. Ophthalmology. Cons. ophthalmologist U.S. Pub. Health Svc., Salt Lake City, 1962-64; pvt. practice Bridgeport, 1964—. Mem. Am. Acad. Ophthalmology, Conn. State Med. Soc., Fairfield County Med. Soc. Republican. Jewish. Home: 24 Glenarden Rd Trumbull CT 06611 Office: 2962 Main St Bridgeport CT 06606

WEINSTEIN, CLEMENT, physician; b. Bklyn., Apr. 11, 1926; s. Samuel and Sadie (Furman) W.; m. Gertrude Caroline Rindsberg, Sept. 23, 1950; children: Roslyn, Fred, Lawrence, Barbara. AB, Columbia Coll., 1947; MD, SUNY, Bklyn., 1950. Intern Maimonides Hosp., Bklyn., 1950-51; resident in medicine Bronx (N.Y.) VA Hosp., 1951, Montefiore Hosp., Bronx, 1954-55; Dazian Found. rsch. fellow L.I. Jewish Hosp., New Hyde Park, N.Y., 1955-56, staff physician, 1956-96; staff physician North Shore U. Hosp., Manhasset, N.Y., 1994—; attending in medicine Jamaica (N.Y.) Hosp., 1956-95, dir. cardiology, 1968-92; geriatrician Grace Plaza of Great Neck, N.Y., 1994-95, Ctr. for Extended Care and Rehab., North Shore U. Hosp., Manhasset, N.Y., 1996—; project coord. Digitelis Investigative Group, Jamaica, N.Y., 1992—. V.p. N.Y. PSR, 1993—. Fellow Am. Coll. Physicians. Home: 69-18 179th St Flushing NY 11365 Office: Ctr Extended Care/Rehab North Shore Univ Hosp 300 Community Dr 16C Manhasset NY 11030

WEINSTEIN, DAVID, physician; b. Miami Beach, Fla., July 9, 1958; s. Henry Robert and Norma Elaine Weinstein; m. Tracy Lynne Gevirtz, Nov. 18, 1990; children: Emery, Sarah. BS, Tulane U., 1980; MD, Mt. Sinai Sch. Medicine, N.Y.C., 1985. Resident Mt. Sinai Hosp., N.Y.C., 1985-90; physician Varady & Weinstein, West Palm Beach, Fla., 1990—; dir. J.F.K. Bladder Control Ctr., Atlantis, Fla., 1993—; chmn. bylaws com. Bethesda Hosp., Boynton Beach, Fla., 1995-96. Fellow ACS; mem. Am. Urol. Assn., S.E. sect. Am. Urol. Assn., Palm Beach Med. Soc. Office: 114 JFK Dr West Palm Beach FL 33462

WEINSTEIN, GERALD D., dermatology educator; b. N.Y.C., Oct. 13, 1936; m. Marcia Z. Weinstein; children: Jeff, Jon, Debbie. BA, U. Pa., 1957, MD, 1961. Diplomate Am. Bd. Dermatology. Intern Los Angeles County Gen. Hosp., 1961-62; clin. assoc. dermatology br. Nat. Cancer Instn. NIH, Bethesda, Md., 1962-64; resident dept. dermatology U. Miami, Fla., 1964-65; asst. prof. Dept. Dermatology U. Miami, Fla., 1966-71, assoc. prof., 1971-74, prof., 1975-79; prof., chmn. dept. dermatology U. Calif., Irvine, 1979—, acting dean Coll. Medicine, 1985-87; attending staff VA Med. Ctr., Long Beach, Calif., 1979—, UCI Med. Ctr., Orange, Calif., 1979—, St. Joseph Hosp., Orange, 1980—. Contbr. articles to profl. jours., chpts. to books. Recipient Lifetime Achievement award Nat. Psoriasis Found., 1994; co-recipient award for psoriasis rsch. Taub Internat. Meml., 1971; NIH spl. postdoctoral fellow, 1965-67. Mem. Am. Acad. Dermatology (chmn. task force on psoriasis 1986—, bd. dirs. 1984-88). Office: U Calif Irvine Coll Medicine Dept Dermatology Irvine CA 92697-2400

WEINSTEIN, HOWARD EUGENE, neurologist; b. Bklyn., Sept. 13, 1946; s. George and Jean (Averbach) W.; m. Susan Katz, 1995; children by previous marriage: Jackie, Stewart. Student, La Salle Coll., Phila., 1964-67; MD, Temple U., Phila., 1971. Diplomate Am. Bd. Psychiatry and Neurology. Intern SUNY, Buffalo, 1971-72; resident, fellow U. Mich., Ann Arbor, 1972-77, mem. exec. faculty neurology, 1975-77; pvt. practice Mesa and Tempe, Ariz., 1979—. Vol. Cantor Temple Emanuel, Tempe, 1982-94, Temple Beth Sholom, Mesa, Ariz., 1994—. Maj. U.S. Army, 1977-79. Fellow Am. Acad. Neurology; mem. Am. Acad. Neurology (Geriat. Sect.), Am. Epilepsy Soc., Am. EEG Soc. Judaism. Office: 1920 E Baseline Tempe AZ 85283

WEINSTEIN, I. BERNARD, oncologist, geneticist, research administrator; b. Madison, Wis., Sept. 9, 1930; married, 1952; 3 children. BS, U. Wis., 1952, MD, 1955. Nat. Cancer Inst. spl. rsch. fellow bacteriology/immunology Harvard Med. Sch./MIT, Boston, 1959-61; career scientist Health Rsch. Coun., City of N.Y., 1961-72; assoc. vis. physician Francis Delafield Hosp., 1961-66; from asst. attending physician to assoc. attending physician Presbyn. Hosp., 1967-81, attending physician, 1981—; from asst. to assoc. prof. medicine Coll. Physicians & Surgeons, divsn. Environ. Sci., N.Y.C., 1978-90; prof. medicine Columbia U., N.Y.C., 1973—, prof. pub. health, 1978—, dir. divsn. oncology, prof. genetics and devel., 1990—, Frode Jensen prof. medicine, dir. comprehensive cancer ctr., 1985—; advisor Lung Cancer Segment, Carcinogenesis Program, Nat. Cancer Inst., 1971-74, Chem. and Molecular Biol. Segment, 1973-76; mem. interdisciplinary comm. program Smithsonian Inst., 1971-74, Pharmacology B Study ect., NIH, 1971-75, numerous sci. and adv. coms. Nat. Cancer Inst., Am. Cancer Soc., 1976-88; advisor Roswell Park Meml. Inst., Buffalo, Brookhaven Nat. Lab., Divsn. Cancer Cause and Prevention, Nat. Cancer Inst., Coun. on Analysis and Projects, Am. Cancer Soc., Internat. Agy. for Rsch. on Cancer, WHO, Lyon, France; Nakasone vis. prof., Tokyo, 1987; GM Cancer Rsch. Found. vis. prof. Internat. Agy. Rsch. Cancer, Lyon, 1988. Assoc. editor Cancer Rsch., 1973-76, 86—, Jour. Environ. Pathology and Toxicology, 1977-84, Jour. Cellular Physiology, 1982-89. Recipient Meltzer medal, 1964, Dlowes award Am. Assn. Cancer Rsch., 1987, Silvio O. Conte award Environ. Health Inst., 1990; Louise Weissberger lectr. U. Rochester, 1981, Mary Ann Swetland lectr. Case Western Res. U., 1983, Daniel Laszlo Meml. lectr. Montefiore Med. Ctr., 1983, Samuel Kuna Disting. lectr. Rutgers U., 1985, Ester Langer lectr. U. Chgo., 1989, Harris Meml. lectr. MIT, 1989; European Molecular Biology Orgn. travel fellow, 1970-71. Mem. AAAS (coun. del. 1985-88, pres. 1990-91), Inst. Medicine/Nat. Acad. Sci., Am. Soc. Microbiology, Internat. Soc. Quantum Biology, Am. Assn. Cancer Rsch., Am. Soc. Clin. Investigation, N.Y. Acad. Sci. Office: Inst Cancer Rsch Columbia Univ 701 W 168th St New York NY 10032

WEINSTEIN, IRWIN MARSHALL, internist, hematologist; b. Denver, Mar. 5, 1926; m. Judith Braun, 1951. Student, Dartmouth Coll., 1943-44, Williams Coll., 1944-45; MD, U. Colo., Denver, 1949. Diplomate Am. Bd. Internal Medicine (assoc. bd. govs. hematology subcom.). Intern Montefiore Hosp., N.Y.C., 1949-50; jr. asst. resident in medicine Montefiore Hosp., 1950-51; sr. asst. resident in medicine U. Chgo., 1951-52, resident in medicine, 1952-53, instr. in medicine, 1953-54, asst. prof. medicine, 1954-55; vis. assoc. prof. medicine U. Calif. Center for Health Scis., L.A., 1955-56, assoc. clin. prof., 1957-60, clin. prof., 1970—; sect. chief in medicine, hematology sect. Wadsworth Gen. Hosp., VA Center, L.A., 1956-59; pvt. practice medicine specializing in hematology and internal medicine Los Angeles, 1959—; mem. staff Cedars-Sinai Med. Center, L.A., 1959—; chief of med. staff Cedars-Sinai Med. Ctr., 1972-74, bd. govs., 1974—; mem. staff U. Calif. Ctr. Health Scis., Wadsworth Gen. Hosp., VA Ctr.; vis. prof. Hadassah Med. Ctr., Jerusalem, 1967; adv. for health affairs to Hon. Alan Cranston, 1971-92; mem. com. on space biology and medicine Space Sci. Bd.; active UCLA Comprehensive Cancer Ctr. Contbr. articles to profl. publs.; editor: (with Ernest Beutler) Mechanisms of Anemia, 1962. Master ACP (gov. So. Calif. Region I 1989-93); fellow Israel Med. Assn. (hon.); mem. AAAS, Am. Fedn. Clin. Rsch., Am. Soc. Hematology (exec. com. 1974-78, chmn. com. on practice 1978-87, mem. council 1974-78), Am. Soc. Internal Medicine, Assn. Am. Med. Colls., Internat. Soc. Hematology, Internat. Soc. Internal Medicine, L.A. Acad. Medicine, L.A. Soc. Nuclear Medicine, Inst. of Medicine NAS, N.Y. Acad. Sci., Reticulo-Endothelial Soc., Royal Soc. Medicine, Western Soc. Clin. Rsch., Alpha Omega Alpha. Office: 8635 W 3rd St Ste 665 Los Angeles CA 90048-6101

WEINSTEIN, JOSEPH MATTHEW, cardiologist; b. White Plains, N.Y., June 11, 1958; s. Lionel Adn Sidel (Bayner) W.; m. Lynne Robin Davis, May 10, 1987 (div. May 1994); 1 child, Jeffrey Phillip. BA, Brown U., 1982, MD, 1992. Intern, resident Boston City Hosp., 1982-85; fellow cardiology Univ. Hosp., Boston, 1985-87; attending physician Cardinal Cushing Hosp., Brockton, Mass., 1987-93, Goddard Meml. Hosp., Stoughton, Mass., 1987-93; chmn. dept. medicine Good Samaritan Med. Ctr., Brockton, 1994—. Contbr. chpt. to book. Fellow Am. Coll. Cardiology; mem. Am. Coll. Physicians, Alpha Omega Alpha, Phi Beta Kappa. Office: 40 Bridgewater Park Med Assocs 9660 Park St Stoughton MA 02172

WEINSTEIN, LOUIS, obstetrics and gynecology educator, researcher; b. Cambridge, Mass., June 8, 1946; s. Edward W. and Pearl F. (Cohen) W.; m. Andrea B. Connor, May 12, 1975; 1 child, Joshua. BS, Bates Coll., 1968; MD, Wake Forest U., 1972. Diplomate Am. Bd. Ob-Gyn., Am. Bd. Maternal-Fetal Medicine. Intern, then resident in ob-gyn. U. Colo., Denver, 1972-76; asst. prof., then assoc. prof. U. Ariz., Tucson, 1978-91; assoc. prof. to prof. ob-gyn., chmn. dept. Med. Coll. Ohio, 1992—. Contbr. numerous articles to med. jours. Lt. comdr. M.C., USNR, 1976-78. Office: Med Coll Ohio 3000 Arlington Ave Toledo OH 43699

WEINSTEIN, MARIE PASTORE, psychologist; b. N.Y.C., Oct. 3, 1940; d. Edward and Sarah (Mancuso) Pastore; children: Arielle Rebecca, Damon Alexander. BA in Polit. Sci. and Lit., Ind. U.; MS in Psychology, L.I. U.; PhD in Ednl. Psychology, CCNY, 1986. Cert. sch. psychologist; lic. psychologist, N.Y. Sch. psychologist evaluation unit Bd. Edn., N.Y.C., 1977-78; dir., adminstr. learning ctr. Guidance Ctr. Flatbush, Bklyn., 1978-82; clin. team coord./psychologist Lorge Upper and Lower Sch., N.Y.C., 1982-85; psychologist devel. disabilities ctr. Roosevelt Hosp., N.Y.C., 1985-87; chief psychologist Blueberry Treatment Ctrs., Bklyn., 1987-89; cons. psychologist Ctr. for Children & Families, St. Albans, N.Y., 1989—; cons. psychologist United Cerebral Palsy Hearst Presch., Bklyn., 1988-89, Charles Drew Day Ctr., Queens Village, N.Y., 1982-85, Warbasse Nursery Sch., Bklyn., 1981-85, YWCA Montessori Sch., 1993-94; adj. asst. prof. Baruch Coll. CUNY, 1989; pvt. practice, Bklyn.; rsch. cons. Children's TV Workshop, N.Y.C., 1979; clin. cons. Bedford Stuyvesant Mental Health Ctr., Bklyn., 1990, Youth Counseling League, N.Y.C., 1993; cons. dist. 2 N.Y.C. Bd. Edn., 1988; guest lectr. Met. Hosp. Dept. Psychiatry, N.Y.C., 1988, Dist. 3 Bd. Edn., 1993; edn. cons. Lit. Vols. N.Y., 1974-76. Contbg. author to children's ency., 1970. Bd. dirs. Artists in Search of. . . . Fellow Am. Orthopsychiat. Assn. (program com. 1990—); mem. APA, Internat. Congress on Child Abuse and Neglect, Manhattan Fedn. Child and Adolescent Svcs. Office: 26 Court St Ste 2112 Brooklyn NY 11242-0103

WEINSTEIN, MARION LOUIS, radiologist; b. Atlanta, Apr. 11, 1944; s. Benjamin Jacob and Dora (Berger) W.; m. Cheryl Struletz, Apr. 1, 1949; 1 child, Joseph David. AB, Emory U., 1966; MD, Med. Coll. Ga., Augusta, 1973. Cert. diagnostic radiologist. Surg. intern U. Fla., Gainesville, 1973-74; resident diagnostic radiology Med. Coll. Ga., Augusta, 1974-77; fellow diagnostic ultrasound Med. Sch. Vanderbilt U., Nashville, 1977-78, asst. prof., chief sect. of diagnostic ultrasound, 1978-79; assoc. Dept. Radiology St. Francis Hosp., Miami Beach, Fla., 1979-83; chmn. Dept. Radiology North Fulton Med. Ctr., Roswell, Ga., 1983-84; assoc. Diagnostic Imaging Specialists, Atlanta, 1984-86; chief Dept. Radiology Heard County Community Hosp., Franklin, Ga., 1984-87; med. dir. Manatee Med. Imaging, Inc., Bradenton, Fla., 1987-91; assoc. Dept. Radiology Hialeah (Fla.) Hosp., 1992—. Author: (with others) Principles of Diagnostic Ultrasound, 2d edit., 1979. With USMCR, 1966-72. Fellow in diagnostic ultrasound and C-T scanning Vanderbilt U. Med. Ctr., 1978. Mem. Radiol. Soc. N. Am., Am. Coll. Radiology, Am. Inst. Ultrasound in Medicine, Am. Roentgen Ray Soc., Greater Miami Radiol. Soc., Fla. Radiol. Soc., Dade County Med. Assn., Fla. Med. Assn. Democrat. Jewish. Office: Hialeah Hospital PO Box 3429 2211 W 60th St Hialeah FL 33016-4410

WEINSTEIN, MICHAEL PAUL, orthopaedic surgeon; b. Pitts., Dec. 17, 1954; s. Sidney and Blanche (Schwartstein) W.; m. Marcy Joan McKown; children: Macklan, Mason, McKenna. BS, U. Pitts., 1976, MD, 1980. Resident in orthopaedic surgery Upstate Med. Ctr., Syracuse, 1981-85; pvt. practice orthopaedic surgery Newport Beach, Calif., 1987—. Jewish. Office: Calif Ortho Specialists 360 San Miguel Dr Ste 701 Newport Beach CA 92660-5927

WEINSTEIN, RALPH ELLIOT, hematologist, oncologist; b. Chgo., Dec. 16, 1954. MD, SUNY, Syracuse, 1982. Diplomate in internal medicine, hematology and oncology Am. Bd. Internal Medicine. Intern Roger Williams Gen. Hosp., Providence, 1982-83, resident in internal medicine, 1983-85; fellow in hematology and oncology U. Conn. Sch. Med., 1985-88; staff in hematology/oncology Good Samaritan Hosp., Portland, Oreg., 1990—, Emanuel Hosp., Portland, 1990—, St. Vincents Hosp., Portland, 1990—. Mem. ACP, AMA, Am. Soc. Clin. Oncology, Am. Soc. Hematology. Office: 2311 NW Northrup St Ste 105 Portland OR 97210-2954

WEINSTEIN, RONALD S., physician, pathologist, educator; b. Schenectady, N.Y., Nov. 20, 1938; s. H. Edward and Shirley (Diamond) W.; m. Mary Dominica Corabi, July 12, 1964; children: Katherine Eiliesh, John Benjamin. B.S., Union Coll., Schenectady, 1960; M.D., Tufts U., 1965. Diplomate: Am. Bd. Pathology; 1972. Chemist Marine Biol. Lab., Woods Hole, Mass., 1960-62; intern Mass. Gen. Hosp., Boston, 1965-66, clin. and research fellow, 1965-70, resident in pathology, 1966-70; dir. Mixter Lab., 1966-70; vice chmn. pathology Aerospace Med. Research Labs., Dayton, Ohio, 1970-72; asso. prof. pathology Tufts U., 1972-75; Harriet Blair Borland prof., chmn. dept. pathology Rush Med. Coll. and Rush-Presbyn.-St. Luke's Med. Center, Chgo., 1975-90; prof., head dept. pathology U. Ariz. and U. Med. Ctr., Tucson, 1990—; dir. Ariz. Telemedicine Program, Tucson, 1996—; teaching fellow Harvard Med. Sch., 1966-70; dir. Central Pathology Lab., Nat. Bladder Cancer Group, 1983-89, mem. editorial bd. Pathology, 1991—, J. Urologic Pathology, 1992—. Mem. editorial bd. Ultrastructural Pathology, 1979—, Human Pathology, 1980—, assoc. editor, 1983-92, mem. editorial bd. Lab. Investigation, 1983—; assoc. editor Advances in Pathology, 1985-91, editor, 1991—; contbr.: articles profl. jours. Served as maj. USAF, 1970-72. Ford Found. fellow, 1959; Congressional intern, 1959; USPHS fellow, 1965-68. Mem. AMa, Am. Soc. Cell Biology, Internat. Acad. pathology (councilor 1980-82, internat. councilor 1982-84), U.S. and Can. Acad. Pathology (pres. 1988-89), Assn. Pathol. (chmn., sec.-treas. 1989-90), Chgo. Pathol. Soc. (pres. 1979-80), Internat. Soc. Urologic Pathology (pres.-elect 1992—), Internat. Coun. Soc. Pathology (v.p. 1992-93). Office: U Ariz 1501 N Campbell Ave Tucson AZ 85724-0001

WEINSTOCK, GARY ALAN, internist, allergist; b. Bronx, N.Y., Aug. 13, 1954; m. Bonnie Siber, Aug. 27, 1978; 2 children. BA, Hofstra U., 1975; MD, Union U., 1979. Diplomate Am. Bd. Internal Medicine, Am. Bd. Allergy and Immunology; lic. MD, N.Y. Resident in internal medicine Cornell Cooperating Hosps., North Shore U. Hosp., 1979-82; fellow in pulmonary diseases Health Scis. Ctr. SUNY at Stony Brook, 1982-83, fellow in allergy and clin. immunology, 1983-86; clin. assoc. Cornell (N.Y.) U. Med. Coll., 1980-82; asst. clin. instr. Dept. of Medicine Health Scis. Ctr., SUNY at Stony Brook, 1982-86; clin. instr. medicine Cornell (N.Y.) U. Med. Coll., 1988-92, clin. asst. prof. medicine, 1992—; provisional attending Dept. of Medicine North Shore U. Hosp., 1986-88, asst. attending Dept. of Medicine, 1988-91, sr. asst. attending Dept. of Medicine, 1991—; teaching ward attending, Med. Svc. at North Shore U. Hosp., 1986—, ann. lectr. to med. housestaff on allergic diseases, 1986—; med. advisor Support for Asthmatic Youth Founding Chpt. of Nat. Network, North Shore U. Hosp., 1989—; med. advisor for adolescent svcs.Asthma and Allergy Found. of Am., 1993—, nat. bd. dirs., 1994—, bd. dirs. N.Y. State, 1994—; lectr. in field. Contbr. articles to profl. jours. and newsletters. Recipient USPHS Individual Nat. Rsch. Svc. award, 1983-86; grantee for Support for Asthmatic Youth, Allen and Hansburys Respiratory Inst., 1991, 92, 93, 94, Fisons, For Preparation of Asthma Ednl. Materials, 1994, 95, Fisons, For Asthma Camp Edn. Programs, 1994. Fellow Am. Acad. Allergy and Immunology; mem. ACP, AMA, Med. Soc. of State of N.Y., Am. Thoracic Soc., Am. Acad. Allergy and Immunology (allied health sect. com. 1993—, travel grant recipient 1985), Nassau County Med. Soc., L.I. Allergy Soc., N.Y. State Allergy Soc. Office: 310 E Shore Rd Ste 308 Great Neck NY 11023

WEINSTOCK, JOEL VINCENT, immunologist; b. Detroit, Mar. 21, 1948; s. Herman and Esther B. (Frazein) W.; m. Allison Lee Rose, July 15, 1979; children: Lisa, Jeffrey, Andrew. BS, U. Mich., 1969; MD, Wayne State U., 1973. Diplomate Am. Bd. Internal Medicine, subspeciality gastroenterology; lic. physician, Mich., Iowa. Straight med. intern Univ. Hosp., Ann Arbor, Mich., 1973-74, resident internal medicine, 1974-76, fellow gastroenterology dept. internal medicine, 1976-78; asst. prof. internal medicine Wayne State U. Sch. Medicine, Detroit, 1978-83, assoc. prof., 1983-86, adj. assoc. prof. dept. immunology and microbiology, 1983-86, vice chief divsn. gastroenterology, 1984-86; assoc. prof., dir. gastroenterology divsn. U. Iowa, Iowa City, 1986-91, prof., dir., 1991—, dir. Ctr. Digestive Diseases, 1990—, dir. divsn. gastroenterology-hepatology, 1986—, dir. Ctr. Digestive Diseases, 1990—; mem. exec. bd. Crohn's and Colitis Found. Am., N.Y.C., 1993—, mem. tng. awards rev. com., 1991-93, chmn., 1993—; chief sect. gastroenterology Hutzel Hosp., Detroit, 1978-84, dir. endoscopy unit, 1978-84, dir. nutritional support svc., 1980-84; vice chief gastroenterology dept. medicine Wayne State U. Sch. Medicine, 1984-86; dir. gastroenterology subspecialty unit Harper Hosp., Detroit, 1984-86, vice-chief gastroenterology, 1984-86; mem.

sci. adv. ang grant rev. com. Crohn's and Colitis Found. Am., 1987—; mem. NIH Task force for developing nat. agenda for IBD rsch., 1989; mem. Lederle award selection com., 1989; mem. study sect. NIH Core Ctr. Rev. Com., 1990, 92; mem. abstract rev. com. ASCI, 1990; vis. prof. Washington U., St. Louis, 1990, U. Tex., Houston, 1991, Cleve. Clinic, 1992, U. Md., Balt., 1993; participant various conferences and meetings; mem. Digestive Diseases Ctr. Planning Com., 19886—; mem. Adult TPN Subcom., 1986—; chmn. coord. com. Ctr. Digestive Diseases, 1986—; mem. grant rev. coms. NIH, 1980—; mem. gastroenterology subspecialty coun. CSCR, 1993—. Mem. editl. bd. Autoimmunity Forum: Gastroenterology Edit., 1989-92; mem. internat. adv. bd. Alimentary Pharmacology and Therapeutics, 1990—; sect. editor Jour. Inflammatory Bowel Disease, 1994; reviewer Am. Jour Gastroenterology, Jour. Clin. Investigation, Jour. Immunology, Jour. Clin. Immunology, Gastroenterology, Digestive Diseases and Scis.; contbr. articles to profl. jours., chpts. to books. Rsch. grantee NIH, 1982—, Sandoz Pharm., 1993, Marion Merrell Dow, 1994, Centocor, 1995. Mem. AAAS, Am. Inst. Nutrition, Am. Soc. Clin. Nutrition, Ctrl. Soc. Clin. Rsch., Am. Soc. Gastrointestinal Endoscopy, Am. Assn. Study Liver Disease, Am. Fedn. Clin. Rsch., Am. Assn. Immunologists, Ileitis and Colitis Found. Am., Am. Soc. Clin. Investigation, Clin. Immunology Soc., Am. Gastroenterological Assn. (rsch. com. 1987-90, chmn. task force rsch. fellowship awards 1989-90, program evaluation com. 1990—), Midwest Gut Club (councillor 1990—), Alpha Omega Alpha. Office: U Iowa Internal Medicine 4607JCP UIHC Iowa City IA 52242

WEINSTOCK, JOSEPH, chemist; b. N.Y.C., Jan. 30, 1928; s. Jack and Pearl (Wedro) W.; m. Mary Jacqueline Leecock, July, 1952 (dec. 1987); children: David, Daniel, Sarah, Rachel, Jonathan, Michael, Joshua, Rebecca, Nathaniel, Jeremiah. BS in Chemistry, Rutgers U., 1949; PhD in Organic Chemistry, U. Rochester, 1952. Rsch. assoc. dept. chemistry Northwestern U., Evanston, Ill., 1952-54, instr. dept. chemistry, 1954-56; from sr. chemist to sr. fellow dept. medicinal chemistry Smith Kline Beecham Pharms., Phila., King of Prussia, Pa., 1956—. Contbr. over 100 articles to Jour. Am. Chem. Soc., Jour. Organic Chemistry, Jour. Medicinal Chemistry, Jour. Pharmacology and Experimental Therapeutics, and others. Chmn. Valley Forge Sewer Authority, Phoenixville, Pa., 1964—. Recipient Sahli award Pa. Mcpl. Authorities Assn. 1990. Mem. Am. Chem. Soc., N.Y. Acad. Sci., AAAS, Sigma Xi. Home: 1234 Pothouse Rd Phoenixville PA 19460-2244

WEINSTOCK, MELVYN, orthodontist; b. Toronto, Ont., Can., Feb. 23, 1941; came to the U.S., 1985; s. Frank and Anne Weinstock. DDS, U. Toronto, Ont., 1964; orthodontic cert., Harvard U., 1969; PhD, McGill U., Montreal, Que., 1972. Postdoctoral fellow Forsyth Dental Ctr., Boston, 1965-66; rsch. fellow Harvard U., Cambridge, Mass., 1966-69, Boston, 1966-69; asst. prof. McGill U., Montreal, 1970-75, assoc. prof., 1975-85; pvt. practice orthodontist St. Petersburg, Tampa, Fla., 1986—, Sarasota, Fla., 1986—; affiliate staff Montreal Gen. Hosp., 1974-85; com. mem., chmn. med. grants rev. bd. Med. Rsch. Coun. Can., Ottawa, 1975-78. Contbr. chpt. to books and articles to profl. jours. Fellow Royal Coll. Dentists (Can.); mem. ADA, Am. Assn. Orthodontics. Office: 7442 N Tamiami Trail Ste B Sarasota FL 34243 Office: #2060 3302 Martin Luther King Blv Tampa FL 33607 Office: 8588 Starkey Rd Ste C Largo FL 34647

WEINTRAUB, ILENE DENISE, internist, endocrinologist; b. N.Y.C., Dec. 20, 1961; d. Samuel and Dorothy (Salvitsky) W.; m. David Alan Tohay, Oct. 26, 1989; children: Jessica, Stephanie. BA, Princeton U., 1983; MD, U. Pitts., 1987. Diplomate Am. Bd. Internal Medicine, Am. Bd. Endocrinology and Metabolism. Attending physician Duke U., Durham, N.C., 1992-93; physician, mem. adv. bd. Joslin Ctr. for Diabetes, MacNeal Hosp., Berwyn, Ill., 1993—. Office: MacNeal Med Ctr Joslin Ctr for Diabetes 3722 S Harlem Blvd Riverside IL 60000

WEINTRAUB, JAMES RUBIN, neurologist; b. Detroit, Apr. 25, 1955; s. Ben A. and Lois Estelle (Rubin) W.; m. Julie Ann Wright, June 7, 1987; children: Jeffrey, Jenna. BS, U. Mich., 1977; postgrad., Wayne State U., 1977-79; DO, U. Osteo. Medicine, 1983. Cert. in neurology and sleep disorders. Intern Oakland Gen. Hosp., Madison Heights, Mich., 1983-84, resident in neurology, 1984-87; fellowship in sleep disorders Henry Ford Hosp., Detroit, 1987; fellowship electromyography Cleve. Clinic, 1987-88; pvt. practice Valley Neurology Assocs., Phoenix, 1988-93, Mich. Head Pain and Neurological Inst., Ann Arbor, Mich., 1993—; clin. prof. Coll. of Osteo. Medicine of the Pacific, Pomona, Calif., 1990—. Recipient Award Mayor of Des Moines, 1980. Mem. AMA, Stroke Coun., Am. Acad. Neurology, Am. Sleep Disorders Assn., Am. Osteo. Assn., Am. Assn. Electro Diagnostic Medicine, Assn. Clin. Neuropsychiatry, Pickwickian Soc. (founding mem. 1992). Republican. Jewish. Home: 1832 Chicory Rdg Ann Arbor MI 48103-9240 Office: Mich Head Pain & Neurological Inst 3120 Professional Dr Ann Arbor MI 48104-5131

WEINTRAUB, JANE ANN, dentist, educator; b. N.Y.C., Nov. 17, 1954; d. Milton I. and Eleanor (Friedman) W. BS, U. Rochester, 1975; DDS, SUNY, Stony Brook, 1979; MPH, Harvard U., 1980, postdoct. cert., 1982. Diplomate Am. Bd. Dental Pub. Health. Resident in dental pub. health Harvard Sch. Dental Medicine, Boston; clin. instr. Harvard U., Boston, 1982-83, N.Y. State Dept. Health, Albany, 1980-81; program analyst Mass. Dept. Pub. Health, Boston, 1982-84; asst. prof. U. Mich., Ann Arbor, 1984-88; asst. prof. U. N.C., Chapel Hill, 1988-90, assoc. prof., 1991-95; Lee Hysan prof. U. Calif., San Francisco, 95—; mem. dental adv. bd. Blue Cross/Blue Shield Mich., Detroit, 1984-88; supr. dentist Mass. Dept. Pub. Health, Boston, 1983-84; instr. Harvard U., 1983-84. Author: Biostats: Data Analysis for Dental Health Care Professionals; edit. bd., reviewer Jour. Pub. Health Dentistry; reviewer Jour. Dental Edn., Jour. Dental Rsch., Community Dentistry Oral Epidemiology; contbr. articles to profl. jours. Mem. ADA, APHA (sect. coun. 1985-88), Am. Assn. Dental Schs., Am. Assn. Pub. Health Dentistry (exec. coun. 1994—), Am. Assn. Women Dentists (Colgate-Palmolive rsch. award com., chmn. mercury exposure com.), Internat. Assn. Dental Rsch. (bd. dirs. behavioral scis. and health svcs. rsch. group 1986-89, program chair-elect 1990, program chair 1991, pres.-elect 1992, pres. 1993, councilor 1994—, chmn. sci. info. com. 1996—), SUNY at Stony Brook Sch. Dental Medicine Alumni Assn. (pres. 1983-85). Office: U Calif San Francisco Sch of Dentistry San Francisco CA 94143-0754

WEINTRAUB, NEAL L., medical educator, cardiologist. Student, Tulane u., 1977-80, MD, 1984. Diplomate Am. Bd. Internal Medicine, Am. Bd. Cardiovasc. Diseases. Resident Emory U., Atlanta, 1984-86; resident U. Ill., Urbana-Champaign, 1986-87, clin. instr. medicine Coll. Medicine, 1987-88, asst. clin. prof. medicine Coll. Medicine, 1988-90; staff physician VA Med. Ctr., Danville, Ill., 1987-90, St. Louis, 1990-91; asst. prof. medicine Sch. Medicine St. Louis U., 1990-95, postdoctoral fellow clin. pharmacology, 1992-94; assoc. cardiology divsn. U. Iowa Coll. Medicine, Iowa City, 1995—. Contbr. articles to profl. jours. Recipient Travel award Am. Coll. Cardiology/Bristol-Myers Squibb, 1994, Clinician Scientist award Am. Heart Assn., 1996. Mem. Alpha Omega Alpha. Office: U Iowa Coll Medicine CV Div Dept Internal Medicine 200 Hawkins Dr Iowa City IA 52242*

WEINTROB, ALEX, psychiatrist; b. Phila., Feb. 6, 1935; s. Joseph and Sophie (Bergen) W.; m. Audry Sue Gartenberg, Sept. 23, 1967; children: Jed, Seth. AB cum laude, Harvard U., 1956; MD, U. Pa., 1960. Diplomate Am. Bd. Psychiatry and Neurology. Instr. in psychiatry Albert Einstein Coll. Medicine, N.Y.C., 1967-72; asst. in psychiatry Beth Israel Med. Ctr., N.Y.C., 1967-72; cons. U.S. Dept. HHS, N.Y.C., 1979-82; assoc. psychiatrist Lenox Hill Hosp., N.Y.C., 1975—; pvt. practice adult child and adolescent psychiatry N.Y.C., 1967—; asst. attending psychiatrist N.Y. Hosp., 1989—; clin. dir. Youth Residence Ctr., Jewish Child Care Assn., 1970-88; panelist N.Y. State Supreme Ct. Panel of Impartial Psychiatrists, N.Y.C., 1987—; clin. asst. prof. psychiatry Cornell U. Med. Coll., N.Y.C., 1989—. Capt. U.S. Army, 1962-64, Korea. Fellow Am. Psychiat. Assn., Am. Acad. Child and Adolscent Psychiatry (councillor 1985-87), Am. Soc. Adolscent Psychiatry (pres.); mem. N.Y. Soc. for Adolscent Psychiatry (pres. 1989-90), N.Y. Coun. on Child and Adolscent Psychiatry (pres. 1986-87), Am. Acad. Psychiatry and the Law. Office: 12 W 96th St New York NY 10025-6509

WEIR, BRYCE KEITH ALEXANDER, neurosurgeon, neurology educator; b. Edinburgh, Scotland, Apr. 29, 1936; came to U.S., 1992; s. Ernest John and Marion (Stewart) W.; m. Mary Lou Lauber, Feb. 25, 1976; children: Leanora, Glyncora, Brocke. BSc, McGill U., Montreal, Que., Can., 1958, MD, CM, 1960, MSc, 1963. Diplomate Am. Bd. Neurol. Surgery, Nat. Bd. Med. Examiners. Intern Montreal Gen. Hosp., 1960-61; resident in neurosurgery Neurological Inst., Montreal, 1962-64, 65-66, N.Y. Neurol. Inst., N.Y.C., 1964-65; neurosurgeon U. Alta., Edmonton, Can., 1967-92, dir. div. neurosurgery, 1982-86, Walter Anderson prof., chmn. dept. surgery, 1986-92; surgeon-in-chief U. Alta. Hosps., 1986-92; Maurice Goldblatt prof. surgery and neurology U. Chgo., 1992—, dir. Brain Rsch. Inst., 1993—; past pres. V Internat. Symposium on Cerebral Vasospasm; mem. neurology A study sect. NIH, 1991-93; invited speaker at over 100 profl. meetings; vis. prof. over 50 univs., including Yale U., Cornell U., Columbia U., Duke U., U. Toronto, U. Calif., San Francisco; over 10 named lectureships, including White lectr. Harvard U., Gainey lectr., Mayo Clinic. Author: Aneurysms Affecting the Nervous System, 1987; mem. editl. bd. Jour. Neurosurgery, chmn. bd., 1993-94; mem. editl. bd. Neurosurgery Quar., Jour. Cerebrovascular Disease; contbr. over 250 articles to med. jours. Named Officer of the Order of Can., 1995. Fellow ACS, Royal Coll. Surgeons Can., Royal Coll. Surgeons Edinburgh (hon.); mem. Am. Surg. Assn., James IV Assn. Surgeons, Am. Acad. Neurol. Surgeons, Soc. Neurol. Surgeons (Grass gold medal 1992). Office: U of Chgo Pritzker Sch of Medicine 5841 S Maryland Ave Chicago IL 60637-1463

WEIR, EDWARD KENNETH, cardiologist; b. Belfast, No. Ireland, Jan. 7, 1943; came to U.S. 1973; s. Thomas Kenneth and Violet Hilda (ffrench) W.; m. Elizabeth Vincent Pearman, May 29, 1971; children: Fergus G., Conor K. BA, U. Oxford, U.K., 1964; MA, BM, BCh, U. Oxford, 1967, DM, 1976. Diplomate Am. Bd. Internal Medicine. Sr. house physician Nuffield Dept. Medicine, Radcliffe Infirmary, Oxford, 1970-71; registrar in cardiology Groote Schuur Hosp., Cape Town, South Africa, 1971-73; postdoctoral rsch. fellow U. Colo., Denver, 1973-75; cons. pediatric cardiologist U. Cape Town Med. Sch., 1975-76; cons. cardiologist U. Natal Med. Sch., Durban, South Africa, 1976-77; assoc. prof. medicine U. Minn., Mpls., 1978-85, prof. medicine, 1985—; staff physician Va. Med. Ctr., Mpls., 1978—; dir. Grover Confs. on Pulmonary Circulation, 1984—. Co-editor: Pulmonary Hypertension, 1984, The Pulmonary Circulation in Health and Disease, 1987, Pulmonary Vascular Physiology and Pathophysiology, 1989, The Diagnosis and Treatment of Pulmonary Hypertension, 1992, Ion Flux in Pulmonary Vascular Control, 1993, The Pulmonary Circulation and Gas Exchange, 1994, Nitric Oxide and Radicals in the Pulmonary Vasculature, 1996. Fulbright scholar, 1973-75; Sr. Internat. Fogarty fellow, 1993. Fellow Am. Coll. Cardiology, Royal Coll. Physicians London; mem. Am. Heart Assn. (Minn. affiliate bd. dirs. 1989-93, Nat. Cardiopulmonary Coun. (exec. com. 1992—), Pulmonary Circulation Found. (treas. 1985—). Office: VA Med Ctr 1 Veterans Dr # 111C Minneapolis MN 55417-2300

WEIR, HENRY SYLVESTER, JR., paramedic; b. Tupelo, Miss., Mar. 7, 1947; s. Henry S. and mary Cecil (Swain) W.; m. Ann Grace Westbrook, June 26, 1969; children: Chris, Chad, Jon. Student, U. Ala., Birmingham, 1979. Assoc. Sci. Emergency Med. Sci. Dir. ambulances Okolona Community Hosp., Okolona, Miss., 1967-74; dir. ambulance svc. Houston Community Hosp., Houston, Miss., 1974-85; paramedic Orange Beach Fire Rescue, Orange Beach, Ala., 1985-89, South Baldwin Hosp. Foley, Ala., 1990—; 1st pres. Miss. Assn. EMTS and Ambulance Svcs., Inc, 1974-78; pres. Am. Ambulance and Resuce Assn., 1975-76, Nat. Assn. First Responders, 1984-88; chief exec. Nat. Assn. First Responders, 1989—. Vice chmn. Chickasaw County Rep., 1982-83; affiliate faculty, Ala. Heart Assn., 1985—. Recipient Gov. George Wallace Commendation, 1987, Gov. Guy Hunt Lifesaving Commendation, 1988, EMT Paramedic 1st runner up, Jour. of EMS, 1988, EMT Paramedic of Yr., Miss. Assn. EMTS 1984, EMT Paramedic Yr. Ala, Nat. Assn. First Responders, 1987. Mem. Am. Ala. Heart Assn., Miss. Heart Assn., Am. Assn. Trauma Specialists, Nat. Registry EMTS. Republican. Baptist. Home: 5334 Armadillo Ave Orange Beach AL 36561-4211

WEIR, THOMAS W(ILSON), dermatologist, dermal pathologist; b. St. Louis, Oct. 12, 1937; s. William Victor and Marion Susan (Wilson) W.; m. Kristina Lee Hagman, Sept. 2, 1961; children—Todd Hagman, Brian Wilson. A.B., Amherst Coll., 1959; M.D., U. Mo., 1963. Diplomate Am. Bd. Dermatology, Am. Bd. Dermal Pathology. Intern Letterman Gen. Hosp., San Francisco, 1963-64; resident in dermatology Temple U., Phila., 1966-69, fellow in dermatopathology, 1968-69. practice medicine specializing in dermatology and dermal pathology, Redmond, Wash., 1970—; clin. asst. prof. med. U. Wash., Seattle, 1970-88, clin. assoc. prof., 1988—; vis. lectr. dept. medicine U. Nairobi, Kenya, 1979-80. Served to capt. M.C., U.S. Army, 1963-66. Fellow Am. Acad. Dermatology, Am. Soc. Dermatopathology, Pacific Dermatol. Assn.; mem. Seattle Dermatol. Soc. (pres. 1974-75). Unitarian. Office: Group Health Cooperative of Puget Sound 2701 156th Ave NE Redmond WA 98052-5513

WEIS, EDMUND BERNARD, JR., orthopaedist, educator; b. Bismarck, N.D., Aug. 4, 1931; s. Edmund Bernard and Margaret Catherine (Rickert) W.; m. Annette Mary Fernandes, Nov. 19, 1973; children: John Paul, Giselle Anne, Susan Ellen, Melanie Elizabeth, Edmund Bernard III, Bronwyn Kristen. Attended, U. Utah, 1949-52; grad., U. Notre Dame, 1953; MD, U. Colo., 1957; MS in Bioengring., Drexel Inst. Tech., 1962; doctoral candidate, Ohio State U., 1968-71; JD, Newport U., 1994. Diplomate Am. Bd. Orthopaedic Surgery; Bar: Calif. 1994. Intern Good Samaritan Hosp., Phoenix, 1957-58; chief vibration and impact br. mercury astronaut crew selection Aerospace Med. Rsch. Labs., Wright-Patterson AFB, Ohio, 1958-66; resident in orthopaedics Ohio State U., Columbus, 1968-71; amputations tng. Dept. Vet. Affairs, Grossinger, N.Y., 1985; pedicle screw fixation tng. Cleve. Rsch. Inst., 1987; thermography tng. Acad. Neuromuscular Thermography, L.A., 1989; surg. lasers tng. Loma Linda (Calif.) U., 1992; rsch. med. officer USAF, Wright-Patterson AFB, Ohio, 1966-68; mem. staff Ohio Vets. Oupatient Ctr., Columbus, 1974-76, N.D. Vets. Hosp., Fargo, 1976-79; mem. staff VA Hosp., Omaha, 1979-85, acting chief rehab., 1983-85; mem. staff, chief orthopaedics VA Hosp., Loma Linda, 1985—; mem. staff Loma Linda Cmty. Hosp., 1985—, chief orthopaedics, 1989-90; mem. staff Loma Linda U. Med. Ctr., 1985—, Redlands (Calif.) Cmty. Hosp., 1986—, San Bernardino (Calif.) Cmty. Hosp., 1990—, Moreno Valley (Calif.) Hosp., 1992—, San Gorgonio Meml. Hosp., Banning, Calif., 1993—; instr. to asst. prof. orthopaedics Ohio State U., 1971-76; assoc. prof. U. N.D., Grand Forks, 1976-79, asst. dean, 1977-79; prof. Creighton U., Omaha, 1979-85; clin. prof. Loam Linda U., 1985—; bioengring. cons. Cox Coronary Heart Inst., Dayton, Ohio, 1962-66, Battelle Meml. Inst., Columbus, 1970-76; orthopaedics cons. Grand Forks AFB Hosp., 1976-79, Ehrling-Berquist AFB Hosp., Omaha, 1979-84, Jour. Bone and Joint Surgery, Waltham, Mass., 1980—; com. mem. Am. Acad. Orthopaedics Emergency Svcs. Contbr. numerous articles to profl. jours.; inventor sonic surg. tool; patentee method and sys. for control of a powered prosthesis. Maj. USAF, Wright-Patterson AFB, 1957-66. Recipient R & D award USAF, 1966, Rsch. award Dept. Vet. Affairs, 1988, U.S. Svc. award, 30 Yr. pin, Jerry L. Pettis Vets. Hosp., 1993; rsch. fellow NIH, 1969-71, travelling fellow Am. Orthopaedics Assn., 1971. Fellow Am. Acad. Orthopaedic Surgeons (Rsch. and Edn. Found. award, 1969); mem. AMA, Orthopaedic Rsch. Soc., San Bernardino County Med. Soc., Calif. Med. Soc., Nat. Assn. Vet. Physicians, N.Am. Spine Soc., Phi Rho Sigma. Home: 30555 7th St Redlands CA 92374 Office: 1800 N Western Ave Ste 300 San Bernardino CA 92411

WEIS, JUDITH SHULMAN, biology educator; b. N.Y.C., May 29, 1941; d. Saul B. and Pearl (Cooper) Shulman; m. Peddrick Weis; children: Jennifer, Eric. BA, Cornell U., 1962; MS, NYU, 1964, PhD, 1967. Lectr. CUNY, 1964-67; asst. prof. Rutgers U., Newark, 1967-71, assoc. prof., 1971-76, prof., 1976—; Congl. sci. fellow U.S. Senate, Washington, 1983-84; mem. grant rev. panel NSF, Washington, 1976-82, program dir., 1988-90; mem. rev. panel EPA, 1984-92; vis. scientist EPA Lab., Gulf Breeze, Fla., 1992. Mem. marine bd. NAS, 1991—. Grantee NOAA, 1977—, N.J. EPA Rsch., 1978-79, 81-83, N.J. Marine Scis. Consortium Rsch., 1987—; NSF fellow, 1962-64. Mem. Am. Inst. for Biol. Scis. (bd. dirs. 1986-88, 89-91), Soc. Environ. Toxicology and Chemistry (bd. dirs. 1990-93), Estuarine Rsch. Fedn., Ecol. Soc. Am., NOW (pres. Essex County 1972), Sierra Club (bd. dirs. N.J. chpt. 1986-88). Office: Rutgers U Dept Biol Scis Newark NJ 07102

WEIS, MERVYN J., physician, gastroenterologist; b. Chgo., June 9, 1940; s. Theodore A. and Anita (Stavins) W.; m. Myra Rubenstein, Nov. 26, 1966 (dec. Nov. 1990); children: Jonathan Mandel, Sari Tova; m. Anita Kagler, Oct. 1992. BA, Northwestern U., 1961, MD, 1965. Diplomate Am. Bd. Internal Medicine. Intern in internal medicine Michael Reese Hosp. and Med. Ctr., Chgo., 1965-66, resident in internal medicine, 1966-67, 69-70, attending physician, 1972-78; fellow in gastroenterology Northwestern U. Med. Ctr., Chgo., 1970-72; attending physician Ravenswood Hosp., Chgo., 1979-83, St. Francis Hosp., Evanston, Ill., 1984-88, Rush North Med. Ctr., Skokie, Ill., 1985-91; attending physician Louis A. Weiss Meml. Hosp., Chgo., 1972—, chmn. divsn. medicine, 1987-89, pres. med. staff, 1989-93, mem. bd. govs., 1987—; cons. in gastroenterology VA Rsch. Hosp., Chgo., 1972-80. Contbr. articles to profl. jours. Capt. U.S. Army, 1967-69. Fellow ACP, Am. Coll. Gastroenterology; mem. AMA, Ill. State Med. Soc., Chgo. Soc. Gastroenterology, Chgo. Med. Soc. Office: 4640 N Marine Dr Ste C 6100 Chicago IL 60640

WEISBERG, AARON, internist, gastroenterologist, consultant, research, educator; b. Bklyn., July 21, 1915; s. Joseph and Yetta (Weisberg) W.; m. Ruth Hannah Mintz, Feb. 7, 1949; children—Harlene Edith, Sharon Esta Weisberg Shapiro. B.A. in Chemistry, NYU, 1935; M.D., Cin. Eclectic Med. Coll., 1939. Diplomate Am. Bd. Internal Medicine. Intern Coney Island Hosp., Bklyn., 1939-41, resident, 1941-42, attending physician, 1946-74, attending physician emeritus, 1974—; dir. medicine Carson C. Peck Meml. Hosp., Bklyn., 1954-70; chief of medicine Meth. Hosp. Bklyn., 1970-74, cons. in medicine and gastroenterology, 1974-86, hon. staff, 1986—; attending staff mem. in medicine and gastroenterology Tampa VA Hosp., 1974—, St. Petersburg (Fla.) Gen. Hosp., 1974—, Palms Pasadena Hosp., St. Petersburg, 1974—; med. dir. Sperry Gyroscope, Clearwater, Fla., 1975-84; clin. asst. prof. internal medicine and gastroenterology and clin. asst. prof. comprehensive medicine U. South Fla., 1975—; cons. gastroenterology Bay Pines (Fla.) VA Hosp. Contbr. numerous articles on cardiology, gastroenterology and cancer to profl. jours.; mem. editorial staff: Colon and Rectal Surgery, 1980—. Served to capt. M.C. U.S. Army, 1942-46. Recipient Gold Medal award Coney Island Hosp., 1972, Silver cert. Meth. Hosp., 1974. Fellow ACP, Am. Coll. Gastroenterology, Internat. Acad. Proctology, Royal Soc. Medicine, Am. Coll Nutrition; mem. Am. Fedn. Clin. Research (sr.), Am. Soc. Gastrointestinal Endoscopy, AMA, Pan Am. Soc., Occupational Med. Assn., Am. Chem. Soc., Am. Heart Assn., Phi Lambda Kappa. Clubs: NYU (N.Y.C.); Seminole Country and Golf. Research on cancer, thymus gland lymphocytes immunity. Office: 6499 38th Ave N Saint Petersburg FL 33710-1656

WEISBERG, LAWRENCE STEPHEN, nephrologist; b. Mt. Vernon, N.Y., Feb. 8, 1950; s. Herman Louis and Irene Susan (Grossman) W.; m. Rebecca Warner Johnson, Sept. 4, 1983; children: Molly Eir Johnson, Anna Laurel Johnson. AB, Washington U., 1971; MD, Temple U., 1981. Resident in internal medicine Hosp. U. Pa., Phila., 1981-84, postdoctoral fellow in nephrology, 1984-87; assoc. investigator Phila. VA Med. Ctr., 1985-87; asst. prof. medicine Robert Wood Johnson Sch. Medicine U. Med. Dentistry of N.J., Camden, 1987-93, assoc. prof., 1993—. Contbr. articles to profl. jours. Rsch. grantee U. Med. Dentistry N.J. Found., 1989. Fellow ACP, Coll. Physicians Phila.; mem. Am. Soc. Nephrology, Internat. Soc. Nephrology, N.J. Soc. Nephrology (pres. 1992-93). Office: U Med Dentistry NJ Robert Wood Johnson Med Sch 401 Haddon Ave Camden NJ 08103

WEISBERG, LYNNE WILLING, psychiatrist, consultant; b. N.Y.C., Apr. 11, 1948; d. Stanley S. and Pearl R. Willing. BA, Barnard Coll., 1969; PhD, U. Mich., 1972; MD, SUNY, Downstate, 1978. Diplomate Am. Bd. Psychiatry and Neurology, Am. Bd. Adolescent Psychiatry. Intern NYU Med. Ctr., 1978-79; resident in adult psychiatry Mt. Sinai Hosp., N.Y.C., 1979-81; fellow in child psychiatry Columbia Med. Ctr., 1981-83; staff psychiatrist Fair Oaks Hosp., Summit, N.J., 1983-85, asst. dir. child and adolescent psychiatry, 1985-88, assoc. dir. child and adolescent psychiatry, 1988-92; dir. child and adolescent outpatient psychiat. svcs. Psychiat. Assocs. N.J. at Fair Oaks Hosp., Summit, 1992—; pvt. practice Morristown, N.J., 1992—; cons. Bonnie Brae Sch., Millington, N.J., 1984-92. Author: When Acting Out Isn't Acting, 1991. Horace Rackham Prize fellow, 1972. Mem. AMA, Med. Soc. N.J. Office: 20 Community Pl Morristown NJ 07960-7501

WEISBERG, SEYMOUR WILLIAM, physician; b. Chgo., Aug. 5, 1910; s. Isaac and Eda (Provus) W.; B.S., U. Chgo., 1932; M.D., Rush Med. Coll., 1936; m. Ella Sperling, Oct. 16, 1949; children—Gerald, Louise. Intern Michael Reese Hosp.; resident Cook County Hosp., Chgo.; practice medicine specializing in internal medicine, Chgo., 1940—; asso. prof. medicine U. Ill. Coll. Medicine, Chgo.; asso. attending physician Cook County Hosp., 1940-44; chief resident tng. unit Chgo. Regional Office VA; mem. attending staff Michael Reese Hosp., Chgo., Louis A. Weiss Meml. Hosp., Chgo., St. Joseph Hosp. Served with AUS, 1944-47. Diplomate Am. Bd. Internal Medicine. Mem. AMA, Ill. Med. Soc., Phi Beta Kappa, Alpha Omega Alpha. Office: 5801 N Sheridan Rd Chicago IL 60660

WEISBERG-SAMUELS, JANET SUSAN, psychologist; b. N.Y.C., Mar. 21, 1940; d. Morris and Vivian (Wank) Weisberg; m. Richard Samuels, Jan. 16, 1983; children—Debra, David. BBA, CCNY, 1960; MS, CUNY, 1966; PhD, Yeshiva U., 1984. Lic. psychologist; cert. sch. psychologist N.Y. State. Psychologist, Bklyn. Jewish Hosp., 1969-75; team leader N.Y. State Dept. Mental Hygiene, N.Y.C., 1977; cons. N.Y.C. Bd. Edn., 1977, Parent-Child Consultation Ctr., 1980—; psychologist Beth Israel Hosp., N.Y.C., 1975-87, acting chief psychologist dept. child psychiatry, 1982-83, dir. Enuresis Clinic, 1981-85; practice in psychology, N.Y.C.; program dir. Brotherhood Synagogue, N.Y.C., 1968-75; dir. tng., 1987—, dept. psychiatry Interfaith Med. Ctr.; clin. faculty Mt. Sinai Sch. Medicine, N.Y.C., 1979—. Pres. Singles divsn. Park Ave. Synagogue, N.Y.C., 1980-83, bd. dirs. Couples Club, 1986—, pres. 1988-90. Mem. Am. Psychol. Assn., N.Y. State Psych. Assn., Eastern Psychol. Assn., Manhattan Psychol. Assn. (exec bd. 1993—). Jewish. Avocations: opera, ballet, museums. Office: 160 E 89th St Apt 1B New York NY 10128-2336

WEISBURGER, JOHN HANS, medical researcher; b. Stuttgart, Germany, Sept. 15, 1921; came to U.S., 1943, naturalized, 1944; s. William and Selma (Barth) W.; children: William, Diane, Andrew. AB, U. Cin., 1947, MS, 1948, PhD, 1949; MD (hon.), U. Umeå, Sweden, 1980. Mem. staff Nat. Cancer Inst., NIH, Bethesda, Md., 1950-61, head carcinogen screening sect., 1961-72; dir. bioassay segment, Carcinogenesis Programs Nat. Cancer Inst., Bethesda, Md., 1971-72; v.p. rsch. Am. Health Found., Valhalla, N.Y., 1972-87; dir. Naylor Dana Inst. for Disease Prevention, Valhalla, 1972-87, dir. emeritus, sr. mem., 1987—; rsch. prof. pathology N.Y. Med. Coll., Valhalla, 1974—; pres. Weisburger Assocs., North White Plains, N.Y., 1987—; mem. biochemistry and nutrition study sect. NIH, 1957-58; mem. interdepartmental panel on carcinogens FDA, USDA, USPHS, 1962-71; chmn. subcom. Nat. Cancer Program Strategic Plan, 1971-74; chmn. carcinogenesis subcom. Nat. Large Bowel Cancer Project, 1972-75; mem. expert panel on nitrites and nitrosamines USDA, 1973-77; chmn. Workshop Colo-rectal Cancer, Unio Internat. Contra Cancrum, Geneva, 1975; mem. Nat. Cancer Inst. Clearinghouse on Environ. Carcinogens, 1976-78; co-chmn. organizing com. U.S.-Japan Coop. Workshop on GI Tract Cancer, 1979, Workshop on Dietary Fats and Fiber in Human Cancer, 1986; chmn. symposium on large bowel cancer 7th congress OMGE, 1982; mem. program com. Internat. Congress of Toxicology III, 1982-83; mem. cancer edn. com. N.Y. Med. Coll., 1983-88; bd. dirs. Westchester div. Am. Cancer Soc., 1983-89; mem. pancreas cancer working group, organ systems program Nat. Cancer Inst., 1985-86; chmn. sci. rev. panel N.J. State Commn. Cancer Rsch., 1988-90; chmn. nutrition and cancer sect. 15th meeting Unio Internt. Contra Cancrum, Hamburg, Germany, 1990; chmn. internat. group Belgian Soc. Psychosocial Aspects of Cancer, Brussels, 1990; internat. lectr. on nutrition and cancer prevention, S.E. Asia, 1991; co-chmn. internat. symposium on health effects of tea, N.Y., 1991; chmn. nutrition and cancer sect. 3d anticarcinogenesis and antimutagenesis conf., Italy, 1991; chmn. study sect. NIH-Nat. Cancer Inst., Bethesda, Md., 1991; co-chmn. mechanisms nutrition cancer European Sch. Oncology, Venice, Italy, 1992; rsch. fellow Japanese Found. for Promotion of Cancer Rsch. Nat. Cancer Ctr. Rsch. Inst, Tokyo, 1992; advisor com. rev. RDA Food and Nutrition Bd. NAS, 1993; lectr. 2d conf. Internat. Fedn. Socs. Toxicologic Pathol., Tours, France, 3d Internat. Symposium Green Tea, Seoul, Korea, 6th Internat. Conf. Carcinogenic Mutagenic N-Aryl Compounds, Internat. Conf. Food Factors, Hamamatsu, Japan, 4th Internat. Yakult Intestinal Flora Symposium, Tokyo, 1995; chmn. workshop tea and health 2d Internat. Congress, Food and Cancer, Edu, The Netherlands, 1996; internat. orgn. com. & lectr. 5th

Internat. Conf. Mech. Antimntag. Anticare, Okayama, Japan, 1996. Assoc. editor Jour. Nat. Cancer Inst., 1960-62, Xenobiotica, 1971—, Archives of Toxicology, 1977-87, Jour. Am. Coll. Toxicology, 1982—, Preventive Medicine, 1988—; mem. internat. editl. adv. bd. Food and Chem. Toxicology, 1967—; assoc. editor Cancer Rsch., 1969-80, mem. cover editl. bd., 1987—; mem. editl. bd. Chemico-Biol. Interactions, 1969-88, Carcinogenesis, 1979-87, Inst. Sci. Info. Atlas of Sci., 1987-89, Cancer Epidemioloyg Biomarkers Prevention, 1991—, Cnacer Detection Prevention, 1994—; mem. guest editl. bd. Japanese Jour. Cancer Rsch., 1987—. With AUS, 1944-46; col. USPHS, 1950-72. Decorated D.S.M., 1964; recipient Meritorious Svc. medal USPHS HEW, 1970, Outstanding Service award Westchester div. Am. Cancer Soc., 1984, Meyer and Anna Prentis award Mich. Cancer Ctr., 1987; named one of 1000 most cited scientists, ISI List, 1981. Leadership plaque N.J. State Commn. Cancer Rsch., 1990. Fellow N.Y. Acad. Scis., Am. Coll. Nutrition; mem. Am. Assn. Cancer Rsch. (rep. to European Assn. Cancer Rsch. 1985-89), Am. Chem. Soc. (com. environ. improvement 1992-94), Am. Gastroent. Am. Conf. Govt. Indsl. Hygienists, Am. Soc. Biochem. Molecular Biologists, Am. Soc. Pharmacology and Exptl. Therapeutics, Am. Soc. Preventive Oncology (founding mem., bd. dirs. 1983-90, Disting. Svc. award 1990), Biochem. Soc. (London, emeritus), Environ. Mutagen Soc., European Assn. Cancer Rsch. (coun. 1985-90), Japan Cancer Assn. (hon. life), Soc. Exptl. Biol. Medicine, Soc. Toxicology (chmn. bd. publs. 1968-71, councilor 1972-74, amb. toxicology Mid-Atlantic divsn. 1990, hon. mem. 1995, Award of Merit 1981), Westchester Chem. Soc. (Disting. Scientist 1996), Sigma Xi, Alpha Chi Sigma (pres. Washington profl. chpt. 1967-68), Phi Lambda Upsilon. Home: 4 Whitewood Rd White Plains NY 10603-1137 Office: Am Health Found Naylor Dana Inst Valhalla NY 10595-1599

WEISDORF, DANIEL JORDAN, physician, hematologist; b. Dec. 10, 1949. AB, Brown U., 1971; MD, Chgo. Med. Sch., 1975. Diplomate Am. Bd. Internal Medicine, Am. Bd. Hematology, Am. Bd. Med. Oncology. Resident in internal medicine Michael Reese Hosp., Chgo., 1975-78; fellow in hematology and med. oncology U. Minn., Mpls., 1978-81, asst. prof. medicine, 1981-89, assoc. prof., 1989-94, prof., 1994—, assoc. dir. Bone Marrow Transplant Program, 1985—; dir. Bone Marrow Transplant Clinic, 1996—. Fellow ACP; mem. Am. Soc. Hematology, Am. Soc. Clin. Oncology. Office: U Minn Hosp Box 480 Mayo Minneapolis MN 55455

WEISFELDT, MYRON LEE, physician, educator; b. Milw., Apr. 25, 1940; s. Simon Charles and Sophia (Price) W.; m. Linda Nan Zaremski, Dec. 29, 1963; children—Ellyn Joy, Lisa Janel, Sara Michelle. Student, Northwester U., 1958-60; BA, Johns Hopkins U., 1962, MD, 1965. Intern and resident Columbia-Presbyn. Med. Ctr., N.Y.C., 1965-67; fellow in cardiology Mass. Gen. Hosp., Boston, 1970-72; asst. prof. medicine Johns Hopkins U., Balt., 1972-78, prof. medicine, 1978-91, Robert L. Levy prof. cardiology, 1979-91; Samuel Bard prof. medicine, chair dept. Columbia-Presbyn. Med. Ctr., N.Y.C., 1991—; dir. cardiology Johns Hopkins Med. Inst., Balt., 1975-91, Peter Belfer Lab. for Johns Hopkins, Ischemic Heart Disease Spl. Ctr. Rsch., 1977-91; nat. pres. Am. Heart Assn., 1989-90; cardiology adv. com. Nat. Heart, Lung and Blood Inst., 1986-90, chmn., 1988-90. Editor: The Aging Heart, 1980; editorial bd. Jour. Clin. Investigation, 1984-88, Circulation, 1980-86, 88—, Jour. Am. Coll. Cardiology, 1987-93, Jour. Molecular and Cellular Cardiology, 1975-80, 86-89, Circulation Rsch., 1988-94. Served with USPHS, 1967-69. NIH grantee, 1977-91. Fellow AAAS, ACP, Am. Coll. Cardiology; mem. Assn. Univ. Cardiologists, Am. Soc. Clin. Investigation, Assn. Am. Physicians, Assn. Prof. Medicine, Phi Beta Kappa, Alpha Omega Alpha, Interurban Clin. Club. Jewish. Home: 47 Havermeyer Rd Irvington NY 10533-2642 Office: Columbia Presbyn Med Ctr 630 W 168th St New York NY 10032-3702

WEISMAN, ADAM MARK, clinical psychologist; b. N.Y.C., Jan. 7, 1959; s. Nelson N. and Selma Cecilia (Winthrop) W. BA in Drama, BS in Psychology, U. Wash., 1982; MA, Kent (Ohio) State U., 1987, PhD, 1991. Lic. psychologist, Calif., Mich., Wash. Psychology asst. Akron (Ohio) Child Guidance Ctr., 1987-88; psychology intern Henry Ford Hosp., Detroit, 1989-90; instr. Kent State U., 1986-89; psychologist asst. Summit County Courthouse, Akron, 1988-90; outreach therapist Neighborhood Svc. Orgn., Detroit, 1990-92; postdoctoral sr. fellow in forensic psychiatry/psychology U. So. Calif., L.A., 1992-94, clin. asst. prof., 1992—; adj. prof. psychology Pepperdine U., Malibu, Calif., 1994—; staff psychologist Parole Clinic Dept. of Corrections, L.A., 1993—; cons. psychologist Patton (Calif.) State Hosp., 1992-94; mem. psychiat.-psychol. panel adult and juvenile Superior Ct., L.A., 1995—, U.S. Dist. Ct., 1995—. Bd. dirs., comm. adv. bd. L.A. Police Dept., 1995—; bd. dirs., pres. Franklin Hills Residents Assn., L.A., 1994—. Recipient Outstanding Civic Svc. award City of L.A., 4th Coun. Dist., 1996. Mem. APA, Wash. State Psychol. Assn., Nat. Register of Health Sci. Providers in Psychology, Forensic Mental Health Assn., Soc. Behavioral Medicine, Am. Acad. Forensic Scis., Am. Psychosomatic Soc., Calif. Coalition on Sex Offenders, Calif. Psychol. Assn., Sex Offenders Roundtable of L.A., Psi Upsilon. Jewish. Office: PO Box 29366 Los Angeles CA 90029-0366

WEISMAN, AVERY DANTO, psychiatrist; b. Detroit, Dec. 13, 1913; s. Alec and Sadie Belle (Danto) W.; m. Erma Carman, Dec. 30, 1950 (dec. 1982); m. Lois London, July 8, 1988. AB, U. Mich., 1935, BS, 1936, MD, 1940. Diplomate Am. Bd. Psychiatry and Neurology. Intern Montefiore Hosp., Pitts., 1940-41; resident in Neurology Wayne County Gen., Eloise, Mich., 1941-42; resident in Neuropath and Neurology Boston City Hosp., 1942-44; resident in psychiatry to sr. psychiatrist Mass. Gen. Hosp., Boston, 1944—; instr. to prof. of psychiatry emeritus Med. Sch. Harvard U., Boston, 1944—; disting. vis. prof. Northwestern U. Med. Sch., 1986-90; numerous vis. professorships. Author 7 books and monographs in field; contbr. articles to profl. publs., chpts. to books. Recipient Deutsch award Boston Psychoanalytic soc., 1950, Sutherland award Sloan Kettering Cancer Ctr., 1982, Disting. Svc. award Yeshiva U., 1983, Avery Weisman Lectureship Found. of thanatology, 1988, Pollin Found. award 1989, Hackett award Acad. Psychosomatic Medicine, 1992. Fellow Am. Psychiat. Assn.; mem. Am. Psychoanalytic Assn., Am. Acad. Neurology, Psychosomatic Acad., Am. Assn. Suicidology (pres. 1977, Dublin award). Jewish. Home: 456 Belmont St Apt 6 Watertown MA 02172-4900 Office: Mass Gen Hosp Boston MA 02114-3104

WEISMAN, DORIS RAY, nurse practitioner, educator; d. Bernard and Beatrice Schuman; m. Herbert Weisman (dec. Jan. 1985). AAS in Nursing, Suffolk County C.C., N.Y., 1976; BS in Pub. Health Adminstrn., SUNY, Saratoga, 1978; BSN, SUNY, Stony Brook, 1986, MSN, 1987. RN, cert. nurse practitioner, cert. instr. basic nursing, cert. AIDS counselor, N.Y., cert. Ambulatory Women's Health. Asst. nursing care coord. St. John's Episcopal Hosp., Smithtown, N.Y., 1977-79; coord. patient svcs. Alert Med. Personnel, Setauket, N.Y., 1980-82; instr. practical nursing Bd. Coop. Ednl. Svcs., Bellport, N.Y., 1982-85; nurse practitioner family planning unit Suffolk County Dept. of Health Svcs., N.Y., 1985-91; clin. instr. Brookhaven Meml. Hosp., Patchogue, N.Y., 1987-91; nurse practitioner gynecology Womens Health, Ronkonkoma, Smithtown, N.Y., 1991—; nurse practitioner gynecology, cytology Univ. Med. Ctr., Stony Brook, 1994—; Primary instr. classroom and clin. evening sessions BOCES III, Dix Hills, N.Y., 1980-83; charge nurse Smithtown Gen. Hosp., N.Y., 1984, instr., rsch. nurse Univ. Hosp., Stony Brook, 1985-87; cons. Hope House Ministries; instr., trainer breast self exam, coord. Breast Health Day Program, Am. Cancer Soc.; lectr. in field. Facilitator Make Today Count Cancer Support Group; founder, facilitator Wondrous Women; mem. resources, info. and guidance com. Am. Cancer Soc. Mission 2000; adv. bd. Breast Cancer Healthy Environ. For A Living Planet. Recipient Vol. of the Year award Am. Cancer Soc., 1991,. Mem. Am. Fertility Soc., N.Am. Menopause Soc., Nurse Practitioners' Assn. of Long Island (pub. rels. com.), Coalition of Nurse Practitioners of N.Y. State, Kappa Gamma-Sigma Theta Tau. Home: 11 Hemlock Dr Miller Place NY 11764 Office: Univ Med Ctr Stony Brook NY 11794-7135

WEISMAN, GARY ANDREW, biochemist; b. Bklyn., June 18, 1951; s. Joseph Herman and Elaine (Melman) W.; m. Sandra Kay Hille, Aug. 4, 1979; children: Laura Joanne, Pamela Michelle, Veronica Evelyn. BS, Polytechnic U., 1972; postgrad., U. Bordeaux, France, 1972-74; PhD, U. Nebr., 1980. Postdoctoral rsch. assoc. Cornell U., N.Y.C., 1980-85; asst. prof. U. Mo., Columbia, 1985-92, assoc. prof., 1992—; spl. reviewer NIH; reviewer NSF, Jour. Membrane Biology and Eur. Jour. Cancer. Contbr. articles to profl. jours. Grantee NIH, 1988, CF Found., 1994—, Am. Diabetes, 1995—. Mem. AAAS, Am. Chem. Soc., Am. Soc. Biochem. and Molecular Biology, Am. Heart Assn., N.Y. Acad. Scis. Home: 1804 University Ave Columbia MO 65201-6004 Office: U Mo Dept Biochemistry M121 Med Scis Bldg Columbia MO 65212

WEISMAN, HERBERT NEAL, dentist, financial planner; b. Mpls., Mar. 12, 1940; s. Sholem and Katherine (Fink) W.; m. Doris Sue Epstein, Dec. 27, 1964; children: David Nathan, Marna Faye. BS, U. Minn., 1962, DDS, 1964; cert. in real estate, LaSalle U., Chgo., 1969; cert., Coll. for Fin. Planning, Denver, 1989. Pvt. practice, St. Louis Park, Minn., 1966—; pres. Miller Supply Co., St. Paul, 1976-77/ v.p. Lebewitz, Weisman, Greene, Mpls., 1982-86; dental ins. cons. Prudential Ins. Co., Mpls., 1988-89; forensic cons. Hennepin County Med. Examiners Office, Mpls., 1988—. Author: So You Want to be Rich, 1994; assoc. editor N.W. Dentistry, 1974-75; contbr. articles to profl. jours. Mem. exec. bd. Jewish Family and Childrens Svc., Mpls., 1982-87; bd. dirs. Adath Jeshuran Synagogue, Mpls., 1983. Capt. USAF, 1964-66. Fellow Acad. Gen. Dentistry (state pres. 1969-70), Royal Soc. Health (Eng.); mem. ADA, Minn. Dental Assn., Mpls. Dental Soc., Inst. Cert. Fin. Planners. Office: 5407 Excelsior Blvd Saint Louis Park MN 55416-2929

WEISMAN, IRVING, social worker, educator; b. N.Y.C., May 6, 1918; s. Max and Sadie (Berkowitz) W.; m. Cyrille Gold, May 1, 1941; children: Seth, Adam. B.S., CCNY, 1939; M.S., U. Buffalo, 1942; Ed.D., Columbia U., 1962. Cert. social worker N.Y. State. Caseworker Nat. Refugee Service, N.Y.C., 1941; warden's asst. Fed. Detention Hdqrs., Bur. Prisons, Dept. Justice, N.Y.C., 1942-43; mil. svc. psychiat. social worker to chief social worker VA, Camden and Union City, N.J., 1946-49; case supr. Altro Health and Rehab. Service, N.Y., 1949-50; field instr., lectr. Columbia U. Sch. Social Work, 1950-57, assoc. prof., 1957-62, prof., 1962-84, prof. emeritus, 1984, adj. prof., 1984, acting dean, 1964-65; assoc. dean Hunter Coll. Sch. Social Work, 1967-69; exec. officer doctoral program social work Grad. Ctr. CUNY, 1975-78; clin. practice William Alanson White Inst., 1976-79; vis. prof. Sch. Social Work, Barry U., 1984-85; adj. prof. Sch. Social Work, San Diego State U., 1988—; UN adv. on social welfare to Ceylon Sri Lanka, 1963-64; sr. Simon research fellow U. Manchester (Eng.), 1970-71; cons. U.S. Office Juvenile Delinquency and Youth Devel., U.S. Children's Bur., NIMH, NIDA, HEW, N.Y.C. Dept. Personnel, Westchester County (N.Y.) Dept. Mental Health, Community Service Soc., Council Social Work Edn., Moblzn. for Youth, N.Y.C., Universidad Católica Madre y Maestra, Santo Domingo, Dominican Republic, 1983-84, United Jewish Appeal-Fedn. Jewish Philanthropies of N.Y.C., 1986-87, U. Puertorriqueña de los Antillas Aguadilla, P.R., 1993; condr. continuing edn. workshops, various univs. Contbr. articles to profl. jours., also monographs. Served with USAAF, 1943-46. HEW and HHS grantee, 1961-62, 64-76, 77-81. Home: 4612 Monongahela St San Diego CA 92117-2415

WEISMAN, MAXWELL NAPIER, psychiatrist, educator; b. N.Y.C., July 9, 1912; s. Morris and Pauline (Malevatsky) W. BS, CCNY, 1930, MA, 1931, PhD, 1936; MD, U. Amsterdam, The Netherlands, 1958. Dir. house plan CCNY, N.Y.C., 1935-41; prof. U. P.R., Rio Piedras, 1946-49; acting dir. vets. edn. P.R. Dept. Instrn., San Juan, 1949-51; dir. community psychiatry Md. Dept. Mental Health, Balt., 1962-68; dir. alcoholism control Md. Dept. Health, Balt., 1968-80, ret., 1980; cons. FAA, Washington, 1975—; cons. Westinghouse Corp., Pitts., 1975—. Co-author: Relapse/Slips, 1983; editor: ARIC, AIDS Med. Glossary, 1995. Fellow Am. Psychiat. Assn. (life); emm. Am. Pub. Health Assn., Md. Med. and Chirurgical Soc., ACLU, Nat. Coun. on Alcoholism. Democrat.

WEISS, ALAN JOHN, plastic surgeon, educator; b. N.Y.C., Sept. 13, 1953; s. William Davis and Laura Weiss; children: David, Sean, Michelle. Student, Tulane U., 1971-74, La. State U., 1974-75; MD, U. P.R., 1981, postgrad., 1981-82; postgrad., N.J. Med. Sch., 1982-83. Diplomate Am. Bd. Plastic Surgery. Intern Sinai Hosp. Balt., 1983-84; resident Providence Hosp., Southfield, Mich., 1985-88; pvt. practice Glen Burnie, Md., 1988—; attending physician North Arundel Hosp., Glen Burnie, 1988—. Fellow ACS. Office: 1600 S Crain Hwy # 508 Glen Burnie MD 21061

WEISS, ALAN NEAL, cardiologist; b. Columbus, Ohio, Oct. 14, 1941. BA, Ohio State U., 1963, MD cum laude, 1966. Diplomate Am. Bd. Internal Medicine, Am. Bd. Internal Medicine and Cardiovascular Diseases. Intern Ohio Sate U. Hosp., Columbus, 1966-67; medical resident Barnes Hosp., Washington U., St. Louis, 1967-70; postgraduate U. Calif. Cardiovascular Inst., San Francisco, 1970-71, trainee in cardiology, 1971-72; chief resident in medicine Barnes Hosp., 1972-73; asst. prof. medicine, cardiovascular divsn. Washington U. Sch. Medicine, St. Louis, 1973-77; pvt. practice Barnes Hosp., 1977-82; assoc. clin. prof. medicine Washington U. Sch. Medicine, 1982-94, clin. prof. medicine, 1994—; staff assoc. in cardiology (myocardial infarction program) USPHS, NIH, Nat. Heart Inst., Bethesda, Md., 1960-69; med. dir. heart station, Barnes Hosp., 1973-77; lectr. health edn. tech., Stanford U., 1983-84; lectr. Internat. Med. Corp., 1983-84. Contbr. articles to profl. jours. Recipient Outstanding Achievement award in medicine, 1966. Fellow Am. Coll. Cardiology; mem. Am. Heart Assn., St. Louis Cardiac Club. Office: Washington U Sch Medicine Barnes Hospital Plaza 16419 East Pavilion Saint Louis MO 63110

WEISS, ALBERT AARON, orthopedic surgeon; b. Phila., Apr. 23, 1948; s. Paul M. and Faye (Adis) W.; m. Karen Corchin, July 18, 1971; children: Jamie I., Keith C. BS, Pa. State U., 1969; MD, Temple U., 1973. Diplomate Am. Bd. Orthop. Surgery. Assoc. prof. orthop. surgery Hahnemann U., Phila., 1979—; chief orthop. surgery Med. Coll. Pa. Hosp., Phila., 1994—; mem. staff Shriners Hops. for Crippled Children, Phila., 1979—. Fellow ACS, Am. Acad. Orthop. Surgeons, Am. Acad. Pediat.; mem. Phila. Orthop. Soc. (pres. 1995-96), Am. Assn. Hand Surgery. Office: Hahnemann U Hosp 230 N Broad St Philadelphia PA 19102

WEISS, ALLAN G., podiatrist; b. Detroit, Nov. 16, 1948; s. Harold and Ruth (Shapiro) W.; m. Geraldine Weiss; children: Max, Katy, Sarah. BS, Mich. State U., 1970; DPM, Ohio Coll. Podiatric Medicine, 1975. Diplomate Am. Bd. Podiatric surgery. Pvt. practice Orange, Calif. Fellow Am. Coll. Foot Surgeons. Office: 1000 W La Veta Ave #19 Orange CA 92668

WEISS, ANDRE, psychiatrist; s. Melchior and Magda (Sziklas) W.; m. Renee Veit, 1952; children: Madeleine Eve Fagan, Stephen Philip. BS, U. Geneva, 1950, MD, 1954. Intern Sewickley Valley (Pa.) Hosp., 1955-56; resident Cen. Islip (N.Y.) State Hosp., 1956; pvt. practice in gen. medicine Aberdeen, Md., 1957-64; resident in psychiatry Sheppard Pratt Hosp., Balt., 1964-67; psychiatrist out patient dept., instr. psychiatry John Hopkins Med. Sch., Balt., 1966-67; med. officer WHO, Geneva, 1968-76; staff psychiatrist Sheppard Pratt Hosp., Balt., 1977-78, Taylor Manor Hosp., Ellicott City, Md., 1984-93, Balt. County Community Mental Health Ctr., Catonsville, Md., 1991—; pvt. practice Geneva, 1978-84, Columbia, Md., 1991—, Silver Spring, Md., 1995—. Author: Typhus in Concentration Camps (Brit. Imperial War Mus. recognition); exhibitor stamp collection (Grand award), 1964. Mem. Am. Psychiat. Assn., Am. Soc. Psychopharmacology. Office: 5438 Smooth Meadow Way Columbia MD 21044-1767 Office: 800 Pershing Dr Silver Spring MD 20910

WEISS, CAROL JULIET, psychiatrist; b. N.Y.C., Mar. 5, 1957; d. Eugene and Rose (Schwartz) Weiss. BA, Wesleyan U., Middletown, Conn., 1977; MD, Johns Hopkins U., Balt., 1983. Diplomate Am. Bd. Psychiatry and Neurology. Intern N.Y. Hosp., N.Y.C., 1983-84; resident Payne Whitney Clinic, N.Y. Hosp., N.Y.C., 1984-87; asst. psychiatrist Payne Whitney Clinic - N.Y. Hosp., N.Y.C., 1983-87; clin. fellow Cornell U., N.Y.C., 1987-89; instr. and clin. affiliate in psychiatry and pub. health Cornell U., 1989-91; clin. asst. prof. in psychiatry and pub. health Cornell U., N.Y.C., 1992—; pvt. practice N.Y.C., 1987—; cons. in field. Contbr. articles to profl. jours., chpts. to books. Mem. Am. Psychiat. Assn., Am. Soc. Addiction Medicine, Am. Med. Soc. on Alcoholism, Phi Beta Kappa. Office: 55 E 72nd St New York NY 10021-4149

WEISS, CHARLES FREDERICK, pharmacologist, pediatrician, retired air force officer; b. Cohoctah, Mich., Apr. 2, 1921; s. Frederick William and Claudius Beehan (Stanard) W.; m. Bernice Pearigen, Aug. 9, 1947; children: Charles S., Paul Frederick, Thomas Barton. BA, U. Mich., 1942; MD, Vanderbilt U., 1949; grad., USAF Sch. Aerospace Medicine, 1952, Indsl. Coll. Armed Forces, 1973. Diplomate Am. Bd. Pediatrics. Commd. 2d lt. USAF, advanced through grades to col.; intern Harper Hosp., Detroit, 1950; resident in pediatrics Children's Hosp. Mich., 1950-52; mini-resident in occupational medicine U. Cin., 1982; pvt. practice in pediatrics Grosse Pointe, Mich., 1953-58; assoc. dir. Parke, Davis and Co., Ann Arbor, Mich., 1958-69; clin. asst. prof. pediatrics/communicable disease U. Mich., 1962-68; assoc. prof. pediatrics, pharmacology, Coll. Pharmacy U. Fla. Coll. Medicine, 1969-73; chief of staff, interin adminstr. Hope Haven Children's Hosp., Jacksonville, Fla., 1974-76; spl. asst., cons. pediatrics, adviser manpower affairs, oversight mgr. drug testing program Office of the Surgeon Gen., USAF, Washington, 1976-83; ret. USAF, 1983; exec. dir. Sunland Ctr., Orlando, Fla., 1984; v.p. med. affairs, chmn. bd. sci. advisors hiMedics, Inc., Hollywood, Fla., 1985-88; dir. planning and devel. Dakle, Inc., Staunton, Va., 1989-92; cons. Siesta Key, Fla., 1989—; clin. assoc. prof. pediatrics U. South Fla. Coll. Medicine, 1992—; cons. SYVA Corp., 1984-85, Key Pharm., Inc., 1983-84, Fla. Dept. HRS, 1984-87, ELAN Pharm. Rsch. Corp., 1991-92; presenter in field; mem. site visit team mental retardation and metabolic diseases NIH, 1970-72. Editor: Pharmacology for the pediatrician, 1971-75; reviewer Military Medicine, 1974—, Pediatrics, 1975—; contbr. articles and abstracts to profl. publs. Med. dir. Fla. Spl. Olympics, 1973, v.p., 1975, med. dir., v.p. 1976, bd. dirs. 1977; bd. dirs. Duval Assn. for Retarded Children, 1973-76; bd. dirs. Pastoral Counseling Ctr., Presbyn. Synod of Suwanee, 1973-76, treas., 1975-76; bd. dirs. Gainesville Open House, 1972-73; ruling elder 1st Presbyn. Ch., Ann Arbor, 1962-65, 67-73, various other coms., Ann Arbor and Gainesville; bd. ushers Nat. Presbyn. Ch., Washington, 1977-84, vice chmn., trustee 1981-84. Col. USAF, 1972-83. Decorated Legion of Merit, 1983. Mem. AMA (Physicians Recognition award), Am. Acad. Pediatrics (com. on sci. mtgs. 1987—, chmn. environ. health com. Fla. chpt. 1990—, Outstanding Svc. award 1986, Pres.' award 1984), Fla. Med. Assn., Fla. Pediatric Soc., Sarasota County Med. Soc., Am. Soc. Clin. Pharmacology and Therapeutics, Soc. Med. Cons. to Armed Svcs., Res. Officers Assn., Ret. Officers Assn., Air Force Assn., Meninak Club Jacksonville, Army and Navy Club, Marine Meml. Club, Order of the Arrow, Rho Chi. Republican. Home and Office: 126 Sandy Hook Rd S Sarasota FL 34242-1685

WEISS, DANIEL LEIGH, physician, pathologist, administrator; b. Long Branch, N.J., July 27, 1923; s. Harry and Liberty (Moisseiff) W.; m. Mary Burns Caudill, May 26, 1951; children: Peter, Leah, Harry. BA, Columbia U., 1943, MD, 1946. Diplomate Nat. Bd. Med. Examiners, Am. Bd. Pathology. Intern, Hosp. for Joint Diseases, N.Y.C., 1946-47; resident, Mt. Sinai Hosp., N.Y.C., 1949-50, 51-53, Beth Israel Hosp., N.Y.C., 1950-51; dir. dept. pathology and lab. medicine D.C. Gen. Hosp., 1953-63; prof. pathology U. Ky., Lexington, 1963-77; exec. sec. Div. Med. Scis., NRC, Nat. Acad. Scis., 1977-82; dep. dir. Affiliated Edn. program svc., Office Acad. Affairs, Dept. Medicine and Surgery, VA, Washington, 1983-87; cons. med. care systems, edn. and rsch. U.S. Pub. Health Svc., Oak Ridge Assoc. U., Booz Allen Hamilton, 1987— ; clin. prof. pathology George Washington U., 1953-63, 79—, Georgetown U., 1953-63, Howard U., 1956-63; vis. prof. U. Kans., U. Ind., U. Copenhagen, U. Oslo, U. Edinburgh, U. Cambridge; U.S. liaison rep. to COGENE (WHO), 1978-82; biomechanics adv. com. U.S. Dept. Transp., 1979-81, interagy. com. on handicapped rsch. USDHEW, 1980-81, com. on nat. standards for medico legal investigation of death Nat. Inst. Justice U.S. Dept. Justice, 1980-82; mem. rev. panel NEH, 1983; cons. ARC, 1980, Fed. Emergency Mgmt. Adminstrn., 1983-87, Med. Sch. Devel., So. Ill. U., Kent State U; cons. office emergency preparedness USDHHS, 1987-90, U.S. Indian Hosp. USPHS, Santa Fe, 1991—. Contbr. articles to profl. jours. Pres., Chamber Music Soc. Central Ky., 1973-75; mem. Lexington Arts Council, 1974-75; bd. dirs. New World Players Chamber Orch., 1982-84, Desert Chorale, Santa Fe, 1994-96. Served from lt. to capt., U.S. Army, 1943-46, 47-49. Recipient Clin. Scientist award, Am. Assn. Clin. Scientists, 1981; Golden Apple, Preclin. Teaching award, U. Ky., 1965; rsch. fellow Life Ins. Med. Rsch. Found., Levy Found. Fellow AAAS, Coll. Am. Pathologists, Am. Soc. Clin. Pathologists, Assn. Clin Scientists; mem. Am. Assn. Pathologists, Internat. Acad. Pathology, Am. Assn. History of Medicine, Soc. Med. Cons. to Armed Forces, Acad. Medicine Washington, Cosmos Club. Home and Office: 5903 Mt Eagle Dr # 418 Alexandria VA 22303-2527 also: #30 County Rd 46 Santa Fe NM 87505-9527

WEISS, EDWARD CRAIG, psychologist; b. Phila., Jan. 20, 1924; s. Arnold and Elizabeth W.; m. Dorothy Earnestine Arant, Aug. 15, 1952; children: Christopher Brent, Leslie Ann. B.A., Temple U., 1948, M.A., 1949; Ph.D., U. Md., 1954. Lic. psychologist, Va. Chief systems analysis br. U.S. Army Human Engring. Lab., Aberdeen Proving Ground, Md., 1954-59; v.p., dir. rsch. Matix Corp., Arlington Va., 1959-67; program dir. NSF, Washington, 1967-81, dir. divsn. info. sci. and tech., 1981-84; sr. scientist Essex Corp., Alexandria, Va., 1984-90; pvt. cons., 1990—; editorial bd. On Line Rev. Editor: The Many Faces of Information Science, 1977. Served with U.S. Army, 1943-46. Mem. Am. Psychol. Assn., Eastern Psychol. Assn., Va. Psychol. Assn., Sigma Xi. Home and Office: 9908 Great Oaks Way Fairfax VA 22030-1607

WEISS, GEORGE ARTHUR, orthodontist; b. Bklyn., Feb. 1, 1921; s. Nathan L. and Ida (Rosenthal) W.; m. Jacqueline Hellermann, Jan. 28, 1945; children: Ellen Joy Weiss Finberg, Leslie Donna Weiss Schoenfeld. BA, Bklyn. Coll., 1941; DDS, Columbia U., 1944, cert. Orthodontics, 1954. Diplomate Am. Bd. of Orthodontics. Dir. dentistry Dental Clinic Southen Japan, Kobe, 1946; chief dentistry Olmstead AFB, Middleburg, Pa., 1947; pvt. practice Orthodontics Bayside, N.Y., 1947—; chief orthodontics Community Svc. Soc., N.Y.C., 1954-57; dir. orthodontics Jamaica (N.Y.) Hosp., 1977—; cons. State Aid Orthodontic Program for Handicapped Children, Suffolk County, N.Y., 1987—. Founder, Oakland Gardens Jewish Ctr., Bayside, N.Y., 1949; Bayside Oaks Jewish Ctr., Bayside, 1954. Major U.S. Army, 1944-48, Japan. Recipient Chemistry award, Am. Inst. Chem., N.Y.C., 1941. Fellow Am. Coll. Dentistry; mem. Am. Bd. Orthodontists, Am. Assn. Orthodontists, Northeastern Soc. Orthodontists, Dental Soc. State of N.Y. (bd. govs. 1976-86, mem. coun. on ins. 1965-75), Queens County Dental Soc. (trustee 1960—, chief adminstr. retirement fund, 1964-72, pres. 1975, Disting. Svc. award, 1988), Old Westbury Golf and Country Club, Alpha Omega Dental Soc. Home and Office: 5901 Springfield Blvd Flushing NY 11364-1938

WEISS, GERSON, physician, educator; b. N.Y.C., Aug. 1, 1939; s. Samuel and Lillian (Wolpe) W.; m. Linda Gordon, Dec. 24, 1959; children: Jonathan, David, Michele, Andrew. B.A., NYU, 1960, M.D., 1964. Diplomate Am. Bd. Ob-Gyn. (mem. div. reproductive endocrinology 1985-90). Intern, fellow dept. medicine Johns Hopkins Sch. Medicine, 1964-65; resident ob-gyn NYU Med. Center, 1964-69; research fellow physiology U. Pitts. Sch. Medicine, 1971-73; asst. prof. ob-gyn NYU Med. Center, 1971-76, asso. prof., 1976-80, prof., 1980-85, dir. div. reproductive endocrinology, 1975-85; prof. ob-gyn U. Med. and Dentistry N.J.-N.J. Med. Sch., 1986—, chmn. dept., 1986—. Mem. editorial bd. Fertility and Sterility Jour., Gyn.-Ob. Investigation; contbr. rsch. articles reproductive endocrinology and gynecology to med. jours. Served to maj. MC U.S. Army, 1969-71. Rsch. grantee NIH, 1975—, United Cerebral Palsy Found., 1977-83, Mellon Found., 1982-85; John Polachek Found. Med. Rsch. fellow. Mem. Am. Coll. Ob-Gyn., Am. Ob-Gyn. Soc., Am. Bd. Ob-Gyn. (bd. dirs. 1993—, ob-gyn. residency rev. com. 1995—), Endocrine Soc. Gynecol. Investigation, N.Y. Obstet. Soc. (pres. 1990-91), N.Y. Gynecol. Soc. (pres. 1989-90), Soc. Study of Reprodn., Phi Beta Kappa, Sigma Xi, Alpha Omega Alpha. Home: 390 1st Ave Apt 11D New York NY 10010-4935 Office: UMDNJ NJ Med Sch Dept Ob-Gyn 185 S Orange Ave Newark NJ 07103-2714

WEISS, HARVEY ALAN, plastic surgeon; b. Detroit, Jan. 29, 1937; children: Michael, Kimberly, David. BS, U. Mich., 1957, MD, 1961. Diplomate Am. Bd. Plastic Surgery; lic. Mich., Ga., Mo. Intern Henry Ford Hosp., Detroit, 1961-62, resident, 1962-68; resident St. Joseph's Mercy Hosp., Ann Arbor, Mich., 1965; pvt. practice Atlanta, 1970—; staff physician Northside Hosp., St. Joseph's Hosp. Maj. USAF, 1968-70. Fellow ACS; mem. Am. Soc. Plastic and Reconstructive Surgery, Soc. Mil. Plastic Surgeons, Southeastern Soc. Plastic Surgeons, Ga. Med. Soc. Plastic Surgeons, Reed O. Dingman Soc. Plastic Surgery. Office: 993-D Johnson Ferry Rd #470 Atlanta GA 30342

WEISS, HARVEY RICHARD, physiology and biophysics educator, researcher; b. Bklyn., May 13, 1943; s. Edgar D. and Frances (Warshavsky) w.; m. Sandra Levy, Aug. 13, 1966; children: Johanna, Andrew. BS, CUNY, 1965; PhD, Duke U., 1969. Postdoctoral fellow Warner-Lambert Rsch. Inst. Columbia U., N.Y.C., 1969-71; mem. grad. program Rutgers U., 1972; from asst. prof. to asst. chmn. U. Medicine and Dentistry of (Piscataway) N.J., 1971-86, prof., dir. heart and brain lab., 1982, acting chair, 1986—; joint adv. com. Robert Wood Johnson Med. Sch., 1972-75, adv. 1st yr. med. students, 1972—, com. of review, 1976-79, curriculum com., co-chmn., 1977-83, radiation safety com., 1980-87, grant review com., 1984-88; seminar com. Rutgers U., 1974,75, exec. com. Physiology Program, 1974-80, 89—; reviewer Nat. Heart Lung and Blood Inst., NIH, Am. Jour. Physiology, Basic Rsch. in Cardiology, Canadian Jour. Physiology and Pharmacology, Cardiovascular Rsch., Circulation Rsch., and others. Grantee NIH, AHA. Office: U of Medicine Dentistry Robert Wood Johnson Med Sch 675 Hoes Ln Piscataway NJ 08854-5635

WEISS, JAMES MOSES AARON, psychiatrist, educator; b. St. Paul, Oct. 22, 1921; s. Louis Robert and Gertrude (Simon) W.; m. Bette Shapera, Apr. 7, 1946; children: Jenny Anne Weiss Ford, Jonathan James. AB summa cum laude, U. Minn., 1941, ScB, 1947, MB, 1949, MD, 1950; MPH with high honors, Yale U., 1951. Diplomate: Am. Bd. Psychiatry and Neurology (examiner 1963-83). Teaching asst. psychology St. Thomas Coll., St. Paul, 1941-42; intern USPHS Hosp., Seattle, 1949-50; resident, fellow psychiatry Yale Med. Sch., 1950-53; from instr. to asst. prof. psychiatry Washington U., St. Louis, 1954-60; mem. faculty U. Mo., 1959—, First Prof. psychiatry, 1961—, founding chmn. dept., 1960-91, prof. community medicine, 1971—, univ. prof. emeritus, 1991—; vis. prof. Inst. Criminology, Cambridge (Eng.) U., 1968-69, All-India Inst. Med. Scis. and U. Malaya, 1984; internat. cons., 1958—; founding co-chmn. Asian-Am. Consortium on Psychiat. Disorders, 1986—; Kohler disting. lectr. St. Louis U., 1988. Author numerous articles in field; editor, co-author: Nurses, Patients, and Social Systems, 1968; corr. editor: Jour. Geriatric Psychiatry, 1967—; founding editor, chmn. bd. Jour. Operational Psychiatry, 1970-90; editorial advisor Community Mental Health Jour., 1979-87; trustee Mo. Rev., 1982-83. Served with M.C., AUS, 1942-46, PTO; to capt. M.C., AUS, 1953-54. Decorated Philippine Liberation medal, 1945; recipient Sir Henry Wellcome award, 1955, Israeli bronze medal, 1963, Basic Books award, 1974, Disting. Service commendation Nat. Council Community Mental Health Ctrs., 1982, 83, 86, Guhleman award for Clin. Excellence U. Mo., 1987, Hon. Achievement award U.Mo., 1991, Disting. Svc. award VA, 1991; named Chancellor's Emissary U. Mo., 1979; faculty fellow Inter-Univ. Council, 1958, sr. research fellow Am. Council Edn. and NSF, 1984. Found. fellow Royal Coll. Psychiatrists; fellow Royal Soc. Medicine, Am. Psychiat. Assn. (life), Am. Pub. Health Assn. (life), Am. Coll. Preventive Medicine (emeritus), Royal Soc. Health, AAAS, Am. Coll. Psychiatrists (life), Am. Assn. Psychoanalytic Physicians (hon.); mem. Assn. Mil. Surgeons U.S. (hon. life), Assn. Western Profs. Psychiatry (chmn. 1970-71), Mo. Acad. Psychiatry (1st pres. 1966-67), Mo. Psychiat. Assn. (life, pres. 1987-88), Assn. de Methodologie et Documentation en Psychiatrie, Mil. Order World Wars, Phi Beta Kappa, Sigma Xi, Psi Chi, Alpha Omega Alpha, Alpha Epsilon Sigma, Gamma Alpha. Clubs: Scholars (Cantab.); Wine Label (London); Yale (St. Louis); Univ. (Columbia). Home: Crow Wing Farm RR 2 Box 2 Columbia MO 65201-9802 Office: U Mo Dept Psychiatry Columbia MO 65212

WEISS, JAYNE SHARI, ophthalmology educator; b. N.Y.C., Mar. 8, 1956; d. Lewis L. and Sally (Brecher) W.; m. Ethan D. Nydorf, Mar. 24, 1990; 1 child, Alana. BA in Biology summa cum laude, SUNY, Buffalo, 1975; MD, Mt. Sinai Sch. Medicine, N.Y.C., 1979. Diplomate Am. Bd. Ophthalmology. Intern in internal medicine Beth Israel Med. Ctr., N.Y.C., 1979-80; resident in ophthalmology Bascom Palmer Eye Inst., Miami, Fla., 1980-83; fellow in eye pathology Mass. Eye & Ear Infirmary-Harvard Med. Sch., Boston, 1983-84; fellow in cornea & external eye diseases Emory U., Atlanta, 1984-85; Fulbright scholar U. Zimbabwe Godfrey Huggins Sch. Medicine, Harare, 1986; asst., then assoc. prof. surgery, dir. cornea svc. U. Mass. Med. Ctr., Worcester, 1986-95; assoc. prof. ophthalmology Wayne State U., Detroit, 1995—, dir. ocular pathology Kresge Eye Inst., 1995—; vis. prof. ophthalmology Tri-Svc. Gen. Hosp., Taipei, Taiwan, 1985; prin. investigator Aesculap Meditec Excimer Laser, Detroit, 1995—. Contbg. author: The Prinicples and Practice of Ophthalmology, 1993: contbr. articles to med. jours.; mem. editl. bd. Cornea Jour., 1995—. Grantee Endocrinology Rsch. Ctr., U. Mass. Med. Ctr., 1988-93, grantee Healey Endowment, 1992. Fellow Am. Acad. Ophthalmology; mem. AMA, Internat. Soc. Refractive Surgeons, Castroviejo Soc., Fulbright Scholar Assn., Phi Beta Kappa, Alpha Omega Alpha. Office: Kresge Eye Inst 4717 St Antoine Detroit MI 48201

WEISS, JEFFREY NEILL, ophthalmologist; b. N.Y.C., June 4, 1952; m. Judith Ann Green. BEE, SUNY, Buffalo, 1972; MD, SUNY, Bklyn., 1976. Diplomate Am. Bd. Ophthalmology, Nat. Bd. Med. Examiners. Intern in surgery Med. Coll. Va., Richmond, 1976-77, resident in ophthalmology, 1977-80; fellow ophthalmologic bioengring. and retina-vitreous Harvard U. and MIT, Boston, 1980-82; fellow in surgery Harvard U. Sch. Medicine, Boston, 1980-82; instr. ophthalmology Harvard U. Sch. Medicine, 1982-87; assoc. investigator Joslin Rsch. Lab., B, 1982-87; dir. Laser Lab., Joslin Diabetes Ctr., B, 1982-87, sr. physician, 1984-87, dep. dir. Beetham eye unit, chief vitreoretinal svc., 1985-87; pvt. practice, Margate, Fla., 1987—. Contbr. articles and abstracts to med. jours., chpts. to books; patentee for protective eye shield, apparatus for detection of diabetes and other abnormalities affecting lens of eye, diabetes detection methods. Named One of Doctors of Yr., South Fla. mag., 1991; grantee Nat Eye Inst., NIH, Lions Club. Mem. Vitreous Soc., Fla. Soc. Ophthalmology, Broward County Ophthalmology Soc., Harvard Club Broward County, Am. Acad. of Ophthalmology. Office: 5800 Colonial Dr Ste 300 Margate FL 33063

WEISS, JEFFREY PAUL, pharmacist, educator; b. Cin., Sept. 19, 1958; s. David Stanford and Judith Ann (Hebenstreit) W.; m. Lorraine Grace Kern, Sept. 11, 1982. BS in Pharmacy, U. Cin., 1983. Cert. pharmacist, Ohio, Fla. Staff pharmacist Christ Hosp., Cin., 1983-84, staff oncology pharmacist, 1984-86, clin. oncology pharmacist, 1986-94, mem. exec. bd. rsch. program Cancer Ctr., 1989-94, dir. Cancer Ctr. Rsch. Pharmacy, 1990-94; retail pharmacist Walt-Mart Pharmacy, Ft. Myers, Fla., 1994-95, Rite-Aid Pharmacy, Ft. Myers, 1995; clin. pharmacy specialist in hematology and oncology Naples (Fla.) Cmty. Hosp., 1995—; adj. instr. pharmacotherapy U. Cin. Coll. Pharmacy, 1984—; trustee Cancer Control Consortium Ohio, Columbus, 1986-87; mem. gastrointestinal cancer com. S.W. Oncology Group, 1990-94; mem. editl. staff Hamilton County Pharm. Assn. Pharmacist Jour., 1984-86. Contbr. abstracts to profl. jours. Mem. profl. edn. com. Cin. br. Am. Cancer Soc., 1984-87. Roche hosp. pharmacy rsch. grantee Roche Pharms., 1985, 87. Mem. Am. Soc. Hosp. Pharmacists (oncology spl. interest group 1984-89, jr. formulary award Cin. chpt. 1982, sr. award 1983), Am. Soc. Hematology, Am. Soc. Clin. Oncology, Fla. Pharmacy Assn., Greater Cin. Soc. Hosp. Pharmacists. Jewish. Office: Naples Cmty Hosp 350 7th St N Naples FL 33940

WEISS, JOSEPH, physician; b. Kosice, Czechoslovakia, June 23, 1913; came to U.S., 1949; s. Abraham Adolf and Johanna (Nagy) W.; m. Eva Farkas, Apr. 24, 1944; 1 child, Julia. MD, Charles U., Prague, Czechoslovakia, 1947. Diplomate Am. Bd. Family Practice. Clin. asst. Charles U., 1947-48; resident in medicine Lebanon Hosp., Bronx, N.Y., 1949-51; clinician N.Y.C. Dept. Health, 1954-85; clin. instr. medicine N.Y. Med. Coll., N.Y.C. and Valhalla, N.Y., 1973-90; bd. dirs. La Guardia-Health Ins. Plan Greater N.Y., 1979-85, chmn. peer rev. com., 1985—; pres. Semmelweis Sci. Soc., N.Y.C., 1973-74; pres. Am.-Hungarian Med. Assn., N.Y.C., 1973-74. Recipient Presdl. Scroll Semmelweis Sci. Soc., 1974, medal Internat. Conv. Pathophysiology, Prague, 1975, Internat. Symposium Cardiomyopathies, Bratislava, Czechoslovakia, 1985. Fellow InterAm. Coll. Physicians and Surgeons, Am. Geriatric Soc., Am. Acad. Family Practice; mem. AMA, N.Y. State Med. Soc., Queens County Med. Soc., N.Y. Acad. Scis. Home: 69-33 170th St Flushing NY 11365-3309

WEISS, JOSEPH FRANKLIN, ophthalmologist; b. Portland, Oct. 24, 1927; s. Henry and Minnie (Kirsch) W.; m. Renee Elizabeth Mertens, June 5, 1965; children: Mathew, Alexander, Heather. BA, Oreg. State Coll., 1952; MD, U. Oreg., 1954. Diplomate Am. Bd. Ophthalmology. Intern U. Chgo. Clinics, 1954-55; med. missionary Overseas Missionary Fellowship, Thailand, 1956-64; resident, ophthalmology Cleve. Met. Hosp., 1964-67; ophthalmologist Hunterdon Med. Ctr., Flemington, N.J., 1968-69, Valley Med. Clinic, Portland, 1970-71, Winona (Minn.) Clinic, 1972-79, Memphis Eye and Cataract Assocs., 1981-96; clin. asst. prof. U. Tenn. Med. Sch., Memphis, 1981-91. Inventor Photostress Tester, 1986. Lt. col. U.S. Army, 1979-81. Recipient Heed fellowship Heed Found., Columbia/Presbyn. Hosp., N.Y.C., 1967. Fellow Am. Acad. Ophthalmology; mem. AMA, Tenn. Med. Assn., Memphis and Shelby County Med. Soc., Memphis Eye Soc. (sec., treas. 1986, pres. 1987), Assn. for Rsch. in Vision and Ophthalmology.

WEISS, JUDITH MIRIAM, psychologist; b. Chgo., June 29, 1939; d. Louis and Annette (Frazin) Schmerling; m. Jon Howard Kaas, May 19, 1963 (div. Dec. 1984); children: Lisa Karen, Jon Michael; m. Stephen Fred Weiss, Dec. 22, 1988. AB in Liberal Arts, Northwestern U., 1961; PhD, Duke U., 1969. Lic. clin. psychologist, Tenn. Postdoctoral fellow U. Wis. Hosp., Madison, 1969-71; neuropsychologist Mental Health Assocs., Madison, 1971-72; asst. prof. George Peabody Coll., Nashville, 1972-77, Vanderbilt U., Nashville, 1972-77; neuropsychologist Comprehensive Clin. Svcs., Nashville, 1977—; advocate, cons. Tenn. Protection and Advocacy, Inc., Nashville, 1976—. Mem. CABLE, Nashville. Mem. APA, Tenn. Psychol. Assn., Internat. Neuropsychol. Assn., Nat. Acad. Neuropsychology, U.s.-China Peoples Friendship Assn., Tenn. Head Injury Assn., B.R.A.I.N., Tenn. Assn. for the Talented and Gifted, Tenn. Assn. Audiologists and Speech-Lang. Pathologists, Nashville Area Psychol. Assn., Coun. for Learning Disabilities, Assn. for Children with Learning Disabilities. Jewish. Home: 893 Stirrup Dr Nashville TN 37221-1918 Office: Comprehensive Clin Svcs 102 Woodmont Blvd Ste 215 Nashville TN 37205-2287

WEISS, KATHLEEN MCKITTRICK, physician; b. Palo Alto, Calif., Oct. 13, 1952; d. Jack Wilson and Amy (Morrison) McKittrick; m. Frederick George Weiss, Sept. 1977. BS, U. Washington, 1974; MD, U. So. Calif., 1978. Diplomate Am. Bd. Internal Medicine. Intern, then resident Kaiser Found. Hosp., Los Angeles, 1978-81; staff physician North West Permanente, Portland, Oreg., 1981-87; gen. practice internal medicine Newberg, Oreg., 1987—. Mem. AcP, Christian Med. Soc. Office: Springbrook NW 2001 Crestview Dr Newberg OR 97132

WEISS, L. LEONARD, pathologist, biophysicist; b. London, June 15, 1928; came to U.S., 1964; m. Maureen A. Weiss, Feb. 23, 1951; children: Gregory, Simon, Emma. MB, BChir, Cambridge U., 1953, MD, 1958, PhD, 1963, ScD, 1971. Lic. in N.Y. State, U.K. Registrar Westminster Hosp., London, 1954-58; scientist Nat. Inst. Med. Rsch., London, 1958-60; cell physiologist Strangeways Rsch. Lab., Cambridge, U.K., 1960-64; dir. dept. exptl. pathology N.Y. State Health Dept. Roswell Pk. Meml. Inst., Buffalo, 1964-93, chief cancer rsch. clinician, 1993—; prof. biophysics, interdisciplinary scis. SUNY, Buffalo, 1965-93, prof. emeritus, 1993—. Author: Metastasis, 1965-91, Watchmaking in England. 1760-1820, 1982. Maj. RAMC, 1960-64, U.K. Fellow Royal Coll. Pathologists, Coll. Am. Pathologists; mem. Youngstown Yacht Club.

WEISS, LINDA WOLFF, health systems administrator; b. Albany, N.Y., Apr. 12, 1953; d. Charles Vincent and Hilda Bertha (Kitzman) Wolff; divorced; 1 child, Russell. AAS, Hudson Valley C.C., Troy, N.Y., 1973; BS, Empire State Coll., 1983; MS in Health Sys. Mgmt., Union Coll., 1987. Staff nuc. medicine technologist VA Med. Ctr., Albany, 1973-83, chief technologist nuc. medicine, 1983-84, asst. chief radiology/nuc. medicine svc., 1984-87, area mgr. emergency medicine preparedness office, 1987-94; area mgr. emergency medicine preparedness office U.S. Dept VA, Albany and Syracuse, N.Y., 1994-96; dir. managed care and planning Upstate N.Y. VA Network, Albany, 1996—; mem. N.Y. State Disaster Preparedness Commn., Albany; charter mem. human needs in disaster standing com., 1989-96, Albany County Local Emergency Preparedness Commn., 1987-96, N.Y. State Vol. Orgns. Active in Disaster, 1989; mem. adj. faculty, tutor Empire State Coll., Albany; investigator Northridge Earthquake Epidemiology Study, 1995-96. Contbg. editor Jour. Clin. Ultrasound, 1981-85, Med. Ultrasound, 1981-85; mem. editl. bd. EMPO News, 1992-96. W.K. Kellogg Found. Ptnrs. fellow in internat. leadership and devel., 1990-93; Leadership VA class, 1996; recipient Dir.'s cert. Hurricane Andrews Response, 1992. Mem. Ptnrs. of the Am. (W.K. Kellogg Found. fellow 1990-93, chair emergency preparedness com. 1991—), Proctor's Theater, Barn Raisers. Lutheran. Office: Upstate NY VA Healthcare PO Box 8980 Albany NY 12208-0980

WEISS, MARIA CRISTINA RODRIGUEZ, cardiovascular nurse; b. San Antonio, Dec. 4, 1949; d. Rodolfo and Gregoria (Gonzales) R.; m. Laurence Rosen, May 12, 1973 (div. Feb. 1980); m. Martin Weiss. Assoc. degree, San Antonio Coll., 1971; BS in Nursing, U. Tex., San Antonio, 1973, postgrad., 1977, 1980—. Lic. nurse, Tex., 1973. Charge nurse Bexar County Hosp., San Antonio, 1973-74; ground floor supr. Luth. Gen. Hosp., San Antonio, 1974; surg. intensive care nurse Audie Murphy Vets. Adminstrn. Hosp., San Antonio, 1974-77; office adminstr., cardiovascular nurse specialist Robert N. Schnitzler, M.D., San Antonio, 1977—; med. cons. papal visit City of San Antonio, 1987, Mayor's Task Force Earthquake Relief, 1985; freelance consulting office mgr., San Antonio, 1977—; freelance fundraiser cons., San Antonio, 1977—; cardiovascular nurse cons. St. Luke's Hosp., Met. Hosp., San Antonio Cmty. Hosp.; lectr. in field, 1979-82. Treas. Yolanda Vera for City Councilwoman, San Antonio, 1986; del. Michael Dukakis for Pres., Bexar County, Tex., 1988; fundraising, phone coord. Judge Roy Barrera for Atty. Gen., 1986; bd. dirs. Arthritis Found., 1982-85, Target 90, San Antonio, 1985-90, Cen. Bario Med. Clin., 1988; active San Antonio Drug Task Force, 1986-88, Health Profls. San Antonio Honoring Mayor Cisneros; steering com. mem. Am. Diabetes Assn., 1986; speakers bur. mem. Am. Heart Assn. Smoking Coalition, 1986, non-smoker coalition speakers bur., Am. Lung Assn., 1986; cmty. liaison St. Joseph's, St. Peter's Children's Homes, 1980-82; adv. bd. San Antonio Handicap Access, 1985; pub. rels. liason United San Antonio, 1982. Named Outstanding Young Woman Am., 1977; recipient Outstanding Accomplishments in Nursing by a Nursing Cons. in Edn. and Health Svcs., 1990. Mem. Am. Heart Assn. (bd. dirs., cardiovascular nursing task force 1977-84, cardiopulmonary resuscitation task force 1980-82, cmty. svc. task force 1980-82, legis. network 1984—, speakers bur. 1986-90, active numerous fundraisers, Outstanding Achievement award 1990), Am. Critical Care Nurses Assn., San Antonio 100, , Spanish Honor Soc., Sigma Theta Tau (Nurse Image Maker award Delta Alpha chpt. 1984).

WEISS, MARTIN HARVEY, neurosurgeon, educator; b. Newark, Feb. 2, 1939; s. Max and Rae W.; m. R. Debora Rosenthal, Aug. 20, 1961; children: Brad, Jessica, Elisabeth. AB magna cum laude, Dartmouth Coll., 1960, BMS, 1961; MD, Cornell U., 1963. Diplomate Am. Bd. Neurol. Surgery (bd. dirs. 1983-89, vice chmn. 1987-88, chmn. 1988-89). Intern Univ. Hosps., Cleve., 1963-64; resident in neurosurgery Univ. Hosps., 1966-70; sr. instr. to asst. prof. neurosurgery Case Western Res. U., 1970-73; asso. prof. neurosurgery U. So. Calif., 1973-76, prof., 1976-78, prof., chmn. dept., 1978—; chmn. neurology B study sect. NIH; mem. residency rev. com. for neurosurgery Accreditation Commn. for Grad. Med. Edn., 1989—, vice chmn., 1991-93, chmn., 1993-95, mem. appeals coun. in neurosurgery, 1995—; Courville lectr. Loma Linda U. Sch. Medicine, 1989; Edgar Kahn vis. prof. U. Mich., 1987; W. James Gardner lectr. Cleve. Clinic, 1993; Edwin Boldrey vis. prof. U. Calif., San Francisco, 1994; hon. guest San Francisco Neurol. Soc., 1994, Australian Neurosurg. Soc., 1996; Arthur Ward vis. prof. U. Wash., 1988; John Raff vis. prof. U. Oreg., 1995; Afrox traveling prof. South African Congress Neurol. Surgeons, 1989; Loyal Davis lectr. Northwestern U., 1990. Author: Pituitary Diseases, 1980; editor-in-chief Clin. Neurosurgery, 1980-83; assoc. editor Bull. L.A. Neurol. Socs., 1976-81, Jour. Clin. Neurosci., 1981—; mem. editl. bd. Neurosurgery, 1979-84, Neurol. Rsch., 1980—, Jour. Neurosurgery, 1987—, chmn., 1995—, assoc. editor, 1996. Served to capt. USAR, 1964-66. Spl. fellow in neurosurgery NIH, 1969-70; recipient Jamieson medal Australasian Neurosurg. Soc., 1996. Mem. ACS (adv. coun. neurosurgery 1985-88), Soc. Neurol. Surgeons, Neurosurg. Soc. Am., Am. Acad. Neurol. Surgery (exec. com. 1988-89, v.p. 1992-93), Rsch. Soc. Neurol. Surgeons, Am. Assn. Neurol. Surgeons (bd. dirs. 1988-91, sec. 1994-97), Congress Neurol. Surgeons (v.p. 1982-83), Western Neurosurg. Soc., Neurosurg. Forum, So. Calif. Neurosurg. Soc. (pres. 1983-84), Phi Beta Kappa, Alpha Omega Alpha. Home: 357 Georgian Rd La Canada-Flintridge CA 91011-3520 Office: 1200 N State St Los Angeles CA 90033-4525

WEISS, MELISSA KATHERINE, physician, educator, administrator; b. Sharon, Mass., Sept. 17, 1960; d. Sam and Donna (Canning) Wilfred; m. Matthew O. Weiss, Nov. 25, 1984; children: Valeri, Sam, Deborah. BS, U. N.H., 1981; MD, U. Nebr., 1983. Diplomate Am. Bd. Family Practice. Intern Brigham Hosp., Boston, 1983, family physician intern, 1984; resident Boston Gen. Hosp., 1985; asst. family medicine Harvard and Boston Coll Hosp., 1986, dir. family medicine, 1987—; Prof. family medicine, Harvard, Boston Coll., 1988—. Author: The Doctor As Parent and Patient, 1990, Family Medicine for The Future, 1993; contbr. many articles to profl. jours. Recipient of the Truth in Publishing award, 1994. Mem. Mass. Med. Soc., Assn. Am. Physicians, Soc. Fam. Physicians, Sigma Xi. Office: Boston Coll. Hosp. 1776 Sergeant Werik Rd Boston MA 02129

WEISS, MICHAEL ELLIOT, physician, educator; b. Mt. Vernon, N.Y., Sept. 25, 1954; s. Leo and Pauline Weiss; m. Leslie Garrison; children: Mia Gabrielle, Hannah Claire. BA in Gen. Studies with high honors, SUNY, Oneonta, 1976; postgrad., Columbia U., 1976; MD, SUNY, Stony Brook, 1981. Diplomate Am. Bd. Med. Examiners, Am. Bd. Internal Medicine, Am. Bd. Allergy and Immunology. Med. lab. technician developmental genetics lab. Albert Einstein Coll. Medicine, 1976-77; resident in internal medicine U. Wis. Hosp., 1981-85; internist Martin Luther King Jr. Health Ctr., Bronx, N.Y., 1984-86; fellow divsn. allergy and clin. immunology Sch. Medicine Johns Hopkins U., Balt., 1986-89; clin. asst. prof. medicine U. Wash., Seattle, 1990—; pvt. practice Redmond (Wash.) Med. Ctr., 1989—; chmn. dept. medicine Evergreen Hosp. Med. Ctr., 1993, chief of staff, 1995. Contbr. articles, abstracts to profl. publs. Nat. Health Svc. Corp. scholar, 1979-81; recipient REgional Health Adminstr.'s award USPHS, 1986, Geigy Fellowship award for clin. rsch., 1987, U.S. Pharmacopeial Fellowship award, 1988; travel grantee Am. Coll. Allergy, 1987, immunology sec. Am. Acad. Pediatrics, 1987, Am. Acad. Allergy and Immunology, 1988. Mem. Am. Acad. Allergy and Immunology (Pres.'s Grant-In-Aid award for clin. rsch. 1989, com. on adverse reaction to antibiotics 1988—, com. on latex allergy, 1991—, com. on undergrad. and grad. med. edn. 1992—), Am. Coll. Allergy and Immunology, Puget Sound Allergy Soc. (sec.-treas. 1991-93, pres. 1993—), Wash. State Allergy Assn., Wash. State Med. Assn. Office: Redwood Med Ctr 8301 161st Ave NE Ste 208 Redwood WA 98052

WEISS, MORRIS MILTON, cardiologist, educator; b. Louisville, Ky., July 18, 1933; s. Morris M. and Evelyn (Brown) W.; m. Gladys Lillian, Dec. 26, 1959; children: Daniel Abraham, John A., Michael Morris; m. Terry Angelia Smith, May 31, 1985; 1 child, David Marshall. MD, U. Louisville, 1958. Intern The Pa. Hosp., Phila., 1958-59; fellow in hypertension U. Pa., Phila., 1959-60; resident in internal medicine Barnes Hosp. Wash. U., St. Louis, 1960-62; to assoc. clin. prof. medicine U. Louisville Sch. Medicine, 1962—; pvt. practice Med. Ctr. Cardiologists, Louisville, 1962—. Lt. col. U.S. Army, 1957-59. Democrat. Jewish. Office: Med Ctr Cardiologists Ste 305 225 Abraham Flexner Way Louisville KY 40204

WEISS, NOEL S., epidemiologist; b. Chgo., Mar. 10, 1943; s. Sidney and Dorothy (Bloom) W.; m. Chu Chen, Oct. 12, 1980; children: Jessica, Jeremy. BA, Stanford U., 1965, MD, 1967; MPH, Harvard U., 1969, DrPH, 1971. Epidemiologist Nat. Ctr. for Health Stats., Rockville, Md., 1971-73; prof. U. Washington, Seattle, 1973—; epidemiologist Fred Hutchinson Cancer Rsch. Ctr., Seattle. Author: Clinical Epidemiology: The Study of the Outcome of Illness, 1986. Recipient Rsch. Career Devel. award Nat. Cancer Inst., 1975, Outstanding Investigator award Nat. Cancer Inst., 1985. Mem. Inst. of Medicine, Am. Pub. Health Assn., Soc. for Epidemiol. Rsch., Am. Epidemiol. Soc. Democrat. Office: U Wash Sch Pub Health and Community Medicine SC-36 Seattle WA 98195*

WEISS, PAUL RICHARD, plastic surgeon; b. Bklyn., July 4, 1942; s. Murray and Belle (Edelman) W.; m. Linda Wayne, Aug. 23, 1964; children: Fredda Susan, Jonathan Michael. BS, Tufts U., 1964; MD, Tulane U., 1969. Diplomate Am. Bd. Surgery, Am. Bd. Plastic Surgery. Intern Bronx Mcpl. Hosp., 1969-70, resident in surgery, 1970-72; resident in surgery Montefiore Med. Ctr., Bronx, 1972-74, resident in plastic surgeon, 1974-76; pvt. practice medicine N.Y.C., 1976—. Fellow ACS (pres. Bronx chpt. 1995-96); mem. Am. Assn. Plastic Surgeons, Am. Soc. Aesthetic Plastic Surgery, Am. Soc. Plastic and Reconstructive Surgery, N.Y. Regional Soc. Plastic Surgeons (pres. 1992-93), Am. Assn. for Hand Surgery, Am. Burn Assn., N.Y. Acad. Medicine. Jewish. Home: 11 Ross Rd Scarsdale NY 10583 Office: 1049 5th Ave Ste 2D New York NY 10028

WEISS, ROBERT FRANKLIN, podiatrist; b. Bridgeport, Conn., May 2, 1946; s. Murray Harold and Sara (Kramer) W.; m. Kathy Barbara Herstein, June 6, 1971; children: Lauren Jennifer, Scott Heath. Student, Norwalk (Conn.) C.C., 1965-67, U. Bridgeport, 1967; DPM, Ohio Coll. Podiatric Medicine, 1971. Diplomate Am. Coun. Cert. Podiat. Physicians and Surgeons, Am. Acad. Pain Mgmt., Am. Bd. Forensic Examiners, Am. Bd. Forensic Medicine; qualified, Am. Bd. Podiatric Orthops. Resident James C. Giuffré Med. Ctr., Phila., 1971-72; chief dept. podiatry St. Joseph Med. Ctr., Stamford, Conn., 1985—; mem. dept. podiatry Stamford Hosp., 1987—, Norwalk Hosp., 1987—; police surgeon Conn. State Police, Meriden, 1985—; cons. sports medicine IBM, White Plains, N.Y., 1985-91, Spl. Olympics World Games, New Haven, 1995; mem. trial adv. com. U.S. Olympic Marathon, Buffalo, 1984, Liberty Park, N.J., 1988. Author: Archives of Podiatric Medicine & Foot Surgery, 1978, 2d edit., 1979; mem. editorial bd. Conn. Runner mag., 1991—; syndicated columnist Sports Medicine & Health, 1980-91; inventor foot support walking and running systems. Founder, mem. Conn. Police Chief Assn., Conn. Law Enforcement Found., 1994—. Fellow Am. Acad. Podiatric Sports Medicine (chmn. credentials and exam. com. 1985-87, Robert Barnes Disting. Svc. award 1988), Am. Soc. Laser Medicine and Surgery; mem. Am. Coll. Foot Surgeons (assoc.), Am. Coll. Foot and Ankle Surgeons (assoc.), Am. Coll. Foot Orthops. and Medicine (assoc.), Am. Coll. Sports Medicine, Am. Med. Athletic Assn., Am. Podiatric Med. Assn., Am. Bd. Forensic Medicine, Am. Coll. Forensic Examiners, Internat. Assn. for Identification (Conn. State divsn.), Internat. Soc. Forensic Podiatrists, Conn. Podiatric Med. Assn. (mem. peer rev. com. 1984-86), Fairfield County Podiatric Med. Assn. Home: 350 Barrack Hill Rd Ridgefield CT 06877-3031 Office: Running Doctor Inc 800 Post Rd Darien CT 06820

WEISS, ROBERT JEROME, psychiatrist, educator; b. West New York, N.J., Dec. 9, 1917; s. Harry and Dora (Samuels) W.; m. Minnie Thompson Moore, Apr. 21, 1945; children—Scott Tillman, James Woodrow, Elizabeth Thompson. Student, Johns Hopkins, 1937; A.B., George Washington U., 1947; M.D., Columbia, 1951; M.A. (hon.), Dartmouth, 1964. Intern Columbia div. Bellevue Hosp., 1951, asst. resident medicine, 1953; resident psychiatry N.Y. Psychiat. Inst., 1954-56; asst. attending Vanderbilt Clinic, 1957-58, Presbyn. Hosp., N.Y.C., 1958-59; chief psychiatry Mary Hitchcock Meml. Hosp., 1959-70; career tchr. trainee Nat. Inst. Mental Health, 1956-58; tchr., research Columbia Coll. Phys. and Surg., 1956-59; prof. psychiatry, chmn. dept. Dartmouth Med. Sch., 1959-70; psychiatrist Beth Israel Hosp., 1988-90; attending physician Presbyn. Hosp., 1975-85, cons. 1985—; vis. prof. comty. medicine Harvard Med. Sch., 1970-75, assoc. dir. comty. health, 1970-95, assoc. dean health care planning; prof. psychiatry and social medicine Columbia Coll. Physicians and Surgeons, 1975-86, also dir. Ctrs. for Comty. Health, 1975-86; De Lamar prof. pub. health practice, dean Columbia U. Sch. Pub. Health, 1980-86, dean and De Lamar prof. of pub. health practice, prof. psychiatry, prof. social medicine, prof. emeritus, 1986—; vis. prof. comty. medicine U. N.Mex. Med. Sch., 1986-89; cons. Nat. Ctr. for Health Svcs. Rsch., 1975-86, NIMH, 1977-86; chmn. psychiatry tng. com. NIMH, 1967-68, mem. coord. panel, 1965-67, ad hoc com. interdisciplinary tng. program, 1966, mem. agenda com., 1966; cons. AT&T, 1990-92; chmn. bd. Academica, 1992, Employee Managed Care Corp., 1994—. Co-editor: Columbia U. Coll. Physicians and Surgeons Complete Home Medical Guide, 1986, editor emeritus 2d and 3d edits., 1989; contbr. articles to profl. jours., chpts. to books. Served to maj. AUS, 1941-46. Recipient Bi-Centennial medal Columbia Coll. Phys. and Surg., 1967. Fellow Am. Psychiat. Assn. (life); mem. Am. Assn. Chmn. Depts. Psychiatry (pres. 1979-80). Home: PO Box 579h Ct Orono ME 04473

WEISS, ROBERT M., urologist, educator; b. N.Y.C., Jan. 13, 1936; s. David and Laura W.; m. Ilana Shemer, May 20, 1973; children—Erik Daniel, Dana Alexandra. B.S. magna cum laude, Franklin and Marshall Coll., Lancaster, Pa., 1957; M.D., SUNY, Bklyn., 1960; M.A. (hon.), Yale

U., 1976. Diplomate: Am. Bd. Urology, Nat. Bd. Med. Examiners. Intern Cornell Med. Div., Bellevue Hosp., N.Y.C., 1960-61; resident in gen. surgery Beth Israel Hosp., N.Y.C., 1961-62; resident in urology Squier Urol. Clinic, Presbyn. Hosp., N.Y.C., 1963-64, 65-67; vs. fellow Columbia U. Coll. Physicians and Surgeons, N.Y.C., 1964-65, adj. assoc. prof. pharmacology, 1975-77, adj. prof. pharmacology, 1977—; mem. faculty Yale U. M,ed. Sch., New Haven, 1967—, prof. urology, 1976-88, prof., chief sect. of urology, 1988—; attending urology Yale-New Haven Hosp., New Haven, 1967-88, head sect. of urology, 1988—; cons. West Haven VA Hosp., Waterbury (Conn.) Hosp. Contbr. articles to med. publs. Served with USAR, 1962-63. Fellow ACS, Am. Acad. Pediatrics; mem. Am. Assn. Genito-Urinary Surgeons, Am. Physiol. Soc., Soc. Gen. Physiologists, Assn. Univ. Urologists, Soc. Pediatric Urology, Am. Urol. Assn., Am. Soc. Clin. Pharmacology and Therapeutics, Internat. Urodynamics Soc., AAAS, Internat. Soc. Dynamics of Upper Urinary Tract, Clin. Soc. Genito-Urinary Surgeons, Phi Beta Kappa, Sigma Xi. *

WEISS, ROBERT MICHAEL, dentist; b. Bklyn., June 5, 1940; s. Henry and Rena (Bluth) W.; (Trustees scholar) L.I. U., 1958-61; DDS, N.Y.U., 1965; postdoctoral cert. LD Pankey Inst. for Advanced Dental Edn., 1979; m. Irene Marilyn Sternick, June 30, 1962; children: Lori Ann, Julie Lynn, Karen Michelle. Pvt. practice dentistry, Avon, Conn., 1967—, pres. Avon Dental Group, P.C., 1972—; nat. cons. Conn. Gen. Ins. Co. for ins. coverage for Gen. Electric Co., 1980—; cons. CNA Ins. Co., 1988—; bd. dirs. Sentinel Bank. Chmn. Children's Dental Health Week, Hartford County, 1971; chmn. Jewish Adult Edn., West Hartford, Conn., 1986-87; trustee Temple Beth Israel, 1983—. Served to capt. USAF, 1965-67. Fellow Acad. Gen. Dentistry, Am. Acad. Gen. Dentistry, Pierre Fauchand Acad. (hon.); mem. ADA, Am. Soc. Preventive Dentistry (pres. Conn. chpt.), Hartford Dental Soc. (mem. exec. com. 1993—, chmn. 100th Anniversary 1996), Conn. State Dental Assn. (ho. of dels. 1992—), Chronic Fatigue Immune Dysfunction Syndrome (Conn. bd. dirs. 1992—), So. New Eng. Assn. Practice Adminstrn., Starnard Beach Assn. (pres. 1984-86). Avon Jr. C. of C. (pres. 1971-72), Pierre Fauchard Acad. (hon. dental soc. fellow), Alpha Omega, Sigma Alpha Mu. Mason. Home: 74 Ferncliff Dr West Hartford CT 06117-1014 Office: 20 W Avon Rd Avon CT 06001

WEISS, ROBERT MICHAEL, dermatologist; b. N.Y.C.; s. Leonard Seymour and Edith Rose (Levine) W.; 1 child, Michael Louis. Ba, U. Pa., 1970; MD, SUNY, Buffalo, 1974. Diplomate Am. Bd. Dermatology. Intern in internal medicine SUNY, Buffalo, 1974-75, resident in internal medicine, 1975-76, resident in dermatology, 1976-79; pvt. practice in dermatology Las Vegas, Nev., 1979—. Fellow Am. Acad. Derrmatology; mem. AMA. Office: Robert M Weiss MD 2300 S Rancho Ste 106 Las Vegas NV 89102

WEISS, SAMUEL ABRAHAM, psychologist, psychoanalyst; b. N.Y.C.; s. Kasiel and Sophie Sima (Schachter) W.; m. Alice Langer, May 20, 1958; children: Benjamin Z., Naomi E., Susan J. BA, Yeshiva U., 1944; MA, NYU, 1948, PhD, 1957. Diplomate in clin. psychology, Am. Bd. Profl. Psychology. Intern Bellevue Psychiat. Hosp., N.Y.C., 1955-56; assoc. rsch. scientist NYU Med. Ctr., N.Y.C., 1956-59, rsch. scientist, 1959-68, assoc. dir. amputee psychology rsch., 1958-66; assoc. prof. psychology Yeshiva U., N.Y.C., 1961-71; psychol. cons. Stern Coll. for Women, Yeshiva U., N.Y.C., 1960-71; psychologist, psychotherapist, psychoanalyst in pvt. practice N.Y.C.; cons. N.Y. State Div. Vocat. Rehab., 1958-73. Contbr. articles to profl. jours. Fellow AAAS (Rosette award 1991), APA (editl. cons. rehab. psychology 1972-80), Am. Psychol. Soc. Jewish. Home: 80-40 Lefferts Blvd Kew Gardens NY 11415-1723 Office: 7 Park Ave Ste 66 New York NY 10016-4330

WEISS, WILLIAM, retired pulmonary medicine and epidemiology educator; b. Phila., July 30, 1919; s. William and Anna (Grossman) W.; m. Esther E. Sabul, June 22, 1941; children: Winifred A., Seth S., Deborah E. BA, U. Pa., 1940, MD, 1944. Clin. dir. pulmonary disease svc. Phila. Gen. Hosp., 1950-74; chest cons. Norristown (Pa.) State Hosp., 1951-60; dir. Pulmonary Neoplasm Rsch. Project, Phila., 1957-67; faculty U. Pa. Grad. Sch. Medicine, Phila., 1952-66, Med. Coll. Pa., Phila., 1952-86; from assoc. prof. to prof. medicine Hahnemann U. Med. Coll., Phila., 1966-84, prof. emeritus, 1984—; cons. to various indsl. cos., Pa., N.J., 1962—. Editor Phila. Medicine, 1976—; mem. editl. bd. Arch. Environ. Health, 1968-86; contbr. more than 110 editls. to profl. jours., 18 chpts. to books. Bd. dirs. Am. Cancer Soc., Phila., 1980-86; cons. on asbestos Bd. Edn., Phila., 1983—; mem. EPA Sci. Review Panel for Health Rsch., Washington, 1980-81, Toxics/Health Effects adv. com. Pa. Dept. Health, 1985-87. Capt. USAF, 1953-55. Recipient Ann. Sci. award Phila. divsn. Am. Cancer Soc., 1979, Cristol award Phila. County Med. Soc., 1989; picture on cover Cancer Rsch., Mar. 1, 1990 for lung cancer rsch. Fellow ACP, Coll. Physicians Phila., Am. Coll. Occupational and Environ. Medicine (merit in authorship award 1974, 85); mem. AMA, Laennec Soc. Phila. (pres. 1970), Phila. Occupational Med. Assn. (pres. 1980-81), Am. Thoracic Soc., Pa. Med. Soc., Phila. County Med. Soc. (Strittmatter award 1991). Home: 3912 Netherfield Rd Philadelphia PA 19129-1014

WEISSBERG, JOSEF HERBERT, psychiatrist; b. N.Y.C., Oct. 25, 1928; s. Bernard and Anna (Spitzer) W.; m. Ann Klein, Dec. 8, 1934; children: Laura, Claire, Edward. Student, Union Coll., 1945-48; MD, Albany Med. Coll., 1952; cert. psychoanalysis, Columbia U., 1962. Diplomate Am. Bd. Psychiatry and Neurology. Intern Roosevelt Hosp., N.Y.C., 1952-53, resident in internal medicine, 1952-54; resident in psychiatry N.Y. State Psychiatric Inst., Columbia Presbyn. Med. Ctr., N.Y.C., 1956-59; assoc. prof. Columbia U., N.Y.C., 1959—; pvt. practic psychiatry N.Y.C., 1959—; dir. tng. dept psychiatry Cath. Med. Ctr. Blkyn. and Queens, Jamaica, N.Y., 1975-78; sr. assoc. attending psychiatrist St. Lukes-Roosevelt Hosp. Ctr., N.Y.C., 1978—; assoc. attending psychiatrist Presbyn. Hosp., N.Y.C., 1959—; dir. Assn. for Short-Term Psychotherapy, N.Y.C., 1980—; cons. psychiatry Met. Life Ins. Co., N.Y.C., 1983-95. Contbr. articles to profl. jours. Capt. USAF, 1954-56. Fellow Am. Psychiat. Assn., Am. Acad. Psychoanalysis (pres. 1991-92, exec. bd. 1987-93, cert. in psychoanalysis). Democrat. Jewish. Home and Office: 103 E 86th St New York NY 10028-1058

WEISSKOPF, BERNARD, pediatrician, child behavior, development and genetics specialist, educator; b. Berlin, Dec. 11, 1929; came to U.S., 1939, naturalized, 1944; s. Benjamin and Bertha (Loew) W.; m. Penelope Allderdice, Dec. 26, 1965; children: Matthew David, Stephen Daniel. BA, Syracuse U., 1951; MD, U. Leiden, Netherlands, 1958. Diplomate Am. Bd. Med. Mgmt. Intern Meadowbrook Hosp., East Meadow, N.Y., 1958-59; resident Meadowbrook Hosp., 1959-60, Johns Hopkins Hosp., Balt., 1962-64; fellow child psychiatry Johns Hopkins U. Sch. Medicine, Balt., 1962-64; asst. prof. pediatrics U. Ill. Coll. Medicine, Chgo., 1964-66; faculty U. Louisville, 1966—, prof. pediatrics, 1970—; also assoc. in psychiatry, pathology and Ob-gyn, dir. Child Evaluation Ctr., Louisville, 1966—; chmn. Gov.'s Adv. Com. Early Childhood, Gov.'s Council on Early Childhood, Ky., 1986-88. Contbr. articles to profl. jours. Trustee Jewish Hosp., Louisville, 1974-77. Served to capt. USAF, 1960-62. Fellow Am. Acad. Pediatrics, Am. Assn. Mental Deficiency; mem. Am. Soc. Human Genetics, So. Soc. Pediatric Rsch., Am. Soc. Law and Medicine, Am. Coll. Physician Execs. Home: 6409 Deep Creek Dr Prospect KY 40059-9422 Office: Child Evaluation Ctr 571 S Floyd St Louisville KY 40202-3830

WEISSMAN, BARBARA MOST, pediatrician; b. Palo Alto, Calif., June 15, 1954; d. Nathan Most and May (Lazarus) Burberick; m. Joseph Daniel Weissman, Aug. 3, 1975; children: Daniel Jacob, David Michael. AB, Cornell U., 1975; MD, Case Western Reserve U., 1980. Diplomate Am. Bd. Psychiatry and Neurology, Am. Bd. Pediatrics. Instr. pediatrics Case Western Reserve U., Cleve., 1985-86, asst. prof. pediatrics, 1986-89; asst. prof. pediatrics Emory U., Atlanta, 1989-94, assoc. prof. pediatrics, 1994—; med. dir. pediatrics Shepherd Spine Ctr., Atlanta, 1989-91; med. dir. rehab. Egleston Children's Hosp. at Emory U., Atlanta, 1985—. Bd. dirs. United Cerebral Palsy, Cleve., 1987-89, Spina Bifida Assn., Atlanta, 1990-94, REACH, Atlanta, 1994—. Fellow Am. Acad. Pediatrics, Am. Soc. Neurorehabilitation, Am. Acad. Cerebral Palsy Devel. Medicine; mem. Am. Acad. Neurology, Child Neurology Soc. Jewish. Office: Emory U Dept of Pediatrics 2040 Ridgewood Dr Atlanta GA 30322

WEISSMAN, EVELYN LEVENSON, surgeon; b. Bklyn., July 4, 1947; d. Alexander and Ethel (Milevsky) Levenson; m. Ira M. Weissman, June 29, 1968; children: Alexander, Rebecca, Gregory, Elizabeth. BS, Bklyn. Coll., 1968; MD, Med. Coll. Pa., 1975. Diplomate Am. Bd. Surgery. Intern, resident Gen. Surgery of Med. Coll. Pa., Phila., 1975-80; fellow in surg. oncology Temple U. Hosp., Phila., 1980-82; surgeon Jefferson County Hosp., Louisville, Ga., 1982-86, Gilman Hosp., St. Marys, Ga., 1986-88, Alice Hyde Hosp., Malone, N.Y., 1988—. Office: 16 4th St Malone NY 12953

WEISSMAN, GAIL KUHN, nursing administrator; b. Sioux City, Iowa. BSN, Vanderbilt U., Nashville, 1960; MA in Nursing, Columbia U., 1963, EdD, 1988; postgrad., Tchr.'s Coll., Columbia U., 1979. Dir. nursing Montefiore Med. Ctr., N.Y.C.; asst. prof. dept. health care mgmt. The Mt. Sinai Hosp. Med. Sch., N.Y.C.; dean Sch. Continuing Edn. The Mt. Sinai Hosp., v.p. nursing; sr. and corp. v.p. Mass. Gen. Hosp., Boston, 1994—; acting chairperson Ctr. for Nursing Rsch. and Edn. Mt. Sinai Sch. Medicine, N.Y.C. Contbr. articles to profl. jours. Named YWCA Woman Achiever, City of N.Y., 1989, Disting. Svc. Alumni award, Vanderbilt U., 1989, So. N.Y. League Nursing Dorothy McMullen-Pisani award, 1989, Jacobi Medallion for Disting. Achievement and Extraordinary Svc. to Hosp., Mt. Sinai Med. Ctr. 1989; recipient Jane Delano Disting. Svc. award N.Y. County RN Assn., 1991. Fellow APHA, NLN, Am. Acad. Nursing, Am. Mgmt. Assn., Am. Hosp. Assn., Am. Orgn. Nurse Execs., Deans and Dirs. of Nursing in Greater N.Y., N.Y. State Nurses Assn., Mass. Orgn. Nursing Execs., Sigma Theta Tau. Home: 276 Marlborough St Boston MA 02116

WEISSMAN, IRVING L., medical scientist; b. Great Falls, Mont., Oct. 21, 1939; married, 1961; 4 children. BS, Mont. State Coll., 1960, DSc (hon.), 1992; MD, Stanford U., 1965. NIH fellow dept. radiology Stanford U., 1965-67, rsch. assoc., 1967-68, from asst. prof. to assoc. prof. dept. pathology, 1969-81, prof. pathology Sch. Medicine, 1981—, prof. devel. biology, 1989—; James McGinnis Meml. lectr. Duke U., 1982; George Feigen Meml. lectr. Stanford U., 1987; Albert Coons Meml. lectr. Harvard U., 1987; Jame Stahlman lectr. Vanderbilt U., 1987; R. E. Smith lectr. U. Tex. Sys. Cancer Ctr., 1988; Chauncey D. Leake lectr. U. Calif., 1989; Harvey lectr. Rockefeller U., 1989; Rose Litman lectr., 1990; sr. Dernham fellow, Calif. divsn. Am. Cancer Soc., 1969-73; mem. immunobiology study sect. NIH, 1976-80; mem. sci. rev. bd. Howard Hughes Med. Inst., 1986—; mem. sci. adv. com. Irvington House Inst., 1987—; co-founder Systemix, Inc., 1988, bd. dirs., 1988—; Karel & Avice Beekhuis prof. cancer biology, 1987; 5th Ann. vis. prof. cancer biology U. Tex. Health Sci. Ctr., 1987; disting. lectr. Western Soc. Clin. Investment, 1990; chmn. U.S.-Japan Immunology Bd., 1992-94; chmn. sci. adv. com. of McLaughlin Rsch. Inst., 1992—, trustee, 1992—; bd. govs. Project Inform, 1995—. Recipient Pasarow award, 1989, Faculty Rsch. award Nat. Am. Cancer Soc., 1974-78, Mont. Conservationist of Yr. Mont. Land Reliance, 1994; named One of Top 100 Alumni Mont. State U., 1993; Josiah Macy Found. scholar, 1974-75. Fellow AAAS; mem. NAS (steering com. NIOM AIDS panel 1985-86), Am. Acad. Arts and Scis., Am. Assn. Immunologists (pres. 1994-95), Am. Assn. Univ. Pathologists, Am. Assn. Pathologists, Am. Soc. Microbiology, Am. Assn. Cancer Rsch., Inst. Immunology. Office: Stanford U Dept Pathology B257 Beckman Ctr Sch Medicine Stanford CA 94305

WEISSMAN, MICHAEL HERBERT, pediatrician, educator; b. Bklyn., Jan. 15, 1942; s. George and Sipora (Silvera) W.; m. Marianne Wastcoat, July 30, 1967; children—Robert, Alexander, Samuel, Sarah, Rachel. B.M.E., Cooper Union, 1963; M.S., Northwestern U., 1965, Ph.D., 1965; M.D., Washington U., St. Louis, 1976. Diplomate Am. Bd. Pediatrics. Intern Bronx Mcpl. Hosp. Ctr., N.Y., 1976-77, resident, 1977-79, chief resident, 1979-80; asst. prof. engring. Carnegie-Mellon U., Pitts., 1967-71, assoc. prof., 1972-73; practice medicine specializing in pediatrics, Mount Kisco, N.Y., 1980—; mem. staff No. Westchester Hosp. Ctr., Mount Kisco, also chief pediats., 1993—, Hosp. of Albert Einstein Coll. Medicine; clin. asst. prof. Albert Einstein Coll. Medicine, 1980—; ptnr. Mt. Kisco Med. Group, P.C., 1981-89, shareholder, 1989—; adj. clin. asst. prof. N.Y. Med. Coll., 1991—. Contbr. articles on bioengring. to profl. jours. Mem. AMA, Am. Acad. Pediats. Office: Mt Kisco Med Group 34 S Bedford Rd Mount Kisco NY 10549-3408

WEISSMAN, RONALD HARLAN, cardiologist; b. White Plains, N.Y., May 24, 1952; s. Morton R. Weissman and Estelle (Hein) Fassler; m. Debra Weissman, June 3, 1979; children: Matthew Adam, Seth Jordan. BA, Trinity Coll., Hartford, Conn., 1974; MD, N.Y. Med. Coll., 1977. Diplomate Am. Bd. Internal Medicine & Cardiovasc. Disease. Intern, resident Long Island Jewish Med. Ctr., New Hyde Park, N.Y., 1977-80; pvt. practice, White Plains; attending physician White Plains Hosp., 1982—, Westchester County Med. Ctr., Valhalla, N.Y., 1982—; attending physician St. Agnes Hosp., White Plains, 1982—, chief divsn. cardiology, 1993—; team physician N.Y. Rangers Hockey Club, N.Y.C., 1983—; bd. dirs. MD Devel. Corp., White Plains, Kings Electronics Co. Inc., Tuckahoe, N.Y. Fellow Am. Coll. Cardiology; mem. ACP. Office: 311 North St White Plains NY 10605

WEISSMAN, RONEE FREEMAN, speech pathologist, tour agency owner; b. N.Y.C., Apr. 16, 1951; d. Jonas Herbert and Marion (Rosen) Freeman; BA magna cum laude, Queens Coll., 1973, MA in Speech Pathology, 1978; m. Eugene Weissman, Jan. 28, 1973; children: Ilana Nicole, Adam Scott. Tchr. high sch. speech, theatre and English, N.Y.C., 1973-75; speech pathologist Byram Hills (N.Y.) Sch. Dist., part-time, 1979-80, E. Ramapo Sch. Dist., Rockland, N.Y., 1981-82; speech pathologist Vis. Therapy Assocs., 1983-84, Children's Village, Dobbs Ferry, N.Y., 1991; owner, v.p., dir. Weissman Teen Tours, Inc., Ardsley, N.Y., 1974—. Youth dir., Sunday sch. tchr. Temple Israel, New Rochelle. Speech and hearing handicapped cert., speech arts cert., N.Y.; lic. speech pathologist, N.Y. Mem. Am. Speech, Lang. and Hearing Assn. (cert. clin. competency), N.Y. State Speech, Lang. and Hearing Assn., Westchester Speech Lang. and Hearing Assn., Am. Camping Assn. (accredited), Phi Beta Kappa, Kappa Delta Pi. Home and Office: 517 Almena Ave Ardsley NY 10502-2127

WEISSMANN, GERALD, medical educator, researcher, writer, editor; b. Vienna, Austria, Aug. 7, 1930; came to U.S., 1938; s. Adolf and Greta (Lustbader) W.; m. Ann Raphael, Apr. 1, 1953; children: Lisa, Andrew. BA with honors, Columbia U., N.Y.C., 1950; MD, NYU, 1954. Diplomate Am. Bd. Internal Medicine. Intern Mt. Sinai Hosp., N.Y.C., 1954-55, asst. resident medicine, 1957-58; chief resident medicine Bellevue Hosp., N.Y.C., 1959-60; fellow depts. biochemistry and medicine Arthritis and Rheumatism Fedn., NYU, 1958-59; rsch. asst. dept. medicine NYU Sch. Medicine, 1959-60, instr. medicine, 1959-62, asst. prof., 1962-65, assoc. prof., 1966-70, prof., 1970—, dir. div. cell biology, 1969-73, dir. div. rheumatology of dept. medicine, 1973—; USPHS spl. rsch. fellow dept. biophysics Strangeways Lab., Cambridge, Eng., 1960-61; sr. investigator Arthritis and Rheumatism Found., N.Y.C., 1961-65; career rsch. scientist Health Rsch. Coun. N.Y.C., 1966-71; instr. physiology Marine Biol. Lab., Woods Hole, Mass., 1973-77, investigator, 1970—, trustee, 1993—; vis. investigator ARC Inst. Animal Physiology, Babraham, Eng., 1964-69, Centre de Physiologie et d'Immunologie Cellulaires, Hosp. St. Antoine, Paris, 1973-74, William Harvey Rsch. Inst., London, 1987; mem. postdoctoral fellowships rev. com. Pfizer Internat., N.Y.C., 1983—; mem. scholarship selection com. Pew Scholars in Biomed. Scis., New Haven, 1984—; lectr. Johns Hopkins U., 1976, 89, Med. Coll. Ga., Augusta, 1980, Med. Coll. Pa., 1988, William Harvey Rsch. Inst., London, 1987, others; nat. adv. bd. Pew Scholars Biomed. Sci., 1984-95. Author: The Woods Hole Cantata, 1995, They All Laughed at Christopher Columbus, 1987, The Doctor With Two Heads, 1990, The Doctor Dilemma, 1992, Democracy and DNA, 1996; editor-in-chief Inflammation, 1975—, Advances in Inflammation Rsch., 1979—, MD Mag., 1989-94; mem. editl. bd. Clin. Immunology and Immunopathology, 1972-88, Advances in Prostaglandin, Thromboxane and Leukotriene Rsch., 1975—, Am. Jour. Medicine, 1976-88, Tissue Reactions, 1979, Immunopharmacology, 1982; contbr. over 300 articles to profl. jours. Capt. M.C., U.S. Army, 1955-57. Recipient Allesandro Robecchi prize Internat. League Against Rheumatism, 1972, Marine Biol. Lab. award, 1974, 1979, U. Bologna medal, Italy, 1978, Lila Gruber Cancer Rsch. award Am. Acad. Dermatology, 1979, Solomon A. Berson Med. Alumni Achievement award NYU, 1980, Merit award NIH, 1987, Centennial award Marine Biol. Lab., 1988, C.M. Plotz award N.Y. Arthritis Found., 1993, others; Guggenheim Found. fellow, N.Y.C., 1973-74. Fellow AAAS; mem. Am. Coll. Rheumatology (pres. 1982-83, Disting. Investigator award 1992), Am. Fedn. Clin. Rsch., Soc. Exptl. Biology and Medicine, Am. Soc. Pharmacology and Exptl. Therapeutics, Am. Soc. Exptl. Pathology, Assn. Am. Immunologists, Am. Soc. Cell Biology, Am. Soc. Clin. Investigation, Am. Soc. Biol. Chemistry and Molecular Biology, Assn. Am. Physicians, Harvey Soc. of N.Y. (pres. 1981-82), Interurban Clin. Club, PEN Am. Ctr., Phi Beta Kappa, Alpha Omega Alpha. Office: NYU Med Ctr Dept Medicine 550 1st Ave New York NY 10016-6481

WEITZEN, EDWIN HYLAN, retired radiologist; b. Balt., Sept. 12, 1917; s. Jacob and Rose (Kramer) W. BA, George Washington U., 1941, MD, 1943. Diplomate Am. Bd. Radiology. Assoc. radiologist Sibley Meml. Hosp., Washington, 1951-58; pvt. practice Silver Spring, Md., 1958-85, ret., 1985. Mem. AMA, Am. Coll. Radiology, N.Y. Acad. Sci., Royal Soc. Medicine. Home: 1005 Dale Dr Silver Spring MD 20910-4102

WEKSLER, MARC EDWARD, physician, educator; b. N.Y.C., Apr. 16, 1937; s. Jacob J. and Lillian W.; m. Babette Barbash; children: David J., Jennifer Lee. B.A., Swarthmore Coll., 1958; M.D., Columbia U., 1962. Intern Bronx (N.Y.) Mcpl. Hosp., 1962-63, resident in medicine, 1963-64; asst. prof. medicine Cornell U. Med. Coll., N.Y.C., 1970-75; asso. prof. Cornell U. Med. Coll., 1975-78, Wright prof. medicine, 1978—, dir. div. geriatrics and gerontology, 1978—; attending physician N.Y. Hosp., Meml. Hosp., N.Y.C.; vis. prof. Pasteur Inst., Paris; cons. NIH, VA, N.Y.C., WHO, Pontifical Acad. Scis., Nat. Acad. Scis.; James Day lectr. Cornell U., 1980; pres. bd. trustees Am. Fedn. Aging Rsch., 1992-94. Editorial bd.: Jour. Clin. Immunology, Annals of Internal Medicine, Proc. Soc. Exptl. Biology and Medicine; asso. editor: Exptl. Aging Research. Founder, pres. Graphic Arts Coun. N.Y.; pres. Am. Fedn. Aging Rsch. Fellow Morgan Libr., Frick Collection. Fellow ACP; mem. Am. Soc. Clin. Investigation, N.Y. Acad. Medicine (chmn. geriatric sect.), Gerontol. Soc. (humanities and arts com.), Assn. Am. Physicians, Interurban Clin. Club, Alpha Omega Alpha. Office: Cornell U Med Coll 1300 York Ave New York NY 10021-4805

WEKSTEIN, DAVID ROBERT, physiology educator, researcher; b. Boston, Feb. 26, 1937; s. Abraham Jacob and Dorothy (Goldschmidt) W.; m. Merle Barbara Weiner, Aug. 31, 1958; children: Lauren Jane, Karen Gail, Debra Susan, Jeffrey Bruce. AB, Boston U., 1957, MA, 1958; PhD, U. Rochester, 1962. Instr. to assoc. prof. physiology U. Ky., Lexington, 1962-81, prof. physiology, 1981—; assoc. dir. Sanders-Brown Ctr. on Aging, Lexington, 1973—, Alzheimer's Disease Rsch. Ctr., Lexington, 1984—. Mem. AAAS, Am. Physiol. Soc., Am. Geriatrics Soc., Gerontol. Soc. Am., Soc. for Exptl. Biology and Medicine, Sigma Xi (pres. local chpt. 1985). Office: U Ky Sanders Brown Ctr on Aging Lexington KY 40536

WELCH, ANTOINETTE, medical technologist; b. Inglewood, Calif., Feb. 15, 1963; d. Gary John and Susan Eileen (Stikeleather) B.; m. Joseph T. Welch, July 1, 1983; children: Tamara Marie, Joseph Thomas IV. Assoc. Med. Lab. Technician, Garland County C.C., Hot Springs, Ark. Med. lab. technician ASCP, 1983—; med. technologist AMT, 1992—.

WELCH, KAREN LUCILLE BRAY, quality management nurse; b. Johnson City, Tenn., Jan. 25, 1955; d. Dale and Frances Evangeline (Barnes) Bray; m. John Arch Johnson, Sept. 3, 1977 (div. Aug. 1984); children: John Mark, Jennifer Marie; m. William Terry Welch, III, Mar. 10, 1995. BS in Nursing, East Tenn. State U., 1977; MS in Nursing, U. Va., 1990. RN, Tenn.; cert. profl. in healthcare quality, Healthcare Quality Cert. Bd.; Cert. in nursing adminstrn., ANA. Major med. unit nurse St. Joseph Hosp., Parkersburg, W.Va., 1977-78; ICU nurse Sts. Mary & Elizabeth Hosp., Louisville, Ky., 1978-78; neonatal ICU nurse Vanderbilt U. Hosp., Nashville, 1979; pub. health nurse Branch-Hillsdale-St. Joseph, Hillsdale, Mich., 1979-81; charge nurse ICU/CCU Hillsdale Hosp., 1981-84; staff nurse VA Med. Ctr., Johnson City, Tenn., 1984-86; head nurse VA Med. Ctr., Johnson City, 1986-90, quality mgmt. RN, 1990—; adj. faculty East Tenn. State U., Johnson City, 1991-93. Mem. Nat. Assn. Healthcare Quality, Tenn. Nurses Assn. (dist. 5, mem. chair 1990-93, 2d v.p. 1994-96, bd. dirs. 1996—, cert. appreciation 1995), Sigma Theta Tau, Phi Kappa Phi. Office: VA Med Ctr Mountain Home TN 37684

WELCH, MICHAEL JOHN, chemistry educator, researcher; b. Stoke-on-Trent, Staffordshire, Eng., June 28, 1939; came to U.S., 1965; s. Arthur John W. and Mary (Welch); m. Teresa Jean Conocchiolli, Apr. 22, 1967 (div. 1979); children: Colin, Lesley. B.A., Cambridge U., Eng., 1961; M.A., Cambridge U., 1964; Ph.D., London U., 1965. Asst. prof. radiation chemistry in radiology Washington U. Sch. Medicine, St. Louis, 1967-70, assoc. prof., 1970-74; assoc. prof. dept. chemistry Washington U. Sch., St. Louis, 1971-75, prof. dept. chemistry, 1978—; prof. radiology Washington U. Sch. Medicine, St. Louis, 1991—, prof. molecular biology and pharmacology, 1993—; dir. radiol. scis. dept. Washignton U., 1990—; mem. diagnostic radiology study sect. NIH, 1986-89, chmn., 1989-91; mem. sci. adv. com. Whitaker Found., 1995—. Author: Introduction to the Tracer Methods, 1972; editor: Radiopharmaceuticals and Other Compoounds Labeled with Shortlived Radionuclides, 1977; assoc. editor Jour. Nuclear Medicine, 1989—; contbr. chpts. to books, more than 400 articles to profl. jours. Recipient Georg Charles de Hevesy Nuclear Medicine Pioneer award, 1992; scholar St. Catharine Coll. Cambridge U., 1958-61. Mem. Soc. Nuclear Medicine (trustee, pres. 1984, Paul C. Aebersold award 1980), Radiopharm. Sci. Coun. (pres. 1980-81), Am. Chem. Soc. (St Louis award 1988, award for nuclear chemistry 1990, Mid-West award 1991), Chem. Soc. London, Radiation Rsch. Soc., Sigma Xi. Home: 1 Spoede Ln Saint Louis MO 63141-7708 Office: Washington U Sch Medicine Edward Mallinckrodt Inst Radiology 510 S Kingshighway Blvd Saint Louis MO 63110-1016

WELCH, NORBERT MICHAEL, JR., urologist; b. Vincennes, Ind., Nov. 5, 1950; s. Norbert Michael and Louise Anna (Berndt) W.; m. Barbara Ann Kroth, July 22, 1978; children: Bryan, Michael, Robert. BS, Ind. U., 1972; MD, Ind. U., Indpls., 1976. Diplomate Am. Bd. Urology. Resident U. Tex. Health Scis. Ctr., Dallas, 1976-82; physician Arnett Clinic, Lafayette, Ind., 1982—. Fellow ACS; mem. Ind. State Med. Assn., Tippecanoe County Med. Soc., Elks. Roman Catholic. Home: 5404 E 200 N Lafayette IN 47905 Office: Arnett Clinic 2600 Greenbush St Lafayette IN 47904

WELCH, OLIVER WENDELL, retired pharmaceutical executive; b. Jacksonville, Tex., Jan. 9, 1930; s. Jackson Andrew and Annie Laura (Trapp) W.; m. Wanda Virginia Urrey, Nov. 14, 1948. BA, Tex. Tech U., 1952; MA, Columbia U., 1958. Pharm. rep., supr. mktg. rsch., manpower devel. Warner Lambert Co., Morris Plains, N.J., 1962-72; mgr. corp. devel. Boehringer Mannheim Corp., N.Y.C., 1972-75; v.p. Biomed. Data Co., N.Y.C., 1975-77; assoc. dir., dep. dir. regulatory affairs Sterling Winthrop Inc., N.Y.C., 1977-94; ret., 1994; cons. Sanofi Winthrop, Inc., N.Y.C., 1995. Mem. Regulatory Affairs Profls. Soc., Drug Info. Assn., Order St. John of Jerusalem. Republican. Episcopalian.

WELCH, WILLIAM BEN, emergency physician; b. Maryville, Mo., June 29, 1954; s. William Verne and Mary Lou (Steins) W.; m. Peggy Patricia Allen, Mar. 24, 1985; children: Jesse Lee, John Michael. BA in Biosci. cum laude, U. Mo., 1976, MD, 1980. Bd. cert. in family practice and emergency medicine. Resident in family practice U. Iowa Hosps. and Clinics, Iowa City, 1980-83; emergency staff physician Fransiscan Sisters Health Care, Danville, Ill., 1983-89; emergency staff physician Level II Trauma Ctr. St. Elizabeth Hosp., Danville, 1983-89; emergency staff physician Level I Trauma Ctr. Carle Found. Hosp., Urbana, Ill., 1989—; clin. asst. prof. U. Ill. Sch. Medicine, Champaign-Urbana, 1989—. Dir. ACLS Ill. chpt. Am. Heart Assn., 1983—, affiliate faculty ACLS Activities, East Cen. Ill., 1986—. Recipient Physician Recognition award AMA, 1984, 87, 90, 93, 96. Fellow Am. Coll. Emergency Physicians. Office: Carlo Clinic Assn 602 W University Urbana IL 61801

WELD, FRANCIS MINOT, cardiologist; b. N.Y.C., Nov. 22, 1939; s. David and Mary Blake (Nichols) W.; m. Helene Singleton Mueller, Oct. 26, 1971; children: Francis M. Jr., Alexandra Singleton, Margaret DuBois. BA, Harvard U., 1961; MD, Columbia U., 1965. Internship internal medicine N.Y. Hosp.-Cornell, N.Y.C., 1965-66, resident internal medicine, 1966-67; sr. asst. surgeon U.S. Pub. Health Svc., Washington, 1967-69; sr. resident medicine N.Y. Hosp.-Cornell, N.Y.C., 1969-70, chiefl resident medicine, 1970-71; fellow in pharmacology Columbia U., N.Y.C., 1971-73, fellow in cardiology, 1973-75, asst. prof. medicine, 1975-82, assoc. clin. prof. medicine,

1982—. Contbr. articles to profl. jours. Grantee Pharm. Mfr. Assn., 1976, N.I.H., Bethesda, Md., 1971-82. Fellow Am. Coll. Physicians, Coun. Clin. Cardiology, Am. Coll. Cardiology, AMA, Am. Soc. Internal Medicine, Century Assn. N.Y. Republican. Presbyterian. Home: 1 E End Ave New York NY 10021-1102 Office: Columbia-Presbyterian/ Eastide 16 E 60th St New York NY 10022-1002

WELDEN, MARY CLARE, nurse; b. Wichita, Kans., Mar. 4, 1943; d. Lee Henry and Betty Clare (Lansdowne) Pates; m. Francis Bernard Hacker, Apr. 18, 1964 (div. Apr. 1978); children: Stephen (dec.), Michael, William. Diploma in nursing, St. Joseph Sch. Nursing, 1964; BS in Healthcare Adminstrn., Okla. City U., 1996. Staff nurse, supr. Richardson (Tex.) Gen. Hosp., 1968-70; supr., obstetrics supr. Collin Meml. Hosp., McKinney, Tex., 1970-77; staff nurse, charge nurse Presbyn. Hosp., Dallas, 1977-81; staff nurse Integris Bapt. Med. Ctr., Oklahoma City, 1981-88, quality assurance nurse, 1988—. Mem. Compassionate Friends. Democrat. Roman Catholic. Home: 1752 Lionsgate Cir Bethany OK 73008-6167 Office: Bapt Med Ctr 3300 NW Expressway St Oklahoma City OK 73112-4999

WELDON, JOHN FRANCIS, anesthesiologist; b. Charleroi, Pa., Aug. 19, 1931; s. Owen Patrick and Ann (O'Toole) W.; m. Dorothy Flaherty, Oct. 3, 1959; children: John P., Maureen Weldon Kamons, Patrick, Sean. BS, U. Pitts., 1953, MD, 1957. Intern St. Joseph Hosp., Pitts., 1957-58; anesthesiology resident Mercy Hosp., Pitts., 1966-68; dir. dept. anesthesiology Mon Valley Hosp., Inc., Monongahela, Pa., 1968-94; pres. med. staff Monongahela Hosp.; cons. S.W. Pa. Heart Assn. Mem. Washington County Med. Soc., Am. Soc. Sr. Physicians, AMA, Pa. Med. Soc., Internat. Assn. Rsch. Svc. Home: 125 Tower St Monongahela PA 15063

WELDON, VIRGINIA V., corporate executive, physician; b. Toronto, Sept. 8, 1935; came to U.S., 1937; d. John Edward and Carolyn Edith (Swift) Verral; children: Ann Stuart, Susan Shaeffer. A.B. cum laude, Smith Coll., 1957; M.D., SUNY-Buffalo, 1962; L.H.D. (hon.), Rush U., 1985. Diplomate Am. Bd. Pediatrics in pediatric endocrinology and metabolism. Intern Johns Hopkins Hosp., Balt., 1962-63, resident in pediatrics, 1963-64; fellow pediatric endocrinology Johns Hopkins U., Balt., 1964-67, instr. pediatrics, 1967-68; instr. pediatrics Washington U., St. Louis, 1968-69, asst. prof., 1969-73, assoc. prof. pediatrics, 1973-79, prof. pediatrics, 1979-89, v.p. Med. Ctr., 1980-89, dep. vice chancellor med. affairs, 1983-89; v.p. sci. affairs Monsanto Co., St. Louis, 1989, v.p. pub. policy, 1989-93, sr. v.p. pub. policy, 1993—; mem. gen. clin. rsch. ctrs. adv. com. NIH, Bethesda, Md., 1976-80, mem. rsch. resources adv. coun., 1980-84; bd. dirs. Gen. Am. Life Ins. Co., Security Equity Life Ins. Co., G.D. Searle & Co.; bd. dirs., advisor Monsanto Co., 1989—. Contbr. articles to sci. jours. Bd. trustees Calif. Inst. Tech., 1996—; commr. St. Louis Zool. Park, 1983-92; bd. dirs., vice chmn. St. Louis Symphony Orch.; bd. dirs. United Way Greater St. Louis, 1978-90, St. Louis Regional Health Care Corp., 1985-91; mem. risk assessment mgmt. commn. EPA, 1992—; mem. Pres.'s Com. of Advisors on Sci. and Tech., 1994—. Fellow AAAS, Am. Acad. Pediatrics; mem. Inst. Medicine, Assn. Am. Med. Colls. (del., chmn. coun. acad. socs. 1984-85, chmn. assembly 1985-86), Am. Pediatric Soc., Nat. Bd. Med. Examiners (bd. dirs. 1987-89), Endocrine Soc., Soc. Pediatric Rsch., St. Louis Med. Soc., Sigma Xi, Alpha Omega Alpha. Roman Catholic. Home: 242 Carlyle Lake Dr Saint Louis MO 63141-7544 Office: Monsanto Co DIA 800 N Lindbergh Blvd Saint Louis MO 63141-7843

WELLER, ELIZABETH BOGHOSSIAN, child and adolescent psychiatrist; b. Aug. 7, 1949; m. Ronald A. Weller, Feb. 18, 1978; children: Andrew, Christine. BS, American U., Beirut, Lebanon, 1971, MD, 1975. Lic. psychiatrist, Lebanon, Mo., Kans., Ohio. Intern Am. U. of Beirut, 1974-75; resident Renard Hosp./Washington U., St. Louis, 1975-78; fellow U. Kans. Med. Ctr., Kansas City, 1978-79; asst. prof. psych. U. Kans. Med. Sch., Kansas City, Kans., 1979-84; chief child/adolescent psychiatry Ohio State U., Columbus, 1985-94, assoc. chair dept. psychiatry, 1994—; cons. Am. Psychiat. Assn. Task Force. Co-author: Psychiatric Disorders in Child/Adolescent, 1990, Current Perspectives on Major Depression Disorders in Children, 1984. Fellow APA, Am. Acad. Child/Adolescent Psychiatry; mem. Kans. Med. Soc., World Federation for Mental Health, Central Ohio Psychiat. Assn., Ohio Psychiat. Assn.,Soc. of Biological Psychiatry. Office: Ohio State U 273 W 12th Ave Columbus OH 43210-1303

WELLER, MALCOLM PHILIP ISADORE, psychiatrist, consultant; b. Manchester, Eng., May 29, 1935; s. Solomon George and Esther (Black) W.; m. Celia Davina Reisler, May 8, 1966; children: Ben Gerald Avrom, Adrian Vivian. MA, Cambridge (Eng.) U., 1958; MB, BS, U. Newcastle (Eng.), 1972. Sr. house officer, registrar to Prof. Sir Martin Roth, Prof. I. Kolvin and Prof. D.W.K. Kay Newcastle Victoria Infirmary, Newcastle Gen. Hosp. and Nuffield Child Psychiat. Unit, 1973-76; cons. Friern Hosp., London, 1981—, Whittington Hosp., London, 1981—, Royal No. Hosp., 1981—; univ. lectr., 1st asst. Charing Cross Hosp. Sch. Medicine, London, 1976-81; hon. sr. lectr. Royal Free Hosp. Sch. Medicine, London, 1981—; vis. scientist Hebrew U., Jerusalem, 1985-89; vice chmn. N.E. Thomas Regional Com. for Hosp. Med. Svcs., 1984—; external examiner Nat. U. Singapore, 1987-88, Manchester U., 1989; hon. med. adviser Nat. Schizophrenia Fellowship, Nat. Schizophrenia Cons., Jewish Assn. for Mentally Ill; course organizer Brit. Postgrad. Med. Fedn. Editor: The Scientific Basis of Psychiatry, 1983, 2d edit., 1992, International Perspectives in Schizophrenia, 1990, Dimensions of Community Care, 1992; contbr. chpts., articles and editorials on schizophrenia, violence and medico-legal issues to med. jours. Chmn. bd. govs. Gosforth Mid. Sch., Newcastle, 1975-76; local authority councillor, Newcastle, 1969-75; mem. com. Laing Art Gallery, 1975-77; concert organizer Newcastle Arts Festival, 1967-70; chmn. CONCERN. Recipient ver Heyden de Lancey prize Cambridge U., 1984, 86, Wilfred Kingdon prize Newcastle U., 1972; Mental Health Found. scholar, 1969; Brit. Coun. travel grantee, 1987. Fellow Royal Coll. Psychiatrists (course organizer), Brit. Psychol. Soc., Royal Soc. Medicine, Collegium Internat. Neuropsychopharmacologium. Jewish. Home: 30 Arkwright Rd, Hampstead NW3 6BH, England Office: 10 Harley St, London WIA IAA, England

WELLER, SHERRILL LYNN, osteopath; b. Flagstaff, Ariz., Mar. 6, 1970; d. David L. and Patricia E. (Riggs) McCormick; m. Christopher Howard Weller, Aug. 19, 1995. BA in Biology and Chemistry, U. San Diego, 1992; postgrad., Western U. Health Scis., Pomona, Calif. Lab. technician U. San Diego, 1989-92; pharmacy technician Flagstaff Med. Ctr., 1992-93. With USN, 1994—. Mem. Am. Acad. Family Practice, Assn. Mil. Surgeons, Assn. Mil. Osteo. Physicians and Surgeons, Officer Spouses Club. Roman Catholic. Home: 418 G Ave Coronado CA 92118

WELLER, THOMAS HUCKLE, physician, emeritus educator; b. Ann Arbor, Mich., June 15, 1915; s. Carl V. and Elsie A. (Huckle) W.; m. Kathleen R. Fahey, Aug. 18, 1945; children: Peter Fahey, Nancy Kathleen, Robert Andrew, Janet Louise. A.B., U. Mich., 1936; M.S., 1937, LL.D. (hon.), 1956; M.D., Harvard, 1940; Sc.D., Gustavus Adolphus U., 1975, U. Mass., 1985; L.H.D., Lowell U., 1977. Diplomate Am. Bd. Pediatrics. Teaching fellow bacteriology Harvard Med. Sch., 1940-41, research fellow tropical medicine, pediatrics, 1947-48, instr. comparative pathology, tropical medicine, 1948-49, asst. prof. tropical pub. health Sch. Pub. Health, 1949-50, assoc. prof., 1950-54, Richard Pearson Strong prof. tropical pub. health, 1954-85, prof. emeritus, 1985—, head dept., 1954-81; intern bacteriology and pathology Children's Hosp., Boston, 1941; intern medicine Children's Hosp., 1942, asst. resident medicine, 1946, asst. dir. research div. infectious diseases, 1949-55; mem. commn. parasitic diseases Armed Forces Epidemiol. Bd., 1953-72, dir., 1953-59. Author sci. papers. Served to maj. M.C. AUS, 1942-46. Recipient E. Mead Johnson award for devel. tissue culture procedures in study virus diseases Am. Acad. Pediatrics, 1953, Kimble Methodology award, 1954, Nobel prize in physiology and medicine, 1954, George Ledlie prize, 1963, Weinstein Cerebral Palsy award, 1973, Stern Symposium honoree, 1972, Bristol award Infectious Diseases Soc. Am., 1980, Gold medal and diploma of honor U. Costa Rica, 1984, First Sci. Achievement award VZV Rsch. Found., 1993. Fellow Am. Acad. Arts and Scis.; mem. Harvey Soc., AMA, Am. Soc. Parasitologists, Am., Royal socs. tropical medicine and hygiene, Am. Pub. Health Assn., AAAS, Am. Epidemiological Soc., Nat. Acad. Scis., Am. Pediatric Soc., Assn. Am. Physicians, Soc. Exptl. Biology and Medicine, Am. Assn. Immunologists. Soc. Pediatric Research, Phi Beta Kappa., Sigma Xi, Alpha Omega Alpha. Home and Office: 56 Winding River Rd Needham MA 02192-1025

WELLISCH, WILLIAM JEREMIAH, social psychology educator; b. Vienna, Austria, July 3, 1938; came to U.S., 1940; s. Max and Zelda (Schanser) W.; m. Geraldine Eve Miller (dec. Feb. 1970); children: Garth Kevin, Miriam Rhoda; m. Claudine Abbey Truman, Sept. 5, 1971; children: Rebecca Colleen, Marcus Joshua, Gabriel Jason. MA in Sociology, U. Mo., 1965, PhD in Sociology, 1968. Researcher urbanization Hemispheric Consultants, Columbia, Mo., 1968-69; cons. to local govt. ofcl on L.Am. Bicultural Consultants, Inc., Denver, 1969-70; prof. Red Rocks Coll., Lakewood, Colo., 1970-76, 77—. Author: Bi-Cultural Development, 1971, Honduras: A Study in Sub-Development, 1978. Mem. citizen's adv. bd. Sta. KCFR Pub. Radio, Denver, 1989—. Republican. Mem. Unification Ch. Home: 2325 Clay St Denver CO 80211-5123 Office: Red Rocks CC 13300 W 6th Ave Lakewood CO 80401

WELLONS, HARRY ALBERT, surgeon, educator; b. Crossville, Tenn., May 9, 1937; s. Harry Alvah and Esther Annie (Lindley) W.; m. Florence Lee Daniel, June 6, 1961; children: Jeannette Lindley, Harry Albert III, Eric Daniel, Patricia Perrow. AB, Guildford Coll., 1957; MD, Med. Coll. Va., 1961. Bd. cert. Am. Bd. Surgery, Am. Bd. Thoracic Surgery. Intern U. Hosp., U. Wis., Madison, 1961-62; resident N.C. Meml. Hosp., Chapel Hill, 1962-66, chief resident, 1965-66; thoracic surgery and sr. clin. trainee Cancer Control Divsn., USPHS, 1966-67; chief resident thoracic and cardiovascular surgery U. Va. Med. Ctr., Charlottesville, 1969-70; from asst. to full prof. surgery U. Va., Charlottesville, 1970-82; clin. prof. surgery, chmn. divsn. thoracic surgery So. Ill. Sch. Medicine, Springfield, 1982-92; pvt. practice in cardiac, thoracic and vascular surgery Springfield, 1982—; Diplomate Am. Bd. Surgery, Am. Bd. Thoracic Surgeons. Contbr. articles to profl. jours. Maj. U.S. Army, 1967-69. Fellow ACS, Am. Coll. Chest Physicians, Am. Coll. Cardiology; mem. AMA, Am. Thoracic Soc., So. Thoracic Surgeons, Am. Assn. for Thoracic Surgery, Internat. Cardiovascular Soc., Am. Heart Assn., Ill. Heart Assn., Sangamon County Heart Assn., So. Thoracic Surg. Assn., So. Surg. Assn., Med. Soc. Va., Muller Surg. Soc., Ill. State Med. Soc., Sangamon County Med. Soc., Alpha Sigma Chi. Home: 1616 W Leland St Springfield IL 62704 Office: Prairie Thoracic & Cardiovascular Surgeons 800 E Carpenter St Springfield IL 62769

WELLS, ANNE JONES, psychotherapist; b. Henderson, N.C., Sept. 16, 1939; d. Ernest Clifford and Gladys (Casey) Jones; m. William D. Wells; divorced; children: Marie Elizabeth, Theodore Ernest. BSN, Emory U., 1962; MS in Psychiat. Nursing, Rutgers U., 1964; PhD in Behavioral Scis., U. Chgo., 1985. RN, Ill.; lic. psychologist, Ill.; lic. marriage and family therapist, Ill. Instr. psychiatric nursing Rutgers U., 1962-64; asst. prof. psychiatric nursing U. Ill., Chgo., 1967-68; rsch. asst. human devel. U. Chgo., 1973; clin. psychology extern Siegel Inst. Michael Reese Hosp. and Med. Ctr., Chgo., 1981-83; clin. trainee, family and child clin. program Family Inst. Chgo., Northwestern Meml. Hosp., 1983-85, asst. team leader, clin. trainee, 1985-86, staff fellow Ctr. for Family Studies, 1986-88; asst. prof. grad. psychiatric nursing U. Ill., Chgo., 1986-88; workshop coord., staff Family Inst., Chgo., 1988-90, sr. clinician, tchr., supr., 1990-91; pvt. practice psychotherapy Chgo. and Evanston, 1991—. Contbr. articles to profl. jours. Mem. APA, Am. Family Therapy Assn., Am. Assn. of Marriage and Family Therapy (approved supr. and clin. mem.), Soc. for Rsch. in Child Devel. Office: 233 E Erie St Ste 601 Chicago IL 60611-2906

WELLS, HERSCHEL JAMES, physician, former hospital administrator; b. Kirkland, Ark., Feb. 23, 1924; s. Alymer James and Martha Thelma (Cross) W.; m. Carmen Ruth Williams, Aug. 5, 1946; children: Judith Alliece Wells Jarecki, Pamela Elliece Wells McKinven, Joanne Olivia Wells Bennett. Student, Emory U., 1941-42, U. Ark., 1942-43; MD, U. Tenn., 1946. Rotating intern, then resident internal medicine Wayne County Gen. Hosp. (and Infirmary), Eloise, Mich., 1946-50; dir. infirmary div. Wayne County Gen. Hosp. (and Infirmary), 1955-65, gen. supt., 1965-74; dir. Wayne County Gen. Hosp. (Walter P. Reuther Meml. Long Term Care Facility), 1974-78; rev. physician DDS, SSA, Traverse City, Mich., 1978—. Served to maj. M.C. AUS, 1948-55. Mem. AMA, Mich. Med. Soc., Am. Fedn. Clin. Rsch., Masons (32 deg.), Alpha Kappa Kappa, Pi Kappa Alpha. Home and Office: 9651 N 3 Rd Copemish MI 49625-9608

WELLS, HUGH H., physician; b. Seneca, S.C., Sept. 7, 1949; s. Hugh H. and Beverly (Carey) W.; m. Peggy Hubbard, June 12, 1971; childen: Brian, Ginger. AB in Chemistry, Duke U., 1971; MD, U. Va., 1975. Cert. Am. Bd. Pediatric, 1979, Am. Bd. Neonatal-Perinatal, 1981. Resident pediatric Med. Ctr. U. N.C., Chapel Hill, 1975-77; fellow neonatology Med. Ctr. U. Va., Charlottesville, 1977-79; co-dir. neonatal svc. Roanoke (Va.) Meml. Hosp., 1979-92, Med. Ctr. for Chilfen at Carilion Roanoke Cmty. Hosp., 1992—. Mem. commn. Early Detection of Hearing Loss in Newborns, Va., 1988—. Fellow Am. Acad. Pediatrics (Va. chpt.), Roanoke Acad. Medicine, Alpha Omega Alpha. Office: Dept Neonatology 102 Highland Ave SE Ste 435 Roanoke VA 24013-2232

WELLS, LIONELLE DUDLEY, pathologist, consultant; b. Winston-Salem, N.C., Feb. 27, 1951. MD, Washington U., St. Louis, 1977. Diplomate Am. Bd. Pathology. Intern Yale New Haven Hosp., 1977-78, resident, 1978-80; resident UCLA Ctr. for Health Scis., Los Angeles, 1980-82; lab dir. Harvard Cmty. Health Plan, 1989—, dir. lab. svcs. New Eng. divsn., 1993—. Fellow Coll. Am. Pathologists, Am. Soc. Cytologists, Am. Coll. Physics Execs. Home: 273 Autumn Ave Duxbury MA 02332-4614 Office: Harvard Community Health Plan 120 Brookline Ave # 200 Boston MA 02215-3905 also: Harvard Pilgrim Health Plan of New Eng One Hoppin St Providence RI 02903

WELLS, LIONELLE DUDLEY, psychiatrist; b. Winnsboro, S.C., Nov. 22, 1921; s. Lionelle Dudley and Mary Wells; m. Mildred Wohltman, June 28, 1945 (dec. 1986); children: Lucia, Lionelle, John, Diane; m. Eilene Bromfield, Sept. 23, 1989. BS, U. S.C., 1943; MD, Med. U. S.C., 1945; grad., Boston Psychoanalytic Inst., 1960. Diplomate Am. Bd. Psychiatry and Neurology; lic. physician, S.C., Mass.; cert. in psychoanalysis. Intern Met. Hosp., N.Y.C., 1945-46; psychiatry resident VA Hosp., North Little Rock, Ark., 1948-50; asst. resident in Psychiatry Graylyn, Bowman-Gray Sch. Medicine, Winston-Salem, 1950-51; instr. psychiatry U. Ark., 1949-51, Mass. Gen. Hosp./Harvard Med. Sch., Boston, 1955-69; clin. instr. psychiatry Harvard Med. Sch., Boston, 1969-78; lectr. psychiatry Boston U. Sch. Medicine, 1977—; asst. clin. prof. psychiatry Harvard Med. Sch., 1978-93; lectr. psychiatry Tufts U. Med. Sch., Boston, Mass., 1981—; cons. staff Newton-Wellesley Hosp., Newton, Mass., 1983-95, hon. staff, 1995—; assoc psychiatrist Mass. Gen. Hosp., Boston, 1975-82, psychiatrist, 1982-96, sr. psychiatrist, 1996—; courtesy staff Waltham Deaconess Hosp. and Med. Ctr., 1977—; cons. Edith Nourse Rogers Meml. VA Med. Ctr., Bedford, Mass., 1966—; cons. in psychiatry VA Outpatient Clinic, Boston, 1959—, others in past; chmn. bd., chief exec. officer Bay State Health Care, 1984-91; nominating com. Am. Managed Care and Rev. Assn., 1988-89, others. Contbr. articles to profl. jours. Recipient Robert Wilson award, Med. U. S.C., 1943, 44. Fellow Am. Coll. Physician Execs., Am. Psychiat. Assn. (life); mem. AMA, Am. Psychoanalytic Assn., Am. Assn. Geriatric Psychiatry, Internat. Gero-Psychiatry Assn., Mass. Psychiat. Soc., Mass. Med. Soc., Boston Psychoanalytic Soc. and Inst., Boston Soc. for Gerontologic Psychiatry (mem. chmn. and dir. 1974-76) Home and Office: 73 Rolling Ln Weston MA 02193-2474

WELLS, SAMUEL ALONZO, JR., surgeon, educator; b. Cuthbert, Ga., Mar. 16, 1936; s. Samuel Alonzo and Martha (Steele) W.; m. Barbara Anne Atwood, Feb. 13, 1964; children: Sarah, Susan. Student, Emory U., 1954-57, M.D., 1961. Diplomate: Am. Bd. Surgery (bd. dirs., exec. com. 1986-89, vice chmn. 1987-88, chmn. 1988-89). Intern Johns Hopkins Hosp., Balt., 1961-62, resident in internal medicine, 1962-63; asst. resident in surgery Barnes Hosp., St. Louis, 1963-64; resident in surgery Duke U., Durham, N.C., 1966-70; guest investigator dept. tumor biology Karolinska Inst., Stockholm, 1967-68; asst. prof. surgery Duke U., Durham, N.C., 1970-72, assoc. prof., 1972-76, prof., 1976-81; clin. assoc. surgery br. Nat. Cancer Inst., NIH, Bethesda, Md., 1964-66, sr. investigator surgery br., 1970-72, cons. surgery br., 1975—; prof., chmn. dept. surgery Washington U., St. Louis, 1981—; dir. Duke U. Clin. Rsch. Ctr., 1978-81. Mem. editl. bd. Annals of Surgery, 1975-93, Surgery, 1975-93, Jour. Surg. Rsch., 1981-93; editor in chief World Jour. Surgery, 1983-92, Current Problems in Surgery, 1989—. Served to lt. comdr. USPHS, 1964-66. Mem. ACS (bd. regents 1989—, residency rev. com. for surgery 1987-93, chmn. 1991-93, vice chmn. 1995—; mem. editl. bd. Current Problems in Surgery 1988—, editor-in-chief 1989—), Am. Surg. Assn. (recorder, mem. coun. 1986-91, pres. 1995-96), Soc. Univ. Surgeons (exec. coun. 1976-78), Soc. Clin. Surgery (treas. 1980-86, v.p. 1986-88, pres. 1988-90), Am. Soc. Clin. Investigation, Inst. of Medicine of NAS, Am. Bd. Surgery (vice chmn. 1987-88, chmn. 1988-89), Nat. Cancer Adv. Bd., Halsted Soc. (pres. 1987), Soc. Surg. Oncology (pres. 1993-94), Alpha Omega Alpha. Home: 46 Westmoreland Pl Saint Louis MO 63108-1244 Office: Washington U Sch Medicine 660 S Euclid Ave Saint Louis MO 63110-1010

WELLS, WINFIELD JOHN, cardiothoracic surgeon; b. Pasadena, Calif., Jan. 11, 1944; s. John Winfield and Ruth (Brown) W.; m. Melinda Wells, Dec. 21, 1968; children: Eric, Amanada. BA, Pomona Coll., Claremont, Calif., 1966; MD, U. So. Calif., L.A., 1970. Diplomate Am. Bd. Surgery, Am. Bd. Thoracic Surgery. Resident, fellow Columbia Presbyn. Hosp., N.Y.C., 1976; cardiothoracic surgeon Myer, Stiles, Lindemitt Med. Group, L.A., 1977-92, U. So. Calif., L.A., 1992—. Fellow ACS; mem. Soc. Thoracic Surgery (councillor at large 1994—), Western Thoracic Surg. Assn. (treas. 1993-96, pres. elect 1996). Office: Childrens Hosp Divsn Cardiothoracic Surg 4650 Sunset Blvd # 66 Los Angeles CA 90027

WELLS-FEDERMAN, CAROL LEE, community health nurse; b. Ilion, N.Y.. AS, Becker Jr. Coll., 1968; BSN cum laude, Boston U., 1976, MEd, 1981; MS, Simmons Coll., 1996. RN, Mass. Owner Carol L. Wells Health Promotion Cons., 1980—; dir. clin. tng. Mind/BodyMed. Inst., 1989-95; assoc. in medicine Harvard Med. Sch., Boston, 1995—; adj. clin. instr., lectr. Simmons Coll. Grad. Sch. Health Studies, 1991—, adj. instr. pub. health Boston U. Sch. Pub. Health, 1990-94. Contbr. articles to profl. jours. Active Big Sister Assn. Boston, 1982-84, Healer's Invitational Yearly Therapeutic Touch Cmty. Svc., Craryville, N.Y., 1987—, Hospice Insvc. Edn. Emerson Hosp., Concord, Mass., 1993-94. Mem. Am. Heart Assn., Mass. Pub. Health Assn. New Eng. Pain Assn., Nurse Healers Profl. Assn. (co-founder Boston chpt.), Assn. Pain Mgmt. Nurses, Soc. Behavioral Medicine, Sigma Theta Tau. Office: Deaconess Hosp One Deaconess Rd Boston MA 02215

WELSH, MARY MCANAW, educator, family mediator; b. Cameron, Mo., Dec. 7, 1920; d. Francis Louis and Mary Matilda (Moore) McA.; m. Alvin F. Welsh, Feb. 10, 1944 (dec.); children: Mary Celia, Clinton F., M. Ann. AB, U. Kans., 1942; MA, Seton Hall U., 1960; EdD, Columbia U., 1971. Reporter, Hutchinson (Kans.) News Herald, 1942-43; house editor Worthington Pump & Machine Corp., Harrison, N.J., 1943-44; tchr., housemaster, coordinator Summit (N.J.) Pub. Schs., 1960-68; prof. family studies N.Mex. State U., Las Cruces, 1972-85; adj. faculty dept. family practice Tex. Tech. Regional Acad. Health Ctr., El Paso, 1978-82, Family Mediation Practice, Las Cruces, 1986—. Mem. AAUW (pres. N.Mex. 1981-83), N.Mex. Council Women's Orgn. (founder, chmn. 1982-83), Delta Kappa Gamma, Kappa Alpha Theta. Democrat. Roman Catholic. Author: A Good Family is Hard to Found, 1972; Parent, Child and Sex, 1970; contbr. articles to profl. jours.; writer, presenter home econs. and family study series KRWG-TV, 1974; moderator TV series The Changing Family in N.Mex./LWV, 1976. Home and Office: PO Box 3483 University Park Las Cruces NM 88003

WELSH, MICHAEL JOHN, cell biologist, researcher, science educator; b. Houston, Oct. 9, 1947; s. Tom Christopher and Clara Marie Welsh; m. Teresa Lynn Winnitoy, Sept. 23, 1978; children: Daniel Alexander, Catherine Samantha Leigh. BSc, Tex A&M U., 1970; PhD, U. Western Ont., London, Can., 1977. Instr. Baylor Coll. Medicine, Houston, 1979; asst. prof. Med. Sch. U. Mich., Ann Arbor, 1979-85, assoc. prof. Med. Sch., 1985-90, prof. Med. Sch., 1990—; rsch. scientist reproductive scis. program U. Mich., 1983—; prof. Mich. Cancer Ctr., 1987—, prof. dept. anesthesiology, 1988—, assoc. chair dept. anatomy and cell biology, 1994—. Contbr. over 75 articles to profl. jours. Baylor Coll. Medicine fellow, 1976; NIH fellow, 1977-79, NIH grantee, 1981—. Mem. AAAS, Am. Soc. for Cell Biology, Soc. for Study of Reprodn. (publs. com. 1990-91), Soc. Toxicology, Am. Assn. Anatomists. Home: 4825 Vorhies Rd Ann Arbor MI 48105-9544 Office: U Mich Med Sch Dept Anatomy & Cell Biology Ann Arbor MI 48109-0616

WELSH, WILLIAM DANIEL, osteopath; b. Balt., May 18, 1950; s. Joseph Leo and Bessie Mary (Tangires) W.; m. Loraine Lynn Barkhaus, July 11, 1985; children: Sean William, Ryan Daniel. Student, Johns Hopkins U., 1971; BS in Biology cum laude, Fairleigh Dickinson U., 1972; DO, Coll. Osteo. Medicine-Surgery, Des Moines, 1975. Diplomate Am. Bd. Osteo. Family Practitioners. Intern Martin Place Hosp., Madison Heights, Mich., 1975-76, resident in internal medicine, 1976-77; pvt. practice, Detroit, 1976-79, Whittier, Calif., 1979—; instr. ACLS, L.A., 1980-92; dir. Family Asthma Forum, L.A., 1982-88; bd. dirs. Whittier Hosp. Med. Ctr., 1981, vice chief staff, 1982-84, med. dir. family asthma forum, 1979-88. med. dir. Summit Place alcohol treatment program,1983-94; med. dir. Mirada Hills Rehab. Hosp., La Mirada, Calif., 1980-88; former clin. preceptor Coll. Osteo. Med. Pacific, Pomona, Calif. Mem. Am. Osteo. Assn., Am. Coll. Osteo. Family Physicians, Osteo. Physicians and Surgeons Calif. Home: 16871 Marina Bay Dr Huntington Beach CA 92649 Office: Friendly Hills HealthCare Network 12291 Washington Blvd Whittier CA 90602

WELTZ, MARTIN DAVID, oncologist, hematologist; b. Phila., Jan. 18, 1948; m. Sharon Frankfort; children: Michael, Adam. BS in Biology, Bklyn. Coll., 1969; DO, U. for Health Scis., 1973. Diplomate Nat. Bd. Med. Examiners for Osteo. Physicians and Surgeons, Am. Bd. Internal Medicine, (subspecialty of med. oncology, subspecialty of hematology). Commd. 2d lt. USMC, 1973, advanced through grades to lt. col., 1981; intern Walter Reed Army Med. Ctr., Washington, 1973-74, resident, 1974-76, fellow hematology and med. oncology sect., 1976-79, attending physician dept. internal medicine, 1979-81, staff hematologist, med. oncologist, dir. med. edn., 1979-80, chief divsn. head Clin. Cancer Chemo-Pharmacology Rsch. Lab., 1979-80, asst. chief, dir. clin. pharmacy hematology-med. oncology, 1980-81; resigned USMC, 1981; pvt. practice, v.p. Hematology-Oncology Cons., Greenbelt, Md., 1983—, v.p., sec., 1986—; v.p., sec., 1986—; attending med.staff AMI Drs. Hosp., Prince George's County, Lanham, Md., 1983, Washington Adventist Hosp., Takoma Park, Md., 1983—, sec.-treas. dept. internal medicine, 1991-94, asst. chmn., 1994; asst. chief hematology/med. oncology Prince Georges Hosp. Ctr., 1986—; staff Laurel Regional Hosp., 1983—, chmn. hematology-med. oncology, 1989—, med. dir. Hospice in Prince George's County, 1989—, chmn. dept. internal medicine, 1989-92, chmn. tumor bd., 1989—, chmn. employees ann. benefit med.-dental staff, 1990—, chmn. med. exec. com., 1993—, pres. med. and dental staff, 1993—, trustee, 1993—; ; bd. dirs. Dimensions Corp., Landover, Md., sec.-treas. bd. dirs., 1990—; pres. Med. Dental Staff laurel Regional Hosp., 1993—; vice chmn. Dept. Internal Medicine, Washington Adventist Hosp., 1994—; sec., treas. Dimensions Health Care Network PHO, 1994—; med. dir. Hospice in Prince Georges County, 1990—; bd. dirs. Universal Health Care Network, Medi-Cen of Md.; bd. dirs., found. chmn. med. exec. com., pres. med.-dental staff Laurel Region Hosp., 1993—; bd. dirs. Dimensions Healthcare Network, Dimensions Health Care Corp. Medi-Cen of Md. and Universal Healthcare Corp., Cancer Care, Inc.; med. dir. hospice, P.G. County, 1992—; chmn., founder tumor bd. Laurel Regional Hosp. and Washington Adventist Hosp., 1988—; chmn. transfusion com. Washington Adventist Hosp., 1990—. Contbr. articles to profl. jours. Bd. dirs. Am. Cancer Soc., Prince George's County, 1981—; med. advisor cansurmount program Am. Cancer Soc., Montgomery County, Md., 1982-90; ring dir. Ea. Regional Karate Tournament, Montgomery Coll., Rockville, Md., 1987—; mem. advisor Md. Blood Ctr., 1987-88; mem. med. adv. bd. Hospice Prince George's County, Largo, Md., 1991—, active archtl. and design com., capital campaign com., bldg. com., 1992—; bd. dirs. Found. Laurel Regional Hosp., 1993—, others. Fellow ACP, Acad. Medicine N.J.; mem. AMA, Am. Soc. Internal Medicine, Am. Soc. Clin. Oncology, Am. Soc. Hematology, Acad. Hospice Physicians, Am. Coll. Clin. Pharmacology, Am. Coll. Osteo. Internists, Am. Soc. Clin. Oncologists, Am. Soc. Clin. Pharmacology and Therapeutics, Am. Soc. Contemporary Medicine and Surgery, Am. Fedn. for Clin. Rsch., Royal Soc. Medicine (London), Md. Osteo. Assn., Oncology Soc. N.J., N.J. Soc. Internal Medicine, N.Y. Acad. Scis., N.Y. Oncology Soc., Md. Soc. Clin. Oncology. Office: Greenway Center Dr Greenbelt MD 20770

WENDA, KLAUS, surgeon; b. Wiesbaden, Germany, Dec. 3, 1952. Recipient Küntscher award, 1989. Office: Klinik Unfall &

Wiederherstellongschirurgie, Horst Schmidt Kliniken, 65799 Wiesbaden Germany

WENDER, MIECZYSŁAW BOGUMIŁ, neurology educator; b. Poznań, Poland, July 8, 1926; s. Mieczysław Henryk and Kamila (Danielec) W.; m. Grażyna Barbara Michałowska, Dec. 3, 1988. Degree, Med. Sch., Poznań, 1951, MD, 1956. Mem. faculty Med. Sch., Poznań, 1948—, docent of neurology, 1961, prorector, 1969-72, dir. dept. neurology, 1963—, prof., 1965—. Contbr. articles to profl. publs. Recipient prize Polish Minister of Health, 1965, 72; named to Polonia Restituta Order, 1969. Mem. Assn. Polish Neuropathologists (pres. 1972-81, pres. com. neurol. scis. 1984-93), Soc. Amis Sci. Poznan (v.p. 1968-85), Deutsche Akad. Naturforscher Leopoldina. Home: Na Stoku 11, Poznań Poland Office: Med Sch, Przybyszewskiego 49, Poznań Poland

WENDORFF, ROBERT HERMAN, osteopathic physician, educator; b. Quincy, Ill., Aug. 23, 1925; s. Herman Amil and Flora A. (Kaempen) W.; m. Jacquelyn L. Hendricks, Nov. 27, 1949 (dec. June 1990); children: Mark Alan, Lesley Gail Wendorff Brown. Student, Knox Coll., 1943-45; DO, Chgo. Coll. Osteopathy, 1948. Rotating intern Lamb Hosp., Denver, 1948-49; pvt. practice gen. family practice physician Denver and Aurora, 1950-77; pvt. practice osteo. manipulative care Denver, 1978—; faculty family practice residency program Presbyn./St. Lukes Hosps., Denver, Aurora, 1970—; dir., faculty Jones Strain-Counter Strain Inc., Boise, Idaho, 1990—. Author: (tchg. manual) Counterstrain Tutorial Manual, 1980. Mem. Am. Osteo. Assn., Colo. Soc. Osteo. Medicine, Am. Acad. Osteopathy (gov. 1981-82), Tri County Osteo. Soc., Denver Osteo. Found., Rocky Mountain Acad. Osteopathy, Valley Country Club. Home: 7167 So Poplar Ln Englewood CO 80112 Office: 496 S Dayton Denver CO 80231

WENDTLAND, MONA BOHLMANN, dietitian, consultant; b. Schulenburg, Tex., Mar. 30, 1930; d. Willy Frank and Leona A. (Bruns) Bohlmann; m. Charles William Ewing, Mar. 8, 1953 (div. Sept. 1975); children: Charles William Jr., Deborah Susan Ewing Richmond; m. William Wolters Wendtland, Jan. 12, 1991. BS in Home Econs., U. Tex., 1952, postgrad., 1952-57. Registered dietitian, Tex. Dietitian sch. lunch program Port Arthur (Tex.) Ind. Sch. Dist., 1952-53; elem. tchr. Portsmouth (Va.) Sch. Dist., 1953-54; dietitian, mgr. lunch room E.M. Scarbrough Dept. Store, Austin, Tex., 1955-57; asst. chief adminstrv. dietitian John Sealy HOsp., Galveston, Tex., 1957-59; chief therapeutic dietitian USPHS Hosp., Galveston, 1959-60, asst. chief dietitian, 1960-62; cons. dietitian Sinton (Tex.) Nursing Home, 1963-65; dietary cons. Deaton Hosp., Galena Park, Tex., 1966-68; dir. food svcs. Nat. Health Enterprises, Houston, 1975-76; dietary cons. to nursing homes and retirement ctrs. Drug Abuse Ctr., Houston, 1976—. Del. Internat. Congress Arts & Comm., 1993. Mem. Am. Dietetic Assn. (registered), Tex. Dietetic Assn., South Tex. Dietetic Assn. (chmn. cons. interest group 1978-79), U. Tex. Home Econs. Assn., Dietitians in Bus. and Industry (nat. rep. to mgmt. practices group 1980-83, treas. Houston chpt. 1980-81, pres. 1981-82, advisor 1983-84), Tex. Gerontol Nutritionists (sec. 1994-95), Tex. Cons. Dietitians in Healthcare Facilities, Tex. Nutrition Coun., Dietary Mgrs. Assn. (advisor Houston dist. 1979-92). Republican. Methodist. Home and Office: 5463 Jason St Houston TX 77096-1238

WENGER, DENNIS R., orthopedist; b. Wadsworth, Ohio, June 18, 1944; s. Morris Rudy and Mabel Naomi (Good) W.; children: Christine, Patrick, Matthew, Anne. BS, Ohio U., 1966; MD, U. Cin., 1970. Resident orthop. U. Iowa, Iowa City, 1971-74; fellow pediatric orthop. Hosp. for Sick Children, Toronto, Can., 1975-76; staff physician Denver Gen. Hosp., 1976-77; asst. chief of staff Tex. Scottish Rite Hosp., Dallas, 1977-84; staff physician orthop. surgery Children's Hosp., San Diego, 1984—; asst. prof. orthop. U. Colo. Med. Ctr., Denver, 1976-77; assoc. prof. orthop. surgery U. Tex., Dallas, 1977-84; assoc. clin. prof. U. Calif. San Diego, 1984-93, clin. prof., 1993—; acad. cons. USN, San Diego, 1984—. Co-author: The Art and Practice of Children's Orthopedics, 1993; editl. bd. mem. Jour. Pediatric Orthop., 1981—; adv. editor Jour. Bone and Joint Surgery, 1986, Jour. Orthop. Rsch., 1985—; bd. editors MVP Video Jour. Orthop., 1994—. Mem. Am. Orthop. Assn., Am. Assn. Orthop. Surgeons, Am. Acad. Pediatrics, Pediatric Orthop. Surgeons N.Am., Scoliosis Rsch. Soc. Office: Pediatric Orthop Ctr 3030 Children's Way #410 San Diego CA 92123

WENGER, DOROTHY MAE, retired dietitian; b. Rozel, Kans., Jan. 20, 1917; d. John Edward and Irene Margaret (McElroy) Franz; m. Edward Lawrence Wenger (dec.); 1 child, Edward Lawrence III; m. Jacob Eric Iverson, 1995. Student, Iowa State Tchrs. Coll., Cedar Falls, 1937-39; BS, Lindenwood Coll. for Women, St. Charles, Mo., 1940; postgrad., U. W.Va., 1941, Columbia U., 1945, 47. Registered dietitian. Dietetic intern Mayo Clinic, Rochester, Minn., 1941, Western Pa. Hosp., Pitts., 1941-42; head dietitian, dir. dept. St. Luke's Hosp., Bluefield, W.Va., 1942-44, Monongalia Gen. Hosp., Morgantown, W.Va., 1944-49, Elyria (Ohio) Meml. Hosp., 1949-57; chief dietitian Lakewood Hosp., Cleve., 1957-58; dir. dietary dept. Beach Hosp., Ft. Lauderdale, Fla., 1959-61, North Broward Med. Ctr., Pompano Beach, Fla., 1961-75; chief dietitian North Broward Med. Ctr., Pompano Beach, 1975-89; ret., 1989; supr. clin. practicum program for student from various schs. including Atlantic Vocat. Sch., Broward Community Coll., Fla. Internat. Coll.; community nutrition lectr. North Broward County Hosp. Dist., 1985-89. Developer dietetic course programs for various levels. Guidance vol. children and adults with dyslexia, 1965—; lector Episc. Ch., 1988—; mem. Bible Study Fellowship Internat., 1990—, St. mary's Guild, 1993—; pres. Order of Daus. of the King, 1995—. Mem. Am. Dietetic Assn., Tri-county Clin. Mgrs., W.Va. Dietetic Assn. (state pres. 1942-44), Greater Miami Dietetic Assn. (adv. com. for dietetic tech. 1974-80), Cons. Dietitians for Long Term Facilities (Fla. state dietetic rep. 1978-79), Fla. Dietetic Assn. (chmn. dist. edn. com. 1975-77), Nat. Honor Soc. (Norfolk, Nebr.), Quota Club (Morgantown), Triangle Club (St. Charles).

WENGER, SIDNEY U., psychiatrist, educator; b. Reading, Pa., Nov. 19, 1913; s. Morris and Tillie (Ullman) W.; m. June F. Klinghoffer, Feb. 12, 1921; 1 child, Robert K. BS, Albright Coll., 1935; MD, Hahnemann Med. Coll., 1939; postgrad. psychoanalysis, Inst. Of Phila. Assn., 1951-56. Diplomate Am. Bd. Psychiatry. Intern Mt. Sinai Hosp., Phila., 1939-41; Resident psychiatry Phila. Psychiat. Ctr., 1941-42, 46-47; clin. prof. psychiatry Med. Coll. Pa., Phila., 1967—; pvt. practice psychiatry and psychoanalysis Phila.; pvt. practice, 1947—; faculty (inactive) Inst. Phila. Assn. Psychoanalysis, 1956—, Med. Coll. of Pa., Phila., 1967—; sr. attending (emeritus) Phila. Psychiat. Ctr., 1947—; cons. Jefferson Park Hosp., Phila., 1980—. Major AUS, 1942-46, NATOUSA. Recipient 50-Yr. Svc. awards Phila. County Med. Soc, 1989, Albert Einstein Med. Ctr., Phila., 1989. Mem. Phila. County Med. Soc., Pa. State Med. Soc., Phila. Assn. for Psychoanalysis, Phila. Psychoanalytic Soc., Am. Psychoanalytic Assn. (cert. in psychoanalysis), Internat. Psychoanalytic Assn., Am. Psychiat. Assn., Phila Psychiat. Soc., Pa. Psychiat. Soc. Office: D129 Presidential Apt Philadelphia PA 19131

WENTS, DORIS ROBERTA, psychologist; b. L.A., Aug. 26, 1944; d. John Henry and Julia (Cole) W. BA, UCLA, 1966; MA, San Francisco State U., 1968; postgrad., Calif. State U., L.A., 1989-90, Claremont (Calif.) Grad. Sch., 1990—. Lic. ednl. psychologist, credentialed sch. psychologist, Calif. Sch. psychologist Diagnostic Sch. for Neurologically Handicapped Children, L.A., 1969-86; pvt. practice Monterey Park, Calif., 1986—; instr. Calif. State U., L.A., 1977. Co-author: Southern California Ordinal Scales of Development, 1977. Mem. Western Psychol. Assn., L.A. World Affairs Coun., L.A. Conservancy, Zeta Tau Alpha (officer Santa Monica alumnae chpt. 1970—, Cert. of Merit 1979), Sigma Xi. Office: Claremont Grad Sch Dept Psychology Claremont CA 91711

WENZ, ROBERT EDWARD, surgeon; b. Berea, Ohio, June 6, 1961; s. Robert George and Marilyn Helen (Fink) W.; m. Margie Ellen Senseman; children: Jennifer Lynn, Eric Andrew. BA magna cum laude, Case Western Res. U., 1983, MD, 1987. Intern Mercy Hosp., Pitts., 1987-88; ophthalmology resident Mt. Sinai Med. Ctr., Cleve., 1989-92; vitreoretinal fellow Kresge Eye Inst., Detroit, 1992-93; pvt. practice vitreoretinal surgery No. Ohio Retinal Consultants, Cleve., 1993—; tchg. faculty Mt. Sinai Med. Ctr., 1993—; diabetic edn. com. Meridia Hillcrest Hosp., Mayfield Heights, Ohio, 1995—. Lectr. in field. Recipient Resident Tchg. award Divsn. Ophthalmology at Mt. Sinai Med. Ctr., 1994. Fellow Am. Acad. Ophthalmology; mem. Cleve. Acad. Medicine, Ohio State Med. Assn., Cleve. Ophthal. Soc., Am. Diabetes Assn. Office: No Ohio Retinal Consultants 2475 E 22d St #405 Cleveland OH 44115-3221 also: 6770 Mayfield Rd #300 Mayfield Heights OH 44124

WENZLER, RICHARD BRUCE, cardiologist; b. Lansing, Mich., June 14, 1955; s. Paul Jordan and Nancy Louise (Uland) W.; m. Jean Valentine Corcoran, Feb. 23, 1985; children: Patrick Jordan, Richard Booth. AB, Ind. U., 1978; MD, Ind. U., Indianapolis, 1981. Diplomate Am. Bd. Internal Medicine, Am. Bd. Cardiovascular Disease. Cardiologist Meridian Med. Cardiology, Indpls., 1988-94, Nasser, Smith & Pinkerton, Danville, Ind., 1995—; dir. CCU, Meth. Hosp. Ind., Indpls., 1993-94; bd. dirs. Hosp./Physician Orgn., Danville, Ind., 1995—. Co-author: (book) Electrocardiography Diagnostic Criteria; contbr. articles to profl. jours. including Jour. Am. Coll. Cardiology, Clin. Rsch. Mem. Am. Heart Assn., Danville, Ind., 1995—. Fellow Am. Coll. Cardiology, Am. Coll. Chest Physicians; mem. AMA, Am. Soc. Nuclear Cardiology. Office: Heart Ctr Hendricks County 112 Hospital Ln Ste 110 Danville IN 46122

WERBACH, MELVYN ROY, physician, writer; b. N.Y.C., Nov. 11, 1940; s. Samuel and Martha (Robbins) W.; m. Gail Beth Leibsohn, June 20, 1967; children: Kevin, Adam. BA, Columbia Coll., N.Y.C., 1962; MD, Tufts U., Boston, 1966. Diplomate Am. Bd. Psychiatry and Neurology. Intern VA Hosp., Bklyn., 1966-67; resident in psychiatry Cedars-Sinai Med. Ctr., L.A., 1969-71; dir. psychol. svcs., clin. biofeedback UCLA Hosp. and Clinics, 1976-80; pres. Third Line Press, 1986—; asst. clin. prof. Sch. Medicine, UCLA, 1978—; mem. nutritional adv. bd. Cancer Treatment Ctrs. Am., 1989-93; mem. adv. com. The Dead Sea Confs., Israel, 1990—. Author: Third Line Medicine, 1986, Nutritional Influences on Illness, 1987, 2d edit., 1993, Nutritional Influences on Mental Illness, 1991, Healing Through Nutrition, 1993; co-author: Botanical Influences on Illness, 1994; mem. editl. bd. Jour. of Nutritional Medicine, 1993—, Health News and Rev., 1991—, Jour. Optimal Nutrition, 1993—, Alt. Medicine Digest, 1994—; mem. internat. adv. bd. Jour. Bodywork and Movement Therapics, 1996—; mem. adv. bd. HealthWorld Online, 1996—; mem. med. adv. bd. Let's Live Mag., 1989-93; columnist Jour. Alt. and Complementary Medicine, 1992—, Townsend Letter for Doctors, 1993—, Australian Jour. Nutrition and Environ. Medicine, 1995—; mem. panel What Doctor's Don't Tell You, 1993—; contbr. articles to med. jours. Mem. Am. Coll. Nutrition, Biofeedback Soc. Calif. (hon. life mem., pres. 1977, Cert. Honor 1985), Australian Coll. Nutritional and Environ. Medicine (hon.).

WERBITT, WARREN, gastroenterologist, educator; b. Phila., Jan. 29, 1939; s. Saull Boris and Pearl (Weiner) W.; m. Drue Natalie Engman Werbitt, Aug. 30, 1964; children: Julie Michele, Jeffrey Brian. BS in Pharmacy, Temple U., 1960; D in Osteopathy, Coll. Osteopathic Medicine, Des Moines, 1966; MD, Med. Coll. Pa., 1973. Diplomate Am. Osteo. Bd. Internal Medicine, also sub-splty. bd. Gastroenterology; diplomate Am. Bd. Internal Medicine, also sub-splty. bd. Gastroenterology. Internship Doctor's Hosp., Columbus, Ohio, 1966-67; residency in internal medicine Doctor's Hosp., Columbus, 1967-68, Cherry Hill (N.J.) Med. Ctr., 1968-69, Mercy Catholic Med. Ctr., Phila., 1969-70; residency in internal medicine Med. Coll. Pa. Hosp., Phila., 1971-72, fellow in gastroenterology, 1970-71, 72-74; instr. Med. Coll. Pa., Phila., 1971—; instr. Phila. Coll. Osteopathic Medicine, 1973-75, chmn. div. gastroenterology, 1975-77; clin. assoc. prof. medicine N.J. Coll. Medicine and Dentistry, 1977—; attending physician and cons. in gastroenterology Med. Coll. Pa., Phila., 1974—, Vet. Adminstrn. Hosp., Phila., 1972-75; chmn. Div. Gastroenterology, Dept. Medicine Phila. Coll. Osteopathic Medicine, 1975-77; chmn. Dept. Medicine Kennedy Meml. Hosp. U. Med. Ctr., Cherry Hill, 1979-81, chmn. subsect. Gastroenterology, 1979-87. Contbg. editor The N.J. Jour. for Ostepathic Physicians and Surgeons, 1980—; mem. scientific adv. com. Phila. chpt. Nat. Found. Ileitis & Colitis, Inc., 1982—; contbr. articles to profl. jours. Recipient Profl. Svc. award Med. Soc. N.J., 1991. Fellow Am. Coll. Physicians, Am. Coll. Gastroenterology, Acad. Med. N.J.; mem. AMA, Am. Soc. Gastrointestinal Endoscopy, Am. Gastroenterology Assn., Am. Soc. Parenteral and Enteric Nutrition, Am. Inst. Ultrasound in Medicine, Phila. Gastrointestinal Rsch. Forum, State Med. Soc. N.J., Camden County Med. Soc., N.J. Endoscopic Soc., Del. Valley Soc. for Gastrointestinal Endoscopy, South Jersey Gastroenterological Soc., Am. Osteopathic Assn., N.J. Soc. Osteopathic Physicians and Surgeons, Am. Coll. Osteopathic Internists, Camden County Osteopathic Assn., Am. Cancer Soc. (bd. dirs. N.J. chpt.), Pres.'s Circle Am. U., N.Y. Acad. Scis., John Sherman Myers Soc., Lambda Omicron Gamma. Office: Profl Gastroenterology Assn 1939 Route 70 E Ste 250 Cherry Hill NJ 08003-4505

WERBLOWSKY, JOSHUA HAROLD, psychiatrist; b. Bklyn., May 25, 1942; s. Israel E. and Bella (Schoffman) W.; m. Joan Goldman, Mar. 18, 1968; children: Yaakov, Ilana, Michal. BA, Yeshiva U., 1963, MD, 1967. Diplomate in psychiatry, forensic psychiatry, geriatric psychiatry, and addiction psychiatry; Am. Bd. Psychiatry and Neurology. Resident in psychiatry Phila. Psychiat. Ctr., 1971; dir. Community Mental Health Dept., Phila., 1972-73; dir. psychiatry Downtown Home for the Aged, Phila., 1972-74; attending psychiatrist Phila. Gen. Hosp., 1975-77; clin. asst. prof. psychiatry Sch. Medicine Hahnemann U., Phila., 1975-94; lectr. in psychiatry Sch. of Medicine U. Pa., Phila., 1975-84; sr. attending psychiatrists Phila. Psychiat. Ctr., 1985—; pvt. practice Phila., 1971—; clin. assoc. prof. psychiatry Med. Coll. Pa., Phila., 1988—, Med. Coll. Pa./Hahneman U., 1994—; psychiat. cons. Fed. Workmen's Compensation Bd., 1983—. Contbr. articles to profl. jours. Fellow Am. Psychiat. Assn., Am. Acad. Forensic Scis.; mem. Am. Assn. Geriatric Psychiatry. Jewish. Home: 509 Waldron Ter Merion Station PA 19066-1325 Office: Presdl Apts Ste D111 Philadelphia PA 19131

WERKMAN, SIDNEY LEE, psychiatry educator; b. Washington, May 3, 1927. A.B., Williams Coll., 1948; M.D., Cornell U., 1952. Diplomate Am. Bd. Psychiatry and Neurology, Am. Bd. Child Psychiatry. Intern U. Va. Hosp., Charlottesville; resident in psychiatry Yale U., 1953-55, St. Elizabeth's Hosp., Washington, 1955-56; assoc. prof. psychiatry George Washington U., Washington, 1960-69; prof. U. Colo. Sch. Medicine, Denver, 1969-87; dir. adolescent psychiatry Children's Hosp. of Washington, 1965-69; clin. prof. Georgetown U. Sch. Medicine, Washington, 1989—; psychiatrist Capital Area Permanente Med. Group, Washington, 1990—; cons. grants NIMH, Washington, 1982—, guest researcher, 1984-85. Author: The Role of Psychiatry in Medical Education, 1966, Only a Little Time: A Chronicle of Dying, 1972, Bringing Up Children Overseas, 1977. Bd. dirs. Med. U. So. Africa, Performing Arts Soc., Washington Concert Operas. Master sgt. U.S. Army. Fellow Commonwealth Fund, Florence, Italy, 1963-64, NEH, 1979. Mem. Am. Psychiat. Assn., Am. Acad. Child Psychiatry, Group for Advancement Psychiatry, Am. Orthopsychiat. Assn. (bd. dirs. 1970-73), Colo. Psychiat. Soc. Office: Ste AG 62 3636 16th St NW Washington DC 20010

WERMAN, BARRY SAMUEL, dermatologist; b. Norwich, Conn., Feb. 18, 1951; s. Hyman and Florence (Meltz) W.; m. Roniel Tyler (div.). BA in Physics, Emory U., 1973, MD cum laude, 1977. Diplomate Am. Bd. Dermatology. Intern N.C. Meml. Hosp., Chapel Hill, 1977-78; resident Grady Meml. Hosp., Atlanta, 1978-81; pvt. practice dermatology Atlanta, 1981—. Contbr. articles to profl. jours. Mem. Am. Acad. Dermatology, Atlanta Dermatology Assn., Ga. Soc. Dermatologists, Phi Beta Kappa, Sigma Pi Sigma, Alpha Omega Alpha. Office: 285 Boulevard NE Ste 335 Atlanta GA 30312-4209

WERNER, ARNOLD, psychiatrist; b. Bklyn., June 8, 1938; m. Elizabeth A. Rederer; 2 children. BS cum laude, Bklyn. Coll., 1959; MD, U. Rochester, 1963. Diplomate Am. Bd. Psychiatry and Neurology in Psychiatry. Intern Vanderbilt U., Nashville, 1964; resident in psychiatry U. Rochester, N.Y., 1964-67, instr. psychiatry, 1966-67; instr. psychiatry Temple U., Phila., 1967-69; asst. prof. Mich. State U., East Lansing, Mich., 1969-72, assoc. prof., 1972-78, prof., 1978—; cons. Gratiot Co. Mental Health Ctr., Alma, 1972-96, Montcalm Ctr. for Behavioral Health, 1996—; coord. Psychosocial Curriculum, 1986-95, gen. practice psychiatry Temple U., 1967-69, Mich. State U., 1969—; dir. home vis. svc. Temple U., 1967-69, psychiat. svcs. Mich. State U. Health Ctr.. 1969-78; dir. consultation liason psychiatry Ingham Med. Ctr., Lansing, 1983-85. Contbr. numerous articles and book reviews to profl. jours., syndicated newspaper columnist, 1969-76. Research grantee NIMH, 1970-71, undergrad. grant, 1980, psychiat. edn. grants. 1982-85; recipient Outstanding Faculty award Sr. Class Council Mich. State U., 1971. Fellow Am. Psychiat. Assn. (com. on pub. info. 1972-75, chmn. 1974-75, peer rev. com. 1975-76, joint commn. on pub. affairs 1976-82, com. on med. student edn., 1982-89, 1994—, sci. program com. 1988-94); mem. Am. Psychosomatic Soc. Office: Mich State U A 228 E Fee Hall East Lansing MI 48824-1316

WERNER, DAVID WILLIAM, psychologist; b. Pitts., Mar. 18, 1952; s. Roy H. and Mable (Clift) W.; m. Maryfrances Gitto, June 6, 1987. BA, Amherst Coll., 1975; EdM, Boston U., 1977; D of Psychology, Mass. Sch. Profl. Psychology, 1983. Cert. drug and alcohol treatment psychologist. Psychotherapist Counseling Clinic Inc., Middletown, R.I., 1977-79; faculty R.I. Jr. Coll., Cranston, 1977-78; exec. dir. Counseling Self-Help Inc., Walpole, Mass., 1982-86; staff psychologist Cutler Counseling Ctr., Norwood, Mass., 1983-85; owner Dedham Psychotherapy, 1988—; pres. New Eng. PsychNet, 1994—; adj. faculty Mass. Sch. Profl. Psychology, Dedham, Mass., 1984-87; cons. Mass. Dept. Mental Health, Boston, 1984—; human rights bd. Norfolk Mental Health, 1986-89. Chair Save Our Swamp, Millis, Mass., 1990-91. Grantee Amherst Coll., 1973. Fellow Am. Acad. Psychologists Treating Addiction (diplomate); mem. APA, Mass. Psychol. Assn., Am. Soc. Psychology and Law. Office: Dedham Psychotherapy Assoc 10 Pearl St Dedham MA 02026-4345

WERNER, GLENN ALLEN, psychologist, supervisor; b. Mpls., June 11, 1955; s. James Allen Werner and Barbara Jean (Prigmeier) Risdall; m. Beth Ann Michnowski, Oct. 1, 1988; children: Brianna Charlene, Brittany Jean. AA in Psychology, Normandale C.C., 1975; BA in Psychology and Speech with honors, St. Cloud (Minn.) State U., 1977, MA in Counseling Psychology and Vocat. Rehab., 1979, B in Elective Studies cum laude, 1982; cert. adult psychiatry, U. Minn., 1984, cert. in indsl. rels., 1989. Lic. psychologist, Minn. Counselor M&R Inc., Mpls., 1974-79; employment placement specialist St. Paul Rehab. Ctr., 1979; sr. vocat. rehab. counselor Minn. Correctional Facility, St. Cloud, 1979-81; psychologist Minn. Security Hosp., St. Peter, 1981-83; clin. psychologist Anoka (Minn.)-Metro Regional Treatment Ctr., 1983-89; psychologist Stillwater Prison, 1989-91; psychologist supr. Cambridge (Minn.) Regional Treatment Ctr., 1991—. Author, illustrator: How to Land A Job- A Guide for Ex-Offenders, 1979. Recipient Exceptional Performance award State of Minn., 1982, 83, 85, 86, 87, 88, 89, 95, 96; nominee for 1st Annual Mo. awards for Health Excellence award, 1989. Mem. Mensa, Psi Chi. Home: 12020 Isanti St NE Blaine MN 55449-7915 Office: care Oakview Cambridge Regional Treatment Ctr 1235 Highway 293 S Cambridge MN 55008-9002

WERNER, HAROLD VINCENT, medical educator; b. Huron, S.D., Aug. 26, 1938; s. Otto and Katharine (Murphy) W.; m. Jacqulyn Hall; children: Carmen, Nicolle, Kurt. BA in Chemistry, Huron Coll., 1961; MA in Biochemistry, U. S.D., 1963; MD, Northwestern U., 1966. Bd. cert. internal medicine, endocrinology-metabolism and geriatrics Am. Bd. Internal Medicine. Intern internal medicine Northwestern U., 1966-67, resident internal medicine, endocrine fellow, 1973-76; postdoctoral rsch. fellow Washington U. Med. Sch., St. Louis, 1967-68, McGill U. Med. Sch., Montreal, Que., Can., 1968-69; rsch. physician Clin. Investigation Ctr. Naval Hosp., Oakland, Calif., 1971-73; asst. prof. dept. medicine and dept. pharmacology U. Mo. Sch. Medicine, Columbia, 1976-80; dir. emergency svcs. St. Mary's and Meml. Hosps., Jefferson City, Mo., 1980-82; pvt. practice Vilamoura, Portugal, 1984-88; Diabetes Ctr. dir. and endocrine practice Ozarks Med. Ctr., Rural Health Clinics, West Plains, Mo., 1990-92; assoc. prof. dept. medicine Tex. Tech. U. Med. Sch., Amarillo, 1992—; cons. for gen. internal medicine and endocrinology/metabolism, investigations divsn. Tex. State Bd. Med. Examiners; acad. clin. cons. hyperlipidemia Merck & Co., Inc., Human Health Divsn. Sect. editor Nutrition-Panhandle Health; editor: The Endocrine Pancreas and Juvenile Diabetes, 1979; contbr. articles to profl. jours. Bd. mem. Amarillo Heart Assn., 1995, 96; pres. Amarillo Internat. Club, 1995, 96. Lt. comdr. USN, 1969-71. Mem. Sigma Xi. Office: Tex Tech Univ Sch Med-Internal Medicine 1400 Wallace Blvd #C Amarillo TX 79106-1708

WERNER, MARLIN SPIKE, speech pathologist and audiologist; b. Portland, Maine, Aug. 15, 1927; s. Leonard Matthews and Margaret (Steele) W.; m. Caroline Emma Paul, Dec. 23, 1985; children: Leo Hart, Joseph Hart. BA in Sociology and Social Work, U. Mo., 1950; ScM in Audiology and Speech Pathology, Johns Hopkins U., 1957; PhD in Speech and Hearing Sci., Ohio State U., 1966. Lic. in audiology, hearing aid dispensing, speech pathology, Hawaii; lic. in audiology and speech pathology, Calif. Audiologist/speech pathologist, dir. Speech and Hearing Ctr. Asheville (N.C.) Orthopedic Hosp., 1960-64; assoc. prof. speech pathology and audiology We. Carolina U., Cullowhee, N.C., 1965-69; assoc. prof. speech pathology, audiology and speech sci. Fed. City Coll. (now U. D.C.), Washington, 1969-73; pres. Friends of Nepal's Hearing Handicapped, Oakland, Calif., 1979-84; audiologist, speech pathologist pvt. practice, Oakland and Lafayette, Calif., 1973-85; pvt. practice Lafayette, 1985-87; pvt. practice speech pathology and audiology Hilo, Hawaii, 1987—; speech and hearing cons. VA Hosp., Oteen, N.C., 1960-64; clin. cons. Speech and Hearing Clinic, Asheville Orthopedic Hosp., 1966-67; lectr., presenter in field. Contbr. articles to profl. jours.; contbr. to Ency. Brit., Am. Heritage Book of Natural Wonders, others. Mem. hearing impaired svcs. task force State of Hawaii Dept. Health, 1987-88; mem. Hawaii County Mayor's Com. for Persons with Disabilities, 1988-94; adv. bd. Salvation Army, 1992; bd. dirs. Hawaii chpt. Am. Arthritis Found.; past pres. Big Island Safety Assn.; mem. Hawaii Gov.'s Bd. Hearing Aid Dealers and Fitters; mem. adv. com., pres. Older Adult Resource Ctr., Laney Coll., Oakland, Calif.; v.p. Hawaii Speleol. Survey; chmn. Hawaii Grotto of Nat. Speleol. Soc., others; mem. adv. bd. Hilo Bay Clinics. MCH fellow Johns Hopkins U., 1954, Pub. Health fellow Ohio State U., 1964. Fellow Nat. Speleological Soc.; mem. AAAS, Am. Speech and Hearing Assn., Acoustical Soc. Am., Calif. Speech and Hearing Assn., Calif. Writers Club (bd. dirs., past pres.), Hawaii Speech/Lang. Hearing Assn. Home: PO Box 11509 Hilo HI 96721-6509 Office: 400 Hualani St Ste 191-a Hilo HI 96720-4378

WERNER, THOMAS LEE, hospital administrator; b. Hazen, N.D., Dec. 8, 1945; married. BA, Union Coll., 1967; MA, U. Nebr., 1969. Asst. dir. pers. Portland (Oreg.) Adventist Med. Ctr., 1971-72; v.p. Verticare Ambulatory Care Program, Portland, 1972-73; adminstr. Tillamook (Oreg.) CountyGen. Hosp., 1973-77, Walla Walla (Wash.)Gen. Hosp., 1977-81; exec. v.p. Fla. Hosp. Med. Ctr., Orlando, 1981-85, pres., 1985—. Office: Fla Hosp Med Ctr 601 E Rollins St Orlando FL 32803-1248*

WERNER, WALLACE JAMES, family physician; b. Sioux Falls, S.D., June 3, 1944; s. Linus Charles and Thelma Blanche (Sayles) W.; m. Susan Katherine Bisbee Werner, May 22, 1971; children: Jeremy James, Nicholas Scott. BA, Augustana Coll., 1966; MD, Northwestern U., 1970. Intern Chgo. Wesley Meml. Hosp., Chgo., 1970-71; physician Manassas (Va.) Med. Ctr., 1974-83; pvt. practice Manassas, 1983—; chief of staff Prince William Hosp. Med. Staff, Manassas, 1991-93, chmn. bylaws com., 1985-91, 93—, chmn. credential com., 1989-91, chmn. dept. of medicine, 1987-91. With U.S. Army, 1972-74. Mem. AMA, Am. Acad. of Family Practice, Va. Med. Soc., Prince William County Med. Soc. Republican. Methodist. Office: W James Werner MD Family Practice 8575 B Sudley Rd Manassas VA 22110

WERNICK, JUSTIN, podiatrist, educator; b. N.Y.C., Feb. 26, 1936; s. Charles and Ethel (Crown) W.; m. Susan Schoenfeld, Oct. 16, 1960 (div.); children: Elissa, Peter. D Podiatric Medicine, N.Y. Coll. Podiatric Medicine, N.Y.C., 1959. Diplomate Am. Bd. Podiatric Orthopedics. Pvt. practice Seaford, N.Y., 1960-78; co-founder, exec. v.p. Langer Biomechanics Group, Inc., Deer Park, N.Y., 1969—; prof. orthopedics N.Y. Coll. Podiatric Medicine, 1969—; mem. adv. bd. Rockport Shoe Co., Marlboro, Mass., 1988-92; lectr. in field, U.S. and abroad. Co-author: A Practical Manual for a Basic Approach to Biomechanics, 1972; guest editor Jour. Current Podiatric Medicine, 1989; editorial adv. Podiatry Tracts; contbr. Clin. Biomedics of the Lower Extremity, 1995. Fellow Am. Coll. Foot Orthopedics, Am. Acad. Podiatric Sports Medicine; mem. Am. Podiatric Med. Assn., N.Y. State Podiatric Med. Assn. (Podiatrist of Yr. award 1976), Nat. Acad. Practice in Podiatry (Disting. Practitioner award 1985). Republican. Jewish. Home: 271 9P Grand Ctrl Pkwy Floral Park NY 11005 Office: Langer Biomechanics Group 450 Commack Rd Deer Park NY 11729-1200

WERNICK, SHELLEY, neurosurgeon; b. Chgo., May 19, 1944; d. Benjamin H. and Rayzle (Friedman) W.; m. Susan Paula Einbinder, June 28,

1970; children: Aaron, Lisa, Robert, Michael. BS in Biology with honors, U. Ill., 1967, MD, 1971. Asst. prof. neurosurgery Med. Coll. Wis., 1976—; neurosurgeon Milw., 1976—; chief pediatric neurosurgery Childrens Hosp., Wis., 1986—; chief neurosurgery St. Michael Hosp., Sinai Samaritan Hosp., Milw., 1986—. Contbr. articles to profl. jours. Capt. USAR, 1971-77. Named Top Milw. Physician Milw. Mag., 1996. Fellow ACS; mem. AMA, Am. Assn. Neurol. Surgeons (joint sect. trauma and critical care, pediatric sect.), Congress of Neurol. Surgeons, Internat. Neurosurg. Soc. Office: Neurosurg Assocs 2350 W Villard Milwaukee WI 53209-5086

WERNTZ, CHARLES LIVINGSTON, III, physician; b. Lower Merion, Pa., Apr. 14, 1963; s. Charles Livingston, Jr. and Sarah T. (Twiggar) W.; m. Donna Irene Ford, June 8, 1996. BS in Commerce and Engring., Drexel U., 1987; DO, Kirksville Coll. Osteo., Medicine, 1996. Cylinder controller M G Industries, Valley Forge, Pa., 1987-90; prodn. scheduler M G Industries, Fairless Hills, Pa., 1990-92. Driver, attendant, Community Ambulance Assn., Ambler, Pa., 1981—; asst. scoutmaster Boy Scouts of Am., Ambler, 1987—; search mgr. Greater Phila. Search and Rescue, Erdenheim, Pa., 1979—. Mem. Am. Assn. of Family Practitioner, Am. Acad. Osteopathy, The Cranial Acad., ASTM. Lutheran. Home: 120 Atwood Rd Erdenheim PA 19038

WERTH, VICTORIA PATRICIA, dermatologist, educator; b. Chgo., Sept. 1, 1954; d. Michael Wolf and Gloria Ruth (Goldsmith) W.; m. Kevin Jon Williams, Jan. 1, 1983; children: Nathan, Erik, Adrienne. BA in Chemistry, Cath. U., 1976, MS in Phys. Chemistry, 1976; MD, Johns Hopkins U., 1980. Diplomate Am. Bd. Internal Medicine, Am. Bd. Dermatology, Am. Bd. Immunodermatology and Immunopathology. Intern in medicine Northwestern Meml. Hosp., Chgo., 1980-81, resident in internal medicine, 1981-83; resident in dermatology NYU, N.Y.C., 1983-86, chief resident in dermatology, 1985-86, rsch. fellow in dermatology, 1986-88, clin. instr. in dermatology, 1986-89, asst. prof. dermatology, 1986-88 ; rsch. collaborator med. dept. Brookhaven Nat. Lab./Assoc. Univs., Inc., 1986-87; asst. prof. dermatology U. Pa. Sch. Medicine, 1989—; chief div. dermatology Phila. VA Hosp., 1989—; lectr. in field. Author: University of Pennsylvania Manual of Dermatologic Diagnosis and Treatment, 1990, In-Conn's Current Therapy, 1991; contbr. articles to profl. publs. Mem. AMA, Am. Coll. Physicians, Am. Acad. Dermatology (task force on govt. medicine), Dermatology Found., Soc. Investigative Dermatology, Am. Coll. Rheumatology, Phi Beta Kappa. Home: 425 Wister Rd Wynnewood PA 19096-1808 Office: VA Hosp Divsn Dermatology University and Woodland Ave Philadelphia PA 19104

WERTHEIMER, MARC JOEL, internist; b. Phila., July 15, 1949; m. Judy Okin; children: Joshua, Sarah. BA, Swarthmore Coll., 1971; MD, Jefferson Med. Coll., 1975. Diplomate Am. Bd. Internal Medicine. Intern Laukenau Hosp., Phila., 1975-76, resident in internal medicine, 1976-78; pvt. practice Media, Pa.; mem. staff Riddle Meml. Hosp.; mem. staff Riddle Meml. Hosp.; med. cons. A Better Chance, Swarthmore, Pa., Crozer-Chester Med. Ctr., 1987—. Mem. Pa. Med. Soc., Delaware County Med. Soc., Phi Beta Kappa, Alpha Omega Alpha. Office: Clin Care Assoc Univ Pa Health Sys Media PA 19063

WERTLIEB, DONALD LAWRENCE, psychologist, educator; b. Washington, Feb. 22, 1952; s. Norman N. and Helen (Rubin) W.; m. Lorre Beth Polinger, Aug. 12, 1973; children: Joshua Michael, Mollie Rebecca, Miriam Tamar. BS in Psychology summa cum laude, Tufts U., 1974, MA in Child Study, 1975; MA in Psychology, Boston U., PhD in Clin. and Community Psychology, 1979. Instr. psychology Harvard U. Med. Sch., Boston, 1978-81, also staff psychologist Judge Baker Guidance Ctr., Boston, 1978-81; asst. prof. Eliot-Pearson dept. child study Tufts U., Medford, Mass., 1981-86, assoc. prof., 1986-89, chmn., 1989—, chmn. dept. edn. interim, 1990-91; sr. rsch. assoc. Harvard U. Community Health Plan, Boston, 1981-87; mem. faculty Inst. for Health Rsch., Harvard Sch. Pub. Health, 1983-87; lectr. dept. social medicine and health policy, Harvard Med. Sch., 1984-89; cons. mental health svcs. Mem. editorial bd. Profl. Psychology, 1979-82, Jour. Applied Devel. Psychology, 1981—, Jour. Clin. Child Psychology, 1981—, Jour. Pediatric Psychology, 1986—. Carmichael prize scholar, 1973; NIMH tng. fellow, 1974-76; NIMH rsch. grantee, 1977-81, 83-86; Office Spl. Edn. tng. grantee, 1981-83; NIH Biomed. Rsch. grantee, 1982; W.T. Grant Found. grantee, 1982-86; lic. psychologist, Mass. Fellow Am. Orthopsychiat. Assn., Am. Psychol. Soc. (charter); mem. APA, Assn. Advancement Psychology, New Eng. Psychol. Assn., Mass. Psychol. Assn., Boston Inst. Devel. Infants and Parents, Soc. Psychol. Study of Social Issues, Soc. Rsch. in Child Devel., Soc. Pediat. Psychology (pres. 1996—), Phi Beta Kappa, Psi Chi.

WERYHA, GEORGES RICHARD, endocrinology educator; b. Strasbourg, France, Sept. 28, 1955; s. Andrew and Marie-Therese (Ursyn-Niemcewicz) W.; m. Bernadette Litzelmann, Feb. 19, 1982; children: Julien, Michel, Etienne. MD, Faculte de Medecine, Nancy, France, 1986, rheumatologist, 1987, endocrinologist, 1989, internist, 1990. Interne des hopitaux C.H.U. de Nancy, 1981-86, chef de clinique, 1986-90, prof., 1991—. Mem. Soc. Francaise d'Endocrinologie, N.Y. Acad. Scis., Am. Diabetes Assn., Am. Soc. for Bone and Mineral Rsch., Endocrine Soc. Office: Service dEndocrinologie CHU, Rue de Morvan, 54500 Vandoeuvre France

WESBURY, STUART ARNOLD, JR., health administration and policy educator; b. Phila., Dec. 13, 1933; s. Stuart Arnold and Jennie (Glazewska) W.; m. June Carol Davis, Feb. 23, 1957; children: Brian, Brent, Bruce, Bradford. BS, Temple U., 1955; MHA, U. Mich., 1960; PhD, U. Fla., 1972. Commd. pharmacist USPHS, 1955, served as adminstrv. officer, hosp. and clinic pharmacist, resigned, 1958; adminstrv. asst. Del. Hosp., 1960-61; asst. adminstr. Bronson Meth. Hosp., 1961-66; assoc. dir., asst. prof. U. Fla. Tchg. Hosp., 1966-67, dir., assoc. prof., 1967-69; v.p. Computer Mgmt. Corp., Gainesville, Fla., 1969-72; dir., prof. grad. studies in health svcs. mgmt. U. Mo., Columbia, 1972-78; pres. Am. Coll. Healthcare Execs., Chgo., 1979-91; sr. v.p. TriBrook Group, Inc., Westmont, Ill., 1992-94; prof. Sch. of Health Adminstrn. and Policy Ariz. State U., Tempe, 1994—. Coauthor: Why We Spend Too Much on Health Care; contbr. articles to profl. jours. Bd. dirs. Health Task, Inc., Atlanta, Blood Sys., Inc., Scottsdale, Ariz., Boys Clubs, Gainesville, Heartland Inst.; chmn. bd. dirs. Mid-Am. chpt. ARC, 1988-91, DuPage County Dist., 1984-87; active Boy Scouts Am.; chmn. adminstrv. bd. Meth. Ch.; trustee Nat. Blood Found.; Rep. Congl. candidate Dist. 13, Ill. Fellow Am. Coll. Health Care Adminstrs. (hon.), Am. Coll. Healthcare Execs. (Silver Medal award 1991); mem. APHA, Am. Hosp. Assn., Hosp. Mgmt. Sys. Soc., Assn. Univ. Programs in Health Adminstrn. (chmn. 1977-78), Am. Assn. Healthcare Cons. (hon.), Rotary (past pres.). Home: 6711 E Camelback Rd Unit 25 Scottsdale AZ 85251-2064 Office: Ariz State Univ Sch Health Adminstrn Policy PO Box 874506 Tempe AZ 85287-4506

WESCHLER, LOUISE BLUMENAUER, physical therapist; b. Albany, N.Y., June 19, 1948; d. Charles Edward and Louise Clara (Jordan) Blumenauer; m. Charles John Weschler, Aug. 28, 1971. AB in Chemistry, Manhattanville Coll., Purchase, N.Y., 1969; MA in Chemistry, U. Chgo., 1973; BS in Phys. Therapy, NYU, N.Y.C., 1978. Tchr., sci. dept. chmn. Aquinas Dominican High Sch., Chgo., 1970-76; lead therapist Riverview Med. Ctr., Red Bank, N.J., 1978-83; contract therapist Bayshore Hosp., Holmdel, N.J., 1984-87, Marlboro Phys. Therapy, Morganville, N.J., 1987—. Mem. Am. Phys. Therapy Assn., Shore Athletic Club N.J. (Athlete of Yr. 1983), Road Runners Club Am., Jersey Shore Touring Soc. Home: 161 Richdale Rd Colts Neck NJ 07722-1315 Office: Marlboro Phys Therapy 100 Campus Dr Morganville NJ 07751-1253

WESCOTT, WILLIAM BURNHAM, oral pathologist, educator; b. Pendleton, Oreg., Nov. 10, 1922; s. Merton Girard and Josephine (Creasey) W.; m. Barbara L., Dec. 31, 1944 (dec. June 12, 1969); children: William Douglas, Diane Elizabeth; m. Gloria Greer-Collins, Aug. 28, 1989. DMD, U. Oreg., Portland, 1951, MS, 1962. Asst. prof. to assoc. dean admin. U. Oreg. Dental Sch., Portland, 1953-72; co-dir. oral disease rsch. VA, Houston, 1972-75; dir. dental edn. ctr. VA, L.A., 1980-85; acting dir. Reg. Med. Edn. Ctr., Birmingham, Ala., 1978-80; chief dental svc. Dept. of Veteran's Affairs, San Francisco, 1985-94; clin. prof. U. Calif., San Francisco, 1994—; dental surgeon, Oreg. Air N.G., Portland, 1954-68; cons. Madigan Army Med. Ctr., Ft. Lewis, W. Va., 1971-74, VA Med. Ctrs., No. Calif., 1985—, prof. pathology Duke U. Med. Sch., 1977-79. Contbr. articles to profl. jours. Dist. chmn. Boys Scouts Am., Portland, 1965-67; bd. dirs. Am. Cancer Soc., Portland, 1964-67; sr. vice comdr. Veterans Foreign Wars Post 5731, Gridley, Calif., 1994—. Lt. Col. U.S. Army, 1942-68. Decorated DFC, USAF, Oreg. N.G. Merit Svc. Medal, Portland. Fellow Am. Acad. Oral and Maxillofacial Pathology, Omicron Kappa Upsilon, Sigma Xi. Home: 437 Justeson Rd Gridley CA 95948 Office: U Calif Sch of Dentistry S 512 San Francisco 3rd & Parnassus San Francisco CA 94143-0424

WESLEY, ROBERT COOK, dental educator; b. Jamestown, Ky., Aug. 19, 1926; s. Hulen Harrison and Bertie Marie (Cook) W.; m. Betty Jean Coffey, Feb. 21, 1953; children: Robert Cook II, Leigh Ann. BA, Berea Coll., 1950; DMD, U. Louisville, 1954. Dentist Berea (Ky.) Hosp., 1954-55; pvt. practice, Berea, 1955-65, Lexington, Ky., 1965-67; vis. prof. U. So. Calif., L.A., 1970-71; mem. faculty U. Ky. Dental Sch., Lexington, 1967—, asst. prof., 1967-72, assoc. prof., 1972—; assoc. prof. Univ. Hosp., Lexington, 1972-93; prof. emeritus, 1993—; vis. prof. U. So. Calif., 1970-71; cons. VA, Lexington, 1971-76. Contbr. articles to dental jours., chpts. to book. With USN, 1944-46, PTO. Mem. ADA, Ky. Dental Assn., Bluegrass Dental Soc., Am. Prosthodontic Soc., Southeastern Acad. Prosthodontics (pres. 1984-85, Fedn. Prosthodontics Orgns. (pres. 1988-89). Office: U Ky Med Pla Lexington KY 40536

WESSLER, STANFORD, physician, educator; b. N.Y.C., Apr. 20, 1917; S. Hugo and Minerva (Miller) W.; m. Margaret Barnet Muhlfelder, Dec. 17, 1942; children—John Stanford, Stephen Lawrence, James Hugh. Grad., Fieldston Sch., N.Y.C., 1934; B.A., Harvard, 1938; M.D., N.Y.U., 1942. From fellow to asst. prof. medicine Harvard U. Med. Sch., 1946-64; from resident to assoc. chief med. svc. Beth Israel Hosp., Boston, 1946-64; prof. medicine Washington U. Sch. Medicine, St. Louis, 1964-74; John L. and Adalaine Simon prof. Washington U. Sch. Medicine, 1966-74; prof. medicine, assoc. dean postgrad. programs NYU Sch. Medicine, 1974-90; physician in chief Jewish Hosp., St. Louis, 1964-74; assoc. physician Barnes Hosp., St. Louis, 1964-74; attending physician NYU Med. Center, Univ. Hosp., N.Y.C., 1974-90, Bellevue Hosp. Center, N.Y.C., 1974-90, Manhattan VA Hosp. Med. Ctr., 1974-90; mem. coms. NRC, Inst. of Medicine, Nat. Heart, Lung and Blood Inst.; bd. dirs. N.Y. Heart Assn., 1980-86; pres. Council Continuing Med. Edn., N.Y., 1979-85. Contbr. articles on vascular disease.; mem. editorial bds. jours. in field. Served with M.C. AUS, 1943-46. Recipient James A. Mitchell award, 1972. Mem. Am. Physiol. Soc., Am. Soc. Clin. Investigation, Assn. Am. Physicians, Am. Heart Assn. (investigator 1955-59, bd. dirs. 1971-76, chmn. publs. com. 1972-76, chmn. coun. on thrombosis 1974-76, v.p. 1974-76, mem. sci. adv. com. 1986-90 Merit award 1978, Disting. Achievement award 1989), Alpha Omega Alpha. Home: 60 Rye Rd Rye NY 10580-2228

WESSMAN, HENRY CLAIR, physical therapist, state agency administrator; b. St. Cloud, Minn., Sept. 17, 1937; s. Henry Claus and Jessie Margaret (Lindberg) W.; m. Lorraine Alice Johnson, Aug. 3, 1957; children: Vicki, Bruce, Valerie, Bradley, Desiree. BS with distinction, U. Minn., 1959, MS in Phys. Therapy/Psychology, 1965; JD, U. N.D., 1989. Bar: N.D.; cert. phys. therapist, Minn., N.D., S.D.; lic. nursing home adminstr., Minn., N.D. Chief phys. therapy St. Francis Hosp., Crookston, Minn., 1959-62; instr. phys. therapy U. Minn., Mpls., 1965-67; chief clin. phys. therapy Northwood (N.D.) Deaconess Hosp. and Home, 1971-89; prof. div. continuing edn. U. N.D., Grand Forks, 1985-92; prof., chmn. phys. therapy U. N.D. Sch. Medicine, 1967-93; exec. dir. Dept. Human Svcs., State of N.D., Bismarck, 1993—; adj. prof. health law U. N.D., Grand Forks, 1990-92; adj. prof. health law/policy U. of Mary, Bismarck, 1993—; fellow health law inst. Cleveland Marshall Law Sch./Cleve. clinic, 1990; expert witness Tech. Assistance Svc. for Attys., Phoenix, 1989-92; corp. bd. dirs. United Hosp., Grand Forks, 1982-92. Contbr. numerous articles to profl. jours. Mayor, City of Grand Forks, 1980-88, mem. City Coun., 1974-80; mem. Ho. of Reps., N.D. State Legislature, Bismarck, 1978-80. Recipient Phys. Therapy Svc. award N.D. Phys. Therapy Assn., 1980; named Outstanding State Legislator, N.D. Wildlife Fedn., 1979, N.D. Health Care Profl. of Yr., Gov.'s Commn. on Employment of People with Disabilities, 1990. Mem. ABA, Am. Phys. Therapy Assn. (accreditation team leader), Am. Pub. Welfare Assn. (dir. 1993—), Am. Coll. Healthcare Adminstrn. Republican. Mem. Evang. Free Ch. Am. Home: 809 Juniper Pl Bismarck ND 58501 Office: ND Dept Human Svcs 600 E Boulevard Ave Bismarck ND 58505

WESSMAN, JOAN FEENEY, nurse administrator; b. Phila., Mar. 28, 1950; d. Walter James and Elizabeth Mary (Nangle) Benns; children: Megan, Kate, Matthew; m. Robert E. Wessman, Apr. 1993. Diploma in nursing, Fairview Gen. Hosp. Sch. Nsg., Cleve., 1971; BS in Nursing, Miami U., Oxford, Ohio, 1981; MS, Ohio State U., 1982. RN, Ohio. Staff nurse Southwest Gen. Hosp., Berea, Ohio, 1971; staff/charge nurse Children's Med. Ctr., Dayton, Ohio, 1971-72, Mercy Hosp., Hamilton, Ohio, 1973-74; supr. McCullough Hyde Meml. Hosp., Oxford, Ohio, 1974-78; staff nurse St. Elizabeth Med. Ctr., Dayton, 1978-79, instr., coord., 1979-80, supr., 1980-83; dir. nursing Miami Valley Hosp., Dayton, 1983-87; sr. v.p. nursing Akron (Ohio) Gen. Med. Ctr., Akron, Ohio, 1987-90; sr. v.p. patient svcs. Akron (Ohio) Gen. Med. Ctr., 1990—; adj. faculty mem. U. Akron, 1987—, Kent (Ohio) State U., 1987—; mem. VHA Cen. Nurse Exec. Task Force, Nat. Nursing Adv. Coun., Health Care Forum; mem. Midwest Alliance in Nursing, 1992—. Adv. bd. mem. Recruitment and Retention Report, 1989—; contbr. articles to profl. jours. Mem. adv. com. ARC, Dayton, 1987; mem. program com. Midwest Alliance in Nursing, 1992—; chair Pvt. Industry Coun., 1991-92, chair, 1992—; mem. adv. bd. Recruitment and Retention Report, 1989—. Recipient Rsch. Incentive award Wright State U., 1986, Excellence in Nursing Leadership award Delta Omega, 1990; Johnson and Johnson Wharton fellow 1991. Mem. AACN, Am. Orgn. Nurse Execs., Am. Hosp. Assn., Ohio Orgn. Nursing Execs. (pres. 1992—), Ohio Hosp. Assn., Ohio Nurses Assn. (del.), Pentagon Coun. (chmn. 1989), Women's Network, Health Care Forum, Nat. League for Nursing, Phi Kappa Phi, Sigma Theta Tau. Episcopalian. Office: Akron Gen Med Ctr 400 Wabash Ave Akron OH 44307-2433

WESSON, DONALD EVERETT, medical educator, physician; b. St. Louis, June 14, 1953; s. Garlen and Rose Marie (Harris) W.; divorced 1984; m. Wanda Jean Ford, July 6,1985; children: David Earl Hasani W., Donald Ernest Hamadi W. BS, MIT, 1974; MD, Baylor Coll. Med., 1978. Med. resident Baylor Coll. Med., Houston, 1978-81; rsch. fellow U. Ill. Med. Sch., Chgo., 1981-83; from instr. to asst. prof. med. Baylor Coll. Med., Houston, 1983-91, assoc. prof. med., 1991-94; prof. med. and physiology Texas Tech U. Health Scis. Ctr., Lubbock, Tex., 1994—. Author (textbooks): Blackwell's Basics in Medicine, 1991, 5th rev. edit. 1995. Mem. adv. bd. Nat. Kidney Found., N.Y.C., 1993—; mem. 100 Black Men of Am., 1994—.

WEST, BOB, pharmaceutical company executive; b. Ellenville, N.Y., Mar. 7, 1931; s. Harry and Elsie May Wicentowsky; m. Betty Parker, May 9, 1957 (div.); children: Debra Ellen, Elizabeth Ann, Sharon Lynn; m. Jacqueline Cutler, Jan. 3, 1982. BS, Union U., 1952; MS, Purdue U., 1954, PhD, 1956; postgrad. mgmt. seminar, U. Chgo., 1972. Pres., dir. research Food, Drug, Chem. Svcs., Stamford, Conn., 1975—; pres., dir. research Bob West Assocs., Inc., Stamford, 1975—; pres. Drug Info. Assn., Phila., 1974-75; sci. adv. bd. Fountain Pharms., Inc., Largo, Fla., 1993—. Editorial bd. Drug Info. Assn. Jour., Phila., 1977-85; contbr. articles to profl. jours. Mem. ASPET, Am. Soc. Toxicology, Acad. Pharm. Scis., Assn. Rsch. Dirs., Drug Info. Assn., Assn. Univ. Tech. Mgrs. Home and office: Food Drug Chem Svcs 3771 Center Way Fairfax VA 22033-2602

WEST, BRANDON ALAN, podiatrist, lawyer, law educator; b. Detroit, July 27, 1960; s. Edgar and Sandra Beth (Ellis) W. BS, Mich. State U., 1982; DPM, Ohio Coll. Podiatric Medicine, Cleve., 1986; JD, Detroit Coll. Law, 1991. Bar: Mich. Podiatric bd. cert. Am. Coll. Podiatric Physicians & Surgeons. Pvt. practice podiatrist Detroit, 1987—, pvt. practice lawyer, 1992—; bus. law instr. Oakland Cmty. Coll., Auburn Hills, Mich., 1992—; small claims mediator Southfield (Mich.) Dist. Ct., 1993—. V.p. Oakbrook Village Condo Assn., Walled Lake, Mich., 1994—. Mem. Mich. Bar Assn. Home: 21120 Constitution Southfield MI 48076 Office: 20400 W Warren Detroit MI 48228

WEST, CHARLES MICHAEL, physician, consultant; b. Ann Arbor, Mich., Jan. 16, 1947; s. Clark Darwin and Ruthann (Asbury) W.; m. Lucia Berger; 1 child, Jonathan Michael. BA, Coll. of Wooster, 1969; MD, U. Cin., 1973. Bd. cert. in internal medicine and infectious diseases. Intern U. Wis., Madison, 1973-74, resident, 1974-76; epidemiologist Ctrs. for Disease Control, Atlanta, 1976-78, Pan Am. Health Orgn., Port of Spain, Trinidad, 1978-80; fellow in infectious diseases U. Colo., Denver, 1980-82; instr. in infectious diseases Nat. Jewish Hosp., Denver, 1982-83; pvt. practice St. Francis Hosp., Topeka, 1983—. Lt. comdr. USPHS, 1976-80. Home: 5700 SW 38th St Topeka KS 66610 Office: C Michael West MD PA 2200 SW 6th St # 107 Topeka KS 66606

WEST, DANIEL JONES, JR., hospital administrator, rehabilitaton counselor, health care consultant, educator; b. Coaldale, Pa., Sept. 19, 1949; s. Daniel J. and Mildred Elizabeth (Kreiger) W.; m. Linda Jean Werdt, Sep. 18, 1971; children: Jeffrey Bryan, Christopher Jones, Danielle K. BS cum laude, Pa. State U., 1971, EdM summa cum laude, 1972, PhD in Counseling Psychology summa cum laude, 1982; postgrad., Montgomery County Community Coll., 1973, Rutgers U., 1974. Diplomate Am. Acad. Behavioral Medicine, Am. Acad. Med. Adminstrs. Adminstr. Good Samaritan Hosp., Pottsville, Pa., 1975-78, asst. v.p. ambulatory svcs., 1978-83; adminstr. MEDIQ, Inc., Scranton (Pa.) State Hosp., 1983-85; pres., CEO HTC Consulting Group, Inc., Gouldsboro, Pa., 1986—; dir., assoc. prof. U. Scranton, 1990—; adj. prof. Pa. State U., 1974-83, U. Scranton, 1983-90, Wilkes Coll., 1986; CEO Medi-Group, Inc., Penn Health Care, Inc., A.I.R., Inc., Med. Sci. Lab., Inc., Lackawanna Med. Group, P.C., Scranton, 1986-91; stockholder, ptnr. Penn Health Care, Inc., 1987—, Health Care Support Svcs., Scranton, 1993—; stockholder, bd. dirs. Northeast Women's Diagnostic Ctr., Scranton, 1989—; regional dir. ops. HCP Consulting Group, Inc., Willow Grove, Pa., 1990—; moderator First Ann. Conf. on Drug and Alcohol Abuse, Bedford, Pa., 1977; mem. adv. com. to rehab. counseling programs Pa. State U., 1983—; numerous positions Stte Bd. of Medicine, Commonwealth of Pa., 1991—; mem. departmental review bd. for rsch. U. Scranton, 1991—; mem. Scranton Temple residency program instnl. rev. bd. Mercy Hosp., 1991—; mem. Fedn. of State Med. Bd. of U.S., Inc., 1994—, mem. editl. adv. bd., 1984-85, voting del. from Pa. for osteopathic bd.; bd. dirs. comm. com. Midwest Regional Med. Bd., 1994—; mem. task force on health care Econ. Devel. Coun. Northeast Pa., 1994—; bd. dirs. Friendship House, 1995—; bd. dirs. Robert Charles Zaloga Found., 1994—; spkr. in field. Author manuals on mgmt. and health care; contbr. articles to profl. jours. Chmn. planning and implementation coun. Schuylkill County Gov.'s Coun. on Drug and Alcohol Abuse, State of Pa., 1973-74; mem. Drug Adv. Task Force, 1973-74, Task Force Child and Family Resource Devel. Program, Schuylkill County, 1973—, Criminal Justice Sys. Task Force, Schuylkill County, 1975—; mem. adv. bd. Holy Family Home Health Care Agy., Schuylkill County, 1977—, chmn. bd. edn. com., 1977—; bd. dirs. St. David's Soc. Schuylkill and Carbon Counties, 1976—, Health Sys. Agy., Northeast Pa., 1977—; mem. instnl. review bd. Cmty. Med. Ctr., 1986—; bd. dirs. Scranton Counseling Ctr., 1990—, mem. long range planning com. and personnel com.; bd. dirs. Telespond Sr. Svcs., Inc., 1991—; mem. Diocesan health care com. Diocese of Scranton, 1992—; mem. steering com. Citizen Advocacy Ctr., AARP Health Advocacy Svcs., 1992—; bd. dirs., v.p. Citizen Advocacy Ctr., Arlington, Va., 1994—; mem. ad hoc com. on children health United Way, 1995—. Recipient Rsch. award Am. Ednl. Rsch. Assn., 1983, Svc. and Leadership award Schuylkill County Drug and Alcohol Exec. Comm., 1982, Dedication and Leadership award Gov.'s Coun. Drug and Alcohol Abuse Drug Adv. Task Force, 1978; Fellow Accreditating Commn. Edn. for Health Svcs. Adminstrn., 1994-95. Fellow Am. Acad. Med. Adminstrs. (editl. com. 1993—), Internat. Acad. Behavioral Medicine, Counseling and Psychotherapy, Inc., Am. Coll. Healthcare Execs. (regents adv. bd. Pa. Area B 1995—), Fedn. State Med. Bds. US, Inc. (editl. com. 1994—), Coll. Osteo. Healthcare Execs. (editl. com. 1991—), Am. Coll. Med. Practice Execs., Am. Coll. Health Care Adminstrs., Assn. Mental Health Adminstrs. (cert., editl. com. 1992—); mem. APHA, AAAS, Nat. Rehab. Assn., Nat. Rehab. Adminstrn. Assn., Am. Hosp. Assn., Med. Group Mgmt. Assn., Hosp. Assn. Pa., Pa. Rehab. Assn., Pa. Med. Group Mgmt. Assn., Phi Kappa Phi, Iota Alpha Delta. Address: RD # 1 Skyline Acres 101 Birch St Gouldsboro PA 18424

WEST, GARY JOHN, physician assistant; b. Albion, Nebr., July 17, 1953; s. John William and Wilma Jean (Hunter) W.; m. Joan Eileen Gasseling, June 3, 1978; children: Kathleen, Bryan, Anna. BS, U. Nebr., 1976. Health aide U. Nebr., Lincoln, 1972-73, health aide coord., 1973-74; physician asst. O'Neill Family Practice, O'Neill, Nebr., 1976-77, Benthack Clinic, Wayne, 1977-93, N.E. Nebr. Med. Group, Wayne, 1993—; physician asst. student health Wayne State Coll., 1977—; active med. staff Providence Med. Ctr., Wayne, 1977—; mem. human and legal rights com. Region IV Svcs., Wayne, 1980-83; guest faculty emergency med. svcs. divsn. N.E. Tech. Coll., Norfolk, Nebr., 1978-92. Pres. St. Mary's Bd. Edn., Wayne, 1983-86; mem., sec. St. Mary's Parish Coun., Wayne, 1986-89; bd. pres., mem. Haven House, Wayne, 1984-95; bd. mem. Wayne child Care Devel. Bd., 1992-95; mem. N.E. Nebr. Emergency Med. Svcs. Adv. Com., 1986-90; CPR instr., instr. trainer ACLS, instr. affiliate faculty Nebr. Heart Assn., 1977-90. Named one of Outstanding Young Men Am., 1983, 844th Point of Light Pres. George Bush, 1991. Fellow Nebr. Acad. Physician Assts. (mem. legis. com. 1984-86, Physician Asst. of Yr. 1995); mem. Am. Acad. Physician Assts., CyclePaths Bicycle Club (founder, pres. 1989—). Roman Catholic. Home: 217 W 11th St Wayne NE 68787 Office: NE Nebr Med Group 615 E 14th Wayne NE 68787

WEST, JAMES EDWARD, surgeon; b. Knoxville, Tenn., Apr. 29, 1939; s. James Paul and Lone Mae (Woods) W.; m. Betsy Lou Renfro, June 10, 1960; children: James E. Jr., Jennifer Lou Frye, Joseph. BS, MD, U. Tenn., 1963. Diplomate Am. Bd. Surgery. Pvt. practice, 1963—; pres. Fedn. State Med. Bds., 1996-97. Maj. U.S. Army, 1969-71, Viet Nam. Named one of Faces of Destiny Montgomery (Ala.) C. of C., 1995. Office: Surgical Clinic of Aniston 901 Leighton Ste 702 Anniston AL 36207-5703

WEST, JOHN BURNARD, physiologist, educator; b. Adelaide, Australia, Dec. 27, 1928; came to U.S., 1969; s. Esmond Frank and Meta Pauline (Spehr) W.; m. Penelope Hall Banks, Oct. 28, 1967; children: Robert Burnard, Joanna Ruth. M.B.B.S., Adelaide U., 1951, M.D., 1958, D.Sc., 1980; Ph.D., London U., 1960; Dr. honoris causa, U. Barcelona, Spain, 1987. Resident Royal Adelaide Hosp., 1952, Hammersmith Hosp., London, 1953-55; physiologist Sir Edmund Hillary's Himalayan Expdn., 1960-61; dir. respiratory research group Postgrad. Med. Sch., London, 1962-67; reader medicine Postgrad. Med. Sch., 1968; prof. medicine and physiology U. Calif. at San Diego, 1969—; Wiltshire lectr., London, 1977, Schwidetzky lectr., 1975, Fleischner lectr., 1977, Robertson lectr. Adelaide U., 1978, McClement lectr. NYU, 1996; leader Am. Med. Rsch. Expdn. to Mt. Everest, 1981; U.S. organizer China-U.S. Conf. on respiratory failure, Nanjing, 1986; mem. life scis. adv. com. NASA, 1985-88, task force sci. uses of space sta., 1984-87, aerospace med. adv. com., 1988-89, chmn. sci. verification com. Spacelab SLS-1, 1983-92; prin. investigator Spacelabs SLS 1, 2, LMS, Neurolab, 1983—; co-investigator European Spacelabs, D2, Euromir, 1987—; mem. commn. on respiratory physiol., 1985—; mem. commn. on clin. physiol., 1991—, mem. commn. gravitation physiol., 1986—; mem. U.S. nat. com. Internat. Union Physiol. Scis., 1984-87; mem. study sect. NIH, chmn., 1973-75; external examiner Nat. U. Singapore, 1995. Author: Ventilation/Blood Flow and Gas Exchange, 1965, Respiratory Physiology-The Essentials, 1974, Translations in Respiratory Physiology, 1975, Pulmonary Pathophysiology-The Essentials, 1977, Translations in Respiratory Physiology, 1977, Bioengineering Aspects of the Lung, 1977, Regional Differences in the Lung, 1977, Pulmonary Gas Exchange (2 vols.), 1980, High Altitude Physiology, 1981, High Altitude and Man, 1984, Everest-The Testing Place, 1985, Best and Taylor's Physiological Basis of Medical Practice, 1985, 91, Study Guide for Best and Taylor, 1985, High Altitude Medicine and Physiology, 1989, The Lung: Scientific Foundations, 1991, Lung Injury, 1992. Recipient Ernest Jung prize for medicine, Hamburg, 1977, Presdl. citation Am. Coll. Chest Physicians, 1977, Reynolds Prize for history Am. Physiol. Soc., 1987; I.J. Flance lectr. Washington U., 1978; G.C. Griffith lectr. Am. Heart Assn., 1978; scholar Macy Found., 1974; Kaiser teaching award 1980; W.A. Smith lectr. Med. Coll. S.C., 1982; S.C., 1982; S. Kronheim lectr. Undersea Med. Soc., 1984; D.W. Richards lectr. Am. Heart Assn., 1980, E.M. Papper lectr. Columbia U., 1981, I.S. Ravdin lectr. ACS, 1982, Burns Amberson lectr. Am. Thoracic Soc., 1984, Harry G. Armstrong lectr. Aerospace Med. Assn., 1984, Annual Space Life Scis. lectr. Federation Associated Socs. of Exptl. Biology, 1991, Hermann Rahn lectr. SUNY Buffalo, 1992, Menkes lectr. Johns Hopkins, 1992, Jeffries Med. Rsch. award AIAA, 1992; Macallum lectr. U. Toronto, Can., 1989, Macleod lectr. Southampton U., U.K., 1990, Bulatto lectr. U. Philippines, Manila, 1990, Mohaideen lectr. L.I. Coll., Bklyn., 1992, Bullard lectr. Uniformed Svcs. U., Bethesda, Md., 1993, Raven lectr. Am. Coll. Sports Medicine, Dallas, 1995; external examiner Nat. U. Singapore, 1995. Fellow Royal Coll. Physicians (London), Royal Australasian Coll. Physicians, Royal Geog. Soc. (London), AAAS (med. sci. nominating com. 1987-93, coun. del. sect. med. scis.), Am. Inst. for Med. and Biol. Engring. (founder fellow 1992), Internat. Soc. for Mountain Medicine (pres. 1991-94); mem. NAS (com. space biology and medicine 1986-90, subcom. on space biology 1984-85, com. advanced space tech. 1992-94, panel on small spacecraft tech. 1994), Nat. Bd. Med. Examiners (physiology test com. 1973-76), Am. Physiol. Soc. (pres. 1984-85, coun. 1981-86, chmn. sct. on history of physiology 1984-92, hist. pubs. adv. com.), Am. Soc. Clin. Investigation, Physiol. Soc. Gt. Britain, Am. Thoracic Soc., Assn. Am. Physicians, Westessn. Physicians, Russian Acad. Sci. (elected fgn. mem.), Explorers Club, Fleischner Soc. (pres. 1985), Harveian Soc. (London), Royal Instn. Gt. Britain, Royal Soc. Medicine (London), Hurlingham Club (London), La Jolla Beach & Tennis Club. Home: 9626 Blackgold Rd La Jolla CA 92037-1110 Office: U Calif San Diego Sch Medicine 0623 Dept Medicine La Jolla CA 92093

WEST, RAYMOND L., nurse; b. Newport News, Va., July 28, 1968; s. Raymond and Louise (Gray) W. AAS cum laude, Thomas Nelson Community Coll., Hampton, Va., 1990; BS cum laude, Med. Coll. Va., 1992. Qualified in Pediat. Advanced Life Support, 1995; cert. pediat. nurse. Staff nurse Williamsburg Commun. Hosp., 1992-93, Children's Hosp. of the Kings Daus., 1993—; mem. Coordinating Coun. Progressive Care Unit, 1995; mem. Progressive Care Unit Logistic Com., 1995; mem. adv. bd. Thomas Nelson C.C. Sch. of Nursing, 1994—. Mem. Sentara Hampton Gen. Hosp. Aux., 1984—, Am. Heart Assn., 1988-89. With USAF, 1987. Mem. AACN, ANA, Nat. League for Nursing, Va. Nurses Assn. (treas. dist. 10 1994—), Va. Commonwealth U.-Med. Coll. Va. Alumni Assn., Thomas Nelson C.C. Alumni Assn., Soc. of Pediatric Nurses, Am. Pediat. Surg. Nurses Assn.

WEST, ROBERT RANYARD, epidemiologist, educator; b. Auchencairn, Scotland, Sept. 15, 1940; s. Ranyard and Jean (Fleming) W. BA, Oxford (Eng.) U., 1963, MA, 1966; PhD, Leeds (Eng.) U., 1969. Tchr. 6th form math. Rugby Sch., 1964; lectr. in physics Mid. East Tech. U., Ankara, 1965; rsch. physicist Leeds U., 1966-69; rsch. fellow Univ. Coll. Cardiff, 1970-72; from lectr. to sr. lectr. to reader in epidemiology Coll. Medicine, U. Wales, Cardiff, 1972—; vis. scientist U. Tampere, Finland, 1975; rsch. scientist WHO, Geneva, 1979; cons. epidemiologist Dept. Health, New Zealand, 1981, WHO, Tanzania, 1986. Author, editor: Cardiac Rehabilitation, 1995; author: Urgent and Emergency Admission to Hospital, 1995; contbr. numerous articles to profl. jours. Rsch. grantee MRC, 1989, NHS, 1989, 94. Fellow Royal Statis. Soc.; mem. Faculty Pub. Health Medicine (hon.), Brit. Cardiac Soc. (audit com. 1990—), Soc. for Social Medicine (com. mem. 1990-94). Office: U Wales, Coll Medicine, Cardiff CF4 4XN, Wales

WEST, ROBERT SUMNER, surgeon; b. Bowman, N.D., Nov. 20, 1935; s. Elmer and Minnie (DeBode) W.; m. Martha W. Hopkins, Mar. 23, 1957; children: Stephen, Christopher, Anna Marie, Catherine, Sarah. BA, U. N.D., 1957, BS in Medicine, 1959; MD, Harvard U., 1961. Diplomate Am. Bd. Surgery. Intern U.S. Naval Hosp., Chelsea, Mass., 1961-62; resident in surgery U. Vt. Med. Ctr. Hosp., 1965-69; pvt. practice Coeur d'Alene, Idaho, 1969—; coroner Kootenai County, Coeur d'Alene, 1984—. Trustee, pres. Coeur d'Alene Sch. Dist. 271 Bd. Edn., 1973-77. Lt. M.C., USN, 1960-65. Fellow ACS (pres. Idaho chpt. 1985, gov. at large); mem. Idaho Med. Assn. (pres. 1989-90, trustee), Kiwanis. Republican. Lutheran. Office: 920 W Ironwood Dr Coeur D Alene ID 83814-2643

WEST, TIMOTHY EUGENE, physician; b. Indpls., Mar. 20, 1948; s. Earl Irvin and Lois L. (Hinds) W.; m. Marcia E. Rives, June 5, 1970; children: Michael, Nathaniel. BS, Harding U., 1970; MD, Ind. U., 1974. Resident Med. U. S.C., Charleston, 1974-78; asst. prof. medicine SUNY, Buffalo, 1981-86; physician pvt. practice, Charleston, 1986—. Fellow Med. U. S.C., 1979-81.

WEST, WARWICK REED, JR., biology educator; b. Evington, Va., Feb. 9, 1922; s. Warwick Reed and Otelia (Woodford) W.; m. Alyce Liggon Johnson, May 29, 1946; children—Warwick Reed III, Leila, Jane. B.S., Lynchburg Coll., 1943; Ph.D., U. Va., 1952. Instr. biology Lynchburg Coll., 1946-49; asst. prof. biology U. Richmond (Va.), 1952-56, assoc. prof., 1956-66, prof., 1966-88, prof. emeritus, 1988—, chmn. dept. biology, 1965-85. Served with USMCR, 1943-46. Mem. AAUP, Va. Acad. Sci., Assn. Southeastern Biologists, Navy League (life mem.), Marine Corps League (life mem.), Sigma Xi. Methodist. Home: 6806 Lakewood Dr Richmond VA 23229-6931

WESTCOTT, JOHN ALLEN, health facility administrator; b. Plainfield, N.J., Aug. 8, 1935; s. John Amos and Frieda (Leonhardt) W.; m. Margarete Braun, June 13, 1957; children: Karen, Kean, Kevin. B Engring. cum laude, Yale U., 1957; MS, Stanford U., 1967. Registered profl. engr., Mass. Commd. ens. USN, 1957, advanced through grades to capt., ret., 1985; v.p. Northwestern Meml. Hosp., Chgo., 1986—. Bd. dirs. United Way, Ventura County, Calif., 1984-85. Home: 675 Revere Rd Glen Ellyn IL 60137

WESTERDAHL, JOHN BRIAN, nutritionist, health educator; b. Tucson, Dec. 3, 1954; s. Jay E. and Margaret (Meyer) W.; m. Doris Mui Lian Tan, Nov. 18, 1989. AA, Orange Coast Coll., 1977; BS, Pacific Union Coll., 1979; MPH, Loma Linda U., 1981. Registered dietitian; chartered herbalist; cert. nutrition specialist. Nutritionist, health educator Castle Med. Ctr., Kailua, Hawaii, 1981-84, health promotion coord., 1984-87, asst. dir. health promotion, 1987-88, dir. health promotion, 1988-89; dir. nutrition and health rsch. Health Sci., Santa Barbara, Calif., 1989-90; sr. nutritionist, project mgr. Shaklee Corp., San Francisco, 1990-96; dir. nutrition Dr. McDougall's Right Foods, Inc., South San Francisco, 1996—; mem. faculty staff, dir. continuing edn. Am. Acad. Nutrition, 1996—; talk show host Nutrition and You, Sta. KGU Radio, Honolulu, 1983-89; nutrition com. mem. Hawaii div. Am. Heart Assn., Honolulu, 1984-87; mem. nutrition study group Govs. Conf. Health Promotion and Disease Prevention for Hawaii, 1985. Editor: Nourish Mag., 1995-96; nutrition editor: Veggie Life Mag., 1995—. Mem. AAAS, Am. Coll. Sports Medicine, Am. Dietetic Assn., Am. Nutritionists Assn., Am. Coll. Nutrition, Soc. for Nutrition Edn., Nat. Wellness Assn., Nutrition Today Soc., Am. Soc. Pharmacognosy, Inst. Food Technologists, Hawaii Nutrition Coun. (v.p. 1983-86,m pres.-elect 1988-89, pres. 1989), Hawaii Dietetic Assn., Calif. Dietetic Assn., N.Y. Acad. Scis., Seventh-day Adventist Dietetic Assn., several other profl. assns. Republican. Seventh-Day Adventist. Office: Dr McDougall's Right Foods 101 Utah Ave South San Francisco CA 94080

WESTERHAUS, CATHERINE K., social worker; b. Corydon, Ind., Oct. 13, 1910; d. Anthony Joseph and Permelia Ann (Mathes) Kannapel; m. George Henry Westerhaus, Apr. 15, 1950. BEd in Music, Kans. U., 1934; MSW, Loyola U., Chgo., 1949. Cert. Acad. Cert. Social Workers. Clin. social worker Friendly Acres Home of Aged, Newton, Kans.; county welfare dir., state adult svcs. supr. Newton-Harvey County, State of Kans.; vol. cert. social worker Newton. Project dir.: Memories of War Years, 1995, The War Years Including Veterans of Harvey County, Kansas, 1995; contbr. articles to profl. jours. With USNR, 1945-46. Named Kans. Social Worker of Yr., 1975. Mem. NASW (cert.), Kans. Soc. Cert. Social Work, Am. Legion (comdr. Wayne G. Austin post 1981-82). Home: 313 W Broadway St Newton KS 67114-2631

WESTERHOLD, RUTH ELIZABETH, psychologist, educator; b. Youngstown, Ohio, Aug. 4, 1926; d. Samuel Gordon and Grace Elizabeth (Green) Meadows; BS, Youngstown U., 1946; postgrad. Ohio U., 1947, U. Ill., 1947-49; PhD, So. Ill. U., 1978; m. Walter Charles Westerhold, June 1, 1949; children: Marsha L., Carl E. Chief clin. psychologist Alton (Ill.) State Hosp., 1952-55; psychologist St. Louis (Mo.) County Spl. Sch. Dist., 1963-68; chief psychologist Kaskaskia Spl. Edn. Dist., Centralia, Ill., 1968-78; dir. learning communications E. Miss. Jr. Coll., Scooba, 1978-83, coordinator instnl. techniques, 1987—, coordinator devel. edn., 1987-88; consulting psychologist div. vocat. rehab. State of Ill., Alton, 1954-55. USPHS fellow, U. Ill., 1947-49. Cert. school psychologist, Mo., Ill. Mem. Soc. Sci. Exploration, Psi Chi Counselor, lectr., writer ethics-morality, health and nutrition, body-mind relationships, child-rearing, family, learning. Home: 1887 Summertree Rd Starkville MS 39759

WESTERMAN, ERIC LANE, epidemiologist; b. Velasco, Tex., June 21, 1946; s. Herman and Helen (Jircik) W.; m. Harriet Virginia Heaps, Apr. 29, 1968; children: Tracey Lynn, Meredith Lane. BS, U. Tex., 1969; MD, Baylor Coll. Medicine, 1972. Diplomate Am. Bd. Internal Medicine and Infectious Diseases. Pvt. practice infectious diseases Tulsa, 1977—; med. dir., v.p. Partnership Health Orgn., Tulsa, 1994—; med. dir. Hillcrest Svc. Co., Tulsa, 1994-95; sr. v.p. Hillcrest Healthcare Sys., Tulsa, 1995—. Fellow Am. Coll. Physicians; mem. Tulsa County Med. Soc.

WESTERMAN, MAXWELL PHILIP, hematologist; b. Sept. 9, 1920; m. Marcia Kahn Gewandter, 1965. BA, Allegheny Coll., 1943; MD, U. Louisville, 1950. Intern U. Pitts. Med. Ctr., 1950-51; resident Phila. Gen. Hosp., 1953-55, chief resident in medicine, 1955-56; NIH trainee and fellow U. Coll. Hosp. Med. Sch., London, 1956-58; instr. in medicine U. Pitts. Sch. Medicine, 1958-61, asst. prof. medicine, 1961-64, rsch. asst. prof. medicine, 1964-68; prof. medicine, chief hematology sect. Chgo. Med. Sch./Mt. Sinai Hosp., 1968-75, vice chmn., dept. medicine, 1972-78; prof. medicine Rush Med. Coll., Chgo., 1975—, Univ. Health Scis./Chgo. Med. Sch., 1987—; chief hematology, oncology Mt. Sinai Hosp., 1968-93, sr. attending physician, 1993—; mem. subcom. on cancer, Chgo. Bd. of Health; bd. trustees Ill. Cancer Coun.; hon. cons. Univ. Coll. Hosp., London, 1978-79; mem. faculty coun., Rush Med. Coll., Chgo.; vis. prof. U. Madrid, 1965, U. Lisbon, 1979, U. Coll. Hosp. Med. Sch., London, 1978-79. Guest editor: (book) Seminars in Hematology: Structure Function and Pathology of the Bone Marrow, 1981; contbr. articles to profl. jours.; designer Westerman-Jensen Marrow Biopsy Needle. With USAF, 1943-45, med. corps, U.S. Army, 1951-53. Recipient rsch. award Interstate Postgrad. Med. Assn., 1960, Sang award for Excellence in Tchg., 1970-72, Morris L. Parker award for Distinction in Med. Rsch., 1974, Lawrence R. Medoff award, 1991; Wellcome Rsch. Travel grantee, U. Coll. hosp. Med. Sch., London, 1981. Mem. Am. Fedn. Clin. Rsch., Am. Soc. Hematology, Am. Soc. Clin. Oncology, Cen. Soc. Clin. Rsch., Internat. Soc. Hematology, Soc. for Exptl. Biology and Medicine, Sigma Xi, Alpha Omega Alpha. Office: Mount Sinai Hosp Hematology/Oncology Unit 15th and California Aves Chicago IL 60608

WESTERMAN, ROBERT NEIL, surgeon; b. St. Louis, June 6, 1942; s. Henry Cornelius and Mildred Elise (Barnett) W.; m. Constance Fuse, May 29, 1972; children: Andrew Barnett, John Charles. AB, Washington U., St. Louis, 1964; MD, St. Louis U., 1968; MBA, Washington U., St. Louis, 1994. Surgeon pvt. practice, St. Louis, 1977—; dir. emergency dept. St. Mary's Health Ctr., St. Louis, 1978-86, dir. employee health svc., 1978-92, dir. dept. surgery, 1992—; sec., treas. med. staff St. Mary's Med. Ctr., 1989, v.p., 1990, pres., 1991; mem. quality measurement com. Greater St. Louis Health Care Alliance, 1992—. Fellow Am. Coll. Surgeons; mem. AMA, Am. Coll. Physician Execs., Mo. State Med. Assn., St. Louis Met. Med. Soc., St. Louis Surg. Soc., Alpha Ometa Alpha. Office: 6744 Clayton Rd Ste 202 Saint Louis MO 63117

WESTERMAN, ROSEMARY MATZZIE, nurse, administrator; b. Sewickley, Pa., May 20, 1949; d. Joseph Edward and Martha (Aquino) Matzzie; m. Philip M. Westerman, Aug. 7, 1971. BSN, Duquesne U., 1971, MSEd, 1975. RN, Pa. Head nurse Dept. Vet. Affairs VA Med. Ctr., Pitts.; assoc. chief, nursing svc., edn. W. S. Middleton Meml. VA Hosp., Madison, Wis.; assoc. chief, nursing svc., edn. Dept. VA Affairs VA Med. Ctr., Chilicothe, assoc. chief nursing svc., long term. care; assoc. chief nurse VA Med. Ctr., Augusta, Ga.; chief nurse VA Med. Ctr., Muskogee, Okla. Active Literacy Vol. of Am. Mem. ANA (cert. nursing adminstrn. advanced), Assoc. Am. Coll. Health Care Execs., Okla. Orgn. Nurse Execs., Okla. Nurses Found., Nursing Orgn. of VA, Okla. Nurses Assn., VA Nurse Execs., Sigma Theta Tau. Home: 1409 E Concord St Broken Arrow OK 74012-9259

WESTFALL, KLLY CAROLINE, medical technologist; b. Pensacola, Fla., Nov. 22, 1967; d. Josh Charles and Janie Sue (Bettis) Carpenter; m. John Raymond Westfall, Feb. 24, 1988; 1 child, Kayla Bryant. Med. Lab. Specialist, Acad. Health Scis., 1987. Cert. med. technologist, Am. Med. Technologists. Med. lab. specialist Bulloch Meml. Hosp., Statesboro, Ga., 1989—. With U.S. Army, 1987-89. Office: Bulloch Meml Hosp 500 E Grady St Statesboro GA 30458

WESTIN, STEINAR, physician; b. Oslo, June 21, 1944; s. Sverre and Karen (Skjeseth) W.; m. Rigmor Austgulen, Dec. 28, 1970 (div. 1985); Kamilla, Johanna, Andreas; m. Lise Skjaak Braek, May 25, 1991. Student, Brandeis U., Mass., 1966-67, U. Bergen, Norway, 1970; MD, U. Trondheim, Norway, 1990. Specialist gen. practice. Jr. registrar Neevengaarden Psychiat. Hosp., 1971; rsch. fellow dept. psychiatry U. Bergen, 1972; gen. practice Asköy Dist., Norway, 1973-78; asst. prof. cmty. medicine and gen. practice U. Trondheim, 1979-83, assoc. prof., 1983-90, prof., 1990—; vis. prof. Royal Australian Coll. Gen. Practitioners, 1995; mem. organizing com. for postgrad. tng. in gen. practice Norwegian Med. Assn., 1986—. Author: Research in General Practice, 1983, The Educational Handbook for General Practitioners, 1985, Problem Solving in General Practice, 1987, Becoming Disabled. A Sociomedical Analysis of Individual Adaptation to Life After Long-Term Unemployment, 1990, Unemployment and Health: Medical and Social Consequences of a Factory Closure in a Ten-Year Controlled Follow-Up Study. A Study From General Practice, 1990; chmn. editl. bd. Jour. Norwegian Med. Assn., 1996—; mem. editl. bd. Brit. Med. Jour., 1995—, European Jour. Gen. Practice, 1994—. Wien/Fulbright scholar Brandeis U., Mass., 1966-67. Mem. Royal Norwegian Soc. Scis. and Letters. Home: Övre Allé 9, N-7016 Trondheim Norway Office: U Trondheim Dept Cmty Med & Gen Practice, Medisinsk Teknisk Senter, N-7005 Trondheim Norway

WESTMAN, JACK CONRAD, child psychiatrist, educator; b. Cadillac, Mich., Oct. 28, 1927; s. Conrad A. and Alice (Pedersen) W.; m. Nancy K. Baehre, July 17, 1953; children—Daniel P., John C., Eric C. M.D., U. Mich., 1952. Diplomate: Am. Bd. Psychiatry and Neurology. Intern Duke Hosp., Durham, N.C., 1952-53; resident U. Mich. Med. Center, 1955-59; dir. Outpatient Services, Children's Psychiatric Hosp., Ann Arbor, Mich., 1961-65; assoc. prof. U. Mich. Med. Sch., 1964-65; coordinator Diagnostic and Treatment Unit, Waisman Center, U. Wis., Madison, 1966-74; prof. psychiatry, 1965—; cons. Joint Commn. on Mental Health of Children, 1967-69, Madison (Wis.) Pub. Schs., 1965-74, Children's Treatment Center, Mendota Mental Health Inst., 1965-69. Author: Individual Differences in Children, 1973, Child Advocacy, 1979, Handbook of Learning Disabilities, 1990, Who Speaks for the Children?, 1991, Licensing Parents, 1994; editor: Child Psychiatry and Human Development; contbr. articles to profl. jours. Vice-pres. Big Bros. of Dane County, 1970-73; v.p. Wis. Assn. Mental Health, 1968-72; co-chmn. Project Understanding, 1968-75. Served with USNR, 1953-55. Fellow Am. Psychiat. Assn., Am. Coll. Psychiatrists, Am. Acad. Child and Adolescent Psychiatry, Am. Orthopsychiat. Assn. (bd. dirs. 1973-76); mem. Am. Assn. Psychiat. Svcs. for Children (pres. 1978-80), Multidisciplinary Acad. Clin. Edn. (pres. 1992—). Home: 1234 Dartmouth Rd Madison WI 53705-2214 Office: 600 Highland Ave Madison WI 53792-0001

WESTOFF, CHARLES FRANCIS, demographer, educator; b. N.Y.C., July 23, 1927; s. Frank Barnett and Evelyn (Bales) W.; m. Joan P. Uszynski, Sept. 11, 1948 (div. Jan. 1969); children: David, Carol; m. Leslie Aldridge, Aug. 1969 (div. Feb. 1993). AB, Syracuse U., 1949, MA, 1950; PhD, U. Pa., 1953. Instr. sociology U. Pa., 1950-52; research assoc. Milbank Meml. Fund, N.Y.C., 1952-55; research assoc. Office Population Research Princeton U., 1955-62, prof. sociology, 1962—, Maurice P. During '22 prof. demographic studies and sociology, 1972—, chmn. dept. sociology, 1965-70, assoc. dir. Office Population Research, 1962-75, dir., 1975-92; assoc. prof. sociology N.Y.U., also chmn. dept. sociology Washington Sq. Coll., 1959-62; vis. sr. fellow East-West Population Inst., Honolulu, 1979, 81; Disting. vis. prof. Am. U., Cairo, 1979; mem. vis. com. Harvard-M.I.T. Joint Center for Urban Studies, 1980-83; exec. dir. Commn. Population growth and Am. Future, 1970-72; mem. adv. com. on population stats. U.S. Bur. Census, 1973-79; chmn. Nat. Com. for Rsch. on 1980 Census, 1981-88; bd. dirs. Alan Guttmacher Inst., 1977-88, 89—; sr. tech. advisor Demographic Health Surveys, 1984—; bd. dirs. Population Resource Ctr., 1985—, Population Ref. Bur., 1988-94, Population Comms. Internat., 1992—; com. on population NAS, 1983-88. Co-author: Family Growth in Metropolitan America, 1961, The Third Child, 1963, College Women and Fertility Values, 1967, The Later Years of Childbearing, 1970, From Now to Zero, 1971, Reproduction in the United States, 1965, 71, Toward the End of Growth: Population in America, 1973, The Contraceptive Revolution, 1976, Demographic Dynamics in America, 1977, Age at Marriage, Age at First Birth and Fertility in Africa, 1992, Unmet Need: 1990-1994, 1994; contbr. artiles on demography and sociology to profl. jours. Fellow Am. Sociol. Assn., Am. Acad. Arts and Scis.; mem. Inst. Medicine Nat. Acad. Sci., Planned Parenthood Fedn. Am. (dir. 1978-81), Population Assn. Am. (bd. dirs. 1960-62, 68-70, 1st v.p. 1972-73, pres. 1974-75), Internat. Union Sci. Study Population. Home: 537 Drakes Corner Rd Princeton NJ 08540-7515

WESTON, HENRY JEFFRAY, pediatrics and child health educator; b. New Plymouth, New Zealand, Sept. 9, 1926; s. Walter Crowley and Constance Lilian (Steuart) W.; m. Patricia Ann Coates, Oct. 7, 1961; children: Margaret Ann, Elizabeth Catherine (dec.), Henry Charles, Patricia Steuart (dec.). Student, U. Otago, 1946-49; MB, ChB, U. New Zealand, 1950; BSc in Geology, Victoria U., 1995. House physician, registrar Wellington Hosp., 1951-54; house physician Royal Postgrad. Med. Sch., Hammersmith Hosp., London, 1955, Brompton Hosp., London, 1955; house physician, cardiac registrar The Hosp. for Sick Children, London, 1956-57, resident asst. physician, 1958-60; cons. pediatrician Wellington, New Zealand, 1960-75; prof. pediats. and child health, chmn. dept. Wellington Sch. Medicine, U. Otago, 1975-92, emeritus prof., 1992—; head pediatric dept., adviser pediatrics Wellington Area Health Bd., 1975-92; pediatric adviser Dept. Health, 1978-92; pediatrician Wellington Hosp., Wellington South, New Zealand, 1992—; pediatrician The Home of Compassion Hosp., 1962-75, Karitane Hosp., 1961-75, Hutt Hosp., 1960-62, Wellington Hosp., 1962-75; examiner pediatrics U. Singapore, 1975, Royal Australasian Coll. Physicians, 1973-83, U. Western Australia, 1981-82, U. Papua New Guinea, 1985-86, U. Malaya, 1988; Colombo plan lectr. pediatrics Auspices of R.A.C.P. U. Singapore, 1975; vis. pediatrician Apia Western Samoa, 1977; leader Ofcl. New Zealand Pediatric Delegation to People's Republic of China, 1981; lectr. in field. Contbr. articles to profl. jours. Col. Royal New Zealand Army Med. Corps, 1948-72. Hon. fellow Australian Coll. Pediatrics; mem. New Zealand Med. Assn., Pediatric Soc. New Zealand, Med. Protection Soc. (New Zealand adviser in pediats. 1991—), Medico-legal Soc., Nurses Edn. & Rsch. Found., Wellington Army Assn., Wellington Golf Club, Gt. Ormond Street Dining Club. Anglican. Home: 6 Hauraki St, Wellington 5, New Zealand Office: Wellington Hosp Capital Health, Riddiford St Pvt Bag 7902, Wellington South New Zealand

WESTOVER, SAMUEL LEE, managed health care executive; b. Soap Lake, Wash., May 30, 1955; s. Gordon Kent Westover and Janice Lelia (Matlock) Jensen; m. Susan Kern, July 13, 1977; children: Michael, S. Fielding, Austin, Clinton, Cassandra. BS in Acctg., Brigham Young U., 1978. Acct. Price Waterhouse, L.A., 1978-80; chief fin. officer, sr. v.p. Maxicare Health Plans, Inc., L.A., 1981-88; chief exec. officer and chief operating officer Western Health Plans, Inc., San Diego, 1988-90; chief fin. officer, sr. v.p. Blue Cross of Calif., Woodland Hills, 1990-93; CFO, sr. v.p. WellPoint Health Networks, Inc., Woodland Hills, 1993; pres., CEO Systemed Inc., Torrance, Calif., 1993—. Office: Systemed Inc 970 W 190th St Ste 400 Torrance CA 90502-1000

WESTPHAL, JOANNE MARIE, enviromental design educator, physician; b. Milw., Mar. 6, 1948; d. John G. Dobronand Ann A. Marks. BS, U. Wis., 1970, MS, 1973, PhD, 1977, MA, 1983; postgrad., Mich. State U., 1995. Lectr. U. Wis., Green Bay, 1971-79; from asst. to assoc. prof. Tex. A & M U., College Station, 1979-86; assoc. prof. Mich. State U., E. Lansing, 1986-96; cons. U.S. Forest Svc., Escanaba, Mich., 1989, Durango, Colo., 1990, Sheridan, Wyo., 1991, regional landscape design Peninsula Town, Traverse City, Mich., 1989—. Editor: (electronic jour.) Landscape Architecture, 1995; mem. adv. bd. Landscape Jour., 1984. Mem. Am. Osteopathic Assn., Am. Soc. Landscape Archs. (Merit award Rsch. 1985, Merit award Planning 1995), Am. Planning Assn., Coun. Educators in Landscape Arch., Internat. Union Forest Researchers.

WESTPHAL, LEONARD WYRICK, health care executive, consultant; b. Kansas City, Mo., Sept. 28, 1946; s. Leonard Henry and Elizabeth (Wyrick) W.; m. Sandra Sanders, Aug. 13, 1972; children: Michael Weston, Margaret Elizabeth. BFA, So. Meth. U., 1969; MA, S.W. Mo. State U., 1972; postgrad., U. Mich., Cen. Mo. State U., Lincoln U. of Mo., Century U. Lic. nursing home adminstr., Mo., Ark. Exec. dir. Dist. III Area Agy. on Aging, Warrensburg, 1972-83; state dir. Mo. Div. of Aging, Jefferson City, Mo., 83-85; spl. asst. to dir. Mo. Dept. Mental Health, Jefferson City, 1985-86; exec. dir. Missouri River Health Care, Jefferson City, 1986-88; health care adminstr., cons., 1988—; continuing edn. instr., mem. adv. coun. continuing edn. SW Mo. State U., 1993—; adj. instr., internship supr. Cen. Mo. State U., Warrensburg, 1974-83; mem. rev. panel State of Mo., 1974-76, HHS, 1984-85; cons. Adminstrn. on Aging, Fed. Emergency Mgmt. Agy., 1977-83; bd. dirs. Mid-Am. Congress on Aging, 1975; chmn. Mo. Gov.'s Task Force, Hearings and Conf. on Alternative Care for Elderly, 1982-83; mem. Mo. Bd. Nursing Home Adminstrs., 1983-85; founder, coord. Older Missourians Craft Festival, 1978-83; pres., v.p. Mo. Alliance Area Agys. on Aging, 1974-76; host radio programs Sta. Kmos-TV, Sta. KCMW-FM, Sta. KWTO, 1993—; mem. adv. com. health care adm. program S.W. Mo. State U.; presenter in field. Author articles in disaster assistance. Mem. Mo. Rep. Com., 1970—, rev. panel United Way, Warrensburg, 1978; mem. coun. ministries lst United Meth. Ch., Warrensburg, 1979-83, mem. adminstrv. coun., 1981-83, pres. Meth. Men, 1982-83; mem. commn. on missions, Wesley United Meth. Ch., Jefferson City, 1984-86, liturgist, 1985-89; mem. ch. and soc. commn. Wesley United Methodist Ch., Springfield, 1989—; pres. PTA, Warrensburg, 1982; coach Little League Football and Basketball, Warrensburg, 1981-82; bd. dirs. Warrensburg Community Betterment, 1976-78; mem. adminstrv. coun., mem. chancel choir Grace United Meth. Ch., Springfield, 1993—. Recipient Boss of Yr. award Warrensburg Jaycees, 1976, svc. recognition Mo. Office Aging, 1977, Mo. Alliance Area Agys. on Aging, 1977, Older Adult Transp. Svc., Columbia, Mo., 1983, Mo. State Fair, 1983, Mo. Dept. Mental Health, 1986; Exceptional Svc. in Disaster Assistance award City of Sedalia, 1977, 80; Outstanding Contbns. award Ret. Sr. Vol. Programs, 1977, 79, Excellence in Adminstrn. award Mo. Office Aging, 1977, Outstanding Svcs. award Hickory County, Mo., 1984, also others. Fellow Am. Coll. Healthcare Adminstrs. (cert.); mem. Am. Coll. Healthcare Execs., Gerontol. Soc. Am., Am. Soc. Pub. Adminstrn., Mo. Alliance for Homecare, Mo. League Nursing Home Adminstrs., Am. Coll. Healthcare Profls., Jefferson City C. of C., Springfield C. of C. (mem. retirement and devel. coms.), Optimists (v.p. Warrensburg 1979-81), Rotary, Elks, Delta Sigma Rho-Tau Kappa Alpha, Delta Chi (alumni advisor, alumni bd. trustees, achievement award). Home: 1420 S Lovers Ln Springfield MO 65804-2123

WESTROPE, MARTHA RANDOLPH, psychologist, consultant; b. Gaffney, S.C., May 19, 1922; d. Gordon Robert and Hannah (Brown) W.; 1 adopted child, Ashley Randolph. BS, Winthrop Coll., 1942; MA, U. N.C., 1944; PhD, State U. of Iowa, Iowa City, 1952. Lic. psychologist, S.C. Pvt. practice Greenville, S.C., 1960—, part-time pvt. practice, 1987—; part-time staff mem. Spartanburg (S.C.) Mental Health Clinic, 1971-73, Greenville Mental Health Ctr., 1974-85, Patrick B. Harris Psychiat. Hosp., Anderson, S.C., 1985-87; med. cons. S.C. Vocat. Rehab. Dept., Greenville, 1987-91, part-time med. cons., 1993—; cons. S.C. Parole Bd. for Psychol. Evaluation, S.C. Dept. Corrections, 1983-87. Mem. Am. Psychol. Assn., Southeastern Psychol. Assn., S.C. Psychol. Assn., Am. Assn. for Advancement of Psychology, Greenville County Mental Health Assn., Am. Group Psychotherapy Assn., Coun. for the Nat. Register of Health Svc. Providers in Psychology. Democrat. Presbyterian. Home: 11 Darien Way Greenville SC 29615-3236 Office: 506 Pettigru St Greenville SC 29601-3117

WETSCH, PEGGY A., nursing informaticist, educator; b. San Diego; d. Harvey William Henry and Helen Catherine (Thorpe) Brink; m. Gearald M. Wetsch, June 26, 1971; children: Brian Gearald, Lynette Kirstiann Nicole. Diploma, Calif. Hosp. Sch. Nursing, 1971; BSN cum laude, Pepperdine U., 1980; MS in Nursing, Calif. State U., L.A., 1985. Cert. in nursing adminstrn., human resource devel. Clin. nurse Orange County Med. Ctr./U. Calif. Irvine Med. Ctr., Orange, Calif., 1971-75; pediatric head nurse U. Calif. Irvine Med. Ctr., 1975-79; clin. nurse educator Palm Harbor Gen./Med. Ctr. Garden Grove, Calif., 1980-81; dir. ednl. svcs. Med. Ctr. of

Garden Grove, 1981-85; dir. edn. Mission Hosp. Regional Med. Ctr., Mission Viejo, Calif., 1986-92; coord. computer and learning resources L.A. Med. Ctr. Sch. Nursing, 1992-95; assoc. part time faculty Saddleback Coll., 1990-94; cons. ptnr. nur.SYS-Edn. systems Cons., 1995—; lectr. statewide nursing program Calif. State U., Dominguez Hills, 1986-92; ednl. cons. Author: (with others) Nursing Diagnosis: Guidelines to Planning Care, 1993, 2d edit., 1994, 3d edit., 1996; contbr. articles to profl. jours. Treas. Orange County Nursing Edn. Coun., 1986-87, 88-90, pres., 1987-88. Mem. ANA, NLN, Am. Nursing Informatics Assn. (pres.-elect 1996—, elections com. So. Calif. chpt. 1994, coord. continuing edn., conf. planning com.), Am. Soc. Health Edn. and Tng., N.am. Nursing Diagnosis Assn. (secondary reviewer Diagnostic Rev. 1989-90, expert adv. panel 1990-92, mem. diagnosis rev. com. 1992-96), Soc. Calif. Nursing Diagnosis Assn. (membership chmn. 1984-92, pres. 1992-94), Nat. Am. Mgmt. Assn. (charter L.A. County, U. So. Calif. Med. Ctr. chpt.), Spina Bifida Assn. Am., Phi Kappa Phi, Sigma Theta Tau (pres. Iota Eta chpt. 1990-92). Home: 1520 San Clemente Ln Corona CA 91720-7949

WETSTONE, HOWARD JEROME, physician, administrator; b. Hartford, Conn., Apr. 27, 1926; s. Murray and Natalie (Tonkonow) W.; m. Roan Joy Horowitz, May 8, 1947; children—Robin Lee Wendehack, Mark Lawrence, Scott Lewis, Jeffrey Bennett. BA, Wesleyan U., 1946; MD, Tufts U., 1951. Intern New Eng. Med. Ctr. Hosp., 1951-52, resident, 1952-53; resident Hartford Hosp., 1953-55, dir. med. rsch., 1958-65, asst. dir. dept. medicine, 1965-72, dir. ambulatory svcs., 1972-84, v.p. corp. med. affairs, 1984-87; v.p. med. affairs Conn. Health System, Hartford, 1987-92; med. dir. MEDSPAN, 1992—; assoc. prof. U. Conn. Med. Sch., Farmington, 1975—; chmn. Med. Delivery Svcs., Inc., 1985-91; mem. Bloomfield Ethics Commn.; chmn. profl. adv. com. Capitol Area Health Consortium; bd. dirs., exec. com., chmn. joint conf. com. Gaylord Hosp., 1994—. Contbr. articles to profl. jours. Mem. Bloomfield Bd. Edn., Conn., 1955-69, chmn., 1961-69; pres. Conn. Assn. Bds. Edn., 1961-63; exec. com. Conn. Pub. TV Corp., Hartford, 1963-87, chmn., 1970-74; pres. Capitol Region Edn. Coun., Hartford, 1965-66; chmn. Govtl. Rels. Com. With USAAF 1946-47. Mem. AMA, Am. Coll. Emergency Physicians, Conn. Hosp. Assn. (hon.), Conn. State Med. Soc. (pres., chmn. legis. com., vice speaker ho. of dels. 1994-95, speaker 1995—), Hartford County Med. Assn. (bd. dirs. 1978-94, pres. 1985-86). Republican. Jewish. Home: 77 Kenwood Cir Bloomfield CT 06002-3435 Office: Conn Health System 55 Farmington Ave Hartford CT 06105-3711

WETTSTEIN, ROBERT MARK, psychiatrist, educator; b. N.Y.C., June 4, 1950; s. Sidney and Bonnie (Baskin) W.; m. Stacey Sayer; children: Zachary Sayer, Emma Rachel. BA in Natural Scis., Johns Hopkins, 1972; MD, UCLA, 1976. Adj. attending dept. psychiatry Rush-Presbyn.-St. Luke's Med. Ctr., Chgo., 1981-83; research coord. Rush-Presbyn.-Consultation Liaison Svc., Chgo., 1981-84; lectr. in psychiatry dept. psychiatry Loyola U. Stritch Sch. Medicine, Maywood, Ill., 1981-84; staff psychiatrist Isaac Ray Ctr.-Rush-Presbyn. St. Luke's Med. Ctr., Chgo., 1981-84; lectr. in psychiatry dept. psychiatry Pritzker Sch. Medicine, Chgo., 1982-84; asst. attending dept. psychiatry Rush-Presbyn.-St. Luke's Med. Ctr., Chgo., 1983-84; asst. prof. dept. psychiatry Rush Med. Coll., Chgo., 1983-84; asst. prof. psychiatry U. Pitts., 1984—; cons. psychiatrist Ill. Dept. Mental Health, Chgo., 1981-84; cons. Mon-Yough Corrections Program, Pitts., 1987—; co-dir. law and psychiatry program Western Psychiat. Inst. and Clinic, Pitts., 1986—. Editor Behavioral Scis. and the Law, 1987—; contbr. psychiatry articles to profl. jours. Recipient Retirement Research Found. award, 1987-88. Mem. Am. Psychiat. Assn., Am. Acad. Psychiatry and the Law (editor newsletter), Am. Soc. Law and Medicine, Internat. Acad. Law and Mental Health. Office: Western Psychiat Inst Ste B103 401 Shady Ave Pittsburgh PA 15206

WETZEL, FRANKLIN TODD, spinal surgeon, educator, researcher; b. Wilmington, Del., Mar. 7, 1955; s. Franklin Huff and Jean Hartman (Clouser) W.; m. Patricia Ann Cassanos, May 23, 1981 (div. June 1993); m. Cathleen Ann Myers, Nov. 21, 1993; 1 child, Colin Todd. AB, Harvard Coll., 1977; MD, U. Pa., 1981. Diplomate Am. Bd. Orthopedic Surgery. Resident Yale U., New Haven, Conn., instr. Med. Sch., 1986-87; fellow S. Henry LaRocca, M.S., New Orleans, 1987-88; asst. prof. Pa. State U., Hershey, 1988-91, assoc. prof., 1991-93; assoc. prof. U. Chgo., 1993—, dir. Spine Ctr., 1993—; reviewer Clin. Orthopaedics, Phila., 1993—. Assoc. editor Spine, 1990—; contbr. articles to profl. jours. Physician Armenian Gen. Benevolent, Hershey, 1988; mem. alumni coun. Wilmington Friends Sch., 1991—. Fellow Am. Acad. Orthopedic Surgery; mem. Cervical Spine Rsch. Soc., N.Am. Spine Soc., Am. Neuromodulation Soc. (bd. dirs. 1994—), Acad. Orthopedic Soc., Am. Pain Soc., Harvard Club (interviewer 1995—), Sigma Xi. Presbyterian. Office: U Chgo Spine Ctr 4646 N Marine Dr Chicago IL 60640

WEY, JONG-SHINN, research laboratory manager; b. Kaohsiung, Taiwan, Oct. 26, 1944; came to U.S. 1968; s. Tan-Ding and Chao (Lee) W.; m. Hseh-Yi Su, 1965; children: John, Nancy. BS in Chem. Engring., Nat. Taiwan U., 1967; PhD, Clarkson U., 1973. Sr. rsch. chemist Eastman Kodak Co., Rochester, N.Y., 1973-80, rsch. assoc., 1980-84, lab. head, 1984-91, sr. lab. head, 1991—. Co-author: Preparation and Properties of Solid State Materials, 1981, Handbook of Industrial Crystallization, 1992. Recipient Jour. award Photographic Sci. and Engring. Fellow Soc. Photographic Scientists and Engrs.; mem. AIChE. Home: 259 Hillary Ln Penfield NY 14526-1646 Office: Eastman Kodak Co Rsch Labs Bldg 59 Rochester NY 14650-1736

WEYANDT, LINDA JANE, anesthetist, hypnotherapist, trauma resolutionist, educator; b. Altoona, Pa., Nov. 5, 1948; d. Charles Leroy and Edna Pearl (Schaefer) W. RN, Phila. Gen. Hosp. Sch. Nursing, 1970; BA, Stephens Coll., 1978; MD, U. Del Noreste, Mex., 1983; postgrad., So. Calif. U., 1995. Cert. trauma resolutionist Am. Inst. Med. and Psychotherapeutic Hypnosis; cert. hypnotherapist Am. Bd. Hypnotherapy. Pvt. practice anesthesia J.L. Med. Svcs., McAllen, Tex., 1986-92; staff anesthetist MD Anderson Hosp., Houston, 1992, VA Hosp., Houston, 1992—; dir., owner Hypnosis and Pain Mgmt. Svcs. of Tex., Houston, 1994—; sr. disabilty analyst, diplomate Am. Bd. Disability Analysts; dir. Associated Hypnotherapy and Pain Mgmt., Houston, 1991; clin. instr. dept. anesthesia Baylor Coll. Medicine, Houston. Contbr. articles to profl. jours. Fellow Am. Bd. Med. Psychotherapists & Psychodiagnosticians (diplomate); mem. Am. Acad. Pain Mgmt. (diplomate), Am. Assn. Behavior Therapists, Biofeedback Soc. Tex., Am. Soc. Clin. Hypnosis, Am. Psychotherapy and Med. Hypnosis Assn. (Advance Med. Hypnosis award 1994), Internat. Soc. Hypnosis Assn., (Australia), Am. Soc. Clin. Hypnosis, Houston Soc. Clin. Hypnosis, Alumna Assn. Stephens Coll., Alumna Assn. Phila. Gen. Hosp., NOW. Office: Associated Hypnotherapy and Pain Mgmt Svcs Tex 6300 W Loop S Ste 333 Bellaire TX 77401

WEYERER, SIEGFRIED BERNHARD, epidemiologist; b. Traunstein, Bavaria, Germany, Aug. 20, 1947; s. Maximilian and Hedwig (Serger) W.; m. Betty (Berniece) Haire, Aug. 13, 1977; children: Margret Kathleen, Jan Curtis. PhD in Psychology and Sociology, U. Salzburg, Austria, 1976; Habilitation in Epidemiology, U. Heidelberg, Germany, 1994. Head dept. psychiat. case register Cen. Inst. Mental Health, Mannheim, Germany, 1985-87; head dept. psychogeriatric rsch. unit Cen. Inst. Mental Health, Mannheim, 1987—; expert in pub. health German Ministry Rsch. and Tech., Bonn, 1991—; expert in pub. health German Ministry Rsch. and Tech., Bonn, 1991—. Author: Psychiatric Epidemiology, 1978, 84; editor: Unemployment, 1986; contbr. articles to profl. jours. Rsch. fellow U. Munich, psychiatric. dept., 1976-85; rsch. grantee German Ministry Rsch. and Tech., Bonn, 1986-89, 93—, rsch. grantee Found. of German Sci. Mem. Am. Pub. Health Assn., German Assn. Gerontology, Assn. European Psychiatrists (sec. gen. epidemiology and social psychiatry 1988—), Internat. Soc. Pharmacoepidemiology, N.Y. Acad. Scis., Soc. for Epidemiologic Rsch. Roman Catholic. Home: Zimmerbachstr 4, D-69469 Weinheim Baden-Wurtt Germany Office: Cen Inst Mental Health, J5 PO Box 122120, D-68072 Mannheim Germany

WEYHING, BURT THOMAS, III, physician; b. Detroit, Feb. 28, 1941; s. Burt Thomas Jr. and Winnifred (Marsh) W.; m. Andrea Egan, Apr. 29, 1966; children: Burt IV, Cornelius, Elizabeth. BS, Wayne State U., 1963, MD, 1967. Diplomate Am. Bd. Radiology, Am. Bd. Nuclear Medicine. Intern Grace Hosp., Detroit, 1967-68, resident in radiology, 1968-71, fellow in radiology, 1971-72, staff radiologist, 1972-80; vice chief of radiology Harper-Grace Hosp., Detroit, 1980-91; chief of radiology Grace Hosp., Detroit, 1991—. Fellow Am. Coll. Radiology (councillor 1990—, fellowship 1988); mem. AMA, Radiol. Soc. N.Am., Am. Roentgen Ray Soc., Wayne State U. Sch. of Medicine Alumni (pres. bd. govs. 1975-84), Alpha Omega Alpha. Home: 158 Kenwood Grosse Point MI 48236 Office: Grace Hosp 6071 W Outer Dr Detroit MI 48235

WEYMULLER, ERNEST ALFRED, JR., surgeon; b. N.Y.C., Dec. 30, 1940; s. Ernest Alfred and Lillian (Saywell) W.; m. Alice Beryl Crowmover, Nov. 8, 1967; children: Ernest A. III, Sims G. BA, Dartmouth Coll., 1962; MD, Harvard U., 1966. Ptnr. Boston ENT Assocs., 1973-78; asst. prof. U. Wash., Seattle, 1978-83, assoc. prof., 1983-88, prof., 1988—, chmn. dept. otolaryngology, 1992—. Author: Altas Head & Neck Reconstruction, 1988, Altas Laryngological Surgery, 1985. Capt. USAF, 1968-70. Fellow Am. Soc. Head and Neck Surgery (treas.-elect 1995—), Am. Layngol. Soc. (editor historian 1995). Office: U Wash Dept Otolaryngology Box 356515 Seattle WA 98195

WHALEN, TIMOTHY JOHN, child and adolescent psychiatrist; b. Columbus, Ohio, May 29, 1960; s. John M. and Nana Lee (Richards) W.; m. Barbara Rhoads, June 18, 1983; children: Elizabeth Anne, Thomas Christopher, Patricia Lee. BS cum laude, Davidson (N.C.) Coll., 1982; MD, Ohio State U., 1986. Resident in family practice Riverside Meth. Hosp., Columbus, 1986-87; resident in psychiatry Johns Hopkins Hosp., Balt., 1987-89, resident child and adolescent psychiat., 1989-90, chief resident child and adolescent psychiat., 1990-91; dir. child and adolescent psychiatry Francis Scott Key Med. Ctr., Balt., 1991-92; med. dir. Am. Day Treatment Ctr. Waldorf (Md.), 1993—; psychiatrist pvt. practice, 1993—; med. dir. Ctr. for Children, LaPlata, Md., 1995—; instr. dept. of psychiatry and behavioral scis., dept. pediatrics Johns Hopkins U., Balt., 1991-95. Mem. AMA, Am. Psychiat. Assn., Am. Acad. Child and Adolescent Psychiatry, Md. Psychiat. Soc. Democrat. Office: 700 Old Line Ctr Ste 308 Waldorf MD 20602

WHALEY, LUCILLE FILLMORE, nursing consultant, educator; b. Garfield, Utah, May 17, 1923; d. Marvin W. and Isabella V. (Bennett) Fillmore; m. Bert A. Whaley, Apr. 5, 1943; children: Kathleen, Maureen. Diploma, St. Marks Hosp. Sch. Nursing, Salt Lake City, 1944; BS, San Jose State Coll., 1962; MS, U. Calif., San Francisco, 1963; EdD, U. So. Calif., 1986. Prof. emeritus nursing San Jose (Calif.) State U., 1963-83; cons. pvt. practice, Sunnyvale, Calif., 1974—. Contbr. articles to profl. jours., books. Mem. ANA, Calif. Nurses Assn., Sigma Theta Tau. Home: 1652 Lachine Dr Sunnyvale CA 94087-4207

WHARAM, MOODY DEWITT, JR., physician, medical educator; b. Washington, July 22, 1941; s. Moody DeWitt Sr. and Ethyl May (Morris) W.; m. Sheila Mairead Reese, June 22, 1968; children: Julia M. J. Franklin, Anne M. BA, Harvard U., 1963; MD, U. Va., 1969. Diplomate Am. Bd. Radiology. Intern in medicine and pediatrics Georgetown U. Med. Ctr., Washington, 1969-70; NIH fellow in radiation oncology U. Calif. Med. Ctr., San Francisco, 1970-73, resident, clin. instr., 1973-74; asst. prof. radiology Sch. Medicine Duke U., Durham, N.C., 1974-75; asst. prof. oncology and radiol. sci. Sch. Medicine Johns Hopkins U., Balt., 1975-80, assoc. prof. oncology, radiol. sci., pediatrics and neurosurgery, 1980-93, prof., 1993—; acting dir. divsn. radiol. oncology Johns Hopkins Oncology Ctr., Balt., 1991-93, dir. divsn. radiol. oncology, 1994—. Lt. (j.g.) USNR, 1963-65. Mem. Am. Coll. Radiology, Am. Soc. Therapeutic Radiology and Oncology, Am. Soc. Clin. Oncology, Internat. Soc. Pediatric Oncology. Roman Catholic. Office: Johns Hopkins Hosp 600 N Wolfe St Baltimore MD 21287-8922

WHARTON, RALPH NATHANIEL, psychiatrist, educator; b. Boston, June 15, 1932; s. Nathaniel Philip and Deeda (Levine) W.; AB cum laude, Harvard U., 1953; MD, Columbia U., 1957, degree in psychoanalysis, 1970; children: Naida, Philip, Laura. Intern, Cornell div. Bellevue Hosp., N.Y.C., 1957-58; resident Columbia-Presbyn. Med. Center, N.Y.C., 1961-64; practice medicine, specializing in psychiatry and psychopharmacology, N.Y.C., 1964—; assoc. psychiatry Coll. Physicians and Surgeons, N.Y.C., 1964-69, asst. prof. clin. psychiatry, 1969-72, assoc. prof., 1972-83, prof., 1984—; sr. rsch. psychiatrist N.Y. State Psychiat. Inst., N.Y.C., 1964-70; assoc. attending in psychiatry Columbia-Presbyn. Hosp., 1970—, ex-officio mem. bd. trustees, pres. Soc. Practitioners Columbia-Presbyn. Med. Center, 1980-82, attending psychiatrist, 1984—; exec. dir. Wharton Fund for Brain Rsch.; med. dir. Black Sea project Macalester Coll., 1994-96. Served with M.C., U.S. Army, 1958-61. Named one of Best Drs., N.Y. mag. Fellow N.Y. Acad. Medicine, Am. Psychiat. Assn., Am. Coll. Psychoanalysts (pres. 1996), Internat. Assn. Study of Pain (founder); mem. AMA (mem. legis. action com.), Soc. Biol. Psychiatry, Royal Soc. Medicine, Lotos Club, Salon de Virtuosi (founding bd. mem.), Harvard Club, Harmonie Club. Author numerous publs. in field. Office: Columbia Presbyn Med Ctr 620 W 168th St New York NY 10032-3702 also: Columbia Presbyn Med Ctr 1070 Park Ave Ste 1D New York NY 10128-1000

WHARTON, WILLIAM POLK, consulting psychologist, retired educator; b. Hopkinsville, Ky.; s. William Polk and Rowena Evelyn (Wall) W.; m. Lillian Marie Andersen, Mar. 11, 1944; 1 child, Christine Evelyn Wharton Leonard. BA, Yale U., 1934; MA, Tchrs. Coll., 1949; PhD, Columbia U., 1952. Diplomate Am. Bd. Profl. Psychology; lic. psychologist, Pa. Rsch. advt. promotion, advt. sales Esquire Inc., N.Y.C., 1934-40; dir. counseling, prof. edn., counseling psychologist Allegheny Coll., Meadville, Pa., 1952-74, emeritus dir. and prof. edn., 1974—; prof., dir. The Ednl. Guidance Clinic, Meadville, 1958-74; pvt. practice cons. psychologist Meadville, 1974—; cons. U.S. Army Edn. Ctr., Ft. Meade, Md., 1960-61; rsch. adv. coun. Ednl. Devel. Ctr., Berea, Ohio, 1971-72; cons. to pres. Alliance Coll., Cambridge Springs, Md., 1975-76. Mem. editorial bd. Psychotherapy, 1966-63; reviewer Jour. Coll. Student Personnel, 1984-88; contbr. articles to profl. jours. Chmn. MH/MR Bd. Crawford County Pa., Meadville, 1970-73; com. chmn., Drug and Alcohol Coun. Crawford County Pa., Meadville, 1973-76; ethics com. chmn. North West Pa. Psychol. Assn., 1975-78; del. Pa. Mental Health Assn. Crawford County, 1978-79. Served U.S. Army, 1940-46; from pvt. to lt. col. USAR, 1964. Psychotherapy Research Group vis. fellow, 1961-62; Romiett Stevens scholar, 1951. Fellow Pa. Psychol. Assn.; mem. Am. Psychol. Assn. (Disting. Contbn. award 1985), Am. Assn. for Counseling and Devel., Nat. Vocat. Guidance Assn., Pa. Coll. Personnel Assn. (chmn. 1956-57), Phi Beta Kappa, Phi Delta Kappa, Kappa Beta Pi, Pi Gamma Mu. Home and Office: 415 N Main St Meadville PA 16335-1510 also (summer): General Delivery Forest Dale VT 05745

WHATMORE, GEORGE BERNARD, physician, clinical neurophysiologist; b. Seattle, Aug. 31, 1917; s. Harry Joseph and Delia (Frolich) W.; BS, U. Wash., 1940, MS, 1941; PhD (Univ. fellow, Rawson fellow, Sheldon fellow), U. Chgo., 1946, MD, 1948; m. Frances Maxwell Beatty, May 28, 1942; children: Pamela Frances, David Blake, Nancy Janice. Intern, King County Hosp., Seattle, 1948-49, resident, 1949-50; resident Lab. Clin. Physiology, Chgo., 1950-51; pvt. practice internal medicine, clin. neurophysiology, functional disorders, Seattle, 1951—; mem. staff Virginia Mason, Swedish, Med.-Dental Bldg. hosps. (all Seattle), 1951—, Eastern State Hosp., Medical Lake, Wash., 1955-58; prin. investigator Pacific N.W. Research Found., Seattle, 1966—. Recipient Ginsburg award U. Chgo., 1946. Mem. AAAS (life), AMA, N.Y. Acad. Sci., Am. Physicians Soc. for Physiologic Tension Control, Internat. Stress and Tension Control Assn., Biofeedback Rsch. Soc., Behavior Therapy and Research Soc., Acad. Psychosomatic Medicine, Assn. for Applied Psychophysiology and Biofeedback, Wash. State Med. Assn., King County Med. Soc., Am., Wash. biofeedback socs., Western Acad. Beaux Arts, Sigma Xi. Author: (with Daniel R. Kohli) Dysponesis: A Neurophysiologic Factor in Functional Disorders, 1968, The Physiopathology and Treatment of Functional Disorders, 1974; A Scientist Looks at Christianity: A Probability Analysis of the Claims and Teachings Attributed to Christ, 2d edit., 1995; contbr. articles to profl. jours. Home: 10524 SE 27th St Bellevue WA 98004-7231 Office: 10524 SE 27th St Bellevue WA 98004-7231

WHEAT, MYRON WILLIAM, JR., cardiothoracic surgeon; b. Sapulpa, Okla., Mar. 24, 1924; s. Myron William and Mary Lee (Hudiburg) W.; m. Erlene Adele Plank, June 12, 1949 (div. June 1970); children: Penelope Louise, Myron William III, Pamela Lynn, Douglas Plank; m. Carol Ann Karmgard, June 18, 1970 (div. Apr. 1996); 1 child, Christopher West. AB, Washington U., St. Louis, 1949; MD cum laude, Washington U., 1951. Diplomate Am. Bd. Surgery, Am. Bd. Thoracic Surgery. Instr., clin. fellow Washington U., St. Louis, 1956-58; asst. prof. surgery U. Fla., Gainesville, 1958-65, prof. surgery, 1965-72; dir. profl. svcs., chief clin. physician U. Fla. Shands Teaching Hosp., Gainesville, 1968-72; prof. surgery, dir. thoracic and cardiothoracic surgery U. Louisville Sch. Medicine, 1972-75; clin. prof. surgery U. Louisville Sch. of Medicine, 1975—; cardiothoracic surgeon Cardiac Surg. Assocs., P.A., St. Petersburg, Fla., 1975-91; cons., thoracic surgery Bay Pine VA Hosp., St. Petersburg, Fla., 1994—; clin. prof. surgery U. So. Fla. Sch. Medicine, Tampa, 1995—; cardiothoracic surgeon Cardiac Surg. Assocs., P.A., Clearwater, Fla., 1991—; clin. prof. surger U. South Fla., 1995—; cons. Bay Pines VA Hosp., St. Petersburg, Fla., 1991—. Author (with others) 14 books; contbr. over 100 articles to profl. jours.; developed drug therapy for acute dissecting aneurysms of the aorta. 1st lt. USAF, 1943-46, ETO. Named First Howard W. Lillenthal Meml. lectr. Mt. Sinai Hosp., 1963; recipient DFC Air medal, Presdl. Citation. Fellow Am. Coll. Cardiology (chmn. bd. govs. 1968-69), Am. Coll. Surgeons (gov.); mem. Am. Surg. Assn., Am. Assn. for Thoracic Surgery, So. Surg. Assn., So. Thoracic Surg. Assn., Soc. Thoracic Surgeons, Soc. Thoracic Surgeons Great Britain and Ireland, Alpha Omega Alpha. Republican. Home and Office: 1772 Long Bow Ln Clearwater FL 34624-6402

WHEATLEY, JAMES W., ophthalmologist; b. Garden City, Kans., May 20, 1945; s. James Elmer and Neada Elizabeth (Engler) W.; m. Linda SuzAnn White, Aug. 27, 1966 (dec. June 1992); children: Troy, Megan. BS in Pharmacy, U. Kans., 1967, MS in Pharmacology, 1969; MD, U. Md., 1976. Diplomate Am. Bd. Ophthalmology. Ophthalmologist Cabarrus Eye Ctr., Concord, N.C., 1980—. Lt. comdr. USNR, 1969-71. Republican. Office: Cabarrus Eye Ctr 500 Lake Concord Rd Concord NC 28025

WHEATLEY, JOSEPH KEVIN, physician, urologist; b. N.Y.C., Jan. 5, 1946; s. Patrick Owen and Catherine (Malloy) W.; m. Anne Johanna Foody, Aug. 22, 1970; children: Joseph, Thomas. BSChemE, Manhattan Coll., 1967; MSChemE, U. Del., 1969; MD, N.J. U. of Medicine, 1974. Diplomate Am. Bd. Urology. Rsch. engr. NASA, Houston, 1965, 66, Exxon, Florham Park, N.J., 1968-69; urology resident Emory Univ., Atlanta, 1975-79, assoc. prof. urology, 1979—; clin. urology practice Urology Assocs., Atlanta, 1986—; chief of urology Kennestone Hosp., Marietta, Ga., 1990-93; medicare care cons. Ga. Found. med. Care, Atlanta, 1982—; tchr. Atlanta VA Med. Ctr., Atlanta, 1979—; mem. hosp. exec. com. Kennestone Hosp., Marietta, 1990-93. Contbr. chpts. to books and articles to profl. jours. Active various Rep. actitives, 1992—. Named Top Drs. in Atlanta Atlanta Mag., 1995-96. Fellow ACS; mem. AMA, Urol. Assn., Urodynamics Soc., Am. Fertility Soc., Soc. of Reproductive Surgeons, Lithotripsy Soc. Roman Catholic. Home: 692 N St Mary's Ln Marietta GA 30064 Office: Urology Assocs 833 Campbell Hill Rd #300 Marietta GA 30060

WHEATON, MARY EDWINA, health facility administrator, educator; b. Clifton, N.Y., Aug. 19, 1950; d. James E. and Beatrice C. (Preston) Potter; m. Gerald B. Wheaton, Sept. 10, 1968; children: Shelley L., Laura Ann. ADN, Chabot Coll., 1986; BSN, Calif. State U., Dominguez Hills, 1995. RN, Calif.; cert. med/surg. nurse. Staff nurse St. Rose Hosp., Hayward, Calif., 1986-88, mem. clin. ladder task force, chairperson rev. bd., 1988-90, charge nurse, 1988-91, mem. nursing standards com., 1990—, chairperson nursing practice com., 1990-92, clin. coord., supr., 1991—; clin. examiner Chabot Coll., Hayward, 1989—. Instr. basic life support Am. Heart Assn., San Ramon, Calif., 1984-86; leader Livermore (Calif.) Girl Scouts U.S., 1976-86, chairperson, 1982-84. Mem. Am. Acad. Med. and Surg. Nursing, Phi Kappa Phi. Baptist.

WHEELAND, DALE N., physician; b. Tucson, Mar. 17, 1953; s. George P. and Buelah M. (Mitchell) W.; m. Christine Ridenour, July 4, 1981; children: Katherine Janelle, Elyse Nicole. BS cum laude, U. Ariz., 1975, MS, 1979; DO, Kirksville Coll. Osteo., 1983. Physician pvt. practice, Tucson, 1984—. Office: Foothills Family Practice 1601 W Ina Rd Tucson AZ 85704

WHEELER, CLARENCE JOSEPH, JR., physician; b. Dallas, Sept. 25, 1917; s. Clarence Joseph Sr. and Sadie Alice (McKinney) W.; m. Alice Mary Freels, Dec. 6, 1942; deceased; m. Patsy Lester Butler, Sept. 2, 1995; children: Stephen Freels, C.J. III, Robert McKinney, Thomas Michael, David Ritchey. BS in Math., So. Meth. U., 1941, BA in Psychology, 1946; MD, John Hopkins U., 1950. Diplomate Am. Bd. Surgery; cert. provider ACLS and advanced trauma life support, Am. Heart Assn. Intern John Hopkins Hosp., Balti., 1950-51; resident in surgery Barnes Hosp., St. Louis, 1951-54; fellow thoracic surgery U. Wis. Hosp., Madison, 1954-56, instr. surgery, 1955-56; attending surgeon Welborne Clinic Baptist Hosp., Evansville, Ind., 1956-57; mem. consulting staff Tex. Children's Hosp., 1957-70; courtesy and consulting staffs Pasadena Hosp., Spring Br. Hosp., others, Houston, 1957-70; mem. active staff Hermann Hosp., Houston, 1957-70, St. Luke's Hosp., Houston, 1957-70, Meth. Hosp., Houston, 1957-70, St. Joseph's Hosp., Houston, 1957-70, Meml. Hosp., Houston, 1957-70, Ben Taub Gen. City/County Hosp., Houston, 1957-70, Diagnostic Hosp., &, 1957-70; attending surgeon Lindley Hosp., Duncan, Okla., 1970-71; sr. attending, chief surgery Gordon Hosp., Lewisburg, Tenn., 1971-73; chief thoracic surgery Lewisburg Community Hosp., 1973-75; mem. active med. staff, med. dir. Carver Family Health Clinic, 1975-82; dir. emergency dept. Meth. Med. Ctr. Ill., Peoria, 1975-82; mem. staff Contract Emergency Med. Care, Houston and Dallas, 1982-88; med. dir. substance abuse unit Terrell (Tex.) State Hosp., 1988-90; med. dir. Schick-Shadel Hosp., Dallas-Ft. Worth, 1991—; med. dir., chief of staff Schick-Shadel Hosp., Ft. Worth, 1991-93; med. dir. Skillman Med. Ctr., Dallas, 1993-95, Centers for Preventative Medicine, Dallas, 1995—; instr. surgery U. Wis. Med. Sch., 1955-56; clin. instr. Baylor Coll. Medicine, Houston, 1959-70; lectr. U. Tex. Postgrad. Sch., Houston, 1957-70; clin. asst. prof. U. Ill. Sch. Medicine, Peoria, 1977-82; sr. med. advisor Thue Tien Province, So. Vietnam, 1968-69; chief of surgery Bien Vien Hué So. Vietnam, 1968-69. Treas. Samuel Clark Red Sch. PTA, Houston, 1959-61; bd. dirs. Salvation Army Boys Club, Houston; mem. Am. Mus. of Nat. History, Met. Mus. Art, Smithsonian Inst., Dallas Symphony Assn., Dallas Opera Soc., Dallas Theatre Ctr., Theatre Three Assn. Capt. USMCR, 1942-45, PTO. Decorated DFC with three stars, Air medal with four stars, Pacific Combat Theatre Ribbon with three stars, Purple Heart, Vietnamese Medal of Health (1st class), Vietnamese Medal Social Welfare, Navy Commendation medal, Presdl. Unit citation medal, Meritorious Bronze Star. Fellow ACS, Am. Coll. Angiology, Am. Coll. Chest Physicians, Royal Soc. Medicine, Internat. Coll. Surgeons, Am. Coll. Gastroenterology, Southea. Surg. Congress, Southwestern Surg. Congress, Internat. Assn. Proctologists; mem. AAAS, AMA, Am. Thoracic Soc., Nat. Tb Assn., Am. Assn. History of Medicine, Am. Soc. Contemporary Medicine and Surgery, Am. Soc. Addiction Medicine (cert.), Am. Heart Assn., Am. Cancer Soc., Am. Soc. Abdominal Surgeons, Marine Corps Officer's Assn., Naval Res. Officer's Assn., Nat. Geog. Soc., Mil. Order of the World Wars, Navy League, Indsl. Med. Assn., So. Med. Assn., Tex. Med. Assn., Tex. Thoracic Soc., Tex. Heart Assn., Tex. Anti-Tb Assn., Postgrad. Med. Assembly So. Tex., St. Louis Med. Soc., Dallas County Med. Soc., Marshall County Med. Soc. (pres.), Harris County Med. Soc., Houston Heart Assn., Houston Gastroent. Soc., Houston Surg. Soc., Greater Dallas Res. Officers Assn., Sierra Club, Rotary, Kappa Sigma, Phi Eta Sigma, Kappa Mu Epsilon, Psi Chi. Episcopalian. Address: 7111 Chipperton Dr Dallas TX 75225-1708 Address: 7111 Chipperton Dr Dallas TX 75225-1708

WHEELER, JOCK R., dean. Dean Ea. Va. Med. Sch. Med. Coll. Hampton Rds. Office: Ea Va Med Sch Med Coll Norfolk Va PO Box 1980 Norfolk VA 23501

WHEELER, MALCOLM HUBERT, surgeon, consultant; b. Marlborough, Wilts, Eng., Apr. 8, 1942; s. Hubert John and Jean Grace (MacDonald) W.; m. Margaret Lynne Davies, Apr. 2, 1968; children: James Malcolm Donald, John Spencer Charles, Richard Alexander Edward. MB BChir, U. Wales, 1965, MD, 1973. Sr. registrar in surgery Cardiff, 1972-76, sr. lectr., cons. surgeon, 1976-81; cons. surgeon Univ. Hosp. Wales, Cardiff, 1981—; guest lectr. Japan Assn. Endocrine Surgeons, Tokyo, 1995; vis. prof. U. Otago, New Zealand, 1995. Editor: Diseases of the Thyroid--Pathophysiology and Management; contbr. articles to med. jours. Steward Ch. in Wales, Cardiff, 1992—. Fellow Royal Coll. Surgeons (Eng., examiner 1994—); mem. Internat. Assn. Endocrine Surgeons (sec./treas. 1991-97), Brit. Assn. Endocrine Surgeons (pres. 1990-91), Surg. Rsch. Soc., Brit. Assn. Gastroenterology, Am. Assn. Endocrine Surgeons (corr. mem.), Royal Soc. Medicine. Home:

Aldbourne House, Cottrell Dr Bonvilston NR, Cardiff CF5 6T4, Wales Office: U Hosp Wales, Dept Surgery, Heath Cardiff Wales

WHEELER, MARILYN GARNSEY, psychotherapist, director; b. Mt. Vernon, N.Y., Sept. 22, 1943; d. Raymond Darwin and Mary (Pavelchek) Garnsey; m. Dan J. Wheeler, Sept. 8, 1962; children: Danny Jr., Maryn Beth, Jennifer Anne. BA magna cum laude, Coll. of St. Rose, 1980; MS and EdS, SUNY, Albany, 1983. Pvt. practice psychotherapist Amsterdam, N.Y., 1981—; exec. dir., therapist Counseling Care & Svcs., Inc., Cohoes, N.Y., 1983—; founder Counseling Care & Svcs., Inc., 1983; mem. adj. faculty SUNY, Albany, 1985—, Antioch/New Eng. Grad. Sch., Keene, N.H., 1991—; cons. Cohoes City Sch. Dist., 1985—. Pres. bd. Rensselaer (N.Y.) Girls Club, 1980-83; elder Second Presbyn. Ch., 1986—, moderator christian edn. com.; bd. dirs. Suburban Albany County Family Self Sufficiency Task Force, 1991—. Mem. AACD, Mental Health Counselors Assn., Kappa Gamma Pi, Delta Epsilon Sigma. Office: Counseling Care & Svcs Inc 22-40 Remsen St Cohoes NY 12047

WHEELER, STEPHEN LEIGH, oral and maxillofacial surgeon; b. Pomona, Calif., Dec. 14, 1951; s. Donald Romick and Barbara (Rowe) W.; m. Lynne Dunahoo, June 17, 1978; children: Jennifer Leigh, Jessica Lynne. BA in Polit. Sci., Stanford U., 1974; DDS, U. So. Calif., 1978. Diplomate Am. Bd. Oral and Maxillofacial Surgery. Resident in oral surgery Los Angeles County-U. So. Calif. Med. Ctr,, L.A., 1978-81; pvt. practice, Encinitas, Calif., 1981—; nat. cons. Interpore Internat., Irvine, Calif., 1994—; admissions interviewer U. So. Calif. Dental Sch., 1975-76; mem. active staff Scripps Meml. Hosp., Encinitas; mem. courtesy staff Scripps Meml. Hosp., La Jolla, Calif.; internat. lectr. and presenter in field of dental implant sys.; dir. West Coast Regional Tng. Ctr., Interpore-IMZ Dental Implant Sys. Contbr. articles to dental jours. Vol. Health Fair Oral Cancer Clinic, Calif. State U., L.A.; participant dental screening San Diego Boy's Club, 1983-84. Mem. ADA, Am. Assn. Oral and Maxillofacial Surgeons, Am. Acad. Implant Dentistry, Marsh Robinson Acad. Oral Surgery, Acad. Osseointegration, Pierre Fauchard dental Honor Acad., Calif. Dental Assn., So. Calif. Soc. Oral and Maxillofacial Surgery (program com. 1990-92), San Diego County Dental Soc. (program chmn. 1987-88, spkr. chmn. nat. meeting 1989-90, bd. dirs. 1990-91), San Dieguito Dental Health Acad. (program chmn. 1983, treas. 1984, v.p. 1985, pres. 1986), San Diego Dental Implant Group (co-founder), Rancho Santa Fe Dental Implant Study Club (founder, pres. 1987), San Diego County Oral Surgery Study Club (program chmn. 1992-93), Paul Revere Study Club, Omicron Kappa Upsilon, Alpha Tau Epsilon. Republican. Office: 310 Santa Fe Dr Ste 112 Encinitas CA 92024

WHEELER, STEVE DEREAL, neurologist; b. Chgo., Sept. 15, 1951; s. Clarence and Tommie L. (Andrews) W.; m. Debra B. Buckingham; children: Winter N., Ryan S., Gabrielle S. Student, Mich. State U., 1970-73; MD, Dartmouth Coll., 1976. Diplomate Am. Bd. Psychiatry and Neurology, Nat. Bd. Med. Examiners; lic. Mich., Ohio, Fla. Intern Thomas Jefferson U., Phila., 1976-77; emergency physician River Dist. Hosp. Emergency Cons., Inc., St. Clair, Mich., 1977-78; fellow Dartmouth Med. Sch., 1978; resident U. Miami, Fla., 1978-81; fellow Washington U., St. Louis, 1981-82; instr. in neurology Med. Coll. Pa., Phila., 1982-83; electroencephalograph reader, attending neurologist VA Med. Ctr., Phila., 1982-83; asst. neurologist, attending neurologist Muscle Clinic U. Hosps. Cleve., 1983-86; electromyographer Rainbow Babies and Children's Hosp., U. Hosps. Cleve., 1983-86; chief neuromuscular diseases divsn., asst. prof. neurology Case Western Res. U., Cleve., 1983-86, co-dir. muscle disease ctr. and lab., 1985-86; clin. assoc. prof. of neurology U. Miami, 1987-89; pvt. practice Miami, 1987—; lectr. Myasthenia Gravis Found., Vermillion, Ohio, 1984, Student Nat. Med. Assn., Cleve., 1983-86; vol. assoc. prof. U. Miami Sch., 1992—, vis. lectr., 1983—; neurology cons. Low Back Pain Team U. Hosps. Cleve., 1984-86; mem. quality assurance com. Coral Reef Hosp., Miami, 1987-88; cons. dir. planning Bapt. Headache Clinic Bapt. Hosp., Miami, 1993—; mem. adminstrv. com. Deering Hosp. Pain Mgmt. Ctr., Miami, 1993-94; mem. sleep diagnostic ctr. com. Bapt. Hosp., 1990-92, 94—, advisor to headache support group, 1995—; lectr. in field. Author (chpt.) Intensive Care For Neurological Trauma and Disease, 1982; contbr. articles to profl. jours. Named Internat. Man Yr., 1991-92; recipient Celebration Excellence Black Achiever award Family Christian Assn. Am., 1992. Fellow Royal Soc. Medicine, Am. Acad. Neurology; mem. Am. Acad. Clin. Neurophysiology, Am. Soc. Internal Medicine, Am. Assn. Study of Headache, Am. Coll. Physicians, Nat. Headache Found., Nat. Chronic Pain Outreach Program, Nat. Stroke Assn., Internat. Headache Soc., Fla. Med. Assn., Fla. Soc. Neurology, Fla. Soc. Internal Medicine, N.Y. Acad. Scis., Muscular Disease Soc. Northeastern Ohio (bd. trustees 1984-86), Dade County Med. Assn., So. Pain Soc., Internat. Assn. Study of Pain, Dartmouth Club Greater Miami, Am. Coun. for Headache Edn. Office: 8950 N Kendall Dr Ste 501 Miami FL 33176-2132

WHEELER, WILLIAM EARL, general surgeon; b. Fort Benning, Ga., Feb. 23, 1952; s. Thomas Harvey and Martha (Donaldson) W.; m. Rebecca Sue Shafer, May 6, 1984; children: Thomas Andrew, William Matthew. AA, East Ctrl. C.C., 1972; BS, Millsaps Coll., 1974; MD, U. Miss., 1977. Diplomate Am. Bd. Surgery. From asst. prof. to assoc. prof. Marshall Univ., Huntington, W.Va., 1983-91; staff surgeon Upstate Carolina Med. Ctr., Gaffney, S.C., 1991—; staff surgeon VA Med. Ctr., Huntington, 1983-91; chief surgical svc., 1985-91; staff and burn surgeon, Cabell Huntington Hosp, 1983-91; staff surgeon St. Mary's Hosp., Huntington, 1983-91; chief surg. sect. Upstate Carolina Med. Ctr., 1994-95; staff surgeon Mary Black Meml. Hosp., Spartanburg, S.C., 1992—; asst. clin. prof. surgery Med. Coll. S.C., Charleston, 1994—. Camp physician, committeeman Boy Scouts Am., Huntington, 1986-91; water safety instr. ARC, Decatur, Miss., 1971-80; elder Limestone Presbyn. Ch., Gaffney, 1994-96, fin. com., 1993-96. Recipient Eagle Scout award, Boy Scouts Am., 1967. Fellow Am. Coll. Surgeons; mem. AMA, Am. Burn Assn., S.C. Med. Assn., So. Med. Assn., Kiwanis. Home: 118 Greenbriar Dr Gaffney SC 29341 Office: 117 E Montgomery St Gaffney SC 29340

WHELAN, JOSEPH L., neurologist; b. Chisholm, Minn., Aug. 13, 1917; s. James Gorman and Johanna (Quilty) W.; m. Gloria Ann Rewoldt, June 12, 1948; children: Joe, Jennifer. Student, Hibbing Jr. Coll., 1935-38; BS, U. Minn., 1940, MB, 1942, MD, 1943. Diplomate Am. Bd. Psychiatry and Neurology. Intern Detroit Receiving Hosp., 1942-43; fellow neurology U. Pa. Hosp., Phila., 1946-47; resident neurology U. Minn. Hosps., Mpls., 1947-49; chief neurology svc. VA Hosp., Mpls., 1949; spl. fellow electroencephalography Mayo Clinic, Rochester, Minn., 1951; practice medicine specializing in neurology Detroit, 1949-73, Petoskey and Gaylord, Mich., 1973-87; asst. prof. Wayne State U., 1957-63; chief neurology svcs. Grace Hosp., St. John's Hosp., Bon Secour Hosp., Detroit; cons. neurologist No. Mich. Hosps., Charlevoix Area Hosp.; instr. Med. Sch. U. Minn., 1949; cons. USPHS, Detroit Bd. Edn. Contbr. articles to profl. jours. Founder, mem. ad hoc Com. to Force Lawyers Out of Govt. Fellow Am. Acad. Neurology (treas. 1955-57), Am. Electroencephalography Soc.; mem. AMA, AAAS, Assn. Rsch. Nervous and Mental Diseases, Soc. Clin. Neurologists, Mich. Neurol. Assn. (sec.-treas. 1967-76, Disting. Physician award 1988), Mich. Med. Soc., No. Mich. Med. Soc., Grosse Pointe (Mich.) Club. Address: 9797 N Twin Lake Rd Mancelona MI 49659-9203

WHELEN, ANDREW CHRISTIAN, microbiologist; b. El Paso, Tex., July 17, 1959; s. Henry James and Frances Annette (Lasiter); m. Jaclyn Kay, Sept. 21, 1991. BS, S.D. State U., 1981; PhD, U. N.D., 1985. Grad. asst. S.D. State U., 1980-82, U. S.D., 1982-83; from grad. asst. to sr. grad. asst. U. N.D., 1983-85; commd. 2d lt. U.S. Army, 1982, advanced through grades to maj., 1993; chief virology Letterman Army Med. Ctr., San Francisco, 1986-88; chief microbiology Landstuhl (Germany) Army Regional Med. Ctr., 1989-93; postdoctoral fellow in microbiology Mayo Clinic, Rochester, Minn., 1993-94; asst. prof. lab. medicine and pathology Mayo Med. Sch., Rochester, Minn., 1994—; dir. microbiology Brooke Army Med. Ctr., San Antonio, Tex., 1995—; adj. faculty San Francisco State U., 1987-88, U. Md., European div., 1989-90, Uniformed Svcs. U. Health Scis., European divsn., 1991-93, 96—. Pres. Jr. Officers Assn., Landstuhl, 1990-91; commr. Installation Softball League, Landstuhl, 1990-91; vol. Spl. Olympics, San Antonio, 1988. Mem. Am. Soc. Microbiology, German-Am. Med. Soc., Soc. Armed Forces Med. Lab. Scientists, Sigma Xi. Home: 1811 E Robinson Ave El Paso TX 79902-2219 Office: Dept Pathology & Area Lab Svcs Brooke Army Med Ctr San Antonio TX 78234

WHELESS, JAMES WARREN, neurologist; b. Glens Falls, N.Y., Apr. 18, 1956; s. True and Ada Adelphine (Bump) W.; m. Annette Carolyn Hyland, Apr. 7, 1982; children: Catherine Elizabeth, Margaret Caroline. BS, U. Okla., Oklahoma City, 1978, MD, 1982. Diplomate Am. Bd. Pediatrics, Am. Bd. Psychiatry and Neurology with spl. qualification in child neurology. Intern, then pediatric resident U. Okla.-Tulsa Med. Coll., 1982-85; fellow in child neurology Northwestern U., Chgo., 1985-88; fellow in clin. neurophysiology/epilepsy Med. Coll. Ga., Augusta, 1988-89; asst. prof. neurology and pediatrics U. Tex., Houston, 1989-95, dir. epilepsy monitoring unit, 1989—, assoc. prof. neurology and pediatrics, 1995—. Contbr. articles, editl. to profl. jours., chpt. to book. Camp physician Kamp Kleidoscope, Livingston, Tex., 1995—. Pres.'s Fund grantee U. Tex.-Houston, 1990, Children's Miracle Network Telethon grantee Hermann Children's Hosp. Fellow Am. Acad. Neurology, Child Neurology Soc.; mem. AMA, Am. Epilepsy Soc., Am. Acad. Pediatrics, Epilepsy Assn. of Houston/Gulf Coast (chmn. profl. adv. bd. 1992-94). Office: U Tex-Houston Dept Neurology 6431 Fannin St Ste 7044 Houston TX 77030

WHETSTONE, MICHAEL M., neuropsychologist, consultant; b. Kansas City, Mo., June 14, 1954; s. Maynard Lee and Jane E. (Smith) W. BA, Park Coll., 1976; MEd, U. Mo., 1980; PhD, U. Iowa, 1985. Lic. Psychologist, Iowa, Mo.; Cert. Rehab. Counselor, Mo. Adminstr., neuropsychologist New Medico Tex., Lindale, 1987-88; adminstr. Meadowbrook Neurologic Treatment Program, Gardner, Kans., 1988-90; neuropsychologist St. John's Regional Health Ctr., Springfield, Mo., 1990—; adj. prof. Forest Inst. Profl. Psychol., Springfield, 1990—; mem. trauma com., St. John's Regional Health Ctr., Springfield, 1990—, rehab. com., 1990—, neuro-ICU com., 1995; surveyor Commn. Accreditation of Rehab. Facilities, 1990—. Mem. Nat. Rehab. Assn., Nat. Acad. Neuropsychology, Nat. Head Injury Assn., Mo. Head Injury Assn. (pres. 1990—, bd. dirs. 1995), Am. Psychol. Assn., Ozark Area Psychol. Assn. Office: St Johns Regional Health Ctr 1235 E Cherokee Springfield MO 65804

WHIDDEN, ROBERT LEE, JR., health care consultant; b. Beverly, Mass., Oct. 10, 1943; s. Robert Lee and Phyllis Alma (Patch) W.; A.B. in English, Harvard U., 1965; m. Lois Ann Lapeza, Mar. 4, 1972. div. dir. Lowell (Mass.) Gen. Hosp., 1970-75; asst. adminstr. Union Hosp., Lynn, Mass., 1975-85; pres. Surgi/1 div., 1984-86, R.L. Whidden and Co., Andover, Mass., 1986—, Query, 1986—, hon. consul, Boston, St. Lucia, 1993—; prin. cons. Charlton Meml. Hosp., Fall River, Mass., 1987—, New Eng. Meml. Hosp., Stoneham, Mass., 1988—; hosp. rep. delegated rev. com. Eastern Mass. Profl. Standards Rev. Orgn., bd. dirs., 1984—; ex-officio mem. Integrated Data Demonstration Grant Com. Blue Cross Mass., 1982—; health care advisor Govt. of Anguilla, Brit. West Indies, 1989-91; cons. health affairs Brit. Dept. Territories, 1990—. Bd. dirs. Lowell Area Continuing Edn. Ctr., Nat. Found. Environ. Control, 1971, Hospice of North Shore, Inc.; bd. dirs., chmn. Northshore Manpower Coalition; mem. corp. edn. adv. bd. North Shore Community Coll., 1981—; mem. North Shore Econ. Coun., 1981—; mem. Mass. Health Data Adv. Council. Nat. Merit scholar, 1960-61. Mem. Am. Coll. Health Care Execs. (diplomate), Mass. Hosp. Assn. (mem. program rev. com. 1982—, chmn. mgmt. com. 1984—, mem. facilities and service com. class of 1987), New Eng. Hosp. Assembly, Am. Soc. Law and Medicine, Health Care Mgmt. Assn., Am. Mgmt. Assn., Phi Beta Kappa. Episcopalian. Clubs: Myopia Polo (patron), Hasty Pudding, Andover Tennis. Home and Office: 3 Spruce Cir Andover MA 01810-4020

WHIFFEN, JAMES DOUGLASS, surgeon, educator; b. N.Y.C., Jan. 16, 1931; s. John Phillips and Lorna Elizabeth (Douglass) W.; child from a previous marriage, Gregory James; m. Sally Vilas Runge, Aug. 21, 1993. B.S., U. Wis., 1952, M.D., 1955. Diplomate: Am. Bd. Surgery. Intern Ohio State U. Hosp., 1955-56; resident U. Wis. Hosp., 1956-57, 59-61; instr. dept. surgery U. Wis. Med. Sch., 1962-64, asst. prof., 1964-67, asso. prof., 1967-71, prof., 1971—, vice chmn. dept., 1970-72, acting chmn., 1972-74; asst. dean Med. Sch., 1975—; mem. exam. council State of Wis. Emergency Med. Services, 1974-77. Bd. dirs. Wis. Heart Assn. Served to lt. comdr. USNR, 1957-59. John and Mary R. Markle scholar in acad. medicine, also; Research Career Devel. award NIH, 1965-75. Fellow A.C.S., Am. Soc. Artificial Internal Organs. Club: Maple Bluff Country. Home: 17 Cambridge Ct Madison WI 53704-5906 Office: 600 Highland Ave Madison WI 53792-0001

WHIFFEN, JOHN ROBERT, orthopaedic surgeon; b. Madison, June 19, 1946; s. John Phillips and Lorna Elizabeth (Douglass) W.; m. Lucy Lee Newman, Oct. 12, 1976; children: Christopher, Jennifer, Elizabeth. BS, U. Wis., 1968; MD, Harvard U., 1971. Diplomate Am. Bd. Orthopaedic Surgery. Orthopaedic resident Harvard U., Boston, 1973-76; pediat. orthopaedic fellow Chgo.-Shriners Hosp., 1978; spinal rsch. fellow Rush-Presbyn. St. Lukes Med. Ctr., Chgo., 1979; orthopaedic spine surgeon Bone & Joint Surgery Assocs., Madison, 1980-84, Madison Orthopaedic Assn., 1984-86, Physicians Plus, Madison, 1986—. Lt. comdr. USN, 1976-78. Fellow Am. Acad. Orthopaedic Surgery; mem. N.Am. Spine Soc., Scoliosis Rsch. Soc. (morbidity's mortality com. 1995—). Office: Physician Plus 1 S Park St Madison WI 53715

WHIMS, LISA ANN, osteopath; b. Akron, Ohio, July 7, 1967; d. Gerald Lloyd and Judith Ann (Poholski) W. BA, Hiram Coll., 1989; DO, Southeastern U. Health Scis., 1993. Diplomate Am. Bd. Osteo. Assn. Intern Palmetto Gen. Hosp., Hialeah, Fla.; resident internal medicine Kennedy Meml. Hosp., Stratford, N.J., osteopath; fellow pulmonary medicine Kennedy Meml. Hosp., Stratford, 1996—. Mem. ACP, Am. Osteo. Assn., Fla. Osteo. Med. Assn., N.J. Assn. Physicians and Surgeons. Home: 1202 Hawthorne Ct Sewell NJ 08080 Office: Kennedy Meml Hosp 18 E Laurel Rd Stratford NJ 08034

WHINERY, MICHAEL ALBERT, physician; b. Watsford, Eng., June 30, 1951; s. Leo Howard and Doris Eileene W. and Alma Piper; m. Tatijana Dunnebier, 1976 (dec. Jan. 1981); m. Judy Renee Wright, Apr. 30, 1982; children: Rhiannon Daire Eileene, Terron Rae Lee. BS, Okla. U., 1976; D of Osteopathy, Okla. State U., 1980. Bd. cert. physician in gen. practice. Intern Hillcrest Health Ctr., Oklahoma City, Okla., 1980-81; with McLoud Clinic, McLoud, Okla.; house physician McLoud Nursing Ctr., 1988—; med. examiner Pottawatomie County Health, McLoud, 1983—. Author: Poetic Voices of America, 1991. Mem. Presdl. Order Merit Nat. Repub. Senatorial Com., Washington, 1991, Presdl. Task Force, 1983—, Senatorial Commn. Repub. Senatorial Inner Circle, Washington, 1991; mem. U.S. Congrl. Adv. Bd., 1993. With USMC, Vietnam. Recipient Acknowledgement of Outstanding Contbn. in Clin. Rsch. award SANDOZ Labs., 1992, Rep. Presdl. Legion of Merit, 1994. Mem. Am. Legion, C. of C., Jr. C. of C., U.S. Senatorial Club (preferred mem.), U.S. Congressional Act Bd. (state advisor 1990-91). Baptist. Office: McLoud Clinic PO Box 520 107 S Main Mc Loud OK 74851

WHIPPLE, ROBERT HARVEY, physical therapist, researcher, educator; b. N.Y.C., May 17, 1942; s. Irwin Robert and Theresa (Taucher) W.; m. Barbara Jean Senkpiel, June 3, 1967; children: Karl, Charlene, Mark, Irene. BA in Biology, U. Rochester, 1964; cert. phys. therapy, Columbia U., 1967; MA in Kinesiology, NYU, 1974. Phys. therapist, supr. rsch. Inst. Rehab. Medicine, N.Y.C., 1966-74; phys. therapist, rsch. scientist NYU, 1974-77; chief phys. therapist Internat. Ctr. for Disabled, N.Y.C., 1977-80; asst. prof. Divsn. Phys. Therapy Ithaca (N.Y.) Coll., 1980-85; assoc. dept. neurology Albert Einstein Coll. Medicine, N.Y.C., 1985-90; asst. prof. neurology dept. U. Conn. Sch. Medicine, Farmington, 1990—; rsch. cons. Dau. of Jacob Geriatric Ctr., Bronx, N.Y., 1985-86; grant reviewer NIH, Bethesda, 1992—. Contbr. articles to profl. jours. Mem. task force on AIDS N.Y. Conf. United Meth. Ch., White Plains, N.Y., 1994—. Mem. Am. Phys. Therapy Assn. (Robert Salant Rsch. award 1985, Excellence in Rsch. award Geriatric sect. 1988, 91). Home: 2105 Quaker Ridge Rd Croton-on-Hudson NY 10520 Office: Balance & Gait Enchancement Univ Conn Health Ctr Farmington CT 06030-6144

WHIPPLE, ROBERT LAFAYETTE, III, cardiologist; b. Atlanta, Nov. 13, 1042; s. Robert Lafayette Jr. and Aileen Eva (Shortley) W.; m. Claire Mary LeBlanc, June 22, 1968; children: Robert L IV, Justin P, Mary Claire. BA, Vanderbilt U., 1963; MD, Emory U., 1967. Diplomate Am. Bd. Internal Medicine, Am. Bd. Cardiovascular Disease; lic. cardiologist Ga. State Bd. Med. Examiners. Intern then resident Grady Meml. Hosp., Atlanta, 1967-69; resident then cardiology fellow Emory U. Hosps., Atlanta, 1973-76; chief resident Crawford Long Hosp., Atlanta, 1975-76; pvt. practice, pres. Cardiology of Ga., P.C., Atlanta, 1976—. Lt. comdre USN, 1969-72, Vietnam. Recipient Eben J. Carey Meml. award Phi Chi, 1964; decorated Bronze star combat V, 1973. Fellow Am. Coll. Cardiology, Coun. Clin. Cardiology, Am. hHart Assn.; mem. AMA, Met. Assn. Atlanta, Alpha Omega Alpha. Home: 1190 W Wesley Rd NW Atlanta GA 30327 Office: Cardiology Ga PC 95 Collier Rd NW Ste 2075 Atlanta GA 30309

WHISNANT, JOSEPH DURWOOD, urologist; b. Winston-Salem, N.C., Sept. 1, 1945; s. Joseph Durwood and Mildred Pauline (Bumparner) W.; m. Betty Anne Stedman, June 24, 1968; children: Jennifer, Rebecca, Rachel. BS, Wake Forest U., 1967; MD, Bowman Gray Sch. Medicine, 1971. Diplomate Am. Bd. Urology. Pvt. practice Rocky Mount, N.C. Maj. USAF, 1971-73. Mem. BCC, Alpha Omega Alpha. Democrat. Baptist. Office: 180 Foy Dr Rocky Mount NC 27804-2417

WHITAKER, AUDIE DALE, hospital laboratory medical technologist; b. Cin., Jan. 19, 1949; s. Audie and Wanda Edith (Weaver) W.; m. Sandra Sue McPhail, Aug. 22, 1970; children: Audie David Nathaniel, Andrea Grace, Alexandra Christine. BA, Olivet Nazarene U., 1971; Degree in Med. Tech., Silver Cross Hosp., Joliet, Ill., 1972. Med. tech. Riverside Hosp., Kankakee, 1971-72, Silver Cross Hosp., Joliet, 1972-77; lab. mgr. Lakeshore Community Hosp., 1977-90; evening lab. supr. Community Hosp., Anderson, Ind., 1990-93; med. technologist Community Hosp. of Anderson, 1990—; lectr. in field. Health care rep. Local Emergency Preparedness Com., Hart, Mich., 1988-90; sec., deacon, bd. dirs. West Shore Christian Fellowship, Muskegon, 1987-90, vice chmn. edn. com., 1988-90; mem. Rep. Nat. Com. S.W. Nazarene Ch. Dist. grantee, 1967, Directed Study grantee, 1970-71, rsch. grantee Sigma Xi, 1993, 95; grad. rsch. grantee Ball State U., 1994, 95. Mem. Am. Soc. Clin. Pathologists. Republican. Home: 1705 N Tillotson Muncie IN 47304-4337 Office: Community Hosp 1515 N Madison Ave Anderson IN 46011-3453

WHITAKER, THOMAS ALEXANDER, ophthalmologist; b. Florence, S.C., Oct. 17, 1944; s. Thomas Lee and Dorothy Blake (Belk) W. BS in Premedicine, Presbyn. Coll., 1966; MD, U. Tenn., 1970. Diplomate Am. Bd. Ophthalmology, Am. Bd. Eye Surgery. Resident U. Ala. and Eye Found. Hosp., Birmingham, 1974-77; ophthalmologist, ptnr. Eye Assocs. S.C., LLC, Myrtle Beach, S.C., 1977—; chief of staff Carolina Regional Surg. Ctr., Myrtle Beach, 1989—; dir. Physicians EyeCare Networks, 1995—; vice chief of staff Grand Strand Gen. Hosp., Myrtle Beach., 1980-81, chief of staff, 1981-82, bd. of trustees, 1982-86. Bd. visitors Presbyn. Coll., Clinton, S.C., 1988-92, trustee, 1993—; bd. dirs. United Way of Horry County, 1988—; elder 1st Presbyn. Ch., Myrtle Beach, 1984-90. Lt. comdr. USNR, 1972-74. Fellow Am. Acad. Ophthalmology, Am. Bd. Eye Surgery; mem. AMA, Am. Coll. Eye Surgeons, Am. Soc. Cataract and Refractive Surgery, Ophthalmic Outpatient Surg. Soc., Contact Lens Assn. Ophthalmology, S.C. Soc. Ophthalmology (past pres.), S.C. Med. Assn., Lions, Rotary. Republican. Home: 9408 Lake Dr Myrtle Beach SC 29572-5006 Office: Ea Carolina Regional Ctr 900 Medical Cir Myrtle Beach SC 29572-4114

WHITAKER, VON BEST, nursing educator; b. New Bern, N.C.; d. Cleveland W. and Lillie (Bryant) Best; m. Roy Whitaker Jr., Aug. 9, 1981; 1 child, Roy Whitaker III. BS, Columbia Union Coll., 1972; MS, U. Md., 1974; MA, U. N.C., 1980, PhD, 1983. Lectr. U. N.C., Chapel Hill, 1981-82; asst. prof. U. Mo., Columbia, Mo., 1982-85; asst. prof. grad. sch. Boston Coll., Newton, Mass., 1985-86; asst. prof. U. Tex. Health Sci. Ctr., San Antonio, 1986-94; assoc. prof. Ga. So. U., Statesboro, 1994—; mem. cataract guideline panel Agy. for Health Care Policy Rsch., 1990-93; rsch. coord. glaucoma svc. Georgia Eye Inst., Savannah. Contbr. articles to profl. jours., chpts. to textbooks; presenter in field. Vol. to prevent blindness. Bush fellowship, 1979-81; recipient Cert. of Appreciation, Prevent Blindness South Tex., 1988, 89. Mem. ANA (cert. community health nurse), APHA, Am. Soc. Ophthalmic Nursing (chair rsch. com.), Assn. Black Faculty in Higher Edn., Nat. Black Nurses Assn., Sigma Theta Tau. Home: 1 Chelmsford Ln Savannah GA 31411

WHITE, AUGUSTUS AARON, III, orthopedic surgeon; b. Memphis, June 4, 1936; s. Augustus Aaron and Vivian (Dandridge) W.; m. Anita Ottemo; children: Alissa Alexandra, Atina Andrea, Annica Akila. AB in Psychology cum laude, Brown U., 1957; MD, Stanford U., 1961; D in Med. Sci., Karolinska Inst., Sweden, 1969; Advanced Mgmt. Program, Harvard U., 1984; DHL (hon.), U. New Haven, 1987. Diplomate Nat. Bd. Examiners, Am. Bd. Orthopaedic Surgery. Intern U. Mich. Hosp., Ann Arbor, 1961-62; asst. resident in gen. surgery Presbyn. Med. Center, San Francisco, 1962-63; asst. resident in orthopaedic surgery Yale Med. Center, New Haven, 1963-65, sr. instr., resident orthopaedic surgery, 1965-66; asst. prof. orthopaedic surgery Yale Med. Sch., 1969-72, assoc. prof., 1972-76, prof., 1977-78, dir. biomech. research dept. orthopedics, 1978-89; prof. orthopedic surgery Harvard Med. Sch., 1978—; orthopedic surgeon-in-chief Beth Israel Hosp., Boston, 1978-91, chief spine surgery divsn., orthopedic surgeon-in chief, 1991-92, emeritus, 1996—; sr. assoc. orthopedic surgery Children's Hosp. Med. Ctr., Boston, 1979-89; assoc. in orthopedic surgery Brigham & Women's Hosp., Boston, 1980-89; cons. div. surgery Sidney Farber Cancer Inst., Boston, 1980—; rschr. biomechanics lab. Beth Israel Hosp.; chair sci. adv. bd., dir. OrthoLogic, Inc., Phoenix; bd. dirs. Am. Shared Hosp. Svcs., San Francisco; cons. orthopaedic surgery West Haven (Conn.) VA Hosp., 1970—, Hill Health Ctr., New Haven, 1970—; chief orthopedic surgery Conn. Health Care Plan, 1976-78; mem. adv. coun. Nat. Inst. Arthritis, Metabolism and Digestive Disease, NIH, 1979-82; mem. admission scom. Yale Med. Sch., 1970-72; presenter, moderator Symposium on Cervical Myelopathy, San Francisco, 1987; chmn. grant rev. com. NIH, 1985; founding mem., bd. overseers Brown U. Sch. of Medicine, 1996—; bd. overseers WGBH Radio/TV, Boston, 1996—. Author: (monograph) Analysis of the Mechanics of the Thoracic Spine in Man, Leprosy, The Foot and The Orthopaedic Surgeon at Am. Acad. Orthopaedic Surgeons, 1970; book Clinical Biomechanics of the Spine, 1978, 2d edit., 1990; Symposium on Idiopathic Low Back Pain, 1982, Your Aching Back-A Doctor's Guide to Relief, 1983, rev. and updated edit., 1990, translated in German, 1992; prin. editor Time/Life Med. Video Back Pain; contbr. articles to profl. jours., chpts. to sci. books. Trustee Brown U., Providence, 1971-76, bd. fellows, 1981-92; trustee Northfield Mt. Hermon Sch., Northfield, Mass., 1976-81; chmn. corp. com. on minority affairs Brown U., Providence, 1981-86, chmn. corp. com. med. edn. med. sch.; mem. bd. dirs. The Partnership, Boston, 1984—. Capt. AUS, 1966-68. Decorated Bronze Star medal; named 1 of 10 Outstanding Young Men U.S. Jr. C. of C., 1969, Selected for Exceptional Black Scientist poster series CIBA-GEIGY Corp., 1982; recipient Martin Luther King, Jr. Med. Achievement award, 1972, Kappa Delta award, nat. prize for outstanding research in orthopaedics field, 1975; nat. award for spinal research Eastern Orthopaedic Assn., 1980; Disting. Service award Northfield Mt. Hermon Sch. Alumni Assn., 1983; William Rogers award Associated Alumni Brown U., 1984; Outstanding Achievement award Delta Upsilon, 1986; Am.-Brit.-Canadian Travelling fellow Am. Orthopedic Assn., 1975. Fellow Am. Acad. Orthopaedic Surgeons, Scoliosis Rsch. Soc.; mem. Orthopaedic Rsch. Soc., Cervical Spine Rsch. Soc., Internat. Soc. for Study Lumbar Spine, Internat. Soc. Orthopaedic Surgery and Traumatology, Nat. Med. Assn. (Orthopaedic Scholar award 1994), Cervical Spine Rsch. Soc. (pres. 1988), N.Am. Spine Soc., Acad. Orthopaedic Soc., Sigma Xi, Sigma Pi Phi.

WHITE, BETTY MAYNARD, retired social worker; b. N.Y.C., May 22, 1922; d. William and Madge (Hooks) Maynard; B.A., Hunter Coll., 1964; M.S.W., Columbia U., 1969; m. Charles E. White, Sept. 8, 1941; 1 child, Charles B. Case worker Bur. Child Welfare, Jamaica, N.Y., 1964-69; supr. foster care Spl. Services for Children, Jamaica, 1969-73, case supr. application sec., family services, group services, 1973-83, supr. III, borough coordinator for Manhattan and Bronx, Office Home Care Services, Div. Med. Rev., 1983-84, dir. div. Med. Rev., 1984; pvt. practice, 1986-90. Mem. Nat. Assn. Social Workers, Acad. Cert. Social Workers, Hunter Coll. Alumni Assn. Democrat. Roman Catholic. Home: 7864 S Leewynn Dr Sarasota FL 34240-9072

WHITE, BILLYE C., nurse, healthcare and quality management consultant; b. Lepanto, Ark., Nov. 28, 1955; d. Howard and Vera (Decanter) Covington; m. David H. White, Apr. 19, 1980. BSN, Ark. State U., Jonesboro, 1978.

RN, Ark.; cert. rehab. RN. Rehab. specialist Systemedic Corp., Little Rock, 1982-90; quality mgmt. dir. N.E. Ark. Rehab., Jonesboro, 1990-96; health care cons. Jonesboro, 1996—; mem. adv. bd. Parenting and Childbirth Edn. Svcs., Jonesboro, 1996; examiner Ark. Quality Award, Little Rock, 1995-96; mem. planning com. Ark. Head Injury Found., 1989-92. Co-leader Regional AIDS Interfaith Network, Jonesboro, 1993—. Mem. Assn. for Practitioners in Infection Control, Assn. Rehab. Nurses, Ark. Risk Mgmt. Assn. (bd. dirs. 1985—), Tenn. Assn. Rehab. (bd. dirs., pres. 1988-90). Baptist. Home: PO Box 444 Jonesboro AR 72403-0444

WHITE, CHARLOTTE SHELTON, oral surgeon; b. Ft. Knox, Ky., Feb. 1, 1951; d. John Paul and Mary Jean (Dowbiggin) Shelton; m. Wade Douglas White, July 28, 1973; 1 child, Benjamin David. AA, Palm Beach Jr. Coll., 1972; DMD, U. Fla., 1983. Diplomate Am. Bd. Oral and Maxillofacial Surgeons. Resident U. Fla., Gainesville, 1983-84; fellow in anesthesia Univ. Hosp., Jacksonville, Fla., 1984-85; intern, resident oral surgery U. Fla. Coll. Dentistry, Jacksonville, 1984-88; from asst. prof. to assoc. prof. U. Fla. Coll. Dentistry, Gainesville, 1988—. Fellow Internat. Coll. Dentists; mem. Am. Dental Assn., Am. Assn. Oral Maxillofacial Surgeons, Am. Assn. Dental Schs., Fla. Soc. Oral and Maxillofacial Surgeons, Am. Soc. Osseointegration, AM. coll. Oral Implantology, Internat. Congress Oral Implantologists, Fla. Dental Assn., Ctrl. Dist. Denal Assn., Alachua County Dental Soc., Fellowship Christian Faculty, Internat. Assn. Dental Rsch., Omicron Kappa Upsilon, Psi Omega. Home: Box 147050 4300 NW 23d Ave Ste 150 Gainesville FL 32614-7050 Office: U Fla Box 100416 JHMHC Gainesville FL 32610-0416

WHITE, CHRISTOPHER JAMES, cardiologist; b. Youngstown, Ohio, Sept. 19, 1952; s. James P. and Joan (Weygandt) W.; m. Janet Lynn Schwartz, May 15, 1987; children: Samantha, Jordan, James, Casey. BA, Oberlin Coll., 1974; MD, Case Western Res. U., 1978. Bd. cert. diplomate cardiovasc. disease. Cath-lab. dir. Letterman Army Med. Ctr., San Francisco, 1983-85, Walter Reed Army Med. Ctr., Washington, 1985-88, Ochsner Clinic, New Orleans, 1988-94; dir. invasive cardiology Health Care Int., Glasgow, Scotland, 1994—. Editor: Interventional Cardiology, 1991, 94; contbr. articles to profl. jours. Maj. U.S. Army, 1978-88. Fellow Am. Coll. Cardiology, European Soc. Cardiology, Am. Soc. Angiography and Intervention; mem. Alpha Omega Alpha. Office: Health Care Int Med Ctr, Beardmore St, Clydebank G81 4HX, Scotland

WHITE, ELIZABETH ANN, occupational health nurse; b. Princeton, Ky., Sept. 5, 1959; d. Bobby Logan and Ginny Lou (McCaslin) Lewis; 1 child, Rebekka Lou Walker. Health Tech. Ctr., Madisonville, Ky., 1993; Student, Hopkinsville Cmty. Coll., Princeton, Ky., 1993—. LPN, Ky. Staff nurse Caldwell County Hosp., Princeton, Ky.; head nurse, pvt. practice Dr. Debra Wilder, Eddyville, Ky.; charge nurse Princeton (Ky.) Health Care Manor. Mem. Village Homemakers Club (activities dir.), Madisonville, Ky. Democrat. Baptist. Home: 709 N Jefferson St Princeton KY 42445

WHITE, EMILY GRUEN, retired psychotherapist; b. Vienna, Austria, Mar. 25, 1921; parents U.S. citizens; d. Hugo and Anne Marian Wallenfels; m. Walter Gruen, Aug. 26, 1944 (div. 1952); 1 child, Marion Gruen Anderson; m. James Charles White, May 30, 1952; children: Anita Bialik, Wallace, Raymond, Margaret Bossen. BA summa cum laude, UCLA, 1943; MA in Child Psychology, U. Iowa, 1945; PhD candidate, U. Calif., Berkeley, 1948. Instr. child devel. U. Minn., Mpls., 1956-58, rsch. fellow in child devel., 1960-62; therapist Neighborhood Counseling Ctr., Mpls., 1976-79; pvt. practice Mpls., 1980-86; ret., 1986; speaker at ch. and sch. groups. Vol. ch. office St. Mary's Greek Orthodox Ch. Mem. Minn. Jung Assn. (bd. dirs.), Community Sts. Martin & Teresa, Phi Beta Kappa. Democrat. Greek Orthodox. Home: 3220 Hennepin Ave Minneapolis MN 55408-3447

WHITE, ERIC MILTON, optometrist; b. Chgo., Sept. 6, 1959; s. Milton George and Nancy Grace (Williams) W.; m. Lorie Ann Fitch, June 27, 1981; children: Tyler, Cameron, Samuel. BA in Physiol. Psychology, U. Calif., San Diego, 1982; BS in Visual Sci., So. Calif. Coll. Optometry, Fullerton, 1984, DO, 1986. Ptnr. DM Rasmussen OD Inc., San Diego, 1986-89; optometrist in pvt. practice San Diego, 1989—; cons. Am. Indian Health Svcs., Lions Optometric Clinic of San Diego, Sharp Hosp. Sr. Citizens Health Ctr., Am. Contact Lenses Adv. Bd., Allergan Medicare Alliance Task Force Com., Tryuson Sys., Dicon Sys., others; lectr., rschr., presenter in field. Contbr. numerous articles to profl. jours. Bd. dirs. So. Calif. chpt. Prevent Blindness Am., 1992—, v.p., 1993-94, pres.-elect., 1994—; active Boy Scouts Am.; chmn. stewardship com. First christian Ch. of El Cajon, 1993-95, trustee, 1993-95. Recipient Appreciation award Nat. Soc. to Prevent Blindness, 1985, 95, Vol. of Yr., United Way/Combined Health Agys., 1995. Mem. Am. Optometric Assn. (Young OD of Yr. 1995), Am. Optometric Found., Sports Vision Assn. Am., Calif. Optometric Assn., So. Calif. Coll. Optometry Alumni Assn. (life), San Diego Optometric Soc., Nat. Eagle Scout Assn. (life). Republican. Home: 1625 Hollow Pl El Cajon CA 92019 Office: Mission Village Med Ctr 2202 Ruffin Rd Ste L San Diego CA 92123

WHITE, EUGENE VADEN, pharmacist; b. Cape Charles, Va., Aug. 13, 1924; s. Paul Randolph and Louise (Townsend) W.; m. Laura Juanita LaFontaine, Aug. 28, 1948; children: Lynda Sue, Patricia Louise. BS in Pharmacy, Med. Coll. Va., 1950; PharM (hon.), Phila. Coll. Pharmacy and Sci., 1966. Pharmacist McKim & Huffman Drug Store, Luray, Va., 1950, Miller's Drug Store, Winchester, Va., 1950-53; pharmacist, ptnr. Shiner's Drug Store, Front Royal, Va., 1953-56; pharmacist, owner Eugene V. White, Pharmacist, P.C., Berryville, Va., 1956—; Sturmer lectr. Phila. Coll. Pharmacy and Sci., 1979; Lubin vis. prof. U. Tenn. Sch. Pharmacy, Memphis, 1974; mem. bd. visitors Sch. Pharmacy, U. Pitts., 1969. Author: The Office-Based Family Pharmacist, 1978; created first office practice in community pharmacy, 1960, developed patient medication profile record, 1960. 2d lt. USAAC, 1943-45. Recipient Nat. Leadership award Phi Lambda Sigma, 1979, Outstanding Pharmacy Alumnus award Med. Coll. Va. Sch. Pharmacy Alumni Assn., 1989; Eugene V. White scholarship named in his honor Shenandoah U. Sch. Pharmacy, 1996. Fellow Am. Coll. Apothecaries (J. Leon Lascoff award 1973); mem. Am. Pharm Assn. (Daniel B. Smith award 1965, Remington Honor medal 1978), Va. Pharm. Assn. (Pharmacist of Yr. award 1966, Outstanding Pharmacist award 1992). Methodist. Office: 1 W Main St Berryville VA 22611-1340

WHITE, GEORGE EDWARD, pedodontist; b. Jamestown, N.Y., July 31, 1941; s. Gordon Ennis and Margaret (Appleyard) W. AB, Colgate U., 1963; DDS, SUNY, Buffalo, 1967; PhD, MIT, 1973; DBA, Century U., 1982. Intern, then resident Children's Hosp., Buffalo, 1967-69; prof., chmn. dept. pediat. dentistry Tufts U. Sch. Dental Medicine, Boston, 1973—; chief dept. oral pediat. New Eng. Med. Center Hosp., Boston, 1973-80; pvt. practice pedodontics, Boston, 1974—; lectr. MIT, 1975-80; cons. Abcor, Inc.; nat., internat. lectr. Nat. Inst. Dental Rsch. grantee, 1973—. Author: Dental Caries: A Multifactorial Disease, 1975, To Stand Alone, 1979; co-author: Maxillofacial Orthopedics: For the Growing Child, 1983; founder, editor-in-chief Jour. Pedodontics, 1976, now named Jour. Clin. Pediat. Dentistry; editor: Clin. Oral Pediatrics, 1979, founder, editor-in-chief Mastering Clin. Pediat. Dentistry, 1993; editor-in-chief Protocols for Clin. Pediat. Dentistry; contbr. articles to profl. jours. Master Acad. Gen. Dentistry; fellow Am. Acad. Pediat. Dentistry, Internat. Coll. Dentistry; mem. Am. Assn. Functional Orthodontist, Northeast Craniomandibular Soc., Platform Soc., Fedn. Dentaire Internationale, Sigma Xi, Omicron Kappa Upsilon. Office: Tufts U Sch Dental Medicine Dept Pediat Dentistry 1 Kneeland St Boston MA 02111-1527

WHITE, GEORGE LOVELLE, JR., health educator, physician assistant; b. Greenville, Miss., Dec. 3, 1948; s. George Lovelle and Catherne Genelle (Simmons) W.; m. Kaylene Thornock, Dec. 3, 1984; children: George Lovelle III, Kaitlin Louise, Kaycee Leigh. AA, West Hills Coll., Coalinga, Calif., 1973; AS, U. Utah, 1974, BS in Health Sci. magna cum laude, 1978, MSPH, 1981, PhD in Health Edn., 1987. Cert. physician asst., ACLS, CPR, advanced trauma life support; registered sanitarian, Utah. Clin. instr. physicians asst. program U. Utah, Salt Lake City, 1978-87, phys. asst., rschr. dept. family and preventive medicine, 1985-87, asst. prof. dept. ophthalomology, dir. rsch., 1987-90; assoc. prof. Ctr. for Cmty. Health U. So. Miss., Hattiesburg, 1990-92, prof. Ctr. Cmty. Health, 1992-95; prof., chair dept. physicians asst. studies U. South Ala. Coll. Allied Health Professions, Mobile, 1995—, chmn. dept. physician asst. studies, 1996—, asst. to dean for clin. rsch., 1995—; cons. to various health and ednl. orgns. including Medi Vision Inc., Boston, 1983-85, Alcon Labs, Inc., Ft. Worth, 1988-90; presenter numerous confs. and orgns. in field. Mem. editl. rev. bd. for various jours. including Physician Asst., 1987-91, Health Values, 1990—, Clin. Revs., 1990—; contbr. numerous articles to profl. jours.and chpts. to books. Chmn. Rep. Voting Dist. 2814, Salt Lake City, 1988-90. With Utah Army Nat. Guard; maj. USAF, 1990-96. Recipient Clin. Teaching award Dept. Family and Preventive Medicine, Salt Lake City, 1988. Fellow Assn. Mil. Surgeons U.S. (life; Physician Asst. award 1996); mem. AAHPER (mem. editl. rev. bd. Health Edn. jour. 1990—), APHA, Am. Acad. Physicians Assts., Am. Soc. Safety Engrs., Sigma Xi, Phi Kappa Phi, Eta Sigma Gamma. Mem. LDS Ch. Office: U So Ala Coll Allied Health Prof Dept Phys Asst Studies 1504 Springhill Ave Ste 4410 Mobile AL 36604-3273

WHITE, HAROLD JACK, pathologist; b. Bklyn., Jan. 4, 1920; s. Abraham and Jennie (Warshawsky) W.; m. Lucette Darby, July 19, 1962; children: Elizabeth, Darby, Matthew, Esther. BS, Harvard U., 1941; MD, U. Geneva, 1952. Diplomate Am. Bd. Pathology. Intern, resident in pathology Yale U. Sch. Medicine, New Haven, 1953-58, fellow, 1957-58; assoc. pathologist Brigham and Women's Hosp., Boston, 1962-66; chief lab. svc. VA Hosp., West Roxbury, Mass., 1962-66, Little Rock, 1966-80; sr. scientist, acting head biomed. sci. dept. GM Rsch. Labs., Warren, Mich., 1980-85, cons., 1985—; prof. pathology, microbiology U. Ark. Med. Sch., Little Rock, 1966—; vis. scientist dept. comparative medicine, MIT, Cambridge, 1988—. Contbr. over 100 articles, abstracts in pathology, microbiology, immunology, toxicology, biomedicine to profl. jours. 1st lt. USAAF, 1942-46. Fellow Coll. Am. Pathologists, Internat. Coll. Pathology. Home: 24 Bass Rocks Rd Gloucester MA 01930-3276 Office: 35 Main St Gloucester MA 01930-5730

WHITE, HARVEY DOUGLAS, cardiologist; b. Awamutu, New Zealand, Nov. 19, 1947; s. Philip Leonard and Estelle Menzies (Smith) W; m. Janette Frances Venus, Feb. 27, 1973; children: Catherine Ann, Michael John. B of Medicine and Surgery, U. Otago, 1973, DSc, 1995. House surgeon Kew Hosp., Invercargill, New Zealand, 1975-75, med. registrar, 1976-78; cardiology registrar Green Lane Hosp., Auckland, New Zealand, 1978-80; assoc. physician Harvard Med. Sch. & Brigham and Women's Hosp., Boston, 1983-84; cardiology specialist Green Lane Hosp., 1985-89, dir. cardiovascular rsch., 1990—, dir. coronary care, 1992—; acting cardiology specialist Green Lane Hosp., 1980-81, hon. med. officer, 1984-88; clin. lectr. U. Auckland Sch. Medicine, 1981; acting cardiologist coronary care unit Auckland Hosp., 1984; clin. lectr. U. Auckland Sch. Medicine, 1992—. Editor: (tech. series) Nat Heart Found. New Zealand, 1990—; mem. editorial bd. Heart, 1996—; contbr. chpts. to books and articles to profl. jours. Overseas clin. fellow Nat. Heart Found. New Zealand, 1980, sr. fellow, 1984-87, rsch. fellow medicine Harvard Med. Sch., 1981-84, clin. rsch. fellow medicine Brigham and Women's Hosp., 1981-84. Fellow Royal Australasian Coll. Physicians (Odlin rsch. fellow 1981), European Soc. Cardiology, Am. Coll. Cardiology. Home: 137 Mountain Rd, Auckland 1003, New Zealand Office: Green Lane Hosp, Green Ln W, Auckland 1003, New Zealand

WHITE, HERBERT CHARLES, psychiatrist; b. Madison, Wis., Nov. 16, 1937; s. Charles Gilbert and Marjorie (Spelman) W.; m. Darlene Rose Kramer, Dec. 17, 1961 (div. Apr. 1976); children: Claire Herdeman, Lesley Nelson, Gwenn White; m. Ardis June, July 11, 1977. BS, Denison U., 1959; DO, Chgo. Coll. Osteo. Medicine, 1964. Bd. cert. Am. Osteo. Bd. Gen. Practice; cert. Am. Med. Soc. on Alcoholism and Other Drug Dependencies, 1987. Intern Traverse City (Mich.) Osteo. Hosp., 1964-65; resident in psychiatry Med. Coll. Wis., Milw., 1991-95; med. dir. addiction program Elmbrook Hosp., Brookfield, Wis., 1972-90, Waukesha (Wis.) Meml. Hosp., 1975-85; med. dir. Kettle Moraine Hosp., Ocondmorool, Wis., 1985-87; med. dir. addiction program Greenbriar Hosp., Greenfield, Wis., 1990-95; dir. behavioral medicine St. Lukes South Shore, Cudahy, Wis., 1995—; med. dir. addiction program Milw. Psychiat. Hosp., 1995—; chair com. on edn. of com. on alcoholism Wis. State Med. Soc., Madison, 1980-90, chair com. alcoholism, 1988-89; asst. clin. prof. in family practice Med. Coll. Wis., 1980—. Contbr. chpt. to book. Bd. dirs. Waukesha (Wis.) Coun. Alcoholism, 1975-83; trustee Prairie Hill Waldberg Sch., Delafield, Wis., 1995—. Mem. AMA, Am. Psychiat. Assn., Am. Osteo. Assn., Am. Med. Soc. Alcoholism. Office: 1220 Dewey Ave Wauwatosa WI 53213

WHITE, JAMEELA ADAMS, family nurse practitioner; b. Rochester, Pa., Oct. 19, 1954; d. Elie James Adams and Alease Rebecca (Waldron) Adams Curry; m. William Harrison White Jr., June 5, 1982; children: William Maurice, Jamel John. BS in Nursing, Hampton U., 1976; MSN, Pace U., 1995. RN, Ohio, N.Y.; family nurse practitioner. Pvt. duty nurse Cleve., 1976-78; asst. head nurse ICU, coronary care unit Brentwood Hosp., Cleve., 1978-79; asst. dir. nursing Astor Gardens Nursing Home, Bronx, N.Y., 1983-84; pub. health nurse Westchester County Health Dept., White Plains, N.Y., 1979-86; mgr. patient service VNS-Home Care, Bronx, 1986-90; home care nurse coord., asst. dir. patient svcs. Wartburg Home LTHHCP, Mt. Vernon, N.Y., 1990-95; FNP United Cerebral Palsy N.Y.S., Inc., N.Y.C., 1995—. Chairperson policy com. Union Child Day Care, Greenburgh, N.Y., 1991-93, mem. edn. com., 1987, bd. dirs., 1991—; pres. nurses unit 1st Bapt. Ch., Elmsford, N.Y., 1987-90; mem. North Elmsford Civic Assn., 1988—, TransAfrica, 1989-92. Recipient N.Y. State Health Svcs. Corps. grant., 1993-95. Mem. NAACP, ANA, N.Y. State Nurses Assn., Nat. Black Child Devel. Assn., Hampton Alumni Assn. (bd. dirs. 1986-91), Chi Eta Phi, Sigma Theta Tau. Democrat. Office: United Cerebral Palsy NYS 330 W 34 St New York NY 10001-2488

WHITE, JAMES EUGENE, general surgeon; b. Thomasville, Ga., Apr. 7, 1959; s. Eugene and Olga Lene (Davis) W.; m. Casi Lin Farner, Oct. 7, 1995. AAS, Med. Coll. Ga., 1979; BS, U. Ga., 1983; MD, Med. Coll. Ga., 1990. Resident in gen. surgery Erlanger Med. Ctr., Chattanooga, 1990-95; chief resident surgery U. Tenn., Chattanooga, 1995-96; pvt. practice Dublin (Ga.) Surg. Assocs., Dublin, Ga., 1996—. Mem. Am. Coll. Surgeons, Soc. Am. Gastrointestinal Endoscopic Surgeons, Southeastern Surg. Congress, Am. Orchid Soc., Phi Kappa Phi. Home: 115 Ovid Dr Dublin GA 31021 Office: Dublin Surg Assocs 508 Academy Ave Dublin GA 31021

WHITE, JERRY GLEN, clinical psychologist; b. Houston, Miss., Dec. 9, 1953; s. Howard G. and M. Louise White. BS, Miss. State U., 1975; MA, U. So. Miss., 1981, PhD, 1984. Lic. psychologist, Ark. Psychology technician Ellisville (Miss.) State Sch., 1975-78; parent educator Ellisville Jaycee Evaluation Ctr., 1978; rsch. asst. U. So. Miss., Hattiesburg, 1981-82; psychologist Profl. Counseling Assts., Little Rock, 1984-92; mem. faculty dept. psychiatry U. Ark. for Med. Scis., Little Rock, 1992—; forensic evaluator Dept. Human Svcs., Little Rock, 1990-91; adj. prof. U. Ark., Little Rock, 1991. Various offices Sierra Club, Hattiesburg, 1976-81, outings leader, Cen. Ark. chpt., 1984-91, chmn., 1988-89, mem. exec. com. Ark. chpt., 1988, 90. Mem. APA, Ark. Psychol. Assn. (legis com.). Office: Ark Children's Hosp Divsn Pediatric Psychiatry 800 Marshall St TPC 5th Fl Little Rock AR 72202

WHITE, JOHN DAVID, retired microbiology researcher; b. Newark, Feb. 14, 1928; s. John Moran and Lily (Levin) W.; m. Irene Ginsberg, Jan. 6, 1950; 1 child, Jonathan L. BA, SUNY, Buffalo, 1948, MA, 1950; PhD in Med. Microbiology, Vanderbilt U., 1953. Microbiologist U.S. Army Biol. Labs., Frederick, Md., 1956-60, chief clin. pathology br., 1961-71; chief ultrastructural pathology U.S. Army Med. Inst. Infectious Dieseases, Frederick, 1972-91; ret., 1991. Contbr. over 50 articles to sci. jours. Bd. dirs. Am. Lung Assn., N.Y.C., 1980-83, pres. 1991-92; bd. dirs. Am. Lung Assn. Md., Timonium, 1968-94, pres. 1972-73. 1st lt. Med. Svc. Corps., U.S. Army, 1953-56.

WHITE, KATHERINE ELIZABETH, retired pediatrician; b. Syracuse, N.Y., Mar. 23, 1920; d. Rufus Macandie and Marguerite Mary (Eselin) W.; m. Nicholas V. Oddo, Feb. 27, 1947 (dec. 1966); 1 child, Sandra S. Qualls. BA, Syracuse U., 1941, MD, 1943. Intern Syracuse U. Med. Ctr., 1944-45; asst. resident Buffalo Children's Hosp., 1945-46, chief resident, 1946-47; instr. pediatrics L.A. Children's Hosp., 1947; pvt. practice Long Beach, Calif., 1947—; mem. med. staff Miller Children's Hosp., Long Beach, 1966—; mem. bd. trustees Miller Children's Hosp., 1970—. Bd. dirs. Children's Clinic, Long Beach, 1968-87. Recipient Meml. Med. Ctr. Found., 1984; Cert. of Recognition, Children's Clinic, 1987, Found. for Children's Health Care, 1987; Humanitarian award Kiwanis, 1990. Fellow Am. Acad. Pediatrics; mem. Calif. Med. Assn., L.A. County Med. Assn., Long Beach Med. Assn., Soroptimist (Woman of Distinction 1989, Hall of Fame award 1990), Phi Beta Kappa. Republican. Roman Catholic. Home: 6354 Riviera Cir Long Beach CA 90815-4767

WHITE, KENNETH JULIUS, pharmacist; b. Ozark, Ala., July 26, 1945; s. Eli David and Irene (Silverman) W.; m. Glenda Carol Sizemore, Oct. 15, 1977; children—Janice, Michael. B.S.A., U. Ga., 1967, B.S.Ph., 1969. Registered pharmacist, Ga., Fla. Pharmacist Reed Drugs, Atlanta, 1969-72, Springhill Pharmacy, Marietta, Ga., 1972-73, Rexall Drugs, Naples, Fla., 1973-75; pharmacist, mgr. K-Mart Corp., Marietta, Ga., 1975—. Treas. pack 795 Cub Scouts, Marietta, 1992; com. mem. troop 795 Boy Scouts of Am., Marietta. Recipient Conchologists of Am. award, 1981. Mem. Am. Pharm. Assn., Ga. Shell Club (pres. 1979-81, corr. sec. 1984-85, Outstanding Exhibit award 1983, Shell of the Show award 1989, recipient DuPont trophy 1990), Kappa Psi (pres. U. Ga. chpt. 1969). Avocations: collecting seashells; speaking to clubs and sch. children. Home: 2587 Ballew Ct Marietta GA 30062-4424 Office: K-Mart 7184 3205A S Cobb Dr Smyrna GA 30080

WHITE, KENNETH SAMUEL, plastic surgeon; b. High Point, N.C., Feb. 19, 1957; s. Hugh Samuel and Margaret (Wyatt) W.; m. Lena Witherspoon, June 9, 1979; children: Stephanie, Ashley, Eric. MD, Bowman Gray Sch. Medicine, 1983. Diplomate Am. Bd. Surgery, Plastic Surgery. Resident in gen. surgery New Hanover Meml. Hosp., 1983-88; resident in plastic surgery Mayo Grad. Sch. Medicine. Mayo Clinic, Rochester, Minn., 1988-90; ptnr. Wilmington (N.C.) Plastic Surgery Specialists, 1990—; bd. dirs. SurgCare, Wilmington; ann. med. mission trips to Dominican Republic, 1992—. Patentee in field. Chmn. adminstrv. bd. Trinity United Meth. Ch., Wilmington, 1993-96. Recipient Young Physicians Cmty. Svc. award N.C., 1996. Fellow ACS (N.C. chpt.); mem. AMA, Am. Soc. Plastic and Reconstructive Surgeons, Southeastern Soc. Plastic and Reconstructive Surgeons, N.C. Med. Soc., New Hanover-Pender Med. Soc. (councilor 1995, vice councilor 1994). Republican. Home: 2230 Waverly Dr Wilmington NC 28403 Office: Wilmington Plastic Surgery 2305 Canterwood Dr Wilmington NC 28401

WHITE, KERR LACHLAN, physician, foundation director; b. Winnipeg, Man., Can., Jan. 23, 1917; s. John Alexander and Ruth Cecelia (Preston) W.; m. Isabel Anne Pennefather, Nov. 26, 1943; children: Susan Isabel, Margot Edith. BA with honors (Oliver Gold medal), McGill U., 1940, M.D., C.M., 1949; M.D. (hon.), U. Leuven, 1978; postgrad., London Sch. Hygiene and Tropical Medicine, 1960; DSc (hon.), McMaster U., 1983. Intern, resident in medicine Mary Hitchcock Meml. Hosp., Hanover, N.H., 1949-52; Hosmer fellow McGill U. and Royal Victoria Hosp., Montreal, Que., Can., 1952-53; asst. prof. medicine U. N.C. Sch. Medicine, Chapel Hill, 1953-57, assoc. prof. medicine and preventive medicine, 1957-62; Commonwealth advanced fellow Med. Rsch. Coun., Social Medicine Rsch. unit London Hosp., 1959-60; chmn., prof. epidemiology and community medicine U. Vt., Burlington, 1962-64; prof. Sch. Hygiene and Pub. Health Johns Hopkins U., Balt., 1965-76, chmn. dept. health care orgn., 1965-72; dir. Inst. Health Care Studies United Hosp. Fund N.Y., 1977-78; dep. dir. health scis. Rockefeller Found., N.Y.C., 1978—; chmn. U.S. Nat. Com. Vital and Health Stats., 1975-79; mem. health adv. panel Office of Tech. Assessment, U.S. Congress, 1975-82; cons. Nat. Ctr. Health Stats., 1967-83, WHO, 1967—. Editor: Manual for Examination of Patients, 1960, Medical Care Research, 1965, Health Care: An International Study, 1976, Epidemiology as a Fundamental Science, 1976, Task of Medicine, 1988, Healing the Schism, 1991; contbr. articles to profl. jours., chpts. to books in field; mem. editl. bd. Med. Care, 1962-73, Inquiry, 1967-79, Internat. Jour. Epidemiology, 1971-81, Internat. Jour. Health Svcs., 1971—. Bd. dirs. Found. for Child Devel., 1969-80; trustee Case-Western Res. U., 1974-79. With Can. Army, 1942-45. Recipient Pew Primary Care Achievement award, 1995. Fellow ACP, AAAS, NAS (Inst. Medicine coun. 1974-76, chmn. membership com. 1975-77), APHA (gov. coun. 1964-68, 71-73, coun. med. care sect. 1962-65), Am. Acad. Preventive Medicine, Am. Heart Assn., Royal Soc. Medicine (hon.); mem. AMA, Internat. Epidemiol. Assn. (hon. life, pres. 1974-77, treas., exec. com. 1964-71, 74-77, coun. 1971-81), Assn. Tchrs. Preventive Medicine (coun. 1963-68), Am. Hosp. Assn. (adv. coun. ednl. and rsch. trust 1965-68), Kerr L. White Inst. Health Svcs. Rsch. (hon. dir. 1995—), Cosmos Club (Washington), Century Club (N.Y.C.), Sigma Xi, Alpha Omega Alpha. Office: Rockefeller Found Div Health Scis 1133 Ave Of The Americas New York NY 10036-6710

WHITE, LAWRENCE L., health services administrator; b. Mpls., Nov. 8, 1943; s. Lawrence Lee and Marjorie Jean (Davis) W.; m. Mary Victoria O'Regan, July 9, 1966; children: Lawrence, Timothy, Jennifer, Erin. BA in Acctg., U. St. Thomas, St. Paul, Minn., 1965; MHA, St. Louis U., 1970. Assoc. adminstr. St. Joseph Mercy Hosp., Sioux City, Iowa, 1973-77; v.p., planning and rsch. Marian Health Ctr., Sioux City, Iowa, 1977-78; asst. adminstr. St. Anthony Hosp., Amarillo, Tex., 1978-80; pres. St. Patrick Hosp., Missoula, Mont., 1980—. Mem. bd. Missoula (Mont.) Area Econ. Devel. Corp., 1984-89; adv. coun. Sch. Bus., U. Mont., 1991-94; pres.'s adv. coun. U. Mont., 1994—; mem. bd. St. Joseph Sch., Missoula, 1993—. Capt. USAF, 1965-73. Mem. Soc. Health and Human Values, Am. Hosp. Assn. (com. mem. 1990—). Roman Catholic. Home: 4411 Fox Farm Rd Missoula MT 59802 Office: St Patrick Hospital 500 W Broadway Missoula MT 59802

WHITE, LESLIE MARY, epidemiologist; b. Huntington, N.Y., July 22, 1954; d. John B. and Inez M. (Montecalvo) W. BS, Mary Washington Coll., 1976; MPH, Johns Hopkins U., 1990; postgrad., U. Md., 1993-95. Microbiologist II Am. Type Culture Collection, Rockville, Md., 1980-83; analyst InterAm. Assocs., Rockville, Md., 1984-86; sr. assoc. Triton Corp., Washington, 1986-87; health analyst Row Scis., Inc., Rockville, 1987-88; rsch. analyst Nat. BioSystems, Rockville, 1988-90; sr. assoc. Clement Internat., Fairfax, Va., 1990-92; project dir. epidemiology Consultants in Epidemiology and Occupational Health, Washington, 1992-93; dir. epidemiology Scis. Internat., Inc., Alexandria, Va., 1993-94; pres. Epidemiology and Health Rsch., Inc., Bethesda, Md., 1994—, Dist. Nuskin/IDN Internat., Bethesda, 1996—. Mem. APHA, U.S. Tennis Assn.(umpire coun.), Soc. Epidemiologic Rsch., Soc. Occupl. and Environ. Health, Bethesda Country Club, Assn. Md. Tennis Ofcls. Home: 7401 Westlake Ter Apt 512 Bethesda MD 20817-6566 Office: Epidemiology and Health Rsch Inc 7401 Westlake Ter Apt 512 Bethesda MD 20817-6566

WHITE, LOWELL E., JR., medical educator; b. Tacoma, Wash., Jan. 16, 1928; s. Lowell E. and Hazel (Conley) W.; m. Margie Mae Lamb, June 21, 1947; children: Henry, Leanna White Maynes, Inger-Britt. B.S. in Pharm., U. Wash., 1951, M.D., 1953. Diplomate Am. Bd. Neurol. Surgery. Intern. N.C. Meml. Hosp., Chapel Hill, 1953-54; resident neurosurgery, asst. to instr. U. Wash., 1954-60, asst. prof., 1960-64, asso. prof., 1964-70; asso. dean U. Wash. (Sch. Medicine), 1965-68; prof., chief div. neurol. surgery U. Fla., 1970-72; prof. U. South Ala., 1972-94, chmn. div. neurosci., 1972-77, ret., 1994; adj. prof. Ala. Sch. of Math. and Sci., 1993-94; chmn. nat. adv. com. Animal Resources NIH, 1966-70; cons. rsch. facilities and resources NIH; cons. divsn. hosp. and med. facilities USPHS; cons. grants adminstrn. policy U.S. Dept. HEW. Contbr. articles profl. jours. Bd. dirs. Mobile County Emergency Med. Svcs. Coun., 1973-82, Mobile cpt. Myasthenia Gravis Found. Am., 1974—, Mobile Mental Health Assn., 1979-89, Spl. Edn. Action Com., 1985—, pres. 1996. With USN, 1946-47, USNR, 1948-66. Guggenheim fellow, 1958-59. Mem. AMA, Am. Assn. Neurol. Surgeons, Am. Assn. Neuropathologists, Am. Acad. Neurol. Surgeons, Soc. for Neurosci., Assn. Am. Med. Colls., Am. Assn. Anatomists, Rsch. Soc. Neurol. Surgeons, Neurosurg. Soc. Ala. (pres. 1975), Skyline Country Club (pres. 1986), Cajal Club. Home: 5750 Huffman Dr N Mobile AL 36693-3013

WHITE, MICHAEL CRAIG, dermatologist; b. Norfolk, Va., Dec. 12, 1954; s. Leland Allen and Lois Lee (Parker) W,; m. Sara Marie Beatty, June 23, 1979; 1 child, Kenneth Michael. BS in Biology, U. Richmond, 1977; MD, Med. Coll. Va., 1981. Diplomat Nat. Bd. Med. Examiners, Am. Bd. Dermatology. Intern USAF Med. Ctr., Keesler AFB, Miss., 1981-82; resident in dermatology Wilford Hall USAF Med. Ctr., San Antonio, 1984-87; pres., founder, clin. dermatologist Danville (Va.) Dermatology Assocs., Inc., 1989—. Maj. USAF, 1981-89. Fellow Am. Acad. Dermatology; mem. AMA, Med. Soc. Va., Danville-Pittsylvania Acad. Medicine, Assn. Mil. Dermatologists. Baptist. Home: 509 Indian Trail Rd Danville VA 24540

Office: Danville Dermatology Assocs 990 Main St Ste 202 Danville VA 24541

WHITE, MORRIS FRANCIS, biochemistry educator; b. Detroit. BS in Chemistry, U. Mich., 1977, MS in Biochemistry, 1979, PhD, 1981. Postdoctoral scholar dept. biol. chemistry U. Mich., Ann Arbor, 1981-82; rsch. fellow in medicine rsch. divsn. Harvard Med. Sch., Boston, 1982-85, instr. in medicine, 1985-87, asst. prof. biochemistry dept. medicine, 1987-92, assoc. prof. biol. chemistry, 1992—; investigator rsch. divsn. Joslin Diabetes Ctr., Boston, 1985—; mem. grant rev. study sects. Juvenile Diabetes Found., 1993—, Am. Diabetes Assn., 1992—, NIH, 1994; speaker in field. Mem. editl. bd. Jour. Biol. Chemistry, 1988-93, Diabetes, 1992—, Molecular Endocrinology, 1994—; contbr. articles to profl. jours. Pew scholar in biomed. scis. Pew Charitable Trusts Phila., 1987-91; recipient Individual Nat. Rsch. Svc. award NIH, 1983-85; Angell scholar U. Mich., 1977. Mem. Am. Diabetes Assn. (Balodimos award 1985-86), Am. Soc. for Biochemistry and Molecular Biology, Endocrine Soc., Juvenile Diabetes Found. Internat. Home: 14 Gretter Rd Roslindale MA 02131-1315 Office: Joslin Diabetes Ctr 1 Joslin Pl Boston MA 02215-5306*

WHITE, PETER ROLAND, plastic surgeon, consultant; b. Birmingham, England, July 9, 1945; Norman Leonard and Gene Elwin (McGrah) W.; m. Elizabeth Susan Graty Bradley, Mar. 23, 1968 (div. 1980); children: Frances Elizabeth, Gordon Michael, Adam Edward; m. Elisabeth Anne Haworth, Dec. 20, 1980. BDS, U. Birmingham, England, 1967. House officer/sr. house officer in dental/oral surgery Dudley Road Hosp., Birmingham, England, 1968, Dental Hosp., Birmingham, 1969-70; with plastic surgery and jaw injuries unit Wordsley, 1970-71; lectr. oral surgery Manchester (England) U., 1971-73; registrar St. Luke's Hosp., Bradford, Yorkshire, England, 1973-74; sr. registrar in oral surgery Liverpool, 1974-77; cons. oral & maxillo-facial surgery Manchester Children's Trust, North Manchester, Rochdale, 1977—; postgrad. dental tutor Rochdale/Oldham, 1980-87, 89-94; treas. North-West Oral Surgery Study Group, 1985—; dep. med. dir. Rochdale NHS Trust, 1994—. Fellow Royal Coll. Surgeons of England, Brit. Assn. Oral & Maxillo-Facial Surgeons; mem. Brit. Dental Assn. (pres. East Lanes, East Cheshire br. 1995-96). Home: 65 Highcroft Way, OL12 9UE Rochdale Lancashire, England Office: 14 St John St, M3 4DZ Manchester England

WHITE, PHILIP HAYDEN, ophthalmologist; b. Natick, Mass., Apr. 4, 1945; s. Harlow Hayden and Rachel Harriet (Wheat) W.; m. Zella Marie Hubbard, Nov. 23, 1974; 1 child, Meridith Leigh. B.A., Dartmouth Coll., 1967; M.D., Tufts U., 1971. Diplomate Am. Bd. Ophthalmology. Intern, Madigan Army Med. Ctr., Tacoma, 1971-72; resident in ophthalmology Brooke Army Med. Ctr., San Antonio, 1976-79; practice medicine specializing in ophthalmology, Sulphur Springs, Tex., 1980—; mem. staff Hopkins County Meml. Hosp., Sulphur Springs, Tex.; treas. Misczellaneous, Inc., Sulphur Springs, 1983—; clin. instr. U. Tex. Med. Sch., Dallas, 1983—. Served to lt. col. U.S. Army, 1971-80, col. Res. Fellow Am. Acad. Ophthalmology; mem. Am. Intraocular Implant Soc., AMA, Tex. Med. Assn., Hopkins Franklin County Med. Soc. (pres. 1987), Classic Car Club Am. Lodge: Shriners, Masons. Avocations: collecting, driving, and exhibiting antique and classic autos. Home: RR 3 Sulphur Springs TX 75482-9803 Office: 109 Medical Cir Sulphur Springs TX 75482-2138

WHITE, RAYMOND PETRIE, JR., dentist, educator; b. N.Y.C., Feb. 13, 1937; s. Raymond Petrie and Mabel Sarah (Shutze) W.; m. Betty Pritchett, Dec. 27, 1961; children—Karen Elizabeth, Michael Wood. Student, Washington and Lee U., 1955-58; D.D.S., Med. Coll. Va., 1962, Ph.D., 1967. Diplomate: Am. Bd. Oral and Maxillofacial Surgery. Postdoctoral fellow anatomy Med. Coll. Va., Richmond, 1962-67; resident in oral surgery Med. Coll. Va., 1964-67; asst. prof. U. Ky., Lexington, 1967-70; asso. prof. U. Ky., 1970-71, chmn. dept. oral surgery, 1969-71; prof., asst. dean adminstrn. Va. Commonwealth U., Richmond, 1971-74; prof. Sch. Dentistry U. N.C., Chapel Hill, 1974—, Dalton L. McMichael disting. prof., 1993—; dean Sch. Dentistry, U. N.C., Chapel Hill, 1974-81, assoc. dean Sch. Medicine, 1981-92; cons. Fayetteville VA Hosp.; mem. staff U.N.C. Hosps., mem. exec. com., 1974—, sec., 1977-78, assoc. chief staff, 1981-92; mem. adv. panel on dentistry U.S. Pharmacopeial Conv., 1985—; sr. program cons. The Robert Wood Johnson Found., 1982-90. Author: (with E.R. Costich) Fundamentals of Oral Surgery, 1971, (with Bell and Proffit) Surgical Correction of Dentofacial Deformities, 1980, (with W.R. Proffit) Surgical Orthodontic Treatment, 1990, (with M.R. Tucker, B.C. Terry, J.E. Van Sickels) Rigid Fixations for Maxillofacial Surgery, 1991; co-editor Internat. Jour. Adult Orthodontics and Orthodontic Surgery, 1985—; asst. editor Jour. Oral and Maxillofacial Surgery, 1993—; contbr. sci. articles to profl. jours. Bd. dirs. Am. Fund for Dental Health, 1978-86, v.p., 1982-85. Recipient Outstanding Tchr. award U. Ky., 1971, Disting. Service award Am. Fund Dental Health, 1987. Mem. ADA, AAAS, N.C. Dental Soc., Internat. Assn. Dental Rsch. (pres. Ky. sect. 1970), Inst. Medicine of NAS, Chalmers J. Lyons Acad. Oral Surgery, Am. Assn. Oral and Maxillofacial Surgeons (gen. chmn. sci. sessions com. 1974-76, Outstanding Svc. award as committeeman 1976, chmn. strategic planning com. 1990-96), N.C. Soc. Oral and Maxillofacial Surgeons, Sigma Xi, Psi Omega, Delta Tau Delta, Alpha Sigma Chi, Sigma Zeta, Psi Omega (Scholarship award 1962), Omicron Kappa Upsilon. Roman Catholic. Home: 1506 Velma Rd Chapel Hill NC 27514-7601 Office: U NC Sch Dentistry Dept Oral/Maxillofacial Surgery Chapel Hill NC 27599-7450

WHITE, RICHARD KINNEY, clinical psychologist, consultant; b. Washington, Dec. 22, 1951; s. Richard Kinney and Patricia (Reed) W.; m. Janis Carol Mallon, July 22, 1989. BA, Clark U., 1973; MA, Cleve. State U., 1975; PhD, SUNY, Buffalo, 1987. Psychology intern Fairhill Mental Health Ctr., Cleve., 1974-75; psychol. assoc. N.E. Mental Health Ctr., Cleve., 1975-77, Psychol. Svcs., Cleve., 1977-80; staff therapist SUNY Buffalo Univ. Counseling Svcs., Amherst, 1985-86; psychologist, treatment team leader Jackson Brook Inst., South Portland, Maine, 1986-88; clin. psychologist in pvt. practice Gorham, Maine, 1988—; grad. instr. SUNY, Buffalo, 1981-84; mem., sec., complaint officer Maine State Bd. Examiners of Psychologists, Augusta, 1990-96; mem. SUNY Buffalo Cmty. Psychology Group, 1981-84. USPHS clin. tng. fellow, 1981; N.Y. State Dept. Mental Health rsch. fellow, 1983. Mem. APA, Maine Psychol. Assn. (award for outstanding profl. svc. in Maine 1994), New Eng. Psychol. Assn., Nat. Register Health Svc. Providers in Psychology, Soc. of Maine Psychologists. Home: 26 Edes Rd Cumberland Center ME 04021 Office: 510 Main St Ste A Gorham ME 04038

WHITE, RICHARD THOMAS, radiologist; b. Binghamton, N.Y., May 10, 1941; s. William Joseph and Winifred (Murphy) W.; divorced; 1 child, Kevin Michael; m. Rory Lynn Leyman. BS, SUNY-Binghamton, 1967; DO, Chgo. Coll. Osteo. Medicine, 1972. Intern Bi County Hosp., Warren, Mich.; staff radiologist Bi-County Hosp., 1977-79; resident Detroit Hosp., Children's Hosp., Detroit, 1973-76; fellow Johns Hopkins Hosp., Balt., 1976; asst. prof. radiology Mich. State U., East Lansing, 1980-84, cons. ultra-sound rsch., 1980-83, cons. nuclear magnetic rsch., 1982-83; asst. prof. radiology U. Tex., Houston, 1984-85, U. Ill., Chgo., 1985-88; chief radiology VA Med. Ctr., Bath, N.Y., 1988—; clin. prof. radiology U. Rochester (N.Y.) Sch. Medicine and Dentistry, 1989—; cons. varsity sports, 1980-84, handicapped athletes Spl. Olympics, Washington, 1978-84, Detroit Red Wings hockey team, 1977-84. Med. dir. Mich. Spl. Olympics Central Mich. U., Mt. Pleasant, 1977-84; bd. dirs. Spl. Olympics, Mt. Pleasant, 1980-84; med. advisor Amateur Hockey Assn. USA, Colorado Springs, Colo., 1980-84. Served with U.S. Army, 1960-63; lt. col. U.S. Army Res., 1990—. Recipient Outstanding Contbn. award Spl. Olympics, 1980; named Team Physician U.S. Nat. Hockey Team, Mich. Amateur Hockey Assn., 1979, 81, 83. Mem. AMA, Am. Osteopath Assn., Radiol. Soc. N.Am., Am. Coll. Radiology, Am. Coll. Med. Imaging, Am. Coll. Sports Medicine, Am. Inst. Ultrasound in Medicine, Am. Acad. Sci., Kiwanis.

WHITE, ROBERT SILLIMAN, psychiatrist; b. New Haven, Conn., Apr. 28, 1947; s. Herbert Palmer and Harriet Sperry (Judd) W.; m. Charlotte Brechbill. BA, Haverford Coll., 1969; MD, U. Va., 1973; cert. psychiatry, Yale U., 1978; postgrad., Inst. Psychoanalysis, New Haven, 1983-90. Cert. Am. Bd. Psychiatry and Neurology. Intern Children's Hosp., Washington, 1973-74; psychiat. resident Yale U. Hosp., 1975-78; Pvt. practice psychiatry New Haven, 1978—; med. dir. Altobello Hosp., Meridan, Conn., 1978-88, St. Raphael's Hosp. Psychiatry Out-patient Clinic, New Haven, 1988—; asst. prof. psychiatry Yale U., New Haven, 1978—. Bd. dirs. Cornerstone Inc., New Haven, 1988—. Mem. Am. Psychiat. Assn., Am. Psychoanalytic Assn., Western New Eng. Psychoanalytic Soc., New Haven County Med. Soc. Home: 128 White Birch Dr Guilford CT 06437-2165 Office: 345 Whitney Ave # 300 New Haven CT 06511-2316

WHITE, RUTH BENNETT, nutritionist, educator; writer; b. Howe, Okla., Aug. 18, 1906; d. Ambrose L. and Sarah A. (Blevins) Bennett; m. Carl Milton White, Aug. 5, 1928; children: Sherril White Spencer, Caroline White Buchanan. B.S. with honors, Okla. Bapt. U., 1928; M.S. (fellow), U. Iowa, 1930; postgrad. Cornell U., 1930-34, Columbia, 1955-56. Teaching fellow Okla. Baptist U., 1925-26; prin. Jr. High Sch., Heavener, Okla., 1926-27; rsch. fellow in chemistry of food, Cornell U., 1930-31; surveyor diets of teenagers, 1931-34; rsch. fellow N.Y. State 4-H Club Camps, summers, 1931-34; instr. nutrition Coll. Home Econs., Cornell U., Ithaca, N.Y., 1931-34; tchr. pub. schs., N.Y.C., 1956-58 Fort Lee (N.J.) High Sch., 1959-60; pub. lectr. foods and nutrition, 1931—; nutrition specialist for community programs Cornell U. N.Y. State Extension, 1931-34, Ankara, Turkey, 1960-61, Lagos, Nigeria, 1962-64; mem. Nat. Commn. on Revision of Home Econs. Curriculum, Fed. Republic of Nigeria, 1961-64. Author: If Food Could Talk, 1932; You and Your Food (text), 4th edit., 1976; Food and Your Future (text), 1972, 3d edit., 1985. Contbr. articles on nutrition to profl. jours. and newspapers. Mem. Leonia (N.J.) Bd. Edn., 1950-54. Recipient Disting. Alumni Achievement award Okla. Baptist U., 1975; named Woman of the Year, San Diego dist. Calif. Home Econs. Assn., 1973, 74; Woman of Achievement award Pres.'s Coun. Womens Svc., Bus. and Profl. Clubs San Diego, 1973, 74. Mem. Am. Home Econs. Assn. (award for profl. contbns. in writng textbooks on food & nutrition 1984), Calif. Home Econs., Assn., Channel Islands Home Econs. Assns., Internat. Fedn. Home Econs. (mem. coun. 1970-76), AAUW (v.p. programs Nashville 1938-40, Urbana, Ill. 1941-43, del. nat. conv. 1984), Soc. Nutrition Edn., Nat. League Am. Pen Women, Pi Lamba Theta, Pi Kappa Delta. Democrat. Address: Health Care Ctr #25 Santa Barbara CA 93105-4839

WHITE, SARAH JOWILLIARD, counselor; b. Oxford, N.C., Sept. 1, 1921; d. John Hiriam and Emma (Redfern) Isham; m. Hamilton B. Carson, Sept. 20, 1945 (div. 1968); 1 child, Lynne Denise. Honor student, Bennett Coll., 1939-42, Cornell U., 1979-82; BA, CCNY, 1973. Clk. N.Y. Dept. Law, N.Y.C., 1948-53; auditor U.S. Fed. Govt. Svc., N.Y.C., 1955-62; postal clk. U.S. Govt., Mt. Vernon, N.Y., 1963-66; prin. N.Y. State Dept. Labor, Mt. Vernon, 1966-88, ret., 1988; youth organizer N.Y. State Careerists Soc., Inc., N.Y.C., 1989—; youth and employment counselor Women in Community Svc., Nat. Coun. Negro Women, Manhattan sect., N.Y.C., 1983—. Vol. Advanced Vocation Edn. Day, Albany, N.Y., 1988; vol., coord. Decade of the Youth, N.Y.C., 1989, 90; corres. sec. Lower East Side United Neighbors, N.Y.C., 1989. Recipient Youth award, 1987, Recognition award, 1987, Internat. Assn. Pers. Employees Youth award, Plaque for Women in Cmty. Svcs., Outstanding Vol. Svc. award Gov. Mario Cuomo, 1994, Outstanding Vol. award, 1991, 92, Outstanding Vol. award Women in Cmty. Svc., 1994, Cert. Appreciation, 1995, Appreciation award South Bronx Job Alumni chpt., 1995, Nat. Coun. Negro Women Recognition award, 1996; named one of N.Y.'s Finest Vols. Women in Cmty. Svcs. Mag., 1994, Woman on the Move, Cable TV, 1994. Mem. NAFE, N.Y. Careerists Soc. (sec., Merit award 1988), Assn. U.S. Govt. Job Corps. (alumni recognition award 1995), Nat. Coun. Negro Women (chairperson, Achievement award 1988-90), Internat. Assn. Pers. Employees, Black Alumni CCNY (pub. rels. com., outstanding award 1989). Democrat. 7th Day Sabbath Keeper House of God.

WHITE, STEVEN KELLY, SR., plastic surgeon, hand surgeon; b. Corona, Calif., Aug. 14, 1953; s. Noel and Helen Catherine (Santoma) W.; m. Ginger Grace Kingsmore, Apr. 18, 1987; children: Elizabeth Ann, Steven Kelly, Jr., Victoria Leigh. BS in Biology, The Citadel, 1975; MD, Med. U. S.C., 1979. Diplomate Am. Bd. Plastic Surgery; cert. gen. surgery. cert. added qualifications surgery of hand; ACLS; BLS. Intern Keesler AFB Med. Ctr., Biloxi, Miss., 1979-80; resident gen. surgery Kessler Med. Ctr., Biloxi, Miss., 1979-81; resident gen. surgery Spartanburg (S.C.) Med. Ctr., 1981-86, chief resident, 1983-84; chief resident Wilford Hall Med. Ctr., San Antonio, 1985-86; chief plastic and reconstructive surgery, staff gen. surgeon, dir. craniofacial anomaly bd., mem. flying ambulatory surg. team Wiesbaden (Ger.) Regional Med. Ctr., 1986-89; pvt. practice Carolina Coastal Plastic and Reconstructive Surgery, P.A., Myrtle Beach, S.C., 1987—; vice chmn. surg. rev. com. Grand Strand Gen. Hosp., 1992-94, mem. staff, chmn. credentials com., 1995-97; mem. staff Loris (S.C.) Cmty. Hosp., Shaw AFB, Conway (S.C.) Hosp.; presenter in field. Contbr. articles to profl. jours. Lt. col. USAF Res., 1975—. Mem. AMA, Am. Soc. Plastic and Reconstructive Surgeons, S.C. Med. Assn. (del. special soc. sect. 1992-96), So. Med. Assn., Soc. Air Force Clin. Surgeons, S.C. Soc. Plastic and Reconstructive Surgeons (sec. 1992, pres. elect 1993), K. of C., Citadel Alumni. Roman Catholic. Home: 98 Holly Ln Myrtle Beach SC 29572 Office: Carolina Coastal Plastic & Reconstructive Surgery PA 1275 21st Ave N Myrtle Beach SC 29577

WHITE, SUSAN VICTORIA, nursing administrator; b. Ocala, Fla., Oct. 7, 1951; d. George and Agnes Victoria (Toffaletti) Spontak. BS in Nursing, U. Fla., 1973, MS in Nursing, 1982, postgrad., 1990—. Cert. critical care nurse. Asst. head nurse ICU Orlando (Fla.) Regional Med. Ctr., 1976-78, patient care coord., 1978-85; quality assurance mgr. Sand Lake Hosp., Orlando, 1985-88, assoc. exec. dir., dir. nursing, 1990-94; bus. sys. analyst Orlando Regional Healthcare Sys., 1995—. Mem. AACN, ANA (cert. nursing adminstrn.), Am. Hosp. Assn., Fla. Nurses Assn., Am. Orgn. of Nurse Execs., Fla. Orgn. Nurse Execs., Ctrl. Fla. Orgn. Nurse Execs., Nat. Quality Assurance Profession, Fla. Utilization Rev. Assn., Am. Coll. Healthcare Execs., Sigma Theta Tau (award for rsch.), Phi Kappa Phi. Home: PO Box 681133 Orlando FL 32868-1133

WHITE, SUSIE MAE, school psychologist; b. Madison, Fla., Mar. 5, 1914; d. John Anderson and Lucy (Crawford) Williams; m. Daniel Elijah White, Oct. 20, 1958 (dec. Sept. 29, 1968). BS, Fla. Meml. Coll., St. Augustine, 1948; MEd, U. Md., 1953; postgrad., Mich. State U., 1955, Santa Fe Community Coll., 1988; Cert. Child Care Supervision, W.T. Loften Edn. Ctr., Gainesville, Fla., 1994. Elem. tchr. Grove Park (Fla.) Elem. Sch., 1943; tchr. Douglas High Sch., High Springs, Fla., 1944-55; sch. psychologist Alachua County Sch. Bd., Gainesville, Fla., 1956-69; coord. social svcs. Alachua County Sch. Bd., Gainesville, 1970; owner, dir. Mother Dear's Child Care Ctr., Gainesville, 1988—. Del. Bapt. World Alliance, Bapt. Conv. Fla., Tokyo, 1970; state dir. leadership Fla. Bapt. Gen. Conv., 1971-85. Recipient Cert. of Appreciation Fla. State Dept. Edn., Tallahassee, 1971, Appreciation for Disting. Svc. award Fla. Gen. Bapt. Conv., Miami, 1979, Hall of Fame award Martin Luther King Jr. Hall of Fame, 1994; The Susie Mae White scholarship fund established Mt. Sinai Congress Christian Edn., 1995. Mem. Nat. Ret. Tchrs. Assn., Alachua County Tchrs. Assn., Fla. Meml. Coll. Nat. Alumni Assn., AAUW, Heroines of Jerico, Masons. Democrat. Office: Child Care Ctr 811 NW 4th Pl Gainesville FL 32601-5049

WHITE, SYLVIA FRANCES, gerontology home care nurse, consultant; b. Dayton, Ohio, May 2, 1952; d. Arthur Francis and Eleanor Ida (Beach) Scarpelli; m. Alan Bruce White, Nov. 28, 1981. BSN, Loyola U., 1975; MPH, U. Ill., Chgo., 1984. Cert. gerontol. nurse; lic. nursing home adminstrn., Ill. Staff nurse Vis. Nurse Assn., Chgo., 1975-80, team leader, 1980-81, supr., 1981-83, dist. adminstr., 1984-86, mgr. North side, 1986-87, dir. patient svcs., 1987; dir. clin. svcs. Kimberly Quality Care, Evanston, Ill., 1987-89; pub. health nurse City of Evanston, Ill., 1989-90; geriatric nurse assoc. City of Evanston, 1990—; cons. surveyor Joint Commn. on Accreditation of Healthcare Orgns., Oakbrook Terrace, Ill., 1988—; vol. Hospice, literacy. Trainer The Arthritis Found., Chgo., 1991-92; mem. Panel Rev. State of Ill. Continuing Edn.; mem. profl. edn. com. Arthritis Found.; hospice vol. Mem. APHA, Ill. Pub. Health Assn., Ill. Home Health Coun., Ill. Alliance for Aging, Zonta, Arthritis Profl. Edn. Com., Nat. Assn. Home Care. Roman Catholic. Home: 222 Sunset Dr Wilmette IL 60091 Office: Evanston Health Dept 2100 Ridge Ave Evanston IL 60201-2796

WHITE, T. KAY, quality assurance professional; b. DuBois, Pa., Feb. 20, 1942; d. Alexander Daniel and Mildred Eileen (Weyant) Mauk; m. Robert George White, May 6, 1971; 1 child, Jennifer Eileen. BSN, Duquesne U., 1967; MS in Nursing Adminstrn., Boston U., 1970. Rn, Fla., Pa. Asst. dir. nursing svc. Altoona (Pa.) Hosp., 1968-69, dir. nursing svc., 1970-73; staff nurse New England Deaconess Hosp., Boston, 1969-70; dir. nursing svc. Med. Ctr., Columbus, Ga., 1973-74, Coral Gables (Fla.) Hosp., 1974-77; asst. adminstr. nursing Cooper Green Hosp., Birmingham, Ala., 1977-79; dir. nursing svc. King's Daughter Hosp., Staunton, Va., 1980-81; dir. nursing Armstrong County Meml. Hosp., Kittanning, Pa., 1981-89; quality assessment coord. Fla. Hosp., Orlando, 1992—. Scholar Dept. Health, Edn. and Welfare, 1969-70, Altoona Hosp. Mem. Fla. Assn. for Healthcare Quality, Nat. Assn. Healthcare Quality Profls. Home: 1949 Westbourne Dr Oviedo FL 32765 Office: Fla Hosp 601 E Rollins Orlando FL 32765

WHITE, TERRY EDWARD, physician; b. Springfield, Mo., May 30, 1954; s. Roy Edward and Eselean (Moffis) W.; m. Susan Marie Peters, Aug. 16, 1981. BA, Drury Coll., 1976; MD, U. Mo., 1980. Diplomate Am. Bd. Physical Medicine and Rehab. Staff physician Lakeshore Hosp., Birmingham, Ala., 1983-86; clin. instr. U. Ala., Birmingham, 1984-86; staff physician Thomas Rehab., Asheville, N.C., 1986—, chief staff, 1987-88, 91-92, 94—, vice chief staff, 1992-94; alternate Medicare State Carrier adv. com., Greensboro, N.C., 1993; bd. dirs. Nationwide Post Polio Support Group, Dallas, N.C., 1992-94; vice chmn. Western N.C. Health Care Provider Coun., 1995—; editl. adv. com. Stroke Rehabilitation. Author: A Patient's and Physician Guide to Late Effects of Polio; mem. editorial staff Stroke Rehabilitation-Patient Education Guide. Named Rehab. Physician Yr., N.C. Med. Soc., 1993. Fellow Am. Acad. Phys. Medicine and Rehab.; mem. N.C. Soc. Phys. Medicine and Rehab. (v.p. 1989-91, pres. 1991-93). Republican. Mem. Christian Ch. Office: Thomas Rehab Hosp 68 Sweeten Creek Rd Asheville NC 28803-2318

WHITE, THOMAS CHARLES, orthopedic surgeon; b. Wooster, Ohio, Feb. 23, 1955; s. Charles Edward and Sally Jane W.; m. Barbara Carnahan, Dec. 16, 1979; children: Stephen Robert, Ashley Louise. BA cum laude, Depauw U., Greencastle, Ind., 1977; MD with distinction, Northwestern U., Chgo., 1981. Diplomate Am. Bd. Orthopedic Surgery. Resident physician Northwestern U. Med. Sch., Chgo., 1981-86; affiliate physician Rockford (Ill.) Clinic Ltd., 1986-89, mem. physician, 1989-94; physician Rockford Meml. Health Svcs. Corp., 1994—; assoc. clin. prof. U. Ill. Coll. Medicine, Rockford, 1989—; chmn. dept. orthopedics Rockford Meml. Hosp., 1993-95, mem. med. exec. com. 1993-95; managed care adv. Rockford Health Sys., 1994. Bd. dirs. Rockford Meml. Hosp. Fellow Am. Acad. Orthopedic Surgeons; mem. AMA, Ill. Orthopedic Soc., Ill. State Med. Soc., Alpha Omega Alpha. Office: Rockford Clinic 2300 N Rockton Rockford IL 61103

WHITE, WILLIAM CLINTON, pathologist; b. Scottsville, Va., Nov. 22, 1911; s. Llewellyn Gordon and Caroline Rebecca (Rawlings) W.; m. Frances Evelyn Daniel, July 2, 1938; children: William Clinton, Elizabeth White Martin. BS, Va. Mil. Inst., 1933; MD, U. Va., 1937. Diplomate Am. Bd. Pathology. Intern, Walter Reed Gen. Hosp., Washington, 1937-39; resident in pathology U. Colo. Med. Ctr., Denver, 1949-53, assoc. prof., 1949-65; med. dir. Los Alamos Hosp., 1946-49; cons. U. Calif. Sci. Labs., Los Alamos, 1949-59; chmn. dept. pathology Denver Gen. Hosp., 1953-65; dir. med. edn. and rsch. Pensacola Found. for Med. Edn. and Research (Fla.), 1965-78; bd. dirs., 1976—; cons. med. edn., emeritus dir. med. edn. Pensacola Edn. Program (Fla.); co-founder, dir. Rocky Mountain Natural Gas Co.; dir. Midwest Nat. Gas Co. Bd. govs. Fellowship Concerned Churchmen, 1982-85, pres., 1983-85. Mem. Selective Service Bd., N.Mex., 1946-49; mem. adv. bd. on cancer to Gov. of Colo., 1960-65; mem. Community Hosp. Council, Fla. Bd. Regents, 1971-74; mem. vestry, chmn. fin. com., sr. warden Christ Ch.; active Salvation Army, Boy Scouts Am. Served to col., M.C., U.S. Army, 1938-46. Recipient cert. of appreciation SSS, 1951; citation of merit Bd. Health and Hosps., Denver, 1963. Mem. AMA, Am. Soc. Clin. Pathologists (counselor), Colo. Soc. Pathology (pres.), Internat. Acad. Pathology (hon. life), Colo. State Med. Soc., Denver Med. Soc., Escambia County Med. Soc. (hon. life), Los Alamos County Med. Soc. (pres.), Andalusia Country Club, Pensacola Country CLub, Rotary Internat., St. Andrew's Soc. (trustee 1981—), Masons, Shriners, K.T. Contbr. articles to profl. jours. Home and Office: 615 Bayshore Dr Apt 101 Pensacola FL 32507-3500

WHITEHAIR, LEO ANTHONY, health scientist, administrator; b. Abilene, Kans., June 13, 1929; s. John Leo and Mary Agnes (Morgan) W.; m. Gloria Mary Vezza, Aug. 9, 1958; children: Kirsten, Robert, Courtney. BS and DVM, Kans. State U., 1953; MS, U. Wis., 1954, PhD, 1962. Diplomate Am. Coll. Vet. Preventive Medicine, Am. Coll. Lab. Animal Medicine (hon.). Commd. 1st lt. USAF, 1954, advanced through grades to lt. col.; vet. officer Aeromed. Lab. Wright-Patterson AFB, Dayton, Ohio, 1954-58; vet. officer nutrition br. Food Inst. of Armed Forces, Chgo., 1961-62; vet. officer, divsn. biology and medicine USAEC, Germantown, Md., 1962-67; health scientist adminstr. animal resources br. div. rsch. resources NIH, Bethesda, Md., 1968-75, dir. regional primate rsch. ctrs. program, 1975-85; adminstr. biomed. rsch. lab. ARC, Rockville, Md., 1985-87; dir. comparative med. program Nat. Ctr. for Rsch. Resources, NIH, Bethesda, 1988—. Contbr. articles to profl. jours. Capt. USPHS, 1967-85. Recipient Helwig-Jennings award Am. Coll. Vet. Preventive Medicine, 1981, Disting. Svc. award Am. Soc. Primatologists, 1994, Charles A. Griffin award Am. Assn. Lab. Animal Sci., 1995; Alumni fellow U. Kans., 1995. Mem. AVMA, D.C. Vet. Medicine Assn. (pres. 1992). Office: NIH Bethesda MD 20892

WHITEHEAD, DAVID LYNN, school counselor; b. Crockett, Tex., Mar. 24, 1950; s. Clifton Baine and Corene (Stowe) W.; m. Joyce Stalmach, June 23, 1973; children: Christopher, Kimberly, Allison. BA with honor, Sam Houston State U., Huntsville, Tex., 1972, MA, 1975. Cert. tchr., speech pathologist, learning disabilities, mental retardation, ednl. diagnostician, counseling, Tex. Speech pathologist Texas City Ind. Sch. Dist., 1972-73; speech pathologist Brenham (Tex.) Ind. Sch. Dist., 1973-75, ednl. diagnostician, 1975-86; ednl. diagnostician Austin County Edn. Coop., Sealy, Tex., 1986-88; sch. counselor Sealy (Tex.) Ind. Sch. Dist., 1988-92; counselor Alton Elem. Sch., Brenham, Tex., 1992—; ednl. cons., Austin County, Tex., 1987-88; reviewer spl. edn. program College Station (Tex.) Ind. Sch. Dist., 1983; feature artist Gov.'s Mansion, State of Tex., Austin, 1985. Pres. Whitehead Cemetery Assn., Grapeland, Tex., 1986-90. Mem. AACD, Tex. Assn. for Counseling and Devel., Ft. Bend County Counseling Assn., Region VI Educational Diagnosticians (pres. Bluebonnet chpt. 1977-78), Nat. Egg Art Guild (SW regional bd. dirs. 1986), Tex. Guild Egg Shell Artists (state pres. 1984-85). Mem. Brethren Ch. Home: RR 1 Box 74 New Ulm TX 78950-9729

WHITEHEAD, JOHN, statistics educator; b. Blackburn, Eng., Jan. 16, 1950; s. Roy and Irene Winifred (Foster) W.; m. Patricia Anne Sowray, Aug. 17, 1974. BA in Math. with 1st class honors, Worcester Coll., Oxford, Eng., 1971; MSc in Probability and Stats., U. Sheffield, Eng., 1972, PhD in Probability and Stats., 1975. Lectr. in math. Chelsea Coll., U. London, 1974-78; lectr. in applied stats. U. Reading, Eng., 1978-82, 84-87, reader in applied stats., 1987-91, prof. applied stats., 1991—, dir. med. and pharm. stats. rsch. unit, 1994—; vis. investigator Fred Hutchinson Cancer Rsch. Ctr., Seattle, 1982-84. Author: The Design and Analysis of Sequential Clinical Trials, 1983, 2d edit., 1992; co-author (with Mrs. H. Brunier): (software) PEST 3, 1993; assoc. editor Biometrics, 1993—. Fellow Royal Statis. Soc., Internat. Statis. Inst.; mem. Internat. Biometric Soc. Office: U Reading Med/Pharm Statis, PO Box 240 Earley Gate, Reading RG6 6FN, England

WHITEHEART, SIDNEY WALDO, medical educator. BS in Biology, Emory U., 1983, BA in Chemistry, 1983; PhD of Biol. Chemistry, Johns Hopkins U., 1989. Rsch. biochemist Merck, Sharp, and Dohme Rsch. Labs., West Point, Pa., 1989-90; postdoctoral fellow Princeton (N.J.) U., 1990-91, Sloan-Kettering Inst., 1991-94; asst. prof. biochemistry U. Ky., Lexington, 1994—; lectr. Marine Biology Labs., Woods Hole, Mass, 1994, U. Heidelberg, Germany, 1995, Washington U., St. Louis, 1995. Contbr. articles to profl. jours. Grantee Am. Heart Assn., 1995-98, Am. Cancer Soc., 1995-97. Mem. AAAS, Am. Soc. Cell Biology, Am. Heart Assn. Sci. Coun. Home: 3434 Fleetwood Dr Lexington KY 40502 Office: Univ Ky Coll Medicine 800 Rose St Lexington KY 40536-0084*

WHITEHILL, JULES LEONARD, surgeon, educator; b. N.Y.C., Mar. 7, 1912; s. Karl and Jenny (Abrahams) W.; m. Muriel Jeannette Berry, Sept. 21, 1943 (dec.); children: Jonathan Robert (dec.), David Carl Evan, Jules

Leonard II (dec.). BS magna cum laude, CCNY, 1931; MD, NYU, 1935. Diplomate Am. Bd. Surgery. Intern, resident, fellow Mt. Sinai Hosp., N.Y.C., 1935-40; assoc. Dr. John Garlock, Dr. Leon Ginzburg, N.Y.C., 1940-42; pvt. practice surgery, chief of surgery Pima County Hosp., Tucson, 1946-60; prof., chair dept. surgery Chgo. Med. Sch., 1960-70, prof. emeritus, 1970—; cons. in field San Diego, 1970—; trustee Chapman Coll., Orange, Calif., 1971-76; chmn. bd. dirs. World Campus Afloat, Orange, 1971-76; bd. visitors, steering com. exec. bd. U. San Diego Med. Sch., 1996—; vis. prof. surgery U. Zagreb, Yugoslavia, 1969. Col. USAF, 1941—, Africa, Italy, France, 3rd gen. comdr. Stroock scholar, N.Y. Regents scholar; Gallatin fellow NYU; Jules Leonard Whitehill chair in surgery named in his honor NYU. Fellow Am. Coll. Surgeons; mem. N.Y. Acad. Sci., Chgo. Surg. Soc., AMA, Internat. Coll. Surgeons (regent, bd. govs.), Royal Soc. Medicine (England), Phi Beta Kappa, Alpha Omega Alpha. Home: 5238 Renaissance Ave San Diego CA 92122

WHITEHOUSE, BRIAN SCOTT, surgeon; b. Boston, June 24, 1962; s. George Gordon and Janet (MacDuff) W.; m. Judith Ann Gooen, Nov. 10, 1990; children: Melissa Jan, Joshua Greg. BS in Neurosci., BA in English, U. Rochester, 1984; MD, Hahnemann U., 1988. Diplomate Am. Bd. Surgery. Intern Montefiore Med. Ctr./Albert Einstein Sch. Medicine, 1988-89, resident, chief resident in gen. surgery, 1989-93; staff surgeon MetroWest Surg. Group, Natick and Framingham, Mass., 1993—. Mem. AMA, Mass. Med. Soc.

WHITEHOUSE, GRAHAM HUGH, radiologist, educator; b. Stanmore, England, Nov. 24, 1939; s. Raymond Hugh and Joyce Miriam Moreton (Powell) W.; m. Jacqueline Meadows Charles, Mar. 22, 1969; children: Richard Hugh, Victoria Jane. MB BS, U. London, 1965. House officer Westminster Hosp., London, 1965-66, registrar X-ray dept., 1967-69; sr. house officer Acton Hosp., London, 1966, St. James Hosp., Balham, London, 1967; sr. registrar United Bristol (Eng.) Hosps., 1969-72; sr. lectr. dept. radiodiagnosis U. Liverpool, Eng., 1972-75, prof. diagnostic radiology, 1976—; asst. prof. dept. radiology U. Rochester, N.Y., 1975-76. Author: Gynaecological Radiology, 1981; co-author: Self Assessment in Diagnostic Radiology, 1986, Exercises in Diagnostic Imaging, 1989, Radiology for Anaesthetists; co-editor: Techniques in Diagnostic Imaging, 1983, 3d edit., 1995; clin. editor Br. Jour. Radiology. Fellow Royal Coll. Radiologists (examiner 1981—), Royal Soc. Medicine (v.p. radiology sect. 1990—), Royal Coll. Physicians of London; mem. Brit. Inst. Radiology. Anglican. Office: Royal Liverpool Univ Hosp, PO Box 147, L69 3BX Liverpool England

WHITEHOUSE, PETER JOHN, neurologist; b. London, May 26, 1949; m. Catherine C.; children: Erin, Meghan, Kirsten. BA magne cum laude, Brown U., 1971; MD, Johns Hopkins U., 1976, PhD, 1977. Diplomate Am. Bd. Psychiatry and Neurology. Clin. clk. Spring Grove State Hosp., Balt., 1973; psychotherapist Johns Hopkins Hosp., Balt., 1974, intern, 1977, resident, 1978-81, instr. depts. neurology and neurosci., 1982-83, dir. brain resource ctr., neuropathology lab., 1982-87, asst. prof. depts. neurology, neurosci., 1983-87; prof. dept. neurology U. Hosps. Cleve. and Case Western Reserve U., 1993—; prof. psychiatry, psychology Case Western Reserve U., 1993%; vis. prof. Nat. Neurological Hosp., London, 1993; assoc. dir. devel. ctr. aging and health Case Western Reserve U., 1990—, dir. divsn. behavioral and geriatric neurology dept. neurology, 1986—; dir. Alzheimer ctr. U. Hosps. Cleve., 1986—; cons. in field. Smithsonian Inst. rsch. grantee, 1970, NIGMS grantee, 1973-77; postdoctoral fellow Boston U. and Harvard U., 1975-76, psychiatry and neurosci. fellow Johns Hopkins Hosp. and Univ., 1981-82, NIH fellow, 1981; vis. scholar Tokyo Met. Inst. Summer Gerontology, Tokyo, 1991; recipient Alfred P. Sloan Rsch. award, 1982-84, Commonwealth Fund award, 1982-87; McKnight Found. award, 1982-85. Office: Alzheimer Ctr U Hosps 12200 Fairhill Rd Cleveland OH 44120

WHITEHURST, LEE ALBERT, physician; b. Greenville, N.C., Mar. 6, 1947; m. Ann Gilliam Dickerson, June 13, 1970; children: Alan Lee, Bradford Dickerson, Amy Craig. BS in Medicine, U. N.C., 1969, MD, 1972. Bd. cert. Am. Acad. Orthopaedic Surgery. Intern in gen. surgery Duke U. Med. Ctr., Durham, N.C., 1972-74; resident in gen. surgery Duke U. Med. Ctr., Durham, 1974-78, resident orthopedics, 1974-78; presenter and lectr. in field. Contbr. articles to profl. jours. Mem. Am. Acad. Orthopedic Surgeons, So. Orthopedic Soc., N.C. Orthopedic Soc., Piedmont Orthopedic Soc. (Kelly award 1991), Am. Med. Soc., So. Med. Soc., N.C. Med. Soc., Wake County Med. Soc. (treas. 1986), N.Am. Spine Soc., N.C. Spine Soc., Alpha Epsilon Delta., Phi Beta Kappa. Office: Triangle Spine & Back Care Ctr 3320 Wake Forst Rd Ste 430 Raleigh NC 27609

WHITELAW, ANDREW GEORGE LINDSAY, neonatologist, educator; b. Derby, Eng., Aug. 31, 1946; arrived in Norway, 1990; s. Robert and Cicely (Ballard) W.; m. Sara Jane Sparks, Sept. 7, 1968 (div. 1987); children: Nicola, Ben, Rebecca; m. Marianne Thoresen, Aug. 4, 1990; 1 child, Thomas. BA in Natural Scis., Cambridge (Eng.) U., 1967, B of Medicine and Surgery, 1971, MD, 1978. Med. qualification, 1971, specialist in pediatrics, 1980. Pediatric resident Northwick Park Hosp., Eng., 1972-73; chief resident Northwick Park Hosp., 1976-78, neonatologist, 1979-81; pediatric resident Hosp. for Sick Children, London, 1974, rsch. fellow, 1975-76; neonatal fellow Hosp. for Sick Children, Toronto, 1978-79; neonatalogist Hammersmith Hosp., Eng., 1981-90, Aker U. Hosp., Oslo, 1990—; assoc. prof. U. Oslo, 1990-95, prof., 1995—; chmn. perinatal working party North West Thames Health, London, 1984-87. Editor: The Very Immature Infant, 1988; editorial bd.: British Jour. Ob-Gyn., 1981-85; assoc. editor Acta Pediatrica, 1996—; contbr. articles to profl. jours. Recipient Rsch. grants Royal Coll. Ob-Gyns., London, 1983, Action Rsch. for the Crippled Child, London, 1985-87, Laerdal Found. for Acute Medicine, Norway, 1989, 92. Fellow Royal Coll. Physicians (London). Office: Aker Univ Hosp, Dept Pediatrics, N-0514 Oslo Norway

WHITESIDES, THOMAS EDWARD, JR., orthopaedic surgeon; b. Gastonia, N.C., Nov. 4, 1929; s. Thomas Edward and Ferne (Bell) W.; m. Peggy Sue Patrick, Jan. 28, 1967; children: William Taylor, Lisa Elizabeth, Edward Patrick, John Thomas. BS, Emory U., 1952, MD, 1955. Diplomate Am. Bd. Orthopaedic Surgeons (dir. 1980-90, trustee 1991—). Resident in orthopaedics Barnes Hosp.-Washington U., St. Louis, 1957-60; asst. prof. surgery Emory U., 1962-66, assoc. prof. surgery, 1966-70, prof. orthopaedic surgery, 1970—, chmn. dept. orthopaedics, 1974-81; instr. orthopaedics Washington U., St. Louis, 1957-60; Alan DeForrest Smith lectr. Columbia U., N.Y.C., 1974; McCarroll lectr. Washington U., St. Louis, 1978, Stein Meml. lectr., 1982; Phesant Meml. lectr. U. So. Calif.; vis. prof. Washington U., Harvard U., Iowa U., U. Pa., others. Author, editor: Evarts Surgery of Musculoskeletal System, 1984, Spine Section, 1984; contbr. numerous articles to profl. jours. Capt.,orthopedit MC, USAF, 1960-62. Recipient Kappa Delta rsch. award, Am. Acad. Orthopaedic Surgeons/Orthopaedic Rsch. Soc., 1980. Mem. Am. Acad. Orthopaedic Surgeons; mem. Am. Orthopaedic Assn., Alpha Omega Alpha. Republican. Presbyterian. Home: 958 Calvert Ln NE Atlanta GA 30319-1202 Office: Emory Clinic Spine Ctr 1265 N Decatur Rd Decatur GA 30033

WHITE-SIMS, SUSANNE TROPEZ, pediatrician, educator; b. New Orleans, Apr. 13, 1949; d. Maxwell Sterling and Ethel (Ross) Tropez; m. James Carnell White, Apr. 10, 1971 (div. 1992); children: Lisa, Janifer, James Carnell; m. Michael Milroy Sims, Feb. 18, 1995. BS, Bennett Coll., 1971; MD, U. N.C., 1975, M.P.H., 1982. Diplomate Am. Bd. Pediatrics. Resident in pediatrics N.C. Meml. Hosp., Chapel Hill, 1975-76, 77-79; pediatrician Darnell Army Hosp., Ft. Hood, Tex., 1976-77; acting dir. pediatric day clinic Wake County Med. Ctr., Raleigh, N.C., 1979-82, dir. pediatric day clinic, 1982-88, dir. teens with tots clinic, 1980-88; asst. prof. pediatrics U. N.C., Chapel Hill, 1982-88, assoc. prof. pediatrics La. State U., New Orleans, 1988—; dir. div. pediatric emergency rm., 1988-89; chief div. ambulatory care, 1989-92, clin. dir. maternal and child health units, 1992, chief divsn. community pediatrics and adolescent medicine, 1992—; pediatrician Shelly Child Devel. Ctr., Raleigh, 1981-88, child med. examiner program, Raleigh, 1979-88; chairperson sch. health com. local chpt. AAP, 1993; adminstrv. bd. chair Cornerstone U.M.C., 1993—, chairperson edn. com., 1991-92; mem. Nat. Com. Sch. Health, 1993—. Contbr. articles to profl. jours. Mem. United Meth. Women. Mem. Walnut Terr. Child Devel. Ctr., Raleigh, 1981-83, chmn., 1982-83; chmn. pastor of parish com. Longview Ch., Raleigh, 1982-84, 87-88, chmn. membership care com.; chmn. edn. com. Cornerstone UMC, 1989-90. Fellow preventive medicine, 1979-82, Faculty Devel. fellow U. N.C. Sch. Medicine, 1985-87. Fellow Am. Acad. Pediatrics (mem. sch. health com.); mem. N.C. Pediatric Soc. (com. child abuse and neglect, adolescent pregnancy), La Pediatric Soc., Ambulatory Pediatric Assn., Adolescent Pregnancy Coalition United Way, Bennett Coll. Alumnae Assn. Democrat.

WHITFIELD, GRAHAM FRANK, orthopedic surgeon; b. Cheam, Surrey, Eng., Feb. 8, 1942; came to U.S., 1969, naturalized, 1975; s. Reginald Frank and Marjorie Joyce (Bennett) W. BSc, King's Coll., U. London, 1963, PhD, Queen Mary Coll., U. London, 1969; MD, N.Y. Med. Coll., 1976. Rsch. scientist Unilever Rsch. Lab., Eng., 1963-66; postdoctoral fellow dept. chemistry Temple U., 1969-71, instr., 1971-72, asst. prof., 1972-73; resident in surgery N.Y. Med. Coll. Affiliated Hosps., N.Y.C., 1976-78, resident in orthopedics, 1978-79, sr. resident in orthopedic surgery, 1979-80, chief resident, 1980-81; attending orthopedic surgeon Good Samaritan Hosp., West Palm Beach, Fla., 1981-87, JFK Med. Ctr., Lake Worth, Fla., 1981—, Palms Wellington Surgical Ctr., West Palm Beach, Fla., 1994—, Wellington Regional Med. Ctr., 1996—; instr. health professions divsn. Nova Southeastern U., North Miami, Fla., 1994-95, clin. asst. prof. dept. surgery, 1995—. Recipient N.Y. Med. Coll. Surg. Soc. award, 1976. Fellow Internat. Coll. Surgeons; mem. AMA, Fla. Med. Assn., Palm Beach County Med. Soc., Royal Inst. Chemistry (Eng.), So. Orthopedic Assn., Fla. Orthopedic Soc., Sigma Xi. Clubs: Beach (Palm Beach), Colette; Brit. Schs. and Univs., Soc. Sons of St. George (N.Y.C.); Govs. of Palm Beaches (West Palm Beach), Explorers' Club (N.Y.C.). Lodges: Rotary, Sovereign Order Knights of St. John. Author: (with Joseph Cohn and Louis Del Guercio) Critical Care Readings, 1981; editorial bd., contbg. editor Hosp. Physician, 1978-82; cons. editor Physician Asst. and Health Practitioner, 1979-82; orthopedic cons. Conv. Reporter, 1980-82; assoc. editor in chief Critical Care Monitor, 1980-82; edit. bd. Complications in Orthopedics, 1986—; practice panel cons. in orthopedic surgery Complications in Surgery, 1982—. Office: 1870 Forest Hill Blvd West Palm Beach FL 33406-8901

WHITING, DAVID ASHBY, dermatologist; b. Johannesburg, Transvaal, South Africa, Sept. 30, 1931; came to U.S. 1977; s. William Rowland and Doris (Ray) W.; m. Diana Julia Kemp, Jan. 30, 1960 (div. 1973); children: Simon, Clare, Martin; m. Harriet Margaret Smith, June 20, 1974. M.B.B.Ch., U. Witwatersrand, South Africa, 1953; M.Med. w/ Dermatology, U. Pretoria, South Africa, 1968; MD, U. Witwatersrand, 1979. Pvt. gen. practice Essex, G.B., 1957-58; pvt. gen. practice Johannesburg, 1958-65, pvt. practice dermatology, 1968-77; med. dir. Baylor Hair Rsch. & Treatment Ctr., Dallas, 1987—; specialist dermatologist Dallas Assoc. Dermatologists, 1979—; vis Pfizer lectr. U. Rhodesia, Salisbury, 1976; vis. Upjohn prof. and lectr., 1990. Contbr. numerous articles to profl. jours.; author chpts. in books. Recipient Silver Award Am. Acad. Dermatology, 1978, Gold award for poster, 1984; Hamilton Maynard Meml. medalist South African Med. Jour., 1978. Mem. Am. Dermatol. Assn., Internat. Soc. Pediatric Dermatologists (treas. 1989), Hair Rsch. Soc. (sec.-treas. 1991-96, pres. 1996—), Dallas Dermatol. Soc., Tex. Dermatol. Soc., Internat. Soc. Tropical Dermatology, Brit. Assn. Dermatologists, St. John's Hosp. Dermatol. Soc., South African Dermatology Soc., Am. Soc. Dermatopathology. Episcopalian. Home: 1 Royal Way Dallas TX 75229-5538 Office: Dallas Assoc Dermatologists 3600 Gaston Ave Ste 1051 Dallas TX 75246-1910

WHITINGTON, PETER FRANK, pediatrics educator, pediatric hepatologist; b. Memphis, May 8, 1947; s. Frank Everett and Mary Lena (Hollingsworth) W.; m. Susan Maurine Hoagland, June 6, 1967; children: Helen Frances, Mary Louise Whitington Mays, Katherine Daphne. BA in Econs., Tulane U., 1968; MD, U. Tenn., Memphis, 1971. Diplomate Am. Bd. Pediatrics, Am. Bd. Pediatric Gastroenterology. Resident in pediatrics, then chief resident U. Tenn. Ctr. for Health Scis., 1972-74, instr., 1975, asst. prof., 1978-81, assoc. prof., 1981-84, chief div. pediatric gastroenterology, 1978-84; rsch. fellow in gastroenterology Johns Hopkins Hosp., Balt., 1975-77; rsch. fellow in gastroenterology dept. pediatrics U. Wis., Madison, 1977-78; assoc. prof. dept. pediat. U. Chgo. Pritzker Sch. Medicine, 1984-87, assoc. prof. depts. pediat. and medicine, 1987-92, prof., 1992—; chief gastroenterology LeBonheur Children's Med. Ctr., Memphis, 1978-84; numerous invited lectures and guest speaker at profl. meetings, workshops, symposia, hosps., confs.; vis. prof. Yale U., New Haven, 1993, U. Torino, Italy, 1994; mem. United Network for Organ Sharing pediatric transplantation com. Nat. Organ Procurement and Transplantation Network, 1992-94; reviewer numerous med. jours. including New Eng. Jour. Medicine, Gastroenterology, Hepatology, Jour. Pediat., Digestive Diseases and Scis., Pediatrics, Transplant. Mem. editl. bd. Jour. Pediatric Gastroenterology and Nutrition, 1991—, Liver Surgery and Transplantation, 1994—; sect. editor Birth Defects Compendium, 1987—; contbr. numerous articles and abstracts to med. jours. Mem. sci. adv. bd. Mid-South chpt. Nat. Found. for Ileitis and Colitis, Memphis, 1983-84; bd. dirs. Liver/Organ Transplant Fund, Memphis, 1983-84, Parents for Ctrl. H.S., Memphis, 1983-84; mem. med. adv. com. Chgo. Met. chpt. Am. Liver Found., 1985—, mem., med. adv. on bd. dirs., 1993—; med. dir. The Johnny Genna Found., Chgo., 1987—. Recipient Cmty. Svc. award NCCJ, Memphis, 1983; postdoctoral rsch. fellow NIH, 1977. Mem. Am. Assn. for Study Liver Diseases, Gastroenterology Rsch. Group, Am. Gastroent. Assn., Soc. for Pediatric Rsch., N.Am. Soc. for Pediatric Gastroenterology and Nutrition, Internat. Gastro-Surg. Club, Chgo. Pediatric Soc. Home: Apt 8 North 5490 South Shore Dr Chicago IL 60615 Office: U Chgo Wyler Children's Hosp 5841 S Maryland Ave MC 4065 Chicago IL 60637-1470*

WHITIS, GRACE RUTH, nursing educator; b. San Antonio, Sept. 14, 1942; d. Allan and Jewel (Conlee) Richardson; m. Robert E. Whitis, Mar. 6, 1965; children: Jay, Jennifer. PhD, U. Tex., 1981; BS, U. Mary Hardin - Baylor, 1968; MS, Baylor U., 1970; MS in Nursing, U. Tex., 1972. Staff nurse Providence Hosp., Waco, Tex., 1965-67; faculty U. Mary Hardin-Baylor, Belton, Tex., 1970-79, prof., dean, 1979-83; prof. nursing Ark State U., Jonesboro, 1993—, chmn. dept., 1985-93; vis. prof. La. Tech. U., Ruston, 1982-84. Contbr. articles to profl. jours. Mem. ANA, Nat. League for Nursing, Ark. Nurses Assn., Soc. Pediatric Nurses, Sigma Theta Tau. Home: 2403 Paula Dr Jonesboro AR 72404 Office: Ark State U PO Box 69 State University AR 72467-0069

WHITLOCK, PAUL AUSTIN, JR., surgeon; b. Carrollton, Ga., Aug. 5, 1942; s. Paul Austin and Martha Louise (Ford) W.; m. Barbara Jean Mohr, Mar. 22, 1969; children: Clarice, Bessie Elizabeth, Paul Austin, Nolan Arthur. BS, U. Ga., 1964; MD, Emory U., 1968. Diplomate Am. Bd. Surgery. Intern Camp Pendleton (Calif.) Naval Hosp., 1968-69; resident in surgery San Diego Naval Hosp., 1969-73; practice medicine specializing in surgery, Statesboro, Ga., 1975—; mem. staff Bulloch Meml. Hosp. 1975—, pres. staff, 1979; deacon First Bapt. Ch., Statesboro, 1987. Served to lt. comdr. M.C., USN, 1968-75. Mem. Bulloch County Ed. Edn., 1989—. Fellow ACS; mem. Ogeechee River Med. Soc. (pres. 1976, 77), Bulloch County C. of C. (pres. 1982), 1st Dist. Med. Soc. (pres. 1981), SAGES, Phi Beta Kappa, Phi Kappa Phi, Alpha Tau Omega. Lodge: Republican. Statesboro Rotary. Lodge Sons Confederate Vets., 1987.

WHITLOCK, ROBERT TURNBULL, gastroenterologist; b. Mt. Airy, N.C., Mar. 29, 1929; s. Coleman Morrison and Gertrude Bryan (Turnbull) W.; m. Joan Catherine McGee, June 19, 1954; children: David, Thomas, Mary Elizabeth, Robert. AB, U. N.C., 1950, MD, 1957. Diplomate Am. Bd. Gastroenterology. Intern, resident, chief resident in medicine Presbyn. Hosp., N.Y.C., 1957-60, 61-62; rsch. fellow Columbia Univ., N.Y.C., 1960-61, 62-64; clin. practice Presbyn. Hosp., 1964-88; prof. clin. medicine Columbia Univ., N.Y.C., 1981—; chief medicine Allen Pavilion Presbyn. Hosp., 1988—. Fellow ACP; mem. AMA, Internat. Assn. Study Liver, Am. Soc. Gastrointestinal Endoscopy, Am. Assn. Study Liver Disease, Am. Gastroenterol. Assn., Phi Beta Kappa, Alpha Omega Alpha. Episcopal. Office: Presbyn Hosp Allen Pavilion 5141 Broadway New York NY 10034

WHITLOW, PATRICK LEE, interventional cardiologist; b. Atlanta, June 26, 1950; s. George and Eloise Whitlow; m. Catherine Elizabeth Widener; children: Laura, Patrick, Katherine. BA in Psychology, U. Va., 1972; MD, Duke U., 1976. Diplomate Am. Bd. Internal Medicine, Am. Bd. Cardiovascular Disease. Intern in internal medicine U. Tex. SW Health Scis. Ctr., Dallas, 1977, resident in internal medicine, 1979; fellowship in cardiology U. Ala., Birmingham, 1981, instr. in medicine divsn. cardiology, 1981-82, asst. prof. medicine, divsn. of cardiology, 1982-86, dir. coronary care unit, 1982-84, dir. cardiac catheterization lab., 1984-86, dir. blood gas analysis lab., 1984-86; dir. coronary care unit The Cleve. Clinic Found., 1986-89, staff dept. cardiology, 1986—, staff dept. of vascular medicine, joint appointment, 1989—, dir. interventional cardiology rsch. lab., 1990—, dir. interventional cardiology, 1991—, staff dept. of molecular cardiology, 1991—; mem. scientific and med. adv. bd. Biocompatibles Ltd., 1994—; mem. scientific adv. bd. Kensey Nash Corp., 1993—; mem. randomized trial adv. com. Heart Technology, Inc./SCIMED, 1993—. Contbr. 100 articles to profl. jours. Recipient numerous grants. Fellow Am. Coll. Cardiology (Ohio Bd. Trustees 1990-94, Young Investigator award 1982); mem. AMA, Am. Heart Assn. (mem. coun. on high blood pressure rsch. and coun. for clin. cardiology, coun. on clin. cardiology 1982—), Advanced Cardiovascular Systems (mem. clin. adv. bd. 1986—), N.Am. Soc. for Cardiac Radiology, Internat. Adreas Grüntzig Soc., Am. Soc. of Anesthesiologists (com. for practice guidelines for sedation and analgesia by nonanesthesiologists 1994—), Omicron Delta Kappa, Phi Beta Kappa. Office: Dept Cardiology F25 Cleveland Clinic Found 9500 Euclid Ave Cleveland OH 44195

WHITMAN, ROY MILTON, psychiatrist; b. N.Y.C., June 6, 1925; s. Jack and Mae (Hoffman) W.; m. Dorothy Louise Yarborough (div. 1965); m. Esther Eve Guttman, May 27, 1968; children: Joy, Bruce, Laura, Rebecca, Michael. BS, Ind. U., 1944, MD, 1946. Intern Kings County Hosp., Bklyn., 1946-47; resident Duke U., Durham, N.C., 1947-48, U. Chgo. Clinics, 1950-52; instr. psychiatry U. Chgo., 1950-52, asst. prof., 1952-54; assoc. prof. Northwestern U., Chgo., 1954-57; assoc. prof. U. Cin., 1957-67, prof., 1967-94, chmn. dept. psychiatry, 1980-89. Author: Dream Psychology and Biology of Dreaming, 1967; contbr. articles to profl. jours. Capt. U.S. Army, 1948-50. Fellow Am. Psychiat. Assn., Am. Coll. Psychoanalysts (pres. 1960—), Ctr. for Advanced Psychoanalytic Studies; mem. Cin. Psychiat. Soc., Sigma Xi. Home: 7137 Fair Oaks Dr Cincinnati OH 45237 Office: U Cin 231 Bethesda Ave Cincinnati OH 45267

WHITMER, KYRA MARIE RIEGLE, nursing researcher; b. Buffalo, Feb. 11, 1940; d. Bervil Howard and Inez Agatha (Tummonds) Riegle; m. Jeffrey Thomas Whitmer. RN, Deaconess Hosp., Buffalo, 1960; BSN, SUNY, Buffalo, 1965; PhD, U. Kans., 1974. Staff nurse, head nurse, in-svc. educator Deaconess Hosp., 1960-65; rsch. assoc., teaching asst. U. Kans. Med. Ctr., Kansas City, 1970-74; asst. prof. nursing, rsch. assoc. Pa. State U., Hershey, 1974-77; assoc. prof. N.Y. State U. Tech., Utica, 1977-78; rsch. assoc. Upstate Med. Ctr., Syracuse, N.Y., 1978-79; rsch. instr., rsch. asst. prof. U. Cin., 1979-88; adj. prof. U. So. Ind., Evansville, 1988-91; nurse researcher Deaconess Hosp., Evansville, 1989-91; adj. faculty LaSalle U., Phila., 1992—; nurse rschr. Fox Chase Cancer Ctr., Phila., 1993—; speaker in field. Contbr. articles to profl. jours. NIH fellow, 1979-82. Mem. ANa, Am. Physiol. Soc., Sigma Theta Tau.

WHITSELL, JOHN CRAWFORD, II, general surgeon; b. St. Joseph, Mo., Dec. 21, 1929; s. Ora Earl and Lorena (Spratt) W. AB, Grinnell Coll., 1950; MD, Washington U., St. Louis, 1954. Diplomate Am. Bd. Surgery, Am. Bd. Thoracic Surgery. From instr. to clin. prof. surgery Cornell U. Med. Ctr., N.Y.C., 1963-70; from asst. attending to attending in surgery N.Y. Hosp., N.Y.C., 1964-70; surg. dir. Rogosin Kidney Ctr. N.Y. Hosp.-Cornell Med. Ctr., N.Y.C., 1973-75; attending in surgery N.Y. Hosp., 1970—; clin. prof. surgery Cornell Med. Coll., 1970—; surg. cons. Rogosin Kidney Ctr., 1975—, Sharon (Conn.) Hosp., 1976—. Contbr. articles to profl. jours. Capt. USAF, 1961-63, Eng. Fellow ACS; mem. Transplantation Soc., N.Y. Surg. Soc., Am. Soc. Transplant Surgeons, N.Y. Soc. for Thoracic Surgery, Soc. Thoracic Surgeons, N.Y. Acad. Medicine, N.Y. Soc. Cardiovascular Surgery, Harvey Soc., Union Club of N.Y., Phi Beta Kappa. Office: 449 E 68th St New York NY 10021-6305

WHITT, DIXIE DAILEY, microbiology educator; b. Longmont, Colo., Mar. 9, 1939; d. Herman Eden and Helen Lurissia (Stanton) Dailey; m. Gregory Sidney Whitt, Aug. 25, 1963. BS, Colo. State U., 1961, PhD, 1965. Postdoctoral trainee Yale U., New Haven, Conn., 1965-68; rsch. biologist, lectr. Yale U., 1968-69; rsch. assoc. U. Ill., Urbana, 1969-87; lectr. basic scis. U. Ill. Coll. Medicine, 1987—. Co-author: (lab. manual) Properties of Bacterial Pathogens, 1990, (textbook) Bacterial Pathogenesis: A Molecular Approach, 1994; contbr. articles to profl. jours. NDEA Title IV fellow, 1961-64, NIH fellow, 1964-65. Fellow Am. Acad. Microbiology; mem. AAAS, Am. Soc. Microbiology (chair membership com. 1995—). Home: 1510 Trails Dr Urbana IL 61801-7052 Office: U Ill Dept Microbiology 407 S Goodwin Ave Urbana IL 61801-3704

WHITTEMORE, PAUL BAXTER, psychologist; b. Framingham, Mass., Apr. 11, 1948; s. Harry Ballou and Margaret (Brown) W.; m. Jane L. Manson, Apr. 22, 1995. BA in Religion, Ea. Nazarene Coll., 1970; MDiv., Nazarene Theol. Sem., 1973; MA in Theology, Vanderbilt U., 1975, PhD in Theology, 1978; PhD in Clin. Psychology, U. Tenn., 1987. Lic. psychologist, Calif. Asst. prof. philosophy and edn. Trevecca Nazarene Coll., Nashville, Tenn., 1973-76; asst. prof. philosophy and theology Point Loma Coll., San Diego, Calif., 1976-80; asst. prof. philosophy Middle Tenn. State U., Murfreesboro, 1980-83; clin. psychology intern. LAC/U. So. Calif. Med. Ctr., L.A., 1986-87; coord. behavior health ctr. Calif. Med. Ctr., L.A., 1987-88; clin. asst. prof. family medicine sch. medicine U. So. Calif., L.A., 1988—; pvt. practice psychologist Newport Beach, Calif., 1989—; mem. behavioral sci. faculty Glendale Adventist Family Practice Residency Program, Glendale, Calif., 1989-90; inpatient group therapist Ingleside Hosp., Rosemead, Calif., 1990-92; founder, pres. The Date Coach, 1992—. Contbr. articles to profl. jours. Recipient Andrew W. Mellon Postdoctoral Faculty Devel. award Vanderbilt U., 1981. Mem. APA, Am. Acad. Religion, Am. Philos. Assn., AAUP (chpt. v.p. 1982-83), Orange County Employee Assistance Profl. Assn. (bd. dirs. 1993—), Orange County Psychol. Assn. (bd. dirs. 1996—). Office: 3901 Macarthur Blvd Ste 200 Newport Beach CA 92660-3011

WHITTEMORE, RONALD P., hospital administrator, retired army officer, nursing educator; b. Saco, Maine, Aug. 10, 1946; s. Ronald B. and Pauline L. (Larson) W.; m. Judy D. McDonald, Feb. 17, 1967; 1 child, Leicia Michelle. BGS, U. S.C., 1974, MEd, 1977; BSN, Med. Coll. Ga., 1975. Enlisted U.S. Army, 1968, advanced through ranks to maj., 1985, ret., 1991; adult/oncology nurse practitioner Martin Army Community Hosp.; asst. head nurse SICU, infection control practitioner Moncrief Army Community Hosp.; infection control practitioner U.S. Army Hosp., Seoul, Korea; chief nurse 2d Combat Support Hosp., Ft. Benning, Ga.; community health nurse Brooke Army Med. Ctr., Ft. Sam Houston, Tex.; comty. health nurse Giessen (Fed. Republic Germany) Mil. Comty.; clin. instr. Eisenhower Army Med. Ctr., Ft. Gordon, Ga.; chief nursing adminstrn. E/N Frankfurt (Germany) Army Med. Ctr.; adminstr., dir. quality improvement Gracewood (Ga.) State Sch. and Hosp., 1995—; instr. Augusta (Ga.) Tech. Inst.; nurse epidemiologist Med. Coll. Ga., Augusta. Mem. ANA, Ga. ANA (3d Dist. honoree, pres. 1983-85), Am. Holistic Nurses Assn., Nat. Assn. Health Care Quality Profls., Sigma Theta Tau. Home: 801 Bon Air Dr Augusta GA 30907 Office: Gracewood State Sch & Hosp Gracewood GA 30812

WHITTEN, WESLEY KINGSTON, retired embryologist; b. Macksville, NSW, Australia, Aug. 1, 1918; s. Alfred Giles and Ethel Ann (Cock) W.; m. Enid Elsbeth Meredith, Dec. 13, 1941; children: Gregory R., Mark G., Jane M., Penelope A. BVSc, U. Sydney (Australia), 1939, BSc, 1941, DSc, 1962. Rsch. scientist CSIRO, Australia, 1946-50; fellow Australian Nat. U., 1950-61; assoc. dir. Nat. Biol. Stand. Lab., Australia, 1961-66; staff scientist Jackson Lab., Bar Harbor, Maine, 1966-80; rsch. assoc. dept. zoology U. Tasmania, Hobart, 1980-89; dir. in vitro fertilization and embryo transfer lab. dept. ob-gyn. U. Tasmania, 1983-86; vis. fellow Australian Nat. U., 1980—; disting. vis. prof. dept. physiology Meml. U. Newfoundland, Can., 1984; vis. scientist dept. clin. scis. Australian Nat. U., 1989-93; associated scientist coop. rsch. ctr. for biol. control of vertebrate pest populations ANU, CSRIO, 1992—; vis. prof. dept. psychology Dalhousie U., Nova Scotia, Can., 1993-94, 96. Discoverer mammalian/mouse pheremones; contbr. articles to profl. jours. Capt. Australian Army, 1940-45. Recipient Marshall medal Soc. for Study of Fertility, 1993, Pioneer award Internat. Soc. for Embryo Transfer, 1995. Fellow Australian Acad. Sci., Australian Inst. Biology.

WHITWORTH, RANDOLPH HOWARD, educator, psychologist; b. Robstown, Tex., May 18, 1929; s. Howard J. and Pearl (Randolph) W.; B.S., U. Tex., Austin, 1951, Ph.D., 1960; m. Selina Morgan, Mar. 17, 1966; children—Kirsten, Randolph T., Caroline S. Asst. prof. psychology Tex. Western Coll., 1960-63; assoc. prof. psychology U. Tex., El Paso, 1963-88, dir. counseling service, 1962-67, asst. dean Coll. Liberal Arts, 1977-83, chmn. dept. psychology, 1983—, prof., 1988—; pvt. practice psychology, El Paso, Tex., 1960—; adj. prof. Tex. Tech. Med. Sch., 1977—. Served with USAF, 1951-55. Mem. APA, Southwestern Psychol. Assn., Rocky Mountain Psychol. Assn., Tex. Psychol. Assn., El Paso Psychol. Assn., Sigma Xi. Contbr. articles to profl. jours. Home: PO Box 13657 El Paso TX 79913-3657 Office: 6006 N Mesa St Ste 500 El Paso TX 79912-4630

WHORTON, M. DONALD, occupational and environmental health physician, epidemiologist; b. Las Vegas, N.Mex., Jan. 25, 1943; s. R.H. and Rachel (Siegal) W.; m. Diana L. Obrinsky, Apr. 9, 1972; children: Matthew Richard, Laura Elizabeth, Julie Hannah. Student, U.S. Naval Acad., 1961-62; B.Biology, N. Mex. Highlands U., 1964; M.D., U. N.Mex., 1968; M.P.H., Johns Hopkins U., 1973. Intern Boston City Hosp., 1968-69; resident in pathology U. N.Mex., Albuquerque, 1969-71; instr., resident in medicine Balt. City Hosp., 1972-74; instr. Johns Hopkins U., Balt.; assoc. dir. div. emergency medicine Balt. City Hosps., 1974-75; clin. asst. prof. div. ambulatory and community medicine Sch. Medicine, U. Calif.-San Francisco, 1975-77; lectr. sch. pub. health program Inst. Indsl. Relations, Ctr. for Labor Research and Edn., 1975-79, med. dir. labor occupational program, 1975-79, assoc. clin. prof. occupational medicine, 1979-88; prin. Environ. Health Assocs., Inc., Oakland, 1978-88; v.p. ENSR Health Scis., 1988-94; pvt. practice Alameda, Calif., 1994—; chmn. adv. com. for hazard evaluation service and info. system Indsl. Relations Dept. State of Calif., 1979-84; cons. in field. Contbr. articles to profl. jours. Recipient Upjohn Achievement award, 1968; Robert Wood Johnson Found. clin. scholar, 1972-74. Fellow Am. Coll. Epidemiology, Am. Coll. Occupational and Environ. Medicine; mem. Am. Pub. Health Assn., Soc. for Occupational and Environ. Health, Am. Coll. Emergency Physicians, Calif. Med. Assn., AAAS, Inst. Medicine, Nat. Acad. Sci., Alpha Omega Alpha. Office: 1135 Atlantic Ave Alameda CA 94501-1145

WHYBROW, PETER CHARLES, psychiatrist, educator; b. Hertforshire, Eng., June 13, 1939; came to U.S., 1964, naturalized, 1975; s. Charles Ernest and Doris Beatrice (Abbott) W.; m. Margaret Ruth Steele, Dec. 11, 1962 (div. 1988); children: Katherine, Helen. Student, Univ. Coll., London, 1956-59; M.B., B.S., Univ. Coll. Hosp. Med. Sch., 1962; diploma psychol. medicine, Conjoint Bd., London, 1968; M.A. (hon.), Dartmouth Coll., 1974, U. Pa., 1984. House officer endocrinology Univ. Coll. Hosp., 1962, sr. house physician psychiatry, 1963-64; house surgeon St. Helier Hosp., Surrey, Eng., 1963; house officer pediatrics Prince of Wales Hosp., London, 1964; resident psychiatry U. N.C. Hosp., 1965-67, instr., research fellow, 1967-68; mem. sci. staff neuropsychiat. research unit Charshalton, Surrey, 1968-69; dir. residency tng. psychiatry Dartmouth Med. Sch., Hanover, N.H., 1969-71; prof. psychiatry Dartmouth Med. Sch., 1970-84, chmn. dept., 1970-78, exec. dean, 1980-83; prof., chmn. dept. psychiatry U. Pa., Phila., 1984—, Ruth Meltzer prof. psychiatry, 1992; psychiatrist-in-chief Hosp. U. Pa., 1984—; dir. psychiatry Dartmouth Hitchcock Affiliated Hosp., 1970-78; vis. scientist NIMH, 1978-79; cons. VA, 1970—, NIMH, 1972— ; chmn. test com. Nat. Bd. Med. Examiners, 1977-84; researcher psychoendrocrinology. Author: Mood Disorders: Toward a New Psychobiology, 1984, The Hibernation Response, 1988; editor: Psychosomatic Medicine, 1977; mem. editl. bd. Cmty. Psychiatry, Psychiat. Times, Directions in Psychiatry, Neuropsychopharmacology; contbr. articles to profl. jours. Recipient Anclote Manor award psychiat. rsch. U. N.C., 1967, Sr. Investigator award nat. Alliance for Rsch. into Schizophrenia and Depression, 1989; Josiah Macy Jr. Found. scholar, 1978-79; fellow Cen. for Advanced Studies in Behavioral Sci., Stanford, 1993-94; recipient Lifetime Investigator award NDMDA, 1996; decorated Knight of Merit, Sovereign Order of St. John of Jerusalem, 1993. Fellow AAAS, Am. Psychiat. Assn., Royal Coll. Psychiatrist (founding mem.), Am. Coll. Psychiatrists, Ctr. Advanced Study of Behavioral Scis.; mem. Assn. Am. Med. Colls., Soc. Psychosomatic Rsch., Am. Assn. Chmn. Depts. Psychiatry (pres. 1977-78), Royal Soc. Medicine, Am. Psychopath Assn., Am. Coll. Neuropsychopharmacology, Soc. Biol. Psychiatry, N.Y. Acad. Scis., Soc. Neurosci., Sigma Xi, Alpha Omega Alpha, Cosmos Club (Washington). Club: Cosmos (Washington). Office: U Pa Dept Psychiatry 305 Blockley Hall Philadelphia PA 19104 also: 135 S 19th St Philadelphia PA 19103-4912

WIATR, CHRISTOPHER L., microbiologist; b. Chgo., Jan. 5, 1948; s. Joseph Thomas and Beatrice Harriet (Kaminski) Wiatr; m. Jeanne Lynn Malecki, Oct. 20, 1978; children: Kelli Jean, Christopher Joseph, Kaycee Lynn, Kirby Ann, Nicholas Aloysius. BS, Ill. Benedictine Coll., 1969; MS, IIT, 1974; PhD, U. Ill., Chgo., 1985. Cert. tchr. Tchr., coach St. Rita High Sch., Chgo., 1969-74; rsch. microbiologist Swift & Co./Esmark/Beatrice Foods, Chgo., 1974-75, lab. mgr., 1975-76, tech. dir. rsch. and quality assurance, 1976-79; sr. microbiologist Nalco Chem. Co. Water and Waste Treatment R & D, Naperville, Ill., 1985-87, sr. rsch. microbiologist, 1988, group leader water rsch., 1989-91; group leader Pulp & Paper Chems. R & D, Naperville, Ill., 1991-94; mgr. microbiology and biochemistry R&D Calgon Corp.-ECCI, Pitts., 1994—; reviewer Nat. Assn. Corrosion Engrs; chmn. biocide session Internat. Water Conf., 1996. Co-author: (book chpt.) Food Preservation by Irradiation, 1978; contbr. articles to profl. jours. Com. Maplebrook I Swim Club, Naperville, 1990-94; Eagle scout, merit badge counselor Boy Scouts Am., 1963—. Named Researcher of Yr., Nalco Chem. Co., 1987. Mem. TAPPI (microbiology and microbiol tech. and water quality com. 1993—), Am. Chem. Soc., Nat. Assn. Corrosion Engrs., Soc. Indsl. Microbiology, Am. Soc. for Microbiology, Sigma Xi (pres. Nalco chpt. 1991-92, session chair microbiology internat. water conf. 1996). Roman Catholic.

WIBELL, LARS BERTIL, physician; b. Stockholm, Feb. 3, 1937; s. Harry Knut and Ebba (Hedlund) W.; m. Monika Forsman (div. 1973); children: Titti, Martin; m. Gunilla Lindmark, Aug. 18, 1980. MD, U. Uppsala, 1964; PhD, U. Uppsala (Sweden), 1974. Assoc. prof. medicine U. Hosp., Uppsala, 1975. Contbr. over 100 sci. papers in nephrology, clin. diabetes and edn. Home: Statarvägen 24, 75245 Uppsala Sweden Office: U Hosp Dept Medicine, Uppsala Sweden

WICK, CAROLYN BROWN, biotechnology consultant; b. Jacksonville, Fla., July 6, 1958; d. John Willoughby and Betty (Butzer) Brown; m. William Owington Wick Jr., Sept. 10, 1983; children: William Ovington III, John Willoughby, Katharine Poole. BA, Williams Coll., 1980; MSc, London Sch. Econs., 1984. Asst. to dir. planning Gibco divsn. Dexter Corp., Chagrin Falls, Ohio, 1980-81, mgr. sales projects, 1981-82, mgr. market rsch., 1982-83; dir. tech. svcs. McCormack Ltd., Milton Keynes, Eng., 1985; rschr. Battelle Meml. Inst., Columbus, Ohio, 1986-88, rsch. scientist, 1988; cons. Bus. Analysis for Biotech., Delaware, Ohio, 1989—; judge Dx Awards for Excellence, Biomed. Mktg. Assn., 1996. Contbr. articles to Genetic Engring. News. Mem. Soc. Indsl. Microbiology (mng. editor jour. 1988-89, symposium convenor 1994-95, chairperson pub. responsibility), Am. Soc. Microbiology. Office: Bus Analysis for Biotech 8722 Olentangy River Rd Delaware OH 43015-9210

WICK, MARK ROBERT, physician, educator; b. Milw., July 23, 1952; s. Robert Howard and Dorothy Edith (Zickuhr) W. BS, Carroll Coll., Waukesha, Wis., 1974; MD, U. Wis., 1978. Diplomate Am. Bd. Pathology in anatomic and clin. pathology, transfusion medicine and dermatopathology. Resident in anatomic pathology, fellow in transfusion Mayo Clinic and Grad. Sch. Medicine, Rochester, Minn., 1978-83; asst. prof. lab. medicine and pathology U. Minn., Mpls., 1983-86, assoc. prof., 1986-89; prof. pathology Washington U., St. Louis, 1989—; del. resident physician sect. AMA, Chgo., 1980-81; project dir. pathology residency in-svc. exam. Am. Soc. Clin. Pathology, Chgo., 1988—; instr. pathology Mayo Med. Sch. and Clinic Found., Rochester, 1980-83. Editor: Pathology of Unusual Malignant Cutaneous Tumors, 1985, Monoclonal Antibodies in Diagnostic Immunohistochemistry, 1988; editor-in-chief Am. Jour. Clin. Pathology, 1990—. Recipient Career Devel. award Am. Cancer Soc., N.Y.C., 1985-88. Fellow Am. Soc. Clin. Pathologists, Coll. Am. Pathologists, Am. Soc. Dermatopathology. Republican. Lutheran. Office: Washington U Med Ctr Ste 300 Peters Bldg 1 Barnes Hosp Plz Saint Louis MO 63110

WICK, PAUL H., psychiatrist; b. Victoria, Tex., Aug. 2, 1936; s. Paul Henry and Bernice (Hummel) W.; m. D'Anna Poole, June 19, 1960; children: Steven, Pamela, Jeffrey. BA, U. Tex., 1957; MD, U. Tex. Med. Br., 1961. Resident in psychiatry U. Tex. Med. Br., Galveston, 1964-67; psychiatrist Tyler (Tex.) Psychiatry Clinic, 1967—; med. dir. Univ. Park Hosp., Tyler, 1985-94; mem. bd. dirs. Tex. Found. for Psychiatric Edn. and Rsch. Mem. citizen's adv. com. Tex. Dept. Mental Health/Mental Retardation, Austin, 1985-86; participant Tex. Assembly of Alcohol Policy, Austin, 1986; bd. dirs. Mental Health Assn. of Tyler, 1978-80. Capt. USAF, 1962-64. Fellow APA (assembly rep.); mem. AMA, Am. Acad. Psychiatry and Law, Assn. Geriatric Psychiatrists, Tex. Med. Assn., Tex. Soc. Psychiat. Physicians (pres. 1990-91), Cen. Neuropsychiatric Assn. Episcopal. Office: Tyler Psychiat Clinic 3300 S Broadway Ave Ste 102 Tyler TX 75701-7849

WICK, ROBERT L., JR., physician; b. Pitts., Oct. 3, 1930; s. Robert L. and Helen Elizabeth (Gollings) W.; married; children: Robert D., Susan E., Douglas M. BS, Va. Mil. Inst., 1951, Carnegie Mellon U., 1955; MD, U. Pitts, 1959; MS, Ohio State U., 1962. Diplomate Am. Bd. Preventive Medicine, Am. Bd. Quality Assurance and Utilization Rev. Physicians, Am. Bd. Forensic Examiners; cert. Am. Soc. Addiction Medicine, Am. Assn. Med. Rev. Officers. Intern South Side Hosp., Pitts., 1959-60; resident physician Ohio State U., 1960-62; chief aerostandards br. FAA, Washington, 1963-65; project engr. Airesearch Corp., L.A., 1965-67; prof. Ohio State U., Columbus, 1967-77; corp. med. dir. Am. Airlines, Dallas-Ft. Worth, 1977-91; med. dir. C.U.R.E., 1993—; vice chmn. med. panel Air Transport Assn., Washington, 1983-88, chmn., 1988-91; chmn. med. adv. com. Internat. Air Transport Assn., Geneva, 1987-88. Editor: Civil Aviation Med. Assn./Bulletin, 1988—; contbr. articles to profl. jours. Pres. Com. on Employment of Handicapped, 1982-91. With U.S. Army, 1951-53, Korea, 1966-67, Vietnam, maj. gen. USAR, 1986-90, Desert Shield, 1990-91. Lovelace Found. fellow, 1962-63; holder 3 aviation world speed records. Fellow Aerospace Med. Assn. (Tamisea award 1975), Am. Coll. Med. Quality (disting.); mem. Civil Aviation Med. Assn. (pres. 1974-75), Flying Physicians Assn. (pres. 1976-77), Internat. Acad. Aviation and Space Medicine (academician), Airlines Med. Dirs. Assn. (pres. 1986-87). Office: 1006 Loch Lomond Dr Arlington TX 76012-2733 Office: Addiction Med Assocs 4801 Brentwood St Fort Worth TX 76112 Office: Med Dir 21800 Oxnard St Ste 550 Woodlands Hills CA 91367

WICKER, JAMES EUGENE, psychologist; b. Whittenburg, Tex., Jan. 26, 1935; s. Elbert Shelton and Mrytle Blanche (Brown) W.; children: Tamra Michelle, David Andrew; m. Dorothy Baldwin, Aug. 9, 1996. AA, Del Mar Coll., 1955; BA in Psychology, U. Tex., 1960, MA, 1962; PhD in Clin. Psychology, Clayton U., 1989. Lic. psychologist, Tex. Electronics technician various cos., Austin, TEx., 1953-57; tech. staff asst. II, research scientist asst. Radiobiol. Lab., U. Tex. and USAF, 1957-64; cons. psychologist, Austin and Ft. Worth, 1962-70; pvt. practice psychology, Ft. Worth, 1970—; spl. instr. psychology U. Tex., 1964; human factors engr. Gen. Dynamics, Ft. Worth, 1964-65, sr. human factors psychologist, 1966-67; dir. Human Factors Lab., 1967-86; psychologist III Counseling Ctr. Tex. Christian U., Ft. Worth, 1987-89; clin. dir. Cherry Ln. Hosp., 1990-91; condr. seminars, lectr., cons. in field. Contbr. articles to profl. jours. Mem. APA, Am. Psychol. Soc., Midwestern Psychol. Assn., Tex. Psychol. Assn., Tarrant County Psychol. Assn. (pres. 1990), Mensa. Republican. Episcopalian. Avocations: hiking, camping, tennis, chess. Address: 3436 Clayton Rd E Fort Worth TX 76116-7342

WICKHAM, JOHN EWART ALFRED, urologist, surgeon, consultant; b. Chichester, Sussex, Eng., Dec. 10, 1927; s. James and Hilda May (Cummins) W.; m. Ann Loney, July 7, 1961; children: Susan, Caroline, Clare. BSc with honours, U. London, 1952, MB, BS, 1955, MS, 1966; MD, U. Gothenburg, 1994. Registrar Royal Postgrad. Med. Sch., London, 1960-62; sr. registrar St. Bartholomews Hosp., London, 1963-67, sr. cons. urology, dir. dept., 1967—; pvt. practice London, 1967—; urologist King Edward VII Hosp., London, 1969—; dir. Inst. Urology and dept. minimal invasive surgery St. Peter' Hosp. and Middlesex Hosp.-U. London, 1980—; cons. urologist RAF, 1970—; cons. surgeon Guy's and Thomas' Hosps., London; bd. dirs. Rencal/c Ltd.; dir. N.E. Thames Lithotripter Unit, 1987—; dir. lithotripter and minimally invasive therapy units London Clinic, 1987—. Editor: Calculous Disease, 1981, Percutaneous Renal Surgery, 1983, Intra-Renal Surgery Lithotripsy II, 1984, Renal Tract Stone, 1989, Minimally Invasive Therapy and Allied Technologies, Jour. Minimally Invasive Therapy; contbr. over 100 articles to med. jours. Recipient J.K. Latimer medal Am. Urol. Assn., 1990, Rovsing medal Danish Surg. Soc., 1993. Fellow Royal Soc. Medicine (pres. urol. sect. 1985), Royal Coll. Surgeons Eng. (Hunterian prof. 1968, Berry medal 1985, Cecil Joll medal 1993), Royal Coll.Physicians London (hon.), Royal Coll. Radiologists Eng. (hon.); mem. Internat. Soc. Endourology (1st pres. 1982), Assn. Surgeons (Cutlers prize and medal 1986), Internat. Soc. Urology, Internat. Soc. Minimally Invasive Therapy (1st pres. 1989), Athenaeum Club London. Home: Stowe Maries, Westcott Nr Dorking RH4 3LR, England Office: 29 Devonshire Pl, London W1N 1PE, England

WICKHAM, M(ARVIN) GARY, optometry educator; b. Ft. Morgan, Colo., Dec. 23, 1942; s. Marvin Gilbert W. and Dorothy Mae (Frazell) West; m. Irene Mary Wilhelm, Mar. 20, 1965. BS, Colo. State U., 1964, MS, 1967; PhD, Wash. State U., 1972. Rsch. physiologist VA, Gainesville, Fla., 1971-74; asst. prof. U. Fla., Gainesville, 1972-74; rsch. physiologist VA, San Diego, 1974-79; asst. rsch. biologist morphology of the eye U. Calif., San Diego, 1974-79; assoc. prof. histology, ocular anatomy and physiology Northeastern State U., Tahlequah, Okla., 1979-85, prof. histology, gen. biology, 1986-88; prof. optometry, histology, human genetics and immunology Northeastern State U., Tahlequah, Okla., ., 1988—; prof. ocular anatomy and physiology and gen. biology Northeastern State U., Tahlequah, Okla.; ad hoc reviewer vision scis. study sects. divsn. rsch. grants NIH, 1990—. Contbr. articles to profl. jours. Recipient Glaucoma Studies grant VA, 1975, Core Em Facility grant, 1977-79, Focal Argon Laser Lesions grant, 1979; Morphology of Mammal Eyes grant NIH, 1980, Computer-Based Image Analysis grantee Nat. Eye Inst., 1990. Mem. AAAS, Soc. Ingegrative Comparative Biology, Am. Inst. Biological Scis., Assn. for Rsch. in Vision and Ophthalmology. Office: Northeastern State U Coll Optometry Tahlequah OK 74464

WICKHAM, ROBERT DEAN, physician; b. Sayre, Pa., Aug. 11, 1923; s. Darley Jenkins and Anna (Dell) W.; m. Louise Jullien, Sept. 24, 1955; children: Louise, Lisa, Leslie, Robert Jr. AB, Drew U., 1947; MD, Albany Med. Coll., 1952. Diplomate Am. Bd. Urology, Nat. Bd. Med. Examiners. Intern Northwestern Med. Ctr., Chgo., 1952-53, surgical resident, 1953-54; resident and chief urology Squire Clinic, Columbia Presbyn., N.Y.C., 1955-57; attending urologist emeritus St. Luke's Roosevelt Med. Ctr., N.Y.C., 1958—; exec. dir., N.Y. section Am. Urological Assn. Inc., 1993—; mem. tech. expert panel resource based relative value study Harvard Sch. Pub. Health; bd. dirs. Trivest Corp.; presenter, lectr. in field. Editorial bd.: Internat. Jour. Urology and Nephrology; contbr. articles to profl. jours. With U.S. Army, 1943-46, WWII, ETO. Decorated Bronze Star with two oak leaf clusters. Mem. AMA, Am. Urol. Assn. (sec., pres. N.Y. sect. 1988-91, recipient Commendation 1991), Am. Assn. Clin. Urologists (pres.-elect to pres. 1991-93), Hungarian Soc. Urology (hon. medal 1991), N.Y. State Urol. Soc., N.Y. State Med. Soc., N.Y. County Med. Soc., N.Y. Acad. Medicine, Soc. for Urology and Engring., Hosp. Grads. Soc., Soc. Urologie Internat., Am. Guild Organists, others. Republican. Office: NY Acad Medicine Am Urol Assn 1216 5th Ave New York NY 10029-5202

WICKWIRE, PATRICIA JOANNE NELLOR, psychologist, educator; b. Sioux City, Iowa; d. William McKinley and Clara Rose (Pautsch) Nellor; m. Robert James Wickwire, Sept. 7, 1957; 1 child, William James. BA cum laude, U. No. Iowa, 1951; MA, U. Iowa, 1959; PhD, U. Tex., Austin, 1971; postgrad. U. So. Calif., UCLA, Calif. State U., Long Beach, 1951-66. Tchr., Ricketts Ind. Schs., Iowa, 1946-48; tchr., counselor Waverly-Shell Rock Ind. Schs., Iowa, 1951-55; reading cons., head dormitory counselor U. Iowa, Iowa City, 1955-57; tchr., sch. psychologist, adminstr. S. Bay Union High Sch. Dist., Redondo Beach, Calif., 1962-82, dir. student svcs. and spl. edn.; cons. mgmt. and edn.; pres. Nellor Wickwire Group, 1981—; mem. exec. bd. Calif. Interagency Mental Health Coun., 1968-72, Beach Cities Symphony Assn., 1970-82; chmn. Friends of Dominguez Hills (Calif.), 1981-85. Lic. ednl. psychologist, marriage, family and child counselor, Calif.; pres. Calif. Women's Caucus, 1993-95. Mem. APA, AAUW (exec. bd., chpt. pres. 1962-72), Nat. Career Devel. Assn. (media chair 1992—), Am. Assn. Career Edn. (pres. 1991—), L.A. County Dirs. Pupil Svcs. (chmn. 1974-79), L.A. County Personnel and Guidance Assn. (pres. 1977-78), Assn. Calif. Sch. Adminstrs. (dir. 1977-81), L.A. County SW Bd. Dist. Adminstrs. for Spl. Edn. (chmn. 1976-81), Calif. Assn. Sch. Psychologists (bd. dirs. 1981-83), Am. Assn. Sch. Adminstrs., Calif. Assn. for Measurement and Evaluation in Guidance (dir. 1981, pres. 1984-85), ACA (chmn. Coun. Newsletter Editors 1989-91, mem. com. on women 1989-92, mem. com. on rsch. and knowledge, 1994—, chmn. 1995—, chmn. 1996—), Assn. Measurement and Eval. in Guidance (Western regional editor 1985-87, conv. chair 1986, editor 1987-90, exec. bd. dirs. 1987-91), Calif. Assn. Counseling and Devel. (exec. bd. 1984—, pres. 1988-89, jour. editor 1990—), Internat. Career Assn. Network (chair 1985—), Pi Lambda Theta, Alpha Phi Gamma, Psi Chi, Kappa Delta Pi, Sigma Alpha Iota. Contbr. articles in field to profl. jours. Office: Calif Assn Counseling 2555 E Chapman Ave Ste 201 Fullerton CA 92631

WIDGEROW, ALAN DAVID, plastic surgeon; b. Johannesburg, South Africa, Nov. 14, 1956; s. Charles and Augusta (Reder) W.; m. Jolyn Sacks, Dec. 9, 1979; children: Davin, Laurelle, Gabriella. MBBCH, U. Witwatersrand, Johannesburg, 1980, MMed in Plastic Surgery, 1990; FCS in Plastic Surgery, Coll. Medicine, South Africa, 1989. Registered specialist plastic & reconstructive surgeon. Cons. head plastic surgery Hillbrow Hosp., South Africa, 1989-90; part time cons. plastic surgery U. Witwatersrand, 1990—; pvt. practice Carstenhof Clinic, Midrand, South Africa, 1990—. Contbr. articles to internat. jours. Lt. South African Army, 1981-82. Mem. Assn. Plastic & Reconstructive Surgeons South Africa (sec. 1990-96, pres. 1996), Am. Soc. Aesthetic Surgeons, Hand Surgery Assn., Lipoplasty Assn., N.Y. Acad. Scis. Office: Carstenhof Clinic, Ste 205 Dane Rd Pvt 896X 54, Midrand 1685, South Africa

WIDIN, GREGORY PETER, biomedical development administrator; b. Plainfield, N.J., Apr. 2, 1952; m. Katharine D. Dawson, May 25, 1974. AB, Kenyon Coll., 1974; PhD, U. Minn., 1979, MS in Mgmt. of Tech., 1992. Postdoctoral fellow Rsch. Lab. Electronics, Cambridge, Mass., 1979-82; supr. 3M, St. Paul, 1982—. Contbr. articles to profl. jours. on aspects of hearing and digital hearing aids. Mem. IEEE, MOT Alumni Assn. (pres. 1994-95). Office: 3M Bldg 270-2N-05 Saint Paul MN 55144

WIDMER, CHARLES GLENN, dentist, researcher; b. Daytona Beach, Fla., Jan. 8, 1955; s. Ernest Clyde and Martha Elizabeth (Hunter) W.; m. Alyson Lynn Byrd, Jul. 11, 1981; children: Kathryn Michelle, Elizabeth Ann. BS, Emory Univ., 1977, DDS, 1981; MS, SUNY, 1983. Asst. prof. Sch. Dentistry Emory Univ., Atlanta, 1983-91; assoc. prof. Coll. Dentistry Univ. Fla., Gainesville, 1991—, acting assoc. dean for rsch., 1996—; reviewer NIH, Washington, 1988-89, 93-94, NIH Reviewer's Res., 1995-99. Contbr. articles to profl. jours. Contbr. Atlanta Zoo, 1985-91. NIH grantee for utilization of Trigeminal Evoked Potentials in dentistry, 1986-92, for orgn. and function of human masseter muscles, 1991—, for methods for conducting temporomandibular joint imaging using MRI, 1988-89, Rsch. Career Devel. award, 1991-96. Mem. ADA, Internat. Assn. Dental Rsch. (sec., treas., v.p., then pres., councilor neurosci. group 1989-95), Assn. Univ. Temporomandibular Disorders and Orofacial Pain Programs (sec., treas., v.p., then pres. 1990-95), Soc. Neurosci., Internat. Brain Rsch. Orgn., N.Y. Acad. Scis. Office: Univ Fla Dept Oral and Maxillofacial Surgery PO Box 100416 Gainesville FL 32610-0416

WIDNER, WILLIAM RICHARD, biology educator, gardener; b. Baxter County, Ark., Apr. 24, 1920; s. Walter Elum and Rena Mae (Long) W.; m. Edna Holcombe Sorelle, Aug. 17, 1962 (div. Feb. 1985); m. Dorothy Anne de Geurin, March 9, 1985. BA, Eastern N.Mex. U., 1942; MS, U. N.Mex., 1948, PhD, 1952. Rsch. asst. biomed. rsch. AEC, Los Alamos, N.Mex., 1948-50; teaching asst. U. N.Mex., Albuquerque, 1950-52; indsl. hygienist AEC, Albuquerque, 1952-55; high sch. tchr. Albuquerque Indian Sch., 1955-56; chmn. biology Howard Payne Coll., Brownwood, Tex., 1956-59; biology prof. Baylor U., Waco, Tex., 1959-89, emeritus prof., 1989—. Capt. USN, 1942-46. Mem. KYCH, Masons (master 1985-86, high priest 1989, dist. dep. grand master dist. 20 1992, order of Silver Trowel 1989, royal order Jesters 1993). Republican. Southern Baptist. Home & Office: 2532 Eldridge Ln Waco TX 76710-1015

WIDYOLAR, SHEILA GAYLE, dermatologist; b. Vancouver, B.C., Can., June 11, 1939; d. Walter Herbert and Olive Louise (O'Neal) Roberts; Kithi K. Widyolar, 1960 (div. 1979); 1 child, Keith. BS, Loma Linda U., 1962; MD, Howard U., 1972. Resident U. Calif., Irvine, 1973-76; dermatologist pvt. practice, Laguna Hills, Calif., 1976—; clin. instr. U. Calif. Sch. Medicine, 1978-86. Pres., bd. dirs. Opera Pacific, Costa Mesa, Calif., 1995-96. Fellow Am. Acad. Dermatology, Am. Soc. Dermatophthology; mem. AMA, Calif. Med. Assn., Dermatological Soc. Orange County (pres. 1983), Alpha Omega Alpha. Office: Ste 403 23911 Calle de Mag Dalena Laguna Hills CA 92653

WIDZER, STEVEN J., pediatric gastroenterologist; b. Cleve., Jan. 11, 1950; s. Ben And Lillian Widzer; m. Helen M. Widzer, June 19, 1971; children: Joshua, Rebecca, Noah. BS, Northwestern U., 1972, MD, 1974. Diplomate Am. Bd. Pediat. Gastroenterology. Resident in pediats. Children's Hosp. of Phila., 1974-76, fellow in pediat. gastroenterology, 1976-78; mem. sect. pediat. gastroenterology St. Christopher's Hosp. of Children, Phila., 1978-84, acting chief, 1984-85, chief, 1985-86; founding ptnr. Widzer and Kelly, Bryn Mawr, Pa., 1986—; asst. prof. pediats. Temple U. Sch. Medicine, Phila., 1978-86, adj. assoc. prof. pediats., 1991—; clin. assoc. prof. pediats. Med. Coll. Pa., Phila., 1987—; assoc. attending staff Bryn Mawr Hosp., 1986—. Contbr. articles to profl. jours. Fellow Am. Acad. Pediats.; mem. N.Am. Soc. for Pediat. Gastroenterology, Chrons and Colitis Found. Am., Am. Gastroent. Assn., Am. Soc. for Parenteral and Enteral Nutrition, Phila. Pediat. Soc. Office: Widzer and Kelly 864 County Line Rd Bryn Mawr PA 19010

WIEBE, MICHAEL EUGENE, microbiologist, cell biologist; b. Newton, Kans., Oct. 1, 1942; s. Austin Roy and Ruth Fern (Stucky) W.; m. Rebecca Ann Doak, June 12, 1965; children: Brandon Clark, Thomas Huntington. BS, Sterling Coll., 1965; PhD, U. Kansas, 1971. Rsch. assoc. Duke U. Med. Ctr., Durham, N.C., 1971-73; asst. prof. Cornell U. Med. Coll., N.Y.C., 1973-81, assoc. prof., 1981-85; assoc. dir. rsch. and devel. N.Y. Blood Ctr., N.Y.C., 1980-83, dir. Leukocyte products, 1983-84; sr. scientist Genentech Inc., South San Francisco, Calif., 1984-88, assoc. dir. medicinal and analytical chemistry, 1988-90, dir. quality control, 1990—; mem. biol. scis. alumni adv. bd. U. Kans., 1994—. Contbr. articles to profl. jours. Mem. bd. trustees Sterling Coll., 1990—, chmn., 1994—. Postdoctoral fellow NIH, 1971-73. Mem. AAAS, Am. Soc. for Microbiology, Am. Soc. Virology, Soc. Exptl. Biology and Medicine, Parenteral Drug Assn. Presbyterian. Home: 44 Woodhill Dr Redwood City CA 94061-1827 Office: Genentech Inc 460 Point San Bruno Blvd South San Francisco CA 94080-4918

WIEBE, RICHARD HERBET, reproductive endocrinologist, educator; b. Herbert, Sask., Can., Dec. 28, 1937; came to U.S., 1971; s. Herbert and Olga Maragratha (Jahnke) W.; m. Jacquelyn Dee Yancy, Aug. 30, 1975; 1 child, Richard Herbert, Jr. MD, U. Sask., 1962. Resident Queen's Univ., Kingston, Ont., Can., 1970; asst. to assoc. prof. Duke U., Durham, N.C., 1972-81; assoc. prof. to prof. U. So. Ala., Mobile, 1981-88; chmn. and prof. Dept. Ob-Gyn. U. S.D., Sioux Falls, 1988-95; chmn., prof. dept. ob-gyn. East Tenn. State U., Johnson City, 1996—; editorial cons., Fertility/Sterility, Birmingham, Ala., 1978—; sec., Univ. Physicians, Sioux Falls, 1991—. Contbr. numerous articles to profl. jours. Recipient, Rsch. Grant, NIH, Ala., 1981-89, Edn./Svc. Grant, USPHS, S.D., 1989—. Mem. ACOG, Assn. Profs. of Ob-Gyn., Am. Soc. Primatologists, Soc. for Gynecol. Investigation, Soc. for Study of Reproduction, Am. Fertility Soc., Endocrine Soc. Home: 4319 Summerfield Dr Piney Flats TN 37686 Office: James H Quillen Sch Med East Tenn State U Dept Ob-Gyn Box 70569 Johnson City TN 37614

WIED, GEORGE LUDWIG, physician; b. Carlsbad, Czechoslovakia, Feb. 7, 1921; came to U.S., 1953, naturalized, 1960; s. Ernst George and Anna (Travnicek) W.; m. Daga M. Graaz, Mar. 19, 1949 (dec. Aug. 1977); m. Kayoko Y. Yamauchi, Nov. 1, 1990. MD, Charles U., Prague, 1945, Hon. Med. Degree, 1995. Intern County Hosp., Carlsbad, Czechoslovakia, 1945; intern U. Chgo. Hosps., 1955; resident in ob-gyn U. Munich, Fed. Republic

Germany, 1946-48; practice medicine specializing in ob-gyn West Berlin, 1948-53; asst. ob-gyn Free U., West Berlin, 1948-52; assoc. chmn. dept. ob-gyn Moabit Hosp., Free U., West Berlin, 1953; asst. prof., dir. cytology U. Chgo., 1954-59, assoc. prof., 1959-65, prof., 1965-91, mem. bd. adult edn., 1964-68, prof. pathology, 1967-91, Blum-Riese prof. ob-gyn, 1968-91, acting chmn. dept. ob-gyn, 1974-75. Editor-in-chief Jour. Reproductive Medicine, Acta Cytologica, Analytical and Quantitative Cytology, Clinical Cytology; editor: Introduction to Quantitative Cytochemistry, Automated Cell Identification and Cell Sorting, Compendium on Clinical Cytology, Compendium on the Computerized Cytology and Histology Laboratory, Compendium on Quality Assurance in Clinical Cytology; sr. editor Gen. and Diagnostic Pathology. Hon. dir. Chgo. Cancer Prevention Ctr., 1959-83; chmn. jury Maurice Goldblatt Cytology award, 1963-92. Recipient Cert. of Merit, U.S. Surgeon Gen., 1952, Maurice Goldblatt Cytology award, 1961, George N. Papanicolaou Cytology award, 1970. Mem. Am. Soc. Cytology (pres. 1965-66), Mex. Soc. Cytology (hon.), Spanish Soc. Cytology (hon.), Brazilian Soc. Cytology (fgn. corr.), Indian Acad. Cytology (hon.), Latin-Am. Soc. Cytology (hon.), Japanese Soc. Cytology (hon.), Internat. Acad. Cytology (pres. 1977-80), German Soc. Cytology (hon.), Ctrl. Soc. Clin. Rsch., Chgo. Path. Soc., Chgo. Gynecol. Soc. (hon.), Am. Soc. Cell Biology, German Soc. Ob-Gyn, Bavarian Soc. Ob-Gyn, German Soc. Endocrinology, Russian Assn. Cytologists (hon.), Swedish Soc. Medicine (hon.), Austrian Soc. Clin. Cytology (hon.), Sigma Xi. Home and Office: 1640 E 50th St Chicago IL 60615-3161

WIEDEMANN, CHARLES LOUIS, dentist; b. Belvidere, N.J., May 6, 1936; s. Charles and Clothilde Paulina (Fischer) W.; m. Jacqueline Burdzy, June 11, 1960; children: Lorraine Carol, Julie Patricia. BA, Rutgers U., 1957; DDS with honors, Fairleigh Dickinson U., 1962; postgrad. student Inst. for Grad. Dentists, 1968-69, U. Pa., 1974-75. Pvt. practice dentistry, Hackettstown, N.J., 1966—; mem., founder dental sect. staff Hackettstown Cmty. Hosp., chief of dentistry, 1973-75, 77-78; dental health dir. Clarence W. Sickles Med. Ctr., Hackettstown, N.J., 1970—; pres. Rexxcom Sys. Electronic Pub. and Computer Software, Co., 1990—; columnist Hackettstown Gazette, 1983-85; co-dir. Stargazer, Board of Ed, Online Mag. telecomms.sys., 1985-86; lectr. Morris County Coll., dental socs. Chmn. Bd. Health, Washington Twp., Morris County, N.J., 1975-78; co-dir. telecomm. sys. Hunterdon Ctrl. Regional H.S., 1989—; presentations to Morris, Warren, and Sussex Counties, N.J. elem. schs. ann., 1966-93. Designer giant talking toothbrush, talking molar. Capt. Dental Corps, AUS, 1962-65. Recipient cert. Stuart L. Isler Found. for Preventive Dentistry, 1986. Fellow Acad. Gen. Dentistry, Am. Endodontic Soc. (Communicator of Yr. award 1983); mem. ADA (panel on quarterly survey of pvt. practitioners 1990-93), Digital Pub. Assn. (founding mem., bd. dirs.), Am. Analgesia Soc., Internat. Analgesia Soc., N.J. Dental Assn. Warren-Sussex Dental Soc., Tri-County Dental Soc., Hackettstown Dental Study Group (co-founder 1974—). Republican. Author: The Now Philosophy for Dentistry, 1972, Fantastic Facts About Dental Health, 1975; (computer software) The Format Machine, 1987, Autofont, 1990, rev. edit. 1996, The Magic Font Machine (Magifont, Magivue, Magishow), 1990, News 1, 1991, Digipad, 1993, The Autofont Titler (for electronic books), 1995; co-author: (computer software) Autodoc, 1990, rev. edit., 1993, Font Mania, 1991, rev. edit., 1996, XL100, 1993, XL2000, 1993, XL2001, 1994, rev. edit. (the XL book edition), 1995, E-Z Book, 1995, Autofont Titler, 1995; author, designer (electronic publishing software) Rexxcom, 1987—; designer computer fonts, modules, graphics simulations; inventor Rexxcom character set, 1992. Editorial adv. panel Dental Econs. Jour., 1979-80; editor DPA News, 1993-95; contbr. articles to profl. jours. and mags.; editor of electronic books, 1995—. Mem. Found. for Motivation in Dentistry (founder, chmn., bd. dirs. 1973—). Mem. Bd. dirs. Digital Pub. Assoc., 1993-95. Office: 110 Mill St Hackettstown NJ 07840

WIEDEN, MARION ANNA, microbiologist; b. Cleve., Oct. 16, 1937; d. Joseph Frank and Anna Barbara (Bohac) Rusnak; B.S., U. Ariz., 1959; m. Walter Carl Wieden, Aug. 8, 1959; children—Mark David, Jill Ann, Matthew Joe. MS, PhD Columbia Pacific U., 1987. Microbiologist, St. Mary's Hosp., Tucson, 1961-63, chief microbiologist, 1963-68; chief microbiology sect. VA Med. Ctr., Tucson, 1968-95; adj. asst prof. med. tech. U. Ariz., 1986—; chmn. Tucson Inter-hosp. Infections Control Com., 1974-77; mem. clin. lab. adv. bd. Ariz. State Dept. Health Services, 1983—. Registered microbiologist and clin. lab. specialist Nat. Registry, Am. Acad. Microbiology. Mem. Am. Soc. Med. Tech. (liaison officer for VA in Ariz.), Ariz. State Soc. Med. Tech. (Cert. of Merit 1975, 78, 79, 80, 83, 85, 89, Cert. of Achievement 1980; Outstanding Contbns. to Microbiology award 1981, 85, 87, 89. Mem. of Yr. award 1981, state dir. 1976-79, 80-81, 88—, program chmn. 1981, 89 conv., gen. chmn. 1983, 85, pres. Tucson chpt. 1980-81), Am. Soc. Microbiology (cert. specialist, chair microbiology sci. assembly 1986-87, 88-89), Ariz. Soc. Microbiology (program chmn. Tucson br. 1979-81), Am. Pub. Health Assn., Assn. Practitioners in Infection Control, Internat. Soc. for Human and Animal Mycology, Am. Soc. Clin. Pathologists (various coms.), Smithsonian Instn., U. Ariz. Alumni Assn., Coccidioidomycosis Study Group, Med. Mycol. Soc. of Ams., Beta Beta Beta, Alpha Delta Pi. Roman Catholic. Contbr. articles to profl. jours. Address: 7180 N Cathedral Rock Pl Tucson AZ 85718-1395

WIEDL-KRAMER, SHEILA COLLEEN, biologist; b. Buffalo, Feb. 19, 1950; d. Frank George and Corinne Ruth (Nuskay) W.; m. Warren J. Kramer, May 8, 1993; one child, Colleen Bryce. B.S., Daemen Coll., 1972; M.S., U. Notre Dame, 1974; Ph.D., SUNY-Buffalo, 1986. Instr., Holy Cross Jr. Coll., South Bend, Ind., 1973-74; research technician SUNY, Buffalo, 1975-78; entomol. asst. N.Y. State Health Dept., 1979-80; entomol. intern Ohio Dept. Health, 1981; prof. natural scis. Trocaire Coll., Buffalo, 1974-85; postdoctoral scientist Am. Cyanamid, Lederle Labs., Pearl River, N.Y., 1985-86, clin. research assoc., 1986-89; assoc. mgr. CIBA Consumer Pharms., Edison, N.J., 1989-90; assoc. dir. clin. projects AKZO/Organon Inc., West Orange, N.J., 1990-95; pres. C. Bryce & Assocs., Flemington, N.J., 1995—; adj. prof. Ramapo Coll. of N.J., 1988—, Rockland Community Coll., 1989—. Mem. N.Y. State Assn. Two-Year Colls., Assn. Gnotobiotics, N.Y. State Archeol. Assn. Club: Notre Dame Alumni. Contbr. articles to profl. jours. Home: 39 Winding Way Flemington NJ 08822 Office: C Bryce & Assocs 39 Winding Way Flemington NJ 08822

WIEDMAN, MICHAEL, ophthalmologist; b. N.Y.C., Oct. 4, 1927; s. Morris and Rose (Green) W.; children: Timothy, Nicholas. AB, U. Vt., 1950, MD, 1954; Cert., Harvard Med. Sch., Boston, 1956. Diplomate Am. Bd. Ophthalmology. Resident U. Hosp., Buffalo, 1954-56, Manh Eye Hosp., N.Y.C., 1954-56; family practice Ky., 1956-57; pvt. practice eye surgery Boston, 1959—; faculty Harvard Med. Sch., Boston, 1960—, Tufts U., 1960—, MIT, Cambridge, 1962-85; Ultima Thule Mount Everest team physician, Nepal, Tibet, 1972-95; med. rsch. dir. Am.-Chinese-Russian Peace Climb Mount Everest, Tibet, 1972-95; rschr. in high altitude disease disease on Mount Everest, Harvard Med. Sch., 1972-96; clin. assoc. Mass. Gen. Hosp. Contbr. articles to profl. jours.; contbr. poetry to Brit. Alpine Jour., Appalachian Mt. Jour.; exhbns. of adventure photography in Paris, Boston, Societé Francaise de Photographic. With U.S. Army Mil. Police, 1946-48. Recipient Best. Dir. in New Eng. award (for Rashomon) Little Theater League; Harvard Med. Sch. grantee, 1972-96. Fellow ACS; mem. New Eng. Ophthalmologic Soc. (treas.), N.E. Med. Assn. (pres.), Explorers Club (N.Y.C.) (fellow), Harvard Travellers Club, Chevalier de Tastevin Soc. Home: 11 W Cedar St Beacon Hill MA 02108 Office: Zero Emerson Pl Boston MA 02114

WIEGAND, STEWART EARLE, dermatologist; b. Detroit, Sept. 28, 1939; s. Wayne Erwin and Miriam Jean (Fairbairn) W.; m. Jimmie Dell Williams, Apr. 2, 1960; children: Brandi, Jill, Vince, Vic, James. BA, U. Tex., 1961; MD, Baylor U., 1965; MS, U. Minn., 1969. Diplomate Am. Bd. Dermatologists. Practice medicine specializing in dermatology Atlanta, 1971—; adj. instr. Emory U., Atlanta, 1969-73, adj. asst. prof., 1977—. Author: Recognition of Dermophytes, 1969, Recognizing Dermatophytes Using pH Indicator Agar, 1974. Pres., organizer Walton (Ga.) Sports Medicine Found., 1984—. Served with USPHS, 1969-71, Nigerian Red Cross. Fellow Am. Coll. Physicians, Am. Acad. Dermatology, Am. Soc. for Dermatol. Surgery; mem. AMA, So. Med. Assn., Med. Assn. Ga., Atlanta Dermatol. Assn., Atlanta Clin. Soc., Med. Assn. Atlanta, Internat. Soc. Tropical Dermatology, Clin. Oncology Assocs. Ga., Inc., Internat. Soc. Dermatol. Surgery, Soc. Investigative Dermatology, Inc., Ga. Soc. Dermatol. Surgeons, Inc. Republican. Presbyterian. Home: 3625 Oak Ln Marietta GA 30062-5353

WIEGNER, ALLEN WALTER, biomedical engineering educator, researcher; b. Bethlehem, Pa., July 22, 1947; s. Howard Jay and Anna (Strouse) W.; m. Sandra A. Waddock, Aug. 26, 1978; 1 child, Benjamin Waddock. SB, SM, MIT, 1970, PhD, 1978. Rsch. assoc. Harvard U. Med. Sch., Boston, 1978-87, asst. prof. neurology (biomed. engring.), 1987—; asst. biomed. engr. Mass. Gen. Hosp., Boston, 1980—; cons. rsch. svc. VA Med. Ctr., 1984—, biomed. engr., 1987—. Contbr. articles, book chpts. to profl. publs. Lt. USPHS, 1970-72. Mem. IEEE (sr.), Biomed. Engring. Soc. (sr.), Soc. for Neurosci. Office: VA Med Ctr Spinal Cord Injury Svc 1400 Vfw Pky West Roxbury MA 02132-4927

WIELGUS, JOHN JAY, biology educator; b. Chgo., May 22, 1945; s. John J. Wielgus and Rosemary (Neimes) Shaffer; m. Carolyn Louise Arnold, Aug. 5, 1972. BA, U. Ill., 1969; MS, Northwestern U., 1974, PhD 1977. Tchr. Morton Upper Grade Ctr., Chgo., 1970-72; prof. Washington and Lee U., Lexington, Va., 1977—. Contbr. articles to profl. jours. Member bd. advisors Rockbridge Mental Health Clinic, Lexington, 1980-82; bd. dirs. Rockbridge Area Conservation Coun., Lexington, 1983-86; co-chair Green Crossroads, Lexington, 1984. Washington & Lee U. grantee, 1977—, Rsch. Corp. grantee, 1985-87. Mem. AAAS. Roman Catholic. Home: RR 1 Box 152J Glasgow VA 24555-9788 Office: Washington & Lee U Dept Of Biology Lexington VA 24450

WIEMANN, MARION RUSSELL, JR. (BARON OF CAMSTER), biologist, microscopist; b. Chesterton, Ind., Sept. 7, 1929; s. Marion Russell and Verda (Peek) W.; 1 child from previous marriage, Tamara Lee (Mrs. Donald D. Kelley). BS, Ind. U., 1959; PhD (hon.), World U. Roundtable, 1991; ScD (hon.), The London Inst, for Applied Rsch., England, 1994, World Academy Germany, 1995. Histo-rsch. technician U. Chgo., 1959, rsch. asst., 1959-62, rsch. technician, 1962-64; tchr. sci. Westchester Twp. Sch., Chesterton, Ind., 1964-66; with U. Chgo., 1965-79, sr. rsch. technician, 1967-70, rsch. technologist, 1970-79; prin. Marion Wiemann & Assocs., cons. R&D, Chesterton, Ind., 1979-89; consultive faculty World U., 1991—, SkyWarn, Nat. Weather Svc., 1993—. Author: Tooth Decay, Its Cause and Prevention Through Controlled Soil Composition, 1985, The Mechanism of Tooth Decay, 1985; contbr. articles to profl. jours. and newspapers. Vice-chmn. The Duneland 4th of July Com., 1987-91; v.p. State Microscopical Soc. Ill., 1969-70, pres., 1970-71. With USN, 1951-53. Recipient Disting. Tech. Communicator award Soc. for Tech. Communication, 1974, Internat. Order Merit (Eng.), 1991; ennobled Royal Coll. Heraldry, Australia, 1991, Highland Laird, Scotland, 1995; named Sagamore of the Wabash Gov. Ind., 1985; McCrone Rsch. Inst. scholar, 1968; named Prof. of Sci. Australian Inst. for Co-Ordinated Rsch., Australia, 1995, knight corps Diplomatique The Sovereign Military Templar Order, 1994; recipient Scouters Key award Boy Scouts Am., 1968, Arrowhead honor, 1968, Albert Einstein Silver medal, Huguenin, Le Locke, Switzerland, Henri Dunant Silver medal with silver bars, 1995, Henri Dunant Silver medal, 1995, medal of honor, England, 1996. Fellow World Lit. Acad.; mem. Internat. Soc. Soil Sci., Order Internat. Fellowship, Internat. Graphoanalysis Soc., Maison Internat. des Intellectuels and Akademie MIDI, VFW (charter mem., bd. dirs., post judge adv. 1986—, apptd. post adj. 1986—, Cross of Malta 1986), Govs. Club. Address: PO Box 532 Chesterton IN 46304-0532

WIEMER, DAVID ROBERT, plastic surgeon; b. Houston, Sept. 16, 1940; m. Beverly Biggs, Feb. 20, 1966; children: D. Robert Jr., J. Bradley. BS in Natural Sci., Okla. State U., 1961; MD, Baylor U., 1965. Intern Ben Taub Gen. Hosp., Houston, 1965-66; resident in gen. surgery Baylor Univ. Coll. Medicine Affiliated Program, Houston, 1966-69, resident in plastic surgery, 1971-74; pvt. practice Wiemer Plastic Surgery, Houston, 1974—; active staff Meth. Hosp., Houston, 1975—, dep. chief divsn. plastic surgery, 1977—, sec. med. staff, 1990-92, pres., 1994-96, bd. dirs., 1990—; dep. chief divsn. plastic surgery VA Med. Ctr., 1977—. Contbr. articles to profl. jours., chpts. to books. Maj. U.S. Army, 1969-71. Mr. Ting Chao grant to Baylor Coll. Medicine, 1993. Mem. ACS, Am. Soc. Plastic and Reconstructive Surgeons, Am. Soc. Aesthetic Plastic Surgery, Assn. Acad. Chmn. and Plastic Surgeons, Tex. Med. Soc. (sec. 1980), Houston Soc. Plastic Surgeons (sec., v.p., pres.), Houston Surg. Soc. (sec., pres.). Presbyterian. Office: Wiemer Plastic Surgery Inc 6560 Fannin #1760 Houston TX 77030

WIENER, JERRY M., psychiatrist; b. Baytown, Tex., May 11, 1933; s. Isidore and Dora L. (Lerner) W.; m. Louise W. Weingarten, Apr. 13, 1964; children—Matthew, Ethan, Ross, Aaron. Student, Rice U., 1952; M.D., Baylor U., 1956; tng. in psychoanalysis, Columbia U. Psychoanalytic Center, 1968. Resident in psychiatry Mayo Clinic, Rochester, Minn., 1957-61, Columbia U. Coll. Physicians and Surgeons, N.Y.C., 1961-62; dir. child and adolescent psychiatry St. Luke's Hosp., N.Y.C., 1962-71; dir. child psychiatry Emory U., Atlanta, 1971-75; chmn. dept. psychiatry Children's Hosp., Washington, 1976-77; prof., chmn. dept. psychiatry George Washington U., 1977—; mem. faculty Washington Psychoanalytic Inst. Editor: Textbook of Child and Adolescent Psychology, 1991, 96, Psychopharmacology in Childhood and Adolescence, 1977, Diagnosis and Psychopharmacology in Childhood and Adolescence, 1995; contbr. articles to profl. jours., chpts. to books. Fellow Am. Psychiat. Assn. (past pres.), Am. Coll. Psychiatrists; mem. Am. Psychoanalytic Assn., Am. Assn. Chmn. Depts. Psychiatry (past pres.), Am. Psychiat. Press, Inc. (chmn. bd. dirs.), Am. Acad. Child and Adolescent Psychiatry (past pres.). Office: George Washington Univ Dept Psychiatry 2150 Pennsylvania Ave NW Washington DC 20037-2396

WIENER, JOSEPH, pathologist; b. Toronto, Can., Sept. 21, 1927; came to U.S., 1949, naturalized, 1960; s. Louis and Minnie (Salem) W.; m. Judith Hesta Ross, June 20, 1954; children: Carolyn L., Adam L. M.D., U. Toronto, 1953. Intern Detroit Receiving Hosp., 1953-54; resident to chief resident pathology Mallory Inst. Pathology, 1954-55; from asst. to assoc. prof. pathology Columbia U., N.Y.C., 1960-68; prof. pathology N.Y. Med. Coll., N.Y.C., 1968-78; prof. pathology Wayne State U., Detroit, 1978—, chmn. dept., 1978-90; cons. NIH, 1970—. Served to capt. M.C. U.S. Army, 1955-57. Grantee: Heart, Lung and Blood Inst., 1971-93; named fellow Coun. for High Blood Pressure Rsch., 1982—. Mem. AAAS, Am. Soc. Investigative Pathology, Am. Soc. Cell Biology, Mich. Path. Soc., Internat. Acad. Pathology, Am. Heart Assn., U.S./Can. Acad. Pathology, Mich. Heart Assn., Alpha Omega Alpha. Office: 540 E Canfield St Detroit MI 48201-1928

WIENER, RUSSELL WARREN, environmental scientist, researcher; b. N.Y.C., June 23, 1952; s. Max and Rhoda (Bruntil) W.; m. Martha E. Smith, Sept. 5, 1982; children: Benjamin, Victoria. Student, Rensselaer Poly. Inst., 1970-71; BS in Biology, Emory U., 1974, MS in Environ. Sci., 1978; PhD in Environ. Health, U. Cin., 1987. Rsch. technician U. N.C., Chapel Hill, 1978-79; aerosol tech. GE, Cin., 1984-86; chief aerosol physics and methods br. U.S. EPA, Research Triangle Park, N.C., 1987—; adj. asst. prof. U. N.C., Chapel Hill, 1989—, N.C. State U., Raleigh, 1994—. Mem. Am. Assn. for Aerosol Rsch. (chair indoor air 1988-94), Am. Indsl. Hygiene Assn., Am. Acad. Indsl. Hygiene. Office: US EPA 79 Alexander Dr MD-77 Research Triangle Park NC 27711

WIERNIK, PETER HARRIS, oncologist, educator; b. Crocket, Tex., June 16, 1939; s. Harris and Molly (Emmerman) W.; m. Roberta Joan Fuller, Sept. 6, 1961; children: Julie Anne, Lisa Britt, Peter Harrison. B.A. with distinction, U. Va., 1961, M.D., 1965; Dr. h.c., U. of Republic, Montevideo, Uruguay, 1982. Diplomate Am. Bd. Internal Medicine, Am. Bd Med. Oncology (mem. writing com. 1981-87). Intern Cleve. Met. Gen. Hosp., 1965-66, resident, 1969-70; resident Osler Svc. Johns Hopkins Hosp., Balt., 1970-71; sr. asst. surgeon USPHS, 1966, advanced through grades to med. dir., 1976; sr. staff assoc. Balt. Cancer Rsch. Ctr., 1966-71, chief sect. med. oncology, 1971-76, chief clin. oncology br., 1976-82, dir., 1976-82; assoc. dir. div. cancer treatment Nat. Cancer Inst., 1976-82; asst. prof. medicine U. Md. Sch. Medicine, Balt., 1971-74, assoc. prof., 1974-76, prof., 1976-82; Gutman prof., chmn. dept. oncology Montefiore Med. Ctr., 1982-94; head divsn. med. oncology Albert Einstein Coll., 1982-94; assoc. dir. for clin. rsch. Albert Einstein Cancer Ctr., 1982-94, 95—; prof. medicine Albert Einstein Coll. Medicine, 1982—; cons. hematology and med. oncology Union Meml. Hosp., Greater Balt. Med. Ctr., Franklin Sq. Hosp.; bd. dirs. Balt. City unit Am. Cancer Soc., 1971-78; chmn. patient care com., 1972-75, mem. profl. edn. and grants com., N.Y.C. divsn., 1983-90, mem. nat. clin. fellowship com., 1984-96; mem. med. adv. com. Nat. Leukemia Assn., 1976-88, chmn. med. adv. com., 1989—; chmn. adult leukemia com. Cancer and Leukemia Group B, 1976-83; prin. investigator Ea. Coop. Oncology Group, 1982-94; chmn. gynecol. oncology com., 1986-88, chmn. leukemia com., 1988-94; sci. cons. Vt. Regional Cancer Ctr., 1987—. Editor: Controversies in Oncology, 1982, Supportive Care of the Cancer Patient, 1983, Neoplastic Diseases of the Blood, 1985, 2d edit., 1991, 3d edit. 1996; assoc. editor Medical Oncology and Tumor Pharmacotherapy, 1987-91, sr. editor, 1991—; assoc. editor onoclogy Am. Jour. Therapeutics, 1994—; co-editor: Year Book of Hematology, 1986—, Handbook of Hematologic and Oncologic Emergencies, 1988, Am. Jour. Med. Scis., 1976-81; N.Am. editor Jour. Cancer Rsch. and Clin. Oncology, 1986-89; mem. editorial bd. Cancer Treatment Reports, 1972-76, Leukemia Rsch., 1977-86, 91—, Leukemia, 1986—, Cancer Clin. Trials, 1977—, Jour. Therapeutic Rsch., 1994—, Hosp. Practice, 1979—, Jour. Clin. Oncology, 1989-91, PDQ Nat. Cancer Inst., 1987-94; sect. editor antineoplastic drugs Jour. Clin. Pharmacology, 1985—; editor-in-chief Medical Oncology, 1993—; also articles, chpt. in books. Recipient Z Soc. award U. Va., 1961, Byrd S. Leavell Hematology award U. Va. Sch. Medicine, 1965. Fellow AAAS, ACP, Am. Coll. Clin. Pharmacology, Internat. Soc. Hematology, Royal Soc. Medicine (London); mem. Am. Soc. Clin. Investigation, Am. Soc. Clin. Oncology (chmn. edn. and tng. com. 1976-79, 84, subcom. on clin. investigation 1980-82, program com. 1990, pub. issues com., 1990-95), Am. Assn. Cancer Rsch., Am. Soc. Hematology, Am. Fedn. Clin. Rsch., Am. Acad. Clin. Toxicology, Internat. Soc. Exptl. Hematology, N.Y. Acad. Sci., Am. Soc. Hosp. Pharmacy, Am. Soc. Clin. Pharmacology and Therapeutics, Am. Radium Soc. (program com. 1987-93, exec. com. 1988-95, publ. com. 1988-92, sec. 1990-91, pres.-elect, 1992-93; pres. 1993-94, Janeway medalist, 1996), Polish Oncology Soc. (hon.), Harvey Soc., Uruguan Hematology Soc. (hon.), European Assn. Cancer Rsch., Phi Beta Kappa (assoc. 1991—), Sigma Xi, Alpha Omega Alpha, Phi Sigma (award 1961). Home: 43 Longview Ln Chappaqua NY 10514-1304 Office: Montefiore Med Ctr 111 E 210th St Bronx NY 10467-2490

WIESCHAUS, ERIC F., molecular biologist, educator; b. June 8, 1947. BS, U. Notre Dame, 1969; PhD in Biology, Yale U., 1974. Rsch. fellow Zool. Inst., U. Zurich, Switzerland, 1975-78; group leader European Molecular Biol. Lab., Germany, 1978-81; from asst. prof. to assoc. prof. Princeton (N.J.) U., 1981-87, prof. biology, 1987—; fellow Lab. de Genetique Moleculaire, France, 1976; vis. rschr. Ctr. Pathobiology, U. Calif., Irvine, 1977; mem. sci. adv. coun. Damon Runyon-Walter Winchell Cancer Fund, 1987-92. Contbr. articles to profl. jours. Recipient Nobel Prize in Medicine, 1995. Fellow Am. Acad. Arts and Scis.; mem. NAS. Office: Princeton U Dept Molecular Biology Princeton NJ 08544

WIESE, NEVA, critical care nurse; b. Hunter, Kans., July 23, 1940; d. Amil H. and Minnie (Zemke) W. Diploma, Grace Hosp. Sch. Nursing, Hutchinson, Kans., 1962; BA in Social Sci., U. Denver, 1971; BSN, Met. State Coll., 1975; MS in Nursing, U. Colo., Denvr, 1978; postgrad., U. N.Mex., 1986—. RN, N.Mex.; CCRN. Cardiac ICU nurse U. N.Mex. Hosp., Albuquerque; coord. critical care edn. St. Vincent Hosp., Santa Fe, charge nurse CCU, clin. nurse III intensive and cardiac care. Recipient Mary Atherton Meml. award for clin. excellence St. Vincent Hosp., 1986. Mem. ANA (cert. med. surg. nurse), AACN (past pres., sec. N.Mex. chpt., Clin. Excellence award 1991), N.Mex. League Nursing (past v.p., bd. dirs., sec., membership com. 1992—).

WIESE, WILLIAM HASTINGS, medicine educator; b. Boston, Nov. 5, 1938; s. Robert George and Esther (Wurst) W.; m. Janislee Arvanites, Jan. 18, 1964; children: Michael, Andrew, Brian. BA, Yale U., 1960; MD, Harvard U., 1964, M in Pub. Health, 1971. Diplomate Am. Bd. Internal Medicine. Resident in medicine Boston City Hosp., 1964-66, 68-69; research assoc. NIH, Bethesda, Md., 1966-68; mem. faculty U. N.Mex., Albuquerque, 1971—; dir. Ctr. for Population Health, 1994-95; mem. test com. Nat. Bd. Med. Examiners, Phila., 1984-87; pres. HealthNet N.Mex., 1985-90. Mem. U.S. Preventive Svcs. Task Force, Washington, 1984-89. Served with USPHS, 1966-68. Mem. APHA, Assn. Tchrs. Preventive Medicine (bd. dirs. 1978-81, 90-93, pres. 1991-92), Coun. on Linkages Between Acad. and Pub. Health Practice, N.Mex. Med. Soc., Greater Albuquerque Med. Assn., Alpha Omega Alpha. Office: U NMex Sch Medicine 2400 Tucker Ave Albuquerque NM 87131

WIESEL, TORSTEN NILS, neurobiologist, educator; b. Upsala, Sweden, June 3, 1924; came to U.S., 1955; s. Fritz Samuel and Anna-Lisa Elisabet (Bentzer) W.; 1 dau., Sara Elisabet. MD, Karolinska Inst., Stockholm, 1954; D Medicine (hon.), Karolinska Inst, Stockholm, 1989; AM (hon.), Harvard U., 1967; ScD (hon.), NYU, 1987, U. Bergen, 1987. Instr. physiology Karolinska Inst., 1954-55; asst. dept. child psychiatry Karolinska Hosp., 1954-55; fellow in ophthalmology Johns Hopkins U., 1955-58, asst. prof. ophthalmic physiology, 1958-59; assoc. in neurophysiology and neuropharmacology Harvard U. Med. Sch., Boston, 1959-60; asst. prof. neurophysiology and neuropharmacology Harvard U. Med. Sch., 1960-64, asst. prof. neurophysiology, dept. psychiatry, 1964-67, prof. physiology, 1967-68, prof. neurobiology, 1968-74, Robert Winthrop prof. neurobiology, 1974-83, chmn. dept. neurobiology, 1973-82; Vincent and Brooke Astor prof. neurobiology, head lab. Rockefeller U., N.Y.C., 1983—, pres., 1992—; Ferrier lectr. Royal Soc. London, 1972; NIH lectr., 1975; Grass lectr. Soc. Neurosci., 1976; lectr. Coll. de France, 1977; Hitchcock prof. U. Calif.-Berkeley, 1980; Sharpey-Schafer lectr. Phys. Soc. London; George Cotzias lectr. Am. Acad. Neurology, 1983. Contbr. numerous articles to profl. jours. Recipient Jules Stein award Trustees for Prevention of Blindness, 1971, Lewis S. Rosenstiel prize Brandeis U., 1972, Friedenwald award Assn. Rsch. in Vision and Ophthalmology, 1975, Karl Spencer Lashley prize Am. Philos. Soc., 1977, Louisa Gross Horwitz prize Columbia U., 1978, Dickson prize U. Pitts., 1979, Nobel prize in physiology and medicine, 1981, W.H. Helmerich III award 1989. Mem. Am. Physiol. Soc., Am. Philos. Soc., AAAS, Am. Acad. Arts and Scis., Nat. Acad. Arts and Scis., Swedish Physiol. Soc., Soc. Neurosci. (pres. 1978-79), Royal Soc. (fgn. mem.), Physiol. Soc. (Eng.) (hon. mem.). Office: Rockefeller U Office Pres 1230 York Ave New York NY 10021-6307*

WIESENBERG, JACQUELINE LEONARDI, medical lecturer; b. West Haven, Conn., May 4, 1928; d. Curzio and Filomena Olga (Turrinziani) Leonardi; m. Russel John Wiesenberg, Nov. 23; children: James Wynne, Deborann Donna. BA, SUNY, Buffalo, 1970, postgrad., 1970-73, 80—. Interviewer, examiner U.S. Dept. Labor, New Haven, 1948-52; sec. W.I. Clark Co., Hamden, Conn., 1952-55; acct. VA Hosp., West Haven, 1956-60; acct.-commissary U.S. Air Force Missle Site, Niagara Falls, N.Y., 1961-62; tchr. Buffalo City Schs., 1970-73, 79; acct. Erie County Social Svcs., Buffalo, 1971-73; lectr., 1973—. Contbr. articles to CAP, U.S. Air Force mag., 1954—. Capt., Nat. Found. March of Dimes, 1969—, com. mem. telethon, 1983-86; den mother Boy Scouts Am., 1961-68; chmn. Meals on Wheels, Town of Amherst, 1975-76; leader, travel chmn. Girl Scouts Am., 1968-77; mem. Nat. Congress Parents and Tchrs., 1957—; heart fund vol. Heart Assn., 1960-86; rep. Am. Diabetes Assn., 1994—, vol. Diabetes collection, 1994-95. Mem. AAUW, NAFE, Internat. Platform Assn., Nat. Parks and Conservation Assn., Am. Astrol. Assn., Nat. Arbor Day Found., Western N.Y. Conf. Aging, Nat. Geographic Soc., The Wilderness Soc., Nat. Trust for Hist. Preservation, The Nature Conservancy, Epsilon Delta Chi. Alpha Iota. Home: 14 Norman Pl Amherst NY 14226-4233

WIESNER, DALLAS CHARLES, immunologist, researcher; b. Brookings, S.D., Mar. 19, 1959; s. Charles Howard Wiesner and Coleen Marie (Hendrickson) Bailey; m. Priscilla Anne Semon, 1992. BS in Microbiology with high honors, S.D. State U., 1982. HIV product devel. tech. Abbott Labs., Diagnostic Div., Abbott Park, Ill., 1985-87; HIV retrocell product mgr. Abbott Labs., Diagnostic Div., North Chicago, Ill., 1987-88; sect. mgr. infectious disease and immunology Abbott Labs., Diagnostic Div., Abbott Park, Ill., 1988-90; mgr. sexually transmitted diseases tech. product devel. Diagnostic div. Abbott Labs., Abbott Park, Ill., 1990-91, sect. mgr. retrovirus tech. product devel., 1991—. Mem. Am. Biog. Inst. Rsch. Assn. (dep. gov.), Am. Soc. for Microbiology, Phi Kappa Phi. Republican. Lutheran. Home: 8716 1st Ave Kenosha WI 53143-6508 Office: Abbott Labs 1 Abbott Park Rd North Chicago IL 60064-3500

WIEST, ELIZABETH HERMAN, nursing educator; b. Lancaster, Pa., July 3, 1936; d. Paul Lester and Elizabeth MacDonald (Woodburn) Herman; m. Donald K. Wiest, Mar. 8, 1980. Diploma Lancaster Gen. Hosp. Sch. Nursing, 1957; BSN, U. Md., 1966, MS, 1968; EdD, U. Wyo., 1980. Staff nurse Lancaster Gen. Hosp., 1957-63, Univ. Hosp., Balt., 1965-66; asst. prof. U. Md., Balt., 1967-74; asst. prof. U. Wyo., Laramie, 1974-80, assoc. prof., 1980-83, dir. off-campus nursing programs, 1983—. Bd. dirs., past chmn. bd. Wyo. affiliate Am. Heart Assn., rep. N.W. Regional Heart Com., 1981-85, mem. edn. and community program com., mem. cardiovascular nursing council of Am. Heart Assn.; exec. bd. Western Council Higher Edn. in Nursing, 1982-85; apptd. to Bd. Health City of Laramie, 1987-93. Gold Heart award Am. Heart Assn. Wyo. USPHS trainee, 1966-67; Kemper scholar, summer 1969. Mem. ANCC (cert. continuing edn. and staff devel., 1992—), LWV (v.p. Laramie chpt.), Am. Nurses Assn. (council on continuing edn.), Western Inst. Nursing, Wyo. Nurses Assn. (pres. Dist. 12 1985-89, bd. dirs. 1985-90, Leadership in Nursing award), Wyo. Commn. Nursing and Nursing Edn. (vice-chmn. 1986-88, bd. dirs. 1989-91, chmn. 1991-95), Lancaster Gen. Hosp. Nurses Alumni Assn., Summer Sch. Alumni Assn. Rutgers Summer Sch. Alcohol Studies, U. Wyo. Alumni Assn., Sigma Theta Tau (v.p. local chpt.), Alpha Pi (pres. local chpt.), Zonta Internat. Republican. Lutheran. Home: 1930 E Sheridan St Laramie WY 82070-4321 Office: U Wyo Sch Nursing PO Box 3065 Laramie WY 82071-3065

WIGDERSON, JONATHAN D., orthopedist; b. Flushing, N.Y., Jan. 27, 1961; s. Jonathan Marks Wigderson and Carol Ann (Lee) Brown; m. Sueanne Nelson, Dec. 3, 1994; 1 child, Jennifer Marie Zagami. BS cum laude, SUNY, Albany, 1982; Do, Ohio U., 1989. Lic. physician, N.Y., N.J., Mich. Orthopedic fellow Booth Meml. Med. Ctr., Flushing, 1991-92; orthopedic resident Peninsula Hosp. Ctr., Far Rockaway, N.Y., 1992—. Mem. Am. Osteo. Assn., Am. Osteo. Acad. Orthopedics, N.Y. Osteo. Orthopedic Assn., Sigma Sigma Phi. Jewish. Home: 21 Rainbow Ln Lindenhurst NY 11757 Office: Peninsula Hosp Ctr 51-15 Beach Channel Dr Far Rockaway NY 11691

WIGGINS, JAMES JOSEPH, family practice physician; b. Pasadena, Calif., Apr. 12, 1960; s. John Lawson and Rita Angela (Cassidy) W. BS, Rutgers U., 1989; DO, Phila. Coll. Osteo. Medicine, 1994. Diplomate Am. Acad. Family Physicians. Chief resident U. Calif.-Davis/Stockton Family Practice Residency Program; osteopath San Joaquin Gen. Hosp., Stockton, Calif., 1994—. Mem. Am. Osteopath. Assn. Home: 1329 Madrona Ave Saint Helena CA 94574 Office: San Joaquin Gen Hosp PO Box 1020 Stockton CA 95201

WIGGINS, JAMES WALTER, mental health center administrator, fire chief; b. Atlanta, Oct. 29, 1949; s. Clifford James and Alice Helen (Kirkland) W.; m. DeLores Eloise Belle Isle, June 18, 1970; children: Kim Cheri, Rodney James. AS, S. Ga. Coll., 1969; BSEd, U. Ga., 1971. Firefighter Jonesboro (Ga.) Fire Dept., 1969-72, capt., 1972-74, asst. chief, 1974-78, fire chief, 1978—; recreation therapist Clayton Mental Health Ctr., Riverdale, Ga., 1971-72, dir. specialized svcs. and activities, 1972-79; asst. dir. Clayton Mental Health/Mental Retardation Substance Abuse, Jonesboro, 1985—; cons. Dept. Human Resources, Stockbridge, Ga., 1974-76. Bd. dirs. Tara Credit Union, Jonesboro, 1978—. Mem. Ga. Assn. Fire Chiefs, Ga. State Firemen's Assn. Baptist. Home: 8201 Creek St Jonesboro GA 30236-3920 Office: Clayton Mental Health Ctr 853 Battlecreek Rd Jonesboro GA 30236-1919

WIGGINS, PATRICIA LEE, physician; b. Scranton, Pa., Oct. 13, 1954; m. B.S. Heir; 2 children. BS, Springfield (Mass.) Coll., 1976; MD, Bowman Gray Sch. Medicine, Winston Salem, N.C., 1980; MPH, U. Calif., Berkeley, 1987. Diplomate Am. Bd. Internal Medicine. Resident Waterbury (Conn.) Hosp., 1980-83; resident. USPHS, Morven, N.C., 1984-86; fellow U. Calif. Davis Med. Ctr., Sacramento, 1986-88; clin. instr. SUNY, Stony Brook, 1988; med. dir. North Bay Work Care, Fairfield, Calif., 1989—; clin. assoc. U. Calif. Davis, Sacramento, 1989—. Mem. Rotary. Office: North Bay Work Care 1010 Nut Tree Rd Ste 200 Vacaville CA 95687

WIGGINS, ROGER C., internist, educator, researcher; b. Tetbury, Eng., May 26, 1945. BA, Cambridge U., Eng., 1968; BChir, Middlesex Hosp. Med. Sch., London, 1971, MB, MA, 1972. House physician dept. medicine The Middlesex Hosp., London, 1971-72; house surgeon Ipswich (Eng.) and East Suffolk Hosps., 1972; sr. house officer Hammersmith Hosp., The Middlesex Hosp., Brompton Hosp., London, 1972-74; rsch. registrar The Middlesex Hosp. Med. Sch., London, 1975-76; postdoctoral fellow Scripps Clinic and Rsch. Found., La Jolla, Calif., 1976-78, rsch. assoc., 1978-79, asst. mem. 1, 1979-81; asst. prof. U. Mich., Ann Arbor, 1981-84, assoc. prof., 1984-90, prof., 1990—, chief nephrology, 1988—, dir. O'Brien Renal Ctr., 1988—, dir. NIH Nephrology Tng. Program, 1988—; lectr., speaker in field. Author chpts. to books; assoc. editor: Jour. Am. Soc. Nephrology, Clin. Sci.; contbr. articles to profl. jours. First Broderip scholar, 1971, Harold Boldero scholar, 1971, James McIntosh scholar, 1971, The Berkeley fellow Gonville and Caius Coll., 1976; recipient Leopold Hudson prize, 1971, The William Henry Rean prize, 1971, Disting. Rsch. Jerome W. Conn award, 1984. Fellow Royal Coll. Physicians (U.K.); mem. Am. Assn. Pathologists, Am. Assn. Immunologists, Am. Soc. Nephrology, Fedn. Clin. Rsch., Am. Soc. Clin. Investigation, Ctrl. Soc. Am. Fedn. Clin. Rsch., Assn. Am. Physicians. Home: 3142 Parkridge Dr Ann Arbor MI 48103-1741 Office: U Mich Nephrology Div 3914 Taubman Ctr Ann Arbor MI 48109-0364

WIGGINS, STEPHANIE DERAN, geriatrics nurse, nursing educator; b. Mobile, Ala., Oct. 12, 1956; d. James Andrew and Mary Frances (Wright) W. A in Nursing, Mobile Coll., 1976; BSN, U. South Ala., 1978; MSN, U. Ala., 1979, DSN in Nursing Svc. Adminstrn., 1990. Cert. BLS instr. Am. Heart Assn.; cert. gerontologist. Float nurse Mobile Infirmary, 1976-81; instr. Mobile Coll., 1979-81; asst. prof. Anna Vaughn Sch. Nursing Oral Roberts U., Tulsa, 1981-85; dir. nursing svc. U. Village Retirement Ctr., Tulsa, 1985-86; chief nurse med.-surg. fl. City of Faith Hosp., Tulsa, 1985-86, dir. home health care, 1986-87, dir. skilled nursing facility, 1986-87; grad. rsch. asst. U. Ala., Birmingham, 1987-89; interim quality assurance coord. Thomas Hosp., Fairhope, Ala., 1989; asst. prof. U. South Ala., Mobile, 1990—. Mem. ANA, Ala. State Nurses Assn. (recruitment and retention com. 1991-95, mem. assessment coord. team 1995, writing com. 1994—, conv. planning com. 1995), Mobile County Nurses Soc. (profl. practice chmn. 1990-92, bd. dirs. 1992—, pres. 1994-95), Oral Roberts U. Anna Vaughn Sch. Nursing Hon. Soc. (pres. 1984-85), Ala. Gerontol. Soc., Sigma Theta Tau (treas. Zeta Gamma chpt. 1991-93, fin. chmn. 1993-95, pres.-elect 1996—), Sigma Phi Omega (Alpha Zeta chpt.). Mem. Assembly of God.

WIGGINS, STEPHEN EDWARD, family practice physician, medical administrator; b. Phila., May 7, 1951; s. Ralph Cannon and Bernice J. (Maslovitz) W.; m. Rebecca del Carmen, Oct. 3, 1992; 1 child, Daniel Stephen. BA, Rutgers U., 1973; MD, Med. Coll. Va., 1977. Diplomate Am. Bd. Family Practice. Resident in family practice Riverside Hosp., Newport News, Va., 1977-80; staff emergency physician North Arundal Hosp., Glen Burnie, Md., 1980-81, So. Md. Hosp. Ctr., Clinton, 1982-84; med. dir. Convenient Health Care, Waldorf, Md., 1984—; ptnr. Old Line Med. Partnership, Waldorf, 1990-96, Convenient Health Care Mgmt., Waldorf, 1989-96; instr. family practice Georgetown U. Sch. Medicine, Washington, 1995-96. Vol. physician and citizen diplomat Gesundheit Inst., Russia, 1991; citizen diplomate U.S.-China Peoples Friendship Assn., China, 1988; vol. physician March of Dimes Walk-a-thon, Md., 1985-86. William Demarest scholar, Rutgers U., New Brunswick, N.J., 1969-73. Fellow Am. Acad. Family Physicians; mem. Med. and Chirurgical Faculty of the State of Md., Md. Acad. Family Physicians, Charles County Med. Soc. Office: Convenient Health Care 640 Old Line Ctr Waldorf MD 20602

WIGHT, DARLENE, retired speech educator; b. Andover, Kans., Jan. 5, 1926; d. Everett John and Claudia (Jennings) Van Biber; m. Lester Delin, Jan. 21, 1950; children: Lester Delin II, Claudia Leigh. AA, Graceland Coll., 1945; BA, U. Kans., 1948, MA, 1952. Permanent profl. cert., Iowa; life tchr.'s cert., Mo. Instr. U. Kans., Lawrence, 1949-50; instr. overseas program U. Md., Munich, 1954; speech pathologist Independence (Mo.) Pub. Sch. Dist., 1958-61; assoc. prof. Graceland Coll., Lamoni, Iowa, 1961-87; cons. Quad-County Sch. Dist., Leon, Iowa, 1966-67, Mt. Ayr (Iowa) Cmty. Sch. Dist., 1967-70; cons. Head Start program SCIAP, Leon, 1972-75, MATURA, Bedford, Iowa, 1973-75. Co-author: Speech Communication Handbook, 1979. Mem. Common Cause, 1989, Friends of Art, Nelson-Atkins Mus. Art, Planned Parenthood, U.S. English, Inc., Habitat for Humanity, Nat. Mus. Women in Arts, Am. Craft Coun. Recipient Award of Merit U. Kans., 1982, Award of Distinction U. Kans., 1947-48. Mem. AAUW, Am. Speech, Lang. and Hearing Assn. (speech pathology clin. competency), Coun. Exceptional Children. Democrat. Mem. Reorganized Latter Day Saints Ch. Office: Graceland Coll Speech Dept Lamoni IA 50140

WIGODNER, BYRON I., pharmaceutical executive; b. Chgo., Ill., Nov. 16, 1952; s. Jerome and Shirley (Simon) W.; m. Ellen Lois Dennen, July 27, 1980; 1 child, Michael. BS in Biology, No. Ill. U., 1974; MBA with distinction, DePaul Grad. Sch., 1979. Profl. sales rep. Sanofi Winthrop Pharms. divsn. Sanofi Winthrop Inc., N.Y.C., 1974-76, regional accounts mgr., 1976-78, med. ctr. rep., 1978-87, divsn. mgr., 1987-94, nat. account mgr., 1994-95, nat. account dir., 1995—; assoc. prof. mktg. Mundelein Coll., Chgo., 1980-91, Webster U., 1993—, Lake Forest Grad. Sch., 1996—; instr. mktg. Coll. of Lake County, 1991-93, Harper Coll., 1992—; adj. instr. Northeastern Ill. Univ., 1981-90. Health bd. commr. Buffalo Grove (Ill.) Bd. Health, 1985—. Mem. Am. Mgmt. Assn., Am. Mktg. Assn., Acad. Health Svcs. Mktg. Home: 2094 Sheridan Rd Buffalo Grove IL 60089-8009

WIGTON, ROBERT SWIFT, medical educator; b. Phila., Jan. 22, 1942; s. Robert Spencer and Marcia Catherine (Swift) W.; m. Deborah Ann Adkins, Jan. 9, 1976. BA, Harvard Coll., 1965; BS, U. Nebr., 1967, MD, 1969, MS, 1973. Diplomate Am. Bd. Internal Medicine. Cert. Nebr. State Bd. Med. Examiners, 1969. Instr. Dept. Physiology U. Nebr. Coll. Medicine, Omaha, 1969-71; asst. prof. Dept. Internal Medicine U. Nebr. Coll. Medicine, 1974-81, dir. House Officer Program, 1976-79, asst. dean for grad. med. edn., 1976-87, assoc. prof. Dept. Internal Medicine, 1981-89, assoc. dean for acad. affairs and grad. med. edn., 1986-93, prof. Dept. Internal Medicine, 1989—, chief Sect. Gen. Internal Medicine, 1993—, assoc. dean for grad. med. edn., 1993—; vis. scholar Dept. Medicine U. Pa. Sch. Medicine, Phila., 1982-83; editl. bds. Med. Decision Making, MD Computing, Jour. Gen. Internal Medicine. Editor: (CD-ROM multimedia text) Procedures in Internal Medicine, 1996; contbr. articles to profl. jours. Fellow ACP (Teaching and Rsch. scholar 1973-76), Am. Coll. Med. Informatics, Soc. for Med. Decision Making (v.p. 1988-89, trustee 1985-88), Soc. Gen. Internal Medicine (coun. 1985-88), Assn. Am. Med. Colls. (regional chair group on ednl. affairs 1994-95), Alpha Omega Alpha (pres. Alpha chpt. 1996—). Office: U Nebr Med Ctr 600 S 42d St Omaha NE 68198

WILANSKY, SUSAN, cardiologist; b. Montreal, Que., Can., Jan. 4, 1953; came to U.S., 1988; d. Douglas L. and Ruth A. (Schelew) W.; m. Michael Jay Markowitz, July 31, 1988; 1 child, Annie; stepchildren: Matthew, Jonah. BSc, U. Toronto, 1975; MD, McMaster U., 1979. Diplomate Am. Bd. Internal Medicine, Cardiology. Intern, resident, cardiologist Toronto We. Hosp., 1979-88; cardiologist The Meth. Hosp., Houston, 1988-90; assoc. dir. Echo Lab. St. Luke's Episc. Hosp./Tex. Heart Inst., Houston, 1990-95, med. dir. Noninvasive Lab., 1995—; asst. prof. U. Toronto, 1986-88, Baylor Coll. Medicine, Houston, 1988-90, clin. asst. prof., 1990—. Contbr. articles to profl. jours. Fellow Am. Coll. Cardiology, Royal Coll. Physicians and Surgeons Can.; mem. Am. Soc. Echocardiography, Am. Heart Assn., Can. Cardiovascular Soc. Office: Hall Garvin Cardio Assocs 6624 Fannin #2480 Houston TX 77030

WILBUR, ANDREW CLAYTON, radiologist; b. Phila., May 30, 1952; s. Richard Sloan and Betty Lou (Fannin) W. AB in Human Biology, Stanford U., 1974; MD, George Washington U., 1978. Diplomate Am. Bd. Radiology. Extern in diagnostic radiology Palo Alto (Calif.) Med. Found., 1978-79; resident in diagnostic radiology U. Ill. Hosp., Chgo., 1979-83, fellow in body imaging, 1983-84; asst. prof. radiology U. Ill. Coll. Medicine, Chgo., 1984-90, assoc. prof., 1990—, dir. body imaging dept. radiology, 1988—, dir. radiology residency program, 1989—. Contbr. articles to profl. jours. Mem. Radiol. Soc. N.Am., Am. Coll. Radiology, Am. Roentgen Ray Soc. Office: Univ of Illinois Hosp M/C 931 1740 W Taylor St Chicago IL 60612

WILBUR, DWIGHT LOCKE, retired physician; b. Harrow-on-the-Hill, Eng., Sept. 18, 1903; came to U.S., 1904; s. Ray Lyman and Marguerite May (Blake) W.; m. Ruth Esther Jordan, Oct. 20, 1928; children—Dwight L., Jordan R., Gregory F. A.B., Stanford U., 1923; M.D., U. Pa., 1926; M.S. in Medicine, U. Minn.-Mpls., 1933; D.Sc. (hon.), Dartmouth Coll., 1973. Diplomate Am. Bd. Internal Medicine. Intern, U. Pa. Hosp., Phila., 1926-28; resident, Mayo Found., Rochester, Minn., 1929-31; staff Mayo Clinic, Rochester, 1931-37; clin. prof. medicine Stanford U., Calif., 1937-68; pvt. practice medicine, San Francisco, 1937-83; physician U.S. Naval Res., Oakland, Calif., 1942-46; clin. prof. medicine emeritus Stanford U., 1968—. Editor, Calif. Medicine, 1946-67. Author (with J.R. Gamble): Chemistry of Digestive Diseases, 1961, Current Concepts of Clinical Gastroenterology, 1965. Contbr. articles to profl. jours. Trustee Mayo Found., 1951-71, emeritus, 1971—. Served to comdr., USNR, 1942-46. Recipient Julius Friedenwald medal, Am. Gastroenterol. Assn., 1961; Spl. Commendation for Outstanding Achievement, U. Minn., 1964; Outstanding Civilian Service medal, Dept. Army, 1966; First Disting. Internist award, Am. Soc. Internal Medicine, 1970. Mem. Calif. Med. Assn. (hon. past pres.), Inst. Medicine Nat. Acad. Scis. (charter), ACP (charter, Alfred Stengel Meml. award 1964, pres. 1958-59, fellow), AMA (pres. 1968-69), Am. Gastroenterologic Assn. (pres. 1954-55). Republican. Club: Commonwealth, Bohemian. Home: 140 Sea Cliff Ave San Francisco CA 94121-1125

WILBUR, RICHARD SLOAN, physician, foundation executive; b. Boston, Apr. 8, 1924; s. Blake Colburn and Mary Caldwell (Sloan) W.; m. Betty Lou Fannin, Jan. 20, 1951; children: Andrew, Peter, Thomas. BA, Stanford U., 1943, MD, 1946; JD, John Marshall Law Sch., 1990. Intern San Francisco County Hosp., 1946-47; resident Stanford Hosp., 1949-51, U. Pa. Hosp., 1951-52; postgrad. tng. U. Mich. Hosp., 1957, Karolinska Sjukhuset, Stockholm, 1960; mem. staff Palo Alto (Calif.) Med. Clinic, 1952-69; dep. exec. v.p. AMA, Chgo., 1969-71, 73-74; asst. sec. for health and environment Dept. Def., 1971-73; sr. v.p. Baxter Labs., Inc., Deerfield, Ill., 1974-76; exec. v.p. Council Med. Splty. Socs., 1976-91, sec. accreditation council for continuing med. edn., 1979-91; asso. prof. medicine Georgetown U. Med. Sch., 1971-77, Stanford Med. Sch., 1952-69; pres. Nat. Resident Matching Plan, 1991-92; chmn. bd. Calif. Med. Assn., 1968-69, Calif. Blue Shield, 1966-68, Am. Medico-Legal Found., 1987—; chmn. bd., CEO Inst. for Clin. Info., 1994—; CEO Medic Alert, 1992-94; pres. Am. Bd. Med. Mgmt., 1992; mem. Am. Bd. Electrodiagnostic Medicine, 1993—. Contbr. articles to med. jours. Vice chmn. Rep. Cen. Com. Santa Clara County, Calif., 1966-89; bd. govs. ARC; chmn. bd. dirs. Medic Alert Found.; bd. dirs. Nat. Adv. Cancer Coun., Nat. Health Coun., 1993—; bd. visitors Drew U. Postgrad. Med. Sch.; chmn. Mid-Am. Blood Svcs. Bd., Lifesource Blood Bank, 1996. With USNR, 1942-49. Recipient Disting. Svc. medal Dept. Def., 1973, scroll of merit Nat. Med. Assn., 1971. Fellow ACP, Am. Coll. Legal Medicine (bd. dirs.), Am. Coll. Physician Execs. (bd. regents 1985-89, pres.-elect 1987, pres. 1988-89), Internat. Coll. Dentistry (hon.); mem. Inst. Medicine, Ill. Med. Assn., Lake County Med. Soc., Am. Gastroent. Assn., Pacific Interurban Clin. Club, Am. Soc. Internal Medicine, Santa Clara County Med. Soc. (hon.), Cedars Club (Soda Springs, Calif.), Union League Phila., Phi Beta Kappa, Alpha Omega Alpha. Home: 985 Hawthorne Pl Lake Forest IL 60045-2217 Office: 207 Westminster Rd Lake Forest IL 60045-1885

WILCHINS, SIDNEY A., gynecologist; b. Paterson, N.J., Feb. 2, 1940; s. Philip Aaron and Esther (Blake) W.; m. Carole Diane Brill, June 23, 1963 (div. Mar. 1985); children: Joan Helen, Edward Victor; m. Estelle Angel, Mar. 15, 1985; children: Jacqueline, Susan. BA in Biol. Scis., Rutgers U., 1961; MD, Georgetown U., 1965. Diplomate Am. Bd. Ob Gyn. Clin. instr. N.J. Med. Sch., Newark, N.J., 1971-73; clin. asst. prof. N.J. Med. Sch., Newark, 1973-78, clin. assoc. prof., 1978—; adj. rsch. prof. N.J. Inst. Tech., Newark, 1978—; assoc. dir. Pilgrim Med. Ctr., Montclair, N.J., 1982-93; med. dir. Ultrasound Diagnostic Sch., Union, N.J., 1989-91, N.J. Menopause Found., 1992—; gynecol. cons. Organon/Akzo, 1991—; med. dir. Gynchoices of Cen. Jersey, 1994—; pres. Soc. of Forensic Obstetricians & Gynecologists, 1994—. Author, editor: Cryosurgery and Medicine, 1990; contbr. articles to profl. jours. Lt. USNR, 1965-69. Fellow ACOG, ACS, N.Y. Acad. Medicine; mem. N.Y. Acad. Scis., Forensic Soc. Ob-Gyn. (pres. 1994-95), Colonia Country Club. Home: 154 Devon Rd Colonia NJ 07067-3205 Office: 14 E Westfield Ave Roselle Park NJ 07204-2208

WILCHINSKY, MARK E., orthopaedic surgeon; b. Bridgeport, Conn., Mar. 18, 1952; s. William and Rita Wilchinsky; children: Jenna, Mark. BS, Fairfield U., 1974; MD, Tulane U., 1975. Diplomate Am. Bd. Orthop. Surgery. Resident in orthopedic surgery U. Mass. Med. Ctr., Worcester; pvt. practice Merritt Orthop. Assocs., Bridgeport, Conn.; asst. prof. orthop. surgery U. Mass. Med. Ctr., Worcester, 1984—. Exec. bd. Goodwill Industries, Bridgeport, 1994—, Burroughs Cmty. Ctr., Bridgeport, 1995—. Fellow Am. Acad. Orthop. Surgeons, Am. Arthroscopy Assn.; mem. New Eng. Orthop. Assn., Ea. Orthop. Assn. Roman Catholic. Office: Merritt Orthopedic Assocs 3909 Main St Bridgeport CT 06606

WILCHUSKY, BERNARD LEONARD, radiologist; b. Port Carbon, Pa., Sept. 9, 1932; s. William Joseph and Helen Anne (Kiselis) W.; m. Leann Cecelia Bartok, July 17, 1959; children: Shari, Mark, Dennis, Jayce; m. Luana Best, June 26, 1988; 1 child, Bernard Jr. BS, U. Pitts., 1955, MD, 1958. Diplomate Am Bd. Radiology. Intern Mercy Hosp., Pitts., 1958-59, resident, 1962-65, staff radiologist, 1965—; pres. Diagnostic Imaging Assocs., Pitts., 1990—; cons. staff Braddock Hosp., Pitts., 1980—; clin. asst. prof. radiology U. Pitts. Sch. Medicine, 1984-90; v.p. med. staff Mercy Hosp., 1984-88. Mem. Am. Coll. Radiology, Radiol. Soc. N.Am., Pa. Radiol. Soc. Roman Catholic. Home: 3466 Palomino Dr Gibsonia PA 15044-8964 Office: Diagnostic Imaging Assocs 2041 Blvd Of The Allies Pittsburgh PA 15219-5801

WILCOX, BENSON REID, cardiothoracic surgeon, educator; b. Charlotte, N.C., May 26, 1932; s. James Simpson and Louisa (Reid) W.; m. Lucinda Holderness, July 25, 1959; children: Adelaide, Alexandra, Melissa, Reid. BA, U. N.C., 1953, MD, 1957. Diplomate Am. Bd. Surgery, Am. Bd. Thoracic Surgery (chmn. 1991-93). Resident Barnes Hosp., St. Louis, 1958-59, N.C. Meml. Hosp., Chapel Hill, 1959-60, 62-64; clin. assoc. Nat. Heart Inst., Bethesda, Md., 1960-62; instr. U. N.C., Chapel Hill, 1963-65, asst. prof., 1965-68, assoc. prof., 1968-71, chief divsn. of cardiothoracic surgery, 1969—, prof., 1971—; cons. NIH Grant Com., Bethesda, 1986-89. Contbr. articles to profl. jours.; author (with others): Atlas of the Heart, 1988, Surgical Anatomy of the Heart, 1992. Pres. Atlantic Coast Conf., Greensboro, N.C., 1980-81; dir. Am. Bd. Thoracic Surgery, 1983-93, chmn., 1991-93. Markle scholar John and Mary Markle Found., 1967; recipient Hadassah Myrtle Wreath award, 1979. Mem. Am. Assn. Thoracic Surgery, Am. Surg. Assn., Soc. Thoracic Surgeons (treas. 1980-86, pres. 1994-95), Soc. Univ. Surgeons, So. Surg. Assn., Thoracic Surgery Dirs. Assn. (pres. 1985-87), Womack Soc. (pres. 1991-93). Democrat. Presbyterian. Office: U NC Med Sch Div Cardiothoracic Surgery 108 Burnett-Womack CB-7065 Chapel Hill NC 27599-7065

WILCOX, CHARLES JULIAN, geneticist, educator; b. Harrisburg, Pa., Mar. 28, 1930; s. Charles John and Gertrude May (Hill) W.; m. Eileen Louise Armstrong, Aug. 27, 1955; children: Marsha Lou, Douglas Edward. BS, U. Vt., 1950; MS, Rutgers U., 1955, PhD, 1959. Registered profl. animal scientist. Dairy farm owner, operator Charlotte, Vt., 1955-56; prof. U. Fla., Gainesville, 1959-95; prof. emeritus, 1995—; cons. in internat. animal agrl. Gt. Britain, France, Sudan, Can., Mex., El Salvador, Ecuador, Brazil, Bolivia, Peru, Colombia, Venezuela, Dominican Republic, Saudi Arabia, Sweden, Norway, 1965—. Author: (with others) Animal Agriculture, 1973, 2d edit., 1980, Improvement of Milk Production in Tropics, 1990; editor: Large Dairy Herd Management, 1978, 93. 1st Lt. U.S. Army, 1951-53, Korea. Decorated Combat Infantryman badge; 3 Korean campaigns. Recipient Disting. Svc. award Fla. Purebred Dairy Assn., 1986, Jr. Faculty award Gamma Sigma Delta, 1988, Sr. Faculty award, 1984, Internat. award for Disting. Svc. to Agr., 1987, Sr. Rsch. Scientist award Sigma Xi, 1994. Mem. Am. Dairy Sci. Assn., Am. Soc. Animal Sci., Brazilian Soc. Genetics (editorial bd. 1979—), Am. Registry Profls. Animal Sci. (examining bd. 1987—), Fla. Holstein Assn. (pres. 1979), Fla. Guernsey Cattle Club (pres. 1974-76). Republican. Office: Univ Fla Dairy and Poultry Sci Dept Gainesville FL 32611-0920

WILCOX, IAN, medical research scientist, cardiology consultant; b. Melbourne, Victoria, Australia, Mar. 19, 1955; s. Max and Patricia Lorraine (Young) W.; m. Christa Ursula Boehm, Nov. 6, 1977; 1 child, Chloe Ursula. B Med. Sci. with honors, U. Newcastle, Eng., 1976, MB, BS, 1979; PhD, U. Sydney, Australia, 1991. House officer Royal Victoria Infirmary, Newcastle, 1980-81; resident med. officer Royal Prince Alfred Hosp., Sydney, NSW, Australia, 1981-83, med. registrar, 1983-84, cardiology registrar, 1984-86, cardiologist Sleep Disorders Unit, 1990—; rsch. fellow Hallstrom Inst. Cardiology Sydney U., 1986-90, sr. rsch. officer Nat. Health and Med. Rsch. Coun., 1990-96; chmn. dept. medicine Strathfield Pvt. Hosp., Sydney, 1996—; cons. cardiologist Shoalhaven Dist. Hosp., Nowra, NSW, 1988—. Contbr. articles to profl. jours. Grantee Nat. Health and Med. Rsch. Coun., 1990-96; med. rsch. scholar Med. Rsch. Coun., Newcastle (Eng.), 1975, postgrad. med. rsch. scholar Nat. Heart Found., Sydney, 1986-89; Bayer Travelling fellow Cardiac Soc., Australia, 1990. Fellow Royal Australian Coll. Physicians; mem. Am. Heart Assn., Cardiac Soc. Australia and New Zealand, Australasian Sleep Rsch. Assn., Med. Defence Union (NSW). Presbyterian. Home: 56 Northcote St, Haberfield, Sydney NSW 2045, Australia Office: Sydney U, Dept Medicine, Sydney NSW 2006, Australia

WILDE, ALAN HUGH, orthopedist; b. Phila., Sept. 7, 1933; s. Norman T. Sr. and Elizabeth (Duthie) W.; m. Marilyn Meyer, June 13, 1958; children: Alan Jr., Douglas, Laurie. AB, U. Pa., 1955; MD, Hannemann U., 1959. Diplomate Am. Bd. Orthopaedic Surgeons. Intern Martin Army Hosp., Ft. Benning, Ga., 1959-60; resident in orthopaedic surgery U. Pitts., 1962-65; fellowship in orthopaedic surgery Edinburgh U., Scotland, 1965; staff dept. orthopaedic surgery Cleve. Clinic, 1966-91, chmn. dept. orthopaedic surgery, 1976-90; bd. gov's. Cleve. Clinic, 1976-80, trustee 1978-80; trustee Orthopaedic Researchand Edn. Found, 1984—. Pres. bd. deacons, trustee Presby. Ch., Cleve. Heights, 1972. Capt. M.C. U.S. Army, 1959-62. Fellow Am. Acad. Orthopaedic Surgeons (chmn. ednl. programming 1984-86), ACS; mem. Am. Orthopaedic Assn. (chmn. N.Am. traveling fellowship com. 1980-86, treas. 1989-94), Am. Shoulder and Elbow Surgeons, Kee Soc., Hip Soc., Mid-Am. Orthopaedic Assn. (1st v.p. 1996). Republican. Club: Cleve. Skating. Home: 2764 Fairmount Blvd Cleveland Heights OH 44118-4018 Office: 2322 E 22d St Cleveland OH 44115

WILDER-SMITH, OLIVER HAMILTON GOTTWALDT, anesthesiologist; b. Frankfurt, Hessen, Germany, Jan. 23, 1956; arrived in Switzerland, 1989; s. Arthur Ernest and Beate Gottwaldt. MBChB, Liverpool (Eng.) U., 1980; Diploma in Anesthesiology, Frankfurt (Germany) U., 1985, MD, 1986. Intern U. Liverpool Hosps., 1980; anesthesiologist Bg-Unfallklinik, Frankfurt, 1981-84, Marburg (Germany) U. Hosp., 1984-86; staff anaesthesiologist Ulm (Germany) U. Hosp., 1986-89, Zieglerspital, Bern, Switzerland, 1989-91, Geneva U. Hosp., 1991—. Author: (with others) Neuroanesthesie et Neuroreanimation Cliniques, 1994; contbr. articles to profl. jours. Mem. European Soc. Anaesthesiology, Internat. Assn. for Study of Pain, Arbeitsgemeinschaft Deutschsprachiger Neuroanasthesisten und Neurointensivmediziner. Office: Geneva U Hosp Dept Anaesthesiology, 24 Rue Micheli du Crest, CH 1211 Geneva 14, Switzerland

WILENSKY, ALLAN S., physician; b. Birmingham, Ala., Jan. 15, 1941; s. Phillip and Louise (Cohen) W.; m. Ilene K. Kamenshine, Mar. 30, 1961; children: Michael, Laurie, Kim. BS, U. Ala., Tuscaloosa, 1961; MD, U. Ala., Birmingham, 1965. Diplomate Am. Bd. Internal Medicine, Bd. Cardiovascular Diseases. Pres. Cardiology, P.C., Birmingham, 1971—; clin. assoc. prof. cardiology U. Ala. Med. Sch., Birmingham, 1977—; past pres. Med. Staff Bapt. Med. Ctr., Princeton, Birmingham, Birmingham Acad. Medicine, Birmingham Cardiovascular Soc. Capt. USAF, 1967-69. Fellow Am. Coll. Cardiology, Am. Coll. Physicians; mem. Phi Beta Kappa. Office: Cardiology PC Ste 307 801 Princeton Ave SW Birmingham AL 35211

WILENTZ, JAMES ROBERT, cardiologist; b. Long Branch, N.J., Sept. 2, 1951; s. Robert N. and Jacqueline (Malino) W.; m. Robin Jane Hyslop Maxwell, Sept. 28, 1991; 1 child, Benjamin. BA, Columbia U., 1972; MD, NYU, 1976. Diplomate Am. Bd. Internal Medicine, Am. Bd. Cardiovascular Disease. Intern, resident, then fellow in medicine Harvard U./Brigham & Women's Hosp., Boston, 1976-82; fellow in cardiology Boston U./Boston City Hosp., 1982-84, staff cardiologist, asst. vis. physician, 1984-85; fellow in interventional cardiology Emory U., Atlanta, 1985-86; asst. chief cardiac cath. lab. Lenox Hill Hosp., N.Y.C., 1986-93; dir. interventional cardiology

Beth Israel Med. Ctr., N.Y.C., 1993—; clin. fellow in medicine Harvard U., 1976-80, rsch. fellow in medicine, 1980-82; instr. in medicine N.Y. Med. Coll., 1986-92; clin. asst. prof. medicine Cornell U. Med. Coll., 1992-93; fellow in medicine Boston U., 1982-84, instr. in medicine, 1984-85. Contbr. articles to profl. publs. Fellow Coun. on Clin. Cardiology Am. Heart Assn. (mem. coun. on arteriosclerosis), Am. Coll. Cardiology; mem. AMA, Mass. Med. Soc., N.Y. Heart Assn., N.Y. State Med. Soc., N.Y. County Med. Soc. Office: Beth Israel Med Ctr 11 Dazian 1st Ave at 16th St New York NY 10003

WILES-LIMAURO, BETH MARIE, trauma nurse, emergency medical technician, paramedic; b. Saranac Lake, N.Y., Oct. 1, 1962; d. Ralph Temple and Genevieve Ardeth (Downs) Wiles; m. Juan Guillermo Castro, Oct. 30, 1982 (div. March 1986); m. Charles Clifton Limauro, July 4, 1995. AS, Broward C.C., Cocoanut Creek, Fla., 1988. RN, EMT, Paramedic, Fla. Mem. Emergency Nurses Assn. (pres.). Methodist.

WILEY, ALBERT LEE, JR., physician, engineer, educator; b. Forest City, N.C., June 9, 1936; s. Albert Lee and Mary Louise (Davis) W.; m. Janet Lee Pratt, June 18, 1960; children: Allison Lee, Susan Caroline, Mary Catherine, Heather Elizabeth. B in Nuclear Engring., N.C. State U., 1958, postgrad., 1958-59; MD, U. Rochester, N.Y., 1963; PhD, U. Wis., 1972. Diplomate Am. Bd. Nuclear Medicine, Am. Bd. Radiology, Am. Bd. Med. Physics. Nuclear engr. Lockheed Corp., Marietta, Ga., 1958; intern in surgery-medicine U. Va. Med. Sch., Charlottesville, 1963-64; resident in radiation therapy Sanford U., Palo Alto, Calif., 1964-65; resident and NCI postdoctoral fellow U. Wis. Hosp., Madison, 1965-68; med. dir. USN Radiol. Def. Lab., San Francisco, 1968-69; staff physician Balboa Hosp., USN, San Diego, 1969-70; asst. prof. radiotherapy M.D. Anderson Hosp. U. Tex., Houston, 1972-73; assoc. dir., clin. dir. radiation oncology U. Wis., Madison, prof. radiology, human oncology, med. physics, 1970-88; prof., chmn. radiation oncology, dir. cancer ctr. East Carolina U. Med. Sch., Greenville, N.C., 1988-93; cons. U.S. NRC, 1981-82, Nat. Cancer Inst., U.S. Dept. VA, 1990-93; advisor, cons. numerous univs. and govt. agys.; mem. Wis. Radioactive Waste Bd., Wis. Gov.'s Coun. on Biotech., Gov.'s Com. on UN. Author more than 140 articles and abstracts on med. physics, environ. health, nuclear medicine, biology and cancer treatment. Rep. candidate for U.S. Congress for 2d Wis. dist., 1982, 84; rep. primary candidate for gov., State of Wis., 1986; mem. Greenville Drug Task Force; bd. dirs. Greenville Salvation Army. Lt. comdr. USNR, ret. Oak Ridge Inst. Nuclear Studies fellow N.C. State U., 1958-59. Fellow Am. Coll. Radiology, Am. Coll. Preventive Medicine, N.C. Inst. Polit. Leadership; mem. IEEE, AMA, AAUP, Am. Assn. Physicists in Medicine, Am. Soc. Therapeutic Radiation Oncologists, Am. Assn. Physics Tchrs., Am. Bd. Sci. in Nuclear Medicine (sec.-treas.), Am. Acad. Health Physics, Am. Cancer Soc. (N.C. bd. dirs.), C. of C., VFW, Vietnam Vets. Am., Am. Legion, Masons, Rotary, Sigma Xi, Tau Beta Pi. Home: Salter Path Rd Box 588 Indian Beach NC 28575 Office: Watson Clinic Radiation Medicine PO Box 95000 Lakeland FL 33805-5000

WILEY, DON CRAIG, biochemistry and biophysics educator; b. Akron, Ohio, Oct. 21, 1944; s. William Childs and Phyllis Rita (Norton) W.; m. Katrin Valgeirsdottir; children: William Valgeir, Lara; children from previous marriage: Kristen D., Craig S. BS in Physics and Chemistry, Tufts U., 1966; PhD in Biophysics, Harvard U., 1971; PhD (hon.), U. Leiden, The Netherlands, 1995; Doctorate (hon.), U. Leiden, Netherlands, 1995. Asst. prof. dept. biochemistry and molecular biology Harvard U., Cambridge, Mass., 1971-75, assoc. prof., 1975-79, prof. biochemistry and biophysics, 1979—, chmn. dept. molecular and cellular biology, 1992-95, investigator Howard Hughes Med. Inst., 1987—; mem. biophys. chemistry study sect. NIH, 1981-85; Shipley Symposium lectr. Harvard Med. Sch., 1985, Peter A. Leermakers Symposium lectr. Wesleyan U., 1986, K.F. Meyer lectr. U. Calif., San Francisco, 1986, John T. Edsall lectr. Harvard U., 1987, Washburn lectr. Boston Mus. Sci., 1987, Harvey lectr. N.Y. Acad. Sci., 1988, XVI Linus Pauling lectr. Stanford U., 1989; rsch. assoc. in medicine Children's Hosp., Boston, 1990—. Contbr. numerous articles to profl. jours. Recipient Ledlie prize Harvard U., 1982, Louisa Gross Horwitz prize Columbia U., 1990, William B. Coley award Cancer Rsch. Inst., 1992, V.D. Mattia award, 1992, Passano Found. Laureate award, 1993, Emil von Behring prize, 1993, Gairdner Found. Internat. award, 1994, Lasker award, 1995; European Molecular Biology fellow, 1976. Fellow NAS (lectr. 1988); mem. AAAS, Am. Acad. Arts and Scis., Am. Chem. Soc. (Nichol's Disting. Symposium lectr. N.E. sect. 1988), Am. Crystallographic Assn., Am. Soc. for Chemistry and Molecular Biology, Am. Soc. for Virology, Biophys. Soc. (Nat. lectr. 1989), Protein Soc. Office: Harvard U Dept Molecular and Cellular Biology 7 Divinity Ave Cambridge MA 02138-2019 also: Children's Hosp Lab of Molecular Medicine 320 Longwood Ave Boston MA 02115-5746

WILEY, JASON LARUE, JR., neurosurgeon; b. Canandaigua, N.Y., Dec. 2, 1917; s. Jason LaRue and Eva Althea (Moore) W.; m. Alma Williams, Jan. 4, 1944 (div. Feb. 1956); children: Robert W., Richard L.; m. Ann Valentine Gerrish, Apr. 14, 1956 (div. July 1979); children: Martha V., Pamela M., Catherine A. Student, Antioch Coll., 1934-37; MD, Harvard U., 1941. Diplomate Am. Bd. Surgery, Am. Bd. Neurol. Surgery. Intern Kings County Hosp., Bklyn., 1941-42; asst. resident surgery Ellis Hosp., Schenectady, N.Y., 1948-49; from asst. to assoc. resident surgery Rochester (N.Y.) Gen. Hosp., 1949-51; from asst. to assoc. to chief resident neurosurgery Yale U. and Hartford Hosp., New Haven and Hartford Conn., 1951-54; practice medicine specializing in neurosurgery Kansa City, Mo., 1954-56, Rochester, 1956—; chief neurosurgery Rochester Gen. Hosp., 1959-71, emeritus neurosurgeon, 1989—; clin. asst. prof. neurosurgery U. Rochester, 1961-88. Mem. Bd. for Profl. Med. Conduct, N.Y. State Dept. Health, Albany, N.Y., 1985—. Served to lt. comdr. USN, 1942-47, PTO. Mem. Med. Soc. County Monroe, Med. Soc. State N.Y., N.Y. State Neurosurg. Soc. (bd. dirs.), Congress Neurol. Surgeons, Am. Assn. Neurol. Surgeons, Canandaigua Yacht Club. Republican. Episcopalian. Office: 1445 Portland Ave Rochester NY 14621-3008

WILEY, JOHN EDWARD, hospital administrator; b. Fontana, Calif., Nov. 23, 1950; s. Clair Vincent and Gladys Viola (Beeler) W.; m. Maryann Valiere Smith, Dec. 4, 1971; children: Scot, Erin, Gina. BA, Calif. State U., 1978, MBA, 1984. Diplomate Am. Coll. Healthcare Execs. Asst. adminstr. Charter Grove Hosp., Corona, Calif., 1975-85, Coll. Hosp., Cerrites, Calif., 1985-86; adminstr. Ramsey Health Care, Enid, Okla., 1986-89; dir. mental health San Bernardino (Calif.) Cmty. Hosp., 1989-90; adminstr., COO Knollwood Ctr., Riverside, Calif., 1990-94; CEO First Hosp. Vallejo, Calif., 1995—; owner Preferred Mgmt., Riverside, 1994—; ind. rep. Trudeau Mktg. Group, Vallejo, 1995—. Mem. Assn. Mental Health Adminstrn. (cert.). Roman Catholic. Office: First Hosp. Vallejo 525 Oregon St Vallejo CA 94590

WILEY, JOHN FREDERICK, physician; b. Goshen, N.Y., July 6, 1963; s. John Preston Jr. and Barbara Teresa (Hick) W.; m. Karen Michele Lee, June 3, 1995. BA in Biology, U. Md., 1985, MD, 1989. Intern Mercy Med. Ctr., Balt., 1989-90, resident, 1990-92; physician pvt. practice, Balt. and Glen Burnie, Md., 1995—. Contbr. chpts. to books. Critical care fellow George Washington U.-NIH, Washington and Bethesda, Md., 1992-95. Mem. AMA, Am. Coll. Physicians, Am. Coll. Chest Physicians, Am. Thoracic Soc., Soc. Critical Care Medicine. Democrat. Roman Catholic. Office: 301 St Paul Pl #818 Baltimore MD 21202

WILEY, MYRA, mental health nurse; b. Lexington, Ala., Jan. 20, 1938; d. Joseph Aaron and Annie Lura (Putnam) Haraway; m. Robert Harold Wiley, Sept. 17, 1960; children: Sonya, Robert, Marie. BSN, U. Ala., Huntsville, 1989. RN, Ala.; cert. in chem. dependency. Nursing asst., night-weekend coord. Upjohn Health Care, Huntsville, 1983-87; nursing asst. North Ala. Rehab. Hosp., Huntsville, 1987-89; staff nurse Humana Hosp., Huntsville, 1989-91; staff nurse counselor Bradford-Parkside, Madison, Ala., 1991-95; relief charge nurse for behavioral health Columbia Med. Ctr. of Huntsville (formerly Crestwood Hosp.), Huntsville, Ala., 1995—. Mem. ANA, Ala. State Nurses Assn., Madison County Nurses Assn, Nat. Consortium Chem. Dependency Nurses, Inc. Baptist.

WILEY, RONALD GORDON, neurologist, neurobiologist, educator; b. Akron, Ohio, Mar. 21, 1947; s. H.J. and Sara Thelma (Moore) W.; m. Virginia Frances Haile; children: Elizabeth Ann, Kathleen, Sara, Allison Christine, Christopher Allen. BS, Northwestern U., 1972, MD with distinction, 1975, PhD in Pharmacology, 1975. Diplomate Am. Bd. Neurology and Psychiatry, Am. Bd. Internal Medicine. Resident in internal medicine Peter Bent Brigham Hosp., Boston, 1975-77; resident in neurology N.Y. Hosp., N.Y.C., 1977-80; fellow in neurobiology Med. Sch. Cornell U., N.Y.C., 1980-82; attending physician in neurology LaGuardia Hosp., N.Y.C., 1980-82; asst. prof. neurology and pharmacology Vanderbilt U., Nashville, 1982-88, assoc. prof. neurology and pharmacology, 1988-94, prof. neurology and pharmacology, 1994—; staff neurologist VA Med. Ctr., Nashville, 1988—; chief neurology svc. Nashville VA Med. Ctr., 1989-90; dir. Lab. Exptl. Neurology VA Med. Ctr., Nashville, 1982—. Co-author: Suicide Transport and Immunolesioning, 1994; author: Neurological Complications of Cancer, 1995; contbr. articles to profl. jours. Troop leader Brownies, Girl Scouts U.S.A., Nashville, 1988-91. Fellow Am. Acad. Neurology; mem. AAAS, Soc. for Neurosci., N.Y. Acad. Sci., Internat. Soc. for Neuroimmunology, Am. Neurol. Assn., Alpha Omega Alpha. Home: 6436 Cloverbrook Dr Brentwood TN 37027-4722 Office: VA Med Ctr Neurology Svc 1310 24th Ave S Nashville TN 37212-2637

WILFORD, BONNIE BAIRD, health policy specialist; b. Chgo., Jan. 11, 1946; d. George Martin and Ruth Eleanor (Anderson) Baird; m. David Edward Wilford, Oct. 2, 1967; children: Heather Lynn, Edward Baird. BA, Knox Coll., 1967; postgrad., Roosevelt U., 1969-71. Staff assoc. Am. Hosp. Assn., Chgo., 1967-70; mgr. plan devel. Blue Cross & Blue Shield Assn., Chgo., 1970-79; dir. dept. substance abuse AMA, Chgo., 1979-91, dir. divsn. clin. sci., 1988-91; ptnr. Wilford & Assocs., healthcare consultants, 1991—; exec. office of the Pres. The White House, 1991-92; cons. Pres.'s Commn. on Model State Drug Laws, 1993-94; dir. Pharm. Policy Project, George Washington U. Med. Ctr., Washington, 1992—. Author: Balancing the Response to Prescription Drug Abuse, 1990, Pharmaceutical Benefits for HIV/AIDS, 1996; editor Pharmaceutical Policy Rev., 1996—; contbr. articles to profl. jours. Recipient Outstanding Svc. award Fla. Task Force on Alcohol and Drug Abuse, 1986, Merit award State of Mo., 1985, Disting. Svc. award U.S. Dept. Health and Human Svcs., 1990. Mem. APHA, Internat. Narcotic Enforcement Officers Assn. (Award of Honor 1985), Assn. for Med. Edn. and Rsch. Substance Abuse, Informal Steering Com. Prescription Drug Abuse (bd. dirs.). Office: CHPR/George Washington U 2021 K St NW Ste 800 Washington DC 20006-1003

WILHELMI, PAUL D., medical technologist; b. Kenmary, N.D., June 4, 1953; s. Carl P. and Odette R. (Dangello) W.; m. Rebecca M. Colomen, Oct. 3, 1974; children: Casey, Jill. AA, N.D. State U.; BS, U. N.D. Lab. mgr. Langdon (N.D.) Hosp., 1974—. Home: 1117 3d St Langdon ND 58249

WILHELMSEN, INGVARD, medical educator; b. Bergen, Norway, Apr. 27, 1949; s. Sverre and Edith Cecilie (Norgaard) W.; m. Ingunn Bergland, Aug. 24, 1974; children: Vera, Ane. PhD, U. Bergen, 1995. Cert. in internal medicine, gastroenterology, psychiatry, Norway. Chief physician dept. medicine Deaconness Home Hosp., Bergen, Norway, 1995—; assoc. prof. U. Bergen, 1996—; head outpatient clinic Deaconness Home Hosp., 1995—. Contbr. articles to profl. jours. Mem. Soc. Behavioral Medicine. Home: Aamundsleitet 31, 5095 Bergen Norway Office: Deaconness Home Hosp, Med Dept, 5009 Bergen Norway

WILHITE, PAMELA JEAN, medical laboratory administrator; b. Sparta, Tenn., July 30, 1954; d. Carl Douglas and Jennie Lee (Roberts) Cannon; m. James Andrew Wilhite, May 19, 1992; 1 child, Kimberly Dionne Henry. Lic. lab. supr., Tenn. Med. lab. technician White County Hosp., Sparta, 1983-88, chief technologist, 1988-94, lab. supr. mgr., 1994—. Home: RR 3 Box 293 Sparta TN 38583-9358

WILK, LAWRENCE HARVEY, orthopaedic surgeon; b. Detroit, June 29, 1933; s. Jacob Oscar and Estelle Ida (Cohen) W.; m. Helen Karen Goldman, July 7, 1957; children: Charles, Patricia, Andrew, Carol. BS in Psychology, U. Mich., 1954, MD, 1958. Diplomate Am. Bd. Orthop. Surgery; lic. physician, Mich., Tex. Intern St. Joseph Mercy Hosp., Ann Arbor, Mich., 1958-59, resident in gen. surgery, 1959-60; resident in orthop. surgery U. Mich. Med. Ctr., Ann Arbor, 1960-63; pvt. practice Corpus Christi, 1965—; med. dir. Ada Wilson Children's Hosp., 1971-78, chief of staff, 1978, active staff to date; active staff Driscoll Found. Children's Hosp., Corpus Christi, Drs. Regional Med. Ctr., Corpus Christi, Meml. Med. Ctr., Corpus Christi, Columbia N.W. Hosp., Robstown, Tex., Bay Area Med. Ctr., Corpus Christi, Spohn South Hosp., Corpus Christi, Sophn Hosp.-South; chief of staff Southside Cmty. Hosp., 1982, chief of surgery, 1991. Contbr. articles to profl. jours. Dist. dir. Disaster Med. Svcs.; chmn. emergency med. svc. com. Coastal Bend Coun. Govts.; mem. Leadership Corpus Christi, Class #1; asst. scoutmaster Troop 218 Boy Scouts Am. Capt. U.S. Army, 1963-65. Fellow ACS; mem. AMA, Tex. Med. Assn., Nueces County Med. Soc., Am. Acad. Orthop. Surgeons, Am. Orthop. Food and Ankle Soc., Tex. Orthop. Assn., Western Orthop. Assn., So. Med. Assn., Nat. Assn. Disability Examiners, Tex. Med. Found., U. Mich. Orthop. Soc., Corpus Christi Surg. Soc., Nat. Eagle Scout Assn. (leadership mem. Gulf Coast coun.), Corpus Christi C. of C., Flying Physicians (pres. Tex. chpt.), Phi Delta Epsilon. Home: 260 Cape Aron Corpus Christi TX 78412 Office: 201 Medical Arts Bldg 1001 Louisiana Pkwy Corpus Christi TX 78404

WILKEN, PAUL WILLIAM, optometrist; b. Sandusky, Ohio, Nov. 14, 1951; s. Carl Anthony and Mary Ellen (Gentry) W.; m. Linda Irene Nierstheimer, Sept. 1, 1973; children: Jennifer, Carl, Michelle, Benjamin. BS, Ohio State U., 1973, OD, 1977. Optometrist John Wasylik, Sandusky, 1977-79; owner Paul W. Wilken, Celina, Ohio, 1979, Van Wert, Ohio, 1987. Author: (newspaper column) Vision Care, 1980-81. Mem. Sch. Curriculum Council, Celina, 1982-84, 1987—; speaker, cons. Mercer County Council on Aging, Mercer County Diabetic Support Group, Celina, 1980—, Joint Twp. Dist. Meml. Hosp. Diabetic Support Group, 1986—, Van Wert County Diabetic Support Group, 1987—; pres. Commn. on Edn., 1989-91; mem. City of Celina Pks. & Recreation Bd., 1994—, pres., 1996—; dist. chmn. Boy Scouts Am., 1994-96. Mem. Am. Optometric Assn., Ohio Optometric Assn., N.W. Ohio Optometric Assn., Ohio State U. Alumni Assn. (life), Epsilon Psi Epsilon (Pledge of Yr. award 1975), Mercer Area C. of C. (trustee 1991-94), Ohio C. of C., Van Wert C. of C., Ohio State U. Alumni Assn. (life), Ohio State U. Optometry Alumni Assn., Mercer County Sportsmans Assn. Republican. Roman Catholic. Lodge: Rotary (charter, sec. 1979-84, pres. 1985-86, govs. rep.1988-89), KC, Moose, Elks. Avocations: flying, motivational speaking. Home: 616 N Main St Celina OH 45822-1463 Office: Wellman Wilken 119 Summit St Celina OH 45822-1023

WILKERSON, LEONARD ALAN, physician; b. St. Louis, May 19, 1950; s. Leonard Leroy and Thelma Elizabeth (Hutt) W.; m. Rebecca Ann LeVeque; children: Stephen Michael, Lea Diane, Stephanie Lynn. BA in Chemistry, William Jewell Coll.; DO, Kirksville Coll. Osteo Med. Commd. ensign USN, 1973, advanced through grades to lt. comdr., 1980; dir. sports medicine clinic Naval Regional Med. Ctr. USN, Bremerton, Wash., 1979-81; asst. chmn. family practice Naval Aerospace Regional Med Ctr USN, Pensacola, Fla., 1981-82, dir. sports medicine clinic Naval Aerospace Regional Med Ctr, 1981-82; resigned USN, 1982; chmn. dept. family practice Fla. Hosp., 1984-88, Osceola Regional Hosp., Kissimmee, 1989-91; chmn. family practice Fla. Hosp.-Kissimmee, 1992-94. Contbr. to profl. publs. Fellow AAFP; mem. Am. Osteo. Acad. Sports Medicine (pres.), Am. Med. Soc. Sports Medicine (bd. dirs.), Osceola County C. of C. (bd. dirs.). Republican. Baptist. Office: Ctr Sports Medicine/Orthopedics/Family Practice 720 Oak Commons Blvd Kissimmee FL 34741-4100

WILKERSON, NORMA NEAHR, nursing educator, researcher. BS, St. Joseph's Coll., Santa Ana, Calif., 1960; ADN cum laude, Orange Coast Coll., 1964; BSN cum laude, Calif. State U., L.A., 1968, MSN cum laude, 1971; PhD in Edn., Curriculum, and Instrn., U. Tex., 1982. RN, Calif., Tex., Wyo. Elem. sch. tchr. various cities, Tex., 1960-62; grad. nurse intern St. Luke's Hosp., Pasadena, Calif., 1964-65; staff, charge nurse pediatrics Santa Rosa (Calif.) Meml. Hosp., 1965-66; staff, charge psychiatric nurse Met. State Hosp., Norwalk, Calif., 1966-68; staff nurse critical care Queen of Angels Hosp., L.A., 1968-69; charge, staff nurse psychiatric care L.A. County U. So. Calif. Med. Ctr., 1969-71; instr. nursing U. Tex., Austin, 1971-73, asst. prof., 1973-83; clin. nurse specialist Maternity Ctr. Brackenridge Hosp., Austin, 1983; assoc. prof. U. Wyo., Laramie, 1984—; staff nurse neonatal ICU Kaiser Med. Ctr., L.A., summer 1975. Co-editor, contbr. books and articles in women's, infants, and children's health. EPDA fellow Calif. State U., L.A., 1969-70. Mem. ANA, Assn. Women's Health, Obstetrics, Neonatal Nurses, Wyo. Nurses Assn. (continuing edn. com. dist. 12, v.p. 1988-92, chair program com., pres. dist. 12 1992-95), Western Inst. Nursing, Sigma Theta Tau (Alpha Phi chpt. counselor 1987), Pi Lambda Theta, Phi Kappa Phi, Kappa Delta Pi.

WILKINS, LUCIEN SANDERS, gastroenterologist; b. Sanford, N.C., Mar. 30, 1942; s. Alexander Betts and Olive Elizabeth (Pittman) W.; m. Freda Barry Hartness, July 16, 1966; children: Lucien Sanders Jr., Elise Perryman. BA, Duke U., 1963; MD, Med. Coll. Va., 1967. Diplomate Am. Bd. Internal Medicine. Intern Medical Coll. Va., Richmond, 1967-68, resident in internal medicine, 1970-72, gastroenterology fellow, 1972-73; clin. gastroenterologist Wilmington (N.C.) Health Assoc., 1973—; vis. physician Hopital St. Croix, Leogane, Haiti, 1979-84; founder Divsn. Gastrointestinal Endoscopy Hopital St. Croix, Leogane, 1984, 1st Endoscopic Ambulatory Surgery Facility in State of N.C., 1990; chmn. dept. medicine New Hanover Regional Med. Ctr., Wilmington, N.C., 1990-92; asst. prof. clin. medicine U. N.C., Chapel Hill, 1974—; bd. dirs. Br. Banking and Trust, Wilmington, 1991—; physican adv. Nat. Found. Ileitis and Colitis, 1976-78. Author: Progeny, 1994. Bd. dirs. Cape Fear Coun. for the Arts, Wilmington, 1976-77, New Hanover Regional Med. Ctr. Found., Wilmington, 1993-95, exec. com., 1994-95, Com. of 100, Wilmington, 1992-95. Lt. comdr. M.C., USN, 1968-70. A. D. Williams rsch. fellow, 1965, Paul Harris fellow Rotary, 1986; winner GTP-L Al Holbert Meml. Race, Sebring, Fla., 1995. Mem. ACP, New Hanover-Pender County Med. Soc. (pres. 1980), Cape Fear Country Club, Surf Club, Hist. Stock Car Racing Group, Figure Eight Island Yacht Club (charter), Wrightsville Beach Ocean Racing Assn. (commodore). Presbyterian. Home: 2215 Lynnwood Dr Wilmington NC 28403-8026 Office: Wilmington Health Assoc 1202 Medical Center Dr Wilmington NC 28401-7307

WILKINS, MAURICE HUGH FREDERICK, biophysicist; b. Pongaroa, New Zealand, Dec. 15, 1916; s. Edgar Henry and Eveline (Whittaker) W.; m. Patricia Ann Chidgey, Mar. 12, 1959; children: Sarah Fenella, George Hugh, Emily Lucy Una, William Henry. PhD, St. John's Coll., Cambridge, 1940; LLD, U. Glasgow, 1972; DSc, Birmingham U., 1992, Trinity Coll., Dublin, 1992. Research with Manhattan Project, U. Calif., Berkeley, 1944; lectr. St. Andrews U., 1945; mem. faculty Kings Coll., London, 1946—, dep. dir. biophysics unit Med. Research Council,, 1955-70, dir. biophysics unit, 1970-72, dir. neurobiology unit, 1972-74, prof. molecular biology, 1962-70, prof. biophysics, 1970-81, also dir. MRC cell biophysics unit (formerly Med. Research Council neurobiology unit), 1974-80. Decorated comdr. Brit. Empire; recipient Albert Lasker award Am. Pub. Health Assn., 1960, Nobel prize for physiology and medicine (with F.H.C. Crick and J.D. Watson), 1962; fellow King's Coll., 1973—. Fellow Royal Soc.; mem. Brit. Biophys. Soc. (past chmn.), Am. Soc. Biol. Chemists (hon.), Brit. Soc. for Social Responsibility in Sci. (pres. 1969), Am. Acad. Arts and Scis. (fgn. hon.).

WILKINS, RICHARD MICHAEL, biology educator; b. Fareham, Hampshire, Eng., Oct. 17, 1942; s. Leslie C.T. and Florence L. (Jackson) W.; m. Mia A. Fontana, Mar., 1969; 1 child, Alexander M. BSc, Exeter U., Exeter, Eng., 1964; MS, U. Wash., 1969, PhD, 1972. Rsch. scientist I.C.I Pharms., Alderley Edge, Eng., 1964-67; teaching and rsch. asst. U. Wash., Seattle, 1967-72; asst. prof. U. P.R., Rio Piedras, P.R., 1972-74; sect. leader May & Baker Ltd., Ongar, Essex, Eng., 1974-76; from lectr. to sr. lectr. Newcastle U., Eng., 1976—; cons. FAO, Rome, UN Indsl. Devel. Orgn., Vienna, Overseas Devel. Adminstrn., London, Agrl. Genetics Co. Editor, Author: Controlled Delivery of Crop Protection Agents, 1990; contbr. numerous articles to profl. jours. Fellow Royal Soc. Chemistry; mem. Controlled Release Soc. (gov. and officer S.C.I. pesticides div., Cert. of Merit 1988), Tropical Agrl. Assn., Am. Chem. Soc., Inst. of Biology London. Office: Newcastle U, Newcastle upon Tyne NE1 7RU, UK

WILKINS, ROBERT HENRY, neurosurgeon, editor; b. Pitts., Aug. 18, 1934; s. George H. and Mary M. (Lemon) W.; m. Gloria A. Kohl, Dec. 28, 1957; children: Michael I., Jeffrey K., Elizabeth A. BS, U. Pitts., 1955, MD, 1959. Diplomate Am. Bd. Neurol. Surgery. Intern, resident gen. surgery Duke U. Med. Ctr., Durham, N.C., 1959-61, resident neurosurgery, 1963-68, asst. prof. neurosurgery, 1968-72, prof. neurosurgery, chief div. neurosurgery, 1976-96; clin. assoc. surgery br. Nat. Cancer Inst., Bethesda, Md., 1961-63; chmn. dept. neurosurgery Scott and White Clinic, Temple, Tex., 1972-75; assoc. prof. neurosurgery U. Pitts., 1975-76; lectr. Cook County Grad. Sch. Medicine, Chgo., 1976—; attending neurosurgeon Durham VA Hosp., 1968-72, 78—; mem. Nat. Adv. Coun. Nat. Inst. Neurol. Disorders and Stroke, 1989-92. Co-editor: Neurosurgery, 2d edit., 3 vols., 1996, Neurosurgery Updates I and II, 1990, 91, Neurosurgery Operative Atlas, 1991—, Principles of Neurosurgery, 1994; editor Clin. Neurosurgery, 1972-75; assoc. editor Surg. Neurology, 1975-76; founding editor Neurosurgery, 1977-82; mem. editl. bd. Jour. Neurosurgery, 1987-96, chmn., 1996—; neurosurgery editor Key Neurology and Neurosurgery, 1993-96, Yr. Book of Neurology and Neurosurgery, 1994—. Recipient Travel award Copenhagen, Nat. Inst. Neurol. Diseases and Blindness, Royal Australasian Coll. Surgeons, Found. lectr. Adelaide 1986. Fellow ACS (gov. 1996); mem. Congress Neurol. Surgeons (pres. 1979-80), Am. Assn. Neurol. Surgeons (treas. 1989-92), So. Neurosurg. Soc. (sec. 1988-91, pres. 1992-93), Soc. Neurol. Surgeons (v.p. 1995-96), Am. Bd. Neurol. Surgery (dir. 1991—, chmn. 1996—), Phi Beta Kappa, Alpha Omega Alpha. Democrat. Episcopalian. Office: Duke U Med Ctr PO Box 3807 Durham NC 27710-3807

WILKINSON, ALAN HERBERT, nephrologist, medical educator; b. Johannesburg, So. Africa, July 11, 1948; came to U.S., 1985; s. Raymond C. and Nonie (Levick) W.; m. Angelika A. E. Adami, Dec. 22, 1973; one child: Rebecca Kate Adami. BS in Physiology, Biochem., Philosophy, U. Witwatersrand, So. Africa, 1969, BS with honors in Biochemistry, 1970, MB, BCh, 1975. Visiting assoc. Dept. Internal Medicine U. Iowa, Iowa City, 1987-88; assoc. prof. of medicine UCLA Sch. Med., L.A., 1988-95, prof. med., 1995—; dir. clin. nephrology UCLA Dept. Med., L.A., 1988-93, dir. kidney and pancreas transplantation, 1993—; bd. dirs. UCLA Ctr. Health Schs., 1994-97. Contbr. articles to profl. jours. Mem. Nat. Kidney Fdn. Steering Comm., U.S. Transplant Games, L.A., 1992. Recipient Exceptional Svc. award, Nat. Kidney Fdn, S.C., 1992. Fellow Nat. Kidney Rsch.; mem. Am. Soc. Transplant Physicians, Internat. Nephrology Soc., Am. Soc. Nephrology, Royal Coll. Physicians (Eng.). Office: UCLA Dept of Med Box 951693 200 Medical Plz Los Angeles CA 90095-1693

WILKINSON, GRANT ROBERT, pharmacology educator; b. Derby, U.K., Aug. 27, 1941; came to U.S., 1966; s. Arthur Henry and Gwendoline Mary (Fox) W.; m. Margaret Kay Fletcher, Aug. 8, 1964 (div. Apr. 1978); children: Grant Russell, Nicole Estelle; m. June Zoe Dass, July 12, 1978 (div. Jan. 1995); children: Tracey Allyson, Ericka Lynne. BSc in Pharmacy, U. Manchester, 1963; PhD, U. London, 1966. Postdoctoral fellow U. Calif., San Francisco, 1966-68; asst. prof. U. Ky., Lexington, 1968-71; asst. prof. Vanderbilt U., Nashville, 1971-73, assoc. prof., 1973-78, prof. of pharmacology, 1978—; cons. NIH, Bethesda, Md., 1972—, NRC, NAS, Washington, 1986-87, 92-94, also pharm. industry: mem. editorial adv. bd. various jours. in field. Author: Drug Metabolism and Disposition: Considerations in Clinical Pharmacology, 1985; contbr. over 200 articles and revs. to profl. publs. Recipient NIH Merit award, 1991. Fellow AAAS (sect. chmn. 1986-87), Am. Assn. Pharm. Sci.; mem. Am. Soc. for Pharmacology and Exptl. Therapeutics, Am. Soc. Clin. Pharmacology and Therapeutics (Rawls-Palmer Progress in Medicine award 1996). Office: Vanderbilt U Dept Pharmacology Nashville TN 37232-6600

WILKINSON, JAMES SPENCER, general physician; b. Wake Forest, N.C., Sept. 26, 1974; s. Robert Watson and Ella Houston (Holding) W.; m. Eva Elizabeth Hitchner, June 21, 1939; children Carol Lynn, James Spencer Jr. MD, U. Pa., 1938, MSc, 1949. Diplomate Am. Bd. Dermatology. Intern Jersey City Med. Ctr., 1939-40, Marine Hosp., Boston, 1940-41; fellow U. Pa. Grad. Sch., Phila., 1946-49; pvt. practice James Wilkinson MD, PA, Raleigh, N.C., 1949—. Capt. U.S. Air Force, 1942-46. Mem. AMA, Raleigh Acad. Medicine, Assn. Mil. Surgeons U.S., Wake County Med. Soc., N.C. Med. Soc., Air Force Assn. Office: James S Wilkinson MD PA 903 W Peace St Raleigh NC 27605

WILKINSON, JOAN KRISTINE, nurse, pediatric clinical specialist; b. Rochester, Minn., June 15, 1953; d. A. Ray and Ruth Audrey (Wegwart) Kubly; m. Robert Morris Wilkinson, June 14, 1975; children: Michael Robert, Kathryn Ann. BS in Nursing, U. Wis., 1975; MS, U. Colo., 1986. RN. Team leader Mendota Mental Health Inst., Madison, Wis., 1975-76; care leader Boulder (Colo.) Psychiat. Inst., 1976-78; pub. health nurse, head nurse Rocky Mountain Poison Ctr., Denver, 1978-83; research teaching asst. U. Colo. Health Scis. Ctr., Denver, 1986-87. Disaster nurse ARC, Boulder, 1976—; participant community service United Way, Denver, 1981-84; vol. nurse Channel 9 Health Fair, Boulder, 1983. Fellow U. Colo. Health Scis. Ctr., 1986; recipient Recognition cert. ARC, Madison, 1978, Gold award United Way, Denver, 1981, Outstanding Citizen award Boulder, 1990, Torch award for outstanding leader Girl Scouts, 1995. Mem. Colo. Nurses Assn. (dist. 12 scholar 1983-86), Am. Nurses Assn., World Health Assn., Sigma Tau Theta. Lutheran. Home: 1195 Hancock Dr Boulder CO 80303-1101 Office: Denver Vis Nurse Assn 3801 E Florida Ste 800 Denver CO 80210

WILKINSON, LOUISE CHERRY, psychology educator, dean; b. Phila., May 15, 1948; m. Alex Cherry Wilkinson; 1 child, Jennifer Cherry. B.A. magna cum laude with honors, Oberlin Coll., 1970; Ed.M., Ed.D., Harvard U., 1974. Prof., chmn. dept. ednl. psychology U. Wis., Madison, 1976-85; prof., exec. officer Grad. Sch. Ph.D. Program CUNY, N.Y.C., 1984-86; prof. II, dean Grad. Sch. Edn. Rutgers U., 1986—; mem. Nat. rev. bd. Nat. Inst. Edn., 1977, 85, 87; cons. Nat. Ctr. for Bilingual Rsch., 1982, 84, U.S. Dept. Edn., 1995-96; adv. bd. Nat. Reading Rsch. Ctr., 1992—. Co-author: Communicating for Learning, 1991; editor: Communicating in Classroom, 1982, Social Context of Instruction, 1984, Gender Influences in the Classroom; mem. editorial bds. and contbr. articles to profl. jours. Fellow Am. Psychol. Assn., Am. Psychol. Soc.; mem. Internat. Assn. for Study Child Lang., Am. Ednl. Rsch. Assn. (v.p. 1990-92, program chair 1997). Home: 3 Andrews Ln Princeton NJ 08540-7633 Office: Rutgers U Grad Sch Edn 10 Seminary Pl New Brunswick NJ 08901-1108

WILKINSON, RALPH RUSSELL, biochemistry educator, toxicologist; b. Portland, Oreg., Feb. 20, 1930; s. Tracy Chandler and Lavern (Russell) W.; m. Evelyn Marie Wickman, Aug. 5, 1956. BA, Reed Coll., 1953; PhD, U. Oreg., 1962; MBA, U. Mo., Kansas City, 1974. Rsch. chemist VA Hosp., Kansas City, Mo., 1973-74; sr. rsch. chemist Midwest Rsch. Inst., Kansas City, 1975-84; prof. Rockhurst Coll., Kansas City, 1985-86, Cleve. Chiropractic Coll., Kansas City, 1987—; cons. in biochemistry, toxicology, environ. impact, tech. assessment, Kansas City, 1984—. Author: (book) Neurotoxins and Neurobiological Function, 1987; contbr. articles to profl. jours. Mem. Southtown Coun., Kansas City, Mo., 1989—, Spina Bifida Assn. Am., Kansas City, 1989—. Recipient NSF fellowship, 1959-60. Mem. Am. Chem. Soc., Sigma Xi. Home: 7911 Charlotte St Kansas City MO 64131

WILKINSON, ROBERT SHAW, JR., physician; b. Bklyn., July 11, 1928; s. Robert Shaw and Melissa Ruth (Royster) W.; m. Carolyn Elizabeth Cobb, June 24, 1951; children: Amy Elizabeth, Karin Lynn, Robert Montague. BA, Dartmouth Coll., 1950; MD, NYU, 1955. Diplomate Am. Bd. Internal Medicine. Intern Kings County Hosp., Bklyn., 1955-56; asst. resident in medicine Upstate Med. Ctr., Syracuse, N.Y., 1958-59, resident in medicine, 1959, rsch. fellow in medicine, 1960-61, asst. instr. in medicine, 1961-62; staff physician Group Health Assn., Washington, 1962-68; prin., pvt. practice in internal medicine Sadin, Wilkinson, Fidler, & Koritzinsky, Washington, 1968—; clin. instr. in medicine George Washington U. Sch. Medicine, Washington, 1962-67, asst. clin. prof. in medicine, 1967-74, assoc. clin. prof. medicine, 1974—; attending physician George Washington U. Hosp., 1962—; med. advisor Inter-Am. Devel. Bank, 1976—. Contbr. articles to Am. Heart Jour., Am. Jour. Cardiology, Circulation. Bd. dirs. Cmty. Fed. Savs. and Loan, Washington, 1974-81, Homemaker Health and Svc., Washington, 1982-85, also mem. adv. bd., 1985—. Capt. U.S. Med. Corps, 1956-58. Recipient Disting. Achievement award (nation's capitol affiliate) Am. Heart Assn., 1986, Alumni award Dartmouth Coll., 1987. Fellow ACP (chmn. credentials com., Gov.'s coun. D.C. chpt. 1996—); mem. AMA, Acad. Medicine Washington D.C. (v.p. 1996—). Democrat. Episcopal. Home: 4827 16th St NW Washington DC 20011 Office: 2141 K St NW Ste 401 Washington DC 20037

WILL, JANE ANNE, psychologist; b. Evansville, Ind., Feb. 6, 1945; d. Edwin Francis and Frances Elizabeth (Patry) W. BA in Edn., St. Benedict's Coll., Ferdinand, Ind., 1968; MA in Edn., MS in Clin. Psychology, U. Evansville, 1973, 1987; MA in Christian Spirituality, Creighton U., 1979; D Psychology, Fla. Tech., Melbourne, 1991. Lic. psychologist, Ind.; joined Sisters of St. Benedict, Inc., Roman Cath. Ch. Tchr. Ireland (Ind.) Jr. H.S., 1969-76, Meml. H.S., Evansville, Ind., 1976-77; dir. recruitment and tng. Sisters of St. Benedict, Inc., Ferdinand, Ind., 1978-84, cons. admissions bd., 1984—; tchr. Mater Dei H.S., Evansville, 1984-88; therapist Osceola Ctr., Kissimme, Fla., 1989-90, Charter Hosp., Kissimme, Fla., 1989-90; intern VA Med. Ctr., St. Louis, 1990-91; clin. psychologist St. Mary's Health Care Svcs., Evansville, 1991—; adj. prof. Bresica Coll., Owensboro, Ky., 1978-80, St. Mary's of the Woods Coll., Terre Haute, Ind., 1980-84. Author jour. Ind. Reading Quarterly, 1973. Bd. dirs. Nat. Formation Dirs., Washington, 1982-84; chairperson region VII Formation Conf., Mich. and Ind., 1982-84. Luise Whiting Bell scholar, 1986. Mem. APA, Ind. Psychol. Assn., Southwestern Ind. Psychol. Assn. (treas. 1992, sec. 1993, v.p. 1994, pres. 1995), Vanderburgh County Mental Health Assn. (bd. dirs. 1994—, v.p. 1996). Roman Catholic. Home: 725 Wedeking Ave Evansville IN 47711-3861

WILL, JERRIE ANN, psychologist; b. Hazleton, Pa., Apr. 6, 1950; d. Gordon John and Doris Griffiths (Brown) W.; m. Gene G. Kuehneman, June 26, 1982 (div. Oct. 1984). BA, Bucknell U., 1971; MA, W.Va. U., 1974, PhD, 1977. Lic. psychologist, Maine. Teaching fellow W.Va. U., Morgantown, 1974-76; clin. psychology intern U. Md. Hosp., Balt., 1976-77; sr. child psychologist Michael Reese Hosp., Chgo., 1977-82; cons. psychologist Ridgeway Psychiat. Hosp., Chgo., 1982-83, Sanford Sch. Dept., Maine, 1983—; pvt. practice Sanford and Wells, Maine, 1984—; team and child psychologist York County Counseling Svcs., Sanford, 1983-85; owner, mgr. Sanford Psychol. Assocs., 1987-95; panelist, reviewer NSF, 1976. Contbr. articles to profl. jours. NIMH Grantee, 1972-75. Mem. APA. Home: 314 Webhannet Dr Wells ME 04090-4225 Office: 100 Main St Sanford ME 04073-3523

WILL, THOMAS ERIC, psychologist; b. Feb. 28, 1949. BA in Edn., Concordia Coll., St. Paul, 1972; MPH, U. Minn., 1980, postgrad. in epidemiology, 1980-81; PsyD with distinction, Forest Inst. Profl. Psychology, Des Plaines, Ill., 1986. Lic. psychologist. Rsch. asst. dept. epidemiology Nat. Cancer Inst. U. Minn., Mpls., 1980-81; mem. crisis intervention staff Forest Psychiat. Hosp., Des Plaines, 1982-83; psychiat. researcher Ill. State Psychiat. Inst., Chgo., 1983-84; psychometrician Evaluation Ctr./U. Chgo. Med. Ctr., 1983-84; health psychologist Group Health, Inc. Mental Health Ctr., Mpls., 1986—; assoc. core faculty Minn. Sch. Profl. Psychology, Mpls., 1988—; adj. asst. prof. Forest Inst. Profl. Psychology, Des Plaines, 1983-85; regional faculty The Fielding Inst., Santa Barbara, Calif., 1991—. Contbr. articles to profl. jours. Recipient grants, Group Health, Inc., 1988. Mem. APA, Nat. Acad. Neuropsychology, Nat. Register of Health Svc. Providers in Psychology, Psi Chi. Office: Health Ptnrs Univ Ave Clinic 2701 University Ave SE Minneapolis MN 55414-3233

WILLARD, FAYE, consumer activist, small business owner, association executive; b. Reinbeck Iowa, Dec. 28, 1921; m. Thomas G. Blackwell, Jr., Mar. 1940 (dec. Mar. 1951); children: Barbara, Janet, Steven. Grad. Strayer Bus. Sch., Washington, 1939. Founder, organizer Am. Assn. Dental Victims, 1977—; consumer activist in dental reform. Office: 3318 E 7th St Long Beach CA 90804-5003

WILLARD, RALPH LAWRENCE, surgery educator, physician, former college president; b. Manchester, Iowa, Apr. 6, 1922; s. Hosea B. and Ruth A. (Hazelrigg) W.; m. Margaret Dyer Dennis, Sept. 26, 1969; children: Laurie, Jane, Ann, H. Thomas. Student, Cornell Coll., 1940-42, Coe Coll., 1945; D.O., Kirksville Coll. Osteo. Medicine, 1949; EdD (hon.), U. North Tex., 1985; ScD (hon.), W.Va. Sch. Osteo. Medicine, 1993. Intern Kirksville Osteo. Hosp., 1949-50, resident in surgery, 1954-57; chmn. dept. surgery Davenport Osteo. Hosp., 1957-68; dean, prof. surgery Kirksville Coll. Osteo. Medicine, 1969-73; asso. dean acad. affairs, prof. surgery Mich. State U. Coll. Osteo. Medicine, 1974-75; dean Tex. Coll. Osteopathic Medicine, 1975-76, pres., 1981-85, prof. surgery, 1985-87; v.p. med. affairs North Tex. State U., Denton, 1976-81; assoc. dean W.Va. Sch. Osteo. Medicine, Lewisburg, 1988-91; mem. Nat. Adv. Council Edn. for Health Professions, 1971-73, Iowa Gov.'s Council Hosps. and Health Related Facilities, 1965-68; chmn. council deans Am. Assn. Colls. Osteo. Medicine, 1970-73, pres., 1979-80. Served with USAAF, 1942-45; Served with USAF, 1952-53; col. USAFR, ret. Decorated D.F.C., Air medal with 4 oak leaf clusters, Meritorious Svc. medal, Legion of Merit; recipient Robert A. Kistner Educator award Am. Assn. Colls. Osteo. Medicine, 1989. Fellow Am. Coll. Physician Execs., Am. Coll. Osteo. Surgeons; mem. Am. Osteo. Assn. (Disting. Svc. cert. 1992), Tex. Osteo. Assn., W.Va. Soc. Osteo. Medicine, Am. Acad. Osteopathy, Acad. Osteo. Dirs. Med. Edn., Aerospace Med. Assn., Flying Physicians Assn., Quiet Birdmen, Davis-Monthan Officers Club, Masons, Shriners, Lewisburg Rotary, Internat. Comanche Soc., Order of Daedalians. Democrat. Episcopalian. Home: PO Box 749 Lewisburg WV 24901-0749 Office: WVa Sch Osteo Medicine 400 N Lee St Lewisburg WV 24901-1128

WILLCUTT, MITCHELL STUART, surgeon assistant; b. Birmingham, Ala.; s. Herman Cleveland and Willene (Lowery) W. BS in Psychology and Biology, U. Montovallo, 1990; BS in Surgery, U. Ala., Birmingham, 1992. Cert. surgeon's asst. Phys. therapy asst. Lakeshore Rehab. Hosp., Birmingham, 1986-89; psychiat. asst. The Children's Hosp., Birmingham, 1990-92; surgeons asst. U. Ala., Birmingham, 1992—; tchr., student dir. Surgeon's Asst. Program, U. Ala. Birmingham, 1992-95. Republican. Baptist. Home: 309 Kenilworth Dr Homewood AL 35209

WILLEMS, RICHARD, molecular biologist; b. Parnu, Estonia, Nov. 28, 1944; s. Leo Endel and Dorrit Regina (Seiling) W.; m. Anne Vainer, May 8, 1970; children: Martin, Kristin. MD, Tartu (Estonia) U., 1968, PhD in Biochemistry, 1972; DSc in Molecular Biology, Moscow U., 1983. Rsch. fellow Tartu U., 1972-75, sr. researcher, 1976-77; vis. scientist Uppsala (Sweden) U., 1975-76, Edinburgh (Scotland) U., 1977-78; sr., prin. researcher Inst. Chem. Physics and Biophysics, Tartu, 1978-85; dir. Estonian Biocentre, Tartu, 1985—; prof. Tartu U., 1986—; mem. Presidium of Acad. Scis., Tallinn, 1987—; v.p. Estonian Acad. Sci., 1995—. Contbr. articles to profl. jours. Bd. dirs. Estonian Soroz Found., 1990-92. Mem. Estonian Acad. Scis., Royal Swedish Acad. Scis. (fgn. mem.), Human Genome Orgn. Home: 126/3 Pallas Str, EE2400 Tartu Estonia Office: Estonian Biocentre, 23 Riia Str, EE2400 Tartu Estonia

WILLETT, WALTER CHURCHILL, epidemiologist, educator; b. Hart, Mich., June 20, 1945; s. Elwin Lintin and Lawain (Churchill) W.; m. Gail Valerae Pettiford, June 11, 1973; children: Amani, Kamali. Student, Mich. State U., 1963-66; MD, U. Mich., 1970; MPH, Harvard U., 1973, PhD, 1980. Diplomate Am. Bd. Internal Medicine. Lectr. in medicine U. Dar es Salaam, Tanzania, 1974-75, head community health dept., 1975-77; fellow clin. epidemiology Channing Lab. Med. Sch., Harvard U., Boston, 1977-80; asst. prof. epidemiology Sch. Pub. Health, Harvard U., Boston, 1980-84, assoc. prof. epidemiology, 1984-88, prof. epidemiology and nutrition, 1988—, chmn. dept. nutrition, 1991—; statis. cons. New Eng. Jour. Medicine, Boston, 1987—. Author: Nutritional Epidemiology, 1989; contbr. over 350 articles to sci. publs. Mem. Am. Epidemiol. Soc., Soc. for Epidemiol. Rsch., Am. Inst. Nutrition, Alpha Omega Alpha. Office: Harvard Sch Pub Health Dept Nutrition 677 Huntington Ave Boston MA 02115-6028

WILLETTE, PAUL A., emergency physician; b. Wakefield, Mass., May 26, 1964; s. Alfred F. and Anne T. (Saterjale) W.; m. Mary C. Willette; children: Spencer, Paul. BS in Biology, Merrimack Coll., 1986; DO, Coll. Osteo. Medicine, Kansas City, Mo., 1990. Diplomate Am. Bd. Emergency Physicians; cert. ACLS, ATLS, PALS. Intern Botsford Gen. Hosp., Farmington Hills, Mich., 1990-91; resident emergency medicine Akron (Ohio) Gen. Med. Ctr., Children's Hosp. Med. Ctr., 1991-94; attending physician emergency medicine Wm. W. Backus Hosp., Norwich, Conn., 1994—; med. dir. Mohegan EMS, Montville, Conn., 1996—. Mem. editl. bd. advisors Emergency Physicians Monthly, 1996—. Mem. Am. Coll. Emergency Physicians, Conn. Coll. Emergency Physicians. Home: 18 Willow Ln East Lyme CT 06333

WILLEY, JAMES LEE, dentist; b. Colorado Springs, Colo., Oct. 26, 1953; s. Elwood James and Dorothy Jean (Norton) W.; m. Catherine Margaret Whitmer, Aug. 23, 1975; children: Andrew James and David Lee (twins). BA, So. Ill. U., 1975; BS in Dentistry, U. Ill., Chgo., 1977, DDS, 1979; MBA, No. Ill. U., 1986. Pvt. practice dentistry Elburn, Ill., 1979—; lectr. Dental Arts Labs., Peoria, Ill., 1981-90. Trustee Paul W. Clopper Meml. Found., 1989—, chmn. fund raising com., 1991—, treas., 1992—; mem. adminstrv. bd. Geneva United Meth. Ch., 1991-92; asst. scoutmaster Boy Scouts Am., Elburn, 1995—; spokesperson Prevent Abuse and Neglect Through Dental Awareness, 1995—; village trustee Village of Elburn, 1995—, mem. fin. com., 1995-96, mem. police com., 1995, mem. pub. works com., 1996. Recipient Certificate of Merit, Swissedent Found., Glendale, Calif., 1983; fellow Clopper Found., 1992. Fellow Am. Endodontic Soc.; mem. ADA (Outstanding Young Dentist Leader award 1992), Ill. State Dental Soc. (alt. del. 1990, spokesperson 1990—, del. 1991-92, dental edn. com. 1991-93, chmn. 1994—, vice speaker ho. of dels. 1992-93), Fox River Valley Dental Soc. (bd. dirs. 1988-93, sec. 1989, treas. 1990, v.p. 1991,pres. 1992), Legis. Interest Com. Ill. Dentists (bd. dirs. 1988—, exec. com. 1989—, 2d v.p. 1991-92, 1st v.p. 1993-94, pres. 1995-96). Home: 711 N 3rd St Elburn IL 60119-9018 Office: 135 S Main St # 7G Elburn IL 60119-9142

WILLHITE, CALVIN CAMPBELL, toxicologist; b. Salt Lake City, Apr. 27, 1952; s. Jed Butler and Carol (Campbell) W.; m. Tandra Pauline Jorgensen, Aug. 14, 1982. BS, Utah State U., 1974, MS, 1977; PhD, Dartmouth Coll., 1980. Toxicologist USDA, Berkeley, Calif., 1980-85, State of Calif., Berkeley, 1985—; adj. assoc. prof. toxicol. Utah State U., 1984-94. Mem. editl. bd. Toxicology and Applied Pharmacology, 1989—; editor N.Y. Acad. Scis., 1993, Toxicology, 1996—, Jour. Toxicological Environ. Health, 1996; contbr. articles on birth defects to profl. jours. Nat. Inst. Child Health and Human Devel. grantee, 1985, 89, 92, March of Dimes Birth Defects Found. grantee, 1987-91, Hoffman LaRoche grantee, 1992-94. Mem. Soc. Toxicology (mem. program com. 1995—, Frank R. Blood award 1986), Teratology Soc. (chair pub. affairs), Am. Conf. Govt. Indsl. Hygienists (TLV com.). Republican. Mem. United Ch. of Christ. Home: 2863 Sanderling Dr Fremont CA 94555 Office: State Calif 700 Heinz Ave Berkeley CA 94710-2721

WILLIAMS, BRYAN, university dean, medical educator; b. Longview, Tex., July 28; s. Lewis Bryan and Margaret Louise (Smart) W.; m. Frances Montgomery, Mar. 31, 1950; children: Harrison, Amy, Philip, Nickolas, Margaret, Lincoln. MD, Southwestern Med. Sch., 1947. Diplomate Am. Bd. Internal Medicine. Pvt. practice Dallas, 1957-70; prof. internal medicine, assoc. dean student affairs Southwestern Med. Sch., 1970-90, prof. internal medicine emeritus, dean student affairs emeritus. Fellow ACP; mem. Inst. Medicine Nat. Acad. Scis. (charter). Home: 3419 Dartmouth Ave Dallas TX 75205-2806

WILLIAMS, CAROL JORGENSEN, social work educator; b. New Brunswick, N.J., Aug. 12, 1944; d. Einar Arthur and Mildred Estelle (Clayton) Jorgensen; m. Oneal Alexander Williams, July 4, 1980. BA, Douglass Coll., 1966; MS in Computer Sci., Stevens Inst. Tech., 1986; MSW, Rutgers U., 1971, PhD in Social Policy, 1981. Child welfare worker Bur. Children's Svcs., Jersey City, 1966-67, Outagamie County Dept. Social Svcs., Appleton, Wis., 1967-69; supr. WIN N.J. Divsn. Youth and Family Svcs., New Brunswick, 1969-70; coord. Outreach Plainfield (N.J.) Pub. Libr., 1972-76; rsch. project dir. County and Mcpl. Govt. Study Commn., N.J. State Legislature, 1976-79; prof. social work Kean Coll. N.J., Union, 1979—; assessment liaison social work program Kean Coll. of N.J., Union, 1987—, dir. MSW program, 1995—; chmn. faculty senate gen. edn. com., Kean Coll. N.J., 1990-94, chmn. faculty senate ad hoc com. for 5-yr. review of gen. edn. program, 1991-93, mem. retention and tenure com. Sch. of Liberal Arts, 1988-94, vice chmn., 1992-94; cons. N.J. div. Youth and Family Svcs., 1979-93, Assn. for Children N.J., 1985-88; cons., evaluator Thomas A. Edison Coll., 1977—, emm. acad. coun. and others. Mem. NOW, Coun. on Social Work Edn. (com. on info. tech.), Nat. Assn. Social Workers (chpt. com. on nominating and leadership identification 1990-92, co-chmn. 1991-92), Kean Coll. Fedn. Tchrs., Assn. Baccalaureate Program Dirs. (mem. com. on info. tech.). Democrat. Clubs: Good Sam (Agoura, Calif.); Outdoor World (Bushkill, Pa.). Home: 32 Halstead Rd New Brunswick NJ 08901-1619 Office: Kean Coll of NJ Social Work Program Morris Ave Union NJ 07083-7117

WILLIAMS, CAROLE ANN, cytotechnologist; b. Duquesne, Pa., Apr. 14, 1934; d. Theodore Wylie and Dorothy Belle (Mehrmann) Williams; BS, Chatham Coll., 1956; postgrad. Case-Western Res. U., 1956-57; MS Calif. State U., 1989. Cytotechnologist, Clin. Path. Lab. of Paul Gross, Pitts., 1957-59; chief cytotechnologist, teaching supr. Presbyn. U. Hosp., Pitts., 1959-63; staff Pathology Lab. of Drs. Armanini & Wegner, Stockton, Calif., 1964; chief cytotechnologist, teaching supr. Hosp. of Good Samaritan, Los Angeles, 1964-89; dir. cytotechnology tng. program UCLA Med. Ctr., 1989—; conductor workshops in field. Mem. Am. Soc. Clin. Pathologists (cytotech. exam. com. bd. registry 1978, mem. bd. govs. 1990-95), Calif. Assn. Cytotechnologists (pres. 1967-68, 72-73), Internat. Acad. Cytology, Am. Soc. Cytopathology (Technologist of Yr. award 1981). Republican. Presbyterian. Home: 2460 Stoner Ave Los Angeles CA 90064-1326 Office: 10833 Le Conte Ave Los Angeles CA 90024

WILLIAMS, CAROLYN ANTONIDES, university dean; b. Louisville, Oct. 27, 1939; d. John Dwight and Dorothy Ida Marie (Hoffman) Antonides; m. Frank Canon Williams, Dec. 26, 1961. BS with honors in Nursing, Tex. Woman's U., 1961; MS in Pub. Health Nursing Edn., U. N.C., 1965, PhD in Epidemiology, 1969. Asst. prof. nursing Emory U., Atlanta, 1968, assoc. prof., 1969, prof., dir. grad. programs and rsch., 1969-71; assoc. prof. nursing, asst. prof. epidemiology U. N.C., Chapel Hill, 1971-81, assoc. prof. nursing, rsch. assoc. Health Svcs. Rsch. Ctr., from 1971, assoc. prof. epidemiology, 1981-84; dean Coll. Nursing, U. Ky., Lexington, 1984—; mem. Pres.'s Commn. Study of Ethical Problems in Medicine and Biomed. and Behavioral Rsch., 1980-82; chair rsch. adv. com. Am. Nurses Found., 1979-81; mem. planning com. study of nursing and nursing edn. Inst. Medicine of NAS, 1980; cons. WHO in S.Am. Mem. editorial bd. Family and Community Health, 1977-90, Advances in Nursing Sci., 1979-88, Internat. Jour. Nursing Studies, 1981—; also articles, chpts. to books. USPHS fellow U. N.C., 1969. Fellow APHA (publs. bd., Young Practitioner award 1973), Am. Acad. Nursing (pres. 1983-85); mem. ANA (chair commn. nursing rsch. 1980-82), Coun. Nurse Researchers, Soc. Epidemiol. Rsch., Delta Omega, Sigma Theta Tau (bd. dirs.). Democrat. Baptist. Office: U Ky Coll Nursing 500 S Limestone St Lexington KY 40506*

WILLIAMS, CECILIA LEE PURSEL, optometrist; b. Lewisburg, Pa., Nov. 15, 1948; d. Lee LaVerne and Geraldine May (Steininger) Pursel; student Lycoming Coll., 1966-68; B.S. (Women's Aux. of Pa. Optometrists scholar 1968-70, Pa. State grantee 1968-70), Pa. Coll. Optometry, 1970, O.D. (Women's Aux. of Pa. Optometrists scholar 1970-72, Pa. State grantee 1970-72), 1972; m. Richard Lee Williams, May 17, 1975; 1 son, Kent Lee. Research optometrist in soft lens materials Gumpelmayer Optik, Vienna, Austria, 1973; optometrist Sterling Optical Co. Contact Lens Center, Washington, 1974-79; pvt. practice optometry, Springfield, Va., 1980—. Recipient Clin. Efficiency award Pa. Coll. Optometry, 1972; lic. and/or cert. optometrist, D.C., Pa., N.Y., N.J., Va. Mem. Optometric Center of Nation's Capital (dir. 1977-80), Am. Optometric Assn., Va. Optometric Assn., No. Va. Optometric Soc., Nat. Honor Soc. for Optometry, Omega Delta. Home: 3600 Wilton Hall Ct Alexandria VA 22310-2176 Office: 6320A Backlick Rd Springfield VA 22150

WILLIAMS, DANIEL T., psychiatrist; b. N.Y.C., Oct. 27, 1944; s. Herbert M. and Charlotte (Turk) W.; m. Marcia Bergtraum, Nov. 25, 1981; children: Harel Michael, Marc Aaron. BA magna cum laude, Columbia U., 1965; MD, Cornell U., 1969. Diplomate Am. Bd. Psychiatry and Neurology. Intern in pediatrics Albert Einstein Med. Ctr., Bronx, N.Y., 1969-70; resident in psychiatry Mt. Sinai Med. Ctr., N.Y.C., 1970-72; fellow in child psychiatry Columbia U.-Presbyn. Med. Ctr., N.Y.C., 1972-74, instr. in clin. psychiatry, 1974-77, asst. in clin. psychiatry, 1977-78, asst. clin. prof. psychiatry, 1978-83, assoc. prof. clin. psychiatry, 1983—, dir. pediatric neuropsychiatry, 1978—. Contbr. articles to profl. jours.; co-editor: (2 vols.) Handbook of Clinical Assessment of Children and Adolescents, 1988; author numerous chpts. in books. Bd. mem. N.Y. Coun. on Child Psychiatry, 1988-90, Epilepsy Inst., N.Y.C., 1980—, A.P. Gold Found., Englewood, N.J., 1988—. Recipient Laughlin award, Outstanding Resident, Nat. Psychiatric Endowment Fund, 1974. Fellow Am Psychiatric Assn., Am. Acad. of Child and Adolescent Psychiatry; mem. Phi Beta Kappa. Office: Columbia-Presbyn Med Ctr 161 Ft Washington Ave New York NY 10032-3713

WILLIAMS, DARRYL MARLOWE, medical educator; b. Denver, Apr. 3, 1938; s. Archie Malvin and Dorothy Merle (Grapes) W.; m. Susan Arlene Moore, June 24, 1966; children: Carol Ruth, Peter Todd, Sarah Elizabeth. Student, U. Colo., 1956-58; BS, Colo. State U., 1993; MD, MS in Anatomy, Baylor U., 1964. Diplomate Am. Bd. Internal Medicine, Am. Bd. Hematology. Intern and resident Baylor Affiliated Hosps., Houston, 1964-66, 67-68; resident U. Utah, Salt Lake City, 1966-67, fellow in hematology, 1968-73, asst. prof., 1973-77; assoc. prof. La State U., Shreveport, 1977-81, prof., 1981-90, chief hematology sect., 1977-85, asst. dean/rsch., 1981-85, dean Sch. Medicine, 1985-90; prof. medicine, dean Sch. Medicine Tex. Tech U. Health Scis. Ctr., Lubbock, 1990-95; prof. medicine office border health and area health edn. Tex. Tech. Health Scis. Ctr., El Paso, 1995—, also bd. dirs., 1995—; dir. med. edn. Cmty. Partnership Tex. Tech. Health Sci. Ctr., El Paso, 1995—; mem. hemophilia adv. com. La. Legislature, Baton Rouge, 1977-83; vice chair La. Lung and Cancer Bd., New Orleans, 1984-90; pres. N.W. La. AIDS Task Force, Shreveport, 1987. Mem. Am. Heart Assn., Lubbock chpt., Shreveport Biracial Commn., 1988, Lubbock Indigent Health Care Coalition Task Force, 1991-92, Health Professions Edn. Adv. Com., Lubbock Friends of Pub. Radio; vice chair health profls. edn. adv. com. Tex. Coord. Bd. Higher Edn., 1992-95. Recipient award Nat. Ski Patrol System, Salt Lake City, 1975. Fellow ACP, Am. Coll. Nutrition; mem. AMA, Am. Soc. Hematology, Am. Inst. Nutrition, Am. Soc. Clin. Nutrition, Tex. Med. Assn. (physicians oncology edn. com.), Royal Soc. Medicine, Alpha Omega Alpha. Office: Tex Tech Health Sci Ctr Health Scis Ctr 4800 Alberta Ave El Paso TX 79905

WILLIAMS, DAVID ALLAN, dentist, educator; b. Dayton, Ohio, June 30, 1949; s. Robert Eugene and Mary Ellen (Moore) W.; m. Diane Elizabeth Costello, Nov. 12, 1993. BS, Mich. State U., 1971; DDS, Case Western Res. U., 1975. Clin. assoc. prof. Northwestern U. Dental Sch., Chgo., 1978—; gen. practice dentistry Northbrook, Ill., 1979—, Chgo., 1980-96. Bd. dirs. United Way of Northbrook. With USN, 1975-78. Armed Forces Health Profls. Scholar, 1972-75. Fellow Acad. Gen. Dentistry; mem. ADA (commn. on dental accreditation), Ill. Dental Soc., Chgo. Dental Soc., Acad. Operative Dentistry, Northbrook Rotary, Delta Tau Delta. Lutheran. Office: Ste 801 666 Dundee Rd Northbrook IL 60062-2734

WILLIAMS, DAVID VANDERGRIFT, organizational psychologist; b. Balt., Feb. 5, 1943; s. Laurence Leighton and Mary Duke (Warfield) W.; m. Diane M. Gayeski, Aug. 23, 1980; 1 child, Evan David Williams. BA, Gettysburg (Pa.) Coll., 1965; MA, Temple U., 1967; PhD, U. Pa., 1971. Asst. prof. psychology Ithaca (N.Y.) Coll., 1970-75, assoc. prof. psychology, 1975—; ptnr. OmniCom Assocs., Ithaca, 1979—; co-dir. Inst. Behavior-Econs., Ithaca, 1993—; cons. and speaker in field. Co-author: Interactive Media, 1985, (multimedia comms.), interactive multimedia software, 1979—; contbr. to books and articles to profl. jours. Bd. dirs. Ctr. for Religion, Ethics and Social Policy, Cornell U., 1975-77, Eco-Justice Task Force, Ithaca, 1975-78; trustee Montessori Sch. Ithaca, 1993—; Alternatives Fed. Credit Union, Ithaca, 1994—. Rsch. fellow U.S. Office of Edn., 1967-70; recipient various grants. Mem. APA, Nat. Soc. for Performance and Instrn., Am. Montessori Soc., Welsh Nat. Gymanfa Ganu Assn., Ithaca Yacht Club, Tau Kappa Epsilon. Office: OmniCom Assocs 407 Coddington Rd Ithaca NY 14850-6011

WILLIAMS, DEREK, JR., pharmaceutical professional; b. Ft. Rucker, Ala., June 25, 1958; s. Derek W. Sr. and Carol E. (Kaufman) W.; m. Penny L. Bradly, Apr. 22, 1991; children: Jason Brian, Courtney Elizabeth. AS, U. Nev., 1981; BA, U. Colo., 1984; MA, U. Nev., 1986; postgrad., Pepperdine U. Rsch. asst. U. Nev., Reno, 1984-86; surgical counselor St. Lukes Hosp., Denver, 1987-89; pub. health advisor Ctrs. for Disease Control, Atlanta,

1989-91; clin. rsch. assoc. Amgen, Inc., Thousand Oaks, Calif., 1991-92, regulatory affairs specialist, 1992—. Named Outstanding Young Men of Am., 1989-90. Mem. Assocs. Clin. Pharmacology, Regulatory Affairs Profls. Soc. Internat. Aids Soc., Am. Pub. Health Assn., Drug Info. Assn., Brit. Inst. Regulatory Affairs. Office: Amgen Inc 1840 De Havilland Dr Thousand Oaks CA 91320-1701

WILLIAMS, DREW DAVIS, surgeon; b. San Augustine, Tex., Jan. 18, 1935; s. Floyd Everett and Villamae (Morehead) W.; m. Marilyn Raus, June 27, 1958; children: Leslie, Cynthia, Matthew, Jennifer, Amelia. BS, Tex. A&M Coll., 1957; MD, U. Tex., 1960; grad., naval flight surgeon, U.S. Naval Sch. Aviation Medicine, Jan.-June, 1963. Diplomate Am. Bd. Surgery, Am. Bd. Quality Assurance and Utilization Rev. Physicians. Intern USPHS Hosp., Seattle, 1960-61; resident in gen. surgery U. Tex. Med. Br., Galveston, 1961-62, 64-68; resident pulmonary svc. M.D. Anderson Hosp., Houston, 3 months, 1968; pvt. practice gen. surgery Baytown, Tex., 1968—; active staff San Jacinto (Tex.) Meth. Hosp., 1968-95, chief of surgery, 1972, 73, pres. med. staff, 1976; mem. courtesy staff Bay Coast Hosp., Baytown, 1968-95; cons. staff Baytown Med. Ctr. Hosp., 1972-95; 1st chmn. dept. surgery in devel. of family practice residency program affiliated with Tex. Med. Sch., Houston, 1977; mem. Tex. State Bd. Med. Examiners, 1983-89, sec.-treas., 1984-88, pres., 1988-89; unit med. dir., clin. instr. dept. preventive medicine and cmty. health U. Tex. Med. Br., Galveston, 1995—. Contbr. articles to med. publs. Flight surgeon USN, 1962-64; lt. comdr. USNR, ret., 1967. Am. Cancer Soc. clin. fellow, 1966-67. Fellow ACS, AMA (Physicians Recognition award), Tex. Med. Assn.; mem. Tex. Med. Found. (fed. peer rev. group), Houston Surg. Soc. (pres. 1994), Southwestern Surg. Congress, Tex. Surg. Soc., Singleton Surg. Soc. (past pres.), Harris County Med. Soc. (chmn. coun. med. splty., mem. exec. bd. 1994), East Harris County Med. Soc. (pres. 1982), Baytown Surg. Soc., Sir William Osler Soc., Am. Cancer Soc. (pres. Baytown chpt. 1970-71), Sons of Republic Tex. (at large life), SAR (past pres. local chpt.), Soc. Descendents of Colonial Clergy, Magna Carta Barons (Somerset chpt.), Colonial Order of the Crown, Sovereign Colonial Soc.-Ams. of Royal Descent, Masons (32 degree), Shriners, KT, Gideons Internat., Phi Beta Pi. Democrat. Mem. Ch. of Christ. Home and Office: 1217 Kilgore Rd Baytown TX 77520-3912

WILLIAMS, GEORGE CHRISTOPHER, biologist, ecology and evolution educator; b. Charlotte, N.C., May 12, 1926; s. George Felix and Margaret (Steuart) W.; m. Doris Lee Calhoun, Jan. 25, 1951; children: Jacques, Sibyl, Judith, Phoebe. AB, U. Calif., Berkeley, 1949; PhD, UCLA, 1955; ScD (hon.), Queen's U., Kingston, Ont., Can., 1995. Instr. and asst. prof. Mich. State U., East Lansing, 1955-60; assoc. prof. dept. ecology and evolution SUNY, Stony Brook, 1960-66, prof., 1966-90; adj. prof. Queens U., Kingston, Ont., Can., 1980—. Author: Adaptation and Natural Selection, 1966, Sex and Evolution, 1975, Natural Selection: Domains, Levels and Challenges, 1992; co-author: Evolution and Ethics, 1989, (with R.M. Nesse) Why We Get Sick: The New Science of Darwinian Medicine, 1995; editor Quar. Rev. Biology, SUNY, 1965—. With U.S. Army, 1944-46. Recipient Eminent Ecologist award Ecol. Soc. Am., 1989, Daniel Giraud Elliot medal Nat. Acad. Sci., 1992; fellow Ctr. Adv. Study Behavioral Sci., Stanford, 1981-82, Guggenheim Found., 1988-89. Fellow AAAS, Soc. Study Evolution (v.p. 1973, pres. 1989), Nat. Acad. Sci., Am. Soc. Ichthyologists and Herpetologists, Am. Soc. Naturalists (editor 1974-79), Icelandic Natural History Soc. Office: SUNY Quarterly Review of Biology Stony Brook NY 11794

WILLIAMS, G(EORGE) MELVILLE, surgeon, medical educator; b. Soochow, China, Nov. 16, 1930; came to U.S., 1940; s. Melville Owens and Annie Lee (Young) W.; m. Lee Logan, June 12, 1955 (div. 1985); children: Curtiss John, Steven Hoyt, Lucy Roxanna, Elizabeth; m. Elizabeth Hopkins, Feb. 14, 1986; m. Elizabeth Hopkins, Feb. 14, 1986 (div.); m. Linda Parsons, Apr. 14, 1996. BA, Oberlin Coll., 1953; MD, Harvard U., 1957. Diplomate Am. Bd. Surgery. Spl. fellow NIH, Melbourne, Australia, 1963-64; instr. surgery Med. Coll. Va., Richmond, 1964-65, asst. prof. surgery, 1965-66, assoc. prof. surgery, 1966-67, prof. surgery, 1967-69; prof. surgery The Johns Hopkins U. Sch. Medicine, Balt., 1969—. Editor: Transplant Rejection. United Network Organ Sharing (pres. 1984-85). Capt. U.S. Army, 1960-62. Grantee NIH, 1969, 82, Am. Heart Assn., 1991. Mem. Am. Surg Assn., The Halsted Soc. (pres. 1983), Am. Soc. Transplant Surgeons (pres. 1982-83), So. Assn. for Vascular Surgery (pres. 1991). Democrat. Methodist. Office: Johns Hopkins Hosp 600 N Wolfe St Baltimore MD 21205-2110

WILLIAMS, GEORGE RAINEY, surgeon, educator; b. Atlanta, Oct. 25, 1926; s. George Rainey and Hildred (Russell) W.; m. Martha Vose, June 16, 1950; children: Bruce, Alden, Margaret, Rainey. Student, U. Tex., 1944-46; B.S., Northwestern U., 1948; M.B., 1950, M.D., 1950. Intern Johns Hopkins Hosp., 1950-51, William Stewart Halsted fellow surgery, 1951-52, asst. resident surgery, 1952-53, asst. resident surgeon, 1955-57, resident surgeon, 1957-58; practice medicine specializing in gen. and thoracic surgery Oklahoma City, 1958—; asst. prof. surgery U. Okla. Health Scis. Center, Oklahoma City, 1958-61; assoc. prof. U. Okla. Health Scis. Center, 1961-63; prof. surgery U. Okla. Health Scis. Center Coll. of Medicine, 1963—, chmn. dept. surgery, 1974—; interim dean U. Okla. Coll. Medicine, 1981-82, 85-86, 88-89; dir. Am. Bd. Surgery, 1975-81, vice chmn., 1979-81. Contbr. articles on gen. and thoracic surgery to profl. jours. Served lt., MC, 3d Inf. Div. AUS, 1953-55. Recipient Disting. Service citation U. Okla., 1982; named to Okla. Hall of Fame, 1986. Fellow ACS (sec. bd. govs. 1985-87, 1st v.p. 1989-90), Soc. Univ. Surgeons, Am. Assn. Thoracic Surgery, So. Surg. Assn., Am. Surg. Assn., Phi Beta Kappa, Delta Kappa Epsilon, Phi Beta Pi, Alpha Epsilon Delta, Alpha Omega Alpha, Pi Kappa Epsilon. Home: 6722 Country Club Dr Oklahoma City OK 73116-4706 Office: U Okla Dept Surgery PO Box 26307 Oklahoma City OK 73126-0307

WILLIAMS, GREGORY EDWARD, industrial hygienist; b. Middletown, Ohio, Sept. 27, 1954; s. Charles Edward and Irene Williams; m. Angela S. Preston, May 27, 1978; children: Matthew J, Rebekah E. BS in Biology, U. Cin., 1976, MS in Indsl. Hygiene, 1978. Cert. indsl. hygienist and safety profl. Corp. indsl. hygiene mgr. corp. auditing & compliance divsn. Caterpillar Inc., Peoria, Ill., 1977-80, indsl. hygiene engr. Mossville Plant and Tech. Ctr., 1980-86, sr. indsl. hygiene engr. corp. med. dept., 1986-95. Mem. Am. Indsl. Hygiene Assn. (pres. Prairie sect. 1981-82, bd. dirs. Prairie sect. 1982-84), Am. Acad. Indsl. Hygiene, Am. Soc. Safety Engrs., Delta Tau Delta. Home: 421 Zook Ct RR #5 Metamora IL 61548-9052 Office: Caterpillar Inc 100 NE Adams St Peoria IL 61629-3315

WILLIAMS, GUY THOMAS, internist; b. Milw., Sept. 12, 1944; s. Guy Sletten and Dorothy Marie (Buchholz) W.; m. Ann Hines Hornback, Aug. 26, 1967; 1 child, Guy Cameron. AB magna cum laude, Notre Dame U., 1966; MD with honors, Northwestern U., 1970. Diplomate Am. Bd. Internal Medicine. Med. resident La. State U., New Orleans, 1973-75; fellow in nephrology Tulane U., New Orleans, 1975-76; med. dir. DePaul Hosp. New Life Ctr., New Orleans, 1977-84; assoc. Drs. Oelsner, Shames & Williams, New Orleans, 1985-89; internist N.W. Fla. Nephrology, Pensacola, 1989-90; pvt. practice Pensacola, 1990-94; mem. staff Tulane U. Hosp., New Orleans, 1994—. Lt. comdr. USPHS, 1971-73. Mem. AMA, ACP, Am. Soc. Internal Medicine, Orleans Parish Med. Soc. Democrat. Home: 6423 S Claiborne Ave New Orleans LA 70125 Office: Tulane U Hosp 1415 Tulane Ave New Orleans LA 70112

WILLIAMS, H. JAMES, rheumatologist; b. Salt Lake City, June 10, 1941; s. Howard James and Silva Florence (Tayler) W.; m. Janet Christensen, Aug. 8, 1967; children: Christopher, Brian, Michael, Julie, Wendy, Rebecca, Deborah. BA in Biology, U. Utah, 1966, MD, 1969. Intern Duke U., 1969-72; chief resident U. Utah, 1972-73; prof. U. Utah, Salt Lake City, 1975—, Thomas E. and Rebecca D Presdl. endowed chair, 1996—; assoc. chmn. dept. internal medicine U. Utah, 1980—, vice chmn., 1975-80, chief divsn. rheumatology, 1990—. Contbr. articles to profl. jours. and chpts. to books; mem. editl. bd. Am. Coll. Rheumatology, 1993—. V.p. Utah chpt. Arthritis Found., Salt Lake City, 1975-76. Major U.S. Army, 1973-75. Fellow Am. Coll. Rheumatology, ACP; mem. Utah State Med. Assocs. Mem. LDS Ch. Home: 2658 Flamingo Dr Salt Lake City UT 84117 Office: 50 N Medical Dr # 4C104 Salt Lake City UT 84132

WILLIAMS, JAMES LEE, JR., optometrist; b. Wilmington, N.C., June 13, 1953; s. James Lee Sr. and Shirley (Brown) W.; m. Ellen Hillary Cooperman, Apr. 29, 1990; children: David Cooper, Lauren Ann. BA cum laude, U. Va., 1975; OD, Pa. Coll. Optometry, 1984. Optometrist Dr. Philip Dobken & Assoc., Richmond, Va., 1992-94, Galeski Optical, Richmond. 1995—. Vol. optometrist for nursing home/home bound, Richmond, 1993-94. Roman Catholic. Home: 1519 Winters Hill Cir Richmond VA 23236

WILLIAMS, JAMES THOMAS, physician, educator; b. Martinsville, Va., Nov. 10, 1933; s. Harry Pemberton and Ruth Ellen (Thomas) W.; m. Jacqueline Cecile Shepard, Apr. 21, 1962; children: Lawrence Dudley, Laurie Cecile. BS, Howard U., 1954, MD, 1958. Diplomate Am. Bd. Internal Medicine, Am. Bd. Endocrinology and Metabolism. Intern Phila. Gen. Hosp., 1958-59; resident in medicine D.C. Gen. Hosp., 1959-60, Freedmen's Hosp., Washington, 1960-62, 64-65; fellow in endocrinology Howard U., Washington, 1965-67, asst. prof. medicine, 1967-74, chief endocrine sect. dept. medicine, 1973-76, assoc. prof. medicine, 1974-85, prof. medicine, 1985—. Capt. U.S. Army, 1962-64. Fellow ACP; mem. Endocrine Soc., Am. Diabetes Assn., Nat. Med. Assn. Democrat. Home: 13414 Tamarack Rd Silver Spring MD 20904-1469 Office: Howard U Hosp 2041 Georgia Ave NW Washington DC 20060-0001

WILLIAMS, JAMIE F., veterinarian, educator; b. San Antonio, Dec. 17, 1955; s. Sherman F. and Jayne (Simmons) W.; 1 child, Tanner. BS in Animal Sci., N.Mex. State U., 1977, MS in Animal Breeding, 1981; DVM, U. Mo. Columbia, 1989. Diplomate Am. Coll. Vet. Radiology. Assoc. veterinarian Mixed Animal Practice, Fulton, Mo., 1989-90; pvt. practice Mo., 1991; resident in radiology Ohio State U., Columbus, 1991-94; asst. prof. vet. radiology La. State U., Baton Rouge, 1994—; cons. Audubon Inst., New Orleans, 1995—. Contbr. articles to profl. jours. Mem. AVMA, Am. Coll. Vet. Radiology (Resident Authored Paper award 1993), Mo. Vet. Med. Assn., Phi Zeta, Gamma Sigma Delta, Phi Kappa Phi. Office: Dept Vet Clin Science La State Univ Baton Rouge LA 70803

WILLIAMS, JOEL MANN, polymer material scientist; b. Suffolk, Va., Apr. 6, 1940; s. Joel Mann and Mildred (Barlow) W.; m. Mary Carol Gregory, Sept. 1, 1962; children: Catherine Reine, Michael Gregory. BS, Coll. William and Mary, 1962; PhD, Northwestern U., 1966. Asst. prof. chemistry U. Minn., Mpls., 1967-68; research chemist E.I. DuPont de Nemours, Waynesboro, Va., 1968-72; mem. staff Los Alamos (N.Mex.) Nat. Lab., 1972-93; contractor Ray Raskin Assocs., 1995—; cons., 1993—. Author: The Electronic Puzzle, 1994, The Delta State: Molecular Carpooling, 1995, Moles, Bits and Cubes, 1996; co-author: Advances in Physical Organic Chemistry, 1968, Analytical Chemistry of Liquid Fuel Sources, 1978, Coal Science and Chemistry, 1986. Fellow NIH, 1963-66, NSF, 1966-67. Mem. Sigma Xi. Republican. Roman Catholic. Clubs: Tennis (Los Alamos) (tres. 1984-86), Mountain Mixers Square Dance (treas. 1977-79), Barranca Mesa Pool Assn. (treas. 1975-76). Home: 51 Zuni St Los Alamos NM 87544-2647

WILLIAMS, JOHN ANDREW, physiology educator, consultant; b. Des Moines, Aug. 3, 1941; s. Harold Southall and Marjorie (Larsen) W.; m. Christa A. Smith, Dec. 26, 1965; children: Rachel Jo, Matthew Dallas. BA, Cen. Wash. State Coll., 1963; MD, U. Wash., Seattle, 1968, PhD, 1968. Staff fellow NIH, Bethesda, Md., 1969-71; research fellow U. Cambridge, Eng., 1971-72; from asst. to prof. physiology U. Calif., San Francisco, 1973-87; prof. physiology, chair dept. physiology, prof. internal medicine U. Mich., Ann Arbor, 1987—; mem. gen. medicine study sect. NIH, Bethesda, 1985-88, DDK-C study sect., 1991-95. Contbr. numerous articles to profl. jours.; editor Am. Jour. Physiology: Gastrointestinal Physiology, 1985-91. Trustee Friends Sch. in Detroit, 1992—. NIH grantee, 1973—. Mem. Am. Physiol. Soc. (Hoffman LaRoche prize 1985, mem. coun. 1996-99), Am. Soc. Cell Biology, Am. Soc. Clin. Investigation, Am. Gastroenterology Assn., Am. Pancreatic Assn. (pres. 1985-86). Democrat. Home: 1115 Woodlawn Ave Ann Arbor MI 48104-3956 Office: Dept Physiology Univ of Mich Med Sch Ann Arbor MI 48109

WILLIAMS, JOHN PHILIP, osteopathic physician; b. Waco, Tex , Nov. 1, 1957; s. Frank and Ginette (Gazell) W.; m. Laurel Karen Stagnitto, Sept. 30, 1984; 1 child, Lauren Katherine. BS, U. New Eng., Biddeford, Maine, 1981; MS, Calif. State U., San Bernardino, 1985; DO, U. New Eng. Coll. Osteo. Med., 1989; internship, Osteo. Hosp. of Maine, Portland, 1990-91; residency, Loma Linda U. Med. Ctr., Calif., 1991-95. Staff physician in internal medicine North Calif. Med. Assnn., Willits, 1994—. Mem. AMA, ACP, Alpha Omega Alpha. Republican. Seventh-day Adventist. Office: 82 Madrone St Willits CA 95490

WILLIAMS, JON EDWARD, clinical psychologist, minister; b. McComb, Miss., May 20, 1937; s. Lloyd Cruise and Pearl (Burris) W.; m. Harley Harris, Dec. 27, 1963; 1 child James Edward. BA cum laude, Millsaps Coll., 1959; MDiv, Union Theol. Sem., 1964; MS, U. Md., 1969, PhD in Clin. Psychology, 1970. Diplomate Am. Bd. Profl. Psychology. Clin. and health psychologist Nat. Security Agy., Fort Meade, Md., 1970-73; exec. dir. Psychol. Svcs. Inc., Annapolis, Md., 1973-93; exec. dir., sr. psychologist Sheppard Pratt Counseling Ctrs., Annapolis, Md., 1993—. Recipient Disting. Svc. award Md. Psychol. Assn., 1985. Fellow Am. Bd Med. Psychotherapists (diplomate); mem. Am. Acad. Behavioral Medicine (diplomate), Am. Bd. Family Psychologists (diplomate), Am. Bd. Managed Care Providers (diplomate), Am. Bd. Vocat. Experts (diplomate), Am. Bd. Sexology (diplomate). Office: Sheppard Pratt Health System 6501 N Charles St PO Box 6815 Baltimore MD 21285

WILLIAMS, JOSIE R., gastroenterologist; b. Paris, Tex., Aug. 25, 1941; d. R. Brooks and Evelyn (Bridges) Williams. RN, Sparks Sch. Nursing, Ft. Smith, Ark., 1962; BS, Tex. A&M U., 1971; MD, U. Tex., San Antonio, 1975. RN, Tex; diplomate Am. Bd. Internal Medicine. Intern Wilford Hall Med. Ctr., Lackland AFB, Tex., 1975-76, resident in internal medicine, 1976-78, fellow in gastroenterology, 1978-80; pvt. practice Paris, Tex., 1982-96; med. dir. cmty. health svcs. John Peter Smith, Ft. Worth, 1996—; chmn. dept. medicine Carswell AFB Hosp., Tex., 1981-82; chmn. dept. medicine med. staff McCuisition Reg. Med. Ctr., Paris, 1985-86, v.p., 1987-89, TMA organized med. staff sect. rep., 1987, chief med. staff, 1989-90; mem. staff Am. Heart Assn. Advanced Life Support Affiliate Facility, Paris, 1987—, course dir., 1983—; bd. dirs. R.A.C.E.-McCuisition Regional Med. Ctr., 1983; pres. Digestive Disease Ctr. Red Bank Valley, 1983-96; med. dir. Cmty. Health Ctrs., John Peter Smith Health Network, Ft. Worth, 1996—. Bd. dirs., pres. Willowcreek Foster Home, Paris, 1988-89; mem. Lamar County A&M Scholarship Bd., 1987; bd. dirs. Paris Edn. Found., 1990—, chmn. Devel. Coun., 1994, Planned Giving Commn.; bd. dirs. Life Anew, 1990—, sec. bd. dirs., 1994. Decorated Air Force Commendation medals (2); named Outstanding Woman of the Yr., YWCA, Paris, 1988. Mem. AMA, ACP, Tex. Med. Assn. (Rural Health Commn. 1990-94, spl. com. on health sys. reform 1992-93, organized med. staff sect. del. 1989-91, Tex. chair 1993-96, coun. on socioecons. 1994-96, chair spl. com. quality and clin. outcomes), Am. Gastroenterology Assn., Lamar Delta County Med. Soc. (alt. del. to Tex. Med. Assn. 1994-95, Tex. alt. del. to AMA 1996—), Am. Soc. Gastrointestinal Endoscopy, Lamar County-Paris C. of C. (agr. bus. com. 1988-90), Lamar County A&M Club, Tex. Physician Svcs. Orgn. (com. mem. 1994—), Alpha Omega Alpha. Lutheran. Office: John Peter Smith Health Network Network 2500 Circle Dr Fort Worth TX 76119

WILLIAMS, JULIE BELLE, psychiatric social worker; b. Algona, Iowa, July 29, 1950; d. George Howard and Leta Maribelle (Durschmidt) W. BA, U. Iowa, 1972, MSW, 1973. Lic. psychologist, ind. clin. social worker, marriage and family therapist, Minn.; lic. social worker, Iowa. Social worker Psychopathic Hosp., Iowa City, 1971-72; OEO counselor YOUR, Webster City, Iowa, 1972; social worker Child Devel. Clinic, Iowa City, 1973; therapist Mid-Eastern Iowa Community Mental Health Ctr., Iowa City, 1973; psychiat. social worker Mental Health Ctr. No. Iowa, Mason City, 1974-79, chief psychiat. social worker, 1979-80; asst. dir. Community Counseling Ctr., White Bear Lake, Minn., 1980-85, dir., 1985—; lectr., cons. in field. NIMH grantee, 1972-73. Mem. NASW (Acad. Cert. Social Workers, Qualified Clin. Social Workers, diplomate), NOW, Am. Orthopsychiat. Assn., Am. Assn. Sex Educators, Counselors and Therapists, Minn. Women Psychologists, Minn. Lic. Psychologists, Phi Beta Kappa. Democrat. Office: 1280 N Birch Lake Blvd White Bear Lake MN 55110

WILLIAMS, LARRY ROSS, surgeon; b. Murphysboro, Ill., July 20, 1952; s. Laurel Ross and Mary Elizabeth (Blankinship) W.; m. Sarah Elizabeth Hecht, June 17, 1978; children: Gretchen Elizabeth, Noelle Louisa. BS, So. Ill. U., 1974; MD, U. Ill., Chgo., 1978, MS, 1982. Resident in surgery U. Ill., Chgo., 1978-83, fellow in surgery, 1983-84; fellow in vascular surgery Northwestern U., Chgo., 1984-85; asst. prof. U. South Fla., Tampa, 1985-92, clin. asst. prof., 1992—; chief vascular surgery Bay Pines VA Hosp., St. Petersburg, Fla., 1985-89; pvt. practice St. Anthony's Hosp., St. Petersburg, 1985—, chief of surgery, 1993-95, pres.-elect med. staff, 1993-95, pres. med. staff, 1996—; bd. govs. Physician-Hosp. Orgn., 1994-95. Contbr. articles to profl. jours. Active First United Meth. Ch., St. Petersburg, 1985—, Vinoy Resort, St. Petersburg, 1992—, Polywogs, St. Petersburg, 1989—. Fellow ACS; mem. Internat. Soc. Cardiovascular Surgery, Soc. Non-Invasive Vascular Technology, Assn. for Acad. Surgery, Pinellas County Med. Soc. (bd. govs. 1994-96), Fla. Med. Assn. (splty. soc. rep. 1994-96), Am. Inst. Ultrasound in Medicine, Fla. Assn. Gen. Surgeons, Peripheral Vascular Surg. Assn., Warren Cole Surg. Soc., So. Assn. for Vascular Surgery, Fla. Vascular Soc. (sec. 1991-94, pres. 1994-95), Fla. Surg. Soc., Southeastern Surg. Congress, Acad. Med. Arts and Scis., Frederick A. Coller Surg. Soc., Soc. for Clin. Vascular Surgery, Fla. Assn. Cardiovascular and Pulmonary Rehab., Phi Eta Sigma, Phi Kappa Phi, Phi Beta Kappa. Office: 1111 7th Ave N Saint Petersburg FL 33705

WILLIAMS, LARRY SCOTT, orthopedic surgeon; b. Salt Lake City, Aug. 16, 1948; s. William Henry and Toni Jean (Allen) W.; m. Shawnie Phillips, Feb. 28, 1974; children: Jason, Jared, Jacob. BA in Biology, U. Utah, 1971, MD, 1975. Diplomate Am. Bd. Orthopedic Surgery. Intern, flight surgeon Univ. Calif., Davis, 1976-79; resident USN Hosp., San Diego, 1979-83; pvt. practice orthopedic surgery San Diego; clin. preceptor U. Calif., San Diego/USN, 1986—. Capt. USNR, 1975-86. Mem. LDS Ch. Address: 4024 Buho Ct San Diego CA 92124-2809

WILLIAMS, LESTER FREDERICK, JR., general surgeon; b. Brockton, Mass., June 28, 1930; s. Lester Frederick Sr. and Frances (Sullivan) W.; m. Sara Jayne Conroy. AB, Brown U., 1952; MD, Boston U., 1956. Diplomate Am. Bd. Surgery. Intern Letterman U.S. Army Hosp., San Francisco, 1956-57; surg. resident Tripler U.S. Army Hosp., Honolulu, 1957-61; surgeon-in-chief U. Hosp., Boston, 1977-84; program dir. Boston U. Affiliated, 1972-84; chmn. div. surgery Boston U., 1972-84; chief of surgery VA Med. Ctr., Nashville, 1985-89; dir. gallstone ctr. Vanderbilt U. Med. Ctr., Nashville, prof. surgery, 1985—; chief of surgery St. Thomas Hosp., Nashville, 1989—; examination cons. Am. Bd. Surgery, 1987—. Editor: Fundamental Approach to Surgical Problems, 1961, Vascular Insufficency of the Bowels, 1970, Vascular Disorders of the Intestinal Tract, 1971, Core Textbook of Surgery, 1972, Self Assessment of Current Knowledge in General Surgery, 1974, Difficult Problems in General Surgery, 1988; contbr. numerous articles to profl. jours. Maj. USAF, 1956-65. USA Rsch. grants, 1965-72, NIH Rsch. grants, 1971—. Fellow ACS; mem. AMA, Am. Assn. for the Surgery of Trauma, Am. Fedn. for Clin. Rsch., Am. Gastroenterol. Assn., Am. Lithotripsy Soc., Am. Motility Soc., Am. Surg. Assn., Am. Trauma Soc., Assn. for Acad. Minority Physicians, Inc., Assn. Program Dirs. in Surgery, Assn. of VA Surgeons, Boston Surg. Soc., Honolulu Surg. Soc., Collegium Internationale Chirurgiae Digestivae, Internat. Assn. for the Surgery of Trauma and Surg. Intensive Care, Internat. Hepato-Biliary-Pancreas Assn., Soc. Univ. Surgeons, So. Surgical Assn., Societe Internationale de Chirurgi, Soc. for Surgery of Alimentary Tract, New England Surgical Soc., Alpha Omega Alpha. Office: Vanderbilt U Med Ctr Garland and 21st Ave Nashville TN 37232-5729

WILLIAMS, LULA MAE, nurse; b. Columbus, Ga., Aug. 12, 1947; d. Roosevelt and Lula Belle (Bridges) W. BS in Nursing, Tuskegee Inst., 1970; M of Nursing, Emory U., 1973. Staff nurse VA Med. Ctr., Tuskegee, Ala., 1971-72, clin. specialist, 1974-77; head nurse VA Med. Ctr., Nashville, 1977-81; asst. chief nurse VA Med. Ctr., Poplar Bluff, Mo., 1981-84; assoc. chief nurse VA Med. Ctr., Perry Point, Md., 1984-85, quality program mgr., 1985-93, risk mgr., 1993—. Contbr. articles to profl. jours. Served to 2d lt. U.S. Army, 1967-70, lt. col. Res. Mem. NAFE, Nat. Assn. for Healthcare Quality, Med. Assn. for Healthcare Quality, Fla. Assn. for Healthcare Quality (program chair-elect Area II 1995-96, program chair 1996—), Soroptomist Internat. (Havre de Grace, Md., corr. sec. 1991-93), Res. Officers Assn., Delta Sigma Theta (Hartford County v.p. 1987, treas. 1988-91, pres. 1991-93, v.p. Clearwater Alumnae chpt. 1995—). Democrat. Mem. Church of Christ.

WILLIAMS, LUTHER STEWARD, science foundation administrator; b. Sawyerville, Ala., Aug. 19, 1940; s. Roosevelt and Mattie B. (Wallace) W.; m. Constance Marie Marion, Aug. 23, 1963; children: Mark Steward, Monique Marie. BA magna cum laude, Miles Coll., 1961; MS, Atlanta U., 1963; PhD, Purdue U., 1968, DSc (hon.), 1987; DSc (hon.), U. Louisville, 1992. NSF lab. asst. Spelman Coll., 1961-62; NSF lab. asst. Atlanta U., 1962-63, instr. biology, faculty rsch. grantee, 1963-64, asst. prof. biology, 1969-70, prof. biology, 1984-87, pres., 1984-87; grad. tchg. asst. Purdue U., West Lafayette, Ind., 1964-65, grad. rsch. asst., 1965-66, asst. prof. biology, 1970-73, assoc. prof., 1973-79, prof., 1979-80, NIH Career Devel. awardee, 1971-75, asst. provost, 1976-80; dean Grad. Sch., prof. biology Washington U., St. Louis, 1980-83; v.p. acad. affairs, dean Grad. Sch. U. Colo., Boulder, 1983-84; Am. Cancer Soc. postdoctoral fellow SUNY-Stony Brook, 1968-69; assoc. prof. biology MIT, 1973-74; spl. asst. to dir. Nat. Inst. Gen. Med. Scis., NIH, Bethesda, Md., 1987-88; dep. dir. Nat. Inst. Gen. Med. Scis. NIH, Bethesda, 1988-89; sr. sci. advisor to dir. NSF, Washington, 1989-90, asst. dir. for edn. and human resources, 1990—; chmn. rev. com. MARC Program, Nat. Inst. Gen. Med. Scis., NIH, 1972-76; grant reviewer NIH, 1971-73, 76, NSF, 1973, 76-80, Med. Research Council of N.Z., 1976; mem. life scis. sreening com. recombinant DNA adv. com. HEW, 1979-81; mem. nat. adv. gen. med. sci. council NIH, 1980-85; mem. adv. com. Office Tech. Assessment, Washington, 1984-87; chmn. fellowship adv. com. NRC Ford Found., 1984-85; mem.-at-large Grad. Record Exam. Bd., 1981-85, chmn. minority grad. edn. com., 1983-85; mem. health, safety and environ. affairs. com. Nat. Labs., U. Calif., 1981-87; mem. adv. panel Office Tech. Assessment, U.S. Congress, 1985-86; mem. fed. task force on women, minorities and the handicapped in sci. and tech., 1987-91; mem. adv. panel to dir. sci. and tech. ctrs. devel. NSF, 1987-88; mem. nat. adv. com. White House Initiative on Historically Black Colls. and Univs. on Sci. and Tech., 1986-89; numerous other adv. bds. and coms. Contbr. sci. articles to profl. jours. Vice chmn. bd. advisors Atlanta Neighborhood Justice Ctr., 1984-87; bd. dirs. Met. Atlanta United Way, 1986-87, Butler St. YMCA, Atlanta, 1985-87; trustee Atlanta Zool. Assn., 1985-87, Miles Coll., 1984-87, Atlanta U., 1984-87, 90-96; mem. nominating com. Dana Found. NIH predoctoral fellow Purdue U., 1966-68. Fellow AAAS, Am. Acad. Microbiology; mem. Am. Soc. Microbiology, Am. Chem. Soc., Am. Soc. Biol. Chemists (mem. ednl. affairs com. 1979-82, com. on equal opportunities for minorities 1972-84), AAAS, N.Y. Acad. Scis. Home: 11608 Split Rail Ct Rockville MD 20852-4423 Office: NSF Education & Human Resources 4201 Wilson Blvd Arlington VA 22230-1803

WILLIAMS, MARGARET LU WERTHA HIETT, nurse; b. Midland, Tex., Aug. 30, 1938; d. Cotter Craven and Mollie Jo (Tarter) Hiett; m. James Troy Lary, Nov. 16, 1960 (div. Jan. 1963); 1 child, James Cotter; m. Tuck Williams, Aug. 11, 1985. BS, Tex. Woman's U., 1960; MA, Tchrs. Coll., N.Y.C., 1964, EdM, 1974, doctoral studies, 1981; postgrad., U. Tex., 1991-92, U. Wis.; cert. completion, U. Wis., Scotland. Cert. clin. nurse specialist, advanced practice nurse; cert. psychiat./mental health nurse, nursing contuining edn. and staff devel. Nurse Midland Meml. Hosp., 1960-63; instr. Odessa (Tex.) Coll., 1963-67; dir. ADNP Laredo (Tex.) Jr. Coll., 1967-70; asst. prof. Pan Am. U., Edinburgh, Tex., 1970-72; rsch. asst. Tchrs. Coll., 1973-74; nursing practitioner St. Luke's Hosp., N.Y.C., 1975-79; sgt. Burns Security, Midland, 1979-81; with Area Builders, Odessa, 1981-83; field supr. We Care Home Health Agy., Midland, 1983-87; clin. educator, supr. Glenwood, A Psychiat. Hosp., Midland, 1987-92; dir. nursing Charter Healthcare Systems, Corpus Christi, Tex., 1992-93; RN III Brown Sch., San Marcos, Tex., 1993—; owner MTW Nursing Consultation, Lockhart, Tex., 1996—, Margaret Hiett Williams RN, CNS, Lockhart, Tex., 1996—; co-owner, operator MTW Med. Legal Cons.; adj. prof. Pace U., 1974-75, S.W. Tex. State U., 1995. Mem. Gov. Richards' Exec. Leadership Coun., 1991-95, re-election steering com., 1994. Recipient Isabelle Hampton-Robb award Nat. League for Nursing, 1976, Achievement award Community Leaders of Am., 1989, Ladies 1st of Midland, 1974. Mem. NAFE, ANA, Tex. Nurses Assn. (pres. dist. 21 1962-65, dist. 32 1970-72), Am. Psychiat. Nurses Assn., Parkland Meml. Hosp. Nurses Alumnae Assn., Tex. Women's U. Alumnae Assn., Midland H.S. Alumni, Bus. and Profl. Women's Club, Mensa,

Lockhart Breakfast Lions Club. Democrat. Office: PO Box 324 Lockhart TX 78644

WILLIAMS, MARIA TARANGO, optometrist; b. Chico, Calif., Feb. 28, 1965; d. Isidro Domingo and Sandra Rae (Tanner) Tarango; m. Joseph Patrick Williams, July 23, 1988. BS, U. Calif., Davis, 1988; OD, U. Calif., Berkeley, 1992. Pvt. practice Marshall H. Kamena, O.D., Livermore, Calif., 1992—, Robert Edelman, M.D., Castro Valley, Calif., 1993—, Randy M. Yamada, O.D., Danville, Calif., 1994—. Recipient J. Harold Bailey award Am. Optometric Found., 1992. Mem. Am. Optometric Assn., Calif. Optometric Assn., Cal Aggie Alumni Assn., Alameda-Contra Costa Counties Optometric Soc. (vision screener 1992—), Optometry Alumni Assn. Office: 1171 Murrieta Blvd Ste 5 Livermore CA 94550

WILLIAMS, MARILYN, health care organization executive; b. Ashland, Ky., July 28, 1950; d. Charley Thurman and Wilma Margaret (Burke) W. BS, Queens Coll., 1971; MS, U. Ala., Birmingham, 1977. Diplomate Am. Coll. Healthcare Execs. Asst. biochemist So. Research Inst., Birmingham, 1972-75; asst. exec. dir. Jefferson County Med. Soc., Birmingham, 1977-78; dir. project rev. Birmingham Regional Health Systems Agy., 1978-80; v.p. planning and regulation Miss. Hosp. Assn., Jackson, 1980-82; v.p. planning, regulation and data Miss. Hosp. Assn., 1982-85; coord. for corp. planning Commn. on Profl. and Hosp. Activities, Ann Arbor, Mich., 1986-89, chief oper. officer, 1990-91; dir. ops. Vis. Nurse Assn., Birmingham, Ala., 1991-93; pres. Future Health Concepts, Birmingham, 1994—; wellness and prevention specialist Choice Behavioral Health Partnership, Birmingham, 1996—; wellness and prevention specialist Choice Behavioral Health Partnership. Contbr. articles to profl. jours. Mem. allocations com. United Way, Jackson, 1985; bd. dirs. Modern Dance Collective, Jackson, 1985; commr. for Housing Authority for Birmingham Dist.; chairperson Magic City Harvest, 1993-94; bd. dirs. A Baby's Place, 1994-95, Positive Maturity, 1994. Richards Co. scholar, 1970; named an Outstanding Young Women of Am., 1974, Woman of Yr. Jackson Bus. and Profl. Women's Club, 1984; recipient Commendation award VA, 1977. Mem. Am. Hosp. Assn., Soc. Hosp. Planning and Mktg., U. Ala. Alumni Assn. Grad. Program in Hosp. and Health Adminstrn., Birmingham Area C. of C. (chair health svcs. com. 1996). Democrat. Home: 1508-G 33rd St S Birmingham AL 35205-2142 Office: Future Health Concepts PO Box 130716 Birmingham AL 35213-0716

WILLIAMS, MARSHALL HENRY, JR., physician, educator; b. New Haven, July 15, 1924; s. Marshall Henry and Henrietta (English) W.; m. Mary Butler, Aug. 27, 1948; children: Stuart, Patricia, Marshall, Frances, Richard. Grad., Pomfret Sch., 1942; B.S., Yale, 1945, M.D., 1947. Diplomate Nat. Bd. Med. Examiners, Am. Bd. Internal Medicine. Intern Presbyn. Hosp., N.Y.C., 1947-48; asst. resident medicine Presbyn. Hosp., 1948-49; asst. resident medicine New Haven Hosp., 1949-50, asst. in medicine, 1950; trainee Nat. Heart Inst., 1950; practice medicine, specializing in internal medicine Bronx, N.Y.; chief respiratory sect., dept. cardiorespiratory diseases Army Med. Service Grad. Sch., Walter Reed Army Med. Center, 1953-55; dir. cardiorespiratory lab. Grasslands Hosp., Valhalla, N.Y., 1955-59; dir. chest svc. Bronx Mcpl. Hosp. Ctr., 1959-94; vis. asst. prof. physiology Albert Einstein Coll. Medicine, Bronx, 1955-59, assoc. prof. medicine and physiology, 1959-66, prof. medicine, 1966-95, prof. emeritus, 1995—; dir. pulmonary div. Montefiore Med. Ctr., Albert Einstein Coll. Medicine, 1981-94. Author: Clinical Applications of Cardiopulmonary Physiology, 1960, Essentials of Pulmonary Medicine, 1982, Consultation in Chest Medicine, 1985; contbr. articles to profl. jours. Served from 1st lt. to capt. U.S. Army, 1950-52. Mem. Am. Physiol. Soc., AAAS, Am. Heart Assn., Westchester Heart Assn (past pres.), Am. Thoracic Soc., Am. Fedn. Clin. Research, N.Y. Acad. Sci., N.Y. Trudeau Soc. (past pres.), Am. Soc. Clin. Investigation, Soc. Urban Physicians (past pres.), N.Y. Tb. and Health Assn. (past dir.), Alpha Omega Alpha. Home: 103 Fox Meadow Rd Scarsdale NY 10583-2301 Office: Albert Einstein Coll Medicine Bronx NY 10461

WILLIAMS, MARTHA SPRING, psychologist; b. Dallas, Oct. 5, 1951; d. Thomas Ayers and Emma Martha (Felmet) Spring; m. James Walter Williams, June 30, 1979; children: Dane Ayers, Jake Austin. BA, East Tex. State U., 1972, MEd, 1974, EdD, 1978. Cert. and lic. psychologist, Tex.; lic. profl. counselor, marriage and family therapist. Tchr. Dallas Ind. Sch.; grad. asst. to dean Coll. Edn. East Tex. State U., 1975-77; intern Terrell State Hosp. Outreach Clinic and Hunt County Clinic, Greenville, Tex., 1975-76, Univ. Counseling Ctr., East Tex. State U., 1976-77; learning dir. Man and His Environ. Program, 1978-85; pvt. practice psychology Dallas, 1981—; adolescent group therapist in-patient psychiat. facility, 1986-91; mem. staff Baylor/Richardson (Tex.) Med. Ctr., clin. dir. allied mental health profls., 1992-94; v.p. for provider rels. Advanced Behavioral Health Care Sys., Inc., 1995—; mem. staff Green Oaks, St. Paul, Seany Behavioral Hosps. Author: (with others) The Role Innovative Woman and Her Positive Impact on Family Functioning, 1981, Women and Intimacy, 1982, Permenstral Syndrome: A Family Affair, 1984, The Expanding Horizons of Traditional Private Pracitce: High Tech High/Touch, 1986, Adolescent Suicide: Consequences of an Anti-Child Society, 1986, Therapist as a Partner, 1987. Nat. del. Dem. Conv., San Francisco, 1984; Dem. county chair Kaufman County, 1993—; mem. state Dem. Exec. Com. 1993—. Mem. APA, Am. Assn. Marriage and Family Therapists, Am. Soc. Clin. Hypnosis. Lutheran. Home: PO Box 1119 Terrell TX 75160-1119 Office: Ste 825 4835 Lyndon B Johnson Fwy Dallas TX 75244-6005

WILLIAMS, MARTIN HOWARD, psychologist; b. N.Y.C., Nov. 1, 1947; s. Alexander Michael and Anne Henrietta (Sonenklar) W.; m. Susan Elizabeth Case, Sept. 1, 1978; children, Rachel, Elizabeth. BA summa cum laude, UCLA, 1968; PhD, U. Calif., Berkeley, 1975. Lic. psychologist, Calif. Predoctoral fellow NSF, U. Calif., Berkeley, 1968-70; psychology intern VA Hosp., Palo Alto, Calif., 1970-71; predoctoral trainee U.S. Pub. Health Svc., Berkeley, 1971-72; psychologist Berkeley Sex Therapy Group, 1973-80, Kaiser Permanente Hosp., Santa Clara, Calif., 1980—, pvt. practice, Los Gatos, Calif., 1980—; quality assurance chair Kaiser Psychiatry Dept., Santa Clara, 1988—; expert witness, pvt. practice, Los Gatos, 1992. Contbr. articles to profl. jours. including Am. Psychologist, Profl. Psychology, Jour. of Personality and Social Behavior. Named Woodrow Wilson fellow, 1968-69. Mem. Am. Psychol. Assn., Am. Psychol. Soc (divsn. psychotherapy 1977—, divsn. ind. practice, 1985—), Am. Psychol. Law Soc., Phi Beta Kappa. Home: 21660 Dorothy Way Los Gatos CA 95030 Office: Paychiatry Dept Kaiser Permanente Hosp 1333 Lawrence Exply Ste 350 Santa Clara CA 95051

WILLIAMS, MARY D(ENNEN), psychologist; b. Cin.; d. Frank Eugene and Katharine Powell (Wiley) D.; children from previous marriage: John Wiley Hartung, Katharine D. Hartung, Denny Hartung. AB, Radcliffe Coll., 1943; MS, U. Vt., 1948; MPA in Pub. Health, U. R.I., 1965; PhD, U. Oreg., 1982. Lic. psychologist, Oreg., Idaho. Instr. zoology U. R.I., Kingston, 1950-51, asst. prof. zoology in Pub. Health, 1957-59; grad. teaching fellow U. Oreg., Eugene, 1978-80; resident psychologist Portland, Oreg., 1982-85; pvt. practice psychologist Portland, 1985—. Mem. APA, Oreg. Psychol. Assn., Portland Psychol. Assn., Oreg. Psychoanalytic Found., Sigma Xi, Pi Sigma Alpha, Phi Kappa Phi.

WILLIAMS, MELVA MAUREEN, medical technologist; b. New Orleans, Sept. 8, 1958; d. Everett Joseph and Melva Dier (Borris) W. BS, Loyola U., New Orleans, 1982; MT, Touro Infirmary Hosp., 1983; MS with honors, Coll. St. Francis, 1992. Non-registered lab. technician Alton Ochsner Med. Found., New Orleans, 1981-82, registered med. technologist, 1983-86, med. tech. supr., 1986-90; tech. dir. Ochsner Med. Found., New Orleans, 1990—. Mem. Am. Soc. Clin. Pathologists (registered med. technologist), La. Soc. Prevention of Cruelty to Animals, Humane Soc. of U.S., Alton Ochsner Med. Found. Soc. Home: 1730 Constantinople St New Orleans LA 70115-4710 Office: Alton Ochsner Med Found 1516 Jefferson Hwy New Orleans LA 70121-2429

WILLIAMS, MICHAEL ALAN, psychologist; b. Cin., May 20, 1948; s. Chester and Gentry Mae (Canada) W.; m. Linda Ann Presswood, Aug. 8, 1970; children: Michael Alan II, Derrick Alexander. BA, U. Cin., 1970, MA, 1971, EdD, 1980. Instr. U. Cin., 1972-75; sch. psychologist Dayton Bd. Edn., Ohio, 1975-78; assoc. prof. Wright State U., Dayton, 1978—, coord. spl. edn. program, 1992—; clin. psychologist Profl. Psychol. Services, Dayton, 1981—; psychol. services coordinator Montgomery County Children's Services, Dayton, 1983-88; psychol. cons. Diversion Alternative for Youth, Dayton, 1990—; program mgr. Head Start Supplementary Tng. Program, Cin., 1973-74; cons. Ohio Luth. Synod, Dayton, 1981-83, Blacks in Govt., Dayton, 1982-85, Montgomery County, Stillwater Health Ctr., Dayton, 1982-86. Co-editor (book): Teaching in a Multicultural Pluralistic Society, 1982, 2d edit., 1987. Treas. Dayton Free Clinic and Counseling Ctr., Dayton, 1983; bd. dirs. Planned Parenthood Assn., Dayton, 1983, Miami Valley Literacy Coun., Dayton, 1990—, Dayton Mediation Ctr., 1995—, S. Cmty., Inc., 1996. Named Outstanding Young Man Am., Jaycees, 1984, Top Ten African-Am. Males, Dayton chpt. Urban League, 1995; McCall Scholarship, 1966-70. Mem. Am. Psychol. Assn., Nat. Assn. Black Psychologists, Nat. Assn. Sch. Psychologists, Dayton Assn. Black Psychologists (v.p. 1986-88, pres. 1988-89), Mental Health Assn. (bd. dirs. 1985), Assn. Tchr. Educators. Home: 4830 Old Hickory Pl Dayton OH 45426-2149 Office: Wright State U 373 Millett Hall Dayton OH 45435

WILLIAMS, MICHAEL JAMES, health care services consultant; b. Royal Oak, Mich., Sept. 23, 1951; s. Robert Burgett and Elizabeth (McGuire) W.; divorced. BA in Police Adminstrn., Wayne State U., 1974, BS in Psychology, 1974; MPA, Calif. State U., Fullerton, 1978. Asst. mgr. Suburban Ambulance Co., Royal Oak, 1970-74; dir. Emergency Med. Services Imperial County, El Centro, Calif., 1974-76, Orange County, Santa Ana, Calif., 1976-80; pres. EMS Systems Design, Irvine, Calif., 1980-89, The Abaris Group, Tustin, 1989—; instr., trainer ACLS, Am. Heart Assn., 1978-80, CPr, 1989—; spl. cons. Hosp. Coun. So. Calif., Calif. Assn. Hosps. and Health Systems; EMS med. coord. trauma emergencies Pyramid Films, Santa Monica, Calif., 1989 (Am. Film Inst. Blue Ribbon award). Contbr. numerous articles to profl. jours. Recipient Recognition award Orange County Emergency Care Commn., 1980, Appreciation award UCI Med. Ctr., Orange, Calif., 1980, Orange County Fire Chiefs Assn., 1980. Mem. Healthcare Fin. Mgmt. Assn., Am. Trauma Soc., Am. Heart Assn. (bd. dirs. Orange County chpt., 1976-82), No. Calif. Healthcare Execs., Orange County Trauma Soc. (bd. dirs. 1981-89, program achievement award, 1987), Internat. Assn. Fire Chiefs (EMS sect.), EMS Adminstrs. Assn. Calif. (founding). Democrat. Office: 700 Yonario Valley Rd # 250 Walnut Creek CA 94596

WILLIAMS, MORGAN LEWIS, pharmacist; b. Summerville, S.C., Feb. 28, 1948; s. Carroll S. and Venie Aline (Pound) W. BS in Pharmacy, U. S.C., 1971; Dipl., Niles Bryant Sch., Sacramento, 1982, Am. Sch. Piano Tuning, Morgan Hill, Calif., 1979. Lic. pharmacist, S.C., N.C.; registered tuner technician. Pharmacist VA Hosp., Columbia, S.C., 1972-75, Med. Ctr. Pharmacy, Florence, S.C., 1975-78, Revco Drugs, Cheraw, S.C., 1978—; organist Mt. Hebron United Meth. Ch., W. Columbia, S.C., 1967-76, Latta (S.C.) United Meth. Ch., 1977-81, Swansea (S.C.) United Meth. Ch., 1983-86, St. David's Episcopal Ch., Cheraw, 1989—; piano technician, Florence, Columbia, Cheraw, 1978—; inst. piano tech. Cheraw, 1991. Asst. editor Lodge Newsletter, Trestle Board, 1985-89. Mem. Piano Technicians Guild (former newsletter editor local chpt., sec./treas.), Am. Guild Orangists, S.C. Pharm. Assn. (pres. 1981-82), Optimist Club, Masons (master 1989, musician 1990—), Am. Pharm. Assn., Order of the Ea. Star, Past Royal Patron of the Order of the Amaranth. Republican. Episcopalian. Office: Revco Drugs 932 Chesterfield Hwy Cheraw SC 29520-7008

WILLIAMS, PATRICIA HELEN, substance abuse services administrator. Grad. RN, Englewood (N.J.) Hosp. Sch. Nursing, 1956; BA in Health Sci., Jersey City State Coll., 1972, BA in Health Adminstrn. magna cum laude, 1973; EdD in Health Edn., Columbia U., 1981, postgrad., 1987. RN, N.J., N.Y. Various health positions, 1958-77; cons. reviewer Choice, Middletown, Conn., 1977-93; dir. health edn. Bergen County Dept. Health Svcs., Paramus, N.J., 1978-81, cons. health edn., 1981-82; asst. prof. community health SUNY Coll. at Old Westbury, Long Island, N.Y., 1981-82; software cons. Healthware: Computer Svcs., 1982-91; asst. prof. health sci. William Paterson Coll., Wayne, N.J., 1982-86; assoc. reviewer Nat. Ctr. for Health Edn., N.Y., 1987-89; dir. Mt. Vernon (N.Y.) Adolescent Pregnancy Svc. Project; dir. substance abuse prevention & health Mt. Vernon Bd. Edn., 1988—; reviewer Globe Fearon Simon & Schuster, Upper Saddle River, N.J.; presenter in field. Contbr. revs. to profl. jours. Trustee Ridgefield (N.J.) Bd. Health, 1985-95, pres., 1990. Mem. APHA, Nat. Ednl. Adminstrs., N.Y. Ednl. Adminstrs., N.Y. State Fedn. Profl. Health Educators. Home: 165 Lake P S Danbury CT 06810-9999 Office: Mt Vernon Pub Schs 165 N Columbus Ave Mount Vernon NY 10553-1101

WILLIAMS, PAUL ALLEN, optometrist; b. Hillsboro, Oreg., June 25, 1962; m. Deneise L. Edwards, Sept. 16, 1989; children: Ashley, Collin. BS, Ill. State U., 1985; OD, Pacific U., 1989. Capt., chief optometry USAF Hosp. Kirtland, Albuquerque, 1989-93; chief optometry So. Ill. U., Springfield, 1993-95; asst. dean clin. affairs Northeastern State U., Tahlequah, Okla., 1995—; co-dir. Ill. Quality Eyecare Network, Yorkville, 1994-95; lectr. in field. Contbr. articles to profl. jours. Recipient Meritorious Svc. medal USAF, 1993, Optometrist of Yr., 1992, Young Optometrist of Yr. Ill. Optometric Assn., 1994, Best Editl. award Optometric Editors Assn., 1993. Fellow Am. Acad. Optometry; mem. Am. Optometric Assn. (vice-chair multidisciplinary sect. 1985-96, chair multidisciplinary practice com., mem. coun. on rsch.), Nat. Rural Health Assn. (mem. membership com.), Armed Forces Optometric Assn. Office: Northeastern State Univ 1001 N Grand Tahlequah OK 74464

WILLIAMS, PHILIP COPELAIN, gynecologist, obstetrician; b. Vicksburg, Miss., Dec. 9, 1917; s. John Oliver and Eva (Copelain) W.; B.S. magna cum laude, Morehouse Coll., 1937; M.D., U. Ill., 1941; m. Constance Shielda Rhetta, May 29, 1943; children—Philip, Susan Carol, Paul Rhetta. Intern, Cook County Hosp., Chgo., 1942-43, resident in ob-gyn, 1946-48; resident in gynecology U. Ill., 1948-49; practice medicine specializing in ob-gyn, Chgo., 1949—; mem. staff St. Joseph Hosp., Ill. Masonic Hosp., Cook County Hosp., McGaw Hosp.; clin. prof. Med. Sch. Northwestern U., Chgo. Bd. dirs. Am. Cancer Soc. Chgo. unit and Ill. div. Served with U.S. Army, 1943-45. Recipient Civic award Loyola U., 1970; Edwin S. Hamilton Interstate Teaching award, 1984; diplomate Am. Bd. Ob-Gyn, Fellow ACS, Internat. Coll. Surgeons; mem. AMA, Chgo., Ill. med. socs., AMA, Chgo. Gynecol. Soc. (treas. 1975-78, pres. 1980-81), Am. Fertility Soc., Inst. Medicine, N.Y. Acad. Scis., AAAS. Presbyn. Clubs: Barclay, Carlton, Plaza. Contbr. articles to profl. jours. Home: 1040 N Lake Shore Dr Chicago IL 60611-1165 Office: 200 E 75th St Chicago IL 60619-2249

WILLIAMS, R. HALLOCK, psychiatrist; b. Ossining, N.Y., Oct. 5, 1929; s. Robert Irving and Carola (Bell) W.; m. Janet M. Corea, June 1, 1957; children: Marcia, Carol, Virginia. BA, Oberlin (Ohio) Coll., 1951; MD, McGill U., Montreal, Can., 1961. Diplomate Am. Bd. Psychiatry and Neurology. Internship The Del. Hosp., Wilmington, 1961-62; residency Norristown (Pa.) State Hosp., 1962-65, staff psychiatrist, 1965-71, clin. dir., 1971-76; pvt. practice Norristown, 1965—; mem. staff Montgomery Hosp., 1969—, Sacred Heart Hosp., 1972-94, Suburban Gen. Hosp., 1994—. With U.S. Army, 1951-53, Korea. Mem. AMA, Pa. Med. Soc., Montgomery County Med. Soc., Am. Psychiat. Assn., Pa. Psychiat. Soc. Democrat. Presbyterian. Home: 629 Manchester Rd Norristown PA 19403-4156 Office: 1651 Markley St Norristown PA 19401

WILLIAMS, RALPH JOSEPH, immuno-hematologist; b. N.Y.C., May 3, 1954; s. Ralph and Connie Williams; m. Felicia Romeo, Oct. 1, 1977. BS, Mercy Coll., 1982; postgrad., NIH, 1978-79. Supr. Montefiori Med. Ctr., Bronx, 1988-89; sr. technologist NYU Med. Ctr., N.Y.C., 1988-90; sr. technologist Bronx (N.Y.) VA Med. Ctr., 1980-88, sect. chief blood bank, 1990—, supr. anatomic pathology and blood bank sect., 1990—. With U.S. Army, 1972-74. Mem. Am. Assn. Blood Banks, Am. Soc. Clin. Pathologists, City of N.Y. Dept. Health, N.Y. Blood Ctr., DAV, Am. Legion. Home: 326 W Madison Ave Dumont NJ 07628-3347 Office: Bronx VA Med Ctr 130 W Kingsbridge Rd Bronx NY 10468-3992

WILLIAMS, RALPH THOMAS, social worker; b. Detroit, Jan. 4, 1946; s. Ralph Winston and Ruth Evelyn (Jones) W.; m. Kerry Jo Hester, Aug. 1968 (div. 1974); children: Lara Michelle, Daniel Christopher (dec.). AA, Crowder Coll., 1967; PhB, Southwestern Coll., 1981; MSW, U. Kans., 1990. Lic. master social worker, Kans., sch. social worker, Kans. Mgr. food svc. Stoffers Food, Chgo., 1968-69; dir. food svc. Saga Food Svc., Bartlesville, Okla., 1969-70, William Newton Meml. Hosp., Winfield, Kans., 1970-88; social worker Crowley County Spl. Svc. Coop., Winfield, 1989-95; social woerk REACH Presch. and Devel. Ctr., Winfield, 1995—. Mem. NASW, Coun. Exceptional Children, Kans. Assn. Sch. Social Workers. Home: 301 W 9th Ave Winfield KS 67156-2726

WILLIAMS, REDFORD BROWN, medical educator; b. Raleigh, N.C., Dec. 14, 1940; s. Redford Brown Sr. and Annie Virginia (Betts) W.; m. Virginia Carter Parrott, August 9, 1940; children: Jennifer Betts, Lloyd Carter. AB, Harvard U., 1963; MD, Yale U., 1967. Diplomate Am. Bd. Internal Medicine. Intern, then resident Yale-New Haven Med. Ctr., 1967-70; sr. surgeon USPHS, Bethesda, Md., 1970-72; asst. prof. Duke U. Med. Ctr., Durham, N.C., 1972, prof. psychiatry, 1977—, prof. psychology, 1990—, dir. behavioral medicine rsch. ctr., 1985—; cons. NIH rev. coms., Bethesda, 1977—. Author: The Trusting Heart, 1989, Anger Kills, 1993; contbr. articles to profl. jours. Dir. N.C. Heart Assn., Chapel Hill, 1980-83. Recipient Rsch. Scientist award NIMH, 1974—; NIH grantee, 1986—. Fellow Soc. Behavioral Medicine (pres. 1984-85, Upjohn Disting. Scientist award 1992), Acad. Behavioral Medicine Rsch. (pres. 1995—); mem. Am. Psychosomatic Soc. (bd. dirs. 1978-81, pres. 1992). Unitarian Universalist. Office: Duke U Med Ctr Box 3926 Durham NC 27710

WILLIAMS, RICHARD DWAYNE, physician, educator; b. Wichita, Kans., Oct. 7, 1944; s. Errol Wayne and Roseanna Jane (Page) W.; m. Beverly Sue Ferguson, Aug. 29, 1964; 1 child, Wendy Elizabeth. BS, Abilene Christian U., 1966; MD, Kans. U., 1970. Diplomate Am. Bd. Urology, Nat. Bd. Med. Examiners. Intern, then resident in gen. surgery U. Minn., Mpls., 1970-72, resident in urology, 1972-76, asst. prof., 1976-79; asst. prof. U. Calif., San Francisco, 1979-84; prof., chmn. dept. urology U. Iowa, Iowa City, 1984—; chief urology VA Med. Ctr., San Francisco, 1979-84, VA Med. Ctr., Iowa City, 1984-88; mem. task force on bd. exams Am. Bd. Urology, 1981-85, guest examiner Oral exams, 1984—, trustee, 1994—; Rubin H. Flocks chair in urology U. Iowa, 1994; mem. nat. adv. coun. NIDDK, NIH. Author: (with others) Advances in Urologic Oncology, 1987, Genitourinary Cancer: Basic and Clinical Aspects, 1987, Adult and Pediatric Urology, 1987, General Urology, 1988, Textbook of Medicine, 1988, also others; editor: Advances in Urologic Oncology, 1987; guest editor Seminars in Urology, 1985, Problems in Urology: Prostate Cancer, 1989; bd. editors Jour. Urology, 1980-88; mem. editorial bd. Urology, Jour. Urology; also articles. Bd. dirs. Iowa chpt. Nat. Kidney Found., bd. sci. advisors 1989—. Major USAR, 1971-77. Bordeau scholar Kans. U. Med. Ctr., 1968-69; NIH, VA, Am. Cancer Soc. grantee. Fellow ACS (chmn. urology sect. No. Calif. chpt. 1980-82, chmn. ann. meeting programs 1988, mem. residency rev. com. urology 1993—, vice chair 1995); mem. AAAS, Iowa Med. Soc., Iowa Urologic Soc., Am. Urologic Assn. (dir. seminar on residency evaluation 1987, bd. editors alt. 1988—, rep. North Ctrl. sect., prodr. slide presentations 1988, recipient prizes 1982, 87, mem. various coms. 1987—), Am. Assn. for Cancer Rsch., Am. Soc. Clin. Oncology, Am. Assn. GU Surgeons, Clin. Soc. Genitourinary Surgeons, Soc. Internat. D'Urologie (U.S. sect.), Soc. Univ. Urologists (chmn. com. on residency evaluation 1986-88, councillor 1987—, pres. 1993), Soc. Surg. Oncology, Soc. Urologic Oncology (chmn. membership com. 1987-90, sec. 1990-91, 91-94, pres.-elect 1995, pres. 1996), Johnson County Med. Soc., Flock's Soc., Western Urologic Forum, Alpha Omega Alpha. Republican. Office: U Iowa Dept Urology 200 Hawkins Dr Iowa City IA 52242-1009

WILLIAMS, ROBERT C., engineering psychologist; b. Berkeley, Calif., Sept. 21, 1954; m. Anne-Marie E. Marz. AA, Macon Jr. Coll., 1982; BS, Gerogia Coll., 1984, MS, 1986. Enlisted USAF, 1972, advanced through grades to staff sgt.; telecommunications operator USAF, Travis AFB, Calif., 1972-74; telecommunications supr. USAF, RAF Greenham Common, Eng., 1974-78; assoc. dir. Pain Evaluation and Treatment Ctr., Macon, Ga., 1986-87; engrng. psychologist U.S. Army, White Sands Missile Range, N.M., 1987—; assoc. dir. dept. psychology Project Life Changes, Milledgville, Ga., 1984-87. Mem. Am. Psychol. Assn., Southeastern Psychol. Assn., Am. Pain Soc., Soc. for Behavioral Medicine, Gamma Beta Phi, Phi Beta Kappa, Ky. Cols. Office: TRAC-WHB US Army Tradoc Analysis Command White Sands Missile Range NM 88002

WILLIAMS, ROBERT CARSON, gastroenterologist; b. Tuscaloosa, Ala., Oct. 28, 1944; s. Robert E. and Clara Gladys (Carson) W.; m. Eunice Padilla, Dec. 27, 1969; children—Robert Bradley, Amy Elizabeth. B.A., David Lipscomb Coll., Nashville, 1965; M.D., U. Tenn., 1968. Diplomate Am. Bd. Internal Medicine, Am. Bd. Gastroenterology. Intern, U. Tex. Teaching Hosp., San Antonio, 1969-70; resident in internal medicine U. Tenn. Hosp., Memphis, 1970-72; fellow in gastroenterology U. Colo. Hosp., Denver, 1972-74; practice medicine, specializing in gastroenterology, Birmingham, Ala., 1976—; v.p. med. staff Med. Ctr. East, 1985-86, pres., 1986-87; bd. dirs. Ea. Health Sys., 1988-94, sec. bd. dirs., 1989-94; bd. dirs. Ala. Health Sys., 1994—. Served to lt. comdr. USNR, 1974-76. Mem. AMA, ACP, Med. Assn. State of Ala., Am. Soc. Gastrointestinal Endoscopy, Am. Coll. Gastroenterology, Birmingham Soc. Internists (v.p. 1992, pres. 1993), Jefferson County Med. Soc. Contbr. articles to profl. jours. Office: 48 Med Park E Ste 357 Birmingham AL 35235

WILLIAMS, RUSSELL DON, social work educator, consultant; b. Chgo., Feb. 13, 1945; s. Henry George Williams and Gertrude Ida (Bartsch) Keener; m. Susan Kay Smith, Dec. 31, 1977; children: Anna, Matthew. BA, U. Ark., Fayetteville, 1968; MSW, U. Ark., Little Rock, 1977. Diplomate Am. Bd. Clin. Social Work; lic. clin. social worker, Ark. Svcs. rep. Ark. Dept. Social Svcs., Ft. Smith, 1973-74; field rep. Ark. Office on Aging, Little Rock, 1974-76; clin. chief social svcs. Human Devel. Ctr., Conway, Ark., 1978-86; from instr. to asst. prof. U. Ark. for Med. Scis., Ft. Smith, 1986—; cons. Brownwood Life Care Ctr., Ft. Smith, 1986—, Meth. Oaks Lodge, Covington Ct., Parkview, Ft. Smith, Ark., New Haven Nursing Homes, Van Buren, Ark., 1988-90. Pres. Ft. Smith Child Abuse Prevention Coun., 1990-94, Multidisciplinary Team on Child Sexual Abuse, Ft. Smith, 1990-91. With U.S. Army, 1969-71. Recipient leadership award Ft. Smith Child Abuse Prevention Coun., 1989. Mem. NASW (pres. Ark. chpt. 1994-96), Soc. Tchrs. Family Medicine, Am. Assn. Mental Retardation (pres. Ark. chpt. 1991-92, Leadership award 1985). Office: Univ Ark for Med Scis Area Health Edn Ctr 612 S 12th St Fort Smith AR 72901

WILLIAMS, RUTH LEE, clinical social worker; b. Dallas, June 24, 1944; d. Carl Woodley and Nancy Ruth (Gardner) W. BA, So. Meth. U., 1966; M Sci.in Social Work, U. Tex., Austin, 1969. Milieu coordinator Starr Commonwealth, Albion, Mich., 1969-73; clin. social worker Katherine Hamilton Mental Health Care, Terre Haute, Ind., 1973-74; clin. social worker, supr. Pikes Peak Mental Health Ctr., Colorado Springs, Colo., 1974-78; pvt. practice social work Colorado Springs, 1978—; pres. Hearthstone Inn, Inc., Colorado Springs, 1978—; practitioner Jin Shin Jyutsu, Colorado Springs, 1978—; pres., v.p. bd. dirs. Premier Care (formerly Colorado Springs Mental Health Care Providers Inc.), 1986-87, chmn. quality assurance com., 1987-89, v.p. bd. dirs., 1992-93. Author, editor: From the Kitchen of The Hearthstone Inn, 1981, 2d rev. edit., 1986, 3d rev. edit., 1992. Mem. Am. Bd. Examiners in Clin. Social Work (charter mem., cert.), Colo. Soc. Clin. Social Work (editor 1976), Nat. Assn. Soc. Workers (diplomate), Nat. Bd. Social Work Examiners (cert.), Nat. Assn. Ind. Innkeepers, So. Meth. U. Alumni Assn. (life). Home: 11555 Howells Rd Colorado Springs CO 80908-3735 Office: 536 E Uintah St Colorado Springs CO 80903-2515

WILLIAMS, SANKEY VAUGHAN, health services researcher, internist; b. San Antonio, Apr. 15, 1944; s. James Sankey and Helen (Long) W.; m. Constance Hess, June 27, 1972; children: Elizabeth Helen, Jennifer Lee. AB, Princeton U., 1966; MD, Harvard U., 1970. Diplomate Am. Bd. Internal Medicine. Intern Hosp. of U. Pa., 1970-71, jr. resident, 1971-72, chief med. resident, 1974-75; assoc. dir. clin. rsch. Ctr. for Study of Aging, U. Pa., 1982-86; assoc. dir. for med. affairs Leonard Davis Inst. for Health Econs., U. Pa., 1978-90; dir. clin. scholars program U. Pa., Phila., 1988-96; prof. health care systems Wharton Sch., U. Pa., Phila., 1989—; prof. medicine U. Pa., Phila., 1989—, chief div. gen. internal medicine, 1992—, Sol Katz prof. medicine, 1992—; commr. Prospective Payment Assessment Commn., U.S. Congress, Washington, 1988-91; chairman health svcs. rsch. devel. grants study sect. Agy. for Health Care Policy and Rsch., 1991-94; counselor for med. affiars to the pres. U. Pa., 1990-92. Co-editor: The Physician's Practice, 1980; author 14 revs, chpt. or editorials; contbr. 35 articles to various sci. jours.

Lt. comdr. USPHS, 1972-74. Recipient Career Devel. award Henry S. Kaiser Family Found., 1981-86. Mem. ACP (diplomate, chmn. clin. privileges com. 1989-93, Am. Fedn. Clin. Rsch. (program chmn. health svcs. rsch. 1985), Soc. for Med. Decision Making (pres. 1985-86), Soc. for Gen. Internal Medicine (coun. 1979-84, editor Jour. Gen. Internal Medicine 1995-2000). Office: Hosp Univ of Pa Divsn Gen Internal Medicine Silverstein 3 Philadelphia PA 19104

WILLIAMS, STUART KONRADD, biomedical educator, researcher; b. Wilmington, Del., Apr. 3, 1952; s. Stuart Konradd and Ann Lee (Mammele) W.; m. Carol Lynn Mraz, July 16, 1976; children—Kyle Clifford, Ross Stuart. B.A., U. Del., 1974, M.S., 1976, Ph.D., 1979. Postdoctoral fellow Yale U. Sch. Med. Pathology, New Haven, 1979-81; asst. prof. Jefferson Med. Coll., Phila., 1981-85, assoc. prof. surgery and dir. research, 1986-91; prof. surgery and physiology, chief sect. surg. biol. dept. surgery, U. Ariz. Health Scis. Ctr., Tucson, 1991—. Mem. Am. Heart Assn. Postdoctoral fellow NSF, 1979; recipient Lamport award Am. Microcirculatory Soc., 1981; Searle scholar Chgo. Community Trust, 1983; Research Career Devel. awardee NIH, 1985. Mem. Am. Soc. Cell Biologists, Microcirculatory Soc., Am. Physiol. Soc. Democrat. Achievements include numerous patents on cell transplantation. Home: 5181 N Circulo Sobrio Tucson AZ 85718-6037 Office: U Ariz Health Sci Ctr PO Box 245084 1501 N Campbell Ave Rm 5334 Tucson AZ 85724-5084

WILLIAMS, THEODORE GLENN, orthopaedic surgeon; b. Cordelle, Ga., Oct. 21, 1939; s. Theodore Hiram and Bannie Laura (Hitchcock) W.; m. Lasseter Dennard, June 30, 1964 (div. Apr. 1976); children: Ted, Lil, Liz, Mia. BSA, U. Ga., 1962; MD, Med. Coll. of Ga., 1966. Diplomate Am. Bd. Orthopedic Surgeons. Resident physician U. Louisville, 1970-74; pvt. practice Orthopaedic Assoc. Inc., Albany, Ga., 1974—; former chief of surgery HCA Palmyra Med. Ctr., Albany, 1985, 86. With USN, 1966-70. Fellow ACS, Am. Acad. Ortho. Surgeons; mem. Ga. Ortho. Soc., Soc. Ortho. Soc., Harkess Traveling Ortho. Soc. Republican. Baptist. Office: Orthopedic Assocs Inc 1105 Palmyra Rd Albany GA 31702-0407

WILLIAMS, THOMAS EUGENE, pharmaceutical executive; b. Texarkana, Ark., May 13, 1936; s. Thomas Earle and Frankie Jo (Garner) W.; m. Peggy Jane O'Neill, May 31, 1958; children: Thomas Eugene, Elizabeth Anne, James David. BA, Yale U., 1958; MD, U. Tex. Southwestern Med. Sch., 1962. Diplomate Am. Bd. Pediatrics, Am. Bd. Pediatric Hematology and Oncology. Rotating intern Hermann Hosp., Houston, 1962-63; pediatric resident Children's Med. Ctr., Dallas, 1963-65; fellow pediatric hematology U. Va. Sch. Medicine, Charlottesville, 1967-68; rsch. assoc. Cancer Rsch. Lab., U. Va., Charlottesville, 1968-69; asst. prof. pediatrics and pathology U. Tex. Health Sci. Ctr. at San Antonio, 1969-72, assoc. prof. pediatrics, asst. prof. pathology, 1972-73, assoc. prof. pediatrics and pathology, 1973-79, assoc. prof. pediatrics, 1985-94; med. dir. Santa Rosa Children's Hosp. Cancer Rsch. and Treatment Ctr., 1974-79, South Tex. Comprehensive Hemophilia Ctr., 1977-79, dir. pediatric bone marrow transplantation program, 1986-93; dir. new drug devel. Orphan Med., Inc., 1994-96; sr. clin. rsch. scientist Burroughs Wellcome Co., 1979-85; clin. assoc. prof. pediatrics U. N.C. Sch. Medicine, 1979-85; clin. fellow bone marrow transplantation program Johns Hopkins U. Sch. Medicine, Balt., 1985. Contbr. articles to med. jours. Served to lt. comdr. USN, 1965-67. Am. Cancer Soc. advanced clin. fellow, 1968-69, 70-72; Am. Soc. Pharmacology and Exptl. Therapeutics travel awardee, 1968. Mem. Am. Soc. Clin. Oncology, Am. Soc. Hematology, Am. Assn. for Cancer Rsch. Episcopalian. Office: 11303 Vance Jackson Rd G6 San Antonio TX 78230-1850

WILLIAMS, THOMAS FRANKLIN, physician, educator; b. Belmont, N.C., Nov. 26, 1921; s. T.F. and Mary L. (Deaton) W.; m. Catharine Carter Catlett, Dec. 15, 1951; children: Mary Wright, Thomas Nelson. BS, U. N.C., 1942; MA, Columbia U., 1943; MD, Harvard U., 1950; DSc (hon.), Med. Coll. Ohio, 1987, U. N.C., 1992. Diplomate Am. Bd. Internal Medicine. Intern Johns Hopkins, Balt., 1950-51; asst. resident physician Johns Hopkins, 1951-53; resident physician Boston VA Hosp., 1953-54; research fellow U. N.C., Chapel Hill, 1954-56; instr. dept. medicine and preventive medicine U. N.C., 1956-57, asst. prof., 1957-61, assoc. prof., 1961-68, prof., 1968; attending physician Strong Meml. Hosp., Rochester, N.Y., 1968—; cons. physician Genesee Hosp., Rochester, N.Y., 1973—, St. Mary's Hosp., Rochester, N.Y., 1974-83, Highland Hosp., Rochester, N.Y., 1973; prof. medicine, preventive medicine and community health U. Rochester, 1968-92, also prof. radiation biology and biophysics, 1968-91, on leave, 1983-91, prof. emeritus, 1992—; mem. adv. bd. U. Rochester (Sch. Medicine and Dentistry), 1968-83; clin. prof. medicine U. Va., 1983-89; lectr. medicine Johns Hopkins U., 1983-89; clin. prof. depts family medicine and medicine Georgetown U., 1983-89; dir. Nat. Inst. on Aging NIH, 1983-91; asst. surgeon gen. USPHS, 1983-91, ret., 1991; attending physician Monroe Community Hosp., Rochester, 1991—, vice chmn. Cmty. Coalition for Long Term Care, 1991—; disting. physician VA Med. Ctr., Canandigua, N.Y., 1995—; med. dir. Monroe Cmty. Hosp., Rochester, 1968-83; mem. rev. coms. Nat. Ctr. for Health Svcs. Rsch.; mem. adv. bd. St. Ann's Home; mem. gov. bd. NRC, 1981-83; sci. dir. Am Fedn. Aging Rsch., 1992—; bd. dirs. Kirkhaven, Nat. Coun. on Aging. Contbr. articles on endocrine disorders, diabetes, health care delivery in chronic illness and aging to profl. publs. Served with USNR, 1943-46. USPHS fellow, 1966-67; Markle scholar, 1957-61. Fellow Am. Pub. Health Assn., ACP; mem. AAAS, Inst. Medicine, NAS (coun. 1980-83, governing bd. 1981-83), Assn. Am. Physicians, N.Y. State Med. Soc., Monroe County Med. Soc., Am. Diabetes Assn. (bd. dir. 1974-80), Am. Fedn. Clin. Rsch., Soc. Exptl. Biology and Medicine, Am. Geriatrics Soc., Am. Gerontol. Soc., Rochester Regional Diabetes Assn. (pres. 1977-79), N.C. Coun. for Human Rels. (chmn. 1963-66), Am. Clin. Climatol. Assn. Episcopalian. Home: 287 Dartmouth St Rochester NY 14607-3202 Office: Monroe Community Hosp Office Med Dir Rochester NY 14620

WILLIAMS, THOMAS HEWETT, orthodontist; b. Chickasha, Okla., Sept. 1, 1936; s. Thurman Herd and Clara Adams (Kramer) W.; m. Darilyn Sue Dutton, Jan. 13, 1979; children: Susan Kay, Tamara Ann, Edward Hewett, Michael Lambert. BS, Okla. U., 1958; DDS, Northwestern U., 1961, MS, 1965. Diplomate Am. Bd. Orthodontists. Practice dentistry specializing in orthodontics Chgo., 1965-95; asst. prof. Northwestern U., Chgo., 1965-83, assoc. prof., 1986-91; dentist specializing in orthodontics Seminole, Okla., 1991—. Served to capt. U.S. Army, 1961-63. Mem. Am. Assn. Orthodontists, Midwestern Soc. Orthodontists (pres. 1991-92), Southwestern Soc. Orthodontists, Okla. Assn. Orthodontists, Ill. Soc. Orthodontists (pres. 1978-79), Charles Tweed Found. Orthodontic Rsch., Internat. Coll. Dentists, Wewoka Country Club. Democrat. Episcopalian. Home: 1 Bogey Ln PO Box 1241 Wewoka OK 74884-1241 Office: 2424 N Milt Phillips Ave Seminole OK 74868 Office: PO Box 1241 Wewoka OK 74884-1241

WILLIAMS, UNA JOYCE, psychiatric social worker; b. Youngstown, Ohio, June 24, 1934; d. Samuel Wilfred and Frances Josephine (Woods) Ellis; children: Wendy Louise, Christopher Ellis, Sharon Elizabeth. BA, U. Ala., 1957; MSW, Adelphi U., 1963. Diplomate CSW, Am. Bd. Examiners in Clin. Social Work, Internat. Acad. Behavioral Medicine, Counseling, Psychotherapy. Dir. Huntington Program for Sr. Citizens; psychiat. social worker-supr. N.Y. State Dept. Mental Hygiene, Suffolk Psychiat. Hosp., Central Islip; info.-referral counselor Mental Health Assn. Nassau County, Hempstead, N.Y.; therapist Madonna Heights Family Clinic, Dix Hills, N.Y.; med. and psychiat. social worker Northport (N.Y.) VA Med. Ctr., psychiat. social worker acute psychiat. treatment svs.; med. social worker dialysis svcs. Northport (N.Y.) Va. Med. Ctr.; cons. on programs for aging Luth. Social Svcs. Mt. N.Y., 1959, sr. citizens cons. Port Jefferson-L.I. Bd. Edn., 1963. Chmn. Huntington Twp. Com. Human Rels., 1970; sec. bd. trustess Unitarian Universalist Fellowship Huntington, 1984. Named Mem. of Yr. Germany Philetelic Soc. Mem. NASW (cert., diplomte), Am. Assn. Family Counselors and Mediators, Germany Philetelic Soc. (pres. chpt. 30, 1990). Home: 316 Lenox Rd Huntington Station NY 11746-2640

WILLIAMS, W. VAIL, psychologist; b. Denver, Apr. 13, 1940; s. Warren J. and Edna M. (Follen) W.; m. Sandra M. Eisenrich (div. 1972); 1 child, Jason; m. Linda Lou Fain, Dec. 27, 1975; children: Ken, Dan, Davis, Jeremiah. BS, Bradley U., 1963, MA, 1964; PhD, U. Okla., 1968. Lic. psychologist, S.D., Colo., Calif. Owner Social Systems Devel., 1970-78; sr. psychologist Ft. Logan Mental Health Ctr., Denver, 1968-74; sr. rsch. assoc. Mental Rsch. Inst., Palo Alto, Calif., 1974-78; assoc. prof. Med. Sch. U. S. D., Sioux Falls, 1978—; chmn. curriuclum and evaluation com. Sch. Medicine U. S.D., Sioux Falls, 1989-92; bd. dirs. Univ. Physicians, U. S.D. Sch. Medicine; cons. Charter Hosp., Sioux Falls, 1989-94; clin. dir. Psychiatry Assocs., 1989—. Contbr. to books and articles to profl. jours. Bd. dirs. S.D. Jr. Football Assn., Sioux Falls, 1988-92, Citizens Against Rape and Violence, Sioux Falls, 1988-89, Post 15 Baseball Program, 1995—. Fellow Am. Orthopsychiat. Assn.; mem. APA, AAAS, S.D. Psychol. Assn. (pres. Div. 1 1993-94), Woodlake Athletic Club. Office: Psychiatry Assoc 4009 W 49th St Ste 308 Sioux Falls SD 57106-5221

WILLIAMS, WILLIAM JOSEPH, physician, educator; b. Bridgeton, N.J., Dec. 8, 1926; s. Edward Carlaw and Mary Hood (English) W.; m. Margaret Myrick Lyman, Aug. 12, 1950 (dec. Aug., 1985) ; children: Susan Lyman, William Prescott, Sarah Robb; m. Karen A. Hughes, Feb. 18, 1989. Student, Bucknell U., 1943-45; MD, U. Pa., 1949. Diplomate: Am. Bd. Internal Medicine. (hematology com. 1976-80). Intern U. Pa., 1949-50, Am. Cancer Soc. research fellow in Biochemistry, 1950-52, resident medicine, 1954-55, assoc. to asst. prof. medicine, 1955-58, assoc. prof. to prof. medicine, chief hematology, 1961-69; sr. instr. microbiology Case Western Res. U., 1952; asst. prof. medicine Washington U., St. Louis, 1959-60; research fellow Oxford U., Eng., 1960-61; mem. hematology tng. com. Nat. Inst. Arthritis and Metabolic Disease, 1964-68, research career program com., 1968-72; chmn. dept. medicine SUNY Health Sci. Ctr., Syracuse, N.Y., 1969-92, prof. medicine, 1969—; interim dean Coll. Medicine SUNY Health Sci. Ctr., Syracuse, 1991-92; vis. scientist Walter and Eliza Hall Inst., Melbourne, Australia, 1980; vis. prof. Monash U., Melbourne, 1980; mem. thrombosis adv. com. Nat. Heart and Lung Inst., 1969-73, chmn., 1971-73; adv. coun. Nat. Arthritis, Metabolism and Digestive Diseases, 1975-79; mem. residency rev. com. internal medicine Accreditation Coun. Grad. Med. Edn., 1983-89, mem. bd. appeals panel for internal medicine, 1989— mem. N.Y. State Coun. Grad. Med. Edn., 1987-89. Editor-in-chief: Hematology, 1972, 4th edit., 1989, Williams Hematology Companion Handbook, 1996; contbr. articles to med. lit. Trustee Everson Mus. Art, 1975-81, 83-89. With USNR, 1944-46, 52-54. Recipient Research Career Devel. award Nat. Heart Inst., 1963-68; Daland fellow Am. Philos. Soc., 1955-57; Markle scholar, 1957-62. Mem. AMA, ACP (gov. Upstate N.Y. 1976-81), Am. Soc. Biol. Chemists, Am. Soc. Clin. Investigation, Assn. Am. Physicians, Am. Clin. and Climatol. Assn., Am. Heart Assn. (council on thrombosis exec. com. 1977-81), Internat. Soc. Thrombosis and Haemostasis, Assn. Profs. Medicine, Am. Soc. Hematology, Interurban Clin. Club (sec. 1964-70), Internat. Hematology Soc., Alpha Omega Alpha. Mem. Soc. Friends. Home: 5160 Peck Hill Rd Jamesville NY 13078-9724 Office: 750 E Adams St Syracuse NY 13210-2306

WILLIAMS, WRIGHT, psychologist, educator; b. Houston, May 10, 1949; s. Marvin Wright and Mary Katherine (Lacey) W.; m. Brenda Eileen Wobig, Apr. 6, 1985 (dec. Nov. 1993); 1 child, Christopher Wright. BA, U. Tex., 1971; MS, Fla. State U., 1976, PhD, 1978. Lic. psychologist, Tex.; cert. group psychotherapist; health service provider in psychology. Clin. psychologist VA Med. Ctr., Houston, 1979—; pvt. practice, Houston, 1980—; asst. prof. Baylor U. Coll. of Medicine, Houston, 1980—; adj. clin. asst. prof. U. Houston, 1982—. Contbr. articles to profl. jours. USPHS/NIMH fellow Fla. State U., 1973-76; recipient Cert. of Recognition, DAV, 1980. Mem. APA (cert. of recognition 1981), Am. Group Psychotherapy Assn., Tex. Psychol. Assn., Houston Psychol. Assn. (exec. com. 1984-93, 95-96, sec.-treas. 1986-87), Houston Group Psychotherapy Soc. (exec. com. 1995-96). Presbyterian. Home: 4126 Falkirk Ln Houston TX 77025-2909 Office: VA Med Ctr Psychology Svc 2002 Holcombe Blvd Houston TX 77030-4211

WILLIAMS-MADDOX, JANICE HELEN, nurse; b. Boston; d. Arthur Hamilton Wade and Edith Josephine (Weekes) Williams; B.S. in Nursing, Boston U., 1957; M.A., Atlanta U. Sch. Edn., 1971; M.Community Health, Emory U., 1976; m. Larry Maddox, May 21, 1977 (dec.). Staff nurse Beth Israel Hosp., Boston, 1957-58, N.Y. Hosp.-Cornell U. Med. Center, N.Y.C., 1958-59; ward supr. Jewish Meml. Hosp., Boston, 1959-61; staff and pvt. duty nurse Mass. Gen. Hosp., Boston, 1961-63; public health nurse Boston Health Dept., 1963-64; intravenous nurse Hughes Spalding Hosp., Atlanta, 1964-66; public health nurse Fulton County (Ga.) Health Dept., 1966-69; sr. tchr. Atlanta Southside Comprehensive Health Center, 1970-73, acting dir. edn., 1973-74, assoc. dir. clin. nursing, 1974-76; asso. dir. mental health planning project So. Region Edn. Bd., Atlanta, 1976-78; nursing cons. Dept. Health and Human Services, Atlanta, 1978-81; head nurse VA Med. Center, Atlanta, 1982-85; br. mgr. Am. Home Health Care of Ga., Inc., Jonesboro, 1985-86; mem. staff Med. Emergency Clinic-Grady Meml. Hosp., 1986-91; project dir. Morehouse Sch. Medicine Initiative, N.K. Kellogg Found., 1991-95; evening coordinator, instr. for innovative practical nursing program for health para-profl. Atlanta Area Tech Sch., 1971-81; mem. admissions com. M. Pub. Health program Emory U. Sch. Medicine, 1979—. Mem. coms., including Women's Day com. Central United Meth. Ch., Atlanta. Recipient spl. recognition Am. Cancer Soc., 1975. Mem. Sigma Theta Tau (Epsilon chpt.).

WILLIAMSON, BARBARA, nursing consultant; b. Phila., May 25, 1951; d. Clifton Calvin and Gertrude (White) W.; 1 child, Kristy Mercedes Williamson Hunt. ADN, C.C. Phila., 1970; BSN, U. Pa., 1973; MSN, St. Joseph's U., 1982. Cert. quality assurance, utilization rev. Staff nurse/charge nurse VA Hosp., Phila., 1970-71; asst. head nurse Met. Hosp., Phila., 1971-72; triage nurse S.E. Phila. Neighborhood Health Ctr., 1974-75, FLWG Health Ctr., Phila., 1976-77; dir. pub. health Montgomery County, Norristown, Pa., 1978-84; nursing cons. med. rev. bd. dept. health and human svcs. Health Care Financing Adminstrn., Phila., 1984-96; nursing cons. peer review orgn., survey and cert. DHHS-HCFA, Gulf Terrace, Pa. 1991—; preceptor grad. studies Villanova U., Norristown, Pa., 1982-84. V.p. West End Civic Assn., Gulf Terrace, 1976-95; bd. dirs., chair, vice chair Phila. Black Women's Health Project, 1984—. Mem. ANA, Pa. Nurses Assn. (commr. nursing practice 1981-82, chair, 1982-83), Am. Bd. Quality Assurance and Utilization Rev. Physicians (mem. fin. com. 1994-95). Home: 183 Lincoln Ave Gulf Terrace PA 19428-2527 Office: 3535 Market St Rm 3200 Philadelphia PA 19104

WILLIAMSON, BRIAN D., cardiac electrophysiologist; b. Farrell, Pa., Sept. 30, 1960; s. W. Raymond and M. Gertrude Williamson; m. Kathy A. Williamson, May 20, 1995. BA, Case Western Res. U., 1982; MD, Ohio State U., 1986. Diplomate Nat. Bd. Medicine Examiners; diplomate in cardiovascular disease and cardiac electrophysiology Am. Bd. Internal Medicine. Intern medicine U. Mich., Ann Arbor, 1986-87, resident medicine, 1987-89, chief medicine resident, 1989-90, cardiology fellow, 1990-92, cardiac electrophysiology fellow, 1992-93, lectr., 1993-94; cardiac electrophysiologist St. Thomas Hosp., Nashville, 1994—; active participant numerous multi-ctr. rsch. trials. Contbr. original rsch. articles in peer-rev. jours. Fellow Am. Coll. Cardiology; mem. Phi Beta Kappa, Alpha Omega Alpha. Office: The Heart Group St Thomas Med Plaza East 4230 Harding Rd Ste 523 Nashville TN 37205

WILLIAMSON, DONALD E., state official; b. Louisville, Miss., June 17, 1955; m. Anita Hudspeth; 1 child, Jonathan Stuart. Student, East Miss. Jr. Coll., 1972-73, Miss. State U., 1973-75; MD cum laude, U. Miss. 1979. Diplomate Am. Bd. Internal Medicine. Intern, resident internal medicine U. Va. Hosp., Charlottesville, 1979-82; with East Miss. State Hosp., Meridian, 1979; state tb control oficer Miss. State Dept. Health, 1982-86; dir. divsn. disease control Ala. Dept. Pub. Health, 1986-88, dir. bur. preventive health svcs., 1988-92, state health officer, 1992—; faculty mem. Injury Control Rsch. Ctr. U. Ala., Birmingham; clin. assoc. prof. dept. internal medicine U. South Ala.; presenter in field. Contbr. articles to profl. jours. Chmn. Ala. Pub. Health Care Authority, Ala. Radiation Adv. Bd. Health; mem. Ala. Commn. Aging, State Bldg. Commn., Statewide Health Coordinating Coun., Ala. Youth Svcs. Bd., Gov.'s Task Force Health Care, 1993, Ala. Child Abuse & Neglect Prevention Bd., Ala. Resource Devel. Com., Ala. Anatomical Bd., Planning and Adv. Coun. Devel. Disabilities, Ala. Bd. Med. Scholarship Awards, Pesticides Adv. Com., Gov.'s Interagy. Coordinating Coun., Ala. Juvenile Justice Coordinating Coun., Emergency Med. Svcs. Adv. Coun., 1986-92, Legis. Adv. Com. AIDS, 1988-90, Atty. Gen.'s Task Force Med.Waste, 1989, Water Resources Adv. Coun., exec. coun. Ala. Children's Svcs. Facilitation Team, 1993—; mem. med. adv. com. ARC. Recipient Mosby Book award, 1979; Pub. Health Leadership Inst. scholar, 1996. Mem. ACP, APHA, Am. Soc. Internal Medicine, Ala. Soc. Internal Medicine, Med. Assn. State Ala., Ala. Pub. Health Assn. (bd. dirs. 1991—, chmn. disease control & epidemiology sect. 1991-92), Phi Theta Kappa, Phi Kappa Phi, alpha Omega Alpha. Home: 813 Lichfield Ct Montgomery AL 36117 Office: Ala Dept Pub Health 434 Monroe St Montgomery AL 36130-3017

WILLIAMSON, DONNA MARIA, pastoral counselor; b. Oswego, N.Y., Feb. 26, 1944; d. Donald Carl and Helen Mary (Saber) Townsley; m. Patrick H. Williamson, July 7, 1962; children: Kevin Patrick, Michael Brian, Timothy Daniel. Grad. pub. schs., Fulton, N.Y. Cert. in clin. pastoral edn., pastoral care, Onondaga Pastoral Counseling Ctr.; weight loss counselor. Chaplain Loretto Geriatric Ctr., Syracuse, 1981-82; hosp. chaplain St. Rose of Lima Parish, Syracuse, 1982-84, pastoral counselor, 1984—; weight loss counselor Nutri-System, Syracuse, 1988-91. Founding mem. Fulton Community Nursery Sch., 1967, Commn. on Women in Ch. and Society, Syracuse, 1984; mem. Alethea, Ctr. on Death and Dying, Inc., Syracuse, 1978, Syracuse Area Domestic Violence Coalition's Religious Task Force, 1993—. Mem. Menninger Found. Roman Catholic. Office: St Rose of Lima Parish 409 S Main St North Syracuse NY 13212

WILLIAMSON, HAROLD E., pharmacologist, educator; b. Racine, Wis., Aug. 8, 1930; s. Harold E. and Grace Mae (McIntyre) W.; m. Joan Louise Chase, Apr. 26, 1957; children: Timothy, Julie, Eric. BS, U. Wis., 1953, PhD, 1959. Project assoc. U. Wis., Madison, 1959-60; from instr. to assoc. prof. U. Iowa, Iowa City, 1960-70, prof., 1970—; vis. scientist U. Bergen, Norway, 1988-89; grant reviewer Am. Heart Assn., St. Louis, 1974-78, Am. Scandinavian Found., N.Y.C., 1988—. Contbr. articles to profl. jours. Grantee NIH, 1961-75, Iowa Heart Assn., 1965-83, 3M, 1986—. Fellow Am. Coll. Clin. Pharmacology; mem. Am. Soc. Pharmacology and Exptl. Therapeutics, Am. Soc. Nephrology, Soc. Exptl. Biology and Medicine, Internat. Soc. Nephrology. Home: 131 S Mt Vernon Dr Iowa City IA 52245-4821 Office: U Iowa 2-252 Bsb Iowa City IA 52242

WILLIAMSON, JO ANN, psychologist; b. Wichita, Kans., Feb. 12, 1951; d. Howard T. Murray and Ferryl Arlene (Rumsey) Fleming; m. James Wallace Johnson, Apr. 5, 1984 (div. 1984); m. Michael R. Williamson, Dec. 21, 1990; children: Wesley, Wade. BA, U. Kans., 1973; MA in Psychology, U. Mo., 1974; PhD in Psychology, Auburn U., 1979. Lic. psychologist, Kans. Clin. asst. prof. Ohio State U., Columbus, 1979-80; asst. prof. Chgo. Med. Sch., 1980-81; psychologist U. Mo., Kansas City, 1981-82; psychologist II Rainbow Mental Health Ctr., Kansas City, 1982-83; pvt. practice Wichita, 1983-86; pres. Jo Ann Murray, Ph.D., P.A., Wichita, 1986-90; psychologist Iowa Meth. Hosp., Des Moines, 1989-90, Hutchinson (Kans.) Correctional Facility, 1990, Cedarvale, Wichita, 1991, Cowley County Mental Health, Winfield, Kans., 1991; mental health psychologist Cowley County, 1991-93; clin. dir. Cowley County Mental Health, 1993—. Contbr. articles to profl. jours. Mem. APA (div. clin. psychology).

WILLIAMSON, MICHAEL DOUGLAS, cardiologist; b. Davenport, Iowa, Nov. 21, 1944; s. Douglas Robert and Beverly Earle (Draper) W.; m. Jean Marie Ferko, June 13, 1970; children: Michael Douglas, Jeffrey, Sarah. Student, U. Iowa, MD, 1970. Diplomate in internal medicine and cardiovascular disease Am. Bd. Internal Medicine; lic. physician, Fla., Iowa, Minn., Calif. Intern Harborview Med. Ctr., Seattle, 1970-71; resident in internal medicine Mayo Clinic, Mayo Grad. Sch. Medicine, Rochester, Minn., 1973-75; fellow in cardiology Mayo Clinic, 1975-77; physician divsn. cardiovascular diseases Morton F. Plant Hosp., Clearwater, Fla., 1977—; cons. cardiology Clearwater Cmty. Hosp., 1978-89; mng. ptnr. Clearwater Cardiovascular Cons. Served to capt. USAF, 1971-73. Fellow ACP, Am. Coll. Cardiology, Am. Heart Assn. (coun. clin. cardiology), Am. Coll. Chest Physicians, Am. Coll. Angiology, Soc. Cardiac Angiology, Am. Soc. Cardiovascular Interventionists; mem. AMA, Pinellas County Med. Soc., Am. Soc. Echocardiography, West Coast (Fla.) Acad. Cardiology, Mayo Alumni Assn. Republican. Roman Catholic. Office: Clearwater Cardiovascular Conss 1100 Clearwater-Largo Rd Largo FL 34640

WILLIAMSON, MICHAEL R., radiologist, educator; b. Mt. Vernon, Ill., Sept. 13, 1948. AB, Washington U., St. Louis, 1971; MD, So. Ill. U., Springfield, 1976. Diplomate Am. Bd. Radiology, Am. Bd. Nuclear Medicine. Intern in internal medicine NCSD, 1976-77, resident in neurology, 1977-78; fellow in nuclear medicine U. Colo., 1981-82; resident in radiology Med. Coll. Va., 1982-84; asst. prof. radiology U. Ark., Little Rock, 1984-88; assoc. prof. U. N.Mex., Albuquerque, 1988-93, prof., 1993—. Author: Gamuts in Ultrasound, 1992, Essentials of Ultrasound, 1996. Recipient grant NIH, 1995. Mem. Soc. Nuclear Medicine (bd. trustees 1994-95). Office: U N Mex Dept Radiology Albuquerque NM 87131

WILLIAMSON, MIRIAM BEDINGER, retired medical librarian; b. Asheville, N.C., Nov. 18, 1919; d. Robert Dabney and Mary Julia (Smith) Bedinger; m. Robert Lewis Williamson Sr., June 9, 1944 (div. June 1969); children: Robert Lewis Jr., John Bedinger, Ellen Richmond, Thomas Reid. BA, Agnes Scott Coll., 1941; MS, Presbyn. Sch. Christian Edn., 1943; postgrad., U. Tenn., 1969. Ch. social worker, kindergarten tchr. N.E. Community Ctr., Italian Presbyn. Mission, Kansas City, Mo., 1943-44; med. librarian Blount Meml. Hosp., Maryville, Tenn., 1972-89, ret. 1989; tchr. vocat. edn. programs, adult reading program Alcoa, Blount County, Maryville sch. systems. Mem. Blount County unit Bread for the World. Grantee Library Medicine, HEW, 1973, HHS, 1981, Blount County unit Am. Cancer Soc., 1982, Blount Meml. Hosp. Aux., 1986-87; recipient Outstanding Service award Vocat. Edn. Dept., 1983, 85. Democrat. Home: 103 Hopi Dr Maryville TN 37804-4331

WILLIAMSON, PAUL RICHARD, medical educator, surgeon; b. Asheville, N.C., Aug. 11, 1956; s. William Cooper and Joyce Lee (Sluder) W. BS in Biology, Wake Forest U., 1978, MD, 1982. Asst. clin. prof. surgery U. Ill., Urbana, 1988-89, U. Fla., Gainesville, 1939—; clin. prof. surgery Orlando (Fla.) Regional Med. Ctr., 1989—, co-dir. colon-rectal fellowship program, 1990—, chief of surgery Sand Lake Divsn., 1991—. Contbr. articles to profl. jours. Fellow ACS, Am. Soc. Colon and Rectal Surgery, So. Med. Assn. (pres., mem. rectal sect. 1994), Phi Beta Kappa. Baptist. Office: Colon Rectal Clinic 110 W Underwood St Orlando FL 32806-1112

WILLIAMSON-STOUTENBURG, JANE SUE, nurse practitioner; b. Davenport, Iowa, Mar. 10, 1949; d. George Baker and Hazel Elaine (Kline) W.; m. Noel Wayne Stoutenburg, Aug. 25, 1979 (div. July 1996); 1 child, Karen. AS, Black Hawk Jr. Coll., East Moline, Ill., 1970; BA, BS, Augustana Coll., 1973, 75; Cert. in Fire Sci., Harper Coll., Palatine, Ill., 1982; AS in Nursing with high honors, Elgin Community Coll., 1987. EMT; cert. paramedic. Srsch. technologist Rush-Presbyn. St. Luke's Med. Ctr., Chgo., 1974-75; acct. supr., pvt. investigator Per Mar Security Inc., Davenport, Iowa, 1975-77; pre-trial release investigator 7th Jud. Ct. Dist., Davenport, Iowa, 1976-77; pharm. rep. Bristol Labs., Syracuse, N.Y., 1977-80; dir. safety tng. Zee Med., Irvine, Calif., 1981-83; tng. specialist ARC, Chgo., 1983-86, Lake County Fire Rescue, Barrington, Ill., 1981—; nurse practitioner Boy Scouts of Am., St. Charles, Ill., 1990—; nurse trainer Buehler YMCA, Palatine, Ill., 1990-92; emergency med. svc. coord. Robbins (Ill.) Fire Dept., 1985—; bd. dirs. Barrington Area Devel. Coun., 1981-90. Author: Academy of Science, 1967, (poetry), 1970. Troop leader Girl Scouts, Barrington, 1990-95; book fair chmn. Lines Sch. PTO, Barrington, 1991-94; camp nurse Boy Scouts Am., Camp Big Timber, Ill., YMCA Camp Duncan, Fox Lake, Ill. Recipient Ill. EMT of the Yr. award, 1989-90, Disting. Svc. award ARC, 1989, Disting. Svc. key Alpha Phi Omega, 1989, Key, Phi Theta Kappa, 1989, Vol. of the Yr. award Chgo. Vol. Bur., 1993, J.C. Penney Golden Flame award, 1993. Mem. Am. Soc. Safety Engrs., Am. Trauma Soc., Am. Acad. Sci., Internat. Soc. Fire Sci. Instrs., Prehosp. Care Providers of Ill., Alpha Phi Omega (mem. bd. dirs. 1995—, publicity com.), P.E.O. Sisterhood. Episcopalian. Office: Lake County Fire Rescue 618 S Northwest Hwy Ste 213 Barrington IL 60010

WILLINGER, RHONDA ZWERN, optometrist; b. Bklyn., Apr. 26, 1962; d. Jerome Max and Jeanette (Zwern) Willinger; m. Wayne Ken Chan, Aug. 26, 1990; 1 child, Jamie S. BS, U. Miami, 1983; OD with honors, New Eng. Coll. Optometry, 1987. Resident in optometry VA Med. Ctr., Bedford,

Mass., 1987-88; pvt. practice, Burlington, Mass., 1988-89; pvt. practice specializing in contact lenses Framingham, Mass., 1989—. Scholar New Coll., U. South Fla., 1979-81; honors scholarship U. Miami, 1981-83. Mem. Am. Optometric Assn. (contact lens sect.), Mass. Soc. Optometrists. Home: 228 Lowell Ave Newton MA 02160-1830 Office: 659 Worcester Rd Framingham MA 01701-5308

WILLINGHAM, WELBORN KIEFER, psychologist, educator; b. Rotan, Tex., Mar. 12, 1928; s. W.B. and Juanita Madge (Eason) W.; m. Mary Maxine McCollum, Aug. 14, 1950; children: Sharon, Douglas, Sheila. BA, Tex. Tech U., 1949; MEd, U. Tex., 1956; PhD, Tex. Tech U., 1964. Tchr., prin. elem. sch. Hale Center, Tex., 1951-53; edn. and tng. officer USAF, Brookley Air Force Base, Ala., 1953-55; tchr., coach Hutchinson Jr. High Sch., Lubbock, Tex., 1955-57; counselor Monterey High Sch., Lubbock, 1957-60; asst. dean students Tex. Tech U., Lubbock, 1963-64; clin. psychologist South Plains Guidance Ctr., Lubbock, 1964-66; from asst. prof. to prof. emeritus Tex. Tech U., Lubbock, 1966—; adj. clin. prof. psychiatry Tex. Tech. U. Health Scis. Ctr., 1983—; cons. psychologist Big Spring (Tex.) VA Med. Ctr., 1990—; mem. allied health staff psychology Meth. Hosp., Lubbock, 1990. Cons. editor Individual Psychology, 1989—; tech. reviewer Tex. Dental Jour., 1989—; contbr. articles to profl. jours. Lt. col. USAFR, 1949-77. Paul Harris fellow Rotary Internat., 1985. Fellow Am. Bd. Med. Psychotherapists (diplomate); mem. N.Am. Soc. Adlerian Psychology (del. assembly 1983-89, chmn. publs. com. 1986-89). Home: 1605 56th St Lubbock TX 79412-2803 Office: Tex Tech U Coll of Edn Lubbock TX 79409

WILLIS, ARNOLD JAY, urologic surgeon, educator; b. Phila., Feb. 12, 1949; s. Alexander and Rosaline May (Dortort) W.; m. Lilian Marie Mortensen, Aug. 29, 1981; children: Adam Mark, Simon Matt, Andreas Morton. BA, Franklin & Marshall U., 1970; MD, Thomas Jefferson Med. Ctr., 1974. Intern George Washington U. Hosp., Washington, 1974-75, resident in surgery, 1975-77, resident in urology, 1977-80; instr. in urology George Washington U. Med. Ctr., Washington, 1980-82, asst. clin. prof., 1982-88, assoc. clin. prof., 1988—; mem. Del Marva Found. Med. care, Washingotn, 1985-90; mem. profl. adv. bd. Nat. Kidney Found., Washington, 1988-92; cons. Caremark Internat., Washington, 1990-93, Managed Care Options, Bethesda, Md., 1993-95. Mem. editl. bd. Health Educator, 1995-96; contbr. articles to sci. jours.; inventor ultrasound guide. Clin. Oncology Tng. grantee NIH, 1974; named Tchr. of Yr., Georgetown Family Practice Residency, 1991. Fellow Internat. Coll. Surgeons (v.p. U.S. sect. 1986—, Washington regent); mem. Am. Urologic Assn., Am. Assn. Clin. Urologists, Washington Urol. Assn. (Resident's prize 1980). Jewish. Home: 2011 Whiteoaks Dr Alexandria VA 22306 Office: 650 Pennsylvania Ave # 450 Washington DC 20003

WILLIS, CARL RAEBURN, JR., pharmaceutical executive; b. Madison, Wis., Apr. 5, 1939; s. Carl Raeburn and Annie Marie (Sjoblom) W.; m. Marilynn Lee Sheron, Oct. 15, 1960 (div. Mar. 1979); children: Bryan Keith, Alexandra Marie, Heather Anne, Shannon Leigh; m. Candace Jane Oldham, Apr. 26, 1980. PhD in Indsl. Pharmacy, Purdue U., 1966, BS in Pharmacy, 1961, MS in Indsl. Pharmacy, 1964. Sr. pharm. chemist Warren-Teed Pharms., Columbus, Ohio, 1966-69; mgr. CIBA/CIBA-Geigy, Summit, N.J., 1969-72; deputy dir. drug regulatory affairs Sterling Drug Inc., N.Y.C., 1972-78; dir. drug regulatory affairs Cooper Labs., Cedar Knolls, N.J., 1978-79; dir. drug regulatory affairs Berlex Labs. Inc., Cedar Knolls, 1979-83, sr. dir. R & D, 1983-84; v.p. ops. Berlex Labs. Inc., Wayne, N.J., 1984-96; v.p. Corp. devel., 1996—. Co-author: Drug & Cosmetic Industry, 1972; guest editorial Pharmaceutical engineering, 1987; contbr. articles to Jour. Pharmaceutical Sci., 1965, 68. Advisor Jr. Achievement, Columbus, 1968, bd. mem., Newark, N.J., 1984-88. Fellow NIMH, 1965-66. Mem. Morristown Airport Pilots Assn., Sigma Xi, Phi Lambda Upsilon, Rho Chi. Office: Berlex Labs Inc 110 E Hanover Ave Cedar Knolls NJ 07927-2095

WILLIS, DEAN NORMAN, surgeon; b. Middleboro, Mass., Aug. 3, 1950; s. Norman Otis and Yvette Willis; m. Eliabeth A. Willis, Oct. 6, 1973; children: Mathew, Mary, Daniel, Michael, David. BA, Assumption Coll., 1972; MD, George Washington U., 1976. Diplomate Am. Bd. Surgery. Intern, resident Yale New Haven (Conn.) Hosp., 1976-81; attending surgeon Lawrence & Meml. Hosp., New London, Conn., 1981—; v.p. med. staff Lawrence & Meml. Hosp., New London, 1994—. Fellow ACS (cancer liaison physician Lawrence & Meml. Hosp. 1993—); mem. AMA, Am. Soc. Gen. Surgeons, Conn. Soc. Bd. Cert. Surgeons, Conn. State Med. Soc. (del. 1990—), New London County Med. Soc. (trustee 1990—), Alpha Omega. Home: 279 N Bridebrook Rd East Lyme CT 06333 Office: Gen Surg Assocs New London Ste 2C 50 Faire Harbour Pl New London CT

WILLIS, ISAAC, dermatologist, educator; b. Albany, Ga., July 13, 1940; s. R.L. and Susie M. (Miller) W.; m. Alliene Horne, June 12, 1965; children: Isaac Horne, Alliric Isaac. BS, Morehouse Coll., 1961, DSc (hon.), 1989; MD, Howard U., 1965. Diplomate Am. Bd. Dermatology. Intern Phila. Gen. Hosp., 1965-66; fellow Howard U., Washington, 1966-67; resident, fellow U. Pa., Phila., 1967-69, assoc. in dermatology, 1969-70; instr. dept. dermatology U. Calif., San Francisco, 1970-72; asst. prof. Johns Hopkins U. and Johns Hopkins Hosp., Balt., 1972-73, Emory U., Atlanta, 1973-77, assoc. prof., 1977-82; prof. Morehouse Sch. Medicine, Atlanta, 1982—, chief dermatology, 1991—; dep. commdr. of 3297th USA Hosp. (1000B), 1990—; attending staff Phila. Gen. Hosp., 1969-70, Moffit Hosp., U. Calif., 1970-72, Johns Hopkins Hosp., Balt. City Hosp., Good Samaritan Hosp., 1972-74, Crawford W. Long Meml. Hosp., Atlanta, 1974—, West Paces Ferry Hosp., 1974—, others; mem. grants rev. panel EPA, 1986—; mem. gen. medicine group IA study sect. NIH, 1985—, mem. nat. adv. bd. Arthritis and Musculoskeletal and Skin Diseases, 1991—; chmn. instl. rev. bd., mem. pharmacy and therapeutic com.; mem. nat. adv. coun. U. Pa. Sch. Medicine, 1995—, charter mem. nat. alumni coun., 1995—; bd. mem. Comml. Bank Gwinnett; West Paces Med. Ctr.; mem. gov.'s commn. on effectiveness and economy in govt. State of Ga. Human Resources Task Force, 1991—; charter mem. Nat. Alumni Adv. Coun. U. Pa. Med. Ctr., 1995—; mem. com. adv. bd. sch. pub. health Emory U., 1994—; cons. in field. Bd. dirs. Heritage Bank, Comml. Bank of Ga., chmn. audit rev. com., 1988—; chmn. State of Ga. Dermatology Found., 1995; bd. dirs. Lupus Specialists, Inc., 1996—, InterVu, Inc., 1995—. Served to col. USAR, 1983—. EPA grantee, 1985—. Author: Textbook of Dermatology, 1971—; Contbr. articles to profl. jours. Chmn. bd. med. dirs. Lupus Erythematrosus Found., Atlanta, 1975-83; bd. dirs. Jacquelyn McClure Lupus Erythematrosus Clinic, 1982—; bd. med. dirs. Skin Cancer Found., 1980—; trustee Friendship Bapt. Ch., Atlanta, 1980-82 . Nat. Cancer Inst. grantee, 1974-77, 78—; EPA grantee, 1980—. Fellow Am. Acad. Dermatolgy, Am. Dermtol. Assn.; mem. AAAS, Soc. Investigative Dermatology, Am. Fedn. Clin. Research, Am. Soc. Photobiology, Am. Med. Assn., Nat. Med. Assn., Internat. Soc. Tropical Dermatology, Pan Am. Med. Assn., Phi Beta Kappa, Omicron Delta Kappa. Clubs: Frontiers Internat., Sportsman Internat. Subspecialties: dermatology; cancer research (medicine). Home: 1141 Regency Rd NW Atlanta GA 30327-2719 Office: NW Med Ctr 3280 Howell Mill Rd NW Ste 342 Atlanta GA 30327-4109

WILLIS, JUDITH BONSIE, health care executive; b. Fort Wayne, Ind.; d. Louis William and Virginia M. (Gardner) Bonsib; divorced; children: Jennifer Lee Willis, Gina Marie Willis, Mathew J., Nathan A., Robert Willis. BA, Ind. U., 1963, MA, 1965; BS in Medicine cum laude, Western Mich. U., 1976. Curriculum coord. Kalamazoo Head Start, Kalamazoo County, 1972-73; physician asst. Kalamazoo, Mich., 1976-78; clin. coord., instr. physician asst. program Western Mich. U., 1977-79; asst. dir. to dir. for rsch. and regional med. edn. Southwestern Mich. Area Health Edn. Ctr., Kalamazoo, 1979-86; asst. to the dean for rsch. Coll. of Human Medicine, Mich. State U., Lansing, 1980-86; healthcare financing adminstrn. Office of Rsch. and Demonstrations, 1986-87; dep. dir. nat. drug policy bd., spl. asst. Fed. Govt., Washington, 1987-88; dir. rsch. Am. Acad. of Physician Assts., Alexandria, Va., 1988-94; pres., CEO Credential Info. and Verification Svcs. Inc., Rockville, 1991—; dir. drug policy rsch. inst. Rand Corp., Santa Monica, 1990—; chair Montgomery County Health Commn., 1992-95, commr., 1991—; mem. primary care network, health rsources svcs. adminstrn. DHHS, 1991-94; dir. Corp. Against Drug Abuse, Washington, 1988—; chair program ovesight bd. Montgomery County Small Bus., 1991-94; mem. health inf. pool adv. bd., econ. adv. coun., Montgomery County, 1990-91; mem. health and drug treatment strategy Office of Drug Control Policy, D.C. Govt., 1989-90; mem. nat. adv. com. Rural hostp. based health care program Robert Wood Johnson Found., Princeton, N.J., 1987-90. Recipient Montgomery County Vol. Recognition award, 1993, 20th Anniversary Outstanding Leadership award AAPA, 1988, Nat. Drug Policy Bd. Recognition award, 1988, Cert. of Appreciation Drug Enforcement Adminstrs., 1987, Presdl. Award for Leadership The Upjohn Co., 1985; Clin. Honors scholarship Ind. U., 1962. Office: CIVS Ste 202 6000 Executive Blvd Rockville MD 20852

WILLIS, ROBERT ADDISON, dentist; b. Wichita, Kans., Apr. 27, 1949; s. Everett Clayton and Mary Ann (Rohlin) W.; m. Janet Sue Jones, Jan. 21, 1968 (div. Dec. 1986); children: Gregory, Jeffrey; m. Sherryl Ann Galloway, Apr. 26, 1991; children: Wes Misak, Wendy Misak. Student, Okaloosa Walton Jr. Coll., Niceville, Fla., 1970-71, Wichita State U., 1972-74; DDS, U. Mo., 1978. Dentist Wellington, Kans., 1978—; cons. Sumner County Regional Hosp., 1980—, Lakeside Lodge Nursing Home, Wellington, 1980—. Bd. dirs. Kans. Babe Ruth Leagues, Inc., dist. commr., 1990—; bd. of elders Calvary Luth. Ch., 1989-94. With USAF, 1968-71. Mem. ADA, Acad. Gen. Dentistry, So. Dist. Dental Soc. (pres. 1980), Kans. Dental Assn. (coun. on peer rev. 1988-89), Wellington Dental Soc. (treas. 1981—), Optimist CLub, Wellington Area C. of C. (com. on indsl. devel. 1992), Am. Legion, Xi Psi Psi. Republican. Home: 620 Circle Dr Wellington KS 67152-3206 Office: 204 E Lincoln Ave Wellington KS 67152-3061

WILLIS, WILLIAM HARRIS, internist, cardiologist; b. St. Augustine, Fla., June 26, 1943; m. Jan Willis; children: Brandon, Patrick. BA in Biology, So. Coll., 1961-65; MD, Loma Linda U., 1969. MD, Fla., Calif., Ala., Tex.; Diplomate Am. Bd. Internal Medicine, Am. Bd. Cardiovascular Diseases, Nat. Bd. Med. Examiners. Intern U. Ala. Hosp. and Clinics, Birmingham, 1969-70, resident, 1970-72; fellowship U. Ala. Med. Ctr., Birmingham, 1972-74, chief fellow of cardiology, 1973-74, instr. in medicine, 1973-74; staff cardiologist USAF Med. Ctr., San Antonio, 1974-76; asst. clin. prof. medicine U. Tex., San Antonio, 1975-76; asst. prof. medicine Loma Linda (Calif.) U. Sch. of Medicine, 1976-78, co-dir. Cardiovascular Labs., 1976-80, assoc. prof. medicine, 1978-84; dir. Cardiology Fellowship Program Loma Linda U. Med. Ctr., 1978-88, dir. Cardiovascular Labs., 1980-89; prof. medicine Loma Linda (Calif.) U. Sch. Medicine, 1984-89; asst. chief cardiology Loma Linda U. Med. Ctr., 1986; med. dir. Loma Linda (Calif.) Internat. Heart Inst., 1988; co-dir. cardiac catheterization lab. Fla. Hosp., Orlando, 1990-96, dir. CCU, 1992-96. Mem. editorial bd. Catheterization and Cardiovascular Diagnosis, 1987-95; reviewer Am. Coll. Cardiology, 1988. Fellow ACP, Am. Coll. Cardiology, Soc. Cardiac Angiography and Interventions (chmn. program com. 1980-88); mem. Soc. Cardiog Angiography and Intervention (bd. dirs. 1989-92). Office: Fla Heart Group PA 1613 N Mills Ave Orlando FL 32803

WILLITTS, LORI ANN, medical surgical nurse; b. Framingham, Mass., May 18, 1971; d. Paul Joseph and Leslee Ann (Pieszchalski) W. BSN, Fairfield U., 1993. RN, Mass., Washington. Staff nurse Metro West Med. Ctr., Framingham, Mass., 1993-94; staff nurse, bone marrow transplant Georgetown U. Hosp., Washington, 1994—. Mem. ANA. Office: Georgetown Univ Hospital 3800 Reservoir Rd Washington DC 20007

WILLKENS, ROBERT FREDERICK, physician; b. Bklyn., July 1, 1927; s. Robert Albert and Christine (Lehreider) W.; children: Garen, Holly, Rebecca, Matthew. BS, Antioch Coll., Yellow Springs, Ohio, 1950; MD, U. Rochester, N.Y., 1954. Diplomate Am. Bd. Internal Medicine; lic. Wash. Intern in medicine King County Hosp., Seattle, 1954-55, asst. resident in medicine, 1955-57; rsch. fellow in arthritis Columbia Presbyn. Med. Ctr., N.Y., 1957-58; chief resident in medicine King County Hosp., Seattle, 1958-59; clin. instr. of medicine U. Wash., Seattle, 1959-61, clin. asst. prof. medicine, 1961-66, clin. assoc. prof. medicine, 1966-73, clin. prof. medicine, 1973—; pres. med. staff King County Hosp., Seattle, 1964-65. Assoc. editor: Bull. of the King County Med. Soc., 1963-68, editor 1969-70; editor: Primary Care Rheumatology, 1990-93; mem. editl. bd. Rheumatic Therapies, 1983-88, Clinical Aspects of Autoimmunity, 1986-88, Arthritis and Rheumatology, 1989—; reviewer: Jour. of Rheumatology, Annals of Internal Medicine, 1980—. Mem. Wash. State Bd. Med. Examiners, 1972-82, chmn. 1975-77; trustee Northwest Pub. Co., 1973-75; mem. Gov.'s Coun. on Aging, 1968-71; mem. exec. bd. A Contemporary Theater, 1963-80, pres. exec. bd. 1964-66, mem. adv. coun. 1980—; mem. bd. dirs. Pike Place Mkt. Found., 1982-92; mem. alumni coun. U. Rochester Sch. Medicine and Dentistry, 1982-85; mem. physician adv. panel Harrington Arthritis Rsch. Ctr., Phoenix, 1982-88, mem. steering com., 1982-88; mem. med. sch. admissions com. U. Wash., 1981-84; mem. strategic planning com. Harborview Med. Ctr., 1983-85, vice chmn. King County Arts Commn., 1986-87, commr. 1984-87. Recipient Mead Johnson Postgraduate Scholar award Am. Coll. Physicians, 1958-59, Disting. Svc. award The Arthritis Found., 1969, Nat. Vol. Svc. Citation award Arthritis Found., 1986, RH Williams Superior Leadership award in Medicine Seattle Acad. Internal Medicine, 1990; Travel grantee Am. Rheumatism Assn., 1965, 67. Master Am. Coll. Rheumatology (mem. edn. coun. 1987-90, CORC liaison 1988-90, mem. mktg. & comm. com. 1989-93, chmn. local arrangements com. 1989-90, mem. program com. 1990); mem. Am. Fedn. for Clin. Rsch., Am. Rheumatism Assn. (mem. conjoint clinics com. 1969-93, mem. mtg. sites com. 1967-68, mem. program com. 1976, 82, 83, 84, 85, 90, vice chmn. edn. coun. 1986-88, chmn. liaison subcom. 1988), Western Soc. for Clin. Investigation, North Pacific Soc. Internal Medicine, Northwest Rheumatism Assn. (v.p. 1970-71, pres. 1972-74), King County Med. Soc. (chmn. program com. 1969-71), Arthritis Found. (Western Wash. chpt. chmn. bd. dirs. 1969-73, mem. rsch. com. 1985-87), Seattle Arthritis Found. (pres. 1967-69). Home: 1307 Willard Ave W Seattle WA 98119

WILLOUGHBY, WILLIAM FRANKLIN, II, physician, researcher; b. Washington, Feb. 4, 1936; s. William Westel and Patricia (DeZychlinska) W.; m. Mary Scott Fishburne, 1963 (div. 1974); children: Westel Woodbury, William Franklin III, Laura Fishburne, Mary Scott; m. Judith Eleanor Barbaras, Oct. 25, 1975; 1 child, Robert Alexander Willoughby. AB, Johns Hopkins U., 1957, MD, 1965, PhD in Microbiology, 1965; grad. with distinction, USAF War Coll., 1985. Diplomate Am. Bd. Pathology. Intern then resident in pathology Johns Hopkins Hosp., 1965-67; asst. prof. depts. pathology and microbiology Case Western Res. U., Cleve.; dir. Virginia Mason Rsch. Ctr., Seattle, 1972-75; assoc. prof. dept. pathology Sch. Medicine, Johns Hopkins U., Balt., 1975-87; prof., chmn. dept. pathology Sch. Medicine, U. S.C., Columbia, 1987-92; prof. dept. pathology Rush U. Coll. Medicine, 1994—; dir. labs. Cook County Hosp., Chgo., 1992—, interim med. dir., 1994-96; prof. dept. pathology Rush Med. Coll., Chgo., 1994—; cons. NIH, Bethesda, Md., 1979—, mem. pathology A study sect., 1982-86; cons. NRC, Washington, 1981-84; mem. Res. Component Med. Coun., Dept. Def., Pentagon, 1991-93; dep. surgeon gen. for res. affairs USAF, Bolling AFB, D.C., 1993-95; asst. surg. gen. USAF, Desert Storm/Desert Shield, 1990-91. Mem. editorial bd. Am. Rev. Respiratory Disease, 1978-84; contbr. articles to profl. jours., reviewer numerous sci. manuscripts. Vestryman Trinity Episcopal Ch., Long Green, Md., 1984-87; bd. dirs. Ctrl. S.C. chpt. ARC, Columbia, 1989-92; bd. fellow Norwich U., 1992-95. Maj. USAFR, 1975-95, advanced through grades to maj. gen., 1992-95. Decorated D.S.M., Legion of Merit, Meritorious Svc. medal; recipient Edwin E. Osgood prize Va. Mason Rsch. Ctr., 1973; Arthritis Found. fellow Scripps Clinic and Rsch. Found., 1967-69; Poncine scholar Poncine Found., 1972-74; NIH rsch. grantee, 1976-91. Fellow Coll. Am. Pathologists; mem. AAAS, Am. Soc. Investigative Pathology, Am. Assn. Immunologists, Am. Soc. Cell Biologists, Internat. Acad. Pathology, Assn. Pathology Chmns., Aerospace Med. Assn., Soc. USAF Flight Surgeons (bd. govs. 1993—), Soc. Cons. to Armed Forces, Am. Thoracic Soc., Assn. Mil. Surgeons U.S., Army Navy Club (Washington), Midtown Tennis Club (Chgo.). Home: 1416A S Federal St Chicago IL 60605-2710 Office: Cook County Hosp Hektoen Inst 627 S Wood St Chicago IL 60612-3810

WILLS, EDWARD MICHAEL, medical and sports video producer; b. Phila., Dec. 12, 1958; s. Edward William and Elizabeth Rosa (Maida) W.; m. Susan Lynn Shaughessy, June 19, 1982; children: Ryan Michael, Eric Matthew, Patrick Thomas, Cory Jonathan. BS in Telecommunications, Kutztown U., 1982. Dir., producer Cable Mgmt. Assn. Inc., Hershey, Pa., 1983-86; producer, editor U. Pitts., 1986—; supervising instr. Milton S. Hershey Sch., Hershey, 1984-85. Producer, editor (sport TV program) Highlights of the Lady Keystone Open, 1984 (CMA Outstanding Achievement award 1984); producer, dir. (sports TV programs) Big Five Basketball, 1984, Big Five Football, 1984; producer, editor (ednl. videos) Magnetic Ressonance Imaging, 1990, Nutrition After Your Liver Transplant, 1990; videographer About Your Heart Surgery, 1988, Partnership for Med. Renaissance, 1987, ACL Treatment Options, 1989; videographer, editor Facial Prosthesis, CNBC, 1990. Communications dir. Candlelighters of Pitts., 1988. Mem. Internat. Learning Forum, Health Scis. Comm. Assn., Planetary Soc. Republican. Presbyterian. Home: 926 Washington St Mc Keesport PA 15132-1653 Office: U Pitts Med Ctr Divsn Creative Svcs 200 Lothrop St Pittsburgh PA 15213-2593

WILMER, HARRY ARON, psychiatrist; b. New Orleans, Mar. 5, 1917; s. Harry Aron and Leona (Schlenker) W.; m. Jane Harris, Oct. 31, 1944; children: Harry, John, Thomas, James, Mary. BS, U. Minn., 1938, MB, 1940, MS, 1940, MD, 1941, PhD, 1944. Intern, Gorgas Hosp., Ancon, C.Z., 1940-41; resident in neurology and psychiatry Mayo Clinic, Rochester, Minn., 1945-49, cons. in psychiatry, 1957-58; physician Palo Alto (Calif.) Clinic, 1949-51; pvt. practice medicine, Palo Alto, 1951-55, 1958-64; prof. psychiatry U. Calif. Med. Sch., San Francisco, 1964-69; sr. psychiatrist Scott & White Clinic, Temple, Tex., 1969-74; prof. psychiatry U. Tex. Health Sci. Ctr., San Antonio, 1974-87; mem. staff Audie Murphy VA Hosp., San Antonio, part-time 1974-82; founder, dir. Internat. Film Festivals on Culture and Psychiatry, U. Tex. Health Sci. Center, 1972-80; founder, pres., dir. Inst. Humanities, Salado, Tex., 1980—; practice medicine, specializing in psychiatry, Salado, Tex., 1982—. Served to capt. M.C., USNR, 1955-57. Guggenheim fellow, Zurich, 1969-70; NRC fellow, Johns Hopkins Hosp., 1944-45. Fellow Am. Psychiat. Assn. (life, emeritus), Am. Coll. Psychiatrists, Am. Acad. Psychoanalysis; mem. AAAS, Internat. Assn. Analytical Psychology, Author: Huber the Tuber, 1942, Corky the Killer, 1945, This is Your World, 1952, Social Psychiatry in Action, 1958, First Book for the Mind, 1963, Vietnam in Remission, 1985, Practical Jung, 1987, Closeness: A Dictionary of Ideas, Vol. I, 1989, Father Mother, 1989; (film) People Need People, 1961, Facing Evil, 1988, Evil, 1989, Creativity, 1990, Creativity Paradoxes and Relflections, 1991, Closeness: Personal and Professional Relations, 1992, Understandable Jung, 1994. Home: 506 S Ridge Rd Mill Creek PO Box 528 Salado TX 76571

WILMERING, KATHY, social worker, clinical nurse specialist; b. St. Louis, Sept. 17, 1958; d. Thomas H. and Jean (Dahm) W. BS in Nursing, St. Louis U., 1981, MSW, 1988; cert. in family therapy, Montlake Inst., Seattle, 1990. Cert. mental health counselor, clin. nurse specialist in Psychiatric Nursing. Nurse Cardinal Glennon Meml. Hosp., St. Louis, 1980-82; lead therapist, nurse Comprehensive Mental Health Ctr., Tacoma, Wash., 1982-86; counsellor Youth Emergency Svcs., St. Louis, 1986-87; nurse Harborview Med. Ctr., Seattle, 1987-93; therapist, community organizer Family Svcs., Seattle, 1988-91; implementer Harborview Mental Health Ctr., Seattle, 1989—; pvt. practice therapist Seattle; adj. faculty Antioch U., 1992—; presenter mental health workshops, 1990—. Mem. Homeless Network Bd., St. Louis, 1986-88, Ford Community Group, St. Louis, 1987-88; mem. task force on housing and homelessness Ch. Coun. Greater Seattle, 1988-91; co-chmn. High Point Svc. Coalition, Seattle, 1989; chmn. pairing project Tacoma Speaker's Bur., 1984-85; vol. nurse Neighborhood Clinic, Tacoma, 1983, Family Care Ctr., St. Louis, 1982. Named Ursuline Acad. Alumni of Yr., 1995. Mem. NASW, N.W. Assn. Advanced Practice Psychiat. Nurses,s Multiple Sclerosis Soc. (accessibility com. 1993—, faculty liaison mountaineers northwest environ. issues course 1994-96), Toastmasters (pres. Seattle 1991-92), City Cantabile Choir. Office: 1900 N Northlake Way Ste 127 Seattle WA 98103-9051

WILMOT, THOMAS RAY, medical entomologist, educator; b. Great Falls, Mont., Sept. 9, 1953; s. Donald D. and Jeanne M. W.; m. Gail A. Ballard, June 26, 1976; children: Lacey A., Eric T. BS in Entomology, Mont. State U., 1975; MS in Entomology, Oreg. State U., 1978; MPH, UCLA, 1984, PhD in Epidemiology, 1986. Inspector Cacade County Pesticide Program, Great Falls, Mont., 1970-75; mgr. Yakima County Mosquito Control, Wash., 1978-80; entomologist Midland County Mosquito Control, Sanford, Mich., 1984—; adj. instr. Saginaw Valley State U., University Center, Mich., 1988—; vector control cons., Midland, Mich., 1988—. Contbr. articles to profl. jours. Mem. Local Emergency Plan Com., Midland, Mich., 1990-96; spkr. Dow Corning Spkrs. Bur., Midland, 1992-96. Pub. Health traineeship USPHS, 1980-84; recipient Achievement award Nat. Assn. Counties, 1994. Mem. Am. Mosquito Control Assn. (mem. editl. bd. 1989-92), Am. Soc. Tropical Medicine and Hygiene, Entomol. Soc. Am. (bd. cert. entomologist), Soc. for Vector Ecology (regional dir. 1990-96), Mich. Mosquito Control Assn. (pres. 1989, disting. svc. award 1994), Phi Kappa Phi. Office: Midland County Mosquito Control 2180 N Meridian Sanford MI 48657

WILMOTH, GREGORY HICKS, psychologist; b. Louisville, Feb. 15, 1947; s. Leslie Hicks and Eileen (O'Doherty) W.; m. Cynthia May Cohen, May 6, 1984; 1 child, Rebecca Lee. BA, U. Ky., 1969; MA, SUNY, Binghamton, 1975, Western Ky. U., 1977; PhD, U. Fla., 1980. Instr. Edison State Coll., Pigua, Ohio, 1975-77; NIMH predoctoral fellow U. Fla., Gainesville, 1977-79, project mgr., 1979-80; asst. prof. U. Md., College Park, 1980-87; pub. policy analyst APA, Washington, 1987-89; analyst-in-charge U.S. Gen. Acctg. Office, Washington, 1989—; cons. U. Md., 1983-84, Quincy Co., Landham, Md., 1983-84. Editor: Psychological Perspectives on Abortion, 1992; mem. editl. bd. Jour. of Social Issues, 1990-93; contbg. author: Family Policy and Abortion, 1991, Moral Reasoning, 1980; contbr. articles to profl. jours. Fellow APA; mem. Coalition for Psychology in the Pub. Interest (pres. 1990-91), Soc. for Population and Environ. Psychology (coun. mem. 1990-93, sec. 1994—), Soc. for Psychol. Study of Social Issues (coun. mem. 1992-93). Office: US General Acctg Office 441 G St NW Washington DC 20548-0001

WILMOTT, ROBERT WILLIAM, pediatrician, educator; b. London, Sept. 12, 1948; came to U.S., 1982; s. William Walter Charles and Rosemary (Moore) W.; m. Susan Jennifer Pitcher; m. Cathryn Maria Clark, Dec. 12, 1981; children: Jennifer, Francesca, Gina, Annabelle. BS, U. Coll. London, 1970, MB, 1973; MD, U. London, 1984. Diplomate Am. Bd. Pediatrics, Pediatric Pulmonary. Clin. dir. pulmonology Children's Hosp. Phila., 1982-86; dir. pulmonary medicine Children's Hosp. Mich., Detroit, 1986-89, Children's Hosp. Med. Ctr., Cin., 1989—; asst. prof. pediatrics U. Pa., Phila., 1981-86; assoc. prof. pediatrics Wayne State U., Detroit, 1986-89, assoc. immunology, 1987-89; assoc. prof. pediatrics U. Cin., 1989—. Editor: Pediatric Clinics of North America, 1994, assoc. editor, Journal of Pediatrics, 1995—; contbr. articles to profl. jours. Bd. trustees Cystic Fybrosis Found., Cin., 1990—, ctr. com., Bethesda, Md., 1990-95, Appreciation award, 1987, 95. Fellow Royal Coll. Physicians, Am. Coll. Chest Physicians, Am. Acad. Pediatrics; mem. AAAS, Am. Thoracic Soc. Office: Children's Hosp Med Ctr 3333 Burnet Ave Cincinnati OH 45229

WILNER, FREEMAN MARVIN, hematologist, oncologist; b. Detroit, June 14, 1926; s. Jack Burton W. and Belle Gertrude (Goldberg) Weeks; m. Marjorie Louise Tewkesbury, Aug. 29, 1948; children: Jeffrey, Robert, Paul, Laura. BS with honors, Wayne State U., 1950, MD, 1953. Diplomate Am. Bd. Internal Medicine, Am. Bd. Hematology, Am. Bd. Oncology. Intern Detroit Receiving Hosp., Detroit, 1953-54, resident, 1954-57, chief med. resident, 1956; pres. Hematology/Oncology Assocs., Royal Oak, Mich., 1974-86, Hematology/Oncology Cons., Mich., 1986—; med. dir. Rose Cance Inst., chief sect. hematology-oncology Rose Cancer Ctr.-William Beaumont Hosp., Royal Oak, Mich., 1972—; presenter, with others, numerous med. seminars; clin. assoc. prof. medicine Wayne State U. Co-author: (with Schneider, John R., Bedell, and Archie) Bleeding and Clotting Disorders, 1981; contbr. articles to profl. jours., case reports and other publs. Bd. dirs. Red Cross Southeastern Mich. Blood Bank, 1991, Karmamous Cancer Inst., 1993. Sgt. USAAF, 1944-47. Recipient Disting. Service Award, School of Medicine , Alumni of Wayne State U., Detroit, 1985; named Tchr. of Yr., House Staff, William Beaumont Hosp., 1969-70, Providence Hosp., 1971. Fellow ACP (Laureate award 1993), Internat. Soc. Hematology, Detroit Acad. Medicine; mem. AMA, Am. Soc. Hematology, Am. Soc. Clin. Oncology, Mich. State Med. Soc., Oakland County Med. Soc., Leukemia Found. Mich. (adv. bd. 1958-79), World Fedn. Hemophilia. Office: Hematology Oncology Cons PC 3601 W 13 Mile Rd Royal Oak MI 48073-6712

WILNER, JOEL M., podiatrist; b. Cleve., July 13, 1957; s. Ronald J. and Shirley (Pearlstein) W.; m. Kelly Marie Wilner, Sept. 16, 1995. BS, U. Colo., 1979; D in Podiatric Medicine, Calif. Coll. Podiatric Med., 1983.

Diplomate foot and ankle surgery Am. Bd. Podiatric Surgery. Resident Tex. Med. Ctr., Houston, 1983-85; podiatrist No. N.Mex. Podiatry Med. Assocs., Santa Fe, 1985—; cons. Santa Fe Capital H.S., 1988—, N.Mex. Med. Rev. Assn., Albuquerque, 1992—; mem. adv. bd. St. Vincent Surg. Ctr., Santa Fe, 1995—. Fellow Am. Coll. Foot and Ankle Surgery., Am. Arthroscopic Assn., Am. Coll. Sports Medicine; mem. Am. Podiatric Med. Assn., N.Mex. Podiatric Medicine Assn. Office: NMex Foot & Ankle Assocs 665 Harkle Rd Santa Fe NM 87505

WILSON, ALBERT JOHN ENDSLEY, III, social gerontologist, administrator, consultant; b. Pitts., Oct. 9, 1934; s. Robert Endsley and Dorothy Mae (Parry) W.; m. Nancy Jean Hooton, Sept. 29, 1955 (div. Mar. 1963); children: Linda Jean, Albert John Endsley IV, Patrick Lee; m. Nera Bernice Kennedy, Nov. 24, 1965. AA in Liberal Arts, St. Petersburg Jr. Coll., 1954; BS in Mgmt., Fla. State U., 1956; MRC, U. Fla., Gainesville, 1958, PhD in Sociology, 1966. Research sociologist Fla. Dept. Health, St. Petersburg, 1961-66; dir. Inst. on Aging, U. So. Fla., Tampa, 1967-74; dep. dir. geriatric ctr. VA, Bay Pines, Fla., 1974-76, cons., Bay Pines and Waco, Tex., 1972-74, 76-77, 79-82; dir. grad. study gerontology Baylor U., Waco, 1978-81; dir., prof. Beard Gerontology Ctr., Lynchburg Coll., Va., 1983-94, prof. emeritus, 1994—; vis. prof. Calif. State U.-Chico, 1976-77; adj. prof. rural sociology Pa. State U., 1978-79; cons. in field; del. White House Conf. on Aging, Washington, 1971; expert witness U.S. Senate Com. on Aging, Washington, 1973; bd. dirs. Adult Care of Central Va., Lynchburg, 1984-87, Alzheimers Disease Support, Lynchburg, 1984-89; mem. geriatric prescription team Cen. Va. Cmty. Svcs. Bd., 1986-94; vice chmn. Va. Gov.'s Adv. Bd. on Aging, 1990-94; bd. dirs. Va. Coalition for the Aging, sec. 1987-88; chmn. adv. coun. Cen. Va. Area Agy. on Aging, 1986-92. Author: Social Services for Older Persons, 1984, revised edit. 1988; also chpt., articles; editor: Total Health and Aging, 1976, Ethical Considerations in Long Term Care, 1977, Centenarians: The New Generation, 1990. V.p. bd. Presbyn. Social Ministries, St. Petersburg, 1972-76, Interfaith Coalition on Aging, Pinellas County, Fla., 1974-76; mem. adv. com. Va. Baptist Hosp. Day Ctr., Lynchburg, 1984-94. Recipient Disting. Faculty Scholar award Lynchburg Coll., 1987, Mildred M. Seltzer Disting. Svc. award Assn. for Gerontology in Higher Edn., 1995; grantee Adminstrn. on Aging, HEW, 1969-72, 71-74, Health Services and Mental Health Adminstrn., USPHS, 1972-73, Calif. Dept. on Aging, 1976-77, Bedford Meml. Found., 1986-87, LWV, 1990-92. Mem. Gerontol. Soc. Am., Nat. Council on Aging, Am. Pub. Health Assn., So. Sociol. Soc., Va. Assn. on Aging (pres. 1985-86, Outstanding Svc. award 1986, Outstanding Educator of Yr. award 1993), So. Gerontol. Soc. (bd. dirs. 1988-90, Pres.'s award 1990). Democrat. Methodist. Avocations: antique and special interest autos, hiking, exploring, traveling. Home: 2024B Nature's Bend Dr Fernandina Beach FL 32034

WILSON, ARTHUR JESS, psychologist; b. Yonkers, N.Y., Oct. 25, 1910; s. Samuel Louis and Anna (Gilbert) W.; BS, NYU, 1935, MA, 1949, PhD, 1961; LLB, St. Lawrence U., 1940; JD, Bklyn. Law Sch., 1967; m. Lillian Moss, Sept. 16, 1941; children—Warren David, Anton Francis. Tchr., Yonkers Pub. Schs., 1935-40; dir. adult edn. Yonkers, 1940-42; supr. vocat. rehab. N.Y. State Dept. Edn., 1942-44; personnel exec. Abraham & Straus, Bklyn., 1946-47; rehab. field sec. N.Y. Tb and Health Assn., 1947-48; dir. rehab. Westchester County Med. Center, Valhalla, N.Y., 1948-67; dir. Manhattan Narcotic Rehab. Center, N.Y. State Drug Abuse Control Commn., 1967-68; clin. psychologist VA Hosp., Montrose, N.Y., 1968-73; pvt. practice clin. psychology, Yonkers, 1973—; cons. N.Y. State Dept. Edn., HEW; spl. lectr. Sch. Pub. Health and Adminstrv. Medicine, Columbia U. and Grad. Sch., N.Y. U.; instr. Westchester Community Coll., Valhalla, N.Y.; selected participant Clin. Study Tour of China, 1980. With USN, 1944-46. Mem. APA, Internat. Mark Twain Soc. (hon.), N.Y. Acad. Scis., N.Y. State Psychol. Assn., Kappa Delta Pi, Phi Delta Kappa, Epsilon Pi Tau. Author: The Emotional Life of the Ill and Injured, 1950; A Guide to the Genius of Cardozo, 1939; The Wilson Teaching Inventory, 1941; also articles. Honored as Westchester Author, Westchester County Hist. Soc., 1957. Home and Office: 4121 NW 88th Ave Apt 204 Coral Springs FL 33065-1820 also: 487 Park Ave Yonkers NY 10703-2121

WILSON, BARBARA MITCHELL, nurse; b. Daytona Beach, Fla., July 11, 1962; d. Joe Hamilton and Mary Joyce (Clark) Mitchell; m. Timothy Steve Wilson, Sept. 24, 1983; children: Michael Timothy, Elizabeth Alene. Diploma, Piedmont Hosp. Sch. Nursing, 1983. RN, CNOR, CRNFA. Nursing asst. Gwinnett Hosp. Sys., Lawrenceville, Ga., 1978-80; staf nurse Piedmont Hosp., Atlanta, 1983-84; staf nurse Gwinnett Hosp. Sys., 1984—, nurse neurosurgery resource, 1984-93, nurse trauma resource, oper. rm., 1991-95, educator oper. rm. nursing, 1994-95; nurse 1st asst. pvt. practice, Atlanta, 1994—; cons. in field. Mem. AORN, ANA, RN First Asst Splty. Assembly (edm. com. 1994-95, governing coun. 1995—, sec. 1995-96, election coord. 1996—), RN First Assts. Ga. (sec./treas. 1995—), Ga. Nurses Assn. Baptist. Home: 415 Clark Lake Estates Grayson GA 30221

WILSON, BRUCE KEITH, men's health nurse; b. Alton, Ill., Aug. 18, 1946; s. Lewis Philip and Ruth Caroline Wilson; m. Karen Loughrey, Aug. 14, 1977; children: Sarah Ann, Andrew James. BSN, U. Tex., San Antonio, 1975, MSN, 1977; PhD, North Tex. State U., Denton, 1987. Cert. in nursing informatics. Coord. Pan Am. U., Edinburg, Tex., 1982-83; house supr. HCA Rio Grande Regional Hosp., McAllen, Tex., 1986-87; program dir. Tex. Southmost Coll., Brownsville, 1983-86; mem. faculty U. Tex.-Pan Am., Edinburg, 1986—. Author: Logical Nursing Math., 1987. With U.S. Army, 1966-68. Mem. ANA, Nat. League for Nursing, Am. Assembly for Men in Nursing, Tex. League for Nursing (bd. dirs. 1993—). Home: 1702 Ivy Ln Edinburg TX 78539-5367 Office: Dept Nursing U Tex-Pan Am Edinburg TX 78539

WILSON, CAROLYN ALICE, internist; b. Norristown, Pa., May 12, 1946; d. William Harper and Helen (Ernst) W.; m. Stephen Varick Dock, Oct. 21, 1989. BA in Psychology, Randolph-Macon Woman's Coll., 1968; BSN, U. Lowell, 1975; MS in Nursing, Med. Coll. of Va., 1979; MPH, MD, Harvard U., East Tenn. State, 1983, 87. Diplomate Am. Bd. Internal Medicine. Unit coord. N.E. Deaconess Hosp., Boston, 1968-75; nursing staff Boston Va. Hosp., 1976-78; nurse practitioner USPHS, 1979-82; nursing staff USPHS Illegal Alien Detention Ctr., El Centro, Calif., 1983, PNS Hosp., Bethel, Alaska, 1984, Holston Valley Med. Ctr., Kingsport, Tenn., 1984-87; physician USPHS Inactive Reserves, 1982—; physician internal medicine Quadrangle Med. Specialists, Greenville, N.C., 1990-93, Stantonsburg Med. Ctr., 1993-94; pvt. practice Greenville, N.C., 1994—. Recipient Community award USPHS, 1981, award Am. Med. Women's Assn., 1987, Ob-gyn award Merch & Co., Inc., 1987. Mem. Alpha Omega Alpha. Home: 103 Ravenwood Dr Greenville NC 27834-6734

WILSON, CHARLES EDWARD, medical records administrator; b. Columbus, Miss., July 13, 1943; s. James Hugh Wilson and Wenonah Elizabeth Marsh Coble; m. Maria Corazon Junio, Nov. 30, 1968 (div. Apr. 1983); children: James Edward, Charles Edward Jr.; m. Susan Salazar Sabino, Oct. 26, 1983. BS, Okla. State U., 1966; MS, Nova U., 1980. Dir. med. records Meml. Med. Ctr., Springfield, Ill., 1972-76, Holy Cross Hosp., Ft. Lauderdale, Fla., 1976-91, Fawcett Meml. Hosp., Port Charlotte, Fla., 1991-94; dir. Wellington Regional Med. Ctr., West Palm Beach, Fla., 1994—; dir., sci. cons. Darn Communications Group and Darn Computer Corp., Boca Raton, Fla., 1981—. Author: Bar Code Applications in Hospitals, 1986. Mem. Broward County Zool. Pk. Commn., Ft. Lauderdale, Fla., 1978. Capt. USAF, 1966-70, Vietnam. Decorated Air Force Commendation medal USAF, 1968, Bronze Star medal USAF, 1970. Mem. AAAS, Am. Med. Record Assn. (registered record adminstr.), Fla. Med. Record Assn., Broward County Med. Record Assn., Cen. Ill. Med. Records Assn. (pres. 1972-74), Am. Legion, VFW. Democrat. Roman Catholic. Home: 8856 NW 76th Pl Fort Lauderdale FL 33321-2436 Office: Wellington Regional Med Ctr 10101 Forest Hill Blvd West Palm Beach FL 33414-6103

WILSON, CHARLES JOHN, university professor; b. Detroit, Oct. 9, 1930; s. Carl John Wilson and Marion Ellen (Leathers) Moran. BA, Albion Coll., 1952; DDS, Northwestern U., 1956; MS, Marquette U., 1961. Diplomate Am. Bd. Quality Assurance and Utilization Rev. Physicians. Pvt. practice dentistry Milw., 1958-67, 78-88; pres. BioRsch., Inc., 1965-87, chmn., 1987—; bd. dirs. State Fin. Bank Milw.; rsch. assoc. Marquette U. Sch. Dentistry, Milw., 1988-92; assoc. clin. prof. U. Wis., Milw., 1983-92, Northwestern U. Dental Sch., Chgo., 1990—; dir. Dental Network Am., Oakbrook Terr., Ill., 1985-88. Capt. U.S. Army, 1956-58. Fellow Internat. Assn. for Dental Rsch., AAAS, Internat. Coll. Dentists; mem. ADA, Wis. Acad. Arts, Scis. and Letters, Fedn. Dentaire Internationale, Am. Acad. Dental Group Practice (past pres.). Republican. Unitarian. Home: 161 E Chicago Ave 44-F Chicago IL 60611-2625 Office: Northwestern U Dental Sch 240 E Huron St Chicago IL 60611-2909

WILSON, CREIGHTON LEMASTER, orthopaedic surgery educator; b. Lambert, Miss., Feb. 6, 1930; m. Virginia Cross Wilson, Oct. 15, 1954; children: Cheighton L. III, Cathy, Camylle. BA, U. Miss., 1950, BS, 1953; MA, U. Ark., 1951; MD, U. Tenn., Memphis, 1954. Diplomate Am. Bd. Orthopaedic Surgery. Intern John Gaston Hosp., 1954-55; resident in gen. surgery Kennedy VA Med. Ctr., Memphis, 1957-58; resident in orthopaedic surgery Jackson Meml. Hosp., Miami, Fla., 1958-59, 60-61, Variety Children's Hosp., Miami, 1959-60; clin. asst. prof. U. Miami Sch. Medicine, 1961-69, clin. assoc. prof., 1969-77, clin. prof., 1977-87 prof. clin. orthopaedics, 1987—; clin. asst., assoc. and prof. orthopaedic surgery U. Miami (Fla.) Sch. Medicine, until 1987, prof. clin. orthopaedics, 1987—. Fellow ACS, Am. Acad. Orthopaedic Surgeons; mem. Fla. Orthopaedic Soc. Office: U Miami Sch Medicine PO Box 016960 Miami FL 33101-6960

WILSON, DIANNE CAROL, nurse; b. Kansas City, Mo., May 17, 1951; d. Lawrence Edward and Jacqueline Jeanene (Bolton) McElyea; m. Abdullah H. Al-Rubaie, Jan. 24, 1970 (div. Mar. 1974); 1 child, Jamal A.; m. Michael Harold Wilson, Jan. 24, 1976. BSN, BA in Sociology, Avila Coll., 1984; MA in Sociology, U. Mo., Kansas City, 1991; MSN, Fort Hays State U., Hays, Kans., 1994; cert. Family Nurse Practitioner, 1994. RN, Mo., Kans., Nebr. Cardiac care nurse Kansas City (Mo.) Area Hosps., 1984-88; home health nurse Kansas City, 1987—; RN cons., med. case mgr. Jewish Vocat. Svcs., Kansas City, 1988-89, Kansas City, 1989-91; faculty Penn Valley Coll., Kansas City, 1991-92, Park Coll., Parkville, Mo., 1993; prin. Avisa Rehab. Case Mgmt., 1989-93; adj. prof. dept. sociology Fort Hays State U., Hays, Kans., 1994; family nurse practitioner Northwest Health Svc., Mound City, Mo., 1995-96; family nurse practitioner Sch. Nursing U. Kans., 1996—; tchr. childbirth edn. rsch. project HCFA, 1988. Vol. Lakeside Nature Ctr., Kansas City, 1990; pres. mother's coun. Boy Scouts Am., Kansas City, 1979-84; originator nursing radio program Sta. KKFI-FM, Kansas City 1989-90. Mem. Kans. Anthrop. Soc., Great Plains Nurse Practitioner Soc. Mona, KSNA, Mo. Coalition of Nurse Practitioners Kans. Alliance of Nurse Practitioners. Home and Office: PO Box 18443 Kansas City MO 64133-8443

WILSON, DONALD EDWARD, physician, educator; b. Worcester, Mass., Aug. 28, 1936; s. Rivers Rivo and Licine (Bradshaw) W.; m. Patricia C. Littell, Aug. 27, 1977; children: Jeffrey D.E., Sean D., Monique, Sheila L. A.B., Harvard U., 1958; M.D., Tufts U., 1962. Diplomate Am. Bd. Internal Medicine. Intern St. Elizabeth Hosp., Boston, 1962-63; resident in medicine, research fellow in gastroenterology VA Hosp. and Lemuel Shattuck Hosp., Boston, 1963-66; assoc. chief gastroenterology Bklyn. Hosp., 1968-71; instr. medicine SUNY Downstate Med. Center, Bklyn., 1968-71; asst. prof. medicine U. Ill., Chgo., 1971-73; asso. prof. U. Ill., 1973-75, prof., 1975-80, acting head dept. medicine, 1976-77; dir. div. gastroenterology U. Ill. Hosp., Chgo., 1971-80; chief of gastroenterology U. Ill. Hosp., 1973-80, physician-in-chief, 1976-77; prof., chmn. dept. medicine SUNY Downstate Med. Center, Bklyn., 1980-91; physician-in-chief State U. and Kings County Hosp., 1980-91; dean, prof. medicine U. Md.Sch. Medicine, Balt., 1991—; vis. prof. medicine U. London, Kings Coll. Med. Sch., 1977-78; mem. gastrointestinal drugs adv. bd. FDA, 1985-87, chmn., 1986-87; mem. Part II test com. Nat. Bd. Med. Examiners, 1985-88; mem. nat. digestive adv. bd. NIH, 1985-87, chmn., 1986-87; mem. gen. clin. rsch. ctrs. com. NIH, 1987—; mem. nat. adv. com. Agy. for Health Care Policy and Rsch., Dept. HHS, 1991—, chmn., 1992—; mem. residency rev. com. for internal medicine Acque, 1993—; mem. nat. com. fgn. med. edn. and accreditation U.S. Dept. Edn., 1994—. Contbr. articles to med. jours. Bd. vis. Harvard Sch. of Pub. Health, 1992-94. Served to capt. M.C., USAF, 1966-68. Recipient Rsch. award HEW, 1971, 74, Rsch. award John A. Hartford Found., Inc., 1972-79, Rsch. award Distilled Spirits Coun. U.S., 1972-74, Rsch. award VA, 1974. Master ACP; mem. NAS, AAAS, Am. Gastroent. Assn., Am. Fedn Clin. Rsch., Am. Assn. Study Liver Disease, Accreditation Coun. Grad. Med. Edn. (rev. com. internal medicine), Central Soc. Clin. Rsch., Central Rsch. Club, Chgo. Soc. Gastroenterology (pres. 1978-79), Digestive Disease Found., Midwest Gut Club, Soc. Exptl. Biology and Medicine, N.Y. Acad. Scis., N.Y. Acad. Medicine, N.Y. Soc. Gastroenterology, Chgo. Soc. Gastrointestinal Endoscopy (pres. 1979-80), Assn. Am. Physicians, Assn. for Acad. Minority Physicians (sec./treas. 1986—), Nat. Med. Assn., Am. Clin. and Climatological Assn., 1994—, Assn. Profs. Medicine (sec.-treas. 1990-91), Inst. of Medicine, Med. Club Bklyn., Sigma Pi Phi (grand boule). Club: Harvard (Chgo., N.Y.C.), 14 West Hamilton St. Club (Balt.), The Ctr. Club, (Balt.). Office: U Md Sch Medicine 655 W Baltimore St Baltimore MD 21201-1509*

WILSON, EDWARD HARLAN, JR., orthopedic surgeon; b. Boston, Nov. 8, 1923; s. Edward Harlan and Dorothy Elizabeth (Hewitt) H.; m. Ruth Sams; children: Edward, Cathlin, Gregory, Elizabeth. AB, Dartmouth Coll., 1944; MD, Ohio State Coll. Medicine, 1947. Diplomate Am. Bd. Orthop. Surgery. Intern Mass. Gen. Hosp., Boston, 1947-48, resident in surgery, 1948-50; resident in orthopedics N.Y. Hosp., N.Y.C., 1950-51; mil. svc. chief divsn. orthop. surgery 320th Gen. Hosp. U.S. Army, Landstuhl, Germany, 1951-52; med. officer 2d aromored divsn. U.S. Army, Mainz, , Germany, 1952-53; resident in orthop. Hosp. for Spl. Surgery, N.Y.C., 1953-56; pvt. practice orthop. surgery San Francisco, 1956—; vice chief dept. orthop. surgery Presbyn. Hosp., San Francisco, 1979—; mem. staff Presbyn. Hosp., San Francisco, chmn. credentials com. pub. rels. com., infection control com., emergency room com.; sec. med. staff; mem. rehab. com. Bd. Trustees, Pacific Med. Ctr.; fee advisor Calif. Blue Shield, 1967-69, cons. SSA, San Francisco, 1981—. Mem. Am. Acad. Orthop. Surgeons (mem. local com. for arrangements nat. meeting 3 yrs.), Am. Coll. Surgeons, Western Orthop. Assn., Calif. Med. Assn., San Francisco Med. Soc. (vice chmn. ins. mediation com.). Office: Presbyn Hosp 2351 Clay St San Francisco CA 94115

WILSON, EMERY ALLEN, university dean, obstetrician-gynecologist, educator; b. Frankfort, Ky., Apr. 8, 1942; s. Emery Lee and Mary Catheryne (Cooper) W.; m. Clara Bullock, June 18, 1966; children: Emily, Bryan. BA, Emory U., 1964; MD, U. Ky., 1968. Diplomate Am. Bd. Ob-Gyn (examiner 1979-89), Am. Bd. Reproductive Endocrinology. Intern, resident U. Ky., 1968-72; instr. Harvard U. Med. Sch., Boston, 1974-76; asst. prof. ob-gyn U. Ky. Coll. Medicine, Lexington, 1976-79, assoc. prof., 1979-81, prof., 1981—, dean, 1987—, dir. Ctr. for Reproductive Medicine, 1983-87; vice chancellor for clin. profession svcs. U. Ky., 1987—; cons. Nat. Inst. Occupational Safety and Health, Cin., 1980-82; dir. Florence Crittendon House, Lexington. 1986-89. Editor: Nutrition in Pregnancy, 1980, Endometriosis, 1987 Professional Management and Practice Management, 1989; author over 100 articles, book chpts., abstracts; reviewer several profl. jours. Maj. USAF, 1972-74. Recipient Acad. Tng. award Ortho Pharms., 1972. Fellow Am. Coll. Obstetricians and Gynecologists; mem. Am. Fertility Soc., Soc. Gynecologic Investigation, Alpha Omega Alpha, Omicron Delta Kappa. Mem. Disciples of Christ Ch. Home: 967 Edgewater Dr Lexington KY 40502-3159 Office: U Ky Coll Medicine 800 Rose St Lexington KY 40536-0001*

WILSON, FRANCES HELEN, occupational therapist; b. Pitts., Oct. 17, 1929; d. J. Vernon and Margaret Hassler (Prugh) Wilson; BA, Conn. Coll., 1951; advanced standing certificate Columbia Sch. Occupational Therapy, 1953. Therapist, Washington County Soc. Crippled Children and Adults, Washington, Pa., 1953-54; staff therapist Oakland VA Hosp., U. Pitts., 1955-66; supr. Occupational Therapy Clinic, Aspinwall VA Hosp., Pitts., 1966-74, 81-85; supr. Occupational Therapy Clinic, Oakland VA Hosp., Pitts., 1974-80. Active Jr. League Pitts., Inc. Mem. Western Pa. (treas. 1967-69), Am. occupational therapy assns., Presbyterian Univ. Hosp. Pitts. Vol. Assn., 1986—. Republican. Presbyterian. Clubs: Conn. Coll. (treas. 1971-94), Twentieth Century (Pitts.). Home: Washington Plz 1116 1420 Centre Ave Pittsburgh PA 15219-3517

WILSON, FRANK LYNDALL, surgeon; b. Oct. 29, 1926; children: Frank L. III, Patricia W. Major; m. Kristina F. Wilson, June 29, 1984. BS, Emory U., 1948, MD, 1952. Diplomate Am. Bd. Surgery, 1960. Surg. intern Univ. Hosps. Cleve., 1952-53; asst. surg. resident Grady Meml. Hosp., Atlanta, 1953, 55-58, chief surg. resident, 1958-59, now mem. surg. staff; pvt. practice surgery, Atlanta, 1959—; chmn. dept. surgery Piedmont Hosp., Atlanta, 1984-91 , also trustee, mem. surg. staff; clin. asst. prof. surgery Emory U. Sch. Medicine; mem. staff Crawford W. Long Meml. Hosp. Trustee Lovett Sch., 1971-79, Piedmont Hosp., 1984-91; chmn. med. div. United Way Atlanta, 1978. Served with USN, 1944-46, 53-55. Fellow ACS (pres. Ga. chpt. 1976-77); mem. Med. Assn. Atlanta (dir. 1977-82, pres. 1980, chmn. med. adv. com. selective service, peer rev. com.), Atlanta Med. Heritage Inc. (pres. 1980-83), Med. Assn. Ga. (vice councilor 1966-68, del.), Ga. Surg. Soc. (pres. 1990-91), So. Med. Assn., AMA, Atlanta Clin. Soc. Rocky Mountain Traumatological Soc. Presbyterian. Club: Piedmont Driving, Highlands Country (N.C.). Office: 95 Collier Rd NW Ste 6015 Atlanta GA 30309-1607

WILSON, FRED M., II, ophthalmologist, educator; b. Indpls., Dec. 10, 1940; s. Fred Madison and Elizabeth (Fredrick) W.; m. Karen Joy Lyman, Sept. 10, 1959 (div. June 1962); 1 child, Teresa Wilson Kulick; m. Claytonia Leigh Pemberton, Aug. 28, 1964; children: Yvonne Wilson Hacker, Jennifer, Benjamin James. AB in Med. Scis., Ind. U., 1962, MD, 1965. Cert. Am. Bd. Ophthalmology. Intern Sacred Heart Hosp., Spokane, Wash., 1965-66; resident in ophthalmology Ind. U., Indpls., 1968-71, fellow in ophthalmology, 1971-72; fellow in ophthalmology F.I. Proctor Found., San Francisco, 1972-73; from asst. prof. to assoc. prof. ophthalmology Ind. U., Indpls., 1972-76, prof. ophthalmology, 1981—; med. dir. Ind. Lions Eye Bank, Inc., Indpls., 1973—; cons. surgeon Ind. U., Indpls., 1973—. Author or editor numerous sci. articles, book chpts. and books on ophthalmology. Lt. comdr. USNR, 1966-68, PTO. Mem. Am. Acad. Ophthalmology (assoc. sec. 1988-93, Sr. Teaching award 1989), Assn. Proctor Fellows, Soc. Heed Fellows, Am. Ophthalmol. Soc., Am. Bd. Ophthalmology (bd. dirs. 1993—), Ill. Soc. Ophthalmology (hon.), Mont. Acad. Ophthalmology (hon.), Pacific-Coast Ophthalmol. Soc. (hon.). Republican. Home: 12262 Crestwood Dr Carmel IN 46033-4323 Office: Ind U Sch Medicine Dept Ophthalmolgy 702 Rotary Cir Indianapolis IN 46202-5133

WILSON, FREDERIC SANDFORD, pharmaceutical company executive; b. Schenectady, NY, Mar. 28, 1944; s. Robert Omer and Isabel May (Sandford) W.; children: Amy Kathleen, Adrienne Ann; m. Judith Ann Goettsche, Feb. 7, 1973; children: Marla Ann, Brian Bennett, Jessica Lea, Jennifer Lynn. BS, Syracuse U., 1968. Acct. exec. Mastropaul Design Inc., Syracuse, N.Y., 1969-70; copy editor Norwich Eaton Pharms., Norwich, N.Y., 1970-72; sales rep. Norwich Eaton Pharms., Gary, Ind., 1972-73; asst. product mgr. Norwich Eaton Pharms., Norwich, 1974-75, mktg. svcs. mgr., 1975-76, product mgr., 1977-81, bus. devel. mgr., 1981-83, sr. product mgr., 1983-85, mgr. med. foods, 1986-89; assoc. mktg. mgr. P&G Pharms., Norwich, 1989-92; dir. profl. rels. P & G Pharms., Cin., 1993—; cons. Sandoz Nutrition Corp., Mpls., 1992. Inventor Jejunostomy Kit, 1981, Vivonex T.E.N. med. food, 1983, Tolerex med. food, 1987. Bd. dirs. Syracuse U. Minority Access Program, 1989-91, Nat. Osteo. Found.; mem. Physician Asst. Found. Mem. Am. Acad. Nurse Practitioners (corp. adv. coun., healthcare industry adv. coun.), Pharms. Assn. for Continuing Med. Edn. (treas., membership chmn.), Am. Acad. of Family Physicians (corp. adv. coun.). Office: P&G Pharms Sharon Woods Tech Ctr 11520 Reed Hartman Hwy Cincinnati OH 45241-2422

WILSON, GAIL ANN, microbiologist, medical technologist; b. Danville, Ill., Jan. 31, 1955; d. Edgar A. and Sylvia J. (Davis) Likins; m. Willis E. Wilson, III, Apr. 9, 1982; 1 child, Sada. Degree, McClennan C.C., 1988; Cert. Lab. Technician, USAF. Cert. med. technologist, 1981. Med. technologist Bexar County Hosp., San Antonio, 1978-79; physicians office technologist various offices, Central, Tex., 1979-93; substitute tchr. Robinson (Tex.) Ind. Sch. Dist., 1991-93; cons. Centex Lab. Cons., Waco, 1991-93; microbiologist Allergan, Waco, 1993—. Dist. pres. Tex. PTA, Robinson, 1996; mem. sch. bd. Robinson Ind. Sch. Dist., 1993-96. Sgt. USAF, 1974-78. Mem. Am. Med. Technologists (cert.), Hist. Waco Found. (historian), Robinson C. of C. (treas. 1994-96). Presbyterian.

WILSON, GERALDINE O'CONNOR, psychologist; b. Hartford, Conn., Oct. 18, 1933; d. Dennis Paul and Florence Marguerite (Sheehan) O'Connor; m. Richard Thomas Wilson, Apr. 12, 1958; children: Susan. Deirdre P., Moira, Megan. BA, Marymount Coll., 1955; MS, So. Conn. State U., 1971, dipl. advanced studies, 1976. Social worker Southbury (Conn.) Tng. Sch., 1956-58; sch. psychologist Waterbury (Conn.) Bd. Edn., 1970-71, Brookfield (Conn.) Bd. Edn., 1971-95; pvt. practice Southbury, 1995—. Mem. Nat. Assn. Sch. Psychologists (cert.), Conn. Assn. Sch. Psychologists (cert., regional dir. 1972-74, treas. 1975-80, newspaper editor 1975-77, practioner of year 1995). Democrat. Roman Catholic. Home and Office: 51 Stillson Rd Southbury CT 06488

WILSON, H. DAVID, dean; b. West Frankfort, Ill., Sept. 13, 1939; m. Jeannette Wilson; children: Jennifer, Jacqueline, Mary Jeanne. AB in Zoology, Wabash Coll., 1961; MD, St. Louis Sch. Medicine, 1966. Diplomate Nat. Bd. Med. Examiners, Am. Bd. Pediatrics. Intern pediatrics Cardinal Glennon Meml. Hosp. for Children, St. Louis U., 1966-67; resident dept. pediatrics U. Ky. Med. Ctr., Lexington, 1967-68, chief resident, 1968-69; NIH rsch. fellow U. Tex. Health Scis. Ctr., Dallas, 1971-73; fellowship Am. Coun. on Edn., 1988-89; dir. admissions Coll. of Medicine, U. Ky., 1986-88; assoc. dean for acad. affairs, prof. Coll. Medicine, U. Ky., 1989-95; dean, prof. U. N.D. Sch. of Medicine, Grand Forks, 1995—; Author: (TV series) For Kids Sake, 1987-88; dir. pediatric infectious diseases U. Ky. Med. Ctr., Lexington, 1973-95, dir. cystic fibrosis care and tchg. ctr., 1975-80, med. dir., clin. virology lab., 1982-95; staff United Hosp., Grand Forks, 1995—; elected univ. senate U. Ky., 1993-96, bd. trustees Gluck Equine Rsch. Found., 1991-95, rules and elections univ. senate standing com., 1991-92, steering com. for U.K. self-study, 1990-95, co-chmn. steering com., 1990-95, chmn. review and search com. for chmn. dept. obstetrics and gynecology, 1990, chmn. curriculum com. Coll. of Medicine, 1989-95; elected acad. coun. of med. ctr. U. Ky. Med. Ctr., 1989-92; lectr. in field. Contbr. numerous articles to profl. jours. Fellow Pediatric Infectious Dieseases Soc.; mem. AMA, Am. Soc. of Microbiology, Am. Thoracic Soc., Am. Acad. Pediatrics, Pan Am. Group for Rapid Viral Diagnosis. Home: 10 Shadyridge Estates Grand Forks ND 58201 Office: U ND Sch of Medicine Rm 1925 501 N Columbia Rd Box 9037 Grand Forks ND 58202-9037

WILSON, HERBERT BENDEL, psychotherapist, counselor; b. Murfreesboro, Tenn., July 29, 1950; s. Rufus Randall and Virginia Lee (Phillips) W.; m Cynthia Lou Miller June 7, 1972 (div. Jan. 1975); 1 child, Rebecca Laurel. BA, Mid. Tenn. State U., 1972, MA, 1984. Lic. profl. counselor; cert. holotropic breathwork practitioner, Tenn. Health Related Bds., Bd. for Certification of Profl. Counselors and Marriage and Family Therapists. Photo journalist Daily News Jour., Murfreesboro, Tenn., 1978-79; counselor Spencer Youth Ctr., Nashville, 1979-82, Koala Adolescent Ctr., Nashville, 1985; substance abuse counselor Opportunity House, Inc., Nashville, 1985-89; psychotherapist Nashville, 1989—. Mem. AACD, Naskville Psychotherapy Inst. (mem. membership com. 1990—). Office: 5600 Brookwood Ter Nashville TN 37205-1451

WILSON, I. DODD, dean; b. St. Peter, Minn., July 10, 1936. AB summa cum laude, Dartmouth Coll., 1958; MD, Harvard U., 1961. Diplomate Am. Bd. Internal Medicine. Intern dept. medicine U. Minn. Hosps., Mpls., 1961-62; med. fellow Dept. of Medicine, 1962-63, 65-66; instr. dept. of medicine U. Minn. Med. Sch., Mpls., 1967-68, asst. prof., 1968-71, assoc. prof., 1971-76, dir. sect. of gastroenterology, 1972-83, vice chmn. dept. of medicine, 1983-86, prof. medicine, 1976-86; dean, prof. medicine U. Ark. Coll. of Medicine, Little Rock, 1986—; exec. vice chancellor U. Ark. Med. Scis., 1994—; mem. Univ. Hosp. Consortium Rsch. Task Force, 1994; adv. bd. UALR Donaghey Project, 1994—; mem. State Crime Lab. Bd., 1992—, chmn. 1991-92; bd. dirs. First Comml. Nat. Bank, Ark. Children's Hosp. Rsch. Inst., Inc.; mem. Ark. Rice Depot Bd., 1988-94; mem. State Med. Examiner's Commn., 1986-90; med. bd. Univ. Hosp., 1986—; mem. chancellor's cabinet U. Ark. for Med. Scis., 1986—; chmn. U. Minn. Clin. Assocs., ad hoc com. for fin matters, 1986; vice chmn. U. Minn. Clin. Assocs., 1986, clin. assoc. exec. com., 1985; mem. univ. com. Univ. Press, 1985-86; clin. assoc. planning and mktg. com. U. Minn., 1985; mem. Hosp. Quality Assurance Steering com., 1984-96, chmn. hosp. utilization mgmt. com., 1985; mem. Univ. Bookstore com., 1985; mem. Univ. Senate, 1985-86; chmn. dept. medicine search com. for Dir. of Gen. Internal Medicine, 1985; chmn. med. sch. search com. head of dept. dermatology U. Minn., 1984, chmn. dept. medicine search com. for dir. pulmonary sect. 1984, mem. hosp. bd. govs. com. on planning and devel., 1983-86, med.=surg. hosp. facilities com., 1982-83, mem. steering com. of self-study task force U. of Minn. Med. Sch., 1982-83, many more coms. Contbr. numerous articles to profl. jours. Lt. USNR, 1963-65. Fellow ACP; mem. AMA, Am. Fedn. for Clin. Rsch., Am. Gastroenterol. Assn., Ctrl. Soc. for Clin. Rsch., Am. Assn. for the Study of Liver Disease, Ark. Med. Soc. (editl. bd. 1988-93, ex-officio mem., coun. 1987—), Pulaski County Med. Soc., Assn. of Am. Med. Colls. (coun. of deans, chair 1995-96, mgmt. edn. program planning com. 1993—, adv. panel on strategic positioning for health care reform 1992—, exec. coun. 1992—, adminstrv. bd. 1992—, DEANS-VA coordinating com. 1990-94, ad hoc com. on nursing svcs. and the tchg. hosp. 1989, adv. com. on medicare regulations for payment of physicians in tchg. hosps. 1989), So. Med. Phi Beta Kappa, Alpha Omega Alpha. Office: Univ Ark for Med Scis Mail Slot #550 4301 W Markham Little Rock AR 72205*

WILSON, JAMES ALLEN, physician; b. Gulfport, Miss., June 17, 1953; s. Herbert and Edna (Gentry) W.; m. D. Roxanne Sones, Aug. 2, 1974; children: Jason, Michelle, Rebecca, Meghan, Matthew. BS in Chemistry, Miss. Coll., 1975; MD, U. Miss., 1978. Diplomate Am. Bd. Urology. Resident in urology U. Fla., Gainesville, 1983; physician, staff urologist Ehrling-Bergquist Hosp. USAF, Omaha, 1983-86; staff urologist Lackland Air Force Base, San Antonio, 1986-88, Watson Clinic LLP, Lakeland, Fla., 1988—. Mem. Am. Urol. Assn., Fla. Urol. Soc. (exec. bd. dirs. 1990—). Home: 1010 N Sugartree Ln Lakeland FL 33813 Office: Watson Clinic LLP 1600 Lakeland Hills Blvd Lakeland FL 33805

WILSON, JAMES MICHAEL, healthcare consultant; b. Harrisburg, Pa., Sept. 14, 1958; s. William J. and Alicemae (Yeager) W.; m. Francine Wilson, Jan. 3, 1987. AA in Liberal Arts, Harrisburg Area C.C., 1979; BS in Pharmacy, Temple U., 1982, MBA in Health Adminstrn., 1986. Pharmacist Wilson's Pharmacy, Linglestown, Pa., 1982-83; adminstrv. asst. Grad. Hosp., Phila., 1983-84; profl. products rep. Roche Labs., Woodlyn, Pa., 1984-86; info. systems analyst Roche Labs., Nutley, N.J., 1986-88, planning mgr., 1988-89; sr. mgr. IMS Am., Totowa, N.J., 1989-90; v.p. SMG Mktg. Group, Chgo., 1990-96; v.p. bus. devel. Med. Data Internat., Inc., 1996—. Author various market studies in field. Fellow Am. Soc. Cons. Pharmacists; mem. Am. Soc. Health System Pharmacists, Acad. Managed Care Pharmacy, Med./Surg. Market Rsch. Group (program chmn. 1991). Republican. Roman Catholic.

WILSON, JAMES MILLER, IV, cardiovascular surgeon, educator; b. Atlanta, Mar. 11, 1946; s. James Miller Wilson III and Sara Sharp. Attended, Emory U.; MD, Duke U., 1971. Diplomate Am. Bd. Surgery, Am. Bd. Thoracic Surgery. Intern N.Y. Hosp., 1971-72; resident N.Y. Hosp.-Cornell Med. Ctr., 1972-73, U. Calif., San Francisco, 1975-80; attending staff Christ Hosp., Cin., 1980—, Bethesda Hosp., Cin., 1980—, Jewish Hosp., Cin., 1980—, Univ. Hosp., Cin., 1982—, Deaconess Hosp, Cin., 1982—; chmn. dept. cardiovasc. surgery Deaconess Hosp., Cin., 1985—; attending staff VA Med Ctr., Cin., 1983—, Children's Hosp., Cin., 1984—, Good Samaritan Hosp., Cin., 1994—; assoc. prof. clin. surgery U. Cin. Coll. Med., 1985—; mem. open heart surgery adv. com., Ohio, 1995—, lectr. in field. Contbr. numerous articles to profl. jours. Lt. Comdr. USN Submarine Svc., 1973-75. Fellow ACS, Am. Coll. Cardiology; mem. AMA, Am. Assn. Thoracic Surgery, Assn. Acad. Surgery, Soc. Thoracic Surgeons, Am. Heart Assn. (mem. cardiovasc. coun.), Ohio State Med. Assn., Cin. Acad. Medicine, Howard C. Nafziger Soc. Office: 311 Straight St Cincinnati OH 45219

WILSON, JANIE MENCHACA, nursing educator, researcher; b. Lytle, Tex., Mar. 15, 1936; m. Patrick W. Wilson; 1 child, Kathryn Lynn Kohlleppel. BSN, Incarnate Word Coll., San Antonio, 1958; MSN, U. Tex., San Antonio, 1973; PhD in Nursing, U. Tex., Austin, 1978. RN. Oper. rm. nurse Santa Rosa Hosp., San Antonio, 1958-59; instr. Brackenridge Hosp. Sch. Nursing, Austin, 1963-66; staff nurse Med. Coll. Ga., Augusta, 1967-68; instr. dept. nursing San Antonio Coll., 1968-72, prof. dept. nursing edn., 1976—; counselor Project GAIN Tex. Nurses Assn., Austin, 1973-76; rsch. assoc. Ctr. for Health Care Rsch. and Evaluation, U. Tex. System, Austin, 1974-75; cons. Nurse Aide Competency Evaluation Program, San Antonio, 1989—; mem. manuscript rev. panel Nursing Rsch., N.Y.C., 1989-91. Contbr. chpts. to books, articles to profl. jours. Bd. dirs. Ctr. for Health Policy Devel., San Antonio, 1988-92; mem. Nat. Adv. Coun. on Nurse Edn. and Practice, 1995—. 1st lt. USAF, 1960-63. Mem. AAUP, ANA (coun. nurse rschrs., coun. cultural diversity, fellow program for ethnic minorities 1975-77), Am. Acad. Nursing, Nat. League Nursing, Nat. Assn. Hispanic Nurses, Sigma Theta Tau. Roman Catholic. Home: 4126 Longvale Dr San Antonio TX 78217-3525 Office: San Antonio Coll 1300 San Pedro Ave San Antonio TX 78212-4201

WILSON, JEAN DONALD, endocrinologist, educator; b. Wellington, Tex., Aug. 26, 1932; s. J.D. and Maggie E. (Hill) W. BA in Chemistry, U. Tex., 1951, MD, 1955. Diplomate: Am. Bd. Internal Medicine. Intern, then resident in internal medicine Parkland Meml. Hosp., Dallas, 1955-58; clin. assoc. Nat. Heart Inst., Bethesda, Md., 1958-60; instr. internal medicine U. Tex. Southwestern Med. Sch., Dallas, 1960-61; prof. U. Tex. Southwestern Med. Sch., 1968—. Editor: Jour. Clin. Investigation, 1972-77. Served as sr. asst. surgeon USPHS, 1958-60. Recipient Amory prize Am. Acad. Arts and Scis., 1977, Fuller prize Am. Urol. Assn., 1983, Lita Annenberg Hazen award, 1986, Dale medal Soc. for Endocrinology, 1991, Pincus medal Worchester Found., 1992. Fellow Royal Coll. Physicians; mem. NAS, Am. Acad. Arts and Scis., Inst. Medicine, Am. Fedn. Clin. Rsch., Am. Soc. Clin. Investigation, Assn. Am. Physicians, Soc. Exptl. Biology and Medicine, Am. Soc. Biochemistry and Molecular Biology, Endocrine Soc. (Oppenheimer award 1972, Koch award 1993). Office: U Tex Southwestern Med Ctr Dept Internal Medicine 5323 Harry Hines Blvd Dallas TX 75235-8857

WILSON, JEREMY SOMERS, gastroenterologist, researcher; b. Sydney, N.S.W., Australia, May 30, 1950; s. Ernest P. and Rosemary (O'Connor) W.; m. Marie Joy McKell; children: Elizabeth, Alexandra. M.B.B.S. with honors, U. Sydney, 1974; MD, U. N.S.W., Sydney, 1984. Diplomate Med. Bd. N.S.W. Intern Royal North Shore Hosp., St. Leonards, N.S.W., Australia, 1974-75; resident and registrar internal medicine Repatriation Gen. Hosp., Concord, N.S.W., 1975-77, gastroenterology registrar, 1977-78; fellow in gastroenterology Prince of Wales and Prince Henry Hosps., N.S.W., 1978-80, accredited specialist in medicine, 1981-83, dir. alcohol and drug svc., 1986-88, staff specialist in gastroenterology, 1988-90, sr. staff specialist in gastroenterology, 1990—; Commonwealth postgrad. rsch. scholar U. N.S.W. and Prince Henry Hosp., 1981-83; NIH Fogarty Internat. fellow, CRB Blackburn travelling fellow RACP and vis. fellow medicine Alcohol Rsch. Ctr., Bronx VA Med. Ctr. and Mt. Sinai Sch. Medicine, N.Y.C., 1983-84, vis. fellow in medicine and fellow in liver disease and clin. nutrition, 1984-85; sr. lectr. cmty. medicine U. N.S.W., 1986-88, sr. lectr., 1988—; lectr. in field; site visitor specialist adv. com. dept. gastroenterology St. Vincent's Hosp., Melbourne, 1990; mem. non-smoking policy com. Eastern Health Svc., 1987, 88, mem. area mgmt. com. divsn. cmty. health, 1986-88, alcohol and drug svc. devel. group, 1987-88; bd. censors Australian Med. Soc. on Alcohol and Drug-Related Problems, 1988-89. Contbr. numerous articles, abstracts to profl. jours., chpts. to books. Mem. animal rsch. rev. panel representing Minister for Health, N.S.W., 1993—; chmn. local organizing com. Australian Gastroenterology Week, Sydney, 1994. Fellow Royal Australasian Coll. Physicians (mem. written exam. com. 1991—); mem. Gastroenterol. Soc. Australia (hon. sec. 1995—, councillor 1993—, mem. abstract selection com. 1987—, mem. rsch. inst. com. 1991—, therapeutics and investigations adv. com. 1991-93, sec. sci. programme com. 1994-95), Am. Gastroenterol. Assn., Australian Med. Assn., Am. Pancreatic Assn., Gastroenterology Rsch. Group, Internat. Assn. Pancreatology, The Gut Found. of Australia, World Congress Gastroenterology (coord. edn. ctr. 1990, mem. social com. 1990, mem. pancreatico-biliary subcom. 1990, Australian Liver Inst. (mgmt. com. 1988-89), Sydney Gut Club (sec. 1987-92). Office: Prince of Wales Hosp, Gastrointestinal Unit, Blacket Bldg, Randwick NSW 2031, Australia

WILSON, JIMMIE ALLEN, hospital administrator; b. Inavale, Nebr., Sept. 15, 1948; s. Francis Walter and Bernice Pauline (Humes) W.; m. Cheryll Lynn Rosenthal Clark, May 12, 1978 (div. Nov. 1990); children: Chad, Jessica; m. Nancy Gail Colston, June 18, 1994; 1 stepchild, Katie. BSBA, U. Nebr., 1970; MS in Health Care Adminstrn., Trinity U., 1987. Cert. adult care home adminstr., Kans. Dept. Health and Environ. Adminstrv. asst., dir. warehousing/transp., dir. compensation/benefits, personnel mgr. Nebr. Meth. Hosp., Omaha, 1970-78; hosp. adminstr. Brodstone Mem. Nuckolls County Hosp., Superior, Nebr., 1978-85; hosp. pres. Susan B. Allen Meml. Hosp., El Dorado, Kans., 1985—; pres., v.p., sec./treas. Hosp. Personnel Mgmt. Assn. of the Midlands, Nebr., 1976-78, Dist. IV Nebr. Hosp. Assn., 1981-83; pres. Dist. 4 Kans. Hosp. Assn., 1992-93. Bd. dirs., officer United Way, El Dorado, Kans., 1986-92, Red Cross, Superior, Nebr., 1979-82, El Dorado, 1992—. Mem. Am. Coll. Health Care Execs., Kans. Assn. Health CAre Execs., Kiwanis, El Dorado C. of C. (ex officio bd. dirs. 1985—). Home: 1704 SW 80th St El Dorado KS 67042 Office: Susan B Allen Meml Hosp 720 W Central El Dorado KS 67042

WILSON, JOHN ANTHONY CLARK, gastroenterologist; b. London, June 11, 1918; s. John Clark and Margaret (Youngson) W.; m. Frances Olwen Thomas, Nov. 2, 1956; children—Anne, Ian, Joy. M.B., Ch.B., U. Edinburgh, 1941. Sr. registrar St. Peters Hosp., Bedford, Eng., 1950-52; sr. house officer Hosp. for Sick Children, London, 1952-53; sr. registrar Royal Infirmary, Stoke on Trent, Eng., 1953-56; 1st asst. Manchester Royal Infirmary, Eng., 1956-60; cons. physician Hope and Salford Royal, Eng., 1960-82; hon. physician Salford Hosps., 1982-88; hon. lectr. in medicine U. Manchester, 1974-82; hon. physician St. Ann's Hospice, Manchester, 1982-86. Inventor coughing belt, 1983. Served with RAF, 1942-46. Recipient Distinction award Dept. Health, 1974. Fellow Royal Coll. Physicians (London), Royal Coll. Physicians (Edinburgh); mem. Eccles Med. Soc. (chmn. 1971-72), Brit. Med. Assn. Mem. United Reform Ch. Club: Manchester Edinburgh U. (pres. 1977-78). Avocations: medical filing; water colors; crosswords. Home: 22 Broad Oak Rd, Worsley Manchester M28 2TG, England

WILSON, JOHN RANDOLPH, cardiologist; b. Boston, Oct. 29, 1948; m. Marguerite, 1977; children: Marisa Lauren, Jonathan Wyndham, Julie Elisabeth. Student, Pomona Coll., 1967-68; BA in History, Stanford U., 1970; MD, Harvard U., 1974; MS, U. Pa., 1989. Intern Cleve. Met. Gen. Hosp., 1974-75, resident, 1975-77; fellow cardiology Hosp. U. Pa., Phila., 1977-79, rsch. fellow cardiology, 1979-80, dir. heart failure program, 1982-91, dir. cardiac exercise and heart failure program, 1986—; asst. prof. medicine U. Pa. Sch. Medicine, Phila., 1980-89, assoc. prof., 1989; prof. Vanderbilt U., Nashville, 1993—, dir. heart failure and heart transplant program. Mem. editl. bd. Am. Jour. Cardiology, 1994—; editl. cons. Circulation and Annals of Internal Medicine, 1982, 88. Recipient Rsch. Career Devel. award NIH, 1986-91, 93-96; merit rev. grantee VA, 1991-94; grantee-in-aid Nat. Am. Heart Assn., 1990-93, 94—. Fellow Am. Coll. Cardiology (mem. editl. bd.); mem. Am. Fedn. Clin. Rsch. (assoc.), Am. Heart Assn. Office: Vanderbilt Univ Med Ctr 315 MRB-2 Nashville TN 37232

WILSON, KATHLEEN GAYLE, family practice physician, naval officer; b. Austin, Tex., Nov. 16, 1956; d. Clarence Vernon Bailey and Dorothy Lucille Widner Yarbro; m. Darrell Wilson, Feb. 29, 1976; children: Jeshua Anthony, Brianna Dianne. AA, U. Md., Europe, 1978; BS with honors, U. Md., College Park, 1985; DO, U. Osteo. Med. and Health Sci., Des Moines, 1991. Diplomate Am. Bd. Family Practice; lic. osteo. physician, Tenn. Intern Nat. Naval Med. Ctr., Bethesda, Md., 1991-92; resident in family practice Naval Hosp., Jacksonville, Fla., 1992-95; mem. family practice staff Naval Hosp., Guantanemo Bay, Cuba, 1995-96; mem. family practice staff Naval Hosp., May Port, Fla., 1996—, advisor, 1986—; adviser LaLeche League Internat., 1986—; disaster preparedness officer Naval Hosp. Command, Guantanemo Bay, 1995-96, brig med. officer, 1995-96. Vol. for migrant phys. U.S. Navy, 1995—. Lt. USNR, 1991—. Recipient scholarships. Republican.

WILSON, LEONARD GILCHRIST, history of medicine educator; b. Orillia, Ont., Can., June 11, 1928; s. George Edward and Mary Agnes (MacPhee) W.; m. Adelia Katherine Hans, June 7, 1969; 1 child, George Edward Hans. B.A., U. Toronto, Can., 1949; M.Sc., U. London, 1955; Ph.D., U. Wis., Madison, 1958. Lectr. Mount Allison U., Sackville, N.B., Can., 1950-53; vis. instr. U. Calif., Berkeley, 1958-59; asst. prof. Cornell U., Ithaca, N.Y., 1959-60; asst. prof. Yale U., New Haven, 1960-65, assoc. prof., 1965-67; prof., head dept. history of medicine U. Minn., Mpls., 1967—. Author: Charles Lyell: The Years to 1841: The Revolution in Geology, 1972, Medical Revolution in Minnesota, 1989; editor: Benjamin Silliman and His Circle, 1979, Sir Charles Lyell's Scientific Journals on the Species Question, 1971; editor Jour. History Medicine and Allied Scis., 1973-82; co-editor: Readings in History of Physiology, 1966; mem. bd. mgrs. Jour. Hist. Medicine, 1962—. Fellow AAAS; mem. Am. Assn. History of Medicine, Am. Hist. Assn., History of Sci. Soc., Minn. Acad. Medicine (pres. 1984-85, sec.-treas. 1989—), Brit. Soc. for the History of Sci., Soc. for the History of natural History. Home: 797 Goodrich Ave Saint Paul MN 55105-3344 Office: U Minn Dept History of Medicine 420 Delaware St SE Minneapolis MN 55455-0374

WILSON, LESLIE, biochemist, cell biologist, biology educator; b. Boston, June 29, 1941; s. Samuel Paul Wilson and Lee (Melniker) Kamerling; m. Carla Helena Van Wingerden, Sept. 9, 1989; children from previous marriage: Sebastian A. Michael, Naomi Beth. BS, Mass. Coll. Pharmacy and Allied Health Scis., 1963; PhD, Tufts U., 1967; postdoctoral study, U. Calif. at Berkeley, 1967-69. Asst. prof. dept. pharmacology Stanford U. Sch. Medicine, 1969-74; assoc. prof. dept. biol. scis. U. Calif., Santa Barbara, 1975-78, prof. biochemistry, 1979—, chmn. dept. biol. scis., 1987-91, head divsn. molecular, cellular, devel. biol., 1992-93; sci. adv. panel mem. cell and devel. biology Am. Cancer Soc., Atlanta, 1984-88; cons. Eli Lilly & Co., Indpls., 1980—. Editor: (book series) Methods in Cell Biology, 1987—; assoc. editor Biochemistry; contbr. numerous rsch. papers to profl. publs. Bd. dirs. Cancer Found. Santa Barbara. Rsch. grantee NIH, 1970—, Am. Cancer Soc., 1986—. Mem. AAAS, Am. Soc. Cell Biology (chmn. sci. program 1977), Am. Soc. Biol. Chemistry and Molecular Biology, Am. Soc. Pharmacology and Exptl. Therapeutics, Am. chem. Soc. Democrat. Office: Univ Calif Dept Biochemistry Santa Barbara CA 93106

WILSON, LINDA ANN, renal dialysis nurse; b. Johnson City, Tenn., Feb. 22, 1947; d. Andrew Jackson and Dorothy (Pate) Robertson; m. William Eugene Wilson, Feb. 17, 1968. Student, U. Tenn., 1969. Cert. nephrology nurse. Nurse Johnson City (Tenn.) Med. Ctr., 1969-73, head nurse renal dialysis, 1973—. Vol. nurse Red Cross. Mem. NAFE, Internat. Platform Assn., Am. Nephrology Nurses Assn., Assn. Nurses Endorsing Transplantation.

WILSON, LINDA SMITH, academic administrator; b. Washington, Nov. 10, 1936; d. Fred M. and Virginia D. (Thompson) Smith; m. Paul A. Wilson, Jan. 22, 1970; 1 dau. by previous marriage: Helen K. Whatley, a stepdau., Beth A. Wilson. B.A., Newcomb Coll., Tulane U., 1957; Ph.D., U. Wis., 1962; HLD (hon.), Tulane U., 1993; DLitt. (hon.), U. Md., 1993. Postdoctoral rsch. assoc. U. Md., College Park, 1962-64, rsch. asst. prof., 1964-67; vis. asst. prof. U. Mo.-St. Louis, 1967-68; asst. to vice chancellor for rsch., asst. vice chancellor for rsch., assoc. vice chancellor for rsch. Washington U., St. Louis, 1968-75; assoc. vice chancellor for rsch. U. Ill., Urbana, 1975-85; assoc. dean Grad. Coll., U. Ill., Urbana, 1978-85; v.p. for rsch. U. Mich., Ann Arbor, 1985-89; pres. Radcliffe Coll., Cambridge, Mass., 1989—; chmn. adv. com. office sci. and engring. pers. NRC, 1990—; mem. dir.'s adv. coun. NSF, Washington, 1980-89, adv. com. edn. and human resources, 1990-95; mem. Nat. Commn. on Rsch., Washington, 1978-80; mem. com. on govt.-univ. relationships NAS, 1981-83, mem. coun. for govt.-univ.-industry rsch. roundtable, 1984-89; mem. rsch. resources adv. coun. NIH, Bethesda, Md., 1978-82, energy rsch. adv. bd. DOE, 1987-90; mem. sci., tech. and states task force Carnegie Commn. on Sci., Tech. and Govt., 1991-92; trustee com. on econ. devel., 1995—, overseer Mus. of Sci., Boston, 1992—. Author book chpts.; contbr. articles to profl. jours. Bd. govs. YMCA, Champaign-Urbana, Ill., 1980-83; mem. adv. bd. Nat. Coalition for Sci. and Tech., Washington, 1983-87; trustee Mass. Gen. Hosp., 1992—; dir. Citizen's Fin. Corp., 1996—. Recipient Centennial award Newcomb Coll., 1986; named One of 100 Emerging Leaders Am. Coun. Edn. and Change, 1978. Fellow AAAS (bd. dirs. 1984-88); mem. NAS (coord. coun. for edn. 1991-93), Am. Chem. Soc. (bd. coun. com. on chemistry and pub. affairs 1978-80), Soc. Rsch. Adminstrs. (Disting. Contbn. to Rsch. Adminstrn. award 1984), Nat. Coun. Univ. Rsch. Adminstrs., Assn. for Biomed. Rsch. (bd. dirs. 1983-86), Inst. Medicine (mem. coun. 1986-89), Am. Coun. Edn. (commn. on women in higher edn. 1991-93, chair 1993), Phi Beta Kappa, Sigma Xi, Alpha Lambda Delta, Phi Delta Kappa, Phi Kappa Phi. Home: 76 Brattle St Cambridge MA 02138-3452 Office: Radcliffe Coll Office of Pres Fay House 10 Garden St Cambridge MA 02138

WILSON, LYN LEONARD, nurse, consultant; b. Fontana, Calif., June 30, 1951; d. William Robert and Wilda M. (Pirl) L.; m. Steven L. Wilson, Nov. 7, 1987; children: Katrina Elaine, Alexander James, Amy Elizabeth. Diploma, St. Francis Sch. Nursing, 1975; BS in Interior Design, Kans. State U., 1984. RN; cert. interior designer. Staff nurse St. Francis Regional Med. Ctr., Wichita, Kans., 1973-81; rsch. nurse U. Kans. Sch. Medicine, 1981-82; staff nurse Sierra Vista Hosp., San Luis Obispo, Calif., 1981, Meml. Hosp., Manhattan, Kans., 1981-84, The St. Mary Hosp., Manhattan, 1982-84; med. planner Widom, Wein, Cohen, L.A., 1984-85; facility programmer Am. Med. Internat., Inc., Beverly Hills, Calif., 1985-86; pres. Lyn Leonard & Assoc., Inc., Fairway, Kans., 1986—. Mem. Inst. Bus. Designers (affiliate). Roman Catholic. Home and Office: 6033 Alhambra St Shawnee Mission KS 66205-3160

WILSON, M. ROY, medical educator; b. Yokohama, Japan, Nov. 28, 1953. BS, Allegheny Coll., 1976; MD, Harvard Med. Sch., 1980; MS in Epidemiology, UCLA, 1990. Diplomate Nat. Bd. Medicine, Am. Bd. Ophthalmology. Intern Harlem Hosp. Ctr., N.Y.C., 1980-81; resident in ophthalmology Mass. Eye & Ear Infirmary/Harvard Med. Sch., Boston, 1981-84, glaucoma, 1984-85; clin. fellow in ophthalmology Harvard Med. Sch., 1980-85, clin. asst. ophthalmology, 1985-86; clin. instr. dept. surgery, Divsn. Ophthalmology Howard U. Sch. Medicine, Washington, 1985-86; asst. prof. ophthalmology UCLA, 1986-91; asst. prof., chief Divsn. Ophthalmology Charles R. Drew U. of Medicine and Sci., L.A., 1986-90, assoc. prof., chief Divsn. Ophthalmology, 1991-94, acad. dean, 1993-95, dean, 1995—, prof., 1994—; prof. UCLA, 1994—; asst. in ophthalmology Mass. Eye and Ear Infirmary, 1985-86; cons. ophthalmologist, Victoria Hosp., Castries, St. Lucia, 1985-86; hosp. appointment, UCLA; chief physician Martin Luther King, Jr. Hosp., L.A., 1986—; project dir. Internat. Eye Found., Ministry of Health, 1985-86; biology lab instr., Allegheny coll., 1975; instr. in biochemistry Harvard U. Summer Sch., 1977-78; instr. Harvard Med. Sch., 1980-85, others; cons. and presenter in field; participant coms. in field. Mem. AMA, Assn. Rsch. in Vision and Ophthalmology, Chandler-Grant Glaucoma Soc., Nat. Med. Assn., Am. Acad. Ophthalmology, Soc. Eye Surgeons Internat. Eye Found., Mass. Eye and Ear Infirmary Alumni Assn., So. Calif. Glaucoma Soc., West Coast Glaucoma Study Club, Assn. Univ. Profs. in Ophthalmology, L.A. Eye Soc., Calif. Med. Assn., Am. Glaucoma Soc., Soc. Epidemiol. Rsch., Am. Pub. Health Assn. Office: 1621 E 120th St Los Angeles CA 90059

WILSON, MARJORIE PRICE, physician, medical commission executive. Student, Bryn Mawr Coll., 1942-45; M.D., U. Pitts., 1949. Intern U. Pitts. Med. Ctr. Hosps., 1949-50; resident Children's Hosp. U. Pitts., 1950-51, Jackson Meml. Hosp., U. Miami Sch. Medicine, 1954-56; chief residency and internship div. edn. svc. Office of Rsch. and Edn., VA, Washington, 1956, chief profl. tng. div., 1956-60, asst. dir. edn. svc., 1960; chief tng. br. Nat. Inst. Arthritis and Metabolic Disease NIH, Bethesda, Md., 1960-63, asst. to assoc. dir. for tng. Office of Dir., 1963-64, assoc. dir. program devel. OPPD, 1967-69, asst. dir. program planning and evaluation, 1969-70; assoc. dir. extramural programs Nat. Libr. Medicine, 1964-67; dir. dept. instl. devel. Assn. Am. Med. Colls., Washington, 1970-81; sr. assoc. dean U. Md. Sch. Medicine, Balt., 1981-86, vice dean, 1986-88, acting dean, 1984; pres., CEO, Ednl. Commn. Fgn. Med. Grads., Phila., 1988-95, emeritus, 1995—; mem. Inst. Medicine Nat. Acad. Scis.,1974—; bd. visitors U. Pitts. Sch. Medicine, 1974—; mem. Nat. Bd. Med. Examiners, 1980-87, 89—; mem. adv. bd. Fogarty Internat. Ctr., 1991—. Contbr. articles to profl. jours. Mem. adv. bd. Robert Wood Johnson Health Policy Fellowships, 1975-87; trustee Analytic Services, Inc., Falls Church, Va., 1976—. Fellow Am. Coll. Physician Execs., AAAS; mem. Assn. Am. Med. Colls., Am. Fedn. Clin. Research, IEEE. Office: Ste 475 2401 Pennsylvania Ave NW Washington DC 20037

WILSON, MARY ELIZABETH, physician, educator; b. Indpls., Nov. 19, 1942; d. Ralph Richard and Catheryn Rebecca (Kurtz) Lausch; m. Harvey Vernon Fineberg, May 16, 1975. AB, Ind. U., 1963; MD, U. Wis., 1971. Diplomate Am. Bd. Internal Medicine, Am. Bd. Infectious Diseases. Tchr. of French and English Marquette Sch., Madison, Wis., 1963-66; intern in medicine Beth Israel Hosp., Boston, 1971-72, resident in medicine, 1972-73, fellow in infectious diseases, 1973-75; physician Albert Schweitzer Hosp., Deschapelles, Haiti, 1974-75, Harvard Health Svcs., Cambridge, Mass., 1974-75; asst. physician Cambridge Hosp., 1975-78; hosp. epidemiologist Mt. Auburn Hosp., Cambridge, 1975-79, chief of infectious diseases, 1978—; adv. com. immunization practices Ctrs. for Disease Control, Atlanta, 1988-92; acad. adv. com. Nat. Inst. Pub. Health, Mex., 1989-91; cons. Ford Found., 1988; instr. in medicine Harvard Med. Sch., Boston, 1975-93, asst. clin. prof., 1994—; asst. prof. depts. epidemiology and population and internat. health Harvard Sch. Pub. Health, 1994—; lectr. Sultan Qaboos U., Oman, 1991; chair Woods Hole Workshop, Emerging Infectious Diseases. Author: A World Guide to Infections: Diseases, Distribution, Diagnosis, 1991; co-editor: (with Richard Levins and Andrew Spielman) Disease in Evolution: Global Changes and Emergence of Infectious Diseases, 1994; mem. editl. bd. Current Issues in Pub. Health; edtl. bd., travel medicine & tropical diseases sect. editor Infectious Diseases in Clinical Practice. Mem. Cambridge Task Force on AIDS, 1987—, Earthwatch, Watertown, Mass., Cultural Survival, Inc., Cambridge; bd. dirs. Horizon Communications, West Cornwall, Conn., 1990. Recipient Lewis E. and Edith Phillips award U. Wis. Med. Sch., 1969, Cora M. and Edward Van Liere award, 1971, Mosby Scholarship Book award, 1971. Fellow ACP, Infectious Diseases Soc. Am., Royal Soc. Tropical Medicine and Hygiene; mem. Am. Soc. Microbiology, N.Y. Acad. Scis., Am. Soc. Tropical Medicine and Hygiene, Mass. Infectious Diseases Soc., Peabody Soc., Internat. Soc. Travel Medicine, Wilderness Med. Soc., Soc. for Vector Ecology, Internat. Union Against Tuberculosis and Lung Disease, Soc. for Epidemiol. Rsch., Sigma Sigma, Phi Sigma Iota, Alpha Omega Alpha. Office: Mt Auburn Hosp 330 Mount Auburn St Cambridge MA 02138-5502

WILSON, MELVIN NATHANIEL, psychology educator; b. St. Louis, Sept. 27, 1948; s. William F. Wilson and Mary Helen (Warder) Thompson; m. Eunice Clark, June 9, 1969 (div. June 1976); 1 child, Jibri-Akil; m. Angela Maria Davis, July 20, 1980. BA, Millikin U., 1970; MA, U. Ill., 1973, PhD, 1977. Asst. prof. U. Houston, 1976-78; vis. asst. prof. U. Ill., Champaign, 1978-79; asst. prof. U. Va., Charlottesville, 1979-86, assoc. prof., 1986—. Author: African American Family Life: Its Structural and Ecological Aspects, 1995; assoc. editor Am. Jour. Cmty. Psychology. Minority Rsch. scholar NSF, 1983-85; fellow Rockefeller Found., 1987, Social Sci. Rsch. Coun., 1991; USPHS grantee, 1970-72. Fellow APA, Am. Psychol. Soc.; mem. Soc. Rsch. on Child Devel., Nat. Coun. Family Rels., Assn. Black Psychologists (life). Office: U Va Psychology Dept Gilmer Hall Charlottesville VA 22903-2477

WILSON, MYRON ROBERT, JR., retired psychiatrist; b. Helena, Mont., Sept. 21, 1932; s. Myron Robert Sr. and Constance Ernestine (Bultman) W. BA, Stanford U., 1954, MD, 1957. Diplomate Am. Bd. Psychiatry and Neurology. Dir. adolescent psychiatry Mayo Clinc, Rochester, Minn., 1965-71; pres. and psychiatrist in chief Wilson Ctr., Faribault, Minn., 1971-86; ret., 1986; chmn. Wilson Ctr., 1986-90; ret., 1990; assoc. clin. prof. psychiatry UCLA, 1985—. Contbr. articles to profl. jours. Chmn., chief exec. officer C.B. Wilson Found., L.A., 1986—; mem. bd. dirs. Pasadena Symphony Orchestra Assn., Calif., 1987. Served to lt. comdr., 1958-60. Fellow Mayo Grad. Sch. Medicine, Rochester, 1960-65. Fellow Am. Psychiat. Assn., Am. Soc. for Adolescent Psychiatry, Internat. Soc. for Adolescent Psychiatry (founder, treas. 1985-88, sec. 1985-88, treas. 1988-92); mem. Soc. Sigma Xi (Mayo Found. chpt.). Episcopalian. Office: Wilson Found 8033 W Sunset Blvd # 4019 West Hollywood CA 90069-1925

WILSON, PAUL TYLER, psychiatrist; b. T'aiku, Shansi, China, Mar. 2, 1932; came to U.S., 1933; s. Samuel Eugene and Alice (Walker) W.; m. Barbara Foley, Feb. 19, 1955; children: Patricia Tyler, Andrea Marie, James Walker. BA, Columbia Coll., 1954; MD, Columbia U., 1961. Diplomate Am. Bd. Psychiatry and Neurology. Intern U. Chgo. Hosp., 1961-62; resident psychiatry U. Mich. Hosp., Ann Arbor, 1962-65; profl. staff Am.

Psychiat. Assn., Washington, 1965-70; psychiatrist Paul T. Wilson, M.D., P.A., Bethesda, Md., 1971—; clin. faculty Georgetown Med. Sch., Washington, 1968-78. Co-author: Money & Information for Mental Health, 1971, Survival Manual for Medical Students, 1982. Fellow Am. Psychiat. Assn.; mem. AAAS, Group for Advancement Psychiatry, Edgemoor Club. Home: 5611 Huntington Pky Bethesda MD 20814-1132 Office: 4401 E West Hwy Bethesda MD 20814-4523

WILSON, PETER RICHARD, consultant geriatrician; b. London, Jan. 14, 1935; s. Jack Marston and Kathleen Penelope Hundley (White) W.; m. Charlotte Elizabeth, July 13, 1962; children: Stuart Marston, Alistair John, Emily Louise. Student, Kings Coll., Wimbledon, Eng., 1947-53, Merton Coll., Oxford, Eng., 1953-57; BM, BCh (hon.), 1960, MA (hon.), 1960. Intern St. Thomas Hosp., London, 1957-61; cons. dept. geriatric medicine Birchwood Severalls Hosp., Colchester, Eng., 1970-95; Mem. exec. coun. Hungtington's Disease Assn.; dir. nursing home elderly mentally ill, Braintree, Eng. Parish councillorr. Fellow Royal Coll. Physicians, Royal Soc. Medicine; mem. Rotary (pres. 1986). Anglican. Home: Vaughans Abberton Rd, Colchester CO2 0LB, England

WILSON, RAYMOND CLARK, former hospital executive; b. Birmingham, Ala., July 8, 1915; s. Raymond Clyde and Lida (Gay) W.; m. Sara Elizabeth Paris, Feb. 17, 1940; children: Margery Jo, Richard Clark, Sara Elizabeth, Raymond Paul. Student, Oglethorpe U., 1933-34, U. Ga., 1934-37, Tulane U., 1948; D.Bus. Adminstrn. (hon.), William Carey Coll. Office mgr. firm C.R. Justi (contractor), Atlanta, 1933-42; paymaster J.A. Jones Constrn. Co., Brunswick, Ga., 1942-45; asst. supt. So. Bapt. Hosp., New Orleans, 1946-53; adminstr. So. Bapt. Hosp., 1953-68, exec. dir., 1969-77; pres. Affiliated Bapt. Hosps., Inc., 1977-80, Health Care Cons. & Mgmt. Services, Inc., 1977-80; ret., 1980; exec. dir. Bapt. Meml. Hosp., Jacksonville, Fla., 1973-77; dir., chmn. La. Health and Indemnity Co.; dir. New Orleans Area Health Planning Council, 1969-74. Bd. dirs. Bapt. Hosp. Found., 1970-78; bd. trustees Crosby Meml. Hosp., 1992-94, chmn., 1993-94. With USAAF, 1945-46. Paul Harris fellow Rotary Found. Fellow Am. Coll. Healthcare Execs. (bd. regents 1972-75); mem. Hosp. Svc. Assn. (bd. dirs., treas. 1953-74), Am. Hosp. Assn. (ho. dels. 1972-75), La. Hosp. Assn. (pres. 1956), New Orleans Hosp. Coun. (pres. 1954-55), Southeastern Hosp. Conf. (pres. 1963), Bapt. Hosp. Assn. (pres. 1964-65). Baptist (trustee, deacon). Home: 200 W Sunnybrook Rd Carriere MS 39426-7831

WILSON, RICHARD PHILIP, ophthalmologist, researcher; b. Frankfurt, Germany, May 22, 1947; came to U.S., 1948; s. Philip Murray and Neva Pearl (Cornelius) W.; m. Karen Lynn Kraus, May 9, 1981; 1 child, Philip Rylan. AB, The Johns Hopkins U., 1969; MD, U. Mo., 1979. Clerkship Community Psychiatry Queens Cliff Mental Health Ctr., North Ryde, Australia, 1973, Psychiatric Hosp., Sidney, Australia, 1973; internal med. clerkship U.S.S. Hope, Maceio, Brazil, 1973; surgery internship U. Va. Hosp., Charlotteville, 1973-74; psychiatry residency Vanderbilt U. Hosp., Nashville, 1974-75; ophthalmology residence then fellowhip The Wills Eye Hosp., Phila., 1975-78, 78-79; from asst. surgeon to attending surgeon Wills Eye Hosp. Glaucoma Svc., 1979—; dir. Glaucoma Svc. Rsch. Lab., Wills Eye Hosp., 1979—; assoc. surgeon, dir. Lankenau Hosp. Glaucoma Svc., Phila., 1984—, 1979-86; opthalmologist TumuTumu Hosp., Presbyn. Ch. East Africa, Keratina, Kenya, 1979; vis. prof. Kenyatta U. Hosp., Nairobi, Kenya, 1979; from asst. prof. to assoc. prof. Thomas Jefferson U. Sch. Med., Phila., 1979—; dir. resident edn. Lankenau Hosp., 1980-87; cons. Saudi Arabian Govt. for King Khaled Eye Spl. Hosp., Riyad, 1982, Am. Acad. Opthalmology, 1985-86; cours. dir. 14th annual Wills Eye Hosp. Glaucoma Conf., 1990. Sect. editor (Glaucoma) Yr. Book of Ophthalmology and Key Ophthalmology, Chgo., 1988-95; editor: Yearbook of Ophthalmology, 1996—; author (videotape) The Management of Combined Cataract and Glaucoma, 1989; reviewer Archives of Ophthalmology, Archives of Internal Medicine, Am. Jour. Opthalmology, Jour. of the AMA, Ophthalmology, Glaucoma; contbr. numerous articles to profl. jours., chpts. to books. Dir. Outreach Program to Kenya, Vol. Ophthalmology Staff, Wills Eye HOsp., 1978—; bd. dirs. Assoc. Svcs. for the Blind, Phila., 1982-84; vol. Emmanuel Eye Ctr., Accra, Ghana, 1996. Mem. AMA (appointed Diagnostic and Therapeutic Tech. Assessment Reference Panel 1990), Am. Acad. of Opthalmology, Am. Glaucoma Soc. (chmn. Profl. Terminology and Codes, 1989-90, rep. to Am. Acad. of Opthalmology CPT Task Force, 1989—), ACS, Pa. Med. Assn., Montgomery County Med. Assn., Opthalmology Club of Phila., Phila. Coll. Physicians, Assn. for Rsch. in Vision and Opthalmology. Democrat. Presbyterian. Home: 243 Beech Hill Rd Wynnewood PA 19096-1122 Office: Glaucoma Svc Wills Eye Hosp 9th And Chestnut St Philadelphia PA 19107-5127

WILSON, ROBERT ALBERT, communications consultant; b. Jamestown, N.Y., Dec. 20, 1936; s. Albert C. and Minnie M. (Leroy) W.; m. Marcia K. Milton, Aug. 22, 1959; children: Jonathan, Kathryn. BA magna cum laude, Colgate U., 1959; diploma, Sch. Advanced Internat Studies, Bologna, Italy, 1960; MA, Johns Hopkins, 1961. News editor/announcer Sta. WJOC, Jamestown, 1953-57; staff reporter Post-Jour., Jamestown, 1958-61; intelligence research specialist U.S. Info. Agy., Washington, 1963-66, sr. editor, 1966-72; sr. assoc. pub. affairs Pfizer, Inc., N.Y.C., 1972-78, assoc. dir. pub. affairs, 1978-81, v.p. pub. affairs, 1981-96; pres. Pfizer Found., Inc., N.Y.C., 1981-95; dir. Nat. Health Coun., 1987-94; chmn. pub. affairs sect. Pharm. Rsch. and Mfrs. Am., 1982-83. Exec. com. Religion in Am. Life, N.Y.C., 1988—; pres. bd. dirs. Conn. Grand Opera & Orch., 1994—. Mem. Pub. Rels. Soc. Am., Riverside Yacht Club, Phi Beta Kappa. Office: Conn Grand Opera and Orch 4 Landmark Sq Stamford CT 06901

WILSON, ROBERT FOSTER, cardiologist, educator; b. Oak Park, Ill., Apr. 30, 1953; s. Robert Foster and Mary Elizabeth (Clark) W.; children: Rebecca, Adam, Jessica. BS, Pa. State U., 1973; MD, U. Iowa, 1977. Diplomate Am. Bd. Internal Medicine with subspecialty in cardiovascular diseases. Resident U. Tex., San Antonio, 1977-80; fellow in cardiovascular disease U. Iowa, Iowa City, 1982-85, asst. prof., 1985-86; asst. prof. U. Minn., Mpls., 1986-91, assoc. prof., 1991—, dir. cardiac catheterization lab., 1991—; chmn. bd. Invasatec, Mpls., Mpls., 1994—. Fellow Am. Heart Assn. (coun. circulation 1991—). Office: U Minn Cardiovascular Divsn 420 Delaware St SE # 508 Minneapolis MN 55455-0374

WILSON, ROBERT GODFREY, radiologist; b. Montgomery, Ala., Mar. 18, 1937; s. Robert Woodridge and Lucille (Godfrey) W.; B.A., Huntingdon Coll., 1957; M.D., Med. Coll. Ala., 1961; m. Dorothy June Waters, Aug. 31, 1957; children—Amy Lucille, Robert Darwin, Robert Woodridge II, Lucy Elizabeth. Intern, Letterman Gen. Hosp., San Francisco, 1961-62; resident in radiology U. Okla. Med. Center, Oklahoma City, 1965-68, clin. instr. in radiology, 1968—; practice medicine specializing in diagnostic and therapeutic radiology, nuclear medicine, Shawnee, Okla., 1968—; mem. med. staff Shawnee Med. Center, Mission Hill Meml. Hosp., Shawnee, 1968—. Served to capt. M.C., USAF, 1960-65. Diplomate Nat. Bd. Med. Examiners, Am. Bd. Radiology, Am. Bd. Nuclear Medicine. Mem. AMA, Okla., Pottawatomie County med. socs., Okla., Greater Oklahoma City radiol. socs., Am. Coll. Radiology, Soc. Nuclear Medicine, Radiol. Soc. N.Am. Methodist. Home: 26 Sequoyah St Shawnee OK 74801-5570 Office: 1110 N Harrison St Shawnee OK 74801

WILSON, ROBERT HENRY, psychologist, educator; b. Abington, Pa., May 18, 1945; s. Robert Henry and Eleanore Mae (Whitaker) W.; m. Karen Bofinger, Dec. 22, 1973. BS in Edn., Shippensburg U., 1967, MS in Counseling Psychology, 1972; MA in Psychology, Lehigh U., 1975. Tchr. Neshaminy Sch. Dist., Langhorne, Pa., 1967—, student assistance program dir., 1985—; pres. RHW Counseling/Consulting, Newtown, Pa., 1983—; mem. state-wide student assistance program com. Dept. Edn., 1988—. Editor: Program and Practices Manual, 1988, 2d edit., 1991. Recipient citation Pa. Ho. of Reps., 1986. 87, 88, 90. U.S. Ho. of Reps., 1988, Presdl. award U.S. Dept. Edn., 1990, 95. Mem. Pa. Assn. Student Assistance Profls. (pres. 1995—), Am. Fedn. Tchrs. (exec. sec. 1980-89), Am. Psychol. Assn. Office: Neshaminy Sch Dist 2001 Old Lincoln Hwy Langhorne PA 19047-3240

WILSON, ROBERT STANLEY EDWARD, physician, researcher; b. Truro, Cornwall, Eng., Nov. 30, 1941; s. Stanley William and Grace Rosetta (Wicks) W.; m. Jacqueline Mary Anne, Mar. 2, 1968; children—Peter Edward, Andrew Robert, Sarah Elizabeth. B.Sc. with honors, U. Bristol, Eng., 1965, M.B., Ch.B. with honors, 1968. House physician Bristol Royal Infirmary, 1968, house surgeon, 1969, sr. house officer in pathology, 1969-70, sr. registrar and tutor, 1973-76; sr. house officer Bristol Gen. Hosp., 1970-71; registrar, tutor Gordon & Westminster Hosp., London, 1971-72, Hammersmith Hosp., London, 1972-73; cons. physician Royal Shrewsbury Hosp., Shropshire, Eng., 1976—, former vice chmn. med. div. and unit mgr.; participant films, radio broadcast. Contbr. numerous articles, chpts. to profl. publs., since 1976 mainly on nebuliser therapy. Chmn. Longden Village Hall, Shropshire, 1979—; sch. gov. Longden Primary Sch., 1981-85, Mary Webb Secondary Sch.; chmn. Shrewsbury Stroke Club, 1981—. Essex County maj. scholar Bristol U., 1962-68. Fellow Royal Coll. Physicians; mem. Brit. Thoracic Assn., West Midlands Thoracic Soc. Liberal. Club: Oswestry Golf (Shropshire). Avocations: farming; golf; philately; watercolor painting; spectator sports. Home: Lower Wood House,, Longden nr Shrewsbury,, Shropshire SY5 8HB, England Office: Royal Shrewsbury Hosp, Mytton Oak Rd, Shrewsbury Shropshire SY3 8XF, England

WILSON, ROGER STANLEY, physician, anesthesiologist; b. Bronx, N.Y., Aug. 30, 1939; s. Floyd Newton and Margaret (Stanley) Wilson; m. Donna Feldmann; children: Susan, Mark. BS cum laude, Trinity Coll., Conn., 1962; MD, N.J. Coll. Medicine, 1966. Diplomate Am. Bd. Anesthesiology, subbd. Critical Care Medicine; lic. physician, N.Y., Mass.; diplomate Nat. Bd. Med. Examiners. Rotating intern Hackensack (N.J.) Hosp., 1966-67; resident in anesthesiology Columbia-Presbyn. Med. Ctr., N.Y.C., 1967-69; vis. fellow in anesthesiology Columbia U., 1969-70; from asst. in anesthesia to anesthetist Mass. Gen. Hosp., Boston, 1970-91; from instr. anesthesia to assoc. prof. Harvard Med. Sch., Boston, 1970-91; attending, chmn. dept. anesthesiology and critical care Meml. Hosp. for Cancer and Allied Diseases, N.Y.C., 1991—; mem. Meml. Sloan-Kettering Cancer Ctr., N.Y.C., 1991—; prof. anesthesiology Cornell U. Med. Coll., N.Y.C., 1991—; assoc. examiner Am. Bd. Anesthesiology, 1978—. Assoc. editor Jour. Cardiothoracic and Vascular Anesthesia, 1986—, Critical Care Medicine, 1990-93; contbr. numerous articles to profl. books; editor, author numerous book chpts. Recipient Henry K. Beecher Clin. Tchr. award Mass. Gen. Hosp., 1977, 84. Mem. Am. Soc. Anesthesiologists, Soc. Critical Care Medicine, Internat. Anesthesia Rsch. Soc., Am. Thoracic Soc., Assn. Univ. Anesthetists, Am. Soc. Critical Care Anesthesiologists, Soc. Cardiovascular Anesthesiologists, N.Y. State Soc. Anesthesiologists, N.Y. State Thoracic Soc., Am. Heart Assn. (coun. on cardiothoracic and vascular surgery), N.Y. County Med. Soc., Med. Soc. State N.Y. Office: Meml Sloan-Kettering Cancer Ctr 1275 York Ave New York NY 10021

WILSON, RUBY LEILA, nurse, educator; b. Punxsutawney, Pa., May 29, 1931; d. Clark H. and Alda E. (Armstrong) W. BS in Nursing Edn., U. Pitts., 1954; MSN, Case Western Res. U., 1959; EdD, Duke U., 1969. Staff nurse, asst. head nurse Allegheny Gen. Hosp., Pitts., 1951-52; night clin. instr., adminstrv. supr. Allegheny Gen. Hosp., 1951-55; staff nurse, asst. head nurse Fort Miley VA Hosp., San Francisco, 1957-58; instr. nursing Duke U. Sch. Nursing, Durham, N.C., 1955-57; asst. prof. med. surg. nursing Duke U. Sch. Nursing, 1959-66, assoc. in medicine, 1963-66, prof. nursing, 1971—, dean sch. nursing., 1971-84, asst. to chancellor for health affairs, 1984—; asst. prof. dept. community and family medicine Duke U. Sch. Medicine, 1971—; cons., vis. prof. Rockefeller Found., Thailand, 1968-71; vis. prof. Case Western Res. U., 1982-84; mem. Gov.'s Commn. on Health Care Reform in N.C., 1994. Contbr. articles to profl. jours. Active N.C. Med. Care Commn., Gov.'s Commn. on N.C. Health Care Reform, 1994—. Fellow Am. Acad. Nursing, Inst. Medicine; mem. ANA, Am. Assn. Colls. Nursing, Am. Assn. Higher Edn., Nat. League Nursing, Assn. for Acad. Health Ctrs. (mem. inst. planning com.), Women's Forum N.C. (bd. dirs. 1984-88, 95—), N.C. Found. for Nursing (pres. 1990-94). Office: Duke U Med Ctr PO Box 3243 Durham NC 27715-3243

WILSON, SAMUEL MAYHEW, surgeon; b. Phila., June 26, 1950; s. Samuel Mack and Lois Elisabeth (Graf) W.; m. Dorothy Hay Barrus, June 9, 1990; children: Elisabeth Hay, Mary Jaudon. BA, Swarthmore Coll., 1972; MS, Drexel U., 1975; MD, Temple U., 1979. Diplomate Am. Bd. Surgery. Resident in surgery Temple U. Hosp., Phila., 1979-84; fellow in vascular surgery Presbyn.-U. Pa. Med. Ctr., Phila., 1984-86; attending surgeon Evang. Cmty. Hosp., Lewisburg, Pa., 1986-88, Albert Einstein Med. Ctr., Phila., 1988-95; attending surgeon Elkins Park (Pa.) Hosp., 1988-95, Frankford Hosp., Phila., 1988-95, JFK Meml. Hosp., Phila., 1988-95; staff surgeon Kent Gen. Hosp., Dover, 1996—; asst. clin. instr. surgery U. Pa. Med. Sch., Phila., 1984-85, assoc. clin. instr., 1985-88; clin. instr. surgery Temple U. Sch. Medicine, Phila., 1988—. Contbr. articles to profl. jours. Active Abington (Pa.) Presbyn. Ch., 1959—. Corp. USMCR, 1972-78. Fellow ACS; mem. AMA (Physician Recognition award), Med. Soc. Del., Kent County Med. Soc., Delaware Valley Vascular Soc., Eastern Vascular Soc. Home: 2 Drake Ct Wyoming DE 19934 Office: 807 S Bradford St Dover DE 19904

WILSON, SHERRY DENISE, speech and language pathologist; b. Rutherford, N.C., Jan. 10, 1963; d. Morris William and Betty Jean (Hudgins) Wilson. AA, Isothermal Community Coll., 1981; BS, Cen. Mo. State U., 1985, MS, 1988. Lic. speech-lang. pathologist, N.C. Speech pathologist DePaul Hosp. Home Health, Cheyenne, Wyo., 1987, 89; coord. handicap svcs., staff speech-lang. pathologist Laramie County Head Start, Cheyenne, 1987-89; speech pathologist, supr., coord., dir. inclusive pre-sch. Ednl. Svcs. Unit # 13, Scottsbluff, 1989-95, project dir. The Early Intervention Demonstration Project, 1991-95; dir. rehab. svc. Brentwood Hills Nursing Ctr. (Beverly Enterprises), Asheville, N.C., 1995—; planning region chair Interagy. coord. Coun. Presch. Spl. Edn., Scottsbluff, Nebr., 1989-93, mem. 1993-95; mem. health adv. bd. Head Start. Gering, Nebr., 1989-91; cons. trainer in field. Founding mem. S.E. Wyo. AIDS Project, Cheyenne, 1989; Odyssey of the Mind coach Gering Jr. H.S., 1989-93; project dir., mem. exec. bd. Cmty. Devel. Coalition, 1994. Named Outstanding Speech Pathologist of Yr., Sigma Alpha Eta, 1985, Two Thousand Notable Am. Women, 1992, 96. Mem. NEA, Am. Speech-Lang.-Hearing Assn. (cert. clin. competence 1989—, Cert. Excellence 1993), Nebr. State Edn. Assn., Coun. for Exceptional Children (early childhood divsn.). Office: Brentwood Hills Nursing Ctr Asheville NC 28804

WILSON, SHERYL A., pharmacist; b. Nashville, Apr. 6, 1957; d. Robert Lewis and Norma Anne (Cox) W. BS in Biology, David Lipscomb U., 1979; BS in Pharmacy, Auburn U., 1985. Lic. pharmacist, Tenn. Student extern/intern East Alabama Med. Ctr., Opelika, Ala., 1982-86; staff pharmacist Metro Nashville Gen. Hosp., 1987-95, PharmaThera, Inc., Nashville, 1995—. Flutist Nashville Community Concert Band, 1973—; preschool tchr. Donelson Ch. of Christ, 1988—. Mem. Am. Pharm. Assn., Am. Soc. Health Sys. Pharmacists, Am. Soc. Parenteral and Enteral Nutrition, Tenn. Soc. Hosp. Pharmacists, Nashville Area Pharmacists Assn. Democrat. Home: 1439 Mcgavock Pike Nashville TN 37216-3231 Office: PharmaThera Inc 1410 Donelson Pike Ste B-3 Nashville TN 37217

WILSON, STEVEN EUGENE, ophthalmologist; b. Oklahoma City, Tex., Dec. 28, 1951; s. Gilford E. and Margie F. (Wheeler) W.; m. Jennifer Jane Lane, Jan. 1, 1995. BA, Calif. State U., Fullerton, 1974; MS in Molecular biology and Biochemistry, U. Calif., Irvine, 1977; MD, U. Calif., San Diego, 1984. Intern in internal medicine Cedars-Sinai Med. Ctr., L.A., 1984-85; resident in ophthalmology Mayo Clinic, Rochester, Minn., 1985-88; fellow in cornea La. State U. Eye Ctr., New Orleans, 1988-90; assoc. prof. U. Tex. Southwestern Med. Sch., Dallas, 1990-95; staff med. dir. Laser Ctrs. Excellence, Cleve. Clinic Found., 1995—; chmn. organizing com. Ocular Cell and Molecular Biology Symposium, Tamarron, Colo., 1996-97. Mem. edtl. bd. Refractive and Corneal Surgery, 1994—, Exptl. Eye Rsch., 1995—; contbr. more than 60 articles to med. jours. Recipient manpower ManPower award Rsch. To Prevent Blindness, 1995, William and Mary Greve internat. rsch. scholar, 1994; grantee Nat Eye Inst., 1992—, Nat. Cancer Inst., 1994—. Fellow Am. Acad. Ophthalmology (honor award 1995); mem. Assn. for Rsch. in Vision and Ophthalmology (program planning com. 1994-95), Internat. Soc. for Refractive Surgery, Internat. Soc. for Eye Rsch., Castroviejo Cornea Soc. Office: Cleve Clinic Found 9500 Euclid Ave Ste A31 Cleveland OH 44095

WILSON, STEVEN PAUL, medical educator; b. New Castle, Pa., Oct. 12, 1950; s. Clarence G. and Mary Elizabeth (Kerr) W.; m. Patricia Rae Forbush, Aug. 14, 1972; 1 child, Ruth Erin Wilson. BS summa cum laude, U. Pitts., 1972; PhD, Duke U., 1976. Asst. med. rsch. prof. Duke U. Med. Ctr., Durham, N.C., 1982-85; asst. prof. U. S.C. Sch. Medicine, Columbia, 1985-89; assoc. prof. U. S.C. Sch. Medicine, 1989—; vis. scientist Wellcome Rsch. Labs., Rsch. Triangle Park, N.C., 1979-81. Contbr. articles to Neuropeptides, FEBS Letters, Jour. Biol. Chemistry, Jour. Neurochemistry; mem. edtl. bd. Jour. Pharmacology and Exptl. Therapeutics 1995-98. NSF fellow, 1972-75, NIH fellow, 1976-79; recipient Stefan Mironescu Rsch. award U. S.C., 1986. Mem. Am. Heart Assn. (basic. sci. coun.), Am. Soc. Neurochemistry, Am. Soc. Pharmacology Experimental Therapeutics, Soc. Neurosci. (S.C. chpt. pres. 1989-90), Phi Beta Kappa. Presbyterian. Office: Dept Pharmacology U SC Sch Med Columbia SC 29208

WILSON, WARNER RUSHING, psychology educator; b. Jackson, Miss., July 27, 1935; s. William Enouch and Ruby (Goyne) W. A.B., U. Chgo., 1956; M.A., U. Ark., 1958; Ph.D., Northwestern U., 1960. Teaching asst. Northwestern U., 1957-60; research psychologist E.I. duPont de Nemours & Co., Wilmington, Del., 1960; asst. prof. U. Hawaii, 1960-65; asso. prof. U. Ala., 1965-73; prof. Wright State U., Dayton, Ohio, 1973-93; pvt. practice Las Vegas, Nev., 1993—; Cons. Bryce State Hosp., Tuscaloosa, Ala., 1966, Ednl. Testing Service, 1968, Tuscaloosa VA Hosp., 1968-74, H.R.B. Singer Co., 1972; Trainee Downey (Ill.) VA Hosp., summer 1959. Contbr. articles to profl. jours. spl. summer fellow in evaluation research Northwestern U., 1973-74, NSF grantee, 1976-78, Johnson Assocs. Postdoctoral Clin. fellow, 1981-82; Research grantee DuPont Co., 1961-62; Research grantee NIMH, 1965, 68-70; Research grantee NSF, 1966-68; Named Outstanding Psychology student U. Ark., 1956-57. Mem. Soc. Exptl. Social Psychology. Home: 2117 Flower Ave N Las Vegas NV 89109 Office: 3376 S Eastern Ave Las Vegas NV 89109-3367

WILSON, WARREN D., neurosurgeon; b. Rome, Ga., July 27, 1948; s. Cayce C. and Margaret (Bradford) W.; m. Beverly Foster, 1973. BA, Rutgers U., 1969; MD, Emory Med. Sch., 1973. Diplomate Am. Bd. Neurological Surgery, Am. Bd. Forensic Examiners. Intern in surgery U. Fla., Gainesville, 1973-74, resident in neurosurgery, 1974-78, teaching fellow neurosci., 1976-78; vice chmn. neurosurgery Harris Hosp., Ft. Worth, 1988-82, 92-94, chmn. neurosurgery, 1982-84, surgeon in chief, 1984-86; cons. neurosurgeon Tex. Med. Found., 1988-93; vice chief of surgery Huguley Hosp., Ft. Worth, 1989-90, chief of surgery, 1990-92; pvt. practice S.W. Neurol. Surgery Assocs., P.A., Ft. Worth. Named Outstanding Neurosurgeon, D mag., 1992. Fellow Am. Bd. Forensic Examiners; mem. Tex. Assn. Neurol. Surgeons (sec. 1986-89, pres.-elect 1990-91, pres. 1991-92, newsletter editor 1986-89), Tex. Med. Assn. (sec. sect. neurol. surgery 1992-93), Tarrant County Soc., Am. Assn. Neurol. Surgeons, Congress Neurol. Surgeons, Mira Vista Country Club. Office: SW Neuro Surgery Assocs PA 800 8th Ave Ste 220 Fort Worth TX 76104

WILSON, WAYNE JEROME, psychology educator; b. Ft. Smith, Ark., Oct. 24, 1932; s. O. B. Wilson and Ora Lee (Luckey) Wilson Rogers. BA, So. Meth. U., Dallas, 1959, MA, 1961; PhD, Tex. Christian U., Ft. Worth, 1965. Prof. psychology Stephen F. Austin State U., Nacogdoches, Tex., 1964—. Author: Good Murders and Bad Murders, 1991, 2d edit., 1996, Sexuality in the Land of Oz, 1994. With U.S. Army, 1953-55. Mem. APA (assoc.), Am. Psychol. Soc. Office: Stephen F Austin State U Psychology Dept Box 4658 Nacogdoches TX 75962

WILSON, WILLIAM PRESTON, psychiatrist, emeritus educator; b. Fayetteville, N.C., Nov. 6, 1922; s. Preston Puckett and Rosa Mae (VanHook) W.; m. Dorothy Elizabeth Taylor, Aug. 21, 1950; children: William Preston, Benjamin V., Karen E., Tammy E., Robert E. B.S., Duke U., 1943, M.D., 1947. Diplomate: Am. Bd. Psychiatry and Neurology (examiner). Intern Gorgas Hosp., Ancon, C.Z.; then resident psychiatry Duke U. Med. Center, later resident neurology, 1949-54; asst. prof. psychiatry Duke U. Med. Sch., 1955-58; asso. prof. psychiatry, dir. psychiat. research U. Tex. Med. Br., Galveston, 1958-60; asso. prof. psychiatry Duke U. Med. Center, 1961-64, head div. clin. neurophysiology, 1961-83, prof. psychiatry, head div. biol. psychiatry, 1964-84, emeritus prof. psychiatry, 1985—; dir. Inst. Christian Growth, Burlington, N.C., 1985—; chief neurophysiol. labs. VA Hosp., Durham, N.C., 1961-76; sec. Am. Bd. Qualification in Electroencephalography, 1971-77; mem. N.C. Gov.'s Task force on Diagnosis and Treatment; mem. med. adv. com. N.C. Found. Mental Health Rsch.; bd. dirs. nat. div. Contact Teleminstry USA, also mem. internat. commn. healing; cons. numerous area hosps.; Finch lectr. Fuller Theol. Sem., Pasadena, Calif., 1974; vis. prof. psychiatry Marshall U. Sch. Medicine, Huntington, W.Va., 1985-89. Co-author: The Grace to Grow; editor: Applications of Electroencephalography in Psychiatry; co-editor: EEG and Evoked Potentials in Psychiatry and Behavioral Neurology; Contbr. med. jours. Mem. ofcl. bd. Asbury United Methodist Ch., Durham; mem. program and curriculum com. United Meth. Ch., 1973-81; trustee Meth. Retirement Home, Durham, N.C.; pres. United Meth. Renewal Services, Inc., 1978-82. Served with AUS, 1943-46. Recipient Ephraim McDowell award Christian Med. Found., 1982, Pioneer in Christian Psychiatry award Congress on Christian Counseling, 1988; named Educator of Yr., Christian Med. and Dental Soc., 1996; EEG Montreal Neurol. Inst. fellow, 1954-55, postdoctoral fellow NIMH. Mem. Am. Psychiatric Assn., So. Psychiatric Assn. (pres. 1977-78), AMA, So. Med. Assn. (chmn. sect. neurology and psychiatry 1970), Med. Soc. N.C., Durham-Orange County Med. Soc. (chmn. student recruitment com. 1965), Soc. Biol. Psychiatry, Am. EEG Soc. (councillor), So. EEG Soc. (pres. 1964), Assn. Research Nervous and Mental Diseases, Am. Epilepsy Soc., AAAS, Am. Acad. Neurology, Sigma Xi, Alpha Omega Alpha. Republican. Club: U.S. Power Squadron (comdr. Durham 1971). Home: 1209 Virginia Ave Durham NC 27705-3263 Office: PO Box 2347 Burlington NC 27216-2347

WILSON, WILLIAM ROBERT, surgeon; b. Norwich, Conn., June 2, 1954; s. William Robert and Margaret Mary (Sullivan) W.; m. Joan Marie Wilson, Apr. 6, 1985; children: William Robert III, Brandon David, Alaina Victoria. AB cum laude, Kenyon Coll., 1976; MD, U. Conn., 1982. Instr. U. Conn., Farmington, 1977-78; resident gen. surgery U. Vt., Mpls., 1982-87; resident in thoracic surgery Case Western Res. U., Oak Lawn, Ill., 1987-89; assoc. staff surgeon Med. Coll. Ohio, Toledo, 1989-90, fellow in pediatric cardiac surgery, 1990-91, asst. prof. surgery and pediatrics, 1991—, chief pediatric cardiac surgery, 1991—; dir. ECMO program Med. Coll. Ohio, 1991—. Contbr. articles to profl. jours. and chpts. to books. Vestry mem. St. Michael's in the Hills, Toledo, 1993-95, adult edn. liaison, 1993—. Fellow ACS; mem. Soc. Thoracic Surgeons, Am. Heart Assn., Midwest Pediatric Cardiology Soc., Toledo Surg. Soc., AMA. Episcopalian. Office: Med Coll Ohio Dept Surgery 3000 Arlington Ave Toledo OH 43614

WILSON, WILLIAM SLATE, general and vascular surgeon, educator; b. Portland, Oreg., June 11, 1937; s. William Miles and Marie Slate (Mecklen) W.; m. A. Davids Morrow, June 2, 1973; children: Megan E., William E. BA, Williams Coll., 1959; MS, MD, U. Oreg., 1964. Diplomate Am. Bd. Surgery. Clin. prof. surgery Oreg. Health Scis. U., 1975—; staff surgeon Salem (Oreg.) Hosp., 1972—; skpr. Ho. Delegates Oreg. Med. Assn., 1985-86, sec. Oreg. Med. Assn., 1982-84. Gen. med. officer USN, 1965-67, Vietnam. Rsch. grantee Am. Cancer Soc., 1961-64. Fellow ACS; mem. Naffziger Surg. Soc. (pres. 1993-94). Republican. Office: The Doctors Clinic 2475 Center St NE Salem OR 97301

WILTON, SUSAN ROTH, ophthalmologist; b. Huntington, N.Y., Aug. 22, 1959; d. Otto William and Anita Louise (Pentola) Roth; m. James Henry Wilton, June 2, 1990. BA, Bucknell U., 1981; MA, U. Ariz., 1985; MD, Med. Coll. Pa., 1989. Diplomate Am. Bd. Ophthalmology. Intern in internal medicine Abington (Pa.) Meml. Hosp., 1989-90; resident in ophthalmology U. Okla., Oklahoma City, 1990-93; assoc. ophthalmologist J.C. Johnston M.D., Inc., Oklahoma City, 1993-94, Saratoga Ophthalmology Assocs., Pottstown, Pa., 1994—. Contbr. articles to profl. jours. Fellow Am. Cancer Soc., 1987. Recipient scholarship William Goldman Found., 1987, Lee Marshall scholarship, 1988, Thomas A. Acers M.D. Excellence in Rsch. award, 1988. Fellow Am. Acad. Ophthalmology, Christian Med. and Dental Soc.; mem. AMA, Christian Ophthalmology Soc., Am. Soc. Cataract and Refractive Soc., Pa. Med. Soc. Office: Sanatoga Ophthalmology Assocs 1560 Medical Dr Pottstown PA 19400

WIN, KHIN SWE, anesthesiologist; b. Rangoon, Burma, Sept. 27, 1934; came to U.S., 1962; d. U Mg and Daw Aye (Kyin) Maung; m. M. Shein

Win, May 28, 1959; children: Tha Shein, Thwe Shein, Maw Shein, Thet Shein, Htoo Shein. Intermediate of Sci. Degree, U. Rangoon, 1954, MB, BS, 1962. Intern Waltham (Mass.) Hosp., 1962-63; resident anesthesiology Boston City Hosp., 1963-65; fellow pediatric anesthesiology New Eng. Med. Ctr. Hosps., Boston, 1965-66; fellow anesthesiology Martin Luther King Jr. Gen. Hosp., L.A., 1978-79; pvt. practice anesthesiology Apple Valley, Calif., 1984—; asst. prof. anesthesiology Martin Luther King Jr./Charles R. Drew Med. Ctr., L.A., 1979-84. Republican. Buddhist. Home: 13850 Pamlico Rd Apple Valley CA 92307-5400 Office: St Mary Desert Valley Hosp Dept Anesthesiology 18300 Us Highway 18 Apple Valley CA 92307-2206

WINANS, ANNA JANE, dietitian; b. Freeport, Ill., June 13, 1939; d. Leo Dale and Gwendolyn Jane White; m. Roger Eugene Winans, Aug. 26, 1967; children: Robert, Jonathan. BS in Dietetics, Iowa State U., 1962. Registered dietitian. Clin. dietitian VA Hosp., Madison, Wis., 1963-67; coord. U. Wis. Hosp., Madison, 1967-69; instr. nutrition Madison Gen. Hosp., 1969-75, Madison Area Coll., 1976-81; nutritionist Women, Infants and Children Nutrition Program, USDA, Fremont, Nebr., 1981—; nutrition cons. area health care facilities, Wis., 1976-81, Nebr., 1985—; food svc. auditor, 1995—. Sec. Chapel Hill Pool Bd., Elkhorn, Nebr., 1987-89; bd. dirs. Homeowner's Assn., Elkhorn, 1989-93; active Elkhorn Woman's Club, 1982—; pres. Elkhorn Libr. Bd., 1989-91, 94. Mem. Am. Dietetic Assn. (registered), Nebr. Dietetic Assn., Omaha Dietetic Assn., PEO, Omicron Nu, Psi Chi. Methodist. Home: 910 S 218th St Elkhorn NE 68022-1938 Office: WIC 626 N D St Fremont NE 68025-5054

WINANS, J(AMES) MERRITT, psychology educator; b. Spokane, Wash., Mar. 1, 1912; s. William Manzon Vernon and Olive Wilson; m. Marjorie Lynch, 1946 (dec.); 1 child, Laurie Elizabeth. PhD, U. Calif., Berkeley, 1950. Lic. psychologist, Calif. Prof. Psychology Bakersfield (Calif.) Coll., 1949-50; prof. Psychology Calif. State U., Sacramento, 1950-78, prof. Psychology emeritus, 1978—; cons. various seminars and workshops in No. Calif., 1950—. Author (book) Effective Members and Successful Groups, 1980; co-author (book) Growing from Infancy to Adulthood, 1958. Lt. comdr., USNR, 1942-46, PTO. Mem. APA, Calif. Psychology Assn. Democrat. Unitarian. Home and Office: 46 Sandburg Dr Sacramento CA 95819-1833

WINBERG, JAN, pediatrician; b. Bollnas, Sweden, Apr. 11, 1923; s. Gottfrid W. and Karin A.R. Winberg; m. Anna Winberg, July 2, 1965; children: Ulla, Per, Maria. MD, Karolinska Inst., 1950, PhD, 1959. Assoc. prof. U. Gothenburg (Sweden), 1959-67, Karolinska Inst., Stockholm, 1967-71; prof. U. UMEA (Sweden), 1972-74; prof. Karolinska Inst., 1974-89, prof. emeritus, 1989—; physician Royal Family of Sweden, 1979-93. Mem. editl. bd. Acta Paediatrica and Infection; contbr. over 300 scientific papers to profl. pubs. With Swedish Navy, 1948—. Mem. European Soc. Pediatric/Nephrology (founder), Internat. Pediatric Nephrology Assn. (founder, hon.), Brit. Assn. Paediat. Nephrology (hon.). Home: Karolinska Hosp, Dept Pediatrics, 171 76 Stockholm Sweden

WINBERRY, JOSEPH PAUL, JR., optometrist; b. Passaic, N.J., Apr. 25, 1957; s. Joseph Paul Sr. and Doris Evelyn (Tiernan) W.; m. Paula Ann Winberry, Oct. 14, 1989. BS, Dickinson Coll., 1979; OD, Ill. Coll. Optometry, 1987. Assoc. optometrist Eye Care Assocs., Harrisburg, Pa., 1987-88; optometrist Sears Optical, York, Pa., 1989-91, Camp Hill (Pa.) Eye Care, Camp Hill, Pa., 1991—; bd. dirs. Tri-County Assn. for Blind, Harrisburg, 1992—. Author The Keystoner newsletter, 1992; contbr. articles to profl. jours. Pres. Dickinson Club Chgo., 1993-87; mem. Big Bros. Chgo., 1985-87; chairperson Alumni Admission Program, Dickinson Coll., 1987—, chmn. 15th class reunion, 1994. Recipient Harold Kohn award Am. Optometric Found., 1987; named one of Outstanding Young Men Am., 1984. Fellow Am. Acad. Optometry; mem. Am. Aptometric Assn., Ctrl. Pa. Optometry Soc. (pres., v.p., sec., treas. 1989—, Optometrist of Yr. 1991), Pa. Optometric Assn. (trustee 1996), Astron. Soc. Harrisburg, KC, Lions (Camp Hill v.p. 1991—), Beta Theta Pi (scholarship 1976). Democrat. Methodist. Home: 134 Lancaster Blvd Mechanicsburg PA 17055 Office: Camp Hill eye Care 1714 Market St Camp Hill PA 17011

WINBURY, MARTIN MAURICE, pharmaceutical executive, educator; b. N.Y.C., Aug. 4, 1918; s. Ervin and Helen (Stein) W.; m. Blanche Mary Simons, July 11, 1942; children: Nancy Ellen, Gail Elizabeth. BS, L.I. U., 1940; MS, U. Md., 1942; PhD, NYU, 1951. Rsch. fellow U. Md., College Park, 1940-42, U.S. Bur. of Mines, College Park, 1942-44; scientist Merck Inst. Therapy Rsch., Rahway, N.J., 1944-47; pharmacologist G. D. Searle, Skokie, Ill., 1947-55; dir. pharmacology Schering Corp., Bloomfield, N.J., 1955-61, Warner Lambert, Morris Plains, N.J., 1961-80; dir. sci. devel. Warner Lambert, Ann Arbor, Mich., 1980-86, ret., 1986; pres. InterPharm, Ann Arbor, 1986—; mem. faculty U. Mich. Med. Sch., Ann Arbor, 1986—. Contbr. articles to profl. jours. Fellow AAAS, Am Coll. Cardiology, N.Y. Acad. Scis.; mem. Am. Soc. Pharmacology and Exptl. Therapy, Am. Heart Assn., Gordon Rsch. Conf. (chmn.). Home: 3600 Windemere Dr Ann Arbor MI 48105-2844 Office: InterPharm PO Box 8335 Ann Arbor MI 48107-8335

WINCHESTER, JAMES FRANK, medicine educator; b. Glasgow, Scotland, Mar. 24, 1944; came to U.S., 1976; s. Alexander Graham and Elizabeth Mary (McKillop) W.; m. Patricia Jane, May 16, 1968; children: J. Craig, Jane E. MB, ChB, Glasgow U., 1969, MD, 1981. Sr. registrar Royal Infirmary, Glasgow, 1974-76; asst. prof. medicine Georgetown U., Washington, 1976-82, assoc. prof., 1982-87, prof., 1987—, acting. dir. divsn. nephrology, 1988-94; attending physician Georgetown U. Med. Ctr., 1976—. Editor: Clinical Management of Poisoning and Drug Overdose, 1983, 1990, 97, Renal Dialysis, 1994; editor-in-chief Replacement of Renal Function by Dialysis, 1996. Chmn. Nat. Kidney Found. of Nat. Capital Area, Washington, 1989. Fellow ACP, Royal Coll. Physicians; mem. Internat. Soc. Peritoneal Dialysis (sec.-treas. 1984—), Am. Soc. Artificial Internal Organs (pres. 1995-96), Nat. Kidney Found. (regional pres. 1991-93, bd. dirs. 1993—), Am. Fedn. Clin. Rsch., Am. Clin. Climatol. Assn., Am. Soc. Transplant Physicians, Am. Soc. Nephrology, Internat. Soc. Nephrology. Office: Georgetown U 3800 Reservoir Rd NW Washington DC 20007-2196

WINCOR, MICHAEL Z., psychopharmacology educator, clinician, researcher; b. Chgo., Feb. 9, 1946; s. Emanuel and Rose (Kershner) W.; m. Emily E.M. Smythe; children: Meghan Heather, Katherine Rose. SB in Zoology, U. Chgo., 1966; PharmD, U. So. Calif., 1978. Rsch. project specialist U. Chgo. Sleep Lab., 1968-75; psychiat. pharmacist Brotman Med. Ctr., Culver City, Calif., 1979-83; asst. prof. U. So. Calif., L.A., 1983—; cons. Fed. Bur. Prisons Drug Abuse Program, Terminal Island, Calif., 1978-81, Nat. Inst. Drug Abuse, Bethesda, Md., 1981, The Upjohn Co., Kalamazoo, 1982-87, 91-92, Area XXIV Profl. Stds. Rev. Orgn., L.A., 1983, Brotman Med. Ctr., Culver City, Calif., 1983-88, SmithKline Beecham Pharms., Phila., 1990-93, Tokyo Coll. of Pharmacy, 1991, G. D. Searle & Co., Chgo., 1992—. Contbr. over 30 articles to profl. jours., chpts. to books, papers presented at nat. and internat. meetings and reviewer. Mem. adv. coun. Franklin Avenue Sch., 1986-89; trustee Sequoyah Sch., 1992-93; mem. tech. com. Ivanhoe Sch., 1993-96. Recipient Cert. Appreciation, Mayor of L.A., 1981, Bristol Labs Award, 1978; Faculty scholar U. So. Calif. Sch. Pharmacy, 1978. Mem. Am. Coll. Clin. Pharmacy (chmn. constn. and bylaws com. 1983-84, mem. credentials com. 1991-93, 95-96, ednl. affairs com. 1994)0, Am. Assn. Colls. Pharmacy (focus group on liberalization profl. curriculum), Am. Soc. Hosp. Pharmacists (chmn. edn. and tng. adv. working group 1985-88, com. on acedemia 1996-97), Am. Pharm. Assn. (del. ann. meeting ho. of dels. 1989), Sleep Rsch. Soc., Am. Sleep Disorders Assn., Calif. Pharmacists Assn. (DuPont Pharma Innovative Pharmacy Practice award 1995), U. So. Calif. Sch. Pharmacy Alumni Assn. (bd. dirs. 1979—), Rho Chi. Office: U So Calif 1985 Zonal Ave Los Angeles CA 90033-1058

WINDER, ALVIN ELIOT, public health educator, clinical psychologist; b. N.Y.C., Feb. 17, 1923; s. Martin Winder and Frances (Erdrick) Isaacson; m. Barbara Ina Dietz, July 19, 1949; children: Mark, Joshua, Sarah, Susan. BA, CUNY, 1947; MS, U. Ill., 1948; PhD, U. Chgo., 1952; MPH, U. Calif., Berkeley, 1980. Lic. clin. psychologist, Mass. Chief psychologist VA Hosp., Downey, Ill., 1953-56; rsch. asst., asst. prof. Clark U., Worcester, Mass., 1956-58; chief psychologist VA Clinic, Springfield, Mass., 1958-61; assoc. prof. psychology Springfield Coll., 1961-63; chmn. psychology dept. Westfield (Mass.) State Coll., 1963-65; assoc. counseling edn. Sch. Edn., U. Mass., Amherst, 1965-69, prof., dir. grad. program div. nursing, 1969-78, prof. Sch. Pub. Health, 1978-93; dir. planning, cons. Springfield (Mass.) Pub. Health Dept., 1993-95; adj. prof. Sch. Pub. Health, Boston U., 1995—; assoc. to exec. sec. Asian Pacific Assn. for Control of Tobacco, 1988—. Author: Introduction to Health Education, 1984, Solid Waste Education Recycling Directory, 1989; editor: Adolescence Contemporary Studies, 1974; guest editor Jour. Applied Behavior, 1970; co-editor: Internat. Quar. of Cmty. Health Edn., 1992—. Sr. selectman Town of Leverett, Mass., 1988-90; Lilly Found. mentor U. Mass., 1989. Grantee U.S. Childrens Bur., 1966, 67, Dexter Found., 1969, NIMH, 1974, Nat. Cancer Inst., 1986-91. Mem. APHA, APA. Home and Office: 84 Booth Rd Dedham MA 02026-5702

WINDHAGER, ERICH ERNST, physiologist, educator; b. Vienna, Austria, Nov. 4, 1928; came to U.S., 1954; s. Maximilian and Bertha (Feitzinger) W.; m. Helga A. Rapant, June 18, 1956; children: Evelyn Ann, Karen Alice. MD, U. Vienna, 1954. Research fellow in biophysics Harvard Med. Sch., Boston, 1956-58; instr. in physiology Cornell U. Med. Coll., N.Y.C., 1958-61; vis. scientist U. Copenhagen, 1961-63; asst. to prof. physiology Cornell U. Med. Coll., N.Y.C., 1963—, Maxwell M. Upson prof. physiology and biophysics, 1978—, chmn. dept. physiology, 1973—. Recipient Homer W. Smith award N.Y. Heart Assn., 1978. Office: Cornell U Med Coll Dept Physiology 1300 York Ave New York NY 10021-4805

WINDHAM, ELDORA BROACH, retired geriatrics nurse; b. Roxboro, N.C., May 24, 1917; d. William Edward and Carrie Oliver (Rice) Broach; m. Milton Eugene Windham, June 17, 1942 (div. 1978); children—Bobbie Almira, Youel Travis, Wray Earle, Twila Janel. R.N., N.C. Pvt. nurse So. Baptist Hosp., New Orleans, 1941-45, 47; supr. Columbia Hosp. (Mo.), 1948-49; ward supr. Community Hosp., Placerville, Calif., 1950-51; missionary nurse, mother Am. Baptist Mission, Assam, India, 1952-61; night supr. obstetrics Person County Meml. Hosp., Roxboro, N.C., 1965-79; charge nurse geriatrics, 1979-93, ret. 1993. Named Dr. Frist Humanitarian Person County Meml. Hosp., 1982. Democrat. Baptist. Home: 2484 Rolling Hills Rd Roxboro NC 27573-7702 Office: Person County Meml Hosp Ridge Rd Roxboro NC 27573

WINDHAM, NANCY QUINTERO, obstetrician, gynecologist; b. Maracaibo, Venezuela, May 18, 1961; came to U.S., 1976; d. George Albert and Jean Louise (Gimbert) Quintero; 1 child, Kathleen Jean. BS, Tulane U., 1982, MD, 1986. Intern Baylor Coll. Medicine, Houston, 1986-87, resident in ob-gyn., 1987-90; pvt. practice ob-gyn. Florence and Darlington, S.C., 1990-91, La Grange, Ga., 1992, Florence, 1993—. Fellow Am. Coll. Obstetricians and Gynecologists (bd. cert.); mem. AMA, S.C. Med. Soc. Office: 901 E Cheves St Ste 300 Florence SC 29506

WINDHAUSER, JOHN WILLIAM, journalism educator; b. Rochester, N.Y., Jan. 30, 1943; s. Milton Edward and Mary Ellen (McDonald) W.; m. Marlene Marie Most. BS, Tri-State U., 1966; MA, Ball State U., 1967; PhD, Ohio U., 1975. Editor, reporter, advt. and pub. relations positions, 1964-77; asst. prof. journalism Colo. State U., Ft. Collins, 1971-77, Bradley U., Peoria, Ill., 1977-78; assoc. prof., dir. research ctr. U. Miss., Oxford, 1978-82; prof. La. State U., Baton Rouge, 1982—; cons. in field; research judge Soc. Profl. Journalists; editorial bd. Journalism Quarterly, Coll. Media Rev., Newspaper Research Jour. Author: The Editorial Process, 1978, 2d edit., 1985; co-editor, co-author: The Media in the 1984 and 1988 Presidential Campaigns, 1991; contbr. numerous articles to profl. jours.; editor Profl. Jour., Coll. Press Rev., 1972-81. Recipient Life Membership award Nat. Council Coll. Publs. Advisers, 1981, Presdl. award Nat. Council Coll. Publs. Advisers, 1973-81. Mem. Assn. for Edn. in Journalism, Speech Communication Assn., The So. Speech Assn. Office: Sch Journalism La State U Baton Rouge LA 70803

WINER, ERIC P., hematologist, oncologist, educator; b. Boston, Dec. 8, 1956; s. Richard Shepherd and Rhoda Ruth (Woogmaster) W.; m. Nancy M. Borstelman, June 23, 1984; children: Jeffrey, Joel, Emily. BA magna cum laude, Yale U., 1978, MD, 1983. Diplomate Nat. Bd. Med. Examiners, Am. Bd. Internal Medicine, Med. Oncology; lic. NC. Intern internal medicine Yale-New Haven Hosp., Conn., 1983-84; resident internal medicine Yale-New Haven Hosp., 1984-86, chief resident, internal medicine, 1986-87; instr. dept. medicine Yale U. Sch. of Medicine, New Haven, 1986-87; staff physician Yale New-Haven Hosp., 1986-87; fellow hematology/oncoolgy Duke U. Med. Ctr., Durham, N.C., 1987-89; assoc. in medicine Duke U. Med. Ctr., Durham, 1989-90, physician, 1989—, asst. prof. medicine divsn. hematology-oncology, 1990-96, assoc. prof., 1996—; cadre mem. psycho-oncology com. Cancer and Leukemia Group B, 1989—, breast com., 1990—, GU working com., 1991-94, clin. econ. working group, 1995—; mem. Cancer Protocol com., Duke U., 1990—, chair psycho-oncology and correleative scis. subcom., 1994—; mem. internal medicine house staff selection com. Duke U., 1991-94, dir. Jordan Inpatient Ward, 1992-95, co-dir. multi-disciplinary breast oncology program, 1993—, mem. hematology-oncology fellowship com.; PI for Duke U. Nat. Surgical Adjuvant Breast Program, 1992—; reviewer Jour. Clin. Oncology, Jour. AMA, Archives of Internal Medicine, Cancer Chemotherapy and Pharmacology, Transplantation, New Eng. Jour. Medicine, Breast Diseases. Contbr. numerous articles, abstracts to profl. jours., chpts. to books. Recipient Kushlan award for outstanding intern, jr. resident Yale U. Sch. Medicine, 1984, 85, Am. Cancer Soc. Career Devel. award, 1991-94, Wendell Rosse award, 1994; grantee: A.W. Mellon Found., 1990-91, Glaxo, Inc. pharmacoecon. divsn., 1991-92, NIH, 1991—. Mem. Am. Soc. Clin. Oncology, Acad. Hospice Physicians, Alpha Omega Alpha. Home: 7 Sinclair Cir Durham NC 27705 Office: Duke U Med Ctr Trent Dr Box3147 Durham NC 27710

WINFIELD, JOHN BUCKNER, rheumatologist, educator; b. Kentfield, Calif., Mar. 19, 1942; s. R. Buckner and Margaret G. (Katterfelt) W.; m. Patricia Nichols (div. 1968); 1 child, Ann Gibson; m. Teresa Lee McGrath, 1969; children: John Buckner III, Virginia Lee. BA, Williams Coll., 1964; MD, Cornell U., 1968. Diplomate Am. Bd. Internal Medicine. Intern in medicine N.Y. Hosp., N.Y.C., 1968-69; staff assoc. LI/Nat. Inst. Allergy and Infectious Diseases NIH, Bethesda, Md., 1969-71; resident in medicine, fellow in rheumatology U. Va. Sch. Medicine, Charlottesville, 1971-73; fellow in immunology Rockefeller U., N.Y.C., 1973-75; asst. prof. medicine U. Va. Sch. Medicine, Charlottesville, 1975-76, assoc. prof. medicine, 1976-78; assoc. prof. medicine U. N.C., Chapel Hill, 1978-81, prof. medicine, 1981—, chief div. rheumatology and immunology, 1978—; dir. Thurston Arthritis Rsch. Ctr. U. N.C. Sch. Medicine, Chapel Hill, 1982—; Smith prof. medicine U. N.C. Sch. Med., Chapel Hill, 1987—; adv. coun. Nat. Inst. Arthritis and Musculoskeletal and Skin Diseases, NIH, 1988-92; chmn. edn. com. Am. Rheumatism Assn., Atlanta, 1980-84; immunol. scis. study sect. NIH, 1979-83, Arthritis Musculoskeletal and Skin study sect., 1992—; vice-chair fellowship com. Arthritis Found., 1982; med. coun. Lupus Found. Am., 1987—. Author more than 100 med. and sci. articles in peer reviewer rheumatology and immunology jours.; mem. editl. bd. Arthritis and Rheumatism, Bull. Rheumatic Diseases, Rheumatology Internat., Clin. Exptl. Rheumatology, Am. Jour. Medicine. Sr. asst. surgeon with USPHS, NIH, Bethesda, Md., 1968-71. Recipient Borden prize Cornell U. Med. Coll., 1964, numerous rsch. grants NIH and Arthritis Found., 1975—, Sr. Investigator award Arthritis Found., 1976-79, Kenan award U. N.C., 1985, NIH merit award, 1992. Fellow ACP; mem. Am. Assn. Immunologists, Am. Coll. Rheumatology, Am. Fedn. Clin. Rsch., Am. Soc. Clin. Investigation, Assn. Am. Physicians, Am. Clin. Climatol. Assn., Chapel Hill Country Club. Republican. Episcopalian. Home: 801 Kings Mill Rd Chapel Hill NC 27514-4920 Office: U NC Sch Medicine Thurston Arthritis Rsch Ctr CB 7280 Rm 3310 Chapel Hill NC 27599

WINFIELD, RAYMOND JOSEPH, JR., urologist; b. Washington, Dec. 28, 1950; s. Raymond Joseph and Marian LaVerne (Dille) W.; m. July 24, 1981; children: Kirsten R., Jordan. BS, Western Mich. U., 1973; B Pharmacy, Ferris State U., Big Rapids, Mich., 1976; MD, U. Caribe, San Juan, P.R., 1980. Pvt. practice, Southfield, Mich. mem. Am. Urol. Assn., North Ctrl. Sect. Am. Urol. Assn., Mich. Br. Am. Urol. Assn., Mich. Med. Soc., Oakland County Med. Soc. Office: Mich Urol Inst PC 22250 Providence Dr Ste 203 Southfield MI 48075

WINFREE, ARTHUR TAYLOR, biologist, educator; b. St. Petersburg, Fla., May 15, 1942; s. Charles Van and Dorothy Rose (Scheb) W.; m. Ji-Yun Yang, June 18, 1983; children: Rachael, Erik from previous marriage. B.Engring. in Physics, Cornell U., 1965; Ph.D. in Biology, Princeton U., 1970. Lic. pvt. pilot. Asst. prof. theoretical biology U. Chgo., 1969-72; assoc. prof. biology Purdue U., West Lafayette, Ind., 1972-79; prof. Purdue U., 1979-86; prof. ecology and evolutionary biology U. Ariz., Tucson, 1986-88, Regents' prof., 1989—; pres., dir. research Inst. Natural Philosophy, Inc., 1979-88. Author: The Geometry of Biological Time, 1980, When Time Breaks Down, 1986, The Timing of Biological Clocks, 1987. Recipient Career Devel. award NIH, 1973-78, The Einthoven award Einthoven Found. and Netherlands Royal Acad. Scis., 1989; NSF grantee, 1966—; MacArthur fellow, 1984-89, John Simon Guggenheim Meml. fellow, 1982. Home: 1210 E Placita De Graciela Tucson AZ 85718-2834 Office: U Ariz Dept Biology 326 BSW Tucson AZ 85721

WING, ANTONY JOHN, nephrologist; b. Oxford, Eng., May 2, 1933; s. Harry John and Helen (Foster) W.; m. Rachel Nora Gray, Jan. 23, 1960; children: Nicola, Mark, Charles, Michael. DM, Oxford U., 1969, BM, BCh, 1956. Registrar St. Thomas Hosp., London, 1964-66; sr. registrar Charing Cross Hosp., London, 1967-68; rsch. fellow Makerere U., Kampala, Uganda, 1968-69; cons. physician St. Thomas Hosp., London, 1969-94; cons. nephrologist St. George's Hosp., London, 1994—; chief med. officer Colonial Mutual Ass. Soc., London, 1980—; chief med.. officer United Friendly Ass. Soc., London, 1988—; examiner Soc. Apothecaries, London, 1970—; chmn. of registry European Diaysis and Transplant Assn., 1976-85, mem. coun., 1985-88. Author: The Renal Unit, 1972, Decision Making in Medicine, 1979; contbr. articles to profl. jours. Mem. governing body Stowe Sch., Buckingham, 1988—; lay reader St. Stephen's Ch., 1979—; chmn. Cicely Northcote Trust, London, 1977-83. With RAF, 1960-64. Fellow Royal Coll. Physicians, Royal Soc. Medicine, Assurance Med. Soc., Soc. of Apothecaries (liveryman), Vincents Club, MCC Club. Mem. Ch. of England. Office: St Georges Hosp, London SW17 0QT, England SE1 7EH

WINGA, EDWARD REES, internist; b. Washington, Iowa, June 26, 1936; s. John Albert and Catherine Eleanor (Rees) W.; m. Sharon Patricia Reynolds, Dec. 27, 1963; children: Daniel, Julie, Andrew. BA, State U. Iowa, 1958, MD, 1962. Diplomate Am. Bd. Internal Medicine. Intern U. Utah Coll. Medicine, Salt Lake City, 1962-63; resident in internal medicine U. Tex. Southwestern Med. Sch., Dallas, 1965-68, fellow in pulmonary disease, 1968-69; staff physician Gundersen Clinic/Lutheran Hosp., La Crosse, Wis., 1969—; chief of staff Lutheran Hosp., 1984-86, med. dir. respiratory therapy, 1982—, rep. to AMA, 1982—. Co-author: Policies and Procedures of a Cardiac Rehabilitation Program — Immediate to Long Term Care, 1978; contbr. articles to profl. jours. Elder First Presbyn. Ch., La Crosse, 1984—. Fellow Am. Coll. Chest Physicians; mem. Am. Thoracic Soc., Am. Sleep Disorders Assn., Nat. Assn. Dirs. of Respiratory Care, Wis. Thoracic Soc., La Crosse County Med. Soc. Office: Gundersen Clinic 1836 South Ave La Crosse WI 54601

WINGARD, DEBORAH LEE, epidemiology educator; b. San Diego, Aug. 20, 1952; d. Peter John and Frances (Castien) W.; m. Pierre Patrick Vaughn, Sept. 4, 1976; children: Brendan, Kyle. BA in Zoology, U. Calif., Berkeley, 1974, MS in Epidemiology, 1976, PhD in Epidemiology, 1980. Rsch. asst. Primary Health Care Project, Berkeley, 1975; rsch. asst. infant health unit Calif. Dept. Health, Berkeley, 1975; rsch. asst. contraceptive drug study Kaiser Permanente Med. Ctr., Walnut Creek, Calif., 1976; rsch. specialist U. Calif., Berkeley, 1976-77, epidemiologist Human Population Lab., 1977-78; asst. prof. epidemiology U. Calif., San Diego, 1980-86, assoc. prof., 1986-95, prof., 1995—; mem. cons. faculty San Diego State U., 1985—; cons. DES Action, USA, Oakland, Calif., 1980, chmn., San Diego, 1982—, co-chmn. nat. com., 1989—; cons. Nat. Inst. on Aging, Bethesda, Md., 1982—; reviewer Am. Jour. Epidemiology, Circulation, Diabetes Care, Jour. AMA, New Eng. Jour. Medicine. Editor Sleep; contbr. numerous articles to profl. jours., chpts. to books. Vice pres. Bencheley-Weinberger Sch. PTA, San Diego, 1989-91, pres., 1991-92; trustee San Diego Jr. Theatre, 1996—. Grantee Nat. Inst. Diabetes, Digestive and Kidney Disease, 1983—, Nat. Inst. on Aging, 1984-89, 90-93, NIH, 1993—. Mem. APHA, Am. Diabetes Assn., Soc. for Epidemiologic Rsch., Am. Heart Assn., Physicians for Social Responsibility, Assn. for Women in Sci. Office: U Calif San Diego 9500 Gilman Dr La Jolla CA 92093-0607

WINGATE, ROBERT LEE, JR., internist; b. Columbia, S.C., May 28, 1936; s. Robert Lee and Helen (Owen) W.; m. Ritanne Cooper, Apr. 19, 1962 (div. 1965); 1 child, Elizabeth Butterfield-Wingate; m. Jeannette DeLatte, Mar. 27, 1968 (div. 1980); children: Laura Owen, Charlotte Cramer. BS, U. S.C., 1957; MD, Med. Coll. S.C., 1961. Intern Cin. Gen. Hosp., 1961-62, jr. resident internal medicine, 1964-65; asst. resident in internal medicine Med. Coll. of Va., Richmond, 1965-66; resident in internal medicine Charity Hosp. of La., New Orleans, 1966-67, resident in neurology, 1967-68; pvt. practice Columbia, 1968-78; PruCare physician Memphis, 1983-85; med. dir. M. Lowennstein and Celanese Corps., Rock Hill, S.C., 1978-80; med. dir. nursing home care unit Dorn VA Hosp., Columbia, 1980-82; med. cons. disability determination div. Vocat. Rehab. S.C., Columbia, 1982-83; cons. Student Health Ctr. U. S.C., Columbia, 1985-86; cons. Urgent Care Ctrs. S.C., 1986-87; pvt. practice Pelion, S.C., 1987-92; staff internist, cons. internal medicine Western Mental Health Inst., Western Institute, Tenn., 1992—; med. dir. Forest Hills Nursing Ctr., Columbia, 1968-78; med. cons. S.C. Commn. for Blind, Columbia, 1970-78, Mid-Carolina Coun. on Alcoholism, Columbia, 1970-74; instr. internal medicine U. S.C. Sch. Medicine, 1980-82; cons. internal medicine and urgent care Pelion Cmty. Care Ctr., 1989-92; instr. Sch. Nursing, Med. Coll. S.C., Winthrop divsn., 1978-80; lectr. in field. Contbr. articles to newspapers. Ofcl. physician Peanut Party S.C., 1990-92. Lt. comdr. M.C., USNR, 1958-66. Grantee Burroughs-Wellcome Co., 1958, Med. Coll. S.C., 1960, Congress of U.S., 1987. Mem. ACP, AMA (physician's recognition award 1969, 74, 79, 85, 86, 94-96, 96-99), Am. Soc. Internal Medicine, Am. Occupational Med. Assn., So. Med. Assn., S.C. Med. Assn., Lexington County Med. Assn., Soc. of 1824, Ruritan, Phi Rho Sigma. Office: Western Mental Health Inst Western Institute TN 38074

WINGO, MARIAN LEE, counselor, therapist; b. Asheville, N.C., Sept. 16, 1944; d. Hugh Albert and Lee Ardis (English) W.; m. Harry C. Davis, Aug. 28, 1966 (div. Sept. 1988); children: Remi, Wade; ptnr. Chris Vinsonhaler, Jan. 22, 1994. BS, Fla. State U., 1966; MS, George Peabody Coll., 1978. Nat. cert. counselor. Owner, dir., trainer, cons. Marian Wingo & Assocs., Ocean Springs, Miss., 1983—; co-owner, dir. Family Counselors Affiliated, Ocean Springs, 1987—; agt./mgr. Chris Vinsonhaler, Ocean Springs. Author: Skills for Rich Living, 1980; columnist Gulf Coast Papers We Are Family. Recipient Outstanding Citizen award Bus. and Profl. Women, San Antonio, 1981, Profl. Devel. Leadership award ASTD, Alexandria, Va., 1984; Today's Woman selectee San Antonio Light, 1980; named Gulf Coast Woman of Achievement, AAUW/Mississippi Gulf Coast C.C., 1991. Mem. AAUW, Assn. Women in Psychology (archivist), Nat. Feminist Therapist Inst. Democrat. Methodist. Office: Family Counselors Affiliated 998 Robinson St Ocean Springs MS 39564-4624

WINHAM, GEORGE KEETH, retired mental health nurse; b. Plain Dealing, La., Nov. 25, 1934; s. Henderson and Lula Mae (Kelly) W.; m. Patricia Annie Weise, Nov. 7, 1959; chldren: Adrian Keeth, George Kevin, Karla Ann. ADN, La. State U., 1974; BS in Health Care, Carolina Christian U., 1986. Cert. chem. dependency nurse specialist; RN, La. Staff nurse preceptor ward 10 VAMC, Shreveport, La., 1992-96, staff nurse ward 10, 1976-88, 96; ret. Overton Brooks VA Med. Ctr., Shreveport, 1996; guest speaker in field. With USAFR, 1982-95. Mem. Drug and Alcohol Nurses Assn., Am. Soc. Pain Mgmt. Nurses, Nat. Fedn. Federal Employees (local treas. 1956, nurse of yr. 1989), Air Force Sgts. Assn., Nat. Consortium Chem. Dependency Nurses, Consol. Assn. Nurses in Substance Abuse, Masons. Baptist. Home: 106 Lancashire Dr Bossier City LA 71111-2023

WINIARSKI, MARK GREGORY, clinical psychologist; b. Buffalo, June 2, 1950; s. Albin Walter and Rose (Dudynic) W.; m. Loretto Kenny, Nov. 20, 1974 (div. 1977); m. Diane Lynn Sturm, May 29, 1988; 1 child, Alex William. BS in Journalism, Northwestern U., 1972; MS in Journalism, Columbia U., 1973; PhD, Fla. State U., 1988. Lic. psychologist, N.Y. Newspaper reporter various newspapers, 1973-81; psychology intern NYU Med. Ctr.-Bellevue Hosp., 1987-88; psychologist Spellman Ctr. for HIV Disease, St. Clare's Hosp., N.Y.C., 1987-90, Blanton-Peale Counseling Ctr., Forest Hills, N.Y., 1988—; psychologist in pvt. practice Forest Hills, N.Y., 1989—, Great Neck, N.Y., 1995—; asst. prof. epidemiology and social medicine Albert Einstein Coll. Medicine, Bronx, 1991—, asst. prof. psychiatry, 1995—; asst. prof. family medicine Albert Einstein Coll. Medicine, 1992—; psychosocial coord. Primary Care & Substance Abuse Project Dept. Family Medicine, Montefiore Med. Ctr., Bronx, 1990-94, project dir. AIDS Mental Health and Primary Care Integration Project, 1991—. Author: AIDS-Related Psychotherapy, 1991; contbr. articles to profl. jours. Mem. Am. Psychol. Assn., Soc. of Behavioral Medicine, N.Y. State Psychol. Assn. Office: Montefiore Med Ctr 111 E 210th St Bronx NY 10467-2490

WINK, MICHAEL, biologist, educator; b. Münstereifel, Fed. Republic Germany, Apr. 10, 1951; s. Alfred and Johanna (Remmen) W.; m. Coralie Oberhoffer, Mar. 11, 1978; children: Leonie, Charlotte, Lucie, Adrian. Diploma in Biology, U. Bonn., Fed. Republic Germany, 1977; Dr. rer. nat., U. Braunschweig, Fed. Republic Germany, 1980, Habilitation, 1985. Scientist U. Braunschweig, 1980-85; Heisenberg fellow U. Munich, 1986-88; assoc. prof. U. Mainz, Fed. Republic Germany, 1988-89; prof. faculty pharmacy and faculty biology U. Heidelberg, Fed. Republic Germany, 1989—; dir. Inst. Pharm. Biology, Heidelberg, 1989—, vice dean, 1990-91, 93—, dean faculty pharmacy, 1991-93. Author four books on ornithology and Lupinen, 1991, Forschung, Anbau und Verwertung, 1992, Fortschritte in der Lupinen forschung und im Lupinenaubau, 1995, PCR im Medizinischen und Biologischen Labor, 1994; contbr. over 260 articles on natural products, chem. ecology, molecular evolution, ornithology, medicinal plants and plant physiology to profl. jours. Recipient Rheinlandtaler award Landschaftsverband Rheinland, Köln, 1988, G. Niethammer award for ornithology. Mem. AAAS, N.Y. Acad. Scis., Brit. Ornithologist's Union, Deutsche Ornithologen Gesellschaft, Gesellschaft fur Biologische Chemie, Internat. Soc. Molecular Evolution, Internat. Soc. Chem. Ecology, Phytochemical Soc. Europe, other sci. socs., Rotary. Office: Inst Pharm Biology, Univ Heidelberg, Im Neuenheimer Feld 364, 69120 Heidelberg Germany

WINKEL, ERWIN CHARLES, II, urologist; b. Houston, July 7, 1934; s. Erwin Charles and Annie (Walther) W.; m. Jacquelyn Yvonne Watson, Sept. 3, 1960; children: Erwin Charles III, Carolyn, Todd. BA, Baylor U., 1956, MD, 1959. Diplomate Am. Bd. Urology. Intern Hermann Hosp., Houston, 1959-60, resident in urology, 1960-62, 64-66, now mem. staff; pvt. practice medicine specializing in urology, Houston, 1966—; a founder North Central Gen. Hosp., Houston, 1974, chief of staff, 1974-75; a founder Houston Northwest Med. Center Hosp., 1973, chief of staff, 1977-78; clin. assoc. in urology U. Tex. Med. Sch., Houston, 1967—. Committeeman Troop 9, Boy Scouts Am., 1952-82, instl. rep., 1960-66, merit badge counsellor, 1967-71; mem. adv. bd. Volunteers of Am., 1968-76. With U.S. Army, 1962-64. Fellow Internat. Coll. Surgeons, ACS; mem. AMA (Physicians Recognition award 1969, 72, 75, 77, 80, 83, 86, 89, 92, 95, 98), Am. Urol. Assn. (continuing edn. 1980, 83, 86, 89, 92, 95, 98), Tex. Urologists Assn., Tex. Med. Assn., Am. Fertility Soc., Am. Geriatrics Soc., Harris County Med. Soc., Houston Urol. Socs., Houston Acad. Medicine. Republican. Methodist. Home: 64 Champions Bend Cir Houston TX 77069-1800 Office: 829 Peakwood Dr Ste 101 Houston TX 77090-2905

WINKELSTEIN, JERRY ALLEN, pediatrician, educator; b. Syracuse, N.Y., Sept. 5, 1940; s. Warren W. and Lillian (Sirkin) W.; m. Marilyn Link, June 21, 1969; children: Beth, Amy. BA, Syracuse U., 1961; MD, Einstein Med. Sch., 1965. Diplomate Am. Bd. Pediatrics. Asst. prof. pediatrics Johns Hopkins U., Balt., 1973-76, assoc. prof., 1976-82, prof., 1982—; dir. div. immunology, dept. pediatrics Johns Hopkins Hosp., Balt., 1981—. Contbr. articles to sci. jours. Chmn. med. adv. com. Immuno Deficiency Found., 1982—. Lt. comdr. USPHS, 1968-70. Recipient Mead-Johnson award Am. Acad. Pediatrics, 1982. Mem. Am. Pediatric Soc., Soc. Pediatric Rsch., Am. Soc. Clin. Investigation, Infectious Disease Soc. Home: 109 Deepdene Rd Baltimore MD 21210-1911 Office: Johns Hopkins Hosp Cmsc # 1103 Baltimore MD 21205

WINKELSTEIN, WARREN, JR, physician, educator; b. Syracuse, N.Y., July 1, 1922; s. Warren and Evelyn (Neiman) W.; children: Rebecca Winkelstein Yamin, Joshua, Shoshana; m. Veva Kerrigan, Feb. 14, 1976. BA, U. N.C., 1942; MD cum laude, Syracuse U., 1947; MPH, Columbia U., 1950. Diplomate Am. Bd. Preventive Medicine. Intern Charity Hosp., New Orleans, 1947-48; with ICA (Vietnam), 1951-53; from dir. div. communicable disease control to 1st dep. comdr. local, environ. health svcs. Erie County Health Dept., 1953-62; from assoc. prof. to prof. SUNY, Buffalo, 1962-68; prof. epidemiology, dean pub. health U. Calif., 1972—. Author: Basic Readings in Epidemiology, 1972; contbr. articles profl. jours. With AUS, 1944-46. Mem. APHA, AAAS, Internat. Am. Epidemiol. Socs., Am. Heart Assn. *

WINKLE, CHARLES WAYNE, psychologist, consultant; b. Sheridan, Ark., Apr. 8, 1948; s. James Charles and Nannie Lovell (Hopson) W.; m. Vicki Lynn Bratton, Apr. 10, 1971; children—Amanda, Megan. B.A., Ouachita U., 1970; M.S., U. Central Ark., 1973; Ed.D., East Tex. State U., 1980. Diplomate Am. Bd. Profl. Psychology; lic. psychologist, Ark., Mo.; diplomate Internat. Acad. Behavioral Medicine Counseling and Psychotherapy; diplomate Bd. Profl. Psychology; cert. law enforcement instr., Ark. Psychol. examiner Western Ark. Counseling and Guidance Ctr., Fort Smith, 1973-78; adminstrv. coordinator Marriage and Family Counseling Ctr., Commerce, Tex., 1979-80; assoc. Smock and Assocs., family therapist, Liberty, Mo., 1981-82; dir. counseling and testing ctr., instr. William Jewell Coll., Liberty, 1980-82; instr. psychology Northwestern Ark. Community Coll., Rogers, 1983-87; psychologist Performance and Diagnostic Clinic, Bentonville, Ark., 1982-86; pvt. practice psychology, Bentonville, 1986-89; program coord. psychology Rebound, Inc., Gallatin, Tenn., 1989-90; psychologist Ozark Ctr., Japlin, Mo., 1990-91, Western Ark. Counseling & Guidance Ctr., Ft. Smith, Ark., 1991—; instr. Westark C.C., 1992—; psychol. cons.; bd. dirs. Northwestern Ark. Crisis Intervention Ctr.; mem. health services adv. com. Northwestern Ark. Head Start. Contbr. articles to profl. mags., weekly column to local newspaper. Chmn. profl. div. United Fund, Bentonville, 1983; deacon Bella Vista Bapt. Ch., Ark., 1983-89; pres.-elect PTA, Bentonville, 1984—. East Tex. State U. grantee, 1979-80; NIMH grantee, 1980; recipient research award Am. Assn. for Marriage and Family Counseling, 1980; named one of Men of Achievement, 1986, Personalities Am., 1986. Served to lt. U.S. Army, 1972-73. Mem. Am. Psychol. Assn., Am. Assn. for Marriage and Family Therapy (clin.), Am. Assn. for Counseling and Devel., Am. Mental Health Counselors Assn., Ark. Assn. Marriage and Family Therapy (bd. dirs.), Gideons Internat. Avocations: writing fiction; fishing; camping; racketball; tennis. Office: PO Box 11818 Fort Smith AR 72917-1818

WINKLEBY, MARILYN A., medical researcher. BA in Social Sci., Calif. State U., Sacramento, 1968, MA in Clin. Psychology, 1974; MPH in Epidemiology/Biostat, U. Calif., Berkeley, 1983, PhD in Epidemiology, 1986. Project dir. cervical cancer screening study UCLA Sch. Pub. Health, 1974-77; co-prin. investigator Calif. Ctr. Sudden Infant Death Syndrome Risk Factor Study, Sch. Medicine, Dept. Cmty. Health U. Calif., Davis, 1977-81, co-investigator cmty. cardiovascular surveillance program, adj. lectr. Sch. Medicine, Dept. Cmty. Health, 1981-82; project coord. epidemiology unit, stress and hypertension study Dept. Epidemiology U. Calif., Berkeley, 1983-87; rsch. epidemiologist Dept. Behavioral and Devel. Pediat. U. Calif., San Francisco, 1986-91; sr. rsch. scientist/prin. investigator Stanford Ctr. Rsch. in Disease Prevention, Stanford U. Sch. of Medicine, Palo Alto, Calif., 1987—; epidemiology cons. SIDS Info. and Counseling Project, Dept. Health, State of Calif., Berkeley, 1980-83; founder, dir. Stanford Med. Youth Sci. Program, 1988—; lectr. divsn. health rsch. and policy, dept. medicine Stanford U., 1989—. Contbr. articles to profl. jours. Bd. dirs. Loaves and Fishes Family Kitchen, San Jose, Calif., 1988-92, Mountain View Cmty. Health Clinic, 1992-95. Fellow Am. Heart Assn. (coun. epidemiology 1989, Established Investigator award 1996). Office: Stanford Ctr Rsch in Disease Prevention 1000 Welch Rd Palo Alto CA 94304-1825*

WINKLER, CUNO, retired nuclear medicine educator; b. Koenigsberg, Prussia, Germany, Sept. 30, 1919; s. Albert and Elizabeth (Schulz) W. MD, U. Hamburg, Fed. Republic Germany, 1951; PhD (hon.), U. Santo Tomas, Manila, 1978. Rsch. fellow Max Planck Inst. Biophysics, Frankfurt, Fed. Republic Germany, 1954-55, Oak Ridge (Tenn.) Inst. Nuclear Studies, 1956-57; sci. asst. in radiology U. Bonn (Fed. Republic Germany) Med. Sch., 1951-54, chief sect. nuclear medicine, 1954-66, asst. prof. nuclear medicine, 1966-72, prof., dir. Inst. Clin. and Exptl. Nuclear Medicine, 1972-87, head rsch. group in radioantibodies, 1986—; prof. emeritus Rhein-Frederik-Wilhelm U., Bonn, 1988—; hon. prof. U. Santo Tomas Med. Sch., 1975; vis. cons. Philippine Heart Ctr. for Asia, Manila, 1978. Author: Nuklearmedizin: Entwicklung-Methoden-Ergebnisse, 1965, Datenverarbeitung in der Nuclearmedizin, 1978; editor: Nuclear Medicine in Clinical Oncology, 1985; contbr. numerous articles to profl. jours. Decorated grand cross (Fed. Republic of Germany); recipient award German Red Cross, 1960, plaque of honour Govt. Rheinland-Westfalen, Germany, 1976, medal George v. Hevesy Found., 1987. Mem. German Soc. Nuclear Medicine, German Soc. Natural Scis. and Physicians, European Assn. Nuclear Medicine, Soc. Nuclear Medicine USA, Rhein-Westfaelische Gesellschaft für Nuklearmedizin (hon., pres. 1978-87), Promotion Medicine Soc. (pres. 1979—). Home: 55 Trierer Str, D-53115 Bonn Germany Office: Inst Nuclear Medicine, Sigmund Freud Str 25, D-53105 Bonn Germany

WINKLER, DOLORES EUGENIA, retired hospital administrator; b. Milw., Aug. 10, 1929; d. Charles Peter and Eugenia Anne (Zamka) Kowalski; m. Donald James Winkler, Aug. 18, 1951; 1 child, David John. Grad., Milw. Bus. Inst., 1949. Acct. Curative Rehab. Ctr., Milw., 1949-60; staff acct. West Allis (Wis.) Meml. Hosp., 1968-70, chief acct., 1970-78, reimbursement analyst, 1978-85, dir. budgets and reimbursement, 1985-95; ret., 1995; mem. adv. coun./fin. com. Tau Home Health Care Agy., Milw., 1981-83. Mem. Healthcare Fin. Mgmt. Assn. (pres. 1989-90, Follmer Bronze award 1980, Reeves Silver award 1986, Muncie Gold award 1989, medal of honor 1993), Inst. Mgmt. Accts. (pres. 1983-84, nat. dir. 1986-88, pres. Mid Am. Regional Coun. 1988-89, award of excellence 1989), Beta Chi Rho (pres. 1948). Home: 12805 W Honey Ln New Berlin WI 53151-2652

WINKLER, GERALD FRANCIS, neurologist; b. Winnipeg, Man., Can., Dec. 8, 1929; came to U.S., 1956, naturalized, 1965; s. Morley and Dorothy (Wire) W.; m. Doris Veiner, Dec. 25, 1957; children: Daniel, Anne, Deborah. MD, U. Man., 1954, MS, 1956. Diplomate Am. Bd. Psychiatry and Neurology. Rotating intern Winnipeg Gen. Hosp., 1953-54; asst. resident medicine Beth Israel Hosp., Boston, 1956-58, asso. neurologist, acting head neurology clinic, 1964-68; resident neurology Mass. Gen. Hosp., 1958-61, asst. in neurology, 1963-66, asst. neurologist, 1966-69, asso. neurologist, 1969—; research fellow Harvard Med. Sch., 1961-63, instr. neurology, 1963-68, asst. clin. prof., 1969—; mem. intersplty. med. adv. com. Mass. Blue Shield, 1978-93, vice chmn., 1986-87. Chmn. bd. trustees Mass chpt. Nat. Multiple Sclerosis Soc., 1976-78; trustee, 1973-78. Fellow Am. Acad. Neurology; mem. AMA, Boston Soc. Psychiatry and Neurology (pres. 1974), Mass. Neurol. Assn. (v.p. 1978-79, pres. 1979-80, 84-85), Mass. Med. Soc. Home: 25 Chesham Rd Brookline MA 02146-5828 Office: Mass Gen Hosp Fruit St Boston MA 02114

WINKLER, GUNTHER, biotechnology executive, drug development expert; b. Laa Thaya, Noe, Austria, Aug. 20, 1957; came to U.S., 1986; s. Kurt and Irmgard (Lahner) W.; m. Maria Toifl, Sept. 11, 1979; children: Claudia, Marc. MS in Biochemistry, U. Vienna, Austria, 1983, PhD in Biochemistry, 1986. Rsch. assoc. Inst. Virology U. Vienna, 1982-86; postdoctoral fellow U. Medicine and Dentistry of N.J., Piscataway, 1986-88; rsch. scientist Biogen, Inc., Cambridge, Mass., 1988-91, dir. med. ops., 1991—; program exec. Biogen, Inc., Cambridge, 1995—; contbr. to sci. confs.; expert presentations on drug devel. strategies and mgmt. of clin. studies, chair clin. confs. Contbr. articles to profl. jours. Recipient Outstanding Achievement award Austrian Soc. Microbiology, 1986. Mem. Am. Mgmt. Assn., Drug Info. Assn., Assocs. Clin. Pharmacology. Home: 8 Churchill Rd Winchester MA 01890-1008 Office: Biogen Inc 14 Cambridge Ctr Cambridge MA 02142

WINKLER, HEINZ K. L., orthopaedic surgeon; b. Vienna, Austria, Feb. 12, 1955; s. Heinrich and Elisabeth (Reichl) W.; m. Angelina Maria Christoforetti, Mar. 19, 1979. MD, U. Vienna, 1982. Med. dir. Bone Bank Baumgartner Hoehe, Vienna, 1987-94; cons. orthopaedic surgeon Orthopaedic Baumgartner Höhe, Vienna, 1991-94, Ortho Danube Hosp., Vienna, 1994—; head Ctrl. Bone Bank Vienna, Danube Hosp., 1994—; prof. orthopaedics Acad. Physiotherapy, Vienna, 1992—; sec. gen. European Assn. Tissue Banks, 1992—; tech. coop. expert Internat. Atomic Energy Agy., 1994—; pres. 3rd European Conf. on Tissue Banking, 1994. Editor: Orthopaedic Allograft Surgery, 1996; inventor dynamic hipendoprosthesis, 1991. Recipient Lectr. award Dankook U., Korea, 1994. Mem. European Assn. Tissue Banks (sec. gen. 1992—), Am. Assn. Tissue Banks, European Assn. Musculoskeletal Transplantation, Argentinian Assn. Orthopaedic Surgery (hon.). Roman Catholic. Home: Oberlaaerstr 314, A-1230 Vienna Austria Office: Danube Hosp SMZO, Langobardenstr 122, A-1220 Vienna Austria

WINKLER, LORRAINE TOBY, psychotherapist, social worker; b. Bronx, N.Y., Oct. 27, 1942; d. Abraham and Sarah (Piperno) W.; m. Eugene Tuch, May 31, 1964 (div. Oct. 1981); children: Sherry, Deborah, David Tuch; m. William J. Lyman, Aug. 26, 1987. BSN, Fairleigh Dickinson U., Rutherford, N.J.; MSW, Rutgers U. RN, N.Y., N.J.; lic. clin. social worker, BCD, Fla., N.Y.; diplomate Nat. Assn. Social Workers, Am. Bd. Examiners. Family therapist spl. unit Div. Youth and Family Svc., 1979-80; clin. specialist Muhlenberg Hosp., Plainfield, N.J., 1980-83; pvt. practice N.J., 1980—; clin. dir., therapist Women's Haven, Paterson, N.J., 1985-86; psychiat. clinician Rahway (N.J.) Hosp., 1985-87; psychotherapist Middlesex Family Svc. Agy., Highland Park, N.J., 1987-89, Ctr. Marriage and Family Counseling, Matawan, N.J., 1987-89; pvt. practice Orlando, Fla., 1980—; mem. Drug Task Force, Somerset, Madison, N.J., 1981, 87-88. Mem. Women's Resource Ctr., Orlando, 1989, 90. Mem. NASW, Acad. Cert. Social Workers, Fla. Soc. Clin. Social Workers (diplomate), Women's Resource Ctr., Orlando C. of C., Rutgers Alumni Assn. Office: Colonial Office Ctr 1310 W Colonial Dr Ste H 12 Orlando FL 32804-7139

WINKLER, SHELDON, dentist, educator; b. N.Y.C., Jan. 25, 1932; s. Ben and Lillian (Barsh) W.; m. Sandra M. Cohen, Aug. 13, 1961; children: Mitchell, Lori. BA, Washington Sq. Coll., 1953; DDS, NYU, 1956. Asst. prof. denture prosthesis NYU Coll. Dentistry, N.Y.C., 1958-61, 66-68, rsch. asst. prof., 1962-63; dir. materials rsch. Consol. Metal Products Industries Inc., Albany, N.Y., 1963-65, cons. materials rsch., 1966-68; asst. prof. removable prosthodontics sch. dentistry SUNY, Buffalo, 1968-70; assoc. prof. SUNY, 1970-79; prof., chmn. dept. prosthodontics Temple U. Sch. Dentistry, Phila., 1979-86, 94—, asst. dean for advanced studies, continuing edn./rsch., 1987-89, acting asst. dean, 1993-95; asst. dir., vis. dentist, dental dept. N.Y. U. Med. Center, Goldwater Meml. Hosp., N.Y.C., 1966-68; attending in prosthodontics E.J. Meyer Meml. Hosp., Buffalo, 1975-79; postgrad. instr. First Dist. Dental Soc. N.Y., N.Y.C., 1963—; cons. Coe Labs., Chgo., 1967-87, Harkness Center, Buffalo, Rosa Coplon Home and Infirmary, Buffalo, 1970-79, Erie Community Coll., Buffalo, 1979—, Lever Bros. Co., N.Y.C., 1981—, VA Hosp., Phila., 1989—; lectr. dept. dental hygiene N.Y.C. Community Coll., 1967-68. Author: (with A. Davidoff and M.H.M. Lee) Dentistry for the Special Patient: The Aged, Chronically Ill and Handicapped, 1972, Essentials of Complete Denture Prosthodontics, 1979, 2d edit., 1988; editor: Resins in Dentistry, 1975, Complete Dentures, 1977, Removable Prosthodontics, 1984; editor Jour. Implant Dentistry, 1990—; contbr. articles to profl. lit.; co-designer McGowan-Winkler complete denture trays. Served as capt. AUS, 1956-58, 61-62. Recipient Outstanding Layman award Vocat. Tech. Alumni and Student Assn., SUNY, Buffalo, 1974, Internat. Edn. award Internat. Congress Oral Implantologists, 1992, journalism award Internat. Coll. Dentists, 1993. Fellow Am. Coll. Dentists, Greater N.Y. Acad. Prosthodontics; mem. ADA, Internat. Assn. Dental Rsch., Am. Assn. Dental Schs., Am. Acad. Implant Prosthodontics, Sci. Rsch. Soc. Am., Acad. Plastics Rsch., Am. Prosthodontic Soc., Am. Soc. Geriatric Dentistry, Internat. Congress of Oral Implantologists, Sigma Xi, Sigma Epsilon Delta, Omicron Kappa Upsilon. Home: 1224 Liberty Bell Dr Cherry Hill NJ 08003-2759 Office: Sch Dentistry Temple U Philadelphia PA 19140

WINKLER, STEVEN ROBERT, hospital administrator; b. Chattanooga, Tenn., Dec. 4, 1953; s. David Wilfred and Margaret (Tepper) W.; m. Monica Sue Nijoka, July 11, 1987; children: Megan Leigh, Sara Elizabeth. BA, Vanderbilt U., 1976; M in Health Adminstrn., Duke U., 1978. Asst. adminstr. Tepper Hosp. and Clinic, Chattanooga, 1978-79, adminstr., 1979-80; assoc. exec. dir. Humana Hosp.-Brandon (Fla.), 1981-83, Humana Hosp.-Bennett, 1983-84; v.p. ops. Baton Rouge Gen. Med. Ctr., 1984-86, v.p. mktg., 1986-88; v.p. risk mgmt. Gen. Health Systems, Baton Rouge, 1988—. V.p. Beth Shalom Synagogue, 1990-93, pres., 1993-95; active Am. Diabetes Assn. (Baton Rouge, state chpts.), Arthritis Found., United Way of Baton Rouge, 1989. Fellow Am. Soc. Healthcare Risk Mgmt. (pres. midsouth region 1990); mem. Am. Coll. Healthcare Execs. (diplomat), Am. Hosp. Assn., Jewish Fedn. Greater Baton Rouge (v.p. 1990, pres. 1992-93), Tipmasters (pres., Tipmaster of Yr. 1989). Office: Gen Health Systems 5757 Corporate Blvd Ste 200 Baton Rouge LA 70808-2571

WINN, H. RICHARD, surgeon. MD, U. Pa., 1968. Diplomate Am Bd. Neurological Surgeons. Intern U. Hosp., Cleve., 1968-69, resident surgery, 1969-70; resident neurolog. surgery U. Hosp. Va., Charlottesville, 1970-74; neurol. surgeon U. Wash. Hosp., Seattle, 1983—; prof., chmn. neurol. surgery U. Wash., Seattle, 1983—. Mem. AMA, Coll. Neurol. Surgery, Am. Assn. Neurol. Surgeons. Office: U Wash Dept Neurosurg 325 9th Ave Box 359766 Seattle WA 98104-2499*

WINN, HUNG NGUYEN, obstetrician, gynecologist, maternal-fetal medicine physician; b. Thanh Hoa, Vietnam, Feb. 11, 1953; came to U.S., 1975; s. Su Cong Nguyen and Diep Thi Truong; m. Lee Nguyen Winn, Aug. 8, 1975; children: John, Jessica, Justin. BA in Biology and Chemistry, Greenville Coll., 1977; MD, U. Ill., Chgo., 1982. Resident in ob-gyn. U. Ill. Peoria, 1982-86, teaching assoc. coll. medicine, 1983-86; fellow in maternal-fetal medicine Yale U. Sch. Medicine, New Haven, 1986-88, instr., 1986-88; asst. prof. ob-gyn Wash. U. Sch. Medicine, St. Louis, 1988-90; maternal-fetal medicine physician Barnes Hosp., St. Louis, 1988-90; dir. maternal-fetal medicine div. St. Louis U., 1990—, assoc. prof. ob-gyn., 1993—. Editor St. Louis Gynecological Soc., 1993—; co-editor: (also co-founder) Jour. of Maternal-Fetal Medicine, (textbook) Clinical Maternal-Fetal Medicine; contbr. articles to profl. jours., chpts. to med. textbooks. Mem. Am. Coll. Obstetricians and Gynecologists, Soc. Perinatologists and Obstetricians. Roman Catholic. Office: St Louis U Sch Medicine St Mary's Health Ctr 6420 Clayton Rd Saint Louis MO 63117-1811

WINN, ROBERT CHEEVER, rehabilitation services professional; b. N.Y.C., Apr. 11, 1939; s. Richard Wilkens and Ella Jane (Mackenzie) W.; m. Margery Ellen Irwin (div. Sept. 1983); children: Elizabeth Jane, Margaret Ruth, Nancy Louise; m. Susan Elizabeth Gengler, June 4, 1988. BA, U. Bridgeport, 1962; MA, Ball State U., 1975. Advanced through grades to maj. USAF, 1963-83; customer support rep. Boeing Mil. Airplanes, Wichita, Kans., 1983-89; counselor Wichita Counseling Ctr., 1988; vocat. rehab. counselor Kans. Rehab. Svcs., Wellington, 1989—. Mem. Sumner County ADA Accsssibility Adv. Bd., 1994—; deacon Hillside Christian Ch., 1991-94, elder, 1995—. Mem. Nat. Rehab. Assn., Kans. Rehab. Assn., Kans. Head Injury Assn., Lions (pres. 1994-95, zone chmn. 1991-92, 94-95), VFW (jr. vice comdr. Derby, Kans. chpt. 1989, adj. 1988), Kans. Rehab. Couselors Assn. (sec., treas. 1994-96). Republican. Home: 924 Bristol Ter Wichita KS 67207-4306 Office: Kans Rehab Svcs 1116 W 8th St Wellington KS 67152-0248

WINNEM, BJØRN MAGNE, anesthesiologist; b. Evenes, Norway, Sept. 21, 1947; s. Erling and Mary Irene (Burchard) W.; m. Dina Navjord, June 25, 1976; children: Marcus, Andreas. Student, U. Vienna, Austria, U. Bergen, Norway, 1967; MD, U. Bergen, Norway, 1976. Cert. anesthesiologist. Resident in surgery SIA, Oslo, Norway, 1976; resident in medicine Torsby (Sweden) Hosp., 1977, Narvik (Norway) Hosp., 1977; physician Narvik Health Authority, 1977-78; clin. resident in anesthesiology U. Trondheim, Norway, 1978-79; resident in anesthesiology U. Tex. Health Sci. Ctr., San Antonio, Tex., 1979; resident anesthesiology and cardiology cardiovascular physiology U. Clin. Trondheim, 1980-83, rsch. fellow, 1984-86; cons. Innherred Sykehus, Levanger, Norway, 1986-87, Lillehammer (Norway) Fylkessykehus, 1987—; head anesthesia, internal care Unprofor Normedcoy, Tuzla, 1994. Contbr. articles to profl. jours. With UN Protection Force, Bosnia-Herzegovina, 1994. Maj. MC, Norwegian Mil., 1994. Recipient Golden Ball, Norwegian Football Assn., 1963; Nat. Rsch. Coun. grantee, 1984-86. Mem. Norwegian Med. Assn., Norwegian Anesthesiology Assn., Scandinavian Anesthesiology Assn., European Soc. Intensive Care Medicine, Itnernat. Trauma Anesthesiology and Critical Care Soc. Home: Sigrid Undsetsvei 8, N 2600 Lillehammer Norway Office: LFS Dept Anesthesiology, A Sandvigsgt 17, N 2600 Lillehammer Norway

WINNIE, GLENNA BARBARA, pediatric pulmonologist; b. Lansing, Mich., Oct. 14; d. Robert John and Irene (Fetchik) W.; m. Jeffrey Alan Cooper, Mar. 17, 1990; children: Robert Jefferson Cooper, David Jamison Cooper. BS, Mich. State U., 1973; MD, Vanderbilt U., 1977. Diplomate Am. Bd. Pediatrics, Am. Bd. Pediatric Pumonology. Resident in pediatrics Case Western Res. U./Babies and Childrens Hosp., Cleve., 1977-79, fellow in pediatric pulmonology, 1979-82; asst. prof. pediatrics Albany (N.Y.) Med. Coll., 1982-90, assoc. prof. pediatrics, 1990-95, head pediatric pulmonology sect., 1982-95; assoc. prof. pediat. U. Pitts., 1995—; dir. Albany Pediat. Pulmonary and Cystic Fibrosis Ctr., 1982-95; adminstrv. dir. pulmonary divsn. Children's Hosp. of Pitts., 1995—, co-dir. Cycstic Fibrosis Ctr., 1995—. Contbr. articles to profl. jours. Bd. dirs. Albany Ronald McDonald Ho., 1986-88. Rsch. grantee Nat. Cystic Fibrosis Found., 1984-86, 88-90, NIH, 1987-93. Mem. Am. Acad. Pediatrics (exec. com. chest sect. 1996—), Am. Thoracic Soc. (rsch. fellowship review com. 1989-92), Capital Dist. Pediatric Soc. (treas. 1985-90, pres. 1990-91), Soc. Pediat. Rsch. Episcopalian. Office: Childrens Hosp of Pitts 3705 Fifth Ave Pittsburgh PA 15213

WINOGRAD, LAWRENCE ALLEN, ophthalmologist; b. Greeley, Colo., Nov. 4, 1933; s. Abe and Edna (Karsh) W.; m. Rochelle Kronsberg, Aug. 21, 1955 (div. 1975); children—Edy, Debra, Joshua, Jonathan; m. Joan Gross, Oct. 12, 1980 (div. 1987). B.A., U. Denver, 1955; M.D., U. Colo., 1958. Diplomate Am. Bd. Ophthalmology; lic., Colo., Calif., Ariz. Intern Los Angeles County Gen. Hosp., 1958-59; resident in ophthalmology U. Colo., 1959-62; practice medicine specializing in ophthalmology, Denver, 1962—; mem. staff St. Anthony Hosp., Denver, 1962—, chief ophthalmology, 1967-76, med. dir. ophthalmic lab., 1971—; clin. instr. U. Colo., 1962-70, asst. clin. prof., 1970-79, assoc. clin. prof., 1979—, clin. prof. ophthalmology, 1995—; med. adv. com. Colo. Soc. Prevention Blindness, 1967-79; pres., founding officer Med. Eye Services of Mountain West, 1971—; sec., exec. sec. Med. Eye Services Am., 1975-82. Editor: New-Insight, 1976-80, The Ophthalmologist, 1976-81, 81-82; cons. editor The Argus, 1983—. Contbr. articles to profl. jours. Served to capt. M.C., USAF, 1962. Mem. Clear Creek County Med. Soc., Colo. Med. Soc., AMA, Colo. Ophthal. Soc. (legis. chmn. 1967-78), Am. Assn. Ophthalmology (nat. sec. 1972-78; speaker ho. of dels. 1978-81), Am. Acad. Ophthalmology, Contact Lens Assn. Ophthalmologists, Colo. Soc. Prevention of Blindness (med. adv. com. 1967-79), Am. Coll. Legal Medicine, Am. Soc. Law and Medicine. Home: 4505 S Yosemite St Apt 416 Denver CO 80237-2528 Office: 1701 S Federal Blvd Denver CO 80219

WINOGRAD, NICHOLAS, chemist; b. New London, Conn., Dec. 27, 1945; s. Arthur Selig Winograd and Winifred (Schaefer) Winograd Mayes; m. Barbara J. Garrison. BS, Rensselaer Poly. Inst., 1967; PhD, Case Western Reserve U., 1970. Asst. prof. chemistry Purdue U., West Lafayette, Ind., 1970-75, assoc. prof. chemistry, 1975-79; prof. chemistry Pa. State U., University Park, 1979-85, Evan Pugh prof. chemistry, 1985—; cons. Shell Devel. Co., Houston, 1975—; mem. chemistry adv. bd. NSF, Washington, 1987-90, analytical chemistry adv. bd., 1986-89. Contbr. articles to profl. jours. A.P. Sloan Found. fellow, 1974; Guggenheim Found. fellow, 1977; recipient Founder's prize Tex. Instruments Found., 1984, Faculty Scholar's Pa. State U., 1985, Bennedetti Pichler award Am. Microchem. Soc., 1991, Outstanding Alumnus award Case Western Res. U., 1991. Fellow AAAS (Sect. award); mem. Am. Chem. Soc. Home: 415 Nimitz Ave State College PA 16801-6412 Office: Pa State U Dept of Chemistry 152 Davey Lab University Park PA 16802-6300

WINOGRAD, SESSILE SARAH, psychotherapist, consultant; b. Providence, June 18, 1928; d. Benjamin and Freda (Shaulson) Mayberg; m. Seymore Winograd, May 27, 1956; children: Yeuhda Leib, Jeffrey Asher. BA in Psychology summa cum laude, U. R.I., 1974, cert. in drug counseling, 1976; MS, Barry U., 1979. Diplomate Am. Bd. Med. Psychotherapists; lic. mental health counselor; nat. cert. counselor; cert. clin.

mental health counselor. Field interviewer Brown U., Providence, 1968-69, med. coder, 1969-71; student counselor continuing edn. for women U. R.I. Ext., Providence, 1970-74; student counselor The Talmudic Coll. Fla., Miami Beach, 1979-84; drug counselor Aleph Inst., Miami Beach, 1979-86; dir. social svcs. Jewish Outreach Project Greater Miami, Inc., Miami, Fla., 1992-93; coord. cancer activities Ctr. for Psychol. Growth, Miami, 1992—; coord. women's cancer recovery program family workshop Miami Heart Inst., Miami Beach, 1992-94; pvt. practice Miami Beach, 1979—, Bklyn., 1994—; cons. Reaching Out for Emergency Help, Brookline, Mass., 1980—, Caring and Sharing, Bklyn., 1984—; lectr. and workshop presenter in field, 1985—; mem. instnl. rev. bd. Guidelines, Inc., Miami, 1991—. Author: Get Help, Get Positive, Get Well: The Aggressive Approach to Cancer Therapy, A Resource Book, 1992, (chpt.) Times of Challenge, 1988. Vice pres. Beth Yeshaye Charities of Miami, Miami Beach, 1980—; cons. Jewish Community Coun. for Russian Immigrants, Miami Beach, 1988—; bd. dirs. Jewish Outreach of Greater Miami, Inc., Miami Beach, 1991—; mem. Neshei Chabad Miami Beach, 1981—. Recipient Pulitzer prize nomination, 1992; named to Barry U. Alumni Hall of Fame, 1994. Mem. ACA, Am. Mental Health Counselor Assn., Gestault-in-Action, Alumni Assn. Barry U., Phi Kappa Phi. Home and Office: 900 Bay Dr Apt 627 Miami FL 33141-5631

WINOKUR, GEORGE, psychiatrist, educator; b. Phila., Feb. 10, 1925; s. Louis and Vera P. Winokur; m. Betty Stricklin, Sept. 15, 1951; children: Thomas, Kenneth, Patricia. A.B., Johns Hopkins U., 1944; M.D., U. Md., 1947. Intern Church Home and Hosp., Balt., 1947-48; asst. resident Seton Inst., Balt., 1948-50; assoc. in neuropsychiatry Washington U., St. Louis, 1950-51; resident in neuropsychiatry Barnes Hosp., St. Louis, 1950-51; asst. prof. psychiatry Washington U., St. Louis, 1955-59, assoc. prof., 1959-66, prof., 1966-71; assoc. psychiatrist Barnes Hosp., 1963-71; cons. in psychiatry Homer G. Phillips Hosp., 1954-64; instr. psychiatry Meharry Med. Coll., Nashville, 1954-55; prof. U. Iowa, Iowa City, 1971—, head dept. psychiatry, 1971-90; dir. Iowa Psychiat. Hosp.; acad. guest U. Zurich, 1984; Louis H. Hohler Meml. lectr. St. Mary's Health Ctr., St. Louis, 1985. Author: Manic Depressive Illness, 1969, Depression: The Facts, 1981, Mania and Depression, A Classification of Syndrome and Disease, 1991, The Natural History of Mania, Depression and Schizophrenia, 1996; mng. editor European Archives of Psychiatry and Neurol. Scis.; chief Am. editor Jour. Affective Disorders, 1979—; mem. editl. bd. 8 profl. jours.; contbr. numerous articles on clin. genetics of affective disorders, alcoholism and schizophrenia to profl. jours. Served to capt. M.C. USAF, 1952-54. Recipient Anna-Monika 1st prize award, 1973, Hofheimer prize, 1972, Samuel W. Hamilton award, 1977, Leonard Crammer Meml. award, 1980, Paul Hoch award, 1981, Vol. Svc. award Nat. Coun. Alcoholism, 1974, Achievement award Am. Acad. Clin. Psychiatrists, 1987, Nelson Urban Rsch. award Mental Health Assn., Iowa, 1988, Lifetime Rsch. award Nat. Depressive and Manic Depressive Assn., 1990, Lifetime Achievement award Internat. Soc. Psychiat. Genetics, 1993, Regents award U. Iowa, 1994, Paul Huston award Iowa Psychiat. Soc., 1994, Gold medal Soc. Biol. Psychiatry, 1984, Lapinlahti medal Helsinki Finland Lapinlahti Hosp. Fellow Am. Psychiat. Assn. (life), Royal Coll. Psychiatrists (hon.); mem. Am. Psychopath. Assn. (pres. 1975-77, Joseph Zubin award 1992), Am. Soc. Human Genetics, Assn. Am. Physicians (hon.), Internat. Group Study of Affective Disorders, Psychiat. Rsch. Soc., Am. Fedn. Clin. Rsch., Assn. Rsch. in Nervous and Mental Disorders, Am. Coll. Neuropsychopharmacology, Societat Catalana de Psiquiatra, Sigma Xi, Tudor and Stewart Club (Balt.). Office: U Iowa Psychiatry Rsch MEB Iowa City IA 52242-1000

WINSHIP, DANIEL HOLCOMB, medicine educator, university dean; b. Houston, July 4, 1933; m. Winnifred Jeneanne Rowold; children: Charles Dwayne, Nancy Ellen, David Rhoads, Rebecca Susan, Molly Beth. BA, Rice U., 1954; MD, U. Tex., Galveston, 1958. Diplomate Am. Bd. Internal Medicine. Intern in internal medicine Ochsner Found. Hosp., New Orleans, 1958-59; asst. resident U. Utah Coll. Medicine, Salt Lake City, 1959-61; fellow in gastroenterology Yale U. Sch. Medicine, New Haven, 1961-63; rsch. fellow med. ethics, fellow law, sci.-medicine program Yale U. Divinity Sch., Yale U. Law Sch., New Haven, 1977; asst. prof., then assoc. prof. medicine Marquette U. Sch. Medicine, Milw., 1963-69; assoc. prof., then prof. U. Mo. Sch. Medicine, Columbia, 1969-84, assoc. dean for VA affairs, 1982-84; prof. U. Kans. Sch. Medicine, Kansas City, 1984-87; assoc. dep. chief med. dir. dept. medicine and surgery VA Ctrl. Office, Washington, 1987-90; prof. medicine, dean Loyola U. Stritch Sch. Medicine, Maywood, Ill., 1990—; gastroenterologist Harry S. Truman Meml. Vets. Hosp., Columbia, 1974-79, chief med. svc., 1979-82, chief staff, 1982-84; chief staff VA Med. Ctr., Kansas City, 1984-86, dir., 1986-87; attending physician Loyola U. Med. Ctr., 1990—, Edward Hines (Ill.) Med. Ctr., 1990—; mem. adv. bd. Greater Chgo. Alliance for Mentally Ill, 1991; pres., bd. dirs. gastroenterology adv. com. VA, 1982-85, chmn. clin. and programs adv. coun., 1988-90; mem. rev. com. Mo. Dept. Mental Health, 1981-82; numerous others. Mem. editl. bd. Clin. Rsch., 1970-73, Annals Clin. Gastroenterology, 1978-83, Gastroenterology: A Weekly Update, 1978-81; assoc. editor Jour. Lab. and Clin. Medicine, 1980-83; contbr. numerous articles and abstracts to med. jours. Bd. dirs. John H. Walters Hospice Ctrl. Mo., 1982-84, chmn., 1983-84. Recipient Outstanding Clin. Tchr. in Medicine award Milwaukee County Hosp. Housestaff, 1964, Golden Apple award Student AMA, 1972, Disting. Svc. medal and award VA, 1990, Ashbel Smith Disting. Alumnus award U. Tex. Med. Br., 1992. Mem. Am. Gastroent. Assn. (com. on rsch. 1975-78, com. on tng. and edn. 1978-81, dir. clin. tchg. project 1990-82, program chmn. motility sect. 1987), Gastroenterology Rsch. Group, Ctrl. Soc. for Clin. Rsch., So. Soc. for Clin. Investigation, Am. Fedn. for Clin. Rsch., Midwest Gut Club (presiding pres. 1980-83), Soc. for Health and Human Values, Inst. Society, Ethics and Life Scis., Sigma Xi, Alpha Omega Alpha (vis. prof. U. Mo. Sch. Medicine 1991, Med. Coll. Wis. 1993). Office: Loyola U Med Ctr 2160 S 1st Ave Maywood IL 60153-3304*

WINSKUNAS, PHILIP FELIX, surgeon; b. Chgo., Aug. 22, 1937; s. Felix C. and Aldona Winskunas. BS, U. Notre Dame, 1959; MD, Loyola U., Chgo., 1963. Diplomate Am. Bd. Surgery, Am. Bd. Thoracic Surgery. Intern L.A. County Hosp., 1963-64; resident in surgery NYU Med. Ctr., 1967-71; resident in thoracic surgery Cook County Hosp., 1972-74; pvt. practice Ill., Wis., 1974-84; asst. prof. surgery U. S.D., 1984—; with VA Hosp., S.D., 1984—. Lt. USN, 1965-67, Vietnam. Fellow ACS. Office: VA Hosp 2501 W 22 St Sioux Falls SD 57117

WINSLET, MARC CHRISTOPHER, surgeon, educator; b. Luton, Bedfordshi, U.K., Feb. 27, 1958; s. Alan John Noel and Eileen Jane (Samm) W.; m. Esther Alice Meli, May 5, 1991; children: Kitty, Harry. M.B.B.S., Royal Free Hosp., London, 1981; MS, U. London, 1988. Sr. house officer St. James/St. Georges Hosps., London, 1983-84; surg. registrar United Hosps., Birmingham, Eng., 1984-85; rsch. fellow Birmingham U., 1985-87; surg. registrar leicester (U.K.) Royal Infirmary, 1987-88; lectr. Queen Elizabeth Hosp., Birmingham, 1988-92; sr. lectr./cons. Royal Free Hosp., London, 1992—, chmn. gen. surgery, divsn. med. dir., 1995; Hunterian prof. Royal Coll. Surgeons, Eng., 1988-89; treas., com. mem. Brit. Stomach Cancer Group, 1994—. Editor Internat. Jour. Colorectal Disease. Fellow Royal Coll. Surgeons (Eng.) (surg. tutor 1993-96), Royal Coll. surgeons (Edinburgh), Brit. Assn. surg. Oncology, Assn. Coloproctology Gt. Britain and Ireland, Assn. Surgeons Gt. Britain and Ireland; mem. Royal Soc. Medicine (mem. coun. sect. coloproctology 1996—). Office: Royal Free Hosp Dept Surgery, Pond St, London NW3 2QG, England

WINSTEAD, CRYSTAL ALLEN, critical care nurse; b. Rocky Mount, N.C., Dec. 28, 1964; d. Joseph Dan and Carolyn (Phillips) Allen; m. Kenneth Wayne Winstead, Sept. 25, 1986. BA in Psychology, Vassar Coll., 1987; BSN, Barton Coll., Wilson, N.C., 1993. RN, N.C.; cert. BLS, EMT. Staff nurse Pitt County Meml. Hosp., Greenville, N.C., 1993—; part time home health nurse Tarheel Home Health, Greenville, 1993—. Mem. ANA, AACCN, N.C. Nurses Assn., Nat. League for Nursing, Home Health Nurses Assn., Sigma Theta Tau. Baptist. Home: PO Box 293 Macclesfield NC 27852

WINSTEAD, DANIEL KEITH, psychiatrist; b. Cin., Dec. 30, 1944; s. Daniel Sebastian and Betty Jane (Kirsch) W.; m. Jennifer Reiner, June 15, 1968; children: Laura Suzanne, Nathaniel Scott. BA, U. Cin., 1966; MD, Vanderbilt U., 1970. Diplomate Am. Bd. Psychiatry and Neurology. Resident U. Cin., 1970-72, fellow, 1972-73; chief VA Med. Ctr. psychiat. svc. Tulane U., New Orleans, 1976-79, dir., consultation/liaison psychiat. tng., 1979-83, dir. psychiatric edn. and residency tng., 1983-87, assoc. prof., 1979-84, prof., 1984—, chmn. dept. psychiatry and neurology, 1987—; chief psychiat. svc. VA Med. Ctr., New Orleans, 1976-80; assoc. chief staff for edn. VA Med Ctr., New Orleans, 1979-87; staff psychiatrist VA Med. Ctr., New Orleans, 1987—; med. dir. Jefferson Parish Substance Abuse Clinic, 1980-81; cons. E.R. Squibb and Sons, 1985-86; vis. physician psychiatry Charity Hosp., New Orleans, 1979-90. Contbr. articles to profl. jours. Maj. U.S. Army, 1973-76. Mem. AMA, Am. Coll. Psychiatrists, Am. Acad. Psychiatry and Law, Am. Psychiat. Assn., La. State Med. Soc., So. Assn. for Rsch. in Psychiatry, Acad. Psychosomatic Medicine, Am. Assn. Chairmen Depts. Psychiatry, Am. Assn. Dirs. Psychiat. Residency Tng., Assn. Acad. Psychiatry, La. Psychiat. Assn. (pres. 1991-92), Soc. Biol. Psychiatry, New Orleans Area Psychiat. Assn., New Orleans Neurol. Soc., Orleans Parish Med. Soc. Republican. Presbyterian. Home: 5348 Bellaire Dr New Orleans LA 70124-1033 Office: Tulane Med Sch 1430 Tulane Ave New Orleans LA 70112-2699

WINSTON, DONNA CAROL, nursing educator, nurse practitioner; b. Cin., Aug. 3, 1938; children: Laura, Gary, Scott, Lindsay. BS, Tex. Christian U., 1978; BBA, U. Cin., 1960; MS, U. Ariz., 1982; PhD, Tex. Woman's U., 1988. Cert. geriatric nurse practitioner, nutritional specialist. Clin. nurse specialist Harris Hosp., Ft. Worth, 1982-84; nursing specialist U. Tex., 1985-86; dir. edn. AMI-North Tex. Med. Ctr., McKinney, 1987; asst. prof. Wayne State U., Detroit, 1988-90, Ariz. State U., Phoenix, 1990-93; geriatric NP in pvt. practice, 1993; adult NP St. Joseph's Med. Ctr., Phoenix, 1994—; cons. Samaritan Corp., 1993, Streich Lang Law Firm, 1995. Mem. Am. Mktg. Assn., Internat. Soc. Human Ethology, Sigma Theta Tau.

WINSTON, STUART A., osteopathic physician, cardiologist, educator; b. Midland, Mich., Oct. 3, 1949; s. Arthur W. Jr. and Kathryn L. (Spaulding) W.; m. Nancy M. Keyser, July 6, 1985. BS, Mich. State U., 1972, DO, 1978. Intern Detroit Osteo. Hosps., 1978-80, resident in medicine, 1980-82; fellow in cardiology Riverside and Detroit Osteo. Hosps., 1982-84; fellow in cardiac electrophysiology U. Calif., San Francisco, 1984; clin. instr. medicine U. Calif. Sch. Medicine, San Francisco, 1984-85; pvt. practice, Des Moines, 1985-88, Ann Arbor, 1988—; instr. medicine U. Mich. Sch. Medicine, Ann Arbor, 1994—; med. dir. Mich. Heart and Vascular Inst., Ann Arbor, 1995—; mem. staff dept. medicine St. Joseph Mercy Hosp., Ann Arbor. Fellow Am. Coll. Cardioloogy (program chmn. sci. session 1996); mem. N.Am. Soc. Pacing and Electrophysiology. Office: Mich Heart PC PO Box 971 MHVI Ste 203 Ann Arbor MI 48106

WINTER, JOAN ELIZABETH, psychotherapist; b. Aiken, S.C., Feb. 24, 1947; d. John S. and Mary Elizabeth (Caldwell) Winter. BS, Ariz. State U., 1970; MSW, Va. Commonwealth U., 1977; EdS, Coll. William and Mary, 1989, EdD, 1993. Lic. clin. social worker, AMFT bd. approved supr., clin. group worker. Va. Counselor Child Psychiatry Hosp., Phoenix, 1969-70, Ariz. Job Coll., Casa Grande, 1970-71; dir. Halfway House, Richmond, Va., 1971-73; state supr. resdl. treatment, Richmond, 1973-75; psycotherapist Med. Coll. Va., Richmond, 1975-76, Va. Commonwealth U., 1976-77; adj. prof., exec. dir. Family Rsch. Project, William and Mary Coll., Richmond, Va., 1979—; dir. Family Inst. Va., Richmond, 1980—; examiner, approved supr. Bd. Behavioral Scis., Commonwealth of Va., 1982—; mem. adj. faculty dept. psychology Coll. William & Mary, Med. Coll. Va.; mem. Avanta Network, Exec. Coun. and Faculty, Nat. Inst. of Drug Abuse, Rsch. Adv. Com. Author: The Phenomenon of Incest, 1977, The Use of Self in Therapy: The Person and Practice of the Therapist, 1987, Family Life of Psychotherapists, 1987 Enhancing the Marital Relationship: Virginia Satir's Parts Party, 1990, Enhancing the Marital Relationship: Virginia Satir's Parts Party, 1991, Family Therapy Research Outcomes: Bowen, Haley and Satir; editor Jour. Couple Therapy; contbr. articles to profl. jours. Diplomate Nat. Assn. Social Workers; mem. Am. Soc. Cert. Social Workers, Am. Family Therapy Assn., Am. Assn. Marriage and Family Therapy (approved supr.), Avanta Network Faculty. Address: 2910 Monument Ave Richmond VA 23221-1404

WINTER, LOEK H. L., radiologist, epidemiologist; b. Voerendaal, The Netherlands, Nov. 30, 1959; s. Ber L. W. Winter and Pia Lammers; m. Gonneke H. A. O. Warnars, May 5, 1990; 1 child, Thomas. DRS, Med. Sch., The Netherlands, 1984; DR, U. Utrecht, The Netherlands, 1991; DRS, Health Scis., The Netherlands, 1996. Bd. cert. radiologist; bd. cert. epidemiologist. Radiologist Reinier de Graat Hosp., Delft, The Netherlands, 1989-93, Onze Lievevrouwe Zieken Hosp., Amsterdam, 1993—; co-founder Plexus NV, Amsterdam, 1991; cons. Good Clin. Practice, Rotterdam, 1996. Mem. NVVRD (advisor 1995). Home: Dorpsstraatg, 1393 NE Nigtevecht The Netherlands Office: Onze Lievevrouwe Zieken Hos, 1o Oosterparkstraat 27g, 1079 HM Amsterdam The Netherlands

WINTER, MILDRED M., educational administrator. BA summa cum laude, Harris Tchrs. Coll.; MEd, U. Mo.; postgrad., Harvard U., U. Cin. Exec. dir. Parents As Tchrs. Nat. Ctr. Inc., St. Louis; tchr., cons., Mo., 1962-68; developer, dir. Ferguson-Florissant Parent-Child Early Edn. Program, Mo., 1969-72; first dir. early childhood edn. Mo. Dept. Elem. and Secondary Edn., 1972-84; sr. lectr. dept. elem. and early childhood edn. U. Mo., St. Louis; cons. in field. Contbr. articles to profl. jours. Named Outstanding Leader in Field of Edn., Mo. House of Reps., 1982, Outstanding Educator and Adv. for Young Children, Mo. Gov. Christopher S. Bond, 1984, Pioneer in Edn., State Bd. Edn., Mo. Dept. Edn., 1991, St. Louis Woman of Achievement in Edn., 1992; cited for Pioneering Leadership in Edn. Resolution, Mo. Senate, 1995; recipient Outstanding Svc. award Assn. Edn. of Young Children, 1984, Vol. Accreditation Leadership award, 1993, Spl. award Nat. Soc. Behavioral Pediat., 1992, Charles A. Dana Pioneering Achievements Health and Edn. Inst. Medicine award NAS, 1995. Office: Parents As Tchrs Nat Ctr Inc 10176 Corporate Sq Dr Ste 230 Saint Louis MO 63132*

WINTER, PETER MICHAEL, physician, anesthesiologist, educator; b. Sverdlovsk, Russia, Aug. 5, 1934; came to U.S., 1938, naturalized, 1944; s. George and Anne Winter; m. Michelle Yakopec, Dec. 28, 1991; children: Karin Anne, Christopher George, Lia Lynn. BA, Cornell U., 1958; MD, U. Rochester, 1962. Intern U. Utah, Salt Lake City, 1962-63; resident in anesthesiology, pharmacology and respiratory physiology Mass. Gen. Hosp., Boston, 1963-65; USPHS fellow Harvard U. Med. Sch., 1964-66; Buswell fellow dept. physiology, asst. prof. SUNY, Buffalo, 1966-69; assoc. prof. dept. anesthesiology Sch. Medicine, U. Wash., Seattle, 1969-74; prof. Sch. Medicine, U. Wash., 1974-79; prof., chmn. dept. anesthesiology and critical care medicine U. Pitts. Sch. Medicine, 1979—, Peter and Eva Safar prof. anesthesiology/critical care med.; anesthesiologist in chief Univ. Health Ctr. Hosps., Pitts. Editorial cons. Anesthesiology; contbr. chpts. to books, papers and abstracts on anesthesia, environ. phys. pharmacology and med. edn. to publs. Served with U.S. Army, 1953-56. Recipient NIH career devel. award, 1971. Mem. AMA, Am. Coll. Chest Physicians, Am. Soc. Anesthesiologists, Royal Soc. Medicine, N.Y. Acad. Scis., Undersea Med. Soc. Internat. Anesthesia Research Soc., Soc. Acad. Anesthesia Chairmen, Assn. Univ. Anesthetists, Morton Soc. Club: Am. Alpine. Office: 3471 5th Ave Ste 910 Pittsburgh PA 15213

WINTER, TERRY DAVID, health services administrator, nurse; b. Amityville, N.Y., Nov. 5, 1952; s. Bernard Leon and Tanja Yvonne (Epstone) W.; m. Antonia Bratt; children: Zachary, Sascha. BA, U. Mich., 1974; BSN, U. Calif., San Francisco, 1979; PHM in Health Policy and Adminstrn., U. Calif., Berkeley, 1990. Staff nurse San Francisco Gen. Hosp., 1979-81; staff nurse, emergency svcs. Herrick Hosp., Berkeley, 1981; staff nurse, emergency svcs. Cmty. Hosp., Santa Rosa, Calif., 1981-86, coord. poison control ctr., 1983-86; outpatient staff nurse Kaiser Permanente, Santa Rosa, 1985-91; intern Marin Cmty. Found., Larkspur, Calif., 1989—; cons. in health policy and demographics Sonoma and Marin Counties, Calif., 1990-92; mgr. HIV svcs. Kaiser Permanente, Santa Rosa, 1991—; cons. to a variety of healthcare orgns. on structure of chronic disease svcs., 1993—. Author: Radiation on the Job--A Manual for Health Workers on Ionizing Radiation, 1981. Office: Kaiser Permanente 401 Bicentennial Way Santa Rosa CA 95403

WINTERMANTEL, ERICH, medical, materials scientist, educator; b. Tuttlingen, Baden-Württ., Germany, May 3, 1956; arrived in Switzerland, 1986; s. Wilhelm and Hilde (Renz) W. Abitur, Gymnasium for Sci., Tuttlingen, 1975; State Diploma in Medicine, U. Tubingen, Fed. Republic Germany, 1981, MD, 1982. Diplomate in sugery. Rsch. fellow U. Toulouse, France, 1979, U. Western Ontario, Can., 1979, U. Montreal, Can., 1980, U. Calif., L.A., 1981; asst. in neurosurgery U. Saarland, Homburg, Fed. Republic Germany, 1983-84, asst. in surgery, 1984-85; asst. in surgery Tech. U. Munich, 1985-86; sr. lectr. Swiss Fed. Inst. of Tech., Zurich, 1986-90, habilitation and pvt. dozent, 1991—, head, 1995—; vis. scientist MIT, 1990, permanent vis. scientist, 1990—, chmn. and prof. biocompatible materials sci. and engring., 1992. Author/editor: Biocompatible Materials Engineering, 1991; patentee in field; contbr. articles to profl. jours./publs.; reviewer scientific jours. Mem. Am. Soc. Artificial Internal Organs, Am. Chem. Soc., Soc. Biomaterials, Materials Rsch. Soc., Internat. Soc. Artificial Internal Organs, Polymer Group of Switzerland, Swiss Soc. Optic and Electron Microscopy, Swiss Soc. Biomed. Engring., German Soc. Biomed. Engring., German Soc. Materials, German Soc. Surgery, Verein Deutscher Ingenieure. Office: Biokompatible Werkstoffe & Bauweisen, Wagistrasse 23, 8952 Schlieren Switzerland

WINTERS, CHARLENE ADRIENNE, nursing educator; b. Long Beach, Calif., Jan. 6, 1952; d. Albert J. and Jean Janis Worrick; m. Don Winters, Jan. 8, 1977; children: John, Scott. AS, Long Beach City Coll., 1976; BS, Calif. State U., Long Beach, 1979, MS, 1984; postgrad., Rush U., 1994—. Staff nurse ICU St. Mary Med. Ctr., Long Beach, 1976-81, clin. educator, 1980-84; asst. prof. Mont. State U., Bozeman, 1984-88, 92—; nursing faculty Salish Kootenai Coll., Pablo, Mont., 1988-92; staff nurse ICU/PAR St. Patrick Hosp., Missoula, Mont., summers, 1986-93. Mem. Am. Assn. Critical Care Nurses, Sigma Theta Tau (Recognition award).

WINTERS, KENNETH JOHN, internist; b. Ridgewood, N.J., Feb. 9, 1954. BS in Biology, Calvin Coll., 1976; MD, Wash. U., St. Louis, 1980. Diplomate Am. Bd. Internal Medicine, Am. Critical Care Medicine, Am. Bd. Cardiovascular Diseases. Resident in internal medicine Barnes Hosp./Wash. U., St. Louis, 1980-83, cardiology fellow, 1987-92; critical care physician St. Lukes Hosp., St. Louis, 1984-87; asst. prof. medicine Wash. U. Sch. Medicine, St. Louis, 1992—; assoc. dir. coronary care unit Barnes Hosp., St. Louis, 1992—; assoc. dir. cardiac cath. lab. Barnes Hosp., St. Louis, 1994—, co-dir. interventional cardiology, 1995—. Author: Washington Manual, 1995. Grantee Am. Heart Assn., 1994-96. Fellow Am. Coll. Cardiology; mem. ACP. Home: 1286 Whispering Pines Dr Saint Louis MO 63146 Office: Washington U Box 8086 660 S Euclid Ave Saint Louis MO 63110

WINTROUB, BRUCE URICH, dermatologist, educator, researcher; b. Milw., Nov. 8, 1943; s. Ernest Bernard and Janet (Zien) W.; m. Marya Kraus, Jan. 20, 1973; children: Annie, Ben, Molly. BA, Amherst Coll., 1965; MD, Washington U., St. Louis, 1969. Diplomate Am. Bd. Internal Medicine, Am. Bd. Dermatology. Intern in medicine Peter Bent Brigham Hosp., Boston, 1969-70, jr. asst. resident in medicine, 1970-71, jr. assoc. in medicine, 1976-80, asst. then attending physician, 1976-81; resident in dermatology Harvard Med. Sch., Boston, 1974-76, instr., 1976-78, asst. prof., 1978-82; assoc. prof. dermatology Sch. Medicine, U. Calif., San Francisco, 1982-85, attending physician med. ctr., 1982—, prof., mem. exec. com. dept. dermatology, 1985-95; chmn. exec. com. dept. dermatology U. Calif., San Francisco, 1985-95; mem. dean's adv. com., governing bd. continuing med. edn., other coms. Sch. Medicine, U. Calif., San Francisco, 1986—; exec. vice dean Sch. Medicine U. Calif., San Francisco, 1995—; assoc.dean Sch. Medicine, U. Calif., Mount Zion, 1990—; dir. Dermatology Assocs., San Francisco, 1982-85; cons. in dermatology Mass. Gen. Hosp., Boston, 1976-82, Beth Israel Hosp. and Children's Hosp. Med. Ctr., Boston, 1978-82, Parker Hill Med. Ctr., Boston, 1980-82; attending physician Robert B. Brigham Hosp. div. Brigham and Women's Hosp., Boston, 1980-81, assoc., 1980-82; chief dermatology svc. Brockton (Mass.) VA Med. Ctr., 1980-82; asst. chief dermatology VA Med. Ctr., San Francisco, 1982-85, mem. space com., 1984-85, dean's adv. com., 1985—, chmn. budget com., 1987—; clin. investigator Nat. Inst. Allergy, Metabolism and Digestive Disease, NIH, 1978. Author: (with others) Biochemistry of the Acute Allergic Reactions, Fifth International Symposium, 1988; contbr. numerous articles, abstracts to profl. jours. NIH clin. fellow and grantee, 1967-69. Fellow Am. Acad. Dermatology (com. evaluations 1985—, coun. govt. liaison 1987—, congress on tech. plannning commn. 1988—, assoc. editor Dialogues in Dermatology jour. 1982-85, Stellwagon prize 1976); mem. Soc. Investigative Dermatology (chmn. pub. rels. com. 1987-88), Assn. Profs. Dermatology (chmn. program com. 1987—, bd. dirs.), Pacific Dermatol. Assn. (chmn. program com. 1987—), San Francisco Dermatol. Soc., Am. Fedn. Clin. Rsch. (chmn. dermatology program 1988-89), Am. Assn. Immunology, Dystrophic Epidermolysis Bullosa Rsch. Am. (bd. dirs. 1981), Internat. Soc. Dermatology, Internat. Soc. Cutaneous Pharmacology (founding mem.), Am. Soc. Clin. Investigation, Skin Pharmacology Soc., Calif. Med. Soc., San Francisco Med. Soc., Clin. Immunology Soc., Dermatology Found., (bd. dirs., exec. com.), AAAS, Am. Assn. Physicians, Calif. Acad. Medicine, Am. Dermatol. Assn., Sigma Xi, Alpha Omega Alpha. Office: Deans Office Sch Medicine U Calif San Francisco 513 Parnassus Ave Rm S224 San Francisco CA 94143-0410

WIPPOLD, FRANZ JOSEPH, II, medical educator; b. St. Louis, Mar. 31, 1951; s. Franz J. and Nelda C. (Cordes) W.; m. Carol Ann Krentz, May 27, 1977; children: Rachel K., Aaron C., Rebecca T. BA, Westminster Coll., 1973; MD, St. Louis U., 1977. Intern in neurology Walter Reed Army Med. Ctr., 1977-78, resident in neurology, 1978-79, resident in radiology, 1979-82; fellow in neuroradiology Mallinckroot Inst. Radiology; dir. MRI Christian Hosp. Northeast, St. Louis, 1986-89; assoc. prof. Mallinckroot Inst., Washington U. Sch. Medicine, St. Louis, 1989—. Author: Practical MRI, 1996. Maj. U.S. Army, 1977-86. Fellow Am. Coll. Angiology; mem. Am. Coll. Neuroradiology (sr.), Am. Coll. Radiology, Am. Roentgen Soc., Radiologic Soc. N.Am., Soc. Magnetic Resonance Imaging, Soc. Magnetic Resonance, Christian Med. Soc., Am. Assn. of Univ. Radiologists. Lutheran. Office: Mallinkroot Inst Radiology 510 S Kings Hwy Saint Louis MO

WIRE, TEDDY KERMIT, psychotherapist; b. Protem, Mo., Feb. 8, 1936; d. Flora (Thornton) Brown; m. Paul W. Wire, May 30, 1953; children: Brenda, Eddie, Patty, Paula. BA, So. Nazarene U., Bethany, Okla., 1971; MEd, U. Ctrl. Okla., 1988. Secondary tchr. Yukon (Okla.) Pub. Schs., 1973-78; asst. mgr. Bethany Rite-Way Printing, 1978-88; psychotherapist Cmty. Counseling Ctr., Oklahoma City, 1989-95, dir. aging svcs., 1995—; adj. prof. psychology So. Nazarene U., 1990-92. Mem. ACA, APA, Am. Soc. on Aging, Phi Delta Lambda. Republican. Mem. Ch. of Nazarene. Home: 3913 Riverside Dr Bethany OK 73008

WIRTH, FREMONT PHILIP, neurosurgeon, educator; b. Nashville, July 23, 1940; s. Fremont P. and Willa (Dean) W.; m. Penelope Simpson, July 25, 1964; children: Fremont Philip II, Andrew Simpson, Carolyn Howe. BA with honors in History, Williams Coll., 1962; MD, Vanderbilt U., 1966. Diplomate Am. Bd. Neurol. Surgery (guest examiner 1989, bd. dirs. 1992—), Nat. Bd. Med. Examiners; cert. advanced trauma life support ACS. Surg. intern Johns Hopkins Hosp., Balt., 1966-67, resident and fellow in surgery, 1967-68; asst. resident in neurosurgery Barnes Hosp., Washington U., St. Louis, 1970-72, fellow in neurosurgery, 1972-74; pvt. practice, Savannah, Ga., 1974—; asst. clin. prof. neurosurgery Med. Coll. Ga., Augusta, 1991—, vis. prof., 1978, 79, 86, 87; mem. staff, neurosurg. ICU, St. Joseph's Hosp., 1974—, dir. 1978—; mem. staff Meml. Med. Ctr., 1974—, dir. rehab., 1983; mem. staff Candler Gen. Hosp., 1974—; med. dir. Head and Spinal Cord Injury Prevention Project for Ga., 1984—; presenter in field, 1970—; vis. prof. U. Md., Balt., 1981, Tufts New Eng. Med. Ctr., Boston, 1982. Series editor (with R.A. Ratcheson) Concepts in Neurosurgery, 1986-93; editor: (with Ratcheson) Neurosurgical Critical Care, Concepts in Neurological Surgery, Vol. 1, 1987, Ruptured Cerebral Aneurysms, Concepts in Neurological Surgery, Vol. 6, 1994; contbr. articles and book revs. to med. jours., chpts. to books. Elder Skidaway Island Presbyn. Ch., 1981-83; mem. pack 57 com. Cub Scouts Am., Savannah, 1979-84; mem. troop 57 com. Boy Scouts Am., Savannah, 1980-85, mem. fin. com. Coastal Empire coun., 1987-90, mem. adv. bd., 1990—; chmn. physicians' solicitation United Way Coastal Empire, 1987; bd. dirs. Think First Found., 1990—. With USPHS, 1968-70. Fellow ACS (bd. govs. 1984-90, sr. mem. trauma com. 1991—); mem. AMA (physician's recognition award 1973-76, 77-79, 80-82, 83-85, 88-91, 91-94, 95—), Congress Neurol. Surgeons (profl. conduct com. 1989—, Disting. Svc. award 1989), Neurol. Soc. Am., Am. Assn. Neurologic Surgeons, Brain Surgery Soc., Ga. Med. Soc., Med. Assn. Ga. (editl. bd. 1987-93), pres. 1995, Ga. Neurosurg. Soc. (exec. com. 1981-88, pres. 1988-89), So. Neurosurg. Soc. (exec. com. 1982-91, pres. 1988-89), Am. Heart

Assn. (fellow stroke coun.). Office: Neurol Inst Savannah 4 E Jackson Blvd Savannah GA 31405-5810

WIRTHLIN, MILTON ROBERT, JR., periodontist; b. Little Rock, July 13, 1932; s. Milton Robert and Margaret Frances (Clark) W.; m. Joan Krieger, Aug. 1, 1954; children: Michael, Steven, Laurie, David, Aina. DDS, U. Calif., San Francisco, 1956, MS, 1968. Commd. ensign USN, 1955, advanced through grades to capt., 1976, retired, 1985; assoc. prof. U. Pacific, San Francisco, 1985-86; assoc. clin. prof. U. Calif., San Francisco, 1986-96, clin. prof., 1996—, dir. postgrad. periodontology, 1996—. Contbr. articles to profl. jours. Asst. scoutmaster Boy Scouts Am., San Bruno, Calif., 1968, com. chmn. Explorer Post, San Francisco, 1981-83; bd. dirs. ARC, Chgo., 1976-81, chiir social svc. com., San Francisco, 1981-83. Decorated Meritorious Svc. medal with 2 gold stars; recipient Gabbs prize U. Calif., 1956. Fellow Internat. Coll. Dentists; mem. Am. Dental Assn., Am. Acad. Perdioontology, Western Soc. Periodontology, Med-Dental Study Guild San Francisco (pres. 1993), Internat. Assn. Dental Rsch., Omicron Kappa Upsilon. Office: U Calif Med Ctr Sch Dentistry San Francisco CA 94143-0762

WISDOM, GUYRENA KNIGHT, psychologist, educator; b. St. Louis, July 27, 1923; d. Gladys Margaret (Hankins) McCullin. AB, Stowe Tchrs. Coll., 1945; AM, U. Ill., 1951; postgrad. St. Louis U., 1952-53, 58, 62; Washington U., St. Louis, 1959-61; U. Chgo., 1966-67; Drury Coll., 1968; U. Mo., 1971-72; Fontbonne Coll., 1973; Harris-Stowe State Coll., 1974, 81-82. Tchr. elem. sch. St. Louis Pub. Sch. System, 1945-63, psychol. examiner, 1963-68, sch. psychologist, 1968-74, cons. spl. edn., 1974-77, supr. spl. edn. dept., 1977-79, coord. staff devel. div., 1979-81; pvt. tutor, 1971-72; sch. psychologist, 1984-85; pvt. practice psychologist, St. Louis, 1985-88; pvt. practice, 1989—; instr. Harris Tchrs. Coll., St. Louis, 1973-74, Harris-Stowe Coll., 1979. Contbr. articles to profl. jours. Mem. Nat. Assn. Sch. Psychologists, Learning Disabilities Assn., Coun. for Exceptional Children, Assn. Supervision and Curriculum Devel., Pi Lambda Theta, Kappa Delta Pi. Roman Catholic. Home: 5046 Wabada Ave Saint Louis MO 63113-1118

WISE, EDMUND JOSEPH, physician assistant, industrial hygienist; b. Pitts., June 18, 1947; s. Edmund Joseph and Marian Elizabeth (Burdelski) W. BA in Biology, Washington and Jefferson Coll., 1969; B of Health Scis., Duke U., 1974; MPH, U. Tenn., 1990. Clin. care tech. II Duke U. Med. Ctr., Durham, N.C., 1971-72; physician asst. Oak Ridge (Tenn.) Nat. Lab., 1974—; mem. toxic substance control act task team Lockheed Martin Energy Sys., Oak Ridge, 1995—; mem. hazardous waste com. Oak Ridge Nat. Lab., 1993—, ergonomics com., 1994—, hearing conservation com., 1984—. Author: History Medical Activities 1/12 Infantry, 1970; co-author: AAPA Guidelines Continuing Medical Education, 1977, ORNL Hazwoper Program Manual, 1993; co-author: (chpt.) Tennessee Academy Constitution and Bylaws, 1976. Mem. malpractice review bd. Tenn. Dept. Pub. Health, Nashville, 1981—. Capt. U.S. Army, 1969-75, Vietnam. Decorated Bronze Star, Combat Med. badge; recipient Gold cert. of Appreciation, Am. Heart Assn., 1983. Fellow Am. Acad. Physician Assts. (house del. 1979, 86, profl. and continuing med. edn. com. 1975-80), Tenn. Acad. Physician Assts. (co-founder, v.p. 1975, pres. 1977); mem. Tenn. Heart Assn. (cert. BCLS, affiliate faculty 1978—), East Tenn. Region Heart Assn. (CPR-Emergency Cardiac Care com. 1980—), Duke U. Alumni Assn., Nat. 4th Infantry Divsn. Assn., Washington and Jefferson Alumni Assn. Republican. Roman Catholic. Home: 1238 Venido Dr Knoxville TN 37932-2598 Office: Oak Ridge Nat Lab Health Divsn PO Box 2008 MS6220 Oak Ridge TN 37831-6220

WISE, HAROLD B., internist, educator; b. Hamilton, Ont., Can., Feb. 14, 1937. MD, U. Toronto, 1961. Physician Prince Albert Clin., Sask., Can., 1962-63; resident Kaiser Found. Hosp., San Francisco, 1963-64, Montefiore Hosp. and Med. Ctr., Bronx, 1964-65; acting dir. ambulatory svc. and home care Morrisania City Hosp., 1965-66; dir. health ctr. Dr. Martin Luther King Jr. Health Ctr., 1966-71; assoc. prof. comty. health Albert Einstein Coll. Medicine, 1970—; Milbank Meml. Fund fellow; dir. internship and residency program social medicine Montefiore Hosp. and Med. Ctr., 1969—, dir. inst. health team devel., 1972; dir. Family Ctr. Health. Mem. Inst. Medicine-NAS, N.Y. Chiropractic Assn. (bd. mem. 1972—). •

WISE, JONATHAN F., ophthalmologist; b. N.Y.C., Mar. 15, 1947; married; two children. BS, Cornell U., 1969; MD, SUNY, 1973. Diplomate Am. Bd. Ophthalmology, Am. Bd. Pediatrics, Nat. Bd. Med. Examiners. From intern pediatrics to fellow in perinatology NYU Hosp./Cornell Med. Ctr., 1973-76; resident in ophthalmology N.Y. Eye and Ear Infirmary, 1976-79; pvt. practice ophthalmology Miami, Hollywood, Fla., 1979—. Office: Hollywood Ophthalmology 3816 Hollywood Blvd Hollywood FL 33021

WISE, ROBERT PHILIP, biopharmacoepidemiologist, clinical pharmacologist; b. Chgo., Oct. 13, 1949; s. Wilfred and Harriet Frances (Traub) W.; m. Izione Santos Silva, Mar. 8, 1980; children: Matthew Raymond, Andrea Louise. BA, Carleton Coll., 1971; MD, Northwestern U., Chgo., 1975; MPH, Harvard U., 1977. Diplomate Am. Bd. Preventive Medicine, Am. Bd. Clin. Pharmacology, Epidemic Intelligence Svc. Student fellow in tropical medicine La. State U., Medellin, Colombia, 1975; med. intern Northwestern Meml. Hosp., Chgo., 1975-76; resident in internat. health Pan Am. Health Orgn., Guatemala, 1977-78; course asst. Harvard Sch. Pub. Health, Boston, 1979-81; cons. pub. health Pragma Corp., Bamako, Mali, 1982; cons. preventive medicine Aurora Assocs., Guinea, Bissau, 1982; cons. pub. health and nutrition Ronco Cons., Guinea, Bissau, 1983; physician, Spanish Clinic Brigham & Women's Hosp., Boston, 1979-83; epidemiologist Ctrs. for Disease Control, Atlanta, 1983-85; pharmacoepidemiologist FDA Ctr. for Drug Evaluation and Rsch., Rockville, Md., 1985-90, FDA Ctr. for Biologics Evaluation and Rsch., Rockville, 1991—; part-time physician Fed. Employee Occupl. Health Clinic, Rockville, 1989-94. Contbr. articles to profl. jours. Bd. dirs. Community Clinic, Inc., Rockville, 1991—. Comdr. USPHS, 1983—. Recipient Citation, Pub. Health Svc., 1990, Achievement medal, 1989. Fellow Am. Coll. Preventive Medicine (Recognition award 1986, 89); mem. APHA, Nat. Coun. Internat. Health, Internat. Soc. Pharmacoepidemiology (bd. dirs. 1995—), Commd. Officers Assn. of USPHS. Jewish. Home: 1612 Auburn Ave Rockville MD 20850-1144 Office: FDA CBER HFM-225 1401 Rockville Pike Rockville MD 20852-1428

WISE, WAYNE CLINTON, nurse anesthetist; b. Edinburg, Tex., June 24, 1951; s. Therman Edsel and Wanda Janice (Cameron) W.; m. Johnnie Fay Haynes, June 25, 1976; children: Richard, Stuart, Katie. BSN, Northwestern State U. La., 1975; MA, Cen. Mich. U., 1978; Cert., U.S. Army Anesthesiology for Army Nurse Corp Officers, 1981. Cert. registered nurse anesthetist. Commd. 1st lt. U.S. Army, 1976, advanced through grades to lt. col., 1993; emergency room charge nurse Terrebonne Parish Gen. Hosp., Houma, La., 1975-76; with Surg. ICU Tripler Army Med. Ctr., Moanalua, Hawaii, 1976-79; with U.S. Army Anesthesia Sch., Ft. Sam Houston, Tex., 1979-81, Fitzsimons Army Med. Ctr., Aurora, Colo., 1984-86; staff CRNA, Affiliate Clin. Faculty Fitzsimons Army Med. Ctr., 1984-86; staff CRNA Reynolds Army Hosp., Ft. Sill, Okla., 1982-84; asst. dir., phase II Anesthesia Sch. Fitzsimons Army Med. Ctr., 1986-88; asst. chief nurse anesthetist Ireland Army Hosp., Ft. Knox, Ky., 1988-89; chief nurse anesthetist Denver Gen. Hosp., 1989-94; staff nurse anesthetist Terrebonne Gen. Med. Ctr., Houma, La., 1994—; affil. clin. faculty U.S. Army, SUNY, Buffalo, 1984-86; assoc. prof. health scis. Tex. Wesleyan U., Ft. Worth, 1986-88; affil. faculty, clin. coord. U. Tex., Houston, 1992-94. Lt. col. U.S. Army Res. Decorated Meritorious Svc. medal U.S. Army, 3 Army Commendation medals, others. Mem. Colo. Assn. Nurse Anesthetists (pres. 1987-88, 91-92), Ky. Assn. Nurse Anesthetists (mem. edn. com. 1988-89), Colo. Assn. Nurse Anesthetists (chmn. program com. 1985-88, 89-91, 92-94), La. Assn. Nurse Anesthetists (program com., govt. rels. com. 1994-96). Republican. Baptist.

WISEMAN, GLORIA DIANA, medical educator, physician; b. N.Y.C.. BS, CCNY, 1977; MD, Columbia U., 1981. Diplomate Nat. Bd. Medical Examiners. Intern and resident in pediatrics NYU Med. Ctr., 1981-84; teaching asst., 1983-84; neonatal-perinatal medicine fellow Babies' Hosp. Columbia U., 1984-86, asst. pediatrician Babies' Hosp., 1984-86, staff assoc., 1984-86; instr. U. Medicine and Dentistry of N.J.-N.J. Med. Sch., 1986-87, asst. prof. clin. pediatrics, 1987-88; neonatology/pediatric attending physician U. Hosp. N.J., 1986-88; rsch. fellow in allergy and immunology Albert Einstein Coll. Medicine, Bronx, N.Y., 1988-91; fellow in allergy and immunology Weiler Hosp. of Albert Einstein Coll. Medicine, Bronx, 1988-91; dir. neonatal-perinatal medicine Englewood (N.J.) Hosp., 1991-96, Holy Name Hosp., N.J., 1996—; asst. attending physician divsn. perinatal medicine Babies' and Children's Hosp. of N.Y., N.Y.C., 1991-96, attending physician divsn. perinatal medicine Columbia-Presbyn. Med. Ctr., N.Y.C., 1996—; divsn. bd. of inquiry faculty of medicine Columbina U., 1978-80; com. of admissions U.M.D.N.J.-N.J. Med. Sch., 1986-88; crit. care com. intensive care nursery U. Hosp. N.J., 1986-88; perinatal morbidity rate mortality com. Englewood Hosp., 1991—, co-chmn. perinatal policy com., 1991-96, pharmacy and therapeutics com., 1992—, future devel. com., 1992-96, ob-gyn. quality improvement com., 1995—, chmn. neonatal intensive care quality assurance com., 1993—; co-chmn. neonatal clin. stds. com., 1994—, level of care design com., 1995-96; asst. attending pediatrician divsn. newborn medicine Mt. Sinai Hosp., 1991-96; asst. prof. pediatrics Mt. Sinai Sch. Medicine/CUNY, 1991-96. Contbr. articles to profl. jours. Recipient Internat. Cultural Diploma of Honor Order Internat. Ambassadors, Internat. Order of Merit Women's Inner Circle of Achievement. Fellow Am. Acad. Pediatrics; mem. AMA (Physician's Recognition awards (2), Am. Acad. Allergy and Immunology, Clin. Immunology Soc., Joint Coun. Allergy and Immunology, N.Y. Perinatal Soc., Babies' Hosp. Alumni Assn., NYU Pediatric Alumni Assn., P&S Columbia U. Alumni Assn., Alumni Orgn. City Coll., Phi Beta Kappa (Gamma chpt.). Office: Holy Name Hosp 718 Teaneck Rd Teaneck NJ 07666

WISENER, LINDA KAY, nurse; b. Tulsa, Mar. 25, 1949; d. Delbert Lee and Kathleen (Claver) Hand; m. David Michael Wisener, June 29, 1968; children: Brandi Renée, Jennifer Ann. ADN, Oklahoma City C.C., 1991. RN, Okla.; cert. CNI, BLS, ACLS, clin. career advancement program. Staff nurse CCU/ICU Bapt. Med. Ctr., Oklahoma City, 1991—, lead nurse post coronary care unit, 1991—, team leader post coronary care unit, intermediate intensive care unit, 1994—. Contbr. poetry to anthologies. Recipient scholarships, Golden Goose award 7 Habits of Highly Effective People. Mem. Nat. Arbor Day Found. Republican. Baptist. Home: Rte 4 Box 195 Tuttle OK 73089

WISH, JAY BARRY, nephrologist, specialist; b. Hartford, Mar. 30, 1950; s. Martin and Evelyn Lillian (Lassman) W.; m. Linda Kristina Hansen, June 29, 1971; (div. 1980); children: Allen Jeremy, Robin Lindsey; m. Diane Elizabeth Perkins, June 5, 1983; children: Jeffrey Bryan, David Phillip. BA, Wesleyan U., 1970; MD, Tufts U., 1974. Diplomate Am. Bd. Internal Medicine, Am. Bd. Nephrology. Resident in medicine New England Med. Ctr., Boston, 1974-79; instr. in medicine Tufts U., Boston, 1978-79; lectr. in health sci. Northeastern U., Boston, 1978-79; asst. prof. of medicine Case Western Res. U., Cleve., 1979-85, assoc. prof. of medicine, 1985-96, prof. medicine, 1996—; dir. hemodialysis U. Hosps. of Cleve., 1980—, dir. continuing edn., 1987-95; chmn. Med. Adv. Bd. Kidney Found. of Ohio, Cleve., 1985-88. Author: Renal Disease and Hypertension, 1982, Disorders of Potassium, 1984, Metabolic Diseases, 1986, Rheumatic Diseases of the Kidney, 1993, Acid-Base and Electrolyte Disorders in the Critically Ill Patient, 1993, Assuring Quality of Care in Dialysis Patients, 1994; contbr. articles to med. jours. Chmn. med. rev. bd. End-Stage Renal Disease Network #22, Pitts., 1982-87, End-State Renal Disease Network #9, Indpls., 1992—; mem. exec. com. Forum of End-Stage Renal Disease Networks, 1992—; bd. dirs. Renal Phys. Assn., 1993—, sec. 1996—; mem. Nat. Kidney Found. Fellow Am. Coll. of Physicians; mem. Cleve. Restoration Soc., Am. Soc. of Nephrology, Internat. Soc. of Nephrology, Alpha Omega Alpha. Democrat. Jewish. Office: U Hosps Cleve 11100 Euclid Ave Cleveland OH 44106-2602

WISHNER, KATHLEEN LAMBERT, physician; b. Modesto, Calif., June 11, 1943; d. Henry Oscar Lambert and Alyce (Littlefield) Lambert Daniells; m. Phillip Andrew Harris, Aug. 4, 1961 (div. 1973); children—Jeffrey John, Michael Lambert; m. William Jay Wishner, May 20, 1973. B.A. cum laude, Calif. State U.-San Francisco, 1963; Ph.D., U. Calif.-San Francisco, 1968; M.D., U. So. Calif., 1976. Diplomate Nat. Bd. Med. Examiners, Am. Bd. Pediatrics, Am. Bd. Pediatric Endocrinology. Intern Children's Hosp. L.A., 1976-77; resident L.A. County/U. So. Calif. Med. Ctr., 1977-78; fellow pediatric endocrinology City of Hope/Harbor-UCLA, 1978-79; asst. prof. U. Minn.-St. Paul, 1968-70, U. So. Calif., L.A., 1970-73; teaching assoc. Georgetown U., Washington, 1973-74; staff physician City of Hope Med Ctr., Duarte, Calif., 1979-81; assoc. clin. prof. U. So. Calif., L.A., 1984-95; clin. prof. medicine U. So. Calif., L.A., 1995—; practice medicine specializing in endocrinology and clin. nutrition, Pasadena, Calif., 1981-95; med. dir. endocrine global bus. unit, Eli Lilly and Co., 1995—; cons. Panel on space sta. ops. medicine NASA, Am. Inst. Biol. Scis., 1983-85. Contbr. articles to profl. jours. NIH grantee, 1969-73, 69-72, 79-81. Mem. Internat. Diabetes Fedn., Am. Diabetes Assn. (dir. So. Calif. affiliate 1982-87, dir. Calif. affiliate 1987-92, pres. 1989-90, nat. bd. dirs. 1988-96, pres. 1994-95, Nat. award 1985), Am. Dietetic Assn. (registered dietitian), Am. Inst. Nutrition, Am. Soc. Clin. Nutrition, European Assn. Study of Diabetes, Am. Acad. Pediats. Democrat. Office: Eli Lilly & Co Lilly Corporate Ctr Indianapolis IN 46285

WISNESKI, SHARON M., critical care nurse, educator; b. Phila., June 22, 1952; d. Charles Edward and Hilda Marie (Riley) Ashley. AS, Wesley Coll., Dover, Del., 1979, BS, 1985; MSN, Widener U., Chester, Pa., 1991, cert. in nursing edn., 1993, postgrad., 1994—. ACLS. Charge nurse, med.-surg. ICU Milford (Del.) Meml. Hosp.; clin. instr. Wesley Coll., Del. Tech. and Community Coll., Dover; critical care per-diem nurse Med. Ctr Del., Newark; instr. nursing Del. State U., Dover, 1991-95, asst. prof., 1995—; part-time staff nurse med. ICU Med. Ctr. of Del., Newark; apptd. rev. bd. Del. Medicaid Drug Utilization Rev. Bd., 1993—; mem. Del. Bd. Nursing Practice Adv. Com., 1994—. Contbr. chpt. to book. Mem. ANA (rev. panelist ANA continuing edn. ind. study 1995—), AACCN (southeastern Pa. chpt.), AAUW, Assn. Black Nursing Faculty, Del. Nurses Assn. (chmn. nursing practice com. 1992, Del. Nurse of Yr. 1993), Inst. Constituent Mems. in Nursing Practice, Sigma Theta Tau, Chi Eta Phi. Home: 336 Pine Valley Rd Dover DE 19904-7113

WISNICKI, JEFFREY LEONARD, plastic surgeon; b. N.Y.C., May 15, 1957; s. Joseph and Lorraine (Justman) W. BS summa cum laude, Rensselaer Poly. Inst., 1976; MD cum laude with honors, Union U., 1980. Diplomate Am. Bd. Plastic Surgery. Intern in surgery Stanford (Calif.) U. Med. Ctr., 1980-81, resident in gen., plastic and reconstructive surgery, 1981-84, chief resident in plastic and reconstructive surgery, 1985-86; fellow in plastic and reconstructive surgery Dartmouth-Hitchcock Med. Ctr., Hanover, N.H., 1984; active staff Good Samaritan Hosp., West Palm Beach, Fla., 1986—, Wellington Regional Hosp., West Palm Beach, 1986—; chief divsn. plastic surgery John F. Kennedy Meml. Hosp., West Palm Beach, 1990-93; chmn. dept. surgery Palms West Hosp., West Palm Beach, 1991-93, chief med. staff, 1994—; clin. instr. surgery U. Calif., San Francisco, 1985; bd. dirs. Interplast, 1985-86, clin. faculty, 1986—; presenter in field. Contbr. chpts. to books and articles to profl. jours. Fellow ACS; mem. Am. Soc. Plastic & Reconstructive Surgeons, Alpha Omega Alpha. Office: 2047 Palm Beach Lakes Blvd West Palm Beach FL 33409

WISNIEWSKI, HENRYK MIROSLAW, pathology and neuropathology educator, research facility administrator, research scientist; b. Luszkowko, Poland, Feb. 27, 1931; came to U.S., 1966; s. Alexander and Ewa (Korthals) W.; m. Krystyna Wylon, Feb. 14, 1954; children: Alexander (dec.), Thomas. MD, Med. Sch., Gdansk, Poland, 1955; PhD in Exptl. Neuropathology, Med. Sch., Warsaw, Poland, 1960; DSc (hon.), Med. Sch., Gdansk, Poland, 1991, Coll. of Staten Island, 1992. From asst. to assoc. prof., head. lab. exptl. neuropathology, assoc. dir. Inst. Neuropathology Polish Acad. Sci., Warsaw, 1958-66; rsch. assoc., from asst. prof. to prof. Albert Einstein Coll. Medicine, N.Y.C., 1966-75; dir. MRC Demyelinating Diseases Unit, Newcastle upon Tyne, Eng., 1974-76; prof. neuropathology SUNY Health Sci. Ctr., Bklyn., 1976—; dir. N.Y. State Inst. Basic Rsch. in Devel. Disabilities, S.I., 1976—; vis. neuropathologist U. Toronto, Ont., Can., 1961-62; vis. scientist Lab. of Neuropathology Nat. Inst. Neurol. and Communicative Diseases and Stroke, NIH, 1962-63; docent Med. Sch., Warsaw, 1965; past mem. Neuology B study sect. NIH; past mem. mental retardation rsch. com. Nat. Inst. Child Health and Human Devel. Mem. editl. bd. Acta Neuropathologica, Neurotoxicology, Jour. Neuropathology and Exptl. Neurology, Devel. Neurosci., Internat. Jour. Geriatric Psychiatry, Alzheimer Disease and Assoc. Disorders Internat. Jour., Brain Sysfunction, Dementia; mem. editl. adv. bd. Neurobiology of Aging; contbr. over 625 articles to profl. jours. and symposia procs. Recipient N.Y.C. Chpt. award Assn. for Help of Retarded Children, 1984, Welfare League award letchworth Village chpt. Assn. for Help of Retarded Children, 1985, Staten Island Chpt. award Benevolent Soc. for Retarded Children, 1986; named Career Scientist, Health Rsch. Coun. of City of N.Y., Honoris Causa Doctor of Sci., Med. Sch., Gdansk, Poland, 1992, Honoris Causa, Doctor of Sci., Coll. of Staten Island, 1992. Fellow AAAS; mem. Am. Assn. Neuropathologists (pres. 1984, Weil award 1969, Moore award 1972), British Soc. Neuropathology, Can. Assn. Neuropathologists, Am. Assn. Retarded Citizens, Assn. Rsch. in Nervous and Mental Disease, Am. Assn. Mental Deficiency, Internat. Soc. Devel. Neuroscis., Soc. Exptl. Neuropathology, World Fedn. Neurology, Sigma Xi. Roman Catholic. Office: NY State Inst Basic Rsch Devel Disabilities 1050 Forest Hill Rd Staten Island NY 10314-6330

WISS, THOMAS ALAN, physician, educator; b. Pana, Ill., July 18, 1950; s. Adolph Joseph II and Betty Jean (Haverfield) W.; m. Gail Marie Frantell, June 24, 1981; children: Emily Christine, Paul Joseph. BS, So. Ill. U., 1979, MD, 1982; RN, Millikin U., 1971. Clin. assoc. prof. medicine SIU Sch. of Medicine, Springfield, Ill., 1990—. 1st lt. U.S. Army, 1971-73. Fellow Am. Coll. Physicians; mem. Am. Soc. Internal Medicine. Office: Capitol Health Care Med 2603 S Sixth St Springfield IL 62703

WITCHER, DANIEL DOUGHERTY, retired pharmaceutical company executive; b. Atlanta, May 17, 1924; s. Julius Gordon and Myrtice Eleanor (Daniel) W.; divorced; children: Beth S., Daniel Dougherty Jr., J. Wright, Benjamin G.; m. Betty Lou Middaugh, Oct. 30, 1982. Student, Mercer U., 1946-47, Am. Grad. Sch. Internat. Mgmt., 1949-50. Regional dir. Sterling Drug Co., Rio de Janeiro and Sao Paulo, Brazil, 1951-56; gen. mgr. Mead Johnson & Co., Sao Paulo, 1956-60; area mgr. Upjohn Internat., Inc., Sao Paulo, 1960-64; v.p. Upjohn Internat., Inc., Kalamazoo, 1964-70, group v.p., 1970-73; pres., gen. mgr. Upjohn Internat., 1973-86; v.p. Upjohn Co., 1973-86, sr. v.p., 1986-89, asst. to pres., 1988-89; chmn. Upjohn Healthcare Svcs., 1982-87; ret., 1989; bd. dirs. Upjohn Co.; trustee Am. Grad. Sch. Internat. Mgmt., 1981—. With USNR, 1943-46. Mem. Pharm. Mfrs. Assn. (chmn. internat. sect. 1981-82, 85-86), Am. Grad. Sch. Internat. Mgmt. Alumni Assn. (pres. 1989-91). Republican. Episcopalian.

WITHERS, HUBERT RODNEY, radiotherapist, radiobiologist, educator; b. Queensland, Australia, Sept. 21, 1932; came to the U.S., 1966; s. Hubert and Gertrude Ethel (Tremayne) W.; m. Janet Macfie, Oct. 9, 1959; 1 child, Genevieve. MBBS, U. Queensland, Brisbane, Australia, 1956; PhD, U. London, 1965, DSc, 1982. Bd. cert. Ednl. Coun. for Fgn. Med. Grads. Intern Royal Brisbane (Australia) and Associated Hosps., 1957; resident in radiotherapy and pathology Queensland Radium Inst. and Royal Brisbane (Australia) Hosp., 1958-63; Univ. Queensland Gaggin fellow Gray Lab., Mt. Vernon Hosp., Northwood, Middlesex, Eng., 1963-65, Royal Brisbane (Australia) Hosp., 1966; radiotherapist Prince of Wales Hosp., Randwick, Sydney, Australia, 1966; vis. rsch. scientist Lab. Physiology, Nat. Cancer Inst., Bethesda, Md., 1966-68; assoc. prof. radiotherapy sect. exptl. radiotherapy U. Tex. Sys. Cancer Ctr. M.D. Anderson Hsop. & Tumor Inst., Houston, 1968-71, prof. radiotherapy, chief sect. sect. exptl. radiotherapy, 1971-80; prof. dir. exptl. radiation oncology dept. radiation oncology UCLA, 1980-89, prof., vice-chair dir. exptl. radiation oncology dept. radiation oncology, 1991-94, Am. Cancer Soc. Clin. Rsch. prof. dept. radiation oncology, 1992—, interim dir. Jonsson Comprehensive Cancer Ctr., 1994-95, chmn. radiation oncology, 1994—; assoc. grad. faculty U. Tex., Grad. Sch. Biomed. Scis, Houston, 1969-73, mem. grad. faculty, 1973-80; prof. dept. radiotherapy Med. Sch., U. Tex. Health Sci. Ctr., Houston, U. Tex. Med. Sch., Houston, 1975-80; prof., dir. Inst. Oncology, The Prince of Wales Hosp., U. NSW, Sydney, Australia, 1989-91; mem. com. mortality mil. pers. present-at-atmosphere tests of nuclear weapons Inst. Medicine, 1993-94; mem. radiation effects rsch. bd. NRC, 1993—; mem. com. neutron dose reporting Internat. Commn. Radiation Units and Measurements, 1982—, mem. report com. clin. dosimetry for neutrons, 1993—; mem. task force non-stochastic effects radiation Internat. Com. Radiation Protection, 1980-84, mem. com. 1, 1993—; mem. radiobiology com. Radiation Therapy Oncology Group, 1979—, mem. dose-time com., 1980-89, mem. gastroenterology com., 1982-89; mem. edn. bd. Royal Australian Coll. Radiology, 1989-91; mem. cancer rsch. coord. com. U. Calif., 1991-95, mem. standing curriculum com. UCLA biomed. physics grad. program, 1983-84; cons. exptl. radiotherapy U. Tex. System Cancer Ctr., 1980—. Mem. Am. editl. bd.: Internat. Jour. Radiat. Oncol. Biol. Phys., 1982-89, 94—, internat. editl. bd., 1989-91; cons. editor: The European Jour. Cancer, 1990-95; editl. bd. dirs.: Endocurietherapy/Hyperthermia Oncology, 1991—, Radiation Oncology Investigations, 1992—; assoc. editor: Cancer Rsch., 1993-94, editl. bd. 1995-97. Mem. Kettering selection com. Gen. Motors Cancer Rsch. Found., 1988-89, chmn., 1989, awards assembly, 1990-94. Recipient Medicine prize Polish Acad. Sci., 1989, Second H.S. Kaplan Disting. Scientist award Internat. Assn. for Radiation Rsch., 1991, Gray medal Internat. Commn. Radiation Units, 1995; named Gilbert H. Fletcher lectr. U. Tex. Sys. Cancer Ctr., 1989, Clifford Ash lectr. Ont. Cancer Inst., Princess Margaret Hosp., 1987, Erskine lectr. Radiol. Soc. N.Am., 1988, Ruvelson lectr. U. Minn., 1988, Milford Schultz lectr. Mass. Gen. Hosp., 1989, Del Regato Found. lectr. Hahnemann U., 1990, Bruce Cain Meml. lectr. New Zealand Soc. Oncology, 1990, others. Fellow Royal Australasian Coll. Radiologists (bd. cert.), Am. Coll. Radiology (bd. cert. therapeutic radiology, adv. com. patterns of care study 1988—, radiation oncology advisory group 1993—, others), Am. Radium Soc. (mem. and credential com. 1986-89, 93-94, treas. 1993-94, pres.-elect 1995-96, pres. 1996—, others), Am. Soc. Therapeutic Radiology and Oncology (awards com. 1993, publs. com. 1993-96, keynote address 1990, 96, Gold medal 1991, others); mem. Nat. Cancer Inst. (various ad-hoc rev. coms. 1970—, radiation study sect. 1971-75, cons. U.S.-Japan Coop. Study high LET Radiotherapy 1975-. emphasis grant rev. com. 1976, clin. cancer ctr. rev. com. 1976-79, toxicology working group 1977-78, reviewer outstanding investigator grants 1984-93, bd. sci. counselors, 1986-88), Nat. Cancer Inst. Can. (adv. com. rsch. 1992-95), Pacific N.W. Radiol. Soc. (hon.), Tex. Radiol. Soc. (hon.), So. Calif. Radiation Oncology Soc. (sec., treas., 1992-94, pres. 1996—), European Soc. Therapeutic Radiology and Oncology (hon.), Polish Oncology Soc. (hon.) Austrian Radiation Oncology Soc. (hon.), Phila. Roentgen Ray Soc. (hon.), Radiation Rsch. Soc. (pres. 1982-83, honors and awards com. 1984-88, ad hoc com. funds utilization 1987-89, adv. com. Radiation Rsch. Jour., 1988—, Failla award 1988). Office: UCLA Med Ctr 10833 LeConte Ave Los Angeles CA 90095-1714

WITHERSPOON, JAMES DONALD, biology educator; b. Springfield, Mo., Dec. 19, 1933; s. Harry H. and Lucy Catherine (Applegate) W.; m. Rebecca Jane Hutto, Jan. 24, 1958; children: Sarah Jane, John Edward. BS, Purdue U., 1955, MS, 1960, PhD, 1963. From instr. to asst. prof. biology Western Md. Coll., Westminster, 1960-68; assoc. prof. Southwestern at Memphis Coll., 1968-76; free-lance writer Phoenix, 1976-82; adj. prof. Grand Canyon Coll., Phoenix, 1982-84, prof., 1984—, chmn. dept. scis., 1985-92, acting chmn. dept. math. and computer scis., 1988-89; coord. allied health Grand Canyon U. (formerly Grand Canyon Coll.), Phoenix, 1992-94, assoc. dean Coll. Sci. and Applied Health, 1994—; cons. Doubleday & Co., Garden City, N.Y., 1960-62, Narco Bio-Sys., Houston, 1972-76; assoc. coord. med. edn. S.W. Kirksville Coll. Osteo. Medicine, 1990-94; leader Am. tchr.: Eszterhazy Karoly Tchrs. Tng. Coll., Hungary, summers 1991-93, Vilnius Pedagogical Univ., Lithuania, summer 1995-96. Author: The Functions of Life, 1970, Human Physiology, 1984, From Field to Lab, 1993; co-author: The Living Laboratory, 1960; co-author numerous tapes and computer programs, 1973-87. Grantee Grass Found., 1962-72, Ariz. Commn. for Postsecondary Edn., 1985-87. Mem. AAAS, Am. Inst. Biol. Scis., Ariz. Alliance for Sci., Maths. and Tech. Edn. (bd. dirs. 1986-88), Sigma Xi. Republican. Presbyterian. Home: 17122 E Grande Blvd Fountain Hills AZ 85268-3224 Office: Grand Canyon U 3300 W Camelback Rd Phoenix AZ 85017-3030

WITHERSPOON, LAURA ELLEN, surgeon; b. Chattanooga, Tenn., Apr. 17, 1959; d. John Knox Jr. and Norma Jean (Cofer) W.; m. Harold David Head, June 16, 1990; children: Scott, Allison. BA, Vanderbilt U., 1981, MD, 1985. Diplomate Am. Bd. Surgery. Resident in surgery Valley Med. Ctr., Fresno, Calif., 1985-90; pvt. practice gen. surgery Chattanooga, 1994—. Maj. USAF, 1990-94. Fellow Am. Coll. Surgeons; mem. AMA, Assn. Women Surgeons, Chattanooga/Hamilton County Med. Soc., Tenn. Med. Assn., Soc. Air Force Clin. Surgeons.

WITHERSPOON, LYNN RALPH, physician; b. Mt. Pleasant, Mich., Nov. 11, 1942; s. Ralph Leo and Kathleen Mae (Williams) W.; m. Glory Ann Smith, Jan. 27, 1980; children: Eric W., Kevin B., Heather A. BA, Fla. State U., 1964; MD, U. Wis., 1968. Diplomate Am. Bd. Nuclear Medicine, Am. Bd. Internal Medicine. With Ochsner Clinic/Alton Ochsner Med. Found., New Orleans, 1974—, dir. radioimmunology lab., 1975—, chmn., dir. med. informatics, 1994—; intern, then resident in internal medicine Ochsner, New Orleans, 1968-70; fellow in nuclear medicine Duke U., Durham, N.C., 1972-74, chief resident in nuclear medicine, 1973-74. Contbr. numerous articles to profl. jours. Elder Jefferson (La.) Presbyn. Ch., 1982—; mem. adv. bd. Sta. WWNO, New Orleans, 1985—. Lt. comdr. USNR, 1970-72. Fellow ACP; mem. Soc. Nuclear Medicine, Southwestern Soc. Nuclear Medicine (v.p. 1980-81, sec. 1983-86, pres. 1988-89), Soc. Nuclear Medicine (trustee 1988-89). Presbyterian. Office: Ochsner Clinic 1514 Jefferson Hwy New Orleans LA 70121-2429

WITHERSPOON, WALTER PENNINGTON, JR., orthodontist, philanthropist; b. Columbia, S.C., Sept. 3, 1938; s. Walter P. and Florence Evelyn (Jones) W.; m. Joyce Ann Smith, Sept. 6, 1970; 1 child, Annie Melissa. BS, U. S.C., 1960; DDS, U. N.C., 1964, MSO, 1969. Bd. qualified Am. Bd. Orthodontics. Pvt. practice in orthodontics, Columbia, 1969—; med. staff Bapt. Med. Ctr., Columbia, 1970—, Lexington County Hosp., West Columbia, 1974—. Hóst Nite Line, Dove Broadcasting Co. Adv. bd. 1st Palmetto Bank and Trust, West Columbia, 1982; mem. adv. bd. First Citizens Bank; candidate S.C. Ho. Reps., 1994; del. S.C. Rep. Com., 1989-96; mem. platform com. S.C. Rep. Party Conv., poll com., 1992; del. Rep. Nat. Conv., Houston, 1992; Rep. nat. committeeman, 1996—; bd. dirs. Southeastern Coll. Assemblies of God, Lakeland, Fla., 1984, Brookland Plantation Home for Boys, Orangeburg, S.C.; pres. Friends of Irmo Libr.; bd. dirs. Irmo-St. Andrew's Coalition of Neighborhood Home Owners' Assns.; chmn. Lexington County Rep. Party; commr. Richland/Lexington Counties Commn. for Tech. Edn., S.C. Commn. on Alcohol and Drug Abuse; bd. dirs. Centerplace for Homeless; active Campbell for Gov., Presdl. Visit-Ticket Com.; amb. Irmo C. of C. Lt. USN, 1964-66. Recipient Century Mem. award Boy Scouts Am., 1984. Mem. ADA, Greater Columbia Dental Assn. (pres. 1975-76), U. N.C. Dental Alumni Assn. (bd. dirs.), S.C. Dental Assn. (ho. of dels. 1971-73, 1991-96, legis. com. 1993), S.C. Orthodontic Assn., Am. Assn. Orthodontists, Sertoma (pres. 1975-76), Am. Legion., So. Assn. Orthodontists, Cen. Dist. Dental Soc., Alston Wilkes Soc. (bd. dirs.). Home: 250 Lancer Dr Columbia SC 29212-1216 Office: 205 Med Cir W Columbia SC 29169

WITHROW, LUCILLE MONNOT, nursing home administrator; b. Alliance, Ohio, July 28, 1923; d. Charles Edward Monnot and Freda Aldine (Guy) Monnot Cameron; m. Alvin Robert Withrow, June 6, 1945 (dec. 1984); children: Cindi Withrow Johnson, Nancy Withrow Townley, Sharon Withrow Hodgkins, Wendel Alvin. AA in Health Adminstrn., Eastfield Coll., 1976. Lic. nursing home adminstr., Tex.; cert. nursing home ombudsman. Held various clerical positions Dallas, 1950-72; office mgr., asst. adminstr. Christian Care Ctr. Nursing Home, Mesquite, Tex., 1972-76; head adminstr. Christian Care Ctr. Nursing Home and Retirement Complex, Mesquite, 1976-91; nursing home ombudsman Tex. Dept. Aging and Tex. Dept. Health, Dallas, 1991-93; legal asst. Law Offices of Wendel A. Withrow, Carrollton, Tex., 1993—; mem. con. on geriatric curriculum devel. Eastfield Coll., Mesquite, 1979, 87; mem. ombudsman adv. com. Sr. Citizens Greater Dallas; nursing home cons.; notary pub., 1995—. Vol. Dallas Arboretum and Bot. Soc., Dallas Summer Musicals Guild; mem. Ombudsman adv. com. Sr. Citizens of Greater Dallas, Health Svcs. Speakers Bur.; charter mem. Stage Show Prodns. Recipient Volunteerism awards Tex. Atty. Gen., 1987, Tex. Gov., 1992. Mem. Tex. Assn. Homes for Aging, Am. Assn. Homes for Aging, Health Svcs. Speakers Bur., White Rock Kiwanis. Republican. Mem. Ch. of Christ. Home: 11344 Lippitt Ave Dallas TX 75218-1922 Office: Law Office of W A Withrow 1120 Metrocrest Dr Ste 200 Carrollton TX 75006-5787

WITHROW, SHEILA KAY, school nurse; b. Dayton, Ohio, Oct. 13, 1959; d. Robert and Shirley Elaine (McGuire) H.; m. James Laurence Withrow, Jr., Aug. 7, 1982; 1 child, Robert Laurence. AAS in Nursing, Miami U., Oxford, Ohio, 1982, BS in Nursing, 1987. RN, Ohio. Staff nurse Children's Hosp. Med. Ctr., Cin., 1982-84; staff nurse Middletown (Ohio) Regional Hosp., 1984-87, adminstrv. clin. coord., 1987-90; clin. coord. Middletown Regional Hosp., 1990-91; sch. nurse Franklin (Ohio) City Schs., 1991—; participant Nursing Grand Rounds The Total Hip Patient, 1986; mem. Patient Care task force, 1988. Mem. Nat. Assn. Sch. Nurses, Ohio Assn. Sch. Nurses. Democrat. Baptist. Home: 205 Leland Ct Middletown OH 45042-3915 Office: Franklin City Schs 150 E 6th St Franklin OH 45005-2555

WITKIN, ARTHUR AARON, psychologist; b. N.Y.C., Aug. 17, 1921; s. Jack and Sadye (Leibowitz) W.; m. Ethel Greenblatt, Feb. 3, 1945 (dec. 1986); children: Jill, Richard, Jeannie. BS, CCNY, 1941, MS, 1943; PhD, NYU, 1956. Lic. psychologist N.Y. State. Chief psychologist Personnel Scis. Ctr., N.Y.C., 1956-92; prof. psychology Queens Coll.-CUNY, 1956—. Author: A Business Executives Guide to Interviewing, 1960. With U.S. Army, 1943-46. Mem. Am. Psychol. Soc., N.Y. State Psychol. Assn. (pres. personnel div. 1980-82, coun. rep. 1988—, McClelland award 1987). Home: 1418 The Colony Hartsdale NY 10530

WITKIN, GEORGIA HOPE, clinical psychologist, lecturer, author. Student Wellesley Coll., 1961-63; BA in Sociology, Barnard Coll., 1965; postgrad. in elem. edn. Hunter Coll., 1967-69; MA in Psychology, New Sch. for Social Rsch., 1970, PhD in Psychology, 1977; postgrad. Psychiat. Inst., 1979. Lic. clin. psychologist, N.Y. Asst. producer Grey Advt., N.Y.C., 1966-68; teaching asst. New Sch. for Social Rsch., 1968-69; adj. lectr. Lehman Coll., CUNY, 1971-72; assoc. prof. dept. social and behavioral sci. SUNY-Valhalla, 1972-86, mem. vis. faculty criminal justice dept., 1978; supr. residency program human sexuality program Mt. Sinai Sch. Medicine, N.Y.C., 1982—, asst. clin. prof. psychiatry, 1985—; staff psychologist dept. ob-gyn. and reproductive sci. Mt. Sinai Med. Ctr., N.Y.C., 1990—; former mem. vis. faculty U. Conn., NYU Coll. Dentistry, also others; former assoc. prof. psychology Westchester Community Coll., Valhalla; presenter at profl. confs., also papers; pvt. practice clin. psychology, N.Y.C.; appeared on various TV shows including Donahue, Today Show, Hour Mag.; host TV program Between the Sexes, CNBC-TV; reporter TV program The Real Story, CNBC-TV; contbr. Today In N.Y., WNBC-TV, Live at Five, WNBC-TV. Author: Human Sexuality, 1982, The Female Stress Syndrome, 1984 (also Dutch, Japan, German, English, Spanish and Australian edits.), rev. edit., 1991, Coping with Stress, 1984, The Male Stress Syndrome, 1986, Quick Fixes and Small Comforts, 1986, Beyond Quick Fixes, 1991, Passions, 1992, The Truth About Women, 1995; columnist Your Emotional Best, Health Mag., also mem. editorial adv. bd.; mem. editorial adv. bd. Jour. Preventive Psychiatry; contbr. articles to profl. publs., mags. and newspapers. Mem. steering com. Westchester Community Coll. Found., 1973-75. NSF fellow, 1978. Mem. AAAS, Soc. for Sex Therapy and Research, Westchester County Psychol. Assn., N.Y. Acad. Scis., Am. Assn. Sex Educators, Counselors and Therapists (cert. sex educator; mem. regional bd., exec. com.), Am. Assn. for Profl. Law Enforcement, Mensa, Criminal Justice Educators Assn. N.Y. State, Am. Soc. Criminology, World Future Soc., N.Y. State United Tchrs., Eastern Psychol. Assn., Am. Med. Writers Assn. Home: 8 E 83rd St Apt 3A New York NY 10028-0418 Office: Mt Sinai Med Coll Dept Psychiatry New York NY 10053

WITKIN, MICHAEL, internist, endocrinologist; b. Panama Canal Zone, Sept. 14, 1938; m. Shelley Dobkin, 1969; children: Karen Ellen, Debra Jo. BA summa cum laude, Wash. & Jefferson Coll., 1960; MD, U. Pa., 1964. Diplomate Am. Bd. Internal Medicine, Am. Bd. Endocrinology and Metabolism. Intern, resident U. N.C., Chapel Hill, 1964-67; endocrine fellow Scripps Clin. & Rsch. Found., La Jolla, Calif., 1967-68; physician Ochsnar Clin., New Orleans, 1971—; internist, endocrinologist Lexington (Ky.) Clin., 1970-71; instr. medicine U. Ky., 1970-71, clin. instr. medicine, Tulane Univ. Sch. Medicine, New Orleans, 1971, clin. asst. prof., 1977, clin. assoc. prof.; lectr. in field. Contbr. articles to profl. pubs. Lt. commdr. USN, 1968-70. Fellow ACP; mem. Endocrine Soc., Alpha Mu Pi Omega, Phi Beta Kappa, Alpha Omega Alpha. Office: Ochsner Clin 1514 Jefferson Hwy New Orleans LA 70121

WITKIN, MILDRED HOPE FISHER, psychotherapist, educator; b. N.Y.C.; d. Samuel and Sadie (Goldschmidt) Fisher; children: Georgia Hope, Roy Thomas, Laurie Phillips, Kimberly, Nicole, Scott, Joshua, Jennifer; m. Jorge Radovic, Aug. 26, 1983. AB, Hunter Coll., MA, Columbia U., 1968; PhD, NYU, 1973. Diplomate Am. Bd. Sexology, Am. Bd. Sexuality; cert. supr. Head counselor Camp White Lake, Camp Emanuel, Long Beach, N.J.; tchr. econs., polit. sci. Hunter Coll. High Sch.; dir., group leader follow-up program Jewish Vacation Assn., N.Y.C.; investigator N.Y.C. Housing Authority; psychol. counselor Montclair State Coll., Upper Montclair, N.J., 1967-68; mem., lectr. Creative Problem-Solving Inst., U. Buffalo, 1968; psychol. counselor Fairleigh Dickinson U., Teaneck, N.J., 1968, dir. Counseling Center, 1969-74; pvt. practice psychotherapy, N.Y.C., also Westport, Conn.; sr. faculty supr., family therapist and psychotherapist Payne Whitney Psychiat. Clinic, N.Y. Hosp., 1973—; clin. asst. prof. dept. psychiatry Cornell U. Med. Coll., 1974—; assoc. dir. sex therapy and edn. program Cornell-N.Y. Hosp. Med. Ctr., 1974—; sr. cons. Kaplan Inst. for Evaluation and Treatment of Sexual Disorders, 1981—; supr. master's and doctoral candidates, NYU, 1975-82; pvt. practice psychotherapy and sex therapy, N.Y.C., also Westport, Conn.; cons. counselor edn. tng. programs N.Y.C. Bd. Edn., 1971-75; cons. Health Info. Systems, 1972-79; vis. prof. numerous colls. and univs.; chmn. sci. com. 1st Internat. Symposium on Female Sexuality, Buenos Aires, 1984. Exhibited in group shows at Scarsdale (N.Y.) Art Show, 1959, Red Shutter Art Studio, Long Beach, 1968. Edn. legislation chmn. PTA, Yonkers, 1955; publicity chmn. United Jewish Appeal, Scarsdale, 1959-65; Scarsdale chmn. mothers com. Boy Scouts Am., 1961-64; mem. Morrow Assn. on Correction N.J., 1969-91; bd. dirs. Girl Scouts of Am. Recipient Bronze medal for svcs. Hunter Coll.; United Jewish Appeal plaque, 1962; Founders Day award N.Y. U., 1973, citation N.Y. Hosp./Cornell U. Med. Ctr., 1990. Fellow Internat. Coun. Sex Edn. and Parenthood of Am. U., Am. Acad. Clin. Sexologists; mem. AAUW, APA, ACA, Assn. Counseling Supervision, Am. Coll. Personnel Assn., Internat. Assn. Marriage and Family Counselors, Am. Coll. Sexuality (cert.), Women's Med. Assn. N.Y.C., N.Y. Acad. Sci., Am. Coll. Pers. Assn. (nat. mem. commn. II 1973-76), Nat. Assn. Women Deans and Counselors, Am. Assn. Sex Educators, Counselors and Therapists (regional bd., nat. accreditation bd., cert. internat. supr.), Soc. for Sci. Study Sex Therapy and Rsch., Eastern Assn. Sex Therapists, Am. Assn. Marriage and Family Counselors, N.J. Assn. Marriage and Family Counselors, Ackerman Family Inst., Am. Personnel and Guidance Assn., Am., N.Y., N.J. psychol. assns., Creative Edn. Found., Am. Assn. Higher Edn., Assn. Counselor Supervision and Edn., Profl. Women's Caucus, LWV, Am. Assn. counseling and Devel., Am. Women's Med. Assn., Nat. Coun. on Women in Medicine, Argentine Soc. Human Sexuality (hon.), Am. Assn. Sexology (diplomate), Conn. Assn. Marriage and Family Therapy, Pi Lambda Theta, Kappa Delta Pi, Alpha Chi Alpha. Author: 45-And Single Again, 1985, Single Again, 1994; contbr. articles to profl. jours. and textbooks; lectr. internat. and nat. workshops, radio and TV. Home: 9 Sturges Commons Westport CT 06880-2832 Office: 35 Park Ave New York NY 10016-3838

WITKOWSKI, MARIANNE, hospital administrator; b. Paloaito, Calif., Jan. 13, 1948; d. James A. and Jane C. (Hagar) Gillis; m. Thomas F. Witkowski, Sept. 1969; children: Susan, Sarah, Peter, Christopher. Grad. nursing diploma, St. Peter's Med Ctr., New Brunswick, N.J., 1969; student, Burlington County Coll., Pemberton, N.J., 1985; BS in Bus. Mgmt., Phila. Coll. Textiles & Sci., 1987. Staff nurse Meml. Hosp. Burlington County, Mt. Holly, N.J., 1969-71; charge nurse, nursing supr. 11-7 specialty Zurbrugg Meml. Hosp., Willingboro, N.J., 1978-81, nursing supr., 3-11 med./surg., 1981-82, asst. DON, 1981-82, asst. v.p. nursing, 1972-85; asst. adminstr. patient care svcs. Kennedy Meml. Hosp., Turnersville, N.J., 1987-94, adminstr., 1994—. Bd. dirs. United Way, 1995, March of Dimes, 1994; chairperson profl. edn. com. Am. Cancer Soc., 1983; mem. Perinatal Coop. Evaluation Com., 1995. Mem. Washington Twp. Rotary. Roman Catholic. Home: 144 E Oak Ave Moorestown NJ 08087 Office: Kennedy Meml Hosps U Med Ctr Washington Twp 435 Hurffville-Cross Keys Turnersville NJ 08012

WITMEYER, RICHARD JAMES, health products executive; b. Bethlehem, Pa., Nov. 28, 1948; s. John Robert and Dora Clarene (Braswell) W.; m. Sally Lynne Godshall, June 7, 1975; children: Flynn Godshall, Catherine Rose. BSChemE, Lehigh U., 1970, MSChemE, 1973; PhD in Materials Engring., N.C. State U., 1978; MBA, Ga. State U., 1985. Jr. process engr. Cities Svc. Corp., Trenton, N.J., 1970-71; process engr. Nat. Starch and Chem. Corp., Plainfield, N.J., 1973-74; rsch. scientist Kimberly-Clark Corp., Neenah (Wis.) and Roswell, Ga., 1977-87; mgr. mktg. Burlington Precision Fabrics Group, Greensboro, N.C., 1987-88; mgr. R&D James River Corp., Greenville, S.C., 1988-90; v.p. sci. affairs London Internat. U.S. Holdings, Regent Hosp. Products Ltd., Greenville, 1990-92; v.p. tech. affairs Standard Textile Co., Cin., 1992-95, Safeskin Corp., San Diego, 1995—; bd. dirs. Bio Barrier Inc., Denver; affiliate mem. Am. Soc. Hosp. Ctrl. Svc. Pers., Atlanta, 1985-87; co. rep. Assn. for the Nonwovens and Disposables Assn., N.y.C., 1987-88. Mem. ASTM (co. rep. 1990-92), Health Industries Mfg. Assn. (adv. bd. 1991-92), Soc. Plastics Engrs., Assn. for Advancement of Med. Instrumentation, Am. Soc. for Quality Control.

WITOVER, STEPHEN BARRY, pediatrician; b. Bklyn., Jan. 7, 1941; s. Nat and Frances (Posner) W.; m. Joyce Bonnie Weiss; children: Julie Lyn, Gary Lee. AB, Adelphi U., 1961; MD, Chgo. Med. Sch., 1965. Intern, resident, chief resident Montefiore Hosp. and Med. Ctr., Bronx, N.Y.; intern to chief resident pediatrics, 1965-68; pres. Merrimack Valley Pediat. Assocs., Billerica, Mass., 1972—; med. dir. Teen Health Svcs. Saints Meml. Hosp., Lowell, Mass., 1974—; chief of pediatrics Teen Health Svcs. St. Johns Hosp., 1982—. Maj. U.S. Army, 1968-70. Office: Merrimack Pediatric Assocs 221 Boston Rd North Billerica MA 01862-2321 also: Merrimack Valley Pediatric Assn 1501 Main St Tewksbury MA 01876

WITTE, CARLTON ROYAL VINCENT, health facility administrator; b. Point Pleasant, N.J., Aug. 29, 1946; s. Carl George and Marion Ida (Pollock) W.; m. Barbara Ann Koontz, Aug. 30, 1969 (div. Mar. 1977); children: Michelle Darlene, Carl Joseph; m. Joyce Ann Smith, Dec. 4, 1977; children: Brett Jonathan, Bryan Christopher, Kristin Ann-Marie. BA in Psychology, U. Tex., 1969; MA in Pub. Adminstrn., U. Okla., 1977; postgrad., Command and Gen. Staff Coll., 1985. Commd. 2d lt. U.S. Army, 1969, advanced through grades to lt. col.; chief patient svcs. Rader Army Health Clinic, Ft. Myer, Va., 1972-73; asst. adminstr. dept. of clinics Forrestal Army Health Clinic, Washington, 1972-74; asst. adminstr. Walter Reed Army Inst. of Rsch., Washington, 1975-78; adminstr. Office of Div. Surgeon, 3d Armored Div., Fed. Republic Germany, 1979-81; assoc. adminstr. Walter Reed Army Med. Ctr., Washington, 1981-84; chief adminstr. Pentagon Health Clinic, Washington, 1984-86; chief patient adminstrn. Walson Army Community Hosp., Ft. Dix, N.J., 1986-90; ret. U.S. Army, 1990; dir. adminstrn. dept. ob-gyn Hershey Med. Ctr., Pa. State U., 1990-92; sr. adminstr. Baltimore City Detention Ctr., Balt., 1992-93; assoc. adminstr. stds. and enforcement long-term care Pa. Dept. Health, Harrisburg, 1993-94; health ins. broker Witte Adv. Svcs., Harrisburg, 1994-96; promotions coord. KRN Radio, WWII 720 AM, Harrisburg, 1995—; chmn. Joint Commn. on Accreditation of Healthcare Orgns. steering com., Walson Hosp., Ft. Dix, 1986-90; cons. Keystone Heath Plan Cen.-Sr. Blue (Medicare HMO), 1996—. Author booklet: Patient Administration Guide-Physicians, 1988; co-author: Patient Administration for Commanders, 1988. Mem. rescue squad, tng. officer Dale City (Va.) Vol. Fire and Rescue, 1975-77; bd. dirs. Pheasant Run, Laurel, Md., 1982-84; charter mem., chmn. liturgy com. St. Joseph's Parish, Ft. Dix, 1988, mem. parish coun., 1988-89; coach Little League, Ft. Dix and South Hanover, Pa., 1989-91; soccer coach South Hanover, pa., 1993-95. Decorated Legion of Merit. Mem. Am. Coll. Health Care Execs., Med. Group Mgmt. Assn., Optimist Internat., Mil. Order of World Wars (perpetual mem.), Mil. Order of Med. Merit. Roman Catholic. Home: 1191 Hillcrest Rd Odenton MD 21113-9999

WITTE, MARLYS HEARST, internist, educator; b. N.Y.C., 1934. MD, NYU Sch. Medicine, 1960. Intern N.C. Meml. Hosp., Chapel Hill, 1960-61; resident Bellevue Hosp. Ctr., N.Y.C., 1961-63; fellow NYU Hosp., Washington U., St. Louis, 1964-66; prof. surgery U. Ariz., 1965-69, 69—; attending internist Ariz. Health Sci. Ctr., Tucson, 1965-69, 69—. Rsch. fellow Am. Heart Assn., 1995-96. Mem. AAAS, Am. Hosp. Assn., Alpha Omega Alpha. Office: U Ariz Coll Medicine 1501 N Campbell Ave Tucson AZ 85724-0001*

WITTHOLT, GUNTER, physician assistant, clinical perfusionist; b. Oldenburg, Germany, May 19, 1936; came to U.S., 1954, naturalized; s. August Heinrich and Elisabeth Anna (Lüdeking) W.; m. G. Eloise Walsh, Nov. 28, 1959; children: Steven Günter, James Jay. AS, CUNY, 1973; student, USPHS Physician Asst. Sch., S.I., N.Y., 1973-74. Cert. cardiopulmonary perfusionist; cert. Am. Bd. Cardiovasc. Perfusion Tech., Nat. Commn. on Cert. Physician Assts.; cert. physician asst. N.Y. Truck driver Mothers Pie Co., Bronx, N.Y., 1958-63; clin. perfusionist Kings County Hosp., Bklyn., 1963-73; physician asst. Comprehensive Rural Health, Elmira, N.Y., 1974-76, Dr. Percy Brazil, Tarrytown, N.Y., 1977-78, Dr. William Jacobson, White Plains, N.Y., 1977-78, Stanfordville (N.Y.) Health Ctr., 1978-93; physician asst. No. Dutchess Hosp., Rhinebeck, N.Y., 1978—, Hyde Park, N.Y., 1993—. With U.S. Army, 1956-58. Mem. Am. Acad. Physician Assts., N.Y. State Soc. Physician Assts., Mid-Hudson Assn. Physician Assts. (past pres.), All Sport Health Club (adv. bd.). Republican. Lutheran. Home: 3 Village Common Fishkill NY 12524 Office: No Dutchess Med Ctr 688 Violet Ave Hyde Park NY 12538

WITTLING, WERNER WOLFGANG, psychology educator, neuropsychologist; b. Neunkirchen, Germany, June 9, 1940; s. Josef and Helene (Haus) W.; m. Christa Bettinger, Aug. 20, 1966; children: Bettina, Arne. Diploma in psychology, U. Saarbrücken, Germany, 1968; PhD, U. Mannheim, Germany, 1974, Habilitation in Psychology, 1983. Cert. psychologist. Head Dept. Counseling Psychology, Saarbrücken, 1969-70; asst. dept. psychology U. Mannheim, 1970-84; lectr. physiol. psychology U. Saarbrücken, 1978-79; prof. clin. psychology U. Trier, Germany, 1978-79; prof., dir. dept. physiol. clin. psychology U. Eichstätt, Germany, 1984—; mem. Adv. Bd. Neuropsychobiology, 1995—. Author: Handbook of Clinical Psychology, 1980, Introduction to Psychology of Perception, 1976; contbr.: Brain Asymmetry, 1995; contbr. articles to profl. jours. including Brain and Cognition, Neuropsychologia, Cortex. Recipient Karin Islinger award Karin Islinger Found., 1974, award European Symposium on Hormone and Drug Assessment in Saliva, 1990. Mem. N.Y. Acad. Scis., German Soc. Psychology, German Psychophysiology Soc. Home: Jean-Mathieu-Strasse 50, D-66540 Neunkirchen Germany Office: Cath Univ Eichstätt, Ostenstrasse 26, D-85071 Eichstätt Germany

WITTMER, JAMES FREDERICK, preventive medicine physician, educator; b. Carlinville, Ill., Dec. 30, 1932; s. Franklin Benjamin and Eva Caroline (Zihlman) W.; m. Juanita Lou Wilkey, June 29, 1962; children: Ellen, Carol, Nancy. MD, Washington U., St. Louis, 1957; MPH, Harvard U., 1961. Diplomate Am. Bd. Preventive Medicine. Intern U. Va. Hosp., Charlottesville, 1857-58; commd. capt. USAF, 1958, advanced through grades to col., 1971; ret., 1979; dean allied health U. Tex. Health Sci. Ctr., San Antonio, 1979-80; asst. med. dir. Conoco Oil Co., Ponca City, Okla., 1980-81; assoc. med. dir. Mobil Oil Corp., N.Y.C., 1981-83; dir. health, environ. and safety ITT, N.Y.C., 1983-95, corp. v.p., 1990-95; clin. prof. medicine Cornell U. Med. Coll., N.Y.C., 1984—; lectr. environ. medicine NYU, N.Y.C., 1984—; adj. prof. U. Tex. Sch. Pub. Health, Houston, 1987—; nat. coord. com. on clin. preventive svcs. USPHS, 1994—. Mem. med. and ins. com. Pres.'s Com. on Employment People with Disabilities, Washington, 1986-94, chmn., 1986-90. Fellow ACP, Am. Coll. Occupational and Environ. Medicine (bd. dirs. 1990—, sec. 1992-94), Am. Coll. Preventive Medicine, Aerospace Med. Assn., N.Y. Acad. Medicine; mem. AMA, Tex. Occupational Med. Assn., Physicians Sci. Soc. Home and Office: 159 Sabine Rd Boerne TX 78006-6217

WITTREICH, WARREN JAMES, psychologist, consultant; b. Weehawken, N.J., Aug. 18, 1929; s. Andrew Otto and Muriel Viola (Wilson) W.; m. Mary Shirley Wells, Sept. 10, 1951 (div. Sept. 7, 1959); children: Michael, Peter; m. Lois Vivian Llewellyn, Sept. 8, 1959; children: Benjamin, Debra, Susie (dec.), Andrea. AB in Psychology summa cum laude, Princeton U., 1951, MA in Psychology, 1953, PhD in Psychology, 1954; PhD in Clin. Psychology, Cath. U., Washington, 1958. Lic. psychologist, Pa. Guest scientist Naval Med. Rsch. Inst., Bethesda, Md., 1953-54; postdoctoral trainee VA, East Orange, N.J., 1954-55; clin. psychologist Lancaster and Phila., Pa., 1955—; exec. v.p. Nat. Analysts, Inc., Phila., 1959-64; pres. Daniel Yankelovich of Pa., Phila., 1964-67; pres., CEO Crossroads Career Planning Corp., Phila., 1967-85; adj. prof., rsch. cons. U. Pa., Phila., 1968-73; CEO Focus Group Assocs. Ltd., Bethlehem, Pa., 1995—; advisor to Sec. of Transp., U.S. Dept. Transp., Washington, 1968-72; expert witness FTC, Washington, 1957, U.S. Congress, Washington, 1959, N.Y. State Supreme Ct., N.Y.C., 1963. Exhibited in 4 one-man shows; 2 commd. paintings; contbr. articles to profl. jours. Worker Robert F. Kennedy Campaign Com., Washington, 1967; mem. Citizens Adv. Com. on Transp. Quality, U.S. Dept. Transp., Washington, 1968-74. Recipient fellowship NSF, 1952-53. Fellow Pa. Psychol. Assn.; mem. APA, Phi Beta Kappa, Sigma Xi. Episcopalian. Home: 1158 W Main St Ste E2-6 Lansdale PA 19446

WITTROCK, MERLIN CARL, educational psychologist; b. Twin Falls, Idaho, Jan. 3, 1931; s. Herman C. and Mary Ellen (Baumann) W.; m. Nancy McNulty, Apr. 3, 1953; children: Steven, Catherine, Rebecca. BS in Biology, U. Mo., Columbia, 1953, MS in Ednl. Psychology, 1956; PhD in Ednl. Psychology, U. Ill., Urbana, 1960. Prof. grad. sch. edn. UCLA, 1960—, founder Ctr. Study Evaluation, chmn. div. ednl. psychology, chmn. faculty, exec. com.; univ. com. on disting. teaching; fellow Ctr. for Advanced Study in Behavioral Scis., 1967-68; vis. prof. U. Wis., U. Ill., Ind. U., Monash U., Australia; bd. dirs. Far West Labs., San Francisco; chmn. com. on evaluation and assessment L.A. Unified Sch. Dist.; mem. nat. adv. panel for math. scis. NRC of NAS, 1988-89; chmn. nat. bd. Nat. Ctr. for Rsch. in Math. Scis. Edn., chmn. charges com. UCLA; adv. bd. Kauffman Found., Kansas City, Mo., 1995—; bd. dirs. Western Edn. Lab. for Edn. Rsch. Author, editor: The Evaluation of Instruction, 1970, Changing Education, 1973, Learning and Instruction, 1977, The Human Brain, 1977, Danish transl., 1980, Spanish transl., 1982, The Brain and Psychology, 1980, Instructional Psychology: Education and Cognitive Processes of the Brain, Neuropsychological and Cognitive Processes of Reading, 1981, Handbook of Research on Teaching, 3d edit., 1986, The Future of Educational Psychology, 1989, Research in Learning and Teaching, 1990, Testing and Cognition, 1991, Generative Science Teaching, 1994, Metacognitiion 1995. Capt. USAF, 1953-55. Recipient Thorndike award for outstanding psychol. rsch., 1987, Disting. Tchr. of Univ. award UCLA, 1990; Ford Found. grantee. Fellow AAAS, APA (pres. divsn. ednl. psychology 1984-85, assn. coun. 1988-91, award for Outstanding Svc. to Ednl. Psychology 1991, 93, Disting. Svc. award for svc. to sci. adv. coun.), Am. Psychol. Soc., (charter fellow), Am. Ednl. Rsch. Assn. (chmn. ann. conv., chmn. publs. 1980-83, assn. coun. 1986-89, bd. dirs. 1987-89, chmn. com. on ednl. TV 1989—, Outstanding Contbns. award 1986, Outstanding Svc. award 1989); mem. Western Edn. Lab. for Edn. Rsch. (bd. dirs.), Phi Delta Kappa. Office: UCLA 3022 Moore Hall Los Angeles CA 90095

WITTY, JOHN BARBER, health care executive; b. Vicksburg, Miss., Mar. 26, 1946; s. Neomah Wilks and Jennie (Barber) W.; m. Susan Deemer, June 26, 1976; children: Justin Michael, Adam David. BA, Miss. State U., 1968; MEd, U. Md., 1972, EdD, 1989. Cert. prin. regular edn. and spl. edn., curriculum coord. spl. edn., tch. spl. edn. K-12, Md. Tchr. Anne Arundel County Pub. Schs., Annapolis, Md., 1972-77; specialist in community affairs Anne Arundel County Pub. Schs., Annapolis, 1977-78, sch. based adminstr., 1978-79, county based adminstr., 1979-87; dir. svcs. devel. Am. Internat. Health Rehab. Svcs., Annapolis, 1987-88, dir. tng. & devel., 1988-89, dir. cost containment svcs., 1989-90, v.p. svcs., 1990-91; chief oper. officer AIIA/Comp Care, Daytona Beach, Fla., 1991-94; pres. Med. Advantage, Orlando, Fla., 1994—; bd. dirs. Anne Arundel County Sheltered Workshop, Glen Burnie, Md., 1987-89. Pres. Rolling Knolls Community Assn., Annapolis, 1980s, Gen.'s Hwy. Coun., Annapolis, 1980s; chmn. Anne Arundel County Stormwater Mgmt. Commn., 1984-85; mem. human rights com. Providence Ctr., 1984-85; pres. Oceantime Condominium Assn., Ocean City, Md., 1984-89, Huntington Community Assn., 1990—. With USN, 1969-72. Recipient Jaycee of Month award, 1975, C. William Brownfield award Annapolis Md. Jaycees, 1975, Jaycee Award of Svc., 1976, Md. State Jaycee award, 1975, 77, Jaycee of Month, 1977, Harold Reece award, 1977. Mem. Rotary, Annapolis Jaycees (v.p., bd. dirs.), Phi Delta Kappa, Kappa Delta Pi, Phi Mu Alpha Sinfonia. Republican. Presbyterian. Home: 2345 Westminster Ter Oviedo FL 32765-7554 Office: Med Advantage 3452 Lake Lynda Dr Ste 250 Orlando FL 32817

WITZ, GISELA, chemist, educator; b. Breslau, Federal Republic of Germany, Mar. 16, 1939; came to U.S., 1955.; d. Gerhardt Witz and Hildegard (Sufeida) Minzak. BA, NYU, 1962, MS, 1965, PhD, 1969. Assoc. rsch. scientist NYU Med. Ctr., N.Y.C., 1970-73, rsch. scientist, 1973-77, asst. prof., 1977-80; asst. prof. Univ. of Medicine and Dentistry of N.J.-Rutgers Med. Sch., Piscataway, N.J., 1980-86; assoc. prof. U. Medicine and Dentistry N.J.-Robert Wood Johnson Med. Sch., Piscataway, 1986-93, prof., 1993—; dep. dir. Joint Grad. Program in Toxicology, Rutgers U./Univ. Medicine and Dentistry of N.J.-Robert Wood Johnson Med. Sch., 1988, assoc. dir. 1992—; cons. Nat. Rsch. Coun., Washington, 1982-83, 85-86. Contbr. articles to profl. jours. Recipient Dupont Teaching award, NYU, 1966; Univ. Scholar, Founders Day award, N.Y. U., 1969. Mem. Am. Assn. Cancer Research, Am. Chem. Soc., Soc. Toxicology, N.Y. Acad. Sci., Sigma Xi. Office: U Medicine and Dentistry NJ Robert Wood Johnson Med Sch Piscataway NJ 08854

WITZEL, LOTHAR GUSTAV, physician, gastroenterologist; b. Mannheim, Fed. Republic of Germany, July 27, 1939; s. Gustav and Martha (Pilger) W. MD, U. Freiburg, Fed. Republic of Germany, 1965; PhD, U. Berlin, 1983. Substitute medicine supt. U. Bern (Switzerland) Med. Sch., 1973-77; dir., med. supt. German Red Cross Hosp., Berlin, 1978-93. Contbr. articles to profl. jours.; patentee in field. Mem. Indian Soc. Gastroenterology (hon.), European Congress Endoscopy (sec. gen. 1981), Swiss Soc. Gastroenterology (corr. mem. 1989, Award of Gastroenterology 1981). Office: Koloniestrasse 21, 13359 Berlin Germany

WITZKE, DAVID JOHN, plastic surgeon, educator; b. Rochester, Minn., Jan. 7, 1951; s. Walton E. and Adeline (Altermatt) W.; m. Barbara-Jo Weko, July 20, 1978; children: Sterling, Mercedes, Beckett, Peyton. BA in Math. summa cum laude, U. Minn., 1973; MD, Mayo Med. Sch., 1977. Diplomate Am. Bd. Surgery, Am. Bd. Plastic Surgery, Nat. Bd. Med. Examiners. Intern gen. surgery Mayo Clinic, 1977-78, resident gen. surgery, 1978-82, resident plastic surgery, 1982-84; rsch. asst. U. Minn., Mpls., 1969-73, Mayo Grad. Sch. Medicine, Rochester, 1973-77; pvt. practice, Sioux Falls, S.D., 1984—; dir. burn unit McKennan Hosp., Sioux Falls, 1986—; clin. instr. surgery U. S.D. Med. Sch., Sioux Falls, 1986—; presenter in field. Contbg. author: Methods in Cell Biology, 1978, Hypertrophic Cardiomyopathy, 1982; contbr. articles to med. jours. Recipient Donald C. Balfour Alumni award, 1978. Fellow ACS; mem. AMA, Am. Soc. Plastic and Reconstructive Surgeons, Am. Soc. Maxillofacial Surgeons, Am. Burn Assn., Am. Cleft Palate Assn., Am. Assn. for Hand Surgery, Am. Soc. for Reconstructive Microsurgery, Internat. Soc. Craniomaxillofacial Surgery, Internat. Congress Plastic and Reconstructive Surgery, Midwestern Assn. Plastic Surgery, Acad. Plastic Surgeons Minn., S.D. Med. Assn., Mayo Clinic Priestley Surg. Soc., Mayo Alumni Assn., Phi Beta Kappa. Office: Plastic Surgery Assocs SD 911 E 20th St Ste 602 Sioux Falls SD 57105

WIVIOTT, WILBERT W., plastic surgeon; b. Milw., May 5, 1927. BS, U. Wis., 1954, MD, 1957, MS, 1961; DDS, Marquette U., 1953. Cert. Am. Bd. Plastic Surgery. Intern Mt. Sinai Hosp., Milw., 1957-58; resident U.S. Vet. Hosp. Wood, Wis., 1958-61; resident in plastic surgery U. Hosps., Madison, 1961-63; plastic surgeon pvt. practice, Milw., 1963—; mem. Milw. Children's Hosp., Milw., Good Samaritan Med. Ctr., St. Michael Hosp., Mt. Sinai Hosp. Served with USNR, 1945-46. Fellow Am. Coll. Surgeons; mem. AMA, Wis. Med. Soc., Milw. County Med. Soc., Wis. Soc. Plastic Surgeons (past pres.), Mid-Western Assn. Plastic Surgeons, Am. Soc. Plastic and Reconstructive Surgeons, Am. Soc. Maxillo-Facial Surgeons (editors com., treas. 1981-83, v.p. 1983-84, pres. 1985-86), Am. Soc. for Aesthetic Plastic Surgeons, Am. Soc. Plastic Surgeons, Wis. Med. Alumni Assn. (past. pres.), Phi Delta Epsilon, Alpha Omega. Office: 8675 N Port Washington Rd Milwaukee WI 53217

WLAZELEK, BRIAN GENE, psychologist; b. Allentown, Pa., Nov. 12, 1957; s. Joseph Wlazelek and Virginia Wlazelek Marone; m. Jeanne Marie Werner, June 21, 1980; children: Kristen Michelle, Sara Renee. BA in Psychology, Temple U., 1979, MEd in Counseling Psychology, 1980; PhD in Counseling Psychology, Lehigh U., 1990. Lic. psychologist, Pa. Therapist Cumberland County Guidance Ctr., Millville, N.J., 1980-81; staff psychologist Atlantic Mental Health Ctr., Atlantic City, N.J., 1981-83, First Hosp. Wyoming Valley, Wilkes-Barre, Pa., 1983-85, Pocono Med. Ctr., East Stroudsburg, Pa., 1985-88; prof. Kutztown (Pa.) U., 1988—; adj. prof. Chestnut Hill Coll., Phila., 1990—; dir. Univ. Counseling Ctr. Sr. cons. Family Life Svcs., Topton, Pa., 1989—. Named Temple Univ. Pres.'s Scholar, 1980. Mem. AACD, APA, Assn. Counseling Ctr. (sec.-treas. 1991-92, pres. 1994-95), N.Am. Soc. Adlerian Psychology, Masons, Rotary (pres. 1992-93), Phi Beta Kappa, Psi Chi, Chi Sigma Iota, Phi Kappa Phi. Lutheran. Home: 58 Rhoades Rd Lenhartsville PA 19534-9595 Office: Kutztown Univ Stratton Adminstrn Bldg Kutztown PA 19530

WŁODARSKI, KRZYSZTOF HENRYK, histologist; b. Warsaw, July 15, 1940; s. Stanisław and Antonina (Wasilewska) W.; m. Jowita Magdalena Mikołajska, Dec. 26, 1966; children: Paweł, Sylwia. Med. degree, Med. Acad., Warsaw, Poland, 1963, MD, 1970, dr.hab., 1981. Rsch. fellow Tissues and Virus Culture Lab. Biomed., Warsaw, 1962-68; lectr., adj. dept. histology Med. Acad. Warsaw, 1968-81, asst. prof. histology, 1981-91, prof. histology, 1991—; rsch. fellow dept. histology U. Liverpool, Eng., 1970-72; assoc. prof. microbiology Wayne State U., Detroit, 1975-76; vis. scientist NIH, NIDR, Bethesda, Md., 1982-83; super referee Bd. Professorship Degree Certification, Warsaw, 1991. Contbr. articles to profl. jours. Roman Catholic. Home: Głogowa 17, 02-639 Warsaw Poland Office: Med Acad Warsaw Histology, Chalubinskiego 5, 02-004 Warsaw Poland

WOEHRLEN, ARTHUR EDWARD, JR., dentist; b. Detroit, Dec. 9, 1947; s. Arthur Edward and Olga (Hewka) W.; m. Sara Elizabeth Heikoff, Aug. 13, 1972; 1 child, Tess Helena. DDS, U. Mich., 1973. Resident in gen. dentistry USAF, 1973-74; gen. practice dentistry Redwood Dental Group, Warren, Mich., 1976—; instr. Sinai Hosp., Detroit, 1977—; chief of dentistry St. John's Hosp., Macomb Ctr., Mt. Clemens, Mich., 1982—; mem. dentistry staff Hutzel Hosp., Warren; reviewer Chubb Ins. Co. (malpractice claims), 1978-89; bd. mem. Mich. Acad. Gen. Dentistry (chmn. State of Mich. Continuing Dental Edn. Accreditation). Contbr. articles on dentistry to profl. jours. Served to capt. USAF, 1973-76. Fellow Internat. Coll. of Oral Implantologists; mem. ADA, Acad. Gen. Dentistry (Master), Mich. Dental Assn., Acad. Gen. Dentistry, Am. Acad. Oral Medicine, Fedn. Dentaire Internationale, Acad. Dentistry for the Handicapped, Am. Acad. Oral Implantologists, Internat. Coll. Oral Implantologists, Macomb Dist. Dental Soc.; panel mem. Am. Arbitration Assn. Republican. Home: 25460 Dundee Rd Royal Oak MI 48067-3018 Office: Redwood Dental Group 13403 E 13 Mile Rd Warren MI 48093-3188

WOELFEL, MARTHA JANE, biology educator; b. San Antonio, July 18, 1948; d. George E. and Norma Marie (Balzen) W. BA cum laude, U. Tex., 1970; postgrad., Ohio State U., 1971-72, U. Ky., 1978-81; MA in Teaching, U. Louisville, 1976. Asst. prof. biology Ky. State U., Frankfort, 1976—, pres. faculty senate, 1985-87, 90-91; acting asst. v.p. for acad. affairs, 1993-94; Tier I trainer Commonwealth of Ky.'s Beginning Tchr. Internship Program, 1990—. Trainer Kentuckiana coun. Girl Scouts U.S.A., 1973—. Recipient Thanks Badge Kentuckiana coun. Girl Scouts U.S.A., 1981, Thanks Badge II, 1996; Muellhaupt fellow Ohio State U., 1972-73. Mem. NSTA, Nat. Assn. Biology Tchrs., Pride of Ky. Sweet Adelines (sect. leader 1981—), Phi Delta Kappa. Democrat. Office: Ky State U E Main St Frankfort KY 40601-2808

WOERNER, ALFRED IRA, medical device manufacturer, educator; b. Jersey City, N.J., Sept. 21, 1935; s. Theodore and Miriam (Mann) W.; m. Margaret R. Martin, Nov. 27, 1959; children: John, Michael, Judith. DME, Stevens Inst., 1956; MS, Stevens, 1961; MBA, NYU, 1965; LLB, LaSalle U., 1963; PhD, Calif. State U., 1990. Gen. program mgr. Becton Dickenson & Co., Ruthuferd, N.J., 1959-63; group v.p., asst. to pres. Howmet Corp., N.Y.C., 1963-69; gen. mgr., v.p. Wide Range Industries, N.Y.C., 1969-72; pres., owner New World Market Ltd., Westwood, N.J., 1972—, Fairfield Surg. Corp., Stanford, Conn., 1972—; cons. Woerner Assocs., Westwood; prof. Fairleigh Dickinson U., Teaneck, N.J., 1969—. Author: Program Management, 1988. Pres. Bd. Edn., Westwood, 1978-86; adv. Stevens Inst. Tech., Hoboken, N.J., 1972-80. Mem. AMA, ASME, Am. Acad. Cons., Am. Statistical Assn. Home: 75 Bergen St Westwood NJ 07675-2332 Office: Fairleigh Dickinson U 1000 River Rd Teaneck NJ 07666-1914

WOFFORD, ELIZABETH DERRICK, pathologist; b. Columbia, S.C., May 13, 1955; d. Homer Edwin and Mary June (Niggel) Derrick; m. John E. Wofford, Apr. 23, 1983; children: John E., Ellison B. BS in Pharmacy, U. S.C., 1977, MS in Organic Chemistry, 1979; MD, Med. U. S.C., 1983. Intern, resident, fellow Vanderbilt U., Nashville, 1983-88; pathologist Bapt. Hosp., Nashville, 1988-89; mem. clin. faculty U. S.C. Sch. Medicine, Columbia, 1990—; staff pathologist Dorn Vets. Hosp., Columbia, 1989-91; pathologist Lexington Med. Ctr., Columbia, S.C., 1991—. Contbr. articles and abstracts to profl. jours. Recipient Merck award Merck Drug Corp., 1977. Fellow Coll. Am. Pathologists; mem. Am. Soc. Clin. Pathologists, AMA, S.C. Med. Assn. Republican. Presbyterian. Home: 2804 Sheffield Rd Columbia SC 29204 Office: Lexington Med Ctr 3720 Sunset Blvd West Columbia SC 29697

WOGAN, GERALD NORMAN, toxicology educator; b. Altoona, Pa., Jan. 11, 1930; s. Thomas B. and Florence E. (Corl) W.; m. Henrietta E. Hoenicke, Aug. 24, 1957; children: Christine F., Eugene E. BS, Juniata Coll., 1951; MS, U. Ill., 1953, PhD, 1957. Asst. prof. physiology Rutgers U., New Brunswick, N.J., 1957-61; asst. prof. toxicology MIT, Cambridge, 1962-65, assoc. prof., 1965-69, prof. toxicology, 1969—, head dept. applied biol. scis., 1979-88, prof. chemistry, 1989—, dir. divsn. toxicology, 1988—; cons. to nat. and internat. govt. agys., industries. NIH grantee, 1963—. Mem. editl. bd. Cancer Rsch., 1971-79, Applied Microbiology, 1971-79, Chem.-Biol. Interactions, 1975-78, Toxicology, Environ. Health, 1974-84, Jour. Nat. Cancer Inst., 1988—; contbr. articles and revs. to profl. jours. Recipient Disting. Alumni award U. Ill. Fellow Am. Acad. Microbiology; mem. AAAS, NAS, Inst. Medicine, Am. Assn. Cancer Rsch., Am. Soc. Pharmacology and Exptl. Therapeutics, Am. Soc. Microbiology, Soc. Toxicology, Am. Inst. Nutrition, Sigma Xi. Office: MIT Divsn of Toxicology 77 Massachusetts Ave Rm 16-333 Cambridge MA 02139-4301

WOHL, ARMAND JEFFREY, cardiologist; b. Phila., Dec. 11, 1946; s. Herman Lewis and Selma (Paul) W.; m. Marylouise Katherine Giangrossi, Sept. 4, 1977; children: Michael Adam, Todd David. Student, Temple U., 1967; MD, Hahnemann U., 1971. Intern Bexar County Hosp., San Antonio, 1971-72; resident in internal medicine Parkland Hosp., Dallas, 1972-74; fellow in cardiology U. Tex. Southwestern Med. Ctr., Dallas, 1974-76; chief of cardiology USAF Hosp. Elmendorf, Anchorage, 1976-78; chief cardiologist Riverside (Calif.) Med. Clin., 1978-79; cardiologist Grossmont Cardiology Med. Group, La Mesa, Calif., 1980-84; pvt. practice, La Mesa, 1985—; chief of cardiology Grossmont Hosp., La Mesa, 1988-90; asst. clin. prof. Sch. Medicine. U. Calif., San Diego, 1990—. Contbr. articles to profl. jours. Bd. dirs. Grossmont Hosp. Dist., 1995—, San Diego County chpt. Am. Heart Assn., 1981-87. Maj. USAF, 1976-78. Fellow Am. Coll. Cardiology (councilor Calif. chpt. 1991—), Am. Coll. Physicians, Coun. on Clin. Cardiology. Office: 5565 Grossmont Center Dr La Mesa CA 91942-3020

WOHL, MARY ELLEN BECK, pediatrician, educator; b. Cleve., June 12, 1932; d. Claude Schaeffer and Ellen Agnes (Manning) Beck; m. Martin Jay Wohl, June 19, 1962; children: Alexander Wilkenson, Laura Ellen. AB, Radcliffe Coll., 1954; MD, Columbia U., 1958. Fellow physiology Harvard Sch. Pub. Health, Boston, 1962-65; assoc. medicine and pulmonary lab. Children's Hosp., Boston, 1965-78, sr. assoc. medicine, 1978—; asst. prof., assoc. prof., prof. pediatrics Harvard Med. Sch., Boston, 1969—. Mem. Am. Coll. Chest Physicians, Am. Pediatric Assn., Am. Physiol. Soc., Acad. Pediatrics, Am. Thoracic Soc., Soc. Pediatric Rsch. Office: 300 Longwood Ave Boston MA 02115

WOHLEB, BERNADETTE MARIE, health facility administrator; b. Bay City, Tex., Jan. 15, 1944; d. George Christian and Eileen Catherine (Ottis) Gassen; m. Roy Edwin Wohleb Jr., Dec. 26, 1964; children: Christopher, Stephen, Catherine. BS in Health Professions, S.W. Tex. State U., 1981; MS in Health Professions, S.W. Tex. Sate U., 1984. Cert. healthcare exec. Supr., coord. support pers. edn. Scott & White Meml. Hosp., Temple, Tex., 1982-85, dir. allied health edn., 1985-88, asst. adminstr., 1988—; dental hygiene adv. bd. Tex. Bd. Dental Examiners, Austin, 1995. Contbr. articles to profl. jours. Bd. dirs. Ralph Wilson Youth Club, Temple, 1989-91, Ronald McDonald House, Temple, 1995; trustee Temple Jr. Coll., 1990—; adv. bd. Women's Resource Ctr., Tex. State Tech. Coll., Waco, 1995—. Mem. Am. Coll. Healthcare Execs. (diplomate), Tex. Hosp. Assn. (AIDS steering com. 1993—), Kiwanis (officer, bd. dirs. 1989-95, pres. 1995-96, Outstanding Kiwanis Advisor award 1989-90, Outstanding Svc. award 1990). Office: Scott & White Meml Hosp 2401 S 31st St Temple TX 76508

WOHLERT, EARL ROSS, health care analyst; b. Phila., Oct. 19, 1963; s. Anton Emil and Dona Lee (Zimmerman) WW.; m. Karen Lynn Bauer, Mar. 12, 1994; 1 child, Ryan Chandler. BA, Hawaii Loa Coll., Kaneohe, 1986; MBA, U. New Haven, 1992. Acct. Yale U. Sch. Medicine, New Haven, 1987-88, fin. analyst, 1988-90, assoc. adminstr. fin., 1990-93, assoc. adminstr. fin. svcs., 1993-95; health care analyst M.D. Health Plan, North Haven, Conn., 1995-96, dir. healthcare analysis, 1996—; mktg. and mgmt. cons. Lt. USNR, 1992. Home: 11 Crofut Rd Orange CT 06477 Office: MD Health Plan 6 Devine St North Haven CT 06473

WOJCIEHOSKI, RANDAL FRANCIS, emergency physician; b. Stevens Point, Wis., Apr. 30, 1960; s. Florian Joseph and Grace (Pehoski) W.; m. Michele Jane Koenig, July 13, 1991; children: Jozef Randal, Kasia Michele. BA, Marquette U., 1982; DPM, N.Y. Coll. Podiatric Medicine, 1986; DO, U. New England, 1989. Staff physician St. Michael's Hosp., Stevens Point, Wis., 1990—, Riverside Med. Ctr., Waupaca, Wis., 1990—; continuing med. edn. com. St. Michael's Hosp., pharmacy and therapeutics com., quality awaurance com.; clin. instr. emergency medicine U. Wis. Med. Sch., Physicians Asst. Program; lectr. in field. Contbr. articles to profl. jours. Med. dir. Portage County Ambulance Svc., med. dir. svc. endotracheal intubation program; med. dir. Portage County First Responders; psychiatric, alcohol and competance med. examiner Portage County Corp. Counsel, Dist. Attys. Office; med. liaison Stevens Point Police/Fire Commn.; med. dir. Waupaca County HAZMAT Drill, 1993; Portage County strategic planning com. Emergency Med. Svcs., 1994-95. Lt. comdr. USNR, 1989—. Am. Coll. Gen. Practitioners Preceptorship grantee, Chgo., 1989. Marquette U. Acad. scholar, Milw., 1978-82, Ctrl. Wis. Health Found. scholar, Stevens Point, 1984; recipient Am. HEart Assn. Good Samaritan award, Wis., 1994. Mem. AMA, Am. Coll. Physicians, Am. Coll. Emergency Physicians, Am. Osteo. Assn., Am. Assn. Physician Specialists, Portage County Med. Soc., Assn. Emergency Physicians (bd. dirs. 1994—). Republican. Roman Catholic. Home: 1066 Martin Island Dr Stevens Point WI 54481 Office: St Michaels Hosp 900 Illinois Ave Stevens Point WI 54481

WOJCIK, EDWARD ADAM, physician; b. Chgo., Dec. 13, 1936; s. Adam Frank and Hattie Mary (Leszciak) W.; m. Celine Theresa Skinner, Oct. 5, 1963; children: Laura, Carol, John. BS, Loyola U., Chgo., 1958; MD, Loyola U., 1962. Diplomate Am. Bd. Orthopaedic Surgery. Intern St. Joseph Hosp., Chgo., 1962-63; resident VA Hosp., Hines, Ill., 1965-69; sr. attending physician La Grange (Ill.) Meml. Hosp., 1973—; bd. mem. athletic trainers Dept. Profl. Regulation, Springfield, Chgo., 1992—. Capt. med. corps U.S. Army, 1963-65. Mayor Daley's Youth Found. scholar Youth Found., Chgo., 1954. Fellow ACS, Am. Acad. Orthopaedic Surgery; mem. AMA, Nat. Fedn. Cath. Physicians (br. pres. 1975), Ill. State Med. Soc., Chgo. Med. Soc. (br. pres. LaGrange 1991-94). Republican. Home: 508 50th Pl Western Springs IL 60558 Office: 1323 Memorial Dr La Grange IL 60525

WOLAHAN, CARYLE GOLDSACK, nursing educator; b. Somerville, N.J., July 27, 1942; d. Wilbur Wood and Jane (Hadley) Goldsack; m. Thomas Warren Hussey, June 26, 1965 (dec. Oct. 1970); 1 child, Timothy Stephen; m. William Kevin Wolahan, Sept. 30, 1983;. BS, Wagner Coll., 1964; MEd, Columbia U., 1973, EdD, 1979. Sch. nurse, tchr. Malverne (N.Y.) Pub. Schs., 1966-67, Dover-Wingdale Pub. Schs., Dover Plains, N.Y., 1967-68; head nurse Harlem Valley State Hosp., Wingdale, N.Y., 1968-69; asst. prof., acting dir. div. nursing Trenton (N.J.) State Coll., 1973-77; assoc. prof., acting dir. Felician Coll., Lodi, N.J., 1979-80, dir. div. nursing, 1982-87; dir. nursing program Stern Coll., Yeshiva U., N.Y.C., 1980-82; assoc. dean Coll. Nursing SUNY Health Sci. Ctr., Bklyn., 1987-91, acting dean Coll. Nursing, 1991-92; dean sch. nursing Adelphi U., 1992—. Contbr. articles to profl. jours., chpts. to books; editor Topics in Clin. Nursing, 1983. Mem. ANA (del. 1978-87), AAUP, N.J. State Nurses Assn. (coun. on edn. 1976-82, chmn. com. on ednl. preparation 1984-88), N.Y. State Nurses Assn. (chair pub. rels. com. 1990-92, spkrs. bur., recruitment com. Dist. 14, 1990, chair coun. on edn.), Nat. League for Nursing (accreditation com. 1985-90, site visitor 1984—), Am. Acad. Nursing, Nursing Edn. Alumni Assn. Tchrs. Coll. (pres. 1990-94), Lake Hopatcong Yacht Club, Sigma Theta Tau. Episcopalian. Home: 341 Maxim Dr Hopatcong NJ 07843-1744

WOLBACH, ALBERT BOGH, JR., family practice physician; b. Allentown, Pa., Sept. 6, 1932; s. Albert Bogh and Gertrude Lillian (Mitchell) W.; m. Shirley Ann Mentzer, Dec. 21, 1957; children: Sheryl Ann, Wendy Sue, Ann Mentzer. AB, U. Pa., 1954; MD, Jefferson Med. Coll., 1958. Diplomate Am. Bd. Family Practice. Intern Lancaster (Pa.) Gen. Hosp., 1958-59; pvt. practice, Ephrata, Pa., 1961—; mem. med. staff Ephrata C.C., 1961—; pres. med. staff Ephrata Hosp., 1969-70, bd. dirs., 1971-86. Contbr. articles to med. jours. Dir. Ephrata Sch. Dist., 1971-83; mem. Ephrata Rep. Com., 1983—. Lt. comdr. USPHS, 1959-61. Mem. Train Collectors Assn. (life, treas. Keystone divsn. 1990—), Masons, Shriners, Nat. Honor Soc., Phi Beta Kappa, Alpha Epsilon Delta. Mem. Ch. of Brethren. Office: 923 W Main St Ephrata PA 17522

WOLCOTT, HUGH DIXON, obstetrics and gynecology educator; b. N.Y.C., Jan. 12, 1946; s. Charles Edmund and Joan Degrau (Loveland) W.; m. Jane Jarrell Smith; children: Allison, James. BS, U.S. Naval Acad., 1967; MSE, Princeton U., 1969; MD, Northwestern U., Chgo., 1979. Diplomate Am. Bd. Ob-Gyn, Am. Bd. Med. Examiners. Commd. ensign USN, 1967, advanced through grades to capt., 1990; aviator, Fighter Squadron 14 Naval Air Station, Oceana, Va., 1971-74; test pilot Naval Air Test Ctr., Patuxent River, Md., 1974-76; staff physician Naval Hosp., Portsmouth, Va., 1984, Jacksonville, Fla., 1984-86; dir. colposcopy and laser clins. Naval Hosp., Portsmouth, Va., 1986-89; dir. ob-gyn. residency program Naval Hosp., Portsmouth, 1989-91, acting chmn. dept. ob-gyn., 1990-91; ret., 1991; asst. prof. Med. Coll. Hampton Roads, Norfolk, Va., 1991—; head dept. ob-gyn. Sentara Hosps., Norfolk, 1996—. Contbr. articles profl. jours. Awarded 1st prize scientific paper by resident physician Am. Coll. Obstetricans and Gynecologists; recipient Guggenheim fellowship Princeton U., 1967-68; Trident scholar U.S. Naval Acad., 1966-67. Fellow Am. Coll. Ob.-Gyns. (chmn. Navy sect. armed forces dist. 1989-91), Assn. Profs. Ob.-Gyns. (assoc.); mem. Am. Assn. Gynecol. Laparoscopists. Episcopalian. Home: 1202 Yancey Cir Virginia Beach VA 23454-2511 Office: Woman Care Ctrs 811 Med Tower 400 Gresham Dr Norfolk VA 23507

WOLCOTT, THOMAS GORDON, marine biology educator; b. San Diego, Dec. 22, 1944; s. Charles Gordon and Gerta (Blodig) W.; m. Donna Lee Riley, Mar. 16, 1968; children: Renee Catherine, Nathaniel Robert. BA in Zoology, U. Calif., Riverside, 1966; PhD in Zoology, U. Calif., Berkeley, 1971. Lectr. U. Calif., Riverside, 1971-72; asst. prof. N.C. State U., Raleigh, 1972-78, assoc. prof., 1978-85, prof. marine earth and atmospheric scis., 1985—; rsch. assoc. Smithsonian Environ. Rsch. Ctr., Edgewater, Md., 1985-87; corp. mem. Bermuda Biol. Sta. for Rsch. Contbr. articles to profl. jours. Grantee NSF, NOAA, U.S. Biol. Survey. Fellow AAAS; mem. Internat. Soc. Biotelemetry, Am. Soc. Zoologists (sec. ecology divsn. 1979-82, edn. com. 1990-93, sec. 1996—), Am. Soc. Limnology and Oceanography, The Crustacean Soc. (gov. bd. 1980, awards com. 1989-92), Sigma Xi. Democrat. Methodist. Office: NC State U Marine Earth & Atmospheric Scis Dept Box 8208 1125 Jordan Hall Raleigh NC 27695

WOLD, PATRICIA NEELY, psychiatrist; b. Lincoln, Nebr., Jan. 1, 1927; d. John Marshall and Edna (Perry) Neely; m. Aaron Wold; children: Marshall, Leo, Miriam. BA, U. Nebr., 1948, MD, 1952. Intern E.J. Meyer Meml. Hosp., Buffalo; resident in psychiatry Mass. Mental Health Ctr., Boston, 1953-55, chief svcs., 1955-56, mem. staff, 1955-56; mem. staff Southard Clinic, Boston, 1956-57, R.I. Mental Hygiene, Providence, 1963-65; med. dir. Farley Community Mental Health Ctr., East Providence, 1965-80; pvt. practice psychiatry Providence, 1965—. Mem. Am. Psychiat. Assn., R.I. Med. Soc., R.I. Med. Women's Assn., R.I. Psychiat. Assn. Office: 355 Thayer St Providence RI 02906-1550

WOLD, WILLIAM SYDNEY, molecular biology educator; b. Pine Falls, Manitoba, Can., Feb. 12, 1944; came to U.S., 1973; s. Roy and Nellie (Yurchison) W.; m. Susan Ann Lees, Dec. 30, 1967; m. Loralee Jane, William Guy, Jessica Ann, Jonathan Evered. BSc, U. Manitoba, 1965, MSc, 1968, PhD, 1973. Postdoctoral fellow St. Louis U., 1973-75, instr., 1975-76, from asst. prof. to prof. molecular biology, 1976-92, prof., chmn. dept. molecular microbiology and immunology, 1992—; reviewer's res. NIH, Washington, 1990—; cons. Genetic Therapy, Inc., 1994. Contbr. articles to Cell Jour., Jour. Biol. Chemistry, Jour. Immunology, others; assoc. editor jour. Virology, 1990—. NIH grantee, 1980—. Mem. AAAS, Am. Soc. Microbiology, Am. Soc. Virology, Internat. Soc. Antiviral Rsch. Office: St Louis U Molecular Microbiology & Immunology 1402 S Grand Saint Louis MO 63104

WOLDEN, JOY LEACH, psychotherapist, divorce mediator, retired; b. Butler, Pa., Nov. 28, 1930; d. Edgar James and Harriet M. (Carle) Leach; m. James V. Sweet, July 12, 1958; children: Stephen, Julia Ritchie, John.; m. Lauritz A. Wolden, June 19, 1988. BA, Carleton Coll., 1952; MS, Va. Commonwealth U., 1954. Psychologist So. Wis. Ctr., Union Grove, 1954-56; adminstrv. dir., psychologist Brown County Guidance Clinic, Green Bay, Wis., 1956-58; psychologist Larue Carter Hosp., Indpls., 1958-59, Washington-Ozaukee Guidance Clinic, West Bend, Wis., 1959-60; psychotherapist Family Svc. Milw., 1983-85, St. Rose Residence, Milw., 1985-88; bd. dirs. Family Svc., Waukesha, Wis., 1976-86; telephone counselor Underground Switchboard, Milw., 1982-84; facilitator parenting and living skills class Childrens Svc. Soc., Milw., 1989-93; psychotherapist, vol. Help Clinic, Waukesha, 1988—. Alumni admissions rep. Carleton Coll., 1982—; chmn. Civil Svc. Commn., Brookfield, Wis., 1988—. Named Outstanding Vol., The Women's Ctr., 1981-84, Mental Health Assn., 1989-93. Mem. P.E.O., Elderhostel (chmn.), Colonial Dames (bd. dirs.), Carleton Alumni Club Milw. (bd. dirs.). Home: 18050 Bonnie Ln Brookfield WI 53045-5429

WOLDMAN, SHERMAN, pediatrician; b. Buffalo, Apr. 1, 1932; s. Joseph Harry and Sadie (Weinstein) W. m. Fern Marlene Weinstein, Dec. 28, 1952; children Deborah Janine Case, Scott Alan, Sabina Heide Muller. BS in Pharmacy Magna Cum Laude, U. Buffalo, 1953, MD with High Hons., 1957. Diplomate Am. Bd. Pediatrics. Intern Millard Fillmore Hosp., Buffalo, 1957-58; resident in pediatrics Children's Hosp., Buffalo, 1958-60; pvt. practice in pediatrics Buffalo, 1961-66, Cheektowaga, N.Y., 1962—; adj. clin. asst. pediatrics, SUNY Sch. Medicine, Buffalo, 1962, clin. assoc.m 1970, clin. asst. prof., 1973, preceptor Sch. Nursing, 1976-82; attending pediatrician Booth Meml. Hosp., Buffalo, 1969-72; sch. physician Williamsville (N.Y.) Ctrl. Schs., 1962-94, chmn. of physicians, 1970-94; courtesy staff St. Joseph Intercomty. Hosp., Cheektowaga, 1963-80, Kenmore (N.Y.) Mercy Hosp., 1963-70, 1974-82, Sisters of Charity Hosp., Buffalo, 1991—, Erie County Med. Ctr., Buffalo, 1979-83, Buffalo Gen. Hosp., 1987-95; provisional staff Mercy Hosp., Buffalo, 1982-83, courtesy staff 1983—. Vol. Leukemia Soc. Am., 1975— , bd. trustees Western N.Y. chpt. 1975—, pres. 1977-79, v.p. 1979-81, mem. profl. edn. com. 1975—, mem. nat. bd. trustees 1978-87, vice chmn. patient aid com., 1980-87; mem. task force on sch. health Erie County (N.Y.) Health Dept; trustee Temple Beth David Ner-Israel, Buffalo, 1964-5. Recipient PREP Fellowship award Am. Acad. Pediatrics, 1979-85; (with Mrs. Fern Woldman) Recognition cert. Cheektowaga C. of C., 1982, Myron L. Woldman Vol. of Yr. award, Leukemia Soc. Am., Western N.Y. chpt. 1987, Disting. Physician award MIllard Fillmore Health System, 1995. Fellow Am. Acad. Pediatrics; mem. Med. Soc. State of N.Y., Buffalo Pediatric Soc. (pres. 1969-70), Gibson Anatomical Soc. (hon.), Med. Soc. County of Erie, N.Y. (chmn. pub. health com. 1978-79), Maimonides Med. Soc. (pres. Buffalo 1982-83), Alpha Omega Alpha, Rho Chi (pres. U. Buffalo chpt. 1952-53), Phi Lambda Kappa (pres. student chpt. 1955-56, alumni 1965, v.p. alumni 1980-81). Office: 4427 Union Rd Cheektowaga NY 14225-2397

WOLF, BARRY ZEV, physician; b. N.Y.C., Dec. 5, 1956; s. Henry and Rae (Spiegel) W.; m. Susan Poleyeff; children: Rachel, Shoshana, Aliza, Etana. BS, Touro Coll., 1978; MD, NYU, 1982. Resident Bellevue Hosp.,

N.Y.C., 1982-85; chief resident N.Y. VA Med. Ctr., N.Y.C., 1985-86; ptnr. Pulmonary Internists, Iselin, N.J., 1988—; chmn. respiratory care com. John F. Kennedy Med. Ctr., Edison, N.J., 1994—, med. dir. respiratory care, 1996—. NYU Med. Ctr. fellow, 1986-88; named one of N.J. Top Doctors, N.J. Monthly, 1996. Fellow Am. Coll. Chest Physicians; mem. AMA, Am. Thoracic Soc. Independent. Jewish. Home: 128 N 8th Ave Highland Park NJ 08904

WOLF, FREDRIC M., educational psychologist; b. Canton, Ohio, Aug. 7, 1945; s. Wayne S. and Anita (Manheim) W.; m. Leora DeLelys Lucas, Sept. 29, 1985; children: Jacob M. Claire D., Adam C.N. BS, U. Wis., 1967; postgrad. Law Sch. Georgetown U., 1967-68; MEd, Kent State U., 1977, PhD, 1980. Instr. math. Cuyahoga C.C., Cleve., 1978-79; rsch. assoc. behavioral scis. Northeastern Ohio U. Med. Coll., Rootstown, 1979-80; rsch. assoc. med. edn. Ohio State U. Coll. Medicine, Columbus 1980-82, clin. asst. prof. pediatrics, 1981-82; asst. prof. postgrad. medicine U. Mich. Med. Sch., Ann Arbor, 1982-87, assoc. prof. 1987-93, prof. 1993—; assoc. dir. edn. Mich. Diabetes Rsch. & Tng. Ctr., Ann Arbor, 1982-84; acting dir. 1984-85; vis. fellow U.K. Cochrane Ctr.; vis. scholar Green Coll., U. Oxford, Eng.; cons. Office Technology Assessment, U.S. Congress, 1987—; dir. Learning Resource Ctr. & Lab. Computing, Cognition, & Clin. Skills, 1990—; cons. Office Rsch. U.S. Dept. Edn., 1986—; cons. Nat. Heart Lung and Blood Inst. NIH, Bethesda, Md., 1985—, Nat. Inst. Deafness & Other Comm. Disorders, Small Bus. Innovation Rsch. Program; cons. NSF, NRC, NAS. Author: Meta-analysis: Quantitative Methods for Research Synthesis, 1986; co-editor: Software for Health Sciences Education: A Resource Catalog, 1994; book rev. editor Medical Decision Making, Editorial Boards: Evaluation & the Health Professions, Medical Decision Making, Cochrane Database of Systematic Reviews; contbr. articles to profl. jours. Vol. Peace Corps, L.Am., 1969-72. Grantee Mich. Dept. Pub. Health, 1984-86, Spencer Found., 1983-84, NIH, 1985—. Fellow APA, Am. Psychol. Soc., Royal Statis. Soc.; mem. AAAS, Am. Ednl. Rsch. Assn., Am. Statis. Assn., Midwestern Ednl. Rsch. Assn. (v.p. 1984-85, pres. 1986-87), Soc. Behavioral Medicine, Soc. Med. Decision Making, Sigma Xi. Office: U Mich Dept Postgrad Medicine G1208 Towsley Ctr Box 0201 Ann Arbor MI 48109-0201

WOLF, GREGORY THOMAS, physician, surgeon; b. Racine, Wis., Apr. 28, 1948; s. Lee J. and Margaret R. (Friedli) W.; m. Suzanne M. Vojtisek, Feb. 14, 1970; children: Michael, Melissa, Jenifer. BS, U. Notre Dame, 1969; MD, U. Mich., 1973. Diplomate AAO-HNS, AAFPRS. Resident in gen. surgery Georgetown U., Washington, 1973-75; resident in otolaryngology Upstate Med. Ctr., Syracuse, N.Y., 1975-78; fellow surgery br. NCI, NIH, Bethesda, Md., 1978-80; from asst. prof. to prof. U. Mich., Ann Arbor, 1980-89, prof., 1989—; chmn. otolaryngology dept. U. Mich., Ann Arbor, 1993—; attending physician Catherine McAuley Health Ctr., Ypsilanti, Mich., 1990—; dir. head and neck oncology U. Mich. Comprehensive Cancer Ctr., Ann Arbor, 1986—. Editor: Head and Neck Oncology, 1984, Head and Neck Oncology Research, 1988. Grantee VA Coop. Studies program, 1984-91, NIH, NIDCD, Univ. Mich., 1996—; named among 400 best cancer specialists Good Housekeeping, 1992. Fellow ACP, Am. Soc. Head Neck Surgery (coun. 1995—); mem. ASCO, Soc. Head Neck Surgeons. Republican. Roman Catholic. Home: 3428 Old Oak Ct Saline MI 48176 Office: Univ Mich 1904 H Taubman Ctr Ann Arbor MI 48109

WOLF, HAROLD HERBERT, pharmacy educator; b. Quincy, Mass., Dec. 19, 1934; s. John I. and Bertha F. (Sussman) W.; m. Joan Z. Silverman, Aug. 11, 1957; children: Gary Jerome, David Neal. B.S., Mass. Coll. Pharmacy, 1956; Ph.D., U. Utah, 1961; LLD (hon.), U. Md., 1994. Asst. prof. pharmacology Coll. Pharmacy Ohio State U., 1961-64, assoc. prof., 1964-69, prof., 1969-76, Kimberly prof., 1975-76, chmn. div. pharmacology, 1973-76; dean Coll. of Pharmacy, U. Utah, Salt Lake City, 1976-89, prof. pharmacology, 1989—, dir. Anticonvulsant Drug Devel. Program, 1989—; vis. prof. U. Sains Malaysia, 1973-74; mem. Nat. Joint Commn. on Prescription Drug Use, 1976-80; mem. NIH rev. com. Biomed. Rsch. Devel. Grant Program, 1978-79; external examiner U. Malaya, 1978, 92, 96, U. Sains Malaysia, 1980. Contbr. articles in field of central nervous system pharmacology and field of pharm. edn. Recipient Alumni Achievement award Mass. Coll. Pharmacy, 1978, Disting. Faculty award U. Utah, 1989, Rosenblatt prize, 1989, Disting. Alumnus award Coll. Pharmacy, U. Utah, 1991. Fellow AAAS, Acad. Pharm. Scis.; mem. Am. Soc. Pharmacology and Exptl. Therapeutics, Am. Pharm. Assn. (task force on edn. 1982-84), Am. Assn. Colls. of Pharmacy (pres. 1977, Disting. Pharmacy Educator award 1988, scholar in residence 1989, chmn. commn. on implementing change in pharmacy edn. 1989-92, 95-96), Am. Soc. Hosp. Pharmacists (commn. on goals 1982-84), Am. Coun. on Pharm. Edn. (bd. dirs. 1985-88), Soc. Neurosci. Jewish. Home: 4512 Bruce St Salt Lake City UT 84124-4720 Office: Univ Utah Coll Pharmacy Salt Lake City UT 84112

WOLF, JAMES STUART, surgeon, administrator; b. Chgo., Mar. 1, 1935; s. Carl Walter and Margaret Vera (Goddard) W.; m. Marjorie Ann Voytilla, July 26, 1958; children: James Stuart, Jr., Anne Elizabeth. AB, Grinnell Coll., 1957; MD, U. Ill., Chgo., 1961. Diplomate Am. Bd. Surgery. Resident in surgery Med. Coll. Va., Richmond, 1967, prof. surgery, 1968-76; chief of surgery McGuire VA Hosp., Richmond, 1968-76; prof. surgery Northwestern U., Chgo., 1976-94, assoc. dean med. edn., 1990-94, emeritus prof. surgery, 1994—; chmn. divsn. transplantation Northwestern U., 1976-91; pres. United Network for Organ Sharing, 1990-91, dir. med. affairs, 1994—; chmn. Regional Bank of Ill., Chgo., 1988-89; vice chmn. Ill. Network for End Stage Renal Disease, Chgo., 1984-88. Bd. dirs. Nat. Kidney Found., Chgo., 1984-91, Chgo. Episcopal Charities, Chgo., 1990-94. Recipient Gift of Life award Nat. Kidney Found., 1992. Fellow Am. Coll. Surgeons; mem. Ctrl. Surg. Soc., Soc. Univ. Surgeons, Am. Soc. Transplant Surgeons, Transplantation Soc., Focus Club Richmond. Republican. Home: 9800 Kingsbridge Rd Richmond VA 23233 Office: United Network forOrgan Sharing 1100 Boulders Pkwy Ste 500 Richmond VA 23225

WOLF, JOHN CHARLES, psychologist; b. St. Louis, Sept. 29, 1943; s. Howard August and Wilda Lucille (French) W.; m. Carole Sue Bruce, Oct. 21, 1967; children—Allan Bruce, Anne Elizabeth. B.S., Stephen F. Austin State U., 1964, M.A., 1967, M.Ed., 1969; Ph.D., N. Tex. State U., 1976. Staff psychologist Lufkin State Sch. for Mentally Retarded, 1966-67; instr. psychology Stephen F. Austin State U., 1967-68; dir. rehab. services Goodwill Industries, Fort Worth, 1969-70; counselor VA Guidance Ctr., Tex. Christian U., Fort Worth, 1970-73; counseling psychologist U.S. VA, Lubbock, Tex., 1978—; adj. instr. psychology South Plains Coll., Lubbock, 1973-91, named outstanding part-time faculty member, 1986-87. Mem. Lubbock County Com. on Employment of Handicapped. Contbr. articles to profl. jours. Bd. dirs. Lubbock Civic Chorale, 1983-85; mem. adv. bd., human svcs. South Plains Coll., 1975-87; vestryman St. Christopher Episcopal Ch., 1982-85, 90-92, 95—; mem. Diocese N.W. Tex. comm. ministry, 1986-91; bd. dirs. Dixie Little League, 1985-87; mem. Gen. Bd. Exam. Chaplains of Episcopal Ch., 1991—; mem. spiritual devel. com. N.W. Tex. Diocese, 1993—. Served with USNR, 1979-83. Recipient Outstanding Performance award VA, 1978, 82, 84-94. Mem. Am. Psychol. Assn., Am. MENSA, N.W. Tex. VA Psychol. Assn. (past pres.), Psi Chi, Kappa Delta Pi. Avocations: Choral singing; golf; hunting. Home: 3312 40th St Lubbock TX 79413-2728 Office: VA Office 4902 34th St Rm 134 Lubbock TX 79410-2342

WOLF, KEVIN JAY, podiatrist; b. Pasadena, Calif., May 25, 1961; s. Jay Roger and Phyllis Louise (Opplinger) W.; m. Ginny Kerwin Weber, Aug. 18, 1984; children: Rebecca, Matthew, William, Patrick. BS, U. Idaho, 1983; DPM, Calif. Coll. Podiatric Medicin, 1987. Podiatrist Fayette Podiatry, Uniontown, Pa., 1989-94; podiatrist, owner Goldsboro Podiatry, Goldsboro, N.C., 1994—. Contbr. articles to profl. jours. Mem. APMA, NCPMS, Kiwanis. Office: Goldsboro Podiatry 907 B Landmark Dr Goldsboro NC 27534

WOLF, LUDWIG, JR., biomedical engineer; b. Chgo., July 24, 1939; s. Ludwig and Paula (Hehl) W.; m. Kathleen Barbara Wroga, Oct. 7, 1972; 1 child, Ximen. BS, Ill. Inst. Tech., 1961, MS, 1963, PhD, 1974. Registered profl. engr., Ill. Rsch. engr. Ill. Inst. Tech. Rsch. Inst., Chgo., 1962-71; dir. Baxter Healthcare Corp., Round Lake, Ill., 1971—. Contbr. articles to sci. jours. NSF fellow, 1961. Mem. ASME, Am. Soc. Artificial Internal Organs, Am. Assn. Blood Banks. Office: Baxter Healthcare Route 120 At Wilson Rd Round Lake IL 60073

WOLF, ROBERT IRWIN, psychoanalyst, art and art therapy educator; b. N.Y.C., Mar. 30, 1947; s. Arthur and Bernice (Rosenwasser) W.; children: Joshua Corey, Rebecca Melissa. B Indsl. Design, Pratt Inst., 1968, M Profl. Studies, 1973. Cert. Am. Bds. for Cert. and Accreditation in Psychoanalysis. Clin. dir. Henry Street Settlement Sch., N.Y.C., 1973-80; prof. art and art therapy Coll. of New Rochelle (N.Y.) Grad. Sch., 1980—; pvt. practice psychoanalysis, art therapy and supervision, N.Y.C., 1974—; dir. Inst. for Expressive Analysis, N.Y.C., 1993-96; vis. prof. art Pratt Inst., Bklyn., 1976—; keynote speaker Delaware Valley Art Therapy Assn., 1979; guest lectr. Ill. Art Therapy Assn., 1980. Contbr. articles to profl. jours., chpt. to book; exhibited sculptures in numerous galleries throughout U.S. Recipient lst place sculpture award Ariel Gallery, N.Y.C., 1989. Mem. Nat. Psychol. Assn. for Psychoanalysis (sr.), Nat. Assn. for Advancement Psychoanalysis (cert.), Coun. Psychoanalytic Psychotherapists, Am. Art Therapy Assn. (registered, contbg. editor Art Therapy 1985—, workshop presenter 1970—), N.Y. Art Therapy Assn. (pres. 1975-76), Westchester Art Therapy Assn. (assoc.). Office: Coll New Rochelle Grad Art Programs New Rochelle NY 10801 also: 27 W 96th St New York NY 10025-6515

WOLF, SHARON ANN, psychotherapist; b. Dallas, May 13, 1951; d. Frank Allan and Ursula (Mohnblatt) W.; 1 child, Allan. BA in Psychology, New Eng. Coll., 1973; MA in Counseling Psychology, Antioch Grad. Sch., 1976; PhD in Clin. Psychology, Union Grad. Sch., 1989. Behavioral spl. ednl. planner Philbrook Children's Learning Ctr., Concord, N.H., 1972; asst. to spl. edn. cons. N.H. Hosp., Concord, 1972-73; spl. edn. planner Rochester (N.H.) Child Devel. Ctr., 1973; counseling practicum Morrill Sch., Concord, N.H., 1973; counseling practicum Contoocook Valley Mental Health Ctr., Henniker, N.H., 1973-74, counseling psychology intern, 1974-76; lab. instr. New Eng. Coll., Henniker, 1973; ednl. and guidance counselor asst. Hillsboro (N.H.)-Deering Sch. Dist., 1973-74; pediatric psychology intern parent-infant devel. program Ctrl. N.H. C.M.H. Ctr., Concord, 1986-87; assoc. psychologist Easter Seal Rehab. Ctr., Manchester, N.H., 1976-80, Ctrl. N.H. Community Mental Health Svcs., Concord, 1980-88; intern forensic psychology Concord Dist. Ct., 1987-88; pvt. practice Northfield, N.H., 1988—; psychol. cons. children and youth program Twin Rivers Counseling Ctr., Franklin, N.H. 1980-83, therapist, 1984-86; therapist Ctrl. N.H. Comm. Mental Health Ctr., 1980-83, Parent-Infant Devel. Program, Concord, N.H., 1983-88. Fellow Am. Orthopsychiat. Assn.; mem. Am. Assn. Suicidology, Am. Assn. Counseling and Devel., New England Coun. on Crime and Delinquency, N.H. Assn. of the Deaf, N.H. Registry of Interpreters for the Deaf. Office: PO Box 253 Tilton NH 03276-0253

WOLF, STEWART GEORGE, JR., physician, medical educator; b. Balt., Jan. 12, 1914; s. Stewart George and Angeline (Griffing) W.; m. Virginia Danforth, Aug. 1, 1942; children: Stewart George III, Angeline Griffing, Thomas Danforth. Student, Phillips Acad., 1927-31, Yale U., 1931-33; A.B., Johns Hopkins U., 1934, M.D., 1938; M.D. (hon.), U. Göteborg, Sweden, 1968. Intern N.Y. Hosp., 1938-39, resident medicine, 1939-42, NRC fellow, 1941-42; rsch. fellow Bellevue Hosp., 1939-42, clin. assoc. vis. neuropsychiatrist, 1946-52; rsch. head injury and motion sickness Harvard neurol. unit Boston City Hosp., 1942-43; asst., then assoc. prof. medicine Cornell U., 1946-52; prof., head dept. medicine U. Okla., 1952-67, Regents prof. medicine, psychiatry and behavioral scis., 1967—, prof. physiology, 1967-69; dir. Marine Biomed. Inst., U. Tex. Med. Br., Galveston, 1969-78; dir. emeritus Marine Biomed. Inst., U. Tex. Med. Br., 1978—, prof. medicine univ., also prof. internal medicine and physiology med. br., 1970-77; prof. medicine Temple U., Phila., 1977—; v.p. med. affairs St. Luke's Hosp., Bethlehem, Pa., 1977-82; dir. Totts Gap Inst., Bangor, Pa., 1958—; supr. clin. activities Okla. Med. Rsch. Found., 1953-55, head psychosomatic and neuromuscular sect., 1952-67, head neurosci. sect., 1967-69; adv. com. Space Medicine and Behavioral Scis., NASA, 1960-61; cons. internal medicine VA Hosp., Oklahoma City, 1952-69; cons. (European Office), Paris, Office Internat. Rsch., NIH, 1963-64; mem. edn. and supply panel Nat. Adv. Commn. on Health Manpower, 1966-67; mem. Nat. Adv. Heart Coun., 1961-65, U.S. Phamacopeia Scope Panel on Gastroenterology, Regent Nat. Libr. Medicine, 1965-69; chmn., 1968-69; mem. Nat. Adv. Environ. Health Scis. Coun., 1978-82; exec. v.p. Frontiers Sci. Found., 1967-69; mem. sci. adv. bd. Muscular Dystrophy Assns. Am., Inc., 1974-91, chmn., 1980-89; mem. gastrointestinal drug adv. com. FDA, 1974-77; bd. Internat. Cardiology Fedn.; mem. bd. visitors dept. biology Boston U., 1978-88; mem. vis. com. Ctr. for Social Rsch., Lehigh U., 1980-90; chmn. adv. com. Wood Inst. on History of Medicine, Coll. Physicians, Phila., 1980-90, mem. program com. Coll. Physicians, 1990-91; dir. Inst. for Advanced Studies in Immunology and Aging, 1988—. Author: Human Gastric Function, 1943, The Stomach, 1965, Social Environment and Health, 1981, others; adv. editor Internat. Dictionary Biology and Medicine, 1978—; editor in chief Integrative Physiol & Behavioral Sci.: The Official Jour. of Pavlovian Soc., 1990—. Pres. Okla. City Symphony Soc., 1956-61; mem. Okla. Sch. of Sci. and Math. Found., 1961—. Recipient Disting. Svc. Citation U. Okla., 1968, Dean's award for disting. med. svc., 1992; Horsley Gantt medal Pavlovian Soc., 1987, Hans Selye award Am. Inst. Stress, 1988, Rsch. award Carolinska Inst., Stockholm, 1994, Wilém Laufberger medal Acad. Scis. of Czech Republic, Citation for sci. and humanitarian achievement The J.E. Purkyně Bohemian Med. Assn. Fellow Am. Psychiat. Assn. (disting., trustee 1992—, Hofheimer prize for rsch. 1952); mem. AMA (coun. mental health 1960-64), Am. Soc. Clin. Investigation, Am. Clin. and Climatol. Assn. (pres. 1975-76), Assn. Am. Physicians, Am. Psychosomatic Soc. (pres. 1961-62), Am. Gastroent. Assn. (rsch. award 1943, pres. 1969-70), Am. Heart Assn. (chmn. com. profl. edn., com. internat. program, awards), Coll. Physicians Phila., Collegium Internat. Activitas Nervosae Superioris (exec. com. 1992—, pres. 1994), Philos. Soc. Tex., Sigma Xi, Alpha Omega Alpha, Omicron Delta Kappa. Club: Cosmos (Washington). Home: 1430 Totts Gap Rd Bangor PA 18013-9716 Office: Totts Med Rsch Labs Bangor PA 18013

WOLF, THOMAS MARK, psychologist, educator; b. Cin., Dec. 25, 1944; s. Herbert and Ursula (Wachtel) W.; m. Valerie Barbara Winchester, Sept. 20, 1969; 1 child, Mark Benjamin. BA, U. Cin., 1966; MA, Miami U., Oxford, Ohio, 1967; PhD, U. Waterloo, Ont., Can., 1971; fellow, St. Louis U., 1974-76. Lic. psychologist, La. From asst. to assoc. prof. SUNY, Cortland, 1970-75; from assoc. to prof. La. State U. Med. Ctr., New Orleans, 1975—; cons. psychologist St. Bernard Group Homes, Chalmette, La., 1979-86, Cen. City Mental Health Clinic, New Orleans, 1980-89, Assoc. Cath. Charities, New Orleans, 1987-89, Child and Adolescent Mental Health Program, New Orleans, 1989-96, New Orleans Target Cities Project, 1996—. Contbr. numerous articles to profl. jours. Mem. APA, La. Psychol. Assn., Soc. Behavioral Medicine, Assn. Am. Med. Colls., Soc. Profl. Well-Being, Nat. Wellness Assn. Democrat. Jewish. Home: 7046 Camp St New Orleans LA 70118-4808 Office: La State U Med Sch Dept Psychiatry 1542 Tulane Ave New Orleans LA 70112-2825

WOLF, WENDY JANE, pediatrician, educator; b. Cin., Jan. 12, 1952; d. John Howell and Jane (Belmeur) W. BA, Denison U., Granville, Ohio, 1974; MD, Ohio State U., 1977. Intern Children's Hosp. of L.A., 1977-78, resident, 1978-80, fellow, 1980-82; faculty physician U. Tex. Med. Br., Galveston, Tex., 1982-93; prof. pediatrics U. Tex. Health Sci. Ctr., Houston, 1993—; pediatric cardiologist U. Tex. Health Sci. Ctr., Houston, 1993—. Fellow Am. Coll. Cardiology, Am. Heart Assn. (bd. mem. Galveston and Houston); mem. Internat. Soc. Heart Rsch., Soc. Pediatric Echocardiography, Alpha Omega Alpha. Office: U Tex Health Sci Ctr 6431 Fannin MSB 3.132 Houston TX 77030

WOLFE, CAROLINE MARGARET, nurse; b. Toledo, Dec. 9, 1943; d. Russet John and Angela Frances (Kelly) DuMont; m. Warren Dwight Wolfe, Dec. 29, 1973; children—Mark Russet, Jeremy Dean, Jason Kelly. Diploma in nursing St. Vincent Hosp., Toledo, 1964; B.S. in Nursing, Mary Manse Coll., Toledo, 1966. RN, Ohio; cert. clin. transplant coord., cert. nephrology nurse. Staff nurse, asst. head nurse ICU, Maumee Valley Hosp., Toledo, 1964-69; asst. head nurse hemodialysis Med. Coll. of Ohio, Toledo, 1969-71, head nurse hemodialysis, 1971-73, head nurse renal unit, 1973-75, staff nurse renal unit, 1978-81, clin. transplant coord., 1981—, sr. cons. Health Systems Concepts, Inc., 1987—. Co-author: (with others) An Instrument to Identify Stressors in Renal Transplant Recipients, 1989. Mem. Am. Nephrology Nurses Assn., N.Am. Transplant Coords. Orgn., Kidney Found. Northwestern Ohio (pres. 1970-72, sec. 1973-74). Democrat. Avocations: skiing, reading, bowling. Home: 5617 Dianne Ct Toledo OH 43623-1076 Office: Med Coll of Ohio PO Box 10008 Toledo OH 43699

WOLFE, LISA HELENE, psychologist; b. Phila., Jan. 15, 1959; d. Stuart and Barbara Joyce (Blumenburg) W. BA, U. Pa., 1981; AM, Harvard U., 1985, PhD, 1989. Lic. psychologist. Teaching fellow Harvard U., 1983-88; psychology intern Mass. Mental Health Ctr., Boston, 1988-89; psychology fellow N.Y. Hosp./Cornell Med. Ctr., White Plains, 1989-91; sr. staff psychologist Met. Hosp., N.Y.C., 1991; staff psychologist Ctr. for Women's Devel.-HRI Hosp., Brookline, Mass., 1992-95; supr. The Trauma Ctr. at Human Resource Inst., Brookline, 1995—; pvt. practice psychology, 1992—. Author: (with others) (book chpt.) The Cognitive Rehabilitation of Learning Disabilities, 1987. Mem. adv. bd. Women's Supported Housing and Empowerment Inc. Mem. APA (divsns. 30, 39), Am. Assn. Applied and Preventive Psychology, Pi Gamma Mu. Office: Watertown MA 02172

WOLFE, MARCI K., optometrist; b. Detroit, Oct. 17, 1957; d. Bennett O. and Betty J. (Hoffman) W.; m. Daniel P. Kramer, Aug. 8, 1982; children: Jeffrey Kramer, Jillian Kramer. Student, Mich. State U., 1975-78; BS, Pa. Coll. Optometry, Phila., 1980, OD, 1982. Optometrist Cumberland Eye Assocs., Vineland, N.J., 1984-88; optometrist, v.p. Marlton (N.J.) Eye Associates, P.C., 1987—; pres. South Jersey Sports Vision ctr., Marlton, 1995—. Treas. Circle of Friends, Cherry Hill, N.J., 1992-94. Mem. Internat. Sports Vision Assn. Office: Marlton Eye Assocs PC 105A Evesboro-Medford Rd Marlton NJ 08053

WOLFERTH, CHARLES CHRISTIAN, surgeon, educator; b. Phila., July 31, 1928; s. Charles Christian and Mary (Comber) W.; m. Mary Fances Halsey; children: Mary, Charles III, John, Catherine. Student, Yale U., 1945-47, St. Joseph's U., 1947-48; MD, U. Pa., 1954. Intern Hosp. U. Pa., 1954-55, resident, 1955-60; adj. prof. surgery Hahnemann U. Hosp., Phila., 1988—; Emilie and Roland T. deHellebranth prof. surgery U. Pa., Phila., 1989—; surgeon-in-chief, chmn. The Grad. Hosp., Phila., 1989—; surg. resident program dir. Grad. Hosp., Phila., 1989—. Co-author: Advances in Trauma, Vols. I thru X, 1986-96. Recipient Proclamation/Appreciation award Bd. Suprs. San Diego, 1987. Fellow ACS (bd. govs. 1988-91, trauma achievement award 1988, outstanding leadership in hosp. categorizaiton Ea. States Com. on Trauma 1988); mem. Am. Trauma Soc. (bd. dirs. 1985-90), Am. Assn. Surg. Trauma, Ea. Surg. Soc., Del. Valley Vascular Soc. (pres. 1979-82), Phila. Acad. Surgery (pres. 1984-85), Internat. Cardiovascular Soc., Soc. Vascular Surgery, Soc. Surgery Alimentary Tract, Soc. Internationale de Chirugie, Phila. Country Club, Merion Golf Club. Office: The Grad Hosp-Dept Surgery Pepper Pavilion 1800 Lombard St Ste 1101 Philadelphia PA 19146-1414

WOLFF, EDWARD, physician; b. N.Y.C., Apr. 15, 1941; s. Julius and Molly W.; m. Marilyn Alice Pels; children: Shanna, Loryn, Kimberly. BS, Muhlenberg Coll., 1958; MD, Georgetown U., 1966. Intern U. Ala. Hosp., Brimingham, 1966-67; resident N.Y. Med. Coll., N.Y.C., 1967-71; physician pvt. practice, Great Neck, N.Y., 1976—; sr. asst. attending North Shore U. Hosp., Manhasset, N.Y.; attending physician St. Francis Hosp. Heart Ctr., Roslyn, N.Y. Contbr. articles to profl. jours. Fellow Am. Coll. Physicians; mem. AMA, N.Y. State Med. Soc., NAssau County Med. Soc. Office: 75 S Midle Neck Rd Great Neck NY 11021

WOLFF, JAMES ALEXANDER, SR., pediatrician, educator; b. N.Y.C., June 19, 1914; s. William Frederick and Blanche Hortense (Reitlinger) W.; m. Janet Loeb, June 24, 1946; children: James Alexander Jr., John K., Barbara Ann Wolff Bullard, Timothy G. BA, Harvard U., 1935; MD, NYU, 1940. Diplomate Am. Bd. Pediatrics, Am. Bd Hematology and Oncology. Prof. pediatrics Coll. Physicians and Surgeons, Columbia U., N.Y.C., 1968-81, prof. emeritus, 1981—; dir. cancer control Comprehensive Cancer Ctr. Columbia U., 1979-81; dir. Valerie Fund Children's Ctr. for Cancer and Blood Disorders, Overlook Hosp., Summit, N.J., 1981-88; ret., 1988; cons. in field. Contbr. articles to profl. jours. Served to capt. U.S. Army, 1942-45, ETO. Decorated Silver Star. Mem. Am. Pediatric Soc., N.Y. Soc. for Study of Blood (pres. 1966-67), Internat. Soc. Pediatric Oncology. Clubs: Harvard U. (N.Y.C.); Edgartown (Mass.) Yacht. Home: 518 Isle Of Capri Dr Fort Lauderdale FL 33301-2440 Other: PO Box 5112 Edgartown MA 02539

WOLFF, RONALD KEITH, toxicologist, researcher; b. Brantford, Ont., Can., July 25, 1946; s. Roy Clifford and Agnes Audrey (Stratton) W.; m. Mary Carole Cromien Wolff, Aug. 26, 1972; children: Mark, Sarah, Andrew, Brian. BS, U. Toronto, 1964-68; MS, 1968-69, PhD, 1969-72. Diplomate Am. Bd. Toxicology, 1983. Rsch. assoc. McMaster U., Hamilton, Can., 1973-76; scientist Lovelace Inhalation Toxicology Rsch. Inst., Albuquerque, N.Mex., 1976-88; rsch. scientist Eli Lilly and Co., Greenfield, Ind., 1988—. Author: (book chpt.) Comprehensive Treatise on Pulmonary Toxicology, 1992; contbr. articles to profl. jours. Recipient Frank Blood award Soc. Toxicology, 1989. Mem. Am. Assn. for Aerosol Rsch., Internat. Soc. Aerosols in Medicine, Soc. Toxicology, Am. Indsl. Hygiene Assn. Office: Lilly Rsch Labs PO Box 708 Greenfield IN 46140-0708

WOLFF, STEVEN, organic chemist; b. N.Y.C., Apr. 15, 1943; s. Werner and Alice (Eckstein) W.; m. Mary Lou Snow, Aug. 25, 1968 (div. 1981); 1 child, Elizabeth; m. Lynne Feigenbaum, Aug. 19, 1984; 1 child, Avery. B.A., Williams Coll., 1965; Ph.D., Yale U., 1970. Postdoctoral fellow Squibb Inst. for Med. Research, New Brunswick, N.J., 1970-71; research assoc. Rockefeller U., N.Y.C., 1971-73, asst. prof., 1973-78, assoc. prof., 1978-87; rsch. leader Hoffmann-La Roche, Nutley, N.J. Mem. Am. Chem. Soc., Royal Soc. Chemistry, InterAm. Photochem. Soc., Phi Beta Kappa. Office: Hoffmann-La Roche 340 Kingsland St Nutley NJ 07110-1150

WOLFF, TERESA TREINEN, educator; b. Sidney, Nebr., Dec. 2, 1950; d. John Neal and Dorothy Catherine (Fehringer) Treinen; m. Albert J. Wolff, Feb. 15, 1980; children: Albert Zeb, Benjamin John. BSN, Creighton U., 1972; MS in Nursing, U. N.Mex., 1979. Staff nurse, head nurse VA Med. Ctr., Omaha and Cheyenne, Wyo.; instr. nursing Laramie County Community Coll., Cheyenne; pub. health planner State Wyo., Cheyenne, pub. health patient care specialist; sr. lectr. U. Wyo., Laramie; past chmn. Wyo. Commn. Nursing and Nursing Edn. Mem. ANA, Wyo. Nurses Assn., Sigma Theta Tau.

WOLFFERS, IVAN, healthcare educator, writer; b. Amersfoort, The Netherlands, May 17, 1948; m. Marion Bloem, June, 1971; 1 child, Kaja. MD, Utrecht State U., The Netherlands, 1975; PhD in Med. Anthropology, Leiden State U., The Netherlands, 1987. Writer Volkskrant Vrij Nederland, Amsterdam, The Netherlands, 1976-83; cons. Novib IOCU, The Hague and Penang, The Netherlands and Malaysia, 1980-85; prof. social medicine Free U., Amsterdam, 1989—; coun. mem. Advice for Min. of Devel. Coop., The Hague, 1990—; cons. in field numerous countries including Indonesia, Vietnam, Thailand, Sri Lanka, Uganda. Author: Medicynen, 1976, 11th edit., 1996, A Short Course for Beginners in Love, 1987 (prize 1987), The Last Traveling Salesman, 1980, Darling, My Darling, 1992. Office: Amsterdam U Dept Soc Med, ud Boechorststr 7, 1081 BT Amsterdam The Netherlands

WOLFLEY, VERN ALVIN, dentist; b. Etna, Wyo., Aug. 4, 1912; s. Rudolf E. and Eliza (Neuenschwander) W.; m. Bernice Michaelson, June 12, 1936; children: Norda Beth Wolfley Brimley, Vern A. Jr., Paul R., Carol Jo Wolfley Bennett. BS, U. Wyo., 1934; BS in Dentistry and DDS, U. Nebr., 1947. Farm mgmt. specialist USDA, 1934-43; placement officer War Relocation Authority, 1943; pvt. practice, Idaho Falls, Idaho, 1947-57, Phoenix, 1957—. Pres. Ariz. Children's Soc., Phoenix, 1960-61. With AUS, 1943; lst lt. USAF, 1954. Mem. ADA (life), Ariz. Dental Assn. (life), Idaho Falls Dental Soc. (pres. 1949-50), Upper Snake River Dental Soc. (pres. 1955-56), Am. Soc. Dentistry for Children (life), Acad. Gen. Dentistry, Internat. Assn. Orthodontics (life), Am. Assn. Functional Orthodontists (charter), Fedn. Dentaire Internat., Cen. Ariz. Dist. Dental Soc. (life), Am. Legion, Lions (v.p. 1956), Omicron Kappa Upsilon, Alpha Zeta. Republican. Mem. LDS Ch. Home: 7819 W Banff Ln Peoria AZ 85381 Office: 2837 W Northern Ave Phoenix AZ 85051-6646

WOLFMAN, ALAN, medical educator, researcher; b. Bronx, N.Y., Mar. 12, 1956; married. Postdoctoral fellow dept. biophysics U. Rochester Med. Ctr., 1988-90; asst. staff dept. cell biology Cleve. Clinic Found., 1990—; adj. prof. dept. biology Cleve. State U., 1994—. Contbr. articles to profl. jours.;

periodic reviewer for Molecular Cellular Biology, Jour. Biol. Chemistry, Biochemistry, BBA; ad hoc reviewer for program project Nat. Inst. Diabetes and Digestive and Kidney Diseases, 1995; invited reviewer for DRTC Pilot Project Ind. U., 1995—; presenter in field. Recipient NIH Postdoctoral fellowship award, 1985-88, Established Investigatorship award Am. Heart Assn., 1996—; NIH First grant, 1988-93, Cell Biology Tng. grant, 1979. Office: Cleve Clinic Found Rsch Inst Dept Cell Biology NC10 9500 Euclid Ave Cleveland OH 44195

WOLFORT, FRANCIS GABRIEL, plastic surgeon; b. N.Y.C., Aug. 6, 1933; s. Francis G. and Margaret M. (Maher) W.; m. Floreen Fazendin, Nov. 28, 1959; children—Ramona, Sean, Maria. BS, MIT, 1954; MD, SUNY, 1958. Diplomate Am. Bd. Surgery, Am. Bd. Plastic Surgery (dir. 1996—). Resident in surgery Boston City Hosp., 1961-66, Mass. Gen. Hosp., 1966-67; resident in plastic surgery Johns Hopkins Hosp., 1967-69, fellow in surgery, asst. prof. surgery, 1969-70; dir. plastic surgery Balt. City Hosp., 1969-70; dir. plastic surgery Cambridge Hosp., Harvard U., 1970—, dir. surg. services, 1976-89, program dir. plastic surg. residency, 1970—; asso. prof. surgery Harvard U. Editor: Acute Hand Injuries-a Multispecialty Approach, 1978, Aesthetic Blepharoplasty, 1995; contbr. articles to med. jours. Served with USN, 1960-62. Fellow ACS, Am. Assn. Plastic Surgeons (trustee 1996), Am. Soc. Surgery of the Hand, Am. Soc. Head and Neck Surgeons; mem. Am. Soc. Plastic and Reconstructive Surgery, Am. Burn Assn., Am. Assn. Surgery of Trauma, Plastic Surgery Rsch. Coun. Home: 33 Monadnock Rd Wellesley MA 02181-1333 Office: Cambridge Hospital 1493 Cambridge St Cambridge MA 02139-1047 : 110 Francis St Boston MA 02215-5501

WOLFSON, DAVID JOHN, pharmacist and researcher; b. Liverpool, Merseyside, U.K., Feb. 21, 1946; s. Myer and Sara (Chmielnicki) W.; m. Eunice Florence Inestone, Mar. 3, 1974; children: Sara, Rebecca, Deborah, Eliot, Nadia. BSc, Liverpool John Moores U., 1969, PhD in Mgmt. Studies, 1985. Pharmacist/sr. pharmacist Walton & Fazakerley Hosps., U.K., 1970-71; dep. chief pharmacist Alder Hey Children's Hosp., U.K., 1971-73; prin. pharmacist Whiston Hosp., Prescot, U.K., 1973-90; dir. Mersey Acad. Pharmacy Practice Unit, Prescot, 1990—; module leader U. Liverpool, 1994—; module leader/rsch. project liaison officer Liverpool John Moores U., 1991—; advisor WHO, 1991—; mem. East Cheshire Prescribing Interface Working Group, 1992-95, St. Helens & Knowsley Drug and Therapeutics Com., 1974—; organising com. Nat. Drug Info. Conf., 1993-94; mem. Med. Benefit/Risk Found., 1994—. Editor: Adverse Drug Reactions, 1994; author/pub.: Alder Hey Book of Children's Doses, 1973; contbr. articles to profl. jours. Recipient Nicholas award Guild Hosp. Pharmacists, 1980, Ciba Geigy award, 1990. Fellow Royal Pharm. Soc. Gr. Britain (vice chmn. BPC Pharmacy Practice Adjudicating Panel 1994—), U.K. Clin. Pharmacy Assn. Jewish. Home: 204 Queens Dr Wavertree, Liverpool L15 6XX, United Kingdom Office: Mersey Acad Pharmacy Practice, Warrington Rd, Prescot L35 5DR, United Kingdom

WOLFSON, JAY, public health educator, consultant, lecturer, lawyer; b. Chgo., July 13, 1952; s. Max Joseph and Ida (Kolender) W.; m. Maxine Loren Coplan, May 4, 1988; children: Alan H., Marc J. AB, U. Ill., 1973; MA, NYU, 1974; MPH, Ind. U., 1975; DrPH, U. Tex., 1981; JD, Stetson Coll., 1993. Asst. prof. health adminstrn. Sch. Pub. Health U. S.C., Columbia, 1978-80; assoc. prof. health adminstrn. Coll. of Pub. Health U. Okla., Oklahoma City, 1981-84; v.p. Health Cost Mgmt., Inc., Tampa, Fla., 1984—; assoc. prof. healthcare, fin. & poicy Coll. Pub. Health, U. South Fla., Tampa, 1991-95; prof. health law and fin. U. South Fla. Coll. Pub. Health, Tampa, 1995—; chair dept. pub. health policy and mgmt. Coll. Pub. Health U. South Fla., dir. Fla. Pub. Health Info. Ctr., 1991—; trustee, chair fin. com. Tampa Gen. Hosp., 1988—; dir. Fla. Pub. Health Info. Ctr., 1990—; vis. prof. Tokyo U. Coll. of Medicine, 1985; sr. fin. cons. Fla. Office of Pub. Counsel, Tallahassee, 1986—; cons. Fla . Dept. Ins., Tallahassee, 1987—, Fla. Dept. Health and Rehab. Svcs., Tallahassee, 1987—, Dun & Bradstreet Co., N.Y.C., 1987—; mem. U.S. Senate Health Care Adv. Com., 1990—; prof. health law and finance Coll. Pub. Health U. South Fla., 1995—. Author: Managing Employee Health Benefits, 1985; contbr. articles to profl. jours. Trustee Hillsborough County Hosp. Authority, Tampa, 1988—. Marcus and Teresa Levi scholar NYU, 1974; W.K. Kellogg Found. fellow, 1983; Sr. Fulbright scholar to Japan, 1985. Mem. Am. Pub. Health Assn., Health Care Fin. Mgmt. Assn. (chair Blue Cross com. 1989—), Am. Coll. Healthcare Execs. Jewish. Office: U South Fla Coll Pub Health 13301 N 30th St Tampa FL 33612-3807

WOLFSON, LAWRENCE AARON, hospital administrator; b. Chgo., July 11, 1941; s. Norman William and Doris D. (Brownstein) W.; m. Cheryl Jean Vogel, Feb. 6, 1987; children: Marc David, Sara Elizabeth, Aaron Michael, Ryan Anthony, Ashley Michelle. BA in Biology, Ind. U., South Bend, 1973, MBA, 1980. Sales rep. Gen. Med. Corp., South Bend, 1973-75, Hoechst-Roussel Pharmaceuticals, Somerville, N.J., 1975-79; purchasing agt. Simon Bros., Inc., South Bend, 1979-81; purchasing mgr. Ingalls Meml. Hosp., Harvey, Ill., 1981-83; dir. purchasing Community Hosp., Munster, Ind., 1983-86; corp. purchasing mgr. Columbus-Cuneo-Cabrini Med. Ctr., Chgo., 1986-88; materials mgmt. cons. South Western Med. Ctr., Chgo., 1988-91; asst. dir. materials mgmt. Michael Reese Hosp. and Med. Ctr., Chgo., 1989-91; dir. material mgmt. Regional Med. Ctr. at Memphis, 1991—; mem. editorial bd. Hosp. Material Mgmt. Quarterly, Aspens Pubs. Cubmaster Cub Scouts, South Bend, 1976-78, Cub Scouts, Cordova, 1995—. With USN, 1961-71. Mem. Am. Soc. Hosp. Materials Mgmt., Healthcare Materials Mgmt. Soc. (regional rep. 1984, cert. profl. in health care material mgmt., Material Mgr. of Yr. 1995), Nat. Assn. Purchasing Mgmt., Am. Soc. Clin. Pathologists (affiliate), Am. Legion, B'nai Brith (pres. 1980-81). Jewish.

WOLFSON, LEONARD LOUIS, bacteriologist, corporate administrator; b. Wilkes-Barre, Pa., Dec. 13, 1922; s. Samuel and Fannie (Schildkraut) W.; m. Doris Constance Rosenfeld; 1 child, Mark David. BS, U. Chgo., 1949, MS, 1951. Research bacteriologist U. Ill., Chgo., 1952-54, Wilson & Co., Chgo., 1954-57; research bacteriologist Nalco Chem. Co., Chgo., 1957-60, group leader, 1961-67; sr. research assoc. Indsl. BioTest Labs., Northbrook, Ill., 1967-70; dir. quality control Will Ross Inc., Milw., 1970-77; pres. Wilro Sci. Labs., Brown Deer, Wis., 1972-78; corp. dir. quality assurance and regulatory affairs Ipco Corp., White Plains, N.Y., 1978-88; cons. med. devices, drugs, cosmetics, health and safety Hartsdale, N.Y., 1988—. Patentee numerous slime control agts.; contbr. articles to profl. jours. Pres. Home Owners Property Assn., Tinley Park, Ill., 1959-61. Mem. Am. Soc. Microbiology, N.Y. Acad. Scis. Democrat. Jewish. Home and Office: 36 Maplewood Rd Hartsdale NY 10530-1624

WOLFZAHN, ANNABELLE FORSMITH, psychologist; b. N.Y.C., Jan. 23, 1932; d. Paul Phillip and Addie (Glassman) Forsmith; m. Herbert Eytan Wolfzahn, Feb. 4, 1956; children: Risa Wolfzahn Herskowitz, Felice, Orna. BA, Hunter Coll., 1953; MA in Counseling Psychology, Manhattan Coll., 1971; PhD in Clin. and Community Psychology, Union Inst., 1979. Cert. sch. psychologist, sch. counselor, N.Y. Counselor for handicapped children Bklyn. Tuberculosis Assn., 1952; social worker Child Placement Svcs., N.Y.C., 1953-58; fellow in social and community psychiatry Albert Einstein Coll. Medicine, 1977-79; intern Bronx (N.Y.) Devel. Svcs., 1977-79; intern head trauma program Rusk Inst., NYU Med. Ctr., 1979; psychologist Creedmore Psychiat. Ctr., 1980-82, Harlem Valley Psychiat. Ctr., 1982-87; clin. coord. of group homes Green Chimneys Children's Svcs., 1987-88; with Ulpan Akiva and Assaf Harofeh Med. Ctr., Tel Aviv U., Israel, 1988-89; nursing home cons., psychotherapist Bklyn. Ctr. for Psychotherapy, 1989-91; pres., coord. Westchester chpt. Vols. for Israel, 1992—; freelance psychologist, counselor, 1994—; mem. workshops in field; mem. staff Mother-Child Home Program of White Plains, N.Y., 1975-76; counselor with multiple sclerosis victims and their families. Contbr. articles to profl. publs. Vol. Vols. for Israel, 1988, 91-92, founder, pres., coord. Westchester Region chpt., 1993—; mem. archaeol. dig Bet Shaan, Israel. Recipient Vol. award White Plains Hosp., 1974-76, John C. Klein Meml. Writing award Newspaper Inst. Am., 1965; Alvin Johnson scholar, 1953. Mem. APA, Westchester County Psychol. Assn., N.Y. Neuropsychology Assn., Am. Mental Health Affiliates of Israel, N.Y. Acad. Scis., Nat. Coun. Jewish Women, Am. Orthopsychiat. Assn. Home and Office: 34 Springdale Rd Scarsdale NY 10583-7329

WOLIN, MICHAEL STUART, physiology educator; b. Bklyn., Sept. 11, 1953; s. Emanuel and Anita (Klein) W.; m. Theresa Marie Burke, Oct. 25, 1987; children: Joshua Mark, Seth Adam, Sarah Rachel. BA in Chemistry, SUNY, Binghamton, 1975; MS, Yale U., 1977, MPhil, 1978, PhD, 1981. NIH Nat. Rsch. Svc. fellow Tulane U. Sch. Medicine, New Orleans, 1981-82, instr. pharmacology, 1982-83; asst. prof. physiology N.Y. Med. Coll., Valhalla, 1983-89, assoc. prof., 1989-95; prof., 1995—; prin. investigator NIH, 1984—. Assoc. editor Am. Jour. Physiology, 1993—; mem. editl. bd. Microcirculation Jour., 1994—. Recipient Merit award NIH, 1996—; Biomed. rsch. scholar C.H. Revson Found., 1983-85. Mem. AAAS, Am. Thoracic Soc. (sci. program com. 1990-95), Am. Heart Assn. (vice chmn. 1995-96, chmn. 1996—, cardiopulmonary coun. 1984—, sci. program com. 1986-93, established investigator 1989-94, cardiovascular rsch. study com. 1992-95, co-chmn. Lung & Devel. Rsch. study com. 1995—, mem. rsch. com. 1995—, Albert Hyman award La. chpt. 1983), Am. Physiol. Soc., Nitric Oxide Soc., Oxygen Soc. Microcirculatory Soc. (chmn. devel. com. 1994-95). Jewish. Home: 40 Goodwin Ave White Plains NY 10607-1014 Office: NY Med Coll Dept Physiology Valhalla NY 10595

WOLINSKY, IRA, nutritionist; b. N.Y.C., Mar. 30, 1938; s. Abraham and Rachel (Stupsky) W.; m. Mary Ann C. Leonard, Jan. 9, 1965; children: Daniella, David. BS, CCNY, 1960; MS, Kans. U., 1965, PhD, 1968. Lectr. Hebrew U., Jerusalem, 1968-74; assoc. prof. Pa. State U., University Park, 1974-79; prof. U. Houston, 1979—. Editor of books and series on nutrition sci., sports nutrition, nutrition methods; contbr. articles to profl. jours. Office: U Houston Dept Human Devel Houston TX 77204

WOLINTZ, ARTHUR HARRY, physician, neuro-ophthalmologist; b. Bklyn., May 30, 1937; s. Louis and Celia (Ragofsky) W.; m. Carol Sue Bergstein, Nov. 28, 1963; children: Robyn Joy, Ellen Sharon. Student, NYU, 1955-58; MD summa cum laude, SUNY, Bklyn., 1962; postgrad., Columbia U., 1967-68. Diplomate Am. Bd. Psychiatry and Neurology, Am. Bd. Ophthalmology; licensee Nat. Bd. Med. Examiners, U. State of N.Y. Intern Maimonides Hosp., Bklyn., 1962-63, jr. resident in medicine, 1963-64; resident Nat. Inst. Neurol. Diseases and Blindness, Bethesda, Md., 1964-66; chief resident Mt. Sinai Hosp., N.Y.C., 1966-67; clin. asst. prof. neurology Downstate Med. Ctr. SUNY, Bklyn., 1968-69, resident in ophthalmology, 1969-71, from asst. prof. to prof., 1971—, prof. clin. ophthalmology and clin. neurology, 1977—, interim chief ophthalmology, 1983, acting regional chmn. dept. ophthalmology, 1984, prof. ophthalmology, 1987—, chmn. dept. ophthalmology, 1987-96; asst. neurologist Presbyn. Hosp., N.Y.C., 1967-68; instr. neuropathology Coll. Physicians and Surgeons Columbia U., N.Y.C., 1967-68; instr. neurology Mt. Sinai Sch. Medicine, N.Y.C., 1967-68; assoc. dir. neurology Maimonides Med. Ctr., Bklyn., 1968-69; asst. neurologist Coney Island Hosp., Bklyn., 1968-69; vis. neurologist Kings County Hosp. Ctr., Bklyn, 1968-69; chief div. ophthalmology and neuro-ophthalmology Kingsbrook Jewish Med. Ctr., Bklyn., 1971, sec. med. and dental staff 1976-77, v.p. 1978-79, pres. 1980-81, dir. ophthalmology 1981; attending physician State Univ. Hosp., Bklyn., 1971, Kings County Hosp. Ctr., Bklyn., 1971; cons. Luth. Med. Ctr., Beth Israel Med. Ctr., Brookdale Hosp. Med. Ctr., Bklyn., L.I. Coll. Hosp., Bklyn., Maimonides Med. Ctr., Cath. Med. Ctr. Bklyn. and Queens, Bklyn. VA Hosp. Author: Essentials of Clinical Neuro-Ophthalmology, 1976; contbr. chpts. to sci. textbooks and handbooks, articles to profl. jours. Treas. Flatbush Jewish Ctr., Bklyn. With USPHS 1964-66. Recipient J. Eugene Chalfin Meml. Lectr. award Alumni Assn. State Univ.-Kings County, 1981, Tchr. of Yr. award dept. ophthalmology Interfaith Med. Ctr., 1988; named Disting. Teaching Prof. SUNY, 1995. Fellow ACP, ACS, Am. Acad. Ophthalmology and Otolaryngology, Am. Acad. Neurology; mem. AMA, Med. Soc. County Kings, Med. Soc. State N.Y., Bklyn. Ophthal. Soc., N.Y. Acad. Medicine, AAAS, Am. Acad. Neurology, Alumni Assn. SUNY (Master Tchr. award 1987, pres.-elect 1989, pres. 1990-91), Oddfellows, Alpha Omega Alpha. Home and Office: 100 Ocean Pky Brooklyn NY 11218-1755

WOLKOW, ALAN EDWARD, chiropractic physician; b. Bklyn., Nov. 9, 1946; s. Benjamin and Leanora (Pliner) W.; m. Terri Lynn Blumenfeld, May 29, 1977; children: Jana, Darren, Michael. AA, CUNY, 1966; BSME, N.Y. Inst. Tech., 1969; postgrad. mech. engring., U. Conn., 1970-71, engr.-in-tng., 1976; DChiropractic cum laude, Life Coll., Marietta, Ga., 1933. Nat. bd. qualified chiropractic orthopedist; cert. CPR; lic. real estate salesman, Ga. Mech. engr. Pratt & Whitney Aircraft Co., East Hartford, Conn., 1969-72, Combustion Engring., Windsor, Conn., 1972-74, Ebasco Svcs., Norcross, Ga., 1974-77, Simons Eastern Co., Decatur, Ga., 1977-79, Austin Co., Atlanta, 1979-80; pvt. practice Wolkow Chiropractic Clinic PC, Duluth, Ga., 1984—; injury prevention cons. Swift Atlanta, Suwanee, Ga., 1987-94. Area coord. Nat. Assn. for Seatbelt Safety,Duluth, 1984—; mem. spkr.'s bur. Ga. Safety Belt Coalition, Atlanta, 1985—, Arthritis Found. Ga., Atlanta, 1987—; asst. advisor B'nai B'rith Youth Orgn., Atlanta, 1978-93. Recipient Cornerstone award PMA, Inc., 1985, Comdr. award, 1986, Chancellor award, 1987; recognition award Found. for Advancement Chiropractic Edn., 1988. Mem. ASME, Am. Chiropractic Assn., Ga. Chiropractic Assn., Nat. Back Found., Am. Coll. Chiropractic Orthopedists, Coun. on Diagnostic Imaging, Parker Chiropractic Resource Found., Kiwanis. Democrat. Jewish. Home: 3754 Loveland Ter Atlanta GA 30341-1742 Office: 1625 Pleasant Hill Rd Ste 170 Duluth GA 30136-5863

WOLLERSHEIM, JANET PUCCINELLI, psychology educator; b. Anaconda, Mont., July 24, 1936; d. Nello J. and Inez Marie (Ungaretti) Puccinelli; m. David E. Wollersheim, Aug. 1, 1959 (div. June 1972); children: Danette Marie, Tod Neil; m. Daniel J. Smith, July 17, 1976. AB, Gonzaga U., 1958; MA, St. Louis U., 1960; PhD, U. Ill., 1968. Lic. psychologist, Mont. Asst. prof. psychology, asst. dir. testing and counseling ctr. U. Mo., 1968-71; prof. psychology U. Mont., Missoula, 1971—, dir. clin. psychology, 1980-87; chair Mont. Bd. Psychologists, 1977-78; cons. Mont. State Prison, 1971-85, Trapper Creek Job Corps, 1973—; pvt. practice, Missoula, 1971—. Author numerous rsch. articles. Bd. dirs. Crisis Ctr., Missoula, 1972-73; mem. profl. adv. bd. Head Start, Missoula, 1972-79. Recipient Disting. scholar award U. Montana, 1991. Fellow Am. Psychol. Assn. (bd. dirs. div. clin. psychology 1990-92); mem. Rocky Mountain Psychol. Assn. (pres. 1983-84), Nat. Council Univ. Dirs. Clin. Psychology (bd. dirs., 1982-88). Roman Catholic. Catholic. Home: 105 Greenwood Ln Missoula MT 59803-2401 Office: 900 N Orange St Ste 201 Missoula MT 59802-2998

WOLLMAN, HARRY, medical educator; b. Bklyn., Sept. 26, 1932; s. Jacob and Florence Roslyn (Hoffman) W.; m. Anne Carolyn Hamel, Feb. 16, 1957; children: Julie Ellen, Emily Jane, Diana Leigh. AB summa cum laude, Harvard Coll., 1954, MD, 1958. Diplomate Am. Bd. Anesthesiology. Intern U. Chgo. Clinics, 1958-59; resident U. Pa., 1959-63, assoc. in anesthesia, 1963-65, mem. faculty, 1965-87, prof. anesthesia, 1970-87, prof. pharmacology, 1971-87, Robert Dunning Dripps prof., chmn. dept. anesthesia, 1972-87; prin. investigator Anesthesia Rsch. Ctr., 1972-78, program dir. Anesthesia Rsch. Tng. Grant, 1972-87; sr. v.p., chief acad. officer, dean Sch. Medicine Hahnemann U., Phila., 1987-92, prof. anesthesiology, 1987-92, prof. pharmacology, 1987-92, univ. prof., 1992—; mem. anesthesia drug panel, drug efficacy study, com. on anesthesia Nat. Acad. Scis.-NRC, 1970-71, com. on adverse reactions to anesthesia drugs, 1971-72; mem. pharm. and toxicology tng. grants com. NIH, 1966-68, anesthesia tng. grants com., 1971-73, surgery, anesthesia and trauma study sect., 1974-78; chmn. com. on studies involving human beings U. Pa., 1972-76, chmn. clin. practice exec. com., 1976-80. Assoc. editor for revs.: Anesthesiology, 1970-75; Contbr. and editor books. Hon. John Harvard scholar Harvard Coll., 1950-53, Harvard Coll. scholar, 1953-54, Detur award, 1951; NIH rsch. traineeship fellow, 1959-63, Pharm. Mfg. Assn. fellow, 1960-61. Mem. AMA, Pa. Soc. Anesthesiologists (pres. 1972-73), Am. Physiol. Soc., Assn. U. Anesthetists (exec. coun. 1971-74, chmn. scientific adv. bd. 1975-77), Soc. Acad. Anesthesia Chairmen (chmn. com. fin. resources 1973-77, pres. 1977-78), Am. Soc. Anesthesiologists, Phila. Soc. Anesthesiologists, Pa. Med. Soc., Phila. County Med. Soc., Am. Dental Soc., Anesthesiology (adv. bd. 1985-90), Assn. Med. Coll., Coll. Physicians Phila., Phi Beta Kappa, Sigma Xi. Home: Mus Towers 1801 Buttonwood St Apt 1020 Philadelphia PA 19130 Office: Hahnemann Univ 3508 Market St Ste 201 Philadelphia PA 19104-3316

WOLLMAN, LEO, physician; b. N.Y.C., Mar. 14, 1914; s. Joseph and Sara (Samrick) W.; m. Eleanor Rakow, Aug. 16, 1936 (dec. 1953); children: Arthur Lee, Bryant Lee; m. Charlotte Kornberg Seidman, Oct. 6, 1954 (div. 1969); m. Ellen Hershenson, Mar. 25, 1985. BS, Columbia U., 1934; MS, NYU, 1938; MD, Royal Coll. Edinburgh, 1942; PhD (hon.), Rochdale, 1972; DSc (hon.), U. Mich., 1973. Diplomate Am. Bd. Hypnosis in Ob-Gyn, Nat. Bd. Acupuncture Medicine, Am. Acad. Pain Mgmt., Am. Bd. Psychiatry and Neurology, Am. Bd. Sexology. Intern Cumberland Hosp., Bklyn., 1942-43; resident Leith Gen. Hosp., 1942; practice medicine specializing in ob-gyn Bklyn., 1944-72; in psychiatry, 1972—; mem. staff Maimonides, Coney Island hosps., Bklyn. Hosp. Ctr., Bklyn., Park East, Mt. Sinai hosps., N.Y.C.; med. dir. acupuncture dept. Lexington Health Facility, N.Y.C. Author: Write Yourself Slim, 1976, Eating Your Way to a Better Sex Life, 1983, numerous articles in profl. jours.; editor-in-chief: Jour. Am. Soc. Psychosomatic Dentistry and Medicine, 1968-83; editor newsletter: Soc. Sci. Study Sex; editor: News Bull. of Inst. for Comprehensive Medicine; assoc. editor: Jour. Sex Research; internat. editor: Latin Am. Jour. Clin. Hypnosis; films I Am Not This Body, 1970, StrangeHer, 1971, Let Me Die a Woman, 1978. Pres. Jewish Com. Coun. Greater Coney Island, 1989—. Recipient Jules Weinstein Ann. Pioneer in Modern Hypnosis award, 1964. Fellow Am. Geriatrics Soc., N.Y. Acad. Scis. (life), Acad. Psychosomatic Medicine (sec. 1965), Soc. Clin. and Exptl. Hypnosis (life), Am. Soc. Clin. Hypnosis (life), Soc. Sci. Study Sex (pres. Eastern region 1979-81), Am. Soc. Psychical Research (life), Am. Med. Writers Assn. (life), Internat. Soc. Comprehensive Medicine, Am. Acad. Psychiatry and Neurology, Am. Coll. Sexology; mem. Nat. Geog. Soc. (life), AAAS (council 1971-73), Am. Assn. Social Psychiatry, Am. Soc. Abdominal Surgeons, Internat. Soc. Nonverbal Psychotherapy, N.Y. State Soc. Med. Research, Royal Medico-Psychol. Assn. (Eng.), N.Y. Soc. for Gen. Semantics, Nat. Assn. on Standard Med. Vocabulary (sec. 1964—), Am. Assn. History Medicine, Am. Assn. Study Headache, Am. Acad. Dental Medicine, Am. Assn. Marriage Counselors, Soc. Med. Jurisprudence, Bklyn. Psychol. Assn., Canadian Soc. for Study Fertility, Am. Fertility Soc. (life), Internat. Fertility Assn., Internat. Soc. for Clin. and Exptl. Hypnosis (life), Am. Soc. Psychosomatic Dentistry and Medicine (pres. 1969-72, exec. dir. 1973-83), Assn. Advancement Psychotherapy, Pan-Am. Med. Assn., Andalusian Soc. Sophrology and Psychosomatic Medicine, Brit. Med. Assn., Bklyn. Acad. Medicine, Internat. Soc. Psychoneuroendocrinology, L.I. Hist. Soc.; also hon. mem. numerous fgn. orgns. Address: 3813 Poplar Ave Brooklyn NY 11224-1301

WOLPE, CLAIRE FOX, civic worker, psychotherapist; b. N.Y.C., June 24, 1909; d. David and Pauline (Hirsch) Fox; A.B., Mills Coll., 1930; M.A., U. So. Calif., 1936, M.S.W., 1965; Ph.D., Marquette U., 1970; postgrad. Smith Coll., summer 1931, Columbia U., summer 1963, U. Mexico City, summer 1964; m. Arthur S. Wolpe, Dec. 25, 1932 (dec. Mar. 1962); children—Ruth (Mrs. Roy Rose), Sheri (Mrs. Jerome Langer). Student advisor Jewish student orgn. UCLA, 1931-33; with Travelers Aid, Los Angeles, 1934; med. social work Los Angeles County Gen. Hosp., 1934-38; with USPHS, 1938; social worker Los Angeles County Health Dept., 1938-39; psychiat. social worker Gateways Psychiat. Hosp. and Mental Health Center, Los Angeles, 1962-63, 65-66; exec. dir. Bay Cities Mental Health Center, Los Angeles, 1966-68; supr. Airport Marina Counseling Service; pvt. practice. Mem. Mayors Com. on Civil Def. 1950-52, Wilshire Coordinating Council, 1954-58; leader Girl Scouts U.S.A., 1954-58; mem. regional bd. NCCJ, 1951-55. Bd. dirs. So. Calif. Mental Health Assn., 1955-58, Los Angeles chpt. A.R.C., 1951-53, Community Relations Conf. So. Calif., 1950-60, Los Angeles Jewish Fedn. Council, 1952-58, B'nai B'rith Anti-Defamation League, 1973—, Hillel Assn., 1973—. Fellow Soc. Clin. Social Workers, Am. Assn. Orthopsychiatry; mem. Nat. Assn. Social Workers, Psychotherapy Assn. So. Calif. (dir. 1967—, pres.-elect 1984), Calif. Marriage, Family and Child Counseling Assn., Group Psychotherapy Assn. So. Calif. (tribute award 1989), Am. Group Psychotherapy Assn., Los Angeles Transactional Analysis Soc. (sec.-treas. 1966-68), Psi Chi. Jewish religion. Mem. B'nai B'rith Women. Home and Office: 234 S Orange Dr Los Angeles CA 90036-3011

WOLTERS, GEORGE JEROME, emergency department physician; b. Phila., Nov. 14, 1954; s. George Jerome and Doris Agnes (Whelan) W.; m. Paige Suzanne Demarest, May 9, 1981; children: Brian, Megan. BS, Widener U., 1975; DO, Phila. Coll. Osteo. Medicine, 1979. Emergency dept. physician Suburban Gen. Hosp., Norristown, Pa., 1983-85; emergency dept. dir. Riddle Meml. Hosp., Media, Pa., 1985—; med. dir. Lower Providence Ambulance, Norristown, 1984-85, RMH Med. Command Facility, Media, 1985—, UMA Ambulance, Lima, Pa., 1990—; pres., founder RNU Emergency Physicians P.C., Media, 1990—. Fellow Am. Coll. Osteopathic Emergency Medicine. Republican. Methodist. Home: 1336 Wexford Dr Westchester PA 19300

WOLTZ, MICHAEL E., physician assistant; b. Shippensburg, Pa., Dec. 9, 1955; s. Gordon Thomas and Mary Eileen (Donohue) W.; m. Dariel DeGennaro, June 19, 1983. AA/AS, Pa. State U., 1983; BS, Hahnemann U., 1985, cert. physician asst., 1985. Physician asst., house officer Med. Coll. of Pa., Phila., 1985-89; physician asst. emergency medicine dept. Hahnemann U., Phila., 1987-89, physician asst. instr., 1987-89; physician asst. emergency medicine dept. Westfield (N.Y.) Meml. Hosp., 1989—, sr. emergency rm. physician asst., 1990—, asst. dir. emergency svcs., 1990—, physician asst. family practice clinic, 1992-96; physician asst. Chatauqua County Health Dept., Mayville, N.Y., 1992-96. With USN/USMC, 1978-81. Fellow Am. Acad. Physician Assts., Alpha Eta. Office: Westfield Meml Hosp 189 E Main St Westfield NY 14787

WOMACK, DEBORAH LYNN, obstetric nurse; b. McMinnville, Tenn., June 12, 1952; d. Archie Elmer and Rose Evelyn (Bratcher) Bivens; m. Carl Michael Womack, July 18, 1970; children: Leah Kristen Womack Miller, Carl Darren, Felicia Hope Womack Young. Grad., State Area Vo-Tech., McMinnville, 1981. LPN, Tenn.; cert. childbirth educator. Intensive care nurse River Park Hosp., McMinnville, 1981; office nurse family practice, McMinnville, 1981-86, obstetrics practice, McMinnville, 1986-94; obstet. nurse River Park Hosp., 1991—, childbirth educator, 1988—; mem. teen pregnancy task force Teen Pregnancy Prevention Coun., McMinnville, 1988-92; RTS Bereavement coord., counselor, 1996—. Sunday sch. tchr. Earleyville Ch. of Christ, 1988-92. Mem. LPN Assn. (local pres. 1991, LPN of Yr. 1991). Home: 381 Swamp Rd Mc Minnville TN 37110

WOMACK, JAMES ARTHUR, physician assistant, educator; b. Dallas, Sept. 23, 1948; s. John Franklin and Mary Lou (Boyd) W.; m. Bonnie Patricia Kindron, Dec. 1, 1972; children: David James, Katherine Elizabeth. A in Med. Sci., Emory U., 1975. Cert. Nat. Commn. on Cert. of Physician Assts., Ga. State Bd. Med. Examiners. Physician asst. Aylett (Va.) Med. Clinic, 1975-76, P&S Clinic, Holdenville, Okla., 1976-84; physician asst., clinic dir. Albany (Ga.) Area Primary Health Care, 1984—; clin. instr. Darton Coll., Albany, 1985—. Staff sgt. USAF, 1969-73. Fellow Am. Acad. Physician Assts. (Rural Physician Asst. of the Yr. 1992), Ga. Assn. Physician Assts., Dougherty County Soc. Physician Assts. (past pres. west 1992-94). Democrat. Baptist. Home: 1709 Whisperwood St Albany GA 31707 Office: Albany Primary Health Care 804 14th Ave Albany GA 31701

WONG, BRIAN R., ophthalmologist; b. Fresno, Calif., Feb. 6, 1961. BA Biochemistry, U. Calif. San Diego, 1983; MD, U. Tex. Med. Br., 1987. Bd. cert. ophthalmologist. Resident, ophthalmology La. State U. Med. Ctr., Shreveport, 1991; fellow reconstructive surgery U. Tex. Health Sci. Ctr., Houston, 1992; asst. prof., dir. Ophthalmic Plastic and Reconstructive Surgery/U. Tex., Galveston, 1992—; bd. dirs. head and neck tumor bd., U. Tex. Med. Br.; speaker in field. Contbg. author book in field. Fellow Am. Acad. Ophthalmology; mem. AMA. Office: Univ Tex Med Br 336 Clinical Scis Bldg G-87 Galveston TX 77550

WONG, DAVID KRISTIAN, orthopedic surgeon; b. San Francisco, July 27, 1959; s. Chong Cheng and Fee Lee (Hong) W.; m. Di Lora Pulliam, May 1, 1989; children: Aubrey, Matthew. BS, U. Calif., Riverside, 1981; MD, U. Okla. Coll. Med., 1986. Diplomate Am. Bd. Orthopedic Surgery. Hand surgeon Okla. Hand Surgery, Oklahoma City, 1992-93, Orthopedic Specialists Tulsa, 1993-95, Ctrl. States Orthopedic Specialists INc., Tulsa, 1995—; physician's adv. com. Okla. Worker's Compensation, 1994, 95. Mem. AMA, Am. Acad. Orthopedic Surgery, Am. Bd. Orthopedic Surgeons, Okla. State Med. Assn. (liaison com. 1993), Tulsa County Med. Soc., Tulsa County Orthopaedic Assn. Office: Ctrl State Ortho Specialist 6585 S Yale Ave #700 Tulsa OK 74136

WONG, DENNIS KA-CHEONG, physician, physical therapist; b. Hong Kong, Hong Kong, Jan. 23, 1954. BA, Columbia U., 1977, cert. in phys. therapy, 1978, MS in Phys. Therapy, 1982; MD, Am. U. of the Caribbean, Montserrat, Brit. West Indies, 1988. Intern internal medicine dept. SUNY Health Sci. Ctr., Bklyn., 1988-89; Nat. Inst. on Disability and Rehab. Rsch. fellow Harvard-MIT Rehab. Engring. Ctr., Cambridge, Mass., 1989-90; resident rehab. medicine dept. Kingsbrook Jewish Med. Ctr., Bklyn., 1990-92, chief resident rehab. medicine dept., 1992—; instr., attending physician dept. rehab. medicine Mt. Sinai Med. Ctr., N.Y.C., 1993-94, pvt. practice, 1994—. Fellow Am. Acad. Phys. Medicine and Rehab.

WONG, EDISON HSING-WEI, physician; b. Kaohsiung, Taiwan, Jan. 26, 1965; came to U.S., 1968; s. David T.M. and Eleanor H.Y. (Yang) W.; m. Pamela Lee Salimeno, Feb. 22, 1992; 1 child, Matthew Thomas. BS, MS, MIT, 1987; MD, Columbia U., 1991. Diplomate Am. Bd. Phys. Medicine and Rehab. Engring. intern GE R & D Ctr., Schenectady, N.Y., 1984-86; intern Maine Med. Ctr., Portland, 1991-92; rehab. medicine resident U. Wash. Med. Ctr., Seattle, 1992-95; co-dir. traumatic brain injury unit Spaulding Rehab. Hosp., Boston, 1995—, med. dir. Assistive Tech. Ctr., 1995—. Editl. bd. Rehab in Rev., 1995—, Joint Centre for Prosthesis and Orthotics and Rehab. Programms in Saudi Arabia, 1995—. Nat. Merit Corp. scholar Esmark, 1982-86. Mem. AMA, Mass. Med. Soc., Foresight Inst., Am. Acad. Phys. Medicine and Rehab. Office: Spaulding Rehab Hosp 125 Nashua St Boston MA 02114

WONG, GARRET S.L., psychiatric/mental health nurse; b. Wailuku, Maui, Hawaii, Dec. 6, 1956; s. William C.N. and Lucy T. (Suzuki) W.; m. Deborah Ruth Gwynup, Apr. 16, 1989 (div. July 1992); 1 child, Sierra Rayn. BA in Psychology, Pacific U., Forest Grove, Oreg., 1979; student, Portland State U., 1981-86; BSN, Oreg. Health Scis. U., Portland, 1993. RN, Oreg. Temporary staffing nurse Clin. Options, Portland, 1993; charge nurse, crisis mgmt. unit Dammasch State U., Wilsonville, Oreg., 1993—. Mem. Oreg. Nurses Assn. Libertarian. Home: 7150 SW Bel-Aire Dr Beaverton OR 97008 Office: Dammasch State Hosp PO Box 38 Wilsonville OR 97070

WONG, IRWIN LANE, physician; b. L.A., Mar. 1, 1960; m. Audrey Julia Young, May 25, 1985; children: Matthew, Alan. BA summa cum laude, UCLA, 1981, MD, 1985. Resident U. Utah, Salt Lake City, 1988-92; fellow U. So. Calif., 1992-94; physician, in reproductive endocrinology and infertility Chandler, Ariz., 1994—. Author articles. Mem. Alpha Omega Alpha. Office: 3200 N Dobson Rd Ste F7 Chandler AZ 85224-9603

WONG, LINDA LOU, surgeon; b. Portland, Oreg., June 14, 1960; d. Livingston M.F. and Rose K.L. Wong. BS in Biology, Stanford U., 1982; MD, U. Calif., Irvine, 1986. Diplomate Am. Bd. Gen. Surgery; lic. physician, Calif., Hawaii. Rschr. dept. urology Stanford (Calif.) U. Med. Ctr., 1980-81; rschr. Cardiovascular Rsch. Lab. Queen's Med. Ctr., Honolulu, 1980-82; rschr. dept. surgery U. Calif.-Irvine, Orange, 1984-86; rschr. dept. surgery Cedars-Sinai Med. Ctr., L.A., 1987-88, gen. surgery resident, 1986-91; transplant fellow liver, kidney, pancreas Calif. Pacific Med. Ctr. Transplant Svcs., San Francisco, 1991-92; dir. liver transplant program St. Francis Med. Ctr., Honolulu, 1993—; asst. prof. surgery U. Hawaii Sch. Medicine, Honolulu, 1993—; gen. transplant surgeon Surg. Assocs., Inc., Honolulu, 1993—; lectr., presenter various orgns. and confs. Contbr. articles to profl. jours. Recipient Pacific Health Rsch. Inst. Scholarship, 1980, Zimmerman Found. Rsch. Scholarship, 1981, Leo Zigler award for excellence in surgery, 1988, 90, 91. Assoc. fellow ACS; mem. AMA, Hawaii Med. Assn., Am. Soc. Artificial Internal Organs, Soc. Organ Sharing, Am. Assn. Study of Liver Diseases, Transplantation Soc., Western Assn. Transplant Surgeons. Office: Surg Assocs Inc 1329 Lusitana St Ste 709 Honolulu HI 96813

WONG, MICHAEL HENRY, anesthesiologist; b. L.A., Feb. 10, 1965; s. Henry and Beulah (Chan) W.; m. Evelyn Wing Han Mark, Dec. 30, 1989; 1 child, Bryce Michael. BS in Biol. Sci., U. So. Calif., 1987; DO, Coll. Osteo. Medicine Pacific, Pomona, Calif., 1991. Intern San Bernardino County Med. Ctr., San Bernardino, Calif., 1991; resident in anesthesiology Loma Linda (Calif.) U. Med. Ctr., 1991-95; dir. anesthesiology South Coast Surgery Ctr., Santa Ana, Calif., 1995—; pres., med. dir. Anesthetix Inc., Huntington Beach, Calif., 1995—, So. Calif. Pain Control Ctr., Inc., Garden Grove, Calif., 1995—. Recipient Alumni Meml. award Coll. Osteo. Medicine of Pacific, 1989. Mem. AMA, Am. Soc. Anesthesiologists, World Tae Kwon Do Fedn. (Dan instr.), Sigma Sigma Phi. Office: So Calif Pain Control Ctr Ste 150 7077 Orangewood Ave Garden Grove CA 92641

WONG, NATHAN DONALD, medicine and epidemiology educator; b. Downey, Calif., Apr. 18, 1961; s. Donald Wah and Mew Lun (Hee) W. BA, Pomona Coll., 1983; MPH, Yale U., 1985, PhD, 1987. Lectr. in medicine Yale U., New Haven, 1987; asst. prof. U. Calif., Irvine, 1988-94, assoc. prof., 1994—, dir. preventive cardiology, dept. medicine, 1991—; assoc. adj. prof. dept. epidemiology UCLA, 1996—; pres., CEO Profl. Rsch. Inst. for Design and Evaluation, Inc., Dana Point, Calif., 1994—; numerous presentations and seminars in field; mem. Prevention 2000 Com., Calif. Dept. Health Svcs., 1995—; interviewed for various publs. and programs, including ABC Eyewitness News, L.A. Times, Orange County Register, CBS News This Morning, Sing Tao Daily, Pacific Rim News Svc., USA Today, N.Y. Times, others; profl. cons. Montebello Schs. Phys. Assessment Program, 1989, Tobacco Resistance Activity Program, Pomona Unified Sch. Dist., 1990-94; Cordis-Webster, Baldwin Park, 1992—, Univ. Heart Imaging, 1994, PacifiCare Wellness Co., Cypress, Calif., 1994—; mem. hypertension study NIH, 1995—, mem. women's health initiative, 1994—; mem. study group Astra-Merck, 1994—. Contbr. articles to profl. jours. Bd. dirs. Am. Heart Assn., 1994—, mem. investigative group fellowship study sect. Greater L.A. affiliate, 1992; mem. adv. bd. Calif. Low-Income Minority Adolescent Nutrition Edn. Program, 1990; mem. Asian/Pacific Islander task force State Dept. Health, 1991; mem. Calif. Senate Hearing Panel on Youth Phys. Edn. and Fitness, 1991; mem. Women's Health Initiative Cmty. Adv. Bd., U. Calif., Irvine, 1994—, vol. Coll. Medicine Health Fair, 1995; vol. Anaheim Sr. Health Fair, 1995; mem. health adv. coun. KOCE 50 TV, 1995. Fellow Am. Coll. Cardiology, Am. Heart Assn. Coun. on Epidemiology and Prevention; mem. Cardiovascular Disease Prevention Coalition. Office: U Calif Dept Medicine C240 MedSci I Irvine CA 92697

WONG, OTTO, epidemiologist; b. Canton, China, Nov. 14, 1947; came to U.S., 1967, naturalized, 1976; s. Kui and Foon (Chow) W.; m. Betty Yeung, Feb. 14, 1970; children: Elaine, Jonathan. BS, U. Ariz., 1970; MS, Carnegie Mellon U., 1972; MS, U. Pitts., 1973, ScD, 1975. Cert. epidemiologist, Am. Coll. Epidemiology, 1982. USPHS fellow U. Pitts., 1972-75; asst. prof. epidemiology Georgetown U. Med. Sch., 1975-78; mgr. epidemiology Equitable Environ. Health Inc., Rockville, Md., 1977-78; dir. epidemiology Tabershaw Occupational Med. Assocs., Rockville, 1978-80; dir. occupational rsch. Biometric Rsch. Inst., Washington, 1980-81; exec. v.p., chief epidemiologist, ENSR Health Scis., Alameda, Calif., 1981-90; chief epidemiologist, pres. Applied Health Scis., San Mateo, Calif., 1991—; cons. WHO, Nat. Cancer Inst., Nat. Inst. Occupl. Safety and Health, Occupl. Safety and Health Adminstrn., Nat. Heart, Lung and Blood Inst., Internat. Agy. for Rsch. on Cancer, U.S. EPA, Ford Motors Co., Gen. Electric, Mobil, Chevron, Union Carbide, Fairfax Hosp., Agy. for Toxic Substances and Disease Registry, Va. U. Ariz. scholar, 1967-68. Fellow Am. Coll. Epidemiology, Human Biology Council; mem. Am. Pub. Health Assn., Biometric Soc., Soc. Epidemiologic Rsch., Phi Beta Kappa, Pi Mu Epsilon. Republican. Contbr. articles to profl. jours. Office: Applied Health Scis PO Box 2078 181 Second Ave Ste 628 San Mateo CA 94401

WONG, PHILLIP ALLEN, osteopathic physician; b. Oakland, Calif., Dec. 8, 1956; s. Timothy Him and Lillian (Lee) W.; m. Lisa Perreautt, Apr. 30, 1983; children: Ashley, Heather. BS in Microbiology and Chemistry, No. Ariz. U., 1979; DO, Kirksville Coll. Osteo. Med., 1983. Intern Kirksville Osteo. Health Ctr., 1983-84; staff family physician USAF, Kirtland AFB, N.Mex., 1984-87; CEO, pvt. practice Albuquerque, 1987—. Capt. USAF, 1984-87. Mem. Am. Acad. Osteopathy (bd. cert. in osteo. manipulative medicine), Am. Osteo. Assn., Am. Coll. Osteo. Family Physicians (bd. cert. family practice), N.Mex. Osteo. Med. Assn. (bd. mem.), Ariz. Acad. Osteopathy (bd. mem.), Cranial Acad. (bd. cert. in cranial in the osteo. field). Office: 10211 Montgomery NE #A Albuquerque NM 87111

WONG, RONALD JAMES, pediatric dental surgeon; b. Fresno, Calif., Dec. 21, 1931; s. Raymond Arthur and Ruth (Moe) W.; B.S., U. So. Calif., 1954, D.D.S., 1956; m. Edith Mok, June 21, 1962 (div. 1986); children: Gary Hunter, Julie, Christy, Carina, Lara, Sabrina. Intern, P.T.A. Clinic, Los Angeles Sch. Dist., 1956-57; resident Greenpark Sch. dental clinic, Chofu, Japan, 1958-59; practice dentistry specializing in pediatric dental surgery, Hollywood, Calif., 1959—; mem. staff Hollywood Presbyn. Hosp.; asst. clin. prof. pedodontics U. So. Calif., Los Angeles, 1959-68; cons. Children's Hosp. Los Angeles, 1960-73, head dental div., 1973-78. Coordinator Lang. Services Archery Venue XXIII Olympics, Los Angeles. Served to capt. USAF, 1957-59. Nat. Amateur Flight Archery Champion U.S.A., 1984; First place winner 25 KG class U.S. Nat. Archery Flight Championship, 1982, Silver Wescott medal No. 2 amateur flight archer in U.S., 1983. Mem. Hollywood, Los Angeles dental socs., Hollywood Acad. Medicine, Am. Stomatological Soc. Japan, Am. Analgesia Soc., Am. Acad. Pedodontics, Am., So. Calif. (pres. 1968-69) socs. dentistry for children, So. Calif., Am. dental assns., Calif. Pedodontic Research Group, Western Pedodontic and Odontic Soc., Am. Endodontic Soc., Am. Hypnodontic Soc., Acad. of Dentistry for the Handicapped, Chinese Am. Citizen's Alliance, Delta Sigma Delta, Alpha Tau Omega. Rotarian. Author: Pedodontic Dental Preparations, 1961. Home: 2415 N Commonwealth Ave Los Feliz CA 90027 Office: 1616 Hillhurst Ave Hollywood CA 90027

WONG, SHAN S., clinical chemist; b. Mankassar, Indonesia, May 10, 1945; came to U.S., 1967; s. Kay K. and Mon L. (Lee) W.; m. Lee-Jun Chang, Feb. 21, 1973; children: Inyork H., I. Hansie. BSc, Oreg. State U., 1970; PhD, Ohio State U., 1974. Vis. asst. prof. Denison U., Granville, Ohio, 1977-78; asst. prof. U. Lowell, Mass., 1978-82, assoc. prof., 1982-84, prof. chemistry, 1984-90; assoc. prof. U. Tex. Med. Sch., Houston, 1990—; sect. chief specimen collection Reference Lab.; chief clin. chemistry Hermann Hosp., Lyndon B. Johnson Gen. Hosp. Author: Chemistry of Protein Conjugation and Cross-linking, 1991; contbr. numerous articles to rsch. publs. McPherson fellow Ohio State U., 1972, recipient Albert L. Henne award, 1971; Samuel A. Talbot Meml. Travel grantee Biophys. Soc., 1974; recipient Young Investigator award Acad. Clin. Lab. Physicians and Scientists, 1986. Mem. Am. Assn. Clin. Chemistry (travel award 1986), Am. Soc. Biochemistry and Molecular Biology, Am. Chem. Soc., Nat. Acad. Clin. Biochemistry. Office: U Tex Health Sci Ctr Pathology PO Box 20708 Houston TX 77225-0708

WONG, STEPHEN WILLIS, ophthalmologist; b. Honolulu, May 11, 1945; s. Robert Tuck and Harriet (Leong) W.; m. Susan Yee, June 11, 1972. BA, Albion Coll., 1968; MD, Jefferson Med. Coll., 1972. Diplomate Am. Bd. Ophthalmology. Intern Lankenau Hosp., Phila., 1972-73; ophthalmology resident Wills Eye Hosp., Phila., 1973-76, retinal-vitreous fellow, 1976-77; asst. prof. Temple U. Sch. Medicine, Phila., 1979-93, assoc. prof., 1993—, dir. resident program, vice chmn. ophthalmology dept., 1979—; cons. USN, Phila., 1979-83. Contbr. articles to med. jours. Lt. comdr. USN, 1977-79. Odd Fellows scholar, 1976-77. Fellow ACS, Am. Acad. Ophthalmology, Phila. Coll. Physicians; mem. AMA. Republican. Office: Temple U Hosp 3401 N Broad St Philadelphia PA 19140

WONG, VINCENT HONG, optometrist; b. San Francisco, May 23, 1963; s. Kim and Helen (Hom) W.; m. Kanako Margaret Tomita, Sept. 3, 1995. AS, City Coll., San Francisco, 1983; BA in Chemistry, San Francisco State U., 1987; BS in Visual Sci., U. Calif., Berkeley, 1991, OD, 1993. Optometrist in pvt. practice North Highlands, Calif., 1993-94, Stockton, Calif., 1994, Placerville, Calif., 1994—, Sacramento, 1995—; vol. at vision screenings Sacramento Valley Optometric Soc., 1993—. Mem. Am. Optometric Assn., Calif. Optometric Assn., Sacramento Valley Optometric Soc.

WONG, WALLACE, medical supplies company executive, real estate investor; b. Honolulu, July 13, 1941; s. Jack Yung Hung and Theresa (Goo) W.; m. Amy Ju, June 17, 1963; children: Chris, Bradley, Jeffery. Student, UCLA, 1960-63. Chmn., pres. South Bay Coll., Hawthorne, Calif., 1965-86; chmn. Santa Barbara (Calif.) Bus. Coll., 1975—; gen. ptnr. W B Co., Redondo Beach, Calif., 1982—; CEO Cal Am. Med. Supplies, Rancho Santa Margarita, Calif., 1986—, Cal Am. Exports, Inc., Rancho Santa Margarita, 1986—, Pacific Am. Group, Rancho Santa Margarita, 1991—; chmn., CEO Alpine, Inc., Rancho Santa Margarita, Calif., 1993—; pres. Bayside Properties, Rancho Santa Margarita, 1993—; bd. dirs. Metrobank, L.A. FFF Enterprises; chmn. bd. 1st Ind. Fin. Group., Rancho Santa Margarita. Acting sec. of state State of Calif., Sacramento, 1982; founding mem. Opera Pacific, Orange County, Calif., 1985; mem. Hist. and Cultural Found., Orange County, 1986; v.p. Orange County Chinese Cultural Club, Orange County, 1985. Named for Spirit of Enterprise Resolution, Hist. & Cultural Found., Orange Country, 1987; recipient resolution City of Hawthorne, 1973. Mem. Westren Accred Schs. & Colls. (v.p. 1978-79), Magic Castle (life), Singapore Club. Office: Alpine Inc 23042 Arroyo Vis Rancho Santa Margarita CA 92688

WONG, WAYNE D., nutritionist; b. San Francisco, May 13, 1950; s. Chaney Noon and La Dean Maryan (Mah) W. m. Betty Lee, Oct. 16, 1977; children: Michael Gabriel, Elizabeth Catherine, Whitney Forbes, Ellesse Florence. BS in Dietetic Adminstrn., U. Calif., Berkeley, 1972; MS in Sch. Bus. Mgmt., Pepperdine U., 1976; student, Nikon Sch. Photography, San Francisco, 1969. Cert. Food Svc. Dir., Calif. Community Coll. tchr.; Registered Dietitian, Sch. Bus. Official, Benefit specialist. Food svc. worker, lab. asst. U. Calif., Berkeley, 1968-69, 70-71; mgmt. intern Mich. State U., East Lansing, 1970; dietetic intern Milw. Pub. Schs., 1972-73; food svc. cons. Trader Vic's, San Francisco, 1973; dir. food svcs. Bakersfield (Calif.) City Sch. Dist., 1973—; instr. Bakersfield Coll., 1978—; cons. Wong, R.D., Bakersfield, 1978—; registered Benefit Specialist Investors Retirement Mgmt., Carpenteria, Calif., 1988—; mem. nat. child nutrition adv. coun. USDA, Washington, 1977-79; 1st v.p. Ptnrs. in Nutrition Coop., Lancaster, Calif., 1988-90; food svc. edn. task force Calif. Dept. Edn., Sacramento, 1979—; project coord. nutrition edn. and tng. exemplary program adoption grant Bakersfield City Sch. Dist., 1982; project dir. basic skills, basic foods course, curriculum and recipe devel. grant Calif. Dept. Edn., 1985, cons. tchg. course, 1985-88; mem. adv. coun. Calif. State U. Long Beach Child Nutrition Program Mgmt. Tng. Ctr., 1991; mem. Sch. Nutrition Adv. Coun., Bakersfield, 1990—; graphics and tech. writing cons. Cal-Pro-Net Ctr., Fresno City Coll., 1995—; program panelist Ptnrs. Nutrition Coop., Am. Sch. Food Svc. Assn., Ann. Nat. Conf., 1995. Author: Food Service Equipment-How Long Should It Last?, 1985; co-author (videotape) Bettermade Plastics, 1991, Recycle: Save Earth's Resources Now; programmer Food Svc. Pers. Database, 1988, Dishmachine Labor and Energy Matrix, 1991; contbr. articles to profl. jours. BBQ fund-raiser co-chmn. Citizens for Yes on Measure B, Bakersfield, 1989; legis. com. Child Nutrition Facilities Act 1975, Sacramento, 1973-76; expert witness State Senate Select Subcom. on Nutrition and Human Needs, Sacramento, 1973; asst. troop leader Boy Scouts Am., Troop 219, San Francisco, 1965-67; participant Chinese Family Life Study U. Calif., Berkeley; dir. polystyrene recycling project Bakersfield City Sch. Dist., 1990; team leader Healthy Kids, Healthy Calif. program Calif. Dept. Edn., 1985-87; sponsor Christian Broadcasting Network Satellite Communications Ctr., 1978; world vision sponsor India Community Devel. Program, 1974-92. Recipient Leadership award Calif. State Dept. Edn., 1987, Outstanding Sch. Lunch Program award USDA, 1989; 1st pl. Calif. Sch. Food Svc. Assn. Country Cook-off, 1983, 84; Toto Wizard nominee Sabatasso Foods, 1985, Best Practice award USDA, 1992. Mem. Am. Dietetic Assn. (Young Dietitian of Yr. 1976), Am. Sch. Food Svc. Assn. (child nutrition mktg. bike ride 1991, Cycle Across Am. for Child Nutrition and Fitness 1993), Am. Running and Fitness Assn., Calif. Assn. Sch. Bus. Ofcls. (photographer 1985, food svc. R&D chmn. 1985-87, recognition 1987, food and nutrition R&D com. 1984), Calif. Sch. Food Svc. Assn. (edn. tng. chmn. 1975-76, wellness awareness bike ride 1990-91, child nutrition bike ride 1991, 1st pl. photo contest 1993, cover photographer assn. jour. Poppyseeds 1992), Sports and Cardiovasc. Nutritionists, Kern County Sch. Food Svc. Assn. (pres. 1987-90, Golden Poppy award 1990), Kern Wheelmen (v.p. 1992), Hour of Power Sparrows Club, Pi Alpha Phi, Omicron Nu. Republican. Baptist. Home: 4901 University Ave Bakersfield CA 93306-1773

WONG, YAU KAI, chemist; b. Hong Kong, Dec. 29, 1960; came to U.S., 1980; s. Chee and An-Ho (Hung) W.; m. Clare Cheung. BS in Chemistry, U. Mo., 1984, MS in Chemistry, 1987; MBA, Rider U., 1994. Rsch. technologist Mass. Gen. Hosp., Boston, 1987-89; quality assurance/quality control specialist Organogeneiss, Inc., Cambridge, Mass., 1989-91; sr. rsch. assoc. Cytogen Corp., Princeton, N.J., 1991-93; analyt. chemist J & J CPI, Skillman, N.J., 1993; supr. analt. chemistry B.W. Mfg. Inc., West Greenwich, R.I., 1993-95; supr. quality control chem. lab. Luitpold Pharms., Inc., Shirley, N.Y., 1995-96. Mem. Am. Chem. Soc. Office: One Luitpold Dr Shirley NY 11967

WONG, YONG-CHUAN, anatomy educator; b. Kuala Lumpur, Selangor, Malaysia, June 7, 1942; s. Beng-Thong and Swee Fatt (Yew) W.; m. Chook-Yee Cho, Dec. 28, 1971; children: Matthew Hong-Yuen, Garry Huong-Chaou. BSc, Nanyang U., Singpore, 1966; MSc, U. Western Ont., London, Can., 1968, PhD, 1971. Lectr. anatomy U. Hong Kong, 1971-77, sr. lectr., 1977-84, reader, 1984—, assoc. dean faculty medicine, 1991—, head dept. anatomy, 1993—; hon. rsch. assoc. U. Birmingham (Eng.), 1974; vis. sr. lectr. Flinders (Australia) U., 1981; vis. prof. U. Chgo., 1977-78, U. Calif., San Francisco, 1988-89. Mem. AAAS, Am. Assn. Cancer Rsch., Am. Anatomists Assn., Can. Assn. Anatomists, Anatomical Soc. Gt. Britain and Ireland, Hong Kong Soc. Study Endocrinology, Hong Kong Inst. Sci., Metabolism and Reprodn., N.Y. Acad. Scis. Office: U Hong Kong Dept Anatomy, 5 Sassoon Rd, Hong Kong Hong Kong

WONGCHAVANICH, NAPISVADEE, internist; b. Bangkok, Thailand, Nov. 24, 1964; d. Pricha and Garnchana (Tanawat) W.; m. Virat Pinyopornpanit, May 23, 1993. MD with honors, Mahidol U., Bangkok, 1988. Cert. Internal Medicine Bd., Thailand. Resident physician dept. internal medicine Chiang Mai U., Thailand, 1988-92; faculty staff internal medicine Bangkok Christian Hosp., 1992-93; intern, resident physician dept. medicine Tex. Tech U. Health Sci. Ctr., Lubbock, 1993-96, chief resident in internal medicine, 1996—. Fellow Royal Coll. Thai Physicians; mem. ACP, AMA, Med. Coun. Thailand, Tex. Med. Assn., Lubbock Crosby Garza. Buddhist. Home: 5302 11th St Apt 137 Lubbock TX 79416-4403

WONG-LIANG, EIRENE MING, psychologist; b. Nassau, Bahamas, Nov. 20, 1961; came to U.S., 1969; d. Menyu and Lim Ming (Chow) Wong; m. Danqing Liang. BA, Trinity U., San Antonio, 1984; PhD, Calif. Sch. Profl. Psychology, 1992. Crisis counselor United Way Crisis Hotline, San Antonio, 1983; lab. asst. Trinity U., 1983; counselor Bayer County Women's Ctr., San Antonio, 1984, Turning Point Juvenile Diversion Project, Garden Grove, Calif., 1985-86; psychol. trainee Wolters Elem. Sch., Fresno, 1987, San Luis Obispo (Calif.) Youth Day Treatment, 1987-88, Calif. Sch. Profl. Psychology Svc. Ctr., Fresno, 1988-89; staff psychologist 314th Med. Ctr., Little Rock, Ark., 1989-93; pvt. practice, clin. psychologist Houston, 1993—. Mem. APA, Am. Soc. Clin. Hypnosis, Nat. Register Health Svc. Providers in Psychology, Tex. Psychol. Assn., Houston Psychol. Assn., Houston Assn. Clin. Hypnosis (charter, exec.), Psi Chi, Zeta Chi (charter, Trinity U. chpt.). Office: 10101 Southwest Fwy Ste 445 Houston TX 77074-1112

WOO, MARY ANN, medical educator. BS in Genetics, U. Calif., Davis, 1976; AA in Nursing, Pasadena (Calif.) City Coll., 1980; BS in Nursing, Mt. St. Mary's Coll., L.A., 1985; M Nursing, UCLA, 1988, D Nursing Sci., 1992. Cert. ACLS, critical care nurse, basic cardiopulmonary resuscitation; RN, Calif. Rsch. asst. dept. animal sci. U. Calif., Davis, 1975-76; tchrs. asst. L.A. Unified Sch. Dist., 1976-77, sch. nurse, 1980-81; tutor dept. biology Pasadena (Calif.) City Coll., 1978-80; staf nurse critical care unit Huntington Meml. Hosp., 1981-88; clin. rsch. nurse IV divsn. cardiology UCLA Med. Ctr., 1988-92, clin. rsch. nurse V, 1992-93, lectr., asst. clin. prof., 1993-94, asst. prof., 1994—; Mem. Pacific S.W. Regional Med. Libr. Svc. Task Force, 1988-89, UCLA Sch. Nursing Instrnl. Resources Com., 1990-92, clin. adv. panel on acute myocardial infarction Calif. Hosp. Outcomes Assessment Project, 1992—; external reviewer Alberta Found. for Nursing Rsch., 1992—; mem. com. on computing UCLA, 1994-95, undergrad. program com. Sch. Nursing, 1995—, Sch. Nursing Distance Learning Project, 1995—, Sch. Nursing Virtual Reality Project, 1995—; lectr. various hosps., schs., orgns. Manuscript reviewer Heart and Lung, 1989—, Am. Jour. Critical Care, 1992—, Progress in Cardiovascular Nursing, 1993—, European Heart Jour., 1994—, Am. Jour. Cardiology, 1995—; mem. editl. bd. Heart and Lung: Jour. Critical Care, 1993—; contbr. articles to profl. jours. Recipient Audrienna M. Moseley fellowship award, 1988-92, scholarship Kaiser Found., 1989, Rsch. awards UCLA Sch. Nursing Alumni Assn., 1990, Sigma Theta Tau, Gamma Tau chpt., 1991, Helene Fuld grant, 1990, Critical Care Nursing rsch. grant Hewlett-Packard/AACCN, 1992-93, grants UCLA, 1994, 95, minigrant UCLA, 1995, Office of Instrnl. Devel. award UCLA, 1995. Mem. AACCN (scholarship com. L.A. chpt. 1990-92), Am. Heart Assn. (program com. Coun. on Cardiovascular Nursing, new investigator award 1st pl. 1993, grant-in-aid 1995). Home: 1701 Camino Lindo South Pasadena CA 91030 Office: UCLA Sch Nursing 700 Tiverton Ave Box 951702 Los Angeles CA 90095-1702*

WOO, PAULINE, cardiologist; b. Hong Kong, Oct. 18, 1963; came to U.S., 1978.; d. William G. and Shu-Fong (Chen) W. BS in Mech. Engring., Stanford U., 1986; MD, Albert Einstein Coll. Medicine, 1991, spl. rsch. diploma, 1991. Diplomate Am. Bd. Internal Medicine. Rsch. engr. IBM Rsch. Divsn., San Jose, Calif., 1985; resident internal medicine CHS-UCLA Med. Ctr., 1991-94; fellow cardiology Harbor-UCLA Med. Ctr., Torrance, 1994—; rschr. in field. Contbr. articles to profl. jours. Mem. AMA, ACP. Home: 3500 Ranch Top Rd Pasadena CA 91107 Office: PO Box 1386 Arcadia CA 91077

WOO, SAVIO LAU CHING, molecular medical geneticist; b. Shaghai, China, Dec. 20, 1944; came to U.S., 1966; s. Kwok-Cheung and Fun-sin (Yu) W.; m. Emily H. Chang, July 14, 1973; children: Audrey C. C., Brian Y.Y. BSc, Loyola Coll., Montreal, Can., 1966; PhD, U. Wash., 1971. Asst. prof. cell biology Baylor Coll. Medicine, Houston, 1975-78, assoc. prof., 1979-83, dir. ctr. for gene therapy, 1991-96, prof., 1984-96, prof. Inst. Molecular Genetics, 1985-96, dir. grad. tng. program cell and molecular biology, 1987-94; assoc. investigator Howard Hughes Med. Inst., Bethesda, Md., 1977-79, investigator, 1979-96; prof., dir. Inst. for Gene Therapy and Molecular Medicine Mount Sinai Sch. Medicine, N.Y.C., 1996—; organizer, 1st chmn. Gordon Conf. on Molecular Genetics, 1985; co-organizer Searle-UCLA Symposium, 1986; organizer 3d Soc. Chinese Bioscientists in Am. Internat. Symposium, 1990; cons. Cooper Lab., Palo Alto, Calif., 1982-84, Zymos Corp., Seattle, 1982-86; sr. sci. advisor Molecular Therapeutics, Inc., West Haven, 1986-92; spl. advisor Gene Medicine, Inc., Woodlands, Tex., 1992-96. Mem. editorial bd. DNA, 1983—, Am. Jour. Human Genetics, 1986-89, Genomics, 1987-95, Biochemistry, 1988-94; U.S. editor: Gene Therapy, 1995—; contbr. over 200 sci. articles to prof. publs. Mem. bd. dirs. March of Dimes Birth Defects Found., Met. Houston chpt., 1979-87. Mem. NIH (study sect. on molecular biology 1983-85, merit award, 1988—), Nat. Inst. Child Health and Human Devel. (bd. sci. counselors 1988-93), Am. Soc. Biol. Chemists, Am. Soc. Cell Biology, N.Y. Acad. Scis., Soc. Study Inborn Errors of Metabolism (D. Noel Raime meml. award 1983).

WOO, SAVIO LAU-YUEN, bioengineering educator; b. Shanghai, China, June 3, 1942; s. Kwok CHong and Fung Sing (Yu) W.; m. Patricia Tak-kit Cheong, Sept. 6, 1969; children: Kirstin Wei-Chi, Jonathan I-Huei. BSME, Chico State U., 1965; MS, U. Wash., 1966, PhD, 1971. Research assoc. U. Wash., Seattle, 1965-70; asst. research prof. U. Calif.-San Diego, La Jolla, 1970-74, assoc. research prof., 1974-75, assoc. prof., 1975-80, prof. surgery and bioengring., 1980-90; vice chmn. for rsch. and dir. MSRC, 1990—; prof. ortho surgery U. Pitts., 1990—, prof. mech. engring., 1990—, Albert B. Ferguson Jr. prof. orthopaedic surgery, 1993—, prin. civil and environ. engring., 1994—, prof. rehab. sci. and tech., 1994—; prin. investigator VA Med. Ctr., San Diego, 1972-90, Pitts., 1990—; cons. bioengr. Children's Hosp., San Diego, 1973-80; cons. med. implant cos., 1978-85; vis. prof. biomechanics Kobe (Japan) U., 1981-82; dir., CEO M&D Coutts Inst. for Joint Reconstrn. and Rsch., 1984-90; mem. sci. adv. com. Whitaker Found., 1986-95, Steadman-Hawkins Sports Medicine Found., 1990—, OsteoArthritis Scis. Inc., 1992-95. Assoc. editor Jour. Biochem. Engring., 1979-87, Jour. Biomechanics, 1978—, Jour. Orthopedic Rsch., 1983-92, Materials Sci. Reports, 1990, Proc. Inst. Mech. Engrs. (Part H), 1990-94; mem. editl. adv. bd. Jour. Orthopedic Rsch., 1993—; internat. adv. bd. Jour. ESSKA, Knee Surgery, Sports Traumatology, Arthroscopy, 1993—; editl. bd. am. Jour. Sports Medicine, 1995—; mem. internat. adv. bd. Jour. Ortho. Sci. Recipient Elizabeth Winston Lanier Kappa Delta award, 1983, 86, awards for excellence in basic sci. rsch. Orthopaedic Rsch. Soc. and Am. Acad. Orthopaedic Surgeons, 1983, 86, 90, 94, O'Donoghue award Am. Orthopaedic Soc. Sports

Medicine, 1990, Wartenweiler Meml. Lectureship, 1987, Citation award Am. Coll. Sports Medicine, 1988, Rsch. Career Devel. award NIH, 1977-82, Muybridge medal Internat. Soc. Internat. Biomechanics, 1995; Japan Soc. Promotion of Sci. fellow, 1981. Fellow ASME (sec., chmn. biomechanics com., chmn. honors com. bioengrig. divsn., mem. exec. com. 1983-88, sec. 1985-86, chmn. 1986-87, H.R. Lissner award 1991), Am. Inst. Med. and Biol. Engrng. (founding fellow, chmn. coll. fellows 1992-94, bd. dirs. 1992-94); mem. NAE, Inst. Medicine NAS, We. Orthopaedic Assn. (hon.), Biomed. Engrng. Soc. (bd. dirs. 1984-86), Am. Acad. Orthopedic Surgeons, Orthopaedic Rsch. Soc. (exec. com. 1983-88, chmn. program com. 1983-84, pres. 1985-86), Am. Soc. Biomechanics (pres. 1985-86, sec. 1977-80, exec. com. 1984-87, Giovanni Borelli award 1993), Internat. Soc. Fractures Repair (bd. dirs. 1986-94, v.p. 1987-90, pres. 1990-92), Can. Orthopedic Rsch. Soc. (hon.), European Orthopedic Rsch. Soc., U.S. Nat. Commn. Biomechanics (chmn. 1994—, exec. com. 1988—). Home: 47 Pleasant View Ln Pittsburgh PA 15238-1859 Office: U Pitts Dept Ortho Surg Liliane Kaufmann Bldg 3471 5th Ave Ste 1010 Pittsburgh PA 15213-3221

WOOD, CHARLES EVANS, physiology educator, researcher; b. San Francisco, May 14, 1952; s. David Alvra and Ora (Bomberger) W.; m. Maureen Keller, Aug. 19, 1979; children: Margaret Aileen, Charles David, Sarah Elizabeth. AB, U. Calif., Berkeley, 1974; PhD, U. Calif., San Francisco, 1980. Asst. prof. U. Fla., Gainesville, 1983-88, assoc. prof., 1988-93; prof., 1993—; mem. human embryology and devel. study sect. NIH, 1995—. Contbr. over 60 articles to profl. jours. and 3 book chpts. for publ. Established investigator Am. Heart Assn., 1988-93, chair peer rev. com. Fla. affiliate, 1996. Grantee NIH, 1983—, Am. Heart Assn., 1983—. Mem. AAAS, N.Y. Acad. Scis., Internat. Soc. Vet. Perinatology, Am. Physiol. Soc. , Soc. for Gynecologic Investigation, Endocrine Soc. Office: U Fla Coll Medicine PO Box 274J Gainesville FL 32602-0274

WOOD, DAVID BRUCE, naturopathic physician; b. Fayetteville, N.C., Jan. 21, 1954; s. Marvin James and Rachel Elenor (Thom) W.; m. Wendy Ann McKiernan, Aug. 1974 (div. Aug. 1976); m. Cheryl Lynn Garbarino, Aug. 17, 1980. BS in Microbiology, U. Wash., 1977; D in Naturopathic Medicine, Bastyr U., Seattle, 1983. Pres., co-founder Trinity Family Health Clinic, Inc., P.S., Edmonds, Wash., 1984—; Spkr. local and nat. TV programs. Singer Sound of Praise Choir, Overlake Christian Ch., Kirkland, Wash., 1987-92; narrator Easter Pagent, 1989; mem. Cedar Park Assembly of God, Bothel, Wash. Mem. Am. Assn. Nutritional Cons., Nat. Health Fedn., Am. Assn. Naturopathic Physicians, Wash. Assn. Naturopathic Physicians (trustee, exec. bd. 1989-92). Home: 13721 Cascadian Way Everett WA 98208-7345 Office: Trinity Family Health Clinic Inc PS 7614 195th St SW Edmonds WA 98026-6260

WOOD, DEBORAH CHRISTINE, critical care nurse, educator; b. Houston, Oct. 20, 1948; d. John Bud and Bettye (Miller) Lawson; m. Billy Ray Wood, May 24, 1977; children: Amy, Mike, John, Daniel. ADN, Trinity Valley Jr. Coll., 1987; BSN, U. Tex., Arlington, 1990; MSN, U. Tex., Tyler, 1994. RN, Tex.; cert. advanced practice nurse, clin. nurse specialist in pediats. Telemetry/stepdown unit staff, charge nurse Mother Frances Hosp., Tyler, 1987-88, staff nurse cardiovasc. ICU, 1987-88, charge nurse cardiovasc. ICU, 1988—; critical care instr. Tyler Jr. Coll., 1992-93, instr. AD nursing program, 1993—. Mem. AACN, Am. Heart Assn. (cardiovascular nursing coun., critical care coun.), Sigma Theta Tau. Roman Catholic.

WOOD, DIRK GREGORY, surgeon, physician; b. Springfield, Ohio, Sept 19, 1953; s. Carlos Paul and Evelyn Cecelia (Bird) W. BA magna cum laude, Urbana (Ohio) U., 1973; MD, UAG Facultad de Medicina, Guadalajara, Mexico, 1980; JD, Capital Law Sch., Columbus, Ohio, 1991. Diplomate Am. Bd. Ob-Gyn, Am. Bd. Forensic Medicine. Intern Bronx (N.Y.) Lebanon Hosp., 1981-82; resident William Beaumont Hosp., Royal Oak, Mich., 1982-86; physician, surgeon Her Care, Inc., Springfield, 1986—; CEO Just What the Doctor Ordered, Springfield, 1992. Coroner Clark County, Ohio, 1991—. Fellow ACS, Am. Coll. Ob-gyn., Internat. Coll. Surgeons, Am. Coll. Legal Medicine, Royal Soc. Medicine (London). Republican. Home: 202 Tuttle Rd Springfield OH 45503-5236 Office: Her Care Inc 2029 E High St Springfield OH 45505-1315

WOOD, DOUGLAS LYNN, medical educator; b. Columbia, Mo., June 24, 1951; s. Cecil Vernon and Wilda Fay (Palmer) W.; m. Julia Ann Sandbothe, May 28, 1977; children: Ethan, Amanda, Paul. BA cum laude with distinction in Biology, Carleton Coll., 1973; MD cum laude, U. Mo., 1977. Diplomate Am. Bd. Internal Medicine, Am. Bd. Cardiovascular Diseases. Asst. prof. medicine Mayo Grad. Sch. Medicine, Rochester, Minn., 1983-91; assoc. prof. medicine Mayo Grad. Sch. Medicine, 1991—; vice-chair dept. medicine Mayo Clinic, Rochester, 1993—, cons. cardiovascular diseases, 1983—. Contbr. articles to profl. jours. Mem. exec. com. cardiac care network Blue Cross/Blue Shield of Minn., Eagan, 1995—; mem. coun. on performance measurement Joint Commn. on Accreditation of Healthcare Orgns., Oakbrook Terrace, Ill., 1995—; mem. CPT editl. panel AMA, Chgo., 1994—; chair fin. coun. St. Pius X Ch., Rochester, 1993—. Fellow ACP, Am. Coll. Cardiology; mem. Am. Coll. Physician Execs., Alpha Omega Alpha, Sigma Xi. Office: Mayo Clinic 200 1st St SW Rochester MN 55906

WOOD, EDWIN CARLYLE, gynecologist; b. Melbourne, Australia, May 28, 1929; s. Carlyle Sandford and Ruth Nellie Wood; m. Judith Badger, Sept. 17, 1957 (div.); children: Gavin Carlyle, Caroline Archer, Simon Alexander; m. Marie Counsel, Oct. 12, 1990. MB BS, Melbourne U., 1952. Resident Royal Women's Hosp., Melbourne, 1954-56, Queen Charlottes and Chelsea Hosp., London, 1957-58; lectr., sr. lectr. Queen Charlotte's & Chelsea Hosp., London, 1959-64; rsch. assoc. Rockefeller Inst., N.Y.C., 1961; chmn. dept. ob.-gyn. Monash U., Melbourne, 1965—; dir. Infertility Med. Ctr., Melbourne, 1978—; chmn. reproductive biology unit Queen Vic Med. Ctr., Melbourne, 1984—, IVF program Monash U., 1978—; found. chmn. med. adv. com. Family Planning Assn., Victoria, Australia, 1970—; dir. Melbourne Gynoscopy Ctr. Author 14 books; contbr. chpts. to books and articles to profl. jours. Decorated comdr. Brit. Empire. Fellow Royal Australian Coll. Ob-Gyns., Royal Coll. Ob-Gyns., Royal Coll. Surgeons (Axel Munthe award for reproductive sci. 1988). Office: Monash Med Ctr Ob-Gyn, 246 Clayton Rd, 284 High St, Ashburton 3147, Australia Office: 284 High St, Ashburton 3147, Australia

WOOD, EMMA S., nursing administrator; b. Lancaster County, Pa., June 20, 1945; d. Moses H. and Elizabeth M. (Shirk) Zimmerman; m. George Wood, Feb. 4, 1977 (dec. July 1989); 1 child, George William Jr. ADN, Edison C.C., 1979; BSN, U. South Fla., 1987, MSN, 1989. RN, Fla.; cert. psychiat. and mental health nurse, cert. profl. in health care quality, clin. specialist in psychiat. mental health. Agy. adminstr., home health nurse VNA of Desoto County, Arcadia, Fla., 1979-81; utilization rev. coord. G. Pierce Wood Meml. Hosp., 1981-85, RN specialist, 1985-89, sr. nurse supr., mgr., 1989-95, nurse educator, 1995—. Mem. ANA, Fla. Nurses Assn., Nat. Assn. for Health Care Quality, Fla. Assn. for Health Care Quality, Am. Psychiat. Nurses Assn., NLN, Sigma Theta Tau. Home: 2808 Caribbean Dr Punta Gorda FL 33982-4302

WOOD, FRANCIS CLARK, JR., medicine educator; b. Phila., Oct. 20, 1928; s. Francis Clark and Mary Louise (Woods) W.; m. Lenora Carolyn Stevenson, Jan. 18, 1958 (dec. 1989); children: Jennie Marilla Wood Sheldon, Amanda Mary Wood Kingsley; m. Thelma Kathryn Philpott, Jan. 5, 1991; 4 stepchildren. AB, Princeton U., 1950; MD, Harvard U., Boston, 1954. Cert. Am. Bd. Internal Medicine, 1963, recert. 1974. Intern King County Hosp., Seattle, 1954-55; med. resident Seattle VA Hosp., 1955-56; med. resident U. Wash., Seattle, 1960-61, mem. faculty dept. medicine, 1961-93, assoc. prof. emeritus, 1993—, program dir. Clin. Rsch. Ctr., 1962-70, assoc. dean Sch. Medicine, 1970-76; chief staff Seattle VA Hosp., 1970-76; dir. physician edn. Providence Med. Ctr., Seattle, 1976-87. Contbr. articles to med. jours., chpts. to books. Lt. (j.g.) USN, 1956-58. Fellow ACP; mem. Endocrine Soc., Am. Diabetes Assn., Wash. State Med. Assn., King County Med. Soc., Wash. Fly Fishing Club. Home: 412 36th Ave Seattle WA 98122-6416 Office: U Wash Dept Medicine Box 356426 Seattle WA 98195

WOOD, JACKIE DALE, physiologist, educator, researcher; b. Picher, Okla., Feb. 16, 1937; s. Aubrey T. Wood and Wilma J. (Coleman) Wood Patterson. BS, Kans. State U., 1964, MS, 1966; PhD, U. Ill., 1969. Asst. prof. physiology Williams Coll., Williamstown, Mass., 1969-71; asst. prof. U. Kans. Med. Ctr., Kansas City, 1971-74, assoc. prof., 1974-78, prof., 1978-79; prof., chmn. dept. physiology Sch. Medicine, U. Nev., Reno, 1979-85; chmn. dept. physiology coll. medicine Ohio State U., Columbus, 1985—; cons. NIH, Bethesda, Md., 1982—. Recipient Research Career Devel. award NIH, 1974, Chancellor's award for teaching excellence U. Kans., 1975; named Hon. Citizen City of Atzugi Japan, 1987; Alexander von Humboldt fellow, W.Ger., 1976. Mem. Am. Physiol. Soc. (assoc. editor 1984-96, rsch. award 1986), Soc. Neurosci., Am. Gastroent. Assn., AAAS, Assn. Chairmen Depts. Physiology. Office: Ohio State U Dept Physiology 300 Hamilton Hall 1645 Neil Ave Columbus OH 43210-1218

WOOD, JAMES H., neurosurgeon, educator; b. Evansville, Ind., Mar. 19, 1948. MD, Johns Hopkins U., 1973. Diplomate Am. Bd. Neurological Surgery. Asst. prof. neurosurgery Emory U., Atlanta, 1981-86, clin. assoc. prof. neurosurgery Med. Coll. Ga., Augusta, 1988—; clin. assoc. surg. neurology br. NIH, Bethesda, 1974-76; chief neurosurgery West Paces Med. Ctr., Atlanta, 1994—, chief surgery, 1996—; vis. prof. Harvard Med. Sch., U. Cin., U. Tenn., Med. Coll. S.C. Editor: (textbooks) Neurobiology of Cerebrospinal Fluid, vol. 1, 1980, vol. 2, 1983, Cerebral Blood Flow, 1987, Carotid Artery Surgery, 1989. Office: Ste 125 3193 Howell Mill Rd NW Atlanta GA 30327

WOOD, JEFFREY JOHN, lawyer; b. Grove City, Pa., Nov. 28, 1952; s. Robert Thomas and Anne Marie W.; m. Carolyn P., Sept. 16, 1977; children: Stephanie, Elaine, Gregory. BA, Juniata Coll., 1976; MEd, Slippery Rock U., 1979; JD, Thomas M. Cooley Law Sch., Lansing, Mich., 1983. Bar: Pa. 1983, U.S. Ct. Appeals (3d, 4th, 6th, 8th, 11th, D.C. and fed. cirs.), U.S. Dist. Ct. (ea., mid., we. dists) Pa., U.S. Supreme Ct., U.S. Claims Ct., U.S. Tax Ct., U.S. Ct. Vet. Appeals, U.S. Ct. Internat. Trade, U.S. Ct. Military Appeals. Program counselor George Jr. Republic, Grove City, Pa., 1976; caseworker, psychologist Pa. Dept. Pub. Welfare, Polk Center, 1976-80; law clk. Lawrence County Ct. Common Pleas, New Castle, 1983-84; mcpl. solicitor, 1985-92, pvt. practice, 1983-92; trust officer Northern Cen. Bank, Williamsport, Pa., 1992-95; chief counsel Pa. Dept. Aging, Gov.'s Office of Gen. Counsel, Harrisburg, 1995—; adj. lectr. Susquehanna U., Selinsgrove, Pa., 1990, 91, Grove City Coll., 1985-88, Butler County C.C., 1984-85, Pa. Coll., Williamsport, 1994. Bd. dirs. day care ctr. St. Paul's United Ch. of Christ, 1989-91; pres. 1987-88; 90-91, ch. coun. , 1989-91; bd. dirs. Selinsgrove Cmty. Libr., 1989-91, pres. 1990-91; adv. bd. Butler County MADD, 1987-88; mem. Synder County Rep. Com., 1988-95, sec. 1990-93; mem. Mercer County Rep. Com., 1984-88; mem. Young Reps. With Pa. NG, 1971-77, 84-85. Mem. Nat. Health Lawyers Assn., Am. Legion. Home: 411 N Broad St Selinsgrove PA 17870-1620

WOOD, LEONARD GEORGE, microbiologist; b. Rochester, N.Y., Apr. 1, 1923; s. William F. and Grace L. (Starrett) W.; m. Elsie Virginia Payne, Apr. 20, 1946; children: Leonard G., Frederick W., Christina, Heather Lee. BS, U. Rochester, 1951; MS, U. Mich., 1952. Bacteriologist Ill. Dept. Pub. Health Lab., Carbondale, 1959—, microbiologist, 1989—, lab. technologist supr., 1991-92, ret., 1992; cons. to dept. wildlife rsch. So. Ill. U. 1992—; field archaeologist State Mus. N.Y., Albany, 1951; pilot Pan Am.-Grace, Lima, Peru, 1945-46. Lt. col. USAF, 1942-72. Mem. AAAS (life), Am. Soc. Microbiology, Ret. Officers Assn. Methodist.

WOOD, MARTHA OAKWELL, obstetrical and gynecological nurse practitioner; b. Chester, Pa., Apr. 19, 1941; d. Albert Edward Jr. and Gertrude Cecelia (Morgan) Warburton; m. Lawrence Dakin Wood, Nov. 22, 1957; children: Lawrence Dakin Jr., Thomas C., Elizabeth W., Michael L., Kathryn M., Scott G. BSN, Neumann coll., 1981; MSN, U. Pa., 1987. RN, Pa. Staff nurse Sacred Heart Med. ctr., Chester, Pa., 1981-84, Crozer-Chester Med. Ctr., 1984-88; clin. instr. obstetrics Neumann Coll., Aston, Pa., 1988, adj. faculty, 1991; instr. maternal-child health Chester County Hosp. Sch. Nursing, West Chester, Pa., 1989-90; adj. clin. instr. Widener U., Chester, 1991; staff devel. specialist Episcopal Hosp., Phila., 1992-93; ob.-gyn. nurse practitioner Camcare Health Corp., Camden, N.J., 1993—, nurse mgr., 1994—; supr. women and children nursing Bryn Mawr (Pa.) Hosp., 1988-89; perinatal nursing support Home Care Obstetrics, Bryn Mawr, 1991-93; manuscript reviewer Lippincott Pub. Co., Phila.; lectr. in field. Educator women's health Women's Assn. for Women's Alternatives, Wawa, Pa., 1990-91; big sister Del. County Pregnancy Ctr.; deaconess North Chester Bapt. Ch., 1991-94. Mem. Pa. Perinatal Assn., Acad. Nurse Practitioners, Assn. Reproductive Health Profls., Assn. Women's Health, Obstetrics, Neonatal Nurses, Sigma Theta Tau (Delta Tau chpt.). Baptist. Home: 103 W Mowry St Chester PA 19013-5023 Office: Camcare Health Corp 3 Cooper Plz Rm 104 Camden NJ 08103-1438

WOOD, MARY JOSEPHINE, physician, radiologist, researcher; b. Pineville, La.; d. Samuel Ray and Bessie Marie (Carter) Baker; m. Charles Donald Wood, Oct. 21, 1949; children: Marie Wiseman, Julia Lucile, Ann Caroline, Charles Martin. BS, U. Ky., 1948; MD, U. Ark., Little Rock, 1966. Diplomate Am. Bd. Radiology, Am. Bd. Nuclear Medicine. Assoc. prof. La. State U. Med. Sch., Shreveport, 1973-87, prof. radiology, 1987—, asst. prof. radiology, 1971-73. Fellow Am. Coll. Nuclear Medicine. Home: La State U Med Ctr Dept Radiology 1501 Kingshighway Shreveport LA 71130

WOOD, MAURICE, medical educator; b. Pelton, Eng., June 28, 1922; came to U.S., 1971; s. Joseph and Eugenie (Lumley) W.; m. Erica Joan Noble, May 1, 1948; children: Roger Lumley, Ashley Michael, Frances Jane. M.B., B.S., U. Durham, Eng., 1945; M.R.C.G.P., Royal Coll. Gen. Practice, London, 1966; F.R.C.G.P., Royal Coll. Gen. Practice, 1975. Diplomate: Am. Bd. Family Practice. Sr. ptnr. med. practice South Shields County, Durham, 1950-71; gen. practice teaching group U. Newcastle, Newcastle-on-Tyne, Eng., 1969-71; gen. clin. asst. dept. psychology-medicine South Shields Gen. Hosp., 1966-71; assoc. prof., dir. research family practice Med. Coll. Va.-Va. Commonwealth U., Richmond, 1971-73, prof., dir. research in family practice, 1973-87, prof. emeritus, 1987—; cons. advisor WHO, Geneva, 1979-90, chmn. working party to develop a classification for primary care, 1979-90; exec. dir. N.Am. Primary Care Rsch. Group, Richmond, 1983-92, past pres., pres. emeritus, 1993—; chmn. com. on cmty. oriented primary care Insts. of Medicine, 1982-84. Assoc. editor: Jour. Family Practice, 1976-83. Recipient award for meritorious svc. Va. Acad. Family Physicians, 1976; Maurice Wood award for career achievement in primary care rsch. foundind in his honor, 1995. Fellow Royal Coll. Gen. Practitioners, Am. Acad. Family Physicians; mem. Inst. Medicine-Nat. Acad. Sci., Soc. Tchrs. Family Medicine (Curtis Hames Career Research award 1984), Inst. of Medicine, NAS, Ambulatory Sentinel Practice Network, Internat. Primary Care Network (treas., bd. mem.). Episcopalian. Lodge: Rotary. Home: Wintergreen Rt 1 Box 672 Roseland VA 22967 Office: MCV-VCU Dept Family Practice PO Box 251 Richmond VA 23202-0251

WOOD, MICHAEL ALLEN, health care executive; b. Mpls., Apr. 4, 1956; s. Lloyd Allen and Mary Frances (Devereaux) W.; m. Jane Mary Selzer, June 5, 1976; children: Jennifer Elizabeth, Jessica Marie. AAS in Cardiopulmonary Tech., Maryville Coll., St. Louis, 1976; BSBA in Fin., Lindenwood Coll., St. Charles, Mo., 1981, MS in Fin., 1982, MBA in Mktg., 1983. Dir. clin. svcs. Health Cons., Inc., St. Louis, 1976-78; adminstrv. dir. Clasen Home Health Care, St. Louis, 1978-83; v.p. mktg. Biomed. Systems Corp., St. Louis, 1983-84; dir. fin. ARA Med. Rehab. Svcs., St. Louis, 1984-85; pres., CEO St. Louis Mgmt. Group, Inc., 1985—, Physicians Healthcare Network, Inc., 1992—; assoc. prof. Lindenwood Coll., 1984—. Contbr. articles to profl. jours. Bd. dirs. Lindenwood Coll. Bd. Overseers, 1988—; bd. dirs. Lindenwood Coll. Alumni Bd., 1986-90; corp. com. Juvenile Diabetes Found., St. Louis, 1989. Mem. St. Louis Soc. Healthcare Planning and Mktg., Med. Group Mgmt. Assn., Mo. Athletic Club, Alpha Sigma Tau. Roman Catholic. Office: St Louis Mgmt Group Inc 1023 Executive Pky Dr Saint Louis MO 63141-6323

WOOD, NANCY ELIZABETH, psychologist, educator; d. Donald Sterret and Orne Louise (Erwin) W. B.S., Ohio U., 1943, M.A., 1947; Ph.D., Northwestern U., Evanston, Ill., 1952. Prof. Case-Western Res. U., Cleve., 1952-60; specialist, expert Dept. HEW, Washington, 1960-62; chief of research Pub. Health, Washington, 1962-64; prof. U. So. Calif., Los Angeles, 1965—; learning disabilities cons., 1960-70; assoc. dir. Cleve. Hearing and Speech Ctr., 1952-60; dir. licensing program Brit. Nat. Trust, London. Author: Language Disorders, 1964, Language Development, 1970, Verbal Learning, 1975 (monograph) Auditory Disorders, 1978, Levity, 1980, Stoneskipping, 1989, Bird Cage, 1994. Pres. faculty senate U. So. Calif., 1987-88. Recipient Outstanding Faculty award Trojan Fourth Estate, 1982, Pres.' Svc. award U. So. Calif., 1992. Fellow Am. Speech and Hearing Assn. (elected, legis. council 1965-68), Am. Psychol. Assn. (cert.), AAAS; mem. Internat. Assn. of Scientists. Republican. Methodist. Office: U So Calif University Park Los Angeles CA 90089

WOOD, NANCY PORTER GUYER, psychotherapist; b. Richmond, Va., Feb. 13, 1943; d. Robert Gregory Porter and Lucy (Van Doren) Oliver; m. Jack Allison, July 17, 1965 (div.); children: Nicole Allison Lysiak, Johnna Allison; m. Chuck Guyer, Oct. 7, 1978; 1 child, Grayson III; m. William R. Wood, Aug. 11, 1994. BA, William and Mary U., 1965; MA, N.C. Cen. U., 1983. Nat. cert. counselor; lic. profl. counselor, N.C. Elem. sch. tchr. Princess Anne County Pub. Schs., Virginia Beach, Va., 1965-67; social worker Luth. Family Svcs., Greensboro, N.C., 1983; counselor U.S. Marine Corps., Parris Island, S.C., 1984; psychotherapist Mental Health Ctr., Opelika, Ala., 1985; family therapist Mental Health Ctr., Pinehurst, N.C., 1986; social worker State of N.C. Juvenile Detention Ctr., Pinehurst, 1987—; pvt. practice psychotherapy Pinehurst and Southport, N.C.; mental health coord. Family and Children's Svcs., Greensboro, N.C., 1993—; pvt. practice psychotherapist Southport, N.C., 1993—; adj. prof. Webster U., Beaufort, S.C., 1983-85; cons. Adolescent Psychiat. Unit The Brunswick Hosp., 1994; family therapist. Editor: Organization and Development Training Manual, 1985. Mem. ACA, C. of C., Lions. Home: PO Box 10445 Southport NC 28461-0445 Office: 107 E 8th St Southport NC 28461

WOOD, PATRICIA ANN, medicine educator, research scientist; b. Mpls., July 17, 1953; d. Lawrence Edward and Helen Gertrude (Canfield) W.; m. William J.M. Hrushesky, June 28, 1985; children: Cassandra Marie Nicole. BS, U. Minn., 1976, MD, 1980, PhD, 1989. Diplomate Am. Bd. Internal Medicine, Am. Bd. Hematology. Intern, resident physician U. Minn., Mpls., 1984-87, med. fellow, 1987-89, med. fellow Albany (N.Y.) Med. Coll., 1989-90; assoc. prof. medicine and pathology Albany Med. Coll., VA Med. Ctr., Albany, 1990—. Recipient Career Devel. award Am. Cancer Soc., 1990, VA Merit award, 1996. Mem. Am. Assn. Cancer Rsch.

WOOD, THOMAS COALE, rehabilitation consultant; b. Flora, Ill., July 11, 1951; s. Cordell Howard and Connie Euphemia (Coale) W.; m. Linda Louise Hefner, Nov. 2, 1974; children: Julia Merritt, Robert Coale. BS in Journalism, U. Colo., 1977; MEd in Counseling and Human Devel. Services, U. Ga., 1982. Cert. rehab. counselor, ins. rehab. specialist, case manager; lic. profl. counselor, Ga. Reporter, Macon Telegraph & News (Ga.), 1978; asst. dir. phys. plant Mercer U., Macon, 1978-81; rehab. coordinator Underwriters Adjusting Co., 1982-84; rehab. cons. Conservco, Macon, 1984-91; pvt. practice rehab. cons. & vocat. expert, Macon, 1991-94; owner The Wood Group, Salem, Va., 1994—. Home: 48 Sawyer Dr Salem VA 24153-6810

WOOD, WILLIAM C., surgeon, medical educator, academic chairman; b. Fairbury, Ill., May 3, 1940; s. William A. and Violet B. (Johnson) W.; m. Judith A. Lindsell, Aug. 15, 1964; children: Kristen Marie, William Andrew, Lindsay Ann. BS cum laude, Wheaton Coll., 1962; MD cum laude, Harvard U., 1966. Asst. prof. Harvard Med. Sch., Boston, 1975-82; asst. prof., chief surg. oncology Mass. Gen. Hosp., Harvard Med. Sch., Boston, 1982-90; prof., chmn. dept. surgery Sch. Medicine Emory U., Atlanta, 1991—; chair breast com. Ea. Coop. Oncology Group, Boston, 1991—; co-chmn. Early Brast Cancer Clin. Trialists Coop. Group, Oxford, Eng., 1995—. Bd. dirs., mem. exec. com. Gordon Conwell Theol. Seminary, S. Hamilton, Mass., 1975—; bd. dirs. Found. Holy Apostles, Atlanta, 1994—. Mem. Am. Soc. Clin. Oncology (bd. dirs. 1995—), Soc. Surg. Oncology (sec. 1995—). Office: Emory U Dept Surgery 1364 Clinton Rd NE Atlanta GA 30322

WOOD, WILLIAM GERARD, anesthesiologist; b. Los Alamos, N.Mex., June 21, 1954; s. William Wayne and Betty Jean (King) W.; children: Ryan, Leah, Emily. BS in Chemistry summa cum laude, U. N.Mex., 1976, MD, 1981. Diplomate Am. Bd. Anesthesiology. Intern in anesthesiology Meth. Med. Ctr., Dallas, 1981-82, U. Tex. SW Med. Ctr., Dallas, 1982-84; staff anesthesiologist USAF, Biloxi, Miss., 1984-86, chief cardiovascular anesthesiology, 1986-88; pvt. practice Bedford (Tex.) Anesthesiology Assocs., 1988-91, Dallas, 1991—; courtesy staff HCA/Columbia North Hills Med. Ctr.; cons. Harris Meth. Continued Care Hosp.; active staff Harris Meth. HEB Hosp. Contbr. articles to profl. jours.; presenter in field. Major, USAF, 1987-88. Recipient AMA Physician Recognition award 1989, 92, 95. Mem. AMA, Am. Soc. Anesthesiologists, Soc. Cardiovascular Anesthesiologists, Soc. Ambulatory Anesthesia, Am. Soc. Regional Anesthesia, Malignant Hyperthermia Assn. of the U.S., Anesthesia Patient Safety Found., Tex. Soc. Anesthesiologists, Tex. Med. Assn., Tarrant County Med. Soc., Dallas County Soc. Anesthesiologists. Republican. Roman Catholic. Office: Pavilion I, Ste 204 221 West Colorado Blvd Dallas TX 75208-2300

WOOD, WILLIAM JARMER, ophthalmologist, educator; b. Lexington, Ky., May 14, 1943; s. W.C.H. and Ruth (Jarmer) W.; children: Lucy Gay, William Jr., Edward Hunt. AB, U. Ky., 1965, MD, 1970. Diplomate Am. Bd. Ophthalmology (examiner). Intern U. Ky. Med. Ctr., Lexington, 1970-71; resident in ophthalmology Wilmer Inst., Johns Hopkins U. Sch. Medicine, Balt., 1971-74; retinal fellow Harvard U., Boston, 1974-75; pvt. practice, Lexington, 1975—; dir. retina svc. U. Ky. Coll. Medicine, 1984-88, clin. prof., 1986—. Contbr. numerous articles to med. jours. Office: Retina and Vitreous Assocs 120 N Eagle Creek Dr Ste 500 Lexington KY 40509-1827

WOODALL, GILBERT EARL, JR., medical administrator; b. Oak Ridge, Tenn., Dec. 21, 1954; m. Sarah Lee Blackburn, Sept., 1989; children: John Sage, Anna Alleen. BA, U. Tenn., 1976; MD, U. Tenn., Memphis, 1977; MS in Pub. Health, Western Ky. U., 1986. Med. dir. GM-Corvette Plant, Bowling Green, Ky., 1982-92, Alliant-Health at Work, Louisville, 1993-94, Jackson Madison-County Gen. Hosp.-Occupl. Medicine, Jackson, Tenn., 1995—. Mem. Mayor's Commn. on Employment and Disability Issues, Bowling Green, 1991, Meharry Med. Sch. Occupational Medicine Residency Adv. Bd., Nashville, 1987-88. Lt. comdr. USNR, 1978-82. Fellow Am. Coll. Occupational and Environ. Medicine (bd. dirs. 1987-90), Am. Coll. Preventive Medicine; mem. Tenn. Med. Assn. Office: JMCGH-Occupational Medicine 708 W Forest Ave Jackson TN 38301

WOODARD, CLARA VERONICA, nursing home official; b. Bayonne, N.J.; d. William George and Lula (Langston) Yelverton; m. John Henry Woodard; children: John Michael, Stephen Jay. Grad., Bayonne Hosp. Sch. Nursing, 1951, Manhattan Sch. Radiology, 1953, NYU-Bellevue Med. Ctr., 1955, Valencia Community Coll., Orlando, Fla. RN, N.J., Fla. Head nurse Bayonne Hosp., 1949-50; office nurse Dr. D.G. Morris, Bayonne, 1951-52; pvt. duty nurse Christ Hosp and Bayonne Hosp., 1954-58; tchr. kindergarten, Nuremburg, Fed. Republic Germany, 1972-73; ICU-CCU nurse Holy Spirit Hosp., Camp Hill, Pa., 1973-74; head nurse Orlando Gen. Hosp., 1974-76, house supr., 1976-78; dir. nurses Winter Park (Fla.) Care Ctr., 1980-83; Medicare coord. Pinar Terrace Manor, Orlando, 1987-92, clin. instr., 1992—, house supr., nurse mgr. Alzheimer unit, 1993—; instr. Valencia Coll., Orlando, Fla. Named Employee of Yr. and Employee of Month, Orlando Gen. Hosp., 1980, Employee of Month, Winter Park Care Ctr., 1983. Mem. NAFE, Nat. League Negro Women. Democrat. Roman Catholic. Home: 2931 De Brocy Way Winter Park FL 32792-4505 Office: Pinar Terrace Manor 7950 Lake Underhill Rd Orlando FL 32822-8229

WOODBURY, LEE VERNON, health care consultant, physician; b. Florence, S.C., Dec. 18, 1949; s. George Sr. and Melvena Candice (White) W.; m. Bernardette Isabelle Freeman, Aug. 25, 1973 (div.); children: Lee Vernon II, Jenifer Candice Elizabeth. BS, Morehouse Coll., 1973; MD, Med. Univ. S.C., 1977. Diplomate Nat. Bd. Med. Examiners. Intern Richland Meml. Hosp., Columbia, S.C., 1977-80, resident in internal medicine, 1980; chief med./surg. svcs. S.C. Dept. Mental Health, Columbia, 1984-86, dir. profl. svcs., 1987-88, facility dir., CEO Tucker Ctr., 1988-92, divsn. dir., long term care, 1992-94, cons. spl. projects, 1994—; chmn. Agy. Pharmacy and Therapeutics Com., Columbia, 1988-94; emergency med. cons. Space Shuttle Landing Team, Edwards AFB, Calif., 1981-83; dir. ICU Edwards AFB Hosp., 1981-83; cons. internal medicine S.C. Dept. Mental Health, Columbia, 1986—. Chmn. bd. dirs. Profl. Health Svcs., Columbia, 1987-90; chmn. bd. trustees First N.E. Bapt. Ch., Columbia, 1988-91; chmn. advisor

Am. Security Coun. Found., Washington, 1982-89; dir. med. group United Way of Midlands, 1991-92; active NAACP, 1993—, Healthy People-2000, 1992—. Maj. USAF, 1980-84. Recipient Recognition award Am. Security Coun. Found., 1983. Mem. S.C. State Employees Assn. (bd. dirs. 1988—). Office: SC Dept Mental Health Office Occupl Health/Safety 2100 Bull St Columbia SC 29202

WOODCOCK, JANET, federal official; b. Washington, Pa., Aug. 29, 1948; d. John and Frances (Crocker) W.; m. Roger Henry Miller, Nov. 16, 1981; children: Kathleen Miller, Susanne Miller. BS cum laude, Bucknell U., 1970; MD, Northwestern U., Chgo., 1977. Diplomate Am. Bd. Internal Medicine. Intern Hershey Med. Ctr./Pa. State U., 1977-78, resident in internal medicine, 1978-80, chief resident in medicine, 1980-81; fellow in rheumatology U. Calif./VA Med. Ctr., San Francisco, 1982-84; instr. medicine divsn. rheumatology and immunology VA Med. Ctr., San Francisco, 1984-85; med. officer divsn. biol. investigational new drugs Ctr. for Biologics Evaluation and Rsch./FDA, Rockville, Md., 1986-87, group leader divsn. biol. investigational new drugs, 1987-88, dep. dir. divsn. biol. investigational new drugs, 1988, dir. divsn. biol. investigational new drugs, 1988-90; dir. Ctr. for Drug Evaluation and Rsch./FDA, Rockville, Md., 1994—; acting dep. dir. Ctr. for Biologics Evaluation and Rsch., FDA, Rockville, Md., 1990-92, dir. office of therapeutics rsch. and rev., 1992-94; dir. Ctr. for Drug Evaluation and Rsch., FDA, Rockville, 1994—; instr. medicine, asst. prof. divsn. gen. internal medicine Hershey Med. Ctr./Pa. State U., 1981; analytical chemist rsch. divsn. A.B. Dick Co., Niles, Ill., 1971-73. Nat. Merit scholar Bucknell U., 1966, Pa. State scholar, 1966; Rsch. fellow Am. Rheumatism Assn.; VA Investigator grantee, 1985. Mem. Alpha Omega Alpha, Alpha Lambda Delta. Office: Dept Health & Human Svc Center Drug Evaluation & Rsch 5600 Fishers Ln Woodmont II Bldg HFD-001 Rockville MD 20857

WOODCOCK, JONATHAN HUGH, health facility director, neurologist; b. Chelsea, Mass., Oct. 17, 1951; s. Hugh Wesson and Ann Harriet (Walker) W.; m. Nancy Margaret Regeness, Dec. 18, 1976; children: Rachel Ann, Mollie Christine, Sarah Margaret. BA, Houghton Coll., 1973; MD, SUNY, Buffalo, 1977. Diplomate Am. Bd. Internal Medicine, Am. Bd. Neurology and Psychiatry in neurology and psychiatry. Resident in internal medicine Case Western Res. Univ. Hosps., Cleve., 1977-79; resident in neurology Mass. Gen. Hosp., Boston, 1979-82; resident in psychiatry McLean Hosp., Belmont, Mass., 1982-84; asst. neurology Mass. Gen. Hosp., Boston, 1984-89; dir. neuropsychiatry unit McLean Hosp., Belmont, 1984-89; med. dir. NeuroBehavioral Inst. of Rockies, Boulder, Colo., 1989-90, Mediplex Rehab-Denver, Thornton, Colo., 1991—; rsch. fellow neurology Mass. Gen. Hosp., 1981-84; instr. psychiatry Harvard Med. Sch., Boston, 1984-89; clin. instr. neurology U. Colo. Health Scis. Ctr., 1992—, asst. clin. prof., 1993—; pres. bd. dirs. Colo. Head Injury Found., 1994-95; mem. profl. adv. bd. Epilepsy Found. Colo., 1991—. Co-author: Impulse Control Disorders, 1986, Behavioral Aspects of Huntington's Disease, 1990. Bd. Overseeing Elders Grace Chapel, Lexington, Mass. 1982-86, assoc. chmn., 1986; bd. dirs. Christian Mission for UN Community 1984—, chmn. 1989—. Mem. APA, Am. Acad. Neurology, Am. Neuropsychiat. Assn., Behavioral Neurology Soc., Am. Soc. Neurorehab. Office: Mediplex Rehab-Denver 8451 Pearl St Denver CO 80229-4804

WOODFIELD, DAVID GRAEME, medical specialist; b. Geraldine, New Zealand, May 9, 1935; s. John Thomas and Mary Elizabeth (Wild) W.; m. Annabell Lynetta Reid, Dec. 15, 1962; children: Belinda, Katherine, Sallyann, Michael. MB ChB, Otago Med. Sch., New Zealand, 1960; PhD, U. Edinburgh, Scotland, 1968. Med. registrar Hosp. Bd., Auckland, New Zealand, 1960-65; rsch. registrar Royal Infirmary, Edinburgh, 1965-68; cons. Govt. of Libya, Tripoli, 1968-70; med. dir. Red Cross Soc. BTS, Papua New Guinea, 1970-76, Regional Blood Svc., Auckland, New Zealand, 1976—; med. adviser Auckland Red Cross Soc., 1979-92; chmn. Med. Aid Abroad, Auckland, 1980, Bapt. City Mission, Auckland, 1978-92; mem. AIDS adv. com. Wellington, N.Z., 1987-93; councillor Internat. Soc. Blood Transfusion, Paris, 1988-92. Contbr. more than 250 articles to profl. jours. Nat. exec. mem. Red. Cross Soc., 1982-84. Fellow Royal Coll. Physicians (Edinburgh), Royal Coll. Physicians (Australia); mem. Australasian Soc. Blood Transfusion (pres. 1993-95), Australasian and S.E. Asian Tissue Typing Assn. (pres. 1989-90), South Pacific Com. Health Rsch. Coun., Rotary Club of Kumeu. Home: 412 Taupaki Rd, Kumeu New Zealand Office: Auckland Regional Blood Svc, Private Bag 92024, Auckland New Zealand

WOODFIELD, DENIS BUCHANAN, health care company executive; b. N.Y.C., Oct. 23, 1933; s. William Frederick and Margery Brunton (Hoyt) W.; m. Rosemary Humphries, Feb. 16, 1963; children: Katherine, Nicholas, Elizabeth. BA, Harvard U., 1954; PhD, Oxford U., 1962. Trainee Chase Manhattan Bank, N.Y.C., 1962-65; analyst Gen. Electric, N.Y.C., 1965-68; banking dir. Pan Am. World Airways, N.Y.C., 1968-74; dir. treasury svcs. Johnson & Johnson, New Brunswick, N.J., 1974-93; exec. dir. P.R. Industries and Svcs. Assn., Princeton, N.J., 1994—; bd. dirs. Br. Schs. and Univs. Found. Author: Surreptitious Printing in England 1550-1640, 1973, English Armorial Bookbindings, 1958. Trustee Princeton Pub. Libr., 1978-92; bd. dirs. Friends of Princeton Univ. Libr., 1994—. Named hon. mem. Sr. Common Room, Lincoln Coll., Oxford U., 1978. Mem. Manorial Soc. Gt. Britain (U.S. chmn. 1981—), Grolier Club (N.Y.C.), Nassau Club (Princeton, N.J.). Episcopalian. Clubs: Grolier (N.Y.C.), Nassau (Princeton, N.J.). Home: 883 Lawrenceville Rd Princeton NJ 08540-4317 Office: PR Industries and Svcs Assn PO Box 7526 Princeton NJ 08543-7526

WOODHOUSE, BERNARD LAWRENCE, pharmacologist, educator; b. Norfolk, Va., Aug. 14, 1936; s. Bernard L. and Marsha Ruth (Blakeney) W., June 6, 1964; children: Donna Anita, Bernadette LaVonne, Dawn Marie. BS, Howard U., 1958, MS, 1963, PhD, 1973. Instr. A&T Coll. of N.C., Greensboro, 1963-64; instr. Savannah (Ga.) State Coll., 1964-70, asst. prof., 1970-73, assoc. prof., 1973-79, prof., 1979—, dir. biology rsch. grants, 1976—, chmn. animal and welfare com., 1976-81. Mem. Savannah (Ga.) Guardsmen, sec., 1989. Grantee NIH, 1975-80, 80-87, Hoffman-La Roche, Inc., Nutley, N.J., 1976-85, 85-90. Mem. Ga. Acad. of Sci., Drug Enforcement Adminstrn, Beta Beta Beta. Democrat. Methodist. Home: 12437 Largo Dr Savannah GA 31419-2056 Office: Savannah State Coll PO Box 20353 Savannah GA 31404-9716

WOODHOUSE, DERRICK FERGUS, ophthalmologist; b. Sutton, Surrey, U.K., May 29, 1927; s. Sydney Carver and Erica (Ferguson) W.; m. Jocelyn Laira Perry, Mar. 9, 1957; children: Karen Tace, Iain Kenrick, Gillian Erica. BM, BCh., Oxford U., Eng., 1951; DO, London Coll., 1956. Intern in medicine, surgery, ophthalmology St. Thomas Hosp., Plymouth, Exeter Hosps., London, 1952-53; registrar in ophthalmology Birmingham (Eng.) Eye. Hosp., 1958-60; sr. registrar in ophthalmology Bristol (Eng.) Eye Hosp., 1960-63; cons. eye surgeon Wolverhampton & Midland Counties Eye Infirmary, Eng., 1963-89; staff opthalmologist Liverpool Hosp., NSW, Australia, 1989—. Contbr. articles to profl. jours.; author: Ophthalmic Nursing, 1980. Mem. Wolverhampton Health Authority, 1970-77; treas. Ophthalmic Nursing Bd., 1970-84, chmn., 1984-88. With RAF, 1953-57. Recipient Gold medal, Nepal Med. Assn., 1989. Fellow Royal Coll. Surgeons, Royal Soc. Medicine, Royal Coll. Ophthalmologists; mem. Irish Coll. Ophthalmologists, Brit. Computer Soc., N.Y. Acad. Scis. Mem. Soc. of Friends.

WOODING, WILLIAM MINOR, medical statistics consultant; b. Waterbury, Conn., Aug. 24, 1917; s. George Lee and Ella Elizabeth (Asher) W.; m. Nina C. Peaslee, May 30, 1940; children: Barbara Lee Wooding Bose, Elizabeth Ann Wooding Kontur. B Chem. Engring. cum laude, Poly. Inst. Bklyn., 1953. Lab. asst. Am. Cyanamid Co., Stamford, Conn., 1941-44, chemist, 1945-50, rsch. chemist, 1950-56, rsch. adminstrv. svcs. coord., 1956-57; asst. chief chemist Revlon Rsch. Ctr., N.Y.C., 1957-60, assoc. rsch. dir., 1960-65; assoc. rsch. dir. Carter-Wallace, Inc., Cranbury, N.J., 1965-67, dir. tech. svcs., 1967-75; dir. statis. svcs. Carter-Wallace, Inc. and Wallace Labs., Cranbury, 1975-82; cons. med. statis. and clin. trials BioStatistics, Swanton, Vt., 1982—; instr. Stat-a-Natrix Inst., Edison, N.J., 1983-86. Author: Planning Pharmaceutical Clinical Trials, 1994. Home and Office: BioStatistics RR 1 Box 4690 Maquam Shore Swanton VT 05488-9736

WOODLE, E. STEVE, transplant surgeon; b. Texarkana, Ark., Jan. 7, 1954; m. Linda Metzger, Sept. 7, 1979; three children. BS summa cum laude, Tex. A&M U., 1976; MD magna cum laude, U. Tex., 1980. Diplomate Am. Bd. Surgery, Am. Coll. Surgeons. Asst. prof. surgery Washington U. Sch. Medicine, St. Louis, 1990-92; asst. prof. surgery & immunology U. Chgo., 1992—; com. mem. Ctr. for Biol. Evaluation and Rsch., FDA, Washington, 1994—. Contbr. over 70 articles to med. and sci. jours. Mem. Am. Soc. Transplant Surgeons, Internat. Transplantation Soc., numerous others. Office: U Chgo Dept Surgery MC 5027 5841 S Maryland Chicago IL 60637

WOODLEY, DAVID TIMOTHY, dermatology educator; b. St. Louis, Aug. 1, 1946; s. Raoul Ramos-Mimosa and Marian (Schlueter) W.; m. Christina Paschall Prentice, May 4, 1974; children: David Thatcher, Thomas Colgate, Peter Paschall. AB, Washington U., St. Louis, 1968; MD, U. Mo., 1973. Diplomate Am. Bd. Internal Medicine, Am. Bd. Dermatology, Nat. Bd. Internal Medicine. Intern Beth Israel Med. Ctr., Mt. Sinai Sch. Medicine, N.Y. Hosp., Cornell U. Sch. Medicine, N.Y.C., 1973-74; resident in internal medicine U. Nebr., Omaha, 1974-76; resident in dermatology U. N.C., Chapel Hill, 1976-78, asst. prof. dermatology, 1983-85, assoc. prof. dermatology, 1985-88; prof. medicine, co-chief div. dermatology Cornell U. Med. Coll., N.Y., 1988-89; prof. and vice chair dept. dermatology Stanford U., 1989-93, Northwestern U., 1993—; research fellow U. Paris, 1978-80; expert NIH, Bethesda, Md., 1983-89; prof., assoc. chmn. dermatology Stanford U Sch. Medicine, 1989-93; chmn. dermatology Sch. Medicine Northwestern U., 1993—. Contbr. chpts. to books and articles in field to profl. jours. Mem. Potomac Albicore Fleet, Washington, 1982-83, Friends of the Art Sch., Chapel Hill, 1983—, Jungian Soc. Triangle Area, Chapel Hill, 1983—. Fellow Am. Acad. Dermatology; mem. Dermatology Found., Am. Soc. for Clin. Research, Soc. Investigative Dermatology, ACP (assoc.), Assn. Physician Poets, Am. Soc. for Clin. Investigation, 1988. Home: 503 W Barry Ave Chicago IL 60657-5416 Office: Northwestern U Med Sch Dept Dermatology 303 E Chicago Ave Chicago IL 60611

WOODMAN, GREY MUSGRAVE, psychiatrist; b. Birmingham, Eng., Jan. 26, 1922; came to U.S., 1959, naturalized, 1963; s. Edward Musgrave and Ida (Cullen) W.; m. Bette Woodman; children: Sheila, Shonagh. BA, U. Oxford (Eng.), 1943, MA, BM, BCh, 1945. Ship's surgeon, 1946-48; intern Whipps Cross Hosp., London, 1948-49, med. registrar, 1951-54, also Newcastle-on-Tyne, Eng., 1951-54; resident in Psychiatry U. Okla. Med. Ctr., 1959-62; staff psychiatrist Western Mo. Mental Health Ctr., Kansas City, 1962-76; med. dir. Mental Health Ctr. Clinton County, Clinton, Iowa, 1976-87; pvt. practice, Clinton, 1976—; founder, dir. Lincolnshire Clinic; mem. staff Jane Lamb Health Ctr., Mercy Hosp. (now Samaritan Health System); staff mem. Comphealth; cons. Mufon. Served with Brit. Merc. Marines, 1946-48. Fellow Royal Soc. Medicine (London, life); mem. AMA (life), Am. Psychiat. Assn. (life), Am. Acad. Med. Hypoanalysts (assoc.), Brit. Med. Assn., World Fedn. Mental Health, Iowa Med. Soc. (past chmn. hospice com.), Internat. Assn. Social Psychiatry. Republican. Episcopalian. Home: 515 N 13th St Clinton IA 52732-4816 Office: Lincolnshire Clinic 223 Wilson Bldg Clinton IA 52732

WOODMANSEE, RAY JAMES, medical case manager, nurse consultant; b. Inglewood, Calif., Aug. 10, 1961; s. Raymond Arthur and Joy Ann (Hardy) W.; m. Jacqueline D'Lynn Tipton, Aug. 18, 1984; children: Joshua Scott, Lauren Noel. BSN cum laude, Azusa Pacific U., 1983. Cert. pub. health nurse, Calif., case mgr.; RN, Calif., Alaska; cert. quality assurance utilization rev. Am. Bd. Quality Assurance and Utilization Rev. Physicians. Nurses aide Driftwood Convalescent Ctr., Torrance, Calif., 1980; nursing tech. Little Co. of Mary Hosp., Torrance, 1982-84, staff nurse acute obs. unit, 1984-85; staff nurse coronary care unit Humana Hosp., Anchorage, 1985-87, cert. medevac nurse medevac team, 1986-89, staff nurse ICU, 1987-89; nurse auditor Fortis Corp., Anchorage, 1989-91; nurse cons. Eagle Ins. Group, Anchorage, 1991-93; nurse, cons., owner Healthcare Evaluations of Alaska, Anchorage, 1991-93; nurse cons., pres. Healthcare Mgmt. Svcs., Inc., Anchorage, 1994—. Dist. del. Alaska Rep. Party, Anchorage, 1992. Mem. NRA, Individual Case Mgmt. Assn. Republican. Pentacostal. Home: 8610 Jupiter Dr Anchorage AK 99507 Office: Healthcare Mgmt Svcs Inc 3820 Lake Otis Pky Ste 111 Anchorage AK 99508-5209

WOODRUFF, CHIVERS RICHARD, JR., physician; b. Birmingham, Ala., Aug. 11, 1944; s. Chivers Richard Sr. and Cherry (Scogin) W.; m. Julia Walls Mariani, Aug. 3, 1968; children: Chivers III, Jake James. BS in Pharm., Samford U., 1967; PhD, U. Ala., Birmingham, 1972, MD, 1974. Diplomate Am. Bd. Med. Examiners, Am. Bd. Family Practice. Pvt. practice Birmingham, 1975—; med. dir. Beverly Health Care Ctr., Birmingham, 1980—, Oak Knoll Nursing Home, Birmingham, 1984—; assoc. prof. of family practice Dept. Family Practice U. Ala., Birmingham, 1980—; intern Birmingham Bapt. Hosp., 1974-75; pres. med. staff Brookwood Hosp., Birmingham, 1989-91, chmn. dept. medicine, 1985-89. Contbr. articles to profl. jours. Recipient physician recognition award AMA, 1992; fellow Am. Found. for Pharm. Edn., 1970-72. Fellow Am. Acad. Family Physicians; mem. So. Med. Assn., Jefferson County Med. Soc., Med. Assn. Ala., Birmingham C. of C. Republican. Mem. Christian Ch. Home: 1206 Cheval Ln Birmingham AL 35216-2037 Office: 200 Montgomery Hwy Birmingham AL 35216

WOODRUFF, DEANNA GLYN, emergency room nurse; b. Newnan, Ga., Sept. 16, 1971; d. Gerald Glen and Sara Elizabeth (Shelnutt) Griffies; m. Tony Woodruff, May 21, 1994. AN magna cum laude, West Ga. Coll., Carrollton, 1992. RN, Ga.; cert. emergency nurse; cert. ACLS, BLS. Emergency rm. nurse West Ga. Coll., Carrollton, 1992—.

WOODRUFF, KAY HERRIN, pathologist, educator; b. Charlotte, N.C., Sept. 22, 1942; d. Herman Keith and Helen Thelma (Tucker) Herrin; m. John T. Lyman, May 3, 1980; children: Robert, Geoffry, Carolyn. BA in Chemistry, Duke U., 1964; MD, Emory U., 1968. Diplomate Am. Bd. Pathology (trustee 1993—). Medicine and pediat. intern U. N.C., Chapel Hill, 1968-69, resident in anatomic pathology, 1969-70; chief resident in anatomic pathology, instr. U. Okla., Oklahoma City, 1970-71, fellow in electron microscopy-pulmonary pathology, instr., 1971-72; chief resident in clin. pathology U. Calif., San Francisco, 1972-74, asst. clin. prof. dept. anatomic pathology, 1974-91, assoc. clin. prof., 1991—; chief electron microscopy VA Hosp., San Francisco, 1974-75, attending clin. cons. dept. anatomic pathology, 1986—; pvt. practice, San Pablo, Calif., 1981—; pres. med. staff Brookside Hosp., San Pablo, 1994, med. dir. Regional Cancer Ctr., 1995—; assoc. pathologist Children's Hosp., San Francisco, 1979-81, St. Joseph's Hosp., San Francisco, 1977-79; cons. pathologist Lawrence Berkeley (Calif.) Lab., 1974-93; med. dir. Bay Area Tumor Inst. Tissue Network, San Pablo, 1989—; asst. clin. prof. pathology health and med. scis. program U. Calif., Berkeley and U. Calif., San Francisco Joint Med. Program, 1985-91, assoc. clin. prof., 1991—, others. Contbr. articles and abstracts to med. jours. Mem. exec. bd. Richmond (Calif.) Quits Smoking, 1986-90, Bay Area Tumor Inst., Oakland, Calif., 1987—; mem. exec. bd. Contra Costa unit Am. Cancer Soc., Walanut Creek, Calif., 1985-87, mem. profl. edn. com., 1985—, mem. pub. edn. com., 1985-86, mem. task force on breast health Calif. div., 1992-93; mem. transfusion adv. com. Irwin Meml. Blood Bank, San Francisco, 1977-83; chmn. transfusion adv. com. Alameda Contra County Blood Bank, 1989-92; commr. Calif. Bd. Med. Quality Assurance, 1978-80. Recipient young investigator award Am. Lung Assn., 1975-77; Outstanding Svc. awards Am. Cancer Soc., 1986, 87, Disting. Svc. award, 1988; Disting. Clin. Tchg. award U. Calif., San Francisco and Berkeley Joint Med. Program, 1987, Outstanding Tchg. award, 1988, Excellence in Basic Sci. Instrn. award, 1990, Excellence in Tchr. Clin. Scis. award, 1993; cert. of recognition Cmty. Svc. Richmond, 1989. Mem. AMA, Coll. Am. Pathologists (editl. bd. CAP Today 1986-90, bd. govs. 1990-96, chair coun. on practice mgmt. 1994), Am. Med. Women's Assn. (exec. bd. 1984-87, regional bd. govs. 1984-87), No. Calif. Women's Med. Assn. (pres. 1982-84), Calif. Soc. Pathologists (bd. dirs. 1988-90), No. Calif. Oncology Group, South Bay Pathology Soc., Am. Assn. Blood Banks, Calif. Med. Assn., Alameda-Contra Costa County Med. Soc., Am. Soc. Clin. Pathology, Calif. Pathology Soc. Office: Brookside Hosp Dept Pathology 2000 Vale Rd San Pablo CA 94806-3808

WOODRUFF, MARTHA JOYCE, home health agency executive; b. Unadilla, Ga., Jan. 3, 1941; d. Metz Loy and Helen (McCorvey) Woodruff. BA, Shorter Coll., 1963; MA, U. Tenn.-Knoxville, 1972. Tchr., Albany H.S. (Ga.), 1963-69; instr. U. Tenn.-Knoxville, 1970-72; asst. prof. Valdosta State Coll. (Ga.), 1972-76; coord. Staff Builders, Atlanta, 1976-78; pres., owner Med. Pers. Pool, Knoxville, 1978-93; owner, pres. Priority Healthcare Svcs, Knoxville, 1993—, Pers. Pool of Knoxville, Inc., 1985-87; mem., adviser Owners Adv. Coun., Pers. Pool of Am., Ft. Lauderdale, Fla., 1980-82; active Altzheimers Assn. Mem. Nat. Coun. on Aging, Nat. Assn. for Adult Daycare, Exec. Women Internat. (bd. dirs. Knoxville chpt. 1996), East Tenn. Women's Polit. Caucus, Tenn. Assn. Home Care, Nat. Assn. Homecare, Knoxville C. of C. (com. for cost containment 1982-85), Blount County C. of C. (retirement com. 1983, mem. indsl. rels. com. 1983). Republican. Methodist.

WOODRUFF, RONALD RUDOLPH, physician assistant; b. Elizabeth, N.J., June 23, 1949; s. Elliott Franklin Woodruff and Charlotte Dorothy Bauer; m. Susan Claire Jackson , Sept. 25, 1970 (div. Dec. 1985); children: Christopher Paul, Jennifer Lyn; m. Julie Greenup, Oct. 3, 1987. BS in Medicine, U. Nebr., 1978. Cert. physician asst. Nat. Commn. on Cert. of Physician Assts. Enlisted USN, 1971-96; hosp. corpsman USN, Jacksonville, Fla., 1994; primary care physician asst. Naval Regional Med. Ctr., Orlando, Fla., 1978-82; emergency medicine physician asst. Naval Regional Med. Ctr., Phila., 1982-88; primary care physician asst. Nat. Naval Med. Ctr., Bethesda, Md., 1988-91; advisor Office of Navy, Surgeon Gen., Washington, 1988-91; emergency medicine physician asst., divsn. officer Naval Air Sta. Agana (Guam) Br. Med. Clinic, 1991-93; clin. coord. physician asst. program Naval Hosp., Camp Pendleton, Calif., 1993-96; ret. USN, 1996; instr., provider ACLS, pediatric ALS, neonatal ALS, BCLS instr.; ambulance instr. EMT. Fellow Am. Acad. Physician Assts. (charter life mem. vets. caucus), Naval Assn. Physician Assts. (pres. 1995—); mem. Assn. Mil. Surgeons of U.S. (life), Tex. Acad. Physician Assts. (affiliate), Oreg. Acad. Physician Assts. (affiliate), Calif. Acad. Physician Assts. (affiliate). Republican. Lutheran. Home: 111 Creekside Terr Boerne TX 78006-5631 Office: Clear Springs Clinic 1529 Hwy 46 New Braunfels TX 78130

WOODS, ALAN CHURCHILL, JR., retired surgery educator; b. Balt., July 1, 1918; s. Alan Churchill and Anne Powel (Byrd) W.; m. Julie Reiner; children: Alan Churchill III, Runyon Colie, Richard C.B., Louise Huntington. AB, Princeton U., 1940; MD, Johns Hopkins U., 1943. Diplomate Am. Bd. Surgery. Intern Johns Hopkins Hosp., Balt., 1943-44, asst. resident in surgery, 1944-45, 48-49, Halsted fellow in surgery, 1949-50; resident Henry Ford Hosp., Detroit, 1948-49; from instr. to assoc. prof. Johns Hopkins U. Sch. Medicine, 1950-88, assoc. prof. emeritus, 1988—; cons. surgeon Union Meml. Hosp., Balt., 1953—, Greater Balt. Med. Ctr., 1953—. Contbr. articles to med. jours. Capt. M.C., AUS, 1946-48. Fellow ACS. Democrat. Episcopalian. Home: 207 Wendover Rd Baltimore MD 21218-1838

WOODS, GERALDINE PITTMAN, health education consultant, educational consultant; b. West Palm Beach, Fla.; d. Oscar and Susie (King) Pittman; m. Robert I. Woods, Jan. 30, 1945; children: Jan, Jerri, Robert I. Student, Talladega Coll., 1938-40, D.Sc. (hon.), 1980; B.S. in Zoology, Howard U., 1942; M.A., Radcliffe Coll. and Harvard U., 1943, Ph.D. in Neuroembryology, 1945; D.Sc. (hon.), Benedict Coll., 1977; HHD (hon.), Howard U., 1989; LHD (hon.), Meharry Med. Coll., 1988; DSc (hon.), Fisk U., 1991, Bennett Coll., 1993. Instr. Howard U., Washington, 1945-46; pres. L.A. chpt. Jack and Jill, 1954-56; pres. Aux. to Med., Dental and Pharm. Assn. of So. Calif., 1951-55, state pres., 1955; past mem. local met. bd. YWCA; mem. nat. adv. coun. Gen. Med. Scis. Inst. NIH, 1964-68, spl. cons., 1969-87; mem. gen. rsch. support program adv. com., div. rsch. resources NIH, 1970-73, 77-78. Mem. regional com. Girl Scouts U.S.A., 1969-75, nat. bd., 1975-78; exec. bd. Cmty. Rels. Conf. So. Calif., 1968-72; exec. com. Leadership Conf. Civil Rights, 1967-70; chmn. Def. Adv. Com. Women in Svcs., 1968; mem. air pollution manpower devel. adv. com. EPA, 1973-75; mem. fgn. svcs. officers selection bds. Dept. State, 1967; mem. Calif. Com. on Public Edn.; mem. Calif. Post Secondary Edn. Commn., 1974-78, vice chmn., 1976; chmn. bd. trustees Howard U., 1975-88; chmn. Howard U. Found., 1984-88; trustee Calif. Mus. Found., Atlanta U., 1974-86; bd. dirs. Ctr. for Ednl. Opportunity at Claremont Colls., Robert Wood Johnson Health Policy Fellowships; mem. Inst. Medicine of NAS, 1974—, Nat. Commn. for Cert. of Physicians Assts., 1974-81; initiated Minority Access to Rsch. Careers, also, Minority Biomed. Rsch. Support program NIH, 1972; co-chmn. internat. conf. Woman to Woman: Single Parenting from a Global Perspective, 1987; video Re: MARC and MBRS programs A Time for Celebration, 1987; bd. dirs. Charles R. Drew U. Medicine and Sci., 1990-93; founder Head Start, L.A., 1965 (award 1985). Named Woman of Yr. Zeta Phi Beta, 1954, one of 20 Famous Black Scientists Nabisco, Black Woman of Achievement Smithsonian Instn., 1981; recipient Meritorious Achievement award Nat. Med. Assn., Inc., 1979, Leadership Achievement award Nat. Assn. Equal Opportunity in Higher Edn., 1987, awards from Pres.'s Coun. of Youth Opportunity, Iota Phi Lambda, Nat. Pan-Hellenic Coun., Howard U. Alumni Assn., So. Calif. Nat. Assn. Colored Women, Calif. Mus. Found., Ch. Christian Fellowship, NIH, Howard U., Delta Sigma Theta, Delta Headstart, 1985, award Calif. State U., 1993, others; one of honorees Dollars and Sense mag. Salute to Am.'s Top 100 Black Business and Profl. Women, 1985; Morehouse Coll. program Rsch. Extravaganza dedicated to her, 1988; named to Gallery of Honor, Assn. Minority Health Profl. Schs., 1990. Mem. NAACP (life), Nat. Coun. Negro Women (life), Golden Key, Phi Beta Kappa, Delta Sigma Theta (pres. R & D Found. 1983-88, nat. pres. 1963-67, ann. Geraldine P. Woods sci. award for Fed. City Alumnae chpt. established in her honor given to an outstanding scientist, Geraldine Pittman Woods Headstart/State Presch. Ctr. dedicated 1993, Mary Church Ferrell award 1979), Delta Sigma Theta. Congregationalist.

WOODS, JAMES STERRETT, toxicologist; b. Lewistown, Pa., Feb. 26, 1940; s. James Sterrett and Jane Smith (Parker) W.; m. Nancy Fugate, Dec. 20, 1969; 1 dau., Erin Elizabeth. AB, Princeton U., 1962; MS, U. Wash., 1968, PhD, 1970; MPH, U. N.C., 1978. Diplomate Am. Bd. Toxicology. Research assoc. dept. Pharmacology Yale U. Sch. Medicine, New Haven, 1970-72; staff fellow environ. toxicology. Nat. Inst. Environ. Health Scis. br. NIH, Research Triangle Park, N.C., 1972-75, head biochem. toxicology sect., 1975-77; program leader environ.-occupational health risk evaluation Battelle Ctrs. for Pub. Health Rsch. and Evaluation, Seattle, 1978—; research prof. U. Wash., Seattle, 1979—. Contbr. articles to profl. jours. Served with USN, 1962-66. Scholar USPHS, 1966-70, Am. Cancer Soc., 1970-72. Mem. AAAS, APHA, Am. Assn. Cancer Rsch., Am. Soc. Pharmacology and Exptl. Therapeutics, N.Y. Acad. Sci., Pacific NW Assn. Toxicologists (founding pres.), Soc. Epidemiology Rsch., Sox. Toxicology, Am. Coll. of Epidemiology. Home: 4516 55th Ave NE Seattle WA 98105-3837 Office: Battelle Research Ctr 4000 NE 41st St Seattle WA 98105-5428

WOODS, JO ELLEN, medical technologist; b. West Union, Ohio, Dec. 17, 1960; d. Jack Ronald and Phyllis Ann (Cooper) Johnson; 1 child Nicholas Tison. ASS, Tyler (Tex.) Jr. Coll., 1985. instr. Universal Pecaution, Columbus. Mem. Health and Safety Com., Columbus, Ohio, 1992—, Hostage Negotiation Team, Columbus, 1996. With Tex. State Guard, 1985-86. Mem. Am. Registry Radiology Technologists, Am. Registry Clin. Radiology Technologists, Ohio Soc. Radiology Technologists. Home: 556 Rocky Fork Blvd Gahanna OH 43230

WOODS, KAREN MARGUERITE, psychologist, human development, institute executive; b. Columbus, Ga., Sept. 17, 1945; d. O. Norman and Nan Catherine (Land) Shands; m. Carl Allen Oberkrom, Sept. 3, 1966 (div. Aug. 1974); children: Kristi Lynn, Jeffrey Michael; m. James Wallace Woods II, Aug. 19, 1978 (div. Feb. 1986); 1 child, Jamie Elizabeth. Student, Mercer U., 1963; BA, William Jewell Coll., 1975; MA, U. Mo., Kansas City, 1976. Lic. psychologist, Mo. Counselor, juvenile officer Platte County Juvenile Ct., Platte City, Mo., 1976-78; sch. psychologist North Kansas City Sch. Dist., Mo., 1978-80; counselor Platte Med. Clinic, Platte City, 1981-84; co-founder/dir. north office Counseling Ctr. for Human Devel., Kansas City, 1984-87; founder, pres. Inst. for Human Devel., Kansas City, 1987—; mem. com. of psychologists State of Mo., 1990—; cons. State Com. of Psychologists, 1990-95, Platte Valley Spl. Edn. Coop., Smithville, Mo., 1984-88; spkr. to area schs. and bus., 1976—, Northland Child Abuse Spkrs. Bur., 1976-78; dir., founder Northland Women's Resource Ctr., Kansas City, 1989—, Northland Women's Resource Ctr., 1989-94. Mem. adv. bd. Mo. Div. Family Services, 1981-83; mem. Northland Child Abuse Task Force, Gladstone, Mo., 1981-83. PEO grantee, 1976; named one of Outstanding Young Women in Am., 1978. Mem. NAFE, Am. Psychol. Assn., Mo. Psychol. Assn., Kansas City Mental Health Assn., Zeta Tau Alpha. Democrat.

Methodist. Club: Clayview Country. Office: Inst for Human Devel 4444 N Belleview Ave Ste 110 Kansas City MO 64116-1507

WOODS, KIMBERLY A., medical technologist; b. Dallas, Nov. 1, 1966; d. Marvin Lloyd and Regina Hattie (Moucka) Adams; m. Robert Scott Woods, Aug. 3, 1991; 1 child, Ryan Scott. AS, Navarro Jr. Coll., Corsicana, Tex., 1987; BS in Biology, East Tex. State U., 1990; ADN, El Centro Coll., Dallas, 1996. Med. technologist Baylor U. Med. Ctr., Dallas, 1986-96; med. technologist, occupls. technician Baylor Works, Ennis, Tex., 1996—; med. technologist P.E.P. Club, 1993-96; lectr. on safety Baylor U., Dallas, 1995-96. Chmn. Nat. Lab. Week Picnic, Dallas, 1993-96. Mem. Beta Sigma Phi (corr. sec. 1990-91, sec. 1992-93, pres. 1993-94, organizer fund raisers 1994-95). Republican. Methodist. Home: 905 Lakeway Ennis TX 95119

WOODS, NANCY FUGATE, women's health nurse, educator. BS, Wis. State U., 1968; MSN, U. Wash., 1969; PhD, U. N.C., 1978. Staff nurse Sacred Heart Hosp., Wis., 1968, Univ. Hosp., Wis., 1969-70, St. Francis Cabrini Hosp., 1970; nurse clinician Yale-New Haven Hosp., 1970-71; instr. nursing Duke U., Durham, N.C., 1971-72, from instr. to assoc. prof., 1972-78; assoc. prof. physiology U. Wash., Seattle, 1978-82, prof. physiology, 1982-84, chairperson dept. parent and child nursing, 1984-90, prof. dept. parent and child nursing, 1990—; dir. Ctr. Women's Health Rsch., U. Wash., Seattle, 1989—; Pres. scholar U. Calif., San Francisco, 1985-86; cons. USPHS, 1984-85, U. Tex., U. Mont, NIH, 1987, Oreg. Health Sci. U., 1985-87, 87-89, Nat. Ctr. Nursing, 1988, Nordic Inst. Nursing Sci., 1990, U. N.C., Chapel Hill, 1990, 91, U. Ariz., 1991, Mont. State U., 1991, Emory U., Atlanta, 1992. Contbr. articles to profl. jours. Fellow ANA, Am. Acad. Nursing; mem. AAUP, APHA, Am. Coll. Epidemiology, Soc. Menstrual Cycle Rsch. (v.p. 1981-82, pres. 1983-85), Soc. Advanced Women's Health Rsch. Office: U Wash Ctr Womens Health Rsch Sch Nursing Seattle WA 98195*

WOODS, ROBERT CHARLES, family practice physician; b. Oklahoma City, Sept. 10, 1948; s. Horace Franklin and Marie (Powell) W.; m. Dawn Ellan Branstine, Oct. 3, 1975; 1 child, Pamela Sue. BS, Okla. State U., 1972; DO, U. Health Scis., 1981. Physician, pres. Buffalo (Mo.) Family Clinic, Inc., 1982—; exec. v.p. Drs. Hosp. Springfield, Mo., 1991-95. Mem. bd. Mo. State Bd. Healing Arts, Jefferson City, 1991—. Sgt. Okla. ANG, 1970-76. Mem. Ozark Dist. Osteo. Assn. (trustee 1984—), Mo. Osteo. Assn. (pres. 1995—, 1st v.p. 1994-95, 2d v.p. 1993-94, trustee 1984—), Am. Osteo. Assn. (del. 1994—). Mem. Ch. Nazarene. Office: Buffalo Family Clinic Inc PO Box 740 Buffalo MO 65622

WOODS, SAMUEL DWIGHT, surgeon; b. Tyro, Kans., Sept. 14, 1930; s. Samuel Branchford and Hattie Harriet (Crawford) W.; m. Marilyn Frances Miller, Sept. 5, 1954 (div. Sept. 1984); children: Steven, Cynthia, Dennis, Donald, Thomas; m. Cynthia Chase Quick Thorne, Oct. 12, 1984. BA, U. Kans., 1952, MD, 1955. Diplomate Am. Bd. Surgery. Surgeon Davis & Woods, Kansas City, Mo., 1963-86, Midwest Surgery, Olathe, Kans., 1986-87, Woods Surg. Care, PA., Olathe, 1987—; chmn. dept. surgery St. Luke's Hosp., Kansas City, Mo., 1979-81; pres. Olathe Med. Ctr. Med. Staff, 1979-80. Mem., chmn. Mid-Am. Comprehensive Health Planning, Kansas City, Mo., 1973-75. Lt. USNR, 1956-58. Fellow Am. Coll. Surgery (sec.-treas. Kansas City chpt. 1992—). Office: Woods Surg Care PA 20375 W 151st St Ste 350 Olathe KS 66061

WOODS, SHERWYN MARTIN, psychiatrist, educator; b. Des Moines, Iowa, June 25, 1932; m. Nancy Bricard. BS with high honors, U. Wis., Madison, 1954, MD with high honors, 1957. Diplomate Am. Bd. Psychiatry and Neurology. Intern Phila. Gen. Hosp., 1957-58; resident in psychiatry U. Wis., Madison, 1958-60, chief resident in psychiatry, 1960-61; instr. psychiatry U. Wis. Med. Sch., Madison, 1961; asst. prof. dept. psychiatry U. So. Calif., L.A., 1963-68, assoc. prof., 1968-74, prof., 1974—; sr. physician LAC-USC Med. Ctr.; asst. instr., instr., now supervising and tng. analyst So. Calif. Psychoanalytic Inst.; vis. prof. U. Wis., 1966-74, U. N.C., 1974, U. B.C., 1977, Pa. State U., 1978, Hebrew U. Med. Sch., Jerusalem, 1979, U. Tex. Med. Sch., 1979, Loma Linda U., 1982, UCLA, 1983, U. Calif.-Davis, 1983; cons. in field. Editl. bd. Contemporary Psychiatry: Jour. Critical Rev., 1981—, Jour. Psychiat. Edn., 1988, Acad. Psychiatry, 1989—; psychiatry editor Med. Grand Rounds, 1982-87; series editor Critical Issues in Psychiatry, 1986-94; reviewer various med. jours.; contbr. articles to profl. jours. Capt. USAF, 1961-63. Grantee NIMH, 1964-66. Fellow Am. Acad. Psychoanalysis, Am. Coll. Psychiatrists, Am. Coll. Psychoanalysts, Am. Psychiat. Assn.; mem. AMA, AAUP, Am. Assn. Dirs. Psychiat. Residency Tng., Am. Psychoanalytic Assn., Assn. Acad. Psychiatry, Assn. Advancement Psychotherapy, Group for Advancement Psychiatry, Internat. Psychoanalytic Assn., Psychiat. Alumni Continuing Edn., So. Calif. Psychiat. Assn., So. Calif. Psychoanalytic Soc., Salerni Collegium. Office: Univ So Calif Sch Medicine 1937 Hospital Pl Los Angeles CA 90033-1071

WOODS, SIMON DARYL SELBY, surgeon; b. Melbourne, Victoria, Australia, Sept. 23, 1955; s. Clifford Selby and June (Wyatt) W.; m. Katherine Ann Spall, June 6, 1981; children: Lachlan, Sally, Amy. HSC, Scotch Coll., Melbourne, Australia, 1971; MBBS, U. Melbourne, 1978. Registered specialist surgeon. Resident Alfred Hosp., Melbourne, Australia, 1979-81, advanced surg. trainee, 1982-85, asst. surgeon, 1988-95, head upper gastrointestinal surgery, 1995—; vis. lectr. surgery Aberdeen (Scotland) U., 1986-87, The Chinese U. Hong Kong, 1987-88; sr. lectr. Monash U., Melbourne, Australia, 1993—. Contbr. chpts. to books. Fellow Royal Australian Coll. Surgeons. Office: Surg Cons Group Ste 44 Cabrini Med Ctr, 183 Wattletree Rd, Malvern 3144 Victoria Australia

WOODS, STEPHEN CHARLES, psychology and medical educator; b. Pasadena, Calif., Feb. 17, 1942; s. Jamie W. and Virginia (Stephens) W.; m. Valerie J. Guest, Feb. 29, 1964 (div. 1985); children: Scott S., Alison J.; m. Evelyn M. Laiche, May 21, 1988. BS in Zoology, U. Wash., 1965, BS in Psychology, 1966, PhD in Psychology and Physiology, 1970. Asst. prof., then assoc. prof. psychology Columbia U., N.Y.C., 1970-73; from asst. prof. to prof. U. Wash., Seattle, 1973-77, prof. psychology and medicine, 1977—, chair dept. psychology, 1981-88, assoc. dean grad. sch. for acad. programs and rsch., 1991—; lectr. various univs. Contbr. articles to profl. jours., chpts. to books. Grantee NIH, 1971—. Fellow Soc. for Study of Ingestive Behavior (pres. 1988-89); mem. Am. Psychol. Assn., Internat. Congress Physiology of Food and Fluid Intake (internat. bd. dirs. 1983-89, pres. 1986-89), N. Am. Assn. for Study of Obesity (bd. dirs. 1984-86). Office: U Wash Dept Psychology # Ni-25 Seattle WA 98195

WOODS, SUSAN LOUISE, nursing educator; b. Los Angeles, Nov. 6, 1946; d. Charles John and Mary Jane (Roach) Blank; m. Thomas W. Glenn, June 8, 1968 (div. 1972); m. James Earl Woods, Aug. 2, 1975; children: Jaime Rose, Jennifer Mary. Diploma in nursing L.A. County/U. So. Calif. Med. Ctr., 1967; BS in Nursing, U. Wash., 1973, MNursing, 1975; PhD Oreg. Health Scis. Ctr., 1991. RN Staff nurse L.A. County/U. So. Calif. Med. Ctr., L.A., 1967-69, Drs. Hosp., Phoenix, 1969-70, VA Hosp., Seattle, 1970-71; head nurse CCU, USPHS Hosp., Seattle, 1971—; from instr. to assoc. prof. nursing U. Wash., Seattle, 1975-93, prof., 1993—, instr. continuing edn., 1975—, assoc. dean acad. programs, 1996—. Author: Cardiac Nursing (AJN Books of Yr. award), 1982, 3rd edit. 1995, Medical Surgical Nursing (AJN Books of Yr. award), 1986, 2d edit. 1991; editor Cardiovascular Medications for Cardiac Nursing, 1990, Cardiovascular Critical Care Nursing, 1983; contbg. author in field. Recipient Nursing Edn. award U. Wash., 1975, disting. alumnus of yr. 1996 Oreg. Health Scis. Univ.; grantee HEW, 1977-79, DHHS, 1981-86. Fellow Am. Heart Assn. (coun. on CVN 1988, K. Lembright award for nursing rsch. 1995); mem. Am. Assn. Critical Care Nurses (award 1985), Am. Heart Assn. (award 1979), Sigma Theta Tau. Republican. Roman Catholic. Home: 3629 1st Ave NW Seattle WA 98107-4904 Office: U Wash Box 357266 Seattle WA 98195-7266

WOODS, WALTER EARL, biomedical manufacturing executive; b. Phila., Sept. 26, 1944; s. Walter Earl and Janet I. (Ferguson) W.; m. Anna Maria Gianfreda, Dec. 4, 1975; children: Jeffrey, Elaine, Roberto, Carlo. BS in Biology, Del. Valley Coll. Sci. and Agr., 1966. Pilot plant operator Shell Chem., Woodbury, N.J., 1966-67; virologist, tissue culturist 1st U.S. Med. Lab., N.Y.C. and Ft. Meade, Md., 1967-69; virologist Merck, Sharpe & Dohme, West Point, Pa., 1969-70; quality control and assurance supr. Richardson-Merrell Inc., Swiftwater, Pa., 1970-74; cons., dir. influenza vaccine mfg. Richardson-Merrell Inc., Naples, Italy, 1974-75; mgr. biol. prodn. Richardson-Merrell Inc., Swiftwater, 1976-78; mgr. biol. prodn. Connaught Labs., Inc., Swiftwater, 1978-81, dir. vaccine mfg., 1982-84, dir. mfg. resource planning, class A rating, 1984-88, dir. product devel. and mgmt., 1989-91; dir. project mgmt., chmn. HIB and Pertussis bus. groups Pasteur Mérieux Connaught, 1991-95; project dir. licensing Acellular Pertussis and Japanese Encepahlitis Vacines, 1992, HIB vaccine, 1993, licensed acP vaccine, Germany, 1994; bus. dir. for license of acellular pertussis vaccine, infant indications; mem. joint devel. com. Merck-Connaught Partnership; corp. sponsor for licensing of DTacP vaccine for infant use, 1996. Bd. dirs. Northeastern Pa. Indsl. Resource Ctr., Wilkes-Barre, Pa., 1988-91. Recipient Banting-Best award, 1989. Mem. ASM, Pharm. Mfrs., Project Mgmt. Inst., Internat. Assn. Biol. Standardization. Home: 53 Deerfield Way Scotrun PA 18355-9637 Office: Connaught Labs Inc PO Box 187 Swiftwater PA 18370-0187

WOOD-SMITH, DONALD, plastic surgeon; b. Sydney, Australia, June 30, 1931; s. William Frederick and Vera Mary; children: Christina Margaret, Donald William, Phillip Raynor. MB, BS, Sydney U., 1954. Diplomate Am. Bd. Plastic Surgury. Surg. resident Lewisham Hosp., Sydney, 1954-56, Royal Marsden Hosp., 1957-58; resident plastic surgery N.Y. U. Hosp. Med. Center, 1960-64, asst. and assoc. attending surgeon, 1964-92; vis. surgeon Bellevue Hosp., 1964-92; chmn. plastic surgery Manhattan Eye Ear and Throat Hosp., 1975-77; assoc. prof. plastic surgery NYU, 1977-84, prof., 1984-92; surgeon, dir. plastic surgery Manhattan Eye Ear and Throat Hosp., 1977-84; cons. plastic surgeon N.Y. Eye and Ear Infirmary, chmn. dept. plastic and reconstructive surgery, 1984—; prof. plastic surgery Columbia Presbyn. Med. Ctr., 1991—. Author: Nursing Care of the Plastic Surgery Patient, 1967, Cosmetic Facial Surgery, 1973; contbr. articles to med. jours. Fellow ACS, Royal Coll. Surgeons of Edinburgh; mem. Am. Assn. Plastic Surgeons, Am. Soc. Plastic and Reconstructive Surgeons, Am. Soc. Maxillofacial Surgeons, N.Y. Acad. Medicine, Brit. Assn. Plastic Surgeons, N.Y. Athletic Club. Republican. Office: 830 Park Ave New York NY 10021

WOODSON, GAYLE ELLEN, otolaryngologist; b. Galveston, Tex., June 9, 1950; d. Clinton Eldon and Nancy Jean (Stephens) W.; m. Kevin Thomas Robbins; children: Nicholas, Gregory, Sarah. BA, Rice U., 1972; MD, Baylor Coll. Medicine, 1975. Diplomate Am. Bd. Otolaryngology (bd. dirs.). Fellow Baylor Coll. Medicine, Houston, 1976, Inst. Laryngology & Otology, London, 1981-82; asst. prof. Baylor Coll. Medicine, 1982-87; asst. attending Harris County Hosp. Dist., Houston, 1982-86; with courtesy staff Saint Luke's Episcopal Hosp., Houston, 1982-87; assoc. attending The Methodist Hosp., Houston, 1982-87; asst. prof. U. Calif. Med. Sch., San Diego, 1987-89; chief otolaryngology VA Med. Ctr., San Diego, 1987-92; assoc. prof. U. Calif. Sch. Med., San Diego, 1989-92; prof. otolaryngology U. Tenn., Memphis, 1993—; mem. staff Bapt. Meml. Hosps., Meth. Hosps., Le Bonheur Children's Hosp.; numerous presentations and lectures in field. Contbr. numerous articles and abstracts to med. jours., also videotapes. Fellow ACS (bd. govs.), Royal Coll. Surgeons, Soc. Univ. Otolaryngologists, Am. Soc. Head and Neck Surgery, Am. Laryngol. Assn., Triological Soc.; mem. AMA, Am. Acad. Otolaryngology-Head and Neck Surgery (bd. dirs.), Am. Med. Women's Assn. (pres. Memphis br.), Soc. Head and Neck Oncologists Eng., Am. Physiol. Soc., Assn. Women Surgeons, Am. Bd. Otolaryngology (bd. dirs., residency rev. com. for otolaryngology), Am. Soc. of Head and Neck Surgeons (coun.). Office: U Tenn Dept Oto/HNS U Calif Med Ctr 956 Court B2-10 Memphis TN 38163

WOODSON, JANE HOLT, educator; b. Norfolk, Va., Sept. 17, 1937; d. R. Garland and Mae Goldie (Morris) Holt; m. William Carter Woodson, 1955; children: Debra Jayne, William Jeffrey, Gregory Holt Woodson (dec.). BS, Lynchburg Coll., 1967; MEd, U. Va., 1973, Edn. Specialist, 1988. Cert. tchr. Va. Tchr., guidance counselor, dir. Bedford County (Va.) Schs., 1967-84; guidance counselor, dir. Amherst County (Va.) Schs., 1984-93; site supr. student tchrs. Lynchburg Coll., 1970-91; cons. Ednl. Cons. Svcs., Lynchburg, 1986-92; coll. bd. adminstr. ETS Amherst County Schs., 1985-89. Author: I Want to Go Home, 1988 (Nat. Honor citation Am. Cancer Soc. 1989), Counseling Families of Terminally Ill Children: An Option-Death at Home, 1990. Vol. Am. Cancer Soc., Leukemia Soc. Mem. NEA, AAUW, Counselors Assn., Va. Assn. for Supervision and Curriculum Devel., Va. Sch. Counselors Assn., Potomac and Chesapeake Assn. of Coll. Admissions Counselors, Phi Delta Kappa, Chi Sigma Iota, Kappa Delta Pi. Home: 4645 Alabama Ave Lynchburg VA 24502-1107

WOODWARD, JAMES KENNETH, pharmacologist; b. Anderson, Mo., Feb. 5, 1938; s. Audley J. and Doris Evelyn (Fields) W.; A.B. in Chemistry, B.S. in Biology, S.W. Mo. State Coll., 1960; postgrad. U. Kans. (USPHS fellow) 1960-62; Ph.D. (USPHS fellow), U. Pa. Sch. Medicine, 1967; m. Kathleen Ruth Winget, June 25, 1960 (div. Nov. 1994); children—Audley J., Kimie Connette; m. Lisa Marie Stuart, Feb. 28, 1996. Pharmacologist, Stine Lab., Newark, Del., 1963-65, research pharmacologist, 1967-71; sr. research pharmacologist Merrell-Nat. Labs., Cin., 1972-73, sect. head, 1973-74, head dept. pharmacology, 1974-78; head dept. pre-clin. pharmacology Merrell Research Center, Merrell Dow Pharms., Inc., 1978-83, assoc. dir. research adminstrn. Merrell Dow Research Inst., 1983-88, dir. biol. devel. Merrell Dow Research Inst., 1988-90, dir. int. reg. affairs, 1990-93; dir. clin. cand. prep. Marion Merrell Dow, 1993, ret., 1993, cons., 1993. USPHS postdoctoral fellow U. Pa., 1967. Pres., Golf Manor Recreation Commn., Cin., 1973-75. Mem. Phila. Physiol. Soc., AAAS. Democrat. Baptist. Patentee antisecretory compounds of imidazoline series. Home: 972 Sheridan Dr Lancaster OH 43130 Office: 2110 E Galbraith Rd Cincinnati OH 45237-1625

WOODWARD, MARY LUCILE, home dialysis nurse, patient educator; b. Carroll, Iowa, June 10, 1951; d. Wilbur John and Lucile Kathryn (Schaefer) Singsank; m. William Callaghan Woodward, Aug. 17, 1974; 1 child, Wesley Charles. Diploma in Nursing, Creighton Meml. St. Joseph's, Omaha, 1972. RN, Nebr.; cert. nephrology nurse, Nephrology Nursing Bd. Staff nurse, charge nurse, acting head nurse St. Joseph's Hosp., Omaha, 1972-78, staff nurse, home peritoneal dialysis trng. nurse, 1978-93; home dialysis charge nurse Dialysis Clinic Inc., Omaha, 1993—; cons. visually impaired Travenal Lab., Deerfield, Ill., 1985; presenter symposium Am. Nephrology Nurses Assn., N.Y., 1987, Tex., 1989; vol. nursing practice advisor Neb. Bd. Nursing, Lincoln, 1990—. contbr. articles to profl. jours. co-leader Cub Scouts of Am., 1990-94. Mem. Am. Nephrology Nursing Assn. (sec./treas. Platte River chpt.), Nat. Kidney Found., Daughters of Seton (sec.). Roman Catholic. Home: 4720 N 109th Circle Omaha NE 68164 Office: Dialysis Clinic Inc 3316 Dodge St Omaha NE 68131

WOODWARD, MICHAEL CLIFFORD, geriatrician, researcher; b. Melbourne, Victoria, Australia, Jan. 6, 1955; s. William John and Sue Mary (Himing) W.; m. Anne Julie Dickins, Nov. 26, 1976; children: Sophy K., Erin C.S., Tess M. MB, BChir, Melbourne U., 1979. Intern, resident med. officer, registrar Royal Melbourne Hosp., 1980-83; registrar Mount Royal Hosp., Victoria, 1984-85; Victoria; specialist physician Repatriation Gen. Hosp., Heidelberg, Victoria, 1988-95; dir. Aged Care Svcs. Austin Repatriation Ctr., Heidelberg, 1995—; chmn. med. adv. coun. MacLeod Hosp., Victoria, 1990-93; mem. Repatriation Pharm. Ref. Com., Canberra, Australia, 1990—; mem. patient care com. Heidelberg Repatriation Hosp., 1990-91. Co-author: Geriatric Medicine, 1991; contbr. chpts. to books, articles to profl. jours. Fellow Royal Australasian Coll. Physicians (sec. com. for physician tng. 1996—, bd. censors 1996—); mem. Australian Assn. Gerontology (pres. Victoria divsn. 1990-94), Australian Soc. for Geriatric Medicine (chairperson edn. & tng. subcom.) Brit. Geriatrics Soc., Am. Geriatrics Soc. Home: 23 McAuley Dr, Rosanna 3084, Australia Office: Heidelberg Repatriation Hos, Aged Care Svcs, Banksia St, Heidelberg West 3081, Australia

WOODWARD, PAMELA ROSE, nurse, healthcare administrator; b. Canton, Ohio, Sept. 18, 1943; d. Wallace Ralph and Ruth Lucille (Hershberger) Hutchison; children: Angela Kay, Alison Rae. Grad. Aultman Hosp. Sch. Nursing, 1965; BS in Edn., Kent State U., 1973; MS in Edn., U. Akron, 1978; EdD U. Akron, 1995. RN, cert. tchr., Ohio. Staff nurse Aultman Hosp., Canton, 1965-66; mem. faculty, supr. Aultman Hosp. and Aultman Hosp. Sch. Nursing, 1966-70, mem. faculty sch. nursing, 1970-79, adminstrv. coordinator research, 1979-81, asst. dir. curriculum, 1981-84, dir. nursing quality assurance and nursing research, 1984-88, dir. quality assurance, 1988-90, assoc. exec. dir. quality assurance officer Ctrl. Mental Health, 1990-91, assoc. exec. dir., 1992—; instr. CPR. Mem. Am. Nursing Assn., Ohio Nursing Assn., Am. Assn. Critical Care Nurses, Emergency Dept. Nurses Assn., Assn. Supervision and Curriculum Devel., Aultman Hosp. Nurses Alumni Assn., Minerva Area Nurses Assn., Sigma Theta Tau, Phi Delta Kappa, Pi Lambda Tau. Presbyterian. Home: 901 Lynnwood Dr Minerva OH 44657-1229 Office: 832 Mckinley Ave Canton OH 44702

WOODWARD, THEODORE ENGLAR, medical educator, internist; b. Westminster, Md., Mar. 22, 1914; s. Lewis Klair and Phoebe Helen (Neidig) W.; m. Celeste Constance Lauve, June 24, 1938; children: William E., R. Craig, Celeste L. Woodward Applefeld. BS, Franklin and Marshall Coll., 1934, DSc (hon.), 1954; MD, U. Md., 1938; DSc (hon.), Western Md. Coll., 1950, Hahnemann U., 1993. Diplomate Am. Bd. Internal Medicine. Asst. prof. medicine U. Md. Sch. Medicine, Balt., 1946-48, assoc. prof., also dir. sect. infectious disease, 1948-54, prof., 1954-83, prof. emeritus, 1983—, chmn. dept., 1954-81; attending physician Balt. VA Med Ctr, 1949—; with Armed Forces Epidemiol. Bd., Washington, 1952-92, mem. commns., 1952-72, pres. bd., 1976-78, 80-92; mem. U.S./Japan Coop. Med. Sci. Program, Washington, 1965—; disting. physician Cen. VA, Washington, 1981-87. Author: Chloramphemicol, 1958, 200 Years of Medicine in Baltimore, 1976, A History of the Department of Medicine, University of Maryland, 1807-1981, 1987, A History of Armed Forces Epidemiological Board, 1940-1990, 1990, Carroll County (Md.) Physicians of the 19th and Early 20th Centuries, 1990, The Armed Forces Epidemiological Board: The History of the Commissions, 1995; contbr. chpts. to textbooks. Life trustee Gilman Sch., Balt., 1955—. Lt. col. Medical Svc. Corp U.S. Army, 1941-46, ETO, PTO. Decorated Order of the Sacred Treasure Gold and Silver Star Govt. of Japan; recipient U.S.A. Typhus Commn. medal Dept. Def., 1945, also Exceptionally Disting. Svc. award, 1990, Outstanding Civilian Svc. medal with oak leaf cluster Dept. Army, 1981. Recipient Disting. Svc. award AMA, 1995. Mem. ACP (master, gov. Md. regent 1969-70, James D. Bruce Meml. award 1970, Disting. Tchr. award 1992), Am. Clin. and Climatol. Assn. (pres. 1969-70), Infectious Disease Soc. Am. (pres. 1976-77, Finland award 1972, Bristol award, Kass award 1991), Inst. Medicine NAS, Elkridge Club (Towson, Md.), Mayo Fellows Assn. (hon.), Hamilton St. Club. Republican. Home: 1 Merrymount Rd Baltimore MD 21210-1908 Office: Balt VA Med Ctr 10 N Green St Baltimore MD 21210

WOODWARD, WILLIAM CHRIS, physician, educator; b. Phila., Sept. 15, 1956; s. William Lee and Alice Bernice (Wenke) W.; children: Matthew James, John Michael. AA, Bucks County C.C., Newtown, Pa., 1976; BA, Temple U., Phila., 1978; D Osteopathy, Phila. Coll. Osteopathic Medicine, Phila., 1982; intern, Univ. Medicine and Dentistry N.J.-SOM, 1982-83, resident internal medicine, 1983-86. Diplomate Am. Bd. Internal Medicine; lic. Pa., N.J., Ky. Emergency medicine attending East Coast Emergency Physicians, Stratford, N.J., 1984-86; med. dir. No. Liberties Med. Ctr., Phila., 1986-88; pvt. practice Phila., 1987-88; med. dir. Doctors To Your Door, Lexington, Ky., 1988-90; pvt. practice Lexington-Fayette County Health Dept., Lexington, Ky., 1988-91, Coventry Family Med. Group, Pottstown, Pa., 1991-94; staff physician Montgomery County Health Dept., Pottstown, Pa., 1992-94; med. dir. Coventry Manor Nursing Home, Pottstown, Pa., 1993-94; tchr. attending Allentown (Pa.) Osteopathic Med. Ctr. Clinics, 1994-95; med. dir. Keystone Hospice, Ft. Washington, Pa., 1995—; staff physician Family Health Ctr. St. Joseph Med. Ctr., 1995—; staff physician Rainbow Home, Wernersville, Pa., 1995—; dir. HIV specialty clinic St. Joseph Med. Ctr., 1995—; dir. amb. care tng. facility Internal Medicine/Primary Care Residency Metro. Hosp., 1986-87; adj. clin. faculty Coll. of Osteopathic Medicine U. New England, 1995—; assoc. dir. Family Practice Residency St. Joseph Med. Ctr., 1995—; adj. clin. faculty Dept. Internal Medicine PCOM, 1995—. Mem. bd. dirs. Keystone Cmty. Blood Bank, 1995—; mem. med. adv. com. Berks AIDS Network, 1995—; founding mem. bd. dirs. and v.p. John A. Woodward Meml. Found., Inc., 1995—. Recipient Med. Resident Essay Competition Am. Coll. Osteopathic Internists, 1987, award Ea. Regional Osteopathic Convention, 1987, Med. Resident Manuscript award Dept. Medicine Univ. Medicine and Dentistry N.J.-SOM, 1986. Mem. AAAS, Am. Med. Dirs. Assn., Am. Osteopathic Assn., Pa. Med. Dirs. Assn., Pa. Osteopathic Med. Assn., Physicians Assn. for AIDS Care. Office: Saint Joseph Med Ctr 200 N 13th St Ste 200 Reading PA 19604

WOODWORTH, HAROLD CYRIL, physician; b. Wells, Minn., Sept. 23, 1920; s. Harry Clark and Martha Meta (Wiecking) W.; AB, Dartmouth Coll., 1942; MD, Harvard U., 1944; PhD, Yale U., 1958; m. Evelyn Eileen Mahon, Aug. 17, 1944; children: Richard, Karl. Intern, Mary Hitchcock Hosp., Hanover, N.H., 1944-45; resident internal medicine, White River Junction, Vt., 1947-48; practice family medicine, Bristol, Vt., 1948-52; chief Microbiology Lab., Ctr. Disease Control, USPHS, Atlanta, 1958-68; county health officer Colbert and Lauderdale Counties, Ala., 1968-75; regional health officer N.W. Ala. Regional Health Dept., Tuscumbia, 1975-81; ret., 1981. Served with USN, 1945-46, 52-54. Recipient Physician's Recognition award AMA, 1979-82; Boss of Yr. award Muscle Shoals Bus. and Profl. Women's Assn., 1980; USPHS postdoctoral fellow, 1955-57, Howard Hughes Med. Inst. fellow, 1957-58. Mem. Am. Pub. Health Assn., Ala. Pub. Health Assn., AAAS, Med. Assn. Ala., Lauderdale County Med. Soc. Methodist. Club: Civitan (Florence, Ala.). Home: 3808 Chisholm Rd Florence AL 35630-6320

WOODWORTH, MARY ESTHER, microbiology educator, consultant; b. Grand Rapids, Mich.; d. Irving and Doris Gertrude (Linsenmeyer) W. BS summa cum laude, U. Mich., 1957; MS, Temple U., 1965, PhD, 1968. Postdoctoral fellow U. Mich., Ann Arbor, 1968-72; rsch. assoc. Syracuse (N.Y.) U., 1972-73; rsch. scientist Johns Hopkins U. Sch. Medicine, Balt., 1973-76; cancer rsch. scientist Roswell Park Meml. Inst., Buffalo, N.Y., 1977-89, acting chair, 1983-84; asst. prof. Roswell Park div. SUNY, Buffalo, 1977-86, assoc. prof., 1986-89; prof. microbiology, dept. chmn. Miami U., Oxford, Ohio, 1989—; bd. dirs. Health Rsch., Inc., Buffalo, 1984-87. Contbr. articles to profl. jours. including Jour. Virology, Jour. Molecular Biology, Molecular Cell Biology, Nucleic Acids Rsch., Biophysics Jour., Jour. Molecular Applied Genetics, Jour. Biol. Chemistry. Recipient Rsch. Career Devel. award NIH, 1978-83. Fellow Am. Acad. Microbiology; mem. AAAS, AAUW, Am. Soc. Microbiology (lectr. 1989-90, com. mem. for genetic and molecular microbiology 1990, chair com. for genetic and molecular microbiology 1992—), Am. Soc. Biochemistry and Molecular Biology, Am. Soc. Virology, Am. Women in Sci., Sigma Xi, Phi Beta Kappa, Phi Kappa Phi. Home: 6313 Bigwood Cir Oxford OH 45056-9271 Office: Miami U Dept Microbiology Oxford OH 45056

WOODWORTH, RONALD STEARNS, osteopathic physician; b. Boston, Oct. 2, 1933; s. Robert Hugo and Helen (Cummings) W.; m. Sigrid Dorn, Aug. 15, 1959; children: (twins) Christopher and Carole, Barbara, Bradford. BS, Springfield Coll., 1956; MA, Columbia Tchrs. Coll., 1959, Tchg. Diploma, 1961; DO, Phila. Coll. of Osteo. Medicine, 1972. Diplomate Am. Osteo. Bd. of Family Practice. Tchr. Malvern (N.Y.) H.S., 1959-62, Montclair (N.J.) State Coll., 1962-67; intern Tricounty Hosp., Springfield, Pa., 1973, emergency physician, 1973-81; emergency physician Riverside Hosp., Wilmington, Del., 1973-78; pvt. practice Bennington, Vt., 1981—; pres.-elect Am. Coll. Osto. Pain Mgmt. and Sclerotheraphy, Wilmington, 1996—. With U.S. Army, 1956-58. Home: Box 327 North Bennington VT 05257 Office: Box 1432 Bennington VT 05201

WOODY, MARY FLORENCE, nursing educator, university administrator; b. Chambers County, Ala., Mar. 31, 1926; d. Hugh Ernest and May Lillie (Gilliland) W.; diploma Charity Hosp. Sch. Nursing, 1947; BS, Columbia U., 1953, M.A., 1955. Staff nurse Wheeler Hosp., Lafayette, Ala., 1947-48; polio nurse Willard Parker Hosp., N.Y.C., 1949; staff nurse, supr. VA Hosp., Montgomery, Ala., 1950-53; faculty mem., field supr., nursing dept. Tchrs. Coll., Columbia U., N.Y.C., 1955-56; asst. dir. nursing Emory U. Hosp., clin. asst. prof. Emory U. Sch. Nursing, Atlanta, 1956-68; asst. dir., dir. nursing Grady Meml. Hosp., Atlanta, 1968-79; founding dean, prof. Sch. Nursing, Auburn (Ala.) U., 1979-84; assoc. dir., dir. nursing Emory U. Hosp., Atlanta, 1984-93; interim dean Sch. Nursing, Emory U., 1992-93; chmn. Ga. Statewide Master Planning Com. for Nursing and Nursing Edn., 1971-75; faculty preceptor patient care adminstrn. Sch. Public Health, U. Minn., 1977-79; mem. bd. dirs. Wesley Woods Found. & Long Term Hosp., 1994—. Recipient Spl. Recognition, 5th Dist. and Ga. Nurses Assn., 1978, 93, Disting. Achievement in Nursing Svc. award Columbia U. Tchrs. Coll.

Alumni Assn., 1992, Jane Van de Vrede Outstanding Svc. to Citizens of Ga. award Ga. League Nursing, Cert. Spl. Recognition award Ga. Nurses Assn., 1993. Fellow Am. Acad. Nursing (charter); mem. Am. Nurses Assn., Nat. League Nursing, Am. Heart Assn., Emory U. Nell Hodgson Woodruff Sch. Nursing Alumni Assn. (hon. 1994), Sigma Theta Tau. Democrat. Chmn. bd. dirs. Am. Jour. Nursing Co., 1978-83. Address: 907 Lenox Hill Atlanta GA 30324-2957

WOODYARD, CLYDE WAYNE, physician assistant; b. Clifton Forge, Va., Feb. 14, 1954; s. John and Wanda Nadine (Saylor) W.; m. Rebbeca Kay Levisay (div. 1992); children: Morgan, Taylor. BA, Catawba Coll., 1976; cert. physician asst., U. Utah, 1984. Med. lab. tech. VA Med. Ctr., Miami, Fla., 1979-82; physician asst. Am. Plasma Mgmt., Salt Lake City, 1984-85, Allergy-Dermatology Assocs., Silver Spring, Md., 1985-88, Jackson River Orthopedics, Low Moor, Va., 1988—; bd. dirs. S.W. Va. Area Health Edn. Ctr., Marion. Contbr. articles to profl. jours. Lt. USN. Fellow Am. Acad. Physician Assts., Va. Acad. Physician Assts., W.Va. Acad. Physician Assts. Home: Rt 1 PO Box 1277 Eagle Rock VA 24085 Office: Jackson River Orthopedics PO Box 194 Low Moor VA 24457

WOOG, JOHN J., plastic surgeon; b. Jamaica, N.Y., Feb. 28, 1958; m. Mary Anna Woog. BS, Pa. State Univ., 1978; MD, Thomas Jefferson Univ., 1980. Diplomate Am. Bd. Ophthalmology. Co-dir. eye plastics & orbit svc. Mass. Eye & Ear Infirmary, Boston, 1985-88; pvt. practice ophthalmology Sloane, Krant, & Finkelstein, Brookline, Mass., 1985-89, Ophthalmic Cons. Boston, 1989—; dir. eye plastics & orbit svc. New England Medical Ctr., Boston, 1988-94, co-dir. eye plastics & orbit svc., 1994—; assoc. clinical prof. Tufts Univ. Sch. Medicine, Boston, 1994—; clinical instr. Harvard Medical Sch., 1989—; bd. dirs. Ophthalmic Cons. Boston, 1989—, Boston Eye Surgery & Laser Ctr., 1992—. Sect. editor: Principles & Practices of Ophthalmology, Eye Trauma, 1994. Fellow Am. Acad. Ophthalmology (Honor award 1994), Am. Soc. Ophthalmic Plastic & reconstructive Surgery (Rsch. award 1985). Office: Ophthalmic Cons Boston 50 Stanford St 6th Fl Boston MA 02114

WOOLDRIDGE, WILFRED ERWIN, physician; b. Springfield, Mo., Mar. 5, 1917; s. Thomas Erwin and Ethel (Spencer) W.; m. Frances Virginia Cowan, Dec. 27, 1942; children: Robert Erwin, Richard Kent. BS, Drury Coll., 1935; MD, Washington U., St. Louis, 1939. Instr. Washington U., 1949-53, Okla. U., Oklahoma City, 1953-65; clin. prof. medicine Mo. U., Columbia, 1965-84, clin. prof. medicine emeritus, 1984—; pres. Assoc. Dermatologists Ltd., Springfield, Mo., 1974-88. Contbr. numerous articles to profl. jours. and mags. Bd. dirs. Springfield Civic Symphony, 1951-55; bd. dirs. Springfield Civic Concert Service, 1951-57, pres., 1957-58, Mid-Am. Singers, 1964-76, founder. Served to capt. AUS, 1944-46. Decorated Bronze Star. Fellow AMA, Am. Acad. Dermatology, Am. Bd. Dermatology. Republican. Episcopalian. Home: 1126 E Stanford St Springfield MO 65807-2058

WOOLF, PAUL DANIEL, physician, educator, researcher; b. N.Y.C., Aug. 14, 1942; s. Irwin and Paula (Cohen) W.; m. Nancy Susan Slater, Dec. 25, 1965; children: David Jeffrey, Karen Elizabeth. BA with honors, U. Pa., 1964; MD, NYU, 1968; MBA, U. Rochester, 1996. Diplomate in endocrinology Am. Bd. Internal Medicine. Intern, resident NYU Med. Ctr./Bellevue Hosp., N.Y.C., 1968-71; instr., fellow U. Rochester (N.Y.) Med. Ctr., 1971-73; asst. prof. medicine U. Rochester, 1975-81, assoc. prof., 1981-89, prof., 1989—, prof. pediatrics, 1992-95, prof. pathology and lab. medicine, 1994—; dir. ambulatory svcs., dept. medicine U. Rochester, 1986-96, acting chief endocrine unit, 1996—. Contbr. more than 80 articles to profl. jours. Lt. comdr. USN, 1971-73. Mellon fellow U. Rochester, 1985-88, Buswell fellow U. Rochester, 1977; recipient Rochester Regional Diabetes award, 1977. Fellow ACP; mem. Am. Fedn. Cin. Rsch. (chair eastern sect. 1981-82), Am. Soc. Clin. Investigation, Am. Thyroid Assn. Office: U Rochester Med Ctr PO Box 693 Rochester NY 14603-0693

WOOLFENDEN, JAMES MANNING, nuclear medicine physician, educator; b. L.A., Nov. 8, 1942. BA with distinction, Stanford U., 1964; MD, U. Wash., 1968. Diplomate Am. Bd. Nuclear Medicine (chmn. credentials com. 1993-94, vice-chmn. examinations com. 1993-95, chmn. exam. com. 1995-96, sec. 1994—), Nat. Bd. Med. Examiners; lic. physician Calif., Ariz., Wash. Med. intern L.A. County-U. So. Calif. Med. Ctr., 1968-69; med. resident West L.A. VA Med. Ctr., 1969-70; nuclear medicine resident L.A. County-U. So. Calif. Med. Ctr., 1972-74; from asst. prof. radiology to assoc. prof. radiology U. Ariz., Tucson, 1974-84, prof. radiology, 1984—; mem. med. staff Univ. Med. Ctr., Tucson, 1974—; cons. VA Med. Ctr., 1974—; cons. med. staff Tucson Med. Ctr., 1975—, Carondelet St. Joseph's Hosp., 1974—, St. Mary's Hosp., Tucson, 1976-90; mem. Nat. Cancer Inst. site visit team NIH, 1976, mem. NHLB Inst. site visit team NIH, 1976, mem. diagnostic radiology study sect., 1993—, chmn., 1995—; mem. med. liaison officer network EPA, 1983—; cons.-tchg. med. staff Kino Cmty. Hosp., 1984-94; med. officer Clin. Ctr., NIH, Bethesda, 1984-85; mem. Ariz. Cancer Ctr., U. Ariz., 1988—, sr. clin. scientist Univ. Heart Ctr., 1990—; Ariz. bd. regents U. Ariz. Presdl. Search Com., 1990-91; chmn. Ariz. Atomic Energy Commn., 1979-80, Ariz. Radiation Regulatory Hearing Bd., 1981—; bd. dirs. Calif. Radioactive Materials Mgmt. Forum, 1989—, chmn.-elect, 1993-94, chmn., 1994-95, Western Forum Edn. in Safe Disposal of Low-Level Radioactive Waste, 1990—, vice chmn., 1991-92, chmn., 1992-94. Manuscript reviewer: Noninvasive Med. Imaging, 1983-84, Jour. Nuclear Medicine, 1985—, Investigative Radiology, 1989-94, Archives of Internal Medicine, 1990—; contbr. book chpts.: Diagnostic Nuclear Medicine, 2d edit., 1988, Adjuvant Therapy of Cancer, 1977, Fundamentals of Nuclear Medicine, 1988, others; contbr. articles and book revs. to profl. publs. Mem. Am. Heart Assn. Coun. on Cardiovasc. Radiology. Maj. U.S. Army, 1970-72, Vietnam. Fellow Am. Coll. Nuclear Physicians (long range planning com. 1981-83, govt. affairs com. 1984—, exec. com. 1987-91, sec. 1989-91, parliamentarian 1991-95, treas. 1996—, mem. publs. com. 1993—, chmn. publs. com. 1993-94, and many others); mem. AMA (diagnostic and therapeutic tech. assessment reference panel 1982—), Am. Fedn. Clin. Rsch., Am. Nuc. Soc., Soc. Nuclear Medicine (com. on audit 1992—, bd. trustees 1992—, Bronze medal for sci. exhibit 1984, bd. dirs., sec.-treas. So. Calif. chpt. 1993-95, chmn.-elect 1995—), Assn. Univ. Radiologists, Pima County Med. Soc., Radiol. Soc. N.Am. Office: Ariz Health Scis Ctr 1501 N Campbell Ave Tucson AZ 85724-5068

WOOLLEY, ADRIAN LYNNE, osteopath; b. Denver, Aug. 5, 1961; d. Norman Charles and Charmaine (Kemp) W. BA in Animal Physiology, U. Calif., San Diego, 1979-84; postgrad., UCLA Ext., 1985-86, L.A. Valley Coll., Van Nuys, Calif., 1985-91; DO, U. Osteo. Medicine and Health Scis., Des Moines, 1995. Student profl. worker L.A. County Dept. Coroner, 1987-90, forensic technician I, 1990, supervising forensic technician, autopsy room supr., liaison, 1991; tchg. asst., embalming technician U. Ostoe. Medicine and Health Scis.-Coll. Osteo. Medicine, Des Moines, 1992-93; chief intern Des Moines Gen. Osteo. Hosp., 1995-96. Student health advocate in birth control and human sexuality U. Calif., San Diego, 1984; coord. health fair for osteo. structural exams, U. Osteo. Medicine and Health Scis.-Coll. Osteo. Medicine, Des Moines, 1992, vol., 1993, table trainer for osteopath in cranial field, 1992-93; mem. choir St. Cyril of Jerusalem Ch., Encino, Calif., 1989-91. Mem. Am. Osteo. Assn., Am. Acad. Osteopathy, The Cranial Acad., Tau Alpha Epsilon (life). Home: 3610 Patricia Dr Apt 11 Urbandale IA 50322

WOOLLEY, FREDRICK ROSS, medical educator; b. Salt Lake City, May 4, 1942; s. Roscoe Hunter and Florence LaDell (Lowry) W.; m. Susan Brown, Sept. 21, 1963; children: Allison Ludlow, Robert, Dianna Chamberlain, Richard, Joseph. BS, U. Utah, 1966; MA, No. Ariz. U., 1969; PhD, Brigham Young U., 1971. Indsl. engr. Kennecott Copper Corp., Salt Lake City, 1966-68; asst. dean student affairs No. Ariz. U., Flagstaff, 1968-69; prof., divsn. chief Sch. of Medicine, U. Utah, Salt Lake City, 1971-89, 91-94; prof. Sch. of Pub. Health, U. Hawaii, Honolulu, 1989-90, prof., dept. chair, 1994—; cons. Utah Dept. of Health, Salt Lake City, 1973-94, Utah Chiefs of Police, Salt Lake City, 1990-94, 96, Honolulu Police Dept., 1994-96. Author: Problem Oriented Nursing, 1974; contbr. articles to profl. jours. Recipient Chief's Recognition award Utah Chiefs of Police Assn., 1994. Mem. Utah Pub. Health Assn. (life, pres. 1975—), Am. Pub. Health Assn. (governing coun.), Assn. of Tchrs. of Preventive Medicine, Coun. on Edn. for Pub. Health (coun.), Phi Kappa Phi, Phi Delta Kappa. Mem. Ch. LDS. Office: U Hawaii Sch Pub Health Biomed T-102 1960 East West Rd Honolulu HI 96822

WOOLLEY, GEORGE WALTER, biologist, geneticist, educator; b. Osborne, Kans., Nov. 9, 1904; s. George Aitcheson and Nora Belle (Jackson) W.; m. Anne Geneva Collins, Nov. 2, 1936; children: George Aitcheson, Margaret Anne, Lawrence Jackson. B.S., Iowa State U., 1930; M.S., U. Wis., 1931, Ph.D., 1935. Fellow U. Wis., 1935-36; mem. staff Jackson Meml. Lab., Bar Harbor, Maine, 1936-49; bd. dirs. Jackson Meml. Lab., 1937-49, v.p. bd., 1943-47, asst. dir. and sci. adminstr., 1947-49, vis. research assoc., 1949—; mem. chief div. steroid biology Sloan-Kettering Inst., N.Y.C., 1949-58, prof. biology, 1949-58; prof. biology Sloan-Kettering Inst. div. Cornell U. Med. Coll., Ithaca, N.Y., 1951—, chief div. human tumor exptl. chemotherapy, 1958-61, chief div. tumor biology, 1961-66; assoc. scientist Sloan-Kettering Inst. Cancer Research, 1966—; health sci. adminstr., program coordinator, head biol. scis. sect. Nat. Inst. Gen. Medical Scis., NIH, 1966-85; cons. Nat. Edn. Service U.S., Washington, 1961—; spl. cons. to Nat. Cancer Inst., NIH, 1956—; Mem. Expert Panel on Carcinogenicity, unio intern. contra cancerum, 1962—; mem. panel com. on growth NRC, 1945-51; mem. several internat. med. congresses. Author chpts. in med. books; mem. editorial bd. Jour. Nat. Cancer Inst., 1947-50. Trustee Dalton Schs., N.Y.C. Fellow AAAS, N.Y. Acad. Sci.; mem. Am. Mus. Natural History, Nat. Sci. Tchrs. Assn. (cons. 1961—), Am. Assn. Cancer Research (dir. 1951-54), Am. Soc. Human Genetics, Mt. Desert Island Biol. Lab., Soc. Exptl. Biology and Medicine, Am. Inst. Biol. Scis., Am. Assn. Anatomists, Am. Genetic Assn., Wis. Acad. Arts Sci. and Letters, Jackson Lab. Assn., Genetics Soc. Am., Environ. Mutagen Soc., Sigma Xi. Clubs: Bar Harbor, Bar Harbor (Maine) Yacht. Home: 5301 Westbard Cir Apt 336 Bethesda MD 20816-1427

WOOLSTON-CATLIN, MARIAN, psychiatrist; b. Seattle, Jan. 20, 1931; d. Howard Brown and Katharine Nichols (Dally) Woolston; m. Randolph Catlin Jr., July 5, 1959; children: Laura Louise, Jennifer Woolston, Randolph III. BA cum laude, Vassar Coll., 1951; MD, Harvard U., 1955. Diplomate Nat. Bd. Medicine. Intern and resident in medicine Children's Hosp., Boston, 1956; resident in psychiatry Mass. Mental Health Ctr., Boston, 1957-59; fellow in child psychiatry Tavistock Clin., London, 1961; commonwealth fellow in child psychiatry Harvard U. at Gaebler Children's Unit, Waltham, Mass., 1975-78, clin. instr. psychiatry, 1978-79; pvt. practice Wellesley Hills, Mass., 1978-91, Medfield, Mass., 1991—; clin. instr. psychiatry Harvard U. at Mass. Mental Health Ctr., Boston, 1957-59, 78-82, Tufts U. at Mass. Mental Health Ctr., 1957-59; mem. exec. bd. Parents' and Children's Svcs., Boston, 1983-86. Designer H.H. Hunnewell Meml. Garden for New England Flower Show Mass. Hort. Soc., 1975 (Ames Cup award). Mem. exec. bd. Ext. Divsn. New Eng. Conservatory Music., 1972-75; charter mem. reuse com. Medfield State Hosp., 1992—. Fellow Am. Acad. Child and Adolescent Psychiatry; mem. AMA, Am. Psychiat. Assn., Mass. Psychiat. Assn., Mass. Med. Soc., Boston Vassar Club (exec. bd. 1963-75), Hills Garden Club Wellesley (exec. bd. and design chief 1973-75). Episcopalian. Home and Office: 314 North St Medfield MA 02052-1204

WOOSLEY, RAYMOND, pharmacology and medical educator; b. Ky., Oct. 2, 1942; m. Julianne B. BS, Western Ky. U., 1964; PhD, U. Louisville, 1967; MD, U. Miami, 1973. Med. lic. Tenn. 1976, D.C. 1988. Intern, resident Vanderbilt U. Hosp., Nashville, 1973-76; sr. pharmacologist, dir. rsch. Meyer (Glaxo) Labs., Ft. Lauderdale, Fla., 1968-71; instr. dept. medicine, pharmacology Vanderbilt U., Nashville, 1976-77, asst. prof., 1977-79, assoc. prof., 1979-84, assoc. dir. clin. rsch. ctr., 1981-88, prof., 1984-88; prof. pharmacology, medicine, chmn. dept. pharmacology Georgetown U. Sch. Medicine, Washington, 1988—, also chief divsn. clin. pharmacology, 1988-94; dir. Inst. for Cardiovascular Scis., Washington, 1995—; researcher in field. Author: Clinical Application of Zinc Metabolism, 1975, Cardiovascular Pharmacology and Therapeutics, 1994; contbr. chpts. to books and articles to profl. jours. NIH Predoctoral fellow NIH, 1964-67, postdoctoral fellow U. Louisville, 1967-68, Vanderbilt U., 1976-77, Am. Coll. Clin. Pharmacology fellow, 1974; Ogden scholar Western Ky. U., 1960-64; recipient Cancer Devel. award in Clin. Pharmacology Pharm. Mfrs. Assn. Found., 1977-80. Fellow Am. Coll. Clin. Pharmacology, Am. Coll. Physicians, Am. Heart Assn. (coun. clin. cardiology 1985—); mem. Am. Soc. Pharmacology & Exptl. Therapeutics (clin. pharmacology exec. com. 1981-92), Am. Fedn. Clin. Rsch., Am. Soc. Clin. Pharmacology and Therapeutics (Rawls-Palmer award 1990), Am. Bd. Clin. Pharmacology, Assn. Med. Sch. Pharmacology (pres. 1996—). Office: Georgetown U Sch Medicine Dept Pharmacology 3900 Reservoir Rd NW Washington DC 20007-2195

WOOTAN, GERALD DON, osteopathic physician, educator; b. Oklahoma City, Nov. 19, 1944; s. Ralph George and Corrinne (Loafman) W. BA, Cen. State U., Edmond, Okla., 1970, BS, 1971; MEd, Cen. State U., 1974; MB, U. Okla., Oklahoma City, 1978; DO, Okla. State U., 1985. Dir. mfg. engring. lab. GE, Oklahoma City, 1965-70; counseling psychologist VA Hosp., Oklahoma City, 1970-76; physician asst. Thomas (Okla.) Med. Clin., 1978-81; pvt. practice, Jenks, Okla., 1986—; intern Tulsa Regional Med. Ctr., 1985-86; assoc. prof. Okla. State U. Coll. Osteo. Medicine, 1986-95, with Springer Clinic, 1995—; sec. Springer Clinic Inc., Tulsa, 1990-91; chmn. gen. practice quality assurance Tulsa Regional Med. Ctr., 1989-91; v.p. New Horizons Counseling Ctr., Clinton, Okla., 1977-81; sr. aviation med. examiner FAA, Tulsa, 1991—; pres. S.W. Diagnostics, Inc., Tulsa, 1989-91, Okla. Edn. Found. Osteo. Medicine, Tulsa, 1988-89; pres., trustee Tulsa Long Term Care Authority. Contbr. articles to profl. jours.; patentee for human restraint. Advancement chmn., chmn. Eagle bd. rev. Boy Scouts Am., Tulsa, 1987-88; trustee Tulsa Long Term Care Authority, 1988-91; trustee Tulsa Community Found. for Indigent Health Care, Inc., 1988-91. With USN, 1962-64. Named Clin. Preceptor of Yr., U. Okla., 1980, Outstanding Alumni award Okla. State U. Coll. Osteo. Medicine, 1990. Mem. Am. Osteo. Assn., Okla. Osteo. Assn., Tulsa Dist. Osteo. Soc. (pres. 1991-92), Am. Acad. Physician Assts., Am. Coll. Gen. Practitioners, Okla. Acad. Gen. Practitioners (v.p.), Am. Coll. Osteo. Family Physicians (bd. cert. 1993, pres. Okla. chpt. 1993-94), Okla. State U. Coll. Osteo. Medicine Alumni Assn. (pres. 1988-89). Home: 4320 E 100th St Tulsa OK 74137-5305 Office: Jenks Health Team 324 W Main St Jenks OK 74037-3747

WORK, HENRY HARCUS, physician, educator; b. Buffalo, Nov. 11, 1911; s. Henry Harcus and Jeannette (Harcus) W.; m. Virginia Codington, Oct. 20, 1945 (dec. Nov. 1991); children—Henry Harcus III, David Codington, William Bruce, Stuart Runyon. A.B., Hamilton Coll., Clinton, N.Y., 1933; M.D., Harvard, 1937. Intern, resident Boston Children's Hosp., 1937-40, Emma P. Bradley Home Providence, 1940, Buffalo Children's Hosp., 1940-42, N.Y. Hosp., 1945-47; psychiat. services adviser, chief U.S. Children's Bur., Washington, 1948-49; assoc. prof. pediatrics U. Louisville, 1949-55; mem. faculty UCLA, 1955-72, prof. psychiatry and pub. health, 1966-72; chief profl. svcs. Am. Psychiat. Assn., Washington, 1972-83; clin. prof. George Washington U., Georgetown U., Uniformed Svcs. U. of Health Scis., U. Md., 1973—. Author: A Guide to Preventive Child Psychiatry, 1965, Minimal Brain Dysfunction: A Medical Challenge, 1967, Psychiatric Emergencies in Childhood, 1967, Crisis in Child Psychiatry, 1975, also articles. Served to capt. AUS, 1942-45. Recipient Simon Wile Award, Amer. Acad. of Child and Adolescent Psychiatry, 1994. Mem. So. Calif. Psychiat. Assn. (pres. 1966-67), Am. Orthopsychiat. Assn. (v.p. 1968-69), Am. Coll. Psychiatry (sec.-gen. 1979-93), Group for Advancement of Psychiatry (pres. 1982-85). Home: 4986 Sentinel Dr Apt 504 Bethesda MD 20816

WORLEY, KAREN BOYD, psychologist; b. Hot Springs, Ark., Apr. 23, 1952; d. Wayne Johnson and Lou (Hull) Boyd; m. Timothy Riker, Sept. 22, 1979; children: Travis, Tyler, Kaitlin, Kelsey. BA, Okla. State U., 1974; PhD, Tex. Tech. U., 1983. Lic. psychologist, Ark. Rsch. asst. Rsch. and Tng. Ctr. for Mentally Retarded Tex. Tech. U., Lubbock, 1974-77, teaching asst., 1977-78; psychology intern Kansas City (Mo.) VA Med. Ctr., 1978-79; psychologist Johnson County Mental Health Ctr., Shawnee Mission, Kans., 1979-81; pvt. practice Pleasant Valley Clinic, Little Rock, 1982—; asst. prof. dept. pediatrics U. of Ark. for Med. Scis., 1991—; mem. Gov.'s Task Force on Child Abuse in Arks., 1983-85, Pulaski County Child Abuse Task Force, 1985, Pulaski County Family Svcs. Rev. Com., 1986-87, Com. to Rev. Investigation Procedures Ark. Children and Family Svcs., 1986, Child Sexual Abuse Network, 1988-93; bd. dirs. Ark. Child Sexual Abuse Edn. Commn., 1985-91, Suspected Child Abuse and Neglect, 1986-92, Ark. Commn. on Child Abuse, Rape and Domestic Violence, 1991—, Victims of Crime Act Bd., 1992—; cons. Mother's Support Group, Parent Ctr., Little Rock, 1983-92. Contbr. articles to profl. publs. Mem. APA, Ark. Psychol. Assn., Nat. Register Health Svc. Providers in Psychology (coun.), Am. Profl. Soc. on Abuse of Children, Assn. for Treatment of Sexual Abusers, Phi Kappa Phi. Methodist. Office: Family Treatment Program 1120 Marshall St Little Rock AR 72202-4600 also: Pleasant Valley Clinic 12361 Hinson Rd North Little Rock AR 72113

WORNER, THERESA MARIE, physician; b. Breckenridge, Minn., Feb. 19, 1948; d. William Daniel and Elizabeth (Stelten) W.; m. Martin Herbst, Mar. 24, 1979. AB, St. Theresa Coll., 1970; MD, U. Minn., 1974. Diplomate Am. Bd. Internal Medicine. Rotating intern Kings County Hosp., Bklyn., 1974-75, resident medicine, 1975-77; fellow VA Med. Ctr., Bronx, N.Y., 1977-78; chief med. sect. Alcoholism treatment program VA Med. Ctr., Bronx, 1978-87; asst. prof. medicine Mt. Sinai Sch. Medicine, N.Y.C., 1984-87; mem. faculty Postgrad. Ctr., 1985-90; physician in charge alcoholism svcs. L.I. Coll. Hosp., Bkyn., 1987-92; assoc. prof. clin. medicine SUNY, Health Sci. Ctr., Bkyn., 1988—; dir. rsch. 32BJ Health Fund, 1992—; clin. assoc. prof. Pub. Health Cornell U. Med. Coll., 1996—; pres./founder Alcohol. Info, 1995; advisor Patient Care Mag., 1984—; cons. REA. Referee Hepatology, 1986, Jour. Study Alcohol, 1984—, Substance Abuse, 1992—, Alcoholism: Clinical and Exptl. Rsch., 1992—, Drug and Alcohol Dependence, 1993—, Drug Therapy, 1994—, Addiction, 1996—; contbr. numerous articles to profl. jours. Active Bronx Bot. Garden, Mus. Modern Art, Met. Mus. Art, Mus. Natural History, Bklyn. Mus. Art, Turtle Bay Civic Assn., Bklyn. Lyric Opera, Empire State Opera, Amato Opera. Grantee Child Welfare Adminstrn., 1991, 92, 93; recipient Physicians Recognition award AMA, 1984, 89, 91, 96, Cert. of Merit Govt. Employees Ins. Co., 1986, PACT Intern Site award, 1991, 92. Fellow ACP; mem. AAAS, Am. Med. Soc. on Alcoholism and Other Drug Dependence, Am. Soc. Internal Medicine, Am. Assn. for Study Liver Diseases (Travel award 1978), N.Y. Acad. Scis., Rsch. Soc. on Alcoholism, Internat. Soc. Biologic Rsch. in Alcoholism. Home: 322 E 50th St New York NY 10022-7902 Office: Rsch Dept 32BJ Health Fund 13th fl 101 Ave of Americas New York NY 10013

WORONOFF, ISRAEL, retired psychology educator; b. Bklyn., Dec. 30, 1926; s. Samuel and Lena (Silberman) W.; m. Fay Goldberg, Feb. 11, 1950; 1 child, Gary. AB in Psychology, U. Mich., 1949, MA in Sociology, 1952, PhD in Edn., 1954. Lic. psychologist, Mich. Instr. Flint (Mich.) Jr. Coll., 1953-54; asst. prof. St. Cloud (Minn.) State Coll., 1954-56; asst. prof. Ea. Mich. U., Ypsilanti, 1956-59, assoc. prof., 1959-62, prof., 1962-92; cons. psychologist Midwest Mental Health Clinic, Dearborn, Mich., 1978-83, Orchard Hills Psychiat. Ctr., Novi, Mich., 1983—. Author: Educator's Guide to Stress Management, 1986. Mem. bd. Jewish Family Svc. of Ann Arbor, 1996—; mem. cmty. rels. com. Jewish Cmty. Assn., Ann Arbor, Mich., 1990-92; v.p. edn. Beth Israel Congregation, Ann Arbor, 1985-87; mem. adv. bd. Mich. Anti-Defamation League of B'nai B'rith, 1958—. Mem. APA, Mich. Psychol. Assn., Am. Edn!. Rsch. Assn. Democrat. Home: 2519 Londonderry Rd Ann Arbor MI 48104-4017

WORRELL, BILLY FRANK, health facility administrator; b. Columbia, Ala., Oct. 12, 1939; s. Beachum Worrell and Madeline (Scott) Wells; children: Jon, Kevin, Heather; m. Lorna Faye Jones, Nov. 26, 1991. A in Bus., Thomas Coll., Thomasville, Ga., 1978; BS magna cum laude, Albany State Coll., 1990, MBA, 1991; MS, LaSalle U., 1995, PhD, 1996. Registered respiratory therapist, respiratory care profl., arterial blood gas technician, neo-natal advanced life support technician. Electrician USN, 1957-60, Newport News (Va.) Shipbldg., 1960-63; mfg. mgr. Lockheed Aircraft, Marietta, Ga., 1963-70, Champion Homes, Thomasville, Ga., 1970-74; salesman Cadillac dealership Thomasville, 1974-76; estimator Knight-Dodson Constrn. Co., Thomasville, 1976-78; adminstr. Ga. Army Nat. Guard, Thomasville, 1978-84; ret., 1984; allied health mgr. Phoebe Putney Meml. Hosp., Albany, 1988-93; dir. cardiopulmonary dept. Mitchell County Hosp., Camilla, Ga., 1994-95; dir. cardiopulmonary contract svcs. Sumter County Hosp., Americus, Ga., 1995—. Columnist newspaper column Lee County Ledger, 1990; actor film and plays. Vol. Salvation Army, Thomasville, 1978-83, Sr. Citizens Group, Thomasville, 1980-83, Kidney Found., Thomasville, 1980-85. Mem. Nat. Bd. Respiratory Care, Ga. Respiratory Care, Toastmasters. Republican. Home: 1142 Philema Rd S Leesburg GA 31763-9314 Office: Sumter County Hospital Americus GA 31709

WORRELL, RICHARD VERNON, orthopedic surgeon, college dean; b. Bklyn., June 4, 1931; s. John Elmer and Elaine (Callender) W.; BA, NYU, 1952; MD, Meharry Med. Coll., 1958; m. Audrey Frances Martiny, June 14, 1958; children: Philip Vernon, Amy Elizabeth. Intern Meharry Med. Coll., Nashville, 1958-59; resident gen. surgery Mercy-Douglass Hosp., Phila., 1960-61; resident orthopedic surgery State U. N.Y. Buffalo Sch. Medicine Affiliated Hosps., 1961-64; resident in orthopedic pathology Temple U. Med. Ctr., Phila., 1966-67; pvt. practice orthopedic surgery, Phila., 1964-68; asst. prof. acting head div. orthopedic surgery U. Conn. Sch. Medicine 1968-70; attending orthopedic surgeon E.J. Meyer Meml. Hosp., Buffalo, Millard Fillmore Hosp., Buffalo, VA Hosp., Buffalo, Buffalo State Hosp.; clin. instr. orthopedic surgery SUNY, Buffalo, 1970-74; chief orthopedic surgery VA Hosp., Newington, Conn., 1974-80; asst. prof. surgery (orthopedics) U. Conn. Sch. Medicine, 1974-77, assoc. prof., 1977-83, asst. dean student affairs, 1980-83; prof. clin. surgery SUNY Downstate Med. Ctr., Bklyn., 1983-86; dir. orthopedic surgery Brookdale Hosp. Med. Ctr., Bklyn., 1983-86; prof. of orthopedics U. N.Mex. Sch. of Medicine, 1986—; dir. orthopedic oncology U. N.Mex. Med. Ctr., 1987—; mem. med. staff U. N.Mex. Cancer Ctr., 1987—; chief orthopedic surgery VA Med. Ctr., Albuquerque, 1987—; cons. in orthopedic surgery Newington (Conn.) Children's Hosp., 1968-70; mem. sickle cell disease adv. com. NIH, 1982-86. Bd. dirs. Big Bros. Greater Hartford. Served to capt. M.C., U.S. Army Res., 1962-69. Diplomate Am. Bd. Orthopedic Surgery, Nat. Bd. Med. Examiners. Fellow ACS, Am. Acad. Orthopedic Surgeons, Royal Soc. Medicine, London; mem. AMA, Am. Orthopaedic Assn., Am. Soc. Clin. Pathologists, Orthopedic Rsch. Soc., Internat. Soc. Orthopedic Surgery and Traumatology, N.Mex. Soc. Clin. Oncology, Internat. Fedn. Surg. Colls. (assoc.), Alpha Omega Alpha. Office: U NMex Sch Medicine Albuquerque NM 87131-5296

WORSHAM, BERTRAND RAY, psychiatrist; b. Atkins, Ark., Feb. 14, 1926; s. Lewis Henry and Emma Lavada (Burris) W.; m. Margaret Ann Dickson, June 4, 1947 (div. 1960); children: Eric Dickson, Vicki Gayle; m. Lynne Ellen Reynolds, Aug. 27, 1976; children: Mary Ellen Clarice, Richard Andrew (dec.). BA, U. Ark., 1951; MD, U. Ark., Little Rock, 1955. Intern Hillcrest Med. Ctr., Tulsa, 1955-56; resident in psychiatry Menninger Sch. Psychiatry, Topeka, 1956-59; pvt. practice, 1959-78; clin. instr. U. Okla. Sch. Medicine, 1965-78; coord. drug and alcohol treatment unit Washington D.C. VA Med. Ctr., 1978-84; med. dir. Norman divsn. Okla. State Vets. Ctr., 1984-89; psychiat. cons. Cmty. Counselling Ctr., Oklahoma City, 1989—; cons. Oklahoma City Vets. Hosp., 1959-72, State Dept. Pub. Health, 1960-65; dir. Cmty. Mental Health Ctr., Shawnee, Okla., 1965-72; mem. staff Coyne Campbell Hosp., 1960-78, Bapt. Med. Ctr., 1960-78, Mercy Health Ctr., 1960-78, Deaconess Hosp., 1963-78, Dr.'s Gen. Hosp., 1963-78, Presbyn. Hosp., 1962-78, U. Health Sci. Ctr., 1962-78, Children's Meml. Hosp., 1968-78, Oklahoma City VA Hosp., 1960-78, Washington D.C. Va. Hosp., 1978-84, Okla. Vets. Ctr., Norman, 1984-89. Mem. Civil Disaster Com., Oklahoma City, 1966, USN League, Okla., 1972—. With USAF, 1944-46; capt. USNR, 1957-86, ret. Fellow Menninger Found., Charles F. Menninger Found.; mem. AMA, Am. Psychiat. Assn. (Okla. dist. br. 1959-78, 84—), Assn. Mil. Surgeons of U.S., Ret. Officers Assn., World Fedn. for Mental Health, Internat. Platform Assn., Washington Psychiat. Assn., No. Va. Mental Health Assn., Masons (32 degree). Republican. Episcopalian. Home: 9915 N Kelley Ave Oklahoma City OK 73131-2022 Office: Cmty Counseling Ctr 1140 N Hudson Ave Oklahoma City OK 73103-3918

WORTH, MELVIN H., surgeon, educator; b. Norwich, Conn., July 14, 1930; s. Melvin H. and Stella E. (Cline) W.; m. Alice Tenzer, May 17, 1953; children: Nancy, David. AB, Clark U., 1950; MD, NYU, 1954. Diplomate Am. Bd. Surgery. Intern Bellevue Hosp., N.Y.C., 1954-55, resident, 1957-61, dir. trauma svc., 1966-79; dir. surgery S.I. U. Hosp., N.Y.C., 1979—; assoc. prof. NYU, N.Y.C., 1968-69; prof. clin. surgery SUNY, Bklyn., 1979—; chmn. trauma designation com. N.Y.C. Emergency Med. Svc., 1990; mem. Office of Profl. Med. Conduct of N.Y. State, 1983—. Vice chmn. N.Y. State Health Rev. and Planning Coun., 1988—. Capt. USMC, 1955-57. Fellow

ACS, Am. Coll. Gastroenterology; mem. Internat. Soc. Surgery, Soc. Am. Gastrointestinal Endoscopic Surgeons, Am. Assn. for Surgery of Trauma, Assn. Acad. Surgery, Soc. Critical Care Medicine, Assn. Surg. Edn., N.Y. Surg. Soc. (pres. 1989), Alpha Omega Alpha. Home: 3003 Van Ness St NW Washington DC 20008-4809 Office: Staten Island U Hosp 475 Seaview Ave Staten Island NY 10305-3436

WORTHAM, EDWIN, V, pediatric ophthalmology; b. Oakland, Calif., May 17, 1954; s. Edwin IV and Georgene (Wise) W.; m. Tammy Lynn Elliott; children: Caroline, Edwin VI. MD, Northwestern U., 1983. Asst. clin. prof. ophthalmology Pacific Med. Ctr., San Francisco, 1988-92; asst. prof. ophthalmology Med. Coll. Va., Richmond, 1992-94; pediatric ophthalmologist Va. Eye Inst., Richmond, 1994—. Inventor in field. Fellow Am. Acad. Ophthalmology, Am. Assn. Pediatric Ophthalmology; mem. Richmond Christian Med. Soc. (sec. 1994-96). Office: Va Eye Inst 400 Westhampton St Richmond VA 23226

WORTHING, LOUIE F., III, plastic surgeon; b. Wharton, Tex., Feb. 28, 1947; s. Louie Fabian Jr. and Imogene (Cogburn) W. BA in Biology, Baylor U., Waco, Tex., 1969; MD, U. Tex., Galveston, 1973. Diplomate Am. Bd. Plastic and Reconstructive Surgery. Owner Aesthetic Biotherapy Ctr., Houston, 1993-95, L. Fabian Worthing III MD PA, Houston, 1980—; bd. trustees, pres. bd. Pallen Corp., Houston. Bd. trustees Houston Grand Opera, 1988-96. Fellow ACS; mem. Am. Soc. Plastic and Reconstructive Surgeons, Am. Soc. Aesthetic Plastic Surgeons, Champions Golf Club, Bentwater Golf Club, Houstonian Club, Univ. Club. Office: 17070 Red Oak Dr # 307 Houston TX 77090

WORTHINGTON, GEORGE MARSHALL, public relations and marketing consultant; b. Houston, Dec. 15, 1953; s. Thomas Eugene and Nancy Ann (Willis) W. BA, Trinity U., San Antonio, 1972; M in Pub. Health & Internat. Affairs, Columbia U., 1978, cert. in mgmt., 1983, MBA, 1993. Writer, analyst Planned Parenthood of N.Y.C., 1978-79, spl. projects coord., 1979-80, mgr., trainer African Family Planning Nurse Practitioner Tng. program, 1980-83; pres. Worthington Assocs. Worldwide, N.Y.C., 1983—. Author: International Compendium of AIDS Programs and Policies, 1989. Alt. rep. mem. numerous non-govt. orgns. UN, UNICEF, UNESCO, WHO, ECOSOC; rep. Internat. Coun. on Disability; bd. dirs. Ednl. Equity Concepts, Ctr. for Independence of Disabled, N.Y.; fonder, mem. working group on AIDS, Non-Govtl. Orgns. Com. on UNICEF; sec. gen. Coun World Orgns. Concerned about AIDS, 1993—. Named one of Outstanding Young Men in Am., 1985, 87; recipient Outstanding Nat. Project award Nat. Inst. Justice, 1984; Jesse Smith Noyes Found. scholar, 1985, Health and Child Survival fellow USAID/Johns Hopkins U., 1991, Charles Revson fellow Columbia U., 1991-92. Mem. Soc. for Internat. Devel. (sec., bd. dirs. 1982-85), Soc. for Ethical Culture (numerous coms.), Am. Pub. Health Assn., Nat. Coun. Internat. Health, Internat. AIDS Soc., Internat. Soc. for AIDS Edn. Democrat. Home and Office: 3D-345 W 21st St New York NY 10011-3059

WORTON, STANLEY IVAN, radiologist, director; b. N.Y.C., Dec. 17, 1932; s. Charles and Ruth (Hirschtritt) W.; m. Joan Kandel, Dec. 17, 1955; children: Marcelle, Debra, Linda, Diane. BA, Cornell U., 1954; MD, Duke U., 1960. Intern Jackson Meml. Hosp., Miami, Fla., 1960-61; resident in radiology Mt. Sinai Hosp., N.Y.C., 1961-64; radiologist Albert Einstein Med. Ctr., Phila., 1964-65, Mt. Siani Hosp., Miami Beach, Fla., 1965-67, Cedars Med. Ctr., Miami, 1967—; bd. dirs. Capital Bank. Member com. Keep Miami Beach Young, 1969. Fellow Am. Coll. Radiology; mem. Dade County Radiologic Soc. (pres.), Fla. Radiologic Soc. (exec. com.). Republican. Jewish. Home: PO Box 12112 Miami FL 33101-2112 Office: Miami Radiology Assocs 1400 NW 12th Ave Miami FL 33136-1003

WOSNITZER, MOREY, urologist; b. Passaic, N.J., Sept. 4, 1929; s. Morris and Ethel (Saltzman) W.; m. Nancy Joell Coplin, Sept. 18, 1978; children: Matthew, Brian. BS, Rutgers U., 1951, MS, 1952; MD, Columbia U., 1956. Diplomate Am. Bd. Urology, Am. Bd. Sexology. Intern in surgery Mt. Sinai Med. Ctr., N.Y.C., 1956-57, asst. resident in surgery, 1957-58; asst. resident in urology Columbia Presbyn. Med. Ctr., N.Y.C., 1958-59, Mass. Gen. Hosp., Boston, 1959-60; resident in urology Peter Bent Brigham Hosp., Boston, 1962-63; pvt. practice Springfield, N.J., 1964—; assoc. in Clin. Urology Columbia U., N.Y.C., 1975—; clin. instr. in Urology Cornell U., N.Y.C., 1989—. Lt. Comdr. USN, 1960-62. Fellow ACS, Internat. Coll. Surgeons, Soc. Urology and Engring., Am. Assn. Clin. Sexologists. Office: 420 Morris Ave Springfield NJ 07081-1149

WOURMS, JOHN PETER BARTON, biology educator; b. N.Y.C., Apr. 30, 1937; s. John Peter and Mary Victoria (Barton) W.; m. Deborah Ruth Deane, June 5, 1972; 1 child, Nicholas Stephen. BS in Biology, Fordham U., 1958, MS in Biology, 1960; PhD in Biol. Scis., Stanford U., 1966. Postdoctoral fellow Harvard U., Cambridge, Mass., 1966-68; asst. prof. zoology McGill U., Montreal, Que., Can., 1968-72; assoc. rsch. scientist, dir. elec.-micro lab. N.Y. Ocean Sci. Lab., Montauk, N.Y., 1972-76; assoc. prof. biol. scis. Clemson (S.C.) U., 1976-80, prof., 1980—; mem. adv. panel in developmental biology NASA, 1984. Author, editor: Genetics of Fishes I, 1976; editor: Reproduction and Development of Sharks, Skates, Rays, and Ratfishes, 1993; assoc. editor: Jour. Exptl. Zoology, 1978-84, Environ. Biology of Fishes, 1982—, Jour. Morphology, 1991—, Acta Zoologica, 1996—. Fellow USPHS-NIH, 1962-66, Am. Cancer Soc., 1966-68, NRC, 1976, Guggenheim Found., 1984-85. Fellow Explorer's Club; mem. Am. Soc. Cell Biology, Am. Soc. Zoologists (divsn. sec. 1983-85, divsn. chair 1996—), Marine Biol. Assn. U.K., Internat. Soc. Developmental Biology. Soc. for Developmental Biology, Am. Soc. Ichthyologists and Herpetologists. Office: Clemson U Dept Biol Scis Clemson SC 29634-1903

WOZNIAK, ROBERT HOWARD, psychology educator; b. San Antonio, Tex., Nov. 1, 1944; s. John Michael and Mary Agnes (Flood) W.; m. Nora Lynn Ashinhurst, Sept. 23, 1967; children: Robert Joel, John Keith. AB, Coll. of Holy Cross, Worcester, Mass., 1966; PhD, U. Mich., 1971. Asst. prof. Inst. Child Devel. U. Minn., Mpls., 1971-76, rsch. assoc., project dir. Rsch., Devel. & Demonstration Ctr. in Edn. Handicapped Children, 1976-78; visiting asst. prof. psychology dept. Tchrs. Coll. Columbia U., N.Y.C., 1979-80; assoc. to full prof., chmn. dept. human devel. Bryn Mawr (Pa.) Coll., 1980-93, prof. dept. psychology, 1993—; cons. Nat. Libr. Medicine, Bethesda, Md., 1990-91. Author: (booklet) Childhood: A Viewer's Guide, 1991; co-compiler: A Century of Serial Publications in Psychology, 1984; editor: Worlds of Childhood, 1993, Roots of Behaviorism, 1993, Behaviorism: The Early Years, 1994, The Evolutionary Origins & Development Psychology, 1995; co-editor: Thinking in Context, 1993, Pure Experience: The Response to William James, 1996; co-host, co-developer: (TV series) Worlds of Childhood: contbr. articles to profl. jours. J. McKeen Cattell Found. fellow, 1986-87. Mem. Jean Piaget Soc. for Study of Cognitive Devel. (pres. 1985-87, bd. dirs. 1981-90), Cheiron Soc. for History of Behavioral Scis. (chmn. exec. com. 1990-93), Soc. for Rsch. in Child Devel. (archivist 1986—). Office: Dept Psychology Bryn Mawr Coll Bryn Mawr PA 19010

WRAITH, JAMES EDMOND, biochemical genetics facility director; b. South Shields, Eng., Oct. 30, 1953; s. James Edmond and Victoria (Vacher) W.; m. Elizabeth Susan Ellison, Aug. 21, 1976; children: Jeffrey, Jennifer, James. MB ChB, Sheffield U., 1977. MRCP, FRCP, London. Clin. fellow Murdoch Inst., Melbourne, Australia, 1986-88; cons. paediatrician Royal Manchester (Eng.) Children's Hosp., 1988-93; dir. Willink Biochem. Genetics Unit, Manchester, 1993—. Contbr. articles on inherited metabolic disease to profl. jours. Mem. Labour Party. Office: Willink Bio Gen Unit-Royal, Manchester Children's Hosp, Manchester M27 4HA, England

WRANNE, BENGT, physiology educator; b. Linköping, Sweden. MD, Uppsala (Sweden) U., 1966, PhD, 1970. Prof. clin. physiology Linköping U., 1994—. Office: Linköping U Hosp, Dept Clin Physiology, 58185 Linköping Sweden

WRAY, BETTY BEASLEY, allergist, immunologist, pediatrician; b. Ga., 1935. MD, Med Coll. Ga., 1960. Diplomate Am. Bd. Allergy and Immunology, Am. Bd. Clin. Lab. Immunology. Intern Talmadge Meml. Hosp., Augusta, Ga., 1960-61, resident in pediatrics, 1962, 64-65, fellow in pediatric allergy, 1966-68; staff mem. U. Hosp., Augusta, Ga., 1974—, Eisenhower Med. Ctr., Augusta, Ga., 1978—; staff mem. Med. Coll. Ga., Augusta, Ga., 1979—, prof. pediatric medicine, chief allergy and immunology; vice-chair dept. pediats. Mem. Am. Acad. Allergy and Immunology, Am. Acad. Pediatrics, Am. Coll. Allergy and Immunology, So. Med. Assn. Office: Med Coll of Georgia Cj # 141 Augusta GA 30912

WRAY, CHARLES HERMAN, surgery educator; b. Orlando Fla., May 9, 1933; s. Charles Adair and Sara Lee (Durham) W.; m. Betty Beasley, Aug. 17, 1957; children: Charles Thomas, Brian Carter, Lee Vaughan, Julienne. AB, Mercer U., 1955; MD, Med. Coll. Ga., Augusta, 1959. Diplomate Am. Bd. Surgery. Intern Univ. Hosp., Augusta, Ga., 1959-60; resident in surgery Med. Coll. Ga. Hosps. and Clinics, 1960-64; instr. surgery Med. Coll. Ga., 1964-66, asst. prof., 1966-70, assoc. prof., 1970-74, prof. surgery, 1974—, vice chmn. surgery, 1985—, v.p. clin. activities, 1993. Co-author: Complications of Vascular Surgery, 1973, Vascular Access for hemodialysis, 1989; co-contbr. articles to profl. jours. Fellow ACS; mem. Internat. Cardiovascular Soc., So. Surg. Assn., Southeastern Surg. Congress, Med. Assn. Ga., Ga. Surg. Soc., Assn. Academic Surgery, Alpha Omega Alpha. Office: Med Coll Ga 1120 15th St Augusta GA 30912

WRAY, CHARLES HERMAN, JR., nursing educator, mental health nurse; b. Leaksville, N.C., Feb. 1, 1950; s. Charles Herman Sr. and Ruby (Cruise) W.; m. Patricia Ann Hall; 1 child, Anne Marie. BSN, U. N.C., 1979; MSN, U. Va., 1985. RN, N.C. Asst. head nurse Children's Psychiat. Unit-Duke U., Durham, N.C., 1985-87; asst. to v.p., dir. nursing Duke Med. Ctr., Durham, 1987-90; course coord. mental health Piedmont C.C., Roxboro, N.C., 1990—. Recipient NIMH traineeship, 1984. Mem. ANA, MENSA, Reed Organ Soc. Episcopalian. Office: Piedmont CC PO Box 1197 Roxboro NC 27573-1197

WRBA, HEINRICH, oncologist, research institute administrator; b. Holleischen, Bohemia, Feb. 14, 1922; s. Johannes and Adolfine (Deridiaux) W.; m. Ingeburg Lohndorf, Aug. 31, 1947; children: Petra, Hannes, Sari, Uta. MD, U. Heidelberg, Germany, 1951, D Natural Scis., 1954. Asst. Univ. Clinics Heidelberg, 1951-56; head dept. exptl. pathology Inst. Pathology, U. Munich, 1956-64; dir. Inst. Exptl. Pathology, German Cancer Rsch. Ctr., Heidelberg, 1964-67; head Inst. Cancer Rsch. U. Vienna, Austria, 1967—, dir. Inst. Applied and Exptl. Oncology, 1983-92, emeritus, 1994—. Contbr. articles to med. jours. With Submarine Svc., German Navy, World War II. Mem. European Orgn. Cancer Rsch. Insts. (founding pres. 1980-83), also others. Office: U Vienna Inst Oncology, Borschkegasse 8 a, A-1090 Vienna Austria

WREN, PAMELA ANNE PORTER, physical therapist; b. Florence, Colo., July 17, 1951; d. Ivan Raymond and Reba Betty (Kintner) Porter; m. Donald Gregory Wren, Nov. 24, 1973; children: Amber Lea, Ashlie Kaye, Alexandria Anne. Student, Hendrix Coll., 1969-71; BS, U. Central Ark., 1973. Lic. physical therapist. Staff phys. therapist, clin. coordinator Meml. Hosp., North Little Rock, Ark., 1973-74; staff phys. therapist Central Baptist Hosp., Little Rock, 1974-75; co-owner, operator Conway Phys. Therapy Clinic, P.A., Ark., 1975—; clin. instr. U. Central Ark. Sch. Phys. Therapy, Conway and Little Rock, 1973—; cert. childbirth educator Prepared Childbirth of Conway, 1976-81. Mem. personnel nominating com. 1st Methodist Ch., Conway, 1977-79, mem. pastor staff rels. com., 1981-82, sec. bd. trustees, 1985-86, chmn., 1987; v.p. Conway Jaycettes, 1975-77; mem. Yokefellows Bible Study, Conway, 1982-84; pres. Conway Ladies Investment Orgn., 1996. Mem. Am. Phys. Therapy Assn. (sec. Ark. chpt. 1977-79), Am. Soc. Psychoprophylaxis in Obstetrics, Internat. Childbirth Educators Assn., LWV (2d v.p. Conway chpt. 1979-82, 1st v.p. 1986). Club: PEO Sisterhood (Conway). Avocations: tennis, swimming, golfing, needlework. Home: 48 Shady Valley Dr Conway AR 72032-3319 Office: Conway Phys Therapy Clinic PA 1404 Caldwell Conway AR 72032

WRETLIND, BENGT MAGNUS, bacteriologist; b. Stockholm, Jan. 5, 1940; m. Marita Kallrot, Jan. 29, 1969; children: Gunnar, Magnus. MD, Karolinska Inst., Stockholm, 1967, PhD, 1977. Cert. clin. bacteriologist, specialist, 1975. Physician Roslagstulls Hosp., Stockholm, 1967-69; physician dept. clin. bacteriology Karolinska Hosp., Stockholm, 1970-85; chief physician Danderyd (Sweden) Hosp., 1985-93; prof. dept. clin. bacteriology Karolinska Instutet at Huddinge Hosp., Sweden, 1993-95; chief phys. Danderyd, 1996—; investigator Naval Med. Rsch. Inst., Bethesda, Md., 1979. Contbr. articles to profl. jours. Mem. Am. Soc. Microbiology, Soc. Gen. Microbiology, Swedish Med. Soc., Swedish Med. Assn. Home: Daldvagen 6, 18162 Lidingo Sweden Office: Huddinge Hosp, Dept Clin Bacteriology, 14186 Huddinge Sweden

WRIGHT, BARBARA EVELYN, microbiologist; b. Pasadena, Calif., Apr. 6, 1926; d. Gilbert Munger Wright and Leta Luella (Brown) Deery. AB, Stanford U., 1947, MA, 1948, PhD, 1951. Biologist NIH, Bethesda, Md., 1953-61; assoc. biochemist Mass. Gen. Hosp., Boston, 1961-69; asst. prof. microbiology Harvard Med. Sch., Boston, 1966-75, assoc. prof., 1975-82; rsch. dir. Boston Biomed. Rsch. Inst., 1967-82; rsch. prof. divsn. biol. scis. U. Mont., Missoula, 1982—; dir. Stella Duncan Rsch. Inst., Missoula, 1982—; cons. Miles Lab., Elkhart, Ind., 1980-84. Author: Critical Variables in Differentiation, 1973; editor: Control Mechanisms in Respiration and Fermentation, 1963; contbr. articles to profl. jours. Grantee NIH, NSF, 1991-96. Mem. AAAS (pres. Pacific divsn. 1984-85), Am. Soc. for Microbiology (Nat. Found. for Microbiology lectr. 1970, divsnl. lectr. 1978), Am. Soc. Biol. Chemists. Home: 1550 Trotting Horse Ln Missoula MT 59801-9220 Office: U Mont DBS Missoula MT 59812

WRIGHT, CAROLE YVONNE, chiropractor; b. Long Beach, Calif., July 12, 1932; d. Paul Burt and Mary Leoan (Staley) Fickes; 1 child, Morgan Michelle. D. Chiropractic, Palmer Coll., Davenport, Iowa, 1976. Instr. Palmer Coll., 1975-76; dir., owner Wright Chiropractic Clinic, Rocklin, Calif., 1978-88, Woodland, Calif., 1980-81; co-owner Ft. Sutter Chiropractic Clinic, Sacramento, 1985-89; owner Wright Chiropractic Health Ctr., Sacramento, 1989—, Capitol Chiropractic, Sacramento, 1993—; cons. in field; lectr., speaker on radio and TV programs, at seminars. Contbr. articles to profl. jours. Co-chmn. Harold Michaels for Congress campaign, Alameda, Calif., 1972; dist. dir. 14th Congl. Dist., 1983—. Mem. Internat Chiropractic Assn. Calif. (bd. dirs. 1978-81, pres. 1983-85), Palmer Coll. Alumni Assn. (Calif. state pres. 1981-83), Rocklin C. of C. (bd. dirs. 1979-81). Republican. Avocations: reading, travel. Home: 1404 Stonebridge Way Roseville CA 95661-5456

WRIGHT, CATHLEEN JANE, medical and surgical nurse; b. Chgo., Mar. 11, 1970; d. James William and Susan Margaret (Grzywacz) W. BSN, Villanova (Pa.) U., 1993. RN, N.J. Staff nurse West Jersey Health System, Camden, N.J., 1993—. Mem. ANA, Acad. Med./Surg. Nurses, Am. Assn. Diabetes Educators, Am. Diabetes Assn., Sigma Theta Tau. Roman Catholic. Home: 139 Wayne Ave Haddonfield NJ 08033 Office: West Jersey Health System 1000 Atlantic Ave Camden NJ 08101

WRIGHT, CHARLES THOMAS, hospital administrator; b. Knoxville, Tenn., Aug. 5, 1951; s. James Barton and Veldia Jesse (Hooper) W.; m. Valerie Fodal, July 20, 1974; children: Heather Lee, Kelly Lynn, Kyle Thomas, Matthew Charles. BS, U. Tenn., 1974; MHA, Ariz. State U., 1982. Rsch. asst. Ariz. State U., Tempe, 1981; adminstrv. resident Providence Hosp., Anchorage, 1982, dir. shared services, 1983-85, asst. adminstr., 1985-90; ex-officio mem. adv. bd. Home Health Care Inc., program devel. com. Home Health Care, Inc., Anchorage, 1984-90; v.p. Mercy Med. Ctr., Roseberg, Oreg., 1990-92; COO Providence Medford (Oreg.) Med. Ctr., 1992-95; CEO Providence Health Sys.-So. Oreg., Medford, 1995—; chair Jackson County Pub. Health Bd. Chmn. fin. com. United Meth. Ch., Chugiak, Alaska, 1984-88, chmn. fin. com., 1986-88; state med. ops. officer Alaska Army N.G., 1986-90, advanced through grades to capt.; ex- officio mem. bd. dirs. Alaska Treatment Ctr., 1985-88. Served to maj. U.S. Army, 1974-80, 90-91, Desert Storm. Decorated Meritorious Svc. medal, Army Commendation medal with 4 oak leaf clusters; Foster McGaw scholar Ctr. for Health Services Adminstrn., Ariz. State U., 1981. Mem Medford-Jackson County C. of C. (bd. dirs.), Beta Gamma Sigma, Phi Kappa Tau. Democrat. Methodist. Home: 2356 Greenbrook St Medford OR 97504-8381 Office: Providence Health Sys-So Oreg 1111 Crater Lake Dr Medford OR 97504

WRIGHT, CHERYL, medical and surgical nurse; b. Ripon, Wis., Apr. 7, 1949; d. Milton William and Dorothy Mae (Ogilvie) W.; m. Ronald Alan Wright, Jan. 16, 1970; children: Mark, Eric, Wendy. AAN, Everett C.C., 1970. RN. Staff nurse St. Luke's Gen. Hosp., Bellingham, Wash., 1970-89; nurse mgr. Roberts Med./Option Care, Bellingham, 1989-96; IV therapy team leader Affiliated Health Svcs., Mt. Vernon, Wash., 1996—. Mem. Intravenous Nurses Soc. Home: 277 Lake Whateam Blvd Bellingham WA 98226 Office: Affiliated Health Svcs 600 E Birchwood Bellingham WA 98225

WRIGHT, CREIGHTON BOLTER, cardiovascular surgeon, educator; b. Washington, Jan. 29, 1939; s. Benjamin Washington and Catherine Adele (Bolter) W.; m. Carolyn Eleanor Craver, Jan. 29, 1966; children: Creighton Bolter, Benson, Kathryn, Elizabeth. BA, Duke U., 1961, MD, 1965; MBA, Xavier U., 1995. Diplomate Am. Bd. Thoracic Surgery, Am. Bd. Surgery, subbd. Gen. Vascular Surgery. Intern, Duke U., Durham, N.C., 1965-66; resident in surgery U. Va., Charlottesville, 1966-71; from asst. prof. to assoc. prof. George Washington U., 1974-76; assoc. prof., then prof. surgery U. Iowa, 1976-81; prof. clin. surgery U. Cin., 1982-89, also clin. prof. surgery Uniformed Services U., 1989—; dir. Dept. of Surgery Jewish Hosp., Cin. Col. USAR, 1966-93; ret., 1993. Decorated Bronze star, Meritorious Svc. medals; recipient Kindred Resident Teaching award, 1967, Golden Apple Teaching award, 1975. Mem. Assn. Acad. Surgery (pres. 1980), Central Surg. Assn., Soc. Univ. Surgeons, Soc. Vascular Surgery, Internat. Soc. Cardiovascular Surgery, Muller Surg. Soc. (pres. 1985-87), Am. Assn. Thoracic Surgery, Soc. Thoracic Surgery, So. Thoracic Surg. Assn., Midwestern Vascular Surg. Soc., Cardiovascular and Thoracic Surgeons, Cin. Surg. Soc. (pres. 1996), Comml. Club, Alpha Omega Alpha, Sigma Chi (Significant Sig award 1993). Editor: Vascular Grafting, 1983; (with others) Venous Trauma, 1983; contbr. articles to profl. jours., chpts. to books. Home: 312 E Second St Covington KY 41011 Office: Cardiovascular & Thoracic Surgeons 2123 Auburn Ave Cincinnati OH 45219

WRIGHT, DANA JACE, nurse, entrepreneur; b. Cleve., Apr. 20, 1952; d. William James and Murl Jean (White) Ewing; m. David Alan Samball, June 22, 1968 (div. Apr. 1971); 1 child, David; m. David M. Wright, July 11, 1981; children: William James, Karen Marie. Assoc. in Nursing, Valencia Community Coll., 1973, AA, 1973; BS in Respiratory Therapy, U. Cen. Fla., 1975; MEd, Auburn U., 1979; D in Nursing, Case Western Res. U., 1982. RN, Fla., Ohio, N.Y., Ga.; cert. emergency med. technician; cert. and registered respiratory therapist; cert. med.-surg. nurse; lic. real estate agt., N.Y. Nursing asst. Holiday Hosp., Orlando, Fla., 1970-71, staff nurse critical care unit, intensive care unit, 1973; pvt. duty nurse Med. Personnel Pool, Orlando, 1973-74; nurse critical care burn team Upjohn, Inc., Augusta, Ga., 1976-77; ednl. dir. dept. respiratory therapy U. Hosp., Augusta, 1975-76; mem. staff respiratory therapy VA Hosp., Augusta, 1976-77; clin. instr. respiratory therapy Med. Coll. Ga., Augusta, 1976-77, Columbus Coll., 1977-78; ednl. dir. respiratory therapy Med. Ctr. Hosp., Columbus, 1977-79; staff nurse, relief supr. Kelly Health Care, Beachwood, Ohio, 1979-81; staff nurse Med. Staff, Inc., Cleve., 1981-83; dir. nursing S.R.T. Med. Staff Inc., Cleve., 1983; pres. Wright Properties, Buffalo, 1987-94, Med. Ctr. Vending, 1994—; part-time nurse Millard Fillmore Suburban Hosp., 1990-91. Treas. Ch. Women's Assn., Snyder, N.Y., 1985-86; mem. nursing resources panel North Ohio Lung Assn., 1981-82; mem. Profl. Parent Network, Buffalo, 1987—. Mem. ANA (alt. del. 1993-94), Am. Assn. Nurses Practicing Independently (assoc.), Nat. Nurses Bus., N.Y. State Nurses Assn. (nurse rsch. cons. 1991-92, 94, chair nurse entrepreneurs 1992-94, WNY regional review team 1992-94), Women's Dental Guild. Republican. Home and Office: 49 Colony Ct Buffalo NY 14226-3507

WRIGHT, DAVID, microbiologist, pathologist; b. London, May 12, 1937; s. Hershal and Ann W.; m. Rosalind Kerstein; 3 children. MBBS, London U., Eng., 1962, MD, 1972. Reader, cons. medical microbiologist, dir. Lyme Lab. Charing Cross Hosp., London, Eng., 1980—. Editor: Molecular & Cellular Biology Series, 1990—, Immunology and Molecular Biology of Sexually Transmitted Diseases, 1990; contbr. articles to profl. jours. Fellow Royal Coll. Pathologists. Office: Charing Cross Hosp Micro Dept, Fulham Palace Road, London W6 8RF, England

WRIGHT, DAVID BRUCE, internist; b. Richmond, Ind., Oct. 16, 1954; s. Donald Herman Sr. and Jean Helen (Walters) W.; m. Cynthia Diane Pleshek, June 21, 1975; children: Timothy Daniel, Paul Aaron, Matthew David, Rachel Elizabeth. BS in Biol. Scis., Fla. Inst. of Tech., 1976; MD, U. South Fla., 1979. Diplomate Am. Bd. Internal Medicine. Chief resident in internal medicine Bapt. Meml. Hosp., Memphis, 1981-82; pvt. practice in internal medicine Cresthaven Internal Medicine Assocs., Memphis, 1985-94, Internal Medicine Assocs. of Cordova (Tenn.), 1994—; assoc. clin. instr. ctr. for health scis. U. Tenn., Memphis, 1985—. Maj. USAF, 1982-85. Eagle Scout Boy Scouts Am., 1972. Mem. Alpha Omega Alpha, Beta Beta Beta.

WRIGHT, DOUGLAS GREGORY, orthopedic surgeon; b. Bklyn., June 16, 1957. BS, U. Ga., 1979; MD, N.Y. Med. Coll., 1983. Asst. prof. U. Pa., Phila., 1989-94; assoc. prof. Wright State U., Dayton, Ohio, 1994—. Mem. Am. Acad. Orthopedic Surgeons, Am. Diabetes Assn., Am. Orthopedic Foot and Ankle Soc., Orthopedic Trauma Assn. Roman Catholic. Office: Wright State U Orthopedics L-200 30 E Apple St Dayton OH 45409

WRIGHT, ELLEN LEE, laboratory manager; b. Atlanta, Sept. 8, 1953; d. Eldon Andre Thompson and Enley Ruth (Buchanan) Derrick; m. Hilary Thomas Wright, Jr., July 4, 1990. AA, Clayton State Coll., Morrow, Ga., 1973; BS, Mulligan Coll., 1975; postgrad., Ga. State U., Atlanta, 1975-87. Cert. Am. Med. Techs., Am. Soc. Clin. Pathologists. Technician Dr. Milton Freedman, Atlanta, 1981; staff technologist Sylvan Grove Hosp., Jackson, Ga., 1981-84, Peachtree Regional Hosp., Newman, Ga., 1984-90; asst. lab. mgr. Fayette Med. Ctr., Fayetteville, Ga., 1990; lab. mgr. PAPP Clinic, Newman, 1990—. Mem. Am. Assn. Clin. Chemists (cert. clin. chemist), Clin. Lab. Mgrs. Assn. Office: PAPP Clinic 15 Cavender St Grantville GA 30220

WRIGHT, ERIC R., physician assistant; b. Fremont, Mich., Apr. 8, 1952; s. Owen Aaron and Ethlyn Emily (Crandall) W.; m. Teresa Christine Harrison, May 3, 1979; 1 child, Natalie Ann. Grad., Hackley Hosp. Sch. Radiol.Tech, Muskegon, Mich., 1975; AS in Physician Assisting with honors, Kettering (Ohio) Coll. Med.Art, 1984. Diplomate Colo. Bd. Med. Examiners. Physician asst. Peak Nine Med. Ctr./Family & Emergency Med. Assocs., Breckenridge, Colo., 1984-85, Richard Wageman, M.D., Monument, Colo., 1985-86, Dennis Caldwell, M.D., Colorado Springs, Colo., 1986-88, Sheldon Ravin, D.O., Skyway Family Practice, Colorado Springs, 1988-90, The People's Clinic, Boulder, Colo., 1990-95, Columbine Family Practice Ctr., Loveland, Colo., 1991-93, Alpine Ear, Nose and Throat, Ft. Collins, Colo., 1993—. Author: PA Protocols: A Guidebook, 1992. Mem. Am. Registry of Radiologic Technologists, Beaven-Black Student Soc. Physician Assts. (v.p. 1982-83), Am. Acad. Physician Assts., Colo. Assn. Physician Assts. (membership chmn. 1990-92), Soc. Physician Assts. in Otolaryngology. SDA. Home: 3411 N Douglas Loveland CO 80538-2574

WRIGHT, ERNEST MARSHALL, physiologist, consultant; b. Belfast, Ireland, June 8, 1940; came to U.S., 1965; BSc, U. London, 1961, DSc, 1978; PhD, U. Sheffield, Eng., 1964. Research fellow Harvard U., Boston, 1965-66; from asst. prof. to full prof. physiology UCLA Med. Sch., 1967—, chmn. dept. physiology, 1987—; cons. NIH, Bethesda, Md., 1982—, Senator Jacob K. Javits neurosci. investigator, 1985. Office: UCLA Sch Med Dept Physiology 10833 Le Conte Ave Los Angeles CA 90095-1751

WRIGHT, FRANCES JANE, educational psychologist; b. Los Angeles, Dec. 22, 1943; d. step-father John David and Evelyn Jane (Dale) Brinegar. BA, Long Beach State U., 1965, secondary tchr. cert., 1966; MA, Brigham Young U., 1968, EdD, 1980; postgrad. U. Nev., 1970, U. Utah, 1972-73; postdoctoral Utah State U., 1985-86. Cert. tchr., adminstr. Utah. Asst. dir. Teenpost Project, San Pedro, Calif., 1966; caseworker Los Angeles County, 1966-67; self-care inservice dir. Utah State Tng. Sch., American Fork, Utah, 1968, vocat. project designer, 1968; tchr. mentally handicapped Santa Ana Unified Schs., Calif., 1968-69; state specialist intellectually handicapped State Office Edn., Salt Lake City, 1969-70; vocat. counselor Manpower, Salt Lake City, 1970-71; tchr. severely handicapped Davis County Schs., Farmington, Utah, 1971-73, diagnostician, 1973-74, resource elem. tchr., 1974-78; instr. Brigham Young U., Salt Lake City, 1976-83; resource tchr. jr. high Davis

County Schs., Farmington, 1978-90; ednl. cons., Murray, Utah, 1973-90; chief ednl. diagnostician Ctr. for Evaluation of Learning and Devel., Layton, Utah, 1989-90; clin. dir. assessment and observation program Idaho Youth Ranch, 1990-95, clin. dir. intake program, 1992-94, supr. family preservation svc./aftercare teams, 1993-95, co-ranch treatment dir. and placement officer, 1995; cons. juvenile correctional dist. 5, 1996—; lectr. in field. Author curriculums in spl. edn.; contbr. articles to profl. jours. Named Profl. of Yr., Utah Assn. for Children with Learning Disabilities, 1985. Mem. Assn. Children/Adults with Learning Disabilities (del. 1979-85, 87, nat. nominating com. 1985-86, nat. bd. dirs. 1988-91), Utah Assn. Children/Adults with Learning Disabilities (exec. bd. 1978-84, profl. adv. bd. 1985-90, coord. LDA orgn. Idaho 1991—), Coun. Exceptional Children (div. learning disabilities, ednl. diagnostics, behavioral disorders), Council Learning Disabilities, Assn. Supervisors and Curriculum Devel. (regional adv.), Windstar Found., Smithsonian Found., Cousteau Soc., Am. Biographical Inst. (life, hon. advisor rsch. bd. advisors nat. div.), Nat. Assn. Sch. Adminstrs. Democrat. Mormon. Lodge: Job's Daughters. Avocations: geneology research, horseback riding, sketching, crafts, reading. Home: 2176 Julie Ln Twin Falls ID 83301 Office: Youth Ctr Juvenile Corrections 2469 Wright Ave Twin Falls ID 83301

WRIGHT, HARRY HERCULES, psychiatrist; b. Charleston, S.C., Jan. 4, 1948; s. Harry Vernon and Agnes Lucile (Simmons) W.; BS, U. S.C., 1970; MD, U. Pa., 1976, MBA, 1976. Resident in psychiatry Wm. S. Hall Psychiat. Inst., Columbia, S.C., 1977-79; adminstrv. fellow in psychiatry NIMH, Rockville, Md., 1979; fellow in child psychiatry William S. Hall Psychiat. Inst., 1979-81, teaching child psychiatrist, 1981—; instr. dept. neuropsychiatry and behavioral sci. U. S.C. Sch. Medicine, 1981-82, asst. prof., 1982-86, assoc. prof., 1986-90, prof., 1990—. Bd. dirs. Carolina Children's Home, 1992; mem. landmarks commn. City of Columbia, 1986. Falk fellow, 1977-79; Laughlin fellow, 1979; recipient Freed award Hall Psychiat. Inst., 1978, Outstanding Service award Sickle Cell Found. Mem. AAAS, Am. Acad. Child Psychiatry, World Psychiat. Assn., World Assn. Infant Mental Health, Am. Soc. Adolescent Psychiatry, Am. Pub. Health Assn., Am. Psychiat. Assn., So. Med. Assn., Riverbank Zool. Soc., Autism Soc. Am., Acad. Orgnl. and Occupl. Psychiatry, Soc. Study Psychiatry and Culture, Omicron Delta Kappa, Sigma Xi. Methodist. Contbr. articles to profl. jours. Home: PO Box 12474 Columbia SC 29211-2474 Office: PO Box PO Box 202 Columbia SC 29202-0202

WRIGHT, HASTINGS KEMPER, surgeon, educator; b. Boston, Aug. 28, 1928; s. Donald M. and Lucia (Durand) W.; m. Nancy E. Howell, June 19, 1954; children: Mark, Kenneth, Barbara, Donald. AB, Harvard U., 1950, MD, 1954, MA, 1973. Diplomate: Am. Bd. Surgery. Intern Univ. Hosps. Cleve., 1954, resident, 1957-61; asst. prof. surgery Western Res. U., Cleve., 1961-66; assoc. prof. surgery Med. Sch. Yale U., New Haven, 1967-72, prof. Med. Sch., 1972-95; prof. surgery emeritus, 1995—; chief gen. surgery Yale-New Haven Hosp., 1968-79, asst. chief surgery, 1979-95. Author: Complications of GI Surgery, 1972; asst. chief editor Archives of Surgery, Chgo., 1977-89. Capt. U.S. Army, 1955-57. Fellow ACS, Am. Surg. Assn.; mem. Soc. Univ. Surgeons (program dir. 1972), Am. Gastroent. Assn., Soc. Surgery Gastrointestinal Tract. Republican. Episcopalian. Clubs: Mory's Assoc. (New Haven); Yale (N.Y.C.). Home: 35 Wood Rd Branford CT 06405-4935 Office: Yale U Med Sch Dept Surgery 333 Cedar St New Haven CT 06510-3206

WRIGHT, JESSE HARTZELL, psychiatrist, educator; b. Altoona, Pa., Sept. 21, 1943; s. Jesse H. and Marion (Stone) W.; m. Susanne Judy Wright, July 9, 1967; children: Andrew, Laura. BS, Juniata Coll., 1965; MD, Jefferson Med. Coll., 1969; PhD, U. Louisville, 1976. Diplomate Am. Bd. Psychiatry and Neurology, Am. Bd. Med. Examiners; lic. psychiatrist, Ky. Asst. prof. U. Louisville, 1975-79, assoc. prof., 1979-87, prof., 1987—; clin. dir. Norton Psychiat. Clinic, Louisville, 1975-83, med. dir., 1983—; resident in psychiatry U. Mich., Ann Arbor, 1970-73; cons. Our Lady of Peace Hosp., Louisville, 1978—, Bapt. Hosp., Louisville, 1979—, Jewish Hosp., Louisville, 1987—. Author first multimedia computer program for psychotherapy, chpts. to books; contbr. articles to prof. jours. Fellow APA; mem. Ky. Psychiat. Assn. (sec. 1979-80, v.p. 1980-81, pres. 1982-83). Home: 15 Indian Hills Trl Louisville KY 40207-1532 Office: Norton Psychiat Clinic 200 E Chestnut St Louisville KY 40202-1822

WRIGHT, JOHN C., II, physician, educator; b. Sodus, N.Y., June 16, 1927; s. John Embry and Frances Louise (Horton) W.; m. Jane A. Atwood, Oct. 27, 1956 (dec. Aug. 1990); children: Kim A., Tamilyn A. Jerilyn A., John C. III. BA, U. Buffalo, 1950; MD, N.Y. Med. Coll., 1955. Diplomate Am. Bd. Family Practice. Intern Waterbury (Conn.) Hosp., 1955-56, resident in medicine, 1956-57; pvt. practice Manchester, Conn., 1957-72; dir. Family Practice Residency Program, Middletown, Conn., 1972-75; asst. prof. dept. cmty. medicine U. Conn., 1972-75; vice chmn., assoc. prof. dept. family practice Wright State U., Dayton, Ohio, 1975-78; assoc. prof. dept. family practice U. Louisville, 1978-92, prof., 1992-95, chmn. dept. family practice, 1978-81, dir. geriatric programs, 1981-92, dir. predoctoral edn., 1978-86, chief geriatric divsn., 1990-92, acting dir. Urban Ctr. on Aging, 1985-91, prof. emeritus, 1995—; med. dir. Hurstbourne Care Ctr. at Stony Brook, Louisville, 1991—, Christian Health Ctr., Louisville, 1985-92; mem. staff St. Anthony Hosp., Louisville, 1978-90, Univ. Hosp., U. Louisville, 1983—, St. Elizabeth Med. Ctr., Dayton, 1976-78, Miami Valley Hosp., Dayton, 1976-78, Good Samaritan Hosp., Dayton, 1976-78, Children's Med. Ctr., Dayton, 1976-78, Frazier Rehab. Ctr. Inc., Louisville, 1986—, Jewish Hosp., Louisville, 1989—, Audubon Hosp., Louisville, 1992—, Kosair Children's Hosp., Louisville, 1990—. Patentee adjustable ski racks, 1979; contbr. articles to profl. jours. Mem. health care and edn. com. Louisville and Jefferson County Bd. Health, 1979-81; mem. vestry St. Francis in the Fields Episc. Ch., 1983-86, mem. choir, 1978-90; founding mem., chair Lifespan: A Teaching Gerontologic Cmty., 1987-90; mem. Nat. Ski Patrol, 1981—. With USNR, 1946-47. Fellow Am. Acad. Family Physicians; mem. AMA, Am. Geriatric Soc., Soc. Tchrs. of Family Medicine, Ky. Med. Assn., Jefferson County Med. Assn., Am. Med. Dirs. Assn. (cert.), Am. Heart Assn. (mem. coun. on epidemiology sect. on hypertension). Home: 3696 Webb Rd Simpsonville KY 40067-6435 Office: U Louisville Dept Family & Cmty Medicine 550 S Jackson St Louisville KY 40202-1622

WRIGHT, JOHN CUSHING, psychology educator, applied animal behaviorist; b. Lakewood, Ohio, May 25, 1947. Student, Ohio U., 1965-67; BA, Wittenberg U., 1970; MA, Miami U., Oxford, Ohio, 1972, PhD, 1976. Cert. applied animal behaviorist. Asst. prof. Berea (Ky.) Coll., 1975-80, Clemson (S.C.) U., 1980-83; assoc. prof. Mercer U., Macon, Ga., 1983-91, prof., 1992—; adj. assoc. prof. dept. anatomy and radiology Sch. Vet. Medicine, U. Ga., Athens; animal behavior cons., Atlanta, 1980—. Editor, pub.: Animal Behavior Cons. Newsletter, 1983—; columnist Animal Behavior the Wright Way, The Heart, Atlanta Humane Soc., 1990-93; contbr. chpts. to books, papers to mtgs. and articles to profl. jours. Fellow Am. Psychol. Soc. (charter); mem. APA, Animal Behavior Soc. (cert. in applied animal behavior, chmn. bd. profl. cert. 1990-94), Southeastern Psychol. Assn., Midwestern Psychol. Assn., Behavior Genetics Assn., Sigma Xi. Office: Mercer U Psychology Dept 1400 Coleman Ave Macon GA 31207

WRIGHT, JOHN ROBERT, pathologist; b. Winnipeg, Man., Can., Aug. 18, 1935; came to U.S., 1961, naturalized, 1968; s. Ross Grant and Anna Marie (Crispin) W.; m. Deanna Pauline Johnson, June 25, 1960; children—Carolyn Deanna, David John. M.D. with honors, U. Man., 1959. Diplomate: Am. Bd. Pathology. Intern Winnipeg Gen. Hosp., 1959-60, resident, 1960-61; resident Balt. City Hosp., 1961-63, Buffalo Gen. Hosp., 1963-64; teaching fellow in medicine U. Man., 1960-61; instr. in pathology, Buswell fellow SUNY-Buffalo, 1965-67, prof. pathology, chmn. dept. pathology, 1974—; asst. chief pathology Balt. City Hosps. and; asst. prof. Johns Hopkins U., 1967-74; cons. Roswell Park Meml. Inst., 1975—, bd. visitors, 1981—, interim dir., 1985-86, chmn. bd. visitors, 1987—. Recipient Louis A. and Ruth Siegel Disting. Teaching award SUNY-Buffalo, 1977, 78, 88, Deans award SUNY, 1987. Mem. AMA, AAAS, Coll. Am. Pathologists, Am. Soc. Investigative Pathologists, Am. Soc. Clin. Pathologists, U.S. and Can. Acad. Pathology, Assn. Pathology Chairmen (pres. 1994-96), Am. Heart Assn., Alpha Omega Alpha. Home: 46 Wynngate Ln Williamsville NY 14221-1840 Office: SUNY 204 Farber Hall Buffalo NY 14214

WRIGHT, KENNETH WESTON, pediatric ophthalmologist; b. L.A., Oct. 25, 1950; s. Harvey Weston and Mary Jo W.; m. Donna Marie; children: Jamie, Matthew, Michael, Lisa, Andrew. BA, Calif. Lutheran Coll., 1972; MD, Boston U., 1977. Intern Harbor Gen. Hosp./UCLA, 1978; resident Doheny Eye Inst., L.A., 1978-81; fellow in pediat. ophthalmology Johns Hopkins Hosp., Balt., 1981, Children's Hosp. Nat. Medicine, Washington, 1982; assoc. prof. U. So. Calif., L.A., 1982-92; pvt. practice, 1992-94; head pediat. ophthalmology/strabismus Cleve. Clinic Found., 1994—. Author, editor: Textbook of Ophthalmology, 1996; editor: Pediatric Ophthalmology & Strabismus, 1995; contbr. articles to profl. jours. Fellow Am. Acad. Pediatrics, Am. Acad. Ophthalmology (com.); mem. Am. Assn. Pediat. Ophthalmology/Strabismus, Wilmer Resident Assn. Office: Cleve Clinic Found 9500 Euclid Ave A31 Cleveland OH 44195

WRIGHT, KIM BRIAN, neurosurgeon; b. Baker, Oreg., Feb. 1, 1953. MD, U. Calif., San Diego, 1979. Intern U. Calif., San Diego, 1979-80; resident in neurosurgery U. Wash., 1980-85; med. staff Providence Med. Ctr., Seattle, Swedish Med. Ctr., Seattle, Highline Cmty. Hosp., Seattle; clin. instr. U. Wash., Seattle. Office: Seattle Neurosurgery Clinic 1600 E Jefferson St Ste 620 Seattle WA 98122-5649

WRIGHT, LABAN JOSEPH, health services administrator; b. Moline, Ill., Sept. 4, 1946; s. Laban Leo and Miriam Ruth (Morgan) W.; m. Sherilyn Kay Grafton-Kennedy, May 6, 1967 (div. Apr. 1987); children: Tiffany Lynn, Laban Joseph; m. Elizabeth Ann Ragland, Nov. 23, 1990. BS, George Washington U., 1978; MA, Webster U., 1983. Commd. ensign U.S. Navy, 1964, advanced through grades to lt comdr., ret., 1985; night adminstr. John Peter Smith Hosp., Ft. Worth, 1985-86; adminstr. Parkside Lodge-Westgate, Denton, Tex., 1986-91; chief fin. officer Burleson Meml. Hosp., Caldwell, Tex., 1991-94; adminstr. Limestone Med. Ctr., Groesbeck, Tex., 1994—. Mem. Tex. Hosp. Assn. (edn. com. 1992—), Ctrl. Tex. Rural Health Assn., Tex. Orgn. Rural and Cmty. Hosp., Am. Mgmt. Assn., Groesbeck C. of C. (bd. dirs. 1995), Groesbeck Noon Lions Club. Methodist. Home: 406 Rocky Creek Groesbeck TX 76642

WRIGHT, PATRICIA LYNN, medical technologist; b. Burkesville, Ky., Oct. 24, 1969; d. Bob and Shirley Helen (Sidwell) W. AS, Lindsey Wilson Coll., 1990. Med. tech. Wayne County Hosp., Monticello, Ky., 1990—. Republican. Methodist. Office: 166 Hospital St Monticello KY 42633

WRIGHT, RICHARD OSCAR, III, pathologist, educator; b. La Junta, Colo., Aug. 9, 1944; s. Richard O. Sr. and Frances R. (Curtiss) W.; m. Bernale Trout, May 31, 1969; children: Lauren Diane, Richard O. IV. BS in Biology, Midwestern State U., 1966; MS in Biology, U. Houston, 1968; DO, U. Health Sci., 1972. Cert. anatomic pathology and lab. medicine Am. Osteo. Bd. Pathology. Sr. attending pathologist Normandy Met. Hosps., St. Louis, 1977-81; sr. attending pathologist Phoenix (Ariz.) Gen. Hosps., 1981—, dir. med. edn., 1989-92; clin. asst. prof. pathology Coll. Osteo. Medicine, Pomona, Calif., 1985—; clin. instr. pathology Ohio U. Coll. Osteo. Medicine, Athens, 1976-77; clin. asst. prof. pathology Kirksville (Mo.) Coll. Osteo. Medicine, 1985-87; vis. lectr. pathology New Eng. Coll. Osteo. Medicine, Biddeford, Maine, 1989-92; cons. pathologist Phoenix (Ariz.) Indian Med. Ctr., 1992-94; adv. bd. Inter Soc. Coun. Pathology, Chgo., 1992—. Active Ariz. Rep. Party, Phoenix, Rep. Nat. Com., Washington; chmn. bd. trustees Phoenix (Ariz.) Gen. Hosp., 1994-95; ex-occicio, mem. bd. trustees, 1995—. Recipient Mead-Johnson award Nat. Osteo. Assn., 1975. Fellow Am. Osteo. Coll. Pathologists (pres. 1989-90, bd. govs. 1984-91), Coll. m. Pathologists; mem. Ariz. Osteo. Med. Assn. Ariz. Soc. Pathologists, Century Club Alumni Assn., AAAS, Alpha Phi Omega, Rho Sigma Chi, Psi Sigma Alpha. Presbyterian. Office: Anatomic Pathology Assoc 19829 N 27th Ave Phoenix AZ 85027-4001

WRIGHT, ROBERT J., health network administrator; b. Evansville, Ind., Mar. 25, 1959; s. Robert F. and Nancy Lou (Parr) W. BS in Acctg., Ind. U., 1981; MBA, U. Chgo., 1986. Auditor Arthur Andersen & Co., Chgo., 1981-85; CFO, Stenograph Corp., Skokie, Ill., 1986-87; COO, Emergency Physican Group, Lincolnshire, Ill., 1987-89; asst. v.p. Med Care HMO, Maywood, Ill., 1989-92; v.p. provider recruitment and retention HealthNetwork, Inc., Oak Brook, Ill., 1992—. Home: 605 N Lyle Ave Elgin IL 60123 Office: HealthNetwork Inc 1420 Kensington Rd Oak Brook IL 60521

WRIGHT, ROY THOMAS, psychologist; b. Bonham, Tex., Apr. 28, 1943; s. Roy Thomas and Nannie Jo (Graham) W.; m. Patricia Kathleen Ryan, Dec. 26, 1965 (div. 1975); m. Mary Pat Carlson, Feb. 16, 1983. BA in Psychology, U. Alaska, College Station, 1968; MEd in Counseling, U Tex. Pan Am., 1980; EdD in Marriage and Family Therapy, East Tex. State U., Commerce, 1985. Lic. marriage and family therapist, profl. counselor, Tex., lic. psychologist Ark. Coord. McAllen (Tex.) Methadone Clinic; child protective svcs. worker Hidalgo County Protective Svcs., Tex., 1974-75; therapist, trainer doctoral interns Hunt Family Svcs. Ctr., Greenville, Tex., 1979-81; psychologist E. Tex. regional Mental Health, Athens, Tex., 1982-85, S.W. Ark. Mental Health, Texarkana, Ark., 1985-89; consulting psychologist APOGEE, Inc., Memphis, Tenn., 1992-94; dir. Sr. Psychol. Assocs., Texarkana, Ark., 1993—, Associated Family Therapists, Texarkana, Ark., 1986—, InfoPsych Profl. Group, Texarkana, Ark., 1995—. Mem. Nat. Counseling Assn., Tex. Counseling Assn., Am. Assn. for Marriage and Family Therapy (clin. mem.), Tex. Assn. for Marriage and Family Therapy (clin. mem.), Am. Assn. Sex Educators, Counselors and Trainers, Am. Assn. Clin. Hypnosis, Ark. Psychol. Assn., Psi Chi. Home: 6109 Ben Burrough Texarkana TX 75503 Office: Assoc Family Therapists 601 Pecan Texarkana AR 75502

WRIGHT, WILLIAM EVAN, physician; b. N.Y.C., Aug. 1, 1946; s. Samuel and Frances Elnora (Perpente) W.; m. Diana Claire Dryer, Aug. 15, 1970; children: Jason William, Elizabeth Garland, Edwin Samuel. BA in Music, U. Rochester, 1968; MD, U. Pa., 1972; MPH, U. Utah, 1979; MS in Physiology, Harvard U., 1980. Diplomate Am. Bd Internal Medicine, Am. Bd. Preventive Medicine, Am. Bd. Occupl. Medicine, Am. Bd. Ind. Med. Examiners; ACOEM cert. med. rev. officer; cert. FAA med. examiner. Intern LDS Hosp., Salt Lake City, 1972-73, resident, 1973-75; resident U. Utah Med. Ctr., Salt Lake City, 1978-79, Harvard Sch. Pub. Health, Boston, 1979-80; asst. prof. U. So. Calif., L.A., 1980-86; med. dir. U.S. DEA, Arlington, Va., 1986-96; program mgr., site med. dir. DynCorp, Reston, Va., 1991-96; regional med. dir. Md. Office of CORE, Boston, 1996—; cons. in field. Contbr. articles to profl. jours. Maj. U.S. Army, 1975-77. Fellow Am. Coll. Physicians, Am. Coll. Occupational and Environ. Health; mem. Alpha Omega Alpha. Home: 6801 Wemberly Way Mc Lean VA 22101

WROBLESKI, DANIEL EDWARD, surgeon; b. Holyoke, Mass., Apr. 25, 1946; s. Edward John and Helen (Cisek) W.; m. Joan Moriarty, June 20, 1970 (div. Dec. 1992); 1 child, Amanda. BS, Trinity Coll., 1969; MD, Columbia U., 1975. Pvt. practice Providence, R.I. Fellow ACS, Am. Soc. Colon and Rectal Surgeons, New Eng. Colon and Rectal Surgery Soc., Providence Surg. Soc. Office: 827 N Main St Providence RI 02904

WU, GUOYAO, nutrition, physiology, and animal science educator; b. China, July 28, 1962; s. Fanjiu Wu and Meixiao Huang; m. Yan Chen, Aug. 7, 1995. BS in Animal Sci., South China Agrl. U., 1982; MS in Animal Nutrition, Beijing (People's Republic of China) Agrl. U., 1984; MS in Animal Biochemistry, U. Alberta, Can., 1986, PhD in Animal Biochemistry, 1989; postgrad. in metabolism/diabetes, McGill U., Mont., Can., 1989-91; postgrad. in biochemistry, Meml. U. Nfld., Can., 1991. Grad. teaching asst. U. Alberta, 1985-88; postdoctoral rschr. Royal Victoria Hosp., McGill U., 1989-91, Meml. U. Newfoundland, 1991; asst. prof. dept. animal sci. and faculty nutrition Tex. A&M U., College Station, 1991-96; assoc. prof. Tex. A&M U., 1996—. Reviewer Amino Acids, Am. Jour. Clin. Nutrition, Am. Jour. Physiology, Analytical Biochemistry, Can. Jour. Physiology and Pharmacology, Diabetes, Diabetologia, Jour. Animal Sci., Jour. Nutrition, Jour. Nutritional Biochemistry, Jour. Cellular Physiology, Metabolism, Poultry Sci., Can. Diabetes Assn., Med. Rsch. Coun. Can., U. Toronto Banting and Best Ctr., Can.; editl. advisor Biochem. Jour., 1993-96; contbr. articles to profl. jours. Grantee Tex. A&M U., 1992—, Ajinomoto Inc., Japan, 1992, USDA, 1992—, Houston Livestock Show and Rodeo, 1992-95, Am. Heart Assn., 1995—; nat. scholarship for grad. studies abroad Ministry Edn. China, 1984-86, grad. tchg. assistantship U. Alta., 1985-88, dissertation fellowship, 1989, Ctr. Rsch. Fund award, 1988, Andrew Stewart Grad. prize, 1989, U. Alberta, Can. Rsch. Inst. fellowship Royal Victoria Hosp., 1988, fellowship Can. Diabetes Assn., 1989, Med. Rsch. Coun. Can. fellow, 1989-91. Mem. AAAS, Am. Diabetes Assn., Am. Inst. Nutrition, Am. Physiol. Soc., Am. Soc. Animal Sci., Biochem. Soc. U.K., Can. Soc. Nutritional Scis., Juv. Diabetes Found. Internat. (grantee 1992-94). Home: 4707 Shoal Creek Dr College Station TX 77845 Office: Tex A&M Univ Dept Animal Sci College Station TX 77843

WU, WILLIAM LUNG-SHEN (YOU-MING WU), aerospace medical engineering design specialist, foreign intelligence analyst; b. Hangchow, Chekiang Province, China, Sept. 1, 1921; came to U.S., 1941, naturalized, 1955; s. Sing-Chih and Mary (Ju-Mei) Wu. AB in Biochemistry, Stanford U., 1943, MD, 1946; MS in Chemistry and Internal Medicine, Tulane U., 1955; diploma, U.S. Naval Sch. Aviation Medicine, Pensacola, Fla., 1956, USAF Sch. Aviation Medicine, USAF Aerospace Med. Ctr., 1961; cert. of tng. in aviation medicine, U. Calif., Berkeley, 1962, 1964. Diplomate Am. Bd. Preventive Medicine, Am. Bd. Internal Medicine, Am. Bd. Psychiatry, Am. Bd. Pathology. Gen. rotating intern U. Iowa Hosps., Iowa City, 1945-46; resident Lincoln (Nebr.) Gen. Hosp., 1946-47, resident in pathology, 1947-48; resident in pathology Bryan Meml. Hosp., Lincoln, 1947-48; fellow, instr. in internal medicine Tulane U., New Orleans, 1948-54; asst. vis. physician Charity Hosp. and Hutchinson Meml. Teaching and Diagnostic and Cancer Detection Clinics, New Orleans, 1948-51, vis. physician, 1951-54; staff physician Holderman (Army) Hosp., Napa, Calif., 1958; staff physician Aviation Space and Radiation Med. Group Gen. Dynamics/Convair, San Diego, 1958-61; aerospace med. specialist, med. monitor for Life Sciences Sect. Gen. Dynamics/Astronautics, San Diego, 1961-65; aerospace med. and bioastronautics specialist Lovelace Found. for Med. Edn. and Rsch., Albuquerque, 1965-68; staff physician Laguna Honda Hosp., San Francisco, 1968-74; ret.; staff physician Kaiser-Permanente Hosp. all-night med. clinic, San Francisco, 1971-73; safety rep. and med. examiner U.S. Civil Aeronaut. Adminstrn., 1959; med. examiner Fed. Aviation Adminstrn., 1961; expert witness in forensic medicine and/or medicolegal jurisprudence for cts. Author 8 books and 100 tech. papers in field. Active mem. Planning, Rsch. and Devel. Commn. Redwood City; bd. dirs. Legal Aid Soc. Santa Clara County, U.S. Congl. Adv. Bd., Am. Security Coun. Found., Little House Sr. Multipurpose Ednl. Ctr.; Life Fellow Royal Soc. of Lichtenstein, Zurich, Switzerland, Oxford Club (N.Y. and Fla.), Royal Coll. of Heraldry. Comdr., flight surgeon M.C., USN, 1954-57. Recipient Gold medal Internat. Inst. Cmty. Svc., 1976, J. Edgar Hoover Gold Disting. Pub. Svc. award Am. Police Hall of Fame, 1991, Albert Einstein Bronze medal Universal Intelligence Data Bank Am., 1986, Cambridge Gold medal, Dedication Insignia. Fellow San Diego Biomed. Rsch. Inst. (bd. dirs. 1961-65, sec. of fellows 1961-62, chmn. of fellows 1963), Inst. Environ. Scis. (chmn. specifications and standards com.), AIAA (mem. nominating com. San Diego sect., plant rep. life sci. sect. 1963-65); mem. IEEE (vice chmn. San Diego chpt. profl. tech. group on biomed. electronics 1962-65), N.Y. Acad. Scis., Internat. Univ. Found. (hon. pres.), Internat. Acad. Found. (hon. registrar-sec.), Computer Club, Sigma Xi, U.S. Naval Inst. (life), Naval League of U.S. West-pac (life), Conss. Nat. Resource Ctr. Network. Home: 250 Budd Ave Apt 219 Campbell CA 95008

WUBAH, DANIEL ASUA, microbiologist; b. Accra, Ghana, Nov. 6, 1960; came to U.S., 1984; s. Daniel Asua and Elizabeth Bruba (Appoe) W.; m. Judith A. Dadson, Dec. 17, 1993; children: Vera, Ewura Abena. MS, U. Akron, 1988; PhD, U. Ga., 1990. Cert. in hazardous waste site ops. and emergency response health and safety. Postdoctoral fellow U.S. EPA Rsch. Lab., Athens, Ga., 1991-92; asst. prof. Towson (Md.) State U., 1992—. Contbr. articles to profl. publs. Sec. African Students Union, U. Ga., Athens, 1988; v.p. Ghana Soc. of Athens, Ga., 1989. Recipient Paul Acquarone award U. Akron, 1985, Palfrey award U. Ga., 1989, Ruska award Southeastern Electron Microscopy Soc., 1989; Faculty Rsch. grantee Towson State U., 1992; grantee NSF, 1993, USDA, 1994. Mem. AAAS, Mycological Soc. of Am., Am. Soc. Microbiology, Med. Mycological Soc. of Am., Internat. Soc. for Human and Animal Mycology. Episcopalian. Home: 28 Stable Run Ct Foxridge MD 21133 Office: Towson State U Dept Biol Scis Towson MD 21204

WUHL, CHARLES MICHAEL, psychiatrist; b. N.Y.C., Sept. 24, 1943; s. Isadore and Sali (Ackner) W.; m. Gail; children—Elise, Amy. M.D., U. Bologna, 1973. Diplomate Am. Bd. Psychiatry and Neurology. Intern, N.Y. Med. Coll., 1975-76, resident in psychiatry, 1976-77; fellow in child psychiatry Columbia Presbyn. Med. Center, 1977-78; practice medicine specializing in psychiatry and child psychiatry, Englewood, N.J., 1978—; attending staff, mem. faculty N.Y. Med. Coll.; psychiatrist NYU, also asst. clin. prof. psychiatry NYU Sch. Medicine. Contbr. to Psychosocial Aspects of Pediatric Care, 1978, World Book Ency., 1980—. Mem. Am. Psychiat Assn., AMA, Am. Acad. Child Psychiatry. Office: 163 Engle St Englewood NJ 07631-2530

WULF, HINNERK F.W., anesthesiologist, educator; b. Kiel, Germany, Jan. 28, 1959; s. Heinrich K. and Jutta O. (Paarmann); m. Patricia Stühmer, Dec. 4, 1987; Kristina, Philipp, Laurids. Physikum, U. Würzburg, Germany, 1979, MD, 1984, anesthesiologist, 1989. Resident Univ. Hosp., Kiel, Germany, 1984-89; cons., lect. Univ. Hosp., Kiel, 1989—. Contbr. articles to profl. jours., chpt. to book. Del. Ärtekammer, Schleswig-Holstein, 1992—. Office: U Hosp Dept Anesthesiology, Schwanenweg 21, D 24105 Kiel Germany

WUNCH, KAREN ELIZABETH, nursing administrator; b. Pasadena, Calif., Aug. 7, 1953; d. William Stuart and Joanne Shirley (Berger) W. BSN, U. Calif., San Francisco, 1975; MS in Nursing, Boston U., 1976. RN, Calif.; CRRN; cert. nursing adminstr. advanced. Mem. nursing staff Univ. Hosp., Boston, 1976; rehab. clin. nurse specialist Sacred Heart Rehab. Hosp., Milw., 1976-81; coor. nursing care Northridge (Calif.) Hosp. Med. Ctr., 1982-88; dir. clin. nursing rehab. Rancho Los Amigos Med Ctr., Downey, Calif., 1988-94, chief nursing officer, 1994, chief nursing officer, dir. profl. svcs., 1995—; mem. adj. clin. faculty Sch. Nursing U. So. Calif., L.A., 1989—. Mem. Nat. League for Nursing, Orgn. Nurse Execs., Am. Congress Rehab. Medicine (1st v.p. 1994—), Assn. Rehab. Nurses (pres. Wis. chpt. 1979), Sigma Theta Tau. Home: 19729 Stagg St Canoga Park CA 91306-2651

WUNDERMAN, LORNA ELLEN, healthcare strategic planner, biostatistician; b. Hollywood, Calif., Mar. 23, 1954; d. Irwin and Gilda Shirley (Margulies) Wunderman; m. Kenneth E. Monroe, Feb. 27, 1987; 1 child, Katie. AA, Foothill Coll., 1972; BS, U. Calif., Berkeley, 1976, MPH, 1978. Cert. Community Coll. tchr., Calif. Research asst. AMA, Chgo., 1978-79, research assoc., 1978-81, dir. dept., cons., 1981-86, exec. asst. to v.p., 1986—, dir. corp. planning, 1987—. Editor: Characteristics of Physicians, 1979, Contbr. articles to med. jours. Grantee Dept. Health and Human Services, Washington, 1979-80, 82, scholar Washington, 1976-78. Mem. The Planning Forum, Am. Statis. Assn., Am. Mktg. Assn., Am. Pub. Health Assn. Avocations: tennis, swimming, traveling. Home: 22299 N Saddle Tree Ln Barrington IL 60010-2428

WURLITZER, FRED PABST, physician, surgeon; b. San Francisco, Dec. 26, 1937; s. Raimund Billings and Pauline (Pabst) W.; m. Lee Jones Wurlitzer (div. Jan. 1991); children: Ricky, Arnisha, Susan, Elena; m. Ann Marie Allan, June 2, 1992; children: Melanie, Heather, Gregory. BA, Stanford U., 1960; MD, U. Cin., 1965; MBA, Golden Gate U., 1985. Diplomate Am. Bd. Gen. Surgery. Intern, resident Highland-Almeda County Hosp., 1965-67; resident in surgery UCLA Sch. Medicine/VA Hosp., 1967-60; fellow in surg. oncology U. Tex./M.D. Anderson Hosp., Houston, 1970-71; instr. surgery U. So. Calif., Los Angeles, 1971-73; physician Pasadena (Calif.) Tumor Inst., 1971-73, San Mateo (Calif.) Med. Clinic, 1973-77; physician in pvt. practice Burlingame, Calif., 1977-84; vol. surgeon various hosps., 1989-93; pres. Wurlitzer Properties, Burlingame, 1976—. Contbr. articles to profl. jours. Comdr. USPHS, 1992—. Recipient Acknowledgement of Outstanding Svc. award Am. Cancer Soc., 1974, Disting. Svc. award Health Vols. Overseas, 1994. Fellow ACS; mem. AMA, Soc. Head and Neck Surgeons, Southwestern Surg. Congress, So. Med. Assn. Unitarian. Home: 18289 Briarswood Kemp TX 75143

WURMSER, LEON, psychiatry educator; b. Jan. 31, 1931; m. Zdenka Koudela; 3 children. MD, U. Zurich, Basel, Switzerland, 1955; student in Psychiatric Tng., U. Basel, 1957-61; student in Psychoanalytic Tng., Balt.-

D.C. Inst., 1966-75. Various adminstrv., teaching and clin. positions, Sheppard Pratt, Balt., 1962-65, Sinai Hosp., Balt., 1966-69, Johns Hopkins U. Hosp., Balt., 1969-71, U. Md., Balt., 1971-83; clin. prof. Psychiatry U. W.Va., Morgantown, from 1983; prof. psychiatry, dir. alcohol and drug abuse program U. Md., 1977-83. Author: Raubmörder and Rauber Kriminalistik, 1959, The Mask of Shame, 1981, The Hidden Dimension, 1978, Flucht vor dem Gewissen, 1987, Die Zerbrochene Wirklichkeit, 1988, Die Maske der Scham, 1990, Das Ratsel des Masochismus, 1993; editor: (with G. Balis et al) Psychiatric Foundations of Medicine, 1978; mem. editorial bd. Substance Abuse Treatment, Forum der Psychoanalyse, Psychoanalytisches Jahrbuch; contbr. some 300 articles to profl. jours. Recipient Lewis B. Hill award Balt.-D.C. Inst. Psychoanalysis, 1975, award for Pioneering Excellence and Achievement, Am. Mental Health Found., 1979-80; named Outstanding Tchr. in Psychiatry, U. Md., 1978-79. Fellow Am. Psychiat. Assn.; mem. Swiss Med. Assn., Swiss Psychiat. Assn., Am. Psychoanalytic Assn. (cert.), Czech Psychoanalytic Soc. (hon.). Home: 904 Crestwick Rd Towson MD 21286-3319 Office: 200 E Joppa Rd Towson MD 21286

WURSTER, DALE ERIC, pharmacy educator; b. Madison, Wis., Jan. 19, 1951; s. Dale Erwin and June M. (Peterson) W.; m. Pamela Ann Marvin, May 31, 1975; children: Elizabeth Ann, Kristin Gail, Dale Edward. BS in Chemistry, U. Wis., 1974; PhD in Phys. Pharmacy, Purdue U., 1979. Asst. prof. Sch. Pharmacy U. N.C., Chapel Hill, N.C., 1979-82; asst. to assoc. prof. Coll. Pharmacy U. Iowa, Iowa City, 1982-95, prof. Coll. Pharmacy, 1996—; cons. to pharm. industry; cons. Nat. Assn. Bds. of Pharmacy, Park Ridge, Ill., 1982—; apptd. to U.S. Pharmacopeial Conv. Com. of Revision, 1995-2000. Contbr. articles to profl. jours. Fed. and indsl. grantee. Mem. Am. Assn. Pharm. Scientists, Am. Chem. Soc., Am. Assn. Colls. Pharmacy, Materials Rsch. Soc., Sigma Xi. Home: 3808 County Down Ln NE North Liberty IA 52317-9388 Office: U Iowa Coll Pharmacy S215 Iowa City IA 52242

WURSTER, DALE ERWIN, pharmacy educator, university dean emeritus; b. Sparta, Wis., Apr. 10, 1918; s. Edward Emil and Emma Sophia (Steingraeber) W.; m. June Margaret Peterson, June 16, 1944; children: Dale Eric, Susan Gay. BS, U. Wis., 1942, PhD, 1947. With faculty U. Wis. Sch. Pharmacy, 1947-71, prof., 1958-71; prof., dean N.D. State U. Coll. Pharmacy, 1971-72, U. Iowa Coll. Pharmacy, Iowa City, 1972-84, prof., 1972—, interim dean, 1991-92, dean emeritus, 1984—; George B. Kaufman Meml. lectr. Ohio State U., 1968; cons. in field; phys. sci. adminstr. U.S. Navy, 1960-63; sci. adv. Wis. Alumni Rsch. Found., 1968-72; mem. revision com. U.S. Pharmacopoeia, 1961-70, pharmacy rev. com. USPHS, 1966-72. Contbr. articles to profl. jours., chpts. to books; patentee in field. With USNR, 1944-46. Recipient Superior Achievement citation Navy Dept., 1964, merit citation U. Wis., 1976; named Hancher Finkbine Medallion Prof. U. Iowa, 1984; recipient Disting. Alumni award U. Wis. Sch. Pharmacy, 1984. Fellow Am. Assn. Pharm. Scientists (founder, sponsor Dale E. Wurster Rsch. award 1990—, Disting. Pharm. Sci. award 1991); mem. Am. Assn. Colls. Pharmacy (exec. com. 1964-66, chmn. conf. tchrs. 1960-61, vis. scientist 1963-70, recipient Disting. Educator award 1983), Acad. Pharm. Scis. (exec. com. 1967-70, chmn. basic pharmaceutics sect. 1965-67, pres. 1975, Indsl. Pharm. Tech. award 1980), Am. Pharm. Assn. (chmn. sci. sect. 1964-65, Rsch. Achievement award 1965), Wis. (Disting. Service award 1971), Iowa Pharmacists Assn. (Robert G. Gibbs award 1983), Wis. Acad. Scis., Arts and Letters, Soc. Investigative Dermatology, Rumanian Soc. Med. Sci. (hon.), Am. Found. Pharm. Edn. (bd. grants 1987-92), Ea. Va. Med. Sch. Contraceptive Rsch. and Devel. Program (tech. adv. com. 1989—), Am. Assn. Pharm. Scientists (Disting. Scientist award 1991), Sigma Xi, Kappa Psi (past officer), Rho Chi, Phi Lambda Upsilon, Phi Sigma. Home: 16 Brickwood Knls NE Iowa City IA 52240-9144

WURTMAN, RICHARD JAY, physician, educator, inventor; b. Phila., Mar. 9, 1938; s. Samuel Richard and Hilda (Schreiber) W.; m. Judith Joy Hirschhorn, Nov. 15, 1959; children: Rachael Elisabeth, David Franklin. A.B., U. Pa., 1956; M.D., Harvard U., 1960. Intern Mass. Gen. Hosp., 1960-61, resident, 1961-62, fellow medicine, 1965-66, clin. assoc. in medicine, 1985—; research assoc., med. research officer NIMH, 1962-67; mem. faculty MIT, Cambridge, 1967—, prof. endocrinology and metabolism, 1970-80, prof. neuroendocrine regulation, 1980-84, Cecil H. Green disting. prof., 1994—; dir. Clin. Rsch. Ctr., MIT, Cambridge, 1985—; prof. neuroscience MIT, 1984-94; lectr. medicine Harvard Med. Sch., 1969—; prof. Harvard-MIT Divsn. Health Scis. and Tech., 1978—; sci. dir. Ctr. for Brain Scis. and Metabolism Charitable Trust, 1981—; invited prof. U. Geneva, 1981; Sterling vis. prof. Boston U., 1981; mem. small grants study sect. NIMH, 1967-69, preclin. psychopharmacology study sect., 1971-75; behavioral biology adv. panel NASA, 1969-72; coun. basic sci. Am. Heart Assn., 1969-74; rsch. adv. bd. Parkinson's Disease Found., 1972-80, Am. Parkinson's Disease Assn., 1978—; com. phototherapy in newborns NRC-Nat. Acad. Scis., 1972-74, com. nutrition, brain devel. and behavior, 1976, mem. space applications bd., 1976-82; mem. task force on drug devel. Muscular Dystrophy Assn., 1980-87; chmn. life scis. adv. com. NASA, 1979-82; chmn. adv. bd. Alzheimer's Disease Assn., 1981-84; assoc. neuroscis. rsch. program MIT, 1974-82; chmn. life scis. adv. bd. USAF, 1985—; Bennett lectr. Am. Neurol. Assn., 1974; Flexner lectr. U. Pa., 1975; founder, chmn. sci. adv. bd. Interneuron Pharms., Inc., 198—; Hans Lindler Meml. lectr. Weizmann Inst., 1993. Author: Catecholamines, 1966; (with others) The Pineal, 1968; editor: (with Judith Wurtman) Nutrition and the Brain, Vols. I and II, 1977, Vols. III, IV, V., 1979, Vol. VI, 1983, Vol. VII, 1986, Vol. VIII, 1990, also numerous other articles and books; mem. editl. bd. Endocrinology, 1967-73, Jour. Pharmacology and Exptl. Therapeutics, 1968-75, Jour. Neural Transmission, 1969-88, Neuroendocrinology, 1969-72, Metabolism, 1970-80, Circulation Research, 1972-77, Jour. Neurochemistry, 1973-82, Life Scis., 1973-81, Brain Rsch., 1977—; holder of approximately 40 U.S. patents on new treatments for diseases and conditions. Recipient Alvarenga prize and lectureship Phila. Coll. Physicians, 1970, CIBA-Geigy Drew award in Biomed. Rsch., 1982, Roger Williams award in Preventive Nutrition, 1987, Roger J. Williams award in Preventive Medicine, 1989, NIMH Merit award, 1989—, Internat. Prize for Modern Nutrition, 1989, Hall of Fame Disting. Alumni award Ctrl. H.S. Phila., 1992; Disting. lectr. Purdue U., 1984; Rufus Cole lectr., Rockefeller U., 1985; Pfizer lectr. NYU Med. Sch., 1985; Grass Fedn. lectr. U. Ga., 1985, Alan Rothballer Meml. lectr., N.Y. Med. Coll., Valhalla, N.Y., 1989, Gretchen Kerr Green lectr in the neuroscis., 1989; Wellcome Vis. Prof. Washington State U., Pullman, 1989; Julius Axelrod Disting. lectr. in neurosci., CUNY, 1990, Sigma Tau Found. lectr. on aging, Rome, 1990, Disting. lectr. in neurosci. La. State U., 1991, McEwen lectr. Queen's U., Ont., 1991; Plenary lectr. 3d Internat. Symposium on Microdialysis, 1993; Hans Lindner Meml. lectr. Weizmann Inst., 1993. Mem. Am. Soc. Clin. Investigation, Endocrine Soc. (Ernst Oppenheim award 1972), Am. Physiol. Soc., Am. Soc. Biol. Chemists, Am. Soc. Pharmacology and Exptl. Therapeutics (John Jacob Abel award 1968), Am. Soc. Neurochemistry, Soc. Neuroscis., Am. Soc. Clin. Nutrition, Am. Inst. Nutrition (Osborne & Mendel award 1982). Club: Harvard (Boston). Home: 300 Boylston St Boston MA 02116-3923 Office: Mass Inst Tech 45 Carleton St # E25-604 Cambridge MA 02142-1323

WURZBERGER, BEZALEL, psychiatrist; b. Medias, Romania, June 28, 1945; came to U.S., 1967; s. Joshua and Isabella (Fulop) W.; m. Gladys Schmidt, Mar. 19, 1971; children: Tamar, David. BA, Columbia U., 1972; MD, Nat. U., Tegucigalpa, Honduras, 1982. Diplomate, Am. Bd. Psychiatry and Neurology. Intern North Gen. Hosp., N.Y.C., 1982-83; resident in psychiatry Creedmoor Psychiat. Ctr., Queens Village, N.Y., 1983-86; clin. psychiat. fellow N.Y. Med. Coll., Valhala, N.Y., 1986-87; staff psychiatrist Glens Falls (N.Y.) Hosp., 1987-92, chmn. dept. psychiatry, 1993—; med. dir., Samaritan Counseling Ctr., Keene, N.Y., 1987—; psychiat. cons., Uihlein Mercy Ctr., Lake Placid, N.Y., 1988—. V.p. Jewish Community Tegucigalpa, 1978-80; bd. dirs. Congregation Shaarey Tefily, Glens Falls, 1989—, v.p., 1993-96, pres., 1996—. Sgt. Israeli Air Force, 1964-67. Mem. AMA, Am. Psychiat. Assn., Soc. Liaison Psychiatry, Acad. Psychosomatic Medicine, Honduran Coll. Physicians. Office: Glens Falls Hosp 80 Park St Glens Falls NY 12801-4413

WUST, CARL JOHN, microbiology and medical biology educator; b. Providence, R.I., July 2, 1928; s. Louis August and Ida (Jauernig) W.; m. Barbara Marion Russin, Sept. 5, 1951 (dec.); children: Carl John, Stephen Louis, Catherine Joanne, Gregory Harold, Elizabeth Diane. BS, Providence Coll., 1950; MS, Brown U., 1953; PhD, Indiana U., 1957. Ordained deacon Roman Cath. Ch. Post-doctoral fellow Yale U., New Haven, Conn., 1957-59; biologist, biochemist Oak Ridge (Tenn.) Nat. Lab., 1959-70; assoc. prof. U. Tenn., Knoxville, Tenn., 1970-74; prof. microbiology U. Tenn., Knoxville, 1974-94, prof. med. biology, 1982-94, prof. emeritus, 1994—. Contbr. articles to profl. jours. Mem. Am. Assn. Immunologists, Am. Soc. for Microbiology, Soc. for Exptl. Biologyand Medicine, Sigma Xi. Roman Catholic. Home: 132 Iroquois Rd Oak Ridge TN 37830-4934 Office: U Tenn Dept Microbiology Knoxville TN 37996

WYATT, ELLIE SHEA, health facility administrator; b. South Weymouth, Mass., Aug. 23, 1960; d. Thomas Wilson and Mary Clare (Neale) Gahan; m. Bradley Jay Wyatt, Apr. 20, 1989. BSN, U. Del., 1982. RN, Colo. Staff nurse telemetry St. Luke's Hosp., Denver, 1982-85; staff nurse IMC Vail (Colo.) Valley Med. Ctr., 1985, managed care mgr., 1994—; staff nurse ICU Beth Israel Hosp., Denver, 1985-87; staff/charge nurse Luth. Med. Ctr., Wheat Ridge, Colo., 1987-89; med. policy analyst I Blue Cross and Blue Shield of Colo./Rocky Mountain Healthcar, Denver, 1989-91, med. policy analyst II, 1991-93, sr. coord. network svcs., 1993-94; cons. in field. Mem. bd. steering com., luncheon chair, race registratio dir. Vail Breast Cancer Awareness Group, 1994—. Mem. Colo. Hosp. Assn. (ex-officio bd. mem. managed care contractors 1994—), Sigma Theta Tau. Home: PO Box 577 Vail CO 81658 Office: Vail Valley Med Ctr 181 W Meadow Dr Vail CO 81657

WYATT, ROSE MARIE, clinical social worker; b. San Angelo, Tex., Feb. 16; d. James Odis and Annie LaVernia (Lott) W. BA, Fisk U., 1957; MS, U. So. Calif., 1963; MA, MSW, U. Chgo., 1972; postgrad., Ill Inst. Tech., 1976—. Elem. tchr. Chgo. Bd. Edn., 1959-63, clin. social worker, 1979—; adult program dir. Chgo. YWCA, 1963-64; youth counselor Chgo. Commn. on Youth Welfare, 1964-66; supervising social worker for Head Start, Chgo. Com. on Urban Opportunity, 1966; social worker Chgo. Commn. on Youth Welfare, 1966-68, Jewish Vocat. Svc., 1968; social worker Sch. Community Rels., Detroit Pub. Schs., 1968-70; social worker United Charities, 1972-74; clin. social worker Rosman-Wyatt and Assocs., Chgo., 1980—, pres., 1981—; instr. dept. corrections Chgo. State U., 1972—. Adv. bd. United Charities, Calumet area, program com. chmn., 1974-80; vol. Assn. of Community Agts. 1968-70, Southside Sr. Citizens Coalition, Chgo., 1963-66, Roseland Health Planning Com., 1974-76, Teen Pregnancy Caucus, 1978-82; mem. social work adv. coun. Chgo. Bd. Edn., 1976. Recipient Outstanding Employee award for med.-social work svcs. Maternal and Child Health Svcs. div. HEW; 1971; Ford Found. scholar Fisk U., 1953-57, U. Chgo. scholar, 1970-72, United Charities scholar, 1970-72. Mem. Nat. Assn. Social Workers, Acad. Cert. Social Workers, Ill. Cert. Social Workers, Chgo. Psychol. Club, Ill Acad. Criminology, NEA, Ill. Assn. Sch. Social Workers, Am. Assn. Mental Deficiency, Qualified Mental Retardation Profls., Fisk U. Alumni Assn., Am. Bridge Assn., Civenos Bridge Club, Alpha Kappa Alpha.

WYATT, RUSSELL SCOTT, optician; b. Kew Gardens, N.Y., July 27, 1948; s. William Douglas and Margaret Mae (Anderson) W.; divorced. BA, U. Pitts., 1970; AS in Vision Care Technology, Miami Dade Cmty. Coll., 1980. Cert. optician Fla. State Bd., 1980. Optician Pearl Vision, Miami, 1980-82, Royal Optical, Mary Esther, Fla., 1987-90, Optiworld, Mary Esther, Fla., 1990-93, White Wilson Med., Ft. Walton Beach, Fla., 1993—. Table tennis tchr. YMCA and Destin (Fla.) Cmty. Ctr., 1992. With USN, 1982-86. Fellow Nat. Acad. Opticianry. Republican. Presbyterian. Home: 1318 Lewis Turner Blvd #18 Fort Walton Beach FL 32547 Office: White Wilson Med Ctr PA 1005 Marwalt Dr Fort Walton Beach FL 32547

WYCOFF, CHARLES COLEMAN, retired anesthesiologist; b. Glazier, Tex., Sept. 2, 1918; s. James Garfield and Ada Sharpe (Braden) W.; m. Gene Marie Henry, May 16, 1942; children: Michelle, Geoffrey, Brian, Roger, Daniel, Norman, Irene, Teresa. AB, U. Calif., Berkeley, 1941; MD, U. Calif., San Francisco, 1943. Diplomate Am. Bd. Anesthesiology. Founder The Wycoff Group of Anesthesiology, San Francisco, 1947-53; chief of anesthesia St. Joseph's Hosp., San Francisco, 1947-52, organizer residency tng. program in anesthesiology, 1950; organizer residency tng. program in anesthesiology San Francisco County Hosp., 1954, chief anesthesia, 1953-54; practice anesthesiology, tchr. Presbyn. Med. Ctr., N.Y.C., 1955-63; asst. prof. anesthesiology Columbia U., N.Y.C., 1955-63; clin. practice anesthesiology St. Francis Meml. Hosp., San Francisco, 1963-84. Producer, dir. films on regional anesthesia; contbr. articles to sci. jours. Scoutmaster Boy Scouts Am., San Francisco, 1953-55. Capt. M.C., U.S. Army, 1945-47. Mem. Alumni Faculty Assn. Sch. Medicine U. Calif.-San Francisco (councilor-at-large 1979-80). Democrat. Home: 394 Cross St Napa CA 94559-3840

WYDRA, FRANK THOMAS, healthcare executive; b. Republic, Pa., May 11, 1939; s. Frank T. and Anne M. (Kois) W.; m. Karen Branch, June 24, 1961; children: Denise Lee, Sheryl Lynn, Frank Thomas III. BS in Mgmt., U. Ill., 1961. V.p. Allied Supermarkets, Inc., Detroit, 1967-75; sr. v.p. HGH Health System, Detroit, 1975-85; pres. Radius Health Care Sysytems, Inc., Detroit, 1983-85; cons. Birmingham, Mich., 1985-88; exec. v.p. The Chi Group, Ann Arbor, Mich., 1988-91; cons. Indsl. Rels. Inc., Detroit, 1991—; lectr. various profl. groups; bd. dirs. Mich. Health Systems Inc., Saber-Salisbury Assocs. Inc., Midwestern Health Ctr., MultiCare Med. Inc., RHS Inc. Author: Learner Controlled Instruction, 1980, (with others) Hospital Survival Guide, 1984, The Cure, 1992; creator 2 mgmt. games Performulations, 1978, The Dynamics of Power and Authority, 1981; contbr. articles to profl. jours. Personnel program advisor Mich. State U. Sch. Labor Relations, 1979-83; chmn. new programs Wayne County Community Coll., Detroit, 1979-80; bd. dirs. Detroit Metro Youth Found., 1980-83, State Mich. Health Occupations Council, Lansing, 1982-85. Capt. U.S. Army, 1961-63. Recipient numerous awards ASTD, Nat. Soc. Performance and Instrn., Mich. SOc. Instructional Tech., Supermarket Inst. Mem. Am. Hosp. Assn., Planning Soc. of Am. Hosp. Assn., Hosp. Personnel Adminstrs. Assn. (pres. 1981-82, numerous awards), Am. Mgmt. Assn., Am. Soc. Hosp. Pers.Adminstrs. (bd. dirs. 1981-83), Mich. Soc. Instrnl. Tech. (life, pres. 1973-74), Mich. Hosp. Assn., Employers Assn. Detroit (bd. dirs. 1982-85), Detroit Athletic Club. Home: 1001 W Glengarry Cir Bloomfield Hills MI 48301-2223

WYER, PETER CHARLES, emergency physician; b. Dolhi, N.Y., July 16, 1943; s. Robert Selden and Wilhelmina (Sebesta) W.; m. Judith Ann Sholdebrand, Mar. 10, 1976. BS, Columbia U., 1970; MD, U. Pa., 1974. Diplomate Am. Bd. Emergency Medicine. Attending emergency medicine physician Wyckoff Hghts. Med. Ctr., Bklyn., 1979-92; pvt. practice Bronx, N.Y., 1981-92; asst. prof. emergency medicine N.Y. Med. Coll., Valhalla, N.Y., 1992—. Pres. Coalition of Comty. of Physicians, Bronx, N.Y., 1990-91. Fellow Am. Coll. Emergency Physicians, N.Y. Acad. Medicine mem. Soc. Acad. Emergency Medicine, Bronx County Med. Soc. (pres. 1995-96).

WYLER, DAVID JOHN, physician, scientist; b. N.Y.C., Dec. 21, 1944; s. Paul and Friedel (Weil) W.; m. Bonnie Jean Hughes (div.); children: Jonathan Michael, Benjamin Aaron; m. Deborah Beth Alport, May 17, 1987; childre: Samuel Alport, Anna Rose. AB cum laude, Brown U., 1966; MD, Harvard U., 1970. Intern, resident U. Calif., San Francisco, 1970-72; clin. assoc. NIH, Bethesda, Md., 1972-75; fellow in infectious disease Mass. Gen. Hosp., 1975-76; sr. investigator Nat. Inst. Allergy and Infectious Diseases, NIH, Bethesda, Md., 1976-79; asst. prof. medicine Sch. Medicine, Johns Hopkins U., Balt., 1978-79; prof. medicine, molecular biology and microbiology Tufts U. and New Eng. Med. Ctr. Hosp., Boston, 1985—; dir. travelers' health svc. New Eng. Med. Ctr. Hosp., 1989-95; cons. NIH, Bethesda, 1975—, Nat. Acad. Scis., Washington, 1991, NSF, Washington, 1982—. Editor (book) Modern Parasite Biology, 1990; contbr. more than 100 sci. articles to profl. jours. Trustee Stoney Hill Farms Homeowners Assn., West Tisbury, Mass., 1989—. Grantee USPHS, 1981—. Fellow ACP, Infectious Diseases Soc. Am.; mem. Am. Soc. Clin. Investigation Am. Fedn. Clin. Rsch., Am. Soc. Tropical Medicine and Hygiene (councillor 1985-87), Am. Soc. Microbiology, Reticuloentothelial Soc., Am. Assn. Immunologists. Democrat. Jewish. Office: New Eng Med Ctr Hosp 750 Washington St Boston MA 02111-1533

WYLER, STEPHEN MARC WOHLFEILER, veterinarian, administrator; b. Bklyn., June 28, 1945; s. Robert and Jessie Carol (Granat) Wohlfeiler. BS, U. Ga., 1967; DVM, U. Bologna, Italy, 1974. Dir. Animal Med. Hosp., Hempstead, N.Y., 1977—. Bd. dirs. Nassau Animal Emergency Clinic, Westbury, N.Y., 1979-88. Mem. AVMA, L.I. Vet. Med. Assn., Assn. Avian Veterinarians. Jewish. Office: Animal Med Hosp 779 Peninsula Blvd Hempstead NY 11550-7222 also: Trylon Vet Care 98-83 Queens Blvd Flushing NY 11374-4351

WYLIE, CHARLES MURRAY, internist, geriatrician, educator; b. Dunfermline, Fife, Scotland, Sept. 20, 1924; came to U.S., 1949; s. Thomas and Mary (Symon) W.; m. Dorothy Joan Marion Hennessy, Jan. 31, 1959; children: Christine, John Adrian, Sheila, Robin. MD, BChir, U. Glasgow, Scotland, 1947; MD, U. Glasgow, 1957; MPH, Johns Hopkins U., 1952, DPH, 1956; DTM, U. London, 1958. Diplomate Am. Bd. Preventive Medicine. Med. intern, resident various hosps., Scotland and Eng., 1947-49; resident in medicine Overlook Hosp., Summit, N.J., 1949-50; health dir. State Dept. Health, Richmond, Va., 1950-53; rsch. assoc. Nat. Commn. on Chronic Illness, Balt., 1953-55; lt. comdr. med. corps U.S.N., 1955-57; from asst. prof. to assoc. prof. Johns Hopkins U., Balt., 1958-67; prof. pub. health adminstrn. U. Mich., Ann Arbor, 1968-86; pvt. practice Ann Arbor, 1986—. Contbr. numerous articles to profl. jours., chpts. to books. Fellow Faculty Cmty. Medicine, Eng., 1972—, Royal Soc. Medicine, London, 1985—. Home: 1607 Dicken Dr Ann Arbor MI 48103 Office: 955 W Eisenhower Cir Ann Arbor MI 48103

WYLIE, JOHN VOORHEES, psychiatrist; b. N.Y.C., Mar. 18, 1941; s. Robert Hawthorn and Jane Deo (Voorhees) W.; m. Ann Gilbert, Dec. 16, 1971; children: John, Alice, Eva, Annabelle. BA, Yale U., 1964; MD, Columbia U., 1969. Diplomate Am. Bd. Psychiatry and Neurology. Surg. intern, then resident Columbia-Presbyn. Hosp., N.Y.C., 1969-71; psychiat. resident Georgetown U. Hosp., Washington, 1972-75; pvt. practice psychiatrist Washington, 1975—; staff psychiatrist Patuxant Instn., Jessup, Md., 1975-78; chmn. dept. psychiatry Sibley Meml. Hosp., Washington, 1988-94. Mem. Am. Psychiat. Assn., Human Behavior and Evolution Soc., Clinico-Pathological Soc. Washington. Episcopalian. Office: 3801 Northampton St NW # 3 Washington DC 20015

WYNN, BRUCE, physician assistant; b. Evarts, Ky., Oct. 9, 1948; s. Sylvan and Ruby Evelyn (Cox) W.; m. Margaret Elaine Beard, Sept. 13, 1968; children: Bruce Clinton, Bradley James. Cert. physician asst., Med. U. S.C., 1976. Cert. physician asst. Nat. Commn. on Cert. of Physician's Assts., Ga. Chief cardiopulmonary therapy Redmond Park Hosp., Rome, Ga., 1974-75; physician asst. Robert T. Connor, M.D., Rome, 1975-84, Rome (Ga.) Gen. Practice, 1984—. Active Gideon Internat., Rome, 1983. Sgt. USMC, 1968-72. Fellow Am. Acad. Physicians' Assts., Ga. Assn. Physicians' Assts. (regional liaison Health Svc. Area region 2 1979-80). Home: 7 Glenrise Terrace NW Rome GA 30165 Office: Rome Gen Practice 101 John Maddox Dr Rome GA 30165

WYNN, DANIEL RICHARD, neurologist. BA in Biology, Reed Coll., 1977; MD, Chgo. Med. Sch., 1983. Bd. cert. neurology with spl. competence on clin. neurophysiology Am. Bd. Psychiatry and Neurology; bd. cert. Am. Bd. Clin. Neurophysiology, Am. Bd. Electrodiagnostic Medicine; diplomate Nat. Bd. Med. Examiners. Resident internal medicine Mayo Grad. Sch. Medicine, Rochester, Minn., 1983-84; resident neurology Mayo Grad. Sch. Medicine, Rochester, 1984-87, fellow EEG, 1987, fellow sleep disorders/polysomnography, 1988; med. dir. Headache Treatment Ctr., Pain Treatment Ctr. Lake Forest (Ill.) Hosp., 1988-90; med. dir. Lake Forest (Ill.) Hosp. Sleep Disorders Ctr., 1990-94; with Cons. in Neurology, Ltd., Wilmette, Ill., 1989—; mem. profl. med. adv. panel Nat. Multiple Sclerosis Soc., Chgo.-Greater Ill. Chpt.; med. dir. The Chgo. Wolves Profl. Hockey Team; clin. instr. internal medicine residency program Ill. Masonic Med. Ctr., Chgo.; lectr. cardiology fellowship program Ill. Masonic Med. Ctr.; com. mem., phys. medicine and rehab. com. Highland Park (Ill.) Hosp.; presenter in field. Contbr. articles to profl. jours. Recipient Melvyn Leichtling Annual Oncology Rsch. award Cook County Hosp., Dept. Ob-gyn., Chgo., 1980; NSF scholar Luther Coll., Decorah, Iowa, 1971. Fellow Am. Bd. Sleep Disorders Medicine (bd. cert., accredited clin. polysomnographer); mem. AMA, Am. Pain Soc., Am. Epilepsy Soc., Am. Electroencephalographic Soc., Am. Assn. Electromyography and Electrodiagnosis, Am. Acad. Neurology, Am. Acad. Clin. Neurophysiology, Ill. State Med. Soc., Internat. Hockey League Physicians Assn., Midwest Pain Soc., Clin. Sleep Soc., Chgo. Med. Soc., Alpha Omega Alpha. Office: Cons in Neurology Ltd Ste 601 1535 Lake Cook Rd Northbrook IL 60062

WYRTZEN, JAMES CHARLES, psychotherapist, academic administrator; b. N.Y.C., Aug. 27, 1942; s. James and Malvina Wyrtzen; BA, Moravian Coll. and Theol. Sem., 1964, MDiv, 1967; DMin, N.Y. Theol. Sem., 1981; Pastoral Care Cert. Blauton Peale Grad Inst., Pastoral Counseling Certificate, 1973; DD, Moravian Theol. Sem., 1991; m. Marcia Metz, Aug. 17, 1975; children: Christy, Andrew Mark, David Christopher. Ordained to ministry United Methodist Ch., 1966; pastor Westhampton Beach (N.Y.), United Meth. Ch., 1967-70, Whitestone (N.Y.) United Meth. Ch., 1970-73; dir. Whitestone Counseling Center, 1973-76, also staff therapist Yorkville (N.Y.) Counseling Center, South Nassau (N.Y.) Family Counseling Inst.; pvt. practice psychotherapy, N.Y.C., 1973—; exec. dir. Center for Creative Living, Allendale, N.J., 1976-88, pres., 1976-88, sr. staff therapist, 1988—; dir. Blanton, Peale Grad. Inst. of the Insts. Religion and Health, 1988—. Pres., Hampton Council Chs., 1969-70; mem. Nat. Mental Health Leadership Forum, 1988-92; trustee Found. mental Health, 1988—. Recipient Cora Dosta Moses Homeltics prize Moravian Theol. Sem., 1967, Distinguished Contribution award, Eastern Region AAPC, 1991, Distinguished Alumnus award, Blauton Peale Inst., 1995. Lic. marriage and family counselor, N.J., Calif. Mem. Am. Assn. Marriage and Family Counselors, Am. Group Psychotherapy Assn., Alumni Assn. Insts. Religion and Health (v.p. 1985-87, pres. 1987-88), Am. Assn. Pastoral Counselors (diplomate, assoc. sec.-treas. 1983-87, mem. exec. com. 1983-92, bd. govs. 1983-92, v.p. 1988-90, pres. 1990-92, chmn. advocacy com. 1992—). Democrat. Home: 42-31 Naugle Dr Fair Lawn NJ 07410-5938 Office: Blanton Peale Grad Inst 3 W 29th St New York NY 10001-4504

WYSOCKI, ANNETTE B., nurse scientist, educator; b. Raleigh, N.C., Dec. 31, 1954; d. Robert Jospeh and Frances (Overton) W.; m. John Nussbaum, May 2, 1987. BSN, East Carolina U., 1978, MSN, 1980; PhD, U. Tex., 1986. Cert. med.-surg. nurse. Staff nurse U. Va., Charlottesville, 1978-79, Seton Med. Ctr., Austin, Tex., 1981-86; rsch. and teaching asst. U. Tex., Austin, 1982-84; sr. rsch. assoc. U. Tex. Southwestern Med. Ctr., Dallas, 1986-87; NIH postdoctoral rsch. fellow U. Tex., Dallas, 1987-89, Cornell U. Med. Coll., N.Y.C., 1989-91; adj. asst. prof. NYU, N.Y.C., 1991—; rsch. asst. prof., dir. nursing rsch. NYU Med. Ctr., N.Y.C., 1991—. Mem. editorial bd. Wounds: A Compendium of Clin. Rsch. and Practice; contbr. articles to profl. jours. Vol. Girl Scouts U.S.A. Am. Nurses Found. scholar; grantee NIH, 1988-91, 93—, Nat. Inst. Nursing Rsch., Am. Nurses Found., 1984-85. Mem. AAAS, Am. Soc. Cell Biology, N.Y. Acad. Scis., Wound Healing Soc., Soc. Investigative Dermatology, Assn. Oper. Rm. Nurses, Sigma Theta Tau. Office: NYU Med Ctr PHL-875 550 1st Ave New York NY 10016-6481

WYSOCKI, BOLESLAW A(NTONI), psychologist, educator; b. Poland, June 10, 1912; s. Wladyslaw and Wiktoria (Mizia) Wysocki; student U. Cracow, U. Edinburgh (Scotland), Cambridge (Eng.) U., Oxford (Eng.) U., 1932-48; Ph.D., U. London (Eng.), 1954. Came to U.S., 1952, naturalized, 1958. Dir. edn. Ministry Edn., Gt. Britain, 1948-52; counselor, tchr. Marquette U., Milw., 1952-55; asso. prof. psychology Alliance (Pa.) Coll., 1955-57, Merrimack (Mass.) Coll., 1957-60, Regis (Mass.) Coll., 1960-62; prof. psychology Newton (Mass.) Coll., 1962-75, Boston Coll., 1975—. Clin. work mental instns., 1952—. Served as mil. psychologist Polish Army, 1943-48. Mem. Am., Mass., Brit. psychol. socs., Polish Inst. Arts and Scis. in Am., AAUP. Contbr. articles to profl. jours. Home: 240 Brattle St Cambridge MA 02138 Office: Boston Coll Dept Psychology Mcguinn Hall Chestnut Hill MA 02167

WYSS, JAMES MICHAEL, neurobiologist, researcher; b. Fort Wayne, Ind., Mar. 11, 1948; s. Alen George and Anne W. (Winicker) W.; m. Gloria Faith Gardels Wyss, Aug. 25, 1973; children: Dana Ann, William Alen, Steven Anthony. AA, Concordia Coll., Ann Arbor, Mich., 1968; BS summa cum laude, Concordia Sr. Coll., Fort Wayne, Ind., 1970; MDiv, Luth. Sch. Theol., Chgo., 1974; PhD, Washington U., St. Louis, Mo., 1976. Instr. Washington Univ., St. Louis, 1974-79; asst. prof. U. Ala. Med. Sch.,

Birmingham, 1979-83, assoc. prof., 1983-88, prof., 1988—, chmn. grad. neurosci. tng. program, 1995—; assoc. dir. Alzheimer's Disease Ctr., Birmingham; chmn. PPL Charities, Inc., St. Louis, 1976-79. Editor: American Dental Anatomy Curriculum, 1989-92, Nat. Bd. Examiners in Optometry, 1992—; contbg. author to profl. jours.; editl bd. Hypertension, 1984-89, Brain Rsch. Bull., 1986-89, Am. Jour. Physiology, 1993—. Chmn. St. Louis Project U.S. Law Enforcement Asst. Adminstrn., St. Louis, 1975-76; sect. chmn First Internat. Workshop on Neurobiology, Bangkok, 1988; interim pastor Trinity Luth. Ch., Birmingham, Ala., 1981--. AP Sloan fellow Washington U., St. Louis, 1976-77. Fellow Coun. High Blood Pressure Rsch. (program com. 1993—); mem. NIH (neurology B study sect. 1985-93, Ala. Heart Assn. (funding rsch. bd. 1982-88, rsch. coun. 1983-86), Soc. Neurosci., Am. Physiol. Soc., Am. Anat. Assn., Ala. Soccer Assn. (head coach girls' state team 1987-89). Home: 1925 Old Creek Trl Birmingham AL 35216-2138 Office: U Ala Dept Cell Biology Birmingham AL 35294-0019

XIN, LI, physiologist; b. Shenyang, Liaoning, People's Republic of China, June 14, 1955; came to U.S., 1989; s. Zhili and Huiming (Wang) X.; m. Huizhong Peng; 1 child, Ryan Xin. MD, China Med. U., Shenyang, Liaoning, People's Republic of China, 1982, MS, 1988. Instr. dept. physiology China Med. U., Shenyang, Liaoning, People's Republic of China, 1983-86, asst. prof. dept. physiology, 1987-89; rsch. asst. prof. dept. physiology U. Tenn., Memphis, 1989-91; rsch. assoc. dept. pharmacology Temple U., Phila., 1992-96, assoc. scientist dept. pharmacology, 1996—; coun. standing mem. Youth Scientists Soc., Shenyang, 1988—. Contbr. articles to profl. jours. Recipient Prize for Excellent Paper, Chinese Physiol. Soc., 1985, Visiting fellowship Boehringer Ingelheim Fonds Found. for Basic Rsch. in Medicine, 1989. Mem. AAAS, Am. Physiol. Soc., N.Y. Acad. Scis., Soc. for Neurosci., Sigma Xi. Home: 114 E Cuthbert Blvd #A-3 Westmont NJ 08108 Office: Temple U Dept of Pharmacology 3420 N Broad St Philadelphia PA 19140-5104

XU, KE-PING, ophthalmologist, educator; b. Shanghai, China, Dec. 22, 1959; d. Xiang-Chen Xu Jue-Min Shen; m. Hai-Ru Long, May 9, 1986; children: Long, Ying. MD, Shanghai Med. U., 1983, MS, 1989. Resident Hua Shan Clin. Coll. Shanghai Med. U., 1983-86, asst. prof., 1990-92, asst. prof. Shanghai First People's Hosp., 1995—; vis. asst. prof. Ichikawa Gen. Hosp. Tokyo Dental Coll., Chiba, Japan, 1992-94. Contbr. articles to profl. jours. Mishima Life Chem. Rsch. grantee, 1993; travel fellow Cornea Ctr. Eye Bank Tokyo Dental Coll., 1996; Uehara Meml. scholar, 1992. Mem. Assn. Rsch. Vision & Ophthalmology. Home: Apt 603 No 23 Ln 530 Bu-Bei Rd, Shanghai 200335, China Office: Shanghai First People's Hosp Dept Opthalmology, 85 Wu-Jin Rd, Shanghai 200080, China

XU, LUO-SHAN, pharmacognosy educator; b. Huxing, Zhejiang, China, May 14, 1932; d. Gong-heng Xu and En-mei Wu; m. Kai-ya Zhou, Aug. 4, 1959; children: Xin, Jin. Diploma undergrad. study, Jiangsu Normal Coll., Suzhou, 1953; diploma grad. study, Eastern China Normal U., Shanghai, 1955. Teaching asst. Kunming (Yunnan) Normal Coll., 1955-56, lectr., 1956-61; lectr. Nanjing (Jiangsu) Coll. Pharmacy, 1961-81, assoc. prof., 1981-86; prof. pharmacognosy China Pharm. U., Nanjing, 1986—. Co-author: Micro-identification of 100 Powder Drugs, 1975 (Nat. Sci. Conf. prize 1978); assoc. chief editor Micro-identification of 380 Powder Drugs, 1986 (Nat. Edn. Com. sci. and tech. 2d prize 1987). Recipient Nat. Sci. and Tech. Progress award, 1992. Mem. China Pharm. Soc. (chmn. Nanjing chpt. for Chinese traditional and natural drugs, sec. Chinese traditional and natural drugs br.). Office: China Pharm U, 24 Tong Jia Xiang, Nanjing 210009, China

XUE, MIAO, dentistry educator, biomaterial scientist; b. Shanghai, China, June 24, 1929; s. Kai-Chang and Gui-zhen (Li) X.; m. Zong-Lan Shen, June 15, 1949; children: Jing-Fang, Jie-Fang. DDS, Shangai Med. U. #2, Peoples Republic China, 1953. Asst. dept. prosthetic dentistry sci. Shanghai Med. U. # 2, 1953-60; lectr., asst. prof. dental material rsch. lab. Shanghai Med. U. # 2, 1960-82, vice head, assoc. prof., 1982-87; vice head, assoc. prof. biomaterial rsch. lab. Shanghai Med. U. # 2, 1982-87; head, prof. dept. dental material sci. Shanghai Med. U. # 2, 1987-91, head, prof. dental material and biomaterial rsch. labs., 1988-91; sr. researcher Nat. Testing Ctr. for Med. Polymer, Shangdong, 1988—; dir. Shanghai Biomaterial Rsch. & Testing Ctr., 1989—. Author: (with others) Science of Applied Dental Material, 1963, Material Science of Prosthetic Dentistry, 1987; editor: China Yearbook of Dentistry, 1984—; chief editor Jour. of Dental Materials and Devices, 1991—. Recipient Cert. of Merit, medal China Ministry Pub. Health, 1960, Merit cert. Shanghai Sci. and Tech. Commn., 1984, 90, 92, State Edn. Commn. China, 1988, 92, China Ministry Pub. Health, 1988, 95, Nat. Govt. Spl. Subsidy, 1992—, Shanghai Advanced Worker award, 1995, award Title Nat. Advanced Sci. & Tech. Rsch. of China. Mem. ASTM, China Dental Material Soc. (bd. dirs.), China Maxillo-facial Implant Soc. (bd. dirs.), Shanghai Biomaterial and Product Adminstrn. (bd. dirs.), Shanghai Biomaterial Com. (chief), Shanghai Assn. for Stomatology (com. mem.), Shanghai Med. Engring. for Stomatology (standing com. mem.), China Shape Memory Alloy Com. (com. mem.), IBC (hon., mem. adv. coun., Cert. Merit 1994), ABI (hon., mem. rsch. bd. advs., 20th Century Achievement award 1994). Office: Shanghai Biomaterial Rsch Ctr, 716 Xie Tu Rd, Shanghai 200023, China

YACOWITZ, HAROLD, biochemist, nutritionist; b. N.Y.C., Feb. 17, 1922; s. Louis and Clara (Kurtzberg) Y.; m. Ann Ruth Barnett, Dec. 31, 1941; children: Caryn R., Richard S., Suzanne Yacowitz Dragan. BS, Cornell U., 1947, M in Nutritional Sci., 1948, PhD, 1950. Rsch. biochemist Parke-Davis Inc., Detroit, 1950-51; assoc. prof. Ohio State U., Columbus, 1951-55; head nutrition rsch. dept. Squibb Inst. for Med. Rsch., New Brunswick, N.J., 1955-59; dir. rsch. Nopco Chem. Co. Inc., Harrison, N.J., 1959-61, Amburgo Co. Inc., Phila., 1961-80; rsch. assoc. Fairleigh Dickinson U., Madison, N.J., 1961-80; pres., dir. rsch. Dr. H. Yacowitz & Co., Piscataway, N.J., 1961—, Animal Identification & Marking Systems Inc., Piscataway, 1982—; pres. Peninsula Investment & Devel. Inc., Cambridge, Md., 1961—; pres., bd. dirs. rsch. Drug Delivery Devices Inc., Piscataway, 1991—. Contbr. articles to profl. jours.; patentee in field. Leader Boy Scouts Am., Ithaca, N.Y., 1946-50, Piscataway, 1955-59. With U.S. Army, 1943-46, ETO, PTO. Grange League Fedn. fellow Cornell U., 1947-48, Robert Gould rsch. fellow, Cornell U., 1949-50, Coun. on Arteriosclerosis fellow Am. Heart Assn., 1970. Fellow N.Y. Acad. Scis. (chmn. sect. biology and medicine 1972-76); mem. Am. Chem. Soc., Am. Inst. Nutrition, Am. Assn. Lab. Animal Scientists, Exptl. Investors Club (New Brunswick, pres. 1955-59). Jewish. Office: Animal Ident Marking Syst Inc 221 2nd Ave Piscataway NJ 08854-3519

YADALAM, KASHINATH GANGADHARA, psychiatrist; b. Bangalore, India, Dec. 17, 1954; came to U.S., 1980; s. Gangadhara N. and Ramarathna G. (Daglur) Y.; m. Jyothi Kashinath, Feb. 26, 1981; children: Akhila, Adithya. MD, Kasturba Med. Coll., Manipal, India, 1977. Diplomate, Am. Bd. Psychiatry and Neurology. Resident in psychiatry U. Nebr., Omaha, 1980-83; clin. fellow psychopharmacology Med. Coll. Pa., Phila., 1983-84; instr. Med. Coll. Pa., 1984-85, asst. prof., 1985-89, dir. neuropsychiatry clinic, 1987-91, assoc. prof., 1989-91; med. dir. Diagnostic and Consultation Ctr. Med. Coll. of Pa.; assoc. dir. The Neuropsychiat. Clinic of La., 1991—; med. dir. Schizophrenia Diagnostic and Consultation Ctr., 1990. Author: (with others) Drug Induced Dysfunction in Psychiatry, 1992; contbr. articles to med. jours. Grantee, NIMH, 1987; recipient Young Investigator award, Internat. Congress Schizophrenia Rsch., Balt., 1987, Young Scientist award Winter Workshop on Schizophrenia, Badgastein, Austria, 1990. Mem. Am. Psychiat. Assn., Am. Coll. Clin. Pharmacology, Nat Alliance of the Mentally Ill. Hindu. Office: 2829 4th Ave Ste 150 Lake Charles LA 70601-7887

YAFFE, STUART ALLEN, physician; b. Springfield, Ill., July 6, 1927; m. Natalie, 1952; children: Scott, Kim Yaffe Schoenburg. BS cum laude, U. Alaska, 1951; MD, St. Louis U., 1956. Diplomate Am. Bd. Family Practice. Intern St. Louis CIty Hosp., 1956-57, resident, 1957-58; physician pvt. practice, 1958—; clin. assoc. prof. So. Ill. U. Sch. Medicine., Springfield, 1971—; ptnr. Springfield Clinic, 1989—. With U.S. Army, 1945-47. Mem. AMA, Am. Acad. Family Physicians, Ill. Acad. Family Physicians, Ill. State Med. Soc., Sangamon County Med. Soc. Office: 1100 Centre West Dr Springfield IL 62704

YAGIELA, JOHN ALLEN, dental educator; b. Washington, July 23, 1947; s. Stanley and Kathryn Marie (Gilkeson) Y.; m. Dolores Jean Mitchell, Mar. 21, 1970; children: Gregory, Leanne. Student, U. Calif., Riverside, 1965-67; DDS, UCLA, 1971, postgrad., 1982-83; PhD in Pharmacology, U. Utah, 1975. Diplomate Am. Dental Bd. Anesthesiology. Asst. prof. dentistry Emory U., Atlanta, 1975-78, assoc. prof., 1978-82; assoc. prof. UCLA, 1982-83, prof., 1983—, assoc. dean acad. and adminstrv. affairs, 1984-89; cons. Astra Pharm. Products Inc., Worcester, Mass., 1982—, VA Wadsworth divsn., L.A., 1983-92, Gen. Med. Co., L.A., 1988—, ADA, Chgo., 1991—. Co-author: Regional Anesthesia of the Oral Cavity, 1981, Local Anesthesia of the Oral Cavity, 1995; co-editor: Pharmacology and Therapeutics for Dentistry, 3d edit., 1989; editor Anesthesia Progress, 1990-95, The Pulse, 1996—; contbr. articles on dental therapeutics to profl. jours. Recipient Award of Achievement Am. Coll. Dentists, 1971; Regents scholar UCLA, 1968-71; Alpha Omega award, 1971. Fellow Am. Dental Soc. Anesthesiology; mem. ADA, AAAS, Internat. Assn. Dental Rsch. (sec.-treas. PTTG group 1984-88, pres.-elect 1989-90, pres. 1990-91), Am. Assn. Dental Schs. (chmn. pharmacology therapeutics sect. 1983), Am. Soc. Dentist Anesthesiolgists (v.p. 1995-96), Omicron Kappa Upsilon. Methodist. Home: 23918 Stagg St West Hills CA 91304 Office: UCLA Sch Dentistry Ctr for Health Scis Los Angeles CA 90095

YAHR, MELVIN DAVID, physician; b. N.Y.C., Nov. 18, 1917; s. Isaac and Sarah (Reigelhaupt) Y.; m. Felice Turtz, May 9, 1948; children—Carol, Nina, Laura, Barbara Anne. A.B., N.Y. U., 1939, M.D., 1943. Diplomate: Am. Bd. Psychiatry and Neurology (pres.). Intern Lenox Hill Hosp., N.Y.C., 1943-44; resident Lenox Hill Hosp., also Montefiore Hosp., Bronx, N.Y., 1947-48; staff Columbia, 1948-73, assoc. prof. clin. neurology, 1957-62, prof. neurology, 1962-70, H.H. Merritt prof. neurology, 1970-73, asst. dean grad. medicine, 1959-67, assoc. dean, 1967-73; asst. neurologist N.Y. Neurol. Inst., 1948-53, assoc. attending neurologist, 1953-60, attending neurologist, 1960-73; Goldschmidt prof. neurology, chmn. dept. neurology Mt. Sinai Med. Center, 1973-92; Aidekman Family Prof. Neurological Rsch., 1992—; exec. dir. Parkinson's Disease Found., 1957-73; panel neurologist N.Y.C. Bd. Edn., 1958-59; mem. com. evalutation drugs in neurology NIH, 1959-60, panel mem. neurol. study sect., 1959-80; mem. com. revisions U.S. Pharmacopea. Assoc. editor: Internat. Jour. Neurology; editor-in-chief Jour. Neural Transmission, 1989—; Archives Neurology, 1964-89. Fellow Am. Acad. Neurology, N.Y. Acad. Medicine, Harvey Soc.; mem. A.M.A. (chmn. com. neurol. disorders in industry), Am. Neurol. Assn. (sec.-treas. 1959-68, pres. 1969), Assn. Research Nervous and Mental Disease, N.Y. State Neurol. Soc., New York County Med. Soc., Am. Epilepsy Soc., Eastern Assn. Electroencephalographers. Office: Mt Sinai School of Med City U Clin Ctr Rsch Parkinson's 5 E 98th St Box 1139 New York NY 10029-6504

YAKATAN, GERALD JOSEPH, pharmaceutical consultant; b. Phila., May 20, 1942; s. Nathan and Bella (Resnick) Y.; m. Una Gittleman, Dec. 20, 1964; children: Nicole Blayne, Brook Noel. BS, Temple U., 1963, MS, 1965; PhD, U. Fla., 1971. Asst. prof. U. Tex., Austin, 1971-76; assoc. prof. U. Tex., 1976-80; dir. pharmacokinetics and drug metabolism Warner Lambert Co., Ann Arbor, Mich., 1980-83; v.p. product devel. Warner Lambert Co., Morris Plains, N.J., 1983-87; exec. v.p. R & D, Immunetech Pharm., San Diego, 1987-90; pres., chief exec. officer Tanabe Rsch. Labs., USA, Inc., San Diego, 1990-95; gen. ptnr. Yakatan & Yakatan, Del Mar, Calif., 1995—. Contbr. articles to profl. jours. NIH fellow, 1965-69, NSF fellow, 1964. Fellow Am. Coll. Clin. Pharmacology (bd. regents 1987—), Am. Assn. Pharm. Sci., Acad. Pharm. Sci.; mem. Am. Acad. Allergy, Athsma & Immunology, Drug Info. Assn., U.S. Profl. Tennis Registry, Fla. Blue Key. Democrat. Jewish. Office: Yakatan & Yakatan 13813 Boquita Dr Del Mar CA 92014-3105

YAKES, BARBARA LEE, occupational and preventive medicine physician, former nurse; b. Detroit; d. Glen Wendel and Marie Louise (Jock) Y.; m. Richard Allen Jankowics, Sept. 12, 1984; 1 child, Allen Glen. BA, Wayne State Univ., 1973, BS in Nursing, 1978; D in Osteopathic medicine, Mich. State Univ., 1986; M in Occupational Health, Harvard Sch. Pub. Health, 1988. Diplomate Am. Bd. Preventive Medicine, Occupational Medicine, Nat. Bd. Osteopathic Medical Examiners. Registered nurse Lafayette Clinic Grace Hosp., Oakwood Hosp., Detroit, 1978-83; internship Mich. Health Ctr., Detroit, 1986-87; resident Harvard Sch. Pub. Health, Boston, 1987-89; plant medical dir. General Motors Corp., Warren, Mich., 1989—. Contbr. articles to profl. jours. Bd. Govs. Acad. scholar Wayne State U., 1969-73; recipient Bubeck OB/GYN award Mich. State U., 1984, Mead-Johnson rsch. award Mead-Johnson Pharm., 1987-88. Fellow Am. Coll. Preventive Medicine; mem. Am. Osteo. Assn., Am. Coll. Occupational and Environ. Medicine, Mich. Assn. Osteo. Physicians and Surgeons, Mich. Occupational Med. Assn., Detroit Inst. Arts Founders Soc., Harvard Club Eastern Mich., Phi Beta Kappa, Sigma Sigma Phi. Office: General Motors Corp Mfg B Bldg Medical Dept 30300 Mound Rd Warren MI 48090-9040

YAKURA, HIDETAKA, immunologist; b. Sapporo, Hokkaido, Japan, Dec. 8, 1947; s. Yasutaroh and Sumiko (Irie) Y. MD, Hokkaido U., 1972, PhD, 1978. Rsch. fellow Farber Cancer Ctr./Harvard Sch. Medicine, Boston, 1976-78; rsch. assoc. Meml. Sloan-Kettering Cancer Ctr., N.Y.C., 1978-83; asst. prof. dept. pathology Asahikawa (Japan) Med. Coll., 1983-85, assoc. prof. dept. pathology, 1985-89; dir., dept. microbiology/immunology Tokyo Met. Inst. for Neurosci., 1989—; vis. investigator Meml. Sloan-Kettering Cancer Ctr., 1988; assoc. scientist Nat. Inst. Neurosci., Nat. Ctr. of Neurology and Psychiatry, Tokyo, 1989—. Mem. Am. Assn. Immunologists, Am. Soc. Microbiology. Office: Tokyo Met Inst Neuroscience, 2-6 Musashidai, Fuchu Tokyo 183, Japan

YALE, JEFFREY FRANKLIN, podiatrist; b. Derby, Conn., Jan. 18, 1943; s. Irving and Bernice (Blume) Y.; m. Lenore Bernsley, Apr. 23, 1987; children: Brian Joseph, Andrew Malcolm, Owen Slade. Student, U. Fla., 1960-62; D of Podiatric Medicine, Ill. Coll. Podiatric Medicine, 1966. Diplomate Am. Bd. Podiatric Surgery, Am. Bd. Podiatric Orthopedics, Am. Bd. Med. Quality Assurance and Utilization Rev. Surg. resident Highland Gen. Hosp., Oakland, Calif., 1966-67; capt. U.S. Army Med. Svc., Fort Ord, Calif., 1967-71; instr. masters level Quinnipiac Coll., Hamden, Conn., 1981; cons. surgeon VA Med. Ctr., West Haven, Conn., 1982—; chmn. podiatric surgery Griffin Hosp., Derby, Conn., 1974—; assoc. clin. prof. U. Osteo. Health Scis., Des Moines, 1982—; chmn. Podiatric Medicine Test Com. Nat. Bd. Podiatric Med. Examiners, 1977-94; pres. Ct. Examining Bd. in Podiatry, 1979, Am. Acad. Podiatric Sports Medicine, 1986; pres. Yale Podiatry Group, P.C., Ansonia, Conn., 1976—; bd. dirs. Podiatry Ins. Co. Am., Brentwood, Tenn., also chmn. underwriting com.; editl. adv. bd. Am. Podiatric Med. Assn., 1992-95. Author: Firm Footings For the Athlete, 1984, The Arthritic Foot, 1984, Yale's Podiatric Medicine, 3d edit., 1987; contbr. numerous sci. articles to profl. jours. Corporator Griffin Hosp., Derby, Conn., 1982. Capt. U.S. Army, 1967-71. Fellow Am. Acad. Podiatric Sports Medicine, Am. Assn. Hosp. Podiatrists, Am. Coll. Foot and Ankle Surgeons; mem. New Haven County Podiatric Med. Assn., Conn. Podiatric Med. Assn., Am. Podiatric Med. Assn., Conn. Pub. Health Assn., Am. Pub. Health Assn. Jewish. Home: 18 Inwood Rd Woodbridge CT 06525-2558 Office: Yale Podiatry Group PC 364 E Main St Ansonia CT 06401-1904

YALE, SEYMOUR HERSHEL, dental radiologist, educator, university dean, gerontologist; b. Chgo., Nov. 27, 1920; s. Henry and Dorothy (Kulwin) Y.; m. Muriel Jane Cohen, Nov. 6, 1943; children: Russell Steven, Patricia Ruth. B.S., U. Ill., 1944, D.D.S., 1945, postgrad., 1947-48. Pvt. practice of dentistry, 1945-54, 56—; asst. clin. dentistry U. Ill., 1948-49, instr. clin. dentistry, 1949-53, asst. prof. clin. dentistry, 1953-54, assoc. prof. dept. radiology Coll. Dentistry, 1956, prof., head dept. Coll. Dentistry, 1957-65, adminstrv. asst. to dean Coll. Dentistry, 1961-63, asst. dean Coll. Dentistry, 1963-64, acting dean Coll. Dentistry, 1964-65, dean, 1965-87, dean emeritus, 1987—; also mem. grad. faculty dept. radiology Coll. Medicine U. Ill., Chgo., prof. dentistry and health resources mgmt. Sch. Pub. Health, 1987—; sr. dental dir. Dental Care Plus Mgmt. Corp., Chgo.; pres., dir. dental edn. Dental Care Plus Mgmt. Ednl. Svcs., Ltd.; health care facilities planner; dir. tng. Dental Technicians Sch., U.S. Naval Tng. Ctr., Bainbridge, md., 1954-56; mem. subcom. 16 Nat. Com. on Radiation Protection; mem. Radiation Protection Adv. Bd., State of Ill., 1971, City of Chgo. Health Sys. Agy.; founder Ctr. for Rsch. in Periodontal Disease and Oral Molecular Biology, 1977; organizer, chmn. Nat. Conf. on Hepatitis-B in Dentistry, 1982; organizer, dir. Univ. Taskforce Primary Health Care Project, U. Ill., Chgo.; chmn. U. Ill.-U. Stockholm-U. Gothenberg Conf. on Geriatrics, 1985; dir. planning AMVETS/UIC Tchg. Nursing Home Project, 1987-91; co-sponsor 1st Egyptian Dental Congress, 1984; adj. prof. Ctr. for Exercise Sci. and Cardiovasc. Rsch., Northeastern Ill. U., Chgo., 1991, Northwestern U. Sch. Dentistry Divsn. Behavioural Scis., Evanston, Ill., 1996—. Editor-in-chief Dental Care Plus Mgmt. Digest, 1995—. Bd. dirs., co-benefactor (with wife) World Heritage Mus., U. Ill., Urbana, 1985; mem. Hillel Bd., U. Ill.-Chgo.; life mem. (with wife) Bronze Circle of Coll. Liberal Arts, U. Ill., Urbana; mem. (with wife) Pres.' Council, U. Ill. Recipient centennial research award Chgo. Dental Soc., 1959; Distinguished Alumnus award U. Ill., 1973; Harry Sicher Meml. Lecture award Am. Coll. Stomologic Surgeons, 1983. Fellow Acad. Gen. Dentistry (hon.), Am. Coll. Dentists; mem. Ill. Dental Soc. (mem. com. on radiology), Chgo. Dental Soc., Internat. Assn. Dental Rsch., Am. Acad. Oral Roentgenology, Am. Dental Assn., Odontographic Soc. Chgo. (Award of Merit 1982), Council Dental Deans State Ill. (chmn.), N.Y. Acad. Scis., Gerontol. Soc. Am., Pierre Fauchard Acad. (Man of Yr. award Ill. sect. 1988), Am. Pub. Health Assn., Gerontol. Soc. Am., Omicron Kappa Upsilon, Sigma Xi, Alpha Omega (hon.). Home: 155 N Harbor Dr Chicago IL 60601-7328 Office: 25 E Washington St Chicago IL 60602

YALOW, ROSALYN SUSSMAN, medical physicist; b. N.Y.C., N.Y., July 19, 1921; d. Simon and Clara (Zipper) Sussman; m. A. Aaron Yalow, June 6, 1943; children: Benjamin, Elanna. A.B., Hunter Coll., 1941; M.S., U. Ill., Urbana, 1942, Ph.D., 1945; D.Sc. (hon.), U. Ill., Chgo., 1974, Phila. Coll. Pharmacy and Sci., 1976, N.Y. Med. Coll., 1976, Med. Coll. Wis., Milw., 1977, Yeshiva U., 1977, Southampton (N.Y.) Coll., 1978, Bucknell U., 1978, Princeton U., 1978, Jersey City State Coll., 1979, Med. Coll. Pa., 1979, Manhattan Coll., 1979, U. Vt., 1980, U. Hartford, 1980, Rutgers U., 1980, Rensselaer Poly. Inst., 1980, Colgate U., 1981, U. So. Calif., 1981, Clarkson Coll., 1982, U. Miami, 1983, Washington U., St. Louis, 1983, Adelphi U., 1983, U. Alta. (Can.), 1983, SUNY, 1984, Tel Aviv U., 1985, Claremont (Calif.) U., 1986, Mills Coll., Oakland, Calif., 1986, Cedar Crest Coll., Allentown, Pa., 1988, Drew U., Madison, N.J., 1988, Lehigh U., 1988; L.H.D. (hon.), Hunter Coll., 1978; DSc. (hon.), San Francisco State U., 1989, Technion-Israel Inst. Tech., Haifa, 1989; DSc (hon.), Med. Coll. Ohio Toledo, 1991; L.H.D. (hon.), Sacred Heart U., Conn., 1978, St. Michael's Coll., Winooski Park, Vt., 1979, Johns Hopkins U., 1979, Coll. St. Rose, 1988, Spertus Coll. Judaica, Chgo., 1988; D. honoris causa, U. Rosario, Argentina, 1980, U. Ghent, Belgium, 1984; D. Humanities and Letters (hon.), Columbia U., 1984; DSc (hon.), Fairleigh Dickinson U., 1992, Conn. Coll., 1992, Smith Coll., Northampton, Mass., 1994, Union Coll., Schenectady, 1994. Diplomate: Am. Bd. Scis. Lectr., asst. prof. physics Hunter Coll., 1946-50; physicist, asst. chief radiosotope service VA Hosp., Bronx, N.Y., 1950-70, chief nuclear medicine, 1970-80, acting chief radioisotope service, 1968-70; research prof. Mt. Sinai Sch. Medicine, CUNY, 1968-74, Disting. Service prof., 1974-79, Solomon A. Berson Disting. prof.-at-large, 1986—; Disting. prof.-at-large Albert Einstein Coll. Medicine, Yeshiva U., 1979-85, prof. emeritus, 1986—; chmn. dept. clin. scis. Montefiore Med. Ctr., Bronx, 1980-85; N.J., 1992, Northampton, Mass.; cons. Lenox Hill Hosp., N.Y.C., 1956-62, WHO, Bombay, 1978; sec. U.S. Nat. Com. on Med. Physics, 1963-67; mem. nat. com. Radiation Protection, Subcom. 13, 1957; mem. Pres.'s Study Group on Careers for Women, 1966-72; sr. med. investigator VA, 1972-92, sr. med. investigator emeritus, 1992—. Co-editor: Hormone and Metabolic Research, 1973-79; editorial adv. council: Acta Diabetologica Latina, 1975-77, Ency. Universalis, 1978—; editorial bd.: Mt. Sinai Jour. Medicine, 1976-79, Diabetes, 1976, Endocrinology, 1967-72; contbr. numerous articles to profl. jours. Bd. dirs. N.Y. Diabetes Assn., 1974. Recipient VA William S. Middleton Med. Research award, 1960; Eli Lilly award Am. Diabetes Assn., 1961; Van Slyke award N.Y. met. sect. Am. Assn. Clin. Chemists, 1968; award A.C.P., 1971; Dickson prize U. Pitts., 1971; Howard Taylor Ricketts award U. Chgo., 1971; Gairdner Found. Internat. award, 1971; Commemorative medallion Am. Diabetes Assn., 1972; Bernstein award Med. Soc. State N.Y., 1974; Boehringer-Mannheim Corp. award Am. Assn. Clin. Chemists, 1975; Sci. Achievement award AMA, 1975; Exceptional Service award VA, 1975; A. Cressy Morrison award N.Y. Acad. Scis., 1975; sustaining membership award Assn. Mil. Surgeons, 1975; Distinguished Achievement award Modern Medicine, 1976; Albert Lasker Basic Med. Research award, 1976; La Madonnina Internat. prize Milan, 1977; Golden Plate award Am. Acad. Achievement, 1977; Nobel prize for physiology/medicine, 1977; citation of esteem St. John's U., 1979; G. von Hevesy medal, 1978; Rosalyn S. Yalow Research and Devel. award established Am. Diabetes Assn., 1978; Banting medal, 1978; Torch of Learning award Am. Friends Hebrew U., 1978; Virchow gold medal Virchow-Pirquet Med. Soc., 1978; Gratum Genus Humanum gold medal World Fedn. Nuclear Medicine or Biology, 1978; Jacobi medallion Asso. Alumni Mt. Sinai Sch. Medicine, 1978; Jubilee medal Coll. of New Rochelle, 1978; VA Exceptional Service award, 1978; Fed. Woman's award, 1961; Harvey lectr., 1966; Am. Gastroenterol. Assn. Meml. lectr., 1972; Joslin lectr. New Eng. Diabetes Assn., 1972; Franklin I. Harris Meml. lectr., 1973; 1st Hagedorn Meml. lectr. Acta Endocrinologica Congress, 1973; Sarasota Med. award for achievement and excellence, 1979; gold medal Phi Lambda Kappa, 1980; Achievement in Life award Ency. Brit., 1980; Theobald Smith award, 1982; Pres.'s Cabinet award U. Detroit, 1982; John and Samuel Bard award in medicine and sci. Bard Coll., 1982; Disting. Research award Dallas Assn. Retarded Citizens, 1982, Nat. Medal Sci., 1988; Abram L. Sachar Silver Medallion Brandeis U., Waltham, Mass., 1989, Disting. Scientist of Yr. award ARCS, N.Y.C., 1989, Golden Scroll award The Jewish Advocate, Boston, 1989, spl. award Clin. Ligand Assay Soc., Washington, 1988, numerous others. Fellow N.Y. Acad. Scis. (chmn. biophysics div. 1964-65), Am. Coll. Radiology (asso. in physics), Clin. Soc. N.Y. Diabetes Assn.; mem. Nat. Acad. Scis., Am. Acad. Arts and Scis., Am. Phys. Soc., Radiation Research Soc., Am. Assn. Physicists in Medicine, Biophys. Soc., Soc. Nuclear Medicine, Endocrine Soc. (Koch award 1972, pres. 1978), Am. Physiol. Soc., (hon.) Harvey Soc., (hon.) Med. Assn. Argentina, (hon.) Diabetes Soc. Argentina, (hon.) Am. Coll. Nuclear Physicians, (hon.) The N.Y. Acad. Medicine, (hon.) Am. Gastroent. Assn., (hon.) N.Y. Roentgen Soc., (hon.) Soc. Nuclear Medicine, Phi Beta Kappa, Sigma Xi, Sigma Pi Sigma, Pi Mu Epsilon, Sigma Delta Epsilon, Tau Beta Pi. Office: VA Hosp 130 W Kingsbridge Rd Bronx NY 10468-3992

YAM, CONSTANCE SHUK-CHEE, dermatologist; b. Hong Kong, July 19, 1940; d. Tung-Lam and Shuzt-Ying (Chan) Y.; children: Christine, Monica. MBBS, U. Hong Kong, 1965. Diplomate Am. Bd. Dermatology. Resident in dermatology Cin. Gen. Hosp., 1969-71; vis. fellow Columbia-Presbyn. Med. Ctr., N.Y.C., 1971-72; pvt. practice Hong Kong, 1973-74, 80—; asst. clin. prof. dermatology U. Cin. Sch. Medicine, 1975-79; pvt. practice Cin., 1976-79; admitting privilege Hong Konh Adventist Hosp., Hong Kong Sanatorium Hosp., Canossa Hosp.; dermatology cons. H.K. Adventist Hosp., 1980-86. Author: Save Your Skin and Stay Young, 1986. Fellow Am. Acad. Dermatology, Am. Soc. for Dermatology Surgery, Hong Kong Acad. Medicine; mem. Internat. Soc. Dermatology Surgery, Internat. Soc. Cosmetic Laser Surgeons, Inc., Hong Kong Coll. Physicians, Am. Acad. Aesthetic and Restorative Surgery. Office: 1203 Melbourne Plz, 33 Queens Rd Ctrl, Hong Kong Hong Kong

YAMABE, SHIGERU, medical educator; b. Tokyo, July 7, 1923; s. Hiroshi and Jyo (Mihara) Y.; m. Takako Naoi, Apr. 2, 1967; 1 child, Yoko. MS, Osaka (Japan) U., 1946, PhD, 1952. Lectr. Osaka U. Med. Sch., 1953-58; prof. Kobe Coll., Nishinomiya, Japan, 1958-89, hon. prof., 1989—; system dir. Drug Rsch. System Internat., Kobe, 1989—; rsch. exec. mbr. Osaka Seijinbyo Med. Ctr., Higashinariku, Osaka, Japan, 1991—; vis. lectr. Tokyo U., Kyoto (Japan) U., 1966-84; vis. prof. dept. microbiology London Hosp. Med. Coll., 1978—, Case Western Res. U., Cleve., 1982, 84, Harvard Med. Sch., Boston, 1988-89; hon. vis. lectr. London Hosp. Med. Coll., 1990—; invited lectr. U. Paris VI, 1992—; vis. sr. scientist Inst. Pathology, Oxford, 1992—; vis. prof. Grad. Sch. Pub. Health U. Pitts., 1993—; sr. sci. advisor Taiho Pharm. Co., Tokyo, 1991—. Author: Bioenergetics, 1968 (award 1970); editor: Research and Development of New Drugs, 1994; internat. jour. editor Antiviral Chemistry and Chemotherapy, 1993—, Jour. Chemotherapy, 1988—; drug designer, inventor Tazobactam antibiotic, 1991, Zaltoprofen anti-inflammatory drug, 1993; 40 patents for cancer and AIDS drugs. Fellow Royal Soc. Medicine; active mem. N.Y. Acad. Sci. Home: 1-2-7 Kamokogahara, Higashinada, Kobe 658, Japan Office: ESS, Hotel Okura Kobe Chuo-ku, Kobe 650, Japan

YAMADA, TADATAKA, internist; b. Tokyo, June 5, 1945. MD, NYU, 1971. Intern Med. Coll. Va. Hosps., Richmond, 1971-72, resident in internal medicine, 1972-74; gastrointestinal fellow UCLA, 1977-79; prof. medicine U. Mich., Ann Arbor; mem. staff U. Mich. Hosp., Ann Arbor. Mem. AAAS, ACP, AAP, AGA, ASCI, IOM. Office: U Mich Gastrointestinal Peptide Rsch 3101 Taubman Ctr Ann Arbor MI 48109-0368*

YAMAMOTO, JOE, psychiatrist, educator; b. Los Angeles, Apr. 18, 1924; s. Zenzaburo and Tomie (Yamada) Y.; m. Maria Fujitomi, Sept. 5, 1947; children: Eric Robert, Andrew Jolyon. Student, Los Angeles City Coll., 1941-42, Hamline U., 1943-45; B.S., U. Minn., 1946, M.B., 1948, M.D., 1949. Asst. prof. dept. psychiatry, neurology, behavioral sci. U. Okla. Med. Center, 1955-58, asst. prof., 1958-60; assoc. prof. dept. psychiatry U. So. Calif. Sch. Medicine, Los Angeles, 1961-69; prof. U. So. Calif. Sch. Medicine, 1969-77, co-dir. grad. edn. psychiatry, 1963-70; prof. UCLA, 1977-94, emeritus prof., 1994—; dir. Psychiat. Outpatient Clinic, Los Angeles County-U. So. Calif. Med. Center, 1958-77; dir. adult ambulatory care services UCLA Neuropsychiat. Inst., 1977-88, chief Lab. for Cross Cultural Studies. Contbr. articles in field to profl. jours. Served to capt., M.C. U.S. Army, 1953-55. Fellow Am. Psychiat. Assn. (life), Pacific Rim Coll. Psychiatrists, Am. Acad. Psychoanalysis (trustee, mem. exec. com., pres. 1978-79), Am. Coll. Psychiatrists, Am. Orthopsychiat. Assn. (pres.-elect 1993-94, pres. 1994-95, past pres.), Am. Assn. for Social Psychiatry (trustee 1981-84, v.p. 1984-86); mem. So. Calif. Psychoanalytic Inst. and Soc. (pres. 1972-73), Soc. for Study of Culture and Psychiatry, Group for Advancement Psychiatry (bd. dirs. 1992-94), Kappa Phi, Alpha Omega Alpha. Office: UCLA Neuro-psychiat Inst 760 Westwood Plz Los Angeles CA 90024-1754

YAMAMOTO, KEITH ROBERT, molecular biologist, educator; b. Des Moines, Feb. 4, 1946. BS, Iowa State U., 1968; PhD, Princeton U., 1973. Asst. prof. biochemistry U. Calif., San Francisco, 1976-79, assoc. prof., 1979-83, prof., 1983—, vice chmn. dept., 1985—, dir. biochemistry and molecular biology program, 1988—; mem. genetic biology rev. panel NSF, Washington, 1984-87; chmn. molecular biology study sect. NIH, Bethesda, Md., 1987-90, mem. nat. adv. coun. for human genome rsch., 1990-91. Co-author: Gene Wars: Military Control over the New Genetic Technologies, 1988; co-editor: Transcriptional Regulation, 1992 ; assoc. editor Jour. Molecular Biology, 1988—, editor Molecular Biology of the Cell, 1991—. Mem. Com. for Responsible Genetics, Boston, 1989—; testifier hearings on biol. warfare com. on govtl. affairs U.S. Senate, Washington, 1989. Recipient Gregory Pincus medal Worchester Found. for Exptl. Biology, 1990; Dreyfus tchr.-scholar, 1982-86. Fellow Am. Acad. Arts and Scis.; mem. AAAS, NAS (panel on sci. responsibility and conduct of rsch. 1990-91), Protein Soc., Am. Soc. for Cell Biology (coun. 1991-92), Am. Soc. for Biochemistry and Molecular Biology (publs. com. 1990-93), Am. Soc. for Devel. Biology. Home: 332 Douglass St San Francisco CA 94114-2452 Office: U Calif San Francisco Dept Biochemistry 513 Parnassus Ave San Francisco CA 94122-2722

YAMANAKA, WENDI SUZUKO, pharmacist; b. Stockton, Calif., July 27, 1957; d. Noboru and Dorothy Chisato (Kaneko) Y. AA in Natural Scis., San Joaquin Delta Coll., 1977; BS in Chemistry and Biology, U. Pacific, 1980, D in Pharmacy, 1983. Lic. pharmacist Calif., Nev. Intern Campus Pharmacy, Stockton, 1981; clin. intern in pharmacy San Joaquin Gen. Hosp., Stockton, 1982; intern pharmacist Drs. Med. Ctr., Modesto, Calif., 1983; pharmacist Payless Drug Stores, San Jose, Calif., 1984—. Mem. Calif. Pharm. Assn., Am. Soc. Hosp. Pharmacists. Buddhist. Home: 5015 Moss Creek Cir Stockton CA 95219-8075

YAMANE, GEORGE MITSUYOSHI, oral diagnosis and radiology educator; b. Honolulu, Aug. 9, 1924; s. Seigi and Tsuta (Moriwaki) Y.; m. Alice Matsuko Nemoto, July 6, 1951; children: Wende Michiko, Linda Keiko, David Kiyoshi. Student, U. Hawaii, 1944; A.B., Haverford Coll., 1946; D.D.S., U. Minn., 1950, Ph.D., 1962. Teaching, research asst. U. Hawaii, Honolulu, 1943-44; teaching asst. div. oral pathology, oral diagnosis Sch. Dentistry, U. Minn., Mpls., 1951-53; asst. prof. oral pathology Coll. Dentistry U. Ill., Chgo., 1957-59; dir. tissue lab. Sch. Dentistry U. Wash., Seattle, 1960-63; asst. prof. oral pathology Sch. Dentistry U. Wash., 1959-63; grad. faculty mem. U. Minn., Mpls., 1963-70; prof., chmn. div. oral diagnosis, oral medicine and oral roentgenology U. Minn., 1963-70; prof., chmn. dept. oral diagnosis and radiology Dental Sch. Univ. of Medicine and Dentistry of N.J., 1970-83; prof. dept. biodental sci. Dental Sch. Coll. of Medicine and Dentistry of N.J., 1983-88, assoc. dean research and postgrad. programs, 1976-79, dir. div. oral and pathobiology, 1988-92, prof. dept oral pathology, biology and diagnosis sci., 1988-92, prof. emeritus, 1992—; cons. Children's Orthopedic Hosp. and Med. Ctr., Seattle, 1960-63, VA Hosp., American Lake, Wash., 1961-63, Mpls., 1964-70; cons. Minn. State Dept. Health, 1965-70, Wyo. State Bd. Health, 1966-70. Contbr. articles to med. and dental jours. Served with AUS. USPHS fellow, 1953-55; recipient Nell S. Talbot Instructorship award Coll. Dentistry U. Ill., 1958; Excellence in Teaching award U. Medicine and Dentistry N.J., 1984, Exceptional Merit award U. Medicine and Dentistry N.J., 1986. Fellow Am. Acad. Oral Pathology, AAAS, Am., Internat. colls. dentists, N.J. Acad. Medicine; mem. Am. Dental Assn., Orgn. Tchrs. Oral Diagnosis (sec.-treas. 1970-73, pres. 1974-75), Am. Acad. Periodontology, Internat. Assn. Dental Research, Am. Assn. Dental Schs., Sigma Xi (pres. Newark chpt. 1985), Omicron Kappa Upsilon, Xi Psi Phi.

YAMANE, STANLEY JOEL, optometrist; b. Lihue, Kauai, Hawaii, Mar. 13, 1943; s. Tooru and Yukiko (Miura) Y.; m. Joyce Mitsuko Tamura; children—Stanley Tooru Aiichi, Karen Margaret. B.S. in Optometry, Pacific U., 1966, O.D., 1966. Diplomate Am. Acad. Optometry. Practice optometry Waipahu, Hawaii, 1967-73; ptnr. with Dr. Dennis M. Kuwabara, 1973-81; ptnr. Drs. Kuwabara & Yamane, Optometrists, Inc., Waipahu, 1981-91; with br. office Drs. Kuwabara & Yamane, Optometrists, Inc., Honolulu; with DBA Eye Care Assocs. of Hawaii, Honolulu, 1989-91; dir. profl. affairs Vistakon, Inc., 1991-92; v.p. profl. affairs Vistakon Inc., 1992—; lectr., cons. in field; sec.-treas. Hawaii Bd. Examiners in Optometry, 1975-76, v.p., 1976-78, pres., 1978-80; mem. adj. faculty Coll. Optometry, Pacific U., 1977-91, Pa. Coll. Optometry, 1981-91, So. Coll. Optometry, 1982-91, U. Mo., St. Louis, 1990-91; bd. dirs. Hawaii Vision Svc. Plan, 1984-91. Cons. editor Optometric Mgmt. Jour., 1981-91, Contact Lens Forum Jour., 1987-91, editor, 1991; contbr. articles to profl. jours. Bd. mgrs. Leeward Oahu Br. YMCA, 1967-70, Hi-Y advisor, 1967-71, mem. Century Club, 1967-91, bd. mgrs. West Oahu Br., 1971-78, gen. chmn. sustaining membership, 1976; 2d v.p. August Ahrens Elem. Sch. PTA, 1969; mem. Leeward Mental Health Adv. Council, 1975-76, Friends of Waipahu Cultural Garden Park Found., 1976—, Aloha council Boy Scouts Am., 1976-91; mem. bus. adv. council Waipahu High Sch., 1976-81, Parent-Tchr.-Community Adv. Council, 1978-80; bd. dirs. Central/Leeward unit Am. Cancer Soc., 1977-80, pub. edn. dir., 1978-79, v.p., 1979-80, founder, chmn. Celebrity Auction, 1980, dir. Oahu Baseline Survey, 1978; bd. dirs. Barbers Point council Navy League Am., 1981-85; profl. bd. advisors U. Houston Inst. for Contact Lens Research. Recipient Merit award Nat. Eye Research Found., 1974, Disting. Service award, 1976. Fellow Am. Acad. Optometry (cornea and contact lens diplomate, vice chair cornea and contact lens sect. 1992-94, chair cornea and contact lens sect. 1994—, sec., 1990-92, vice chair ethics com. 1991-92, corp. support for Jour. com. 1981, chair diplomate awards com. 1988-90), AAAS, Am. Optometric Assn. (ann. congress del. 1978, pub. health com. 19738, optometric paraoptometric personnel com. 1978-79, contact lens project team 1979-80, task force on R&D 1984-87, contact lens sect. coun. 1988-92, sec., 1989-90, vice chair 1990-91, chair elect 1991-92, numerous coms.), Leeward Oahu Jaycees (Disting. Service award 1969, Top Outstanding Young Man award 1975), Hawaii State Jaycees, Am. Optometric Found. (bd. dirs. 1981-91 , chmn. task force clin. research 1981-83, nominations com. 1982, treas. 1985-86, sec., 1987-88, pres.-elect, 1988-89, pres. 1989-90), Am. Pub. Health Assn., Better Vision Inst., Coll. Optometrists in Vision Devel., Hawaii Optometric Assn. (corr. sec. 1968-70, state newsletter editor 1968-70, rec. sec. 1971, 2d v.p. 1972, pres. 1974-75; Man of Yr. 1975, Optometrist of Yr. 1979), Internat. Optometric & Optical League, Internat. Soc. Contact Lens Rsch., Brit. Contact Lens Assn., Japan Contact Lens Acad., Nat. Assn. of the Professions, Nat. Eye Research Found. (fellow Internat. Orthokeratology sect.; editorial bd. Contacto Jour. 1979, contact lens cert. com. 1981-85), Nat. Fedn. Ind. Bus., Optometric Cons. in Contact Lens Optometric Extension Program Found. (chmn. study group 1969-70, state dir. 1971-73), Optometric Hist. Soc., Optometric Polit. Action Coms., Soc. Contact Lens Specialists, Hawaii Assn. Children with Learning Disabilities, Hawaii Assn. Intellectually Gifted Children (pub. relations chmn. 1st Ann. State Conf. 1975, legis. lobbyist 1975-76), Waipahu Bus. Assn. (bd. dirs. 1974-78, chmn. pub. relations 1974-75, legis. lobbyist 1974-75, pres. 1974-75), Nat. Acad. Practice in Optometry (mem.-at-large on exec. com., disting. practitioner in optometry). Democrat. Baptist. Home: 8609 Autumn Green Dr Jacksonville FL 32256-9560 Office: Vistakon Inc Vp Profl Affairs 4500 Salibury Rd Ste 300 Jacksonville FL 32216-0954

YAMAOKA, TETSUO, psychology educator; b. Fukuoka, Japan, Feb. 25, 1936; s. Kenzoh and Yasue (Kudoh) Y.; m. Yohko Akizuki, Oct. 6, 1969; 1 child, Ryohji. MLitt, Kyushu U., Fukuoka, Japan, 1962, DLitt, 1976. Asst. Kyushu U., 1967-70; lectr. Komazawa U., Tokyo, 1970-73, asst. prof., 1973-79, chief prof., 1979-81; prof. psychology Kanazawa (Japan) U., 1981—. Author: Psychology of Zen, 1977, Introduction to Psychology, 1980, Study of Mental Self-Control, 1981; contbr. articles to profl. jours. Mem. Assn. Japanese Ednl. Psychology, Japanese Psychol. Assn., Japanese Group Dynamics Assn., Japanese Ergonimics Assn. Office: Kanazawa U 1-1 Marunouchi, Kakuma, Kanazawa 920-01, Japan

YAMAZI, YUKIO, health facility administrator, virology educator; b. Nagoya, Aichi, Japan, Jan. 3, 1923; s. Torataro and Kameki (Higashiyama) Y.; m. Sumako Higashiyama, Oct., 1947; children: Mitsuko Hinata, Yaeko Nishida. MB, Nippon Med. Sch., Tokyo, 1947, D in Med. Sci., 1953. Tech. ofcl. NIH, Tokyo, 1948-49, Nat. Hygienic Inst., Tokyo, 1949-60; assoc. prof. microbiology Nippon Med. Sch., 1960-71; prof. microbiology and immunology Nippon (Japan) Med. Sch., 1971-88, prof. emeritus, 1988—; rsch. assoc. epidemiology pub. health Yale U., New Haven, 1968-70; med. dir. Hohsen Clinic, Tokyo, 1988-91; vis. prof. Chiang Mai (Thailand) U., 1986—; dir. Internat. Good Will Found. of Japan, Tokyo, 1974—; med. dir. Sayama (Japan) Good Will Hosp., 1991—. Author: Medical Microbiology and Immunology, 1985; co-author: Viral Diseaes in Southeast Asia and West Pacific, 1982, Virus Diseases in Asia, 1988. Ministry of Edn. grantee, 1980, 86, WHO grantee, 1988. Fellow Japan Assn. Internat. Health, Japan Assn. Infectious Diseases, Japan Soc. of Allergology, Soc. Japanese Virologists, Japan Soc. Chemotherapy, Japanese Soc. Bacteriology; mem. Am. Soc. Microbiology. Mem. Christian Ch. Home: 1-28-7 Sakae, Tachikawa 190, Tokyo Office: Sayama Good Will Hosp, 428-1 Aoyogi, Sayama Saitama 35019, Japan

YAMBE, TOMOYUKI, medical educator; b. Sendai, Miyagi, Japan, May 7, 1959; s. Takasi and Yoshiko (Oka) Y.; m. Ikuko Takahashi, Sept. 29, 1986; children: Ken-ichiro, Yui, Rei, Ryui. MD, Tohoku U., Sendai, 1985, PhD, 1990. Instr. rsch. inat. tbc. and cancer Tohoku U., Sendai, 1992-93, instr. Inst. Devel. Aging and Cancer, 1993—. Mem. Japanese Soc. Artificial Organs (bd. trustee, Young Investigators award 1988, Presdl. award 1993), Japan Soc. Med. Electronics and Biol. Engring. (editl. trustee). Home: 4-1 Seiryo-machi Aoba-ku, Sendai 980, Japan

YAN, BING, biophysicist; b. Jinan, Shandong, China, Oct. 5, 1957; s. Baolin Yan and Shizhen Huang; m. Siaomei Sun, Apr. 21, 1984; 1 child, Patrick S. BS, Shandong U., Jinan, 1981; MA, Columbia U., 1987, MPhil, 1990, PhD, 1990. Rsch. fellow Cambridge (Eng.) U., 1990-91; rsch. assoc. U. Tex. Med. Sch., Houston, 1991-93; asst. fellow Sandoz Pharm. Corp., East Hanover, N.J., 1993-95, assoc. fellow, 1995—. Contbr. articles to profl. publs. Columbia U. fellow, 1986-90. Mem. Am. Chem. Soc., N.Y. Acad. Scis., Biophys. Soc. U.S.A. (Talbert award 1990), Protein Soc. Office: Sandoz Pharm Corp 59 Rt 10 East Hanover NJ 07936

YAN, SAU-CHI BETTY, biochemist; b. Hong Kong, Nov. 25, 1954; d. Ming Yan and Choo-Chen Woo; m. Victor J. Chen, Feb. 29, 1980; 1 child, Heidi I. BS, Ctrl. Mo. State U., 1975; PhD, Iowa State U., 1980. Postdoctoral fellow St. Paul-Ramsey Med. Ctr., 1980-82; postdoctoral fellow med. sch. U. Tex., Houston, 1982-84; sr. biochemist Eli Lilly & Co., Indpls., 1985-88, sr. scientist, 1989-93, sr. rsch. scientist, 1993—. Patentee in field; contbr. articles to profl. jours. Bd. dirs. A Children's Habitat, Indpls., 1994. Mem. AAAS, Am. Soc. Biochemistry, Molecular Biology, Protein Soc., Soc. Chinese Bioscientists Am. Office: Eli Lilly & Co 307 W Mccarty St # Dc1543 Indianapolis IN 46225-1235

YANAGITANI, ELIZABETH, optometrist; b. Ogden, Utah, Nov. 24, 1953; d. Katsuyoshi and Yaeko (Watanabe) Y. AS, Weber State Coll., Ogden, Utah, 1974; BA magna cum laude, U. Utah, 1976; OD, Pacific U., Forest Grove, Oreg., 1980. Externship Tripler Army Med Ctr., Schofield Barracks, Hawaii, 1979; staff optometrist Gen. Med., San Diego, 1984-89, San Ysidro Health Ctr., Calif., 1985-87, 91—, Logan Heights Family Health Ctr., San Diego, 1989-91; assoc. of pvt. office Chula Vista, Calif., 1985—; asst. instr. Am. Bus. Coll., San Diego, 1982. Recipient Gates Meml. award Nat. Eye Rsch. Found., 1980; scholar Weber State Coll., 1972-73, U. Utah, 1975, Project award Beta Sigma Kappa, 1980. Mem. San Diego County Optometric Soc. (v.p. 1985), Calif. Optometric Soc. (del. to leadership conf. 1985), Achievement Through Vision/COVD (pres. 1990), Phi Kappa Phi.

YANCEY, ASA GREENWOOD, SR., physician; b. Atlanta, Aug. 19, 1916; s. Arthur H. and Daisy L. (Sherard) Y.; m. Carolyn E. Dunbar, Dec. 28, 1944; children: Arthur H. II, Carolyn L., Caren L., Asa Greenwood Jr. BS, Morehouse Coll., 1937, ScD (hon.), 1991; MD, U. Mich., 1941; ScD (hon.), Howard U., 1991. Diplomate Am. Bd. Surgery. Intern City Hosp., Cleve., 1941-42; resident Freedmen's Hosp., Washington, 1942-45, U.S. Marine Hosp., Boston, 1945; instr. surgery Meharry Med. Coll., 1946-48; chief surgery VA Hosp., Tuskegee, Ala., 1943-58; chief surgery of Hughes Spalding Pavilion, 1958-72; pvt. practice specializing in surgery Atlanta, 1958-86; med. dir. Grady Meml. Hosp., Atlanta, 1972-89; mem. staff Hughes Spalding Hosp., St. Joseph Hosp., Emory U. Hosp., up to 1986-88; asst. prof. surgery Emory U., 1958-72, assoc. prof., 1972-75, prof. surgery, 1975-86, prof. emeritus, 1986—, assoc. dean Emory U. Sch. Medicine, 1972-89; clin. prof. surgery Morehouse Sch. Medicine, 1985—. Contbr. articles to profl. jours. Mem. Atlanta Bd. Edn., 1967-77, Fulton-De Kalb Hosp. Authority; trustee Body for Grady Meml. Hosp., 1989-93. 1st lt. M.C., AUS, 1942. Fellow ACS, Am. Surg. Assn.; mem. Nat. Med. Assn. (1st v.p. 1988-89, trustee 1960-66, editorial bd. jour. 1964-80), Inst. Medicine of NAS, So. Surg. Assn. Baptist. Home and Office: 2845 Engle Rd NW Atlanta GA 30318-7216

YANCEY, ELEANOR GARRETT, retired crisis intervention clinician; b. Ga., Oct. 24, 1933; adopted d. Overton LaVerne Garrett; m. Robert Grady Yancey, Nov. 10, 1961 (div. Apr. 1968); children: Katherine La Verne, David Shawn. Student, High Mus. Art Inst., 1952-53, Ga. State U., 1953-55, 78; BA, La Grange Coll., 1958. Social worker, case worker Fulton County Dept. Family and Children's Svcs., Atlanta, 1957-61; asst. tchr. Atlanta (Ga.) Bd. Edn., 1973-85; mental health crisis intervention clinician Dekalb County Bd. Health, Decatur, 1985-95, acting dir. crisis intervention, 1988-90; ret., 1995. Performed summer stock, 1969-70. Performed with Rogers & Co., 1969, 70; band booster pres. Henry Grady High Sch., Atlanta, 1977-78, v.p. PTA, 1978-79; pres. PTA Morningside Elem. Sch., Atlanta, 1977; grand juror Dekalb County, Decatur, 1983; active Sesquicentennial Celebration of Ala. Statehood. Mem. Kappa Kappa Iota (Lambda chpt. state pres. 1987-88, Eta pres. local chpt. 1992—). Democrat. Home: 3425 Regalwoods Dr Doraville GA 30340-4019

YANCEY, KIM BRUCE, dermatology researcher; b. Atlanta, Nov. 25, 1952; s. Andrew Jackson and Edrie Mae (Johnson) Y. BS, U. Ga. 1974; MD, Med. Coll. Ga., 1978. Diplomate Am. Bd. Dermatology. Intern dept. internal medicine Med. Coll. Ga., Augusta, 1978-79, resident dept. dermatology, 1979-81; med. staff fellow dermatology br. NIH, Bethesda, Md., 1981-84, sr. staff fellow dermatology br., 1984-85, sr. investigator dermatology br., 1993—; asst. prof. dept. dermatology Uniformed Svcs. U. Health Scis., Bethesda, 1985-87, assoc. prof. dept. dermatology, 1987-93, acting chmn. dept. dermatology, 1990-93; cons. Nat. Naval Med. Ctr., Bethesda, 1985—, Walter Reed Army med. ctr., Washington, 1985—. Author monographs and sci. manuscripts; contbr. articles to profl. jours. Rsch. grantee NIH, 1986—, collaborative rsch. grantee NATO, 1988-93. Fellow Am. Acad. Dermatology (editorial bd. 1986-93); mem. AMA, Am. Bd. Dermatology, Am. Dermatol. Assn. (Young Leadership award 1986), Soc. Investigative Dermatology (bd. dirs. 1982-84, co-chmn. ea. region 1990-92), Am. Fedn. Clin. Rsch., Dermatology Found., Washington Dermatol. Soc. Methodist. Office: NIH Nat Cancer Inst Derm Br Bldg 10 Rm 12n238 10 Center Dr MSC 1908 Bethesda MD 20892-1908

YANG, HSIN-MING, immunologist; b. Taipei, Taiwan, Dec. 2, 1952; came to U.S., 1980; s. Sze Piao and Yun-Huan (Chang) Y.; m. Yeasing Yeh, June 28, 1980; children: Elaine, Albert. BS, Nat. Taiwan U., 1976, MS, 1983; PhD, U. Wash., 1985. Rsch. assoc. Tri-Svc. Gen. Hosp., Taipei, 1979-80; fellow Scripps Clinic and Rsch. Found., La Jolla, Calif., 1986-88, sr. rsch. assoc., 1988-90; asst. prof. U. Nebr. Med. Ctr., Omaha, 1990-91; sr. rsch. scientist Pacific Biotech, Inc., San Diego, 1991-95; mgr. Scantibodies Lab., Inc., Santee, Calif., 1995—; lectr. Yun-Pei Coll. Med. Tech., Shinchiu, Taiwan, 1979-80. Contbr. articles to profl. jours., chpt. to book; inventor in field; patentee on analyte detection device including a hydrophobic barrier for improved fluid flow. Joseph Drown Found. fellow, 1986, Nat. Cancer Ctr. fellow, 1987-88. Mem. Am. Assn. for Cancer Rsch., Am. Assn. Clin. Chemistry, N.Y. Acad. Scis. Office: Scantibodies Lab Inc 9336 Abraham Way Santee CA 92071

YANG, JERRY ZEREN, internist, obstetrician, gynecologist, educator; b. Xi Chong, Sichuan, China, July 2, 1958; came to U.S., 1989; s. Di De and Suhua (Zeng) Y.; m. Li-Ling Liao, Mar. 30, 1964. MD, West China U. of Med. Scis., Chengdu, Sichuan, 1983, MS, 1986. Intern West China U. of Med. Scis., Chengdu, 1982-83, resident, 1983-88, asst. prof., 1986-88, lectr., 1988-94, assoc. prof., 1994—; postdoctoral fellow U. Calif., San Francisco, 1989-92; fellow Stanford U., 1992-96; mem. staff dept. internal medicine Kaiser Permanente Hosps., Santa Clara, Calif., 1996—. Assoc. editor-in-chief An English-Chinese Dictionary of Ob/Gyn, 1989; contbr. articles to profl. jours. Cheng's scholar U. Calif., 1989; Nat. Com. of Scis. of Beijing, 1987. Mem. Chinese Assn. of Ob./Gyn., Anti-Cancer Assn. of China. Office: Kaiser Permanente Hosp Dept Internal Medicine Santa Clara CA 95051

YANG, JIE, radiologist, dentist; b. Nindu, Peoples Republic of China, Sept. 15, 1963; came to the U.S., 1993; s. Biqing and Guixiu (Cui) Y.; m. Xianghong Zhang, July 29, 1989; 1 child, Sherry Z.M. DDS, Shanghai 2d Med. U., 1984; M Med Sci, Beijing Med. U., 1990; MS, U. Iowa, 1996, cert., 1996. Oral surgeon and radiologist Jiangxi (Peoples Republic of China) Med. Coll., 1984-87; resident Beijing Med. U., 1987-90; pvt. practice as dentist Bangkok, 1990-93; rsch. assoc. Asian Inst. Technology, Bangkok, 1990-93; resident, teaching asst. U. Iowa, Iowa City, 1993—. Contbr. articles to profl. jours. Mem. Am. Acad. Oral and Maxillofacial Radiology, Chinese Assn. Oral and Maxillofacial Radiology. Office: U Iowa Dept OPRM Coll of Dentistry Iowa City IA 52242

YANG, LEE CHHAO YEIGN, osteopath; b. Battambang, Cambodia, June 8, 1965; came to U.S., 1979; s. Phiev Ear and Siem Heng Ly; m. Muzette Ly, July 3, 1994. BA, Calif. State U. Fullerton, 1989; DO, Chgo. Coll. Osteo. Medicine, 1993. Osteopath Mich. Capital Med. Ctr., Lansing. Mem. Am. Osteo. Assn. Office: Mich Capital Med Ctr 2727 Pennsylvania Lansing MI 48910

YANG, RALPH TZU-BOW, chemical engineering educator, researcher; b. Chung King, China, Sept. 18, 1942; came to U.S., 1965, naturalized, 1976; s. Chen Pei and Wei (Gee) Y.; m. Frances H. Chang, Dec. 23, 1972; children—Michael, Robert. BS, Nat. Taiwan U., 1964; MS, Yale U., 1968, PhD, 1971. Rsch. assoc. Argonne Nat. Lab., Ill., 1972-73; sci. Aluminum Co. of Am., Pitts., 1973-74; group leader Brookhaven Nat. Lab., Upton, N.Y., 1974-78; assoc. prof. SUNY-Buffalo, 1978-82, prof., 1982—, chmn. chem. engring. dept., 1990-95; Praxair prof. chem. engring., chair, 1993-95, prof., chmn. chem. engring. dept. U. Mich., 1995—; cons. in field. Author: Gas Separation by Adsorption Processes, 1987. Contbr. articles to profl. jours. Patentee in field. Research grantee NSF, 1980—, Dept. Energy, 1980—, Alcoa Found., 1979-81. Fellow Am. Inst. Chem. Engring. (William H. Walker award for excellence in contbn. to chem. engring. lit., 1991, Inst. award for Excellence in Gases Tech. 1996); mem. Am. Chem. Soc. (Ind. Engring. Chem. Rsch. jour. adv. bd. 1991-93), Am. Carbon Soc. (adv. bd. 1985—), Am. Soc. Engring. Edn., Internat. Adsorption Soc. (adv. bd. Jour. of Adsorption 1993—), Adsorption Sci. and Tech. (adv. bd. 1986—). Office: U Mich Dept Chem Engring Ann Arbor MI 48109

YANG, ROBERT KUO-HOW, pharmaceutical and nutritional product development; b. Shanghai, China, May 25, 1944; children: Stephen, Julie. BS, Chung-Hsing Provincial U., Taichung, Taiwan, 1967; MS, Marquette U., 1972; PhD, SUNY, Buffalo, 1975. Resh. assoc. Hooker Chem. Corp., Grand Island, N.Y., 1975-1978; sr. mgr. Warner-Lambert Co., Morris Plains, N.J., 1978-92; tech. cons. Actimed Labs., Burlington, N.J., 1992—, Fuisz Technologies, Ltd., Chantilly, Va., 1993—; tech. cons. Princeton Separations, Inc., Adelphia, N.J., 1994—, Pacific Inds., Inc., Phila., 1994—. Patentee in field. Com. chmn. Adv. Com. for Minority Advancement, Morris Plains, 1989-92; pres. Christian Testimony, Inc., Morris Plains, 1988-92; mem. Innovation Team, Morris Plains, 1986-87. Lt. with Armed Forces, 1967-68, China. Mem. Am. Chem. Soc. Republican. Home: 14 Northgate Village Burlington NJ 08016 Office: Fuisz Technologies Ste 100 3810 Concorde Parkway Chantilly VA 22021

YANG, WILLIAM, pediatrician, researcher; b. Qingdao, Shandong, China, Mar. 13, 1948; came to U.S., 1962; s. Maurice and Xing-Qing (Wang) Y.; m. Susan Terozita Depoliti, May 5, 1985; children: William Simone Jr., Adrienne C., Stephen C. BA in Math., Chemistry, U. Calif., Irvine, 1969; PhD in Chemistry, U. Ill., Chgo., 1973; MD, U. Chgo., 1976. Diplomate Nat. Bd. Med. Examiners, Am. Bd. Pediatrics. Intern in pediatrics Children's Hosp., Phila., 1976-77, resident in pediatrics, 1977-78, fellow in pediatric endocrinology and metabolism, 1978-81; asst. prof. pediatrics U. Pa., Phila., 1981-82; assoc. dir. clin. investigations research and devel. div. Smith Kline & French, Phila., 1982-84, med. dir. Far East, China, 1985-87; clin. assoc. Childrens Hosp. of Phila., 1982—; assoc. med. dir. research and devel. div. Berlex Labs., Cedar Knolls, N.J., 1984-85; med. dir. Ams., Far East, South Africa internat. div. Smith, Kline & French Labs., Phila., 1988-89; area med. dir. Japan, East Asia Smith Kline Beecham Pharms., Phila., 1989-93; v.p. pharm. devel. Pharmagenesis, Palo Alto, Calif., 1994—. Contbr. articles to profl. jours. Recipient Young Investigator award NIH, 1982. Mem. AMA, Am. Chem. Soc. Home: 370 Sycamore Ave Merion Station PA 19066-1539 Office: Pharmagenesis 3183 Porter Dr Palo Alto CA 94304-1213

YANG, XIAOMING, radiologist; b. Anshan, Liaoning, China, Feb. 7, 1955; arrived in Finland, 1989; s. Jirong and Chunren (Li) Y.; m. Hongxiu Ji, June 24, 1986; children: Kristiina Ou, Karoliina Xue. B Med. Sci., Suzhou (China) Med. Coll., 1983; M Med. Sci., Peking Union Med. Coll., Beijing, China, 1986; PhD, Kuopio (Finland) U., 1991. Med. diplomat, China, Finland. Resident, reschr. Peking Union Med. Coll. Hosp., Beijing, 1983-88; vis. physician Cardiovascular Disease Inst., Beijing, 1987-88; vis. physician, rschr. Loma Linda (Calif.) U. Med. Ctr., 1988-89; resident, rschr. Kuopio U. Hosp., 1989-96; attending physician, docent Kuipio U. Hosp., Finland, 1996—. Contbr. articles to profl. jours. Mem. Cardiovascular and Interventional Radiol. Soc. Europe, European Assn. Radiology, Finnish Med. Assn. Office: Kuopio U Hosp, Dept Clin Radiology PL 1777, FIN70211 Kuopio Finland

YANG, YANG, research scientist; b. Kaohsiung, Taiwan, Nov. 7, 1958; came to U.S., 1985; s. Shun-Wen and Huang-Yin Yang; m. Danmei Lee, May 30, 1987. BS in Physics, Nat. Cheng Kung U., 1982; MS in Physics, U. Mass., 1988, PhD in Physics, 1992. Rsch. asst. U. Mass., Lowell, 1989-91; rsch. assoc. U. Calif., Riverside, 1991-92; rsch. scientist UNIAX Corp., Santa Barbara, Calif., 1992—. Contbr. articles to profl. jours. Mem. Am. Phys. Soc., Material Rsch. Soc. Office: UNIAX Corp 6780 Crotona Dr Santa Barbara CA 93117

YANIV, MOSHE, molecular biology educator; b. Petach-Tikva, Israel, Nov. 7, 1938; arrived in France, 1964; s. Zvi and Haya (Grodensky) Yanishesky; m. Josette Rouviere, Sept. 1969; children: Gil, Karine. MSc, Hebrew U., Jerusalem, 1961; PhD, Paris U., 1969. Prof. molecular biology Inst. Pasteur, Paris, 1987—, head unit, 1976—, chmn. dept. molecular biology, 1985-87, chmn. dept. biotech., 1993-95; vice chmn. Embo Coun., Heidelberg, Germany, 1991-95, chmn., 1996; mem. assembly GM Cancer Rsch. Found., N.Y., 1990-94. Mem. French Acad. Sci. (Charles-Leopold Mayer prize 1995), Academia Europaea. Recipient Rosen prize for Cancerology, Found. Med. Rsch., 1983. Home: 159 Rue Blomet, 75015 Paris France Office: Inst Pasteur, 25 Rue du Docteur Roux, 75724 Paris Cedex 15, France

YANKAUER, ALFRED, physician, educator; b. N.Y.C., Oct. 12, 1913; s. Alfred Sr. and Teresa (Loewy) Y.; m. Marian Wynn, May 22, 1948; children: Kenneth and Douglas (twins). BA, Dartmouth Coll., 1934; MD, Harvard U., 1938; MPH, Columbia U., 1947. Diplomate Am. Bd. Pediatrics, Am. Bd. Preventive Medicine and Pub. Health. Health officer N.Y.C. Dept. Health, 1947-50; asst. commr. of health Rochester (N.Y.) Health Bur., 1950-52; dir. MCH Bur. N.Y. State Dept. Health, Albany, 1952-61; WHO prof. child health Madras (India) Med. Sch., 1957-59; regional advisor Pan-Am. Health Orgn./WHO, Washington, 1961-66; sr. rsch. assoc. Sch. of Pub. Health Harvard U., Boston, 1966-73; prof. family and community health and pediatrics Med. Sch. U. Mass., Worcester, 1973—; asst. prof. health Cornell U. Med. Coll., N.Y.C., 1947-50; med. dir. pediatric nurse practitioner program Mass. Gen.Hosp./Northeastern U. Coll. of Nursing, Boston, 1972-79. Editor Am. Jour. Pub. Health, 1975-90; contbr. over 200 articles to profl. jours. Mem. health adv. com. Pub. Affairs Commn., N.Y.C., 1980-88; bd. dirs. Am. Social Health Commn., Research Triangle Park, N.C., 1984-90, chmn. rsch. adv. com., 1990—. Maj., M.C., U.S. Army, 1941-45, ETO. Fellow Am. Acad. Pediatrics (Jop Lewis Smith award 1979); mem. APHA (Excellence award 1990), Mass. Pub. Health Assn. (Zemuel Shatluck award 1987). Democrat. Office: U Mass Med Ctr 55 Lake Ave N Worcester MA 01655-0309

YANKEE, RONALD AUGUST, health facility administrator; b. Franklin, Mass., May 24, 1934; s. Theodore H. and Georgia C. (Webb) Y. BS, Tufts U., 1956; MD, Yale Med. Sch., 1960. Sr. investigator Nat. Cancer Inst., Bethesda, Md., 1963-74; dir. blood bank Dana Farber Cancer Inst., Boston, 1974-79; med. dir. R.I. Blood Ctr., Providence, 1979—; assoc. prof. Harvard Med. Sch., Boston, 1974-79; prof. medicine Brown U., Providence, 1979—. Office: Rhode Island Blood Ctr 405 Promenade St Providence RI 02908

YANNAS, IOANNIS VASSILIOS, polymer science and engineering educator; b. Athens, Apr. 14, 1935; s. Vassilios Pavlos and Thalia (Sarafoglou) Y.; m. Stamatia Frondistou (div. Oct. 1984); children: Tania, Alexis. AB, Harvard U., 1957; SM, MIT, 1959; MS, Princeton U., 1965, PhD, 1966. Asst. prof. mech. engring. MIT, Cambridge, 1966-68, duPont asst. prof., 1968-69, assoc. prof., 1969-78, prof. polymer sci. and engring. dept. mech. engring., 1978—, prof., dept. materials sci. and engring., 1983—; prof. Harvard-MIT Div. Health Scis. and Tech., Cambridge, 1978—; vis. prof. Royal Inst. Tech., Stockholm, 1974. Mem. editorial bd. Jour. Biomed. Materials Rsch., 1986—, Jour. Materials Sci. Materials Medicine, 1990—, Tissue Engineering, 1994—; contbr. over 100 tech. articles. to profl. jours.; 13 patents in field. Recipient awards for design of first successful artificial skin for treatment of massively burned patients, including Founders award Soc. for Biomaterials, 1982, Clemson award Soc. for Biomaterials, 1992, Fred O. Conley award Soc. Plastics Engrs., 1982, award in medicine and genetics Sci. Digest/Cutty Sark, 1982, Doolittle award Am. Chem. Soc., 1988; fellow Pub. Health Svc., Princeton U., 1963, Shriners Burns Inst., Mass. Gen. Hosp., Boston, 1980-81. Fellow Am. Inst. Chemists, Am. Inst. Med. and Biol. Engrs. (founding mem.), Biomaterials Sci. and Engring.; mem. Inst. Medicine of Nat. Acad. Scis. Office: MIT Bldg 3-334 77 Massachusetts Ave Cambridge MA 02139-4301

YANO, SABURO, health facility adviser; b. Osaka, Japan, May 20, 1928; m. Kimi Morikawa, May 3, 1954; children: Jun-Ichi, Kenji. MD, Osaka U., 1953, PhD, 1959. Assoc. prof. Osaka U. Med. Sch., 1974-76; prof. Toyama (Japan) Med. & Pharm. U., 1976-91; prof. emeritus Toyama (Japan) Med. & Pham. U., 1991—; dir. Toneyama Nat. Hosp., Osaka, 1991-94. Home: 2-18-10 Miyata, Takatsuki 569-11, Japan

YAO, FUN-SUN FRANK, anesthesiologist; b. Changhwa, Taiwan, Feb. 23, 1942; came to U.S., 1972; s. Sui-Lin and Ju-Hsiang (Ko) Y.; m. Baw-Chyr Yao, Nov. 11, 1969; children: Tong-Yi, Ning-Yen, Titania. MD, Nat. Taiwan U. Med. Coll., 1968. Am. Coll. Anesthesiologists, 1975. Resident in surgery Nat. Taiwan U. Hosp., Taipei, 1969-72; surgical intern Maimonides Hosp., Bklyn., 1972-73; resident anesthesia Cornell Med. Ctr. N.Y. Hosp., N.Y.C., 1973-75, fellow anesthesia, 1975-76; instr. anesthesiology Cornell U. Med. Coll., N.Y.C., 1976-77, asst. prof. anesthesiology, 1977-85, assoc. prof. anesthesiology, 1985—; atending anesthesiologist The N.Y. Hosp., N.Y.C., 1983—. Editor Anesthesiology Problem-Oriented Patient Management, 1983, 88, 93. Fellow Am. Coll. Anesthesiologists, N.Y. Acad. Medicine, N.Y. Acad. Sci.; mem. Am. Soc. Anesthesiology, N.Y. Soc. Anesthesiologists, Soc. Cardiovascular Anesthesiologists, Internat. Anesthesia Rsch. Soc. Buddhist. Office: 525 E 68th St New York NY 10021-4873

YAO, GUANGBI, immunologist, hepatologist, research administrator; b. Changshou, Jiangsu, China, Sept. 25, 1931; s. Zhu-jiu Yao and Qi-ya Zhang; m. Qingyi Sun, Oct. 3, 1959; children: Mu, Qian. MD, Shanghai Med. U., People's Republic China, 1954. Dir. Jing An Clin. Immunology Rsch. Ctr. Jin An Qu Cen. Hosp., Shanghai, 1982—. Editor-in-chief Chinese Jour. Digestion, 1991—, Liver, 1996—; editor: Clin. Hepatology, 1959, Advances in Hepatology, 1964, Lectures: Recent Advances in Internal Medicine, 1991, Recent Progress in Liver Disease, 1992. Recipient Model Worker award Shanghai Mcpl. Govt., 1983, Outstanding Scientist award, 1991. Mem. Internat. Assn. Study Liver, Asian Pacific Assn. Study of Liver, Chinese Soc. Internal Medicine (pres. Shanghai br. 1986-95), Chinese Med. Assn. (v.p. Shanghai br. 1985-95), Chinese Soc. Gastroenterology (v.p. 1991—). Office: Jing An Qu Cen Hosp, 259 Xi Kang Rd, Shanghai People's Republic of China 200040

YAO, TITO GO, physician; b. Manila, May 30, 1943; came to U.S., 1970, naturalized, 1984; s. Vicente and Sin Keng (Go) Y.; M.D., Far Eastern U., Manila, 1969; m. Lilia Ytem, July 3, 1976; children—Robert James, Richard. Diplomate Am. Bd. Pediatrics, Am. Bd. Quality Assurance. Intern, Evang. Deaconess Hosp., Milw., 1970-71; resident in pediatrics T.C. Thompson Children's Hosp., Chattanooga, 1971-72, Methodist Hosp., Bklyn., 1972-73; fellow St. Christopher Hosp. Children, Phila., 1973-74, Cook County Children's Hosp., Chgo., 1974-75; dir. GSK Med. Center, Chgo., 1976—, chmn. Loretto Hosp. dept. pediatrics, 1988—; dir. RJ Med. Center, Chgo., 1980—; mem. staff Norwegian Am. Hosp., Loretto Hosp., St. Anthony's Hosp. Fellow Am. Acad. Pediatrics, Am. Coll. Utilization Rev. Physicians; mem. AMA (Physician Recognition award 1973—), Assn. Philippine Physicians Practicing in Am., Ill. Med. Assn., Am. Assn. Individual Investors, Chgo. Med. Soc., Chgo. Pediatric Soc. Office: 5351 W North Ave Chicago IL 60639 also: 5140 W Chicago Ave Chicago IL 60651-2903

YAP, JESUS F., JR., cardiologist; b. The Philippines, May 21, 1944; came to U.S., 1968; s. Jesus N. and Rosalina (Fulay) Y.; m. Nancy L. Moore; children: Rosalina, Robert, Stephen. Student, U. The Philippines, 1964, MD, 1968. Intern St. Peter's Hosp., Albany, N.Y., 1968-69, resident in medicine, 1969-72; fellow in cardiology Norwalk (Conn.) Hosp., 1972-74, chief of echocardiography, 1974-76; attending med. staff St. Joseph Hosp., Stamford, Conn., 1974—, Stamford (Conn.) Hosp., 1974—; chief cardiology St. Joseph Hosp., 1977—, asst. dir. medicine, vice chief of staff, 1994—, dir. Heart Inst., 1995—; clin. instr. medicine N.Y. Med. Coll., N.Y.C., 1975—. Mem. Nat. Rep. Com., Washington, 1989, Conn. Rep. Com., Hartford, 1990. Fellow Am. Coll. Cardiology, Am. Coll. Chest Physicians, Am. Heart Assn., Am. Coll. Angiology; mem. AMA, Fairfield County Med. Assn. Republican. Roman Catholic. Office: Cardiology Assocs 1275 Summer St Stamford CT 06905

YARBOROUGH, MARK ALAN, urologist; b. Wilmington, N.C., Feb. 6, 1957; s. Francis Aubrey Yarborough (dec.) and Doris Felder Rogers; m. Robin Campbell, June 11, 1983; 1 child, Perry Alan. BS, Clemson U., 1979; MD, Med. U. S.C., 1983. Bd. cert. Am. Bd. Urology. Intern U. Ky.; resident U. Ala., Birmingham; chief urology St. Joseph's Hosp., Asheville, N.C., 1991; med. advisor Life After Cancer, Asheville, 1994—; bd. mem. provider com. WNC Health Alliance, Asheville, 1995; sec. Buncombe County Med. Soc., Asheville, 1995. Fellow ACS; mem. AMA, Am. Urol. Assn., N.C. Med. Soc. Episcopalian. Office: Asheville Urol Assocs 1 Doctors Pk Asheville NC 25801

YARBROUGH, KATHRYN DAVIS, public health nurse; b. Montrose, Colo., Aug. 31, 1947; d. L.O. and V. Jean (Dunn) Davis; m. James H. Yarbrough, Aug. 8, 1970; children: James, Jason. Diploma, Good Samaritan Hosp. Sch. Nursing, Phoenix, 1971; BSN, Kennesaw State Coll., 1996. RN, Ga.; cert. NAACOG. Supr. Cherokee County Health Dept., Canton, Ga., 1976—. Den mother Boy Scouts Am., Canton, 1986-87; bd. dirs. Cancer soc., Canton, 1987—, Cherokee County Violence Ctr., 1990, First Steps Bd., 1993—, Cherokee County Advocacy Ctr., 1994—; HIV cons. ARC, Canton, 1988—, disaster vol., Cherokee County, 1993—; co-chair Early Intervention Coun., Canton, 1991-93; mem. Leadership Cherokee, 1994, Interagy Coun., 1994; mem. Blue Ridge Jud. Cir. Domestic Violence Task Force. Mem. Svc. League Cherokee County (hon.). Methodist. Office: Cherokee County Health Dept 1219 Univeter Rd Canton GA 30115-8261

YARBROUGH, MARY GALE, hospital administrator; b. Ellis County, Tex., Feb. 15, 1946; d. Emmitt Ward and Ruthie Lee (McBrayer) McClendon; m. Orville Leon Yarbrough, Feb. 20, 1936; 1 child, Kyle William. B in Nursing, San Jose State U., 1975; M in Sci., U. Calif., 1977. Infection control practitioner VA Hosp., Palo Alto, Calif., 1970-78; dir. nursing O'Connor Hosp., San Jose, Calif., 1978-83; assoc. adminstr. City of Hope Nat. Med. Ctr., Duarte, Calif., 1983-86; exec. v.p., chief ops. officer Mercy Hosp. and Med. Ctr., San Diego, 1986—; clin. faculty UCLA, 1983—, U. Calif., San Francisco, 1978-83, U. San Diego, 1986—. Editor: Infection Control: An Integrated Approach, 1983; author, contributor Contemporary Strategies for Human Resource Mgmt., 1987, Nursing Skills and Evaluation, 1983, APIC Curriculum for Infection Control Practitioner, 1983. Sec., bd. dirs. Arcadia (Calif.) Jr. All Am. Football League, 1984-85. Recipient Tribute to Women in Industry award YWCA, 1987. Mem. Am. Soc. for Nursing Adminstrs., Calif. Soc. for Nursing Service (chmn.), Assn. for Practitioners in Infection Control (pres. 1976). Lodge: Rotary. Office: Mercy Hosp and Med Ctr 4077 5th Ave San Diego CA 92103-2105

YARBROUGH, TERRY PINCKNEY, physician; b. Columbia, S.C., Apr. 2, 1940; s. Dabney Randolph and Frances Horton (Colcock) Y.; m. Alexandra Mayo, Aug. 28, 1965; children: Alexandra, Laurens. MD, Med. Coll. of Va., 1965. Intern U. of Tex. Med. Br., Galveston, 1965-66; resident in internal medicine Med. Coll. Va., Richmond, 1968-71; pvt. practice Internal Medicine of Portsmouth Ltd., 1971—. Capt. USAR, 1966-68. Mem. ACP, Am. Coll. of Cardiology, Coun. Clin. Cardiology, Am. Heart Assn., Am. Soc. of Internal Medicine, Med. Soc. of Va. Episcopalian. Office: Internal Medicine ofPortsmouth Ltd 3300 High Portsmouth VA 23707

YARGER, JAMES GREGORY, chemical company regulatory administrator; b. Waverly, Iowa, Sept. 15, 1951; s. Glen Virgil and Lillian Maxine Yarger; m. Jeannie Rae Van Vickle; children: Benjamin, Jason. BA, U. Iowa, 1974; PhD, Brandeis U., 1981. Notary Public, Ill. Postdoctoral fellow Harvard U., Cambridge, Mass., 1981-83; sr. rsch. scientist Miles Inc., Elkhart, Ind., 1983-87; staff scientist Amoco Tech. Co., Naperville, Ill., 1987-92, sr. rsch. scientist and regulatory affairs officer, 1993-94; mgr. regulatory affairs, quality control and quality sys., 1994-95; dir. quality control-regulatory affairs Cambridge Chem., Inc., Germantown, Wis., 1996—. Contbr. chpts. to books, articles to profl. jours. including Biol. Chemistry, Molecular and Cellular Biology, Devels. in Indsl. Microbiology, Jour. Cell Sci., Poultry Sci. Participant Gov.'s Voluntary Action Program, Ind., 1987; pres. Hunters Woods Homeowners Assn., St. Charles, Ill., 1991, Charlemagne Homeowners Assn., St. Charles, 1992; dep. registrar Kane County, Ill.,1 993-96. Am. Cancer Soc. fellow, 1981-83. Mem. Am. Soc. Quality Control, Regulatory Affairs Profls. Soc., Sigma Xi. Home: W71N391 Cedar Pointe Ave Cedarburg WI 53012 Office: Cambridge Chem Inc N115W 19392 Edison Dr PO Box 67 Germantown WI 53022

YARMOLINSKY, ADAM, educator; b. N.Y.C., Nov. 17, 1922; s. Avrahm and Babette (Deutsch) Y.; m. Harriet Leslie Rypins, 1945 (div. 1981); children: Sarah Franklin, Tobias, Benjamin Levi, Matthew Jonas; m. Jane Cox Vonnegut, 1984 (dec.); m. Sarah Ames Ellis, 1990. AB, Harvard U., 1943; LLB, Yale U., 1948. Bar: N.Y. 1949, D.C. 1952; U.S. Supreme Ct. 1955. Law clk. to Judge C.E. Clark U.S. Ct. Appeals (2d cir.), 1948-49; assoc. Root, Ballantine, Harlan, Bushby & Palmer, N.Y.C., 1949-50; law clk. to Justice Stanley Reed U.S. Supreme Ct., 1950-51; assoc. Cleary, Gottlieb, Friendly & Ball, Washington, 1951-55; dir. Washington office Fund for the Republic, Inc., 1955-56, sec., 1956-57; pub. affairs editor Doubleday & Co., Inc., 1957-59; cons. pvt. founds., 1959-60, spl. asst. sec. of def., 1961-64; dep. dir. Pres.'s. Anti-Poverty Task Force, 1964; chief U.S. Emergency Relief Mission to Dominican Republic, 1965; prin. dep. asst. sec. def. for internat. security affairs, 1965-66; prof. law Harvard U.; mem. inst. politics John F. Kennedy Sch. Govt., 1966-72; (on leave, 1970-72); chief exec. officer Welfare Island Devel. Corp., 1971-72; Ralph Waldo Emerson univ. prof. U. Mass., 1972-77; counselor ACDA, 1977-79; of counsel Fort & Schlefer, Washington, 1979—; prof. policy scis. grad. program U. Md. Balt. County, Balt., 1985-93, acting provost, 1986-87, provost, 1987-93; regents prof. pub. policy U. Md. System, 1993—; lectr. Am. U. Law Sch., 1951-56, Yale U. Law Sch., 1958-59; adj. prof. Georgetown U. Law Ctr., 1984-85; cons. Office Tech. Assessment, 1974-77; mem. gov.'s adv. coun. Mass. Comprehensive Health Planning Agy., 1972-76; nat. adv. com. Inst. for Rsch. on Poverty, 1972-77; mem. Governing Coun. Wye Faculty Seminar; moderator Aspen Inst. Exec. Seminars, 1976—, Troutbeck Ednl. Leadership Program, 1984—, Oxford Aspen Seminars, 1986-89. Author: Recognition of Excellence, 1960, The Military Establishment, 1971, Paradoxes of Power, 1983; editor: Case Studies in Personnel Security, 1955, Race and Schooling in the City, 1980; editor: (with Nicholas Farnham) Rethinking Liberal Education, 1995; spl. corr. The Economist, London, 1956-60; contbr. articles to profl. jours. Trustee Bennington Coll., 1984—, chmn., 1986-88; trustee Robert F. Kennedy Meml., Vera Inst. Justice, 1967—, New Directions Edn. Fund, 1979-82, Ctr. for Nat. Policy, 1984—, Am. Sch. Tangiers, 1979-89, Ocean Rsch. and Edn. Soc., 1980-85, Coalition for Nat. Svc., 1986—, Coun. Econ. Priorities, 1990-93, Hospice Care of D.C., 1990—, vice chair Ind. Sector, 1980-84, 89-95, 96—, chmn. gov. rels. com., 1989-92, vice chmn. bd., 1994-95; trustee Com. for Nat. Security, 1983, chmn. bd., 1986-91; chmn. bd. Lawyers Alliance for World Security, 1995—; trustee PACT, 1995—. Recipient Disting. Pub. Svc. medal Dept. Def., 1966. Fellow Am. Acad. Arts and Scis.; mem. Assn. Bar City of N.Y. (chmn. com. sci. and law 1984-87), Am. Law Inst. (life), Hudson Inst., Internat. Inst. Strategic Studies, Inst. Medicine of NAS (charter mem., coun. 1970-77, com. on human rights 1978-89), Coun. on Fgn. Rels., Century (N.Y.C.), Cosmos (D.C.). Office: UMBC 1000 Hilltop Cir Baltimore MD 21250

YARMUSH, MARTIN LEON, biochemical and biomedical engineering educator; b. Bklyn., Oct. 8, 1952; s. Rubin Wolf and Rosalyn (Mann) Y.; children: Rubin, Gabriel, Joshua. BA, Yeshiva U., 1975; PhD, Rockefeller U., 1979; MD, Yale U., 1984. Assoc. rsch. prof. chem. engring. MIT, Cambridge, 1984-88; prof. biochem. engring., dep. chmn. dept. chem. engring. Rutgers U., Piscataway, N.J., 1988-95; Helen Andrus Benedict prof. surgery and bioengring. Harvard Med. Sch., Boston, 1995—; dir. ctr. engring. medicine Mass. Gen. Hosp., Boston, 1995—; dir. rsch. Boston Shriners Burns Hosp., 1995—; cons. Ortho Diagnostic, Union Carbide, Pharmacia. Recipient nat. rch. svc. award NIH, 1984, rsch. career devel. award, 1989, Presdl. Young Investigator award NSF, 1988, Trustees award for excellence in rsch. Rutgers U., 1992, Hoechst Celanese Innovative Rsch. award, 1993; Lucille P. Markey scholar, 1985, Am. Inst. for Med. and. Biol. Engring. fellow, 1992. Mem. AMA, Am. Chem. Soc., Am. Inst. Chem. Engrs., Am. Assn. Immunologists, Am. Soc. Cell Biology, Am. Soc. for Artificial Internal Organs. Jewish. Office: Mass Gen Hosp Bigelow 1401 55 Fruit St Boston MA 02114

YARYAN, RUBY BELL, psychologist; b. Toledo, Apr. 28, 1938; d. John Sturges and Susan (Bell) Y.; m. John Frederick Buenz, Jr., Dec. 15, 1962 (div. 1968). AB, Stanford U., 1960; PhD, U. London, 1968. Lic. clin. psychologist; diplomate Am. Bd. Psychology. Rsch. dir., univ. radio and tv U. Calif., San Francisco, 1968-70; dir. delinquency coun. U.S. Dep. Justice, Washington, 1970-73; evaluation dir. Office of Criminal Justice Planning, Sacramento, Calif., 1973-76; CAO project mgr. San Diego (Calif.) County, 1977-92; dir. devel. svcs. Childhelp USA, Woodland Hills, Calif., 1992-94; rsch. coord. Neuropsychiat. Inst. and Hosp. UCLA, 1986-87; exec. dir. Centinela Child Guidance Clinic, Inglewood, Calif., 1987-89; clin. dir. Nat. Found. Emotionally Handicapped, North Hills, Calif., 1990-93; pvt. practice Beverly Hills, Calif., 1973—; psychologist Sr. Psychology Svcs., North L.A. County, 1994—; cons. White House Conf. Children, Washington, 1970; mem. Nat. Adv. Com. Criminal Justice Standards and Goals, Washington, 1973; clin. affiliation UCLA Med. Ctr. Contbr. articles to profl. jours.; chpts. to books and monographs in field. Chair Human Svcs. Commn., City of West Hollywood, Calif., 1986; first vice-chair United Way/Western Region, L.A., 1988; mem. planning-allocations-rsch. coun. United Way, San Diego, 1980-82. Grantee numerous fed., state and local govt. orgns. Mem. Am. Psychol. Assn., Western Psychol. Assn., Calif. Psychol. Assn., Am. Orthopsychiat. Assn., Am. Profl. Soc. on Abuse of Children, Phi Beta Kappa. Episcopalian. Office: 337 S Beverly Dr Ste 107 Beverly Hills CA 90212-4307

YASREBI, HOSEIN, surgeon; b. Kashan, Iran, Apr. 28, 1939; came to U.S., 1965; s. Abulhasan and Tooran (Arbab) Y.; m. Kadijeh Darbani, May 18, 1973; children: Leila, Mona, Sara. M.D., U. Tehran, 1964. Intern St. Vincent's Med. Ctr., Jacksonville, Fla., 1965; resident JHEP program in gen. surgery Univ. Hosp. of Jacksonville, 1966-70, now mem. staff; pvt. practice medicine specializing in bariatric surgery, Jacksonville, 1972—; mem. staff Meth. Hosp., Jacksonville, also pres. med. staff, 1991, St. Luke's Hosp., Jacksonville, Meml. Med. Ctr., Jacksonville; asst. clin. prof. U. Fla. Fellow ACS; mem. AMA, Fla. Med. Assn., Southeasrn Surg. Congress. Fellow ACS. Past pres. Islamic Center N.E. Fla. Home: 7078 San Fernando Pl Jacksonville FL 32217-3401

YASUDA, MINEO, anatomy educator; b. Kyoto, Japan, July 8, 1937; s. Minoru and Misao (Mochizuki) Y.; m. Iku Akira, Aug. 25, 1968; children: Kumi, Wakana. MD, Kyoto U., 1962, PhD, 1975. Lic. MD, 1963. Instr. anatomy Faculty Medicine Kyoto U., 1963-71, asst. prof. anatomy, 1971-75; head dept. perinatology Inst. Devel. Rsch. Aichi (Japan) Prefectural Colony, 1975-77; prof. anatomy Sch. Medicine Hiroshima (Japan) U., 1977—. Author: Congenital Malformations, 1974, Modern Trends in Human Genetics, 1975, Clinical Human Embryology, 1983; editor Jour. Congenital Anomalies, 1990—. Mem. Teratology Soc., Internat. Soc. Dvel. Biologists, Japanese Teratology Soc. (pres. 1983, bd. dirs. 1977—), Japanese Assn. Anatomists (councilor 1977—, bd. dirs. 1992—), Japanese Soc. Toxicol. Scis. (councilor 1977—), Japan Soc. Human Genetics (councilor 1987—). Home: 13-20 Yahata 2-chome, Fuchu-cho, Aki-gun 735, Japan Office: Hiroshima U Sch Medicine, 2-3 Kasumi 1-chome Minamiku, Hiroshima 734, Japan

YASUDA, YUZURU, neurologist; b. Kyoto, Japan, May 7, 1949; S. Saburo and Shigeko (Kuriyama) Terada; m. Hiroko Suwa, Jan. 15, 1983; children: Ken, Noriko. MD, Kyoto U., 1983. Bd. cert. diplomate in neurology. Intern Kyoto Univ. Sch. Medicine, 1977-78, Kitano Hosp., Osaka, Japan, 1978-79; sub-chief dept. neurology Kyoto City Hosp., 1983-90; chief dept. neurology Otsu Red Cross Hosp., Japan, 1990—. Author: Neurology, 1986, Journal of Neurology, Neurosurgery and Psychiatry, 1990, European Neurology, 1993, Clinical Neurology and Neurosurgery, 1994. Mem. Japanese Soc. Neurology, Japanese Soc. Internal Medicine, Japanese Soc. Neuropathology. Home: 62-4 Takenokaido-cho, Takehana Yamashina-ku Kyoto 607, Japan Office: Otsu Red Cross Hosp, Dept Neurology, 1-1-35 Nagara, Otsu 520, Japan

YATES, HARRY ROBERT, JR., internist; b. Roanoke, Va., Sept. 21, 1926; s. Harry Robert and Edith Marrion (Davis) Y.; m. Mary Stewart Gills, Sept. 4, 1948; children: Anne Leigh (Yates) Farmer, Susan Davis (Yates) Claytor, Harry R. III. BA, U. Va., 1947, MD, 1951. Diplomate Am. Bd. Internal Medicine. Chief of medicine Roanoke (Va.) Meml. Hosp., 1965-68, chief of staff, 1968-69; assoc. clin. prof. medicine U. Va., 1970-90. Lt. USNR, 1953-54. Fellow Am. Coll. of Physicians; mem. Am. Soc. Gastrointestinal Endoscopy, Norfolk So. Physicians Assn., AMA, Med. Soc. Va. Republican. Presbyterian. Home: 2812 Rosalind Ave SW Roanoke VA 24014-3218

YATES, JAMES ARTHUR, plastic surgeon; b. Butler, Pa., June 5, 1935; s. Adolph Walter and Laura Marie (De Foggie) Y.; m. Debra Lynne Stringer, June 19, 1983; 1 child, Jamie Dale Yates Reynolds. BA, Cornell U., 1956; MD, U. Md., Balt., 1960. Diplomate Am. Bd. Plastic Surgery, Nat. Bd. Med. Examiners, Am. Bd. Surgery; lic. physician, Pa., Ohio, R.I. Intern Cleve. Clinic Hosp., 1960-61, resident in gen. surgery, 1961-62; resident in gen. surgery U. Pitts. Med. Ctr., 1963-65; resident in plastic surgery R.I. Hosp., 1966-67, chief resident, 1967-68; pvt. practice Plastic Surg. Ctr. Ltd., Camp Hill, Pa., 1968—; teaching fellow gen. surgery U. Pitts. Med. Ctr., 1963-65, instr. gen. surgery, 1965-66; clin. instr. plastic surgery Milton S. Hershey (Pa.) Med. Ctr., 1968—; staff maxillofacial and plastic surgery dept. Harrisburg (Pa.) Hosp., 1968—; chief plastic and aesthetic surgery dept. Holy Spirit Hosp., Camp Hill, 1968—; staff Polyclinic Med. Ctr., Harrisburg, 1968—, Seidle Meml. Hosp., Mechanicsburg, Pa., Cmty. Gen. Osteo. Hosp., Harrisburg, Mechanicsburg Rehab. Hosp., Carlisle (Pa.) Hosp.; med. dir. Grandview Surgery and Laser Ctr., Camp Hill; cons. Harrisburg State Hosp.; physician surveyor Am. Assn. Ambulatory Health Care, Am. Assn. for Ambulatory Plastic Surgery; physician trainer plastic surgery residency program Am. Coll. Osteo. Surgery. Contbr. articles to profl. jours.; adv. bd. Town and Country Mag. Police commr. West Shore Regional Police Dept.; mem. credentialling com. Keystone Health Plan; mem. task force on ambulatory surgery Pa. Dept. Health;mem. coun. Lemoyne (Pa.) Borough Coun., v.p.; credentialing officer Freedom Health Care HMO. Fellow ACS; mem. AMA, Pa. Med. Soc., Am. Burn Assn., Am. Soc. Plastic and Reconstructive Surgeons, Am. Burn Victim Found., Am. Soc. Aesthetic Plastic Surgery, Vail Cosmetic Surgery Soc., Pa. Plastic Surgery Soc., Am. Soc. Automobile Medicine, Northeastern Soc. Plastic Surgeons, Royal Soc. Medicine, Lipolysis Soc. N.Am., Internat. Soc. Clin. Plastic Surgeons, South Ctrl. Pa. Regional Med. Dirs., Am. Coll. Physician Execs. Republican. Roman Catholic. Home: 833 Kiehl Dr Lemoyne PA 17043 Office: Plastic Surgery Ctr Ltd 205 Grandview Ave Camp Hill PA 17011

YATES, RALPH A., physician; b. Waukegan, Ill., May 11, 1948; s. Torbin F. and Florence G. (Olson) Y.; m. Laurie Yates, Oct. 16, 1971; children: Trevor A., Rebecca A. BS, U.S. Coast Guard Acad., 1970; DO, Kirksville Coll. Osteopathic, 1979. Diplomate Am. Coll. Osteopathic Family Physician; certificate of added qualification in sports medicine. Attending physician Beaumont Family Medical Clinic, Portland, Oreg., 1980-90, Columbia Family Medical Assocs., Portland, Oreg., 1990—, Multi Sport Medicine Inc., Portland, Oreg., 1986—; clinical instr. dept. family medicine Oreg. Health Sci. Univ., Portland, Oreg., 1994—; clinical asst. prof. family medicine Coll. Osteopathic Medicine of the Pacific, Pamona, Calif., 1980—; team physician Portland Winter Hawks World Jr. Profl. Hockey, Portland, 1986—, Portland Rage Roller Hockey Internat., Portland, 1994—, Portland Lightening Bolts Spring Football League, Portland, 1991. Editor: Oregon Cycling, 1985—; columnist Oregon Distance Runner, 1985—. Physician bd. mem. Am. Diabetes Assn., Portland, 1985-86; co-chmn. Lewis & Clark Chpt. ADA, 1996. With USCG, 1970-75. Nat. judge for Schering Asthma Athlete Scholarship program, 1990-92. Mem. Am. Coll. Osteopathic Family Physicians, Am. Coll. Sports Medicine, Am. Medical Soc. Sports Medicine, Am. Osteopathic Assn., Multnomax County Medical Soc., Oreg. Medical Assn., Am. Diabetes Assn., Osteopathic Physicians/Surgeons Oreg., Sigma Sigma Phi. Office: 3510 NE 122nd Ste 201 Portland OR 97230

YATES, TOMMY EUGENE, pathologist; b. Newton, Miss., Nov. 6, 1963; s. Norman Eugene and Patsy Ann (Truhitt) Y.; m. Shannon Jackson, Sept. 6, 1986; children: Thomas J., Madison Nicole. BS in Med. Tech., U. So. Miss., 1985; DO, W.Va. Sch. Osteo. Medicine, 1993. Med. tech. Med. Path Lab, Meridian, Miss., 1987-89; intern U. South Ala. Med. Ctr., Mobile, 1994-95, resident in anatomic and clin. pathology, 1995—. Soccer coach Daphne (Ala.) Youth Soccer, 1993—; coach Daphne Youth Baseball, 1995—. Present Day Club scholar, 1981. Mem. AMA, Coll. Am. Pathologists (mem. stds. com. 1995-96), Am. Acad. Forensic Scis., Am. Soc. Clin. Pathologists. Republican. Baptist. Home: 121 Michael Loop Daphne AL 36526 Office: U South Ala Med Ctr Pathology Dept 2451 Fillingin St Mobile AL 36617

YATES, WILLIAM ALBERT, physician, hospital administrator; b. Ottawa, Ont., Can., Nov. 16, 1929; came to U.S., 1954; s. John Frederick and Mary Edna Irene (Stedman) Y.; m. Patricia Eileen Ellis, Aug. 23, 1953; children: Jeffrey, Donald, Cynthia, Scott. MDCM, Queen's Coll., Kingston, Ont., 1954. Diplomate Am. Bd. Surgery. Internship Conemaugh Valley Meml. Hosp., Johnstown, Pa., 1954-55; residency in gen. surgery Mercy Hosp., Pitts., 1955-59; chmn. dept. surgery Lee Hosp., Johnstown, Pa., 1959-88, v.p. med. affairs, 1988—, med. dir. occupational health, 1990-96; ret., 1996. Chmn. United Fund, Johnstown, 1976. Flight lt. RCAF, 1950-53. Fellow ACS. Republican. Home: 305 Resty Ct Johnstown PA 15905-1643

YATES, ZOLA LYNNE, psychiatric and mental health nurse practitioner; b. Keokuk, Iowa, Dec. 16, 1939; d. Robert William and Kathryn Caralyn

(Schneider) Y. Diploma, Christ Hosp. Sch. Nursing, Cin., 1961; BSN, U. Cin., 1965, MSN, 1967. RN, Ohio; cert. psychiat./mental health nurse practitioner. Instr. U. Cin. Coll. Nursing, 1967-72, Bethesda Hosp. Sch. Nursing, Cin., 1972-74; supr. psychiat. nursing VA Med. Ctr., Cin., 1974-75; dir. nursing edn. U. Cin. Hosp., 1975-79; dir. nursing svc. Glades Gen. Hosp., Belle Glade, Fla., 1979-84; asst. dir. psychiat. nursing U. Tex. Med. Br., Galveston, 1986-87; dir. quality assurance/risk mgmt. Cypress Creek Hosp., Houston, 1987-89; clin. specialist Starbranch Psychiatry Assocs., Houston, 1990-91; psychiat./mental health nurse practitioenr Douglas County Health Dept., Roseburg, Oreg., 1993—; pvt. practice Valley View Counseling, Roseburg, 1993—; cons. nursing adminstrn., Houston, 1992, cons. nursing insvc. edn., Houston, 1992; clin. preceptor advanced nursing practice Tex. Women's U., Houston, 1991. Mem. Assn. Advanced Practice Psychiatry Nurses, Douglas County Assn. Nurse Practitioners. Democrat. Episcopalian. Home: 1348 SE Court Roseburg OR 97470 Office: Valley View Counseling 1701 W Harvard Roseburg OR 97470

YATES-BUCKLES, JEANNETTE KEBER, prosthodontics educator; b. Hackensack, N.J., Dec. 22, 1942; d. Richard Sigmund and Jeannette Ida (Zweil) Keber; m. Edward Scott Yates, Mar. 18, 1961 (div. June 1979); m. Kenneth Peter Buckles, Oct. 17, 1987; children: Darlene Denise, Edward Scott Jr. A. Applied Sci., Union Coll., 1972; student, Fairleigh Dickinson U., 1972-74; DMD, U. Dentistry and Medicine N.J., Newark, 1977. Postgrad. resident Mt. Sinai Hosp., N.Y.C., 1977-78; assoc. dentist Wayne (N.J.) Dental Group, 1978, Fairfield (N.J.) Dental Group, 1978-79; pvt. practice dentistry Hackensack, 1979—; assoc. prof. prosthodontics Fairleigh Dickinson U. Dental Sch., Teaneck, N.J., 1979-90; attending dentist Hackensack Med. Ctr., 1979-89. Fellow Acad. Gen. Dentistry (award 1987); mem. N.J. Women Dentists Study Group (v.p. 1980-82), N.J. Network Bus. and Profl. Women (v.p. 1985-87, bd. dirs. 1984-92). Republican. Scientologist. Office: 67 Summit Ave Hackensack NJ 07601-1262

YATSU, FRANK M., neurologist, educator; b. L.A., Nov. 28, 1932; s. Frank K. and Helen Amano Yatsu; m. Michiko Y., Sept. 10, 1955; 1 child, Carolyn E. AB, Brown U., 1955; MD, Case-Western Res. U., 1959. Intern Univ. Hosp., Cleve., 1959-60, resident in medicine, 1960-61; resident in neurology Neurol. Inst., N.Y.C., 1961-63; fellow in neurology Albert Einstein Coll. Medicine, N.Y.C., 1964-65; from asst. to assoc. prof. neurology U. Calif., San Francisco, 1967-75; chair dept. neurology Oreg. Health Scis. Ctr., Portland, Oreg., 1975-82; chair dept. neurology U. Tex., Houston, 1982-95, chair emeritus, 1995—, prof. dept. neurology, 1995—; chair neurology program project com. NIH, Bethesda, 1969-74. Mem. editl. bd. Neurology, Stroke, Annals of Neurology, 1971—. Lt. comdr. USN, 1965-67. Fellow Am. Acad. Neurology (mem. legis. com. Mpls. 1978-92); mem. Am. Neurol. Assn. (councilor), World Fedn. Neurology (mem. nominating com.). Office: U Tex Dept Neurology 6431 Fannin St Houston TX 77030

YATSUSHIRO, GUY NATHAN, internist, geriatrician, educator; b. Honolulu, May 5, 1953; s. Yasu O. and Yuriko Yatsushiro; m. Patricia Lane. BA, U. Hawaii, 1976, MD, 1980. Diplomate Am. Bd. Internal Medicine, Am. Bd. Geriatrics. Asst. prof. medicine U. Hawaii, Honolulu, 1994—. Mem. AMA, ACP, Am. Soc. Internal Medicine. Office: 1914 S King St Ste 201 Honolulu HI 96826

YAU, EDWARD TINTAI, toxicologist, pharmacologist; b. Canton, China, Dec. 29, 1944; came to U.S., 1967; s. Wing S. and Fong K. (Wong) Y.; m. Assumpta Koo, July 3, 1979; 1 child, Jonathan C. BS in Biology, Bapt. Coll., Hong Kong, 1967; PhD in Pharmacology, U. Miss., 1974. Diplomate Am. Bd. Toxicology. Postdoctoral fellow, then asst. prof. Purdue U., West Lafayette, Ind., 1974-77; toxicology supr. Wyeth Labs., Great Valley, Pa., 1977-79; sr. toxicologist CIBA-GEIGY Corp., Summit, N.J., 1979-82, mgr., 1982-86, asst. dir., 1986-88, dir., 1988-92, exec. dir., 1993—; adj. prof. U. Miss., Oxford, 1989-92, 95—. Contbr. articles to sci. publs. Recipient NSF award, 1970. Mem. Am. Chem. Soc., Am. Coll. Toxicology, Soc. Toxicology, Teratology Soc., Sigma Xi. Republican. Baptist. Home: 67 Grant Ave Clifton NJ 07011-3522 Office: CIBA-GEIGY Corp 556 Morris Ave Summit NJ 07901-1330

YAU, KING-WAI, neuroscientist, educator; b. Canton, Kwangtung, China, Oct. 27, 1948; came to U.S., 1968; s. Tin-Man and Wai-Hing (Chan) Y.; m. Crystal Lin, Dec. 27, 1975; children: Emily, Jason. AB, Princeton U., 1971; PhD, Harvard U., 1976. Rsch. assoc. Stanford (Calif.) U., 1976-79, Cambridge (Eng.) U., 1979-80; from asst. prof. to prof. U. Tex. Med. Br., Galveston, 1980-86; prof. neurosci. Johns Hopkins Sch. Medicine, Balt., 1986—; investigator Howard Hughes Med. Inst., Balt., 1986—. Recipient Rank prize in optoelectronics, London, 1980, Rsch. Career Devel. award NIH, 1981-86, Merit award, 1992-96, Alcon Rsch. Inst. award, 1996. Mem. Soc. Neurosci., Soc. Gen. Physiologists, Assn. Rsch. Vision and Opthalmology (Friedenwald award 1993), Biophys. Soc., Physiol. Soc. (U.K.). Office: Johns Hopkins U Sch Med 725 N Wolfe St Baltimore MD 21205-2105

YAWATA, YOSHIHITO, hematologist, oncologist educator; b. Kamakura, Kanagawa, Japan, Feb. 7, 1936; s. Yoshio and Chieko (Kawaguchi) Y.; m. Ayumi Takinami; children: Makoto, Masami. MD, Yokohama U., Japan, 1961; PhD, U. Tokyo, Japan, 1967. Bd. cert. in internal medicine, hematology/oncology. Clin. fellow U. Tokyo, Japan, 1962-64, rsch. fellow, 1964-69; rsch. specialist UCLA, 1969-71; rsch. fellow U. Minn., Mpls., 1971-72, asst. prof., 1972-74; assoc. prof. Kawasaki Med. Sch., Kurashiki, Japan, 1974-77, prof. medicine, 1977—; com. mem. Idiopathic Disorders of Hematopoietic Organs for Japanese Ministry of Health and Welfare, 1974—; prin. investigator Japan-France Coop. Study by Japan Soc. for Promotion of Sci., 1992-94. Author: Red Cell Enzymology, 1963-70, Red Cell Membrane Researches, 1971—; mem. editorial bd. Jour. of Lab. and Clin. Medicine; editor-in-chief Kawasaki Med. Jour. Grantee Japanese Ministry of Edn., Sci. and Culture, 1970—. Mem. Am. Soc. Hematology, Internat. Soc. Hematology, Am. Fedn. Clin. Rsch., Japan Soc. Hematology, Japan Soc. Clin. Hematology, Japanese Soc. Internal Medicine. Home: 1342-343 Nishisaka, Kurashiki 70101, Japan Office: Kawasaki Med Sch, 577 Matsushima, Kurashiki 70101, Japan

YAZDI, NASSER NADOSHANI, pediatrician; b. Tehran, Iran, Mar. 21, 1929; s. Mohammad and Akram (Barzin) Y.; m. Shirin Laleh, Feb. 12, 1968; 1 child, Reza Nadoshani. BSc, McPherson Coll., Kans., 1956; MD, U. West Berlin, Germany, 1960. Diplomate Am. Bd. Pediatrics. Pediatric resident Allegheny Gen. Hosp., Pitts., 1961, St. Francis Hosp., Pitts., 1961-62, Children's Meml. Hosp., Chgo., 1962-63; fellow in pediatric allergy Children's Asthma Rsch. Inst. and Hosp., Denver, 1963-65; pvt. practice pediatrics and allergy Tehran, 1965—; med. inspector Ministry of Labour, Tehran, 1965-74; shareholder, gen. mgr. Tehran Med. Ctr. for Children, 1970—, lectr. in allergy/immunology to date. Author: Change of Haemoglobene, 1956. Mem. AMA, Am. Acad. Allergy, Denver Med. Assn., Iranian Soc. Pediatrics, Med. Coun. of Islamic Republic of Iran. Muslim. Office: 849 Enghelab Ave, 15916 Tehran Iran

YAZICI, HASAN, rheumatologist, educator; b. Istanbul, Turkey, Mar. 22, 1945; s. Bedi and Muzehher (Torun) Y.; m. Berrin Karaogul, June 12, 1969; children: Yusuf, Hakan, Emin. MD, U. Istanbul, 1969. Diplomate in internal medicine and rheumatology Am. Bd. Internal Medicine. Intern Albert Einstein Hosp., Phila., 1979-70; resident in medicine U. Nebr., Omaha, 1970-72; resident in medicine, fellow in rheumatology Creighton U., Omaha, 1972-74; dozent, chief div. rheumatology Cerrahpasa Med. Faculty, U. Istanbul, 1978-88, prof., chief divsn. rheumatology, 1988—; gen. sec. European League Against Rheumatism, Zurich, 1995—; mem. exec. com. med. scis. div. Sci. and Tech. Rsch. Coun. Turkey, Ankara, 1990-94. Co-editor: Vasculitides, 1995; mem. editorial bd. Clin. and Exptl. Rheumatology, 1988—; occasional newspaper columnist; contbr. chpt. to book, articles to profl. jours. Lt. Turkish Army, 1976. Mem. Turkish Acad. Scis. (coun. 1995—), Brit. Soc. for Rheumatology, Soc. for Rsch. and Edn. in Rheumatology of Turkey (founding mem., pres. 1994—). Home: Safa Sok 17/4, 81310 Istanbul Turkey Office: Cerrahpasa Med Faculty, Aksarzy, 34303 Istanbul Turkey

YAZIGI, ROBERTO FERNANDO, obstetrician-gynecologist; b. Santiago, Chile, Apr. 10, 1947; s. Roberto D. Yazigi and Margarita R. Id; m. Myriam S. Waissbluth, July 10, 1977; children: Viviana, Carolina. MD, Cath. U., Santiago, Chile, 1972; degree in ob-gyn., Roswell Park Meml. Inst., Buffalo, 1978. Bd. cert. in ob-gyn., bd. cert. gynecologic oncology. Tchg. fellow Harvard Med. Sch., Boston, 1973-76; asst. prof. U. Catolica, Santiago, 1978-82, 85-86, Harvard Med. Sch., Boston, 1983-84; assoc. prof. U. Tex., Dallas, 1986-91; pvt. practice Clinica Las Condes, Santiago, 1991—; head gynecol. oncology U. Tex., Dallas, 1986-91, dir. gynecol. oncology fellowship program, 1987-91; head gynecol. oncology Clinica Las Condes, Santiago, 1991—, dir. ob-gyn., 1995—. Co-author: Textbook of Gynecology, 1984, Manual of Gynecological Oncology and Gynecology, 1989, Basic Gynecology of Obstetrics, 1993, (supplement) Williams Obstetrics, 1990. Gynecology Oncology fellow Harvard U., 1976. Fellow ACOG, Soc. Gynecologic Oncology. Home: Cerro Las Arañas 12383, La Dehesa Santiago, Chile Office: Clinica Las Condes, Lo Fontecilla 441, Santiago Chile

YAZULLA, STEPHEN, neurobiology educator; b. Jersey City, Sept. 3, 1945; s. Stephen Sr. and Elsie Alvina (Smith) Y.; m. Margaret Ann Stanley, Apr. 23, 1983; children: Lisa, Debra; stepchildren: Caroline, Marie. BS in Psychology, U. Scranton, Pa., 1967; MA in Psychology, U. Del., 1969, PhD in Psychology, 1971. Postdoctoral fellow U. Del., Newark, 1971-72, Harvard U., Cambridge, Mass., 1972-74; asst. prof. SUNY, Stony Brook, 1974-79, assoc. prof., 1979-86, prof., 1986—; vis. prof. Nat. Netherlands Acad. of Arts and Scis., 1996; mem. study sect. divsn. rsch. grants NIH, Bethesda, Md., 1985-90, mem. res. rev. bd., 1990—; dir. Electron Microscopy Facilities, SUNY, 1986—. Author chpts. in books; mem. editorial bd. Visual Neurosci., 1990-92, assoc. editor, 1993—; mem. editorial bd. Jour. Neurocytology, 1992—; contbr. numerous articles to profl. jours. NIH fellow U. Del./Harvard U., 1971-74; grantee NIH, 1976—, NSF, 1990-92. Mem. Assn. Rsch. in Vision and Ophthalmology, Internat. Brain Rsch. Orgn., N.Y. Acad. SCis., Soc. for Neurosci., Sigma Xi. Republican. Roman Catholic. Office: SUNY Stony Brook Dept Neurology Stony Brook NY 11794

YEAGER, CLIFFORD A., health facility administrator; b. Granite City, Ill., July 23, 1953; s. Carl E. and Lula M. (Barnestable) Y.; m. Cheryl D. Mahurin, July 13, 1979; children: Jason, Christopher. BSN, So. Ill. U., 1979, MBA, 1988. RN, Mo. Nurse St. Mary's Hosp.s, East St. Louis, Mo., 1982-83, Lucy Lee Hosp., Poplar Bluff, Mo., 1983-86; ancillary group mgr. Lucy Lee Hosp., 1986-87, chief operating officer, 1987-93; chief operating officer Columbia (Mo.) Regional Med. Ctr., 1993-94; CEO Twin Rivers Regional Med. Ctr., Kennett, Mo., 1994—. Office: Twin Rivers Regional Med Ctr 1301 1st St Kennett MO 63857

YEAGER, JOSEPH CORNELIUS, consulting psychologist, behavioral researcher; b. Pitts., Jan. 5, 1940; s. Joseph Jacob and Elizabeth Zane (Singleton) Y.; m. Linda Dianne Sommer, Sept. 1, 1983; children: Rachel, Benjamin, Jerimiah. BA, Thiel Coll., 1963; MS, U. Pitts., 1967, PhD, 1969. Dir. human resource devel. USAIR, Pitts., 1964-70; dir. profl. pers. ETS, Princeton, N.J., 1970-74; internal cons. Pfizer Co., N.Y.C., 1974-84; pres. Linguistechs, New Hope, Pa., 1981—. Author: Thinking about Thinking, 1985, The Goal Strategy Book, 1990, What They Didn't Teach Sales 101, 1990, (video) Psychology of Friendly Persuasion, 1984. Recipient Martin Luther King award Music and Arts Soc., Pitts., 1974. Mem. APA, Am. Psychol. Soc., Human Factors Soc. Office: Linguistechs Luxembourg Ctr 503 Corporate Dr Langhorne PA 19047

YEAGER, LEONA BRANDES, physician, educator; b. Manville, Ill., June 24, 1908; d. Alberta and Augusta (Irrgang) Brandes; m. Edwin Macy Yeager, June 20, 1936; children: Georgia, Jans. BA, North Central Coll., 1929; MA, Northwestern U., 1943, MD, 1944. Diplomate Am. Bd. Internal Medicine. Dir. student health Northwestern U., Evanston, Ill., 1946-77; prof. clin. medicine Northwestern U., Evanston, 1970-77, emeritus prof. clin. medicine, 1977—; sr. physician Evanston Twp. Hosp., 1946-77, emeritus physician, 1977—; attending physician Cook County Hosp., Chgo., 1946-77. Contbr. articles to profl. jours. Pres. Sun City (Ariz.) Area Interfaith, 1985, Sun City Interfaith Services Aux., 1987—; dir. Coll. Health Nurse Practitioner Program, Evanston, 1975-79; alumni regent Northwestern U., 1986-89. Recipient Disting. Alumnus award North Cen. Coll., 1963. Fellow Am. Coll. Health Assn. (pres. 1964, Hitchcock award 1970, Boynton award 1976); mem. AMA, Inst. of Medicine, Geriatric Soc., Nat. Conf. on Aging, Sun Cities Physician Club (pres. 1989-90). Clubs: Lakes (Sun City); Mich. Shores (Wilmette, Ill.). Home: 10606 W Emerald Pt Sun City AZ 85351-2742

YEATTS, DOROTHY ELIZABETH FREEMAN, nurse, retired county official, educator; b. Richmond, Va., Jan. 19, 1925; d. Robert Franklin and Elizabeth Bell (Wiggins) Freeman; m. Roy Earl Yeatts, Nov. 27, 1948; children: Martha Jane Yeatts Couch, Robert Patrick. Diploma in nursing, Stuart Circle Hosp., Richmond, Va., 1947; BS in Nursing, Coll. William and Mary, 1947; cert. pub. health nursing supr., U. N.C., 1974. RN, Va., N.C. Vis. nurse Instructive Vis. Nurses Assn., Richmond, 1947-49; maternity nurse N.C. Bapt. Hosp., Winston-Salem, 1969-71; pub. health nurse I. Forsyth County Health Dept., Winston-Salem, 1971-72, pub. health nurse coord., 1972-74, pub. health nurse supr., 1974-78; instr. ARC, Winston-Salem, 1978-93; vol. Am. Red Cross, 1993—. Pres. Buckingham Park Garden Club, Richmond, 1956-58; elder Trinity Presbyn. Ch., Winston-Salem, 1978-81, Sunday sch. tchr., 1960-84, circle bible moderator, 1984—; bd. dirs. Forsyth Cancer Soc., Winston-Salem, 1980-86; vol. ARC. Republican. Home: 703 Devon Ct Winston Salem NC 27104-1269

YEE, AMY SUMEI, educator; b. San Francisco, Sept. 22, 1958; d. Robert Shee Hong and Sim Kuen (Wong) Y.; m. K. Eric Paulson, July 7, 1984; 1 child, Christopher. AB in Biochemistry, U. Calif., Berkeley, 1980; PhD in Biochemistry, U. Calif., Davis, 1985. Postdoctoral fellowship molecular cell biology Rockefeller U., 1986-89; assoc. Howard Hughes Med. Inst., 1989; asst. prof. Tufts U. Sch. Medicine, Boston, 1990—; guest investigator Rockefeller U., 1989; NIH reviewer, 1994. Contbr. articles to profl. jours. Recipient Alumni scholarship U. Calif., Berkeley, 1976-78, Jastro-Shields Grad. fellowship U. Calif., Davis, 1981-83, 84-85, NIH Tng. grant U. Calif., Davis, 1982-83, Michael Swackhammer Rsch. fellowship U. Calif., Davis, 1984, Am. Cancer Soc. Postdoctoral fellowship Rockefeller U., 1986-89; recipient Am. Cancer Soc. Jr. Faculty Rsch. award Tufts U., 1991-94, Established Investigator award Am. Heart Assn., 1996. Mem. Am. Soc. Biochemistry and Molecular Biology. Office: Tufts Univ Sch Medicine 136 Harrison Ave Boston MA 02111-1800*

YEE, DARLENE, gerontological health educator; b. N.Y.C., Sept. 19, 1958; d. Jimmy Tow and Yuen Hing (Chin) Y. BA in Biology, Barnard Coll., 1980; MS in Gerontology, Coll. New Rochelle, 1981; MS in Health Edn., Columbia U., 1984, EdD in Health Edn., 1985. Cert. Nat. Commn. Health Edn. Asst. dir. biology lab. Barnard Coll., N.Y.C., 1980-83; rsch. assoc. safety rsch. and edn. project Columbia U. Tchrs. Coll., N.Y.C., 1983-85; asst. prof. health and phys. edn. York Coll., N.Y.C., 1985-88; cons. Transp. Rsch. Bd., NAS, Washington, 1987, N.Y. State Dept. Edn., Albany, 1987, U.S. Dept. Edn., Washington, 1991; assoc. prof. clin. gerontology health edn. and promotion U. Tex. Med. Br., Galveston, 1988-90; assoc. prof. health edn. San Francisco State U., 1990-93; prof. health edn., 1994-95; prof. gerontology San Francisco State U., 1995—. Contbr. articles to profl. jours. Mem. Am. Coll. Health Care Adminstrs., Gerontol. Soc. Am., Am. Soc. on Aging, Assn. for Advancement Health Edn., Nat. Coun. on Aging, Sigma Xi. Home: 40 Meadow Park Cir Belmont CA 94002-2947 Office: San Francisco State U Gerontology Programs 20 Tapia Dr San Francisco CA 94132-1717

YEE, ROBERT DONALD, ophthalmologist; b. Peking, China, Feb. 21, 1945; came to U.S., 1947, naturalized, 1947; s. James and Marian Y.M. (Li) Y.; m. Linda Margaret Neil, June 28, 1968; children—Jillian Neil, Allison Betram. A.B., Harvard U., 1966, M.D., 1970. Diplomate Am. Bd. Ophthalmology. Intern, U. Rochester, N.Y., 1970-71; resident in ophthalmology Jules Stein Eye Inst., UCLA, 1971-74; fellow in neuro-ophthalmology Nat. Eye Inst., Bethesda, Md., 1974-76; chief ophthalmology Harbor-UCLA Med. Ctr., Torrance, Calif., 1976-80; asst. prof. ophthalmology Sch. Medicine, UCLA, 1976-78, assoc. prof., 1978-82, prof., 1982-87; prof., chmn. dept. ophthalmology Ind. U. Sch. Medicine, Indpls., 1987—. Mem. editorial bd. Investigative Ophthalmology and Visual Sci., 1982—, von Graefe's Archives of Ophthalmology, 1983-89. Author numerous med. research papers. Served as lt. comdr. USPHS, 1974-75. Fulbright scholar, 1966; NIH grantee, 1976—; Dolly Green Research scholar, 1984-86; Feldman endowed chair ophthalmology UCLA, 1984-87. Fellow ACS, Am. Ophthal. Soc., Am. Acad. Ophthalmology; mem. Assn. Rsch. in Ophthalmology and Vision (chmn. eye movement sect. 1981, 87, trustee 1996—), Ind. Acad. Opthalmology, Chinese Am. Ophthal. Soc. (pres. 1996—), Ind. Med. Soc., Indpls. Ophthal. Soc., Phi Beta Kappa, Alpha Omega Alpha. Office: Ind U Med Ctr 702 Rotary Cir Indianapolis IN 46202-5133

YEE, THOMAS, neurologist; b. Hong Kong, May 10, 1960; came to U.S., 1969; s. Gin Ying and Siu Ching (Yiu) Y. BS in Physiology, U. Calif., Davis, 1983; DO, Coll. Osteo. Med. The Pacific, Pomona, Calif., 1987. Diplomate Am. Bd. Electrodiagnostic Medicine, Am. Bd. Psychiatry and Neurology. Intern Wilson Meml. Hosp., Johnson City, N.Y., 1987-88, resident, 1988; resident U. Calif.-Davis, Martinez, 1989-92, fellow in neurology, 1992-93, fellow in clin. neurophysiology, 1993-94; fellow in neuromuscular Calif. Pacific Med. Ctr., San Francisco, 1994-95; cons. Merced (Calif.) Cmty. Med. Ctr., 1993—, VA Palo Alto (Calif.) Health Care Sys., 1996—. Contbr. articles to profl. jours. Mem. Am. Osteo. Assn., Am. Acad. Neurology, Am. Assn. Electrodiagnostic Medicine, Am. Clin. Neurophysiology Soc., ARC, Pi Mu Epsilon, Phi Kappa Phi. Office: VA Palo Alto Health Care Sys Neurology 127 3801 Miranda Ave Palo Alto CA 94304

YEN, JENG HSIEN, physician, educator; b. Yuen-Lin County, Republic of China, Oct. 3, 1956; s. Wan Ting and Yu Chih (Chen) Y.; m. Shu Jui Hu, May 10, 1991; 2 children. MD, Kaosuing (Taiwan) Med. Coll., Republic of China, 1983, MSc, 1988, PhD, 1996. Chief resident Kaohsuing Med. Coll., 1986-87, vis. staff mem., 1987—, lectr., 1988-96, asst. prof., 1996—. Recipient Outstanding Paper award R&D Found. of Immunology, 1990, 91, Rotary Internat., 1990. Mem. Rheumatology Assn. Republic of China, Soc. Internal Medicine Republic of China, Chinese Soc. Immunology. Office: Kaosuing Med Coll, 100 Shih-Chuan 1st Rd, 807 Kaohsuing Taiwan Republic of China

YEN, SAMUEL S(HOW)-C(HIH), obstetrics and gynecology educator, reproductive endocrinologist; b. Beijing, Feb. 22, 1927; s. K.Y. and E.K. Yen; children: Carol Amanda, Dolores Amelia, Margaret Rae. BS, Cheeloo U., China, 1949; MD, U. Hong Kong, 1954, DSc, 1980. Diplomate Am. Bd. Ob-Gyn (bd. examiners 1973-78), Am. Bd. Reproductive Endocrinology (bd. examiners 1976-82). Intern Queen Mary Hosp., Hong Kong, 1954-55; resident Johns Hopkins U., Balt., 1956-60; assoc. prof. reproductive biology Case Western Res. U., Cleve., 1970—; prof. ob-gyn U. Calif., San Diego, 1972-83, chmn. dept. reproductive medicine, 1972-83, prof. reproductive medicine, 1983—; dir. reproductive endocrinology U. Calif. Med. Ctr., San Diego, 1983—, W.R. Persons chair, 1987; assoc. dir. obstetrics Univ. Hosp., Cleve., 1968-70; DeGroof lectr., 1987; Van Campenhaut lectr. Can. Fertility and Andrology Soc., 1995. Editor: Reproductive Endocrinology Physiology, Pathophysiology and Clinical Management, 1978, 2d rev. edit., 1986, 3d edit., 1991; mem. editorial bd. Endocrine Revs., 1984—. Recipient Axel Munthe Found. award, 1982, Simpson medal U. Edinburgh, Scotland, 1996; Oglebay fellow, 1968-69. Fellow Royal Coll. Ob-Gyn., Royal Coll. Obstetricians and Gynecologists (ad eundem, London); mem. NAS Inst. Medicine, Assn. Am. Physicians, Soc. for Gynecol. Investigation (pres. 1981, Disting. Scientist award 1992), Endocrine Soc. (Rorer Clin. Investigator award 1992). Office: U Calif-San Diego Reproductive Medicine # 0633 La Jolla CA 92093

YENDREK, RONALD JOHN, psychiatrist; b. Farrell, Pa., July 14, 1963; s. John Julius Jr. and Veronica Diana Maria (Kurtz) Y.; m. Angela Marzullo, Nov. 5, 1990. BS in Biology, Youngstown State U., 1985; DO, Ohio U., 1989. Diplomate Nat. Bd. Osteopathic Med. Examiners. Intern Youngstown (Ohio) Osteo. Hosp., 1989-90; family practitioner pvt. practice, Brookfield, Ohio, 1990-91; resident Ohio State U., Columbus, 1991-95; psychiatrist Ravenna (Ohio) Meml. Hosp., 1995—; med. dir. Partial Psychiat. Outpatient Progra, Ravenna, 1995—, Cath. Family Charity Ctr. Family Counseling, Kent, Ohio, 1996—. Mem. AMA, APA, Am. Osteo Assn., Ohio Osteo. Assn., Ohio Psychiat. Assn., Mensa, U.S. Chess Fedn., Maine Collectors Club. Roman Catholic. Office: 401 Devon Pl Ste 230 Bath OH 44210

YERBY, ALONZO SMYTHE, health services administrator, educator; b. Augusta, Ga., Oct. 15, 1921; s. Rufus Garvin and Wilhelmina Ethlyn (Smythe) Y.; m. Monteal Monica May, Sept. 17, 1943; children—Mark, Lynne, Kristen. B.S., U. Chgo., 1941; M.D., Meharry Med. Coll., 1946; M.P.H., Harvard, 1948. Diplomate: Am. Bd. Preventive Medicine. Intern Coney Island Hosp., Bklyn.; resident in preventive medicine Health Ins. Plan N.Y., 1950-53; exec. dir. med. services N.Y.C. Dept. Health; med. welfare adminstr. N.Y.C. Dept. Welfare, 1960-65; commr. of hosps. N.Y.C., 1965-66; prof. health services adminstrn. Harvard Sch. Pub. Health, Boston, 1966-82; dep. asst. sec. health for intergovtl. affairs Dept. Health and Human Services, Washington, 1980-81; prof., dir. div. health services adminstrn. Uniformed Services U. of Health Scis., Bethesda, Md., 1982—; cons. Bur. Family Services, Nat. Center Health Services Research, HEW, WHO; mem. Nat. Adv. Commn. on Health Manpower, 1966-67, HEW Adv. Com. on Relationships with State Health Agys., 1963-66, Nat. Profl. Standards Rev. Council, 1978-80; vis. scientist USA-USSR Exchange Program, 1967, 79. Author: Community Medicine in England and Scotland, 1976. Served with AUS, 1943-46. Fellow Am. Pub. Health Assn.; mem. Am. Coll. Preventive Medicine, Inst. Medicine of Nat. Acad. Scis., N.Y. Acad. Medicine. Club: Harvard (N.Y.C.). Home: 466 Park Dr # 1 Boston MA 02215-3750

YERGER, GRETCHEN M., nurse; married; 3 children. Diploma in nursing, Genesee Hosp. Sch. Nursing, Rochester, N.Y., 1970. RN, N.Y., cert. reproductive endocrinology, infertility nurse, ANCC; cert. HIV counselor. Staff nurse labor and delivery room Genesee Hosp., 1970-71, Columbia Hosp. for Women, Washington, 1970-72; staff nurse labor and delivery room Binghamton (N.Y.) Gen. Hosp., 1973-74, 76-82, post-partum staff nurse, 1974-76; staff nurse labor and delivery room United Health Svcs., Johnson City, N.Y., 1982-89, staff nurse Perinatal Ctr., 1989—; HIV counselor. Home: 2941 Holly Ln Endwell NY 13760

YESALIS, CHARLES EDWARD, health policy and administration educator, exercise and sport science educator; b. Evanston, Ill., Oct. 14, 1946; s. Charles Edward and Ethel Marie (Johnson) Y.; m. Diane Elizabeth Grabb, Dec. 1, 1967; 1 child, Marcy Marie. BS, U. Mich., 1969, MPH, 1972; ScD, Johns Hopkins U., 1975. Instr. Johns Hopkins U. Sch. Hygiene & Pub. Health, Balt., 1975-76; asst. prof. U. Iowa Coll. Medicine, Iowa City, 1976-80, assoc. prof., 1980-86; prof. Pa. State U. Coll. Health & Human Devel., University Park, 1986—. Editor: Anabolic Steroids in Sport and Exercise, 1993. Home: PO Box 10668 State College PA 16805-0668 Office: Pa State Univ 115 Henderson Bldg University Park PA 16802

YESSENOW, RANDALL SCOTT, plastic surgeon; b. Lima, Ohio, Oct. 1, 1958; s. Paul and Gayle Yessenow; children: Lauren, Courtney. BS, Case Western Res. U., 1980; MD, Ohio State U., 1984. Diplomate Am. Bd. Otolaryngology, Am. Bd. Plastic Surgery, Nat. Bd. Med. Examiners; lic. physician Iowa, Okla., Calif., Ind., Ill. Intern U. Iowa Hosp. and Clinics, Iowa City, 1984-85, resident otolaryngology, head and neck surgery, 1985-89; resident plastic surgery U. Okla. Health Scis. Ctr., Oklahoma City, 1989-91; surgeon Office of H. Weinberg, M.D., Munster, Ind., 1991, Office of D. Pesavento, M.D., Merrillville, Ind., 1992-95, Advanced Ctr. for Plastic and Hand surgery, P.C., Merrillville, 1995—; lectr. in field. Contbr. articles to profl. jours. Samuel J. Roessler Med. Rsch. scholar, 1981, 84. Fellow ACS, Internat. Coll. surgeons, Am. Acad. Otolaryngology - Head and Neck Surgery; mem. Am. Soc. Plastic and Reconstructive Surgeons (youngn plastic surgeons com. 1993—, CPT com. 1994—), Landacre Soc. Office: Adv Ctr Plastic/Hand Surg 333 W 89th Ave #W5 Merrillville IN 46410

YEUNG, CHAP-YUNG, pediatrics educator; b. Hong Kong, Dec. 29, 1936; s. Him and Lai-Yin (Pang) Y.; m. Helen Kwan-sik Chiu; children: Rae Sukman, Jane Suk-Cheung. M.B., B.S., U. Hong Kong, 1961. Cons. pediatrician Queen Elizabeth Hosp., Hong Kong, 1970-72; asst. prof. pediatrics McMaster U., Can., 1972-76, assoc. dir. neonatal services, 1974-76; cons. Scarborough Centenary Hosp., Ont., Can., 1977-80; pediatric cons. Govt. of Hong Kong, 1980—; prof., chair dept. pediatrics U. Hong Kong, 1980—; chief pediatric svc. Queen Mary Hosp., Tsan Yuk Maternity Hosp., Duchess of Kent Children's Hosp; hon. adviser Assn. Child Health and Devel.,

1985—, Spastics Assn. Hong Kong, 1985—, Beijing-Hong Kong Acad. Exchange Ctr.; v.p. Hong Kong Coll. Physicians, 1987-91; founding pres. Hong Kong Coll. Pediatricians, 1991—. Commonwealth med. scholar, 1966-68; Commonwealth fellow, Melbourne, 1970. Fellow Royal Australiasian Coll. Physicians Royal Coll. Physicians Can., Royal Coll. Physicians, London, Edinburgh, Glasgow, Ireland; mem. Assn. Maternal and Neonatal Health (pres. 1984—), Internat. Coll. Pediatricians, Brit. Pediatric Assn., Am. Pediatric Soc. (hon.), Can. Med. Assn., Hong Kong Med. Assn. Home: Grantham Hosp, A12 Sr Staff Quarters, Hong Kong Hong Kong Office: U Hong Kong Queen Mary Hosp, Dept Pediatrics, Hong Kong Hong Kong

YIENGPRUKSAWAN, ANUSAK, surgical oncologist; came to U.S., 1984; m. Melanie Hall. MD, Tohoku U., Sendai, Japan, 1978. Diplomate Am. Bd. Surgery. Resident Columbia U. Affiliate Harlem Hosp., N.Y.C., 1984-89; surg. oncology fellow Meml. Sloan-Kettering Cancer Ctr., N.Y.C., 1989-91; attending surgeon, chief div. surg. oncology Meth. Hosp., Bklyn., 1991-94; attending surgeon Englewood (N.J.) Hosp., 1994—, Ridgewood (N.J.) Valley Hosp., 1995—; dir. endoscopic ultrasound lab The Meth. Hosp., Bklyn., 1991-94, Englewood (N.J.) Med. Ctr., Endoscopic Ultrasaound Sect., 1995—, Ridgewood Valley Hosp. surg. ultrasound divsn. Author: Ultrasound, Endoscopic Ultrasound, Cancer Surgery. Japanese Min. Edn. scholar, 1972-82; Japanese Coun. for Med. Tng. Fellowship Program grantee, Tokyo, 1982-84. Fellow Am. Soc. Gastrointestinal Endoscopy, Soc. Am. Gastrointertinal Endoscopic Surgeons; mem. AMA, Am. Inst. Ultrasonic Med., Bklyn. Surg. Soc. Office: 145 Prospect St Ridgewood NJ 07450

YILMA, TILAHUN DANIEL, virology educator, veterinary researcher; b. Bulki, Gemugofa, Ethiopia, Dec. 15, 1943; parents Wolde-Ab Yilma and Getenesh Negewo. BS in Vet. Sci., U. Calif., Davis, 1968, DVM, 1970, PhD in Microbiology, 1977. Head vet. scv. Min. Agr., Harar, Ethiopia, 1970-71; lectr. UNDP/FAO of the UN Sch. for Animal Health Assts., DebreZeit, Ethiopia, 1971-72; rsch. assoc. USDA, Greenport, N.Y., 1977-79; asst. prof. vet. microbiology, pathology Wash. State U., Pullman, 1980-85, assoc. prof. vet. microbiology, pathology, 1985-86; prof. virology U. Calif., Davis, 1986—. Patentee in field. Recipient Ciba-Geigy prize Ciba-Geigy Ltd., 1990, Beecham award, 1988. Office: U Calif Sch Vet Medicine Davis CA 95616

YIM, HERBERT KAMAKAKAOPUA, hospital administrator; b. Honolulu, Oct. 13, 1933; s. Herbert Ah Choy and Mary (Wharton) Y.; m. Josselyn Ku'Uleipualikolehua O'Sul livan, May 18, 1957; children: Jon. Mathhew, Mark, Luis, Robert, Tiare Malia, Lydia. BA in zoology, U. Hawaii, 1955; M in hosp. adminstrn., Baylor U., 1971. Lic. nursing home administrator, Hawaii. Commd. 2d lt. U.S. Army, 1955, advanced through grades to col., 1976, ret., 1979; assoc. adminstr. Rehab. Hosp. Pacific, Honolulu, 1979-84; hosp. adminstr. Kauai Vets. Meml. Hosp., Waimea, Hawaii, 1984-87, Lana'i Cmty. Hosp., Lana'i City, Hawaii, 1994—; pres., CEO Molokai Gen. Hosp., Kaunakakai, Hawaii, 1987-92; bd. trustee Healthcare Assocs. Hawaii, Honolulu, 1995—; faculty nurse master's program U. Phoenix, Honolulu, 1992—; health planning com. mem. State Health Planning and Devel. Agy., Honolulu, 1992—. Bd. dirs. Prince Kuhio Hawaiian Civic Club, Honolulu, 1978-84; Ahahui 'Olelo Hawaii mem. U. Hawaii, Honolulu, 1979-82. Mem. Am. Hosp. Assn., Am. Health Care Assn., Healthcare Assn. Hawaii, Acad. Hawaiian Arts and Culture, Rotary. Home: 660 Akahi St Lana'i City HI 96763 Office: Lana'i Cmty Hosp PO Box 797 Lana'i City HI 96763

YIN, BEATRICE WEI-TZE, medical researcher; b. Taipei, Taiwan, Mar. 9, 1959; came to U.S., 1970; d. Chuan Keun and Ming Hsien (Huang) Y. BS, CUNY, Flushing, 1982, MS, 1988. Rsch. asst. Meml. Sloan-Kettering Cancer Ctr., N.Y.C., 1982—. Inventor Monoclonal antibodies to human gastrointestinal cancers, 1992. Office: Meml Sloan Kettering Cancer Ctr 1275 York Ave New York NY 10021-6007

YIN, RAYMOND WAH, radiologist; b. Canton, Republic of China, July 2, 1938; came to U.S., 1972; m. Jean Youe Mok, Jan. 29, 1967; children: Linda, Dany, Judy. MD, Sun Yat Sen U., Canton, 1961, Nat. Taiwan U., 1965. Diplomate Am. Bd. Radiology, Am. Bd. Nuclear Medicine. Intern Victoria Gen. Hosp., Dalhausie U., Halifax, Nova Scotia, Can., 1967-68; resident Royal Victoria Hosp., McGill U., Montreal, Que., 1968-72; staff radiologist St. Francis Hosp., Hartford, 1972-75; radiologist St. Joseph Hosp., Bloomington, Ill., 1975-89, Mennonite Brakaw Hosp., Normal, Ill., 1975—; practice medicine specializing in radiology Bloomington, 1975—; asst. prof. radiology U. Ill., Peoria, 1980—, So. Ill. U., 1988—; vis. prof. Sun Yat Sen U. Sch. Med. Scis. Fellow Royal Coll. Physicians of Can. Home: 4210 E Quail Ave Las Vegas NV 89120

YIP, WILLIAM CHIN-LING, pediatric cardiologist, consultant; b. Singapore, Nov. 8, 1950; s. Tung-Hoong Soo Yip and Chi-Yong Linly Lee; m. Ting-Fei Ho, Sept. 25, 1979; 3 children. MBBS, U. Singapore, 1974, M in Medicine (Pediatrics), 1978; AM, Acad. Medicine Singapore, 1982; MD, Nat. U. Singapore, 1986; diploma in child health, Royal Coll. Physicians, London, 1980. House officer Singapore Gen. Hosp., 1974-75, univ. trainee dept. pediats., 1977-78, lectr. dept. pediats., 1978-82, sr. lectr., 1982-87; assoc. prof., cons. Nat. Univ. Hosp., Singapore, 1987-88; cons. pediat. cardiologist Gleneagles Hosp., Singapore, 1988—; vis. cons. Inst. Health Sch. Health Scis., Singapore, 1982-88, Ministry of Edn., Singapore, 1984, Nat. Univ. Hosp., Singapore, 1988—; dir. Singapore Baby and Child Clinic, Singapore, 1988—. Author, editor book chpts.; contbr. articles to profl. jours. Capt. Singapore Armed Forces, 1975-77; capt. Res.; capt. Sinapore Civil Def. Res., 1993—. Recipient Long Svc. medal St. John Ambulance Brigade, 1981. Fellow Acad. Medicine Singapore, Royal Coll. Physicians (Edinburgh); mem. AAAS (internat.), Royal Coll. Physicians (Eng.), Singapore Pediat. Soc. (v.p., Haridas Meml. Lectr. gold medal 1983), Am. Inst. Ultrasound in Medicine, Singapore Med. Assn., Singapore Cardiac Soc., N.Y. Acad. Scis. Office: Singapore Baby and Child Clinic, 4/6 Napier Rd # 07-01-03, Singapore 1025, Singapore

YIUM, JACKSON JOE, nephrologist, educator; b. Dallas, May 31, 1935; m. Mildred Elizabeth Yium. MD, U. Tex., 1962. Diplomate Am. Bd. Internal Medicine, Am. Bd. Nephrology, Tex. Bd. Med. Examiners, Tenn. Bd. Med. Examiners, Ga. Bd. Med. Examiners. Intern Barnes Hosp., St. Louis, Miss., 1962-63; resident Barnes Hosp., St. Louis, 1963-64; resident Baylor Coll. Medicine Affiliate Hosps., Houston, 1966-68, nephrology fellow, 1968-70; asst. in medicine Washington U. Sch. Medicine, St. Louis, 1962-64; asst. instr. medicine Baylor Coll. Medicine, 1966-68, asst. prof. medicine and ob-gyn., 1970-73; assoc. clin. prof. medicine U. Tenn. Clin. Edn. Ctr., Chattanooga, 1973-82, acting chief medicine, 1977-78; vice chmn. dept. medicine U. Tenn., 1978-85; med. dir. Dialysis Clinic, Inc., Chattanooga, 1973—; chief nephrology sect. and hemodialysis unit Erlanger Med. Ctr., Chattanooga, 1973—; co-dir. Erlanger Regional Kidney Transplant Ctr., 1989—; clin. prof. medicine U. Tenn. Health Sci. Ctr., Chattanooga, 1982-90, prof. medicine, 1990—; med. dir. Dialysis Clinics Inc., Chattanooga. Capt. USAF-MC, 1964-66. Home: 1101 East Brow Rd Signal Mountain TN 37377 Office: Nephrology Assocs Ste 1111 Med Ctr Plaza Chattanooga TN 37403

YKI-JÄRVINEN, HANNELE, medical educator, endocrinologist; b. Helsinki, Finland, Feb. 25, 1956; arrived in U.S., 1994; d. Yrjö Olavi and Gerda Lydia Erika (Holmberg) Y. MD, U. Helsinki, 1981, PhD, 1984. Rsch. fellow Finnish Acad. of Sci., Helsinki, 1983-85, scientist, 1987-88, sr. scientist, 1989-90; resident in internal medicine Helsinki U., 1990-93, resident in endocrinology, 1993-94; asst. prof. medicine Dept. Med. Divsn. of Diabetes, U. Tex., San Antonio, 1994—; prof. Acad. Finland, 1995—; vis. assoc. scientist Clin. Diabetes and Nutrition sect. NIH, Phoenix, 1985-87; lectr. numerous confs. and univs. Editl. bd. mem. Am. Jour. of Physiology, 1995—, Endocrinology and Metabolism, 1994—; contbr. articles to profl. jours. including Lancet, Jour. Clin. Invest, Am. Jour. Physiol., New Eng. Jour. Medicine, Diabetes, Acta Endocrinology, Diabetologia, Metabolism, Am. Jour. Medicine, Jour. Intern Medicine, Haemost, others. Recipient Anders Jahre Medisinske prize, 1995. Mem. Internat. Diabetes Fedn. (chairperson sci. com. 16th meeting), Finnish Diabetes Rsch. Soc. (sec.), Finnish Med. Assn., Finnish Med. Soc. (Young Investigators award 1989), Finnish Diabetes Rsch. Soc. Duodecim, (sec., bd. founders 1990—), Finnish Internal Medicine Soc., Finnish Endocrine Soc., European Assn. for Study of Diabetes (Minkowski award 1993), Scandinavian Soc. for Study of Diabetes (Young Investigator award 1989), Am. Diabetes Assn. Office: U Tex Health Sci Ctr 7703 Floyd Curl Dr San Antonio TX 78284-6200*

YOCHIM, PAUL DAVID, anesthesiologist; b. Erie, Pa., Sept. 8, 1954; s. Robert Anthony and Lucille (Pitetti) Y.; m. Susan Elizabeth Pettersen, Sept. 15, 1985; children: Jenny Leigh, Daniel James. BS in Biology, Mercyhurst Coll., Erie, Pa., 1976; DO, Kirksville (Mo.) Coll., 1982. Resident Montefiore Med. Ctr., Bronx, N.Y., 1987-90; physician dept emergency medicine Metro Health Ctr., Erie, Pa., 1983-87; anesthesiologist Med. Ctr. Anesthesiologists, Louisville, Ky., 1990—. Mem. med. team Goodwill Games, St. Petersburg, Russia, 1994. Mem. AMA, Am. Soc. Anesthesiologists, Am. Internat. Healthcare Alliance (det. to hosp. 122 St. Petersburg), Ky. Med. Assn., Jefferson County Med. Soc. Democrat. Lutheran. Home: 3112 Springstead Cir Louisville KY 40241

YODAIKEN, RALPH E., pathologist, occupational medicine physician; b. Johannesburg, Republic of South Africa, 1928. BS, U. Witwatersrand, Republic of South Africa, 1956; MPH, Johns Hopkins U., 1976. Bd. cert. pathology, bd. cert. forensic pathology. Intern Coronation Hosp., Johannesburg, 1956-57; resident U. Witwatersrand Med. Ctr., 1957-58, Johannesburg Gen. Hosp., 1958; assoc. pathologist Buffalo Gen. Hosp., 1965-67; mem. staff Cin. Gen. Hosp., 1968-71; rsch. assoc. Johns Hopkins U. Sch. Hygiene and Pub. Health, Balt., 1976—; sr. staff mem. Nat. Inst. Occupational Safety and Health, Washington, 1977—, chmn. sr. adv. staff, 1983; dir. office occupational medicine Occupational Safety and Health Adminstrn., U.S. Dept. Labor, Bethesda, 1983-91, sr. med. advisor, 1991—; lectr. U. Witwatersrand, 1958-63; adj. asst. prof. pathology, SUNY Buffalo, 1963-67; adj. assoc. prof. U. Cin., 1968-71; adj. prof., adj. assoc. prof. medicine Emory U., Atlanta, 1971-75; adj. clin. prof. George Washington U., 1975—. Served to lt. Israeli Army, 1948-50. Fellow Coll. Am. Pathologists, Am. Coll. Occupational and Environ. Health.

YODER, DAVID E., medical educator, speech, language pathologist; b. Shipshewana, Ind., July 16, 1932; m. Dee Yoder; children:, Lisa, Eric. BA in Speech Comm., Goshen Coll., 1954; MA in Speech Pathology, Northwestern U., 1955; PhD in Speech Pathology and Audiology, U. Kans., 1965. Asst. prof. Colo. State U., Ft. Collins, 1965-68; asst. prof. U. Wis., Madison, 1968-71, assoc. prof., 1971-73, chair dept. comm. disorders, 1973-78, prof., 1973-86; prof. speech and hearing scis. U. N.C., Chapel Hill, 1986—, clin. prof., Sch. Edn., 1986-95, dir. Ctr. Literacy & Disability Studies, 1989-92, assoc. dir. policy studies, 1993—. Co-author: Contemporary Issues in Language Intervention, 1983, Decision Making in Speech-Language Pathology, 1988; co-editor: Language Intervention with the Retarded: Developing Strategies, 1972, Handbook of Speech-Language-Pathology and Audiology, 1988; contbr. numerous articles to profl. jours., chpts. to books; presenter in field of child language disorders, psycholinguistics, autmentative and alternative communication, literacy development, and multicultural awareness; editl. cons. DCCD Pub. of Coun. for Exceptional Children, 1972-74; editl. bd. Topics in Lang. Disorders, 1980-95, Clinics in Communication Disorders, 1991-94; editl. cons. Jour. Speech and Hearing Devel., 1965-72; editor Colo. Speech and Hearing Assn. Jour., 1967-68; editl. cons. Am. Jour. Mental Deficiency, 1972-75; editor Jour. Augmentative and Alternative Communication, 1984-86; contbg. editor Communication Outlook, 1980—. Am. Assn. on Mental Deficiency fellow, 1976; Walker-Bascom prof. in communicative disorders, 1980-86; recipient honors of Wis. Speech-Lang.-Hearing Assn., 1986, Culture for Svc. award Goshen Coll. Outstanding Alumnus, 1992. Fellow Am. Speech and Hearing Assn. (extensive com. work, conv. activity); v.p. for clin. affairs 1979-81, exec. bd. 1983-85, pres. 1984, Honor award 1995), Am. Assn. Mental Retardation (v.p. speech pathology-audiology divsn. 1972-75, v.p. exec.com. 1972-75, extensive com. work and conv. activity), Internat. Soc. Augmentative and Alternative Comms. (bd. dirs. 1982-86, 92-95, extensive conf. work); mem. Internat. Assn. Logopedics and Phoniatrics (chmn. com. augmentative and alternative comm. 1984-90), U.S. Soc. for Augmentative and Alternative Comm. (co-founder, first pres. 1989, exec. bd. 1989-91, bd. dirs. 1990—), N.C. Speech-Hearing-Lang. Assn. (extensive com., conf. and conv. activity), N.C. Augmentative Comm. Assn. (planning com. 1990-93). Office: Univ NC Dept Med Allied Health Prof Speech and Hearing Scis Chapel Hill NC 27599-7120

YODER, MARY JANE WARWICK, psychotherapist; b. Corryton, Tenn., Nov. 20, 1933; d. Harry Alonzo and Mary Luzelle (Furches) Warwick; m. Edwin Milton Yoder, Jr., Nov. 1, 1958; children: Anne Daphne, Edwin Warwick. BA, U. N.C., Chapel Hill, 1956; MFA, U. N.C., Greensboro, 1969; MSW, Va. Commonwealth U., 1987; cert. individual psychotherapy, Smith Coll., 1991. Lic. ind. clin. social worker, D.C.; lic. clin. social worker, Va. Editorial asst. Harper & Bros., N.Y.C., 1956-57; flight attendant Pan Am. Airlines, N.Y.C., 1957-59; adj. faculty mem. in ballet Guilford Coll., Greensboro, 1961-64; ballet tchr., adminstr. Jane Yoder Sch. of Ballet, Greensboro, 1964-75; homilitics listener Va. Theol. Sem., Alexandria, 1978-80; social worker, dance therapist Woodbine Nursing Ctr., Alexandria, 1983-87; staff psychotherapist D.C. Inst. Mental Health, 1987-92; pvt. practice Capitol Hill Ctr. Individual and Family Therapy, 1992—. Ballet and book critic Greensboro Daily News, 1961-75. Dancer, choreographer Greensboro Civic Ballet, 1961-75. Mem. Nat. Assn. Social Workers, Greater Washington Soc. for Clin. Social Work, Inc., Washington Sch. Psychiatry, Washington Soc. for Jungian Psychology, Jungian Venture, Army-Navy Country Club. Episcopalian. Office: Capitol Hill Ctr Individual and Family Therapy 530 7th St SE Washington DC 20003-2768

YODER, STANLEY JONAS, orthopedic surgeon; b. Belleville, Pa., Aug. 13, 1938; s. Moses Aaron and Kathryn Barbara Y.; children: Stanley Phillip, Julie Beth. BA, Goshen (Ind.) Coll., 1960; MD, Jefferson Med. Coll., Phila., 1964. Diplomate Am. Bd. Orthop. Surgery. Intern Geisingermedica Ctr., Danville, Pa., 1964-65, resident, 1968-72; orthop. surgeon Billings (Mont.) Clinic, 1972-78, Centre Orthop., State College, Pa., 1978-93, U. Orthop. & Sports Medicine Ctr., State College, Pa., 1993—; cons. Mont. Ctr. Handicapped, Billings, 1976-78; team physician Rocky Mountain Coll., Billings, 1973-78; chief of staff Rehab. Hosp., Pleasan Gap, Pa., 1986-92. Pres. Boalsburg (Pa.) Village Conservancy, 1989. Lt. comdr USPHS, 1965-68. Fellow Am. Acad. Orthop. Surgeons; mem. Pan Pacific Surg. Assn., Pa. Med. Soc., Centre County Med. Soc. (pres. 1978—), Interstate Orthop. Soc., Ea. Orthop. Assn. Republican. Mennonite. Home: 404 W Main St Boalsburg PA 16827 Office: Univ Orthop & Sports Medicine Ctr 101 Regent Ct State College PA 16801-7965

YODER WISE, PATRICIA SNYDER, nurse, educator; b. Wadsworth, Ohio, July 2, 1941; d. Belford Grant and Leona Cora (Mohler) Snyder; m. Robert Thomas Wise, Feb. 17, 1973; children: Doreen Ellen, Deborah Ann. BSN, Ohio State U., 1963; MSN, Wayne State U., 1968; EdD, Tex. Tech U., 1984. Cert. gerontol. nurse and nursing adminstr., RN, Tex., Ohio. Rsch. asst. Wayne State U., Detroit, 1968; ednl. dir. Ohio Nurses' Assn., Columbus, 1968-72; asst. dir. nursing Mt. Clemens (Mich.) Gen. Hosp., 1972-73; assoc. prof., head of nursing Ferris State Coll., Big Rapids, Mich., 1975-77; asst. prof., assoc. prof., dir. continuing edn. U. Colo., Denver, 1977-79; assoc. dean, assoc. prof. Sch. Nursing, Tex. Tech U. Health Scis. Ctr., Lubbock, 1979-86, assoc. dean, prof., 1986-87, interim assoc. dean grad. program, 1986-89, exec. assoc. dean, prof. nursing, 1989-92, interim dean, prof., 1992-93; dean, prof. Sch. Nursing, 1993—; prin. p.t. Wylan Assocs., Lubbock, 1989—; mem. acad. adv. panel on nursing Health and Scis. Network, 1983-92, Nurses Coalition, 1982-92; bd. dirs. RN Polit. Action Com., 1989-93. Editor Jour. Continuing Edn. in Nursing, 1986—. Fellow Am. Acad. Nursing; mem. ANA (site visitor continuing edn. 1982-88), Tex. Nurses Assn. (bd. dirs. 1989-93, pres. dist. 18 1987-89, pres. 1995—), Coun. Continuing Edn., Am. Nurses Found. (Tchg. Excellence award 1968), Tex. Nurses Found. (pres. 1992-95), Sigma Theta Tau (grantee). Home: 3713 95th St Lubbock TX 79423-3811

YOGANATHAN, AJIT PRITHIVIRAJ, biomedical engineer, educator; b. Colombo, Sri Lanka, Dec. 6, 1951; came to U.S., 1973; s. Ponniah and Mangay (Navaratnam) Y. BSChemE with honors, Univ. Coll., U. London, 1973; PhDChemE, Calif. Tech. U., 1978. Engring. asst. Shell Oil Refinery, Stanlow, Eng., 1972; teaching asst. Calif. Inst. Tech., 1973-74, 1976, rsch. fellow, 1977-79; asst. prof. Ga. Inst. Tech., 1979-83, assoc. prof., 1983-88, chmn. bioengring. com., 1984-88, prof. chem. engring., 1988-94, dir. Bioengring. Ctr., 1989—, prof. mech. engring., 1989-94, co-dir. Emory U.-Ga. Tech. Biomed. Tech. Ctr., 1992—, Regents prof., 1994—; adj. assoc. prof. U. Ala., 1985—. Founding fellow Am. Inst. Med. & Biol. Engring., 1992; recipient Edwin Walker prize Brit. Inst. Mech. Engrs., 1988, Humboldt fellowship, 1985, Am. Heart Assn.-Ga. Affiliate Rsch. Investigatorship award, 1980-83, Calif. Inst. Tech. fellowship, 1973-77, Goldsmid Medal and prize Univ. Coll., 1973, 72, Brit. Coun. scholarship, 1971-73. Mem. AICE, ASME, Biomed. Engring. Soc., Am. Soc. Echocardiography (dir. 1987-91). Office: Sch of Chem Engring Ga Tech U Atlanta GA 30332

YOGEV, SARA, psychologist; b. Tel Aviv, May 23, 1946; came to U.S., 1975; d. Israel and Cila (Fink) Frankel; m. Ram Yogev, Oct. 2, 1967; children: Eldad, Shelly, Tomer. BA, Hebrew U., 1965-69, MA, 1970-73; PhD, Northwestern U., Evanston, Ill., 1976-79. Cert. clin. psychologist, Ill. Clin. experience dist. sch. psychologist Office Edn. and Culture, Jerusalem, Israel, 1968-71; intern. Beer Yaakov Psychiatric Hosp., Israel, 1971-72; asst. dir. Dept. Psychology, Hebrew U., Jerusalem, Israel, 1972-73; psychotherapist Mental Health Ctr., Hebrew U., Jerusalem, Israel; clin. psychologist Inst. Psychoanalysis, Jerusalem, Israel, 1973-75; psychotherapist, supr. Youth and Family Services, Ill., 1977-80; pvt. practice psychology Skokie, Ill., 1981—; academic experience instr. counseling psychology, 1977-79, asst. prof., Northwestern U., 1979-82, research psychologist at the rank asst. prof., 1983-86, visiting scholar, Ctr. Urban Affairs and Policy Research, 1987. Contbr. articles to profl. jours. and books. Mem. American Assn. for Marriage and Family Therapy, American Psyhological Assn., Nat. Register Health Service. Jewish. Office: # 32 5225 Old Orchard Rd Skokie IL 60077-1027

YOKOYAMA, KAZUSHIGE KAZUNARI, biomedical engineer, researcher; b. Takeura, Shiraoi, Japan, Mar. 11, 1951; s. Toshio and Fumiko (Sato) Y.; m. Tomoko Ohta, Mar. 25, 1976; children: Kyosuke, Hiroaki. BA, Shizuoka (Japan) U., 1973; MA, U. Tokyo, 1976, PhD, 1979. Jr. rsch. scientist Beckman Rsch. Inst., City of Hope, Duarte, Calif., 1983-85; rsch. scientist Riken, Tsukuba, Japan, 1985; head DNA bank Riken, Tsukuba, 1993; vis. lectr. Hiroshima (Japan) U., 1993-94, Tokushima (Japan) U., 1995-96; hon. prof. China Med. U., Shenyang, 1995; vice dir. Gene Diagnosis Ctr., Shenyang, 1995. Author: Antisense RNA and DNA, 1992 (medal 1992). Buddhist. Office: Riken, 3-1-1 Koyadai, 305 Tsukuba Ibaraki, Japan

YOKOYAMA, YUZURU, educator, social worker; b. Sapporo, Japan, Mar. 10, 1958; s. Hiroshi and Keiko (Murayama) Y. BA, Doshisha U., Kyoto, Japan, 1980, MA, 1982; MSW, U. Calif., Berkeley, 1985; PhD, U. Wash., Seattle, 1989. Asst. prof. Japan Welfare Acad., Sapporo, Japan, 1989-91, Osaka Prefecture U. Sch. of Social Welfare, Sakai, Japan, 1991-96, Hokusei Gakuen U. Sch. of Social Welfare, 1996—. Contbr. articles to profl. jours. Translator Keiro Nursing Home, Seattle, 1987-88; vol. Japanese Am. Svcs. in East Bay, Berkeley, 1982-88, Asian Community Mental Health Svcs., Oakland, Calif., 1982-83. Mem. NASW, Japan Welfare Studies, Internat. Coun. Social Welfare, Internat. Coun. of Psychologists, Inter-Univ. Consortium Social Devel., Japanese Community Welfare Studies. Home: #506 7-28 2 Jiyo, 4-chome 24 ken Nishi-ku, Sapporo 063, Japan Office: Gakuen U Sch of Social Welfare, 312 Chome Oxachi Nishi Atsubetsu Ku, Sapporo 009, Japan

YOLLICK, BERNARD LAWRENCE, otolaryngologic surgeon; b. Toronto, Mar. 24, 1922; came to U.S., 1949; s. Samuel and Beatrice (Roth) Y.; m. Liny L. Pajgin, 1947; children: Ingrid, Eric Lyf. Sr. Matriculation, Harbord Collegiate Inst., Toronto, 1939; MD, U. Toronto, 1945. Diplomate Am. Bd. Surgery, Am. Bd. Otolaryngology. Intern Sunnybrook Hosp., toronto, 1945-46; resident D.C. Gen. Hosp., Washington, 1950, St. Louis County Hosp., Clayton, Mo., 1952-53; Am. Cancer Soc. fellow M.D. Anderson Cancer Hosp., Houston, 1953-54; resident in pathology Cook County Hosp., Chgo., 1949; surgeon Houston, 1953-59; fellowship in otolaryngology VA Hosp., Dallas, 1960-63; prof. anatomy Baylor Med. Sch., Houston, 1953-59, U. Tex. Dental Sch., Houston, 1953-59, Baylor Coll. Dentistry, Dallas, 1987-90; mem. staff Children's Med. Ctr., Dallas, 1990—; mem. staff, chief dept. otolaryngology St. Paul Med. Ctr., Dallas, 1990—. Contbr. articles to profl. jours. Served to capt. Royal Can. Army Med. Corps, 1942-45. Recipient fellowship Am. Cancer Soc., 1953. Fellow Am. Coll. Surgeons; mem. Tex. Otolaryn. Assn. (pres. 1979).

YONKER, RICHARD AARON, rheumatologist; b. Phila., Aug. 8, 1952. BA, George Washington U., 1974; DO, Coll. Osteopathic Medicine, 1978. Diplomate Am. Bd. Internal Medicine, Am. Bd. Rheumatology. Rheumatologist Sarasota (Fla.) Arthritis Ctr., 1984—. Fellow Am. Coll. Rheumatology; mem. Am. Osteopathic Assn., Fla. Med. Assn., Fla. Osteopathic Med. Assn., Fla. Rheumatology Soc., Sarasota County Med. Soc. Office: Sarasota Arthritis Ctr 3500 S Tamiami Trl Sarasota FL 34239

YONTS, CHARLES GLENN, psychologist; b. Hazard, Ky., July 10, 1957; s. Newton Wesley and Maulta (Sizemore) Y.; m. Sharon Elaine Stacy, Sept. 26, 1982; 1 child, Charles Wesley. BS in Psychology with distinction, Ea. Ky. U., 1979, MS in Clin. Psychology, 1981, MBA, 1984. Cert. with autonomous functioning in clin. psychology Ky. Bd. Psychology. Staff psychologist Ky. River Mental Health/Mental Retardation Ctr., Hazard, 1981-82; pvt. practice clin. psychology Somerset and Berea, Ky., 1982—; dir. psychology Oakwood, Somerset, 1985—; profl. expert in mental retardation Oakwood, 1987—; condr. numerous workshops in field. Contbr. articles to profl. jours. Bd. dirs. Regional Ky. chpt. Am. Heart Assn., Somerset, 1994—; pres. Oakhill Elem. Pulaski Sch. PTA, Somerset, 1994-95; deacon Beacon Hill Bapt. Ch., Somerset, 1989—. Mem. Am. Assn. Mental Retardation, Southeastern Psychol. Assn. Democrat. Home: 5011 Ash Valley Dr Somerset KY 42501 Office: Oakwood 2441 S Hwy 27 Somerset KY 42501

YOO, JAMES H., radiation oncologist, nuclear medicine physician; b. South Korea, Dec. 13, 1941; came to U.S., 1968; s. Ki S. and Ki O. (Lee) Y.; m. Esther Cha Yoo, Sept. 3, 1968; children: James, Thomas, Andrew. BSE, Seoul (Korea) Nat. U., 1964, MSE, 1968; PhD, Tex. Tech. U., 1971; MD, U. Tex., San Antonio, 1982. Diplomate Am. Bd. Radiology, Am. Bd. Nuclear Medicine. Pediatric intern U. Tex. Health Sci. Ctr., San Antonio, 1982-83, resident in nuclear medicine, 1983-87; resident in radiation oncology Temple U./Tufts Med. Sch.-New Eng. Med. Ctr., Boston, 1987-90; asst. staff physician City of Hosp Med. Ctr., Duarte, Calif., 1990-91; staff radiation oncologist dept. vets. affairs East Orange (N.J.) Med. Ctr., 1991—; rsch. staff physician ECOG, 1992—, mem. Radiation Oncology sect., 1995—. Chmn., pres. Korean Ednl. Com., N.Y. and N.J., 1995—; chmn. bd. dirs. Hankook Coll., 1995—; elder Korean Bahn Sok Ch., Livingston, N.J., 1993—. Maj. M.C. USAR, 1983-95. Fellow N.J. Acad. Medicine; mm. ASTRO. Presbyterian. Office: East Orange VA Med Ctr 385 Tremont Ave East Orange NJ 07018

YOO, TAIWOO, family physician; b. Seoul, Korea, June 7; m. Yongsoon C. Chung, Apr. 7, 1984; children: Edward H., Christopher J. MD, Seoul (Korea) Nat. U., 1980, M Med. Sci., 1983, PhD, 1990; MS in Epidemiology, Bowman Gray Sch. Medicine, 1989. Diplomate Korean Bd. Family Practice. Resident in family practice Seoul Nat. U. Hosp., 1980-83, asst. prof. family practice, 1990—, dir. family practice residency, 1990—; postgrad. fellow U. Minn., Mpls., 1984-85; family practice resident U. Hosp. of Cleve., 1985-88; fellow family and cmty. medicine Bowman Gray Sch. Medicine, Winston-Salem, N.C., 1988-89; dir. family medicine Kyunghee U. Med. Ctr., Seoul, 1989-90. Author: The Family Structure and Dynamics in Shin D,ed, 1991, Introduction to Clinical Preventive Medicine, 1994; editor: Textbook of Family Medicine, 1995. Rsch. grantee Ciba-Geigy Ltd., 1992, Pasteur Dairy, 1995, Ministry Info. and Comms., 1995. Mem. Am. Acad. Family Physicians, Soc. Tchrs. Family Medicine, Soc. Prospective Medicine. Home: 111-108 Hanshin, Apt Donamdong Sungbukgu, Seoul 136-060, Korea Office: Seoul Nat U Coll Medicine, Dept Family Medicine, Seoul 110-744, Korea

YOOD, HAROLD STANLEY, internist; b. Plainfield, N.J., Feb. 23, 1920; s. Raphael and Netta (Newcorn) Y.; m. Helen H. Hull, Nov. 8, 1941; children: Pamela, Patricia Yood Herskovitz, Paula Yood Peterson, Andrew H. BA, U. Va., 1940, MD, 1943. Intern Syracuse (N.Y.) U. Med. Ctr., 1943; pvt. practice Plainfield, N.J., 1946-91; med. dir. Cen. Jersey Individual Physicians Assn.; staff dept. medicine Muhlenberg Hosp., 1946—, pres. staff, 1980-86, cons., 1991-95, emeritus, 1995—. Contbr. articles to Jour. Med. Soc. N.J., Communication for Ciba, others. Bd. govs. Muhlenberg Regional

Med. Ctr., 1980-86, exec. com.; trustee, v.p. United Way Plainfield/Fanwood, 1975-81; bd. dirs. United Way Union County, 1978-81; pres. Jewish Community Ctr., Plainfield, 1970-71; v.p. Jewish Fedn. Cen. N.J., 1971-73, Cen. N.J. Jewish Home for Aged, 1973-80. Capt. M.C. AUS, 1944-45, ETO. Decorated Purple Heart, Croix de Guerre (France), Croix de Guerre (Belgium). Fellow Am. Coll. Gastroenterology (sr.), Am. Coll. Angiography (ret.), Internat. Coll. Angiology (ret.); mem. AMA, Med. Soc. N.J. (governing coun. hosp. med. staff sect. 1983-92, chmn. 1988-90; trustee 1989-90), Union County Med. Soc., Plainfield Area Med. Assn., Am. Coll. Physician Execs., Lions (life). Office: CJIPA 1133 Park Ave Plainfield NJ 07060-3006

YORK, JAMES LESTER, research scientist; b. Peoria, Ill., Nov. 12, 1942; s. Wayne Mills and Lucy (Aupperle) Y.; m. Patricia Mary Stanton, Aug. 22, 1970; children: Benjamin, Nora. AB, Bradley U., 1965; PhD, U. Ill., Chgo., 1972. Postdoctoral trainee SUNY, Buffalo, 1972-74, rsch. assoc. prof. psychology, 1981—; rsch. scientist Rsch. Inst. on Addictions, Buffalo, 1974—; referee for sci. jours. Psychopharmacology, Alcohol, Alcoholism, Pharmacology-Biochemistry-and-Behavior, Physiology and Behavior, Behavioral Pharmacology. Contbr. articles to profl. publs. Grantee Nat. Inst. Alcohol Abuse and Alcoholism, 1976, 87, 90, 91, N.Y. State Health Rsch. Coun., 1978, 80. Mem. Rsch. Soc. Alcoholism, Soc. Stimulus Properties of Drugs, Am. Soc. Pharmacology and Exptl. Therapeutics, Internat. Soc. Biomed. Rsch. on Alcoholism, Gerontology Soc. Am. Home: 783 Chestnuthill Rd East Aurora NY 14052 Office: Rsch Inst on Addictions 1021 Main St Buffalo NY 14203-1016

YORK, JANET BREWSTER, nurse, family and sex therapist, sculptor; b. N.Y.C., Mar. 5, 1941; d. Edward Cox and Janet Stone Brewster; AA with honors, Briarcliff Coll., 1961; RN with highest honors, U. Iowa, 1965; BA summa cum laude, Marymount Manhattan Coll., 1975; MA with honors, N.Y. U., 1978; m. Albert Thompson York, Mar. 31, 1962 (dec.); children: Clifton Gaston, Torrance Brewster; 1 adopted child, Justin Brigham. Nurse, Manhattan Eye, Ear and Throat Hosp., N.Y.C., 1966-74; nurse, counselor Washington Free Clinic, 1969-71; family therapist Ackerman Family Inst., N.Y.C., 1976-80; sex therapist N.Y. Med. Coll., Flower Fifth Ave Hosp., N.Y.C., 1976-80; individual practice family and sex therapy, N.Y.C., 1978—; supervisory staff grad. edn. program in human sexuality N.Y.U. Med. Ctr., 1982—; sculptor, 1988—. Bd. dirs. Spence/Chapin Adoption Agy., Manhattan Eye, Ear and Throat Hosp. Vita fellow Internat. Coun. of Sex Edn. and Parenthood, Am. U., 1981; recipient Evelyn Monte Sculpture award, 1988, 94, Ellsworth Howell Art Sculpture award, 1991, 93. Mem. Am. Soc. for Sex Therapy and Research, Am. Assn. Sex Edn., Counseling and Therapy, Soc. for Sci. Study Sex, Sex Info. and Edn. Council U.S., Am. Assn. Marriage and Family Therapists, Nat. Assn. Women Artist, Am. Medallic Soc., Nantucket Art Assn., Walker Art Ctr., Nat. Mus. Women in the Arts. Clubs: Lawrence Beach, Rockaway Hunting, N.Y.U, Millbrook. Represented in permanent collection The Dog Mus. of Am., St. Louis; contbr. articles to profl. jours.; also videotape Death as a Part of Life. Home: 155 E 72nd St New York NY 10021-4371

YORK, WILLIAM CALVIN, physician; b. Gallipolis, Ohio, July 13, 1954; s. Charles Calvin and Rosalie (Kinney) Y.; m. Lynn Marie Rogers; m. Elizabeth Rose Dynesius, June 2, 1995; children: Shelby Lynn, Rachel Autumn. BS in Biology, Jacksonville U., 1978; DO, W.Va. Sch. Osteo. Medicine, 1982. Family practice/EM Jenkings (Ky.) Cmty. Hosp., 1984-85; med. examiner Dept. Justice, Washington, 1984—. Author (screenplay) The Sojata Sequence, 1989. Lt. USN, 1983-84. Mem. Vietnam Vets. Am., Am. Legion. Home: 2032 WSR 16 Green Cove Springs FL 32043 Office: MFT Inc 2648B Sunrise Village Dr Orange Park FL 32073

YOSHIMOTO, NAOMI, nurse; b. Puunene, Hawaii, Feb. 7, 1951; d. Herbert Toshio and Lillian Mitsue (Yakabe) Y. BS, Brigham Young U., 1973; MS, U. Hawaii, 1983. RN, Utah, Hawaii. Staff nurse Kaiser Med. Found., Honolulu, 1973-75, Latter-Day Saints Hosp., Salt Lake City, 1975-78, Queen's Med. Ctr., Honolulu, 1979, 85, 96—; mgr. health service Brigham Young U., Laie, Hawaii, 1979-80; staff nurse Straub Clinics and Hosp. Inc., Honolulu, 1980-83, 1984-87; clin. nurse specialist Kuakini Med. Cen., Honolulu, 1983-84; instr. nursing Sch. Nursing U. Hawaii, Honolulu, 1985; quality assurance and health edn. coordinator Best Care, Honolulu, 1987-89; unit supr. Straub Clinics and Hosp., Inc., Honolulu, 1989-92; instr. Nursing Dept. Kapiolani C.C., Honolulu, 1992—. Various positions Ch. Jesus Christ Latter-Day Saints, Honolulu. Mem. ANA, AACN, Am. Assn. Neurosci. Nurses, Phi Kappa Phi. Home: 1532 Halekoa Dr Honolulu HI 96821-1125

YOSHIMOTO, YUHEI, neurosurgeon; b. Osaka, Japan, July 27, 1957; s. Ichiji and Michiko (Ihara) Y.; m. Noriko Akazawa, Oct. 28, 1990; children: Sohta, Satomi. MD, Tokyo U., 1983, PhD, 1994. Bd. cert. neurosurgeon. Resident Tokyo U., 1983-84; sr. resident Tokyo Police Hosp., 1984—, Higashi Yokohama (Japan) Hosp., 1988—, Tokyo Teishin Hosp., 1990—; lectr. Tokyo U., 1992—; asst. prof. Dokkyo U., Tochigi, Japan, 1994—. Contbr. articles to profl. jours. Mem. Japan Neurosurg. Soc. Office: Dokkyo U Sch Medicine Dept Neurosurgery, 880 Kitakobayashi Mibu, Shimotsuga Tochigi 321-02, Japan

YOSHIOKA, MASANORI, pharmaceutical sciences educator; b. Iwagi, Japan, Sept. 4, 1941; s. Takeo and Toshiko (Tasaka) Y.; m. Masae Kurahashi, Mar. 23, 1943; children: Shima, Nami. BA, Showa Coll. Pharm. Scis., Tokyo, 1965; M., U. Tokyo, 1967, PhD, 1970. Cert. pharmacist. Assoc. faculty pharm. sci. U. Tokyo, 1970-73, lectr. faculty pharm. sci., 1977-83, assoc. prof. faculty pharm. sci., 1983; prof. faculty pharm. sci. Setsunan U., Osaka, Japan, 1983—; lectr. faculty medicine Hiroshima U., Hiroshima, Japan, 1985-87, 92, 94; rsch. assoc. sch. medicine Yale U., New Haven, 1970-72; vis. scientist cancer inst. Cairo U., 1980-81; vis. prof. Paris U. XI, Orsay, France, 1986-87, Technion-Israel Inst. Tech., Haifa, 1987. Editor Bunseki, 1981-83, Biogenic Amines, 1983-91, Chem. & Pharm. Bull., 1987-89, 92—, Progress in HPLC, vol. 4, 1989. Mem. com. Japan Soc. for the Promotion Sci., Tokyo, 1980—. Mem. Pharm. Soc. Japan, Japan Soc. for Analytical Chemistry, Japan Soc. Clin. Chemistry, Internat. Soc. Toxinology (Frankfurt am Main, Fed. Republic Germany), N.Y. Acad. Scis., Rotary. Home: 6-15 Otokoyamayoshii, Yawata Kyoto 614, Japan Office: Setsunan U Faculty Pharm, Sci 52 3 Nagaotogecho, Hirakata 573 01, Japan

YOSHITAKE, AKIRA, chemical company researcher, pharmacist; b. Kyoto, Japan, Oct. 9, 1937; s. Haruo and Masa (Adachi) Y.; m. Tomoko Kodama, May 2, 1962; children: Harumi, Naomi. BS, Kyoto U., 1960, MS, 1962, PhD, 1966. Cert. pharmacist. Rsch. assoc. U. Wis., Madison, 1967-69; postdoctoral fellow UCLA, 1969-70, U. B.C., Vancouver, Can., 1970-71; rsch. assoc. Sumitomo Chem. Co., Ltd., Osaka, Japan, 1971-85, sr. rsch. assoc., rsch. mgr., 1986—; lectr. Kyoto U., 1971-72, 85—; cons. Protection of Environment of Kyoto City, 1990—. Inventor, patentee in cytotoxic agts., others; contbr. over 100 articles to profl. jours. Mem. Am. Chem. Soc., Japanese Soc. Pharm. Scis., Internat. Soc. for Study of Xenobiotics, Japanese Soc. for Study of Xenobiotics, Pesticide Sci. Soc. Japan, Environ. Mutagen Soc. Japan, Japanese Soc. Nuclear Medicine, Japan Radioisotope Assn. Home: 6 Izumigawacho Shimogamo, Sakyo-ku, Kyoto 606, Japan Office: Sumitomo Chem Co Ltd, 1-98 Chome Kasugadenaka, Osaka 554, Japan

YOSHIUCHI, ELLEN HAVEN, childbirth educator; b. Newark, Apr. 15, 1949; d. Michael Joseph and Adeline V. (Lindblom) Haven; m. Takeshi Yoshiuchi, Dec. 1, 1973; children: Teri Takumi, Niki Noboru. BA summa cum laude, CUNY, 1980; M Profl. Studies in Human Rels., N.Y. Inst. Tech., 1991. Cert. bereavement svcs. counselor. Pvt. practice childbirth edn., 1983-89; program asst. parent/family edn. St. Luke's/Roosevelt Hosp. Ctr., N.Y.C., 1989-93, mem. faculty parent/family edn. program, 1990—; mem. faculty Family Ctr. at Riverdale Neighborhood House, Bronx, N.Y., 1991—; mem. perinatal bereavement com. St. Luke's/Roosevelt Hosp. Ctr., N.Y.C., 1989—; mem. bd. trustees Pan Asian Repertory Theater, N.Y., 1996—. Editor ASPO/N.Y.C. News, 1983-86; contbr. articles to profl. jours. Fellow Am. Coll. Childbirth Educators; mem. ACA, Internat. Childbirth Edn. Assn., Assn. Specialists in Group Work, N.Y. State Perinatal Assn., Am. Soc. for Psychoprophylaxis in Obstetrics/Lamaze (cert. tchr., pres. N.Y.C. chpt. 1987-91, nominating com. 1991-93, dir. ednl. program 1991-93).

YOTHER, ANTHONY WAYNE, critical care nurse, nurse manager; b. Anniston, Ala., Jan. 30, 1964; s. Johnny Wayne and Carol Sue (Bradshaw) Y. BSN, Jacksonville State U., 1987; MSN, U. Ala., Birmingham, 1992; MS in Health Care Policy and Adminstrn., Mercer U., 1994. Cert. med.-surg. nursing, med.-surg. clin. specialist, nursing adminstrn., adult critical care nursing, pediatric adv. life support. ICU mgr. Grady Health Sys., Atlanta, 1994—. Mem. ANA (cert.), AACCN (cert.), Am. Heart Assn., Ga. Nurses Assn., Laurleen B. Wallace Coll. Nursing Alumni Assn. (v.p. 1988-90, pres. 1990-92), U. Ala.-Birmingham Alumni Assn., Mercer U. Alumni Assn., Jacksonville State U. Alumni Assn., Sigma Theta Tau Internat.

YOTIS, WILLIAM W., microbiologist; b. Almyros, Thessaly, Greece, Jan. 17, 1930; came to U.S., 1948; s. Vasilios and Aspasia (Papapostolou) Y.; m. Eleonora Colon-Valez, Aug. 9, 1957; children: William W., Athena, Victor. BS, Wayne State U., 1954; PhD, Northwestern U., 1960. Instr. Med. Sch. Loyola U., Chgo., 1960-62, asst. prof. microbiology, 1963-66, assoc. prof., 1967-72; prof. Med. Sch. Loyola U., Maywood, Ill., 1973—; vis. scientist Argonne (Ill.) Nat. Lab., 1978-86; mem. editorial bd. Applied and Environ. Microbiology, Washington, 1977-85, Infection and Immunity, Washington, 1987-89. Author: Isoelectric Focusing of Microbial Proteins, 1977, Review of Microbiology and Immunobiology, 1989, Advances in Steroid Biochemistry and Pharmacology, vol. III, 1972; contbr. numerous articles to profl. jours. Mem. Am. Soc. Microbiology, Am. Assn. Dental Rsch., N.Y. Acad. Sci. (editor 1974). Greek Orthodox. Home: 1160 Clippers Way Tarpon Springs FL 34689

YOUKER, JAMES EDWARD, radiologist; b. Cooperstown, N.Y., Nov. 13, 1928; s. Bliss Jacob and Marian (Ostrander) Y.; children—Elizabeth Ann, James David. A.B., Colgate U., 1950; M.D., U. Buffalo, 1954. Diplomate: Am. Bd. Radiology. Intern U. Minn., Mpls., 1954-55; resident in radiology U. Minn., 1955-56, 58-60; resident in pathology Georgetown U., Washington, 1958; pvt. practice medicine, specializing in radiology Corpus Christi, Tex., 1956-58; asst. prof. radiology Med. Coll. Va., Richmond, 1961-63; research fellow U. Lund, Malmo, Sweden, 1963-64; asst. prof. radiology U. Calif., San Francisco, 1964-67; asso. prof. U. Clif., 1967-68; prof., chmn. dept. radiology Med. Coll. Wis., Milw., 1968—; dir. dept. radiology Milwaukee County Gen. Hosp., Milw., 1968—; chmn. dept. radiology Froedtert Meml. Luth. Hosp., 1979—; served with Project Hope, Indonesia, 1961; cons./lectr. VA Hosp., Richmond, 1961-63, San Francisco, 1964-68, Martinez, Calif., 1964-68; cons./lectr. Letterman Army Med. Center, San Francisco, 1964-68, Oakknoll Naval Hosp., Oakladn, Calif., 1964-68, VA Hosp., Wood, Wis., 1968—, Gt. Lakes Naval Hosp., Chgo., 1968—; vis. prof. U. Calif. Sch. Medicine, San Francisco, 1974, Stanford U. Sch. Medicine, Palo Alto, Calif., 1976; vis. physician dept cardiology St. Vincent's Hosp., Melbourne, Australia, 1974-75; mem. com. diagnosis breast cancer task force NIH, 1975-79; Head Physicians for Ford; chmn. health and med. sci. tech. com. for program planning com. North Div. High Sch., 1979; bd. dirs. Med. Coll. Wis., 1986—, mem. residency rev. commn. for radiology, 1985—. Editorial adv. bd.: Critical Revs. in Radiologic Scis; editorial bd.: Postgrad. Radiology; reviewer: Am. Jour. Roentgenology; assoc. reviewer Radiol.; assoc. editor: Cardiovascular Diseases, 1985—; contbr. numerous articles to profl. jours. Served with M.C. USN, 1956-58. N.Y. State Regents scholar, 1946; Buffalo Found. scholar, 1952; grantee USPHS; grantee Squibb Pharms.; grantee Nat. Cancer Inst.; grantee others. Fellow Am. Coll. Radiology (bd. chancellors 1978—, vice-chmn. commn. on cancer 1972-74, chmn./mem. numerous coms., v.p. 1983-84); mem. Am. Assn. Physicians Assts. (adv. bd.), Am. Cancer Soc. (coms. Milw. br.), Am. Heart Assn. Council on Cardiovascular Radiology, AMA, Am. Roentgen Ray Soc. (adv. com. research and edn.), Assn. Univ. Radiologists (chmn. govt. affairs com. 1978-79), Med. Soc. Milwaukee County (hosp. med. staff liaison com. 1978-79), Milw. Acad. Medicine, Milw. Roentgen Ray Soc., Soc. Chairmen Acad. Radiolgy Depts. (pres. 1972, coms.), Soc. Gastrointestinal Radiology, Vail Creative Concepts Conf. (co-founder), Wis. Med. Soc., Wis. Radiol. Soc. (dir., chmn. technician affairs com.). Republican. Clubs: Univ. (Milw.); Chenequa Country. Office: Milw County Hosp 8700 W Wisconsin Ave Milwaukee WI 53226-3512*

YOUMANS, WILLIAM BARTON, physiologist; b. Cin., Feb. 3, 1910; s. Charles Trimble and Lucy May (Gardiner) Y.; m. Cynthia McCreary Holbrook, Nov. 24, 1932; children: William Barton, Carol Anne, Charles Gilbert. BS, Western Ky. State Coll., Bowling Green, 1932; MS, Western Ky. State Coll., 1933; PhD, U. Wis., 1938; MD, U. Oreg., 1944 Intern Henry Ford Hosp., Detroit, 1944-45; instr. biology Western Ky. U., Bowling Green, 1932-35; rsch. asst. physiology U. Wis., Madison, 1935-36; instr. physiology U. Wis., 1936-38; instr. physiology to assoc. prof. physiology U. Oreg. Med. Sch., Portland, 1938-42; prof. physiology U. Oreg. Med. Sch., 1942-46, head physiology dept., 1946-52; prof. and chmn. dept. physiology U. Wis., Madison, 1952-71; prof. physiology U. Wis., 1971-76, prof. emeritus, 1976—; mem. physiology study sect. USPHS, 1952-56, mem. tng. grant and fellowship rev. panels, 1956-60, 60-64. Author: Nervous and Neurohumoral Regulation of Intestinal Motility, 1949, Hemodynamics in Failure of the Circulation, 1951, Basic Medical Physiology, 1952, Fundamentals of Human Physiology, 1957, others; contbr. articles to profl. jours. Recipient Meritorious Achievement award, U. Oreg. Med. Sch. Alumni Assn., 1967, Emeritus Faculty award, U. Wis. Med. Alumni Assn., 1985. Fellow AAAS; mem. Am. Physiol. Soc., Am. Soc. Pharmacology and Exptl. Therapeutics, Am. Heart Assn., Alpha Omega Alpha, Phi Sigma, Gamma Alpha. Home: 118 Klahanie View Ln Port Angeles WA 98363-8300

YOUNATHAN, MARGARET TIMS, nutritionist, educator; b. Clinton, Miss., Apr. 25, 1926; d. Peter Asbury and Eula Lee (Tatum) Tims; BA, U. So. Miss., 1946, BS, 1950; MS, U. Tenn., 1951; PhD, Fla. State U., 1958; m. Ezzat S. Younathan, Aug. 11, 1958; children: Janet Nadya, Carol Miriam. Instr., food and nutrition Oreg. State U., 1951-55; postdoctoral rsch. assoc. Fla. State U., 1958-59; sr. nutritional cons. Ark. Dept. Health, Little Rock, 1962-68; instr. pediatrics U. Ark. Sch. Medicine, Little Rock, 1962-65, asst. prof. pediatrics, 1965-68; assoc. prof. food and nutrition Sch. Human Ecology, La. State U., 1971-79, prof., 1979-94; ret. 1994; internat. nutrition work in Sierra Leone, 1984, Jamaica, 1987. La. State U. Coun. on Rsch. summer faculty grantee, 1980; research grantee Lou Ana Foods, Inc, 1987. Mem. Inst. Food Technologists, Am. Inst. Nutrition, Am. Dietetic Assn., Am. Home Econs. Assn., La. Home Econs. Assn. (pres. dist. D. 1981-82, Disting. Home Economist award 1988), Sigma Xi, Phi Kappa Phi, Gamma Sigma Delta, Omicron Nu, Phi Upsilon Omicron. Mem. Christian Ch. (Disciples of Christ). Contbr. articles on food and nutrition rsch. to profl. jours. Home: 1048 Castle Kirk Dr Baton Rouge LA 70808-6023 Office: Sch Human Ecology La State U Baton Rouge LA 70803

YOUNG, BRUCE P., physician; b. N.Y., Jan. 26, 1955; married; two children: Caroline, Stoddard. BA, Hamilton Coll., 1976; MD, Rutgers Med. Sch., 1980. Diplomate Nat. Bd. Med. Examiners; cert. Am. Acad. Orthopaedic Surgeons, Workman's Compensation. Intern Albert Einstein-Montefiore Coll. Medicine, Bronx, 1980-81; resident in orthopaedic surgery Rutgers Med. Sch., 1981-85; various positions to chief of surgery North Broward Med. Ctr., Pompano Beach, Fla., 1985—; staff Boca Raton Community Hosp., Fla., 1993—, West Boca Med. Ctr., Fla.; chief surgery North Broward Med. Ctr. Fellow Am. Acad. Orthopaedic Surgeons; mem. AMA, Broward County Med. Assn., Fla. Med. Assn. Office: Lighthouse Orthopaedics 1821 NE 25th St Lighthouse Point FL 33064

YOUNG, DAVID VERN, surgeon; b. Bryan, Tex., May 5, 1949; s. LeVern Benjamin and Mary Frances (Smith) Y.; m. Neta Ann Hendricks; children: Sarah, John. BA, Calif. Bapt. Coll., 1969; MD, U. Calif., San Francisco, 1973. Diplomate Am. Bd. Surgery. Rotating intern Valley Med. Ctr./U. Calif. San Francisco, Fresno, Calif., 1973-74, resident in surgery, 1974-78; missionary surgeon Jiblah Bapt. Hosp., Yemen, 1979-81, 83-85, Ajloun Bapt. Hosp., Jordan, 1981-82; postgrad. fellow in surgery VA Hosp., Fresno, 1982-83; pvt. practice surgery Fresno, 1985—; chair dept. surgery Fresno Cmty. Hosp., 1990, v.p. med. staff, 1991; pres. med. staff Cmty. Hosps. of Ctrl. Calif., Fresno, 1992; exec. com. Fresno Cmty. and Com. Hosp. Ctrl. Calif., 1989-94; pres. Comty. Surg. Group, 1996—. Contbr. articles to profl. jours. Organizer, mem. Christian Health Care Network, Fresno, 1989—; deacon Harvard Terr. Bapt. Ch., Fresno, 1985-90; mem. leadership team Cmty. Bible Ch., Fresno, 1993-95. Named Alumnus of Yr., Calif. Bapt. Coll., 1989. Fellow ACS; mem. Calif. Med. Assn., Christian Med./Dental Soc. Republican. Office: 110 N Valeria Ste 401 Fresno CA 93720

YOUNG, DONALD ROY, pharmacist; b. Belfast, Pa., Oct. 7, 1935; s. Roy Clifford and Gladys Nicholas (Ealer) Y.; m. Joyce Anne Waldridge; children: Donald, Lynda, David. BS in Pharmacy, U. Md., Balt., 1957. Pharmacist Brookside Rhodes Drugs Co., Newark, Del., 1956-57; pharmacist, mgr. Newark Rhodes Drugs Co., 1957-64; pharmacist, owner, mgr. Hudson's Pharmacy, St. Michaels, Md., 1964—; bd. dirs., officer St. Michaels Bank; treas. Calvert Drug Co. Balt., 1970-76. Pres. St. Michaels Improvement Corp., 1966—. Mem. Nat. Assn. Retail Druggists, Ea. Shore Pharm. Assn. (pres. 1967-68, 82-86), Talbot County C. of C. (Outstanding Small Bus. Man of Yr. award 1989), St. Michaels Bus. Assn. (pres.), U. Md. Sch. Pharmacy Alumni Assn. (life), Isaac Walton League, Miles River Yacht Club, Rotary (pres. St. Michaels 1970, Most Outstanding Mem. award 1988, Paul Harris fellow award 1995), Elks, Masons (32 degree, master 1969-70, apptd. jr. grand deacon of Grand Line 1989-90). Republican. Methodist. Home: PO Box 130 118 Tricefields Rd Saint Michaels MD 21663 Office: Hudsons Pharmacy PO Box 130 Saint Michaels MD 21663

YOUNG, DONALD STIRLING, clinical pathology educator; b. Belfast, N. Ireland, Dec. 17, 1933; s. John Stirling and Ruth Muir (Whipple) Y.; m. Silja Meret; children: Gordon, Robert, Peter. MB, ChB, U. Aberdeen, Scotland, 1957; PhD in Chem. Pathology, U. London, 1962. Terminable lectr. materia medica U. Aberdeen, 1958-59; fellow Postgrad. Med. Sch., U. London, 1959-62, registrar, 1962-64; vis. scientist NIH, Bethesda, Md., 1965-66; chief clin. chemistry service NIH, 1966-77; head clin. chemistry sect. Mayo Clinic, Rochester, Minn., 1977-84; prof. pathology and lab. medicine U. Pa., 1984—; dir. William Pepper Lab. Hosp. of U. Pa., 1984—; past bd. dirs. Nat. Com. Clin. Lab. Standards. Co-editor: Drug Interference and Drug Metabolism in Clinical Chemistry, 1976, Clinician and Chemist, 1979, Chemical Diagnosis of Disease, 1979, Drug Measurement and Drug Effects in Laboratory Health Science, 1980, Interpretation of Clinical Laboratory Tests, 1985, Effects of Drugs on Clinical Laboratory Tests, 1995, Effects of Preanalytical Variables on Clinical Laboratory Tests, 1996. Recipient Dir.'s award NIH, 1977, Gerard B. Lambert award, 1974-75, MDS Health Group award Can. Soc. Clin. Chemists, 1978; Roman lectr. Australian Assn. Clin. Biochemists, 1979; Jendrassik award Hungarian Soc. Clin. Pathologists, 1985, ATB award Italian Soc. Clin. Biochemistry, 1987. Mem. Am. Assn. Clin. Chemistry (J.H. Roe award Capital sect. 1973, Bernard Gerulat award N.J. sect. 1977, Ames award 1977, Van Slyke award N.Y. met. sect. 1985, J.G. Reinhold award Phila. sect. 1993, past pres.), Internat. Fedn. Clin. Chemists (past pres.), Acad. Clin. Lab. Physicians and Scientists (past exec. com.), Assn. Clin. Biochemists (Ciba-Corning lectr. 1985). Home: 1116 Remington Rd Wynnewood PA 19096-4045 Office: Hosp U Pa 3400 Spruce St Philadelphia PA 19104-4283

YOUNG, DOUGLAS ALAN, physiologist, research scientist; b. Mpls., Sept. 1, 1955; s. LeRoy and Lovie (Jackson) Y.; m. Leslie Henderson, Aug. 9, 1980; children: Paige, Blair. BA, St. Olaf Coll., 1977; PhD, Washington U., 1983. Postdoctoral fellow Washington U. Med. Sch., St. Louis, 1983-86, rsch. asst. prof., 1986-87; asst. fellow Sandoz Pharm. Corp., East Hanover, N.J., 1987-89; assoc. fellow Sandoz Rsch. Inst., Sandoz Pharm. Corp., East Hanover, N.J., 1989-91, sr. assoc. fellow, 1991-92, fellow, sect. head, 1992-94; group leader Bristol-Meyers Squibb Pharm. Rsch. Inst., Princeton, N.J., 1994-96, assoc. dir. metabolism, 1996—. Contbr. over 30 sci. articles to profl. jours. Mem. AAAS, Am. Diabetes Assn.(bd. dirs. N.J. affiliate, Feasibility award 1986), Am. Physiol. Soc. Office: Bristol-Myers Squibb PO Box 4500 Princeton NJ 08543-4000

YOUNG, ELIZABETH BELL, consultant; b. Franklinton, N.C., July 2, 1929; d. Joseph H. and Eulalia V. (Miller) B.; m. Charles A. Young, Nov. 27, 1964. BA, N.C. Cen. U., 1948, MA, 1950; PhD, Ohio State U., 1959. Cert. speech pathologist; cert. audiologist. Chairperson dept. English Barber Scotia Coll., Concord, N.C., 1949-52; dir. speech area, prof. Talladega (Ala.) Coll., 1954-56; dir. speech clinic, prof. Va. State U., Petersburg, 1956-57; prof. Fla. A&M U., Tallahassee, 1959; chmn. dept. English Fayetteville (N.C.) State U., 1959-63; speech pathologist, rsch. asst. Howard U. Sch. Dentistry, Washington, 1963-64; prof., chairperson dept. English U. Md.-East Shore, Princess Anne, Md., 1965-66; prof., supr. Speech Clinic Cath. U. Am., Washington, 1966-79; congl. staff aide U.S. Ho. of Reps., Washington, 1981-82, 88-90; prof. speech U. D.C., Washington, 1983-84; cons. nat. and local orgns. Washington, 1985-88, 90—; lectr. over 250 speeches, seminars and workshops; speechwriter, cons. Nat. Assn. Equal Opportunity in Higher Edn., Washington, 1990. Contbr. articles to profl. jours. Fundraiser, pub. rels. polit. candidates, 1963-90; mem. bd. United Negro Coll. Fund, 1970-80, D.C. Gen. Hosp. Handicapped Intervention Program, 1970-91. Recipient Citations and Certs. of Achievement community and nat. orgns., 1959-90. Fellow Am. Speech-Lang.-Hearing Assn.; mem. Pub. Mems. Assn. (bd. mem. 1980-91), Ohio State U. Alumni Assn., N.C. Cen. U. Alumni Assn. Democrat. Baptist.

YOUNG, FRANCIS ALLAN, psychologist; b. Utica, N.Y., Dec. 29, 1918; s. Frank Allan and Julia Mae (McOwen) Y.; m. Judith Wadsworth Wright, Dec. 21, 1945; children—Francis Allan, Thomas Robert. B.S., U. Tampa, 1941; M.A., Western Res. U., 1945; Ph.D., Ohio State U., 1949. Instr. Wash. State U., Pullman, 1948-50; asst. prof. Wash. State U., 1950-56, assoc. prof., 1956-61, prof. psychology, 1961-88, dir. primate rsch. ctr., 1957-88, prof., dir. emeritus, 1988—; vis. prof. ophthalmology U. Oreg., Portland, 1964; asst. dir. U. Wash. Regional Primate Ctr., dir. primate field sta., 1966-68; vis. prof. pharmacology U. Uppsala (Sweden) Med. Sch., 1971; vis. prof. optometry U. Houston, 1979-80. Editor: (with Donald B. Lindsley) Early Experience and Visual Information Processing in Perceptual and Reading Disorders, 1970; contbr. chpts. to books, numerous articles to profl. jours. Named Disting. Psychologist State of Wash., Wash. Psychol. Assn., 1973; recipient Paul Yarwood Meml. award Calif. Optometric Assn., 1978; Apollo award Am. Optometric Assn., 1980; Nat. Acad. Sci.-NRC sr. postdoctoral fellow in physiol. psychology U. Wash., 1956-57; research grantee NSF, 1950-53; research grantee USAF, 1965-72; research grantee NIH, 1960-78. Home: 344 NW Webb St Pullman WA 99163-3150 Office: Wash State U Psychology Dept Pullman WA 99164-1170

YOUNG, FRANK COLEMAN, JR., ophthalmologist; b. Clinton, S.C., Oct. 24, 1934; s. Frank Coleman and Lois Susan (Adair) Y.; m. JoAnn Marlene Addy, July 1, 1960; children—Frank C. III, Jonelle Susan, Frances Ann. B.A., B.S., Presbyn. Coll., 1956; M.D., Med. Coll. S.C., 1960. Diplomate Am. Bd. Ophthalmology. Intern, Brooke Gen. Hosp., Ft. Sam Houston, Tex., 1960-61, resident, 1963-66; commd. 2d lt. U.S. Army, 1956, advanced through grades to col., 1975, resigned, 1970, retired from USAR 1994; practice medicine specializing in ophthalmology, 20/20 Ophthalmic Assocs., P.A., Montgomery, Ala., 1970-1994—; mem. staff Bapt. Med. Ctr., v.p. medical affairs, Bapt . Med Ctr., 1994, mem. Am. Acad. Ophthalmology, ACS, AMA. Presbyterian. Home: 3165 Rolling Rd Montgomery AL 36111-1740 Address: PO Box 11010 Montgomery AL 36111

YOUNG, FRANKLIN, nutritional biochemistry educator, researcher; b. Beijing, China, Feb. 1, 1928; came to U.S., 1950, naturalized, 1967; s. Andrew On-Yin and Helen (Loh) Y.; m. Kathlina Patanella. Student U. Shanghai, 1946-48; AB, Mercer U., 1951; BS, U. Fla., 1952, M. Agr., 1954, PhD, 1960. Cert. nutrition specialist. Grad. research fellow U. Fla., Gainesville, 1958-60; post doctoral research fellow, 1960-61; research assoc. Bowman Gray Sch. Medicine, Winston-Salem, N.C., 1961-65, research instr., 1965-66; assoc. prof. U. Hawaii, Honolulu, 1968-83; prof. nutritional biochemistry, chmn. and researcher cardiovascular diseases and hypertension U. Utah, Salt Lake City, 1983-85; prof. nutritional biochemistry West Chester U., Pa., 1985—. Contbr. articles to profl. jours. Mem. Am. Inst. Nutrition, Sigma Xi, Gamma Sigma Delta (charter mem., treas. 1970-71), Phi Kappa Phi, Phi Sigma. Office: West Chester U Dept Health West Chester PA 19383

YOUNG, GRACE MAY-EN, pediatrician; b. Pitts.. AB, Harvard U., 1977; MD, Columbia U., 1981. Diplomate Am. Bd. Pediat. Emergency Medicine, Am. Bd. Pediat. Asst. prof. pediat. George Washington U. Sch. Medicine, Washington, 1986-90, NYU Sch. Medicine, N.Y.C., 1990-93; assoc. prof. pediat. U. Md. Sch. Medicine, Balt., 1993—. Office: Univ Md Med Ctr Pediat Emergency Dept 22 S Greene St # N1W45 Baltimore MD 21201

YOUNG, HENRY E., medical educator; b. Dayton, Ohio, Dec. 5, 1951; s. Henry O. and Lucille M. Y.; m. Valerie E. Achorn, May 16, 1976; 1 child,

Katherine. BS in Biology, Ohio State U., 1974; MS in Zoology, U. Ark., 1977; PhD, Tex. Tech. U., 1983. Instr.biochemistry Rush-Presbyn.-St. Luke's Med. Ctr., Chgo., 1987-88; asst. prof. anatomy Mercer U. Sch. Medicine, Macon, Ga., 1988-95, asst. prof. surgery, 1988-93, assoc. prof. anatomy, pediatrics, 1995—. Inventor in field. NIH Postdoctoral fellow biochemistry Case Western Res. U., Cleve., 1983-85, Muscular Dystrophy Assn. postdoctoral fellow, 1985-87; recipient Hooding award Excellence in Teaching and Rsch. Mercer U. Med. Sch., 1993, 94. Mem. Nat. Coun. Adoptable Children, Ga. Coun. Adoptable Children. Home: 195 Ashton Dr Macon GA 31220 Office: Mercer U Sch Medicine 1550 College St Macon GA 31207

YOUNG, HENRY T., family medicine physician; b. Ferriday, La., May 31, 1955; s. Henry Thomas and Hazel (Edwards) Y.; m. Crista M., Apr. 7, 1979; children: Henry T. III, Sarah M., Michael J. BS, La. Coll., 1977; MD, La. State U., 1981. Diplomate Am. Bd. Family Practice. Intern, resident in family practice La. State U., Shreveport, 1981-84; pvt. practice family medicine Jonesville, Denham Spring, La., 1984—; med. dir. Harvest Manor, Denham Springs, 1994-96; clin. preceptor La. State U., New Orleans, 1984—, Baton Rouge Gen. Health Sys., 1995—. Pres. Livingston Parish chpt. Am. Cancer Soc. Fellow Am. Acad. Family Practice; mem. Am. Med. Dir.'s Assn., La. Acad. Family Practice, East Baton Rouge Parish Med. Soc., La. Med. Dir.'s Assn., La. State Med. Soc. Baptist. Office: Family Health La Inc. 1113 S Range Ave Ste D Denham Springs LA 70726-4822

YOUNG, JAMES JULIUS, university administrator, former army officer; b. Fort Ringgold, Tex., Nov. 28, 1926; s. John Cooper and Violet Thelma (Ohl) Y.; m. June Agnes Hillstead, Dec. 17, 1948; children: Robert Michael, Steven Andrew, Patrick James, Mary Frances. B.S., U. Md., 1960; M.H.A., Baylor U., 1962; Ph.D. in Hosp. and Health Adminstrn, U. Iowa, 1969. Commd. 2d lt. U.S. Army, 1947, advanced through grades to brig. gen., 1977; comdr., med. ops. officer, dir. tng. field med. units in European Command, 1949-53; comdr. Mil. Med. Leadership Sch., 1953-54; med. advisor (Nationalist Army of China), 1955-57; asst. adminstr. Fitzsimons Army Med. Center, 1957-60; med. plans and ops. officer (US Forces), Korea, 1962-63; sr. field med. instr., chief field med. service Med. Field Service Sch., 1963-66; dir. health care orgn. and mgmt. analysis Office of Surgeon Gen., 1969-71; dir. med. plans and ops. directorate Office of the Surgeon, Military Assistance Command, Vietnam, 1971-72; exec. officer, chief adminstrv. services Silas Hays Army Hosp., 1973-74; military health analyst, military health care study OMB, Exec. Office of Pres., 1974-76; dep. dir. resources mgmt. and cons. for health care adminstrn. Office of Surgeon Gen., 1976-77; chief Med. Services Corps, U.S. Army and; dir. resources mgmt. Office of Surgeon Gen., 1977-81; ret., 1981; instr. U. Iowa, 1967-69; asst. prof., preceptor Baylor U., 1973-74; vice chancellor for health affairs W.Va. Bd. Regents, Charleston, 1982-87; dean sch. of allied health scis. U. Tex. Health Sci. Ctr., San Antonio, 1987-90, interim dean Sch. Medicine, 1988-89, dean Sch. Medicine, 1989—; cons. to Min. of Health, Republic of Vietnam, 1971-72; adj. prof. Baylor U., 1977-81, George Washington U., 1975-76, W.Va. U., 1986; prof. U. Tex. health Sci. Ctr., San Antonio, 1989—. Contbr. articles to profl. jours. Decorated D.S.M., Legion of Merit, Meritorious Service medal and; others; recipient Walter Reed medallion for service, 1981; Army Med. Dept. medallion for contribution to health service, 1981. Mem. APHA, Coun. Deans, Assn. of Am. Med. Colls., Assn. Mil. Surgeons (chmn. med. svc. sect. 1978), Assn. U.S. Army, Interag. Inst. Fed. Health Execs., Phi Kappa Tau. Roman Catholic. Home: 1610 Anchor Dr San Antonio TX 78213-1943 Office: U Tex Health Sci Ctr Office Of Dean Med Sch San Antonio TX 78284

YOUNG, JAMES OLIVER, dentist, communication company executive; b. Parris Island, S.C., Apr. 19, 1945; s. William Oliver and Ruth Cherokee (Risner) Y.; m. Virginia Evelyn Koontz; children: Amy Robyn, Jenny Elizabeth, Thomas William. BS, Southeast State U., Okla., 1967; DDS, Baylor U., 1972. Practice dentistry, Ardmore, Okla., 1972-93; v.p. Cherokee Telephone Co., Calera, Okla., 1963—, pres., 1994—; v.p. Cherokee Cellular, Inc., 1989—; pres. Communication Equipment Co., Calera, 1984—, Cherokee Telephone Co., Calera, Okla., 1994. Trustee Ardmore Devel. Authority, 1980-85; bd. dirs. Ardmore Community Concerts Assn., 1980-90, Salvation Army, 1990-91; scoutmaster Boy Scouts Am., pres. Arbuckle Area coun., 1994, 95; mem. Okla. state adv. bd. Easter Seal Soc. Named one of Outstanding Young Men Am., 1981. Fellow Acad. Gen. Dentistry, Acad. of Dentistry Internat.; mem. ADA, Okla. Dental Assn., Ind. Dentists of So. Okla. (pres. 1986), Okla. C. of C. (bd. dirs. 1984-85). Republican. Episcopalian. Lodge: Masons. Avocations: skiing, sailing. Home: 2207 Ridgeway St Ardmore OK 73401-3405 Office: PO Box 445 Calera OK 74730-0445

YOUNG, JAY MAITLAND, product manager health care products; b. Louisville, Nov. 26, 1944; s. Clyde Dudley and Olive May (Tyas) Y. BA in Chemistry and Math magna cum laude, Vanderbilt U., 1966; MS in Biochemistry, Yale U., 1967, MPhil in Phys. Chemistry, 1968, PhD in Chemistry, 1971. Asst. prof. chemistry Bryn Mawr (Pa.) Coll., 1970-76; rsch. biochemist Abbott Labs., Abbott Park, Ill., 1977-78; project mgr. physiolog. diagnostics Abbott Labs., Abbott Park, 1978-80, project mgr. cancer product devel., 1980-82, internat. clin. specialist sci. affairs, 1982-85, clin. project mgr. physiol. diag. quality and sci. support, 1986-90, staff quality assurance and sci. support, 1990-93, fertility, pregnancy, thyroid mgr., quality and sci. support, 1993-95; fertility, pregnancy, thyroid, cancer mgr., product quality assurance Abbott Labs., Abbott Park, 1995—; cons. Inst. for Cancer Rsch., Fox Chase, Phila., 1974, vis. scientist, 1975-76; honors examiner Swarthmore Coll., 1973, 74; mem. vis. evaluation com., 1975; presenter to med. groups on cancer markers, viral hepatitis and epidemiology of Aids, 1982-84. Contbr. articles to profl. jours.; patentee in med. field. Predoctoral fellow NSF, Yale U., 1966-70; postdoctoral fellow, NIH, U. Oxford, 1971-72; grantee NSF, NATO Travel grant, U. Salford, Eng., 1974. Mem. Am. Med. Writers Assn. Office: Abbott Labs Dept 9FK AP31 200 Abbott Park Rd Abbott Park IL 60064

YOUNG, JOHN KARL, anatomist, educator; b. Mpls., Aug. 15, 1951; s. Lloyd William and Pearl Johanna (Newstrom) Y.; m. Paula Jean Spesock, July 2, 1977; children: Michael Christian, Matthew Thomas. Student, U. So. Calif., L.A., 1968; BS, Cornell U., 1972; PhD, UCLA, 1977. Postdoctoral fellow U. Minn., Mpls., 1977-79; asst. prof. Howard U., Washington, 1979-85, assoc. prof., 1985—. Author: Cells, 1990, Plasticity in the Nervous System, 1992, Hormones, 1994, Development, Aging and Disease, 1994; contbr. articles to profl. jours. Mem. Am. Assn. Anatomists, Am. Physiol. Assn. Office: Howard U Dept Anatomy 520 W St NW Washington DC 20001-2337

YOUNG, JOHN LEONARD, psychiatrist, educator; b. Huntington, Ind., Apr. 26, 1943; s. Jay Alfred and Anne Elizabeth (Neff) Y. BA, Stonehill Coll., 1966; ThM, U. Notre Dame, 1970, MS, 1974; MD, Stanford U., 1977. Diplomate Am. Bd. Psychiatry and Neurology, Am. Bd. Forensic Psychiatry; joined Congregation of Holy Cross, ordained priest Roman Cath. Ch., 1971. Resident in medicine Norwalk (Conn.) Hosp., 1977-78; resident in psychiatry Yale U. Med. Sch., New Haven, 1978-81, postdoctoral fellow, 1981-82, asst. prof. psychiatry, 1982-88, asst. clin. prof., 1989-92, assoc. clin. prof., 1992—; unit chief Whiting Forensic Inst., Middletown, Conn., 1989—; supr. Pastoral Ctr., New Haven, 1979-86; mem. ethics com. Hosp. of St. Raphael, New Haven, 1982—; jour. reviewer Hosp. and Cmty. Psychiatry, 1988—. Contbr. articles to med. jours. Trustee Stonehill Coll., North Easton, Mass., 1972-90; bd. dirs. King's Coll., Wilkes-Barre, Pa., 1983—, Hill Health Ctr., New Haven, 1983-85; cons. law revision com. Conn. Ho. of Reps., Hartford, 1983-85. Recipient President's medal Stonehill Coll., 1980; Stanford U. Med. Alumni Assn. scholar, 1976. Mem. Am. Psychiat. Assn., Am. Acad. Psychiatry and Law, Am. Chem. Soc., Internat. Assn. for Forensic Psychotherapy, Soc. for Sci. Study Religion. Home: 203 Maple St New Haven CT 06511-4048 Office: Whiting Forensic Inst PO Box 70 Middletown CT 06457-0070

YOUNG, JULIA REGINA, medical technologist; b. Jacksonville, N.C., Aug. 16, 1960; d. Andrew and Catherine Pataki. BS in Med. Tech., Gannon U., 1982. Med. technologist Preston Meml. Hosp., Kingwood, W.Va., 1982-83, St. Francis Med. Ctr., Pitts., 1983-89; med. lab. tech. program dir. Pa. State U., New Kensington, 1989—; mem. adv. bd. Lenape Vo-Tech., Ford City, Pa., 1989—, lab technician program Pitts. Pub. Schs., 1995—; mem. program rev. for accreditation Nat. Accreditation Agy. for Clin. Lab. Scis., Chgo., 1989—. Mem. Am. Soc. Clin. Pathologists. Office: Pa State U 3550 7th St Rd New Kensington PA 15068

YOUNG, LARRY DALE, medical psychologist; b. Fountain Head, Tenn., Dec. 13, 1948; s. Finley Odell and Hattie Frances (Hickey) Y.; m. Sandra Annette Tice, Dec. 27, 1970; children: Abigail Dawn, Matthew Edward Louis. BA, David Lipscomb Coll., 1970; MS, U. Ga., 1972; PhD, Harvard U., 1979. Asst. prof. U. Miss., Oxford, 1978-80; asst. prof. med. psychology Bowman Gray Sch. Medicine, Wake Forest U., Winston-Salem, N.C., 1980-90, assoc. prof., 1990-96, prof., 1996—, acting head med. psychology program, 1989-90; site surveyor Commn. on Accreditation of Rehab. Facilities, Tucson, 1984—. Assoc. editor: Biofeedback and Self-Regulation; former mem. editorial bd. Annals of Behavioral Medicine, 1994—; contbr. articles to profl. jours. Bd. dirs. Piedmont Health Systems Agy., Greensboro, N.C., 1984-87. Mem. Am. Psychol. Assn., Assn. for Advancement Behavior Therapy, Soc. for Psychophysiol. Research, Southeastern Psychol. Assn., Soc. Behavioral Medicine, Assn. Applied Psychophysiology and Biofeedback, Am. Pain Soc., Internat. Assn. Study Pain, Assn. Med. Sch. Prof. Psychology, Phi Beta Kappa. Office: Wake Forest U Bowman Gray Sch Medicine Dept Anesthesia Pain Control Ctr Medical Center Blvd Winston Salem NC 27157

YOUNG, LIONEL WESLEY, radiologist; b. New Orleans, Mar. 14, 1932; s. Charles Henry and Ethel Elsie (Johnson) Y.; m. Florence Inez Brown, June 24, 1957; children: Tina Inez, Lionel Thomas, Owen Christopher. BS in Biology, St. Benedict's Coll., Atchison, Kans., 1953; MD, Howard U., 1957. Diplomate Am. Bd. Radiology. Intern Detroit Receiving Hosp., Wayne State Univ. Coll. of Medicine, 1957-58; resident Strong Meml. Hosp., U. Rochester (N.Y.) Med. Ctr., 1958-61; pediatric radiologist, assoc. prof. radiology and pediatrics U. Rochester Med. Ctr., 1965-75; prof. radiology and pediatrics U. Pitts., 1975-86; dir. radiology and pediatrics Children's Hosp. of Pitts., 1980-86; chmn. radiology Children's Hosp. Med. Ctr. of Akron (Ohio), 1986—, Children's Hosp. and Northeastern Ohio U. Coll. Medicine, Rootstown, 1987—; pres. Akron Pediatric Radiologists, 1986—. Lt. comdr. USN, 1961-63. Mem. Am. Coll. Radiology (mem. coun., steering com.), Soc. for Pediatric Radiology. Democrat. Roman Catholic. Office: Division of Pediatric Radiology Loma Linda Univ Children's Hosp 11234 Anderson St Loma Linda CA 92354

YOUNG, LUCY HWA-YUE, physician, retina surgeon; b. Taipei, Taiwan, Dec. 8, 1957; came to U.S., 1974; d. TsenMen Young and PeiLan Liu; m. Henning A. Gaissert, Aug. 12, 1989; children: Anna Gaissert, Philipp Gaissert. BS in Biology, U. Wis., 1977, MD, 1981; PhD, Harvard U., 1984. Diplomate Am. Bd. Ophthalmology. Intern Framingham (Mass.) Union Hosp., 1984-85; resident in ophthalmology Mass. Eye and Ear Infirmary, Boston, 1985-88, retina fellow, 1988-90; instr. in ophthalmology Mass. Eye and Ear Infirmary/Harvard U., Boston, 1990-92, asst. prof. ophthalmology, 1992—; mem. utilization review Mass. Eye and Ear Infirmary, 1990—, pharmacy com., 1993—. Contbr. articles to profl. jours. Recipient grant Mass. Lions Eye Rsch. Found., 1992, 93, 94, 95, 96, grant NIH, 1994-99. Fellow Am. Coll. Surgeons; mem. Am. Acad. Ophthalmology, Assn. for Rsch. in Vision and Ophthalmology, New Eng. Ophthal. Soc., Retina Soc., Mass. Soc. Eye Physicians and Surgeons, Soc. for Neurosci. Office: Mass Eye and Ear Infirmary 243 Charles St Boston MA 02114

YOUNG, MARGARET ALETHA MCMULLEN (MRS. HERBERT WILSON YOUNG), social worker; b. Vossburg, Miss., June 13, 1916; d. Grady Garland and Virgie Aletha (Moore) McMullen; BA cum laude, Columbia Bible Coll., 1949; grad. Massey Bus. Coll., 1958; MSW, Fla. State U., 1965; postgrad. Jacksonville U., 1961-62, Tulane U., 1967; m. Herbert Wilson Young, Aug. 19, 1959. Dir. Christian edn. Eau Claire Presbyn. Ch., Columbia, S.C., 1946-51; tchr. Massey Bus. Coll., Jacksonville, Fla., 1954-57, office mgr., 1957-59; social worker, unit supr. Fla. div. Family Svcs., St. Petersburg, 1960-66, dist. casework supr., 1966-71; social worker, project supr., program supr. Project Playpen, Inc., 1971-81, pres. bd., 1982-83, cons., 1986-89; pvt. practice family counselor, 1982—; mem. coun. Child Devel. Ctr., 1983-89; mem. transitional housing com., Religious Community Svcs., 1984-90. Mem. Acad. Cert. Social Workers, Nat. Assn. Social Workers (pres. Tampa Bay chpt. 1973-74), Fla. Assn. for Health and Social Services (pres. chpt. 1971), Nature Conservancy, Eta Beta Rho. Democrat. Presbyn. Rotary Ann (pres. 1970-71). Home: Presbyterian Home CMR 13 201 W 9th North St Summerville SC 29483-6721

YOUNG, MARTIN D., parasitologist; b. Moreland, Ga., July 4, 1909; s. Joe Hugh and Jennie Sue (Martin) Y.; m. GeDelle Brabham, July 18, 1938; children: Martin Brabham, Margaret Cope (Mrs. Anderson). B.S., Emory U., 1931, M.S., 1932, D.Sc. (hon.), 1963; Sc.D., Johns Hopkins U., 1937; D.Sc. (hon.), Mich. State U., 1975, U. Fla., 1985. Diplomate: Am. Acad. Microbiology, Med. Lab. Parasitology. Prof. biology, head dept. Jr. Coll., Augusta, Ga., 1932-34; prof. health East State Tchrs. Coll., Johnson City, Tenn., 1939; staff NIH, USPHS, Columbia, S.C., 1937-61; parasitologist dir. malaria lab., 1941-50, dir. sect. on epidemiology, 1950-61, in charge imported malaria studies, 1943-46, dir. malaria survey of Liberia, 1948; asst. chief Lab. Parasite Chemotherapy, NIH, 1961-62; assoc. dir. Nat. Inst. Allergy and Infectious Diseases, 1962-64; dir. Gorgas Meml. Lab., 1964-74; dir. research Gorgas Meml. Inst., 1972-74, research asso., 1974-78; cons. Health Dept., C.Z., 1964-74; vis. rsch. prof. parasitology Coll. Vet. Medicine; adj. rsch. prof. immunology, med. microbiology and medicine Med. Coll., U. Fla., Gainesville, 1974—; vis. prof. microbiology Ala. Med. Ctr.; clin. prof. med. parasitology La. State U. Med. Sch., 1967-76; prof. extraordinario ad-honorem Faculty Medicine, U. Panama; vis. prof. Meml. U., St. John's Nfld., Can., 1977; hon. rsch. assoc. Smithsonian Tropical Rsch. Inst., 1966-74; mem. adv. on malaria to WHO-Pan-Am. Health Orgn., 1957-62, 65-68; mem. expert panel on malaria WHO, 1950-84; WHO cons. malaria, Rumania, 1961; ICA cons. on Govt. India malaria control program, 1957; mem. malaria commn., commn. on parasitic diseases, commn. on environ. health Armed Forces Epidemiological Bd., 1965-73; cons. Malaria Control Strategy for Tropical Africa, AID, 1980; cons. on internat. devel. to NRC Bd. Sci. and Tech., 1984. Chmn. editorial bd., editor pro tem: Am. Jour. Tropical Medicine and Hygiene, 1959, mem. editorial bd., 1960-63; asst. editor: Jour. Wildlife Disease, 1981-84, mem. editorial bd., 1985-87; contbr. numerous articles in parasitology, prin. human malaria, to sci., publs., books. Mem. Columbia (S.C.) Bd. Health, 1960-61; bd. dirs. Gorgas Meml. Inst. Tropical and Preventive Medicine, 1977-83, mem. adv. sci. bd., 1983—. Decorated grand officer Order Manuel Amador Guerrero Panama, 1974; co-recipient Jefferson award S.C. Acad. Sci. for especially meritorious paper, 1946, 52, 61 ann. meetings; recipient Rockefeller Pub. Service award, 1953; Darling medal and prize WHO, 1963; Gorgas medal Assn. Mil. Surgeons U.S., 1974; Cert. of Merit Gorgas Meml. Inst., 1974; Cert. of Appreciation, Surgeon Gen. U.S. Army, 1974. Fellow AAAS (councilor 1947-48, 52-55), Royal Soc. Tropical Medicine and Hygiene (local sec. 1962-64, 84—); hon. fellow Nat. Soc. India for Malaria and Other Mosquito-borne Diseases; mem. Nat. Malaria Soc. (sec.-treas. 1946-50, del. 4th internat. congress on tropical med. and malaria, Washington 1948, pres. elect 1952), Am. Soc. Parasitologists (del. to 6th Internat. congresses on Tropical Medicine and Malaria, Lisbon 1958, councillor 1947-50, editorial bd. 1951-54, pres. 1965, emeritus), Am. Soc. Tropical Med. and Hygiene (pres. 1952, del. 5th Internat. Congress Tropical Medicine and Malaria, Istanbul 1953, rep. Nat. Acad. Sci. 1962-65, Le Prince medal 1976, Craig lectr. 1985), Am. Soc. Profs. Biology (v.p. 1949-50), Emory U. Alumni Assn. (nat. v.p. from grad. sch. 1947-48), Assn. Southeastern Biologists (councillor 1941-42, sec.-treas. 1942-46, pres. 1947-48, emeritus), S.C. Acad. Sci. (councilor 1941, v.p. 1948-49, pres. 1949-50, emeritus), Australian Soc. Parasitology, Soc. Protozoologists, Internat. Primatology Soc., Wildlife Disease Assn., Am. Acad. Microbiology, Asociación Panameña de Microbiologiá, Sigma Xi, Phi Zeta, Gamma Alpha, Phi Sigma. Methodist. Clubs: Rotary, Torch. Home: 610 NW 89th St Gainesville FL 32607-1453

YOUNG, MARVIN RICHARD, dermatologist, educator; b. Monroe, Wash., Apr. 5, 1935; s. Julian Giliat and Margaret Alice (Anderson) Y.; m. Judith Yvonne Heitkemper, Dec. 27, 1958; children: John Edward, Leslie Elizabeth. BA, U. Oreg., Eugene, 1957; MD, Oreg. Health Scis. U., Portland, 1959. Diplomate Am. Bd. Dermatology. Intern Phila. Gen. Hosp., 1959-60; dermatology resident Oreg. Health Sci. U., 1960-65; pvt. practice Seattle, 1965-88, Minor & James Med., Seattle, 1988-96; clin. instr., asst. prof., assoc. prof., clin. prof. derm. U. Wash. Sch. Medicine, 1965—. Contbr. med. articles to profl. jours. Lt. comdr. USNR, 1960-62. Fellow Am. Acad. Dermatology; mem. AMA, Seattle Dermatol. Soc. (pres. 1975), Wash. State Med. Assn. (pres. 1991), King County Med. Soc. (pres. 1984).

YOUNG, MICHAEL C., allergist, immunologist, pediatrician; b. Chgo., July 10, 1953; s. Koon C. and Siu Fun (Hui) Y.; m. Karen Lee Young, Apr. 7, 1979; 1 child, Liane. AB cum laude, Harvard Coll., 1975; MD, Yale U., 1979. Diplomate Am. Bd. Allergy and Immunology, Am. Bd. Pediatrics, Nat. Bd. Med. Examiners. Resident pediatrics Children's Hosp., Boston, 1979-82, fellow in allergy and immunology, 1982-84, asst. in medicine (immunology), attending physician, 1984—; clin. instr. pediatrics Harvard Med. Sch., Boston, 1984—; mem. active staff South Shore Hosp., South Weymouth, Mass., 1985—. Contbr. articles to profl. jours. Recipient Nat. Rsch. Svc. award NIH, 1982-84. Fellow Am. Coll. Allergy and Immunology (Parke Davis Allergy Fellows award 1983), Am. Acad. Allergy and Immunology, Am. Coll. Chest Physicians, Am. Acad. Pediatrics; mem. New Eng. Soc. Allergy, Mass. Allergy Soc. (pres. 1992-94), Mass. Med. Soc. Office: South Shore Allergy & Asthma Specialists 851 Main St South Weymouth MA 02190

YOUNG, MICHAEL WARREN, geneticist, educator; b. Miami, Fla., Mar. 28, 1949; s. Lloyd George and Mildred (Tillery) Y.; m. Laurel Ann Eckhardt, Dec. 27, 1978; children: Natalie, Arissa. BA, U. Tex., 1971, PhD, 1975. NIH postdoctoral fellow Med. Sch., Stanford (Calif.) U., 1975-77; asst. prof. genetics The Rockefeller U., N.Y.C., 1978-83, assoc. prof., 1984-88, prof., 1988—; investigator Howard Hughes Med. Inst., N.Y.C., 1987—; head Rockefeller unit NSF Sci. and Tech. Ctr. Biol. Timing, 1991—; mem. adv. panel on genetic biology NSF, Washington, 1983-87; spl. advisor Am. Cancer Soc., N.Y.C., 1985—; spl. reviewer genetics study sect. NIH, Bethesda, Md., 1990—, mem. cell biology study sect., 1993—. Contbr. articles to profl. jours. Meyer Found. fellow, N.Y.C., 1978-83. Fellow N.Y. Soc. Fellows; mem. AAAS, Genetics Soc. Am., Am. Soc. Microbiologists, N.Y. Acad. Scis., Harvey Soc. Home: PO Box 37 Saddle River NJ 07458-0037 Office: The Rockefeller Univ 1230 York Ave New York NY 10021-6307

YOUNG, NEAL STUART, internist, hematologist, public health physician; b. N.Y.C., Apr. 13, 1947; s. Everett and Renee (Perl) Y.; m. Genoveffa Franchini, Aug. 1, 1982; children: Andrea, Massimo, Giorgio. AB, Harvard U., 1967; MD, Johns Hopkins U., 1971. Diplomate Am. Bd. Internal Medicine. Intern, then resident Mass. Gen. Hosp., Boston, 1971-73; commd. officer USPHS, 1973, advanced through grades to capt.; clin. assoc. Nat. Inst. ADDK, NIH, Bethesda, Md., 1973-75; fellow in hematology Barnes Hosp., St. Louis, 1975-76; vis. expert Nat. Heart, Lung and Blood Inst., NIH, Bethesda, 1976-81, sr. investigator, 1978-83, sect. chief cardiology sect., 1983-93, br. chief hematology br., 1993—; cons. to various industries and law firms; Haddock lectr., P.R., 1985; Bennett meml. lectr., Mt. Sinai Med. Ctr.,N.Y.C., 1991; Corsi meml. lectr., Florence, Italy, 1992; Castle lectr. Harvard U., 1994; Asseler lectr. U. Calif., San Francisco, 1995. Author: Aplastic Anemia, Acquired and Inherited, 1994; editor numerous books on bone marrow failure, viral infections of marrow; assoc. editor Blood; contbr. over 200 articles and revs. to med. jours., chpts. to books. Fellow ACP; mem. Am. Soc. Clin. Investigation (councillor), Am. Soc. Hematology, Am. Assn. Physicians. Home: 4400 17th St NW Washington DC 20011 Office: NIH Bldg 10 Rm 7C103 900 Rockville Pike Bethesda MD 20892-1652

YOUNG, PAUL ANDREW, anatomist; b. St. Louis, Oct. 3, 1926; s. Nicholas A. and Olive A. (Langford) Y.; m. Catherine Ann Hofmeister, May 14, 1949; children—Paul, Robert, David, Ann, Carol, Richard, James, Steven, Kevin, Michael. B.S., St. Louis U., 1947, M.S., 1953; Ph.D., U. Buffalo, 1957. Asst. in anatomy U. Buffalo, 1953, instr. anatomy, 1957; asst. prof. anatomy St. Louis U., 1957, asso. prof., 1966, prof., 1972—, chmn. dept., 1973—. Author: (with B.D. Bhagat and D.E. Biggerstaff) Fundamentals of Visceral Innervation, 1977, (with P.H. Young) Basic Clinical Neuroanatomy, 1996, also computer assisted neurological anatomy tutorials; contbr. articles to profl. publs. Recipient Golden Apple award Student AMA, 1974, Teaching award Acad. Sci. St. Louis, 1993. Mem. Am. Assn. Anatomists, Am. Assn. Clin. Anatomists, Soc. Neurosci., Sigma Xi, Alpha Omega Alpha. Office: St Louis U Dept Anatomy & Neurobiology 1402 S Grand Blvd Saint Louis MO 63104-1004

YOUNG, PAUL HENRY, neurosurgeon; b. St. Louis, Feb. 18, 1950; s. Paul Andrew and Catherine Ann (Hofmeister) Y.; m. Mary Ann Fayfrie, Aug. 12, 1972; children: Julie, Jennifer, Jason, Jacquelyn. BA in Chemistry, St. Louis U., 1971, MD, 1975. Diplomate Am. Bd. Neurol. Surgery; lic. Mo., Ill. Intern Harbor Gen. Hosp., Torrance, Calif., 1975-76; resident surgery St. Louis U. Hosps., 1976-77; fellow neurol. microvascular surgery U. Zurich, Switzerland, 1980-81; asst. prof. St. Louis U. Sch. Medicine, 1981-83, asst. clin. prof. neurosurgery and anatomy, 1983-91, assoc. clin. prof., 1991—; dir. Microsurgery and Brain Rsch. Inst.; bd. dirs. Practical Anatomy and Surg. technique Workshop, founder, pres. 1991-94; attending physician St. Mary's Health Ctr., 1981—, St. Anthony's Med. Ctr., 1982—. Author: Microsurgery of the Cervical Spine, 1991; co-author: Guide for Basic Neurological Anatomy, 1983 (update yearly), Microneurosurgery, vol. I-Anatomy, 1984, vol. 2-Aneurysms, 1984, vol. IVA, 1994, vol. IVB-Brain Tumors, 1995, Lumbar Microdiscectomy, 1989; presenter in field; contbr. articles to profl. jours. Mem. AMA, Am. Assn. Neurol. Surgeons, Am. Heart Assn., Nat. Stroke Assn. (sci. adv. bd.), Soc. Neurosci., N.Am. Skull Base Soc. (founder), Congress Neurol. Surgeons, So. Med. Soc., Mo. State Med. Assn., St. Louis Met. Med. Soc., St. Louis Soc. Neuroscis., St. Louis Surg. Soc., Health Vols. Overseas, Mo. Doctors for Life, KC (DuBourg coun.), St. Louis Zoo Friends Assn., St. Louis Sci. Ctr., Friends of St. Louis Art Mus., Beta Beta Beta, Sigma Xi. Roman Catholic. Office: Microsurgery & Brain Rsch 6725 Chippewa Saint Louis MO 63109

YOUNG, ROBERT JOHN, physician assistant; b. Lynn, Mass., Nov. 27, 1948; s. Harvey Joseph and Thelma Ruth (Burnham) Y.; m. Mary-Jo Sadowski, May 1, 1976. Student, Mass. Coll. Pharmacy, 1966-68; cert., U.S. Med. Ctr., 1975. Nat. Commn. on Cert. of Physician Assts. Program dir. Big Bros. and Big Sisters Danbury (Conn.) Youth Svcs., 1978-80; physician asst. Fairfield Hills Hosp., Newtown, Conn., 1980-86, Southbury (Conn.) Tng. Sch., 1986—; conf. mgr. Conn. Acad. Physician Asst., Cromwell, 1986-95; clin. instr. Quinnipiac Coll., Hamden, Conn., 1995—. Editor (newsletter) Conn APA News, 1994—. Student mentor program coord. Quinnipiac Coll., Hamden, 1994—. With USN, 1968-72. Recipient Outstanding Svc. to Healthcare award Conn. State Legis., Hartford, 1986, 89. Fellow Am. Acad. Physician Assts., Conn. Acad. Physician Assts. (pres. 1986); mem. New Eng. Hist. Geneal. Soc., Peabody Essex Mus. Home: 18 Golden Hill Rd Danbury CT 06811-4633

YOUNG, RONALD FREDERICK, neurosurgeon; b. Buffalo, Jan. 4, 1939; s. Frederick Earl and Ruth Henrietta (Cowan) Y.; m. Sheila Marie Young, June 23, 1962 (div. 1990); children: Scott Ronald, Anne Louise, Karen Lynn. BA, SUNY, Buffalo, 1961, MD, 1965. Diplomate Am. Bd. Neurol. Surgery. Intern in surgery U. Minn Hosp., Mpls., 1965-66; resident in neurosurgery VA Hosp., Longbeach, Calif., 1966-67; resident in neurosurgery SUNY, Syracuse, 1969-73, asst. prof. neurosurgery, 1973-77; assoc. prof. UCLA, 1977-85; prof. neurosurgery U. Calif., Irvine, 1986-93; chief of neurosurgery U. Calif. Med. Ctr., Irvine, 1986-93; clin. prof. U. Calif., Irvine, 1993—; dir. N.W. Gamma Knife Ctr. and N.W. Neurosci. Inst. Northwest Hosp., Seattle, 1993—; Elizabeth Crosby Meml. lectr. U. Mich., Ann Arbor, 1990. Author: Spinal Cord Injury, 1981; contbr. articles to med. jours. Capt. USAF Med. Corps, 1967-69. Recipient Kongress medal German Neurosurg. Soc., 1982. Fellow Am. Coll. Surgeons; mem. Western Neurosurg. Soc. (v.p. 1990-91, pres. 1993-94), Am. Acad. Pain Medicine (sec. 1991—), Am. Assn. Neurol. Surg., Congress Neurol. Surgery, Soc. Univ. Neurosurgeons (pres. 1996-97), Santa Fe Neurosci. Inst. (bd. dirs. 1983—), Am. Acad. Neurosurgery, Soc. of Neurol. Surgeons. Office: NW Hosp Gamma Knife Ctr 1560 N 115th St Ste G-5 Seattle WA 98133

YOUNG, STEPHEN R., health facility executive; b. Pitts., Apr. 2, 1940; s. Isaac Carl and Jeanette (Rabinowitz) Y.; m. Barbara Shullman, June 30, 1963; children: Joel Michael, Jodi Faye. BS in Pharmacy, U. Pitts., 1962; MBA, Cornell U., 1968. Registered pharmacist, Pa., N.Y. Chief pharmacy svc. U.S. Naval Hosp., Agana, Guam, 1963-66; adminstrv. resident Sloan

Kettering Cancer Ctr., N.Y.C., 1967; asst. adminstr. St. Joseph Mercy Hosp., Ann Arbor, Mich., 1968-75; exec. v.p. St. Michael Hosp., Milw., 1975-86, pres., 1989—; pres. Elmbrook Meml. Hosp., Brookfield, Wis., 1986-89. Lt. USNR, 1963-66. Fellow Am. Coll. Healthcare Execs.; mem. Wis. Hosp. Assn. (bd. dirs. 1990—), Hosp. Coun. Greater Milw. Area (chmn. 1993-94), Med. Coll. Wis. Affiliated Hosps. (pres. bd. dirs. 1994—). Home: 10433 N Pine Ridge Dr Mequon WI 53092 Office: St Michael Hosp 2400 W Villard Ave Milwaukee WI 53209

YOUNG, STEVEN DOUGLAS, chemist; b. Morristown, N.J., July 29, 1956; s. Frederick Crest and Joyce Elaine Y.; m. Mary Beth Szymula. BS, Stevens Inst. of Technology, 1978; PhD, U. Calif., Berkeley, 1982. Sr. rsch. chemst Merck Rsch. Labs., West Point, Pa., 1982-87, rsch. fellow, 1987-91, sr. rsch. fellow, 1991-95, sr. investigator, 1995—. Author: (book) Drug Discovery Technologies, 1990, Perspectives in Drug Discovery and Design, Vol. 1, 1993. Mem. Am. Chem. Soc., Sigma Xi. Republican. Presbyterian. Office: Merck & Co Sunneytown Pike (26-410) West Point PA 19486

YOUNG, TERI ANN BUTLER, pharmacist; b. Littlefield, Tex., Aug. 22, 1958; d. Doyle Wayne and Bettie May (Lair) Butler; m. James Oren Young, Aug. 1, 1981; children: Andrew Wayne, Aaron Lee. BS in Pharmacy, Southwestern Okla. State U., 1981. Staff pharmacist St. Mary of Plains Hosp., Lubbock, Tex., 1981-84; staff pharmacist West Tex. Hosp., Lubbock, 1984-85, asst. dir. pharmacy, 1985-86; pharmacist cons. for nursing homes Billy D. Davis & Assocs., Lubbock, 1986—; relief pharmacist Prescription Lab., Med. Pharmacy and Foster Infusion Care, Lubbock, 1987-89; staff pharmacist Univ. Med. Ctr., 1990—, diabetic teaching pharmacist, 1995—; relief pharmacist West Tex. Hosp., 1986-91, Highland Hosp., 1990—, Med. Infusion Technology, 1992—. Mem. Lubbock Area Soc. of Hosp. Pharmacists (sec., treas. 1982-83), Lubbock Area Pharm. Assn., West Tex. Pharm. Assn., Am. Soc. Hosp. Pharmacists, Pilot Internat., Lubbock Genealogical Soc. Republican. Baptist. Lodge: Eastern Star. Home: 7410 Toledo Ave Lubbock TX 79424-2214 Office: Univ Med Ctr 602 Indiana Ave Lubbock TX 79415-3364

YOUNG, VERNON ROBERT, nutrition, biochemistry educator; b. Rhyl, Wales, Nov. 15, 1937; married, 1966; 5 children. BS, U. Reading, 1959; diploma in agr., Cambridge U., 1960; PhD in Nutrition, U. Calif., Davis, 1965. Lectr. nutritional biochemistry MIT, Cambridge, Mass., 1965-66, asst. prof. physiology chemistry, 1966-72, assoc. prof., 1972-76, prof. nutritional biochemistry, 1976—; program mgmt. human nutrition competitive rsch. grants program USDA, 1980-81; assoc. program dir. MIT Clin. Rsch. Ctr., Cambridge, Mass., 1985-87; biochemist dept. surgery Mass. Gen. Hosp. & Harvard Med. Sch., Boston, 1987—; sr. vis. scientist USDA Human Nutrition Ctr. Aging, Tufts U., 1988—. Recipient Rank prize in nutrition, 1989. Mem. NAS, Am. Inst. Nutrition (Mead Johnson award 1973, Borden award 1982), Am. soc. Clin. Nutrition (McCollum award 1987), Nutrition Soc., Gerontology Soc. Am., Am. Chem. Soc. Office: MIT Dept Nutritional Biochem Bldg E18 Rm 613 50 Ames St Cambridge MA 02139*

YOUNGBERG, ROBERT LOVETT, psychologist; b. Lynn, Mass., Jan. 9, 1962; s. Robert Curtis and Maureen Timothea (Lovett) Y.; m. Denise Ann Dunne; 1 child, Cassidy Ann. BS, Boston Coll., 1984, MA, 1986; PhD, Temple U., 1995. Sr. clinician Choate Hosp. Crisis Team, Woburn, Mass., 1986-88; rsch. specialist U. Pa. Med. Sch., Phila., 1989-91; clin. fellow McLean Hosp. Harvard Med. Sch., Belmont, Mass., 1993-95, Mass. Gen. Hosp./Harvard Med. Sch., 1994-96, Lahey Clinic, Burlington, Mass., 1996—. Recipient scholarship Boston Coll. Alumni Assn., 1984-86; grantee Found. for Cognitive Therapy and Rsch., U. Pa., 1991. Fellow Am. Counseling Assn.; mem. APA (assoc.), Soc. for Advancement Rsch. in Clin. Psychology (student), Am. Assn. Suicidology. Roman Catholic. Home: 24 Long Dr Westboro MA 01581 Office: McLean Hosp Mill St Belmont MA 02106

YOUNGDAHL, PATRICIA LUCY, psychologist, educator; b. Cape Girardeau, Mo., Sept. 8, 1927; d. George B. and Alta Mae (Crites) Lucy; m. James E. Youngdahl, June 13, 1948 (div. Apr. 1974); children: Jay, Kristi, Lincoln, Sara. AA, Stephens Coll., 1946; BA, Washington U. (Mo.), 1948, MA, 1950; PhD, Fla. Inst. Tech., 1985. Lic. psychologist, Ark. Assoc. exec. dir. Social Planning Coun., St. Louis, 1950-52; instr. psychology U. Ark., Fayetteville, 1958-59, psychol. examiner Med. Ctr., Little Rock, 1961-64, asst. prof. Med. Scis. Campus, Little Rock, 1975—, dir. child clin. psychology internship tng. program. Author: (with others) How to Use Transactional Analysis in the Public Schools, 1974, (with others) Arkansas Divorce Simplified, 1994. Mem. exec. com. Pulaski County Dem. Com., Little Rock, 1972—, State Dem. Party, 1980—; chmn. Ark. for Kennedy, 1979-80; del. Nat. Dem. Conv. 1976, 80, 84; chmn. Ark. Women's Polit. Caucus, 1973-83; appted. to Com. Profl. Conduct, Ark. Named to 100 Ark. Women of Achievement Ark. Press Women's Assn., 1980; apptd. by gov. to Pygmalion Commn. for Alternative Edn., 1993. Mem. Ark. Psychol. Assn., Am. Psychol. Assn. (assoc.). Unitarian-Universalist Ch. Home: 7108 Rockwood Rd Little Rock AR 72207-1708 Office: Childrens Hosp 800 Marshall St Little Rock AR 72202-3510

YOUNGER, KENNETH MARVIN, ophthalmologist; b. Indpls., Nov. 28, 1944; s. Howard and Pearl (Lazar) Y.; m. Jenny B. Younger, Sept. 3, 1967; children: Robin Younger Hubley, Joe. BA in Med. Sci., Ind. U., 1966, MD, 1969. Diplomate Am. Bd. Ophthalmology. Intern UCLA Affiliated Hosps., 1970; resident in ophthalmology Ind. U. Sch. Medicine, Indpls., 1975; pvt. practice Med. Eye Specialists, Bozeman, Mont., 1975—; adj. prof. Mont. State U., Bozeman, 1975—; pres., med. dir. Same Day Surgery Ctr., Bozeman, 1985—; bd. dirs. Mont. Low Vision Svc. Mem., chmn. sch. bd. Anderson Sch. Dist. 41, Bozeman, 1980-86. Capt. USAF, 1970-72. Fellow Am. Acad. Ophthalmology (assoc. examiner); mem. Am. Soc. Cataract and Refractive Surgery, Mont. Acad. Ophthalmology. Office: Med Eye Specialists 300 N Willson Ste 1003 Bozeman MT 59715

YOUNG LIVELY, SANDRA LEE, nurse; b. Rockport, Ind., Dec. 31, 1943; d. William Cody and Flora Juanita (Carver) Thorpe; m. Kenneth Leon Doom, May 4, 1962 (div. 1975); children: Patricia, Anita, Elizabeth, Melissa, Kenny. AS, Vincennes U., 1979, student, U. So. Ind., 1987—. Nursing aide, nurse Forest Del Nursing Home, Princeton, Ind., 1975-80; charge nurse Welborn Bapt. Hosp., Evansville, Ind., 1979-80, 82-83; staff nurse Longview Regional Hosp., Tex., 1980-82; dir. home health Roy H. Laird Meml. Hosp., Kilgore, Tex., 1984-86; med. post-coronary nurse Mercy Hosp., Owensboro, Ky., 1987, Dept. of Corrections charge nurse, Branchville Tng. Ctr., Tell City, Ind, 1987-90; charge nurse dept. mental health Evansville (Ind.) State Hosp., 1990—; staff nurse, asst. dir. Leisure Lodge Home Health, Overton, Tex., 1983-84. Grantee Roy H. Laird Meml. Hosp., 1986. Mem. NAFE, Menniger Found., Vincennes U. Alumni Assn., Internat. Platform Assn. Avocations: writing, research, cake decorating, house plants. Home: 614 Gilmer Rd Apt 251 Longview TX 75604 Office: Evansville State Hosp 3400 Lincoln Ave Evansville IN 47714-0147

YOUNT, KIM ALLEN, dentist; b. Leavenworth, Kans., Apr. 30, 1954; s. Robert Eugene and Barbara Jean (Gee) Y.; m. Debra Jo Walker, Feb. 20, 1990; children: Jacob Allen, Lucas Arthur, Kimberly Ann. AA, Johnson County C.C., 1974; BS in Biology, U. Mo., 1976, DDS, 1981. Lic. Practitioner Dental Bd., Kans., Mo. Landscape designer Rieke Nursery, Shawnee, Kans., 1974-80; clin. dentistry instr. U. Mo., Kansas City, 1981; gen. practice dentistry Rolling Fork, Miss., 1982-83, Liberal, Kans., 1983—. Mem. Profl. Devel. Coun., Liberal, 1995. Mem. ADA, Miss. Dental Assn., Ducks Unltd., S.W. Dental Study Club, Psi Omega. Republican. Home: 2300 S Holly Dr Liberal KS 67901-2085 Office: 1411 W 15th St Ste 301 Liberal KS 67901-2285

YOUSUFF, SARAH SAFIA, physician; b. Binghampton, N.Y., Dec. 8, 1960; d. Mohamed and Razia (Sivaramasastry) Y.; m. Donald John Sudy, Aug. 7, 1993. BA in Zoology, U. Tex., Austin, 1982; MD, U. Tex., 1988. Diplomate Am. Bd. Anesthesiology, Am. Bd. Pain Medicine. Fellow in med. mgmt. U. N.C., Chapel Hill, 1992-93; resident in anesthesiology U. Wash., Seattle, 1988-92; staff anesthesiologist Krōn Med., Research Triangle Park, N.C., 1992-94; med. dir. dept. anesthesiology Southwest Hosp., Little Rock, Ark., 1994-96; pres. Southwest Anesthesia Assocs., Little Rock, 1994-95; ptnr. Pain Cons. Ark., 1995—; dir. Southwest Pain Mgmt. Clinic, Little Rock, 1995—. capt. USAR, 1990—. Mem. AMA, Am. Soc. Anesthesiology, Am. Coll. Physician Execs., Ark. Med. Soc., Pulaski County Med. Soc., Internat. Spinal Injection Soc., Internat. Assn. for Study of Pain, Am. Acad. of Pain Medicine, Am. Soc. of Regional Anesthesia. Home: 18 Edenfield Cv Little Rock AR 72212-2667 Office: Southwest Pain Mgmt Clinic 11401 Interstate 30 Little Rock AR 72209

YOW, ANGIE JONES, practical nurse, orthopedics; b. Sanford, N.C., Aug. 7, 1972; d. Jimmy Boyd and Annie Louise (Godfrey) Jones; m. Jonathan Jones Yow, Feb. 16, 1990. Degree in practical nursing, Sandhills Cmty. Coll., Pinehurst, N.C., 1993. LPN, N.C. LPN, respiratory fl. U. N.C. Hosps., Chapel Hill, 1993; LPN, orthopedic clinic Pinehurst (N.C.) Surg. Clinic, 1993—; mem. com. to help patients understand diagnostic tests, Moore Regional Hosp., Pinehurst, 1993-94. St. Joseph's scholar, Pinehurst, 1993. Republican. Baptist. Home: Rt 3 Box 7C-5 Cameron NC 28326

YU, JEN, medical educator; b. Taipei, Taiwan, Jan. 23, 1943; came to U.S., 1969; s. Chin Chuan and Shiu Lan (Lin) Y.; m. Janet Chen, June 16, 1973; children—Benjamin, Christopher. M.D., Nat. Taiwan U., 1968; Ph.D. in Physiology, U. Pa., 1972. Diplomate Am. Bd. Phys. Medicine and Rehab. Intern. Phila. Gen. Hosp., 1972-73; resident in phys. medicine and rehab. Hosps. U. Pa., 1973-75; asst. prof. dept. phys. medicine and rehab. U. Pa. Sch. Medicine, Phila., 1975-76, U. Tex. Health Sci. Ctr., San Antonio, 1976-79, assoc. prof., 1979-81; prof. dept. phys. medicine and rehab. U. Calif.-Irvine Coll. Medicine, 1981-82, prof., chmn. dept. phys. medicine and rehab., 1982—. Contbr. articles to med. jours. Mem. Am. Acad. Phys. Medicine and Rehab., Am. Congress Rehab. Medicine, Assn. Acad. Physiatrists, Am. Assn. Anatomists, Soc. for Neurosci. Office: U Calif Irvine Med Ctr Dept Phys Medicine and Rehab 101 The City Dr Orange CA 92863-3298

YU, JOSEPH SEKIGUCHI, radiologist; b. Sao Paulo, Brazil, July 27, 1960; came to U.S., 1969; s. Thomas Hung Chang and Teiko (Sekiguchi) Y.; m. Cynthia Marie Anderson, May 11, 1991; 1 child, Sarah Michelle. BS, Ohio State U., 1983, MD, 1987. Diplomate Am. Bd. Radiology, Nat. Bd. Med. Examiners. Staff radiologist U. Calif. San Diego, 1993; chief osteoradiologist Ohio State U. Med. Ctr., Columbus, 1994—. Contbr. articles to profl. jours. Mem. Radiol. Soc. N.Am. Office: Ohio State Univ Med Ctr 450 W 10th Ave Columbus OH 43210

YU, LUCY CHA, science educator; b. Champaign, Ill., Aug. 10, 1937; d. Shih Tsun and Tsue-Hwa (Ho) Cha; m. Francis T.S. Yu, June 15, 1962; children: Peter Tou, Ann G.C., Edward H. BS, U. Mich., 1962, MALS, 1972, PhD, 1981. Asst. libr., dir. Sch. Pub. Health Libr. U. Mich., Ann Arbor, 1972-80; assoc. prof. Pa. State U., University Park, 1981-91, prof., 1991—; rsch. assoc., rsch. scientist Inst. Policy Rsch. and Evaluation, University Park, 1982—; vis. prof. Johns Hopkins U., Balt., 1992; vis. scientist Nat. Ctr. for Health Stats., Washington, 1992. Contbr. articles to profl. jours. Mem. APHA (officer gerontol. health sect. 1992-95), Am. Gerontol. Health Assn.

YU, ROBERT KUAN-JEN, biochemistry educator; b. Chungking, China, Jan. 27, 1938; came to U.S., 1962; s. Shin-cheng and June Chien-yu (Tsao) Y.; m. Helen Chow, July 1, 1972; children: David S., Jennifer S. BS, Tunghai U., Taiwan, 1960; PhD, U. Ill., 1967; Med.ScD. (hon.), Tokyo, 1980; MA (hon.), Yale U., 1985. Rsch. assoc., instr. Albert Einstein Coll. Medicine, Bronx, 1967-72; asst. prof. Yale U., New Haven, 1973-75, assoc. prof., 1975-82, prof., 1983-88; prof. biochemistry, chmn. dept. Va. Commonwealth U., Richmond, 1988—; mem. study sect. NIH, Washington, 1980-84; mem. Bd. Lab. Svcs., Va., 1994—. Editor: Gangioside Structure Function and Biomedical Potential, 1984, New Trends in Ganglioside Research, 1988; contbr. over 470 articles to profl. publs. Josiah Macy scholar, 1979; grantee NIH, 1975—; recipient Va. Outstanding Scientist of Yr. award, 1995, Jacob Javits award NIH, 1984-91, Alexander von Humboldt award, 1990. Mem. AAAS, Am. Soc. Cell Biology, Am. Soc. Neurochemistry (mem. coun. 1983-86, 91—), Internat. Soc. Neurochemistry, Soc. Neurosci., Am. Soc. Biochemistry and Molecular Biology, Am. Chem. Soc., N.Y. Acad. Sci. Home: 306 Cheswick Ln Richmond VA 23229-7660 Office: Va Commonwealth Univ Medical College Virginia Richmond VA 23298-0614

YU, VICTOR LIN-KAI, physician, educator; b. Mpls., Jan. 9, 1943; s. Robert S.H. and Victoria (Hsiao) Y.; m. Deborah Lin, June 19, 1971; children: Chen Ming, Kwan Ting. BA, Carleton Coll., 1965; MD, U. Minn., 1970. Internship and residency U. Colo., Denver, 1970-72; residency Stanford U., Palo Alto, Calif., 1974, postdoctoral fellow, 1975-77; prof. medicine U. Pitts., 1978—; chmn. bd. sci. counselors NIH, 1986-92; chief infectious disease sect. VA Med. Ctr., Pitts., 1981—; disting. lectr. Am. Soc. Microbiology, 1988; Malia lectr. Shadyside Hosp., 1992; Berris lectr. U. Toronto, 1993; Rubin lectr. Berkshire AHEC. Contbr. rsch. on Legionnaires' disease to sci. publs. Recipient Disting. Rsch. award Am. Legion, 1982, Health Svcs. Rsch. Found., 1984; named disting. scientist Chinese Med. Soc., Taipei, Taiwan, 1988; recipient Gold medal for Outstanding Contbn. to Sci., Fed. Exec. Bd., 1993, Citation of Merit, Allegheny County, Pa., 1993. Fellow ACP; mem. Orgn. Chinese Ams. (officer Pitts. sect. 1978—). Home: 87 Longue Vue Dr Pittsburgh PA 15228-1538 Office: U Pitts Divsn Infectious Disease 501 Kaufmann Bldg Pittsburgh PA 15213

YUAN, JUNYING, medical educator, researcher; b. Shanghai, China. BS, Fudan U., Shanghai, 1982; PhD in Neurosci., Harvard U., 1989. Postdoctoral trainee in devel. biology MIT, 1989-90; instr. medicine Harvard U., 1990-91, asst. prof. medicine and program in neurosci., 1992-96, asst. prof. cell biology and program in neurosci., 1996—; asst. geneticist Cardiovasc. Rsch. Ctr. Mass. Gen. Hosp., 1990-96. Mem. editl. bd. Current Biology, 1996; ad hoc reviewer NIH Human Embryology and Devel. 2 Study Sect., 1995, regular reviewer, 1996—; patentee in field; contbr. articles to profl. jours.; presenter in field. Recipient Wilson S. Stone Meml. award MD Anderson Cancer Ctr. U. Tex., 1994, Established Investigator award Am. Heart Assn., 1996—; Ryan fellow Harvard Med. Sch., 1985-89. Office: Harvard Med Sch Dept Cell Biology 240 Longwood Ave Boston MA 02115

YUAN, XIAO-JIAN, medical researcher, educator; b. Xintian, Hunan, People's Republic of China, May 9, 1963; s. Tian-Lin Yuan and Li-Hua Chen. MD, Suzhou (China) Med. Coll., 1983; PhD in Physiology, Peking Union Med. Coll., Beijing, 1993; postgrad., U. Md., 1993. Intern Suzhou Med. Coll. Hosp., 1982-83; resident Lanzhou (China) Med. Coll Hosp., 1983-84; mem. sci. cadre Office Sci. and Tech. Gansu Environ. Protection Bur., Lanzhou, 1984; rsch. assoc. dept. environ. medicine Gansu Inst. Environ. Scis., Lanzhou, 1984-85; postdoctoral fellow dept. physiology and medicine U. Md. Sch. Medicine, Balt., 1988-93, rsch. asst. prof. dept. physiology, 1993-96, rsch. asst. prof. divsn. pulmonary and critical care med., 1993-96, asst. prof., 1996—; lectr. in field; ad hoc reviewer grant applications NIH, 1995-96, study section mem. Am. Heart Assn., 1995-99; ad hoc reviewer rsch. grant applications Wellcome Trust (London), 1995, U.S. Dept. Vets. Affairs, 1995. Author: Olympic Complete Words, 1988; editorial asst. Gansu Assn. Environ. Scis., 1984-85; contbr. articles to profl. jours. Parker B. Francis fellow, 1994-97. Mem. AAAS, Am. Heart Assn. (Md. affiliate rsch. fellow 1990-92, grantee 1990-92, 93-95, 96—, Cournand and Comroe Young Investigator award 1995), Am. Physiol. Soc. (Giles F. Filley Meml. award 1995, Rsch. Career Enhancement award 1995), Am. Thoracic Soc., Biophys. Soc., Chinese Assn. Physiol. Sci. (editorial asst. 1987-88), Soc. Chinese Bioscientists in Am., Soc. Biophysicists in A. (Dr. C.W. Dunker award 1993). Home: 6810 Maple Leaf Ct Apt 202 Baltimore MD 21209 Office: U Md Sch Medicine Div Pulmonary Medicine 10 S Pine St MSTF 800 Baltimore MD 21201

YUDIS, MELVIN, physician; b. Phila., May 11, 1937; s. George and Sylvia (Chernoff) Y.; divorced; children: David, Heidi Jo, Jonathan. AB, Temple U., 1959; MD, Jefferson Med. Coll., 1963. Diplomate Am. Bd. Internal Medicine in internal medicine and nephrology, NAt. Bd. Med. Examiners. Intern straight med. Jefferson Med. Coll. Hosp., Phila., 1963-64; resident internal medicine Hahnemann Med. Coll. and Hosp., Phila., 1964-66, NIH postdoctoral fellow in renology and vascular diseases, 1966-67; physician-in-chief sect. nephrology dept. medicine Abington Meml. Hosp., 1969—; attending nephrologist dept. medicine Holy Redeemer Hosp., Meadowbrook, Pa., 1969—; attending physician dept. medicine subsect. nephrology Nazareth Hosp., Phila., 1969—; coun. rep. End Stage Renal Disease Network, 1978—, sec.-treas., 1985, 86, 87, chmn. water purity com, network rep. to State of Pa. presciption drug com., mem. network 4 transplant and organ procurement com., 1994—. Contbr. articles to profl. jours. Lt. comdr. M.C., USN, 1967-69. Mem. AMA, ACP, Am. Soc. Nephrology, Am. Soc. Artificial and Internal Organs, Am. Soc. Internal Medicine, Internal Soc. Nephrology, Nat. Kidney Found., Am. Coll. Cardiology, Pan Am. Med. Assn., Am. Heart Assn. (mem. exec. com. Montgomery County br. 1974—), Renal Physicians Assn., Internat. Soc. Peritoneal Dialysis, Montgomery County Med. Soc., J. Marion Sims Soc., Pa. Soc. Internal Medicine, Greater Del. Valley Kidney Adv. Coun., Del. Valley Soc. Nephrologists, Pa. Soc. Nephrology (councilor). Office: Hypertension-Nephrology Assocs 3940 B Commerce Ave Willow Grove PA 19090

YUDOFSKY, STUART CHARLES, medical educator; b. Louisville, Ky., July 17, 1944; s. Joseph A. and Dorothy Charlotte (Krotzki) Y.; m. Beth Koster, June 19, 1976; children: Elissa, Lynn, Emily. BA, NYU, 1966; MD, Baylor Coll. Medicine, 1970. Am. Bd. of Psychiatry and Neurology. Intern Albert Einstein Coll. of Medicine, Jacobi Hosp., N.Y.C., 1970-71; resident in psychiatry Columbia U. Coll. of Physicians and Surgeons, Presbyn. Hosp., N.Y.C., 1971-74; instr. in clin. psychiatry Columbia U. Coll. of Physicians and Surgeons, N.Y.C., 1974-77, asst. prof. clin. psychiatry, 1977-81, acting vice chmn. and vice chair dept. of psychiatry, 1981-84, assoc. prof. clin. psychiatry, 1981-88; prof., chmn. dept. psychiatry U. Chgo., 1988-91; prof., chmn. dpet. psychiatry Baylor Coll. of Medicine, Houston, 1991—; chief psychiatry svc. Meth. Hosp., Houston, 1991—; com. on programs Am. Coll. Psychiatrists, 1995—. Editor: Textbook of Neuropsychiatry, 1987, 2d edit., 1992; Textbook of Psychiatry, 1988, 2d edit., 1994; author: What You Need to Know about Psychiatric Drugs, 1992; Principles of the Psychiatric Evaluation, 1991; editor-in-chief Jour. of Neurpsychiatry and Clin. Neuroscis., 1988—. Falk fellow Am. Psychiatric Assoc., 1979; named Tchr. of Yr. U.S. Psychiat. and Mental Health Congress, 1993. Mem. The Mental Health Assn. of Houston and Harris County (bd. dirs. 1991—, Ima Hogg award 1995), Phi Beta Kappa. Office: Baylor Coll of Medicine Dept Psychiatry One Baylor Plaza Houston TX 77030

YUN, DANIEL DUWHAN, physician, foundation administrator; b. Chinjoo, Korea, Jan. 20, 1933; came to U.S., 1959, naturalized, 1972; s. Kapryong and Woo Im Yun; m. Rebecca Sungja Choi, Apr. 13, 1959; children: Samuel, Lois, Caroline, Judith. BS, Coll. Sci. and Engring., Yon-Sei U., 1954, MD, 1958; student U. Pa., 1963, PhD Barrington U., 1995. Intern, Quincy (Mass.) City Hosp., 1960; resident and fellow Presbyn.-U. Pa. Med. Ctr., Phila., 1961-65; med. dir. Paddon Meml. Hosp., Nfld., Labrador, Can., 1965-66; dir. spl. care unit Elkins Park (Pa.) Hosp., 1967-79; founder, pres. Philip Jaisohn Meml. Found., Inc., Elkins Park, Pa., 1975-85, also med. dir., trustee; clin. prof. medicine U. Xochicalco, 1978; faculty Med. Coll. Pa.-Hahnemann U. Mem. Bd. Asian Studies Found., U.S. Senatorial Bus. Adv. Bd.; mem. home safety com. Mayor's Commn. on Svcs to Aging, Phila.; trustee United Way of Southeastern Pa., co-founder Rep. Presdl. Task Force; mem. U.S. Congl. Adv. Bd.; cons. on Korean affairs Phila. City Coun.; hon. mem. adv. coun. Peaceful Unification Policy of Korea; chmn. bd. Korean-Am. Christian Broadcasting of Phila.; mem. Phila. Internat. City Coord. Com.; commr. Pa. Human Rels. Commn., 1991—; founder, pres. Korean Heritage Found., 1991—; amb. City of Phila., 1991. Recipient Phila. award-Human Rights award, 1981, Disting. Community Svc. award Phila. Dist. Atty., 1981, medal of Merit Presdl. Task Force, 1981, Medal of Nat. Order, Republic of Korea, 1984, Nat. Dong Baek medal Republic of Korea, 1987, award City Coun. Phila., 1987, Gov.'s Pa. Heritage awards, 1990, commendation award Pa. Senate, 1991, award Asian Law Ctr., 1991, Republican Senatorial Medal of Freedom, 1994; named to Legion of Honor, The Chapel of Four Chaplains, named Amb. City of Phila., 1991. Mem. AMA, Am. Soc. Internal Medicine, Am. Coll. Cardiology, Am. Heart Assn. (mem. council on clin. cardiology), Pa. Med. Soc., Phila. County Med. Soc., Royal Soc. Health, Am. Coll. Internat. Physicians, World Med. Assn., Fedn. State Med. Bds., Am. Law Enforcement Officers' Assn., Am. Fedn. Police, Internat. Culture Soc. Korea (hon.), Am. Soc. Contemporary Medicine and Surgery. Home: 3903 Somers Dr Huntingdon Valley PA 19006-1913 Office: 60 Township Line Rd Elkins Park PA 19027-2220

YUNICH, ALBERT MANSFELD, physician; b. Ruvno, Russia, June 15, 1909; s. Max A. and Bessie (Feldman) Y.; arrived in U.S., 1911; B.A., Cornell U., 1931, M.D., 1935; Sc.D. (hon.), Albany Med. Coll., 1985; m. Mary Lynn Aronson, June 9, 1935. Intern, Albany Med. Center Hosp., 1935-36, resident, 1936-39; fellow in gastroenterology Mt. Sinai Hosp., N.Y.C., 1939-40; instr. medicine Albany Med. Coll., 1940-42, asst. clin. prof. gastroenterology, 1942-52, assoc. clin. prof., 1952-65, clin. prof. gastroenterology, 1967-76, clin. prof. gastroenterology emeritus, 1977—, sr. physician, gastroenterologist Albany Med. Center Hosp.; cons. gastroenterology St. Peter's Hosp., VA Hosp., Albany. V.p. Albany Symphony Orch., 1960-64; mem. exec. com. Albany County unit Am. Cancer Soc., 1974-78; chmn. Mary and Gene Sarazen Scholarship Fund, Siena Coll., 1978; trustee Nat. Jewish Hosp., Denver, 1965-75. Diplomate Am. Bd. Internal Medicine and Gastroenterology. Fellow Am. Coll. Gastroenterology (life); mem. Albany County Med. Soc., Med. Soc. State N.Y., AMA, Am. Coll. Gastroenterology, Am. Soc. Internal Medicine, Pan-Am. Med. Assn., Alpha Omega Alpha. Jewish. Clubs: Fort Orange, Colonie Country. Contbr. articles to med. jours. Home: Heritage Rd # 222 Guilderland NY 12084-9314 Office: Albany Med Coll Albany NY 12208

YUNIS, JORGE JOSE, anatomy, pathology, and microbiology educator; b. Sincelejo, Colombia, Oct. 5, 1933; s. José and Victoria (Turbay) Y.; m. Malvina Torbay, Jan. 15, 1994; children by previous marriage: George, Olga, Karl, Amira, Omar. MD, Complutense U., Madrid, 1956, PhD, 1957. Gen. practice medicine Barranquilla, Colombia, 1957-59; resident in clin. pathology U. Minn., Mpls., 1959-62, resident in anat. pathology, 1962-64, mem. faculty, 1965-89, prof., 1969-89, dir. grad. studies of lab. medicine, 1969-74, dir. grad. studies of pathology, 1972-74, chmn. human genetics com. for health scis., 1972-77; mem. faculty Hahnemann U., Phila., 1989-92, prof. dept. neoplastic diseases, 1989-92, vice chmn., assoc. dir. Inst. for Cancer and Blood Diseases, 1989-92, dir. Human Genetics and Molecular Biology Div., 1989-92, prof. dept. pathology, 1991-92; prof. depts. anatomy, pathology, microbiology & immunology Thomas Jefferson U. Med. Coll., Phila., 1993—; dir. cancer biol., dept. anatomy, pathology, cell biology Thomas Jefferson U. Med. Col., Phila., 1993—; vis. prof. numerous univs. Author: Human Chromosome Method, 1965, 75, Biochemical Methods in Red Cell Genetics, 1969, Molecular Pathology, 1975, New Chromosomal Syndromes, 1977, Molecular Structure Human Chromosomes, 1977, Esencia Humana, 1995; contbr. more than 250 articles to profl. jours. Named Clin. Prof. of Yr. Harvard Med. Sch., 1987; honored by Colombian Parliament, Bogota, 1986, 93, Colombian Med. Schs. Assn., 1993. Mem. Leukemia Soc. Am. (trustee 1983-88), Colombian Acad. Medicine. Office: Jefferson Med Coll 1020 Locust St Philadelphia PA 19107-6731

YURT, ROGER WILLIAM, medical educator, physician; b. Louisville, June 8, 1945; s. Albert William and Mary Louise (McGrath) Y.; m. Joan A. Terry, Sept. 3, 1971; children: Jennifer, Daniel, Gregory. BS in Biology, Loyola U., New Orleans, 1967; MD, U. Miami, 1972. Diplomate Nat. Bd. Med. Examiners. Intern Parkland Meml. Hosp.-Southwestern Med. Sch., U. Tex.-Dallas, 1972-73, resident in surgery, 1973-74; postdoctoral fellow in medicine Robert B. Brigham Hosp.-Harvard U. Med. Sch., Boston, 1974-77; postdoctoral trainee NIH, 1975-77; resident in surgery, then chief resident in surgery N.Y. Hosp.-Cornell Med. Ctr., N.Y.C., 1977-79, acting dir. Burn Ctr., dir. rsch., 1982-83, dir. Trauma Ctr., 1992—, prof. surgery, 1982-92, prof. surgery, 1992—, The Johnson & Johnson Disting. prof. surgery, 1995—, vice chmn. dept. surgery Cornell U. Med. Coll., 1987—, acting chmn., 1991-93, dir. Burn Ctr., 1995—; acting surgeon-in-chief, The N.Y. Hosp., 1991-93; clin. asst. prof. surgery Uniformed Services U. of Health Sci., Bethesda, Md., 1980-82; clin. asst. prof. gen. surgery Health Sci. Ctr., U. Tex.-San Antonio, 1981-82; chmn. burn com., mem. bd. dirs. Regional Emergency Med. Services of N.Y., 1982-84, mem. trauma ctr. adv. com., 1984—, chmn., 1995—, N.Y. Bklyn. ACS Com. Trauma, 1994—; dir. Mulhearn Research Lab., N.Y.C., 1982—. Editor: Infections in Surgery, 1981-88; contbr. articles to med. jours. Served to maj. M.C., U.S. Army, 1979-82. Grantee United Health Found., 1968-69, NIH, 1984-87; fellow Sch. Medicine, U. Miami, summer 1969-71, USPHS, 1973-75; Irma Hirschl Trust Career Scientist award, 1984-88. Mem. Am. Surg. Assn. Surg. Infection Soc. (charter, chmn. membership com., sec. 1987-90, pres. 1991-92), Assn. Acad. Surgery, Soc. Univ. Surgeons, Internat. Surg. Soc., Am. Assn. for Surgery of Trauma, Ea. Assn. for Surgery of Trauma, Alpha Omega

Alpha, Omicron Delta Kappa. Roman Catholic. Office: Cornell U Medical Coll 1300 York Ave New York NY 10021-4805

YUSPA, STUART HOWARD, cancer etiologist; b. Balt., July 19, 1941. BS, Johns Hopkins U., 1962; MD, U. Md., 1966. Diplomate Am. Bd. Internal Medicine. Intern Hosp. U. Pa., 1966-67; rsch. assoc. cancer Nat. Cancer Inst., 1967-70; res. internal medicine Hosp. U. Pa., 1970-72; sr. investigator cancer Nat. Cancer Inst., 1972—; chief divsn. cancer etiology Lab. Cellular Carcinogenesis & Tumor Promotion, 1981—. Editor-in-chief Molecular Carcinogenesis. Named Montagna Lectr., 1988; recipient Lila Gruber Cancer Rsch. award, 1989, Elizabeth Miller Meml. Lectr. award, 1990. Mem. AAAS, Am. Assn. Cancer Rsch. (G.H.A. Clowes Meml. award 1993), Am. Soc. Cell Biology, Soc. Investigative Dermatology. Office: National Cancer Institute 9000 Rockville Pike Bldg 37 Bethesda MD 20892

YUTSIS, PAVEL I., physician; b. Odessa, USSR, Sept. 3, 1947; came to U.S., 1980; s. Isaac Yakov and Feiga Mordkovna (Linetsky) Y.; m. Lilia Davidovna Grinman, Feb. 1, 1974; children: Maxim, Francine. Degree, Odessa Med. Sch., 1966; MD, Voronezh State Med. Inst., 1975. Pediatric resident Gen. Hosp., Voronezh, 1975-76, chmn. Dept. Pediatrics, attending physician, 1976-77; pediatric neurology fellow Coll. Hosp., Perm, USSR, 1977; asst. prof. Dept. Pediatrics Children's Hosp., Perm, 1977-78; attending pediatrician, chmn. Pediatric Infectious Disease Gen. Hosp., Odessa, USSR, 1979; nursing asst. Overlook Hosp., Summit, N.J., 1981-83; pediatric resident St. Joseph Hosp. and Med. Ctr., Paterson, N.J., 1983-86; med. dir./pediatrics allergy and immunology Rivpen Med. Ctr., Bklyn., 1986-87; clin. nutrition, allergy & immunology, clin. ecology World Health Med. Group, N.Y.C., 1988-89; clin. ecology Heart Bio Ctr., Westbury, N.Y., 1989-90; med. dir. Advanced Preventive Med. Group, Bkln., 1988—; dir. Dept. Clin. Ecology Atkins Ctr. for Complementary Medicine, N.Y.C., 1990—, Corsello Ctr., N.Y.C., 1994—; talk show host Sta. WEVD-AM. Contbr. articles to profl. jours. Lectr. in field. Lt. Russian Army. Mem. Am. Acad. Environ. Medicine, Am. Coll. for the Advancement in Medicine, Found. for the Advancement of Innovative Medicine (sec., bd. trustees). Jewish. Office: APMG Med Associates 1309 W 7th St Brooklyn NY 11204-4830

ZABEL, ROBERT ALGER, retired educator, scientist; b. Boyceville, Wis., Mar. 11, 1917; s. William Rudolph and Grace Freedom (Leonard) Z.; m. Norma Livingston Hallock, July 22, 1944; children—Virginia Ellen, Margaret Anne, Grace Marilyn, John William, Robert Alger. B.S., U. Minn., 1938, postgrad., 1939-41; M.S., N.Y. State U. Coll. Forestry, Syracuse, 1943, Ph.D., 1947. Teaching fellow botany N.Y. State U. Coll. Forestry, 1940-42, 46-47; forest pathologist N.E. Expt. Sta., 1957, asst. prof. forest pathology, 1947-52, assoc. prof., 1953-55, head dept. botany, pathology, 1955—, assoc. dean biol. scis., undergrad. instrn., 1964—, assoc. dean instrn. and biol. scis., 1965-70, v.p. acad. affairs, 1970-73, prof., 1954-85; ret., 1985; mem. com., adv. bd. Army R & D, NRC; wood technologist USAAF, 1942-43. Contbr. articles to profl. publs. Served to capt. USMCR, 1943-46. Fellow Soc. Am. Foresters; mem. Forest Products Research Soc., Soc. Am. Microbiology, Am. Inst. Biol. Scis., A.A.A.S., Am. Phytopath. Soc., Sigma Xi, Alpha Zeta, Gamma Sigma Delta. Home: 4563 Broad Rd Syracuse NY 13215-2403

ZABLE, MARIAN MAGDELEN, physician assistant, consultant; b. Beaver Dam, Wis., Oct. 13, 1933; d. John Joseph and Agatha Mary (Eschlie) Fernbach; m. Jerome Edward Zable, July 30, 1960 (div. 1970); children: Terrence, Andrea, Michael. BS, U. Wis., 1964; Physician Asst., U. Fla., 1975. Tchr. Brown Deer (Wis.) Sch. System, 1964, Orange County (Fla.) Schs., 1965-70; curriculum devel., adminstr. So. Coll., Orlando, Fla., 1970-72; physician asst., asst. dir. Longevity Ctr., Orlando, 1977; physician asst. Pritikin Longevity Ctr., Miami, Fla., 1978-83, Cardiovascular Assocs., Kissimmee, Fla., 1984-92; pres., physician asst., cons. Physician's Svcs., Inc., Orlando, 1986—. Mem. Am. Acad. Physician Assts., Fla. Acad. Physician Assts. Home: 3407 Trentwood Blvd Orlando FL 32812-4850 Office: Tai Poinciana Clinic 2 Doverplum Ave Poinciana FL 34759-3409

ZACHERT, VIRGINIA, psychologist, educator; b. Jacksonville, Ala., Mar. 1, 1920; d. R.E. and Cora H. (Massee) Z. Student, Norman Jr. Coll., 1937; AB, Ga. State Woman's Coll., 1940; MA, Emory U., 1947; PhD, Purdue U., 1949. Diplomate: Am. Bd. Profl. Psychologists. Statistician Davison-Paxon Co., Atlanta, 1941-44; research psychologist Mil. Contracts, Auburn Research Found., Ala. Poly. Inst.; indsl. and research psychologist Sturm & O'Brien (cons. engrs.), 1958-59; research project dir. Western Design, Biloxi, Miss., 1960-61; self-employed cons. psychologist Norman Park, Ga., 1961-71, Good Hope, Ga., 1971—; rsch. assoc. med. edn. Med. Coll. Ga., Augusta, 1963-65, assoc. prof., 1965-70, rsch. prof., 1970-84, rsch. prof. emeritus, 1984—, chief learning materials divsn., 1973-84, faculty senate, 1976-84, acad. coun., 1976-82, pres. acad. coun., 1983, sec., 1978; mem. Ga. Bd. Examiners Psychologists, 1974-79, v.p., 1977, pres. 1978; adv. bd. Comdr. Gen. ATC USAF, 1967-70; cons. Ga. Silver Haired Legislature, 1980-86, senator, 1987-93, pres. protem, 1987-88, pres., 1989-93, rep., spkr. protem, 1993—; govs. appointee Ga. Coun. on Aging, 1988-96; U.S. Senate mem. Fed. Coun. on the Aging, 1990-93; senator appointee White House Conf. on Aging, 1995. Author: (with P.L. Wilds) Essentials of Gynecology-Oncology, 1967, Applications of Gynecology-Oncology, 1967. Del. White House Conf. on Aging, 1981, 95. Served as aerologist USN, 1944-46;aviation psychologist USAF, 1949-54. Fellow AAAS, Am. Psychol. Assn.; mem. AAUP (chpt. pres. 1977-80), Sigma Xi. (chpt. pres. 1980-81). Baptist. Home: 1126 Highland Ave Augusta GA 30904-4628 Office: Med Coll Ga Dept Ob-Gyn Augusta GA 30912

ZAEPFEL, GLENN PETER, psychologist; b. N.Y.C., Feb. 15, 1951; s. Walter Henry and Lillian Adair (Kovach) Z.; m. Linda Carrie Grinton, June 1, 1974; children: Peter, Caroline, Christine. BA, U. S.C., 1973; MEd, Ga. State U., 1980, PhD, 1986. Milieu therapist Peachtree-Parkwood Hosp., Atlanta, 1978-80; dir. Roswell St. Counseling Ctr., Marietta, Ga., 1980-84; dir. counseling and psychol. svcs. DeKalb Pain Control and Rehab. Ctr., Decatur, Ga., 1981-85; pvt. practice psychology, Columbia, S.C., 1985—; Author: He Wins, She Wins, 1994; founder, program dir. Bapt. Med. Ctr. Pain Mgmt. Program, Columbia, 1985-87; founder, pres. Columbia Counseling Ctr., P.A., 1986—; dir. behav. health Carolina Primary Care, L.L.C., adv. bd. mem. Mem. Am. Psychol. Assn., Christian Assn. for Psychol. Studies, Am. Rehab. Counseling Assn., Am. Assn. Counseling and Devel., Am. Bd. Med. Psychotherapists. Republican. Presbyterian. Club: Sinfonia Fraternity (Columbia). Avocations: sports, music. Home: 1153 Scotts Hill Rd Chapin SC 29036-8974 Office: 900 Saint Andrews Rd Columbia SC 29210-5816 also: 601 Polo Rd Columbia SC 29223-2905 also: 122 Powell Dr Lexington SC 29072-9203

ZAFAR, MOHAMMED JAULIKAR, physician; b. Vaniyambadi, Madras, India, Apr. 19, 1958; m. Nazneen Nikhat, May 16, 1982; children: Fouzaan Zafar, Adnan Zafar. MD, Madras Med. Coll., India, 1982; postgrad. in internal medicine, U. Madras, 1985-87. Diplomate Am. Bd. Psychiatry and Neurology (neurology and clin. neurophysiology). Intern Univ. Madras, India, 1981-82; resident in pediatric medicine Inst. of Child Health, Madras, 1982; resident in internal medicine Apollo Hosp., Madras, 1983-85; intern in internal medicine U. Mo. Hosp. and Clinics, 1987-88; chief resident in neurology U. Mo. Hosp. and Clinics/VA Med. Ctr., Columbia, 1987-90; fellow assoc., clin. neurophysiology dept. neurology U. Iowa Hosps. and Clinics, Iowa City, 1991-92; instr. clin. neurology, U. Mo., Mich. State U. Contbr. articles to profl. jours. and publs. Mem. Am. Acad. Neurology, AMA, Am. Soc. Neuroimaging, Mich. State Med. Soc., Kalamazoo Acad. Medicine, Am. Acad. Clin. Neurophysiology. Home: 7482 Dunross Dr Kalamazoo MI 49002-7882 Office: Kalamazoo Neurology PC Ste 229 1717 Shaffer Kalamazoo MI 49001

ZAFFARONI, ALEJANDRO C., biochemist, medical research company executive; b. Montevideo, Uruguay, Feb. 27, 1923; came to U.S., 1944; s. Carlos and Luisa (Alfaro) Z.; m. Lyda Russomanno, July 5, 1946; children—Alejandro A., Elisa. B., U. Montevideo, 1943; Ph.D. in Biochemistry, U. Rochester, 1949; Doctorate (hon.), U. Republic, Montevideo, 1983; M.Divinity, Cen. Bapt. Seminary, 1987. Dir. biochem. research Syntex S.A., Mexico City, 1951-54, v.p., dir. research, 1954-56; exec. v.p., dir. Syntex Corp., Palo Alto, Calif., 1956-68; pres. Syntex Labs. Inc., Palo Alto, Calif., 1962-68, Syntex Research, Palo Alto, Calif., 1962-68; founder, co-chmn. ALZA Corp., Palo Alto, Calif., 1968—, also CEO; founder, mem. policy bd. and exec. com. DNAX Research Inst. of Molecular and Cellular Biology, Inc., Palo Alto, Calif., 1980—, chmn., 1980-82; founder, chmn., chief exec. officer Affymax, N.V., Palo Alto, 1989—; chmn. Internat. Psoriasis Research Found., Palo Alto; incorporator Neuroscis. Research Found. MIT, Brookline, Mass.; bd. govs. Weizmann Inst. Sci., Rehovot, Israel; mem. pharm. panel of com. on tech. and internat. econs. and trade issues Nat. Acad. Engring. Office of Fgn. Sec. and Assembly of Engring., Washington; hon. prof. biochemistry Nat. U. Mex., 1957, U. Montevideo, 1959. Contbr. numerous articles to profl. jours.; patentee in field. Recipient Barren medal Barren Found., Chgo., 1974; Pres.'s award Weizmann Inst. Sci., 1978; Chem. Pioneer award Am. Inst. Chemists, Inc., 1979, National Medal of Technology, 1995. Fellow Am. Acad. Arts and Scis., Am. Pharm. Assn.; mem. AAAS, Am. Chem. Soc., Am. Found. Pharm. Edn., Am. Inst. Chemists, Inc., Am. Soc. Biol. Chemists, Inc., Am. Soc. Microbiology, Am. Soc. Pharmacology and Exptl. Therapeutics, Biomed. Engring. Soc., Calif. Pharmacists Assn., Internat. Pharm. Fedn., Internat. Soc. Chronobiology, Internat. Soc. Study of Biol. Rhythms, Soc. Exptl. Biology and Medicine, Sociedad Mexicana de Nutricion y Endocrinologia, Biochem. Soc. Eng., Endocrine Soc., Internat. Soc. Research in Biology of Reproduction, N.Y. Acad. Scis., Christian Legal Soc. (Mo. bd. dirs. 1973—), Tau Kappa Epsilon (internat. pres. 1953-57). *

ZAFREN, KEN, physician; b. Cin., Oct. 12, 1953; s. Herbert Cecil and Miriam (Koenigsberg) Z.; m. Christina Tower, June 29, 1984. BA in Math., New Coll., Sarasota, Fla., 1975; MD, U. Wash., 1984. Diplomate Nat. Bd. Med. Examiners, Am. Bd. Emergency Medicine. Transitional intern Presbyn.-St. Luke's Med. Ctr., Denver, 1985-86; pvt. practice Anchorage, 1986-91, Kern Med Ctr, Bakersfield, Calif., 1991-94; emergency physician Alaska Regional Hosp., Anchorage, 1994—, Providence Hosp., Anchorage, 1994—; med. dir. Lake Clark Nat. Park, 1996—, Denali Nat Park Mountaineering Rangers, 1996—; asst. med. dir. North Care, 1990-91; mem. Alaska Mountain Rescue Group, 1988—, chmn., 1991, med. dir., 1994—; U.S. rep. to med. commn. of Internat. Commn. for Alpine Rescue, 1995—. Mem. Rocky Mountain Rescue Group, Boulder, 1976-80, Mountain Rescue Council, Seattle, 1979-83. NIH tng. grantee, 1979-83; grand prize winner 1988 MD Magazine photo contest. Fellow Am. Coll. Emergency Physicians, Am. Acad. Emergency Medicine; mem. Am. Alpine Club, Mountaineering Club Alaska (bd. dirs. 1990-91), Himalayan Rescue Assn. (life, assoc. dir. USA 1993—), Wilderness Med. Soc. (bd. dirs. 1991-96).

ZAGAR, ERIS A., oncology nurse; b. Pittsburg, Kans., Nov. 13, 1956; d. Frank and Eris Marie (Darigo) Z. BSN, Pitts. State U., 1978; MSN, U. Mo., 1988. RN. Charge nurse St. Francis Hosp. & Med. Ctr., Topeka; edn. nurse I U. Mo. Hosp. & Clinics, Columbia, charge nurse, staff nurse IV short stay ctr.; oncology clin. nurse specialist Holston Med. Group, Ellis Fischel Cancer Ctr., Columbia. Mem. ANA, Oncology Nursing Soc., Sigma Theta Tau. Office: Ellis Fischel Cancer Ctr 115 Bus Loop 70 W Columbia MO 65203

ZAGON, IAN STUART, neuroscience and anatomy educator, researcher; b. N.Y.C., Mar. 28, 1943; s. Benjamin and Beatrice (Shaffer) Z.; m. Eileen Kostel, Nov. 26, 1964. BS, U. Wis., 1965; MS, U. Ill., 1969; PhD, U. Colo., 1972. Asst. prof. biol. structure U. Miami, Fla., 1972-74; asst. prof. anatomy Pa. State U., Hershey, 1974-78, prof. genetics, 1975—, assoc. prof., 1978-85, prof., 1985-91, prof. cell and molecular biology and neurosci., 1984—, prof. neurosci. and anatomy, 1991—; cons. Nat. Inst. on Drug Abuse, Rockville, Md., 1980—; cons., reviewer NIH, Bethesda, Md., 1984—; grant reviewer Am. Heart Assn. of Pa., 1985—, mem. rsch. com., 1988—, bd. dirs., 1992—, v.p., 1993—. Author: Maternal Substance Abuse and the Developing Nervous System, 1992, Receptors in the Developing Nervous System, 1993; mem. editl. bd. Brain Rsch. Bull., 1980—, sect. editor, 1994—; mem. editl. bd. Physiology and Behavior, 1987—, Pharmacology, Biochemistry and Behavior, 1989—, Advances in Neuroimmunology, 1990, Internat. Jour. Devel. Neurosci., 1987-89, Brain Rsch., 1992—, Devel. Brain Rsch., 1992—; contbr. numerous articles to med. and profl. jours.; patentee on growth factors and devel. cancer. Grantee, NIH, Am. Cancer Soc., Nat. Inst. Drug Abuse. Mem. Am. Soc. Cell. Biology, Soc. for Neurosci., Assn. for Rsch. in Vision and Ophthalmology. Office: Pa State U Coll of Medicine PO Box 850 Hershey PA 17033-0850

ZAGOREN, ALLEN JEFFREY, surgeon; b. Bklyn., May 17, 1947; s. Max and Harriett (Feldman) Z.; m. Gail Marie Sarcinella, Feb. 20, 1977. BA in Biology, Hofstra U., 1969; DO, Phila. Coll. Osteo. Medicine, 1975. Diplomate Am. Bd. Osteo. Surgery, Nat. Bd. Examiners Osteo.-Med. Surgery. Intern Stratford (N.J.) div. John F. Kennedy Meml. Hosp., 1975-76; resident Cherry Hill (N.J.) Med. Ctr., 1976-80; assoc. prof. surgery U. Medicine and Dentistry, Piscataway, N.J., 1980-82; practice osteo. medicine specializing in surgery Rose Clinic, Des Moines, 1982-94, Capitol Hill Surgery, Des Moines, 1994—; mem. staff Mercy Hosp. Med. Ctr., Des Moines; practice osteo. medicine specializing in surgery Capitol Hill Surgery, Des Moines; chmn. dept. surgery Des Moines Gen. Hosp., 1985-91, Madison County Meml. Hosp., Winterset, Iowa; adj. prof. surgery and nutrition U. Osteo. Medicine; assoc. prof. pharmacy Drake U.; lectr. in field; mem. Nat. Bd. Examiners in Osteo. Medicine and Surgery; mem. surg. rev. com. Bd. Med. Examiners of Iowa, 1996—; med. dir. Wound Care Ctr., 1996, program dir. gen. surgery residency, 1993—. Contbr. articles to profl. jours.; creator videotapes (with others). Bd. dirs. Des Moines Gen. Hosp. Found., sec., 1986-93; active Iowa Found. for Med. Care, Nutritional Coun. Iowa; chmn. bd. dirs. Des Moines Gen. Found., 1991-94; trustee Tiffereth Israel Synagogue, 1992. Grantee SKF Labs., Phila., 1986, Norwich (N.Y.) Eaton Labs., 1986, Ross Labs., 1995, 96. Fellow Am. Coll. Osteo. Surgeons (rsch., nutritional support, visual aids coms., chair rsch. com. 1991-92, 1st Prize awards 1982, 83), Am. Coll. Nutrition, Internat. Coll. Surgeons; mem. Am. Osteo. Soc., Am. Soc. Gastrointestinal Endoscopy, Iowa Osteo. Med. Assn. (pres. 1994-95, chmn. constrn. and v.p. bylaws coms. 1992, trustee), Polk County Med. Soc. (treas. 1991-93), Am. Soc. Parenteral and Enteral Nutrition (bd. dirs. 1986, chmn. various coms.), Iowa and Nebr. Soc. Parenteral and Enteral Nutrition (pres. 1990-92), Nat. Wildlife Fedn. (chair com. postgrad. edn. Iowa Health Reform Project 1993), Iowa Health Leadership Consortium (CEO com.), Smithsonian Instn., Airplane Owners and Pilots Assn., Iowa Nebr. Nutrition Soc. (pres. 1990-92). Jewish. Office: Capitol Hill Surgery 1300 Des Moines St Des Moines IA 50309

ZAGOREN, JOY CARROLL, health facility director, researcher; b. N.Y.C., Oct. 31, 1933; d. Murray Morris and Celia (Donner) Rossman; m. Robert H. Zagoren, June 29, 1958 (div. 1988); children: Glenn, Robin; m. Robert Henry Chester, Apr. 1, 1988; children: Peter, Lisabeth, Melinda, Cecily, Kate. BS, NYU, 1957; MS, Adelphi U., 1969; PhD with distinction, NYU, 1981. Sec. sch. faculty Great Neck (N.Y.) Pub. Schs., 1957-71; rsch. scientist Inst. Psychobiol. Studies, Queens Village, N.Y., 1968-71; rsch. assoc. Albert Einstein Coll. Medicine, Bronx, N.Y., 1971-84; asst. prof. Sch. Medicine SUNY, Stony Brook, 1984-86; dir. Seriatum, N.Y.C., 1991—; ptnr. Winter Tree Collection; chmn. Esrath Nashim Hosp., 1986—; med. bd. dirs. Sarah Herzog Meml. Hosp., 1994—. Editor: The Node of Ranvier, 1984; contbr. articles to profl. jours. Chair Peace Corps Svc. Coun., Tri-State, 1965-75; pres. Kidney Found. L.I., N.Y., 1965-77; v.p. United Cmty. fund L.I., 1970-83; bd. dirs. Jerusalem Mental Health Ctr., N.Y.C., 1986—; mem. med. bd. dirs. Sarah Herzog Meml. Hosp., hon. chair dinner, 1995, chair dinner, 1996. Recipient post doctoral fellowship NIH, 1982-84, svc. awards Kidney Found., Kiwanis, and others, 1970-87; named Disting. Alumnus of Yr., Adelphi U., 1986. Mem. AAAS, ACA, N.Y. Acad. Sci., Am. Assn. Neuropathology, Esrath Nashim Hosp. (chairperson 1986—, apptd. med. bd. dirs. 1994. Democrat. Jewish. Home: 405 E 82nd St New York NY 10028-6038 Office: Seriatum PO Box 396 Livingston Manor NY 12758-0396

ZAGORZYCKI, MARIA TERESA, physician; b. Trenton, N.J., Dec. 18, 1953; d. John M. and Janina Zofia (Jaworski) Z. BA in Biochemistry with distinction in all subjects, Cornell U., 1975; MD, George Washington U., 1979. Diplomate Am. Bd. Ob-Gyn. Intern UCLA Hosp., 1979-80, resident in ob-gyn., 1980-82, chief resident in ob-gyn., 1982-83, asst. clin. prof. ob-gyn, 1983—. Fellow Am. Coll. Ob-Gyn, Inter-Am. Coll. Physicians and Surgeons; mem. Am. Fertility Soc., Am. Med. Women's Assn., Am. Assn. Gynecologic Laproscopists, Los Angeles County Obstetrical and Gynecol. Soc., Phi Delta Epsilon. Club: Cornell of So. Calif. Office: 16500 Ventura Blvd Ste 414 Encino CA 91436-2062

ZAHAVI, JOSEPH MATHEW, physician, researcher; b. Jerusalem, Israel, Dec. 24, 1932; s. Meir and Hana (Levy) Z.; m. Miriam Weiss, June 7, 1960; children: Meir, Itai-Zvi. MD, Hebrew U. Sch. Medicine, Jerusalem, 1960; grad. cert., Tel-Aviv U., 1967. Resident Ichilov Hosp., Tel-Aviv, 1960-67, temporary chief physician, 1967-71, permanent chief physician, 1971-75, dir. dept. medicine, day clinic, 1980—; dir. dept. medicine Naharryah Govt. Hosp., 1975-76; hon. cons. thrombosis unit King's Coll. Hosp., London, 1977-80. Capt. Israeli Res. Corps, 1974-87. Recipient Am. Physician fellowship Israeli Med. Assn., 1972, 73, Chief Scientist Office grants Ministry of Health, Israel, 1974, 75, 82, 83, 86, 89, 90, G. Meirbaum Fund grants Tel-Aviv U. Sch. Medicine, 1982, 83, 85, J. Tiber Fund grant Tel-Aviv U. Sch. Medicine, 1985, Dr. Schauder Fund Tel-Aviv U. Sch. Medicine, 1987. Mem. AAAS, Israeli Soc. Internal Medicine, Am. Coll. Chest Physicians, Internat. Soc. Thrombosis and Hemostasis, Internat. Soc. Internal Medicine, Am. Heart Assn. Coun. on Thrombosis, Mediterranean League Against Thromboembolic Diseases, Brit. Med. Assn., Israeli Soc. for Atherosclerotic Rsch., N.Y. Acad. Scis., Internat. Union Agiology, Internat. Arteriosclerosis Soc. Home: 11 Bavli St, Tel-Aviv 62331, Israel Office: Day Clinic Dept Medicine, Ichilov Hosp, Tel Aviv 64239, Israel

ZAHLER, STANLEY ARNOLD, genetics educator; b. N.Y.C., May 28, 1926; s. Irving and Clara (Heimowitz) Z.; m. Eleanor Janette Haugness, Nov. 1, 1952; children: Kathy Ann, Diane Louise, Peter Irving. Student, CCNY, 1941-44; AB, NYU, 1948; MS, U. Chgo., 1950, PhD, 1952. Postdoctoral fellow USPHS, Urbana, Ill., 1952-54; asst. prof. U. Wash., Seattle, 1954-59; from asst. prof. to prof. Cornell U., Ithaca, N.Y., 1959-93, chair sect. genetics and devel., 1990-94, prof. emeritus microbial genetics, 1994—; cons. in field. Ens. USNR, 1944-46. Mem. Am. Soc. Microbiology (various offices 1960-85). Office: Cornell U Biotech Bldg Ithaca NY 14853

ZAIMAN, K. ROBERT, dentist; b. Cin., Oct. 19, 1944; s. Noboru Gary and Toshiko (Matsuyama) Z.; m. Kimberly Ann Sass, Nov. 6, 1976; children: Kara Jean, Matthew Robert. Student, Creighton U., Omaha, 1962-64, DDS, 1968. Asst. prof. Creighton U. Sch. Dentistry, Omaha, 1971-73, assoc. prof., 1973-75; pvt. practice dentistry Omaha, 1971—. Past v.p., bd. dirs. Japanese-Am. Citizens League, Omaha, 1977-86; bd. elders King of Kings Luth. Ch., 1990—. Lt. comdr. USN, 1964-71. Fellow Acad. Gen. Dentistry (pres. 1976-77, nat. del. 1971-76), Acad. Continuing Edn.; mem. ADA, Omaha Dist. Dental Soc. (treas. 1980-85, bd. dirs. 1968—), Nebr. Dental Assn. (del. 1971—), Omaha Study Club (pres.), Delta Sigma Delta (pres. 1973-74). Office: 10841 Q St Ste 109 Omaha NE 68137-3701

ZAJAC, ANN L., chiropractor; d. Frank and Doris Zajac; children: Christopher, Gregor, Joseph Flood. BA, Worcester (Mass.) State Coll., 1969; MEd, Loyola U., 1972; BS, Nat. Coll. Chiropractic, 1985, D of Chiropractic, 1987. Tchr. Dist. 218, Ill., 1969-74, Moraine Valley Cmty. Coll., Ill., 1990-91; pvt. practice Tinley Park, Ill., 1987—. Lectr. chamber meetings, Tinley Park, 1980—, other civic orgns.; chairperson Renew, Orland Park, 1981-83. Mem. Ill. Chiropractic Soc., Tinley Park C. of C., Orland Park C. of C., Am. Bus. Women's Assn. (ednl. chairperson). Office: 7050 W 183rd St Tinley Park IL 60477

ZAJICEK-COLEMAN, EVA MARIA, psychologist, consultant, trainer; b. Boston, Lincolnshire, Eng., Apr. 5, 1951; d. Karel and Marie Erhart Zajicek; m. John Coleman, June 16, 1979; children: Joanna Marie, Laura Jane. BA in Psychology with honors, Manchester (Eng.) U., 1972; MA in Psychology of Counselling & Psychotherapy, Antioch U., London, 1988; PhD in Psychology, London U., 1986. Registered psychotherapist. Statistician, systems analyst Brit. Oxygen Co., Wolverhampton, 1972-73; rsch. asst. Family Rsch. Unit, London, 1974-82; gen. practice surgery counsellor, G.P. practice, Hove, 1986—; pvt. practice, Ditchling, Eng., 1988—; trustee Trust for Study Adolescence, Brighton, Eng., 1989-95; lectr. Brighton Poly., 1988-90; cons. Brit. Rail, Watford, 1990-91; mgr. Threshold Women's Counselling Svc., 1991—. Co-author: Pregnancy: A Psychological Social Study, 1981; rev. editor Brit. Jourr. Guidance and Counselling, 1990—; also articles. Trustee Chalvington Trust, Seaford, Eng., 1980-91. Mem. Brit. Assn. Counselling, Brit. Psychol. Soc. (chartered).

ZAJONC, ROBERT B(OLESLAW), psychology educator; b. Lodz, Poland, Nov. 23, 1923; came to U.S., 1949, naturalized, 1953; s. Mieczyslaw and Anna (Kwiatkowska) Z.; m. Donna Benson, June 20, 1953 (div. 1981); children: Peter Clifford, Michael Anton, Joseph Robert; m. Hazel Markus, May 25, 1982; 1 child, Krysia Courcelle Markus. Ph.D., U. Mich., 1955; Dr. hon. causa, U. Louvain, 1984, U. Warsaw, 1989. Asst. prof. psychology U. Mich., 1955-60, assoc. prof., 1960-63, prof., 1963-94, Charles Horton Cooley Disting. prof. psychology, 1983-94, rsch. scientist Inst. for Social Rsch., 1960-83, dir., 1989; prof. psychology Stanford (Calif.) U., 1994—; directeur d'études Maison des Sciences de L'Homme, Paris, 1985-86; vis. prof. U. Oxford, 1971-72. Author: Social Psychology: An Experimental Approach, 1965; editor: Animal Social Psychology, 1970; assoc. editor: Jour. Personality and Social Psychology, 1960-66. Guggenheim fellow, 1978-79; Fulbright fellow, 1962-63; recipient Disting. Prof. award of social sci., 1983. Fellow AAAS (co-recipient Psychol. prize 1976), APA (Disting. Sci. Contbrn. award 1978), Japan Soc. Promotion of Sci., N.Y. Acad. Scis.; mem. Soc. for Exptl. Social Psychology (Disting. Scientist award 1986), Polish Acad. Scis. (fgn.). Office: Stanford U Dept Psychology Jordan Hall Stanford CA 94305

ZAK, HENRY LEON, oral surgeon; b. Lancaster, N.Y., Sept. 12, 1923; s. Leon and Lottie (Ogrodowicz) Z.; m. Virginia E. Boron, Aug. 24, 1949; children: Henry Stephen, Claudia Cynthia, Christopher Paul. DDS, St. Louis U. Sch. Dentistry, 1946; BS, Baylor Coll. Dentistry, 1960; MS in Oral Surgery, Baylor U., 1960; MS in Forensic Scis., George Washington U., 1976. Diplomate Am. Bd. Oral Surgery, N.Y. State Bd. Oral Surgery. Intern surgery Cin. Gen. Hosp., 1947-48; gen. practice dentistry, 1948-51; post dental surgeon Army Arctic Tgn. Ctr., Big Delta, Alaska, 1952-54; chief oral surgery USA Hosp., Ft. Hood, Tex., 1954-57; resident in oral surgery Brooke Army Gen. Hosp., San Antonio, 1958-60; chief oral surgery Schofield Barracks, Hawaii, 1960-63, USA Hosp., Ft. Lee, Va., 1963-67, 93d Evacuation Hosp., Long Biah, Vietnam, 1967-68, USA Hosp., Ft. Belvoir, Va., 1968-71; ret. U.S. Army Dental Corps, 1971; oral surgeon Group Health Assn., 1971-78; pvt. practice oral surgery, 1978—. Mem. AAAS, Am. Soc. Oral Surgeons, Am. Dental Assn., N.Y. State Dental Soc., Internat. Platform Assn., 8th Dist. Dental Soc. State N.Y., Omicron Kappa Upsilon. Home: 8204 East Blvd Dr Alexandria VA 22308

ZAKHARIA, GEORGE FARID, urologist; b. Tripoli, Lebanon, Jan. 17, 1959; came to U.S., 1985; s. Farid Nakhle and Alice Saba (Daoura) Z. BSc, Am. U. of Beirut, Lebanon, 1980, MD, 1985. Diplomate Am. Bd. Urology. Intern in surgery SUNY Health Sci. Ctr., Syracuse, 1985-86, resident in urology, 1986-91; urologist staff VA Hosp., Fresno, Calif., 1992-94; pvt. practice Wichita (Kans.) Urology Group, 1994—. Christian. Home and Office: 2848 N Cypress Wichita KS 67226

ZALCBERG, JOHN RAYMOND, medical oncologist; b. Melbourne, Australia, Feb. 6, 1952; s. Abram and Irene (Kurc) Z.; m. Lynette Glenda Moses, Dec. 7, 1975; children: Nicole, David. MB BS, U. Melbourne, 1975, PhD, 1984. Sessional oncologist Austin and Repatriation Hosps., Victoria, 1985-86; dir. med. oncology Heidelberg Repatriation Hosp., Victoria, 1986-95; dir. Cancer Svc. Austin and Repatriation Med. Ctr., 1995—; profl. assoc. Dept. Medicine U. Melbourne, 1995—; cons. mem. Eastern Coop. Oncology Group, Denver, 1992—; exec. sec. Lorne Cancer Conf., 1987—; chmn. sr. med. staff. assocs., Austin and Repat. Med. Ctr., 1995—. Contbr. numerous articles to sci. jours. Chmn. ethics com. Montefiore Home for the Aged, Melbourne, 1992—; chmn. cancer rsch. group Clin. Oncol. Soc. Australia, 1992-94. Recipient numerous grants for rsch. and study. Fellow Royal Australasian Coll. Physicians. Jewish. Office: Austin - Repatriation Med Ctr, Banksia St, Melbourne 3081, Australia

ZALESKI, BRIAN WILLIAM, chiropractor; b. Trenton, N.J., Oct. 27, 1962; s. Joseph Rudolph and Roseline (Moore) Z.; m. Petra Gertrude Tucker, Apr. 10, 1983; children: Natasha Reneé, Tatyana Amber. Student, Def. Lang. Inst., Monterey, Calif., 1980-81; BS, Palmer Coll., 1992, D of Chiropractic, 1992. Indsl. disability evaluator, Calif.; qualified med. evaluator, Calif. Grad. rschr. Palmer Coll. of Chiropractice, Davenport, Iowa, 1991-92; chiropractor Peninsula Spinal Care, Daly City, Calif., 1992, Creekside Family Chiropractic, Vacaville, Calif., 1992—; prin. investigator, presenter Internat. Conf. on Spinal Manipulation, 1992. Baseball umpire Iowa High Schs., Davenport, 1989-92, Men's Sr. League, Davenport, 1989-91, No. Calif. Umpires Assn., San Mateo, Calif., 1992; mem. adv. bd. Solano Serve Our Srs. Recipient scholarship Internat. Chiropractors Assn., 1989, 90, Cecil M. Grogan scholarship Palmer Internat. Alumni Assn., 1991, Alma Nielsen scholarship Internat. Chiropractors Assn. Aux., 1991, Student Rsch. grant Palmer Coll. Chiropractic, 1992; named to Dean's List, 1991-92. Mem. Internat. Chiropractors Assn. (coun. on chiropractic pediatrics), Calif. Chiropractic Assn. (net masters com., ins. rels. com.), Assn. for History of Chiropractic, Palmer Internat. Alumni Assn., Napa/Solano Chiropractic Soc. (pres.), Calif. Chiropractic Assn., Masons, Delta Sigma Chi, Chi Rho Theta. Republican. Office: Creekside Family Chiropractic 3000 Alamo Dr Ste 108 Vacaville CA 95687-6345

ZALESKI, JAN FRANCISZEK, biochemist; b. Bytom, Poland, Feb. 3, 1949; came to U.S., 1979; s. Stanislaw and Maria (Fliska) Z.; m. Margaret M. Toczkowska, Dec. 28, 1971; children: Marta, Monika. MS in Biochemistry, U. Warsaw, Poland, 1971, PhD in Biochemistry, 1978. Rsch. assoc., asst. prof., assoc. prof. U. Warsaw Inst. Biochemistry, 1971-82; vis. scientist Roswell Park Meml. Inst., Buffalo, 1979-82; assoc. scientist Okla. Med. Rsch. Found., Oklahoma City, 1982-85; rsch. assoc. U. Pa. Med. Sch., Phila., 1985-88; vis. scientist Great Lakes Lab., Buffalo, 1988; rsch. assoc. prof. Rutgers U. Sch. Pharmacy, New Brunswick, N.J., 1989—; cons. J.A. Haley Vets. Hosp., Tampa, 1985, Great Lakes Lab., Buffalo, 1988, Wyeth-Ayerst Rsch., Princeton, 1994. Contbr. articles to profl. jours., chpts. to books. Co-recipient awards Ministry Sci. and Higher Edn., Warsaw, 1978, Polish Acad. Scis., Warsaw, 1979. Mem. Internat. Soc. Study of Xenobiotics, Am. Soc. Biochemistry and Molecular Biology. Office: Rutgers U Lab Cell & Biochem Toxicology 41 Gordon Rd Piscataway NJ 08854-5945

ZALEZNIK, ABRAHAM, psychoanalyst, management specialist, educator; b. Phila., Jan. 30, 1924; s. Isadore and Anna (Appelbaum) Z.; m. Elizabeth Ann Aron, June 24, 1945; children: Dori Faith, Ira Harry. AB in econs., Alma Coll., 1945, DLitt (hon.), 1992; MBA, Harvard U., 1947, DCS, 1951; grad., Boston Psychoanalytic Soc. and Inst., 1965. Research asst. Harvard U. Grad. Sch. Bus. Adminstrn., 1947-48, instr., 1948-51, asst. prof., 1951-56, assoc. prof., 1956-61, prof., 1961—, Cahners-Rabb prof. social psychology of mgmt., 1967-83, Konosuke Matsushita prof. leadership, 1983-90, Konosuke Matsushita prof. leadership emeritus, 1990—; research fellow Boston Psychoanalytic Soc. and Inst., 1965-68, mem. faculty, 1972—; pvt. practice psychoanalysis Boston, 1968—; cons. to mgmt.; chmn. bd. King Ranch; vice chmn. bd. Ogden Corp.; bd. dirs. Ardco, Inc., Timberland Co., Freedom Newspapers, Inc., Am. Greetings, Butchers, Inc. Author: Human Dilemmas of Leadership, 1966, (with Manfred F.R. Kets de Vries) Power and the Corporate Mind, 1975, The Managerial Mystique, 1989, An Executive Guide to Motivating People, 1990, Learning Leadership, 1992; contbr. articles to profl. jours. Trustee Beth Israel Hosp., Boston, 1968—. Served with USN, 1942-46. Mem. Boston Psychoanalytic Soc., Am. Psychoanalytic Assn. (cert.), Am. Sociol. Assn., Tavern Club (Boston), Belmont Country Club (Mass.). Home: 170 N Ocean Blvd Palm Beach FL 33480 Office: Harvard University Business School Boston MA 02163 also: Ogden Corp 2 Pennsylvania Plz New York NY 10121

ZALZAL, GEORGE HABIB, pediatric otolaryncologist; b. Brumana, Lebanon, Apr. 28, 1954; s. Habib George and Minerva Alfred (Younis) Z.; m. Vivian Lynn Malouf, July 19, 1987; children: Habib George, Pierre George. BS, Am. U. of Beirut, 1975, MD, 1979. Diplomate Nat. Bd. Med. Examiners, Am. Bd. Otolaryngology. Intern Am. U. of Beirut Sch. of Medicine and Med. Ctr., 1978-79, resident in surgery, 1979-80, resident in otolaryngology, 1980-83; fellow in pediatric otolaryngology U. Cin. Coll. Medicine, Children's Hosp. Med. Ctr., 1983-85, instr., 1985-86; active staff otolaryngology Children's Hosp. Med. Ctr., Cin., 1985-86, Christian Holmes Hosp., Cin., 1985-86; asst. prof. George Washington U. Sch. Medicine, Washington, 1986-91, assoc. prof. surgery and pediatrics, 1991—, tenure, 1993—; attending staff otolaryngology Children's Nat. Med. Ctr., Washington, 1986—, chmn. dept. otolaryngology, 1994—; attending staff otolaryngology George Washington U. med. Ctr., 1986—; cons. staff otolaryngology Walter Reed Army Med. Ctr., Washington, 1986—. Contbr. articles to profl. jours., publs. Rsch. grantee in field. Mem. Lebanese Order Physicians, Am. U. of Beirut Med. Alumni (pres. Otolaryngology Head and Neck Surgery Assn. 1992—), AMA, Assn. Rsch. on Otolaryngology, Washington Met. Ear, Nose and Throat-HEad and Neck Soc., Am. Soc. Pediatric Otolaryngology, Am. Acad. Otolaryngology Head and Neck Surgery, Soc. for Ear, Nose and Thorat Advancement in Children. Home: 7541 Pepperell Dr Bethesda MD 20817-4653 Office: Children's Nat Med Ctr Pediatric Otolaryngology 111 Michigan Ave NW Washington DC 20010-2970

ZAMBITO, RAYMOND FRANCIS, oral surgeon, educator; b. N.Y.C., Nov. 9, 1926; s. John and Lucy (Mecca) Z.; m. Dorothy M. Sikoryak, Apr. 23, 1960; children: Mary Lucille, Paul Michael, Christine Marie, John Raymond, Michael Sikoryak, Peter Ignatius. Student, Bklyn. Coll., 1943-44; B.S., U. Scranton, 1948; DDS, NYU, 1953, cert. in oral surgery, 1956; MA in Adminstrn. in Higher Edn., Columbia U., 1968, EdD, 1978; MBA in Health Care Mgmt., Adelphi U., 1978; DSc honoris causa, Seton Hall U., 1994. Diplomate Am. Bd. Oral and Maxillofacial Surgery. Intern in oral surgery Kings County Hosp. Ctr., Bklyn., 1956-57; resident in gen. anesthesiology Jewish Chronic Disease Hosp., Bklyn., 1957; resident in oral surgery and anesthesiology Cook County Hosp., Chgo., 1957-59; practice gen. dentistry Kings Park, N.Y., 1953-55, Chgo., 1958-59; oral surgery Bklyn., 1959-61, Williston Park, N.Y., 1961-66, N.Y.C., 1966-68, Jamaica, N.Y., 1968—; asst. dept. of oral and maxillo-facial surgery U. Ill. Coll. Dentistry, 1958-59; instr. Sch. of Dental and Oral Surgery, Columbia U., N.Y.C., 1961-66; chief of svc. in dept. dentistry St. Francis Hosp., Roslyn, N.Y., 1963-66; cons. in oral surgery and dental dept. adminstrn., 1975-85; asst. attending oral surgeon Kings County Hosp. Ctr., Bklyn., 1959-62; attending oral surgeon L.I. Jewish Med. Ctr., New Hyde Park, N.Y., 1962-71; asst. attending oral surgeon Queens Hosp. Ctr., Jamaica, N.Y., 1964-65; assoc. attending oral surgeon Elmhurst (N.Y.) Gen. Hosp. 1965-66; attending oral surgeon and dir. dentistry and oral surgery Lincoln Hosp., 1966-68; asst. prof. of dental surgery Albert Einstein Coll. of Medicine, Yeshiva U., 1966-68, asst. clin. prof., 1968-73; oral surgeon-in-charge Cath. Med. Ctr. of Bklyn., 1968—; cons. in oral and maxillo-facial surgery St. Joseph's Hosp. and Med. Ctr., Paterson, N.J., 1976—; asst. prof. dept. oral surgery and anesthesiology Fairleigh Dickinson U. Sch. of Dentistry, Hackensack, N.J., 1971-72, prof., 1972-89, coordinator dir. hosp. dentistry, 1972-89; adj. assoc. prof. of clin. pharmacy and dentistry Bklyn. Coll. of Pharmacy, 1976-77; cons. oral surgeon Suffolk State Sch., Melville, N.Y., 1965-71; dir. Spl. Dental Clinic for the Handicapped, Bur. of the Handicapped, Cath. Charities, Bklyn., 1973-75; mem. Cath. Med. Mission Bd., Mission OAAC Surgery, Dominican Rep., 1991—, summers 92-96. Co-editor: Hospital Dental Practice, A Manual, 1978, Immunology and Infectious Diseases of the Mouth, Head, and Neck, 1991, Manual of Dental Therapeutics, 1991; editor-in-chief Jour. Hosp. Dental Practice, 1973-80; contbr. articles on oral surgery and dental edn. to profl. jours. Lectr. Christian Life Communities movement to secondary schs. and colls., various states, 1962—; tchr. confrat. religious classes, 1964-85; mem. parish coun. St. Gertrude's Roman Cath. Ch., Bayville, N.Y., 1969-72, chmn., 1971-72; founder, chmn. Fedn. Lay Orgns., Diocese of Rockville Centre, 1968-72; pres. David Park Civic Assn., 1966-67; couns. Nat. Coun. Cath. Men, Washington, 1967--72. With USN, 1944-46, capt. Dental Corps, USNR ret. Decorated knight Order of Malta in U.S.; grantee HEW, 1967-70, 85-88. Fellow Am. Coll. of Dentists, Internat. Coll. Dentists, Am. Pub. Health Assn., Am. Dental Soc. of Anesthesiology, L.I. Acad. of Odontology; mem. Am. Soc. of Oral and Maxillofacial Surgeons, Am. Dental Assn. (mem. rev. com. coun. on hosp. and instnl. dental svcs. 1975—, cons. coun. on dental edn. 1973—), N.Y. State Soc. of Oral Surgeons (alt. del. to Am. Soc. Oral Surgeons), Am. Acad. Oral Pathology, Am. Acad. of History of Dentistry, N.Y. State Dental Soc. of Anesthesiology (pres. 1964), Am. Assn. Of Hosp. Dentists, Cath. Dentists Guild (pres. 1955-56), Am. Hosp. Assn. (mem. coun. on profl. svcs. 1976-78), Am. Coll. Oral and Maxillo Facial Surgeons (v.p. 1976-79), Christian Med. Soc., Internat. Assn. of Oral Surgeons, Nat. Fedn. of Christian Life Communities (pres. nat. fedn. 1971-73), del. to internat. gen. assembly in Rome, 1967, an Republic, 1970), Omicron Kappa Upsilon. Home: 603 Bayville Rd Locust Valley NY 11560-1207 Office: Cath Med Ctr Bklyn and Queens 88-25 153rd St Jamaica NY 11432-3731

ZAMBONI, WILLIAM ARNOLD, plastic and reconstructive surgeon, lab director; b. Reno, Nev., Dec. 10, 1958; s. Roger and Judy (Young) Z.; m. Karen Burke, Apr. 9, 1988. BS, U. Nev., 1980, MD, 1984. Diplomate Am. Bd. Surgery, Am. Bd. Plastic Surgery. Intern So. Ill. U. Sch. Medicine, Springfield, 1984-85, gen. surg. resident, 1985-89, resident in plastic surgery, 1989-91; asst. prof. surgery So. Ill. U., Springfield, 1991-94, chief sect. hyperbaric medicine, dir. hyperbaric rsch. lab., 1991-94; assoc. prof., chief divsn. plastic surgery U. Nev., Las Vegas, 1994—, dir microsurgical and hyperbaric rsch. lab., 1994—. Author: (textbook) Applications of Hyperbaric Oxygen Therapy in Plastic Surgery, 1995; co-author Handbook of Hand Therapy, 1992, Hyperbaric Medicine Practice, 1994, Plastic Surgery: The Requisites, 1993, Orthopedic Clinics of North America, 1993; contbr. numerous articles to profl. pubs. including Surgical Forum vol. XLVI, Plastic Reconstructive Surgery, others. Mem. med. adv. com. Nev. Donor Network, 1995-96. Recipient Jr. Faculty Rsch. award U. Nev., 1994-95; NIH grantee, 1994-99, Ctrl. Rsch. Com. grantee, 1993-94, Hyperbaric Rsch. and Devel. grantee, 1993, over twenty other grants. Fellow ACS; mem. AMA, Am. Soc. Plastic and Reconstructive Surgery (newsmedia spokesperson 1995—, plastic surgery edn. found. DATA com. 1994—, breast reconstruction advocacy project 1995-96), Am. Soc. Aesthetic Plastic Surgery, Am. Coll. Hyperbaric Medicine, Plastic Surgery Rsch. Coun., Undersea and Hyperbaric Med. Soc. (exec. com. sec. 1991-92, clin. trials com. 1993-94). Roman Catholic. Office: U Nev Sch Med 2040 West Charleston No 601 Las Vegas NV 89012

ZAMBUTO, RAYMOND PETER, biomedical engineer; b. N.Y.C., Apr. 30, 1945; s. Peter John and Mary Ann (Benevegna) Z.; m. Janet Marie Vieira, July 25, 1970; children: Peter A., Joseph R., Mary H. BSEE, Poly. Inst. Bklyn., 1967, MS in Biol. Engring., 1970. Cert. clin. engr. Engring. cons. St. Vincent's Hosp., N.Y.C., 1968; biomed. engr. Lockheed Electronics Co., Hyattsville, Md., 1969; sr. med. engr. Mass. Gen. Hosp., Boston, 1969-72; asst. dir. Mass. Hosp. Assn., Burlington, 1972-74; pres. Tech. in Medicine, Inc., Milford, Mass., 1974—. Patentee refreshed display with EKG, 1974; contbr. articles to profl. jours. and chpts. to books. Cubmaster, com. chmn. Boy Scouts Am., Ashland, Mass., 1982-83; PTO pres. Ashland Pub. Schs., 1982-84; mem. parish coun. St. Cecilia Ch., Ashland, 1990—; mem. biotech. adv. bd. Minuteman Regional Vocat. High Sch., Lexington, Mass., 1991-92. NIH trainee, 1968, spl. fellow, 1969. Fellow Am. Soc. for Healthcare Engring. (sr., shared clin. engring. com. 1975-93, joint task force for JCAHO quality indicator 1992-93); mem. Assn. for Advancement of Med. Instrumentation, Smaller Bus. Assn. N.E., Nat. Fire Protection Assn. Office: Tech in Medicine Inc 115 Water St Milford MA 01757

ZAMECNIK, PAUL CHARLES, oncologist, medical research scientist; b. Cleve., Ohio, Nov. 22, 1912; m.; 3 children. AB, Dartmouth Coll., 1933; MD, Harvard U., 1936; DSc (hon.), U. Utrecht, 1966, Columbia U., 1971, Harvard U., 1982, Roger Williams Coll., 1983, Dartmouth Coll., 1988, U. Mass., 1994. Resident Huntington Meml. Hosp. Harvard U., Boston, MA, 1936-37; intern. U. Hosps., Cleve., Ohio, 1938-39; Moseley traveling fellow Carlsberg Labs. Harvard U., Copenhagen, 1939-40; Finney-Howell fellow Rockefeller Inst., 1941-42; instr., assoc. prof. Harvard U., 1942-56, Collis P. Huntington prof., 1956-79; dir. J.C. Warren Labs., 1956-79; chmn. exec. com. Dept. Medicine Harvard U., 1955-61; emeritus prof. oncological medicine Sch. Medicine, 1979—; prin. sci. Worcester Found. Experimental Biology, 1979—; physician Mass. Gen. Hosp., 1956-79, hon. physician, 1979—; vis. fellow dept. chemistry Calif. Tech. U., 1952; vis. Commonwealth scholar U. Cambridge, 1962. Recipient Warren Triennial prize, 1946, 50, James Ewing award, 1962, Borden award, 1965, Am. Cancer Soc. Nat. award, 1968, Passano award, 1970, Nat. medal of sci. NSF, 1991, Hudson Hoagland award, 1992, City of Medicine award, Durham, N.C., 1995, Enterprize 2000 award City of Worcester, Mass., 1996. Mem. NAS, Am. Acad. Arts and Sci., Am. Soc. Biol. Chemists, Am. Assn. Cancer Rsch. (pres. 1964-65), Assn. Am. Physicians, Interurban Club, Peripatetic Club. Office: Worcester Found Exptl Biology 222 Maple Ave Shrewsbury MA 01545-2732

ZAMINSKY, LAUREL JIL, rehabilitation nurse, case manager; b. Atlanta, Dec. 30, 1963. BSN, Fla. State U., 1986. RN, Fla.; registered rehab. provider, Fla. RN rehab. case mgr. Bethesda Meml. Hosp., Boynton Beach, Fla., 1993—. Mem. ANA, Assn. Rehab. Nurses, Fla. Nurses Assn., Palm Coast Assn. Rehab. Nurses. Office: Bethesda Memorial Hospital Attn Employ Med 2815 S Seacrest Blvd Boynton Beach FL 33435

ZAMORA, SERGIO MARTIN, plastic surgeon; b. Guadalajara, Mexico, Feb. 25, 1963; came to U.S., 1989; s. Mario and Gloria (Morales) Z.; m. Desiree Vincent, Apr. 25, 1991; 1 child, Sergio Adrian. BS, Auonomous U. Guadalajara, 1982, MD, 1986. Intern, resident surgery U. S.C., 1990-96; fellow plastic surgery U. Utah, Salt Lake City, 1996—; cons. Hyperbaric & Undersea Orgn., 1993—. Home: 1620 Atlantic Dr Columbia SC 29210

ZAMRINI, EDWARD YOUSSEF, behavioral neurologist; b. Cairo, Apr. 27, 1958; s. Joseph Boutros and Therese Edouard Zamrini; m. Cynthia Lynn Douglass, Oct. 2, 1993; 1 child, Omar Edward. BSc, Am. U. Beirut, 1980, MD, 1984. Dir. geriatric neuropsychiatry program VA Med. Ctr., Augusta, Ga., 1990—. Contbr. articles to profl. jours. Mem. AMA, ACP, N.Y. Acad. Scis., Am. Acad. Neurology, Alzheimer's Disease and Related Disorders Assn. (bd. dirs. 1990-95, chair edn. com. 1990-92, columnist 1989-94, pres. Augusta chpt. 1993-94), Amnesty Internat. (chpt. rep. 1990). Office: VA Med Ctr 1 Freedom Way Augusta GA 30904-6258

ZANARDELLI, JOHN JOSEPH, healthcare services executive; b. Monongahela, Pa., July 27, 1950; s. John and Linda (Lazzari) Z.; m. Suzanne King, Jan. 29, 1972; children: Brandon John, Stephen William, Robyn Lynn. AA, Community Coll. Allegheny Cty, Pitts., 1970; AS in Acctg., Community Coll. Allegheny Cty., Pitts., 1991; BS in Edn., California U. Pa., 1972; MPH, U. Pitts., 1979, cert. acct., 1994. Rsch. asst. grad. sch. pub. health U. Pitts., 1973-78; adminstrv. resident Cen. Med. Ctr. & Hosp., Pitts., 1978-79; vice chmn., sec., dir. Allegheny Mountain Health Enterprises, Inc., Oil City, Pa., 1985-88; exec. v.p. Oil City Area Health Ctr., Inc., 1979-88; exec. v.p., chief oper. officer Grane Healthcare, Inc., Pitts., 1988-90; adminstr., chief oper. officer Southwood Psychiat. Hosp., Inc., Pitts., 1990-91; exec. dir. Allegheny Sr. Care, Pitts., Pa., 1991-92; exec. dir., CEO United Meth. Svcs. for the Aging, 1993—; preceptor health adminstrn. program grad. schs. in pub. health and bus. U. Pitts., 1980—; pres. HCPP, Inc., Pitts., 1983—. Fellow Am. Coll. Healthcare Execs. Home: 2997 Greenwald Rd Bethel Park PA 15102-1615 Office: Asbury Heights 700 Bower Hill Rd Pittsburgh PA 15243-2098

ZANCA, JANE ANN, medical writer, editor; b. New Orleans, Aug. 30, 1946; d. John Richard and Marjorie Jane (Garcia) Z.; div.; children: Jesse Alexander Battey, Amanda Kathleen Battey. BA in Eng. Lit. & Creative Writing, Agnes Scott Coll., 1983; postgrad., Ga. State U., 1983-84. Writer, editor, researcher Goodlife Mag., Atlanta, 1985-86; instr. writing De Kalb Coll., Clarkston, Ga., 1986-89, Emory U., Atlanta, 1987-88; med. editor Arthritis & Rheumatism Jour., Atlanta, 1986-89; med. writer, editor Am. Cancer Soc., Atlanta, 1989—. Co-author: The Cancer Recovery Eating Plan, 1995; contbr. poems and fiction to profl. pubs. Vol. instr. Atlanta Inroads Program for Minority Students, 1995—: vol. DeKalb County Spl. Populations, Mason Mill Center, Ga., 1989—. Recipient Silver award Nat. Health Info. Awards, Merit award, 1995; named 1st pl. short fiction Ga. State U., 1986. Mem. Am. Med. Writers Assn., Am. Assn. Cancer Educators. Mem. Soc. of Friends. Office: Am Cancer Soc 1599 CLifton Rd NE Atlanta GA 30329

ZANDE, ELIZABETH A., health services administrator; b. Tupper Lake, N.Y., Feb. 2, 1962; d. John Henry and Carol Naoma (Elliott) Fitzpatrick; m. Robert James Zande, Oct. 26, 1984; children: Matthew A., Michael John. AA, Canton ATC, 1981; BS, SUNY, Plattsburgh, 1983; postgrad., Am. Health Info. Mgmt. Sys., 1992; BS in Records Adminstrn., Stephens Coll., 1994. Registered records adminstr., N.Y. Dir. med. records Mercy Healthcare Ctr., Tupper Lake, 1990-94; provider contracting rep. Pacificare Mil. Health Sys., Austin, Tex., 1994—; records adminstr. Fed. Prision, RayBrook, N.Y., 1994-96. Democrat. Roman Catholic. Home: 22 Bushey Ave Tupper Lake NY 12986

ZANDER, GAILLIENNE GLASHOW, psychologist; b. Bklyn., Apr. 7, 1932; d. Saul and Anna (Karasik) G.; m. A.J. Zander, Aug. 5, 1952; children: Elizabeth L., Caroline M., Catherine A. MusB, U. Wis., 1953, MS, 1970; PhD, Marquette U., 1984. Diplomate Am. Bd. Forensic Examiners. Music tchr. Wis. Sch. Systems, 1953-65; psychol. asst. Vernon Psychol. Labs., Chgo., 1965-70; psychologist Milw. Pub. Schs., 1970-92, CESA 19, Kenosha, Wis., 1977-78; pvt. practice psychology Milw., 1980—. Fellow Am. Orthopsychiat. Assn.; mem. APA, Wis. Psychol. Assn., Psychologists Assn. in Milw. Pub. Schs. (rep., v.p., pres.), Am. Acad. Pain Mgmt. (diplomate). Home: 13750 Carson Ct Brookfield WI 53005-4989 also: Cooper Resource Ctr 20860 Watertown Rd Waukesha WI 53186-1872

ZANDER, JANET ADELE, psychiatrist; b. Miles City, Mont., Feb. 19, 1950; d. Adelbert William and Valborg Constance (Buckneberg) Z.; m. Mark Richard Ellenberger, Sept. 16, 1979; 1 child, Evan David Zander Ellenberger. BA, St. Olaf Coll., 1972; MD, U. Minn., 1976. Diplomate Am. Bd. Psychiatry and Neurology. Resident in psychiatry U. Minn., Mpls., 1976-79, fellow in psychiatry, 1979-80, asst. prof. psychiatry, 1981—; staff psychiatrist St. Paul (Minn.) Ramsey Med. Ctr., 1980—, dir. edn. in psychiatry, 1980—, dir. inpatient psychiatry, 1986—; vice chair Dept. Psychiatry St. Paul Ramsey Med. Ctr., 1991-96; bd. dirs. Perry Assurance. Contbr. research articles to sci. jours. Sec. Concentus Musicus Bd. Dirs., St. Paul, 1981-89; mem. property com. St. Clement's Episcopal Ch., St. Paul, 1985. Mem. Am. Psychiat. Assn., Am. Med. Women's Assn., Minn. Psychiat. Soc. (ethics com. 1985-87, women's com. 1985-87, coun. 1994-96), Minn. Med. Assn., Ramsey County Med. Soc. (bd. dirs. 1994—). Democrat. Home: 230 Crestway Ln West Saint Paul MN 55118-4424 Office: St Paul Ramsey Med Ctr 640 Jackson St Saint Paul MN 55101-2502

ZANGENEH, FEREYDOUN, pediatrics educator, pediatric endocrinologist; b. Tehran, Iran, July 11, 1937; came to U.S., 1962, 86; married. MD, U. Tehran, Iran, 1961. Diplomate Am. Bd. Pediatrics and Pediatric Endocrinology. Intern Washington Hosp. Ctr., 1962; resident in pediatrics U. Chgo. Hosps. & Clinics, 1963-65; fellow in pediatric endocrinology Children's Memorial Hosp., Chgo., 1965-66, U. Wash., Seattle, 1966-68; asst. prof. to prof. U. Tehran, Iran, 1968-86; assoc. prof. pediatrics Marshall U. Sch. of Medicine, Huntington, W.Va., 1986-89; assoc. prof. pediatrics W.Va. U., Charleston, 1989-95, prof. pediatrics, 1995—, dir. pediatric endocrinology, 1989—, prof. pediatrics., 1995—; instr. pediatrics U. Wash., Seattle, 1967-68; dir. dept. endocrinology Children's Hosp. Med. Ctr., Tehran, Iran, 1968-86; dir. pediatric endocrinology Marshall U. Sch. Medicine, Huntington, 1986-89; mem. W.Va. Adv. Com. on Newborn Metabolic Screening, W.Va. Adv. Com. on Diabetes Mellitus. Author: (with others) Pediatric Endocrinology and Metabolism; contbr. articles and abstracts to profl. jours. Bd. dirs., rsch. com., camp com. Am. Diabetes Assn., W.Va. affiliate, Charleston, active in Huntington W.Va. affiliate, 1986-89; bd. dirs. Diabetes Camp of W.Va. Capt. Iranian Army Med. Corps, 1969-71. Recipient Gharib Rsch. award, Iranian Pediatric Soc., Tehran, 1976. Fellow Am. Acad. Pediatrics, Am. Coll. Endocrinology; mem. Internat. Pediatric Assn. (adv. expert panel 1977-83), Union Mid. Ea. and Mediterranean Pediatric Socs. (exec. coun. 1979-85), Lawson Wilkins Pediatric Endocrine Soc., Endocrine Soc., Am. Assn. Clin. Endocrinologists. Office: WVa U Dept Pediatrics 830 Pennsylvania Ave Ste 104 Charleston WV 25302-3389

ZANIBONI, ALBERTO PIERPAOLO, oncologist, consultant; b. Brescia, Italy, Oct. 10, 1959; s. Mario Zaniboni and Grazia Bottazzi; m. Chiara Favretto, May 15, 1991; 1 child, Benedetta. MD summa cum laude, Faculty Medicine, Brescia, 1984; oncology specialist summa cum laude, Statal U., Milan, Italy, 1986; haematology specialist, Statal U., Pavia, Italy, 1991. Fellow Nat. Cancer Inst., Milan, 1986; fellow oncology dept. Ospedale San Giovanni, Bellinzona, 1989; fellow thoracic oncology dept. Meml. Sloan-Kettering Cancer Ctr., N.Y.C., 1989; asst. oncologist Spedali Civili, Brescia, 1989—; oncology cons. Schering Plough Corp., Milan, 1993—, Azienda 14, Iseo, Italy, 1996—, Istituto Mario Negri, Milan, 1988—; mem. sci. com. Gruppo Italiano Studio Carcinomi Apparato Digerente, Milan, 1990—. Contbr. numerous articles to profl. jours. Asst. physician Carabinieri, Milan, 1985-86. Grantee Regione Lombardia, 1993. Mem. Am. Soc. Clin. Oncology, Am. Assn. Cancer Rsch. (corr.), European Soc. Med. Oncology. Home: Via Gabriele Rosa 3, 25121 Brescia Italy Office: Spedali Civili Oncologia Medica, Piazzale Spedali Civili 1, 25100 Brescia Italy

ZANNA, MARTIN THOMAS, physician; b. Mpls., Apr. 2, 1947; s. Peter J. and Mary L. (Peck) Z. AB, Harvard U., 1969, MPH, 1976; MD, U. Minn., 1973. Diplomate Am. Bd. Preventive Medicine. Resident in pub. health N.J. State Dept. Health, 1974-77, acting dir. chronic disease svcs., 1976-79, dir. chronic disease svcs., 1979-81; med. adminstr. Fla. Dept. Health and Rehab. Svcs., Tallahassee, 1981-82; med. cons. N.J. Medicaid, Trenton, 1982—, chief med. cons., 1990—; mem. Fla. Cancer Coun., 1981-82, Fla. Bd. Med. Examiners, 1982; mem. N.J. Hypertension Study Group, 1977-81; chmn. grad. med. edn. com. N.J. State Dept. Health, 1993—. Participant Fla. Gov.'s Mission to Haiti, 1982; mem. divsn. profl. edn. Am. Cancer Soc., 1976-81. Fellow Am. Coll. Preventive Medicine; mem. Am. Pub. Health Assn., Harvard Club (Boston), Harvard Faculty Club (Cambridge). Home: # 11 201 Salem Ct Princeton NJ 08540 Office: NJ State Dept Health & Sr Svcs CN 360 Trenton NJ 08625-0360

ZANOWIAK, PAUL, pharmacy educator; b. Little Falls, N.J., July 11, 1933; s. Harry and Susan (Kreel) Z.; m. Elizabeth Adele Bertsch, Nov. 19, 1957; children: Matthew Gregory, Jennifer Anne, Tamara Joan, Patricia Elizabeth. BS in Pharmacy, Rutgers U., 1954, MS, 1957; PhD, U. Fla., 1959. Registered pharmacist, Pa. Instr. pharmacy U. Fla., Gainesville, 1958-59; R&D chemist Noxzema Corp., Balt., 1959-64; asst. then assoc. prof. W.Va. U., Morgantown, 1964-71; prof. pharmaceutics Temple U., Phila., 1971—, asst. to dean, 1971-72, actin dean pharmacy, 1972-74, chair dept., 1971-81, dir. div. continuing edn., 1981—. Me. bd. edn. Jenkintown (Pa.) Sch. Dist., 1974—, pres., 1987-88. Mem. Am. Pharm. Assn., Am. Soc. Health Sys. Pharmacists, Am. Assn. Colls. Pharmacy (bd. dirs. 1978-80), Am. Assn. Pharm. Scientists, Pa. Pharm. Assn. (pres. 1989-90), Nat. Assn. Retail Druggists, Montgomery County Pharm. Assn., Phila. Pharmacy Forum, Sigma Xi, Rho Chi (pres. 1986-88). Office: Temple U Sch Pharmacy 3307 N Broad St Philadelphia PA 19140-5193

ZAPPACOSTA, ANTHONY R., physician; b. Phila., Oct. 1, 1944. MD, Hahaemann Medical Coll., 1969. Diplomate Am. Bd. Internal Medicine, Am. Bd. Nephrology. Chief nephrology sect. The Bryn Mawr Hosp., Bryn Mawr, Pa., 1974—. Author: CAPD, 1984. Mem. Am. Soc. Nephrology.

ZAPPIA, SISTER MARY ROQUETA, retired social services professional, volunteer; b. Clifton, Ariz., Sept. 25, 1915; d. Joseph Rocco and Guilia M. (Casetto) Z. RN, St. Mary's Sch. Nursing, Tucson, 1936; BSNE, San Francisco Coll. for Women, 1946; MSW, Ariz. State U., 1970. RN, Ariz., Calif.; registered social worker, Calif.; joined Sisters of Mercy, Roman Cath. Ch., 1941. Supr. St. Mary's Hosp., San Francisco, 1941-46; social worker St. Mary's Hosp. Clinics, San Francisco, 1941-46; instr. sociology, social problems, supr. St. Joseph's Hosp., Phoenix, 1946-53; supr. St. Joseph's Hosp. Mercy Clinics, Phoenix, 1953-66, med. social worker, 1970-83; social worker, adminstr. St. John's Hosp. Nursing Home, Oxnard, Calif., 1966-68; field instr. social work Ariz. State U., Tempe, 1970—. Cons. Transient Aid Ctr., St. Vincent de Paul, Phoenix, 1983—, Kimberly Home Healthcare, Phoenix, 1982—; mem. Sisters of Mercy, Burlingame, Calif., 1941—. Mem. NASW, St. Vincent de Paul Soc. Democrat. Roman Catholic. Home: 525 W Earll Dr Apt 117 Phoenix AZ 85013-4328 Office: St Vincent de Paul Transien Aid Ctr 420 W Watkins St Phoenix AZ 85003-2830

ZARBIN, MARCO ATTILIO, ophthalmologist, surgeon, educator; b. Milan, Nov. 20, 1956; came to the U.S., 1958; s. Gino Franco and Adriana Virginia (Corasaniti) Z.; m. Christine Zarbin (Godfrey), Aug. 19, 1984. BA summa cum laude, Dartmouth Coll., 1978; MD, PhD, Johns Hopkins U., 1984. Diplomate Am. Bd. Ophthalmology. Resident Johns Hopkins Hosp., Balt., 1985-88, fellow vitreoretinal surgery, 1988-89, chief resident opthalmology, 1989, fellow retinal vascular disease, 1990; asst. prof. ophthalmology U. Calif., San Francisco, 1990-93; chair dept. ophthalmology N.J. Med. Sch., Newark, 1994—; mem. sci. adv. bd. Found. Fighting Blindness, Hunt Valley, Md., 1995—. Fellow Am. Acad. Ophthalmology (Honor award 1995), Retina Soc.; mem. Assn. for Rsch. in Vision and Ophthalmology, Phi Beta Kappa, Alpha Omega Alpha. Office: NJ Med Sch Dept Ophthalmology 90 Bergen St Newark NJ 07103-2499

ZARET, BARRY LEWIS, cardiologist, medical educator; b. N.Y.C., Oct. 3, 1940; s. Irving Z. and Beatrice (Fader) Zaret; m. Myrna Zimmerman, June 23, 1963; children: Adam L., Elliot C., Owen M. B.S., Queens Coll., 1962; M.D., NYU, 1966; M.A., Yale U., 1982. Diplomate: Am. Bd. Internal Medicine. Intern Bellevue Hosp., N.Y.C., 1966-67, resident, 1967-79; research fellow John Hopkins U., Balt., 1969-71; asst. prof. medicine Yale U., New Haven, 1973-76, assoc. prof. medicine and diagnostic radiology, 1976, chief sect. cardiology, 1978—, assoc. prof. medicine and diagnostic radiology, 1980-82, prof. medicine and diagnostic radiology, 1982-84; Robert W. Berliner prof. medicine Yale U., 1984—, assoc. chair clin. affairs dept. internal medicine, 1994—; mem. staff Yale-New Haven Med. Ctr. Mem. editorial bd. Am. Jour. Cardiology, 1977—, Jour. Am. Coll. Cardiology, 1986-91, 92—, Jour. Cardiac Imaging, 1986—, Circulation, 1993; assoc. editor: Yearbook of Nuclear Medicine, 1980-95; editor-in-chief Jour. Nuclear Cardiology, 1993—; contbr. articles to profl. jours. Recipient Casimir Funk award Soc. Mil. Surgeons, 1973; recipient Herrman Blumgart Pioneer award New Eng. chpt. Soc. Nuclear Medicine, 1978. Fellow Am. Coll. Cardiology, Coun. Clin. Cardiology, Am. Heart Assn., Coun. Circulation, Am. Heart Assn., Am. Physiology Soc.; mem. Am. Soc. Clin. Investigation, Am. Fedn. Clin. Rsch., Assn. Am. Physicians, Soc. Nuclear Medicine, Am. Soc. Nuclear Cardiology, Assn. Univ. Cardiologists, Assn. Profs. Cardiology (pres. 1992), Phi Beta Kappa, Alpha Omega Alpha, Interurban Clin. Club. Jewish. Home: 15 Cassway Rd Woodbridge CT 06525-1214 Office: Yale U Sch Medicine 333 Cedar St # 3fmp New Haven CT 06520-8017

ZARETSKY, ROBERT, surgeon; b. Bklyn., Oct. 2, 1932; s. Jacob and Rose Zaretsky; m. Audrey Edith Eichner, Aug. 2, 1953; children: Jay, Steven, Joy. BA, Lehigh U., 1954; MD, Chgo. Med. Sch., 1958. Intern Mt. Sinai Hosp., N.Y.C., 1958-59, resident in orthopedic surgery, 1960-63; resident in gen. surgery Bklyn. VA Hosp., 1959-60; pvt. practice N.Y.C., 1963-91, Sports Medicine and Rehab. Therapy, N.Y.C., 1991—; asst. clin. prof. orthopaedic surgery Mt. Sinai Med. Sch., N.Y.C., 1967—, assoc. attending, 1963—; attending orthopedic surgeon Beth Israel North Hosp., N.Y.C., 1977—. Contbr. articles to profl. jours. Capt. N.Y. NG, 1961-66. Recipient award Hoffman LaRoche, 1958, Appleton award Appleton Crofts, 1958, award Mosby Pubs., 1958. Fellow Am. Acad. Orthopaedic Surgeons, ACS; mem. Arthroscopy Assn. N.Am., Internat. Arthroscopy Assn. Office: Sports Medicine Rehab Thera 134 E 93d St New York NY 10128

ZARICZNYJ, BASILIUS, orthopedic surgeon; b. Ukraine, Aug. 31, 1924; came to U.S., 1951; s. Alex and Maria (Kostiw) Z.; m. Stefania Pidburny, Aug. 21, 1954; children: Marta, Stephanie Christine, Andrea Maria, Mark B. MD, U. Bonn, Germany, 1951. Diplomate Am. Bd. Orthopedic Surgery. Resident St. Luke's Hosp., Chgo., 1954-56, Univ. Hosps., Oklahoma City, 1955-56; fellow in orthopedics Northwestern U., Chgo., 1957; asst. prof. Sch. Medicine U. Okla., Oklahoma City, 1957-58; orthopedic surgeon Springfield, Ill., 1958—; clin. prof. Sch. Medicine So. Ill. U., Springfield, Ill., 1973-85, acting chmn. divsn. orthopedic surgery, 1972-75, chief sports medicine sect., 1975-82, program chmn. sports injury symposium, 1977-79, 82, 83; mem. sports medicine com. Ill. State Med. Soc., 1979-80; chmn. dept. orthopedic surgery St. John's and Meml. Hosps., Springfield, 1970-79; program chmn. Med. Congress of World Fedn. of Ukrainian Med. Assn., Dniepropetrovsk, 1994, Odessa, Ukraine, 1996; presenter Am. Acad. Orthopedic Surgeons, Miami, Fla., 1961, N.Y., 1969, San Francisco, 1971, Washington, 1972, Las Vegas, 1973, 77, Anaheim, Calif., 1983, Chgo. Orthopedic Soc., 1967, 76, O'Donoghue Okla. Orthopedic Alumni Assn., Oklahoma City, 1972, 75, 78, Internat. Soc. for Orthopedic Surgery and Traumatology, XII World Congress, Tel Aviv, 1972, Copenhagen, 1975, Kyoto, Japan, 1978, So. Ill U. Sch. Medicine, Springfield, 1977, 79, 80, 82, Ill. State Orthopedic Soc., Chgo., 1978, ACS, Chgo., 1979, Am. Orthopedic Soc. for Sports Medicine, Atlanta, 1980, Big Sky, Mont., 1980,, Lake Tahoe, Nev., 1981, Clin. Orthopedic Soc., Chgo., 1987, World Fedn. Ukrainian Med. Assn., Kiev, Ukraine, 1990, U. Lviv, Ukraine, 1990, 11th Congress of Orthopedic Surgeons of Ukraine, Kharkiv, 1991, 4th Congress of World Fedn. of Ukrainian Med. Assn., Kharkiv, 1992, among others. Mem. editl. bd. Jour. Ukrainan Med. Assn. N.Am., 1977-95; contbr. articles to profl. jours. Fellow Am. Acad. Orthopedic Surgery; mem. AMA, Ill. Orthopedic Soc., Internat. Soc. Orthopedic Surgery and Traumatology, Am. Orthopedic Soc. for Sports Medicine, Internat. Soc. of the Knee, Mid-Am. Orthopedic Assn., Ukrainian Acad. and Profl. Assn. Pres. 1985-89), Sangamon County Med. Soc., Chgo. Orthopedic Soc. Home and Office: 125 Oakmont Dr Springfield IL 62704

ZARINCZUK, JAMES, family physician; b. Montreal, Que., Can., Feb. 21, 1947; s. Nick and Sophie Zarinczuk; m. Yoshiko Otti, Nov. 27, 1991. BSc, McGill U., Montreal, 1968, MD in Cmty. Medicine, 1972; MPH, U. South Fla., 1991. Diplomate Am. Bd. Family Practice, Am. Bd. Preventive Medicine. Asst. prof. N.E. Ohio Coll. Medicine, Akron, 1978-80; commd. capt. U.S. Army, 1980, advanced through grades to col., 1992; staff Silas B. Hays Army Cmty. Hosp., Monterey, Calif., 1980-85; hosp. comdr. 43d MASH, Pyongtaek, South Korea, 1985-86; clinic comdr. 133 Gen. Dispensary, Bamberg, Germany, 1985-88; regimental surgeon 11th Armored Calvary Regiment, Fulda, Germany, 1988-90; resident in aerospace medicine USAF Sch. Aerospace Medicine, San Antonio, 1991-92; dir. U.S. Army Aeromed. Activity, Daleville, Ala., 1992-95; staff Eisenhower Army Med. Ctr., Augusta, Ga., 1995—; asst. prof. McGill U., 1972-78. Fellow Aerospace Med. Assn. (assoc.), Am. Assn. Family Physicians, Assn. Mil. Surgeons Uniformed Svcs. Roman Catholic. Home: 420 Wicklow Ln Augusta GA 30909-3628 Office: Eisenhower Army Med Ctr Directorate of Primary Care Svcs Fort Gordon GA 30905-5650

ZARINS, CHRISTOPHER KRISTAPS, surgery educator, vascular surgeon; b. Tukums, Latvia, Dec. 2, 1943; came to U.S., 1946; s. Richard A. and Maria (Rozenbergs) Z.; m. Zinta Zarins, July 8, 1967; children: Daina, Sascha, Karina. BA, Lehigh U., 1964; MD, Johns Hopkins U., 1968. Surgery residency U. Mich., Ann Arbor, 1968-74; asst. prof. surgery U. Chgo., 1976-79, assoc. prof. surgery, 1979-82, prof. surgery, 1983-93, chief of vascular surgery, 1978-93; prof. surgery, chmn. divsn. vascular surgery Stanford (Calif.) U., 1993—, acting chmn. Dept. of Surgery, 1995—. Author: Essays In Surgery, 1986, Atlas of Vascular Surgery, 1988; editor Jour. of Surg. Rsch., 1982-95; contbr. articles to profl. jours. Pres. Latvian Med. Found., Boston, 1991. Lt. comdr. USN, 1974-76. Grantee NIH, NSF. Mem. Am. Surg. Soc., Soc. for Clin. Surgery, Soc. for Vascular Surgery, Internat. Soc. for Cardiovascular Surgery, Soc. of Univ. Surgeons, Latvian Nat. Acad. of Scis., Latvian Vascular Surg. Soc. (pres. 1989). Office: Stanford U Med Ctr Divsn Vascular Surgery 300 Pasteur Dr # H3630 Stanford CA 94305-5450

ZARRA, THOMAS JOSEPH, emergency, pediatric critical care nurse; b. Belleville, N.J., July 13, 1958; s. Joseph A. and Phyllis (DiNorcia) Z.; m. Donna Marie Zarra, Sept. 26, 1982; children: Brian James, Kristen Marie. AAS paramedic, Essex County Coll., 1981; cert. paramedic, U. Med. and Den. of N.J., 1981; diploma, Englewood Hosp., 1987. RN, N.J.; CEN; cert. trauma nurse care course, BCLS, ACLS, pediatric advanced life support instr. Paramedic MICU Wayne (N.J.) Gen. Hosp., 1984-87; emergency staff nurse Englewood (N.J.) Hosp., 1987-88; mobile intensive care paramedic, nurse Mountainside Hosp., Montclair, 1981—; staff nurse emergency dept. Atlantic City Med. Ctr., 1988-92, staff nurse pediatric spl. care unit, 1992-94, pediatric patient care mgr., 1994—; N.J. gov.'s apptd. mem. Emergency Med. Svcs. Adv. Coun. for Children. Recipient award for lifesaving care Fairfield Twp., 1983, award in prehosp. care N.J. Dept. Health, 1983, Essex County Dept. Correction, 1992. Mem. Emergency Nurse's Assn., Assn. Diploma Schs. Profl. Nursing (exec. bd. dirs. 1991-92). Home: 202 Buffalo Ave Somers Point NJ 08244-2239

ZARRETT, MARY ANN, mental health professional, educator, consultant; b. Big Clifty, Ky., July 8, 1949; d. Julius Forest and Gladys Mae (Hawkins) Duvall; m. Robert Warren Zarrett, Dec. 27, 1969 (div. Aug. 1983); children: Rob Warren, Elizabeth Duvall. BSN, U. Ky., 1971; MS in Counseling, Ctrl. Mo. State U., 1977; MA in Human and Orgnl. Devel., The Fielding Inst., 1994, PhD in Human and Orgnl. Systems, 1996. RN, N.D.; nat. cert. counselor. Rsch., cataloging and circulation asst. U. Ky. Med. Ctr. Library, Lexington, 1969-71; nurse aide Taylor Manor Nursing Home, Versailles, Ky., 1970; self-employed Burlington, Vt., 1971-74; per diem nurse psychiat. ward St. Luke's Hosp., Fargo, N.D., 1988-92; counselor, instr. Moorhead State U., Fargo, 1985-89, asst. prof., 1990—, dir. tng. Counseling Ctr., 1987-90, outreach coord., 1989-90, affirmative action officer, 1992; cons. Minn. Army N.G. through Met. State U., 1987; cons. Pathways/U.S. West, 1990—; orgnl. cons., 1990—. Adv. bd. mem. Compassionate Friends Fargo, N.D., 1986—; chmn. music Plymouth Congregational Ch., Fargo, 1986-88; chmn. Fargo Clinic Art Gallery, 1982-84. Mem. ACA, Minn. Assn. Specialists in Group Work, Am. Mental Health Counselors Assn., Nat. Orgnl. Devel. Network, Phi Kappa Phi. Republican. Congregationalist. Office: Moorhead State U Counseling Ctr Moorhead MN 56560

ZASTUDIL, ROBERT GENE, JR., physician's assistant; b. Lajes AFB, Azores, Portugal, Jan. 4, 1957; s. Robert Gene Sr. and Maria M. (Olivera) Z.; m. Susan Lee Lubeck, May 8, 1982; children: Amanda Sue, Joshua Paul. BS in Hosp. Admin., George Washington U., Washington, D.C., 1991, BS in Health Scis., 1994. Commd. ensign USN, Va., 1975—; physician asst. student USN, San Antonio, Tex., 1992-93, San Diego, 1993-94; physician asst. USN, Little Creek, Va., 1994—. Active Dendbergh PTA, 1991—. Fellow Am. Assn. Physician Assts., Navy Assn. Physician Assts. Republican. Roman Catholic.

ZATLIN, GABRIEL STANLEY, physician; b. N.Y.C., Dec. 5, 1935; s. Samuel and Bernice (Morgenstern) Z.; m. Linda M. Gertner, Dec. 29, 1959 (div. 1973); children: Jonathan Reid, Andrew Evan; m. Lorna G. Schofield, May 14, 1983; 1 child, Sarah Schofield. BS, U. Miami, Coral Gables, Fla., 1956; MD, Washington U., St. Louis, 1960. Diplomate Am. Bd. Pediatrics, Am. Bd. Family Practice. Intern St. Louis Children's Hosp., 1960-61, resident, 1961-62; resident Children's Hosp. Med. Ctr., Boston, 1965-66, Downstate Med. Ctr., Bklyn., 1979-81; Epidemiologist Ctrs. for Disease Control, Atlanta, 1962-64; pvt. practice Atlanta, 1966-73; cons. Pertamina, Jakarta, Indonesia, 1974-76; field dir. African Health Tng. Project, Yaounde, Cameroun, 1976-77; assoc. dir. Brown U. Health Svcs., Providence, 1977-79; asst. prof. Downstate Med. Ctr., Bklyn., 1981-82; assoc. dir. St. Mary Hosp. Family Practice, Hoboken, N.J., 1982-88; dir. St. Mary Hosp. Family Practice, 1988-92; clin. assoc. prof. Downstate Med. Ctr., Bklyn., 1992-95, dir. family practice residency program, 1993-95; faculty family practice residency program Beth Israel Hosp., 1995—. Contbr. articles to profl. jours.; cons. Resident/Staff Physician jour., 1985—, VIS jour., 1986—. With USPHS, 1962-64. Fellow Am. Acad. Pediatrics; mem. Am. Acad. Family Practice, Soc. for Adolescent Medicine. Office: Inst for Urban Family Prac 16 E 16th St New York NY 10003

ZATUCHNI, JACOB, internal medicine educator; b. Phila., Oct. 8, 1920. AB in Chemistry, Temple U., 1941, MD, 1944. Cert. cardiovascular diseases Am. Bd. Internal Medicine. Intern Jewish Hosp., Phila., 1944-45; resident diseases of the chest Eagleville (Pa.) Sanatorium, 1945-47; resident internal medicine Temple U. Hosp., Phila., 1947-50; internist Temple U. Sch. Medicine, Phila., 1950; instr. medicine Temple U. Sch. Medicine and Hosp., Phila., 1950-54, asst. prof. medicine, 1954-58, assoc. prof. medicine, 1958-61, chief cardiac clinic B, 1959-60, prof. clin. medicine, 1962-66, prof. medicine, 1966-87, prof. emeritus, 1987—; clin. asst. medicine Episcopal Hosp., 1950-53, assoc. in medicine, 1953-59, teaching chief medicine, 1959-67, head sect. cardiovascular disease, 1967-82, dir. dept. medicine, 1974-82, head heart sta., 1982-87, attending physician, 1982-87; sr. diagnostician Pa. Hosp., 1987—, dir. clin. svcs. cardiovascular sect., 1987—; clin. prof. medicine U. Pa. Sch. Medicine, 1988—. Author: Notes on Physical Diagnosis, 1964; contbr. articles to profl. jours. Fellow ACP, Am. Coll. Chest Physicians, Am. Coll. Cardiology; mem. AMA, Am. Heart Assn. (fellow coun. clin. cardiology), Phila. Coll. Physicians, N.Y. Acad. Scis., Am. Fedn. for Clin. Rsch., Heart Assn. Southeastern Pa. (bd. govs.), Am. Phoracic Soc., Pa. Med. Soc., Philadelphia County Med. Soc. (standing com. on med. edn., standing com. med. econs., standing com. profl. rels. and grievances), So. Med. Assn., Am. Soc. Nuclear Medicine, Am. Soc. Echocardiography, Pyramid Honor Soc., Sigma Xi, Alpha Omega Alpha. Office: Pa Cardiol Assoc Ltd 801 Spruce St Philadelphia PA 19107-5701

ZAVON, MITCHELL RALPH, physician; b. N.Y.C., May 9, 1923; s. Irving and Claire (Gutterman) Z.; m. Betty Berthold, June 24, 1976; children by previous marriage: Peter, Dan, Juliet, Barbara. Student, Cornell U., 1940-43, Harvard U., 1943-44; M.D., Boston U., 1945-49; postgrad. Duke U., 1951-52, U. Cin., 1956-58. Diplomate Am. Bd. Med. Examiners, Am. Bd. Preventive Medicine, Am. Bd. Indsl. Hygiene. Intern, Wilson Meml. Hosp., Johnson City, N.Y.; surgeon USPHS, Washington, 1950-56; asst. to clin. prof. U. Cin., 1956-71 clin prof. Industrial med. asst. clin. prof. med.; asst. health commr. Cin. Health Dept., 1956-74; med. dir. Ethyl Corp., Baton Rouge, 1974-76; dir. health Occidental Chem. Corp., Niagara Falls, N.Y., 1976-86; pres., med. dir. Agatha Corp., 1968—; mem., cons., del. Threshold Limits Com., 1962-87 ; mem., cons. Biol. Indeces Com., 1982-96 . Contbr. articles to profl. jours. Bd. dirs. HART; Soc.; mem. consulting staffs Niagara Falls Meml. Hosp, pres. Place-to-Be, 1978-83; mem. Cincinnatus Assocs., 1969-74. Fellow APHA, Am. Coll. Occupl. and Environ. Medicine, Am. Indsl. Hygiene Assn.; mem. AMA, AAAS, Am. Assn. Adv. Scis., NY. State Med. Soc., Niagara County Med. Soc.; Am. Conference on Govtl. Indsl. Hygienists. Unitarian. Office: Agatha Corp 4497 Lower River Rd Lewiston NY 14092-1056 Other: PO Box 58425 Cincinnati OH 45258-0425

ZAWACKI, BRUCE EDWIN, surgeon, ethicist; b. Northampton, Mass., Dec. 6, 1935. BS, Coll. of the Holy Cross, 1957; MD, Harvard U., 1961; MA, U. So. Calif., 1986. Diplomate Am. Bd. Surgery. Dir. burn study br. U.S. Army Inst. Surg. Rsch., San Antonio, 1968; gen. surgeon So. Calif. Permanente Med. Group, Panorama City, 1969-71; dir. burn ctr. LAC and U. So. Calif. Med. Ctr., L.A., 1971—; assoc. prof. surgery U. So. Calif. Sch. Medicine, L.A., 1975—; assoc. prof. religion U. So. Calif. Sch. Religion, L.A., 1992—; chair ethics resource com. LAC and U. So. Calif. Med. Ctr., L.A., 1988—. Contbr. articles to profl. jours. Served to maj. U.S. Army, 1967-68. Mem. Am. Burn Assn. (2d v.p., bd. trustees 1992-93), Soc. for Health and Human Values, L.A. Surg. Soc., Internat. Soc. for Burn Injuries. Office: LAC & USC Med Ctr 1200 N State St Rm 12-650 Los Angeles CA 90033-4525

ZAWADA, EDWARD THADDEUS, JR., physician, educator; b. Chgo., Oct. 3, 1947; s. Edward Thaddeus and Evelyn Mary (Kovarek) Z.; m. Nancy Ann Stephen, Mar. 26, 1977; children: Elizabeth, Nicholas, Victoria, Alexandra. BS summa cum laude, Loyola U., Chgo., 1969; MD summa cum laude, Loyola-Stritch Sch. Medicine, 1973. Diplomate Am. Bd. Internal Medicine, Am. Bd. Nephrology, Am. Bd. Nutrition, Am. Bd. Critical Care, Am. Bd. Geriatrics, Am. Bd. Clin. Pharm. Intern UCLA Hosp., 1973, resident, 1974-76; asst. prof. medicine UCLA, 1978-79, U. Utah, Salt Lake City, 1979-81; assoc. prof. medicine Med. Coll. Va., Richmond, 1981-83; assoc. prof. medicine, physiology & pharmacology U. S.D. Sch. Medicine, Sioux Falls, 1983-86, Freeman prof., chmn. dept. Internal Medicine, 1987—, chief div. nephrology and hypertension, 1983-88, pres. univ. physician's practice plan, 1992—; chief renal sect. Salt Lake VA Med. Ctr., 1980-81; asst. chief med. service McGuire VA Med. Ctr., Richmond, 1981-83. Editor: Geriatric Nephrology and Urology, 1984; contbr. articles to profl. publs. Pres. Minnehaha div. Am. Heart Assn., 1984-87, pres. Dakota affiliate Am. Heart Assn., 1989-91. VA Hosp. System grantee, 1981-85, 85-88; Health and Human Svcs. grantee Pub. Health Scvs. Rsch. Adminstrn. Bureau Health Profl., 1993—. Fellow ACP, Am. Coll. Chest Physicians, Am. Coll. Nutrition, Am. Coll. Clin. Pharmacology, Internat. Coll. Angiology, Am. Coll. Angiology, Am. Coll. Clin. Pharmacology, Royal Soc. Medicine; mem. Internat. Soc. Nephrology, Am. Soc. Nephrology, Am. Soc. Pharmacology and Exptl. Therapeutics, Am. Physiol. Soc., Am. Inst. Nutrition, Am. Soc. Clin. Nutrition, Am. Geriatric Soc., Westward Ho Country Club. Democrat. Roman Catholic. Home: 2908 S Duchess Ave Sioux Falls SD 57103-4826 Office: U SD Sch Medicine 1400 W 22nd St Sioux Falls SD 57105-1505

ZAWADSKY, PETER MICHAEL, medical administrator, pediatrician; b. New Brunswick, N.J., Oct. 26, 1942; s. Peter Michael and Annie Zawadsky. AB, Rutgers Coll., 1964; MD, Harvard U., 1968. Diplomate Am. Bd. Pediatrics. Advanced through grades to col. U.S. Army, 1971-94, staff pediatrician, 1971-84; chief pediat. infectious diseases Walter Reed Army Med. Ctr., Washington, 1984-92, asst. chief dept. pediat., 1992-94; dir. pediat. Regional Inst. for Children and Adolescents, Rockville, Md., 1994—. Organist Walter Reed Meml. Chapel. Decorated Legion of Merit, U.S. Army, 1994. Fellow Am. Acad. Pediat. Home: 9429 Chatteroy Pl Montgomery Village MD 20879 Office: RICA-Rockville 15000 Broschart Rd Rockville MD 20850

ZAWIRSKA, BOZENNA STANISLAWA, pathologist; b. Zbaraz, Poland, June 30, 1923; d. Hipolit and Helena (Pitullej) Z. MD, Med. Acad. Wroclaw, 1956. Vice dean Med. Acad. Wroclaw, 1968-70, vice dir. Biostructure Inst., 1970-81, head chair and dept. pathology, 1979-90, cons. prof. pathology, 1991—. Author: Neoplasma, 1981, Environmental Research, 1981, Gastroenterology, 1983, Zbl.allg.Path., 1968. Recipient awards Polish Ministry of Health, 1969, 83, 90, Rector of Med. Acad. Wroclaw, 1951-89. Mem. Polish Soc. Pathology (v.p. 1976-79), Polish Soc. Physicians, European Assn. Cancer Rsch., European Soc. Pathology. Home: Sklodowskiej-Curie 15/35, Wroclaw Poland 50-381 Office: Med Acad, ul Marcinkowskiego 1, Wroclaw Poland 50-368

ZAX, MELVIN, psychologist, educator; b. Cambridge, Mass., Apr. 14, 1928; s. Joseph and Sadie (Kirshner) Z.; m. Ruth Leah Vogel, Apr. 23, 1977; children: Jeffrey S., David B., Jonathan B. A.B., Boston U., 1951, A.M., 1952; Ph.D., U. Tenn., 1955. Clin. psychologist U. Tenn., Knoxville, 1955-56; staff psychologist St. Elizabeths Hosp., Washington, 1956-57; asst. to assoc. prof. psychology U. Rochester, N.Y., 1957-62; assoc. prof. psychology, 1962-67; prof. U. Rochester, N.Y., 1967-93, prof. emeritus, 1993—; pvt. practice, 1973—; chmn. exptl. and spl. tng. rev. com. NIMH, 1970-71. Author: (with G. Stricker) Patterns of Psychopathology, 1963, (with E.L. Cowen) Abnormal Psychology: Changing Conceptions, 1972, (with G.A. Specter) An Introduction to Community Psychology, 1974, (with M. Nichols) Catharsis in Psychotherapy, 1977; editor: (with Stricker) The Study of Abnormal Behavior: Selected Readings, 1964, (with Cowen and E.A. Gardner) Emergent Approaches to Mental Health Problems, 1967, (with D. Dorr and J. Bonner) The Psychology of Discipline, 1983; adv. editor Jour. Cons. and Clin. Psychology, 1965-81; contbr. articles to profl. jours. Served with AUS, 1946-47. NIMH spl. research fellow Psykologisk Inst., Copenhagen, 1966-67. Fellow Am. Psychol. Assn.; mem. Eastern Psychol. Assn., AAUP, Phi Beta Kappa, Sigma Xi, Phi Kappa Phi. Home: 27 Sky Ridge Dr Rochester NY 14625-2167 Office: 625 Panorama Trl Bldg 2 Rochester NY 14625-2432

ZAZECKIS, THOMAS MICHAEL, neuropsychologist, clinical psychologist; b. Berwyn, Ill.; s. Anthony Michael and Norma Rose (Mattas) Z.; m. Anne P. Heroux Brennan, May 5, 1970 (div. May 10, 1979); children: Michelle, Michael; m. Donna Lee Danielson, June 5, 1993; stepchildren: Nicholas Smith, Alexis Smith. BA in Biology, Lewis U., 1970; MA in Clin. Psychology, U. Ariz., 1980, PhD in Clin. Psychology, 1983; postgrad. in Neuropsychology, U. Tex., Houston, 1989. Lic. psychologist, Tex. Commd. 2d lt. USAF, 1976, advanced through grades to maj., 1989; clin. psychologist Sheppard AFB, Wichita Falls, Tex., 1983-87; chief psychology svc. Hellenikon AFB, Athens, Greece, 1987-89; postdoctoral fellow U. Tex. Health Sci. Ctr., Houston, 1989-90; chief psychology svc. Sheppard AFB, 1990—. Contbr. articles to profl. jours. Bd. dirs. Child Advs., Wichita Falls, 1990—. Mem. APA, Aerospace Med. Assn., Am. Soc. Clin. Hypnosis, Air Force Soc. Clin. Psychologists. Home: 4406 Ridgemont Dr Wichita Falls TX 76309 Office: USAF 82 Med Group 149 Hart St Ste 100 Sheppard AFB TX 76311

ZAZULA, BERNARD MEYER, physician administrator; b. Bklyn., July 7, 1941; s. Harry and Clara (Serchuk) Z.; m. Elise Hoch, Aug. 2, 1966; children: Rona, Harold. BA, Yeshiva Coll., 1961; MD, Albert Einstein Coll., 1965; MPH, Columbia U., 1976. Diplomate Nat. Bd. Med. Examiners, Am. Bd. Preventive Medicine; med. lic., N.Y.; cert. in pub. health and gen. preventive medicine. Intern, resident in pediats. Kings County Hosp., Bklyn., 1965-68; sub-dist. med. officer of health Ministry of Health, Jerusalem, 1971-73; dist. health officer N.Y.C. Dept. Health, 1973-74, dir. Bur. for Handicapped Children, 1975-86; med. dir. Medicaid program N.Y.C. Human Resources Adminstrn., 1986—; cons. dept. medicine Flushing (N.Y.) Hosp., 1989-93; tchg. staff Wyckoff Heights Hosp., Queens, N.Y., 1993—. Mem., bd. dirs. Queens Valley Homeowners' Civic Assn., Flushing, 1985-91, Young Israel of Kew Gardens Hills, N.Y., 1983-91. Maj. U.S. Army, 1968-70, Vietnam. Fellow N.Y. Acad. Medicine; mem. APHA, Queens County Med. Soc. (pres. 1995-96), Med. Soc. State of N.Y. (chmn. ethics com. 1992—), Alumni Assn. Albert Einstein Coll. Medicine (nat. pres. 1991-93). Jewish. Home: 144-05 70th Rd Flushing NY 11367 Office: Med Assistance Program 330 W 34th St New York NY 10001

ZEA-IRIARTE, WALTER LEOPOLDO, gastroenterologist, educator; b. Guatemala, Nov. 13, 1959; arrived in Japan, 1991.; s. Walter Leopoldo Zea-Vivar and Clara Luz Iriarte-Beteta. MD, San Carlos U., Guatemala, 1986; PhD, Nagasaki (Japan) U., 1996. Diplomate Guatemalan Coll. Physicians and Surgeons. Resident in internal medicine San Juan de Dios Gen. Hosp., Guatemala, 1985-88; fellow in tropical medicine Inst. Tropical Medicine, Nagasaki (Japan) U. Sch. Medicine, 1989-90; fellow in gastroenterology 2nd Dept. Internal Medicine, Nagasaki U. Sch. of Medicine, 1991-96, fellow in gastrointestinal endoscopy, 1991-96; fellow in gastrointestinal pathology Dept. of Pathology, Atomic Disease Inst., Nagasaki U. Sch. of Medicine, 1991-96, asst. prof., 1996—; mgmt. mem. bd. Med. and Surgeons' Coll. Guatemala, 1987-88. Contbr. articles to profl. jours. Mem. Am. Coll. Gastroenterology (in-tng.), Am. Roentgen Ray Soc. (in-tng.), Soc. Minimally Invasive Therapy (in-tng.). Roman Catholic. Office: Atomic Bomb Disease Inst, Nagasaki U Sakamoto-1-12-4, 852 Nagasaki Japan

ZEDLER, EMPRESS YOUNG, psychologist; b. Abilene, Tex., Nov. 9, 1908; d. William James and Edith (Deaver) Young; m. Paul Louis Zedler, June 5, 1928. B.A., U. Tex., 1928, M.A., 1948, Ph.D., 1952. Chairperson dept. spl. edn. Southwest Tex. State U., San Marcos, 1960-78, disting. prof. emeritus, 1988—; pvt. practice child psychologist, Luling, Tex., 1978-94; ret. 1994. Fellow Am. Speech Lang. and Hearing Assn., Acad. Cerebral Palsy and Rehabilitative Medicine; mem. Assn. Children's Learning Disabilities (Founders Gold Key award), Am. Psychol. Assn., Tex. Psych. Assn., Tex. Speech Lang. and Hearing Assn. (Internat. award), Acad. Aphasia, Phi Beta Kappa. Episcopalian. Club: Country (Austin). Author: Listening for Speech Sounds, 1955; (with others) Principles of Childhood Learning Disabilities, 1972. Home: 1100 S Laurel Ave Luling TX 78648-3507

ZEFFREN, JACOB MAYER, physician; b. St. Louis. BA, Yeshiva U., 1971; MD, St. Louis U., 1975. Resident Beth Israel Med. Ctr., N.Y.C., 1975-78; pvt. practice St. Louis, 1980-83; asst., assoc. dir. clin. oncology Hoffman-LaRoche, Inc., Nutley, N.J., 1983-91, dir. drug safety, 1991—; instr. clin. medicine Washington U. Sch. Medicine, St. Louis, 1981-85; clin. instr. medicine U. Medicine & Dentistry N.J., 1987-94, clin. asst. prof., 1994—. Oncology and rsch. fellow Meml. Sloan-Kettering Cancer Ctr., N.Y.C., 1978-80, rsch. fellow. Office: Hoffman-LaRoche Inc 340 Kingsland St Nutley NJ 07110

ZEGARELLI, EDWARD VICTOR, retired dental educator, researcher; b. Utica, N.Y., Sept. 9, 1912; s. Frank Anthony and Maria Josephine (Ambroselli) Z.; m. Irene Marie Ceconi, June 17, 1939; children: Edward V., David J., Philip E., Peter J. AB, Columbia U., 1934, DDS, 1937, DSc (hon.), 1983; MS, U. Chgo., 1942. Staff Sch. Dental and Oral Surgery, Columbia U., 1937-78, asst. instr., then successively instr., asst. prof., asso. prof., head diagnosis and roentgenology, 1947-58, chmn. com. dental research, 1956-78, Dr. Edwin S. Robinson prof. dentistry, 1958, prof. dentistry, dir. div. stomatology, 1958-78, acting dean, 1973, dean, 1974-78, dean emeritus, 1979—; Edward V. Zegarelli prof. dentistry, 1993—; chmn. sect. hosp. dental services Columbia-Presbyn. Med. Center; dir. and attending dentist dental service Presbyn. Hosp., 1974-79, also mem. exec. com. of med. bd., 1974-76; police surgeon N.Y.C., 1968-89; chmn. exam. com. N.E. Regional Bd. Dental Examiners, 1969-90; cons. VA, Washington; Weisberger Meml. lectr. Harvard U., 1969, Mershon Meml. lectr., 1970, Ralph L. Spaulding Meml. lectr., 1972; deans com. Montrose VA Hosp.; cons. East Orange, Kingsbridge VA hosps., Westchester Med. Ctr., Valhalla, N.Y., USPHS, Phelps Meml. Hosp., Tarrytown, N.Y., Vassar Bros. Hosp., Poughkeepsie, Bur. Medicine, FDA, Council on Dental Therapeutics; area cons. VA; cons.-lectr. U.S. Naval Dental Sch., Bethesda, Md., 1970-78; pres. N.Y. State Bd. Dental Examiners, 1970-71; chmn. exam. rev. com. N.E. Regional Bd. Dental Examiners, 1969-90; Samuel Charles Miller Meml. lectr., 1976; mem. council deans Am. Assn. Dental Schs., 1973-79; mem. postgrad. edn. com. N.Y.C. Cancer Com.; mem. profl. edn. and grants com. N.Y.C. div. Am. Cancer Soc., 1963-73; chmn. panel on drugs in dentistry NAS, NRC, FDA; mem. N.Y. State Health Research Council, N.Y. Commn. on Health Manpower; chmn. bd. govs. (dental) Gen. Health Ins.,

N.Y.C. Contbg. author: The Thyroid, Medical Roentgenology, Current Pediatric Therapy, Cancer of Head and Neck; author: (with others) Pharmacotherapeutics of Oral Disease, 1964, Clinical Stomatology, 1966, Diagnosis of Diseases of Mouth and Jaws, 1969, 2d edit., 1978; also articles on mouth, jaw bone disease. Bd. dirs. Hist. Soc. Tarrytowns, 1983, United Way Tarrytowns, 1983, YMCA of Tarrytowns, 1984, Phelps Meml. Hosp. Hospice Agy, 1986. Recipient Austin Sniffen medal 9th Dist. Dental Soc., 1961; Columbia U. Dental Alumni Research award, 1963; Jarvie-Burkhart medal N.Y. Dental Soc., 1970; Samuel J. Miller medal Am. Acad. Oral Medicine, 1976; Henry Spenadel award 1st Dist. Dental Soc., 1979; Man of Yr. award C. of C. Tarrytowns and Irvington, 1983; Man of Achievement award Americans for Italian Migration, 1984; named Disting. Practitioner mem. Nat. Acads. Practice, 1986. Fellow Am. Coll. Dentists (William J. Gies medal 1981), N.Y. Acad. Dentistry, Internat. Coll. Dentists, 9th Dist. Dental Soc.; mem. Am. Acad. Oral Pathology, Am. Assn. for Cancer Edn. (charter), Am. Assn. Dental Examiners (Dentist Citizen of Yr. award 1978), Orgn. Tchrs. Oral Diagnosis, N.Y. Acad. Scis., N.Y. Dental Soc. (chmn. council sci. research 1956-71), Greater N.Y. Acad. Prosthodontics (hon.), Guatemala Dental Soc. (hon.), Am. Dental Assn. (mem. council dental therapeutics 1963-69, vice chmn. 1969), Columbia Dental Alumni Assn., William Jarvie Research Soc., Internat. Assn. Dental Research, AAAS, Nat. Italian-Am. Found., Sigma Xi (chpt. pres. 1974-76), Omicron Kappa Upsilon (sec. treas. Columbia chpt. 1944-57, pres. 1959-60), Sigma Phi Alpha., Knight Malta. Lodge: Rotary (pres. 1985-86) (Tarrytown). Home: 120 Gory Brook Rd Tarrytown NY 10591

ZEGLIN, CAROLE ANN, medical educator; b. Morgantown, W.Va., Feb. 19, 1949; d. Edward Tilden and Marietta (Walls) Stemple; m. Daniel F. Zeglin, Oct. 1, 1971; children: Christianna and Timothy. Degree in med. technology, Franklin Sch. Sci. and Arts, 1969. Med. technologist Meml. Gen. Hosp., Elkins, W.Va., 1968-70; med. technologist Frick Cmty. Hosp., Mt. Pleasant, Pa., 1970-73, cons., 1996; med. technologist F.V. Maida, P.C., Mt. Pleasant, Pa., 1980-94, cons., 1992-95; instr. Douglas Sch. Bus., Monessen, Pa., 1994-95; instr., dept. head med. asst. program Western Sch. Health/Bus., Monroeville, Pa., 1995—; instr. and cons. Westmoreland County C.C., Youngwood, Pa., 1996—. Mem. Boston Coll. Parents Club, Chestnut Hill, Mass., 1994—. Mem. Am. Med. Technologists (nat. and state chpts.). Roman Catholic.

ZEHR, WAYNE DANIEL, mail order pharmaceutical company executive; b. Lowville, N.Y., May 22, 1954; s. Reginald and Nina (Widrick) Z.; m. Ann M. Phreaner, July 30, 1977; 1 child, Jordan D. BS in Pharmacy, Bklyn. Coll. Pharmacy, 1977; JD, Widener U., 1993. Bar: Pa. Pharmacist Dounough Pharmacy, 1977-78; asst. mgr. Rea & Derick Pharmacy, 1978-80, mgr., 1980-83; asst. mgr. Weis Markets pharmacy, 1983-84, mgr., 1984-87; purchasing mgr. Ctrl. Fill, Inc. (CFI), 1988-90, adminstrv. mgr., 1990—, attorney, 1993—. Sec. West Hanover twp. planning commn., 1995—. Mem. ABA (regional finalist negotiation 1991, client counseling 1992), Pa. Bar Assn., Dauphin County Bar Assn. Home: 6972 Sterling Rd Harrisburg PA 17112-8909 Office: Central Fill Inc 31st Revere St Harrisburg PA 17111

ZEIGER, HERBERT EVAN, JR., neurosurgeon; b. Landgale, Ala., Aug. 23, 1949; s. H. Evan Sr. and Imogene (Morris) Z.; m. Margaret Swift Shook, Feb. 25, 1984; children: H. Evan III, Ashley Shook, Douglas Shook. BA, Samford U., 1971; MD, U. Ala., 1974. Diplomate Am. Bd. Neurol. Surgery. Intern Carraway Meth. Med. Ctr., Birmingham, 1975-76; resident Washington U. Med. Sch./ Barnes Hosp., St. Louis, 1976-81; attending neurosurgeon Carraway Meth. Med. Ctr., Birmingham, Ala., 1987—; assoc. prof. neurosurgery U. Ala., Brimingham, 1981-87; attending neurosurgeon Norwood Clinic, Brimingham, 1987—. Author: Stroke and the Extracranial Vessels, 1983; contbr. articles to profl. jours. Bd. dirs. Ala. Family Alliance, Birmingham, 1989—, Children's Harbor, Birmingham, 1993-96, Salvation Army, Birmingham, 1990—. Fellow U. Western Ont. London, Can., 1981. Fellow Am. Coll. Surgeons; mem. Am. Assn. Neurol. Surgeons, So. Neurosurg. Soc., Neurosurg. Soc. Ala (pres. 1988-90), Birmingham Surg. Soc., Congress Neurol. Surgeons, Jefferson County Med. Soc. (pres.-elect, v.p. 1995—), Rotary (fellow com. 1990). Presbyterian. Home: 3009 Canterbury Ln Birmingham AL 35223 Office: Norwood Clinic Inc 1528 Carraway Blvd Birmingham AL 35234

ZEIGLER, VICKI LYNN, pediatrics nurse; b. Hampton, S.C., May 26, 1961; d. Richard Jackson and Miriam Banner (Smith) Z.; m. Paul Crawford Gillette, Feb. 1, 1992. BSN, Med. U. of S.C., 1982, MSN, 1991. RN, S.C.; cert. spl. competency in cardiac pacing for non-physicians N.Am. Soc. Pacing and Electrophysiology. Staff nurse pediatrics Med. U. S.C., Charleston, 1983-85, nurse clinician pediatric cardiology, 1985-91, pediatric arrhythmia/pacemaker case mgr., 1992-94, pediatric arrhythmia nurse specialist, 1994-96; pediat. arrhythmia case mgr. Cook Children's Med. Ctr., Ft. Worth, 1996—; BLS instr. Am. Heart Assn., Columbia, S.C. Contbr. articles to profl. jours. Recipient Young Investigator award Sigma Theta Tau. Mem. AACN, Assn. for Care of Children's Health, North Am. Soc. of Pacing and Electrophysiology, Am. Heart Assn. Coun. of Cardiovascular Nursing, Sigma Theta Tau. Republican. Office: Cook Childrens Med Ctr Cardiology Dept 801 7th Ave Fort Worth TX 76104-2796

ZEILMAKER, GERARDUS HENDRIKUS, biologist, professor; b. Haarlem, The Netherlands, Nov. 12, 1936. PhD in Biology, U. Amsterdam, The Netherlands, 1964. Rsch. biologist Netherlands Cancer Inst., Amsterdam, 1958-69; prof. physiology Erasmus U., Rotterdam, The Netherlands, 1969—; cons. in field. Editor: Frozen Storage of Laboratory Animals, 1983. Office: Erasmus U, PO Box 1738, 2061 LL Bloemendaal The Netherlands

ZEISEL, STEVEN H., nutrition educator; b. N.Y.C., July 16, 1950. BS in Life Sci., MIT, 1971; MD, Harvard Med. Sch., 1975; PhD in Nutrition/Natural Endocrine, MIT, 1980. Asst. Children's Hosp., Boston, 1980-81; asst. prof. pathology and pediatrics Boston U. Sch. Medicine, 1982-87, assoc. prof., 1987-90, prof., 1990-91; prof. dept. pediatrics U. N.C., Chapel Hill, 1990—, prof., chair dept. nutrition, 1990—; chair med. edn. com. Am. Soc. Clin. Nutrition, 1995—; chair joint membership com. AIN/ASCN, 1992-94; mem. study sect. Clin. Nutrition Rsch. units NIH, 1993-95; del. Assn. AMCCAS, 1991—. Editor-in-chief Jour. Nutritional Biochemistry. Mem. Am. Inst. Nutrition, Am. Soc. Clin. Nutrition, Am. Soc. Parenteral and Enteral Nutrition, Am. Coll. Nutrition, Am. Pub. Health Assn., Soc. Pediatric Rsch. Office: U NC Dept Nutrition # 7400 Sch Pub Health/Sch Medicine McGavran Greenberg Hall Chapel Hill NC 27599-7400

ZEITELS, JERROLD ROY, plastic surgeon; b. N.Y.C., Apr. 2, 1955; s. Harry Lewis and Natalie R. (Rabinowitz) Z.; m. Susan Mary Hatfield, Sept. 15, 1981; children: Lauren, Rebecca. BA, U. Pa., 1976; MD, U. Chgo., 1980. Diplomate Am. Bd. Gen. Surgery, Plastic Surgery, Hand Surgery. Resident gen. surgery U. Mich., Ann Arbor, 1984-85; resident plastic surgery U. Pa., Phila., 1985-87; plastic surgeon Assocs. Plastic & Aesthetic Surgery, Westfield, N.J., 1987—; attending physician Overlook Hosp., Summit, N.J., 1987—, Rahway (N.J.) Hosp., 1987—, Union (N.J.) Hosp., 1987—. Contbr. articles to profl. jours. Fellow ACS; mem. AMA, Am. Assn. Hand Surgery, N.J. Soc. Plastic Surgery (mem.-at-large), Phi Beta Kappa. Office: Assocs Plastic & Aesthetic Surgery 522 E Broad St Westfield NJ 07090

ZELAC, RONALD EDWARD, physicist; b. Chgo., Jan. 22, 1941. BS in engring. physics summa cum laude, U. Ill., 1962, MS in physics, 1964; MS in envirno. health, U. Mich., 1965; PhD in environ. engring., U. Fla., 1970. Diplomate Am. Bd. Health Physics, Am. Bd. Medical Physics. Chief health physicist IIT Rsch. Inst., Chgo., 1965-68; radiation physicist Mercy Medical Ctr., Chgo., 1965-68; asst., assoc. prof. Temple U., Phila., 1970-92, radiation safety officer, 1970-91; adj. assoc. prof. U. Pa., Phila., 1980-86; assoc. vice provost Temple U., Phila., 1987-91; sr. physicist and mgr. tech. Landauer Inc., Glenwood, Ill., 1991—; adj. prof. Northwestern U., Evanston, Ill., 1991—, Temple U., 1992—; cons. Wyeth-Ayerst Rsch., Radnor, Pa., Princeton, N.J., 1971—, Presby. U. Pa. Med. Ctr., Phila., 1974-86, Mobile Rsch. Devel. Corp., Paulsboro, Princeton, 1977—, Rhone-Poulenc Rorer Cen. Rsch., Ft. Washington, Collegeville, Pa., 1986—. Editor: A Guide to Personnel Monitoring, 1993; contbr. articles to profl. jours. Fellow Phi Kappa Phi, 1962-63, U.S. AEC, 1964-65, USPHS, 1968-70. Mem. Health Physics Soc. (com. mem. 1978-79), Campus Safety Assn., Am. Assn. Physicists in Medicine, Am. Coll. Medical Physics, Sigma Xi (v.p., pres. 1984-88). Home: 860 N Dewitt Pl Apt 1307 Chicago IL 60611-1722 Office: Landauer Inc 2 Science Rd Glenwood IL 60425-1531

ZELDES, ILYA MICHAEL, forensic scientist, lawyer; b. Baku, Azerbaidjan, USSR, Mar. 15, 1933; came to U.S., 1976; s. Michael B. and Pauline L. (Ainbinder) Z.; m. Emma S. Kryss, Nov. 5, 1957; 1 child, Irina Zeldes Rieser. JD, U. Azerbaidjan, Baku, 1955; PhD in Forensic Scis., U. Moscow, 1969. Expert-criminalist Med. Examiner's Bur., Baku, 1954-57; rsch. assoc. Criminalistics Lab., Moscow, 1958-62; sr. rsch. assoc. All-Union Sci. Rsch. Inst. Forensic Expertise, Moscow, 1962-75; chief forensic scientist S.D. Forensic Lab., Pierre, 1977-93; owner Forensic Scientist's Svcs., Pierre, 1977-93. Author: Physical-Technical Examination, 1968, Complex Examination, 1971, The Problems of Crime, 1981; contbr. numerous articles to profl. publs. in Australia, Austria, Bulgaria, Can., Eng., Germany, Holland, India, Ireland, Israel, Rep. of China, Taiwan, U.S. and USSR. Mem. Internat. Assn. Identification (rep. S.D. chpt. 1979-93, chmn. forensic lab. analysis subcom. 1991-96), Assn. Firearm and Tool Mark Examiners (emeritus). Home: 5735 Foxlake Dr Apt 1 Fort Myers FL 33917-5651

ZELDIS, STEVEN MARTIN, cardiologist; b. Bklyn., June 11, 1946; s. Milton E. and Norma (Gratz) Z.; m. Roberta L. Weiss, June 8, 1974; children: Mark, Beth. BA, U. Rochester, 1968; MD, Yale U., 1972. Diplomate Am. Bd. Internal Medicine, Am. Bd. Cardiovascular Diseases. Intern Yale-New Haven (Conn.) Hosp., 1972-73, resident, 1973-75; cardiology fellow U. Pa., Phila., 1975-77; dir. non-invasive cardiology Long Island Jewish Med. Ctr., New Hyde Park, N.Y., 1977-81; asst. prof. medicine SUNY, Stony Brook, 1977-87, assoc. prof. medicine, 1987—; acting chief cardiology Nassau Hosp., Mineola, N.Y., 1981-84; chief cardiology Winthrop U. Hosp., Mineola, 1981-93, dir. med. edn., 1991—. Recipient Leadership award, Am. Heart Assn., Nassau, N.Y., Long Island Heart Coun. Fellow Clin. Coun. Am. Heart Assn., Am. Coll. of Physicians, Am. Coll. Cardiology (key contact com. 1991), Am. Coll. Chest Physicians. Office: Winthrop U Hosp Div Cardiology Mineola NY 11577

ZELENY, MARJORIE PFEIFFER (MRS. CHARLES ELLINGSON ZELENY), psychologist; b. Balt., Mar. 31, 1924; d. Lloyd Armitage and Mable (Willian) Pfeiffer; BA, U. Md., 1947; MS, U. Ill., 1949; postgrad., 1951-54; m. Charles Ellington Zeleny, Dec. 11, 1950 (dec.); children: Ann Douglas, Charles Timberlake. Vocational counseling psychologist VA, Balt., 1947-48; asst. U. Ill. at Urbana, 1948-50, research asso. Bur. Research, 1952-53; chief psychologist dept. neurology and psychiatry Ohio State U. Coll. Medicine, Columbus, 1950-51; research psychologist, cons., Tucson, Washington, 1954—. Mem. Am., D.C. psychol. assns., AAAS, Southeastern Psychol Assn., DAR, Nat. Soc. Daus. Colonial Wars, Nat. Soc. Colonial Dames XVII Century, Nat. Soc. Descendants of Early Quakers, Nat. Soc. Daus. of Am. Colonists, Nat. Soc. Dames of Ct. of Honor, Nat. Soc. U.S. Daus. of 1812, Mortar Bd., Delta Delta Delta, Sigma Delta Epsilon, Psi Chi, Sigma Tau Epsilon. Roman Catholic. Home: 6825 Wemberly Way Mc Lean VA 22101-1534

ZELINKA, DIANE MARIE, optometrist; b. Wilkes-Barre, Pa., May 18, 1967; d. Leonard John and Helen Mary (Frank) Z.; m. David Gary Jupiter, Sept. 24, 1994. BS summa cum laude, Wilkes Coll., 1989; OD, Pa. Coll. Optometry, 1992. Cert. optometrist, Pa., Del. Pvt. practice, Wilmington and Seaford, Del., 1993—. Mem. adv. bd. 1st State Cmty. Action, Georgetown, Del., 1994; mem. eye health program Lions Club, Georgetown, 1994-95. Mem. Am. Optometric Assn. (vision USA program 1994-95), Del. Optometric Assn. Democrat. Roman Catholic. Home: 1412 Dalmation Pl Apt T2 Belcamp MD 21017 Office: Del Eye Surgeons PA 1100 Grant Ave Wilmington DE 19805

ZELLMER, MARK RICHARD, physician assistant program administrator; b. Dubuque, Iowa, June 7, 1954; s. Richard and Minona Zellmer; m. Debra A. Daehn, June 24, 1978; children: Timothy M.J., Bethany N.S. BA in Chemistry, Natural Sci., Augsburg Coll., 1976; MA in Sci. Edn., Coll. of St. Thomas, 1977; BS in Medicine, U. Iowa, 1983. Cert. physician asst., Nat. Commn. of Cert. of Physician Assts.; cert. ACLS instr. EMT Dumont (Iowa) Ambulance Svc., 1979-80; instr., coord. EMT course Kirkwood C.C., Cedar Rapids, Iowa, 1981; EMT-paramedic Mercy Hosp./Area Ambulance, Cedar Rapids, Iowa, 1980-83; physician asst. Park Clinic, Allison, Iowa, 1983-87, Interstate Clinic, Red Wing, Minn., 1987-93; physician asst. program dir. U. S.D. Sch. Medicine, Vermillion, 1993-95, U. Wis., LaCrosse, 1995—; physician asst. Gundersen Clinic-Hillsboro, Wis., 1995—; mem. rural health adv. com. Minn. Dept. Health, St. Paul, 1992-93; presenter in field. Mem. parish nurse com. Our Savior's Luth. Ch., LaCrosse, 1996; Luth. campus ministry dir. com. U. Wis., LaCrosse, 1996. Fellow Am. Acad. Physician Assts (chpt. and mem. rels. com. 1991-93, external liaison NRHA 1993), Minn. Acad. Physician Assts. (pres., legis. chair 1988, Presdl. award 1990, 93), Wis. Acad. Physician Assts. (physician asst. program liaison 1995); mem. Assn. Physician Assts. Programs (assoc.). Home: 723 Cliffwood Ln La Crosse WI 54601 Office: Univ Wis Dept Clin Sci Physician Asst Program 1725 State St La Crosse WI 54601

ZELLNER, DAVID CARL, physician, educator; b. Castalia, Ohio, June 3, 1929; s. Harrison C. and Elsie (Steward) Z.; m. Constance Lou Williams, June 25, 1955; children: Cathy, James, Karen. BA, Oberlin Coll., 1951; MD, Case Western Res. U., 1955. Diplomate Am. Bd. Internal Medicine, Am. Bd. Hematology, Am. Bd. Med. Oncology. Intern Cin. Gen. Hosp., 1955-56; resident in medicine U. Cin., 1958-60, fellow in cardiology 1960-61, fellow hematology, 1961-62, asst. prof. medicine, 1964-69, instr. medicine, 1962-64, assoc. prof. medicine, 1969-74, prof. medicine, 1974—, acting dir. hematology divsn., 1972-76. Capt. Med. Corps, U.S. Army, 1956-58. Fellow ACP; mem. AAAS, Am. Soc. Hematology, Am. Soc. Clin. Oncology, Am. Fedn. Clin. Rsch. Office: U Cin Med Arts Bldg Ste 6000 222 Piedmont Ave Cincinnati OH 45219-4223

ZEMANKIEWICZ, STANISLAW, orthopaedic surgeon; b. Lwow, Poland, Sept. 26, 1942; came to U.S., 1982; s. Kazimierz and Maria (Dykiel) Z.; m. Elizabeth Bayor, Mar. 3, 1973; children: Peter, Paul. MD, Silesian Med. Sch., Katowice, Poland, PhD, 1981. Diplomate Am. Bd. Orthop. Surgery. Adj. prof. orthop. Silesian Med. Sch., 1978-81; orthop. surgeon Polk Gen. Hosp., Bartow, Fla., 1983-85, chief orthop. dept., 1986—; pvt. practice Bartow, 1983—; mem. residence review U. South Fla., Tampa, 1985-86. Contbr. articles to profl. jours.; author book. Sgt. Polish Air Force, 1962-64. Recipient Silver Crest, Polish Senate, 1966. Mem. Fla. Orthop. Soc. Republican. Roman Catholic. Home: 1043 Candlewood Dr Lakeland FL 33813 Office: Bartow Memorial Hospital Dept Orthop Surgery Bartow FL

ZEMEL, NORMAN PAUL, orthopedic surgeon; b. Bklyn., Oct. 15, 1939; s. Nathan M. and Mary (Sklarevsky) Z.; m. Mary P. Kane. BSN, Rutgers U., 1961; MD, Thomas Jefferson Med. Sch., 1965. Bd. cert. orthopaedic surgery with added qualification in hand surgery Am. Bd. Orthopaedic Surgery. Orthopaedic surgery resident Northwestern U., Chgo., 1969-73; hand surgery fellow Boyes Hand Fellowship, L.A., 1973-74; hand surgery physician Boyes, Stark, Ashworth, L.A., 1974-88, Kerlan-Jobe Orthopaedic Clinic, Inglewood, Calif., 1989—; clin. assoc. prof. dept. orthopaedics U. So. Calif. Sch. Medicine, L.A., 1977—. Contbr. chpts. to books and articles to profl. jours. Lt. USNR, 1966-68, Vietnam. Mem. ACS, Am. Acad. Orthopaedic Surgery (bd. councilors), Am. Soc. for Surgery of the Hand, Western Orthopaedic Assn. (pres. L.A. chpt. 1993-94), Soc. Internat. de Orthopedique et de Traumatologie. Office: Kerlan-Jobe Orthopaedic Clinic 501 E Hardy St Ste 300 Inglewood CA 90301

ZEMTSOV, ALEXANDER, dermatology and biochemistry educator; b. Baku, USSR, Nov. 9, 1959; came to U.S., 1977; s. Ilya and Marya (Dubinsky) Z.; m. Tali Giveon, Oct. 17, 1987; children: Raquel Karen, Gregory Ethan. BA magna cum laude, Temple U., 1981; MSc, U. Pa., 1982; MD with honors, NYU, 1986. Diplomate Am. Bd. Dermatology. Intern, then resident Cleve. Clinic Hosp. Found., 1989-90; assoc. prof. biochemistry and molecular biology Ind. U. Sch. Medicine, Muncie, 1995—. Editor Skin Rsch. and Tech. Jour.; contbr. articles to profl. jours. and books. Recipient Am. Soc. Dermatol. Surgery award, 1989; Cert. Appreciation, Ohio Dermatol. Soc., 1990. Fellow Am. Acad. Dermatology, Am. Contact Dermatitis Soc.; mem. Soc. Magnetic Resonance, Internat. Soc. for Digital Imaging of Skin (pres.), Kiwanis, Lubbock Club. Jewish. Office: University Dermatology Ctr 2525 University Ave #402 Muncie IN 47303

ZENG, FAN-GANG, neuroscientist; b. Jiujiang, China, Feb. 20, 1964; s. Qin-Biao and Mei-Li Zeng; m. Ruby Xiong, Aug. 18, 1987. BS, U. Sci. and Tech., Hefei, 1982; MS, Academia Sinica, Shanghai, 1985; PhD, Syracuse (N.Y.) U., 1990. Rsch. assoc. House Ear Inst., L.A., 1990-92, asst. scientist, 1992-94, dir. auditory perception lab., 1994—; ad hoc mem. NIH Study Sect., Md., 1995-96; adj. prof. Henan Med. U., 1994—. Editl. cons. Jour. Speech and Hearing Rsch., 1993—. Recipient NIH first award, Md., 1994—, doctoral award Syracuse U., 1991. Mem. AAAS, IEEE, Assn. Otolaryngology, Acoustical Soc. Am. Office: House Ear Inst 2100 W 3rd St Los Angeles CA 90057

ZENG, ZHAO-BANG, geneticist, educator; b. Wuhan, China, Dec. 8, 1957; came to the U.S., 1986; s. Guangming and Yulan (Ni) Z.; m. Jia Ma, Sept. 9, 1983; 1 child, Jiemin. BS, Huazhong Agrl. U., 1981; PhD, U. Edinburgh, 1986. Asst. lectr. Huazhong Agrl. U., Wuhan, 1982-83; postdoctoral rsch. assoc. N.C. State U., Raleigh, 1986-90, vis. asst. prof., 1990-91, rsch. asst. prof., 1992-94; rsch. assoc. prof., 1994—; adj. prof. Hunzhong Agrl. U., Wuhan, China, 1995—. Assoc. editor Genetics, 1994—, Theoretical Population Biology, 1995—; contbr. articles and revs. to profl. jours. Grantee NIH, 1990—, NSF, 1993—, USDA, 1994—. Mem. Am. Soc. Genetics, Soc. for Study Evolution, Biometric Soc., Phi Kappa Phi, Sigma Xi. Home: 112 Kirkfield Dr Cary NC 27511-6815 Office: NC State U Dept Statistics Box 8203 Raleigh NC 27695

ZENILMAN, MICHAEL E., surgeon, educator; b. Far Rockaway, N.Y., Mar. 14, 1958; s. David and Dorothy Zenilman; m. Marilyn Idell, 1980. BS with highest honors, SUNY, Stony Brook, 1980; MD summa cum laude, SUNY, Bklyn., 1984. Diplomate Am. Bd. Surgery. Resident in surgery, fellow, then chief resident Barnes Hosp.-Washington U. Sch. Medicine, St. Louis, 1984-91; asst. prof. surgery, chief geriatric surgery Johns Hopkins U. Sch. Medicine, Balt., 1991-93; assoc. prof., chief of surgery Albert Einstein Sch. Medicine, Bronx, N.Y., 1993—. Contbr. articles on surgery and basic sci. to sci. jours. Fellow ACS; mem. Assn. Acad. Surgery, Soc. for Surgery Alimentary Tract, Am. Gastroent. Assn., Phi Beta Kappa, Alpha Omega Alpha. Office: Montefiore Med Pk 1575 Blondell Ave Ste 125 Bronx NY 10461-2601

ZENNER, HANS PETER, otolaryngologist; b. Essen, Germany, Nov. 13, 1947; s. Hans and Eleonore (Lang) Z.; m. Birgit Zenner, 1977; 4 children. MD, U. Mainz, Germany, 1972, PhD, 1974; Dr.habil., U. Wuerzburg, Germany, 1981. Wiss. asst. U. Wuerzburg, 1974-81, dozent, 1981-86, prof., 1986-88; prof. orolaryngology, chmn. dept. U. Tübingen, Germany, 1988—; vis. scientist U. Mich., Ann Arbor, 1985, Washington U., St. Louis, 1987. Author: Allergologie, 1987, Therapie HNO, 1993, Physiologie; editor: All. Atemwegserkrank., 1988. Pres. Inst. Sonderhoerhilfe, Munich, 1990—; advisor Govt. of Germany, 1992—. Recipient Troeltsch award German Acad. Otolayngology, 1982, Sandor-Cseresmes medal Hungarian Triological Soc., 1985, Four Centennial prize, U. Würzburg, 1985, Leibniz award German Rsch. Coun., 1986, Haymann prize German Triological Soc., 1988. Mem. Rotary. Home: Silcherstr 5, W-7400 Tübingen Germany Office: U Tübingen Dept Otolaryngology, SilcherstraBe 5, 72076 Tübingen Germany

ZEPLOWITZ, FRANKLIN, surgeon; b. Buffalo, Sept. 30, 1933; s. Abraham and Ida (Shapiro) Z.; m. Piera Esther SaLama, June 17, 1962; children: David M., Lynn F. Grad., SUNY, Buffalo, 1954, MD, 1958. Diplomate Am. Bd. Surgery. Intern Buffalo Gen. Hosp., 1958-59, resident surgery, 1959-62; chief resident surgery Youngstown (Ohio) Hosp., 1962-63; commd. U.S. Army N.G., 1959, commd. officer, resigned, 1970; pvt. practice in general surgery U.S. Army N.G., Buffalo, 1963—; instr. surgery, mem. dean's nat. adv. coun. SUNY Sch. Medicine; chief of staff O.L.U. Hosp., Buffalo, 1994—. Fellow ACS; mem. Buffalo Surg. Soc. (pres. 1991-92), Med. Soc. State of N.Y. (state and fed. legis. coms., ho. of dels.), Erie County Med. Soc. (former chmn. legis. com., exec. bd., sec.-treas. 1994, v.p. 1995-96, pres.-elect 1996-97), SUNY Buffalo Sch. Medicine Alumni Assn. (past pres.), James Platt White Soc. (chmn. 1996). Office: 2083 S Park Ave Buffalo NY 14220-2148

ZEPPA, GUILLERMO ESTEBAN, neurologist; b. Cordoba, Argentina, Jan. 16, 1964; s. Juan Carlos and Catalina Laura (Verde-Paz) Z.; m. Maria Alejandra Pastore, Dec. 23, 1987; 1 child, Ignacio. MD, Nat. U. Cordoba, 1986. Resident in neurology Hosp. Cordoba, 1987-90, chief resident, 1990-92; fellow movement disorders unit Hosp. Clinic i Provincial, Barcelona, 1992; instr. in neurology Nat. U. Cordoba, 1989-94; attending neurologist Hosp. Privado, Cordoba, 1992—; cons. neurologist Hosp. Cordoba, 1993—. Scholar Inst. de Coperacion Iberoamericano, 1992. Mem. Argentine Neurol. Soc., Internat. Movement Disorders Soc., Am. Acad. Neurology (movement disorders sect.). Roman Catholic. Home: Obispo Trejo 835 11B, 5000 Cordoba Argentina Office: Hosp Privado, Naciones Unidas 346, 5016 Cordoba Argentina

ZERELLA, JOSEPH T., pediatric surgeon; b. Youngstown, Ohio, Mar. 7, 1941; s. Atilio and Ann (Capuzello) Z.; m. Diana Isabelle Talbot, Aug. 5, 1967; children—Ann, Michael, Mark. B.S., Northwestern U., 1962, M.D., 1966. Diplomate Am. Bd. Surgery, Am. Bd. Pediatric Surgery. Intern Med. Coll. Wis., Milw., 1966-67, resident in surgery, 1967-68, 70-73; tng. fellow in pediatric surgery Children's Hosp. Med. Ctr., Cin., 1973-75; staff pediatric surgeon Phoenix Children's Hosp., 1975—; staff Ariz. Children's Hosp., Phoenix, 1975—; pvt. practice medicine specializing in pediatric surgery, Phoenix, 1975—; mem. staff Good Samaritan Hosp., Phoenix, 1975—, sect. chief pediatric surgery, 1979—; mem. staff St. Joseph's Hosp., Phoenix, 1975—, sect. chief pediatric surgery, 1980—; Contbr. articles to profl. jours. Served as capt. U.S. Army, 1968-70. Fellow ACS, Am. Acad. Pediatrics, Am. Pediatric Surg. Assn., Pacific Assn. Pediatric Surgeons. Roman Catholic. Office: Saguaro Children's Surgery Ltd 1301 E Mcdowell Rd Ste 100 Phoenix AZ 85006-2605

ZERHOUNI, ELIAS ADAM, radiologist, educator; b. Algeria, Apr. 12, 1951; s. Mohamed and Yamna (Raahmouni) Z.; m. Nadia Zerhouni, Oct. 25, 1975; children: Djillali, Yasmin, Adam. MD, U. Algiers, 1975. Diplomate Am. Bd. Radiology. Asst. prof. radiology Ea. Va. Med. Sch., 1981-83, assoc. prof., 1983-85; instr. Johns Hopkins U., Balt., 1978-79, asst. prof., 1979-81, assoc. prof., 1985-92, prof., 1992—, chmn., 1995—; cons. Nat. Cancer Inst., NHLBI, U. Utah Radiology strategic planning, The White House, Washington, 1985-88; centennial lectr. Swedish Royal Acad. Radiology, Stockholm, 1994. Patentee in field. Recipient Lauterbur award for MRI Resonance, 1989, 93, Hounsfield award for CT Resonance, 1991. Mem. Am. Heart Assn. (coun. mem.), Radiological Soc. N. Am., Soc. Thoracic Radiology (founding), Soc. Computed Body Tomography, Soc. Magnetic Resonance in Medicine (bd. trustees), Fleischner Soc. Office: Johns Hopkins U JHOC Rm 4210 601 N Caroline St Baltimore MD 21287-0842

ZERR, DEAN A., family nurse practitioner; b. Quinter, Kans., Aug. 10, 1947; s. Ludwig and Frances (Selensky) Z. BSN, RN, Ft. Hays State U., 1971, MSN, 1995; cert. nurse clinician, Wichita State U., 1974. RN, Kans.; advanced registered nurse practitioner; cert. nursing adminstr. Staff nurse rehab./pediatrics Hadley Regional Med. Ctr., Hays, Kans., 1971-72, charge nurse surg. floor, 1972-73, head nurse surg. floor, nursing supr., 1976-79; adminstr. Phillips County Health Dept., Phillipsburg, Kans., 1974-76, DON Rawlins County Hosp., Atwood, Kans., 1979-81; DON Trego County Lempke Meml. Hosp., WaKeeney, Kans., 1981-83; staff nurse emergency dept. St. Catherine Hosp., Garden City, Kans., 1983-86, charge nurse emergency dept., 1986-87, unit mgr. emergency dept., 1987-91; family nurse practitioner United Meth. Wester Kans. Mex. Am. Mins. Health Clinic, Garden City, 1991-93; asst. prof. grad. studies program Ft. Hays State U., Hays, Kans., 1993—. Founding trustee Kans. Nurses Found. Mem. ANA (cert. nursing adminstr., state del. conv. 1974), Emergency Nurses Assn., Kans. State Nurses Assn. (bd. dirs.), Kans. State Bd. Nursing (v.p. 1990-91, pres. 1991-93, Kans. del. to Nat. Coun. State Bds. Nursing Ann. Conv. 1990, 92), Kans. State Troopers Assn. (assoc.), Kans. Sheriff's Assn. (hon.), Am. Fedn. Law Enforcement Officers (assoc.), Ft. Hays State U. Alumni Assn. (life), Ft. Hays State U. Nursing Alumni Assn. (founding pres.). Home: 1311 Eisenhower Rd Hays KS 67601-2531

ZERZAN, CHARLES JOSEPH, JR., gastroenterologist; b. Portland, Oreg., Dec. 1, 1921; s. Charles Joseph and Margaret Cecelia (Mahony) Z.;

BA, Wilamette U., 1948; MD, Marquette U., 1951; m. Joan Margaret Kathan, Feb. 7, 1948; children: Charles Joseph, Michael, Kathryn, Paul, Joan, Margaret, Terrance, Phillip, Thomas, Rose, Kevin, Gregory. Commd. 2d. lt., U.S. Army, 1940, advanced through grades to capt., 1945, ret., 1946, re-enlisted, 1951, advanced through grades to lt. col., M.C., 1965; intern Madigan Gen. Hosp., Ft. Lewis, Wash., 1951-52; resident in internal medicine Letterman Gen. Hosp., San Francisco, 1953-56, Walter Reed Gen. Hosp., Washington, 1960-61; chief of medicine Rodriquez Army Hosp., 1957-60, U.S. Army Hosp., Fort Gordon, Calif., 1962-65; chief gastroenterology Fitzsimmons Gen. Hosp., Denver, 1965-66; chief profl. services U.S. Army Hosp., Ft. Carson, Colo., 1967-68; dir. continuing med. edn. U. Oreg., Portland, 1968-73; ptnr. Permanente Clinic, Portland, 1973—; assoc. clin. prof. medicine U. Oreg., 1973—; individual practice medicine, specializing in gastroenterology, Portland, 1968-92; staff Northwest Permanente, P.C., dir., 1980-83. Mem. Portland Com. Fgn. Rels., 1986—, bd. dirs., 1994—. Decorated Legion of Merit, Army Commendation medal with oak leaf cluster; Meritorious Alumnus award Oreg. Health Scis. U., 1990. Diplomate Am. Bd. Internal Medicine. Fellow A.C.P.; mem. Am. Gastroenterol. Assn., Oreg. Med. Assn. (del. Clackamas County), Ret. Officers Assn. Republican. Roman Catholic. Home and Office: 6364 SE Mcnary Rd Portland OR 97267-5119

ZETS, JEFFREY MICHAEL, physician; b. Youngstown, Ohio, Apr. 17, 1964; s. Myron Michael and Bernadette (Layshock) Z.; m. Andrea Suzanne Flak, Aug. 24, 1991. MD, Northeastern Ohio U., 1988. Attending physician Mt. Sinai Med. Ctr., Cleve., 1991—. Fellow Am. Coll. Emergency Physicians; mem. AMA, Am. Heart Assn. (affiliate), Ohio State Med. Assn. Republican. Home: 336 Danbury Ln Richmond Heights OH 44143 Office: Mt Sinai Med Ctr 1 Mt Sinai Dr Cleveland OH 44106

ZEVON, SANFORD S., cardiologist, educator; b. Bklyn., Oct. 16, 1932; s. Murray Franklin and Celia (Karlin) Z.; m. Madeline Isaacs, Jan. 17, 1960; children: Paul Rubin, Daniel William, Lawrence Benjamin. BA, U. Ill., 1954; MD, SUNY, Bklyn., 1958. Diplomate Nat. Bd. Med. Examiners, Am. Bd. Internal Medicine; lic. physician N.Y., Calif. Intern Jewish Hsop. Bklyn., 1958-59, resident, 1959-60; resident Mt. Zion Hosp., San Fracisco, 1960-61; resident Montefiore Hosp., Bronx, 1961-62, trainee, 1962-67, adj. attending physician, 1967—; asst. clin. prof. medicine Albert Einstein Coll. Medicine, Bronx, 1981—; attending physician White Plains (N.Y.) Hosp. Med. Ctr., 1972—, chief divsn. cardiology, 1978-95, chief emeritus, mem. med. bd., 1981-84; cons. in field. Contbr. articles to profl. jours. Trustee Westchester Health Care Found., Inc., 1977-81; physicians chmn. United Way White Plains, 1976-78, bd. dirs., 1978-80; bd. dirs. Main St. Theatre, White Plains, 1980-81. Fellow ACP, Am. Coll. Cardiology, Am. Heart Assn. (coun. clin. cardiology), N.Y. Cardiol. Soc.; mem. AMA (physicians Recognition award 1976, 96), Am. Soc. Echocardiography, N.Y. Med. Soc., Westchester County Med. Soc., Westchester Heart Assn. (med. adv. com. 1977-7(0. Office: 33 Davis Ave White Plains NY 10605-1015

ZGOURIDES, GEORGE DEAN, psychology educator; b. Houston, May 21, 1961; s. Ted John and Katherine Louise (Palios) Z. BA, Rice U., 1982, MusM, 1985; MA, Trinity U., San Antonio, 1986; Psychology D, Pacific U., Forest Grove, Oreg., 1989. Lic. clin. psychologist, Tex., Ariz. Resident in psychology Tualatin Valley Mental Health Ctr., Portland, Oreg., 1989-90; instr. Pacific U., 1989-90; asst. prof. U. Portland, 1990—; pastoral resident U. Portland, 1991—. Author: Don't Let Them Psych You Out!, 1993, Human Sexuality, 1996; co-author: Anxiety Disorders, 1991; contbr. articles to profl. jours.; composer 2 orch. poeces (premiers 1985, 89), also numerous classical and liturigal works, 1983—. pastoral resident U. Portland, 1991—; asst. pastor Portsmouth Trinity Luth. Ch., 1996—. Will Rice fellow Rice U., 1982; scholar Am. Hellenic Progressive Assn., 1987. Mem. Coun. Tchrs. Undergrad. Psychology, Am. Assn. Christian Counselors. Office: U Portland Dept Psychology 5000 N Willamette Blvd Portland OR 97203-5743

ZHANG, FA, research chemist; b. Jining, Nei Mong, China, Sept. 4, 1958; came to U.S., 1989; s. Cheng Jian and Feng Ying (Liu) Z.; m. Guang-Mei Li, July 15, 1985; children: Henry, Jerry. BSc, Lanzhou (China) U., 1981, MSc, 1984, PhD, 1987. Lectr. Lanzhou U., 1988; postdoctoral fellow Queensland U., Brisbane, Australia, 1989; sr. rschr. U. Okla., Oklahoma City, 1990-94; rsch. chemist Am. Cyanamid Co., Princeton, N.J., 1995—. Contbr. articles on mechanisms of aging, Parkinson's disease and alcoholism to sci. jours. Rsch. grantee Nat. Lab. Applied Organic Chemistry, Lanzhou, 1987. Mem. Am. Chem. Soc., Chinese Chem. Soc. Office: Am Cyanamid Co PO Box 400 Princeton NJ 08543

ZHANG, YUAN FU, microbiologist; b. Huan Shi, Hubei, People's Republic of China, Mar. 15, 1940; s. You Wen Zhang and Xiu Ying Wu; m. Ji Ya Chen; children: Xiao Young, Yong jin, Fan Zhang. B in Medicine, Wu Han Univ., Hubei, 1964. Asst. prof. Inst. of Epidemiology and Microbiology/ China Acad. for Preventive Medicine, Beijing, 1964-78, assoc. prof., head of rsch. group, 1978—; vis. scholar Ctrs. for Disease Control, Atlanta, 1984-85, Temple U., Phila., 1985-87, Technion-Israel Inst. Tech., 1995-96; vis. scholar dept. genetics and microbiology Vrije U. Brussels, 1996. Author: Sequence Analysis, 1985; inventor in field; research in medical microbiology, molecular microbiology, monoclonal antibody, construction of plasmid, and others. Fellow China Assn. for Microbiologists; mem. China Assn. for Exptl. Animals. Home: 18 Bldg RM 6 23 (A) Qi Li, Zhuang Rd/Fengtai, 100071 Beijing People's Republic of China Office: Inst Epidemiology/Microbiology, PO Box 5 Changping, 102206 Beijing People's Republic of China

ZHAO, JI-YUAN, surgeon, orthopedist; b. Hinghua City, Jiangsu, China, Dec. 6, 1926; m. Liu Qing-Ling, May 4, 1960; 3 children. MD, Nanjing Med. U., 1953. Intern Nanjing People's Drum-Tower Hosp., 1952-53; surgeon Jining People's Hosp., 1954-58; surgeon-in-chief Jinxiang People's Hosp., 1958-83, assoc. prof., 1983-93, prof., 1993—. Contbr. articles to profl. jours. Mem. Jining Surg. Club, Chinese Med. Club. Office: Jining Peoples Hosp, Dept of Surgery, Jinxiang 272200, China

ZHAO, XI, medical researcher; b. Nanjing, China, Nov. 3, 1955; came to U.S., 1986; s. Xiang Ming and Ming Zhen (Ma) Zhao; m. Brien Wilson; 1 child, Steve. BS, Nanjing (China) Normal U., 1983; MS, Chinese Acad. Scis., Shanghai, 1986; PhD, Ohio State U., 1989. V.p. R&D Baekon, Inc., Fremont, Calif., 1989-92; rsch. scientist Stanford (Calif.) Med. Ctr., 1990-94; prof. Chinese Acad. Preventive Medicine, Beijing, 1994—; pres., chief sci. officer InCell, Inc., Santa Clara, Calif., 1991—. Contbr. articles to profl. jours. and books; 3 patents pending. Recipient 2nd prize Chinese Soc. Ultrastructure, 1983, award ICSABER Soc., 1988, 1st prize Bennett Rsch. Soc., 1989, award Katharine McCormick Fund, 1990. Mem. AAAS, Am. Soc. Cell Biology, Am. Soc. Bone and Mineral Rsch., Soc. Chinese Bioscientists in Am., Los Gatos Yacht Club, Los Gatos S & R Club. Office: InCell Inc 2310 Walsh Ave Santa Clara CA 95051

ZHUO, MIN, neurobiology educator; b. Xia Pu, People's Republic of China, Nov. 25, 1964; came to U.S., 1988; s. Zi-Jing and Wan-Ru (Huang) Z.; m. Kelly Bin Wei, Apr. 27, 1993. BS, Chinese Inst. Sci. Tech., 1985; MS, Shanghai Inst. Physiology, 1987; PhD, U. Iowa, 1992. Vis. scientist U. Iowa, 1988-89; postdoctoral fellow Columbia U., N.Y.C., 1992-93; rsch. assoc. Howard Hughes Med. Inst. Columbia U., 1993-95, Stanford U., 1995-96; asst. prof. dept. anesthesiology Washington U., St. Louis, 1996—. Contbr. articles and abstracts to profl. jours. Mem. Soc. for Neurosci., Internat. Assn. for Study of Pain (Travel award 1990), Am. Pain Soc. (Travel awards 1990, 91, 92), AAAS. Office: Washington U Dept Anesthesiology Saint Louis MO 63110-1093

ZICKUHR, CLYDE WILLIAM, health care industry executive; b. Milw., Sept. 5, 1934; s. William and Margaret (Vincent) Z.; m. Lila M. Rauch, Oct. 5, 1957; children—Cathy Ann, Karen, Patricia. B.S. in B.A., Marquette U., 1957; M.B.A., Xavier Coll., 1979. Vice pres. product mgmt. Will Ross, Inc., Milw., 1966-68; pres. Badger Labs., Jackson, Wis., 1968-71; v.p. planning G.D. Searle/Will Ross, Milw., 1971-75, v.p., gen. mgr. Kenwood div., 1975-78, White Knight div., 1978-79; pres. Crocker Fels Co., Cin., 1979-84, 95—; pres. ABCO, 1982-84; pres. Mich. Health Systems, Inc., Ann Arbor, 1984—; mem. merchandise com. Abco Buying Co., Milw., 1982—; bd. dirs. Chi Group, Mich. Health Systems, Inc. (ex-oficio). Editorial adv. bd. Med. Products-Salesmen Trade Jour., Chgo., 1983—. Bd. dirs. Clear Lake Shores, Inc., Manitowish Waters, Wis., 1972—. Office: Michigan Health Systems Inc 1900 Section Rd Cincinnati OH 45237

ZIDE, IRENE LOIS, endocrinologist; b. N.Y.C., July 25, 1950; d. Benjamin and Tina (Burman) Schmulowitz; m. Arnold Zide, Nov. 14, 1973; children: Stephen, Daniel, Julie, Joshua. BA, Bklyn. Coll., 1972; MD, Med. Coll. Pa., 1979. Intern Abington Meml. Hosp., 1979-80; resident in internal medicine Booth Meml. Med. Ctr., 1980-82; fellow in endocrinology Mount Sinai Hosp., Bronx, N.Y., 1983-85; attending endocrinologist Elmhurst Hosp., Queens, N.Y., 1985-88, L.I. Jewish Med. Ctr., 1988—; physician Women's Health Ctr., Bethpage, N.Y., 1986-89; pvt. practice Woodmere, N.Y., 1989—. Fellow Am. Coll. Endocrinologists. Office: 10 Brower Ave Woodmere NY 11598

ZIEGLER, CHRISTINE BERNADETTE, psychology educator, consultant; b. Syracuse, N.Y., Mar. 22, 1951; d. Salvatore and Beverlie (Hopkins) Capozzi; m. Steven Jon Ziegler, Jan. 7,1979;1 child. Justin. Bs, SUNY, Brockport, 1978; MS, Syracuse U., 1980, PhD, 1982. Adj. asst. prof. SUNY, Cortland, N.Y., 1983-86, Syracuse (N.Y.) U., 1984-86, LeMoyne Coll., Syracuse, 1986-87; rsch. cons. Syracuse (N.Y.) U., 1982-86; assoc. prof. Kennesaw (Ga.) State Coll., 1987—; dean continuing edn. East Cobb Mid. Sch.; parent facilitator Ga. Coun. Child Abuse, Atlanta, 1990—; cons. Dissertation Rsch. UGA, Atlanta; cons. aggression reduction tng. N.W. Regional Hosp., Rome, Ga.; presenter numerous profl. confs. in field. Reviewer for Teaching of Psychology Jour., Jour. Undergrad. Rsch.; contbr. articles to profl. jours. Mem. Juvenile Ct. Panel, Health Children's Initiative; mem. sch. adv. com., Marietta, Ga., 1989, mem. sch. bond com., 1989. Recipient fellowship Syracuse U., 1982. Mem. APA, AAAS, NAS, Ga. Psychol. Assn., Southeastern Psychol. Assn., Soc. Philosophy and Psychology, Soc. for Rsch. in Child Devel., Psychology Club (advisor), Blue Key (chpt. v.p.). Home: 1408 Dewberry Trl Marietta GA 30062-4013 Office: Kennesaw State College 3455 Steve Frey Rd Kennesaw GA 30144

ZIEGLER, EKHARD ERICH, pediatrics educator; b. Saalfelden, Austria, Apr. 12, 1940; children: Stefan, Gabriele, Lena. M.D., U. Innsbruck, Austria, 1964. Diplomate: Am. Bd. Pediatrics. Intern U. Innsbruck, 1966-67, resident in pediatrics, 1967-68 70-71, resident in pharmacology, 1964-66, asst. dept. pediatrics, 1970-73; vis. instr. pediatrics U. Iowa, Iowa City, 1968-70, asst. prof. pediatrics, 1973-76, assoc. prof., 1976-81, prof., 1981—; mem. nutrition study sect. NIH, 1988-92. Recipient Nutrition award Am. Acad. Pediactrics, 1988. Mem. Am. Soc. Clin. Nutrition, Soc. Pediatric Research, Soc. Exptl. Biology and Medicine, N.Am. Soc. Pediatric Gastroenterology, Midwest Soc. Pediatric Research, Am. Pediatric Soc., The Nutrition Soc., N.Y. Acad. Scis., Am. Acad. Pediatrics. Club: Univ. Athletic (Iowa City). Office: U Iowa Dept Pediatrics Iowa City IA 52242

ZIEGLER, JANET CASSARO, holistic health nurse; b. Bklyn., Oct. 26, 1946; d. Dominic Michael and Rose (Locascio) Cassaro; m. Paul Dennis Ziegler, Nov. 1, 1970; children: Paul Dennis, Daniel Peter, Michael Tyson. BSN, D'Youville Coll., 1968; M in Nursing, U. Pitts., 1975. Instr. Norfolk (Va.) State Coll., 1970-72; instr. nursing Pa. State U., 1989—; pvt. practice in childbirth edn. Va., 1971-72, Pitts., 1972-81; clin. nurse specialist Vis. Nurse Assn. Allegheny County, Pitts., 1975-83; nurse-healer pvt. practice, Pitts., 1982—; educator, cons. Am. Soc. Psychoprophylaxis in Obstetrics, Pitts., 1971-81; practitioner, educator Clin. Hypnosis, Pitts., 1982—, Biofeedback Inst. Am., Wheat Ridge, Colo., 1983—; practitioner, cons., educator Therapeutic Touch, Pitts., 1981—. Served to lt. USN, 1968-70. Mem. Am. Holistic Nurses Assn., Nurse Healer's Profl. Assocs. (bd. trustees), Biofeedback and Behavioral Medicine Assn. of Western Pa., Assn. Clin. Nurse Specialists, Aloha Internat., People's Med. Soc., Inst. Noetic Scis. Republican. Roman Catholic. Home: 4566 Dogwood Dr Allison Park PA 15101-1135 Office: 5200 Centre Ave Ste 706 Pittsburgh PA 15232-1302

ZIEGLER, WILLIAM FRANCIS, osteopath. BS in Chemistry, Wagner Coll., 1986; DO, U. Osteo. Medicine, 1990. Lab. instr. U. Osteo. Medicine and Health Scis., Des Moines, 1987-88; intern Union (N.J.) Hosp., 1990-91; resident in ob.-gyn. Med. Ctr. Del., Wilmington, 1991-95; fellow in reproductive endrocrinology and infertility U. Vt., Burlington, 1995—. Recipient Pharm. Resident Membership award, 1986, Frank K. Bobbot Meml. award in Chemistry, 1985, Ortho Resident Thesis Writing award, 1995, Zeneca Resident Writing award, 1995. Mem. Am. Chem. Soc. (v.p. Wagner Coll. chpt. 1982-86), Am. Coll. Ob.-Gyn. (vice chmn. jr. fellows dist. III chmn. 1991-93), Del. Med. Soc., Del. Osteo. Med. Soc., Am. Fertility Soc., Sigma Sigma Phi, Tri Beta. Office: 1 S Prospect St Burlington VT 05401

ZIELIŃSKI, JERZY, urologist; b. Ruda, Bucovina, Romania, May 6, 1914; s. Jzydor Rathauser and Nora Maria (Weinreb) Z.;m. Maria Magdalena Grzymalska, Dec. 31, 1940; children: Maria Magdalena, Christine, Eva. Diploma, U. Lwow (Poland), 1937; DSc, U. Wroclaw (Poland), 1949; Habilitation, U. Katowice (Poland), 1962, D honoris causa, 1991. Resident State Hosp., Lwow, 1937-38; resident dept. urology State Hosp., Warsaw, Poland, 1938-39; sr. resident dept. urology Mcpl. Hosp., Lwow, 1939-41; cons. urologist Outpatients Clinic, Lwow, 1941-42; sr. resident Mil. Hosp. Katowice, Clin. Surgery and Urology, Bytom, Zabrze, Katowice, 1945-64; head clinic Clinic Urology, Sch. Medicine, Katowice, 1964-84; cons. urologist outpatients dept. Urol. Clinic, Katowice, 1984—; med. adv. bd. Ministry Health, Warsaw, 1978-82; v.p. Silesian Sch. Medicine, Katowice, 1980-81. Prin. author, editor: Urological Oncology 3d edit., 1986; co-author: Urological Radiology, 1977; editor, co-author (textbook) Urology (3 vols.), 1992, Environmental Dangers and Local Diseases in Upper Silesia, Ethics in Medicine and Science, 1992; contbr. articles on urol. oncology and traumatology to profl. jours. Pres. Silesian Inter-High Sch. Soc., 1988—; v.p. Anti-Cancer Soc., Gliwice, Inst. Oncology, 1985—. Maj., M.C., Polish mil., 1948-56. Recipient Order Polonia Restituta, Ministry Health, 1972, Officer's Cross Order Polonia Restituta, Pres. Polish Rep., 1995, diploma Australian Polcul Found. for merits in devel. of Polish ind. culture, 1992. Fellow European Assn. Urology (mgmt. com. 1982-86), Internat. Assn. Urology; mem. Polish Med. Assn. (pres. 1970-74), Polish Soc. Urology (hon., pres. 1974-78), French Soc. Urology, German Soc. Urology (corr.), Tcheco-Slovakian Sci. Assn. (hon.). Democrat. Roman Catholic. Home: 30 Sklodowska-Curie str Apt 9, 40058 Katowice Poland Office: Silesian Sch Medicine, Cinic Urology, 9 Strzelecka Str, 40073 Katowice Poland

ZIENTY, FERDINAND BENJAMIN, chemical company research executive, consultant; b. Chgo., Mar. 21, 1915; s. Albert Frank and Rose Cecelia (Przypyszny) Z.; BS, U. Ill., 1935; MS, U. Mich., 1936, PhD, 1938; m. Claylain Lorraine Cawiezell, Apr. 14, 1945; children: Jane Zienty Wheeler, Donald Ferd. Research chemist organic chems. div. Monsanto Co., St. Louis, 1938-40, research group leader, 1940-47, asst. dir. research, 1947-50, asso. dir. research, 1950-56, dir. research, 1956-60, dir. advanced organic chems. research, 1960-64, mgr. research and devel., 1964-79, dir. chemistry bio med program, 1979-83, dir. research Health Care div., 1983, cons., 1983—, v.p. research George Lueders & Co. subs. Monsanto Co., St. Louis, 1968-70. Recipient Hodel, Saltiel, Hodel prize for scholarship, 1935, Sesquicentennial award U. Mich., 1967; Disting. Alumnus award U. Mich. Coll. Pharmacy, 1981. Fairchild scholar, 1935, Frederick Stearns fellow, 1936-37. Fellow AAAS, N.Y. Acad. Scis., Acad. Scis. of St. Louis (trustee); mem. Am. Chem. Soc., Am. Inst. Chem. Engrs., Am. Pharm. Assn., Inst. Food Technologists, Mo. Acad. Sci., Soc. Chem. Industry (London). Clubs: Triple A Country, Univ. Club. St. Louis. Contbr. articles to profl. jours. Patentee in field. Home and Office: 850 Rampart Dr Saint Louis MO 63122-1644

ZIERDT, CHARLES HENRY, microbiologist; b. Pitts., Apr. 24, 1922; s. Conrad Henry and Nancy Leora (Harshberger) Z.; m. Margaret May Wise, June 1, 1942 (div. 1962); children—Charles Henry, Jr., Carolyn, Douglas, Richard; m. Willadene Smith, Sept. 30, 1967. B.S., Pa. State U., 1943; M.S., U. Mich., 1945; Ph.D., George Washington U., 1967. Rsch. assoc. Parke-Davis & Co., Detroit, 1945-48; microbiologist Henry Ford Hosp., Detroit, 1948-53, USPHS, Detroit, 1953-56; rsch. microbiologist NIH, Bethesda, Md., 1956—. Scientist sponsor U. Md., 1975—; instr. Found. Advanced Edn. Scis., Bethesda, 1978—. Author: Glucose Nonfermenting Gram Negative Bacteria in Clinical Microbiology, 1978; Non-fermentative Gram Negative Rods: Laboratory Identification and Clinical Aspects, 1985; McGraw-Hill Yearbook of Science and Technology, 1986; Diagnostic Procedures for Bacterial Infections, 1987; contbr. over 100 articles to profl. jours. Patentee in field. Active PTA. Fellow Am. Acad. Microbiology; mem. Am. Soc. Microbiology (chpt. pres. 1976), U.S. Fedn. Culture Collections (membership chmn. 1985), Avanti Owners Assn. Internat., Mensa, Model A Ford Club of Am. (Fairfax, Va. chpt. pres. 1985), Model T Ford Club Internat., Sigma Xi. Republican. Achievements include the classification and pathogenesis of Blastocystis Hominis, an intestinal protozoan parasite of man. Avocations: gardening; antique car restoration, church historian. Home: 4100 Norbeck Rd Rockville MD 20853-1869 Office: NIH Bethesda MD 20816

ZIERLER, KENNETH, physiologist, physician, educator; b. Balt., Sept. 5, 1917; s. Joseph and Betsey (Levie) Z.; m. Margery Shapiro, June 8, 1941; children: Peggy Zierler Rosenthal, Linda Zierler Jucovy, Sally, Amy, Michael K. AB, Johns Hopkins U., 1936, postgrad., 1936-37; MD, U. Md., 1941. Intern medicine Sinai Hosp., Balt., 1941-42; asst. resident, resident NYU div. Goldwater Meml. Hosp., N.Y.C., 1942-43; fellow, prof. medicine Johns Hopkins U. Med. Sch., Balt., 1946-72, prof. physiology, medicine, 1969-72, 73—; assoc. prof. environ. medicine Johns Hopkins Sch. Hygiene and Pub. Health, Balt., 1956-64; asst. physician to physician Johns Hopkins Hosp., Balt., 1946-72, physician-in-charge dept. phys. therapy, 1950-57, chemist-in-charge, 1957-68, physician, 1973—; dir. Inst. for Muscle Disease, N.Y.C., 1972-73; adj. prof. Rockefeller U., N.Y., 1972-73, Cornell Med. Sch., N.Y., 1972-73; mem. adv. com. on physiology, Office of Naval Rsch., Am. Inst. Biol. Scis., 1964-76, chmn., 1964-72; mem. panel of space biology and medicine Pres.'s Sci. Adv. Com., 1967; cons. task group on tracer kinetics Internat. Commn. on Radiol. Units and Measurements, 1966; mem. cardiovascular B study sect. NIH, 1972-76; co-chmn. rating com. rev. of doctoral programs in biol. scis. N.Y. State Commr. Edn., 1983—. Contbr. 239 sci. papers to profl. jours.; mem. editl. bd. Johns Hopkins Hosp. bull., 1956-67, Johns Hopkins Med. Jour., 1967-70, Jour. Clin. Investigations, 1959-64; mem. editorial bd. Circulation Rsch., 1962-67, co-editor, 1966, substitute editor, 1968, assoc. editor, 1968-77; mem. editorial com. Ann. Rev. Physiology, 1971-75; assoc. editor Medicine, 1963-72. Capt. med. corps U.S. Army, 1943-46, ETO, MTO. Decorated Bronze Star; Career scholar Muscular Dystrophy Assn., 1973-91. Mem. Am. Soc. for Clin. Investigations, Assn. Am. Physicians, Endocrine Soc., Am. Diabetes Assn. Office: Johns Hopkins Med Sch Blalock Bldg Rm 904 600 N Wolfe St Baltimore MD 21287-4904

ZIFERSTEIN, ISIDORE, psychoanalyst, educator, consultant; b. Klinkowitz, Bessarabia, Russia, Aug. 10, 1909; came to U.S., 1920; s. Samuel David and Anna (Russler) Z.; m. Barbara Shapiro, June 21, 1935; children: D. Gail, J. Dan. BA, Columbia U., 1931, MD, 1935; PhD, So. Calif. Psychoanalytic Inst, 1977. Intern Jewish Hosp. of Bklyn., N.Y., 1935-37; staff psychiatrist Mt. Pleasant (Iowa) State Hosp., 1937-41; chief resident psychiatrist Psychiat. Inst. of Grasslands Hosp. of Westchester County, Valhalla, N.Y., 1941-44; pvt. practice, psychoanalysis and psychiatry N.Y.C., 1944-47, L.A., 1947—; mem. faculty So. Calif. Psychoanalytic Inst., L.A., 1951-70, mem. bd. trustees, 1953-57, mem. edn. com., 1953-57; cons. L.A. (Calif.) Psychiat. Svcs., 1954-63; researcher The Psychiat. & Psychosomatic Rsch. Inst., Mt. Sinai Hosp., L.A., 1955-65; assoc. clin. prof. of psychiatry Univ. So. Calif., L.A., 1960-64, Univ. Calif., L.A., 1970-77; rsch. cons. Postgrad. Ctr. for Mental Health, N.Y.C., 1962-75; attending staff dept. psychiatry Cedars-Sinai Med. Ctr., L.A., 1975—; psychiat. cons. Iowa State Penitentiary, Ft. Madison; lectr. on transcultural psychiatry, group psychotherapy and group dynamics UCLA, U. Calif., Berkeley, USC, U. Wash., Willamette Coll., Eugene, Oreg., U. Oreg., U. B.C., U. Md., U. Wis., U. Judaism, U. Mex., Wayne State U., U. Pitts., Chgo. Med. Coll., Ctr. for Study of Democratic Instns., U. Leningrad, Bekhterev Psychoneurol. Rsch. Inst., Leningrad, BBC, San Francisco State Coll., others. Contbr. over 65 articles to Am. Jour. Psychiatry, Am. Jour. Orthopsychiatry, Internat. Jour. Group Psychotherapy, Praxis Der Kinderpsychologie Und Kinderpsychiatrie, and others. Bd. dirs. Viewer-Sponsored TV Found., L.A., 1960, Nat. Assn. for Better Broadcasting, L.A., 1962-75, ACLU So. Calif. chpt., L.A., 1962-77; pres. Peace Edn. Coun., Pasadena, Calif., 1960; del. to state conv. Calif. Dem. Coun., Sacramento, 1960; mem. del. to Soviet Union, Promoting Enduring Peace, New Haven, 1959; participant Conf. of Scientists for Peace, Oslo, Norway, 1962; del. to "Pacem in Terris" Convocation, SANE, N.Y.C., 1963, mem. nat. bd., 1970-74, and many others. Recipient Pulitzer scholarship award Pulitzer Found., N.Y.C., 1927, Green Prize for Outstanding scholarship Columbia Coll., N.Y.C., 1930, Peace award Women for Legis. Action, L.A., 1962, grant for rsch. in transcultural psychiatry Founds. Fund for Rsch. in Psychiatry, New Haven, 1963, grant for continuing rsch. in transcultural psychiatry NIMH, Bethesda, Md., 1969, Pawlowski Peace Prize, Pawlowski Peace Found., Inc., Wakefield, Mass., 1974. Fellow Am. Psychiat. Assn. (life, fellowship medal 1970), AAAS (life); mem. AMA (life), Am. Psychoanalytic Assn. (life, cert. in psychoanalysis by bd. profl. standards), Internat. Psychoanalytical Assn., World Fedn. for Mental Health, Westside Jewish Culture Club (lectr.), Physicians for Social Responsibility, Sierra Club, Nat. Wildlife Fedn., Environ. Def. Fund, Common Cause, MADD, Phi Beta Kappa. Democrat. Jewish. Office: 3150 E Tropicana Ave # C351 Las Vegas NV 89121-7315

ZIFF, JOEL DAVID, psychologist; b. Mpls., June 19, 1947; s. Samuel J. and Helen (Geffen) Z.; m. Elizabeth Rosenzweig, Jan. 1, 1992. BA, Columbia U., 1969; MAT, Harvard U., 1971; EdD, U. Mass., 1979. Lic. psychologist, Mass. Pvt. practice Newton, Mass., 1975—; faculty Mass. Sch. Profl. Psychology, Dedham, Mass., 1987-88; adj. faculty Lesley Coll., Cambridge, Mass., 1986—. Author: The Classroom Meeting: An Alternative Approach to Management and Discipline, 1979, Everyone's Picking On Me!, 1978, Mirrors in Time: A Psycho-Spiritual Journey Through the Jewish year; contbr. articles to profl. jours. Mem. APA, Mass. Psychol. Assn., Internat. Transactional Analysis Assn., Am. Soc. for Clin. Hypnosis, Soc. for Clin. And Exptl. Hypnosis.

ZIFF, MORRIS, internist, rheumatologist, educator; b. N.Y.C., Nov. 19, 1913; s. Benjamin and Ethel (Seldowitz) Z.; m. Jacqueline Mae Miller, Dec. 10, 1978; children: Edward B., David R. BS, NYU, 1934, PhD, 1937, MD, 1948. Intern Bellevue Hosp., N.Y.C., 1948-49, resident in internal medicine, 1949-50, attending physician, 1950-58; asst. prof. medicine NYU, 1954-57, assoc. prof., 1957-58; Ashbel Smith prof. internal medicine U. Tex. Health Sci. Ctr., Dallas, 1958-84, Ashbel prof. emertus internal medicine, 1984—, Morris Ziff prof. rheumatology, 1982—; dir. Harold C. Simmons Arthritis Rsch. Ctr., Dallas, 1983-84; attending physician Parkland Meml. Hosp., Dallas, 1958—; mem. med. staff Zale-Lipshy Univ. Hosp., Dallas, 1989—; cons. Dallas VA Hosp., Brooke Army Hosp., 1964-75, William Beaumont Army Hosp., 1965-76. Contbr. over 250 articles to sci. jours., chpts. to books. Recipient Heberden medal Heberden Soc. London, 1964, Rsch. Career award USPHS, 1962-84, Marchman award Dallas So. Med. Soc., 1968, Disting. Svc. award Arthritis Found., 1968, Disting. Alumni Sci. award NYU, 1966, Carol Nachman prize in rheumatology, 1974, World Internat. Conf. on Inflammation prize, 1986. Fellow ACP; mem. Assn. Am. Physicians, Am. Soc. Clin. Investigation, Am. Assn. Immunologists, Am. Coll. Rheumatology (master, Bunim medal 1982, Gold medal 1988), N.Y. Acad. Medicine (Klemperer medal 1991), Harvey Soc., Phi Beta Kappa, Sigma Xi, Alpha Omega Alpha. Home: 11116 Pinocchio Dr Dallas TX 75229-4031 Office: U Tex Health Sci Ctr Health Sci Ctr 5323 Harry Hines Blvd Dallas TX 75235-9030

ZIFF, ROBERT ALAN, obstetrician, gynecologist; b. N.Y.C., Oct. 8, 1952; s. Paul and Iera A. (Ginsbourg) Z.; m. Susan Marion Fox, Oct. 22, 1978. BA, SUNY, Albany, 1973; MD, Rutgers U., 1978. Diplomate Nat. Bd. Med. Examiners. Intern in ob-gyn Lenox Hill Hosp., N.Y.C., 1978-79, resident in ob-gyn, 1979-82; pvt. practice specializing in ob-gyn N.Y.C., 1982-84, Marion, S.C., 1984; coord. med. edn. in ob-gyn Lenox Hill Hosp., N.Y.C., 1982-84; clin. Inst. N.Y. Med. Coll., N.Y.C., 1982-84; mem. utilization rev. com. English Park Med. Ctr., Marion, 1985-88, chief staff, 1987-88; mem. peer svcs. rev. bd. S.C. Peer Rev. Orgn., Inc., 1986-89, Carolina Med. Rev., 1989—. Contbr. articles to profl. jours. Fellow Royal Soc. Medicine, Am. Coll. Ob-Gyns., Am. Coll. Surgeons; mem. Am. Med. Soc., Am. Soc. Colposcopy and Cervical Pathology, S.C. Med. Soc., Hugh R.K. Barber Alumni Assn., Soc. Gynecologic Laparoscopists. Home: 325 Carolina Rd Loris SC 29569-5335 Office: PO Box 67 Loris SC 29569-0067 Office: 800 25th Ave S North Myrtle Beach SC 29582-4358

ZIGLER, EDWARD FRANK, psychologist, educator; b. Kansas City, Mo., Mar. 1, 1930; s. Louis and Gertrude (Gleitman) Z.; m. Bernice Gorelick,

Aug. 28, 1955; 1 child, Scott. BA, U. Mo.-Kansas City, 1954; PhD, U. Tex., 1958; MA (hon.), Yale, 1967; DSc (hon.), Boston Coll., 1985; LHD (hon.), Bank St. Coll. Edn., 1989, U. New Haven, 1991, St. Joseph Coll., 1991; PhD (hon.), U. Mo., 1993, CUNY, 1995; Hon. degree, CUNY, 1995; LLD (hon.), Gonzaga U., 1995. Psychol. intern Worcester (Mass.) State Hosp., 1957-59; asst. prof. psychology U. Mo., 1958-59; mem. faculty Yale U., 1959—, prof. psychology and child study center, 1967—, Sterling prof., 1976—, dir. child devel. program, 1961-76, chmn. dept. psychology, 1973-74; head psychology sect. Yale Child Study Center, 1967—; dir. Bush Center in Child Devel. and Social Policy, 1977—; chief Children's Bur. NEW, Washington, 1970-72; cons. in field, 1962—; mem. nat. steering com. Project Head Start, 1965-70, chmn. 15th anniversary Head Start com., 1980; mem. nat. adv. com. Nat. Lab. Early Childhood Edn., 1967-70; nat. rsch. adv. bd. Nat. Assn. Retarded Children, 1968-73; nat. rsch. coun. Project Follow-Through, 1968-70; chmn. adv. com. Vietnamese Children's Resettlement, 1975; mem. Pres.'s Com. on Mental Retardation, 1980; joint appointee Yale U. Sch. Medicine, 1982—, chmn. Yale Infant Care Leave Commn., 1983-85, Parents as Tchrs., 1986—; mem. adv. com. Head Start Quality and Expansion, 1993; mem. adv. com. on svcs. for families with infants and toddlers HHS, 1994. Author, co-author, editor books and monographs; contbr. articles to profl. jours. Served with AUS, 1951-53. Recipient Gunnar Dybwad Disting. scholar in behavioral and social sci. award Nat. Assn. Retarded Children, 1964, 69, Social Sci. Aux. award, 1962, Alumni Achievement award U. Mo., 1965, Alumnus of Yr. award, 1972, C. Anderson Aldrich award Am. Acad. Pediatrics, 1985, Nat. Achievement award Assn. for Advancement of Psychology, 1985, Dorothea Lynde Dix Humanitarian award for svc. to handicapped Elwyn Inst., 1987, Sci. Leadership award Joseph P. Kennedy Jr. Found., 1990, Mensa Edn. and Rsch. Found. award for excellence, 1990, Nat. Head Start Assn. award, 1990 Founders award, 1995, Bldg. dedication Edward Zigler Head Start Ctr., 1990, As They Grow award in edn. Parents mag., 1990, Excellence in Edn. award Pi Lambda Theta, 1991, Friend of Edn. award Conn. Edn. Assn., 1991, Loyola-Mellon Social Sci. award 1991, Pres.'s award Conn. Assn. Human Svcs., 1991, Harold W. McGraw, Jr. prize in edn., 1992, Disting. Achievement in Rsch. award Internat. Assn. Sci. Study of Mental Deficiency, 1992, Disting. Svc. award Coun. Chief State Sch. Officers, 1993, Outstanding Fed. Leadership in Support of Head Start Rsch., Adminstrn. on Children, Youth and Families, 1993, Child and Family Advocacy award Parents as Tchrs. Nat. Ctr., 1994, Distinction award U. Pa. Edn. Alumni Assn., 1994; named Hon. Commr. Internat. Yr. of Child, 1979. Fellow Am. Orthopsychiat. Assn. (Blanche F. Ittleson award 1989, pres. 1993-94), Am. Psychol. Assn. 9pres. div. 7 1974-75, G. Stanley Hall award 1979, award for disting. contbns. to psychology in pub. interest 1982, Nicholas Hobbs award 1985, award for disting. profl. contbns. to knowledge 1986, Edgar A. Doll award 1986, award for disting. contbn. to cmty. psychology and cmty. mental health 1989); mem. Inst. Medicine of NAS, AAAS, Am. Acad. Mental Retardation (career rsch. award 1982), Soc. Psychol. Study Social Issues (Kurt Lewin Meml. award 1995), Zero to Three (Dolley Madison award 1995), P.R. Head Start Assn. (outstanding leadership award 1995). Home: 177 Ridgewood Ave North Haven CT 06473-4442 Office: Yale U Dept Psychology PO Box 208205 2 Hillhouse Ave New Haven CT 06520-8205

ZIL, JOHN STEPHEN, psychiatrist, physiologist; b. Chgo., Oct. 8, 1947; s. Stephen Vincent and Marilyn Charlotte (Jackson) Zilius; 1 child, Charlene-Elena. BS magna cum laude, U. Redlands, 1969; MD, U. Calif., San Diego, 1973; MPH, Yale U., 1977; JD with honors, Jefferson Coll., 1985. Intern, resident in psychiatry and neurology U. Ariz., 1973-75; fellow in psychiatry, advanced fellow in social and community psychiatry, Yale community cons. to Conn. State Dept. Corrections, Yale U., 1975-77, instr. psychiatry and physiology, 1976-77; instr. physiology U. Mass., 1976-77; acting unit chief Inpatient and Day Hosp. Conn. Mental Health Ctr., Yale-New Haven Hosp. Inc., 1975-76, unit chief, 1976-77; asst. prof. psychiatry U. Calif., San Francisco, 1977-82, assoc. prof. psychiatry and medicine, 1982-86, vice-chmn. dept. psychiatry, 1983-86; adj. prof. Calif. State U., 1985-87; assoc. prof. bioengring. U. Calif., Berkely and San Francisco, 1982-92, clin. faculty, Davis, 1991—; chief psychiatry and neurology VA Med. Ctr., Fresno, Calif., 1977-86, prin. investigator Sleep Rsch. & Physiology Lab., 1980-86; dir. dept. psychiatry and neurology U. Calif.-San Francisco, Fresno-Cen. San Joaquin Valley Med. Edn. Program and Affiliated Hosps. and Clinics, 1983-86; chief psychiatrist State of Calif. Dept. Corrections cen. office, 1986—; chmn. State of Calif. Inter-Agy. Tech. Adv. com. on Mentally Ill Inmates & Parolees, 1986-92; mem. med. adv. com. Calif. State Personnel Bd., 1986—; appointed councillor Calif. State Mental Health Plan, 1988-93; cons. Nat. Inst. Corrections, 1992—; invited faculty contbr. and editor Am. Coll. Psychiatrist's Resident in Tng. Exam., 1981—. Author: The Case of the Sleepwalking Rapist, 1992, Mentally Disordered Criminal Offenders, 5 vols., 1989, reprinted, 1991; contbg. author: The Measurement Mandate: On the Road to Performance Improvement in Health Care, 1993; assoc. editor Corrective and Social Psychiatry Jour., 1978—, referee, 1980—, reviewer, 1981—; contbr. articles in field to profl. jours. Nat. Merit scholar, 1965; recipient Nat. Recognition award Bank of Am., 1965, Julian Lee Roberts award U. Redlands, 1969, Kendall award Internat. Symposium in Biochemistry Research, 1970, Campus-Wide Profl. Achievement award U. Calif., 1992, Career Achievement award U. Redlands, 1994. Fellow Royal Soc. Health, Am. Assn. Social Psychiatry; mem. Am. Assn. Mental Health Profls. in Corrections (nat. pres. 1978—), Calif. Scholarship Fedn. (past pres.), AAUP, Am. Psychiat. Assn., Nat. Council on Crime and Delinquency, Am. Pub. Health Assn., Delta Alpha, Alpha Epsilon Delta. Office: PO Box 163359 Sacramento CA 95816-9359

ZILVETI, CARLOS BENJAMIN, preventive medicine physician, pediatrician; b. Sucre, Bolivia, June 14, 1928; came to U.S., 1956; s. Carlos and Marina (De La Reza) Z.; m. Halina J. Daszewski, Sept. 8, 1957 (div. Sept. 1976); 1 child: Carlos Joseph III; m. Vita Palazzolo, Sept. 5, 1987. BS, Sacred Heart Coll., Sucre, Bolivia, 1946; MD, U. San Francisco Xavier, Sucre, Bolivia, 1954; MPH, Yale U., 1966. Physician in rural medicine Bolivian Power Co., La Paz, 1955; intern in pediats. and gen. medicine Hosp. Obrero V.P.E., La Paz, 1956; asst. resident in pediats. St. Luke's Hosp., Meml. Cancer Ctr., Woman's Hosp., N.Y.C., 1957-58, Hosp. of St. Raphael, New Haven, Conn., 1958-59; pvt. practice New Haven, Conn., 1960-63; dir. maternal-child health New Haven Dept. Health, 1964-74; regional med. officer South and Ctrl. Am. Peace Corps, Bogota, Colombia, 1975-76; regional med. officer West Africa Peace Corps, Liberia, Ghana, Togo, 1976-79; chief environ. medicine Wilford Hall Med. Ctr. USAF, San Antonio, 1979-83, cons. preventive and occupl. medicine, 1983-91; ret. USAF, 1991, cons. aerospace-preventive medicine; cons. FDA, HEW, Washington, 1966-75; cons. to Headstart Am. Acad. Pediats., Stanford-Norwalk, Conn., 1968-75; regional med. officer, sci. attache West Africa U.S. Dept. State. Contbr. articles to profl. jours. Chmn. gov.'s task force Conn. State Dept. HEalth, Hartford, 1969-75. Fellow Am. Acad. Pediats. (emeritus), Am. Coll. Preventive Medicine; mem. APHA, AMA, New Eng. Pub. Health Assn., Conn. Acad. Preventive Medicine, Am. Occupl. Med. Assn. Home: 9222 Dover Ridge San Antonio TX 78250-3557

ZIMBARDO, PHILIP GEORGE, psychologist, educator, writer; b. N.Y.C., Mar. 23, 1933; s. George and Margaret (Bisicchia) Z.; m. Christina Maslach, Aug. 10, 1972; children: Zara, Tanya; 1 son by previous marriage, Adam. AB, Bklyn. Coll., 1954; MS, Yale U., 1955, PhD, 1959. Asst. prof. psychology Yale U., New Haven, 1959-61, NYU, N.Y.C., 1961-67; vis. assoc. prof. psychology Columbia U., N.Y.C., 1967-68; prof. psychology Stanford (Calif.) U., 1968—; pres. P.G. Zimbardo, Inc., San Francisco. Author: Cognitive Control of Motivation, 1969, Canvassing or Peace, 1970, Psychology and You, 1976, Shyness, What It Is, What To Do About It, 1977, Influencing Attitudes and Changing Behavior, rev. edit., 1977, The Shyness Workbook, 1979, A Parent's Guide to the Shy Child, 1981, The Psychology of Attitude Change and Social Influence, 1991, Psychology and Life, rev. edit., 1996. Pres. Montclair Ter. Assn., 1975—; sr. project advisor Exploratorium, 1993; host, writer, gen. acad. advisor PBS-TV series Discovering Psychology, 1987-90. Ctr. for Advanced Study of Behavioral Scis. fellow, 1971; recipient Peace medal Tokyo Police Dept., 1972, City Medal of Honor, Salamanca, Spain, Disting. Tchr. award Am. Psychol. Found., 1975. Mem. APA (Presdl. citation Discovery Psychology series 1994), AAAS, AAUP, Internat. Congress Psychology, Western Psychol. Assn. (pres. 1983), Ea. Psychol. Assn., Calif. Psychol. Assn. (Disting. Contbn. to Rsch. award 1978), Can. Psyuchol. Assn., Soc. for Psychol. Study of Social Issues, Soc. for Clin. and Exptl. Hypnosis, Sigma Xi, Phi Beta Kappa, Psi Chi. Roman Catholic. Home: 25 Montclair Ter San Francisco CA 94109-1517 Office: Stanford U Psychology Dept Stanford CA 94305

ZIMENT, IRWIN, medical educator; b. England, 1936. MB BChir, Cambridge U., 1961. Intern, resident England, 1961-64, USA, 1964-65; resident Bronx Mcpl. Hosp. Ctr., 1965-66; dir. respiratory therpay Harbor Gen. Hosp., Torrance, Calif., 1968-75; chief medicine Olive View-UCLA Med. Ctr., 1975—, med. dir., 1994—; prof. medicine UCLA Sch. Medicine, 1980—. Contbr. articles to profl. jours. Infectious Disease fellow Wadsworth VA Hosp., L.A., 1966-68. Mem. Am. Thoracic Soc. (din. problems assembly chmn. 1981-82 , resp. bd. med. advisors 1986-90), Am. Coll. Chest Physicians (mem. editl. bd.), Nat. Assn. Med. Dir. Respiratory Care (founding mem., vice pres. 1978, treas. 1979-81, bd. dirs. 1983-89), Calif Thoracic Soc. (pres. 1980-81, various coms. 1970-85), L.A. Lung Assn. (various coms. 1969-86). Office: Olive View-UCLA Med Ctr Med Adminstrn Rm 2C138 14445 Olive View Dr Sylmar CA 91342-1495

ZIMET, LLOYD, health planner, educator; b. Bklyn., Oct. 5, 1951; s. Victor R. and Marcia (Sorkin) Z. BA, Whittier (Calif.) Coll., 1973; MA, U. Md., 1983, PhD, 1984; MPH, NYU, 1989. Head basketball coach Aarhus (Denmark) U., 1973-78, 80-82, 85-86; resident dir. U. Md., College Park, 1978-80; sports supr. Montgomery County (Md.) Dept. of Recreation, 1978, 82-84; dir. health promotion Optimal Fitness Inc., N.Y.C., 1986-91; cons. cmty. and occupational health, 1991—; dir. edn. AIDS Ctr. of Queens (N.Y.) County, 1989-90; dir. Patricia Manning Meml. Fund childhood cancer Am. Cancer Soc., Queens, 1988-95; mem. AIDS adv. com. N.Y.C. Bd. of Edn., 1989-90; mem. adv. bd. Adolescent Health Network, Queens, 1989-90. Bd. govs. U.S. Amateur Boxing Fedn., Colorado Springs, Colo., 1988-91; bd. dirs. Met. Amateur Boxing Fedn., N.Y.C., 1988-91. Fellow Soc. Pub. Health Educators; mem. APHA, APA.

ZIMMER, ALF CONRAD, psychology educator; b. Bevensen, Lower Saxony, Fed. Republic of Germany, Nov. 2, 1943; s. Adolf and Margarete (Kleybolte) Z.; m. Margot Schürings, Dec. 16, 1970 (div. July 1980); m. Katharina Dahmen, Oct. 14, 1988; m. Sebastian, Fabian. Diploma in Psychology, Westf. Wilhelms U., Münster, Fed. Republic of Germany, 1971, PhD, 1973, PhD habilitation, 1982. Rsch. asst. Eberhard Karls U., Tübingen, Fed. Republic of Germany, 1971-73; asst. prof Bayrische Landesuniv., Regensburg, Fed. Republic of Germany, 1973-76; assoc. prof. Ossietzky U., Oldenburg, Fed. Republic of Germany, 1976-80; visiting scholar Stanford U., Calif., 1980-83; assoc. prof. Westfälische Wilhelms U., Münster, 1980-84; full prof. Bayrische Landesuniv., Regensburg, 1984—; v.p. U. Regensburg, 1992—; mem. Acad. Senate of Univ., Regensburg, 1974-76, 90-94; chmn. dept. psychology, Münster, 1982-83, dept. philosophy II, Regensburg, 1988-90; chmn. Dept. Psychology, Regensburg, 1984-88. Author: Multivariate Statistics, 1979, Criteria of Traffic Safety, 1996; editor: Wolfgang Köhler Centennial, 1988, Qualitative Aspects of Decision Making, 1996; contbr. articles to profl. jours. Recipient Univ. medal Trieste U. dept. physics, 1990, Univ. medal U. Odessa, 1992. Fellow Gestalt Theory and Application (governing bd. 1982-86, mng. editor 1984-91); mem. Am. Psychol. Soc., Dt. Gesellschaft Psychology (Early Career award 1975), N.Y. Acad. Scis., Psychonomic Soc. Home: Müllerstr 4, 93059 Regensburg Germany Office: Bayrische Landesuniv, Psychology Dept Univ, 93040 Regensburg Germany

ZIMMER, DANIEL R., physician assistant; b. Appleton, Wis., Jan. 26, 1947; s. Jacob and Edith Mary (Schwalen) Z.; m. Irene Stanley, July 7, 1977. BA, U. Wis., Oshkosh, 1969. Cert. physician asst. Physician asst. Alyeska Pipeline Svc. Co., Fairbanks, Alaska, 1974-77, Cmty. Emergency Svcs., Appleton, 1977-79, Thousand Oaks (Calif.) Med. Group, 1980-88, Kaiser Permanente, Woodland Hills, Calif., 1988—; tchr. Emporer's Acupuncture Coll., Santa Monica, Calif., 1987-88. Served with U.S. Army, 1969-71, Vietnam. Recipient Acad. Excellence award Marshfield (Wis.) Clinic Physician Asst. Program, 1974. Fellow Am. Acad. Physician Assts. Office: Kaiser Permanente 5601 DeSoto Ave Woodland Hills CA 91367

ZIMMER, PHYLLIS ARN, nursing educator; b. Syracuse, N.Y.; m. Hal Zimmer, Aug. 5, 1972. BSN, U. Rochester, 1972, Cert. Med. Nurse Practitioner, 1974; MN, U. Wash., 1982. Cert. family nurse practitioner. Nurse practitioner Jordan Health Ctr., Rochester. N.Y., 1972-76, Jewish Hosp. St. Louis, 1976-78, Warren County Family Planning Clinic, Warrenton, Mo., 1978-80; faculty sch. nursing U. Wash., Seattle, 1983—; coord. family nurse practitioner master's program U. Wash., 1994—; pvt. practice nurse practitioner Seattle, 1985-93; ptnr. FnP Assocs., 1993—; cons. Agy. for Health Care Policy and Rsch., 1994, Nat. Health Svc. Corps. 1994. Contbr. articles to profl. jours. Mem. AWHONN, ANA, Nat. Orgn. Nurse Practitioner Faculties (chair edn. com. 1989-90, bd. dirs. 1990—, v.p. 1991-92, pres. 1992-93), Am. Coll. Nurse Practitioners (pres. 1995—), Wash. Nurses Assn. Advanced RN Practitioners United, Sigma Theta Tau. Home: 2647 134th Ave NE Bellevue WA 98005-1813

ZIMMERMAN, BARRY JOSEPH, educational psychology educator, researcher; b. Sheboygan, Wis., Nov. 23, 1942; s. Victor J. and Ida M. (Dekeyser) Z.; m. Diana J. Conley, Aug. 6, 1966; children: Kristin L., Shana M. BA, U. Ariz., 1965, PhD, 1969; MA, N.Mex. State U., 1966. Lic. psychologist, Ariz. Asst. prof. U. Ariz., Tucson, 1970-72, assoc. prof., 1972-74; assoc. prof. grad. sch. CUNY, 1974-78, prof. grad. sch., 1978-96, disting. prof., 1996—; head human learning Devel. and Instrn. Area; vis. scholar Stanford (Calif.) U., 1991; co-investigator Columbia Coll. Physicians and Surgeons, N.Y.C., 1987—. Co-author: Social Learning and Cognition, 1978; co-editor: Functions of Language and Cognition, 1979, Self-Regulated Learning and Academic Achievement, 1989, Self-Regulation of Learning and Performance, 1994; mem. editl. bd. Devel. Rev., 1980—, Merrill-Palmer Quar., 1979-80, Contemporary Ednl. Psychology, 1975-90, 95—, Jour. Applied Devel. Psychology, 1983-90, Am. Ednl. Rsch. Jour., 1992—, Jour. Ednl. Psychology, 1993—; editor jour. issue Self-Regulated Learning, 1990. Bd. dirs. Am. Lung Assn., 1988-90, coun. mem., 1991-93, chmn. sch. health com., 1988-92, rsch. coord. com., 1989-91. Rsch. Support grantee Nat. Inst. Heart, Lung and Blood, 1987—. Fellow APA (divsn. 7, 15, 16, pres.-elect divsn. 15 1995—), Am. Psychol. Soc.; mem. AAUP, Am. Ednl. Rsch. Assn. (asst. chmn. divsn. C 1991-92), Am. Thoracic Soc. (chmn. behavioral sci. assembly 1991-93), Soc. for Rsch. in Child Devel., Leonia Tennis Club. Office: CUNY Grad Sch 33 W 42nd St New York NY 10036-8003

ZIMMERMAN, BETH ANN, nurse, quality management coordinator; b. Ft. Monroe, Va., Oct. 13, 1962; d. Robert Lee and Judy Ann (Hughes) Nesselroad; m. George Chadwick Zimmerman, Nov. 12, 1994. Diploma, Jewish Hosp. Sch. Nursing, Cin., 1984; cert., Zavier U., Cin., 1991; student, Mt. St. Joseph Coll., Cin., 1996—. RN, Ohio; cert. facilitator tng., profl. healthcare quality, ambulatory perianesthesia. Staff nurse, coord. quality mgmt. Mercy Ambulatory Ctr., Fairfield, Ohio, 1984—; presenter confs. in field. Mem. editl. rev. bd. Jour. Healthcare Quality, 1995-96. Mem. Nat. Assn. Healthcare Quality, Ohio Assn. Healthcare Quality, Southwestern Ohio Assn. Healthcare Quality (past pres.). Office: Mercy Ambulatory Surgery Ctr 2990 Mack Rd Fairfield OH 45014

ZIMMERMAN, DAVID RADOFF, journalist, author; b. Chgo., Aug. 10, 1934; s. Leo M. and Sarah (Radoff) Z.; m. Veva Jeanne Hampton, Oct. 12, 1966; children: Jacob Ben, Tobias Eli. Student, U. Chgo., 1950-52; A.B. cum laude, Brandeis U., 1955; postgrad., U. Paris, 1955. Editor Hyde Park Herald, Chgo., 1954; copy boy New York Daily News, 1956-57; editorial asst. New York Post, 1957-61; freelance editor, 1961-62; editor New York Acad. Medicine, 1962-63; sr. writer Med. World News, 1963-69; med. columnist Ladies Home Jour., 1967-80; freelance author, 1969—; sci. reporter Newsday, 1985-86; pres. David Zimmerman, Inc.; pub. Probe Newsletter; tchr. mag. writing CCNY, 1972-73; adj. in sci. writing Columbia U. Grad. Sch. Journalism, 1983-95; instr. New Sch. Social Rsch., 1994—. Author: Rh, The Intimate History of a Disease and Its Conquest, 1973, To Save a Bird in Peril, 1975 (Christopher award 1976), The Essential Guide to Nonprescription Drugs, 1983, Zimmerman's Complete Guide to Nonprescription Drugs, 1992. World Wildlife Fund rsch. grantee, 1974, Fund for Investigative Journalism grantee, 1978, Coun. for Advancement of Sci. Writing grantee, 1980-81; Knight fellow in specialized journalism, 1991, journalist fellow Maine Biol. Labs., 1994, U. Va. Ethics in Genetics fellow, 1995-96. Mem. Am. Soc. Journalists and Authors (pres. 1972-74), Nat. Assn. Sci. Writers (exec. com. 1977-82, treas. 1982). Address: 139 W 13th St # 6 New York NY 10011-7856

ZIMMERMAN, DELANO ELMER, physician; b. Fond du Lac, Wis., Mar. 21, 1933; s. Elmer Herbert and Agatha Angeline (Freund) Z.; m. Nancy Margaret Garry, Aug. 13, 1966; children: Kate Zimmerman Lennard, Joseph, Nick. BS, U. Wis., 1961, MD, 1965. Diplomate Am. Soc. Profl. Disability Cons. Intern, Hennepin County Hosp., Mpls., 1965,; physician, surgeon Winnebago (Wis.) State Hosp., 1966-67; gen. practice medicine, Neenah, Wis., 1967-73; emergency room physician Community Emergency Svcs. , Appleton, 1973-77, Meml. Med. Center, Springfield, Ill., 1977-92; faculty So. Ill. U. Sch. Medicine, Springfield, 1977—; past bd. dirs. nominating com. Sangamon Valley chpt. ARC. With USN, 1951-56. Mem. Am. Coll. Emergency Physicians, Ill. Coll. Emergency Physicians (bd. dirs., awards com., fin. com., mem.-at-large, govt. affairs com.), Soc. for Acad. Emergency Medicine. Roman Catholic. Home: The Cottage 1467 Cowling Bay Rd Neenah WI 54956-9205

ZIMMERMAN, JANICE F., nursing administrator; b. Ft. Madison, Iowa, May 3, 1951; d. Earl Roy and V. Kathryn (Allcock) Thye; m. Leonard L. Zimmerman, Nov. 18, 1978; children: Bobby Showers, Lindsay. Diploma, St. Luke's Sch. Nursing, Sioux City, Iowa, 1973; BSN, U. Mo., 1979. RN, Mo. Staff nurse U. Mo. Hosp., Columbia; supr. patient care, coord. nursing edn., outpatient mgr. St. Mary's Health Ctr., Jefferson City, Mo. Mem. ANA, Mo. Nurses Assn., Soc. Ambulatory Care Profls., Sigma Theta Tau. Home: 216 Franklin St Holts Summit MO 65043-2504

ZIMMERMAN, JEFFREY, psychologist; b. N.Y.C., Jan. 19, 1954. BS in Psychology, Am. U., Washington, 1975; MA in Clin. Psychology, U. Miss., 1978, PhD in Clin. Psychology, 1980. Staff therapist United Social & Mental Health Svcs., Willamantic, Conn., 1980-81; psychologist, chief psychologist dept. rehab. medicine Mt. Sinai Hosp., Hartford, Conn., 1981-85; dir. Conn. Psychol. Group, P.C., Avon, Conn., 1985—. Mem. Am. Psychol. Assn., Conn. Psychol. Assn. (coun. rep. 1988-90, pres. 1993-94). Office: Conn Psychol Group PC 40 Dale Rd Avon CT 06001-3612

ZIMMERMAN, LINDA J., psychologist; b. Meyersdale, Pa., Mar. 6, 1953; d. Charles Hilbert and Elsie Mae (Will) Burk; m. Timothy Karl Zimmerman, July 19, 1975; children: Tara Lynn, Julie Erin. BS, Indiana U. of Pa., 1974; MA, Slippery Rock U., 1989; PsyD, U. Pitts., 1995. Cert. sch. psychologist, Pa.; lic. counseling psychologist, Pa. Substitute tchr. North Allegheny Schs., Wexford, Pa., 1985-89; therapist Staunton Clinic/Sewickley (Pa.) Valley Hosp., 1989-91, North Hills Psychol. Assocs., Gibsonia, Pa., 1991-93; psychologist in pvt. practice Pitts., 1993—. Mem. Children's Issues Roundtable, Pitts., 1988—; bd. dirs. Western Pa. Com. for Prevention of Child Abuse, Pitts., 1991-95; staff parish com. Ingomar (Pa.) United Meth. Ch., 1995-96. Mem. APA, Pa. Psychol. Assn., Greater Pitts. Psychol. Assn. Republican. Office: Ste 306B 300 McKnight Park Dr Pittsburgh PA 15237

ZIMMERMAN, SOL SHEA, pediatrician; b. N.Y.C., June 25, 1948; s. Isaac and Estera (Berkowicz) Z.; m. Diana F. Zimmerman, Aug. 8, 1971; children: Jeffrey, Steven, Andrew. AB, Columbia U., 1968; MD, NYU, 1972. Diplomate Am. Bd. Pediats.; pediat. critical care medicine. Intern dept. pediats. NYU-Bellevue Hosp. Ctr., N.Y.C., 1972-73, resident dept. pediats., 1973-75, chief resident dept. pediats., 1977-78, asst. prof. clin. pediats., 1978-83, assoc. prof. clin. pediats., 1983—, dir. pediat. critical care medicine, 1978—, assoc. dir. dept. pediats., 1985—; pres. Pediat. Assocs. N.Y.C., P.C., 1978—. Editor, author: (textbook) Critical Care Pediatrics, 1985. Chmn. com. on heart, health in the young N.Y.C. affiliate Am. Heart Assn., 1987-93. Maj. USAF MC, 1975-77. Fellow Am. Acad. Pediats., Am. Coll. Chest Physicians, Critical Care Medicine; mem. N.Y. Soc. Pediat. Critical Care Medicine (v.p. 1989-91, pres. 1991-93), Alpha Omega Alpha. Office: Pediat Assocs of NYC PC 317 E 34th St New York NY 10016

ZIMMERMAN, THOM JAY, ophthalmologist, educator; b. Lincoln, Ill., Oct. 5, 1942; s. Kenneth Earl and Georgia Rosemary (Taylor) Z.; m. Tinker Steiner; 1 child, Jessica. BS in Zoology, U. Ill., 1964; MD, U. Ill., Chgo., 1968; PhD in Pharmacology, U. Fla., 1976. Diplomate Nat. Bd. Med. Examiners, Am. Bd. Ophthalmology. Intern St. Lukes Hosp., Chgo., 1968-69; resident U. Fla. Coll. Medicine, Dept. Ophthalmology, Gainesville, 1971-74, corneal fellow, 1974-75, glaucoma fellow, 1976-77; acting chmn. dept. ophthalmology La. State U., New Orleans, 1977; assoc. prof. ophthalmology and pharmacology Ochsner Clinic, New Orleans, 1977-79; prof. pharmacology and toxicology U. Louisville, 1986—, prof., chmn. dept. ophthalmology, 1986—; ophthalmic cons. (glaucoma) USPHS Hosp., New Orleans, 1977-82; cons. Nat. Adv. Eye Council and NEI, 1983; U.S. rep. for exec. com. Pan-Am. Glaucoma Soc., 1983-85; chmn. glaucoma symposium of Nat. Soc. to Prevent Blindness, 1988; guest lectr. numerous profl. socs. and confs. Author 6 books and numerous editorials; contbr. sci. articles to profl. jours.; mem. editorial bd. Jour. Continuing Edn. in Ophthalmology, 1977—, Annals of Ophthalmology, 1978—, Advances in Therapy, 1986—; contbr. book chpts., abstracts. Served with USPHS, 1969-71. Recipient Will F. Lyon award Presbyn.-St. Lukes Hosp., 1969; Robert E. McCormick scholar Research to Prevent Blindness Inc., 1978; grantee Nat. Eye Inst., 1978-84, 85-86; delivered Culler Meml. lecture, Ohio State U., 1986. Fellow Am. Coll. Clin. Pharmacology; mem. AMA (Physician's Recognition award 1971, 73, 75, 77, 79, 81, 83), Assn. for Research in Vision and Ophthalmology, Am. Soc. for Clin. Pharmacology and Therapeutics, Am. Soc. Contemporary Ophthalmology, Internat. Glaucoma Congress, Am. Acad. Ophthalmology, La.-Miss. Ophthalmology Soc., Research to Prevent Blindness Ophthalmologic Assn., So. Med. Assn., Can. Implant Soc., Ky. Med. Assn., Ky. Acad. Eye Physicians and Surgeons, Louisville Acad. Ophthalmology, Jefferson County Med. Soc., Alpha Omega Alpha. Home: 389 Mockingbird Valley Rd Louisville KY 40207-1337 Office: Univ of Louisville Dept Ophthalmology 301 E Muhammad Ali Blvd Louisville KY 40202-1511

ZIMNY, MARILYN LUCILE, anatomist, educator; b. Chgo., Dec. 12, 1927; d. John and Lucile Ruth (Andryske) Z. BA, U. Ill., 1948; MS, Loyola U., Chgo., 1951, PhD, 1954. Asst. prof. anatomy La. State U. Med. Ctr., New Orleans, 1954-59, assoc. prof., 1959-64, prof., 1964-75, prof., acting head, 1975-76, prof., head, 1976—, acting dean sch. grad. studies, 1989-90, dean sch. grad. studies and vice-chancellor for academic affairs, 1990—; vis. prof. anatomy U. Costa Rica Sch. Medicine, 1961, 62; chmn. La. Edn. Quality Support Fund Planning Com., State of La., Bd. Regents, 1993—; mem. So. Regional Edn. Bd., Regional Consortium of State higher Edn. Health Affairs Ofcls., 1993—. Grantee, NIH, 1958-72, 88-89, Arthritis Found., 1969-72, Schlieder Ednl. Found., 1972-75, Frost Found., 1975-78, NSF, 1982-83. Mem. AAAS, Am. Assn. Anatomists (mem. exec. com. 1981-85, program sec. 1990-94), Am. Physiol. Soc., Assn. Anatomy Chmn. (pres. 1983), Electron Microscopic Soc. Am., Am. Assn. Dental Schs. (sect. anat. scis.), Assn. Rsch. in Vision and Ophthalmology, Am./Internat. Assn. Dental Rsch., Omicron Kappa Upsilon, Alpha Omega Alpha. Home: 3330 Esplanade Ave New Orleans LA 70119-3132 Office: La State U Med Ctr Resource Ctr New Orleans LA 70112

ZIMOLONG, BERNHARD MICHAEL, psychologist, educator; b. Breslau, Germany, Apr. 26, 1944; s. Hans Joachim and Hiltraud (John) Z.; m. Ursula Eva-Maria Herbst, Aug. 5, 1966; 1 child, Andreas. Diploma, U. Munster, Germany, 1970; PhD, U. Braunschweig, Germany, 1974, habilitation, 1981. Asst. prof. U. Braunschweig, 1972-82; prof. U. Bochum, Germany, 1984—; speaker Spl. Rsch. Ctr. 1987, 1992-95; vis. prof. Purdue U., West-Lafayette, Ind., 1983-84, Decision Rsch., Eugene, Oreg., 1988-89. Author books on engring. psychology, human reliability, safety mgmt. and occupational health and safety; contbr. articles to profl. jours. Lt. German Army, 1964-66. Grantee Heisenberg Deutsche Forschungsgemeinschaft, 1982-84. Mem. Human Factors Soc., Deutsche Gesellschaft Psychologie. Office: Ruhr U Bochum, Dept Psychology, 44780 Bochum Germany

ZINBERG, STANLEY, physician, educator; b. N.Y.C., Aug. 18, 1934; s. Phillip M. and Etta (Beck) Z.; m. Margaret T. McNally; children: Lloyd M., Randi Ellen, Gregory A. BA, Columbia Coll., 1955; MD, SUNY, 1959; MS, NYU, 1990. Diplomate Am. Bd. Obstetrics and Gynecology. Intern Cornell Med. div. Bellevue Hosp., N.Y.C., 1959-60; resident in ob-gyn. NYU Bellevue Med. Ctr., N.Y.C., 1960-64; assoc. prof. ob-gyn. NYU Sch. Medicine, N.Y.C., 1966—; chief gynecology Bellevue Hosp., N.Y.C., 1975-81; mem. staff NYU Hosp., 1966-93; chief ob-gyn. N.Y. Downtown Hosp.,

N.Y.C., 1981-93; dir. practice activities Am. Coll. Obstetricians & Gynecologists, Washington, 1994—; examiner Am. Bd. Ob-gyn., 1976—; mem. Residency Rev. Com. for Ob-gyn., 1987-92; chmn. faculty coun. NYU Sch. Medicine, N.Y.C., 1978-79; pres. med. staff N.Y. Downtown Hosp., 1991-92. Contbr. articles to profl. jours. Capt. U.S. Army, 1964-66. Fellow ACOG (Manhattan sect. chmn. 1979-82, dir. practice activities 1994—), N.Y. Obstet. Soc. (pres. 1989-90), N.Y. Acad. Medicine (chmn. sect. on ob-gyn. 1985-86), N.Y. Gynecol. Soc.; mem. Am. Coll. Physician Execs., Assn. Profs. of Gynecology and Obstetrics (affiliate), Soc. Alumni Bellevue Hosp., Bellevue Obstet. and Gynecol. Soc. (pres. 1988-92), N.Y. State Bd. for Profl. Med. Conduct. Home: Apt 1416 700 New Hampshire Ave NW Washington DC 20037-2406 Office: Am Coll Ob-Gyn 409 12th St SW Washington DC 20024-2188

ZINCKE, HORST, urologist; b. Frankfurt, Germany, Apr. 20, 1937; came to U.S., 1969; m. Maren Zincke; children: Marian, M. Tanja. MD, U. Frankfurt am Main, 1966; PhD, U. Giessen, 1983. Urologist Mayo Clinic, Rochester, Minn., 1975-94; urologist, transplantation surgeon Mayo Clinic, Rochester, 1995—; chmn. dept. urologic surgery, head uro-oncol. surgery, co-dir. renal transplantation program Health Care Internat., Clydebank, Scotland, 1994; prof. Mayo Clinic, Rochester, 1984, 95, Named Professorship, 1993. Editl. bd. mem. Transplantation Procs., Progres en Urologie, Oncology Reports; reviewer Jour. Urology, Urology, Jour. Lab. and Clin. Medicine, Transplantation, Jour. N.Y. State Medicine, Mayo Clinic Procs., Jour. Endourology. Fellow ACS; mem. AMA, Am. Soc. Transplant Surgeons, Transplantation Soc., Assn. Minn. Immunologists, Minn. Urologic Soc., Zumbro Valley Med. Soc., Soc. Internat. Urology (U.S. sect.), Soc. Urologic Oncology, Urologic Soc. of Transplantation, Wis. Urologic Soc. (hon.), Chilean Urologic Soc. (corr.), Soc. Pelvic Surgeons, Priestley Soc., Chilean Urologic Soc. (hon.), Pan-Pacific Surg. Assn., Sigma Xi. Office: Mayo Clinic Dept Urology 200 1st St SW Rochester MN 55905

ZINGALE, ROBERT G., surgeon; b. Bklyn., Feb. 9, 1957; s. Joseph and Theresa Zingale; m. Christine A. Smith, Oct. 4, 1986; children:Jillian, Kara, Alec. BS cum laude, Pace U., 1979; MD, SUNY, Bklyn., 1983. Diplomate Am. Bd. Surgery, Surg. Crit. Care, Nat. Bd. Med. Examiners. Resident Maimonides Med. Ctr., Bklyn., 1983-88; trauma fellow Coney Island Hosp, Bklyn., 1988-89; attending physician, dir. trauma Huntington (N.Y.) Hosp., 1989—; attending physician Nassau County Med. Ctr., East Meadow, N.Y., 1991—; clin. instr. SUNY, Stony Brook, 1991—; clin. asst. prof. surgery N.Y. Med. Coll./North Shore U. Hosp., Valhalla, 1993—. Contbr. articles to profl. jours. Fellow ACS, Suffolk Acad. Medicine; mem. AMA, Soc. Laparoendoscopic Surgeons, Am. Soc. Gen. Surgeons, N.Y. Met. Breast Cancer Grop, Med. Soc. N.Y., Suffolk County Med. Soc. Office: Huntington Med Group 180 E Pulaski Rd Huntington Station NY 11746-1915

ZINGALE, SALVATORE ANTHONY, clinical psychologist; b. Catania, Italy, Nov. 12, 1950; came to U.S., 1966; s. Giuseppe and Amelia (Stivala) Z.; m. Aurelia Catalano, June 7, 1975; children: Amanda, David. BA, Bloomfield Coll., 1972; MS, Vanderbilt U., 1978, PhD, 1981. Diplomate Am. Bd. Med. Psychotherapists; lic. clin. psychologist, Tenn. Pvt. practice Nashville, 1986—; pres. Psychol. Health Cons. P.C., Nashville, 1995—; sr. psychology cons. Rebound Head Trauma Rehab. Ctr., Gallatin, Tenn., 1986-90; adj. faculty psychology internship tng. program Vanderbilt U., Nashville, 1988-92; cons. Bapt. Hosp. Rehab. Ctr., Nashville, 1990-92. Bd. editors Am. Jour. Clin. Biofeedback, 1981-84; contbr. articles to profl. jours. Capt. U.S. Army, 1981-86, major USAR, 1986—. Mem. APA, Tenn. Psychol. Assn. (sustaining), Nashville Area Psychol. Assn. (charter). Roman Catholic. Office: 110 29th Ave N Nashville TN 37203-1401

ZINKERNAGEL, ROLF MARTIN, immunology educator; b. Basle, Switzerland, Jan. 6, 1944; s. Robert W. and Suzanne (Staehlin) Z.; m. Kathrin G. Lüdin, Mar. 11, 1968; children: Christine, Annelies, Martin. MD, U. Basel, 1968. Intern in surgery Claraspital, Basel, 1968-69; postdoctoral Inst. Biochemistry, Lausanne, 1970-72, Dept. Microbiology, ANU, Canberra, Australia, 1973-75; asst. prof. Dept. Immunopathology, Scripps U., La Jolla, Calif., 1975-80, mem., 1978-79; assoc. prof. Dept. Pathology, Div. Exptl. Pathology, U. Zurich, 1979-92; full prof. Dept. Pathology, Inst. Exptl. Immunology, U. Zurich, 1992—. Editorial bd. Exptl. Cell Biology, 1976-88, Immunogenetics, 1977—, Parasite Immunology, 1978-84, Jour. of Immunology, 1978-80, Thymus, 1979-89, Antiviral Rsch., 1980-88, Jour. of Exptl. Medicine, 1981-84, Cellular Immunology, 1983—, European Jour. of Immunology, 1981—, Jour. of Environ. Pathology Toxicology and Oncology, 1981—, Internat. Jour. of Microbiology, 1983—, and others. Recipient Albert Lasker Award for Basic Med. Rsch., 1995. Mem. Swiss Soc. of Allergy and Immunology, Australian Soc. for Immunology, Am. Assn. of Immunoloigsts, Am. Assn. of Pathologists, Scandinavian Soc. of Immunology (hon.), Soc. Française d'Immunolgie (hon.), Swiss Soc. of Pathology, Swiss Soc. of Microbiology, Swiss Soc. of Cell and Molecular Biology, Acadmia Euopea, Internat. Soc. for Antiviral Rsch., ENI European Network of Immunol. Instns., Deutsche Gesellschaft fur Immunologie, Deutsche Gesellschaft fur Virologie, others. Office: Dept Pathology Inst, Exptl Immunology, U Hosp, 8091 Zurich Switzerland

ZINKIN, LEWIS DAVID, physician; b. N.Y.C., Apr. 28, 1945; s. Solomon B. and Margaret (Tovim) Z.; m. Rochelle Ellen Dershowitz, July 7, 1968; children: Donniel, Ephraim, Gila, Hillel, Adina. BA, Yeshiva U., 1966; MD, N.J. Coll. Med., 1970. Lic. physician, N.J. Surg. intern St. Vincent's Hosp., N.Y.C., 1970-71, gen. surg. resident, 1973-77; colon and rectal surg. fellow Greater Balt. Med. Ctr., 1977-78; attending physician R.W. Johnson U. Hosp., New Brunswick, N.J., 1978—, St. Peters Med. Ctr., New Brunswick, N.J., 1978—; clin. assoc. prof. R.W. Johnson Med. Sch., New Brunswick, 1980-96. Pres. Congl. Ohr Torah, Edison, N.J., 1993-96. Lt. USN, 1971-73. Mem. Am. Cancer Soc. (chmn. N.J.). Jewish. Office: Brier Hill Ct B-3 East Brunswick NJ 08816

ZINOBER, JOAN WAGNER, consulting psychologist, management consultant; b. Los Angeles, July 30, 1944; d. Leonard Issac and Maida (Prenn) Wagner; m. Peter Wolfson Zinober, June 13, 1971; children: Brett Wagner, Scott Wagner, Bryan Wagner. BA, Mich. State U., 1965; MA, U. Conn., 1967, PhD in Psychology, 1970; MBA, Fla. Inst. Tech., 1983. Lic. psychologist, Fla. Asst. prof. NYU, 1969-71; rsch. coord. U.S. Dept. Health and Human Svcs., Washington, 1971-72; dir. rsch. & evaluation Hillsborough Cmty. Mental Health Ctr., Tampa, 1972-80, dir. Fla. Consortium, Tampa, 1977-80; pres. Zinober and Assocs., Tampa, 1980-91; mng. ptnr. Ctr. for the Professions, 1991—; clin. asst. prof. psychiatry U. South Fla. Med. Sch., 1973-84; chmn. rsch. coun. Nat. Coun. of Cmty. Mental Health Ctrs., Washington, 1978-80. Editor: A Trust of Evaluation, 1980; contbr. numerous articles to profl. jours. NIMH grantee, 1977-80, contracts, 1981, developer, presenter numerous workshops, 1975—. Mem. ABA (Disting. Writing award 1993, mem. leadership sch. quality improvement task force), APA, ASTD, The Fla. Bar (prof. stress com., editor Lawyering Skills Bulletin), Med. Group Mgmt. Assn., Athena Soc. (bd. dirs.), Fla. Psychol. Assn., Soc. Psychologists in Mgmt. (bd. mem.).

ZIPES, DOUGLAS PETER, cardiologist, researcher; b. White Plains, N.Y., Feb. 27, 1939; s. Robert Samuel and Josephine Helen (Weber) Z.; m. Marilyn Joan Jacobus, Feb. 18, 1961; children: Debra, Jeffrey, David. B.A. cum laude, Dartmouth Coll., 1961, B.Med. Sci., 1962; M.D. cum laude, Harvard Med. Sch., 1964. Diplomate Am. Bd. Internal Medicine (mem. subsplty. bd. cardiovascular disease 1989—, chmn., 1995—, chmn. com. cert. in clin. cardiac electrophysiology 1989-96). Intern, resident, fellow in cardiology Duke U. Med. Ctr., Durham, N.C., 1964-68; vis. scientist Masonic Med. Research Lab., Utica, N.Y., 1970-71; asst. prof. medicine Ind. U. Sch. Medicine, Indpls., 1970-73, assoc. prof., 1973-76, prof., 1976-94, prof. pharmacology and toxicology, 1993—, disting. prof. medicine, 1994—; dir. Divsn. of Cardiology Krannert Inst. Cardiology, Ind. U. Sch. Medicine, 1995—; cons.; mem. cardiology adv. com. NIH, 1991-94. Author: Comprehensive Cardiac Care, 7th edit., 1991; editor: Slow Inward Current, 1980, Cardiac Electrophysiology and Arrhythmias, 1985, Nonpharmacological Therapy of Tachyarrhythmias, 1987, Cardiac Electrophysiology From Cell to Bedside, 1990, 2d edit., 1994; co-editor: Treatment of Heart Diseases, 1992, Ablation of Cardiac Arrhythmias, 1994, Antiarrhythmic Therapy: A Pathophysiologic Approach, 1994; mem. editl. bd. Circulation, 1974-78, 83—, Am. Jour. Cardiology, 1979-82, 88—, Am. Jour. Medicine, 1979-90, Jour. Am. Coll. Cardiology, 1983, Am. Heart Jour., 1977—, PACE, 1977—, Circulation Rsch., 1983-90, Am. Jour. Noninvasive Cardiology, 1985-89, Jour. Electrophysiology, 1987-89, Cardiovascular Drugs and Therapy, 1986-93, Japanese Heart Jour., 1989—, Jour. Cardiovascular Pharmacology and Therapeutics, 1994—, Jour. Cardiovascular Pharmacology, 1995—, Cardiovascular Therapeutics, 1995, Current Clin. Trials, 1995; editor-in-chief: Progress in Cardiology, 1988-92, Jour. Cardiovascular Electrophysiology, 1990—, Cardiology in Rev., 1992—, Contemporary Treatments of Cardiovascular Disease, 1996; contbr. numerous articles to med. pubs.; patentee cardioverter, elec. prevention of arrhythmia, discrimination of atrial fibrillation and fixation of implantable devices. Pres., bd. dirs. Indpls. Opera Co., 1983-85; mem. study sect. NIH, Washington, 1977-81; mem. nat. merit rev. bd. VA, 1982-85, Cardiology Adv. Com. NHLBL, 1991-94, chmn. steering com. AVID. Recipient Disting. Achievement award Am. Heart Assn., 1989. Fellow ACP, Am. Coll. Cardiology (chmn. ACC/AHA subcom. to assess EP studies, chmn. young investigators award com. 1988-94, trustee 1992—, mem. nominating com. 1993, Disting. Scientist award 1996), Am. Heart Assn. (exec. com. 1980-88, sci. sessions program 1983-86, 96—, chmn. various coms., chmn. 1995, bd. dirs. Internat. Cardiology Found. 1993—, bd. dirs. 1994—, chmn. emergency cardiac care com.); mem. Am. Soc. Clin. Investigation, Assn. Univ. Cardiologists (v.p. 1994, pres. 1995), Assn. Am. Physicians, Am. Physiol. Soc., Cardiac Electrophysiology Soc. (pres. 1985-86), N.Am. Soc. Pacing and Electrophysiology (pres. 1988-90, trustee 1990—, Disting. Scientist award 1995), InterAm. Soc. Cardiology (1st v.p. 1995—), Ind. Cardiac Electrophysiology Soc. (founder). Home: 10614 Winterwood Carmel IN 46032-9688 Office: Ind U Sch Medicine 1100 W Michigan St Indianapolis IN 46202-5208

ZIPF, ROBERT EUGENE, JR., legal medicine consultant, pathologist; b. Dayton, Ohio, Sept. 18, 1940; s. Robert Eugene and Meriam (Murr) Z.; m. Nancy J. Gaskell, Sept. 11, 1965; children: Karin Lorene, Marjorie Kristine. BA, DePauw U., 1962; MD, Ohio State U., 1966. Diplomate Am. Bd. Pathology. Intern, Miami Valley Hosp., Dayton, Ohio, 1966-67; dir. forensic pathology Duke U. Med. Ctr., Durham, N.C., 1967-72; dir. radioisotope pathology Riverside Meth. Hosp., Columbus, 1974-78; dep. coroner, forensic pathologist Franklin County, Columbus, 1974-78; regional forensic pathologist State of N.C., Rocky Mount, 1978—; chmn. pathology Nash Gen. Hosp., Rocky Mount, 1978—; clin. asst. prof. East Caroline U. Med. Sch., Greenville, N.C., 1979—; adj. prof. Atlantic Christian Coll., Wilson, N.C., 1980-89, dir. Sch. Med. Tech., 1983-89; cons. in field. Contbr. articles to profl. jours. Trustee, United Fund, 1979-84; mem. Mayor's Com. on Drug and Substance Abuse, 1987—. Maj. USAF, 1972-74. Fellow Am. Soc. Clin. Pathologist, Am. Acad. Forensic Scientists; mem. Assn. Clin. Scientists, Am. Coll. Nuclear Medicine, N.C. Med. Soc., N.Y. Acad. Scis. (pres. Lab. Users Group 1988-90, 92), SMS (clin. adv. bd. 1988-91, lab. advisors bd. 1989-91), Nash County Med. Soc. (pres. 1995). Home: 120 Newby Ct Rocky Mount NC 27804-3322 Office: Nash Gen Hosp Pathology Lab Rocky Mount NC 27804

ZIPF, WILLIAM BYRON, pediatric endocrinologist, educator; b. Dayton, Ohio, Mar. 20, 1946; s. Robert Eugene and Merium (Murr) Z.; m. Joanne Fisher, Sept. 20, 1969; children: William Byron Jr., Thanda Lynn, Robert E. II. BA, Denison U., 1968; MD, Ohio State U., 1972. Diplomate Nat. Bd. Med. Examiners, Am. Bd. Pediatrics, Am. Bd. Pediatric Endocrinology. Intern in pediatrics Mott Children's Hosp./U. Mich., Ann Arbor, 1972-73, resident in pediatrics, 1973-75, clin. fellow in pediatric endocrinology, 1975-76, rsch. fellow, 1976-78; asst. prof. dept. pediatrics and physiology Ohio State U., Columbus, 1978-83, assoc. prof., 1983-89, prof., 1989—; dir. clin. study ctr. Children's Hosp./Ohio State U., Columbus, 1982—, vice-chmn. dept. pediatrics, 1989—, dir. pediatric endocrinology, 1990—. Contbr. chpts. on endocrine diseases of children to books, articles to profl. jours. Grantee NIH, 1980-84, Cystic Fibrosis Found., 1987-92. Fellow Am. Acad. Pediatrics, Nat. Med. Bd.; mem. Soc. Pediatric Rsch., Endocrine Soc., Lawson Wilkins Soc. Pediatric Endocrinolgoy. Office: Childrens Hosp 700 Childrens Dr Columbus OH 43205-2666

ZIPKIN, JEFFREY WARREN, urologist; b. Akron, Ohio, July 17, 1951; s. Morris A. and Alice (Jaffe) Z.; m. Susan Silverman, Nov. 5, 1978; children: Elise, Mollie, Ariel, Derek. BA, U. Mich., 1972, MA, 1973; MD, Ohio State U., 1977. Resident Boston, 1977-79, Cin., 1979-83; urologist Urology Assocs. Southwestern Ohio, Inc., Cin., 1983—. Contbr. articles to profl. jours. Fellow AMA, Am. Urol. Assn.; mem. Ohio State Med. Assn. Jewish. Office: Urology Assoc SW Ohio Inc 10475 Reading Rd #206 Cincinnati OH 45241

ZIRKLE, JOHN WILLIAM, internist; b. Morristown, Tenn., June 19, 1945; s. James W. and Anna L. (Patrick) Z.; m. Eva K. Ergenbright, June 14, 1969; children: Anne K., Sarah P. BS, BA, Carson-Newman Coll., 1966; MD, U. N.C., 1970. Diplomate Am. Bd. Internal Medicine. Intern U. Va. Med. Ctr., Charlottesville, 1970-71, resident, 1974-76, chief resident in medicine, 1976-77, fellow in hematology, 1977-79; pvt. practice Milligan Clinic, Jefferson City, Tenn., 1979—. Contbr. articles to profl. jours. Elder 1st Presbyn. Ch., Jefferson City. Lt. comdr. USNR, 1971-74. Fellow ACP; mem. Am. Soc. Internal Medicine, Knoxville Soc. Internal Medicine (treas. 1991-92), Am. Med. Soc., Va. Soc. Hematology and Oncology. Office: 1810 Bishop Ave Ste C Jefferson City TN 37760-1997

ZIROLI, DARRELL MARK, physician assistant; b. Erie, Pa., Nov. 18, 1956; s. Guiliano Gilbert and Bernadette Ann (Wieczkowski) Z.; m. Mary Lou Hannah, Aug. 29, 1981; children: Andrew Mark, Christina Danielle. Student, Behrend Coll., Erie, Pa., 1974-75; BS, Gannon U., Erie, 1978; BS/Assocs., U.Ala., Birmingham, 1981. Cert. surgeon's asst. and physician asst., Ala. Mental health technician St. Vincent's Hosp., Erie, 1978-79; surgeon's asst. Henry Ford Hosp., Detroit, 1981-83, The Eye Ctr., New Port Richey, Fla., 1983-84, Eye Ctr. Fla., Ft. Myers, 1984-93, Ala. Neurosurgeons, Birmingham, 1993-94; physician asst. Cardiovascular Assocs., Birmingham, 1994—; tchr. ocular anesthesia Eye Ctr. Fla., Ft. Myers, 1989-93. Fellow Am. Acad. Physician Assts. Republican. Home: 5236 Memory Ln Mount Olive AL 35117 Office: Cardiovascular Assocs 880 Montclair Rd Birmingham AL 35213

ZIRPS, FOTENA ANATOLIA, psychologist, researcher; b. Pitts., Mar. 27, 1958; d. George T. and Barbara F. (Skinner) Z. BA, U. Akron, 1983, MA, 1987; PhD, Fla. State U., 1990. Sch. psychologist Canton (Ohio) City Schs., 1985-86; sch. psychologist Leon County Schs., Tallahassee, 1986-88, program evaluator, 1988-90; cons. Evaluation Systems Design, Inc., Tallahassee, 1990-91; pres. Zirps, Vella and Assocs., Inc., Tallahassee, 1991—; dir. program evaluation Families First, Atlanta, 1991-94; assoc. prof. Fla. Mental Health Inst. U. South Fla., 1995—; Fla. mental health coord. Fla. Mental Health Inst.-U. South Fla., 1995—; coord. spl. studies for children Comprehensive Cmty. Mental Health Program-U. South Fla., 1995—; tchr. Fla. State U., Tallahassee, summers 1988-91, grant coord., 1989-90; cons. hild Welfare League Am.; coord. spl. studies Comprehensive Cmty. Mental Health Svcs. Children with Severe Emotional Disturbances. Author: Sun and Moon, 1991, Doing It Right th First Time: A Model Quality Assurance foı Human Services Agencies, 1994, (with others) Computer Models of Reading, 1989; author, cartoonist: (slides show/audio tape) Human Rights, 1986; co-inventor: (games) Beauty Pageant, Alien Abduction; editor, co-author: Quality Improvement Program and Program Evaluation in Child Welfare: Managing into the Next Century; panel standards writers Coun. on Accreditation Svcs. for Families and Children, Inc. Chmn. grad. student adv. com. Fla. State, 1986-88. Mem. Am. Psychol. Assn., Am. Evaluation Assn., Am. Ednl. Rsch. Assn. (Disting. Presenter 1991), Nat. Coun. Rsch. in Child Welfare, Fla. Ednl. Rsch. Assn. (Disting. Author 1990). Quaker. Office: U South Fla Fla Mental Health Inst 13301 Bruce B Downs Blvd Tampa FL 33612-3899

ZISKIND, ALAN, managed healthcare consultant, physician; b. N.Y.C., Jan. 12, 1932; s. Edward and Rose (Finson) Z.; m. Barbara Schiff; Dec. 28, 1952; children: Andrew, Mark, Michael. AB, Columbia Coll., 1953; MD cum laude, Boston U., 1957; MPH, Harvard U., 1964. Diplomate Am. Bd. Pediatrics. Pvt. practice pediatrics Belmont, Mass., 1960-88; med. dir. Prudential HealthCare Sys., Boston, 1986-91; v.p. Health New Eng., Springfield, Mass., 1991-94; pres. The Ziskind Group, Wilbraham, Mass., 1994—; malpractice tribunal Commonwealth Mass., Boston, 1982—; cons. hosp. rev. program Medicaid Divsn. Dept. Pub. Welfare, 1979—; instr. Boston U. Sch. Medicine, 1963—; asst. pediatrics Harvard MEd. Sch., Boston, 1960—. Mem. Am. Coll. Physican Execs., New. Eng. Pediat. Soc., Mass. Med. Soc. Office: The Ziskind Group 6 Briar Cliff Dr Wilbraham MA 01095

ZISKIND, ANDREW A., cardiologist; b. Boston, Aug. 31, 1958; s. Alan and Barbara (Schiff) Z.; m. Geraldynn Landry, May 16, 1990; children: Katherine, Becky. AB, Bowdoin Coll., 1980; MD, U. Pa., 1984. Diplomate Am. Bd. Cardiology, Am. Bd. Internal Medicine. Intern, resident Mass. Gen. Hosp., Boston, 1984-87, fellow in cardiology, 1987-90; asst. prof. medicine U. Md., Balt., 1990-96, assoc. prof., 1996—; dir. cardiac catheterization lab. U. Md., 1990-95, dir. cardiac network, 1995—. Fellow Am. Coll. Cardiology, Am. Coll. Physicians, Soc. Cardiac Angiography & Interventions; mem. Am. Coll. Physicians Execs., Am. Fedn. Clin. Rsch. Home: 4106 Long Green Rd Glen Arm MD 21057 Office: 250 W Pratt St Ste 880 Baltimore MD 21201

ZISMAN, LAWRENCE S., internist; b. 1959. MD, Albert Einstein Coll. Medicine, 1987. Postdoctoral fellow U. Colo. Health Sci. Ctr. Recipient Clinician Scientist award Am. Heart Assn., 1995-96. Office: U Colo 5483 E Utah Pl Denver CO 80222-3948*

ZISSMAN, JOSHUA, healthcare consultant; b. Princeton, N.J., Apr. 10, 1953; s. Daniel Abraham and Harriet Mildred (Russcol) Z.; m. Joan Alison Becker, May 2, 1947; 1 child, Elizabeth Fredette. BA cum laude, NYU, 1982; MBA in Health Adminstrn., Temple U., 1994. Sr. staff asst. Abington (Pa.) Meml. Hosp.; cons. Med. Advisors, Inc., Ft. Washington, Pa.; mem. program com. Greater Phila. Health Assembly. Bd. dirs. Laurel House, Norristown, Pa. Recipient Frontline Leadership award Zenger-Miller Assocs., 1992, Chairperson's award Temple U., 1994. Mem. Am. Coll. Healthcare Execs. (assoc.), Nat. Assn. Health Care Quality, Am. Hosp. Assn., Hosp. Assn. Pa., Pa. Assn. Health Care Quality. Office: Med Advisors Inc 501 Office Center Dr #248 PO Box 1537 Fort Washington PA 19034

ZITEK, BROOK E., psychiatrist; b. Akron, Ohio, July 12, 1960; s. Anton and Beth Ellen (Morehouse) Z. DO, Ohio U., 1986. Gen. psychiatrist Deaconess Hosp., Billings, Mont., 1991-92, Yellowstone Treatment Ctrs., Billings, 1992-95, Locumtenens, Mont. and Ohio, 1993-95, Deaconess Behavioral Health Clinic, Billings, 1995—; cons. in field. Mem. Yellowstone Valley Citizens Coun., Billings, 1994—, PRIDE, 1994—. Recipient Steinbrenner Scholarly Presentation award Cleve. Clinic Found., 1990. Mem. Am. Psychiat. Assn., Mont. Osteo. Assn., Mont. Psychiat. Assn. Office: Deaconess Billings Clinic Health Systems 2800 Tenth Ave North Billings MT 59107

ZITRIN, CHARLOTTE MARKER, psychiatrist, educator, researcher; b. N.Y.C., Sept. 30, 1918; d. Abraham and Regina (Adler) Marker; m. Arthur Zitrin, Oct. 4, 1942; children: Richard Alan, Elizabeth Ann. BA cum laude, NYU, 1939, MD, 1943. Diplomate Am. Bd. Med. Examiners. Intern Kings County Hosp., 1943-44; resident in pediatrics Bellevue Hosp., 1944-45; asst. in pediatrics NYU Bellevue Med. Ctr., 1945-46, from rsch. fellow to asst. prof. pediatrics, 1948-58; attending physician pediatrics L.I. Jewish Hosp., 1958-60; resident in psychiatry Hillside Hosp., 1960-63, clin. asst., 1964-65; supervising psychiatrist Hillside Hosp. Div. L.I. Jewish Med. Ctr., Glen Oaks, N.Y., 1965—, dir. Behavior Therapy Clinic, 1970-89; ret., dir. Phobia Clinic, 1972-89; ret.; asst. clin. prof. pediatrics NYU-Bellevue Med. Ctr., 1958-60; asst. prof. clin. psychiatry dept. psychiatry and Behavioral Scis. Ctr., SUNY, Stony Brook, 1973-81, clin. assoc. prof., 1982-89; assoc. prof. psychiatry Albert Einstein Coll. Medicine, 1989—; lectr. in field. Contbr. articles to med. jours. Fellow Am. Psychiat. Assn., Am. Psychopath. Assn., Nassau County Acad. Med.; mem. AAAS, Assn. Advancement Behavior Therapy, Nassau County Med. Soc., Nassau County Psychiat. Soc., N.Y. Acad. Scis., N.Y. State Med. Soc., Psi Chi. Office: 56 Ruxton Rd Great Neck NY 11023-1529

ZITSMAN, JEFFREY LEONARD, pediatric surgeon; b. Springfield, Ohio, Jan. 17, 1951; s. Bernard Charles and Gloria Rosalie (Levy) Z.; m. Arlene Joy Mellitz, June 24, 1975 (div. Feb. 1987); children: Rachel Hannah, Noah Chaim; m. Elaine Janine Abrams, Oct. 23, 1988; children: Jonah Samuel, Tobias Gabriel. Student, U. Cin., 1968-70; AB in Natural Scis., Johns Hopkins U., 1972; MD, Tufts U., 1976. Diplomate Am. Bd. of Surgery; spl. qualifications in pediatric surgery, surg. critical care. Resident in surgery New Eng. Med. Ctr., Boston, 1976-81; resident in pediatric surgery Babies Hosp., N.Y.C., 1983-85; asst. prof. surgery Robert Wood Johnson Med. Sch., New Brunswick, N.J., 1985-88; asst. prof. clin. surgery Columbia U., N.Y.C., 1988-91; asst. prof. surgery N.Y. Med. Coll., Valhalla, N.Y., 1991—. Contbr. med. articles to profl. jours. and chpt. to book. Mem. ACS, Am. Acad. Pediatrics, Am. Pediatric Surg. Assn. Office: Lincoln Hosp Dept of Surgery 234 E 149th St Bronx NY 10451 also: 688 White Plains Rd Scarsdale NY 10583

ZITT, MYRON J., allergist, immunologist; b. N.Y.C., Sept. 15, 1939; s. Arthur and Bertha (Grossman) Z.; m. Jeanne Patricia Schwartz, Oct. 9, 1966; 1 child, Jonathan. BS, Trinity Coll., 1960; MD, SUNY, Bklyn., 1965. Bd. cert. Am. Bd. Internal Medicine, Am. Bd. Allergy & Immunology. Intern L.I. Coll. Hosp., Bklyn., 1965-66, resident, 1966-68; asst. chief allergy-immunology Queens L.I. Med. Group, North Babylon, N.Y., 1972—; dir. adult allergy clinic Nassau County Med. Ctr., East Meadow, N.Y., 1979—; assoc. clin. prof. SUNY, Stpny Brook, 1984—. Co-editor: (guidebook) Healthcare Reform Managed Care, 1994; mem. editl. bd. Annals of Allergy-Asthma-Immunology, 1995—. Maj. USAF, 1969-72. Allergy-Immunology fellow Duke U., Durham, N.C., 1968-69. Fellow Am. Coll. Allergy, Asthma & Immunology (regent 1992-95), Am. Acad. Allertgy, Asthma & Immunology, Nassau Acad. Medicine; mem. Am. Thoracic Soc., L.I. Allergy Soc. (pres. 1989-91). Home: 9 Cypress Dr Woodbury NY 11797 Office: Queens LI Med Group 300 Bayshore Rd North Babylon NY 11703

ZIZIC, THOMAS MICHAEL, physician, educator; b. Milw., Dec. 9, 1939; s. Michael Mitchell Zizic and Dorothy (Batas) Ciric; m. Karen Owens, June 15, 1962 (div. Sept. 1967); m. Martha Ann Ardos, Nov. 22, 1967; children: Lara Ann, Kristine Michelle. BS, U. Wis., 1961; MD, Johns Hopkins U., 1965. Intern Johns Hopkins Hosp., Balt., 1965-66, asst. resident, 1966-67, fellow in internal medicine, 1969-71, instr. dept. medicine, 1971-73, asst. prof. medicine, 1971-81, assoc. prof. medicine, 1981—; pvt. practice, Balt., 1988—; co-dir. Chesapeake Osteoporosis Ctr., Balt., 1988—; dir. med. affairs Murray Electronics, 1993—; v.p. med. quality care Physicians Quality Care, 1995—; pres. U.S. Osteoporosis Network, Inc., 1996—; cons. in field. Contbr. numerous articles and abstracts to profl. jours. V.p. Md. chpt. Arthritis Found., Balt., 1976-77; chmn. Md. Commn. on Arthritis and Related Diseases, 1986-90. Fellow Am. Coll. Rheumatology, 1986; Md. Soc. Rheumatic Diseases (pres. 1975-76), D.C. Rheumatism Assn., Balt. City Med. Soc., Johns Hopkins Hosp. Med. Soc., Arthritis Found. (fellow 1971-73, v.p. 1976-77, med. and sci. com. 1977-79, chmn. profl. edn. com. 1977-78, govtl. affairs com. 1979-83), Phi Beta Kappa, Phi Kappa Phi, Phi Eta Sigma. Office: 5601 Loch Raven Blvd Baltimore MD 21237

ŽIŽKA, ZDENĚK, biologist, researcher; b. Prague, Czech Republic, Jan. 21, 1944; s. Bedřich and Ružena (Žrámková) Ž.; m. Eva Nováková, Jan. 11, 1980; 1 child, Zdeněk. Diploma, Charles U., 1967, RNDr, 1970; PhD, Acad. Scis. Prague, 1975. Scientist Inst. Entomology, Acad. Scis., Prague, 1967-84; scientist Inst. Microbiology, Acad. Scis., Prague, 1985—, head labor, 1988-90. Contbr. over 120 articles to profl. jours. Head Youth Biol. Coub in Youth Ctr. Neratovice, 1974—. Capt. Czech Mil., 1968-88. Acad. Scis. grantee, 1992-94. Fellow Czech Zool. Soc., Czech. Soc. Microbiology, Czech. Soc. Electron Microscopy. Home: Blanická 13, 120 00 Prague 2, Czech Republic Office: Academy of Sciences, Inst of Microbiology, Vídeňská 1083, 142 20 Prague Czech Republic

ZLOTOWSKI, MARTIN, psychologist; b. Lodz, Poland, Aug. 10, 1934; s. Pawel and Helen Z.; m. Judith Ann Lifschitz, May 17, 1974; children: David, Steven, Laura. BA, NYU, 1955; MA, Mich. State U., 1958, PhD, 1960. Research assoc. Grad. Sch. Public Health, U. Pitts., 1960-61; research assoc., lectr. Boston U., 1961-62; staff psychologist VA Hosp., Coatesville, Pa., 1962-65, unit chief, 1965-73; clin. dir. St. Mary Providence, 1966-70; assoc. prof. spl. edn. West Chester (Pa.) U., 1973—, grad. coord., 1987—; dir. Counseling Assocs., Paoli, Pa., 1973-85, exec. dir., 1985—. V.p. Victim

Witness Services Chester County, 1976-77. Fellow Phila. Soc. Clin. Psychologists (pres. 1978-79, sec. human services ctr. 1982), Phila. Psychol. Assn., Am. Orthopsychiat. Assn.; mem. APA, Mental Health Assn. S.E. Pa. Democrat. Jewish. Home: 605 Eagle Rd Wayne PA 19087-3437

ŻMUDZKI, JAN, toxicology educator, veterinarian, researcher; b. Wrocław, Poland, Nov. 1, 1947; s. Edmund and Ludwika (Rudnicka) Ż; m. Bożena Giza, Dec. 21, 1971; children: Jacek, Justyna. DVM, Coll. Vet. Medicine, Wrocław, 1971; PhD, Vet. Rsch. Inst., Pulawy, Poland, 1978. Rsch. asst. Vet. Rsch. Inst., 1971-73, rsch. assoc., 1973-78, asst. prof. toxicology, 1978-87, assoc. prof., 1987-91, prof., 1991—, head dept., 1993—; vis. scientist U. Tenn., Knoxville, 1980-81, Tex. A&M U., College Station, 1982-85. Recipient award Polish Soc. Pharmacology, 1979, Polish Ministry Agr., 1988. Mem. Polish Soc. Vet. Sci. (chpt. v.p. 1987-88, chpt. pres. 1989-91), Polish Soc. Toxicology (chpt. v.p. 1987-90). Office: Vet Rsch Inst, Partyzantów 57, 24-100 Pulawy Poland

ZOGRAFI, GEORGE, pharmacologist, educator; b. N.Y.C., Mar. 13, 1936; married; 4 children. BS, Columbia U., 1956; MS, U. Mich., 1958, PhD in Pharm. Chemistry, 1961; DS (hon.), Columbia U., 1976. Asst. prof. pharmacology Columbia U., N.Y.C., 1961-64; from asst. prof. to assoc. prof. U. Mich., Ann Arbor, 1964-72; rsch. fellow Am. Found. Pharm. Edn., 1970-71; Pheiffer rsch. fellow Utrecht (The Netherlands) U., 1970-71; prof. pharmacology U. Wis., Madison, 1972—, dean, 1975-80. Mem. AAAS, NAS (Inst. Medicine), Am. Pharm. Assn. (Ebert prize 1984), Am. Chem. Soc., Am. Assn. Pharm. Scientists, Internat. Pharm. Fedn., Internat. Assn. Colloid and Interface Scientists, Am. Inst. Hist. Pharm., Sigma Xi. Office: U Wis Sch Pharmacology 425 N Charter St Madison WI 53706*

ZOLESSI, SERGIO LUIS, orthopedic surgeon; b. Montevideo, Uruguay, Jan. 29, 1944; s. Horacio Luis and Yolanda Orfilia (Britos) Z.; m. Maria Merdeces Bruquetas, Aug. 20, 1969; children: Mariana, Martin Horacio, Veronica, Pablo Sergio, Magdalena. MD, U. Montevideo, 1973, postgrad., 1976. Anatomy dissector faculty medicine U. Montevideo, 1964-69; intern practitioner hosps. Ministerio de Salud Publica, Montevideo, 1971-77; intern practitioner Banco de Seguros del Estado, Montevideo, 1972-77; orthopedic surgeon Banco de Protesis, Montevideo, 1976—, Hosp. de Rivera, Uruguay, 1977-90, Asistencial Medica de Rivera, 1977—; phys. end. supr. Adminstrn. Nat. Edn., Rivera, 1983—. Author: Actas Societad Rioplatense de Traumatologica, 1980, Actas Congreso Slaut, 1981. Mem. conv. Pardito Nat., Rivero, 1984. Mem. Soc. Trauatologia Uruguay, Soc. Medicina Rivera (sec. 1988—). Roman Catholic. Home: Jose Enruqie Rd 1275, 40000 Rivera Uruguay Office: Asistencial Medica, Faustino Carambula 1169, 40000 Rivero Uruguay

ZOLLER, MICHAEL, otolaryngologist, educator; b. New Orleans, July 21, 1947; s. Harry and Mildred (Daitch) Z.; m. Linda Kramer, Dec. 21, 1974; children: Rebecca, Jonathan. BS, U. New Orleans, 1968; MD, Tulane U., 1972. Resident in gen. surgery Jewish Hosp., St. Louis, 1972-74, Washington U. Sch. Medicine; resident in otolaryngology Mass. Eye and Ear Infirmary, Harvard U., Boston, 1974-77; pres. Ear, Nose and Throat Assocs., Savannah, Ga., 1977—; asst. clin. prof. surgery Med. Coll. Ga., Augusta, 1982-96; assoc. clin. prof. surgery, 1996—; co-dir. otoneurology dept. St. Joseph's Hosp., Savannah, 1994—. Chmn. med. divsn. United Way, Savannah, 1990, chmn. profl. divsn., 1991, 94, 95; v.p. Am. Cancer Soc., Savannah, 1994, bd. dirs., 1993—, pres. Chatham County Unit, 1996; bd. dirs. Savannah Country Day Sch., 1993—, chmn. ann. campaign, 1995-96; pres. Savannah Jewish Fedn., 1991-93. Recipient Young Leadership award Savannah Jewish Fedn., 1985, Boss of Yr. award Savannah Jaycees, 1993, Celebrate Savannah award for outstanding contbns. to Savannah, Ga. Guardian, 1996; Harvard U. Med. Sch. fellow, 1976-77. Fellow ACS; mem. AMA, Am. Acad. Head and Neck Soc., Am. Neurotology Soc., Ga. Med. Soc. (v.p. endowment fund 1996, sec. endowment fund 1992, pres. 1992, John B. Rabun Cmty. Svc. award 1995), 1st Dist. Med. Assn. (pres. 1987-88), Med. Assn. Ga. (bd. dirs., mem. ho. dels., Ga. Cup award 1993, Ayest-Wyeth Cmty. Svc. award 1996), So. Med. Assn., Ga. Soc. Otolaryngology (sec.-treas. 1995-96), Savannah C. of C. Office: Ear Nose and Throat Assocs 5201 Frederick St Savannah GA 31405-4501

ZOLLI, FRANCIS ALBERT, chiropractor; b. Jersey City, July 24, 1954; s. Albert John and Angela Mary (Ricciardore) Z.; m. Adelia Marie Russo, Sept. 1, 1984. BS in Psychology, St. Peter's Coll., Jersey City, 1976; Dr. Chiropractic, N.Y. Chiropractic Coll., Glen Head, 1979; postgrad., U. Bridgeport, 1993—. Diplomate Nat. Bd. Chiropractic Examiners; lic. dr. of chiropractic, N.Y., N.J. Clinic dir. N.Y. Chiropractic Coll., Glen Head, 1980-82, dir. clin. scis., 1984-87, dean students, 1987, v.p. for devel., 1988-89; chmn. chiropractic coll. comm. U. Bridgeport, 1989, dean Coll. Chiropractic, 1990—. Editor: Symptomatology and Differential Diagnosis, 1986; author: Chiropractic Concepts in Healing, 1984; contbr. articles to profl. jours. Adv. bd. Bloomfield (N.J.) Coll., 1994—. Recipient Testimonial, N.Y. Chiropractic Coll., 1987. Fellow Internat. Coll. Chiropractic; mem. Am. Chiropractic Assn., Found. for Chiropractic Edn. and Rsch., No. N.J. Chiropractic Soc., Acad. for Gen. Practice of Chiropractic, Coun. on Chiropractic Edn. (bd. dirs. 1994—), Assn. of Chiropractic Colls. (bd. dirs. 1994—). Office: Univ of Bridgeport College of Chiropractic 75 Linden Ave Bridgeport CT 06601

ZOLLINGER, RICHARD WILLIAM, surgeon, educator; b. Millersport, Ohio, Jan. 10, 1912; s. William Milton and Hattie Almyra (Zartman) Z.; m. Mary Louise Torbert, Sept. 4, 1938; children: Ann, Barbara, Leslie, Diana, Richard II. BA, Ohio State U., 1933; MD, Harvard U., 1936. Diplomate Am. Bd. Surgery. Intern L.I. Coll. Hosp., Bklyn., 1936-37; asst. resident surgery Ohio State U., Columbus, 1937-38, resident in gynecology, 1938-39, resident in rsch. surgery, 1939-40, resident in thoracic surgery, 1940-41, clin. prof. surgery emeritus; dir. med. edn. Mt. Carmel Med. Ctr., Columbus, 1950-60, chmn. dept. surgery, 1960-77. Author: Country Boy, 1991, Surgeons Journal, 1992, Reminiscence, 1993; contbr. articles to profl. jours. Maj. USAAC, 1942-46. Mem. AMA, ACS (pres. Ohio chpt. 1968), Western Surg. Assn. (v.p. 1976-77), Ctrl. Surg. Assn., Ea. Surg. Soc. (pres. 1974-75), Soc. for Surgery of Alimentary Tract, Columbus Country Club (past pres), Jefferson Golf and Country Club. Office: 130 S Davis Ste 203 Columbus OH 43222

ZOOK, BERNARD CHARLES, pathology educator, administrator, researcher; b. Beach, N.D., Nov. 1, 1935; s. Frank N. and Elizabeth Ferne (Kramer) Z.; m. Elinore A. (Schillo), Oct. 1, 1955; children—Bernita, Melinda, Andrew. B.S., Colo. State U., 1962, D.V.M., 1963; postgrad. Harvard Med. Sch., 1963-68, Northeastern U., Boston, 1966. Diplomate Am. Coll. Veterinary Pathologists. From research fellow to asst. in pathology Harvard Med. Sch., Boston, 1963-68; from research fellow to assoc. pathologist Angell Meml. Animal Hosp., Boston, 1963-69; asst. prof. George Washington U., Washington, 1969-74, assoc. prof., 1974-83, prof. pathology, 1983—; cons. comml. orgns. Contbr. articles on heart disease, poisoning, radiation injury and other med. conditions to profl. jours. Vol. Seneca council Boy Scouts Am., 1981-84. Research fellow Smithsonian Instn., 1969—; grantee NIH, 1967-68, Murray Corp., 1981-85, Nat. Cancer Inst., 1975-86, Population Council, 1981-85, Motorola Corp., 1991—. Mem. AVMA, AAAS, Radiation Research Soc., Soc. Toxicologic Pathologists, Nat. Soc. Med. Research (bd. dirs. 1981-86), Beta Beta Beta, Phi Zeta. Republican. Roman Catholic. Club: Bridge. Lodge: K.C. Avocations: music; painting. Office: George Washington U Med Ctr 2300 I St NW Washington DC 20037-2337

ZOOK, ELVIN GLENN, plastic surgeon, educator; b. Huntington County, Ind., Mar. 21, 1937; s. Glenn Hardman and Ruth (Barton) Z.; m. Sharon Kay Neher, Dec. 11, 1960; children—Tara E., Leigh A., Nicole L. B.A., Manchester Coll., 1959; M.D., Ind. U., 1963. Diplomate Am. Bd. Surgery, Am. Bd. Thoracic Surgery, Am. Bd. Plastic Surgery. Intern Meth. Hosp., Indpls., 1963-64; resident in gen. and thoracic surgery Ind. U. Med. Center, Indpls., 1964-69; resident in plastic surgery Ind. U. Hosp., Indpls., 1969-71; asst. prof. plastic surgery Ind. U. Hosp., 1971-73; asso. prof. surgery So. Ill. U., Springfield, 1973-75; prof. So. Ill. U., 1975—, chmn. div. plastic surgery, 1973—; mem. staff Meml. Med. Center, St. Johns Hosp., Springfield. Contbr. articles to med. jours. Mem. AMA, Assn. Acad. Surgery, Am. Soc. Plastic and Reconstructive Surgery (sec. 1988-91, v.p. 1991-92, pres.-elect 1992-93, pres. 1993-94), Midwestern Soc. Plastic and Reconstructive Surgery (pres. 1986-87), ACS, Sangamon County Med. Soc. (pres. 1987), Am. Cleft Palate Assn., Am. Assn. Plastic Surgery (trustee 1987-90), Plastic Surgery Rsch. Coun. (chmn. 1981), Am. Burn Assn., Ill. Surg. Soc., Am. Soc. Surgery Hand (coun.), Am. Bd. of Plastic Surgery (sec.-treas. 1988-91, chmn. 1991-92), Am. Soc. Aesthetic Plastic Surgery, Am. Soc. Surgery of Trauma, Assn. Acad. Chmn. Plastic Surgery (pes. 1986-87), Am. Surg. Assn., RRC for Plastic Surgery, Sangamo Club, Springfield Med. Club, Island Bay Yacht Club. Presbyterian. Clubs: Sangamo, Springfield Med, Island Bay Yacht. Home: 42 Hazel Dell Springfield IL 62707-9507 Office: 800 N Rutledge St Springfield IL 62702-4911

ZOOK, MARTHA FRANCES HARRIS, retired nursing administrator; b. Topeka, Nov. 15, 1921; d. Dwight Thacher and Helen Muriel (Houston) Harris; m. Paul Warren Zook, July 2, 1948 (dec. 1995); children: Mark Warren (dec.), Mary Elizabeth Zook Hughey. RN, Meriden (Conn.) Hosp. Sch. Nursing, 1947; student U. Kans., 1948-49, Kans. State U., 1960-61, Barton County Community Coll., 1970-73; BA, Stephens Coll., 1977; postgrad. Ft. Hays State U., 1978-79. Staff nurse Stormont Hosp., Topeka, 1947-48; staff nurse Watkins Meml. Hosp., Lawrence, Kans., 1948-49; nursing supr. Larned State Hosp., 1949-53, sect. supr., 1956-57, dir. nursing, 1958-61, 83-86; sect. nurse Sedgewick Sect., 1961-76, clin. instr. nursing edn., 1976-77, dir. nursing edn., 1977-83; clinic nurse for podiatrist; sect. supr. Dillon Bldg., Larned, 1957-58; Vol. Am. Cancer Soc., ARC, Larned Grade Sch. Children's Drug Info. Program. Mem. AAUW, Sacred Heart Altar Soc. Democrat. Roman Catholic. Home: 1109 Johnson Ave Larned KS 67550-2232

ZOON, KATHRYN EGLOFF, biochemist; b. Yonkers, N.Y., Nov. 6, 1948; d. August R. and Violet T. (Pollock) Egloff; BS, Rensselaer Poly. Inst., 1970; PhD Johns Hopkins U., 1975; m. Robert A. Zoon, Aug. 22, 1970; children: Christine K, Jennifer R. Interferon rsch. fellow NIH, Bethesda, Md., 1975-77, staff fellow, 1977-79, sr. staff fellow, 1979-80; sr. staff fellow div. biochem. biophysics Bur. Biologics, FDA, Bethesda, 1980-83; rsch. chemist divsn. biochem. biophysics, 1983-84, rsch. chemist divsn. virology, 1984-88, rsch. chemist div. cytokine biology, Ctr. for Biologics Evaluation and Rsch., FDA, 1988—, div. dir., 1989-92; dir. Ctr. for Biologics Evaluation and Rsch., 1992—; lectr. NIH, 1994, Reigelman Lecturship, 1994. N.Y. State Regents fellow, 1970; Person of the Yr. award Biopharm, 1992, 95 Pub. Svc. award Genetic Engring. News, 1994; Presdl. Meritorious Exec. Rank award, 1994. Mem. Am. Soc. Biochemistry and Molecular Biology, Internat. Soc. Interferon Rsch., Internat. Soc. Cytokine Rsch. Roman Catholic. Contbr. numerous articles on research in biol. chemistry to sci. jours.; sect. editor Jour. Interferon Research, 1980—. Office: CBER 1401 Rockville Pike Rockville MD 20852-1428*

ZORUMSKI, CHARLES F., psychiatrist, neuroscientist, educator; b. St. Louis, June 24, 1952; s. Charles F. and Cecilia J. (Bronakowski) Z.; m. Teresa J. Adams, Apr. 28, 1979; children: Erik C., Ian C. AB in Chemistry, St. Louis U., 1974, MD, 1978. Diplomate Am. Bd. Psychiatry and Neurology. Resident in psychiatry Washington U. Med. Sch., St. Lois, 1982, instr. in psychiatry, 1982-84, asst. prof., 1984-90, assoc. prof. neurobiology, 1987-90, assoc. prof. psychiatry and neurbiology, 1990-93, prof. psychiatry and neurobiology, 1993—, assoc. vice chmn. for rsch., 1992—; ad hoc mem. grant rev. study sect. NIH, Washington, 1994—. Mem. editl. bd. Neurobiology of Disease, 1995; contbr. over 120 articles to sci. publs.; patentee in field. Asst. varsity soccer coach St. Louis U., 1984—; youth soccer and youth basketball coach. Recipient Physician Scientist award NIMH, 1987-92, Rsch. Career Devel. award NIMH, 1992—; neuroscis. fellow Klingenstein Found., 1987-90. Fellow Am. Psychopathologic Assn.; mem. Am. Psychiat. Assn., Soc. for Neurosci., Ea. Mo. Psychiat. Assn., Assn. for Convulsive Therapy. Office: Washington U Med Sch Dept Psychiatry 4940 Children's Pl Saint Louis MO 63110

ZSIGMOND, ELEMER KALMAN, anesthesiologist; b. Budapest, Hungary, May 16, 1930; came to U.S., 1956, naturalized, 1966; s. Elemer Zeykvary and Terez (Kartori) Z.; m. Kathryn Fogarasi, Oct. 19, 1953; 1 son, Zoltan William. M.D., U. Budapest, 1955. Diplomate: Am. Bd. Anesthesiology. Intern Med. Clinics, U. Budapest, 1954-55; intern Allegheny Gen. Hosp., Pitts., 1960-61, resident in anesthesiology, 1961-63, clin. anesthesiologist, dir. anesthesiology research labs., 1966-68; resident in internal medicine Hosp. Sztalinvaros and Cardiac Sanatorium, Balatonfured, Hungary, 1955-56; res. assoc., anesthesia rsch. lab. Mercy Hosp., Pitts., 1957-60; prof. anesthesiology Med. Sch., U. Mich., Ann Arbor, 1968-79; prof. anesthesiology U. Ill. Med. Sch., Chgo., 1979-95, prof. emeritus, 1995—; mem. staff Univ. Hosp., U. Ill., Chgo. Contbr. over 300 articles on anesthesiology, neuropharmacology, and pulmonary physiology to profl. jours. Fellow Am. Coll. Anesthesiologists, Am. Coll. Clin. Pharmacologists; mem. Am. Soc. Anesthesiologists, Internat. Anesthesia Research Soc., N.Y. Acad. Sci., AAAS, AMA, Ill. Med. Soc., Cook County Med. Soc. Home: 6611 N Longmeadow Ave Chicago IL 60646-3207 Office: U Ill Med Ctr Ste 3214B 1740 W Taylor St Chicago IL 60612-7232

ZUBE-MILES, BARBARA J., rehabilitation nurse; b. Visalia, Calif., May 1, 1952; d. George D. and Elaine (Sabath) Amromin; m. Edward; children: Nicholas, Adam. BSN, U. Mo., 1985. Cert. rehab. RN. Staff nurse, outpatient care coord., referral nurse spec. Rusk Rehab. Ctr., U. Mo., Columbia; presented paper Chronicity and Progressive Self-Care Agency, 1990-91, A Rehabilitative Approach to Chronic Pain Management, 1993. Designer poster for 1st Internat. Self-Care Deficit Nursing Theory Conf., 1989. Mem. Assn. Rehab. Nurses (past pres. Cen. Mo. chpt.), Mo. Nurses Assn., Sigma Theta Tau (Alpha Iota chpt.), Phi Kappa Phi, Golden Key Soc.

ZUBER, RANDOLPH CLARK, urologist; b. Dallas, Apr. 4, 1941; s. Oran H. and Minnie M. (Cuthbertson) Z.; m. Billie Gayle Schumacher, June 20, 1964; children: Randolph Blake, Rustin Kurt. BA, U. Tex., 1963; MD, U. Tex. Med. Br., 1967; AAPS, Amarillo Jr. Coll., 1961. Diplomate Am. Bd. Urology. Intern Kans. U. Med. Ctr., 1967-68, resident in urology, 1969-72; practice medicine specializing in urology, Kerrville, Tex., 1974—; bishop Ch. of Christ, 1983-93; mem. urologic cultural exchange to Peoples Republic of China People to People Found., 1987. Founding dir., past pres. Hill County Right to Life; chmn. steering com. Kerr Country YMCA, 1990. Served to maj. USAF, 1972-74. Recipient Disting. Leadership award, cert. of Excellence Leadership Kerr County, 1989. Fellow ACS; mem. Am. Urol. Assn. (Tex. rep., bd. dirs. south cen. sect. 1990-96), Tex. Urol. Soc. (pres. 1988-89, bd. dirs. 1996—), Tex. Med. Assn. Office: 710 Water St Ste 300 Kerrville TX 78028

ZUBER, WILLIAM FREDERICK, thoracic and vascular surgeon; b. New Orleans, Dec. 30, 1932; s. Frederick and Bertie B. (Seale) Z.; m. Norma Burns Keen, Sept. 27,1958; children: William Frederick, Michael Craig, Kimberly, Karen. MD, Tulane U., 1956. Diplomate Am. Bd. Surgery with subspecialty in thoracic and vascular surgery. Teaching fellow Temple U., Phila., 1963-64; asst. prof. U. So. Calif., L.A., 1967-82; pvt. practice Ventura, Calif.; cons. Ventura County Med. Ctr., 1966—, chief surgery, 1973, 83-84, chief of staff, 1986-87; chief surgery Cmty. Meml. Hosp., Ventura, 1977, 85, 93, chief of staff, 1979. Contbr. articles to profl. jours. Pres. Am. Heart Assn., Ventura, 1972. Capt. M.C. U.S. Army, 1959-61. Mem. ACS, Internat. Cardiovascular Soc., Soc. Thoracic Surgeons, So. Calif. Vascular Surg. Soc. Office: 2856 Cabrillo #201 Ventura CA 93003

ZUBKOFF, MICHAEL, medical educator; b. N.Y.C., June 2, 1944; s. Harry and Catherine (O'Brien) Z.; children: Steven, Joel, Lisa; m. Leslee Ann Michaels, 1991. BA, Am. Internat. Coll., 1965, LLD (hon.), 1981; MA, Columbia U., 1966, cert. Internat. Fellow program, 1966, PhD, 1968. MA (hon.), Dartmouth Coll., 1980. Research assoc. conservation human resources Columbia U., N.Y.C., 1966-67; assoc. prof. econs. Fisk U., Nashville, 1967-70; assoc. prof. health econs., assoc. chmn. dept. family and community health Meharry Med. Coll., Nashville, 1967-75; assoc. prof. econs. Vanderbilt U., Nashville, 1970-75; prof. econs. and mgmt. Amos Tuck Sch. Bus., chmn. dept. community and family medicine Med. Sch. Dartmouth Coll., Hanover, N.H., 1975—; mem. inst. medicine Nat. Acad. Scis., 1982—, mem. assembly engrs. inst. med. com. on tech. and health care, 1977-79, grad. med. ednl. nat. adv. com., 1977-81, com. on grad.-med. edn. programs for mil. services Nat. Acad. Scis., 1980-82, nat. research council commn. on human resources Nat. Acad. Scis., 1980-84, com. on aging soc. Nat. Acad. Scis., 1984-89; corr. com. human rights Nat. Acad. Scis., 1983—, nat. rsch. coun. com. computer tech. and svc. sector productivity Nat. Acad. Scis., 1991-94; instr. econs. Harvard U., Yale U., and Columbia U., 1967-68. Co-author: Urban Health Services: The Case of New York, 1971, Consumer Incentives for Health Care, 1974, Health: A Victim of Cause of Inflation, 1976, Framework for Government Intervention in the Health Sector, 1978, Hospital Cost Containment: Selected Notes for Public Policy, 1980, Problem Based Learning of Social Science & Humanities by Fourth Year Medical Students, 1986, The Medical Outcomes Study: An Application of Methods for Monitoring the Results of Medical Care, 1989, Measuring Functional Status & Well Being: The Medical Outcomes Study Approach, 1992, Health Society & The Physician: Problem Based Learning of Social Sciences & Humanities, 1993; contbr. numerous articles to profl. jours. del., health spokesman White House Summit on Inflation, 1974. Fellow Woodrow Wilson Found., 1964-66, Fulbright Found., 1967-68, USPHS, 1966-67. Mem. Am. Econ. Assn., Am. Pub. Health Assn. Home: RR 1 Fairlee VT 05045-9801 Office: Dartmouth Med Sch Dept of Community & Family Med Strasenburgh Hall 2nd Fl Rm 203 Hanover NH 03755

ZUBROFF, LEONARD SAUL, surgeon; b. Minersville, Pa., Mar. 27, 1925; s. Abe and Fannie (Freedline) Z.; BA, Wayne State U., 1945, MD, 1949. Diplomate Am. Bd. Surgery. Intern Garfield Hosp., Washington, 1949-50, resident in surgery, 1951-55, chief resident surgery, 1954-55; pvt. practice medicine specializing in surgery, 1958-76; med. dir. Chevrolet Gear and Axle Plant, Chevrolet Forge Plant, GM, Detroit, 1977-78, divisional med. dir. Detroit Diesel Allison div., 1978-87, regional med. dir. GM, 1987-89; ret., 1989; bd. trustees LeVine Found.; mem. staff Hutzel Hosp., Detroit Meml. Hosp.; chief of surgery, chief profl. svcs. N.E. Air Command, Pepperell AFB, Newfoundland. With USAF, 1956-58. Fellow ACS; mem. Acad. Surgery Detroit, Coll. Occupational and Environ. Medicine, Mich. Occupational Med. Assn. (pres. 1990-91), Detroit Occupational Physicians Assn. (former pres.), Masons (33 degree), Phi Lambda Kappa. Home and Office: 22511 Bellwood Dr South Southfield MI 48034

ZUBROW, SIDNEY N., internist; b. Phila., Aug. 30, 1913; s. Nathan and Sara (Kantrowitz) Z.; m. Molly Cohen; m. Betzy Zubrow Cohen, Diane Zubrow Sand. BA, U. Pa., 1934; MD, Hahnemann Med. Coll., 1938. Diplomate am. Bd. Internal Medicine. Intern Mt. Sinai Hosp., Phila., 1938-39; pvt. practice, 1956—; assoc. prof. medicine Med. Sch. U. Pa., Phila., 1973—; cons. to dept. internal medicine Pa. Hosp., Phila., 1973. Maj. U.S. Army, 1942-46. Named Physician of Yr. Phila. County Med. Soc., 1981. Fellow ACP, Phila. Coll. Physicians; mem. AMA, Phila. County Med. Soc., Pa. Med. Soc., Jewish Acad. Arts and Scis. Republican. Jewish. Home: 1820 Rittenhouse Sq Philadelphia PA 19103-5832 Office: 501 S 8th St Philadelphia PA 19106-4001

ZUCCO, RONDA KAY, addictions program manager; b. Peoria, Ill., Apr. 3, 1960; d. Richard Leon Zucco. BA, So. Ill. U., 1981. Cert. addictions profl.; internat. cert. alcohol and drug counselor. Counselor Spl. Supportive Svcs., So. Ill. U., Carbondale, 1981-83; substance abuse counselor Interventions, Chgo., 1984-86; addictions counselor Parkside at BroMenn, Bloomington, Ill., 1986-89; dir. continuing care/sr. counselor Fla. Hosp. (formerly Parkside), Orlando, Fla., 1989-95, cmty. rels. rep. Ctr. for Psychiatry, 1995; addictions program mgr. Charter Behavioral Health Sys., Kissimmee, Fla., 1995—; tng. instr. for group facilitation Parkside/Fla. Hosp., 1989-95; presenter seminars in field, bd. dirs. Ill. Cert. Bd. Addiction Profls., Bloomington, 1986-89. Vol. ARC, Cardondale, 1978-81, crisis hotline Jackson County Cmty. Mental Health Ctr., Cardondale, 1981, Alliance for the Mentally Ill Greater Orlando, 1995—, Coalition for the Homeless, Orlando, 1995—; active AIDS Spkr.'s BUr., BroMenn Healthcare, Bloomington, Ill., 1986-89. State of Ill. Gen. Assembly scholar, 1977-81. Mem. Am. Mktg. Assn., Am. Assn. for Counseling and Devel., Am. Mental Health Counselors Assn., Fla. Alcohol and Drug Abuse Assn., Fla. Prevention Assn., Nat. Businesswomen's Leadership Assn., C. of C. Greater Orlando, Kappa Delta Pi, Chi Sigma Iota. Home: 10600 Bloomfield Dr Apt 311 Orlando FL 32825

ZUCKER, ARNOLD HARRIS, psychiatrist; b. Bklyn., July 29, 1930; s. Charles Israel and Bertha (Leff) Z.; m. Marilyn Pistreich, June 10, 1962; children: Harvey, Deborah, Shoshanna, David. BA, Bklyn. Coll., 1950; MD, SUNY, Bklyn., 1954; cert. psychoanalysis, Columbia U. Psychoanalytic Ctr, 1971. Diplomate, Am. Bd. Psychiatry and Neurology. Intern USPHS, Staten Island, N.Y., 1954-55; resident Kings County Hosp., Bklyn., 1955-56, Southwestern Med. Sch., Dallas, 1958-59, Albert Einstein Coll. Medicine, Bronx, N.Y., 1959-60; asst. clin. prof. psychiatry Albert Einstein Coll. Medicine, 1960-72; pvt. practice Mt. Vernon, N.Y., 1960—; assoc. attending psychiatrist, Mt. Vernon Hosp.; assoc. prof. pastoral counseling, Iona Coll., New Rochelle, N.Y., 1968—. Contbr. articles to profl. jours. Surgeon, USPHS, 1956-58. Fellow Am. Psychiat. Assn. (life), Am. Acad. Psychoanalysis (life); mem. Am. Psychoanalytic Assn., Assn. Psychoanalytic Medicine, AMA, Westchester Psychoanalytic Soc., Phi Beta Kappa. Democrat. Jewish. Office: 120 E Prospect Ave Mount Vernon NY 10550-2205

ZUCKER, HOWARD ALAN, pediatric cardiologist, intensivist, anesthesiologist; b. N.Y.C., Sept. 6, 1959; s. Saul and Phyllis (Goldblatt) Z.. BS, McGill U., Montreal, Quebec, Can., 1979; MD, George Washington U., 1982. Diplomate Am. Bd. Pediatrics, subspecialties in pediatric critical care, pediatric cardiology, Am. Bd. Anesthesiology, subspecialty in anesthesia critical care. Pediatric intern Johns Hopkins Hosp., Balt., 1982-83, pediatric resident, 1983-85; anesthesiology resident Hosp. of U. Pa., Phila., 1985-87; pediatric critical care fellow Children's Hosp. of Phila., 1987-88; asst. prof. anesthesiology and pediatrics Yale U. Sch. Medicine, New Haven, Conn., 1988-90; pediatric cardiology fellow Children's Hosp., Harvard Med. Sch., Boston, 1990-92; asst. prof. pediatrics and anesthesiology Columbia U. Coll. Physicians and Surgeons, N.Y.C., 1992—; pediat. dir. ICU, dir. pediatric transport Columbia Presbyn. Med. Ctr. Babies & Children's Hosp. N.Y., N.Y.C., 1992—; involved with crew tng. of NASA Space Shuttle STS-1 Mission, 1978-80; rsch. affiliate, Man-vehicle Lab, MIT. Chmn. bd. Terre Verte Found., Inc. Named Person of Week ABC World News Tonight, 1993. Fellow Am. Acad. Pediatrics, Am. Coll. Cardiology, Am. Coll. Chest Physicians; mem. AMA, Am. Soc. Anesthesiologists, Am. Heart Assn., Soc. Critical Care Medicine. Jewish. Home: 100 Winston Dr Apt 12G Cliffside Park NJ 07010-3240 Office: Columbia Presbyn Med Ctr Babies & Childrens Hosp NY 3959 Broadway New York NY 10032-1537

ZUCKER, JEAN MAXSON, nurse; b. Dunmore, Pa., Aug. 9, 1925; d. Earl L. and Florence M. (Cromwell) Maxson; R.N., Kings County Hosp. Center, 1948; cert. gerontol. nurse; children—Lawrence F., Pamela J., Diane K. Pvt. duty nurse various locations, N.Y., N.J., 1959-64; indsl. nurse Bendix Corp., Eatontown, N.J., 1955; asst. head nurse Point Pleasant Hosp., N.J., 1964-66; head nurse intensive and coronary care unit VA Hosp., Ft. Howard, Md., 1974-78; clin. nurse USPHS Hosp., Balt., 1978-81; nursing supr. VA Hosp. Center, Ft. Howard, 1981-94; clin. nurse VAMC, Ft. Howard, 1994—; tchr. in field. Mem. Am., Md. nurses assns., Am. Assn. Critical Care Nurses, NOW. Democrat. Methodist.

ZUCKER, ROBERT STEPHEN, neurophysiologist, neurobiology educator; b. Phila., Apr. 18, 1945; s. Irving Aaron and Dorothy Ruth (Pittenturf) Z.; m. Glenda Anita Teal, Sept. 1, 1968 (div. Apr. 1982); 1 child, David Aaron; m. Susan Henrietta Schwartz, Jan. 3, 1983; children: Mark Daniel Isaac, Ariel Dana. SB in Physics, MIT, 1966; PhD in Neurol. Sci., Stanford U., 1971. Asst. prof. physiology U. Calif., Berkeley, 1974-80, assoc. prof., 1980-85, prof., 1985-90, prof. neurobiology, 1990—; vis. investigator Univ. Coll., London, 1971-73, Nat. Ctr. Sci. Rsch., Gif-sur-Yvette, France, 1973-74; corp. mem. Marine Biology Lab., Woods Hole, Mass., 1981—; mem. bd. sci. counselors Nat. Inst. Neurol. and Communicative Disorders and Stroke, Washington, 1982; mem. study sects. NIH, 1983-84, 90-91, 93; mem. NIH Reviewer's Rsch., 1994—; Nachshen meml. lectr. U. Md., 1992. Mem. editl. bd. Jour. Neurobiology, 1982-86, Jour. Neurosci., 1989-94; contbr. articles to profl. jours. Recipient Jacob Javits award, 1987-94; fellow Helen Hay Whitney Found., NIH, NSF, NATO, Alfred P. Sloan Found.; grantee NIH, NSF, 1976. Mem. AAAS, AAUP, ACLU, Soc. Neurosci., Biophys. Sci., Union Concerned Scientists, Common Cause, Sierra Club, Sigma Xi. Democrat. Jewish. Home: 1236 Oxford St Berkeley CA 94709-1423 Office: U Calif Dept Molecular Cell Bi Berkeley CA 94720

ZUCKERBRAUN, JOEL, optometrist; b. Norwich, Conn., Oct. 29, 1956; s. Leonard and Irene Ada (Liebenau) Z. BA, Clark U., 1978; OD, New Eng. Coll. Optometry, Boston, 1982. Pvt. practice, Springfield, Mass., 1982-95, Jewett City, Conn., 1983—. Bd. dirs., v.p. Rope Ferry Common Condominium Assn., Waterford, Conn., 19944-95. Mem. Am. Optometric Assn., Conn. Assn. Optometrists, Lions (treas. Griswold, Conn. 1988-89, pres. 1989-90). Office: PO Box 338 8 N Main St Jewett City CT 06351

ZUCKERMAN, BARRY, medical educator. Prof., chmn. dept. pediatrics Boston U. Sch. Medicine; mem. Nat. Commn. on Children, Carnegie Commn. on Mtg. the Needs of Young Children.; bd. dirs. Zero to Three, Nat. Ctr. for Clin. Infant Programs, Nat. Ctr. Children in Poverty. Recipient Nat. Leadership Award Children's Def. Fund, 1994. Office: Boston City Hosp Dept Peds Dowling 3 S Boston MA 02215*

ZUCKERMAN, JOSEPH L., pediatrician; b. Memphis, Dec. 9, 1926; s. Max and Annie (Goldberg) Z.; m. Sylvia Hodes, Mar. 12, 1950; children: Laurence, Janet. BA, Vanderbilt U., 1947, MD, 1950. Pediatrician Comprehensive Med. Care, Chattanooga. Office: Comprehensive Med Care 3905 Webb Rd Chattanooga TN 37416

ZUCKERMAN, KENNETH STUART, hematology and oncology educator, researcher; b. Columbus, Ohio, June 22, 1946; s. Louis and Harriette Claire (Swartz) Z.; m. Lynn Shapiro, June 21, 1970; children: Jodi, Josh. BS, U. Mich., 1968; MD, Ohio State U., 1972. Resident internal medicine Ohio State U., Columbus, 1972-75; fellow hematology subspecialty Harvard U., Peter Bent Brigham Hosp., Boston, 1975-78; asst. prof. internal medicine U. Mich., Ann Arbor, 1978-82, assoc. prof. internal medicine, 1982-83; assoc. dir. Simpson Meml. Rsch. Inst., Ann Arbor, 1982-83; assoc. prof. medicine U. Ala., Birmingham, 1983-85, prof. medicine, 1985-93, dep. dir. div. hematology and oncology, 1983-90; scientist Comprehensive Cancer Ctr. Ala., Birmingham, 1983-85, sr. scientist, 1985-93; prof. internal medicine U. So. Fla., Tampa, 1993—; dir. div. med. oncology and hematology U. South Fla., Tampa, 1993—; chief medicine svc., dir. Hemopoietic Growth Control Program H. Lee Moffitt Cancer Ctr., Tampa, 1993—; Harold H. Davis Prof. of Cancer Rsch. U. South Fla., 1994—, prof. biochemistry and molecular biology, 1995—; cons. NIH, 1979—; vis. scientist Chester Beatty Labs., London, 1987-88; mem. VA Merit Rev. Bd. Hematology, 1993—, chmn., 1995—. Am. Cancer Soc. scholar in cancer rsch., 1988; NIH rsch. grantee, 1977—. Mem. AAAS, ACP (MKSAP X hematology com. 1992-95), Am. Soc. Clin. Investigation, Am. Fedn. Med. Rsch., Am. Soc. Hematology (subcom. on erythropoletin and cell proliferation 1983-86, chmn. myelodysplasia and myeloproliferative disorders edn. program 1991-92, chmn. scientific program com., 1994; govt. affairs and pub. policy com. 1995—), Internat. Soc. Exptl. Hematology (membership com. 1982-85, nominating com. 1985-88, 89-92, editl. bd. 1983-89), Am. Assn. for Cancer Rsch., Am. Soc. for Microbiology, So. Blood Club (pres. 1996—). Jewish. Home: 15610 Cochester Dr Tampa FL 33647-1155 Office: Divsn Med Oncology-Hematology U South Fla Moffit Cancer Ctr 12902 Magnolia Dr Tampa FL 33612-9497

ZUCKERMAN, SIDNEY, retired allergist, immunologist; b. N.Y.C., May 2, 1918; s. Max and Rose (Katz) Z.; m. Irene Elinor Cohen, Oct. 27, 1945; children: Elaine, Laurie, Jed, Amy. BA, Columbia Coll., 1939; MD, N.Y. Med. Coll., 1943. Diplomate Am. Bd. Internal Medicine, Am. Bd. Allergy and Immunology. Chief medicine 72d Sta. Hosp. US Army Med. Corps., Sendai, Japan, 1945-47; med. dir. Ford Instrument Co. divsn. Sperry Corp., N.Y.C., 1947-60; pvt. practice N.Y.C., 1947-91; med. dir. Sperry Rand Corp., Great Neck, N.Y., 1960-90. Capt. U.S. Army Med. Corps., 1945-47, Japan. Fellow ACP, Am. Coll. Allergists and Immunologists, Am. Acad. Allergy and Immunology, Am. Coll. Occupational Medicine, Am. Assn. Cert. Allergists; mem. Masons (jr. warden). Home: 4140 Bocaire Blvd Boca Raton FL 33487-1148

ZUFI, DAVID, plastic surgeon; b. Perth, Australia, July 9, 1928; m. Judith Edna Friedlander, Sept. 1, 1972. MB, BS, U. Melbourne, Australia, 1951. Diplomate Am. Bd. Surgery, Am. Bd. Plastic Surgery. Intern Royal Perth Hosp., Australia; resident Larkin Hosp. (now Healthcare South), Miami, Fla., $D; pvt. practice Miami, Fla., 1973—; plastic surgeon Cedars Med. Ctr., Miami, North Shore Med. Ctr., Miami, Larkin Hosp. Fellow Royal Coll. Surgeons (London), Royal Australasian Coll. Surgeons; mem. Am. Soc. Plastic and Reconstructive Surgeons. Home: 641 Reinante Ave Coral Gables FL 33156 Office: 8955 SW 87th Ct Ste 110 Miami FL 33176-2264

ZUGERMAN, CHARLES, dermatology; b. Phila., Mar. 23, 1945; s. Isadore and Florence (Blaskey) Z.; m. Shelley, Nov. 16, 1949; children: David, Ashley. BA, U. Pa., 1967; MD, Temple U., 1972. Diplomate Am. Bd. Dermatology, Nat. Bd. Med. Examiners. Assoc. prof. dermatology Northwestern U., Chgo., 1977-82; pvt. practice dermatology Chgo., 1982—; from assoc. to attending physician dept. dermatology Northwestern Meml. Hosp., 1977-84; cons. VA Adminstrn. Lakeside Hosp. Fellow Am. Acad. Dermatology; mem. Am. Occupl. Medicine Assn., Noah Worcester Dermatol. Soc., Ctrl. States Occupl. Medicine Assn., Soc. for Investigative Dermatology. Office: 676 N St Clair Chicago IL 60611

ZUHDI, NAZIH, surgeon; b. Beirut, May 19, 1925; came to U.S., 1950; s. Omar and Lutfiye (Atef) Z.; children by previous marriage: Omar, Nabil; m. Annette McMichael; children: Adam, Leyla, Zachariah. BA, Am. U., Beirut, 1946, MD, 1950. Diplomate Am. Bd. Surgery, Am. Bd. Thoracic Surgery. Intern St. Vincent's Hosp., S.I., N.Y., 1950-51, Presbyn.-Columbia Med. Ctr., N.Y.C., 1951-52; resident Kings County SUNY Med. Ctr., N.Y.C., 1952-56; fellow SUNY Downstate Med. Ctr., Bklyn., 1953-54; resident Univ. Hosps., Mpls., 1956; resident Univ. Hosp., Oklahoma City, 1957-58, practice surgery specializing in cardiovascular and thoracic, 1958-87, practice in heart transplantation, lung transplantation and heart-lung transplantation, 1985—; founder, dir. Transplantation Inst. Bapt. Med. Ctr., 1984—, transplantation surgeon in chief Bapt. Hosp., Oklahoma City; founder, chmn. Okla. Cardiovascular Inst., Oklahoma City, 1983-84, Okla. Heart Ctr., Oklahoma City, 1984-85. Contbg. author Cardiac Surgery, 1967, 2d edit., 1972; contbr. articles to profl. jours.; developer numerous med. devices, techniques, rsch. and publs. on cardiopulmonary bypass, internal hypothermia, assisted circulation, heart surgery and transplantation of thoracic organs; developer heart-lung machines; designer, use of exptl. plastic bypass hearts; originator use of banked citrated blood for cardiopulmonary bypass for open heart surgery, of clin. non-hemic primes of heart-lung machines producing intentional hemodilution, at present, the universally accepted principle of cardiopulmonary bypass for partial and total body perfusion; researcher in cardiovascular studies. Named Hon. Citizen, Brazil; named to Okla. Hall of Fame, 1994; Muslim scholar, lectr.; NCCJ Humanitarian honoree, 1996. Fellow ACS; mem. AMA, NCCJ (Humanitarian award 1996), Am. Thoracic Soc., Okla. Thoracic Soc., So. Med. Assn., Okla. Med. Assn., Internat. Coll. Angiology, Am. Coll. Chest Physicians, Oklahoma City C. of C., Oklahoma County Med. Soc., Oklahoma City Clin. Soc., Okla. Surg. Assn., Oklahoma City Surg. Soc., Southwestern Surg. Congress, Am. Coll. Cardiology, Am. Soc. Artificial Internal Organs, Soc. Thoracic Surgeons (founding mem.), Am. Assn. for Thoracic Surgery, Internat. Cardiovasc. Soc., Okla. State Heart Assn., Osler Soc., So. Thoracic Surg. Assn., Lillehei Surg. Soc., Internat. Soc. Heart Transplantation, Dwight Harken's Founder's Group Cardiac Surgery, Internat. Soc. Cardiothoracic Surgery (Japan, founder), Am. Soc. Transplant Surgeons, Milestones of Cardiology of Am. Coll. Cardiology, Okla. City Golf and Country Club, Okla. Hall of Fame. Home: 7305 Lancet Ct Oklahoma City OK 73120-1430

ZUIDEMA, GEORGE DALE, surgeon; b. Holland, Mich., Mar. 8, 1928; s. Jacob and Reka (Dalman) Z.; m. Joan K. Houtman, June 2, 1953; children: Karen Sue, David Jay, Nancy Ruth, Sarah Kay. A.B., Hope Coll., 1949, D.Sc. (hon.), 1969; M.D., Johns Hopkins U., 1953. Diplomate: Am. Bd. Surgery. Intern Mass. Gen. Hosp., 1953-54, asst. resident surgeon, then chief resident surgeon, 1954, 57, 58, 59; asst. prof. surgery, then assoc. prof. U. Mich. Sch. Medicine, 1960-64; prof. surgery, dir. dept. Johns Hopkins Sch. Medicine; also surgeon in chief Johns Hopkins Hosp., 1964-84; prof. surgery, vice provost med. affairs U. Mich., 1984-94; Cons. Walter Reed Army Med. Center, Sinai Hosp., Balt., Balt. City Hosp., Clin. Center of NIH; chmn. Study on Surg. Services for U.S., 1970-75. Editor: (with O.H. Gauer) Gravitational Stress in Aerospace Medicine, 1961; (with G.L. Nardi) Surgery-A Concise Guide to Clinical Practice, 1961, 4th edit., 1982; (with R.D. Judge and J. Fitzgerald) Physical Diagnosis, 1963, 4th edit., 1982; (with W.F. Ballinger and R.B. Rutherford) Management of Trauma, 1968, 3d edit., 1979, 4th edit., 1985; (with L. Schlossberg) Atlas of Human Functional Anatomy, 1977, 2d edit., 1980, 3d edit., 1986, Shackelford's Surgery of the Alimentary Tract, 4th edit., 1996; editor Jour. Surg. Rsch., 1966-72, assoc. editor, mem. editl. bd., 1972—; mem. editl. bd. Surgery Ann., 1968—, Surgery, 1970—, co-editor in chief, 1975—. Bd. dirs. Md. divsn. Am. Cancer Soc., 1964-68; trustee William Beaumont Hosp., Royal Oak, Mich., Hope Coll., Holland, Mich. Capt. M.C., USAF, 1954-56. John and Mary R. Markle scholar academic medicine, 1961-66; recipient Henry Russell award U. Mich., 1963. Fellow ACS, Royal Coll. Surgeons Ireland (hon.); mem. Assn. Am. Med. Colls., Ctrl. Soc. Clin. Rsch., Soc. Univ. Surgeons, Am. Surg. Assn., So. Surg. Assn., Soc. Clin. Surgery, Soc. Vascular Surgery, Internat. Cardiovascular Surgery, Halsted Soc., Nat. Inst. Medicine, Assn. Acad. Surgeons (pres. 1967-69), Allen O. Whipple Soc., Coun. on Grad. Med. Edn., Phi Beta Kappa, Tri Beta, Alpha Omega Alpha. Home: 11 Haverhill Ct Ann Arbor MI 48105-1406 Office: U Mich M4100 Med Sci I Ann Arbor MI 48109-0608

ZUKER, GILBERT ARNOLD, surgeon; b. Niagara Falls, Can., Nov. 16, 1933; s. Philip and Esther (Stein) Z.; m. Elaine Susan Adler, Dec. 9, 1961; children: Amy Lyn, Shari Rae, Tara Jane. MD, U. Toronto, 1959. Diplomate Am. Bd. Surgery. Intern New Mt. Sinai Hosp., Toronto, 1959-60; fellow in surgery Mayo Clinic, Rochester, Minn., 1960-64; chief resident in surgery New Mt. Sinai Hosp., Toronto, 1964-65; pvt. practice Scarborough Centenary Hosp., West Hill, Ont., Can., 1965-79, Fountain Valley (Calif.) Regional Hosp., 1979—; pres. med. staff Scarborough Centenary Hosp., 1976-79; chmn. dept. surgery Fountain Valley Regional Hosp., 1984-89. Fellow ACS, Royal Coll. of Surgeons; mem. Orange County Med. Assn., Calif. Med. Assn., Alpha Omega Alpha, Phi Delta Epsilon. Office: 11160 Warner Ave #305 Fountain Valley CA 92708

ZUKIN, PAUL, health research educator; b. L.A., Dec. 26, 1919; s. Ernest Zukin and Lena Victoria Rosenkranz; m. Mary Jane Zukin, July 3, 1942; children: Barbara, James Henry, Donald Demetrius. BA in Psychology, UCLA, 1941; MD, U. Calif., San Francisco, 1944; MPH in Med. Care Orgn., UCLA, 1966; postgrad., Harvard U., 1972, Mass. Gen. Hosp.-Harvard U., 1979, Hammersmith Hosp.-U. London, 1980. Diplomate Am. Bd. Internal Medicine. Intern L.A. County Gen. Hosp., 1944-45; resident in internal medicine L.A. County Harbor Gen. Hosp. & Wadsworth VA Hosp., 1947-50; pvt. practice specializing in internal medicine Beverly Hills, Calif., 1950-66; dir. health and human factors Litton Internat. Devel. Corp., Greece and Turkey, 1967-69; dir. health svcs. rsch. and tng. Divsn. Comty. Health Svcs., L.A. County, 1970-74; prof. medicine, preventive medicine and pub. health UCLA, 1970-74; v.p., med. dir. Kaiser Found. Internat., Oakland, Calif., 1974-80; pres. Health Mgmt. Corp., Piemont, Calif., 1980-93; clin. prof. dept. health rsch. and policy Stanford (Calif.) U. Sch. Medicine, 1993—; cons. WHO Health Svcs., Turkey, 1973, Nepal, 1973, Burma, 1973; dir. feasibility study for prepaid health program USAID, South Korea, 1977; med. programmer Dr. Torres Hosp. Devel. Project, Saipan, 1980; dir. Health Comms. Project, Pacific Basin, 1982-91; evaluator rural health improvement project USAID, Niger, 1981;cons. Water Resource Devel. Project, Kitui Province, Kenya, 1982; cons. Taabo Dam Hosp., Ivory Coast, 1975-79; planner, cons. rural primary health care project PAHO/USAID, Brazil, 1972; cons. cost containment, revenue generation and health svcs. improvement, Am. Samoa, 1981-84, numerous other health-related projects for internat. orgns., nat. govts. and pvt. sector. Contbr. numerous articles to profl. jours. and internat. presentations. Capt. U.S. Army M.C., 1945-47. Fellow ACP, APHA, Am. Coll. Preventive Medicine; mem. AMA, Calif. Med. Assn., Greek Med. Assn., Alameda-Contra Costa County Med. Assn., Soc. for Internat. Devel. (pres. No. Calif. chpt. 1977, 78), Delta Omega.

ZUKOWSKI, BARBARA WANDA, clinical social work psychotherapist; b. Queens, N.Y., Apr. 30, 1957; d. Stanley F. and Domicille K. (Trzebuchowska) Z. BS in Psychology, Bklyn. Coll., 1984; MSW, NYU, 1986; student, Bklyn. Coll. Conservatory Mus., 1982-84; student classical guitar, Am. Inst. Guitar, N.Y.C., 1982-84, 90—. Lic. social worker, N.Y. Clin. social worker on-site program Staten Island (N.Y.) Children's Community Mental Health Soc., 1986-87; clin. social worker Cath. Charities Diocese of Bklyn., 1984-85, 87-89, N.Y.C. Health & Hosps. Corp., Bklyn., 1989-92; child therapist Program for Devel. Human Potential Office of Cath. Edn., Diocese of Bklyn., 1992—; pvt. practice as dream analyst and psychotherapist, Bklyn., 1989—; developer children's creative arts therapy groups for social work use Cath. Charities Diocese of Bklyn., 1988-89. Singer/songwriter, guitarist, rec. artist, Cosmic Shindig, 1994, Emily, 1996. Music minister Pax Christi Met. N.Y., 1990-93. Mem. NASW, NARAS, Broadcast Music Internat., Songwriters Guild of Am. Home: 144 Driggs Ave # 3 Brooklyn NY 11222-4202

ZUMO, BILLIE THOMAS, biologist; b. Cheyenne, Wyo., Sept. 25, 1936; d. Thomas Elias and Katherine A. (Pappas); m. Charles Vincent, Aug. 21, 1959; 1 child, Thomas J. BA, U. Wyo., Laramie, 1958; MA, U. No.Colo., Greeley, 1963. Cert. tchr. Tchr. Carey Jr. H.S., Cheyenne, 1958-61, 61-63; English language tchr. McCormick Jr. H.S., Cheyenne, 1961; biology tchr. Laramie County C.C., Cheyenne; tchr. Central H.S., Cheyenne, 1963; exec. bd. Sch. Dist. curriculum adv., 1982-85; chmn. sci. dept., 1990—; mem. faculty adv. com. Central High Sch., 1988—, mem. prin. screening com., 1990-91. Football statis. Cen. Football Team, Cheyenne, 1976—; lay mem. rsch. com. of the Pharmacy Theraputics Com., 1985; judge sch. dist. sci. fair, Cheyenne, 1987-88; ch. choir dir., Cheyenne. Recipient Disting. Svc. award Sts. Constandine and Helen Orthodox Ch., 1979, Disting. Svc. award as choir dir. Archbishop Iakovas, N.Y., 1988. Mem. Nat. Assn. Biology Tchrs. (state rep. 1992—), NEA, Cheyenne Tchrs. Edn. Assn., Wyo. Edn. Assn., Nat. Forum of Greek Orthodox Musicians, Ladies Philoptochos Soc. of Denver Diocese (treas. 1989-93, 1st v.p. 1993-95, pres. 1995—), AAUW, Phi Delta Kappa. Democrat. Eastern Greek Orthodox. Home: 900 Ranger Dr Cheyenne WY 82009-2535 Office: Cen High Sch 5500 Education Dr Cheyenne WY 82009-4008

ZUMOFF, BARNETT, endocrinologist, medical researcher; b. Bklyn., June 1, 1926; s. Abraham and Stella (Zumoff) Z.; m. Selma Silver, Nov. 11, 1951; children: Janine, Francine, Linda. AB, Columbia U., 1945; postgrad., Albany Med. Coll., 1945-47; MD, L.I. Coll. Medicine, 1949. Diplomate Am. Bd. Internal Medicine, Am. Bd. Endocrinology and Metabolism. Rotating intern, med. resident Bklyn. Jewish Hosp., 1949-50, 51; straight med. intern Mass. Meml. Hosp., 1950-51; resident pathology Bklyn. VA Hosp., 1954-55; resident medicine univ. svc. Kings County Hosp., 1954-55; spl. fellow medicine, clin. asst. medicine Meml. Ctr., 1955-57; clin. asst. medicine Kings County Hosp., 1957-62; asst. Sloan-Kettering Inst., 1957-60, assoc., 1960-62; asst. medicine James Ewing Hosp., 1959-62, assoc. attending physician div. neoplastic medicine, 1961-63; attending physician dept. oncology, 1963-82; attending physician dept. medicine Montefiore Med. Ctr., 1977-82, 87—, Hosp. for Joint Diseases-Orthopedic Inst., 1981—; attending physician and chief div. endocrinolog and metabolism dept. medicine Beth Israel Med. Ctr., N.Y.C., 1981—; instr. in medicine Cornell U. Med. Coll., 1958-62; asst. prof. Albert Einstein Coll. Medicine, 1965-71, assoc. prof., 1971-78, prof., 1978-82, 94—; vis. prof., 1987-94; prof. Mt. Sinai Sch. Medicine, 1982-94; adj. prof., 1994—; asst. dir. Clin. Rsch. Ctr., Montefiore Hosp., 1961-76, dir. 1976-81, dir. cancer endocrinology, 1976-84, sr. investigator Inst. Steroid Rsch., 1963-81; vis. physician Rockefeller U. Hosp., 1978-84; adj. attending physician Mt. Sinai Med. Ctr., 1988—. Mem. editl. bd. Jour. Clin. Endocrinology and Metabolism, 1971-76, Anticancer Rsch., 1981—, Breast Disease-An Internat. Jour., 1987—; translator Yiddish poetry; contbr. over 250 articles to profl. jours. Pres. Workmen's Cir., 1984-88, 92-96, The Forward Assn., 1991-92, 95—; co-pres. Congress for Jewish Culture, 1989—; active Atran Found., 1987—. With M.C., USAF, 1951-82, brig. gen. Res. ret. Decorated Legion of Merit, Combat Readiness medal, Meritorious Svc. medal, Air Force Commendation medal. Fellow ACP; mem. AMA, AAAS, Am. Heart Assn. (coun. on arteriosclerosis), Am. Soc. Clin. Investigation, Endocrine Soc., Aerospace Med. Assn., Am. Diabetes Assn. (profl. sect.), Am. Fedn. Clin. Rsch., Assn. Mil. Surgeons U.S., Soc. Med. Cons. Armed Forces, Soc. USAF Flight Surgeons, N.Y. Diabetes Assn. Home: 3710 Bedford Ave Brooklyn NY 11229-1704 Office: Beth Israel Med Ctr Div Endocrinolgy Metabolism 1st Ave At 16th St New York NY 10003

ZUMPE, DORIS, ethologist, researcher, educator; b. Berlin, May 18, 1940; came to U.S., 1972; d. Herman Frank and Eva (Wagner) Z. BSc, U. London, 1961, PhD, 1970. Asst. to K.Z. Lorenz, Max-Planck-Inst. für Verhaltensphysiologie, Seewiesen, Fed. Republic Germany, 1961-64; rsch. asst. and assoc., lectr. Inst. Psychiatry, U. London, 1965-72; rsch. assoc. Emory U. Sch. Medicine, Atlanta, 1972-74, asst. prof. psychiatry (ethology), 1974-77, assoc. prof., 1977-87, prof., 1987—; reviewer NSF, 7 sci. jours. Contbr. over 140 articles to profl. jours. NIMH grantee, 1971—. Mem. AAAS, Internat. Soc. Psychoneuroendocrinology, Internat. Primatological Soc., Internat. Soc. for Human Ethology, Soc. for Study of Reprodn., Am. Soc. Primatologists, N.Y. Acad. Scis., Earl Music Am., Viola da Gamba Soc. Am. Office: Emory U Sch Medicine Dept Psychiatry Atlanta GA 30322

ZUMWALT, ROSS EUGENE, forensic pathologist, educator; b. Goodrich, Mich., July 18, 1943; s. Paul Lawrence and Lila Ann (Birky) Z.; m. Theresa Ann Schar, Sept. 12, 1970 (div. Apr. 1988); children: Christopher Todd, Tenley Ann; m. Cheryl Lynn Willman, Sept. 4, 1988; 1 child, David Willman Zumwalt. BA, Wabash Coll., 1967; MD, U. Ill., 1971. Diplomate in anat. and forensic pathology Am. Bd. Pathology. Intern, resident in pathology Mary Bassett Hosp., Cooperstown, N.Y., 1971-73; resident in anat. and forensic pathology Southwestern Med. Sch., Dallas, 1973-76; asst. med. examiner Dallas County, Dallas, 1974-76; staff pathologist, dir. labs. Naval Regional Med. Ctr., Camp Lejeune, N.C., 1976-78; dep. coroner Cuyahoga County, Cleve., 1978-80, Hamilton County, Cin., 1980-86; assoc. prof. pathology U. Cin. Sch. Medicine, 1980-86; prof. pathology U. N.Mex. Sch. Medicine, Albuquerque, 1987—; chief med. investigator Office of Med. Investigator, Albuquerque, 1991—; trustee Am. Bd. Pathology, Tampa, Fla., 1993—. Lt. comdr. USN, 1976-78. Fellow Am. Acad. Forensic Scis., Coll. Am. Pathologists; mem. AMA, Nat. Assn. Med. Examiners (bd. dirs. 1984—, pres. 1995-96), Am. Soc. Clin. Pathologists, Am. and Can. Acad. Pathologists. Office: Office of Med Investigator 700 Camino de Salud Albuquerque NM 87131 Also: 819 El Alhambra Cir NW Albuquerque NM 87107-6301

ZUNICH, JANICE, pediatrician, geneticist, educator, administrator; b. New Kensington, Pa., Sept. 2, 1953; d. Nick and Mary (Zivkovich) Z.; m. Milan Katic, June 20, 1981; children: Nikola Ilija, Milana. BS, Ohio State U., 1974, MD, 1978. Diplomate Am. Bd. Pediatrics, Nat. Bd. Med. Examiners, Am. Bd. Med. Genetics (clin. genetics, clin. cytogenetics). Lab. technician Community Hosp., Lorain, Ohio, summer 1974, Ohio State U. Hosp., Columbus, 1974-75; intern then resident in pediatrics Columbus (Ohio) Children's Hosp., 1978-81; genetics fellow Luth. Gen. Hosp., Park Ridge, Ill., 1981-83; asst. prof. pediats. W.Va. U. Med. Ctr., Morgantown, 1983-85, assoc. dir. cytogenetics, 1984-85; clin. assoc. prof. med. genetics, dir. Genetics Ctr. N.W. Ctr. Med. Edn., Ind. U. Sch. Medicine, Gary, 1985—; genetics cons. Community Hosp., Munster, Ind., Porter Meml. Hosp., Valparaiso, Ind., St. Anthony Med. Ctr., Crown Point, Ind., Meth. Hosp., Gary and Merrillville, Ind., St. Margaret Hosp., Hammond, Ind. Contbr. articles to profl. jours. Mem. med. com. Planned Parenthood, N.W.-N.E. Ind., Merrillville, 1987—; mem. adv. com. N.W. Ind. Sickle Cell Found., Gary, 1987—; mem. med. adv. com. Svcs. for Children with Spl. Health Care Needs, Indpls., 1989-92; mem. adv. bd. Parent Edn. Ctr., Whiting, Ind., 1988—. Named Person of Yr., Down Syndrome Assn. N.W. Ind., Highland, 1988; Charles F. Whitten fellow Sickle Cell Found. N.W. Ind., 1990. Fellow Am. Acad. Pediatrics; mem. Am. Soc. Human Genetics, Ind. State Med. Assn., Lake County Med. Soc., Great Lakes Regional Genetics Group (financing. genetics svcs. sub-com. 1988—), Phi Beta Kappa, Alpha Epsilon Delta. Eastern Orthodox. Office: NW Ctr for Med Edn 3400 Broadway Gary IN 46408-1101

ZUPUNSKI-TURNER, LESLEY, geriatrics nurse; b. Vancouver, Wash., July 3, 1952; d. Nick D. and Elsie Elvina (Shay) Zupunski; m. William Morgan Turner, Feb. 14, 1983 (dec.). BSN, Ea. Wash. U., 1988. RN, Wash. Staff nurse cardiac critical care Sacred Heart Med. Ctr., Spokane, Wash.; night charge nurse Regency North, Spokane; supr. St. Brendan, Spokane; nurse Beverly Nursing Network, Portland, Oreg.; dir. nursing svcs. Hillhaven Nursing Home, Vancouver, Wash.; resident care mgr. Hill Haven Corp, Beaverton, Oreg. Mem. Sigma Theta Tau.

ZURLINE, WILLIAM JOHN, physician assistant; b. Chickasha, Okla., Mar. 1, 1949; s. Joseph C. and Ada Josephine (Stibbens) Z.; m. Thaylia Sue Pearcy, Mar. 25, 1972; children: Matt Wayne, Mark Randall, Mignon Ellen. BS in Biochemistry, Okla. State U., 1972; BS in Health, Okla. U., 1975. Nat. cert. physician asst. Respiratory tech. Grady Meml. Hosp., Chickasha, 1966-72; respiratory/ventilator tech. Bapt. Med. Ctr., Oklahoma City, 1972-73; physician asst. Abilene (Tex.) Pediats., 1974-81, Meml. Hosp., Frederick, Okla., 1981-88, Atoka (Okla.) Meml. Hosp., 1988-92, Maysville (Okla.) Med. Ctr., 1992—; tech. med. dir. com. EMS State Health Dept., Oklahoma City, 1986-91. With Nat. Guards, 1977-81. Mem. Am. Assn. Physician Assocs., Okla. Assn. Physician Assocs. (Physician Asst. of the Yr. 1992), Am. Heart Assn. (ACLS instr. 1983—, affiliate faculty BLS 1990—), Okla. Rural Health Assn. (bd. dirs. 1994—), Maysville C. of C. (pres. 1995). Roman Catholic. Home: PO Box 673 Maysville OK 73057 Office: Maysville Med Ctr 605 Main PO Box 660 Maysville OK 73057

ZUSMER, TODD RUSSELL, osteopath; b. East Meadow, N.J., Sept. 28, 1967; s. Noel Robert and Roxanne (Hirsch) Z. BA in Psychology, U. Tex., 1989; DO, Nova So. U., 1996. Mental health technician Oaks Treatment Ctr., Austin, Tex., 1988-89. Jewish. Home: 1050 92d St # 3 Bay Harbor Isle FL 33154

ZUSPAN, FREDERICK PAUL, obstetrician, gynecologist, educator; b. Richwood, Ohio, Jan. 20, 1922; s. Irl Goff and Kathryn (Speyer) Z.; m. Mary Jane Cox, Nov. 23, 1943; children: Mark Frederick, Kathryn Jane, Bethany Anne. BA, Ohio State U., 1947, MD, 1951. Intern Univ. Hosps., Columbus, Ohio, 1951-52; resident Univ. Hosps., 1952-54; resident Western Res. U., Cleve., 1954-56, Oblebay fellow, 1958-60, asst. prof., 1958-60; chmn. dept. bo-gyn. McDowell (Ky.) Meml. Hosp., 1956-58, chief clin. svcs., 1957-58; prof., chmn. dept. ob-gyn. Med. Coll. Ga., Augusta, 1960-66; Joseph Boliver DeLee prof. ob-gyn., chmn. dept. U. Chgo., 1966-75; obstetrician, gynecologist in chief Chgo. Lying-In Hosp., 1966-75; prof., chmn. dept. ob-gyn. Ohio State U., Columbus, 1975-87, R.L. Meiling prof. ob-gyn. Sch. Medicine, 1984-90, prof. emeritus, 1991—. Founding editor Lying In, Jour. Reproductive Medicine; editor-in-chief Am. Jour. Ob-Gyn. and Ob-Gyn. Reports, (with Lindheimer and Katz) Hypertension in Pregnancy, 1976, Current Developments in Perinatology, 1977, (with Quilligan) Operative Obstetrics, 1981, 89, Manual of Practical Obstetrics, 1981, 90, Clin. and Exptl. Hypertension in Pregnancy, 1979-86, (with Rayburn) Drug Therapy in Ob-Gyn., 1981, 3rd edit., 1992; editor: (with Christian) Controversies in Obstetrics and Gynecology; contbr. articles to med. jours., chpts. to books. Pres. Barren Found., 1974-76. With USNR, 1942-43; 1st lt. USMCR, 1943-45. Decorated DFC, Air medal with 10 oak leaf clusters. Mem. Soc. Gynecol. Investigation, Chgo. Gynecol. Soc., Am. Assn. Ob-Gyn., Columbus Ob-Gyn. Soc. (pres. 1984-85), Am. Acad. Reproductive Medicine (pres.), Am. Coll. Obstetricians and Gynecologists, Assn. Profs. of Gynecology and Obstetrics (pres. 1972), South Atlantic Assn. Obstetricians and Gynecologists (Found. prize for rsch. 1962), Ctrl. Assn. Ob-Gyn. (cert. of merit, rsch. prize 1970), Am. Soc. Clin. Exptl. Hypnosis (exec. sec. 1968, v.p. 1970), Soc. Gynecol. Investigation, Internat. Soc. Study of Hypertension in Pregnancy (pres. 1981-83), Am. Gynecology and Obstetrics Soc. (pres. 1986-87), Soc. Perinatal Obstetrics, Perinatal Rsch. Soc., Sigma Xi, Alpha Omega Alpha, Alpha Kappa Kappa. Home: Upper Arlington 2400 Coventry Rd Columbus OH 43221-3754

ZVETINA, JAMES RAYMOND, pulmonary physician; b. Chgo., Oct. 14, 1913; s. John and Jennie (Albrecht) Z.; m. Florence Courtney, Feb. 4, 1944. BS, Loyola U., 1940; MD, U. Ill., 1943. Intern West Suburban Hosp., Oak Park, Ill., 1944, resident physician, 1944-45; asst. ward med. officer USNH, NOB, Norfolk, Va., 1945; staff physician Pulmonary TB Svc. VA Med. Hosp., Hines, Ill., 1946-54; asst. chief Pulmonary Svc. VA Med. Hosp., Hines, Ill., 1954-68, sect. chief, 1968-88, attending physician, 1988-91, cons., 1992—; clin. prof. medicine Coll. Medicine, U. Ill., Chgo., 1978—; mem. adv. bd. Coll. Medicine, U. Ill., 1985—; rep. Rsch. Conf. in Pulmonary Disease, VA Armed Forces, 1946-74. Contbr. articles to profl. jours. V.p. Chgo. Cath. Physicians, 1979, pres., 1978. Comdr. USNR, 1945-46, med. officer USNR, ret. Recipient Svc. award 40 Yrs. VA Adminstrn., 1985, Svc.

award 30 Yrs. U. Ill. Med. Sch., 1978. Fellow Am. Coll. Chest Physicians; mem. AMA, Ill. State Med. Soc. (Fifty Yr. club), Chgo. Med. Soc., Third Order of St. Dominic. Roman Catholic. Home: 96 Forest Ave Riverside IL 60546-1977 Office: VA Hines Hines IL 60141

ZWANGER, JEROME, physician; b. N.Y.C., Apr. 4, 1923; s. Benjamin and Evelyn Z.; m. Bernice E. Lomazov, May 22, 1955; children: Susan, Roberta, Melissa, Betsy. AB, U. Pa., 1943; MD, Chgo. Med. Sch., 1947. Diplomate Am. Bd. Radiology. Intern Wyckoff Heights Hosp., Bklyn., 1947-49; resident L.I. Coll. Hosp., Bklyn., 1949-52; practice medicine specializing in radiology; asst. dir. dept. radiology L.I. Coll. Hosp., N.Y., 1953-54; radiologist L.I. Jewish Hosp., 1955-60; dir. radiology Cen. Gen. Hosp., Plainview, N.Y., 1961—, also bd. dirs.; asst. prof. clin. radiology SUNY, Stony Brook, 1974-80. Bd. dirs. Nassau Physicians Rev. Orgn., 1975-78; governing bd. Nassau-Suffolk Health Systems Agy.; mem. N.Y. State Bd. Medicine. Mem. vis. com. Met. Mus. Art, Phila. Art Mus.; bd. overseers Sch. Arts and Scis., U. Pa. Fellow Am. Coll. Radiology (councilor 1975—), Nassau Acad. Medicine (founder); mem. AMA, Med. Soc. N.Y., Nassau County Med. Soc. (pres.), Radiol. Soc. N.Am., N.Y. State Radiol. Soc. (pres. 1986-87), L.I. Radiol. Soc. (past pres.), U. Pa. Alumni Assn. (trustee 1977—). Office: 126 Hicksville Rd Massapequa NY 11758-5822

ZWANGER, MARK L., surgeon, educator; b. Somerville, N.J.. MD, Thomas Jefferson U., 1982; MBA, Wharton Coll., Phila., 1989. Residency dir. Thomas Jefferson U. Hosp., Phila.; resident in emergency medicine Wayne State U., Detroit; asst. prof. surgery Thomas Jefferson U. Hosp., Phila. Office: Thomas Jefferson Univ Hosp 239 Thompson Bldg Philadelphia PA 19147

ZWEIMAN, BURTON, physician, scientist, educator; b. N.Y.C., June 7, 1931; s. Charles and Gertrude (Levine) Z.; m. Claire Traig, Dec. 30, 1962; children: Amy Beth, Diane Susan. AB, U. Pa., 1952, MD, 1956. Diplomate Am. Bd. Internal Medicine, Am. Bd. Allergy & Immunology. Intern Mt. Sinai Hosp., N.Y.C.; Hosp. U. Pa., Bellevue Hosp. Ctr. Hosp. U. Pa., Bellevue Hosp. Center, 1957-60; fellow NYU Sch. Medicine, 1960-61; mem. faculty dept. medicine U. Pa. Sch. Medicine, Phila., 1963—; prof. medicine, chief allergy and immunology divsn. U. Pa. Sch. Medicine, 1975—; cons. U.S. Army, NIH; co-chmn. Am. Bd. Allergy and Immunology, 1979-81. Editor Jour. Allergy Clin. Immunology, 1988-93; contbr. articles to med. jours. Served with M.C., USNR, 1961-63. Allergy Found. Am. fellow, 1959-61. Fellow ACP, Am. Acad. Allergy, Asthma and Immunology (past pres.); mem. Am. Assn. Immunologists, Am. Fedn. Clin. Rsch., Phi Beta Kappa, Alpha Omega Alpha. Office: U Pa Sch Medicine 512 Johnson Pavilion 36th and Hamilton Walk Philadelphia PA 19104-1999

ZWIBELMAN, JAY SCOTT, neurologist; b. St. Louis, Mar. 22, 1962; s. Irvin Robert and Sally (Lite) Z.; m. Andrea Marie Peterson, Aug. 17, 1985; children: Hannah Nicole, Zachary Alan, Ethan Anton. BA, MD, U. Mo., Kansas City, 1986. Diplomate Am. Bd. Neurology. Intern, then resident in neurology U. Wis. Hosp. and Clinics, Madison, 1986-89, chief resident, 1989-90; fellow in pain mgmt. Harvard U.-Mass. Gen. Hosp., Boston, 1990-91; pvt. practice, Kansas City, 1991-93, Shawnee Mission, Kans., 1993—. Mem. AMA, Am. Acad. Neurology, Am. Pain Soc. Home: 8817 Norwood Leawood KS 66206 Office: Neurology Cons 8800 W 75th St Ste 100 Shawnee Mission KS 66204

ZWICKE, DIANNE LYNN, internist, cardiologist, educator; b. Marshfield, Wis., Oct. 27, 1952; d. Edward Raymond and Donna Mae (Erickson) Z. Diploma in nursing, St. Joseph's Hosp., Marshfield, 1973; BS in Nursing, Marquette U., 1975; MD, U. N.C., 1982. Diplomate Am. Bd Internal Medicine, subspecialty cert. in cardiovascular diseases. Resident in internal medicine U. Wis.-Marshfield Clinic-St. Joseph's Hosp., 1982-84, chief resident, 1984-85; fellow in cardiology U. Wis. Clin. Campus-Sinai Samaritan Med. Ctr., Milw., 1985-87, assoc. prof. medicine, 1987—; mem. active staff in cardiology and emergency medicine U. Wis. Cliin. Campus-Sinai Samaritan Med. Ctr., Milw., 1987—; clin. instr. surgery emergency-trauma svcs. Med. Coll. Wis., Milw; attending staff St. Luke's Hosp., St. Francis Hisp., St. Michael's Hosp., West Allis Meml. Hosp., Milw.; bd. govs., mem. State Wis. Nat. Faculty Am. Heart Assn.; presenter in field. Contbr. articles and abstracts to med. jours. Fellow ACP, Am. Coll. Cardiology, Am. Coll. Chest Physicians; mem. Soc. Critical Care Medicine, Wis. Med. Soc. (chmn. on continuing med. edn. 1987), Milw. County Med. Soc. (med. dir. cardiovascular fellowship tng. program, med. dir. women's heart care program and pulmonary hypertension program), Sigma Theta Tau. Democrat. Lutheran. Office: U Wis Clin Campus 950 N 12th St Milwaukee WI 53233-1306

ZYDOWICZ, DANIEL ALAN, internist; b. Cleve., Nov. 29, 1946; s. Alphonse J. and Jane V. (Strelecki) Z.; m. Madolane Sablar Dean, June 22, 1968; children: Mark, Sara. BS in Biology, John Carroll U., 1968; MD, St. Louis U., 1972. Diplomate Am. Bd. Internal Medicine, Am. Bd. Infectious Diseases. Intern Hennepin County Med. Ctr., Mpls., 1972-73; med. staff USPHS Indian Health Svc., Pawnee, Okla., 1973-74, Anchorage, Alaska, 1974-75; resident in internal medicine Hennepin County Med. Ctr., 1975-78; infectious disease fellow U. Minn./Hennepin County Med. Ctr., 1978-80; pvt. practice Intermed Consultants, Edina, Minn., 1980—; med. staff, dir. infection control Riverside Med. Ctr., 1985—; med. staff Fairview Southdale Hosp., chief internal medicine 1991. Lt. comdr. USPHS, 1973-75. Mem. Am. Soc. Internal Medicine, Infectious Disease Soc. Am., Am. Soc. Microbiology, Hennepin County Med. Soc. Roman Catholic. Office: Intermed Consultants 6363 France Ave S #400 Edina MN 55435